CASTLE CONNOLLY

AMERICA'S TOP DOCTORS®

A CASTLE CONNOLLY GUIDE

13TH EDITION

The Best in American Medicine

America's trusted source for identifying Top Doctors

The selection of medical providers for inclusion in this book was based in part on opinions solicited from physicians, nurses, and other health care professionals. The author and publishers cannot assure the accuracy of information provided to them by third parties, since such opinions are necessarily subjective and may be incomplete. The omission from this book of particular health care providers does not mean that such providers are not competent or reputable.

The purpose of this book is educational and informational. It is not intended to replace the advice of your physician or to assist the layman in diagnosing or treating illness, disease, or injury. Following the advice or recommendations set forth in this book is entirely at the reader's own risk. The author and publishers cannot ensure accuracy of, or assume responsibility for, the information in the book as such information is affected by constant change. Liability to any person or organization for any loss or damage caused by errors or omissions in this book is hereby disclaimed. Whenever possible, readers should consult their own primary care physician when selecting health care providers, including any selection based upon information contained in this book. In order to protect patient privacy the names of patients cited in anecdotes throughout the book have been omitted.

The confidence of our readers in our editorial integrity is crucial to the success of the Castle Connolly Guides. Any use of the Castle Connolly name, or of any list or listing (or portion of either) from any Castle Connolly Guide, for advertising or for any commercial purpose, without prior written consent, is strictly prohibited and may result in legal action.

For more information, please contact:

Castle Connolly Medical Ltd., 42 West 24th St, New York, New York 10010
212-367-8400x110
E-mail: info@castleconnolly.com
Web site: http://www.castleconnolly.com.

Library of Congress Control Number: 2013919419
ISBN 1-883769-68-X 978-1-883769-68-0 (paperback)
Printed in the United States of America

Table of Contents

About the Publishers....xxix

Medical Advisory Board....xxxi

Foreword....xxxii

Introduction....1

Using This Guide To Find Top Specialists....5

Maximizing Your First Appointment With A Top Doctor....21

Utilizing Special Resources....25

How To Use This Guide....37

Locating A Specialist....37

Geographic Regions And States....38

Medical Specialties....41

Descriptions And Abbreviations....42

The Training Of A Specialist....49

Partnership For Excellence Program....53

List Of Participating Hospitals....**54**

Cleveland Clinic Foundation....55

Continuum Health Partners....56

Fox Chase Cancer Center....57

Hospital for Special Surgery....58

The Johns Hopkins Hospital....59

Maimonides Medical Center....60

Moffitt Cancer Center....61

Mount Sinai Medical Center....62

New England Baptist Hospital....63

New York Eye & Ear Infirmary....64

NewYork-Presbyterian Hospital....65

North Shore-LIJ Health System....66

NorthShore University Health System....67

NYU Langone Medical Center....68

Penn Medicine....69

St. Francis Hospital -The Heart Center 70
Wills Eye Hospital 71

Physician Listings 73

Adolescent Medicine....75
New England....76
Mid Atlantic....76
Midwest....77
Great Plains & Mountains....77
Southwest....78
West Coast & Pacific....78

Allergy & Immunology 79
New England....80
Mid Atlantic....80
Southeast....82
Midwest....83
Southwest....85
West Coast & Pacific....85

Cardiovascular Disease......**87**

Cardiovascular Disease......**88**

New England......88

Mid Atlantic......91

Southeast......97

Midwest......100

Great Plains & Mountains......107

Southwest......107

West Coast & Pacific......110

Cardiac Electrophysiology......**112**

New England......112

Mid Atlantic......114

Southeast......116

Midwest......117

Great Plains & Mountains......119

Southwest......119

West Coast & Pacific......119

Interventional Cardiology......**120**

New England......120

Mid Atlantic......121

Southeast......124

Midwest......125

Great Plains & Mountains......127

Southwest......127

West Coast & Pacific......128

Centers of Excellence

Cardiovascular Disease

Continuum Health Partners......129

Maimonides Medical Center......130

Mount Sinai Medical Center......131-132

NewYork-Presbyterian Hospital......133

NorthShore University Health System......134

NYU Langone Medical Center......135

Penn Medicine....136
Cardiac Electrophysiology
Mount Sinai Medical Center 137
NYU Langone Medical Center 138
Interventional Cardiology
Mount Sinai Medical Center 139
NYU Langone Medical Center 140
St. Francis Hospital - The Heart Center 141-142

Child Neurology....143
New England....144
Mid Atlantic....145
Southeast....147
Midwest....148
Great Plains & Mountains....150
Southwest....150
West Coast & Pacific....151
Centers of Excellence
Mount Sinai Medical Center....153

Clinical Genetics 155
New England....156
Mid Atlantic....156
Southeast....159
Midwest....160
Great Plains & Mountains....161
Southwest....161
West Coast & Pacific....162
Centers of Excellence
Mount Sinai Medical Center....165

Colon & Rectal Surgery 167
New England....168
Mid Atlantic....169
Southeast....171
Midwest....173

Great Plains & Mountains 175
Southwest 176
West Coast & Pacific 177
Centers of Excellence
Cleveland Clinic 179
Mount Sinai Medical Center 180
NYU Langone Medical Center 181

Dermatology 183
New England 184
Mid Atlantic 186
Southeast 191
Midwest 194
Great Plains & Mountains 197
Southwest 198
West Coast & Pacific 200
Centers of Excellence
Cleveland Clinic 203
Mount Sinai Medical Center 204
NYU Langone Medical Center 205

Endocrinology, Diabetes & Metabolism 207
New England 208
Mid Atlantic 210
Southeast 215
Midwest 218
Great Plains & Mountains 222
Southwest 222
West Coast & Pacific 223
Centers of Excellence
Cleveland Clinic 227
Mount Sinai Medical Center 228

Gastroenterology 229
New England 230
Mid Atlantic 232

Southeast 241
Midwest..........246
Great Plains & Mountains..........252
Southwest 252
West Coast & Pacific..........255

Centers of Excellence

Cleveland Clinic..........259
Mount Sinai Medical Center..........260
NewYork-Presbyterian Hospital..........261
NYU Langone Medical Center..........262

Geriatric Medicine 263

New England..........264
Mid Atlantic..........264
Southeast..........265
Midwest..........266
Great Plains & Mountains..........267
Southwest..........267
West Coast & Pacific..........267

Centers of Excellence

Maimonides Medical Center..........269
Mount Sinai Medical Center..........270
NYU Langone Medical Center..........271

Gynecologic Oncology..........273

New England..........274
Mid Atlantic..........276
Southeast..........280
Midwest..........284
Great Plains & Mountains..........287
Southwest..........287
West Coast & Pacific..........290

Centers of Excellence

Cleveland Clinic..........293
Mount Sinai Medical Center..........294

Hand Surgery **295**
New England 296
Mid Atlantic 297
Southeast 300
Midwest 302
Great Plains and Mountains 304
Southwest 304
West Coast & Pacific 305
Centers of Excellence
Cleveland Clinic 307
Mount Sinai Medical Center 308
NYU Langone Medical Center 309

Hematology & Medical Oncology **311**
Hematology **312**
New England 312
Mid Atlantic 313
Southeast 318
Midwest 320
Great Plains & Mountains 324
Southwest 325
West Coast & Pacific 327
Medical Oncology **330**
New England 330
Mid Atlantic 336
Southeast 354
Midwest 365
Great Plains & Mountains 375
Southwest 378
West Coast & Pacific 384
Centers of Excellence
Hematology
Cleveland Clinic 395
NYU Langone Medical Center 396

Medical Oncology
Maimonides Medical Center 397
Moffitt Cancer Center 398
Mount Sinai Medical Center 399-400
NewYork-Presbyterian Hospital 401
NorthShore University Health System 402
NYU Langone Medical Center 403
Penn Medicine 404

Hospice & Palliative Medicine 405
New England 406
Mid Atlantic 406
Southeast 407
Midwest 407
Great Plains & Mountains 408
Southwest 408
West Coast & Pacific 408

Infectious Disease 411
New England 412
Mid Atlantic 412
Southeast 415
Midwest 417
Great Plains & Mountains 419
Southwest 419
West Coast & Pacific 420
Centers of Excellence
Cleveland Clinic 422
Mount Sinai Medical Center 423

Internal Medicine 425
Mid Atlantic 426
Southeast 426
Midwest 427
Great Plains & Mountains 427
West Coast & Pacific 427

Centers of Excellence
Mount Sinai Medical Center 428
NYU Langone Medical Center 429

Maternal & Fetal Medicine 431
New England 432
Mid Atlantic 433
Southeast 436
Midwest 437
Great Plains & Mountains 440
Southwest 440
West Coast & Pacific 441
Centers of Excellence
Cleveland Clinic 444
Mount Sinai Medical Center 445-446

Neonatal-Perinatal Medicine 447
New England 448
Mid Atlantic 448
Southeast 450
Midwest 451
Great Plains & Mountains 452
Southwest 453
West Coast & Pacific 453
Centers of Excellence
Mount Sinai Medical Center 455

Nephrology 457
New England 458
Mid Atlantic 458
Southeast 461
Midwest 462
Southwest 465
West Coast & Pacific 466
Centers of Excellence
Cleveland Clinic 468

Mount Sinai Medical Center....469-470

Neurological Surgery....471

New England....472

Mid Atlantic....474

Southeast....483

Midwest....488

Great Plains & Mountains....494

Southwest....495

West Coast & Pacific....498

Centers of Excellence

Cleveland Clinic....503

Mount Sinai Medical Center....504

NewYork-Presbyterian Hospital....505

NYU Langone Medical Center....506

Penn Medicine....507

Neurology....509

New England....510

Mid Atlantic....512

Southeast....523

Midwest....527

Great Plains & Mountains....534

Southwest....535

West Coast & Pacific....538

Centers of Excellence

Cleveland Clinic....543

Continuum Health Partners....544

Maimonides Medical Center....545

Mount Sinai Medical Center....546-548

North Shore-LIJ Health System....549

NorthShore University Health System....550

NYU Langone Medical Center....551

Penn Medicine....552

Nuclear Medicine **553**
Mid Atlantic 554
Southeast 555
Midwest 556
Southwest 557
West Coast & Pacific 557
Centers of Excellence
Cleveland Clinic 558

Obstetrics & Gynecology **559**
New England 560
Mid Atlantic 560
Southeast 562
Midwest 563
Great Plains & Mountains 566
Southwest 566
West Coast & Pacific 567
Centers of Excellence
Cleveland Clinic 568
Maimonides Medical Center 569
Mount Sinai Medical Center 570-571
Penn Medicine 572

Ophthalmology **573**
New England 574
Mid Atlantic 575
Southeast 586
Midwest 593
Great Plains & Mountains 601
Southwest 601
West Coast & Pacific 604
Centers of Excellence
Cleveland Clinic 611
Mount Sinai Medical Center 612
New York Eye & Ear Infirmary 613
Wills Eye Hospital 614

Orthopaedic Surgery **615**

New England 616
Mid Atlantic 620
Southeast 635
Midwest 639
Great Plains & Mountains 646
Southwest 647
West Coast & Pacific 649

Centers of Excellence

Cleveland Clinic 655
Hospital for Special Surgery 656
Mount Sinai Medical Center 657
New England Baptist Hospital 658
NorthShore University Health System 659
NYU Hospital for Joint Diseases 660
Penn Medicine 661

Otolaryngology **663**

New England 665
Mid Atlantic 668
Southeast 677
Midwest 682
Great Plains & Mountains 689
Southwest 691
West Coast & Pacific 694

Centers of Excellence

Cleveland Clinic 699
Mount Sinai Medical Center 700-701
New York Eye & Ear Infirmary 702
NYU Langone Medical Center 703

Pain Medicine **705**

New England 706
Mid Atlantic 706
Southeast 708
Midwest 709

Great Plains & Mountains 711
Southwest 711
West Coast & Pacific 712

Centers of Excellence

Cleveland Clinic 715
Mount Sinai Medical Center 716

Pathology 717

New England 718
Mid Atlantic 720
Southeast 725
Midwest 727
Great Plains & Mountains 729
Southwest 730
West Coast & Pacific 731

Pediatrics 737

Pediatrics 740

New England 740
Mid Atlantic 740
Southeast 741
Midwest 741
Southwest 742
West Coast & Pacific 742

Pediatric Allergy & Immunology 743

New England 743
Mid Atlantic 743
Southeast 744
Midwest 745
Great Plains & Mountains 745
Southwest 746
West Coast & Pacific 746

Pediatric Cardiology 747

New England 747
Mid Atlantic 748
Southeast 751

Midwest....752
Great Plains & Mountains....753
Southwest....754
West Coast & Pacific....754
Pediatric Critical Care Medicine....755
Mid Atlantic....755
Midwest....755
Great Plains & Mountains....755
Southwest....755
West Coast & Pacific....756
Pediatric Endocrinology....756
New England....756
Mid Atlantic....757
Southeast....759
Midwest....760
Great Plains & Mountains....761
West Coast & Pacific....761
Pediatric Gastroenterology....762
New England....762
Mid Atlantic....763
Southeast....764
Midwest....765
Great Plains & Mountains....767
Southwest....768
West Coast & Pacific....768
Pediatric Hematology-Oncology....769
New England....769
Mid Atlantic....771
Southeast....777
Midwest....781
Great Plains & Mountains....786
Southwest....787
West Coast & Pacific....789
Pediatric Infectious Disease....792
New England....792

Mid Atlantic....793
Southeast....794
Midwest....795
Southwest....796
West Coast & Pacific....797
Pediatric Nephrology....797
New England....797
Mid Atlantic....797
Southeast....798
Midwest....799
West Coast & Pacific....800
Pediatric Otolaryngology....801
New England....801
Mid Atlantic....802
Southeast....803
Midwest....803
Great Plains & Mountains....805
Southwest....805
West Coast & Pacific....805
Pediatric Pulmonology....806
New England....806
Mid Atlantic....806
Southeast....808
Midwest....808
Great Plains & Mountains....810
Southwest....810
West Coast & Pacific....810
Pediatric Rheumatology....811
New England....811
Mid Atlantic....811
Southeast....812
Midwest....813
Southwest....813
Pediatric Surgery....813
New England....813

Mid Atlantic 814
Southeast 817
Midwest 819
Great Plains & Mountains 821
Southwest 821
West Coast & Pacific 823
Pediatric Urology 824
New England 824
Mid Atlantic 824
Southeast 825
Midwest 826
Great Plains & Mountains 828
Southwest 828
West Coast & Pacific 828
Centers of Excellence
Pediatrics
Cleveland Clinic 829
Maimonides Medical Center 830
Mount Sinai Medical Center 831
New York Eye & Ear Infirmary 832
NewYork-Presbyterian Hospital 833
North Shore-LIJ Health System 834
NYU Langone Medical Center 835
Pediatric Cardiology
Mount Sinai Medical Center 836
NYU Langone Medical Center 837
Pediatric Critical Care Medicine
Mount Sinai Medical Center 838
NYU Langone Medical Center 839
Pediatric Emergency Medicine
Mount Sinai Medical Center 840
NYU Langone Medical Center 841
Pediatric Endocrinology
Mount Sinai Medical Center 842
NYU Langone Medical Center 843

Pediatric Gastroenterology
Mount Sinai Medical Center 844
NYU Langone Medical Center 845
Pediatric Hematology-Oncology
Mount Sinai Medical Center 846
NYU Langone Medical Center 847
Pediatric Infectious Disease
NYU Langone Medical Center 848
Pediatric Nephrology
Mount Sinai Medical Center 849
NYU Langone Medical Center 850
Pediatric Otolayngology
Mount Sinai Medical Center 851
NYU Langone Medical Center 852
Pediatric Pulmonology
Mount Sinai Medical Center 853
NYU Langone Medical Center 854
Pediatric Radiology
NYU Langone Medical Center 855
Pediatric Rheumatology
Mount Sinai Medical Center 856
NYU Langone Medical Center 857
Pediatric Surgery
Mount Sinai Medical Center 858
NYU Langone Medical Center 859

Physical Medicine & Rehabilitation 861
New England 862
Mid Atlantic 862
Southeast 866
Midwest 867
Great Plains & Mountains 870
Southwest 870
West Coast & Pacific 872

Centers of Excellence
Cleveland Clinic 873
Mount Sinai Medical Center 874
NYU Langone Medical Center 875

Plastic Surgery 877
New England 878
Mid Atlantic 880
Southeast 888
Midwest 892
Great Plains & Mountains 897
Southwest 898
West Coast & Pacific 901
Centers of Excellence
Cleveland Clinic 907
Johns Hopkins Hospital 908
Mount Sinai Medical Center 909
New York Eye & Ear Infirmary 910

Preventive & Occupational Medicine 911
Occupational Medicine 912
Mid Atlantic 912
Southwest 912
Preventive Medicine 912
Mid Atlantic 912
Southeast 913
Centers of Excellence
Occupational Medicine
Mount Sinai Medical Center 914
Preventive Medicine
Mount Sinai Medical Center 915-917

Psychiatry 919
Psychiatry 920
New England 920
Mid Atlantic 922

Southeast 927
Midwest 929
Great Plains & Mountains 931
Southwest 931
West Coast & Pacific 932
Addiction Psychiatry 936
New England 936
Mid Atlantic 936
Midwest 937
Great Plains & Mountains 937
Southwest 938
Child & Adolescent Psychiatry 938
New England 938
Mid Atlantic 939
Southeast 941
Midwest 941
Great Plains & Mountains 942
Southwest 943
West Coast & Pacific 943
Geriatric Psychiatry 944
Mid Atlantic 944
Southeast 945
Midwest 945
Great Plains & Mountains 946
West Coast & Pacific 946
Centers of Excellence
Psychiatry
Cleveland Clinic 947
Mount Sinai Medical Center 948
NYU Langone Medical Center 949
Child & Adolescent Psychiatry
Mount Sinai Medical Center 950
NYU Langone Medical Center 951
Geriatric Psychiatry
Mount Sinai Medical Center 952

Pulmonary Disease **953**
New England 954
Mid Atlantic 956
Southeast 961
Midwest 964
Great Plains & Mountains 967
Southwest 968
West Coast & Pacific 969
Centers of Excellence
Cleveland Clinic 973
Mount Sinai Medical Center 974

Radiation Oncology **975**
New England 976
Mid Atlantic 978
Southeast 983
Midwest 988
Great Plains & Mountains 992
Southwest 993
West Coast & Pacific 995
Centers of Excellence
Cleveland Clinic 999
Continuum Health Partners 1000
Mount Sinai Medical Center 1001-1002
NYU Langone Medical Center 1003
Penn Medicine 1004

Radiology **1005**
Diagnostic Radiology **1007**
New England 1007
Mid Atlantic 1008
Southeast 1012
Midwest 1014
Great Plains & Mountains 1016
Southwest 1016
West Coast & Pacific 1017

Neuroradiology **1019**
New England 1019
Mid Atlantic 1020
Southeast 1021
Midwest 1023
Great Plains & Mountains 1025
Southwest 1025
West Coast & Pacific 1025
Vascular & Interventional Radiology **1027**
New England 1027
Mid Atlantic 1027
Southeast 1029
Midwest 1030
Great Plains & Mountains 1031
Southwest 1032
West Coast & Pacific 1032
Centers of Excellence
Diagnostic Radiology
Cleveland Clinic 1034
NYU Langone Medical Center 1035
Vascular & Interventional Radiology
Mount Sinai Medical Center 1036
NewYork-Presbyterian Hospital 1037

Reproductive Endocrinology **1039**
New England 1040
Mid Atlantic 1041
Southeast 1045
Midwest 1046
Great Plains & Mountains 1049
Southwest 1049
West Coast & Pacific 1051
Centers of Excellence
Cleveland Clinic 1054
Mount Sinai Medical Center 1055

Rheumatology **1057**
New England 1058
Mid Atlantic 1059
Southeast 1063
Midwest 1064
Great Plains & Mountains 1066
Southwest 1066
West Coast & Pacific 1067
Centers of Excellence
Cleveland Clinic 1069
Mount Sinai Medical Center 1070
NYU Langone Medical Center 1071

Sports Medicine **1073**
New England 1074
Mid Atlantic 1074
Southeast 1076
Midwest 1077
Great Plains & Mountains 1078
Southwest 1078
West Coast & Pacific 1079
Centers of Excellence
Cleveland Clinic 1080
Mount Sinai Medical Center 1081

Surgery **1083**
New England 1084
Mid Atlantic 1089
Southeast 1103
Midwest 1111
Great Plains & Mountains 1122
Southwest 1123
West Coast & Pacific 1130
Centers of Excellence
Cleveland Clinic 1139
Fox Chase Cancer Center 1140

Moffitt Cancer Center....1141
Mount Sinai Medical Center....1142-1143
Penn Medicine....1144

Thoracic & Cardiac Surgery....1145
New England....1146
Mid Atlantic....1149
Southeast....1160
Midwest....1166
Great Plains & Mountains....1172
Southwest....1173
West Coast & Pacific....1177
Centers of Excellence
Mount Sinai Medical Center....1182-1183
NYU Langone Medical Center....1184

Urology....1185
New England....1186
Mid Atlantic....1188
Southeast....1196
Midwest....1202
Great Plains & Mountains....1206
Southwest....1207
West Coast & Pacific....1210
Centers of Excellence
Cleveland Clinic....1215
Mount Sinai Medical Center....1216-1217
NYU Langone Medical Center....1218

Vascular Surgery....1219
New England....1220
Mid Atlantic....1221
Southeast....1225
Midwest....1226
Great Plains & Mountains....1228
Southwest....1229

West Coast & Pacific 1230
Centers of Excellence
Maimonides Medical Center 1231
Mount Sinai Medical Center 1232
NYU Langone Medical Center 1233

Appendices

Appendix A: Medical Boards 1237
Appendix B: Self-Designated Medical Specialties 1247
Appendix C: Hospital Listings 1251
Appendix D: Selected Resources 1313
Appendix E: Source of Quality Data on Hospitals 1319

Indices

Subject Index 1322
Specialty & Special Expertise Index 1327
Alphabetical Listing of Doctors 1501
Acknowledgements 1569
Corporate Products 1571
Corporate Membership for Employers 1571
The New Movers Program 1572
Healthcare Solutions 1573
Strategic Relationships 1576
Everyday Health 1576
Sharecare 1577
Vitals 1578
Castle Connolly Lifestream MD 1579
Empowered Medical 1580
DrScore.com 1581
Grandparents.com 1582
Consumer's Medical Resource (CMR) 1583
Gluten-Free Directory 1584
National Physician of the Year Awards 1585
Castle Connolly and Social Media 1595
Doctor-Patient Advisor for Individual Consumers 1597
Premium Membership at www.CastleConnolly.com 1597
Other Products and Services from Castle Connolly 1598

About The Publishers

John K. Castle, the Chairman of Castle Connolly Medical Ltd., has spent much of the last three decades involved with healthcare institutions and issues. Mr. Castle served as Chairman of the Board of New York Medical College for eleven years, an institution where he served on the Board of Trustees for twenty-two years.

Mr. Castle has been extensively involved in other healthcare and voluntary activities as well. He served for five years as a commissioner and officer of the Joint Commission formerly known as (JCAHO), the body which accredits most public and private hospitals throughout the United States. Mr. Castle has also served as a trustee of five different hospitals in the metropolitan New York region, including NewYork Presbyterian Hospital, where he continues to serve.

Mr. Castle has also served as the Chairman of the Columbia Presbyterian Science Advisory Council and as a Director of the Whitehead Institute for Biomedical Research. He is a Fellow of New York Academy of Medicine and has served as a Trustee of the Academy. He was Chairman of the United Hospital Fund of New York's Capital Campaign and continues as Director Emeritus of the United Hospital Fund. He is a Life Member of the MIT Corporation, the governing body of the Massachusetts Institute of Technology.

Mr. Castle received his bachelor's degree from the Massachusetts Institute of Technology, his MBA as a Baker Scholar with High Distinction from Harvard, and two Honorary Doctorate degrees.

Mr. Castle's goal, as is the goal of Dr. John Connolly and all the Castle Connolly team, is to publish ***America's Top Doctors®*, *America's Top Doctors® for Cancer*, *Top Doctors: New York Metro Area***, and other materials as well as build websites to help the public identify the very best in healthcare resources.

John J. Connolly, Ed.D., - the nation's foremost expert on identifying top physicians, is the President & CEO of Castle Connolly Medical Ltd. publisher of *America's Top Doctors®* and other consumer guides to help people find the best healthcare. He is also Vice-Chairman of Castle Connolly Graduate Medical Ltd., which publishes review manuals to assist resident physicians and fellows in preparing for their board exams.

Dr. Connolly served as President of New York Medical College, the nation's second largest private medical college, for more than ten years. He is a Fellow of the New York Academy of Medicine, a Fellow of the New York Academy of Sciences, a Director of the Northeast Business Group on Health, a member of the President's Council of the United Hospital Fund, and a member of the Board of the American Swiss Foundation.

Dr. Connolly has served as trustee of two hospitals and as Chairman of the Board of one. He is extensively involved in healthcare and community activities and has served on a number of voluntary and corporate boards including the Board of the American Lyme Disease Foundation, of which he is a founder and past chairman, and the Culinary Institute of America for over 20 years where he is now Chairman Emeritus. He also served as a director and Chairman of the Professional Examination Service and is presently on the board of the American Swiss Foundation. His current corporate board service includes: Baker and Taylor; Air Methods Corporation; Dearborn Risk Management and the Advisory Board of the Hudson Group. Past board positions include Morton's of Chicago and Marie Callendar's-Perkins Restaurant Group. He holds a Bachelor of Science degree from Worcester State College, a Master's degree from the University of Connecticut, and a Doctor of Education degree in College and University Administration from Teacher's College, Columbia University, honorary doctorates (LHD) from Mercy College and Worcester State University.

Over the years, Dr. Connolly has served on the boards of, and as an officer of, numerous not-for-profit organizations including: President, Sullivan County Association for Retarded Children; Director and Chairman United Way of Dutchess County; Director and Founding Chairman Dutchess County Industrial Development Agency; Director and Founder Dutchess County Economic Development Association, President, Westchester County Historical Society.

Medical Advisory Board

Castle Connolly Medical Ltd. is pleased to have associated with a distinguished group of medical leaders who offer invaluable advice and wisdom in our efforts to assist consumers in making good healthcare choices. We thank each member of the Medical Advisory Board for their valuable contributions.

Jeremiah A. Barondess, M.D.
President Emeritus
New York Academy of Medicine,
Professor of Clinical Medicine
Emeritus, Weill-Cornell Medical
College

Menard M. Gertler, M.D., D.Sc.
Clinical Professor of Medicine
Cornell University Medical School

Yutaka Kikkawa, M.D.
Professor and Chairman (Emeritus)
Department of Pathology
University of California
Irvine College of Medicine

Edward D. Miller, M.D.
Dean/CEO Emeritus
Johns Hopkins Medicine
Professor of Anesthesiology &
Critical Care Medicine

Ronald Pion, M.D.
Chairman and CEO
Medical Telecommunications
Associates

Leon G. Smith, M.D.
Chairman of Medicine
St. Michael's Medical Center, NJ

Ralph Snyderman, M.D.
Former President and CEO
Duke University Health System

Roger Bulger, M.D.
National Institutes of Health (Ret.)

Leo Hennikoff, M.D.
President and CEO (Ret.)
Rush Presbyterian-St. Luke's
Medical Center

David Paige, M.D.
Professor
Bloomberg School of Public Health
John Hopkins University

Richard L. Reece, M.D.
Editor
Physician Practice Options

Helen Smits, M.D.
Former Deputy Director
Health Care Financing
Administration (HCFA)

Foreword

The challenge of finding the best healthcare is a formidable one for most Americans and for others who seek medical care in the United States. While this country offers the best medical care in the world, many people are overwhelmed by its complexity and bureaucracy.

While most of us are fortunate and never need to venture beyond our local communities to find medical specialists able to meet our healthcare needs, the needs of many patients cannot be met in their local areas. For them, the search for the top specialists can be as important as life itself!

This great nation is fortunate in possessing some of the world's leading medical centers and specialty hospitals where cutting edge research is conducted and innovative new therapies are practiced daily. These health centers employ and train many of the world's most skilled physicians. The organization which I formerly headed, the Association of Academic Health Centers, serves as a forum of exchange for these centers of medical excellence and, therefore, I know them well. However, I also know well the difficulty and challenges that patients and their families face in identifying and locating the tremendous wealth of medical talent and dedication that lies within the walls of these outstanding facilities.

Castle Connolly Medical Ltd. has dedicated extensive time and resources to identify-ing the best healthcare this nation has to offer. They have done this not to serve physicians or hospitals, but to serve healthcare consumers. Their efforts will be vital and important resources to Americans and others who seek the best medical care available in this country—wherever it is being practiced.

Roger Bulger, M.D.
Former President, Association of Academic Health Centers (AAHC)
Washington DC

Top Doctors Make A Difference

Top Doctors Make A Difference

Introduction

There are times in life when the nature of a disease or medical condition that afflicts you or a loved one warrants identifying the top doctor—the very best specialist anywhere in the nation—to diagnose or treat that particular medical problem. At times like these, you need Castle Connolly's ***America's Top Doctors***®, the national guide designed to assist you under just these circumstances.

While the overall quality of medical care throughout the United States is generally of very high quality and in many places is superb, there are still those rare, complex or extremely difficult problems that demand resources beyond the ordinary or that require talents that are exceptional.

This guide identifies those top medical specialists throughout the country who possess the skill and experience to address these problems. Top specialists who provide excellent care tend to be located predominantly, although not exclusively, at major medical centers, specialty hospitals and leading teaching hospitals. These exceptional physicians are acknowledged as such by their peers and are recognized for their expertise by the medical profession.

The top specialists we have identified are not the only excellent physicians who are caring for patients in this nation. Since there are more than 720,000 doctors in the United States, we cannot identify every top specialist. Therefore, we have included narrative to assist those using this guide who may not find the specialist they need within its listings. Clearly, there are many primary care physicians and other well-trained specialists in communities and hospitals throughout the United States.

Most physicians in this guide are board certified not only in a specialty, but also in a subspecialty or in multiple subspecialties. Board or subspecialty certification alone, however, does not distinguish them from excellent specialists at hospitals in your community, many of whom are also board certified in both a specialty and a subspecialty.

However, the majority of physicians included in this guide have trained at the top medical centers under medical pioneers who possess state-of-the-art knowledge in a specific disease or problem and have often devised new techniques and therapeutic approaches, many of which are life-saving procedures or cures. These doctors most often practice their science and art at leading hospitals and, more specifically, in programs at hospitals that are recognized for their excellence in a given field. Many others have been trained at leading centers in other nations since the U.S. is not alone in pioneering new medical knowledge, although its position as the leader in "high-tech" medicine is generally acknowledged.

Another major characteristic distinguishing the majority of physicians in this guide from those at local hospitals is their continued focus and training. Rather than practicing at a community hospital (or even at a leading regional hospital) and developing a general, broad-based practice, these physicians continued their training in a particular disease, syndrome or subspecialty to such a degree that they developed extensive knowledge and unique skills in treating that particular problem.

Often that focused, advanced training is accompanied by active involvement in clinical research. This is an additional reason why the physicians listed in this guide are located at only a few hundred of the more than six thousand hospitals in the United States. It is difficult, although not impossible, to conduct important clinical research in isolation or without an environment supportive of research. It takes time, money, residents, research associates, technicians, equipment and more to produce significant clinical research. Certainly there have been individuals who have made important and lasting contributions to research with little or none of this support, but those instances are rare. Today, for the most part, major advances in medicine occur in the labs and on the floors of major medical centers and specialty hospitals, in medical schools and in clinical labs created and financed for that purpose by commercial enterprises.

How Physicians Were Selected For Inclusion In This Guide

Castle Connolly's Top Doctors™ selection process begins with surveys of physicians and healthcare professionals. Each year, Castle Connolly surveys thousands of physicians and other healthcare professionals and asks them to identify excellent doctors in every specialty in their region and throughout the nation. When we began the research for the first edition of America's Top Doctors® 20 years ago, we surveyed over 230,000 of the nation's leading medical specialists, department chairs, residency program directors, vice presidents of medical affairs and presidents of the nation's leading medical centers and specialty hospitals. In addition to mail and online surveys, the Castle Connolly physician-led research team makes thousands of phone calls each year, talking with leading specialists, chairs of clinical departments and vice presidents of medical affairs, seeking to identify top specialists for every disease and procedure.

The Castle Connolly physician-led research team carefully reviews the credentials of every physician being considered for inclusion in Castle Connolly Guides, magazine features and website. The review includes, among other factors, scrutiny of medical education, training, hospital appointments, administrative posts, professional achievements, and malpractice and disciplinary history. Information on outcomes, procedure volume and malpractice is becoming increasingly available, but the public disclosure varies from state to state. Castle Connolly uses its best efforts to gather the information that is available and use it effectively. Ultimately, however, it is the professional judgment of the Castle Connolly editors, the Chief Medical and Research Officer and the research staff, which determines Castle Connolly Top Doctor™ selection.

Physicians may also be removed from the Castle Connolly lists if, in the judgment of the selection team, that is warranted. Some of the reasons physicians are removed include retirement, change in practice (taking a full time administrative post, for example), unavailability to patients, malpractice or disciplinary issues, negative physician or patient feedback, professional demeanor or a change in the "mix" of specialists Castle Connolly will present for a given community. Being removed from a Castle Connolly list does not necessarily indicate something negative about the physician.

Castle Connolly does not claim to identify every excellent physician in the nation or a region; it is impossible to identify them all. Those identified by Castle Connolly are clearly among the very best in the nation. That is why our guides, websites and other distribution channels for this critical information describe a process whereby consumers can identify excellent physicians using their own efforts. Furthermore, there are many excellent physicians on the regional level, especially in primary care, that are not included in this guide. Included in this guide are the nation's top referral specialists and those skilled at treating a specific condition or disease; they are found primarily at teaching hospitals, major medical centers and leading specialty hospitals.

How do we accomplish this enormous task? Over the years, the Castle Connolly physician-led research team developed its extensive database of physicians across the nation through periodic mail, telephone and email surveys. This cumulative database is systematically maintained and continuously updated. Surveyed physicians nominate top doctors in both their own and related specialties – especially those to whom they would refer their own patients. Each year this database is supplemented by further mail surveys and telephone interviews with leaders in the various medical specialties and leading physicians at major medical centers.

To augment our large mail, telephone and online polling process, additional surveys are conducted among the following carefully selected groups: directors of graduate medical programs, directors of clinical services at member hospitals of the Council of Teaching Hospitals (COTH), board members of medical specialty academies, associations and societies and deans and chairs of departments at medical schools

Building on years of prior research, thousands of top doctors included in earlier editions of our guides are invited to offer their nominations for Castle Connolly ***America's Top Doctors***®. Beginning in 2011, and moving forward, the nomination process invited every licensed MD and DO across the country to participate. This involved contacting over 50,000 physicians and healthcare executives, a nationwide distribution of nomination notifications via various media channels and partnering with US News and World Report as a means of expanding our process to physicians across the country.

More than 48,000 physicians have been nominated through this process this year. Extensive biographical forms were sent to those physicians most frequently nominated for completion. After careful review of their professional backgrounds, the Castle Connolly research staff conducted further research to check disciplinary, certification and license histories.

We do not intentionally include physicians simply because they have important titles. While a position as a chief of service or a department head at a teaching hospital is an important post, such positions are achieved through a combination of many talents including administrative skills, seniority and factors that are not as important for inclusion in this guide as is skill in clinical care. The same is true of leaders of county medical societies, professional associations or even specialty groups. While these are significant positions and acknowledge a leadership among peers, these titles are not essential to clinical skill recognition.

The same perspective applies to research expertise. Many physicians listed in the Guide are engaged in clinical research and make significant contributions to their fields, with some devoting a substantial portion of their time to research. However, we avoided including those physicians who solely conduct research and who do not provide patient care.

The result of this extensive research effort is a list of outstanding, highly skilled physicians who are recognized as among the best in their specialties and in the nation; a list which consumers/patients can use to find the very best specialists to meet their particular needs.

Lastly, this book differs from the regional Castle Connolly Guides in two important ways. First, Castle Connolly ***America's Top Doctors® 13th Edition*** is national, not regional, in scope. Second, the regional Guides are based on the generally accurate premise that healthcare is local and most people find their healthcare where they live and work. However, Castle Connolly ***America's Top Doctors® 13th Edition*** is designed to meet the needs of those people who cannot find the right specialists locally but who can and will travel anywhere in the country to be cared for by a top specialist at an outstanding hospital. This guide will assist readers in that important search and, for that reason, does not include primary care physicians.

Using This Guide To Find Top Specialists

This guide is organized and planned to be as user-friendly as possible. Still, as with anything as complex as medical specialties, subspecialties and the myriad of diseases and problems that specialists treat, there needs to be a system to organize the physicians' names, the diseases and problems they manage and their special expertise.

To organize the specialists in this guide, we have followed the American Board of Medical Specialties (ABMS) format. The ABMS is the authoritative body for the recognition of medical specialties. Without the ABMS as the official controlling body there would be hundreds of unregulated medical specialties.

The ABMS recognizes twenty-five specialties and more than ninety subspecialties. The listing of ABMS specialties and subspecialties can be found in Appendix A. In addition to ABMS recognized specialties, there are at least one hundred other groups calling themselves "medical specialists" that are not recognized by the ABMS. Some of these groups are working toward recognition and have exams and other standards for membership. Others are organizations of physicians interested in a particular problem or area of medicine that exist to exchange information but have no intention of seeking ABMS recognition. Some groups calling themselves "boards" really have little authority or meaningful standards. Thus, while a physician may state he/she is, for example, a specialist in cosmetic surgery, there is no ABMS recognized specialty by that name. Therefore, you have no idea whether this physician has any special training and expertise or is simply trying to recruit paying patients to a lucrative aspect of surgical practice.

You can get information on a doctor's credentials from the doctor, from the doctor's hospital (Medical Affairs Office) or from your health plan if a doctor is in the network. You can also get this information from numerous Web sites, including www.castleconnolly.com. You can check on a physician's board certification by calling the ABMS at (866) 275-2267 or by logging on to its Web site at www.abms.org.

If you seek a particular type of specialist or subspecialist, turn to the section of this guide covering that medical specialty or subspecialty. There you will be able to further restrict your search to a specific geographic region or, if you prefer, to search throughout the nation.

To make your search easier, we have organized the specialties and subspecialties into the following regions: New England, Mid Atlantic, Midwest, Southeast, Southwest, Great Plains and Mountains, and West Coast and Pacific. To find an outstanding cardiologist in St. Louis, for example, look under Cardiovascular Disease and then under the Midwest region. (See Pages 38-39 for geographical regions and states.)

A second way to use this guide is to look at the Special Expertise Index, which lists the areas of special expertise of included physicians. This list of special expertise indicates more than 2,000 medical topics including diseases, therapeutic approaches and techniques. You can look up the particular disease, problem or technique you are interested in and locate a physician in that manner. We assume that many people using this guide will know what their particular problem is and will begin their exploration with this index. However, we encourage you to read the entire text since it will help you to better understand how to find the right physician for yourself or a family member, especially if one is not found in this guide.

Choosing An Appropriate Specialist

It may seem that choosing the correct specialist to treat a particular medical problem is simply a matter of finding a top doctor in a specific medical specialty. For treatment of a problem with your vision, you would choose an ophthalmologist. A skin or hair problem would require treatment by a dermatologist and a broken bone would need the care of an orthopaedic surgeon.

Sometimes, however, the type of specialist needed may not be obvious. For example, back surgery may be performed by either an orthopaedic surgeon or a neurosurgeon. Different aspects of sports medicine, as another example, are practiced by orthopaedic surgeons who treat sports-related injuries in both adults and children, pediatricians who treat only children or internists and family practitioners whose focus is on prevention of injuries.

In some cases, several specialists with expertise in different areas of medical practice all become involved in treating the same patient's health problem. For example, a person with diabetes might need care from an endocrinologist, a cardiologist and an ophthalmologist. In other situations, doctors trained in different specialties may use varied approaches or differing therapies to manage a disease or condition. Such is the case, for example, with prostate cancer: a patient could be treated by a urologist, a medical oncologist, or a radiation oncologist. The urologist might provide the patient with a surgical treatment option, while the medical oncologist would treat the patient with chemotherapy and the radiotherapist would use radiation therapy and/or radioactive seed implantation. All approaches could be successful, or one might be preferable to another, depending on the patient and his condition. Therefore, a wise patient will thoroughly explore all options before making a choice.

Finding the right specialist is also important in terms of the quality of your care. For example, many orthopaedic surgeons will operate on hands, but it is clearly preferable to have someone trained and certified specifically in hand surgery (a subspecialty of both orthopaedic surgery and plastic surgery) to perform that delicate surgery. Similarly, a dermatologist may indicate that his/her practice includes cosmetic surgery; however, there is no approved ABMS dermatology subspecialty or fellowship training in cosmetic surgery. While many dermatologists do pursue additional training in cosmetic surgery, it should be understood that dermatologic practice is limited to cutaneous procedures ranging from the removal of skin tumors to laser resurfacing. On the other hand, some board certified otolaryngologists have additional training that enables them to perform cosmetic surgery procedures on the head and neck.

Choosing the right type of specialist is as important as selecting the right doctor. For example, the diagnosis of melanoma, a very serious, potentially life threatening form of skin cancer, is missed in many cases. Therefore, if you have a skin lesion that might possibly be melanoma, you should be certain that the pathologist reading your slides is board certified in the subspecialty of dermatopathology.

These examples illustrate this important principle: always seek the best healthcare. Look for the best-trained doctors, not those who simply can do the job. That doesn't mean that you need to consult a doctor listed in this guide every time you have a health problem. It does mean you should be certain that the physicians who care for you, whether in your community or at a world-class medical center, are trained appropriately and are qualified to provide the care you require. Remember, when it comes to healthcare no one wants second best!

Given this complexity, how do you find the right specialist to provide your care? The first and most important person to look to for guidance is your primary care physician. He/she will assess your medical condition, determine the appropriate type of specialist to recommend and perhaps refer you to a specific doctor or doctors. You should always ask your primary care physician why a particular specialist is being recommended, since that specialist may be a colleague in your doctor's medical group or may be the only (or the most conveniently located) specialist of the type in your health plan. Ask how well your primary care physician knows the specialist, whether they have a long-standing professional relationship and if other patients referred to the specialist had successful outcomes. Be sure to ask for several recommendations, if possible, to provide you with some choice among specialists.

If you do not have a primary care doctor, try to learn as much as you can about your medical problem and the type of specialist best suited to treat it. However, keep in mind that many diseases or conditions present with symptoms that often are indistinguishable from those of other diseases or conditions, making them difficult to diagnose precisely even for physicians armed with the results of diagnostic tests.

Judging The Qualifications Of A Physician

The specialists listed in Castle Connolly ***America's Top Doctors***® are clearly among the best in the nation and have been identified through a rigorous research process and thorough screening by the Castle Connolly research team. Through our extensive surveys and research we have done much of the work in finding a top referral specialist for you. But how do you judge the qualifications of a physician who may not be listed in this Guide? If you are trying to find a specialist on your own, how should you go about it? How can you tell when a physician has the appropriate training in a specialty and how do you distinguish what is meaningful and what is not from among all those plaques and certificates on a doctor's wall?

The following pages will outline that process for you. In fact, what is written here reflects much of the logic that underlies the selection of physicians for this book.

The following material will help you not only in finding a top specialist in this Guide, but it also should be helpful to you in choosing among the many specialists, primary care doctors and other physicians that you will need to consult throughout your life.

The reality is that few of us see only one doctor in our lifetime. Each of us may be cared for by a primary care physician, an ophthalmologist, an orthopaedic surgeon, a dermatologist, a surgeon or a number of other specialists. The choices can be many and they can be among the most important choices that we make in our lives.

Education

Your review of your prospective doctor's education and training should begin with medical school. While you may feel that the institution at which someone earned a bachelor's degree could be an indication of the quality of the doctor, most people in the medical field do not believe it plays a major role. A degree from a highly selective undergraduate college or university will help an aspiring doctor gain admission to a medical school, but once there, all students are peers. However, the information on undergraduate colleges, if important to you, is available in *The Official ABMS Directory of Board Certified Medical Specialists*® and other medical directories.

American medical schools are highly standardized, at least in terms of basic quality. A group known as the Liaison Committee for Medical Education (LCME) accredits all U.S. medical schools that grant medical degrees (MDs) and osteopathic degrees (DOs). Most also are accredited by the appropriate state agency, if one exists, and by regional accrediting agencies that accredit colleges and universities of all kinds.

Furthermore, U.S. medical schools have universally high standards for admission, including success on the undergraduate level and on the Medical College Admissions Tests (MCATs). Although frequently criticized for being slow to change and for training too many specialists, the system of medical education in the United States has insured high quality in medical practice. One recent positive change is a strong effort in most medical schools to diversify the composition of the student body. While these schools have been less successful in enrolling racial minorities, the number of women in U.S. medical schools has increased to the point that women now make up about 50 percent of most classes. In certain specialties preferred by women medical graduates (pediatrics, for example) it is possible that in coming years the majority of specialists will be female.

Most doctors practicing in the United States are graduates of U.S. medical schools, but there are two other groups of doctors who make up a relatively significant portion of the total physician population. They are (1) foreign nationals who graduated from foreign schools and (2) U.S. nationals who graduated from foreign schools. (Canadian medical schools are not considered foreign). Those two groups comprise almost one-third of physicians in practice in the U.S.

Foreign Medical Graduates

Foreign medical schools vary greatly in quality. Even some of the oldest and finest European schools have become virtually "open door," with huge numbers of unscreened students making teaching and learning difficult. Others are excellent and provided the model for our system of medical education.

The fact that someone graduated from a foreign school does not mean that he/she is a poor doctor. Foreign schools, like U.S. schools, produce good doctors and poor doctors. Foreign medical graduates must pass the same exam taken by U.S. graduates for licensure, but the failure rate for foreign graduates is significantly higher. In the first year of using the new United States Medical Licensing Exam (USMLE), 93 percent of U.S. medical school graduates passed Step II, the clinical exam, as compared with 39 percent of the foreign graduates. It is clear that the quality of foreign schools, if not individual doctors, is not the same as U.S. medical schools, at least as measured by our standards. Nonetheless, many communities and patients have been well served by foreign medical graduates practicing in this country—often in areas where it has been difficult to attract graduates of American schools. In fact, almost one-third of physicians practicing in the U.S. are foreign trained.

In addition, many foreign medical schools and their teaching hospitals are world renowned for their leadership in medical care, research and teaching and many of the technologies and techniques we utilize in the U.S. today have been developed and perfected in foreign countries.

Residency

Most doctors practicing today have at least three years of postgraduate training (following the MD or DO) in an approved residency program. This not only is an important step in the process of becoming a competent doctor, but it is also a requirement for board (specialty) certification. Most people assume that a prospective doctor needs to complete a three-year residency program to obtain a medical license. That is not an accurate assumption! New York State, for example, requires only one postgraduate year. However, since all approved residencies last at least three years and some, such as those in neurosurgery, general surgery, orthopaedic surgery and urology, may extend for five or more years, it is important to know the details of a doctor's training. Licensure alone is not enough of a basis upon which to make a decision.

Without undertaking extensive and detailed research on every residency program, the best assessment you can make of a doctor's residency program is to see if it took place in a large medical center whose name you recognize. The more prestigious institutions tend to attract the best medical students, sometimes regardless of the quality of the individual residency program. If in doubt about a doctor's training, ask the doctor if the residency he/she completed was in the specialty of the practice; if not, ask why not.

It is also important to be certain that a doctor completed a residency that has been approved by the appropriate governing board of the specialty, such as the American Board of Surgery, the American Board of Radiology, or the American Osteopathic Board of Pediatrics. These board groups are listed in Appendix A. If you are really concerned about a doctor's training, you should call the hospital that offered the residency and ask if the residency program was approved by the appropriate specialty group. If still in doubt, consult the publication *Directory of Graduate Medical Education Programs*, often called the "green book," found in medical school or hospital libraries, which lists all approved residencies.

Board Certification

With an MD or DO degree and a license, an individual may practice in any medical specialty with or without additional training. For example, doctors with a license but no special training may call themselves cardiologists, pediatricians or gynecologists. This is why board certification is such an important factor. The American Board of Medical Specialties (ABMS) recognizes 25 specialties and more than 90 subspecialties. Visit www.abms.org or call 866-275-2267 for more information. Eighteen boards certify in 106 specialties under the aegis of the American Osteopathic Association (AOA). Visit www.osteopathic.org or call 800-621-1773 for more information. Doctors who have qualified for such specialization are called board certified; they have completed an approved residency and passed the board's exam. (See Appendix A for the approved ABMS and AOA lists). While many doctors who are not board certified do call themselves "specialists," board certification is the best standard by which to measure competence and training. Throughout this Guide a description of each specialty and subspecialty is provided as an introduction to the listing of physicians in that specialty.

You can be confident that doctors who are board certified have, at a minimum, the proper training in their specialty and have demonstrated their proficiency through supervision and testing. While there are many non-board certified doctors who are highly competent, it is more difficult to assess the level of their training. While board certification alone does not guarantee competence, it is a standard that reflects successful completion of an appropriate training program. If it is impossible to find a doctor in your area who is board certified in a particular subspecialty, for example, geriatric medicine or sports medicine, at least be certain the physician is board certified in a related specialty such as internal medicine or orthopaedic surgery.

Board certified doctors are referred to as Diplomates of the Board. Some of the colleges of medical specialties (e.g., the American College of Radiology, the American College of Surgeons) have multiple levels of recognition. The first is basic membership and the second, more prestigious and difficult to obtain, is status as a Fellow. Fellowship status in the colleges is meaningful and is based on experience, professional achievement and recognition by one's peers, including extensive experience in patient care. It should be viewed as a significant professional qualification.

Board Eligibility

Many doctors who have been more recently trained are waiting to take the boards. They are sometimes described as "board eligible," a common term that the ABMS advocates abandoning because of its ambiguity. Board eligible means that the doctor has completed an approved residency and is qualified to sit for the related board's exam.

Each member board of the ABMS has its own policy regarding the use and recognition of the board eligible term. Therefore, the description "board eligible" should not be viewed as a genuine qualification, especially if a doctor has been out of medical school long enough to have taken the certification exam. To the boards, a doctor is either board certified or not. Furthermore, most of the specialty boards permit unlimited attempts to pass the exam and, in some cases, doctors who have failed the exam twice or even ten times continue to call themselves board eligible. In osteopathic medicine, the board eligible status is recognized only for the first six years after completion of a residency.

In addition to the approved lists of specialties and subspecialties of the ABMS and AOA, there are a wide variety of other doctors and groups of doctors who call themselves specialists. At present there are at least 100 such groups called "self-designated medical specialties." They range from doctors who are working to create a recognized body of knowledge and subspecialty training to less formal groups interested in a particular approach to the practice of medicine. These groups may or may not have standards for membership. There is no way to determine the true extent of their members' training and neither the ABMS or the AOA recognizes them. While you should be cautious of doctors who claim they are specialists in these areas, many do have advanced training and the groups at least offer a listing of people interested in a particular approach to medical care. Rely on board certification to assure yourself of basic competence, and use membership in one of these groups to indicate strong interest and possible additional training in a particular aspect of medicine. A list of these self-designated medical specialties may be found in Appendix B.

Recertification

A relatively new focus of the specialty boards is the area of recertification. Until recently, board certification lasted for an unlimited time. Now, almost all the boards have put time limits on the certification period. For example, in Internal Medicine and Anesthesiology, the time limit is ten years; in Family Practice, six, and under some circumstances, seven years. These more stringent standards reflect an increasing emphasis on recertification by both the medical boards and state agencies responsible for licensing doctors.

Since the policies of the boards vary widely, it is a good procedure to ask a doctor if certification was awarded and when. If the date was seven to ten years ago, ask if he/she has been recertified. Unfortunately, many boards permit "grandfathering," whereby already certified doctors do not have to be recertified, and recertification requirements apply only to newly certified doctors. Appendix A contains a list of the names and addresses of the boards and the certification period for each board specialty. Even if recertification is not required, it is good professional practice for doctors to undertake the process. It assures you, the patient, that they are attempting to stay current.

Many states have a continuing medical education requirement for doctors. These states typically require a minimum number of continuing medical education (CME) credits for a doctor to maintain a medical license. Seven states require 150 CME credits over a three-year period. Osteopathic doctors are required to take 120 hours of CME credits within three years to maintain certification.

Fellowships

The purpose of a fellowship is to provide advanced training in the clinical techniques and research of a particular specialty. Fellowships usually, but not always, are designed to lead to board certification in a subspecialty such as cardiology, which is a subspecialty of internal medicine. Many physicians listed in this Guide have had fellowship training. In the U.S. there are a variety of fellowship programs available to doctors, which fall into two broad categories: approved and unapproved. Approved fellowships are those that are approved by the appropriate medical specialty board (e.g., the American Board of Radiology) and lead to subspecialty certificates. Fellowship programs that are unapproved are often in the same areas of training as those that are approved, but they do not lead to subspecialty certificates. Unfortunately, all too often, an unapproved fellowship exists only to provide relatively inexpensive labor for the research and/or patient care activities of a clinical department in a medical school or hospital. In such cases, the learning that takes place is secondary and may be a good deal less than in an approved fellowship. On the other hand, any fellowship is better than none at all and some unapproved fellowships have that status for a valid reason that should not reflect negatively on the program. For example, the fellowship may have been recently created, with approval being sought. To check that a fellowship is an approved one, call the hospital where the training took place or call the medical board for that specialty.

Some physicians may have completed more than one fellowship and may be boarded in two or more subspecialties. Also, some physicians may pursue fellowship training and subspecialty certification, but then choose to practice in their primary field of certification. For example, a doctor who is board certified in internal medicine also may have obtained board certification in cardiology, but may choose to practice primarily internal medicine rather than cardiology. For the most part, the physicians in this Guide practice in their subspecialties.

Professional Reputation

There are doctors who meet every professional standard on paper, but who are simply not good doctors. In all probability the medical community has ascertained that and, while the individual may still practice medicine, his/her reputation will reflect that collective assessment. There are also doctors who are outstanding leaders in their fields because of research or professional activities but who are not particularly strong, or perhaps even active, in patient care. It is important to distinguish that kind of professional reputation from a reputation as a competent, caring doctor in delivering patient care, or in the case of this Guide, as an outstanding practitioner in a given specialty.

Hospital Appointment

Most doctors are on the medical staff of one or more hospitals and are known as "attendings;" some are not. If a doctor does not have admitting privileges or is not on the attending staff of a hospital, you may wish to consider choosing a different doctor. It can be very difficult to ascertain whether or not the lack of hospital appointment is for a good reason. For example, it is understandable that some doctors who are raising families or heading toward retirement choose not to meet the demands (meetings, committees, etc.) of being an attending. However, if you need care in a hospital, the lack of such an appointment means that another doctor will have to oversee that care. In some specialties, such as dermatology and psychiatry, doctors may conduct their entire practice in the office and a hospital appointment is not as essential, or as good a criterion for assessment, as in other specialties.

While mistakes are made, most hospitals are quite careful about admissions to their medical staffs. The best hospitals are highly selective, so a degree of screening (or "credentialing") has been done for you. In other words, the best doctors practice at the best hospitals. Since caring for a patient in a hospital is often a team effort involving a number of specialists, the reputation of the hospital to which the doctor admits patients carries special weight. Hospital medical staffs review their colleagues' credentials and authorize performance of specific procedures. In addition, they typically review and reappoint their medical staff every two or three years. In effect, this is an additional screening to protect patients. It is especially true of hospitals that have what are known as closed staffs, where it is impossible to obtain admitting privileges unless there is a vacancy that the administration and medical staff deem necessary to fill. If you are having a surgical procedure and are concerned about the doctor's skill or experience, it may be worthwhile to call the Medical Affairs office at the doctor's hospital to see if he/she is authorized to perform that procedure in that hospital.

The reasons for a hospital's selectivity are easy to understand: no hospital wishes to expose itself to liability and every hospital wants to have the best reputation possible in order to attract patients. Obviously, the quality of the medical staff is immensely important in creating that reputation.

Physicians listed in this guide are primarily on the staffs of major medical centers, usually teaching hospitals, and leading specialty hospitals, e.g. children's, cancer, heart, psychiatric, etc. There are many excellent physicians on the staffs of community hospitals that call themselves "medical centers," but they are not physicians who typically attract complex cases and referrals from outside their area.

To learn about a hospital visit its website. It is also useful to review a hospital's accreditation status under the Joint Commission on the Accreditation of Healthcare Organizations at www.JCAHO.com. A new website created by the federal government, www.hospitalcompare.hhs.gov, offers some measures of comparative hospital quality and may be of interest as well. U.S. News & World Report also offers its authoritative guide to the best hospitals in the U.S., which is available at http://health.usnews.com/best-hospitals.

A last and very important reason why a hospital appointment is an essential requirement in your choice of doctor is that some states permit doctors to practice without malpractice insurance. If you are injured as a result of a doctor's poor care, you could be without recourse. However, few hospitals permit doctors to practice in them unless they carry malpractice insurance. This not only protects the hospital, but the patient as well.

Medical School Faculty Appointment

Many doctors have appointments on the faculties of medical schools. There is a range of categories from "straight" appointments, meaning full-time appointment as professor, associate professor, assistant professor or instructor, to clinical ranks that may reflect lesser degrees of involvement in teaching or research. If someone carries what is known as a straight academic rank (i.e. "professor of surgery," without clinical in the title), this usually means that the individual is engaged full-time in medical school research, teaching activities and patient care. The title "clinical professor of surgery" usually indicates a less direct involvement in medical school activities such as teaching and research.

Doctors who are full-time academicians may be in the forefront of new techniques and research, but they are not necessarily better doctors. Nonetheless, you would be assured that they have the support of other faculty, residents and medical students.

When you are seeking a subspecialist, a doctor's relationship to a medical school becomes more meaningful since medical school faculties tend to be made up of subspecialists. You are less likely to find large numbers of general or primary care practitioners engaged full-time on a medical school faculty. The newest approaches and techniques in medicine, for the most part, are explored and developed by medical school faculties in their laboratories and clinical practice settings. This is where they practice their subspecialties, as well as teach and conduct research. Such leading specialists are not necessarily better doctors than community doctors; rather, they are trained to provide a different kind of medical care. Obviously the type of medical care users of this guide are seeking is that different kind of care available primarily from top subspecialists at leading hospitals and medical centers.

Medical Society Membership

Most medical society memberships sound very prestigious and some are; however, there are many societies that are not selective and which virtually any doctor can join. In addition, membership in many of the more prestigious societies is based on research and publication or on leadership in the field and may have little to do with direct patient care. While it is clearly an honor to be invited to join these groups, membership may be less than helpful in discerning whether a doctor can deliver the excellent clinical care you require.

Experience

Experience is difficult to assess. Obviously, in most cases, an older doctor has more experience; on the other hand, a younger doctor has been more recently immersed in the challenge of medical school, residency, or even a fellowship, and may be the most up-to-date. If a doctor is board certified, you may assume that assures at least a minimal amount of experience, but since it could be as little as a year, check the date of graduation from medical school or completion of residency to know precisely how long a doctor has been in practice.

There is a good deal of evidence that there is a positive relationship between quantity of experience and quality of care. It may be that, the more a doctor performs a procedure, the better he/she becomes at it. That is why it is important to ask a doctor about his or her experience with the procedure that you need. Does the doctor see and treat similar cases every day, every week or only rarely? Of course, with some rare diseases, rarely is the only possible answer, but it is relative frequency that is critical. Major metropolitan areas, especially New York and San Francisco, became leaders in the treatment of AIDS because of the number of patients seen in those metropolitan areas. Doctors in the suburbs of New York City (especially in New York's Westchester, Nassau and Suffolk counties) and in Fairfield County, Connecticut became leaders in the research and treatment of Lyme disease because that region is the epicenter of the disease.

In some states, data is available on volume or numbers of certain procedures performed at hospitals. Likewise, The Leapfrog Group (www.leapfroggroup.org) compares hospitals' performance on the national standards of safety, quality and efficiency - areas of healthcare that are most relevant to consumers and this information is later used to improve hospital quality, save healthcare spending and assist hospital employees with purchasing strategies. The federal government has posted outcome data for hospitals, but for a limited number of procedures, on a website www.hospitalcompare.hhs.gov/hospital-search.aspx. There is a good deal of controversy, however, on the validity and usefulness of such data. Opponents cite the fact that some of the data is produced from Medicare patient records only and, thus, is based solely on an elderly population that does not represent the total activity of a hospital or doctor. Proponents of the use of such volume data agree that it is not perfect, but suggest it can be one useful criterion in selecting the best places to receive care for these specific problems. Other helpful sites include www.whynotthebest.org and www.leapfroggroup.org.

The one type of experience you should specifically want to know about is that dealing with any special procedure, particularly a surgical one, that has recently been developed and introduced into practice. For example, in the 1980's many doctors using laparoscopic cholecystectomy, a then new surgical technique for removing gallbladders, experienced a high percentage of problems because they were not properly trained. This prompted the American Board of Surgery to announce new standards for the training of surgeons using this technique. Do not hesitate to ask about your doctor's training in a procedure and how frequently and with what degree of success he/she has performed it. Practice may not lead to perfection, but it does improve skills and enhance the probability of success.

In some cases, relatively young doctors have recently completed residency or fellowship training under recognized leaders who have developed new approaches or techniques for dealing with a particular problem. They may have learned the new techniques from their mentors and may be far ahead of the field (and ahead of more senior and distinguished colleagues) in using those approaches. So age and experience must be considered and weighed along with other factors when choosing a physician.

Second Opinions

Second opinions are a valuable medical tool, too infrequently used in many instances and overused in others. Clearly, you do not want to seek another doctor's opinion on every ailment or problem that you face, but a second opinion should be pursued in the following situations:

- before major surgery
- if the diagnosis is serious or life threatening
- if a rare disease is diagnosed
- if a diagnosis is uncertain
- if the number of tests or procedures recommended might be excessive
- if a test result has serious implications (e.g., a positive Pap smear)
- if the treatment suggested is risky or expensive
- if you are uncomfortable with the diagnosis and/or treatment
- if a course of treatment is not successful
- if you question your doctor's competence
- if your insurance company requires it

Most doctors will be supportive if you request a second opinion and many will recommend it. In many cases, insurance companies will pay for second opinions, but check ahead of time to make sure your insurance plan does cover them. In an HMO you may have to be more assertive because one way HMOs control costs is by limiting second opinions. Often, the opinion of a second doctor will confirm the opinion of the first, but the reassurance may be worth the time and extra cost. On the other hand, if the second opinion differs from the first, you have two alternatives: seek the opinion of a third doctor, or educate yourself as much as possible by talking to both doctors, reading up on the problem, and trusting your instincts about which diagnosis is correct.

Office And Practice Arrangements

Although clearly not as important as training or reputation, a specialist's office and practice arrangements often are of significance to patients. Practice arrangements include office hours, office location, billing procedures and accessibility among the many factors that result in how well the office is run.

Some specialists only will see new patients who are referred to them by another doctor. Therefore, you may need to have your treating physician contact the specialist's office to arrange for your initial visit. Your health plan may also require that your primary care doctor provide a referral.

If English is not your first language, it may be advisable to determine whether someone in the specialist's office speaks your primary language or if a translator can be present during appointments. This will ease communication and assure that all questions, responses and instructions are understood.

Accessibility of the specialist's office may be a concern if you are wheelchair-bound, are elderly or cannot climb stairs or negotiate narrow corridors. Convenient parking may also be important to you.

Other arrangements that may need to be made in advance of your first visit or discussed with the specialist's office staff concern payment. You may wish to ask the following:

- Does the specialist accept your health insurance coverage?
- Is the specialist within your plan's network and will you need to pay a co-payment? Or, is the specialist out-of-network and will you have to pay for your care out-of-pocket, meet a deductible or submit a form for reimbursement?
- Are credit cards an acceptable mode of payment?
- Does the specialist accept Medicare, Medicaid or no-fault insurance? Does the specialist treat workers' compensation cases?

- If you are a non-resident of the United States, will you need to arrange for the transfer or exchange of currency to pay the specialist's fee?

When you are choosing a top specialist, these issues may be of lesser or greater importance, depending on the problem and type of care warranted. If you are traveling a great distance to have a specific procedure performed by a top specialist at a major medical center, continuing long-term monitoring or follow-up care by that physician may not be required or may not be feasible and such things as office practice arrangements are of less importance. On the other hand, if you have a chronic problem that needs to be monitored with follow-up care provided by the same top specialist, then such issues as accessibility of the doctor's office, appointment hours, waiting times and courtesy and professionalism of the staff become more significant.

Personal Chemistry

One element of the doctor-patient relationship that we stress in our guides is chemistry between doctor and patient, a part of which is often referred to as a doctor's "bedside manner." While this factor is of major import in a long-term relationship such as one you would have with your primary care physician, it is of less importance when you see a specialist only once or twice. However, since many people using this book may have chronic conditions that require ongoing care, it is important to give the matter some consideration.

It is vital that there is a sense of mutual trust and respect between patient and doctor; a judgment that individuals must make for themselves. Among the many talented doctors listed in this guide, there are very likely some to whom you would relate well and others with whom you may not feel as comfortable.

Patients prefer doctors who listen, demonstrate concern, are responsive to patient needs and spend sufficient time with them. The qualities of physicians in this regard, even the excellent ones in this guide, vary immensely.

You, the patient, are the only one who can assess these qualities because individuals react differently to various personalities. It is important for you to carefully judge your feelings towards a physician, especially if you are embarking on a long-term relationship. You should feel you can be open, trusting and responsive to your physician and that your relationship will be a positive one. Otherwise, find another doctor, since not doing so could adversely affect your care.

Once you have used this guide to identify the top specialist(s) best suited to treat your condition, there is much you can do to maximize the value of your first visit.

Top Doctors Make a Difference

The Best in American Medicine
www.CastleConnolly.com

Maximizing Your First Appointment With A Top Doctor

After your research is done and you've secured an appointment for an initial consultation with a top doctor known for his/her expertise in the diagnosis or treatment of your particular medical condition, what should you do?

Whether your visit to the specialist's office is a car ride or a plane trip away, there undoubtedly will be arrangements to make before your appointment. You may have to take time off from work, arrange for childcare while you are away and make travel plans and hotel reservations, but there are a number of other important steps to take to assure that you and the specialist make the best use of the time you spend together.

Have you done everything you can to prepare yourself and the specialist for the consultation? The following checklist will help you maximize the value of your visit to the specialist and will go a long way toward focusing you on the task at hand—getting the best advice or treatment for your health problem from one of the top doctors in the medical specialty related to your condition.

Gathering The Facts

- Does the specialist have all the information needed to make a diagnosis of or treatment plan for your condition?
- Have your medical records, test results and X-rays been sent ahead of time to allow for their review by the specialist in advance of your first appointment?
- Have you written out your medical history, including that of your siblings, parents and grandparents, emphasizing the particular problem for which you are visiting this specialist?
- Are you prepared with a written list of questions?
- Do you understand the answers?

A specialist becoming newly involved in your care needs to learn as much as possible about the state of your health in a very limited time. Since top doctors are extremely busy people with many demands on their time, you should make certain that all relevant records and case summaries are obtained and sent to the specialist well in advance of your appointment.

Obtaining Your Records

All healthcare providers, including hospitals, doctors and their staffs, are under legal obligation to maintain the privacy of your medical records. In order to obtain release of those records, you must make a request in writing. If you need to obtain records from a number of providers, you should write one clear and concise letter authorizing release of your records and including your name, address, telephone number, date of birth, identification number and any other identifying information such as a hospital chart number. You then can make photocopies of this letter, but be sure to sign and date each copy as if it were an original. You also may want to specifically name those test results (e.g., pathology slides) or X-ray films (not just written reports or summaries) that must be included in addition to making a general request for your records. It's also a good idea to indicate the date of your appointment so the office staff can respond in a timely manner.

Although state laws require the timely release of medical records, hospital medical records departments and doctors' offices often take several weeks to pull and review patient charts and get them in the mail either to you or to another doctor. In addition to written authorization, you may be asked to pay the costs involved in copying your records, test results and X-ray films because many doctors' offices will not release the originals. Consider placing a call in advance to determine the procedure for releasing your records, how long you can expect it to take and the costs involved so that you can save time by including payment with your release authorization letter. Be sure to allow sufficient time in advance of your consultation appointment for your request to be processed. Since you often must wait several weeks for an appointment with a specialist, allow at least that amount of time to obtain your records.

Even after making your written requests, you should follow up each letter with a telephone call to be sure that your records actually are sent. You should not assume that your request for records will be promptly fulfilled by an often overburdened, although well-intentioned, office staff.

Remember, the more information the specialist has about your condition, the fewer repeat or additional tests or procedures you will need to undergo, the lower the costs of your consultation and, most important, the more expeditiously the specialist will be able to render an opinion.

The Facts And Only The Facts

Be thorough and organized in documenting your personal and familial medical histories, the medications you take and in relaying information about your condition. Even seemingly minor bits of information may provide subtle clues to the nature of your medical problem and the optimal way in which to treat it. It's also advisable to bring a list with you of names, addresses and telephone numbers of all physicians who have cared for you, especially those you have seen regarding your current medical problem.

Even though thoroughness is essential to presenting a clear picture of your medical condition, bear in mind that the specialist needs to get to your core health concerns as quickly as possible. Therefore, if you have a complex medical history, you may want to ask your current doctors to provide treatment summaries in addition to copies of your medical records. Hospital records should include your admission history and physical exam, dictated consultation and operation notes and discharge summaries for all hospitalizations. You may also be able to get a cumulative lab and X-ray summary for your hospital stays.

Unlike X-rays, which can be copied at reasonable cost, original pathology slides must be transported by mail or hand-carried. Your specialist may wish to have the pathologist with whom he/she works speak directly with the pathologist who initially interpreted your slides as part of the process of evaluating your case.

Being Prepared

You are likely to be a bit nervous when you meet with the specialist you have chosen. Anxiety about your health and concern about your future care may cause you to forget information you should provide or miss hearing or understanding important information that the specialist communicates. Therefore, you may want to write down all relevant information so that you do not leave out anything of importance when you meet with the specialist or complete forms in the office. You also may want to write out your questions in advance so you don't forget anything.

To avoid leaving out important details of your condition or past treatment, prepare a concise, chronological summary before your consultation takes place. You may wish to type it and provide a copy to the specialist for inclusion in your chart. Highlight major medical results or significant events in the course of an illness or treatment if these will enlighten the doctor about your condition. Your personal perspective on the state of your health is vital to a full understanding of your medical problem.

It is possible that the specialist will use language that you do not understand or may speak quickly assuming certain knowledge on your part about your condition or its treatment. Don't hesitate to ask for clarification as often or repeatedly as you may need to in order to fully comprehend what you are being told. If you are concerned that you may forget what the doctor tells you, ask the doctor's permission to take notes or ask if you might bring along a tape recorder so you can later replay what was said, especially any instructions you are given. You may prefer to bring along a relative or close friend to serve as a "second set of ears," but, again, seek the doctor's permission to do so in advance of your appointment.

Following this process will assure that you and the specialist you are consulting get the most from your appointment. After all, you both have the same goal: restoring you to optimal health and well being.

What To Do If You Can't Get An Appointment

At times it may be difficult, perhaps even impossible, to secure an appointment with the specific specialist you have identified. There are a number of reasons why this may occur. For example, the specialist may not be taking any new patients or may have such a busy schedule that it takes several weeks or months to get an appointment. He/she may only see patients during very limited hours because of teaching, research or other responsibilities or currently may have other limitations related to the acceptance of new patients.

However, bear in mind that the doctors in this guide are the leaders in their specialties and therefore they work with and train the very best and brightest in their specialties. So, if you are unable to consult with a particular doctor, consider making an appointment with one of his/her outstanding colleagues. You can do this by asking a member of the doctor's office staff to refer you to an associate who is a member of the practice group or to another excellent physician who is specially trained to address your particular medical issue.

You can be comfortable knowing that you will receive high quality care from another specialist who practices in the same top setting.

Utilizing Special Resources

The following information on special resources has been included to meet the needs of healthcare consumers who have extraordinarily difficult or unique health problems, and have been unable to identify the resources to address their problems. These patients and their doctors may need to search for very new, cutting-edge, perhaps even experimental and not yet approved therapies. In such cases the search may lead to clinical trials; tests of new drugs and new medical devices or innovative therapeutic approaches. Fortunately, these situations are rare, but when they do occur, they are critical.

In addition to the outstanding private and public hospitals recognized in this guide, the U.S. government maintains its own unique, expert source of patient care and clinical research at the National Institutes of Health (NIH). In fact, the NIH operates its own hospital at which the care provided is usually related to clinical studies its researchers are undertaking.

In addition to those at the NIH, clinical trials also are conducted at leading medical centers and other organizations throughout the country. These facilities may be testing a new drug therapy, a new use for an existing medication or a medical device to deal with a problem that is not being resolved through the use of more traditional approaches.

This section will guide you in utilizing these special resources.

The Clinical Trial As A Treatment Option

For some patients the best medical treatment may only be available through clinical trials (also called treatment studies), which are designed to develop improved ways to use current medical treatments or to find new medical treatments by studying their effects on humans. Treatments are studied to determine if they are safe, effective and better treatments than conventional or standard therapies. Only if they meet all three of these criteria are they made available to the general public.

Many people are frightened by the term "clinical trial" because it conveys the notion of being a "guinea pig" in an experiment. Contrary to popular belief, however, most new treatments are extensively studied by scientists in the laboratory before they are ever tested by physicians in clinical settings. Among the factors that keep patients from participating in clinical trials are: lack of awareness about clinical trials as a treatment option; fear of side effects or adverse reactions to treatment; refusal of insurance companies to pay for experimental treatments; failure of a physician to inform the patient about clinical trials; difficulty finding suitable clinical trials; unavailability of clinical trials for certain medical problems; distance of the patient from major medical centers conducting clinical trials; disruption of personal and family life; and the decision to stop medical treatment altogether.

Despite these and other obstacles, many people do seek out clinical trials. One of the most pressing reasons to participate is the opportunity to obtain treatment that might not be available otherwise. New medical treatments can offer participants hope for a cure, an extended lifespan, or an improvement in how they feel. Some participants also take comfort in knowing that others may benefit from their contribution to medical knowledge.

Deciding if a clinical trial is the right treatment option for you is no simple matter. Certainly, you will want to talk about it with your doctor(s) and other professionals involved in your care, as well as with family members and friends. But in order to fully benefit from what others have to say — based on either their professional knowledge or personal experience — you need to understand exactly what a clinical trial is and what your role as a volunteer will be.

Understanding Clinical Trials

Clinical trials are conducted for just about every medical condition, including life-threatening diseases such as AIDS or cancer; chronic illnesses such as diabetes and asthma; psychiatric disorders such as depression or anxiety; behavioral problems such as smoking and substance abuse; and even common ailments such as hair loss and acne. Chances are, there is at least one trial (and probably more) that may be appropriate for you.

With more than 100 different types of cancer, it is understandable that a large number of clinical trials are cancer-related. Extensive information about clinical trials for cancer can be found on www.cancer.gov, the Web site of the National Cancer Institute (NCI). NCI is part of the NIH. CenterWatch, an online clinical trials listing service, identifies over 14,000 clinical trials that are actively recruiting patients. Veritas Medicine, another useful online organization, allows individuals to perform personalized searches of its clinical trials database. See Appendix D for "Selected Resources" for more information on clinical trials.

When choosing a clinical trial you should determine the factors that are most important to you. For instance, patients generally prefer to participate in trials near their homes so that they can maintain their usual day-to-day activities, be surrounded by family and friends and avoid travel and lodging costs. If travel or temporary relocation becomes necessary, try to find a trial site that is near to some family member or friend or one that is in a locale similar to your own city or town. Many organizations, such as the National Cancer Institute, will work with patients and their families to identify support networks for them wherever they participate.

Questions to ask the trial's sponsor about eligibility criteria:

- What are the inclusion and exclusion criteria for the clinical trial(s) I am considering?
- How can I improve my chances of being accepted?
  Can I change my health plan to one that will cover the trial's costs?
  Can I relocate to another city or state?
- If I am not eligible for one trial, what other trials are being conducted for my condition?
- Will I be paid for my time or reimbursed for my out-of-pocket expenses?

Participating In A Clinical Trial

Clinical trials are conducted by a research team led by a principal investigator (usually a physician) and are comprised of physicians, nurses and other health professionals such as social workers, psychologists and nutritionists. As a participant you may be required to commit a fair amount of time to a clinical trial, often more than with standard treatment. Initially, you will probably be given a physical examination and asked for your medical history. During the trial, you will have regular or periodic visits to the trial site which may include diagnostic and laboratory tests. You also may be asked to follow fixed schedules for medications and other interventions and to keep detailed records of your symptoms and health condition. Generally, clinical trials last from six to twenty-six weeks, though some (called maintenance trials) can last up to a year to determine if a treatment will prevent the relapse of a medical condition.

Participants in clinical trials should remain under the care of their regular physician(s) since clinical trials tend to provide short-term treatment for a specific medical condition and do not generally provide comprehensive primary care. In fact, some trials require that a patient's regular physician sign a consent form before the patient is enrolled. In addition, your regular physician can collaborate with the research team to make sure there are no adverse reactions between your other medications or treatments and the investigational treatment.

Questions to ask the research team or your physician about your role in a clinical trial:

- Who are the members of the health team?
  Who will be in charge of my care?
- How long will the trial last?
- How does treatment in the trial compare with or differ from the standard treatment?
- Will I be hospitalized? How often? For how long a period of time?
- What will occur during each visit?
  What treatments or procedures will I be given?
- Will I still be able to see my regular physician(s)?
  Will my doctor and the research team collaborate?
- Can I be put in touch with other patients who have participated in this trial?

Weighing The Benefits And Risks Of A Clinical Trial

If you are considering participation in a clinical trial, you need to consider the medical, emotional and financial ramifications of participation. Of course, the obvious benefit of a clinical trial is the chance that a new treatment may improve your health and prognosis. You will have access to drugs and other medical interventions before they are widely available to the public and you will obtain expert and specialized medical care at leading healthcare facilities. Many patients receive an added psychological benefit by taking an active role in their treatment.

It is important to bear in mind that some medical interventions used in clinical trials may carry potential risks depending upon the type of treatment and the patient's condition. While many side effects or adverse reactions are temporary (such as hair loss and nausea caused by some anti-cancer drugs), other more serious reactions can be permanent and even life-threatening (for example, heart, liver or kidney damage).

Deciding whether or not to participate in a clinical trial is often a matter of determining if the trial's potential benefits outweigh its possible risks. This is a highly personal decision that may be difficult to make in situations involving experimental treatment in which limited medical information may be available.

Questions to ask the research team about the benefits and risks of a clinical trial:

- What other treatment option(s) do I have at this time?
  Is there any chance that a more promising treatment may be available soon?
- What are the short and long-term benefits and risks as compared with standard treatment?
- Will I experience any known side effects or adverse reactions?
  Will these be temporary, long-term or permanent?
  Relatively minor or perhaps life-threatening?
- If I am harmed in any way by the new treatment, what other treatments will I be entitled to?
  Who will pay for subsequent treatment?

Getting Information On Clinical Trials

The more information you have about a clinical trial, the easier it will be to make a decision about whether or not it is right for you, and the more confident you will be that you made an appropriate decision. In addition to the "Selected Resources" appendix in this guide, the staff at your local public library, community hospital, or major medical center can assist you in locating the information you need from books, consumer organizations and on the Internet.

Learning About The National Institutes Of Health(NIH)

The National Institutes of Health (NIH) comprise one of the world's leading medical research centers and the Federal government's principal agency for biomedical research. An agency of the United States Department of Health, United States Public Health Service, NIH encompasses 25 separate institutions and centers with its main campus located in Bethesda, Maryland. Research is also conducted at several field units across the country and abroad.

Patient Care At The NIH

The Warren Grant Magnuson Clinical Center, NIH's principal medical research center and hospital located in Bethesda, Maryland, provides medical care only to patients participating in clinical research programs. Two categories of patients participate in the Clinical Center studies: children and adults who wish to improve their own health, such as those with newly diagnosed medical problems, ongoing medical problems or family history of disease; and healthy volunteers wishing to advance knowledge about the causes, progress and treatment of disease. The patient's case must fit into an ongoing NIH research project for which the patient has the precise kind or stage of illness under investigation. General diagnostic and treatment services common to community hospitals are not available.

The Magnuson Clinical Center is the world's largest biomedical research hospital and ambulatory care facility, housing 1,600 laboratories conducting basic and clinical research. There are 1,200 tenured physicians, dentists and researchers on staff along with 660 nurses and 570 allied healthcare professionals (dieticians, imaging technologists, medical technologists, medical records and clerical staff, pharmacists and therapists).

The Center's hospital is specially designed for medical research and accommodates 540 carefully selected patients who are participating in clinical research programs. Its 350-bed facility has 24 inpatient care units to which 7,000 patients are admitted annually. The Center also has an Ambulatory Care Research Facility (ACRF) that serves 68,000 outpatient visits each year. A new facility, called the Mark O. Hatfield Clinical Research Center, which began accepting patients in early 2005, has 242 beds for inpatient care and 90 day-hospital stations for outpatient care. The Mark O. Hatfield Center carries out the latest biomedical research that results in new forms of disease diagnosis, prevention and treatment, which is then incorporated into improved methods of patient care.

This is a fine example of Translational Medicine where excellent research discoveries are translated into new and improved methods of clinical treatment. In other words, the laboratory discoveries are brought to the bedside.

The Clinical Center also maintains a Children's Inn for pediatric outpatients and their families. This family-centered residence operates 24 hours a day, 7 days a week, 365 days a year.

In an effort to bring clinical research to the community, NIH supports approximately 80 General Clinical Research Centers (GCRCs) around the country, located within hospitals of major academic medical centers.

It is important to note that, as part of the federal government, the Warren Grant Magnuson Clinical Center provides treatment in clinical trials at no cost to its patients. In some cases, patients receive a stipend to help cover the costs of traveling to Bethesda for treatment and follow-up care. Travel costs for the initial screening visit, however, are not covered.

Areas Of Clinical Study At The NIH

At the Magnuson Clinical Center alone, NIH physician-scientists conduct nearly 1,000 studies each year. Among the areas of study are cancer and related diseases.

Not all of these clinical areas are under investigation at any given time, however. The Patient Recruitment and Public Liaison Office (PRPL) at the NIH Clinical Center assists patients, their families and their physicians in obtaining information about participation in NIH clinical trials. Trained nurses are available to answer questions about the research programs and admission procedures.

Cancer Care At The Warren Grant Magnuson Clinical Center

The National Cancer Institute (NCI) is the largest of the biomedical research institutes and centers at NIH. There, clinical studies are designed to evaluate new and promising ways to prevent, detect, diagnose and treat cancer. The Warren Grant Magnuson Clinical Center provides a separate outpatient division for cancer patients and also has several designated inpatient units.

If you are interested in entering a cancer study at the Magnuson Clinical Center (or at the General Clinical Research Centers), you should first discuss treatment options with a physician. As a general rule, patients interested in participating in clinical studies must be referred by a physician. However, in some instances, self-referral may be permitted.

Patients with medical problems other than cancer or healthy volunteers who wish to participate in a clinical study should contact the particular NIH institute responsible for the clinical area involved.

Cancer Care At The NCI Clinical Centers And Comprehensive Cancer Centers

You may also obtain clinical oncology services (education, screening, diagnosis or treatment) or participate in clinical trials at one of the 22 Cancer Centers or 39 Comprehensive Cancer Centers designated by the NCI for their scientific excellence and extensive resources devoted to cancer and cancer-related problems. Centers are located in 32 states, with the majority of sites in California, New York and Pennsylvania. You can find out about clinical trials at the NCI-designated centers by contacting NCI's Clinical Studies Support Center (CSSC) or by calling each center directly. Information about other cancer-related services at these centers also may be obtained from the center itself. For more information, you can visit the National Cancer Institute's website at www.cancer.gov.

Top Doctors Make A Difference

How To Use This Guide

Locating A Specialist

This guide is organized to make finding the right specialists for you or your loved ones as simple as possible. Physicians' biographies are presented by specialty and are organized by geographic region within each specialty or subspecialty. Thus, you may search for a particular type of specialist or subspecialist in one or more regions or throughout the nation.

A second way to locate the right specialist is to use the **"Specialty & Special Expertise Index"** beginning on page 1327. This index is organized according to diseases, conditions, procedures or techniques as well as the doctor's specialty. For example, you can locate a top specialist for diabetes or for Mohs' surgery by looking for those terms in the **"Specialty & Special Expertise Index."**

If you already know a specialist's name, you can find his/her listing by using the **"Alphabetical Listing of Doctors"** beginning on page 1501.

SAMPLE PHYSICIAN LISTING

Smith, John MD [Ped] - **Spec Exp:** Asthma Allergy; **Hospital:** Children's Hosp (page 120);
Name [Specialty] | Special Expertise(s) | Admitting Hospital & Hospital Information Page

Address: 300 Ridge Road Boston, MA 12345; **Phone:** (617) 555-2343; **Board Cert:** Ped 75;
Office Address | Office Phone | Board Certification(s)

Med School: Harvard Med Sch 70; **Resid:** Ped, Children's Hosp 73;
Medical School | Residency(ies)

Fellow: AM, Children's Hosp 74; **Fac Appt:** Assoc Prof Ped, The Med Sch
Fellowship(s) | Faculty Appointment

Geographic Regions And States

To assist you in using Castle Connolly ***America's Top Doctors***® in the most efficient and effective manner, the Guide is divided into seven geographic regions. This will help you to locate a specialist in your local or neighboring region. For example, if you live in Mississippi in the Southeast region and you are willing and able to travel to Louisiana in the Southwest region to consult with a specialist in neurology, you can review just those two regions, under the section headed "NEUROLOGY." However, if you prefer to review the information on neurologists throughout the country, you can search the entire neurology section. Or, you can consult the "SPECIAL EXPERTISE INDEX" in the back of this Guide and choose a neurologist who has specific expertise to meet your particular needs.

The geographic regions are as follows:

- New England
- Mid Atlantic
- Southeast
- Midwest
- Great Plains and Mountains
- Southwest
- West Coast and Pacific

The states that are included in each region are listed on the following page and a map of the regions is also provided. Please note that not all regions are represented in all specialties. For example, in "Geriatric Psychiatry" there are no listings in the Southwest region.

West Coast and Pacific:
Alaska
California
Hawaii
Nevada
Oregon
Washington

Great Plains and Mountains:
Colorado
Idaho
Kansas
Montana
Nebraska
North Dakota
South Dakota
Utah
Wyoming

Southwest:
Arizona
Arkansas
Louisiana
New Mexico
Oklahoma
Texas

Midwest:
Illinois
Indiana
Iowa
Michigan
Minnesota
Missouri
Ohio
Wisconsin

New England:
Connecticut
Maine
Massachusetts
New Hampshire
Rhode Island
Vermont

Mid Atlantic:
Delaware
Maryland
New Jersey
New York
Pennsylvania
Washington, DC
West Virginia

Southeast:
Alabama
Florida
Georgia
Kentucky
Mississippi
North Carolina
South Carolina
Tennessee
Virginia

Top Doctors Make A Difference

Medical Specialties

In the pages that follow, each list of doctors in a medical specialty or subspecialty is preceded by a brief description of that specialty (or subspecialty) and the training required for board certification.

Critical Care Medicine has been excluded because in emergency situations there is neither time nor opportunity for choice. A number of other specialities not relevant to most patients (e.g., Forensic Psychiatry) have not been included as well.

The following descriptions of medical specialties and subspecialties were provided by the American Board of Medical Specialties (ABMS), an organization comprised of the 24 medical specialty boards that provide certification in 25 medical specialties. A complete listing of all specialists certified by the ABMS can be found in *The Official ABMS Directory of Board Certified Medical Specialists*, and is published by *Marquis Who's Who*. It is available (either in a multi-volume directory or on CD-ROM) in most public libraries, hospital libraries, university libraries and medical libraries. The ABMS also operates a toll-free phone line at 1-866-275-2267 and a website at www.abms.org to verify the certification status of individual doctors.

The following important policy statement, approved by the ABMS Assembly on March 19, 1987, remains valid.

The Purpose Of Certification

The intent of the certification process, as defined by the member boards of the American Board of Medical Specialties, is to provide assurance to the public that a certified medical specialist has successfully completed an approved educational program and an evaluation, including an examination process designed to assess the knowledge, experience and skills requisite to the provision of high quality patient care in that specialty.

Medical Specialty and Subspecialty Descriptions and Abbreviations

The following medical specialties and subspecialties are indicated in the doctors' listings by their abbreviations. Specialties are indicated in bold, subspecialties in italics, and the three primary care specialties in bold capitals. To review the official American Board of Medical Specialties (ABMS) organization of specialties, refer to Appendix A.

Addiction Psychiatry — *AdP*

Deals with habitual psychological and physiological dependence on a substance or practice which is beyond voluntary control.

Adolescent Medicine — *AM*

Involves the primary care treatment of adolescents and young adults.

Allergy & Immunology — **A&I**

Diagnosis and treatment of allergies, asthma, and skin problems such as hives and contact dermatitis.

Cardiac Electrophysiology (Clinical) — *CE*

Involves complicated technical procedures to evaluate heart rhythms and determine appropriate treatment for them.

Cardiovascular Disease — *Cv*

Involves the diagnosis and treatment of disorders of the heart, lungs, and blood vessels.

Child & Adolescent Psychiatry — *ChAP*

Deals with the diagnosis and treatment of mental diseases in children and adolescents.

Child Neurology — *ChiN*

Diagnosis and medical treatment of disorders of the brain, spinal cord, and nervous system in children.

Clinical Genetics — **CG**

Deals with identifying the genetic causes of inherited diseases and ailments and preventing, when possible, their occurrence.

Colon and Rectal Surgery — **CRS**

Surgical treatment of diseases of the intestinal tract, colon and rectum, anal canal, and perianal area.

Dermatology — **D**

Diagnosis and treatment of benign and malignant disorders of the skin, mouth, external genitalia, hair and nails, as well as a number of sexually transmitted diseases.

Diagnostic Radiology — *DR*

Involves the study of all modalities of radiant energy in medical diagnoses and therapeutic procedures utilizing radiologic guidance.

Endocrinology, Diabetes & Metabolism — *EDM*

Involves the study and treatment of patients suffering from hormonal and chemical disorders.

Gastroenterology *Ge*

The study, diagnosis and treatment of diseases of the digestive organs including the stomach, bowels, liver, and gallbladder.

Geriatric Medicine *Ger*

Deals with diseases of the elderly and the problems associated with aging.

Geriatric Psychiatry *GerPsy*

Involves the diagnosis, prevention, and treatment of mental illness in the elderly.

Gynecologic Oncology *GO*

Deals with cancers of the female genital tract and reproductive systems.

Hematology *Hem*

Involves the diagnosis and treatment of diseases and disorders of the blood, bone marrow, spleen, and lymph glands.

Hospice and Palliative Medicine *H&PM*

Palliative care relieves the suffering and provides the best quality of life to people suffering from serious and severe chronic illness. Hospice care focuses on the palliation of a terminally ill patient's symptoms and also provides passionate support to both the patient and their surrounding loved ones.

Infectious Disease *Inf*

The study and treatment of diseases caused by a bacterium, virus, fungus, or animal parasite.

INTERNAL MEDICINE **IM**

Diagnosis and nonsurgical treatment of diseases, especially those of adults. Internists may act as primary care specialists, highly trained family doctors, or they may subspecialize in specialties such as cardiology or nephrology.

Interventional Cardiology *IC*

A cardiologist with special training who uses minimally invasive and non-surgical procedures to treat cardiovascular diseases.

Maternal & Fetal Medicine *MF*

Involves the care of women with high-risk pregnancies and their unborn fetuses.

Medical Oncology *Onc*

Refers to the study and treatment of tumors and other cancers.

Neonatal-Perinatal Medicine *NP*

Involves the diagnosis and treatments of infants prior to, during, and one month beyond birth.

Nephrology *Nep*

Concerned with disorders of the kidneys, high blood pressure, fluid and mineral balance, dialysis of body wastes when the kidneys do not function, and consultation with surgeons about kidney transplantation.

Neurological Surgery **NS**

Involves surgery of the brain, spinal cord, and nervous system.

Neurology **N**
Diagnosis and medical treatment of disorders of the brain, spinal cord, and nervous system.

Neuroradiology *NRad*
Involves the utilization of imaging procedures during diagnosis as they relate to the brain, spine and spinal cord, head, neck, and organs of special sense in adults and children.

Nuclear Medicine **NuM**
Evaluation of the functions of all the organs in the body and treatment of thyroid disease, benign and malignant tumors, and radiation exposure through the use of radioactive substances.

OBSTETRICS & GYNECOLOGY **ObG**
Deals with the medical aspects of and intervention in pregnancy and labor and the overall health of the female reproductive system.

*Occupational Medicin*e *OM*
Concentrates on the effect of the work environment on the health of employees.

Ophthalmology **Oph**
Diagnosis and treatment of diseases of and injuries to the eye.

Orthopaedic Surgery **OrS**
Involves operations to correct injuries which interfere with the form and function of the extremities, spine, and associated structures.

Otolaryngology **Oto**
Explores and treats diseases in the interrelated areas of the ears, nose and throat.

Pain Medicine *PM*
Involves providing a high level of care for patients experiencing problems with acute or chronic pain in both hospital and ambulatory settings.

Pathology **Path**
A doctor trained to examine tissues specimens microscopically and clinical laboratory tests, to diagnose and monitor diseases.

Pediatric Cardiology *PCd*
Involves the diagnosis and treatment of heart disease in children.

Pediatric Critical Care Medicine *PCCM*
Involves the care of children who are victims of life threatening disorders such as severe accidents, shock, and diabetes acidosis.

Pediatric Endocrinology *PEn*
Involves the study and treatment of children with hormonal and chemical disorders.

Pediatric Gastroenterology *PGe*
The study, diagnosis, and treatment of diseases of the digestive tract in children.

Pediatric Hematology-Oncology *PHO*

The study and treatment of cancers of the blood and blood-forming parts of the body in children.

Pediatric Infectious Disease *PInf*

The study and treatment of diseases caused by a virus, bacterium, fungus, or animal parasite in children.

Pediatric Nephrology *PNep*

Deals with the diagnosis and treatment of disorders of the kidneys in children.

Pediatric Otolaryngology *PO*

Involves the diagnosis and treatment of disorders of the ear, nose, and throat which affect children.

Pediatric Pulmonology *PPul*

Involves the diagnosis and treatment of diseases of the chest, lungs, and chest tissue in children.

Pediatric Rheumatology *PRhu*

Involves the treatment of diseases of the joints and connective tissues in children.

Pediatric Surgery *PS*

Treatment of disease, injury, or deformity in children through surgical techniques.

Pediatric Urology *Ped Uro*

Treatment of urologic congenital anomalies, and childhood and adolescent acquired urologic problems such as disease and trauma.

PEDIATRICS **Ped**

Diagnosis and treatment of diseases of childhood and monitoring of the growth, development, and well-being of preadolescents.

Physical Medicine & Rehabilitation **PMR**

The use of physical therapy and physical agents such as water, heat, light electricity, and mechanical manipulations in the diagnosis, treatment, and prevention of disease and body disorders.

Plastic Surgery **PlS**

Involves reconstructive and cosmetic surgery of the face and other body parts.

Preventive Medicine **PrM**

A specialty focusing on the prevention of illness and on the health of groups rather than individuals.

Psychiatry **Psyc**

Examination, treatment, and prevention of mental illness through the use of psychoanalysis and/or drugs.

Pulmonary Disease *Pul*

Involves the diagnosis and treatment of diseases of the chest, lungs, and airways.

Radiation Oncology *RadRO*

Involves the use of radiant energy and isotopes in the study and treatment of disease, especially malignant cancer.

Reproductive Endocrinology *RE*

Deals with the endocrine system (including the pituitary, thyroid, parathyroid, adrenal glands, placenta, ovaries, and testes) and how its failure relates to infertility.

Rheumatology *Rhu*

Involves the treatment of diseases of the joints, muscles, bones and associated structures.

Sports Medicine *SM*

Refers to the practice of an orthopaedist or other physician who specializes in injuries to the bone or other soft tissues (muscles, tendons, ligaments) caused by participation in athletic activity.

Surgery **S**

Treatment of disease, injury, and deformity by surgical procedures.

Surgery of the Hand *HS*

Involves providing appropriate care for all structures in the upper extremity directly affecting the hand and wrist function.

Thoracic and Cardiac Surgery **T&CS**

Involves surgery on the heart, lungs, and chest area.

Urology **U**

Diagnosis and treatment of diseases of the genitals in men and disorders of the urinary tract and bladder in both men and women.

Vascular & Interventional Radiology *VIR*

Involves diagnosing and treating diseases by percutaneous methods guided by various radiologic imaging modalities.

Vascular Surgery *VascS*

Involves the operative treatment of disorders of the blood vessels excluding those to the heart, lungs, or brain.

Top Doctors Make A Difference

Top Doctors Make A Difference

The Training Of A Specialist

Excerpted from "Which Medical Specialist For You?" American Board of Medical Specialties, Evanston, IL, Revised 2000

Everyone knows that a "medical doctor" is a physician who has had years of training to understand the diagnosis, treatment and prevention of disease. The basic training for a physician specialist includes four years of premedical education in a college or university, four years of medical school, and after receiving the M.D. degree, at least three years of specialty training under supervision (called a "residency"). Training in subspecialties can take an additional one to three years.

Some specialists are primary care doctors such as family physicians, general internists and general pediatricians. Other specialists concentrate on certain body systems, specific age groups, or complex scientific techniques developed to diagnose or treat certain types of disorders. Specialties in medicine developed because of the rapidly expanding body of knowledge about health and illness and the constantly evolving new treatment techniques for disease.

A subspecialist is a physician who has completed training in a general medical specialty and then takes additional training in a more specific area of that specialty called a subspecialty. This training increases the depth of knowledge and expertise of the specialist in that particular field. For example, cardiology is a subspecialty of internal medicine, pediatric surgery is a subspecialty of surgery and pediatrics, and child and adolescent psychiatry is a subspecialty of psychiatry. The training of a subspecialist within a specialty requires an additional one or more years of full-time education.

The training, or residency, of a specialist begins after the doctor has received the M.D. degree from a medical school. Resident physicians dedicate themselves for three to seven years to full-time experience in hospital and/or ambulatory care settings, caring for patients under the supervision of experienced specialists. Educational conferences and research experience are often part of that training. In years past, the first year of post-medical school training was called an internship, but is now called residency.

Licensure

The legal privilege to practice medicine is governed by state law and is not designed to recognize the knowledge and skills of a trained specialist. A physician is licensed to practice general medicine and surgery by a state board of medical examiners after passing a state or national licensure examination. Each state or territory has its own procedures to license physicians and sets the general standards for all physicians in that state or territory.

Who Credentials A Specialist And Subspecialist?

Specialty boards certify physicians as having met certain published standards. There are 24 specialty boards that are recognized by the American Board of Medical Specialties (ABMS) and the American Medical Association (AMA). All of the specialties and subspecialties recognized by the ABMS and the AMA are listed in the brief descriptions that follow. Remember, a subspecialist first must be trained and certified as a specialist.

In order to be certified as a medical specialist by one of these recognized boards a physician must complete certain requirements. Generally, these include:

1 Completion of a course of study leading to the M.D. or D.O. (Doctor of Osteopathy) degree from a recognized school of medicine.

2 Completion of three to seven years of full-time training in an accredited residency program designed to train specialists in the field.

3 Many specialty boards require assessments and documentation of individual performance from the residency training director, or from the chief of service in the hospital where the specialist has practiced.

4 All of the ABMS Member Boards require that a person seeking certification have an unrestricted license to practice medicine in order to take the certification examination.

5 Finally, each candidate for certification must pass a written examination given by the specialty board. Fifteen of the 24 specialty boards also require an oral examination conducted by senior specialists in that field. Candidates who have passed the exams and other requirements are then given the status of "Diplomate" and are certified as specialists. A similar process is followed for specialists who want to become subspecialists.

All of the ABMS Member Boards now, or will soon, issue only time-limited certificates which are valid for six to ten years. In order to retain certification, diplomates must become "recertified," and must periodically go through an additional process involving continuing education in the specialty, review of credentials and further examination. Boards that may not yet require recertification have provided voluntary recertification with similar requirements.

How To Determine If A Physician Is A Certified Specialist

Certified specialists are listed in *The Official ABMS Directory of Board Certified Medical Specialists* published by *Marquis Who's Who*. The ABMS Directory can be found in most public libraries, hospital libraries, university libraries and medical libraries, and is also available on CD-ROM. Alternatively, you could ask for that information from your county medical society, the American Board of Medical Specialties, or one of the specialty boards.

The ABMS operates a toll free number (1-866-275-2267) to verify the certification status of individual physicians. Additionally, information about the ABMS organization and links to an electronic directory of certified specialists can be accessed through the ABMS Web site at www.abms.org.

Almost all board certified specialists also are members of their medical specialty societies. These societies are dedicated to furthering standards, practice and professional and public education within individual medical specialties. Some, such as the American College of Surgeons and the American College of Obstetricians and Gynecologists, require board certification for full membership. A physician who has attained full membership is called a "Fellow" of the society and is entitled to use this designation in all formal communications such as certificates, publications, business cards, stationery and signage. Thus, "John Doe, M.D., F.A.C.S." (Fellow of the American College of Surgeons) is a board certified surgeon. Similarly, F.A.A.D. (Fellow of the American Academy of Dermatology) following the M.D. or D.O. in a physician's title would likely indicate board certification in that specialty.

The Partnership For Excellence Program

Among the more than 6,000 acute care and specialty hospitals in the United States, many have extraordinary capabilities for superior patient care. These hospitals, renowned for their use of state-of-the-art equipment and up-to-the-minute technology, also attract outstanding physicians and other healthcare professionals. Many of their physicians are among those in the listings in this Guide.

To assist you in your search for top specialists and to supplement the information contained in the physician listings that follow, we invited a select group of these fine institutions to profile their services, special programs and centers of excellence in the *Partnership for Excellence* program. This special section contains pages sponsored by the included hospitals. This paid sponsorship program is totally separate from the physician selection process, which is based upon nominations by physicians and a completely independent review by our physician led research team.

The *Partnership for Excellence* program provides an overview of the programs and services offered by the included hospitals with information related to their accreditation and sponsorship. Most also provide their physician referral numbers, should you wish to ask the hospitals for recommendations of doctors not listed in Castle Connolly ***America's Top Doctors***® 13th Edition.

In addition to the *Partnership for Excellence* program, profiled hospitals were also invited to highlight their special programs or services that focus on a particular disease or medical condition. These can be found in the "Centers of Excellence" sections that are interspersed throughout this book following the medical specialties and/or subspecialties to which they relate. Sponsored pages in the centers of excellence sections reflect the depth of commitment of these hospitals, which provide the staff, resources and financial support necessary to develop these special programs.

By visiting our website **www.CastleConnolly.com**, you may also link to the websites of these outstanding hospitals for even more detailed information on their cancer programs. We believe you will find this informaton helpful in your search for the best healthcare—from both physicians and hospitals—throughout the United States!

Participating Hospitals

- Cleveland Clinic Foundation
- Continuum Health Partners
- Fox Chase Cancer Center
- Hospital for Special Surgery
- The Johns Hopkins Hospital
- Maimonides Medical Center
- Moffitt Cancer Center
- Mount Sinai Medical Center
- New England Baptist Hospital
- New York Eye & Ear Infirmary
- New York-Presbyterian Hospital
- North Shore-LIJ Health System
- NorthShore University Health System
- NYU Langone Medical Center
- Penn Medicine
- St. Francis Hospital -The Heart Center
- Willis Eye Hospital

Cleveland Clinic

Every life deserves world class care.

Cleveland Clinic is one of the largest and busiest health centers in America. Founded in 1921, it integrates clinical and hospital care with research and education in a private, non-profit group practice. Cleveland Clinic is ranked among the top four hospitals in America in *U.S. News & World Report's* annual survey, and is ranked No. 1 in America for heart care.

At Cleveland Clinic and Cleveland Clinic Florida, more than 3,000 full-time salaried physicians representing 120 medical specialties and subspecialties provide for more than 5.1 million outpatient visits and over 157,000 hospital admissions a year, for patients from throughout the United States and more than 80 countries. A major inpatient and outpatient surgery center, it performs more than 200,000 cases a year.

The main campus of Cleveland Clinic occupies 55 buildings on 166 acres east of downtown Cleveland, Ohio. Cleveland Clinic also includes a system of eight full-service Community Hospitals, and 16 family health and surgery centers in surrounding communities.

Cleveland Clinic has a growing international presence. It serves patients at Cleveland Clinic Canada, in Toronto and at the Lou Ruvo Center for Brain Health in Las Vegas. It manages Sheikh Kahlifah Medical City, in Abu Dhabi, and is in the process of constructing Cleveland Clinic Abu Dhabi – a comprehensive clinic and hospital in Dubai.

Cleveland Clinic was founded by four physicians who had served in World War I and hoped to replicate the organizational efficiency of military medicine. They established Cleveland Clinic as a not-for-profit group practice with a mission of patient care, research and education. Cleveland Clinic has grown through the years by adhering to that model.

Cleveland Clinic's integrated structure enables it to control costs, measure and improve quality, and provide access to high-quality healthcare services across a broad regional system.

Cleveland Clinic
9500 Euclid Ave.
Cleveland, OH 44195

Offering Same-Day Appointments
Call 866.320.4573

Treatment Guides
Cleveland Clinic has developed comprehensive treatment guides for many diseases and conditions. To download our free treatment guides, visit clevelandclinic.org/treatmentguides.

Online Medical Second Opinion
Call 216.444.3223 or
800.223.2273 ext. 43223 or
email eclevelandclinic@ccf.org

Out-of-State Patients Assistance
Call 800.223.2273, ext. 55580 or
email medicalconcierge@ccf.org

Visit Us At:
clevelandclinic.org

Follow Us On:
Facebook
facebook.com/clevelandclinic

Twitter
@ClevelandClinic

You Tube
youtube.com/clevelandclinic

Health Hub
clevelandclinic.org/HealthHub

Sponsorship: Voluntary Not-for-profit **Beds:** 2,180 certified beds
Accreditation: Joint Commission of Accreditation of Healthcare Organizations (JCAHO), Accreditation Council for Graduate Medical Education, Medical Society of New York, in conjunction with the Accreditation Council for Continuing Medical Education

A STRONG PARTNERSHIP WITH A PROUD HERITAGE

Continuum Health Partners is a partnership of five venerable health care providers: Beth Israel Medical Center in Manhattan, Beth Israel Brooklyn, St. Luke's Hospital, Roosevelt Hospital, and The New York Eye and Ear Infirmary. Each of the five partner institutions was established more than a century ago by individuals committed to improving health and health care in their communities. Today, the system represents over 4,000 physicians and dentists and is superbly equipped to respond to the health care needs of the populations we serve. Our providers also see patients in group and private practice settings and in ambulatory centers in New York City and Westchester County.

LOCATIONS

Continuum Health Partners has campuses in Manhattan and Brooklyn. Beth Israel Medical Center has two divisions: the Milton and Caroll Petrie Division on the East Side, and Beth Israel Brooklyn. The Phillips Ambulatory Care Center, a state-of-art outpatient center, is located at Union Square. St. Luke's Hospital is in Morningside Heights and Roosevelt Hospital is in the Columbus Circle and Lincoln Center neighborhoods on the West Side. The New York Eye and Ear Infirmary is located on Second Avenue and 14th street.

ACADEMIC AFFILIATIONS

Beth Israel Medical Center is the University Hospital and Manhattan Campus for the Albert Einstein College of Medicine. St. Luke's-Roosevelt Hospital Center is an Academic Affiliate of Columbia University College of Physicians and Surgeons. The New York Eye and Ear Infirmary is the primary teaching center of the New York Medical College and affiliated teaching hospitals in the areas of ophthalmology and otolaryngology.

FOX CHASE
CANCER CENTER
TEMPLE HEALTH

333 Cottman Avenue
Philadelphia, PA 19111-2497
Phone: 1-888-FOX CHASE • Fax: 215-728-2702
www.foxchase.org

Sponsorship	Affiliate of Temple Health
Beds	100 licensed beds
Accreditation	The Joint Commission; American Hospital Association; American College of Surgeons Commission on Cancer with commendation; College of American Pathology; American College of Radiology; American Nurses Credentialing Center's Magnet designation

Overview

Fox Chase Cancer Center, part of the Temple University Health System, is one of the leading cancer research and treatment centers in the United States. Founded in 1904 in Philadelphia as one of the nation's first cancer hospitals, Fox Chase was also among the first institutions to be designated a National Cancer Institute Comprehensive Cancer Center in 1974. Fox Chase researchers have won the highest awards in their fields, including two Nobel Prizes. Fox Chase physicians are also routinely recognized in national rankings, and the Center's nursing program has received Magnet status for nursing excellence three consecutive times, having been the first hospital in Pennsylvania and the nation's first cancer hospital to earn this distinction from the American Nurses Credentialing Center. Today, Fox Chase conducts a broad array of nationally competitive basic, translational, and clinical research, with special programs in cancer prevention, detection, survivorship, and community outreach.

- Fox Chase's 100-bed hospital is one of the few in the country devoted entirely to adult cancer care.
- Fox Chase sees nearly 7,200 new patients a year. Annual hospital admissions exceed 4,800, and outpatient visits to physicians total more than 92,000 a year.
- Fox Chase's board-certified specialists are recognized nationally and internationally in medical, radiation and surgical oncology, diagnostic imaging, diagnostic pathology, pain management, oncology nursing and oncology social work.
- The staff provides a coordinated approach to meet the treatment needs of each patient. Special multidisciplinary centers provide consultations and treatment recommendations for specific types of cancer.
- The nursing staff of specially trained oncology nurses maintains excellent nurse-to-patient ratios.
- Fox Chase investigators have received numerous awards and honors, including Nobel Prizes in medicine and chemistry, a Kyoto Prize, a Lasker Clinical Research Award, memberships in the National Academy of Sciences and General Motors Cancer Research Foundation Prizes.
- Fox Chase maintains the first known cancer affiliate network in the United States. Established in 1986, Fox Chase Cancer Center Partners is a select group of 17 community hospitals in Pennsylvania and New Jersey with Fox Chase-affiliated cancer programs.
- Fox Chase is a founding member of the National Comprehensive Cancer Network, an alliance of the nation's leading academic cancer centers that is dedicated to improving the quality and effectiveness of cancer care.

**For more about Fox Chase physicians and services,
visit our website, www.foxchase.org, or call 1-888-FOX CHASE.**

HOSPITAL
FOR
**SPECIAL
SURGERY**

HOSPITAL FOR SPECIAL SURGERY

535 East 70th Street • New York, NY 10021
Physician Referral: 800.854.0071 • www.HSS.edu
Facebook, Twitter and YouTube @ HSpecialSurgery

Sponsorship: Private, Non-Profit
Beds: 205
Accreditation: The Joint Commission
Web Site: HSS.edu

HSS.edu
Every Musculoskeletal Specialty.
One Comprehensive Web Site.

FIRST IN ITS FIELD

Founded in 1863, Hospital for Special Surgery is a leading tertiary care academic medical center for orthopedics, rheumatology, and rehabilitation.

PIONEERS IN ORTHOPEDIC SURGERY

HSS performs more joint replacements than any other hospital in the world, and more hip and knee procedures than any other hospital in the nation. Surgeries that are rare at other hospitals are routine procedures here. HSS pioneered designs and surgical techniques for the modern artificial knee replacement in the 1970's and has been leading total knee replacement ever since. HSS also pioneered minimally invasive spine surgery techniques that reduce the need for spinal fusion. Our surgeons are also innovators in hand, elbow, shoulder, and spine surgery techniques and are leading experts in arthroscopy and hip preservation.

GLOBAL LEADERS IN RHEUMATOLOGY

HSS rheumatologists are international authorities, academic leaders, and pioneering researchers in rheumatological and autoimmune conditions. They are recognized for their depth of experience in diagnosing and treating the full spectrum of rheumatological diseases, including osteoarthritis, lupus, antiphospholipid syndrome, rheumatoid arthritis, scleroderma, vasculitis, gout, and pediatric inflammatory arthritis, and are valued resources for evaluation of patients who are diagnostic dilemmas. Cutting edge research and treatment centers include the Mary Kirkland Center for Lupus Research, the Barbara Volcker Center for Women and Rheumatic Diseases, the Inflammatory Arthritis Center, the Scleroderma, Vasculitis, & Myositis Center, and the Osteoporosis and Metabolic Bone Health Center.

WORLD'S MOST EXPERIENCED MUSCULOSKELETAL RADIOLOGISTS

HSS is the world's largest academic center dedicated to musculoskeletal imaging. Our experts developed novel MRI techniques that detect early failure of joint arthroplasty and implants. HSS innovations in ultrasound and MRI also allow earlier diagnosis of autoimmune conditions and arthritis.

RECOGNIZED FOR QUALITY

HSS has one of the lowest surgical complication rates in the country as well as top scores for patient safety. For the fourth consecutive year, HSS was recognized by the state for having an infection rate that is significantly lower than the New York State average for hip replacement. 95% of our hip and knee replacement patients receive regional anesthesia, shown to provide superior outcomes with less pain and complications, compared to 11% elsewhere. 92% of patients say they would recommend HSS to their friends and family, compared to 71% for other U.S. hospitals.

Ranked #1 in the Nation for Orthopedics in *U.S.News & World Report* "Best Hospitals" 2013-14 issue. Among the top ranked in Orthopedics & Rheumatology for 23 consecutive years

First hospital in NY State to receive Magnet Recognition for Nursing Excellence by the American Nurses Credentialing Center three consecutive times

Official Hospital of the NY Mets, NY Giants, NY Knicks, NY Liberty, NY Red Bulls, The PGA of America, New York Road Runners for the ING New York City Marathon, St. John's Athletics, CUNY Athletic Conference, and other professional and college teams

Designated as the first National Medical Center of the United States Olympic Committee's National Medical Network

Maimonides Medical Center

4802 Tenth Avenue
Brooklyn, New York 11219
Phone: 718.283.6000
Physician Referral:
888.MMC.DOCS (662.3627)
www.maimonidesmed.org

Sponsorship: Voluntary, Not-for-Profit
Beds: 711 acute, 70 psychiatric
Accreditation: The Joint Commission
American College of Surgeons
American Council for
Graduate Medical Education (ACGME)

Maimonides Medical Center is the Brooklyn clinical campus of the Albert Einstein College of Medicine and is among the largest independent teaching hospitals in the U.S. training more than 400 fellows and residents each year. Widely recognized for major achievements in medical technology and patient safety, Maimonides conducts clinical trials for new treatments and therapies, and is cited for clinical excellence by numerous health care evaluation services.

CENTERS OF EXCELLENCE

Cancer Center

The Maimonides Cancer Center offers a fully integrated approach which includes prevention, screening, diagnostics, treatment, palliative care and clinical research. Staffed by leading physicians, nurses and social workers, the Center provides compassionate, patient-centered, state-of-the-art care.

Heart & Vascular Center

Heart Services

Maimonides is in the top 2% of hospitals in the nation for heart attack outcomes. Its renowned Heart & Vascular Center includes Catheterization Labs, state-of-the-art Hybrid ORs, an Electrophysiology Lab, two ICUs, a Chest Pain Observation Unit, Advanced Cardiac Care Unit, Congestive Heart Failure Program, and Atrial Fibrillation Center.

Vascular Services

The Division of Vascular & Endovascular Surgery offers comprehensive services for patients with vascular disease and associated conditions. In 2013, a new Aortic Program was created. The accreditation of our Vascular Diagnostics Laboratory assures the highest possible standards of care.

Jaffe Stroke Center

The Jaffe Stroke Center at Maimonides received the *Gold Plus Quality Award* from the American Stroke Association. Currently the site of clinical trials for new stroke medications, medical devices and protocols, the Stroke Center offers interventional neuroradiology techniques and telemedicine.

Infants & Children's Hospital

The Maimonides Infants & Children's Hospital of Brooklyn, one of only five accredited children's hospitals in NYC, includes comprehensive inpatient services and more than 30 pediatric subspecialties. The Children's Hospital also has a Child Life Program, Pediatric ICU, Neonatal ICU and Pediatric ER.

Stella & Joseph Payson Birthing Center

Maimonides delivers more babies than any other hospital in New York State. With excellent outcomes, the Payson Birthing Center includes a Perinatal Testing Center, offers the services of doulas, and includes midwifery in a home-like setting using the most advanced technology.

Geriatrics Program

Maimonides serves one of the oldest populations in New York State, with one in four patients over the age of 75. The Geriatrics Program is fully equipped to meet the special needs of seniors and encompasses inpatient and outpatient services.

MOFFITT CANCER CENTER

BEDS:	206
SPONSORSHIP:	Free-standing cancer center, not-for-profit corporation
ACCREDITATIONS:	The Joint Commission, Foundation for the Accreditation of Cellular Therapy, College of American Pathologists, American College of Surgeons Commission on Cancer, American College of Radiology and the National Accreditation Program for Breast Centers, among others

Moffitt is the only National Cancer Institute-designated Comprehensive Cancer Center based in Florida and the No. 1 cancer hospital in the state, according to the *U.S. News & World Report* "Best Hospitals" ranking. Moffitt is licensed for 206 beds, 36 of which are dedicated to the blood and marrow transplantation unit. Moffitt has one of the largest blood and marrow transplant programs in the Southeast, performing more than 400 transplants a year. The Cancer Center has an outpatient clinic with a complete digital imaging center, a radiation therapy department, infusion center, 14 operating rooms, two research buildings, and off-site locations including a screening center for high-risk patients and a 50,000-square-foot outpatient center. Our specialized clinical research unit is dedicated to phase I and early-phase II clinical trials and supports projects with intensive pharmacokinetics and correlative laboratory studies.

Moffitt supports a staff of physicians, known as the Moffitt Medical Group. Most are fellowship trained and are among the best in their respective fields. Physicians, including residents and interns, total more than 300.

Moffitt Cancer Center trains more oncologists than any other institution in the state and has been designated a Statutory Teaching Hospital by the Florida Agency for Health Care Administration.

Our clinical services are organized into disease-oriented interdisciplinary programs with a full complement of services. Moffitt is at the forefront of personalized medicine with its commitment to Total Cancer Care® – a system designed to enable researchers and treatment teams to identify and meet all of the needs of patients and their families. Personalized treatments are a key element to improving cancer outcomes at Moffitt.

REFERRAL INFORMATION: To make an appointment, please call 1-888-MOFFITT or visit MOFFITT.org

MOFFITT CANCER CENTER
12902 MAGNOLIA DRIVE, TAMPA, FL

MOFFITT CANCER CENTER AT INTERNATIONAL PLAZA
4101 JIM WALTER BOULEVARD, TAMPA, FL

H. LEE MOFFITT CANCER CENTER & RESEARCH INSTITUTE
AN NCI COMPREHENSIVE CANCER CENTER

MOFFITT CANCER CENTER®

CLOSER TO OUR PATIENTS.
CLOSER TO A CURE.®

The Mount Sinai Medical Center

Mount Sinai

One Gustave L. Levy Place
Fifth Avenue and 100th Street
New York, NY 10029-6574

Physician Referral:
1-800-MD-SINAI (637-4624)
www.mountsinai.org

Sponsorship: Voluntary Not-for-Profit
Beds: 1,171
Accreditation:
The Joint Commission; Commission for Accreditation of Rehabilitation Facilities;
Magnet Award for Nursing Excellence

For over 160 years, The Mount Sinai Medical Center in New York City has been committed to delivering outstanding health care to patients locally and globally. Encompassing both The Mount Sinai Hospital and Icahn School of Medicine at Mount Sinai, the institution is a leader in medical breakthroughs, innovations in care, and translational research. The Icahn School of Medicine has consistently been ranked by *U.S. News & World Report* as one of the nation's top 20 medical schools, and it is among the top five in the nation in National Institutes of Health funding per investigator. The Mount Sinai Hospital is nationally ranked as one of the top 25 hospitals in 7 specialties in the 2013-2014 "Best Hospitals" issue of *U.S. News & World Report*. Mount Sinai's Kravis Children's Hospital also ranks in seven out of ten pediatric specialties by *U.S. News & World Report*.

Under the direction of Valentin Fuster, MD, PhD, **Mount Sinai Heart** incorporates world-class resources, interdisciplinary programs, and innovative approaches to prevent and treat cardiovascular diseases. In New York State, our Cardiac Catheterization Laboratory was deemed both the busiest and the safest, with the lowest 30-day risk-adjusted mortality rate for percutaneous coronary interventions (PCI). Building on the expertise of our internationally renowned cardiologists, interventionalists, and cardiac surgeons, we provide patients with the most advanced evidence-based medicine, treatments, and personalized care.

The Tisch Cancer Institute coordinates a full-service diagnostic and treatment program for cancer patients, treating cancer of the liver, breast, prostate, and head and neck, as well as hematological malignancies, such as myeloproliferative disorders. Our **Dubin Breast Center** provides advanced detection and treatment - and addresses every aspect of breast health – all in one centralized location. This year, the **Derald H. Ruttenberg Treatment Center**, our outpatient cancer facility, will double in size upon its move to the new **Leon and Norma Hess Center for Science and Medicine**. In addition, the Hess Center will house two full floors dedicated to cancer research.

The Recanati/Miller Transplantation Institute is one of the few places in the country to provide multi-organ transplantation. We were the first in New York State to perform many combined transplant procedures, including liver and kidney transplantation, pediatric liver transplantation, and living adult-and pediatric-donor liver transplantation.

The Department of Genetics and Genomic Sciences conducts basic research, trains fellows who specialize in research or counseling, and educates the next generation of doctors and genetic counselors in cutting-edge precision medicine techniques. **The Mount Sinai Genetic Testing Laboratory** is the leading referral center for clinical genetics and metabolic disorders in the New York tri-state area and one of the largest newborn screening referral centers in the United States. Our Department's genetic testing lab and medical genetics clinic provide expert diagnostic, therapeutic, and counseling services for patients and families with genetic disorders, birth defects, and pregnancy loss.

NEW ENGLAND BAPTIST™ HOSPITAL

Expertise in *motion*

New England Baptist Hospital
125 Parker Hill Avenue
Boston, MA 02120
Physician Referral: **1-855-370-6324**
nebh.org

New England Baptist Hospital (NEBH) is one of the few hospitals across the country and the only hospital in New England to specialize exclusively in musculoskeletal care. NEBH offers nationally recognized expertise in orthopedic surgery, neurosurgery and non-surgical treatments with an exceptional blend of advanced medical knowledge and superb patient care.

Joint Replacement Program: Our reputation as a national leader in joint replacements was built by pioneering innovative surgical techniques and implants. Today, the program is one of the most comprehensive programs in the country equipped to perform replacements on all patients, including those with more unique issues such as deformities, failed implants and revisions, and tertiary problems.

Spine Care Center: The NEBH Spine Center physiatrists (medical specialists in Physical Medicine and Rehabilitation) are experts in the evaluation, treatment and management of spinal disorders. Following evaluation, our physiatrists provide extensive education and information so patients can make an informed decision about surgical and non-surgical treatment options.

Sports Medicine: We deliver the highest quality sports care tailored to each individual's needs and goals. We treat professional and elite athletes including the World Champion Boston Celtics, World Cup soccer players and Olympic athletes and offer this same high level of care to amateur and recreational athletes.

NEBH offers musculoskeletal specialty expertise in all fields of Medicine to support complex cases and high risk patients. Our Musculoskeletal Radiologists and Anesthesiologists are dedicated exclusively to the needs of the orthopedic patient, ensuring accurate diagnosis and protocols designed to reduce operative and post-operative pain.

Consistently ranked as a top hopital in the nation for orthopedics *US News and World Report*

Six-time Guardian of Excellence /Summit Award Winner For Patient Satisfaction by *Press Ganey*

Recipient of the 2013 Patient Safety Excellence Award from *Healthgrades* (Top 5% in the nation for patient safety)

Recipient of the 2013 Outstanding Patient Experience Award from *Healthgrades* (Top 10% in the nation for patient experience)

Becker's Hospital Review 101 Top Hospitals wih Orthopedic Programs

---

Proud to be the Official Hospital of the Boston Celtics and to provide services to many student and professional athletes from across the country.

NY Eye & Ear Infirmary

THE NEW YORK EYE AND EAR INFIRMARY

310 East 14th Street
New York, New York 10003
Tel. 212.979.4000 Fax. 212.228.0664
www.nyee.edu

BEDS:	**69; Operating Rooms: 19; Surgical Cases: 31,000+ a year**
Sponsorship:	**Voluntary Not-for-Profit**
Accreditation:	**The Joint Commission**
	College of American Pathologists

GENERAL OVERVIEW

The New York Eye and Ear Infirmary is one of the world's leading facilities for the diagnosis and treatment of diseases of the eyes, ears, nose, throat and related conditions. Founded in 1820, it is the first and most historic specialty hospital in the nation, as well as one of the busiest.

ACADEMIC AFFILIATIONS

The New York Eye and Ear Infirmary has some of the nation's most competitive and highly regarded residency programs in Ophthalmology and Otolaryngology/ Head & Neck Surgery, plus more than two dozen post-graduate fellowships in subspecialties of Ophthalmology, Otolaryngology and Plastic & Reconstructive Surgery. NYEE is an affiliated teaching hospital of New York Medical College. The Accreditation Council for Continuing Medical Education has awarded NYEE's Institute for Continuing Medical Education its highest accreditation status – "Accreditation with Commendation" as a provider of continuing medical education for physicians.

THE MEDICAL STAFF

The Medical Staff includes more than 600 board-certified attending physicians and surgeons throughout the metropolitan area. Many are renowned for their breakthrough research introducing widely practiced techniques.

SPECIALTIES

Ophthalmology: Within this area are comprehensive eye care, cataract, cornea & external disease, refractive surgery, eye trauma, glaucoma, pediatric glaucoma, low vision, neuro-ophthalmlogy, ophthalmic oncology, ophthalmic pathology, oculoplastic & orbital surgery, pediatric ophthalmology & strabismus, retinal vitreous, and uveitis/ocular immunology. Laser treatments, photographic and imaging services, and electrophysiological testing are among the most advanced anywhere.

Otolaryngology: The department is in the forefront of treatment modalities using highly sophisticated endoscopic and laser equipment. Subspecialties include rhinology, laryngology, head & neck surgery, otology/neurotology, facial plastic surgery, pediatric otolaryngology, audiology, speech therapy and hearing aid dispensing.

Plastic & Reconstructive Surgery: Microsurgical capabilities and premium patient accommodations provide an optimum environment for facial plasty, liposuction, breast surgery and repair of defects from disease or trauma.

RELATED SERVICES

New York Eye Trauma Center: An advanced program for emergency treatment of eye injuries, it also is the Eye Injury Registry of New York State and leading collector of data which will help develop preventative strategies.

Ambulatory Surgery: A comprehensive Ambulatory Surgery Center is designed to expedite admission testing, pre-op preparation and post-op recovery in an efficient and comfortable setting.

Pediatric Specialty Care: Services of eye and ear, nose and throat specialists are coordinated with other professional and support staff especially sensitive to the youngest patients.

RESEARCH AND EDUCATION

The New York Eye and Ear Infirmary is a national and international leader in research in its specialties, achieving many "firsts" in successful surgical procedures and medical treatments. Laboratories include Cell Culture, Ocular Imaging, and Microsurgical Education. Over a hundred studies and clinical trials are currently being conducted.

Physician Referral: Call 1.800.449.HOPE (4673)

NewYork-Presbyterian

Affiliated with Columbia University College of Physicians and Surgeons and Weill Cornell Medical College

NewYork-Presbyterian Hospital
Columbia University Medical Center
622 West 168th Street
New York, NY 10032

NewYork-Presbyterian Hospital
Weill Cornell Medical Center
525 East 68th Street
New York, NY 10065

1-877-NYP-WELL (1-877-697-9355) www.nyp.org

Sponsorship: Voluntary Not-for-Profit
Beds: 2,409
Accreditation: Joint Commission on Accreditation of Healthcare Organizations (JCAHO), Commission on Accreditation of Rehabilitation Facilities (CARF) and College of American Pathologists (CAP)

The #1 hospital in New York. 13 years running. Once again, we are proud to be named the top-ranked hospital in the New York metro area. NewYork-Presbyterian placed higher on the Honor Roll of 'America's Best Hospitals' than any other hospital in the region. This is the 13th consecutive year that we've been recognized to the Honor Roll by *U.S. News & World Report*. NewYork-Presbyterian has the most physicians listed in *New York Magazine's* "Best Doctors" issue and is recognized for having more top doctors than any other hospital in the nation.

Overview

NewYork-Presbyterian Hospital, based in New York City, is the nation's largest not-for-profit, non-sectarian hospital, with 2,409 beds. The Hospital has nearly 2 million inpatient and outpatient visits in a year, including about 13,000 deliveries and nearly 300,000 visits to its emergency departments. NewYork-Presbyterian's 6,000 affiliated physicians and 19,618 staff provide state-of-the-art inpatient, ambulatory and preventive care in all areas of medicine. The Hospital enjoys a unique affiliation with two of the nation's leading Ivy League medical schools—Columbia University College of Physicians and Surgeons and the Joan and Sanford I. Weill Medical College of Cornell University.

NewYork-Presbyterian Hospital Features Renowned CENTERS OF EXCELLENCE Including:

Morgan Stanley Children's Hospital and the Komansky Center for Children's Health— One of the largest, most comprehensive children's hospitals in the world, providing highly sophisticated pediatric medical, surgical, and intensive care services in a family-friendly, compassionate environment.

NewYork-Presbyterian Cancer Centers—Through a multidisciplinary team approach, we deliver seamless care and offer the latest therapeutic options and clinical trials for all cancer types.

NewYork-Presbyterian Digestive Disease Services—Our collaborative team manages and treats patients with digestive cancers and nonmalignant digestive diseases, such as inflammatory bowel disease, pancreatic and biliary disorders, and colorectal cancer with compassionate care.

NewYork-Presbyterian Heart—Advances in cardiac care—from clinical cardiology, to interventional procedures, to surgical solutions—offer outstanding outcomes to adult and pediatric heart patients.

NewYork-Presbyterian Neuroscience Centers—Expert teams provide the most sophisticated diagnostic and treatment services for Alzheimer's disease, multiple sclerosis, Parkinson's disease, aneurysms, epilepsy, brain tumors, strokes, and other neurological disorders.

NewYork-Presbyterian Psychiatry—NewYork-Presbyterian Hospital's behavioral health and psychiatric services for adults, children, and adolescents offer a full continuum of programs at all levels of care.

NewYork-Presbyterian Transplant Institute—Our experts are internationally known for performing adult and pediatric heart, liver, kidney, pancreas, lung, bone marrow/stem cell, and intestinal and ex vivo transplantation.

NewYork-Presbyterian Vascular Care Center—We provide comprehensive, multidisciplinary preventive, diagnostic, and treatment services for aortic aneurysm, carotid artery disease, blood clots, and peripheral vascular diseases.

William Randolph Hearst Burn Center—NewYork-Presbyterian Hospital is home to the largest and busiest burn center in the nation, caring for more than 5,000 patients annually.

In addition, we offer extraordinary expertise, comprehensive programs, and specialized resources in the fields of AIDS, reproductive medicine and infertility, trauma care, and women's health.

NorthShore University HealthSystem
Evanston Hospital Glenbrook Hospital Highland Park Hospital Skokie Hospital
A teaching affiliate of the University of Chicago Pritzker School of Medicine

NorthShore University HealthSystem
2650 Ridge Avenue, Evanston, IL 60201
Patient Access: (847) 364-6400
Physician Referral: (847) 570-5020
northshore.org

NorthShore University HealthSystem provides comprehensive, fully integrated healthcare to the Chicago region with a vast network of medical experts, four award-winning hospitals and 2,200 affiliated physicians. Many of NorthShore's physicians are on faculty at the University of Chicago Pritzker School of Medicine. Through **NorthShore's collaboration with Mayo Clinic**, patients have access to two leading teams, working together on the most complex cases.

NorthShore Medical Group is an 850-plus physician network that offers both primary and specialty care at more than 100 offices throughout Cook and Lake Counties.

NorthShore Kellogg Cancer Center has specialists in every type of cancer and includes often overlooked components of cancer care, such as nutrition and psychological support.

NorthShore Cardiovascular Services delivers comprehensive treatment of heart disease, with particular strengths in interventional cardiology, radiology, clinical cardiology, cardiac and vascular surgery.

NORTHSHORE UNIVERSITY HEALTHSYSTEM CENTERS OF EXCELLENCE:

- Kellogg Cancer Center
- Cardiovascular Services
- Gastroenterology Services
- Orthopaedic Services
- Neurological Institute

The board-certified physicians at **NorthShore Gastroenterology Services** treat a wide range of digestive disorders. They are committed to early diagnosis and prevention of colorectal, esophageal and pancreatic cancers and other GI conditions.

NorthShore Orthopaedic Services provides complete care for any orthopaedic challenge, using the latest techniques, including minimally invasive, computer-aided and customized surgical procedures. Their treatment plans focus on immediate relief and long-term recovery.

NorthShore Neurological Institute is renowned for finding innovative answers to difficult neurological challenges like Parkinson's, multiple sclerosis, epilepsy, brain tumors and concussions.

With nearly 1,000 active research studies, **NorthShore Research Institute** is at the forefront of medical advancement, speeding findings from the lab to clinical trial.

NorthShore's advanced Electronic Medical Record system connects everyone caring for a patient, allowing them to share up-to-date treatment information. **NorthShore*Connect*** lets patients view test results, email doctors, schedule appointments, renew prescriptions and more, online or through a mobile app.

NorthShore University HealthSystem's comprehensive care is making make life healthier for Chicagoland families.

NYU Langone
MEDICAL CENTER

550 First Avenue *(at 31st Street)*
New York, NY 10016

www.NYULMC.org

Physician Referral: **888-7-NYU-MED** *(888-769-8633)*

NYU LANGONE MEDICAL CENTER

NYU Langone Medical Center—a world-class, patient-centered, integrated, academic medical center—is one of the nation's premier destinations for excellence in patient care, biomedical research, and medical education. Located in the heart of Manhattan, NYU Langone is composed of Tisch Hospital, its flagship acute care facility; the Hospital for Joint Diseases, a dedicated inpatient orthopaedic hospital; Hassenfeld Children's Hospital, a comprehensive pediatric hospital supporting a full array of children's health services; Rusk Rehabilitation, the #1 rehab program in New York since *U.S. News & World Report* began its hospital rankings in 1989; and a growing ambulatory care network with locations throughout Manhattan, the outer boroughs, and the tri-state area, bringing services directly to where its patients live and work.

In a culture where treating the whole person and not simply the disease is the norm, NYU Langone Medical Center is renowned for clinical excellence across a wide array of specialties, including cancer, cardiology, cardiac and vascular surgery, musculoskeletal (including orthopaedics and rehabilitation), neurosurgery and children's services.

An integral part of NYU Langone, NYU School of Medicine has trained thousands of physicians and scientists who have helped to shape the course of medical history and enrich the lives of countless people since 1841. NYU Langone's tri-fold mission to serve, teach, and discover is achieved 365 days a year. For more information, go to www.NYULMC.org, Facebook, Twitter, and YouTube.

For more than two centuries, Penn physicians and scientists have been committed to the highest standards of patient care, education and research. That commitment has been recognized throughout the Greater Philadelphia region and across the nation.

Penn Medicine received $397 million in research grant funding from the National Institutes of Health in 2011, making Penn the third highest funded medical school in the country. *U.S. News & World Report* also consistently ranks Penn Medicine, the Perelman School of Medicine and the School of Nursing among the nation's best.

What Sets Penn Apart?

Penn's physicians and scientists are united in the health system's mission to expand the frontiers of medicine through new discoveries in the detection, treatment and prevention of human disease. Because they develop and test new treatments through clinical trials, their patients gain access to the very latest advances and future generations will benefit from the work they do today.

Penn continues to lead the way in discovering new treatment methods for diseases once considered incurable, including groundbreaking research in cancer, cardiac, neurosciences, orthopaedics, genetics and imaging. Over the past 30 years, Penn physicians and scientists have participated in many important discoveries, including:

- The first general vaccine against pneumonia.
- The introduction of total intravenous feeding.
- The development of cognitive therapy.
- The development of magnetic resonance imaging and other imaging technologies.
- The development of a treatment for patients with chronic lymphocytic leukemia using genetically engineered versions of their own T-cells.
- The development of techniques to minimize complications associated with Transcatheter Aortic Valve Replacement.
- Pioneering new procedures in robotic-assisted surgery.

Locations

Patients are seen at:

- Hospital of the University of Pennsylvania
- Penn Presbyterian Medical Center
- Pennsylvania Hospital
- Penn Medicine Bucks County
- Penn Medicine Cherry Hill
- Penn Medicine Media
- Penn Medicine Radnor
- Penn Medicine Rittenhouse
- Penn Medicine Valley Forge
- Penn Medicine Woodbury Heights
- Penn's primary care physician network provides services in the local communities in Bucks, Chester, Delaware, Montgomery and Philadelphia counties in Pennsylvania and in Southern New Jersey.
- Hospice and home care services are provided by Penn Home Care and Hospice Services.

On the Web

Visit **PennMedicine.org** for the latest patient education with explanation of surgical procedures and follow-up care, screening tools, drug interactions and descriptions, as well as an encyclopedia of health information.

For more information or to schedule an appointment, call 800.789.PENN (7366) or visit PennMedicine.org.

St. Francis Hospital, The Heart Center®
Catholic Health Services
At the heart of health

100 Port Washington Blvd.
Roslyn, New York 11576
www.stfrancisheartcenter.com
(516) 562-6000
1-888-HEARTNY

St. Francis Hospital, The Heart Center® is New York State's only specialty designated cardiac center and a nationally recognized leader in cardiac care. Founded in 1922 by the Franciscan Missionaries of Mary, the Hospital is an innovator in the delivery of specialized cardiovascular services in an environment where excellence and compassion are emphasized. St. Francis also offers a nationally recognized program in non-cardiac surgery, including some of the most advanced technology and minimally invasive techniques available for vascular, prostate, ear-nose-throat (ENT), abdominal, oncologic, gastrointestinal, and orthopedic surgery and procedures.

Cardiac Diagnostics and Treatment

St. Francis Hospital performs one of the highest volumes of cardiac surgical, interventional and arrhythmia procedures in the nation and has been consistently recognized for its outstanding quality of care. In 2013-14, St. Francis Hospital was ranked one of America's top 10 hospitals in cardiology and heart surgery by *U.S. News & World Report*.

Cardiac surgery: In 2012, 1,337 open-heart surgeries were performed at St. Francis Hospital. The Hospital's cardiothoracic surgical staff has the combined experience of over 16,000 open-heart procedures in the last 10 years alone and are experts in all types of heart surgery, from conventional, open-heart bypass to off-pump coronary artery bypass (OPCAB) to the newest, minimally invasive valve procedures, including surgical techniques designed to treat certain cardiac arrhythmias or irregular heart rhythms.

Cardiac catheterization: In 2012, St. Francis interventional cardiologists performed 10,025 cardiac catheterizations and 2,719 percutaneous coronary interventions (angioplasty with stents) and other cardiac and peripheral vascular interventions. The Hospital is also recognized as one of the East Coast's highest volume centers for catheter-based techniques to repair congenital heart defects.

Arrhythmia and Pacemaker Center: St. Francis has a leading national program for pacemaker implantation and the diagnosis and treatment of cardiac rhythm abnormalities. The Center has unparalleled expertise in radiofrequency cardiac ablation, including treatment of atrial fibrillation.

Research and Technology: At the St. Francis Cardiac Research Institute, a team of world-renowned researchers is working with the latest noninvasive imaging technology, including advanced techniques and world-class expertise in cardiac CT angiography, cardiac magnetic resonance imaging (MRI), cardiac PET/CT and three-dimensional echocardiography. This multimodality approach to investigating the heart's function and disease processes is aimed at improving methods of diagnosing heart disease.

Broad-Based Excellence

St. Francis Hospital is also ranked one of America's best hospitals in ear, nose and throat; gastroenterology and GI surgery; geriatrics; neurology and neurosurgery; orthopedics; pulmonology; and urology by *U.S. News & World Report*. In 2012, the Hospital opened a new Cancer Institute, which brings together all of the essential elements for an integrated approach to treating cancer with the Hospital's signature commitment to quality and compassionate care.

Physician referral:	**1-888-HEARTNY**
Sponsorship:	Voluntary not-for-profit
Beds:	306
Accreditation:	Awarded accreditation from the Joint Commission.

Wills Eye Hospital has more ophthalmologists listed in Castle Connolly's *America's Top Doctors® 2013* than any hospital in the U.S.

With more than 200 ophthalmologists on staff, Wills Eye's clinical expertise, state-of-the-art diagnostic testing, and advanced surgical capabilities make it a worldwide referral center where more than 300,000 patients are treated annually. Today, we continue to shape the science and medicine of ophthalmology, thanks to our talented, skilled physicians and staff who are dedicated to improving and preserving sight.

Complex Ocular Surgery Center

In the Wills Eye surgical suite, every member of the surgical team strives to provide world-class care. Patients with complicated eye problems have the comfort of knowing that our ophthalmologists have the advanced skills, knowledge, and expertise that can lead to superior outcomes in complex cases.

Diagnostic Testing Center

Our specialized testing center is one of the largest such facilities in the country and assists Wills Eye physicians in the diagnosis and treatment of ocular disease. Testing procedures include: visual fields, optical coherence tomography, ultrasounds, electrophysiology, and anterior segment imaging.

Eye Emergency Department

As the Philadelphia region's only emergency eye care center and one of the few remaining 24/7 eye emergency departments in the country, Wills Eye's Emergency Department provides state-of-the-art care at our Center City location. We treat a wide range of eye problems, from infections to major trauma, and support many community and local hospitals in the region that cannot offer in-depth ophthalmic emergency coverage on their own.

Research

One of the core strengths at Wills Eye is the close connection between innovative research and advanced patient care. Our ophthalmologists pursue research that can be translated quickly to clinical care in areas such as glaucoma, ocular cancers, retinal and corneal diseases.

Wills Eye Surgical Network

Our clinical expertise and dedication to patient care is available at Wills Eye's flagship location in Center City Philadelphia and at our network of same-day surgical centers throughout the Tri-State region. All of our facilities are designed to provide patients with a high quality, safe and comfortable experience.

Medical Services

Cataract & Primary Eye Care: Comprehensive eye exams, cataract surgery, cataract screenings.
Cornea: Treatment for disorders of the cornea, and laser vision correction to treat nearsightedness, astigmatism, and farsightedness.
Glaucoma: One of the largest glaucoma treatment centers in the U.S., featuring a multi-pronged approach of surgical techniques, devices, and medicines to tackle glaucoma-related vision loss and blindness.
Neuro-Ophthalmology: Diagnosis and treatment of disorders affecting the nerves and muscles in and around the eye, as well as ocular manifestations of conditions such as thyroid eye disease.
Ocular Oncology: Largest eye cancer center in the U.S. providing treatment for common and rare cancers.
Oculoplastic & Orbital Surgery: Treatment of the area in and around the eye, specifically for the eyelids, orbit, and tear duct systems.
Pediatric Ophthalmology & Ocular Genetics: Management of eye problems in children, including strabismus, amblyopia, cataracts, and glaucoma, and research into new treatments. Family-oriented team evaluations and treatment of genetic eye and systemic disorders.
Retina: Comprehensive management of medical and surgical diseases that affect the retina, such as age-related macular degeneration and diabetic retinopathy.

Top Doctors Make A Difference

Physician Listings

Top Doctors Make A Difference

Adolescent Medicine

a subspecialty of Pediatrics

An internist or pediatrician who specializes in adolescent medicine is a multidiciplinary healthcare specialist trained in the unique physical, psychological and social characteristics of adolescents, their healthcare problems and needs.

Training Required: Three years in internal medicine OR three years in pediatrics *plus* additional training and examination for certification in adolescent medicine

ADOLESCENT MEDICINE

New England

Emans, Sarah Jean H MD [AM] - **Spec Exp:** Pediatric Gynecology; Adolescent Gynecology; **Hospital:** Children's Hospital - Boston; **Address:** Childrens Hosp, Dept Adolescent Med, 300 Longwood Ave, Boston, MA 02115-5724; **Phone:** 617-355-7170; **Board Cert:** Pediatrics 1993; Adolescent Medicine 2009; **Med School:** Harvard Med Sch 1970; **Resid:** Pediatrics, Chldns Hosp 1973; **Fellow:** Adolescent Medicine, Chldns Hosp 1975; **Fac Appt:** Prof Ped, Harvard Med Sch

Mid Atlantic

Adger Jr, Hoover MD [AM] - **Spec Exp:** Addiction/Substance Abuse; Opiate Addiction; **Hospital:** Johns Hopkins Hosp (page 59); **Address:** Johns Hopkins Harriet Lane Clinic, 200 N Wolfe St, rm 2065, Rubenstein Child Hlth Bldg, Baltimore, MD 21287; **Phone:** 443-287-8944; **Board Cert:** Pediatrics 1986; Adolescent Medicine 2009; **Med School:** Case West Res Univ 1979; **Resid:** Pediatrics, Cincinnati Chldns Hosp Med Ctr 1982; **Fellow:** Adolescent Medicine, UCSF Med Ctr 1984; **Fac Appt:** Prof Ped, Johns Hopkins Univ

Chambers, Christopher V MD [AM] - **Spec Exp:** Metabolic Syndrome; Sexually Transmitted Diseases; **Hospital:** Thomas Jefferson Univ Hosp; **Address:** Jefferson Univ Physicians - Family Med, 833 Chestnut St E, Ste 301, Philadelphia, PA 19107; **Phone:** 215-955-7190; **Board Cert:** Family Medicine 2008; Adolescent Medicine 2011; **Med School:** Duke Univ 1980; **Resid:** Family Medicine, Thomas Jefferson Univ Hosp 1983; **Fellow:** Adolescent Medicine, UCSF Med Ctr 1985; **Fac Appt:** Prof FMed, Jefferson Med Coll

Ginsburg, Kenneth R MD [AM] - **Spec Exp:** Behavioral Disorders; Adolescent Behavior-High Risk; **Hospital:** Chldns Hosp of Philadelphia; **Address:** Chldns Hosp Philadelphia, Main Bldg, 3400 Civic Ctr Blvd Fl 11, Philadelphia, PA 19104; **Phone:** 215-590-3537; **Board Cert:** Adolescent Medicine 2009; **Med School:** Albert Einstein Coll Med 1987; **Resid:** Pediatrics, Chldns Hosp 1990; **Fac Appt:** Prof Ped, Univ Pennsylvania

Murray, Pamela J MD [AM] - **Spec Exp:** Adolescent Gynecology; Menstrual Disorders; **Hospital:** Ruby Memorial - WVU Hosp; **Address:** WVU Hosp - Phys Ofc Ctr, 1 Med Ctr Drive, Morgantown, WV 26506; **Phone:** 304-598-4835; **Board Cert:** Pediatrics 1983; Adolescent Medicine 2009; **Med School:** Med Coll PA 1978; **Resid:** Pediatrics, Chldns Hosp 1981; **Fellow:** Public Health, Univ New South Wales Affil Hosps 1987; **Fac Appt:** Prof Ped, W VA Univ

Rudy, Bret J MD [AM] - **Spec Exp:** HIV in Adolescents; AIDS/HIV; **Hospital:** NYU Langone Med Ctr (page 68), Bellevue Hosp Ctr; **Address:** 145 E 32nd St, rm 1408, 14th Fl Penthouse, New York, NY 10016; **Phone:** 212-263-6425; **Board Cert:** Adolescent Medicine 2009; **Med School:** Univ Pittsburgh 1985; **Resid:** Pediatrics, Chldns Hosp 1988; **Fellow:** Hematology & Oncology, Chldns Hosp 1989; Internal Medicine, Chldns Hosp 1994

Slap, Gail B MD [AM] - **Spec Exp:** Chronic Illness; Developmental Disorders; **Hospital:** Chldns Hosp of Philadelphia; **Address:** Chldns Hosp Philadelphia, Main Bldg, 3400 Civic Ctr Blvd, Philadelphia, PA 19104; **Phone:** 215-590-5868; **Board Cert:** Internal Medicine 1980; Adolescent Medicine 2004; **Med School:** Univ Pennsylvania 1977; **Resid:** Internal Medicine, Hosp Univ Penn - UPHS 1980; **Fellow:** Adolescent Medicine, Chldns Hosp 1982; **Fac Appt:** Prof Ped, Univ Pennsylvania

Midwest

Bravender, Terrill D MD [AM] - **Spec Exp:** Eating Disorders; Nutrition; **Hospital:** Nationwide Chldn's Hosp; **Address:** 495 E Main St, Columbus, OH 43215; **Phone:** 614-722-2450; **Board Cert:** Pediatrics 2011; Adolescent Medicine 2007; **Med School:** Univ Mich Med Sch 1992; **Resid:** Pediatrics, Duke Med Ctr 1996; **Fellow:** Adolescent Medicine, Chldns Hosp 1998; **Fac Appt:** Asst Prof Med, Ohio State Univ

Garofalo, Robert MD [AM] - **Spec Exp:** AIDS/HIV in Adolescents; Sexually Transmitted Diseases; Preventive Medicine; Gay/Lesbian/Transgender Health; **Hospital:** Lurie Chldn's Hosp-Chicago; **Address:** Lurie Chldn's Hosp-Adolescent Med, 225 E Chicago Ave, Box 161, Chicago, IL 60614; **Phone:** 773-303-6056; **Board Cert:** Adolescent Medicine 2009; **Med School:** NYU Sch Med 1992; **Resid:** Pediatrics, Chldn's Hosp 1995; **Fellow:** Pediatrics, Harvard/Boston Chldn's Hosp 1997; Adolescent Medicine, Harvard/Boston Chldn's Hosp 2001; **Fac Appt:** Assoc Prof Ped, Northwestern Univ

Kokotailo, Patricia K MD [AM] - **Hospital:** Univ WI Hosp & Clins; **Address:** UW Hlth Clins, Univ Statn Clin, 2880 University Ave, Ste 9010, Madison, WI 53705; **Phone:** 608-263-6421; **Board Cert:** Pediatrics 1987; Adolescent Medicine 2009; **Med School:** Northwestern Univ 1982; **Resid:** Pediatrics, Johns Hopkins Hosp 1985; **Fellow:** Adolescent Medicine, Johns Hopkins Hosp 1989; **Fac Appt:** Prof Ped, Univ Wisc

Sigman, Garry S MD [AM] - **Spec Exp:** Eating Disorders; Obesity; Behavorial Disorders; **Hospital:** Loyola Univ Med Ctr; **Address:** Loyola Outpatient Ctr, 2160 S First Ave, Maywood, IL 60153; **Phone:** 708-327-9119; **Board Cert:** Pediatrics 1983; Adolescent Medicine 2009; **Med School:** Wayne State Univ 1978; **Resid:** Pediatrics, Chldns Hosp of MI 1981; **Fellow:** Adolescent Medicine, Strong Meml Hosp 1983; **Fac Appt:** Assoc Prof Ped, Loyola Univ-Stritch Sch Med

Singh, Nimi MD [AM] - **Spec Exp:** Anxiety & Depression; Eating Disorders; Nutrition; **Hospital:** Univ Minn Med Ctr, Fairview - West Bank Campus; **Address:** Fairview Chldns Clinic, 2535 University Ave SE, Minneapolis, MN 55414; **Phone:** 612-672-2350; **Board Cert:** Pediatrics 2009; **Med School:** Mount Sinai Sch Med 1989; **Resid:** Pediatrics, Rainbow Babies & Chldns Hosp 1992; **Fellow:** Adolescent Medicine, Univ Wash Med Ctr 1996; **Fac Appt:** Asst Prof Ped, Univ Minn

Great Plains and Mountains

Bermudez, Ovidio B MD [AM] - **Spec Exp:** Eating Disorders; Obesity; Nutrition; **Hospital:** Denver Health Med Ctr; **Address:** Eating Recovery Ctr, 8140 E Fifth Ave, Denver, CO 80230; **Phone:** 877-825-8584; **Board Cert:** Pediatrics 2012; Adolescent Medicine 2009; **Med School:** Dominican Republic 1985; **Resid:** Pediatrics, Med Coll Penn Hosp 1988; **Fellow:** Adolescent Medicine, Univ Alabama Affil Hosp 1990; **Fac Appt:** Clin Prof Ped, Univ Colorado

Kaplan, David W MD [AM] - **Spec Exp:** Anxiety Disorders; Adolescent Gynecology; Depression; **Hospital:** Chldn's Hosp - Aurora (CO); **Address:** Chldns Hosp, 13123 E 16th Ave, Aurora, CO 80045; **Phone:** 720-777-6131; **Board Cert:** Pediatrics 1975; Public Health & Genl Preventive Med 1980; Adolescent Medicine 2009; **Med School:** Case West Res Univ 1970; **Resid:** Pediatrics, Univ Colorado Med Ctr 1973; Adolescent Medicine, Chldns Hosp Med Ctr 1975; **Fellow:** Public Health & Genl Preventive Med, Harvard Sch Pub Hlth 1976; **Fac Appt:** Prof Ped, Univ Colorado

Sigel, Eric J MD [AM] - **Spec Exp:** Eating Disorders; Addiction/Substance Abuse; Depression; Aggression Disorders; **Hospital:** Chldn's Hosp - Aurora (CO); **Address:** Children's Hosp, Adolescent Med Clinic, 13123 E 16th Ave, Aurora, CO 80045; **Phone:** 720-777-6131; **Board Cert:** Pediatrics 2007; Adolescent Medicine 2012; **Med School:** Case West Res Univ 1989; **Resid:** Pediatrics, Rainbow Babies & Chldns Hosp 1992; **Fellow:** Adolescent Medicine, Chldns Hosp 1995; **Fac Appt:** Assoc Prof Ped, Univ Colorado

Southwest

Hergenroeder, Albert C MD [AM] - **Spec Exp:** Pediatric & Adolescent Sports Medicine; Eating Disorders; Obesity; Adolescent Gynecology; **Hospital:** Texas Chldns Hosp; **Address:** TCH-Adolescent & Sports Med Service, TCH Clinical Care Ctr Fl 11, 6701 Fannin St, Houston, TX 77030; **Phone:** 832-822-4887; **Board Cert:** Pediatrics 1993; Sports Medicine 2004; Adolescent Medicine 2009; **Med School:** Univ Pittsburgh 1980; **Resid:** Pediatrics, Duke Univ Med Ctr 1983; **Fellow:** Adolescent Medicine, Univ Wash Affil Hosp 1985; **Fac Appt:** Prof Ped, Baylor Coll Med

West Coast and Pacific

Anderson, Martin M MD [AM] - **Spec Exp:** Clinical Trials; Obesity; **Hospital:** UCLA Ronald Reagan Med Ctr; **Address:** UCLA Med Ctr, Dept Pediatrics, 200 UCLA Medical Plaza, Ste 265, Los Angeles, CA 90095; **Phone:** 310-825-0867; **Board Cert:** Pediatrics 1986; Adolescent Medicine 2009; **Med School:** UC Davis 1980; **Resid:** Pediatrics, Mott Chldns Hosp 1983; **Fellow:** Adolescent Medicine, UCSF Med Ctr 1986; UCLA Med Ctr 1998; **Fac Appt:** Prof Ped, UCLA

Irwin Jr, Charles E MD [AM] - **Spec Exp:** Eating Disorders; Adolescent Gynecology; **Hospital:** UCSF Med Ctr; **Address:** UCSF Chldns Hosp, 400 Parnassus Ave Fl 2, San Francisco, CA 94143; **Phone:** 415-353-2002; **Board Cert:** Pediatrics 1993; **Med School:** UCSF 1971; **Resid:** Pediatrics, UCSF Med Ctr 1974; **Fellow:** Adolescent Medicine, UCSF Med Ctr 1977; **Fac Appt:** Prof Ped, UCSF

Staggers, Barbara C MD [AM] - **Spec Exp:** Adolescent Behavior-High Risk; **Hospital:** Chldns Hosp - Oakland; **Address:** 5400 Telegraph Ave, Oakland, CA 94618; **Phone:** 510-428-3387; **Board Cert:** Adolescent Medicine 2011; **Med School:** UCSF 1980; **Resid:** Pediatrics, Chldns Hosp 1983; **Fellow:** Adolescent Medicine, UCSF Med Ctr 1985

Allergy & Immunology

An allergist-immunologist is trained in evaluation, physical and laboratory diagnosis and management of disorders involving the immune system. Selected examples of such conditions include asthma, anaphylaxis, rhinitis, eczema and adverse reactions to drugs, foods and insect stings as well as immune deficiency diseases (both acquired and congenital), defects in host defense and problems related to autoimmune disease, organ transplantation or malignancies of the immune system. As our understanding of the immune system develops, the scope of this specialty is widening.

Training programs are available at some medical centers to provide individuals with expertise in both allergy/immunology and adult rheumatology, or in both allergy/immunology and pediatric pulmonology. Such individuals are candidates for dual certification.

Training Required: Two years in allergy/immunology OR prior certification in internal medicine or pediatrics *plus* additional training and examination

Allergy & Immunology

New England

Castells, Maria C MD/PhD [A&I] - **Spec Exp:** Drug Allergy; Food Allergy; Anaphylaxis; Mast Cell Diseases; **Hospital:** Brigham & Women's Hosp; **Address:** Brigham & Women's Hosp, Allergy Div, 850 Boylston St, Ste 540, Chestnut Hill, MA 02467; **Phone:** 617-732-9850; **Board Cert:** Internal Medicine 2004; Allergy & Immunology 2005; **Med School:** Spain 1979; **Resid:** Internal Medicine, Kansas Univ Med Ctr 1988; Allergy & Immunology, Medical Coll Virginia 1990; **Fac Appt:** Assoc Prof Med, Harvard Med Sch

MacLean, James A MD [A&I] - **Spec Exp:** Asthma; Allergy; Urticaria; **Hospital:** Mass Genl Hosp, N Shore Med Ctr - Salem Hosp; **Address:** Asthma & Allergy Affiliates, 114 Highland Ave, Salem, MA 01970; **Phone:** 978-745-3711; **Board Cert:** Internal Medicine 1988; Allergy & Immunology 2011; **Med School:** McGill Univ 1985; **Resid:** Internal Medicine, Royal Victoria Hosp 1989; **Fellow:** Allergy & Immunology, Mass Genl Hosp 1991; Immunopathology, Mass Genl Hosp 1994; **Fac Appt:** Asst Prof A&I, Harvard Med Sch

Umetsu, Dale T MD/PhD [A&I] - **Spec Exp:** Asthma; Immune Deficiency; Eczema; Food Allergy; **Hospital:** Children's Hospital - Boston; **Address:** Boston Chldns Hosp, Allergy & Immunology, 300 Longwood Ave, Fegan 6, Boston, MA 02115; **Phone:** 617-919-2439; **Board Cert:** Pediatrics 1984; Allergy & Immunology 1985; **Med School:** NYU Sch Med 1979; **Resid:** Pediatrics, Chldns Hosp 1982; **Fellow:** Allergy & Immunology, Chldns Hosp 1984; **Fac Appt:** Prof Ped, Harvard Med Sch

Wong, Johnson T MD [A&I] - **Spec Exp:** Asthma; Rhinosinusitis; Urticaria; Immune Deficiency; **Hospital:** Mass Genl Hosp, Newton - Wellesley Hosp; **Address:** 8 Hawthorne Pl, Ste 104, Boston, MA 02114; **Phone:** 617-742-5730; **Board Cert:** Internal Medicine 1983; Allergy & Immunology 1985; **Med School:** UCSF 1980; **Resid:** Internal Medicine, UCLA-Wadsworth VA Hosp 1983; **Fellow:** Allergy & Immunology, Mass Genl Hosp 1986; **Fac Appt:** Asst Prof Med, Harvard Med Sch

Mid Atlantic

Buchbinder, Ellen M MD [A&I] - **Spec Exp:** Asthma & Allergy; Rhinitis; Hives; Food & Drug Allergy; **Hospital:** Mt Sinai Med Ctr (page 62); **Address:** 111 E 88th St, Ste 1-B, New York, NY 10128; **Phone:** 212-410-3246; **Board Cert:** Internal Medicine 1981; Allergy & Immunology 1983; **Med School:** Tulane Univ 1978; **Resid:** Internal Medicine, New England Deaconess Hosp 1981; **Fellow:** Allergy & Immunology, Mass Genl Hosp 1983; **Fac Appt:** Asst Clin Prof Med, Mount Sinai Sch Med

Chandler, Michael J MD [A&I] - **Spec Exp:** Asthma; Sinus Disorders; Airway Disorders; **Hospital:** Mt Sinai Med Ctr (page 62); **Address:** City Allergy, 115 E 61st St Fl 12, New York, NY 10065; **Phone:** 212-486-6715; **Board Cert:** Internal Medicine 1984; Allergy & Immunology 1987; **Med School:** Wayne State Univ 1981; **Resid:** Internal Medicine, Northwestern Meml Hosp 1984; **Fellow:** Allergy & Immunology, Northwestern Meml Hosp 1986; **Fac Appt:** Asst Clin Prof Med, Mount Sinai Sch Med

Cunningham-Rundles, Charlotte MD/PhD [A&I] - **Spec Exp:** Immunotherapy; Immunodeficiency Disorders; **Hospital:** Mt Sinai Med Ctr (page 62); **Address:** Mt Sinai Hosp, Dept of Med-Allergy & Immunology, 5 E 98th St Fl 11, New York, NY 10029; **Phone:** 212-659-9268; **Board Cert:** Internal Medicine 1972; **Med School:** Columbia P&S 1969; **Resid:** Internal Medicine, Bellevue Hosp Ctr 1972; **Fellow:** Allergy & Immunology, NYU Med Ctr 1974; **Fac Appt:** Prof Med, Mount Sinai Sch Med

Ein, Daniel MD [A&I] - **Spec Exp:** Asthma & Allergy; Sinus Disorders; Food Allergy; Immune Deficiency; **Hospital:** G Washington Univ Hosp; **Address:** Med Faculty Assoc Allergy & Sinus Ctr, 2300 M St NW Fl 2 - Ste 200, Washington, DC 20037; **Phone:** 202-741-2770; **Board Cert:** Internal Medicine 1980; Allergy & Immunology 1989; **Med School:** Albert Einstein Coll Med 1964; **Resid:** Internal Medicine, Mass Genl Hosp 1969; **Fellow:** Immunology, Natl Cancer Inst 1968; **Fac Appt:** Clin Prof A&I, Geo Wash Univ

Fishman, Henry J MD [A&I] - **Spec Exp:** Asthma & Allergy; **Address:** Fishman Allergy & Asthma, 2141 K St, Ste 206, Washington, DC 20037; **Phone:** 202-833-3500; **Board Cert:** Internal Medicine 1982; Allergy & Immunology 1985; **Med School:** Univ Rochester 1979; **Resid:** Internal Medicine, Geo Wash Med Ctr 1982; **Fellow:** Allergy & Immunology, Georgetown Univ Hosp 1984; **Fac Appt:** Asst Clin Prof Med, Georgetown Univ

Kaliner, Michael A MD [A&I] - **Spec Exp:** Asthma & Allergy; Sinusitis; Rhinitis; **Hospital:** MedStar Washington Hosp Ctr; **Address:** Institute for Asthma and Allergy, 6515 hillmead Rd, bethesda, MD 20817; **Phone:** 301-986-9262; **Board Cert:** Internal Medicine 1974; Allergy & Immunology 1993; **Med School:** Univ MD Sch Med 1967; **Resid:** Internal Medicine, UCSF Med Ctr 1970; **Fellow:** Allergy & Immunology, Harvard Univ Affil Hosp 1973; **Fac Appt:** Clin Prof Med, Geo Wash Univ

Mazza, David S MD [A&I] - **Spec Exp:** Asthma; Sinus Disorders; Eczema; **Hospital:** St. Luke's - Roosevelt Hosp Ctr - Roosevelt Div (page 56); **Address:** 7 Lexington Ave, Ste P3, New York, NY 10010-5517; **Phone:** 212-677-7170; **Board Cert:** Pediatrics 1983; Allergy & Immunology 2008; **Med School:** Univ VT Coll Med 1977; **Resid:** Pediatrics, NYU-Bellevue Hosp 1980; **Fellow:** Pediatric Allergy & Immunology, Bellevue Hosp 1982; **Fac Appt:** Asst Prof Ped, Columbia P&S

Metcalfe, Dean D MD [A&I] - **Spec Exp:** Mast Cell Diseases; Anaphylaxis; **Hospital:** Natl Inst of Hlth - Clin Ctr; **Address:** Natl Inst Allergy & Infectious Disease, Allergic Disease Lab, MS 1881, 10 Center Drive Bldg 10 - rm 11C207, Bethesda, MD 20892-1881; **Phone:** 301-496-2165; **Board Cert:** Internal Medicine 1975; Allergy & Immunology 1977; Rheumatology 1980; **Med School:** Univ Tenn Coll Med 1972; **Resid:** Internal Medicine, Univ Mich Hosps 1974; Allergy & Immunology, Natl Inst Allergy & Infectious Dis-NIH 1977; **Fellow:** Rheumatology, Peter Bent Brigham Hosp 1979

Phillips, S. Michael MD [A&I] - **Spec Exp:** Allergy; Autoimmune Disease; Immunodeficiency Disorders; **Hospital:** Penn Presby Med Ctr - UPHS (page 69), Hosp Univ Penn - UPHS (page 69); **Address:** Penn Presby Med Ctr - Allergy/Immunology, 51 N 39th St, Mutch Bldg - Fl 5, Philadelphia, PA 19104-2640; **Phone:** 215-662-2775; **Board Cert:** Internal Medicine 1974; Allergy & Immunology 1979; **Med School:** Univ Wisc 1966; **Resid:** Internal Medicine, Hosp Univ Penn - UPHS 1968; **Fellow:** Immunology, Hosp Univ Penn - UPHS 1969; Immunology, Brigham & Women's Hosp 1972; **Fac Appt:** Prof Med, Univ Pennsylvania

Shepherd, Gillian M MD [A&I] - **Spec Exp:** Food & Drug Allergy; Rhinosinusitis & Asthma; Urticaria; Insect Allergies; **Hospital:** NY-Presby/Weill Cornell Med Ctr, NY (page 65); **Address:** 235 E 67th St, Ste 203, New York, NY 10065; **Phone:** 212-288-9300; **Board Cert:** Internal Medicine 1979; Allergy & Immunology 1981; **Med School:** NY Med Coll 1976; **Resid:** Internal Medicine, Lenox Hill Hosp 1979; **Fellow:** Allergy & Immunology, New York Hosp-Cornell 1981; **Fac Appt:** Assoc Clin Prof Med, Cornell Univ-Weill Med Coll

Slankard, Marjorie L MD [A&I] - **Spec Exp:** Sinus Disorders; Asthma; Food Allergy; **Hospital:** NY-Presby/Columbia Univ Med Ctr, NY (page 65), Valley Hosp; **Address:** 51 W 51st St, Ste 360, New York, NY 10019; **Phone:** 212-326-8410; **Board Cert:** Internal Medicine 1974; Allergy & Immunology 1977; **Med School:** Univ MO-Columbia Sch Med 1971; **Resid:** Internal Medicine, New York Hosp 1974; **Fellow:** Allergy & Immunology, New York Hosp-Cornell 1976; Neoplastic Diseases, Mount Sinai Med Ctr 1980; **Fac Appt:** Clin Prof Med, Columbia P&S

Southeast

Benenati, Susan V MD [A&I] - **Spec Exp:** Asthma; Latex Allergy; Sinus Disorders; Nasal Allergy; **Hospital:** Baptist Hosp of Miami, South Miami Hosp; **Address:** 6705 Red Rd, Ste 318, Coral Gables, FL 33143; **Phone:** 305-665-1623; **Board Cert:** Internal Medicine 1988; Allergy & Immunology 2011; **Med School:** Univ S Fla Coll Med 1984; **Resid:** Internal Medicine, Indiana Univ Med Ctr 1988; **Fellow:** Allergy & Immunology, Johns Hopkins Hosp 1990

DeShazo, Richard D MD [A&I] - **Spec Exp:** Immunodeficiency Disorders; Allergy; Rheumatology; Pediatric Allergy & Immunology; **Hospital:** Univ Mississippi Med Ctr, G.V. (Sonny) Montgomery VA Med Ctr - Jackson; **Address:** Univ Mississippi Med Ctr, Dept Med, 768 Lakeland Drive LJ Bldg, Jackson, MS 39216; **Phone:** 601-815-1078; **Board Cert:** Internal Medicine 1974; Allergy & Immunology 1977; Rheumatology 1982; Geriatric Medicine 2005; **Med School:** UAB Sch Med 1971; **Resid:** Internal Medicine, Walter Reed Genl Hosp 1974; **Fellow:** Microbiology, Walter Reed Army Inst Rsch 1975; Clinical Immunology, Walter Reed Genl Hosp 1977; **Fac Appt:** Prof Med, Univ Miss

Friedman, Stuart A MD [A&I] - **Spec Exp:** Asthma; Sinus Disorders; Allergy; **Hospital:** Boca Raton Regl Hosp, Delray Med Ctr; **Address:** 5162 Linton Blvd, Ste 201, Delray Beach, FL 33484; **Phone:** 561-495-2580; **Board Cert:** Internal Medicine 1980; Allergy & Immunology 1983; **Med School:** Spain 1976; **Resid:** Internal Medicine, Winthrop Univ Hosp 1980; **Fellow:** Immunology, Univ Cincinnati Med Ctr 1982

Ledford, Dennis K MD [A&I] - **Spec Exp:** Asthma; **Hospital:** Florida Hosp - Tampa, Tampa Genl Hosp; **Address:** Allergy, Asthma & Immunology Assocs, 13801 Bruce B Downs Blvd, Ste 502, Tampa, FL 33613; **Phone:** 813-971-9743; **Board Cert:** Internal Medicine 1980; Rheumatology 1984; Allergy & Immunology 1985; Clinical & Laboratory Immunology 1986; **Med School:** Univ Tenn Coll Med 1976; **Resid:** Internal Medicine, Univ Hosp 1980; **Fellow:** Rheumatology, NYU-Bellevue Hosp 1982; Allergy & Immunology, Univ S FL Affil Hosp 1985; **Fac Appt:** Prof A&I, Univ S Fla Coll Med

Lieberman, Phillip L MD [A&I] - **Spec Exp:** Asthma; Rhinitis; Anaphylaxis; **Hospital:** Baptist Memorial Hospital-Memphis, Methodist Univ Hosp - Memphis; **Address:** Allergy & Asthma Care, 7205 Wolf River Blvd, Ste 200, Germantown, TN 38138; **Phone:** 901-757-6100; **Board Cert:** Internal Medicine 1970; Allergy & Immunology 2013; **Med School:** Univ Tenn Coll Med 1965; **Resid:** Internal Medicine, Memphis City Hosps 1969; **Fellow:** Allergy & Immunology, Northwestern Univ Affil Hosp 1971; **Fac Appt:** Clin Prof A&I, Univ Tenn Coll Med

Lockey, Richard F MD [A&I] - **Spec Exp:** Asthma & Allergy; Rhinitis; Immune Deficiency; Hereditary Angioedema; **Hospital:** Florida Hosp - Tampa, Tampa Genl Hosp; **Address:** Allergy, Asthma, & Immunology Assocs, 13801 Bruce B Downs Blvd, Ste 502, Tampa, FL 33613; **Phone:** 813-971-9743; **Board Cert:** Internal Medicine 1970; Allergy & Immunology 1974; **Med School:** Temple Univ 1965; **Resid:** Internal Medicine, Univ Michigan Med Ctr 1968; **Fellow:** Allergy & Immunology, Univ Michigan Med Ctr 1970; **Fac Appt:** Prof Med, Univ S Fla Coll Med

Markert, M Louise MD/PhD [A&I] - **Spec Exp:** DiGeorge Syndrome; Immunodeficiency Disorders; **Hospital:** Duke Univ Hosp; **Address:** Research Park 4, 109B, 6 Circuit Drive, Durham, NC 27710; **Phone:** 919-684-6263; **Board Cert:** Allergy & Immunology 1987; Pediatrics 1987; Diagnostic Lab Immunology 1988; **Med School:** Duke Univ 1982; **Resid:** Pediatrics, Duke Univ Med Ctr 1984; **Fellow:** Allergy & Immunology, Duke Univ Med Ctr 1987; **Fac Appt:** Assoc Prof PS, Duke Univ

Pacin, Michael P MD [A&I] - **Spec Exp:** Insect Allergies; Asthma; Rhinitis; **Hospital:** Baptist Hosp of Miami, South Miami Hosp; **Address:** FL Ctr Allergy & Asthma Care, 9035 Sunset Drive, Ste 202, Miami, FL 33173; **Phone:** 305-279-3366; **Board Cert:** Internal Medicine 1974; Allergy & Immunology 1979; **Med School:** Washington Univ, St Louis 1969; **Resid:** Internal Medicine, Jewish Hosp 1971; Internal Medicine, Jackson Meml Hosp 1972; **Fellow:** Allergy & Immunology, VA Hosp 1974

Sundy, John S MD/PhD [A&I] - **Spec Exp:** Asthma; Allergic Rhinitis; Immunotherapy; Gout; **Hospital:** Duke Univ Hosp, Durham Regional Hosp; **Address:** 1821 Hillandale Rd, Ste 25A, Durham, NC 27705; **Phone:** 919-668-7630; **Board Cert:** Internal Medicine 2006; Allergy & Immunology 2009; Rheumatology 2008; **Med School:** Hahnemann Univ 1991; **Resid:** Internal Medicine, Duke Univ Med Ctr 1993; **Fellow:** Rheumatology, Duke Univ Med Ctr 1996; Allergy & Immunology, Duke Univ Med Ctr 1998; **Fac Appt:** Asst Prof Med, Duke Univ

Midwest

Ballas, Zuhair K MD [A&I] - **Hospital:** Univ Iowa Hosp & Clins; **Address:** UIHC Dept of Internal Med, 200 Hawkins Drive, Iowa City, IA 52242; **Phone:** 319-356-8133; **Board Cert:** Internal Medicine 1977; Allergy & Immunology 1981; Diagnostic Lab Immunology 1988; **Med School:** Amer Univ Beirut 1974; **Resid:** Internal Medicine, Rutgets Med Sch Affil Hosp 1975; Internal Medicine, Jefferson Univ Hosp 1976; **Fellow:** Allergy & Immunology, Johns Hopkins Univ Hosp 1978; Allergy & Immunology, Fred Hutchinson Cancer Rsch Ctr 1980; **Fac Appt:** Prof A&I, Univ Iowa Coll Med

Bernstein, David Isaac MD [A&I] - **Spec Exp:** Occupational Asthma; Asthma; Rhinosinusitis; **Hospital:** Univ Cincinnati Med Ctr; **Address:** 8444 Winton Rd, Cincinnati, OH 45231; **Phone:** 513-931-0775; **Board Cert:** Internal Medicine 1980; Allergy & Immunology 1983; Diagnostic Lab Immunology 1988; **Med School:** Univ Cincinnati 1977; **Resid:** Internal Medicine, Cleveland Clinic 1980; **Fellow:** Allergy & Immunology, Northwestern Meml Hosp 1982; **Fac Appt:** Clin Prof Med, Univ Cincinnati

Bernstein, Jonathan A MD [A&I] - **Spec Exp:** Asthma; Occupational Asthma; Drug Allergy; Eczema; **Hospital:** Univ Cincinnati Med Ctr; **Address:** 8444 Winton Rd, Cincinnati, OH 45267-0563; **Phone:** 513-931-0775; **Board Cert:** Internal Medicine 1988; Allergy & Immunology 2011; **Med School:** Univ Cincinnati 1985; **Resid:** Internal Medicine, Cleveland Clinic 1988; **Fellow:** Allergy & Immunology, Northwestern Meml Hosp 1990; **Fac Appt:** Assoc Prof Med, Univ Cincinnati

Grammer, Leslie C MD [A&I] - **Spec Exp:** Asthma; Sinusitis; Drug Allergy; Food Allergy; **Hospital:** Northwestern Meml Hosp; **Address:** Northwestern Med Faculty Fdn, Ambulatory Care Ctr, 675 N St Clair, Ste 18-250, Chicago, IL 60611-5975; **Phone:** 312-695-8624; **Board Cert:** Internal Medicine 1979; Allergy & Immunology 1981; Diagnostic Lab Immunology 1986; Occupational Medicine 1989; **Med School:** Northwestern Univ 1976; **Resid:** Internal Medicine, Northwestern Meml Hosp 1979; **Fellow:** Allergy & Immunology, Northwestern Meml Hosp 1981; **Fac Appt:** Prof Med, Northwestern Univ

Greenberger, Paul A MD [A&I] - **Spec Exp:** Asthma; Anaphylaxis; Drug Allergy; Food Allergy; **Hospital:** Northwestern Meml Hosp, Jesse Brown VA Med Ctr; **Address:** Northwestern Med Faculty Fdn, Ambulatory Care Ctr, 675 N St Clair Fl 18 - Ste 18-250, Chicago, IL 60611; **Phone:** 312-695-8624; **Board Cert:** Internal Medicine 1976; Allergy & Immunology 1979; Diagnostic Lab Immunology 1986; **Med School:** Indiana Univ 1973; **Resid:** Internal Medicine, Jewish Hosp 1976; **Fellow:** Allergy & Immunology, Northwestern Meml Hosp 1978; **Fac Appt:** Prof A&I, Northwestern Univ-Feinberg Sch Med

Jost, Barbara Capes MD [A&I] - **Spec Exp:** Sinusitis; Drug Allergy; **Hospital:** St. Luke's Hosp - Chesterfield, MO, Barnes-Jewish Hosp; **Address:** Internal Medicine Assocs, South Medical Bldg, Ste 5009, 224 S Woods Mill Rd, Chesterfield, MO 63017; **Phone:** 314-878-6260; **Board Cert:** Internal Medicine 2011; Allergy & Immunology 2005; **Med School:** St Louis Univ 1998; **Resid:** Internal Medicine, Barnes Jewish Hosp 2001; Allergy & Immunology, Barnes Jewish Hosp 2005

Korenblat, Phillip E MD [A&I] - **Spec Exp:** Allergy; Asthma; Anaphylaxis; Airway Disorders; **Hospital:** Barnes-Jewish West County Hosp, Missouri Baptist Med Ctr; **Address:** 1040 N Mason Rd, Ste 115, St Louis, MO 63141-6361; **Phone:** 314-542-0606; **Board Cert:** Internal Medicine 1971; Allergy & Immunology 1974; **Med School:** Univ Ark 1960; **Resid:** Internal Medicine, Barnes Jewish Hosp 1965; **Fellow:** Allergy & Immunology, Scripps Clin Rsch Fdn 1966; **Fac Appt:** Clin Prof A&I, Washington Univ, St Louis

Li, James Tung-Chieh MD [A&I] - **Spec Exp:** Asthma; Allergy; **Hospital:** St. Mary's Hosp - Rochester MN (Mayo), Rochester Methodist Hosp; **Address:** Mayo Clinic, Div Allergic Diseases, 200 First St SW, Box W15A, Rochester, MN 55905; **Phone:** 507-284-4966; **Board Cert:** Internal Medicine 1984; Allergy & Immunology 1985; **Med School:** Duke Univ 1981; **Resid:** Internal Medicine, Duke Univ Hosp 1984; **Fellow:** Allergy & Immunology, Mayo Med Ctr & Clin 1985; **Fac Appt:** Prof Med, Mayo Med Sch

Routes, John M MD [A&I] - **Spec Exp:** Immunodeficiency Disorders; Asthma; Allergy; **Hospital:** Chldns Hosp - Wisconsin; **Address:** Chldns Hosp of Wisconsin, 9000 W Wisconsin Ave, Ste 440B, Milwaukee, WI 53226; **Phone:** 414-266-6840; **Board Cert:** Internal Medicine 1984; Allergy & Immunology 1987; **Med School:** Indiana Univ 1981; **Resid:** Internal Medicine, Univ Utah Affil Hosps 1984; **Fellow:** Allergy & Immunology, Natl Jewish Hosp 1989; Infectious Disease, Natl Jewish Hosp 1990; **Fac Appt:** Prof Ped, Med Coll Wisc

Sanders, Georgiana MD [A&I] - **Spec Exp:** Asthma; Food Allergy & Eczema; Rhinitis; Pediatric Allergy & Immunology; **Hospital:** Univ Michigan Med Ctr; **Address:** Univ MI Allergy Specialty Clin, 24 Frank Lloyd Wright Dr, Ste H-2100, Ann Arbor, MI 48105; **Phone:** 734-936-5634; **Board Cert:** Pediatrics 1982; Allergy & Immunology 1985; **Med School:** Univ Cincinnati 1975; **Resid:** Pediatrics, Chldns Hosp 1978; Pediatrics, Boston City Hosp 1979; **Fellow:** Allergy & Immunology, Univ of MI Hosp 1984; **Fac Appt:** Asst Clin Prof Med, Univ Mich Med Sch

Tillinghast, Jeffrey Paul MD [A&I] - **Hospital:** Barnes-Jewish Hosp; **Address:** 1040 N Mason Rd, Ste 115, St Louis, MO 63141; **Phone:** 314-542-0606; **Board Cert:** Internal Medicine 1984; Allergy & Immunology 1987; **Med School:** Washington Univ, St Louis 1980; **Resid:** Internal Medicine, Barnes Hospital 1983; **Fellow:** Allergy & Immunology, Natl Inst Health 1985; **Fac Appt:** Assoc Prof Med, Washington Univ, St Louis

Tobin, Mary MD [A&I] - **Spec Exp:** Food Allergy; Irritable Bowel Syndrome; **Hospital:** Rush Univ Med Ctr; **Address:** Rush Univ Consultants-A & I, 1725 W Harrison St, Ste 117, Chicago, IL 60612; **Phone:** 312-942-6296; **Board Cert:** Internal Medicine 1980; Allergy & Immunology 1983; **Med School:** Rush Med Coll 1977; **Resid:** Internal Medicine, Rush Univ Med Ctr 1981; **Fellow:** Allergy & Immunology, Rush Univ Med Ctr 1983; **Fac Appt:** Assoc Prof Med, Rush Med Coll

Wood, John A MD [A&I] - **Spec Exp:** Asthma; **Hospital:** St. Luke's Hosp - Chesterfield, MO; **Address:** Internal Med Assocs, 224 S Woods Mill Rd, Ste 500 S, Chesterfield, MO 63017; **Phone:** 314-878-6260; **Board Cert:** Internal Medicine 1972; Pulmonary Disease 1978; Allergy & Immunology 1979; **Med School:** Univ Okla Coll Med 1968; **Resid:** Internal Medicine, Univ Hosp 1970; Internal Medicine, Barnes Hosp-Wash Univ Sch Med 1971; **Fellow:** Pulmonary Disease, Wash Univ Sch Med 1977; Allergy & Immunology, Wash Univ Sch Med 1977; **Fac Appt:** Asst Prof Med, Washington Univ, St Louis

Southwest

Freeman, Theodore M MD [A&I] - **Spec Exp:** Insect Allergies; Asthma; Rhinitis; **Hospital:** Methodist Hosp-San Antonio; **Address:** 5282 Medical Drive, Ste 500, San Antonio, TX 78229; **Phone:** 210-614-7594; **Board Cert:** Internal Medicine 1983; Allergy & Immunology 1987; Clinical & Laboratory Immunology 1988; **Med School:** Univ S Fla Coll Med 1980; **Resid:** Internal Medicine, Keesler Med Ctr 1983; **Fellow:** Allergy & Immunology, Wilford Hall Med Ctr 1986; Diagnostic Lab Immunology, Mass Genl Hosp 1987; **Fac Appt:** Assoc Prof Med, Uniformed Srvs Univ, Bethesda

Gruchalla, Rebecca S MD/PhD [A&I] - **Spec Exp:** Asthma & Allergy; Drug Allergy; Immunodeficiency Disorders; **Hospital:** UT Southwestern Med Ctr at Dallas, Chldns Med Ctr of Dallas; **Address:** Div Allergy & Immunology, 5303 Harry Hines Blvd, Dallas, TX 75390-8872; **Phone:** 214-645-2800; **Board Cert:** Internal Medicine 1988; Allergy & Immunology 2012; **Med School:** Univ Tex SW, Dallas 1985; **Resid:** Internal Medicine, Hosp Univ Penn 1988; **Fellow:** Allergy & Immunology, Univ Tex SW Med Ctr 1991; **Fac Appt:** Prof Med, Univ Tex SW, Dallas

Lewis, John C MD [A&I] - **Spec Exp:** Asthma; Rhinosinusitis; Mast Cell Diseases; Eosinophil Disorders; **Hospital:** Mayo Clinic - Scottsdale; **Address:** Mayo Clin-Div Allergy & Immunology, 13400 E Shea Blvd, Scottsdale, AZ 85259-5404; **Phone:** 480-301-4284; **Board Cert:** Internal Medicine 1985; Allergy & Immunology 2011; **Med School:** Loyola Univ-Stritch Sch Med 1982; **Resid:** Internal Medicine, Wilford Hall Med Ctr 1985; **Fellow:** Allergy & Immunology, Mayo Clin 1990; **Fac Appt:** Asst Prof Med, Mayo Med Sch

Schubert, Mark S MD/PhD [A&I] - **Spec Exp:** Asthma & Allergy; Sinus Disorders; **Hospital:** Banner Good Samaritan Regl Med Ctr - Phoenix, St. Joseph's Hosp & Med Ctr - Phoenix; **Address:** Allergy Asthma Clin, 300 W Clarendon Rd, Ste 120, Phoenix, AZ 85013-2517; **Phone:** 602-277-3337; **Board Cert:** Internal Medicine 1987; Allergy & Immunology 2009; **Med School:** Univ Ariz Coll Med 1983; **Resid:** Neurological Surgery, Barrow Neurological Inst 1985; Internal Medicine, Banner Good Samaritan Regl Med Ctr 1987; **Fellow:** Allergy Immunology & Rheumatology, Stanford Univ Hosp & Clins 1989; **Fac Appt:** Assoc Clin Prof Med, Univ Ariz Coll Med

Wong, Duane W MD [A&I] - **Spec Exp:** Pediatric Allergy & Immunology; **Hospital:** Phoenix Children's Hosp, Mercy Gilbert Med Ctr; **Address:** Arizona Allergy Assocs, 348 E Virginia Ave, Phoenix, AZ 85004; **Phone:** 480-897-6992; **Board Cert:** Allergy & Immunology 2012; Pediatrics 2010; **Med School:** Northwestern Univ-Feinberg Sch Med 1984; **Resid:** Pediatrics, Chldns Hosp 1986; Pediatrics, Chdns Hosp 1987; **Fellow:** Allergy & Immunology, Chldns Hosp 1989

West Coast and Pacific

Altman, Leonard C MD [A&I] - **Spec Exp:** Urticaria; Asthma; Sinusitis; Allergy; **Hospital:** Univ Wash Med Ctr, Seattle Chldns Hosp; **Address:** 9725 3rd Ave NE, Ste 500, Seattle, WA 98115; **Phone:** 206-527-1200; **Board Cert:** Internal Medicine 1975; Allergy & Immunology 1979; **Med School:** Harvard Med Sch 1969; **Resid:** Internal Medicine, Univ Wash Affil Hosps 1971; Internal Medicine, Univ Wash Affil Hosps 1975; **Fellow:** Allergy & Immunology, Natl Inst Hlth 1974; **Fac Appt:** Clin Prof Med, Univ Wash

Henderson Jr, William R MD [A&I] - **Spec Exp:** Allergy; Asthma & Allergy; **Hospital:** Univ Wash Med Ctr; **Address:** UW Medicine at South Lake Union, 850 Republican St, Seattle, WA 98109; **Phone:** 206-598-4615; **Board Cert:** Internal Medicine 1976; Allergy & Immunology 1979; **Med School:** UCSF 1973; **Resid:** Internal Medicine, Stanford Med Ctr 1975; Internal Medicine, Natl Inst Hlth 1976; **Fellow:** Allergy & Immunology, Natl Inst Hlth 1978; **Fac Appt:** Prof A&I, Univ Wash

Montanaro, Anthony MD [A&I] - **Spec Exp:** Asthma; Allergy; Immunodeficiency Disorders; **Hospital:** OR Hlth & Sci Univ; **Address:** OHSU, Div Allergy & Clin Immunology, 3181 SW Sam Jackson Park Rd, MC OP-34, Portland, OR 97239-2098; **Phone:** 503-494-4300; **Board Cert:** Internal Medicine 1981; Allergy & Immunology 1993; Rheumatology 1984; **Med School:** Univ Wash 1978; **Resid:** Internal Medicine, Scripps Mercy Hosp & Med Ctr 1981; **Fellow:** Allergy Immunology & Rheumatology, OR Hlth & Sci Univ 1983; **Fac Appt:** Prof Med, Oregon Hlth & Sci Univ

Ostrom, Nancy K MD [A&I] - **Spec Exp:** Asthma & Allergy; **Hospital:** Rady Children's Hosp - San Diego; **Address:** Allergy & Asthma Medical & Research Ctr, 5776 Ruffin Rd, San Diego, CA 92123; **Phone:** 858-292-1144; **Board Cert:** Pediatrics 1984; Allergy & Immunology 1987; **Med School:** Mayo Med Sch 1980; **Resid:** Pediatrics, Mayo Clinic 1983; **Fellow:** Allergy & Immunology, Mayo Clinic 1985; **Fac Appt:** Assoc Clin Prof Ped, UCSD

Spector, Sheldon Laurence MD [A&I] - **Spec Exp:** Asthma; Clinical Trials; Allergy; **Hospital:** UCLA Ronald Reagan Med Ctr, Santa Monica - UCLA Med Ctr & Ortho Hosp; **Address:** California Allergy & Asthma Med Grp, 11645 Wilshire Blvd, Ste 1155, Los Angeles, CA 90025; **Phone:** 310-966-9022; **Board Cert:** Internal Medicine 1974; Allergy & Immunology 1980; **Med School:** Wayne State Univ 1964; **Resid:** Internal Medicine, Mt Sinai Hosp 1966; Internal Medicine, UCLA Med Ctr 1969; **Fellow:** Allergy & Immunology, Natl Jewish Hosp-Rsch Ctr 1971; **Fac Appt:** Clin Prof Med, UCLA

Tamaroff, Marc A MD [A&I] - **Spec Exp:** Sinus Disorders; Asthma; Rhinitis; Immune Deficiency; **Hospital:** Long Beach Meml Med Ctr, Miller Children's Hosp; **Address:** Allergy & Asthma Care Ctr, 3816 Woodruff Ave, Ste 209, Long Beach, CA 90808-2147; **Phone:** 562-496-4749; **Board Cert:** Internal Medicine 1979; Allergy & Immunology 1983; **Med School:** Univ Ariz Coll Med 1974; **Resid:** Internal Medicine, St Mary Med Ctr 1977; **Fellow:** Allergy & Immunology, UCLA Med Ctr 1979; **Fac Appt:** Assoc Clin Prof Med, UCLA

Cardiovascular Disease

a subspecialty of Internal Medicine

Cardiovascular Disease: An internist specializing in diseases of the heart, lungs and blood vessels and manages complex cardiac conditions such as heart attacks and life-threatening, abnormal heartbeat rhythms.

Cardiac Electrophysiology: A field of special interest within the subspecialty of cardiovascular disease which involves intricate technical procedures to evaluate heart rhythms and determine appropriate treatment for them.

Interventional Cardiology: An area of medicine within the subspecialty of cardiology which uses specialized imaging and other diagnostic techniques to evaluate blood flow and pressure in the coronary arteries and chambers of the heart, and uses technical procedures and medications to treat abnormalities that impair the function of the heart.

Training Required: Three years in internal medicine *plus* additional training and examination for certification in cardiovascular disease, clinical electrophysiology or interventional cardiology

Cardiovascular Disease

New England

Balady, Gary J MD [Cv] - **Spec Exp:** Preventive Cardiology; **Hospital:** Boston Med Ctr; **Address:** Boston Med Ctr, Cardiovascular Ctr, 732 Harrison Ave, Preston Family Bldg Fl 3, Boston, MA 02118; **Phone:** 617-638-7490; **Board Cert:** Internal Medicine 1982; Cardiovascular Disease 1985; **Med School:** UMDNJ-Rutgers Med Sch 1979; **Resid:** Internal Medicine, Boston Univ Med Ctr 1982; **Fellow:** Cardiovascular Disease, Boston Univ Med Ctr 1985; **Fac Appt:** Prof Med, Boston Univ

Cabin, Henry S MD [Cv] - **Spec Exp:** Interventional Cardiology; Cardiac Catheterization; **Hospital:** Yale-New Haven Hosp; **Address:** Yale Cardiology, 11 Harrison Ave, Branford, CT 06405; **Phone:** 203-483-8300; **Board Cert:** Internal Medicine 1978; Cardiovascular Disease 1983; **Med School:** Yale Univ 1975; **Resid:** Internal Medicine, Yale-New Haven Hosp 1978; **Fellow:** Research, Natl Heart Lung & Blood Inst 1981; Cardiovascular Disease, Yale-New Haven Hosp 1982; **Fac Appt:** Prof Med, Yale Univ

Catherwood, Edward MD [Cv] - **Spec Exp:** Pulmonary Hypertension; **Hospital:** Dartmouth - Hitchcock Med Ctr; **Address:** Dartmouth-Hitchcock Medical Ctr, Div Cardiology, 1 Medical Center Drive, Lebanon, NH 03756; **Phone:** 603-650-5724; **Board Cert:** Internal Medicine 1978; Cardiovascular Disease 1981; Critical Care Medicine 2009; **Med School:** Jefferson Med Coll 1975; **Resid:** Internal Medicine, Hahnemann Univ Hosp 1978; **Fellow:** Cardiovascular Disease, Hahnemann Univ Hosp 1980; **Fac Appt:** Assoc Prof Med, Dartmouth Med Sch

DeNofrio, David MD [Cv] - **Spec Exp:** Transplant Medicine-Heart; Heart Failure; **Hospital:** Tufts Med Ctr; **Address:** Tufts Med Ctr, Heart Failure & Cardiac Transplant Ctr, 800 Washington St, Box 5931, Boston, MA 02111; **Phone:** 617-636-8068; **Board Cert:** Internal Medicine 2011; Cardiovascular Disease 2005; Advanced Heart Failure & Transplant Cardiology 2012; **Med School:** Tufts Univ 1988; **Resid:** Internal Medicine, Barnes Hosp 1991; **Fellow:** Cardiovascular Disease, Duke Univ Med Ctr 1994; **Fac Appt:** Assoc Prof Med, Tufts Univ

Diver, Daniel J MD [Cv] - **Spec Exp:** Angioplasty; Coronary Artery Disease; Stroke; **Hospital:** St. Francis Hosp & Med Ctr; **Address:** St Francis Care, Hoffman Heart, 114 Woodland St, Hartford, CT 06105; **Phone:** 860-714-4019; **Board Cert:** Internal Medicine 1984; Cardiovascular Disease 1989; **Med School:** Johns Hopkins Univ 1981; **Resid:** Internal Medicine, Johns Hopkins Hosp 1984; **Fellow:** Cardiovascular Disease, Beth Israel Deaconess Med Ctr 1987; **Fac Appt:** Prof Med, Univ Conn

Hutter Jr, Adolph M MD [Cv] - **Hospital:** Mass Genl Hosp; **Address:** MGH Cardiology Dept, 55 Fruit St, Yawkey Ctr, rm 5B, Boston, MA 02114; **Phone:** 617-726-2884; **Board Cert:** Internal Medicine 1969; Cardiovascular Disease 1971; **Med School:** Univ Wisc 1963; **Resid:** Internal Medicine, Strong Meml Hosp 1968; **Fellow:** Cardiovascular Disease, Mass Genl Hosp 1970; **Fac Appt:** Prof Med, Harvard Med Sch

Johnson, Paula A MD [Cv] - **Spec Exp:** Heart Disease in Women; Women's Health; **Hospital:** Brigham & Women's Hosp; **Address:** Brigham & Womens Hosp, 850 Boylston St, Chestnut Hill, MA 02467; **Phone:** 857-307-4000; **Board Cert:** Internal Medicine 1988; Cardiovascular Disease 2011; **Med School:** Harvard Med Sch 1985; **Resid:** Internal Medicine, Brigham & Womens Hosp 1988; **Fellow:** Cardiovascular Disease, Brigham & Womens Hosp 1991; **Fac Appt:** Prof Med, Harvard Med Sch

Kirshenbaum, James M MD [Cv] - **Spec Exp:** Cardiac Catheterization; Coronary Artery Disease; Congestive Heart Failure; **Hospital:** Brigham & Women's Hosp; **Address:** Brigham & Womens Hosp, Cardiovascular Div, 75 Francis St, Boston, MA 02115; **Phone:** 857-307-1967; **Board Cert:** Internal Medicine 1982; Cardiovascular Disease 1985; **Med School:** Harvard Med Sch 1979; **Resid:** Internal Medicine, Peter Bent Brigham Hosp 1982; **Fellow:** Cardiovascular Disease, Brigham & Womens Hosp 1985; **Fac Appt:** Assoc Prof Med, Harvard Med Sch

Konstam, Marvin A MD [Cv] - **Spec Exp:** Transplant Medicine-Heart; Heart Failure; Coronary Angioplasty/Stents; **Hospital:** Tufts Med Ctr; **Address:** Tufts Med Ctr, Cardiovacular Ctr, 800 Washington St, Box 108, Boston, MA 02111; **Phone:** 617-636-6293; **Board Cert:** Internal Medicine 1979; Cardiovascular Disease 1981; Diagnostic Radiology 1980; Advanced Heart Failure & Transplant Cardiology 2010; **Med School:** Columbia P&S 1975; **Resid:** Diagnostic Radiology, Mass Genl Hosp 1978; Internal Medicine, Mass Genl Hosp 1979; **Fellow:** Cardiovascular Disease, Brigham & Women's Hosp 1981; **Fac Appt:** Prof Med, Tufts Univ

Kuvin, Jeffrey T MD [Cv] - **Spec Exp:** Preventive Cardiology; Congenital Heart Disease; Echocardiography; **Hospital:** Tufts Med Ctr; **Address:** Tufts Med Ctr, Cardiovascular Ctr, 800 Washington St, Box 315, Boston, MA 02111; **Phone:** 617-636-5846; **Board Cert:** Internal Medicine 2005; Cardiovascular Disease 2009; **Med School:** Emory Univ 1992; **Resid:** Internal Medicine, New England Med Ctr 1996; **Fellow:** Cardiovascular Disease, New England Med Ctr 1999; **Fac Appt:** Assoc Prof Med, Tufts Univ

Liang, Bruce T MD [Cv] - **Spec Exp:** Ischemic Heart Disease; Congestive Heart Failure; Heart Valve Disease; **Hospital:** Univ of Conn Hlth Ctr, John Dempsey Hosp; **Address:** UConn Health Center, 263 Farmington Ave, Farmington, CT 06030-2202; **Phone:** 860-679-3343; **Board Cert:** Internal Medicine 1985; Cardiovascular Disease 1987; **Med School:** Harvard Med Sch 1982; **Resid:** Internal Medicine, Hosp Univ Penn 1985; **Fellow:** Cardiovascular Disease, Brigham & Womens Hosp 1987; **Fac Appt:** Prof Med, Univ Conn

Loscalzo, Joseph MD/PhD [Cv] - **Spec Exp:** Coronary Artery Disease; Peripheral Vascular Disease; **Hospital:** Brigham & Women's Hosp; **Address:** Brigham & Women's Hosp, Div Cardiology, 75 Francis St, Boston, MA 02115; **Phone:** 617-732-6340; **Board Cert:** Internal Medicine 1981; Cardiovascular Disease 1983; **Med School:** Univ Pennsylvania 1978; **Resid:** Internal Medicine, Peter Bent Brigham Hosp 1981; **Fellow:** Cardiovascular Disease, Brigham & Women's Hosp 1983; **Fac Appt:** Prof Med, Harvard Med Sch

Manning, Warren J MD [Cv] - **Spec Exp:** Heart Valve Disease; Echocardiography; Cardiomyopathy; **Hospital:** Beth Israel Deaconess Med Ctr - Boston; **Address:** Beth Israel Deacones Med Ctr, 330 Brookline Ave, Boston, MA 02215-5400; **Phone:** 617-667-2192; **Board Cert:** Internal Medicine 1986; Cardiovascular Disease 1989; Echocardiography 2006; **Med School:** Harvard Med Sch 1983; **Resid:** Internal Medicine, Beth Israel Hosp 1986; **Fellow:** Cardiovascular Disease, Beth Israel Hosp 1989; **Fac Appt:** Prof Med, Harvard Med Sch

O'Gara, Patrick T MD [Cv] - **Spec Exp:** Heart Valve Disease; Coronary Artery Disease; Aortic Diseases & Dissection; **Hospital:** Brigham & Women's Hosp; **Address:** Brigham & Womens Hosp, Cardiovascular Div, Cardiovascular Div, 70 Francis St, Boston, MA 02115; **Phone:** 857-307-1990; **Board Cert:** Internal Medicine 1981; Cardiovascular Disease 1983; **Med School:** Northwestern Univ 1978; **Resid:** Internal Medicine, Mass Genl Hosp 1981; **Fellow:** Cardiovascular Disease, Mass Genl Hosp 1983; Research, Natl Heart Lung & Blood Inst 1986; **Fac Appt:** Prof Med, Harvard Med Sch

Pfeffer, Marc Alan MD [Cv] - **Hospital:** Brigham & Women's Hosp; **Address:** Brigham & Women's Hosp, Cardiovascular Div, 75 Francis St, Boston, MA 02115; **Phone:** 617-732-5681; **Board Cert:** Internal Medicine 1979; Cardiovascular Disease 1981; Advanced Heart Failure & Transplant Cardiology 2010; **Med School:** Univ Okla Coll Med 1976; **Resid:** Internal Medicine, Brigham & Women's Hosp 1979; **Fellow:** Cardiovascular Disease, Brigham & Women's Hosp 1980; **Fac Appt:** Prof Med, Harvard Med Sch

Ridker, Paul M MD [Cv] - **Spec Exp:** Coronary Artery Disease; Preventive Cardiology; Cholesterol/Lipid Disorders; **Hospital:** Brigham & Women's Hosp; **Address:** Southern Jamaica Plain Health Ctr, 640 Centre St, Jamaica Plains, MA 02130; **Phone:** 617-278-0869; **Board Cert:** Internal Medicine 1989; **Med School:** Harvard Med Sch 1986; **Resid:** Internal Medicine, Brigham & Women's Hosp 1989; **Fellow:** Cardiovascular Disease, Brigham & Women's Hosp 1991; **Fac Appt:** Assoc Prof Med, Harvard Med Sch

Roberts, Barbara H MD [Cv] - **Spec Exp:** Heart Disease in Women; Preventive Cardiology; **Hospital:** Miriam Hosp; **Address:** The Miriam Hosp - Women's Cardiac Ctr, 164 Summit Ave, Fain Med Bldg, Providence, RI 02906; **Phone:** 401-793-5750; **Board Cert:** Internal Medicine 1975; Cardiovascular Disease 1975; **Med School:** Case West Res Univ 1968; **Resid:** Internal Medicine, Yale-New Haven Hosp 1971; **Fellow:** Cardiovascular Disease, PB Brigham Hosp-Harvard 1975; **Fac Appt:** Assoc Clin Prof Med, Brown Univ

Stevenson, Lynne W MD [Cv] - **Spec Exp:** Heart Failure; Transplant Medicine-Heart; **Hospital:** Brigham & Women's Hosp; **Address:** Brigham & Women's Hospital, 75 Francis St, Boston, MA 02115; **Phone:** 617-732-7141; **Board Cert:** Internal Medicine 1982; Cardiovascular Disease 1985; Advanced Heart Failure & Transplant Cardiology 2012; **Med School:** Stanford Univ 1979; **Resid:** Internal Medicine, UCLA Med Ctr 1982; **Fellow:** Cardiovascular Disease, UCLA Med Ctr 1984; **Fac Appt:** Prof Med, Harvard Med Sch

Thompson, Paul D MD [Cv] - **Spec Exp:** Preventive Cardiology; Cholesterol/Lipid Discorders; Coronary Artery Disease; Hypertension; **Hospital:** Hartford Hosp; **Address:** 85 Jefferson St, Ste 704, Hartford, CT 06106; **Phone:** 860-545-1695; **Board Cert:** Internal Medicine 1976; Cardiovascular Disease 2011; **Med School:** Tufts Univ 1973; **Resid:** Internal Medicine, Tufts New England Med Ctr 1975; **Fellow:** Cardiovascular Disease, Tufts New England Med Ctr 1976; Cardiovascular Disease, Stanford Univ Med Ctr 1978

Williams, David O MD [Cv] - **Spec Exp:** Cardiac Catheterization; **Hospital:** Brigham & Women's Hosp; **Address:** Brigham & Women's Hosp, Cardiovascular Div, 1620 Tremont St Fl 3, Boston, MA 02115; **Phone:** 857-307-1987; **Board Cert:** Internal Medicine 1972; Cardiovascular Disease 1975; **Med School:** Hahnemann Univ 1969; **Resid:** Internal Medicine, Hahnemann Univ Hosp 1972; **Fellow:** Cardiovascular Disease, UC Davis Med Ctr 1974; **Fac Appt:** Prof Med, Brown Univ

Zusman, Randall M MD [Cv] - **Spec Exp:** Hypertension; Cholesterol/Lipid Disorders; Atrial Fibrillation; Coronary Artery Disease; **Hospital:** Mass Genl Hosp; **Address:** Mass Genl Hosp, Yawkey Ctr, 55 Fruit St, Ste 5B, Boston, MA 02114; **Phone:** 617-726-7790; **Board Cert:** Internal Medicine 1976; Cardiovascular Disease 1983; **Med School:** Yale Univ 1973; **Resid:** Internal Medicine, Mass General Hosp 1978; **Fellow:** Cardiovascular Disease, Mass General Hosp 1979; **Fac Appt:** Assoc Prof Med, Harvard Med Sch

Mid Atlantic

Andersen, Holly S MD [Cv] - **Spec Exp:** Preventive Cardiology; Women's Health; Mitral Valve Prolapse; **Hospital:** NY-Presby/Weill Cornell Med Ctr, NY (page 65); **Address:** 425 E 61st St Fl 6, New York, NY 10065; **Phone:** 212-752-2000; **Board Cert:** Internal Medicine 2012; Cardiovascular Disease 2005; **Med School:** Univ Rochester 1989; **Resid:** Internal Medicine, NY Presby-Cornell Med Ctr 1992; **Fellow:** Cardiovascular Disease, NY Presby-Cornell Med Ctr 1995; **Fac Appt:** Assoc Clin Prof Med, Cornell Univ-Weill Med Coll

Blumenthal, David S MD [Cv] - **Spec Exp:** Heart Valve Disease; Preventive Cardiology; Coronary Artery Disease; **Hospital:** NY-Presby/Weill Cornell Med Ctr, NY (page 65); **Address:** 407 E 70th St, Fl 1, New York, NY 10021-5302; **Phone:** 212-861-3222; **Board Cert:** Internal Medicine 1978; Cardiovascular Disease 1981; **Med School:** Cornell Univ-Weill Med Coll 1975; **Resid:** Internal Medicine, NY Hosp 1978; Internal Medicine, NY Hosp 1981; **Fellow:** Cardiovascular Disease, Johns Hopkins Hosp 1980; **Fac Appt:** Clin Prof Med, Cornell Univ-Weill Med Coll

Blumenthal, Roger S MD [Cv] - **Spec Exp:** Preventive Cardiology; Hypertension; Cardiovascular Disease/Young Adult; **Hospital:** Johns Hopkins Hosp (page 59); **Address:** Johns Hopkins Preventive Cardiology Ctr, 10755 N Falls Rd, Ste 360, Lutherville, MD 21093; **Phone:** 410-583-2740; **Board Cert:** Internal Medicine 1988; Cardiovascular Disease 2003; **Med School:** Cornell Univ-Weill Med Coll 1985; **Resid:** Internal Medicine, Johns Hopkins Hosp 1988; **Fellow:** Cardiovascular Disease, Johns Hopkins Hosp 1992; **Fac Appt:** Prof Med, Johns Hopkins Univ

Borer, Jeffrey S MD [Cv] - **Spec Exp:** Heart Valve Disease; Heart Failure; Nuclear Cardiology; Coronary Artery Disease; **Hospital:** SUNY Downstate Med Ctr (Univ Hosp Brooklyn), NY-Presby/Weill Cornell Med Ctr, NY (page 65); **Address:** SUNY Downstate Med Ctr, Div Cardiology, Howard Gilman Institute, 635 Madison Ave Fl 3, New York, NY 10022; **Phone:** 212-289-7777; **Board Cert:** Internal Medicine 1973; Cardiovascular Disease 1975; **Med School:** Cornell Univ-Weill Med Coll 1969; **Resid:** Internal Medicine, Mass Genl Hosp 1971; **Fellow:** Cardiovascular Disease, Natl Heart, Lung & Blood Inst 1974; Cardiovascular Disease, Guy's Hosp 1975; **Fac Appt:** Prof Med, SUNY Downstate

Bove, Alfred A MD/PhD [Cv] - **Spec Exp:** Diving Medicine; Heart Failure; Sports Medicine; **Hospital:** Temple Univ Hosp; **Address:** Temple Univ Hosp, Div Cardiology, 3401 N Broad St, Parkinson Pavillon, Fl 9, Philadelphia, PA 19140; **Phone:** 215-707-9259; **Board Cert:** Internal Medicine 1971; Cardiovascular Disease 1983; Undersea & Hyperbaric Medicine 2010; **Med School:** Temple Univ 1966; **Resid:** Internal Medicine, Temple Univ Hosp 1970; **Fellow:** Cardiovascular Disease, Temple Univ Hosp 1972; Physiology, Mayo Clin 1973; **Fac Appt:** Prof Emeritus Med, Temple Univ

Brozena, Susan C MD [Cv] - **Spec Exp:** Transplant Medicine-Heart; Congestive Heart Failure; Heart Disease in Women; **Hospital:** Hosp Univ Penn - UPHS (page 69); **Address:** Penn Cardiac Care, 250 King of Prussia Rd, Ste 2B, Radnor, PA 19087; **Phone:** 610-902-2273; **Board Cert:** Internal Medicine 1984; Cardiovascular Disease 2011; Advanced Heart Failure & Transplant Cardiology 2010; **Med School:** Temple Univ 1981; **Resid:** Internal Medicine, Temple Univ Hosp 1984; **Fellow:** Cardiovascular Disease, Temple Univ Hosp 1986; **Fac Appt:** Assoc Prof Med, Univ Pennsylvania

Coppola, John T MD [Cv] - **Spec Exp:** Cardiac Catheterization; Angioplasty; **Hospital:** NYU Langone Med Ctr (page 68), Bellevue Hosp Ctr; **Address:** 275 7th Ave Fl 3, New York, NY 10001; **Phone:** 646-660-9999; **Board Cert:** Internal Medicine 1981; Cardiovascular Disease 1983; Interventional Cardiology 2009; **Med School:** NY Med Coll 1978; **Resid:** Internal Medicine, St Vincent Catholic Med Ctr 1981; **Fellow:** Cardiovascular Disease, St Vincent Catholic Med Ctr 1983

Dangas, George MD/PhD [Cv] - **Spec Exp:** Acute Coronary Syndromes; Angioplasty & Stent Placement; Endovascular Therapy; Percutaneous Vascular Interventions; **Hospital:** Mt Sinai Med Ctr (page 62), Mount Sinai Hosp of Queens (page 62); **Address:** Cardiovascular Med Assocs, 1190 5th Ave, rm GP1 South, New York, NY 10029; **Phone:** 212-241-7014; **Board Cert:** Interventional Cardiology 2009; Cardiovascular Disease 2007; Vascular Medicine 2006; Endovascular Medicine 2005; **Med School:** Greece 1989; **Resid:** Internal Medicine, Miriam Hosp 1994; **Fellow:** Cardiovascular Disease, Mount Sinai Med Ctr 1997; Interventional Cardiology, Mount Sinai Med Ctr 1998; **Fac Appt:** Prof Med, Mount Sinai Sch Med

Devereux, Richard B MD [Cv] - **Spec Exp:** Marfan's Syndrome; **Hospital:** NY-Presby/Weill Cornell Med Ctr, NY (page 65); **Address:** 525 E 68th St, rm K-415, New York, NY 10065; **Phone:** 212-746-4655; **Board Cert:** Internal Medicine 1974; Cardiovascular Disease 1977; **Med School:** Univ Pennsylvania 1971; **Resid:** Internal Medicine, New York Hosp 1974; **Fellow:** Cardiovascular Disease, Hosp Univ Penn - UPHS 1976; **Fac Appt:** Prof Med, Cornell Univ-Weill Med Coll

Edmundowicz, Daniel MD [Cv] - **Spec Exp:** Preventive Cardiology; Cholesterol/Lipid Disorders; **Hospital:** Jeanes Hosp, Temple University Hosp-Episcopal Campus; **Address:** 3401 N Broad St, Parkinson Pavilion, 9th FL, Philadelphia, PA 19140; **Phone:** 215-707-9259; **Board Cert:** Internal Medicine 2005; Cardiovascular Disease 2009; **Med School:** Hahnemann Univ 1990; **Resid:** Internal Medicine, Temple Univ Hosp 1993; **Fellow:** Cardiovascular Disease, UPMC 1996; **Fac Appt:** Assoc Prof Med, Univ Pittsburgh

Eisen, Howard J MD [Cv] - **Spec Exp:** Transplant Medicine-Heart; Congestive Heart Failure; **Hospital:** Hahnemann Univ Hosp; **Address:** Drexel Cardiology, 230 N Broad St, Ste 740, Philadelphia, PA 19102; **Phone:** 215-762-4200; **Board Cert:** Internal Medicine 1984; Cardiovascular Disease 1987; Advanced Heart Failure & Transplant Cardiology 2010; **Med School:** Univ Pennsylvania 1981; **Resid:** Internal Medicine, Hosp Univ Penn - UPHS 1984; **Fellow:** Cardiovascular Disease, Barnes-Jewish Hosp 1987; **Fac Appt:** Prof Med, Drexel Univ Coll Med

Follansbee, William P MD [Cv] - **Spec Exp:** Nuclear Cardiology; Amyloid Heart Disease; Nuclear Cardiology; Scleroderma; **Hospital:** UPMC Presby, Pittsburgh; **Address:** UPMC Heart & Vascular Inst, 200 Lothrop St, Ste 429, Pittsburgh, PA 15213; **Phone:** 412-647-3437; **Board Cert:** Internal Medicine 1977; Cardiovascular Disease 1981; **Med School:** Univ Pennsylvania 1974; **Resid:** Internal Medicine, Hosp Univ Penn 1978; **Fellow:** Cardiovascular Disease, Hosp Univ Penn 1980; **Fac Appt:** Prof Med, Univ Pittsburgh

Friedman, Sanford J MD [Cv] - **Spec Exp:** Preventive Cardiology; **Hospital:** Mt Sinai Med Ctr (page 62); **Address:** 941 Park Ave, New York, NY 10028; **Phone:** 212-988-3772; **Board Cert:** Internal Medicine 1980; Cardiovascular Disease 1977; **Med School:** Tufts Univ 1971; **Resid:** Internal Medicine, Mt Sinai Hosp 1974; **Fellow:** Cardiovascular Disease, Mt Sinai Hosp 1976; **Fac Appt:** Assoc Clin Prof Med, Mount Sinai Sch Med

Fuster, Valentin MD/PhD [Cv] - **Spec Exp:** Coronary Artery Disease; Heart Valve Disease; Congenital Heart Disease; Preventive Cardiology; **Hospital:** Mt Sinai Med Ctr (page 62); **Address:** Cardiovascular Med Assocs, 1190 Fifth Ave Fl 1, New York, NY 10029-6500; **Phone:** 212-241-7911; **Board Cert:** Internal Medicine 1976; Cardiovascular Disease 1977; **Med School:** Spain 1967; **Resid:** Internal Medicine, Mayo Clin 1972; Cardiovascular Disease, Mayo Clin 1974; **Fellow:** Cardiovascular Disease, Univ Edinburgh 1971; **Fac Appt:** Prof Med, Mount Sinai Sch Med

Garcia, Mario J MD [Cv] - **Spec Exp:** Echocardiography-Transesophageal; Echocardiography; **Hospital:** Montefiore Med Ctr-Moses Campus, NY; **Address:** Montefiore Einstein Heart/Cardiovascular Care, 111 E 210th St, Bronx, NY 10467; **Phone:** 718-920-4172; **Board Cert:** Internal Medicine 2003; Cardiovascular Disease 2003; **Med School:** Dominican Republic 1986; **Resid:** Internal Medicine, St Vincent's Med Ctr 1990; **Fellow:** Nuclear Cardiology, Mass Genl Hosp 1994; Cardiovascular Disease, Cleveland Clinic 1996; **Fac Appt:** Prof Med, Albert Einstein Coll Med

Gardin, Julius M MD [Cv] - **Spec Exp:** Echocardiography; Geriatric Cardiology; Preventive Cardiology; Cholesterol/Lipid Disorders; **Hospital:** Hackensack Univ Med Ctr; **Address:** Hackensack Univ Med Ctr, Dept Medicine, 30 Prospect Ave, 1 Main, Ste 1647, Hackensack, NJ 07601; **Phone:** 551-996-3500; **Board Cert:** Internal Medicine 1975; Cardiovascular Disease 1977; **Med School:** Univ Mich Med Sch 1972; **Resid:** Internal Medicine, Univ Mich Hosp 1975; **Fellow:** Cardiovascular Disease, Georgetown Univ Hosp 1977; **Fac Appt:** Prof Med, UMDNJ-Univ Med Dent NJ

Gliklich, Jerry MD [Cv] - **Spec Exp:** Heart Valve Disease; Arrhythmias; **Hospital:** NY-Presby/Columbia Univ Med Ctr, NY (page 65); **Address:** NY-Presby, Heart Ctr, 173 Fort Washington Ave, Ste 606, New York, NY 10032; **Phone:** 212-305-5588; **Board Cert:** Internal Medicine 1978; Cardiovascular Disease 1981; **Med School:** Columbia P&S 1975; **Resid:** Internal Medicine, NY-Presby/Weill Cornell Med Ctr 1978; **Fellow:** Cardiovascular Disease, NY-Presby/Columbia Univ Med Ctr 1981; **Fac Appt:** Clin Prof Med, Columbia P&S

Goldberg, Nieca MD [Cv] - **Spec Exp:** Women's Health; Preventive Cardiology; Heart Disease in Women; **Hospital:** NYU Langone Med Ctr (page 68), Lenox Hill Hosp (page 66); **Address:** Joan H. Tisch Ctr for Women's Hlth, 207 E 84th St, New York, NY 10028; **Phone:** 212-289-2045; **Board Cert:** Internal Medicine 1987; Cardiovascular Disease 2005; **Med School:** SUNY Downstate 1984; **Resid:** Internal Medicine, St. Luke's - Roosevelt Hosp Ctr - Roosevelt Div 1987; **Fellow:** Cardiovascular Disease, SUNY Downstate Affil Hosp 1990; **Fac Appt:** Assoc Clin Prof Med, NYU Sch Med

Goodman, Dennis A MD [Cv] - **Spec Exp:** Preventive Cardiology; Cholesterol/Lipid Disorders; Complementary Medicine; **Hospital:** NYU Langone Med Ctr (page 68), Lenox Hill Hosp (page 66); **Address:** 635 Madison Ave, Fl 3, New York, NY 10022; **Phone:** 212-784-5998; **Board Cert:** Internal Medicine 1984; Cardiovascular Disease 1989; Integrative Medicine 2006; **Med School:** South Africa 1979; **Resid:** Internal Medicine, Montefiore Med Ctr 1984; **Fellow:** Cardiovascular Disease, Baylor Coll Med 1987; **Fac Appt:** Assoc Clin Prof Med, NYU Sch Med

Gottdiener, John S MD [Cv] - **Spec Exp:** Echocardiography; **Hospital:** Univ of MD Med Ctr; **Address:** 110 S Paca St Fl 7, Baltimore, MD 21201; **Phone:** 410-328-6072; **Board Cert:** Internal Medicine 1975; Cardiovascular Disease 1979; **Med School:** Georgetown Univ 1970; **Resid:** Internal Medicine, Univ NC Hosp 1972; **Fellow:** Cardiovascular Disease, Georgetown Univ Hosp 1976; **Fac Appt:** Prof Med, Univ MD Sch Med

Gottlieb, Stephen Scott MD [Cv] - **Spec Exp:** Heart Failure; Transplant Medicine-Heart; **Hospital:** Univ of MD Med Ctr; **Address:** Univ Maryland Med Ctr, Cardiology, 419 W Redwood St, Ste 600, Baltimore, MD 21201; **Phone:** 410-328-8788; **Board Cert:** Internal Medicine 1984; Cardiovascular Disease 1987; Advanced Heart Failure & Transplant Cardiology 2010; **Med School:** Brown Univ 1981; **Resid:** Internal Medicine, Univ Chicago Hosps 1984; **Fellow:** Cardiovascular Disease, Mt Sinai Hosp 1985; **Fac Appt:** Prof Med, Univ MD Sch Med

Greenberg, Mark A MD [Cv] - **Spec Exp:** Interventional Cardiology; Cardiac Catheterization; Heart Valve Disease; **Hospital:** Montefiore Med Ctr-Moses Campus, NY; **Address:** 111 E 210th St, Division of Cardiology, Bronx, NY 10467; **Phone:** 718-920-4212; **Board Cert:** Internal Medicine 1976; Cardiovascular Disease 1979; **Med School:** Univ IL Coll Med 1973; **Resid:** Internal Medicine, Montefiore Med Ctr 1976; **Fellow:** Cardiovascular Disease, Montefiore Med Ctr 1979; **Fac Appt:** Clin Prof Med, Albert Einstein Coll Med

Halperin, Jonathan L MD [Cv] - **Spec Exp:** Vascular Disease; Atrial Fibrillation; **Hospital:** Mt Sinai Med Ctr (page 62); **Address:** Cardiology Associates, 1190 Fifth Ave, New York, NY 10029; **Phone:** 212-241-7243; **Board Cert:** Internal Medicine 1980; Cardiovascular Disease 1981; **Med School:** Boston Univ 1975; **Resid:** Internal Medicine, Boston Univ Med Ctr 1977; **Fellow:** Vascular Medicine, Boston Univ Med Ctr 1978; Cardiovascular Disease, Boston Univ Med Ctr 1980; **Fac Appt:** Prof Med, Mount Sinai Sch Med

Herling, Irving M MD [Cv] - **Spec Exp:** Cholesterol/Lipid Disorders; Preventive Cardiology; Heart Valve Disease; **Hospital:** Lankenau Hosp; **Address:** Lankenau Heart & Vascular Grp, 100 E Lancaster Ave, Ste 450, Wynnewood, PA 19096; **Phone:** 484-572-0112; **Board Cert:** Internal Medicine 1977; Cardiovascular Disease 1979; **Med School:** Univ Pennsylvania 1974; **Resid:** Internal Medicine, Hosp Univ Penn - UPHS 1977; **Fellow:** Cardiovascular Disease, Hosp Univ Penn - UPHS 1979

Horn, Evelyn M MD [Cv] - **Spec Exp:** Pulmonary Hypertension; Heart Failure; Ventricular Assist Device (LVAD); **Hospital:** NY-Presby/Weill Cornell Med Ctr, NY (page 65); **Address:** 520 E 70th St Starr Bldg Fl 4 - Ste 443, New York, NY 10021; **Phone:** 212-746-2381; **Board Cert:** Internal Medicine 1983; Cardiovascular Disease 1985; Advanced Heart Failure & Transplant Cardiology 2010; **Med School:** Mount Sinai Sch Med 1980; **Resid:** Internal Medicine, Mt Sinai Hosp 1983; **Fellow:** Cardiovascular Disease, Cedars-Sinai Med Ctr 1985; **Fac Appt:** Clin Prof Med, Cornell Univ-Weill Med Coll

Inra, Lawrence A MD [Cv] - **Spec Exp:** Coronary Artery Disease; Preventive Cardiology; Cholesterol/Lipid Disorders; Hypertension; **Hospital:** NY-Presby/Weill Cornell Med Ctr, NY (page 65), Hosp For Special Surgery (page 58); **Address:** 407 E 70th St, New York, NY 10021; **Phone:** 212-249-1011; **Board Cert:** Internal Medicine 1979; Cardiovascular Disease 1981; **Med School:** Johns Hopkins Univ 1976; **Resid:** Internal Medicine, Presby/Weill Cornell Med Ctr 1979; **Fellow:** Cardiovascular Disease, Mt Sinai Med Ctr 1981; **Fac Appt:** Assoc Clin Prof Med, Cornell Univ-Weill Med Coll

Jessup, Mariell MD [Cv] - **Spec Exp:** Congestive Heart Failure; Transplant Medicine-Heart; **Hospital:** Hosp Univ Penn - UPHS (page 69), Penn Presby Med Ctr - UPHS (page 69); **Address:** Penn Heart & Vascular Ctr, 2 East, Perelman Ctr, 3400 Civic Center Blvd, Philadelphia, PA 19104; **Phone:** 215-615-0800; **Board Cert:** Internal Medicine 1979; Cardiovascular Disease 2011; Advanced Heart Failure & Transplant Cardiology 2010; **Med School:** Hahnemann Univ 1976; **Resid:** Internal Medicine, Hahnemann Hosp 1979; **Fellow:** Cardiovascular Disease, Hosp Univ Penn 1982; **Fac Appt:** Prof Med, Univ Pennsylvania

Katz, Stuart D MD [Cv] - **Spec Exp:** Heart Failure; Transplant Medicine-Heart; **Hospital:** NYU Langone Med Ctr (page 68); **Address:** NYU Cardiology Assocs, 530 First Ave Skirball Bldg - Ste 9U, New York, NY 10016; **Phone:** 212-263-7751; **Board Cert:** Internal Medicine 1986; Cardiovascular Disease 1989; Advanced Heart Failure & Transplant Cardiology 2010; **Med School:** SUNY Downstate 1983; **Resid:** Internal Medicine, Johns Hopkins Bayview Med Ctr 1986; **Fellow:** Cardiovascular Disease, Montefiore Med Ctr-Moses Campus 1989; **Fac Appt:** Prof Med, NYU Sch Med

Kostis, John B MD [Cv] - **Spec Exp:** Coronary Artery Disease; Hypertension; Cholesterol/Lipid Disorders; **Hospital:** Robert Wood Johnson Univ Hosp - New Brunswick; **Address:** 125 Paterson St, CAB Bldg - Fl 5 - Ste 5200, New Brunswick, NJ 08901; **Phone:** 732-235-7685; **Board Cert:** Internal Medicine 1973; Cardiovascular Disease 1973; **Med School:** Greece 1960; **Resid:** Internal Medicine, Evanglismos Hosp 1964; Internal Medicine, Cumberland Med Ctr 1967; **Fellow:** Cardiovascular Disease, Philadelphia Genl Hosp 1969; **Fac Appt:** Prof Med, UMDNJ-RW Johnson Med Sch

Landzberg, Joel S MD [Cv] - **Spec Exp:** Preventive Cardiology; Coronary Artery Disease; Heart Failure; Heart Valve Disease; **Hospital:** Hackensack Univ Med Ctr, Valley Hosp; **Address:** Westwood Cardiology Associates, 333 Old Hook Rd, Ste 200, Westwood, NJ 07675-3200; **Phone:** 201-664-0201; **Board Cert:** Internal Medicine 1986; Cardiovascular Disease 1989; Interventional Cardiology 2012; **Med School:** Columbia P&S 1983; **Resid:** Internal Medicine, Vanderbilt Univ Hosp 1986; **Fellow:** Cardiology Research, Moffit Hosp 1987; Cardiovascular Disease, Brigham & Womens Hosp 1991; **Fac Appt:** Assoc Clin Prof Med, UMDNJ-NJ Med Sch, Newark

Mather, Paul J MD [Cv] - **Spec Exp:** Heart Failure; Transplant Medicine-Heart; **Hospital:** Thomas Jefferson Univ Hosp; **Address:** Jefferson Univ Phys-Cardiology, 925 Chestnut St, Mezzanine Level, Philadelphia, PA 19107; **Phone:** 215-955-5050; **Board Cert:** Cardiovascular Disease 2005; Advanced Heart Failure & Transplant Cardiology 2012; **Med School:** Temple Univ 1988; **Resid:** Internal Medicine, Temple Univ Hosp 1991; **Fellow:** Cardiovascular Disease, Temple Univ Hosp 1994; **Fac Appt:** Assoc Prof Med, Jefferson Med Coll

Meller, Jose MD [Cv] - **Spec Exp:** Preventive Cardiology; Coronary Artery Disease; Heart Disease in Pregnancy; Heart Valve Disease; **Hospital:** Mt Sinai Med Ctr (page 62); **Address:** 941 Park Ave, New York, NY 10028; **Phone:** 212-988-3772; **Board Cert:** Internal Medicine 1973; Cardiovascular Disease 1975; **Med School:** Chile 1969; **Resid:** Internal Medicine, Elmhurst Hosp 1971; Internal Medicine, Mt Sinai Med Ctr 1972; **Fellow:** Cardiovascular Disease, Mt Sinai Med Ctr 1974; **Fac Appt:** Clin Prof Med, Mount Sinai Sch Med

Pichard, Augusto D MD [Cv] - **Spec Exp:** Interventional Cardiology; Cardiac Catheterization; Angioplasty & Stent Placement; Percutaneous Valve Repair; **Hospital:** MedStar Washington Hosp Ctr; **Address:** 110 Irving St NW, Ste 4B1, Washington, DC 20010; **Phone:** 202-877-5975; **Board Cert:** Internal Medicine 1975; Cardiovascular Disease 1977; **Med School:** Chile 1969; **Resid:** Internal Medicine, Univ Chile 1970; Internal Medicine, Catholic Univ 1971; **Fellow:** Cardiovascular Disease, Cleveland Clin 1973; **Fac Appt:** Prof Med, Georgetown Univ

Poon, Michael MD [Cv] - **Spec Exp:** Coronary Artery Disease; Pulmonary Hypertension; Cardiac CT Angiography; Cardiac Imaging; **Hospital:** Stony Brook Univ Med Ctr, Mt Sinai Med Ctr (page 62); **Address:** 70 Bowery, Ste 303, New York, NY 10013; **Phone:** 212-925-4088; **Board Cert:** Cardiovascular Disease 2007; Cardiovascular Computed Tomography 2008; **Med School:** Mount Sinai Sch Med 1987; **Resid:** Internal Medicine, Mount Sinai Med Ctr 1991; **Fellow:** Cardiovascular Disease, Mount Sinai Med Ctr 1993; **Fac Appt:** Prof Med, SUNY Stony Brook

Reis, Steven E MD [Cv] - **Spec Exp:** Heart Disease in Women; Congestive Heart Failure; Metabolic Syndrome; Preventive Cardiology; **Hospital:** UPMC Presby, Pittsburgh, Magee-Womens Hosp - UPMC; **Address:** UPMC Cardiovascular Inst at Univ Ctr, 120 Lytton Ave, Ste 100B, Pittsburgh, PA 15213; **Phone:** 412-802-3000; **Board Cert:** Internal Medicine 2011; Cardiovascular Disease 2000; **Med School:** Harvard Med Sch 1987; **Resid:** Internal Medicine, Brigham & Womens Hosp 1990; **Fellow:** Cardiovascular Disease, Johns Hopkins Hosp 1994; **Fac Appt:** Assoc Prof Med, Univ Pittsburgh

Russell, Stuart D MD [Cv] - **Spec Exp:** Heart Failure; Transplant Medicine-Heart; **Hospital:** Johns Hopkins Hosp (page 59); **Address:** Johns Hopkins Heart and Vascular Inst, 600 N Wolfe St, Baltimore, MD 21287; **Phone:** 410-955-5708; **Board Cert:** Internal Medicine 2006; Cardiovascular Disease 2007; Advanced Heart Failure & Transplant Cardiology 2010; **Med School:** Univ Wash 1991; **Resid:** Internal Medicine, Johns Hopkins Hosp 1994; **Fellow:** Cardiovascular Disease, Duke Univ Med Ctr 1997; **Fac Appt:** Assoc Prof Med, Johns Hopkins Univ

Saunders, Elijah MD [Cv] - **Spec Exp:** Hypertension-Complex; Coronary Artery Disease; **Hospital:** Univ of MD Med Ctr; **Address:** Univ MD Med Sch, Div Hypertension, 419 W Redwood St, Ste 620, Baltimore, MD 21201; **Phone:** 410-328-4366; **Med School:** Univ MD Sch Med 1960; **Resid:** Internal Medicine, Univ Maryland Med Ctr 1963; **Fellow:** Cardiovascular Disease, Univ Maryland Med Ctr 1965; **Fac Appt:** Prof Med, Univ MD Sch Med

Schulman, Steven P MD [Cv] - **Spec Exp:** Acute Coronary Syndromes; **Hospital:** Johns Hopkins Hosp (page 59); **Address:** Johns Hopkins Medicine, 601 N Caroline St, Outpatient Center Fl 7, Baltimore, MD 21287; **Phone:** 410-955-7378; **Board Cert:** Internal Medicine 1986; Cardiovascular Disease 1989; **Med School:** Johns Hopkins Univ 1981; **Resid:** Internal Medicine, Johns Hopkins Hosp 1984; **Fellow:** Cardiovascular Disease, Johns Hopkins Hosp 1988; **Fac Appt:** Assoc Prof Med, Johns Hopkins Univ

Schwartz, Allan MD [Cv] - **Hospital:** NY-Presby/Columbia Univ Med Ctr, NY (page 65); **Address:** 173 Fort Washington Ave, Ste 4-600C, New York, NY 10032; **Phone:** 212-305-5367; **Board Cert:** Internal Medicine 1977; Cardiovascular Disease 1979; **Med School:** Columbia P&S 1974; **Resid:** Internal Medicine, Columbia-Presby Med Ctr 1976; **Fellow:** Cardiovascular Disease, Mass Genl Hosp 1978; **Fac Appt:** Clin Prof Med, Columbia P&S

Schwartz, William J MD [Cv] - **Spec Exp:** Coronary Artery Disease; Cardiac Catheterization; Congestive Heart Failure; **Hospital:** Mt Sinai Med Ctr (page 62); **Address:** Mt Sinai Multispecialty Physicians, 150 E 77th St, Ste 1E, New York, NY 10075; **Phone:** 212-439-6000; **Board Cert:** Internal Medicine 1978; Cardiovascular Disease 1981; **Med School:** Albert Einstein Coll Med 1975; **Resid:** Internal Medicine, Bronx Municipal Hosp 1978; **Fellow:** Cardiovascular Disease, Bronx Municipal Hosp 1981; **Fac Appt:** Asst Prof Med, Mount Sinai Sch Med

Shlofmitz, Richard A MD [Cv] - **Spec Exp:** Interventional Cardiology; Cardiac Catheterization; **Hospital:** St. Francis Hosp - The Heart Ctr (page 70); **Address:** 100 Port Washington Blvd, Ste 105, Vizza Pavilion, Roslyn, NY 11576; **Phone:** 516-390-9640; **Board Cert:** Internal Medicine 1984; Cardiovascular Disease 1987; **Med School:** NYU Sch Med 1980; **Resid:** Internal Medicine, N Shore Univ Hosp 1984; **Fellow:** Cardiovascular Disease, Presby/Columbia Univ Med Ctr 1987

Silvestry, Frank E MD [Cv] - **Spec Exp:** Heart Valve Disease; Percutaneous Valve Repair; Echocardiography; **Hospital:** Hosp Univ Penn - UPHS (page 69); **Address:** Penn Heart & Vascular Ctr, Perelman Ctr Ground Fl, 3400 Civic Ctr Blvd, Philadelphia, PA 19104; **Phone:** 215-615-4949; **Board Cert:** Cardiovascular Disease 2008; Echocardiography 2003; **Med School:** Univ Pennsylvania 1990; **Resid:** Internal Medicine, Hosp Univ Penn - UPHS 1994; **Fellow:** Cardiovascular Disease, Hosp Univ Penn - UPHS 1997; **Fac Appt:** Assoc Prof Med, Univ Pennsylvania

Slater, William R MD [Cv] - **Spec Exp:** Arrhythmias; Heart Valve Disease; Cardiac Electrophysiology; **Hospital:** NYU Langone Med Ctr (page 68); **Address:** NYU Medical Ctr, Div Cardiology, 530 First Ave Skirball Bldg - Ste 9U, New York, NY 10016; **Phone:** 212-263-7463; **Board Cert:** Internal Medicine 1981; Cardiovascular Disease 1985; **Med School:** Harvard Med Sch 1978; **Resid:** Internal Medicine, Bellevue Hosp Ctr 1981; **Fellow:** Cardiovascular Disease, Mt Sinai Hosp 1984; Cardiovascular Disease, Mass Genl Hosp/Brigham & Womens Hosp 1986; **Fac Appt:** Assoc Prof Med, NYU Sch Med

Steingart, Richard M MD [Cv] - **Spec Exp:** Heart Failure; Heart Disease in Cancer Patients; Cardiac Effects of Cancer/Cancer Therapy; Amyloid Heart Disease; **Hospital:** Meml Sloan-Kettering Canc Ctr; **Address:** 1275 York Ave, New York, NY 10065; **Phone:** 212-639-8488; **Board Cert:** Internal Medicine 1977; Cardiovascular Disease 1979; **Med School:** Mount Sinai Sch Med 1974; **Resid:** Internal Medicine, Yale-New Haven Hosp 1977; **Fellow:** Cardiovascular Disease, Mt Sinai Med Ctr 1979; **Fac Appt:** Prof Med, Cornell Univ-Weill Med Coll

Tenenbaum, Joseph MD [Cv] - **Spec Exp:** Heart Valve Disease; Coronary Artery Disease; Atrial Fibrillation; Critical Care; **Hospital:** NY-Presby/Columbia Univ Med Ctr, NY (page 65); **Address:** 173 Ft Washington Ave, MHC Bldg - Fl 4 - Ste 606, Irving Pavilion, New York, NY 10032; **Phone:** 212-305-5288; **Board Cert:** Internal Medicine 1977; Cardiovascular Disease 1979; **Med School:** Harvard Med Sch 1974; **Resid:** Internal Medicine, Columbia-Presby Med Ctr 1977; **Fellow:** Cardiovascular Disease, Mt Sinai Hosp 1979; **Fac Appt:** Prof Med, Columbia P&S

Waxman, Harvey L MD [Cv] - **Spec Exp:** Arrhythmias; Cardiac Catheterization; Heart Valve Disease; **Hospital:** Penn Presby Med Ctr - UPHS (page 69); **Address:** Philadelphia Heart Inst, 51 N 39th St, Ste 400, Philadelphia, PA 19104; **Phone:** 215-662-9189; **Board Cert:** Internal Medicine 1977; Cardiovascular Disease 1979; **Med School:** Mount Sinai Sch Med 1974; **Resid:** Internal Medicine, Bellevue Hosp Ctr 1977; **Fellow:** Cardiovascular Disease, Jackson Meml Hosp 1979; Cardiac Electrophysiology, Hosp Univ Penn - UPHS 1980; **Fac Appt:** Clin Prof Med, Univ Pennsylvania

Weitz, Howard H MD [Cv] - **Spec Exp:** Preventive Cardiology; **Hospital:** Thomas Jefferson Univ Hosp; **Address:** Jefferson Univ Phys-Dept Cardiology, 925 Chestnut St, Mezzanine Level, Philadelphia, PA 19107; **Phone:** 215-955-5050; **Board Cert:** Internal Medicine 1981; Cardiovascular Disease 1985; **Med School:** Thomas Jefferson Univ 1978; **Resid:** Internal Medicine, Thomas Jefferson Univ Hosp 1982; **Fellow:** Cardiovascular Disease, Thomas Jefferson Univ Hosp 1984; **Fac Appt:** Prof Med, Thomas Jefferson Univ

Southeast

Bashore, Thomas M MD [Cv] - **Spec Exp:** Heart Valve Disease; Pulmonary Hypertension; Congenital Heart Disease-Adult; Pericardial Disease; **Hospital:** Duke Univ Hosp; **Address:** DUMC, Box 3012, Durham, NC 27710-0001; **Phone:** 919-684-2407; **Board Cert:** Internal Medicine 1975; Cardiovascular Disease 1977; **Med School:** Ohio State Univ 1972; **Resid:** Internal Medicine, NC Meml Hosp 1975; **Fellow:** Cardiovascular Disease, Duke Univ Med Ctr 1977; **Fac Appt:** Prof Med, Duke Univ

Bass, Theodore A MD [Cv] - **Spec Exp:** Interventional Cardiology; Coronary Artery Disease; **Hospital:** UF Hlth Jacksonville; **Address:** Shands Jacksonville, Cardiology Dept, 655 W 8th St ACC Bldg Fl 5, Jacksonville, FL 32209; **Phone:** 904-244-2655; **Board Cert:** Internal Medicine 1979; Cardiovascular Disease 1981; Interventional Cardiology 2011; **Med School:** Brown Univ 1976; **Resid:** Internal Medicine, Mayo Clin 1979; **Fellow:** Cardiovascular Disease, Univ Hosp 1981; **Fac Appt:** Prof Med, Univ Fla Coll Med

Borzak, Steven L MD [Cv] - **Spec Exp:** Coronary Artery Disease; Arrhythmias; Heart Failure; Cholesterol/Lipid Disorders; **Hospital:** JFK Med Ctr - Atlantis, Bethesda Memorial Hosp; **Address:** FL Cardiology Grp, 110 JFK Drive, Ste 110, Atlantis, FL 33462; **Phone:** 561-641-9541; **Board Cert:** Internal Medicine 1987; Cardiovascular Disease 2011; **Med School:** Univ IL Coll Med 1984; **Resid:** Internal Medicine, Michael Reese Hosp 1988; **Fellow:** Cardiovascular Disease, Brigham & Womens Hosp 1991; **Fac Appt:** Prof Med, Nova SE Univ, Coll Osteo Med

Bourge, Robert C MD [Cv] - **Spec Exp:** Heart Failure; Pulmonary Hypertension; Transplant Medicine-Heart; Nuclear Cardiology; **Hospital:** UAB Hosp; **Address:** University of Alabama at Birmingham, 1900 University Blvd, 321k, THT Bldg, Birmingham, AL 35294-0001; **Phone:** 205-934-3624; **Board Cert:** Internal Medicine 1982; Cardiovascular Disease 1985; Nuclear Medicine 1987; **Med School:** Louisiana State U, New Orleans 1979; **Resid:** Internal Medicine, Univ Alabama Hosps 1982; Nuclear Medicine, Univ Alabama Hosps 1985; **Fellow:** Cardiovascular Disease, Univ Alabama Hosps 1984; **Fac Appt:** Prof Med, UAB Sch Med

Byrd III, Benjamin F MD [Cv] - **Spec Exp:** Congenital Heart Disease; Echocardiography; Heart Valve Disease; **Hospital:** Vanderbilt Univ Med Ctr; **Address:** Vanderbilt Heart & Vascular Inst, 1215 21st Ave, MCE South Tower, Ste 5209, Nashville, TN 37232; **Phone:** 615-322-2318; **Board Cert:** Internal Medicine 1981; Cardiovascular Disease 1983; **Med School:** Vanderbilt Univ 1977; **Resid:** Psychiatry, Harvard/Mass Mental Hlth 1979; Internal Medicine, Vanderbilt Univ Hosp 1981; **Fellow:** Cardiovascular Disease, Vanderbilt Univ Hosp 1983; Cardiovascular Disease, UCSF Med Ctr 1984; **Fac Appt:** Prof Med, Vanderbilt Univ

Califf, Robert M MD [Cv] - **Spec Exp:** Coronary Artery Disease; Cholesterol/Lipid Disorders; Heart Failure; **Hospital:** Duke Univ Hosp; **Address:** 200 Trent Drive, 1117 Davison Bldg, DUMC 3701, Durham, NC 27710; **Phone:** 919-668-8820; **Board Cert:** Internal Medicine 1984; Cardiovascular Disease 1985; **Med School:** Duke Univ 1978; **Resid:** Internal Medicine, UCSF Med Ctr 1980; **Fellow:** Cardiovascular Disease, Duke Univ Med Ctr 1983; **Fac Appt:** Prof Med, Duke Univ

Chizner, Michael A MD [Cv] - **Spec Exp:** Preventive Cardiology; Coronary Artery Disease; Cardiac Catheterization; Coronary Angioplasty/Stents; **Hospital:** Broward Hlth Med Ctr, Broward Hlth Imperial Point; **Address:** 1625 SE 3rd Ave, Ste 300, Fort Lauderdale, FL 33316; **Phone:** 954-355-5001; **Board Cert:** Internal Medicine 1977; Cardiovascular Disease 1979; **Med School:** Cornell Univ 1974; **Resid:** Internal Medicine, New York Hosp 1977; **Fellow:** Cardiovascular Disease, Georgetown Univ 1979; **Fac Appt:** Clin Prof Med, Univ Miami Sch Med

Clements Jr, Stephen D MD [Cv] - **Spec Exp:** Cardiac Catheterization; Echocardiography; Heart Failure; **Hospital:** Emory Univ Hosp; **Address:** Emory Clin, Cardiology Dept, 1365A Clifton Rd NE, Ste 2200, Atlanta, GA 30322; **Phone:** 404-778-3468; **Board Cert:** Internal Medicine 1971; Cardiovascular Disease 1975; **Med School:** Med Coll GA 1966; **Resid:** Internal Medicine, Grady Meml Hosp 1970; **Fellow:** Cardiovascular Disease, Emory Univ Hosp 1971; **Fac Appt:** Prof Med, Emory Univ

Corrigan, Victor E MD [Cv] - **Spec Exp:** Cardiac Catheterization; Interventional Cardiology; Transplant Medicine-Heart; **Hospital:** Piedmont Hosp; **Address:** Piedmont Heart Inst, 275 Collier Rd, Ste 300, Atlanta, GA 30309; **Phone:** 404-605-2800; **Board Cert:** Internal Medicine 1986; Cardiovascular Disease 1989; Interventional Cardiology 2009; **Med School:** Med Coll GA 1983; **Resid:** Internal Medicine, Emory Univ Hosp 1986; **Fellow:** Cardiovascular Disease, Emory Univ Hosp 1988

Hare, Joshua M MD [Cv] - **Spec Exp:** Heart Failure; Stem Cell Therapy in Heart Failure; **Hospital:** Univ of Miami Hosp; **Address:** Univ Miami Hosp, Cardiology Dept, 1295 NW 14th St South Bldg Fl 2 - Ste A, Miami, FL 33125; **Phone:** 305-243-5554; **Board Cert:** Cardiovascular Disease 2006; **Med School:** Johns Hopkins Univ 1988; **Resid:** Internal Medicine, Johns Hopkins Hosp 1991; **Fellow:** Cardiovascular Disease, Brigham & Womens Hosp 1993; **Fac Appt:** Prof Med, Univ Miami Sch Med

Harrison, J Kevin MD [Cv] - **Spec Exp:** Interventional Cardiology; Heart Valve Disease; **Hospital:** Duke Univ Hosp; **Address:** 7408 Duke North Hosp, Durham, NC 27710; **Phone:** 919-681-3763; **Board Cert:** Internal Medicine 1988; Cardiovascular Disease 2012; Interventional Cardiology 2003; **Med School:** NYU Sch Med 1984; **Resid:** Internal Medicine, Johns Hopkins Hosp 1987; **Fellow:** Cardiovascular Disease, Duke Univ Med Ctr 1990; **Fac Appt:** Prof Med, Duke Univ

Iskandrian, Ami E MD [Cv] - **Spec Exp:** Nuclear Cardiology; Coronary Artery Disease; Heart Valve Disease; **Hospital:** UAB Hosp; **Address:** Univ Alabama-Birmingham, 318 LHRB, 1900 University Blvd, Birmingham, AL 35294-0006; **Phone:** 205-934-0545; **Board Cert:** Internal Medicine 1974; Cardiovascular Disease 1975; Nuclear Cardiology 1999; **Med School:** Iraq 1965; **Resid:** Internal Medicine, Univ Baghdad Affil Hosp 1971; Internal Medicine, Hahnemann Univ Hosp 1973; **Fellow:** Cardiovascular Disease, Hahnemann Univ Hosp 1975; **Fac Appt:** Prof Med, UAB Sch Med

Limacher, Marian C MD [Cv] - **Spec Exp:** Preventive Cardiology; Heart Disease in Women; Women's Health; Echocardiography; **Hospital:** UF Hlth Shands Hosp; **Address:** Cardiovascular Ctr, 1600 SW Archer Rd, rm M 409, Gainesville, FL 32610; **Phone:** 352-273-9308; **Board Cert:** Internal Medicine 1980; Cardiovascular Disease 1983; **Med School:** St Louis Univ 1977; **Resid:** Internal Medicine, Baylor Coll Med Affil Hosp 1980; **Fellow:** Cardiovascular Disease, Baylor Coll Med Affil Hosp 1983; **Fac Appt:** Prof Med, Univ Fla Coll Med

Linton, MacRae F MD [Cv] - **Spec Exp:** Cholesterol/Lipid Disorders; Preventive Cardiology; Metabolic Syndrome; **Hospital:** Vanderbilt Univ Med Ctr; **Address:** Vanderbilt Heart & Vascular Inst, 1215 21st Ave S, MCE South Tower, Ste 5209, Nashville, TN 37204; **Phone:** 615-322-2318; **Board Cert:** Internal Medicine 1988; **Med School:** Univ Tenn Coll Med 1985; **Resid:** Internal Medicine, Vanderbilt Univ Med Ctr 1988; **Fellow:** Endocrinology, UCSF Med Ctr 1991; **Fac Appt:** Prof Med, Vanderbilt Univ

Litwin, Sheldon E MD [Cv] - **Spec Exp:** Cardiovascular Imaging; Echocardiography; Cardiac MRI; Cardiac CT Angiography; **Hospital:** Georgia Regents Med Ctr-Augusta; **Address:** Georgia Regents Cardiovascular Ctr, 1003 Chafee Ave, Augusta, GA 30912; **Phone:** 706-721-2426; **Board Cert:** Internal Medicine 2003; Cardiovascular Disease 2003; **Med School:** Washington Univ, St Louis 1985; **Resid:** Internal Medicine, Univ Arizona Med Ctr 1988; **Fellow:** Cardiovascular Disease, Beth Israel Hosp-Harvard 1991; **Fac Appt:** Prof Med, Med Coll GA

Nocero Jr, Michael A MD [Cv] - **Spec Exp:** Nuclear Cardiology; **Hospital:** Florida Hosp - Orlando; **Address:** Central FL Cardiology Grp, 1745 N Mills Ave, Ste 100, Orlando, FL 32803; **Phone:** 407-841-7151 x1111; **Board Cert:** Internal Medicine 1972; Cardiovascular Disease 1976; **Med School:** NYU Sch Med 1966; **Resid:** Internal Medicine, Bellevue Hosp 1971; **Fellow:** Cardiovascular Disease, Bellevue Hosp 1973

O'Connor, Christopher M MD [Cv] - **Spec Exp:** Heart Failure; **Hospital:** Duke Univ Hosp; **Address:** Duke Univ Med Ctr, 2301 Erwin Rd, Durham, NC 27710; **Phone:** 919-681-6195; **Board Cert:** Internal Medicine 1988; Cardiovascular Disease 1989; **Med School:** Univ MD Sch Med 1983; **Resid:** Internal Medicine, Duke Univ Med Ctr 1988; **Fellow:** Cardiovascular Disease, Duke Univ Med Ctr 1989; **Fac Appt:** Prof Med, Duke Univ

Oparil, Suzanne MD [Cv] - **Spec Exp:** Hypertension; Heart Disease in Women; **Hospital:** UAB Hosp; **Address:** UAB Cardiology, 703 19th St S, Zeigler Rsch Bldg, rm 1034, Birmingham, AL 35294; **Phone:** 205-801-7563; **Board Cert:** Internal Medicine 1970; **Med School:** Columbia P&S 1965; **Resid:** Internal Medicine, NY-Presby/Columbia Univ Med Ctr 1967; Internal Medicine, Mass Genl Hosp 1968; **Fellow:** Cardiovascular Disease, Mass Genl Hosp 1971; **Fac Appt:** Prof Med, UAB Sch Med

Pepine, Carl J MD [Cv] - **Spec Exp:** Coronary Artery Disease; Hypertension; Heart Disease in Women; **Hospital:** UF Hlth Shands Hosp; **Address:** UF Hlth, Cardiology Dept, 4037 NW 86th Terr Fl 2, Gainesville, FL 32606; **Phone:** 352-265-0139; **Board Cert:** Internal Medicine 1971; Cardiovascular Disease 1973; **Med School:** UMDNJ-NJ Med Sch, Newark 1966; **Resid:** Internal Medicine, Jefferson Univ Hosp 1968; Internal Medicine, Naval Hosp 1969; **Fellow:** Cardiovascular Disease, Naval Hosp 1971; **Fac Appt:** Prof Emeritus Med, Univ Fla Coll Med

Phillips III, Harry R MD [Cv] - **Spec Exp:** Cardiac Catheterization; **Hospital:** Duke Univ Hosp; **Address:** Duke Univ Med Ctr, 2301 Erwin Rd, Durham, NC 27710; **Phone:** 919-681-4804; **Board Cert:** Internal Medicine 1978; Cardiovascular Disease 1979; Interventional Cardiology 2011; **Med School:** Duke Univ 1975; **Resid:** Internal Medicine, Mass Genl Hosp 1977; **Fellow:** Cardiovascular Disease, Mass Genl Hosp 1979; **Fac Appt:** Prof Med, Duke Univ

Powers, Eric R MD [Cv] - **Spec Exp:** Heart Valve Disease; Interventional Cardiology; Coronary Artery Disease; **Hospital:** MUSC Med Ctr; **Address:** MUSC Heart & Vascular Ctr, 25 Courtenay Drive, Ashley River Tower Fl 7, Charleston, SC 29425-5920; **Phone:** 843-792-1952; **Board Cert:** Internal Medicine 1977; Cardiovascular Disease 1979; **Med School:** Harvard Med Sch 1974; **Resid:** Internal Medicine, Mass Genl Hosp 1976; **Fellow:** Cardiovascular Disease, Mass Genl Hosp 1979; **Fac Appt:** Prof Med, Med Univ SC

Rogers, Joseph G MD [Cv] - **Spec Exp:** Congestive Heart Failure; Transplant Medicine-Heart; **Hospital:** Duke Univ Hosp; **Address:** Duke Univ Med Ctr, 200 Trent Dr, Clinic 2G, Durham, NC 27710; **Phone:** 919-681-3398; **Board Cert:** Cardiovascular Disease 2005; Advanced Heart Failure & Transplant Cardiology 2012; **Med School:** Univ Nebr Coll Med 1988; **Resid:** Internal Medicine, Univ Nebraska Med Ctr 1991; **Fellow:** Cardiovascular Disease, Wash Univ Med Ctr 1995; **Fac Appt:** Assoc Prof Med, Duke Univ

Smith, Andrew L MD [Cv] - **Spec Exp:** Transplant Medicine-Heart; Heart Failure; **Hospital:** Emory Univ Hosp, Emory Univ Hosp Midtown; **Address:** Emory Ctr for Heart Failure/Transplant, 1365 Clifton Rd NE, Ste 2115, Atlanta, GA 30322; **Phone:** 404-778-5544; **Board Cert:** Internal Medicine 1987; Cardiovascular Disease 2012; Advanced Heart Failure & Transplant Cardiology 2010; **Med School:** Emory Univ 1984; **Resid:** Internal Medicine, Temple Univ Hosp 1987; **Fellow:** Cardiovascular Disease, Temple Univ 1990; **Fac Appt:** Prof Med, Emory Univ

Smith Jr, Sidney C MD [Cv] - **Spec Exp:** Coronary Artery Disease; Invasive Cardiology; **Hospital:** NC Memorial Hosp - UNC; **Address:** 300 Meadowmont Village Cir, Ste 313, Chapel Hill, NC 27517; **Phone:** 919-966-7244; **Board Cert:** Internal Medicine 1972; Cardiovascular Disease 1973; **Med School:** Yale Univ 1967; **Resid:** Internal Medicine, Peter Bent Brigham Hosp 1969; **Fellow:** Cardiovascular Disease, Peter Bent Brigham Hosp 1971; **Fac Appt:** Prof Med, Univ NC Sch Med

Vetrovec, George MD [Cv] - **Spec Exp:** Interventional Cardiology; **Hospital:** Med Coll of VA Hosp; **Address:** 1200 E Broad St, rm 607, Box 980036, West Hospital, Richmond, VA 23298; **Phone:** 804-828-8885; **Board Cert:** Internal Medicine 1974; Cardiovascular Disease 1977; Interventional Cardiology 2010; **Med School:** Univ VA Sch Med 1970; **Resid:** Internal Medicine, Med Coll Virginia Hosp 1974; **Fellow:** Cardiovascular Disease, Med Coll Virginia Hosp 1976; **Fac Appt:** Prof Med, Med Coll VA

Vignola, Paul MD [Cv] - **Spec Exp:** Interventional Cardiology; **Hospital:** Watauga Med Ctr; **Address:** The Cardiology Center, Appalachian Regional Healthcare System, 175 Mary St, Boone, NC 28607; **Phone:** 828-264-9664; **Board Cert:** Internal Medicine 1974; Cardiovascular Disease 1977; Interventional Cardiology 2009; **Med School:** Yale Univ 1971; **Resid:** Internal Medicine, Yale-New Haven Hosp 1974; **Fellow:** Cardiovascular Disease, Mass Genl Hosp 1976

Wells, Gretchen L MD/PhD [Cv] - **Spec Exp:** Heart Valve Disease; Congenital Heart Disease-Adult; Heart Disease in Pregnancy; Cardiac Effects of Chemotherapy; **Hospital:** Wake Forest Baptist Med Ctr; **Address:** Wake Forest Baptist Med Ctr, Dept Cardiology, Medical Center Blvd, Winston-Salem, NC 27157-1045; **Phone:** 336-716-6674; **Board Cert:** Cardiovascular Disease 2010; **Med School:** UAB Sch Med 1994; **Resid:** Internal Medicine, Wake Forest Univ Med Ctr 1997; **Fellow:** Cardiovascular Disease, Wake Forest Univ Med Ctr 2000; **Fac Appt:** Assoc Prof Med, Wake Forest Univ

Midwest

Bonow, Robert O MD [Cv] - **Spec Exp:** Heart Valve Disease; Coronary Artery Disease; Cardiomyopathy; **Hospital:** Northwestern Meml Hosp; **Address:** Northwestern Bluhm Cardiovascular Inst, 675 N St Clair St, Galter 19-100, Chicago, IL 60611; **Phone:** 312-695-4965; **Board Cert:** Internal Medicine 1976; Cardiovascular Disease 1981; **Med School:** Univ Pennsylvania 1973; **Resid:** Internal Medicine, Hosp Univ Penn 1976; **Fellow:** Cardiovascular Disease, Natl Inst Health-NHLBI 1979; **Fac Appt:** Prof Med, Northwestern Univ

Braverman, Alan C MD [Cv] - **Spec Exp:** Marfan's Syndrome; Aortic Diseases & Dissection; Aneurysm; Heart Valve Disease; **Hospital:** Barnes-Jewish Hosp; **Address:** Wash Univ Med Sch, Div Cardiovascular Disease, 660 S Euclid Ave, Box 8086, St Louis, MO 63110; **Phone:** 314-362-1291; **Board Cert:** Internal Medicine 1988; Cardiovascular Disease 2011; **Med School:** Univ MO-Kansas City 1985; **Resid:** Internal Medicine, Brigham & Womens Hosp 1988; Internal Medicine, Brigham & Womens Hosp 1991; **Fellow:** Cardiovascular Disease, Brigham & Womens Hosp 1990; **Fac Appt:** Prof Med, Washington Univ, St Louis

Burket, Mark W MD [Cv] - **Spec Exp:** Peripheral Vascular Disease; Coronary Artery Disease; Percutaneous Vascular Interventions; **Hospital:** Univ of Toledo Med Ctr; **Address:** 28442 E River Rd, Ste 110, Perrysburg, OH 43551; **Phone:** 419-383-3697; **Board Cert:** Internal Medicine 1982; Cardiovascular Disease 1985; **Med School:** Ohio State Univ 1979; **Resid:** Internal Medicine, Ohio State Univ 1982; **Fellow:** Cardiovascular Disease, Med Coll Ohio 1985; **Fac Appt:** Prof Med, Med Univ Ohio at Toledo

Cerqueira, Manuel MD [Cv] - **Spec Exp:** Cardiac Imaging; Nuclear Cardiology; Coronary Artery Disease; **Hospital:** Cleveland Clin (page 55); **Address:** Cleveland Clinic, 9500 Euclid Ave, Desk JB3, Cleveland, OH 44195; **Phone:** 216-444-2665; **Board Cert:** Internal Medicine 1981; Nuclear Medicine 1984; Cardiovascular Disease 1989; **Med School:** NYU Sch Med 1976; **Resid:** Internal Medicine, Bellevue Hosp Ctr 1980; Cardiovascular Disease, Yale-New Haven Hosp 1982; **Fellow:** Nuclear Medicine, Yale-New Haven Hosp 1983

Chaitman, Bernard R MD [Cv] - **Spec Exp:** Nuclear Cardiology; Echocardiography; **Hospital:** St. Louis Univ Hosp; **Address:** SLUCare, Div Cardiology, Univ Club Tower, 1034 S Brentwood Blvd, Ste 1120, St Louis, MO 63117; **Phone:** 314-977-4663; **Board Cert:** Internal Medicine 1973; Cardiovascular Disease 1975; **Med School:** McGill Univ 1969; **Resid:** Internal Medicine, Royal Victoria Hosp 1972; **Fellow:** Cardiovascular Disease, Univ Oregon Hosps 1974; Cardiovascular Disease, Univ Montreal 1975; **Fac Appt:** Prof Med, St Louis Univ

Connolly, Heidi M MD [Cv] - **Spec Exp:** Congenital Heart Disease; Heart Disease in Pregnancy; **Hospital:** Mayo Med Ctr & Clin - Rochester; **Address:** Mayo Clin, Div Cardiovasc Disease, 200 First St SW, Rochester, MN 55905; **Phone:** 507-284-1226; **Board Cert:** Internal Medicine 1989; Cardiovascular Disease 2011; **Med School:** Ireland 1986; **Resid:** Internal Medicine, Mayo Clin 1989; **Fellow:** Cardiovascular Disease, Mayo Clin 1991; **Fac Appt:** Prof Med, Mayo Med Sch

Cooper, Christopher J MD [Cv] - **Spec Exp:** Interventional Cardiology; **Hospital:** Univ of Toledo Med Ctr; **Address:** 28442 E River Rd, Ste 110, Perrysburg, OH 43551; **Phone:** 419-383-3697; **Board Cert:** Internal Medicine 2004; Cardiovascular Disease 2005; Interventional Cardiology 2009; **Med School:** Univ Cincinnati 1988; **Resid:** Internal Medicine, Brigham & Womens Hosp 1991; **Fellow:** Cardiovascular Disease, Brigham & Women's Hosp-Harvard Med Sch 1994

Davidson, Michael MD [Cv] - **Spec Exp:** Preventive Cardiology; Cholesterol/Lipid Disorders; **Hospital:** Univ of Chicago Med; **Address:** 150 E Huron St, Avenue Hotel Bldg, Ste 900, Chicago, IL 60611; **Phone:** 773-834-4150; **Board Cert:** Internal Medicine 1984; Cardiovascular Disease 1987; **Med School:** Ohio State Univ 1981; **Resid:** Internal Medicine, Rush Presby-St Lukes Med Ctr 1984; **Fellow:** Cardiovascular Disease, Rush Presby-St Lukes Med Ctr 1986; **Fac Appt:** Clin Prof Med, Univ Chicago-Pritzker Sch Med

Eagle, Kim A MD [Cv] - **Spec Exp:** Aortic Diseases & Dissection; Acute Coronary Syndromes; Heart Attack; Peripheral Vascular Disease; **Hospital:** Univ Michigan Med Ctr; **Address:** Univ MI Cardiovascular Ctr, 1500 E Medical Ctr Drive, Ste 2131, Ann Arbor, MI 48109; **Phone:** 734-998-7400; **Board Cert:** Internal Medicine 1982; Cardiovascular Disease 1987; **Med School:** Tufts Univ 1979; **Resid:** Internal Medicine, Yale-New Haven Hosp 1983; **Fellow:** Cardiovascular Disease, Mass Genl Hosp-Harvard 1986; **Fac Appt:** Asst Prof Med, Univ Mich Med Sch

Fintel, Dan MD [Cv] - **Spec Exp:** Coronary Artery Disease; Cholesterol/Lipid Disorders; Nuclear Cardiology; **Hospital:** Northwestern Meml Hosp; **Address:** Bluhm Cardiovascular Inst, 675 N St Clair St Fl 19 - Ste 100, Chicago, IL 60611; **Phone:** 312-695-2745; **Board Cert:** Internal Medicine 1982; Cardiovascular Disease 1985; **Med School:** Harvard Med Sch 1979; **Resid:** Internal Medicine, Mt Sinai Med Ctr 1982; **Fellow:** Cardiovascular Disease, Johns Hopkins Hosp 1985; **Fac Appt:** Assoc Prof Med, Northwestern Univ

Geltman, Edward M MD [Cv] - **Spec Exp:** Congestive Heart Failure; Transplant Medicine-Heart; Non-Invasive Cardiology; **Hospital:** Barnes-Jewish Hosp, Barnes-Jewish West County Hosp; **Address:** Washington Univ Sch of Med, Cardiovascular Division, 660 S Euclid Ave, Box 8086, St Louis, MO 63110; **Phone:** 314-454-7687; **Board Cert:** Internal Medicine 1974; Cardiovascular Disease 1979; Advanced Heart Failure & Transplant Cardiology 2010; **Med School:** NYU Sch Med 1971; **Resid:** Internal Medicine, Bellevue Hosp 1974; **Fellow:** Cardiovascular Disease, Barnes Jewish Hosp 1978; **Fac Appt:** Prof Med, Washington Univ, St Louis

Gibbons, Raymond J MD [Cv] - **Spec Exp:** Nuclear Cardiology; Heart Attack; **Hospital:** Mayo Med Ctr & Clin - Rochester; **Address:** Mayo Clin, Div Cardiovasc Disease, 200 First St SW, Rochester, MN 55905; **Phone:** 507-284-2541; **Board Cert:** Internal Medicine 1979; Cardiovascular Disease 1981; **Med School:** Harvard Med Sch 1976; **Resid:** Internal Medicine, Mass Genl Hosp 1978; **Fellow:** Cardiovascular Disease, Duke Univ Med Ctr 1981; **Fac Appt:** Prof Med, Mayo Med Sch

Grubb, Blair P MD [Cv] - **Spec Exp:** Autonomic Disorders; **Hospital:** Univ of Toledo Med Ctr, St. Vincent's Mercy Med Ctr - Toledo; **Address:** Heart & Vascular Ctr, 3000 Arlington Rd, Toledo, OH 43614-2598; **Phone:** 419-383-3963; **Board Cert:** Internal Medicine 1985; Cardiovascular Disease 1987; **Med School:** Dominican Republic 1980; **Resid:** Internal Medicine, Grtr Baltimore Med Ctr 1985; **Fellow:** Cardiovascular Disease, MS Hershey Med Ctr/Penn State 1987; Cardiac Electrophysiology, MS Hershey Med Ctr/Penn State 1988; **Fac Appt:** Prof Med, Med Univ Ohio at Toledo

Hauptman, Paul J MD [Cv] - **Spec Exp:** Heart Failure; **Hospital:** St. Louis Univ Hosp; **Address:** SLUCare Div Cardiology, Univ Club Tower, 1034 S Brentwood Blvd, Ste 1120, Saint Louis, MO 63117; **Phone:** 314-977-4663; **Board Cert:** Cardiovascular Disease 2003; **Med School:** Cornell Univ 1987; **Resid:** Internal Medicine, Brigham and Women's Hosp 1990; **Fellow:** Cardiovascular Disease, Mount Sinai Med Ctr 1992; Cardiovascular Disease, Brigham and Women's Hosp 1993; **Fac Appt:** Prof Med, St Louis Univ

Hayes, Sharonne N MD [Cv] - **Spec Exp:** Heart Disease in Women; Preventive Cardiology; Cholesterol/Lipid Disorders; Echocardiography; **Hospital:** Mayo Med Ctr & Clin - Rochester; **Address:** Mayo Clin-Women's Heart Clinic, 200 First St SW, Rochester, MN 55905; **Phone:** 507-284-3683; **Board Cert:** Internal Medicine 1986; Cardiovascular Disease 1989; **Med School:** Northwestern Univ 1983; **Resid:** Internal Medicine, Mayo Clin 1986; **Fellow:** Cardiovascular Research, Mayo Clin 1987; Cardiovascular Disease, Mayo Clin 1990; **Fac Appt:** Prof Med, Mayo Med Sch

Heroux, Alain MD [Cv] - **Spec Exp:** Transplant Medicine-Heart; Heart Failure; **Hospital:** Loyola Univ Med Ctr; **Address:** 2160 S 1st Ave Bldg 111, Maywood, IL 60153; **Phone:** 708-327-2738; **Med School:** Canada 1981; **Resid:** Internal Medicine, Laval Univ Med Ctr 1985; Cardiovascular Disease, Royal Victory Hosp 1987; **Fellow:** Heart Transplant, Univ Virginia Med Coll 1989; **Fac Appt:** Prof Med, Loyola Univ-Stritch Sch Med

Jaffe, Allan S MD [Cv] - **Spec Exp:** Ischemic Heart Disease; Heart Disease & Depression; **Hospital:** Mayo Med Ctr & Clin - Rochester; **Address:** Mayo Clinic, Div Cardiovascular Disease, 200 First St SW, Gonda 5-468, Rochester, MN 55905; **Phone:** 507-284-1648; **Board Cert:** Internal Medicine 1976; Cardiovascular Disease 1979; **Med School:** Univ MD Sch Med 1973; **Resid:** Internal Medicine, Barnes Hosp 1975; Internal Medicine, Wash Univ 1976; **Fellow:** Cardiovascular Disease, Barnes Hosp 1978; **Fac Appt:** Prof Med, Mayo Med Sch

Johnson, Maryl R MD [Cv] - **Spec Exp:** Congestive Heart Failure; Transplant Medicine-Heart; **Hospital:** Univ WI Hosp & Clins, Meriter Hosp; **Address:** Univ Wisconsin Hosp/Clins-Cardio, 600 Highland Ave, MS 5710, Madison, WI 53792-0001; **Phone:** 608-263-0080; **Board Cert:** Internal Medicine 1981; Cardiovascular Disease 1983; Advanced Heart Failure & Transplant Cardiology 2012; **Med School:** Univ Iowa Coll Med 1977; **Resid:** Internal Medicine, Univ Iowa Hosp 1981; **Fellow:** Cardiovascular Disease, Univ Iowa Hosp 1982; **Fac Appt:** Prof Med, Univ Wisc

Kereiakes, Dean J MD [Cv] - **Spec Exp:** Coronary Angioplasty/Stents; Congestive Heart Failure; Interventional Cardiology; **Hospital:** Christ Hosp, The - Cincinnati; **Address:** Ohio Heart & Vascular Center, 2123 Auburn Ave, Ste 136, Cincinnati, OH 45219; **Phone:** 513-721-8881; **Board Cert:** Internal Medicine 1981; Cardiovascular Disease 1985; **Med School:** Univ Cincinnati 1978; **Resid:** Internal Medicine, UCSF Med Ctr 1982; Internal Medicine, Mass Genl Hosp 1981; **Fellow:** Cardiovascular Disease, UCSF Med Ctr 1984; Coronary Angioplasty, Sequoia Hosp 1984; **Fac Appt:** Clin Prof Med, Ohio State Univ

Klein, Lloyd W MD [Cv] - **Spec Exp:** Coronary Artery Disease; Angiography-Coronary; Interventional Cardiology; Coronary Syndrome-Acute; **Hospital:** Gottlieb Meml Hosp, Adv Illinois Masonic Med Ctr; **Address:** Clinical Cardiology Associates, 675 W North Ave, Fl 4 - Ste 406, Melrose Park, IL 60160; **Phone:** 708-681-7862; **Board Cert:** Internal Medicine 1980; Cardiovascular Disease 1983; Interventional Cardiology 2009; **Med School:** Univ Cincinnati 1977; **Resid:** Internal Medicine, Albert Einstein/Municipal Hosp 1980; **Fellow:** Cardiovascular Disease, Mt Sinai Hosp 1982; **Fac Appt:** Prof Med, Rush Med Coll

Liao, James MD [Cv] - **Spec Exp:** Cholesterol/Lipid Disorders; Peripheral Vascular Disease; Non-Invasive Cardiology; **Hospital:** Univ of Chicago Med; **Address:** Univ Chicago Med Ctr-Cardiology, 5758 S Maryland Ave, Chicago, IL 60637; **Phone:** 773-702-9461; **Board Cert:** Internal Medicine 1988; Cardiovascular Disease 2004; **Med School:** UCSF 1985; **Resid:** Internal Medicine, Brigham & Women's Hosp 1988; **Fellow:** Cardiovascular Disease, Mass Genl Hosp 1991; **Fac Appt:** Prof Med, Univ Chicago-Pritzker Sch Med

Mehlman, David J MD [Cv] - **Spec Exp:** Echocardiography; Heart Valve Disease; Coronary Artery Disease; **Hospital:** Northwestern Meml Hosp; **Address:** Northwestern Bluhm Cardiovascular Inst, 675 N St Clair St, Galter Bldg Fl 19 - Ste 100, Chicago, IL 60611; **Phone:** 312-695-4965; **Board Cert:** Internal Medicine 1976; Cardiovascular Disease 1979; **Med School:** Johns Hopkins Univ 1973; **Resid:** Internal Medicine, Johns Hopkins Hosp 1976; **Fellow:** Cardiovascular Disease, Univ Chicago Hosps 1978; **Fac Appt:** Assoc Prof Med, Northwestern Univ

Nishimura, Rick A MD [Cv] - **Spec Exp:** Echocardiography; Pericardial Disease; **Hospital:** Mayo Med Ctr & Clin - Rochester, St. Mary's Hosp - Rochester MN (Mayo); **Address:** Mayo Clinic, 200 First St SW, Gonda 5-368, Rochester, MN 55905; **Phone:** 507-284-8342; **Board Cert:** Internal Medicine 1981; Cardiovascular Disease 1983; **Med School:** Rush Med Coll 1978; **Resid:** Internal Medicine, Mayo Clin 1980; **Fellow:** Cardiovascular Disease, Mayo Clin 1983; **Fac Appt:** Prof Med, Mayo Med Sch

Nissen, Steven E MD [Cv] - **Spec Exp:** Cholesterol/Lipid Disorders; Intravascular Ultrasound; Cardiac Intensive Care; **Hospital:** Cleveland Clin (page 55); **Address:** 9500 Euclid Ave, Desk J2-3, Cleveland, OH 44195; **Phone:** 216-445-6852; **Board Cert:** Internal Medicine 1981; Cardiovascular Disease 1983; **Med School:** Univ Mich Med Sch 1978; **Resid:** Internal Medicine, UC Davis Med Ctr 1981; **Fellow:** Cardiovascular Disease, Chandler Med Ctr 1983

O'Neill, William W MD [Cv] - **Spec Exp:** Interventional Cardiology; Heart Valve Disease; **Hospital:** Henry Ford Hosp; **Address:** Center for Structural Heart Disease, 2799 W Grand Blvd Fl K-14, Detroit, MI 48202; **Phone:** 313-916-1878; **Board Cert:** Internal Medicine 1980; Cardiovascular Disease 1983; **Med School:** Wayne State Univ 1977; **Resid:** Internal Medicine, Wayne State Univ Affil Hosps 1980; **Fellow:** Cardiovascular Disease, Univ Mich Med Ctr 1982; **Fac Appt:** Assoc Prof Med, Univ Mich Med Sch

Raff, Gilbert L MD [Cv] - **Spec Exp:** Cardiac CT Angiography; Cardiac MRI; **Hospital:** Beaumont Hosp-Royal Oak; **Address:** 3601 W 13 Mile Rd, Royal Oak, MI 48073; **Phone:** 248-898-1767; **Board Cert:** Internal Medicine 1978; Cardiovascular Disease 1981; **Med School:** UC Davis 1975; **Resid:** Internal Medicine, Univ Michigan Hosp 1978; **Fellow:** Cardiovascular Disease, UCSF Med Ctr 1981; **Fac Appt:** Prof Med, Oakland Univ-William Beaumont Med Sch

Rahko, Peter S MD [Cv] - **Spec Exp:** Congestive Heart Failure; Heart Valve Disease; Echocardiography; Echocardiography-Transesophageal; **Hospital:** Univ WI Hosp & Clins, Meriter Hosp; **Address:** UW Heart & Vascular Clin, 600 Highland Ave, rm G7-343, MC 3248, Madison, WI 53792-3248; **Phone:** 608-263-1530; **Board Cert:** Internal Medicine 1982; Cardiovascular Disease 1985; **Med School:** Univ Minn 1979; **Resid:** Internal Medicine, Indiana Univ Med Ctr 1982; **Fellow:** Cardiovascular Disease, Univ Pittsburgh Med Ctr 1985; **Fac Appt:** Prof Med, Univ Wisc

Reiss, Craig MD [Cv] - **Spec Exp:** Ischemic Heart Disease; Heart Valve Disease; Preventive Cardiology; Coronary Artery Disease; **Hospital:** St. Luke's Hosp - Chesterfield, MO; **Address:** St Lukes Hosp, 226 S Woods Mill Rd, Ste 47 West, Chesterfield, MO 63017; **Phone:** 314-434-3278; **Board Cert:** Internal Medicine 1986; Cardiovascular Disease 1989; **Med School:** Univ MO-Kansas City 1983; **Resid:** Internal Medicine, Brigham & Women's Hosp 1989; **Fellow:** Cardiovascular Disease, Brigham & Women's Hosp 1988

Rich, Stuart MD [Cv] - **Spec Exp:** Pulmonary Hypertension; Heart Failure; **Hospital:** Univ of Chicago Med; **Address:** 5758 S Maryland Ave, Chicago, IL 60637; **Phone:** 773-702-9461; **Board Cert:** Internal Medicine 1978; Cardiovascular Disease 1981; **Med School:** Loyola Univ-Stritch Sch Med 1974; **Resid:** Internal Medicine, Barnes-Jewish Hosp 1978; **Fellow:** Cardiovascular Disease, Univ Chicago Hosp 1980; **Fac Appt:** Prof Med, Rush Med Coll

Rihal, Charanjit S MD [Cv] - **Spec Exp:** Acute Coronary Syndromes; Coronary Artery Disease; Interventional Cardiology; **Hospital:** Mayo Med Ctr & Clin - Rochester; **Address:** 200 First St SW, MB 4-506, Rochester, MN 55905; **Phone:** 507-255-2440; **Board Cert:** Internal Medicine 1989; Cardiovascular Disease 2011; Interventional Cardiology 2009; **Med School:** Canada 1985; **Resid:** Internal Medicine, Mayo Clin 1989; **Fellow:** Cardiovascular Disease, Mayo Clin 1991; Interventional Cardiology, Mayo Clin 1993; **Fac Appt:** Prof Med, Mayo Med Sch

Rosenbush, Stuart W MD [Cv] - **Spec Exp:** Cardiac Catheterization; Coronary Angioplasty/Stents; Coronary Artery Disease; Heart Failure; **Hospital:** Rush Univ Med Ctr, Skokie Hosp/NorthShore Univ Hlth Syst (page 67); **Address:** Univ Cardiologists, 1725 W Harrison St, Ste 1159, Chicago, IL 60612-3835; **Phone:** 312-942-5020; **Board Cert:** Internal Medicine 1979; Cardiovascular Disease 1981; **Med School:** Univ IL Coll Med 1976; **Resid:** Internal Medicine, Michael Reese Hosp 1979; **Fellow:** Cardiovascular Disease, Rush Presby-St Lukes Med Ctr 1981; **Fac Appt:** Asst Prof Med, Rush Med Coll

Safian, Robert D MD [Cv] - **Spec Exp:** Interventional Cardiology; **Hospital:** Beaumont Hosp-Royal Oak; **Address:** Beaumont Academic Heart & Vascular Grp, 3601 W 13 Mile Rd Fl 3, Royal Oak, MI 48073; **Phone:** 248-898-4163; **Board Cert:** Internal Medicine 1983; Cardiovascular Disease 1987; Interventional Cardiology 2010; **Med School:** Univ Fla Coll Med 1979; **Resid:** Pathology, Univ Miami Med Ctr 1981; Internal Medicine, UCSD Med Ctr 1983; **Fellow:** Cardiovascular Disease, Beth Israel Hosp-Harvard 1987

Sanborn, Timothy MD [Cv] - **Spec Exp:** Interventional Cardiology; Gene Therapy-Cardiac Angiogenesis; Heart Valve Disease; Carotid Artery Stent Placement; **Hospital:** Evanston Hosp/NorthShore Univ Hlth Sys (page 67); **Address:** NorthShore Medical Group, Evanston Hosp, 1000 Central St, Ste 800, Evanston, IL 60201; **Phone:** 847-570-2250; **Board Cert:** Internal Medicine 1980; Cardiovascular Disease 2003; Interventional Cardiology 2009; **Med School:** Northwestern Univ 1977; **Resid:** Internal Medicine, Boston City Hosp 1980; **Fellow:** Cardiovascular Disease, Boston Univ Med Ctr 1983; **Fac Appt:** Clin Prof Med, Northwestern Univ

Shapiro, Jerrold MD [Cv] - **Spec Exp:** Echocardiography; Preventive Cardiology; **Hospital:** Swedish Covenant Hosp; **Address:** 4801 W Peterson Ave, Ste 610, Chicago, IL 60646; **Phone:** 773-283-5900; **Board Cert:** Internal Medicine 1976; Cardiovascular Disease 1977; **Med School:** Univ IL Coll Med 1968; **Resid:** Internal Medicine, Ill Masonic Med Ctr 1972; **Fellow:** Cardiovascular Disease, Northwestern Meml Hosp 1974

Shea, Richard J MD [Cv] - **Spec Exp:** Heart Valve Disease; Echocardiography; Nuclear Cardiology; Echocardiography-Transesophageal; **Hospital:** Franciscan St. Francis Hlth-Indianapolis; **Address:** Franciscan Hlth, Indiana Heart Phys, 5330 E Stop 11 Road, Indianapolis, IN 46237; **Phone:** 317-893-1664; **Board Cert:** Cardiovascular Disease 2009; **Med School:** Georgetown Univ 1989; **Resid:** Internal Medicine, Fitzsimons Army Med Ctr 1992; **Fellow:** Cardiovascular Disease, Washington Hosp Ctr 1999

Simon, Daniel I MD [Cv] - **Spec Exp:** Interventional Cardiology; **Hospital:** UH Case Med Ctr; **Address:** UH Case Medical Center, 11100 Euclid Ave, Cleveland, OH 44106-5038; **Phone:** 216-844-5347; **Board Cert:** Cardiovascular Disease 2003; Interventional Cardiology 2010; **Med School:** Harvard Med Sch 1987; **Resid:** Internal Medicine, Brigham & Womens Hosp 1989; **Fellow:** Cardiovascular Disease, Brigham & Womens Hosp 1992; Interventional Cardiology, Beth Israel Med Ctr 1995

Sorrentino, Matthew MD [Cv] - **Spec Exp:** Preventive Cardiology; Hypertension; **Hospital:** Univ of Chicago Med; **Address:** 5758 S Maryland Ave, Chicago, IL 60637; **Phone:** 773-702-9461; **Board Cert:** Internal Medicine 1987; Cardiovascular Disease 2011; **Med School:** Univ Chicago-Pritzker Sch Med 1984; **Resid:** Internal Medicine, Univ Chicago Hosps 1989; **Fellow:** Cardiovascular Disease, Univ Chicago Hosps 1991; **Fac Appt:** Assoc Prof Med, Univ Chicago-Pritzker Sch Med

Stein, James H MD [Cv] - **Spec Exp:** Preventive Cardiology; Echocardiography; Cholesterol/Lipid Disorders; **Hospital:** Univ WI Hosp & Clins; **Address:** UW Heart & Vascular Clin, 600 Highland Ave, rm G7-343, MC 3248, Madison, WI 53792; **Phone:** 608-263-1530; **Board Cert:** Internal Medicine 2003; Cardiovascular Disease 2007; **Med School:** Yale Univ 1990; **Resid:** Internal Medicine, Univ Chicago Affil Hosps 1993; **Fellow:** Cardiovascular Disease, Rush Univ Med Ctr 1996; **Fac Appt:** Prof Med, Univ Wisc

Stewart, William James MD [Cv] - **Spec Exp:** Heart Valve Disease; Echocardiography; **Hospital:** Cleveland Clin (page 55); **Address:** Div Cardiovascular Medicine, 9500 Euclid Ave, Desk J1-5, Cleveland, OH 44195; **Phone:** 216-444-5923; **Board Cert:** Internal Medicine 1980; Cardiovascular Disease 1983; **Med School:** Univ Cincinnati 1977; **Resid:** Internal Medicine, Univ Mich Hosp 1980; **Fellow:** Cardiovascular Disease, Boston Univ Med Ctr 1982; Cardiovascular Disease, Mass Genl Hosp 1984; **Fac Appt:** Prof Med, Cleveland Cl Coll Med/Case West Res

Volgman, Annabelle Santos MD [Cv] - **Spec Exp:** Heart Disease in Women; Arrhythmias; Atrial Fibrillation; Preventive Cardiology; **Hospital:** Rush Univ Med Ctr, Rush Oak Park Hosp; **Address:** Rush Heart Ctr for Women, 1725 W Harrison St, Professional Bldg, Ste 1159, Chicago, IL 60612; **Phone:** 312-942-5020; **Board Cert:** Cardiovascular Disease 2006; **Med School:** Columbia P&S 1984; **Resid:** Internal Medicine, Univ Chicago Hosps 1987; **Fellow:** Cardiovascular Disease, Northwestern Meml Hosp 1989; Cardiac Electrophysiology, Northwestern Meml Hosp 1990; **Fac Appt:** Prof Med, Rush Med Coll

von der Lohe, Elisabeth MD [Cv] - **Spec Exp:** Heart Disease in Women; Interventional Cardiology; Pulmonary Hypertension; **Hospital:** IU Health Methodist Hosp; **Address:** Krannert Inst Cardiology, 1801 N Senate Blvd, Ste E4000, Indianapolis, IN 46202; **Phone:** 317-962-0561; **Board Cert:** Interventional Cardiology 2013; Cardiovascular Disease 2011; **Med School:** Germany 1978; **Resid:** Internal Medicine, Marien Hosp 1981; **Fellow:** Cardiovascular Disease, Klinikum Aachen 1986; **Fac Appt:** Clin Prof Med, Indiana Univ

Wagoner, Lynne E MD [Cv] - **Spec Exp:** Congestive Heart Failure; Heart Disease in Women; Transplant Medicine-Heart; Pulmonary Hypertension; **Hospital:** Mercy Hosp - Fairfield; **Address:** 3000 Mack Rd, Ste 100, Fairfield, OH 45014; **Phone:** 513-751-4222; **Board Cert:** Internal Medicine 1989; Cardiovascular Disease 2003; Advanced Heart Failure & Transplant Cardiology 2012; **Med School:** E Carolina Univ 1986; **Resid:** Internal Medicine, Pitt Co Meml Hosp/E Carolina Univ 1989; **Fellow:** Cardiovascular Disease, Univ Utah Affil Hosp 1994; **Fac Appt:** Assoc Prof Med, Univ Cincinnati

Walsh, Mary N MD [Cv] - **Spec Exp:** Heart Disease in Women; Nuclear Cardiology; Congestive Heart Failure; Transplant Medicine-Heart; **Hospital:** St. Vincent Indianapolis Hosp; **Address:** St Vincent, Cardiology Dept, 8333 Naab Rd, Ste 400, Indianapolis, IN 46260; **Phone:** 317-338-6666; **Board Cert:** Internal Medicine 1986; Cardiovascular Disease 2011; Advanced Heart Failure & Transplant Cardiology 2010; **Med School:** Univ Minn 1983; **Resid:** Internal Medicine, UT Southwestern Med Ctr 1986; **Fellow:** Cardiovascular Disease, Wash Univ Phys 1989; **Fac Appt:** Asst Clin Prof Med, Indiana Univ

Webb, Gary D MD [Cv] - **Spec Exp:** Congenital Heart Disease-Adult; **Hospital:** Cincinnati Chldns Hosp Med Ctr; **Address:** The Heart Inst, Cincinatti Chldn's Hosp, 3333 Burnett Ave, MC 2003, Cincinatti, OH 45229; **Phone:** 513-803-7329; **Med School:** McGill Univ 1967; **Resid:** Internal Medicine, Royal Victoria Hosp 1972; **Fellow:** Cardiovascular Disease, Toronto Genl Hosp 1974

Wilkoff, Bruce L MD [Cv] - **Spec Exp:** Defibrillator Cable Extraction; Pacemakers; **Hospital:** Cleveland Clin (page 55); **Address:** Cleveland Clinic, 9500 Euclid Ave, Desk J2-2, Cleveland, OH 44195; **Phone:** 216-444-6697; **Board Cert:** Internal Medicine 1982; Cardiovascular Disease 1985; **Med School:** Ohio State Univ 1979; **Resid:** Internal Medicine, Univ Hosps 1982; **Fellow:** Cardiovascular Disease, Univ Hosps 1984; Research, Ohio State Univ Med Ctr 1986; **Fac Appt:** Prof Med, Cleveland Cl Coll Med/Case West Res

Williams, Eric S MD [Cv] - **Spec Exp:** Ischemic Heart Disease; Acute Coronary Syndromes; Echocardiography; Cardiomyopathy; **Hospital:** IU Health Methodist Hosp; **Address:** Krannert Inst Cardiology, 1801 N Senate Blvd, Ste E4000, Indianapolis, IN 46202; **Phone:** 317-962-0500; **Board Cert:** Internal Medicine 1974; Cardiovascular Disease 1977; **Med School:** Indiana Univ 1971; **Resid:** Internal Medicine, IU Hlth Hosp 1973; **Fellow:** Cardiovascular Disease, IU Hlth Hosp 1975; **Fac Appt:** Prof Med, Indiana Univ

Williams Sr, Kim A MD [Cv] - **Spec Exp:** Nuclear Cardiology; Coronary Artery Disease; **Hospital:** Harper Univ Hosp; **Address:** Wayne St Univ Sch Med, Harper Univ Hosp, 3990 John R St, 4 Hudson, Detroit, MI 48201; **Phone:** 313-745-2620; **Board Cert:** Internal Medicine 1982; Cardiovascular Disease 2009; Nuclear Medicine 1986; **Med School:** Univ Chicago-Pritzker Sch Med 1979; **Resid:** Internal Medicine, Emory Univ Affil Hosp 1982; **Fellow:** Cardiovascular Disease, Univ Chicago 1984; Nuclear Medicine, Univ Chicago 1986; **Fac Appt:** Prof Med, Wayne State Univ

Young, James B MD [Cv] - **Spec Exp:** Transplant Medicine-Heart; Heart Failure; Ventricular Assist Device (LVAD); Amyloid Heart Disease; **Hospital:** Cleveland Clin (page 55); **Address:** 9500 Euclid Ave, Desk J3-4, Cleveland, OH 44195; **Phone:** 216-444-2333; **Board Cert:** Internal Medicine 1977; Cardiovascular Disease 1979; **Med School:** Baylor Coll Med 1974; **Resid:** Internal Medicine, Baylor Affil Hosp 1977; Internal Medicine, Methodist Hosp 1980; **Fellow:** Cardiovascular Disease, Baylor Affl Hosp 1979

Great Plains and Mountains

Anderson, Jeffrey L MD [Cv] - **Spec Exp:** Arrhythmias; Cholesterol/Lipid Disorders; Cardiac MRI; **Hospital:** LDS Hosp, Salt Lake Regional Med Ctr; **Address:** Intermountain Med Ctr, 5121 S Cottonwood St, Murray, UT 84107-5701; **Phone:** 801-507-4000; **Board Cert:** Internal Medicine 1975; Cardiovascular Disease 1979; Cardiac Electrophysiology 2012; **Med School:** Harvard Med Sch 1972; **Resid:** Internal Medicine, Mass Genl Hosp 1974; **Fellow:** Research, Natl Inst Hlth 1976; Cardiovascular Disease, Stanford Univ Med Ctr 1978; **Fac Appt:** Prof Med, Univ Utah

Lindenfeld, JoAnn MD [Cv] - **Spec Exp:** Congestive Heart Failure; Transplant Medicine-Heart; Heart Disease in Women; **Hospital:** Univ Colorado Hosp; **Address:** 12605 E 16th Ave, Ste B120, Aurora, CO 80045; **Phone:** 720-848-5300; **Board Cert:** Internal Medicine 1976; Cardiovascular Disease 2011; Advanced Heart Failure & Transplant Cardiology 2010; **Med School:** Univ Mich Med Sch 1973; **Resid:** Internal Medicine, UCSD Med Ctr 1976; **Fellow:** Cardiovascular Disease, UT Hlth Sci Ctr 1979; **Fac Appt:** Prof Med, Univ Colorado

Southwest

Abi-samra, Freddy M MD [Cv] - **Spec Exp:** Arrhythmias; Atrial Fibrillation; **Hospital:** Ochsner Med Ctr-New Orleans; **Address:** Oschner Med Ctr, Dept Cardiology, 1514 Jefferson Hwy Fl 3rd, Clin Twr, New Orleans, LA 70121; **Phone:** 504-842-4145; **Board Cert:** Internal Medicine 1984; Cardiovascular Disease 1985; **Med School:** Lebanon 1979; **Resid:** Internal Medicine, Amer Univ Med Ctr 1981; Cardiovascular Disease, Metro Genl Hosp 1984; **Fellow:** Hypertension, Cleveland Clin 1982; Cardiac Electrophysiology, Cleveland Clin 1986

Alpert, Joseph S MD [Cv] - **Spec Exp:** Coronary Artery Disease; **Hospital:** Univ Arizona Med Ctr-Univ Campus; **Address:** Univ Arizona Sarver Hrt Ctr, 1501 N Campbell Ave Fl 6, Tuscon, AZ 85724; **Phone:** 520-626-2763; **Board Cert:** Internal Medicine 1973; Cardiovascular Disease 1975; **Med School:** Harvard Med Sch 1969; **Resid:** Internal Medicine, Brigham & Women's Hosp 1973; **Fellow:** Cardiovascular Disease, Brigham & Women's Hosp 1975

Ballantyne, Christie M MD [Cv] - **Spec Exp:** Preventive Cardiology; Cholesterol/Lipid Disorders; **Hospital:** Methodist Hosp - Houston; **Address:** Methodist Hospital, DeBakey Heart & Vascular Ctr, 6565 Fannin St, Houston, TX 77030; **Phone:** 713-790-5800; **Board Cert:** Internal Medicine 1985; Cardiovascular Disease 1987; **Med School:** Baylor Coll Med 1982; **Resid:** Internal Medicine, Univ Tex SW Med Ctr 1985; **Fellow:** Cardiovascular Disease, Baylor Coll Med 1988; **Fac Appt:** Prof Med, Baylor Coll Med

Carabello, Blase A MD [Cv] - **Spec Exp:** Heart Valve Disease; **Hospital:** DeBakey VA Med Ctr-Houston; **Address:** St Lukes Medical Center, 6720 Bertner Ave, Houston, TX 77030; **Phone:** 713-794-7070; **Board Cert:** Internal Medicine 1977; Cardiovascular Disease 1979; **Med School:** Temple Univ 1973; **Resid:** Internal Medicine, Mass Genl Hosp 1976; **Fellow:** Cardiovascular Disease, Peter Bent Brigham Hosp 1978; **Fac Appt:** Prof Med, Baylor Coll Med

Freeman, Gregory L MD [Cv] - **Spec Exp:** Interventional Cardiology; **Hospital:** Methodist Hosp-San Antonio; **Address:** Methodist Cardiology Clinic, 4411 Medical Drive, Ste 300, San Antonio, TX 78229; **Phone:** 210-614-5400; **Board Cert:** Internal Medicine 1979; Cardiovascular Disease 1983; **Med School:** Loyola Univ-Stritch Sch Med 1976; **Resid:** Internal Medicine, Cook County Hosp 1979; **Fellow:** Cardiovascular Disease, Loyola Univ Med Ctr 1981; Research, UCSD Sch Med 1983

Gould, K Lance MD [Cv] - **Spec Exp:** Preventive Cardiology; PET Imaging; Cholesterol/Lipid Disorders; **Hospital:** Meml Hermann Hosp - Texas Med Ctr; **Address:** Univ Texas - PET Imaging Ctr, 6431 Fannin St, rm 4.256 MSB, Houston, TX 77030-1501; **Phone:** 713-500-6611; **Med School:** Case West Res Univ 1964; **Resid:** Internal Medicine, Univ Wash Med Ctr 1967; Cardiovascular Disease, Univ Wash Med Ctr 1964; **Fellow:** Cardiovascular Disease, Univ Wash Med Ctr 1971; **Fac Appt:** Prof Med, Univ Tex, Houston

Krajcer, Zvonimir MD [Cv] - **Spec Exp:** Peripheral Vascular Disease; Carotid Artery Disease; Aneurysm-Abdominal & Thoracic Aortic; **Hospital:** St. Luke's Episcopal Hosp-Houston; **Address:** 6624 Fannin St, Ste 2780, Houston, TX 77030; **Phone:** 713-790-9401; **Board Cert:** Internal Medicine 1975; Cardiovascular Disease 1977; **Med School:** Slovenia 1970; **Resid:** Internal Medicine, Northwestern Medical Ctr 1974; **Fellow:** Cardiovascular Disease, St Luke's Episcopal Hosp 1977; **Fac Appt:** Clin Prof Med, Baylor Coll Med

Massin, Edward K MD [Cv] - **Spec Exp:** Congestive Heart Failure; Transplant Medicine-Heart; Coronary Artery Disease; **Hospital:** St. Luke's Episcopal Hosp-Houston; **Address:** Cardiology Consultants Houston, 6624 Fannin St, Ste 2310, Houston, TX 77030-2335; **Phone:** 713-796-2668; **Board Cert:** Internal Medicine 1973; Cardiovascular Disease 1973; **Med School:** Washington Univ, St Louis 1965; **Resid:** Internal Medicine, Barnes Hosp 1967; **Fellow:** Cardiovascular Disease, Univ CO Med Ctr 1971; **Fac Appt:** Clin Prof Med, Baylor Coll Med

McPherson, David D MD [Cv] - **Spec Exp:** Echocardiography; Congenital Heart Disease-Adult; Heart Valve Disease; Echocardiography-Transesophageal; **Hospital:** Meml Hermann Hosp - Texas Med Ctr; **Address:** UT Adult Congenital Heart Disease, 6410 Fannin St, Ste 600, Houston, TX 77030; **Phone:** 832-325-7216; **Board Cert:** Internal Medicine 2005; Cardiovascular Disease 2007; **Med School:** Univ Alberta 1978; **Resid:** Internal Medicine, Dalhousie Univ Hosp 1981; **Fellow:** Cardiovascular Disease, Dalhousie Univ 1983; Cardiovascular Disease, Univ Iowa 1984; **Fac Appt:** Prof Med, Univ Tex, Houston

Nagueh, Sherif F MD [Cv] - **Spec Exp:** Echocardiography; Heart Failure; **Hospital:** Methodist Hosp - Houston; **Address:** Methodist DeBakey Heart & Vascular Ctr, 6550 Fannin St, Ste 1901, Smith Tower, Houston, TX 77030; **Phone:** 713-441-1100; **Board Cert:** Internal Medicine 2003; Cardiovascular Disease 2007; **Med School:** Egypt 1986; **Resid:** Internal Medicine, Baylor Coll Med 1993; **Fellow:** Cardiovascular Disease, Baylor Coll Med 1996; **Fac Appt:** Prof Med, Cornell Univ-Weill Med Coll

Quinones, Miguel A MD [Cv] - **Spec Exp:** Echocardiography; Heart Valve Disease; **Hospital:** Methodist Hosp - Houston; **Address:** Methodist DeBakey Heart & Vascular Ctr, 6550 Fannin St, rm 1901, Smith Tower, Houston, TX 77030; **Phone:** 713-441-1100; **Board Cert:** Internal Medicine 1972; Cardiovascular Disease 1974; **Med School:** Puerto Rico 1968; **Resid:** Internal Medicine, Harlem Hosp 1971; **Fellow:** Cardiovascular Disease, Baylor Coll Med 1974; **Fac Appt:** Prof Med, Cornell Univ-Weill Med Coll

Ramee, Stephen R MD [Cv] - **Spec Exp:** Interventional Cardiology; Angioplasty; Carotid Artery Stent Placement; Renovascular Disease; **Hospital:** Ochsner Med Ctr-New Orleans; **Address:** Ochsner Med Ctr, Dept Cardiology, 1514 Jefferson Hwy Fl 3, Clin Twr, New Orleans, LA 70121; **Phone:** 504-842-3727; **Board Cert:** Internal Medicine 1983; Cardiovascular Disease 1985; **Med School:** Geo Wash Univ 1980; **Resid:** Internal Medicine, Letterman Army Med Ctr 1983; **Fellow:** Cardiovascular Disease, Letterman Army Med Ctr 1985

Smart, Frank W MD [Cv] - **Spec Exp:** Congestive Heart Failure; Transplant Medicine-Heart; Ventricular Assist Device (LVAD); Pulmonary Hypertension; **Hospital:** Ochsner Med Ctr-West Bank, Touro Infirm; **Address:** LSU Health Care Network, 3700 Saint Charles Ave, New Orleans, LA 70112; **Phone:** 504-412-1366; **Board Cert:** Internal Medicine 1988; Cardiovascular Disease 2001; Advanced Heart Failure & Transplant Cardiology 2010; **Med School:** Louisiana State U, New Orleans 1985; **Resid:** Internal Medicine, Ochsner Fdn Hosp 1988; **Fellow:** Cardiovascular Disease, Baylor Coll Med 1991; **Fac Appt:** Prof, Louisiana State U, New Orleans

Snyder, David W MD [Cv] - **Spec Exp:** Cardiac Electrophysiology; **Hospital:** E Jefferson Genl Hosp; **Address:** E Jefferson Cardiology Consultants, 4200 Houma Blvd Fl 2, Metairie, LA 70011; **Phone:** 504-454-4102; **Board Cert:** Internal Medicine 1978; Cardiovascular Disease 1981; **Med School:** Duke Univ 1975; **Resid:** Internal Medicine, Barnes-Jewish Hosp 1979; **Fellow:** Cardiovascular Disease, Barnes-Jewish Hosp 1981

Stainback III, Raymond F MD [Cv] - **Spec Exp:** Stroke; Coronary Artery Disease; Heart Valve Disease; Echocardiography-Transesophageal; **Hospital:** St. Luke's Episcopal Hosp-Houston; **Address:** Hall-Garcia Cardiology Assoc, 6624 Fannin St Ste 2480, Houston, TX 77030-2309; **Phone:** 713-529-5530; **Board Cert:** Cardiovascular Disease 2007; **Med School:** Baylor Coll Med 1987; **Resid:** Internal Medicine, Vanderbilt Univ Med Ctr 1990; **Fellow:** Cardiovascular Disease, Vanderbilt Univ Med Ctr 1993; Echocardiography, UCSF Med Ctr 1995; **Fac Appt:** Assoc Clin Prof Med, Baylor Coll Med

Thames, Marc D MD [Cv] - **Spec Exp:** Coronary Artery Disease; Congestive Heart Failure; **Hospital:** Scottsdale Hlthcare - Shea; **Address:** Cardiovascular Consultants, 3805 E Bell Rd, Ste 3100, Phoenix, AZ 85032-3356; **Phone:** 602-867-8644; **Board Cert:** Internal Medicine 1974; Cardiovascular Disease 1979; **Med School:** Med Coll VA 1970; **Resid:** Internal Medicine, Brigham & Women's Hosp 1974; **Fellow:** Cardiology Research, Brigham & Women's Hosp 1975; Cardiovascular Disease, Mayo Clin 1977

Wilansky, Susan MD [Cv] - **Spec Exp:** Heart Disease in Women; Heart Disease in Pregnancy; Echocardiography; Heart Valve Disease; **Hospital:** Mayo Clinic - Phoenix; **Address:** Mayo Clinic, Div Cardiology, 13400 E Shea Blvd, Scottsdale, AZ 85259; **Phone:** 480-301-8200; **Board Cert:** Cardiovascular Disease 1989; **Med School:** McMaster Univ 1979; **Resid:** Internal Medicine, Univ Toronto Affil Hosp 1983; **Fellow:** Cardiovascular Disease, Univ Toronto 1985; Echocardiography, Univ Toronto 1986; **Fac Appt:** Assoc Prof Med, Mayo Med Sch

Zoghbi, William A MD [Cv] - **Spec Exp:** Echocardiography; **Hospital:** Methodist Hosp - Houston; **Address:** Methodist DeBakey Heart & Vascular Ctr, 6550 Fannin St, Ste 1901, Smith Tower, Houston, TX 77030; **Phone:** 713-441-1100; **Board Cert:** Internal Medicine 1982; Cardiovascular Disease 1985; **Med School:** Meharry Med Coll 1979; **Resid:** Internal Medicine, Baylor Coll Affil Hosps 1982; **Fellow:** Cardiovascular Disease, Baylor Coll Med 1985

West Coast and Pacific

Bairey-Merz, Cathleen Noel MD [Cv] - **Spec Exp:** Preventive Cardiology; Heart Disease in Women; Ischemic Heart Disease; **Hospital:** Cedars-Sinai Med Ctr; **Address:** Cedars-Sinai Women's Heart Ctr, 127 S San Vicente Blvd, Ste A3600, Los Angeles, CA 90048; **Phone:** 310-423-9680; **Board Cert:** Internal Medicine 1984; Cardiovascular Disease 1987; **Med School:** Harvard Med Sch 1981; **Resid:** Internal Medicine, UCSF Med Ctr 1984; **Fellow:** Cardiovascular Disease, Cedars-Sinai Med Ctr 1987; **Fac Appt:** Prof Med, UCLA

Blanchard, Daniel G MD [Cv] - **Spec Exp:** Echocardiography; Hypertension; **Hospital:** UCSD Med Ctr; **Address:** UCSD Sulpizio Cardiovascular Ctr, 9434 Medical Center Drive, La Jolla, CA 92037; **Phone:** 858-657-8530; **Board Cert:** Internal Medicine 1988; **Med School:** UCSD 1985; **Resid:** Internal Medicine, UCSD Med Ctr 1988; **Fellow:** Cardiovascular Disease, USCD Med Ctr 1991; **Fac Appt:** Prof Med, UCSD

Budoff, Matthew J MD [Cv] - **Spec Exp:** Cholesterol/Lipid Disorders; Preventive Cardiology; Cardiac Imaging; **Hospital:** LAC - Harbor - UCLA Med Ctr; **Address:** 21840 S Normandy St, Ste 850, Torrance, CA 90502; **Phone:** 310-222-5101; **Board Cert:** Internal Medicine 2003; Cardiovascular Disease 2007; **Med School:** Geo Wash Univ 1990; **Resid:** Internal Medicine, UCLA/Harbor Med Ctr 1993; **Fellow:** Cardiovascular Disease, UCLA/Harbor Med Ctr 1997; **Fac Appt:** Prof Med, UCLA

Dichek, David A MD [Cv] - **Spec Exp:** Coronary Artery Disease; Gene Therapy; **Hospital:** Univ Wash Med Ctr; **Address:** UWMC-Regl Heart Ctr, 1959 NE Pacific St, Box 356171, Seattle, WA 98195; **Phone:** 206-598-4300; **Board Cert:** Internal Medicine 1987; Cardiovascular Disease 2004; **Med School:** UCLA 1984; **Resid:** Internal Medicine, Mass Genl Hosp 1987; **Fellow:** Cardiovascular Disease, NIH/Johns Hopkins Hosp 1992; **Fac Appt:** Prof Med, Univ Wash

Edelen, John S MD [Cv] - **Spec Exp:** Angioplasty & Stent Placement; Interventional Cardiology; **Hospital:** Alta Bates Summit Med Ctr-Alta Bates Campus; **Address:** Berkeley Cardiovascular Med Grp, 3300 Webster St Fl 4 - Ste 410, Oakland, CA 94609; **Phone:** 510-549-4220; **Board Cert:** Internal Medicine 1974; Cardiovascular Disease 1975; Interventional Cardiology 2001; **Med School:** Columbia P&S 1969; **Resid:** Internal Medicine, Columbia-Presby Med Ctr 1971; **Fellow:** Cardiovascular Disease, Pacific Med Center 1975

Elkayam, Uri MD [Cv] - **Spec Exp:** Heart Failure; Heart Disease in Pregnancy; Heart Valve Disease; Coronary Artery Disease; **Hospital:** LAC & USC Med Ctr; **Address:** Healthcare Consultation Center II, 1520 San Pablo St, Ste 1000, Los Angeles, CA 90033; **Phone:** 323-442-7669; **Board Cert:** Internal Medicine 1989; Cardiovascular Disease 2009; **Med School:** Israel 1973; **Resid:** Internal Medicine, Tel Aviv Sourasky Med Ctr 1976; **Fellow:** Cardiovascular Disease, Albert Einstein Hosp 1978; Cardiovascular Disease, Cedars Sinai Med Ctr 1979; **Fac Appt:** Prof Med, USC Sch Med

Fishbein, Daniel P MD [Cv] - **Spec Exp:** Congestive Heart Failure; Transplant Medicine-Heart; **Hospital:** Univ Wash Med Ctr; **Address:** UWMC-Regl Heart Ctr, 1959 NE Pacific St, Box 356171, Seattle, WA 98195; **Phone:** 206-685-3895; **Board Cert:** Internal Medicine 1983; Cardiovascular Disease 1987; **Med School:** Albert Einstein Coll Med 1980; **Resid:** Internal Medicine, Univ Wash Med Ctr 1983; **Fellow:** Cardiovascular Disease, Univ Wash Med Ctr 1987; Interventional Cardiology, Univ Wash Med Ctr 1989; **Fac Appt:** Prof Med, Univ Wash

Fonarow, Gregg C MD [Cv] - **Spec Exp:** Cardiomyopathy; Heart Failure; Preventive Cardiology; Clinical Trials; **Hospital:** UCLA Ronald Reagan Med Ctr; **Address:** 100 UCLA Medical Plaza, Ste 630E, Los Angeles, CA 90095; **Phone:** 310-825-8816; **Board Cert:** Cardiovascular Disease 2003; **Med School:** UCLA 1987; **Resid:** Internal Medicine, UCLA Med Ctr 1990; **Fellow:** Cardiovascular Disease, UCLA Med Ctr 1993; **Fac Appt:** Prof Med, UCLA

French, William J MD [Cv] - **Spec Exp:** Heart Failure; Interventional Cardiology; Coronary Artery Disease; **Hospital:** LAC - Harbor - UCLA Med Ctr; **Address:** Harbor-UCLA Med Ctr, 1000 W Carson St, Torrance, CA 90509-2004; **Phone:** 310-222-2415; **Board Cert:** Internal Medicine 1973; Cardiovascular Disease 1979; Interventional Cardiology 2012; **Med School:** Univ VT Coll Med 1968; **Resid:** Internal Medicine, Harlem Hosp Ctr 1971; Internal Medicine, Grad Hosp Univ Penn Affil Hosp 1972; **Fellow:** Critical Care Medicine, Hollywood Pres Hosp-USC 1975; Cardiovascular Disease, Harbor-UCLA Med Ctr 1977; **Fac Appt:** Prof Med, UCLA

Hunt, Sharon Ann MD [Cv] - **Spec Exp:** Transplant Medicine-Heart; **Hospital:** Stanford Univ Hosp & Clins; **Address:** Stanford Univ Div Cardiovascular Med, 300 Pasteur Drive, CVRB 265, Stanford, CA 94305; **Phone:** 650-498-6605; **Board Cert:** Internal Medicine 1977; Cardiovascular Disease 2011; Advanced Heart Failure & Transplant Cardiology 2010; **Med School:** Stanford Univ 1972; **Resid:** Internal Medicine, Stanford Univ Hosp 1974; **Fellow:** Cardiovascular Disease, Stanford Univ 1976; **Fac Appt:** Prof Med, Stanford Univ

Johnson, Allen D MD [Cv] - **Spec Exp:** Congenital Heart Disease-Adult; Congestive Heart Failure; **Hospital:** Scripps Green Hosp; **Address:** Scripps Clinic-Torrey Pines, 10666 N Torrey Pines Rd, MS SW 206, La Jolla, CA 92037; **Phone:** 858-554-8836; **Board Cert:** Internal Medicine 1973; Cardiovascular Disease 1973; **Med School:** Johns Hopkins Univ 1965; **Resid:** Internal Medicine, Johns Hopkins Hosp 1979; **Fellow:** Cardiovascular Disease, UCSD Med Ctr 1972; **Fac Appt:** Clin Prof Med, Univ SD Sch Med

Judelson, Debra R MD [Cv] - **Spec Exp:** Hypertension; Cholesterol/Lipid Disorders; Heart Disease in Women; Preventive Cardiology; **Hospital:** Cedars-Sinai Med Ctr, Brotman Med Ctr; **Address:** Cardiovascular Med Group of Southern CA, 414 N Camden Drive, Ste 1100, Beverly Hills, CA 90210-4532; **Phone:** 310-278-3400 x155; **Board Cert:** Internal Medicine 1979; Cardiovascular Disease 1981; **Med School:** Harvard Med Sch 1976; **Resid:** Internal Medicine, Kaiser Foundation Hosp 1979; **Fellow:** Cardiovascular Disease, Kaiser Foundation Hosp 1981

Kaul, Sanjiv MD [Cv] - **Spec Exp:** Cardiac Imaging; Echocardiography; Coronary Artery Disease; Preventive Cardiology; **Hospital:** OR Hlth & Sci Univ; **Address:** OHSU, Dept Cardiology, 3181 SW Sam Jackson Park Rd, MC UHN62, Portland, OR 97239; **Phone:** 503-494-8750; **Board Cert:** Internal Medicine 1980; Cardiovascular Disease 1983; **Med School:** India 1975; **Resid:** Internal Medicine, Univ Vermont Med Ctr 1980; **Fellow:** Cardiovascular Disease, UCLA Ronald Reagan Med Ctr 1982; Cardiovascular Disease, Mass Genl Hosp 1983; **Fac Appt:** Prof Med, Oregon Hlth & Sci Univ

Kobashigawa, Jon A MD [Cv] - **Spec Exp:** Transplant Medicine-Heart; Congestive Heart Failure; Heart Valve Disease; Cardiac Catheterization; **Hospital:** Cedars-Sinai Med Ctr; **Address:** California Heart Ctr, 8536 Wilshire Blvd Fl 3 - Ste 302, Beverly Hills, CA 90211; **Phone:** 310-248-8300; **Board Cert:** Internal Medicine 1983; Cardiovascular Disease 1987; Advanced Heart Failure & Transplant Cardiology 2012; **Med School:** Mount Sinai Sch Med 1980; **Resid:** Internal Medicine, UCLA Med Ctr 1983; **Fellow:** Cardiovascular Disease, UCLA Med Ctr 1986; **Fac Appt:** Clin Prof Med, UCLA

Lewis, Sandra J MD [Cv] - **Spec Exp:** Heart Disease in Women; Preventive Cardiology; Congestive Heart Failure; **Hospital:** Legacy Good Samaritan Med Ctr, Legacy Emanuel Hosp; **Address:** NW Cardiovascular Inst, 2222 NW Lovejoy St, Ste 606, Portland, OR 97210; **Phone:** 503-229-7554; **Board Cert:** Internal Medicine 1980; Cardiovascular Disease 1985; **Med School:** Stanford Univ 1977; **Resid:** Internal Medicine, Stanford Univ Hosp & Clins 1980; **Fellow:** Cardiovascular Disease, Stanford Univ Hosp & Clins 1983; **Fac Appt:** Assoc Clin Prof Med, Oregon Hlth & Sci Univ

Redberg, Rita F MD [Cv] - **Spec Exp:** Echocardiography; Heart Disease in Women; Preventive Cardiology; **Hospital:** UCSF Med Ctr; **Address:** UCSF Cardiology, 535 Mission Bay Blvd S, San Francisco, CA 94158; **Phone:** 415-353-2873; **Board Cert:** Internal Medicine 1985; Cardiovascular Disease 1989; **Med School:** Univ Pennsylvania 1982; **Resid:** Internal Medicine, Columbia-Presby Med Ctr 1985; **Fellow:** Cardiovascular Disease, Columbia-Presby Med Ctr 1988; **Fac Appt:** Prof Med, UCSF

Schnittger, Ingela MD [Cv] - **Spec Exp:** Echocardiography; Echocardiography-Transesophageal; **Hospital:** Stanford Univ Hosp & Clins; **Address:** 300 Pasteur Drive, rm H2157, Stanford, CA 94305-5233; **Phone:** 650-723-5196; **Board Cert:** Internal Medicine 1980; Cardiovascular Disease 1983; **Med School:** Sweden 1975; **Resid:** Internal Medicine, Stanford Univ Hosp 1980; **Fellow:** Cardiovascular Disease, Stanford Univ 1983; **Fac Appt:** Prof Med, Stanford Univ

Shah, Prediman K MD [Cv] - **Spec Exp:** Coronary Artery Disease; Cholesterol/Lipid Disorders; Preventive Cardiology; Heart Valve Disease; **Hospital:** Cedars-Sinai Med Ctr; **Address:** Cedars-Sinai Med Ctr, 8700 Beverly Blvd, Ste A3600, Los Angeles, CA 90048; **Phone:** 310-423-3884; **Board Cert:** Internal Medicine 1975; Cardiovascular Disease 1977; **Med School:** India 1969; **Resid:** Internal Medicine, All India Inst Med Scis 1971; Internal Medicine, Montefiore Hosp 1974; **Fellow:** Cardiovascular Disease, Montefiore Hosp 1976; Research, Cedars Sinai Med Ctr 1977; **Fac Appt:** Prof Med, UCLA

Skolnick, Alan E MD [Cv] - **Spec Exp:** Nuclear Cardiology; **Hospital:** Providence Alaska Med Ctr; **Address:** Alaska Hrt Inst, 3841 Piper St, Ste T-100, Anchorage, AK 99508; **Phone:** 907-561-3211; **Board Cert:** Internal Medicine 2002; Cardiovascular Disease 2005; Nuclear Cardiology 1998; **Med School:** Albert Einstein Coll Med 1989; **Resid:** Internal Medicine, Beth Israel Deaconess Med Ctr 1992; **Fellow:** Cardiovascular Disease, Boston Med Ctr 1994

Tobis, Jonathan Marvin MD [Cv] - **Spec Exp:** Interventional Cardiology; Angioplasty; Cardiac Catheterization; Heart Valve Disease; **Hospital:** UCLA Ronald Reagan Med Ctr, Santa Monica - UCLA Med Ctr & Ortho Hosp; **Address:** 100 UCLA Medical Plaza, Ste 630W, Los Angeles, CA 90095; **Phone:** 310-825-9011; **Board Cert:** Internal Medicine 1976; Cardiovascular Disease 1979; Interventional Cardiology 2009; **Med School:** Albert Einstein Coll Med 1973; **Resid:** Internal Medicine, Lincoln Hosp 1975; Internal Medicine, Univ CA Irvine Med Ctr 1976; **Fellow:** Cardiovascular Disease, Univ CA Irvine Med Ctr 1978; **Fac Appt:** Prof Med, UCLA-David Geffen Sch Med

Topol, Eric J MD [Cv] - **Spec Exp:** Genetic Arrhythmias; **Hospital:** Scripps Meml Hosp - La Jolla; **Address:** Scripps Clin Torrey Pines, 3344 N Torrey Pines Ct, MS SGM 300, La Jolla, CA 92037; **Phone:** 858-554-5708; **Board Cert:** Internal Medicine 1982; Cardiovascular Disease 1985; **Med School:** Univ Rochester 1979; **Resid:** Internal Medicine, UCSF Med Ctr 1982; **Fellow:** Cardiovascular Disease, Johns Hopkins Hosp 1985

Cardiac Electrophysiology

New England

Buxton, Alfred E MD [CE] - **Spec Exp:** Arrhythmias; **Hospital:** Beth Israel Deaconess Med Ctr - Boston; **Address:** BIDMC Department of Cardiology, 330 Brookline Ave, Shapiro 7, Boston, MA 02215; **Phone:** 617-667-8800; **Board Cert:** Internal Medicine 1977; Cardiovascular Disease 1981; Cardiac Electrophysiology 2012; **Med School:** Univ Pennsylvania 1973; **Resid:** Internal Medicine, Hosp Univ Penn 1978; **Fellow:** Cardiovascular Disease, Hosp Univ Penn 1980; Cardiac Electrophysiology, Hosp Univ Penn 1981; **Fac Appt:** Assoc Prof Med, Harvard Med Sch

Donahue, J. Kevin MD [CE] - **Spec Exp:** Arrhythmias; Catheter Ablation; Defibrillators; Ventricular Tachycardia Ablation; **Hospital:** UMass Memorial Med Ctr; **Address:** UMass Meml Med Ctr, Dept Cardiovascular Med, 55 Lake Ave N, Worcester, MA 01655-0002; **Phone:** 508-334-3452; **Board Cert:** Cardiovascular Disease 2009; Cardiac Electrophysiology 2011; **Med School:** Washington Univ, St Louis 1992; **Resid:** Internal Medicine, Hosp Univ Penn 1994; **Fellow:** Cardiovascular Disease, Johns Hopkins Hosp 1999; Cardiac Electrophysiology, Johns Hopkins Hosp 1999; **Fac Appt:** Prof Med, Univ Mass Sch Med

Epstein, Laurence M MD [CE] - **Spec Exp:** Arrhythmias; Defibrillator Cable Extraction; Defibrillators; Pacemakers; **Hospital:** Brigham & Women's Hosp; **Address:** Brigham & Women's Hosp, 70 Francis St, Fl 3, Clinic C, Boston, MA 02115; **Phone:** 857-307-4000; **Board Cert:** Internal Medicine 1989; Cardiovascular Disease 2012; Cardiac Electrophysiology 2012; **Med School:** Univ Chicago-Pritzker Sch Med 1985; **Resid:** Internal Medicine, UCSF Med Ctr 1988; **Fellow:** Cardiovascular Disease, Hosp Univ Penn 1991; Cardiac Electrophysiology, UCSF Med Ctr 1992; **Fac Appt:** Assoc Prof Med, Harvard Med Sch

Estes III, N.A. Mark MD [CE] - **Spec Exp:** Arrhythmias; **Hospital:** Tufts Med Ctr; **Address:** Tufts Medical Ctr, 800 Washington St, Box 197, Boston, MA 02111; **Phone:** 617-636-6156; **Board Cert:** Internal Medicine 1980; Cardiovascular Disease 1983; Cardiac Electrophysiology 2012; **Med School:** Univ Cincinnati 1977; **Resid:** Internal Medicine, Beth Israel Deaconess Hosp 1980; **Fellow:** Cardiovascular Disease, New England Med Ctr 1982; Cardiac Electrophysiology, Mass General Hosp 1983; **Fac Appt:** Prof Med, Tufts Univ

Josephson, Mark Eric MD [CE] - **Spec Exp:** Arrhythmias; **Hospital:** Beth Israel Deaconess Med Ctr - Boston; **Address:** Beth Israel Deaconess Med Ctr, 330 Brookline Ave, Boston, MA 02215; **Phone:** 617-667-8800; **Board Cert:** Internal Medicine 1973; Cardiovascular Disease 1975; **Med School:** Columbia P&S 1969; **Resid:** Internal Medicine, Mt Sinai Med Ctr 1971; **Fellow:** Cardiovascular Disease, Hosp Univ Penn 1975; **Fac Appt:** Prof Med, Harvard Med Sch

Link, Mark S MD [CE] - **Spec Exp:** Arrhythmias; Ventricular Tachycardia Ablation; Heart Disease in Athletes; Sudden Death Prevention; **Hospital:** Tufts Med Ctr; **Address:** Tufts Med Ctr, 800 Washington St, Box 197, Boston, MA 02111; **Phone:** 617-636-5902; **Board Cert:** Internal Medicine 1989; Cardiovascular Disease 2007; Cardiac Electrophysiology 2008; **Med School:** Tufts Univ 1986; **Resid:** Internal Medicine, NY Presby Hosp/Columbia 1989; **Fellow:** Cardiovascular Disease, New England Med Ctr 1996; Cardiac Electrophysiology, New England Med Ctr 1997; **Fac Appt:** Prof Med, Tufts Univ

Ruskin, Jeremy N MD [CE] - **Spec Exp:** Arrhythmias; Atrial Fibrillation; **Hospital:** Mass Genl Hosp; **Address:** Cardiac Arrhythmia Service, Mass General Hosp, 55 Fruit St, Boston, MA 02114; **Phone:** 617-726-8514; **Board Cert:** Internal Medicine 1974; Cardiovascular Disease 1975; Cardiac Electrophysiology 2003; **Med School:** Harvard Med Sch 1971; **Resid:** Internal Medicine, Beth Israel Deaconess Med Ctr 1973; **Fellow:** Cardiovascular Disease, Mass Genl Hosp 1975; Cardiac Electrophysiology, US Public Hlth Service Hosp; **Fac Appt:** Assoc Prof Med, Harvard Med Sch

Stevenson, William G MD [CE] - **Spec Exp:** Arrhythmias; **Hospital:** Brigham & Women's Hosp; **Address:** Brigham & Womens Hosp, Cardiovascular Div, 75 Francis St, Boston, MA 02115; **Phone:** 857-307-4000; **Board Cert:** Internal Medicine 1982; Cardiovascular Disease 1985; Cardiac Electrophysiology 2005; **Med School:** Tulane Univ 1979; **Resid:** Internal Medicine, UCLA Med Ctr 1982; **Fellow:** Cardiovascular Disease, UCLA Med Ctr 1984; Cardiac Electrophysiology, UCLA Med Ctr 1985; **Fac Appt:** Prof Med, Harvard Med Sch

Mid Atlantic

Berger, Ronald D MD/PhD [CE] - **Spec Exp:** Catheter Ablation; **Hospital:** Johns Hopkins Hosp (page 59); **Address:** Johns Hopkins Medicine, 601 N Caroline St, Outpatient Center Fl 7, Baltimore, MD 21287; **Phone:** 443-997-0270; **Board Cert:** Cardiovascular Disease 2004; Cardiac Electrophysiology 2006; **Med School:** Harvard Med Sch 1987; **Resid:** Internal Medicine, Brigham & Women's Hosp 1990; **Fellow:** Cardiovascular Disease, Johns Hopkins Hosp 1993; **Fac Appt:** Prof Med, Johns Hopkins Univ

Callans, David J MD [CE] - **Spec Exp:** Arrhythmias; Pacemakers; **Hospital:** Hosp Univ Penn - UPHS (page 69); **Address:** Hosp Univ Penn - Cardiology, 3400 Spruce St, Founders Bldg - Fl 9, Philadelphia, PA 19104; **Phone:** 215-662-6052; **Board Cert:** Internal Medicine 1989; Cardiovascular Disease 2005; Cardiac Electrophysiology 2005; **Med School:** Johns Hopkins Univ 1986; **Resid:** Internal Medicine, Hosp Univ Penn 1989; **Fellow:** Cardiovascular Disease, Hosp Univ Penn 1993; Cardiac Electrophysiology, Hosp Univ Penn 1994; **Fac Appt:** Prof Med, Univ Pennsylvania

Chinitz, Larry A MD [CE] - **Spec Exp:** Arrhythmias; Pacemakers; Defibrillators; Atrial Fibrillation; **Hospital:** NYU Langone Med Ctr (page 68); **Address:** Heart Rhythm Ctr, 403 E 34th St Fl 4, New York, NY 10016-6402; **Phone:** 212-263-7149; **Board Cert:** Internal Medicine 1982; Cardiovascular Disease 1985; **Med School:** NYU Sch Med 1979; **Resid:** Internal Medicine, Bellevue Hosp Ctr 1983; **Fellow:** Cardiovascular Disease, NYU Med Ctr/Bellevue Hosp Ctr 1985; Cardiac Electrophysiology, Montefiore Hosp 1986; **Fac Appt:** Assoc Prof Med, NYU Sch Med

Cohen, Martin B MD [CE] - **Spec Exp:** Arrhythmias; Pacemakers; Defibrillators; Coronary Angioplasty/Stents; **Hospital:** Westchester Med Ctr, White Plains Hosp; **Address:** Westchester Heart & Vascular, 19 Bradhurst Ave Fl 3 - Ste 3850 South, Hawthorne, NY 10532-2140; **Phone:** 914-909-6900; **Board Cert:** Internal Medicine 1983; Cardiovascular Disease 1985; Cardiac Electrophysiology 2006; Interventional Cardiology 2004; **Med School:** SUNY Downstate 1980; **Resid:** Internal Medicine, Univ Hosp 1983; **Fellow:** Cardiovascular Disease, Univ Hosp 1985; Interventional Cardiology, Westchester Co Med Ctr 1986; **Fac Appt:** Assoc Prof Med, NY Med Coll

Curtis, Anne B MD [CE] - **Spec Exp:** Arrhythmias; Pacemakers; Defibrillators; **Hospital:** Buffalo Genl Hosp; **Address:** 3980 Sheridan Drive, Fl 6, Dent Tower, Amherst, NY 14226; **Phone:** 716-961-9900; **Board Cert:** Internal Medicine 1982; Cardiovascular Disease 1985; Cardiac Electrophysiology 2012; **Med School:** Columbia P&S 1979; **Resid:** Internal Medicine, Columbia- Presby Hosp 1982; **Fellow:** Cardiovascular Disease, Duke Univ Med Ctr 1985; Cardiac Electrophysiology, Duke Univ Med Ctr 1986; **Fac Appt:** Prof Med, SUNY Buffalo

Epstein, Andrew E MD [CE] - **Spec Exp:** Arrhythmias; Defibrillators; Catheter Ablation; Genetic Arrhythmias; **Hospital:** Hosp Univ Penn - UPHS (page 69), VA Med Ctr - Philadelphia; **Address:** Hosp Univ Penn - Dept Cardiology, 3400 Spruce St Founders Bldg Fl 9, Philadelphia, PA 19104; **Phone:** 215-615-5455; **Board Cert:** Internal Medicine 1980; Cardiovascular Disease 1983; Cardiac Electrophysiology 2006; **Med School:** Univ Rochester 1977; **Resid:** Internal Medicine, Barnes-Jewish Hosp 1980; **Fellow:** Cardiovascular Disease, UAB Hosp 1982; **Fac Appt:** Prof Med, Univ Pennsylvania

Gomes, Joseph Anthony MD [CE] - **Spec Exp:** Arrhythmias; Heart Attack; Atrial Fibrillation; Pacemakers; **Hospital:** Mt Sinai Med Ctr (page 62); **Address:** Cardiovascular Medicine Assocs, 1190 Fifth Ave, 1-South, Guggenheim Pavilion, New York, NY 10029-6500; **Phone:** 212-241-7272; **Board Cert:** Internal Medicine 1974; Cardiovascular Disease 1975; **Med School:** India 1969; **Resid:** Internal Medicine, Mt Sinai Med Ctr 1973; **Fellow:** Cardiovascular Disease, Mt Sinai Med Ctr 1975; Cardiac Electrophysiology, USPHS Cardio-Pulmonary Lab 1976; **Fac Appt:** Prof Med, Mount Sinai Sch Med

Halperin, Henry R MD [CE] - **Spec Exp:** Catheter Ablation; Pacemakers; **Hospital:** Johns Hopkins Hosp (page 59); **Address:** The Johns Hopkins Hospital, 601 N Caroline St, Outpatient Center Fl 7, Baltimore, MD 21287; **Phone:** 410-955-2412; **Board Cert:** Internal Medicine 1981; Cardiovascular Disease 1983; Cardiac Electrophysiology 2009; **Med School:** Louisiana State U, Shrevport 1977; **Resid:** Internal Medicine, LSU Charity Hosp 1980; **Fellow:** Cardiovascular Disease, Johns Hopkins Hosp 1983; **Fac Appt:** Prof Med, Johns Hopkins Univ

Iwai, Sei MD [CE] - **Spec Exp:** Arrhythmias; Atrial Fibrillation; Radiofrequency Ablation; **Hospital:** Westchester Med Ctr; **Address:** Westchester Heart & Vascular, 19 Bradhurst Ave Fl 3 - Ste 3850 South, Valhalla, NY 10595; **Phone:** 914-909-6900; **Board Cert:** Internal Medicine 1997; Cardiovascular Disease 2011; Cardiac Electrophysiology 2001; **Med School:** Columbia P&S 1994; **Resid:** Internal Medicine, NY-Presby/Columbia Univ Med Ctr 1997; **Fellow:** Cardiovascular Disease, NY-Presby/Weill Cornell Med Ctr 2000; Cardiac Electrophysiology, NY-Presby/Weill Cornell Med Ctr 2001; **Fac Appt:** Prof Med, NY Med Coll

Lerman, Bruce MD [CE] - **Spec Exp:** Catheter Ablation; Atrial Fibrillation; Defibrillators; Arrhythmias; **Hospital:** NY-Presby/Weill Cornell Med Ctr, NY (page 65); **Address:** NY Presby/Weill Cornell Med Ctr, 520 E 70th St, Starr 4, New York, NY 10021-9800; **Phone:** 212-746-2169; **Board Cert:** Internal Medicine 1980; Cardiovascular Disease 1985; Cardiac Electrophysiology 2012; **Med School:** Loyola Univ-Stritch Sch Med 1977; **Resid:** Internal Medicine, Northwestern Univ Hosp 1980; Internal Medicine, Univ Michigan Med Ctr 1981; **Fellow:** Cardiovascular Disease, Hosp Univ Penn 1982; Cardiovascular Disease, Johns Hopkins Hosp 1983; **Fac Appt:** Prof Med, Cornell Univ-Weill Med Coll

Levine, Joseph H MD [CE] - **Spec Exp:** Arrhythmias; Sudden Death Prevention; Atrial Fibrillation; Pacemakers; **Hospital:** St. Francis Hosp - The Heart Ctr (page 70); **Address:** 100 Port Washington Blvd, Roslyn, NY 11576; **Phone:** 516-622-1011; **Board Cert:** Internal Medicine 1983; Cardiovascular Disease 1987; Cardiac Electrophysiology 2003; **Med School:** Univ Rochester 1980; **Resid:** Internal Medicine, Yale-New Haven Hosp 1983; **Fellow:** Cardiovascular Disease, Johns Hopkins Hosp 1986; Cardiac Electrophysiology, Hosp U Penn 1987

Marchlinski, Francis E MD [CE] - **Spec Exp:** Pacemakers; Arrhythmias; **Hospital:** Hosp Univ Penn - UPHS (page 69); **Address:** Hosp Univ Penn, Div Cardiology, 3400 Spruce St Founders Bldg Fl 9, Philadelphia, PA 19104-4206; **Phone:** 215-662-6005; **Board Cert:** Internal Medicine 1979; Cardiovascular Disease 1981; Cardiac Electrophysiology 2012; **Med School:** Univ Pennsylvania 1976; **Resid:** Internal Medicine, Hosp Univ Penn - UPHS 1979; **Fellow:** Cardiovascular Disease, Hosp Univ Penn - UPHS 1982; **Fac Appt:** Prof Med, Univ Pennsylvania

Mehta, Davendra MD/PhD [CE] - **Spec Exp:** Arrhythmias; Congenital Heart Disease-Adult; Atrial Fibrillation; Heart Failure; **Hospital:** Mt Sinai Med Ctr (page 62); **Address:** Cardiovascular Medicine Assocs, 1190 Fifth Ave, 1-South, Guggenheim Pavilion, New York, NY 10029-6501; **Phone:** 212-241-3559; **Board Cert:** Cardiovascular Disease 2009; Cardiac Electrophysiology 2009; **Med School:** India 1976; **Resid:** Internal Medicine, Leicester Royal Infirmary 1983; **Fellow:** Cardiovascular Disease, Groby Road Hosp 1986; Electrocardiography, St George's Hosp 1989; **Fac Appt:** Prof Med, Mount Sinai Sch Med

Naccarelli, Gerald V MD [CE] - **Spec Exp:** Pacemakers; Arrhythmias; **Hospital:** Penn State Milton S Hershey Med Ctr; **Address:** Penn State Heart & Vascular Inst, 500 University Drive, UPC I Bldg, Ste 600, MS HO47, Hershey, PA 17033; **Phone:** 717-531-3907; **Board Cert:** Internal Medicine 1979; Cardiovascular Disease 1981; **Med School:** Penn State Coll Med 1976; **Resid:** Internal Medicine, NC Bapt Hosp 1978; Internal Medicine, Hershey Med Ctr 1979; **Fellow:** Cardiovascular Disease, Indiana Univ Med Ctr 1982; **Fac Appt:** Prof Med, Penn State Coll Med

Tomaselli, Gordon F MD [CE] - **Spec Exp:** Arrhythmias; Sudden Death Prevention; **Hospital:** Johns Hopkins Hosp (page 59); **Address:** Johns Hopkins Medicine, 601 N Caroline St, Outpatient Center Fl 7, Baltimore, MD 21287; **Phone:** 410-955-2774; **Board Cert:** Internal Medicine 1985; Cardiovascular Disease 1989; Cardiac Electrophysiology 2005; **Med School:** Albert Einstein Coll Med 1982; **Resid:** Internal Medicine, UCSF Med Ctr 1985; **Fellow:** Cardiovascular Disease, Johns Hopkins Hosp 1989; **Fac Appt:** Prof Med, Johns Hopkins Univ

Southeast

DeLurgio, David B MD [CE] - **Spec Exp:** Arrhythmias; Atrial Fibrillation; Sudden Death Prevention; Heart Failure; **Hospital:** Emory Univ Hosp Midtown, Emory Univ Hosp; **Address:** Emory Univ Hosp Midtown, 550 Peachtree St NE Fl 6, Atlanta, GA 30308; **Phone:** 404-686-2504; **Board Cert:** Cardiovascular Disease 2007; Cardiac Electrophysiology 2008; **Med School:** UCLA 1990; **Resid:** Internal Medicine, Emory Univ Hosp 1993; **Fellow:** Cardiovascular Disease, UCLA Med Ctr 1995; **Fac Appt:** Assoc Prof Med, Emory Univ

DiMarco, John P MD/PhD [CE] - **Spec Exp:** Arrhythmias; Pacemakers; Defibrillators; **Hospital:** Univ of Virginia Hlth Sys; **Address:** Univ Virginia Hlth Scis Ctr, 1215 Lee St, Charlottesville, VA 22908-0158; **Phone:** 434-924-2031; **Board Cert:** Internal Medicine 1978; Cardiovascular Disease 1981; Cardiac Electrophysiology 2005; **Med School:** Case West Res Univ 1975; **Resid:** Internal Medicine, Mass Genl Hosp 1977; Critical Care Medicine, Case West Res Univ 1978; **Fellow:** Cardiovascular Disease, Mass Genl Hosp 1980; Cardiac Electrophysiology, Mass Genl Hosp 1981; **Fac Appt:** Prof Med, Univ VA Sch Med

Ellenbogen, Kenneth A MD [CE] - **Spec Exp:** Arrhythmias; Pacemakers; Defibrillators; **Hospital:** VCU Med Ctr, Henrico Doctors Hosp; **Address:** VCU Med Ctr, 1200 E Marshall St, Richmond, VA 23298; **Phone:** 804-828-7565; **Board Cert:** Internal Medicine 1983; Cardiovascular Disease 1985; Cardiac Electrophysiology 2005; **Med School:** Johns Hopkins Univ 1980; **Resid:** Internal Medicine, Johns Hopkins Hosp 1983; **Fellow:** Cardiovascular Disease, Duke Univ Med Ctr 1986; **Fac Appt:** Prof Med, Med Coll VA

Interian Jr, Alberto MD [CE] - **Spec Exp:** Arrhythmias; Sudden Death Prevention; Pacemakers; **Hospital:** Mercy Hosp, Jackson Meml Hosp; **Address:** Mercy Hosp, Arrhythmia & Syncope Ctr, 3641 S Miami Ave, Ste 221, Miami, FL 33133; **Phone:** 305-285-2642; **Board Cert:** Internal Medicine 1985; Cardiovascular Disease 1987; **Med School:** Univ Miami Sch Med 1982; **Resid:** Internal Medicine, Jackson Meml Hosp 1985; **Fellow:** Cardiovascular Disease, Jackson Meml Hosp 1988; **Fac Appt:** Prof Med, Univ Miami Sch Med

Onufer, John R MD [CE] - **Spec Exp:** Atrial Fibrillation; Catheter Ablation; Pacemakers; Defibrillators; **Hospital:** Henrico Doctors Hosp; **Address:** Virginia Cardiovascular Specialists, 7611 Forest Ave, Ste 100, Richmond, VA 23229; **Phone:** 804-288-4827; **Board Cert:** Internal Medicine 1987; Cardiovascular Disease 2011; Cardiac Electrophysiology 2012; **Med School:** Washington Univ, St Louis 1984; **Resid:** Internal Medicine, Barnes Jewish Hosp 1987; **Fellow:** Cardiovascular Disease, Washington Univ 1990; Cardiac Electrophysiology, Washington Univ 1991

Sorrentino, Robert A MD [CE] - **Spec Exp:** Arrhythmias; Defibrillators; Pacemakers; Heart Failure; **Hospital:** Georgia Regents Med Ctr-Augusta; **Address:** GA Regents, Heart & Cardiovascular Svcs, 1120 15th St BBR Bldg - rm 6513B, Augusta, GA 30912; **Phone:** 706-721-2426; **Board Cert:** Internal Medicine 1988; Cardiovascular Disease 2002; Cardiac Electrophysiology 2008; **Med School:** Albany Med Coll 1985; **Resid:** Internal Medicine, Duke Univ Hosp 1988; **Fellow:** Cardiovascular Disease, Duke Univ Hosp 1991; **Fac Appt:** Prof Med, Med Coll GA

Midwest

Anderson, Mark E MD/PhD [CE] - **Spec Exp:** Arrhythmias; **Hospital:** Univ Iowa Hosp & Clins; **Address:** 200 Hawkins Drive GH Bldg, Iowa City, IA 52242-1081; **Phone:** 319-356-2745; **Board Cert:** Internal Medicine 2005; Cardiovascular Disease 2005; **Med School:** Univ Minn 1989; **Resid:** Internal Medicine, Stanford Univ Med Ctr 1991; **Fellow:** Cardiovascular Disease, Stanford Univ Sch Med 1994; Cardiac Electrophysiology, Stanford Univ Sch Med 1996; **Fac Appt:** Prof Med, Univ Iowa Coll Med

Asirvatham, Samuel J MD [CE] - **Spec Exp:** Atrial Fibrillation; **Hospital:** Mayo Med Ctr & Clin - Rochester, Rochester Methodist Hosp; **Address:** 200 1st St SW, Mary-Brig Bldg Fl 4 - Ste 523, Rochester, MN 55905; **Phone:** 507-293-3376; **Board Cert:** Internal Medicine 2007; Cardiovascular Disease 2008; Cardiac Electrophysiology 2010; **Med School:** India 1991; **Resid:** Internal Medicine, Univ WI Hosp & Clins 1994; **Fellow:** Cardiovascular Disease, OU Med Ctr 1998; Cardiac Electrophysiology, Mayo Clin 2000; **Fac Appt:** Prof Med, Mayo Med Sch

Faddis, Mitchell N MD/PhD [CE] - **Spec Exp:** Arrhythmias; **Hospital:** Barnes-Jewish Hosp; **Address:** Barnes-Jewish Hosp, Dept Cardiology, 4921 Parkview Pl Fl 8th - Ste A, St Louis, MO 63110; **Phone:** 314-362-1291; **Board Cert:** Internal Medicine 2006; Cardiovascular Disease 2009; Cardiac Electrophysiology 2010; **Med School:** Washington Univ, St Louis 1993; **Resid:** Internal Medicine, Barnes-Jewish Hosp 1996; **Fellow:** Cardiovascular Disease, Barnes-Jewish Hosp 1998; **Fac Appt:** Assoc Prof Med, Washington Univ, St Louis

Goldberger, Jeffrey MD [CE] - **Spec Exp:** Defibrillators; Pacemakers; Catheter Ablation; **Hospital:** Northwestern Meml Hosp; **Address:** Bluhm Cardiovascular Inst, 675 N St Clair St, Galter Pavilion Fl 19 - Ste 100, Chicago, IL 60611; **Phone:** 312-695-4965; **Board Cert:** Internal Medicine 1987; Cardiovascular Disease 1989; Cardiac Electrophysiology 2012; **Med School:** Albert Einstein Coll Med 1984; **Resid:** Internal Medicine, Bronx Municipal Hosp 1987; **Fellow:** Cardiovascular Disease, UCSF Med Ctr 1990; **Fac Appt:** Prof Med, Northwestern Univ-Feinberg Sch Med

Hayes, David L MD [CE] - **Spec Exp:** Pacemakers; **Hospital:** Mayo Med Ctr & Clin - Rochester; **Address:** Mayo Clinic, 200 1st St SW, Rochester, MN 55905; **Phone:** 507-284-2511; **Board Cert:** Internal Medicine 1980; Cardiovascular Disease 1981; **Med School:** Univ MO-Kansas City 1977; **Resid:** Internal Medicine, Mayo Clin 1980; **Fellow:** Cardiovascular Disease, Mayo Clin 1982; **Fac Appt:** Prof Med, Mayo Med Sch

Knight, Bradley P MD [CE] - **Spec Exp:** Arrhythmias; Pacemakers; Atrial Fibrillation; **Hospital:** Northwestern Meml Hosp; **Address:** Northwestern Meml Hosp, 675 N St Clair, Galter 19-100, Chicago, IL 60611; **Phone:** 312-926-2148; **Board Cert:** Cardiovascular Disease 2007; Cardiac Electrophysiology 2008; **Med School:** Ohio State Univ 1990; **Resid:** Internal Medicine, Univ Michigan Hosp 1993; **Fellow:** Cardiovascular Disease, Univ Mich Med Sch 1995; Cardiac Electrophysiology, Univ Mich Med Sch 1997; **Fac Appt:** Prof Med, Northwestern Univ-Feinberg Sch Med

Lindsay, Bruce MD [CE] - **Spec Exp:** Arrhythmias; **Hospital:** Cleveland Clin (page 55); **Address:** Cleveland Clinic, 9500 Euclid Ave, Desk J2-2, Cleveland, OH 44195; **Phone:** 216-444-4293; **Board Cert:** Internal Medicine 1980; Cardiovascular Disease 1987; Cardiac Electrophysiology 2012; **Med School:** Jefferson Med Coll 1976; **Resid:** Internal Medicine, Univ Michigan Med Ctr 1980; **Fellow:** Cardiovascular Disease, Barnes-Jewish Hosp 1985

Love, Charles J MD [CE] - **Spec Exp:** Defibrillator Cable Extraction; Pacemakers; **Hospital:** OSU Wexner Med Ctr; **Address:** Heart & Lung Inst, 473 W 12 Ave Fl 2, Columbus, OH 43210; **Phone:** 614-293-4942; **Board Cert:** Internal Medicine 1986; Cardiovascular Disease 1989; Cardiac Electrophysiology 2004; **Med School:** Univ Pittsburgh 1983; **Resid:** Internal Medicine, Ohio State Univ Hosp 1986; **Fellow:** Cardiac Electrophysiology, Ohio State Univ Hosp 1988; **Fac Appt:** Prof Med, Ohio State Univ

Cardiac Electrophysiology

Miller, John M MD [CE] - **Spec Exp:** Arrhythmias; Catheter Ablation; Atrial Fibrillation; Ventricular Tachycardia Ablation; **Hospital:** IU Health Methodist Hosp; **Address:** Krannert Inst Cardiology, 1801 N Senate Blvd, Ste E4000, Indianapolis, IN 46202; **Phone:** 317-962-0500; **Board Cert:** Internal Medicine 1982; Cardiovascular Disease 1985; Cardiac Electrophysiology 2003; **Med School:** Penn State Coll Med 1979; **Resid:** Internal Medicine, NC Meml Hosp 1982; **Fellow:** Cardiovascular Disease, Hosp Univ Penn 1985; **Fac Appt:** Prof Med, Indiana Univ

Morady, Fred MD [CE] - **Spec Exp:** Arrhythmias; WPW Syndrome; **Hospital:** Univ Michigan Med Ctr; **Address:** U of M Cardiology, Cardiovascular Ctr, Fl 3, 1500 E Med Ctr Drive, SPC5856, Ann Arbor, MI 48109; **Phone:** 734-647-7321; **Board Cert:** Internal Medicine 1978; Cardiovascular Disease 1981; Cardiac Electrophysiology 2005; **Med School:** UCSF 1975; **Resid:** Internal Medicine, UCSF Med Ctr 1978; **Fellow:** Cardiovascular Disease, UCSF Med Ctr 1980; **Fac Appt:** Prof Med, Univ Mich Med Sch

Prystowsky, Eric N MD [CE] - **Spec Exp:** Arrhythmias; Catheter Ablation; Atrial Fibrillation; **Hospital:** St. Vincent Indianapolis Hosp; **Address:** St Vincent, Cardiology Dept, 8333 Naab Rd, Ste 400, Indianapolis, IN 46260; **Phone:** 317-338-6024; **Board Cert:** Internal Medicine 1976; Cardiovascular Disease 1979; Cardiac Electrophysiology 2005; **Med School:** Mount Sinai Sch Med 1973; **Resid:** Internal Medicine, Mount Sinai Med Ctr 1976; **Fellow:** Cardiovascular Disease, Duke Univ Hosp 1979

Schuger, Claudio D MD [CE] - **Spec Exp:** Arrhythmias; Defibrillators; **Hospital:** Henry Ford Hosp; **Address:** Henry Ford Hosp, Div Cardiology, 2799 W Grand Blvd, Ste 322, Detroit, MI 48202; **Phone:** 313-916-2417; **Board Cert:** Cardiac Electrophysiology 2008; Cardiovascular Disease 2007; **Med School:** Argentina 1977; **Resid:** Internal Medicine, Hacarmel Hosp 1982; **Fellow:** Cardiovascular Disease, Bikur Cholim Hosp 1985; Cardiac Electrophysiology, Harper Univ Hosp 1990; **Fac Appt:** Prof Med, Wayne State Univ

Tchou, Patrick J MD [CE] - **Spec Exp:** Arrhythmias; **Hospital:** Cleveland Clin (page 55); **Address:** Dept Cardiology, 9500 Euclid Ave, Desk J2-2, Cleveland, OH 44195; **Phone:** 216-444-6792; **Board Cert:** Internal Medicine 1982; Cardiovascular Disease 1985; Cardiac Electrophysiology 2012; **Med School:** Case West Res Univ 1979; **Resid:** Internal Medicine, Metro Genl Hosp 1982; **Fellow:** Cardiovascular Disease, Metro Genl Hosp 1984; Research, Mt Sinai Med Ctr 1985; **Fac Appt:** Prof Med, Ohio State Univ

Waldo, Albert Leon MD [CE] - **Spec Exp:** Arrhythmias; Syncope; Long QT Interval Syndrome; Atrial Fibrillation; **Hospital:** UH Case Med Ctr; **Address:** University Hospitals Case Medical Center, 11100 Euclid Ave, MS LKS-5038, Cleveland, OH 44106-1736; **Phone:** 216-844-7690; **Board Cert:** Internal Medicine 1971; Cardiovascular Disease 1975; **Med School:** SUNY Downstate 1962; **Resid:** Internal Medicine, Baltimore City Hosp 1965; Internal Medicine, Kings Co Hosp 1966; **Fellow:** Cardiovascular Disease, Columbia Presby Med Ctr 1968; Cardiac Electrophysiology, Columbia Presby Med Ctr 1969; **Fac Appt:** Prof Med, Case West Res Univ

Wilber, David J MD [CE] - **Spec Exp:** Atrial Fibrillation; Catheter Ablation; Sudden Death Prevention; **Hospital:** Loyola Univ Med Ctr; **Address:** Loyola Univ Med Ctr, Cardiovascular Inst, 2160 S First Ave Bldg 110 - rm 6232, Maywood, IL 60153; **Phone:** 708-216-2642; **Board Cert:** Internal Medicine 1980; Cardiovascular Disease 1985; Cardiac Electrophysiology 2013; **Med School:** Northwestern Univ 1977; **Resid:** Internal Medicine, Northwestern Meml Hosp 1980; **Fellow:** Cardiovascular Disease, Univ MI Hosp 1984; Cardiac Electrophysiology, Mass Genl Hosp 1986; **Fac Appt:** Prof Med, Loyola Univ-Stritch Sch Med

Great Plains and Mountains

Lewkowiez, Laurent MD [CE] - **Spec Exp:** Arrhythmias; Ventricular Tachycardia Ablation; Atrial Fibrillation; **Hospital:** Exempla Saint Jos. Hosp.-Denver; **Address:** Kaiser Permanente Med Grp, 2045 Franklin St, Denver, CO 80205; **Phone:** 303-338-4545; **Board Cert:** Cardiovascular Disease 2010; Cardiac Electrophysiology 2003; **Med School:** Univ SC Sch Med 1992; **Resid:** Internal Medicine, Univ Colorado Affil Hosp 1996; **Fellow:** Cardiovascular Disease, Univ Colorado Affil Hosp 1999; Cardiac Electrophysiology, Univ Colorado Affil Hosp 2001; **Fac Appt:** Asst Prof Med, Univ Colorado

Sauer, William H MD [CE] - **Spec Exp:** Catheter Ablation; Pacemakers; Defibrillators; **Hospital:** Univ Colorado Hosp; **Address:** 12605 E 16th Avenue, MS B-120, Anschutz In-Patient Pavilion, Aurora, CO 80045; **Phone:** 720-848-6510; **Board Cert:** Cardiovascular Disease 2006; Cardiac Electrophysiology 2007; **Med School:** Univ Pennsylvania 1999; **Resid:** Internal Medicine, Hosp Univ Penn 2001; **Fellow:** Cardiovascular Disease, Hosp Univ Penn 2004; Cardiac Electrophysiology, Hosp Univ Penn 2005; **Fac Appt:** Assoc Prof Med, Univ Colorado

Southwest

Natale, Andrea MD [CE] - **Spec Exp:** Arrhythmias; Atrial Fibrillation; **Hospital:** St. David's Med Ctr; **Address:** Texas Cardiac Arrhythmia Institute, 3000 N IH 35, Ste 700, Austin, TX 78705; **Phone:** 512-807-3150; **Board Cert:** Cardiovascular Disease 2012; Cardiac Electrophysiology 2012; **Med School:** Italy 1985; **Resid:** Internal Medicine, Univ Rome Med Ctr 1989; **Fellow:** Cardiovascular Disease, Univ Western Ontario 1992; Cardiac Electrophysiology, Sinai Samaritan Med Ctr/Univ WI 1994

Shen, Win-Kuang MD [CE] - **Spec Exp:** Arrhythmias; Catheter Ablation; Defibrillators; Autonomic Disorders; **Hospital:** Mayo Clinic - Phoenix; **Address:** 5777 E Mayo Blvd, Phoenix, AZ 85054; **Phone:** 480-342-0348; **Board Cert:** Internal Medicine 1986; Cardiovascular Disease 2011; Cardiac Electrophysiology 2012; **Med School:** NY Med Coll 1983; **Resid:** Internal Medicine, Mayo Clin 1986; **Fellow:** Cardiovascular Disease, Mayo Clin 1988; Cardiac Electrophysiology, Duke Univ Hosp 1991; **Fac Appt:** Prof Med, Mayo Med Sch

West Coast and Pacific

Cannom, David S MD [CE] - **Spec Exp:** Arrhythmias; Atrial Fibrillation; **Hospital:** Good Samaritan Hosp - LA, California Hosp Med Ctr; **Address:** Los Angeles Cardiology Assocs, 1245 Wilshire Blvd, Ste 703, Los Angeles, CA 90017; **Phone:** 213-977-0419; **Board Cert:** Internal Medicine 1980; Cardiovascular Disease 1975; **Med School:** Univ Minn 1967; **Resid:** Internal Medicine, Yale-New Haven Hosp 1972; **Fellow:** Cardiovascular Disease, Stanford Univ 1975; **Fac Appt:** Clin Prof Med, UCLA

Feld, Gregory K MD [CE] - **Spec Exp:** Atrial Fibrillation; **Hospital:** UCSD Med Ctr; **Address:** UCSD Sulpizio Cardiovascular Ctr, 9434 Medical Center Drive, La Jolla, CA 92037; **Phone:** 858-657-8530; **Board Cert:** Internal Medicine 1980; Cardiovascular Disease 1983; Cardiac Electrophysiology 2012; **Med School:** Dartmouth Med Sch 1977; **Resid:** Internal Medicine, Wadsworth VA Hosp 1981; **Fellow:** Cardiothoracic Research, Wadsworth VA Hosp 1984; **Fac Appt:** Prof Med, UCSD

Cardiac Electrophysiology

Gang, Eli S MD [CE] - **Spec Exp:** Arrhythmias; Pacemakers; Defibrillators; **Hospital:** Cedars-Sinai Med Ctr, Brotman Med Ctr; **Address:** Cardiovascular Med Grp of Southern CA, 414 N Camden Drive, Ste 1100, Beverly Hills, CA 90210; **Phone:** 310-278-3400; **Board Cert:** Internal Medicine 1978; Cardiovascular Disease 1981; **Med School:** Columbia P&S 1975; **Resid:** Internal Medicine, Roosevelt Hosp 1978; **Fellow:** Cardiovascular Disease, Columbia Presby Hosp 1981; **Fac Appt:** Clin Prof Med, UCLA

Higgins, Steven MD [CE] - **Spec Exp:** Arrhythmias; Defibrillators; **Hospital:** Scripps Meml Hosp - La Jolla, Tri-City Med Ctr - Oceanside; **Address:** 9850 Genesee Ave, Ste 940, La Jolla, CA 92037; **Phone:** 858-658-0088; **Board Cert:** Internal Medicine 1982; Cardiovascular Disease 1985; Cardiac Electrophysiology 2003; **Med School:** Univ Rochester 1979; **Resid:** Internal Medicine, Univ CO Med Ctr 1982; **Fellow:** Cardiovascular Disease, Univ CO Med Ctr 1985

Swerdlow, Charles D MD [CE] - **Spec Exp:** Atrial Fibrillation; Arrhythmias; Pacemakers; Defibrillators; **Hospital:** Cedars-Sinai Med Ctr, UCLA Ronald Reagan Med Ctr; **Address:** Cardiovascular Med Grp of Southern CA, 414 N Camden Drive, Ste 1100, Beverly Hills, CA 90210; **Phone:** 310-278-3400; **Board Cert:** Internal Medicine 1979; Cardiovascular Disease 1981; Cardiac Electrophysiology 2004; **Med School:** Harvard Med Sch 1976; **Resid:** Internal Medicine, LAC-Harbor Genl Hosp 1979; **Fellow:** Cardiovascular Disease, Stanford Univ Med Ctr 1981; **Fac Appt:** Clin Prof Med, UCLA

Wang, Paul J MD [CE] - **Spec Exp:** Arrhythmias; Atrial Fibrillation; Defibrillators; **Hospital:** Stanford Univ Hosp & Clins; **Address:** Stanford Univ Cardiovascular Med, 300 Pasteur Drive, rm A260, Stanford, CA 94305; **Phone:** 650-723-7111; **Board Cert:** Internal Medicine 1986; Cardiovascular Disease 1989; Cardiac Electrophysiology 2002; **Med School:** Columbia P&S 1983; **Resid:** Internal Medicine, NY Presby-Columbia Med Ctr 1986; **Fellow:** Cardiovascular Disease, Brigham & Women's Hosp 1989; **Fac Appt:** Prof Med, Stanford Univ

Interventional Cardiology

New England

Gibson, C Michael MD [IC] - **Spec Exp:** Acute Coronary Syndromes; Clinical Trials; **Hospital:** Beth Israel Deaconess Med Ctr - Boston; **Address:** Beth Israel Deaconess Med Ctr, 185 Pilgrim Rd, Room Deaconess 319, Boston, MA 02215; **Phone:** 617-632-7753; **Board Cert:** Internal Medicine 1989; **Med School:** Univ Chicago-Pritzker Sch Med 1986; **Resid:** Internal Medicine, Brigham & Womens Hosp 1989; Internal Medicine, Brigham & Womens Hosp 1993; **Fellow:** Cardiovascular Disease, Beth Israel Deaconess Med Ctr 1992; **Fac Appt:** Assoc Prof Med, Harvard Med Sch

Jacobs, Alice K MD [IC] - **Spec Exp:** Cardiac Catheterization; Heart Disease in Women; **Hospital:** Boston Med Ctr; **Address:** Boston Med Ctr, 732 Harrison Ave Fl 3, Boston, MA 02118; **Phone:** 617-638-8707; **Board Cert:** Internal Medicine 1978; Endocrinology 1979; Cardiovascular Disease 1985; **Med School:** St Louis Univ 1975; **Resid:** Internal Medicine, St Louis Univ Hosp 1977; **Fellow:** Endocrinology, UCSD Med Ctr 1980; Cardiovascular Disease, Boston Med Ctr 1982; **Fac Appt:** Prof Med, Boston Univ

Kimmelstiel, Carey D MD [IC] - **Spec Exp:** Cardiac Catheterization; Heart Failure; **Hospital:** Tufts Med Ctr; **Address:** Tufts Med Ctr, Cardiovascular Ctr, 800 Washington St, rm 264, Boston, MA 02111-1526; **Phone:** 617-636-5914; **Board Cert:** Cardiovascular Disease 1989; Internal Medicine 1985; Interventional Cardiology 2009; **Med School:** SUNY Downstate 1982; **Resid:** Internal Medicine, Kings Co Hosp/SUNY Downstate 1986; **Fellow:** Cardiovascular Disease, UMass Memorial Med Ctr 1989; Interventional Cardiology, Tufts-New Engl Med Ctr 1990; **Fac Appt:** Assoc Prof Med, Tufts Univ

Laham, Roger J MD [IC] - **Spec Exp:** Angioplasty; **Hospital:** Beth Israel Deaconess Med Ctr - Boston; **Address:** Beth Israel Deaconess Med Ctr, Cardiovascular Services, 330 Brookline Ave, Boston, MA 02215; **Phone:** 617-667-8800; **Board Cert:** Internal Medicine 2004; Cardiovascular Disease 2005; Interventional Cardiology 2010; **Med School:** Amer Univ Beirut 1989; **Resid:** Internal Medicine, Duke Univ Med Ctr 1992; **Fellow:** Cardiovascular Disease, Beth Israel Deaconess Med Ctr 1994; Interventional Cardiology, Beth Israel Deaconess Med Ctr 1996; **Fac Appt:** Assoc Prof Med, Harvard Med Sch

Palacios, Igor F MD [IC] - **Spec Exp:** Interventional Cardiology; **Hospital:** Mass Genl Hosp; **Address:** Mass Genl Hosp, Cardiac Unit, 55 Fruit St, GRB 800, Boston, MA 02114; **Phone:** 617-726-8424; **Board Cert:** Internal Medicine 1979; Cardiovascular Disease 1981; Interventional Cardiology 2009; **Med School:** Venezuela 1969; **Resid:** Cardiovascular Disease, Hosp Univ de Caracas 1973; **Fellow:** Cardiovascular Disease, Mass Genl Hosp-Harvard 1980; **Fac Appt:** Assoc Prof Med, Harvard Med Sch

Rosenfield, Kenneth MD [IC] - **Spec Exp:** Angioplasty & Stent Placement; **Hospital:** Mass Genl Hosp; **Address:** MGH Interventional Cardiology Associates, 55 Fruit St, Boston, MA 02114; **Phone:** 617-724-1935; **Board Cert:** Internal Medicine 1985; Cardiovascular Disease 1989; Interventional Cardiology 2013; **Med School:** Univ Mass Sch Med 1982; **Resid:** Internal Medicine, Kaiser Fdn Hosp 1985; **Fellow:** Cardiovascular Disease, New Eng Med Ctr 1988; Interventional Cardiology, St Elizabeth's Med Ctr 1989

Zelman, Richard B MD [IC] - **Spec Exp:** Angioplasty & Stent Placement; **Hospital:** Cape Cod Hosp; **Address:** 40 Quinlan Way, Ste 104, Hyannis, MA 02601; **Phone:** 508-862-7645; **Board Cert:** Internal Medicine 1986; Cardiovascular Disease 1989; Interventional Cardiology 2009; **Med School:** Univ Tex, San Antonio 1983; **Resid:** Internal Medicine, Brigham & Womens Hosp 1986; **Fellow:** Cardiovascular Disease, Brigham & Womens Hosp 1989

Mid Atlantic

Chang, Gene MD [IC] - **Spec Exp:** Cardiac Catheterization; Angioplasty & Stent Placement; Atrial Septal Defect; **Hospital:** Penn Presby Med Ctr - UPHS (page 69); **Address:** Philadelphia Heart Inst, 51 N 39th St, Fl 4, Ste 400, Philadelphia, PA 19104; **Phone:** 215-662-9000; **Board Cert:** Cardiovascular Disease 2008; Interventional Cardiology 2009; **Med School:** Tufts Univ 1991; **Resid:** Internal Medicine, New England Deaconess Hosp 1995; **Fellow:** Cardiovascular Disease, Hosp Univ Penn 1998; Interventional Cardiology, Hosp Univ Penn 1999; **Fac Appt:** Asst Clin Prof Med, Univ Pennsylvania

Cohen, Howard A MD [IC] - **Spec Exp:** Angioplasty; Ventricular Assist Device (LVAD); **Hospital:** Temple Univ Hosp; **Address:** Temple Univ-Interventional Cardiology, 3401 N Broad St Fl 9, Philadelphia, PA 19140; **Phone:** 215-707-2230; **Board Cert:** Internal Medicine 1974; Cardiovascular Disease 1977; **Med School:** NYU Sch Med 1970; **Resid:** Internal Medicine, Bellevue Hosp Ctr 1974; **Fellow:** Cardiovascular Disease, Johns Hopkins Hosp 1976; **Fac Appt:** Clin Prof Med, Temple Univ

Interventional Cardiology

Gray, William A MD [IC] - **Spec Exp:** Peripheral Vascular Disease; Percutaneous Valve Repair; Coronary Artery Disease; Mitral Valve Surgery; **Hospital:** NY-Presby/Columbia Univ Med Ctr, NY (page 65); **Address:** Ctr for Interventional Vascular Therapy, 161 Fort Washington Ave, Fl 6th, New York, NY 10032; **Phone:** 212-305-7060; **Board Cert:** Internal Medicine 1987; Interventional Cardiology 2011; Vascular Medicine 2004; **Med School:** Temple Univ 1984; **Resid:** Internal Medicine, Rhode Island Hosp/Brown Univ 1988; **Fellow:** Cardiovascular Disease, Brown Univ 1992; **Fac Appt:** Assoc Prof Med, Columbia P&S

Herrmann, Howard C MD [IC] - **Spec Exp:** Cardiac Catheterization; Angioplasty & Stent Placement; Heart Valve Disease; Atrial Septal Defect; **Hospital:** Hosp Univ Penn - UPHS (page 69), Penn Presby Med Ctr - UPHS (page 69); **Address:** Penn Heart & Vascular Ctr, Perelman Ctr for Advanced Medicine, 3400 Civic Center Blvd, 2 East, Philadelphia, PA 19104; **Phone:** 215-662-2180; **Board Cert:** Internal Medicine 1984; Cardiovascular Disease 1987; Interventional Cardiology 2009; **Med School:** Harvard Med Sch 1981; **Resid:** Internal Medicine, Mass General Hosp 1984; **Fellow:** Cardiovascular Disease, Mass General Hosp 1987; **Fac Appt:** Prof Med, Univ Pennsylvania

Lee, Joon S MD [IC] - **Spec Exp:** Cardiac Catheterization; **Hospital:** UPMC Presby, Pittsburgh; **Address:** UPMC Presbyterian, Div Cardiology, 200 Lothrop St, Ste A333, Pittsburgh, PA 15213; **Phone:** 412-647-1385; **Board Cert:** Internal Medicine 2005; Cardiovascular Disease 2005; Interventional Cardiology 2009; **Med School:** Duke Univ 1988; **Resid:** Internal Medicine, Mass General Hosp 1991; **Fellow:** Cardiovascular Disease, Mass General Hosp 1996; **Fac Appt:** Asst Prof Med, Univ Pittsburgh

Leon, Martin B MD [IC] - **Hospital:** NY-Presby/Columbia Univ Med Ctr, NY (page 65); **Address:** 161 Ft Washington Ave, Irving Pavillion Fl 6 - Ste 607, New York, NY 10032; **Phone:** 212-305-7060; **Board Cert:** Internal Medicine 1979; Cardiovascular Disease 1983; **Med School:** Yale Univ 1975; **Resid:** Internal Medicine, Yale-New Haven Hosp 1978; **Fellow:** Cardiovascular Disease, Yale-New Haven Hosp 1980

Mehran, Roxana MD [IC] - **Spec Exp:** Cardiac Catheterization; Acute Coronary Syndrome; Arrhythmias; **Hospital:** Mt Sinai Med Ctr (page 62); **Address:** Cardiocascular Medicine Associates, 1190 5 Ave S, Guggenheim Pavilion, New York, NY 10029; **Phone:** 212-659-9691; **Board Cert:** Cardiovascular Disease 2011; Interventional Cardiology 2011; **Med School:** Grenada 1987; **Resid:** Internal Medicine, Univ Conn Hlth Ctr 1991; **Fellow:** Cardiovascular Disease, Mount Sinai Med Ctr 1994; Interventional Cardiology, Mount Sinai Med Ctr 1995; **Fac Appt:** Prof Med, Mount Sinai Sch Med

Moses, Jeffrey W MD [IC] - **Spec Exp:** Angiography-Coronary; Angioplasty & Stent Placement; Heart Valve Disease; **Hospital:** NY-Presby/Columbia Univ Med Ctr, NY (page 65); **Address:** 161 Ft Washington Ave, Herbert Irving Pavillion Fl 6th, New York, NY 10032; **Phone:** 212-305-7060; **Board Cert:** Internal Medicine 1977; Cardiovascular Disease 1981; Interventional Cardiology 2009; **Med School:** Univ Pennsylvania 1974; **Resid:** Internal Medicine, Penn Presby Med Ctr 1977; **Fellow:** Cardiovascular Disease, Penn Presby Med Ctr 1980

Parikh, Manish A MD [IC] - **Spec Exp:** Coronary Angioplasty/Stents; **Hospital:** Lenox Hill Hosp (page 66); **Address:** 51 W 51st St, Ste 330, New York, NY 10019; **Phone:** 212-326-8532; **Board Cert:** Cardiovascular Disease 2010; Interventional Cardiology 2010; **Med School:** UMDNJ-NJ Med Sch, Newark 1990; **Resid:** Internal Medicine, New York Hosp 1993; **Fellow:** Cardiovascular Disease, New York Hosp 1997; **Fac Appt:** Asst Prof Med, Cornell Univ-Weill Med Coll

Petrossian, George A MD [IC] - **Spec Exp:** Carotid Artery Stent Placement; Peripheral Vascular Disease; Coronary Angioplasty/Stents; Renovascular Disease; **Hospital:** St. Francis Hosp - The Heart Ctr (page 70), South Nassau Comm Hosp; **Address:** 1405 Old Northern Blvd, 1st Floor, Roslyn, NY 11576-1353; **Phone:** 516-484-6777; **Board Cert:** Internal Medicine 1986; Cardiovascular Disease 1989; Interventional Cardiology 2010; **Med School:** Mount Sinai Sch Med 1983; **Resid:** Internal Medicine, Columbia-Presby Med Ctr 1987; **Fellow:** Cardiovascular Disease, Columbia -Presby Med Ctr 1989; Interventional Cardiology, Mass Genl Hosp 1990

Reiner, Jonathan S MD [IC] - **Spec Exp:** Angioplasty & Stent Placement; **Hospital:** G Washington Univ Hosp; **Address:** GWU Med Faculty Assocs, 2150 Pennsylvania Ave NW, rm 4-417, Washington, DC 20037; **Phone:** 202-741-3333; **Board Cert:** Internal Medicine 1989; Cardiovascular Disease 2004; Interventional Cardiology 2011; **Med School:** Georgetown Univ 1986; **Resid:** Internal Medicine, North Shore Univ Hosp 1989; **Fellow:** Cardiovascular Disease, George Wash Univ Sch Med 1993; **Fac Appt:** Prof Med, Geo Wash Univ

Resar, Jon R MD [IC] - **Spec Exp:** Percutaneous Coronary Intervention; Percutaneous Valve Repair; Congenital Heart Disease-Adult; Angioplasty; **Hospital:** Johns Hopkins Hosp (page 59); **Address:** Johns Hopkins Hosp, Dept Cardiology, 601 N Caroline St, Baltimore, MD 21287; **Phone:** 410-614-1132; **Board Cert:** Internal Medicine 1988; Cardiovascular Disease 2011; Interventional Cardiology 2009; **Med School:** Med Coll Wisc 1985; **Resid:** Internal Medicine, Johns Hopkins Hosp 1988; **Fellow:** Cardiovascular Disease, Johns Hopkins Hosp 1991; Interventional Cardiology, Johns Hopkins Hosp 1992; **Fac Appt:** Assoc Prof Med, Johns Hopkins Univ

Roubin, Gary MD/PhD [IC] - **Spec Exp:** Coronary Angioplasty/Stents; Carotid Artery Stent Placement; Peripheral Vascular Disease; **Hospital:** St. Luke's - Roosevelt Hosp Ctr - St Luke's Hosp (page 56); **Address:** 425 W 59th St, Ste 9A, New York, NY 10019; **Phone:** 212-523-7200; **Med School:** Australia 1975; **Resid:** Internal Medicine, Royal Prince Albert Hosp 1979; Cardiovascular Disease, Hallstrom Inst of Cardiology 1981; **Fellow:** Cardiology Research, Natl Heart Fdn 1983; Interventional Cardiology, Emory Univ 1985; **Fac Appt:** Clin Prof Med, NYU Sch Med

Shani, Jacob MD [IC] - **Spec Exp:** Cardiac Catheterization; Angioplasty & Stent Placement; Percutaneous Valve Repair; Aortic Valve Replacement; **Hospital:** Maimonides Med Ctr (page 60); **Address:** Maimonides Med Ctr-Cardiology, 4802 10th Ave, Brooklyn, NY 11219-2844; **Phone:** 718-283-7480; **Board Cert:** Internal Medicine 1981; Cardiovascular Disease 1983; Interventional Cardiology 2009; **Med School:** Israel 1977; **Resid:** Internal Medicine, Maimonides Med Ctr 1981; **Fellow:** Cardiovascular Disease, Beth Israel Hosp 1983; **Fac Appt:** Prof Med, NYU Sch Med

Sharma, Samin K MD [IC] - **Spec Exp:** Angioplasty & Stent Placement; Heart Valve Disease; **Hospital:** Mt Sinai Med Ctr (page 62); **Address:** Mount Sinai Hosp, div Cardiology, 5 E 98th St Fl 1, New York, NY 10029; **Phone:** 212-427-1540; **Board Cert:** Internal Medicine 1986; Cardiovascular Disease 1989; **Med School:** India 1978; **Resid:** Internal Medicine, SMS Hosp 1982; Internal Medicine, NYU Downtown Hosp 1986; **Fellow:** Cardiovascular Disease, City Hosp Ctr at Elmhurst 1988; Interventional Cardiology, Mt Sinai Hosp 2000; **Fac Appt:** Prof Med, Mount Sinai Sch Med

Shorofsky, Stephen R MD/PhD [IC] - **Spec Exp:** Arrhythmias; **Hospital:** Univ of MD Med Ctr; **Address:** UMMC-Div of Cardiology, 22 S Greene St, rm N3W77, Baltimore, MD 21201; **Phone:** 410-328-6056; **Board Cert:** Internal Medicine 1988; Cardiac Electrophysiology 2004; **Med School:** Univ Chicago-Pritzker Sch Med 1985; **Resid:** Internal Medicine, Univ Chicago Hosps 1988; **Fellow:** Cardiovascular Disease, Univ Chicago Hosps 1991; Cardiac Electrophysiology, Univ Chicago Hosps 1994; **Fac Appt:** Prof Med, Univ MD Sch Med

Stone, Gregg W MD [IC] - **Spec Exp:** Angioplasty & Stent Placement; Coronary Artery Disease; **Hospital:** NY-Presby/Columbia Univ Med Ctr, NY (page 65); **Address:** 161 Fort Washington Ave, Irving Pavillion Fl 6 - Ste 607, New York, NY 10032; **Phone:** 212-305-7060; **Board Cert:** Internal Medicine 1985; Cardiovascular Disease 1987; **Med School:** Johns Hopkins Univ 1982; **Resid:** Internal Medicine, NY Hosp-Cornell Medical Ctr 1985; **Fellow:** Cardiovascular Disease, Cedars-Sinai Medical Ctr 1988; Coronary Angioplasty, Mid-America Heart Inst 1989; **Fac Appt:** Prof Med, Columbia P&S

Southeast

Applegate, Robert J MD [IC] - **Spec Exp:** Cardiac Catheterization; Angioplasty; **Hospital:** Wake Forest Baptist Med Ctr; **Address:** Medical Ctr Blvd, Janeway Tower Fl 7th, Winston-Salem, NC 27157-1045; **Phone:** 336-716-6674; **Board Cert:** Internal Medicine 1983; Cardiovascular Disease 1987; Interventional Cardiology 2009; **Med School:** Univ VA Sch Med 1980; **Resid:** Internal Medicine, Oregon Hlth Sci Univ Hosp 1983; **Fellow:** Pharmacology, Univ Texas Hlth Sci Ctr 1984; Cardiovascular Disease, Univ Texas Hlth Sci Ctr 1986; **Fac Appt:** Prof Med, Wake Forest Univ

Bittl, John A MD [IC] - **Spec Exp:** Cardiac Catheterization; Invasive Cardiology; **Hospital:** Munroe Regional Med Ctr; **Address:** Ocala Heart Inst, 1500 SW 1st Ave, Ocala, FL 34471; **Phone:** 352-351-7206; **Board Cert:** Internal Medicine 1982; Cardiovascular Disease 1985; Interventional Cardiology 2011; **Med School:** Johns Hopkins Univ 1979; **Resid:** Internal Medicine, UCLA Med Ctr 1982; **Fellow:** Cardiovascular Disease, Brigham & Womens Hosp 1984

Douglas Jr, John S MD [IC] - **Spec Exp:** Angioplasty & Stent Placement; Cardiac Catheterization; Coronary Artery Disease; **Hospital:** Emory Univ Hosp; **Address:** Emory Univ Hosp, Cardiology Dept, 1364 Clifton Rd, rm F606, Atlanta, GA 30322; **Phone:** 404-727-7040; **Board Cert:** Internal Medicine 1972; Cardiovascular Disease 1975; Interventional Cardiology 2009; **Med School:** Washington Univ, St Louis 1967; **Resid:** Internal Medicine, NC Meml Hosp 1969; Internal Medicine, Grady Meml Hosp 1972; **Fellow:** Cardiovascular Disease, Emory Univ Hosp 1974; **Fac Appt:** Prof Med, Emory Univ

Fromkin, Kenneth R MD [IC] - **Spec Exp:** Angioplasty & Stent Placement; Coronary Artery Disease; Cardiac Catheterization; Acute Coronary Syndromes; **Hospital:** Cleveland Clin - Weston (page 55); **Address:** Cleveland Clinic Florida, 2950 Cleveland Clinic Blvd, Weston, FL 33331-3609; **Phone:** 954-659-5290; **Board Cert:** Cardiovascular Disease 2011; Interventional Cardiology 2012; **Med School:** Univ Chicago-Pritzker Sch Med 1994; **Resid:** Internal Medicine, Yale-New Haven Hosp 1997; **Fellow:** Cardiovascular Disease, New York Hosp-Cornell 2000; Interventional Cardiology, New York Hosp-Cornell 2001

Kandzari, David E MD [IC] - **Spec Exp:** Angioplasty & Stent Placement; Peripheral Vascular Disease; Clinical Trials; **Hospital:** Piedmont Hosp; **Address:** Piedmont Heart Inst, 275 Collier Rd NW, Ste 300, Atlanta, GA 30309; **Phone:** 404-605-2800; **Board Cert:** Cardiovascular Disease 2003; Interventional Cardiology 2005; **Med School:** Duke Univ 1995; **Resid:** Internal Medicine, Johns Hopkins Hosp 1998; **Fellow:** Cardiovascular Disease, Duke Univ Hosp 2002; Interventional Cardiology, Duke Univ Hosp 2004

Khawaja, Shazib N MD [IC] - **Spec Exp:** Peripheral Vascular Disease; Vascular Medicine; Echocardiography; Nuclear Cardiology; **Hospital:** Tanner Med Ctr; **Address:** Tanner Heart & Vascular Specialists, 705 Dixie St, Ste 401, Carrollton, GA 30117; **Phone:** 770-836-9326; **Board Cert:** Cardiovascular Disease 2012; Interventional Cardiology 2003; **Med School:** Univ S Ala Coll Med 1995; **Resid:** Internal Medicine, Albany Med Ctr 1998; **Fellow:** Cardiovascular Disease, Dartmouth-Hitchcock Med Ctr 2001; Interventional Cardiology, Univ Minn Med Ctr 2002; **Fac Appt:** Asst Clin Prof Med, Emory Univ

Leesar, Massoud MD [IC] - **Spec Exp:** Percutaneous Coronary Intervention; Peripheral Vascular Disease; **Hospital:** UAB Hosp; **Address:** The Kirklin Clin, 2000 6th Ave S, Birmingham, AL 35233; **Phone:** 205-934-7898; **Board Cert:** Internal Medicine 1989; Cardiovascular Disease 2010; Interventional Cardiology 2013; **Med School:** Iran 1980; **Resid:** Internal Medicine, Univ Toronto Affil Hosp 1987; Internal Medicine, Waterbury Hosp 1989; **Fellow:** Cardiovascular Disease, Detroit Med Ctr-Sinai Grace 1992; Interventional Cardiology, Univ Louisville Hosp 1994; **Fac Appt:** Prof Med, UAB Sch Med

Matar, Fadi MD [IC] - **Spec Exp:** Angioplasty; Peripheral Vascular Disease; **Hospital:** Tampa Genl Hosp, St. Joseph's Hosp - Tampa; **Address:** FCI Heart Ctr, 509 S Armenia Ave, Ste 200, Tampa, FL 33609; **Phone:** 813-353-1515; **Board Cert:** Cardiovascular Disease 2007; Interventional Cardiology 2009; **Med School:** Amer Univ Beirut 1987; **Resid:** Internal Medicine, Maryland Genl Hosp 1990; **Fellow:** Cardiovascular Disease, Washington Hosp 1994; **Fac Appt:** Asst Prof Med, Univ S Fla Coll Med

Morris, Douglas C MD [IC] - **Spec Exp:** Angioplasty; Cardiac Catheterization; Heart Valve Disease; **Hospital:** Emory Univ Hosp, Emory Univ Hosp Midtown; **Address:** Emory Clin, Cardiology Dept, 1365A Clifton Rd NE, Ste 2200, Atlanta, GA 30322; **Phone:** 404-778-5299; **Board Cert:** Internal Medicine 1973; Cardiovascular Disease 1975; **Med School:** Baylor Coll Med 1968; **Resid:** Internal Medicine, Vanderbilt Univ Med Ctr 1970; Internal Medicine, Vanderbilt Univ Med Ctr 1973; **Fellow:** Cardiovascular Disease, Emory Univ Hosp 1975

Reddy, Bhagat K MD [IC] - **Spec Exp:** Angioplasty & Stent Placement; Carotid Artery Stent Placement; Peripheral Vascular Disease; Intravascular Ultrasound; **Hospital:** Piedmont Hosp; **Address:** Piedmont Heart Institute, 275 Collier Rd NW, Ste 300, Atlanta, GA 30309; **Phone:** 404-605-2800; **Board Cert:** Cardiovascular Disease 2012; Interventional Cardiology 2003; Endovascular Medicine 2005; **Med School:** India 1995; **Resid:** Internal Medicine, Robert Packer Hosp 1999; **Fellow:** Cardiovascular Disease, Med Coll OH Affil Hosp 2002; Interventional Cardiology, Vanderbilt Univ Med Ctr 2003

Midwest

Bach, Richard G MD [IC] - **Spec Exp:** Cardiac Catheterization; Acute Coronary Syndromes; Cardiomyopathy-Hypertrophic; **Hospital:** Barnes-Jewish Hosp; **Address:** Washington Univ Sch Med, Cardiovascular Div, 660 S Euclid Ave, Campus Box 8086, St Louis, MO 63110; **Phone:** 314-362-1963; **Board Cert:** Internal Medicine 1987; Cardiovascular Disease 2011; Interventional Cardiology 2010; **Med School:** NYU Sch Med 1984; **Resid:** Internal Medicine, Bellvue Hosp/NYU Med Ctr 1987; **Fellow:** Cardiovascular Disease, Bellvue Hosp/NYU Med Ctr 1990; Interventional Cardiology, NYU Med Ctr 1991; **Fac Appt:** Assoc Prof Med, Washington Univ, St Louis

Dieter, Robert S MD [IC] - **Spec Exp:** Vascular Medicine; Peripheral Vascular Disease; Angioplasty & Stent Placement; Renal Artery Stenosis; **Hospital:** Loyola Univ Med Ctr; **Address:** Loyola Univ MC, Dept Cardiology, 2160 S First Ave EMS Bldg, Maywood, IL 60153; **Phone:** 708-216-4466; **Board Cert:** Internal Medicine 2010; Cardiovascular Disease 2012; Interventional Cardiology 2003; **Med School:** Univ IL Coll Med 1996; **Resid:** Internal Medicine, UIC Med Ctr 1999; Cardiovascular Disease, Univ Wisconsin 2002; **Fellow:** Interventional Cardiology, Univ Wisconsin; Vascular Medicine, Georgetown Univ; **Fac Appt:** Asst Prof Med, Loyola Univ-Stritch Sch Med

Ellis, Stephen G MD [IC] - **Spec Exp:** Angioplasty & Stent Placement; Angiogenesis; **Hospital:** Cleveland Clin (page 55); **Address:** Cleveland Clinic, Dept Cardiology, 9500 Euclid Ave, Desk J2-3, Cleveland, OH 44195; **Phone:** 216-445-6712; **Board Cert:** Internal Medicine 1981; Cardiovascular Disease 1985; Interventional Cardiology 2009; **Med School:** UCLA 1978; **Resid:** Internal Medicine, Cedars-Sinai Med Ctr 1981; **Fellow:** Cardiovascular Disease, Stanford Univ Med Ctr 1985; Interventional Cardiology, Emory Univ Hosp 1986; **Fac Appt:** Prof Med, Cleveland Cl Coll Med/Case West Res

Feldman, Ted E MD [IC] - **Spec Exp:** Patent Foramen Ovale; **Hospital:** Evanston Hosp/NorthShore Univ Hlth Sys (page 67); **Address:** Northshore Medical Group, 9977 Woods Drive Fl 3, Skokie, IL 60077; **Phone:** 847-663-8410; **Board Cert:** Internal Medicine 1981; Cardiovascular Disease 1985; Interventional Cardiology 2009; **Med School:** Indiana Univ 1978; **Resid:** Internal Medicine, Rush-Presby-St Lukes Hosp 1982; **Fellow:** Cardiovascular Disease, Univ Chicago 1985; **Fac Appt:** Clin Prof Med, Northwestern Univ

Henry, Timothy D MD [IC] - **Spec Exp:** Acute Coronary Syndromes; Angiogenesis; **Hospital:** Abbott - Northwestern Hosp; **Address:** 920 E 28th St, Ste 300, MS 33300, Minneapolis, MN 55407; **Phone:** 612-863-3900; **Board Cert:** Internal Medicine 1985; Cardiovascular Disease 1989; **Med School:** UCSF 1982; **Resid:** Internal Medicine, Univ Colorado Hosp 1985; **Fellow:** Cardiovascular Disease, Univ Minnesota 1990; Interventional Cardiology, Univ Minnesota 1991; **Fac Appt:** Prof Med, Univ Minn

Holmes Jr, David R MD [IC] - **Spec Exp:** Heart Attack; Acute Coronary Syndromes; Angioplasty & Restenosis; **Hospital:** Mayo Med Ctr & Clin - Rochester; **Address:** Mayo Clinic, Div Cardiovasc Dis, 200 First St SW, Rochester, MN 55905; **Phone:** 507-255-2504; **Board Cert:** Internal Medicine 1974; Cardiovascular Disease 1977; Interventional Cardiology 2009; **Med School:** Med Coll Wisc 1971; **Resid:** Internal Medicine, Mayo Clinic 1974; **Fellow:** Cardiovascular Disease, Mayo Clinic 1977; **Fac Appt:** Prof Med, Mayo Med Sch

Lasala, John M MD/PhD [IC] - **Spec Exp:** Coronary Artery Disease; Coronary Angioplasty/Stents; Cardiac Catheterization; Aortic Diseases & Dissection; **Hospital:** Barnes-Jewish Hosp; **Address:** Washington Univ Sch Med, 660 S Euclid Ave, Box 8086, St Louis, MO 63110; **Phone:** 314-747-4535; **Board Cert:** Internal Medicine 1986; Cardiovascular Disease 1989; Interventional Cardiology 2009; **Med School:** Univ Conn 1983; **Resid:** Internal Medicine, Barnes-Jewish Hosp 1986; **Fellow:** Cardiovascular Disease, Yale-New Haven Hosp 1989; Interventional Cardiology, Yale-New Haven Hosp 1990; **Fac Appt:** Assoc Prof Med, Washington Univ, St Louis

Leya, Fred MD [IC] - **Spec Exp:** Aneurysm-Aortic; Arrhythmias; Coronary Artery Disease; Heart Valve Disease; **Hospital:** Loyola Univ Med Ctr; **Address:** Loyola Ctr for Heart & Vasc Med, 2160 S 1st Ave Bldg 110 - rm 6210, Maywood, IL 60153; **Phone:** 708-216-4225; **Board Cert:** Internal Medicine 1982; Cardiovascular Disease 1983; Interventional Cardiology 2009; **Med School:** Poland 1977; **Resid:** Internal Medicine, Northwestern Univ/Columbus Hosp 1981; **Fellow:** Cardiovascular Disease, Loyola Univ Med Ctr 1983; **Fac Appt:** Prof Med, Loyola Univ-Stritch Sch Med

Lopez, John J MD [IC] - **Spec Exp:** Cardiac Catheterization; Coronary Artery Disease; Heart Valve Disease; **Hospital:** Loyola Univ Med Ctr; **Address:** Loyola Univ Med Ctr-Cardiology, 2160 S First Ave Bldg 110 - Ste 6210, Maywood, IL 60153; **Phone:** 708-216-4720; **Board Cert:** Cardiovascular Disease 2005; Interventional Cardiology 2009; **Med School:** Columbia P&S 1989; **Resid:** Internal Medicine, Beth Israel Hosp 1992; **Fellow:** Cardiovascular Disease, Beth Israel Hosp 1995; Interventional Cardiology, Beth Israel Hosp 1999; **Fac Appt:** Prof Med, Loyola Univ-Stritch Sch Med

Schreiber, Theodore L MD [IC] - **Spec Exp:** Coronary Angioplasty/Stents; Carotid Artery Disease; Aortic Diseases & Dissection; **Hospital:** Harper Univ Hosp; **Address:** Harper Univ Hosp, 3990 John R St, Webber Bldg - Ste 9370, Detroit, MI 48201; **Phone:** 313-745-7025; **Board Cert:** Internal Medicine 1981; Cardiovascular Disease 1983; **Med School:** Cornell Univ-Weill Med Coll 1978; **Resid:** Internal Medicine, NY Hosp-Cornell Med Ctr 1981; **Fellow:** Cardiovascular Disease, NY Hosp-Cornell Med Ctr 1983; **Fac Appt:** Assoc Prof Med, Wayne State Univ

Whitlow, Patrick MD [IC] - **Spec Exp:** Cardiac Catheterization; **Hospital:** Cleveland Clin (page 55); **Address:** Cleveland Clinic, Dept Cardiology, 9500 Euclid Ave, Desk J2-3, Cleveland, OH 44195; **Phone:** 216-444-1746; **Board Cert:** Internal Medicine 1979; Cardiovascular Disease 1981; **Med School:** Duke Univ 1976; **Resid:** Internal Medicine, Parkland Meml Hosp 1979; **Fellow:** Cardiovascular Disease, Univ Alabama Hosp 1979

Great Plains and Mountains

Carroll, John D MD [IC] - **Spec Exp:** Heart Valve Disease; Congenital Heart Disease-Adult; Coronary Artery Disease; **Hospital:** Univ Colorado Hosp; **Address:** Univ Colorado, Dept Cardiology, 12605 E 16th Ave, MC B120, Aurora, CO 80045; **Phone:** 720-848-5300; **Board Cert:** Internal Medicine 1979; Cardiovascular Disease 1981; Interventional Cardiology 2009; **Med School:** Univ Chicago-Pritzker Sch Med 1976; **Resid:** Internal Medicine, Tufts-New Engl Med Ctr 1979; **Fellow:** Cardiovascular Disease, Tufts-New Engl Med Ctr 1981; **Fac Appt:** Prof Med, Univ Colorado

Southwest

Bailey, Steven R MD [IC] - **Spec Exp:** Coronary Artery Disease; Angioplasty & Stent Placement; Congenital Heart Disease; Heart Valve Disease; **Hospital:** Univ Hosp-San Antonio; **Address:** UTHSCSA, Cardiology Dept, 8300 Floyd Curl Drive Fl 3, San Antonio, TX 78229; **Phone:** 210-567-4601; **Board Cert:** Internal Medicine 1981; Cardiovascular Disease 1983; Interventional Cardiology 2009; **Med School:** Oregon Hlth & Sci Univ 1978; **Resid:** Internal Medicine, Fitzsimmons AMC 1981; **Fellow:** Cardiovascular Disease, Fitzsimmons AMC 1983; **Fac Appt:** Prof Med, Univ Tex, San Antonio

Feldman, Marc D MD [IC] - **Spec Exp:** Cardiac Catheterization; **Hospital:** Univ Hosp-San Antonio; **Address:** UTHSCSA, Cardiology Dept, 8300 Floyd Curl Drive Fl 3, San Antonio, TX 78229; **Phone:** 210-450-4888; **Board Cert:** Internal Medicine 1984; Cardiovascular Disease 1989; Interventional Cardiology 2010; **Med School:** Univ Pennsylvania 1981; **Resid:** Internal Medicine, Univ Chicago Med Ctr 1984; **Fellow:** Cardiovascular Disease, Beth Israel Deaconess Med Ctr 1987; **Fac Appt:** Prof Med, Univ Tex, San Antonio

Kleiman, Neal S MD [IC] - **Spec Exp:** Angioplasty & Stent Placement; **Hospital:** Methodist Hosp - Houston; **Address:** Methodist DeBakey Cardiology Assocs, 6550 Fannin St, Ste 1901, Smith Tower, Houston, TX 77030; **Phone:** 713-441-1100; **Board Cert:** Internal Medicine 1984; Cardiovascular Disease 1987; Interventional Cardiology 2009; **Med School:** Columbia P&S 1981; **Resid:** Internal Medicine, Baylor Affil Hosp 1984; **Fellow:** Interventional Cardiology, Baylor Coll Med 1987; **Fac Appt:** Assoc Prof Med, Cornell Univ-Weill Med Coll

Perin, Emerson C MD/PhD [IC] - **Spec Exp:** Stem Cell Therapy in Heart Failure; Angiogenesis; **Hospital:** St. Luke's Episcopal Hosp-Houston; **Address:** Southwest Cardiology Consultants, 6624 Fannin St, Ste 2220, Houston, TX 77030; **Phone:** 713-791-9400; **Board Cert:** Internal Medicine 1988; Cardiovascular Disease 2010; **Med School:** Brazil 1983; **Resid:** Internal Medicine, Jackson Meml Hosp 1988; **Fellow:** Cardiovascular Disease, St Lukes Episcopal Hosp 1991; **Fac Appt:** Asst Prof Med, Baylor Coll Med

Smalling, Richard W MD/PhD [IC] - **Spec Exp:** Coronary Artery Disease; Peripheral Vascular Disease; Heart Valve Disease; Congenital Heart Disease; **Hospital:** Meml Hermann Hosp - Texas Med Ctr; **Address:** 6410 Fannin St, Ste 600, Houston, TX 77030-1501; **Phone:** 832-325-7211; **Board Cert:** Internal Medicine 1978; Cardiovascular Disease 1981; Interventional Cardiology 2009; **Med School:** Univ Tex, Houston 1975; **Resid:** Internal Medicine, UCSD Med Ctr 1978; **Fellow:** Cardiovascular Disease, UCSD Med Ctr 1980; **Fac Appt:** Prof Med, Univ Tex, Houston

West Coast and Pacific

Greene, Robert M MD [IC] - **Spec Exp:** Cardiac Catheterization; Acute Coronary Syndromes; **Hospital:** Alta Bates Summit Med Ctr-Alta Bates Campus, Alta Bates Summit Med Ctr-Oakland; **Address:** Berkeley Cardiovascular Med Grp, 3300 Webster St Fl 4, Oakland, CA 94609; **Phone:** 510-549-4220; **Board Cert:** Internal Medicine 1976; Cardiovascular Disease 1977; Interventional Cardiology 2009; **Med School:** UCSF 1972; **Resid:** Internal Medicine, Wadsworth VA Hosp 1975; **Fellow:** Cardiovascular Disease, UCLA Med Ctr 1977

Mahmud, Ehtisham MD [IC] - **Spec Exp:** Cardiac Catheterization; Carotid Artery Stent Placement; Stem Cell Therapy in Heart Failure; Gene Therapy; **Hospital:** UCSD Med Ctr; **Address:** 9434 Medical Center Drive, MC 7784, La Jolla, CA 92037; **Phone:** 858-657-8030; **Board Cert:** Cardiovascular Disease 2010; Interventional Cardiology 2011; **Med School:** Univ Alberta 1989; **Resid:** Internal Medicine, UC San Diego 1995; **Fellow:** Cardiovascular Disease, UC San Diego 1999; Interventional Cardiology, Emory Univ Hosp 2000; **Fac Appt:** Prof Med, UCSD

Teirstein, Paul S MD [IC] - **Spec Exp:** Coronary Angioplasty/Stents; Heart Valve Disease; **Hospital:** Scripps Green Hosp; **Address:** Scripps Clinic, 10666 N Torrey Pines Rd, La Jolla, CA 92037; **Phone:** 858-554-9905; **Board Cert:** Internal Medicine 1983; Cardiovascular Disease 1987; Interventional Cardiology 2009; **Med School:** Mount Sinai Sch Med 1980; **Resid:** Internal Medicine, Brigham & Womens Hosp 1983; **Fellow:** Cardiovascular Disease, Stanford Univ Hosp 1986; Interventional Cardiology, Mid-Amer Heart Inst 1987

Yeung, Alan C MD [IC] - **Spec Exp:** Mitral Valve Surgery; Coronary Artery Disease; **Hospital:** Stanford Univ Hosp & Clins; **Address:** Stanford Univ Med Ctr, Div Interventional Cardiology, 300 Pasteur Drive, rm H2103, MC 5218, Stanford, CA 94305-5218; **Phone:** 650-723-0180; **Board Cert:** Internal Medicine 1987; Cardiovascular Disease 1989; Interventional Cardiology 2010; **Med School:** Harvard Med Sch 1984; **Resid:** Internal Medicine, Mass Gen Hosp 1987; **Fellow:** Cardiovascular Disease, Brigham & Womens Hosp 1990; **Fac Appt:** Prof Med, Stanford Univ

Maimonides
Medical Center

Maimonides Heart & Vascular Center

4802 Tenth Avenue
Brooklyn, New York 11219
Phone: 718.283.7489 • Fax: 718.635.7505
www.maimonidesmed.org/cardiac

The Cardiac Institute and Division of Vascular and Endovascular Surgery were integrated in 2013 to form the Maimonides Heart & Vascular Center.

Heart Services

Having pioneered numerous heart care innovations through the years, the Heart & Vascular Center offers diagnostic studies and therapeutic treatments, procedures and surgeries. It has been ranked by the Centers for Medicare and Medicaid Services among the few hospitals which have achieved excellent ratings in both heart attack and heart failure patient outcomes.

Cardiology

Headed by Jacob Shani, MD, the Department of Cardiology is among the most published and respected in the field, the Maimonides cardiology team continuously sets higher standards for patient care. The division has participated in numerous NIH-sponsored cardiac drug trials, and our Congestive Heart Failure (CHF) Program is among the most effective in the nation.

Interventional Cardiology

Numerous therapeutic devices have been developed and implemented here. Our Electrophysiology Lab has a superb record of achievement in diagnosing and treating arrhythmias. Close collaboration with the Department of Emergency Medicine ensures that chest pain patients are evaluated immediately, and that interventional procedures are used to stop heart attacks in progress whenever necessary.

Cardiothoracic Surgery

The Maimonides Division of Cardiothoracic Surgery has an illustrious history, setting a national standard for advances in cardiothoracic. Under the direction of Greg Ribakove, MD, minimally invasive and robotic heart surgeries, as well as advanced procedures such as LVAD and TAVI, are offered in state-of-the-art facilities, including a hybrid OR. In collaboration with Electrophysiology, Cardiothoracic Surgery has established an Atrial Fibrillation Center of Excellence. Maimonides provides one of the most prestigious cardiothoracic residency programs in the U.S.

Historic Moments

- In 1967, the first successful human heart transplant in the nation was performed at Maimonides.
- The intra-aortic balloon pump was developed here in 1970.
- Surgical techniques that protect the spine during cardiothoracic surgery were perfected here in 1982.
- Revolutionary cardiac catheterization devices were invented here in 1992 and 1997.
- Maimonides was the first hospital in the U.S. to implement fully automatic external cardiac defibrillators in 2001.

The Centers for Medicare and Medicaid Services, an agency of the federal government, recently published the latest data on 30-day mortality rates for hospitals across the country. Maimonides Medical Center achieved better-than-expected results in all three categories measured – heart attack, heart failure and pneumonia – a distinction only 25 hospitals in the U.S. achieved.

Maimonides Medical Center

The right care.
Right here.

www.maimonidesmed.org/cardiac

Mount Sinai

THE MOUNT SINAI MEDICAL CENTER

Cardiothoracic Surgery

One Gustave L. Levy Place
Fifth Avenue and 100th Street
New York, NY 10029-6574

Physician Referral: 1-800-MD-SINAI (637-4624)
www.mountsinai.org

THE DEPARTMENT OF CARDIOTHORACIC SURGERY at Mount Sinai is one of the nation's most prestigious programs. **In 2013, *U.S. News & World Report* ranked our cardiology and heart surgery service 13th in the country.** Cardiothoracic surgical patients benefit from an integrated and personalized care plan designed in coordination with expert cardiologists, anesthesiologists, perfusionists, and intensive care physicians. Mount Sinai is a quaternary referral center, meaning its surgeons often operate on the sickest and most complicated patients.

The Mitral Valve Repair Reference Center is one of the largest and most advanced in the nation. The superiority of mitral valve repair over replacement with a mechanical or bioprosthetic valve is now well established. Directed by David H. Adams, MD, Mount Sinai's Mitral Valve Repair Reference Center offers patients one of the highest percentages of successful valve repair in the world. In patients with mitral valve prolapse, our success rate in avoiding valve replacement approaches 100 percent. Our physicians are experts in mitral valve repair for patients with advanced cardiomyopathy. For patients who have associated atrial fibrillation, we offer the latest in concomitant arrhythmia surgery, including the MAZE procedure. Mitral valve repair with minimally invasive approaches is also performed when appropriate. Learn more about our Reference Center at www.mitralvalverepair.org.

The Cardiac Transplant and Assist Program, one of the largest in the nation, is under the direction of Anelechi Anyanwu, MD. We have been involved in the field of mechanical cardiac assistance from its inception, and have experience with most of the available FDA-approved devices. We have also played an active role in multi-institutional studies exploring permanent mechanical heart support.

Transcatheter Aortic Valve Replacement/Implantation (TAVR/TAVI) Program offers breakthrough treatment. Our physicians have been performing TAVR/TAVI for two years, with patients coming from around the world for this treatment. We were the first institution in the country to implant the Medtronic CoreValve Transcatheter Aortic Valve replacement device, and we are the first hospital in New York State able to implant both the Edwards Sapien Valve and the Medtronic CoreValve. These minimally invasive treatments spare patients from open-heart surgery and offer quicker recovery and return to daily activities. Our TAVR/TAVI program is led by Dr. David Adams, the National Co-Principal Investigator of the United States FDA pivotal trial of the Medtronic CoreValve Transcatheter Aortic Valve replacement device, and Dr. Samin Sharma, Director of Clinical Cardiology and Interventional Cardiology.

Pediatric and Congenital Cardiac Surgery Program achieves exceptional results. Led by Dr. Khanh Nguyen, patients from newborns to young adults are cared for in this program, which has achieved outstanding results with challenging problems by incorporating the most advanced techniques available. Part of only three active pediatric heart transplant centers in the state, our program also provides support for very sick hearts in infants and older children, using Extra-Corporeal Membrane Oxygenators (ECMO) or Ventricular Assist Devices (VAD). The care extended to the patient and family is supported by an outstanding multidisciplinary team. Superb post-operative care is provided in a dedicated Pediatric Cardiac Surgical Intensive Care Unit, under the direction of pediatric cardiologists, intensivists, and surgeons.

LEADING SURGEONS, UNPARALLELED POSSIBILITIES

The Department of Cardiothoracic Surgery at Mount Sinai is chaired by David H. Adams, MD, the Marie-Josée and Henry R. Kravis Professor. Dr. Adams is a world-renowned mitral repair surgeon. Anelechi Anyanwu, MD, leads one of the largest ventricular assist device and heart transplant centers in the country. He is also an expert in complex and re-operative valve surgery. Paul Stelzer, MD, is a specialist in aortic root surgery whose experience with the Ross procedure is unmatched, exceeding 20 years and 500 cases. These leaders work in concert with other members of Mount Sinai Heart, which is under the direction of world-renowned cardiologist Valentin Fuster, MD, PhD, to deliver unparalleled possibilities for patients with cardiovascular disease.

NewYork-Presbyterian

Affiliated with Columbia University College of Physicians and Surgeons and Weill Cornell Medical College

NewYork-Presbyterian Hospital
Columbia University Medical Center
622 West 168th Street
New York, NY 10032

NewYork-Presbyterian Hospital
Weill Cornell Medical Center
525 East 68th Street
New York, NY 10065

1-877-NYP-WELL (1-877-697-9355) **www.nyp.org/heart**

NewYork-Presbyterian Heart

In 2013-2014, NewYork-Presbyterian Hospital's heart and heart surgery program was ranked 3rd in the nation in the annual "Best Hospitals" survey conducted by *U.S. News & World Report*™. NewYork-Presbyterian has leading clinical programs for patients with coronary artery disease and a wide range of other heart disorders, with particular expertise in the management of:

- Aortic aneurysms, acute dissections, and trauma, with rapid diagnosis and effective medical and surgical interventions
- Heart failure, featuring a robust mechanical circulatory support program. Patients come from all over the world for placement of ventricular assist devices to be used long-term or as a bridge to transplant. NewYork-Presbyterian Hospital/Columbia University Medical Center is one of the world's leading institutions for heart transplantation and is one of the few centers offering patients a total artificial heart
- Adults with congenital heart disorders: echocardiography, interventional cardiac catheterization, interventional electrophysiology, and surgery. NewYork-Presbyterian's adult congenital heart surgeons are among the world's best for complex congenital heart surgery and cardiac transplantation. Related care is provided by specialists in high-risk pregnancy, genetics, fetal echocardiography, GI and liver disease, pulmonary, and hematology
- Cardiac rhythm abnormalities, with experienced electrophysiologists who diagnose and treat atrial fibrillation and other arrhythmias using pacemakers, implantable cardioverter defibrillators, ablation, and novel approaches to restore normal heart rhythm
- Valve disorders: using minimally invasive surgical approaches whenever possible. NewYork-Presbyterian Hospital doctors pioneered transcatheter aortic valve replacement (TAVR), and continue to perform more TAVR procedures than any other center in the country. Our investigators led the PARTNER Trial, which showed that TAVR is as effective as conventional open-heart surgery for reducing mortality among high-risk patients with aortic stenosis. We are also participating in the EVEREST II clinical trial, evaluating a new device to repair mitral valve leakage
- Heart disorders in the elderly: NewYork-Presbyterian Hospital surgeons have earned a reputation for performing heart surgery on the very elderly (over age 80), achieving excellent outcomes
- Patients who require surgery may receive treatment using a robotic approach, delivered using the Siemens Artis zeego® medical imaging system. This system provides surgeons with exceptional visualization of blood vessels.

A Reputation for Excellence

At NewYork-Presbyterian Hospital, the optimal care of patients with heart disease is achieved by combining an experienced team of clinicians with the latest advances in technology. Basic science and clinical research efforts are aimed at developing more effective ways to prevent, diagnose, and treat cardiac disorders. NewYork-Presbyterian Hospital features renowned cardiac care programs in the following areas:

- Cardiac diagnostics
- Electrophysiology
- Clinical cardiology
- Interventional cardiology
- Cardiac assist devices
- Cardiothoracic surgery, including transplantation
- Mitral valve repair

NewYork-Presbyterian Hospital is designated by the Society of Chest Pain Centers as an Accredited Chest Pain Center, dedicated to reducing heart-related deaths by improving the response time for the diagnosis and treatment of chest pain.

NorthShore
University HealthSystem

Cardiovascular Services

NorthShore Cardiovascular Services
2650 Ridge Avenue, Evanston, IL 60201
(847) 570-2250
northshore.org/cardio

NorthShore University HealthSystem's Cardiovascular Services improve the lives of thousands of patients every year, using advanced surgical and nonsurgical procedures. Personalized treatment programs focus on each patient's individual needs.

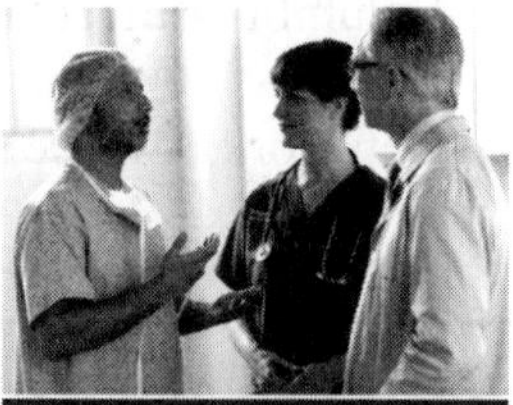

CARDIOVASCULAR SERVICES SPECIALTIES:

- Cardiovascular Surgery
- Electrophysiology
- Heart Failure Program
- Lipid and Preventive Cardiology Program
- Interventional Cardiology
- Heart Valve Program (including TAVR)
- Clinical Cardiology
- Women's Heart Health
- Cardiac Imaging

Multidisciplinary Care, Leading Experts

NorthShore's cardiovascular team is comprised of world-class experts in every cardiac specialty. Their multidisciplinary team of dedicated experts includes interventional cardiologists, cardiac electrophysiologists, clinical cardiologists, cardiac surgeons, advanced practice nurses and physician assistants, all committed to providing patients with quality, accessible care.

The team includes more than 10 Castle Connolly-recognized cardiologists and cardiovascular surgeons who specialize in a full spectrum of innovative surgical procedures. They employ advanced techniques, including non-invasive procedures, leading-edge equipment and interventional drug therapies. NorthShore's cardiac imaging centers specialize in advanced cardiac imaging, including 3D transthoracic echocardiograms, stress testing and electrocardiograms.

Under the new leadership of Jorge Saucedo, MD, Division Head of Cardiology, and Paul Pearson, MD, PhD, Division Chief of Cardiovascular Surgery, NorthShore is launching five advanced, sub-specialty cardiac surgery programs over the next year, enhancing its already robust research and academic agenda. And through NorthShore's collaboration with Mayo Clinic, patients have access to the combined strength of two leading teams of cardiovascular specialists. Together, they treat the most complex cases.

Life-Saving Research

NorthShore University HealthSystem is one of the nation's preeminent academic medical centers, committed to developing life-saving innovations. Ted E. Feldman, MD, internationally recognized for his interventional cardiology work, is helping keep NorthShore at the forefront of research. Dr. Feldman is the global principal investigator on the effort to develop second-generation transcatheter aortic valve replacement devices. The specialists at Cardiovascular Services also conduct a wide range of clinical trials to offer patients earlier access to medical advances.

NYU Langone
MEDICAL CENTER

CARDIAC AND VASCULAR INSTITUTE
550 First Avenue *(at 31st Street)*
New York, NY 10016
www.NYULMC.org
Physician Referral: **888-7-NYU-MED** *(888-769-8633)*

CARDIAC AND VASCULAR INSTITUTE

The Cardiac and Vascular Institute (CVI) at NYU Langone Medical Center continues to advance new techniques for repairing heart valves, curing heart rhythm disorders, and treating aortic diseases and congestive heart failure. We care for both adults and children. CVI is consistently ranked among the leading heart and heart surgery centers in *U.S. News & World Report's annual 'Best Hospitals'* rankings.

Cardiac Catheterization CVI offers superior catheter-based diagnosis and evaluation of cardiac health. Our laboratory provides a full range of procedures to evaluate, diagnose, and provide treatment options.

Cardiac Rehabilitation and Prevention The Joan and Joel Smilow Cardiopulmonary Rehabilitation and Prevention Center provides individualized treatment plans through NYU Langone's Rusk Rehabilitation, in a state-of-the-art and comfortable facility.

Cardiac Surgery NYU Langone is a nationally recognized leader in advanced surgical treatments for adult and congenital heart disease. We have world-renowned expertise in mitral valve repair, aortic valve replacement and aortic aneurysm repair, as well as specializing in high-risk and elderly patients.

Cardiology The Leon H. Charney Division of Cardiology is a leader in cardiovascular patient care, biomedical research, and education. We are advancing the field of cardiovascular medicine through a variety of innovative collaborations.

Congenital Heart Disease The pediatric and adult congenital cardiac program treats patients of all ages with inherited and acquired cardiac defects. We have a highly experienced team of specialists in pediatric and adult cardiology, pediatric interventional cardiology, congenital cardiac surgery, neonatal and pediatric cardiac intensive care, pediatric cardiac anesthesiology, nursing, and extracorporeal perfusion.

Heart Failure A multidisciplinary team offers the most advanced care for heart failure including echocardiograms, pacemaker and defibrillator implantations, open heart surgeries, and left ventricular assist devices.

Nuclear Cardiology/Stress The Nuclear Cardiology/Stress Laboratory performs a range of tests that assist cardiologists in the assessment and diagnosis of heart disease.

Vascular Surgery We offer diagnostic and treatment for patients with conditions ranging from arterial aneurysms to deep vein thrombosis, as well as carotid stenosis and limb salvage including minimally invasive vein surgery, endovascular aortic surgery, thoracic aneurysm correction and abdominal aneurysm interventions.

Mount Sinai

THE MOUNT SINAI MEDICAL CENTER

Cardiac Electrophysiology

One Gustave L. Levy Place
Fifth Avenue and 100th Street
New York, NY 10029-6574

Physician Referral: 1-800-MD-SINAI (637-4624)
www.mountsinai.org

Cardiac Electrophysiology

Ranked #13 in the United States for cardiology and heart surgery by *U.S. News & World Report*, Mount Sinai is a recognized leader in the treatment of abnormal heart rhythms, also known as cardiac electrophysiology. Our clinical leadership, innovative research, and leading-edge therapies continually draws patients from around the world to seek treatment with us.

A major referral destination, our **HELMSLEY CENTER FOR ELECTROPHYSIOLOGY** offers the full range of therapies for all types of arrhythmia, from common arrhythmias such as atrial fibrillation to challenging ones as ventricular tachycardia. We combine technology, technique, and expertise to deliver the highest-quality and most advanced care. Mount Sinai specialists are skilled in performing the most delicate arrhythmia procedures, even those not attempted at most hospitals. Our patients can feel assured they've chosen a center that offers every available treatment for cardiac arrhythmias, as well as experts who can tailor those treatments for the most customized care.

COMBINING SCIENCE WITH PERSONALIZED CARE

The Center for Electrophysiology continues its leadership through various research studies with the goal of developing superior technologies. In fact, Mount Sinai is currently the lead center on several multinational clinical trials exploring new arrhythmia procedures, keeping us on the cutting edge and offering access to the most advanced treatments.

Advancing the Treatment of Arrhythmias

Mount Sinai has been leading the development of new arrhythmia technologies since 1909, when one of our physicians became the first in the United States to use an electrocardiogram. Today the Center for Electrophysiology provides the full spectrum of therapies, including procedures that implant devices for regulating heart rhythms (such as Pacemakers and ICDs) to procedures that use catheters for fixing the source of the abnormal heartbeat (called ablations).

To make ablations safer and more effective, our center was the first in the country to use several breakthrough technologies, including a visually guided laser balloon catheter in 2009 and the TactiCath force-sensing catheter in 2011, as well as a new generation of visually guided catheter in 2012. Vivek Reddy, MD, Director of our Cardiac Arrhythmia Service, was the first physician in the world to use several new ablation techniques, such as the cryoballoon catheter and robotic navigation. Also, Drs. Reddy and Dukkipati were the first in the US to perform a suture-based catheter ligation of the left atrial appendage (to prevent stroke in AF) in 2009.

NYU Langone MEDICAL CENTER

CARDIAC AND VASCULAR INSTITUTE
550 First Avenue *(at 31st Street)*
New York, NY 10016
www.NYULMC.org
Physician Referral: **888-7-NYU-MED** *(888-769-8633)*

CARDIAC AND VASCULAR INSTITUTE

The Cardiac and Vascular Institute (CVI) at NYU Langone Medical Center continues to advance new techniques for repairing heart valves, curing heart rhythm disorders, and treating aortic diseases and congestive heart failure. We care for both adults and children. CVI is consistently ranked among the leading heart and heart surgery centers in *U.S. News & World Report's annual 'Best Hospitals'* rankings.

Cardiac Catheterization CVI offers superior catheter-based diagnosis and evaluation of cardiac health. Our laboratory provides a full range of procedures to evaluate, diagnose, and provide treatment options.

Cardiac Rehabilitation and Prevention The Joan and Joel Smilow Cardiopulmonary Rehabilitation and Prevention Center provides individualized treatment plans through NYU Langone's Rusk Rehabilitation, in a state-of-the-art and comfortable facility.

Cardiac Surgery NYU Langone is a nationally recognized leader in advanced surgical treatments for adult and congenital heart disease. We have world-renowned expertise in mitral valve repair, aortic valve replacement and aortic aneurysm repair, as well as specializing in high-risk and elderly patients.

Cardiology The Leon H. Charney Division of Cardiology is a leader in cardiovascular patient care, biomedical research, and education. We are advancing the field of cardiovascular medicine through a variety of innovative collaborations.

Congenital Heart Disease The pediatric and adult congenital cardiac program treats patients of all ages with inherited and acquired cardiac defects. We have a highly experienced team of specialists in pediatric and adult cardiology, pediatric interventional cardiology, congenital cardiac surgery, neonatal and pediatric cardiac intensive care, pediatric cardiac anesthesiology, nursing, and extracorporeal perfusion.

Heart Failure A multidisciplinary team offers the most advanced care for heart failure including echocardiograms, pacemaker and defibrillator implantations, open heart surgeries, and left ventricular assist devices.

Nuclear Cardiology/Stress The Nuclear Cardiology/Stress Laboratory performs a range of tests that assist cardiologists in the assessment and diagnosis of heart disease.

Vascular Surgery We offer diagnostic and treatment for patients with conditions ranging from arterial aneurysms to deep vein thrombosis, as well as carotid stenosis and limb salvage including minimally invasive vein surgery, endovascular aortic surgery, thoracic aneurysm correction and abdominal aneurysm interventions.

Mount Sinai

THE MOUNT SINAI MEDICAL CENTER

Interventional Cardiology/ Cath Lab Treatments

One Gustave L. Levy Place
Fifth Avenue and 100th Street
New York, NY 10029-6574

Physician Referral: 1-800-MD-SINAI (637-4624)
www.mountsinai.org

INTERVENTIONAL CARDIOLOGY/ CATH LAB TREATMENTS

Ranked among the top 13 hospitals for heart services by *U.S. News & World Report*, 2013 Mount Sinai Heart is celebrated internationally as a world leader in all facets of cardiology care and research. Our **Cardiac Catheterization Laboratory** ranks among the nation's best and busiest, offering expert diagnosis, state-of-the-art technology, and unparalleled excellence in care and patient safety. It has achieved the highest safety rating among New York State's 54 institutions that perform percutaneous coronary interventions (PCI), a minimally invasive heart procedure commonly known as angioplasty. No other hospital has matched this level of patient safety rating for both emergency and non-emergency cases since public reporting of PCI results began in 1994, per the New York State Department of Health.

Mount Sinai's multidisciplinary interventional cardiology team, patient volume, and procedural offerings continue to expand significantly, as the **Cath Lab** has performed more than 5,500 interventions a year for the last five years. This upward momentum has also drawn an increase in complex cases. Stable interventional growth with declining complications–despite increasing complexity of cases–has been achieved at Mount Sinai Heart through seamless teamwork and dedication to treating each individual patient, taking into account his or her medical history, type and status of condition and lifestyle.

MULTIDISCIPLINARY CARDIAC CATHETERIZATION TEAM

The Cath Lab's multidisciplinary team of interventionalists, nurses, technicians and support staff is committed to continuous quality improvement and providing excellent patient care. Constant communication and adherence of protocols have enabled our team to achieve an unprecedented level of patient safety. Additionally, world-class research physicians have recently joined the team to further our studies of the underlying causes of heart disease and develop targeted tools and procedures to treat its many permutations.

EXCELLENCE IN FULL RANGE OF INTERVENTIONAL CARDIOLOGY PROCEDURES

Patients ranging from pediatrics to geriatrics come to Mount Sinai's Catheterization Laboratory from all over the world for interventional procedures to help restore the pathway to the heart. This includes routine diagnostics and procedures such as angioplasties, and stents (including drug-eluting stents) to the full spectrum of techniques for complex cases. Our team is internationally recognized for our vast expertise in the following complex procedures:

- Rotational atherectomy
- PCI for CTO (chronic total occlusion, or chronic blockage)
- Left main stenting for unprotected left main coronary artery (LMCA) disease
- TAVI/TAVR (transcatheter aortic valve implementation/replacement)
- Balloon valvuloplasty: aortic and mitral

NYU Langone MEDICAL CENTER

CARDIAC AND VASCULAR INSTITUTE
550 First Avenue *(at 31st Street)*
New York, NY 10016
www.NYULMC.org
Physician Referral: **888-7-NYU-MED** *(888-769-8633)*

CARDIAC AND VASCULAR INSTITUTE

The Cardiac and Vascular Institute (CVI) at NYU Langone Medical Center continues to advance new techniques for repairing heart valves, curing heart rhythm disorders, and treating aortic diseases and congestive heart failure. We care for both adults and children. CVI is consistently ranked among the leading heart and heart surgery centers in *U.S. News & World Report's annual 'Best Hospitals'* rankings.

Cardiac Catheterization CVI offers superior catheter-based diagnosis and evaluation of cardiac health. Our laboratory provides a full range of procedures to evaluate, diagnose, and provide treatment options.

Cardiac Rehabilitation and Prevention The Joan and Joel Smilow Cardiopulmonary Rehabilitation and Prevention Center provides individualized treatment plans through NYU Langone's Rusk Rehabilitation, in a state-of-the-art and comfortable facility.

Cardiac Surgery NYU Langone is a nationally recognized leader in advanced surgical treatments for adult and congenital heart disease. We have world-renowned expertise in mitral valve repair, aortic valve replacement and aortic aneurysm repair, as well as specializing in high-risk and elderly patients.

Cardiology The Leon H. Charney Division of Cardiology is a leader in cardiovascular patient care, biomedical research, and education. We are advancing the field of cardiovascular medicine through a variety of innovative collaborations.

Congenital Heart Disease The pediatric and adult congenital cardiac program treats patients of all ages with inherited and acquired cardiac defects. We have a highly experienced team of specialists in pediatric and adult cardiology, pediatric interventional cardiology, congenital cardiac surgery, neonatal and pediatric cardiac intensive care, pediatric cardiac anesthesiology, nursing, and extracorporeal perfusion.

Heart Failure A multidisciplinary team offers the most advanced care for heart failure including echocardiograms, pacemaker and defibrillator implantations, open heart surgeries, and left ventricular assist devices.

Nuclear Cardiology/Stress The Nuclear Cardiology/Stress Laboratory performs a range of tests that assist cardiologists in the assessment and diagnosis of heart disease.

Vascular Surgery We offer diagnostic and treatment for patients with conditions ranging from arterial aneurysms to deep vein thrombosis, as well as carotid stenosis and limb salvage including minimally invasive vein surgery, endovascular aortic surgery, thoracic aneurysm correction and abdominal aneurysm interventions.

St. Francis Hospital, The Heart Center®
Catholic Health Services
At the heart of health

100 Port Washington Blvd.
Roslyn, New York 11576
www.stfrancisheartcenter.com
(516) 562-6000
1-888-HEARTNY

A Leader in Cardiac Care
St. Francis Hospital, The Heart Center® is New York State's only specialty designated cardiac center and is one of the busiest heart centers in the nation. Located in Roslyn, New York, on Long Island's North Shore, St. Francis is ranked among the top 10 hospitals in the United States for cardiology and heart surgery by *U.S. News & World Report*. It is the seventh consecutive year that *U.S. News* has named St. Francis one of the best hospitals in America. In 2013-14, the Hospital was also nationally ranked in ear, nose and throat; gastroenterology and GI surgery; geriatrics; neurology and neurosurgery; orthopedics; pulmonology; and urology.

St. Francis Hospital:

- Has a highly experienced team of physicians and surgeons with one of the largest volumes in the nation for cardiac surgery, interventional cardiology, and arrhythmia procedures

- Offers innovative approaches to cardiac surgery, including minimally invasive procedures and off-pump coronary artery bypass surgery, designed to minimize trauma and reduce surgical complications

- Performs one of the region's highest volumes of catheter-based techniques to correct congenital heart defects such as atrial septal defects (ASDs), ventricular septal defects (VSDs), and patent foramen ovale (PFO)

- Operates a nationally recognized Arrhythmia and Pacemaker Center staffed with electrophysiologists with over a decade of experience in radiofrequency ablation, a permanent cure for certain arrhythmias, including atrial fibrillation

- Maintains a high volume center for the implantation of cardiac pacemakers and defibrillators

- Offers a world-class program in cardiac imaging that fully integrates all technologies, including advanced methods in cardiac MRI, coronary CT angiography, PET/CT and three-dimensional echocardiography

- Has earned the Magnet designation for excellence in nursing services, an honor achieved by only 7 percent of hospitals in the U.S.

- Is a premier center for clinical trials and studies of the application of image-guided methods of diagnosis and treatment of heart disease, such as CoreValve, eValve, CREST, and Symplicity

St. Francis Hospital has outstanding patient satisfaction ratings, and is top-ranked for patients saying they would recommend the Hospital to family and friends.

"Our large cardiac caseload and our growing research program put us in an excellent position to introduce new techniques that can benefit thousands of people in need each year."

–Alan D. Guerci, M.D.
President and Chief Executive Officer
Catholic Health Services of Long Island

St. Francis Hospital, The Heart Center®
Catholic Health Services
At the heart of health

100 Port Washington Blvd.
Roslyn, New York 11576
www.stfrancisheartcenter.com
(516) 562-6000
1-888-HEARTNY

Noninvasive Cardiac Imaging
Using the latest in noninvasive cardiac imaging technology, St. Francis Hospital's physicians can evaluate blood flow, heart muscle strength, anatomy, and coronary artery blockages, allowing them to more effectively guide a patient's course of treatment.

Among the most recent advances in St. Francis Hospital's range of services are:

Coronary CT Angiography
St. Francis Hospital was the first hospital on Long Island to offer Multidetector Computed Tomography (MDCT) for noninvasive coronary artery imaging. Now, with more advanced technology and personalized design of imaging protocols for each individual, St. Francis can minimize radiation exposure for every patient.

Cardiac MRI
The only center on Long Island with a dedicated Cardiac MRI program and world-class expertise in cardiac MRI, St. Francis Hospital uses MRI to evaluate heart anatomy, function, blood flow, scarring, and inflammation using advanced techniques on two state-of-the-art scanners. Cardiac MRI allows physicians to evaluate effects of heart attack and coronary artery blockages and non-coronary causes of heart failure to determine whether or not patients will benefit from heart surgery or other therapies. World-renowned cardiac MRI authority Nathaniel Reichek, M.D., leads St. Francis Hospital's clinical and research applications of cardiac MRI.

Three-Dimensional Echocardiography
St. Francis Hospital is an internationally recognized leader in three-dimensional echocardiography for quantifying the effects of heart disease. By creating three-dimensional reconstructions of the heart and blood flow within it, this technology provides diagnostic information that surpasses that available with conventional echocardiography in many patients.

Nuclear Imaging
Conventional nuclear imaging involves the injection of nuclear isotopes and imaging by a gamma camera that circles the patient's body, improving the accuracy of stress testing. St. Francis Hospital offers the latest advances in nuclear cardiology, such as positron emission tomography of the heart with CT attenuation correction (PET/CT). The nuclear cardiology laboratory at St. Francis Hospital is also a leader in developing new types of computer analysis to improve the value of all forms of cardiac nuclear imaging, and was among the first facilities in the U.S. to receive accreditation from The Intersocietal Commission for the Accreditation of Nuclear Medicine Laboratories.

Noninvasive Imaging at St. Francis Hospital
Noninvasive imaging services at St. Francis Hospital include:

- Multidetector computed tomographic coronary angiography
- Cardiac MRI
- SPECT/CT nuclear Imaging
- Cardiac PET/CT imaging
- Transesophageal echocardiography
- Three-dimensional echocardiography
- Stress testing with nuclear, echocardiographic or MRI imaging.

The St. Francis Cardiac Imaging Program also supports the Hospital's nationally recognized programs in surgical and interventional cardiology, performing monitoring transesophageal echocardiography during surgical and transarterial valve replacements, catheter treatment of leaky heart valves and minimally invasive treatment to prevent stroke due to cardiac blood clots in atrial fibrillation.

In addition, St. Francis Hospital uses its leading-edge noninvasive imaging technology in its research programs on cardiovascular disease. Drawing on its depth of experience with various imaging modalities, the Hospital has launched a multi-disciplinary effort at its Cardiac Research Institute to improve methods for the diagnosis and treatment of cardiac disease. Past research efforts at the Hospital include The St. Francis Heart Study – a pioneering effort and the largest study of CT calcium scoring to be conducted at any single center – which first demonstrated the value of CT calcium scoring for atherosclerotic plaque detection as a tool in cardiac risk evaluation.

Child Neurology

a subspecialty of Neurology

A neurologist specializes in the diagnosis and treatment of all types of disease or impaired function of the brain, spinal cord, peripheral nerves, muscles and autonomic nervous system, as well as the blood vessels that relate to these structures. A child neurologist has special skills in the diagnosis and management of neurologic disorders of the neonatal period, infancy, early childhood and adolescence.

Training Required: Four years

Child Neurology

New England

Darras, Basil T MD [ChiN] - **Spec Exp:** Neuromuscular Disorders; Cerebral Palsy; **Hospital:** Children's Hospital - Boston; **Address:** Boston Chldn's Hosp, Neurology, Fegan 11, 300 Longwood Ave, Boston, MA 02115; **Phone:** 617-355-8235; **Board Cert:** Clinical Genetics 1987; Pediatrics 1988; Child Neurology 1992; Neuromuscular Medicine 2008; **Med School:** Greece 1977; **Resid:** Pediatrics, Nassau County Med Ctr 1982; Child Neurology, Tufts-New England Med Ctr 1985; **Fellow:** Clinical Genetics, Yale Univ Sch Med 1988; **Fac Appt:** Prof N, Harvard Med Sch

Griesemer, David A MD [ChiN] - **Spec Exp:** Epilepsy/Seizure Disorders; Brain Injury; **Hospital:** Tufts Med Ctr, Floating Hosp for Children at Tufts Med Ce; **Address:** Tufts Med Ctr, 800 Washington St, Box 330, Boston, MA 02111; **Phone:** 617-636-8100; **Board Cert:** Child Neurology 1992; **Med School:** Johns Hopkins Univ 1976; **Resid:** Pediatrics, Johns Hopkins Hosp 1978; **Fellow:** Child Neurology, Univ Michigan Hosp 1985; **Fac Appt:** Prof N, Tufts Univ

Holmes, Gregory L MD [ChiN] - **Spec Exp:** Epilepsy/Seizure Disorders; **Hospital:** FAHC - Med Ctr Campus; **Address:** Fletcher Allen Neurology, 111 Colchester Ave, Medical Ctr East Pavilion 4, Burlington, VT 05401; **Phone:** 802-847-2788; **Board Cert:** Pediatrics 1979; Neurology 1980; **Med School:** Univ VA Sch Med 1974; **Resid:** Pediatrics, Yale-New Haven Hosp 1976; **Fellow:** Pediatric Neurology, Univ Virginia 1979; **Fac Appt:** Prof N, Univ VT Coll Med

Mandelbaum, David E MD/PhD [ChiN] - **Spec Exp:** Epilepsy/Seizure Disorders; Neonatal Neurology; Autism; **Hospital:** Rhode Island Hosp, Women & Infants Hosp of RI; **Address:** Dept of Neurology, 593 Eddy St, George Bldg - Fl 1, Providence, RI 02903; **Phone:** 401-444-5685; **Board Cert:** Child Neurology 1987; Pediatrics 1987; Clinical Neurophysiology 2013; Neurodevelopmental Disabilities 2011; **Med School:** Columbia P&S 1980; **Resid:** Pediatrics, Yale-New Haven Hosp 1982; Neurology, Neuro Inst-Columbia 1983; **Fellow:** Child Neurology, Neuro Inst-Columbia 1985; **Fac Appt:** Prof N, Brown Univ

Pomeroy, Scott L MD/PhD [ChiN] - **Spec Exp:** Neuro-Oncology; Brain Tumors; **Hospital:** Children's Hospital - Boston, Dana-Farber Cancer Inst; **Address:** Boston Chldn's Hosp, 300 Longwood Ave, Dept Neurology-Fegan 11, Boston, MA 02115; **Phone:** 617-355-6386; **Board Cert:** Child Neurology 1988; **Med School:** Univ Cincinnati 1982; **Resid:** Pediatrics, Chldns Hosp 1984; Neurology, St. Louis Chldn's Hosp/Wash Univ 1985; **Fellow:** Neurological Biology, Wash Univ Hosp 1990; Pediatric Neurology, St. Louis Chldn's Hosp/Wash Univ 1990; **Fac Appt:** Prof N, Harvard Med Sch

Sahin, Mustafa MD/PhD [ChiN] - **Spec Exp:** Tuberous Sclerosis; Cerebrovascular Malformations; Sturge-Weber Syndrome; **Hospital:** Children's Hospital - Boston; **Address:** Boston Chldn's Hosp, 300 Longwood Ave, Fegan 11, Boston, MA 02115; **Phone:** 617-355-8994; **Board Cert:** Child Neurology 2011; **Med School:** Yale Univ 1995; **Resid:** Pediatrics, Chldns Hosp 1997; Child Neurology, Chldns Hosp 2000; **Fac Appt:** Assoc Prof N, Harvard Med Sch

Shaywitz, Bennett A MD [ChiN] - **Spec Exp:** Learning Disorders; Dyslexia; Headache; **Hospital:** Yale-New Haven Hosp; **Address:** Yale New Haven Chldns Hosp-Ped Neurology Dept, 1 Park St Fl 2, West Pavilion, New Haven, CT 06510; **Phone:** 203-785-4641; **Board Cert:** Pediatrics 1968; Child Neurology 1973; **Med School:** Washington Univ, St Louis 1963; **Resid:** Pediatrics, Bronx Muni Hosp Ctr 1967; **Fellow:** Child Neurology, Albert Einstein Coll Med 1970; **Fac Appt:** Prof Ped, Yale Univ

Mid Atlantic

Allen, Jeffrey MD [ChiN] - **Spec Exp:** Neuro-Oncology; Brain Tumors; Neurofibromatosis; **Hospital:** NYU Langone Med Ctr (page 68); **Address:** Hassenfeld Childrens Ctr, 160 E 32nd St Fl 2 - Ste L3, New York, NY 10016; **Phone:** 212-263-9907; **Board Cert:** Child Neurology 1977; **Med School:** Harvard Med Sch 1969; **Resid:** Pediatrics, Montreal Chldns Hosp 1973; Pediatric Neurology, Montreal Neur Inst/McGill 1976; **Fac Appt:** Prof Ped, NYU Sch Med

Bergman, Ira MD/PhD [ChiN] - **Spec Exp:** Complex Diagnosis; Neuro-Oncology; **Hospital:** Chldns Hosp of Pittsburgh - UPMC; **Address:** Chldns Hosp Pittsburgh, 4401 Penn Ave Fl 8, Pittsburgh, PA 15224; **Phone:** 412-692-5520; **Board Cert:** Pediatrics 1981; Child Neurology 1980; **Med School:** Univ Chicago-Pritzker Sch Med 1974; **Resid:** Pediatrics, Mass Genl Hosp 1978; **Fellow:** Neurology, Mass Genl Hosp 1980; **Fac Appt:** Assoc Prof Ped, Univ Pittsburgh

Crawford, Thomas O MD [ChiN] - **Spec Exp:** Neuromuscular Disorders; Muscular Dystrophy; Ataxia Telangiectasia; **Hospital:** Johns Hopkins Hosp (page 59); **Address:** Johns Hopkins Pediatric Specialty Clinic, 200 N Wolfe St, Ste 2158, Baltimore, MD 21287; **Phone:** 410-955-4259; **Board Cert:** Pediatrics 1986; Child Neurology 1990; **Med School:** USC Sch Med 1980; **Resid:** Pediatrics, LAC-USC Med Ctr 1984; Child Neurology, Chldns Hosp 1987; **Fellow:** Neuromuscular Medicine, Johns Hopkins Hosp 1988; **Fac Appt:** Assoc Prof N, Johns Hopkins Univ

DeVivo, Darryl C MD [ChiN] - **Spec Exp:** Metabolic Disorders; Neuromuscular Disorders; Spinal Muscular Atrophy (SMA); **Hospital:** NY-Presby/Columbia Univ Med Ctr, NY (page 65); **Address:** Neurological Inst, 710 W 168th St, Ste NI 201, New York, NY 10032; **Phone:** 212-305-5244; **Board Cert:** Child Neurology 1972; **Med School:** Univ VA Sch Med 1964; **Resid:** Pediatrics, Mass Genl Hosp 1966; Neurology, Mass Genl Hosp 1967; **Fellow:** Neurology, Natl Inst Hlth 1969; Child Neurology, Chldns Hosp 1970; **Fac Appt:** Prof N, Columbia P&S

Hartman, Adam L MD [ChiN] - **Spec Exp:** Epilepsy; **Hospital:** Johns Hopkins Hosp (page 59); **Address:** Pediatric Epilepsy Ctr, 600 N Wolfe St, Meyer 2-147, Baltimore, MD 21287; **Phone:** 410-955-9100; **Board Cert:** Child Neurology 2006; **Med School:** Northwestern Univ-Feinberg Sch Med 1994; **Resid:** Pediatrics, National Naval Med Ctr 1997; Child Neurology, Johns Hopkins Med Ctr 2005; **Fellow:** Epilepsy, Johns Hopkins Hosp 2007; **Fac Appt:** Asst Prof N, Johns Hopkins Univ

Ichord, Rebecca N MD [ChiN] - **Spec Exp:** Stroke in Children; Brain Injury; **Hospital:** Chldns Hosp of Philadelphia; **Address:** Chldns Hosp, 3400 Civic Ctr Blvd, Wood Bldg Fl 6, Philadelphia, PA 19104-4318; **Phone:** 215-590-4142; **Board Cert:** Pediatrics 1984; Child Neurology 1992; **Med School:** Geo Wash Univ 1979; **Resid:** Pediatrics, Chldns Natl Med Ctr 1983; **Fellow:** Developmental-Behavioral Pediatrics, Johns Hopkins Hosp 1985; Child Neurology, Johns Hopkins Hosp 1991; **Fac Appt:** Assoc Prof N, Univ Pennsylvania

Kosofsky, Barry E MD/PhD [ChiN] - **Spec Exp:** Developmental Disorders; Autism; Stroke; **Hospital:** NY-Presby/Weill Cornell Med Ctr, NY (page 65); **Address:** Cornell Med Ctr, Dept Pediatrics, 505 E 70th St, Helmsley Tower Fl 3, New York, NY 10021; **Phone:** 212-746-3321; **Board Cert:** Child Neurology 1993; **Med School:** Johns Hopkins Univ 1985; **Resid:** Pediatrics, Chldns Hosp 1987; Child Neurology, Mass Genl Hosp 1990; **Fellow:** Neurological Biology, Mass Genl Hosp 1992; **Fac Appt:** Prof Ped, Cornell Univ-Weill Med Coll

Legido, Agustin MD/PhD [ChiN] - **Spec Exp:** Mitochondrial Disorders; Neonatal Neurology; Epilepsy; **Hospital:** St. Christopher's Hosp for Chldn; **Address:** St Christopher's Hosp Chldn, Dept Neurology, 3601 A St, Philadelphia, PA 19134; **Phone:** 215-427-5452; **Board Cert:** Pediatrics 2011; Child Neurology 1991; **Med School:** Spain 1980; **Resid:** Pediatrics, St. Christopher's Hosp for Chldn 1989; Neurology, Med Coll PA Affil Hosp 1990; **Fellow:** Child Neurology, Chldns Hosp 1988; **Fac Appt:** Prof Ped, Drexel Univ Coll Med

Maytal, Joseph MD [ChiN] - **Spec Exp:** Epilepsy/Seizure Disorders; Migraine; **Hospital:** Steven & Alexandra Cohen Chldn's Med Ctr of NY (page 66); **Address:** Div Pediatric Neurology, 410 Lakeville Rd, Ste 105, Lake Success, NY 11042; **Phone:** 516-465-5255; **Board Cert:** Pediatrics 1986; Child Neurology 1988; **Med School:** Israel 1979; **Resid:** Pediatrics, Brookdale Univ Hosp Med Ctr 1983; Child Neurology, Montefiore Med Ctr-Einstein Campus 1986; **Fellow:** Neurophysiology, Montefiore Med Ctr-Einstein Campus 1987; **Fac Appt:** Clin Prof N, Albert Einstein Coll Med

Mink, Jonathan W MD/PhD [ChiN] - **Spec Exp:** Movement Disorders; Tourette's Syndrome; Dystonia; **Hospital:** Golisano Chldn's Hosp, Univ Rochester Strong Meml Hosp; **Address:** Golisano Chldns Hosp, Child Neurology, 601 Elmwood Ave, Box 631, Rochester, NY 14642; **Phone:** 585-275-2808; **Board Cert:** Child Neurology 2007; **Med School:** Washington Univ, St Louis 1989; **Resid:** Neurology, Barnes-Jewish Hosp 1992; **Fellow:** Pediatric Neurology, Chldns Hosp 1994; **Fac Appt:** Prof N, Univ Rochester

Nass, Ruth D MD [ChiN] - **Spec Exp:** Autism; ADD/ADHD; Learning Disorders; Migraine; **Hospital:** NYU Langone Med Ctr (page 68); **Address:** 1 Park Ave Fl 7, New York, NY 10016; **Phone:** 212-263-6622; **Board Cert:** Pediatrics 1980; Child Neurology 1981; **Med School:** Albert Einstein Coll Med 1975; **Resid:** Pediatrics, NY-Presby/Weill Cornell Med Ctr 1977; Child Neurology, NY-Presby/Weill Cornell Med Ctr 1980; **Fellow:** Neurology, NY-Presby/Weill Cornell Med Ctr 1982; **Fac Appt:** Prof N, NYU Sch Med

Packer, Roger J MD [ChiN] - **Spec Exp:** Brain Tumors; Neurofibromatosis; **Hospital:** Chldns Natl Med Ctr; **Address:** 111 Michigan Ave NW, MS 20010, Washington, DC 20010-2978; **Phone:** 202-476-6230; **Board Cert:** Child Neurology 1982; Pediatrics 1982; **Med School:** Northwestern Univ 1976; **Resid:** Pediatrics, Chldns Med Ctr 1978; Neurology, Chldns Hosp-Univ Penn 1981; **Fac Appt:** Prof N, Geo Wash Univ

Phillips, Peter C MD [ChiN] - **Spec Exp:** Brain Tumors; Neuro-Oncology; Neurofibromatosis; **Hospital:** Chldns Hosp of Philadelphia; **Address:** Chldn's Hosp Philadelphia, 34th St & Civic Center Blvd, CTRB Bldg - Ste 4027, Philadelphia, PA 19104; **Phone:** 215-590-5188; **Board Cert:** Pediatrics 1985; Child Neurology 1986; **Med School:** Univ Conn 1978; **Resid:** Pediatrics, Chldns Hosp 1980; Neurology, Neuro Inst 1983; **Fellow:** Child Neurology, Meml Sloan Kettering Cancer Ctr 1986; **Fac Appt:** Prof Ped, Univ Pennsylvania

Riviello Jr, James J MD [ChiN] - **Spec Exp:** Epilepsy/Seizure Disorders; Epilepsy in Tuberous Sclerosis; Electrical Status Epilepticus Of Sleep; **Hospital:** Morgan Stanley Children's Hosp of NY-Presby, NY (page 65); **Address:** NY-Presby, Child Neurology, 180 Fort Washington Ave, rm 542, New York, NY 10032; **Phone:** 646-426-3876; **Board Cert:** Pediatrics 1984; Child Neurology 1985; Clinical Neurophysiology 2006; **Med School:** Tufts Univ 1978; **Resid:** Pediatrics, St Christopher Hosp Chldn 1980; Neurology, Temple Univ Hosp 1983; **Fellow:** Pediatric Neurology, St Christopher Hosp Chldn 1983; **Fac Appt:** Prof N, Columbia P&S

Santos, Cesar C MD [ChiN] - **Spec Exp:** Epilepsy; Sleep Disorders; Stroke in Children; Clinical Trials; **Hospital:** MedStar Georgetown Univ Hosp; **Address:** Georgetown Univ Hosp, Peds-Child Neuro, 3800 Reservoir Rd NW, Pasquerilla Healthcare Ctr, Fl 2, Washington, DC 20007; **Phone:** 202-444-8518; **Board Cert:** Child Neurology 2004; Clinical Neurophysiology 2005; **Med School:** Philippines 1982; **Resid:** Pediatrics, St Lukes Roosevelt Hosp 1988; **Fellow:** Pediatric Neurology, Duke Univ Hosp 1991; Neurophysiology, Duke Univ Hosp 1992; **Fac Appt:** Prof Ped, Wake Forest Univ

Shinnar, Shlomo MD/PhD [ChiN] - **Spec Exp:** Epilepsy/Seizure Disorders; Infantile Spasms-West Syndrome; **Hospital:** Montefiore Med Ctr-Moses Campus, NY; **Address:** Montefiore Med Ctr, Pediatric Neurology and Epilepsy, 111 E 210th St, Fl 4, Bronx, NY 10467; **Phone:** 718-920-4378; **Board Cert:** Neurology 1984; Pediatrics 1984; Clinical Neurophysiology 2005; **Med School:** Albert Einstein Coll Med 1978; **Resid:** Pediatrics, Johns Hopkins Hosp 1980; Neurology, Johns Hopkins Hosp 1983; **Fac Appt:** Prof N, Albert Einstein Coll Med

Southeast

Dure IV, Leon S MD [ChiN] - **Spec Exp:** Huntington's Disease; Tourette's Syndrome; Movement Disorders; **Hospital:** Children's Hosp AL, UAB Hosp; **Address:** UAB Pediatric Neurology, 1600 7th Ave S, CHB 314, Birmingham, AL 35233-0011; **Phone:** 205-996-7850; **Board Cert:** Child Neurology 1991; **Med School:** Baylor Coll Med 1984; **Resid:** Pediatrics, NY-Presby/Columbia Univ Med Ctr 1986; Child Neurology, TX Chldns Hosp 1989; **Fellow:** Child Neurology, Univ Michigan Med Ctr 1990; **Fac Appt:** Prof N, UAB Sch Med

Finkel, Richard S MD [ChiN] - **Spec Exp:** Neuromuscular Disorders; **Hospital:** Nemours Chldns Hosp - Orlando; **Address:** Nemours Chldns Clin-Neurology, 1717 S Orange Ave, Ste 100, Orlando, FL 32806; **Phone:** 407-650-7715; **Board Cert:** Pediatrics 1984; Child Neurology 1986; Neuromuscular Medicine 2008; **Med School:** Washington Univ, St Louis 1978; **Resid:** Pediatrics, Chldns Hosp 1980; **Fellow:** Neurology, Brigham & Womens Hosp 1983; **Fac Appt:** Clin Prof Ped, Univ Pennsylvania

Greenwood, Robert S MD [ChiN] - **Spec Exp:** Neurofibromatosis; Epilepsy; **Hospital:** NC Memorial Hosp - UNC; **Address:** 101 Manning Drive, CB #7025, Chapel Hill, NC 27599; **Phone:** 919-966-2528; **Board Cert:** Pediatrics 1974; Child Neurology 1979; **Med School:** Univ Tex Med Br, Galveston 1968; **Resid:** Pediatrics, St Louis Chldns Hosp 1971; Child Neurology, St Louis Chldns Hosp 1975; **Fellow:** Child Neurology, St Louis Chldns Hosp 1977; **Fac Appt:** Prof N, Univ NC Sch Med

Lavenstein, Bennett L MD [ChiN] - **Spec Exp:** Movement Disorders; Neuromuscular Disorders; **Hospital:** Chldns Natl Med Ctr, Inova Fairfax Hosp for Chldn; **Address:** 3023 Hamaker Ct, Ste 300, Fairfax, VA 22031; **Phone:** 571-226-8380; **Board Cert:** Pediatrics 1977; Child Neurology 1979; **Med School:** Univ MD Sch Med 1974; **Resid:** Pediatrics, Univ of MD Hlth System 1977; Neurology, Georgetown Univ Hosp 1979; **Fellow:** Neuromuscular Medicine, Natl Inst Hlth; **Fac Appt:** Assoc Clin Prof N, Univ VA Sch Med

Tennison, Michael MD [ChiN] - **Spec Exp:** Epilepsy; Headache; Neurophysiology; Neurogenetics; **Hospital:** NC Memorial Hosp - UNC; **Address:** 101 Manning Dr, CB 7025 Drive, Chapel Hill, NC 27599-7025; **Phone:** 919-966-2528; **Board Cert:** Pediatrics 1979; Child Neurology 1983; **Med School:** Harvard Med Sch 1975; **Resid:** Pediatrics, Harbor UCLA Med Ctr 1978; Neurology, Univ NC Hosp 1981; **Fellow:** Clinical Neurophysiology, Univ NC Hosp 1984; **Fac Appt:** Prof N, Univ NC Sch Med

Wheless, James W MD [ChiN] - **Spec Exp:** Epilepsy/Seizure Disorders; **Hospital:** Le Bonheur Chldns Med Ctr, St. Jude Children's Research Hosp; **Address:** 848 Adams Ave, Ste L-400, Memphis, TN 38103; **Phone:** 901-287-5060; **Board Cert:** Pediatrics 1987; Child Neurology 1989; Clinical Neurophysiology 2007; **Med School:** Univ Okla Coll Med 1982; **Resid:** Pediatrics, Univ Oklahoma Med Ctr 1985; **Fellow:** Pediatric Neurology, Chldns Meml Hosp 1988; Epilepsy, Med Coll Georgia Affil Hosp 1989; **Fac Appt:** Prof N, Univ Tenn Coll Med

Midwest

Brunstrom-Hernandez, Janice MD [ChiN] - **Spec Exp:** Cerebral Palsy; **Hospital:** St. Louis Chldns Hosp; **Address:** Washington Univ Sch Med, Dept Ped Neuro, 660 S Euclid Ave, Box 8111, St Louis, MO 63110; **Phone:** 314-454-6120; **Board Cert:** Child Neurology 2005; **Med School:** Med Coll VA 1987; **Resid:** Neurology, St Louis Chldns Hosp 1989; Neurology, Barnes Jewish Hosp 1990; **Fellow:** Child Neurology, St Louis Chldns Hosp 1995; **Fac Appt:** Asst Prof N, Washington Univ, St Louis

Cohen, Bruce H MD [ChiN] - **Spec Exp:** Epilepsy; Mitochondrial Disorders; **Hospital:** Akron Children's Hosp; **Address:** Akron Children's Hosp, NeuroDevelopmental Science Ctr, 215 W Bowery St, Akron, OH 44308; **Phone:** 330-543-8050; **Board Cert:** Child Neurology 1990; **Med School:** Albert Einstein Coll Med 1982; **Resid:** Pediatrics, Chldns Hosp 1984; Child Neurology, Neurologic Inst-Columbia 1987; **Fellow:** Pediatric Neuro-Oncology, Chldns Hosp 1989; **Fac Appt:** Prof Ped, NE Ohio Univ

Edgar, Terence S MD [ChiN] - **Spec Exp:** Neuromuscular Disorders; Cerebral Palsy; Epilepsy; **Hospital:** St. Vincent Hosp - Green Bay; **Address:** Prevea Hlth - Allouez Hlth Ctr, 1821 S Webster Fl 3, Green Bay, WI 54301; **Phone:** 920-272-1270; **Board Cert:** Pediatrics 2010; Child Neurology 2006; **Med School:** South Africa 1984; **Resid:** Pediatrics, Univ Wisconsin Hosp & Clin 1995; Child Neurology, Univ Wisconsin Hosp & Clin 1996; **Fellow:** Neuromuscular Disease, Univ Wisconsin Hosp & Clin 1996; Epilepsy, Mayo Clin 2010

Epstein, Leon G MD [ChiN] - **Spec Exp:** Migraine; **Hospital:** Lurie Chldn's Hosp-Chicago; **Address:** Lurie Chldn's Hosp, Div Neurology, 2515 N Clark St, Fl 8, Chicago, IL 60614; **Phone:** 773-880-4352; **Board Cert:** Child Neurology 1979; **Med School:** Wayne State Univ 1973; **Resid:** Neurology, St Josephs Mercy Hosp 1974; Neurology, Univ Arizona Med Ctr 1976; **Fellow:** Neurology, Columbia Presby Med Ctr 1978; **Fac Appt:** Prof Ped, Northwestern Univ

Hershey, Andrew D MD/PhD [ChiN] - **Spec Exp:** Headache; Migraine; **Hospital:** Cincinnati Chldns Hosp Med Ctr; **Address:** Cincinnati Childn's Hosp-Neurology, 3333 Burnet Ave, MC 2015, Cincinnati, OH 45229; **Phone:** 513-636-4222; **Board Cert:** Child Neurology 2008; Headache Medicine 2006; **Med School:** Washington Univ, St Louis 1992; **Resid:** Pediatrics, St Louis Children's Hosp 1994; Neurology, Barnes-Jewish Hosp 1995; **Fellow:** Pediatric Neurology, St Louis Children's Hosp 1997; **Fac Appt:** Prof Ped, Univ Cincinnati

Keating, Gesina F MD [ChiN] - **Spec Exp:** Brain Tumors; Spinal Tumors; Cancer Survivors-Late Effects of Therapy; Chiari's Deformity; **Hospital:** Mayo Med Ctr & Clin - Rochester; **Address:** 200 First St SW, Mayo Clinic, Rochester, MN 55905; **Phone:** 507-284-9974; **Board Cert:** Child Neurology 2008; **Med School:** Mayo Med Sch 1991; **Resid:** Pediatrics, Vanderbilt Univ Med Ctr 1993; Child Neurology, Mayo Clinic 1996; **Fellow:** Pediatric Neuro-Oncology, Beth Israel Med Ctr 1997

Kohrman, Michael H MD [ChiN] - **Spec Exp:** Epilepsy; Seizure Disorders; Sleep Disorders; Tuberous Sclerosis; **Hospital:** Univ Chicago Med-Comer Chldn's Hosp; **Address:** Univ Chicago-Comer Chldn's Hosp, 5841 S Maryland Ave, rm C391, MS 3055, Chicago, IL 60637; **Phone:** 773-702-6487; **Board Cert:** Child Neurology 1987; Pediatrics 1987; Clinical Neurophysiology 2013; Sleep Medicine 2007; **Med School:** Rush Med Coll 1981; **Resid:** Pediatrics, Univ Chicago/Wyler Chldns Hosp 1983; **Fellow:** Pediatric Neurology, Univ Chicago Hosp 1986; Electroencephalography, Univ Chicago Hosp 1987; **Fac Appt:** Prof N, Univ Chicago-Pritzker Sch Med

Kotagal, Suresh MD [ChiN] - **Spec Exp:** Sleep Disorders/Apnea; **Hospital:** Mayo Med Ctr & Clin - Rochester, St. Mary's Hosp - Rochester MN (Mayo); **Address:** Mayo Clinic, 200 First St SW, Rochester, MN 55905-0002; **Phone:** 507-266-0774; **Board Cert:** Pediatrics 1979; Child Neurology 1982; Sleep Medicine 2009; **Med School:** India 1974; **Resid:** Pediatrics, Chldns Hosp 1976; Child Neurology, St Louis Univ Hosp 1979; **Fellow:** Sleep Medicine, Stanford Univ 1982; **Fac Appt:** Prof N, Mayo Med Sch

Kovnar, Edward H MD [ChiN] - **Spec Exp:** Epilepsy/Seizure Disorders; Neurophysiology; Developmental Disorders; **Hospital:** Chldns Hosp - Wisconsin; **Address:** Aurora Advn Hlthcare, 3003 W Good Hope Rd, Milwaukee, WI 53209-0996; **Phone:** 414-352-8828; **Board Cert:** Pediatrics 1984; Child Neurology 1984; Clinical Neurophysiology 2004; Neurodevelopmental Disabilities 2005; **Med School:** Washington Univ, St Louis 1977; **Resid:** Pediatrics, Chldns Hosp 1979; Neurology, Barnes Hosp 1980; **Fellow:** Pediatric Neurology, Chldns Hosp 1982; Clinical Neurophysiology, Chldns Hosp 1991

Noetzel, Michael Justin MD [ChiN] - **Spec Exp:** Cerebral Palsy; Brain Injury; Movement Disorders; **Hospital:** St. Louis Chldns Hosp; **Address:** Washington Univ Ped Neurology Ctr, 660 S Euclid Ave, Box 8111, St Louis, MO 63110; **Phone:** 314-454-6120; **Board Cert:** Child Neurology 1984; Pediatrics 1984; **Med School:** Univ VA Sch Med 1977; **Resid:** Pediatrics, St Louis Chldns Hosp 1979; Neurology, Barnes Hosp 1980; **Fellow:** Child Neurology, St Louis Chldns Hosp 1982; **Fac Appt:** Prof Ped, Washington Univ, St Louis

Nordli Jr, Douglas R MD [ChiN] - **Spec Exp:** Epilepsy; **Hospital:** Lurie Chldn's Hosp-Chicago; **Address:** Lurie Chldn's Hosp-Epilepsy Ctr, 225 E Chicago Ave, Box 29, Chicago, IL 60611; **Phone:** 312-227-3540; **Board Cert:** Child Neurology 1990; **Med School:** Columbia P&S 1984; **Resid:** Pediatrics, Babies Hosp 1986; Child Neurology, Neuro Inst/Columbia-Presby Med Ctr 1989; **Fellow:** Clinical Neurophysiology, Neuro Inst/Columbia-Presby Med Ctr 1990; **Fac Appt:** Prof N, Northwestern Univ

Patterson, Marc C MD [ChiN] - **Spec Exp:** Neurogenetics; Developmental Disorders; Metabolic Disorders; **Hospital:** Mayo Med Ctr & Clin - Rochester; **Address:** Mayo Clinic, Div Child & Adolescent Neurology, 200 First St SW, Rochester, MN 55905; **Phone:** 507-284-3351; **Board Cert:** Child Neurology 2004; Neurodevelopmental Disabilities 2011; **Med School:** Australia 1981; **Resid:** Neurology, Univ Queenland 1988; Child Neurology, Mayo Clinic 1990; **Fellow:** Metabolic Neurology, Natl Inst Health 1992; Pediatrics, Mayo Cilnic 1993; **Fac Appt:** Prof N, Mayo Med Sch

Scher, Mark S MD [ChiN] - **Spec Exp:** Epilepsy; Neonatal Neurology; **Hospital:** UH Rainbow Babies & Chldns Hosp, UH Case Med Ctr; **Address:** UH Rainbow Babies & Children's Hospital, Pediatric Neurology, 11100 Euclid Ave, Cleveland, OH 44106; **Phone:** 216-844-3691; **Board Cert:** Pediatrics 1986; Child Neurology 1983; **Med School:** SUNY Downstate 1976; **Resid:** Pediatrics, NY Presby Hosp 1978; **Fellow:** Pediatric Neurology, Univ MN Med Ctr 1981; Research, Stanford Univ Med Ctr 1983; **Fac Appt:** Prof N, Case West Res Univ

Sivaswamy, Lalitha MD [ChiN] - **Spec Exp:** Headache; Migraine; **Hospital:** Chldns Hosp of Michigan; **Address:** Children's Hosp Michigan, Dept Neurology, 3901 Beaubien Blvd, Detroit, MI 48201; **Phone:** 313-993-2596; **Board Cert:** Child Neurology 2006; Headache Medicine ; **Med School:** India 1989; **Resid:** Pediatrics, Henry Ford Hosp 1996; **Fellow:** Genetics, Chldns Hosp British Columbia 1998; Child Neurology, Chldns Hosp Michigan 2005; **Fac Appt:** Assoc Prof Ped, Univ Mich Med Sch

Tonsgard, James MD [ChiN] - **Spec Exp:** Neurofibromatosis; **Hospital:** Univ Chicago Med-Comer Chldn's Hosp; **Address:** Univ Chicago-Comer Chldn's Hosp, 5721 S Maryland Ave, Chicago, IL 60637; **Phone:** 773-702-6487; **Board Cert:** Pediatrics 1981; **Med School:** Yale Univ 1975; **Resid:** Pediatrics, Yale-New Haven Hosp 1977; Neurology, Univ Chicago Hosp 1980; **Fellow:** Child Neurology, Univ Chicago Hosp 1981; **Fac Appt:** Assoc Prof Ped, Univ Chicago-Pritzker Sch Med

Tuxhorn, Ingrid E MD [ChiN] - **Spec Exp:** Epilepsy; Gravet Syndrome; **Hospital:** UH Rainbow Babies & Chldns Hosp, UH Case Med Ctr; **Address:** UH Rainbow Babies & Children's Hospital, Pediatric Epileptology, 11100 Euclid Ave, MS 6009, Cleveland, OH 44106; **Phone:** 216-286-6644; **Board Cert:** Pediatrics 1985; **Med School:** Africa 1975; **Resid:** Pediatrics, Baystate Med Ctr 1982; Pediatrics, Yale-New Haven Hosp 1983; **Fellow:** Pediatric Neurology, U Mass Meml Med Ctr 1990; Neurophysiology, Cleveland Clinic 1992

Wiznitzer, Max MD [ChiN] - **Hospital:** UH Rainbow Babies & Chldns Hosp; **Address:** Rainbow Babies & Chldns Hosp, Pediatric Neurology, 11100 Euclid Ave, Cleveland, OH 44106; **Phone:** 216-844-3691; **Board Cert:** Pediatrics 1982; Child Neurology 1986; Neurodevelopmental Disabilities 2004; **Med School:** Northwestern Univ 1977; **Resid:** Pediatrics, Chldns Hosp Med Ctr 1980; **Fellow:** Developmental-Behavioral Pediatrics, Cincinnati Med Ctr 1981; Pediatric Neurology, Chldns Hosp 1984; **Fac Appt:** Assoc Prof Ped, Case West Res Univ

Wyllie, Elaine MD [ChiN] - **Spec Exp:** Epilepsy/Seizure Disorders; **Hospital:** Cleveland Clin (page 55); **Address:** Cleveland Clinic, Epilepsy Center, 9500 Euclid Ave, Desk S5-1, Cleveland, OH 44195; **Phone:** 216-444-5559; **Board Cert:** Pediatrics 1982; Child Neurology 1986; **Med School:** Indiana Univ 1978; **Resid:** Pediatrics, Indiana Univ Med Ctr 1980; Pediatrics, Case West Med Ctr 1981; **Fellow:** Neurophysiology, Cleveland Clinic 1984; Pediatric Neurology, Cleveland Clinic 1985

Yamada, Kelvin A MD [ChiN] - **Spec Exp:** Epilepsy; **Hospital:** St. Louis Chldns Hosp; **Address:** Washington Univ Ped Neurology Ctr, 660 S Euclid Ave, Box 8111, Saint Louis, MO 63110; **Phone:** 314-454-6120; **Board Cert:** Pediatrics 2011; Child Neurology 1990; Clinical Neurophysiology 2004; Sleep Medicine 2007; **Med School:** Baylor Coll Med 1983; **Resid:** Pediatrics, Baylor Coll Affil Hosp 1985; Neurology, Barnes-Jewish Hosp 1986; **Fellow:** Child Neurology, St Louis Chldn's Hosp 1990; **Fac Appt:** Assoc Prof N, Washington Univ, St Louis

Great Plains and Mountains

Bale Jr, James F MD [ChiN] - **Spec Exp:** Infections-Neurologic; Infections-Congenital; **Hospital:** Primary Children's Med Ctr, Univ Utah Hlth Care; **Address:** Primary Chldns Med Ctr, 100 N Mario Capecchi Drive, Salt Lake City, UT 84113; **Phone:** 801-587-7575; **Board Cert:** Pediatrics 2002; Child Neurology 1982; **Med School:** Univ Mich Med Sch 1975; **Resid:** Pediatrics, Univ Utah Hosps 1977; Neurology, Univ Utah Hosps 1980; **Fellow:** Infectious Disease, Univ Utah Hosps 1981; Neurovirology, UCSF-VA Med Ctr 1982; **Fac Appt:** Prof N, Univ Utah

Southwest

Filipek, Pauline A MD [ChiN] - **Spec Exp:** Autism; Autism in Infants; Developmental Disorders; **Hospital:** Children's Meml Hermann Hosp; **Address:** Autism Ctr-Childrens Learning Institute, 7000 Fannin St, Ste 2453, Houston, TX 77030; **Phone:** 713-500-3600; **Board Cert:** Pediatrics 1985; Child Neurology 2010; **Med School:** Georgetown Univ 1980; **Resid:** Pediatrics, Univ Mass Med Ctr 1983; Child Neurology, Mass Genl Hosp 1986; **Fellow:** Neuroimaging, Mass Genl Hosp 1987; **Fac Appt:** Prof Ped, Univ Tex, Houston

Iannaccone, Susan T MD [ChiN] - **Spec Exp:** Neuromuscular Disorders; **Hospital:** Chldns Med Ctr of Dallas, UT Southwestern Med Ctr at Dallas; **Address:** Children's Medical Ctr, 2350 Stemmons Frwy, Ste 5074, Dallas, TX 75207; **Phone:** 214-456-5220; **Board Cert:** Pediatrics 1975; Child Neurology 1976; **Med School:** SUNY Hlth Sci Ctr 1969; **Resid:** Pediatrics, St Louis Chldns Hosp 1972; Neurology, Strong Meml Hosp 1975; **Fellow:** Neurology, Strong Meml Hosp 1975; **Fac Appt:** Prof N, Univ Tex SW, Dallas

Sharp, Gregory B MD [ChiN] - **Spec Exp:** Epilepsy; **Hospital:** UAMS Med Ctr, Arkansas Chldns Hosp; **Address:** 1 Children's Way, Little Rock, AR 72202; **Phone:** 501-364-1850; **Board Cert:** Pediatrics 2011; Child Neurology 1993; **Med School:** Univ Ark 1984; **Resid:** Pediatrics, Univ Ark Chldns Hosp 1987; **Fellow:** Pediatric Neurology, Mayo Clinic 1990; **Fac Appt:** Prof Ped, Univ Ark

West Coast and Pacific

Ashwal, Stephen MD [ChiN] - **Hospital:** Loma Linda Chldns Hosp; **Address:** Pediatric Neuroscience Ctr, 2195 Club Ctr Drive, Ste A, San Bernadino, CA 92408; **Phone:** 909-835-1810; **Board Cert:** Pediatrics 1975; Child Neurology 1978; **Med School:** NYU Sch Med 1970; **Resid:** Pediatrics, Bellevue Hosp 1973; **Fellow:** Child Neurology, Univ Minn Med Ctr 1976; **Fac Appt:** Prof Ped, Loma Linda Univ

Fisher, Paul G MD [ChiN] - **Spec Exp:** Neuro-Oncology; Brain Tumors; **Hospital:** Lucile Packard Chldn's Hosp; **Address:** Stanford Cancer Ctr-Dept Neurology, 750 Welch Rd, Ste 206, Palo Alto, CA 94304; **Phone:** 650-497-8953; **Board Cert:** Child Neurology 2008; **Med School:** UCSF 1989; **Resid:** Pediatrics, Johns Hopkins Univ Hosp 1991; Neurology, Johns Hopkins Univ Hosp 1994; **Fellow:** Neuro-Oncology, Children's Hosp 1995; **Fac Appt:** Prof Ped, Stanford Univ

Gospe Jr, Sidney M MD/PhD [ChiN] - **Spec Exp:** Epilepsy/Seizure Disorders; Neuromuscular Disorders; Neurotoxicology; **Hospital:** Seattle Chldns Hosp; **Address:** Seattle Children's Hospital, 4800 Sand Point Way NE, MS MB.7.410, Seattle, WA 98105; **Phone:** 206-987-2078; **Board Cert:** Pediatrics 2005; Child Neurology 2010; **Med School:** Duke Univ 1981; **Resid:** Pediatrics, Baylor Coll Med 1983; **Fellow:** Child Neurology, Baylor Coll Med 1986; **Fac Appt:** Prof N, Univ Wash

Haas, Richard H MD [ChiN] - **Spec Exp:** Mitochondrial Disorders; Neurometabolic Disorders; **Hospital:** UCSD Med Ctr, Rady Children's Hosp - San Diego; **Address:** UCSD Sch Med, Div Ped Neuro, 9500 Gilman Drive, MC 0935, La Jolla, CA 92093-0935; **Phone:** 858-966-5819; **Board Cert:** Child Neurology 1983; Pediatrics 1985; **Med School:** England, UK 1972; **Resid:** Pediatrics, Univ London 1979; Child Neurology, Univ Colo Hlth Sci Ctr 1981; **Fellow:** Biochemical Mental Retardation, Univ Colo Hlth Sci Ctr 1983; **Fac Appt:** Prof Ped, UCSD

Lott, Ira T MD [ChiN] - **Spec Exp:** Down Syndrome; **Hospital:** Chldns Hosp Orange Co, UC Irvine Med Ctr; **Address:** CHOC Childrens Neurology Ctr, 1120 W La Veta Ave, Ste 125, Orange, CA 92868-3874; **Phone:** 714-509-7601; **Board Cert:** Pediatrics 1975; Child Neurology 1977; **Med School:** Ohio State Univ 1967; **Resid:** Pediatrics, Mass Genl Hosp 1969; **Fellow:** Research, Natl Inst Hlth 1971; Neurology, Harvard-Mass Genl Hosp 1974; **Fac Appt:** Prof N, UC Irvine

Mitchell, Wendy G MD [ChiN] - **Spec Exp:** Epilepsy/Seizure Disorders; Opsoclonus-Ataxia in Children; Neurodegenerative Disorders; **Hospital:** Chldns Hosp - Los Angeles; **Address:** Chldns Hosp Los Angeles, Dept Neuro, 4650 Sunset Blvd, MS 82, Los Angeles, CA 90027-6062; **Phone:** 323-361-2498; **Board Cert:** Pediatrics 1978; Child Neurology 1983; **Med School:** UCSF 1973; **Resid:** Pediatrics, Moffit Hosp-UCSF 1975; Child Neurology, Univ North Carolina 1976; **Fellow:** Behavioral Pediatrics, Mt Zion Med Ctr 1978; **Fac Appt:** Prof N, USC Sch Med

Pinter, Joseph D MD [ChiN] - **Spec Exp:** Down Syndrome; Tourette's Syndrome; **Hospital:** Doernbecher Chldns Hosp/OHSU; **Address:** OHSU, Dept Child Neurology, 707 SW Gaines Rd, MC CDRCP, Portland, OR 97239; **Phone:** 503-494-5856; **Board Cert:** Child Neurology 2008; **Med School:** UCLA 1990; **Resid:** Pediatrics, Univ Washington/Cedars Sinai Med Ctr 1993; Child Neurology, Chldn's Hosp 1996; **Fellow:** Neurological Science, UCSF Med Ctr 1999; **Fac Appt:** Assoc Prof N, Oregon Hlth & Sci Univ

Roddy, Sarah M MD [ChiN] - **Spec Exp:** Tourette's Syndrome; ADD/ADHD; **Hospital:** Loma Linda Chldns Hosp; **Address:** Pediatric Neuroscience Ctr, 2195 Club Ctr Drive, Ste A, San Bernadino, CA 92408; **Phone:** 909-835-1810; **Board Cert:** Child Neurology 1987; Pediatrics 1987; **Med School:** Loma Linda Univ 1980; **Resid:** Pediatrics, Loma Linda Univ Med Ctr 1983; **Fellow:** Pediatric Neurology, Loma Linda Univ Med Ctr 1986; **Fac Appt:** Assoc Prof N, Loma Linda Univ

Rosser, Tena L MD [ChiN] - **Spec Exp:** Neurocutaneous Disorders; Neurofibromatosis; Tuberous Sclerosis; **Hospital:** Chldns Hosp - Los Angeles; **Address:** Chldns Hosp Los Angeles, Dept Neurology, 4650 Sunset Blvd, MS 82, Los Angeles, CA 90027-6062; **Phone:** 323-361-2471; **Board Cert:** Pediatrics 2007; Child Neurology 2003; **Med School:** Univ NC Sch Med 1996; **Resid:** Pediatrics, Chldn's Natl Med Ctr 1999; **Fellow:** Child Neurology, Chldn's Natl Med Ctr 2003; **Fac Appt:** Asst Prof N, USC-Keck School of Medicine

Sankar, Raman MD/PhD [ChiN] - **Spec Exp:** Epilepsy/Seizure Disorders; Headache; Migraine; **Hospital:** Mattel Chldns Hosp at UCLA, UCLA Ronald Reagan Med Ctr; **Address:** UCLA Sch Med-Div Ped Neurology, 10833 Le Conte Ave, rm 22-474, Los Angeles, CA 90095; **Phone:** 310-825-6196; **Board Cert:** Child Neurology 2005; **Med School:** Tulane Univ 1986; **Resid:** Pediatrics, Chldns Hosp 1988; Neurology, UCLA Med Ctr 1989; **Fellow:** Child Neurology, UCLA Med Ctr 1991; **Fac Appt:** Prof Ped, UCLA

Trauner, Doris A MD [ChiN] - **Spec Exp:** Autism; Speech Disorders; **Hospital:** Rady Children's Hosp - San Diego; **Address:** Rady Chldn's Specialists, 8010 Frost St, Ste 400, San Diego, CA 92123; **Phone:** 858-966-5819; **Board Cert:** Pediatrics 1978; Child Neurology 1979; Neurodevelopmental Disabilities 2011; **Med School:** Med Coll VA 1972; **Resid:** Pediatrics, UCSD Med Ctr 1974; Neurology, UCSD Med Ctr 1975; **Fellow:** Child Neurology, Univ Chicago 1977; **Fac Appt:** Prof Ped, UCSD

Zupanc, Mary L MD [ChiN] - **Spec Exp:** Epilepsy; **Hospital:** Chldns Hosp Orange Co; **Address:** CHOC Childrens Neurology Ctr, 1120 W La Veta Ave, Ste 125, Orange, CA 92868-3874; **Phone:** 714-509-7602; **Board Cert:** Pediatrics 1985; Child Neurology 2010; Clinical Neurophysiology 2006; **Med School:** UCLA 1979; **Resid:** Pediatrics, Univ Wash Med Ctr 1981; Pediatrics, UCLA-Harbor Med Ctr 1982; **Fellow:** Pediatric Neurology, Univ Wisconsin 1985

Top Doctors Make A Difference

Clinical Genetics

A specialist trained in diagnostic and therapeutic procedures for patients with genetically-linked diseases. This specialist uses modern cytogenetic, radiologic and biochemical testing to assist in specialized genetic counseling, implements needed therapeutic interventions and provides prevention through prenatal diagnosis.

A clinical geneticist demonstrates competence in providing comprehensive diagnostic, management and counseling services for genetic disorders.

A medical geneticist plans and coordinates large scale screening programs for inborn errors of metabolism, hemoglobinopathies, chromosome abnormalities and neural tube defects.

Training Required: Two or four years

CLINICAL GENETICS

New England

Bale, Allen E MD [CG] - **Spec Exp:** Cancer Genetics; **Hospital:** Yale-New Haven Hosp; **Address:** Yale-New Haven, Genetics Dept, 333 Cedar St SHM Bldg - rm 329, New Haven, CT 06510; **Phone:** 203-764-8400; **Board Cert:** Internal Medicine 1983; Clinical Genetics 1987; Clinical Molecular Genetics 2010; **Med School:** Univ Mass Sch Med 1979; **Resid:** Internal Medicine, Western Penn Hosp 1983; **Fellow:** Medical Genetics, Natl Inst Hlth-Clin Ctr 1987; **Fac Appt:** Prof CG, Yale Univ

Bianchi, Diana MD [CG] - **Spec Exp:** Prenatal Genetic Diagnosis; Fetal Abnormalities; Twin to Twin Transfusion Syndrome (TTTS); **Hospital:** Tufts Med Ctr; **Address:** Tufts Med Ctr, Div of Genetics, 800 Washington St, Box 394, Boston, MA 02111; **Phone:** 617-636-1468; **Board Cert:** Pediatrics 1985; Clinical Genetics 1987; Neonatal-Perinatal Medicine 1987; **Med School:** Stanford Univ 1980; **Resid:** Pediatrics, Chldns Hosp 1983; **Fellow:** Neonatology, Chldns Hosp 1986; Clinical Genetics, Harvard Med Sch 1987; **Fac Appt:** Prof Ped, Tufts Univ

Holmes, Lewis B MD [CG] - **Spec Exp:** Birth Defects; Inherited Disorders; Prenatal Diagnosis; **Hospital:** Mass Genl Hosp, Brigham & Women's Hosp; **Address:** Mass Genl Hosp, Dept Pediatrics, 175 Cambridge St Fl 5 - rm 504, Boston, MA 02114; **Phone:** 617-726-1742; **Board Cert:** Pediatrics 1968; Clinical Genetics 1982; **Med School:** Duke Univ 1963; **Resid:** Pediatrics, Mass Genl Hosp 1965; **Fellow:** Pediatric Endocrinology, Mass Genl Hosp 1966; **Fac Appt:** Prof Ped, Harvard Med Sch

Mahoney, Maurice J MD [CG] - **Spec Exp:** Fetal Therapy; Prenatal Diagnosis; **Hospital:** Yale-New Haven Hosp; **Address:** Yale Genetics Consultation Serv, 333 Cedar St, rm WWW330, New Haven, CT 06520-8005; **Phone:** 203-785-2661; **Board Cert:** Pediatrics 1967; Clinical Genetics 1982; Clinical Biochemical Genetics 1982; **Med School:** Univ Pittsburgh 1962; **Resid:** Pediatrics, Johns Hopkins Hosp 1965; Pediatrics, Childrens Hosp 1966; **Fellow:** Clinical Genetics, Yale Univ Sch Med 1970; **Fac Appt:** Prof CG, Yale Univ

Pauker, Susan P MD [CG] - **Spec Exp:** Prenatal Diagnosis; Marfan's Syndrome; **Hospital:** Brigham & Women's Hosp; **Address:** Harvard Vanguard Med Associates, 133 Brookline Ave, Boston, MA 02215-3904; **Phone:** 617-421-3320; **Board Cert:** Pediatrics 1976; Clinical Genetics 1987; **Med School:** Tufts Univ 1971; **Resid:** Pediatrics, Mass Genl Hosp 1973; **Fellow:** Clinical Genetics, Mass Genl Hosp 1975; **Fac Appt:** Assoc Clin Prof Ped, Harvard Med Sch

Seashore, Margretta R MD [CG] - **Spec Exp:** Inherited Metabolic Disorders; Inborn Errors of Metabolism; **Hospital:** Yale-New Haven Hosp; **Address:** 1 Park St, New Haven, CT 06520-8005; **Phone:** 203-785-2660 x1; **Board Cert:** Pediatrics 1970; Clinical Biochemical Genetics 1982; Clinical Genetics 1982; **Med School:** Yale Univ 1965; **Resid:** Pediatrics, Yale-New Haven Hosp 1968; **Fellow:** Clinical Genetics, Yale-New Haven Hosp 1970; **Fac Appt:** Prof CG, Yale Univ

Mid Atlantic

Anyane-Yeboa, Kwame MD [CG] - **Spec Exp:** Dysmorphology; Prenatal Diagnosis; **Hospital:** Morgan Stanley Children's Hosp of NY-Presby, NY (page 65); **Address:** Morgan Stanley Chldn's Hosp NY, 3959 Broadway, rm 718N, New York, NY 10032; **Phone:** 212-305-6731; **Board Cert:** Pediatrics 1979; Clinical Genetics 1982; **Med School:** Ghana 1972; **Resid:** Pediatrics, Harlem Hosp Ctr 1977; **Fellow:** Clinical Genetics, Columbia P&S 1980; **Fac Appt:** Assoc Prof Ped, Columbia P&S

Bialer, Martin G MD/PhD [CG] - **Spec Exp:** Marfan's Syndrome; Neurofibromatosis; Metabolic Genetic Disorders; Cancer Genetics; **Hospital:** Steven & Alexandra Cohen Chldn's Med Ctr of NY (page 66), NS-LIJ Hlth Sys (page 66); **Address:** 1554 Northern Blvd, Ste 204, Manhasset, NY 11030; **Phone:** 516-365-3996; **Board Cert:** Pediatrics 1987; Clinical Biochemical Genetics 1990; Clinical Genetics 1990; **Med School:** Med Univ SC 1983; **Resid:** Pediatrics, N Shore Univ Hosp 1986; **Fellow:** Clinical Genetics, Univ of VA Hlth Sys 1989; **Fac Appt:** Clin Prof Ped, NYU Sch Med

Chung, Wendy Kay MD [CG] - **Spec Exp:** Cancer Genetics; Metabolic Genetic Disorders; **Hospital:** NY-Presby/Columbia Univ Med Ctr, NY (page 65); **Address:** 3959 Broadway Ave, New York, NY 10032; **Phone:** 212-305-6731; **Board Cert:** Clinical Genetics 2002; Clinical Molecular Genetics 2005; **Med School:** Cornell Univ 1998; **Resid:** Clinical Genetics, NY-Presby/Columbia Univ Med Ctr 2002; **Fellow:** Genetics, NY-Presby/Columbia Univ Med Ctr 2003; **Fac Appt:** Asst Prof Ped, Columbia P&S

Davis, Jessica G MD [CG] - **Spec Exp:** Marfan's Syndrome; Mental Retardation; Neurofibromatosis; Ehlers-Danlos Syndrome; **Hospital:** NY-Presby/Weill Cornell Med Ctr, NY (page 65), Hosp For Special Surgery (page 58); **Address:** 505 E 70th St, Box 128, New York, NY 10065; **Phone:** 646-962-2205; **Board Cert:** Clinical Genetics 1984; **Med School:** Columbia P&S 1959; **Resid:** Pediatrics, St Luke's Hosp 1962; Clinical Genetics, Albert Einstein Coll Med Affil Hosp 1965; **Fellow:** Cytogenetics, Albert Einstein Coll Med Affil Hosp 1966; Pediatrics, Albert Einstein Col Med Affil Hosp 1968; **Fac Appt:** Assoc Clin Prof Ped, Cornell Univ-Weill Med Coll

Desnick, Robert J MD/PhD [CG] - **Spec Exp:** Inherited Metabolic Disorders; Lysosomal Diseases; Gaucher Disease; Porphyria; **Hospital:** Mt Sinai Med Ctr (page 62); **Address:** Mount Sinai Med Ctr, Icahn Med Inst, 1425 Madison Ave, Fl 14, rm 14-34, Box 1498, New York, NY 10029; **Phone:** 212-659-6700; **Board Cert:** Clinical Genetics 1982; Clinical Biochemical Genetics 1982; Clinical Molecular Genetics 2009; **Med School:** Univ Minn 1971; **Resid:** Pediatrics, Univ Minn Affil Hosp 1973; **Fac Appt:** Prof Emeritus CG, Mount Sinai Sch Med

Desposito, Franklin MD [CG] - **Spec Exp:** Birth Defects; Genetic Disorders; **Hospital:** Univ Hosp (Newark), Saint Barnabas Med Ctr; **Address:** 90 Bergen St, Ste 5400, Newark, NJ 07103; **Phone:** 973-972-3300; **Board Cert:** Pediatrics 1986; Clinical Genetics 1982; Clinical Cytogenetics 1990; Clinical Molecular Genetics 2010; **Med School:** Ros Franklin Univ/Chicago Med Sch 1957; **Resid:** Pediatrics, Long Island Jewish Hosp 1961; **Fellow:** Hematology, Univ Wisc Sch Med 1963; **Fac Appt:** Prof Ped, UMDNJ-NJ Med Sch, Newark

Driscoll, Deborah A MD [CG] - **Spec Exp:** Prenatal Genetic Diagnosis; Fetal Abnormalities; **Hospital:** Hosp Univ Penn - UPHS (page 69); **Address:** Hosp Univ Penn - UPHS, Dept Obstetrics & Gynecology, 3400 Spruce St, 5 Dulles, Philadelphia, PA 19104; **Phone:** 215-662-3232; **Board Cert:** Obstetrics & Gynecology 2013; Clinical Genetics 1990; **Med School:** NYU Sch Med 1983; **Resid:** Obstetrics & Gynecology, Hosp Univ Penn - UPHS 1987; **Fellow:** Clinical Genetics, Hosp Univ Penn - UPHS 1989; **Fac Appt:** Prof ObG, Univ Pennsylvania

Gilbert, Fred MD [CG] - **Spec Exp:** Cancer Genetics; Dysmorphology; **Hospital:** NY-Presby/Weill Cornell Med Ctr, NY (page 65), Brooklyn Hosp Ctr; **Address:** Pediatric Genetics, 240 Willoughby St, Ste 9K, Brooklyn, NY 11201; **Phone:** 718-250-6227; **Board Cert:** Clinical Genetics 1982; Clinical Cytogenetics 1982; **Med School:** Albert Einstein Coll Med 1966; **Resid:** Internal Medicine, Barnes Hosp 1968; Internal Medicine, Natl Inst Hlth 1971; **Fellow:** Clinical Genetics, Yale-New Haven Hosp 1974; **Fac Appt:** Assoc Prof Ped, Cornell Univ-Weill Med Coll

Kronn, David F MD [CG] - **Spec Exp:** Bone Disorders-Metabolic; Bone Disorders-Inherited; **Hospital:** Westchester Med Ctr, Children's & Women's Phys.of Westchester; **Address:** Regional Medical Genetics, 503 Grasslands Rd, Ste 200, Valhalla, NY 10595; **Phone:** 914-304-5280; **Board Cert:** Clinical Genetics 2010; Clinical Biochemical Genetics 2010; **Med School:** Ireland 1989; **Resid:** Pediatrics, NYU Med Ctr 1996; **Fellow:** Clinical Genetics, NYU Med Ctr 1996; **Fac Appt:** Assoc Prof CG, NY Med Coll

Marion, Robert W MD [CG] - **Spec Exp:** Spina Bifida; Williams Syndrome; Marfan's Syndrome; Down Syndrome; **Hospital:** Montefiore Med Ctr-Moses Campus, NY, Blythedale Children's Hosp; **Address:** 3415 Bainbridge Ave, Bronx, NY 10467; **Phone:** 718-741-2323; **Board Cert:** Pediatrics 1985; Clinical Genetics 1987; **Med School:** Albert Einstein Coll Med 1979; **Resid:** Pediatrics, Einstein Affil Hosp 1982; **Fellow:** Clinical Genetics, Einstein Affil Hosp 1984; **Fac Appt:** Prof Ped, Albert Einstein Coll Med

Ostrer, Harry MD [CG] - **Spec Exp:** Genetic Disorders; Hereditary Cancer; **Hospital:** Montefiore Med Ctr-Wakefield Campus, NY; **Address:** Albert Einstein College of Medicine, 1300 Morris Park Ave, Ullman Blg, rm 819, Bronx, NY 10461; **Phone:** 718-430-8605; **Board Cert:** Clinical Genetics 1984; Pediatrics 1985; Clinical Cytogenetics 1990; Clinical Molecular Genetics 2010; **Med School:** Columbia P&S 1976; **Resid:** Pediatrics, Johns Hopkins Hosp 1978; Clinical Genetics, Johns Hopkins Hosp 1984; **Fellow:** Molecular Genetics, Natl Inst Health 1981; **Fac Appt:** Prof Path, Albert Einstein Coll Med

Pyeritz, Reed E MD/PhD [CG] - **Spec Exp:** Marfan's Syndrome; Hereditary Hemorrhagic Telangiectasia; Inherited Disorders; **Hospital:** Hosp Univ Penn - UPHS (page 69), Chldns Hosp of Philadelphia; **Address:** Perelman Ctr-Med Genetics, 3400 Civic Ctr Blvd, South Pavilion Fl 1, Philadelphia, PA 19104; **Phone:** 215-662-4740; **Board Cert:** Internal Medicine 1978; Clinical Genetics 1982; **Med School:** Harvard Med Sch 1975; **Resid:** Internal Medicine, Brigham & Women's Hosp 1978; Clinical Genetics, Johns Hopkins Hosp 1982; **Fac Appt:** Prof CG, Univ Pennsylvania

Rosenbaum, Kenneth MD [CG] - **Spec Exp:** Birth Defects; **Hospital:** Chldns Natl Med Ctr, Shady Grove Adven Hosp; **Address:** Chldns Natl Med Ctr, Dept Med Genetics, 111 Michigan Ave NW, Ste 1950, Washington, DC 20010; **Phone:** 202-476-6287; **Board Cert:** Pediatrics 1976; Clinical Genetics 1982; Clinical Cytogenetics 1982; **Med School:** Univ Louisville Sch Med 1971; **Resid:** Pediatrics, Childrens Natl Med Ctr 1974; **Fellow:** Clinical Genetics, Johns Hopkins Hosp 1977; **Fac Appt:** Assoc Prof Ped, Geo Wash Univ

Wasserstein, Melissa MD [CG] - **Spec Exp:** Phenylketonuria (PKU); Fabry's Disease; Metabolic Genetic Disorders; **Hospital:** Mt Sinai Med Ctr (page 62); **Address:** Mt Sinai Med Ctr, Clin Genetics, 1428 Madison Ave, rm AB1-12, New York, NY 10029; **Phone:** 212-241-6947; **Board Cert:** Pediatrics 2010; Clinical Biochemical Genetics 2010; **Med School:** NYU Sch Med 1992; **Resid:** Pediatrics, Mt Sinai Med Ctr 1995; **Fellow:** Clinical Genetics, Mt Sinai Med Ctr 1997; **Fac Appt:** Assoc Prof CG, Mount Sinai Sch Med

Zackai, Elaine MD [CG] - **Spec Exp:** Craniosynostosis; Cytogenetic Disorders; **Hospital:** Chldns Hosp of Philadelphia; **Address:** Chldns Hosp Philadelphia, Dept Clin Genetics, 3400 Civic Ctr Blvd, rm 8C05, Philadelphia, PA 19104; **Phone:** 215-590-2920; **Board Cert:** Pediatrics 1977; Clinical Genetics 1982; Clinical Cytogenetics 1982; **Med School:** NYU Sch Med 1968; **Resid:** Pediatrics, Chldns Hosp 1970; **Fellow:** Clinical Genetics, Chldns Hosp 1971; Clinical Genetics, Yale Univ Med Sch 1972; **Fac Appt:** Prof Ped, Univ Pennsylvania

Southeast

Driscoll, Daniel J MD/PhD [CG] - **Spec Exp:** Prader-Willi Syndrome; Obesity-Pediatric; Angelman Syndrome; **Hospital:** UF Hlth Shands Hosp; **Address:** UF Hlth, Pediatric Genetics, 1600 SW Archer Rd, Ste M346, Gainesville, FL 32610; **Phone:** 352-294-5050; **Board Cert:** Pediatrics 1987; Clinical Genetics 1990; Clinical Cytogenetics 1990; **Med School:** Albany Med Coll 1983; **Resid:** Pediatrics, Johns Hopkins Hosp 1986; **Fellow:** Clinical Genetics, Johns Hopkins Hosp 1989; **Fac Appt:** Prof Ped, Univ Fla Coll Med

Jayakar, Parul MD [CG] - **Spec Exp:** Neurogenetics; **Hospital:** Univ of Miami Hosp, Baptist Hosp of Miami; **Address:** Miami Chldns Hosp, Brain Inst, 3100 SW 62nd Ave Fl 3, Miami, FL 33155; **Phone:** 786-624-4717; **Board Cert:** Clinical Genetics 2004; Pediatrics 2004; Clinical Genetics 2010; Clinical Biochemical Genetics 2005; **Med School:** India 1978; **Resid:** Internal Medicine, Lady Hardinge Med Sch 1980; Clinical Genetics, Jackson Meml Hosp 1992

Korf, Bruce R MD/PhD [CG] - **Spec Exp:** Inherited Disorders; Neurogenetics; Neurofibromatosis; **Hospital:** UAB Hosp; **Address:** UAB Dept Genetics, Kirklin Clin, 720 20th St S, KAUL 230, Birmingham, AL 35294-0024; **Phone:** 205-934-4983; **Board Cert:** Clinical Genetics 1984; Child Neurology 1986; Pediatrics 1988; Clinical Molecular Genetics 2010; **Med School:** Cornell Univ-Weill Med Coll 1980; **Resid:** Pediatrics, Chldns Hosp 1982; Child Neurology, Chldns Hosp 1985; **Fellow:** Clinical Genetics, Chldns Hosp 1985; **Fac Appt:** Prof CG, UAB Sch Med

Shoffner IV, John M MD [CG] - **Spec Exp:** Mitochondrial Disorders; Angelman Syndrome; Prader-Willi Syndrome; Neurogenetics; **Hospital:** Northside Hosp, Chldns Hlthcare Atlanta @ Scottish Rite; **Address:** Med Neurogenetics Lab, 5505 Peachtree Dunwoody Rd, Ste 580, Atlanta, GA 30342; **Phone:** 678-225-0222; **Board Cert:** Neurology 1992; Clinical Molecular Genetics 2013; Clinical Biochemical Genetics 2013; **Med School:** Emory Univ 1985; **Resid:** Neurology, Emory Univ Hosp 1989; **Fac Appt:** Assoc Prof CG, Emory Univ

Stevenson, Roger E MD [CG] - **Spec Exp:** Birth Defects; Mental Retardation; **Hospital:** Self Regional Healthcare; **Address:** Greenwood Genetic Ctr, 113 Gregor Mendel Cir, Research Bldg, Greenwood, SC 29646; **Phone:** 864-941-8146; **Board Cert:** Pediatrics 1971; Clinical Genetics 1982; Clinical Cytogenetics 1984; **Med School:** Wake Forest Univ 1966; **Resid:** Pediatrics, Johns Hopkins Hosp 1969; **Fellow:** Clinical Genetics, Johns Hopkins Hosp 1972

Sutphen, Rebecca MD [CG] - **Spec Exp:** Genetic Disorders; Hereditary Cancer; Cancer Risk Assessment; **Hospital:** Moffitt Canc Ctr (page 61); **Address:** 3650 Spectrum Blvd, MDC 221, Tampa, FL 33612; **Phone:** 813-396-9224; **Board Cert:** Clinical Molecular Genetics 2010; Clinical Genetics 2010; **Med School:** Temple Univ 1990; **Resid:** Pediatrics, All Children's Hosp 1993; **Fellow:** Clinical Genetics, Univ S Fla Coll Med 1995; **Fac Appt:** Prof CG, Univ S Fla Coll Med

Ward, Jewell C MD/PhD [CG] - **Spec Exp:** Inborn Errors of Metabolism; Metabolic Genetic Disorders; Phenylketonuria (PKU); Reproductive Genetics; **Hospital:** Le Bonheur Chldns Med Ctr; **Address:** UT Le Bonheur Pediatric Specialists, 51 N Dunlap St, Ste 400, Memphis, TN 38105; **Phone:** 901-866-8818; **Board Cert:** Clinical Genetics 1982; Clinical Biochemical Genetics 1982; **Med School:** Indiana Univ 1971; **Resid:** Pediatrics, Ohio's Chldns Hosp 1974; **Fellow:** Medical Genetics, Indiana Univ Affil Hosp 1975; Medical Genetics, Johns Hopkins Univ Hosp 1979; **Fac Appt:** Prof Ped, Univ Tenn Coll Med

Midwest

Bartholomew, Dennis W MD [CG] - **Spec Exp:** Genetic Disorders; **Hospital:** Nationwide Chldn's Hosp; **Address:** Nationwide Chldn's Hosp: Timken Hall, 700 Children's Drive Fl 2, Columbus, OH 43205; **Phone:** 614-722-3537; **Board Cert:** Pediatrics 1986; Clinical Biochemical Genetics 1990; Clinical Genetics 1987; **Med School:** Northwestern Univ 1980; **Resid:** Pediatrics, David Grant Med Ctr 1983; **Fellow:** Genetics, Johns Hopkins Hosp 1987; **Fac Appt:** Assoc Clin Prof Ped, Ohio State Univ

Burton, Barbara MD [CG] - **Spec Exp:** Marfan's Syndrome; Phenylketonuria (PKU); Lysosomal Diseases; Inborn Errors of Metabolism; **Hospital:** Lurie Chldn's Hosp-Chicago, Northwestern Meml Hosp; **Address:** Lurie Chldn's Hosp, Dept Genetics, 225 E Chicago Ave, Box 59, Chicago, IL 60611; **Phone:** 312-227-6120; **Board Cert:** Pediatrics 1978; Clinical Genetics 1982; Clinical Biochemical Genetics 1982; **Med School:** Northwestern Univ 1973; **Resid:** Pediatrics, Chldns Meml Hosp 1975; **Fellow:** Clinical Genetics, Chldns Meml Hosp 1977; **Fac Appt:** Prof Ped, Northwestern Univ

Charrow, Joel MD [CG] - **Spec Exp:** Biochemical Genetics; Lysosomal Diseases; Neurofibromatosis; **Hospital:** Lurie Chldn's Hosp-Chicago; **Address:** Lurie Chldn's Hosp-Div Genetics, 225 E Chicago Ave, Box 59, Chicago, IL 60611; **Phone:** 312-227-6120; **Board Cert:** Pediatrics 1980; Clinical Genetics 1982; Clinical Biochemical Genetics 1987; **Med School:** Mount Sinai Sch Med 1976; **Resid:** Pediatrics, Chldns Meml Hosp 1979; **Fellow:** Clinical Genetics, Chldns Meml Hosp-Northwestern Univ 1981; **Fac Appt:** Prof Ped, Northwestern Univ

Hainline, Bryan E MD/PhD [CG] - **Spec Exp:** Inborn Errors of Metabolism; Metabolic Genetic Disorders; Mitochondrial Disorders; **Hospital:** Riley Hosp for Children; **Address:** 975 W Walnut St, Ste 130, Indianapolis, IN 46202; **Phone:** 317-274-3966; **Board Cert:** Pediatrics 1988; Clinical Biochemical Genetics 2009; Clinical Molecular Genetics 1990; Clinical Genetics 1990; **Med School:** Duke Univ 1981; **Resid:** Pediatrics, St Louis Chldn's Hosp 1985; **Fellow:** Medical Genetics, Washington Univ School of Med 1988

Pergament, Eugene MD/PhD [CG] - **Spec Exp:** Prenatal Genetic Diagnosis; Down Syndrome; Genetic Preimplantation Diagnosis; **Hospital:** Northwestern Meml Hosp; **Address:** 680 N Lake Shore Drive, Ste 1230, Chicago, IL 60611; **Phone:** 312-981-4400; **Board Cert:** Clinical Genetics 1982; Clinical Cytogenetics 1984; **Med School:** Univ Chicago-Pritzker Sch Med 1970; **Resid:** Pediatrics, Univ Chicago 1972; **Fac Appt:** Prof ObG, Northwestern Univ

Saal, Howard M MD [CG] - **Spec Exp:** Craniofacial Disorders; Cleft Palate/Lip; Neurofibromatosis; **Hospital:** Cincinnati Chldns Hosp Med Ctr; **Address:** Chldns Hosp Med Ctr, Div Human Genetics, 3333 Burnet Ave Bldg E5 - rm 5430, MC 4006, Cincinnati, OH 45229-3039; **Phone:** 513-636-4760; **Board Cert:** Clinical Genetics 1984; Clinical Cytogenetics 1984; Pediatrics 1985; **Med School:** Wayne State Univ 1979; **Resid:** Pediatrics, Univ Conn Hlth Ctr 1982; **Fellow:** Medical Genetics, Univ Washington Med Ctr 1984; **Fac Appt:** Prof Ped, Univ Cincinnati

Shulman, Lee P MD [CG] - **Spec Exp:** Prenatal Diagnosis; Ovarian Cancer; **Hospital:** Northwestern Meml Hosp; **Address:** 250 E Superior St, rm 05-2174, Division Clinical Genetics, Chicago, IL 60611; **Phone:** 312-472-4683; **Board Cert:** Obstetrics & Gynecology 2012; Clinical Genetics 1990; **Med School:** Cornell Univ 1983; **Resid:** Obstetrics & Gynecology, N Shore Univ Hosp 1987; **Fellow:** Reproductive Genetics, Univ TN Med Ctr 1989; **Fac Appt:** Prof ObG, Northwestern Univ

Weaver, David D MD [CG] - **Spec Exp:** Bone Disorders-Inherited; Genetic Disorders; Inherited Disorders; Weaver Syndrome; **Hospital:** Riley Hosp for Children, IU Health North Hosp; **Address:** IU Hlth, Med & Molecular Genetics, 975 W Walnut St, rm IB130, Indianapolis, IN 46202-5251; **Phone:** 317-274-3966; **Board Cert:** Pediatrics 1978; Clinical Genetics 1982; **Med School:** Oregon Hlth & Sci Univ 1966; **Resid:** Pediatrics, OR Hlth Sci Univ 1972; **Fellow:** Clinical Genetics, Univ Wash Med Ctr 1974; Metabolic Diseases, OR Hlth Sci Univ 1976; **Fac Appt:** Prof Emeritus CG, Indiana Univ

Whelan, Alison MD [CG] - **Spec Exp:** Gynecologic Cancer Risk; Colon & Rectal Cancer Risk; Hereditary Cancer; **Hospital:** Barnes-Jewish Hosp, St. Louis Chldns Hosp; **Address:** 4921 Parkview Pl Fl 8 - Ste C, St Louis, MO 63110; **Phone:** 314-454-6093; **Board Cert:** Internal Medicine 1989; Clinical Genetics 2010; **Med School:** Washington Univ, St Louis 1986; **Resid:** Internal Medicine, Barnes Hosp 1989; Pediatrics, Wash Univ Sch Med 1994; **Fellow:** Research, Wash Univ Sch Med 1991; Clinical Genetics, Wash Univ Sch Med 1994; **Fac Appt:** Prof Med, Washington Univ, St Louis

Great Plains and Mountains

Carey, John C MD [CG] - **Spec Exp:** Birth Defects; Hearing Loss; Chromosome Disorders; **Hospital:** Primary Children's Med Ctr, Univ Utah Hlth Care; **Address:** Div Med Genetics, 50 N Med Drive Bldg SOM - rm 2C412, Salt Lake City, UT 84132; **Phone:** 801-581-8943; **Board Cert:** Pediatrics 1979; Clinical Genetics 1982; **Med School:** Georgetown Univ 1972; **Resid:** Pediatrics, UCSF Med Ctr 1975; **Fellow:** Clinical Genetics, UCSF Med Ctr 1979; **Fac Appt:** Prof Ped, Univ Utah

Hoyme, H Eugene MD [CG] - **Spec Exp:** Fetal Alcohol Syndrome; Cytogenetic Disorders; Dysmorphology; **Hospital:** Sanford USD Med Ctr; **Address:** Sanford Children's Specialty Clinic, 1600 W 22nd St, Sioux Falls, SD 57117-5039; **Phone:** 605-312-1000; **Board Cert:** Pediatrics 1980; Clinical Genetics 1984; Clinical Cytogenetics 1987; **Med School:** Univ Chicago-Pritzker Sch Med 1976; **Resid:** Pediatrics, UCSD Med Ctr 1979; **Fellow:** Dysmorphology, UCSD Med Ctr 1981; **Fac Appt:** Prof Ped, Univ SD Sch Med

Southwest

Andersson, Hans C MD [CG] - **Spec Exp:** Pediatric Clinical Genetics; Inherited Metabolic Disorders; Lysosomal Diseases; **Hospital:** Tulane Med Ctr, Womens & Chldns Hosp-Lafayette; **Address:** Haywood Genetics Ctr SL-31, Tulane Univ Medical School, 1430 Tulane Ave, New Orleans, LA 70112; **Phone:** 504-988-5229; **Board Cert:** Clinical Genetics 1990; Clinical Biochemical Genetics 2010; Clinical Molecular Genetics 1990; **Med School:** Tulane Univ 1984; **Resid:** Pediatrics, Tulane Univ Med Ctr 1987; **Fellow:** Clinical Genetics, NIH 1991; Research, Univ Gottingen 1993; **Fac Appt:** Prof Ped, Tulane Univ

Craigen, William J MD/PhD [CG] - **Spec Exp:** Biochemical Genetics; Mitochondrial Disorders; **Hospital:** Texas Chldns Hosp, Ben Taub Genl Hosp; **Address:** Texas Children's Genetic Clinic, 6701 Fannin St, Fl 16, MC CC 1560, Houston, TX 77030; **Phone:** 832-822-4280; **Board Cert:** Clinical Genetics 2010; Clinical Biochemical Genetics 2010; **Med School:** Baylor Coll Med 1988; **Resid:** Pediatrics, Baylor Coll Med 1990; Pediatrics, Baylor Coll Med 1992; **Fellow:** Clinical Genetics, Baylor Coll Med 1990; **Fac Appt:** Prof CG, Baylor Coll Med

Cunniff, Christopher M MD [CG] - **Spec Exp:** Developmental Disorders; Sexual Differentiation Disorders; Fetal Alcohol Syndrome; **Hospital:** Univ Arizona Med Ctr-Univ Campus; **Address:** Univ Ariz Dept Pediatric Genetics, 1501 N Campbell Ave, Tucson, AZ 85724; **Phone:** 520-626-5175; **Board Cert:** Pediatrics 2010; Clinical Genetics 1990; **Med School:** UAB Sch Med 1984; **Resid:** Pediatrics, FAHC - Med Ctr Campus 1987; **Fellow:** Clinical Genetics, UCSD Med Ctr 1989; **Fac Appt:** Prof Ped, Univ Ariz Coll Med

Mulvihill, John J MD [CG] - **Spec Exp:** Genetic Disorders; Neurofibromatosis; Fertility in Cancer Survivors; **Hospital:** Chldns Hosp OU Med Ctr; **Address:** Chldn's Hosp-OU Med Ctr, Dept Pediatric Genetics, 1200 N Children's Ave, Ste 12100, Oklahoma City, OK 73104; **Phone:** 405-271-2006; **Board Cert:** Pediatrics 1975; Clinical Genetics 1982; **Med School:** Univ Wash 1969; **Resid:** Pediatrics, Johns Hopkins Hosp 1974; **Fellow:** Research, NCI-Natl Inst Hlth 1972; **Fac Appt:** Prof CG, Univ Okla Coll Med

Northrup, Hope MD [CG] - **Spec Exp:** Biochemical Genetics; Neurogenetics; Dysmorphology; Spina Bifida; **Hospital:** Meml Hermann Hosp - Texas Med Ctr, LBJ General Hosp; **Address:** UT Physicians-Div Med Genetics, 6431 Fannin St, MS 3.144, Houston, TX 77030; **Phone:** 713-500-5760; **Board Cert:** Pediatrics 1988; Clinical Genetics 1990; Clinical Biochemical Genetics 1990; **Med School:** Med Univ SC 1983; **Resid:** Pediatrics, Chldns Med Ctr-Univ Tex SW 1986; **Fellow:** Medical Genetics, Inst Molec Gene-Baylor Coll Med 1989; **Fac Appt:** Prof Ped, Univ Tex, Houston

Plon, Sharon E MD/PhD [CG] - **Spec Exp:** Hereditary Cancer; Cancer Risk Assessment; **Hospital:** Texas Chldns Hosp, St. Luke's Episcopal Hosp-Houston; **Address:** Texas Chldn's Hosp, 1102 Bates St, MC FC1200, Houston, TX 77030; **Phone:** 832-824-4539; **Board Cert:** Clinical Genetics 2010; **Med School:** Harvard Med Sch 1987; **Resid:** Internal Medicine, Univ Washington Affil Hosp 1988; **Fellow:** Molecular Genetics, National Cancer Inst 1990; Medical Genetics, Fred Hutchinson Cancer Research Ctr 1993; **Fac Appt:** Prof CG, Baylor Coll Med

West Coast and Pacific

Boles, Richard G MD [CG] - **Spec Exp:** Mitochondrial Disorders; Vomiting-Cyclic; **Hospital:** Chldns Hosp - Los Angeles; **Address:** UCLA Med Genetics Dept, 4650 Sunset Blvd, MS 90, Los Angeles, CA 90027; **Phone:** 323-361-2178; **Board Cert:** Clinical Genetics 2010; Clinical Biochemical Genetics 2010; Pediatrics 2009; **Med School:** UCLA 1987; **Resid:** Pediatrics, Harbor-UCLA Med Ctr 1990; **Fellow:** Genetics and Metabolism, Yale Univ 1993; **Fac Appt:** Assoc Prof Ped, USC Sch Med

Cassidy, Suzanne MD [CG] - **Spec Exp:** Prader-Willi Syndrome; Connective Tissue Disorders; Neurocutaneous Disorders; **Hospital:** UCSF Med Ctr; **Address:** 533 Parnassus Ave, rm U-100A, San Francisco, CA 94143; **Phone:** 415-476-2757; **Board Cert:** Pediatrics 1982; Clinical Genetics 1983; **Med School:** Vanderbilt Univ 1976; **Resid:** Pediatrics, Univ Wash Affil Prgms 1979; **Fellow:** Clinical Genetics, Univ Wash 1981; **Fac Appt:** Prof Ped, UC Irvine

Curry, Cynthia J MD [CG] - **Hospital:** Chldns Hosp Central CA, Comm Regl Med Ctr - Fresno; **Address:** 2900 Fresno St, Ste 101, Fresno, CA 93701; **Phone:** 559-227-4472; **Board Cert:** Pediatrics 1973; Clinical Genetics 1982; **Med School:** Yale Univ 1967; **Resid:** Pediatrics, Univ Wash Orth Chldns Hosp 1969; Pediatrics, Univ Minn Hosp 1970; **Fellow:** Dysmorphology, UCSF Med Ctr 1976; **Fac Appt:** Prof CG, UCSF

Falk, Rena E MD [CG] - **Spec Exp:** Prenatal Diagnosis; Mental Retardation; Prenatal Genetic Diagnosis; **Hospital:** Cedars-Sinai Med Ctr; **Address:** Cedars Sinai Med Ctr, Dept Med Genetics, 8700 Beverly Blvd, PACT Bldg, Ste 400, Los Angeles, CA 90048; **Phone:** 310-423-9914; **Board Cert:** Pediatrics 1976; Clinical Genetics 1982; Clinical Cytogenetics 1984; **Med School:** UCLA 1971; **Resid:** Pediatrics, Cedars-Sinai Med Ctr 1973; **Fellow:** Clinical Genetics, UCLA Med Schl 1975; Molecular Biology, UCLA 1977

Graham Jr, John M MD [CG] - **Spec Exp:** Dysmorphology; Craniofacial Disorders; Mental Retardation; Vascular Malformations; **Hospital:** Cedars-Sinai Med Ctr; **Address:** Cedars Sinai Med Ctr, Dept Med Genetics, 8700 Beverly Blvd, PACT Bldg, Ste 400, Los Angeles, CA 90048; **Phone:** 310-423-9909; **Board Cert:** Pediatrics 1982; Clinical Genetics 1982; **Med School:** Med Univ SC 1975; **Resid:** Pediatrics, Boston Chldns Hosp-Harvard 1977; **Fellow:** Developmental-Behavioral Pediatrics, Boston Chldns Hosp 1978; Dysmorphology, Univ Wash 1980

Grody, Wayne W MD/PhD [CG] - **Spec Exp:** Genetic Disorders; Hereditary Cancer; **Hospital:** UCLA Ronald Reagan Med Ctr; **Address:** UCLA School Medicine, Div, Med Genetic & Molecular Pathology, 10833 Le Conte Ave, Los Angeles, CA 90095-1732; **Phone:** 310-206-6581; **Board Cert:** Anatomic & Clinical Pathology 1987; Clinical Genetics 1990; Clinical Biochemical Genetics 1990; Molecular Genetic Pathology 2001; **Med School:** Baylor Coll Med 1977; **Resid:** Pathology, UCLA Med Ctr 1986; **Fellow:** Clinical Genetics, UCLA Med Ctr 1987; **Fac Appt:** Prof CG, UCLA

Hudgins, Louanne MD [CG] - **Spec Exp:** Congenital Anomalies-Limb; Prenatal Diagnosis; **Hospital:** Stanford Univ Hosp & Clins; **Address:** Stanford Univ Med Ctr, Div Medical Genetics, 300 Pasteur Drive, rm H315, Stanford, CA 94305; **Phone:** 650-723-6858; **Board Cert:** Clinical Genetics 2010; **Med School:** Univ Kansas 1984; **Resid:** Pediatrics, UConn Hlth Science Ctr 1987; **Fellow:** Clinical Genetics, Univ Connecticut 1990; **Fac Appt:** Prof Ped, Stanford Univ

Jonas, Adam J MD [CG] - **Spec Exp:** Inherited Metabolic Disorders; Genetic Disorders; **Hospital:** LAC - Harbor - UCLA Med Ctr; **Address:** Harbor-UCLA Med Ctr, Div Med Genetics, 1000 W Carson St, Box 17, Torrance, CA 90509-2910; **Phone:** 310-222-2301; **Board Cert:** Pediatrics 1982; Clinical Biochemical Genetics 1987; Clinical Genetics 1990; **Med School:** UCSD 1976; **Resid:** Pediatrics, Chldns Ortho Hosp 1978; Pediatrics, Univ Hosp 1979; **Fellow:** Genetics and Metabolism, UCSD Sch Med 1982; **Fac Appt:** Prof Ped, UCLA

Jones, Marilyn C MD [CG] - **Spec Exp:** Dysmorphology; Craniofacial Disorders; **Hospital:** Rady Children's Hosp - San Diego, UCSD Med Ctr; **Address:** 7920 Frost St, Ste 200, San Diego, CA 92123-2746; **Phone:** 858-966-5840; **Board Cert:** Pediatrics 1979; Clinical Genetics 1982; **Med School:** Columbia P&S 1974; **Resid:** Pediatrics, UCSD Med Ctr 1978; Clinical Genetics, UCSD Med Ctr 1979

Morris, Colleen A MD [CG] - **Spec Exp:** Williams Syndrome; Inherited Disorders; Fetal Alcohol Syndrome; **Hospital:** Univ Med Ctr - Las Vegas; **Address:** Univ Nevada Sch Medicine, Dept Pediatrics/Genetics, 2040 W Charleston Blvd, Ste 401, Las Vegas, NV 89102; **Phone:** 702-671-2200; **Board Cert:** Pediatrics 1986; Clinical Genetics 1987; **Med School:** Loyola Univ-Stritch Sch Med 1981; **Resid:** Pediatrics, Phoenix Hosp 1984; **Fellow:** Clinical Genetics, Univ Utah Sch Med 1986; **Fac Appt:** Prof Ped, Univ Nevada

Nussbaum, Robert MD [CG] - **Spec Exp:** Genetic Disorders; **Hospital:** UCSF Med Ctr; **Address:** Inst Human Genetics, 1600 Divisadero St Fl 2, San Francisco, CA 94143; **Phone:** 415-885-7779; **Board Cert:** Internal Medicine 1978; Clinical Genetics 1982; Clinical Molecular Genetics 2013; **Med School:** Harvard Med Sch 1975; **Resid:** Internal Medicine, Barnes Hosp 1978; **Fellow:** Clinical Genetics, Baylor Univ 1983

Randolph, Linda M MD [CG] - **Spec Exp:** Prenatal Genetic Diagnosis; **Hospital:** Chldns Hosp - Los Angeles, Van Nuys Comm Hosp; **Address:** UCLA Med Genetics Dept, 4650 Sunset Blvd, MS 90, Los Angeles, CA 90027; **Phone:** 323-361-2178; **Board Cert:** Pediatrics 1987; Clinical Genetics 1987; Clinical Cytogenetics 1990; **Med School:** Geo Wash Univ 1982; **Resid:** Pediatrics, Chldns Natl Med Ctr 1985; **Fellow:** Clinical Molecular Genetics, Harbor-UCLA Med Ctr/Cedar-Sinai Med Ctr 1989; **Fac Appt:** Asst Prof Ped, USC-Keck School of Medicine

Seaver, Laurie H MD [CG] - **Spec Exp:** Birth Defects; Fetal Alcohol Syndrome; Dysmorphology; Prenatal Diagnosis; **Hospital:** Kapiolani Med Ctr for Women & Chldn, Queen's Med Ctr - Honolulu; **Address:** Hawaii Community Genetics, 1441 Kapiolani Blvd, Ste 1800, Honolulu, HI 96814; **Phone:** 808-973-3403; **Board Cert:** Pediatrics 2012; Clinical Genetics 2010; **Med School:** Univ Ariz Coll Med 1987; **Resid:** Pediatrics, Univ Ariz Med Ctr 1990; **Fellow:** Clinical Genetics, Univ Ariz Coll Med 1993; **Fac Appt:** Assoc Prof Ped, Univ Hawaii JA Burns Sch Med

Weitzel, Jeffrey N MD [CG] - **Spec Exp:** Hereditary Cancer; **Hospital:** City of Hope Natl Med Ctr; **Address:** City of Hope Cancer Ctr, 1500 E Duarte Rd, Duarte, CA 91010; **Phone:** 626-256-8662; **Board Cert:** Internal Medicine 1986; Medical Oncology 1989; Clinical Genetics 2010; **Med School:** Univ Minn 1983; **Resid:** Internal Medicine, Univ Minn Hosps 1986; Hematology, Hammersmith Hosp 1987; **Fellow:** Hematology & Oncology, Tufts-New England Med Ctr 1992; Clinical Genetics, Tufts-New England Med Ctr 1996; **Fac Appt:** Assoc Clin Prof Med, USC Sch Med

Wilcox Jr, William R MD/PhD [CG] - **Spec Exp:** Inborn Errors of Metabolism; Skeletal Dysplasia; Fabry's Disease; Rare Genetic Disorders; **Hospital:** Cedars-Sinai Med Ctr; **Address:** Cedars Sinai Med Ctr, Dept Med Genetics, 8700 Beverly Blvd, PACT Bldg, Ste 400, Los Angeles, CA 90048; **Phone:** 310-423-9914; **Board Cert:** Clinical Genetics 2010; Clinical Biochemical Genetics 2010; Clinical Molecular Genetics 2010; **Med School:** UCLA 1988; **Resid:** Pediatrics, UCLA Med Ctr 1991; **Fellow:** Clinical Genetics, Cedars-Sinai Med Ctr 1994; **Fac Appt:** Prof Ped, UCLA

Top Doctors Make A Difference

Colon & Rectal Surgery

A colon and rectal surgeon is trained to diagnose and treat various diseases of the intestinal tract, colon, rectum, anal canal and perianal area by medical and surgical means. This specialist also deals with other organs and tissues (such as the liver and gallbladder) involved with primary intestinal disease.

Colon and rectal surgeons have the expertise to diagnose and often manage anorectal conditions such as hemorrhoids, fissures (painful tears in the anal lining), abscesses and fistulae (infections located around the anus and rectum) in the office setting. They also treat problems of the intestine and colon and perform endoscopic procedures to evaluate and treat problems such as cancer, polyps (precancerous growths) and inflammatory conditions.

Training Required: Six years (including general surgery)

Colon & Rectal Surgery

New England

Bleday, Ronald MD [CRS] - **Spec Exp:** Colon & Rectal Cancer; **Hospital:** Brigham & Women's Hosp, Dana-Farber Cancer Inst; **Address:** Brigham & Women's Hosp, Dept Surgery, 75 Francis St Fl 3 - Ste A, Boston, MA 02115; **Phone:** 617-732-8460; **Board Cert:** Surgery 2009; Colon & Rectal Surgery 2011; **Med School:** McGill Univ 1982; **Resid:** Surgery, Rhode Island Hosp 1989; Surgical Oncology, Brigham & Womens Hosp 1986; **Fellow:** Endoscopy, Mass Genl Hosp 1990; Colon & Rectal Surgery, Univ Minn Hosp 1991; **Fac Appt:** Assoc Prof S, Harvard Med Sch

Hackford, Alan W MD [CRS] - **Hospital:** Steward St Elizabeth's Med Ctr-Boston; **Address:** St Elizabeth's Medical Office, 11 Nevins St MOB Bldg Fl 2 - Ste 201, Boston, MA 02135; **Phone:** 617-789-2442; **Board Cert:** Colon & Rectal Surgery 1985; Surgery 2012; **Med School:** Univ Conn 1977; **Resid:** Surgery, New England Med Ctr 1982; **Fellow:** Colon & Rectal Surgery, Lahey Clinic 1984; **Fac Appt:** Prof S, Tufts Univ

Harnsberger, Jeffrey R MD [CRS] - **Spec Exp:** Colon & Rectal Cancer; Inflammatory Bowel Disease; **Hospital:** Elliot Hosp, Dartmouth - Hitchcock Med Ctr; **Address:** Dartmouth-Hitchcock Manchester, 100 Hitchcock Way, Manchester, NH 03104; **Phone:** 603-695-2840; **Board Cert:** Surgery 2011; Colon & Rectal Surgery 2005; **Med School:** Med Coll OH 1987; **Resid:** Surgery, Dartamouth-Hitchkock Med Ctr 1992; **Fellow:** Colon & Rectal Surgery, St Louis Univ Med Ctr 1993; **Fac Appt:** Asst Prof S, Dartmouth Med Sch

Hyman, Neil H MD [CRS] - **Spec Exp:** Inflammatory Bowel Disease; Colon & Rectal Cancer; **Hospital:** FAHC - Med Ctr Campus; **Address:** Fletcher Allen Surgery, 111 Colchester Ave, Main Pavilion, Fl 5, Burlington, VT 05401; **Phone:** 802-847-3339; **Board Cert:** Surgery 2008; Colon & Rectal Surgery 2011; **Med School:** Univ VT Coll Med 1984; **Resid:** Surgery, Mt Sinai Med Ctr 1990; **Fellow:** Colon & Rectal Surgery, Cleveland Clin 1992; **Fac Appt:** Prof S, Univ VT Coll Med

Longo, Walter E MD [CRS] - **Spec Exp:** Colon & Rectal Cancer; Gastrointestinal Surgery; Inflammatory Bowel Disease; **Hospital:** Yale-New Haven Hosp; **Address:** Yale, Colon & Rectal Surgery Dept, 800 Howard Ave Fl 3, New Haven, CT 06510; **Phone:** 203-785-2616; **Board Cert:** Surgery 2011; Colon & Rectal Surgery 2006; **Med School:** NY Med Coll 1984; **Resid:** Surgery, Yale-New Haven Hosp 1990; **Fellow:** Research, Yale-New Haven Hosp 1988; Colon & Rectal Surgery, Cleveland Clin 1991; **Fac Appt:** Prof S, Yale Univ

Nagle, Deborah A MD [CRS] - **Spec Exp:** Colon & Rectal Cancer; Anal Cancer; Laparoscopic Surgery; **Hospital:** Beth Israel Deaconess Med Ctr - Boston; **Address:** BIDMC - Colon & Rectal Surgery, 330 Brookline Ave, Boston, MA 02215; **Phone:** 617-667-4159; **Board Cert:** Colon & Rectal Surgery 2006; Surgery 2004; **Med School:** Univ Pennsylvania 1988; **Resid:** Surgery, Graduate Hosp 1993; Colon & Rectal Surgery, Thos Jefferson Univ Hosp 1994; **Fac Appt:** Prof CRS, Univ Pennsylvania

Read, Thomas E MD [CRS] - **Spec Exp:** Colon & Rectal Cancer; Inflammatory Bowel Disease; Laparoscopic Surgery; Diverticulitis; **Hospital:** Lahey Hosp & Med Ctr; **Address:** Lahey Clin, Dept Colon & Rectal Surgery, 41 Mall Rd, Ste 6W-Clin, Burlington, MA 01805; **Phone:** 781-744-8971; **Board Cert:** Surgery 2005; Colon & Rectal Surgery 2008; **Med School:** UCSF 1988; **Resid:** Surgery, UCSF Med Ctr 1995; **Fellow:** Colon & Rectal Surgery, Lahey Clinic 1996; **Fac Appt:** Prof S, Tufts Univ

Roberts, Patricia L MD [CRS] - **Spec Exp:** Diverticulitis; Colon & Rectal Cancer; Inflammatory Bowel Disease; Crohn's Disease; **Hospital:** Lahey Hosp & Med Ctr; **Address:** Lahey Clin, Dept Colon & Rectal Surgery, 41 Mall Rd, Ste 6W-Clin, Burlington, MA 01805; **Phone:** 781-744-8243; **Board Cert:** Colon & Rectal Surgery 2003; **Med School:** Boston Univ 1981; **Resid:** Surgery, Boston City Hosp 1986; **Fellow:** Colon & Rectal Surgery, Lahey Clinic 1988; **Fac Appt:** Prof S, Tufts Univ

Schoetz Jr, David J MD [CRS] - **Spec Exp:** Inflammatory Bowel Disease/Crohn's; Colon & Rectal Cancer; Incontinence-Fecal; Anorectal Disorders; **Hospital:** Lahey Hosp & Med Ctr; **Address:** Lahey Clinic Med Ctr, Dept Colon & Rectal Surg, 41 Mall Rd, Ste 6W-Clin, Burlington, MA 01805-0001; **Phone:** 781-744-8889; **Board Cert:** Surgery 2001; Colon & Rectal Surgery 2009; **Med School:** Med Coll Wisc 1974; **Resid:** Surgery, Boston Univ Med Ctr 1981; **Fellow:** Colon & Rectal Surgery, Lahey Clin 1982; **Fac Appt:** Prof S, Tufts Univ

Shah, Nishit S MD [CRS] - **Spec Exp:** Anorectal Disorders; Colon & Rectal Cancer; Inflammatory Bowel Disease; **Hospital:** Rhode Island Hosp, Miriam Hosp; **Address:** University Surgical Associates, 2 Dudley St, Ste 370, Providence, RI 02905; **Phone:** 401-553-8322; **Board Cert:** Surgery 2010; Colon & Rectal Surgery 2013; **Med School:** England, UK 1989; **Resid:** Surgery, Univ Pittsburgh Med Ctr 1995; **Fellow:** Colon & Rectal Surgery, Cleveland Clinic 1996; Colon & Rectal Surgery, Univ Illinois

Shellito, Paul C MD [CRS] - **Spec Exp:** Colon & Rectal Cancer; Ulcerative Colitis; Anorectal Disorders; **Hospital:** Mass Genl Hosp; **Address:** Mass Genl Hosp, 15 Parkman St, Ste 460, Boston, MA 02114-3117; **Phone:** 617-724-0365; **Board Cert:** Surgery 2012; Colon & Rectal Surgery 1994; **Med School:** Harvard Med Sch 1977; **Resid:** Surgery, Mass Genl Hosp 1980; Surgery, Mass Genl Hosp 1983; **Fellow:** Colon & Rectal Surgery, Univ Minn Hosp & Clin 1985; **Fac Appt:** Asst Prof S, Harvard Med Sch

Mid Atlantic

Efron, Jonathan E MD [CRS] - **Spec Exp:** Colon & Rectal Cancer; Incontinence-Fecal; Inflammatory Bowel Disease; Anorectal Disorders; **Hospital:** Johns Hopkins Hosp (page 59); **Address:** Johns Hopkins, Surgery Dept, 600 N Wolfe St Blalock Bldg - Ste 618, Baltimore, MD 21287; **Phone:** 410-955-7323; **Board Cert:** Surgery 2008; Colon & Rectal Surgery 2009; **Med School:** Univ MD Sch Med 1993; **Resid:** Surgery, LIJ Med Ctr 1999; **Fellow:** Colon & Rectal Surgery, Cleveland Clin 2000; Research, Cleveland Clin 2001; **Fac Appt:** Assoc Prof S, Johns Hopkins Univ

Eisenstat, Theodore E MD [CRS] - **Spec Exp:** Colon Cancer; Inflammatory Bowel Disease; Anorectal Disorders; Hemorrhoids; **Hospital:** Robert Wood Johnson Univ Hosp - New Brunswick, JFK Med Ctr - Edison; **Address:** Robert Wood Johnson Med Group, Clinical Academic Bldg, 125 Paterson St, Ste 4100, New Brunswick, NJ 08901; **Phone:** 732-235-7920; **Board Cert:** Surgery 1974; Colon & Rectal Surgery 1994; **Med School:** NY Med Coll 1968; **Resid:** Surgery, Thomas Jefferson Univ Hosp 1971; Surgery, Pennsylvania Hosp 1973; **Fellow:** Colon & Rectal Surgery, Muhlenberg Med Ctr 1978; **Fac Appt:** Clin Prof S, UMDNJ-RW Johnson Med Sch

Fry, Robert D MD [CRS] - **Spec Exp:** Colon & Rectal Cancer; Rectal Cancer/Sphincter Preservation; Ulcerative Colitis; Anorectal Disorders; **Hospital:** Pennsylvania Hosp-UPHS (page 69), Hosp Univ Penn - UPHS (page 69); **Address:** Pennsylvania Hospital, Div Colon & Rectal Surgery, 301 S Eighth St, Ste 4D, Philadelphia, PA 19106-4023; **Phone:** 215-662-2078; **Board Cert:** Surgery 2006; Colon & Rectal Surgery 1998; **Med School:** Washington Univ, St Louis 1972; **Resid:** Surgery, Barnes Jewish Hosp 1977; **Fellow:** Colon & Rectal Surgery, Cleveland Clinic 1978; **Fac Appt:** Prof S, Univ Pennsylvania

Gearhart, Susan L MD [CRS] - **Spec Exp:** Colon & Rectal Cancer-Hereditary; Incontinence-Fecal; Inflammatory Bowel Disease/Crohn's; **Hospital:** Johns Hopkins Hosp (page 59); **Address:** Johns Hopkins, Surgery Dept, 600 N Wolfe St Blalock Bldg - Ste 618, Baltimore, MD 21287; **Phone:** 410-955-7323; **Board Cert:** Surgery 2011; Colon & Rectal Surgery 2012; **Med School:** Loyola Univ-Stritch Sch Med 1993; **Resid:** Surgery, John Hopkins Hosp 2000; **Fellow:** Colon & Rectal Surgery, Cleveland Clin 2002; **Fac Appt:** Asst Prof S, Johns Hopkins Univ

Goldstein, Scott D MD [CRS] - **Spec Exp:** Colon & Rectal Cancer; Inflammatory Bowel Disease; Laparoscopic Surgery; **Hospital:** Thomas Jefferson Univ Hosp; **Address:** Jefferson Dept Surgery, 1100 Walnut St, Ste 500, Philadelphia, PA 19107; **Phone:** 215-955-5869; **Board Cert:** Surgery 2007; Colon & Rectal Surgery 1985; **Med School:** SUNY Buffalo 1978; **Resid:** Surgery, Lenox Hill Hosp 1983; **Fellow:** Colon & Rectal Surgery, UMDNJ Affil Hosps 1984; **Fac Appt:** Asst Prof S, Thomas Jefferson Univ

Gorfine, Stephen R MD [CRS] - **Spec Exp:** Anal Disorders & Reconstruction; Hemorrhoids; Rectal Cancer; Anal Cancer; **Hospital:** Mt Sinai Med Ctr (page 62); **Address:** 25 E 69th St, New York, NY 10021-4925; **Phone:** 212-517-8600; **Board Cert:** Internal Medicine 1981; Surgery 2007; Colon & Rectal Surgery 1988; **Med School:** Univ Mass Sch Med 1978; **Resid:** Internal Medicine, Mt Sinai Hosp 1981; Surgery, Mt Sinai Hosp 1985; **Fellow:** Colon & Rectal Surgery, Ferguson Hosp 1987; **Fac Appt:** Clin Prof S, Mount Sinai Sch Med

Guillem, Jose G MD [CRS] - **Spec Exp:** Colon & Rectal Cancer; Rectal Cancer/Sphincter Preservation; Colon & Rectal Cancer-Hereditary; Peritoneal Mucinous Carcinomatosis; **Hospital:** Meml Sloan-Kettering Canc Ctr; **Address:** 1275 York Ave, New York, NY 10065; **Phone:** 212-639-8278; **Board Cert:** Surgery 2004; Colon & Rectal Surgery 2005; **Med School:** Yale Univ 1983; **Resid:** Surgery, Columbia-Presby Med Ctr 1990; **Fellow:** Colon & Rectal Surgery, Lahey Clinic 1991; **Fac Appt:** Prof CRS, Cornell Univ-Weill Med Coll

Marks, John H MD [CRS] - **Spec Exp:** Laparoscopic Surgery; Colon & Rectal Cancer; Inflammatory Bowel Disease; Minimally Invasive Surgery; **Hospital:** Lankenau Hosp, Bryn Mawr Hosp; **Address:** Medical Office Bldg West, Ste 330, 100 E Lancaster Ave, Wynnewood, PA 19096; **Phone:** 610-645-9093; **Board Cert:** Surgery 2004; Colon & Rectal Surgery 2008; **Med School:** Jefferson Med Coll 1989; **Resid:** Surgery, Thomas Jefferson Univ Hosp 1994; Colon & Rectal Surgery, Thomas Jefferson Univ Hosp 1995; **Fellow:** Laparoscopic Surgery, Hosp St Roche 1996

Medich, David S MD [CRS] - **Spec Exp:** Colon & Rectal Cancer; Ulcerative Colitis; Inflammatory Bowel Disease/Crohn's; **Hospital:** UPMC Passavant-McCandless; **Address:** 9100 Babcock Blvd, Ste 4828, Pittsburgh, PA 15237; **Phone:** 877-684-7189; **Board Cert:** Surgery 2004; Colon & Rectal Surgery 2006; **Med School:** Ohio State Univ 1987; **Resid:** Surgery, Univ Pittsburgh Med Ctr 1990; **Fellow:** Research, Univ Pittsburgh 1993; Colon & Rectal Surgery, Cleveland Clinic 1994; **Fac Appt:** Assoc Prof CRS, Univ Pittsburgh

Milsom, Jeffrey W MD [CRS] - **Spec Exp:** Laparoscopic Surgery; Inflammatory Bowel Disease/Crohn's; Colon & Rectal Cancer & Surgery; **Hospital:** NY-Presby/Weill Cornell Med Ctr, NY (page 65); **Address:** NY Cornell Med Ctr, Div Colorectal Surg, 1315 York Ave Fl 2, New York, NY 10065-5304; **Phone:** 646-962-2993; **Board Cert:** Colon & Rectal Surgery 1986; **Med School:** Univ Pittsburgh 1979; **Resid:** Surgery, St Luke's-Roosevelt Hosp 1981; Surgery, Univ Virginia Med Ctr 1984; **Fellow:** Colon & Rectal Surgery, Ferguson Hosp 1985; **Fac Appt:** Prof S, Cornell Univ-Weill Med Coll

Pello, Mark J MD [CRS] - **Spec Exp:** Colon & Rectal Cancer; Inflammatory Bowel Disease; Laparoscopic Surgery; **Hospital:** Cooper Univ Hosp; **Address:** 3 Cooper Plaza, Ste 411, Camden, NJ 08103; **Phone:** 856-968-7478; **Board Cert:** Surgery 2007; Colon & Rectal Surgery 1980; **Med School:** Jefferson Med Coll 1975; **Resid:** Surgery, Cooper Med Ctr 1979; Colon & Rectal Surgery, Wm Beaumont Hosp 1980; **Fac Appt:** Assoc Prof S, UMDNJ-RW Johnson Med Sch

Procaccino Jr, John A MD [CRS] - **Spec Exp:** Inflammatory Bowel Disease/Crohn's; Colon & Rectal Cancer; Anorectal Disorders; Colon & Rectal Cancer-Familial Polyposis; **Hospital:** N Shore Univ Hosp (page 66), Long Is Jewish Med Ctr (page 66); **Address:** Chief, Div of Colon & Rectal Surg, 900 Northern Blvd, Ste 100, Great Neck, NY 11021; **Phone:** 516-730-2100; **Board Cert:** Surgery 2009; Colon & Rectal Surgery 2011; **Med School:** NYU Sch Med 1984; **Resid:** Surgery, N Shore Univ Hosp 1989; **Fellow:** Colon & Rectal Surgery, Cleveland Clin 1990; **Fac Appt:** Asst Clin Prof S, Cornell Univ-Weill Med Coll

Stein, David E MD [CRS] - **Spec Exp:** Colon & Rectal Cancer & Surgery; Laparoscopic Surgery; Inflammatory Bowel Disease; Cancer Risk Assessment; **Hospital:** Hahnemann Univ Hosp, St. Francis Hosp; **Address:** 219 N Broad St Fl 8, Philadelphia, PA 19107; **Phone:** 215-762-1545; **Board Cert:** Surgery 2003; Colon & Rectal Surgery 2004; **Med School:** SUNY Downstate 1997; **Resid:** Surgery, Thom Jefferson Univ Hosp 2002; **Fellow:** Colon & Rectal Surgery, Cleveland Clin 2003; **Fac Appt:** Assoc Prof S, Drexel Univ Coll Med

Steinhagen, Randolph M MD [CRS] - **Spec Exp:** Colon & Rectal Cancer & Surgery; Crohn's Disease; Hemorrhoids; Ulcerative Colitis; **Hospital:** Mt Sinai Med Ctr (page 62), St. John's Riverside Hosp-Andrus Pavil; **Address:** Div Colon & Rectal Surgery, 5 E 98th St Fl 14 - Ste D, Box 1259, New York, NY 10029-6501; **Phone:** 212-241-3547; **Board Cert:** Surgery 2012; Colon & Rectal Surgery 1985; **Med School:** Wayne State Univ 1977; **Resid:** Surgery, Mount Sinai Hosp 1982; **Fellow:** Colon & Rectal Surgery, Cleveland Clinic 1983; **Fac Appt:** Prof S, Mount Sinai Sch Med

Weiser, Martin R MD [CRS] - **Spec Exp:** Colon & Rectal Cancer; Laparoscopic Surgery; Cancer Surgery; **Hospital:** Meml Sloan-Kettering Canc Ctr; **Address:** Meml Sloan-Kettering Cancer Ctr, 1275 York Ave, Ste C1075, New York, NY 10065; **Phone:** 646-639-6698; **Board Cert:** Surgery 2009; Colon & Rectal Surgery 2012; **Med School:** Univ Chicago-Pritzker Sch Med 1991; **Resid:** Surgery, Brigham & Women's Hosp 1998; Colon & Rectal Surgery, Mount Sinai Med Ctr 2002; **Fellow:** Research, Harvard Med Sch 1995; Surgical Oncology, Meml Sloan Kettering Cancer Ctr 2000; **Fac Appt:** Assoc Prof S, Cornell Univ-Weill Med Coll

Whelan, Richard L MD [CRS] - **Spec Exp:** Laparoscopic Surgery; Colon & Rectal Cancer; Colonoscopy; Diverticulitis; **Hospital:** St. Luke's - Roosevelt Hosp Ctr - Roosevelt Div (page 56), NY-Presby/Columbia Univ Med Ctr, NY (page 65); **Address:** St Luke-Roosevelt Hosp, 425 W 59th St, Ste 7B, Brodsky Bldg, New York, NY 10019; **Phone:** 212-523-8172; **Board Cert:** Colon & Rectal Surgery 1989; **Med School:** Columbia P&S 1982; **Resid:** Surgery, NY-Presby/Columbia Univ Med Ctr 1987; **Fellow:** Colon & Rectal Surgery, Univ Minn Med Ctr 1988; **Fac Appt:** Prof S, Columbia P&S

Southeast

Beck, Sandra J MD [CRS] - **Hospital:** Univ of Kentucky Albert B. Chandler Hosp; **Address:** Univ Kentucky Chandler Hosp, Dept Surgery, 800 Rose St, Lexington, KY 40536; **Phone:** 859-257-3253; **Board Cert:** Surgery 2011; Colon & Rectal Surgery 2012; **Med School:** Wright State Univ 1995; **Resid:** Surgery, Allegheny Genl Hosp 2001; **Fellow:** Colon & Rectal Surgery, Cleveland Clin 2002; **Fac Appt:** Assoc Prof S, Univ KY Coll Med

Galandiuk, Susan MD [CRS] - **Spec Exp:** Colon & Rectal Cancer; Inflammatory Bowel Disease/Crohn's; **Hospital:** Univ of Louisville Hosp, Norton Hosp; **Address:** Univ Surgical Assocs, 401 E Chestnut St, Ste 710, Louisville, KY 40202; **Phone:** 502-583-8303; **Board Cert:** Surgery 2008; Colon & Rectal Surgery 2011; **Med School:** Germany 1982; **Resid:** Surgery, Cleveland Clinic Fdn 1988; **Fellow:** Research, Univ Louisville Hosp 1989; Colon & Rectal Surgery, Mayo Clinic 1990; **Fac Appt:** Prof CRS, Univ Louisville Sch Med

Golub, Richard W MD [CRS] - **Spec Exp:** Colon & Rectal Cancer; Laparoscopic Surgery; Hemorrhoids; **Hospital:** Sarasota Meml Hosp, Doctors Hosp - Sarasota; **Address:** Intercoastal Surgical Grp, 3333 Cattlemen Rd, Ste 206, Sarasota, FL 34332; **Phone:** 941-341-0042; **Board Cert:** Colon & Rectal Surgery 2011; **Med School:** Albert Einstein Coll Med 1984; **Resid:** Surgery, Stony Brook Univ Med Ctr 1990; **Fellow:** Colon & Rectal Surgery, Grant Med Ctr 1991

Hartmann, Rene F MD [CRS] - **Spec Exp:** Laparoscopic Surgery; Rectovaginal Fistula; Colon Cancer; Inflammatory Bowel Disease; **Hospital:** Baptist Hosp of Miami, Jackson Meml Hosp; **Address:** JMG Specialty Phys, 9195 Sunset Drive, Ste 230, Miami, FL 33173; **Phone:** 305-271-0300; **Board Cert:** Colon & Rectal Surgery 1994; **Med School:** Venezuela 1971; **Resid:** Surgery, Jackson Meml Hosp 1976; Surgery, Orange Meml Hosp 1977; **Fellow:** Colon & Rectal Surgery, Grant Hosp 1978; **Fac Appt:** Assoc Clin Prof S, Univ Miami Sch Med

Mantyh, Christopher R MD [CRS] - **Spec Exp:** Colon & Rectal Cancer & Surgery; Rectal Cancer/Sphincter Preservation; Incontinence-Fecal; Colon & Rectal Cancer-Familial Polyposis; **Hospital:** Duke Univ Hosp; **Address:** Duke Univ Med Ctr, 200 Trent Drive, Durham, NC 27710; **Phone:** 919-681-3977; **Board Cert:** Surgery 2008; Colon & Rectal Surgery 2010; **Med School:** Univ Wisc 1991; **Resid:** Surgery, Duke Univ Med Ctr 1998; **Fellow:** Colon & Rectal Surgery, Cleveland Clinic 1999; **Fac Appt:** Assoc Prof CRS, Univ Wisc

Marcet, Jorge E MD [CRS] - **Spec Exp:** Colon & Rectal Cancer; Crohn's Disease; Anal Disorders & Reconstruction; **Hospital:** Tampa Genl Hosp; **Address:** USF Surgery Dept, 1 Tampa General Cir, Ste F-145, Tampa, FL 33606; **Phone:** 813-844-4545; **Board Cert:** Surgery 2010; Colon & Rectal Surgery 2011; **Med School:** Cornell Univ-Weill Med Coll 1985; **Resid:** Surgery, St Lukes-Roosevelt Med Ctr 1990; **Fellow:** Colon & Rectal Surgery, St Lukes-Roosevelt Med Ctr 1990; Colon & Rectal Surgery, St Lukes-Roosevelt Med Ctr 1991; **Fac Appt:** Prof S, Univ S Fla Coll Med

Nogueras, Juan J MD [CRS] - **Spec Exp:** Colon & Rectal Cancer; Hereditary Colon Cancer; Incontinence-Fecal; Inflammatory Bowel Disease/Crohn's; **Hospital:** Cleveland Clin - Weston (page 55); **Address:** Cleveland Clin, Colorectal Surgery Dept, 2950 Cleveland Clinic Blvd, Desk22, Weston, FL 33331; **Phone:** 954-659-5251; **Board Cert:** Surgery 2007; Colon & Rectal Surgery 2012; **Med School:** Jefferson Med Coll 1982; **Resid:** Surgery, NY-Presby/Columbia Univ Med Ctr 1987; **Fellow:** Colon & Rectal Surgery, Univ Minn Med Ctr 1991

Sands, Laurence R MD [CRS] - **Spec Exp:** Colon & Rectal Cancer; Incontinence-Fecal; Crohn's Disease; **Hospital:** Univ of Miami Hosp & Clins/Sylvester Comp Canc Ctr; **Address:** UHlth, Colon & Rectal Surgery Dept, 1475 NW 12th Ave, Miami, FL 33136; **Phone:** 305-243-9110; **Board Cert:** Colon & Rectal Surgery 2009; Surgery 2004; **Med School:** Northwestern Univ 1990; **Resid:** Surgery, Einstein Med Ctr 1995; **Fellow:** Colon & Rectal Surgery, Cleveland Clin 1996; **Fac Appt:** Prof S, Univ Miami Sch Med

Vernava III, Anthony M MD [CRS] - **Spec Exp:** Colon & Rectal Cancer; Colon & Rectal Cancer-Familial Polyposis; Inflammatory Bowel Disease; Crohn's Disease; **Hospital:** Physicians Regl Hlthcare Med Ctr-Pine Ridge; **Address:** Physicians Regl Med Grp, 6101 Pine Ridge Rd, Naples, FL 34119; **Phone:** 239-348-4531; **Board Cert:** Surgery 2007; Colon & Rectal Surgery 1989; **Med School:** St Louis Univ 1982; **Resid:** Surgery, St Louis Univ Med Ctr 1987; **Fellow:** Colon & Rectal Surgery, Univ MN Med Ctr 1988; Colon & Rectal Surgery, Natl Cancer Ctr 1989

Wexner, Steven D MD [CRS] - **Spec Exp:** Colon & Rectal Cancer; Laparoscopic Surgery; Inflammatory Bowel Disease/Crohn's; Incontinence-Fecal; **Hospital:** Cleveland Clin - Weston (page 55); **Address:** Cleveland Clinic, 2950 Cleveland Clinic Blvd, Weston, FL 33331-3609; **Phone:** 954-659-5251; **Board Cert:** Surgery 2005; Colon & Rectal Surgery 2006; **Med School:** Cornell Univ 1982; **Resid:** Surgery, Roosevelt Hosp 1987; **Fellow:** Colon & Rectal Surgery, Univ Minnesota 1988; **Fac Appt:** Prof S, FAU/Schmidt Coll Med

Midwest

Abcarian, Herand MD [CRS] - **Spec Exp:** Rectal Cancer/Sphincter Preservation; Inflammatory Bowel Disease; Anorectal Disorders; Incontinence-Fecal; **Hospital:** Univ of IL Med Ctr at Chicago, Gottlieb Meml Hosp; **Address:** Univ of IL Med Ctr, Division of Colorectal Surgery, 840 S Wood St, Fl 5, Ste 518, MS 958, Chicago, IL 60612; **Phone:** 312-413-2708; **Board Cert:** Surgery 1972; Colon & Rectal Surgery 1972; **Med School:** Iran 1965; **Resid:** Surgery, Cook County Hosp 1971; Colon & Rectal Surgery, Cook County Hosp 1972; **Fac Appt:** Prof S, Univ IL Coll Med

Birnbaum, Elisa H MD [CRS] - **Spec Exp:** Colon & Rectal Cancer; Inflammatory Bowel Disease/Crohn's; Pelvic Organ Prolapse; Rectovaginal Fistula; **Hospital:** Barnes-Jewish Hosp; **Address:** 4921 Parkview Pl, St Louis, MO 63110; **Phone:** 314-454-7177; **Board Cert:** Surgery 2009; Colon & Rectal Surgery 2011; **Med School:** Univ IL Coll Med 1985; **Resid:** Surgery, LIJ Med Ctr 1990; **Fellow:** Colon & Rectal Surgery, Barnes Jewish Hosp 1991; **Fac Appt:** Prof S, Washington Univ, St Louis

Church, James Michael MD [CRS] - **Spec Exp:** Colon & Rectal Cancer; Colon & Rectal Cancer-Familial Polyposis; Desmoid Tumors; Incontinence-Fecal; **Hospital:** Cleveland Clin (page 55); **Address:** 9500 Euclid Ave, A Bldg - Fl 3, Cleveland, OH 44195; **Phone:** 216-444-6536; **Med School:** New Zealand 1974; **Resid:** Surgery, Aukland Hosps 1980; **Fellow:** Research, Aukland Hosps 1983; Colon & Rectal Surgery, Cleveland Clinic 1984; **Fac Appt:** Prof CRS, Cleveland Cl Coll Med/Case West Res

Delaney, Conor P MD/PhD [CRS] - **Spec Exp:** Laparoscopic Surgery; Colon & Rectal Cancer; Inflammatory Bowel Disease/Crohn's; Rectal Cancer/Sphincter Preservation; **Hospital:** UH Case Med Ctr; **Address:** Univ Hosp Case Med Ctr, Dept Surgery-Colorectal, 11100 Euclid Ave, MS 5047, Cleveland, OH 44106; **Phone:** 216-844-8087; **Board Cert:** Surgery 1998; Colon & Rectal Surgery 1998; **Med School:** Ireland 1989; **Resid:** Surgery, Univ Hosp 1993; Surgery, Univ Hosp 1999; **Fellow:** Research, Univ Pittsburgh 1995; Colon & Rectal Surgery, Cleveland Clinic 2000; **Fac Appt:** Prof S, Cleveland Cl Coll Med/Case West Res

Dietz, David W MD [CRS] - **Spec Exp:** Colon & Rectal Cancer; Anal Cancer; Anorectal Disorders; Pelvic Floor Disorders; **Hospital:** Cleveland Clin (page 55); **Address:** Cleveland Clinic, Colorectal Surgery, 9500 Euclid Ave, Desk A30, Cleveland, OH 44195; **Phone:** 216-445-6597; **Board Cert:** Surgery 2010; Colon & Rectal Surgery 2012; **Med School:** Jefferson Med Coll 1993; **Resid:** Surgery, Cleveland Clinic 1999; Colon & Rectal Surgery, Cleveland Clinic 2001

Foley, Eugene F MD [CRS] - **Spec Exp:** Colon & Rectal Cancer; Ulcerative Colitis; **Hospital:** Univ WI Hosp & Clins; **Address:** Univ WI Hosp & Clins, 600 Highland Ave, Box 7375, Madison, WI 53792-7375; **Phone:** 608-263-2521; **Board Cert:** Surgery 2003; Colon & Rectal Surgery 2005; **Med School:** Harvard Med Sch 1985; **Resid:** Surgery, Beth Israel Deaconess Med Ctr 1991; **Fellow:** Colon & Rectal Surgery, Lahey Clin 1993; **Fac Appt:** Prof S, Univ Wisc

Lavery, Ian C MD [CRS] - **Spec Exp:** Colon & Rectal Cancer; Inflammatory Bowel Disease; Pediatric Gastrointestinal Surgery; **Hospital:** Cleveland Clin (page 55); **Address:** 9500 Euclid Ave, Desk A30, Cleveland, OH 44195; **Phone:** 216-444-6930; **Board Cert:** Colon & Rectal Surgery 1998; **Med School:** Australia 1967; **Resid:** Surgery, Princess Alexandra Hosp 1974; Colon & Rectal Surgery, Cleveland Clinic 1977; **Fac Appt:** Prof S, Case West Res Univ

Lederman, Eric D MD [CRS] - **Spec Exp:** Colon & Rectal Cancer; Anorectal Disorders; Crohn's Disease; Diverticulitis; **Hospital:** Missouri Baptist Med Ctr; **Address:** Suburban Surgical Assocs, 555 N New Ballas Rd, Ste 265, St Louis, MO 63141-6886; **Phone:** 314-991-4644; **Board Cert:** Surgery 2008; Colon & Rectal Surgery 2010; **Med School:** Washington Univ, St Louis 1992; **Resid:** Surgery, Albany Med Ctr 1999; **Fellow:** Colon & Rectal Surgery, St Louis Univ Hosp 2001

Lowry, Ann C MD [CRS] - **Spec Exp:** Anal Sphincter Repair; Rectovaginal Fistula; Inflammatory Bowel Disease; **Hospital:** Fairview Southdale Hosp, Abbott - Northwestern Hosp; **Address:** 1055 W Gate Drive, Ste 190, St Paul, MN 55114; **Phone:** 651-312-1700; **Board Cert:** Colon & Rectal Surgery 2013; **Med School:** Tufts Univ 1977; **Resid:** Surgery, New England Med Ctr 1982; **Fellow:** Colon & Rectal Surgery, Univ Minn Affil Hosp 1987; **Fac Appt:** Clin Prof S, Univ Minn

Ludwig, Kirk A MD [CRS] - **Spec Exp:** Colon & Rectal Cancer & Surgery; Pelvic Organ Prolapse; Rectal Cancer/Sphincter Preservation; Incontinence-Fecal; **Hospital:** Froedtert & Med Coll WI; **Address:** Dept Surgery, 9200 W Wisconsin Ave, Milwaukee, WI 53226; **Phone:** 414-805-5783; **Board Cert:** Surgery 2005; Colon & Rectal Surgery 2007; **Med School:** Univ Cincinnati 1988; **Resid:** Surgery, Med Coll Wisc 1994; **Fellow:** Colon & Rectal Surgery, Cleveland Clin 1996; **Fac Appt:** Assoc Prof S, Med Coll Wisc

Madoff, Robert D MD [CRS] - **Spec Exp:** Colon & Rectal Cancer; Inflammatory Bowel Disease; Incontinence/Pelvic Floor Disorders; **Hospital:** Univ Minn Med Ctr, Fairview - West Bank Campus; **Address:** 420 Delaware St SE, Minneapolis, MN 55455; **Phone:** 612-624-9708; **Board Cert:** Colon & Rectal Surgery 2002; **Med School:** Columbia P&S 1979; **Resid:** Surgery, Univ Minn Hosps 1987; **Fellow:** Colon & Rectal Surgery, Univ Minn Hosps 1988; **Fac Appt:** Prof S, Univ Minn

Mutch, Matthew G MD [CRS] - **Spec Exp:** Colon & Rectal Cancer; Inflammatory Bowel Disease; Incontinence/Pelvic Floor Disorders; Rectovaginal Fistula; **Hospital:** Barnes-Jewish Hosp; **Address:** 4921 Parkview Pl, St Louis, MO 63110-1010; **Phone:** 314-454-7177; **Board Cert:** Surgery 2012; Colon & Rectal Surgery 2013; **Med School:** Washington Univ, St Louis 1994; **Resid:** Surgery, Barnes Jewish Hosp 2001; **Fellow:** Research, Barnes Jewish Hosp 1998; Colon & Rectal Surgery, Lahey Clinic 2002; **Fac Appt:** Assoc Prof S, Washington Univ, St Louis

Nelson, Heidi MD [CRS] - **Spec Exp:** Colon & Rectal Cancer; Gastrointestinal Cancer; **Hospital:** Mayo Med Ctr & Clin - Rochester, Rochester Methodist Hosp; **Address:** Mayo Clinic, 200 First St SW, Rochester, MN 55905; **Phone:** 507-284-2511; **Board Cert:** Surgery 2007; Colon & Rectal Surgery 1989; **Med School:** Univ Wash 1981; **Resid:** Surgery, Oregon Hlth Sci Univ Hosp 1987; Colon & Rectal Surgery, Oregon Hlth Sci Univ Hosp 1985; **Fellow:** Colon & Rectal Surgery, Mayo Clinic 1988; **Fac Appt:** Prof S, Mayo Med Sch

Orkin, Bruce A MD [CRS] - **Spec Exp:** Colon & Rectal Cancer; Laparoscopic Surgery; Robotic Surgery; Microsurgery; **Hospital:** Rush Univ Med Ctr; **Address:** Rush Univ Surgeons, Professional Bldg, 1725 W Harrison St, Ste 810, Chicago, IL 60612; **Phone:** 312-942-7780; **Board Cert:** Colon & Rectal Surgery 2010; Surgery 2008; **Med School:** Univ Minn 1981; **Resid:** Surgery, UCLA Med Ctr 1983; Surgery, Mayo Clinic 1986; **Fellow:** Surgical Research, Mayo Clinic 1988; Colon & Rectal Surgery, Cleveland Clinic 1989; **Fac Appt:** Prof S, Rush Med Coll

Pemberton, John H MD [CRS] - **Spec Exp:** Inflammatory Bowel Disease/Crohn's; Colon & Rectal Cancer; **Hospital:** Rochester Methodist Hosp, St. Mary's Hosp - Rochester MN (Mayo); **Address:** Mayo Clinic, Div Colon & Rectal Surg, 200 First St SW, Gonda Bldg, rm 9-205, Rochester, MN 55905; **Phone:** 507-284-2359; **Board Cert:** Surgery 2001; Colon & Rectal Surgery 1985; **Med School:** Tulane Univ 1976; **Resid:** Surgery, Mayo Clinic 1983; **Fellow:** Colon & Rectal Surgery, Mayo Clinic 1984; **Fac Appt:** Prof S, Mayo Med Sch

Rafferty, Janice F MD [CRS] - **Spec Exp:** Colon & Rectal Cancer; Ulcerative Colitis; Crohn's Disease; Anal Disorders & Reconstruction; **Hospital:** Christ Hosp, The - Cincinnati, Univ Cincinnati Med Ctr; **Address:** UC Physicians Colon & Rectal Surgery, 2123 Auburn Ave, Ste 524, Cincinnati, OH 45219; **Phone:** 513-929-0104; **Board Cert:** Surgery 2004; Colon & Rectal Surgery 2008; **Med School:** Ohio State Univ 1988; **Resid:** Surgery, Univ Cincinnati Hosp 1995; Colon & Rectal Surgery, Barnes Jewish Hosp 1996; **Fac Appt:** Prof S, Univ Cincinnati

Remzi, Feza H MD [CRS] - **Spec Exp:** Colon & Rectal Cancer & Surgery; Inflammatory Bowel Disease; Laparoscopic Surgery; **Hospital:** Cleveland Clin (page 55); **Address:** Cleveland Clinic, 9500 Euclid Ave, Dept A30, Cleveland, OH 44195; **Phone:** 216-445-5020; **Board Cert:** Surgery 2006; Colon & Rectal Surgery 2007; **Med School:** Turkey 1989; **Resid:** Colon & Rectal Surgery, Cleveland Clinic 1996; Colon & Rectal Surgery, Cleveland Clinic 1997

Saclarides, Theodore J MD [CRS] - **Spec Exp:** Rectal Cancer/Sphincter Preservation; Laparoscopic Surgery; Inflammatory Bowel Disease; **Hospital:** Loyola Univ Med Ctr; **Address:** Loyola Univ Med Ctr, 2160 S First Ave, Maywood, IL 60153; **Phone:** 708-327-2846; **Board Cert:** Surgery 2007; Colon & Rectal Surgery 1989; **Med School:** Univ Miami Sch Med 1982; **Resid:** Surgery, Rush Univ Med Ctr 1987; **Fellow:** Colon & Rectal Surgery, Mayo Clinic 1988; **Fac Appt:** Prof S, Rush Med Coll

Senagore, Anthony MD [CRS] - **Spec Exp:** Laparoscopic Surgery; Colon & Rectal Cancer; Anorectal Disorders; Inflammatory Bowel Disease/Crohn's; **Hospital:** Covenant HealthCare, St. Mary's Med Ctr of Saginaw; **Address:** CMU Midwestern Surgical Assocs, 912 S Washington Ave, Ste 1, Saginaw, MI 48601; **Phone:** 989-790-1001; **Board Cert:** Surgery 2006; Colon & Rectal Surgery 2009; Surgical Critical Care 2006; **Med School:** Mich State Univ 1981; **Resid:** Surgery, Butterworth Hosp 1987; Colon & Rectal Surgery, Ferguson Hosp 1989; **Fac Appt:** Prof S, Central Michigan Univ Coll Med

Stryker, Steven J MD [CRS] - **Spec Exp:** Colon & Rectal Cancer; Inflammatory Bowel Disease; Laparoscopic Surgery; **Hospital:** Northwestern Meml Hosp; **Address:** 676 N Saint Clair St, Ste 1525A, Chicago, IL 60611-2862; **Phone:** 312-943-5427; **Board Cert:** Surgery 2004; Colon & Rectal Surgery 1986; **Med School:** Northwestern Univ 1978; **Resid:** Surgery, Northwestern Meml Hosp 1983; **Fellow:** Colon & Rectal Surgery, Mayo Clinic 1985; **Fac Appt:** Assoc Clin Prof S, Northwestern Univ

Trudel, Judith L MD [CRS] - **Spec Exp:** Colon & Rectal Cancer; Anorectal Disorders; **Hospital:** St. John's Hosp-Maplewood MN, St. Joseph's Hosp; **Address:** Colon & Rectal Surgery Assocs, 1055 Westgate Drive, Ste 190, St Paul, MN 55114; **Phone:** 651-312-1620; **Board Cert:** Surgery 2007; Colon & Rectal Surgery 2006; **Med School:** Canada 1979; **Resid:** Surgery, Montreal Genl Hosp 1984; **Fellow:** Colon & Rectal Surgery, Cleveland Clin 1986; **Fac Appt:** Assoc Prof S, Univ Minn

Wise, Paul E MD [CRS] - **Spec Exp:** Colon & Rectal Cancer & Surgery; Minimally Invasive Surgery; Colon & Rectal Cancer-Hereditary; Inflammatory Bowel Disease; **Hospital:** Barnes-Jewish Hosp, Barnes-Jewish West County Hosp; **Address:** 1040 N Mason Rd, Ste 120, Creve Coeur, MO 63141; **Phone:** 314-454-7177; **Board Cert:** Surgery 2004; Colon & Rectal Surgery 2005; **Med School:** Johns Hopkins Univ 1996; **Resid:** Surgery, Vanderbilt Univ Med Ctr 2003; **Fellow:** Colon & Rectal Surgery, Barnes-Jewish Hosp 2004; **Fac Appt:** Assoc Prof S, Washington Univ, St Louis

Wolff, Bruce G MD [CRS] - **Spec Exp:** Inflammatory Bowel Disease; Crohn's Disease; Colon & Rectal Cancer; **Hospital:** Mayo Med Ctr & Clin - Rochester; **Address:** Mayo Clinic, 200 First St SW, Rochester, MN 55905; **Phone:** 507-284-2511; **Board Cert:** Colon & Rectal Surgery 2001; **Med School:** Duke Univ 1973; **Resid:** Surgery, NY Hosp-Cornell Med Ctr 1981; **Fellow:** Colon & Rectal Surgery, Mayo Clinic 1982; **Fac Appt:** Prof S, Mayo Med Sch

Great Plains and Mountains

Blatchford, Garnet J MD [CRS] - **Spec Exp:** Colon Cancer; Anal Disorders & Reconstruction; **Hospital:** Methodist Hosp - Omaha, Bergan Mercy Med Ctr-Alegant Hlth; **Address:** 9850 Nicholas St, Ste 100, Omaha, NE 68114; **Phone:** 402-343-1122; **Board Cert:** Colon & Rectal Surgery 2009; **Med School:** Univ Nebr Coll Med 1983; **Resid:** Surgery, Univ Nebraska Med Ctr 1988; Colon & Rectal Surgery, Creighton Univ 1990; **Fac Appt:** Assoc Prof S, Creighton Univ

Schatz, Lisa Shawn MD [CRS] - **Spec Exp:** Gastrointestinal Surgery; Colon & Rectal Cancer & Surgery; **Hospital:** Rose Med Ctr; **Address:** Rocky Mountain Surgical Assocs, 4545 E 9th Ave, Ste 460, Denver, CO 80220; **Phone:** 303-388-2922; **Board Cert:** Surgery 2011; Colon & Rectal Surgery 2012; **Med School:** Case West Res Univ 1995; **Resid:** Surgery, Univ Hosps of Cleveland 2000; Colon & Rectal Surgery, Alton Ochsner Med Ctr 2002; **Fac Appt:** Assoc Clin Prof CRS, Univ Colorado

Thorson, Alan G MD [CRS] - **Spec Exp:** Colon & Rectal Cancer; Rectal Cancer/Sphincter Preservation; Incontinence-Fecal; Laparoscopic Surgery; **Hospital:** Nebraska Meth Hosp, Bergan Mercy Med Ctr-Alegant Hlth; **Address:** 9850 Nicholas St, Ste 100, Omaha, NE 68114-2191; **Phone:** 402-343-1122; **Board Cert:** Colon & Rectal Surgery 1999; **Med School:** Univ Nebr Coll Med 1979; **Resid:** Surgery, Univ Nebraska Affil Hosp 1984; Colon & Rectal Surgery, Univ Minn Affil Hosp 1985; **Fac Appt:** Clin Prof S, Creighton Univ

Williams, Shauna Tseu MD [CRS] - **Spec Exp:** Ulcerative Colitis; **Hospital:** St. Alphonsus Regl Med Ctr; **Address:** 1072 N Liberty St, Ste 201, Boise, ID 83704; **Phone:** 208-377-2273; **Board Cert:** Surgery 2009; Colon & Rectal Surgery 2010; **Med School:** Univ Hawaii JA Burns Sch Med 1984; **Resid:** Surgery, Univ Oregon Hlth Sci Ctr 1990; **Fellow:** Colon & Rectal Surgery, Mayo Clinic 1991

Southwest

Bailey, H Randolph MD [CRS] - **Spec Exp:** Rectal Cancer/Sphincter Preservation; Inflammatory Bowel Disease; Incontinence-Fecal; Endometriosis-Intestine; **Hospital:** Methodist Hosp - Houston, St. Luke's Episcopal Hosp-Houston; **Address:** Colon & Rectal Clinic, Smith Tower, 6550 Fannin St, Ste 2307, Houston, TX 77030-2717; **Phone:** 713-790-9250; **Board Cert:** Surgery 1974; Colon & Rectal Surgery 2004; **Med School:** Univ Tex SW, Dallas 1968; **Resid:** Surgery, Hermann Hosp 1973; **Fellow:** Colon & Rectal Surgery, Ferguson-Droste Hosp 1974; **Fac Appt:** Clin Prof S, Univ Tex, Houston

Beck, David E MD [CRS] - **Spec Exp:** Colon & Rectal Cancer; Minimally Invasive Surgery; Inflammatory Bowel Disease; **Hospital:** Ochsner Med Ctr-New Orleans; **Address:** Ochsner Med Ctr, Div Colorectal Surg, 1514 Jefferson Hwy Fl 4, New Orleans, LA 70121-2429; **Phone:** 504-842-4060; **Board Cert:** Colon & Rectal Surgery 1987; **Med School:** Univ Miami Sch Med 1979; **Resid:** Surgery, Wilford Hall USAF Med Ctr 1984; **Fellow:** Colon & Rectal Surgery, Cleveland Cllin 1986; **Fac Appt:** Prof S, Louisiana State U, New Orleans

Fleshman Jr, James W MD [CRS] - **Spec Exp:** Colon & Rectal Cancer; Laparoscopic Surgery; Inflammatory Bowel Disease; Robotic Surgery; **Hospital:** Baylor Univ Med Ctr-Dallas; **Address:** Colon & Rectal Surgical Assocs, 3410 Worth St, Ste 235, Dallas, TX 75246; **Phone:** 214-820-8768; **Board Cert:** Colon & Rectal Surgery 2012; Surgery 2002; **Med School:** Washington Univ, St Louis 1980; **Resid:** Surgery, Barnes-Jewish Hosp 1986; **Fellow:** Colon & Rectal Surgery, Univ Toronto 1987

Haas, Eric M MD [CRS] - **Spec Exp:** Laparoscopic Surgery; Colon & Rectal Cancer; Inflammatory Bowel Disease/Crohn's; Incontinence-Fecal; **Hospital:** Methodist Hosp - Houston, Woman's Hosp TX; **Address:** 7900 Fannin St, Ste 2700, Houston, TX 77054; **Phone:** 713-790-0600; **Board Cert:** Surgery 2012; Colon & Rectal Surgery 2013; **Med School:** Univ Tex, Houston 1997; **Resid:** Surgery, St Joseph Hosp 2002; **Fellow:** Colon & Rectal Surgery, Univ TX Affil Hosp 2003

Heppell, Jacques P MD [CRS] - **Spec Exp:** Colon & Rectal Cancer; Inflammatory Bowel Disease; Anorectal Disorders; **Hospital:** Mayo Clinic - Phoenix; **Address:** Mayo Clinic, 5777 E Mayo Blvd, Phoenix, AZ 85054; **Phone:** 480-342-2697; **Board Cert:** Surgery 2004; Colon & Rectal Surgery 1995; **Med School:** Univ Montreal 1974; **Resid:** Surgery, Univ Montreal Affil Hosps 1979; **Fellow:** Colon & Rectal Surgery, Mayo Clinic 1983; **Fac Appt:** Prof S, Mayo Med Sch

Hicks, Terry C MD [CRS] - **Spec Exp:** Colon & Rectal Cancer; **Hospital:** Ochsner Med Ctr-New Orleans; **Address:** Ochsner Med Ctr, Div Colorectal Surg, 1514 Jefferson Hwy, Fl 4, New Orleans, LA 70121-2429; **Phone:** 504-842-5884; **Board Cert:** Colon & Rectal Surgery 2002; **Med School:** Univ Tex, San Antonio 1977; **Resid:** Surgery, Univ Louisville Med Ctr 1982; Colon & Rectal Surgery, Ochsner Clinic 1983; **Fac Appt:** Clin Prof S, Louisiana State U, New Orleans

Huber Jr, Philip J MD [CRS] - **Spec Exp:** Colon & Rectal Cancer; Inflammatory Bowel Disease; **Hospital:** Med City Dallas Hosp, TX Hlth Presby Hosp Dallas; **Address:** 8160 Walnut Hill Ln, Ste 306, Dallas, TX 75231; **Phone:** 214-345-8060; **Board Cert:** Colon & Rectal Surgery 1993; **Med School:** Columbia P&S 1972; **Resid:** Surgery, Parkland Meml Hosp 1977; **Fellow:** Colon & Rectal Surgery, Presby Hosp 1978; **Fac Appt:** Prof CRS, Univ Tex SW, Dallas

Young-Fadok, Tonia M MD [CRS] - **Spec Exp:** Laparoscopic Surgery; Crohn's Disease; Ulcerative Colitis; Colon & Rectal Cancer; **Hospital:** Mayo Clinic - Phoenix; **Address:** Mayo Clinic Hosp, 5777 E Mayo Blvd, MCSB 3rd Fl, Phoenix, AZ 85054; **Phone:** 480-342-2697; **Board Cert:** Surgery 2006; Colon & Rectal Surgery 2009; **Med School:** England, UK 1987; **Resid:** Surgery, St Elizabeths Med Ctr 1995; **Fellow:** Colon & Rectal Surgery, Mayo Clinic 1997; Laparoscopic Surgery, Mayo Clinic 1997; **Fac Appt:** Prof S, Mayo Med Sch

West Coast and Pacific

Beart Jr, Robert W MD [CRS] - **Spec Exp:** Colon & Rectal Cancer; Rectal Cancer/Sphincter Preservation; **Hospital:** Glendale Mem Hosp & Hlth Ctr; **Address:** Colorectal Surgery Inst, 222 W Eulalia St, Ste 100A, Glendale, CA 91204; **Phone:** 818-244-8161; **Board Cert:** Colon & Rectal Surgery 1995; **Med School:** Harvard Med Sch 1971; **Resid:** Surgery, Univ Colo Med Ctr 1976; Colon & Rectal Surgery, Mayo Clinic 1978; **Fellow:** Transplant Surgery, Univ Colo Med Ctr 1975; **Fac Appt:** Prof Emeritus S, USC Sch Med

Chiu, Yanek S MD [CRS] - **Hospital:** CA Pacific Med Ctr-Pacific Campus; **Address:** 3838 California St, Ste 616, San Francisco, CA 94118; **Phone:** 415-668-0411; **Board Cert:** Colon & Rectal Surgery 1997; **Med School:** Boston Univ 1971; **Resid:** Surgery, Boston Med Ctr 1976; **Fellow:** Colon & Rectal Surgery, Mayo Clinic 1978; **Fac Appt:** Assoc Clin Prof CRS, UCSF

Coutsoftides, Theodore MD [CRS] - **Spec Exp:** Laparoscopic Surgery; Inflammatory Bowel Disease; Anal Sphincter Repair; **Hospital:** St. Joseph's Hosp - Orange; **Address:** 1310 W Stewart Drive, Ste 605, Orange, CA 92868-3857; **Phone:** 714-532-2544; **Board Cert:** Colon & Rectal Surgery 1977; **Med School:** Israel 1970; **Resid:** Surgery, Cleveland Clinic 1973; Surgery, Royal Victoria Hosp 1976; **Fellow:** Colon & Rectal Surgery, Cleveland Clinic 1977; **Fac Appt:** Assoc Prof S, UC Irvine

Lee, Patrick Y H MD [CRS] - **Hospital:** Providence Portland Med Ctr, Legacy Good Samaritan Med Ctr; **Address:** Surgical Specialty Grp, Colon & Rectal Clin, 9155 SW Barnes Rd, Ste 839, Portland, OR 97225; **Phone:** 503-222-1615; **Board Cert:** Surgery 2004; Colon & Rectal Surgery 2007; **Med School:** Northwestern Univ-Feinberg Sch Med 1988; **Resid:** Surgery, OR Hlth & Sci Univ 1994; **Fellow:** Colon & Rectal Surgery, Cleveland Clin 1995

Medwell, Steven MD [CRS] - **Spec Exp:** Colon & Rectal Cancer & Surgery; Ulcerative Colitis; Crohn's Disease; **Hospital:** Swedish Med Ctr-First Hill-Seattle; **Address:** Polyclinic-First Hill, 1145 Broadway, Seattle, WA 98122; **Phone:** 206-860-4440; **Board Cert:** Colon & Rectal Surgery 1978; **Med School:** Indiana Univ 1973; **Resid:** Surgical Pathology, Swedish Med Ctr 1977; **Fellow:** Colon & Rectal Surgery, Ferguson Hosp 1978; **Fac Appt:** Assoc Clin Prof CRS, Univ Wash

Ramamoorthy, Sonia L MD [CRS] - **Spec Exp:** Colon & Rectal Cancer; Diverticulitis; Incontinence/Pelvic Floor Disorders; Inflammatory Bowel Disease; **Hospital:** UCSD Med Ctr; **Address:** 3855 Health Sciences Drive, MC 0987, La Jolla, CA 92093; **Phone:** 858-822-6277; **Board Cert:** Surgery 2012; Colon & Rectal Surgery 2005; **Med School:** Boston Univ 1996; **Resid:** Surgery, UCSD Med Ctr 2001; **Fellow:** Colon & Rectal Surgery, Barnes-Jewish Hosp 2002; Research, UCSD Med Ctr 2006; **Fac Appt:** Assoc Prof S, UCSD

Sokol, Thomas P MD [CRS] - **Spec Exp:** Colon & Rectal Cancer & Surgery; Incontinence-Fecal; Constipation; Gastrointestinal Motility Disorders; **Hospital:** Cedars-Sinai Med Ctr; **Address:** 8737 Beverly Blvd, Ste 402, Los Angeles, CA 90048-1828; **Phone:** 310-854-3580; **Board Cert:** Colon & Rectal Surgery 2008; **Med School:** Ros Franklin Univ/Chicago Med Sch 1980; **Resid:** Surgery, Habor UCLA Med Ctr 1985; **Fellow:** Colon & Rectal Surgery, Carle Fdn Hosp/Univ Ill 1986; **Fac Appt:** Assoc Clin Prof S, UCLA

Stamos, Michael J MD [CRS] - **Spec Exp:** Rectal Cancer/Sphincter Preservation; Laparoscopic Surgery; Inflammatory Bowel Disease; Colon & Rectal Cancer; **Hospital:** UC Irvine Med Ctr; **Address:** UC Irvine Med Ctr, Div Colon & Rectal Surg, 101 The City Drive, 22c Bldg, Orange, CA 92868; **Phone:** 714-456-6262; **Board Cert:** Surgery 2010; Colon & Rectal Surgery 2012; **Med School:** Case West Res Univ 1985; **Resid:** Surgery, Jackson Meml Hosp 1990; **Fellow:** Colon & Rectal Surgery, Ochsner Clinic 1991; **Fac Appt:** Prof S, UC Irvine

Varma, Madhulika G MD [CRS] - **Spec Exp:** Colon & Rectal Cancer & Surgery; Inflammatory Bowel Disease; Pelvic Floor Disorders; Laparoscopic Surgery; **Hospital:** UCSF - Mt Zion Med Ctr; **Address:** Center for Colorectal Surgery, 2330 Post St, Ste 260, San Francisco, CA 94115-1799; **Phone:** 415-885-3606; **Board Cert:** Colon & Rectal Surgery 2010; Surgery 2007; **Med School:** Brown Univ 1991; **Resid:** Surgery, UCSF Med Ctr 1998; **Fellow:** Colon & Rectal Surgery, Univ Minnesota Med Ctr 2000; Research, UCSF Med Ctr 2001; **Fac Appt:** Prof S, UCSF

Welton, Mark L MD [CRS] - **Spec Exp:** Ulcerative Colitis; Crohn's Disease; Colon & Rectal Cancer; Anal Cancer; **Hospital:** Stanford Univ Hosp & Clins, Lucile Packard Chldn's Hosp; **Address:** The Cancer Ctr, 875 Blake Wilbur Drive, Stanford, CA 94305; **Phone:** 650-498-6000; **Board Cert:** Surgery 2012; Colon & Rectal Surgery 2005; **Med School:** UCLA 1984; **Resid:** Surgery, UCLA Med Ctr 1992; **Fellow:** Colon & Rectal Surgery, Barnes Jewish Hosp 1993; **Fac Appt:** Prof S, Stanford Univ

Wong, Ronald J MD [CRS] - **Spec Exp:** Laparoscopic Surgery; **Hospital:** Queen's Med Ctr - Honolulu; **Address:** Queen's Physicians' Office Bldg 1, 1380 Lusitana St, rm 614, Honolulu, HI 96813; **Phone:** 808-524-1856; **Board Cert:** Surgery 2008; **Med School:** Univ Hawaii JA Burns Sch Med 1981; **Resid:** Surgery, Univ Hawaii 1985; Surgery, Catholic Med Ctr 1987; **Fellow:** Research, Cornell Univ Med Ctr 1988; Colon & Rectal Surgery, Suburban Hosp 1989; **Fac Appt:** Clin Prof S, Univ Hawaii JA Burns Sch Med

Worsey, Michael J MD [CRS] - **Spec Exp:** Colon & Rectal Cancer; **Hospital:** Scripps Meml Hosp - La Jolla; **Address:** Advanced Surgical Assocs, 9834 Genesee Ave, Ste 201, La Jolla, CA 92037; **Phone:** 858-558-2272; **Board Cert:** Surgery 2009; Colon & Rectal Surgery 2008; **Med School:** England, UK 1985; **Resid:** Surgery, Bristol Royal Infirm/Royal Gwent Hosp 1989; Surgery, Univ Pittsburgh Med Ctr 1997; **Fellow:** Colon & Rectal Surgery, Cleveland Clin 1998

Cleveland Clinic

Every life deserves world class care.

Cleveland Clinic
Digestive Disease Institute
9500 Euclid Ave.
Cleveland, OH 44195

Colorectal Surgery

Cleveland Clinic's Digestive Disease Institute (DDI) is one of the largest digestive programs in the country and is ranked No. 2 in the nation by *U.S. News & World Report*. DDI was one of the first to fully integrate its departments of Bariatric Surgery, Colorectal Surgery, Gastroenterology & Hepatology, General Surgery and Nutrition. Combining these disciplines in one location facilitates unprecedented patient care, multidisciplinary education and collaborative research. In 2012, DDI physicians performed over 18,000 surgical cases and close to 60,000 endoscopic cases. Transplant surgeons completed over 150 digestive disease-related organ transplants, including liver, pancreas and intestinal transplantation, achieving outstanding outcomes.

Highlights of the Department of Colorectal Surgery:

- The first ileoanal pouch for ulcerative colitis was performed at Cleveland Clinic in the 1980s.
- Our colorectal surgeons performed the world's first colon resection entirely through a single incision in the belly button in 2008.
- We performed the world's first single-incision procto-colectomy and ileoanal pouch anastomosis (removing the entire large intestine and rectum) in 2009, leaving only a coin-sized scar in the patient's abdomen.
- We have an international reputation for excellence in inflammatory bowel disease, performing the most Crohn's disease operations, especially the bowel-conserving strictureplasty. We also perform the world's highest volume of J-Pouch surgeries and are the nation's largest referral center for repairing failed pelvic pouches.
- Our team performs more colon and rectal cancer surgeries than any other hospital in Ohio and one of the highest volumes in the nation.
- Led by a team of female physicians, our pelvic floor center treats the entire spectrum of bowel disorders, including fecal incontinence and chronic constipation.

Offering Same-Day Appointments
Call 866.320.4573

Treatment Guides
Cleveland Clinic has developed comprehensive treatment guides for many diseases and conditions. To download our free treatment guides, visit clevelandclinic.org/treatmentguides.

Online Medical Second Opinion
Call 216.444.3223 or 800.223.2273 ext. 43223 or email eclevelandclinic@ccf.org

Out-of-State Patients Assistance
Call 800.223.2273, ext. 55580 or email medicalconcierge@ccf.org

Visit Us At:
clevelandclinic.org

Follow Us On:

Facebook
facebook.com/clevelandclinic

Twitter
@ClevelandClinic

You Tube
youtube.com/clevelandclinic

Health Hub
clevelandclinic.org/HealthHub

NYU Langone
MEDICAL CENTER

550 First Avenue *(at 31st Street)*
New York, NY 10016

www.NYULMC.org

Physician Referral: **888-7-NYU-MED** *(888-769-8633)*

GASTROENTEROLOGY

NYU Langone Medical Center is dedicated to the diagnosis and treatment of patients with diseases of the gastrointestinal tract. Physicians draw on their extensive knowledge and experience in the diagnosis and management of inflammatory bowel disease, peptic ulcer disease, esophageal disorders, gastrointestinal cancer, and liver, biliary and pancreatic diseases. Laser, laparoscopic, endoscopic, and other minimally invasive options are available, and we specialize in the following areas:

Colorectal Cancer

The Medical Center offers the most advanced screening options available for the diagnosis of colon cancer. Additionally, physicians continue to investigate colorectal cancer in special populations such as women, veterans, immigrants, minorities and patients with HIV, and offer the use of standard and virtual colonoscopy for the detection of colorectal polyps and cancer.

Esophageal Diseases

The Esophageal Disease Center offers patients state-of-the-art diagnosis and treatment of esophageal disorders. The Center focuses on gastroesophageal reflux disease, esophageal motility disorders, Barrett's esophagus, adenocarcinoma of the esophagus and swallowing disorders. It also offers diagnostic studies on esophageal manometry, impedance testing for swallowing, pH catheter and impedance testing for reflux and BRAVO capsule pH testing, as well as such therapies as Barrett's ablation and esophageal dilations.

Gastrointestinal Cancers

Cancer Institute physicians treat patients with all types of gastrointestinal cancers, including those of the esophagus, stomach, colon/rectum, small intestine, liver, pancreas, gallbladder, and biliary tract. They also treat individuals with complex recurring disease, including those originally treated elsewhere. Patients have the opportunity to participate in numerous clinical trials.

Complex Treatments and Diagnosis

Our physicians are highly experienced in the use of enteroscopy and capsule endoscopy for the diagnosis of gastrointestinal bleeding of unknown origin. They have special interest in the diagnosis and treatment of patients with complex pancreatic-biliary disease through the use of ERCP and endoscopic ultrasound.

Liver Lesions and Adrenal Tumors

Our team treats liver lesions with painless radiofrequency ablation and are highly skilled in laproscopic adrenalectomies.

Top Doctors Make A Difference

Dermatology

A dermatologist is trained to diagnose and treat pediatric and adult patients with benign and malignant disorders of the skin, mouth, external genitalia, hair and nails, as well as a number of sexually transmitted diseases. The dermatologist may have additional training and experience in the diagnosis and treatment of skin cancers, melanomas, moles and other tumors of the skin, the management of contact dermatitis and other allergic and nonallergic skin disorders, and in the recognition of the skin manifestations of systemic (including internal malignancy) and infectious diseases. Dermatologists may have special training in dermatopathology and in the surgical techniques used in dermatology. They also have expertise in the management of cosmetic disorders of the skin such as hair loss and scars, and the skin changes associated with aging.

Training Required: Four years.

Certification in the following subspecialties requires additional training and examination.

Dermatopathology: A dermatopathologist has the expertise to diagnose and monitor diseases of the skin including infectious, immunologic, degenerative and neoplastic diseases. This entails the examination and interpretation of specially prepared tissue sections, cellular scrapings and smears of skin lesions by means of routine and special (electron and fluorescent) microscopes.

Pediatric Dermatology: A dermatologist trained to diagnose and treat pediatric patients with dermatologic diseases.

Dermatology

New England

Anderson, Richard Rox MD [D] - **Spec Exp:** Birthmarks/Hemangiomas; Pediatric Dermatology; Laser Surgery; **Hospital:** Mass Genl Hosp; **Address:** Dermatology Laser Center, 50 Staniford St, Ste 250, Boston, MA 02114; **Phone:** 617-724-6960; **Board Cert:** Dermatology 2009; **Med School:** Harvard Med Sch 1984; **Resid:** Dermatology, Mass Genl Hosp 1991; **Fellow:** Dermatologic Research, Mass Genl Hosp 1988; **Fac Appt:** Assoc Prof D, Harvard Med Sch

Arndt, Kenneth A MD [D] - **Spec Exp:** Skin Laser Surgery; Cosmetic Dermatology; **Hospital:** Beth Israel Deaconess Med Ctr - Boston, New England Bapt Hosp (page 63); **Address:** Skincare Physicians, 1244 Boylston St, Ste 302, Chestnut Hill, MA 02467; **Phone:** 617-731-1600; **Board Cert:** Dermatology 1966; **Med School:** Yale Univ 1961; **Resid:** Dermatology, Mass Genl Hosp 1965; **Fellow:** Dermatology, Harvard Med Sch 1965; **Fac Appt:** Clin Prof D, Harvard Med Sch

Bolognia, Jean L MD [D] - **Spec Exp:** Melanoma; Skin Cancer; **Hospital:** Yale-New Haven Hosp; **Address:** Yale, Dermatology Dept, 2 Church St S, Ste 305, New Haven, CT 06519; **Phone:** 203-789-1249; **Board Cert:** Dermatology 2009; **Med School:** Yale Univ 1980; **Resid:** Internal Medicine, Yale-New Haven Hosp 1982; Dermatology, Yale-New Haven Hosp 1985; **Fellow:** Dermatology, Yale-New Haven Hosp 1987; **Fac Appt:** Prof D, Yale Univ

Dover, Jeffrey MD [D] - **Spec Exp:** Cosmetic Dermatology; Skin Laser Surgery; **Hospital:** Beth Israel Deaconess Med Ctr - Boston, New England Bapt Hosp (page 63); **Address:** Skincare Physicians, 1244 Boylston St, Ste 302, Chesnut Hill, MA 02467; **Phone:** 617-731-1600; **Board Cert:** Dermatology 1985; **Med School:** Univ Ottawa 1981; **Resid:** Dermatology, Univ Toronto 1984; Dermatology, St Johns Hosp 1985; **Fellow:** Dermatology, Mass Genl Hosp 1987; **Fac Appt:** Assoc Prof D, Yale Univ

Dufresne, Raymond G MD [D] - **Spec Exp:** Mohs' Surgery; Skin Cancer; **Hospital:** Rhode Island Hosp; **Address:** University Dermatology, 593 Eddy St, APC 10, Providence, RI 02903; **Phone:** 401-444-7024; **Board Cert:** Internal Medicine 1983; Dermatology 1986; **Med School:** Vanderbilt Univ 1980; **Resid:** Internal Medicine, Vanderbilt Univ Med Ctr 1983; Dermatology, Vanderbilt Univ Med Ctr 1986; **Fellow:** Mohs Surgery, Cleveland Clinic 1988; **Fac Appt:** Asst Prof D, Brown Univ

Edelson, Richard L MD [D] - **Spec Exp:** Cutaneous Lymphoma; Immune Deficiency-Skin Disorders; **Hospital:** Yale-New Haven Hosp; **Address:** Yale, Dermatology Dept, 2 Church St S, Ste 305, New Haven, CT 06519; **Phone:** 203-789-1249; **Board Cert:** Dermatology 1977; **Med School:** Yale Univ 1970; **Resid:** Dermatology, Mass Genl Hosp 1972; Dermatology, Natl Inst Hlth-Clin Ctr 1975; **Fac Appt:** Prof D, Yale Univ

Fewkes, Jessica L MD [D] - **Spec Exp:** Mohs' Surgery; Skin Cancer-Head & Neck; Melanoma-Head & Neck; Cosmetic Dermatology; **Hospital:** Mass Eye & Ear Infirm; **Address:** Facial & Cosmetic Surgery Center, Mass Eye & Ear Infirmary, 243 Charles St, 9th Fl, Boston, MA 02114; **Phone:** 617-573-3789; **Board Cert:** Dermatology 1982; **Med School:** UCSF 1978; **Resid:** Dermatology, Mass Genl Hosp 1982; **Fellow:** Mohs Surgery, Duke Univ Med Ctr 1983; **Fac Appt:** Asst Prof D, Harvard Med Sch

Gellis, Stephen MD [D] - **Spec Exp:** Pediatric Dermatology; Melanoma; Pigmented Lesions; **Hospital:** Children's Hospital - Boston; **Address:** Boston Chldn's Hosp, Dept Dermatology, 300 Longwood Ave Fegan Bldg Fl 6, Boston, MA 02115; **Phone:** 617-355-6117; **Board Cert:** Pediatrics 1978; Dermatology 1979; Pediatric Dermatology 2006; **Med School:** Harvard Med Sch 1973; **Resid:** Pediatrics, Chldn's Hosp 1976; Dermatology, Mass Genl Hosp 1978; **Fac Appt:** Asst Prof D, Harvard Med Sch

Gilchrest, Barbara A MD [D] - **Spec Exp:** Photoaging; Melanoma; Skin Cancer; **Hospital:** Boston Med Ctr; **Address:** Boston Univ Cosmetic & Laser Center, 725 Albany St, Ste B8, Boston, MA 02118; **Phone:** 617-638-7420; **Board Cert:** Internal Medicine 1975; Dermatology 1978; **Med School:** Harvard Med Sch 1971; **Resid:** Internal Medicine, Boston City Hosp 1973; Dermatology, Harvard Med Sch Affil Hosp 1976; **Fellow:** Photo Biology, Harvard Med Sch Affil Hosp 1975; **Fac Appt:** Prof D, Boston Univ

Gottlieb, Alice B MD/PhD [D] - **Spec Exp:** Psoriasis; Psoriatic Arthritis; Atopic Dermatitis; Clinical Trials; **Hospital:** Tufts Med Ctr; **Address:** Tufts Med Ctr, 800 Washington St, Box 114, Boston, MA 02111; **Phone:** 617-636-0156; **Board Cert:** Internal Medicine 1982; Dermatology 2011; Rheumatology 1984; **Med School:** Cornell Univ-Weill Med Coll 1980; **Resid:** Internal Medicine, New York Hosp 1982; Dermatology, New York Hosp 1993; **Fellow:** Rheumatology, Hosp Special Surgery 1984; **Fac Appt:** Prof D, Tufts Univ

Kane, Kay S MD [D] - **Spec Exp:** Pediatric Dermatology; **Hospital:** Children's Hospital - Boston; **Address:** Boston Chldn's Hosp, 300 Longwood Ave Fegan Bldg Fl 6, Boston, MA 02115; **Phone:** 617-355-6126; **Board Cert:** Dermatology 2005; **Med School:** Harvard Med Sch 1993; **Resid:** Dermatology, Mass General Hosp 1997; **Fac Appt:** Asst Prof D, Harvard Med Sch

Kupper, Thomas S MD [D] - **Spec Exp:** Melanoma; Cutaneous Lymphoma; Skin Cancer; **Hospital:** Brigham & Women's Hosp, Dana-Farber Cancer Inst; **Address:** Dana Farber Cancer Institute, 450 Brookline Ave Fl 11, Boston, MA 02115; **Phone:** 617-632-6869; **Board Cert:** Dermatology 1989; **Med School:** Yale Univ 1981; **Resid:** Surgery, Yale-New Haven Hosp 1983; Dermatology, Yale-New Haven Hosp 1989; **Fac Appt:** Prof D, Harvard Med Sch

Leffell, David J MD [D] - **Spec Exp:** Mohs' Surgery; Melanoma; Cutaneous Lymphoma; Skin Laser Surgery; **Hospital:** Yale-New Haven Hosp; **Address:** Yale, Surgical Dermatology Dept, 40 Temple St, Ste 5A, New Haven, CT 06510; **Phone:** 203-785-3466; **Board Cert:** Internal Medicine 1984; Dermatology 2009; **Med School:** McGill Univ 1981; **Resid:** Internal Medicine, NY-Presby/Weill Cornell Med Ctr 1984; Dermatology, Meml Sloan-Kettering Cancer Ctr 1986; **Fellow:** Dermatology, Yale-New Haven Hosp 1987; Dermatologic Surgery, Univ Michigan Med Ctr 1988; **Fac Appt:** Prof D, Yale Univ

Maloney, Mary E MD [D] - **Spec Exp:** Mohs' Surgery; Skin Cancer; Dermatologic Surgery; **Hospital:** UMass Memorial Med Ctr; **Address:** UMass Meml Med Ctr-Hahnemann Campus, 281 Lincoln St Fl 4, Worcester, MA 01605; **Phone:** 508-334-5962; **Board Cert:** Dermatology 1982; **Med School:** Univ VT Coll Med 1977; **Resid:** Internal Medicine, Hartford Hospital 1979; Dermatology, Dartmouth-Hitchcock Med Ctr 1982; **Fellow:** Dermatologic Surgery, UCSF Med Ctr 1983; **Fac Appt:** Prof D, Univ Mass Sch Med

Neel, Victor A MD/PhD [D] - **Spec Exp:** Mohs' Surgery; Skin Cancer; Cosmetic Dermatology; **Hospital:** Mass Genl Hosp; **Address:** Mass General Hosp, Dermatology Assocs, 50 Staniford St, Ste 270, Boston, MA 02114; **Phone:** 617-726-1869; **Board Cert:** Dermatology 2009; **Med School:** Cornell Univ-Weill Med Coll 1995; **Resid:** Pediatrics, Rhode Island Hosp 1997; Dermatology, Rhode Island Hosp 2000; **Fellow:** Mohs Surgery, UCLA Med Ctr 2001; **Fac Appt:** Asst Prof D, Harvard Med Sch

Olbricht, Suzanne M MD [D] - **Spec Exp:** Skin Cancer; Mohs' Surgery; Muir-Torre Syndrome; **Hospital:** Lahey Hosp & Med Ctr; **Address:** Lahey Clinic, Dept Dermatology Surgery, 20 Wall St, Burlington, MA 01805; **Phone:** 781-744-8348; **Board Cert:** Internal Medicine 1979; Dermatology 1983; **Med School:** Baylor Coll Med 1976; **Resid:** Internal Medicine, Mass General Hosp 1979; Dermatology, Mass General Hosp 1983; **Fellow:** Mohs Surgery, Mass General Hosp 1991; **Fac Appt:** Assoc Prof D, Harvard Med Sch

Stern, Robert S MD [D] - **Spec Exp:** Psoriasis; Phototherapy; Drug Allergy; Skin Cancer; **Hospital:** Beth Israel Deaconess Med Ctr - Boston; **Address:** Beth Israel Deaconess Med Ctr, Dept Dermatology, 330 Brookline Ave, Boston, MA 02215-5400; **Phone:** 617-667-3689; **Board Cert:** Dermatology 1977; **Med School:** Yale Univ 1970; **Resid:** Dermatology, Mass Genl Hosp 1976; **Fellow:** Epidemiology, NIH 1973; **Fac Appt:** Prof D, Harvard Med Sch

Tsao, Hensin MD/PhD [D] - **Spec Exp:** Melanoma; Melanoma Genetics; Skin Cancer; **Hospital:** Mass Genl Hosp; **Address:** Mass Genl Hosp, Dept Dermatology, 50 Staniford St Fl 2 - Ste 200, Boston, MA 02114-2543; **Phone:** 617-726-2914; **Board Cert:** Dermatology 2006; **Med School:** Columbia P&S 1993; **Resid:** Dermatology, Brigham & Women's Hosp 1996; **Fellow:** Dermatology, Mass Genl Hosp 1997; **Fac Appt:** Assoc Prof D, Harvard Med Sch

Mid Atlantic

Alster, Tina S MD [D] - **Spec Exp:** Skin Laser Surgery; Scar Revision; Birthmarks/Hemangiomas; **Hospital:** MedStar Georgetown Univ Hosp; **Address:** Washington Inst of Derm Laser Surg, 1430 K St NW, Ste 200, Washington, DC 20005; **Phone:** 202-628-8855; **Board Cert:** Dermatology 1990; **Med School:** Duke Univ 1986; **Resid:** Dermatology, Yale Univ 1989; **Fellow:** Dermatologic Laser Surgery, Boston Univ Hosp 1990; **Fac Appt:** Clin Prof D, Georgetown Univ

Anhalt, Grant J MD [D] - **Spec Exp:** Oral Dermatology; Pemphigus; Autoimmune Disease; Blistering Diseases; **Hospital:** Johns Hopkins Hosp (page 59); **Address:** Hopkins at Green Spring Station, 10751 Falls Rd, Ste 304, Lutherville, MD 21093; **Phone:** 410-321-5900; **Board Cert:** Dermatology 2009; Clinical & Laboratory Dematologic Immunology 1987; **Med School:** Canada 1975; **Resid:** Internal Medicine, Hlth Scis Ctr 1977; Dermatology, Univ Mich Med Ctr 1980; **Fellow:** Immunological Dermatology, Univ Mich Med Ctr 1981; **Fac Appt:** Prof D, Johns Hopkins Univ

Avram, Marc R MD [D] - **Spec Exp:** Hair Restoration/Transplant; Skin Laser Surgery; Cosmetic Dermatology; Botox Therapy; **Hospital:** NY-Presby/Weill Cornell Med Ctr, NY (page 65); **Address:** 905 5th Ave, MS 10021, New York, NY 10021-2650; **Phone:** 212-734-4007; **Board Cert:** Dermatology 2012; Hair Restoration Surgery 2007; **Med School:** SUNY Downstate 1989; **Resid:** Dermatology, Mass Genl Hosp 1994; **Fac Appt:** Clin Prof D, Cornell Univ-Weill Med Coll

Belsito, Donald V MD [D] - **Spec Exp:** Contact Dermatitis; Cutaneous Lymphoma; Psoriasis; Atopic Dermatitis; **Hospital:** NY-Presby/Columbia Univ Med Ctr, NY (page 65); **Address:** Columbia Dermatology Associates, 51 W 51st St, Fl 3, Ste 390, New York, NY 10019; **Phone:** 212-305-5293; **Board Cert:** Internal Medicine 1979; Dermatology 1983; Clinical & Laboratory Dematologic Immunology 1985; **Med School:** Cornell Univ-Weill Med Coll 1976; **Resid:** Internal Medicine, Case West Res Univ Hosps 1979; Dermatology, NYU Med Ctr 1982; **Fellow:** Dermatologic Research, NYU Med Ctr 1983; **Fac Appt:** Prof D, Columbia P&S

Bernstein, Robert M MD [D] - **Spec Exp:** Hair Restoration/Transplant; Hair Loss in Women; Hair Transplant-Robotic Surgery; **Hospital:** NY-Presby/Columbia Univ Med Ctr, NY (page 65); **Address:** 110 E 55th St, Fl 11, New York, NY 10022; **Phone:** 212-826-2400; **Board Cert:** Dermatology 1982; Hair Restoration Surgery 1998; **Med School:** UMDNJ-NJ Med Sch, Newark 1978; **Resid:** Dermatology, Einstein Affil Hosp 1982; **Fac Appt:** Clin Prof D, Columbia P&S

Bickers, David R MD [D] - **Spec Exp:** Skin Cancer-Consult by Referral Only; **Hospital:** NY-Presby/Columbia Univ Med Ctr, NY (page 65); **Address:** 51 W 51st St, Ste 390, New York, NY 10104; **Phone:** 212-326-8465; **Board Cert:** Dermatology 2006; **Med School:** Univ VA Sch Med 1967; **Resid:** Dermatology, NYU Med Ctr 1974; **Fac Appt:** Prof D, Columbia P&S

Bondi, Edward E MD [D] - **Spec Exp:** Skin Cancer; Melanoma; **Hospital:** Hosp Univ Penn - UPHS (page 69); **Address:** Perelman Center-Dept Dermatology, 3400 Civic Center Blvd, Ste 330-S, Philadelphia, PA 19104; **Phone:** 215-662-2737; **Board Cert:** Dermatology 1978; **Med School:** Hahnemann Univ 1974; **Resid:** Dermatology, Hosp Univ Penn 1978; **Fac Appt:** Assoc Prof D, Univ Pennsylvania

Brandt, Fredric S MD [D] - **Spec Exp:** Botox Therapy; Cosmetic Dermatology; **Address:** Laser & Skin Surgery Ctr, 323 E 34th St Fl 2, New York, NY 10016; **Phone:** 212-889-7096; **Board Cert:** Internal Medicine 1978; Dermatology 1981; **Med School:** Hahnemann Univ 1975; **Resid:** Internal Medicine, NYU Sch Med Affil Hosp 1978; Dermatology, Jackson Meml Hosp 1981

Braun III, Martin MD [D] - **Spec Exp:** Skin Cancer; **Hospital:** MedStar Washington Hosp Ctr; **Address:** Braun Dermatology Associates, 2112 F St NW, Ste 701, Washington, DC 20037; **Phone:** 202-293-7618; **Board Cert:** Dermatology 1977; Dermatopathology 1982; **Med School:** Univ MD Sch Med 1970; **Resid:** Dermatology, Univ Mich Med Ctr 1976; **Fellow:** Mohs Surgery, Precept w/ Dr Frederic Mohs 1975; **Fac Appt:** Clin Prof D, Geo Wash Univ

Brodland, David G MD [D] - **Spec Exp:** Mohs' Surgery; Skin Cancer; Reconstructive Surgery-Skin; **Hospital:** UPMC Shadyside; **Address:** Shadyside Medical Bldg, 5200 Centre Ave, Ste 303, Pittsburgh, PA 15232; **Phone:** 412-681-9400; **Board Cert:** Dermatology 1989; **Med School:** Southern IL Univ 1985; **Resid:** Dermatology, Mayo Clinic 1989; **Fellow:** Mohs Surgery, UPMC Shadyside 1990; **Fac Appt:** Asst Prof D, Univ Pittsburgh

Bronin, Andrew MD [D] - **Spec Exp:** Melanoma; Skin Cancer; Complex Diagnosis; **Hospital:** Greenwich Hosp, Yale-New Haven Hosp; **Address:** 4 Rye Ridge Plaza, Rye Brook, NY 10573-2820; **Phone:** 914-253-8080; **Board Cert:** Dermatology 1981; **Med School:** NY Med Coll 1975; **Resid:** Dermatology, New York Hosp 1979; **Fac Appt:** Assoc Clin Prof D, Yale Univ

Brown, Marc D MD [D] - **Spec Exp:** Skin Cancer; Mohs' Surgery; Melanoma; **Hospital:** Univ Rochester Strong Meml Hosp; **Address:** University Dermatology Associates, 601 Elmwood Ave, Rochester, NY 14642; **Phone:** 585-275-9208; **Board Cert:** Dermatology 2009; **Med School:** Georgetown Univ 1979; **Resid:** Internal Medicine, Strong Meml Hosp/Univ Rochester 1982; Dermatology, Univ Mich Hosps 1987; **Fellow:** Cutaneous Oncology, Univ Mich Hosps 1989

Cohen, Bernard A MD [D] - **Spec Exp:** Pediatric Dermatology; Skin Laser Surgery; Hemangiomas; Vascular Malformations; **Hospital:** Johns Hopkins Hosp (page 59); **Address:** Johns Hopkins, Ped Dermatology Dept, Rubenstein Child Health Bldg, 200 N Wolfe St, Ste 2107, Baltimore, MD 21287; **Phone:** 410-955-2049; **Board Cert:** Pediatrics 1982; Dermatology 1984; Pediatric Dermatology 2004; **Med School:** Johns Hopkins Univ 1977; **Resid:** Pediatrics, Johns Hopkins Hosp 1980; Dermatology, Johns Hopkins Hosp 1984; **Fac Appt:** Prof D, Johns Hopkins Univ

Cohen, Steven R MD [D] - **Spec Exp:** Occupational Skin Diseases; Contact Dermatitis; Psoriasis; **Hospital:** Montefiore Med Ctr-Moses Campus, NY; **Address:** 3514 Bainbridge Ave Fl 1, Bronx, NY 10467; **Phone:** 866-633-8255; **Board Cert:** Dermatology 2009; **Med School:** Univ Pennsylvania 1971; **Resid:** Dermatology, Yale-New Haven Hosp 1977; **Fac Appt:** Prof D, Albert Einstein Coll Med

Cotsarelis, George MD [D] - **Spec Exp:** Hair Loss; Scalp Disorders; **Hospital:** Hosp Univ Penn - UPHS (page 69); **Address:** Perelman Ctr for Advanced Medicine, 3400 Civic Center Blvd, Ste 330-1 South, Philadelphia, PA 19104; **Phone:** 215-662-2737; **Board Cert:** Dermatology 2010; **Med School:** Univ Pennsylvania 1987; **Resid:** Dermatology, Hosp Univ Penn 1992; **Fellow:** Dermatology, Hosp Univ Penn; **Fac Appt:** Prof D, Univ Pennsylvania

DeLeo, Vincent A MD [D] - **Spec Exp:** Contact Dermatitis; **Hospital:** St. Luke's - Roosevelt Hosp Ctr - Roosevelt Div (page 56), Beth Israel Med Ctr - Petrie Div (page 56); **Address:** 1090 Amsterdam Ave, Fl 11, New York, NY 10025; **Phone:** 212-523-5898; **Board Cert:** Dermatology 2009; **Med School:** Louisiana State U, New Orleans 1969; **Resid:** Dermatology, NY-Presby/Columbia Univ Med Ctr 1976; **Fac Appt:** Clin Prof D, Columbia P&S

Dzubow, Leonard M MD [D] - **Spec Exp:** Mohs' Surgery; Skin Cancer; Melanoma; **Hospital:** Riddle Meml Hosp, Crozer - Chester Med Ctr; **Address:** 101 Chesley Drive, Georgetown Bldg, Media, PA 19063; **Phone:** 484-621-0082; **Board Cert:** Internal Medicine 1978; Dermatology 2009; **Med School:** Univ Pennsylvania 1975; **Resid:** Internal Medicine, Hosp Univ Penn 1978; Dermatology, NYU-Skin Cancer Unit 1980; **Fellow:** Mohs Surgery, NYU-Skin Cancer Unit 1981; **Fac Appt:** Prof D, Univ Pennsylvania

Geronemus, Roy G MD [D] - **Spec Exp:** Skin Cancer; Mohs' Surgery; Cosmetic Dermatology; **Hospital:** New York Eye & Ear Infirm (page 64), NYU Langone Med Ctr (page 68); **Address:** Laser Skin Surgical Ctr of NY, 317 E 34th St, Ste 11N, New York, NY 10016-4974; **Phone:** 212-686-7306; **Board Cert:** Dermatology 1983; **Med School:** Univ Miami Sch Med 1979; **Resid:** Dermatology, NYU-Skin Cancer Unit 1983; **Fellow:** Mohs Surgery, NYU-Skin Cancer Unit 1984; **Fac Appt:** Clin Prof D, NYU Sch Med

Gordon, Marsha L MD [D] - **Spec Exp:** Cosmetic Dermatology; Botox Therapy; Facial Rejuvenation; **Hospital:** Mt Sinai Med Ctr (page 62); **Address:** 5 E 98th St Fl 5, New York, NY 10029-6574; **Phone:** 212-241-9728; **Board Cert:** Dermatology 1988; **Med School:** Univ Pennsylvania 1984; **Resid:** Dermatology, Mt Sinai Med Ctr 1988; **Fac Appt:** Clin Prof D, Mount Sinai Sch Med

Greenbaum, Steven S MD [D] - **Spec Exp:** Mohs' Surgery; Skin Cancer; Cosmetic Dermatology; Dermatologic Surgery; **Hospital:** Thomas Jefferson Univ Hosp, Hahnemann Univ Hosp; **Address:** 1528 Walnut St, Ste 1101, Philadelphia, PA 19102; **Phone:** 215-735-4994; **Board Cert:** Dermatology 1987; **Med School:** Tulane Univ 1983; **Resid:** Dermatology, Henry Ford Hosp 1987; **Fellow:** Mohs Surgery, UCSF Med Ctr 1988; **Fac Appt:** Clin Prof D, Drexel Univ Coll Med

Grossman, Melanie MD [D] - **Spec Exp:** Skin Laser Surgery; Facial Rejuvenation; Body Contouring; Cosmetic Dermatology; **Hospital:** NY-Presby/Columbia Univ Med Ctr, NY (page 65); **Address:** 161 Madison Ave, Ste 4NW, New York, NY 10016-5405; **Phone:** 212-725-8600; **Board Cert:** Dermatology 2010; **Med School:** NYU Sch Med 1988; **Resid:** Internal Medicine, Yale-New Haven Hosp 1989; Dermatology, Columbia-Presby Med Ctr 1992; **Fellow:** Laser Surgery, Mass Genl Hosp 1995; **Fac Appt:** Asst Clin Prof D, Columbia P&S

Halpern, Allan C MD [D] - **Spec Exp:** Skin Cancer; Melanoma; Melanoma Early Detection/Prevention; **Hospital:** Meml Sloan-Kettering Canc Ctr; **Address:** Memorial Sloan-Kettering Cancer Ctr, 160 E 53rd St, Fl 2, New York, NY 10022; **Phone:** 212-610-0766; **Board Cert:** Internal Medicine 1984; Dermatology 1988; **Med School:** Albert Einstein Coll Med 1981; **Resid:** Internal Medicine, Montefiore Hosp 1985; Dermatology, Hosp Univ Penn 1989; **Fellow:** Epidemiology, Hosp Univ Penn 1989; **Fac Appt:** Assoc Prof Med, Cornell Univ-Weill Med Coll

James, William D MD [D] - **Spec Exp:** Acne; Rosacea; Travel Medicine; Contact Dermatitis; **Hospital:** Hosp Univ Penn - UPHS (page 69); **Address:** Perelman Ctr for Advanced Medicine, 3400 Civic Center Blvd, Ste 330-S, Philadelphia, PA 19104; **Phone:** 215-662-2737; **Board Cert:** Dermatology 1981; Diagnostic Lab Immunology 1985; **Med School:** Indiana Univ 1977; **Resid:** Dermatology, Letterman Army Med Ctr 1981; **Fac Appt:** Prof D, Univ Pennsylvania

Kalb, Robert E MD [D] - **Spec Exp:** Psoriasis; Phototherapy; **Hospital:** Buffalo Genl Hosp; **Address:** Buffalo Med Group, 325 Essjay Rd, Ste 210, Williamsville, NY 14221; **Phone:** 716-630-1102; **Board Cert:** Dermatology 1986; **Med School:** SUNY Downstate 1982; **Resid:** Dermatology, Columbia Presby Med Ctr 1986; **Fac Appt:** Clin Prof D, SUNY Buffalo

Kress, Douglas W MD [D] - **Spec Exp:** Pediatric Dermatology; **Hospital:** Chldns Hosp of Pittsburgh - UPMC; **Address:** Chldn's Dermatology Ctr, 11279 Perry Hwy, Ste 108, Wexford, PA 15090; **Phone:** 724-933-9190; **Board Cert:** Dermatology 2006; Pediatric Dermatology 2004; **Med School:** Jefferson Med Coll 1992; **Resid:** Dermatology, UPMC 1996; **Fellow:** Pediatric Dermatology, Chldns Hosp 2003; **Fac Appt:** Assoc Clin Prof D, Univ Pittsburgh

Kriegel, David A MD [D] - **Spec Exp:** Mohs' Surgery; Skin Cancer; **Hospital:** Mt Sinai Med Ctr (page 62); **Address:** Manhattan Ctr for Dermatology, 250 W 57th St, Ste 825, New York, NY 10107-0809; **Phone:** 212-489-6669; **Board Cert:** Dermatology 2003; **Med School:** Boston Univ 1987; **Resid:** Dermatology, New England Med Ctr 1991; **Fellow:** Mohs Surgery, Stony Brook Univ Hosp 1993; **Fac Appt:** Assoc Prof D, Mount Sinai Sch Med

Lebwohl, Mark G MD [D] - **Spec Exp:** Skin Cancer; Psoriasis; Pseudoxanthoma Elasticum; **Hospital:** Mt Sinai Med Ctr (page 62); **Address:** Dermatology Assocs, 5 E 98th St Fl 5, New York, NY 10029-6501; **Phone:** 212-241-9728; **Board Cert:** Internal Medicine 1981; Dermatology 1983; **Med School:** Harvard Med Sch 1978; **Resid:** Internal Medicine, Mt Sinai Hosp 1981; Dermatology, Mt Sinai Hosp 1983; **Fellow:** Dermatology, Mt Sinai Hosp 1983; **Fac Appt:** Prof D, Mount Sinai Sch Med

Lessin, Stuart R MD [D] - **Spec Exp:** Cutaneous Lymphoma; Skin Cancer; Melanoma Risk Assessment; Mycosis Fungoides; **Hospital:** Bryn Mawr Hosp; **Address:** Bryn Mawr Skin & Cancer Inst, 919 Conestoga Rd, Bldg 2 - Ste 106, Rosemont, PA 19010; **Phone:** 610-525-5028; **Board Cert:** Dermatology 1986; **Med School:** Temple Univ 1982; **Resid:** Dermatology, Hosp Univ Penn 1986; **Fellow:** Molecular Biology, Wistar Inst 1987; **Fac Appt:** Prof Emeritus D, Temple Univ

Lowitt, Mark H MD [D] - **Spec Exp:** Acne; Eczema; Psoriasis; Skin Cancer; **Hospital:** Greater Baltimore Med Ctr; **Address:** 6565 N Charles St, Ste 315, Baltimore, MD 21204; **Phone:** 410-321-1195; **Board Cert:** Dermatology 2003; **Med School:** Tulane Univ 1987; **Resid:** Internal Medicine, New England Deaconess Hosp 1990; **Fellow:** Dermatology, Univ MD Med Ctr 1993; **Fac Appt:** Assoc Clin Prof D, Univ MD Sch Med

Miller, Stanley J MD [D] - **Spec Exp:** Skin Cancer; Mohs' Surgery; Melanoma; **Hospital:** Univ of MD-St. Joseph Med Ctr, Univ of MD Med Ctr; **Address:** 1104 Kenilworth Drive, Ste 201, Charles Towson Bldg, Towson, MD 21204; **Phone:** 443-279-0340; **Board Cert:** Dermatology 2009; **Med School:** Univ VT Coll Med 1984; **Resid:** Dermatology, UCSD Med Ctr 1989; **Fellow:** Dermatologic Surgery, Univ Penn Hlth System 1991; **Fac Appt:** Asst Prof D, Johns Hopkins Univ

Nigra, Thomas P MD [D] - **Spec Exp:** Hair Loss; Psoriasis; Skin Cancer; Vitiligo; **Hospital:** MedStar Washington Hosp Ctr, MedStar Natl Rehab Hosp; **Address:** 110 Irving St, rm 2B-44, Washington, DC 20010; **Phone:** 202-877-6227; **Board Cert:** Dermatology 1973; **Med School:** Univ Pennsylvania 1967; **Resid:** Dermatology, Mass Genl Hosp 1973; Dermatology, Natl Inst of Health 1971; **Fac Appt:** Clin Prof D, Geo Wash Univ

Orlow, Seth J MD/PhD [D] - **Spec Exp:** Pediatric Dermatology; Birthmarks/Hemangiomas; Psoriasis/Eczema; **Hospital:** NYU Langone Med Ctr (page 68); **Address:** NYU Dermatologic Assocs, Faculty Practice Twr, 530 First Ave Fl 7 - Ste 7R, New York, NY 10016-6402; **Phone:** 212-263-5889; **Board Cert:** Dermatology 2009; Pediatric Dermatology 2004; **Med School:** Albert Einstein Coll Med 1986; **Resid:** Pediatrics, Mt Sinai Med Ctr 1987; Dermatology, Yale-New Haven Hosp 1989; **Fellow:** Pediatric Dermatology, Yale-New Haven Hosp 1990; **Fac Appt:** Prof D, NYU Sch Med

Prioleau, Philip G MD [D] - **Spec Exp:** Melanoma; Skin Cancer; Mohs' Surgery; **Hospital:** NY-Presby/Weill Cornell Med Ctr, NY (page 65); **Address:** 1035 Fifth Ave, Ste C, New York, NY 10028; **Phone:** 212-794-3548; **Board Cert:** Surgery 1973; Anatomic Pathology 1979; Dermatopathology 1980; Dermatology 1983; **Med School:** Med Univ SC 1967; **Resid:** Surgery, Univ VA Med Ctr 1972; Plastic Surgery, Duke Univ Hosp 1975; **Fellow:** Dermatopathology, Barnes Jewish Hosp 1980; Dermatology, NYU Med Ctr 1981; **Fac Appt:** Assoc Clin Prof D, Cornell Univ-Weill Med Coll

Ramsay, David L MD [D] - **Spec Exp:** Cutaneous Lymphoma; Skin Cancer; Mycosis Fungoides; **Hospital:** NYU Langone Med Ctr (page 68); **Address:** 530 1st Ave, Ste 7G, New York, NY 10016-6402; **Phone:** 212-683-6283; **Board Cert:** Dermatology 1974; **Med School:** Indiana Univ 1969; **Resid:** Dermatology, NYU Med Ctr 1973; **Fellow:** Dermatology, Univ Illinois Hosp 1974; **Fac Appt:** Clin Prof D, NYU Sch Med

Ratner, Desiree MD [D] - **Spec Exp:** Mohs' Surgery; Skin Cancer; **Hospital:** Beth Israel Med Ctr - Petrie Div (page 56); **Address:** 325 W 15th St, New York, NY 10011; **Phone:** 212-367-0145; **Board Cert:** Dermatology 2003; **Med School:** Johns Hopkins Univ 1989; **Resid:** Internal Medicine, Beth Israel Deaconess Med Ctr 1990; Dermatology, Univ Michigan Med Ctr 1993; **Fellow:** Mohs Surgery, New England Med Ctr 1994; Mohs Surgery, Lahey Clinic 1995; **Fac Appt:** Prof D, Columbia P&S

Rigel, Darrell S MD [D] - **Spec Exp:** Melanoma; Skin Cancer; Cosmetic Dermatology; **Hospital:** NYU Langone Med Ctr (page 68); **Address:** 35 E 35th Street, Ste 208, New York, NY 10016-3823; **Phone:** 212-684-5964; **Board Cert:** Dermatology 1983; **Med School:** Geo Wash Univ 1978; **Resid:** Dermatology, NYU Med Ctr 1982; **Fellow:** Dermatologic Surgery, NYU Med Ctr 1983; **Fac Appt:** Clin Prof D, NYU Sch Med

Rook, Alain H MD [D] - **Spec Exp:** Cutaneous Lymphoma; Immune Deficiency-Skin Disorders; Mycosis Fungoides; Cutaneous T-cell Lymphoma; **Hospital:** Hosp Univ Penn - UPHS (page 69); **Address:** Perelman Center-Dept Dermatology, 3400 Civic Center Blvd, Ste 330-S, Philadelphia, PA 19104-4283; **Phone:** 215-662-2737; **Board Cert:** Internal Medicine 1979; Nephrology 1980; Dermatology 2011; **Med School:** Univ Mich Med Sch 1975; **Resid:** Internal Medicine, McGill Affil Hosp 1977; Dermatology, Hosp Univ Penn 1989; **Fellow:** Nephrology, McGill Univ 1979; Immunology, NIH 1986; **Fac Appt:** Prof D, Univ Pennsylvania

Schultz, Neal B MD [D] - **Spec Exp:** Cosmetic Dermatology; Melanoma Early Detection/Prevention; Skin Laser Surgery; Tattoo Removal; **Hospital:** Mt Sinai Med Ctr (page 62); **Address:** Park Avenue Skin Care, 1130 Park Ave, New York, NY 10128; **Phone:** 212-369-9600; **Board Cert:** Dermatology 1978; **Med School:** Columbia P&S 1973; **Resid:** Internal Medicine, Mt Sinai Hosp 1975; Dermatology, Mt Sinai Hosp 1978; **Fac Appt:** Clin Prof D, Mount Sinai Sch Med

Shupack, Jerome L MD [D] - **Spec Exp:** Rare Skin Disorders; Psoriasis; Eczema; Blistering Diseases; **Hospital:** NYU Langone Med Ctr (page 68); **Address:** 530 1st Ave, HCC 7F, New York, NY 10016-6402; **Phone:** 212-263-7344; **Board Cert:** Dermatology 1970; **Med School:** Columbia P&S 1963; **Resid:** Internal Medicine, Mt Sinai Hosp 1965; Dermatology, NYU Med Ctr 1970; **Fac Appt:** Prof D, NYU Sch Med

Soter, Nicholas A MD [D] - **Spec Exp:** Urticaria; Psoriasis; Vasculitis; Phototherapy; **Hospital:** NYU Langone Med Ctr (page 68); **Address:** 240 E 38th St, Fl 12, New York, NY 10016-6402; **Phone:** 212-263-5015; **Board Cert:** Dermatology 1970; Diagnostic Lab Immunology 1985; **Med School:** Univ Tex SW, Dallas 1965; **Resid:** Dermatology, Baylor Med Ctr 1968; Dermatology, Mass Genl Hosp 1969; **Fellow:** Immunology, Harvard Med Sch 1973; **Fac Appt:** Prof D, NYU Sch Med

Stanley, John R MD [D] - **Spec Exp:** Blistering Diseases; Pemphigus; **Hospital:** Hosp Univ Penn - UPHS (page 69); **Address:** Perelman Ctr for Advanced Medicine, 3400 Civic Center Blvd, Ste 330 - 1 South, Philadelphia, PA 19104; **Phone:** 215-662-2737; **Board Cert:** Dermatology 1978; Clinical & Laboratory Dematologic Immunology 1985; **Med School:** Harvard Med Sch 1974; **Resid:** Dermatology, NYU Med Ctr 1978; **Fac Appt:** Prof D, Univ Pennsylvania

Werth, Victoria P MD [D] - **Spec Exp:** Autoimmune Disease; Lupus/SLE; Connective Tissue Disorders; Blistering Diseases; **Hospital:** Hosp Univ Penn - UPHS (page 69), VA Med Ctr - Philadelphia; **Address:** Perelman Ctr for Advanced Medicine, 3400 Civic Ctr Blvd, Ste 330 - 1 South, Philadelphia, PA 19104; **Phone:** 215-662-2737; **Board Cert:** Internal Medicine 1983; Dermatology 1986; Diagnostic Lab Immunology 1989; **Med School:** Johns Hopkins Univ 1980; **Resid:** Internal Medicine, Northwestern Meml Hosp 1983; Dermatology, NYU Med Ctr 1986; **Fellow:** Immunological Dermatology, NYU 1988; **Fac Appt:** Prof D, Univ Pennsylvania

Yan, Albert C MD [D] - **Spec Exp:** Pediatric Dermatology; Hemangiomas; Genetic Disorders-Skin; Atopic Dermatitis; **Hospital:** Chldns Hosp of Philadelphia, Hosp Univ Penn - UPHS (page 69); **Address:** Chldns Hosp of Philadelphia, Div Dermatology, 3550 Market St Fl 2, Philadelphia, PA 19104; **Phone:** 215-590-2169; **Board Cert:** Pediatrics 2011; Dermatology 2008; Pediatric Dermatology 2004; **Med School:** Univ Pennsylvania 1993; **Resid:** Pediatrics, Chldns Hosp 1996; Dermatology, Hosp Univ Penn - UPHS 1999; **Fac Appt:** Assoc Prof Ped, Univ Pennsylvania

Zitelli, John MD [D] - **Spec Exp:** Mohs' Surgery; Skin Cancer; Melanoma; Reconstructive Surgery-Skin; **Hospital:** UPMC Shadyside; **Address:** Shadyside Medical Bldg, 5200 Centre Ave, Ste 303, Pittsburgh, PA 15232; **Phone:** 412-681-9400; **Board Cert:** Dermatology 2009; **Med School:** Univ Pittsburgh 1976; **Resid:** Dermatology, UPMC Shadyside 1979; **Fellow:** Mohs Surgery, Univ Wisconsin Hosp 1980; **Fac Appt:** Assoc Clin Prof D, Univ Pittsburgh

Southeast

Amonette, Rex A MD [D] - **Spec Exp:** Skin Cancer; Mohs' Surgery; **Address:** Memphis Dermatology Clin, 1455 Union Ave, Memphis, TN 38104-6727; **Phone:** 901-726-6655; **Board Cert:** Dermatology 1974; **Med School:** Univ Ark 1966; **Resid:** Dermatology, Univ Tenn Med Ctr 1971; **Fellow:** Mohs Surgery, NYU Med Ctr 1972; **Fac Appt:** Clin Prof D, Univ Tenn Coll Med

Brody, Harold J MD [D] - **Spec Exp:** Cosmetic Dermatology; Dermatologic Surgery; Facial Rejuvenation; Skin Laser Surgery-Resurfacing; **Hospital:** Emory Univ Hosp; **Address:** 1218 W Paces Ferry Rd, Ste 200, Atlanta, GA 30327; **Phone:** 404-525-7409; **Board Cert:** Dermatology 1978; **Med School:** Med Univ SC 1974; **Resid:** Dermatology, Emory Univ Hosp 1978; **Fac Appt:** Clin Prof D, Emory Univ

Burton III, Claude S MD [D] - **Spec Exp:** Skin Laser Surgery; **Hospital:** Duke Univ Hosp; **Address:** 200 Trent Dr, Clinic 3K, Durham, NC 27710; **Phone:** 919-684-3432; **Board Cert:** Internal Medicine 1982; Dermatology 1984; **Med School:** Duke Univ 1979; **Resid:** Internal Medicine, Duke Univ Med Ctr 1982; Dermatology, Duke Univ Med Ctr 1984; **Fac Appt:** Prof D, Duke Univ

Callen, Jeffrey P MD [D] - **Spec Exp:** Lupus/SLE; Dermatomyositis; Vasculitis; Psoriasis; **Hospital:** Univ of Louisville Hosp, Kosair Chldn's Hosp; **Address:** 310 E Broadway, Ste 200, Louisville, KY 40202; **Phone:** 502-583-1749; **Board Cert:** Internal Medicine 1975; Dermatology 2009; **Med School:** Univ Mich Med Sch 1972; **Resid:** Internal Medicine, Univ Mich Med Ctr 1975; Dermatology, Univ Mich Med Ctr 1977; **Fac Appt:** Prof D, Univ Louisville Sch Med

Camisa, Charles MD [D] - **Spec Exp:** Psoriasis; Oral Dermatology; Lichen Planus; Cutaneous T-cell Lymphoma; **Address:** Riverchase Dermatology, 261 9th St S, Naples, FL 34102; **Phone:** 239-216-4337; **Board Cert:** Dermatology 1981; Clinical & Laboratory Dematologic Immunology 1987; **Med School:** Mount Sinai Sch Med 1977; **Resid:** Dermatology, NYU Med Ctr 1981; **Fac Appt:** Assoc Prof D, Univ S Fla Coll Med

Cohen, Bernard H MD [D] - **Spec Exp:** Hair Restoration/Transplant; Hair Loss; **Address:** Hair Loss Ctr, 550 Biltmore Way, Ste 870, Coral Gables, FL 33134; **Phone:** 305-443-9977; **Board Cert:** Dermatology 1972; Hair Restoration Surgery ; **Med School:** Columbia P&S 1967; **Resid:** Dermatology, NYU Med Ctr 1971

Cook, Jonathan L MD [D] - **Spec Exp:** Skin Cancer; Mohs' Surgery; Reconstructive Surgery-Skin; Skin Laser Surgery; **Hospital:** Duke Univ Hosp; **Address:** 5324 McFarland Drive, Ste 400, Durham, NC 27707; **Phone:** 919-419-4945; **Board Cert:** Dermatology 2005; **Med School:** Med Univ SC 1992; **Resid:** Dermatology, Emory Univ Hosp 1996; **Fellow:** Dermatologic Surgery, Hosp Univ Penn 1997; **Fac Appt:** Prof D, Duke Univ

Eichler, Craig J MD [D] - **Spec Exp:** Skin Cancer; Dermatologic Surgery; **Hospital:** Physicians Regl Hlthcare Med Ctr-Pine Ridge; **Address:** 6101 Pine Ridge Rd, Naples, FL 34119; **Phone:** 239-348-4325; **Board Cert:** Dermatology 2003; **Med School:** Univ Fla Coll Med 1989; **Resid:** Dermatology, Univ Texas Med Branch 1993

Elmets, Craig A MD [D] - **Spec Exp:** Psoriasis/Eczema; Phototherapy; Contact Dermatitis; Photodynamic Therapy; **Hospital:** UAB Hosp, Birmingham VA Med Ctr; **Address:** 1530 3rd Ave S, EFH Bldg, rm 414, Birmingham, AL 35294; **Phone:** 205-996-7546; **Board Cert:** Internal Medicine 1978; Dermatology 2009; Clinical & Laboratory Dematologic Immunology 1989; **Med School:** Univ Iowa Coll Med 1975; **Resid:** Internal Medicine, U Kansas Med Ctr 1978; Dermatology, U Iowa Hosps 1980; **Fellow:** Immunological Dermatology, U Texas SW Hlth Sci Ctr 1982; **Fac Appt:** Prof D, UAB Sch Med

Fenske, Neil A MD [D] - **Spec Exp:** Skin Cancer; Melanoma; Psoriasis; **Hospital:** Moffitt Canc Ctr (page 61), Tampa Genl Hosp; **Address:** USF, Dermatology Dept, 13330 USF Laurel Drive Fl 6, Tampa, FL 33612; **Phone:** 813-974-4744; **Board Cert:** Dermatology 1977; Dermatopathology 1984; **Med School:** St Louis Univ 1973; **Resid:** Dermatology, Univ WI Hosp & Clins 1977; **Fac Appt:** Prof Med, Univ S Fla Coll Med

Garrett, Algin MD [D] - **Spec Exp:** Skin Cancer; Mohs' Surgery; **Hospital:** Med Coll of VA Hosp; **Address:** Stonypoint Med Pk, 9000 Stonypoint Pkwy Fl 2, Richmond, VA 23235; **Phone:** 804-560-8991; **Board Cert:** Dermatology 1983; **Med School:** Penn State Coll Med 1978; **Resid:** Internal Medicine, VA Med Ctr 1980; Dermatology, VCU Med Ctr 1983; **Fellow:** Mohs Surgery, Cleveland Clin 1988; **Fac Appt:** Prof D, Va Commonwealth Univ Sch Med

Green, Howard A MD [D] - **Spec Exp:** Mohs' Surgery; Skin Cancer; **Hospital:** St. Mary's Med Ctr - W Palm Bch; **Address:** 120 Butler St, Ste A, West Palm Beach, FL 33407-6106; **Phone:** 561-659-1510; **Board Cert:** Internal Medicine 1988; Dermatology 2011; **Med School:** Boston Univ 1985; **Resid:** Internal Medicine, Jefferson Univ Hosp 1988; Dermatology, Harvard Affil Hosps 1992; **Fellow:** Mohs Surgery, Boston Univ Med Ctr 1993

Grichnik, James M MD/PhD [D] - **Spec Exp:** Melanoma; Skin Cancer; **Hospital:** Univ of Miami Hosp & Clins/Sylvester Comp Canc Ctr; **Address:** 1501 NW 10th Ave, BRB Bldg, rm 912, Miami, FL 33136; **Phone:** 305-243-6045; **Board Cert:** Dermatology 2003; **Med School:** Harvard Med Sch 1990; **Resid:** Dermatology, Duke Univ Med Ctr 1994; **Fac Appt:** Prof D, Univ Miami Sch Med

Johr, Robert MD [D] - **Spec Exp:** Pigmented Lesions; Melanoma; Pediatric Dermatology; **Hospital:** Boca Raton Regl Hosp; **Address:** 1050 NW 15th St, Ste 201A, Boca Raton, FL 33486; **Phone:** 561-368-4545; **Board Cert:** Dermatology 1981; **Med School:** Mexico 1975; **Resid:** Dermatology, Roswell Park Cancer Ctr 1977; Dermatology, Metro Med Ctr 1979; **Fac Appt:** Clin Prof D, Univ Miami Sch Med

Jorizzo, Joseph L MD [D] - **Spec Exp:** Rheumatologic Dermatology; Immune Deficiency-Skin Disorders; Complex Diagnosis; Dermatomyositis; **Hospital:** Wake Forest Baptist Med Ctr, NY-Presby/Weill Cornell Med Ctr, NY (page 65); **Address:** Wake Forest Baptist Dermatology, 4618 Country Club Rd, Winston-Salem, NC 27104; **Phone:** 336-716-3926; **Board Cert:** Dermatology 1979; **Med School:** Boston Univ 1975; **Resid:** Dermatology, UNC Meml Hosp 1979; **Fellow:** Dermatology, Dermatology Inst 1980; **Fac Appt:** Prof D, Wake Forest Univ

Kirsner, Robert S MD/PhD [D] - **Spec Exp:** Wound Healing/Care; Leg Ulcers; **Hospital:** Univ of Miami Hosp; **Address:** Univ Miami, Dermatology Dept, 1295 NW 14th St South Bldg - Ste M, Miami, FL 33125; **Phone:** 305-243-6704; **Board Cert:** Dermatology 2005; **Med School:** Univ Miami Sch Med 1988; **Resid:** Internal Medicine, Univ Miami-Jackson Meml Hosp 1990; Dermatology, Univ Miami-Jackson Meml Hosp 1995; **Fellow:** Wound Healing, Univ Miami-Jackson Meml Hosp 1992; **Fac Appt:** Prof D, Univ Miami Sch Med

Leshin, Barry MD [D] - **Spec Exp:** Skin Cancer; Mohs' Surgery; **Address:** 1450 Professional Park Drive, Ste 150, Winston-Salem, NC 27103; **Phone:** 336-724-2434; **Board Cert:** Dermatology 2009; **Med School:** Univ Tex, Houston 1981; **Resid:** Dermatology, Univ Iowa Hosp 1985; **Fellow:** Dermatologic Surgery, Univ Iowa Hosp 1986; **Fac Appt:** Clin Prof PlS, Wake Forest Univ

McMichael, Amy J MD [D] - **Spec Exp:** Hair Loss; Ethnic Skin Disorders; Pigmented Lesions; Skin Cancer; **Hospital:** Wake Forest Baptist Med Ctr; **Address:** Wake Forest Baptist Med Ctr, 4618 Country Club Rd, Winston-Salem, NC 27104; **Phone:** 336-716-3926; **Board Cert:** Dermatology 2013; **Med School:** Univ Pennsylvania 1990; **Resid:** Dermatology, Univ Mich Hosps 1994

Nouri, Keyvan MD [D] - **Spec Exp:** Mohs' Surgery; Skin Cancer; Cutaneous Lymphoma; **Hospital:** Univ of Miami Hosp & Clins/Sylvester Comp Canc Ctr; **Address:** UHlth, Dermatology Mohs Unit, 1295 NW 14th St South Bldg Fl 2, Miami, FL 33136; **Phone:** 305-243-4183; **Board Cert:** Dermatology 2005; **Med School:** Boston Univ 1993; **Resid:** Dermatology, Univ Miami Hosp 1997; **Fellow:** Dermatologic Surgery, NYU Med Ctr 1999; **Fac Appt:** Prof D, Univ Miami Sch Med

Olsen, Elise A MD [D] - **Spec Exp:** Cutaneous Lymphoma; Hair Loss; Hirsutism; **Hospital:** Duke Univ Hosp; **Address:** Duke Univ Med Ctr, Box 3294, Durham, NC 27710; **Phone:** 919-684-3432; **Board Cert:** Dermatology 1983; **Med School:** Baylor Coll Med 1978; **Resid:** Internal Medicine, Univ NC Meml Hosp 1980; Dermatology, Duke Univ Med Ctr 1983; **Fac Appt:** Prof D, Duke Univ

Russell, Mark A MD [D] - **Spec Exp:** Skin Cancer; Mohs' Surgery; Dermatologic Surgery; Nail Diseases; **Hospital:** Univ of Virginia Hlth Sys; **Address:** Univ VA Hlth Sys, Dept Dermatology, 1221 Lee St, PCC Bldg Fl 3, Box 800718, Charlottesville, VA 22908; **Phone:** 434-924-5599; **Board Cert:** Dermatology 2005; Dermatopathology 2001; **Med School:** Ohio State Univ 1993; **Resid:** Dermatology, Vanderbilt Univ Med Ctr 1997; **Fellow:** Mohs Surgery, Vanderbilt Univ Med Ctr 1999; Dermatopathology, Univ VA Hlth Sys 2000; **Fac Appt:** Assoc Prof D, Univ VA Sch Med

Sherertz, Elizabeth F MD [D] - **Spec Exp:** Eczema; Contact Dermatitis; Occupational Skin Diseases; **Hospital:** Waccamaw Community Hosp, Georgetown Meml Hosp; **Address:** Dermatology Assoc of Waccamaw, Waccamaw Medical Park-East, 4033 Highway 17 Bypass, Ste 105, Murrells Inlet, SC 29576; **Phone:** 843-652-8110; **Board Cert:** Dermatology 1982; **Med School:** Univ VA Sch Med 1978; **Resid:** Dermatology, Duke Univ Med Ctr 1982; **Fac Appt:** Clin Prof D, Wake Forest Univ

Sobel, Stuart A MD [D] - **Spec Exp:** Skin Cancer; Cosmetic Dermatology; Pemphigus; Skin Laser Surgery; **Hospital:** Meml Regl Hosp, Joe DiMaggio Chldns Hosp; **Address:** 4340 Sheridan St, Ste 101, Hollywood, FL 33021-3511; **Phone:** 954-983-5533; **Board Cert:** Dermatology 2009; **Med School:** Tufts Univ 1972; **Resid:** Dermatology, Mt Sinai Hosp 1976

Sokoloff, Daniel O MD [D] - **Spec Exp:** Skin Cancer; Cosmetic Dermatology; **Hospital:** Good Sam Med Ctr - W Palm Beach, St. Mary's Med Ctr - W Palm Bch; **Address:** Palm Beach Dermatology, 4475 Medical Center Way, Ste 2, West Palm Beach, FL 33407; **Phone:** 561-863-1000; **Board Cert:** Dermatology 1982; **Med School:** Geo Wash Univ 1977; **Resid:** Dermatology, Baylor Med Ctr 1982

Thiers, Bruce H MD [D] - **Spec Exp:** Cutaneous Lymphoma; Skin Cancer; Psoriasis; **Hospital:** MUSC Med Ctr; **Address:** 135 Rutledge Ave, MS 578, Fl 11, Charleston, SC 29425; **Phone:** 843-792-9784; **Board Cert:** Dermatology 1978; **Med School:** SUNY Buffalo 1974; **Resid:** Dermatology, SUNY Buffalo Med Ctr 1978; **Fac Appt:** Prof D, Med Univ SC

Midwest

Arpey, Christopher J MD [D] - **Spec Exp:** Mohs' Surgery; Skin Cancer; Skin Laser Surgery; Wound Healing/Care; **Hospital:** Mayo Med Ctr & Clin - Rochester; **Address:** Mayo Clinic - Dept Dermatology, 200 First St SW, Rochester, MN 55905; **Phone:** 507-284-2536; **Board Cert:** Dermatology 2011; Internal Medicine 1989; **Med School:** Univ Rochester 1986; **Resid:** Internal Medicine, Univ Iowa Hosps & Clinics 1989; Dermatology, Univ Hosps 1992; **Fellow:** Mohs Surgery, Univ Iowa Hosps & Clinics 1994; **Fac Appt:** Prof D, Mayo Med Sch

Bailin, Philip L MD [D] - **Spec Exp:** Mohs' Surgery; Skin Laser Surgery; Skin Cancer; **Hospital:** Cleveland Clin (page 55); **Address:** Dermatology & Plastic Surg Inst, 9500 Euclid Ave, MC A-60, Cleveland, OH 44195; **Phone:** 216-444-2115; **Board Cert:** Dermatology 1975; **Med School:** Northwestern Univ 1968; **Resid:** Dermatology, Cleveland Clin 1974; **Fellow:** Dermatopathology, Armed Forces Inst Pathology 1975; Mohs Surgery, Univ Wisc Hosp & Clin

Barbosa, Victoria H MD [D] - **Spec Exp:** Ethnic Skin Disorders; Hair Loss; Pigmented Lesions; Acne; **Hospital:** Rush Univ Med Ctr; **Address:** Rush Univ Med Ctr, 30 N Michigan Ave, Ste 1429, Chicago, IL 60602; **Phone:** 312-407-0000; **Board Cert:** Dermatology 2007; **Med School:** Yale Univ 1994; **Resid:** Dermatology, Yale-New Haven Hosp 1998; **Fac Appt:** Asst Prof D, Rush Med Coll

Bayliss, Susan J MD [D] - **Spec Exp:** Pediatric Dermatology; Eczema; Vascular Malformations; Hemangiomas/Birthmarks; **Hospital:** St. Louis Chldns Hosp; **Address:** St Louis Chldns Hosp, 1 Children's Pl, rm 3N48, St Louis, MO 63110; **Phone:** 314-454-6187; **Board Cert:** Dermatology 1982; Pediatric Dermatology 2006; **Med School:** Univ Tex Med Br, Galveston 1974; **Resid:** Pediatrics, St Louis Chldns Hosp 1977; Dermatology, Geisinger Medical Center 1982; **Fac Appt:** Prof Med, Washington Univ, St Louis

Cornelius, Lynn A MD [D] - **Spec Exp:** Melanoma; **Hospital:** Barnes-Jewish Hosp; **Address:** 4921 Parkview Pl, Ste 5B, St. Louis, MO 63110; **Phone:** 314-362-2643; **Board Cert:** Dermatology 1989; **Med School:** Univ MO-Columbia Sch Med 1984; **Resid:** Dermatology, Barnes Jewish Hosp-Wash Univ 1989; **Fellow:** Immunological Dermatology, Emory Univ Med Ctr 1992; **Fac Appt:** Assoc Prof D, Washington Univ, St Louis

Crutchfield III, Charles E MD [D] - **Spec Exp:** Skin Cancer; Psoriasis; Eczema; Cosmetic Dermatology; **Hospital:** Regions Hosp - St Paul; **Address:** Crutchfield Dermatology, 1185 Town Ctr Drive, Ste 101, Eagan, MN 55123; **Phone:** 651-209-3600; **Board Cert:** Dermatology 2008; **Med School:** Mayo Med Sch 1994; **Resid:** Dermatology, Univ Minnesota Affil Hosp 1998; **Fac Appt:** Clin Prof D, Univ Minn

Fivenson, David P MD [D] - **Spec Exp:** Blistering Diseases; Wound Healing/Care; Lupus/SLE; Behcet's Syndrome; **Hospital:** St. Joseph Mercy Hosp - Ann Arbor; **Address:** 3001 Miller Rd, Ann Arbor, MI 48103; **Phone:** 734-222-9630; **Board Cert:** Dermatology 1989; Clinical & Laboratory Dematologic Immunology 1991; **Med School:** Univ Mich Med Sch 1984; **Resid:** Dermatology, Univ Cincinnati Med Ctr 1989; **Fellow:** Immunological Dermatology, UCSD Med Ctr 1986; **Fac Appt:** Assoc Clin Prof D, Mich State Univ

Fosko, Scott W MD [D] - **Spec Exp:** Mohs' Surgery; Skin Cancer; Dermatologic Surgery; **Hospital:** St. Louis Univ Hosp; **Address:** 1755 S Grand Blvd, Ste 210, St Louis, MO 63104; **Phone:** 314-256-3420; **Board Cert:** Internal Medicine 1989; Dermatology 2012; **Med School:** Univ MD Sch Med 1986; **Resid:** Internal Medicine, Univ Va Med Ctr 1989; Dermatology, Yale-New Haven Hosp 1992; **Fellow:** Mohs Surgery, Hosp UPenn 1993; **Fac Appt:** Prof D, St Louis Univ

Garden, Jerome M MD [D] - **Spec Exp:** Skin Laser Surgery; Facial Rejuvenation; Vascular Birthmarks; **Hospital:** Northwestern Meml Hosp; **Address:** 150 E Huron St, Ste 1200, Chicago, IL 60611; **Phone:** 312-280-0890; **Board Cert:** Dermatology 1984; **Med School:** Northwestern Univ 1980; **Resid:** Internal Medicine, Northwestern Univ Affil Hosp 1981; Dermatology, Northwestern Univ Affil Hosp 1984; **Fac Appt:** Prof D, Northwestern Univ

Hanke, C. William MD [D] - **Spec Exp:** Mohs' Surgery; Skin Laser Surgery; Cosmetic Dermatology; Photodynamic Therapy; **Hospital:** St. Vincent Carmel Hosp; **Address:** Laser & Skin Surgery Ctr, 13400 N Meridian St, Ste 290, Carmel, IN 46032; **Phone:** 317-660-4900; **Board Cert:** Dermatology 2009; Dermatopathology 1982; **Med School:** Univ Iowa Coll Med 1971; **Resid:** Dermatology, Cleveland Clin 1978; Dermatopathology, Indiana Univ 1982; **Fellow:** Mohs Surgery, Cleveland Clin 1979; **Fac Appt:** Clin Prof D, Indiana Univ

Hruza, George J MD [D] - **Spec Exp:** Skin Laser Surgery; Mohs' Surgery; Cosmetic Surgery; Xeroderma Pigmentosum; **Hospital:** St. Luke's Hosp - Chesterfield, MO, St. Louis Univ Hosp; **Address:** 1001 Chesterfield Pkwy E, Ste 101, St Louis, MO 63017; **Phone:** 314-878-3839; **Board Cert:** Dermatology 1986; **Med School:** NYU Sch Med 1982; **Resid:** Dermatology, NYU Med Ctr-Skin Cancer Unit 1986; **Fellow:** Laser Surgery, Mass Genl Hosp-Harvard 1987; Mohs Surgery, Univ Wisc Affil Hosp 1988; **Fac Appt:** Clin Prof D, St Louis Univ

Johnson, Timothy M MD [D] - **Spec Exp:** Melanoma; Mohs' Surgery; Skin Cancer; **Hospital:** Univ Michigan Med Ctr; **Address:** Univ Michigan Comprehensive Cancer Ctr, 1500 E Med Ctr Drive Fl 1, Ann Arbor, MI 48109; **Phone:** 734-936-6360; **Board Cert:** Dermatology 1988; **Med School:** Univ Tex, Houston 1984; **Resid:** Dermatology, Univ Texas Med Ctr 1988; **Fellow:** Cutaneous Oncology, Univ Mich Med Ctr 1989; Mohs Surgery, Univ Oregon Hlth Sci Ctr 1990; **Fac Appt:** Prof D, Univ Mich Med Sch

Krunic, Aleksandar L MD [D] - **Spec Exp:** Mohs' Surgery; Skin Cancer; Melanoma; Dermatologic Surgery; **Hospital:** Univ of IL Med Ctr at Chicago; **Address:** Univ Illinois Med Ctr, Derm Ctr, 1801 W Taylor St, Ste 3E, Chicago, IL 60612; **Phone:** 312-996-8666; **Board Cert:** Dermatology 2003; **Med School:** Yugoslavia 1988; **Resid:** Dermatology, Univ Chicago Hosp 2003; **Fellow:** Dermatologic Surgery, Duke Univ Med Ctr 1997; Mohs Surgery, Univ Texas SW Med Ctr 2004; **Fac Appt:** Assoc Clin Prof D, Univ IL Coll Med

Lim, Henry W MD [D] - **Spec Exp:** Phototherapy; Vitiligo; Cutaneous Lymphoma; Skin Cancer; **Hospital:** Henry Ford Hosp; **Address:** Henry Ford Hosp, Dept Derm, 3031 W Grand Blvd, Ste 800, Detroit, MI 48202-3141; **Phone:** 313-916-4060; **Board Cert:** Dermatology 2005; Clinical & Laboratory Dematologic Immunology 1985; **Med School:** SUNY Downstate 1975; **Resid:** Dermatology, NYU Med Ctr 1979; **Fellow:** Immunological Dermatology, NYU Med Ctr 1980; **Fac Appt:** Prof Path, Wayne State Univ

Liu, Vincent MD [D] - **Hospital:** Univ Iowa Hosp & Clins; **Address:** Univ Iowa Hosp, Dermatology Clin, 200 Hawkins Drive, Iowa City, IA 52242; **Phone:** 319-356-7546; **Board Cert:** Dermatology 2009; Dermatopathology 2001; **Med School:** Univ Pennsylvania 1996; **Resid:** Dermatology, Mass Genl Hosp 2000; **Fellow:** Dermatopathology, Mass Genl Hosp 2001; **Fac Appt:** Assoc Clin Prof D, Univ Iowa Coll Med

Lucky, Anne W MD [D] - **Spec Exp:** Pediatric Dermatology; Acne; **Hospital:** Cincinnati Chldns Hosp Med Ctr; **Address:** Dermatology Associates of Cincinnati, 7691 Five Mile Rd, Ste 312, Cincinnati, OH 45230; **Phone:** 513-232-3332; **Board Cert:** Pediatrics 1975; Pediatric Endocrinology 1978; Dermatology 1981; Pediatric Dermatology 2004; **Med School:** Yale Univ 1970; **Resid:** Pediatrics, Boston Chldns Hosp 1973; Dermatology, Yale-New Haven Hosp 1981; **Fellow:** Pediatric Endocrinology, Natl Inst Hlth 1976; **Fac Appt:** Prof D, Univ Cincinnati

Mutasim, Diya F MD [D] - **Spec Exp:** Immune Deficiency-Skin Disorders; Dermatopathology; Autoimmune Disease; **Hospital:** Univ Cincinnati Med Ctr; **Address:** 222 Piedmont Ave, Ste 5300, Cincinnati, OH 45219; **Phone:** 513-475-7630; **Board Cert:** Dermatology 1990; Immunopathology 1991; Dermatopathology 1993; **Med School:** Lebanon 1979; **Resid:** Dermatology, Johns Hopkins Hosp 1989; **Fellow:** Immunological Dermatology, Johns Hopkins Hosp 1985; **Fac Appt:** Prof D, Univ Cincinnati

Neuburg, Marcelle MD [D] - **Spec Exp:** Mohs' Surgery; Skin Cancer; Pigmented Lesions; **Hospital:** Froedtert & Med Coll WI; **Address:** Clinical Cancer Ctr-Dermatology Dept, 9200 W Wisconsin Ave, Milwaukee, WI 53226; **Phone:** 414-805-5300; **Board Cert:** Internal Medicine 1985; Dermatology 1988; **Med School:** Oregon Hlth & Sci Univ 1982; **Resid:** Internal Medicine, MedStar Georgetown Univ Hosp 1985; Dermatology, Boston Med Ctr 1988; **Fellow:** Mohs Surgery, Tufts New England Med Ctr 1990; **Fac Appt:** Prof D, Med Coll Wisc

Otley, Clark C MD [D] - **Spec Exp:** Mohs' Surgery; Skin Cancer; Skin Cancer in Transplant Patients; Dermatologic Surgery; **Hospital:** Mayo Med Ctr & Clin - Rochester; **Address:** Mayo Clinic, 200 First St SW, Rochester, MN 55905; **Phone:** 507-284-2536; **Board Cert:** Dermatology 2013; **Med School:** Duke Univ 1991; **Resid:** Dermatology, Mass Genl Hosp 1995; **Fellow:** Dermatologic Surgery, Mayo Clinic 1996; **Fac Appt:** Assoc Prof D, Mayo Med Sch

Paller, Amy S MD [D] - **Spec Exp:** Genetic Disorders-Skin; Immune Deficiency-Skin Disorders; Atopic Dermatitis; Pediatric Dermatology; **Hospital:** Lurie Chldn's Hosp-Chicago; **Address:** Lurie Children's Hosp, 225 E Chicago Ave, Box 107, Chicago, IL 60611; **Phone:** 312-227-6060; **Board Cert:** Pediatrics 1982; Dermatology 2007; Pediatric Dermatology 2004; **Med School:** Stanford Univ 1978; **Resid:** Pediatrics, Chldns Meml Hosp 1981; Dermatology, Northwestern Meml Hosp 1983; **Fellow:** Research, Univ NC Hosp 1984; **Fac Appt:** Prof D, Northwestern Univ

Rhodes, Arthur R MD [D] - **Spec Exp:** Melanoma; Melanoma Risk Assessment; Melanoma Early Detection/Prevention; Pediatric Dermatology; **Hospital:** Rush Univ Med Ctr; **Address:** Rush Univ Dermatology Patient Svcs, 1725 W Harrison St, Ste 264, Chicago, IL 60612; **Phone:** 312-942-2195; **Board Cert:** Internal Medicine 1972; Dermatology 2009; **Med School:** Columbia P&S 1969; **Resid:** Internal Medicine, Beth Israel Hosp 1972; Dermatology, Mass Genl Hosp 1978; **Fac Appt:** Prof D, Rush Med Coll

Shea, Christopher R MD [D] - **Spec Exp:** Melanoma; Cutaneous Lymphoma; Pigmented Lesions; Dermatopathology; **Hospital:** Univ of Chicago Med; **Address:** Univ of Chicago Medicine, Ctr for Advanced Medicine, 5758 S Maryland Ave, Chicago, IL 60637; **Phone:** 773-834-1348; **Board Cert:** Dermatology 2009; Dermatopathology 1991; Anatomic Pathology 1998; **Med School:** Georgetown Univ 1983; **Resid:** Dermatology, Mass Genl Hosp 1989; Anatomic Pathology, Georgetown Univ Hosp 1981; **Fellow:** Dermatology, Harvard-Mass Genl Hosp 1989; Dermatopathology, NY-Presby/Weill Cornell Med Ctr 1991; **Fac Appt:** Prof D, Univ Chicago-Pritzker Sch Med

Treadwell, Patricia A MD [D] - **Spec Exp:** Pediatric Dermatology; Vascular Birthmarks; **Hospital:** Riley Hosp for Children; **Address:** Riley Hosp, Ped Dermatology Dept, 705 Riley Hospital Drive, Ste 1300, Indianapolis, IN 46202; **Phone:** 317-944-2801; **Board Cert:** Pediatrics 1982; Dermatology 1983; **Med School:** Cornell Univ-Weill Med Coll 1977; **Resid:** Pediatrics, Riley Hosp Chldn 1980; Dermatology, IU Hlth Hosp 1983; **Fac Appt:** Prof D, Indiana Univ

Voorhees, John MD [D] - **Spec Exp:** Psoriasis; Photoaging; **Hospital:** Univ Michigan Med Ctr; **Address:** Univ Michigan, Dept Dermatology, 1500 E Med Ctr Drive, Taubman Ctr, Level 1, Ann Arbor, MI 48109-5314; **Phone:** 734-936-4054; **Board Cert:** Dermatology 1970; **Med School:** Univ Mich Med Sch 1963; **Resid:** Dermatology, Univ Mich Hosp 1969; **Fac Appt:** Prof D, Univ Mich Med Sch

Witman, Patricia Mary MD [D] - **Spec Exp:** Pediatric Dermatology; **Hospital:** Nationwide Chldn's Hosp; **Address:** Nationwide Chldns Hosp, 555 S 18th St, Columbus, OH 43205; **Phone:** 614-722-5777; **Board Cert:** Dermatology 2007; Pediatric Dermatology 2006; **Med School:** Med Coll Wisc 1994; **Resid:** Dermatology, Froedtert Meml Hosp 1998; **Fellow:** Pediatric Dermatology, UCSF Med Ctr 2002

Wood, Gary S MD [D] - **Spec Exp:** Cutaneous Lymphoma; Melanoma; Skin Cancer; Parapsoriasis; **Hospital:** Univ WI Hosp & Clins, Wm S Middleton Mem Vet Hosp-Madison; **Address:** Univ Wisconsin Health, Dept Dermatology, 1 S Park St, Fl 7, Madison, WI 53715-1375; **Phone:** 608-287-2620; **Board Cert:** Anatomic Pathology 1983; Dermatology 1986; Dermatopathology 1987; **Med School:** Univ IL Coll Med 1979; **Resid:** Anatomic Pathology, Stanford Univ Med Ctr 1983; Dermatology, Stanford Univ Med Ctr 1985; **Fellow:** Immunopathology, Stanford Univ Med Ctr 1981; **Fac Appt:** Prof D, Univ Wisc

Zelickson, Brian D MD [D] - **Spec Exp:** Skin Laser Surgery; **Hospital:** Fairview Southdale Hosp; **Address:** 825 Nicollet Mall, Med Arts Bldg - Ste 1002, Minneapolis, MN 55402; **Phone:** 612-338-0711; **Board Cert:** Dermatology 2009; **Med School:** Mayo Med Sch 1986; **Resid:** Dermatology, Mayo Clinic 1990; **Fac Appt:** Asst Prof D, Univ Minn

Great Plains and Mountains

Bowen, Glen M MD [D] - **Spec Exp:** Melanoma; Cutaneous Lymphoma; Clinical Trials; Mohs' Surgery; **Hospital:** Univ Utah Hlth Care, Cottonwood Hosp & Med Ctr; **Address:** Huntsman Canc Inst, 2000 Circle of Hope, Ste 2400, Salt Lake City, UT 84132; **Phone:** 801-585-0197; **Board Cert:** Dermatology 2013; **Med School:** Univ Utah 1990; **Resid:** Dermatology, Univ MI Med Ctr 1993; **Fellow:** Immunological Dermatology, Univ MI Med Ctr 1995; Mohs Surgery, Univ Utah Affil Hosps 2001; **Fac Appt:** Assoc Prof D, Univ Utah

Krueger, Gerald G MD [D] - **Spec Exp:** Psoriasis; **Hospital:** Univ Utah Hlth Care; **Address:** Univ Utah Hlth Sci Ctr, Dept Derm, 30 N 1900 E, rm 4A330 SOM, Salt Lake City, UT 84132; **Phone:** 801-581-6465; **Board Cert:** Dermatology 1973; **Med School:** Loma Linda Univ 1966; **Resid:** Dermatology, Univ Colorado Med Ctr 1972; **Fac Appt:** Prof D, Univ Utah

Sontheimer, Richard D MD [D] - **Spec Exp:** Immune Deficiency-Skin Disorders; Lupus/SLE; Dermatomyositis; **Hospital:** Univ Utah Hlth Care; **Address:** Univ Hlth Care, Dept Dermatology, 30 N 1900 E, rm 4A330, Salt Lake City, UT 84132; **Phone:** 801-581-6465; **Board Cert:** Internal Medicine 1976; Dermatology 1979; Clinical & Laboratory Dematologic Immunology 1985; **Med School:** Univ Tex SW, Dallas 1972; **Resid:** Internal Medicine, Univ Utah Affil Hosps 1976; Dermatology, Parkland Meml Hosp 1979; **Fellow:** Research, Southwestern Med Sch 1978; **Fac Appt:** Prof D, Univ Utah

Southwest

Carney, John M MD [D] - **Spec Exp:** Mohs' Surgery; Skin Cancer; **Address:** 11321 Interstate 30, Ste 201, Little Rock, AR 72209; **Phone:** 501-455-4700; **Board Cert:** Dermatology 1984; **Med School:** Northwestern Univ 1979; **Resid:** Dermatology, U Hosps/Case West Res U 1984; **Fellow:** Physiology, Harvard Med Sch 1985; Dermatologic Surgery, Univ Tenn Med Ctr 1986

Cather, Jennifer C MD [D] - **Spec Exp:** Psoriasis; **Hospital:** Baylor Univ Med Ctr-Dallas; **Address:** Modern Dermatology, 9101 N Central Expy, Ste 160, Dallas, TX 75231; **Phone:** 214-265-1818; **Board Cert:** Dermatology 2008; **Med School:** Univ Tex SW, Dallas 1994; **Resid:** Dermatology, UT Derm Hosp 2000; **Fellow:** Research, MD Anderson Canc Ctr 1997

Cockerell, Clay J MD [D] - **Spec Exp:** Dermatopathology; **Hospital:** UT Southwestern Med Ctr at Dallas; **Address:** 5939 Harry Hines Blvd, Ste 100, Dallas, TX 75390-9191; **Phone:** 214-645-2400; **Board Cert:** Dermatology 2008; Dermatopathology 1986; **Med School:** Baylor Coll Med 1981; **Resid:** Dermatology, NYU Langone Med Ctr 1985; **Fellow:** Dermatopathology, NYU Langone Med Ctr 1986; **Fac Appt:** Clin Prof DP, Univ Tex SW, Dallas

Duvic, Madeleine MD [D] - **Spec Exp:** Cutaneous Lymphoma; Skin Cancer; Alopecia Areata; **Hospital:** UT MD Anderson Canc Ctr; **Address:** Derm Dept-MD Anderson Cancer Ctr, 1400 Pressler St - Unit 1452, Houston, TX 77030; **Phone:** 713-792-6800; **Board Cert:** Dermatology 1981; Internal Medicine 1982; **Med School:** Duke Univ 1977; **Resid:** Dermatology, Duke Univ Med Ctr 1980; Internal Medicine, Duke Univ Med Ctr 1982; **Fellow:** Geriatric Medicine, Duke Univ Med Ctr 1984; **Fac Appt:** Prof D, Univ Tex, Houston

Hansen, Ronald C MD [D] - **Spec Exp:** Pediatric Dermatology; **Hospital:** Phoenix Children's Hosp; **Address:** Phoenix Chldns Hosp, Dermatology Clin F, 1919 E Thomas Rd, Phoenix, AZ 85006; **Phone:** 602-933-0895; **Board Cert:** Pediatrics 1974; Dermatology 1980; **Med School:** Univ Iowa Coll Med 1968; **Resid:** Pediatrics, Chldns Hosp 1970; Pediatrics, Stanford Univ Hosp & Clins 1972; **Fellow:** Dermatology, Univ Ariz Coll Med Affil Hosp 1980; **Fac Appt:** Prof D, Univ Ariz Coll Med

Levy, Moise L MD [D] - **Spec Exp:** Pediatric Dermatology; Vascular Birthmarks; Genetic Disorders-Skin; Blistering Diseases; **Hospital:** Dell Children's Med Ctr of Central Texas; **Address:** 1301 Barbara Jordan Blvd, Ste 200, Pediatrics Bldg, Ste 200, Austin, TX 78723; **Phone:** 512-628-1920; **Board Cert:** Pediatrics 1985; Dermatology 1986; Pediatric Dermatology 2004; **Med School:** Univ Tex, Houston 1979; **Resid:** Pediatrics, Univ Tex Affil Hosp 1983; Dermatology, Baylor Coll Med 1986; **Fac Appt:** Clin Prof D, Baylor Coll Med

Lim Quan, Katherine K MD [D] - **Spec Exp:** Mohs' Surgery; Skin Cancer; **Hospital:** Chandler Regional Med Ctr; **Address:** Valley Skin Cancer Surgery, 1100 S Dobson Rd, Ste 223, Chandler, AZ 85286; **Phone:** 480-214-0388; **Board Cert:** Dermatology 2006; **Med School:** Northwestern Univ 1992; **Resid:** Dermatology, Mayo Clinic 1996; **Fellow:** Dermatologic Surgery, Mayo Clinic 1997

Linder, Jennifer L MD [D] - **Spec Exp:** Mohs' Surgery; Skin Cancer; Cosmetic Dermatology; **Address:** Linder Dermatology & Skin Cancer Ctr, 6710 E Camelback Rd, Ste 220, Scottsdale, AZ 85251; **Phone:** 480-946-7939; **Board Cert:** Dermatology 2003; **Med School:** Washington Univ, St Louis 1999; **Resid:** Dermatology, Thomas Jeff U Hosp 2003; **Fellow:** Dermatologic Surgery, Mohs College 2004

Menter, M Alan MD [D] - **Spec Exp:** Psoriasis; Cosmetic Dermatology; Eczema; **Hospital:** Baylor Univ Med Ctr-Dallas, UT Southwestern Med Ctr at Dallas; **Address:** 3900 Junius St, Ste 145, Dallas, TX 75246; **Phone:** 972-386-7546; **Board Cert:** Dermatology 1978; **Med School:** South Africa 1966; **Resid:** Dermatology, Pretoria Genl Hosp 1971; Dermatology, Guys Hosp 1972; **Fellow:** Dermatology, St Johns Hosp 1973; Dermatology, Univ Texas SW 1979; **Fac Appt:** Clin Prof D, Univ Tex SW, Dallas

Orengo, Ida F MD [D] - **Spec Exp:** Mohs' Surgery; Skin Cancer; Melanoma; **Hospital:** Methodist Hosp - Houston, DeBakey VA Med Ctr-Houston; **Address:** Baylor Dermatology, 1977 Butler Blvd, Ste E6.200, Houston, TX 77030; **Phone:** 713-798-6925; **Board Cert:** Dermatology 2009; **Med School:** Baylor Coll Med 1987; **Resid:** Dermatology, Baylor Coll Med 1991; **Fellow:** Dermatologic Surgery, Harvard Med Sch/Mass Genl Hosp 1992; **Fac Appt:** Prof D, Baylor Coll Med

Perone, Jennifer Beth MD [D] - **Spec Exp:** Mohs' Surgery; Cosmetic Dermatology; **Hospital:** UT Southwestern Med Ctr at Dallas; **Address:** Surgical Dermatology Assoc, One Forest Medical Plaza, 12200 Park Central Drive, Ste 215, Dallas, TX 75251; **Phone:** 972-239-6999; **Board Cert:** Dermatology 2011; **Med School:** NYU Sch Med 1999; **Resid:** Dermatology, Duke Univ Med Ctr 2003; **Fellow:** Mohs Surgery, UT Southwestern Med Ctr-Dalla 2006

Pitts, Jeanette M MD [D] - **Spec Exp:** Mohs' Surgery; Skin Cancer; Melanoma; Skin Laser Surgery; **Hospital:** Univ Arizona Med Ctr-Univ Campus; **Address:** Univ Arizona Cancer Ctr, North Campus, 3838 N Campbell Ave, Tucson, AZ 85719-1454; **Phone:** 520-694-2873; **Board Cert:** Dermatology 2009; **Med School:** Univ Kansas 1996; **Resid:** Dermatology, Emory Univ 1998; **Fellow:** Mohs Surgery, Hershey Med Ctr 1999; **Fac Appt:** Assoc Clin Prof Med, Univ Ariz Coll Med

Taylor III, R. Stan MD [D] - **Spec Exp:** Mohs' Surgery; Melanoma; Skin Cancer; **Hospital:** UT Southwestern Med Ctr at Dallas, Parkland Hlth & Hosp Sys; **Address:** Univ Tex SW Med Sch, Dept Derm, 5323 Harry Hines Blvd, Dallas, TX 75390-7208; **Phone:** 214-645-8950; **Board Cert:** Dermatology 1989; **Med School:** Univ Tex Med Br, Galveston 1985; **Resid:** Dermatology, Univ Mich Med Ctr 1989; **Fellow:** Immunological Dermatology, Univ Mich Med Ctr 1990; Mohs Surgery, Oregon Hlth Sci Univ 1991; **Fac Appt:** Prof D, Univ Tex SW, Dallas

Wheeland, Ronald G MD [D] - **Spec Exp:** Skin Laser Surgery; Mohs' Surgery; Cosmetic Dermatology; Cutaneous Lymphoma; **Hospital:** Univ Arizona Med Ctr-Univ Campus; **Address:** 12345 E Summer Trail, Tucson, AZ 85749; **Phone:** 520-404-1516; **Board Cert:** Dermatology 2009; Dermatopathology 1978; **Med School:** Univ Ariz Coll Med 1973; **Resid:** Dermatology, Univ OK Affil Hosp 1977; **Fellow:** Dermatopathology, Univ Oklahoma 1978; Mohs Surgery, Cleveland Clinic 1984; **Fac Appt:** Prof Emeritus D, Univ Ariz Coll Med

West Coast and Pacific

Bennett, Richard G MD [D] - **Spec Exp:** Mohs' Surgery; Skin Cancer; Hidradenitis Suppurativa; Dermatofibrosarcoma Protruberans; **Hospital:** Keck Med Ctr of USC, UCLA Ronald Reagan Med Ctr; **Address:** 1301 20th St, Ste 570, Santa Monica, CA 90404-2080; **Phone:** 310-315-0171; **Board Cert:** Dermatology 1975; **Med School:** Case West Res Univ 1970; **Resid:** Dermatology, Hosp Univ Penn 1974; **Fellow:** Mohs Surgery, NYU Med Ctr 1977; **Fac Appt:** Clin Prof D, UCLA

Berg, Daniel MD [D] - **Spec Exp:** Skin Cancer; Mohs' Surgery; Skin Laser Surgery; Hair Restoration/Transplant; **Hospital:** Univ Wash Med Ctr; **Address:** 1229 Madison St, Ste 1090, Seattle, WA 98104; **Phone:** 206-215-3300; **Board Cert:** Dermatology 2009; **Med School:** Univ Toronto 1985; **Resid:** Internal Medicine, Sunnybrook Med Ctr 1988; Dermatology, Duke Univ Hosp 1991; **Fellow:** Dermatologic Surgery, Univ Toronto 1992; Dermatologic Surgery, Univ British Columbia 1994; **Fac Appt:** Prof D, Univ Wash

Cunningham, Bari B MD [D] - **Spec Exp:** Pediatric Dermatology; Birthmarks/Hemangiomas; Laser Surgery; **Hospital:** Rady Children's Hosp - San Diego; **Address:** Comprehensive Dermatology Grp, 477 N El Camino Real, Ste C204, Encinitas, CA 92024; **Phone:** 760-634-3376; **Board Cert:** Dermatology 2006; Pediatric Dermatology 2006; **Med School:** Emory Univ 1992; **Resid:** Dermatology, Northwestern Meml Hosp 1995; **Fellow:** Pediatric Dermatology, Chldn's Meml Hosp 1996

Eichenfield, Lawrence F MD [D] - **Spec Exp:** Pediatric Dermatology; Atopic Dermatitis; Vascular Birthmarks; **Hospital:** Rady Children's Hosp - San Diego, UCSD Med Ctr; **Address:** Ped & Adolescent Dermatology, 8010 Frost St, Ste 602, San Diego, CA 92123-4204; **Phone:** 858-966-6795; **Board Cert:** Dermatology 2009; Pediatric Dermatology 2004; **Med School:** Mount Sinai Sch Med 1984; **Resid:** Pediatrics, Chldns Hosp 1987; Dermatology, Hosp Univ Penn 1991; **Fac Appt:** Prof Ped, UCSD

Fitzpatrick, Richard E MD [D] - **Spec Exp:** Cosmetic Dermatology; Skin Laser Surgery-Resurfacing; Hair Restoration/Transplant; **Address:** GBK Cosmetic Laser Dermatology, 9339 Genesee Ave, Ste 300, San Diego, CA 92121; **Phone:** 858-657-1002; **Board Cert:** Dermatology 2003; **Med School:** Emory Univ 1970; **Resid:** Dermatology, UCLA Med Ctr 1978; **Fac Appt:** Assoc Clin Prof D, UCSD

Frieden, Ilona J MD [D] - **Spec Exp:** Pediatric Dermatology; Vascular Birthmarks; Hemangiomas; **Hospital:** UCSF - Mt Zion Med Ctr; **Address:** UCSF, Dept Dermatology, 1701 Divisadero St, Fl 3, Box 0316, San Francisco, CA 94115; **Phone:** 415-353-7800; **Board Cert:** Dermatology 2005; Pediatrics 1983; Pediatric Dermatology 2004; **Med School:** UCSF 1977; **Resid:** Pediatrics, UCSF Med Ctr 1980; Dermatology, UCSF Med Ctr 1983; **Fac Appt:** Clin Prof D, UCSF

Friedlander, Sheila F MD [D] - **Spec Exp:** Pediatric Dermatology; Infectious Disease; **Hospital:** Rady Children's Hosp - San Diego, UCSD Med Ctr; **Address:** Ped & Adolescent Dermatology, 8010 Frost St, Ste 602, San Diego, CA 92123; **Phone:** 858-966-6795; **Board Cert:** Pediatrics 1984; Dermatology 1990; Pediatric Dermatology 2004; **Med School:** Univ Chicago-Pritzker Sch Med 1979; **Resid:** Pediatrics, Bronx Municipal Hosp 1983; Dermatology, UCLA Med Ctr 1990; **Fellow:** Infectious Disease, Montefiore Med Ctr 1986; **Fac Appt:** Clin Prof Ped, UCSD

Glogau, Richard Gordon MD [D] - **Spec Exp:** Cosmetic Dermatology; Skin Laser Surgery; Mohs' Surgery; Botox Therapy; **Hospital:** UCSF Med Ctr; **Address:** 350 Parnassus Ave, Ste 400, San Francisco, CA 94117; **Phone:** 415-564-1261; **Board Cert:** Dermatology 2009; Dermatopathology 1982; **Med School:** Harvard Med Sch 1973; **Resid:** Dermatology, UCSF Med Ctr 1977; **Fellow:** Dermatologic Surgery, UCSF Med Ctr 1978; **Fac Appt:** Clin Prof D, UCSF

Greenway Jr, Hubert T MD [D] - **Spec Exp:** Skin Cancer; Mohs' Surgery; Melanoma; **Hospital:** Scripps Green Hosp; **Address:** Scripps Clin, Div Mohs' Surgery, 10666 N Torrey Pines Rd, La Jolla, CA 92037; **Phone:** 858-554-8646; **Board Cert:** Dermatology 1982; **Med School:** Med Coll GA 1974; **Resid:** Dermatology, Naval Hosp 1982; **Fellow:** Mohs Surgery, Univ Wisconsin Med Ctr 1983

Grimes, Pearl E MD [D] - **Spec Exp:** Pigmented Lesions; Ethnic Skin Disorders; Vitiligo; Cosmetic Dermatology; **Hospital:** UCLA Ronald Reagan Med Ctr; **Address:** 5670 Wilshire Blvd, Ste 650, Los Angeles, CA 90036; **Phone:** 323-467-4389; **Board Cert:** Dermatology 1979; **Med School:** Washington Univ, St Louis 1974; **Resid:** Dermatology, Howard Univ Hosp 1979; **Fac Appt:** Clin Prof D, UCLA

Hanifin, Jon M MD [D] - **Spec Exp:** Atopic Dermatitis; **Hospital:** OR Hlth & Sci Univ; **Address:** OHSU, Dept Dermatology, 3303 SW Bond Ave, MC CH16D, Portland, OR 97239; **Phone:** 503-418-3376; **Board Cert:** Dermatology 1970; **Med School:** Univ Wisc 1965; **Resid:** Dermatology, UCSF Med Ctr 1969; **Fellow:** Clinical & Laboratory Immunology, UCSF Med Ctr 1970; **Fac Appt:** Prof D, Oregon Hlth & Sci Univ

Kilmer, Suzanne L MD [D] - **Spec Exp:** Skin Laser Surgery-Resurfacing; Facial Rejuvenation; Cosmetic Dermatology; **Hospital:** Mercy General Hosp - Sacramento; **Address:** The Laser & Skin Surgery Center, 3835 J St, Sacramento, CA 95816-5520; **Phone:** 916-456-0400; **Board Cert:** Dermatology 2009; **Med School:** UC Davis 1987; **Resid:** Dermatology, UC Davis Med Ctr 1991; **Fellow:** Laser Surgery, Mass Genl Hosp 1992; **Fac Appt:** Asst Clin Prof D, UC Davis

Kim, Youn Hee MD [D] - **Spec Exp:** Cutaneous Lymphoma; Skin Cancer; **Hospital:** Stanford Univ Hosp & Clins; **Address:** 875 Blake Wilbur Drive, Clinic A, Palo Alto, CA 94304; **Phone:** 650-498-6000; **Board Cert:** Dermatology 1989; **Med School:** Stanford Univ 1984; **Resid:** Dermatology, Metropolitan Hosp 1989; **Fac Appt:** Prof D, Stanford Univ

Koo, John Ying Ming MD [D] - **Spec Exp:** Psoriasis/Eczema; Photosensitive Skin Diseases; Phototherapy; Psychodermatology; **Hospital:** UCSF Med Ctr; **Address:** Psoriasis Day Treatment Ctr, 515 Spruce St, San Francisco, CA 94118; **Phone:** 415-476-4702; **Board Cert:** Dermatology 1988; Psychiatry 1988; **Med School:** Harvard Med Sch 1981; **Resid:** Psychiatry, UCLA Neur Psyc Inst 1985; Dermatology, UCSF Med Ctr 1988; **Fac Appt:** Prof D, UCSF

Lask, Gary P MD [D] - **Spec Exp:** Cosmetic Dermatology; Mohs' Surgery; Skin Laser Surgery-Resurfacing; Scar Revision; **Hospital:** UCLA Ronald Reagan Med Ctr; **Address:** 16260 Ventura Blvd, Ste 530, Encino, CA 91436; **Phone:** 818-788-4022; **Board Cert:** Dermatology 1983; **Med School:** Mexico 1977; **Resid:** Dermatology, ML King Jr-Drew Med Ctr 1983; **Fellow:** Mohs Surgery, ML King Jr-Drew Med Ctr 1984; **Fac Appt:** Clin Prof D, UCLA

Nghiem, Paul T MD/PhD [D] - **Spec Exp:** Merkel Cell Carcinoma; Skin Cancer; **Hospital:** Univ Wash Med Ctr; **Address:** Seattle Cancer Care Alliance, 825 Eastlake Ave E, Fl 4, Box 358050, Seattle, WA 98195; **Phone:** 206-288-1024; **Board Cert:** Dermatology 2009; **Med School:** Stanford Univ 1994; **Resid:** Dermatology, Mass Gen Hosp 1998; **Fellow:** Research, Harvard Univ 2002; **Fac Appt:** Assoc Prof D, Univ Wash

Richardson, Timothy F MD [D] - **Spec Exp:** Mohs' Surgery; Skin Cancer; **Hospital:** Eisenhower Med Ctr; **Address:** Mirage Dermatology, 36867 Cook St, Ste 101, Palm Desert, CA 92211; **Phone:** 760-341-1999; **Board Cert:** Internal Medicine 1987; Dermatology 2004; **Med School:** Georgetown Univ 1983; **Resid:** Internal Medicine, Loma Linda Univ Med Ctr 1986; Dermatology, Loma Linda Univ Med Ctr 1994; **Fellow:** Mohs Surgery, Loma Linda Univ Med Ctr 1995

Rubin, Mark G MD [D] - **Spec Exp:** Skin Laser Surgery; Cosmetic Dermatology; **Hospital:** UCSD Med Ctr; **Address:** Lasky Skin Center, 153 S Lasky Drive, Ste 1, Beverly Hills, CA 90212; **Phone:** 310-556-0119; **Board Cert:** Dermatology 1985; **Med School:** Jefferson Med Coll 1981; **Resid:** Dermatology, Henry Ford Hosp 1985; **Fac Appt:** Assoc Prof D, UCSD

Swanson, Neil A MD [D] - **Spec Exp:** Skin Cancer; Mohs' Surgery; Reconstructive Surgery-Skin; Cosmetic Dermatology; **Hospital:** OR Hlth & Sci Univ, VA Medical Center - Portland; **Address:** 3303 SW Bond Ave, MC CH-5D, Portland, OR 97239; **Phone:** 503-418-3376; **Board Cert:** Dermatology 1980; **Med School:** Univ Rochester 1976; **Resid:** Dermatology, Univ Michigan Med Ctr 1979; **Fellow:** Dermatology, UCSF Med Ctr 1980; **Fac Appt:** Prof D, Oregon Hlth & Sci Univ

Swetter, Susan M MD [D] - **Spec Exp:** Melanoma; Melanoma Early Detection/Prevention; Skin Cancer; **Hospital:** Stanford Univ Hosp & Clins, VA Hlth Care Sys - Palo Alto; **Address:** Stanford Univ Med Ctr, Dept Dermatology, 875 Blake Wilbur Dr, Clinic A, MC 5820, Stanford, CA 94305; **Phone:** 650-498-6000; **Board Cert:** Dermatology 2001; **Med School:** Univ Pennsylvania 1990; **Resid:** Dermatology, Stanford U Med Ctr 1994; **Fac Appt:** Prof D, Stanford Univ

Woodley, David T MD [D] - **Spec Exp:** Autoimmune Disease; Blistering Diseases; Psoriasis; Acne; **Hospital:** Keck Med Ctr of USC; **Address:** USC Dermatology, 1520 San Pablo St, Los Angeles, CA 90033; **Phone:** 323-442-6200; **Board Cert:** Dermatology 1982; Internal Medicine 1976; Clinical & Laboratory Dematologic Immunology 1993; **Med School:** Univ MO-Columbia Sch Med 1973; **Resid:** Internal Medicine, Univ Nebraska Med Ctr 1976; Dermatology, Univ NC Med Ctr 1978; **Fellow:** Dermatologic Research, Univ Paris 1980; **Fac Appt:** Prof D, USC-Keck School of Medicine

Cleveland Clinic

Every life deserves world class care.

Dermatology

Cleveland Clinic's Department of Dermatology, part of the Dermatology & Plastic Surgery Institute, offers a full array of subspecialized care for adult and pediatric patients. Our physicians diagnose and treat all disorders of the skin, hair and nails, whether primary or related to an underlying systemic illness, including industrial-related conditions.

Volume-Leading Mohs Center

The department offers a full range of procedures in the subspecialty area of dermatologic surgery. These include Mohs micrographic surgery for high-risk skin cancers (including local tissue reconstruction), laser surgery, chemical peels, soft tissue augmentation, Botox® injections, hair transplant and liposuction. We performed more than 2,000 Mohs procedures in the past year alone. Additionally, our Cutaneous Care Center provides outpatient treatment, rather than hospitalization, for patients with extensive, severe or chronic skin diseases utilizing phototherapy and excimer laser treatment. Staff dermatologists and residents are involved in research, either institutionally or through industrial support of clinical trials.

Cleveland Clinic's Department of Dermatology provides expertise in the diagnosis and management of the full spectrum of dermatologic conditions, as well as an extensive range of cosmetic evaluations and surgeries. We continue to meet our community responsibility through active participation in skin cancer screening and other activities related to National Skin Cancer Week. The Department of Dermatology also provides medical missionary assistance in developing countries. We continuously strive to improve outcomes in dermatology, not just for the patients who entrust us with their care today, but for future generations.

Cleveland Clinic
Dermatology & Plastic Surgery Institute
9500 Euclid Ave.
Cleveland, OH 44195

Offering Same-Day Appointments
Call 866.320.4573

Treatment Guides
Cleveland Clinic has developed comprehensive treatment guides for many diseases and conditions. To download our free treatment guides, visit clevelandclinic.org/treatmentguides.

Online Medical Second Opinion
Call 216.444.3223 or 800.223.2273 ext. 43223 or email eclevelandclinic@ccf.org

Out-of-State Patients Assistance
Call 800.223.2273, ext. 55580 or email medicalconcierge@ccf.org

Visit Us At:
clevelandclinic.org

Follow Us On:
Facebook
facebook.com/clevelandclinic

Twitter
@ClevelandClinic

You Tube
youtube.com/clevelandclinic

Health Hub
clevelandclinic.org/HealthHub

Mount Sinai

THE MOUNT SINAI MEDICAL CENTER
Dermatology

One Gustave L. Levy Place
Fifth Avenue and 100th Street
New York, NY 10029-6574

Physician Referral: 1-800-MD-SINAI (637-4624)
www.mountsinai.org

The Mount Sinai **DEPARTMENT OF DERMATOLOGY** has one of the most comprehensive programs for skin health and the treatment of skin diseases in the nation. In addition to our offices at Mount Sinai Hospital, the department has satellite offices throughout New York City.

Skin Cancer
Our department is at the forefront of research in the treatment and prevention of skin cancer. Our Mohs surgeons, Drs. Hooman Khorasani and David Kriegel perform state-of-the-art surgical treatment and repairs for all types of skin cancer.

Dr. Orit Markowitz uses new imaging techniques for the early diagnosis and prevention of melanoma. We are one of the few dermatology departments with optical coherence tomography (OCT) technology, Molemax technology and Melafind systems. The latter devices are useful for evaluating non-melanoma skin cancers and pigmented lesions and for following and diagnosing melanoma.

Drs. Czernik, Goldenberg, Goldstein, Lamb, Lebwohl, Levitt, Markowitz, Shim-Chang, and Zeichner have expertise in the diagnosis, prevention, and treatment of all skin cancers and have developed many of the treatments currently in use to prevent and treat cancerous and precancerous skin lesions. We also treat one of the largest groups of patients with cutaneous T-cell lymphoma.

General Dermatology
Psoriasis:
Our faculty number among the country's leading experts in psoriasis, including our Department Chairman, Dr. Mark Lebwohl, and Drs. Norman Goldstein, Gary Goldenberg, Jacob Levitt, Annette Czernik and Angela Lamb. Our center includes a state-of- the-art phototherapy unit, an infusion center for intravenous treatments, an excimer laser therapy unit, and a research center where many new therapies available for psoriasis are tested.

Autoimmune and inflammatory skin diseases:
We have one of the largest centers for inflammatory skin diseases where we treat psoriasis, atopic dermatitis and contact dermatitis. Dr. Emma Guttman is doing clinical research in new targeted therapies for severe atopic dermatitis. Dr. Suhail Hadi is one of the most experienced in the use of the excimer laser for psoriasis and vitiligo. Our faculty also includes three renowned acne experts, Drs. Angela Lamb, Joshua Zeichner, and Susan Bershad.

Our bullous disease center is run by Drs. Jacob Levitt and Annette Czernik. We are one of the few dermatology departments in the nation with its own infusion unit, so patients may be treated either as outpatients in the infusion unit or as inpatients at The Mount Sinai Medical Center.

Pediatric and Adolescent Dermatology
Our faculty treats all ages for skin. Dr. Susan Bershad is a board-certified pediatric and adolescent dermatologist. Dr. Lauren Geller is trained in pediatrics and in pediatric dermatology and is board-certified in dermatology. Dr. Emma Guttman is a trailblazer in research on atopic dermatitis and other forms of eczema.

Cosmetic Dermatology Center
We were one of the first programs in the nation to have a procedural dermatology fellowship, which is run by Drs. David Kriegel and Hooman Khorasani. Along with Drs. Marsha Gordon, Heidi Waldorf, Gary Goldenberg, Joshua Zeichner, and Helen Shim-Chang, our team is renowned for noninvasive skin rejuvenation combining topical regimens, soft tissue fillers, botulinum toxin, photodynamic therapy and laser and radio frequency devices. Members of our faculty perform liposuction, blepharoplasty, microdermabrasion, laser hair removal, sclerotherapy, skin tightening procedures, laser removals of tattoos, and pigmented and vascular lesions as well as laser resurfacing such as fraxel and total Fx.

NYU Langone
MEDICAL CENTER

550 First Avenue *(at 31st Street)*
New York, NY 10016

www.NYULMC.org

Physician Referral: **888-7-NYU-MED** *(888-769-8633)*

DERMATOLOGY

The Ronald O. Perelman Department of Dermatology is a national and international leader in dermatology, employing the most advanced science and medicine to diagnose and treat skin disorders. The Department provides high-quality dermatologic care and conducts research into some of the most significant dermatologic problems. We also collaborate with experts from The Cancer Institute at NYU Langone. Services include adult and pediatric medical dermatology, dermatologic/skin cancer surgery and cosmetic dermatology. We specialize in the following areas:

Dermatologic / Skin Cancer Surgery and Cosmetic Dermatology

NYU Langone Medical Center's dermatologists provide specialized care for the treatment of malignant and benign skin lesions and offer cutting-edge therapies for aesthetic and cosmetic concerns.

General Dermatology

Dermatologic associates offer multi-subspecialty dermatology care in private office settings for patients with disorders of the skin, hair, and nails, including inflammatory skin diseases such as psoriasis and lupus, cancers and other skin tumors, hair loss, infections and allergic skin diseases such as eczema, contact dermatitis and hives.

Pediatric and Adolescent Dermatology

The Medical Center also boasts a specialized professional practice dedicated to the treatment of diseases affecting the skin, hair, and nails of infants, children and adolescents. These disorders include acne, atopic dermatitis/eczema, hair loss, hemangiomas, moles, birthmarks, vitiligo and genetic disorders affecting the skin.

Charles C. Harris Skin and Cancer Unit / Dermatology Clinical Trials Unit

The Charles C. Harris Skin and Cancer Unit at the Ambulatory Care Center is an outpatient dermatology teaching center combining unique patient care with superior medical education. Resident and attending physicians provide diagnosis and treatment of skin diseases that include acne, eczema and warts as well as complex medical conditions such as connective tissue disorders, pigmented lesions, skin allergies and skin cancers.

Dermatopathology

Highly trained dermatopathologists at the Medical Center examine skin tissues submitted by physicians from biopsies and surgeries to diagnose skin diseases and malignancies. One of the busiest academic skin pathology units in the country, the Dermatopathology section of the Department also provides consultative services for the review of skin pathology specimens performed elsewhere.

Top Doctors Make A Difference

Endocrinology, Diabetes & Metabolism

a subspecialty of Internal Medicine

An internist who concentrates on disorders of the internal (endocrine) glands such as the thyroid and adrenal glands. This specialist also deals with disorders such as diabetes, metabolic and nutritional disorders, pituitary diseases, menstrual and sexual problems.

Training Required: Three years in internal medicine *plus* additional training and examination for certification in endocrinology, diabetes and metabolism.

Endocrinology, Diabetes & Metabolism

New England

Abrahamson, Martin J MD [EDM] - **Spec Exp:** Diabetes; **Hospital:** Beth Israel Deaconess Med Ctr - Boston; **Address:** Joslin Diabetes Ctr, 1 Joslin Pl, Ste 260, Boston, MA 02215; **Phone:** 617-309-2501; **Board Cert:** Internal Medicine 2005; Endocrinology, Diabetes & Metabolism 2005; **Med School:** South Africa 1977; **Resid:** Internal Medicine, Groote Schuuer Hosp-Univ Cape Town 1983; **Fellow:** Endocrinology, Diabetes & Metabolism, Groote Schuuer Hosp-Univ Cape Town 1985; Research, Univ Cape Town 1987; **Fac Appt:** Assoc Prof Med, Harvard Med Sch

Axelrod, Lloyd MD [EDM] - **Spec Exp:** Diabetes; **Hospital:** Mass Genl Hosp; **Address:** MGH Diabetes Unit, 50 Staniford St Fl 3 - Ste 340, Boston, MA 02114; **Phone:** 617-726-8722; **Board Cert:** Internal Medicine 1973; Endocrinology, Diabetes & Metabolism 1973; **Med School:** Harvard Med Sch 1967; **Resid:** Internal Medicine, Brigham & Womens Hosp 1969; Internal Medicine, Mass Genl Hosp 1971; **Fellow:** Endocrinology, Diabetes & Metabolism, Brigham & Womens Hosp 1970; Endocrinology, Diabetes & Metabolism, Mass Genl Hosp 1972; **Fac Appt:** Assoc Prof Med, Harvard Med Sch

Beaser, Richard S MD [EDM] - **Spec Exp:** Diabetes; **Hospital:** Beth Israel Deaconess Med Ctr - Boston; **Address:** Joslin Diabetes Ctr, One Joslin Pl, Boston, MA 02215; **Phone:** 617-732-2665; **Board Cert:** Internal Medicine 1980; **Med School:** Boston Univ 1977; **Resid:** Internal Medicine, Univ Mass Med Ctr 1980; **Fellow:** Diabetes, Joslin Clinic 1981; Endocrinology, Lahey Clinic 1982; **Fac Appt:** Assoc Clin Prof Med, Harvard Med Sch

Bhasin, Shalender MD [EDM] - **Spec Exp:** Reproductive Endocrinology-Male; Sexual Dysfunction; **Hospital:** Brigham & Women's Hosp; **Address:** Brigham & Womens Hosp, Endocrine Div, 221 Longwood Ave, Ste RF2, Boston, MA 02115; **Phone:** 617-732-5661; **Board Cert:** Internal Medicine 1981; Endocrinology, Diabetes & Metabolism 2008; **Med School:** India 1976; **Resid:** Internal Medicine, Northwestern Univ Med Ctr 1981; **Fellow:** Endocrinology, Diabetes & Metabolism, Harbor-UCLA Med Ctr 1984

Biller, Beverly M K MD [EDM] - **Spec Exp:** Pituitary Disorders; Cushing's Syndrome; Acromegaly; **Hospital:** Mass Genl Hosp; **Address:** Neuroendocrine Clinic Center, Zero Emerson Pl, Ste 112, Boston, MA 02114-3117; **Phone:** 617-726-7948; **Board Cert:** Internal Medicine 1986; Endocrinology 1989; **Med School:** Univ Okla Coll Med 1983; **Resid:** Internal Medicine, Beth Israel Deaconness Hosp 1986; **Fellow:** Endocrinology, Diabetes & Metabolism, Mass Genl Hosp 1989; **Fac Appt:** Assoc Prof Med, Harvard Med Sch

Braverman, Lewis E MD [EDM] - **Spec Exp:** Thyroid Disorders; **Hospital:** Boston Med Ctr; **Address:** Boston Med Ctr, Dept Endocrinology, Diabetes & Nutrition, 732 Harrison Ave Fl 2, Boston, MA 02118-2309; **Phone:** 617-638-7470; **Board Cert:** Internal Medicine 1963; Nuclear Medicine 1972; **Med School:** Johns Hopkins Univ 1955; **Resid:** Internal Medicine, Boston City Hosp 1960; **Fellow:** Endocrinology, Boston City Hosp 1962; **Fac Appt:** Prof Med, Boston Univ

Comi, Richard J MD [EDM] - **Spec Exp:** Diabetes; Hypoglycemia; Thyroid Disorders; Pituitary Disorders; **Hospital:** Dartmouth - Hitchcock Med Ctr; **Address:** Dartmouth-Hitchcock Med Ctr, Dept Endocrinology, 1 Med Ctr Drive, Ste 5C, Lebanon, NH 03756; **Phone:** 603-650-8630; **Board Cert:** Internal Medicine 1983; Endocrinology 1987; **Med School:** Harvard Med Sch 1980; **Resid:** Internal Medicine, Mass Genl Hosp 1983; **Fellow:** Endocrinology & Diabetes, Natl Inst Hlth 1986; **Fac Appt:** Assoc Prof Med, Dartmouth Med Sch

Cushing, Gary W MD [EDM] - **Spec Exp:** Thyroid Disorders; **Hospital:** Lahey Hosp & Med Ctr; **Address:** Lahey Hosp & Med Ctr, 4 West Endocrinology, 41 Mall Rd, Burlington, MA 01805; **Phone:** 781-744-2088; **Board Cert:** Internal Medicine 1983; Endocrinology 1985; **Med School:** Univ Mass Sch Med 1980; **Resid:** Internal Medicine, St Vincent Hosp 1983; **Fellow:** Endocrinology, Beth Israel Hosp 1985; **Fac Appt:** Assoc Clin Prof Med, Tufts Univ

Daniels, Gilbert H MD [EDM] - **Spec Exp:** Thyroid Disorders; Parathyroid Disease; Thyroid Cancer; Adrenal Cancer; **Hospital:** Mass Genl Hosp; **Address:** MGH Thyroid Associates, 15 Parkman St WACC Bldg - Ste 730S, Boston, MA 02114; **Phone:** 617-726-8430; **Board Cert:** Internal Medicine 1972; Endocrinology, Diabetes & Metabolism 1975; **Med School:** Harvard Med Sch 1966; **Resid:** Internal Medicine, Mass Genl Hosp 1972; **Fellow:** Biochemistry, Natl Inst Hlth 1970; Endocrinology, Diabetes & Metabolism, UCSF Med Ctr 1971; **Fac Appt:** Prof Med, Harvard Med Sch

Holick, Michael F MD/PhD [EDM] - **Spec Exp:** Bone Disorders-Metabolic; Osteoporosis; Calcium Disorders; Nutrition; **Hospital:** Boston Med Ctr; **Address:** Boston Med Ctr, 732 Harrison Ave Fl 2, Boston, MA 02118; **Phone:** 617-638-7470; **Board Cert:** Internal Medicine 1979; **Med School:** Univ Wisc 1976; **Resid:** Internal Medicine, Mass Genl Hosp 1979; **Fellow:** Endocrinology, Mass Genl Hosp 1980; **Fac Appt:** Prof Med, Boston Univ

Inzucchi, Silvio E MD [EDM] - **Spec Exp:** Diabetes; Pituitary Disorders; Growth Hormone Disorder-Adult; Cholesterol/Lipid Disorders; **Hospital:** Yale-New Haven Hosp; **Address:** Yale Diabetes Center, 789 Howard Ave, Dana Clinic Bldg fl 2, New Haven, CT 06520; **Phone:** 203-737-1932; **Board Cert:** Internal Medicine 1988; Endocrinology, Diabetes & Metabolism 2006; **Med School:** Harvard Med Sch 1985; **Resid:** Internal Medicine, Yale-New Haven Hosp 1988; **Fellow:** Endocrinology, Diabetes & Metabolism, Yale-New Haven Hosp 1994; **Fac Appt:** Prof Med, Yale Univ

Kahn, Barbara B MD [EDM] - **Spec Exp:** Obesity; Nutrition; **Hospital:** Beth Israel Deaconess Med Ctr - Boston; **Address:** Beth Israel Deaconess Medical Ctr, 330 Brookline Ave, Boston, MA 02215; **Phone:** 617-735-3324; **Board Cert:** Internal Medicine 1980; Endocrinology, Diabetes & Metabolism 1985; **Med School:** Stanford Univ 1977; **Resid:** Internal Medicine, UC Davis Med Ctr 1980; **Fellow:** Endocrinology, Diabetes & Metabolism, Natl Inst Hlth 1982; **Fac Appt:** Prof Med, Harvard Med Sch

Kronenberg, Henry M MD [EDM] - **Spec Exp:** Bone Disorders-Metabolic; Parathyroid Disease; **Hospital:** Mass Genl Hosp; **Address:** MGH Endocrine Associates, 15 Parkman Street, Wang AC 730A, Boston, MA 02114; **Phone:** 617-726-8720; **Board Cert:** Internal Medicine 1973; Endocrinology, Diabetes & Metabolism 1975; **Med School:** Columbia P&S 1970; **Resid:** Internal Medicine, Mass Genl Hosp 1972; **Fellow:** Endocrinology, Mass Genl Hosp 1975; **Fac Appt:** Prof Med, Harvard Med Sch

Larsen, Philip Reed MD [EDM] - **Spec Exp:** Thyroid Disorders; **Hospital:** Brigham & Women's Hosp; **Address:** 221 Longwood Ave Fl 2, Boston, MA 02115; **Phone:** 617-732-5666; **Board Cert:** Internal Medicine 1970; **Med School:** Columbia P&S 1963; **Resid:** Internal Medicine, NY Presby-Columbia Med Ctr 1965; Internal Medicine, Cincinnati General Hosp 1967; **Fellow:** Endocrinology, NIH 1968; Endocrinology, Cincinnati General Hosp 1969; **Fac Appt:** Prof Med, Harvard Med Sch

LeBoff, Meryl S MD [EDM] - **Spec Exp:** Osteoporosis; Bone Disorders-Metabolic; **Hospital:** Brigham & Women's Hosp; **Address:** 221 Longwood Ave Fl 2, Boston, MA 02115; **Phone:** 617-732-5666; **Board Cert:** Internal Medicine 1979; Endocrinology, Diabetes & Metabolism 1981; **Med School:** UMDNJ-NJ Med Sch, Newark 1975; **Resid:** Internal Medicine, USC Med Ctr 1979; **Fellow:** Endocrinology, Brigham & Womens Hosp 1982; **Fac Appt:** Assoc Prof Med, Harvard Med Sch

Lechan, Ronald M MD/PhD [EDM] - **Spec Exp:** Pituitary Disorders; Hypothalamic Dysfunction; Endocrine Cancers; Adrenal Disorders; **Hospital:** Tufts Med Ctr; **Address:** Tufts Medical Ctr, 800 Washington St, Box 268, Boston, MA 02111; **Phone:** 617-636-5689; **Board Cert:** Internal Medicine 1979; Endocrinology, Diabetes & Metabolism 1981; **Med School:** Univ VT Coll Med 1976; **Resid:** Internal Medicine, Beth Israel Hosp 1978; **Fellow:** Endocrinology, Diabetes & Metabolism, Tufts Med Ctr 1981; **Fac Appt:** Prof Med, Tufts Univ

Levine, Robert A MD [EDM] - **Spec Exp:** Thyroid Cancer; Thyroid Disorders; Thyroid Ultrasound; **Hospital:** St. Joseph Hosp & Trauma Ctr; **Address:** Thyroid Center of New Hampshire, 5 Coliseum Ave, Ste 209, Nashua, NH 03063; **Phone:** 603-881-7141; **Board Cert:** Internal Medicine 1984; Endocrinology, Diabetes & Metabolism 1987; **Med School:** Univ Conn 1981; **Resid:** Internal Medicine, Mt Auburn Hosp 1984; **Fellow:** Endocrinology, Yale-New Haven Hosp 1987

Nathan, David M MD [EDM] - **Spec Exp:** Diabetes; **Hospital:** Mass Genl Hosp; **Address:** MGH Diabetes Center, 50 Staniford St Fl 3, Box 340, Boston, MA 02114; **Phone:** 617-726-8722; **Board Cert:** Internal Medicine 1978; Endocrinology, Diabetes & Metabolism 1981; **Med School:** Mount Sinai Sch Med 1975; **Resid:** Internal Medicine, Brigham & Women's Hosp 1978; **Fellow:** Endocrinology, Diabetes & Metabolism, Mass Genl Hosp 1980; **Fac Appt:** Prof Med, Harvard Med Sch

Pearce, Elizabeth N MD [EDM] - **Spec Exp:** Thyroid Disorders; **Hospital:** Boston Med Ctr; **Address:** Boston Med Ctr, Dept Endocrinology, Diabetes & Nutrition, 732 Harrison St Fl 2, Boston, MA 02118; **Phone:** 617-638-7470; **Board Cert:** Endocrinology, Diabetes & Metabolism 2012; **Med School:** Harvard Med Sch 1997; **Resid:** Internal Medicine, Beth Israel Deaconess Med Ctr 2000; **Fellow:** Endocrinology, Diabetes & Metabolism, Boston Med Ctr 2003; **Fac Appt:** Assoc Prof Med, Boston Univ

Ross, Douglas S MD [EDM] - **Spec Exp:** Thyroid Disorders; Thyroid Cancer; **Hospital:** Mass Genl Hosp; **Address:** Mass General Hosp, Thyroid Associates, 15 Parkman St WAC Bldg - Ste 730 S, Boston, MA 02114; **Phone:** 617-726-3872; **Board Cert:** Internal Medicine 1980; Endocrinology, Diabetes & Metabolism 1983; **Med School:** Harvard Med Sch 1977; **Resid:** Internal Medicine, Mass General Hosp 1980; **Fellow:** Endocrinology, Mass General Hosp 1983; **Fac Appt:** Prof Med, Harvard Med Sch

Seely, Ellen Wells MD [EDM] - **Spec Exp:** Pregnancy & Endocrine Disorders; Diabetes in Pregnancy; Diabetes in Women; Thyroid Disorders in Pregnancy; **Hospital:** Brigham & Women's Hosp; **Address:** Brigham & Womens Hosp, Endocrine Div, 221 Longwood Ave, Ste RF2, Boston, MA 02115; **Phone:** 617-732-5661; **Board Cert:** Internal Medicine 1984; Endocrinology, Diabetes & Metabolism 1987; **Med School:** Columbia P&S 1981; **Resid:** Internal Medicine, Brigham & Womens Hosp 1984; **Fellow:** Endocrinology, Diabetes & Metabolism, Brigham & Womens Hosp 1987; **Fac Appt:** Prof Med, Harvard Med Sch

Mid Atlantic

Ball, Douglas W MD [EDM] - **Spec Exp:** Thyroid Cancer; **Hospital:** Johns Hopkins Hosp (page 59); **Address:** Johns Hopkins, Endocrinology Dept, 601 N Caroline St Fl 7, Baltimore, MD 21287; **Phone:** 410-955-4926; **Board Cert:** Internal Medicine 1987; **Med School:** Geo Wash Univ 1984; **Resid:** Internal Medicine, UPMC 1987; **Fellow:** Endocrinology, Diabetes & Metabolism, Johns Hopkins Hosp 1991; **Fac Appt:** Assoc Prof Med, Johns Hopkins Univ

Bergman, Donald MD [EDM] - **Spec Exp:** Osteoporosis; Thyroid Disorders; Calcium Disorders; Paget's Disease of Bone; **Hospital:** Mt Sinai Med Ctr (page 62); **Address:** 1199 Park Ave, Ste 1F, New York, NY 10128; **Phone:** 212-876-7333; **Board Cert:** Internal Medicine 1975; Endocrinology, Diabetes & Metabolism 1977; **Med School:** Jefferson Med Coll 1971; **Resid:** Obstetrics & Gynecology, Mt Sinai Hosp 1972; Internal Medicine, Mt Sinai Hosp 1975; **Fellow:** Endocrinology, Diabetes & Metabolism, Mt Sinai Hosp 1977; **Fac Appt:** Clin Prof Med, Mount Sinai Sch Med

Bilezikian, John P MD [EDM] - **Spec Exp:** Osteoporosis; Bone Disorders-Metabolic; **Hospital:** NY-Presby/Columbia Univ Med Ctr, NY (page 65); **Address:** Columbia Metabolic Bone Disease Program, Harkness Pavilion, 180 Ft Washington Ave Fl 9 - Ste 904, New York, NY 10032; **Phone:** 212-305-2663; **Board Cert:** Internal Medicine 1975; Endocrinology, Diabetes & Metabolism 1977; **Med School:** Columbia P&S 1969; **Resid:** Internal Medicine, NY-Presby/Columbia Univ Med Ctr 1975; **Fellow:** Endocrinology, Diabetes & Metabolism, Natl Inst Health 1977; **Fac Appt:** Prof Med, Columbia P&S

Blum, Conrad B MD [EDM] - **Spec Exp:** Cholesterol/Lipid Disorders; Thyroid Disorders; Diabetes; **Hospital:** NY-Presby/Columbia Univ Med Ctr, NY (page 65); **Address:** 51 W 51 St, rm 360, New York, NY 10022-1002; **Phone:** 212-326-8421; **Board Cert:** Internal Medicine 1976; Endocrinology, Diabetes & Metabolism 1977; **Med School:** Northwestern Univ 1971; **Resid:** Internal Medicine, Brigham & Women's Hosp 1976; **Fellow:** Endocrinology, Diabetes & Metabolism, Northwestern Meml Hosp 1977; **Fac Appt:** Clin Prof Med, Columbia P&S

Bockman, Richard S MD/PhD [EDM] - **Spec Exp:** Bone Disorders-Metabolic; Osteoporosis; Parathyroid Disease; Paget's Disease of Bone; **Hospital:** Hosp For Special Surgery (page 58), NY-Presby/Weill Cornell Med Ctr, NY (page 65); **Address:** 519 E 72nd St, Ste 206, New York, NY 10021; **Phone:** 212-606-1458; **Board Cert:** Internal Medicine 1975; **Med School:** Yale Univ 1968; **Resid:** Internal Medicine, NYU Langone Med Ctr 1973; **Fellow:** Endocrinology, Diabetes & Metabolism, NY-Presby/Weill Cornell Med Ctr 1975; **Fac Appt:** Prof Med, Cornell Univ-Weill Med Coll

Brillon, David J MD [EDM] - **Spec Exp:** Diabetes; Thyroid Disorders; Clinical Trials; **Hospital:** NY-Presby/Weill Cornell Med Ctr, NY (page 65); **Address:** Cornell-Weill Physicians-Endocrinology, 525 E 68th St Fl 20, Baker Pavilion, New York, NY 10065; **Phone:** 212-746-6290; **Board Cert:** Internal Medicine 1983; Endocrinology, Diabetes & Metabolism 1987; **Med School:** Brown Univ 1980; **Resid:** Internal Medicine, Rochester Genl Hosp 1983; **Fellow:** Endocrinology, Rochester Genl Hosp 1986; Endocrinology, Diabetes & Metabolism, UCSD Med Ctr 1988; **Fac Appt:** Clin Prof Med, Cornell Univ-Weill Med Coll

Burman, Kenneth D MD [EDM] - **Spec Exp:** Thyroid Disorders; Thyroid Cancer; **Hospital:** MedStar Washington Hosp Ctr; **Address:** Wash Hosp Ctr, Endocrinology Section, 110 Irving St NW, rm 1A-50B, Washington, DC 20010; **Phone:** 202-877-0333; **Board Cert:** Internal Medicine 1973; Endocrinology, Diabetes & Metabolism 1975; **Med School:** Univ MO-Columbia Sch Med 1970; **Resid:** Internal Medicine, Barnes Hosp 1972; **Fellow:** Endocrinology, Diabetes & Metabolism, Walter Reed Hosp 1974; **Fac Appt:** Prof Med, Georgetown Univ

Calvi, Laura M MD [EDM] - **Spec Exp:** Neuroendocrinology; Pituitary Disorders; **Hospital:** Univ Rochester Strong Meml Hosp; **Address:** Univ Rochester Med Ctr, Endocrinology, 601 Elmwood Ave, Box 693, Rochester, NY 14642; **Phone:** 585-275-2901; **Board Cert:** Endocrinology, Diabetes & Metabolism 2010; **Med School:** Harvard Med Sch 1995; **Resid:** Internal Medicine, Mass Genl Hosp 1998; **Fellow:** Endocrinology, Mass Genl Hosp 2000; **Fac Appt:** Assoc Prof Med, Univ Rochester

Cooper, David S MD [EDM] - **Spec Exp:** Thyroid Disorders; **Hospital:** Johns Hopkins Hosp (page 59); **Address:** Johns Hopkins, Endocrinology Dept, 601 N Caroline St Fl 7, Baltimore, MD 21287; **Phone:** 410-502-4926; **Board Cert:** Internal Medicine 1987; Endocrinology, Diabetes & Metabolism 2008; **Med School:** Tufts Univ 1973; **Resid:** Internal Medicine, Barnes-Jewish Hosp 1976; **Fellow:** Endocrinology, Mass Genl Hosp 1978; **Fac Appt:** Prof Med, Johns Hopkins Univ

Davies, Terry F MD [EDM] - **Spec Exp:** Thyroid Disorders in Pregnancy; Graves' Disease; Hashimoto's Disease; Thyroid Cancer; **Hospital:** Mt Sinai Med Ctr (page 62), VA Hudson Valley-FDR/Montrose; **Address:** 5 E 98th St, Box 1055, New York, NY 10029-6500; **Phone:** 212-241-7975; **Med School:** England, UK 1971; **Resid:** Internal Medicine, Univ Newcastle Affil Hosp 1975; **Fellow:** Endocrinology, Diabetes & Metabolism, Univ Newcastle Affil Hosp 1977; Endocrinology, Diabetes & Metabolism, Natl Inst Hlth 1979; **Fac Appt:** Prof Med, Mount Sinai Sch Med

Dobs, Adrian S MD [EDM] - **Spec Exp:** Hormonal Disorders; Hypogonadism-Male; Metabolic Disorders; Complementary Medicine; **Hospital:** Johns Hopkins Hosp (page 59); **Address:** Johns Hopkins, Endocrinology Dept, 1830 E Monument St, Ste 328, Baltimore, MD 21287; **Phone:** 410-955-9270; **Board Cert:** Internal Medicine 1981; Endocrinology 1987; **Med School:** Albany Med Coll 1978; **Resid:** Internal Medicine, Montefiore Med Ctr 1982; **Fellow:** Endocrinology, Johns Hopkins Hosp 1984; **Fac Appt:** Prof Med, Johns Hopkins Univ

Donner, Thomas W MD [EDM] - **Spec Exp:** Diabetes; Heart Disease in Diabetic Patients; **Hospital:** Johns Hopkins Hosp (page 59); **Address:** Johns Hopkins Comprehensive Diabetes Ctr, 601 N Caroline St, Ste 2008, Baltimore, MD 21287; **Phone:** 410-955-7139; **Board Cert:** Internal Medicine 1989; Endocrinology, Diabetes & Metabolism 2007; **Med School:** Univ VA Sch Med 1986; **Resid:** Internal Medicine, Univ MD Med Ctr 1989; **Fellow:** Endocrinology, Diabetes & Metabolism, Univ MD Med Ctr 1991; **Fac Appt:** Assoc Prof Med, Johns Hopkins Univ

Greene, Loren Wissner MD [EDM] - **Spec Exp:** Thyroid Disorders; Osteoporosis; Pituitary Disorders; Diabetes; **Hospital:** NYU Langone Med Ctr (page 68), NY-Presby/Lower Manhattan Hosp (page 65); **Address:** 650 First Ave, Fl 7th, New York, NY 10016-6402; **Phone:** 212-263-7449; **Board Cert:** Internal Medicine 1978; Endocrinology, Diabetes & Metabolism 1981; **Med School:** NYU Sch Med 1975; **Resid:** Internal Medicine, Bellevue Hosp Ctr-NYU 1978; **Fellow:** Endocrinology, Bellevue Hosp Ctr-NYU 1980; **Fac Appt:** Assoc Clin Prof Med, NYU Sch Med

Greenspan, Susan L MD [EDM] - **Spec Exp:** Osteoporosis; Osteoporosis in Men; **Hospital:** UPMC Presby, Pittsburgh; **Address:** Univ Pittsburgh, Osteoporosis Ctr, 3471 Fifth Ave, Kaufmann Bldg - Ste 1110, Pittsburgh, PA 15213; **Phone:** 412-692-2220; **Board Cert:** Internal Medicine 1982; Endocrinology, Diabetes & Metabolism 1987; **Med School:** Harvard Med Sch 1979; **Resid:** Internal Medicine, Beth Israel Hosp 1982; **Fellow:** Endocrinology, Mass Genl Hosp 1985; Geriatric Medicine, Beth Israel Hosp 1986; **Fac Appt:** Prof Med, Univ Pittsburgh

Haber, Richard S MD [EDM] - **Spec Exp:** Thyroid Disorders; Thyroid Cancer; Parathyroid Disease; Parathyroid Cancer; **Hospital:** Mt Sinai Med Ctr (page 62); **Address:** Mt Sinai Med Ctr, Dept Medicine, Div of Endocrinology, 5 E 98th St Fl 11, New York, NY 10029; **Phone:** 212-241-7975; **Board Cert:** Endocrinology, Diabetes & Metabolism 1983; Internal Medicine 1980; **Med School:** NYU Sch Med 1977; **Resid:** Internal Medicine, SUNY Health Sci Ctr 1980; **Fellow:** Endocrinology, Diabetes & Metabolism, NY Presby-Columbia Med Ctr 1983; **Fac Appt:** Prof Med, Mount Sinai Sch Med

Jacobs Jr, Thomas P MD [EDM] - **Spec Exp:** Adrenal Disorders; Pituitary Disorders; Calcium Disorders; Thyroid Disorders; **Hospital:** NY-Presby/Columbia Univ Med Ctr, NY (page 65); **Address:** 161 Fort Washington Ave, rm 210, MS 10032, New York, NY 10032-3713; **Phone:** 212-305-5578; **Board Cert:** Internal Medicine 1973; Endocrinology, Diabetes & Metabolism 1975; **Med School:** Johns Hopkins Univ 1968; **Resid:** Internal Medicine, Columbia Presby Hosp 1973; **Fellow:** Endocrinology, Diabetes & Metabolism, Univ Wash Med Ctr 1975; **Fac Appt:** Clin Prof Med, Columbia P&S

Kleinberg, David L MD [EDM] - **Spec Exp:** Pituitary Disorders; Neuroendocrinology; **Hospital:** NYU Langone Med Ctr (page 68); **Address:** 650 1st Ave Fl 4, New York, NY 10016; **Phone:** 212-263-6772; **Board Cert:** Internal Medicine 1972; Endocrinology 1975; **Med School:** Univ Miami Sch Med 1966; **Resid:** Internal Medicine, Maimonides Med Ctr 1968; Internal Medicine, NY-Presby/Columbia Univ Med Ctr 1971; **Fellow:** Endocrinology, Diabetes & Metabolism, NY-Presby/Columbia Univ Med Ctr 1970; **Fac Appt:** Prof Med, NYU Sch Med

Korytkowski, Mary T MD [EDM] - **Spec Exp:** Diabetes; Diabetes Clinical Trials; Hormonal Disorders; **Hospital:** UPMC Presby, Pittsburgh; **Address:** Center for Diabetes & Endocrinology, 3601 Fifth Ave, Ste 3B, Faulk Med Bldg, Pittsburgh, PA 15213-3403; **Phone:** 412-586-9714; **Board Cert:** Internal Medicine 1985; Endocrinology, Diabetes & Metabolism 1989; **Med School:** Univ NC Sch Med 1982; **Resid:** Internal Medicine, Johns Hopkins Hosp 1985; **Fellow:** Endocrinology, Diabetes & Metabolism, Sinai Hosp/Johns Hopkins Hosp 1988; **Fac Appt:** Prof Med, Univ Pittsburgh

Ladenson, Paul W MD [EDM] - **Spec Exp:** Thyroid Disorders; Thyroid Cancer; **Hospital:** Johns Hopkins Hosp (page 59); **Address:** Johns Hopkins Hosp, Div Endocrinology & Metabolism, 1830 E Monument St, rm 333, Baltimore, MD 21287; **Phone:** 410-502-4926; **Board Cert:** Internal Medicine 1978; Endocrinology, Diabetes & Metabolism 1981; **Med School:** Harvard Med Sch 1975; **Resid:** Internal Medicine, Mass Genl Hosp 1978; **Fellow:** Endocrinology, Diabetes & Metabolism, Mass Genl Hosp 1980; **Fac Appt:** Prof Med, Johns Hopkins Univ

Lipson, Ace MD [EDM] - **Spec Exp:** Diabetes; Thyroid Disorders; Pituitary Disorders; Adrenal Disorders; **Hospital:** G Washington Univ Hosp; **Address:** 1120 19th St NW, Ste 200, Washington, DC 20036; **Phone:** 202-296-3443; **Board Cert:** Internal Medicine 1976; Endocrinology, Diabetes & Metabolism 1979; **Med School:** Washington Univ, St Louis 1973; **Resid:** Internal Medicine, George Washington Univ Med Ctr 1976; **Fellow:** Endocrinology, Johns Hopkins Hosp 1978; **Fac Appt:** Clin Prof Med, Geo Wash Univ

Maclaren, Noel Keith MD [EDM] - **Spec Exp:** Diabetes; Obesity; Thyroid Disorders; Addison's Disease; **Hospital:** Lenox Hill Hosp (page 66), NY-Presby/Weill Cornell Med Ctr, NY (page 65); **Address:** Bioseek Endocrine Clinic, 200 W 57th St, Ste 605, New York, NY 10019; **Phone:** 212-371-0658; **Board Cert:** Pediatrics 1977; Pediatric Endocrinology 1978; **Med School:** New Zealand 1963; **Resid:** Internal Medicine, Wellington Public Hosp 1967; **Fellow:** Pediatric Endocrinology, Johns Hopkins Hosp 1973; Pediatric Endocrinology, Univ MD Hosp 1974; **Fac Appt:** Prof Ped, Cornell Univ-Weill Med Coll

Mandel, Susan J MD [EDM] - **Spec Exp:** Thyroid Disorders; Thyroid Cancer; Thyroid Disorders in Pregnancy; Thyroid Ultrasound; **Hospital:** Hosp Univ Penn - UPHS (page 69); **Address:** Penn Endocrinology, Perelman Ctr for Advanced Medicine, 3400 Civic Ctr Blvd Fl 4-West, Philadelphia, PA 19104; **Phone:** 215-662-2300; **Board Cert:** Internal Medicine 1989; Endocrinology 2011; **Med School:** Columbia P&S 1986; **Resid:** Internal Medicine, Columbia Presby Med Ctr 1989; **Fellow:** Endocrinology, Brigham & Womens Hosp 1992; **Fac Appt:** Prof Med, Univ Pennsylvania

McConnell, Robert J MD [EDM] - **Spec Exp:** Thyroid Disorders; Thyroid Ultrasound; **Hospital:** NY-Presby/Columbia Univ Med Ctr, NY (page 65); **Address:** 161 Fort Washington Ave, Ste 210, New York, NY 10032-3713; **Phone:** 212-305-5579; **Board Cert:** Internal Medicine 1978; Endocrinology, Diabetes & Metabolism 1981; **Med School:** Columbia P&S 1973; **Resid:** Internal Medicine, Barnes Hosp 1975; **Fellow:** Endocrinology, Diabetes & Metabolism, Columbia-Presby Hosp 1978; **Fac Appt:** Clin Prof Med, Columbia P&S

Roberts, Michelle M MD [EDM] - **Spec Exp:** Osteoporosis; **Hospital:** UPMC Presby, Pittsburgh; **Address:** Center for Diabetes & Endocrinology, Faulk Medical Bldg, 3601 Fifth Ave, Ste 3B, Pittsburgh, PA 15213; **Phone:** 412-586-9714; **Board Cert:** Internal Medicine 1986; Endocrinology, Diabetes & Metabolism 1989; **Med School:** Duke Univ 1983; **Resid:** Internal Medicine, Univ Pittsburgh Med Ctr 1986; **Fellow:** Endocrinology, Diabetes & Metabolism, Univ Pittsburgh 1989; **Fac Appt:** Assoc Prof Med, Univ Pittsburgh

Rodbard, Helena W MD [EDM] - **Spec Exp:** Diabetes; Gynecomastia; Metabolic Disorders; **Hospital:** Shady Grove Adven Hosp; **Address:** 3200 Tower Oaks Blvd, Ste 250, Rockville, MD 20852; **Phone:** 301-770-7373; **Board Cert:** Internal Medicine 1981; Endocrinology, Diabetes & Metabolism 1983; **Med School:** Brazil 1972; **Resid:** Internal Medicine, MedStar Washington Hosp Ctr 1981; **Fellow:** Endocrinology, Diabetes & Metabolism, Natl Inst Hlth-Clin Ctr 1979; Endocrinology, Diabetes & Metabolism, G Washington Univ Hosp 1982

Schutta, Mark H MD [EDM] - **Spec Exp:** Diabetes; Diabetes Prevention; Hypoglycemia; **Hospital:** Hosp Univ Penn - UPHS (page 69); **Address:** Penn Rodebaugh Diabetes Ctr, Perelman Ctr for Advanced Medicine, 3400 Civic Center Blvd, 4 West, Philadelphia, PA 19104; **Phone:** 215-662-2300; **Board Cert:** Endocrinology, Diabetes & Metabolism 2002; **Med School:** Jefferson Med Coll 1993; **Resid:** Internal Medicine, T Jefferson Univ Hosp 1996; **Fellow:** Endocrinology, Diabetes & Metabolism, Hosp Univ Penn 1999; **Fac Appt:** Assoc Prof Med, Univ Pennsylvania

Schwartz, Stanley S MD [EDM] - **Spec Exp:** Diabetes; Metabolic Syndrome; Thyroid Disorders; **Hospital:** Lankenau Hosp, Bryn Mawr Hosp; **Address:** 233 E Lancaster Ave, Ste 305, Ardmore, PA 19003-2321; **Phone:** 610-642-6800; **Board Cert:** Internal Medicine 1976; Endocrinology, Diabetes & Metabolism 1979; **Med School:** Univ Chicago-Pritzker Sch Med 1973; **Resid:** Internal Medicine, Hosp Univ Penn 1976; **Fellow:** Endocrinology, Diabetes & Metabolism, Univ Chicago 1978; **Fac Appt:** Prof Emeritus Med, Univ Pennsylvania

Seplowitz, Alan H MD [EDM] - **Spec Exp:** Thyroid Disorders; Cholesterol/Lipid Disorders; Diabetes; **Hospital:** NY-Presby/Columbia Univ Med Ctr, NY (page 65); **Address:** 161 Fort Washington Ave, Ste 4-422, New York, NY 10032-3729; **Phone:** 212-305-5503; **Board Cert:** Internal Medicine 1975; Endocrinology 1977; **Med School:** Columbia P&S 1972; **Resid:** Internal Medicine, Columbia-Presby Med Ctr 1974; **Fellow:** Lipid Metabolism, Natl Inst Hlth 1976; Endocrinology, Diabetes & Metabolism, Columbia-Presby Med Ctr 1978; **Fac Appt:** Assoc Prof Med, Columbia P&S

Siris, Ethel S MD [EDM] - **Spec Exp:** Osteoporosis; Paget's Disease of Bone; Bone Disorders-Metabolic; **Hospital:** NY-Presby/Columbia Univ Med Ctr, NY (page 65); **Address:** 180 Ft Washington Ave, HP Bldg Fl 9 - Ste 903, New York, NY 10032-3710; **Phone:** 212-305-9531; **Board Cert:** Internal Medicine 1974; Endocrinology, Diabetes & Metabolism 1977; **Med School:** Columbia P&S 1971; **Resid:** Internal Medicine, NY-Presby/Columbia Univ Med Ctr 1974; **Fellow:** Research, Natl Inst of Hlth - Clin Ctr 1976; Endocrinology, Diabetes & Metabolism, NY-Presby/Columbia Univ Med Ctr 1977; **Fac Appt:** Prof Med, Columbia P&S

Snyder, Peter J MD [EDM] - **Spec Exp:** Pituitary Tumors; Reproductive Endocrinology-Male; Neuroendocrine Tumors; **Hospital:** Hosp Univ Penn - UPHS (page 69); **Address:** Penn Endocrinology, Perelman Ctr for Advanced Medicine, 3400 Civic Center Blvd, 4-West, Philadelphia, PA 19104; **Phone:** 215-662-2300; **Board Cert:** Internal Medicine 1972; Endocrinology, Diabetes & Metabolism 1972; **Med School:** Harvard Med Sch 1965; **Resid:** Internal Medicine, Beth Israel Hosp 1970; **Fellow:** Endocrinology, Diabetes & Metabolism, Hosp Univ Penn 1971; **Fac Appt:** Prof Med, Univ Pennsylvania

Surks, Martin I MD [EDM] - **Spec Exp:** Thyroid Disorders; **Hospital:** Montefiore Med Ctr-Moses Campus, NY, N Central Bronx Hosp; **Address:** 3400 Bainbridge Ave Fl 2, Bronx, NY 10467; **Phone:** 866-633-8255; **Board Cert:** Internal Medicine 1967; Endocrinology, Diabetes & Metabolism 1977; **Med School:** NYU Sch Med 1960; **Resid:** Internal Medicine, Montefiore Med Ctr 1962; Internal Medicine, VA Hosp 1964; **Fellow:** Research, Natl Inst Arthritis-Metabolic Disease 1966; **Fac Appt:** Prof Med, Albert Einstein Coll Med

Tuttle, R Michael MD [EDM] - **Spec Exp:** Thyroid Cancer; **Hospital:** Meml Sloan-Kettering Canc Ctr; **Address:** Meml Sloan Kettering Cancer Ctr, 1275 York Ave, New York, NY 10065; **Phone:** 646-888-2716; **Board Cert:** Endocrinology, Diabetes & Metabolism 2004; **Med School:** Univ Louisville Sch Med 1987; **Resid:** Internal Medicine, DD Eisenhower Army Med Ctr 1990; **Fellow:** Endocrinology, Diabetes & Metabolism, Madigan Army Med Ctr 1993; **Fac Appt:** Prof Med, Cornell Univ-Weill Med Coll

Wartofsky, Leonard MD [EDM] - **Spec Exp:** Thyroid Cancer; **Hospital:** MedStar Washington Hosp Ctr; **Address:** 110 Irving St NW, Washington, DC 20010-2975; **Phone:** 202-877-3109; **Board Cert:** Internal Medicine 1971; Endocrinology, Diabetes & Metabolism 1972; **Med School:** Geo Wash Univ 1964; **Resid:** Internal Medicine, Barnes Jewish Hosp 1966; Internal Medicine, Montefiore Med Ctr 1967; **Fellow:** Endocrinology, Diabetes & Metabolism, Boston City Hosp 1969; **Fac Appt:** Prof Med, Georgetown Univ

Wondisford, Frederic E MD [EDM] - **Spec Exp:** Diabetes-Adult & Pediatric; **Hospital:** Johns Hopkins Hosp (page 59); **Address:** Johns Hopkins, CMSC 10-113, 600 N Wolfe St, Baltimore, MD 21287; **Phone:** 410-502-5761; **Board Cert:** Internal Medicine 1986; Endocrinology, Diabetes & Metabolism 1989; **Med School:** NE Ohio Univ 1983; **Resid:** Internal Medicine, U Hosps/Case Western Res U 1986; **Fellow:** Endocrinology, NIH Clin Ctr 1989; **Fac Appt:** Prof Med, Johns Hopkins Univ

Xing, Michael M MD/PhD [EDM] - **Spec Exp:** Thyroid Disorders; Thyroid Cancer; **Hospital:** Johns Hopkins Hosp (page 59); **Address:** Johns Hopkins, Endocrinology Dept, 601 N Caroline St Fl 7, Baltimore, MD 21287; **Phone:** 410-502-6888; **Board Cert:** Internal Medicine 2010; Endocrinology, Diabetes & Metabolism 2003; **Med School:** China 1984; **Resid:** Internal Medicine, Greater Baltimore Med Ctr 2000; **Fellow:** Endocrinology, Johns Hopkins Hosp 2003; **Fac Appt:** Assoc Prof Med, Johns Hopkins Univ

Southeast

Ain, Kenneth B MD [EDM] - **Spec Exp:** Thyroid Cancer; Thyroid Disorders; **Hospital:** Univ of Kentucky Albert B. Chandler Hosp, Lexington VA Med Ctr; **Address:** Univ KY Med Ctr, 800 Rose St, rm MN524, Lexington, KY 40536-0298; **Phone:** 859-323-3778; **Board Cert:** Internal Medicine 1984; Endocrinology, Diabetes & Metabolism 1987; **Med School:** Brown Univ 1981; **Resid:** Internal Medicine, Hahnemann Univ Hosp 1984; **Fellow:** Endocrinology, Univ Chicago 1986; Thyroid Oncology, Natl Inst of Hlth - Clin Ctr 1990; **Fac Appt:** Prof Med, Univ KY Coll Med

Barrett, Eugene J MD/PhD [EDM] - **Spec Exp:** Diabetes; Diabetic Vascular Disease Prevention; Thyroid Disorders; **Hospital:** Univ of Virginia Hlth Sys; **Address:** Univ VA Hlth Sys, 415 Ray C Hunt Drive, Charlottesville, VA 22903; **Phone:** 434-924-1825; **Board Cert:** Internal Medicine 1978; **Med School:** Univ Rochester 1975; **Resid:** Internal Medicine, Strong Meml Hosp 1977; **Fellow:** Endocrinology, Diabetes & Metabolism, Yale-New Haven Hosp 1980; **Fac Appt:** Prof Med, Univ VA Sch Med

Buse, John B MD/PhD [EDM] - **Spec Exp:** Diabetes; **Hospital:** NC Memorial Hosp - UNC; **Address:** UNC Highgate Specialty Center, 5316 Highgate Drive, Ste 125, Chapel Hill, NC 27513; **Phone:** 919-484-1015; **Board Cert:** Internal Medicine 1989; Endocrinology, Diabetes & Metabolism 2011; **Med School:** Duke Univ 1986; **Resid:** Internal Medicine, Univ Chicago Hosps 1988; **Fellow:** Endocrinology, Diabetes & Metabolism, Univ Chicago Hosps 1991; **Fac Appt:** Prof Med, Univ NC Sch Med

Clore, John N MD [EDM] - **Spec Exp:** Diabetes; Hypoglycemia; Pancreatic Islet Cell Transplant; **Hospital:** Med Coll of VA Hosp; **Address:** Medical Specialties Clinic, 417 N 11th St, Richmond, VA 23298; **Phone:** 804-828-2161; **Board Cert:** Internal Medicine 1985; Endocrinology, Diabetes & Metabolism 1989; **Med School:** Med Coll VA 1982; **Resid:** Internal Medicine, Med Coll VA Hosp 1985; **Fellow:** Endocrinology, Diabetes & Metabolism, Med Coll VA Hosp 1988; **Fac Appt:** Prof Med, Va Commonwealth Univ Sch Med

Dalkin, Alan C MD [EDM] - **Spec Exp:** Bone Disorders-Metabolic; Osteoporosis; **Hospital:** Univ of Virginia Hlth Sys; **Address:** Univ VA Hlth Sys, 415 Ray C Hunt Drive, Charlottesville, VA 22903; **Phone:** 434-924-1825; **Board Cert:** Internal Medicine 1987; Endocrinology 1989; **Med School:** Univ Mich Med Sch 1984; **Resid:** Internal Medicine, Univ Chicago Hosps 1987; **Fellow:** Endocrinology, Diabetes & Metabolism, Univ MI Hosp 1990; **Fac Appt:** Prof Med, Univ VA Sch Med

Feinglos, Mark MD [EDM] - **Spec Exp:** Diabetes; Thyroid Disorders; **Hospital:** Duke Univ Hosp; **Address:** DUMC, Box 3921, Durham, NC 27710-0001; **Phone:** 919-684-4005; **Board Cert:** Internal Medicine 1976; Endocrinology, Diabetes & Metabolism 1977; **Med School:** McGill Univ 1973; **Resid:** Internal Medicine, Duke Univ Med Ctr 1975; **Fellow:** Endocrinology, Diabetes & Metabolism, Duke Univ Med Ctr 1978; **Fac Appt:** Prof Med, Duke Univ

Goodman, Neil F MD [EDM] - **Spec Exp:** Reproductive Endocrinology; Polycystic Ovarian Syndrome; Hormonal Disorders; Infertility; **Address:** 9150 SW 87th Ave, Ste 210, Miami, FL 33176; **Phone:** 305-595-6855; **Board Cert:** Internal Medicine 1973; Endocrinology, Diabetes & Metabolism 1975; **Med School:** Columbia P&S 1970; **Resid:** Internal Medicine, Beth Israel Deaconess Med Ctr 1972; **Fellow:** Endocrinology, Mass Genl Hosp 1974; **Fac Appt:** Clin Prof Med, Univ Miami Sch Med

Koch, Christian A MD [EDM] - **Spec Exp:** Endocrine Cancers; Thyroid Cancer; Pituitary Disorders; **Hospital:** Univ Mississippi Med Ctr; **Address:** 2500 N State St, Jackson, MS 39216; **Phone:** 601-984-5495; **Board Cert:** Endocrinology, Diabetes & Metabolism 2011; Internal Medicine 2010; **Med School:** Germany 1991; **Resid:** Internal Medicine, Ohio State Univ Hosp 1997; **Fellow:** Endocrinology, Natl Inst Hlth 2001; **Fac Appt:** Prof Med, Univ Miss

Lilienfeld, Howard S MD [EDM] - **Spec Exp:** Endocrine Cancers; Thyroid Cancer; **Hospital:** Moffitt Canc Ctr (page 61); **Address:** H Lee Moffitt Cancer Ctr, Dept Endocrinology, 12902 Magnolia Drive, Tampa, FL 33612; **Phone:** 813-745-3636; **Board Cert:** Internal Medicine 1975; Endocrinology, Diabetes & Metabolism 1977; **Med School:** Dalhousie Univ 1972; **Resid:** Internal Medicine, Dalhousie Univ Hosp 1975; **Fellow:** Endocrinology, Diabetes & Metabolism, Wellesly Hosp/Univ Toronto 1976; Nuclear Medicine, St Michael's Hosp/Univ Toronto 1977; **Fac Appt:** Asst Prof Med, Univ S Fla Coll Med

Marshall, John C MD/PhD [EDM] - **Spec Exp:** Reproductive Endocrinology; Pituitary Disorders; Polycystic Ovarian Syndrome; Neuroendocrinology; **Hospital:** Univ of Virginia Hlth Sys; **Address:** Univ VA Hlth Sys, 450 Ray C Hunt Drive, Charlottesville, VA 22908; **Phone:** 434-924-2431; **Board Cert:** Internal Medicine 1978; Endocrinology, Diabetes & Metabolism 1981; **Med School:** England, UK 1965; **Resid:** Neurology, Natl Hosp Queen Square 1968; Cardiovascular Disease, Natl Heart Hosp 1969; **Fellow:** Endocrinology, Diabetes & Metabolism, Hammersmith Hosp 1972; Endocrinology, Diabetes & Metabolism, UCLA Med Ctr 1974; **Fac Appt:** Prof Med, Univ VA Sch Med

Nestler, John E MD [EDM] - **Spec Exp:** Polycystic Ovarian Syndrome; Diabetes; **Hospital:** Med Coll of VA Hosp; **Address:** Medical College of Virginia/Department of Internal Medicine, Box 980663, Richmond, VA 23298-0663; **Phone:** 804-828-2161; **Board Cert:** Internal Medicine 1982; Endocrinology 1985; **Med School:** Univ Pennsylvania 1979; **Resid:** Internal Medicine, Med Coll Virginia 1983; **Fellow:** Endocrinology, Hosp Univ Penn 1985; **Fac Appt:** Prof Med, Med Coll VA

Ober, K Patrick MD [EDM] - **Spec Exp:** Diabetes; **Hospital:** Wake Forest Baptist Med Ctr; **Address:** Medical Center Blvd, Winston-Salem, NC 27157; **Phone:** 336-713-7251; **Board Cert:** Internal Medicine 1977; Endocrinology, Diabetes & Metabolism 1979; **Med School:** Univ Fla Coll Med 1974; **Resid:** Internal Medicine, NC Baptist Hosp 1976; **Fellow:** Endocrinology & Metabolism, NC Baptist Hosp 1978; **Fac Appt:** Prof Med, Wake Forest Univ

Ovalle, Fernando MD [EDM] - **Spec Exp:** Diabetes; **Hospital:** UAB Hosp, Birmingham VA Med Ctr; **Address:** UAB Kirklin Clinic, 2000 6th Ave S, MCDC Clinic, Fl 4, Birmingham, AL 35233; **Phone:** 205-934-4171; **Med School:** Mexico 1989; **Resid:** Internal Medicine, Henry Ford Hosp 1995; **Fellow:** Endocrinology, Diabetes & Metabolism, Barnes Hosp-Wash Univ 1997; **Fac Appt:** Prof Med, UAB Sch Med

Powers, Alvin C MD [EDM] - **Spec Exp:** Diabetes; Thyroid Disorders; **Hospital:** Vanderbilt Univ Med Ctr, TN Valley Healthcare Sys-Nashville; **Address:** Vanderbilt Diabetes Ctr, 1215 21st Ave S, Med Ctr East, South Tower, Ste 8210, Nashville, TN 37232-0202; **Phone:** 615-343-8332; **Board Cert:** Internal Medicine 1982; Endocrinology, Diabetes & Metabolism 1985; **Med School:** Univ Tenn Coll Med 1979; **Resid:** Internal Medicine, Duke Univ Med Ctr 1982; **Fellow:** Endocrinology, Diabetes & Metabolism, Joslin Diabetes Ctr 1983; Endocrinology, Diabetes & Metabolism, Mass Genl Hosp 1985; **Fac Appt:** Prof Med, Vanderbilt Univ

Skyler, Jay S MD [EDM] - **Spec Exp:** Diabetes; **Hospital:** Univ of Miami Hosp, Jackson Meml Hosp; **Address:** Univ Miami, Diabetes Rsch Inst, 1450 NW 10th Ave, Ste 3054, Miami, FL 33136; **Phone:** 305-243-6146; **Board Cert:** Internal Medicine 1972; Endocrinology, Diabetes & Metabolism 1973; **Med School:** Jefferson Med Coll 1969; **Resid:** Internal Medicine, Duke Univ Hosp 1971; **Fellow:** Endocrinology, Diabetes & Metabolism, Duke Univ Hosp 1973; **Fac Appt:** Prof Med, Univ Miami Sch Med

Thorner, Michael MD [EDM] - **Spec Exp:** Cushing's Syndrome; Growth Hormone Disorder-Adult; Metabolic Syndrome; Pituitary Disorders; **Hospital:** Univ of Virginia Hlth Sys; **Address:** Univ VA Hlth Sys, 415 Ray C Hunt Drive, Charlottesville, VA 22903; **Phone:** 434-982-3297; **Med School:** England, UK 1970; **Resid:** Internal Medicine, Univ London Affil Hosp 1972; **Fellow:** Endocrinology & Metabolism, Univ London Affil Hosp 1974; **Fac Appt:** Prof Med, Univ VA Sch Med

Vance, Mary Lee MD [EDM] - **Spec Exp:** Pituitary Disorders; Neuroendocrinology; **Hospital:** Univ of Virginia Hlth Sys; **Address:** Univ VA Hlth Sys, 415 Ray C Hunt Drive, Charlottesville, VA 22903; **Phone:** 434-982-3591; **Board Cert:** Internal Medicine 1980; **Med School:** Louisiana State U, New Orleans 1977; **Resid:** Internal Medicine, Baylor Univ Med Ctr 1980; **Fellow:** Endocrinology, Univ VA Hlth Sys 1983; **Fac Appt:** Prof Med, Univ VA Sch Med

Weissman, Peter N MD [EDM] - **Spec Exp:** Diabetes; **Hospital:** Baptist Hosp of Miami; **Address:** Endocrinology Assocs, 7867 N Kendall Drive, Ste 80, Miami, FL 33156; **Phone:** 305-595-0777; **Board Cert:** Internal Medicine 1972; Endocrinology, Diabetes & Metabolism 1972; **Med School:** NYU Sch Med 1966; **Resid:** Internal Medicine, Barnes-Jewish Hosp 1969; **Fellow:** Geriatric Medicine, Gerontology Rsch Ctr 1970; Endocrinology, Diabetes & Metabolism, Univ Michigan Hosp 1972; **Fac Appt:** Assoc Clin Prof Med, Univ Miami Sch Med

Midwest

Bahn, Rebecca S MD [EDM] - **Spec Exp:** Graves' Disease; Graves' Disease-Eye; **Hospital:** Mayo Med Ctr & Clin - Rochester; **Address:** Mayo Clin, Div Endocrinology, 200 First St SW, Rochester, MN 55905; **Phone:** 507-284-1600; **Board Cert:** Internal Medicine 1985; Endocrinology, Diabetes & Metabolism 1987; **Med School:** Mayo Med Sch 1981; **Resid:** Internal Medicine, Mayo Clin 1984; **Fellow:** Endocrinology, Diabetes & Metabolism, Mayo Clin 1986; **Fac Appt:** Prof Med, Mayo Med Sch

Brennan, Michael D MD [EDM] - **Spec Exp:** Thyroid Disorders; Diabetes; **Hospital:** Mayo Med Ctr & Clin - Rochester; **Address:** Mayo Clin, Div Endocrinology, 200 First St SW, Rochester, MN 55905; **Phone:** 507-284-1600; **Board Cert:** Internal Medicine 1975; Endocrinology, Diabetes & Metabolism 1977; **Med School:** Ireland 1969; **Resid:** Internal Medicine, Henry Ford Hosp 1972; Internal Medicine, Mayo Clin 1975; **Fellow:** Endocrinology, Diabetes & Metabolism, Mayo Clin 1977; **Fac Appt:** Prof Med, Mayo Med Sch

Broadstone, Vasti Lima MD [EDM] - **Spec Exp:** Diabetes; Weight Management; **Hospital:** Floyd Meml Hosp & Hlth Svcs; **Address:** Floyd Meml-Joslin Diabetes Ctr Affil, 2019 State St, New Albany, IN 47150; **Phone:** 812-949-5700; **Board Cert:** Internal Medicine 1987; **Med School:** Brazil 1976; **Resid:** Internal Medicine, Wright State Univ Affil Hosps 1981; **Fellow:** Endocrinology, Diabetes & Metabolism, Univ Louisville Affil Hosps 1984

Burmeister, Lynn MD [EDM] - **Spec Exp:** Thyroid Disorders; Hashimoto's Disease; Graves' Disease; **Hospital:** Univ Minn Med Ctr, Fairview - West Bank Campus; **Address:** Univ Minnesota Physicians, 516 Delaware St SE, Clinic 6A, Minneapolis, MN 55455; **Phone:** 612-625-8690; **Board Cert:** Internal Medicine 1988; **Med School:** Univ Minn 1985; **Resid:** Internal Medicine, Univ Minn Med Ctr 1988; **Fellow:** Endocrinology, Univ Minn Med Ctr 1989; **Fac Appt:** Assoc Prof Med, Univ Minn

Clutter, William E MD [EDM] - **Spec Exp:** Endocrine Cancers; Calcium Disorders; Bone Disorders-Metabolic; **Hospital:** Barnes-Jewish Hosp, Washington Univ Phys; **Address:** 4921 Parkview Pl, Ste 5C, St Louis, MO 63110; **Phone:** 314-362-3500; **Board Cert:** Internal Medicine 1978; Endocrinology, Diabetes & Metabolism 1981; **Med School:** Ohio State Univ 1975; **Resid:** Internal Medicine, Barnes Jewish Hosp 1978; **Fellow:** Endocrinology, Diabetes & Metabolism, Barnes Jewish Hosp 1980; **Fac Appt:** Assoc Prof Med, Washington Univ, St Louis

Cohen, Robert M MD [EDM] - **Spec Exp:** Diabetes; Metabolic Disorders; **Hospital:** Univ Cincinnati Med Ctr; **Address:** Univ Cincinnati Physicians, 222 Piedmont Ave, Ste 6000, Cincinnati, OH 45219; **Phone:** 513-475-7400; **Board Cert:** Internal Medicine 1981; Endocrinology, Diabetes & Metabolism 1983; **Med School:** Univ Rochester 1978; **Resid:** Internal Medicine, Rush-Presby-St Lukes Hosp 1981; **Fellow:** Endocrinology, Univ Chicago Med Ctr 1984; **Fac Appt:** Assoc Prof Med, Univ Cincinnati

Cryer, Philip E MD [EDM] - **Spec Exp:** Diabetes; Hypoglycemia; **Hospital:** Barnes-Jewish Hosp, St. Louis Chldns Hosp; **Address:** Wash Univ Sch Med, Div Endo, Metab & Lipid Rsch, 660 S Euclid Ave, Box 8127, St Louis, MO 63110-1093; **Phone:** 314-362-3500; **Board Cert:** Internal Medicine 1972; Endocrinology, Diabetes & Metabolism 1972; **Med School:** Northwestern Univ 1965; **Resid:** Internal Medicine, Barnes Jewish Hosp 1972; **Fellow:** Endocrinology, Diabetes & Metabolism, Barnes Hosp-Wash Univ 1968; **Fac Appt:** Prof Med, Washington Univ, St Louis

D'Alessio, David A MD [EDM] - **Spec Exp:** Diabetes; **Hospital:** Univ Cincinnati Med Ctr; **Address:** Univ Cincinnati Physicians, 222 Piedmont Ave, Ste 6000, Cincinnati, OH 45219; **Phone:** 513-475-7400; **Board Cert:** Internal Medicine 1986; Endocrinology, Diabetes & Metabolism 1989; **Med School:** Univ Wisc 1983; **Resid:** Internal Medicine, Temple Univ Med Ctr 1986; **Fellow:** Endocrinology, Univ Washington Med Ctr 1990; **Fac Appt:** Assoc Prof Med, Univ Cincinnati

Econs, Michael J MD [EDM] - **Spec Exp:** Osteoporosis; Paget's Disease of Bone; Bone Disorders-Metabolic; **Hospital:** IU Hlth Univ Hosp; **Address:** IU Hlth, Endocrinology Dept, 550 N University Blvd, Ste 2180, Indianapolis, IN 46202; **Phone:** 317-274-1339; **Board Cert:** Internal Medicine 1986; Endocrinology, Diabetes & Metabolism 1989; **Med School:** UCSF 1983; **Resid:** Internal Medicine, Univ MD Med Ctr 1986; **Fellow:** Endocrinology, Duke Univ Hosp 1989; **Fac Appt:** Prof Med, Indiana Univ

Ehrmann, David A MD [EDM] - **Spec Exp:** Polycystic Ovarian Syndrome; Diabetes; **Hospital:** Univ of Chicago Med; **Address:** Center for Advanced Medicine, 5758 S Maryland Ave, Fl 5 - Ste 5A, Chicago, IL 60637; **Phone:** 773-702-6138; **Board Cert:** Internal Medicine 1985; Endocrinology, Diabetes & Metabolism 1987; **Med School:** Univ Mich Med Sch 1982; **Resid:** Internal Medicine, Univ Mich Med Ctr 1985; **Fellow:** Endocrinology, Diabetes & Metabolism, Univ Chicago Hosps 1987; **Fac Appt:** Assoc Prof Med, Univ Chicago-Pritzker Sch Med

Emanuele, Mary Ann MD [EDM] - **Spec Exp:** Diabetes; Osteoporosis; Thyroid Disorders; Parathyroid Disease; **Hospital:** Loyola Univ Med Ctr; **Address:** Loyola Outpatient Center, Medical Specialties Fl 3, 2160 S First Ave, Maywood, IL 60153-3304; **Phone:** 708-216-0160 x2; **Board Cert:** Internal Medicine 1978; Endocrinology, Diabetes & Metabolism 1983; **Med School:** Loyola Univ-Stritch Sch Med 1975; **Resid:** Internal Medicine, Univ Hawaii Med Ctr 1978; **Fellow:** Endocrinology, Edward Hines Jr VA Hosp 1980; **Fac Appt:** Prof Med, Loyola Univ-Stritch Sch Med

Emanuele, Nicholas V MD [EDM] - **Hospital:** Edward Hines, Jr. VA Hosp; **Address:** Hines VA Hosp Bldg 200 Fl 4, 5000 S 5th Ave, Hines, IL 60141; **Phone:** 708-202-2445; **Board Cert:** Internal Medicine 1975; Endocrinology 1979; **Med School:** Northwestern Univ 1967; **Resid:** Internal Medicine, Hines VA Hosp 1974; **Fellow:** Endocrinology, Northwestern Univ Affil Hosp 1976

Hammer, Gary D MD/PhD [EDM] - **Spec Exp:** Adrenal Cancer; Adrenal Disorders; **Hospital:** Univ Michigan Med Ctr; **Address:** Univ Michigan Comprehensive Cancer Ctr, 1500 E Medical Ctr Drive Fl 1 - rm 1127, Ann Arbor, MI 48109-2200; **Phone:** 734-647-8906; **Board Cert:** Endocrinology, Diabetes & Metabolism 2007; **Med School:** Tufts Univ 1992; **Resid:** Internal Medicine, UCSF Med Ctr 1994; **Fellow:** Endocrinology & Metabolism, UCSF Med Ctr 1997; **Fac Appt:** Prof Med, Univ Mich Med Sch

Herman, William H MD [EDM] - **Spec Exp:** Diabetes; **Hospital:** Univ Michigan Med Ctr; **Address:** U-M Metabolism, Endocrinology & Diabetes, East Ann Arbor Health & Geriatrics Ctr, 4260 Plymouth Rd Fl 1, Ann Arbor, MI 48109; **Phone:** 734-764-6831; **Board Cert:** Internal Medicine 1982; Endocrinology, Diabetes & Metabolism 1989; **Med School:** Boston Univ 1979; **Resid:** Internal Medicine, Univ Mich Med Ctr 1982; **Fellow:** Preventive Medicine, Ctrs Disease Control 1985; Endocrinology, Diabetes & Metabolism, Univ Mich Med Ctr 1988; **Fac Appt:** Prof Med, Univ Mich Med Sch

Jensen, Michael D MD [EDM] - **Spec Exp:** Eating Disorders/Obesity; Nutrition; **Hospital:** Mayo Med Ctr & Clin - Rochester; **Address:** Mayo Clin, Div Endocrinology, 200 First St SW, Rochester, MN 55905; **Phone:** 507-284-1600; **Board Cert:** Internal Medicine 1982; Endocrinology, Diabetes & Metabolism 1985; **Med School:** Univ MO-Kansas City 1979; **Resid:** Internal Medicine, Mayo Clin 1982; **Fellow:** Endocrinology, Diabetes & Metabolism, Mayo Clin 1985; **Fac Appt:** Prof Med, Mayo Med Sch

Kennedy, Laurence MD [EDM] - **Spec Exp:** Diabetes; Adrenal Disorders; Acromegaly; Pituitary Disorders; **Hospital:** Cleveland Clin (page 55); **Address:** Cleveland Clinic, 9500 Euclid Ave, MC F20, Cleveland, OH 44195; **Phone:** 216-445-8645; **Med School:** Northern Ireland 1972; **Resid:** Internal Medicine, Belfast City Hosp 1976; **Fellow:** Endocrinology & Diabetes, Royal Victoria Hosp 1978; Endocrinology, Univ Florida Affil Hosp 1980

Khosla, Sundeep MD [EDM] - **Spec Exp:** Osteoporosis; Bone Disorders-Metabolic; **Hospital:** Mayo Med Ctr & Clin - Rochester; **Address:** Mayo Clin, Div Endocrinology, 200 First St SW, Rochester, MN 55905; **Phone:** 507-284-1600; **Board Cert:** Internal Medicine 1985; Endocrinology 1987; **Med School:** Harvard Med Sch 1982; **Resid:** Internal Medicine, Mass Genl Hosp 1985; **Fellow:** Endocrinology, Diabetes & Metabolism, Mass Genl Hosp 1988; **Fac Appt:** Prof Med, Mayo Med Sch

Kopp, Peter A MD [EDM] - **Spec Exp:** Thyroid Cancer; Pituitary Disorders; Parathyroid Disease; McCune-Albright Syndrome; **Hospital:** Northwestern Meml Hosp; **Address:** Northwestern Medical Faculty Foundation, 675 N St Clair St, Ste 14-100, Galter Pavillion, Chicago, IL 60611; **Phone:** 312-695-7970; **Board Cert:** Internal Medicine 2003; Endocrinology, Diabetes & Metabolism 2004; **Med School:** Switzerland 1985; **Resid:** Internal Medicine, Regl Hosp 1988; Internal Medicine, Bern Univ Hosp 1992; **Fellow:** Endocrinology, Diabetes & Metabolism, Bern Univ Hosp 1990; Endocrinology, Diabetes & Metabolism, Northwestern Univ Hosp 1997; **Fac Appt:** Assoc Prof Med, Northwestern Univ-Feinberg Sch Med

Lash, Robert W MD [EDM] - **Spec Exp:** Osteoporosis; Diabetes; Diabetes in Pregnancy; Thyroid Disorders; **Hospital:** Univ Michigan Med Ctr; **Address:** UM Metabolism, Endocrinology, Diabetes, Domino's Farms Lobby C, Ste 1300, 24 Frank Lloyd Wright Drive, Ann Arbor, MI 48106; **Phone:** 734-936-5504; **Board Cert:** Internal Medicine 1987; Endocrinology, Diabetes & Metabolism 1989; **Med School:** Albert Einstein Coll Med 1984; **Resid:** Internal Medicine, UCSF Med Ctr 1987; **Fellow:** Endocrinology, Natl Inst Hlth 1990; **Fac Appt:** Clin Prof Med, Univ Mich Med Sch

Mazzone, Theodore MD [EDM] - **Spec Exp:** Diabetes; Cholesterol/Lipid Disorders; **Hospital:** Evanston Hosp/NorthShore Univ Hlth Sys (page 67); **Address:** Northshore Medical Group, Endocrinology Dept, 1000 Central St, Ste 800, Chicago, IL 60201; **Phone:** 847-663-8540; **Board Cert:** Internal Medicine 1980; Endocrinology, Diabetes & Metabolism 2011; **Med School:** Northwestern Univ 1977; **Resid:** Internal Medicine, UCLA Med Ctr 1980; **Fellow:** Endocrinology, Diabetes & Metabolism, Univ Wash Med Ctr 1983; **Fac Appt:** Clin Prof Med, Univ Chicago-Pritzker Sch Med

McGill, Janet B MD [EDM] - **Spec Exp:** Diabetes; Thyroid Disorders; **Hospital:** Barnes-Jewish Hosp; **Address:** Center for Advanced Disease, 4921 Parkview Pl Fl 13 - Ste B, St Louis, MO 63110-1010; **Phone:** 314-747-7300; **Board Cert:** Internal Medicine 1983; Endocrinology, Diabetes & Metabolism 1987; **Med School:** Mich State Univ 1979; **Resid:** Internal Medicine, William Beaumont Hosp 1984; **Fellow:** Endocrinology, Diabetes & Metabolism, William Beaumont Hosp 1985; Diabetes, Washington Univ 1987; **Fac Appt:** Assoc Prof Med, Washington Univ, St Louis

McMahon, M Molly MD [EDM] - **Spec Exp:** Nutrition; Diabetes; **Hospital:** Mayo Med Ctr & Clin - Rochester; **Address:** Mayo Clin, Div Endocrinology, 200 First St SW, Rochester, MN 55905; **Phone:** 507-284-1600; **Board Cert:** Internal Medicine 1985; Endocrinology, Diabetes & Metabolism 1987; **Med School:** Univ Wisc 1981; **Resid:** Internal Medicine, Med Coll Wisconsin 1984; **Fellow:** Endocrinology, Diabetes & Metabolism, Mayo Clinic 1987; Nutrition, New Eng Deaconess Hosp 1988; **Fac Appt:** Prof Med, Mayo Med Sch

Philipson, Louis H MD/PhD [EDM] - **Spec Exp:** Diabetes; **Hospital:** Univ of Chicago Med; **Address:** Univ Chicago Kovler Diabetes Ctr, 5758 S Maryland Ave DCAM Bldg - Ste 5A, Chicago, IL 60637; **Phone:** 773-702-6138; **Board Cert:** Internal Medicine 1989; **Med School:** Univ Chicago-Pritzker Sch Med 1986; **Resid:** Internal Medicine, Univ Chicago Med Ctr 1989; **Fellow:** Endocrinology, Diabetes & Metabolism, Univ Chicago Med Ctr 1991; **Fac Appt:** Prof Med, Univ Chicago-Pritzker Sch Med

Semenkovich, Clay F MD [EDM] - **Spec Exp:** Cholesterol/Lipid Disorders; Diabetes; Thyroid Disorders; Adrenal Disorders; **Hospital:** Barnes-Jewish Hosp; **Address:** Center for Advanced Disease, 4921 Parkview Pl Fl 13 - Ste B, St Louis, MO 63110; **Phone:** 314-747-7300; **Board Cert:** Internal Medicine 1984; Endocrinology, Diabetes & Metabolism 1987; **Med School:** Washington Univ, St Louis 1981; **Resid:** Internal Medicine, Barnes-Jewish Hosp 1984; **Fellow:** Endocrinology, Diabetes & Metabolism, Wash Univ Hosp 1986; **Fac Appt:** Prof Med, Washington Univ, St Louis

Smith, Steven A MD [EDM] - **Spec Exp:** Diabetes; **Hospital:** Mayo Med Ctr & Clin - Rochester; **Address:** Mayo Clin, Div Endocrinology, 200 1st St SW, Rochester, MN 55905; **Phone:** 507-284-1600; **Board Cert:** Internal Medicine 1981; Endocrinology, Diabetes & Metabolism 1987; **Med School:** Med Coll GA 1978; **Resid:** Internal Medicine, Meml Med Ctr 1981; **Fellow:** Endocrinology, Mayo Clin 1987; **Fac Appt:** Prof Med, Mayo Med Sch

Sowers, James R MD [EDM] - **Spec Exp:** Diabetes; Hypertension; Cholesterol/Lipid Disorders; **Hospital:** Univ of Missouri Hlth Care; **Address:** UMC, Dept Internal Med, 1 Hosp Drive, rm D109, Columbia, MO 65212; **Phone:** 573-882-2573; **Board Cert:** Internal Medicine 1974; Endocrinology, Diabetes & Metabolism 1977; **Med School:** Univ MO-Columbia Sch Med 1971; **Resid:** Internal Medicine, St Johns Mercy Med Ctr 1974; **Fellow:** Endocrinology, Wadsworth VA Hosp Ctr-UCLA 1976; **Fac Appt:** Prof Med, Univ MO-Columbia Sch Med

Watts, Nelson B MD [EDM] - **Spec Exp:** Osteoporosis; Bone Disorders-Metabolic; Paget's Disease of Bone; Gorham-Stout Disease; **Hospital:** Jewish Hosp - Kenwood - Cincinnati; **Address:** 4760 E Galbraith Rd, Ste 212, Cincinnati, OH 45236; **Phone:** 513-686-2663; **Board Cert:** Internal Medicine 1972; Endocrinology, Diabetes & Metabolism 1985; **Med School:** Univ NC Sch Med 1969; **Resid:** Internal Medicine, Charlotte Meml Hosp 1972; **Fellow:** Endocrinology, Diabetes & Metabolism, NC Meml Hosp 1970; **Fac Appt:** Prof Med, Univ Cincinnati

Weiss, Roy E MD/PhD [EDM] - **Spec Exp:** Cushing's Syndrome; Pituitary Disorders; Thyroid Disorders; Pediatric Endocrinology; **Hospital:** Univ of Chicago Med; **Address:** Univ Chicago, Sect, Adult/Ped Endo-Diabetes-Metabolism, 5788 S Maryland Ave, Ste 5A, Chicago, IL 60637; **Phone:** 773-702-9266; **Board Cert:** Endocrinology, Diabetes & Metabolism 2011; **Med School:** Israel 1985; **Resid:** Internal Medicine, Univ Chicago Hosp 1988; **Fellow:** Endocrinology, Diabetes & Metabolism, Univ Chicago Hosp 1990; **Fac Appt:** Prof Med, Univ Chicago-Pritzker Sch Med

Werner, Phillip L MD [EDM] - **Spec Exp:** Diabetes; Thyroid Disorders; **Hospital:** Adv Luth Genl Hosp; **Address:** Advocate Medical Group, Nesset Pavilion-Endocrinology Dept, 1775 W Ballard Rd Fl 2, Park Ridge, IL 60068; **Phone:** 847-318-2400; **Board Cert:** Internal Medicine 1975; Endocrinology 1977; **Med School:** Univ IL Coll Med 1972; **Resid:** Internal Medicine, Univ IL Med Ctr 1975; **Fellow:** Endocrinology, Diabetes & Metabolism, Univ Wash Med Ctr 1977; **Fac Appt:** Assoc Clin Prof Med, Ros Franklin Univ/Chicago Med Sch

Zimmerman, Robert S MD [EDM] - **Spec Exp:** Diabetes; **Hospital:** Cleveland Clin (page 55); **Address:** Cleveland Clinic-Diabetes Ctr, 10685 Carnegie Ave, Cleveland, OH 44106; **Phone:** 216-444-9428; **Board Cert:** Internal Medicine 1984; Endocrinology, Diabetes & Metabolism 1987; **Med School:** Johns Hopkins Univ 1981; **Resid:** Internal Medicine, Duke Univ Hosp 1984; **Fellow:** Endocrinology, Mayo Clinic 1987

Great Plains and Mountains

Eckel, Robert H MD [EDM] - **Spec Exp:** Cholesterol/Lipid Disorders; Eating Disorders/Obesity; Diabetes; Cardiovascular Disease; **Hospital:** Univ Colorado Hosp; **Address:** 12605 E 16th Ave, Ste B120, Anschutz Medical Campus, Aurora, CO 80045; **Phone:** 720-848-5300; **Board Cert:** Internal Medicine 1976; Endocrinology, Diabetes & Metabolism 2008; **Med School:** Univ Cincinnati 1973; **Resid:** Internal Medicine, Univ Wisconsin Hosps 1976; **Fellow:** Endocrinology, Diabetes & Metabolism, Univ Wash Med Ctr 1979; **Fac Appt:** Prof Med, Univ Colorado

Recker, Robert Roy MD [EDM] - **Spec Exp:** Osteoporosis; Diabetes; Endocrinology; **Hospital:** Alegent Creighton Univ Med Ctr, Omaha VA Med Ctr; **Address:** Creighton Univ Med Ctr, Div Endocrinology, 601 N 30th St, Ste 4820, Omaha, NE 68131; **Phone:** 402-280-4470; **Board Cert:** Internal Medicine 1971; **Med School:** Creighton Univ 1963; **Resid:** Internal Medicine, Creighton Affil Hosps 1969; **Fellow:** Endocrinology, Diabetes & Metabolism, Creighton Univ 1971; **Fac Appt:** Prof Med, Creighton Univ

Ridgway III, Eli Chester MD [EDM] - **Spec Exp:** Thyroid Cancer; Thyroid Disorders; Pituitary Disorders; **Hospital:** Univ Colorado Hosp; **Address:** Univ CO Hosp, Endocrinology Dept, 1635 Aurora Court, MS F732, Aurora, CO 80045; **Phone:** 720-848-2650; **Board Cert:** Internal Medicine 1972; Endocrinology 1973; **Med School:** Univ Colorado 1968; **Resid:** Internal Medicine, Mass Genl Hosp 1970; **Fellow:** Endocrinology, Mass Genl Hosp 1972; **Fac Appt:** Prof Med, Univ Colorado

Southwest

Brown, Jeffrey S MD [EDM] - **Spec Exp:** Thyroid Disorders; Diabetes; Osteoporosis; Adrenal Disorders; **Hospital:** Methodist Hosp - Houston, Spring Branch Med Ctr-CLOSED; **Address:** 909 Dairy Ashford St, Ste 205, Houston, TX 77079-5309; **Phone:** 281-589-2681; **Board Cert:** Internal Medicine 1979; Endocrinology, Diabetes & Metabolism 1981; **Med School:** Univ Hlth Scis, Chicago Med Sch 1976; **Resid:** Internal Medicine, LIJ Hosp 1979; **Fellow:** Endocrinology, Univ TX Hlth Ctr 1981; **Fac Appt:** Assoc Prof Med, Univ Tex, Houston

Cunningham, Glenn R MD [EDM] - **Spec Exp:** Diabetes; Hypogonadism; Erectile Dysfunction; **Hospital:** St. Luke's Episcopal Hosp-Houston; **Address:** 6620 Main St, Ste 1180, Houston, TX 77030; **Phone:** 713-798-2500; **Board Cert:** Internal Medicine 1972; Endocrinology, Diabetes & Metabolism 1972; **Med School:** Univ Okla Coll Med 1966; **Resid:** Internal Medicine, Duke Univ Med Ctr 1970; Internal Medicine, VA Hosp 1971; **Fellow:** Endocrinology, Duke Univ Med Ctr 1970; **Fac Appt:** Prof Med, Baylor Coll Med

Gagel, Robert F MD [EDM] - **Spec Exp:** Thyroid Cancer; **Hospital:** UT MD Anderson Canc Ctr; **Address:** MD Anderson Cancer Ctr, 1515 Holcombe Blvd, Unit 1463, FCT Bldg Fl 12, Houston, TX 77030; **Phone:** 713-563-4400; **Board Cert:** Internal Medicine 1975; Endocrinology 1977; **Med School:** Ohio State Univ 1971; **Resid:** Internal Medicine, New England Med Ctr 1973; **Fellow:** Endocrinology, New England Med Ctr 1975; Research, Harvard Med Sch 1981; **Fac Appt:** Prof Med, Univ Tex, Houston

Lavis, Victor R MD [EDM] - **Spec Exp:** Diabetes; **Hospital:** UT MD Anderson Canc Ctr; **Address:** MD Anderson Cancer Ctr, 1515 Holcombe Blvd, Unit 1461, Houston, TX 77030; **Phone:** 713-792-2841; **Board Cert:** Internal Medicine 1969; Endocrinology, Diabetes & Metabolism 2008; **Med School:** Stanford Univ 1962; **Resid:** Internal Medicine, Boston Cty Hosp 1964; Internal Medicine, UCLA Med Ctr 1967; **Fellow:** Endocrinology, Diabetes & Metabolism, Univ Washington 1970; **Fac Appt:** Clin Prof Med, Univ Tex, Houston

Robbins, Richard J MD [EDM] - **Spec Exp:** Thyroid Cancer; Pituitary Tumors; Pituitary Disorders; **Hospital:** Methodist Hosp - Houston; **Address:** 6550 Fannin St, Ste 1001, Houston, TX 77030; **Phone:** 713-441-6640; **Board Cert:** Internal Medicine 1978; Endocrinology, Diabetes & Metabolism 1983; **Med School:** Creighton Univ 1975; **Resid:** Internal Medicine, New York Hosp 1978; **Fellow:** Endocrinology, New England Med Ctr 1981; **Fac Appt:** Prof Med, Cornell Univ-Weill Med Coll

Rubenfeld, Sheldon MD [EDM] - **Spec Exp:** Thyroid Cancer; Thyroid Disorders; Diabetes; **Hospital:** St. Luke's Episcopal Hosp-Houston, Methodist Hosp - Houston; **Address:** 7515 S Main St, Ste 690, Houston, TX 77030; **Phone:** 713-795-5750; **Board Cert:** Internal Medicine 1976; Endocrinology, Diabetes & Metabolism 1979; **Med School:** Georgetown Univ 1971; **Resid:** Internal Medicine, Baylor Affil Hosps 1976; **Fellow:** Endocrinology, Baylor Affil Hosps 1978; **Fac Appt:** Clin Prof Med, Baylor Coll Med

Sherman, Steven I MD [EDM] - **Spec Exp:** Thyroid Cancer; Endocrine Cancers; **Hospital:** UT MD Anderson Canc Ctr; **Address:** MD Anderson Cancer Ctr, 1515 Holcombe Blvd, Unit 435, Houston, TX 77030; **Phone:** 713-792-2840; **Board Cert:** Internal Medicine 1988; Endocrinology, Diabetes & Metabolism 2007; **Med School:** Johns Hopkins Univ 1985; **Resid:** Internal Medicine, Johns Hopkins Hosp 1988; **Fellow:** Endocrinology, Diabetes & Metabolism, Johns Hopkins Hosp 1991; **Fac Appt:** Prof Med

Waguespack, Steven G MD [EDM] - **Spec Exp:** Thyroid Cancer; Pituitary Tumors; Hereditary Endocrine Cancers; **Hospital:** UT MD Anderson Canc Ctr; **Address:** UT MD Anderson Cancer Center, Dept of Endocrine Neoplasia, 1515 Holcombe Blvd, MS 1461, Houston, TX 77030; **Phone:** 713-563-4400; **Board Cert:** Endocrinology, Diabetes & Metabolism 2012; Pediatric Endocrinology 2011; **Med School:** Univ Tex, Houston 1994; **Resid:** Internal Medicine & Pediatrics, Indiana Univ Hosps 1998; **Fellow:** Endocrinology, Diabetes & Metabolism, Indiana Univ Hosps 2002; Pediatric Endocrinology, Riley Chldns Hosp 2002; **Fac Appt:** Assoc Prof Med, Univ Tex, Houston

West Coast and Pacific

Ahmann, Andrew J MD [EDM] - **Spec Exp:** Diabetes; Clinical Trials; **Hospital:** OR Hlth & Sci Univ; **Address:** OHSU, Div Endocrinology, 3181 SW Sam Jackson Park Rd, MC PPV05, Portland, OR 97239; **Phone:** 503-494-3273; **Board Cert:** Internal Medicine 1983; Endocrinology, Diabetes & Metabolism 1987; **Med School:** Univ Colorado 1980; **Resid:** Internal Medicine, Fitzsimons Army Med Ctr 1983; **Fellow:** Endocrinology, Diabetes & Metabolism, Walter Reed Army Med Ctr 1986; **Fac Appt:** Prof Med, Oregon Hlth & Sci Univ

Akatsu, Haruko MD [EDM] - **Spec Exp:** Thyroid Cancer; Thyroid Disorders; Diabetes; Metabolic Disorders; **Hospital:** Stanford Univ Hosp & Clins; **Address:** Stanford Univ Div Endocrinology, 300 Pasteur Drive, Ste A-175, Stanford, CA 94305; **Phone:** 650-723-6961; **Board Cert:** Endocrinology, Diabetes & Metabolism 2003; **Med School:** Brown Univ 1994; **Resid:** Internal Medicine, Stanford Univ Med Ctr 1997; **Fellow:** Endocrinology, Stanford Univ 1999; **Fac Appt:** Assoc Clin Prof Med, Stanford Univ

Berkson, Richard A MD [EDM] - **Spec Exp:** Diabetes; Thyroid Disorders; **Hospital:** St. Mary Med Ctr - Long Beach, Long Beach Meml Med Ctr; **Address:** 1868 Pacific Ave, Long Beach, CA 90806-6113; **Phone:** 562-595-4718; **Board Cert:** Internal Medicine 1975; Endocrinology, Diabetes & Metabolism 1977; **Med School:** SUNY Buffalo 1972; **Resid:** Internal Medicine, SUNY Buffalo Affil Hosp 1975; **Fellow:** Endocrinology, Diabetes & Metabolism, Joslin Clin 1976; Endocrinology, Diabetes & Metabolism, UCLA Med Ctr 1977; **Fac Appt:** Assoc Clin Prof Med, UCLA

Edelman, Steven V MD [EDM] - **Spec Exp:** Diabetes; **Hospital:** UCSD Med Ctr; **Address:** 1110 Camino Del Mar, Ste B, Del Mar, CA 92014; **Phone:** 858-755-5683; **Board Cert:** Internal Medicine 1986; Endocrinology, Diabetes & Metabolism 2003; **Med School:** UC Davis 1982; **Resid:** Internal Medicine, UCLA-San Fernando 1985; **Fellow:** Diabetes, The Joslin Clin 1986; Endocrinology, Diabetes & Metabolism, The Lahey Clin 1987; **Fac Appt:** Prof Med, UCSD

Fitzgerald, Paul A MD [EDM] - **Spec Exp:** Thyroid Disorders; Diabetes; Pheochromocytoma; Pituitary Tumors; **Hospital:** UCSF Med Ctr; **Address:** 350 Parnassus Ave, Ste 710, San Francisco, CA 94117-3685; **Phone:** 415-665-1136; **Board Cert:** Internal Medicine 1975; Endocrinology, Diabetes & Metabolism 1981; **Med School:** Jefferson Med Coll 1972; **Resid:** Internal Medicine, Presby Med Ctr-Univ Colo 1975; **Fellow:** Endocrinology, Diabetes & Metabolism, UCSF Med Ctr 1978; **Fac Appt:** Clin Prof Med, UCSF

Heber, David MD [EDM] - **Spec Exp:** Nutrition & Cancer Prevention; Nutrition & Disease Prevention/Control; Nutrition & Obesity; **Hospital:** UCLA Ronald Reagan Med Ctr; **Address:** UCLA Ctr for Human Nutrition, 900 Veteran Ave, rm 12-217, Los Angeles, CA 90095-1742; **Phone:** 310-206-1987; **Board Cert:** Internal Medicine 1976; Endocrinology, Diabetes & Metabolism 1977; **Med School:** Harvard Med Sch 1973; **Resid:** Internal Medicine, LAC Harbor Genl Hosp 1975; **Fellow:** Endocrinology, Diabetes & Metabolism, LAC Harbor Genl Hosp 1978; **Fac Appt:** Prof Med, UCLA

Hirsch, Irl B MD [EDM] - **Spec Exp:** Diabetes; **Hospital:** Univ Wash Med Ctr; **Address:** Univ Wash Med Ctr, Diabetes Care Ctr, 4225 Roosevelt Way NE, Ste 101, Box 354691, Seattle, WA 98195; **Phone:** 206-598-4882; **Board Cert:** Internal Medicine 1987; Endocrinology, Diabetes & Metabolism 1989; **Med School:** Univ MO-Columbia Sch Med 1984; **Resid:** Internal Medicine, Mt Sinai Med Ctr 1987; **Fellow:** Metabolism, Washington Univ 1989; **Fac Appt:** Prof Med, Univ Wash

Hoffman, Andrew R MD [EDM] - **Spec Exp:** Pituitary Disorders; Pituitary Tumors; Neuroendocrinology; **Hospital:** Stanford Univ Hosp & Clins, VA Hlth Care Sys - Palo Alto; **Address:** 300 Pasteur Drive, rm A-175, Stanford, CA 94305-5103; **Phone:** 650-723-6961; **Board Cert:** Internal Medicine 1979; Endocrinology 1981; **Med School:** Stanford Univ 1976; **Resid:** Internal Medicine, Mass Genl Hosp 1978; **Fellow:** Endocrinology, Natl Inst Hlth 1980; **Fac Appt:** Prof Med, Stanford Univ

Kamdar, Vikram V MD [EDM] - **Spec Exp:** Diabetes; Diabetic Leg/Foot; Thyroid Disorders; **Hospital:** Santa Monica - UCLA Med Ctr & Ortho Hosp, UCLA Ronald Reagan Med Ctr; **Address:** 2020 Santa Monica Blvd, Ste 550, Santa Monica, CA 90404; **Phone:** 310-828-1050; **Board Cert:** Internal Medicine 1978; Endocrinology, Diabetes & Metabolism 1979; **Med School:** India 1971; **Resid:** Internal Medicine, Lemuel Shattuck Hosp 1972; **Fellow:** Endocrinology, Diabetes & Metabolism, Cedars-Sinai Med Ctr 1975; **Fac Appt:** Assoc Clin Prof Med, UCLA

Kandeel, Fouad MD/PhD [EDM] - **Spec Exp:** Thyroid Cancer; Endocrine Cancers; Neuroendocrinology; **Hospital:** City of Hope Natl Med Ctr; **Address:** City of Hope, Div Endocrinology, 1500 E Duarte Rd, Duarte, CA 91010; **Phone:** 626-256-4673; **Med School:** Egypt 1969; **Resid:** Internal Medicine, Birmingham & Midland Hosp for Women 1972; **Fellow:** Endocrinology, Diabetes & Metabolism, Queen Elizabeth Hosp 1975; **Fac Appt:** Assoc Clin Prof Med, UCLA

Katznelson, Laurence MD [EDM] - **Spec Exp:** Pituitary Disorders; Acromegaly; Cushing's Syndrome; Neuroendocrine Tumors; **Hospital:** Stanford Univ Hosp & Clins, Lucile Packard Chldn's Hosp; **Address:** Stanford Comprehensive Cancer Ctr, 875 Blake Wilbur Drive, MC 5826, Stanford, CA 94305; **Phone:** 650-736-2062; **Board Cert:** Internal Medicine 1988; **Med School:** UCLA 1985; **Resid:** Internal Medicine, Hosp Univ Penn 1988; **Fellow:** Endocrinology, Mass Genl Hosp 1991; **Fac Appt:** Assoc Prof Med, Stanford Univ

Klonoff, David C MD [EDM] - **Spec Exp:** Diabetes; **Hospital:** Mills-Peninsula Med Ctr; **Address:** 1720 El Camino Real, Ste 130, Burlingame, CA 94010; **Phone:** 650-697-4345; **Board Cert:** Internal Medicine 1980; Endocrinology, Diabetes & Metabolism 1981; **Med School:** UCSF 1976; **Resid:** Internal Medicine, UCLA Med Ctr 1978; Internal Medicine, UCSF Hosps 1979; **Fellow:** Endocrinology, Diabetes & Metabolism, Metab Rsch Unit-UCSF Med Ctr 1981; **Fac Appt:** Clin Prof Med, UCSF

Melmed, Shlomo MD [EDM] - **Spec Exp:** Pituitary Tumors; Acromegaly; Pituitary Disorders; **Hospital:** Cedars-Sinai Med Ctr; **Address:** Cedars-Sinai Med Ctr, 127 S San Vicente Blvd, Ste A6600, Los Angeles, CA 90048; **Phone:** 310-423-2830; **Board Cert:** Internal Medicine 1979; Endocrinology, Diabetes & Metabolism 1983; **Med School:** South Africa 1970; **Resid:** Internal Medicine, Sheba Med Ctr 1976; **Fellow:** Endocrinology, Diabetes & Metabolism, Wadsworth VA Hosp 1980; **Fac Appt:** Prof Med, UCLA

Orwoll, Eric S MD [EDM] - **Spec Exp:** Osteoporosis; Osteoporosis in Men; Bone Disorders-Metabolic; **Hospital:** OR Hlth & Sci Univ; **Address:** OHSU, Div Endocrinology, 3181 SW Sam Jackson Park Rd, MC PPV05, Portland, OR 97239; **Phone:** 503-494-3273; **Board Cert:** Internal Medicine 1977; Endocrinology, Diabetes & Metabolism 1979; **Med School:** Univ MD Sch Med 1974; **Resid:** Internal Medicine, Providence Portland Med Ctr 1977; **Fellow:** Endocrinology, Diabetes & Metabolism, OR Hlth & Sci Univ 1979; **Fac Appt:** Prof Med, Oregon Hlth & Sci Univ

Peters, Anne L MD [EDM] - **Spec Exp:** Diabetes; **Hospital:** Keck Med Ctr of USC; **Address:** USC Westside Center for Diabetes, 150 N Robertson Blvd, Ste 210, Beverly Hills, CA 90211; **Phone:** 310-657-3030; **Board Cert:** Internal Medicine 1986; Endocrinology 1989; Endocrinology, Diabetes & Metabolism 2010; **Med School:** Univ Chicago-Pritzker Sch Med 1983; **Resid:** Internal Medicine, Stanford Univ Med Ctr 1985; Internal Medicine, Harbor-UCLA Med Ctr 1986; **Fellow:** Endocrinology, Diabetes & Metabolism, Cedars-Sinai Med Ctr 1988; **Fac Appt:** Prof Med, USC-Keck School of Medicine

Rushakoff, Robert J MD [EDM] - **Spec Exp:** Diabetes; **Hospital:** UCSF - Mt Zion Med Ctr; **Address:** UCSF-Mt Zion Med Ctr, 1600 Divisadero St, Ste C430, Box 1616, San Francisco, CA 94143-1616; **Phone:** 415-885-3868; **Board Cert:** Internal Medicine 1985; Endocrinology, Diabetes & Metabolism 1989; **Med School:** Med Coll Wisc 1982; **Resid:** Internal Medicine, Mt Zion Hosp Med Ctr 1985; **Fellow:** Endocrinology, Mt Zion Hosp/Cell Biol 1986; Endocrinology, Cedars-Sinai Med Ctr 1987; **Fac Appt:** Prof Med, UCSF

Singer, Peter A MD [EDM] - **Spec Exp:** Thyroid Disorders; Pituitary Disorders; **Hospital:** Keck Med Ctr of USC; **Address:** 1520 San Pablo St, Ste 1000, Los Angeles, CA 90033; **Phone:** 323-442-5100; **Board Cert:** Internal Medicine 1972; Endocrinology, Diabetes & Metabolism 1973; **Med School:** UCSF 1965; **Resid:** Internal Medicine, LAC-USC Med Ctr 1971; **Fellow:** Endocrinology, Diabetes & Metabolism, LAC-USC Med Ctr 1973; **Fac Appt:** Clin Prof Med, USC Sch Med

Swerdloff, Ronald S MD [EDM] - **Spec Exp:** Reproductive Endocrinology-Male; Pituitary Disorders; **Hospital:** LAC - Harbor - UCLA Med Ctr; **Address:** 1000 W Carson St, Box 446, Torrance, CA 90509-2910; **Phone:** 310-222-1867; **Board Cert:** Internal Medicine 1968; Endocrinology 1972; **Med School:** UCSF 1962; **Resid:** Internal Medicine, Univ Washington Hosp 1964; Internal Medicine, UCLA 1966; **Fellow:** Endocrinology, Diabetes & Metabolism, NIH Gerontology Branch 1968; Endocrinology, Diabetes & Metabolism, Harbor-UCLA Med Ctr 1969; **Fac Appt:** Prof Med, UCLA

Woeber, Kenneth A MD [EDM] - **Spec Exp:** Thyroid Disorders; **Hospital:** UCSF - Mt Zion Med Ctr; **Address:** Endocrine Clinic at Mt. Zion, 2200 Post St, Ste C-432, Campus Box 1640, San Francisco, CA 94143-1640; **Phone:** 415-885-7574; **Board Cert:** Internal Medicine 1980; Endocrinology, Diabetes & Metabolism 1973; **Med School:** South Africa 1957; **Resid:** Internal Medicine, Johannesburg Hosp 1962; **Fellow:** Endocrinology, Diabetes & Metabolism, Harvard/Boston City Hosp 1964; **Fac Appt:** Prof Med, UCSF

Cleveland Clinic

Every life deserves world class care.

Endocrinology, Diabetes and Metabolism

Cleveland Clinic's Endocrinology & Metabolism Institute is committed to providing the highest quality healthcare for patients with diabetes, endocrine or metabolic disorders. Our staff includes endocrinologists, endocrine surgeons, metabolic specialists, diabetes and thyroid experts and a cardiologist, as well as diabetes educators, dietitians, nurse practitioners and clinical nurse specialists. We are ranked No. 2 in the nation by *U.S. News & World Report* — the highest ranking in Ohio.

We Offer Specialized Endocrine Clinics

The Endocrinology & Metabolism Institute has an array of disease-specific clinics, including:

- Thyroid/parathyroid disorders
- Pituitary disorders
- Post-pancreas transplant care
- Liver/adrenal tumor care
- Type 1 and Type 2 diabetes
- Calcium disorders
- Preventive cardiology
- Transition endocrine (pediatric to adult)

Leading Thyroid Center

Our Thyroid Center is designed so that all specialists work together as a team to accurately and proactively diagnose and treat all forms of thyroid disorders, including thyroid cancer. We have been the leader in incorporating fine needle aspirations and ultrasounds into the realm of endocrinology.

We also offer nationally recognized pituitary care and enhanced diabetes care. Cleveland Clinic is one of the top centers in the U.S. for volume of pituitary surgeries at an institution.

Additionally, we take on all of the clinical challenges that chronic disease management continues to offer as we seek to develop healthier communities.

Cleveland Clinic
Endocrinology &
Metabolism Institute
9500 Euclid Ave.
Cleveland, OH 44195

Offering Same-Day Appointments
Call 866.320.4573

Treatment Guides
Cleveland Clinic has developed comprehensive treatment guides for many diseases and conditions. To download our free treatment guides, visit clevelandclinic.org/treatmentguides.

Online Medical Second Opinion
Call 216.444.3223 or
800.223.2273 ext. 43223 or
email eclevelandclinic@ccf.org

Out-of-State Patients Assistance
Call 800.223.2273, ext. 55580 or
email medicalconcierge@ccf.org

Visit Us At:
clevelandclinic.org

Follow Us On:
Facebook
facebook.com/clevelandclinic

Twitter
@ClevelandClinic

You Tube
youtube.com/clevelandclinic

Health Hub
clevelandclinic.org/HealthHub

Gastroenterology

a subspecialty of Internal Medicine

An internist who specializes in diagnosis and treatment of diseases of the digestive organs including the stomach, bowels, liver and gallbladder. This specialist treats conditions such as abdominal pain, ulcers, diarrhea, cancer and jaundice and performs complex diagnostic and therapeutic procedures using endoscopes to see internal organs.

Training Required: Three years in internal medicine *plus* additional training and examination for certification in gastroenterology.

Gastroenterology

New England

Aslanian, Harry R MD [Ge] - **Spec Exp:** Endoscopic Ultrasound; Esophageal Cancer; Pancreatic Cancer; Rectal Cancer; **Hospital:** Smilow Cancer Hosp at Yale-New Haven; **Address:** Smilow Cancer Hosp, Interventl Endoscopy, 20 York St Fl 4, New Haven, CT 06510; **Phone:** 203-200-5083; **Board Cert:** Gastroenterology 2012; **Med School:** Brown Univ 1996; **Resid:** Internal Medicine, Mayo Clin 1999; **Fellow:** Gastroenterology, Yale-New Haven Hosp 2002; Endoscopy, Yale-New Haven Hosp 2003; **Fac Appt:** Assoc Prof Med, Yale Univ

Butterly, Lynn MD [Ge] - **Spec Exp:** Colonoscopy; Endoscopy; Colon & Rectal Cancer Detection; Colon & Rectal Cancer-Familial Polyposis; **Hospital:** Dartmouth - Hitchcock Med Ctr; **Address:** Dartmouth-Hitchcock Med Ctr, Dept Gastro, 1 Med Ctr Drive, Lebanon, NH 03756; **Phone:** 603-650-5030; **Board Cert:** Internal Medicine 1983; Gastroenterology 1985; **Med School:** Harvard Med Sch 1979; **Resid:** Internal Medicine, Mass Genl Hosp 1983; **Fellow:** Gastroenterology, Mass Genl Hosp 1985; **Fac Appt:** Asst Prof Med, Dartmouth Med Sch

Chung, Daniel C MD [Ge] - **Spec Exp:** Colonoscopy; Colon & Rectal Cancer-Familial Polyposis; Pancreatic Cancer (Familial); Pancreatic Endocrine Tumors; **Hospital:** Mass Genl Hosp; **Address:** Mass Genl Hosp, Gastroenterology Assocs, 55 Fruit St Blake Bldg Fl 4, Boston, MA 02114; **Phone:** 617-726-3544; **Board Cert:** Gastroenterology 2003; **Med School:** Harvard Med Sch 1988; **Resid:** Internal Medicine, Mass Genl Hosp 1991; **Fellow:** Gastroenterology, Mass Genl Hosp 1995; **Fac Appt:** Assoc Prof Med, Harvard Med Sch

Chung, Raymond T MD [Ge] - **Spec Exp:** Transplant Medicine-Liver; Liver Disease; Hepatitis C; **Hospital:** Mass Genl Hosp; **Address:** Mass General Hosp, 55 Fruit St Blake Bldg Fl 4, Boston, MA 02114; **Phone:** 617-724-6006; **Board Cert:** Internal Medicine 1989; Gastroenterology 2007; Transplant Hepatology 2008; **Med School:** Yale Univ 1986; **Resid:** Internal Medicine, Johns Hopkins Hosp 1989; **Fellow:** Gastroenterology, Mass Genl Hosp 1983; **Fac Appt:** Assoc Prof Med, Harvard Med Sch

Dienstag, Jules L MD [Ge] - **Spec Exp:** Liver Disease; Hepatitis; Transplant Medicine-Liver; **Hospital:** Mass Genl Hosp; **Address:** Mass Genl Hosp, GI Unit, 55 Fruit St, Warren Bldg - Fl 10, Boston, MA 02114-2622; **Phone:** 617-726-7450; **Board Cert:** Internal Medicine 1975; **Med School:** Columbia P&S 1972; **Resid:** Internal Medicine, Univ Chicago-Billings Hosp 1974; **Fellow:** Virology, Natl Inst Hlth 1976; Gastroenterology, Mass Genl Hosp 1978; **Fac Appt:** Prof Med, Harvard Med Sch

Farraye, Francis A MD [Ge] - **Spec Exp:** Endoscopy; Inflammatory Bowel Disease; Colon & Rectal Cancer Detection; Diarrheal Diseases; **Hospital:** Boston Med Ctr; **Address:** Boston Med Ctr, Div Gastroenterology, 830 Harrison Ave Moakley Bldg Fl 2, Ste 2100, Boston, MA 02118; **Phone:** 617-638-6525; **Board Cert:** Gastroenterology 1989; Internal Medicine 1985; **Med School:** Albert Einstein Coll Med 1982; **Resid:** Internal Medicine, Beth Israel Hosp 1985; **Fellow:** Gastroenterology, Beth Israel Hosp 1988

Fisher, Rosemarie Louise MD [Ge] - **Spec Exp:** Nutrition; Nutrition in Bowel Disorders; Inflammatory Bowel Disease/Crohn's; Endoscopy; **Hospital:** Yale-New Haven Hosp, St. Mary's Hosp - Waterbury; **Address:** 20 York St, Tompkins Bldg - Ste 236, New Haven, CT 06510; **Phone:** 203-688-1449; **Board Cert:** Internal Medicine 1975; Gastroenterology 1977; **Med School:** Tufts Univ 1971; **Resid:** Internal Medicine, Montefiore Med Ctr 1973; **Fellow:** Gastroenterology, Yale-New Haven Hosp 1975; **Fac Appt:** Prof Med, Yale Univ

Friedman, Lawrence S MD [Ge] - **Spec Exp:** Liver Disease; **Hospital:** Newton - Wellesley Hosp, Mass Genl Hosp; **Address:** Newton-Wellesley Hosp, Dept Medicine, 2014 Washington St, Newton, MA 02462; **Phone:** 617-243-5480; **Board Cert:** Internal Medicine 1981; Gastroenterology 2005; **Med School:** Johns Hopkins Univ 1978; **Resid:** Internal Medicine, Johns Hopkins Hosp 1981; **Fellow:** Gastroenterology, Mass Genl Hosp 1984; **Fac Appt:** Prof Med, Harvard Med Sch

Gordon, Stuart R MD [Ge] - **Spec Exp:** Pancreatic & Biliary Disease; Pancreatic/Biliary Endoscopy (ERCP); Endoscopic Ultrasound; **Hospital:** Dartmouth - Hitchcock Med Ctr; **Address:** Dartmouth-Hitchcock Medical Center, One Medical Center Drive, Lebanon, NH 03756; **Phone:** 603-650-5261; **Board Cert:** Internal Medicine 2002; Gastroenterology 2005; **Med School:** Columbia P&S 1988; **Resid:** Internal Medicine, Dartmouth-Hitchcock Med Ctr 1991; **Fellow:** Gastroenterology, Dartmouth-Hitchcock Med Ctr 1994; **Fac Appt:** Assoc Prof Med, Dartmouth Med Sch

Kaplan, Lee M MD/PhD [Ge] - **Spec Exp:** Obesity; Weight Management; Liver Disease; **Hospital:** Mass Genl Hosp; **Address:** MGH Gastroenterology Associates, 55 Fruit St Bldg 4, Boston, MA 02114-2517; **Phone:** 617-724-6007; **Board Cert:** Gastroenterology 1987; Internal Medicine 1984; **Med School:** Albert Einstein Coll Med 1981; **Resid:** Internal Medicine, Mass Genl Hosp 1984; **Fellow:** Gastroenterology, Mass Genl Hosp 1987; **Fac Appt:** Assoc Prof Med, Harvard Med Sch

Kelsey, Peter B MD [Ge] - **Spec Exp:** Endoscopy; Pancreatic & Biliary Disease; **Hospital:** Mass Genl Hosp; **Address:** Mass Genl Hosp, 55 Fruit St, Blake Bldg Fl 4, Boston, MA 02114-2621; **Phone:** 617-724-6044; **Board Cert:** Gastroenterology 1985; Internal Medicine 1982; **Med School:** Columbia P&S 1979; **Resid:** Internal Medicine, NY Presby/Columbia Med Ctr 1982; **Fellow:** Gastroenterology, Mass Genl Hosp 1984; **Fac Appt:** Asst Prof Med, Harvard Med Sch

La Mont, J Thomas MD [Ge] - **Spec Exp:** Clostridium Difficile Disease; Inflammatory Bowel Disease; **Hospital:** Beth Israel Deaconess Med Ctr - Boston; **Address:** BIDMC,Div of Gastroenterology/GI East, 330 Brookline Ave, Ste 101, Boston, MA 02215; **Phone:** 617-667-8377; **Board Cert:** Internal Medicine 1972; Gastroenterology 1975; **Med School:** Univ Rochester 1965; **Resid:** Internal Medicine, UCLA Ronald Reagan Med Ctr 1971; **Fellow:** Gastroenterology, Mass Genl Hosp 1973; **Fac Appt:** Prof Med, Harvard Med Sch

Lichtenstein, David R MD [Ge] - **Spec Exp:** Pancreatic & Biliary Disease; Peptic Acid Disorders; Endoscopic Therapies; **Hospital:** Boston Med Ctr; **Address:** Boston Med Ctr, 830 Harrison Ave Moakley Bldg - Ste 2100, Boston, MA 02118; **Phone:** 617-638-6525; **Board Cert:** Internal Medicine 1988; Gastroenterology 2004; **Med School:** Univ Pennsylvania 1985; **Resid:** Internal Medicine, Duke Univ Med Ctr 1988; **Fellow:** Gastroenterology, Beth Israel Hosp 1990; Advanced Endoscopy, Duke Univ Med Ctr 1992; **Fac Appt:** Assoc Prof Med, Univ Pennsylvania

Mason, Joel B MD [Ge] - **Spec Exp:** Nutrition in Acute Illness; Nutrition in Bowel Disorders; Nutrition & Cancer Prevention; Inflammatory Bowel Disease; **Hospital:** Tufts Med Ctr; **Address:** Tufts Med Ctr, Div Gastroenterology/Hepatology, 800 Washington St, Ste 239, Boston, MA 02111-1513; **Phone:** 617-636-5883; **Board Cert:** Internal Medicine 1984; Gastroenterology 1987; **Med School:** Univ Chicago-Pritzker Sch Med 1981; **Resid:** Internal Medicine, Univ Iowa Hosps 1984; **Fellow:** Gastroenterology, Univ Chicago Hosps 1986; Nutrition, Univ Chicago Hosps 1986; **Fac Appt:** Prof Med, Tufts Univ

Nunes, David P MD [Ge] - **Spec Exp:** Liver Disease; Hepatitis; **Hospital:** Boston Med Ctr; **Address:** Boston Med Ctr, Div Gastroenterology, 830 Harrison Ave Mokley Bldg Fl 2, Ste 2100, Boston, MA 02118; **Phone:** 617-638-6525 x3; **Board Cert:** Internal Medicine 2006; Gastroenterology 2007; **Med School:** Ireland 1984; **Resid:** Internal Medicine, Dublin Voluntary Hosp 1987; **Fellow:** Gastroenterology, Federated Dublin Volunt Hosps 1989; **Fac Appt:** Assoc Prof Med, Boston Univ

Proctor, Deborah D MD [Ge] - **Spec Exp:** Inflammatory Bowel Disease; Colon Cancer Screening; Endoscopy; **Hospital:** Yale-New Haven Hosp; **Address:** Yale Medical Group, 40 Temple St, Ste 1A, New Haven, CT 06519; **Phone:** 203-785-4138; **Board Cert:** Gastroenterology 2003; **Med School:** Univ Cincinnati 1982; **Resid:** Internal Medicine, Beth Israel Hosp 1990; **Fellow:** Gastroenterology, Beth Israel Hosp 1992; **Fac Appt:** Prof Med, Yale Univ

Rothstein, Richard I MD [Ge] - **Spec Exp:** Gastroesophageal Reflux Disease (GERD); Swallowing Disorders; Barrett's Esophagus; Endoscopy; **Hospital:** Dartmouth - Hitchcock Med Ctr; **Address:** Dartmouth-Hitchcock Med Ctr, Div Gastroenterology, 1 Medical Center Drive, Lebanon, NH 03756; **Phone:** 603-650-5261; **Board Cert:** Internal Medicine 1983; Gastroenterology 1987; **Med School:** Boston Univ 1980; **Resid:** Internal Medicine, Univ Mass Med Ctr 1983; **Fellow:** Gastroenterology, Dartmouth-Hitchcock Med Ctr 1985; **Fac Appt:** Prof Med, Dartmouth Med Sch

Siegel, Corey A MD [Ge] - **Spec Exp:** Ulcerative Colitis; Crohn's Disease; Colonoscopy; Inflammatory Bowel Disease; **Hospital:** Dartmouth - Hitchcock Med Ctr; **Address:** Dartmouth-Hitchcock Med Ctr, Gastroenterology & Hepatology Div, 1 Medical Ctr Drive, Lebanon, NH 03756; **Phone:** 603-650-5261; **Board Cert:** Gastroenterology 2005; **Med School:** Tufts Univ 1998; **Resid:** Internal Medicine, Dartmouth-Hitchcock Med Ctr 2002; **Fellow:** Gastroenterology, Dartmouth-Hitchcock Med Ctr 2005; Inflammatory Bowel Disease, Mass Genl Hosp 2005; **Fac Appt:** Asst Prof Med, Dartmouth Med Sch

Weinstock, Joel V MD [Ge] - **Spec Exp:** Endoscopy; Inflammatory Bowel Disease; **Hospital:** Tufts Med Ctr; **Address:** Tufts Med Ctr, Div Gastroenterology & Hepatology, 800 Washington St, rm 233, Boston, MA 02111; **Phone:** 617-636-5883; **Board Cert:** Internal Medicine 1976; Gastroenterology 1979; **Med School:** Wayne State Univ 1973; **Resid:** Internal Medicine, Univ Hosp Michigan 1976; **Fellow:** Gastroenterology, Univ Hosp Michigan 1978; **Fac Appt:** Prof Med, Tufts Univ

Mid Atlantic

Al-Kawas, Firas H MD [Ge] - **Spec Exp:** Pancreatic & Biliary Disease; **Hospital:** MedStar Georgetown Univ Hosp; **Address:** GI Division Georgetown Hosp, 3800 Reservoir Rd NW Fl 2 - Ste M2025, Washington, DC 20007; **Phone:** 202-444-1670; **Board Cert:** Internal Medicine 1979; Gastroenterology 1983; **Med School:** Syria 1974; **Resid:** Internal Medicine, Georgetown Univ Hosp 1979; **Fellow:** Gastroenterology, VA Med Ctr 1981; **Fac Appt:** Prof Med, Georgetown Univ

Albert, Michael B MD [Ge] - **Spec Exp:** Inflammatory Bowel Disease; Ulcerative Colitis; Endoscopy; Colon Cancer Screening; **Hospital:** G Washington Univ Hosp; **Address:** DC Gastroenterology, 2131 K St NW, Ste 800A, Washington, DC 20037; **Phone:** 202-223-5544; **Board Cert:** Internal Medicine 1985; Gastroenterology 1987; **Med School:** Johns Hopkins Univ 1982; **Resid:** Internal Medicine, Mayo Clinic 1984; Internal Medicine, Duke Univ Med Ctr 1985; **Fellow:** Gastroenterology, G Washington Univ Med Ctr 1987; **Fac Appt:** Prof Med, Geo Wash Univ

Aronchick, Craig A MD [Ge] - **Spec Exp:** Colonoscopy; Colon Cancer Screening; **Hospital:** Pennsylvania Hosp-UPHS (page 69); **Address:** Wills Surgery Center, 3340 S Broad St, Philadelphia, PA 19145; **Phone:** 267-354-2632; **Board Cert:** Internal Medicine 1981; Gastroenterology 1983; **Med School:** Temple Univ 1978; **Resid:** Internal Medicine, Temple Univ Hosp 1981; **Fellow:** Gastroenterology, Hosp Univ Penn 1983

Benjamin, Stanley B MD [Ge] - **Spec Exp:** Gastrointestinal Motility Disorders; Esophageal Disorders; Gastroesophageal Reflux Disease (GERD); **Hospital:** MedStar Georgetown Univ Hosp; **Address:** GUMC - Second Floor, Main Hospital, 3800 Reservoir Rd NW, rm M2210, Washington, DC 20007; **Phone:** 202-444-1669; **Board Cert:** Internal Medicine 1977; Gastroenterology 1979; **Med School:** Univ Pittsburgh 1974; **Resid:** Internal Medicine, Natl Naval Med Ctr 1977; **Fellow:** Gastroenterology, Natl Naval Med Ctr 1979; **Fac Appt:** Prof Med, Georgetown Univ

Borum, Marie L MD [Ge] - **Spec Exp:** Colon Cancer Screening; AIDS/HIV-Gastrointestinal Complications; Women's Health; Liver Disease; **Hospital:** G Washington Univ Hosp; **Address:** MFA Dept Medicine, 2150 Pennsylvania Ave NW Fl 3, Washington, DC 20037; **Phone:** 202-741-3333; **Board Cert:** Internal Medicine 1988; Gastroenterology 2011; **Med School:** UMDNJ-Rutgers Med Sch 1985; **Resid:** Internal Medicine, G Washington Univ Med Ctr 1988; **Fellow:** Gastroenterology, G Washington Univ Med Ctr 1991; **Fac Appt:** Prof Med, Geo Wash Univ

Brandt, Lawrence MD [Ge] - **Spec Exp:** Inflammatory Bowel Disease; Clostridium Difficile Disease; **Hospital:** Montefiore Med Ctr-Moses Campus, NY; **Address:** 3400 Bainbridge Ave Fl 2, Bronx, NY 10467-2401; **Phone:** 866-633-8255; **Board Cert:** Internal Medicine 1972; Gastroenterology 2006; **Med School:** SUNY Downstate 1968; **Resid:** Internal Medicine, Mt Sinai Med Ctr 1972; **Fellow:** Gastroenterology, Mt Sinai Med Ctr 1972; **Fac Appt:** Prof Emeritus Med, Albert Einstein Coll Med

Brown Jr, Robert S MD [Ge] - **Spec Exp:** Hepatitis; Liver Disease; Transplant Medicine-Liver; Autoimmune Liver Disease; **Hospital:** NY-Presby/Columbia Univ Med Ctr, NY (page 65), NY-Presby/Weill Cornell Med Ctr, NY (page 65); **Address:** Ctr for Liver Disease & Transplantation, 622 W 168th St PH Bldg Fl 14 - rm 105, New York, NY 10032; **Phone:** 212-305-1305; **Board Cert:** Internal Medicine 2012; Gastroenterology 2005; Transplant Hepatology 2010; **Med School:** NYU Sch Med 1989; **Resid:** Internal Medicine, Beth Israel Deaconess Med Ctr 1992; **Fellow:** Gastroenterology, UCSF Med Ctr 1994; Hepatology, UCSF Med Ctr 1995; **Fac Appt:** Prof Med, Columbia P&S

Canto, Marcia I MD [Ge] - **Spec Exp:** Endoscopy; Endoscopic Ultrasound; Pancreatic Cancer-Early Detection; **Hospital:** Johns Hopkins Hosp (page 59); **Address:** Johns Hopkins Gastroenterology, 10700 Charter Drive, Charter Med Bldg, Ste 310, Columbia, MD 21044; **Phone:** 410-715-0350; **Board Cert:** Internal Medicine 1989; Gastroenterology 2008; **Med School:** Philippines 1985; **Resid:** Internal Medicine, SUNY Upstate Med Univ Hosp 1989; **Fellow:** Gastroenterology, SUNY Upstate Med Univ Hosp 1993; **Fac Appt:** Prof Med, Johns Hopkins Univ

Carr-Locke, David L MD [Ge] - **Spec Exp:** Pancreatic/Biliary Endoscopy (ERCP); Pancreatic & Biliary Disease; Endoscopy; **Hospital:** Beth Israel Med Ctr - Petrie Div (page 56); **Address:** 10 Union Square E, Ste 2G, New York, NY 10003; **Phone:** 212-420-4015; **Board Cert:** Internal Medicine 1974; **Med School:** England, UK 1972; **Resid:** Obstetrics & Gynecology, Orsett Hosp 1974; Internal Medicine, Leicester Hosp 1976; **Fellow:** Gastroenterology, Leicester Hosp 1978; Research, New Eng Baptist Hosp 1979; **Fac Appt:** Prof Med, Albert Einstein Coll Med

Cohen, Jonathan MD [Ge] - **Spec Exp:** Pancreatic/Biliary Endoscopy (ERCP); Colonoscopy; Barrett's Esophagus; Gastrointestinal Cancer; **Hospital:** NYU Langone Med Ctr (page 68); **Address:** Concorde Medical Group, 232 E 30th St, New York, NY 10016-8202; **Phone:** 212-889-5544; **Board Cert:** Gastroenterology 2005; **Med School:** Harvard Med Sch 1990; **Resid:** Internal Medicine, Beth Israel Hosp 1993; **Fellow:** Gastroenterology, UCLA Med Ctr 1995; Endoscopy, Wellesley Hosp 1995; **Fac Appt:** Clin Prof Med, NYU Sch Med

Cohen, Lawrence B MD [Ge] - **Spec Exp:** Gastroesophageal Reflux Disease (GERD); Esophageal Disorders; Colon & Rectal Cancer; Endoscopy; **Hospital:** Mt Sinai Med Ctr (page 62); **Address:** 311 E 79th St, Ste 2A, New York, NY 10075; **Phone:** 212-996-6633; **Board Cert:** Internal Medicine 1981; Gastroenterology 1983; **Med School:** Hahnemann Univ 1978; **Resid:** Internal Medicine, Mt Sinai Med Ctr 1981; **Fellow:** Gastroenterology, Mt Sinai Med Ctr 1983; **Fac Appt:** Clin Prof Med, Mount Sinai Sch Med

DeCross, Arthur J MD [Ge] - **Spec Exp:** Inflammatory Bowel Disease; Ulcerative Colitis; Crohn's Disease; **Hospital:** Univ Rochester Strong Meml Hosp; **Address:** 180 Saw Grass Drive, Ste 230, Rochester, NY 14620; **Phone:** 585-275-4711; **Board Cert:** Gastroenterology 2003; **Med School:** Albany Med Coll 1988; **Resid:** Internal Medicine, Univ Rochester Strong Meml Hosp 1991; **Fellow:** Gastroenterology, Univ Virginia Med Ctr 1994; **Fac Appt:** Assoc Prof Med, Univ Rochester

Di Marino Jr, Anthony J MD [Ge] - **Spec Exp:** Celiac Disease; Gastroesophageal Reflux Disease (GERD); Esophageal Disorders; Crohn's Disease; **Hospital:** Thomas Jefferson Univ Hosp; **Address:** 132 S 10th St, Ste 480, Div Gastroenterology, Philadelphia, PA 19107; **Phone:** 215-955-2728; **Board Cert:** Internal Medicine 1977; Gastroenterology 1972; **Med School:** Hahnemann Univ 1968; **Resid:** Internal Medicine, Hahnemann Univ Hosp 1970; Internal Medicine, Hosp Univ Penn 1971; **Fellow:** Gastroenterology, Hosp Univ Penn 1973; **Fac Appt:** Prof Med, Thomas Jefferson Univ

Dieterich, Douglas T MD [Ge] - **Spec Exp:** Hepatitis; AIDS/HIV-Gastrointestinal Complications; Liver Disease; Endoscopy; **Hospital:** Mt Sinai Med Ctr (page 62); **Address:** 5 E 98th St Fl 11, New York, NY 10029; **Phone:** 212-241-7270; **Board Cert:** Internal Medicine 1981; Gastroenterology 1987; **Med School:** NYU Sch Med 1978; **Resid:** Internal Medicine, Bellevue Hosp Ctr 1981; **Fellow:** Gastroenterology, Bellevue Hosp Ctr 1983; **Fac Appt:** Prof Med, Mount Sinai Sch Med

Falk, Gary W MD [Ge] - **Spec Exp:** Barrett's Esophagus; Achalasia; Esophageal Disorders; Eosinophilic Esophagitis; **Hospital:** Hosp Univ Penn - UPHS (page 69); **Address:** 9 Penn Tower/One Convention Ave, Fl 9, Philadelphia, PA 19104; **Phone:** 215-662-4279; **Board Cert:** Internal Medicine 1983; Gastroenterology 1985; **Med School:** Univ Rochester 1980; **Resid:** Internal Medicine, George Washington Univ Hosp 1983; **Fellow:** Gastroenterology, Univ Michigan Med Ctr 1986; **Fac Appt:** Prof Med, Univ Pennsylvania

Fisher, Robert S MD [Ge] - **Spec Exp:** Gastrointestinal Motility Disorders; Peptic Acid Disorders; Gastrointestinal Functional Disorders; **Hospital:** Temple Univ Hosp; **Address:** 3401 N Broad St, Philadelphia, PA 19140; **Phone:** 215-707-3433; **Board Cert:** Internal Medicine 1971; Gastroenterology 1973; **Med School:** Univ Pennsylvania 1964; **Resid:** Internal Medicine, Temple Univ Med Ctr 1970; **Fellow:** Gastroenterology, Hosp Univ Penn 1972

Freiman, Hal MD [Ge] - **Spec Exp:** Gastroesophageal Reflux Disease (GERD); Colon Cancer Screening; Irritable Bowel Syndrome; Hepatitis; **Hospital:** Beth Israel Med Ctr - Petrie Div (page 56), NYU Langone Med Ctr (page 68); **Address:** 59 W 12th St, Ste 1D, New York, NY 10011-8520; **Phone:** 212-206-0074; **Board Cert:** Internal Medicine 1981; Gastroenterology 1983; **Med School:** Albany Med Coll 1978; **Resid:** Internal Medicine, St Vincent's Hosp 1981; **Fellow:** Gastroenterology, Westchester Co Med Ctr 1983

Gerdes, Hans MD [Ge] - **Spec Exp:** Endoscopy; Endoscopic Ultrasound; Barrett's Esophagus; Gastrointestinal Cancer; **Hospital:** Meml Sloan-Kettering Canc Ctr; **Address:** 1275 York Avenue, New York, NY 10065; **Phone:** 212-639-7108; **Board Cert:** Internal Medicine 1987; Gastroenterology 1989; **Med School:** Cornell Univ-Weill Med Coll 1983; **Resid:** Internal Medicine, New York Hosp 1986; **Fellow:** Gastroenterology, Meml Sloan Kettering Cancer Ctr 1989; **Fac Appt:** Prof Med, Cornell Univ-Weill Med Coll

Giardiello, Francis MD [Ge] - **Spec Exp:** Colon Cancer; Colon & Rectal Cancer-Familial Polyposis; Cancer Risk Assessment; **Hospital:** Johns Hopkins Hosp (page 59); **Address:** Johns Hopkins, Gastroenterology Dept, 1830 E Monument St, rm 431, Baltimore, MD 21205; **Phone:** 410-955-2635; **Board Cert:** Internal Medicine 1983; Gastroenterology 1985; **Med School:** Tufts Univ 1980; **Resid:** Internal Medicine, Univ Michigan Med Ctr 1983; **Fellow:** Gastroenterology, Johns Hopkins Hosp 1985; **Fac Appt:** Prof Med, Johns Hopkins Univ

Ginsberg, Gregory G MD [Ge] - **Spec Exp:** Pancreatic/Biliary Endoscopy (ERCP); Endoscopy; Endoscopic Ultrasound; Barrett's Esophagus; **Hospital:** Hosp Univ Penn - UPHS (page 69); **Address:** Perelman Ctr for Advanced Medicine, 3400 Civic Center Blvd, South Pavilion, 4th Fl, Philadelphia, PA 19104; **Phone:** 215-349-8222; **Board Cert:** Gastroenterology 2000; **Med School:** Jefferson Med Coll 1987; **Resid:** Internal Medicine, Georgetown Univ Med Ctr 1990; **Fellow:** Gastroenterology, Georgetown Univ 1992; Therapeutic Endoscopy, Georgetown Univ 1993; **Fac Appt:** Prof Med, Univ Pennsylvania

Goggins, Michael MD [Ge] - **Spec Exp:** Pancreatic Cancer-Early Detection; **Hospital:** Johns Hopkins Hosp (page 59); **Address:** Johns Hopkins, Gastroenterology Dept, 2360 W Joppa Rd, Ste 205, Lutherville, MD 21093; **Phone:** 410-933-7495; **Med School:** Ireland 1988; **Resid:** Internal Medicine, St James's Hosp 1990; **Fellow:** Gastroenterology, St James's Hosp 1992; **Fac Appt:** Assoc Prof Med, Johns Hopkins Univ

Green, Peter H R MD [Ge] - **Spec Exp:** Celiac Disease; Endoscopy; Colonoscopy; Malabsorption Syndrome; **Hospital:** NY-Presby/Columbia Univ Med Ctr, NY (page 65); **Address:** Celiac Dis Ctr, Harkness Bldg, 180 Fort Washington Ave, Ste 936, New York, NY 10032-3713; **Phone:** 212-305-5590; **Med School:** Australia 1970; **Resid:** Internal Medicine, North Shore Med Ctr 1974; **Fellow:** Gastroenterology, North Shore Med Ctr 1976; Gastroenterology, Beth Israel Deaconess Med Ctr 1977; **Fac Appt:** Prof Med, Columbia P&S

Greenwald, Bruce D MD [Ge] - **Spec Exp:** Endoscopic Ultrasound; Barrett's Esophagus; Esophageal Cancer; Clinical Trials; **Hospital:** Univ of MD Med Ctr; **Address:** Univ MD Med Ctr Div Gastroenterology, 22 S Greene St, Fl 3, rm N3W62, Baltimore, MD 21201; **Phone:** 410-328-8731; **Board Cert:** Gastroenterology 2000; **Med School:** Univ MD Sch Med 1987; **Resid:** Internal Medicine, Univ Virginia Hlth Sys 1990; **Fellow:** Gastroenterology, Univ Maryland Med Ctr 1992; **Fac Appt:** Prof Med, Univ MD Sch Med

Haber, Gregory B MD [Ge] - **Spec Exp:** Endoscopy; Pancreatic/Biliary Endoscopy (ERCP); Endoscopic Ultrasound; Barrett's Esophagus; **Hospital:** Lenox Hill Hosp (page 66); **Address:** 100 E 77th St Fl 2, New York, NY 10075; **Phone:** 212-434-6279; **Med School:** Univ Toronto 1970; **Resid:** Internal Medicine, Univ Toronto Med Ctr 1975; **Fellow:** Gastroenterology, Univ Toronto Med Ctr 1978

Haluszka, Oleh MD [Ge] - **Spec Exp:** Pancreatic/Biliary Endoscopy (ERCP); Gastrointestinal Cancer; Endoscopic Ultrasound; Endoscopic Therapies; **Hospital:** Temple Univ Hosp; **Address:** Temple Univ Div Gastroenterology, 3401 N Broad St, Parkinson Pavilion, Ste 831, Philadelphia, PA 19140; **Phone:** 215-707-9577; **Board Cert:** Internal Medicine 1987; Gastroenterology 2011; **Med School:** Uniformed Srvs Univ, Bethesda 1982; **Resid:** Internal Medicine, US Naval Hosp 1987; **Fellow:** Gastroenterology, US Naval Hosp 1990; Endoscopy, Med Coll Wisconsin 1993; **Fac Appt:** Assoc Clin Prof Med, Temple Univ

Herrine, Steven K MD [Ge] - **Spec Exp:** Liver Disease; Hepatitis C; Transplant Medicine-Liver; **Hospital:** Thomas Jefferson Univ Hosp; **Address:** Jefferson Div Gastroenterology, 132 S 10th St, Ste 480, Philadelphia, PA 19107; **Phone:** 215-955-8900; **Board Cert:** Internal Medicine 2003; Gastroenterology 2005; Transplant Hepatology 2006; **Med School:** Jefferson Med Coll 1990; **Resid:** Internal Medicine, Hosp Univ Penn 1993; **Fellow:** Gastroenterology, Thos Jefferson Univ Hosp 1995; **Fac Appt:** Prof Med, Thomas Jefferson Univ

Hoops, Timothy C MD [Ge] - **Spec Exp:** Gastrointestinal Cancer; Endoscopy; Cancer Risk Assessment; **Hospital:** Penn Presby Med Ctr - UPHS (page 69); **Address:** Penn Presbyterian Med Ctr, Wright-Saunders Bldg, Ste 218, 51 N 39th St, Philadelphia, PA 19104; **Phone:** 215-662-8900; **Board Cert:** Internal Medicine 1984; Gastroenterology 1987; **Med School:** Univ IL Coll Med 1981; **Resid:** Internal Medicine, Univ Colorado Affil Hosp 1984; **Fellow:** Gastroenterology, Univ Colorado 1986; **Fac Appt:** Clin Prof Med, Univ Pennsylvania

Infantolino, Anthony MD [Ge] - **Spec Exp:** Interventional Endoscopy; Gastrointestinal Cancer; Endoscopic Ultrasound; Barrett's Esophagus; **Hospital:** Thomas Jefferson Univ Hosp; **Address:** Jefferson Div Gastroenterology, 132 S 10th St, Main Bldg, Ste 480, Philadelphia, PA 19107; **Phone:** 215-955-8900; **Board Cert:** Internal Medicine 1988; Gastroenterology 2012; **Med School:** UMDNJ-RW Johnson Med Sch 1985; **Resid:** Internal Medicine, Thom Jefferson Univ Hosp 1988; **Fellow:** Gastroenterology, Graduate Hosp-UPHS 1991; **Fac Appt:** Assoc Clin Prof Med, Thomas Jefferson Univ

Itzkowitz, Steven H MD [Ge] - **Spec Exp:** Colon & Rectal Cancer; Colon & Rectal Cancer Detection; Inflammatory Bowel Disease; Hereditary Cancer; **Hospital:** Mt Sinai Med Ctr (page 62); **Address:** 5 E 98th St, Box 1625, New York, NY 10029-6501; **Phone:** 212-241-4299; **Board Cert:** Internal Medicine 1982; Gastroenterology 1985; **Med School:** Mount Sinai Sch Med 1979; **Resid:** Internal Medicine, Bellevue Hosp/NYU Med Ctr 1982; **Fellow:** Gastroenterology, UCSF Med Ctr 1984; **Fac Appt:** Prof Med, Mount Sinai Sch Med

Jacobson, Ira M MD [Ge] - **Spec Exp:** Liver & Biliary Disease; Hepatitis; Hepatitis C; **Hospital:** NY-Presby/Weill Cornell Med Ctr, NY (page 65); **Address:** 1305 York Ave Fl 4, New York, NY 10021-5016; **Phone:** 646-962-4040; **Board Cert:** Internal Medicine 1982; Gastroenterology 2009; Transplant Hepatology 2006; **Med School:** Columbia P&S 1979; **Resid:** Internal Medicine, UCSF Med Ctr 1982; **Fellow:** Gastroenterology, Mass Genl Hosp 1984; **Fac Appt:** Prof Med, Cornell Univ-Weill Med Coll

Kalloo, Anthony N MD [Ge] - **Spec Exp:** Endoscopy; Pancreatic Disease; **Hospital:** Johns Hopkins Hosp (page 59); **Address:** Johns Hopkins, Gastroenterology Dept, 2360 W Joppa Rd, Ste 205, Lutherville, MD 21093; **Phone:** 410-933-7495; **Board Cert:** Internal Medicine 1985; Gastroenterology 1987; **Med School:** Jamaica 1979; **Resid:** Internal Medicine, Howard Univ Hosp 1985; **Fellow:** Gastroenterology, VA Med Ctr 1987; **Fac Appt:** Prof Med, Johns Hopkins Univ

Kantsevoy, Sergey V MD/PhD [Ge] - **Spec Exp:** Pancreatic Disease; Endoscopic Ultrasound; Pancreatic/Biliary Endoscopy (ERCP); Endoscopic Therapies; **Hospital:** Mercy Med Ctr - Baltimore; **Address:** Mercy Med Ctr, Gastroenterology Dept, 301 St Paul Pl, Ste 718, Baltimore, MD 21202; **Phone:** 410-332-9356; **Board Cert:** Gastroenterology 2011; **Med School:** Russia 1983; **Resid:** Internal Medicine, Bronx-Lebanon Hosp Ctr 1995; Internal Medicine, Washington Hosp Ctr 1997; **Fellow:** Gastroenterology, Johns Hopkins Hosp 2000; **Fac Appt:** Asst Prof Med, Johns Hopkins Univ

Kastenberg, David M MD [Ge] - **Spec Exp:** Gastrointestinal Cancer; Capsule Endoscopy; Celiac Disease; Nutrition & Cancer Prevention; **Hospital:** Thomas Jefferson Univ Hosp; **Address:** Jefferson Univ Physicians-Div GI, 132 S 10th St, Main Bldg - Ste 480, Phildelphia, PA 19107; **Phone:** 215-955-8900; **Board Cert:** Internal Medicine 2010; Gastroenterology 2000; **Med School:** NYU Sch Med 1987; **Resid:** Internal Medicine, Temple Univ Hosp 1990; **Fellow:** Gastroenterology, Thomas Jefferson Univ Hosp 1992; **Fac Appt:** Assoc Prof Med, Jefferson Med Coll

Katz, Philip O MD [Ge] - **Spec Exp:** Gastroesophageal Reflux Disease (GERD); Swallowing Disorders; Barrett's Esophagus; Esophageal Disorders; **Hospital:** Einstein Med Ctr; **Address:** 5401 Old York Rd, Klein Bldg - Ste 202, Philadelphia, PA 19141; **Phone:** 215-456-8210; **Board Cert:** Internal Medicine 1981; Gastroenterology 1987; **Med School:** Bowman Gray 1978; **Resid:** Internal Medicine, NC Baptist Hosp 1981; **Fellow:** Gastroenterology, Bowman Gray 1986; **Fac Appt:** Clin Prof Med, Thomas Jefferson Univ

Kochman, Michael L MD [Ge] - **Spec Exp:** Endoscopy; Pancreatic/Biliary Endoscopy (ERCP); Gastrointestinal Cancer; Pancreatic Disease; **Hospital:** Hosp Univ Penn - UPHS (page 69), Penn Presby Med Ctr - UPHS (page 69); **Address:** Perelman Ctr Advanced Medicine, 3400 Civic Center Blvd, South Pavilion Fl 4, Philadelphia, PA 19104; **Phone:** 215-349-8222; **Board Cert:** Internal Medicine 1989; Gastroenterology 2013; **Med School:** Univ IL Coll Med 1986; **Resid:** Internal Medicine, Univ Illinois Med Ctr 1990; **Fellow:** Gastroenterology, Univ Michigan 1993; Endoscopic Ultrasound, Indiana Univ 1992; **Fac Appt:** Prof Med, Univ Pennsylvania

Korsten, Mark A MD [Ge] - **Spec Exp:** Constipation; Gastrointestinal Motility Disorders; Spinal Cord Injury & Colonic Motility; Liver Disease; **Hospital:** James J. Peters VA Med Ctr-Bronx; **Address:** 130 W Kingsbridge Rd, Ste 3H, Bronx, NY 10468; **Phone:** 718-584-9000 x6753; **Board Cert:** Internal Medicine 1973; Gastroenterology 1975; **Med School:** Yale Univ 1970; **Resid:** Internal Medicine, Mt Sinai Med Ctr 1973; **Fellow:** Gastroenterology, Mt Sinai Med Ctr 1975; **Fac Appt:** Prof Med, Mount Sinai Sch Med

Kotler, Donald P MD [Ge] - **Spec Exp:** Esophageal Disorders; Nutrition & AIDS; Hepatitis; **Hospital:** St. Luke's - Roosevelt Hosp Ctr - St Luke's Hosp (page 56); **Address:** 1111 Amsterdam Ave, SR 12, New York, NY 10025; **Phone:** 212-523-3670; **Board Cert:** Internal Medicine 1976; Gastroenterology 1979; **Med School:** Albert Einstein Coll Med 1973; **Resid:** Internal Medicine, Jacobi Med Ctr 1976; **Fellow:** Gastroenterology, Hosp Univ Penn - UPHS 1978; **Fac Appt:** Prof Med, Columbia P&S

Kowalski, Thomas E MD [Ge] - **Spec Exp:** Pancreatic Disease; Biliary Disease; Pancreatic/Biliary Endoscopy (ERCP); Endoscopic Ultrasound; **Hospital:** Thomas Jefferson Univ Hosp; **Address:** Jefferson Div Gastroenterology, 132 S 10th St, Main Bldg - Ste 480, Philadelphia, PA 19107; **Phone:** 215-955-8900; **Board Cert:** Internal Medicine 2003; Gastroenterology 2003; **Med School:** SUNY Buffalo 1988; **Resid:** Internal Medicine, Johns Hopkins Hosp 1991; **Fellow:** Gastroenterology, Hosp Univ Penn 1993; Advanced Endoscopy, Hosp Univ Penn 1994; **Fac Appt:** Assoc Prof Med, Thomas Jefferson Univ

Kurtz, Robert C MD [Ge] - **Spec Exp:** Pancreatic Cancer (Familial); Gastrointestinal Cancer; Endoscopy; Cancer Prevention; **Hospital:** Meml Sloan-Kettering Canc Ctr; **Address:** 1275 York Ave, New York, NY 10065; **Phone:** 212-639-7620; **Board Cert:** Internal Medicine 1971; Gastroenterology 1977; **Med School:** Jefferson Med Coll 1968; **Resid:** Internal Medicine, NY Hosp/Meml Sloan Kettering Cancer Ctr 1971; **Fellow:** Gastroenterology, Meml Sloan Kettering Cancer Ctr 1973; **Fac Appt:** Prof Med, Cornell Univ-Weill Med Coll

Lebwohl, Oscar MD [Ge] - **Spec Exp:** Endoscopy; Inflammatory Bowel Disease/Crohn's; Ulcerative Colitis; Gastrointestinal Cancer; **Hospital:** NY-Presby/Columbia Univ Med Ctr, NY (page 65); **Address:** 161 Fort Washington Ave, rm 420, New York, NY 10032-3713; **Phone:** 212-305-5363; **Board Cert:** Internal Medicine 1975; Gastroenterology 1977; **Med School:** Harvard Med Sch 1972; **Resid:** Internal Medicine, Mt Sinai Med Ctr 1975; **Fellow:** Gastroenterology, Columbia-Presby Med Ctr 1976; Hepatology, Mt Sinai Med Ctr 1977; **Fac Appt:** Prof Med, Columbia P&S

Lewis, Blair MD [Ge] - **Spec Exp:** Endoscopy; Capsule Endoscopy; **Hospital:** Mt Sinai Med Ctr (page 62); **Address:** 1067 5th Ave, New York, NY 10128-0101; **Phone:** 212-369-6600; **Board Cert:** Internal Medicine 1985; Gastroenterology 1987; **Med School:** Albert Einstein Coll Med 1982; **Resid:** Internal Medicine, Montefiore Med Ctr 1985; **Fellow:** Gastroenterology, Mt Sinai Med Ctr 1987; **Fac Appt:** Clin Prof Med, Mount Sinai Sch Med

Lichtenstein, Gary R MD [Ge] - **Spec Exp:** Inflammatory Bowel Disease; Crohn's Disease; Ulcerative Colitis; **Hospital:** Hosp Univ Penn - UPHS (page 69); **Address:** Perelman Ctr for Advanced Medicine, 3400 Civic Center Blvd, South Pavilion, 4th Fl, Philadelphia, PA 19104; **Phone:** 215-349-8222; **Board Cert:** Internal Medicine 1987; Gastroenterology 1989; **Med School:** Mount Sinai Sch Med 1984; **Resid:** Internal Medicine, Duke Univ Med Ctr 1987; **Fellow:** Gastroenterology, Hosp Univ Penn 1990; **Fac Appt:** Prof Med, Univ Pennsylvania

Lightdale, Charles J MD [Ge] - **Spec Exp:** Barrett's Esophagus; Gastrointestinal Cancer; Endoscopic Ultrasound; **Hospital:** NY-Presby/Columbia Univ Med Ctr, NY (page 65); **Address:** Columbia-Presby Med Ctr, Irving Pavilion, 161 Fort Washington Ave, rm 812, New York, NY 10032-3713; **Phone:** 212-305-3423; **Board Cert:** Internal Medicine 1972; Gastroenterology 1973; **Med School:** Columbia P&S 1966; **Resid:** Internal Medicine, Yale-New Haven Hosp 1968; Internal Medicine, NY Hosp-Cornell 1969; **Fellow:** Gastroenterology, NY Hosp-Cornell 1973; Gastroenterology & Nutrition, Meml Sloan-Kettering Cancer Ctr 1973; **Fac Appt:** Prof Med, Columbia P&S

Lipshutz, William H MD [Ge] - **Spec Exp:** Inflammatory Bowel Disease/Crohn's; Colonoscopy; Esophageal Disorders; Gastroesophageal Reflux Disease (GERD); **Hospital:** Pennsylvania Hosp-UPHS (page 69); **Address:** 230 W Washington Square Fl 4, Philadelphia, PA 19106; **Phone:** 215-829-3561; **Board Cert:** Internal Medicine 1972; Gastroenterology 1973; **Med School:** Univ Pennsylvania 1967; **Resid:** Internal Medicine, Pennsylvania Hosp 1972; **Fellow:** Gastroenterology, Univ Penn 1971

Magun, Arthur M MD [Ge] - **Spec Exp:** Hepatitis; Ulcerative Colitis; Endoscopy; Crohn's Disease; **Hospital:** NY-Presby/Columbia Univ Med Ctr, NY (page 65); **Address:** 161 Fort Washington Ave, Herbert Irving Pavillion Fl 3 - rm 338, New York, NY 10032-3713; **Phone:** 212-305-5287; **Board Cert:** Internal Medicine 1980; Gastroenterology 1983; **Med School:** Mount Sinai Sch Med 1977; **Resid:** Internal Medicine, Presby/Columbia Univ Med Ctr 1980; **Fellow:** Gastroenterology, Presby/Columbia Univ Med Ctr 1983; **Fac Appt:** Clin Prof Med, Columbia P&S

Markowitz, David D MD [Ge] - **Spec Exp:** Gastroesophageal Reflux Disease (GERD); Esophageal Disorders; **Hospital:** NY-Presby/Columbia Univ Med Ctr, NY (page 65); **Address:** 161 Ft Washington Ave, Ste 853, New York, NY 10032; **Phone:** 212-305-1024; **Board Cert:** Internal Medicine 1988; Gastroenterology 2011; **Med School:** Columbia P&S 1985; **Resid:** Internal Medicine, Presby/Columbia Univ Med Ctr 1988; **Fellow:** Gastroenterology, Presby/Columbia Univ Med Ctr 1991; **Fac Appt:** Assoc Prof Med, Columbia P&S

Metz, David C MD [Ge] - **Spec Exp:** Peptic Acid Disorders; Neuroendocrine Tumors; Gastroesophageal Reflux Disease (GERD); Gastrointestinal Motility Disorders; **Hospital:** Hosp Univ Penn - UPHS (page 69); **Address:** Perelman Ctr for Advanced Medicine, 3400 Civic Center Blvd, South Pavilion, 4th Fl, Philadelphia, PA 19104; **Phone:** 215-349-8222; **Board Cert:** Internal Medicine 1989; Gastroenterology 2011; **Med School:** South Africa 1982; **Resid:** Internal Medicine, Albert Einstein Med Ctr 1988; **Fellow:** Gastroenterology, Natl Inst Hlth 1991; **Fac Appt:** Prof Med, Univ Pennsylvania

Miskovitz, Paul F MD [Ge] - **Spec Exp:** Endoscopy; Liver Disease; Biliary Disease; **Hospital:** NY-Presby/Weill Cornell Med Ctr, NY (page 65); **Address:** 635 Madison Ave, Fl 17, New York, NY 10022; **Phone:** 212-717-4966; **Board Cert:** Internal Medicine 1978; Gastroenterology 1981; **Med School:** Cornell Univ-Weill Med Coll 1975; **Resid:** Internal Medicine, Presby/Columbia Univ Med Ctr 1978; **Fellow:** Gastroenterology, Presby/Columbia Univ Med Ctr 1980; **Fac Appt:** Clin Prof Med, Cornell Univ-Weill Med Coll

Okolo III, Patrick I MD/PhD [Ge] - **Spec Exp:** Liver Cancer; Pancreatic Cancer; Gastrointestinal Cancer; Clinical Trials; **Hospital:** Johns Hopkins Hosp (page 59); **Address:** John Hopkins, Gastroenterology Dept, 2360 W Joppa Rd, Ste 205, Lutherville, MD 21093; **Phone:** 410-933-7495; **Board Cert:** Internal Medicine 2004; Gastroenterology 2008; **Med School:** Nigeria 1988; **Resid:** Internal Medicine, IU Hlth Univ Hosp 1994; **Fellow:** Gastroenterology, John Hopkins Hosp 1997; **Fac Appt:** Assoc Prof Med, Johns Hopkins Univ

Pasricha, P. Jay MD [Ge] - **Spec Exp:** Swallowing Disorders-Botox Therapy; Gastrointestinal Motility Disorders; Pancreatic Disease; Gastroparesis; **Hospital:** Stanford Univ Hosp & Clins; **Address:** Stanford Univ Hosp & Clins, Ctr Neurogastroenterology, 4940 Eastern Ave, Ste A-505, Baltimore, MD 21224-5309; **Phone:** 410-550-1793; **Board Cert:** Internal Medicine 1988; Gastroenterology 2006; **Med School:** India 1983; **Resid:** Internal Medicine, DC Genl Hosp 1988; **Fellow:** Pulmonary Disease, New England Med Ctr 1990; Gastroenterology, Johns Hopkins Hosp 1992; **Fac Appt:** Prof Med, Stanford Univ

Peikin, Steven R MD [Ge] - **Spec Exp:** Endoscopy; Endoscopic Ultrasound; Colon Cancer Screening; Nutrition; **Hospital:** Cooper Univ Hosp; **Address:** Cooper Digestive Health Inst, 501 Fellowship Rd, Ste 101, Mt Laurel, NJ 08054; **Phone:** 856-642-2133; **Board Cert:** Internal Medicine 1977; Gastroenterology 1979; **Med School:** Jefferson Med Coll 1974; **Resid:** Internal Medicine, UCSF Med Ctr 1977; **Fellow:** Gastroenterology, Mass Genl Hosp 1980; **Fac Appt:** Prof Med, UMDNJ-RW Johnson Med Sch

Pezzone, Michael A MD/PhD [Ge] - **Spec Exp:** Irritable Bowel Syndrome; Inflammatory Bowel Disease; Pain-Pelvic; **Hospital:** Washington Hosp, The, UPMC Presby, Pittsburgh; **Address:** Manifold Professional Bldg #3, 86 Wellness Way, Washington, PA 15301; **Phone:** 724-503-4637; **Board Cert:** Internal Medicine 2007; Gastroenterology 2010; **Med School:** Univ Pittsburgh 1994; **Resid:** Internal Medicine, Univ Pittsburgh Med Ctr 1997; **Fellow:** Gastroenterology, Univ Pittsburgh Med Ctr 2000; **Fac Appt:** Assoc Prof Med, Univ Pittsburgh

Pochapin, Mark B MD [Ge] - **Spec Exp:** Pancreatic Cancer; Endoscopic Ultrasound; Colon & Rectal Cancer Detection; **Hospital:** NYU Langone Med Ctr (page 68); **Address:** NYU Women's Ctr, 207 E 84th St Fl 2, New York, NY 10028; **Phone:** 646-501-6760; **Board Cert:** Gastroenterology 2004; **Med School:** Cornell Univ-Weill Med Coll 1988; **Resid:** Internal Medicine, NY Hosp-Cornell Med Ctr 1991; **Fellow:** Gastroenterology, Montefiore Med Ctr 1993; **Fac Appt:** Prof Med, Cornell Univ-Weill Med Coll

Ravich, William J MD [Ge] - **Spec Exp:** Achalasia; Barrett's Esophagus; Esophageal Cancer; Swallowing Disorders; **Hospital:** Johns Hopkins Hosp (page 59), Greater Baltimore Med Ctr; **Address:** 10751 Falls Rd, Ste 401, Lutherville, MD 21093; **Phone:** 410-616-2840; **Board Cert:** Internal Medicine 1978; Gastroenterology 1981; **Med School:** Ros Franklin Univ/Chicago Med Sch 1975; **Resid:** Internal Medicine, Montefiore Hosp 1978; **Fellow:** Gastroenterology, Johns Hopkins Hosp 1981; **Fac Appt:** Assoc Prof Med, Johns Hopkins Univ

Reddy, K Rajender MD [Ge] - **Spec Exp:** Liver Disease; Transplant Medicine-Liver; Hepatitis; **Hospital:** Hosp Univ Penn - UPHS (page 69); **Address:** Perelman Ctr for Advanced Medicine, 3400 Civic Center Blvd, South Pavilion, 4th Fl, Philadelphia, PA 19104; **Phone:** 215-349-8222; **Board Cert:** Internal Medicine 1980; Gastroenterology 1983; Transplant Hepatology 2006; **Med School:** India 1972; **Resid:** Internal Medicine, NY Med Coll Hosps 1980; Gastroenterology, Johnson City Hosp 1982; **Fellow:** Hepatology, Univ Miami 1983; **Fac Appt:** Prof Med, Univ Pennsylvania

Reynolds, James C MD [Ge] - **Spec Exp:** Gastroesophageal Reflux Disease (GERD); Gastrointestinal Motility Disorders; Barrett's Esophagus; **Hospital:** Hahnemann Univ Hosp; **Address:** Drexel Gastroenterology Assocs, 219 N Broad St Fl 5, Philadelphia, PA 19107; **Phone:** 215-762-6220; **Board Cert:** Internal Medicine 1980; Gastroenterology 1985; **Med School:** Univ Fla Coll Med 1977; **Resid:** Internal Medicine, New York Hosp 1980; **Fellow:** Gastroenterology, Hosp Univ Penn 1983; **Fac Appt:** Prof Med, Drexel Univ Coll Med

Sass, David MD [Ge] - **Spec Exp:** Liver Disease; Transplant Medicine-Liver; **Hospital:** Thomas Jefferson Univ Hosp; **Address:** Jefferson U Physicians, Gastroenterology, 132 S 10 St, Main Bldg, Ste 480, Philadelphia, PA 19107; **Phone:** 215-955-8900; **Board Cert:** Transplant Hepatology 2006; Gastroenterology 2003; Internal Medicine 2009; **Med School:** South Africa 1992; **Resid:** Internal Medicine, Albert Einstein Med Ctr 1998; **Fellow:** Gastroenterology, Univ Pittsburgh Med Ctr 2003; Transplant Hepatology, Univ Pittsburgh Med Ctr 2004; **Fac Appt:** Assoc Prof Med, South Africa

Scherl, Ellen MD [Ge] - **Spec Exp:** Inflammatory Bowel Disease; Crohn's Disease; Ulcerative Colitis; **Hospital:** NY-Presby/Weill Cornell Med Ctr, NY (page 65); **Address:** 1315 York Ave, Mezzanine Level, New York, NY 10021; **Phone:** 212-746-5077; **Board Cert:** Internal Medicine 1983; **Med School:** NY Med Coll 1977; **Resid:** Internal Medicine, Beth Israel Med Ctr 1981; **Fellow:** Gastroenterology, Mt Sinai Med Ctr 1983; **Fac Appt:** Prof Med, Cornell Univ-Weill Med Coll

Schiano, Thomas D MD [Ge] - **Spec Exp:** Liver Disease; Transplant Medicine-Liver; Transplant Medicine-Bowel; Hepatitis; **Hospital:** Mt Sinai Med Ctr (page 62); **Address:** 5 E 98th St Fl 12, Box 1104, MS 10029, New York, NY 10029; **Phone:** 212-241-8035; **Board Cert:** Transplant Hepatology 2006; Gastroenterology 2005; **Med School:** Mexico 1987; **Resid:** Internal Medicine, Maimonides Med Ctr 1992; Gastroenterology, Temple Univ 1995; **Fellow:** Nutrition, Meml Sloan-Kettering Cancer Ctr 1993; Hepatology, Mt Sinai Med Ctr 1996; **Fac Appt:** Prof Med, Mount Sinai Sch Med

Shike, Moshe MD [Ge] - **Spec Exp:** Gastrointestinal Cancer; Nutrition & Cancer Prevention; Endoscopy; **Hospital:** Meml Sloan-Kettering Canc Ctr, NY-Presby/Weill Cornell Med Ctr, NY (page 65); **Address:** 1275 York Ave, New York, NY 10065; **Phone:** 212-639-7230; **Board Cert:** Internal Medicine 1977; Gastroenterology 1981; **Med School:** Israel 1975; **Resid:** Internal Medicine, Mt Auburn Hosp 1977; **Fellow:** Gastroenterology, Toronto Genl Hosp 1981; **Fac Appt:** Prof Med, Cornell Univ-Weill Med Coll

Slivka, Adam MD/PhD [Ge] - **Spec Exp:** Pancreatic & Biliary Disease; Pancreatic Cancer; Pancreatic/Biliary Endoscopy (ERCP); **Hospital:** UPMC Presby, Pittsburgh; **Address:** Digestive Disorders Center, 200 Lothrop St, 3rd Fl-PUH D-Wing, Pittsburgh, PA 15213; **Phone:** 412-647-8666; **Board Cert:** Gastroenterology 2005; **Med School:** Mount Sinai Sch Med 1988; **Resid:** Internal Medicine, Brigham & Womens Hosp 1991; **Fellow:** Gastroenterology, Brigham & Womens Hosp 1994; **Fac Appt:** Asst Prof Med, Univ Pittsburgh

Tobias, Hillel MD [Ge] - **Spec Exp:** Liver Disease; Hepatitis B & C; Liver & Biliary Disease; **Hospital:** NYU Langone Med Ctr (page 68); **Address:** 232 E 30th St, New York, NY 10016-8202; **Phone:** 212-889-5544; **Board Cert:** Internal Medicine 1967; Gastroenterology 1979; Transplant Hepatology 2006; **Med School:** Washington Univ, St Louis 1960; **Resid:** Internal Medicine, Bellevue Hosp Ctr 1963; Hepatology, Royal Free Hosp 1965; **Fellow:** Hepatology, Mt Sinai Hosp 1967; **Fac Appt:** Prof Med, NYU Sch Med

Waye, Jerome D MD [Ge] - **Spec Exp:** Endoscopy; Colon Cancer; Colonoscopy; **Hospital:** Mt Sinai Med Ctr (page 62), Lenox Hill Hosp (page 66); **Address:** 650 Park Ave, New York, NY 10065; **Phone:** 212-439-7779; **Board Cert:** Internal Medicine 1965; Gastroenterology 1970; **Med School:** Boston Univ 1958; **Resid:** Internal Medicine, Mt Sinai Hosp 1961; **Fellow:** Gastroenterology, Mt Sinai Hosp 1962; **Fac Appt:** Clin Prof Med, Mount Sinai Sch Med

Weinberg, David S MD [Ge] - **Spec Exp:** Colonoscopy; Cancer Risk Assessment; Cancer Prevention; Endoscopy; **Hospital:** Fox Chase Cancer Ctr (page 57); **Address:** Fox Chase Cancer Ctr, Dept Medicine, 333 Cottman Ave, Ste P3179, Philadelphia, PA 19111; **Phone:** 215-214-1424; **Board Cert:** Gastroenterology 2006; **Med School:** Cornell Univ-Weill Med Coll 1989; **Resid:** Internal Medicine, Beth Israel Hosp 1992; **Fellow:** Gastroenterology, Hosp Univ Penn 1995; Epidemiology, Hosp Univ Penn 1995; **Fac Appt:** Prof Med, Temple Univ

Southeast

Abreu, Maria T MD [Ge] - **Spec Exp:** Inflammatory Bowel Disease; Ulcerative Colitis; Crohn's Disease; **Hospital:** Univ of Miami Hosp; **Address:** Univ Miami Hosp, Gastroenterology Dept, 1475 NW 12th Ave, Miami, FL 33136; **Phone:** 305-243-8644; **Board Cert:** Gastroenterology 2005; **Med School:** Univ Miami Sch Med 1990; **Resid:** Internal Medicine, Brigham & Womens Hosp 1992; **Fellow:** Gastroenterology, UCLA Med Ctr 1995; **Fac Appt:** Prof Med, Univ Miami Sch Med

Baillie, John MD [Ge] - **Spec Exp:** Pancreatic/Biliary Endoscopy (ERCP); **Hospital:** Carteret Genl Hosp; **Address:** 300 Penny Ln, Moorehead, NC 28557; **Phone:** 252-648-8712; **Med School:** Scotland, UK 1977; **Resid:** Internal Medicine, Victoria Infirmary 1981; **Fellow:** Gastroenterology, Univ of Minnesota Med Ctr 1984; Gastroenterology, Middlesex Hospital 1988; **Fac Appt:** Prof Med, Wake Forest Univ

Barkin, Jamie S MD [Ge] - **Spec Exp:** Pancreatic & Biliary Disease; Gastrointestinal Cancer; Endoscopy; **Hospital:** Mount Sinai Med Ctr - Miami; **Address:** Mount Sinai, Gastroenterology Dept, 4300 Alton Rd Gumenick Bldg - Ste 2522, Miami Beach, FL 33140; **Phone:** 305-674-2240; **Board Cert:** Internal Medicine 1973; Gastroenterology 1975; **Med School:** Univ Miami Sch Med 1970; **Resid:** Internal Medicine, Univ Miami Hosp 1973; **Fellow:** Gastroenterology, Univ Miami Hosp 1975; **Fac Appt:** Prof Med, Univ Miami Sch Med

Berg, Carl L MD [Ge] - **Spec Exp:** Transplant Medicine-Liver; Liver Disease; **Hospital:** Duke Univ Hosp; **Address:** DUMC, Box 3923, Durham, NC 27710; **Phone:** 919-684-6437; **Board Cert:** Internal Medicine 1989; Gastroenterology 2012; Transplant Hepatology 2008; **Med School:** Washington Univ, St Louis 1986; **Resid:** Internal Medicine, Barnes-Jewish Hosp 1989; **Fellow:** Gastroenterology, Brigham & Women's Hosp 1992; **Fac Appt:** Prof Med, Duke Univ

Bloomer, Joseph R MD [Ge] - **Spec Exp:** Porphyria; Liver Disease; Transplant Medicine-Liver; Hepatitis B; **Hospital:** UAB Hosp, UAB Highlands Hosp; **Address:** UAB Liver Center, 1918 University Blvd, MCLM 284, Birmingham, AL 35294-0005; **Phone:** 205-975-5676; **Board Cert:** Internal Medicine 1972; **Med School:** Case West Res Univ 1966; **Resid:** Internal Medicine, UCSF Med Ctr 1968; **Fellow:** Hepatology, Yale Univ 1972; **Fac Appt:** Prof Med, UAB Sch Med

Branch, Malcolm S MD [Ge] - **Spec Exp:** Endoscopy; Pancreatic/Biliary Endoscopy (ERCP); Pancreatic & Biliary Disease; Colonoscopy; **Hospital:** Duke Univ Hosp; **Address:** DUMC-Div Gastroenterology, Box 3662, Durham, NC 27710; **Phone:** 919-684-3140; **Board Cert:** Internal Medicine 1987; Gastroenterology 2012; **Med School:** Med Coll GA 1984; **Resid:** Internal Medicine, Univ Texas Hlth Science Ctr 1987; **Fellow:** Gastroenterology, Duke Univ Med Ctr 1991; **Fac Appt:** Prof Med, Duke Univ

Brazer, Scott R MD [Ge] - **Spec Exp:** Gastroesophageal Reflux Disease (GERD); Colon Cancer Screening; **Hospital:** Durham Regional Hosp; **Address:** 249 E NC 54, Ste 200, Durham, NC 27713; **Phone:** 919-806-8322; **Board Cert:** Internal Medicine 1984; Gastroenterology 1987; **Med School:** Case West Res Univ 1981; **Resid:** Internal Medicine, Duke Univ Med Ctr 1984; **Fellow:** Gastroenterology, Duke Univ Med Ctr 1987

Castell, Donald O MD [Ge] - **Spec Exp:** Esophageal Disorders; Swallowing Disorders; **Hospital:** MUSC Med Ctr; **Address:** MUSC Digestive Disease Ctr, 25 Courtenay Drive, ART-7100A, MC CMS290, Charleston, SC 29425; **Phone:** 843-876-4265; **Board Cert:** Internal Medicine 1977; Gastroenterology 1970; **Med School:** Geo Wash Univ 1960; **Resid:** Internal Medicine, US Naval Hosp 1965; **Fellow:** Gastroenterology, Tufts Univ 1969; **Fac Appt:** Prof Med, Univ SC Sch Med

DeVault, Kenneth MD [Ge] - **Spec Exp:** Gastroesophageal Reflux Disease (GERD); Esophageal Disorders; **Hospital:** Mayo - Jacksonville; **Address:** Mayo Clin, Gastroenterology Dept, 4500 San Pablo Rd S Davis Bldg Fl 6, Jacksonville, FL 32224; **Phone:** 904-953-2272; **Board Cert:** Internal Medicine 1989; Gastroenterology 2003; **Med School:** Wake Forest Univ 1986; **Resid:** Internal Medicine, Vanderbilt Univ Med Ctr 1989; **Fellow:** Gastroenterology, Thomas Jefferson Univ Med Ctr 1992; **Fac Appt:** Prof Med, Mayo Med Sch

Diehl, Anna Mae E MD [Ge] - **Spec Exp:** Liver Disease; **Hospital:** Duke Univ Hosp; **Address:** DUMC South, Div Gastroenterology, 200 Trent Drive, Ste 03107, Box 3913, Durham, NC 27710; **Phone:** 919-684-4173; **Board Cert:** Internal Medicine 1981; Gastroenterology 1983; **Med School:** Georgetown Univ 1978; **Resid:** Internal Medicine, Johns Hopkins Hosp 1981; **Fellow:** Gastroenterology, Johns Hopkins Hosp 1983; **Fac Appt:** Prof Med, Duke Univ

Drossman, Douglas A MD [Ge] - **Spec Exp:** Gastrointestinal Motility Disorders; Pain-Abdominal/Functional; Gastrointestinal Functional Disorders; **Hospital:** NC Memorial Hosp - UNC; **Address:** Drossman Gastroenterology, 55 Vilcom Center Drive, Ste 110, Chapel Hill, NC 27514; **Phone:** 919-929-7790; **Board Cert:** Internal Medicine 1973; Gastroenterology 1979; **Med School:** Albert Einstein Coll Med 1970; **Resid:** Internal Medicine, NC Meml Hosp 1972; Internal Medicine, Bellevue Hosp Ctr-NYU 1973; **Fellow:** Psychiatry, Univ Rochester 1976; Gastroenterology, NC Meml Hosp-UNC 1978; **Fac Appt:** Prof Med, Univ NC Sch Med

Elliott, Norman L MD [Ge] - **Spec Exp:** Enteroscopy-Small Bowel; Endoscopy; **Hospital:** Emory Univ Hosp Midtown, Piedmont Hosp; **Address:** Atlanta Gastroenterology Assocs, 550 Peachtree St NE, Ste 1600, Atlanta, GA 30308; **Phone:** 404-881-1094; **Board Cert:** Internal Medicine 1982; Gastroenterology 1985; **Med School:** Yale Univ 1979; **Resid:** Internal Medicine, Emory Univ Hosp 1982; **Fellow:** Gastroenterology, UAB Hosp 1985; **Fac Appt:** Asst Clin Prof Med, Emory Univ

Estores Jr, David S MD [Ge] - **Spec Exp:** Barrett's Esophagus; Swallowing Disorders; Esophageal Cancer; **Hospital:** UF Hlth Shands Hosp; **Address:** UFHlth, Gastroenterology Dept, 2000 SW Archer Drive Fl 3, Gainesville, FL 32608; **Phone:** 352-265-0139; **Board Cert:** Internal Medicine 1989; Gastroenterology 2011; **Med School:** Philippines 1985; **Resid:** Internal Medicine, St Lukes Hosp 1989; **Fellow:** Gastroenterology, UPMC-Presby 1992; **Fac Appt:** Asst Prof Med, Univ S Fla Coll Med

Forsmark, Christopher MD [Ge] - **Spec Exp:** Pancreatic/Biliary Endoscopy (ERCP); Celiac Disease; Pancreatic Disease; Endoscopy; **Hospital:** UF Hlth Shands Hosp; **Address:** UF Hlth, Gastroenterology Dept, 1600 SW Archer Rd Fl 3, Gainesville, FL 32610; **Phone:** 352-273-9400; **Board Cert:** Internal Medicine 1986; Gastroenterology 2006; **Med School:** Johns Hopkins Univ 1983; **Resid:** Internal Medicine, UCSF Med Ctr 1987; **Fellow:** Gastroenterology, USCF Med Ctr 1990; **Fac Appt:** Prof Med, Univ Fla Coll Med

Fried, Michael W MD [Ge] - **Spec Exp:** Transplant Medicine-Liver; Liver Disease; Hepatitis; **Hospital:** NC Memorial Hosp - UNC; **Address:** 101 Manning Drive, Chapel Hill, NC 27599; **Phone:** 919-966-2516; **Board Cert:** Internal Medicine 1987; Gastroenterology 1989; **Med School:** Israel 1984; **Resid:** Internal Medicine, SUNY Upstate Med Ctr 1987; **Fellow:** Gastroenterology, SUNY Upstate Med Ctr 1989; Hepatology, NIH 1993; **Fac Appt:** Prof Med, Univ NC Sch Med

Hawes, Robert H MD [Ge] - **Spec Exp:** Endoscopic Ultrasound; Pancreatic/Biliary Endoscopy (ERCP); Pancreatic Disease; **Hospital:** Florida Hosp - Orlando; **Address:** FL Hosp, Gastroenterology Dept, 601 E Rollins St, Orlando, FL 32803; **Phone:** 407-303-2570; **Board Cert:** Internal Medicine 1985; Gastroenterology 1987; **Med School:** Indiana Univ 1980; **Resid:** Internal Medicine, IU Hlth Hosp 1984; **Fellow:** Gastroenterology, IU Hlth Hosp 1985; **Fac Appt:** Prof Med, Med Univ SC

Hoffman, Brenda J MD [Ge] - **Spec Exp:** Endoscopic Ultrasound; Gastrointestinal Cancer; Colon & Rectal Cancer-Familial Polyposis; Endoscopic Therapies; **Hospital:** MUSC Med Ctr, R H Johnson VA Med Ctr - Charleston; **Address:** 25 Courteney Street St ART Bldg Fl 7, ART7100A, Ste 7095, MSC290, Charleston, SC 29425; **Phone:** 843-876-4265; **Board Cert:** Internal Medicine 1986; Gastroenterology 1989; **Med School:** Univ KY Coll Med 1983; **Resid:** Internal Medicine, MUSC Med Ctr 1987; **Fellow:** Gastroenterology, Med Univ SC 1989; **Fac Appt:** Prof Med, Med Univ SC

Isaacs, Kim L MD/PhD [Ge] - **Spec Exp:** Inflammatory Bowel Disease; Crohn's Disease; Ulcerative Colitis; **Hospital:** NC Memorial Hosp - UNC; **Address:** 101 Manning Dr, 1st FL, GI Clinic, Chapel Hill, NC 27599-7080; **Phone:** 919-966-2511; **Board Cert:** Internal Medicine 1987; Gastroenterology 2011; **Med School:** SUNY Stony Brook 1984; **Resid:** Internal Medicine, Univ NC Hosps 1987; **Fellow:** Gastroenterology, Univ NC Hosps 1991; **Fac Appt:** Prof Med, Univ NC Sch Med

Koch, Kenneth L MD [Ge] - **Spec Exp:** Gastrointestinal Motility Disorders; Gastroparesis; Esophageal Disorders; **Hospital:** Wake Forest Baptist Med Ctr; **Address:** Medical Ctr Blvd, Winston-Salem, NC 27157; **Phone:** 336-713-7777; **Board Cert:** Internal Medicine 1978; Gastroenterology 1983; **Med School:** Univ Iowa Coll Med 1975; **Resid:** Internal Medicine, Penn State Hershey Med Ctr 1978; **Fellow:** Gastroenterology, Univ Florida Affil Hosp 1980; **Fac Appt:** Prof Med, Univ NC Sch Med

Lambiase, Louis R MD [Ge] - **Spec Exp:** Pancreatic Disease; Endoscopic Ultrasound; Pain-Abdominal/Functional; Liver Disease; **Hospital:** Erlanger Med Ctr; **Address:** 979 E 3rd St, Ste C-825, Chattanooga, TN 37403; **Phone:** 423-778-4830; **Board Cert:** Internal Medicine 2002; Gastroenterology 2003; **Med School:** Univ Miami Sch Med 1987; **Resid:** Internal Medicine, Presbyterian/VA Hosps 1990; **Fellow:** Gastroenterology, Univ Fla 1993; **Fac Appt:** Prof Med, Univ Tenn Coll Med

Liddle, Rodger A MD [Ge] - **Spec Exp:** Pancreatic Disease; Hormone Secreting Tumors; **Hospital:** Duke Univ Hosp, Durham VA Med Ctr; **Address:** Duke Box 3913, 303 Sands Bldg, Durham, NC 27710; **Phone:** 919-681-6380; **Board Cert:** Internal Medicine 1981; Gastroenterology 1983; **Med School:** Vanderbilt Univ 1978; **Resid:** Internal Medicine, UCSF Med Ctr 1981; **Fellow:** Gastroenterology, UCSF Med Ctr 1984; **Fac Appt:** Prof Med, Duke Univ

Lind, Christopher D MD [Ge] - **Spec Exp:** Gastroesophageal Reflux Disease (GERD); Swallowing Disorders; Biliary Disease; Gastrointestinal Motility Disorders; **Hospital:** Vanderbilt Univ Med Ctr; **Address:** Vanderbilt Digestive Disease Center, 1301 Medical Center Drive, The Vanderbilt Clinic, Ste 1660, Nashville, TN 37232-5280; **Phone:** 615-322-0128; **Board Cert:** Internal Medicine 1984; Gastroenterology 1987; **Med School:** Vanderbilt Univ 1981; **Resid:** Internal Medicine, Univ Virginia Hosps 1984; **Fellow:** Gastroenterology, Shands/Univ Florida 1986; Gastroenterology, Univ Virginia 1988; **Fac Appt:** Prof Med, Vanderbilt Univ

Martin, Paul MD [Ge] - **Spec Exp:** Liver Disease; Hepatitis; Transplant Medicine-Liver; **Hospital:** Univ of Miami Hosp; **Address:** Univ Miami Hosp, Gastroenterology Dept, 1321 NW 14th St, Ste 510, Miami, FL 33125; **Phone:** 305-243-5787; **Board Cert:** Internal Medicine 1984; Gastroenterology 2011; Transplant Hepatology 2006; **Med School:** Ireland 1978; **Resid:** Internal Medicine, St Vincents Hosp 1982; Internal Medicine, Univ Alberta 1984; **Fellow:** Gastroenterology, Queen Univ 1986; Hepatology, Natl Inst Hlth 1989; **Fac Appt:** Prof Med, Univ Miami Sch Med

Mertz, Howard R MD [Ge] - **Spec Exp:** Endoscopic Ultrasound; Irritable Bowel Syndrome; Inflammatory Bowel Disease; **Hospital:** Saint Thomas West Hosp - Nashville; **Address:** Nashville Gastrointestinal Specialists, 4230 Harding Rd, Ste 309W, Nashville, TN 37205; **Phone:** 615-383-0165; **Board Cert:** Internal Medicine 1989; Gastroenterology 2012; **Med School:** Baylor Coll Med 1986; **Resid:** Internal Medicine, Johns Hopkins Hosp 1989; **Fellow:** Gastroenterology, UCLA Med Ctr 1991; **Fac Appt:** Asst Clin Prof Med, Vanderbilt Univ

Plevy, Scott MD [Ge] - **Spec Exp:** Inflammatory Bowel Disease; Crohn's Disease; Ulcerative Colitis; **Hospital:** NC Memorial Hosp - UNC; **Address:** 101 Manning Dr, 1st FL, GI Clinic, Chapel Hill, NC 27599; **Phone:** 919-966-2511; **Board Cert:** Gastroenterology 2007; **Med School:** Columbia P&S 1988; **Resid:** Internal Medicine, Brigham-Womens Hosp 1991; **Fellow:** Gastroenterology, UCLA Med Ctr 1992; Inflammatory Bowel Disease, Cedars Sinai Med Ctr 1994; **Fac Appt:** Assoc Prof Med, Univ NC Sch Med

Porayko, Michael K MD [Ge] - **Spec Exp:** Liver Disease; Transplant Medicine-Liver; Liver Cancer; Hepatitis-Chronic; **Hospital:** Vanderbilt Univ Med Ctr; **Address:** Digestive Disease Center, 1301 Medical Center Drive, Ste 1660, Nashville, TN 37232; **Phone:** 615-322-0128; **Board Cert:** Internal Medicine 1984; Gastroenterology 1987; Transplant Hepatology 2006; **Med School:** Univ IL Coll Med 1981; **Resid:** Internal Medicine, MSU Affil Hosps 1984; **Fellow:** Gastroenterology, Lahey Clinic/New England Deaconess Hosp 1987; Hepatology, Mayo Clinic 1988; **Fac Appt:** Prof Med, Vanderbilt Univ

Raiford, David S MD [Ge] - **Spec Exp:** Autoimmune Liver Disease; Steatohepatitis; Transplant Medicine-Liver; **Hospital:** Vanderbilt Univ Med Ctr; **Address:** Vanderbilt Digestive Disease Center, 1301 Medical Ctr Drive, Ste 1660, Nashville, TN 37232-5280; **Phone:** 615-322-0128; **Board Cert:** Internal Medicine 1989; Gastroenterology 2011; Transplant Hepatology 2006; **Med School:** Johns Hopkins Univ 1985; **Resid:** Internal Medicine, Johns Hopkins Hosp 1989; **Fellow:** Gastroenterology, Johns Hopkins Hosp 1991; **Fac Appt:** Prof Med, Vanderbilt Univ

Rao, Satish S.C. MD/PhD [Ge] - **Spec Exp:** Gastrointestinal Motility Disorders; Incontinence-Fecal; Chest Pain-Non Cardiac; Gastroesophageal Reflux Disease (GERD); **Hospital:** Georgia Regents Med Ctr-Augusta; **Address:** GA Regents, Gastroenterology Dept, 1120 15th St, rm BBR2538, Augusta, GA 30912; **Phone:** 706-721-9522; **Board Cert:** Gastroenterology 2008; **Med School:** India 1978; **Resid:** Internal Medicine, Sunderland Hosps 1982; Internal Medicine, York Dist Hosp 1984; **Fellow:** Royal Hallamshire Hosp 1986; Gastroenterology, Royal Liverpool Hosp 1988; **Fac Appt:** Prof Med, Med Coll GA

Reuben, Adrian MD [Ge] - **Spec Exp:** Liver Disease; Hepatitis C; Liver Failure; **Hospital:** MUSC Med Ctr; **Address:** MUSC GI & Hepatology, 25 Courtenay Drive, ART 7100A, MC MSC 290, Charleston, SC 29403; **Phone:** 843-792-6982; **Med School:** England, UK 1969; **Resid:** Internal Medicine, National Heart 1972; Gastroenterology, Hammersmith Hosps; **Fellow:** Hepatology, Guy's Hosp; **Fac Appt:** Prof Med, Med Univ SC

Sartor, Ryan B MD [Ge] - **Spec Exp:** Inflammatory Bowel Disease; **Hospital:** NC Memorial Hosp - UNC; **Address:** 101 Manning Dr, 1st FL, GI Clinic, Chapel Hill, NC 27599; **Phone:** 919-966-2511; **Board Cert:** Internal Medicine 1978; Gastroenterology 1981; **Med School:** Baylor Coll Med 1974; **Resid:** Internal Medicine, Baylor Affil Hosp 1977; **Fellow:** Gastroenterology, Univ NC Hosps 1981; **Fac Appt:** Prof Med, Univ NC Sch Med

Scudera, Peter L MD [Ge] - **Spec Exp:** Colon & Rectal Cancer Detection; Pancreatic/Biliary Endoscopy (ERCP); Hepatitis-Chronic; **Hospital:** Inova Fair Oaks Hosp, Inova Fairfax Hosp; **Address:** Gastroenterology Assocs of Northern VA, 3700 Joseph Siewick Drive, Ste 308, Fairfax, VA 22033; **Phone:** 703-698-8960; **Board Cert:** Internal Medicine 1987; Gastroenterology 1989; **Med School:** Cornell Univ-Weill Med Coll 1984; **Resid:** Internal Medicine, New York Hosp 1987; **Fellow:** Gastroenterology, New York Hosp-Cornell 1989; **Fac Appt:** Asst Clin Prof Med, Geo Wash Univ

Seidner, Douglas L MD [Ge] - **Spec Exp:** Nutrition; Malabsorption Syndrome; Nutrition in Bowel Disorders; Endoscopy; **Hospital:** Vanderbilt Univ Med Ctr; **Address:** Vanderbilt Ctr Human Nutrition, 1211 21st Ave S, Med Arts Bldg - Ste 514, Nashville, TN 37232; **Phone:** 615-936-1288; **Board Cert:** Internal Medicine 1986; Gastroenterology 2000; **Med School:** SUNY Upstate Med Univ 1983; **Resid:** Internal Medicine, New England Deaconess Hosp 1986; **Fellow:** Nutrition & Metabolism, New England Deaconess Hosp 1987; Gastroenterology, George Washington Univ 1989; **Fac Appt:** Assoc Prof Med, Vanderbilt Univ

Shiffman, Mitchell L MD [Ge] - **Spec Exp:** Transplant Medicine-Liver; Hepatitis C; Liver Disease; Liver Cancer; **Hospital:** Bon Secours St Mary's Hosp, Bon Secours Mary Immaculate Hosp; **Address:** 5855 Bremo Rd, Ste 509, Richmond, VA 23226; **Phone:** 804-977-8920; **Board Cert:** Internal Medicine 1986; Gastroenterology 1989; **Med School:** SUNY Upstate Med Univ 1983; **Resid:** Internal Medicine, Med Coll Va Hosp 1986; **Fellow:** Gastroenterology, Med Coll Va Hosp 1988; **Fac Appt:** Clin Prof Med, Eastern VA Med Sch

Smoot, Duane T MD [Ge] - **Spec Exp:** Colon & Rectal Cancer Detection; Gastrointestinal Cancer; Peptic Acid Disorders; **Hospital:** Nashville Genl Hosp; **Address:** Meharry Med Grp, Dept Internal Med, 1005 TB Todd Jr Blvd, Nashville, TN 37208; **Phone:** 615-327-6277; **Board Cert:** Internal Medicine 1987; Gastroenterology 2003; **Med School:** Howard Univ 1983; **Resid:** Internal Medicine, Univ MD Hosp 1986; **Fellow:** Gastroenterology, Univ MD Hosp 1989; **Fac Appt:** Prof Med, Meharry Med Coll

Vaezi, Michael F MD/PhD [Ge] - **Spec Exp:** Gastroesophageal Reflux Disease (GERD); Esophageal Disorders; Achalasia; **Hospital:** Vanderbilt Univ Med Ctr; **Address:** Vanderbilt Digestive Disease Center, 1301 Medical Ctr Drive, Ste 1660, Nashville, TN 37232; **Phone:** 615-322-0128; **Board Cert:** Internal Medicine 2007; Gastroenterology 2009; **Med School:** UAB Sch Med 1992; **Resid:** Internal Medicine, Univ AL-Birmingham Med Ctr 1995; **Fellow:** Gastroenterology, Cleveland Clin 1996; **Fac Appt:** Prof Med, Vanderbilt Univ

Wilcox, C. Mel MD [Ge] - **Spec Exp:** Pancreatic & Biliary Disease; Zollinger-Ellison Syndrome; Endoscopic Therapies; Pancreatic/Biliary Endoscopy (ERCP); **Hospital:** UAB Hosp; **Address:** UAB-Div Gastroenterology, 1808 7th Ave S, Boshell Bldg, rm 380, Birmingham, AL 35294-0007; **Phone:** 205-996-4744; **Board Cert:** Internal Medicine 1986; Gastroenterology 2007; **Med School:** Med Coll GA 1983; **Resid:** Internal Medicine, Univ Alabama Affil Hosp 1986; **Fellow:** Gastroenterology, UCSF Med Ctr 1990; **Fac Appt:** Prof Med, UAB Sch Med

Yanda, Randy J MD [Ge] - **Spec Exp:** Interventional Endoscopy; Pancreatic/Biliary Endoscopy (ERCP); Colon Cancer Screening; **Hospital:** Piedmont Hosp; **Address:** Digestive Hlthcare, 95 Collier Rd NW, Ste 4055, Atlanta, GA 30309; **Phone:** 404-355-3200; **Board Cert:** Internal Medicine 1987; Gastroenterology 2011; **Med School:** Univ Iowa Coll Med 1984; **Resid:** Internal Medicine, UCSF Med Ctr 1987; **Fellow:** Gastroenterology, UCSF Med Ctr 1990

Younossi, Zobair MD [Ge] - **Spec Exp:** Liver Disease; **Hospital:** Inova Fairfax Hosp; **Address:** Ctr for Liver Diseases, Fairfax Hosp, 3300 Gallows Rd, Claude Moore Bldg, Falls Church, VA 22042; **Phone:** 703-776-3182; **Board Cert:** Gastroenterology 2005; Transplant Hepatology 2006; **Med School:** Univ Rochester 1989; **Resid:** Internal Medicine, Scripps Clin & Rsch Fdn 1992; **Fellow:** Gastroenterology, Scripps Clin & Rsch Fdn 1995; **Fac Appt:** Prof Med, Va Commonwealth Univ Sch Med

Midwest

Bacon, Bruce Raymond MD [Ge] - **Spec Exp:** Hepatitis C; Hepatic Iron Metabolism; Liver Disease; **Hospital:** St. Louis Univ Hosp, SSM St Mary's Hlth Ctr - St Louis; **Address:** 3660 Vista Ave, Ste 302, St Louis, MO 63110-2540; **Phone:** 314-577-6000; **Board Cert:** Internal Medicine 1978; Gastroenterology 2008; Transplant Hepatology 2006; **Med School:** Case West Res Univ 1975; **Resid:** Internal Medicine, Metro Genl Hosp 1978; **Fellow:** Gastroenterology, Metro Genl Hosp 1982; **Fac Appt:** Prof Med, St Louis Univ

Barnes, David S MD [Ge] - **Spec Exp:** Biliary Disease; Hepatitis; Liver Disease; Transplant Medicine-Liver; **Hospital:** Cleveland Clin (page 55); **Address:** Cleveland Clinic, Div Gastroenterology, 9500 Euclid Ave, Ste A-51, Cleveland, OH 44195; **Phone:** 216-444-1764; **Board Cert:** Internal Medicine 1984; Gastroenterology 1987; Transplant Hepatology 2006; **Med School:** Univ NC Sch Med 1981; **Resid:** Internal Medicine, Univ Mass Med Ctr 1984; **Fellow:** Gastroenterology, Case Western Reserve Univ 1985

Baron, Todd H MD [Ge] - **Spec Exp:** Endoscopy; Pancreatic/Biliary Endoscopy (ERCP); **Hospital:** Mayo Med Ctr & Clin - Rochester; **Address:** Mayo Clin, Div Gastroenterology, 200 First St SW Fl 9, Rochester, MN 55905; **Phone:** 507-284-2174; **Board Cert:** Internal Medicine 1989; Gastroenterology 2003; **Med School:** Univ Fla Coll Med 1986; **Resid:** Internal Medicine, Univ Alabama Med Ctr 1990; **Fellow:** Gastroenterology, Univ Alabama Med Ctr 1993; Advanced Endoscopy, Duke Univ Med Ctr 1993; **Fac Appt:** Prof Med, Mayo Med Sch

Brown, Kimberly A MD [Ge] - **Spec Exp:** Liver Disease; Transplant Medicine-Liver; Hepatitis C; Liver Cancer; **Hospital:** Henry Ford Hosp; **Address:** Henry Ford Hosp, Dept Gastroenterology, 2799 W Grand Blvd Fl K16, Detroit, MI 48202-2608; **Phone:** 313-916-8865; **Board Cert:** Internal Medicine 1988; Gastroenterology 2012; Transplant Hepatology 2006; **Med School:** Wayne State Univ 1985; **Resid:** Internal Medicine, Univ Michigan Med Ctr 1989; **Fellow:** Gastroenterology, Univ Michigan Med Ctr 1992

Chari, Suresh T MD [Ge] - **Spec Exp:** Pancreatic Disease; **Hospital:** Mayo Med Ctr & Clin - Rochester; **Address:** Mayo Clin, Div Gastroenterology, 200 First St SW Fl 9, Rochester, MN 55905; **Phone:** 507-284-2141; **Board Cert:** Gastroenterology 2009; **Med School:** India 1982; **Resid:** Internal Medicine, Univ Arizona Hlth Sci Ctr 1996; **Fellow:** Gastroenterology, Mayo Clin 1999; **Fac Appt:** Prof Med, Mayo Med Sch

Chey, William D MD [Ge] - **Spec Exp:** Gastrointestinal Motility Disorders; Gastrointestinal Functional Disorders; Peptic Acid Disorders; Gastroesophageal Reflux Disease (GERD); **Hospital:** Univ Michigan Med Ctr; **Address:** 3912 Taubman Center, SPC5362, Ann Arbor, MI 48109-5362; **Phone:** 734-936-4775; **Board Cert:** Internal Medicine 1989; Gastroenterology 2003; **Med School:** Emory Univ 1986; **Resid:** Internal Medicine, Emory Univ Med Ctr 1989; **Fellow:** Gastroenterology, Univ Mich Hosps 1993; **Fac Appt:** Prof Med, Univ Mich Med Sch

Cominelli, Fabio MD/PhD [Ge] - **Spec Exp:** Inflammatory Bowel Disease/Crohn's; Ulcerative Colitis; **Hospital:** UH Case Med Ctr, Louis Stokes Cleveland VA Med Ctr-Wade Park Campus; **Address:** Univ Hosps Case Medical Ctr, Div Gastroenterology, 11100 Euclid Ave, Cleveland, OH 44106-5066; **Phone:** 216-844-7344; **Med School:** Italy 1983; **Resid:** Internal Medicine, Careggi Hosp/Univ Italy 1986; **Fellow:** Gastroenterology, Harbor-UCLA Med Ctr 1989; **Fac Appt:** Prof Med, Case West Res Univ

Crippin, Jeffrey S MD [Ge] - **Spec Exp:** Transplant Medicine-Liver; Liver Disease; Liver Failure; Gastrointestinal Cancer; **Hospital:** Barnes-Jewish Hosp; **Address:** Barnes Jewish Hosp, Div Gastroenterology, 4921 Parkview Pl, Ste 8C, St Louis, MO 63110; **Phone:** 314-454-8160; **Board Cert:** Internal Medicine 1987; Gastroenterology 2011; Transplant Hepatology 2006; **Med School:** Univ Kansas 1984; **Resid:** Internal Medicine, Kansas Univ Med Ctr 1988; **Fellow:** Gastroenterology, Mayo Clinic 1991; **Fac Appt:** Assoc Prof Med, Washington Univ, St Louis

Di Bisceglie, Adrian M MD [Ge] - **Spec Exp:** Hepatitis C; Hepatitis; Liver Cancer; **Hospital:** St. Louis Univ Hosp; **Address:** St Louis Univ, Div Gastroenterology, 1402 S Grand Blvd, St Louis, MO 63110; **Phone:** 314-577-6000; **Board Cert:** Internal Medicine 2012; Transplant Hepatology 2010; **Med School:** South Africa 1977; **Resid:** Internal Medicine, Baragwanath Hosp 1984; **Fellow:** Hepatology, Natl Inst Hlth 1988; **Fac Appt:** Prof Med, St Louis Univ

Early, Dayna S MD [Ge] - **Spec Exp:** Colon & Rectal Cancer Detection; Endoscopic Ultrasound; Endoscopic Therapies; **Hospital:** Barnes-Jewish Hosp, Barnes-Jewish West County Hosp; **Address:** Center for Advanced Medicine, 4921 Parkview Pl Fl 8, Saint Louis, MO 63110; **Phone:** 314-747-3969; **Board Cert:** Internal Medicine 2003; Gastroenterology 2005; **Med School:** Univ MO-Columbia Sch Med 1990; **Resid:** Internal Medicine, Vanderbilt Univ Med Ctr 1993; **Fellow:** Gastroenterology, Vanderbilt Univ Med Ctr 1995; **Fac Appt:** Prof Med, Washington Univ, St Louis

Edmundowicz, Steven A MD [Ge] - **Spec Exp:** Endoscopy; Biliary Disease; Pancreatic Disease; Pancreatic Cancer; **Hospital:** Barnes-Jewish Hosp; **Address:** Washington Univ Sch Med, Div Gastroenterology, 660 S Euclid Ave, Box 8124, St Louis, MO 63110; **Phone:** 314-747-2066; **Board Cert:** Internal Medicine 1986; Gastroenterology 1989; **Med School:** Jefferson Med Coll 1983; **Resid:** Internal Medicine, Barnes Hosp 1986; **Fellow:** Gastroenterology, Barnes Hosp/Wash Univ 1989; **Fac Appt:** Prof Med, Washington Univ, St Louis

Elliott, David E MD/PhD [Ge] - **Spec Exp:** Celiac Disease; Inflammatory Bowel Disease/Crohn's; Intestinal Parasites; **Hospital:** Univ Iowa Hosp & Clins; **Address:** UIHC Ctr for Digestive Diseases, 200 Hawkins Drive, Iowa City, IA 52242; **Phone:** 319-356-4060; **Board Cert:** Internal Medicine 2003; Gastroenterology 2003; **Med School:** Wayne State Univ 1988; **Resid:** Internal Medicine, Johns Hopkins Hosp 1991; **Fellow:** Gastroenterology, Univ Iowa Hosps 1993; **Fac Appt:** Assoc Prof Med, Univ Iowa Coll Med

Elta, Grace H MD [Ge] - **Spec Exp:** Pancreatic & Biliary Disease; **Hospital:** Univ Michigan Med Ctr; **Address:** Univ Michigan Hlth Sys, 1500 E Medical Ctr Drive, Taubman Ctr, rm 3912, Ann Arbor, MI 48109-0362; **Phone:** 734-647-5944; **Board Cert:** Internal Medicine 1980; Gastroenterology 1983; **Med School:** Univ Mich Med Sch 1977; **Resid:** Internal Medicine, New England Med Ctr 1980; **Fellow:** Gastroenterology, New England Med Ctr 1982; **Fac Appt:** Prof Med, Univ Mich Med Sch

Gholam, Pierre M MD [Ge] - **Spec Exp:** Liver Disease; Transplant Medicine-Liver; **Hospital:** UH Case Med Ctr; **Address:** UH Case Medical Ctr, 11100 Euclid Ave, Cleveland, OH 44106; **Phone:** 216-844-5387; **Board Cert:** Gastroenterology 2012; Transplant Hepatology 2006; Internal Medicine 2011; **Med School:** Lebanon 1996; **Resid:** Internal Medicine, St Lukes-Roosevelt Hosp 1999; **Fellow:** Gastroenterology, St Lukes-Roosevelt Hosp 2002; **Fac Appt:** Asst Prof Med, Case West Res Univ

Goldberg, Michael J MD [Ge] - **Spec Exp:** Pancreatic Cancer; Colon & Rectal Cancer; **Hospital:** Evanston Hosp/NorthShore Univ Hlth Sys (page 67), Glenbrook Hosp/NorthShore Univ Hlth Syst (page 67); **Address:** NorthShore Medical Group-Evanston Hosp, 1000 Central St, Ste 615, Evanston, IL 60201; **Phone:** 847-657-1900; **Board Cert:** Internal Medicine 1978; Gastroenterology 1981; **Med School:** Univ IL Coll Med 1975; **Resid:** Internal Medicine, Univ Illinois Hosp 1978; **Fellow:** Gastroenterology, Tufts-New England Med Ctr 1981; **Fac Appt:** Clin Prof Med, Univ Chicago-Pritzker Sch Med

Gostout, Christopher MD [Ge] - **Spec Exp:** Endoscopy; **Hospital:** Mayo Med Ctr & Clin - Rochester; **Address:** Mayo Clin, Div Gastroenterology, 200 First St SW Fl 9, Rochester, MN 55905; **Phone:** 507-284-2141; **Board Cert:** Internal Medicine 1979; Gastroenterology 1981; **Med School:** SUNY Downstate 1976; **Resid:** Internal Medicine, Mayo Clin 1979; **Fellow:** Gastroenterology, Mayo Clin 1981

Hanauer, Stephen B MD [Ge] - **Spec Exp:** Inflammatory Bowel Disease; Crohn's Disease; Ulcerative Colitis; Clinical Trials; **Hospital:** Univ of Chicago Med; **Address:** University of Chicago Medicine, 5841 S Maryland Ave, Chicago, IL 60637-1426; **Phone:** 773-702-1466; **Board Cert:** Internal Medicine 1980; Gastroenterology 2010; **Med School:** Univ IL Coll Med 1977; **Resid:** Internal Medicine, Univ Chicago Hosps 1980; **Fellow:** Gastroenterology, Univ Chicago Hosps 1982; **Fac Appt:** Prof Med, Univ Chicago-Pritzker Sch Med

Jensen, Donald M MD [Ge] - **Spec Exp:** Transplant Medicine-Liver; Hepatitis C; Liver & Biliary Disease; Liver Cancer; **Hospital:** Univ of Chicago Med; **Address:** Univ of Chicago, Ctr for Liver Disease, 5841 S Maryland Ave, MC 9015, Chicago, IL 60637; **Phone:** 773-702-2300; **Board Cert:** Internal Medicine 1975; Gastroenterology 1981; **Med School:** Univ IL Coll Med 1972; **Resid:** Internal Medicine, Rush Presby St Lukes Hosp 1975; Gastroenterology, Rush Presby St Lukes Hosp 1976; **Fellow:** Gastroenterology, King's Coll Hosp 1978; **Fac Appt:** Prof Med, Univ Chicago-Pritzker Sch Med

Jonnalagadda, Sreenivasa S MD [Ge] - **Spec Exp:** Pancreatic/Biliary Endoscopy (ERCP); Endoscopic Ultrasound; Interventional Endoscopy; **Hospital:** St. Luke's Hosp of Kansas City, St. Luke's South; **Address:** St Luke's GI Specialists, 4401 Wornall Rd, Kansas City, MO 64111; **Phone:** 913-932-3709; **Board Cert:** Internal Medicine 2005; Gastroenterology 2007; **Med School:** India 1990; **Resid:** Internal Medicine, St. Louis Univ Hlth Sci Ctr 1995; **Fellow:** Gastroenterology, Truman Med Ctr 1997; Advanced Endoscopy, Wellesley Hosp 1998; **Fac Appt:** Prof Med, Univ MO-Kansas City

Kahrilas, Peter J MD [Ge] - **Spec Exp:** Esophageal Disorders; Swallowing Disorders; **Hospital:** Northwestern Meml Hosp; **Address:** 675 N St Clair, Fl 17, Ste 250, Chicago, IL 60611; **Phone:** 312-695-5620; **Board Cert:** Internal Medicine 1982; Gastroenterology 1987; **Med School:** Univ Rochester 1979; **Resid:** Internal Medicine, Univ Hosp 1982; **Fellow:** Gastroenterology, Northwestern Meml Hosp 1984; Research, Med Coll Wisconsin 1986; **Fac Appt:** Prof Med, Northwestern Univ

Konicek, Frank J MD [Ge] - **Spec Exp:** Endoscopy; Inflammatory Bowel Disease/Crohn's; Pancreatic Disease; Liver Disease; **Hospital:** Swedish Covenant Hosp, Adv Illinois Masonic Med Ctr; **Address:** 3004 N Ashland Ave, Chicago, IL 60657-3012; **Phone:** 773-871-4600; **Board Cert:** Internal Medicine 1977; Gastroenterology 1975; **Med School:** Loyola Univ-Stritch Sch Med 1963; **Resid:** Internal Medicine, St Francis Hosp 1965; Internal Medicine, Hines VA Hosp 1969; **Fellow:** Gastroenterology, Hines VA Hosp 1971; **Fac Appt:** Clin Prof Med, Loyola Univ-Stritch Sch Med

Kwo, Paul Y MD [Ge] - **Spec Exp:** Hepatitis B & C; Transplant Medicine-Liver; Liver Disease; **Hospital:** IU Hlth Univ Hosp; **Address:** University Hosp, Ste 1710, 550 N University Blvd, Indianapolis, IN 46202; **Phone:** 317-944-8660; **Board Cert:** Gastroenterology 2005; Transplant Hepatology 2006; **Med School:** Wayne State Univ 1988; **Resid:** Internal Medicine, Univ MD Med Ctr 1991; **Fellow:** Gastroenterology, Mayo Clinic 1995; **Fac Appt:** Prof Med, Indiana Univ

La Russo, Nicholas F MD [Ge] - **Spec Exp:** Transplant Medicine-Liver; Liver & Biliary Disease; **Hospital:** St. Mary's Hosp - Rochester MN (Mayo), Rochester Methodist Hosp; **Address:** Mayo Clinic, Div Gastroenterology, 200 First St SW, Guggenheim Bldg Fl 17 - rm 21D, Rochester, MN 55905; **Phone:** 507-284-1006; **Board Cert:** Internal Medicine 1972; Gastroenterology 1979; **Med School:** NY Med Coll 1969; **Resid:** Internal Medicine, Mayo Clinic 1972; **Fellow:** Gastroenterology, Mayo Clinic 1975; **Fac Appt:** Prof Med, Mayo Med Sch

Lashner, Bret A MD [Ge] - **Spec Exp:** Inflammatory Bowel Disease; **Hospital:** Cleveland Clin (page 55); **Address:** 2049 E 100th St Crile Bldg, Desk A-31, Cleveland, OH 44195; **Phone:** 216-444-6536; **Board Cert:** Internal Medicine 1983; Gastroenterology 1985; **Med School:** NYU Sch Med 1980; **Resid:** Internal Medicine, Temple Univ Hosp 1983; **Fellow:** Gastroenterology, Univ Chicago Med Ctr 1986

Levy, Michael J MD [Ge] - **Spec Exp:** Pancreatic/Biliary Endoscopy (ERCP); Endoscopic Ultrasound; **Hospital:** Mayo Med Ctr & Clin - Rochester; **Address:** 200 First St SW Fl 9, Rochester, MN 55905; **Phone:** 507-284-2141; **Board Cert:** Gastroenterology 2009; **Med School:** Univ SC Sch Med 1991; **Resid:** Internal Medicine, New Hanover Regl Med Ctr 1994; **Fellow:** Gastroenterology, Univ S Alabama Hlth Sys 1996; **Fac Appt:** Prof Med, Mayo Med Sch

Loftus Jr, Edward V MD [Ge] - **Spec Exp:** Inflammatory Bowel Disease; Crohn's Disease; Ulcerative Colitis; Microscopic Colitis; **Hospital:** Mayo Med Ctr & Clin - Rochester; **Address:** Mayo Clin, Div Gastroenterology, 200 First St SW Fl 9, Rochester, MN 55905; **Phone:** 507-284-2141; **Board Cert:** Internal Medicine 2003; Gastroenterology 2005; **Med School:** Univ Pennsylvania 1988; **Resid:** Internal Medicine, Temple Univ Hosp 1991; **Fellow:** Gastroenterology, Mayo Clinic 1995; **Fac Appt:** Prof Med, Mayo Med Sch

Lucey, Michael R MD [Ge] - **Spec Exp:** Liver Disease; Transplant Medicine-Liver; **Hospital:** Univ WI Hosp & Clins; **Address:** Univ WI Hosp - Dept Gastroenterology, 1685 Highland Ave, Centennial Bldg Fl 4, Madison, WI 53705-2281; **Phone:** 608-263-7322; **Board Cert:** Gastroenterology 2011; Transplant Hepatology 2006; **Med School:** Ireland 1976; **Resid:** Internal Medicine, Fed Dublin Vol Hosps 1983; Gastroenterology, St Bartholomews Hosp/Kings Coll Hosp 1983; **Fellow:** Hepatology, Kings Coll Hosp 1985; Gastroenterology, Univ Michigan Med Ctr 1987; **Fac Appt:** Prof Med, Univ Wisc

Meiselman, Mick S MD [Ge] - **Spec Exp:** Pancreatic & Biliary Disease; Barrett's Esophagus; Gastrointestinal Cancer; **Hospital:** Evanston Hosp/NorthShore Univ Hlth Sys (page 67), Glenbrook Hosp/NorthShore Univ Hlth Syst (page 67); **Address:** Kellogg Cancer Center, 2650 Ridge Ave, Fl 2, Evanston, IL 60201; **Phone:** 847-570-2030; **Board Cert:** Internal Medicine 1982; Gastroenterology 1985; **Med School:** Northwestern Univ 1979; **Resid:** Internal Medicine, Cedars-Sinai Hosp 1982; **Fellow:** Gastroenterology, UCSF Med Ctr 1984; **Fac Appt:** Asst Clin Prof Med, Univ Chicago-Pritzker Sch Med

Murray, Joseph A MD [Ge] - **Spec Exp:** Celiac Disease; Esophageal Disorders; **Hospital:** Mayo Med Ctr & Clin - Rochester; **Address:** Mayo Clin, Div Gastroenterology, 200 First St SW Fl 9, Rochester, MN 55905; **Phone:** 507-284-2141; **Board Cert:** Internal Medicine 2009; Gastroenterology 2010; **Med School:** Ireland 1983; **Resid:** Internal Medicine, St Laurences Hosp 1986; Gastroenterology, Beaumont Hosp 1988; **Fellow:** Gastroenterology, Univ Iowa Hosp & Clins 1990; **Fac Appt:** Prof Med, Mayo Med Sch

Owyang, Chung MD [Ge] - **Spec Exp:** Gastrointestinal Motility Disorders; Digestive Disorders; **Hospital:** Univ Michigan Med Ctr; **Address:** Univ Michigan Hlth Sys, 1500 E Medical Ctr Drive, Taubman Ctr, rm 3912, Ann Arbor, MI 48109-0362; **Phone:** 734-647-5944; **Board Cert:** Internal Medicine 1976; Gastroenterology 1981; **Med School:** McGill Univ 1972; **Resid:** Internal Medicine, Montreal Genl Hosp 1975; **Fellow:** Gastroenterology, Mayo Grad Sch 1978; **Fac Appt:** Prof Med, Univ Mich Med Sch

Pfau, Patrick R MD [Ge] - **Spec Exp:** Barrett's Esophagus; Endoscopy; **Hospital:** Univ WI Hosp & Clins; **Address:** Univ WI Hosp - Dept Gastroenterology, 1685 Highland Ave, Centennial Bldg Fl 4, Madison, WI 53705; **Phone:** 608-263-4033; **Board Cert:** Gastroenterology 2010; **Med School:** Northwestern Univ-Feinberg Sch Med 1994; **Resid:** Internal Medicine, Pennsylvania Hosp-UPHS 1997; **Fellow:** Gastroenterology, Pennsylvania Hosp-UPHS 2000; **Fac Appt:** Assoc Prof Med, Univ Wisc

Reichelderfer, Mark MD [Ge] - **Spec Exp:** Endoscopy; Inflammatory Bowel Disease; **Hospital:** Univ WI Hosp & Clins; **Address:** Univ WI Hosp - Dept Gastroenterology, 1685 Highland Ave, Centennial Bldg Fl 4, Madison, WI 53705-2281; **Phone:** 608-263-4033; **Board Cert:** Internal Medicine 1977; Gastroenterology 1979; **Med School:** Columbia P&S 1974; **Resid:** Internal Medicine, Bassett Med Ctr 1977; **Fellow:** Gastroenterology, Univ Wisc Hosps & Clins 1979; **Fac Appt:** Prof Med, Univ Wisc

Rex, Douglas K MD [Ge] - **Spec Exp:** Colonoscopy; Endoscopic Ultrasound; Colon & Rectal Cancer Detection; Inflammatory Bowel Disease; **Hospital:** IU Hlth Univ Hosp; **Address:** IU Hlth, Gastroenterology Dept, 550 N University Blvd, Ste 4100, Indianapolis, IN 46202; **Phone:** 317-948-9763; **Board Cert:** Internal Medicine 1985; Gastroenterology 1987; **Med School:** Indiana Univ 1980; **Resid:** Internal Medicine, IU Hlth Hosp 1982; Internal Medicine, IU Hlth Hosp 1985; **Fellow:** Gastroenterology, IU Hlth Hosp 1984; **Fac Appt:** Prof Med, Indiana Univ

Schulze, Konrad S MD [Ge] - **Spec Exp:** Gastroesophageal Reflux Disease (GERD); Peptic Acid Disorders; Gastroparesis; **Hospital:** Univ Iowa Hosp & Clins; **Address:** UIHC Ctr for Digestive Diseases, 200 Hawkins Drive, Iowa City, IA 52242; **Phone:** 319-356-4060; **Board Cert:** Internal Medicine 1987; Gastroenterology 1975; **Med School:** Germany 1968; **Resid:** Psychiatry, Boston City Hosp 1971; Internal Medicine, Montreal Genl Hosp 1974; **Fellow:** Gastroenterology, Univ Iowa 1977; **Fac Appt:** Prof Med, Univ Iowa Coll Med

Semrad, Carol E MD [Ge] - **Spec Exp:** Celiac Disease; Diarrheal Diseases; Malabsorption Syndrome; Nutrition; **Hospital:** Univ of Chicago Med; **Address:** 5841 S Maryland Ave, rm S401, MC 4080, Chicago, IL 60637; **Phone:** 773-702-6921; **Board Cert:** Internal Medicine 1985; Gastroenterology 1987; **Med School:** Columbia P&S 1982; **Resid:** Internal Medicine, Columbia-Presby Med Ctr 1985; **Fellow:** Gastroenterology, Columbia-Presby Med Ctr 1986; **Fac Appt:** Assoc Prof Med, Univ Chicago-Pritzker Sch Med

Shaker, Reza MD [Ge] - **Spec Exp:** Swallowing Disorders; Gastrointestinal Motility Disorders; Gastroesophageal Reflux Disease (GERD); Pancreatic/Biliary Endoscopy (ERCP); **Hospital:** Froedtert & Med Coll WI, Clement J Zablocki VA Med Ctr; **Address:** Froedtert Med Coll Wisconsin-Dept Gastro, 9200 W Wisconsin Ave, rm E4510, Milwaukee, WI 53226; **Phone:** 414-955-6840; **Med School:** Iran 1975; **Resid:** Internal Medicine, Kingsbrook Jewish Med Ctr 1985; **Fellow:** Gastroenterology, Med Coll Wisc Affil Hosp 1988; **Fac Appt:** Prof Med, Univ Wisc

Sherman, Stuart MD [Ge] - **Spec Exp:** Pancreatic & Biliary Disease; Endoscopy; Pancreatic/Biliary Endoscopy (ERCP); **Hospital:** IU Hlth Univ Hosp; **Address:** IU Hlth, Gastroenterology Dept, 550 N University Blvd, rm 1634, Indianapolis, IN 46202; **Phone:** 317-944-0925; **Board Cert:** Internal Medicine 1985; Gastroenterology 2011; **Med School:** Washington Univ, St Louis 1982; **Resid:** Internal Medicine, UPMC Presby Hosp 1985; **Fellow:** Gastroenterology, UCLA Med Ctr 1989; **Fac Appt:** Prof Med, Indiana Univ

Silverman, William B MD [Ge] - **Spec Exp:** Pancreatic/Biliary Endoscopy (ERCP); Liver Disease; **Hospital:** Univ Iowa Hosp & Clins; **Address:** UIHC Ctr for Digestive Diseases, 200 Hawkins Drive, Iowa City, IA 52242; **Phone:** 319-356-4060; **Board Cert:** Internal Medicine 1988; Gastroenterology 2008; **Med School:** Belgium 1984; **Resid:** Internal Medicine, Lutheran General Hosp 1987; **Fellow:** Gastroenterology, Case Western Res Univ 1989; Gastroenterology, Indiana Univ Hosp 1990; **Fac Appt:** Prof Med, Univ Iowa Coll Med

Te, Helen MD [Ge] - **Spec Exp:** Liver Disease; Transplant Medicine-Liver; Hepatitis; **Hospital:** Univ of Chicago Med; **Address:** 5841 S Maryland Ave, Box MC 7120, Chicago, IL 60637; **Phone:** 773-702-2395; **Board Cert:** Internal Medicine 2006; Gastroenterology 2011; Transplant Hepatology 2006; **Med School:** Philippines 1992; **Resid:** Internal Medicine, Rush Presby Hosp 1996; **Fellow:** Gastroenterology, Univ Chicago Hosp 2000; **Fac Appt:** Assoc Prof Med, Univ Chicago-Pritzker Sch Med

Tremaine, William J MD [Ge] - **Spec Exp:** Inflammatory Bowel Disease/Crohn's; Ulcerative Colitis; Irritable Bowel Syndrome; **Hospital:** Mayo Med Ctr & Clin - Rochester, St. Mary's Hosp - Rochester MN (Mayo); **Address:** Mayo Clin, Div Gastroenterology, 200 First St SW, Mayo E-9, Rochester, MN 55905; **Phone:** 507-284-2468; **Board Cert:** Internal Medicine 1979; Gastroenterology 1981; **Med School:** Univ Miss 1976; **Resid:** Internal Medicine, Mayo Clin 1980; **Fellow:** Gastroenterology, Mayo Clin 1981; **Fac Appt:** Prof Med, Mayo Med Sch

Vanagunas, Arvydas D MD [Ge] - **Spec Exp:** Peptic Acid Disorders; Colon Cancer Screening; Endoscopy; **Hospital:** Northwestern Meml Hosp; **Address:** 675 N St Clair St, Ste 17-250, Chicago, IL 60611; **Phone:** 312-695-5620; **Board Cert:** Internal Medicine 1977; Gastroenterology 1981; **Med School:** Univ IL Coll Med 1973; **Resid:** Internal Medicine, Northwestern Meml Hosp 1976; Internal Medicine, VA Lakeside Hosp 1977; **Fellow:** Gastroenterology, Northwestern Meml Hosp 1980; **Fac Appt:** Prof Med, Northwestern Univ

Vargo II, John J MD [Ge] - **Spec Exp:** Endoscopy; Barrett's Esophagus; Pancreatic/Biliary Endoscopy (ERCP); Pancreatic Disease; **Hospital:** Cleveland Clin (page 55); **Address:** Cleveland Clinic, 9500 Euclid Ave, Desk A-31, Cleveland, OH 44195; **Phone:** 216-445-5012; **Board Cert:** Internal Medicine 1988; **Med School:** Univ Rochester 1985; **Resid:** Internal Medicine, Montefiore Hosp 1988; **Fellow:** Gastroenterology, Cleveland Clinic 1990

Vege, Santhi S MD [Ge] - **Spec Exp:** Pancreatic Disease; **Hospital:** Mayo Med Ctr & Clin - Rochester; **Address:** Mayo Clin, Div Gastroenterology, 200 First St SW Fl 9, Rochester, MN 55905; **Phone:** 507-284-2141; **Board Cert:** Internal Medicine 2007; **Med School:** India 1975; **Resid:** Internal Medicine, Govt Genl Hosp 1978; Internal Medicine, Mayo Clin 1997; **Fellow:** Gastroenterology, Post Grad Inst 1981; Gastroenterology, Mayo Clin 1998; **Fac Appt:** Prof Med, Mayo Med Sch

Wald, Arnold MD [Ge] - **Spec Exp:** Constipation; Gastrointestinal Motility Disorders; Irritable Bowel Syndrome; Incontinence-Fecal; **Hospital:** Univ WI Hosp & Clins; **Address:** Univ WI Hosp - Dept Gastroenterology, 1685 Highland Ave, Centennial Bldg Fl 4, Madison, WI 53705-2281; **Phone:** 608-263-1995; **Board Cert:** Internal Medicine 1972; Gastroenterology 1975; **Med School:** SUNY Downstate 1968; **Resid:** Internal Medicine, SUNY Downstate Med Ctr (Univ Hosp Brooklyn) 1972; **Fellow:** Gastroenterology, Johns Hopkins Hosp 1975; **Fac Appt:** Prof Med, Univ Wisc

Waxman, Irving MD [Ge] - **Spec Exp:** Gastrointestinal Cancer; Pancreatic Cancer; Endoscopy; Interventional Endoscopy; **Hospital:** Univ of Chicago Med; **Address:** 5758 S Maryland Ave, MC 9028, Chicago, IL 60637; **Phone:** 773-702-1459; **Board Cert:** Internal Medicine 1988; Gastroenterology 2003; **Med School:** Mexico 1985; **Resid:** Internal Medicine, New Eng Deaconess Hosp 1988; **Fellow:** Gastroenterology, Georgetown Univ Med Ctr 1991; Endoscopy, Univ Academic Med Ctr 1991; **Fac Appt:** Prof Med, Univ Chicago-Pritzker Sch Med

Wiesner, Russell H MD [Ge] - **Spec Exp:** Transplant Medicine-Liver; **Hospital:** Mayo Med Ctr & Clin - Rochester; **Address:** Mayo Clin, Div Gastroenterology, 200 First St SW Fl 9, Rochester, MN 55905; **Phone:** 507-284-2141; **Board Cert:** Internal Medicine 1978; Gastroenterology 1981; **Med School:** Med Coll Wisc 1975; **Resid:** Internal Medicine, Mayo Clin 1978

Wolfe, M Michael MD [Ge] - **Hospital:** MetroHealth Med Ctr; **Address:** MetroHealth Med Ctr, Dept Medicine, 2500 MetroHealth Drive, rm G-575, Cleveland, OH 44109; **Phone:** 216-778-8266; **Board Cert:** Internal Medicine 1979; Gastroenterology 1981; **Med School:** Ohio State Univ 1976; **Resid:** Internal Medicine, Med Coll Penn Hosp 1979; **Fellow:** Gastroenterology, Univ Florida Hosps 1982; **Fac Appt:** Prof Med, Case West Res Univ

Great Plains and Mountains

Fang, John C MD [Ge] - **Spec Exp:** Endoscopy; Esophageal Disorders; Irritable Bowel Syndrome; Barrett's Esophagus; **Hospital:** Univ Utah Hlth Care; **Address:** 50 N Med Drive, Clinic 3, Salt Lake City, UT 84132; **Phone:** 801-581-2215; **Board Cert:** Gastroenterology 2008; **Med School:** Washington Univ, St Louis 1989; **Resid:** Internal Medicine, Temple Univ Hosp 1992; **Fellow:** Gastroenterology, Univ VA Hlth Sci Ctr 1995; **Fac Appt:** Prof Med, Univ Utah

Hunter, Ellen B MD [Ge] - **Spec Exp:** Hepatitis; Liver Disease; Transplant Medicine-Liver; **Hospital:** St. Luke's Boise Med Ctr; **Address:** Idaho Gastroenterology Assocs, 425 W Vannock St, Boise, ID 83702; **Phone:** 208-343-6458; **Board Cert:** Internal Medicine 1986; Gastroenterology 1989; **Med School:** Georgetown Univ 1983; **Resid:** Internal Medicine, Vanderbilt Univ Med Ctr 1986; **Fellow:** Gastroenterology, Mayo Clinic 1989

Levine, Joel B MD [Ge] - **Spec Exp:** Colon & Rectal Cancer Detection; Colonoscopy; Gastroesophageal Reflux Disease (GERD); **Hospital:** Denver Health Med Ctr; **Address:** Denver Hlth, Digestive & Liver Clin, 700 Delaware St, Davis Pav Fl 3, Denver, CO 80204; **Phone:** 303-602-6170; **Board Cert:** Internal Medicine 1973; Gastroenterology 1977; **Med School:** SUNY Downstate 1969; **Resid:** Internal Medicine, Univ Chicago Med Ctr 1971; Internal Medicine, Mass Genl Hosp 1974; **Fellow:** Gastroenterology, Mass Genl Hosp 1977

Shah, Raj J MD [Ge] - **Spec Exp:** Pancreatic/Biliary Endoscopy (ERCP); **Hospital:** Univ Colorado Hosp; **Address:** Univ CO Hosp, 1635 Aurora Ct, MS F735, Aurora, CO 80045; **Phone:** 720-848-2775; **Board Cert:** Gastroenterology 2010; **Med School:** NE Ohio Univ 1994; **Resid:** Internal Medicine, Univ of Pittsburgh Med Ctr 1997; **Fellow:** Gastroenterology, Univ Hosps of Cincinnati 2000; Advanced Endoscopy, Maine Med Ctr 2001; **Fac Appt:** Assoc Prof Med, Univ Colorado

Sorrell, Michael F MD [Ge] - **Spec Exp:** Transplant Medicine-Liver; Hepatitis; Liver Tumors; Liver Disease; **Hospital:** Nebraska Med Ctr; **Address:** 983285 Nebraska Medical Ctr, Omaha, NE 68198-3285; **Phone:** 402-559-7912; **Board Cert:** Internal Medicine 1972; **Med School:** Univ Nebr Coll Med 1959; **Resid:** Internal Medicine, Univ Nebraska Hosp 1968; Gastroenterology, Univ Nebraska Hosp 1969; **Fellow:** Hepatology, New Jersey Coll Med 1971; **Fac Appt:** Prof Med, Univ Nebr Coll Med

Young, Renee L MD [Ge] - **Spec Exp:** Inflammatory Bowel Disease; Crohn's Disease; **Hospital:** Nebraska Med Ctr; **Address:** Univ Nebraska Medical Ctr, 982000 Nebraska Medical Center, Omaha, NE 68198-2000; **Phone:** 402-559-2270; **Board Cert:** Internal Medicine 1986; Gastroenterology 2011; **Med School:** Univ Nebr Coll Med 1983; **Resid:** Internal Medicine, Univ Nebraska Med Ctr 1986; **Fellow:** Gastroenterology, Univ Nebraska Med Ctr 1990; **Fac Appt:** Assoc Prof Med, Univ Nebr Coll Med

Southwest

Anderson, Karl E MD [Ge] - **Spec Exp:** Porphyria; Liver Disease; **Hospital:** UT Med Br at Galveston(John Sealy Hosp); **Address:** 301 University Blvd, Galveston, TX 77555-1109; **Phone:** 409-772-4661; **Board Cert:** Internal Medicine 1972; Gastroenterology 1972; **Med School:** Johns Hopkins Univ 1965; **Resid:** Internal Medicine, Vanderbilt Univ Hosp 1967; Internal Medicine, New York Hosp 1968; **Fellow:** Gastroenterology, New York Hosp-Cornell 1970; **Fac Appt:** Prof Med, Univ Tex Med Br, Galveston

Balart Jr, Luis A MD [Ge] - **Spec Exp:** Hepatitis C; Liver Disease; **Hospital:** Tulane Med Ctr; **Address:** Tulane Univ Med Ctr, Dept Gastro, 1430 Tulane Ave, Ste SL35, New Orleans, LA 70112; **Phone:** 504-988-5800; **Board Cert:** Internal Medicine 1976; Gastroenterology 1981; **Med School:** Cuba 1973; **Resid:** Internal Medicine, Naval Regl Med Ctr 1976; **Fellow:** Gastroenterology, Ochsner Med Ctr 1981; Hepatology, Rancho Los Amigos Natl Rehab Ctr 1982; **Fac Appt:** Prof Med, Tulane Univ

Boland, Clement R MD [Ge] - **Spec Exp:** Colon & Rectal Cancer Detection; Hereditary Cancer; Cancer Genetics; **Hospital:** Baylor Univ Med Ctr-Dallas; **Address:** GI Canc Rsch Lab, 3500 Gaston Ave, Ste 250, Dallas, TX 75246; **Phone:** 214-820-2692; **Board Cert:** Internal Medicine 1978; Gastroenterology 1981; **Med School:** Yale Univ 1973; **Resid:** Internal Medicine, USPHS Hosp 1978; **Fellow:** Gastroenterology, UCSF Med Ctr 1981; **Fac Appt:** Clin Prof Med, Univ Tex SW, Dallas

Boyer, Thomas D MD [Ge] - **Spec Exp:** Liver Disease; Hepatitis; Transplant Medicine-Liver; **Hospital:** Univ Arizona Med Ctr-Univ Campus; **Address:** Univ Med Ctr, Div Gastroenterology, 1501 N Campbell Ave, Tucson, AZ 85724; **Phone:** 520-626-5952; **Board Cert:** Internal Medicine 1975; Gastroenterology 1977; Transplant Hepatology 2008; **Med School:** USC-Keck School of Medicine 1969; **Resid:** Internal Medicine, LAC & USC Med Ctr 1974; **Fellow:** Hepatology, USC Affil Hosp 1976; Gastroenterology, UCSF Med Ctr 1978; **Fac Appt:** Prof Med, Univ Ariz Coll Med

Bresalier, Robert Scott MD [Ge] - **Spec Exp:** Gastrointestinal Cancer; Peptic Acid Disorders; Cancer Prevention; **Hospital:** UT MD Anderson Canc Ctr; **Address:** MD Anderson Canc Ctr, Gastroenterology, Hepatology & Nutrition, 1515 Holcombe Blvd - Unit 1466, Houston, TX 77030; **Phone:** 713-745-4340; **Board Cert:** Internal Medicine 1981; Gastroenterology 1983; **Med School:** Univ Chicago-Pritzker Sch Med 1978; **Resid:** Internal Medicine, Barnes Hosp-Washington Univ 1981; **Fellow:** Gastroenterology, UCSF Med Ctr 1983; **Fac Appt:** Prof Med, Univ Tex, Houston

Bulat, Robert S MD [Ge] - **Hospital:** Tulane Med Ctr; **Address:** Tulane Univ Med Ctr, Dept Gastro, 1430 Tulane Ave, Ste SL35, New Orleans, LA 70112; **Phone:** 504-988-5800; **Board Cert:** Gastroenterology 2010; **Med School:** McMaster Univ 1990; **Resid:** Internal Medicine, Univ Toronto Med Ctr 1993; **Fellow:** Gastroenterology, McMaster Univ 1995; Gastroenterology, McMaster Univ 1997; **Fac Appt:** Prof Med, Tulane Univ

Cunningham, John T MD [Ge] - **Spec Exp:** Pancreatic Cancer; Biliary Disease; Pancreatic/Biliary Endoscopy (ERCP); **Hospital:** Univ Arizona Med Ctr-Univ Campus; **Address:** Univ Medical Ctr, Div Gastroenterology, 1501 N Campbell Ave, rm 6402, Tucson, AZ 85724-5028; **Phone:** 520-626-8659; **Board Cert:** Internal Medicine 1975; Gastroenterology 1977; **Med School:** Med Coll VA 1970; **Resid:** Internal Medicine, MUSC Med Ctr 1975; **Fellow:** Gastroenterology, MUSC Med Ctr 1977; **Fac Appt:** Prof Med, Univ Ariz Coll Med

Das, Ananya MD [Ge] - **Spec Exp:** Endoscopy; Endoscopic Ultrasound; Pancreatic/Biliary Endoscopy (ERCP); Gastrointestinal Cancer; **Hospital:** Mercy Gilbert Med Ctr; **Address:** Arizona Ctr for Digestive Hlth, 2680 S Val Vista Drive Bldg 4 - Ste 116, Gilbert, AZ 85295; **Phone:** 480-507-5678; **Board Cert:** Gastroenterology 2008; **Med School:** India 1987; **Resid:** Internal Medicine, SUNY Downstate Med Ctr 1996; **Fellow:** Gastroenterology, Cleveland Clin 1998; Endoscopy, Cleveland Clin 2000; **Fac Appt:** Prof Med, Mayo Med Sch

Faigel, Douglas O MD [Ge] - **Spec Exp:** Pancreatic/Biliary Endoscopy (ERCP); Endoscopic Ultrasound; Pancreatic & Biliary Disease; Gastrointestinal Cancer; **Hospital:** Mayo Clinic - Scottsdale; **Address:** Mayo Clinic-Gastroenterology, 13400 E Shea Blvd, Scottsdale, AZ 85259; **Phone:** 480-301-6990; **Board Cert:** Internal Medicine 2003; Gastroenterology 2005; **Med School:** Univ Pennsylvania 1990; **Resid:** Internal Medicine, UCSF Med Ctr 1993; **Fellow:** Gastroenterology, U Penn Hosp 1995; **Fac Appt:** Assoc Prof Med, Mayo Med Sch

Fallon, Michael B MD [Ge] - **Spec Exp:** Liver Disease; Hepatitis C; **Hospital:** Meml Hermann Hosp - Texas Med Ctr; **Address:** Univ TX Professional Bldg, 6400 Fannin, Houston, TX 77030; **Phone:** 713-704-6800; **Board Cert:** Internal Medicine 1988; Gastroenterology 2011; Transplant Hepatology 2008; **Med School:** Univ VA Sch Med 1984; **Resid:** Internal Medicine, Yale-New Haven Hosp 1988; **Fellow:** Gastroenterology, Yale-New Haven Hosp 1990; **Fac Appt:** Prof Med, Univ Tex, Houston

Fleischer, David E MD [Ge] - **Spec Exp:** Esophageal Cancer; Barrett's Esophagus; Endoscopy; **Hospital:** Mayo Clinic - Scottsdale; **Address:** Mayo Clinic-Gastroenterology, 13400 E Shea Blvd, Scottsdale, AZ 85259; **Phone:** 480-301-6990; **Board Cert:** Internal Medicine 1975; Gastroenterology 1977; **Med School:** Vanderbilt Univ 1970; **Resid:** Internal Medicine, Metro Genl Hosp 1975; **Fellow:** Gastroenterology, Harbor-UCLA Med Ctr 1977; **Fac Appt:** Prof Med, Mayo Med Sch

Galati, Joseph S MD [Ge] - **Spec Exp:** Liver Disease; Transplant Medicine-Liver; Hepatitis C; Liver Cancer; **Hospital:** Methodist Hosp - Houston, St. Luke's Episcopal Hosp-Houston; **Address:** 6560 Fannin St, Ste 2050, Houston, TX 77030; **Phone:** 713-794-0700; **Board Cert:** Gastroenterology 2005; **Med School:** Grenada 1987; **Resid:** Internal Medicine, Kings Co Hosp 1991; **Fellow:** Gastroenterology, Univ Nebraska Med Ctr 1994; Transplant Hepatology, Univ Nebraska Med Ctr 1994; **Fac Appt:** Asst Prof Med, Univ Tex, Houston

Glombicki, Alan P MD [Ge] - **Spec Exp:** Hepatitis; Transplant Medicine-Liver; Digestive Disorders; **Hospital:** Methodist Hosp - Houston, Meml Hermann Hosp - Texas Med Ctr; **Address:** 6550 Fannin St, Ste 2301, Smith Tower, Houston, TX 77030; **Phone:** 713-796-8627; **Board Cert:** Internal Medicine 1986; Gastroenterology 1987; **Med School:** Univ IL Coll Med 1981; **Resid:** Internal Medicine, Baylor Affil Hosp 1984; Hepatology, Baylor Affil HOsp 1987; **Fellow:** Gastroenterology, Baylor Coll Med 1986; **Fac Appt:** Assoc Prof Med, Univ Tex, Houston

Leighton, Jonathan A MD [Ge] - **Spec Exp:** Capsule Endoscopy; Inflammatory Bowel Disease; Ulcerative Colitis; **Hospital:** Mayo Clinic - Scottsdale; **Address:** Mayo Clin - Dept Gastroenterology, 13400 E Shea Blvd, Scottsdale, AZ 85259; **Phone:** 480-301-6990; **Board Cert:** Internal Medicine 1984; Gastroenterology 2011; **Med School:** Univ Ariz Coll Med 1981; **Resid:** Internal Medicine, UT Affil Hosp 1984; **Fellow:** Gastroenterology & Nutrition, UT Affil Hosp 1987; Research, UT Affil Hosp 1991; **Fac Appt:** Prof Med, Mayo Med Sch

Poordad, Fred F MD [Ge] - **Spec Exp:** Liver Disease; Hepatitis B & C; Transplant Medicine-Liver; **Address:** Digestive Diseases Center of Sout Texas, 607 Camden St, Ste 108, San Antonio, TX 78215; **Phone:** 210-253-3426; **Board Cert:** Gastroenterology 2005; Transplant Hepatology 2006; **Med School:** Canada 1990; **Resid:** Internal Medicine, St Thomas Med Ctr/Ohio State Univ Med Ctr 1993; **Fellow:** Gastroenterology, MUSC Hlth 1995; Hepatology, Johns Hopkins Hosp 2005

Raju, Gottumukkala S MD [Ge] - **Spec Exp:** Colon Cancer; **Hospital:** UT MD Anderson Canc Ctr; **Address:** UT MD Anderson Cancer Center, 1400 Pressler Blvd, Houston, TX 77230; **Phone:** 713-792-2330; **Board Cert:** Gastroenterology 2007; **Med School:** India 1986; **Resid:** Internal Medicine, Cleveland Clin 1995; **Fellow:** Gastroenterology, Univ Iowa Hosp & Clin 1997; Endoscopy, Beth Israel Deaconess Hosp 1998; **Fac Appt:** Prof Med, Univ Tex, Houston

Schiller, Lawrence R MD [Ge] - **Spec Exp:** Diarrheal Diseases; Gastrointestinal Functional Disorders; Gastrointestinal Motility Disorders; **Hospital:** Baylor Univ Med Ctr-Dallas; **Address:** Digestive Health Associates of Texas, 712 N Washington Ave, Ste 200, Dallas, TX 75246; **Phone:** 214-545-3990; **Board Cert:** Internal Medicine 1976; Gastroenterology 1981; **Med School:** Jefferson Med Coll 1972; **Resid:** Internal Medicine, Temple Univ Hosp 1976; **Fellow:** Gastroenterology, Univ Texas Hlth Sci Ctr 1980; **Fac Appt:** Clin Prof Med, Univ Tex SW, Dallas

Speeg, Kermit V MD/PhD [Ge] - **Spec Exp:** Transplant Medicine-Liver; **Hospital:** Univ Hosp-San Antonio; **Address:** Dept Gastroenterology, 7703 Floyd Curl Drive, MC 7878, San Antonio, TX 78229-3900; **Phone:** 210-567-4879; **Board Cert:** Internal Medicine 1976; **Med School:** Univ Tex SW, Dallas 1972; **Resid:** Internal Medicine, Vanderbilt Univ Hosp 1974; **Fellow:** Gastroenterology, Vanderbilt Univ Hosp 1977; **Fac Appt:** Prof Med, Univ Tex, San Antonio

Stump, David L MD [Ge] - **Hospital:** Methodist Hosp-San Antonio; **Address:** Gastroenterology Clinic Of San Antonio, 8550 Datapoint Drive, Ste LL 100, San Antonio, TX 78229-3436; **Phone:** 210-615-8308; **Board Cert:** Internal Medicine 1983; Gastroenterology 1985; **Med School:** Indiana Univ 1980; **Resid:** Internal Medicine, Indiana Univ Med Ctr 1983; **Fellow:** Gastroenterology, UT San Antonio 1985

Vierling, John M MD [Ge] - **Spec Exp:** Liver Disease; Transplant Medicine-Liver; Autoimmune Liver Disease; Hepatitis B & C; **Hospital:** St. Luke's Episcopal Hosp-Houston; **Address:** Baylor Clinic, 6620 Main St, Ste 1475, Houston, TX 77030; **Phone:** 832-355-1400; **Board Cert:** Internal Medicine 1975; Gastroenterology 1979; Transplant Hepatology 2006; **Med School:** Stanford Univ 1972; **Resid:** Internal Medicine, Strong Meml Hosp 1974; Hepatology, Natl Inst Hlth 1977; **Fellow:** Gastroenterology, UCSF 1978; **Fac Appt:** Prof Med, Baylor Coll Med

West Coast and Pacific

Cello, John P MD [Ge] - **Spec Exp:** Endoscopy; Colonoscopy; Capsule Endoscopy; Pancreatic/Biliary Endoscopy (ERCP); **Hospital:** San Francisco Genl Hosp, UCSF Med Ctr; **Address:** San Francisco Genl Hosp-UCSF, 1001 Potrero Ave, Ste NH3D, San Francisco, CA 94110; **Phone:** 415-206-8822; **Board Cert:** Internal Medicine 1972; Gastroenterology 1977; **Med School:** Harvard Med Sch 1969; **Resid:** Internal Medicine, Peter Bent Brigham Hosp 1972; **Fellow:** Gastroenterology, UCSF Med Ctr 1977; **Fac Appt:** Prof Med, UCSF

Chang, Kenneth J MD [Ge] - **Spec Exp:** Gastrointestinal Cancer; Endoscopic Ultrasound; Interventional Endoscopy; Barrett's Esophagus; **Hospital:** UC Irvine Med Ctr; **Address:** Comprehensive Digestive Disease Ctr, 101 The City Drive S, Bldg 22C, Rt 99 - rm 106, Orange, CA 92868; **Phone:** 714-456-6187; **Board Cert:** Internal Medicine 1988; Gastroenterology 2011; **Med School:** Brown Univ 1985; **Resid:** Internal Medicine, Rhode Island Hosp 1988; **Fellow:** Gastroenterology, UC Irvine Med Ctr 1990; **Fac Appt:** Clin Prof Med, UC Irvine

Dea, Stanley MD [Ge] - **Spec Exp:** Endoscopy; Pancreatic/Biliary Endoscopy (ERCP); Capsule Endoscopy; Endoscopic Ultrasound; **Hospital:** Olive View-UCLA Med Ctr, VA Greater Los Angeles Hlthcare Sys; **Address:** 14445 Olive View Drive, rm 2B-182, Sylmar, CA 91342; **Phone:** 818-364-3205; **Board Cert:** Internal Medicine 2004; Gastroenterology 2008; **Med School:** Univ Chicago-Pritzker Sch Med 1990; **Resid:** Internal Medicine, Harbor-UCLA Med Ctr 1993; **Fellow:** Gastroenterology, UCLA Med Ctr 1995; **Fac Appt:** Clin Prof Med, UCLA-David Geffen Sch Med

Eisen, Glenn M MD [Ge] - **Spec Exp:** Endoscopy; Liver Disease; Barrett's Esophagus; **Hospital:** Providence St Vincent Med Ctr; **Address:** Peterkort Med Offc-West Hills, 9701 SW Barnes Rd, Ste 300, Portland, OR 97225; **Phone:** 503-297-8081; **Board Cert:** Gastroenterology 2006; **Med School:** Albert Einstein Coll Med 1987; **Resid:** Internal Medicine, Mt Sinai Med Ctr 1991; **Fellow:** Gastroenterology, Duke Univ Hosp 1996; **Fac Appt:** Clin Prof Med, Oregon Hlth & Sci Univ

Ellis, Jonathan C MD [Ge] - **Hospital:** Cedars-Sinai Med Ctr; **Address:** Tower Digestive Health Medical Group, 9090 Wilshire Blvd, Ste 101, Beverly Hills, CA 90211; **Phone:** 310-550-0400; **Board Cert:** Internal Medicine 1985; Gastroenterology 1989; **Med School:** Stanford Univ 1982; **Resid:** Internal Medicine, Cedars Sinai Med Ctr 1986; **Fellow:** Gastroenterology, UCLA 1988; **Fac Appt:** Assoc Prof Med, UCLA

Fennerty, M. Brian MD [Ge] - **Spec Exp:** Gastroesophageal Reflux Disease (GERD); **Hospital:** OR Hlth & Sci Univ; **Address:** Digestive Hlth, Ctr for Hlth & Healing, 3303 SW Bond Ave, MC CH6D, Portland, OR 97239; **Phone:** 503-494-4373; **Board Cert:** Internal Medicine 1984; Gastroenterology 2008; **Med School:** Creighton Univ 1980; **Resid:** Internal Medicine, Naval Hosp 1984; **Fellow:** Gastroenterology, Arizona Hlth Sci Ctr 1988; **Fac Appt:** Prof Med, Oregon Hlth & Sci Univ

Gerson, Lauren B MD [Ge] - **Spec Exp:** Gastroesophageal Reflux Disease (GERD); Barrett's Esophagus; Esophageal Disorders; Capsule Endoscopy; **Hospital:** Stanford Univ Hosp & Clins; **Address:** 900 Blake Wilbur Drive, Palo Alto, CA 94305; **Phone:** 650-736-5555; **Board Cert:** Gastroenterology 2012; **Med School:** SUNY Buffalo 1990; **Resid:** Internal Medicine, California Pacific Med Ctr 1993; **Fellow:** Gastroenterology, Stanford Univ Med Ctr 1995; **Fac Appt:** Assoc Prof Med, Stanford Univ

Gish, Robert MD [Ge] - **Spec Exp:** Liver Cancer; Transplant Medicine-Liver; Hepatitis; Clinical Trials; **Hospital:** UCSD Med Ctr; **Address:** UCSD Liver Transplant Ctr, 200 W Arbor Drive, San Diego, CA 92103; **Phone:** 619-543-5415; **Board Cert:** Internal Medicine 1984; Gastroenterology 1987; Transplant Hepatology 2006; **Med School:** Univ Kansas 1980; **Resid:** Internal Medicine, UCSD Med Ctr 1983; **Fellow:** Gastroenterology, UCLA Med Ctr 1988; **Fac Appt:** Clin Prof Med, UCSD

Gluck, Michael MD [Ge] - **Spec Exp:** Pancreatic/Biliary Endoscopy (ERCP); Inflammatory Bowel Disease; Pancreatic & Biliary Disease; Eosinophilic Esophagitis; **Hospital:** Virginia Mason Med Ctr; **Address:** 1100 Ninth Ave, Seattle, WA 98101; **Phone:** 206-223-2319; **Board Cert:** Internal Medicine 1984; Gastroenterology 1989; **Med School:** UCLA 1981; **Resid:** Internal Medicine, Univ Wash Med Ctr 1984; **Fellow:** Gastroenterology, Univ Wash Med Ctr 1986

Han, Steven-Huy MD [Ge] - **Spec Exp:** Transplant Medicine-Liver; Hepatitis B & C; Liver Disease; **Hospital:** UCLA Ronald Reagan Med Ctr; **Address:** Dumont-UCLA Liver Transplant Center, Pfleger Liver Institute, 200 UCLA Medical Plaza, Ste 214, Los Angeles, CA 90095; **Phone:** 310-794-7788; **Board Cert:** Gastroenterology 2008; Transplant Hepatology 2006; **Med School:** Albany Med Coll 1990; **Resid:** Internal Medicine, Santa Clara Valley Med Ctr 1993; **Fellow:** Hepatology, USC 1996; Gastroenterology, UCLA 1998; **Fac Appt:** Assoc Prof Med, UCLA

Kimmey, Michael B MD [Ge] - **Spec Exp:** Pancreatic/Biliary Endoscopy (ERCP); Endoscopy; Endoscopic Ultrasound; Inflammatory Bowel Disease; **Hospital:** St. Joseph Med Ctr - Tacoma, St. Anthony Hosp -Gig Harbor; **Address:** Tacoma Digestive Disease Ctr, 1112 6th Ave, Ste 200, Tacoma, WA 98405; **Phone:** 253-272-8664; **Board Cert:** Internal Medicine 1982; Gastroenterology 1987; **Med School:** Washington Univ, St Louis 1979; **Resid:** Internal Medicine, Univ Wash Med Ctr 1982; **Fellow:** Gastroenterology, Univ Wash Med Ctr 1987; **Fac Appt:** Clin Prof Med, Univ Wash

Kozarek, Richard A MD [Ge] - **Spec Exp:** Pancreatic Disease; Pancreatic/Biliary Endoscopy (ERCP); Inflammatory Bowel Disease; **Hospital:** Virginia Mason Med Ctr; **Address:** 1100 Ninth Ave, Seattle, WA 98111; **Phone:** 206-223-2319; **Board Cert:** Internal Medicine 1977; Gastroenterology 1979; **Med School:** Univ Wisc 1973; **Resid:** Internal Medicine, Good Samaritan Hosp 1976; **Fellow:** Gastroenterology, Univ Arizona/ VA Hosp 1978; **Fac Appt:** Clin Prof Med, Univ Wash

Loomba, Rohit MD [Ge] - **Spec Exp:** Liver Disease; Transplant Medicine-Liver; **Hospital:** UCSD Med Ctr; **Address:** UCSD Med Ctr, Dept Gastroenterology, 9350 Campus Point Drive, La Jolla, CA 92037; **Phone:** 619-543-6834; **Board Cert:** Internal Medicine 2004; Gastroenterology 2009; **Med School:** India 1999; **Resid:** Internal Medicine, St Luke's Hosp 2004; **Fellow:** Hepatology, Natl Inst Hlth 2007; Gastroenterology, UCSD Med Ctr 2009; **Fac Appt:** Assoc Prof Med, UCSD

Mittal, Ravinder K MD [Ge] - **Spec Exp:** Gastrointestinal Motility Disorders; Esophageal Disorders; Swallowing Disorders; **Hospital:** UCSD Med Ctr; **Address:** 9350 Campus Point Drive, La Jolla, CA 92037; **Phone:** 619-543-6834; **Board Cert:** Internal Medicine 1982; Gastroenterology 1985; **Med School:** India 1978; **Resid:** Internal Medicine, Lincoln Hosp 1982; **Fellow:** Gastroenterology, Yale-New Haven Hosp 1985; **Fac Appt:** Prof Med, UCSD

Ostroff, James W MD [Ge] - **Spec Exp:** Pancreatic/Biliary Endoscopy (ERCP); Pancreatic Disease; Colonoscopy; **Hospital:** UCSF Med Ctr, UCSF - Mt Zion Med Ctr; **Address:** 350 Parnassus Ave, Ste 410, San Francisco, CA 94117-3608; **Phone:** 415-502-2112; **Board Cert:** Internal Medicine 1980; Gastroenterology 1983; **Med School:** Cornell Univ-Weill Med Coll 1977; **Resid:** Internal Medicine, NY Hosp-Cornell Med Ctr 1980; **Fellow:** Gastroenterology, UCSF Hosps 1982; **Fac Appt:** Prof Med, UCSF

Petrini, John L MD [Ge] - **Spec Exp:** Endoscopy; **Hospital:** Santa Barbara Cottage Hosp; **Address:** Sansum Clinic, 317 W Pueblo St, Santa Barbara, CA 93105; **Phone:** 805-898-3120; **Board Cert:** Internal Medicine 1980; Gastroenterology 1983; **Med School:** UCSF 1977; **Resid:** Internal Medicine, Emory Univ Hosp 1980; **Fellow:** Gastroenterology, UCLA Wadsworth VA Hosp 1982; **Fac Appt:** Assoc Clin Prof Med, USC-Keck School of Medicine

Roth, Bennett E MD [Ge] - **Spec Exp:** Gastroesophageal Reflux Disease (GERD); Inflammatory Bowel Disease/Crohn's; Irritable Bowel Syndrome; Esophageal Disorders; **Hospital:** UCLA Ronald Reagan Med Ctr; **Address:** UCLA Digestive Disease Center, Peter Morton Building, 200 UCLA Medical Plaza, Ste 365-C, Los Angeles, CA 90095; **Phone:** 310-825-1597; **Board Cert:** Internal Medicine 1972; Gastroenterology 1975; **Med School:** Hahnemann Univ 1968; **Resid:** Internal Medicine, Hosp Univ Penn 1971; **Fellow:** Gastroenterology, UCLA Med Ctr 1974; **Fac Appt:** Prof Med, UCLA

Sandborn, William J MD [Ge] - **Spec Exp:** Inflammatory Bowel Disease; Ulcerative Colitis; Crohn's Disease; **Hospital:** UCSD Thornton Hosp, UCSD Med Ctr; **Address:** 9350 Campus Point Drive, La Jolla, CA 92037; **Phone:** 858-657-7423; **Board Cert:** Gastroenterology 2003; **Med School:** Loma Linda Univ 1987; **Resid:** Internal Medicine, Loma Linda Univ 1990; **Fellow:** Gastroenterology, Mayo Clinic 1993; **Fac Appt:** Prof Med, UCSD

Savides, Thomas MD [Ge] - **Spec Exp:** Gastrointestinal Cancer; Barrett's Esophagus; Colonoscopy; Endoscopic Ultrasound; **Hospital:** UCSD Med Ctr; **Address:** 9350 Campus Point Drive, La Jolla, CA 92037; **Phone:** 619-543-6834; **Board Cert:** Internal Medicine 2003; Gastroenterology 2003; **Med School:** UCSD 1987; **Resid:** Internal Medicine, UCLA Med Ctr 1990; **Fellow:** Gastroenterology, UCLA Med Ctr 1993; Gastroenterology, Indiana Univ Med Ctr 1994; **Fac Appt:** Clin Prof Med, UCSD

Schembre, Drew MD [Ge] - **Spec Exp:** Celiac Disease; Colon & Rectal Cancer-Familial Polyposis; Esophageal Cancer; Pancreatic Cancer; **Hospital:** Swedish Med Ctr-First Hill-Seattle; **Address:** Swedish Gastroenterology, 1221 Madison St, Ste 1220, Arnold Pavilion, Seattle, WA 98104; **Phone:** 206-215-4250; **Board Cert:** Internal Medicine 2003; Gastroenterology 2005; **Med School:** UMDNJ-NJ Med Sch, Newark 1988; **Resid:** Internal Medicine, U Utah Affil Hosps 1991; **Fellow:** Gastroenterology, U Utah Affil Hosps 1995

Surawicz, Christina MD [Ge] - **Spec Exp:** Clostridium Difficile Disease; Infectious Diarrhea; **Hospital:** Harborview Med Ctr; **Address:** 410 9th Ave, Box 359866, Seattle, WA 98104; **Phone:** 206-744-7070; **Board Cert:** Internal Medicine 1976; Gastroenterology 1979; **Med School:** Univ KY Coll Med 1973; **Resid:** Internal Medicine, Univ Washington Med Ctr 1976; **Fellow:** Gastroenterology, Univ Washington Med Ctr 1979; **Fac Appt:** Prof Med, Univ Wash

Targan, Stephan R MD [Ge] - **Spec Exp:** Inflammatory Bowel Disease; **Hospital:** Cedars-Sinai Med Ctr; **Address:** Cedars-Sinai IBD Ctr, 8730 Alden Drive, Ste #E-204, Los Angeles, CA 90048; **Phone:** 310-423-4100; **Board Cert:** Internal Medicine 1974; Infectious Disease 1976; Gastroenterology 1979; **Med School:** Johns Hopkins Univ 1971; **Resid:** Internal Medicine, Harbor-UCLA Med Ctr 1976; **Fellow:** Infectious Disease, Harbor-UCLA Med Ctr 1976; Gastroenterology, UCLA Med Ctr 1978; **Fac Appt:** Prof Med, UCLA

Zaman, Atif MD [Ge] - **Spec Exp:** Liver Disease; Hypertension; Hepatitis; **Hospital:** OR Hlth & Sci Univ; **Address:** OHSU, Ctr for Hlth & Healing, 3303 SW Bond Ave, MC CH6D, Portland, OR 97201; **Phone:** 503-494-4373; **Board Cert:** Gastroenterology 2008; **Med School:** Tufts Univ 1991; **Resid:** Internal Medicine, Baylor Coll Affil Hosp 1994; **Fellow:** Gastroenterology, OR Hlth & Sci Univ 1998; **Fac Appt:** Prof Med, Oregon Hlth & Sci Univ

Cleveland Clinic
Digestive Disease Institute
9500 Euclid Ave.
Cleveland, OH 44195

Gastroenterology

Cleveland Clinic's Digestive Disease Institute (DDI) is one of the largest digestive programs in the country and is ranked No. 2 in the nation by *U.S. News & World Report*. DDI was one of the first to fully integrate its departments of Bariatric Surgery, Colorectal Surgery, Gastroenterology & Hepatology, General Surgery, and Nutrition. Combining these disciplines in one location facilitates unprecedented patient care, multidisciplinary education and collaborative research. In 2012, DDI physicians performed over 18,000 surgical cases and close to 60,000 endoscopic cases. Transplant surgeons completed over 150 digestive disease-related organ transplants, including liver, pancreas and intestinal transplantation, achieving outstanding outcomes.

Highlights of our Department of Gastroenterology :

- We have a state-of-the-art endoscopy facility designed to improve patient satisfaction while emphasizing both safety and quality.
- Our advanced endoscopy team performs a range of endoscopic procedures annually, including endoscopic retrograde cholangiopancreatography, endoscopic ultrasound and percutaneous endoscopic gastrostomy.
- Our Center for Swallowing & Esophageal Disorders offers comprehensive treatment for swallowing and esophageal disorders.
- DDI developed the world's first Pouchitis Clinic.
- The section of Comprehensive Gastroenterology focuses on typically underserved disorders such as small bowel diseases, including celiac disease.
- Our liver specialists have the experience and expertise to accurately diagnose and treat all forms of liver disease, including viral hepatitis, fatty liver, alcoholic liver disease, autoimmune liver diseases, genetic liver diseases and liver cancer.

Offering Same-Day Appointments
Call 866.320.4573

Treatment Guides
Cleveland Clinic has developed comprehensive treatment guides for many diseases and conditions. To download our free treatment guides, visit clevelandclinic.org/treatmentguides.

Online Medical Second Opinion
Call 216.444.3223 or 800.223.2273 ext. 43223 or email eclevelandclinic@ccf.org

Out-of-State Patients Assistance
Call 800.223.2273, ext. 55580 or email medicalconcierge@ccf.org

Visit Us At:
clevelandclinic.org

Follow Us On:
Facebook
facebook.com/clevelandclinic

Twitter
@ClevelandClinic

You Tube
youtube.com/clevelandclinic

Health Hub
clevelandclinic.org/HealthHub

NewYork-Presbyterian

Affiliated with Columbia University College of Physicians and Surgeons and Weill Cornell Medical College

NewYork-Presbyterian Hospital
Columbia University Medical Center
622 West 168th Street
New York, NY 10032

Center for Advanced Digestive Care
NewYork-Presbyterian Hospital
Weill Cornell Medical Center
525 East 68th Street
New York, NY 10065

1-877-NYP-WELL (1-877-697-9355) www.nyp.org/digestive

NewYork-Presbyterian Digestive Disease Services

Since 2010, NewYork-Presbyterian Hospital's gastroenterology program has ranked among the top ten in the nation in the annual "Best Hospitals" survey conducted by *U.S. News & World Report*™. NewYork-Presbyterian's Digestive Disease Services feature a collaborative team approach, an exceptional track record of routine and advanced procedures, prevention programs, and basic science and clinical research aimed at developing novel therapies.

- Interventional endoscopic procedures to treat disorders such as pancreatic cancer, pancreatitis, biliary and pancreatic stones, Barrett's esophagus, and polyps.
- Endoscopic sewing and radiofrequency ablation for gastroesophageal reflux disease (GERD).
- Minimally invasive surgical approaches, including single-incision, endolumenal, "needlescopic" procedures and combined endoscopic laparoscopic surgery (CELS).
- The Center for Liver Disease and Transplantation achieves extraordinary outcomes in living and deceased liver transplant and features laparoscopic removal of living donor liver tissue for select cases.
- Colorectal surgery is enhanced by the state-of-the-art Siemens Artis zeego® medical imaging system. This system provides real-time, more accurate 3-D images of the body and enables surgeons to transition seamlessly from diagnosis to surgical remedy.

Patients benefit from a range of routine diagnostic tests such as endoscopy, colonoscopy, and flexible sigmoidoscopy, as well as laparoscopy to diagnose and stage digestive cancers. Interventional endoscopic approaches are also available, including:

- Endoscopic retrograde cholangiopancreatography (ERCP) to evaluate the ducts of the gallbladder, pancreas, and liver.
- Endoscopic ultrasound (EUS) to diagnose pancreatic disorders and stage esophageal, gastric, and rectal cancers. NewYork-Presbyterian Hospital is one of only a few centers using EUS for needle aspiration of pancreatic cysts and tumors.
- Cholangioscopy to evaluate stones or strictures in the pancreatic or bile ducts.
- Double-balloon and spiral enteroscopy to investigate possible intestinal bleeding.
- Probe-based confocal laser endomicroscopy to enhance the early detection and treatment of cancers and precancerous conditions.
- Endoscopic stenting to relieve obstructions and improve symptoms.

Comprehensive and Compassionate Care

Patients who come to NewYork-Presbyterian Hospital benefit from a personalized multidisciplinary approach to the care of:

- Cancers of the esophagus, liver, pancreas, colon, stomach, and rectum
- Inflammatory bowel diseases (Crohn's disease and ulcerative colitis)
- Liver disease, including fatty liver and cirrhosis and hepatitis B and C
- Esophageal disorders, such as GERD and Barrett's esophagus
- Disorders of the pancreas, gallbladder, and bile ducts
- Celiac disease
- Polyps, particularly in the colon
- Peptic ulcer and other stomach diseases
- Anal and rectal diseases
- Obesity (through weight loss surgery)
- Type 2 diabetes (through metabolic surgery)

NYU Langone
MEDICAL CENTER

550 First Avenue *(at 31st Street)*
New York, NY 10016

www.NYULMC.org

Physician Referral: **888-7-NYU-MED** *(888-769-8633)*

GASTROENTEROLOGY

NYU Langone Medical Center is dedicated to the diagnosis and treatment of patients with diseases of the gastrointestinal tract. Physicians draw on their extensive knowledge and experience in the diagnosis and management of inflammatory bowel disease, peptic ulcer disease, esophageal disorders, gastrointestinal cancer, and liver, biliary and pancreatic diseases. Laser, laparoscopic, endoscopic, and other minimally invasive options are available, and we specialize in the following areas:

Colorectal Cancer

The Medical Center offers the most advanced screening options available for the diagnosis of colon cancer. Additionally, physicians continue to investigate colorectal cancer in special populations such as women, veterans, immigrants, minorities and patients with HIV, and offer the use of standard and virtual colonoscopy for the detection of colorectal polyps and cancer.

Esophageal Diseases

The Esophageal Disease Center offers patients state-of-the-art diagnosis and treatment of esophageal disorders. The Center focuses on gastroesophageal reflux disease, esophageal motility disorders, Barrett's esophagus, adenocarcinoma of the esophagus and swallowing disorders. It also offers diagnostic studies on esophageal manometry, impedance testing for swallowing, pH catheter and impedance testing for reflux and BRAVO capsule pH testing, as well as such therapies as Barrett's ablation and esophageal dilations.

Gastrointestinal Cancers

Cancer Institute physicians treat patients with all types of gastrointestinal cancers, including those of the esophagus, stomach, colon/rectum, small intestine, liver, pancreas, gallbladder, and biliary tract. They also treat individuals with complex recurring disease, including those originally treated elsewhere. Patients have the opportunity to participate in numerous clinical trials.

Complex Treatments and Diagnosis

Our physicians are highly experienced in the use of enteroscopy and capsule endoscopy for the diagnosis of gastrointestinal bleeding of unknown origin. They have special interest in the diagnosis and treatment of patients with complex pancreatic-biliary disease through the use of ERCP and endoscopic ultrasound.

Liver Lesions and Adrenal Tumors

Our team treats liver lesions with painless radiofrequency ablation and are highly skilled in laproscopic adrenalectomies.

Geriatric Medicine

a subspecialty of Internal Medicine or Family Practice

An internist or family physician with special knowledge of the aging process and special skills in the diagnostic, therapeutic, preventive and rehabilitative aspects of illness in the elderly. This specialist cares for geriatric patients in the patient's home, the office, long-term care settings such as nursing homes and the hospital.

Family Medicine

A family physician is concerned with the total healthcare of the individual and the family, and is trained to diagnose and treat a wide variety of ailments in patients of all ages. The family physician receives a broad range of training that includes internal medicine, pediatrics, obstetrics and gynecology, psychiatry and geriatrics. Special emphasis is placed on prevention and the primary care of entire families, utilizing consultations and community resources when appropriate.

Training Required: Three years in internal medicine or family practice *plus* additional training and examination for certification in geriatric medicine.

Geriatric Medicine

New England

Cooney Jr, Leo M MD [Ger] - **Spec Exp:** Geriatric Functional Assessment; Rheumatology; Mobility Evaluation & Treatment; **Hospital:** Yale-New Haven Hosp; **Address:** Yale-New Haven Hosp, Adler Geriatric Assessment Ctr, 20 York St, New Haven, CT 06510; **Phone:** 203-688-2204; **Board Cert:** Internal Medicine 1974; Rheumatology 1978; **Med School:** Yale Univ 1969; **Resid:** Internal Medicine, Boston Med Ctr 1971; Internal Medicine, Boston Med Ctr 1974; **Fellow:** Rheumatology, Boston Med Ctr 1975; **Fac Appt:** Prof Med, Yale Univ

Lipsitz, Lewis Arnold MD [Ger] - **Spec Exp:** Falls in the Elderly; Hypertension; Hypotension; Syncope; **Hospital:** Beth Israel Deaconess Med Ctr - Boston, Hebrew Senior Life; **Address:** Beth Israel Med Ctr, Gerontology, 110 Francis St, Ste 1A, Boston, MA 02215; **Phone:** 617-632-8696; **Board Cert:** Internal Medicine 1980; Geriatric Medicine 2009; **Med School:** Univ Pennsylvania 1977; **Resid:** Internal Medicine, Beth Israel Hosp 1980; **Fellow:** Geriatric Medicine, Mass Genl Hosp 1983; **Fac Appt:** Prof Med, Harvard Med Sch

Tinetti, Mary E MD [Ger] - **Spec Exp:** Falls in the Elderly; Geriatric Functional Assessment; **Hospital:** Yale-New Haven Hosp; **Address:** Yale-New Haven Hosp, Adler Geriatric Assessment Ctr, 20 York St, New Haven, CT 06510; **Phone:** 203-688-6361; **Board Cert:** Internal Medicine 1981; **Med School:** Univ Mich Med Sch 1978; **Resid:** Internal Medicine, Univ Minnesota Affil Hosp 1981; **Fellow:** Geriatric Medicine, Univ Rochester Affil Hosp 1984; **Fac Appt:** Prof Med, Yale Univ

Mid Atlantic

Bloom, Patricia A MD [Ger] - **Spec Exp:** Complementary Medicine; Dementia; **Hospital:** Mt Sinai Med Ctr (page 62); **Address:** Martha Stewart Ctr for Living, 1440 Madison Ave, New York, NY 10029-6542; **Phone:** 212-659-8552; **Board Cert:** Internal Medicine 1978; Geriatric Medicine 2011; **Med School:** Univ Minn 1975; **Resid:** Internal Medicine, Montefiore Med Ctr 1978; **Fac Appt:** Assoc Prof Med, Mount Sinai Sch Med

Burton, John R MD [Ger] - **Hospital:** Johns Hopkins Bayview Med Ctr (page 59); **Address:** Johns Hopkins, Geriatric Med Dept, 5505 Hopkins Bayview Cir, Baltimore, MD 21224; **Phone:** 410-550-0925; **Board Cert:** Internal Medicine 1980; Nephrology 1974; Geriatric Medicine 2005; **Med School:** McGill Univ 1965; **Resid:** Internal Medicine, Baltimore City Hosp 1971; **Fellow:** Nephrology, Mass Genl Hosp 1972; **Fac Appt:** Prof Med, Johns Hopkins Univ

Callahan, Eileen H MD [Ger] - **Spec Exp:** Frail Elderly; Preventive Medicine; Dementia; **Hospital:** Mt Sinai Med Ctr (page 62); **Address:** Martha Stewart Ctr for Living, 1440 Madison Ave, New York, NY 10029; **Phone:** 212-659-8552; **Board Cert:** Internal Medicine 2004; Geriatric Medicine 2008; **Med School:** UMDNJ-NJ Med Sch, Newark 1991; **Resid:** Internal Medicine, St Vincents Cath Med Ctr 1994; **Fellow:** Geriatric Medicine, Mt Sinai Med Ctr 1996; **Fac Appt:** Assoc Prof Med, Mount Sinai Sch Med

Finucane, Thomas E MD [Ger] - **Spec Exp:** Pain Management; Swallowing Disorders; Ethics; **Hospital:** Johns Hopkins Bayview Med Ctr (page 59), Johns Hopkins Hosp (page 59); **Address:** Johns Hopkins, Geriatric Med Dept, 5505 Hopkins Bayview Cir, Baltimore, MD 21224; **Phone:** 410-550-0925; **Board Cert:** Internal Medicine 1982; Geriatric Medicine 2008; **Med School:** Emory Univ 1978; **Resid:** Internal Medicine, G Washington Univ Hosp 1982; **Fac Appt:** Prof Med, Johns Hopkins Univ

Gambert, Steven R MD [Ger] - **Spec Exp:** Endocrinology; Osteoporosis; **Hospital:** Univ of MD Med Ctr; **Address:** Univ MD Med Ctr, Geriatric Med Dept, 22 S Greene St, rm N3E09, Baltimore, MD 21201; **Phone:** 410-328-1143; **Board Cert:** Internal Medicine 1978; **Med School:** Columbia P&S 1975; **Resid:** Internal Medicine, Dartmouth-Hitchcock Med Ctr 1977; **Fellow:** Geriatric Medicine, Beth Israel Deaconess Med Ctr 1979; Endocrinology, Beth Israel Deaconess Med Ctr 1979; **Fac Appt:** Prof Med, Univ MD Sch Med

Lachs, Mark S MD [Ger] - **Spec Exp:** Abuse/Neglect; **Hospital:** NY-Presby/Weill Cornell Med Ctr, NY (page 65); **Address:** Irving Sherwood Wright Med Ctr on Aging, 1484 First Ave, New York, NY 10075; **Phone:** 212-746-7000; **Board Cert:** Internal Medicine 1988; Geriatric Medicine 2002; **Med School:** NYU Sch Med 1985; **Resid:** Internal Medicine, Hosp Univ Penn - UPHS 1988; **Fellow:** Geriatric Medicine, Yale-New Haven Hosp 1990; **Fac Appt:** Prof Med, Cornell Univ-Weill Med Coll

Resnick, Neil M MD [Ger] - **Spec Exp:** Voiding Dysfunction; Incontinence; **Hospital:** UPMC Presby, Pittsburgh, UPMC Shadyside; **Address:** 3471 5th Ave, Kaufmann Bldg, Ste 500, Pittsburgh, PA 15213-3313; **Phone:** 412-692-2364; **Board Cert:** Internal Medicine 1980; Geriatric Medicine 2009; **Med School:** Stanford Univ 1977; **Resid:** Internal Medicine, Beth Israel Hosp 1980; **Fellow:** Geriatric Medicine, Harvard Univ 1982; Urodynamics, Harvard Univ 1984; **Fac Appt:** Prof Med, Univ Pittsburgh

Studenski, Stephanie A MD [Ger] - **Spec Exp:** Balance Disorders; Mobility Evaluation & Treatment; Falls in the Elderly; **Hospital:** UPMC Presby, Pittsburgh; **Address:** 3471 Fifth Ave, Kaufman Medical Bldg, Ste 500, Pittsburgh, PA 15213; **Phone:** 412-692-2360; **Board Cert:** Internal Medicine 1982; Rheumatology 1984; Geriatric Medicine 2002; **Med School:** Univ Kansas 1979; **Resid:** Internal Medicine, Duke Univ Med Ctr 1982; **Fellow:** Rheumatology, Duke Univ Med Ctr 1984; Geriatric Medicine, Duke Univ Med Ctr 1986; **Fac Appt:** Prof Med, Univ Pittsburgh

Southeast

Greganti, Mac Andrew MD [Ger] - **Spec Exp:** Diagnostic Problems; Dementia; **Hospital:** NC Memorial Hosp - UNC; **Address:** Univ NC Sch of Medicine,Dept Med, 125 MacNider Bldg CB#7005, Chapel Hill, NC 27599-7005; **Phone:** 919-966-3063; **Board Cert:** Internal Medicine 1987; **Med School:** Univ Miss 1972; **Resid:** Internal Medicine, Strong Meml Hosp 1975; **Fac Appt:** Prof Med, Univ NC Sch Med

Hanson, Laura C MD [Ger] - **Spec Exp:** Frailty Syndrome; Palliative Care; **Hospital:** NC Memorial Hosp - UNC; **Address:** UNC Sch Med, 5003 Old Clinic Bldg, CB 7550, Chapel Hill, NC 27599; **Phone:** 919-966-5945 x251; **Board Cert:** Internal Medicine 1989; Geriatric Medicine 2012; Hospice & Palliative Medicine 2008; **Med School:** Harvard Med Sch 1986; **Resid:** Internal Medicine, Brigham & Womens Hosp 1988; Internal Medicine, Univ NC Hosp 1989; **Fellow:** Geriatric Medicine, Univ NC Hosp 1991; **Fac Appt:** Assoc Prof Med, Univ NC Sch Med

Lyles, Kenneth W MD [Ger] - **Spec Exp:** Bone Disorders-Metabolic; Tumoral Calcinosis; Parathyroid Disease; Osteoporosis; **Hospital:** Duke Univ Hosp, Durham VA Med Ctr; **Address:** 200 Trent Dr, Clinic A, Durham, NC 27710; **Phone:** 919-660-7520; **Board Cert:** Internal Medicine 1977; Endocrinology 1979; Geriatric Medicine 2010; **Med School:** Med Coll VA 1974; **Resid:** Internal Medicine, VA Commonwealth Univ Med Ctr 1977; **Fellow:** Endocrinology, Diabetes & Metabolism, Duke Univ Med Ctr 1979; Geriatric Medicine, Duke Univ/VA Med Ctr 1981; **Fac Appt:** Prof Med, Duke Univ

Palmer, Robert M MD [Ger] - **Spec Exp:** Geriatric Functional Assessment; Dementia; **Hospital:** Sentara Norfolk Genl Hosp; **Address:** 825 Fairfax Ave Fl 2 - rm 201, Norfolk, VA 23507; **Phone:** 757-446-7040; **Board Cert:** Internal Medicine 1975; Geriatric Medicine 2009; **Med School:** Univ Mich Med Sch 1971; **Resid:** Internal Medicine, LA County Med Ctr 1975; **Fellow:** Geriatric Medicine, UCLA Med Ctr 1986

Midwest

Carr, David B MD [Ger] - **Spec Exp:** Polypharmacology; Alzheimer's Disease; **Hospital:** Barnes-Jewish Hosp; **Address:** Wash Univ Sch Med, Div Geriatrics, 4921 Parkview Pl, Ste 6c, St Louis, MO 63110; **Phone:** 314-286-1967; **Board Cert:** Internal Medicine 1989; Geriatric Medicine 2012; **Med School:** Univ MO-Columbia Sch Med 1985; **Resid:** Internal Medicine, Mich State Univ Affil Hosps 1988; **Fellow:** Geriatric Medicine, Duke Univ 1990; **Fac Appt:** Prof Med, Washington Univ, St Louis

Dale, Lowell C MD [Ger] - **Spec Exp:** Tobacco Abuse; Nutrition; **Hospital:** Mayo Med Ctr & Clin - Rochester; **Address:** Mayo Clinic, 200 First St SW, Rochester, MN 55905; **Phone:** 507-284-2439; **Board Cert:** Internal Medicine 1984; **Med School:** Univ Minn 1981; **Resid:** Internal Medicine, Mayo Clin 1984; **Fellow:** Internal Medicine, Mayo Clin 1985; **Fac Appt:** Assoc Prof Med, Mayo Med Sch

Duthie Jr, Edmund H MD [Ger] - **Spec Exp:** Geriatric Functional Assessment; **Hospital:** Froedtert & Med Coll WI, Clement J Zablocki VA Med Ctr; **Address:** Froedtert & Med Coll WI - Div Geriatrics, 9200 W Wisconsin Ave Fl 5, Milwaukee, WI 53226; **Phone:** 414-805-0728; **Board Cert:** Internal Medicine 1979; Geriatric Medicine 2008; **Med School:** Georgetown Univ 1976; **Resid:** Internal Medicine, Med Coll Wisc Affil Hosps 1979; **Fellow:** Geriatric Medicine, Jewish Inst Geri Care-SUNY 1980; **Fac Appt:** Prof Med, Med Coll Wisc

Flaherty, Joseph H MD [Ger] - **Spec Exp:** Drugs & Aging; **Hospital:** St. Louis Univ Hosp; **Address:** 1402 S Grand Blvd, rm M238, St Louis, MO 63104; **Phone:** 314-977-6055; **Board Cert:** Internal Medicine 2003; Geriatric Medicine 2006; **Med School:** St Louis Univ 1990; **Resid:** Internal Medicine, Kansas City Univ Med Ctr 1993; **Fellow:** Geriatric Medicine, St Louis Univ 1995; **Fac Appt:** Assoc Prof Med, St Louis Univ

Morley, John E MD [Ger] - **Spec Exp:** Endocrinology; Menopause-Male; Alzheimer's Disease; Frailty Syndrome; **Hospital:** St. Louis Univ Hosp; **Address:** St Louis Univ Hlth Sci Ctr, Div Ger Med, 3660 Vista Ave, Ste 204, St Louis, MO 63110; **Phone:** 314-977-6157; **Board Cert:** Internal Medicine 1978; Endocrinology, Diabetes & Metabolism 1981; Geriatric Medicine 2008; **Med School:** South Africa 1972; **Resid:** Internal Medicine, Johannesburg Genl Hosp 1974; Internal Medicine, Baragwanath Hosp 1976; **Fellow:** Endocrinology, Diabetes & Metabolism, Wadsworth VA Hosp-UCLA 1979; **Fac Appt:** Prof Med, St Louis Univ

Sachs, Greg A MD [Ger] - **Spec Exp:** Dementia; Alzheimer's Disease; Palliative Care; **Hospital:** IU Hlth Univ Hosp; **Address:** IU Hlth, Senior Care Ctr, 1050 Wishard Blvd Fl 4, Indianapolis, IN 46202; **Phone:** 317-630-8000; **Board Cert:** Internal Medicine 1988; Geriatric Medicine 2010; Hospice & Palliative Medicine 2010; **Med School:** Yale Univ 1985; **Resid:** Internal Medicine, Univ Chicago Med Ctr 1987; **Fellow:** Geriatric Medicine, Univ Chicago Med Ctr 1990; **Fac Appt:** Prof Med, Indiana Univ

Thomas, David R MD [Ger] - **Spec Exp:** Wound Healing/Care; Nutrition; Frail Elderly; **Hospital:** St. Louis Univ Hosp, Des Peres Hosp; **Address:** 3900 S Grand Blvd, St Louis, MO 63118; **Phone:** 314-771-5800; **Board Cert:** Internal Medicine 1975; Geriatric Medicine 2009; **Med School:** Univ Miss 1971; **Resid:** Internal Medicine, Univ Miss Med Ctr 1975; **Fellow:** Geriatric Medicine, Johns Hopkins Hosp 1988; **Fac Appt:** Prof Med, St Louis Univ

Great Plains and Mountains

Schwartz, Robert S MD [Ger] - **Spec Exp:** Diabetes; Hormonal Disorders; Nutrition; **Hospital:** Univ Colorado Hosp, VA Eastern CO Health Care Sys-Denver; **Address:** Anschutz Outpatient Pav, 1635 Aurora Ct Fl 5, MS F750, Aurora, CO 80045; **Phone:** 720-848-3400; **Board Cert:** Internal Medicine 1977; Endocrinology 1981; **Med School:** Ohio State Univ 1974; **Resid:** Internal Medicine, Univ Wash Med Ctr 1977; **Fellow:** Endocrinology, Diabetes & Metabolism, Univ Wash Med Ctr 1980; **Fac Appt:** Prof Med, Univ Colorado

Supiano, Mark A MD [Ger] - **Spec Exp:** Hypertension; Geriatric Functional Assessment; **Hospital:** Univ Utah Hlth Care; **Address:** Univ Utah, Geriatrics Div, 30 N 1900 E, AB 193 SOM, Salt Lake City, UT 84132; **Phone:** 801-587-9103; **Board Cert:** Internal Medicine 1985; Geriatric Medicine 2009; **Med School:** Univ Wisc 1982; **Resid:** Internal Medicine, Univ Mich Med Ctr 1985; **Fellow:** Geriatric Medicine, Univ Mich Med Ctr 1986; **Fac Appt:** Prof Med, Univ Utah

Southwest

Dyer, Carmel B MD [Ger] - **Spec Exp:** Elder Abuse; Dementia; Delirium; Geriatric Functional Assessment; **Hospital:** Meml Hermann Hosp - Texas Med Ctr, LBJ General Hosp; **Address:** Center Forg Aging, 6700 West Loop St, Ste 130, Bellaire, TX 77401; **Phone:** 713-486-5150; **Board Cert:** Geriatric Medicine 2000; **Med School:** Baylor Coll Med 1988; **Resid:** Internal Medicine, Baylor Affil Hosps 1991; **Fellow:** Geriatric Medicine, Baylor Affil Hosps 1993; **Fac Appt:** Prof Med, Univ Tex, Houston

Lipschitz, David A MD/PhD [Ger] - **Spec Exp:** Preventive Medicine; Nutrition; **Hospital:** Saline Meml Hosp; **Address:** Saline Meml Hosp-Healthy Aging Ctr, 1 Medical Park Drive, Ste 305, Medical Office B Bldg, Benton, AR 72015; **Phone:** 855-690-9355; **Board Cert:** Internal Medicine 1975; Hematology 1976; **Med School:** South Africa 1966; **Resid:** Internal Medicine, Johannesburg Genl Hosp 1972; **Fellow:** Hematology, Univ Washington Med Ctr 1974; Internal Medicine, Montefiore Hosp 1975; **Fac Appt:** Prof Med, Univ Ark

Raji, Mukaila A MD [Ger] - **Spec Exp:** Memory Disorders; Cognitive Loss in Aging; **Hospital:** UT Med Br at Galveston(John Sealy Hosp); **Address:** UTMB Geriatric Clinics, 400 Harborside Drive, Ste 100, Galveston, TX 77550; **Phone:** 409-772-3373; **Board Cert:** Internal Medicine 2009; Geriatric Medicine 2009; **Med School:** Nigeria 1987; **Resid:** Internal Medicine, Washington Hosp Ctr 1997; **Fellow:** Geriatric Medicine, Duke Univ Med Ctr 1999; **Fac Appt:** Prof Med, Univ Tex Med Br, Galveston

Wei, Jeanne MD/PhD [Ger] - **Spec Exp:** Cardiovascular Disease; **Hospital:** UAMS Med Ctr, John L McClellan VA Med Ctr; **Address:** UAMS Thomas A Lyon Longevity Ctr, 4301 W Markham St, Little Rock, AR 72205; **Phone:** 501-686-6219; **Board Cert:** Internal Medicine 1978; Cardiovascular Disease 1979; **Med School:** Univ IL Coll Med 1975; **Resid:** Internal Medicine, Johns Hopkins Hosp 1977; **Fellow:** Cardiovascular Disease, Johns Hopkins Hosp 1979; Research, Natl Inst Aging 1979; **Fac Appt:** Prof Med, Univ Ark

West Coast and Pacific

Abrass, Itamar B MD [Ger] - **Spec Exp:** Geriatric Endocrinology; Endocrinology; Diabetes; **Hospital:** Harborview Med Ctr, Univ Wash Med Ctr; **Address:** Harborview Med Ctr, 325 9th Ave, Box 359860, Seattle, WA 98104; **Phone:** 206-744-4191; **Board Cert:** Internal Medicine 1974; Endocrinology, Diabetes & Metabolism 1975; **Med School:** UCSF 1966; **Resid:** Internal Medicine, NY-Presby/Columbia Univ Med Ctr 1968; **Fellow:** Endocrinology, Diabetes & Metabolism, UCSD Med Ctr 1971; **Fac Appt:** Prof Med, Univ Wash

McCormick, Wayne MD [Ger] - **Spec Exp:** Dementia; AIDS/HIV; **Hospital:** Harborview Med Ctr, Univ Wash Med Ctr; **Address:** Harborview Med Ctr, 325 9th Ave, Box 359860, Seattle, WA 98104; **Phone:** 206-744-4191; **Board Cert:** Internal Medicine 1986; Geriatric Medicine 2012; Public Health & Genl Preventive Med 1992; Hospice & Palliative Medicine 2010; **Med School:** Washington Univ, St Louis 1983; **Resid:** Internal Medicine, Michael Reese Hosp 1987; **Fellow:** Geriatric Medicine, Univ Wash Med Ctr 1990; **Fac Appt:** Prof Med, Univ Wash

Reuben, David B MD [Ger] - **Spec Exp:** Geriatric Functional Assessment; **Hospital:** UCLA Ronald Reagan Med Ctr, Santa Monica - UCLA Med Ctr & Ortho Hosp; **Address:** Peter Morton Medical Building, 200 UCLA Medical Plaza, Ste 420, Los Angeles, CA 90095; **Phone:** 310-206-8272; **Board Cert:** Internal Medicine 1980; Geriatric Medicine 2005; **Med School:** Emory Univ 1977; **Resid:** Internal Medicine, Rhode Island Hosp 1980; **Fellow:** Geriatric Medicine, UCLA Med Ctr 1987; **Fac Appt:** Prof Med, UCLA

Tenover, Joyce S MD/PhD [Ger] - **Spec Exp:** Polypharmacology; Dementia; Depression; **Hospital:** VA Hlth Care Sys - Palo Alto; **Address:** VA Palo Alto HCS, GRECC (182B), 3801 Miranda Ave, Palo Alto, CA 94304-1290; **Phone:** 650-493-5000 x66946; **Board Cert:** Internal Medicine 1983; Geriatric Medicine 2008; **Med School:** Geo Wash Univ 1980; **Resid:** Internal Medicine, Univ Wash Affil Hosps 1983; Internal Medicine, VA Med Ctr 1984; **Fellow:** Geriatric Medicine, VA Med Ctr 1987; **Fac Appt:** Clin Prof Med, Geo Wash Univ

Maimonides Medical Center

GERIATRICS PROGRAM

4802 Tenth Avenue
Brooklyn, New York 11219
Phone: 718.283.7071 • Fax: 718.635.6417
www.maimonidesmed.org/geriatrics

Maimonides serves one of the oldest populations in New York State, with one quarter of our patients over the age of 75. The Geriatrics Program at Maimonides is fully equipped to meet the special needs of this growing population. Directed by Barbara Paris, MD, the program encompasses inpatient and outpatient services, featuring the Acute Care for Elderly (ACE) Unit and the Safe at Home program. The staff is focused on the continuity, coordination, quality and dignity of care provided.

Patient Evaluation

ACE Unit services focus on acute medical care and account for the complex needs of hospitalized elderly patients. Special attention is given to the assessment of memory loss and understanding the underlying causes of geriatric syndromes that result in falls, incontinence and frailty. Psychosocial issues affecting elderly patients, such as loneliness and end-of-life care, are also addressed.

Wound Care and Hyperbaric Center

Elderly patients can often have wounds that do not heal easily, which is why we have a dedicated wound care team available. Individualized wound treatment is dependent upon the type and severity of the wound. Treatments include conventional and advanced wound dressings, antibiotic therapy, protective footwear, and hyperbaric oxygen therapy.

Safe at Home Program

The Safe at Home program actively manages the care of the frail elderly so that they may live at home and within their communities. The program is designed to identify patients aged 75 years and older who are at high risk during the transitional period from hospital to home; provide them with coordinated comprehensive care after the transition from hospital to home; actively engage family caregivers and community support networks; increase patient satisfaction with their care during this transitional period; and reduce re-hospitalizations, emergency room visits and nursing home placements.

Outpatient Geriatric Services

Our geriatric team offers comprehensive assessment and primary care services throughout Southern Brooklyn.

Relying heavily on evidence-based medicine, Maimonides Medical Center has been commended for outstanding services by a number of independent rating organizations. Earlier this year, Maimonides was named a Distinguished Hospital for Clinical Excellence by HealthGrades – one of only three hospitals in the metropolitan area; the American Stroke Association bestowed its Gold Plus Achievement Award on the hospital; and the American Hospital Association once again named it a Most Wired hospital.

Maimonides Medical Center
The right care.
Right here.

www.maimonidesmed.org/geriatrics

Mount Sinai

THE MOUNT SINAI MEDICAL CENTER
Geriatrics and Palliative Care

One Gustave L. Levy Place
Fifth Avenue and 100th Street
New York, NY 10029-6574

Physician Referral: 1-800-MD-SINAI (637-4624)
www.mountsinai.org

THE BEST IN CLINICAL CARE

In recognition of the care offered to older patients, The Mount Sinai Medical Center's **BROOKDALE DEPARTMENT OF GERIATRICS AND PALLIATIVE MEDICINE** is cited time and time again among the finest in the nation. In 2013, *U.S. News & World Report* ranked our geriatrics specialty #4 and our medical school program #1 in the United States.

We offer a full spectrum of patient care, including a specialized inpatient care team for the elderly to minimize complications sometimes associated with an older person's hospital stay, a primary care geriatrics practice for older adults living in the community, a hospital-based consultation service for patients throughout Mount Sinai, a number of community-linked programs and partnerships, and a palliative care team dedicated to ensuring the highest quality care and support for patients and families facing serious illnesses.

The Martha Stewart Center for Living, a modern facility designed by renowned architect C.C. Pei, provides clinical care and education for patients and serves as a training ground for physicians. Our newly opened Wiener Family Palliative Care Unit, the only one of its kind in Manhattan, provides inpatient care for patients and families facing serious and life-threatening illness.

Groundbreaking Research—Mount Sinai's researchers continue to advance the understanding, prevention, and treatment of age-related disorders. The extensive research on aging conducted by the Brookdale Department of Geriatrics and Palliative Medicine includes studies on health services, medical decision making and ethical dilemmas, palliative care, the neurobiology of aging, and clinical interventions to promote independence in old age. The department's expertise serves as a renowned educational resource for all Mount Sinai affiliates and other institutions in teaching geriatrics and palliative medicine to medical students, medical residents, geriatrics and palliative care fellows, established physicians, and health profession trainees in other disciplines.

History Of Excellence—The Mount Sinai Medical Center is a pioneer in geriatric medicine. In 1909, a Mount Sinai physician coined the term "geriatrics," and in 1914, he wrote the first textbook on medical care for older adults. Today, the Brookdale Department of Geriatrics and Palliative Medicine continues to break new ground, offering comprehensive care, disease prevention, and the promotion of healthy and productive aging. The department's enhanced expertise in assessing and managing patients with dementia greatly complements its established, interdisciplinary approach to patient care, in which medical staff and social workers address each patient's needs as a team.

THE FIRST FREESTANDING DEPARTMENT OF GERIATRICS AT A U.S. MEDICAL SCHOOL

Mount Sinai's Brookdale Department of Geriatrics and Palliative Medicine was the first freestanding department of geriatrics established by a U.S. medical school, and it continues to be one of the very best. It offers unparalleled inpatient and outpatient care, as well as numerous treatment programs designed to meet the unique needs of older adults. Mount Sinai is also home to world-class researchers dedicated to advancing our understanding of Alzheimer's disease and other common geriatric conditions. At the department's heart are its patients. The geriatricians of The Mount Sinai Medical Center work hard to improve life and longevity for New York's elderly.

NYU Langone MEDICAL CENTER

550 First Avenue *(at 31st Street)*
New York, NY 10016

www.NYULMC.org

Physician Referral: **888-7-NYU-MED** *(888-769-8633)*

INTERNAL MEDICINE

Internal medicine physicians at NYU Langone Medical Center are dedicated to treating the whole patient, and not just their disease. Our team addresses both the physical and psychological aspects of health and disease through clear communication and a fully integrated regimen of care. We specialize in the following areas:

Primary and Specialized Healthcare
General Internal Medicine offers a multidisciplinary medical approach to treating illnesses involving the heart, lungs, gastrointestinal tract, joints, bones, muscles, endocrine organs and kidneys. A wide range of laboratory, imaging and advanced diagnostic testing, ranging from throat cultures to the complex mapping of the electrical surface of the heart, is available on-site or by referral. Comprehensive women's healthcare, including cancer screening and osteoporosis prevention and treatment, is also available. We offer a variety of convenient office locations in Manhattan and the surrounding metropolitan area.

Geriatrics
Our geriatric specialists provide comprehensive and multidisciplinary care, consultation and follow-up for elderly patients ranging from prevention and healthy aging to the treatment and care of chronic conditions including dementia, functional impairment and degenerative disorders.

Top Doctors Make A Difference

Gynecologic Oncology

a subspecialty of Obstetrics & Gynecology

An obstetrician/gynecologist who provides consultation and comprehensive management of patients with gynecologic cancer, including those diagnostic and therapeutic procedures necessary for the total care of the patient with gynecologic cancer and resulting complications.

Training Required: Four years *plus* two years in clinical practice before certification in obstetrics and gynecology is complete *plus* additional training and examination in gynecologic oncology.

Gynecologic Oncology

New England

Azodi, Masoud MD [GO] - **Spec Exp:** Laparoscopic Surgery; Ovarian Cancer-Early Detection; Uterine Cancer; Vulvar & Vaginal Cancer; **Hospital:** Smilow Cancer Hosp at Yale-New Haven; **Address:** Smilow Cancer Hosp, Gynecologic Oncology, 25 Park St, Ste B, New Haven, CT 06519; **Phone:** 203-785-4013; **Board Cert:** Gynecologic Oncology 2012; Obstetrics & Gynecology 2012; **Med School:** Wright State Univ 1992; **Resid:** Obstetrics & Gynecology, Aultman Hosp 1996; **Fellow:** Gynecologic Oncology, Yale-New Haven Hosp 1999; **Fac Appt:** Assoc Prof ObG, Yale Univ

Berkowitz, Ross S MD [GO] - **Spec Exp:** Gynecologic Cancer; **Hospital:** Brigham & Women's Hosp, Dana-Farber Cancer Inst; **Address:** Brigham & Women's Hospital, Div Gynecologic Oncology, 75 Francis St, Ste A3150, Boston, MA 02115; **Phone:** 617-732-8840; **Board Cert:** Obstetrics & Gynecology 1981; Gynecologic Oncology 1982; **Med School:** Boston Univ 1973; **Resid:** Surgery, Brigham and Women's Hosp 1975; Obstetrics & Gynecology, Brigham and Women's Hosp 1978; **Fellow:** Gynecologic Oncology, Brigham and Women's Hosp 1980; **Fac Appt:** Prof ObG, Harvard Med Sch

Brewer, Molly A MD [GO] - **Spec Exp:** Ovarian Cancer; Gynecologic Cancer; Gynecologic Cancer-Rare; **Hospital:** Univ of Conn Hlth Ctr, John Dempsey Hosp, Middlesex Hosp; **Address:** Univ Conn Hlth Ctr, Div Gyn Oncology, 263 Farmington Ave, MC2875, Farmington, CT 06032-2875; **Phone:** 860-679-2100; **Board Cert:** Obstetrics & Gynecology 2012; Gynecologic Oncology 2012; **Med School:** SUNY Upstate Med Univ 1991; **Resid:** Obstetrics & Gynecology, Oregon Hlth Scis Ctr 1995; **Fellow:** Gynecologic Oncology, MD Anderson Cancer Ctr 1997; **Fac Appt:** Prof ObG, SUNY Upstate Med Univ

Cain, Joanna M MD [GO] - **Spec Exp:** Cervical Cancer; Ovarian Cancer; Uterine Cancer; Women's Health; **Hospital:** UMass Mem Med Ctr-Memorial Campus; **Address:** UMass Meml Med Ctr-Dept of Ob/Gyn, 119 Belmont St Jaquith Bldg Fl 2, Worcester, MA 01605; **Phone:** 508-334-1377; **Board Cert:** Obstetrics & Gynecology 2012; Gynecologic Oncology 2012; **Med School:** Creighton Univ 1977; **Resid:** Obstetrics & Gynecology, Univ Washington Med Ctr 1981; **Fellow:** Gynecologic Oncology, Meml Sloan Kettering Cancer Ctr 1983; Clinical Ethics, Univ Washington; **Fac Appt:** Prof ObG, Univ Mass Sch Med

Cosin, Jonathan A MD [GO] - **Hospital:** Hosp of Central CT at New Britain, Hartford Hosp; **Address:** 440 New Britian Ave, Plainville, CT 06062; **Phone:** 860-826-1101; **Board Cert:** Obstetrics & Gynecology 2012; Gynecologic Oncology 2012; **Med School:** NY Med Coll 1991; **Resid:** Obstetrics & Gynecology, Baystate Med Ctr 1995; **Fellow:** Gynecology, Meml Sloan Kettering Cancer Ctr 1993; Gynecologic Oncology, Univ Minnesota Hosp 1998; **Fac Appt:** Asst Prof ObG, Georgetown Univ

DeMars, Leslie R MD [GO] - **Spec Exp:** Gynecologic Cancer; Laparoscopic Surgery; **Hospital:** Dartmouth - Hitchcock Med Ctr; **Address:** Dartmouth-Hitchcock Med Ctr, Gyn-Oncology, 1 Medical Center Drive, Lebanon, NH 03756; **Phone:** 603-653-3525; **Board Cert:** Obstetrics & Gynecology 2012; Gynecologic Oncology 2012; **Med School:** Univ VT Coll Med 1987; **Resid:** Obstetrics & Gynecology, Univ NC Hosp 1991; **Fellow:** Gynecologic Oncology, Univ NC Hosp 1994; **Fac Appt:** Assoc Prof ObG, Dartmouth Med Sch

Granai III, Cornelius O MD [GO] - **Spec Exp:** Gynecologic Cancer; Complementary Medicine; International Health; **Hospital:** Women & Infants Hosp of RI, Kent Hosp; **Address:** Women & Infants Hosp, Womens Oncology Program, 101 Dudley St, Providence, RI 02905; **Phone:** 401-453-7520; **Board Cert:** Obstetrics & Gynecology 2012; Gynecologic Oncology 2012; **Med School:** Univ VT Coll Med 1977; **Resid:** Obstetrics & Gynecology, Tufts-New England Med Ctr 1981; **Fellow:** Gynecologic Oncology, Tufts Univ 1983; **Fac Appt:** Prof ObG, Brown Univ

Muto, Michael G MD [GO] - **Spec Exp:** Ovarian Cancer; Cervical Cancer; Vulvar & Vaginal Cancer; Robotic Surgery; **Hospital:** Brigham & Women's Hosp, Dana-Farber Cancer Inst; **Address:** Brigham & Women's Hosp, Div Gynecologic Oncology, 75 Francis St, Ste A3173, Boston, MA 02115; **Phone:** 617-732-8840; **Board Cert:** Obstetrics & Gynecology 2012; Gynecologic Oncology 2012; **Med School:** Univ Mass Sch Med 1983; **Resid:** Obstetrics & Gynecology, Brigham & Women's Hosp 1987; **Fellow:** Gynecologic Oncology, Brigham & Women's Hosp 1990; **Fac Appt:** Assoc Prof ObG, Harvard Med Sch

Rutherford, Thomas J MD [GO] - **Spec Exp:** Ovarian Cancer; Uterine Cancer; Ovarian Cancer-Early Detection; Cervical Cancer; **Hospital:** Smilow Cancer Hosp at Yale-New Haven; **Address:** Smilow Cancer Hosp, Gynecologic Oncology, 25 Park St, Ste B, New Haven, CT 06519; **Phone:** 203-200-4176; **Board Cert:** Obstetrics & Gynecology 2012; Gynecologic Oncology 2012; **Med School:** Med Coll OH 1989; **Resid:** Obstetrics & Gynecology, Cooper Univ Hosp 1993; **Fellow:** Gynecologic Oncology, Yale-New Haven Hosp 1995; **Fac Appt:** Prof ObG, Yale Univ

Santin, Alessandro MD [GO] - **Spec Exp:** Immunotherapy; Ovarian Cancer; Vulvar & Vaginal Cancer; **Hospital:** Yale-New Haven Hosp; **Address:** Yale Gynecologic Oncology, 35 Park St Fl 1, New Haven, CT 06520; **Phone:** 203-200-4176; **Med School:** Italy 1989; **Resid:** Obstetrics & Gynecology, Univ Brescia Sch Med 1993; **Fellow:** Gynecologic Oncology, UC Irvine Med Ctr 1995; Gynecologic Oncology, UAMS Med Ctr 2000; **Fac Appt:** Prof ObG, Yale Univ

Schorge, John O MD [GO] - **Spec Exp:** Ovarian Cancer; Uterine Cancer; Cervical Cancer; Minimally Invasive Surgery; **Hospital:** Mass Genl Hosp; **Address:** Mass General Hosp, Gillette Ctr for Gynecologic Oncology, 55 Fruit St, Ste YAW 9E, Boston, MA 02114; **Phone:** 617-724-6899; **Board Cert:** Obstetrics & Gynecology 2012; Gynecologic Oncology 2012; **Med School:** Vanderbilt Univ 1993; **Resid:** Obstetrics & Gynecology, Brigham & Women's Hosp 1997; **Fellow:** Gynecologic Oncology, Brigham & Women's Hosp 2000; **Fac Appt:** Assoc Prof ObG, Harvard Med Sch

Schwartz, Peter E MD [GO] - **Spec Exp:** Ovarian Cancer; Uterine Cancer; Gynecologic Surgery-Complex; Cervical Cancer; **Hospital:** Smilow Cancer Hosp at Yale-New Haven; **Address:** Smilow Cancer Hosp, Gynecology Oncology, 20 York St, New Haven, CT 06510; **Phone:** 203-785-4014; **Board Cert:** Obstetrics & Gynecology 1973; Gynecologic Oncology 1979; **Med School:** Albert Einstein Coll Med 1966; **Resid:** Obstetrics & Gynecology, Yale-New Haven Hosp 1970; **Fellow:** Gynecologic Oncology, UT MD Anderson Cancer Ctr 1975; **Fac Appt:** Prof ObG, Yale Univ

Silasi, Dan-Arin MD [GO] - **Spec Exp:** Robotic Surgery; **Hospital:** Yale-New Haven Hosp; **Address:** Yale, Gynecologic Oncology, 25 Park St, Ste B, New Haven, CT 06513; **Phone:** 203-737-6214; **Board Cert:** Obstetrics & Gynecology 2012; Gynecologic Oncology 2012; **Med School:** Romania 1993; **Resid:** Otolaryngology, Univ Med & Pharm 1999; Obstetrics & Gynecology, UT Hlth Sci Ctr 2005; **Fellow:** Gynecologic Oncology, Yale-New Haven Hosp 2006; **Fac Appt:** Asst Prof ObG, Yale Univ

Tarraza, Hector M MD [GO] - **Spec Exp:** Gynecologic Cancer; **Hospital:** Maine Med Ctr; **Address:** Maine Medical Partners, 100 Campus Drive, Ste 125, Scarborough, ME 04074; **Phone:** 207-883-0069; **Board Cert:** Obstetrics & Gynecology 2012; Gynecologic Oncology 2012; **Med School:** Harvard Med Sch 1981; **Resid:** Obstetrics & Gynecology, Mass Genl Hosp 1985; **Fellow:** Gynecologic Oncology, Mass Genl Hosp 1987; **Fac Appt:** Prof ObG, Tufts Univ

Gynecologic Oncology

Mid Atlantic

Abbas, Fouad M MD [GO] - **Spec Exp:** Gynecologic Cancer; Ovarian Cancer; Cervical Cancer; **Hospital:** Sinai Hosp - Baltimore; **Address:** Sinai Hosp, Gynecologic Onc Dept, 2411 W Belvedere Ave, Ste 206, Baltimore, MD 21215; **Phone:** 410-601-9030; **Board Cert:** Obstetrics & Gynecology 2012; Gynecologic Oncology 2012; **Med School:** Univ MD Sch Med 1986; **Resid:** Obstetrics & Gynecology, Johns Hopkins Hosp 1990; **Fellow:** Gynecologic Oncology, Johns Hopkins Hosp 1992; **Fac Appt:** Asst Prof ObG, Univ MD Sch Med

Abu-Rustum, Nadeem R MD [GO] - **Spec Exp:** Ovarian Cancer; Uterine Cancer; Cervical Cancer; Vulvar Disease/Cancer; **Hospital:** Meml Sloan-Kettering Canc Ctr; **Address:** 1275 York Ave, Ste H-1308, New York, NY 10065; **Phone:** 212-639-7051; **Board Cert:** Obstetrics & Gynecology 2012; Gynecologic Oncology 2012; **Med School:** Lebanon 1990; **Resid:** Obstetrics & Gynecology, Greater Baltimore Med Ctr 1994; **Fellow:** Gynecologic Oncology, Meml Sloan-Kettering Cancer Ctr 1997; **Fac Appt:** Prof ObG, Cornell Univ-Weill Med Coll

Alexander, Margaret N MD [GO] - **Spec Exp:** HPV-Human Papilloma Virus; Vaccine Therapy; Laparoscopic Surgery; **Hospital:** Sibley Mem Hosp; **Address:** 9100 Old Georgetown Rd, Bethesda, MD 20814; **Phone:** 301-564-4966; **Board Cert:** Obstetrics & Gynecology 2012; **Med School:** Yale Univ 1986; **Resid:** Obstetrics & Gynecology, Yale-New Haven Hosp 1994; **Fellow:** Gynecologic Oncology, Georgetown Univ Hosp 1997; **Fac Appt:** Asst Prof ObG, Geo Wash Univ

Barakat, Richard R MD [GO] - **Spec Exp:** Robotic Surgery; Ovarian Cancer; Uterine Cancer; Cervical Cancer; **Hospital:** Meml Sloan-Kettering Canc Ctr; **Address:** 1275 York Ave, rm H1305, New York, NY 10065; **Phone:** 646-497-9055; **Board Cert:** Obstetrics & Gynecology 2012; Gynecologic Oncology 2012; **Med School:** SUNY Hlth Sci Ctr 1985; **Resid:** Obstetrics & Gynecology, Bellevue Hosp 1989; **Fellow:** Gynecologic Oncology, Meml Sloan Kettering Cancer Ctr 1991; **Fac Appt:** Prof ObG, Cornell Univ-Weill Med Coll

Barnes, Willard MD [GO] - **Spec Exp:** Pelvic Tumors; Gynecologic Cancer; **Hospital:** MedStar Georgetown Univ Hosp; **Address:** Georgetown Univ Hosp, Lombardi Cancer Ctr, Dept Gyn Oncology, 3800 Reservoir Rd NW, Washington, DC 20007-2194; **Phone:** 202-444-2114; **Board Cert:** Obstetrics & Gynecology 2012; Gynecologic Oncology 2012; **Med School:** Univ Miss 1979; **Resid:** Obstetrics & Gynecology, Univ Miss Med Ctr 1983; **Fellow:** Gynecologic Oncology, Georgetown Univ Med Ctr 1985; **Fac Appt:** Assoc Prof ObG, Georgetown Univ

Barter, James MD [GO] - **Spec Exp:** Laparoscopic Surgery; Ovarian Cancer; Robotic Surgery; **Hospital:** Holy Cross Hospital - Silver Spring; **Address:** Womens Hlth Specialists, 6301 Executive Blvd, Rockville, MD 20852; **Phone:** 301-770-4967; **Board Cert:** Obstetrics & Gynecology 2012; Gynecologic Oncology 2012; **Med School:** Univ VA Sch Med 1977; **Resid:** Internal Medicine, Univ Kentucky Med Ctr 1979; Obstetrics & Gynecology, Duke Univ Hosp 1983; **Fellow:** Gynecologic Oncology, UAB Hosp 1985; **Fac Appt:** Clin Prof ObG, Geo Wash Univ

Boice, Charles R MD [GO] - **Spec Exp:** Ovarian Cancer; Cervical Cancer; **Hospital:** MedStar Franklin Square Hosp; **Address:** 10301 Georgia Ave, Ste 205, Silver Springs, MD 20902; **Phone:** 301-592-1600; **Board Cert:** Obstetrics & Gynecology 1981; Gynecologic Oncology 1982; **Med School:** Loma Linda Univ 1973; **Resid:** Obstetrics & Gynecology, LAC & USC Med Ctr 1973; Surgery, City Hope Natl Med Ctr 1978; **Fellow:** Oncology, UT MD Anderson Cancer Ctr 1980; **Fac Appt:** Assoc Clin Prof ObG, Univ Wash

Burger, Robert A MD [GO] - **Spec Exp:** Ovarian Cancer; Uterine Cancer; Cervical Cancer; Gestational Trophoblastic Disease; **Hospital:** Pennsylvania Hosp-UPHS (page 69), Jeanes Hosp; **Address:** Pennsylvania Hosp, Gynecologic Oncology, Penn Medicine Washington Square, 800 Walnut St Fl 10, Philadelphia, PA 19107; **Phone:** 800-789-7366; **Board Cert:** Obstetrics & Gynecology 2012; Gynecologic Oncology 2012; **Med School:** NYU Sch Med 1988; **Resid:** Obstetrics & Gynecology, Hosp Univ Penn 1992; **Fellow:** Gynecologic Oncology, UC Irvine Med Ctr 1996

Caputo, Thomas A MD [GO] - **Spec Exp:** Cervical Cancer; Ovarian Cancer; Uterine Cancer; Vulvar Disease/Cancer; **Hospital:** NY-Presby/Weill Cornell Med Ctr, NY (page 65); **Address:** NY Presby Hosp-Weill Cornell, 525 E 68th St, Ste J-130, New York, NY 10021; **Phone:** 212-746-3179; **Board Cert:** Obstetrics & Gynecology 1993; Gynecologic Oncology 1977; **Med School:** UMDNJ-NJ Med Sch, Newark 1965; **Resid:** Obstetrics & Gynecology, Martland Hosp 1969; **Fellow:** Gynecologic Oncology, Emory Univ Hosp 1975; **Fac Appt:** Clin Prof ObG, Cornell Univ-Weill Med Coll

Carlson Jr, John A MD [GO] - **Spec Exp:** Gynecologic Cancer; Ovarian Cancer; Gynecologic Surgery-Complex; **Hospital:** Virtua West Jersey Hosp - Voorhees; **Address:** 200 Bowman Drive, Ste E315, Voorhees, NJ 08043; **Phone:** 856-247-7310; **Board Cert:** Obstetrics & Gynecology 1981; Gynecologic Oncology 1982; **Med School:** Georgetown Univ 1974; **Resid:** Obstetrics & Gynecology, Hosp Univ Penn 1978; **Fellow:** Gynecologic Oncology, MD Anderson Cancer Ctr 1980; **Fac Appt:** Prof ObG, Drexel Univ Coll Med

Chi, Dennis S MD [GO] - **Spec Exp:** Ovarian Cancer; Uterine Cancer; Cervical Cancer; Gynecologic Surgery-Complex; **Hospital:** Meml Sloan-Kettering Canc Ctr; **Address:** 1275 York Ave, New York, NY 10065; **Phone:** 212-639-5016; **Board Cert:** Obstetrics & Gynecology 2012; Gynecologic Oncology 2012; **Med School:** NYU Sch Med 1990; **Resid:** Obstetrics & Gynecology, NYU Med Ctr 1994; **Fellow:** Gynecologic Oncology, Meml Sloan Kettering Cancer Ctr 1997; **Fac Appt:** Prof ObG, NYU Sch Med

Cornelison, Terri L MD/PhD [GO] - **Spec Exp:** Gynecologic Cancer; Ovarian Cancer; Clinical Trials; **Hospital:** Johns Hopkins Hosp (page 59); **Address:** Johns Hopkins, Gynecologic Onc Svc, 601 N Caroline St Fl 8, Baltimore, MD 21287; **Phone:** 443-997-0400; **Board Cert:** Obstetrics & Gynecology 2012; Gynecologic Oncology 2012; **Med School:** Yale Univ 1985; **Resid:** Obstetrics & Gynecology, Beth Israel Deaconess Med Ctr 1989; **Fellow:** Gynecologic Oncology, Roswell Park Cancer Inst 1992; **Fac Appt:** Asst Prof ObG, Johns Hopkins Univ

Curtin, John P MD [GO] - **Spec Exp:** Uterine Cancer; Ovarian Cancer; Laparoscopic Surgery; Gestational Trophoblastic Disease; **Hospital:** NYU Langone Med Ctr (page 68); **Address:** NYU Clin Cancer Ctr, 240 E 38th St, Fl 19, New York, NY 10016-6402; **Phone:** 212-731-5345; **Board Cert:** Obstetrics & Gynecology 2012; Gynecologic Oncology 2012; **Med School:** Creighton Univ 1979; **Resid:** Obstetrics & Gynecology, Univ Minn Med Ctr 1984; **Fellow:** Gynecologic Oncology, Meml Sloan-Kettering Cancer Ctr 1988; **Fac Appt:** Prof ObG, NYU Sch Med

Dottino, Peter R MD [GO] - **Spec Exp:** Laparoscopic Surgery; Gynecologic Cancer; Uterine Cancer; Ovarian Cancer; **Hospital:** Mt Sinai Med Ctr (page 62), Maimonides Med Ctr (page 60); **Address:** The Group for Women, 800-A 5th Ave, Ste 405, New York, NY 10065; **Phone:** 212-888-8439; **Board Cert:** Obstetrics & Gynecology 2012; Gynecologic Oncology 2012; **Med School:** Georgetown Univ 1979; **Resid:** Obstetrics & Gynecology, SUNY Downstate Med Ctr 1983; **Fellow:** Gynecologic Oncology, Mt Sinai Hosp 1986; **Fac Appt:** Assoc Clin Prof ObG, Mount Sinai Sch Med

Dunton, Charles J MD [GO] - **Spec Exp:** Ovarian Cancer; Uterine Cancer; Cervical Cancer; Gynecologic Surgery-Complex; **Hospital:** Lankenau Hosp; **Address:** Main Line Gyn Oncology, 100 E Lancaster Ave, Medical Office Bldg East, Ste 661, Wynnewood, PA 19096; **Phone:** 610-649-8085; **Board Cert:** Obstetrics & Gynecology 2012; Gynecologic Oncology 2012; **Med School:** Jefferson Med Coll 1980; **Resid:** Obstetrics & Gynecology, Lankenau Hosp 1984; **Fellow:** Gynecologic Oncology, Hosp Univ Penn 1989; **Fac Appt:** Prof ObG, Jefferson Med Coll

Edwards, Robert P MD [GO] - **Spec Exp:** Ovarian Cancer; Gynecologic Cancer; Cervical Cancer; Clinical Trials; **Hospital:** Magee-Womens Hosp - UPMC; **Address:** Univ Pittsburgh Physicians, 300 Halket St, Ste 2130, Pittsburgh, PA 15213; **Phone:** 412-641-1153; **Board Cert:** Obstetrics & Gynecology 2012; Gynecologic Oncology 2012; **Med School:** Univ Pittsburgh 1984; **Resid:** Obstetrics & Gynecology, Magee-Womens Hosp 1989; **Fellow:** Gynecologic Oncology, Univ Alabama Affil Hosp 1993; **Fac Appt:** Prof ObG, Univ Pittsburgh

Fields, Abbie L MD [GO] - **Spec Exp:** Fertility Preservation in Cancer; Robotic Surgery; Cancer Genetics; Pelvic Reconstruction; **Hospital:** MedStar Washington Hosp Ctr; **Address:** Washington Hospital Center, 110 Irving St NW, rm 5B-33B, Washington, DC 20010; **Phone:** 202-877-2391; **Board Cert:** Obstetrics & Gynecology 2012; Gynecologic Oncology 2012; **Med School:** Ohio State Univ 1987; **Resid:** Obstetrics & Gynecology, Northwestern Meml Hosp 1991; **Fellow:** Gynecologic Oncology, Johns Hopkins Hosp 1993

Fishman, David A MD [GO] - **Spec Exp:** Gynecologic Cancer; Ovarian Cancer-Early Detection; Minimally Invasive Surgery; **Hospital:** Mt Sinai Med Ctr (page 62); **Address:** 5 E 98th St, Fl 2, New York, NY 10029; **Phone:** 212-241-7952; **Board Cert:** Obstetrics & Gynecology 2011; Gynecologic Oncology 2011; **Med School:** Texas Tech Univ 1988; **Resid:** Obstetrics & Gynecology, Yale-New Haven Hosp 1992; **Fellow:** Gynecologic Oncology, Yale-New Haven Hosp 1994; **Fac Appt:** Prof ObG, Mount Sinai Sch Med

Giuntoli II, Robert Lawrence MD [GO] - **Spec Exp:** Gynecologic Cancer; Ovarian Cancer; Gestational Trophoblastic Disease; Immunotherapy; **Hospital:** Johns Hopkins Hosp (page 59); **Address:** Johns Hopkins, Gynecologic Onc Svc, 601 N Caroline St Fl 8, Baltimore, MD 21287; **Phone:** 443-997-0400; **Board Cert:** Obstetrics & Gynecology 2012; Gynecologic Oncology 2012; **Med School:** Univ Pennsylvania 1994; **Resid:** Obstetrics & Gynecology, Duke Univ Med Ctr 1998; **Fellow:** Gynecologic Oncology, Mayo Clin 2002; **Fac Appt:** Asst Prof ObG, Johns Hopkins Univ

Herzog, Thomas J MD [GO] - **Spec Exp:** Cervical Cancer; Gynecologic Cancer; Laparoscopic Surgery; Ovarian Cancer; **Hospital:** NY-Presby/Columbia Univ Med Ctr, NY (page 65); **Address:** Herbert Irving Pavilion, 161 Fort Washington Ave, Fl 8, rm 837, New York, NY 10032; **Phone:** 212-305-3410; **Board Cert:** Obstetrics & Gynecology 2012; Gynecologic Oncology 2012; **Med School:** Univ Cincinnati 1986; **Resid:** Obstetrics & Gynecology, Good Samaritan Hosp 1990; **Fellow:** Gynecologic Oncology, Barnes Jewish Hosp/Wash Univ 1993; **Fac Appt:** Prof ObG, Columbia P&S

Kelley III, Joseph L MD [GO] - **Spec Exp:** Breast Cancer; Ovarian Cancer; Cervical Cancer; Gynecologic Cancer; **Hospital:** Magee-Womens Hosp - UPMC; **Address:** Univ Pittsburgh Physicians, Div Gyn Oncology, 300 Halket St, Ste 1750, Pittsburgh, PA 15213; **Phone:** 412-641-5411; **Board Cert:** Obstetrics & Gynecology 2012; Gynecologic Oncology 2012; **Med School:** St Louis Univ 1985; **Resid:** Obstetrics & Gynecology, Magee-Womens Hosp 1989; **Fellow:** Gynecologic Oncology, MD Anderson Cancer Ctr 1991; **Fac Appt:** Prof ObG, Univ Pittsburgh

King, Stephanie A MD [GO] - **Spec Exp:** Minimally Invasive Gynecologic Surgery; Ovarian Cancer; Uterine Cancer; Cervical Cancer; **Hospital:** Fox Chase Cancer Ctr (page 57), Jeanes Hosp; **Address:** Fox Chase Cancer Ctr-Div Gyn Oncology, 333 Cottman Ave, Philadelphia, PA 19111; **Phone:** 215-728-5628; **Board Cert:** Obstetrics & Gynecology 2012; Gynecologic Oncology 2012; **Med School:** Univ Pennsylvania 1983; **Resid:** Obstetrics & Gynecology, Hosp Univ Penn 1988; **Fellow:** Gynecologic Oncology, Hosp Univ Penn 1990

Koulos, John P MD [GO] - **Spec Exp:** Uterine Cancer; Ovarian Cancer; Cervical Cancer; Vulvar & Vaginal Cancer; **Hospital:** Beth Israel Med Ctr - Petrie Div (page 56); **Address:** Beth Israel Hosp Cancer Ctr, 10 Union Square E, Ste 4C, New York, NY 10003; **Phone:** 212-844-5729; **Board Cert:** Obstetrics & Gynecology 2012; Gynecologic Oncology 2012; **Med School:** Northwestern Univ 1978; **Resid:** Obstetrics & Gynecology, Northwestern Univ Med Sch 1982; **Fellow:** Gynecologic Oncology, Meml Sloan Kettering Cancer Ctr 1984; **Fac Appt:** Assoc Prof ObG, Albert Einstein Coll Med

Lele, Shashikant B MD [GO] - **Spec Exp:** Ovarian Cancer; Reconstructive Surgery; Pelvic Surgery-Complex; **Hospital:** Roswell Park Canc Inst, Buffalo Genl Hosp; **Address:** Roswell Park Cancer Inst, Elm & Carlton Streets, Buffalo, NY 14263; **Phone:** 716-845-5855; **Board Cert:** Obstetrics & Gynecology 1976; Gynecologic Oncology 1979; **Med School:** India 1968; **Resid:** Obstetrics & Gynecology, JJ Hosp-Grant Med Ctr 1970; Obstetrics & Gynecology, Mt Sinai Hosp 1973; **Fellow:** Gynecologic Oncology, Roswell Park Cancer Inst 1976; **Fac Appt:** Clin Prof ObG, SUNY Buffalo

Lin, Jeffrey Y MD [GO] - **Spec Exp:** Gynecologic Cancer; Cervical Cancer; Ovarian Cancer; **Hospital:** Sibley Mem Hosp, G Washington Univ Hosp; **Address:** Sibley Ctr for GYN Oncology, 5255 Loughboro Rd NW Fl 4, Washington, DC 20016; **Phone:** 202-243-5295; **Board Cert:** Obstetrics & Gynecology 2012; Gynecologic Oncology 2012; **Med School:** Albany Med Coll 1984; **Resid:** Obstetrics & Gynecology, George Washington Med Ctr 1988; **Fellow:** Gynecologic Oncology, Univ Rochester Med Ctr 1991; **Fac Appt:** Prof ObG, Geo Wash Univ

Martino, Martin MD [GO] - **Spec Exp:** Robotic Surgery; Minimally Invasive Surgery; **Hospital:** Lehigh Valley Hosp; **Address:** Gynecologic Oncology Specialists, 1240 S Cedar Crest Blvd, Ste 403, Allentown, PA 18103; **Phone:** 610-402-3650; **Board Cert:** Obstetrics & Gynecology 2011; Gynecologic Oncology 2012; **Med School:** Hahnemann Univ 1998; **Resid:** Obstetrics & Gynecology, RWJ Univ Hosp 1999; Gynecologic Oncology, Meml Sloan-Kettering Canc Ctr 2003; **Fellow:** Gynecologic Oncology, H Lee Moffitt Cancer Ctr 2004

Morgan, Mark A MD [GO] - **Spec Exp:** Laparoscopic Surgery; Gynecologic Surgery-Complex; Gynecologic Cancer; Uro-Gynecology; **Hospital:** Hosp Univ Penn - UPHS (page 69), Jeanes Hosp; **Address:** Pennsylvania Hosp, 801 Spruce St Fl 7, Philadelphia, PA 19107; **Phone:** 215-829-2345; **Board Cert:** Obstetrics & Gynecology 2012; Gynecologic Oncology 2012; **Med School:** SUNY Downstate 1982; **Resid:** Obstetrics & Gynecology, Hosp Univ Penn 1986; **Fellow:** Gynecologic Oncology, Hosp Univ Penn 1988; **Fac Appt:** Clin Prof ObG, Univ Pennsylvania

Nagarsheth, Nimesh MD [GO] - **Spec Exp:** Cervical Cancer; Ovarian Cancer; Uterine Cancer; Vaginal Cancer; **Hospital:** Mt Sinai Med Ctr (page 62), Englewood Hosp & Med Ctr; **Address:** Ruttenberg Treatment Ctr, 1470 Madison Ave, New York, NY 10029; **Phone:** 212-241-1111; **Board Cert:** Obstetrics & Gynecology 2007; Gynecologic Oncology 2007; **Med School:** Mount Sinai Sch Med 1997; **Resid:** Obstetrics & Gynecology, Duke Univ Med Ctr 1997; **Fellow:** Gynecologic Oncology, Mt Sinai Med Ctr 2004; **Fac Appt:** Assoc Prof ObG, Mount Sinai Sch Med

Odunsi, Adekunle O MD/PhD [GO] - **Spec Exp:** Ovarian Cancer; Gynecologic Cancer; Immunotherapy; Clinical Trials; **Hospital:** Roswell Park Canc Inst, Buffalo Genl Hosp; **Address:** Roswell Park Cancer Inst, Elm and Carlton Streets, Buffalo, NY 14263; **Phone:** 716-845-5855; **Board Cert:** Obstetrics & Gynecology 2012; Gynecologic Oncology 2012; **Med School:** Nigeria 1984; **Resid:** Obstetrics & Gynecology, Rosie Maternity & Addenbrookes Hosps 1990; Obstetrics & Gynecology, Yale-New Haven Hosp 1999; **Fellow:** Gynecologic Oncology, Roswell Park Cancer Inst 2001; **Fac Appt:** Prof ObG, SUNY Buffalo

Randall, Thomas C MD [GO] - **Spec Exp:** Gynecologic Cancer; Robotic Surgery; **Hospital:** Pennsylvania Hosp-UPHS (page 69); **Address:** Penn Gyn Oncology at Pennsylvania Hosp, 801 Spruce St, Fl 7, Philadelphia, PA 19107; **Phone:** 215-829-2345; **Board Cert:** Obstetrics & Gynecology 2012; Gynecologic Oncology 2012; **Med School:** Johns Hopkins Univ 1987; **Resid:** Obstetrics & Gynecology, Johns Hopkins Hosp 1991; **Fellow:** Gynecologic Oncology, Hosp Univ Penn 1992; **Fac Appt:** Assoc Clin Prof ObG, Univ Pennsylvania

Rosenblum, Norman G MD/PhD [GO] - **Spec Exp:** Ovarian Cancer; Uterine Cancer; Vulvar Disease/Cancer; Endometrial Cancer; **Hospital:** Thomas Jefferson Univ Hosp; **Address:** 925 Chesnut St, Ste 320A, Philadelphia, PA 19107-5127; **Phone:** 215-955-6200; **Board Cert:** Obstetrics & Gynecology 2012; Gynecologic Oncology 2012; **Med School:** Jefferson Med Coll 1978; **Resid:** Obstetrics & Gynecology, Hosp Univ Penn 1982; **Fellow:** Gynecologic Oncology, Hosp Univ Penn 1984; **Fac Appt:** Prof ObG, Jefferson Med Coll

Rubin, Stephen C MD [GO] - **Spec Exp:** Ovarian Cancer; Uterine Cancer; Cervical Cancer; Gynecologic Cancer-Rare; **Hospital:** Hosp Univ Penn - UPHS (page 69); **Address:** Jordan Ctr for Gynecologic Cancer, Perelman Ctr for Advanced Medicine, 3400 Civic Center Blvd, 3 West, Philadelphia, PA 19104-4283; **Phone:** 215-662-3318; **Board Cert:** Obstetrics & Gynecology 2012; Gynecologic Oncology 2012; **Med School:** Univ Pennsylvania 1976; **Resid:** Obstetrics & Gynecology, Hosp Univ Penn 1980; **Fellow:** Gynecologic Oncology, Hosp Univ Penn 1982; **Fac Appt:** Prof ObG, Univ Pennsylvania

Steren, Albert J MD [GO] - **Spec Exp:** Robotic Surgery; **Hospital:** Holy Cross Hospital - Silver Spring; **Address:** Womens Hlth Specialists, 6301 Executive Blvd, Rockville, MD 20852; **Phone:** 301-770-4967; **Board Cert:** Obstetrics & Gynecology 2012; Gynecologic Oncology 2012; **Med School:** Geo Wash Univ 1987; **Resid:** Obstetrics & Gynecology, John Hopkins Hosp 1991; **Fellow:** Gynecologic Oncology, Univ Miami Hosp 1994

Southeast

Alvarez, Ronald D MD [GO] - **Spec Exp:** Gynecologic Cancer; Ovarian Cancer; Robotic Surgery; Cervical Cancer; **Hospital:** UAB Hosp, Brookwood Med Ctr; **Address:** Univ Alabama, Div Gyn Oncology, 619 19th St S, Birmingham, AL 35249; **Phone:** 205-934-4986; **Board Cert:** Obstetrics & Gynecology 2007; Gynecologic Oncology 2007; **Med School:** Louisiana State U, New Orleans 1983; **Resid:** Obstetrics & Gynecology, Univ Alabama Hosp 1987; **Fellow:** Gynecologic Oncology, Univ Alabama Hosp 1990; **Fac Appt:** Prof ObG, UAB Sch Med

Berchuck, Andrew MD [GO] - **Spec Exp:** Ovarian Cancer; Uterine Cancer; **Hospital:** Duke Univ Hosp; **Address:** Duke Univ Med Center, Box 3079, Durham, NC 27710; **Phone:** 919-684-3765; **Board Cert:** Obstetrics & Gynecology 2012; Gynecologic Oncology 2012; **Med School:** Case West Res Univ 1980; **Resid:** Obstetrics & Gynecology, Case Western Res Univ Hosp 1984; **Fellow:** Gynecology, UT Southwestern Affil Hosp 1985; Gynecologic Oncology, Meml Sloan-Kettering Cancer Ctr 1987; **Fac Appt:** Prof ObG, Duke Univ

Bicher, Annette MD [GO] - **Spec Exp:** Ovarian Cancer; Laparoscopic Surgery; **Hospital:** Inova Fairfax Hosp, Suburban Hosp; **Address:** Mid-Atlantic Pelvic Surgery Assocs, 3289 Woodburn Rd, Ste 320, Annandale, VA 22003; **Phone:** 703-698-7100; **Board Cert:** Obstetrics & Gynecology 2012; Gynecologic Oncology 2012; **Med School:** Univ Mich Med Sch 1987; **Resid:** Obstetrics & Gynecology, George Washington Univ Med Ctr 1991; **Fellow:** Research, NCI-NIH 1992; Gynecologic Oncology, MD Anderson Cancer Ctr 1994; **Fac Appt:** Asst Prof ObG, Geo Wash Univ

Cantuaria, Guilherme HC MD/PhD [GO] - **Spec Exp:** Robotic Surgery; Minimally Invasive Gynecologic Surgery; Endometrial Cancer; Ovarian Cancer; **Hospital:** Northside Hosp; **Address:** University Gynecology Oncology, 960 Johnson Ferry Rd, Ste 130, Atlanta, GA 30342; **Phone:** 404-300-2990; **Board Cert:** Obstetrics & Gynecology 2013; Gynecologic Oncology 2013; **Med School:** Brazil 1992; **Resid:** Obstetrics & Gynecology, Jackson Meml Hosp 1997; **Fellow:** Gynecologic Oncology, Jackson Meml Hosp 2000; **Fac Appt:** Assoc Clin Prof ObG, Morehouse Sch Med

Clarke-Pearson, Daniel L MD [GO] - **Spec Exp:** Gynecologic Surgery-Complex; Gynecologic Cancer; Vulvar & Vaginal Cancer; Gestational Trophoblastic Disease; **Hospital:** NC Memorial Hosp - UNC, Wesley Long Comm Hosp; **Address:** NC Women's Hospital, 101 Manning Drive, Chapel Hill, NC 27599; **Phone:** 919-966-5280; **Board Cert:** Obstetrics & Gynecology 2006; Gynecologic Oncology 2006; **Med School:** Case West Res Univ 1975; **Resid:** Obstetrics & Gynecology, Duke Univ Med Ctr 1979; **Fellow:** Gynecologic Oncology, Duke Univ Med Ctr 1981; **Fac Appt:** Prof ObG, Univ NC Sch Med

Creasman, William T MD [GO] - **Spec Exp:** Uterine Cancer; Ovarian Cancer; Gynecologic Cancer-Rare; Clinical Trials; **Hospital:** MUSC Med Ctr; **Address:** MUSC-Dept ObGyn, 96 Jonathan Lucas St CSB 634, Charleston, SC 29425; **Phone:** 843-792-8627; **Board Cert:** Obstetrics & Gynecology 1991; Gynecologic Oncology 1974; **Med School:** Baylor Coll Med 1960; **Resid:** Obstetrics & Gynecology, Rochester Med Ctr 1967; **Fellow:** Gynecologic Oncology, Anderson Hosp Tumor Inst 1969; **Fac Appt:** Prof ObG, Med Univ SC

Duska, Linda R MD [GO] - **Spec Exp:** Cervical Cancer; Gynecologic Cancer; Gynecologic Surgery-Complex; Ovarian Cancer; **Hospital:** Univ of Virginia Hlth Sys; **Address:** Univ VA Hlth System, Box 800712, Div Gynecologic Oncology, 1215 Lee St, Charlottesville, VA 22908; **Phone:** 434-924-1851; **Board Cert:** Obstetrics & Gynecology 2011; Gynecologic Oncology 2011; Hospice & Palliative Medicine 2012; **Med School:** NYU Sch Med 1991; **Resid:** Obstetrics & Gynecology, Johns Hopkins Hosp 1995; **Fellow:** Gynecologic Oncology, Mass Genl Hosp 1998; **Fac Appt:** Assoc Prof ObG, Univ VA Sch Med

Finan, Michael A MD [GO] - **Spec Exp:** Ovarian Cancer; Cervical Cancer; Uterine Cancer; **Hospital:** Univ of S AL Med Ctr, Mobile Infirmary Med Ctr; **Address:** 1660 Springhill Ave, Mobile, AL 36604; **Phone:** 251-665-8000; **Board Cert:** Obstetrics & Gynecology 2012; Gynecologic Oncology 2012; **Med School:** Louisiana State U, New Orleans 1986; **Resid:** Obstetrics & Gynecology, H Lee Moffitt Cancer Ctr 1990; **Fellow:** Gynecologic Oncology, H Lee Moffitt Cancer Ctr 1992; **Fac Appt:** Prof Onc, Univ S Ala Coll Med

Fiorica, James V MD [GO] - **Spec Exp:** Breast Cancer; Uterine Cancer; **Hospital:** Sarasota Meml Hosp; **Address:** First Physician's Group, 1888 Hillview St, Sarasota, FL 34239; **Phone:** 941-917-8383; **Board Cert:** Obstetrics & Gynecology 2012; Gynecologic Oncology 2012; **Med School:** Tufts Univ 1982; **Resid:** Obstetrics & Gynecology, Univ South Fla Affil Hosp 1986; **Fellow:** Gynecologic Oncology, Univ South Fla Affil Hosp 1989; Breast Disease, Tufts Univ 1990; **Fac Appt:** Clin Prof ObG, Univ S Fla Coll Med

Ghamande, Sharad A MD [GO] - **Spec Exp:** Ovarian Cancer; Gynecologic Surgery-Complex; Clinical Trials; **Hospital:** Georgia Regents Med Ctr-Augusta, Univ Hosp - Augusta; **Address:** MCG Hlth Cancer Ctr, Gynecologic Onc, 1411 Laney Walker Blvd, Augusta, GA 30912; **Phone:** 706-721-6744; **Board Cert:** Obstetrics & Gynecology 2012; Gynecologic Oncology 2012; **Med School:** India 1990; **Resid:** Obstetrics & Gynecology, Boston Med Ctr 1997; **Fellow:** Gynecologic Oncology, Roswell Park Cancer Inst 2000; **Fac Appt:** Assoc Prof ObG, Med Coll GA

Havrilesky, Laura J MD [GO] - **Spec Exp:** Ovarian Cancer; **Hospital:** Duke Univ Hosp; **Address:** Duke Univ Med Ctr, Gyn Oncology, Box 3079, Durham, NC 27710; **Phone:** 919-684-3765; **Board Cert:** Obstetrics & Gynecology 2012; Gynecologic Oncology 2012; **Med School:** Duke Univ 1995; **Resid:** Obstetrics & Gynecology, Duke Univ Med Ctr 1999; **Fellow:** Gynecologic Oncology, Duke Univ Med Ctr 2002; **Fac Appt:** Assoc Prof ObG, Duke Univ

Horowitz, Ira R MD [GO] - **Spec Exp:** Laparoscopic Surgery; Ovarian Cancer; Cervical Cancer; **Hospital:** Emory Univ Hosp, Emory Univ Hosp Midtown; **Address:** Emory Clinic, 1365A Clifton Rd NE Fl 4, Atlanta, GA 30322; **Phone:** 404-778-3401; **Board Cert:** Obstetrics & Gynecology 2012; Gynecologic Oncology 2012; **Med School:** Baylor Coll Med 1980; **Resid:** Obstetrics & Gynecology, Baylor Affil Hosp 1984; **Fellow:** Gynecologic Oncology, Johns Hopkins Hosp 1987; **Fac Appt:** Prof ObG, Emory Univ

Kohler, Matthew F MD [GO] - **Spec Exp:** Gynecologic Surgery-Complex; Gynecologic Cancer; Gestational Trophoblastic Disease; **Hospital:** MUSC Med Ctr; **Address:** MUSC Med Ctr-Women's Hlth Ob/Gyn, 86 Jonathan Lucas St, MS 957, Charleston, SC 29425; **Phone:** 843-792-9300; **Board Cert:** Obstetrics & Gynecology 2012; Gynecologic Oncology 2012; **Med School:** Duke Univ 1987; **Resid:** Obstetrics & Gynecology, Duke Univ Med Ctr 1991; **Fellow:** Gynecologic Oncology, Duke Univ Med Ctr 1994; **Fac Appt:** Assoc Prof ObG, Med Univ SC

Lambrou, Nicholas C MD [GO] - **Spec Exp:** Robotic Surgery; Uterine Cancer; Ovarian Cancer; Cervical Cancer; **Hospital:** South Miami Hosp, Mount Sinai Med Ctr - Miami; **Address:** 6200 Sunset Drive, Ste 502, Miami, FL 33143; **Phone:** 305-430-6969; **Board Cert:** Obstetrics & Gynecology 2012; Gynecologic Oncology 2012; **Med School:** Boston Univ 1996; **Resid:** Obstetrics & Gynecology, Johns Hopkins Hosp 2000; **Fellow:** Gynecologic Oncology, Univ Miami/Jackson Meml Hosp 2003; **Fac Appt:** Assoc Prof ObG, Univ Miami Sch Med

Lancaster, Johnathan M MD/PhD [GO] - **Spec Exp:** Ovarian Cancer; Cancer Genetics; Gene Therapy; **Hospital:** Moffitt Canc Ctr (page 61); **Address:** H Lee Moffitt Cancer Ctr, Womens Onc, 12902 Magnolia Drive, Ste 3057, Tampa, FL 33612; **Phone:** 813-745-3980; **Board Cert:** Obstetrics & Gynecology 2012; Gynecologic Oncology 2012; **Med School:** Wales, UK 1997; **Resid:** Obstetrics & Gynecology, Duke Univ Hosp 2000; **Fellow:** Gynecologic Oncology, Duke Univ Hosp 2003; **Fac Appt:** Assoc Prof ObG, Univ S Fla Coll Med

Lentz, Samuel S MD [GO] - **Spec Exp:** Gynecologic Cancer; Pelvic Reconstruction; Incontinence; Incontinence-Fecal; **Hospital:** Wake Forest Baptist Med Ctr; **Address:** Wake Forest Baptist Med Ctr, Div Gyn Oncology, Medical Center Blvd, Winston-Salem, NC 27157; **Phone:** 336-716-6673; **Board Cert:** Obstetrics & Gynecology 2012; Gynecologic Oncology 2012; **Med School:** Wake Forest Univ 1978; **Resid:** Obstetrics & Gynecology, NC Baptist Hosp 1982; **Fellow:** Gynecologic Oncology, Mayo Clinic 1989; **Fac Appt:** Prof ObG, Wake Forest Univ

Lucci, Joseph A MD [GO] - **Spec Exp:** Cervical Cancer; HPV-Human Papilloma Virus; **Hospital:** Univ of Miami Hosp & Clins/Sylvester Comp Canc Ctr, Jackson Meml Hosp; **Address:** UHlth, Gynecologic Oncology Dept, 1475 NW 12th Ave, Ste 3500, Miami, FL 33136; **Phone:** 305-243-2233; **Board Cert:** Obstetrics & Gynecology 2012; Gynecologic Oncology 2012; **Med School:** Univ Tex, Houston 1984; **Resid:** Obstetrics & Gynecology, St Joseph Med Ctr 1988; **Fellow:** Gynecologic Oncology, UC Irvine Med Ctr 1992; **Fac Appt:** Clin Prof ObG, Univ Miami Sch Med

Makhija, Sharmila K MD [GO] - **Spec Exp:** Ovarian Cancer; Cervical Cancer; Uterine Cancer; **Hospital:** Univ of Louisville Hosp, Norton Hosp; **Address:** James Graham Brown Cancer Ctr, 529 S Jackson St Fl 3, Louisville, KY 40202; **Phone:** 502-561-7220; **Board Cert:** Obstetrics & Gynecology 2012; Gynecologic Oncology 2012; **Med School:** UAB Sch Med 1992; **Resid:** Obstetrics & Gynecology, Univ Louisville Hosp 1996; **Fellow:** Gynecologic Oncology, Meml Sloan Kettering Cancer Ctr 1999; **Fac Appt:** Prof ObG, Univ Louisville Sch Med

Modesitt, Susan C MD [GO] - **Spec Exp:** Gynecologic Cancer; Ovarian Cancer; Vulvar Disease/Cancer; Obesity; **Hospital:** Univ of Virginia Hlth Sys; **Address:** Emily Couric Clinical Cancer Center, 1240 Lee St, Charlottesville, VA 22903; **Phone:** 434-924-5197; **Board Cert:** Obstetrics & Gynecology 2012; Gynecologic Oncology 2012; **Med School:** Univ VA Sch Med 1995; **Resid:** Obstetrics & Gynecology, Univ NC Hlth Care System 1999; **Fellow:** Gynecologic Oncology, Univ TX-MD Anderson Cancer Ctr 2002; **Fac Appt:** Assoc Prof ObG, Univ VA Sch Med

Orr Jr, James W MD [GO] - **Spec Exp:** Gynecologic Cancer; **Hospital:** Lee Memorial Hlth Systems, Naples Comm Healthcare System; **Address:** FL Gynecologic Oncology, Regional Cancer Ctr, 8931 Colonial Ctr Drive, Ste 400, Fort Myers, FL 33905; **Phone:** 239-334-6626; **Board Cert:** Obstetrics & Gynecology 2008; Gynecologic Oncology 2008; **Med School:** Univ VA Sch Med 1976; **Resid:** Obstetrics & Gynecology, UAB Hosp 1980; **Fellow:** Gynecologic Oncology, UAB Hosp 1982; **Fac Appt:** Clin Prof ObG, Univ S Fla Coll Med

Penalver, Manuel A MD [GO] - **Spec Exp:** Gynecologic Cancer; Cervical Cancer; Pelvic Tumors; **Hospital:** Doctors' Hosp - Coral Gables (FL), Baptist Hosp of Miami; **Address:** Doctors Hosp, Ob/Gyn Dept, 5000 University Drive, Ste 3300, Coral Gables, FL 33146; **Phone:** 305-663-7001; **Board Cert:** Obstetrics & Gynecology 2012; Gynecologic Oncology 2012; **Med School:** Univ Miami Sch Med 1977; **Resid:** Obstetrics & Gynecology, Jackson Meml Hosp 1982; **Fellow:** Gynecologic Oncology, Jackson Meml Hosp 1984

Poliakoff, Steven R MD [GO] - **Spec Exp:** Ovarian Cancer; Minimally Invasive Surgery; Cancer Genetics; Robotic Surgery; **Hospital:** Mount Sinai Med Ctr - Miami, South Miami Hosp; **Address:** 6280 Sunset Drive, Ste 502, South Miami, FL 33143; **Phone:** 305-596-0870; **Board Cert:** Obstetrics & Gynecology 1983; **Med School:** Univ NC Sch Med 1975; **Resid:** Obstetrics & Gynecology, Johns Hopkins Hosp 1979; **Fellow:** Gynecologic Oncology, Jackson Meml Hosp 1981

Runowicz, Carolyn D MD [GO] - **Spec Exp:** Ovarian Cancer; Cervical Cancer; Breast Cancer; **Hospital:** Jackson N Med Ctr; **Address:** 11200 S W 8th St SW, MS 33199, AHC2 Bldg - Fl 6 - Ste 693, Miami, FL 33199; **Phone:** 305-348-4372; **Board Cert:** Obstetrics & Gynecology 2012; Gynecologic Oncology 2012; **Med School:** Jefferson Med Coll 1977; **Resid:** Obstetrics & Gynecology, Mount Sinai Med Ctr 1981; **Fellow:** Gynecologic Oncology, Mount Sinai Med Ctr 1983; **Fac Appt:** Prof ObG, FIU Coll Med

Soper, John T MD [GO] - **Spec Exp:** Gynecologic Cancer; Gynecologic Surgery-Complex; Gestational Trophoblastic Disease; **Hospital:** NC Memorial Hosp - UNC, Rex HlthCare; **Address:** Div Gyn-Onc, Dept OB/GYN, Physicians Office Bldg, B103, 170 Manning Drive, Chapel Hill, NC 27599-7572; **Phone:** 919-966-1195; **Board Cert:** Obstetrics & Gynecology 2012; Gynecologic Oncology 2012; **Med School:** Univ Iowa Coll Med 1978; **Resid:** Obstetrics & Gynecology, Univ Utah Med Ctr 1982; **Fellow:** Duke Univ Med Ctr 1985; **Fac Appt:** Prof ObG, Univ NC Sch Med

Spann Jr, Cyril O MD [GO] - **Spec Exp:** Gynecologic Cancer; Ovarian Cancer; Robotic Surgery; **Hospital:** Grady Hlth Sys, Emory Univ Hosp Midtown; **Address:** Grady Hlth Sys, Ob/Gyn Dept, 69 Jesse Hill Jr Drive, Ste 400, Atlanta, GA 30303; **Phone:** 404-778-3401; **Board Cert:** Obstetrics & Gynecology 2012; Gynecologic Oncology 2012; **Med School:** Meharry Med Coll 1981; **Resid:** Obstetrics & Gynecology, Emory Univ Med Ctr 1985; **Fellow:** Gynecologic Oncology, NC Meml Hosp 1989; **Fac Appt:** Prof ObG, Emory Univ

Valea, Fidel A MD [GO] - **Spec Exp:** Cervical Cancer; Laparoscopic Surgery; **Hospital:** Duke Univ Hosp; **Address:** Duke Univ Med Ctr, Box 3079, Durham, NC 27710; **Phone:** 919-684-3765; **Board Cert:** Obstetrics & Gynecology 2012; Gynecologic Oncology 2012; **Med School:** SUNY Stony Brook 1985; **Resid:** Surgery, Univ NC Hosps 1987; Obstetrics & Gynecology, Univ NC Hosps 1990; **Fellow:** Gynecologic Oncology, Univ NC Hosps 1992; **Fac Appt:** Assoc Prof ObG, Duke Univ

Van Nagell Jr, John R MD [GO] - **Spec Exp:** Ovarian Cancer; Cervical Cancer; **Hospital:** Univ of Kentucky Albert B. Chandler Hosp; **Address:** Markey Cancer Ctr, Div Gyn Onc, Whitney-Hendrickson Bldg, 800 Rose St, Fl 3, Lexington, KY 40536; **Phone:** 859-323-5553; **Board Cert:** Obstetrics & Gynecology 1973; Gynecologic Oncology 1976; **Med School:** Univ Pennsylvania 1967; **Resid:** Obstetrics & Gynecology, Univ Kentucky Med Ctr 1971; **Fellow:** Gynecologic Oncology, Univ Kentucky 1973; **Fac Appt:** Prof ObG, Univ KY Coll Med

Midwest

Cliby, William A MD [GO] - **Spec Exp:** Ovarian Cancer; Robotic Surgery; Uterine Cancer; Gynecologic Cancer; **Hospital:** Mayo Med Ctr & Clin - Rochester; **Address:** Mayo Clinic, 200 First St SW, Rochester, MN 55905; **Phone:** 507-266-9323; **Board Cert:** Obstetrics & Gynecology 2011; Gynecologic Oncology 2011; **Med School:** Univ VT Coll Med 1987; **Resid:** Obstetrics & Gynecology, Duke Univ Med Ctr 1991; **Fellow:** Gynecologic Oncology, Mayo Clinic 1994; Cancer Research, Fred Hutchinson Cancer Rsch Ctr 1997; **Fac Appt:** Prof ObG, Mayo Med Sch

Copeland, Larry J MD [GO] - **Spec Exp:** Ovarian Cancer; Uterine Cancer; Gynecologic Cancer; Gynecologic Cancer-Rare; **Hospital:** Arthur G James Cancer Hosp & Research Inst, OSU Wexner Med Ctr; **Address:** 320 W 10th Ave, Starling L Bldg, Ste M210, Columbus, OH 43210; **Phone:** 614-293-7642; **Board Cert:** Obstetrics & Gynecology 2012; Gynecologic Oncology 2012; **Med School:** Univ Western Ontario 1973; **Resid:** Obstetrics & Gynecology, McMaster Univ Affil Hosps 1977; **Fellow:** Gynecologic Oncology, MD Anderson Cancer Ctr-Univ Tex 1979; **Fac Appt:** Prof ObG, Ohio State Univ

Fowler, Jeffrey M MD [GO] - **Spec Exp:** Laparoscopic Surgery; Gynecologic Cancer; Robotic Surgery; Pelvic Reconstruction; **Hospital:** OSU Wexner Med Ctr; **Address:** OSU Gynecologic Oncology, 3651 Ridge Mill Drive, Hilliard, OH 43026; **Phone:** 614-293-3873; **Board Cert:** Obstetrics & Gynecology 2013; Gynecologic Oncology 2013; **Med School:** Northwestern Univ 1985; **Resid:** Obstetrics & Gynecology, Ohio State Univ Hosp 1989; **Fellow:** Gynecologic Oncology, Cedars-Sinai Med Ctr-UCLA 1991; **Fac Appt:** Prof ObG, Ohio State Univ

Gostout, Bobbie S MD [GO] - **Hospital:** Mayo Med Ctr & Clin - Rochester, St. Mary's Hosp - Rochester MN (Mayo); **Address:** 200 First St SW, Rochester, MN 55905; **Phone:** 507-538-8400; **Board Cert:** Obstetrics & Gynecology 2012; Gynecologic Oncology 2012; **Med School:** Mayo Med Sch 1986; **Resid:** Obstetrics & Gynecology, Mayo Med Ctr & Clin 1991; **Fellow:** Research, Mayo Med Ctr & Clin 1993; Gynecologic Oncology, Mayo Med Ctr & Clin 1996; **Fac Appt:** Asst Prof ObG, Mayo Med Sch

Hurteau, Jean A MD [GO] - **Spec Exp:** Ovarian Cancer; Uterine Cancer; Cervical Cancer; Minimally Invasive Surgery; **Hospital:** Evanston Hosp/NorthShore Univ Hlth Sys (page 67), Highland Park Hosp/NorthShore Univ Hlth Syst (page 67); **Address:** Kellogg Cancer Ctr, 2650 Ridge Ave, Evanston, IL 60201; **Phone:** 847-570-2639; **Board Cert:** Obstetrics & Gynecology 2012; Gynecologic Oncology 2012; **Med School:** Univ Montreal 1985; **Resid:** Obstetrics & Gynecology, Univ Toronto Affil Hosp 1990; **Fellow:** Cancer Research, Natl Cancer Inst 1992; Gynecologic Oncology, Duke Univ Med ctr 1995; **Fac Appt:** Clin Prof ObG, Univ Chicago-Pritzker Sch Med

Johnston, Carolyn M MD [GO] - **Spec Exp:** Gynecologic Surgery-Complex; Cervical Cancer; **Hospital:** Univ Michigan Med Ctr; **Address:** Univ Michigan Comprehensive Cancer Ctr, 1500 E Med Ctr Drive, rm 5902, Ann Arbor, MI 48109-0276; **Phone:** 734-647-8906; **Board Cert:** Obstetrics & Gynecology 2012; Gynecologic Oncology 2012; **Med School:** Yale Univ 1984; **Resid:** Obstetrics & Gynecology, Univ Chicago Hosp 1988; **Fellow:** Gynecologic Oncology, Mount Sinai Hosp 1990; **Fac Appt:** Assoc Clin Prof ObG, Univ Mich Med Sch

Lengyel, Ernst MD/PhD [GO] - **Spec Exp:** Ovarian Cancer; Uterine Cancer; **Hospital:** Univ of Chicago Med; **Address:** Univ Chicago Med Ctr, Dept Gyn Onc, 5841 S Maryland Ave, rm L-264, MC 2050, Chicago, IL 60637; **Phone:** 773-702-6722; **Board Cert:** Obstetrics & Gynecology 2012; Gynecologic Oncology 2012; **Med School:** Germany 1992; **Resid:** Obstetrics & Gynecology, Hosp of Univ Munich 2000; **Fellow:** Gynecologic Oncology, UCSF Med Ctr 2003; **Fac Appt:** Prof ObG, Univ Chicago-Pritzker Sch Med

Lurain III, John R MD [GO] - **Spec Exp:** Gestational Trophoblastic Disease; Uterine Cancer; Ovarian Cancer; Cervical Cancer; **Hospital:** Northwestern Meml Hosp; **Address:** Northwestern Medical Faculty Foundation, 250 E Superior St, Fl 4, rm 420, Chicago, IL 60611-3056; **Phone:** 312-695-0990; **Board Cert:** Obstetrics & Gynecology 1977; Gynecologic Oncology 1981; **Med School:** Univ NC Sch Med 1972; **Resid:** Obstetrics & Gynecology, Univ Pittsburgh Magee-Womens Hosp 1975; **Fellow:** Gynecologic Oncology, Roswell Park Cancer Inst 1979; **Fac Appt:** Prof ObG, Northwestern Univ

Moore, David H MD [GO] - **Spec Exp:** Cervical Cancer; Ovarian Cancer; Clinical Trials; Robotic Surgery; **Hospital:** Franciscan St. Francis Hlth-Indianapolis, Community Hosps - Indianapolis; **Address:** Franciscan Hlth, Cancer Ctr, 8111 S Emerson Ave, Ste 204, Indianapolis, IN 46237; **Phone:** 317-528-2555; **Board Cert:** Obstetrics & Gynecology 2012; Gynecologic Oncology 2012; **Med School:** Indiana Univ 1982; **Resid:** Obstetrics & Gynecology, IU Hlth Hosp 1986; **Fellow:** Gynecologic Oncology, Univ N Carolina 1988

Mutch, David G MD [GO] - **Spec Exp:** Gynecologic Cancer; Pelvic Reconstruction; **Hospital:** Barnes-Jewish Hosp; **Address:** 4911 Barnes Jewish Hosp Plaza, CB 8064, St Louis, MO 63110; **Phone:** 314-362-3181; **Board Cert:** Obstetrics & Gynecology 2012; Gynecologic Oncology 2012; **Med School:** Washington Univ, St Louis 1980; **Resid:** Obstetrics & Gynecology, Barnes Hosp-Wash Univ 1984; **Fellow:** Gynecologic Oncology, Duke Univ Med Ctr 1987; **Fac Appt:** Prof ObG, Washington Univ, St Louis

Potkul, Ronald K MD [GO] - **Spec Exp:** Ovarian Cancer; Cervical Cancer; Robotic Surgery; Vulvar & Vaginal Cancer; **Hospital:** Loyola Univ Med Ctr; **Address:** Loyola Univ Med Ctr, 2160 S 1st Ave Bldg 112 - rm 267, Maywood, IL 60153; **Phone:** 708-327-3500; **Board Cert:** Obstetrics & Gynecology 2012; Gynecologic Oncology 2012; **Med School:** Univ Chicago-Pritzker Sch Med 1981; **Resid:** Obstetrics & Gynecology, Univ Chicago Hosps 1984; **Fellow:** Gynecologic Oncology, Georgetown Univ Hosp 1988; **Fac Appt:** Prof ObG, Loyola Univ-Stritch Sch Med

Powell, Matthew A MD [GO] - **Spec Exp:** Cervical Cancer; Ovarian Cancer; Vulvar & Vaginal Cancer; **Hospital:** Barnes-Jewish Hosp, Missouri Baptist Med Ctr; **Address:** Washington Univ Sch Med, Dept Ob/Gyn, 4911 Barnes Jewish Hosp Plaza, Box 8064, St Louis, MO 63110; **Phone:** 314-362-3181; **Board Cert:** Obstetrics & Gynecology 2011; Gynecologic Oncology 2011; **Med School:** Mich State Univ 1995; **Resid:** Obstetrics & Gynecology, Ohio State Univ Hosp & Clins 1999; **Fellow:** Gynecologic Oncology, Barnes-Jewish Hosp 2002; **Fac Appt:** Assoc Prof ObG, Washington Univ, St Louis

Rader, Janet S MD [GO] - **Spec Exp:** Cervical Cancer; Ovarian Cancer; Uterine Cancer; **Hospital:** Froedtert & Med Coll WI; **Address:** Med Coll of Wisconsin, Dept OB/GYN, 9200 W Wisconsin Ave, Milwaukee, WI 53226; **Phone:** 414-805-6606; **Board Cert:** Obstetrics & Gynecology 2012; Gynecologic Oncology 2012; **Med School:** Univ MO-Columbia Sch Med 1983; **Resid:** Obstetrics & Gynecology, Michael Reese Hosp & Med Ctr 1988; **Fellow:** Gynecologic Oncology, Johns Hopkins Hosp 1992; **Fac Appt:** Prof ObG, Washington Univ, St Louis

Reynolds, R Kevin MD [GO] - **Spec Exp:** Laparoscopic Surgery; Fertility Preservation in Cancer; Cervical Cancer; **Hospital:** Univ Michigan Med Ctr; **Address:** Univ Michigan Comprehensive Cancer Ctr, 1500 E Med Ctr Drive, Ann Arbor, MI 48109; **Phone:** 734-764-9106; **Board Cert:** Obstetrics & Gynecology 2012; Gynecologic Oncology 2012; **Med School:** Univ New Mexico 1982; **Resid:** Obstetrics & Gynecology, Univ Vt Hosp 1986; **Fellow:** Gynecologic Oncology, Univ Mich Med Ctr 1991; **Fac Appt:** Prof ObG, Univ Mich Med Sch

Rice, Laurel W MD [GO] - **Spec Exp:** Ovarian Cancer; Uterine Cancer; Cervical Cancer; **Hospital:** Univ WI Hosp & Clins; **Address:** 600 Highland Ave, Ste H4-612, Madison, WI 53792; **Phone:** 608-263-3194; **Board Cert:** Obstetrics & Gynecology 2012; Gynecologic Oncology 2012; **Med School:** Univ Colorado 1983; **Resid:** Obstetrics & Gynecology, Brigham & Women's Hosp 1988; **Fellow:** Gynecologic Oncology, Brigham & Women's Hosp 1991; **Fac Appt:** Assoc Prof ObG, Univ VA Sch Med

Rodriguez, Gustavo C MD [GO] - **Spec Exp:** Ovarian Cancer; Cancer Prevention; Ovarian Cancer-Early Detection; **Hospital:** Evanston Hosp/NorthShore Univ Hlth Sys (page 67), Highland Park Hosp/NorthShore Univ Hlth Syst (page 67); **Address:** Kellogg Cancer Ctr, 2650 Ridge Ave, Evanston, IL 60201; **Phone:** 847-570-2639; **Board Cert:** Obstetrics & Gynecology 2012; Gynecologic Oncology 2012; **Med School:** Univ IL Coll Med 1985; **Resid:** Obstetrics & Gynecology, Univ Illinois Med Ctr 1989; **Fellow:** Gynecologic Oncology, Duke Univ Med Ctr 1991; **Fac Appt:** Assoc Clin Prof ObG, Univ Chicago-Pritzker Sch Med

Rose, Peter G MD [GO] - **Spec Exp:** Cervical Cancer; Ovarian Cancer; Uterine Cancer; **Hospital:** Cleveland Clin (page 55), MetroHealth Med Ctr; **Address:** Cleveland Clin, 9500 Euclid Ave A-81, Cleveland, OH 44195; **Phone:** 216-444-1712; **Board Cert:** Obstetrics & Gynecology 2012; Gynecologic Oncology 2012; **Med School:** Boston Univ 1981; **Resid:** Surgery, Vanderbilt Univ Med Ctr 1983; Obstetrics & Gynecology, Ohio State Univ Med Ctr 1986; **Fellow:** Gynecologic Oncology, Roswell Park Cancer Inst 1988; **Fac Appt:** Prof ObG, Case West Res Univ

Rotmensch, Jacob MD [GO] - **Spec Exp:** Gynecologic Cancer; Ovarian Cancer; Cervical Cancer; Uterine Cancer; **Hospital:** Rush Univ Med Ctr; **Address:** Univ Gynecologic Oncology Assocs, 1725 W Harrison St, Professional Bldg, Ste 1010, Chicago, IL 60612; **Phone:** 312-942-6300; **Board Cert:** Obstetrics & Gynecology 2012; Gynecologic Oncology 2012; **Med School:** Meharry Med Coll 1977; **Resid:** Obstetrics & Gynecology, Johns Hopkins Hosp 1981; **Fellow:** Gynecologic Oncology, Johns Hopkins Hosp 1984; **Fac Appt:** Prof ObG, Rush Med Coll

Schink, Julian C MD [GO] - **Spec Exp:** Ovarian Cancer; **Hospital:** Northwestern Meml Hosp; **Address:** Northwestern Medical Faculty Foundation, 250 E Superior St, Ste 420, Chicago, IL 60611; **Phone:** 312-695-0990; **Board Cert:** Obstetrics & Gynecology 2012; Gynecologic Oncology 2012; **Med School:** Univ Tex, San Antonio 1982; **Resid:** Obstetrics & Gynecology, Northwestern Meml Hosp 1986; **Fellow:** Gynecologic Oncology, UCLA Med Ctr 1988; **Fac Appt:** Prof ObG, Northwestern Univ

Stehman, Frederick B MD [GO] - **Spec Exp:** Clinical Trials; Gynecologic Cancer; **Hospital:** IU Hlth Univ Hosp, Wishard Hlth Srvs; **Address:** IU Hlth, Cancer Ctr, 535 Barnhill Drive, rm 436, Indianapolis, IN 46202; **Phone:** 317-944-2130; **Board Cert:** Obstetrics & Gynecology 2005; Gynecologic Oncology 2003; **Med School:** Univ Mich Med Sch 1972; **Resid:** Obstetrics & Gynecology, Univ Kansas Med Ctr 1975; Surgery, Univ Kansas Med Ctr 1977; **Fellow:** Gynecologic Oncology, UCLA Med Ctr 1979; **Fac Appt:** Prof Emeritus ObG, Indiana Univ

Waggoner, Steven MD [GO] - **Spec Exp:** Ovarian Cancer; Cervical Cancer; Uterine Cancer; **Hospital:** UH Case Med Ctr; **Address:** UH MacDonald Women's Hosp, Dept Ob/Gyn & Gyn Oncology, 11100 Euclid Ave, rm 7133, Cleveland, OH 44106; **Phone:** 216-844-3954; **Board Cert:** Obstetrics & Gynecology 2012; Gynecologic Oncology 2012; **Med School:** Univ Wash 1984; **Resid:** Obstetrics & Gynecology, Univ Chicago Hosps 1988; **Fellow:** Gynecologic Oncology, Georgetown Univ Med Ctr 1991; **Fac Appt:** Prof ObG, Case West Res Univ

Yamada, S Diane MD [GO] - **Spec Exp:** Ovarian Cancer; Uterine Cancer; Cervical Cancer; Minimally Invasive Surgery; **Hospital:** Univ of Chicago Med; **Address:** Ctr for Advanced Medicine, 5758 S Maryland Ave Fl 3 - Ste H, Chicago, IL 60637; **Phone:** 773-702-6123; **Board Cert:** Obstetrics & Gynecology 2012; Gynecologic Oncology 2012; **Med School:** UCLA 1991; **Resid:** Obstetrics & Gynecology, Harbor-UCLA Med Ctr 1995; **Fellow:** Gynecologic Oncology, Cedar-Sinai Med Ctr 1996; Gynecologic Urology, UC Irvine Med Ctr 1999; **Fac Appt:** Prof ObG, Univ Chicago-Pritzker Sch Med

Great Plains and Mountains

Davidson, Susan MD [GO] - **Spec Exp:** Gynecologic Cancer; **Hospital:** Univ Colorado Hosp; **Address:** 12631 E 17th Ave, B 198-4, Aurora, CO 80045; **Phone:** 303-724-2066; **Board Cert:** Obstetrics & Gynecology 2012; Gynecologic Oncology 2012; **Med School:** Univ Tex, San Antonio 1984; **Resid:** Obstetrics & Gynecology, Univ Texas Med Ctr 1988; **Fellow:** Gynecologic Oncology, Meml Sloan Kettering Cancer Ctr 1990; **Fac Appt:** Assoc Prof ObG, Univ Colorado

Remmenga, Steven W MD [GO] - **Spec Exp:** Ovarian Cancer; Cervical Cancer; Gynecologic Cancer; **Hospital:** Nebraska Med Ctr; **Address:** 983255 Nebraska Medical Center, Omaha, NE 68198-3255; **Phone:** 402-559-5068; **Board Cert:** Obstetrics & Gynecology 2012; Gynecologic Oncology 2012; **Med School:** Univ Nebr Coll Med 1981; **Resid:** Obstetrics & Gynecology, Naval Hospital 1986; **Fellow:** Gynecologic Oncology, Walter Reed Army Med Ctr 1990; **Fac Appt:** Prof ObG, Univ Nebr Coll Med

Soisson, Andrew P MD [GO] - **Spec Exp:** Cervical Cancer; HPV-Human Papilloma Virus; **Hospital:** Univ Utah Hlth Care, LDS Hosp; **Address:** Huntsman Canc Hosp, 1950 Circle of Hope, Salt Lake City, UT 84112; **Phone:** 801-585-0100; **Board Cert:** Obstetrics & Gynecology 2006; Gynecologic Oncology 2006; **Med School:** Georgetown Univ 1981; **Resid:** Obstetrics & Gynecology, Madigan Army Med Ctr 1987; **Fellow:** Gynecologic Oncology, Duke Univ Hosp 1991; **Fac Appt:** Prof ObG, Univ Utah

Southwest

Bodurka, Diane C MD [GO] - **Spec Exp:** Ovarian Cancer; Pelvic Surgery-Complex; **Hospital:** UT MD Anderson Canc Ctr; **Address:** UT MD Anderson Canc Ctr, Dept Gynecologic Oncology, 1155 Herman Pressler, Box 1362, Houston, TX 77230-1439; **Phone:** 713-792-6810; **Board Cert:** Gynecologic Oncology 2012; Obstetrics & Gynecology 2012; **Med School:** Georgetown Univ 1990; **Resid:** Obstetrics & Gynecology, Univ AL Affil Hosps 1995; **Fellow:** Gynecologic Oncology, MD Anderson Canc Ctr 1999; **Fac Appt:** Prof ObG, Univ Tex, Houston

Borst, Matthew P MD [GO] - **Spec Exp:** Ovarian Cancer; **Hospital:** Banner Good Samaritan Regl Med Ctr - Phoenix; **Address:** Phoenix-Biltmore Cancer Ctr, 2222 E Highland Ave, Ste 400, Phoenix, AZ 85016; **Phone:** 602-277-4868; **Board Cert:** Obstetrics & Gynecology 2012; Gynecologic Oncology 2012; **Med School:** Med Coll VA 1984; **Resid:** Obstetrics & Gynecology, Cook Co Hosp 1988; **Fellow:** Gynecologic Oncology, U AL Med Ctr 1992; **Fac Appt:** Asst Clin Prof ObG, Univ Ariz Coll Med

Braly, Patricia S MD [GO] - **Spec Exp:** Ovarian Cancer; Breast Cancer; **Hospital:** St. Tammany Parish Hosp, E Jefferson Genl Hosp; **Address:** Women's Cancer Care, 606 W 12th Ave, Covington, LA 70433; **Phone:** 985-892-2252; **Board Cert:** Gynecologic Oncology 1985; Obstetrics & Gynecology 1994; **Med School:** UC Irvine 1976; **Resid:** Obstetrics & Gynecology, UC Irvine Med Ctr 1980; **Fellow:** Gynecologic Oncology, UC Irvine Med Ctr 1983

Burke, Thomas W MD [GO] - **Spec Exp:** Uterine Cancer; Vulvar & Vaginal Cancer; **Hospital:** UT MD Anderson Canc Ctr; **Address:** UT MD Anderson Canc Ctr, 1400 Pressler Street, Unit 1485, Houston, TX 77030-4009; **Phone:** 713-792-7695; **Board Cert:** Obstetrics & Gynecology 2012; Gynecologic Oncology 2012; **Med School:** Tulane Univ 1978; **Resid:** Obstetrics & Gynecology, Tripler Army Med Ctr 1983; **Fellow:** Gynecologic Oncology, Walter Reed Natl Military Med Ctr 1987; **Fac Appt:** Prof ObG, Univ Tex, Houston

Burnett, Alexander F MD [GO] - **Spec Exp:** Laparoscopic Surgery; Fertility Preservation in Cancer; Gynecologic Cancer; **Hospital:** UAMS Med Ctr; **Address:** 4301 W Markham St, Slot 793, Little Rock, AR 72205; **Phone:** 501-686-8522; **Board Cert:** Obstetrics & Gynecology 2012; Gynecologic Oncology 2012; **Med School:** Georgetown Univ 1986; **Resid:** Obstetrics & Gynecology, Georgetown U Affil Hosps 1990; **Fellow:** Gynecologic Oncology, Georgetown U Affil Hosps 1993; **Fac Appt:** Assoc Prof ObG, Univ Ark

Chambers, Setsuko K MD [GO] - **Spec Exp:** Gynecologic Cancer; Ovarian Cancer; Breast Cancer Risk Assessment; **Hospital:** Univ Arizona Med Ctr-Univ Campus; **Address:** Arizona Cancer Center, 1515 N Campbell Ave, Tucson, AZ 85724; **Phone:** 520-626-9285; **Board Cert:** Obstetrics & Gynecology 2012; Gynecologic Oncology 2012; **Med School:** Brown Univ 1980; **Resid:** Obstetrics & Gynecology, Yale-New Haven Hosp 1984; **Fellow:** Gynecologic Oncology, Yale-New Haven Hosp 1986; **Fac Appt:** Prof ObG, Univ Ariz Coll Med

Fromm, Geri-Lynn MD [GO] - **Spec Exp:** Cervical Cancer; Ovarian Cancer; Gestational Trophoblastic Disease; **Hospital:** St. Luke's Episcopal Hosp-Houston, Woman's Hosp TX; **Address:** 7580 Fanning St, Ste 335D, Houston, TX 77054; **Phone:** 713-665-0404; **Board Cert:** Obstetrics & Gynecology 2012; Gynecologic Oncology 2012; **Med School:** Northwestern Univ 1981; **Resid:** Obstetrics & Gynecology, Magee-Womens Hosp - UPMC 1986; **Fellow:** Gynecologic Oncology, UT MD Anderson Canc Ctr 1990; **Fac Appt:** Assoc Clin Prof ObG, Baylor Coll Med

Gershenson, David M MD [GO] - **Spec Exp:** Ovarian Rare & Borderline Tumors; Fertility Preservation in Cancer; Sex Cord-Stromal Tumors; **Hospital:** UT MD Anderson Canc Ctr, St. Luke's Episcopal Hosp-Houston; **Address:** UT MD Anderson Cancer Ctr, 1515 Holcombe Ave, Unit 1362, Houston, TX 77030; **Phone:** 713-745-2565; **Board Cert:** Obstetrics & Gynecology 2012; Gynecologic Oncology 2012; **Med School:** Vanderbilt Univ 1971; **Resid:** Obstetrics & Gynecology, Yale-New Haven Hosp 1975; **Fellow:** Gynecologic Oncology, MD Anderson Cancer Ctr 1979; **Fac Appt:** Prof ObG, Univ Tex, Houston

Hatch, Kenneth D MD [GO] - **Spec Exp:** Cervical Cancer; Uro-Gynecology; Pelvic Organ Prolapse Repair; **Hospital:** Univ Arizona Med Ctr-Univ Campus, Northwest Med Ctr Tucson; **Address:** Arizona Cancer Center, 1515 N Campbell Ave, Tucson, AZ 85724; **Phone:** 520-626-9285; **Board Cert:** Obstetrics & Gynecology 1993; Gynecologic Oncology 1981; **Med School:** Univ Nebr Coll Med 1971; **Resid:** Obstetrics & Gynecology, U AL Med Ctr 1976; **Fellow:** Gynecologic Oncology, U AL Med Ctr 1978; **Fac Appt:** Prof ObG, Univ Ariz Coll Med

Kline, Richard C MD [GO] - **Spec Exp:** Ovarian Cancer; Cervical Cancer; Uterine Cancer; Vulvar & Vaginal Cancer; **Hospital:** Ochsner Med Ctr-New Orleans; **Address:** Ochsner Clinic Foundation, 1514 Jefferson Hwy, Benson Cancer Ctr, New Orleans, LA 70121; **Phone:** 504-842-4165; **Board Cert:** Obstetrics & Gynecology 2012; Gynecologic Oncology 2012; **Med School:** Louisiana State U, New Orleans 1980; **Resid:** Obstetrics & Gynecology, Ochsner Fdn Hosp 1984; **Fellow:** Gynecologic Oncology, MD Anderson Cancer Ctr 1986

Levenback, Charles F MD [GO] - **Spec Exp:** Vulvar Disease/Cancer; Cervical Cancer; Gynecologic Cancer; **Hospital:** UT MD Anderson Canc Ctr; **Address:** UT MD Anderson Cancer Ctr, 1515 Holcombe Ave, Unit 1362, Houston, TX 77030; **Phone:** 713-745-2563; **Board Cert:** Obstetrics & Gynecology 2012; Gynecologic Oncology 2012; **Med School:** Mount Sinai Sch Med 1983; **Resid:** Obstetrics & Gynecology, Albert Einstein Affil Hosp 1987; **Fellow:** Gynecologic Oncology, Meml Sloan Kettering Cancer Ctr 1989; **Fac Appt:** Prof ObG, Univ Tex, Houston

Lu, Karen H MD [GO] - **Spec Exp:** Ovarian Cancer; Ovarian Cancer-Early Detection; Uterine Cancer; Cancer Genetics; **Hospital:** UT MD Anderson Canc Ctr; **Address:** Univ of Texas MD Anderson Cancer Ctr, 1515 Holcombe Blvd Unit 1362, Houston, TX 77030; **Phone:** 713-745-8902; **Board Cert:** Obstetrics & Gynecology 2012; Gynecologic Oncology 2012; **Med School:** Yale Univ 1991; **Resid:** Obstetrics & Gynecology, Brigham & Women's Hosp 1994; **Fellow:** Gynecologic Oncology, Brigham & Women's Hosp 1999; **Fac Appt:** Prof ObG, Yale Univ

Magrina, Javier MD [GO] - **Spec Exp:** Gynecologic Cancer; Endometriosis; Hysterectomy Alternatives; Robotic Surgery; **Hospital:** Mayo Clinic - Phoenix; **Address:** Mayo Clinic Gynecology, 5779 E Mayo Blvd, Phoenix, AZ 85054; **Phone:** 480-342-2668; **Board Cert:** Obstetrics & Gynecology 1994; Gynecologic Oncology 1982; **Med School:** Spain 1972; **Resid:** Obstetrics & Gynecology, Mayo Clinic 1977; **Fellow:** Gynecologic Oncology, U Ks Affil Hosps 1980; **Fac Appt:** Prof ObG, Mayo Med Sch

Mannel, Robert S MD [GO] - **Spec Exp:** Laparoscopic Surgery; Ovarian Cancer; Clinical Trials; **Hospital:** OU Med Ctr; **Address:** Stephenson Cancer Ctr, 800 NE 10th St, Ste 2100, Oklahoma City, OK 73104; **Phone:** 405-271-7770; **Board Cert:** Obstetrics & Gynecology 2012; Gynecologic Oncology 2012; **Med School:** Univ Tex Med Br, Galveston 1982; **Resid:** Obstetrics & Gynecology, Scott & White Hosp 1986; **Fellow:** Gynecologic Oncology, UC Irvine Med Ctr 1989; **Fac Appt:** Prof ObG, Univ Okla Coll Med

Miller, David Scott MD [GO] - **Spec Exp:** Gynecologic Cancer; Cervical Cancer; Uterine Cancer; **Hospital:** UT Southwestern Med Ctr at Dallas; **Address:** Simmons Cancer Ctr, Gynecological Onc, 2201 Inwood Rd, Ste 106, Dallas, TX 75390; **Phone:** 214-645-4673; **Board Cert:** Obstetrics & Gynecology 2012; Gynecologic Oncology 2012; **Med School:** Univ Okla Coll Med 1977; **Resid:** Obstetrics & Gynecology, Hosp Univ Penn 1981; **Fellow:** Reproductive Endocrinology, UCSD Med Ctr 1982; Gynecologic Oncology, Stanford Univ Hosp & Clins 1985; **Fac Appt:** Prof ObG, Univ Tex SW, Dallas

Siller, Barry S MD [GO] - **Spec Exp:** Cervical Cancer; **Hospital:** Meml Hermann Hosp - Texas Med Ctr; **Address:** 915 Gessner Rd, Ste 400, Medical Plaza 3, Houston, TX 77024; **Phone:** 713-242-2575; **Board Cert:** Obstetrics & Gynecology 2012; Gynecologic Oncology 2012; **Med School:** Baylor Coll Med 1988; **Resid:** Obstetrics & Gynecology, UAB Med Ctr 1993; **Fellow:** Gynecologic Oncology, UAB Med Ctr 1997

Singh, Diljeet K MD [GO] - **Spec Exp:** Gynecologic Cancer; Ovarian Cancer; Ovarian Cancer-Early Detection; **Hospital:** Banner Gateway Med Ctr; **Address:** 2946 E Banner Gateway Drive, Gilbert, AZ 85234; **Phone:** 480-256-3609; **Board Cert:** Obstetrics & Gynecology 2013; Gynecologic Oncology 2013; **Med School:** Northwestern Univ-Feinberg Sch Med 1991; **Resid:** Obstetrics & Gynecology, Johns Hopkins Hosp 1996; **Fellow:** Gynecologic Oncology, MD Anderson Cancer Ctr 1999

Smith, Donna M MD [GO] - **Spec Exp:** Cervical Cancer; Ovarian Cancer; **Hospital:** Scottsdale Healthcare Thompson Peak; **Address:** Arizona Oncology, Biltmore Cancer Ctr, 2222 E Highland Ave, Ste 400, Phoenix, AZ 85016; **Phone:** 602-253-5300; **Board Cert:** Obstetrics & Gynecology 2007; Gynecologic Oncology 2007; **Med School:** Univ MO-Kansas City 1980; **Resid:** Obstetrics & Gynecology, Emory Univ Hosp 1984; **Fellow:** Gynecologic Oncology, Georgetown Univ Med Ctr 1987

Sood, Anil K MD [GO] - **Spec Exp:** Gynecologic Cancer; Ovarian Cancer; **Hospital:** UT MD Anderson Canc Ctr; **Address:** Univ Texas MD Anderson Cancer Ctr, 1515 Holcombe Blvd Unit 1362, Houston, TX 77030-4000; **Phone:** 713-792-8340; **Board Cert:** Obstetrics & Gynecology 2012; Gynecologic Oncology 2012; **Med School:** Univ NC Sch Med 1991; **Resid:** Obstetrics & Gynecology, Univ FL Med Ctr 1995; **Fellow:** Gynecologic Oncology, Univ Iowa Hosps & Clin 1998

Walker, Joan L MD [GO] - **Spec Exp:** Ovarian Cancer; Cervical Cancer; Uterine Cancer; Gynecologic Cancer; **Hospital:** OU Med Ctr; **Address:** Stephenson Cancer Ctr, 800 NE 10th St, Ste 2100, Oklahoma City, OK 73104; **Phone:** 405-271-7770; **Board Cert:** Obstetrics & Gynecology 2012; Gynecologic Oncology 2012; **Med School:** UCLA 1982; **Resid:** Obstetrics & Gynecology, Hosp Univ Penn 1986; **Fellow:** Gynecologic Oncology, UC-Irvine Med Ctr 1990; **Fac Appt:** Prof ObG, Univ Okla Coll Med

West Coast and Pacific

Berek, Jonathan S MD [GO] - **Spec Exp:** Ovarian Cancer; Uterine Cancer; Cervical Cancer; Vulvar & Vaginal Cancer; **Hospital:** Stanford Univ Hosp & Clins; **Address:** Stanford Women's Cancer Center, 900 Blake Wilbur Drive, Stanford, CA 94305; **Phone:** 650-498-6004; **Board Cert:** Obstetrics & Gynecology 2009; Gynecologic Oncology 2009; **Med School:** Johns Hopkins Univ 1975; **Resid:** Obstetrics & Gynecology, Brigham & Womens Hosp 1979; **Fellow:** Gynecologic Oncology, UCLA Sch Med 1981; **Fac Appt:** Prof ObG, Stanford Univ

Berman, Michael L MD [GO] - **Spec Exp:** Gynecologic Cancer; Cervical Cancer; **Hospital:** UC Irvine Med Ctr, Long Beach Meml Med Ctr; **Address:** UC Irvine Health Gynecologic Oncology, 101 The City Drive S, Pavilion III, Orange, CA 92868; **Phone:** 714-456-8000; **Board Cert:** Obstetrics & Gynecology 2005; Gynecologic Oncology 2005; **Med School:** Geo Wash Univ 1967; **Resid:** Obstetrics & Gynecology, GW Univ Hosp 1969; Obstetrics & Gynecology, LAC-Harbor Hosp 1974; **Fellow:** Gynecologic Oncology, UCLA Med Ctr 1976; **Fac Appt:** Prof ObG, UC Irvine

Bristow, Robert E MD [GO] - **Spec Exp:** Ovarian Cancer; Gynecologic Cancer; **Hospital:** UC Irvine Med Ctr; **Address:** UC Irvine Health Gynecologic Oncology, 101 The City Drive S, Pavilion III, Orange, CA 92868; **Phone:** 714-456-8000; **Board Cert:** Obstetrics & Gynecology 2012; Gynecologic Oncology 2012; **Med School:** USC Sch Med 1991; **Resid:** Obstetrics & Gynecology, Johns Hopkins Hosp 1995; **Fellow:** Gynecologic Oncology, UCLA Med Ctr 1998; **Fac Appt:** Prof ObG, UC Irvine

Carney, Michael E MD [GO] - **Spec Exp:** Gynecologic Cancer; Pelvic Surgery-Complex; Minimally Invasive Surgery; **Hospital:** Kapiolani Med Ctr for Women & Chldn, Queen's Med Ctr - Honolulu; **Address:** Kapiolani Womens Cancer Ctr, 1319 Punahou St, Ste 640, Honolulu, HI 96826; **Phone:** 808-983-6090; **Board Cert:** Obstetrics & Gynecology 2012; Gynecologic Oncology 2012; **Med School:** Loyola Univ-Stritch Sch Med 1990; **Resid:** Obstetrics & Gynecology, Duke Univ Hosp 1994; **Fellow:** Gynecologic Oncology, Duke Univ Hosp 1999; **Fac Appt:** Assoc Clin Prof ObG, Univ Hawaii JA Burns Sch Med

Chan, John CK MD [GO] - **Spec Exp:** Ovarian Cancer; Gene Therapy; Clinical Trials; **Hospital:** UCSF Med Ctr; **Address:** UCSF Medical Center, 1600 Divisidaro St, San Francisco, CA 94143-1702; **Phone:** 415-353-9600; **Board Cert:** Obstetrics & Gynecology 2012; Gynecologic Oncology 2012; **Med School:** UCLA 1995; **Resid:** Obstetrics & Gynecology, UC Irvine Med Ctr 1999; **Fellow:** Gynecologic Oncology, UC Irvine 2003; **Fac Appt:** Assoc Prof ObG, UCSF

Goff, Barbara A MD [GO] - **Spec Exp:** Ovarian Cancer; Uterine Cancer; Cervical Cancer; Gynecologic Surgery-Complex; **Hospital:** Univ Wash Med Ctr; **Address:** Univ Washington, Dept Gyn/Onc, 825 Eastlake Ave E, MS G3-100, Seattle, WA 98109; **Phone:** 206-288-2273; **Board Cert:** Obstetrics & Gynecology 2012; Gynecologic Oncology 2012; **Med School:** Univ Pennsylvania 1986; **Resid:** Obstetrics & Gynecology, Mass Genl Hosp/Brigham & Womens Hosp 1990; **Fellow:** Gynecologic Oncology, Mass Genl Hosp 1993; **Fac Appt:** Prof ObG, Univ Wash

Greer, Benjamin E MD [GO] - **Spec Exp:** Gynecologic Cancer; **Hospital:** Univ Wash Med Ctr; **Address:** Seattle Cancer Care Alliance, 825 Eastlake Ave E, MS G3-100, Seattle, WA 98109; **Phone:** 206-288-2273; **Board Cert:** Obstetrics & Gynecology 2002; Gynecologic Oncology 2002; **Med School:** Univ Pennsylvania 1966; **Resid:** Obstetrics & Gynecology, Univ Colorado Hosp 1971; **Fac Appt:** Prof ObG, Univ Wash

Husain, Amreen MD [GO] - **Spec Exp:** Cervical Cancer; Women's Health; **Hospital:** Stanford Univ Hosp & Clins; **Address:** Stanford Comprehensive Cancer Ctr, 900 Blake Wilbur Drive, Stanford, CA 94305; **Phone:** 650-498-6004; **Board Cert:** Obstetrics & Gynecology 2013; Gynecologic Oncology 2013; **Med School:** NY Med Coll 1991; **Resid:** Obstetrics & Gynecology, Cornell Univ Med Ctr/NY Hosp 1995; **Fellow:** Gynecologic Oncology, Meml Sloan-Kettering Cancer Ctr 2000; **Fac Appt:** Assoc Prof ObG, Stanford Univ

McGonigle, Kathryn F MD [GO] - **Spec Exp:** Gynecologic Cancer; Gynecologic Surgery; **Hospital:** Northwest Hosp - Seattle; **Address:** Women's Cancer Care of Seattle, 1560 N 115 St Med Office Bldg - Ste 101, Seattle, WA 98133; **Phone:** 206-368-6806; **Board Cert:** Obstetrics & Gynecology 2011; Gynecologic Oncology 2011; **Med School:** St Louis Univ 1984; **Resid:** Obstetrics & Gynecology, UCSD Med Ctr 1988; **Fellow:** Gynecologic Oncology, UCLA Med Ctr 1993; **Fac Appt:** Asst Clin Prof ObG, Univ Wash

Muntz, Howard G MD [GO] - **Spec Exp:** Robotic Surgery; Ovarian Cancer; Gynecologic Surgery-Complex; Gestational Trophoblastic Disease; **Hospital:** Northwest Hosp - Seattle; **Address:** Women's Canc Care Seattle, 1560 N 115th St, Ste 101, Seattle, WA 98133; **Phone:** 206-368-6806; **Board Cert:** Obstetrics & Gynecology 2012; Gynecologic Oncology 2012; **Med School:** Harvard Med Sch 1984; **Resid:** Obstetrics & Gynecology, Brigham & Womens Hosp 1989; **Fellow:** Gynecologic Oncology, Mass General Hosp 1992; **Fac Appt:** Assoc Clin Prof ObG, Univ Wash

Pejovic, Tanja MD/PhD [GO] - **Spec Exp:** Ovarian Cancer; Gynecologic Cancer-Rare; Uterine Cancer; Cervical Cancer; **Hospital:** OR Hlth & Sci Univ; **Address:** OHSU, Ctr Womens Hlth, 3181 SW Sam Jackson Park Rd, Portland, OR 97239; **Phone:** 503-418-4500; **Board Cert:** Obstetrics & Gynecology 2012; Gynecologic Oncology 2012; **Med School:** Yugoslavia 1984; **Resid:** Gynecologic Oncology, Lund Univ Affil Hosp 1995; Obstetrics & Gynecology, Yale-New Haven Hosp 2000; **Fellow:** Gynecologic Oncology, Yale-New Haven Hosp 2003; **Fac Appt:** Assoc Prof ObG, Oregon Hlth & Sci Univ

Plaxe, Steven C MD [GO] - **Spec Exp:** Ovarian Cancer; Uterine Cancer; Cervical Cancer; Gestational Trophoblastic Disease; **Hospital:** UCSD Med Ctr; **Address:** Moores Cancer Center, 3855 Health Sciences Drive, La Jolla, CA 92093-0987; **Phone:** 858-822-6199; **Board Cert:** Obstetrics & Gynecology 2012; Gynecologic Oncology 2012; **Med School:** Mount Sinai Sch Med 1981; **Resid:** Obstetrics & Gynecology, Yale-New Haven Hosp 1985; **Fellow:** Gynecologic Oncology, Mt Sinai Med Ctr 1988; **Fac Appt:** Prof ObG, UCSD

Smith, Lloyd Herbert MD/PhD [GO] - **Spec Exp:** Ovarian Cancer; Uterine Cancer; Vulvar Disease/Cancer; Vaginal Cancer; **Hospital:** UC Davis Med Ctr; **Address:** UC Davis Cancer Center, 4501 X St, Sacramento, CA 95817-2307; **Phone:** 916-734-6945; **Board Cert:** Obstetrics & Gynecology 2012; Gynecologic Oncology 2012; **Med School:** UC Davis 1981; **Resid:** Obstetrics & Gynecology, UC Davis Med Ctr 1985; **Fellow:** Gynecologic Oncology, Stanford Univ Hosp 1988; **Fac Appt:** Prof ObG, UC Davis

Spirtos, Nicola Michael MD [GO] - **Spec Exp:** Gynecologic Cancer; Ovarian Cancer; **Hospital:** Sunrise Hosp & Med Ctr, Univ Med Ctr - Las Vegas; **Address:** 3131 La Canada St, Ste 241, Las Vegas, NV 89169; **Phone:** 702-693-6870; **Board Cert:** Obstetrics & Gynecology 2012; Gynecologic Oncology 2012; **Med School:** Northwestern Univ 1980; **Resid:** Obstetrics & Gynecology, Women's Hosp LAC-USC Med Ctr 1984; **Fellow:** Gynecologic Oncology, Stanford Univ Affil Hosp 1987; **Fac Appt:** Prof ObG

Stern, Jeffrey L MD [GO] - **Spec Exp:** Laparoscopic Surgery; Vulvar Disease/Cancer; **Hospital:** Alta Bates Summit Med Ctr-Alta Bates Campus; **Address:** Womens Cancer Ctr Northern Calif, 2001 Dwight Way, Berkley, CA 94704; **Phone:** 510-204-5770; **Board Cert:** Obstetrics & Gynecology 1983; Gynecologic Oncology 1984; **Med School:** SUNY Upstate Med Univ 1976; **Resid:** Obstetrics & Gynecology, Johns Hopkins Hosp 1980; **Fellow:** Gynecologic Oncology, USC Med Ctr 1982

Teng, Nelson NH MD/PhD [GO] - **Spec Exp:** Ovarian Cancer; Clinical Trials; **Hospital:** Stanford Univ Hosp & Clins; **Address:** Dept Gyn Oncology, 900 Blake Wilbur Drive, Palo Alto, CA 94304; **Phone:** 650-498-6004; **Board Cert:** Obstetrics & Gynecology 2003; Gynecologic Oncology 2003; **Med School:** Univ Miami Sch Med 1977; **Resid:** Obstetrics & Gynecology, UCLA Med Ctr 1981; **Fellow:** Gynecologic Oncology, Stanford Univ Sch Med 1984; **Fac Appt:** Assoc Prof ObG, Stanford Univ

THE MOUNT SINAI MEDICAL CENTER

Gynecologic Oncology

Mount Sinai

One Gustave L. Levy Place
Fifth Avenue and 100th Street
New York, NY 10029-6574

Physician Referral: 1-800-MD-SINAI (637-4624)
www.mountsinai.org

The Mount Sinai Medical Center's **DIVISION OF GYNECOLOGIC ONCOLOGY** was founded in 1967 before the discipline received official designation as a subspecialty of The American Board of Obstetrics and Gynecology. Since then, we've been at the forefront treating all gynecologic cancers the most common forms of cancer in women after breast, lung, and colon cancers–a fact recognized by *U.S. News & World Report* as it named us among the top medical centers in the country for both cancer and gynecology in its 2013-2014 "Best Hospitals" issue.

Our surgeons were early adaptors of the new robotic surgical systems now in place—years before most centers used the systems. These minimally invasive surgeries offer shorter hospital stays, less scarring, and a faster return to normal activity than other forms of surgery. Approximately 60 percent of our surgeries are now performed using a minimally invasive approach.

To deliver the highest quality, most comprehensive care, we work closely with our colleagues at Mount Sinai's Tisch Cancer Institute as well as with those in diagnostic and interventional radiology, genetics, radiation therapy, palliative care, behavioral medicine, nutrition, and physical therapy. Practicing at the Derald H. Ruttenberg Cancer Center, relocated in 2012 to our beautiful and expansive Leon and Norma Hess Center for Science and Medicine, we manage surgical patients, provide consultations, and administer chemotherapy in a unified and intimate setting designed to ensure patient privacy and comfort. Our nurses are specifically trained in cancer treatment , and we have on-site oncology pharmacists.

Our services include cancer screening, early detection, therapy, and post-treatment surveillance for cancers of the cervix, fallopian tube, ovary, uterus, vagina and vulva.

ACCESS TO CLINICAL TRIALS

As a member of the Gynecologic Oncology Group (GOG), we offer our patients exposure to national clinical trials for the treatment of gynecologic cancers. Mount Sinai physicians have been pioneers in investigating optimal chemotherapeutic regimens leading to significant improvements in outcomes. Current investigations and clinical trials are available for patients with ovarian, uterine, cervical, and endometrial cancers.

Treatments We Provide

We provide a comprehensive range of treatments for gynecologic malignancies and complex benign gynecologic conditions. These include:

- Laser and laparoscopic surgeries
- Lymphadenectomy
- Ovarian cytoreduction and debulking
- Port implantation
- Urologic and bowel surgery

Hand Surgery

a subspecialty of Orthopaedics, Surgery or Plastic Surgery

A specialist trained in the investigation, preservation and restoration by medical, surgical and rehabilitative means of all structures of the upper extremity directly affecting the form and function of the hand and wrist.

For more information about the mentioned specialties or those physicians, see **Orthopaedic Surgery, Surgery** or **Plastic Surgery** section(s).

Training Required: Five years (including general surgery) in orthopaedics *plus* two years in clinical practice before final certification is achieved *plus* additional training and examination in hand surgery OR five to seven years in plastic surgery *plus* additional training and examination in hand surgery.

Hand Surgery

New England

Belsky, Mark R MD [HS] - **Spec Exp:** Arthritis; Sports Injuries; Elbow Surgery; Dupuytren's Contracture; **Hospital:** Newton - Wellesley Hosp; **Address:** 2000 Washington St, Green Bldg, Ste 201, Newton, MA 02462-1629; **Phone:** 617-965-4263; **Board Cert:** Orthopaedic Surgery 1982; Hand Surgery 2011; **Med School:** Tufts Univ 1974; **Resid:** Surgery, Peter Bent Brigham Hosp 1976; Orthopaedic Surgery, Tufts-New England Med Ctr 1979; **Fellow:** Hand Surgery, Roosevelt Hosp 1980; **Fac Appt:** Clin Prof OrS, Tufts Univ

Cassidy, Charles MD [HS] - **Spec Exp:** Hand & Upper Extremity Surgery; Elbow Surgery; **Hospital:** Tufts Med Ctr; **Address:** Tufts Medical Ctr, 800 Washington St, Box 306, Boston, MA 02111; **Phone:** 617-636-5150; **Board Cert:** Hand Surgery 2007; Orthopaedic Surgery 2007; **Med School:** Northwestern Univ 1987; **Resid:** Orthopaedic Surgery, Tufts Univ Med Ctr 1993; **Fellow:** Hand Surgery, Tufts Univ Med Ctr 1995; **Fac Appt:** Assoc Prof OrS, Tufts Univ

Jupiter, Jesse B MD [HS] - **Spec Exp:** Upper Extremity Trauma; Hand Surgery; Fractures-Non Union; **Hospital:** Mass Genl Hosp, Newton - Wellesley Hosp; **Address:** Mass General Hospital, 55 Fruit St, Yawkey Center, Ste 2100, Boston, MA 02114; **Phone:** 617-726-5100; **Board Cert:** Orthopaedic Surgery 1982; **Med School:** Yale Univ 1972; **Resid:** Surgery, Mass Genl Hosp 1976; Orthopaedic Surgery, Mass Genl Hosp 1979; **Fellow:** Trauma, Univ of Basle Affil Hosp 1980; Hand Surgery, Univ Louisville Affil Hosp 1981; **Fac Appt:** Prof OrS, Harvard Med Sch

Sampson, Christian E MD [HS] - **Spec Exp:** Hand Injuries; Hand & Fingers Vascular Surgery; **Hospital:** Brigham & Women's Hosp; **Address:** Brigham & Women's Hosp, Div Plastic Surg, 75 Francis St, Boston, MA 02115; **Phone:** 617-732-6297; **Board Cert:** Plastic Surgery 2004; Hand Surgery 2012; **Med School:** Boston Univ 1986; **Resid:** Surgery, Boston Med Ctr 1991; Plastic Surgery, Brigham & Women's Hosp 1993; **Fellow:** Hand Surgery, St Luke's Roosevelt Hosp 1994; **Fac Appt:** Asst Prof PlS, Harvard Med Sch

Swigart, Carrie R MD [HS] - **Spec Exp:** Hand & Wrist Surgery; Elbow Surgery; **Hospital:** Yale-New Haven Hosp; **Address:** 800 Howard Ave, Fl 1, New Haven, CT 06520; **Phone:** 203-785-3851; **Board Cert:** Orthopaedic Surgery 2011; Hand Surgery 2011; **Med School:** Univ Pennsylvania 1991; **Resid:** Surgery, Yale-New Haven Hosp 1992; Orthopaedic Surgery, Yale-New Haven Hosp 1996; **Fellow:** Hand Surgery, St Lukes-Roosevelt Med Ctr 1997; **Fac Appt:** Asst Prof OrS, Yale Univ

Thomson, J Grant MD [HS] - **Spec Exp:** Carpal Tunnel Syndrome; Hand Reconstruction; Microsurgery; Elbow Surgery; **Hospital:** Yale-New Haven Hosp; **Address:** Yale Plastic Surgery, 800 Howard Ave Fl 4, New Haven, CT 06519; **Phone:** 203-737-5130; **Board Cert:** Hand Surgery 2004; Plastic Surgery 2004; **Med School:** McGill Univ 1983; **Resid:** Surgery, Montreal Genl Hosp 1988; Plastic Surgery, Montreal Genl Hosp 1990; **Fellow:** Hand Surgery, Barnes Jewish Hosp 1991; **Fac Appt:** Assoc Prof PlS, Yale Univ

Waters, Peter Michael MD [HS] - **Spec Exp:** Brachial Plexus Palsy; Hand-Congenital Anomaly; **Hospital:** Children's Hospital - Boston; **Address:** Boston Chldn's Hosp, Dept Ortho Surgery, 300 Longwood Ave, Fegan 2, Boston, MA 02115-5724; **Phone:** 617-355-6021; **Board Cert:** Orthopaedic Surgery 2012; Hand Surgery 2012; **Med School:** Tufts Univ 1981; **Resid:** Pediatrics, Mass Genl Hosp 1983; Orthopaedic Surgery, Harvard Combined Prog 1988; **Fellow:** Hand Surgery, Brigham/Chldns Hosp 1989; **Fac Appt:** Assoc Prof OrS, Harvard Med Sch

Weiss, Arnold-Peter MD [HS] - **Spec Exp:** Carpal Tunnel Syndrome; Wrist Surgery; Elbow Replacement; **Hospital:** Rhode Island Hosp; **Address:** Univ Orthopedics, 2 Dudley St, Ste 200, Providence, RI 02905-3248; **Phone:** 401-457-1520; **Board Cert:** Orthopaedic Surgery 2004; Hand Surgery 2004; **Med School:** Johns Hopkins Univ 1985; **Resid:** Orthopaedic Surgery, Johns Hopkins Hosp 1990; **Fellow:** Hand Surgery, Indiana Hand Ctr 1991; **Fac Appt:** Prof OrS, Brown Univ

Mid Atlantic

Athanasian, Edward A MD [HS] - **Spec Exp:** Bone & Soft Tissue Tumors; Hand & Upper Extremity Tumors; **Hospital:** Hosp For Special Surgery (page 58), Meml Sloan-Kettering Canc Ctr; **Address:** Hospital for Special Surgery, 523 E 72nd St Fl 4th, New York, NY 10021; **Phone:** 212-606-1962; **Board Cert:** Orthopaedic Surgery 2008; Hand Surgery 2008; **Med School:** Columbia P&S 1988; **Resid:** Surgery, Beth Israel Deaconess Hosp 1989; Orthopaedic Surgery, Hosp Special Surgery 1993; **Fellow:** Hand Surgery, Mayo Clinic 1994; Orthopaedic Oncology, Meml Sloan Kettering Cancer Ctr 1995; **Fac Appt:** Assoc Clin Prof OrS, Cornell Univ-Weill Med Coll

Baratz, Mark E MD [HS] - **Spec Exp:** Upper Extremity Surgery; Elbow Reconstruction; Carpal Tunnel Syndrome; **Hospital:** Select Specialty Hosp of Pittsburgh-UPMC; **Address:** UPMC, Orthopaedic Specialists, 125 N Franklin Drive, Ste 1B, Washington, PA 15301; **Phone:** 877-471-0935; **Board Cert:** Orthopaedic Surgery 2004; Hand Surgery 2004; **Med School:** Univ Pittsburgh 1984; **Resid:** Orthopaedic Surgery, UPMC 1990; **Fellow:** Orthopaedic Research, UPMC 1987; Hand Surgery, Med Coll Penn 1991

Beredjiklian, Pedro K MD [HS] - **Spec Exp:** Hand & Wrist Surgery; Arthroscopic Surgery; Elbow Reconstruction; **Hospital:** Riddle Meml Hosp, Thomas Jefferson Univ Hosp; **Address:** Rothman Institute, 1118 W Baltimore Pike, Media, PA 19063; **Phone:** 800-321-9999; **Board Cert:** Orthopaedic Surgery 2011; Hand Surgery 2011; **Med School:** Columbia P&S 1992; **Resid:** Orthopaedic Surgery, Hosp Univ Penn 1997; **Fellow:** Hand & Microvascular Surgery, Hosp Special Surgery 1998; **Fac Appt:** Assoc Prof OrS, Thomas Jefferson Univ

Bozentka, David J MD [HS] - **Spec Exp:** Hand & Upper Extremity Surgery; Elbow Surgery; **Hospital:** Penn Presby Med Ctr - UPHS (page 69); **Address:** Penn Orthopaedic Institute, I Cupp Pavilion, 51 N 39th St, Philadelphia, PA 19104; **Phone:** 215-349-5773; **Board Cert:** Orthopaedic Surgery 2006; Hand Surgery 2006; **Med School:** Jefferson Med Coll 1987; **Resid:** Orthopaedic Surgery, W Virgina Univ Hosp 1992; **Fellow:** Hand Surgery, Hosp Univ Penn 1993; **Fac Appt:** Assoc Prof OrS, Univ Pennsylvania

Brushart, Thomas M MD [HS] - **Spec Exp:** Hand & Upper Extremity Surgery; Peripheral Nerve Surgery; Carpal Tunnel Syndrome; **Hospital:** Johns Hopkins Hosp (page 59); **Address:** Johns Hopkins, Hand Surgery Dept, 601 N Caroline St, rm 5221, Baltimore, MD 21287; **Phone:** 410-955-9663; **Board Cert:** Orthopaedic Surgery 1985; **Med School:** Harvard Med Sch 1978; **Resid:** Orthopaedic Surgery, Mass Genl Hosp 1981; **Fellow:** Hand Surgery, Curtis Hand Ctr 1983; **Fac Appt:** Prof OrS, Johns Hopkins Univ

Carlson, Michelle Gerwin MD [HS] - **Spec Exp:** Sports Injuries; Hand & Upper Extremity Surgery; Arthritis; Pediatric Hand Surgery; **Hospital:** Hosp For Special Surgery (page 58), NY-Presby/Weill Cornell Med Ctr, NY (page 65); **Address:** 523 E 72nd St, Fl 4, rm 439, New York, NY 10021; **Phone:** 212-606-1546; **Board Cert:** Orthopaedic Surgery 2007; Hand Surgery 2007; **Med School:** Cornell Univ-Weill Med Coll 1987; **Resid:** Orthopaedic Surgery, Hosp Special Surg 1992; **Fellow:** Hand Surgery, Hosp Special Surg 1993; **Fac Appt:** Assoc Prof OrS, Cornell Univ-Weill Med Coll

Culp, Randall MD [HS] - **Spec Exp:** Microsurgery; Hand & Upper Extremity Surgery; Elbow Surgery; **Hospital:** Thomas Jefferson Univ Hosp, Lankenau Hosp; **Address:** Philadelphia Hand Center, 700 S Henderson Rd, Ste 200, King of Prussia, PA 19406; **Phone:** 610-768-5959; **Board Cert:** Orthopaedic Surgery 2011; Hand Surgery 2011; **Med School:** Penn State Coll Med 1982; **Resid:** Orthopaedic Surgery, Hosp Univ Penn 1987; **Fellow:** Hand Surgery, Hosp Univ Penn 1988; **Fac Appt:** Prof OrS, Jefferson Med Coll

Eglseder Jr, W. Andrew MD [HS] - **Spec Exp:** Hand & Upper Extremity Surgery; Trauma; Hand Reconstruction; **Hospital:** Univ of MD Med Ctr; **Address:** Univ MD Shock Trauma Ctr, 22 S Greene St, Baltimore, MD 21201; **Phone:** 410-328-6284; **Board Cert:** Orthopaedic Surgery 2010; Hand Surgery 2010; **Med School:** Univ MD Sch Med 1982; **Resid:** Orthopaedic Surgery, Univ Maryland Med Ctr 1987; **Fellow:** Hand Surgery, Univ Louisville Med Ctr 1989; **Fac Appt:** Assoc Prof OrS, Univ MD Sch Med

Glickel, Steven Z MD [HS] - **Spec Exp:** Hand & Wrist Surgery; Elbow Surgery; Peripheral Nerve Surgery; **Hospital:** St. Luke's - Roosevelt Hosp Ctr - Roosevelt Div (page 56); **Address:** 1000 10th Ave Fl 3, New York, NY 10019-1147; **Phone:** 212-523-7590; **Board Cert:** Orthopaedic Surgery 1985; Hand Surgery 2010; **Med School:** Harvard Med Sch 1976; **Resid:** Surgery, NY-Presby/Columbia Univ Med Ctr 1978; Orthopaedic Surgery, Brigham & Women's Hosp 1981; **Fellow:** Hand Surgery, St. Luke's - Roosevelt Hosp Ctr - Roosevelt Div 1983; Research, NY-Presby/Columbia Univ Med Ctr 1982; **Fac Appt:** Clin Prof OrS, Columbia P&S

Goitz, Robert J MD [HS] - **Spec Exp:** Hand & Upper Extremity Surgery; **Hospital:** UPMC Mercy, Pittsburgh; **Address:** Kaufman Medical Bldg, Ste 1010, 3471 Fifth Ave, Pittsburgh, PA 15213; **Phone:** 412-605-3324; **Board Cert:** Orthopaedic Surgery 2011; Hand Surgery 2012; **Med School:** Johns Hopkins Univ 1992; **Resid:** Orthopaedic Surgery, Univ Pittsburgh Med Ctr 1997; **Fac Appt:** Assoc Prof OrS, Univ Pittsburgh

Hotchkiss, Robert N MD [HS] - **Spec Exp:** Wrist Surgery; Elbow Reconstruction; Dupuytren's Contracture; **Hospital:** Hosp For Special Surgery (page 58); **Address:** 523 E 72nd St Fl 4, New York, NY 10021-4099; **Phone:** 212-606-1964; **Board Cert:** Orthopaedic Surgery 2010; Hand Surgery 2010; **Med School:** Johns Hopkins Univ 1980; **Resid:** Surgery, Johns Hopkins Hosp 1982; Orthopaedic Surgery, Johns Hopkins Hosp 1985; **Fellow:** Hand Surgery, Union Meml Hosp 1987; **Fac Appt:** Assoc Prof OrS, Cornell Univ-Weill Med Coll

Imbriglia, Joseph E MD [HS] - **Spec Exp:** Arthritis; Carpal Tunnel Syndrome; Shoulder Surgery; Rotator Cuff Surgery; **Hospital:** UPMC Passavant-McCandless, UPMC Shadyside; **Address:** 6001 Stonewood Drive, Wexford, PA 15090-7380; **Phone:** 724-933-3850; **Board Cert:** Orthopaedic Surgery 1977; Hand Surgery 2010; **Med School:** Hahnemann Univ 1970; **Resid:** Surgery, Univ Pittsburgh Med Ctr 1972; Orthopaedic Surgery, Columbia Presby Med Ctr 1975; **Fellow:** Hand Surgery, Columbia Presby Med Ctr 1976; **Fac Appt:** Clin Prof OrS, Univ Pittsburgh

Kozin, Scott H MD [HS] - **Spec Exp:** Congenital Hand Deformities; Brachial Plexus Palsy-Pediatric; Spinal Cord Injury-Pediatric; Tendon Surgery; **Hospital:** Philadelphia Shriners Hosp; **Address:** Shriners Hosp for Children, 3551 N Broad St, Philadelphia, PA 19140; **Phone:** 215-430-4288; **Board Cert:** Orthopaedic Surgery 2005; Hand Surgery 2005; **Med School:** Hahnemann Univ 1986; **Resid:** Orthopaedic Surgery, Albert Einstein Med Ctr 1991; **Fellow:** Hand Surgery, Mayo Clinic 1992; **Fac Appt:** Assoc Prof OrS, Temple Univ

Kulick, Roy G MD [HS] - **Spec Exp:** Carpal Tunnel Syndrome; Arthritis; Tendon Surgery; Hand & Upper Extremity Surgery; **Hospital:** Montefiore Med Ctr-Einstein Campus, NY; **Address:** Dept Orthopaedic Surgery, 1250 Waters Pl Fl 11, Bronx, NY 10461; **Phone:** 718-920-2060; **Board Cert:** Orthopaedic Surgery 1980; Hand Surgery 2011; **Med School:** Cornell Univ-Weill Med Coll 1973; **Resid:** Surgery, St. Luke's - Roosevelt Hosp Ctr - Roosevelt Div 1975; Orthopaedic Surgery, NY-Presby/Columbia Univ Med Ctr 1978; **Fellow:** Hand Surgery, Hosp for Special Surgery 1979; **Fac Appt:** Assoc Prof OrS, Albert Einstein Coll Med

Lane, Lewis B MD [HS] - **Spec Exp:** Carpal Tunnel Syndrome; Arthritis; Sports Injuries; Hand Reconstruction; **Hospital:** N Shore Univ Hosp (page 66); **Address:** University Orthopaedics, 611 Northern Blvd, Ste 200, Great Neck, NY 11021; **Phone:** 516-723-2663; **Board Cert:** Orthopaedic Surgery 1981; Hand Surgery 2010; **Med School:** Columbia P&S 1974; **Resid:** Surgery, NY Hosp 1975; Orthopaedic Surgery, Hosp Special Surgery 1979; **Fellow:** Research, Hosp Special Surgery 1976; Hand Surgery, St Lukes-Roosevelt Hosp Ctr 1980; **Fac Appt:** Prof OrS, Hofstra N Shore-LIJ Sch Med

Lee, W. P. Andrew MD [HS] - **Spec Exp:** Reconstructive Surgery; Cartilage Damage; Transplant-Hand; Pediatric Hand Surgery; **Hospital:** Johns Hopkins Hosp (page 59); **Address:** Johns Hopkins, Plastic Surgery Dept, 601 N Caroline St, rm 8152F, Baltimore, MD 21287; **Phone:** 410-997-9466; **Board Cert:** Hand Surgery 2005; Plastic Surgery 2005; **Med School:** Johns Hopkins Univ 1983; **Resid:** Surgery, Johns Hopkins Hosp 1989; Plastic Surgery, Mass Genl Hosp 1991; **Fellow:** Microsurgery, Johns Hopkins Hosp 1987; Hand Surgery, Indiana Hand Ctr 1993; **Fac Appt:** Prof OrS, Johns Hopkins Univ

Lubahn, John D MD [HS] - **Spec Exp:** Microsurgery; **Hospital:** UPMC Hamot, St. Vincent Hlth Ctr; **Address:** 300 State St, Ste 205, Erie, PA 16507; **Phone:** 814-456-6022; **Board Cert:** Orthopaedic Surgery 2010; Hand Surgery 2010; **Med School:** Case West Res Univ 1975; **Resid:** Surgery, Univ Rochester Med Ctr 1977; Orthopaedic Surgery, Univ Rochester Med Ctr 1980; **Fellow:** Hand Surgery, Univ Louisville Hosp 1981

Melone Jr, Charles P MD [HS] - **Spec Exp:** Wrist Surgery; Fractures; **Hospital:** Beth Israel Med Ctr - Petrie Div (page 56); **Address:** Hand Surgery Ctr, 321 E 34th St, New York, NY 10016; **Phone:** 212-340-0000; **Board Cert:** Orthopaedic Surgery 1976; Hand Surgery 2004; **Med School:** Georgetown Univ 1969; **Resid:** Surgery, Nassau Univ Med Ctr 1971; Orthopaedic Surgery, Nassau Univ Med Ctr 1974; **Fellow:** Hand Surgery, NYU Langone Med Ctr 1975; **Fac Appt:** Prof OrS, Albert Einstein Coll Med

Osterman, A Lee MD [HS] - **Spec Exp:** Upper Extremity Surgery; Wrist Surgery; Neuromuscular Disorders; **Hospital:** Thomas Jefferson Univ Hosp; **Address:** Philadelphia Hand Ctr, 700 S Henderson Rd, Ste 200, King of Prussia, PA 19406-4207; **Phone:** 610-768-5959; **Board Cert:** Orthopaedic Surgery 1980; **Med School:** Univ Pennsylvania 1973; **Resid:** Orthopaedic Surgery, Hosp Univ Penn 1978; **Fellow:** Hand Surgery, Hosp Univ Penn 1979; Microvascular Surgery, Duke Univ Med Ctr 1980; **Fac Appt:** Prof OrS, Jefferson Med Coll

Raphael, James S MD [HS] - **Spec Exp:** Reconstructive Microvascular Surgery; Upper Extremity Trauma; Limb Surgery/Reconstruction; **Hospital:** Einstein Med Ctr, Thomas Jefferson Univ Hosp; **Address:** Einstein Med Ctr, Willowcrest Bldg Fl 4, 5501 Old York Rd, Philadelphia, PA 19141; **Phone:** 215-456-7900; **Board Cert:** Orthopaedic Surgery 2007; Hand Surgery 2007; **Med School:** SUNY Upstate Med Univ 1988; **Resid:** Orthopaedic Surgery, Mt Sinai Hosp 1993; **Fellow:** Hand Surgery, Thomas Jefferson Univ Hosp/Philadelphia Hand Ctr 1994; **Fac Appt:** Assoc Clin Prof OrS, Jefferson Med Coll

Raskin, Keith B MD [HS] - **Spec Exp:** Wrist/Hand Injuries; Arthritis; Carpal Tunnel Syndrome; Elbow Surgery; **Hospital:** NYU Langone Med Ctr (page 68), NYU Hosp For Joint Dis; **Address:** 317 E 34th St, Fl 3, New York, NY 10016; **Phone:** 212-263-4263; **Board Cert:** Orthopaedic Surgery 2013; Hand Surgery 2013; **Med School:** Geo Wash Univ 1983; **Resid:** Orthopaedic Surgery, NYU Langone Med Ctr 1988; **Fellow:** Hand Surgery, Union Mem Hosp 1989; **Fac Appt:** Assoc Clin Prof OrS, NYU Sch Med

Rosenwasser, Melvin P MD [HS] - **Spec Exp:** Carpal Tunnel Syndrome; Sports Injuries; Elbow Surgery; Trauma; **Hospital:** NY-Presby/Columbia Univ Med Ctr, NY (page 65); **Address:** New York Orthopedic Hosp Assocs, 622 W 168th St, PH 11, rm 1150, New York, NY 10032; **Phone:** 212-305-8036; **Board Cert:** Orthopaedic Surgery 1999; Hand Surgery 2011; **Med School:** Columbia P&S 1976; **Resid:** Surgery, St. Luke's - Roosevelt Hosp Ctr - Roosevelt Div 1979; Orthopaedic Surgery, NY-Presby/Columbia Univ Med Ctr 1982; **Fellow:** Hand Surgery, NY-Presby/Columbia Univ Med Ctr 1983; **Fac Appt:** Prof OrS, Columbia P&S

Sotereanos, Dean G MD [HS] - **Spec Exp:** Hand & Upper Extremity Surgery; Elbow Surgery; **Hospital:** Allegheny Genl Hosp; **Address:** 1307 Federal St Fl 2, Pittsburgh, PA 15212; **Phone:** 412-359-4263; **Board Cert:** Orthopaedic Surgery 2013; Hand Surgery 2013; **Med School:** Hahnemann Univ 1984; **Resid:** Surgery, Univ Pittsburgh Med Ctr 1986; Orthopaedic Surgery, Univ Pittsburgh Med Ctr 1989; **Fellow:** Hand Surgery, Duke Univ Med Ctr 1990; **Fac Appt:** Assoc Prof OrS, Univ Pittsburgh

Strauch, Robert J MD [HS] - **Spec Exp:** Hand Reconstruction; Hand & Elbow Nerve Disorders; Hand & Wrist Surgery; Elbow Surgery; **Hospital:** NY-Presby/Columbia Univ Med Ctr, NY (page 65); **Address:** New York Orthopedic Hosp Assocs, 622 W 168th St, PH 11, rm 1119, New York, NY 10032; **Phone:** 212-305-4272; **Board Cert:** Orthopaedic Surgery 2005; Hand Surgery 2005; **Med School:** Columbia P&S 1986; **Resid:** Orthopaedic Surgery, NY-Presby/Columbia Univ Med Ctr 1991; **Fellow:** Hand Surgery, Indiana Hand Ctr 1992; **Fac Appt:** Prof OrS, Columbia P&S

Thoder, Joseph J MD [HS] - **Spec Exp:** Wrist/Hand Injuries; Trauma; **Hospital:** Temple Univ Hosp; **Address:** Temple Orthopaedics & Sports Medicine, 11000 Roosevelt Blvd, Philadelphia, PA 19116; **Phone:** 215-214-6655; **Board Cert:** Orthopaedic Surgery 2011; Hand Surgery 2011; **Med School:** Temple Univ 1982; **Resid:** Orthopaedic Surgery, Temple Univ Hosp 1987; **Fellow:** Hand & Microvascular Surgery, Thos Jefferson Univ Hosp 1988; **Fac Appt:** Prof OrS, Temple Univ

Wolfe, Scott W MD [HS] - **Spec Exp:** Wrist Surgery; Nerve Disorders/Surgery; Fractures; **Hospital:** Hosp For Special Surgery (page 58); **Address:** Hosp for Special Surgery, 535 E 70 St, New York, NY 10021; **Phone:** 212-606-1529; **Board Cert:** Orthopaedic Surgery 2013; Hand Surgery 2013; **Med School:** Cornell Univ-Weill Med Coll 1984; **Resid:** Surgery, St. Luke's - Roosevelt Hosp Ctr - Roosevelt Div 1986; Orthopaedic Surgery, Hosp Special Surg 1989; **Fellow:** Hand & Microvascular Surgery, Presby/Columbia Univ Med Ctr 1990; **Fac Appt:** Prof OrS, Cornell Univ-Weill Med Coll

Southeast

Badia, Alejandro MD [HS] - **Spec Exp:** Hand & Upper Extremity Surgery; Shoulder Surgery; Elbow Surgery; Wrist Surgery; **Address:** 3650 NW 82nd Ave, Ste 103, Doral, FL 33166; **Phone:** 305-227-4263; **Board Cert:** Orthopaedic Surgery 2009; Hand Surgery 2009; **Med School:** NYU Sch Med 1989; **Resid:** Orthopaedic Surgery, NYU Med Ctr 1995; **Fellow:** Hand Surgery, Allegheny Genl Hosp 1997; Trauma 1998

Carneiro, Ronaldo MD [HS] - **Spec Exp:** Carpal Tunnel Syndrome; Arthritis; Dupuytren's Contracture; Hand & Wrist Surgery; **Hospital:** Physicians Regl Hlthcare Med Ctr-Pine Ridge; **Address:** 8340 Collier Blvd, Ste 303, Naples, FL 34114; **Phone:** 239-348-4040; **Board Cert:** Plastic Surgery 1990; **Med School:** Brazil 1970; **Resid:** Surgery, Union Meml Hosp 1975; Plastic Surgery, Allentown & Sacred Heart Hosp Ctr 1977; **Fellow:** Hand Surgery, Jackson Meml Hosp 1977; Plastic Surgery, Univ Miami Hosp 1978; **Fac Appt:** Assoc Clin Prof PlS, Univ S Fla Coll Med

Cendales, Linda C MD [HS] - **Spec Exp:** Transplant-Hand; Microsurgery; Reconstructive Surgery; Carpal Tunnel Syndrome; **Hospital:** Emory Univ Hosp, Emory Univ Hosp Midtown; **Address:** Emory Transplant Ctr, 1365 Clifton Rd NE B Bldg Fl 6, Atlanta, GA 30322; **Phone:** 404-727-0701; **Med School:** Mexico 1992; **Resid:** Surgery, Hosp Genl 1996; Hand Surgery, Natl Inst Orthopaedics 1997; **Fellow:** Hand & Microvascular Surgery, Kleinert Inst, Univ Louisville 2001; Transplant Surgery, Natl Inst Hlth 2004; **Fac Appt:** Asst Prof S, Emory Univ

Friedman, David W MD [HS] - **Spec Exp:** Hand Reconstruction; Arthritis; Microsurgery; Sports Injuries; **Hospital:** Cleveland Clin - Weston (page 55); **Address:** Cleveland Clin, Hand Surgery Dept, 2950 Cleveland Clinic Blvd, Weston, FL 33331; **Phone:** 954-659-5430; **Board Cert:** Plastic Surgery 2009; Hand Surgery 2008; **Med School:** Univ Tex SW, Dallas 1988; **Resid:** Surgery, UMDNJ Affil Hosp 1994; Plastic Surgery, NYU Med Ctr 1996; **Fellow:** Hand Surgery, NYU Med Ctr 1997

Greene, Thomas L MD [HS] - **Spec Exp:** Arthritis; Peripheral Nerve Surgery; Arthroscopic Surgery; Tendon Surgery; **Hospital:** Tampa Genl Hosp, St. Joseph's Hosp - Tampa; **Address:** 2727 W Dr Martin Luther King Jr Blvd, Ste 560, Tampa, FL 33607-6009; **Phone:** 813-873-0337; **Board Cert:** Orthopaedic Surgery 1983; Hand Surgery 2010; **Med School:** Ohio State Univ 1975; **Resid:** Surgery, Univ Michigan Med Ctr 1977; Orthopaedic Surgery, Univ Michigan Med Ctr 1980; **Fellow:** Hand Surgery, St Vincent's Hosp 1981

Grossman, John A.I. MD [HS] - **Spec Exp:** Brachial Plexus Palsy; Peripheral Nerve Surgery; Congenital Hand Deformities; **Hospital:** Miami Children's Hosp, NYU Hosp For Joint Dis; **Address:** 8940 N Kendall Drive, Ste 904E, Miami, FL 33176; **Phone:** 305-666-2004; **Board Cert:** Plastic Surgery 1989; **Med School:** Univ VA Sch Med 1978; **Resid:** Surgery, Cleveland Clin 1982; Plastic Surgery, E Virginia Affil Hosp 1985; **Fellow:** Hand Surgery, French Hand Inst 1983; **Fac Appt:** Assoc Clin Prof OrS, NYU Sch Med

Hunt III, Thomas R MD [HS] - **Spec Exp:** Hand & Wrist Surgery; Arthritis; Trauma; Hand Reconstruction; **Hospital:** UAB Hosp; **Address:** UAB Orthopaedic Surgery, 1313 13th St S, Ste 201, Birmingham, AL 35205-5327; **Phone:** 205-930-8339; **Board Cert:** Orthopaedic Surgery 2006; Hand Surgery 2006; **Med School:** Vanderbilt Univ 1986; **Resid:** Orthopaedic Surgery, Univ Kansas Med Ctr 1992; **Fellow:** Hand Surgery, Hosp Univ Penn 1993; **Fac Appt:** Prof S, UAB Sch Med

Koman, L. Andrew MD [HS] - **Spec Exp:** Pediatric Hand Surgery; Vascular Disease-Upper Extremity; Pain-Nerve Injury; **Hospital:** Wake Forest Baptist Med Ctr; **Address:** 131 Miller St, Winston-Salem, NC 27103; **Phone:** 336-716-8094; **Board Cert:** Orthopaedic Surgery 1981; Hand Surgery 2010; **Med School:** Duke Univ 1974; **Resid:** Surgery, Duke Univ Med Ctr 1975; Orthopaedic Surgery, Duke Univ Med Ctr 1979; **Fellow:** Hand Surgery, Duke Univ Med Ctr 1980; **Fac Appt:** Prof OrS, Wake Forest Univ

Peljovich, Allan E MD [HS] - **Spec Exp:** Brachial Plexus Palsy; Cerebral Palsy; Trauma; Congenital Limb Deformities; **Hospital:** Northside Hosp, Chldns Hlthcare Atlanta @ Scottish Rite; **Address:** Hand & Upper Extremity Ctr, 980 Johnson Ferry Rd NE, Ste 1020, Atlanta, GA 30342; **Phone:** 404-255-0226; **Board Cert:** Hand Surgery 2003; **Med School:** Univ Pennsylvania 1992; **Resid:** Orthopaedic Surgery, Case Western Reserve Univ Hosp 1998; **Fellow:** Hand Surgery, Brigham & Womens Hosp/Chldns Hosp 1999; Hand Surgery, MetroHealth Med Ctr 2000

Midwest

Bishop, Allen T MD [HS] - **Spec Exp:** Microsurgery; Brachial Plexus Palsy; **Hospital:** Mayo Med Ctr & Clin - Rochester; **Address:** Mayo Clin, Div Hand Surgery, 200 First St SW, Rochester, MN 55905; **Phone:** 507-284-0475; **Board Cert:** Orthopaedic Surgery 2010; Hand Surgery 2010; **Med School:** Mayo Med Sch 1981; **Resid:** Orthopaedic Surgery, Mayo Clin 1986; **Fellow:** Hand Surgery, St Vincent Hosp 1987; **Fac Appt:** Prof OrS, Mayo Med Sch

Carroll IV, Charles MD [HS] - **Spec Exp:** Carpal Tunnel Syndrome; Dupuytren's Contracture; Elbow Surgery; Shoulder Surgery; **Hospital:** Northwestern Meml Hosp, Evanston Hosp/NorthShore Univ Hlth Sys (page 67); **Address:** NOI NorthShore Orthopaedic Inst, 680 N Lakeshore Drive, Ste 924, Chicago, IL 60611; **Phone:** 312-664-6848; **Board Cert:** Orthopaedic Surgery 2011; Hand Surgery 2011; **Med School:** Univ MD Sch Med 1982; **Resid:** Surgery, Johns Hopkins Hosp 1984; Orthopaedic Surgery, Johns Hopkins Hosp 1987; **Fellow:** Hand Surgery, Indiana Univ Med Ctr 1988; Shoulder Surgery, Univ Western Ontario 1988; **Fac Appt:** Assoc Clin Prof OrS, Northwestern Univ-Feinberg Sch Med

Chung, Kevin Chi MD [HS] - **Spec Exp:** Reconstructive Surgery; Hand & Microvascular Surgery; Upper Extremity Trauma; Nail Surgery; **Hospital:** Univ Michigan Med Ctr; **Address:** 24 Frank Lloyd Wright Drive, Ann Arbor, MI 48105; **Phone:** 734-998-6022; **Board Cert:** Hand Surgery 2007; Plastic Surgery 2007; **Med School:** Emory Univ 1987; **Resid:** Surgery, Univ Tex Hlth Sci Ctr 1992; Plastic Surgery, Univ Michigan Hosp 1994; **Fellow:** Hand Surgery, Curtis Hand Ctr-Union Meml Hosp 1995; **Fac Appt:** Prof S, Univ Mich Med Sch

Cohen, Mark S MD [HS] - **Spec Exp:** Hand Surgery; Wrist Surgery; Elbow Surgery; **Hospital:** Rush Univ Med Ctr; **Address:** Midwest Orthopedics at Rush, 1611 W Harrison St, Ste 400, Chicago, IL 60612; **Phone:** 312-243-4244; **Board Cert:** Orthopaedic Surgery 2006; Hand Surgery 2006; **Med School:** Harvard Med Sch 1986; **Resid:** Orthopaedic Surgery, UCSD Med Ctr 1992; **Fellow:** Hand Surgery, Indiana Hand Ctr 1993; **Fac Appt:** Prof OrS, Rush Med Coll

DeSilva, Stephen P MD [HS] - **Hospital:** Henry Ford Hosp, Henry Ford- W Bloomfield Hosp; **Address:** Henry Ford Hosp, 2799 W Grand Blvd, Ste K12, Detroit, MI 48202; **Phone:** 248-661-7195; **Board Cert:** Orthopaedic Surgery 2012; Hand Surgery 2012; **Med School:** Johns Hopkins Univ 1983; **Resid:** Orthopaedic Surgery, Mayo Clinic 1988; **Fellow:** Hand Surgery, Union Meml Hosp 1989; **Fac Appt:** Prof OrS, Wayne State Univ

Failla, Joseph M MD [HS] - **Spec Exp:** Hand Reconstruction; **Hospital:** Providence Hosp - Southfield, Huron Valley-Sinai Hosp; **Address:** Farmbrook Med Complex Bldg 1 - Ste 201, 29829 Telegraph Rd, Southfield, MI 48034; **Phone:** 248-352-4263; **Board Cert:** Orthopaedic Surgery 2011; Hand Surgery 2011; **Med School:** SUNY Buffalo 1982; **Resid:** Orthopaedic Surgery, SUNY 1987; **Fellow:** Hand Surgery, Mayo Clinic 1988

Fischer, Thomas J MD [HS] - **Spec Exp:** Microsurgery; Elbow Reconstruction; Fractures-Complex; Wrist Surgery; **Hospital:** St. Vincent Indianapolis Hosp, IU Health Methodist Hosp; **Address:** Indiana Hand to Shoulder Ctr, 8501 Harcourt Rd, Indianapolis, IN 46260; **Phone:** 317-875-9105; **Board Cert:** Orthopaedic Surgery 2010; Hand Surgery 2010; **Med School:** Indiana Univ 1979; **Resid:** Orthopaedic Surgery, Univ Wash Med Ctr 1984; **Fellow:** Hand Surgery, Hand Surg Assocs 1985; Hand Surgery, Duke Univ Hosp 1986; **Fac Appt:** Assoc Clin Prof OrS, Indiana Univ

Gelberman, Richard H MD [HS] - **Spec Exp:** Tendon Surgery; Peripheral Nerve Surgery; **Hospital:** Barnes-Jewish Hosp; **Address:** Wash Univ Sch Med, Dept Orthopaedics, 4921 Parkview Pl Fl 6th - Ste A, St Louis, MO 63110; **Phone:** 314-747-2500; **Board Cert:** Orthopaedic Surgery 2007; Hand Surgery 2007; **Med School:** Univ Tenn Coll Med 1969; **Resid:** Surgery, Univ Wisc Med Ctr 1975; **Fellow:** Hand Surgery, Duke Univ Med Ctr 1977; Pediatric Orthopaedic Surgery, Chldns Hosp-Harvard 1986; **Fac Appt:** Prof OrS, Washington Univ, St Louis

Graham, Thomas J MD [HS] - **Spec Exp:** Hand & Wrist Surgery; Elbow Surgery; Sports Injuries; Wrist/Hand Injuries; **Hospital:** Cleveland Clin (page 55); **Address:** Cleveland Clin-Dept Orthopedics, MC GCIC-10, 9500 Euclid Ave, Cleveland, OH 44195; **Phone:** 216-444-6260; **Board Cert:** Orthopaedic Surgery 2007; Hand Surgery 2007; **Med School:** Univ Cincinnati 1988; **Resid:** Orthopaedic Surgery, Univ Michigan Med Ctr 1993; **Fellow:** Hand Surgery, Indiana Hand Ctr 1994

Hastings II, Hill MD [HS] - **Spec Exp:** Wrist Surgery; Elbow Reconstruction; Fractures & Tendon Transfers; Arthritis; **Hospital:** St. Vincent Indianapolis Hosp, IU Health Methodist Hosp; **Address:** Indiana Hand to Shoulder Ctr, 8501 Harcourt Rd, Indianapolis, IN 46260; **Phone:** 317-875-9105; **Board Cert:** Orthopaedic Surgery 1982; Hand Surgery 2010; **Med School:** USC Sch Med 1974; **Resid:** Surgery, Univ Colorado Hosp 1976; Orthopaedic Surgery, Mass Genl Hosp 1980; **Fellow:** Hand Surgery, St Vincent Hosp 1981; **Fac Appt:** Clin Prof OrS, Indiana Univ

Kleinman, William B MD [HS] - **Spec Exp:** Upper Extremity Surgery-Pediatric; Congenital Hand Deformities; Wrist Reconstruction; Hand Reconstruction; **Hospital:** St. Vincent Indianapolis Hosp, IU Health Methodist Hosp; **Address:** Indiana Hand to Shoulder Ctr, 8501 Harcourt Rd, Indianapolis, IN 46260; **Phone:** 317-875-9105; **Board Cert:** Orthopaedic Surgery 1979; **Med School:** Cornell Univ-Weill Med Coll 1972; **Resid:** Surgery, Univ Colorado Hosp 1974; Orthopaedic Surgery, NY Orthopaedic Hosp 1977; **Fellow:** Hand Surgery, NY-Presby/Columbus Univ Med Ctr 1978; Microvascular Surgery, Duke Univ Hosp 1979; **Fac Appt:** Clin Prof OrS, Indiana Univ

Light, Terry R MD [HS] - **Spec Exp:** Hand-Congenital Anomaly; Hand Injuries-Pediatric; Arthritis; Thumb-Absence; **Hospital:** Loyola Univ Med Ctr, Shriners Hosp for Children-Chicago; **Address:** Loyola Univ Med Ctr, Dept Ortho Surg, 2160 S First Ave, Maguire Bldg, rm 1700, Maywood, IL 60153-5590; **Phone:** 708-216-4570; **Board Cert:** Orthopaedic Surgery 1979; Hand Surgery 2010; **Med School:** Ros Franklin Univ/Chicago Med Sch 1973; **Resid:** Orthopaedic Surgery, Yale-New Haven Hosp 1977; **Fellow:** Hand Surgery, Hartford Combined Prog 1977; **Fac Appt:** Prof OrS, Loyola Univ-Stritch Sch Med

Mass, Daniel MD [HS] - **Spec Exp:** Tendon Surgery; Shoulder Reconstruction; Elbow Reconstruction; Wrist Surgery; **Hospital:** Univ of Chicago Med; **Address:** 5841 S Maryland Ave, MC 3079, Chicago, IL 60637; **Phone:** 773-834-3531; **Board Cert:** Orthopaedic Surgery 2007; Hand Surgery 2007; **Med School:** Univ Chicago-Pritzker Sch Med 1975; **Resid:** Orthopaedic Surgery, Univ Chicago Hosp 1979; **Fellow:** Hand Surgery, St Francis Hosp 1980; **Fac Appt:** Prof S, Univ Chicago-Pritzker Sch Med

Mih, Alexander D MD [HS] - **Spec Exp:** Pediatric Hand Surgery; Congenital Hand Deformities; Hand Reconstruction-Pediatric; Microsurgery; **Hospital:** IU Hlth Univ Hosp, Riley Hosp for Children; **Address:** Indiana Hand to Shoulder Ctr, 8501 Harcourt Rd, Indianapolis, IN 46260; **Phone:** 317-875-9105; **Board Cert:** Orthopaedic Surgery 2013; Hand Surgery 2013; **Med School:** Johns Hopkins Univ 1984; **Resid:** Orthopaedic Surgery, Mayo Clinic 1989; **Fellow:** Hand Surgery, Indiana Hand Ctr 1990; **Fac Appt:** Assoc Prof OrS, Indiana Univ

Nagle, Daniel J MD [HS] - **Spec Exp:** Wrist Surgery; Carpal Tunnel Syndrome; Cubital Tunnel Syndrome; **Hospital:** Northwestern Meml Hosp; **Address:** Chicago Ctr for Surgery of the Hand, 737 N Michigan Ave, Ste 700, Chicago, IL 60611; **Phone:** 312-337-6960; **Board Cert:** Orthopaedic Surgery 2007; Hand Surgery 2007; **Med School:** Belgium 1978; **Resid:** Orthopaedic Surgery, Northwestern Univ Affil Hosp 1983; **Fellow:** Hand Surgery, Christine Kleinert 1984; **Fac Appt:** Prof OrS, Northwestern Univ

Putnam, Matthew D MD [HS] - **Spec Exp:** Wrist Surgery; Fracture Deformities/Arm; Arthritis; Nerve Disorders/Surgery; **Hospital:** Univ Minn Med Ctr, Fairview - West Bank Campus; **Address:** 2512 S 7th St, rm 102, Minneapolis, MN 55454; **Phone:** 612-273-9400; **Board Cert:** Orthopaedic Surgery 2008; Hand Surgery 2008; **Med School:** Dartmouth Med Sch 1977; **Resid:** Surgery, Roosevelt Hosp 1979; Orthopaedic Surgery, Univ Pittsburgh 1984; **Fellow:** Hand Surgery, NYOH 1985; **Fac Appt:** Prof OrS, Univ Minn

Seitz Jr, William H MD [HS] - **Spec Exp:** Hand & Upper Extremity Surgery; Shoulder Surgery; Elbow Surgery; Wrist Surgery; **Hospital:** Lutheran Med Ctr - Cleveland, Cleveland Clin (page 55); **Address:** 1730 W 25th St, Ste 2C, Cleveland, OH 44113; **Phone:** 216-363-2331; **Board Cert:** Orthopaedic Surgery 2008; Hand Surgery 2008; **Med School:** Columbia P&S 1979; **Resid:** Surgery, St Vincents Med Ctr 1981; Orthopaedic Surgery, Columbia-Presby Med Ctr 1984; **Fellow:** Hand & Microvascular Surgery, Columbia-Presby Med Ctr 1985; **Fac Appt:** Prof OrS, Case West Res Univ

Steinmann, Scott P MD [HS] - **Spec Exp:** Shoulder Surgery; Elbow Surgery; Brachial Plexus Palsy; Reconstructive Microvascular Surgery; **Hospital:** Mayo Med Ctr & Clin - Rochester; **Address:** Mayo Clin, Dept Hand Surgery, 200 1st St SW, Rochester, MN 55905; **Phone:** 507-284-4577; **Board Cert:** Orthopaedic Surgery 2004; Hand Surgery 2004; **Med School:** Cornell Univ-Weill Med Coll 1988; **Resid:** Orthopaedic Surgery, Hosp Special Surgery 1992; **Fellow:** Shoulder Surgery, NY-Presby/Columbia Univ Med Ctr 1995; Hand Surgery, Mayo Clin 1998; **Fac Appt:** Prof OrS, Mayo Med Sch

Stern, Peter J MD [HS] - **Spec Exp:** Hand & Wrist Surgery; Microsurgery; **Hospital:** Good Samaritan Hosp - Cincinnati, Univ Cincinnati Med Ctr; **Address:** Hand Surgery Specialists, 538 Oak St, Ste 200, Cincinnati, OH 45219; **Phone:** 513-961-4263; **Board Cert:** Orthopaedic Surgery 2011; Hand Surgery 2011; **Med School:** Washington Univ, St Louis 1970; **Resid:** Surgery, Beth Israel Hosp 1972; Orthopaedic Surgery, Harvard Combined Prgm 1977; **Fellow:** Hand Surgery, Univ Louisville Hosps 1979; **Fac Appt:** Prof OrS, Univ Cincinnati

Great Plains and Mountains

Idler, Richard S MD [HS] - **Spec Exp:** Upper Extremity Surgery; Microsurgery; Fractures; **Hospital:** Penrose Hosp, St. Francis Med Ctr; **Address:** Colorado Springs Orthopaedic Grp, 3010 N Circle, Ste 100b, Colorado Springs, CO 80909; **Phone:** 719-632-7669; **Board Cert:** Orthopaedic Surgery 1985; Hand Surgery 2010; **Med School:** Dartmouth Med Sch 1975; **Resid:** Surgery, UCLA Med Ctr 1977; Plastic Surgery, UCLA Med Ctr 1978; **Fellow:** Orthopaedic Surgery, Mass Genl Hosp 1981; Hand Surgery, St Vincent Hosp 1982

Southwest

Breidenbach III, Warren C MD [HS] - **Spec Exp:** Transplant-Hand; **Hospital:** Univ Arizona Med Ctr-Univ Campus; **Address:** UPH Clin at Alvernon, 707 N Alvernon Way Fl 2 - Ste 201, Tucson, AZ 85711; **Phone:** 520-694-8888; **Board Cert:** Plastic Surgery 1988; Hand Surgery 2012; **Med School:** Univ Calgary 1975; **Resid:** Surgery, McGill Affil Hosp 1979; Plastic Surgery, McGill Affil Hosp 1981; **Fellow:** Microsurgery, Eastern Va Med Sch Affil Hosp 1982; Hand Surgery, Kleinert Inst 1984; **Fac Appt:** Prof PlS, Univ Ariz Coll Med

Collins, Evan D MD [HS] - **Spec Exp:** Hand & Upper Extremity Surgery; Wrist/Hand Injuries; Elbow Surgery; Joint Reconstruction; **Hospital:** Methodist Hosp - Houston; **Address:** Methodist Hospital, Dept Orthopaedics, 6560 Fannin St, Scurlock Twr Fl 4 Ste 410, Houston, TX 77030; **Phone:** 713-441-3535; **Board Cert:** Orthopaedic Surgery 2011; Hand Surgery 2011; **Med School:** SUNY Downstate 1992; **Resid:** Surgery, Baylor Affil Hosp 1997; **Fellow:** Hand Surgery, Baylor College Med 1999

Ezaki, Marybeth MD [HS] - **Spec Exp:** Hand-Congenital Anomaly; Hand Reconstruction-Pediatric; **Hospital:** Texas Scottish Rite Hosp for Chldn; **Address:** 2222 Welborn St, Dallas, TX 75219; **Phone:** 214-559-7842; **Board Cert:** Orthopaedic Surgery 1985; **Med School:** Yale Univ 1977; **Resid:** Orthopaedic Surgery, Univ Tex SW Med Ctr 1982; **Fellow:** Hand Surgery, Weyham Pk Hosp 1982; **Fac Appt:** Prof OrS, Univ Tex SW, Dallas

Moneim, Moheb S MD [HS] - **Spec Exp:** Microsurgery; Hand Injuries; Peripheral Nerve Surgery; Arthritis; **Hospital:** Univ Hosp - New Mexico; **Address:** 1101 Medical Arts Rd Bldg 5, Dept Orthopedics, MSC10-5600, Albuquerque, NM 87131; **Phone:** 505-272-4107; **Board Cert:** Orthopaedic Surgery 1998; Hand Surgery 2010; **Med School:** Egypt 1963; **Resid:** Orthopaedic Surgery, Duke Univ Med Ctr 1975; **Fellow:** Hand Surgery, Hosp for Spec Surgery 1976; **Fac Appt:** Prof OrS, Univ New Mexico

Rayan, Ghazi M MD [HS] - **Spec Exp:** Microsurgery; Congenital Limb Deformities; Arthritis; **Hospital:** INTEGRIS Baptist Med Ctr - OK, OU Med Ctr; **Address:** 3366 Northwest Expressway, D Bldg - Ste 700, Oklahoma City, OK 73112-4439; **Phone:** 405-945-4888; **Board Cert:** Orthopaedic Surgery 2000; **Med School:** Egypt 1973; **Resid:** Surgery, S Baltimore Genl Hosp 1977; Orthopaedic Surgery, Union Meml Hosp 1980; **Fellow:** Hand & Microvascular Surgery, Union Meml Hosp 1980; **Fac Appt:** Clin Prof OrS, Univ Okla Coll Med

West Coast and Pacific

Abrams, Reid A MD [HS] - **Spec Exp:** Hand & Upper Extremity Surgery; Elbow Reconstruction; Fractures & Tendon Transfers; Carpal Tunnel Syndrome; **Hospital:** UCSD Med Ctr; **Address:** UCSD Med Ctr, Dept Orthopaedic Surgery, 200 W Arbor St, San Diego, CA 92103; **Phone:** 858-657-8200; **Board Cert:** Orthopaedic Surgery 2012; Hand Surgery 2012; **Med School:** Univ Colorado 1982; **Resid:** Orthopaedic Surgery, Univ Colo Med Ctr 1987; **Fellow:** Pediatric Orthopaedic Surgery, Chldns Hosp Hlth Ctr 1988; Hand Surgery, Brigham & Womens Hosp 1989; **Fac Appt:** Prof OrS, UCSD

Atkinson, Robert E MD [HS] - **Spec Exp:** Arthritis; Arthroscopic Surgery; Nerve Disorders/Surgery; **Hospital:** Queen's Med Ctr - Honolulu, Kapiolani Med Ctr @ Pali Momi; **Address:** Orthopedic Associates, 1401 S Beretanis St, Ste 750, Honolulu, HI 96814; **Phone:** 808-521-8128; **Board Cert:** Orthopaedic Surgery 1985; **Med School:** Jefferson Med Coll 1977; **Resid:** Orthopaedic Surgery, Hosp Special Surgery 1982; **Fellow:** Hand Surgery, Mass Genl Hosp 1983; **Fac Appt:** Clin Prof OrS, Univ Hawaii JA Burns Sch Med

Chang, James MD [HS] - **Spec Exp:** Hand & Upper Extremity Surgery; Reconstructive Surgery; Pediatric Hand Surgery; Peripheral Nerve Surgery; **Hospital:** Stanford Univ Hosp & Clins; **Address:** SUMC Hand & Upper Extremity Surgery, 450 Broadway St, Pavilion A, Fl 2, Redwood City, CA 94063-6120; **Phone:** 650-723-5256; **Board Cert:** Plastic Surgery 2009; Hand Surgery 2011; **Med School:** Yale Univ 1993; **Resid:** Plastic Surgery, Stanford Univ Med Ctr 1998; **Fellow:** Hand Surgery, UCLA Med Ctr 2000; **Fac Appt:** Prof PlS, Stanford Univ

Godzik, Cathleen A MD [HS] - **Spec Exp:** Congenital Hand Deformities; Sports Injuries; Dupuytren's Contracture; Arthritis; **Hospital:** Good Samaritan Hosp - LA, California Hosp Med Ctr; **Address:** 1245 Wilshire Blvd, Ste 611, Los Angeles, CA 90017; **Phone:** 213-482-6100; **Board Cert:** Orthopaedic Surgery 2012; Hand Surgery 2012; **Med School:** NY Med Coll 1981; **Resid:** Surgery, Brown Univ Sch Med 1983; Orthopaedic Surgery, Univ Conn Sch Med 1985; **Fellow:** Hand Surgery, Joseph Boyes-USC 1987

Hanel, Douglas P MD [HS] - **Spec Exp:** Reconstructive Microvascular Surgery; Hand-Congenital Anomaly; Elbow Reconstruction; **Hospital:** Harborview Med Ctr, Seattle Chldns Hosp; **Address:** Harborview Med Ctr, 908 Jefferson St, Fl 6, Box 359798, Seattle, WA 98104; **Phone:** 206-744-3462; **Board Cert:** Orthopaedic Surgery 2007; Hand Surgery 2007; **Med School:** St Louis Univ 1977; **Resid:** Orthopaedic Surgery, St Louis Univ Hosp 1982; **Fellow:** Hand Surgery, Univ Louisville Hosp 1983; Microsurgery, Univ Louisville Hosp 1983; **Fac Appt:** Prof OrS, Univ Wash

Hentz, Vincent R MD [HS] - **Spec Exp:** Brachial Plexus Palsy; Dupuytren's Contracture; Hand & Upper Extremity Surgery; Pediatric Hand Surgery; **Hospital:** Stanford Univ Hosp & Clins; **Address:** Hand & Upper Extremity Surgery, 450 Broadway St, Pavilion A Fl 2, Redwood City, CA 94063; **Phone:** 650-723-5256; **Board Cert:** Plastic Surgery 2007; Hand Surgery 2002; **Med School:** Univ Fla Coll Med 1968; **Resid:** Plastic Surgery, Stanford Univ Hosp 1974; **Fellow:** Hand Surgery, Roosevelt Hosp 1975; **Fac Appt:** Prof Emeritus S, Stanford Univ

Jones, Neil F MD [HS] - **Spec Exp:** Hand Reconstruction-Pediatric; Nerve Disorders/Surgery; Tendon Surgery; Toe-to-Hand Transfer; **Hospital:** UC Irvine Med Ctr, Chldns Hosp Orange Co; **Address:** 101 The City Drive S, Pavillion 3, Orange, CA 92868; **Phone:** 714-456-7012; **Board Cert:** Plastic Surgery 1985; **Med School:** England, UK 1974; **Resid:** Surgery, Radcliffe Infirmary 1979; Plastic Surgery, Univ Mich Med Ctr 1981; **Fellow:** Plastic Surgery, The London Hosp 1982; Hand & Microvascular Surgery, Mass Gen Hosp 1983; **Fac Appt:** Prof OrS, UC Irvine

Meals, Roy A MD [HS] - **Spec Exp:** Hand & Wrist Surgery; **Hospital:** UCLA Ronald Reagan Med Ctr; **Address:** 1033 Gayley Ave, Ste 104, Los Angeles, CA 90024; **Phone:** 310-824-1262; **Board Cert:** Orthopaedic Surgery 1980; Hand Surgery 2010; **Med School:** Vanderbilt Univ 1971; **Resid:** Surgery, Johns Hopkins Hosp 1973; Orthopaedic Surgery, Johns Hopkins Hosp 1978; **Fellow:** Hand Surgery, Mass Genl Hosp 1979; **Fac Appt:** Clin Prof S, UCLA

Slutsky, David J MD [HS] - **Spec Exp:** Preiser's Disease; Keinbocks Disease; Microsurgery; Arthroscopic Surgery; **Hospital:** LAC - Harbor - UCLA Med Ctr, Torrance Memorial Med Ctr; **Address:** The Slutsky Hand & Wrist Inst, 2808 Columbia St, Torrance, CA 90503; **Phone:** 310-618-9922; **Board Cert:** Orthopaedic Surgery 2012; Hand Surgery 2012; **Med School:** Univ Manitoba 1981; **Resid:** Orthopaedic Surgery, Univ Manitoba Med Ctr 1987; **Fellow:** Hand & Microvascular Surgery, Loma Linda Univ Med Ctr 1989; **Fac Appt:** Asst Prof OrS, UCLA

Szabo, Robert M MD [HS] - **Spec Exp:** Peripheral Nerve Surgery; Hand Injuries; Hand & Upper Extremity Tumors; Shoulder Reconstruction; **Hospital:** UC Davis Med Ctr, Mercy General Hosp - Sacramento; **Address:** UC Davis, Dept Orthopaedics, 4860 Y St, Ste 1700, Sacramento, CA 95817; **Phone:** 916-734-3678; **Board Cert:** Orthopaedic Surgery 2009; Hand Surgery 2009; **Med School:** SUNY Buffalo 1977; **Resid:** Surgery, Mt Sinai Hosp 1979; Orthopaedic Surgery, Mt Sinai Hosp 1982; **Fellow:** Hand Surgery, UCSD Med Ctr 1983; Epidemiology, UC Berkeley 1995; **Fac Appt:** Prof OrS, UC Davis

Trumble, Thomas MD [HS] - **Spec Exp:** Nerve Disorders/Surgery; Upper Extremity Trauma; Elbow Surgery; Hand & Wrist Surgery; **Hospital:** Overlake Hosp Med Ctr; **Address:** Bellevue Bone and Joint Physicians, 1632 116th Ave NE, Ste C, Bellevue, WA 98004; **Phone:** 425-458-5543; **Board Cert:** Orthopaedic Surgery 2009; Hand Surgery 2009; **Med School:** Yale Univ 1979; **Resid:** Orthopaedic Surgery, Yale-New Haven Hosp 1984; **Fellow:** Hand Surgery, Duke Univ Med Ctr 1984; Reconstructive Microsurgery, Mass Genl Hosp 1985; **Fac Appt:** Prof Emeritus S, Univ Wash

NYU Langone
MEDICAL CENTER

550 First Avenue *(at 31st Street)*
New York, NY 10016
www.NYULMC.org/orthosurgery
Physician Referral: **888-7-NYU-MED** *(888-769-8633)*

ORTHOPAEDIC SURGERY

The Department of Orthopaedic Surgery at NYU Langone Medical Center continues to be recognized as a national leader, **ranked #5 in the nation by *U.S. News & World Report's* 2013-2014 "Best Hospitals" survey**. Our physicians combine extensive experience with cutting-edge research and technology to address bone and joint problems that affect a patient's quality of life. The expertise of our world-class orthopaedists represents the full range of subspecialty areas including **Adult Reconstructive, Sports Medicine and Primary Care Sports Medicine, Spine, Shoulder & Elbow, Foot & Ankle, Hand Surgery, Trauma & Fracture, Orthopaedic Oncology, and Pediatric Orthopaedics**; additional areas of specialization include minimally-invasive surgery and robotic-assisted joint replacement.

Premier Areas of Expertise

Joint Replacement Center physicians evaluate degenerative joint conditions caused by arthritis, injuries, congenital problems and general wear-and-tear to determine the best course of treatment. Our surgeons are experts in knee, hip and shoulder replacements, complex joint revisions, and minimally invasive surgeries, conducting more than 3,000 procedures annually. The experts in our **Hip Center** also specialize in the cutting-edge, minimally invasive anterior total hip replacement technique.

The Spine Center provides conservative care for lower back and neck pain, scoliosis, osteoporosis, problems associated with failed previous surgery, idiopathic disorders, growth disorders, neuromuscular disease, degenerative and congenital conditions, and traumatic deformity. Our surgeons perform over 2,000 procedures a year, including minimally invasive spinal fusions.

Hand Center specialists diagnose and offer operative and non-operative care for a wide range of upper extremity conditions, including fractures, congenital anomalies, soft tissue and skeletal trauma, degenerative and rheumatoid arthritis, sports-related injuries, vascular disorders, tumors and occupational disorders.

Sports Medicine and Primary Care Sports Medicine physicians treat sports-related injuries or conditions of the knee, shoulder, elbow and ankle, using joint preservation techniques as well as surgical procedures. Our patients range from athletes playing at the high school, college and professional levels to recreational athletes/active individuals from every age group.

(continued)

Top Doctors Make A Difference

Hematology & Medical Oncology

a subspecialty of Internal Medicine

Hematology: An internist with additional training who specializes in diseases of the blood, spleen and lymph glands. This specialist treats conditions such as anemia, clotting disorders, sickle cell disease, hemophilia, leukemia and lymphoma.

Medical Oncology: An internist who specializes in the diagnosis and treatment of all types of cancer and other benign and malignant tumors. This specialist decides on and administers chemotherapy for malignancy, as well as consulting with surgeons and radiotherapists on other treatments for cancer.

Training Required: Three years in internal medicine *plus* additional training and examination for certification in hematology or medical oncology.

HEMATOLOGY

New England

Anderson, Kenneth C MD [Hem] - **Spec Exp:** Multiple Myeloma; Hematologic Malignancies; **Hospital:** Dana-Farber Cancer Inst, Brigham & Women's Hosp; **Address:** Dana Farber Cancer Inst, 450 Brookline Ave, Ste M557, Boston, MA 02215; **Phone:** 617-632-2144; **Board Cert:** Internal Medicine 1980; **Med School:** Johns Hopkins Univ 1977; **Resid:** Internal Medicine, Johns Hopkins Hosp 1980; **Fellow:** Hematology & Oncology, Dana Farber Cancer Inst 1983; **Fac Appt:** Prof Med, Harvard Med Sch

Ballen, Karen K MD [Hem] - **Spec Exp:** Leukemia; Bone Marrow Transplant; **Hospital:** Mass Genl Hosp; **Address:** Mass General Hospital, 55 Fruit St, Ste 120, Ste 120, Boston, MA 02114; **Phone:** 617-724-1124; **Board Cert:** Internal Medicine 1989; Medical Oncology 2003; Hematology 2004; **Med School:** Dartmouth Med Sch 1986; **Resid:** Internal Medicine, Beth Israel Deaconess Med Ctr 1989; **Fellow:** Hematology & Oncology, Brigham & Women's Hosp 1992; **Fac Appt:** Assoc Prof Med, Harvard Med Sch

Comenzo, Raymond L MD [Hem] - **Spec Exp:** Plasma Cell Disorders; Stem Cell Transplant; Amyloidosis; POEMS Syndrome; **Hospital:** Tufts Med Ctr; **Address:** Tufts Medical Center, 800 Washington St, Box 826, Boston, MA 02111; **Phone:** 617-636-6454; **Board Cert:** Internal Medicine 1989; Hematology 2004; Blood Banking Transfusion Medicine 1992; **Med School:** Boston Univ 1986; **Resid:** Internal Medicine, Boston City Hosp 1989; **Fellow:** Hematology & Oncology, New Engl Med Ctr 1991; **Fac Appt:** Prof Med, Tufts Univ

Meehan, Kenneth MD [Hem] - **Spec Exp:** Bone Marrow Transplant; **Hospital:** Dartmouth - Hitchcock Med Ctr; **Address:** Norris Cotton Cancer Ctr, Dartmouth-Hitchcock Med Ctr, 1 Medical Center Drive, Lebanon, NH 03756; **Phone:** 603-650-4628; **Board Cert:** Internal Medicine 1989; Hematology 2004; **Med School:** Georgetown Univ 1986; **Resid:** Internal Medicine, Georgetown Univ 1989; **Fellow:** Hematology & Oncology, Dartmouth-Hitchcock Med Ctr 1992; **Fac Appt:** Assoc Prof Med, Dartmouth Med Sch

Miller, Kenneth B MD [Hem] - **Spec Exp:** Bone Marrow Transplant; Leukemia; Myelodysplastic Syndromes; Paroxysmal Nocturnal Hemoglobinuria; **Hospital:** Tufts Med Ctr; **Address:** Tufts Med Ctr, Dept Medicine, 800 Washington St, Box 245, Boston, MA 02111; **Phone:** 617-636-2600; **Board Cert:** Internal Medicine 1976; Hematology 1980; **Med School:** NY Med Coll 1972; **Resid:** Internal Medicine, NYU Med Ctr/VA Hosp 1976; **Fellow:** Hematology, Tufts Med Ctr 1979; **Fac Appt:** Prof Med, Tufts Univ

Richardson, Paul G MD [Hem] - **Spec Exp:** Multiple Myeloma; **Hospital:** Dana-Farber Cancer Inst, Brigham & Women's Hosp; **Address:** Dana Farber Cancer Inst, 450 Brookline Ave, Ste 1B30, Boston, MA 02215; **Phone:** 617-632-2127; **Board Cert:** Medical Oncology 2012; **Med School:** England, UK 1986; **Resid:** Internal Medicine, Baystate Med Ctr 1994; **Fellow:** Medical Oncology, Dana Farber Cancer Inst 1995; Hematology, Beth Israel Deaconess Med Ctr 1997; **Fac Appt:** Assoc Prof Med, Harvard Med Sch

Schiffman, Fred J MD [Hem] - **Spec Exp:** Hematologic Malignancies; Anemia-Cancer Related; Bleeding/Coagulation Disorders; **Hospital:** Miriam Hosp; **Address:** Comp Cancer Ctr at Miriam Hospital, 164 Summit Ave, Fain-3, Providence, RI 02906; **Phone:** 401-793-2920; **Board Cert:** Internal Medicine 1979; Hematology 1982; Medical Oncology 1987; **Med School:** NYU Sch Med 1973; **Resid:** Internal Medicine, Yale-New Haven Hosp 1979; **Fellow:** Hematology, Yale-New Haven Hosp 1981; **Fac Appt:** Prof Med, Brown Univ

Spitzer, Thomas R MD [Hem] - **Spec Exp:** Bone Marrow Transplant; Leukemia; **Hospital:** Mass Genl Hosp; **Address:** Mass General Hospital, 55 Fruit St, Ste 120, Boston, MA 02114; **Phone:** 617-724-1124; **Board Cert:** Internal Medicine 1977; Medical Oncology 1983; Hematology 1984; **Med School:** Univ Rochester 1974; **Resid:** Internal Medicine, NYew York Hosp-Cornell Med Ctr 1977; Internal Medicine, Mem Sloan Kettering Cancer Ctr 1977; **Fellow:** Hematology & Oncology, Case West Res Univ 1983; **Fac Appt:** Prof Onc, Harvard Med Sch

Stone, Richard M MD [Hem] - **Spec Exp:** Leukemia; Leukemia-Acute Lymphoblastic; **Hospital:** Dana-Farber Cancer Inst, Brigham & Women's Hosp; **Address:** Dana Farber Cancer Inst, 450 Brookline Ave, Boston, MA 02215; **Phone:** 617-632-1906; **Board Cert:** Internal Medicine 1984; Medical Oncology 2008; Hematology 1988; **Med School:** Harvard Med Sch 1981; **Resid:** Internal Medicine, Brigham & Womens Hosp 1984; **Fellow:** Medical Oncology, Dana-Farber Cancer Inst 1987; **Fac Appt:** Prof Med, Harvard Med Sch

Mid Atlantic

Abrams, Charles S MD [Hem] - **Spec Exp:** Bleeding/Coagulation Disorders; Thrombotic Disorders; **Hospital:** Hosp Univ Penn - UPHS (page 69); **Address:** Penn Blood Center, 3 Dulles, 3400 Spruce St, Philadelphia, PA 19104; **Phone:** 215-573-3288; **Board Cert:** Internal Medicine 1987; Medical Oncology 1989; Hematology 2005; **Med School:** Yale Univ 1984; **Resid:** Internal Medicine, Hosp Univ Penn 1987; **Fellow:** Hematology & Oncology, Hosp Univ Penn 1988; **Fac Appt:** Prof Med, Univ Pennsylvania

Allen, Steven Lee MD [Hem] - **Spec Exp:** Bleeding/Coagulation Disorders; Leukemia & Lymphoma; Multiple Myeloma; Gaucher Disease; **Hospital:** N Shore Univ Hosp (page 66), Long Is Jewish Med Ctr (page 66); **Address:** Monter Cancer Ctr, 450 Lakeville Rd, Lake Success, NY 11042; **Phone:** 516-734-8959; **Board Cert:** Internal Medicine 1980; Hematology 1982; Medical Oncology 1983; **Med School:** Johns Hopkins Univ 1977; **Resid:** Internal Medicine, NY Hosp-Cornell 1980; **Fellow:** Hematology & Oncology, NY Hosp-Cornell 1983; **Fac Appt:** Prof Hem & Onc, Hofstra N Shore-LIJ Sch Med

Baer, Maria R MD [Hem] - **Spec Exp:** Leukemia; Myelodysplastic Syndromes; Myeloproliferative Disorders; **Hospital:** Univ of MD Med Ctr; **Address:** Univ MD Med Ctr, Greenebaum Cancer Ctr, 22 S Greene St, rm S9D08, Baltimore, MD 21201; **Phone:** 410-328-7904; **Board Cert:** Internal Medicine 1983; Hematology 1984; **Med School:** Johns Hopkins Univ 1979; **Resid:** Internal Medicine, Vanderbilt Univ Hosp 1982; **Fellow:** Hematology, Vanderbilt Univ Hosp 1985; **Fac Appt:** Prof Hem & Onc, Univ MD Sch Med

Brodsky, Robert A MD [Hem] - **Spec Exp:** Hematologic Malignancies; Autoimmune Disease; Graft vs Host Disease; **Hospital:** Johns Hopkins Hosp (page 59); **Address:** Johns Hopkins, Hematology Dept, 720 Rutland Ave, Ross Bldg, rm 1025, Baltimore, MD 21205; **Phone:** 410-955-8964; **Board Cert:** Hematology 2006; **Med School:** Hahnemann Univ 1989; **Resid:** Internal Medicine, Vanderbilt Univ Hosp 1991; **Fellow:** Hematology, Vanderbilt Univ Hosp 1994; Medical Oncology, Johns Hopkins Hosp 1997; **Fac Appt:** Prof Med, Johns Hopkins Univ

Cheson, Bruce D MD [Hem] - **Spec Exp:** Leukemia & Lymphoma; Hematologic Malignancies; **Hospital:** MedStar Georgetown Univ Hosp; **Address:** GUMC-Lombardi Cancer Ctr, 3800 Reservoir Rd NW, Podium A, Washington, DC 20007; **Phone:** 202-444-7932; **Board Cert:** Internal Medicine 1974; Hematology 1976; **Med School:** Tufts Univ 1971; **Resid:** Internal Medicine, Univ Virginia Hosp 1974; **Fellow:** Hematology, New England Med Ctr Hosp 1976; **Fac Appt:** Prof Med, Georgetown Univ

Diuguid, David L MD [Hem] - **Spec Exp:** Bleeding/Coagulation Disorders; **Hospital:** NY-Presby/Columbia Univ Med Ctr, NY (page 65); **Address:** 161 Ft Washington Ave, Irving Bldg Fl 10, New York, NY 10032; **Phone:** 212-305-0527; **Board Cert:** Internal Medicine 1982; Hematology 1986; Medical Oncology 1985; **Med School:** Cornell Univ-Weill Med Coll 1979; **Resid:** Internal Medicine, Boston Med Ctr 1983; **Fellow:** Hematology & Oncology, New England Bapt Hosp 1986; **Fac Appt:** Assoc Prof Med, Columbia P&S

Filicko-O'Hara, Joanne E MD [Hem] - **Spec Exp:** Hematologic Malignancies; Leukemia & Lymphoma; Bone Marrow Transplant; Myeloproliferative Disorders; **Hospital:** Thomas Jefferson Univ Hosp; **Address:** Jefferson Univ Physicians, 925 Chestnut St, Ste 420, Phildelphia, PA 19107; **Phone:** 215-955-8874; **Board Cert:** Hematology 2009; Medical Oncology 2010; **Med School:** Hahnemann Univ 1992; **Resid:** Internal Medicine, Thomas Jefferson Univ Hosp 1995; **Fellow:** Hematology & Oncology, Thomas Jefferson Univ Hosp 1998; **Fac Appt:** Assoc Prof Onc, Jefferson Med Coll

Friedman, Alan L MD [Hem] - **Spec Exp:** Leukemia & Lymphoma; Myelodysplastic Syndromes; Multiple Myeloma; **Hospital:** Einstein Med Ctr, Jeanes Hosp; **Address:** Albert Einstein Med Ctr, 5501 Old York Rd Braemer Bldg Fl 2 - Ste 1, Philadelphia, PA 19141; **Phone:** 215-456-3880; **Board Cert:** Internal Medicine 1978; Hematology 1982; Medical Oncology 1981; **Med School:** Hahnemann Univ 1975; **Resid:** Internal Medicine, Albert Einstein Med Ctr 1978; **Fellow:** Medical Oncology, Meml Sloan-Kettering Cancer Ctr 1980; Hematology, Thomas Jefferson Univ Hosp 1981

Fruchtman, Steven M MD [Hem] - **Spec Exp:** Myeloproliferative Disorders; Polycythemia Rubra Vera; **Address:** 1150 Park Ave, Ste Medical, New York, NY 10128; **Phone:** 212-427-7700; **Board Cert:** Internal Medicine 1980; Hematology 1984; **Med School:** NY Med Coll 1977; **Resid:** Internal Medicine, Univ Hosp 1981; **Fellow:** Hematology, Mount Sinai Med Ctr 1984; Hematology, Meml Sloan Kettering Cancer Ctr 1985; **Fac Appt:** Assoc Prof Hem & Onc, NY Med Coll

Goldberg, Jack MD [Hem] - **Spec Exp:** Leukemia; Lymphoma; Multiple Myeloma; Paroxysmal Nocturnal Hemoglobinuria; **Hospital:** Penn Presby Med Ctr - UPHS (page 69), Hosp Univ Penn - UPHS (page 69); **Address:** Abramson Cancer Ctr at Penn-Presby Hosp, 51 N 39th St, Medical Arts Bldg, Ste 103A, Philadelphia, PA 19104; **Phone:** 215-662-9801; **Board Cert:** Internal Medicine 1976; Hematology 1980; Medical Oncology 1989; **Med School:** SUNY Upstate Med Univ 1973; **Resid:** Internal Medicine, Boston Univ Hosp 1975; **Fellow:** Hematology & Oncology, SUNY Syracuse 1977; **Fac Appt:** Clin Prof Onc, Univ Pennsylvania

Gruenstein, Steven MD [Hem] - **Spec Exp:** Hematologic Malignancies; Gastrointestinal Cancer; Lung Cancer; **Hospital:** Mt Sinai Med Ctr (page 62); **Address:** 12 E 86th St, Central Park Hematology/Oncology, New York, NY 10028-0506; **Phone:** 212-861-6660; **Board Cert:** Internal Medicine 1988; **Med School:** Italy 1984; **Resid:** Internal Medicine, Metropolitan Hosp Ctr 1987; **Fellow:** Hematology & Oncology, Beth Israel Med Ctr 1990; **Fac Appt:** Assoc Clin Prof Med, Mount Sinai Sch Med

Isola, Luis M MD [Hem] - **Spec Exp:** Anemia-Aplastic; Hodgkin's Lymphoma; Multiple Myeloma; **Hospital:** Mt Sinai Med Ctr (page 62); **Address:** Ruttenberg Treatment Ctr, 1470 Madison Ave Fl 3rd, New York, NY 10029; **Phone:** 212-824-8709; **Board Cert:** Internal Medicine 1986; Hematology 1988; **Med School:** Argentina 1979; **Resid:** Internal Medicine, Ctr for Med Education 1983; **Fellow:** Hematology, Mt Sinai Med Ctr 1985; **Fac Appt:** Prof Med, Mount Sinai Sch Med

Jurcic, Joseph G MD [Hem] - **Spec Exp:** Leukemia; Myelodysplastic Syndromes; Clinical Trials; **Hospital:** NY-Presby/Columbia Univ Med Ctr, NY (page 65); **Address:** 161 Fort Washington Ave, Garden Level, New York, NY 10032; **Phone:** 646-317-5077; **Board Cert:** Medical Oncology 2005; Hematology 2008; **Med School:** Univ Pennsylvania 1988; **Resid:** Internal Medicine, Barnes Hosp 1991; **Fellow:** Hematology & Oncology, Meml Sloan Kettering Cancer Ctr 1994; **Fac Appt:** Clin Prof Med, Columbia P&S

Kempin, Sanford J MD [Hem] - **Spec Exp:** Bleeding/Coagulation Disorders; Leukemia; Lymphoma; Thrombotic Disorders; **Hospital:** Beth Israel Med Ctr - Petrie Div (page 56); **Address:** 325 W 15th St, New York, NY 10011; **Phone:** 212-604-6010; **Board Cert:** Internal Medicine 1976; Medical Oncology 1977; Hematology 1978; **Med School:** Belgium 1971; **Resid:** Internal Medicine, Lemuel Shattuck Hosp 1972; **Fellow:** Hematology, St Jude Chldns Rsch Hosp 1975; Medical Oncology, Meml Sloan Kettering Cancer Ctr 1976; **Fac Appt:** Asst Prof Hem & Onc, Albert Einstein Coll Med

Kessler, Craig M MD [Hem] - **Spec Exp:** Bleeding/Coagulation Disorders; Hemophilia; Hematologic Malignancies; **Hospital:** MedStar Georgetown Univ Hosp; **Address:** GUMC, Lombardi Cancer Ctr, 3800 Reservoir Rd NW, Podium A, Washington, DC 20007; **Phone:** 202-444-8676; **Board Cert:** Internal Medicine 1976; Hematology 1980; **Med School:** Tulane Univ 1973; **Resid:** Internal Medicine, Ochsner Fdn Hosp 1976; **Fellow:** Hematology, Johns Hopkins Hosp 1978; **Fac Appt:** Prof Med, Georgetown Univ

Luger, Selina M MD [Hem] - **Spec Exp:** Myelodysplastic Syndromes; Leukemia; Leukemia-Chronic Myeloid; Stem Cell Transplant; **Hospital:** Hosp Univ Penn - UPHS (page 69); **Address:** Perelman Center For Advanced Medicine, West Pavilion, 2nd Fl, 3400 Civic Center Blvd, Philadelphia, PA 19104; **Phone:** 215-662-6348; **Board Cert:** Hematology 2006; **Med School:** Canada 1987; **Resid:** Internal Medicine, Univ Pittsburgh Med Ctr 1990; **Fellow:** Hematology & Oncology, Pennsylvania Hosp-UPHS 1993; **Fac Appt:** Prof Hem & Onc, Univ Pennsylvania

Mangan, Kenneth F MD [Hem] - **Spec Exp:** Bone Marrow Transplant; Hematologic Malignancies; Anemia-Aplastic; Paroxysmal Nocturnal Hemoglobinuria; **Hospital:** Jeanes Hosp, Temple Univ Hosp; **Address:** Temple BMT Program, Friends Hall Physicians Bldg, 7604 Central Ave, Lower Level, Philadelphia, PA 19111-2499; **Phone:** 215-214-3129; **Board Cert:** Internal Medicine 1976; Hematology 1978; **Med School:** Geo Wash Univ 1973; **Resid:** Internal Medicine, G Washington Univ Hosps 1976; **Fellow:** Hematology, Tufts-New England Med Ctr 1979; **Fac Appt:** Prof Hem & Onc, Temple Univ

Marks, Stanley M MD [Hem] - **Spec Exp:** Leukemia; Lymphoma; Multiple Myeloma; **Hospital:** UPMC Shadyside, UPMC Presby, Pittsburgh; **Address:** UPMC- Hillman Cancer Ctr, 5115 Centre Ave, Fl 3, Pittsburgh, PA 15232; **Phone:** 412-235-1020; **Board Cert:** Internal Medicine 1976; Hematology 1978; **Med School:** Univ Pittsburgh 1973; **Resid:** Internal Medicine, Presby Univ Hosp 1976; **Fellow:** Hematology & Oncology, Brigham Hosp/Dana Farber Cancer Ctr 1978; **Fac Appt:** Clin Prof Hem & Onc, Univ Pittsburgh

Maslak, Peter G MD [Hem] - **Spec Exp:** Leukemia; Stem Cell Transplant; Myelodysplastic Syndromes; Clinical Trials; **Hospital:** Meml Sloan-Kettering Canc Ctr; **Address:** 1275 York Avenue, New York, NY 10065; **Phone:** 212-639-5518; **Board Cert:** Internal Medicine 1987; Hematology 2000; Medical Oncology 1989; **Med School:** Mount Sinai Sch Med 1984; **Resid:** Internal Medicine, Univ Michigan Med Ctr 1987; Internal Medicine, Meml Sloan Kettering Cancer Ctr 1991; **Fellow:** Hematology & Oncology, Meml Sloan Kettering Cancer Ctr 1990; **Fac Appt:** Clin Prof Med, Cornell Univ-Weill Med Coll

Mears, John Gregory MD [Hem] - **Spec Exp:** Lymphoma; Leukemia; Multiple Myeloma; **Hospital:** NY-Presby/Columbia Univ Med Ctr, NY (page 65); **Address:** 161 Ft Washington Ave, Ste 923, New York, NY 10032; **Phone:** 212-305-3506; **Board Cert:** Internal Medicine 1976; Hematology 1978; **Med School:** Columbia P&S 1973; **Resid:** Internal Medicine, Boston Univ Med Ctr 1975; **Fellow:** Hematology & Oncology, Columbia-Presby Med Ctr 1978; **Fac Appt:** Clin Prof Hem & Onc, Columbia P&S

Millenson, Michael M MD [Hem] - **Spec Exp:** Leukemia & Lymphoma; Thromboembolic Disorders; Hematologic Malignancies; **Hospital:** Fox Chase Cancer Ctr (page 57); **Address:** Fox Chase Cancer Center, 333 Cottman Ave, Philadelphia, PA 19111; **Phone:** 215-728-2600; **Board Cert:** Internal Medicine 1987; **Med School:** Temple Univ 1984; **Resid:** Internal Medicine, Temple Univ Hosp 1987; **Fellow:** Hematology & Oncology, Beth Israel Hosp 1991

Porter, David L MD [Hem] - **Spec Exp:** Leukemia; Bone Marrow Transplant; Lymphoma; Gene Therapy; **Hospital:** Hosp Univ Penn - UPHS (page 69); **Address:** Perelman Ctr for Advanced Medicine Fl 2, 3400 Civic Center Blvd, 2 West, Philadelphia, PA 19104; **Phone:** 215-615-5858 x2; **Board Cert:** Hematology 2006; **Med School:** Brown Univ 1987; **Resid:** Internal Medicine, Boston Univ Hosp 1990; **Fellow:** Hematology & Oncology, Brigham & Womens Hosp 1993; **Fac Appt:** Prof Hem & Onc, Univ Pennsylvania

Rai, Kanti R MD [Hem] - **Spec Exp:** Leukemia; Lymphoma; Multiple Myeloma; **Hospital:** NS-LIJ Hlth Sys (page 66), Long Is Jewish Med Ctr (page 66); **Address:** Long Island Jewish Med Ctr, Div Hem-Onc, CLL Research & Treatment Program, 410 Lakeville Rd, Ste 212, New Hyde Park, NY 10042; **Phone:** 718-470-4050; **Board Cert:** Pediatrics 1959; **Med School:** India 1955; **Resid:** Pediatrics, Lincoln Hosp 1958; Pediatrics, North Shore Univ Hosp 1959; **Fellow:** Hematology, LI Jewish Med Ctr 1960; **Fac Appt:** Prof Onc, Hofstra N Shore-LIJ Sch Med

Rao, A Koneti MD [Hem] - **Spec Exp:** Bleeding/Coagulation Disorders; Thromboembolic Disorders; Platelet Disorders; Inherited Disorders; **Hospital:** Temple Univ Hosp; **Address:** 3401 N Broad St Fl 4th, Philadelphia, PA 19140; **Phone:** 215-707-4684; **Board Cert:** Internal Medicine 1977; Hematology 1980; **Med School:** India 1973; **Resid:** Internal Medicine, Thom Jeff Univ Hosp 1977; **Fellow:** Hematology & Oncology, Temple Univ Hosp 1978; Hematology, Thom Jeff Univ Hosp 1979; **Fac Appt:** Prof Hem & Onc, India

Raphael, Bruce Gordon MD [Hem] - **Spec Exp:** Lymphoma; Leukemia; Multiple Myeloma; Anemia; **Hospital:** NYU Langone Med Ctr (page 68), Bellevue Hosp Ctr; **Address:** NYU Clinical Cancer Ctr, 240 E 38th St, Fl 19, New York, NY 10016-6402; **Phone:** 212-731-5185; **Board Cert:** Internal Medicine 1978; Hematology 1980; Medical Oncology 1981; **Med School:** McGill Univ 1975; **Resid:** Internal Medicine, Jewish Genl Hosp 1977; **Fellow:** Medical Oncology, Meml Sloan Kettering Cancer Ctr 1978; Hematology, NYU Med Ctr 1980; **Fac Appt:** Clin Prof Med, NYU Sch Med

Rapoport, Aaron P MD [Hem] - **Spec Exp:** Leukemia; Lymphoma; Multiple Myeloma; **Hospital:** Univ of MD Med Ctr; **Address:** Univ MD Med Ctr, Greenebaum Cancer Ctr, 22 S Greene St, rm N9E12, Baltimore, MD 21201; **Phone:** 410-328-1230; **Board Cert:** Internal Medicine 1989; Hematology 2012; **Med School:** Harvard Med Sch 1986; **Resid:** Internal Medicine, Univ Rochester Strong Meml Hosp 1989; **Fellow:** Hematology, Univ Rochester Strong Meml Hosp 1992; **Fac Appt:** Prof Med, Univ MD Sch Med

Rowley, Scott D MD [Hem] - **Spec Exp:** Stem Cell Transplant; Bone Marrow Transplant; Graft vs Host Disease; **Hospital:** Hackensack Univ Med Ctr; **Address:** John Pheuer Cancer Ctr, 92 2nd St, Ste 230, Hackensack, NJ 07601; **Phone:** 551-996-8297; **Board Cert:** Internal Medicine 1981; Medical Oncology 1983; Hematology 1984; **Med School:** Univ Mass Sch Med 1978; **Resid:** Internal Medicine, Rhode Island Hosp 1981; **Fellow:** Hematology & Oncology, Rhode Island Hosp 1984; **Fac Appt:** Assoc Prof Med, UMDNJ-NJ Med Sch, Newark

Savage, David G MD [Hem] - **Spec Exp:** Stem Cell Transplant; Bone Marrow Transplant; Lymphoma; **Hospital:** NY-Presby/Columbia Univ Med Ctr, NY (page 65); **Address:** 177 Fort Washington Ave, Millstein Bldg - Fl 6, rm 435, New York, NY 10032; **Phone:** 212-305-9783; **Board Cert:** Internal Medicine 1977; Hematology 1982; Medical Oncology 1985; **Med School:** Columbia P&S 1974; **Resid:** Internal Medicine, Harlem Hosp/Columbia Presby Med Ctr 1977; **Fellow:** Hematology & Oncology, Harlem Hosp/Columbia Presby Med Ctr 1982; **Fac Appt:** Prof Med, Columbia P&S

Schuster, Michael W MD [Hem] - **Spec Exp:** Bone Marrow Transplant; Hematologic Malignancies; Myelodysplastic Syndromes; Anemia-Aplastic; **Hospital:** Stony Brook Univ Med Ctr; **Address:** Stony Brook Univ Cancer Ctr, 3 Edmund D Pellegrino Rd, Stony Brook, NY 11794; **Phone:** 631-444-3577; **Board Cert:** Internal Medicine 1984; Hematology 1986; **Med School:** Dartmouth Med Sch 1980; **Resid:** Internal Medicine, Beth Israel Deaconess Med Ctr 1983; **Fellow:** Hematology & Oncology, Beth Israel Deaconess Med Ctr 1987; **Fac Appt:** Prof Hem & Onc, SUNY Stony Brook

Schuster, Stephen J MD [Hem] - **Spec Exp:** Lymphoma; Bone Marrow Transplant; **Hospital:** Hosp Univ Penn - UPHS (page 69); **Address:** Abramson Cancer Ctr, Perelman Ctr, West Pavilion Fl 2, 3400 Civic Ctr Blvd, Philadelphia, PA 19104; **Phone:** 215-615-5858; **Board Cert:** Internal Medicine 1984; Hematology 1986; Medical Oncology 1989; **Med School:** Jefferson Med Coll 1981; **Resid:** Internal Medicine, Pennsylvania Hosp 1984; **Fellow:** Hematology & Oncology, Thomas Jefferson Univ Hosp 1986; **Fac Appt:** Assoc Prof Med, Univ Pennsylvania

Slease, Robert B MD [Hem] - **Spec Exp:** Hematologic Malignancies; Hodgkin's Lymphoma; Stem Cell Transplant; Clinical Trials; **Hospital:** Christiana Hosp; **Address:** CCHS, Hematology, 4701 Ogletown-Stanton Rd, Ste 4200, Newark, DE 19713; **Phone:** 302-737-7700; **Board Cert:** Internal Medicine 1975; Hematology 1978; **Med School:** Univ Kansas 1972; **Resid:** Internal Medicine, Natl Naval Med Ctr 1975; **Fellow:** Hematology, Natl Naval Med Ctr 1977; **Fac Appt:** Clin Prof Med, Jefferson Med Coll

Soff, Gerald A MD [Hem] - **Spec Exp:** Bleeding/Coagulation Disorders; Thrombotic Disorders; Hematologic Disorders in Cancer Patients; Anemia; **Hospital:** Meml Sloan-Kettering Canc Ctr; **Address:** MSKCC Div Hematology, 1275 York Ave Fl 4 - Ste 6, New York, NY 10065; **Phone:** 212-639-2335; **Board Cert:** Internal Medicine 1984; Hematology 1988; **Med School:** Johns Hopkins Univ 1981; **Resid:** Internal Medicine, Med Coll Virginia Affil Hosp 1984; **Fellow:** Hematology & Oncology, Beth Israel Deaconess Med Ctr 1988

Spivak, Jerry L MD [Hem] - **Spec Exp:** Myeloproliferative Disorders; Polycythemia Rubra Vera; Leukemia; Anemia; **Hospital:** Johns Hopkins Hosp (page 59); **Address:** 720 Rutland Ave, Traylor Bldg - Fl 9 - Ste 924, Baltimore, MD 21205; **Phone:** 410-955-5454; **Board Cert:** Internal Medicine 1971; Hematology 1974; **Med School:** Cornell Univ 1964; **Resid:** Internal Medicine, Johns Hopkins Hosp 1966; Internal Medicine, Johns Hopkins Hosp 1972; **Fellow:** Hematology, Natl Cancer Inst 1968; Hematology, Johns Hopkins Hosp 1971; **Fac Appt:** Prof Hem & Onc, Johns Hopkins Univ

Strair, Roger MD/PhD [Hem] - **Spec Exp:** Leukemia; Lymphoma; Bone Marrow Transplant; Multiple Myeloma; **Hospital:** Robert Wood Johnson Univ Hosp - New Brunswick; **Address:** Cancer Inst of NJ, 195 Little Albany St, New Brunswick, NJ 08903; **Phone:** 732-235-7464; **Board Cert:** Internal Medicine 1984; Hematology 1986; Medical Oncology 1987; **Med School:** Albert Einstein Coll Med 1981; **Resid:** Internal Medicine, Brigham & Women's Hosp 1984; **Fellow:** Hematology & Oncology, Brigham & Women's Hosp 1988; **Fac Appt:** Assoc Prof Med, UMDNJ-RW Johnson Med Sch

Streiff, Michael B MD [Hem] - **Spec Exp:** Bleeding/Coagulation Disorders; Polycythemia Rubra Vera; Clinical Trials; Hemophilia; **Hospital:** Johns Hopkins Hosp (page 59); **Address:** Johns Hopkins, Hematology Dept, 601 N Caroline St Fl 7, Baltimore, MD 21287; **Phone:** 410-955-3142; **Board Cert:** Medical Oncology 2005; Hematology 2004; **Med School:** Johns Hopkins Univ 1988; **Resid:** Internal Medicine, Shands at Univ FL 1991; **Fellow:** Hematology & Oncology, Johns Hopkins Hosp 1994; **Fac Appt:** Assoc Prof Med, Johns Hopkins Univ

Tallman, Martin S MD [Hem] - **Spec Exp:** Leukemia; **Hospital:** Meml Sloan-Kettering Canc Ctr; **Address:** Meml Hematology Lymphoma Grp, 1275 York Ave, Ste H-719, Box 380, New York, NY 10065; **Phone:** 212-639-3842; **Board Cert:** Internal Medicine 1983; Medical Oncology 1987; Hematology 1988; **Med School:** Ros Franklin Univ/Chicago Med Sch 1980; **Resid:** Internal Medicine, Evanston Hosp 1983; **Fellow:** Medical Oncology, Fred Hutchinson Cancer Ctr 1987; **Fac Appt:** Prof Med, Cornell Univ-Weill Med Coll

Van Besien, Koen W MD/PhD [Hem] - **Spec Exp:** Lymphoma; Stem Cell Transplant; **Hospital:** NY-Presby/Weill Cornell Med Ctr, NY (page 65); **Address:** Stem Cell Transplant Program, 520 E 70th St, Starr Bldg, Ste 303, New York, NY 10021; **Phone:** 212-746-2048; **Board Cert:** Internal Medicine 2005; Medical Oncology 2005; Hematology 2006; **Med School:** Belgium 1984; **Resid:** Internal Medicine, Univ Leuven Med Ctr 1987; **Fellow:** Hematology & Oncology, Indiana Univ Med Ctr 1990; **Fac Appt:** Prof Hem & Onc, Cornell Univ-Weill Med Coll

Wisch, Nathaniel MD [Hem] - **Spec Exp:** Lymphoma; Breast Cancer; Leukemia; Anemia-Cancer Related; **Hospital:** Lenox Hill Hosp (page 66), Mt Sinai Med Ctr (page 62); **Address:** Central Park Hematology & Oncology, 12 E 86th St, New York, NY 10028-0506; **Phone:** 212-861-6660; **Board Cert:** Internal Medicine 1965; Hematology 1972; Medical Oncology 1977; **Med School:** Northwestern Univ 1958; **Resid:** Internal Medicine, VA Hosp 1960; Internal Medicine, Montefiore Hosp 1961; **Fellow:** Hematology & Oncology, Mount Sinai Hosp 1964; **Fac Appt:** Clin Prof Med, Mount Sinai Sch Med

Yanovich, Saul MD [Hem] - **Spec Exp:** Bone Marrow Transplant; **Hospital:** Univ of MD Med Ctr; **Address:** Univ of Maryland Greenebaum Cancer Ctr, 22 S Greene St, rm N9E12, Baltimore, MD 21201; **Phone:** 410-328-1230; **Board Cert:** Internal Medicine 1980; Hematology 1976; Medical Oncology 1981; **Med School:** Colombia 1970; **Resid:** Internal Medicine, Univ Miami-Jackson Meml Hosp 1974; Hematology, Univ Miami-Jackson Meml Hosp 1976; **Fellow:** Oncology, Dana Farber Canc Ctr 1978; **Fac Appt:** Prof Med, Univ MD Sch Med

Southeast

Adams-Graves, Patricia MD [Hem] - **Spec Exp:** Sickle Cell Disease; **Hospital:** Univ of Tennesee Med Ctr, Regional Med Ctr - Memphis; **Address:** 956 Court Ave, rm F 210, Memphis, TN 38163; **Phone:** 901-448-6820; **Board Cert:** Internal Medicine 1989; **Med School:** Univ Louisville Sch Med 1986; **Resid:** Internal Medicine, Univ Louisville Affil Hosp 1989; **Fellow:** Hematology & Oncology, Univ Tennessee Hlth Science Ctr 1993; **Fac Appt:** Assoc Prof Med, Univ Tenn Coll Med

Bigelow, Carolyn L MD [Hem] - **Spec Exp:** Bone Marrow Transplant; Sickle Cell Disease; Leukemia; **Hospital:** Univ Mississippi Med Ctr; **Address:** Univ Mississippi Med Ctr-Div Hematology, 2500 N State St, Jackson, MS 39216; **Phone:** 601-984-5615; **Board Cert:** Internal Medicine 1982; Hematology 1988; **Med School:** Univ Miss 1979; **Resid:** Internal Medicine, Univ Mississippi Med Ctr 1982; **Fellow:** Hematology & Oncology, Univ Washington Med Ctr 1987; **Fac Appt:** Prof Med, Univ Miss

Blaustein, Arnold S MD [Hem] - **Spec Exp:** Hematologic Malignancies; Lymphoma; **Hospital:** Mount Sinai Med Ctr - Miami; **Address:** Mount Sinai Comp Cancer Ctr, 4306 Alton Rd Fl 3, Miami Beach, FL 33140; **Phone:** 305-535-3300; **Board Cert:** Internal Medicine 1972; Hematology 1974; Medical Oncology 1977; **Med School:** Univ MD Sch Med 1966; **Resid:** Pathology, Mount Sinai Med Ctr 1968; Internal Medicine, Hosp U Penn 1972; **Fellow:** Hematology & Oncology, Hosp U Penn 1974; **Fac Appt:** Assoc Clin Prof Med, Univ Miami Sch Med

Copelan, Edward A MD [Hem] - **Spec Exp:** Leukemia; Myelodysplastic Syndromes; Bone Marrow Transplant; Multiple Myeloma; **Hospital:** Carolinas Med Ctr; **Address:** Levine Cancer Inst, 1021 Morehead Medical Drive, Ste 3100, Charlotte, NC 28204; **Phone:** 980-442-5300; **Board Cert:** Internal Medicine 1980; Hematology 1982; Medical Oncology 1983; **Med School:** Tufts Univ 1977; **Resid:** Internal Medicine, Ohio State Univ Hosp 1980; **Fellow:** Hematology & Oncology, Ohio State Univ Hosp 1983; Bone Marrow Transplant, UCLA Med Ctr; **Fac Appt:** Clin Prof Med, Univ NC Sch Med

Djulbegovic, Benjamin MD/PhD [Hem] - **Spec Exp:** Multiple Myeloma; Lymphoma; Myeloproliferative Disorders; Clinical Trials; **Hospital:** Moffitt Canc Ctr (page 61); **Address:** H Lee Moffitt Cancer Ctr, Hematology, 12902 Magnolia Drive, Tampa, FL 33612; **Phone:** 813-745-8986; **Board Cert:** Hematology 2004; **Med School:** Bosnia 1976; **Resid:** Internal Medicine, Univ Med Ctr 1983; Internal Medicine, Univ Louisville Hosp 1988; **Fellow:** Hematology & Oncology, Univ Louisville Hosp 1990

Greer, John P MD [Hem] - **Spec Exp:** Leukemia & Lymphoma; Cutaneous T-cell Lymphoma; Stem Cell Transplant; Hematologic Malignancies; **Hospital:** Vanderbilt Univ Med Ctr; **Address:** Vanderbilt Ingram Cancer Ctr, 1301 Medical Center Drive, Ste 3297, Nashville, TN 37232; **Phone:** 615-936-8422; **Board Cert:** Pediatrics 1985; Internal Medicine 1979; Hematology 1984; Medical Oncology 1985; **Med School:** Vanderbilt Univ 1976; **Resid:** Internal Medicine, Tulane Univ Med Ctr 1979; Pediatrics, Med Coll Virginia Hosps 1981; **Fellow:** Hematology & Oncology, Vanderbilt Univ Med Ctr 1984; **Fac Appt:** Prof Med, Vanderbilt Univ

Holland, H Kent MD [Hem] - **Spec Exp:** Bone Marrow & Stem Cell Transplant; Hematologic Malignancies; **Hospital:** Northside Hosp; **Address:** Blood & Marrow Transplant Group of GA, Tower at Northside Hosp, 5670 Peachtree Dunwoody Rd, Ste 1000, Atlanta, GA 30342; **Phone:** 404-255-1930; **Board Cert:** Internal Medicine 1985; Medical Oncology 1987; Hematology 1988; **Med School:** Univ Tex SW, Dallas 1982; **Resid:** Internal Medicine, NY-Presby/Weill Cornell Med Ctr 1985; **Fellow:** Hematology & Oncology, Johns Hopkins Hosp 1988

Komrokji, Rami S MD [Hem] - **Spec Exp:** Myelodysplastic Syndromes; Leukemia-Myeloid; Lymphoma, Non-Hodgkin's; Clinical Trials; **Hospital:** Moffitt Canc Ctr (page 61); **Address:** H Lee Moffitt Cancer Ctr, Hematology, 12902 Magnolia Drive, Tampa, FL 33612; **Phone:** 813-745-8986; **Board Cert:** Hematology 2004; Medical Oncology 2004; **Med School:** Jordan 1996; **Resid:** Internal Medicine, Case Western Univ Affil Hosp 2001; **Fellow:** Hematology & Oncology, Univ Rochester Strong Meml Hosp 2004; **Fac Appt:** Assoc Prof

Ortel, Thomas L MD/PhD [Hem] - **Spec Exp:** Bleeding/Coagulation Disorders; Thrombotic Disorders; **Hospital:** Duke Univ Hosp; **Address:** Duke Box 3422, 0563 Stead Bldg, Durham, NC 27710; **Phone:** 919-684-5350; **Board Cert:** Internal Medicine 1988; Hematology 2012; **Med School:** Indiana Univ 1985; **Resid:** Internal Medicine, Duke Univ Med Ctr 1988; **Fellow:** Hematology & Oncology, Duke Univ Med Ctr 1991; **Fac Appt:** Prof Med, Duke Univ

Powell, Bayard L MD [Hem] - **Spec Exp:** Leukemia; Myelodysplastic Syndromes; **Hospital:** Wake Forest Baptist Med Ctr; **Address:** Wake Forest Baptist Med Ctr, Medical Ctr Blvd-Cancer Ctr, Winston-Salem, NC 27157-1082; **Phone:** 336-716-7970; **Board Cert:** Internal Medicine 1983; Medical Oncology 1985; **Med School:** Univ NC Sch Med 1980; **Resid:** Internal Medicine, NC Baptist Hosp 1983; **Fellow:** Hematology & Oncology, Wake Forest Univ Sch Med 1986; **Fac Appt:** Prof Med, Wake Forest Univ

Rosenblatt, Joseph D MD [Hem] - **Spec Exp:** Lymphoma; Leukemia; Multiple Myeloma; Lymphomas-Rare; **Hospital:** Univ of Miami Hosp & Clins/Sylvester Comp Canc Ctr, Jackson Meml Hosp; **Address:** Sylvester Comprehensive Cancer Ctr, 1475 NW 12th Ave, D8-4, Ste 3300, Miami, FL 33136; **Phone:** 305-243-4860; **Board Cert:** Internal Medicine 1983; Medical Oncology 1985; **Med School:** UCLA 1980; **Resid:** Internal Medicine, UCLA Med Ctr 1983; **Fellow:** Hematology & Oncology, UCLA 1986; **Fac Appt:** Prof Onc, Univ Miami Sch Med

Schwartzberg, Lee S MD [Hem] - **Spec Exp:** Breast Cancer; Lung Cancer; Stem Cell Transplant; **Hospital:** Baptist Memorial Hospital-Memphis; **Address:** West Clinic, 100 N Humphreys Blvd, Memphis, TN 38120; **Phone:** 901-683-0055; **Board Cert:** Internal Medicine 1983; Medical Oncology 1985; Hematology 1986; **Med School:** NY Med Coll 1980; **Resid:** Internal Medicine, North Shore Univ Hosp 1983; Internal Medicine, Meml Sloan Kettering Cancer Ctr 1985; **Fellow:** Hematology & Oncology, Meml Sloan Kettering Cancer Ctr 1984; Hematology & Oncology, Meml Sloan Kettering Cancer Ctr 1987; **Fac Appt:** Assoc Prof Med, Univ Tenn Coll Med

Sokol, Lubomir MD/PhD [Hem] - **Spec Exp:** Lymphoma; Hematologic Malignancies; Leukemia-Chronic Lymphocytic; Cutaneous T-cell Lymphoma; **Hospital:** Moffitt Canc Ctr (page 61), Tampa Genl Hosp; **Address:** H Lee Moffitt Cancer Ctr & Rsch Inst, 12902 Magnolia Drive, Tampa, FL 33612; **Phone:** 813-745-8212; **Board Cert:** Internal Medicine 2000; Medical Oncology 2002; Hematology 2003; **Med School:** Czech Republic 1981; **Resid:** Radiation Oncology, Charles Univ 1984; Internal Medicine, LSU Med Ctr 1999; **Fellow:** Radiation Oncology, Charles Univ 1990; Hematology & Oncology, USF Med Ctr 2002; **Fac Appt:** Assoc Prof Hem & Onc, Czech Republic

Telen, Marilyn J MD [Hem] - **Spec Exp:** Sickle Cell Disease; Anemias & Red Cell Disorders; Transfusion Medicine; **Hospital:** Duke Univ Hosp; **Address:** Duke Box 2615, 333 Med Sci Res Bldg, Durham, NC 27710; **Phone:** 919-684-5378; **Board Cert:** Internal Medicine 1980; Hematology 1984; **Med School:** NYU Sch Med 1977; **Resid:** Internal Medicine, Erie Co Med Cr 1980; **Fellow:** Hematology, Duke Univ Med Ctr 1983; **Fac Appt:** Prof Med, Duke Univ

Williams, Michael E MD [Hem] - **Spec Exp:** Lymphoma; Multiple Myeloma; Leukemia; Mantle Cell Lymphoma; **Hospital:** Univ of Virginia Hlth Sys; **Address:** Univ VA Hlth Sys, Div Hematology/Oncology, 1215 Lee St, Charlottesville, VA 22908-0716; **Phone:** 434-924-9637; **Board Cert:** Internal Medicine 1982; Medical Oncology 1987; Hematology 2009; **Med School:** Univ Cincinnati 1979; **Resid:** Internal Medicine, Univ VA Hlth Sys 1983; **Fellow:** Hematology & Oncology, Univ VA Hlth Sys 1986; **Fac Appt:** Prof Med, Univ VA Sch Med

Zuckerman, Kenneth S MD [Hem] - **Spec Exp:** Myeloproliferative Disorders; Anemia-Aplastic; Myelodysplastic Syndromes; Leukemia; **Hospital:** Moffitt Canc Ctr (page 61), Tampa Genl Hosp; **Address:** H Lee Moffitt Cancer Center, 12902 USF Magnolia Drive, Tampa, FL 33612-9416; **Phone:** 813-745-8090; **Board Cert:** Internal Medicine 1975; Hematology 1978; **Med School:** Ohio State Univ 1972; **Resid:** Internal Medicine, Ohio State Univ Hosps 1975; **Fellow:** Hematology, Peter Bent Brigham Hosp/Harvard Univ 1978; **Fac Appt:** Prof Med, Univ S Fla Coll Med

Midwest

Baron, Joseph M MD [Hem] - **Spec Exp:** Bleeding/Coagulation Disorders; Lymphoma; Myeloproliferative Disorders; **Hospital:** Univ of Chicago Med; **Address:** 5758 S Maryland Ave, Chicago, IL 60637-1463; **Phone:** 773-702-6149; **Board Cert:** Internal Medicine 1969; Hematology 1972; Medical Oncology 1975; **Med School:** Univ Chicago-Pritzker Sch Med 1962; **Resid:** Internal Medicine, Univ Chicago Hosps 1964; Internal Medicine, Univ Chicago Hosps 1967; **Fellow:** Hematology, Univ Chicago Hosps 1968; **Fac Appt:** Assoc Prof Med, Univ Chicago-Pritzker Sch Med

Blinder, Morey A MD [Hem] - **Spec Exp:** Bleeding/Coagulation Disorders; Anemia; Sickle Cell Disease; **Hospital:** Barnes-Jewish Hosp; **Address:** 4921 Parkview Pl, B, 7, St Louis, MO 63110; **Phone:** 314-362-7216; **Board Cert:** Internal Medicine 1984; Hematology 1988; Medical Oncology 1987; **Med School:** St Louis Univ 1981; **Resid:** Internal Medicine, Univ Illinois Hosp 1984; **Fellow:** Hematology & Oncology, Univ Wash Med Ctr 1986; **Fac Appt:** Assoc Prof Med, Washington Univ, St Louis

Blum, Kristie MD [Hem] - **Spec Exp:** Lymphoma; Lymphoma, Non-Hodgkin's; Lymphomas-Rare; **Hospital:** OSU Wexner Med Ctr; **Address:** B315 Starling-Loving Hall, 320 W 10th Ave, Columbus, OH 43210; **Phone:** 614-293-8508; **Board Cert:** Medical Oncology 2004; Hematology 2004; **Med School:** Univ Miami Sch Med 1997; **Resid:** Internal Medicine, Univ VA Hlth Sci Ctr 2000; **Fellow:** Hematology & Oncology, Vanderbilt Univ Med Ctr 2001; Hematology & Oncology, Wash Univ Affil Hosp 2003; **Fac Appt:** Asst Prof Med, Ohio State Univ

Bockenstedt, Paula MD [Hem] - **Spec Exp:** Bleeding/Coagulation Disorders; Leukemia; Von Willebrand's Disease; **Hospital:** Univ Michigan Med Ctr; **Address:** Univ Michigan Comprehensive Cancer Ctr, 1500 E Med Ctr Dr, MIB, rm C-344, Ann Arbor, MI 48109-8048; **Phone:** 734-936-6393; **Board Cert:** Internal Medicine 1981; Hematology 1984; **Med School:** Harvard Med Sch 1978; **Resid:** Internal Medicine, Brigham-Womens Hosp 1981; **Fellow:** Hematology, Brigham-Womens Hosp 1984; **Fac Appt:** Assoc Clin Prof Med, Univ Mich Med Sch

Byrd, John C MD [Hem] - **Spec Exp:** Leukemia-Chronic Lymphocytic; **Hospital:** Arthur G James Cancer Hosp & Research Inst; **Address:** 300 W 10th Ave, Fl 2nd, Columbus, OH 43210; **Phone:** 614-293-3196; **Board Cert:** Hematology 2007; **Med School:** Univ Ark 1991; **Resid:** Internal Medicine, Walter Reed AMC 1994; **Fellow:** Hematology & Oncology, Walter Reed AMC 1997; **Fac Appt:** Assoc Prof Med, Ohio State Univ

DiPersio, John F MD/PhD [Hem] - **Spec Exp:** Bone Marrow Transplant; Hematologic Malignancies; Leukemia; **Hospital:** Barnes-Jewish Hosp; **Address:** Alvin J. Siteman Cancer Center, 4921 Parkview Pl, Ste 7B, St Louis, MO 63110; **Phone:** 314-454-8306; **Board Cert:** Internal Medicine 1984; Medical Oncology 1987; Hematology 1988; **Med School:** Univ Rochester 1980; **Resid:** Internal Medicine, Parkland Meml Hosp 1984; **Fellow:** Hematology & Oncology, UCLA Med Ctr 1987; **Fac Appt:** Prof Med, Washington Univ, St Louis

Farag, Sherif S MD/PhD [Hem] - **Spec Exp:** Multiple Myeloma; Leukemia & Lymphoma; Bone Marrow Transplant; Stem Cell Transplant; **Hospital:** IU Hlth Univ Hosp; **Address:** IU Hlth, Cancer Ctr, 550 N University Blvd Fl 5, Indianapolis, IN 46202; **Phone:** 317-944-0920; **Med School:** Australia 1984; **Resid:** Internal Medicine, Univ Melbourne Med Ctr 1987; **Fellow:** Hematology, St Vincents Hosp 1990; Bone Marrow Transplant, Roswell Park Cancer Inst 1991; **Fac Appt:** Assoc Prof Med, Indiana Univ

Gertz, Morie A MD [Hem] - **Spec Exp:** Multiple Myeloma; Amyloidosis; Waldenstrom's Macroglobulinemia; Plasma Cell Disorders; **Hospital:** Mayo Med Ctr & Clin - Rochester, Rochester Methodist Hosp; **Address:** 200 1st St SW, Rochester, MN 55905; **Phone:** 507-284-3725; **Board Cert:** Internal Medicine 1979; Hematology 1982; Medical Oncology 1983; **Med School:** Loyola Univ-Stritch Sch Med 1975; **Resid:** Internal Medicine, St Lukes Hosp 1979; **Fellow:** Hematology & Oncology, Mayo Clin 1982; **Fac Appt:** Prof Hem & Onc, Mayo Med Sch

Gordon, Leo I MD [Hem] - **Spec Exp:** Lymphoma, Non-Hodgkin's; Hodgkin's Lymphoma; Leukemia-Chronic Lymphocytic; Mantle Cell Lymphoma; **Hospital:** Northwestern Meml Hosp; **Address:** Northwestern Meml Faculty Foundation, 676 N St Clair St, Ste 850, Chicago, IL 60611-3124; **Phone:** 312-695-4546; **Board Cert:** Internal Medicine 1976; Hematology 1978; Medical Oncology 1979; **Med School:** Univ Cincinnati 1973; **Resid:** Internal Medicine, Univ Chicago Hosps 1976; **Fellow:** Hematology, Univ Minnesota Hosps 1978; Hematology & Oncology, Univ Chicago Hosps 1979; **Fac Appt:** Prof Med, Northwestern Univ-Feinberg Sch Med

Gregory, Stephanie A MD [Hem] - **Spec Exp:** Lymphoma; Leukemia; Plasma Cell Disorders; Multiple Myeloma; **Hospital:** Rush Univ Med Ctr; **Address:** Rush University Medical Center, 1725 W Harrison St, Ste 834, Chicago, IL 60612; **Phone:** 312-942-5982; **Board Cert:** Internal Medicine 1972; Hematology 1972; **Med School:** Med Coll PA Hahnemann 1965; **Resid:** Internal Medicine, Rush/Presby-St Luke's Med Ctr 1969; **Fellow:** Hematology, Rush/Presby-St Luke's Med Ctr 1972; **Fac Appt:** Prof Med, Rush Med Coll

Grever, Michael R MD [Hem] - **Spec Exp:** Hematologic Malignancies; Leukemia; Drug Development; Clinical Trials; **Hospital:** OSU Wexner Med Ctr; **Address:** 395 W 12th Ave, Doan Tower, rm 392, Columbus, OH 43210; **Phone:** 614-293-8724; **Board Cert:** Internal Medicine 1975; Medical Oncology 1979; Hematology 1988; **Med School:** Univ Pittsburgh 1971; **Resid:** Internal Medicine, Univ Pittsburgh Hosp 1974; **Fellow:** Hematology & Oncology, Ohio State Univ 1978; **Fac Appt:** Prof Med, Ohio State Univ

Habermann, Thomas M MD [Hem] - **Spec Exp:** Lymphoma; Hodgkin's Lymphoma; Leukemia; **Hospital:** Mayo Med Ctr & Clin - Rochester; **Address:** Mayo Clin, 200 1st St SW, Rochester, MN 55905; **Phone:** 507-284-3159; **Board Cert:** Internal Medicine 1982; Hematology 1984; **Med School:** Creighton Univ 1979; **Resid:** Internal Medicine, Mayo Clinic 1982; **Fellow:** Hematology, Mayo Clinic 1985; **Fac Appt:** Prof Med, Mayo Med Sch

Juckett, Mark B MD [Hem] - **Spec Exp:** Bone Marrow Transplant; **Hospital:** Univ WI Hosp & Clins; **Address:** Dept Hematology, 600 Highland Ave, Ste H4-534, Madison, WI 53792; **Phone:** 608-265-1700; **Board Cert:** Hematology 2004; Medical Oncology 2005; **Med School:** Univ Louisville Sch Med 1987; **Resid:** Internal Medicine, Univ Minn Med Ctr, Fairview - West Bank Campus 1991; **Fellow:** Hematology & Oncology, Univ Minn Med Ctr, Fairview - West Bank Campus 1994; **Fac Appt:** Assoc Prof Med, Univ Wisc

Kraut, Eric H MD [Hem] - **Spec Exp:** Hematologic Malignancies; Leukemia; Drug Development; Clinical Trials; **Hospital:** OSU Wexner Med Ctr; **Address:** 320 W 10th Ave, A358 SL, Columbus, OH 43210; **Phone:** 614-293-2887; **Board Cert:** Internal Medicine 1975; Medical Oncology 1977; Hematology 1978; **Med School:** Temple Univ 1972; **Resid:** Internal Medicine, Univ Pittsburgh Hosp 1975; **Fellow:** Hematology & Oncology, Ohio State Univ Hosp 1977; **Fac Appt:** Prof Med, Ohio State Univ

Kuriakose, Philip MD [Hem] - **Spec Exp:** Leukemia; **Hospital:** Henry Ford Hosp; **Address:** Henry Ford Hosp, Hematology/Oncology, 2799 W Grand Blvd, K13, Detroit, MI 48202; **Phone:** 313-916-1841; **Board Cert:** Internal Medicine 2009; Medical Oncology 2012; Hematology 2012; **Med School:** India 1990; **Resid:** Internal Medicine, Christian Med Coll 1992; Internal Medicine, Henry Ford Hosp 1994; **Fellow:** Hematology & Oncology, Mayo Clinic 1995

Larson, Richard A MD [Hem] - **Spec Exp:** Leukemia & Lymphoma; Bone Marrow Transplant; Myelodysplastic Syndromes; **Hospital:** Univ of Chicago Med; **Address:** University of Chicago Medicine, 5841 S Maryland Ave, MS 2115, Chicago, IL 60637; **Phone:** 773-702-6149; **Board Cert:** Internal Medicine 1980; Hematology 1982; Medical Oncology 1983; **Med School:** Stanford Univ 1977; **Resid:** Internal Medicine, Univ Chicago Med Ctr 1980; **Fellow:** Hematology & Oncology, Univ Chicago Med Ctr 1983; **Fac Appt:** Prof Hem & Onc, Univ Chicago-Pritzker Sch Med

Litzow, Mark R MD [Hem] - **Spec Exp:** Bone Marrow Transplant; Leukemia; **Hospital:** Mayo Med Ctr & Clin - Rochester; **Address:** Mayo Clinic, Div Hematology, 200 First St SW, Rochester, MN 55905; **Phone:** 507-284-5362; **Board Cert:** Internal Medicine 1983; Hematology 1988; Medical Oncology 1989; Hospice & Palliative Medicine 2012; **Med School:** Univ Chicago-Pritzker Sch Med 1980; **Resid:** Internal Medicine, Mayo Clinic 1984; **Fellow:** Medical Oncology, Mayo Clinic 1990; **Fac Appt:** Asst Prof Med, Mayo Med Sch

Maciejewski, Jaroslaw P MD/PhD [Hem] - **Spec Exp:** Anemia-Aplastic; Hematologic Malignancies; Stem Cell Transplant; **Hospital:** Cleveland Clin (page 55); **Address:** Cleveland Clinic, 9500 Euclid Ave, Desk R40, Cleveland, OH 44195; **Phone:** 216-445-5962; **Med School:** Germany 1990; **Resid:** Internal Medicine, Univ Nevada Med Ctr 1997; **Fellow:** Hematology, Natl Inst Hlth 2000; **Fac Appt:** Prof Med, Case West Res Univ

McGlave, Philip B MD [Hem] - **Spec Exp:** Leukemia; Bone Marrow Transplant; **Hospital:** Fairview Lakes Med Ctr; **Address:** Univ Minn, Dept Med, Div Hem/Onc Transplanatation, 420 Delaware St SE, Minneapolis, MN 55455; **Phone:** 612-273-2800; **Board Cert:** Internal Medicine 1977; Hematology 1980; **Med School:** Univ IL Coll Med 1974; **Resid:** Internal Medicine, Univ Minnesota Med Ctr 1977; **Fellow:** Hematology & Oncology, Univ Minnesota Med Ctr 1980; **Fac Appt:** Prof Med, Univ Minn

Milhem, Mohammed M MD [Hem] - **Spec Exp:** Bone Cancer; Bone Marrow Transplant; Sarcoma; Melanoma; **Hospital:** Univ Iowa Hosp & Clins; **Address:** Univ Iowa Hosp & Clinics, 200 Hawkins Drive, rm C32 GH, Iowa City, IA 52242; **Phone:** 319-356-4200; **Board Cert:** Hematology 2003; Medical Oncology 2003; **Med School:** Jordan 1995; **Resid:** Internal Medicine, Univ IL Med Ctr 2000; **Fellow:** Hematology & Oncology, Univ IL Med Ctr 2003; Bone Marrow Transplant, Univ IL Med Ctr 2004; **Fac Appt:** Assoc Prof Hem & Onc, Univ Iowa Coll Med

Nand, Sucha MD [Hem] - **Spec Exp:** Myelodysplastic Syndromes; Myeloproliferative Disorders; Leukemia; Lymphoma, Non-Hodgkin's; **Hospital:** Loyola Univ Med Ctr; **Address:** Loyola University Medical Center, Cardinal Bernardin Cancer Ctr, 2160 S First Ave, Bldg 112, rm 342, Maywood, IL 60153-3304; **Phone:** 708-327-3217; **Board Cert:** Internal Medicine 1979; Medical Oncology 1981; Hematology 1982; **Med School:** India 1971; **Resid:** Physical Medicine & Rehabilitation, Northwestern Meml Hosp 1976; Internal Medicine, North Chicago VA Hosp 1978; **Fellow:** Hematology & Oncology, Northwestern Meml Hosp 1981; **Fac Appt:** Prof Hem & Onc, Loyola Univ-Stritch Sch Med

Palascak, Joseph E MD [Hem] - **Spec Exp:** Hemophilia; Bleeding/Coagulation Disorders; Thrombotic Disorders; **Hospital:** Univ Cincinnati Med Ctr; **Address:** Barrett Center, 234 Goodman St Fl 2, Cincinnati, OH 45219; **Phone:** 513-475-8500; **Board Cert:** Internal Medicine 1975; Hematology 1978; **Med School:** Jefferson Med Coll 1968; **Resid:** Internal Medicine, Thomas Jefferson Univ Hosp 1971; **Fellow:** Hematology, Thomas Jefferson Univ Hosp 1972; **Fac Appt:** Assoc Prof Med, Univ Cincinnati

Porcu, Pierluigi MD [Hem] - **Spec Exp:** Lymphoma; Lymphoma, Non-Hodgkin's; Immunotherapy; **Hospital:** OSU Wexner Med Ctr; **Address:** 320 W 10th Ave, B320 Starling Loving Hall, Columbus, OH 43210; **Phone:** 614-293-2268; **Board Cert:** Medical Oncology 2011; **Med School:** Italy 1987; **Resid:** Internal Medicine, Indiana Univ Hosp 1996; **Fellow:** Hematology & Oncology, Indiana Univ Hosp 1999; **Fac Appt:** Assoc Prof Med, Ohio State Univ

Rondelli, Damiano MD [Hem] - **Spec Exp:** Stem Cell Transplant; Bone Marrow Transplant; Hematologic Malignancies; Sickle Cell Disease; **Hospital:** Univ of IL Med Ctr at Chicago; **Address:** UIC Cancer Ctr, 1818 W Taylor St, Ste 1E, Chicago, IL 60612; **Phone:** 312-413-3547; **Med School:** Italy ; **Resid:** Internal Medicine, Univ Bologna/Inst of Hematology; **Fellow:** Hematology, Univ Bologna/Inst of Hematology; **Fac Appt:** Prof Med, Univ IL Coll Med

Roodman, G. David MD/PhD [Hem] - **Spec Exp:** Multiple Myeloma; Hematologic Malignancies; **Hospital:** IU Hlth Univ Hosp; **Address:** IU Hlth, Cancer Ctr, 980 W Walnut St, Ste C312, Indianapolis, IN 46202; **Phone:** 317-278-6255; **Board Cert:** Internal Medicine 1978; Hematology 1980; **Med School:** Univ KY Coll Med 1973; **Resid:** Internal Medicine, Univ Minn Med Ctr 1978; **Fellow:** Hematology, Univ Minn Med Ctr 1980; **Fac Appt:** Prof Hem & Onc, Indiana Univ

Singhal, Seema MD [Hem] - **Spec Exp:** Multiple Myeloma; **Hospital:** Northwestern Meml Hosp; **Address:** Northwestern Div Hematology/Oncology, 676 N St Clair St, Ste 2100, Chicago, IL 60611; **Phone:** 312-695-0990; **Board Cert:** Internal Medicine 2005; **Med School:** India 1989; **Resid:** Internal Medicine, King Edward Meml Hosp 1991; **Fellow:** Bone Marrow Transplant, Hadassah Univ Hosp 1992; Hematology, Royal Marsden Hosp 1996; **Fac Appt:** Prof Med, Northwestern Univ

Stiff, Patrick J MD [Hem] - **Spec Exp:** Bone Marrow Transplant; Leukemia; Ovarian Cancer; Vaccine Therapy; **Hospital:** Loyola Univ Med Ctr, Gottlieb Meml Hosp; **Address:** Cardinal Bernand Cancer Ctr, 2160 S First Ave Bldg 112, Maywood, IL 60153; **Phone:** 708-327-3148; **Board Cert:** Internal Medicine 1978; Medical Oncology 1981; Hematology 1982; **Med School:** Loyola Univ-Stritch Sch Med 1975; **Resid:** Internal Medicine, Cleveland Clinic Fdn 1978; **Fellow:** Hematology & Oncology, Meml Sloan Kettering Cancer Ctr 1981; **Fac Appt:** Prof Hem & Onc, Loyola Univ-Stritch Sch Med

Stock, Wendy MD [Hem] - **Spec Exp:** Leukemia; Myelodysplastic Syndromes; **Hospital:** Univ of Chicago Med; **Address:** Univ Chicago Med Ctr, 5841 S Maryland, MC 2115, Chicago, IL 60637; **Phone:** 773-834-8982; **Board Cert:** Internal Medicine 1988; Hematology 2012; **Med School:** Rush Med Coll 1985; **Resid:** Internal Medicine, Univ Chicago Med Ctr 1988; **Fellow:** Hematology & Oncology, Univ Chicago Med Ctr 2001; **Fac Appt:** Prof Med, Univ Chicago-Pritzker Sch Med

Tefferi, Ayalew MD [Hem] - **Spec Exp:** Myeloproliferative Disorders; Leukemia; **Hospital:** Mayo Med Ctr & Clin - Rochester; **Address:** 200 1st St SW, Rochester, MN 55905; **Phone:** 507-538-1068; **Board Cert:** Internal Medicine 1986; Hematology 1988; **Med School:** Greece 1982; **Resid:** Internal Medicine, St Josephs Hosp 1986; **Fellow:** Hematology, Mayo Clinic 1988; **Fac Appt:** Prof Hem & Onc, Mayo Med Sch

Uberti, Joseph P MD/PhD [Hem] - **Spec Exp:** Bone Marrow Transplant; Stem Cell Transplant; **Hospital:** Barbara Ann Karmanos Cancer Inst; **Address:** Barbara Ann Karmanos Cancer Inst, 4100 John R St, MC HW04H0, Detroit, MI 48201; **Phone:** 313-576-8760; **Board Cert:** Internal Medicine 1986; Medical Oncology 1989; **Med School:** Wayne State Univ 1983; **Resid:** Internal Medicine, Detroit Receiving Hosp 1986; **Fellow:** Hematology & Oncology, Wayne State Univ Hosps 1988; **Fac Appt:** Prof Med, Wayne State Univ

Winter, Jane N MD [Hem] - **Spec Exp:** Lymphoma, Non-Hodgkin's; Hodgkin's Lymphoma; Bone Marrow Transplant; Langerhans Cell Histiocytosis (LCH); **Hospital:** Northwestern Meml Hosp; **Address:** Northwestern Univ - Div Hem/Oncology, 675 N St Clair St, Ste 2100, Chicago, IL 60611-2927; **Phone:** 312-695-0990; **Board Cert:** Internal Medicine 1980; Hematology 2008; Medical Oncology 1983; **Med School:** Univ Pennsylvania 1977; **Resid:** Internal Medicine, Univ Chicago Hosps 1980; **Fellow:** Hematology & Oncology, Columbia Presby Hosp 1981; Hematology & Oncology, Northwestern Meml Hosp 1983; **Fac Appt:** Prof Hem & Onc, Northwestern Univ

Great Plains and Mountains

Lind, Stuart E MD [Hem] - **Spec Exp:** Lymphoma; Bleeding/Coagulation Disorders; **Hospital:** Univ Colorado Hosp; **Address:** Anschutz Cancer Pavilion, 1665 Aurora Ct, Ste 2004, Aurora, CO 80045; **Phone:** 720-848-0300; **Board Cert:** Internal Medicine 1979; Hematology 1982; Medical Oncology 1981; Blood Banking Transfusion Medicine 2007; **Med School:** NYU Sch Med 1976; **Resid:** Internal Medicine, Northwestern Meml Hosp 1979; **Fellow:** Hematology & Oncology, Mass Genl Hosp 1981; Blood Banking, Univ Colorado Hosp 2007; **Fac Appt:** Prof Hem & Onc, Univ Colorado

Rodgers III, George M MD/PhD [Hem] - **Spec Exp:** Hematopathology; Anemia-Cancer Related; Bleeding/Coagulation Disorders; **Hospital:** Univ Utah Hlth Care; **Address:** Univ Utah Med Ctr - Div Hematology, 30 N 1900 E, rm 5C402, Salt Lake City, UT 84132; **Phone:** 801-585-3229; **Board Cert:** Internal Medicine 1979; Hematology 1982; Pathology 1984; **Med School:** Tulane Univ 1976; **Resid:** Internal Medicine, Baylor Affil Hosps 1979; **Fellow:** Hematology, UCSF Med Ctr 1982; **Fac Appt:** Prof Med, Univ Utah

Vose, Julie M MD [Hem] - **Spec Exp:** Lymphoma; **Hospital:** Nebraska Med Ctr; **Address:** 987680 Nebraska Med Ctr, Emile @ 42nd St, Omaha, NE 68198-7630; **Phone:** 402-559-5600; **Board Cert:** Internal Medicine 1987; Medical Oncology 2011; Hematology 2012; **Med School:** Univ Nebr Coll Med 1984; **Resid:** Internal Medicine, Univ Nebraska Med Ctr 1987; **Fellow:** Hematology & Oncology, Univ Nebraska Med Ctr 1990; **Fac Appt:** Prof Med, Univ Nebr Coll Med

Southwest

Adams, Roberta H MD [Hem] - **Spec Exp:** Bone Marrow Transplant; Stem Cell Transplant; Sarcoma; **Hospital:** Phoenix Children's Hosp, Mayo Clinic - Phoenix; **Address:** Phoenix Chldns Hosp-Hematology/Oncology Dept, 1919 E Thomas Rd, Phoenix, AZ 85016; **Phone:** 602-546-0920; **Board Cert:** Pediatrics 1986; Pediatric Hematology-Oncology 2009; **Med School:** Columbia P&S 1981; **Resid:** Pediatrics, Chldns Hosp 1984; **Fellow:** Pediatric Hematology-Oncology, Univ of Utah Affil Hosp 1990; **Fac Appt:** Asst Prof Med, Mayo Med Sch

Barlogie, Bart MD/PhD [Hem] - **Spec Exp:** Bone Marrow Transplant; Plasma Cell Disorders; Multiple Myeloma; Castleman's Disease; **Hospital:** UAMS Med Ctr; **Address:** UAMS-Myeloma Inst Rsch & Therapy, 4301 West Markham St, Slot 816, Little Rock, AR 72205; **Phone:** 501-686-8230; **Med School:** Germany 1969; **Resid:** Internal Medicine, Univ Muenster Med Sch; **Fellow:** Medical Oncology, MD Anderson Cancer Ctr-Tumor Inst 1976; **Fac Appt:** Prof Med, Univ Ark

Brenner, Malcolm K MD/PhD [Hem] - **Spec Exp:** Gene Therapy; Bone Marrow Transplant; **Hospital:** Methodist Hosp - Houston, Texas Chldns Hosp; **Address:** 6701 Fannin St, Ste 1410, Houston, TX 77030; **Phone:** 832-824-4671; **Med School:** England, UK 1975; **Resid:** Internal Medicine, Cambridge Univ Affil Hosps 1979; **Fellow:** Immunology, Clin Rsch Ctr 1984; Hematology & Oncology, Royal Free Hosp 1986; **Fac Appt:** Prof Med, Baylor Coll Med

Champlin, Richard E MD [Hem] - **Spec Exp:** Bone Marrow Transplant; Stem Cell Transplant; Leukemia & Lymphoma; **Hospital:** UT MD Anderson Canc Ctr; **Address:** MD Anderson Canc Ctr, Stem Cell Transplantation Ctr, 1515 Holcombe Blvd, Unit 0423, Houston, TX 77030; **Phone:** 713-792-6100; **Board Cert:** Internal Medicine 1978; Hematology 1980; Medical Oncology 1981; **Med School:** Univ Chicago-Pritzker Sch Med 1975; **Resid:** Internal Medicine, LAC - Harbor - UCLA Med Ctr 1978; **Fellow:** Hematology & Oncology, LAC - Harbor - UCLA Med Ctr 1981; **Fac Appt:** Prof Med, Univ Tex, Houston

Cobos, Everardo MD [Hem] - **Spec Exp:** Bone Marrow Transplant; Bleeding/Coagulation Disorders; **Hospital:** Univ Med Ctr-Lubbock; **Address:** SCRTC Dept, 3601 4th St, MS 9410, Lubbock, TX 79430; **Phone:** 806-775-8600 x222; **Board Cert:** Internal Medicine 1985; Medical Oncology 1987; Hematology 1988; **Med School:** Univ Tex, San Antonio 1981; **Resid:** Internal Medicine, Letterman Army Med Ctr 1985; **Fellow:** Hematology & Oncology, Letterman Army Med Ctr 1988; **Fac Appt:** Prof Hem & Onc, Texas Tech Univ

Cooper, Barry MD [Hem] - **Spec Exp:** Leukemia; Lymphoma; Bleeding/Coagulation Disorders; **Hospital:** Baylor Univ Med Ctr-Dallas; **Address:** TX Oncology, 3410 Worth St, Ste 400, Dallas, TX 75246-2096; **Phone:** 214-370-1002; **Board Cert:** Internal Medicine 1974; Medical Oncology 1977; Hematology 1978; **Med School:** Johns Hopkins Univ 1971; **Resid:** Internal Medicine, Johns Hopkins Hosp 1974; **Fellow:** Metabolism, Natl Inst Health 1977; Hematology, Brigham & Women's Hosp 1978; **Fac Appt:** Clin Prof Med, Univ Tex SW, Dallas

Cortes, Jorge E MD [Hem] - **Spec Exp:** Leukemia; Myelodysplastic Syndromes; Myeloproliferative Disorders; **Hospital:** UT MD Anderson Canc Ctr; **Address:** UT MD Anderson Canc Ctr, Leukemia Ctr, 1515 Holcombe Blvd, Unit 428, Houston, TX 77030; **Phone:** 713-792-8760; **Med School:** Mexico 1986; **Resid:** Internal Medicine, Instituto Nacional de la Nutricion 1989; **Fellow:** Hematology, UT MD Anderson Canc Ctr 1992; Hematology & Oncology, UT MD Anderson Canc Ctr 1995; **Fac Appt:** Prof Med, Univ Tex, Houston

Emanuel, Peter D MD [Hem] - **Spec Exp:** Lymphoma; Leukemia; Hodgkin's Lymphoma; Multiple Myeloma; **Hospital:** UAMS Med Ctr; **Address:** 4301 W Markham St, Slot 623, Little Rock, AR 72205; **Phone:** 501-526-2272; **Board Cert:** Internal Medicine 1988; **Med School:** Univ Wisc 1985; **Resid:** Internal Medicine, UAB Med Ctr 1988; **Fellow:** Hematology & Oncology, UAB Med Ctr 1991; **Fac Appt:** Prof Med, Univ Ark

Fonseca, Rafael MD [Hem] - **Spec Exp:** Multiple Myeloma; **Hospital:** Mayo Clinic - Scottsdale, Mayo Clinic - Phoenix; **Address:** Mayo Clinic-Hematology Div, 13400 E Shea Blvd, Scottsdale, AZ 85259; **Phone:** 480-301-7085; **Board Cert:** Hematology 2010; **Med School:** Mexico 1991; **Resid:** Internal Medicine, Jackson Meml Med Ctr 1994; **Fellow:** Hematology & Oncology, Mayo Clinic 1998; **Fac Appt:** Prof Med, Mayo Med Sch

Garcia-Manero, Guillermo MD [Hem] - **Spec Exp:** Myelodysplastic Syndromes; Leukemia; Leukemia-Myeloid; Clinical Trials; **Hospital:** UT MD Anderson Canc Ctr; **Address:** UT MD Anderson Cancer Ctr, Dept Leukemia, Cancer Medical Division, 1515 Holcombe Blvd, Unit 428, Houston, TX 77030; **Phone:** 713-563-2000; **Board Cert:** Internal Medicine 1996; Hematology 1999; Medical Oncology 1999; **Med School:** Spain 1991; **Resid:** Internal Medicine, Thomas Jefferson Hosp 1996; **Fellow:** Hematology & Oncology, Thomas Jefferson Hosp 1999; **Fac Appt:** Prof Hem & Onc, Univ Tex, Houston

Kantarjian, Hagop M MD [Hem] - **Spec Exp:** Leukemia; **Hospital:** UT MD Anderson Canc Ctr; **Address:** MD Anderson Canc Ctr, Dept Leukemia, Unit 428, 1400 Holcombe Blvd, Houston, TX 77030; **Phone:** 713-792-7026; **Board Cert:** Internal Medicine 1983; Medical Oncology 1985; **Med School:** Amer Univ Beirut 1979; **Resid:** Internal Medicine, Univ TX MD Anderson Canc Ctr 1983; **Fellow:** Hematology & Oncology, Univ TX MD Anderson Canc Ctr 1985; **Fac Appt:** Prof Med, Univ Tex, Houston

Keating, Michael MD [Hem] - **Spec Exp:** Leukemia-Chronic Lymphocytic; **Hospital:** UT MD Anderson Canc Ctr; **Address:** MD Anderson Canc Ctr, 1400 Holcombe Blvd, Unit 428, Houston, TX 77030-4000; **Phone:** 713-745-2376; **Med School:** Australia 1966; **Resid:** Internal Medicine, St Vincents Hosp 1970; **Fellow:** Hematology, MD Anderson Canc Ctr 1975; **Fac Appt:** Prof Med, Univ Tex, Houston

Lin, Weei-Chin MD/PhD [Hem] - **Spec Exp:** Hematologic Malignancies; Bleeding/Coagulation Disorders; **Hospital:** Ben Taub Genl Hosp; **Address:** One Baylor Plaza, MARB Bldg - rm R410, MS 187, Houston, TX 77030; **Phone:** 713-526-4243; **Med School:** Taiwan 1986; **Resid:** Internal Medicine, Duke Univ Med Ctr 1996; **Fellow:** Hematology & Oncology, Duke Univ Med Ctr 1999; **Fac Appt:** Assoc Prof Hem & Onc, Baylor Coll Med

Lyons, Roger M MD [Hem] - **Spec Exp:** Leukemia & Lymphoma; Multiple Myeloma; Bleeding/Coagulation Disorders; Platelet Disorders; **Hospital:** Methodist Hosp-San Antonio, Methodist Spec & Transpl Hosp; **Address:** 4411 Medical Drive, Ste 100, San Antonio, TX 78229-3325; **Phone:** 210-595-5300; **Board Cert:** Internal Medicine 1981; Hematology 1982; **Med School:** Canada 1967; **Resid:** Internal Medicine, Winnipeg Genl Hosp 1969; Internal Medicine, Barnes-Jewish Hosp 1972; **Fellow:** Hematology, Washington Univ Phys 1975; **Fac Appt:** Clin Prof Med, Univ Tex, San Antonio

Mesa, Ruben A MD [Hem] - **Spec Exp:** Myeloproliferative Disorders; Myelodysplastic Syndromes; Leukemia; **Hospital:** Mayo Clinic - Scottsdale, Select Specialty Hosp-Phoenix; **Address:** Mayo Clinic-Hematology Dept, 13400 E Shea Blvd, Scottsdale, AZ 85259; **Phone:** 480-301-8335; **Board Cert:** Internal Medicine 2008; Hematology 2011; Medical Oncology 2002; **Med School:** Mayo Med Sch 1995; **Resid:** Internal Medicine, Mayo Clinic 1998; **Fellow:** Hematology & Oncology, Mayo Clinic 2003; **Fac Appt:** Prof Hem & Onc, Mayo Med Sch

Munker, Reinhold MD [Hem] - **Spec Exp:** Leukemia & Lymphoma; Bone Marrow Transplant; Hematologic Malignancies; **Hospital:** Louisiana State Univ Hosp; **Address:** LSU Health Shreveport, Feist-Weiller Cancer Ctr, 1501 Kings Hwy, Shreveport, LA 71130; **Phone:** 318-813-1016; **Board Cert:** Internal Medicine 2004; Hematology 2006; **Med School:** Germany 1979; **Resid:** Internal Medicine, Univ Clinic of Grosshaden 1989; **Fellow:** Hematology & Oncology, Univ Clinic of Grossharden 1993; Blood Banking, Univ Clinic of Grossharden 1997; **Fac Appt:** Assoc Prof Med, Louisiana State U, Shrevport

Stewart, Alexander Keith MD [Hem] - **Spec Exp:** Multiple Myeloma; Waldenstrom's Macroglobulinemia; Amyloidosis; Clinical Trials; **Hospital:** Mayo Clinic - Scottsdale; **Address:** Mayo Clinic-Hematology Div, 13400 E Shea Blvd, Scottsdale, AZ 85259; **Phone:** 480-301-7085; **Med School:** Scotland, UK 1984; **Resid:** Internal Medicine, Kingston Genl Hosp 1988; Hematology, Toronto Genl Hosp 1990; **Fellow:** Hematology Research, New England Med Ctr 1992; **Fac Appt:** Prof Med, Mayo Med Sch

Strauss, James F MD [Hem] - **Spec Exp:** Bleeding/Coagulation Disorders; Leukemia; Lymphoma; **Hospital:** TX Hlth Presby Hosp Dallas; **Address:** TX Oncology, 8220 Walnut Hill Ln Bldg 2 - Ste 700, Dallas, TX 75231; **Phone:** 214-739-4175; **Board Cert:** Internal Medicine 1976; Hematology 1978; Medical Oncology 1981; **Med School:** NYU Sch Med 1972; **Resid:** Internal Medicine, Baylor Univ Med Ctr 1976; **Fellow:** Hematology, Univ Texas SW Med Ctr 1978

Yeager, Andrew M MD [Hem] - **Spec Exp:** Bone Marrow & Stem Cell Transplant; Graft vs Host Disease; Leukemia; **Hospital:** Univ Arizona Med Ctr-Univ Campus; **Address:** Arizona Cancer Ctr, 1515 N Campbell Ave, Ste 2956, Tucson, AZ 85724-5024; **Phone:** 520-626-3191; **Board Cert:** Pediatrics 1979; Pediatric Hematology-Oncology 1980; **Med School:** Johns Hopkins Univ 1975; **Resid:** Pediatrics, Johns Hopkins Hosp 1978; Pediatrics, Johns Hopkins Hosp 1982; **Fellow:** Pediatric Hematology-Oncology, Johns Hopkins Hosp 1980; **Fac Appt:** Prof Med, Univ Ariz Coll Med

West Coast and Pacific

Damon, Lloyd E MD [Hem] - **Spec Exp:** Leukemia; Lymphoma; Stem Cell Transplant; **Hospital:** UCSF Med Ctr; **Address:** UCSF Comprehensive Cancer Ctr, 400 Parnassus Ave, Ste A-502, San Francisco, CA 94143; **Phone:** 415-353-2421; **Board Cert:** Internal Medicine 1985; Medical Oncology 1987; Hematology 1988; **Med School:** Univ Mich Med Sch 1982; **Resid:** Internal Medicine, UCSF Med Ctr 1985; **Fellow:** Hematology & Oncology, UCSF Med Ctr 1988; **Fac Appt:** Prof Med, UCSF

DeLoughery, Thomas G MD [Hem] - **Spec Exp:** Thrombotic Disorders; Myeloproliferative Disorders; Bleeding/Coagulation Disorders; Platelet Disorders; **Hospital:** OR Hlth & Sci Univ; **Address:** 3303 SW Bond Ave, MC CH7M, Portland, OR 97239; **Phone:** 503-494-6594; **Board Cert:** Internal Medicine 1988; Blood Banking Transfusion Medicine 1995; Medical Oncology 2011; Hematology 2002; **Med School:** Indiana Univ 1985; **Resid:** Internal Medicine, OR Hlth & Sci Univ 1988; **Fellow:** Hematology & Oncology, OR Hlth & Sci Univ 1991; **Fac Appt:** Prof Med, Oregon Hlth & Sci Univ

Forman, Stephen J MD [Hem] - **Spec Exp:** Lymphoma; Leukemia; Bone Marrow Transplant; Breast Cancer; **Hospital:** City of Hope Natl Med Ctr; **Address:** City Hope Natl Med Ctr, Dept Hematology, 1500 E Duarte Rd, rm 3002, Duarte, CA 91010-3012; **Phone:** 626-256-4673; **Board Cert:** Internal Medicine 1977; **Med School:** USC Sch Med 1974; **Resid:** Internal Medicine, LAC-Harbor-UCLA Med Ctr 1976; **Fellow:** Hematology, LAC-USC Med Ctr 1978; Hematology, City of Hope Med Ctr 1979; **Fac Appt:** Clin Prof Med, USC Sch Med

Heinrich, Michael C MD [Hem] - **Spec Exp:** Hematologic Malignancies; Sarcoma; Gastrointestinal Stromal Tumors; **Hospital:** VA Medical Center - Portland, OR Hlth & Sci Univ; **Address:** 3710 SW US Veteran's Hospital Rd, MC P3RND19, Portland, OR 97239; **Phone:** 503-220-8262 x51169; **Board Cert:** Internal Medicine 1987; Hematology 2010; Medical Oncology 2011; **Med School:** Johns Hopkins Univ 1984; **Resid:** Internal Medicine, Oreg Hlth Scis Univ 1988; **Fellow:** Hematology & Oncology, Oreg Hlth Scis Univ 1991; **Fac Appt:** Prof Med, Oregon Hlth & Sci Univ

Kipps, Thomas J MD/PhD [Hem] - **Spec Exp:** Leukemia; Lymphoma, Non-Hodgkin's; **Hospital:** UCSD Med Ctr; **Address:** Moores UCSD Cancer Ctr, 3855 Health Sciences Drive, La Jolla, CA 92093; **Phone:** 858-822-6100; **Board Cert:** Internal Medicine 1982; Hematology 1984; **Med School:** Harvard Med Sch 1979; **Resid:** Internal Medicine, Stanford Univ Med Ctr 1981; **Fellow:** Hematology & Oncology, Stanford Univ Med Ctr 1984; **Fac Appt:** Prof Med, UCSD

Leung, Lawrence L MD [Hem] - **Spec Exp:** Bleeding/Coagulation Disorders; **Hospital:** Stanford Univ Hosp & Clins, VA Hlth Care Sys - Palo Alto; **Address:** Stanford Cancer Center - Hematology, 875 Blake Wilbur Drive, Palo Alto, CA 94305; **Phone:** 650-498-6000; **Board Cert:** Internal Medicine 1978; Hematology 2009; Medical Oncology 1981; **Med School:** Columbia P&S 1975; **Resid:** Internal Medicine, New York Hosp 1978; **Fellow:** Hematology & Oncology, New York Hosp/Cornell 1981; **Fac Appt:** Prof Med, Stanford Univ

Levine, Alexandra M MD [Hem] - **Spec Exp:** Lymphoma; AIDS Related Cancers; AIDS/HIV; **Hospital:** City of Hope Natl Med Ctr; **Address:** City of Hope National Medical Center, 1500 E Duarte Rd, Duarte, CA 91010; **Phone:** 626-471-7213 x60213; **Med School:** USC Sch Med 1971; **Resid:** Internal Medicine, LAC-USC Med Ctr 1974; **Fellow:** Hematology & Oncology, Grady Meml Hosp-Emory Univ 1975; Hematology, LAC-USC Med Ctr 1978; **Fac Appt:** Prof Med, USC Sch Med

Lill, Michael MD [Hem] - **Spec Exp:** Stem Cell Transplant; Lymphoma; Hematologic Malignancies; **Hospital:** Cedars-Sinai Med Ctr; **Address:** Samuel Oschin Cancer Center, 8700 Beverly Blvd, Ste AC 1070, Los Angeles, CA 90048; **Phone:** 310-423-1160; **Med School:** Australia 1982; **Resid:** Internal Medicine, Sir Charles Gairdner Hospital 1985; **Fellow:** Hematology, Royal Perth Hospital 1989; Hematopathology, Sir Charles Gairdner Hosp 1989; **Fac Appt:** Prof Hem & Onc, UCLA

Linenberger, Michael L MD [Hem] - **Spec Exp:** Bone Marrow Transplant; Bleeding/Coagulation Disorders; Multiple Myeloma; Leukemia & Lymphoma; **Hospital:** Univ Wash Med Ctr; **Address:** Seattle Cancer Care Alliance, 825 Eastlake Ave E, Seattle, WA 98109-1023; **Phone:** 206-288-1260; **Board Cert:** Internal Medicine 1985; Hematology 1988; **Med School:** Univ Kansas 1982; **Resid:** Internal Medicine, Rhode Is Hosp 1985; **Fellow:** Hematology, Univ Wash Med Ctr 1988; **Fac Appt:** Assoc Prof Med, Univ Wash

Maziarz, Richard MD [Hem] - **Spec Exp:** Leukemia; Immunotherapy; Bone Marrow Transplant; Lymphoma; **Hospital:** OR Hlth & Sci Univ; **Address:** OHSU Ctr Hematologic Malignancies, 3181 SW Sam Jackson Park Rd, Multnomah Pavilion, Portland, OR 97239; **Phone:** 503-494-4606; **Board Cert:** Internal Medicine 1982; Hematology 1988; Medical Oncology 1989; **Med School:** Harvard Med Sch 1979; **Resid:** Internal Medicine, Univ Hosp 1982; **Fellow:** Hematology & Oncology, Brigham & Womens Hosp 1988; **Fac Appt:** Prof Hem & Onc, Oregon Hlth & Sci Univ

Mitchell, Beverly S MD [Hem] - **Spec Exp:** Hematologic Malignancies; Leukemia; Lymphoma; **Hospital:** Stanford Univ Hosp & Clins; **Address:** Stanford Cancer Center, 875 Blake Wilbur Drive, Stanford, CA 94305-5456; **Phone:** 650-725-9621; **Board Cert:** Internal Medicine 1973; Hematology 1978; **Med School:** Harvard Med Sch 1969; **Resid:** Internal Medicine, U Wash Med Ctr 1973; **Fellow:** Metabolism, U Zurich 1975; Hematology & Oncology, U Michigan 1977; **Fac Appt:** Prof Med, Stanford Univ

Nademanee, Auayporn P MD [Hem] - **Spec Exp:** Lymphoma; Hematologic Malignancies; Clinical Trials; **Hospital:** City of Hope Natl Med Ctr; **Address:** City of Hope National Medical Center, 1500 Duarte Rd, Duarte, CA 91010; **Phone:** 626-256-4673; **Board Cert:** Hematology 1982; Medical Oncology 1983; Internal Medicine 1978; **Med School:** Thailand 1973; **Resid:** Internal Medicine, Touro Infirm-Tulane Univ 1978; **Fellow:** Hematology & Oncology, Sepulveda VA Hosp 1980; Hematology & Oncology, USC Med Ctr 1981; **Fac Appt:** Prof Med, UCLA

Negrin, Robert S MD [Hem] - **Spec Exp:** Bone Marrow Transplant; **Hospital:** Stanford Univ Hosp & Clins; **Address:** Blood and Marrow Transplant Clinic, 875 Blake Wilbur Drive, Clinic E, Stanford, CA 94305; **Phone:** 650-498-6000; **Board Cert:** Internal Medicine 1987; Hematology 2007; **Med School:** Harvard Med Sch 1984; **Resid:** Internal Medicine, Stanford Univ Hosp 1987; **Fellow:** Hematology, Stanford Univ Hosp 1990; **Fac Appt:** Prof Med, Stanford Univ

O'Donnell, Margaret R MD [Hem] - **Spec Exp:** Leukemia; Clinical Trials; **Hospital:** City of Hope Natl Med Ctr; **Address:** City of Hope National Med Ctr, 1500 E Duarte Rd, Duarte, CA 91010; **Phone:** 800-826-4673; **Board Cert:** Internal Medicine 1978; Hematology 1980; Medical Oncology 1979; **Med School:** Med Coll PA 1974; **Resid:** Internal Medicine, Montreal Genl Hosp 1976; Hematology, Royal Victoria Hosp-Montreal 1977; **Fellow:** Hematology & Oncology, Fred Hutchinson Cancer Ctr 1979

Petersdorf, Stephen H MD [Hem] - **Spec Exp:** Lymphoma; Myelodysplastic Syndromes; Leukemia; **Hospital:** Univ Wash Med Ctr; **Address:** Seattle Cancer Care Alliance, 825 Eastlake Ave E, MS E2102, Seattle, WA 98109-1023; **Phone:** 206-288-6202; **Board Cert:** Internal Medicine 1986; Hematology 2011; Medical Oncology 2011; **Med School:** Brown Univ 1983; **Resid:** Internal Medicine, Univ Washington Med Ctr 1986; **Fellow:** Hematology & Oncology, Univ Washington Med Ctr 1989; **Fac Appt:** Assoc Prof Med, Univ Wash

Saven, Alan MD [Hem] - **Spec Exp:** Leukemia; Lymphoma; **Hospital:** Scripps Green Hosp; **Address:** Scripps Green Hosp, Hematology, 10666 N Torrey Pines Rd, MS 312, La Jolla, CA 92037; **Phone:** 858-554-9489; **Board Cert:** Internal Medicine 1987; Medical Oncology 1989; **Med School:** South Africa 1982; **Resid:** Internal Medicine, Albert Einstein Med Ctr 1986; **Fellow:** Hematology & Oncology, Scripps Clinic 1987

Schiller, Gary J MD [Hem] - **Spec Exp:** Leukemia; **Hospital:** UCLA Ronald Reagan Med Ctr; **Address:** UCLA Oncology Center, 200 UCLA Medical Plaza, Ste 120, Los Angeles, CA 90095; **Phone:** 310-206-6909; **Board Cert:** Internal Medicine 1987; Medical Oncology 1989; Hematology 2010; **Med School:** USC Sch Med 1984; **Resid:** Internal Medicine, UCLA Med Ctr 1987; **Fellow:** Hematology & Oncology, UCLA Med Ctr 1990; **Fac Appt:** Prof Med, UCLA

Snyder, David S MD [Hem] - **Spec Exp:** Leukemia; Bone Marrow Transplant; Myeloproliferative Disorders; **Hospital:** City of Hope Natl Med Ctr; **Address:** City of Hope National Medical Center, 1500 E Duarte Rd, Duarte, CA 91010-3012; **Phone:** 626-256-4673 x62692; **Board Cert:** Internal Medicine 1980; Hematology 1984; **Med School:** Harvard Med Sch 1977; **Resid:** Internal Medicine, Beth Israel Deaconess Med Ctr 1980; **Fellow:** Immunology, Harvard Med Sch 1982; Hematology & Oncology, New England Bapt Hosp 1984

Medical Oncology

New England

Antin, Joseph H MD [Onc] - **Spec Exp:** Bone Marrow Transplant; Stem Cell Transplant; Anemia-Aplastic; Myelodysplastic Syndromes; **Hospital:** Brigham & Women's Hosp, Dana-Farber Cancer Inst; **Address:** Dana-Farber Cancer Institute, 450 Brookline Ave, rm D1B30, Boston, MA 02215; **Phone:** 617-632-3245; **Board Cert:** Internal Medicine 1981; Medical Oncology 1983; Hematology 1984; **Med School:** Cornell Univ-Weill Med Coll 1978; **Resid:** Internal Medicine, Brigham & Women's Hosp 1981; **Fellow:** Hematology & Oncology, Brigham & Womens Hosp/Dana Farber 1984; **Fac Appt:** Prof Onc, Harvard Med Sch

Azzoli, Christopher G MD [Onc] - **Spec Exp:** Lung Cancer; Lung Cancer (advanced); **Hospital:** Mass Genl Hosp; **Address:** MGH Cancer Ctr, 32 Fruit St, Yawkey Bldg, rm 7E, Boston, MA 02114; **Phone:** 617-724-4000; **Board Cert:** Internal Medicine 2009; Medical Oncology 2001; **Med School:** Johns Hopkins Univ 1996; **Resid:** Internal Medicine, Johns Hopkins Hosp 1999; **Fellow:** Medical Oncology, Meml Sloan Kettering Cancer Ctr 2002; **Fac Appt:** Asst Prof Med, Harvard Med Sch

Birrer, Michael J MD/PhD [Onc] - **Spec Exp:** Ovarian Cancer; Clinical Trials; Gynecologic Cancer; **Hospital:** Mass Genl Hosp; **Address:** Mass General Hospital, 55 Fruit St, Ste YAW 9E, Boston, MA 02114; **Phone:** 617-724-4000; **Board Cert:** Internal Medicine 1985; Medical Oncology 1987; **Med School:** Albert Einstein Coll Med 1982; **Resid:** Internal Medicine, Mass General Hosp 1985; **Fellow:** Medical Oncology, Natl Inst of Hlth - Clin Ctr 1987; **Fac Appt:** Prof Med, Harvard Med Sch

Bubley, Glenn J MD [Onc] - **Spec Exp:** Prostate Cancer; Testicular Cancer; **Hospital:** Beth Israel Deaconess Med Ctr - Boston; **Address:** BIDMC-Div of Hematology/Oncology, 330 Brookline Ave Shapiro Bldg Fl 9, Boston, MA 02215; **Phone:** 617-735-2062; **Board Cert:** Internal Medicine 1980; Medical Oncology 1983; **Med School:** Mich State Univ 1977; **Resid:** Internal Medicine, St Francis Hosp 1980; **Fellow:** Hematology & Oncology, Beth Israel Deaconess Med Ctr 1983; **Fac Appt:** Assoc Prof Med, Harvard Med Sch

Burstein, Harold J MD [Onc] - **Spec Exp:** Breast Cancer; **Hospital:** Dana-Farber Cancer Inst, Brigham & Women's Hosp; **Address:** Dana-Farber Cancer Inst, 450 Brookline Ave Yawkey Bldg Fl 12, Boston, MA 02215; **Phone:** 617-632-4587; **Board Cert:** Medical Oncology 2010; **Med School:** Harvard Med Sch 1994; **Resid:** Internal Medicine, Mass Genl Hosp 1997; **Fellow:** Medical Oncology, Dana Farber Cancer Inst 2000; **Fac Appt:** Assoc Prof Med, Harvard Med Sch

Canellos, George P MD [Onc] - **Spec Exp:** Lymphoma-Second Opinion; Hodgkin's Disease-Second Opinion; **Hospital:** Dana-Farber Cancer Inst, Brigham & Women's Hosp; **Address:** Dana Farber Cancer Inst, 450 Brookline Ave, Dana 1B-14, Boston, MA 02215; **Phone:** 617-632-3470; **Board Cert:** Internal Medicine 1967; Hematology 1972; Medical Oncology 1973; **Med School:** Columbia P&S 1960; **Resid:** Internal Medicine, Mass Genl Hosp 1963; Internal Medicine, Mass Genl Hosp 1966; **Fellow:** Medical Oncology, Natl Cancer Inst 1965; Hematology, Royal Post Graduate Sch of Med 1967; **Fac Appt:** Prof Med, Harvard Med Sch

Come, Steven E MD [Onc] - **Spec Exp:** Breast Cancer; Hodgkin's Lymphoma; **Hospital:** Beth Israel Deaconess Med Ctr - Boston, Dana-Farber Cancer Inst; **Address:** Beth Israel Deaconess Hosp, 330 Brookline Ave, Ste CC913, Boston, MA 02215-5400; **Phone:** 617-667-4599; **Board Cert:** Internal Medicine 1975; Medical Oncology 1979; **Med School:** Harvard Med Sch 1972; **Resid:** Internal Medicine, Beth Israel Hosp 1977; **Fellow:** Medical Oncology, Natl Cancer Inst 1976; **Fac Appt:** Assoc Prof Onc, Harvard Med Sch

DeVita Jr, Vincent T MD [Onc] - **Spec Exp:** Lymphoma Consultation; Hodgkin's Disease Consultation; **Hospital:** Yale-New Haven Hosp; **Address:** Yale, Cancer Ctr, 333 Cedar St, rm FMP117, New Haven, CT 06520; **Phone:** 203-737-1010; **Board Cert:** Internal Medicine 1974; Hematology 1972; Medical Oncology 1973; **Med School:** Geo Wash Univ 1961; **Resid:** Internal Medicine, Geo Washington Univ Hosp 1963; Internal Medicine, Yale-New Haven Hosp 1966; **Fellow:** Medical Oncology, Natl Cancer Inst 1965; **Fac Appt:** Prof Med, Yale Univ

Dizon, Don S MD [Onc] - **Spec Exp:** Gynecologic Cancer; Breast Cancer; Cancer Survivors-Late Effects of Therapy; Sexual Health in Cancer Survivors; **Hospital:** Mass Genl Hosp; **Address:** Mass General Hospital, 55 Fruit St, Yawkey 9E, Boston, MA 02114; **Phone:** 617-724-4000; **Board Cert:** Internal Medicine 2008; Medical Oncology 2012; **Med School:** Univ Rochester 1995; **Resid:** Internal Medicine, Yale-New Haven Hosp 1998; **Fellow:** Oncology, Meml Sloan Kettering Cancer Ctr 2001; **Fac Appt:** Asst Prof Onc, Harvard Med Sch

Erban III, John K MD [Onc] - **Spec Exp:** Breast Cancer; Hematologic Malignancies; Stem Cell Transplant; **Hospital:** Tufts Med Ctr; **Address:** Tufts Med Ctr, 800 Washington St, Box 245, Boston, MA 02111; **Phone:** 617-636-8077; **Board Cert:** Internal Medicine 1984; Medical Oncology 1989; Hematology 2010; **Med School:** Tufts Univ 1981; **Resid:** Internal Medicine, Hosp Univ Penn 1984; **Fellow:** Hematology & Oncology, New England Med Ctr 1990; **Fac Appt:** Prof Onc, Tufts Univ

Ernstoff, Marc Stuart MD [Onc] - **Spec Exp:** Melanoma; Genitourinary Cancer; Skin Cancer; **Hospital:** Dartmouth - Hitchcock Med Ctr; **Address:** 1 Medical Center Drive, Lebanon, NH 03756; **Phone:** 603-650-5534; **Board Cert:** Internal Medicine 1981; Medical Oncology 1989; **Med School:** NYU Sch Med 1978; **Resid:** Internal Medicine, Albert Einstein Coll Med 1981; **Fellow:** Medical Oncology, Yale Univ Affil Hosp 1984; **Fac Appt:** Prof Med, Dartmouth Med Sch

Flaherty, Keith T MD [Onc] - **Spec Exp:** Melanoma-Advanced; Clinical Trials; **Hospital:** Mass Genl Hosp; **Address:** Mass Genl Cancer Ctr Hematology/Oncology, 55 Fruit St, Ste YAW-9E, Boston, MA 02114; **Phone:** 617-724-4800; **Board Cert:** Medical Oncology 2003; **Med School:** Johns Hopkins Univ 1997; **Resid:** Internal Medicine, Brigham & Women's Hosp 2000; **Fellow:** Hematology & Oncology, Pennsylvania Hosp-UPHS 2002

Foss, Francine M MD [Onc] - **Spec Exp:** Cutaneous T-cell Lymphoma; Stem Cell Transplant; Graft vs Host Disease; Multiple Myeloma; **Hospital:** Smilow Cancer Hosp at Yale-New Haven; **Address:** Smilow Cancer Hosp, Hematology, 35 Park St Fl 7, New Haven, CT 06520; **Phone:** 203-200-4363; **Board Cert:** Internal Medicine 1985; Medical Oncology 1987; **Med School:** Univ Mass Sch Med 1982; **Resid:** Internal Medicine, Brigham & Womens Hosp 1985; **Fellow:** Medical Oncology, Natl Cancer Inst 1988; **Fac Appt:** Prof Med, Yale Univ

Freedman, Arnold S MD [Onc] - **Spec Exp:** Lymphoma; Bone Marrow Transplant; Stem Cell Transplant; **Hospital:** Brigham & Women's Hosp, Dana-Farber Cancer Inst; **Address:** Dana-Farber Cancer Inst, 450 Brookline Ave, Dana-2, Boston, MA 02115; **Phone:** 617-582-9086; **Board Cert:** Internal Medicine 1982; Medical Oncology 1985; **Med School:** Univ Mass Sch Med 1979; **Resid:** Internal Medicine, Memorial Hosp 1982; **Fellow:** Medical Oncology, Dana Farber Cancer Inst 1985; **Fac Appt:** Assoc Prof Med, Harvard Med Sch

Fuchs, Charles S MD [Onc] - **Spec Exp:** Gastrointestinal Cancer; Esophageal Cancer; **Hospital:** Dana-Farber Cancer Inst, Brigham & Women's Hosp; **Address:** Dana Farber Cancer Inst, 450 Brookline Ave, Ste D1220, Boston, MA 02215; **Phone:** 617-632-5840; **Board Cert:** Internal Medicine 1989; Medical Oncology 2012; **Med School:** Harvard Med Sch 1986; **Resid:** Internal Medicine, Brigham & Womens Hosp 1989; **Fellow:** Hematology & Oncology, Dana Farber Cancer Inst 1992; **Fac Appt:** Prof Med, Harvard Med Sch

Garber, Judy E MD [Onc] - **Spec Exp:** Breast Cancer; Breast Cancer Genetics; Cancer Risk Assessment; **Hospital:** Dana-Farber Cancer Inst, Brigham & Women's Hosp; **Address:** Dana Farber Cancer Inst, 450 Brookline Ave, Boston, MA 02215; **Phone:** 617-632-5961; **Board Cert:** Internal Medicine 1984; Medical Oncology 1987; Hematology 1988; **Med School:** Yale Univ 1981; **Resid:** Internal Medicine, Brigham & Womens Hosp 1984; **Fellow:** Hematology & Oncology, Brigham & Womens Hosp/Dana Farber Cancer Inst 1988; Cancer Epidemiology, Dana Farber Cancer Inst 1990; **Fac Appt:** Assoc Prof Med, Harvard Med Sch

Garnick, Marc B MD [Onc] - **Spec Exp:** Prostate Cancer; Testicular Cancer; Bladder Cancer; **Hospital:** Beth Israel Deaconess Med Ctr - Boston; **Address:** Beth Israel Deaconess Med Ctr, SCC9, 330 Brookline Ave, Boston, MA 02215; **Phone:** 617-735-2062; **Board Cert:** Internal Medicine 1976; Medical Oncology 1979; **Med School:** Univ Pennsylvania 1972; **Resid:** Internal Medicine, Hosp Univ Penn 1974; **Fellow:** Research, Natl Inst Hlth 1976; Medical Oncology, Dana-Farber Cancer Inst 1978; **Fac Appt:** Clin Prof Med, Harvard Med Sch

George, Suzanne MD [Onc] - **Spec Exp:** Bone Tumors; Sarcoma-Soft Tissue; **Hospital:** Dana-Farber Cancer Inst, Brigham & Women's Hosp; **Address:** Dana-Farber Cancer Inst, 450 Brookline Ave, rm D1212, Boston, MA 02215; **Phone:** 617-632-5122; **Board Cert:** Medical Oncology 2011; **Med School:** Univ Mass Sch Med 1995; **Resid:** Internal Medicine, Univ NC Hlth Sys 1997; **Fellow:** Hematology & Oncology, New England Med Ctr 2001; **Fac Appt:** Asst Prof Med, Harvard Med Sch

Haddad, Robert I MD [Onc] - **Spec Exp:** Head & Neck Cancer; **Hospital:** Dana-Farber Cancer Inst, Brigham & Women's Hosp; **Address:** Dana Farber Cancer Inst - Oncology, 450 Brookline Ave, Boston, MA 02215; **Phone:** 617-632-3090; **Board Cert:** Medical Oncology 2011; **Med School:** Lebanon 1995; **Resid:** Internal Medicine, St Luke's Roosevelt Med Ctr 1998; **Fellow:** Hematology & Oncology, Univ Maryland Cancer Ctr 2000; **Fac Appt:** Assoc Prof Onc, Harvard Med Sch

Herbst, Roy S MD/PhD [Onc] - **Spec Exp:** Lung Cancer; Thoracic Cancers; Drug Development; Clinical Trials; **Hospital:** Smilow Cancer Hosp at Yale-New Haven; **Address:** Smilow Cancer Hosp, Thoracic Oncology, 20 York St Fl 4, New Haven, CT 06504; **Phone:** 203-200-5864; **Board Cert:** Medical Oncology 2007; **Med School:** Cornell Univ-Weill Med Coll 1991; **Resid:** Internal Medicine, Brigham & Womens Hosp 1994; **Fellow:** Medical Oncology, Dana Farber Cancer Inst 1996; **Fac Appt:** Prof Med, Univ Tex, Houston

Hochberg, Ephraim P MD [Onc] - **Spec Exp:** Lymphoma; Hodgkin's Lymphoma; Lymphomatoid Granulomatosis; **Hospital:** Mass Genl Hosp; **Address:** Mass General Hospital, 55 Fruit St, Ste YAW 9A, Boston, MA 02114; **Phone:** 617-724-4000; **Board Cert:** Medical Oncology 2013; Hematology 2004; **Med School:** Case West Res Univ 1996; **Resid:** Internal Medicine, Brigham & Women's Hosp 1999; **Fellow:** Hematology & Oncology, Dana Farber Cancer Inst 2002

Hochster, Howard S MD [Onc] - **Spec Exp:** Gastrointestinal Cancer; Gynecologic Cancer; Colon & Rectal Cancer; **Hospital:** Smilow Cancer Hosp at Yale-New Haven; **Address:** Smilow Cancer Hosp, GI Cancer Dept, 35 Park St, Ste NP8-202, New Haven, CT 06520; **Phone:** 203-200-4422; **Board Cert:** Internal Medicine 1983; Medical Oncology 1985; Hematology 1986; **Med School:** Yale Univ 1980; **Resid:** Internal Medicine, NYU Med Ctr 1983; **Fellow:** Hematology & Oncology, NYU Med Ctr 1985; Medical Oncology, Jules Bordet Inst 1986; **Fac Appt:** Prof Med, Yale Univ

Hollister Jr, Dickerman MD [Onc] - **Spec Exp:** Breast Cancer; Lung Cancer; Colon Cancer; Leukemia & Lymphoma; **Hospital:** Greenwich Hosp; **Address:** 77 Lafayette Pl, Ste 200, Greenwich, CT 06830; **Phone:** 203-863-3737; **Board Cert:** Internal Medicine 1978; Hematology 1980; Medical Oncology 1981; **Med School:** Univ VA Sch Med 1975; **Resid:** Internal Medicine, NY-Presby/Weill Cornell Med Ctr 1978; **Fellow:** Hematology & Oncology, NY-Presby/Weill Cornell Med Ctr 1981; **Fac Appt:** Asst Clin Prof Med, Yale Univ

Johnson, Bruce E MD [Onc] - **Spec Exp:** Lung Cancer; Thoracic Cancers; Mesothelioma; **Hospital:** Dana-Farber Cancer Inst, Brigham & Women's Hosp; **Address:** Dana-Farber Cancer Institute, 450 Brookline Ave, Boston, MA 02215; **Phone:** 617-632-4790; **Board Cert:** Internal Medicine 1982; Medical Oncology 1985; **Med School:** Univ Minn 1979; **Resid:** Internal Medicine, Univ Chicago Hosps 1982; **Fellow:** Medical Oncology, Natl Cancer Inst 1985; **Fac Appt:** Prof Onc, Harvard Med Sch

Kantoff, Philip W MD [Onc] - **Spec Exp:** Genitourinary Cancer; Prostate Cancer; Testicular Cancer; **Hospital:** Dana-Farber Cancer Inst, Brigham & Women's Hosp; **Address:** Dana Farber Cancer Inst, 450 Brookline Ave, Dana 1230, Boston, MA 02215; **Phone:** 617-632-4622; **Board Cert:** Internal Medicine 1982; Medical Oncology 1989; **Med School:** Brown Univ 1979; **Resid:** Internal Medicine, NYU/Bellevue Hosp 1982; **Fellow:** Molecular Genetics, Natl Inst of Hlth - Clin Ctr 1986; Hematology & Oncology, Dana Farber Cancer Inst 1988; **Fac Appt:** Prof Onc, Harvard Med Sch

Kaufman, Peter A MD [Onc] - **Spec Exp:** Breast Cancer; Clinical Trials; **Hospital:** Dartmouth - Hitchcock Med Ctr; **Address:** DHMC, Dept Hem-Onc, One Medical Center Drive, Lebanon, NH 03756; **Phone:** 603-653-6181; **Board Cert:** Internal Medicine 1986; Medical Oncology 1989; **Med School:** NYU Sch Med 1983; **Resid:** Internal Medicine, Duke Univ Med Ctr 1986; **Fellow:** Hematology & Oncology, Duke Univ Med Ctr 1989; **Fac Appt:** Assoc Prof Med, Dartmouth Med Sch

Lacy, Jill MD [Onc] - **Spec Exp:** Colon & Rectal Cancer; Gastrointestinal Cancer; Pancreatic Cancer; Esophageal Cancer; **Hospital:** Smilow Cancer Hosp at Yale-New Haven; **Address:** Smilow Cancer Hosp, GI Cancer Dept, 35 Park St, Ste NP8-202, New Haven, CT 06520; **Phone:** 203-200-4422; **Board Cert:** Internal Medicine 1982; Medical Oncology 2005; **Med School:** Yale Univ 1978; **Resid:** Internal Medicine, Yale-New Haven Hosp 1981; **Fellow:** Medical Oncology, Yale-New Haven Hosp 1985; **Fac Appt:** Assoc Prof Onc, Yale Univ

Legare, Robert D MD [Onc] - **Spec Exp:** Breast Cancer; Breast Cancer Risk Assessment; **Hospital:** Women & Infants Hosp of RI; **Address:** Women & Infants Hosp, 101 Dudley St, Providence, RI 02905; **Phone:** 401-453-7540; **Board Cert:** Internal Medicine 2005; Hematology 2006; Medical Oncology 2008; **Med School:** Tufts Univ 1990; **Resid:** Internal Medicine, Yale-New Haven Hosp 1992; **Fellow:** Hematology & Oncology, Brigham & Womens Hosp 1996; **Fac Appt:** Assoc Prof Med, Brown Univ

Lilenbaum, Rogerio C MD [Onc] - **Spec Exp:** Thoracic Cancers; Lung Cancer; **Hospital:** Smilow Cancer Hosp at Yale-New Haven; **Address:** Smilow Cancer Hosp, Thoracic Oncology, 20 York St Fl 4, New Haven, CT 06510; **Phone:** 203-200-5864; **Board Cert:** Internal Medicine 2005; Hematology 2008; Medical Oncology 2007; **Med School:** Brazil 1986; **Resid:** Internal Medicine, Univ Hosp 1989; **Fellow:** Hematology & Oncology, Washington Univ Phys 1992; Medical Oncology, UCSD Med Ctr 1994

Lynch Jr, Thomas J MD [Onc] - **Spec Exp:** Lung Cancer; Thoracic Cancers; **Hospital:** Smilow Cancer Hosp at Yale-New Haven; **Address:** Smilow Cancer Hosp, Thoracic Oncology, 35 Park St Fl 4, New Haven, CT 06510; **Phone:** 203-688-5864; **Board Cert:** Internal Medicine 1989; Medical Oncology 2003; **Med School:** Yale Univ 1986; **Resid:** Internal Medicine, Mass Genl Hosp 1989; **Fellow:** Medical Oncology, Dana Farber Cancer Inst 1991; **Fac Appt:** Assoc Prof Med, Yale Univ

Mathew, Paul MD [Onc] - **Spec Exp:** Prostate Cancer; Genitourinary Cancer; **Hospital:** Tufts Med Ctr; **Address:** Tufts Med Ctr, Div Hematology-Oncology, 800 Washington St, Box 245, Boston, MA 02111; **Phone:** 617-636-8483; **Board Cert:** Hematology 2004; Medical Oncology 2003; **Med School:** Nigeria 1985; **Resid:** Internal Medicine, Cook Co Hosp 1990; **Fellow:** Hematology & Oncology, Mayo Clinic 1994; **Fac Appt:** Assoc Prof Onc, Tufts Univ

Matulonis, Ursula A MD [Onc] - **Spec Exp:** Gynecologic Cancer; Ovarian Cancer; Breast Cancer; Fertility Preservation in Cancer; **Hospital:** Dana-Farber Cancer Inst; **Address:** Dana Farber Cancer Inst, 450 Brookline Ave, Fl 14, Boston, MA 02215; **Phone:** 617-632-2334; **Board Cert:** Medical Oncology 2000; **Med School:** Albany Med Coll 1987; **Resid:** Internal Medicine, Univ Pittsburgh Med Ctr 1990; **Fellow:** Medical Oncology, Dana Farber Cancer Inst 1993; **Fac Appt:** Assoc Prof Med, Harvard Med Sch

Mayer, Robert J MD [Onc] - **Spec Exp:** Colon & Rectal Cancer; Gastrointestinal Cancer; **Hospital:** Dana-Farber Cancer Inst, Brigham & Women's Hosp; **Address:** Dana Farber Cancer Inst, 450 Brookline Ave, Boston, MA 02215; **Phone:** 617-632-3474; **Board Cert:** Internal Medicine 1973; Medical Oncology 1975; Hematology 1976; **Med School:** Harvard Med Sch 1969; **Resid:** Internal Medicine, Mt Sinai Hosp 1971; Hematology & Oncology, Natl Cancer Inst 1974; **Fellow:** Dana Farber Cancer Inst 1976; **Fac Appt:** Prof Onc, Harvard Med Sch

Petrylak, Daniel P MD [Onc] - **Spec Exp:** Testicular Cancer; Prostate Cancer; Bladder Cancer; Kidney Cancer; **Hospital:** Yale-New Haven Hosp, Greenwich Hosp; **Address:** Yale Smilow Cancer Center, 35 Park St, New Haven, CT 06520; **Phone:** 203-200-4822; **Board Cert:** Internal Medicine 2001; Medical Oncology 2003; **Med School:** Case West Res Univ 1985; **Resid:** Internal Medicine, Jacobi Med Ctr 1988; **Fellow:** Oncology, Meml-Sloan Kettering Cancer Ctr 1991; **Fac Appt:** Prof Onc, Yale Univ

Pusztai, Lajos MD [Onc] - **Spec Exp:** Breast Cancer; **Hospital:** Smilow Cancer Hosp at Yale-New Haven; **Address:** Yale, Breast Cancer, 35 Park St, North Pav 1, New Haven, CT 06510; **Phone:** 203-200-2328; **Board Cert:** Medical Oncology 2011; **Med School:** Hungary 1987; **Resid:** Internal Medicine, St Marys Hosp 1996; **Fellow:** Medical Oncology, UT MD Anderson Cancer Ctr 1999; **Fac Appt:** Prof Med, Yale Univ

Ryan, David P MD [Onc] - **Spec Exp:** Colon Cancer; Pancreatic Cancer; Gastrointestinal Cancer; **Hospital:** Mass Genl Hosp; **Address:** Mass General Hospital, 55 Fruit St, Ste YAW 7E, Boston, MA 02114; **Phone:** 617-724-4000; **Board Cert:** Medical Oncology 2009; **Med School:** Columbia P&S 1992; **Resid:** Internal Medicine, NY-Presby/Columbia Univ Med Ctr 1996; **Fellow:** Hematology & Oncology, Mass Genl Hosp 1998; **Fac Appt:** Assoc Prof Med, Harvard Med Sch

Saif, M Wasif MD [Onc] - **Spec Exp:** Pancreatic Cancer; Colon & Rectal Cancer; Gastrointestinal Cancer; **Hospital:** Tufts Med Ctr; **Address:** Tufts Medical Ctr, 800 Washington St, Box 245, Boston, MA 02111; **Phone:** 617-636-5627; **Board Cert:** Medical Oncology 2012; **Med School:** Pakistan 1992; **Resid:** Internal Medicine, Univ Conn Med Ctr 1998; **Fellow:** Hematology & Oncology, Natl Cancer Inst 2001; **Fac Appt:** Asst Clin Prof Med, Tufts Univ

Schnipper, Lowell E MD [Onc] - **Spec Exp:** Breast Cancer; **Hospital:** Beth Israel Deaconess Med Ctr - Boston; **Address:** BIDMC-Div of Hematology/Oncology, 330 Brookline Ave Shapiro Bldg Fl 9, Boston, MA 02215; **Phone:** 617-667-1921; **Board Cert:** Internal Medicine 1973; Medical Oncology 1983; **Med School:** SUNY Downstate 1968; **Resid:** Internal Medicine, Yale-New Haven Hosp 1970; Medical Oncology, Natl Cancer Inst 1973; **Fellow:** Hematology & Oncology, Barnes Jewish Hosp 1974; **Fac Appt:** Prof Med, Harvard Med Sch

Shulman, Lawrence N MD [Onc] - **Spec Exp:** Breast Cancer; **Hospital:** Dana-Farber Cancer Inst, Brigham & Women's Hosp; **Address:** Dana-Farber Cancer Inst, 450 Brookline Ave, DANA 1608, Boston, MA 02215; **Phone:** 617-632-2277; **Board Cert:** Internal Medicine 1978; Medical Oncology 1981; Hematology 1982; **Med School:** Harvard Med Sch 1975; **Resid:** Internal Medicine, Beth Israel Hosp 1977; **Fellow:** Hematology & Oncology, Beth Israel Hosp 1980; **Fac Appt:** Assoc Prof Onc, Harvard Med Sch

Smith, Matthew R MD/PhD [Onc] - **Spec Exp:** Prostate Cancer; **Hospital:** Mass Genl Hosp; **Address:** Mass Genl Hosp, Hematology/Oncology, 55 Fruit St, Ste YAW 7E, Boston, MA 02114; **Phone:** 617-724-5257; **Board Cert:** Medical Oncology 2007; **Med School:** Duke Univ 1992; **Resid:** Internal Medicine, Brigham & Women's Hosp 1994; **Fellow:** Medical Oncology, Dana Farber Cancer Inst 1997; **Fac Appt:** Assoc Prof Med, Harvard Med Sch

Soiffer, Robert J MD [Onc] - **Spec Exp:** Stem Cell Transplant; Bone Marrow Transplant; Leukemia; Lymphoma; **Hospital:** Dana-Farber Cancer Inst, Brigham & Women's Hosp; **Address:** Dana-Farber Cancer Inst, 450 Brookline Ave Dana Bldg - rm D2-032, Boston, MA 02215; **Phone:** 617-632-3667; **Board Cert:** Internal Medicine 1986; Medical Oncology 1989; **Med School:** NYU Sch Med 1983; **Resid:** Internal Medicine, Brigham & Women's Hosp 1986; **Fellow:** Medical Oncology, Dana-Farber Cancer Inst 1989; **Fac Appt:** Prof Onc, Harvard Med Sch

Strauss, Gary M MD [Onc] - **Spec Exp:** Lung Cancer; Thoracic Cancers; Melanoma; Breast Cancer; **Hospital:** Tufts Med Ctr; **Address:** Tufts Med Ctr, Div of Hem/Oncology, 800 Washington St, Box 245, Boston, MA 02111; **Phone:** 617-636-5291; **Board Cert:** Internal Medicine 1975; Medical Oncology 1979; Hematology 1980; **Med School:** Yale Univ 1972; **Resid:** Internal Medicine, Boston City Hosp 1974; Internal Medicine, Mass Genl Hosp 1977; **Fellow:** Medical Oncology, Natl Cancer Inst 1976; Hematology & Oncology, Mass General Hosp 1979; **Fac Appt:** Prof Med, Tufts Univ

Strenger, Rochelle MD [Onc] - **Spec Exp:** Breast Cancer; Hematologic Malignancies; Lymphoma; **Hospital:** Miriam Hosp, Rhode Island Hosp; **Address:** Comprehensive Cancer Ctr-Miriam Hosp, 164 Summit Ave, Fain 3, Providence, RI 02906; **Phone:** 401-793-2920; **Board Cert:** Internal Medicine 1986; Medical Oncology 2009; **Med School:** Albert Einstein Coll Med 1982; **Resid:** Internal Medicine, Brigham & Womens Hosp 1985; **Fellow:** Hematology & Oncology, Brigham & Womens Hosp 1988

Sweeney, Christopher J MD [Onc] - **Spec Exp:** Genitourinary Cancer; Prostate Cancer; Testicular Cancer; **Hospital:** Dana-Farber Cancer Inst; **Address:** Dana Farber Cancer Inst, 450 Brookline Ave, Ste D-1230, Boston, MA 02215; **Phone:** 617-632-4524; **Board Cert:** Medical Oncology 2011; **Med School:** Australia 1993; **Resid:** Internal Medicine, Gundersen Lutheran Med Ctr 1997; **Fellow:** Hematology & Oncology, Indiana Univ Med Ctr 2000; **Fac Appt:** Assoc Prof Onc, Harvard Med Sch

Sznol, Mario MD [Onc] - **Spec Exp:** Immunotherapy; Drug Development; Melanoma; **Hospital:** Smilow Cancer Hosp at Yale-New Haven; **Address:** Smilow Cancer Hosp, Melanoma, 333 Cedar St, rm SMP130, New Haven, CT 06520; **Phone:** 203-200-6622; **Board Cert:** Internal Medicine 1985; Medical Oncology 1987; **Med School:** Baylor Coll Med 1982; **Resid:** Internal Medicine, Baylor Coll Med 1985; **Fellow:** Medical Oncology, Mount Sinai Med Ctr 1987; **Fac Appt:** Prof Onc, Yale Univ

Taplin, Mary Ellen MD [Onc] - **Spec Exp:** Prostate Cancer; Prostate Cancer (advanced); Genitourinary Cancer; **Hospital:** Dana-Farber Cancer Inst, Brigham & Women's Hosp; **Address:** Dana Farber Cancer Inst, 450 Brookline Ave, Ste D-1230, Boston, MA 02215; **Phone:** 617-632-3237; **Board Cert:** Internal Medicine 1989; Hematology 2006; Medical Oncology 2003; **Med School:** Univ Mass Sch Med 1986; **Resid:** Internal Medicine, Univ Mass Med Ctr 1990; **Fellow:** Hematology & Oncology, Beth Israel Deaconess Med Ctr 1993; **Fac Appt:** Assoc Prof Med, Harvard Med Sch

Torti, Frank M MD [Onc] - **Spec Exp:** Prostate Cancer; Urologic Cancer; **Hospital:** Univ of Conn Hlth Ctr, John Dempsey Hosp; **Address:** Univ Connecticut Hlth Ctr, 263 Farmington Ave, Farmington, CT 06030-1920; **Phone:** 860-679-2594; **Board Cert:** Internal Medicine 1978; Medical Oncology 1979; **Med School:** Harvard Med Sch 1974; **Resid:** Internal Medicine, Beth Israel Hosp 1976; **Fellow:** Medical Oncology, Stanford Univ Med Ctr 1979; **Fac Appt:** Prof Med, Univ Conn

Verschraegen, Claire F MD [Onc] - **Spec Exp:** Cancers-Rare & Unusual; Drug Discovery; Gynecologic Cancer; Sarcoma; **Hospital:** FAHC - Med Ctr Campus; **Address:** Vermont Cancer Center, 89 Beaumont Ave, Ste Given, rm E214, Burlington, VT 05405; **Phone:** 802-656-5487; **Board Cert:** Medical Oncology 2000; **Med School:** Belgium 1982; **Resid:** Internal Medicine, Bordet 1985; Internal Medicine, Univ Texas 1991; **Fellow:** Cancer Research, Stehlin Fdn for Cancer Research 1988; Oncology, MD Anderson Cancer Ctr 1994

Vredenburgh, James J MD [Onc] - **Spec Exp:** Brain Tumors; Gliomas; Brain Tumors-Metastatic; **Hospital:** St. Francis Hosp & Med Ctr; **Address:** St Francis/Mount Sinai Regl Cancer Ctr, Hematology/Onc Dept, 114 Woodland St Fl 2, Hartford, CT 06105; **Phone:** 860-714-5554; **Board Cert:** Internal Medicine 1986; Hematology 1988; Medical Oncology 1989; **Med School:** Univ VT Coll Med 1983; **Resid:** Internal Medicine, St Francis Med Ctr 1986; **Fellow:** Hematology & Oncology, Dartmouth-Hitchcock Med Ctr 1989

Weisberg, Tracey MD [Onc] - **Spec Exp:** Breast Cancer; **Hospital:** Maine Med Ctr; **Address:** Maine Ctr for Cancer Medicine, 100 Campus Drive, Unit 108, Scarborough, ME 04074; **Phone:** 207-396-7600; **Board Cert:** Internal Medicine 1987; Medical Oncology 1989; **Med School:** SUNY Stony Brook 1983; **Resid:** Internal Medicine, Mount Sinai Hosp 1985; Internal Medicine, Hartford Hosp 1986; **Fellow:** Medical Oncology, Yale Univ Hosp 1988

Winer, Eric P MD [Onc] - **Spec Exp:** Breast Cancer; **Hospital:** Dana-Farber Cancer Inst, Brigham & Women's Hosp; **Address:** Dana Farber Cancer Inst, 450 Brookline Ave Yawkey Bldg - Ste 1250, Boston, MA 02215; **Phone:** 617-632-6876; **Board Cert:** Internal Medicine 1987; Medical Oncology 1989; **Med School:** Yale Univ 1983; **Resid:** Internal Medicine, Yale-New Haven Hosp 1987; **Fellow:** Hematology & Oncology, Duke Univ Med Ctr 1989; **Fac Appt:** Prof Med, Harvard Med Sch

Mid Atlantic

Aghajanian, Carol A MD [Onc] - **Spec Exp:** Ovarian Cancer; Gynecologic Cancer; Trophoblastic Tumors; **Hospital:** Meml Sloan-Kettering Canc Ctr; **Address:** 300 E 66th St, New York, NY 10065; **Phone:** 646-888-4217; **Board Cert:** Internal Medicine 2012; Medical Oncology 2005; **Med School:** SUNY Downstate 1989; **Resid:** Internal Medicine, Mt Sinai Med Ctr 1992; **Fellow:** Medical Oncology, Meml Sloan Kettering Cancer Ctr 1995; **Fac Appt:** Prof Med, Cornell Univ-Weill Med Coll

Ahlgren, James D MD [Onc] - **Spec Exp:** Gastrointestinal Cancer; Carcinoid Tumors; Neuroendocrine Tumors; **Hospital:** G Washington Univ Hosp; **Address:** 2150 Pennsylvania Ave NW, Ste 1-100, Washington, DC 20037-3201; **Phone:** 202-741-2478; **Board Cert:** Internal Medicine 1980; Medical Oncology 1989; **Med School:** Georgetown Univ 1977; **Resid:** Internal Medicine, Georgetown Univ Hosp 1979; **Fellow:** Medical Oncology, Georgetown Univ Hosp 1981; **Fac Appt:** Prof Med, Geo Wash Univ

Aisner, Joseph MD [Onc] - **Spec Exp:** Lung Cancer; Solid Tumors; Thymoma; Mesothelioma; **Hospital:** Robert Wood Johnson Univ Hosp - New Brunswick; **Address:** Cancer Inst of New Jersey, 195 Little Albany St, New Brunswick, NJ 08903-2681; **Phone:** 732-235-7464; **Board Cert:** Internal Medicine 1973; Medical Oncology 1975; **Med School:** Wayne State Univ 1970; **Resid:** Internal Medicine, Georgetown Univ Hosp 1972; **Fellow:** Medical Oncology, Natl Cancer Inst 1975; **Fac Appt:** Prof Med, UMDNJ-RW Johnson Med Sch

Algazy, Kenneth M MD [Onc] - **Spec Exp:** Lung Cancer; Head & Neck Cancer; Hematologic Malignancies; **Hospital:** Hosp Univ Penn - UPHS (page 69), VA Med Ctr - Philadelphia; **Address:** Hosp Univ Pennsylvania, 3400 Convention Ave, The Perelman Ctr, Fl 2, Philadelphia, PA 19104; **Phone:** 215-615-5810; **Board Cert:** Internal Medicine 1972; Hematology 1974; Medical Oncology 1979; **Med School:** Temple Univ 1969; **Resid:** Internal Medicine, Strong Meml Hosp 1972; **Fellow:** Hematology & Oncology, Johns Hopkins Hosp 1974; **Fac Appt:** Clin Prof Onc, Temple Univ

Ambinder, Richard F MD/PhD [Onc] - **Spec Exp:** Lymphoma; Hodgkin's Lymphoma; AIDS Related Cancers; **Hospital:** Johns Hopkins Hosp (page 59); **Address:** Johns Hopkins Hosp, Sidney Kimmel Comp Cancer Ctr, 401 N Broadway, Ste 1343, Baltimore, MD 21231; **Phone:** 410-955-8964; **Board Cert:** Internal Medicine 1982; Medical Oncology 1985; **Med School:** Johns Hopkins Univ 1979; **Resid:** Internal Medicine, Johns Hopkins Hosp 1981; **Fellow:** Internal Medicine, Johns Hopkins Hosp 1982; Medical Oncology, Johns Hopkins Hosp 1985; **Fac Appt:** Prof Med, Johns Hopkins Univ

Arlen, Philip M MD [Onc] - **Spec Exp:** Prostate Cancer-Vaccine Therapy; Vaccine Therapy-Clinical Trials Only; Clinical Trials Only; **Hospital:** Natl Inst of Hlth - Clin Ctr, Walter Reed Natl Military Med Ctr; **Address:** Natl Cancer Inst-Ctr for Cancer Rsch, Laboratory of Tumor Immunology & Bio, 10 Center Drive, Bldg 10, rm 809, Bethesda, MD 20892-1750; **Phone:** 301-496-4343; **Board Cert:** Medical Oncology 2008; **Med School:** Med Coll GA 1991; **Resid:** Internal Medicine, Georgia Baptist Hlth Care Syst 1994; **Fellow:** Hematology & Oncology, Emory Univ Med Ctr 1997; Oncology Research, Natl Cancer Inst-NIH 1999

Armstrong, Deborah K MD [Onc] - **Spec Exp:** Gynecologic Cancer; Breast Cancer; Ovarian Cancer-Early Detection; Breast Cancer Genetics; **Hospital:** Johns Hopkins Hosp (page 59); **Address:** Sidney Kimmel Comp Cancer Ctr, 401 N Broadway, Ste 1343, Baltimore, MD 21231; **Phone:** 410-955-8964; **Board Cert:** Internal Medicine 1987; Medical Oncology 2007; **Med School:** Geo Wash Univ 1984; **Resid:** Internal Medicine, Univ Pittsburgh 1987; **Fellow:** Medical Oncology, Johns Hopkins Hosp 1993; **Fac Appt:** Assoc Prof Med, Johns Hopkins Univ

Astrow, Alan B MD [Onc] - **Spec Exp:** Ovarian Cancer; Breast Cancer; **Hospital:** Maimonides Med Ctr (page 60); **Address:** Maimonides Cancer Ctr, 6300 8th Ave, Brooklyn, NY 11220; **Phone:** 718-765-2653; **Board Cert:** Internal Medicine 1983; Hematology 1986; Medical Oncology 1987; **Med School:** Yale Univ 1980; **Resid:** Internal Medicine, Boston City Hosp 1983; **Fellow:** Hematology & Oncology, NYU Med Ctr 1986; **Fac Appt:** Assoc Clin Prof Med, NY Med Coll

Atkins, Michael B MD [Onc] - **Spec Exp:** Melanoma; Kidney Cancer; Immunotherapy; **Hospital:** MedStar Georgetown Univ Hosp; **Address:** Lombardi Comprehensive Cancer Ctr, 3800 Reservoir Rd NW, Washington, DC 20007; **Phone:** 202-444-2223; **Board Cert:** Internal Medicine 1983; Medical Oncology 1987; **Med School:** Tufts Univ 1980; **Resid:** Internal Medicine, New England Med Ctr 1983; **Fellow:** Hematology & Oncology, New England Med Ctr 1987; **Fac Appt:** Prof Onc, Georgetown Univ

Attas, Lewis MD [Onc] - **Spec Exp:** Breast Cancer; Lymphoma; Bleeding/Coagulation Disorders; Gaucher Disease; **Hospital:** Englewood Hosp & Med Ctr, Holy Name Med Ctr; **Address:** 350 Engle St, Englewood, NJ 07631; **Phone:** 201-568-5250; **Board Cert:** Internal Medicine 1985; Medical Oncology 1987; Hematology 1988; Hospice & Palliative Medicine 2012; **Med School:** Mount Sinai Sch Med 1982; **Resid:** Internal Medicine, Montefiore Hosp Med Ctr 1985; **Fellow:** Hematology & Oncology, North Shore Univ Hosp 1988; **Fac Appt:** Assoc Clin Prof Med, Mount Sinai Sch Med

Axelrod, Rita S MD [Onc] - **Spec Exp:** Head & Neck Cancer; Lung Cancer; Complementary Medicine; **Hospital:** Thomas Jefferson Univ Hosp; **Address:** 925 Chestnut St Fl 3, Philadelphia, PA 19107; **Phone:** 215-955-8874; **Board Cert:** Internal Medicine 1976; Medical Oncology 1977; Hematology 1978; **Med School:** NYU Sch Med 1970; **Resid:** Internal Medicine, Med Coll Georgia Hosps 1973; **Fellow:** Hematology & Oncology, Hosp Univ Penn 1975; **Fac Appt:** Assoc Clin Prof Med, Thomas Jefferson Univ

Bajorin, Dean F MD [Onc] - **Spec Exp:** Genitourinary Cancer; Bladder Cancer; Testicular Cancer; Clinical Trials; **Hospital:** Meml Sloan-Kettering Canc Ctr; **Address:** 1275 York Avenue, New York, NY 10065; **Phone:** 646-422-4333; **Board Cert:** Internal Medicine 1981; Medical Oncology 1985; **Med School:** NY Med Coll 1978; **Resid:** Internal Medicine, Hartford Hosp 1981; **Fellow:** Medical Oncology, Meml Sloan Kettering Ctr 1985; **Fac Appt:** Prof Med, Cornell Univ-Weill Med Coll

Bashevkin, Michael L MD [Onc] - **Spec Exp:** Solid Tumors; Hematologic Malignancies; **Hospital:** Maimonides Med Ctr (page 60); **Address:** Hematology Oncology Assocs, 1660 E 14th St, Ste 501, Brooklyn, NY 11229; **Phone:** 718-382-8500 x501; **Board Cert:** Internal Medicine 1976; Hematology 1978; Medical Oncology 1979; **Med School:** SUNY Downstate 1973; **Resid:** Internal Medicine, VA Med Ctr 1976; **Fellow:** Hematology & Oncology, Maimonides Med Ctr 1979

Belani, Chandra P MD [Onc] - **Spec Exp:** Lung Cancer; Drug Discovery; **Hospital:** Penn State Milton S Hershey Med Ctr; **Address:** Penn State Hershey Cancer Inst, 500 University Drive, PSHCI Bldg Fl 1, Hershey, PA 17033; **Phone:** 717-531-1078; **Board Cert:** Internal Medicine 1986; Medical Oncology 1987; **Med School:** India 1978; **Resid:** Internal Medicine, SMS Med Hosp 1981; Internal Medicine, Good Samaritan/Univ MD Hosps 1985; **Fellow:** Hematology & Oncology, Univ Maryland Hosp 1987; **Fac Appt:** Prof Onc, Penn State Coll Med

Belenkov, Elliot Michael MD [Onc] - **Spec Exp:** Solid Tumors; **Hospital:** Mt Sinai Med Ctr (page 62), Lenox Hill Hosp (page 66); **Address:** 178 E 85th St, Fl 4, New York, NY 10028; **Phone:** 212-472-5500; **Board Cert:** Internal Medicine 1987; Medical Oncology 2011; **Med School:** Russia 1976; **Resid:** Psychiatry, Metro Hospital 1983; Internal Medicine, Metro Hospital 1986; **Fellow:** Hematology, Lenox Hill Hosp 1988; **Fac Appt:** Asst Clin Prof Onc, Cornell Univ-Weill Med Coll

Biggs, David D MD [Onc] - **Spec Exp:** Breast Cancer; Kidney Cancer; Melanoma; Skin Cancer; **Hospital:** Christiana Hosp; **Address:** Med Oncology Hematology Consultants, 4701 Ogletown-Stanton Rd, Ste 3400, Newark, DE 19713; **Phone:** 302-366-1200; **Board Cert:** Internal Medicine 1988; Hematology 2012; Medical Oncology 2012; **Med School:** Univ Kansas 1984; **Resid:** Internal Medicine, Med Coll Wisconsin 1989; **Fellow:** Hematology & Oncology, Hosp Univ Penn 1991; **Fac Appt:** Asst Clin Prof Med

Bosl, George J MD [Onc] - **Spec Exp:** Testicular Cancer; **Hospital:** Meml Sloan-Kettering Canc Ctr; **Address:** 1275 York Avenue, New York, NY 10065; **Phone:** 212-639-8473; **Board Cert:** Internal Medicine 1976; Medical Oncology 1979; **Med School:** Creighton Univ 1973; **Resid:** Internal Medicine, NY Hosp 1975; Internal Medicine, Meml Sloan-Kettering Cancer Ctr 1977; **Fellow:** Medical Oncology, Univ Minn Hosps 1979; **Fac Appt:** Prof Med, Cornell Univ-Weill Med Coll

Brentjens, Renier J MD [Onc] - **Spec Exp:** Leukemia; Leukemia-Chronic Lymphocytic; T cell Immune Therapy; Cancer Immune Therapy; **Hospital:** Meml Sloan-Kettering Canc Ctr; **Address:** Meml Sloan Kettering Cancer Ctr, 1275 York Ave Fl 4 - Ste 3, New York, NY 10021; **Phone:** 212-639-5279; **Board Cert:** Medical Oncology 2002; **Med School:** SUNY Buffalo 1996; **Resid:** Internal Medicine, Yale-New Haven Hosp 1999; **Fellow:** Medical Oncology, Meml Sloan Kettering Cancer Ctr 2001; **Fac Appt:** Assoc Prof Med, Cornell Univ-Weill Med Coll

Brufsky, Adam M MD/PhD [Onc] - **Spec Exp:** Breast Cancer; **Hospital:** Magee-Womens Hosp - UPMC, UPMC Presby, Pittsburgh; **Address:** 300 Halket St, Ste 4628, Pittsburgh, PA 15213; **Phone:** 412-641-6500; **Board Cert:** Internal Medicine 2004; Medical Oncology 2005; **Med School:** Univ Conn 1990; **Resid:** Internal Medicine, Brigham & Womens Hosp 1992; **Fellow:** Medical Oncology, Dana Farber Cancer Inst 1995; Bone Marrow Transplant, Dana Farber Cancer Inst 1993; **Fac Appt:** Asst Prof Med, Univ Pittsburgh

Carabasi, Matthew H MD [Onc] - **Spec Exp:** Bone Marrow Transplant; Stem Cell Transplant; Leukemia & Lymphoma; Hematologic Malignancies; **Hospital:** Thomas Jefferson Univ Hosp; **Address:** Jefferson Univ Physicians, Div Medical Oncology, 925 Chestnut St, Fl 4, Philadelphia, PA 19107; **Phone:** 215-955-8963; **Board Cert:** Internal Medicine 1983; Medical Oncology 1987; **Med School:** Jefferson Med Coll 1980; **Resid:** Internal Medicine, Hahnemann Univ Hosp 1984; **Fellow:** Hematology & Oncology, Meml Sloan-Kettering Cancer Ctr 1988; Research, Meml Sloan-Kettering Cancer Ctr 1989; **Fac Appt:** Prof Onc, Jefferson Med Coll

Carducci, Michael A MD [Onc] - **Spec Exp:** Urologic Cancer; Drug Discovery & Development; Clinical Trials; Palliative Care; **Hospital:** Johns Hopkins Hosp (page 59); **Address:** Johns Hopkins Hosp, Sidney Kimmel Cancer Ctr, 401 N Broadway, Ste 1343, Baltimore, MD 21231; **Phone:** 410-955-8964; **Board Cert:** Internal Medicine 2011; Medical Oncology 2005; **Med School:** Wayne State Univ 1988; **Resid:** Internal Medicine, Univ Colorado Hlth Sci Ctr 1992; **Fellow:** Medical Oncology, Johns Hopkins Hosp 1995; **Fac Appt:** Prof Onc, Johns Hopkins Univ

Celano, Paul MD [Onc] - **Spec Exp:** Gynecologic Cancer; Genitourinary Cancer; Breast Cancer; Clinical Trials; **Hospital:** Greater Baltimore Med Ctr, Johns Hopkins Hosp (page 59); **Address:** Sandra & Malcolm Berman Cancer Inst, 6569 N Charles St, Ste 205, Baltimore, MD 21204; **Phone:** 443-849-3051; **Board Cert:** Internal Medicine 1984; Medical Oncology 1987; **Med School:** Mount Sinai Sch Med 1981; **Resid:** Internal Medicine, Thos Jefferson Univ Hosp 1984; **Fellow:** Medical Oncology, Johns Hopkins Hosp 1987; **Fac Appt:** Asst Prof Onc, Johns Hopkins Univ

Chachoua, Abraham MD [Onc] - **Spec Exp:** Lung Cancer; Thoracic Cancers; Solid Tumors; **Hospital:** NYU Langone Med Ctr (page 68); **Address:** NYU Clinical Cancer Ctr, 160 E 34th St Fl 2, New York, NY 10016; **Phone:** 212-731-5388; **Med School:** Australia 1978; **Resid:** Internal Medicine, Alfred Hosp 1982; **Fellow:** Hematology & Oncology, Alfred Hosp 1985; Hematology & Oncology, NYU Med Ctr 1988; **Fac Appt:** Assoc Prof Med, NYU Sch Med

Chapman, Paul B MD [Onc] - **Spec Exp:** Melanoma; Immunotherapy; Clinical Trials; Vaccine Therapy; **Hospital:** Meml Sloan-Kettering Canc Ctr; **Address:** 300 E 66th St, New York, NY 10065; **Phone:** 646-888-4162; **Board Cert:** Internal Medicine 1984; Medical Oncology 1987; **Med School:** Cornell Univ-Weill Med Coll 1981; **Resid:** Internal Medicine, Univ Chicago Hosps 1984; **Fellow:** Medical Oncology, Meml Sloan-Kettering Cancer Ctr 1987; **Fac Appt:** Prof Med, Cornell Univ-Weill Med Coll

Chu, Edward MD [Onc] - **Spec Exp:** Colon & Rectal Cancer; Gastrointestinal Cancer; Clinical Trials; **Hospital:** UPMC Shadyside, UPMC Presby, Pittsburgh; **Address:** Univ of Pittsburgh Cancer Institute, 5150 Centre Ave, Fl Fifth, rm 571, Univ of Pittsburgh Cancer Institute, Pittsburgh, PA 15232; **Phone:** 412-648-6589; **Board Cert:** Internal Medicine 1986; Medical Oncology 1989; **Med School:** Brown Univ 1983; **Resid:** Internal Medicine, Roger Williams Hosp 1987; **Fellow:** Medical Oncology, Natl Cancer Inst 1992; **Fac Appt:** Prof Onc, Univ Pittsburgh

Claxton, David F MD [Onc] - **Spec Exp:** Leukemia; Bone Marrow Transplant; Hematologic Malignancies; Anemia-Aplastic; **Hospital:** Penn State Milton S Hershey Med Ctr; **Address:** 500 University Drive, rm T4422, Hershey, PA 17033; **Phone:** 717-531-8678; **Board Cert:** Internal Medicine 1984; Medical Oncology 2004; **Med School:** McGill Univ 1978; **Resid:** Internal Medicine, Royal Victoria Hosp 1984; **Fellow:** Hematology, Royal Victoria Hosp 1986; Medical Oncology, UT-MD Anderson Cancer Ctr 1989

Cohen, Gary I MD [Onc] - **Spec Exp:** Hematologic Malignancies; Stem Cell Transplant; Melanoma; Breast Cancer; **Hospital:** Greater Baltimore Med Ctr; **Address:** GBMC-Sandra & Malcolm Berman Cancer Inst, 6569 N Charles St, Ste 201, Baltimore, MD 21204; **Phone:** 443-849-3051; **Board Cert:** Internal Medicine 1978; Hematology 1982; Medical Oncology 1985; **Med School:** Univ MD Sch Med 1975; **Resid:** Internal Medicine, SUNY Buffalo Genl Hosp 1978; **Fellow:** Hematology & Oncology, VA Medical Ctr 1981

Cohen, Philip MD [Onc] - **Spec Exp:** Breast Cancer; **Hospital:** MedStar Georgetown Univ Hosp; **Address:** Lombardi Cancer Ctr, 3800 Reservoir Rd NW, Washington, DC 20007; **Phone:** 202-444-2198; **Board Cert:** Internal Medicine 1973; Medical Oncology 1975; Hematology 1976; **Med School:** Harvard Med Sch 1970; **Resid:** Internal Medicine, Mass Genl Hosp 1973; **Fellow:** Hematology & Oncology, Natl Cancer Inst 1976; **Fac Appt:** Assoc Prof Med, Geo Wash Univ

Cohen, Roger B MD [Onc] - **Spec Exp:** Head & Neck Cancer; Lung Cancer; Drug Discovery & Development; Clinical Trials; **Hospital:** Hosp Univ Penn - UPHS (page 69); **Address:** Perelman Ctr for Advanced Medicine, 3400 Civic Center Blvd, 2 West, Philadelphia, PA 19104; **Phone:** 215-662-4469; **Board Cert:** Internal Medicine 1984; Hematology 1986; Medical Oncology 2005; **Med School:** Harvard Med Sch 1980; **Resid:** Internal Medicine, Mt Sinai Hosp 1982; Hematology, Mt Sinai Hosp 1986; **Fellow:** Research, Sloan Kettering Canc Inst 1985; Medical Oncology, Natl Canc Inst 1993; **Fac Appt:** Prof Med, Univ Pennsylvania

Cohen, Seymour M MD [Onc] - **Spec Exp:** Breast Cancer; Melanoma; Lung Cancer; Lymphoma; **Hospital:** Mt Sinai Med Ctr (page 62); **Address:** 1150 5th Ave, New York, NY 10128; **Phone:** 212-249-9141; **Board Cert:** Internal Medicine 1971; Medical Oncology 1973; **Med School:** Univ Pittsburgh 1962; **Resid:** Internal Medicine, Montefiore Med Ctr 1964; Internal Medicine, Mount Sinai Med Ctr 1965; **Fellow:** Hematology, Mount Sinai Med Ctr 1966; Hematology & Oncology, LI Jewish Hosp 1969; **Fac Appt:** Assoc Clin Prof Onc, Mount Sinai Sch Med

Coleman, Morton MD [Onc] - **Spec Exp:** Leukemia & Lymphoma; Hodgkin's Lymphoma; Multiple Myeloma; Waldenstrom's Macroglobulinemia; **Hospital:** NY-Presby/Weill Cornell Med Ctr, NY (page 65); **Address:** 407 E 70th St, Fl 3, New York, NY 10021-5302; **Phone:** 212-517-5900; **Board Cert:** Internal Medicine 1971; Hematology 1972; Medical Oncology 1973; **Med School:** Med Coll VA 1963; **Resid:** Internal Medicine, Grady Meml Hosp-Emory 1965; Internal Medicine, NY-Presby/Cornell Univ Med Ctr 1968; **Fellow:** Hematology & Oncology, NY-Presby/Cornell Univ Med Ctr 1970; **Fac Appt:** Clin Prof Hem & Onc, Cornell Univ-Weill Med Coll

Cristofanilli, Massimo MD [Onc] - **Spec Exp:** Breast Cancer; Breast Cancer-Inflammatory; **Hospital:** Thomas Jefferson Univ Hosp; **Address:** Jefferson University Hospital, 925 Chestnut St, Ste 320A, Philadelphia, PA 19107; **Phone:** 215-955-8874; **Board Cert:** Medical Oncology 2010; **Med School:** Italy 1986; **Resid:** Internal Medicine, Cabrini Med Ctr 1996; **Fellow:** Medical Oncology, MD Anderson Cancer Ctr 1998; **Fac Appt:** Prof Med, Univ Pennsylvania

Cullen, Kevin MD [Onc] - **Spec Exp:** Head & Neck Cancer; **Hospital:** Univ of MD Med Ctr; **Address:** Greenebaum Cancer Ctr, 22 S Greene St, rm N9E22, Baltimore, MD 21201; **Phone:** 410-328-5506; **Board Cert:** Internal Medicine 1986; Medical Oncology 1989; **Med School:** Harvard Med Sch 1983; **Resid:** Internal Medicine, Beth Israel Hosp 1986; Internal Medicine, Hammersmith Hosp 1985; **Fellow:** Medical Oncology, Natl Cancer Inst 1988

Czuczman, Myron S MD [Onc] - **Spec Exp:** Hodgkin's Lymphoma; Multiple Myeloma; Leukemia-Chronic Lymphocytic; Clinical Trials; **Hospital:** Roswell Park Canc Inst, Buffalo Genl Hosp; **Address:** Roswell Park Cancer Institute, Elm & Carlton Sreets, Buffalo, NY 14263; **Phone:** 716-845-1643; **Board Cert:** Internal Medicine 1988; **Med School:** Penn State Coll Med 1985; **Resid:** Internal Medicine, North Shore Univ Hosp 1988; **Fellow:** Hematology & Oncology, Meml Sloan-Kettering Cancer Ctr 1991; **Fac Appt:** Prof Med, SUNY Buffalo

Daly, Mary B MD/PhD [Onc] - **Spec Exp:** Breast Cancer; Breast Cancer Risk Assessment; Cancer Prevention; Cancer Genetics; **Hospital:** Fox Chase Cancer Ctr (page 57); **Address:** Fox Chase Cancer Ctr, 333 Cottman Ave, Philadelphia, PA 19111; **Phone:** 215-728-2791; **Board Cert:** Internal Medicine 1981; Medical Oncology 1983; **Med School:** Univ NC Sch Med 1978; **Resid:** Internal Medicine, Univ TX Hlth Sci Ctr 1981; **Fellow:** Medical Oncology, Univ TX Hlth Sci Ctr 1983; **Fac Appt:** Prof Med, Temple Univ

Dawson, Nancy MD [Onc] - **Spec Exp:** Prostate Cancer; Kidney Cancer; Bladder Cancer; **Hospital:** MedStar Georgetown Univ Hosp; **Address:** Lombardi Cancer Ctr, 3800 Reservoir Rd NW, Washington, DC 20007; **Phone:** 202-444-9094; **Board Cert:** Internal Medicine 1982; Hematology 1984; Medical Oncology 1985; **Med School:** Georgetown Univ 1979; **Resid:** Internal Medicine, Walter Reed AMC 1982; **Fellow:** Hematology & Oncology, Walter Reed AMC 1985; **Fac Appt:** Prof Med, Georgetown Univ

Dickler, Maura N MD [Onc] - **Spec Exp:** Breast Cancer; Clinical Trials; **Hospital:** Meml Sloan-Kettering Canc Ctr; **Address:** 300 E 66th St, New York, NY 10065; **Phone:** 646-888-5456; **Board Cert:** Medical Oncology 2008; **Med School:** Univ Chicago-Pritzker Sch Med 1991; **Resid:** Internal Medicine, Univ Chicago Hosps 1994; **Fellow:** Medical Oncology, Meml Sloan Kettering Cancer Ctr 1998; **Fac Appt:** Assoc Prof Med, Cornell Univ-Weill Med Coll

DiPaola, Robert S MD [Onc] - **Spec Exp:** Genitourinary Cancer; Prostate Cancer; Urologic Cancer; **Hospital:** Robert Wood Johnson Univ Hosp - New Brunswick; **Address:** Cancer Inst of New Jersey, 195 Little Albany St, New Brunswick, NJ 08903-2681; **Phone:** 732-235-3336; **Board Cert:** Internal Medicine 2011; Medical Oncology 2005; **Med School:** Univ Utah 1988; **Resid:** Internal Medicine, Duke Univ Med Ctr 1991; **Fellow:** Hematology & Oncology, Univ Penn Hosp 1994; **Fac Appt:** Assoc Prof Med, UMDNJ-RW Johnson Med Sch

Domchek, Susan M MD [Onc] - **Spec Exp:** Breast Cancer; Breast Cancer Genetics; Breast Cancer Risk Assessment; **Hospital:** Hosp Univ Penn - UPHS (page 69); **Address:** Abramson Cancer Ctr, Perelman Ctr, 3 West, 3400 Civic Center Blvd, Philadelphia, PA 19104; **Phone:** 215-615-3360; **Board Cert:** Medical Oncology 2011; **Med School:** Harvard Med Sch 1995; **Resid:** Internal Medicine, Mass Genl Hosp 1998; **Fellow:** Medical Oncology, Dana Farber Cancer Inst 2001; **Fac Appt:** Assoc Prof Med, Univ Pennsylvania

Donehower, Ross Carl MD [Onc] - **Spec Exp:** Pancreatic Cancer; Colon Cancer; Prostate Cancer; **Hospital:** Johns Hopkins Hosp (page 59); **Address:** Johns Hopkins Hosp, Sidney Kimmel Comp Cancer Ctr, 410 N Broadway, Ste 1343, Baltimore, MD 21231; **Phone:** 410-955-8964; **Board Cert:** Internal Medicine 1977; Medical Oncology 1979; **Med School:** Univ Minn 1974; **Resid:** Internal Medicine, Johns Hopkins Hosp 1976; **Fellow:** Medical Oncology, Natl Inst Hlth 1980; **Fac Appt:** Prof Med, Johns Hopkins Univ

Doroshow, James H MD [Onc] - **Spec Exp:** Drug Discovery & Development; Colon Cancer; Breast Cancer; **Hospital:** Natl Inst of Hlth - Clin Ctr; **Address:** National Cancer Inst, Div Cancer Treatment & Diagnosis, 31 Center Dr, Bldg 31-rm 3A44, Bethesda, MD 20892-2440; **Phone:** 301-496-4291; **Board Cert:** Internal Medicine 1976; Medical Oncology 1977; **Med School:** Harvard Med Sch 1973; **Resid:** Internal Medicine, Mass Genl Hosp 1975; **Fellow:** Medical Oncology, Natl Cancer Inst 1978

Eisenberger, Mario MD [Onc] - **Spec Exp:** Prostate Cancer; **Hospital:** Johns Hopkins Hosp (page 59); **Address:** Johns Hopkins Hosp, Sidney Kimmel Comp Cancer Ctr, 410 N Broadway, Ste 1343, Baltimore, MD 21231; **Phone:** 410-614-3511; **Board Cert:** Internal Medicine 1976; Medical Oncology 1979; **Med School:** Brazil 1972; **Resid:** Internal Medicine, Michael Reese Hosp 1975; **Fellow:** Hematology, Michael Reese Hosp 1976; Medical Oncology, Jackson Meml Hosp/Univ Miami 1979; **Fac Appt:** Prof Med, Johns Hopkins Univ

Emens, Leisha A MD/PhD [Onc] - **Spec Exp:** Breast Cancer; Immunotherapy; **Hospital:** Johns Hopkins Hosp (page 59); **Address:** Johns Hopkins Hosp, Sidney Kimmel Comp Cancer Ctr, 410 N Broadway, Ste 1343, Baltimore, MD 21231; **Phone:** 410-955-8964; **Board Cert:** Internal Medicine 2008; Medical Oncology 2011; Hematology 2002; **Med School:** Baylor Coll Med 1995; **Resid:** Internal Medicine, Univ Tex Southwestern Med Ctr 1998; **Fellow:** Medical Oncology, Johns Hopkins Hosp 2001; Research, Natl Cancer Inst 1993; **Fac Appt:** Assoc Prof Onc, Johns Hopkins Univ

Engstrom, Paul F MD [Onc] - **Spec Exp:** Neuroendocrine Tumors; Gastrointestinal Cancer; Colon & Rectal Cancer; **Hospital:** Fox Chase Cancer Ctr (page 57); **Address:** Fox Chase Cancer Ctr, Medical Oncology, 333 Cottman Ave, Philadelphia, PA 19111; **Phone:** 215-728-2986; **Board Cert:** Internal Medicine 1969; Medical Oncology 1973; **Med School:** Univ Minn 1962; **Resid:** Internal Medicine, Univ Minn Hosp 1965; **Fac Appt:** Prof Med, Temple Univ

Ettinger, David S MD [Onc] - **Spec Exp:** Lung Cancer; Sarcoma; Clinical Trials; **Hospital:** Johns Hopkins Hosp (page 59); **Address:** Bunting Blaustein Cancer Rsch Bldg, 1650 Orleans St, rm G88, Baltimore, MD 21287-0013; **Phone:** 410-955-8847; **Board Cert:** Internal Medicine 1976; Medical Oncology 1977; **Med School:** Univ Louisville Sch Med 1967; **Resid:** Internal Medicine, Mayo Clin 1971; **Fellow:** Medical Oncology, Johns Hopkins Hosp 1975; **Fac Appt:** Prof Onc, Johns Hopkins Univ

Fine, Howard A MD [Onc] - **Spec Exp:** Brain Tumors; Neuro-Oncology; **Hospital:** NYU Langone Med Ctr (page 68); **Address:** NYU Cancer Institute, 160 E 34th St, New York, NY 10016; **Phone:** 212-731-5089; **Board Cert:** Internal Medicine 1987; Medical Oncology 1989; **Med School:** Mount Sinai Sch Med 1984; **Resid:** Internal Medicine, Hosp Univ Penn 1987; **Fellow:** Medical Oncology, Dana Farber Cancer Ctr 1989; **Fac Appt:** Prof Onc, NYU Sch Med

Fine, Robert Lance MD [Onc] - **Spec Exp:** Pancreatic Cancer; Drug Development; Pituitary Tumors; Clinical Trials; **Hospital:** NY-Presby/Columbia Univ Med Ctr, NY (page 65); **Address:** 650 W 168th St Black Bldg, Fl 20 - Ste 20-05, New York, NY 10032; **Phone:** 212-305-1168; **Board Cert:** Internal Medicine 1983; Medical Oncology 1985; **Med School:** Univ Chicago-Pritzker Sch Med 1979; **Resid:** Internal Medicine, Stanford Univ Med Ctr 1982; **Fellow:** Medical Oncology, National Cancer Inst 1985; **Fac Appt:** Assoc Prof Med, Columbia P&S

Fisher, Richard I MD [Onc] - **Spec Exp:** Lymphoma; Hodgkin's Lymphoma; **Hospital:** Fox Chase Cancer Ctr (page 57); **Address:** 333 Cottman Ave, Philadelphia, PA 19111; **Phone:** 215-728-2625; **Board Cert:** Internal Medicine 1973; Medical Oncology 1977; **Med School:** Harvard Med Sch 1970; **Resid:** Internal Medicine, Mass Genl Hosp 1972; **Fac Appt:** Prof Onc, Temple Univ

Flomenberg, Neal MD [Onc] - **Spec Exp:** Bone Marrow Transplant; Stem Cell Transplant; Leukemia & Lymphoma; Hematologic Malignancies; **Hospital:** Thomas Jefferson Univ Hosp; **Address:** Jefferson Dept Medical Oncology, 925 Chestnut St Fl 3, Philadelphia, PA 19107; **Phone:** 215-955-8874; **Board Cert:** Internal Medicine 1979; Medical Oncology 1981; Hematology 1982; **Med School:** Jefferson Med Coll 1976; **Resid:** Internal Medicine, Montefiore Med Ctr 1979; **Fellow:** Hematology & Oncology, Meml Sloan Kettering Cancer Ctr 1982; **Fac Appt:** Prof Med, Thomas Jefferson Univ

Forastiere, Arlene A MD [Onc] - **Spec Exp:** Esophageal Cancer; Head & Neck Cancer; **Hospital:** Johns Hopkins Hosp (page 59); **Address:** Johns Hopkins Hosp, Sidney Kimmel Comp Cancer Ctr, 410 N Broadway, Ste 1343, Baltimore, MD 21231; **Phone:** 410-955-8964; **Board Cert:** Internal Medicine 1978; Medical Oncology 1981; **Med School:** NY Med Coll 1975; **Resid:** Internal Medicine, Albert Einstein Med Ctr 1977; Internal Medicine, Univ Conn Hlth Ctr 1978; **Fellow:** Medical Oncology, Meml Sloan-Kettering Cancer Ctr 1980; **Fac Appt:** Prof Med, NY Med Coll

Fox, Kevin R MD [Onc] - **Spec Exp:** Breast Cancer; **Hospital:** Hosp Univ Penn - UPHS (page 69); **Address:** Abramson Cancer Ctr, Perelman Ctr for Advanced Medicine, 3400 Civic Center Blvd, 3 West, Philadelphia, PA 19104; **Phone:** 215-662-7469; **Board Cert:** Internal Medicine 1985; Medical Oncology 1987; **Med School:** Johns Hopkins Univ 1981; **Resid:** Internal Medicine, Johns Hopkins Hosp 1984; **Fellow:** Hematology & Oncology, Hosp Univ Penn 1987; **Fac Appt:** Prof Med, Univ Pennsylvania

Friedberg, Jonathan W MD [Onc] - **Spec Exp:** Lymphoma; Hodgkin's Lymphoma; Clinical Trials; **Hospital:** Univ Rochester Strong Meml Hosp; **Address:** James P Wilmot Cancer Ctr, 601 Elmwood Ave, Box 704, Rochester, NY 14642-8704; **Phone:** 585-275-5823; **Board Cert:** Hematology 2010; **Med School:** Harvard Med Sch 1994; **Resid:** Internal Medicine, Mass Genl Hosp 1997; **Fellow:** Hematology & Oncology, Dana Farber/Partners Cancer Ctr 1999; **Fac Appt:** Prof Med, Univ Rochester

Gabrilove, Janice L MD [Onc] - **Spec Exp:** Myelodysplastic Syndromes; Leukemia; Hematologic Malignancies; Myeloproliferative Disorders; **Hospital:** Mt Sinai Med Ctr (page 62); **Address:** Mount Sinai Med Ctr-Dept Hem/Onc, One Gustave L Levy Pl, Box 1079, New York, NY 10029-6574; **Phone:** 212-241-9650; **Board Cert:** Internal Medicine 1980; Medical Oncology 1983; **Med School:** Mount Sinai Sch Med 1977; **Resid:** Internal Medicine, Columbia-Presby Med Ctr 1980; **Fellow:** Hematology & Oncology, Meml Sloan-Kettering Cancer Ctr 1983; **Fac Appt:** Prof Med, Mount Sinai Sch Med

Gelmann, Edward P MD [Onc] - **Spec Exp:** Prostate Cancer; Bladder Cancer; Kidney Cancer; **Hospital:** NY-Presby/Columbia Univ Med Ctr, NY (page 65); **Address:** Columbia Univ Med Ctr, Milstein Hosp Bldg 6-435, 177 Fort Washington Ave, New York, NY 10032; **Phone:** 212-305-8610; **Board Cert:** Internal Medicine 1979; Medical Oncology 1981; **Med School:** Stanford Univ 1976; **Resid:** Internal Medicine, Univ Chicago Hosps 1979; **Fellow:** Medical Oncology, National Cancer Inst 1981; **Fac Appt:** Prof Med, Columbia P&S

Glick, John H MD [Onc] - **Spec Exp:** Breast Cancer; Hodgkin's Lymphoma; Lymphoma, Non-Hodgkin's; **Hospital:** Hosp Univ Penn - UPHS (page 69); **Address:** Abramson Cancer Ctr, Perelman Ctr for Advanced Medicine, 3400 Civic Center Blvd, 3 South, Philadelphia, PA 19104; **Phone:** 215-662-6065; **Board Cert:** Internal Medicine 1973; Medical Oncology 1975; **Med School:** Columbia P&S 1969; **Resid:** Internal Medicine, Presbyterian Hosp 1971; **Fellow:** Medical Oncology, Natl Cancer Inst 1973; Medical Oncology, Stanford Univ 1974; **Fac Appt:** Prof Onc, Univ Pennsylvania

Goldstein, Lori J MD [Onc] - **Spec Exp:** Breast Cancer; Breast Cancer-Novel Therapies; **Hospital:** Fox Chase Cancer Ctr (page 57); **Address:** Fox Chase Cancer Ctr, Dept Med Oncology, 333 Cottman Ave, Philadelphia, PA 19111; **Phone:** 215-728-2689; **Board Cert:** Internal Medicine 1985; Medical Oncology 2012; **Med School:** SUNY Upstate Med Univ 1982; **Resid:** Internal Medicine, Presby Univ Hosp 1985; **Fellow:** Medical Oncology, Natl Cancer Inst/NIH 1990; **Fac Appt:** Prof Med, Temple Univ

Goy, Andre MD [Onc] - **Spec Exp:** Lymphoma; Hodgkin's Lymphoma; **Hospital:** Hackensack Univ Med Ctr; **Address:** 92 2nd St, Hackensack, NJ 07601; **Phone:** 201-996-5900; **Med School:** France 1988; **Resid:** Internal Medicine, Grenoble Univ Med Ctr 1992; **Fellow:** Hematology & Oncology, Grenoble Univ Med Ctr 1993

Grana, Generosa MD [Onc] - **Spec Exp:** Breast Cancer; Cancer Genetics; Cancer Prevention; **Hospital:** Cooper Univ Hosp, Lourdes Med Ctr of Burlington Co; **Address:** 900 Centennial Blvd, Ste M, Voorhees, NJ 08043; **Phone:** 856-325-6750; **Board Cert:** Internal Medicine 1988; Medical Oncology 2011; **Med School:** Northwestern Univ 1985; **Resid:** Internal Medicine, Temple Univ Hosp 1988; **Fellow:** Hematology & Oncology, Fox Chase Cancer Ctr 1992; **Fac Appt:** Assoc Prof Med, UMDNJ-RW Johnson Med Sch

Grossbard, Michael L MD [Onc] - **Spec Exp:** Lymphoma; Gastrointestinal Cancer; Breast Cancer; **Hospital:** St. Luke's - Roosevelt Hosp Ctr - Roosevelt Div (page 56), Beth Israel Med Ctr - Petrie Div (page 56); **Address:** 1000 10th Ave, Fl 11, Ste C02, St Luke's-Roosevelt Hospital, New York, NY 10019; **Phone:** 212-523-5419; **Board Cert:** Internal Medicine 1989; Medical Oncology 2011; **Med School:** Yale Univ 1986; **Resid:** Internal Medicine, Mass Genl Hosp 1989; **Fellow:** Medical Oncology, Dana Farber Cancer Inst 1991; **Fac Appt:** Clin Prof Hem & Onc, Columbia P&S

Grossman, Stuart MD [Onc] - **Spec Exp:** Brain Tumors; Neuro-Oncology; Pain-Cancer; **Hospital:** Johns Hopkins Hosp (page 59); **Address:** David Koch Cancer Rsch Bldg, 1550 Orleans St, Ste 1-M16, Baltimore, MD 21287; **Phone:** 410-955-8964; **Board Cert:** Internal Medicine 1976; Medical Oncology 1983; **Med School:** Univ Rochester 1973; **Resid:** Internal Medicine, Strong Meml Hosp 1976; **Fellow:** Medical Oncology, Johns Hopkins Hosp 1981; **Fac Appt:** Prof Med, Johns Hopkins Univ

Gulley, James L MD/PhD [Onc] - **Spec Exp:** Prostate Cancer-Vaccine Therapy; Vaccine Therapy-Clinical Trials Only; Clinical Trials Only; **Hospital:** Natl Inst of Hlth - Clin Ctr; **Address:** NIH Center for Cancer Research, 10 Center Drive, MSC 1750, Bldg 10-rm 13N208, Bethesda, MD 20892; **Phone:** 301-435-2956; **Board Cert:** Medical Oncology 2010; **Med School:** Loma Linda Univ 1995; **Resid:** Internal Medicine, Emory Univ Med Ctr 1998; **Fellow:** Medical Oncology, Natl Cancer Inst-NIH 2000

Haas, Naomi S Balzer MD [Onc] - **Spec Exp:** Genitourinary Cancer; Kidney Cancer; Clinical Trials; Prostate Cancer; **Hospital:** Hosp Univ Penn - UPHS (page 69); **Address:** Penn Hematology/Oncology, 3400 Spruce St, Philadelphia, PA 19104; **Phone:** 215-662-7402; **Board Cert:** Internal Medicine 1988; Medical Oncology 2005; **Med School:** NE Ohio Univ 1985; **Resid:** Internal Medicine, Abington Meml Hosp 1988; **Fellow:** Hematology & Oncology, Fox Chase Cancer Ctr 1989; **Fac Appt:** Assoc Prof Med, Univ Pennsylvania

Hageboutros, Alexandre MD [Onc] - **Spec Exp:** Gastrointestinal Cancer; Lung Cancer; Colon & Rectal Cancer; **Hospital:** Cooper Univ Hosp; **Address:** 900 Centennial Blvd, Ste M, Voorhees, NJ 08043-4689; **Phone:** 856-325-6750; **Board Cert:** Hematology 2004; Medical Oncology 2005; **Med School:** Lebanon 1987; **Resid:** Internal Medicine, Cooper Hosp 1991; **Fellow:** Hematology & Oncology, Temple Univ Hosp 1992; Hematology & Oncology, Fox Chase Cancer Ctr 1994; **Fac Appt:** Assoc Prof Med, UMDNJ-NJ Med Sch, Newark

Henry, David H MD [Onc] - **Spec Exp:** AIDS Related Cancers; **Hospital:** Pennsylvania Hosp-UPHS (page 69); **Address:** 230 W Washington Square Fl 2, Philadelphia, PA 19106; **Phone:** 215-829-6088; **Board Cert:** Internal Medicine 1978; Hematology 1980; Medical Oncology 1981; **Med School:** Univ Pennsylvania 1975; **Resid:** Internal Medicine, Hosp Univ Penn 1978; **Fellow:** Hematology & Oncology, Hosp Univ Penn 1978; **Fac Appt:** Clin Prof Med, Univ Pennsylvania

Himelstein, Andrew L MD [Onc] - **Spec Exp:** Leukemia & Lymphoma; Palliative Care; **Hospital:** Christiana Hosp; **Address:** Medical Onc/Hem Consultants, 4701 Ogletown-Stanton Rd, Ste West 3400, Helen Graham Cancer Ctr, Newark, DE 19713; **Phone:** 302-366-1200; **Board Cert:** Internal Medicine 1988; Hematology 2010; Medical Oncology 2011; Hospice & Palliative Medicine 2010; **Med School:** Washington Univ, St Louis 1985; **Resid:** Internal Medicine, Mt Sinai Hosp 1988; **Fellow:** Hematology & Oncology, Colum-Presby Univ Hosp 1991; **Fac Appt:** Asst Clin Prof Onc, Thomas Jefferson Univ

Hogan, Thomas F MD [Onc] - **Spec Exp:** Urologic Cancer; Kidney Cancer; Genitourinary Cancer; **Hospital:** Ruby Memorial - WVU Hosp; **Address:** Mary Babb Randolph Cancer Ctr, One Medical Ctr Drive, Morgantown, WV 26506-8110; **Phone:** 304-598-4552; **Board Cert:** Internal Medicine 1975; Medical Oncology 1977; Anatomic Pathology 1997; **Med School:** Med Coll VA 1972; **Resid:** Internal Medicine, Thomas Jefferson Univ Hosp 1975; **Fellow:** Medical Oncology, Univ Wisconsin Affil Hosp 1977; **Fac Appt:** Prof Med, W VA Univ

Holcombe, Randall F MD [Onc] - **Spec Exp:** Gastrointestinal Cancer; Liver Cancer; Clinical Trials; Pancreatic Cancer; **Hospital:** Mt Sinai Med Ctr (page 62); **Address:** The Ruttenberg Treatment Ctr, 1470 Madison Ave, New York, NY 10029; **Phone:** 212-241-6756; **Board Cert:** Internal Medicine 1986; Medical Oncology 2003; Hematology 2012; **Med School:** UMDNJ-NJ Med Sch, Newark 1983; **Resid:** Internal Medicine, Brigham & Womens Hosp 1986; **Fellow:** Hematology, Brigham & Women's Hosp 1989; Medical Oncology, Brigham & Women's Hosp 1989; **Fac Appt:** Prof Onc, Mount Sinai Sch Med

Holland, James F MD [Onc] - **Spec Exp:** Breast Cancer; Pancreatic Cancer; **Hospital:** Mt Sinai Med Ctr (page 62); **Address:** Mount Sinai Med Ctr, 1 Gustave Levy Pl, Box 1079, New York, NY 10029; **Phone:** 212-241-4495; **Board Cert:** Internal Medicine 1955; **Med School:** Columbia P&S 1947; **Resid:** Internal Medicine, Columbia-Presby Hosp 1949; Internal Medicine, Francis Delafield Hosp 1952; **Fellow:** Medical Oncology, Francis Delafield Hosp 1953; **Fac Appt:** Prof Med, Mount Sinai Sch Med

Horwitz, Steven M MD [Onc] - **Spec Exp:** Cutaneous T-cell Lymphoma; Hodgkin's Lymphoma; Lymphoma, Non-Hodgkin's; Clinical Trials; **Hospital:** Meml Sloan-Kettering Canc Ctr; **Address:** Meml Sloan-Kettering Cancer Ctr, 1275 York Ave, New York, NY 10065; **Phone:** 212-639-3045; **Board Cert:** Medical Oncology 2011; **Med School:** Case West Res Univ 1993; **Resid:** Internal Medicine, Strong Memorial Hosp 1996; **Fellow:** Medical Oncology, Stanford Univ Med Ctr 1999

Hudis, Clifford A MD [Onc] - **Spec Exp:** Breast Cancer; **Hospital:** Meml Sloan-Kettering Canc Ctr; **Address:** 300 E 66th St, BAIC Bldg, New York, NY 10065; **Phone:** 646-888-5449; **Board Cert:** Internal Medicine 1986; Medical Oncology 2011; **Med School:** Med Coll PA Hahnemann 1983; **Resid:** Internal Medicine, Hosp Univ Penn 1987; **Fellow:** Medical Oncology, Meml Sloan Kettering Cancer Ctr 1991; **Fac Appt:** Prof Med, Cornell Univ-Weill Med Coll

Ilson, David H MD/PhD [Onc] - **Spec Exp:** Esophageal Cancer; Colon & Rectal Cancer; Mesothelioma; Unknown Primary Cancer; **Hospital:** Meml Sloan-Kettering Canc Ctr; **Address:** 300 E 66th St, New York, NY 10065; **Phone:** 646-888-4183; **Board Cert:** Internal Medicine 1989; Medical Oncology 2012; **Med School:** NYU Sch Med 1986; **Resid:** Internal Medicine, Bellevue-NYU Sch Med 1989; **Fellow:** Medical Oncology, Meml Sloan Kettering Hosp 1992; **Fac Appt:** Assoc Prof Med, Cornell Univ-Weill Med Coll

Isaacs, Claudine J MD [Onc] - **Spec Exp:** Breast Cancer; Breast Cancer Risk Assessment; **Hospital:** MedStar Georgetown Univ Hosp; **Address:** Lombardi Comprehensive Cancer Ctr, 3800 Reservoir Road NW, Washington, DC 20007; **Phone:** 202-444-3677; **Board Cert:** Medical Oncology 2003; **Med School:** McGill Univ 1987; **Resid:** Internal Medicine, Montreal Genl Hosp 1990; Hematology & Oncology, McGill Univ Hosp 1992; **Fellow:** Medical Oncology, Georgetown Univ Med Ctr 1993; **Fac Appt:** Prof Onc, Georgetown Univ

Kelly, W Kevin DO [Onc] - **Spec Exp:** Prostate Cancer; Urologic Cancer; Solid Tumors; **Hospital:** Thomas Jefferson Univ Hosp; **Address:** 925 Chestnut St, Ste 220A, Philadelphia, PA 19107; **Phone:** 215-955-8874; **Board Cert:** Medical Oncology 2003; **Med School:** Philadelphia Coll Osteo Med 1986; **Resid:** Internal Medicine, Albert Einstein Med Ctr 1990; **Fellow:** Hematology & Oncology, Meml Sloan Kettering Cancer Ctr 1993

Kelsen, David Paul MD [Onc] - **Spec Exp:** Gastrointestinal Cancer; Neuroendocrine Tumors; Unknown Primary Cancer; Merkel Cell Carcinoma; **Hospital:** Meml Sloan-Kettering Canc Ctr; **Address:** 300 E 66th St Fl 10, New York, NY 10065; **Phone:** 646-888-4179; **Board Cert:** Internal Medicine 1976; Medical Oncology 1979; **Med School:** Hahnemann Univ 1972; **Resid:** Internal Medicine, Temple Univ Hosp 1976; **Fellow:** Medical Oncology, Meml Sloan Kettering Cancer Ctr 1978; **Fac Appt:** Prof Med, Cornell Univ-Weill Med Coll

Kemeny, Nancy E MD [Onc] - **Spec Exp:** Colon Cancer; Rectal Cancer; Liver Cancer; **Hospital:** Meml Sloan-Kettering Canc Ctr; **Address:** 300 E 66th St Fl 10, New York, NY 10065; **Phone:** 646-888-4180; **Board Cert:** Internal Medicine 1974; Medical Oncology 1981; **Med School:** UMDNJ-NJ Med Sch, Newark 1971; **Resid:** Internal Medicine, St Luke's Hosp 1974; **Fellow:** Medical Oncology, Mem Sloan Kettering Cancer Ctr 1976; **Fac Appt:** Prof Med, Cornell Univ-Weill Med Coll

Kirkwood, John M MD [Onc] - **Spec Exp:** Melanoma; Immunotherapy; **Hospital:** UPMC Shadyside, UPMC Presby, Pittsburgh; **Address:** UPMC Hillman Cancer Center, 5117 Centre Ave, Pittsburgh, PA 15213-1862; **Phone:** 412-623-7707; **Board Cert:** Internal Medicine 1976; Medical Oncology 1981; **Med School:** Yale Univ 1973; **Resid:** Internal Medicine, Yale-New Haven Hosp 1976; **Fellow:** Medical Oncology, Dana Farber Cancer Inst 1979; **Fac Appt:** Prof Med, Univ Pittsburgh

Kohn, Elise C MD [Onc] - **Spec Exp:** Ovarian Cancer; Gynecologic Cancer; Clinical Trials; **Hospital:** Natl Inst of Hlth - Clin Ctr; **Address:** NIH-Medical Oncology Branch, 9000 Rockville Pike Bldg 10 - rm 12N226, Bethesda, MD 20892; **Phone:** 301-496-9336; **Board Cert:** Internal Medicine 1986; Medical Oncology 1989; **Med School:** Univ Mich Med Sch 1983; **Resid:** Internal Medicine, Michigan Hosp & Med Ctr 1986; **Fellow:** Medical Oncology, NCI-NIH Clin Ctr 1989

Kressel, Bruce R MD [Onc] - **Spec Exp:** Lung Cancer; **Hospital:** G Washington Univ Hosp, Sibley Mem Hosp; **Address:** Washington Oncology-Hematology Center, 2141 K St NW, Ste 707, Washington, DC 20037; **Phone:** 202-293-5382; **Board Cert:** Internal Medicine 1976; Medical Oncology 1977; Hematology 1978; **Med School:** Tufts Univ 1973; **Resid:** Internal Medicine, George Washington Univ Med Ctr 1976; **Fellow:** Medical Oncology, George Washington Univ Med Ctr 1977; Hematology, George Washington Univ Med Ctr 1978; **Fac Appt:** Clin Prof Hem & Onc, Geo Wash Univ

Kris, Mark G MD [Onc] - **Spec Exp:** Lung Cancer; Mediastinal Tumors; Thymoma; Thoracic Cancers; **Hospital:** Meml Sloan-Kettering Canc Ctr; **Address:** 300 E 66th St, New York, NY 10065; **Phone:** 646-888-4197; **Board Cert:** Internal Medicine 1980; Medical Oncology 1983; **Med School:** Cornell Univ-Weill Med Coll 1977; **Resid:** Internal Medicine, New York Hosp 1980; **Fellow:** Medical Oncology, Meml Sloan Kettering Cancer Ctr 1983; **Fac Appt:** Prof Med, Cornell Univ-Weill Med Coll

Laheru, Daniel A MD [Onc] - **Spec Exp:** Pancreatic Cancer; Gastrointestinal Cancer; Vaccine Therapy; **Hospital:** Johns Hopkins Hosp (page 59); **Address:** Bunting Blaustein Cancer Rsch Bldg, 1650 Orleans St, rm 4M09, Baltimore, MD 21287-0013; **Phone:** 410-955-8974; **Board Cert:** Medical Oncology 2010; **Med School:** Baylor Coll Med 1995; **Resid:** Internal Medicine, Univ Utah Hosp & Clinics 1998; **Fellow:** Medical Oncology, Johns Hopkins Hosp 1998; **Fac Appt:** Assoc Prof Med, Johns Hopkins Univ

Langer, Corey J MD [Onc] - **Spec Exp:** Lung Cancer; Head & Neck Cancer; Mesothelioma; Thoracic Cancers; **Hospital:** Hosp Univ Penn - UPHS (page 69); **Address:** Abramson Cancer Ctr, Perelman Ctr for Advanced Medicine, 3400 Civic Center Blvd, 2 West, Philadelphia, PA 19104; **Phone:** 215-615-5121; **Board Cert:** Internal Medicine 1984; Hematology 1986; Medical Oncology 1987; **Med School:** Boston Univ 1981; **Resid:** Internal Medicine, Graduate Hosp 1984; Hematology & Oncology, Presby Hosp 1986; **Fellow:** Medical Oncology, Fox Chase Cancer Ctr 1987; **Fac Appt:** Prof Med, Univ Pennsylvania

Leighton Jr, John C MD [Onc] - **Spec Exp:** Gastrointestinal Cancer; Liver Cancer; Breast Cancer; **Hospital:** Einstein Med Ctr, Jeanes Hosp; **Address:** Albert Einstein Med Ctr, 9880 Bustleton Ave, Ste 208, Philadelphia, PA 19415; **Phone:** 215-827-1570; **Board Cert:** Internal Medicine 2012; Medical Oncology 2005; Hematology 2006; **Med School:** Temple Univ 1989; **Resid:** Internal Medicine, Albert Einstein Med Ctr 1993; **Fellow:** Hematology & Oncology, Fox Chase Cancer Ctr 1995

Levine, Ellis G MD [Onc] - **Spec Exp:** Breast Cancer; Testicular Cancer; Bladder Cancer; Prostate Cancer; **Hospital:** Roswell Park Canc Inst; **Address:** Roswell Park Cancer Institute, Elm & Carlton Streets, Buffalo, NY 14263-0001; **Phone:** 716-845-2300; **Board Cert:** Internal Medicine 1982; Medical Oncology 1985; **Med School:** Univ Pittsburgh 1979; **Resid:** Internal Medicine, Univ Minn Hosps 1982; **Fellow:** Medical Oncology, Univ Minn 1985; **Fac Appt:** Assoc Prof Med, SUNY Buffalo

Maki, Robert G MD/PhD [Onc] - **Spec Exp:** Sarcoma; Gastrointestinal Stromal Tumors; Desmoid Tumors; **Hospital:** Mt Sinai Med Ctr (page 62); **Address:** The Ruttenberg Treatment Ctr, 1470 Madison Ave, New York, NY 10029-6574; **Phone:** 212-241-6756; **Board Cert:** Internal Medicine 2005; Medical Oncology 2007; **Med School:** Cornell Univ-Weill Med Coll 1992; **Resid:** Internal Medicine, Brigham & Womens Hosp 1995; **Fellow:** Medical Oncology, Dana-Farber Cancer Inst 1998; **Fac Appt:** Prof Onc, Mount Sinai Sch Med

Marshall, John L MD [Onc] - **Spec Exp:** Gastrointestinal Cancer; Drug Development; **Hospital:** MedStar Georgetown Univ Hosp; **Address:** Lombardi Cancer Ctr, 3800 Reservoir Rd NW, Washington, DC 20007; **Phone:** 202-444-7064; **Board Cert:** Medical Oncology 2003; **Med School:** Univ Louisville Sch Med 1988; **Resid:** Internal Medicine, Georgetown Univ Hosp 1991; **Fellow:** Medical Oncology, Georgetown Univ Hosp 1993; **Fac Appt:** Assoc Prof Med, Georgetown Univ

Masters, Gregory A MD [Onc] - **Spec Exp:** Lung Cancer; Esophageal Cancer; Thoracic Cancers; **Hospital:** Christiana Hosp; **Address:** Med Oncology Hematology Consultants, 4701 Ogletown-Stanton Rd, Ste 3400, Newark, DE 19713; **Phone:** 302-366-1200; **Board Cert:** Internal Medicine 2003; Medical Oncology 2005; **Med School:** Northwestern Univ 1990; **Resid:** Internal Medicine, Hosp Univ Penn 1993; **Fellow:** Medical Oncology, Univ Chicago Med Ctr 1995; **Fac Appt:** Assoc Prof Med, Thomas Jefferson Univ

Mintzer, David M MD [Onc] - **Spec Exp:** Breast Cancer; Gastrointestinal Cancer; Head & Neck Cancer; Palliative Care; **Hospital:** Pennsylvania Hosp-UPHS (page 69); **Address:** Pennsylvania Hematology/Oncology Assocs, 230 W Washington Square, Fl 2, Philadelphia, PA 19106; **Phone:** 215-829-6088; **Board Cert:** Internal Medicine 1980; Hematology 1982; Medical Oncology 1983; Hospice & Palliative Medicine 2012; **Med School:** Jefferson Med Coll 1977; **Resid:** Internal Medicine, Pennsylvania Hosp 1980; **Fellow:** Hematology, Jefferson Univ Hosp 1982; Medical Oncology, Meml Sloan Kettering Cancer Ctr 1984; **Fac Appt:** Clin Prof Med, Univ Pennsylvania

Moore, Anne MD [Onc] - **Spec Exp:** Breast Cancer; **Hospital:** NY-Presby/Weill Cornell Med Ctr, NY (page 65); **Address:** Weill Cornell Breast Ctr, 425 E 61st St Fl 8, New York, NY 10065; **Phone:** 212-821-0550; **Board Cert:** Internal Medicine 1973; Hematology 1976; Medical Oncology 2008; **Med School:** Columbia P&S 1969; **Resid:** Internal Medicine, Cornell Univ Med Ctr 1973; **Fellow:** Medical Oncology, Rockefeller Univ 1976; **Fac Appt:** Prof Med, Cornell Univ-Weill Med Coll

Morginstin, Mark S DO [Onc] - **Spec Exp:** Hematologic Malignancies; Breast Cancer; **Hospital:** Einstein Med Ctr, Jeanes Hosp; **Address:** AEMC, Cancer Ctr, 5501 Old York Rd Fl 1, Philadelphia, PA 19141; **Phone:** 215-456-3880; **Board Cert:** Internal Medicine 2003; Medical Oncology 2008; Hematology 2009; **Med School:** UMDNJ Sch Osteo Med 1996; **Resid:** Internal Medicine, Albert Einstein Med Ctr 1999; **Fellow:** Hematology & Oncology, Univ Conn Hlth Ctr 2008

Motzer, Robert J MD [Onc] - **Spec Exp:** Kidney Cancer; Testicular Cancer; **Hospital:** Meml Sloan-Kettering Canc Ctr; **Address:** 1275 York Avenue, New York, NY 10065; **Phone:** 646-422-4312; **Board Cert:** Internal Medicine 1984; Medical Oncology 1987; **Med School:** Univ Mich Med Sch 1981; **Resid:** Internal Medicine, Meml Sloan Kettering Cancer Ctr 1984; **Fellow:** Medical Oncology, Meml Sloan Kettering Cancer Ctr 1987; **Fac Appt:** Assoc Prof Med, Cornell Univ-Weill Med Coll

Muggia, Franco M MD [Onc] - **Spec Exp:** Gynecologic Cancer; **Hospital:** NYU Langone Med Ctr (page 68); **Address:** NYU Clinical Cancer Ctr, 160 E 34th St Fl 4, New York, NY 10016; **Phone:** 212-731-5433; **Board Cert:** Internal Medicine 1968; Medical Oncology 1973; Hematology 1974; **Med School:** Cornell Univ-Weill Med Coll 1961; **Resid:** Internal Medicine, Hartford Hosp 1964; **Fellow:** Hematology & Oncology, Francis A Delafield Hosp 1967; **Fac Appt:** Prof Med, NYU Sch Med

Nanus, David M MD [Onc] - **Spec Exp:** Prostate Cancer; Bladder Cancer; Testicular Cancer; Genitourinary Cancer; **Hospital:** NY-Presby/Weill Cornell Med Ctr, NY (page 65); **Address:** NY Hosp-Cornell Med Ctr,Payson Pavillion, 525 E 68th St, Fl 3, Ste 341, New York, NY 10021; **Phone:** 646-962-2072; **Board Cert:** Internal Medicine 1985; Medical Oncology 1987; **Med School:** Univ Hlth Scis, Chicago Med Sch 1982; **Resid:** Internal Medicine, Bronx Muni Hosp 1985; **Fellow:** Medical Oncology, Meml Sloan Kettering Canc Ctr 1989; **Fac Appt:** Prof Onc, Cornell Univ-Weill Med Coll

Nissenblatt, Michael J MD [Onc] - **Spec Exp:** Breast Cancer; Colon Cancer; Lung Cancer; Hereditary Cancer; **Hospital:** Robert Wood Johnson Univ Hosp - New Brunswick, St. Peter's Univ Hosp; **Address:** Central Jersey Oncology Ctr, 1 Brier Hill Ct, East Brunswick, NJ 08816; **Phone:** 732-390-7750; **Board Cert:** Internal Medicine 1976; Medical Oncology 1979; **Med School:** Columbia P&S 1973; **Resid:** Internal Medicine, Johns Hopkins Hosp 1976; **Fellow:** Medical Oncology, Johns Hopkins Hosp 1978; **Fac Appt:** Clin Prof Onc, UMDNJ-RW Johnson Med Sch

Norton, Larry MD [Onc] - **Spec Exp:** Breast Cancer; **Hospital:** Meml Sloan-Kettering Canc Ctr; **Address:** 300 E 66th St, BAIC Bldg Fl 9 - Ste 933, New York, NY 10065; **Phone:** 646-888-5438; **Board Cert:** Internal Medicine 1975; Medical Oncology 1977; **Med School:** Columbia P&S 1972; **Resid:** Internal Medicine, Bronx Muni Hosp 1975; **Fellow:** Medical Oncology, Natl Cancer Inst 1977; **Fac Appt:** Prof Med, Cornell Univ-Weill Med Coll

O'Connor, Owen A MD/PhD [Onc] - **Spec Exp:** Hodgkin's Lymphoma; Lymphoma, Non-Hodgkin's; Drug Development; Clinical Trials; **Hospital:** NY-Presby/Columbia Univ Med Ctr, NY (page 65); **Address:** Columbia Doctors Midtown, 51 W 51st St, Ste 200, New York, NY 10019; **Phone:** 212-326-5720; **Board Cert:** Internal Medicine 2004; Medical Oncology 2005; **Med School:** UMDNJ-RW Johnson Med Sch 1994; **Resid:** Internal Medicine, NY-Presby/Weill Cornell Univ Med Ctr 1996; **Fellow:** Medical Oncology, Memorial Sloan-Kettering Cancer Ctr 2000; **Fac Appt:** Asst Clin Prof Med, Columbia P&S

O'Reilly, Eileen M MD [Onc] - **Spec Exp:** Pancreatic Cancer; Neuroendocrine Tumors; Colon & Rectal Cancer; **Hospital:** Meml Sloan-Kettering Canc Ctr, NY-Presby/Weill Cornell Med Ctr, NY (page 65); **Address:** Meml Sloan-Kettering Cancer Ctr, 300 E 66th St, rm 1021, New York, NY 10065; **Phone:** 646-888-4182; **Med School:** Ireland 1990; **Resid:** Internal Medicine, St Vincent's Hosp 1994; **Fellow:** Hematology & Oncology, St Vincent's Hosp 1995; Medical Oncology, Memorial Sloan-Kettering Cancer Ctr 1997; **Fac Appt:** Assoc Prof Onc, Cornell Univ-Weill Med Coll

Offit, Kenneth MD [Onc] - **Spec Exp:** Cancer Genetics; Breast Cancer; Lymphoma; Hodgkin's Disease Consultation; **Hospital:** Meml Sloan-Kettering Canc Ctr; **Address:** Meml Sloan-Kettering Cancer Ctr, 1275 York Ave, Box 192, New York, NY 10065; **Phone:** 646-888-4050; **Board Cert:** Internal Medicine 1985; Medical Oncology 1987; **Med School:** Harvard Med Sch 1982; **Resid:** Internal Medicine, Lenox Hill Hosp 1985; **Fellow:** Medical Oncology, Meml Sloan Kettering Cancer Ctr 1987; Hematology, Meml Sloan Kettering Cancer Ctr 1988; **Fac Appt:** Prof Med, Cornell Univ-Weill Med Coll

Oh, William K MD [Onc] - **Spec Exp:** Genitourinary Cancer; Prostate Cancer; Testicular Cancer; Adrenal Cancer; **Hospital:** Mt Sinai Med Ctr (page 62); **Address:** Ruttenberg Treatment Center, 1470 Madison Ave, New York, NY 10029; **Phone:** 212-659-5429; **Board Cert:** Medical Oncology 2009; **Med School:** NYU Sch Med 1992; **Resid:** Internal Medicine, Brigham & Womens Hosp 1995; **Fellow:** Medical Oncology, Dana-Farber Cancer Inst 1997; **Fac Appt:** Prof Onc, Mount Sinai Sch Med

Oratz, Ruth MD [Onc] - **Spec Exp:** Breast Cancer; **Hospital:** NYU Langone Med Ctr (page 68), Lenox Hill Hosp (page 66); **Address:** The Women's Oncology & Wellness Practice, 345 E 37th St, Ste 202, New York, NY 10016; **Phone:** 212-400-4904; **Board Cert:** Internal Medicine 1985; Medical Oncology 1989; **Med School:** Albert Einstein Coll Med 1982; **Resid:** Internal Medicine, Bellevue Hosp 1985; **Fellow:** Medical Oncology, Bellevue Hosp 1988; **Fac Appt:** Assoc Clin Prof Med, NYU Sch Med

Oster, Martin W MD [Onc] - **Spec Exp:** Breast Cancer; Gastrointestinal Cancer; Head & Neck Cancer; Lung Cancer; **Hospital:** NY-Presby/Columbia Univ Med Ctr, NY (page 65); **Address:** NY Presby Hosp-Columbia University Med Ctr, 161 Fort Washington Ave, New York, NY 10032-3713; **Phone:** 212-305-8231; **Board Cert:** Internal Medicine 1974; Medical Oncology 1975; **Med School:** Columbia P&S 1971; **Resid:** Internal Medicine, Mass Genl Hosp 1973; **Fellow:** Medical Oncology, Natl Cancer Inst/NIH 1976; **Fac Appt:** Assoc Clin Prof Onc, Columbia P&S

Parnes, Howard L MD [Onc] - **Spec Exp:** Cancer Prevention; Prostate Cancer; Bladder Cancer; **Hospital:** Natl Inst of Hlth - Clin Ctr; **Address:** NCI Div of Cancer Prevention, 9609 Medical Center Drive, Rockville, MD 20850; **Phone:** 240-276-7045; **Board Cert:** Internal Medicine 1984; Medical Oncology 1987; **Med School:** UMDNJ-NJ Med Sch, Newark 1981; **Resid:** Internal Medicine, Baltimore City Hosps 1984; **Fellow:** Medical Oncology, Univ MD Cancer Ctr 1987

Pasmantier, Mark W MD [Onc] - **Spec Exp:** Lung Cancer; Ovarian Cancer; Breast Cancer; Lymphoma; **Hospital:** NY-Presby/Weill Cornell Med Ctr, NY (page 65); **Address:** 407 E 70th St, Fl 3, New York, NY 10021-5302; **Phone:** 212-517-5900; **Board Cert:** Internal Medicine 1972; Hematology 1974; Medical Oncology 1975; **Med School:** NYU Sch Med 1966; **Resid:** Internal Medicine, Harlem Hosp 1970; **Fellow:** Hematology, Montefiore Med Ctr 1971; Medical Oncology, NY Hosp 1972; **Fac Appt:** Clin Prof Med, Cornell Univ-Weill Med Coll

Pavlick, Anna C DO [Onc] - **Spec Exp:** Melanoma; Skin Cancer; Sarcoma; **Hospital:** NYU Langone Med Ctr (page 68), Bellevue Hosp Ctr; **Address:** NYU Cancer Inst, 160 E 34th St Fl 9, New York, NY 10016; **Phone:** 212-731-5431; **Board Cert:** Medical Oncology 2008; **Med School:** UMDNJ Sch Osteo Med 1990; **Resid:** Internal Medicine, Hackensack Med Ctr 1993; **Fellow:** Hematology & Oncology, Meml Sloan Kettering Cancer Ctr 1996; **Fac Appt:** Assoc Prof Med, NYU Sch Med

Pecora, Andrew L MD [Onc] - **Spec Exp:** Stem Cell Transplant; Myelodysplastic Syndromes; Melanoma; Immunotherapy; **Hospital:** Hackensack Univ Med Ctr; **Address:** 92 2nd St, Hackensack, NJ 07601; **Phone:** 201-996-5900; **Board Cert:** Internal Medicine 1986; Hematology 1988; Medical Oncology 1989; **Med School:** UMDNJ-NJ Med Sch, Newark 1983; **Resid:** Internal Medicine, New York Hosp 1986; **Fellow:** Hematology & Oncology, Meml Sloan Kettering Cancer Ctr 1988; **Fac Appt:** Prof Med, UMDNJ-NJ Med Sch, Newark

Perry, David J MD [Onc] - **Spec Exp:** Gastrointestinal Cancer; Lung Cancer; Clinical Trials; **Hospital:** MedStar Washington Hosp Ctr; **Address:** Washington Hosp Ctr-Dept Med Oncology, 110 Irving St NW, rm C-2151, Washington, DC 20010; **Phone:** 202-877-2843; **Board Cert:** Internal Medicine 1979; Medical Oncology 1981; Hematology 1982; **Med School:** Univ Pennsylvania 1974; **Resid:** Internal Medicine, Walter Reed AMC 1979; **Fellow:** Hematology & Oncology, Walter Reed AMC 1982; **Fac Appt:** Assoc Prof Med, Eastern VA Med Sch

Pfister, David G MD [Onc] - **Spec Exp:** Head & Neck Cancer; Laryngeal Cancer; Thyroid Cancer; Immunotherapy; **Hospital:** Meml Sloan-Kettering Canc Ctr; **Address:** 300 E 66th St Fl 14, New York, NY 10065; **Phone:** 646-888-4232; **Board Cert:** Internal Medicine 1985; Medical Oncology 1989; **Med School:** Univ Pennsylvania 1982; **Resid:** Internal Medicine, Hosp Univ Penn 1985; **Fellow:** Epidemiology, Yale-New Haven Hosp 1987; Hematology & Oncology, Meml Sloan Kettering Cancer Ctr 1989; **Fac Appt:** Assoc Prof Med, Cornell Univ-Weill Med Coll

Pienta, Kenneth J MD [Onc] - **Spec Exp:** Prostate Cancer; **Hospital:** Johns Hopkins Hosp (page 59); **Address:** Johns Hopkins Hosp, Sidney Kimmel Comprehensive Cancer Ctr, 401 N Broadway, Baltimore, MD 21231; **Phone:** 410-502-1336; **Board Cert:** Medical Oncology 2011; **Med School:** Johns Hopkins Univ 1986; **Resid:** Internal Medicine, Univ Chicago Hosps 1988; **Fellow:** Medical Oncology, Johns Hopkins Hosp 1991; **Fac Appt:** Prof Onc, Johns Hopkins Univ

Posner, Marshall R MD [Onc] - **Spec Exp:** Head & Neck Cancer; Skin Cancer-Head & Neck; **Hospital:** Mt Sinai Med Ctr (page 62); **Address:** The Ruttenberg Treatment Ctr, 1470 Madison Ave, New York, NY 10029; **Phone:** 212-659-5461; **Board Cert:** Internal Medicine 1978; Medical Oncology 1981; **Med School:** Tufts Univ 1975; **Resid:** Internal Medicine, Boston City Hosp 1978; **Fellow:** Oncology, Dana-Farber Cancer Inst 1981; **Fac Appt:** Prof Onc, Mount Sinai Sch Med

Raptis, George MD [Onc] - **Spec Exp:** Breast Cancer; **Hospital:** N Shore Univ Hosp (page 66), Long Is Jewish Med Ctr (page 66); **Address:** 450 Lakeville Rd, Monter Cancer Ctr A Bldg, Lake Success, NY 11042; **Phone:** 516-734-8900; **Board Cert:** Medical Oncology 2003; **Med School:** Mount Sinai Sch Med 1987; **Resid:** Internal Medicine, Mt Sinai Med Ctr 1990; **Fellow:** Hematology & Oncology, Meml Sloan-Kettering Canc Ctr 1993; **Fac Appt:** Assoc Prof Med, Hofstra N Shore-LIJ Sch Med

Remick, Scot C MD [Onc] - **Spec Exp:** AIDS Related Cancers; Clinical Trials; Drug Development; Thyroid Cancer; **Hospital:** Ruby Memorial - WVU Hosp; **Address:** WVU Mary Babb Randolph Cancer Ctr, 1801 RCB Health Sciences Center S, Box 9300, Morgantown, WV 26506-9300; **Phone:** 304-598-4552; **Board Cert:** Internal Medicine 1985; Medical Oncology 1987; **Med School:** NY Med Coll 1982; **Resid:** Internal Medicine, Johns Hopkins Hosp 1985; **Fellow:** Medical Oncology, Univ Wisconsin Clin Canc Ctr 1988; **Fac Appt:** Prof Onc, W VA Univ

Ruggiero, Joseph T MD [Onc] - **Spec Exp:** Gastrointestinal Cancer; **Hospital:** NY-Presby/Weill Cornell Med Ctr, NY (page 65); **Address:** 1305 York Ave, Fl 12, New York, NY 10021-4635; **Phone:** 646-962-6200; **Board Cert:** Internal Medicine 1980; Hematology 1982; Medical Oncology 1983; **Med School:** NYU Sch Med 1977; **Resid:** Internal Medicine, New York Hosp 1980; **Fellow:** Hematology & Oncology, New York Hosp/Cornell 1983; **Fac Appt:** Assoc Clin Prof Onc, Cornell Univ-Weill Med Coll

Saltz, Leonard B MD [Onc] - **Spec Exp:** Colon & Rectal Cancer; Gastrointestinal Cancer & Rare Tumors; Neuroendocrine Tumors; Unknown Primary Cancer; **Hospital:** Meml Sloan-Kettering Canc Ctr; **Address:** Memorial Sloan Kettering Cancer Center, 300 E 66th St, rm 1049, New York, NY 10065; **Phone:** 646-888-4181; **Board Cert:** Internal Medicine 1986; Hematology 1988; Medical Oncology 1989; **Med School:** Yale Univ 1983; **Resid:** Internal Medicine, New York Hosp 1986; **Fellow:** Hematology, New York Hosp-Cornell/Rockefeller Univ 1988; Oncology, New York Hosp-Cornell/Rockefeller Univ 1989; **Fac Appt:** Assoc Prof Med, Cornell Univ-Weill Med Coll

Scheinberg, David A MD/PhD [Onc] - **Spec Exp:** Leukemia; Immunotherapy; Vaccine Therapy; **Hospital:** Meml Sloan-Kettering Canc Ctr; **Address:** 1275 York Avenue, New York, NY 10065; **Phone:** 646-888-2190; **Board Cert:** Internal Medicine 1986; Medical Oncology 2005; **Med School:** Johns Hopkins Univ 1983; **Resid:** Internal Medicine, NY Hosp-Cornell Med Ctr 1986; **Fellow:** Medical Oncology, Meml Sloan Kettering Cancer Ctr 1989; **Fac Appt:** Prof Med, Cornell Univ-Weill Med Coll

Scher, Howard I MD [Onc] - **Spec Exp:** Genitourinary Cancer; Prostate Cancer; Bladder Cancer; Immunotherapy; **Hospital:** Meml Sloan-Kettering Canc Ctr; **Address:** 1275 York Avenue, New York, NY 10065; **Phone:** 646-422-4330; **Board Cert:** Internal Medicine 1979; Medical Oncology 1985; **Med School:** NYU Sch Med 1976; **Resid:** Internal Medicine, Bellevue Hosp 1980; **Fellow:** Medical Oncology, Meml Sloan Kettering Cancer Ctr 1983; **Fac Appt:** Prof Med, Cornell Univ-Weill Med Coll

Schilder, Russell J MD [Onc] - **Spec Exp:** Gynecologic Cancer; Cervical Cancer; Ovarian Cancer; Drug Development; **Hospital:** Thomas Jefferson Univ Hosp, Methodist Hosp; **Address:** 925 Chestnut St Fl 3, Philadelphia, PA 19107; **Phone:** 215-955-8874; **Board Cert:** Internal Medicine 1986; Hematology 1988; Medical Oncology 1989; **Med School:** Univ Miami Sch Med 1983; **Resid:** Internal Medicine, Temple Univ Hosp 1986; **Fellow:** Hematology & Oncology, Fox Chase Cancer Ctr 1989; **Fac Appt:** Prof Med, Jefferson Med Coll

Schuchter, Lynn M MD [Onc] - **Spec Exp:** Melanoma; Breast Cancer; Clinical Trials; **Hospital:** Hosp Univ Penn - UPHS (page 69); **Address:** Abramson Cancer Ctr, Perelman Ctr for Advanced Medicine, 3400 Civic Center Blvd, 4 West, Philadelphia, PA 19104; **Phone:** 215-615-5858; **Board Cert:** Internal Medicine 1985; Medical Oncology 1989; **Med School:** Ros Franklin Univ/Chicago Med Sch 1982; **Resid:** Internal Medicine, Michael Reese Hosp 1985; **Fellow:** Medical Oncology, Johns Hopkins Hosp 1989; **Fac Appt:** Assoc Prof Med, Univ Pennsylvania

Silverman, Lewis R MD [Onc] - **Spec Exp:** Myelodysplastic Syndromes; Leukemia & Lymphoma; Multiple Myeloma; **Hospital:** Mt Sinai Med Ctr (page 62); **Address:** Ruttenberg Treatment Ctr, 1470 Madison Ave Fl 3, New York, NY 10029; **Phone:** 212-241-6756; **Board Cert:** Internal Medicine 1981; Hematology 1986; Medical Oncology 1987; **Med School:** Belgium 1978; **Resid:** Internal Medicine, Metropolitan Hosp Ctr 1980; Internal Medicine, Montefiore Med Ctr 1981; **Fellow:** Hematology, Montefiore Med Ctr 1982; Medical Oncology, Mt Sinai Med Ctr 1984; **Fac Appt:** Assoc Prof Med, Mount Sinai Sch Med

Smith, Thomas Joseph MD [Onc] - **Spec Exp:** Breast Cancer; Palliative Care; **Hospital:** Johns Hopkins Hosp (page 59); **Address:** Johns Hopkins Hosp, Sidney Kimmel Comp Cancer Ctr, 600 N Wolfe St, Blalock 371, Baltimore, MD 21287; **Phone:** 410-955-2091; **Board Cert:** Internal Medicine 1982; Medical Oncology 1987; Hospice & Palliative Medicine 2008; **Med School:** Yale Univ 1979; **Resid:** Internal Medicine, Hosp Univ Penn 1982; **Fellow:** Medical Oncology, Med Coll Virginia 1987; **Fac Appt:** Prof Med, Va Commonwealth Univ Sch Med

Socinski, Mark A MD [Onc] - **Spec Exp:** Lung Cancer; **Hospital:** UPMC Shadyside; **Address:** Hillman Cancer Ctr, 5115 Centre Ave Fl 2, Pittsburgh, PA 15232; **Phone:** 412-692-4724; **Board Cert:** Internal Medicine 1988; Medical Oncology 2012; **Med School:** Univ VT Coll Med 1984; **Resid:** Internal Medicine, Beth Israel Hosp 1986; **Fellow:** Medical Oncology, Dana-Farber Cancer Inst 1989; **Fac Appt:** Prof Med, Univ Pittsburgh

Speyer, James L MD [Onc] - **Spec Exp:** Ovarian Cancer; Breast Cancer; **Hospital:** NYU Langone Med Ctr (page 68), Bellevue Hosp Ctr; **Address:** 160 E 34th St Fl 4, New York, NY 10016-4750; **Phone:** 212-731-5432; **Board Cert:** Internal Medicine 1977; Hematology 1978; Medical Oncology 1979; **Med School:** Johns Hopkins Univ 1974; **Resid:** Internal Medicine, Columbia-Presby Med Ctr 1976; Hematology, Columbia-Presby Med Ctr 1977; **Fellow:** Medical Oncology, Natl Cancer Inst 1979; **Fac Appt:** Prof Med, NYU Sch Med

Spriggs, David R MD [Onc] - **Spec Exp:** Ovarian Cancer; Drug Development; Uterine Cancer; Gynecologic Cancer; **Hospital:** Meml Sloan-Kettering Canc Ctr; **Address:** 300 E 66th St, New York, NY 10021; **Phone:** 646-888-4223; **Board Cert:** Internal Medicine 1981; Medical Oncology 2006; **Med School:** Univ Wisc 1977; **Resid:** Internal Medicine, Columbia-Presby Hosp 1981; **Fellow:** Medical Oncology, Dana-Farber Cancer Inst 1985; **Fac Appt:** Prof Med, Cornell Univ-Weill Med Coll

Staddon, Arthur P MD [Onc] - **Spec Exp:** Sarcoma; **Hospital:** Pennsylvania Hosp-UPHS (page 69); **Address:** Pennsylvania Oncology/Hematology Assocs, 230 W Washington Square Fl 2, Philadelphia, PA 19106; **Phone:** 215-829-6088; **Board Cert:** Internal Medicine 1975; Medical Oncology 1979; Hematology 1980; **Med School:** Univ Pennsylvania 1972; **Resid:** Internal Medicine, Hosp Univ Penn 1975; **Fellow:** Hematology & Oncology, Hosp Univ Penn 1980; **Fac Appt:** Clin Prof Med, Univ Pennsylvania

Stadtmauer, Edward A MD [Onc] - **Spec Exp:** Bone Marrow & Stem Cell Transplant; Leukemia & Lymphoma; Multiple Myeloma; Amyloidosis; **Hospital:** Hosp Univ Penn - UPHS (page 69); **Address:** Abramson Cancer Ctr, Perelman Ctr for Advanced Medicine, 3400 Civic Center Blvd Fl 2, Philadelphia, PA 19104; **Phone:** 215-662-7910; **Board Cert:** Internal Medicine 1986; Hematology 1988; Medical Oncology 1989; **Med School:** Univ Pennsylvania 1983; **Resid:** Internal Medicine, Bronx Muni Hosp 1986; **Fellow:** Hematology & Oncology, Hosp Univ Penn 1989; **Fac Appt:** Prof Onc, Univ Pennsylvania

Stoopler, Mark Benjamin MD [Onc] - **Spec Exp:** Lung Cancer; Esophageal Cancer; Unknown Primary Cancer; **Hospital:** NY-Presby/Columbia Univ Med Ctr, NY (page 65); **Address:** 161 Fort Washington Ave, Ste 936, New York, NY 10032-3713; **Phone:** 212-305-8230; **Board Cert:** Internal Medicine 1978; Medical Oncology 1981; **Med School:** Cornell Univ-Weill Med Coll 1975; **Resid:** Internal Medicine, North Shore Univ Hosp 1978; Internal Medicine, NY Meml Hosp 1978; **Fellow:** Medical Oncology, Meml-Sloan Kettering Cancer Ctr 1980; **Fac Appt:** Assoc Clin Prof Onc, Columbia P&S

Straus, David J MD [Onc] - **Spec Exp:** Lymphoma; Multiple Myeloma; Hodgkin's Lymphoma; **Hospital:** Meml Sloan-Kettering Canc Ctr; **Address:** 1275 York Ave, Box 406, New York, NY 10065; **Phone:** 212-639-8365; **Board Cert:** Internal Medicine 1972; Hematology 1976; Medical Oncology 1977; **Med School:** Marquette Sch Med 1969; **Resid:** Internal Medicine, Montefiore Med Ctr 1972; **Fellow:** Hematology, Beth Israel Hosp/Brigham Hosp 1974; Medical Oncology, Meml Sloan Kettering Cancer Ctr 1976; **Fac Appt:** Prof Onc, Cornell Univ-Weill Med Coll

Sun, Weijing MD [Onc] - **Spec Exp:** Gastrointestinal Cancer; Pancreatic Cancer; Esophageal Cancer; **Hospital:** UPMC Presby, Pittsburgh, UPMC Shadyside; **Address:** Hillman Cancer Center, 5115 Centre Ave Fl 2, Pittsburgh, PA 15232; **Phone:** 412-692-4724; **Board Cert:** Medical Oncology 2011; **Med School:** China 1982; **Resid:** Internal Medicine, Loyola Univ Med Ctr 1998; **Fellow:** Hematology & Oncology, Hosp Univ Penn 2001; **Fac Appt:** Prof Med, Univ Pittsburgh

Tagawa, Scott T MD [Onc] - **Spec Exp:** Prostate Cancer; Bladder Cancer; Kidney Cancer; Urologic Cancer; **Hospital:** NY-Presby/Weill Cornell Med Ctr, NY (page 65); **Address:** NY Presby-Weill Cornell Med Ctr, 525 E 68th St, Box 403, New York, NY 10065; **Phone:** 646-962-2072; **Board Cert:** Medical Oncology 2005; Hematology 2006; **Med School:** USC-Keck School of Medicine 1998; **Resid:** Internal Medicine, USC Med Ctr 2002; **Fellow:** Hematology & Oncology, USC Med Ctr 2005; **Fac Appt:** Assoc Clin Prof Onc, Cornell Univ-Weill Med Coll

Tap, William D MD [Onc] - **Spec Exp:** Sarcoma; Sarcoma-Soft Tissue; Ewing's Sarcoma; Bone Tumors; **Hospital:** Meml Sloan-Kettering Canc Ctr; **Address:** 300 E 66th St Fl 10, New York, NY 10065; **Phone:** 646-888-4163; **Board Cert:** Internal Medicine 2003; Hematology 2006; Medical Oncology 2006; **Med School:** Thomas Jefferson Univ 2000; **Resid:** Internal Medicine, Vanderbilt Univ Med Ctr 2003; **Fellow:** Hematology & Oncology, UCLA Med Ctr 2006

Tester, William MD [Onc] - **Spec Exp:** Lung Cancer; Prostate Cancer; **Hospital:** Einstein Med Ctr; **Address:** AEMC Cancer Center , 1st Floor, 5501 Old York Rd, Philadelphia, PA 19141; **Phone:** 215-456-3880; **Board Cert:** Internal Medicine 1980; Medical Oncology 1983; Hematology 1986; **Med School:** Hahnemann Univ 1977; **Resid:** Internal Medicine, Albert Einstein Med Ctr 1980; **Fellow:** Medical Oncology, NIH-Natl Cancer Inst 1982; Hematology, Georgetown Univ 1983; **Fac Appt:** Clin Prof Onc, Thomas Jefferson Univ

Tkaczuk, Katherine H MD [Onc] - **Spec Exp:** Breast Cancer; **Hospital:** Univ of MD Med Ctr; **Address:** Greenebaum Cancer Ctr, 22 S Greene St, rm S9D12, Baltimore, MD 21201; **Phone:** 410-328-7904; **Board Cert:** Medical Oncology 2011; **Med School:** Poland 1984; **Resid:** Internal Medicine, St Agnes Hosp 1989; **Fellow:** Hematology & Oncology, Univ Maryland Cancer Ctr 1992; **Fac Appt:** Prof Med, Univ MD Sch Med

Toppmeyer, Deborah L MD [Onc] - **Spec Exp:** Breast Cancer; Hereditary Cancer; **Hospital:** Robert Wood Johnson Univ Hosp - New Brunswick; **Address:** Cancer Inst of New Jersey, 195 Little Albany St, New Brunswick, NJ 08903; **Phone:** 732-235-9692; **Board Cert:** Internal Medicine 1988; Medical Oncology 2006; **Med School:** Albany Med Coll 1985; **Resid:** Internal Medicine, Univ Pittsburgh Hlth Ctr Hosp 1988; **Fellow:** Medical Oncology, Dana Farber Cancer Inst 1993; **Fac Appt:** Assoc Prof Med

Trump, Donald L MD [Onc] - **Spec Exp:** Prostate Cancer; Genitourinary Cancer; Drug Discovery & Development; Clinical Trials; **Hospital:** Roswell Park Canc Inst; **Address:** Roswell Park Cancer Institute, Elm and Carlton Streets, Buffalo, NY 14263; **Phone:** 716-845-2300; **Board Cert:** Internal Medicine 1973; Medical Oncology 1977; **Med School:** Johns Hopkins Univ 1970; **Resid:** Internal Medicine, Johns Hopkins Hosp 1975; **Fellow:** Medical Oncology, Johns Hopkins Hosp 1974; **Fac Appt:** Prof Med, SUNY Buffalo

Vahdat, Linda T MD [Onc] - **Spec Exp:** Breast Cancer; Breast Cancer-Novel Therapies; Clinical Trials; **Hospital:** NY-Presby/Weill Cornell Med Ctr, NY (page 65); **Address:** 425 E 61st St Fl 8, New York, NY 10065; **Phone:** 212-821-0644; **Board Cert:** Medical Oncology 2005; **Med School:** Mount Sinai Sch Med 1987; **Resid:** Internal Medicine, Mt Sinai Hosp 1990; **Fellow:** Hematology & Oncology, Meml Sloan Kettering Cancer Ctr 1994; **Fac Appt:** Prof Med, Cornell Univ-Weill Med Coll

Vaughn, David J MD [Onc] - **Spec Exp:** Testicular Cancer; Bladder Cancer; Prostate Cancer; Genitourinary Cancer; **Hospital:** Hosp Univ Penn - UPHS (page 69); **Address:** Abramson Cancer Ctr, Perelman Ctr for Advanced Medicine, 3400 Civic Center Blvd, 4 West, Philadelphia, PA 19104; **Phone:** 215-615-5858; **Board Cert:** Medical Oncology 2003; **Med School:** Harvard Med Sch 1987; **Resid:** Internal Medicine, New York Hosp 1990; **Fellow:** Hematology & Oncology, Hosp Univ Penn 1993; **Fac Appt:** Prof Onc, Univ Pennsylvania

Vinciguerra, Vincent P MD [Onc] - **Spec Exp:** Breast Cancer; Gastrointestinal Cancer; Lung Cancer; Cancer Prevention; **Hospital:** N Shore Univ Hosp (page 66), Glen Cove Hosp (page 66); **Address:** Monter Cancer Ctr, 450 Lakeville Rd, Lake Success, NY 11042; **Phone:** 516-734-8954; **Board Cert:** Internal Medicine 1971; Hematology 1974; Medical Oncology 1975; **Med School:** Georgetown Univ 1966; **Resid:** Internal Medicine, NY Hosp-Cornell 1969; Internal Medicine, N Shore Univ Hosp 1971; **Fellow:** Hematology & Oncology, NY Hosp-Cornell 1973; Hematology & Oncology, N Shore Univ Hosp 1974; **Fac Appt:** Prof Med, NYU Sch Med

von Mehren, Margaret MD [Onc] - **Spec Exp:** Sarcoma; Melanoma; Immunotherapy; Gastrointestinal Stromal Tumors; **Hospital:** Fox Chase Cancer Ctr (page 57); **Address:** Fox Chase Cancer Ctr, Dept Med Oncology, 333 Cottman Ave, Philadelphia, PA 19111-2434; **Phone:** 215-728-2814; **Board Cert:** Medical Oncology 2007; **Med School:** Albany Med Coll 1989; **Resid:** Internal Medicine, NYU Med Ctr 1993; **Fellow:** Hematology & Oncology, Fox Chase Cancer Ctr 1996; **Fac Appt:** Assoc Prof Med, Temple Univ

Waintraub, Stanley E MD [Onc] - **Spec Exp:** Breast Cancer; Bleeding/Coagulation Disorders; **Hospital:** Hackensack Univ Med Ctr; **Address:** 92 2nd St, Hackensack, NJ 07601; **Phone:** 201-996-5864; **Board Cert:** Internal Medicine 1980; Hematology 1982; Medical Oncology 1983; **Med School:** NY Med Coll 1977; **Resid:** Internal Medicine, Metropolitan Hosp Ctr 1980; **Fellow:** Hematology, Montefiore Hosp Med Ctr 1982; Medical Oncology, Meml Sloan Kettering Cancer Ctr 1983

Weiner, Louis M MD [Onc] - **Spec Exp:** Gastrointestinal Cancer; Immunotherapy; Liver Cancer; **Hospital:** MedStar Georgetown Univ Hosp; **Address:** Lombardi Cancer Ctr, 3800 Reservoir Rd NW, Washington, DC 20007; **Phone:** 202-444-2198; **Board Cert:** Internal Medicine 1980; Medical Oncology 1985; **Med School:** Mount Sinai Sch Med 1977; **Resid:** Internal Medicine, Univ Vermont Med Ctr Hosp 1980; **Fellow:** Hematology & Oncology, New England Med Ctr 1983; **Fac Appt:** Prof Med, Georgetown Univ

Wetzler, Meir MD [Onc] - **Spec Exp:** Leukemia; Leukemia-Chronic Myeloid; Myelodysplastic Syndromes; Myeloproliferative Disorders; **Hospital:** Roswell Park Canc Inst, Buffalo Genl Hosp; **Address:** Roswell Park Cancer Inst, Elm and Carlton Streets, Buffalo, NY 14263; **Phone:** 716-845-7617; **Board Cert:** Internal Medicine 2011; Medical Oncology 2003; **Med School:** Israel 1980; **Resid:** Internal Medicine, Kaplan Hosp 1986; **Fellow:** Medical Oncology, MD Anderson Cancer Ctr 1992; **Fac Appt:** Prof Med, SUNY Buffalo

Wilson, Wyndham MD [Onc] - **Spec Exp:** Lymphoma; **Hospital:** Natl Inst of Hlth - Clin Ctr; **Address:** National Cancer Inst, 9000 Rockville Pike, Bldg 10 - rm 4N-115, Bethesda, MD 20892; **Phone:** 301-435-2415; **Board Cert:** Internal Medicine 1985; Medical Oncology 1987; **Med School:** Stanford Univ 1981; **Resid:** Internal Medicine, Stanford Univ Affil Hosp 1984; **Fellow:** Oncology, Natl Cancer Inst-NIH 1987

Wolchok, Jedd D MD/PhD [Onc] - **Spec Exp:** Melanoma; Immunotherapy; Clinical Trials; Vaccine Therapy; **Hospital:** Meml Sloan-Kettering Canc Ctr; **Address:** Meml Sloan Kettering Cancer Ctr, 1275 York Ave, New York, NY 10065; **Phone:** 646-888-2395; **Board Cert:** Medical Oncology 2011; **Med School:** NYU Sch Med 1994; **Resid:** Internal Medicine, NYU Med Ctr 1997; **Fellow:** Medical Oncology, Meml Sloan-Kettering Canc Ctr 2000

Wolff, Antonio C MD [Onc] - **Spec Exp:** Breast Cancer; Drug Development; **Hospital:** Johns Hopkins Hosp (page 59); **Address:** Bunting Blaustein Cancer Rsch Bldg, 1650 Orleans St, rm 1-189, Baltimore, MD 21287; **Phone:** 410-583-2970; **Board Cert:** Medical Oncology 2000; **Med School:** Brazil 1986; **Resid:** Internal Medicine, Mt Sinai Med Ctr 1991; **Fellow:** Hematology & Oncology, Washington Univ Med Ctr 1992; Medical Oncology, Johns Hopkins Hosp 1995; **Fac Appt:** Prof Med, Johns Hopkins Univ

Zelenetz, Andrew D MD/PhD [Onc] - **Spec Exp:** Lymphoma; **Hospital:** Meml Sloan-Kettering Canc Ctr; **Address:** 205 E 64th St, New York, NY 10065; **Phone:** 212-639-2656; **Board Cert:** Medical Oncology 2009; **Med School:** Harvard Med Sch 1984; **Resid:** Internal Medicine, Stanford Univ Med Ctr 1988; **Fellow:** Medical Oncology, Stanford Univ Med Ctr 1991; **Fac Appt:** Asst Prof Med, Cornell Univ-Weill Med Coll

Southeast

Anthony, Lowell B MD [Onc] - **Spec Exp:** Gastrointestinal Cancer; Carcinoid Tumors; Neuroendocrine Tumors; **Hospital:** Univ of Kentucky Albert B. Chandler Hosp; **Address:** UK HealthCare, Markey Cancer Ctr, Whitney Hendrickson Bldg, 800 Rose St Fl 1, Lexington, KY 40536; **Phone:** 866-340-4488; **Board Cert:** Internal Medicine 1983; Medical Oncology 1989; **Med School:** Vanderbilt Univ 1979; **Resid:** Internal Medicine, Vanderbilt Univ Med Ctr 1982; **Fellow:** Medical Oncology, Vanderbilt Univ Med Ctr 1985; **Fac Appt:** Prof Onc, Louisiana State U, New Orleans

Antonia, Scott J MD/PhD [Onc] - **Spec Exp:** Kidney Cancer; Lung Cancer; Thoracic Cancers; **Hospital:** Moffitt Canc Ctr (page 61); **Address:** H Lee Moffitt Cancer Ctr, Thoracic Clin, 12902 Magnolia Drive, Tampa, FL 33612; **Phone:** 813-745-2677; **Board Cert:** Medical Oncology 2006; **Med School:** Univ Conn 1989; **Resid:** Internal Medicine, Yale-New Haven Hosp 1991; **Fellow:** Medical Oncology, Yale-New Haven Hosp 1994; **Fac Appt:** Prof Med, Univ S Fla Coll Med

Arteaga, Carlos L MD [Onc] - **Spec Exp:** Breast Cancer; **Hospital:** Vanderbilt Univ Med Ctr; **Address:** Vanderbilt Hematology Oncology, 2220 Pierce Ave, 683 Preston Rsch Bldg, Nashville, TN 37232-6838; **Phone:** 615-322-2064; **Board Cert:** Internal Medicine 1984; Medical Oncology 1989; **Med School:** Ecuador 1980; **Resid:** Internal Medicine, Grady Meml Hosp 1984; **Fellow:** Hematology & Oncology, Univ TX Hlth Sci Ctr 1987; **Fac Appt:** Prof Med, Vanderbilt Univ

Balducci, Lodovico MD [Onc] - **Spec Exp:** Genitourinary Cancer; Breast Cancer; **Hospital:** Moffitt Canc Ctr (page 61); **Address:** H Lee Moffitt Cancer Ctr, Senior Adults, 12902 Magnolia Drive, Tampa, FL 33612; **Phone:** 813-745-8658; **Board Cert:** Internal Medicine 1987; Hematology 1978; Medical Oncology 1979; **Med School:** Italy 1968; **Resid:** Internal Medicine, Univ Mississippi Med Ctr 1976; Hematology & Oncology, Univ Mississippi Med Ctr 1979; **Fellow:** Internal Medicine, A Gemelli Genl Hosp 1970; **Fac Appt:** Prof Onc, Univ S Fla Coll Med

Benedetto, Pasquale W MD [Onc] - **Spec Exp:** Genitourinary Cancer; Bone Tumors; Gastrointestinal Cancer; Pancreatic Cancer; **Hospital:** Univ of Miami Hosp & Clins/Sylvester Comp Canc Ctr; **Address:** SCCC, Med Oncology Dept, 1475 NW 12th Ave, Ste 3310, Miami, FL 33136; **Phone:** 305-243-6604; **Board Cert:** Internal Medicine 1979; Medical Oncology 1981; Hematology 1982; **Med School:** Cornell Univ-Weill Med Coll 1976; **Resid:** Internal Medicine, Johns Hopkins Hosp 1979; **Fellow:** Medical Oncology, Meml Sloan-Kettering Cancer Ctr 1981; **Fac Appt:** Prof Med, Univ Miami Sch Med

Berlin, Jordan D MD [Onc] - **Spec Exp:** Gastrointestinal Cancer; Pancreatic Cancer; Liver Cancer; Colon Cancer; **Hospital:** Vanderbilt Univ Med Ctr; **Address:** Vanderbilt Ingram Cancer Ctr, 2220 Pierce Ave, Ste 1710, Nashville, TN 37232-6307; **Phone:** 615-986-8422; **Board Cert:** Internal Medicine 2002; Medical Oncology 2005; **Med School:** Univ IL Coll Med 1989; **Resid:** Internal Medicine, Univ Cincinnati Med Ctr 1992; **Fellow:** Medical Oncology, Univ Wisconsin 1995; **Fac Appt:** Prof Med, Vanderbilt Univ

Bernard, Stephen A MD [Onc] - **Spec Exp:** Gastrointestinal Cancer; Palliative Care; Clinical Trials; **Hospital:** NC Memorial Hosp - UNC; **Address:** 170 Manning Drive Fl 3rd - rm 3105, Chapel Hill, NC 27599-7305; **Phone:** 919-966-0000; **Board Cert:** Internal Medicine 1987; Medical Oncology 1979; Hospice & Palliative Medicine 2008; **Med School:** Univ NC Sch Med 1973; **Resid:** Internal Medicine, Columbia-Presby Med Ctr 1976; **Fellow:** Hematology & Oncology, Wash Univ Hosps 1978; **Fac Appt:** Prof Onc, Univ NC Sch Med

Blackwell, Kimberly L MD [Onc] - **Spec Exp:** Breast Cancer; Clinical Trials; **Hospital:** Duke Univ Hosp; **Address:** Duke Univ Med Ctr, Box 3893, Durham, NC 27710; **Phone:** 919-668-6688; **Board Cert:** Medical Oncology 2010; **Med School:** Mayo Med Sch 1994; **Resid:** Internal Medicine, Duke Univ Med Ctr 1997; **Fellow:** Medical Oncology, Duke Univ Med Ctr 2000; **Fac Appt:** Assoc Prof Med, Duke Univ

Blobe, Gerard C MD/PhD [Onc] - **Spec Exp:** Pancreatic Cancer; Colon & Rectal Cancer; Clinical Trials; **Hospital:** Duke Univ Hosp; **Address:** Duke Univ, Box 91004, Durham, NC 27708; **Phone:** 919-668-6688; **Board Cert:** Internal Medicine 2009; Medical Oncology 2011; **Med School:** Duke Univ 1995; **Resid:** Internal Medicine, Brigham & Women's Hosp 1997; **Fellow:** Medical Oncology, Dana-Farber Cancer Inst 2000; **Fac Appt:** Prof Onc, Duke Univ

Bolger, Graeme B MD [Onc] - **Spec Exp:** Prostate Cancer; Testicular Cancer; **Hospital:** UAB Hosp; **Address:** 2540 North Pavilion, 1802 6th Ave S, Birmingham, AL 35294; **Phone:** 205-934-2992; **Board Cert:** Internal Medicine 1984; Medical Oncology 2011; **Med School:** McGill Univ 1981; **Resid:** Internal Medicine, Johns Hopkins Hosp 1984; **Fellow:** Medical Oncology, F Hutchinson Cancer Rsch 1985; Oncology, Sloan-Kettering Cancer Ctr 1992; **Fac Appt:** Assoc Prof Med, UAB Sch Med

Boston, Barry MD [Onc] - **Spec Exp:** Gastrointestinal Cancer; Genitourinary Cancer; Prostate Cancer; **Hospital:** St. Francis Hosp - Memphis, Methodist Univ Hosp - Memphis; **Address:** Boston Baskin Cancer Foundation, 7945 Wolf River Blvd, Ste 300, Germantown, TN 38138; **Phone:** 901-752-6131; **Board Cert:** Internal Medicine 1974; Medical Oncology 1977; **Med School:** Louisiana State U, New Orleans 1971; **Resid:** Internal Medicine, Univ Tenn Hosp-VA Hosp 1973; Hematology, Univ Tenn Hosp-VA Hosp 1973; **Fellow:** Medical Oncology, Yale New Haven Hosp 1975; **Fac Appt:** Assoc Prof Med, Univ Tenn Coll Med

Brenin, Christiana M MD [Onc] - **Spec Exp:** Breast Cancer; **Hospital:** Univ of Virginia Hlth Sys; **Address:** Univ VA Hlth System, Box 800716, Div Hematology/Oncology, 1215 Lee St, Charlottesville, VA 22908; **Phone:** 434-924-8552; **Board Cert:** Internal Medicine 2003; Medical Oncology 2008; **Med School:** NY Med Coll 1990; **Resid:** Internal Medicine, Northwestern Meml Hosp 1993; **Fellow:** Hematology & Oncology, Northwestern Meml Hosp 1996; **Fac Appt:** Assoc Prof Med, Univ VA Sch Med

Brescia, Frank J MD [Onc] - **Spec Exp:** Palliative Care; Breast Cancer; Gastrointestinal Cancer; Ethics; **Hospital:** MUSC Med Ctr; **Address:** MUSC Med Ctr- Women's Hlth Ob/Gyn, 86 Jonathan Lucas St, Charleston, SC 29425; **Phone:** 843-792-9300; **Board Cert:** Internal Medicine 1974; Medical Oncology 1975; Hospice & Palliative Medicine 2012; **Med School:** UMDNJ-NJ Med Sch, Newark 1968; **Resid:** Internal Medicine, North Shore Univ Hosp 1970; **Fellow:** Medical Oncology, Meml Sloan Kettering Cancer Ctr 1974; **Fac Appt:** Prof Med, Med Univ SC

Burris III, Howard A MD [Onc] - **Spec Exp:** Drug Discovery & Development; Breast Cancer; Pancreatic Cancer; Clinical Trials; **Hospital:** Centennial Med Ctr; **Address:** Tennessee Oncology, 250 25th Ave N, Ste 100, Nashville, TN 37203; **Phone:** 615-320-5090; **Board Cert:** Internal Medicine 1988; Medical Oncology 2011; **Med School:** Univ S Ala Coll Med 1985; **Resid:** Internal Medicine, Brooke Army Med Ctr 1988; **Fellow:** Medical Oncology, Brooke Army Med Ctr 1991

Carey, Lisa A MD [Onc] - **Spec Exp:** Breast Cancer; **Hospital:** NC Memorial Hosp - UNC; **Address:** Univ North Carolina-Div Hem/Onc, 170 Manning Drive, Fl 3rd, POB Campus Box 7305, Chapel Hill, NC 27599-7300; **Phone:** 919-843-6814; **Board Cert:** Internal Medicine 2003; Medical Oncology 2007; **Med School:** Johns Hopkins Univ 1990; **Resid:** Internal Medicine, Johns Hopkins Hosp 1993; **Fellow:** Oncology, Johns Hopkins Hosp 1996; **Fac Appt:** Prof Hem & Onc, Univ NC Sch Med

Carpenter Jr, John T MD [Onc] - **Spec Exp:** Breast Cancer; **Hospital:** UAB Hosp; **Address:** The Kirklin Clinic, 2000 6th Ave S, Birmingham, AL 35233; **Phone:** 205-934-5077; **Board Cert:** Internal Medicine 1972; Hematology 1981; Medical Oncology 1975; **Med School:** Tulane Univ 1968; **Resid:** Internal Medicine, Grady Meml Hosp 1971; **Fellow:** Hematology & Oncology, Emory Univ 1973; **Fac Appt:** Prof Med, UAB Sch Med

Chanan-Khan, Asher A MD [Onc] - **Spec Exp:** Multiple Myeloma; Leukemia-Chronic Lymphocytic; **Hospital:** Mayo - Jacksonville; **Address:** Mayo Clin, Hematology/Oncology Dept, 4500 San Pablo Rd, Jacksonville, FL 32224; **Phone:** 904-953-7290; **Med School:** Pakistan 1993; **Resid:** Internal Medicine, Harlem Hosp Ctr 1997; **Fellow:** Hematology & Oncology, NYU Med Ctr 1999

Chao, Nelson J MD [Onc] - **Spec Exp:** Bone Marrow Transplant; Lymphoma; Leukemia; **Hospital:** Duke Univ Hosp; **Address:** Duke Univ Med Ctr, Box 3961, Durham, NC 27710; **Phone:** 919-668-1002; **Board Cert:** Internal Medicine 1984; Medical Oncology 1987; **Med School:** Yale Univ 1981; **Resid:** Internal Medicine, Stanford Univ Med Ctr 1984; **Fellow:** Oncology, Stanford Univ Med Ctr 1987; **Fac Appt:** Prof Med, Duke Univ

Chung, Ki Young MD [Onc] - **Spec Exp:** Gastrointestinal Cancer; **Hospital:** Greenville Meml Hosp; **Address:** Cancer Ctrs of the Carolinas, 120 Dillon Drive, Spartanburg, SC 29307; **Phone:** 864-699-5700; **Board Cert:** Medical Oncology 2004; **Med School:** Univ NC Sch Med 1995; **Resid:** Internal Medicine, Sinai Hosp 1999; **Fellow:** Hematology & Oncology, Meml Sloan Kettering Cancer Ctr 2003

Colon-Otero, Gerardo MD [Onc] - **Spec Exp:** Ovarian Cancer; Breast Cancer; Hematologic Malignancies; Pancreatic Cancer-Acinar Cell; **Hospital:** Mayo - Jacksonville; **Address:** Mayo Clin, Breast Clin, 4500 San Pablo Rd, Jacksonville, FL 32224; **Phone:** 904-953-2272; **Board Cert:** Internal Medicine 1982; Hematology 1984; Medical Oncology 1985; **Med School:** Puerto Rico 1979; **Resid:** Internal Medicine, Mayo Clin 1982; **Fellow:** Hematology, Mayo Clin 1984; Medical Oncology, Univ Virginia Hlth Sys 1986; **Fac Appt:** Assoc Prof Med, Mayo Med Sch

Conry, Robert M MD [Onc] - **Spec Exp:** Melanoma; Lung Cancer; Colon & Rectal Cancer; Sarcoma; **Hospital:** UAB Hosp; **Address:** The University of Alabama at Birmingham, The Kirklin Clinic at Acton Road, 2145 Bonner Way, Birmingham, AL 35243; **Phone:** 205-978-0250; **Board Cert:** Medical Oncology 2011; **Med School:** UAB Sch Med 1987; **Resid:** Internal Medicine, Univ Alabama Hosp 1990; **Fellow:** Medical Oncology, Univ Alabama Hosp 1993; **Fac Appt:** Assoc Prof Med, UAB Sch Med

Crawford, Jeffrey MD [Onc] - **Spec Exp:** Lung Cancer; **Hospital:** Duke Univ Hosp; **Address:** Duke Univ Med Ctr, Box 3476, Durham, NC 27710; **Phone:** 919-668-6688; **Board Cert:** Internal Medicine 1977; Hematology 1980; Medical Oncology 1981; **Med School:** Ohio State Univ 1974; **Resid:** Internal Medicine, Duke Univ Med Ctr 1977; **Fellow:** Hematology & Oncology, Duke Univ Med Ctr 1981; **Fac Appt:** Prof Med, Duke Univ

De Simone, Philip MD [Onc] - **Spec Exp:** Colon Cancer; Pancreatic Cancer; **Hospital:** Univ of Kentucky Albert B. Chandler Hosp; **Address:** Markey Cancer Ctr, Dept Med Onc, 800 Rose St, Whitney-Hendrickson Bldg, Lexington, KY 40536; **Phone:** 859-257-4488; **Board Cert:** Internal Medicine 1972; Hematology 1974; **Med School:** Univ VT Coll Med 1967; **Resid:** Internal Medicine, Univ Kentucky Med Ctr 1972; **Fellow:** Hematology & Oncology, Univ Kentucky Med Ctr 1974; **Fac Appt:** Prof Med, Univ KY Coll Med

Dunphy II, Frank R MD [Onc] - **Spec Exp:** Lung Cancer; Head & Neck Cancer; **Hospital:** Duke Univ Hosp; **Address:** Duke Univ Med Ctr, Box 3685, Durham, NC 27710; **Phone:** 919-668-6688; **Board Cert:** Internal Medicine 1984; Hematology 1986; Medical Oncology 1989; **Med School:** Louisiana State U, New Orleans 1979; **Resid:** Internal Medicine, Louisiana St Univ Hosp 1983; **Fellow:** Hematology & Oncology, Louisiana St Univ Hosp 1985; **Fac Appt:** Assoc Prof Med, Duke Univ

Flinn, Ian W MD/PhD [Onc] - **Spec Exp:** Leukemia; Lymphoma; Bone Marrow Transplant; Multiple Myeloma; **Hospital:** Centennial Med Ctr; **Address:** Tennessee Oncology, 250 25th Ave N, Ste 412, Nashville, TN 37203; **Phone:** 615-986-7600; **Board Cert:** Hematology 2007; Medical Oncology 2008; **Med School:** Johns Hopkins Univ 1990; **Resid:** Internal Medicine, Univ Michigan Med Ctr 1993; **Fellow:** Hematology & Oncology, Johns Hopkins 1996

Forero-Torres, Andres MD [Onc] - **Spec Exp:** Lymphoma; Breast Cancer; **Hospital:** UAB Hosp; **Address:** The Kirklin Clinic, 2000 6th Ave S, Birmingham, AL 35233; **Phone:** 205-934-5077; **Med School:** Colombia 1982; **Resid:** Internal Medicine, Javeriana Univ 1987; **Fellow:** Medical Oncology, Javeriana Univ 1991; **Fac Appt:** Prof Med, UAB Sch Med

Fracasso, Paula M MD/PhD [Onc] - **Spec Exp:** Gynecologic Cancer; Breast Cancer; **Hospital:** Univ of Virginia Hlth Sys; **Address:** UVA-Emily Couric Cancer Ctr, 1240 Lee St, Charlottesville, VA 22903; **Phone:** 434-243-6143; **Board Cert:** Internal Medicine 1987; Medical Oncology 2003; **Med School:** Yale Univ 1984; **Resid:** Internal Medicine, Beth Israel Hosp 1987; **Fellow:** Cancer Research, Mass Inst Tech 1989; Hematology & Oncology, Tufts-New England Med Ctr 1991; **Fac Appt:** Prof Med, Univ VA Sch Med

Friedman, Henry S MD [Onc] - **Spec Exp:** Neuro-Oncology; Brain & Spinal Cord Tumors; Gliomas; **Hospital:** Duke Univ Hosp; **Address:** Preston R Tisch Brain Tumor Ctr, 047 Baker House, Trent Drive, DUMC, Box 3624, Durham, NC 27710; **Phone:** 919-684-5301; **Board Cert:** Pediatrics 1982; Pediatric Hematology-Oncology 1982; **Med School:** SUNY Upstate Med Univ 1977; **Resid:** Pediatrics, SUNY Upstate Med Ctr 1980; **Fellow:** Pediatric Hematology-Oncology, Duke Univ Med Ctr 1983; **Fac Appt:** Prof Neuro-Onc, Duke Univ

Garst, Jennifer L MD [Onc] - **Spec Exp:** Lung Cancer; Cancer Survivors-Late Effects of Therapy; Clinical Trials; Thoracic Cancers; **Hospital:** Duke Raleigh Hosp, Duke Univ Hosp; **Address:** Duke Raleigh Cancer Ctr, 3404 Wake Forest Rd, Ste 100, Raleigh, NC 27609; **Phone:** 919-954-3050; **Board Cert:** Internal Medicine 2008; Medical Oncology 2011; **Med School:** Med Coll GA 1990; **Resid:** Internal Medicine, Univ SW Texas Hosp 1993; **Fellow:** Hematology & Oncology, Duke Univ Med Ctr 1996; **Fac Appt:** Prof Med, Duke Univ

George, Daniel J MD [Onc] - **Spec Exp:** Prostate Cancer; Kidney Cancer; **Hospital:** Duke Univ Hosp; **Address:** Duke Univ Med Ctr, Box 102002, Durham, NC 27710; **Phone:** 919-668-8108; **Board Cert:** Medical Oncology 2007; **Med School:** Duke Univ 1992; **Resid:** Internal Medicine, Johns Hopkins Hosp 1995; **Fellow:** Medical Oncology, Johns Hopkins Hosp 1998; **Fac Appt:** Assoc Prof S, Duke Univ

Geyer Jr, Charles E MD [Onc] - **Spec Exp:** Breast Cancer; Clinical Trials; **Hospital:** VCU Med Ctr; **Address:** VCU Med Ctr N Hosp, Dalton Oncology Clin, 1300 E Marshall St, Richmond, VA 23298; **Phone:** 804-828-5116; **Board Cert:** Internal Medicine 1983; Medical Oncology 1987; **Med School:** Texas Tech Univ 1980; **Resid:** Internal Medicine, Baylor Affil Hosps 1983; **Fellow:** Medical Oncology, Baylor Affil Hosps 1985; **Fac Appt:** Prof Med, Va Commonwealth Univ Sch Med

Godley, Paul A MD/PhD [Onc] - **Spec Exp:** Prostate Cancer (advanced); Testicular Cancer; Penile Cancer; Bladder Cancer; **Hospital:** NC Memorial Hosp - UNC; **Address:** UNC Hematology/Oncology, POB, Campus Box 7305, 3rd Floor, 170 Manning Drive, Chapel Hill, NC 27599; **Phone:** 919-966-4431; **Board Cert:** Internal Medicine 1987; Medical Oncology 2002; **Med School:** Harvard Med Sch 1984; **Resid:** Internal Medicine, Univ Hosps 1987; **Fellow:** Epidemiology, Univ NC Sch of Public Hlth 1989; Hematology & Oncology, Univ NC Hosps 1991; **Fac Appt:** Assoc Prof Med, Univ NC Sch Med

Graham II, Mark L MD [Onc] - **Spec Exp:** Breast Cancer; Breast Cancer Genetics; **Hospital:** WakeMed Cary; **Address:** Waverly Hematology/Oncology, 300 Ashville Ave, Ste 310, Cary, NC 27518; **Phone:** 919-233-8585; **Board Cert:** Internal Medicine 1989; **Med School:** Mayo Med Sch 1982; **Resid:** Internal Medicine, Duke Univ Med Ctr 1985; **Fellow:** Medical Oncology, Univ CO Hlth Sci Ctr 1990; Medical Oncology, Mayo Clinic 1991; **Fac Appt:** Assoc Clin Prof Med, Univ NC Sch Med

Greco, F Anthony MD [Onc] - **Spec Exp:** Lung Cancer; Unknown Primary Cancer; **Hospital:** Centennial Med Ctr; **Address:** Tennessee Oncology, 250 25th Ave N, Ste 100, Nashville, TN 37203; **Phone:** 615-320-5090; **Board Cert:** Internal Medicine 1975; Medical Oncology 1977; **Med School:** W VA Univ 1972; **Resid:** Internal Medicine, Univ West Virginia Hosp 1974; **Fellow:** Medical Oncology, Natl Cancer Inst 1976

Grosh, William W MD [Onc] - **Spec Exp:** Melanoma; Sarcoma; Neuroendocrine Tumors; **Hospital:** Univ of Virginia Hlth Sys; **Address:** Univ VA Hlth Sys, Box 800716, 1215 Lee St, Multistory Bldg - rm 6012, Charlottesville, VA 22908; **Phone:** 434-924-1904; **Board Cert:** Internal Medicine 1978; Medical Oncology 1985; **Med School:** Columbia P&S 1974; **Resid:** Internal Medicine, Vanderbilt Univ Med Ctr 1977; **Fellow:** Medical Oncology, Vanderbilt Univ Med Ctr 1983; **Fac Appt:** Assoc Prof Med, Univ VA Sch Med

Hande, Kenneth R MD [Onc] - **Spec Exp:** Unknown Primary Cancer; Sarcoma; Carcinoid Tumors; Drug Development; **Hospital:** Vanderbilt Univ Med Ctr, VA Tennessee Valley Healthcare System-Alvin C. Yor; **Address:** Vanderbilt Hematology/Oncology, 2220 Pierce Ave, 777 Preston Rsch Bldg, Nashville, TN 37232-6307; **Phone:** 615-936-8422; **Board Cert:** Internal Medicine 1975; Medical Oncology 1977; **Med School:** Johns Hopkins Univ 1972; **Resid:** Internal Medicine, Barnes-Jewish Hosp 1974; **Fellow:** Medical Oncology, Natl Cancer Inst 1977; **Fac Appt:** Prof Med, Vanderbilt Univ

Hurd, David MD [Onc] - **Spec Exp:** Lymphoma; Leukemia; Bone Marrow Transplant; **Hospital:** Wake Forest Baptist Med Ctr; **Address:** Medical Ctr Blvd, Winston-Salem, NC 27157-1082; **Phone:** 336-713-5440; **Board Cert:** Internal Medicine 1977; Medical Oncology 1981; **Med School:** Univ IL Coll Med 1974; **Resid:** Internal Medicine, Univ Minn Hosp 1977; **Fellow:** Medical Oncology, Univ Minn Hosp 1979; **Fac Appt:** Prof Med, Wake Forest Univ

Jahanzeb, Mohammad MD [Onc] - **Spec Exp:** Breast Cancer; Lung Cancer; Clinical Trials; **Hospital:** Boca Raton Regl Hosp, Univ of Miami Hosp & Clins/Sylvester Comp Canc Ctr; **Address:** 1192 E Newport Center Drive, Ste 100, Deerfield Beach, FL 33442; **Phone:** 954-698-3665; **Board Cert:** Medical Oncology 2003; Hematology 2005; **Med School:** Pakistan 1986; **Resid:** Internal Medicine, New Britain Genl Hosp 1990; **Fellow:** Hematology & Oncology, Washington Univ 1993; **Fac Appt:** Prof Med, Univ Miami Sch Med

Jillella, Anand MD [Onc] - **Spec Exp:** Bone Marrow Transplant; Leukemia; Lymphoma; Multiple Myeloma; **Hospital:** Georgia Regents Med Ctr-Augusta; **Address:** GA Regents Med Ctr, Hematology/Oncology, 1120 15th St, rm BA5407, Augusta, GA 30912; **Phone:** 706-721-2505; **Board Cert:** Medical Oncology 2007; **Med School:** India 1985; **Resid:** Internal Medicine, Med Coll Georgia 1992; **Fellow:** Medical Oncology, Yale-New Haven Hosp 1996; **Fac Appt:** Prof Med, Med Coll GA

Khuri, Fadlo Raja MD [Onc] - **Spec Exp:** Lung Cancer; Head & Neck Cancer; Thyroid Cancer; Salivary Gland Tumors; **Hospital:** Emory Univ Hosp, Grady Hlth Sys; **Address:** 1365 Clifton Road Rd NE, C Bldg, Ste 3000, Atlanta, GA 30322; **Phone:** 404-778-1900; **Board Cert:** Medical Oncology 2008; **Med School:** Columbia P&S 1989; **Resid:** Internal Medicine, Boston City Hosp 1992; **Fellow:** Hematology & Oncology, Tufts Univ 1995; **Fac Appt:** Prof Hem & Onc, Emory Univ

Kraft, Andrew S MD [Onc] - **Spec Exp:** Prostate Cancer; Sarcoma; Drug Development; Clinical Trials; **Hospital:** MUSC Med Ctr; **Address:** MUSC Hollings Cancer Ctr, 86 Jonathan Lucas St, Charleston, SC 29425; **Phone:** 843-792-8284; **Board Cert:** Internal Medicine 1980; Medical Oncology 1985; **Med School:** Univ Pennsylvania 1975; **Resid:** Internal Medicine, Mt Sinai Hosp 1979; **Fellow:** Hematology & Oncology, Natl Cancer Inst 1985; **Fac Appt:** Prof Med, Med Univ SC

Kucuk, Omer MD [Onc] - **Spec Exp:** Genitourinary Cancer; Nutrition in Cancer Therapy; Prostate Cancer; Nutrition & Cancer Prevention/Control; **Hospital:** Emory Univ Hosp; **Address:** Emory Winship Cancer Inst, 1365C Clifton Rd NE, Ste 2110, Atlanta, GA 30322; **Phone:** 404-778-1900; **Board Cert:** Internal Medicine 1978; Hematology 1984; Medical Oncology 1989; **Med School:** Turkey 1975; **Resid:** Internal Medicine, St Francis Hosp 1978; **Fellow:** Hematology & Oncology, Northwestern Univ 1981; **Fac Appt:** Prof Hem & Onc, Emory Univ

Lawson, David H MD [Onc] - **Spec Exp:** Melanoma; **Hospital:** Emory Univ Hosp; **Address:** Emory Winship Cancer Institute, 1365C Clifton Rd NE, Ste 2110, Atlanta, GA 30322; **Phone:** 404-778-1900; **Board Cert:** Internal Medicine 1977; Medical Oncology 1979; **Med School:** Emory Univ 1974; **Resid:** Internal Medicine, Emory Univ Hosps 1977; **Fellow:** Medical Oncology, Emory Univ 1979; **Fac Appt:** Assoc Prof Hem & Onc, Emory Univ

Lesser, Glenn J MD [Onc] - **Spec Exp:** Neuro-Oncology; Brain Tumors; **Hospital:** Wake Forest Baptist Med Ctr; **Address:** Wake Forest Univ-Div Hematolgy/Oncology, Medical Center Blvd, Winston-Salem, NC 27157-1082; **Phone:** 336-713-5440; **Board Cert:** Medical Oncology 2007; **Med School:** Penn State Coll Med 1987; **Resid:** Internal Medicine, NC Baptist Hosp/Bowman Gray Sch Med 1991; **Fellow:** Medical Oncology, Johns Hopkins Hosp 1995; **Fac Appt:** Prof Hem & Onc, Wake Forest Univ

Limentani, Steven A MD [Onc] - **Spec Exp:** Breast Cancer; Clinical Trials; **Hospital:** Carolinas Med Ctr; **Address:** 1100 S Tryon St, Ste 400, Charlotte, NC 28203; **Phone:** 704-446-9046; **Board Cert:** Internal Medicine 1989; Medical Oncology 2011; Hematology 2012; **Med School:** Tufts Univ 1986; **Resid:** Internal Medicine, New England Deaconess Hosp 1989; **Fellow:** Hematology & Oncology, New England Med Ctr 1992

Lippman, Marc E MD [Onc] - **Spec Exp:** Breast Cancer; **Hospital:** Univ of Miami Hosp & Clins/Sylvester Comp Canc Ctr; **Address:** SCCC, Med Oncology, 1475 NW 12th Ave Fl 3, Miami, FL 33136; **Phone:** 305-243-1000; **Board Cert:** Internal Medicine 1987; Endocrinology 1975; Medical Oncology 1977; **Med School:** Yale Univ 1968; **Resid:** Internal Medicine, Johns Hopkins Hosp 1970; **Fellow:** Medical Oncology, Natl Cancer Inst 1973; Endocrinology, Yale-New Haven Hosp 1974; **Fac Appt:** Prof Med, Univ Miami Sch Med

List, Alan F MD [Onc] - **Spec Exp:** Myelodysplastic Syndromes; Leukemia; **Hospital:** Moffitt Canc Ctr (page 61); **Address:** 12902 Magnolia Drive, Tampa, FL 33612-9497; **Phone:** 813-745-7101; **Board Cert:** Internal Medicine 1983; Medical Oncology 1985; Hematology 1986; **Med School:** Univ Pennsylvania 1980; **Resid:** Internal Medicine, Good Samaritan Hosp 1983; Oncology, Vanderbilt Univ Med Ctr 1985; **Fellow:** Hematology, Vanderbilt Univ Med Ctr 1986; **Fac Appt:** Prof Med, Univ S Fla Coll Med

Lossos, Izidore MD [Onc] - **Spec Exp:** Lymphoma; Hodgkin's Lymphoma; Leukemia; Lymphomas-Rare; **Hospital:** Univ of Miami Hosp & Clins/Sylvester Comp Canc Ctr, Jackson Meml Hosp; **Address:** Univ Miami - Sylvester Comp Cancer Ctr, 1475 NW 12th Ave, D8-4, Miami, FL 33136; **Phone:** 305-243-4785; **Med School:** Israel 1987; **Resid:** Internal Medicine, Hadassah Univ Hosp 1995; **Fellow:** Hematology & Oncology, Hadassah Univ Hosp 1997; Medical Oncology, Stanford Univ 2001; **Fac Appt:** Prof Hem & Onc, Univ Miami Sch Med

Lutzky, Jose MD [Onc] - **Spec Exp:** Melanoma; Prostate Cancer; **Hospital:** Mount Sinai Med Ctr - Miami; **Address:** Mount Sinai Comp Cancer Ctr, 4306 Alton Rd Fl 3, Miami Beach, FL 33140; **Phone:** 305-535-3300; **Board Cert:** Internal Medicine 1985; Medical Oncology 1987; Hematology 1988; **Med School:** Brazil 1980; **Resid:** Internal Medicine, Mount Sinai Med Ctr 1985; **Fellow:** Hematology & Oncology, Columbia-Presby Med Ctr 1988; **Fac Appt:** Asst Clin Prof Med, Univ Miami Sch Med

Lyckholm, Laurel J MD [Onc] - **Spec Exp:** Neuro-Oncology; Palliative Care; **Hospital:** VCU Med Ctr, Med Coll of VA Hosp; **Address:** Dalton Oncology Clinic, 1300 E Marshall St, Richmond, VA 23219; **Phone:** 804-828-7999; **Board Cert:** Internal Medicine 1989; Medical Oncology 2003; Hematology 2004; Hospice & Palliative Medicine 2008; **Med School:** Creighton Univ 1985; **Resid:** Internal Medicine, Creighton Univ 1989; **Fellow:** Hematology & Oncology, Univ IA Hosp 1992; Medical Ethics, Univ Chicago 1996; **Fac Appt:** Assoc Prof Med, Med Coll VA

Lyman, Gary H MD [Onc] - **Spec Exp:** Breast Cancer; **Hospital:** Duke Univ Hosp; **Address:** Duke Cancer Institute, Hock Plaza, 2424 Erwin Rd, Ste 205, Durham, NC 27705; **Phone:** 919-668-6688; **Board Cert:** Internal Medicine 1987; Medical Oncology 1977; Hematology 1978; **Med School:** SUNY Buffalo 1972; **Resid:** Internal Medicine, Univ North Carolina Hosp 1974; **Fellow:** Medical Oncology, Roswell Park Meml Inst 1976; Biostatistics, Harvard Med Sch 1982; **Fac Appt:** Prof Med, Duke Univ

Lynch Jr, James W MD [Onc] - **Spec Exp:** Lymphoma; Hodgkin's Disease Consultation; Hodgkin's Lymphoma; Lymphoma, Non-Hodgkin's; **Hospital:** UF Hlth Shands Hosp; **Address:** Shands Hlthcare, Div Hematology/Oncology, 2000 SW Archer Rd, Gainesville, FL 32608; **Phone:** 352-265-0725; **Board Cert:** Internal Medicine 1987; Medical Oncology 2012; **Med School:** Eastern VA Med Sch 1984; **Resid:** Internal Medicine, Univ FL/Shands Hosp 1987; **Fellow:** Medical Oncology, Natl Cancer Inst 1991; **Fac Appt:** Prof Med, Univ Fla Coll Med

Marcom, Paul Kelly MD [Onc] - **Spec Exp:** Breast Cancer; Clinical Trials; Cancer Genetics; **Hospital:** Duke Univ Hosp; **Address:** Duke Univ Med Ctr, Box 3147, Durham, NC 27710; **Phone:** 919-684-3877; **Board Cert:** Internal Medicine 2003; Medical Oncology 2005; **Med School:** Baylor Coll Med 1989; **Resid:** Internal Medicine, Duke Univ Med Ctr 1992; **Fellow:** Hematology & Oncology, Duke Univ Med Ctr 1995; **Fac Appt:** Assoc Prof Med, Duke Univ

McGuire III, William P MD [Onc] - **Spec Exp:** Gynecologic Cancer; Ovarian Cancer; Uterine Leiomyosarcoma; **Hospital:** Inova Fairfax Hosp; **Address:** 3300 Gallows Rd, Fall's Church, VA 22042; **Phone:** 703-970-6545; **Board Cert:** Internal Medicine 1974; Medical Oncology 1981; **Med School:** Baylor Coll Med 1971; **Resid:** Internal Medicine, Yale-New Haven Hosp 1973; **Fellow:** Medical Oncology, Natl Cancer Inst 1976; **Fac Appt:** Clin Prof Med, Univ MD Sch Med

Miller, Antonius A MD [Onc] - **Spec Exp:** Lung Cancer; **Hospital:** Wake Forest Baptist Med Ctr, W.G. (Bill) Hefner VA Med Ctr; **Address:** Wake Forest University, Comprehensive Cancer Center, Medical Center Blvd, Winston-Salem, NC 27157; **Phone:** 336-713-4392; **Med School:** Germany 1977; **Resid:** Internal Medicine, Univ Essen Med Sch 1979; Internal Medicine, Univ TN Med Ctr 1987; **Fellow:** Hematology & Oncology, UT MD Anderson Cancer Ctr 1981; **Fac Appt:** Prof Onc, Wake Forest Univ

Miller, Donald M MD/PhD [Onc] - **Spec Exp:** Melanoma; Lung Cancer; **Hospital:** Univ of Louisville Hosp; **Address:** James Graham Brown Cancer Center, 529 S Jackson St, Louisville, KY 40202; **Phone:** 502-562-4790; **Board Cert:** Internal Medicine 1979; **Med School:** Duke Univ 1973; **Resid:** Internal Medicine, Peter Bent Brigham Hosp 1975; **Fellow:** Internal Medicine, Peter Bent Brigham Hosp 1978; Medical Oncology, Natl Cancer Inst 1979; **Fac Appt:** Prof Onc, Univ Louisville Sch Med

Moore, Joseph O MD [Onc] - **Spec Exp:** Leukemia; Hodgkin's Lymphoma; Lymphoma, Non-Hodgkin's; Neuroendocrine Tumors; **Hospital:** Duke Univ Hosp; **Address:** Duke Univ Med Ctr, 1 Tent Drive, rm 25153, Box 3872, Morris Bldg, Durham, NC 27710; **Phone:** 919-684-8964; **Board Cert:** Internal Medicine 1975; Medical Oncology 1977; **Med School:** Johns Hopkins Univ 1970; **Resid:** Internal Medicine, Johns Hopkins Hosp 1975; **Fellow:** Hematology & Oncology, Duke Univ Med Ctr 1977; **Fac Appt:** Prof Med, Duke Univ

Morgan, David S MD [Onc] - **Spec Exp:** Leukemia & Lymphoma; Hodgkin's Lymphoma; AIDS Related Lymphoma; **Hospital:** Vanderbilt Univ Med Ctr; **Address:** Vanderbilt Hematology/Oncology, 2220 Pierce Ave, 777 Preston Research Bldg, Nashville, TN 37232-6307; **Phone:** 615-936-8422; **Board Cert:** Internal Medicine 2003; Medical Oncology 2008; **Med School:** Vanderbilt Univ 1990; **Resid:** Internal Medicine, Yale-New Haven Hosp 1993; **Fellow:** Medical Oncology, Stanford Univ Med Ctr 1997; **Fac Appt:** Assoc Prof Med, Vanderbilt Univ

Muss, Hyman B MD [Onc] - **Spec Exp:** Breast Cancer; Breast Cancer in Elderly; **Hospital:** NC Memorial Hosp - UNC; **Address:** UNC Hematology/Oncology, Physicians Office Bldg, 170 Manning Drive Fl 3, Box CB 7305, Chapel Hill, NC 27599; **Phone:** 919-966-4431; **Board Cert:** Internal Medicine 1973; Hematology 1974; Medical Oncology 1975; **Med School:** SUNY Downstate 1968; **Resid:** Internal Medicine, Peter Bent Brigham Hosp 1970; **Fellow:** Hematology & Oncology, Peter Bent Brigham Hosp 1974; Hematology & Oncology, Dana-Farber Cancer Ctr 1974; **Fac Appt:** Prof Onc, Univ NC Sch Med

Nabell, Lisle M MD [Onc] - **Spec Exp:** Breast Cancer; Head & Neck Cancer; **Hospital:** UAB Hosp; **Address:** The Kirklin Clinic, 2000 6th Ave S, Birmingham, AL 35233; **Phone:** 205-934-5077; **Board Cert:** Medical Oncology 2000; **Med School:** Univ NC Sch Med 1987; **Resid:** Internal Medicine, Univ Alabama Hosp 1990; **Fellow:** Hematology & Oncology, Univ Alabama Hosp 1992; **Fac Appt:** Assoc Prof Med, UAB Sch Med

O'Regan, Ruth M MD [Onc] - **Spec Exp:** Breast Cancer; Breast Cancer Risk Assessment; Cancer Prevention; Clinical Trials; **Hospital:** Emory Univ Hosp, Grady Hlth Sys; **Address:** Emory Winship Cancer Inst, 1365C Clifton Rd NE, Ste 2110, Atlanta, GA 30322; **Phone:** 404-778-1900; **Board Cert:** Medical Oncology 2010; **Med School:** Ireland 1988; **Resid:** Internal Medicine, Med Coll Wisconsin 1995; Internal Medicine, Northwestern Univ Hosp 1999; **Fellow:** Medical Oncology, Northwestern Univ 1998; **Fac Appt:** Prof Hem & Onc, Emory Univ

Pao, William MD/PhD [Onc] - **Spec Exp:** Thoracic Cancers; Lung Cancer; **Hospital:** Vanderbilt Univ Med Ctr; **Address:** Vanderbilt Ingram Cancer Ctr, 2220 Pierce Ave, Ste 1710, Nashville, TN 37232-6307; **Phone:** 615-936-8422; **Board Cert:** Medical Oncology 2003; **Med School:** Yale Univ 1998; **Resid:** Internal Medicine, New York Hosp 2000; **Fellow:** Medical Oncology, Meml Sloan Kettering Canc Ctr 2004; **Fac Appt:** Prof Med, Vanderbilt Univ

Pasche, Boris C MD/PhD [Onc] - **Spec Exp:** Colon & Rectal Cancer; Gastrointestinal Cancer; Hereditary Cancer; **Hospital:** UAB Hosp; **Address:** The Kirklin Clinic, 2000 6th Ave S, Birmingham, AL 35233; **Phone:** 205-934-5077; **Board Cert:** Medical Oncology 2008; **Med School:** Sweden 1986; **Resid:** Internal Medicine, NY Hosp/Cornell Med Ctr 1994; **Fellow:** Hematology & Oncology, Sloan Kettering Cancer Ctr 1996; **Fac Appt:** Prof Med, UAB Sch Med

Perez, Edith A MD [Onc] - **Spec Exp:** Breast Cancer; Breast Cancer Risk Assessment; Clinical Trials; **Hospital:** Mayo - Jacksonville; **Address:** Mayo Clin, Breast Clin, 4500 San Pablo Rd, Jacksonville, FL 32224; **Phone:** 904-953-7283; **Board Cert:** Internal Medicine 1983; Hematology 1986; Medical Oncology 1987; **Med School:** Univ Puerto Rico 1979; **Resid:** Internal Medicine, Loma Linda Univ Med Ctr 1982; **Fellow:** Hematology & Oncology, Martinez VA Hosp 1987; **Fac Appt:** Prof Med, Mayo Med Sch

Posey III, James A MD [Onc] - **Spec Exp:** Gastrointestinal Cancer; Colon Cancer; Liver Cancer; Biliary Cancer; **Hospital:** UAB Hosp; **Address:** The Kirklin Clinic, 2000 6th Ave S, Birmingham, AL 35233; **Phone:** 205-934-5077; **Board Cert:** Medical Oncology 2012; **Med School:** Howard Univ 1991; **Resid:** Internal Medicine, Georgetown U Med Ctr 1994; **Fellow:** Hematology & Oncology, Georgetown U Med Ctr 1997; **Fac Appt:** Assoc Prof Med, UAB Sch Med

Ready, Neal E MD/PhD [Onc] - **Spec Exp:** Lung Cancer; Head & Neck Cancer; Clinical Trials; **Hospital:** Duke Univ Hosp; **Address:** Duke Univ Med Ctr, Box 3198, Durham, NC 27710; **Phone:** 919-668-6688; **Board Cert:** Internal Medicine 1989; Hematology 2005; Medical Oncology 2005; **Med School:** Vanderbilt Univ 1986; **Resid:** Internal Medicine, Rhode Island Hosp 1989; **Fellow:** Hematology, Rhode Island Hosp 1992; Medical Oncology, New England Med Ctr 1994

Robert, Nicholas J MD [Onc] - **Spec Exp:** Breast Cancer; **Hospital:** Inova Fairfax Hosp; **Address:** Virginia Cancer Specialists, 8503 Arlington Blvd, Ste 400, Fairfax, VA 22031; **Phone:** 703-280-5390; **Board Cert:** Internal Medicine 1978; Anatomic Pathology 1979; Medical Oncology 1981; Hematology 1984; **Med School:** McGill Univ 1974; **Resid:** Internal Medicine, Royal Victoria Hosp 1976; Pathology, Mass Genl Hosp 1979; **Fellow:** Hematology, Peter Bent Brigham Hosp 1980; Medical Oncology, Dana Farber Cancer Inst 1981

Robert-Vizcarrondo, Francisco MD [Onc] - **Spec Exp:** Lung Cancer; Mesothelioma; Drug Development; Clinical Trials; **Hospital:** UAB Hosp; **Address:** The Kirklin Clinic, 2000 6th Ave S, Birmingham, AL 35233; **Phone:** 205-934-5077; **Board Cert:** Internal Medicine 1973; Medical Oncology 1975; Hematology 1976; **Med School:** Puerto Rico 1969; **Resid:** Internal Medicine, Univ PR Hosp 1972; Hematology, Univ PR Hosp 1974; **Fellow:** Medical Oncology, Univ AL Hosps 1976; **Fac Appt:** Prof Hem & Onc, UAB Sch Med

Romond, Edward H MD [Onc] - **Spec Exp:** Breast Cancer; Hemophilia; **Hospital:** Univ of Kentucky Albert B. Chandler Hosp; **Address:** Univ of KY Med Ctr, Div of Medical Oncol, CC413 Markey Cancer Center, 800 Rose St, Lexington, KY 40536; **Phone:** 859-323-6522; **Board Cert:** Internal Medicine 1980; Hematology 1984; Medical Oncology 1983; **Med School:** Univ KY Coll Med 1977; **Resid:** Internal Medicine, Michigan State Univ Hosps 1980; **Fellow:** Hematology & Oncology, Michigan State Univ 1983; **Fac Appt:** Prof Onc, Univ KY Coll Med

Schwartz, Michael A MD [Onc] - **Spec Exp:** Lymphoma; Prostate Cancer; Breast Cancer; **Hospital:** Mount Sinai Med Ctr - Miami; **Address:** Mount Sinai Med Ctr, Hematology/Oncology, 4306 Alton Rd Fl 3, Miami Beach, FL 33140; **Phone:** 305-535-3310; **Board Cert:** Internal Medicine 1989; Medical Oncology 2004; Hematology 2004; **Med School:** UMDNJ-RW Johnson Med Sch 1986; **Resid:** Internal Medicine, Mount Sinai Med Ctr 1989; **Fellow:** Hematology & Oncology, Meml Sloan-Kettering Cancer Ctr 1992; **Fac Appt:** Asst Clin Prof Med, Univ Miami Sch Med

Serody, Jonathan S MD [Onc] - **Spec Exp:** Breast Cancer Vaccine Therapy; Clinical Trials; Lymphoma; **Hospital:** NC Memorial Hosp - UNC; **Address:** Lineberger Comprehensive Cancer Ctr, 450 West Drive, CB 7295, Chapel Hill, NC 27599-7295; **Phone:** 919-966-8644; **Board Cert:** Internal Medicine 1989; Hematology 2007; **Med School:** Univ VA Sch Med 1986; **Resid:** Internal Medicine, Univ NC Med Ctr 1989; **Fellow:** Hematology, Univ NC Med Ctr 1992; Bone Marrow Transplant, Fred Hutchinson Transplant Program 1993; **Fac Appt:** Prof Med, Univ NC Sch Med

Shea, Thomas MD [Onc] - **Spec Exp:** Bone Marrow Transplant; Lymphoma; Leukemia; **Hospital:** NC Memorial Hosp - UNC; **Address:** Univ N Carolina, Dept Medicine, 170 Manning Drive, CB 7305, Chapel Hill, NC 27599; **Phone:** 919-966-7746; **Board Cert:** Internal Medicine 1982; Hematology 1984; Medical Oncology 1985; **Med School:** Univ NC Sch Med 1978; **Resid:** Internal Medicine, Beth Israel Deaconess Med Ctr 1982; **Fellow:** Hematology & Oncology, Beth Israel Deaconess Med Ctr 1985; Bone Marrow Transplant, Dana Farber Cancer Inst 1988; **Fac Appt:** Prof Med, Univ NC Sch Med

Sherman, Carol A MD [Onc] - **Spec Exp:** Lung Cancer; Thoracic Cancers; **Hospital:** MUSC Med Ctr; **Address:** MUSC Hematology/Oncology, 173 Ashley Ave, MS 365, Charleston, SC 29425; **Phone:** 843-792-9621; **Board Cert:** Internal Medicine 1987; Medical Oncology 1989; **Med School:** Univ Mass Sch Med 1984; **Resid:** Internal Medicine, Univ Mass Med Ctr 1987; **Fellow:** Hematology & Oncology, Univ Mass Med Ctr 1989; **Fac Appt:** Assoc Prof Med, Med Univ SC

Shin, Dong Moon MD [Onc] - **Spec Exp:** Head & Neck Cancer; Mesothelioma; Thymoma; Lung Cancer; **Hospital:** Emory Univ Hosp; **Address:** Emory Winship Cancer Inst, 1365 C Clifton Rd NE, Ste 3094, Atlanta, GA 30322; **Phone:** 404-778-1900; **Board Cert:** Internal Medicine 1985; Medical Oncology 1989; **Med School:** South Korea 1975; **Resid:** Internal Medicine, Cook Co Hosp 1985; **Fellow:** Medical Oncology, UT-MD Anderson Cancer Ctr 1988; **Fac Appt:** Prof Hem & Onc, Emory Univ

Sosman, Jeffrey A MD [Onc] - **Spec Exp:** Melanoma; Skin Cancer; Immunotherapy; Drug Discovery; **Hospital:** Vanderbilt Univ Med Ctr; **Address:** Vanderbilt Ingram Cancer Ctr, 2220 Pierce Ave, Ste 1710, Nashville, TN 37232-6307; **Phone:** 615-936-8422; **Board Cert:** Anatomic Pathology 1985; Internal Medicine 1987; Medical Oncology 1989; **Med School:** Albert Einstein Coll Med 1981; **Resid:** Anatomic Pathology, Univ Chicago Hosps 1985; Internal Medicine, Univ Wisconsin Hosp 1986; **Fellow:** Medical Oncology, Univ Wisconsin 1989; **Fac Appt:** Prof Med, Vanderbilt Univ

Sotomayor, Eduardo M MD [Onc] - **Spec Exp:** Lymphoma; Gene Therapy; Vaccine Therapy; Clinical Trials; **Hospital:** Moffitt Canc Ctr (page 61); **Address:** H Lee Moffitt Cancer Ctr, 12902 Magnolia Drive, MS FOB3, Tampa, FL 33612; **Phone:** 813-745-3980; **Board Cert:** Medical Oncology 2009; **Med School:** Peru 1988; **Resid:** Internal Medicine, Univ Miami Hosp 1995; **Fellow:** Immunology, Univ Miami Hosp 1992; Oncology, Johns Hopkins Hosp 1998; **Fac Appt:** Assoc Prof Med, Univ S Fla Coll Med

Stone, Joel A MD [Onc] - **Spec Exp:** Lung Cancer; Breast Cancer; **Hospital:** St. Vincent's Med Ctr - Riverside (Jacksonville); **Address:** Cancer Specialists of North Florida, 2 Shircliff Way, Ste 800, Jacksonville, FL 32204; **Phone:** 904-388-2619; **Board Cert:** Internal Medicine 1977; Medical Oncology 1979; **Med School:** Univ VA Sch Med 1974; **Resid:** Internal Medicine, Univ KY Med Ctr 1977; **Fellow:** Hematology & Oncology, Emory Univ Hosp 1979

Sutton, Linda Marie MD [Onc] - **Spec Exp:** Breast Cancer; Palliative Care; **Hospital:** Duke Univ Hosp; **Address:** University Tower, 3100 Tower Blvd, Ste 600, Durham, NC 27707; **Phone:** 919-419-5005; **Board Cert:** Internal Medicine 2012; Medical Oncology 2003; **Med School:** Univ Mass Sch Med 1987; **Resid:** Internal Medicine, Montefiore Med Ctr 1990; **Fellow:** Hematology & Oncology, Duke Univ Med Ctr 1993

Thigpen, James T MD [Onc] - **Spec Exp:** Gynecologic Cancer; Breast Cancer; Lung Cancer; **Hospital:** Univ Mississippi Med Ctr; **Address:** 350 W Woodrow Wilson Ave, Jackson, MS 39216; **Phone:** 601-984-5590; **Board Cert:** Internal Medicine 1972; Hematology 1974; Medical Oncology 1975; **Med School:** Univ Miss 1969; **Resid:** Internal Medicine, Univ Miss Med Ctr 1971; **Fellow:** Hematology & Oncology, Univ Miss Med Ctr 1973; **Fac Appt:** Prof Med, Univ Miss

Troner, Michael B MD [Onc] - **Spec Exp:** Head & Neck Cancer; Urologic Cancer; **Hospital:** Baptist Hosp of Miami; **Address:** Baptist Hosp, 8940 N Kendall Drive, Ste 300E, Miami, FL 33176; **Phone:** 305-595-2141; **Board Cert:** Internal Medicine 1972; Medical Oncology 1973; **Med School:** SUNY Downstate 1968; **Resid:** Internal Medicine, Univ MD Med Ctr 1971; **Fellow:** Medical Oncology, Univ Miami Hosp 1973

Vaughan, William P MD [Onc] - **Spec Exp:** Bone Marrow Transplant; Hematologic Malignancies; **Hospital:** UAB Hosp; **Address:** 1900 University Blvd, Tinsley Harrison Tower 541, Birmingham, AL 35294-0007; **Phone:** 205-975-0837; **Board Cert:** Internal Medicine 1975; Medical Oncology 1979; **Med School:** Univ Conn 1972; **Resid:** Internal Medicine, Univ Chicago Hosps 1975; **Fellow:** Oncology, Johns Hopkins Hosp 1977; **Fac Appt:** Prof Hem & Onc, UAB Sch Med

Waller, Edmund K MD [Onc] - **Spec Exp:** Bone Marrow & Stem Cell Transplant; Leukemia; Testicular Cancer; **Hospital:** Emory Univ Hosp; **Address:** Emory Winship Cancer Inst, Hem/Onc, 1365 Clifton Rd NE C Bldg, Atlanta, GA 30322; **Phone:** 404-778-1900; **Board Cert:** Internal Medicine 1988; Medical Oncology 2006; **Med School:** Cornell Univ 1985; **Resid:** Internal Medicine, Stanford Univ Hosp & Clins 1988; **Fellow:** Oncology, Stanford Univ Hosp & Clins 1992; **Fac Appt:** Prof Hem & Onc, Emory Univ

Weber, Jeffrey S MD/PhD [Onc] - **Spec Exp:** Melanoma; **Hospital:** Moffitt Canc Ctr (page 61); **Address:** H Lee Moffitt Cancer Ctr, 12902 Magnolia Ave, Tampa, FL 33612; **Phone:** 813-745-2007; **Board Cert:** Internal Medicine 1983; Medical Oncology 1987; **Med School:** NYU Sch Med 1980; **Resid:** Internal Medicine, UCSD Med Ctr 1983; **Fellow:** Medical Oncology, Natl Cancer Inst 1990; **Fac Appt:** Assoc Prof Med, USC Sch Med

Weiss, Geoffrey R MD [Onc] - **Spec Exp:** Gastrointestinal Cancer; Genitourinary Cancer; Melanoma; **Hospital:** Univ of Virginia Hlth Sys; **Address:** Univ VA Hlth System, Box 800716, Div Hematology/Oncology, 1215 Lee St, Charlottesville, VA 22908-0716; **Phone:** 434-243-0066; **Board Cert:** Internal Medicine 1977; Medical Oncology 1981; **Med School:** St Louis Univ 1974; **Resid:** Internal Medicine, Temple Univ Hosp 1978; **Fellow:** Medical Oncology, Dana-Farber Canc Inst 1982; **Fac Appt:** Prof Med, Univ VA Sch Med

Wingard, John R MD [Onc] - **Spec Exp:** Bone Marrow Transplant; Leukemia; Multiple Myeloma; Lymphoma; **Hospital:** UF Hlth Shands Hosp; **Address:** Shands Hosp-Division of Hematology, 1600 SW Archer Rd, Gainesville, FL 32610; **Phone:** 352-265-0111 x29452; **Board Cert:** Internal Medicine 1976; Medical Oncology 1983; **Med School:** Johns Hopkins Univ 1973; **Resid:** Internal Medicine, Memphis City Hosps 1976; Internal Medicine, VA Hosp 1977; **Fellow:** Medical Oncology, Johns Hopkins Hosp 1979; **Fac Appt:** Prof Med, Univ Fla Coll Med

Yunus, Furhan MD [Onc] - **Spec Exp:** Multiple Myeloma; Lymphoma; **Hospital:** Methodist Univ Hosp - Memphis, Baptist Memorial Hospital-Memphis; **Address:** Boston Baskin Cancer Foundation, 7945 Wolf River Blvd, Ste 300, Germantown, TN 38138; **Phone:** 901-722-3627; **Board Cert:** Medical Oncology 2008; **Med School:** Pakistan 1986; **Resid:** Internal Medicine, Methodist Hosp 1993; **Fellow:** Hematology & Oncology, Univ Ariz Coll Med Affil Hosp 1995; **Fac Appt:** Asst Prof Med, Univ Tenn Coll Med

Midwest

Abraham, Jame MD [Onc] - **Spec Exp:** Breast Cancer; Clinical Trials; **Hospital:** Cleveland Clin (page 55); **Address:** Taussig Cancer Inst, 9500 Euclid Ave, Cleveland, OH 44195; **Phone:** 216-444-6833; **Board Cert:** Internal Medicine 2007; Medical Oncology 2010; **Med School:** India 1991; **Resid:** Internal Medicine, Univ Conn Sch Med Affil Hosps 1997; **Fellow:** Medical Oncology, Natl Cancer Inst 1999; Hematology, Natl Heart Lung & Blood Inst 2000; **Fac Appt:** Prof Onc, W VA Univ

Adelstein, David J MD [Onc] - **Spec Exp:** Head & Neck Cancer; Esophageal Cancer; Lung Cancer; **Hospital:** Cleveland Clin (page 55); **Address:** Cleveland Clinic, Taussig Cancer Inst, 9500 Euclid Ave, R35, Cleveland, OH 44195; **Phone:** 216-444-9310; **Board Cert:** Internal Medicine 1978; Medical Oncology 1981; Hematology 1982; **Med School:** NYU Sch Med 1975; **Resid:** Internal Medicine, Univ Hosps Cleveland 1978; **Fellow:** Hematology & Oncology, Univ Hosps Cleveland 1981; **Fac Appt:** Prof Med, Cleveland Cl Coll Med/Case West Res

Albain, Kathy S MD [Onc] - **Spec Exp:** Breast Cancer; Lung Cancer; Cancer Survivors-Late Effects of Therapy; **Hospital:** Loyola Univ Med Ctr; **Address:** Loyola Univ Med Ctr, 2160 S First Ave Bldg 112 - Ste 109, Maywood, IL 60153-5590; **Phone:** 708-327-3102; **Board Cert:** Internal Medicine 1981; Medical Oncology 1983; **Med School:** Univ Mich Med Sch 1978; **Resid:** Internal Medicine, Univ Illinois Med Ctr 1981; **Fellow:** Hematology & Oncology, Univ Chicago Med Ctr 1984; **Fac Appt:** Prof Onc, Loyola Univ-Stritch Sch Med

Albertini, Mark R MD [Onc] - **Spec Exp:** Melanoma; Melanoma-Advanced; Immunotherapy; **Hospital:** Univ WI Hosp & Clins, Wm S Middleton Mem Vet Hosp-Madison; **Address:** UW Carbone Canc Ctr, 600 highland Ave Fl K6 - rm 530 CSC, Madison, WI 53792-5669; **Phone:** 608-265-1700; **Board Cert:** Internal Medicine 1987; Medical Oncology 2002; **Med School:** Univ VT Coll Med 1984; **Resid:** Internal Medicine, Univ Wisc Hosps Clins 1987; **Fellow:** Medical Oncology, Univ Wisc Hosps Clins 1991; **Fac Appt:** Assoc Prof Onc, Univ Wisc

Benson III, Al B MD [Onc] - **Spec Exp:** Colon Cancer; Gastrointestinal Cancer; Liver Cancer; Pancreatic Cancer; **Hospital:** Northwestern Meml Hosp, Jesse Brown VA Med Ctr; **Address:** Northwestern Meml Hosp-Div Hem/Onc, 675 N St Clair St Fl 21 - Ste 100, Chicago, IL 60611; **Phone:** 312-695-0990; **Board Cert:** Internal Medicine 1979; Medical Oncology 1983; **Med School:** SUNY Buffalo 1976; **Resid:** Internal Medicine, Univ Wisc Hosps 1979; **Fellow:** Medical Oncology, Univ Wisc Hosps 1984; **Fac Appt:** Prof Med, Northwestern Univ

Bishop, Michael R MD [Onc] - **Spec Exp:** Leukemia & Lymphoma; Stem Cell Transplant; Lymphoma, Non-Hodgkin's; Multiple Myeloma; **Hospital:** Univ of Chicago Med; **Address:** Univ Chicago Medicine-Hem/Onc, 5841 S Maryland Ave, Chicago, IL 60637; **Phone:** 773-702-8222; **Board Cert:** Internal Medicine 1989; Medical Oncology 2011; **Med School:** Univ IL Coll Med 1985; **Resid:** Internal Medicine, Northwestern Meml Hosp 1988; **Fellow:** Hematology & Oncology, Loyola Univ Med Ctr 1991; **Fac Appt:** Prof Med, Univ Chicago-Pritzker Sch Med

Bitran, Jacob D MD [Onc] - **Spec Exp:** Breast Cancer; Bone Marrow Transplant; Lung Cancer; **Hospital:** Adv Luth Genl Hosp; **Address:** Oncology Specialists, 1700 Luther Ln, Park Ridge, IL 60068-1270; **Phone:** 847-268-8200; **Board Cert:** Internal Medicine 1974; Medical Oncology 1977; Hematology 1986; **Med School:** Univ IL Coll Med 1971; **Resid:** Pathology, Rush-Presby St Lukes Hosp 1973; Internal Medicine, Michael Reese Hosp 1975; **Fellow:** Hematology & Oncology, Univ Chicago Hosps 1977; **Fac Appt:** Prof Onc, Ros Franklin Univ/Chicago Med Sch

Bolwell, Brian J MD [Onc] - **Spec Exp:** Bone Marrow Transplant; Hematologic Malignancies; **Hospital:** Cleveland Clin (page 55); **Address:** 9500 Euclid Ave, Ste R-32, Desk R32, Cleveland, OH 44195; **Phone:** 216-444-6922; **Board Cert:** Internal Medicine 1985; Medical Oncology 1987; **Med School:** Case West Res Univ 1981; **Resid:** Internal Medicine, Univ Hosp 1984; **Fellow:** Hematology & Oncology, Hosp Univ Penn 1987; **Fac Appt:** Prof Med, Cleveland Cl Coll Med/Case West Res

Bonomi, Philip D MD [Onc] - **Spec Exp:** Lung Cancer; Thymoma; Mesothelioma; **Hospital:** Rush Univ Med Ctr; **Address:** Rush University Medical Center, 1725 W Harrison St, Ste 821, Chicago, IL 60612; **Phone:** 312-942-5904; **Board Cert:** Internal Medicine 1975; Medical Oncology 1977; **Med School:** Univ IL Coll Med 1970; **Resid:** Internal Medicine, Geisinger Med Ctr 1975; **Fellow:** Medical Oncology, Rush Presby-St Luke's Med Ctr 1977; **Fac Appt:** Prof Med, Rush Med Coll

Brockstein, Bruce E MD [Onc] - **Spec Exp:** Head & Neck Cancer; Sarcoma; Melanoma; **Hospital:** Evanston Hosp/NorthShore Univ Hlth Sys (page 67), Highland Park Hosp/NorthShore Univ Hlth Syst (page 67); **Address:** Evanston Hospital - Northshore Med Grp, Kellogg Cancer Ctr, 2650 Ridge Ave, Evanston, IL 60201; **Phone:** 847-570-2112; **Board Cert:** Internal Medicine 2003; Medical Oncology 2005; **Med School:** Univ Chicago-Pritzker Sch Med 1990; **Resid:** Internal Medicine, Hosp Univ Penn 1993; **Fellow:** Hematology & Oncology, Univ Chicago Hosps 1996; **Fac Appt:** Assoc Clin Prof Onc, Univ Chicago-Pritzker Sch Med

Buckner, Jan Craig MD [Onc] - **Spec Exp:** Brain Tumors; Neuro-Oncology; **Hospital:** Mayo Med Ctr & Clin - Rochester; **Address:** Mayo Clinic, 200 First St SW, Rochester, MN 55905; **Phone:** 507-284-4320; **Board Cert:** Internal Medicine 1983; Medical Oncology 1985; **Med School:** Univ NC Sch Med 1980; **Resid:** Internal Medicine, Butterworth Hosp 1983; **Fellow:** Medical Oncology, Mayo Clinic 1985; **Fac Appt:** Prof Med, Mayo Med Sch

Budd, G. Thomas MD [Onc] - **Spec Exp:** Breast Cancer; **Hospital:** Cleveland Clin (page 55); **Address:** Cleveland Clinic, Taussig Cancer Ctr, 9500 Euclid Ave, Desk R35, Cleveland, OH 44195; **Phone:** 216-444-6480; **Board Cert:** Internal Medicine 1980; Medical Oncology 1983; **Med School:** Univ Kansas 1977; **Resid:** Internal Medicine, Cleveland Clinic 1980; **Fellow:** Hematology & Oncology, Cleveland Clinic 1982

Carbone, David MD/PhD [Onc] - **Spec Exp:** Lung Cancer; Mesothelioma; Thymoma; **Hospital:** OSU Wexner Med Ctr; **Address:** 320 W 10th Ave, rm B402, Starling Loving Hall, Columbus, OH 43210; **Phone:** 614-293-6786; **Board Cert:** Internal Medicine 1988; Medical Oncology 2011; **Med School:** Johns Hopkins Univ 1985; **Resid:** Internal Medicine, Johns Hopkins Hosp 1988; **Fellow:** Medical Oncology, Natl Cancer Inst 1991; **Fac Appt:** Prof Onc, Ohio State Univ

Chapman, Robert A MD [Onc] - **Spec Exp:** Lung Cancer; **Hospital:** Henry Ford Hosp; **Address:** Henry Ford Hospital, 2799 W Grand Blvd Fl K13, Detroit, MI 48202; **Phone:** 313-916-1841; **Board Cert:** Internal Medicine 1985; Medical Oncology 1989; **Med School:** Cornell Univ-Weill Med Coll 1976; **Resid:** Internal Medicine, Henry Ford Hosp 1979; **Fellow:** Medical Oncology, Meml Sloan Kettering Cancer Ctr 1981

Chitambar, Christopher R MD [Onc] - **Spec Exp:** Lymphoma; Leukemia; Breast Cancer; **Hospital:** Froedtert & Med Coll WI; **Address:** Div Neoplastic Dis, 9200 W Wisconsin Ave, Milwaukee, WI 53226-3522; **Phone:** 414-805-4600; **Board Cert:** Internal Medicine 1980; Hematology 1982; Medical Oncology 1983; **Med School:** India 1977; **Resid:** Internal Medicine, Univ Med Ctr Brackenridge 1980; **Fellow:** Hematology & Oncology, Univ CO Hlth Sci Ctr 1983; **Fac Appt:** Prof Med, Med Coll Wisc

Clamon, Gerald H MD [Onc] - **Spec Exp:** Lung Cancer; Palliative Care; **Hospital:** Univ Iowa Hosp & Clins; **Address:** Holden Comprehensive Cancer Ctr, Med Onc, 200 Hawkins Drive, Ste C32GH, Iowa City, IA 52242; **Phone:** 319-384-8442; **Board Cert:** Internal Medicine 1976; Medical Oncology 1979; **Med School:** Washington Univ, St Louis 1971; **Resid:** Internal Medicine, Barnes Hosp 1976; **Fellow:** Research, Natl Cancer Inst 1974; Medical Oncology, Univ Iowa Hosp & Clinics 1977; **Fac Appt:** Prof Med, Univ Iowa Coll Med

Clark, Joseph I MD [Onc] - **Spec Exp:** Kidney Cancer; Melanoma; Head & Neck Cancer; **Hospital:** Loyola Univ Med Ctr, Edward Hines, Jr. VA Hosp; **Address:** Cardinal Bernardin Cancer Ctr, Loyola Univ Med Ctr, 2160 S First Ave, rm 346, Maywood, IL 60153-5500; **Phone:** 708-327-3217; **Board Cert:** Medical Oncology 2006; **Med School:** Loyola Univ-Stritch Sch Med 1989; **Resid:** Internal Medicine, Loyola Univ Med Ctr/Hines VA Hosp 1992; **Fellow:** Hematology & Oncology, Fox Chase Cancer Ctr/Temple Univ Hosp 1995; **Fac Appt:** Prof Med, Loyola Univ-Stritch Sch Med

Cleary, James F MD [Onc] - **Spec Exp:** Palliative Care; Head & Neck Cancer; **Hospital:** Univ WI Hosp & Clins; **Address:** UW Carbone Canc Ctr, 600 Highland Ave CSC Bldg - rm K6-546, Madison, WI 53792; **Phone:** 608-262-5223; **Board Cert:** Hospice & Palliative Medicine 2011; **Med School:** Australia 1984; **Resid:** Internal Medicine, Royal Adelaide Hosp 1987; **Fellow:** Medical Oncology, Royal Adelaide Hosp 1990; **Fac Appt:** Assoc Prof Med, Univ Wisc

Clinton, Steven K MD/PhD [Onc] - **Spec Exp:** Genitourinary Cancer; Prostate Cancer; Nutrition & Cancer Prevention/Control; **Hospital:** OSU Wexner Med Ctr; **Address:** 320 W 10th Ave, rm 456 SL, Columbus, OH 43210; **Phone:** 614-293-6196; **Board Cert:** Internal Medicine 1987; **Med School:** Univ IL Coll Med 1984; **Resid:** Internal Medicine, Univ Chicago Hosps 1987; **Fellow:** Medical Oncology, Dana-Farber Cancer Inst/Harvard 1991; **Fac Appt:** Prof Med, Ohio State Univ

Cobleigh, Melody A MD [Onc] - **Spec Exp:** Breast Cancer; **Hospital:** Rush Univ Med Ctr; **Address:** Rush Univ Med Ctr, 1725 W Harrison St, Ste 821, Chicago, IL 60612-3828; **Phone:** 312-942-5904; **Board Cert:** Internal Medicine 1979; Medical Oncology 1981; **Med School:** Rush Med Coll 1976; **Resid:** Internal Medicine, Rush Presby-St Lukes Med Ctr 1979; **Fellow:** Medical Oncology, Indiana Univ Hosp 1981; **Fac Appt:** Prof Med, Rush Med Coll

Cooney, Kathleen A MD [Onc] - **Hospital:** Univ Michigan Med Ctr; **Address:** Univ Michigan Comprehensive Cancer Ctr, 1500 E Medical Center Drive, Ann Arbor, MI 48109; **Phone:** 734-647-8903; **Board Cert:** Internal Medicine 1987; Medical Oncology 2011; **Med School:** Univ Pennsylvania 1984; **Resid:** Internal Medicine, Univ Michigan Med Ctr 1987; Internal Medicine, Univ Michigan Med Ctr 1988; **Fellow:** Hematology & Oncology, Univ Michigan Med Ctr 1991; **Fac Appt:** Prof U, Univ Mich Med Sch

Dowlati, Afshin MD [Onc] - **Spec Exp:** Lung Cancer; Thoracic Cancers; **Hospital:** UH Case Med Ctr; **Address:** UH Seidman Cancer Ctr, 11100 Euclid Ave, Cleveland, OH 44106; **Phone:** 216-844-3951; **Board Cert:** Internal Medicine 2010; Medical Oncology 2011; **Med School:** Belgium 1992; **Resid:** Internal Medicine, Univ Liege 1996; **Fellow:** Hematology & Oncology, Case Western/Univ Hosps 1998; **Fac Appt:** Assoc Prof Med, Case West Res Univ

Dreicer, Robert MD [Onc] - **Spec Exp:** Prostate Cancer; Kidney Cancer; Bladder Cancer; Testicular Cancer; **Hospital:** Cleveland Clin (page 55); **Address:** 9500 Euclid Ave, Desk R35, MS R35, Cleveland, OH 44195; **Phone:** 216-445-4623; **Board Cert:** Internal Medicine 1986; Medical Oncology 1989; **Med School:** Univ Tex, Houston 1983; **Resid:** Internal Medicine, Ind Univ Med Ctr 1986; **Fellow:** Medical Oncology, Univ Wisconsin Hosp 1989; **Fac Appt:** Prof Onc, Cleveland Cl Coll Med/Case West Res

Einhorn, Lawrence H MD [Onc] - **Spec Exp:** Testicular Cancer; Lung Cancer; Urologic Cancer; **Hospital:** IU Hlth Univ Hosp; **Address:** IU Hlth, Cancer Ctr, 535 Barnhill Drive Fl 2, Indianapolis, IN 46202; **Phone:** 317-944-0920; **Board Cert:** Internal Medicine 1972; Medical Oncology 1975; **Med School:** UCLA 1967; **Resid:** Internal Medicine, IU Health Affil Hosp 1969; **Fellow:** Hematology & Oncology, IU Health Affil Hosp 1972; Hematology & Oncology, MD Anderson Cancer Ctr 1973; **Fac Appt:** Prof Med, Indiana Univ

Ellis, Matthew J MD/PhD [Onc] - **Spec Exp:** Breast Cancer; **Hospital:** Barnes-Jewish Hosp; **Address:** Washington University, 4921 Parkview Pl, St Louis, MO 63110; **Phone:** 314-747-1171; **Board Cert:** Internal Medicine 2004; Medical Oncology 2005; **Med School:** England, UK 1984; **Resid:** Internal Medicine, Hammersmith Hosp 1988; **Fellow:** Research, Georgetown Univ Med Ctr 1992; Medical Oncology, Georgetwon Univ Med Ctr 1994; **Fac Appt:** Prof Med, Washington Univ, St Louis

Ensminger, William D MD/PhD [Onc] - **Spec Exp:** Gastrointestinal Cancer; Liver Cancer; Clinical Trials; **Hospital:** Univ Michigan Med Ctr; **Address:** Univ Michigan Comprehensive Cancer Ctr, 1500 E Medical Center Drive Fl B1, Ann Arbor, MI 48109; **Phone:** 734-647-8902; **Board Cert:** Internal Medicine 1976; Medical Oncology 1979; **Med School:** Harvard Med Sch 1973; **Resid:** Internal Medicine, Beth Israel Hosp 1975; **Fellow:** Medical Oncology, Dana Farber Cancer Inst 1977; **Fac Appt:** Prof Med, Univ Mich Med Sch

Fleming, Gini F MD [Onc] - **Spec Exp:** Breast Cancer-Novel Therapies; Gynecologic Cancer; Ovarian Cancer; **Hospital:** Univ of Chicago Med; **Address:** Univ Chicago Med Ctr, 5841 S Maryland Ave, MC 2115, Chicago, IL 60637-1470; **Phone:** 773-702-6149; **Board Cert:** Internal Medicine 1988; Medical Oncology 2012; **Med School:** Univ IL Coll Med 1985; **Resid:** Internal Medicine, Univ Chicago Hosps 1988; **Fellow:** Hematology & Oncology, Univ Chicago Hosps 1992; **Fac Appt:** Prof Med, Univ Chicago-Pritzker Sch Med

Flynn, Patrick J MD [Onc] - **Spec Exp:** Hematologic Malignancies; Colon & Rectal Cancer; Clinical Trials; Breast Cancer; **Hospital:** Abbott - Northwestern Hosp, Fairview Southdale Hosp; **Address:** 910 E 26th St, Ste 200, Minneapolis, MN 55404; **Phone:** 612-884-6300; **Board Cert:** Internal Medicine 1978; Medical Oncology 1981; Hematology 1982; **Med School:** Univ Minn 1975; **Resid:** Internal Medicine, Hennepin Co Med Ctr 1978; **Fellow:** Hematology & Oncology, Univ Minnesota Hosp 1981

Gaynor, Ellen MD [Onc] - **Spec Exp:** Breast Cancer; Gastrointestinal Cancer; Prostate Cancer; **Hospital:** Loyola Univ Med Ctr; **Address:** Loyola Bernardin Cancer Center, 2160 S First Ave Bldg 112 - rm 108, Maywood, IL 60153-3328; **Phone:** 708-327-3214; **Board Cert:** Internal Medicine 1982; Hematology 1986; Medical Oncology 1985; **Med School:** Univ Wisc 1978; **Resid:** Internal Medicine, Loyola Univ Med Ctr 1982; **Fellow:** Hematology & Oncology, Univ Chicago Med Ctr 1984; **Fac Appt:** Prof Med, Loyola Univ-Stritch Sch Med

Gerson, Stanton L MD [Onc] - **Spec Exp:** Leukemia; Lymphoma, Non-Hodgkin's; Stem Cell Transplant; Multiple Myeloma; **Hospital:** UH Case Med Ctr; **Address:** Seidman Cancer Ctr, 11000 Euclid Ave Wearn Bldg, rm 151, MS 5065, Cleveland, OH 44106-5065; **Phone:** 216-844-8565; **Board Cert:** Internal Medicine 1980; Hematology 1982; Medical Oncology 1983; **Med School:** Harvard Med Sch 1977; **Resid:** Internal Medicine, Hosp Univ Penn 1980; **Fellow:** Hematology & Oncology, Hosp Univ Penn 1983; **Fac Appt:** Prof Hem & Onc, Case West Res Univ

Goldberg, Richard M MD [Onc] - **Spec Exp:** Colon & Rectal Cancer; Neuroendocrine Tumors; Gastrointestinal Cancer; Anal Cancer; **Hospital:** OSU Wexner Med Ctr; **Address:** 300 W Tenth Ave, Ste 519, Columbus, OH 43210; **Phone:** 614-366-6355; **Board Cert:** Internal Medicine 1982; Medical Oncology 1985; **Med School:** SUNY Upstate Med Univ 1979; **Resid:** Internal Medicine, Emory Univ Med Ctr 1982; **Fellow:** Medical Oncology, Georgetown Univ Med Ctr 1984; **Fac Appt:** Prof Med, Ohio State Univ

Gradishar, William J MD [Onc] - **Spec Exp:** Breast Cancer; **Hospital:** Northwestern Meml Hosp; **Address:** Northwestern Meml Hosp-Div Hem/Onc, 675 N St Clair St Fl 21 - Ste 100, Chicago, IL 60611; **Phone:** 312-695-0990; **Board Cert:** Internal Medicine 1985; Medical Oncology 1989; **Med School:** Univ IL Coll Med 1982; **Resid:** Internal Medicine, Michael Reese Hosp 1985; **Fellow:** Hematology & Oncology, Univ Chicago Hosps 1990; **Fac Appt:** Prof Med, Northwestern Univ

Harris, Lyndsay N MD [Onc] - **Spec Exp:** Breast Cancer; **Hospital:** UH Case Med Ctr; **Address:** Univ Hosp Case Med Ctr, Div of Hem/Onc, 11100 Euclid Ave, Cleveland, OH 44106; **Phone:** 216-844-3302; **Board Cert:** Medical Oncology 2010; **Med School:** Univ Alberta 1988; **Resid:** Internal Medicine, Univ Alberta Hosp 1991; **Fellow:** Medical Oncology, Univ British Columbia Faculty of Med 1993; Breast Cancer, Georgetown Univ Hosp 1994; **Fac Appt:** Prof Med, Case West Res Univ

Hayes, Daniel F MD [Onc] - **Spec Exp:** Breast Cancer; **Hospital:** Univ Michigan Med Ctr; **Address:** Univ Michigan Comprehensive Cancer Ctr, 1500 E Medical Ctr Drive, Ste SPC 5916, Ann Arbor, MI 48109-5942; **Phone:** 734-936-6000; **Board Cert:** Internal Medicine 1982; Medical Oncology 1985; **Med School:** Indiana Univ 1979; **Resid:** Internal Medicine, Parkland Meml Hosp 1982; **Fellow:** Medical Oncology, Dana Farber Cancer Inst 1985; **Fac Appt:** Prof Med, Univ Mich Med Sch

Hoffman, Philip C MD [Onc] - **Spec Exp:** Lung Cancer; Breast Cancer; **Hospital:** Univ of Chicago Med, Little Company of Mary Hosp & Hlth Care Ctrs; **Address:** 5841 S Maryland Ave, MC 2115, Chicago, IL 60637-1447; **Phone:** 773-834-7424; **Board Cert:** Internal Medicine 1975; Hematology 1980; Medical Oncology 1981; **Med School:** Jefferson Med Coll 1972; **Resid:** Internal Medicine, Hosp Univ Penn 1975; **Fellow:** Hematology & Oncology, Univ Chicago Hosps 1980; **Fac Appt:** Prof Med, Univ Chicago-Pritzker Sch Med

Hussain, Maha H MD [Onc] - **Spec Exp:** Prostate Cancer; Bladder Cancer; Testicular Cancer; Genitourinary Cancer; **Hospital:** Univ Michigan Med Ctr; **Address:** Univ Michigan Cancer Ctr, 1500 E Medical Ctr Drive, Ann Arbor, MI 48109; **Phone:** 734-936-8903; **Board Cert:** Internal Medicine 1986; Medical Oncology 1989; **Med School:** Iraq 1980; **Resid:** Internal Medicine, Wayne State Univ Affil Hosps 1986; **Fellow:** Medical Oncology, Wayne State Univ Affil Hosps 1989; **Fac Appt:** Prof Med, Univ Mich Med Sch

Ingle, James N MD [Onc] - **Spec Exp:** Breast Cancer; **Hospital:** Mayo Med Ctr & Clin - Rochester, Rochester Methodist Hosp; **Address:** Mayo Clinic, 200 First St SW,, Gonda Bldg - Fl 10, Rochester, MN 55905-0001; **Phone:** 507-284-4857; **Board Cert:** Internal Medicine 1974; Medical Oncology 1975; **Med School:** Johns Hopkins Univ 1971; **Resid:** Internal Medicine, Johns Hopkins Hosp 1976; Medical Oncology, Natl Cancer Inst 1975; **Fac Appt:** Prof Hem & Onc, Mayo Med Sch

Kalaycio, Matt E MD [Onc] - **Spec Exp:** Leukemia; Bone Marrow Transplant; **Hospital:** Cleveland Clin (page 55); **Address:** Taussig Cancer Ctr, 9500 Euclid Ave, Desk R35, Cleveland, OH 44195; **Phone:** 216-444-3705; **Board Cert:** Internal Medicine 2002; Hematology 2004; Medical Oncology 2005; **Med School:** W VA Univ 1988; **Resid:** Internal Medicine, Mercy Hosp 1991; **Fellow:** Hematology & Oncology, Cleveland Clinic 1994; **Fac Appt:** Prof Med, Cleveland Cl Coll Med/Case West Res

Kalemkerian, Gregory P MD [Onc] - **Spec Exp:** Lung Cancer; Mesothelioma; Thymoma; **Hospital:** Univ Michigan Med Ctr; **Address:** Univ Michigan Comprehensive Cancer Ctr, 1500 E Medical Center Drive, B1-363, Ann Arbor, MI 48109; **Phone:** 734-232-6046; **Board Cert:** Internal Medicine 1988; Medical Oncology 2011; **Med School:** Northwestern Univ 1985; **Resid:** Internal Medicine, Northwestern Meml Hosp 1988; **Fellow:** Medical Oncology, Johns Hopkins Hosp 1993; **Fac Appt:** Prof Onc, Univ Mich Med Sch

Kaminski, Mark S MD [Onc] - **Spec Exp:** Lymphoma; Bone Marrow Transplant; Drug Development; Clinical Trials; **Hospital:** Univ Michigan Med Ctr; **Address:** Univ Michigan Comprehensive Cancer Ctr, 1500 E Medical Ctr Drive, B1-358, Ann Arbor, MI 48109; **Phone:** 734-647-8901; **Board Cert:** Internal Medicine 1981; Medical Oncology 1983; **Med School:** Stanford Univ 1978; **Resid:** Internal Medicine, Barnes Hosp 1981; **Fellow:** Medical Oncology, Stanford Univ Med Ctr 1985; **Fac Appt:** Prof Med, Univ Mich Med Sch

Kindler, Hedy Lee MD [Onc] - **Spec Exp:** Pancreatic Cancer; Mesothelioma; Gastrointestinal Cancer; **Hospital:** Univ of Chicago Med; **Address:** Univ of Chicago Medical Ctr, 5841 S Maryland Ave, Chicago, IL 60637-1470; **Phone:** 773-702-4400; **Board Cert:** Medical Oncology 2005; **Med School:** SUNY Buffalo 1989; **Resid:** Internal Medicine, UCLA Med Ctr 1992; **Fellow:** Medical Oncology, Meml Sloan Kettering Cancer Ctr 1995; **Fac Appt:** Assoc Prof Onc, Univ Chicago-Pritzker Sch Med

Krishnamurthi, Smitha S MD [Onc] - **Spec Exp:** Gastrointestinal Cancer; Colon & Rectal Cancer; **Hospital:** UH Case Med Ctr; **Address:** UH Seidman Cancer Ctr, 11100 Euclid Ave, Cleveland, OH 44106; **Phone:** 216-844-1006; **Board Cert:** Internal Medicine 2006; Medical Oncology 2008; **Med School:** Univ Pennsylvania 1993; **Resid:** Internal Medicine, Univ Penn Affil Hosps 1996; **Fellow:** Medical Oncology, Johns Hopkins Hosp 1996; **Fac Appt:** Asst Prof Med, Case West Res Univ

Kuzel, Timothy M MD [Onc] - **Spec Exp:** Kidney Cancer; Melanoma; Cutaneous Lymphoma; **Hospital:** Northwestern Meml Hosp; **Address:** Northwestern Meml Hosp, 675 N St Clair St Fl 21 - Ste 100, Chicago, IL 60611; **Phone:** 312-695-0990; **Board Cert:** Internal Medicine 1987; Hematology 2010; Medical Oncology 1989; **Med School:** Univ Mich Med Sch 1984; **Resid:** Internal Medicine, McGraw MC-Northwestern Univ 1987; **Fellow:** Hematology & Oncology, McGraw MC-Northwestern Univ 1990; **Fac Appt:** Prof Med, Northwestern Univ

Lazarus, Hillard M MD [Onc] - **Spec Exp:** Bone Marrow & Stem Cell Transplant; Leukemia & Lymphoma; Multiple Myeloma; **Hospital:** UH Case Med Ctr; **Address:** 11100 Euclid Ave, Cleveland, OH 44106; **Phone:** 216-844-3969; **Board Cert:** Internal Medicine 1977; Medical Oncology 1979; Hematology 1980; **Med School:** Univ Rochester 1974; **Resid:** Internal Medicine, Univ Hosps 1977; **Fellow:** Hematology & Oncology, Univ Hosps 1979; **Fac Appt:** Prof Onc, Case West Res Univ

Loehrer, Patrick J MD [Onc] - **Spec Exp:** Thymoma; Genitourinary Cancer; Pancreatic Cancer; Esophageal Cancer; **Hospital:** IU Hlth Univ Hosp; **Address:** IU Hlth, Cancer Ctr, 535 Barnhill Drive Fl 2, Indianapolis, IN 46202; **Phone:** 317-944-0920; **Board Cert:** Internal Medicine 1981; Medical Oncology 2006; **Med School:** Rush Med Coll 1978; **Resid:** Internal Medicine, Rush Presby-St Lukes Hosp 1981; **Fellow:** Medical Oncology, IU Health Affil Hosp 1983; **Fac Appt:** Prof Med, Indiana Univ

Logie, Keith W MD [Onc] - **Spec Exp:** Leukemia & Lymphoma; Kidney Cancer; Solid Tumors; **Hospital:** IU Health North Hosp; **Address:** Central Indiana Cancer Ctrs, 10212 Lantern Road, Fishers, IN 46037; **Phone:** 317-841-5656; **Board Cert:** Internal Medicine 1980; Medical Oncology 1983; **Med School:** Univ VA Sch Med 1977; **Resid:** Internal Medicine, Univ Rochester Strong Meml Hosp 1980; **Fellow:** Medical Oncology, Univ Rochester Strong Meml Hosp 1982

Loprinzi, Charles L MD [Onc] - **Spec Exp:** Breast Cancer; **Hospital:** Mayo Med Ctr & Clin - Rochester; **Address:** Mayo Clinic, Dept Med Oncology, 200 First St SW, Rochester, MN 55905-0001; **Phone:** 507-284-4320; **Board Cert:** Internal Medicine 1982; Medical Oncology 1985; **Med School:** Oregon Hlth & Sci Univ 1979; **Resid:** Internal Medicine, Maricopa Co Hosp 1982; **Fellow:** Medical Oncology, Univ Wisconsin Med Ctr 1984; **Fac Appt:** Prof Med, Mayo Med Sch

Markowitz, Sanford D MD [Onc] - **Spec Exp:** Colon & Rectal Cancer; Hereditary Cancer; **Hospital:** UH Case Med Ctr; **Address:** UH Seidman Cancer Ctr, 11100 Euclid Ave, Cleveland, OH 44106; **Phone:** 216-844-3951; **Board Cert:** Internal Medicine 1984; Medical Oncology 1987; **Med School:** Yale Univ 1980; **Resid:** Internal Medicine, Univ Chicago Hosp 1984; **Fellow:** Medical Oncology, Natl Cancer Inst 1986; **Fac Appt:** Prof Med, Case West Res Univ

Meropol, Neal J MD [Onc] - **Spec Exp:** Gastrointestinal Cancer; Colon Cancer; Pancreatic Cancer; **Hospital:** UH Case Med Ctr; **Address:** 11100 Euclid Ave, Wearn Bldg, rm 145, Cleveland, OH 44106; **Phone:** 216-983-4752; **Board Cert:** Internal Medicine 1988; Medical Oncology 2011; **Med School:** Vanderbilt Univ 1985; **Resid:** Internal Medicine, Univ Hosps/Case West Res 1988; **Fellow:** Hematology & Oncology, Hosp Univ Penn 1992; **Fac Appt:** Prof Onc, Case West Res Univ

O'Brien, Timothy E MD [Onc] - **Spec Exp:** Gastrointestinal Cancer; Colon & Rectal Cancer; Multiple Myeloma; Lung Cancer; **Hospital:** MetroHealth Med Ctr; **Address:** MetroHealth Cancer Care Ctr, 2500 MetroHealth Drive, Ste C-2100, Cleveland, OH 44109-1998; **Phone:** 216-778-5802; **Board Cert:** Medical Oncology 2007; Hematology 2008; **Med School:** Univ Rochester 1989; **Resid:** Internal Medicine, Univ Hosps 1992; **Fellow:** Hematology & Oncology, Univ Hosps 1997; **Fac Appt:** Assoc Prof Med, Case West Res Univ

Olopade, Olufunmilayo I MD [Onc] - **Spec Exp:** Breast Cancer; Hereditary Cancer; Breast Cancer Genetics; Cancer Risk Assessment; **Hospital:** Univ of Chicago Med; **Address:** Univ Chicago Med Ctr, 5841 S Maryland Ave, MC 2115, Chicago, IL 60637-1470; **Phone:** 773-702-6149; **Board Cert:** Internal Medicine 1986; Medical Oncology 1989; **Med School:** Nigeria 1980; **Resid:** Internal Medicine, Cook Co Hosp 1986; **Fellow:** Hematology & Oncology, Univ Chicago Hosps 1991; **Fac Appt:** Prof Med, Univ Chicago-Pritzker Sch Med

Ozer, Howard MD [Onc] - **Spec Exp:** Lymphoma; **Hospital:** Univ of IL Med Ctr at Chicago; **Address:** Univ Illinois Med Ctr, Dept Onc, 1818 W Taylor St, Ste 1E, Chicago, IL 60612; **Phone:** 312-355-1625; **Board Cert:** Internal Medicine 1979; **Med School:** Yale Univ 1975; **Resid:** Internal Medicine, Mass Genl Hosp 1977; **Fellow:** Hematology & Oncology, PB Brigham/Dana Farber Cancer Inst 1979; **Fac Appt:** Prof Med, Univ IL Coll Med

Peace, David J MD [Onc] - **Spec Exp:** Prostate Cancer; Vaccine Therapy; Leukemia & Lymphoma; Immunotherapy; **Hospital:** Univ of IL Med Ctr at Chicago, MacNeal Hosp; **Address:** 1801 W Taylor St, Ste 1E, Chicago, IL 60612; **Phone:** 312-413-1507; **Board Cert:** Internal Medicine 1983; Medical Oncology 1987; **Med School:** Univ Pittsburgh 1980; **Resid:** Internal Medicine, Univ Pittsburgh Med Ctr 1983; **Fellow:** Hematology & Oncology, Univ Washington Med Ctr 1988

Peereboom, David M MD [Onc] - **Spec Exp:** Neuro-Oncology; Brain Tumors; Drug Development; **Hospital:** Cleveland Clin (page 55); **Address:** Cleveland Clin, Solid Tumor Dept, 9500 Euclid Ave, Cleveland, OH 44195; **Phone:** 216-445-6068; **Board Cert:** Internal Medicine 1989; Medical Oncology 2004; **Med School:** Med Coll VA 1986; **Resid:** Internal Medicine, Univ Hosp 1990; **Fellow:** Medical Oncology, Johns Hopkins Hosp 1993; **Fac Appt:** Assoc Prof Onc, Cleveland Cl Coll Med/Case West Res

Peterson, Bruce MD [Onc] - **Spec Exp:** Lymphoma; Leukemia; **Hospital:** Univ Minn Med Ctr, Fairview - West Bank Campus; **Address:** Univ of Minnesota, 424 Harvard St, Minneapolis, MN 55455; **Phone:** 612-625-5411; **Board Cert:** Internal Medicine 1974; Medical Oncology 1977; **Med School:** Univ Minn 1971; **Resid:** Internal Medicine, Fletcher Allen Hlthcare 1973; Internal Medicine, Fairview-Univ Med Ctr 1974; **Fellow:** Medical Oncology, Fairview-Univ Med Ctr 1977; **Fac Appt:** Prof Med, Univ Minn

Petruska, Paul J MD [Onc] - **Spec Exp:** Leukemia & Lymphoma; Solid Tumors; **Hospital:** St. Louis Univ Hosp; **Address:** SLU, Dept Hem/Onc, 3655 Vista Ave, St Louis, MO 63110; **Phone:** 314-577-6057; **Board Cert:** Internal Medicine 1972; Hematology 1974; Medical Oncology 1979; **Med School:** St Louis Univ 1967; **Resid:** Internal Medicine, St. Louis Hosp 1969; Internal Medicine, St. Louis Hosp 1972; **Fellow:** Hematology & Oncology, St. Louis Hosp 1974; **Fac Appt:** Prof Med, St Louis Univ

Pohlman, Brad L MD [Onc] - **Spec Exp:** Lymphoma; Lymphoma, Non-Hodgkin's; Bone Marrow Transplant; **Hospital:** Cleveland Clin (page 55); **Address:** Cleveland Clinic, Taussig Cancer Inst, 9500 Euclid Ave, Desk R35, Cleveland, OH 44195; **Phone:** 216-444-6833; **Board Cert:** Internal Medicine 1988; **Med School:** Indiana Univ 1985; **Resid:** Internal Medicine, Univ Wisc Hosp 1988; **Fellow:** Hematology, Univ Minn Hosp 1992

Ratain, Mark J MD [Onc] - **Spec Exp:** Solid Tumors; Drug Discovery & Development; **Hospital:** Univ of Chicago Med; **Address:** Univ Chicago Med Ctr, 5841 S Maryland Ave, MC 2115, Chicago, IL 60637; **Phone:** 773-702-6149; **Board Cert:** Internal Medicine 1983; Hematology 1986; Medical Oncology 1985; **Med School:** Yale Univ 1980; **Resid:** Internal Medicine, Johns Hopkins Hosp 1983; **Fellow:** Hematology & Oncology, Univ Chicago Hosp 1986; **Fac Appt:** Prof Med, Univ Chicago-Pritzker Sch Med

Richards, Jon M MD/PhD [Onc] - **Spec Exp:** Melanoma; **Hospital:** Adv Luth Genl Hosp, Skokie Hosp/NorthShore Univ Htlh Syst (page 67); **Address:** Center for Advanced Care, 1700 Luther Ln Fl 2, Park Ridge, IL 60068; **Phone:** 847-268-8200; **Board Cert:** Medical Oncology 2007; **Med School:** Cornell Univ-Weill Med Coll 1983; **Resid:** Internal Medicine, Univ Chicago Hosps 1985; **Fellow:** Hematology & Oncology, Univ Chicago Hosps 1988; **Fac Appt:** Assoc Prof Med, Univ IL Coll Med

Rosen, Steven T MD [Onc] - **Spec Exp:** Hematologic Malignancies; Breast Cancer; Leukemia & Lymphoma; **Hospital:** Northwestern Meml Hosp; **Address:** Northwestern Meml Hosp, 675 N St Clair St Fl 21 - Ste 100, Chicago, IL 60611; **Phone:** 312-695-0990; **Board Cert:** Internal Medicine 1979; Medical Oncology 1981; Hematology 1984; **Med School:** Northwestern Univ 1976; **Resid:** Internal Medicine, Northwestern Univ Hosp 1979; **Fellow:** Medical Oncology, Natl Cancer Inst 1981; **Fac Appt:** Prof Med, Northwestern Univ

Roth, Bruce J MD [Onc] - **Spec Exp:** Prostate Cancer; Bladder Cancer; Testicular Cancer; Kidney Cancer; **Hospital:** Barnes-Jewish Hosp, Barnes-Jewish West County Hosp; **Address:** Washington University Physicians, 5225 Midamerica Plaza, MS 63129, St Louis, MO 63110; **Phone:** 314-747-1171; **Board Cert:** Internal Medicine 1983; Medical Oncology 1985; **Med School:** St Louis Univ 1980; **Resid:** Internal Medicine, Indiana Univ Med Ctr 1983; **Fellow:** Hematology & Oncology, Indiana Univ Med Ctr 1986; **Fac Appt:** Prof Onc, Washington Univ, St Louis

Salgia, Ravi MD/PhD [Onc] - **Spec Exp:** Lung Cancer; Mesothelioma; Thoracic Cancers; **Hospital:** Univ of Chicago Med; **Address:** Univ Chicago Medical Ctr, 5841 S Maryland Ave, MC 2115, Chicago, IL 60637; **Phone:** 773-702-6149; **Board Cert:** Medical Oncology 2006; **Med School:** Loyola Univ-Stritch Sch Med 1987; **Resid:** Internal Medicine, Johns Hopkins Hosp 1990; **Fellow:** Medical Oncology, Dana-Farber Cancer Inst 1993; **Fac Appt:** Prof Med, Univ Chicago-Pritzker Sch Med

Schiffer, Charles A MD [Onc] - **Spec Exp:** Leukemia; Lymphoma; Multiple Myeloma; **Hospital:** Barbara Ann Karmanos Cancer Inst, Harper Univ Hosp; **Address:** Karmanos Cancer Inst, Cancer Research Ctr, 4100 John R St, Detroit, MI 48201; **Phone:** 800-527-6266; **Board Cert:** Internal Medicine 1972; Medical Oncology 1973; **Med School:** NYU Sch Med 1968; **Resid:** Internal Medicine, Bellevue-NY VA Hosp-NYU 1972; **Fellow:** Medical Oncology, Natl Cancer Inst 1974; **Fac Appt:** Prof Med, Wayne State Univ

Schwartz, Burton S MD [Onc] - **Spec Exp:** Lymphoma; Breast Cancer; **Hospital:** Abbott - Northwestern Hosp; **Address:** 910 E 26th St, Ste 200, Minneapolis, MN 55404; **Phone:** 612-884-6300; **Board Cert:** Internal Medicine 1980; Hematology 1976; Medical Oncology 1977; **Med School:** Meharry Med Coll 1968; **Resid:** Internal Medicine, Michael Reese Hosp 1971; **Fellow:** Hematology, Univ Minn Hosp 1976; **Fac Appt:** Clin Prof Med, Univ Minn

Shapiro, Charles L MD [Onc] - **Spec Exp:** Breast Cancer; **Hospital:** Arthur G James Cancer Hosp & Research Inst; **Address:** 1145 Olentangy River Rd Fl 4, Columbus, OH 43212; **Phone:** 614-293-0066; **Board Cert:** Internal Medicine 1987; Medical Oncology 2005; **Med School:** SUNY Buffalo 1984; **Resid:** Internal Medicine, Temple Univ Hosp 1987; **Fellow:** Medical Oncology, Dana-Farber Cancer Inst 1991; **Fac Appt:** Assoc Prof Med, Ohio State Univ

Shields, Peter G MD [Onc] - **Spec Exp:** Hematologic Malignancies; **Hospital:** OSU Wexner Med Ctr; **Address:** Ohio State Univ Med Ctr, 300 W 10th Ave, Ste 519, Columbus, OH 43201; **Phone:** 614-688-6563; **Board Cert:** Medical Oncology 1989; **Med School:** Mount Sinai Sch Med 1983; **Resid:** Internal Medicine, G Washington Univ Hosp 1986; **Fellow:** Hematology & Oncology, G Washington Univ Hosp 1990; **Fac Appt:** Prof Med, Ohio State Univ

Silver, Samuel M MD/PhD [Onc] - **Spec Exp:** Hematologic Malignancies; Bleeding/Coagulation Disorders; Porphyria; Myeloproliferative Disorders; **Hospital:** Univ Michigan Med Ctr, VA Ann Arbor Healthcare Sys; **Address:** Univ Michigan Med Ctr/Cancer Ctr, 4101 Med Sci I C- Wing, 1301 Catherine St, Ann Arbor, MI 48109-5624; **Phone:** 734-764-2204; **Board Cert:** Internal Medicine 1982; Medical Oncology 1985; Hematology 1984; **Med School:** Cornell Univ-Weill Med Coll 1979; **Resid:** Internal Medicine, UCSF-Moffit Hosp 1982; **Fellow:** Hematology & Oncology, Hosp Univ Penn 1985; **Fac Appt:** Clin Prof Onc, Univ Mich Med Sch

Silverman, Paula MD [Onc] - **Spec Exp:** Breast Cancer; **Hospital:** UH Case Med Ctr, UH Ahuja Med Ctr (OH); **Address:** UH Seidman Cancer Ctr, 11100 Euclid Ave, Cleveland, OH 44106; **Phone:** 216-844-8510; **Board Cert:** Internal Medicine 1984; Medical Oncology 1989; **Med School:** Case West Res Univ 1981; **Resid:** Internal Medicine, Univ Hosps 1984; **Fellow:** Hematology & Oncology, Case Western Res Univ 1987; **Fac Appt:** Assoc Prof Med, Case West Res Univ

Smith, Mitchell R MD/PhD [Onc] - **Spec Exp:** Lymphoma; Leukemia-Chronic Lymphocytic; Hodgkin's Lymphoma; Multiple Myeloma; **Hospital:** Cleveland Clin (page 55); **Address:** Cleveland Clinic-Taussig Cancer Inst, 9500 Euclid Ave, Cleveland, OH 44195; **Phone:** 866-223-8100; **Board Cert:** Internal Medicine 1985; Medical Oncology 1987; Hematology 1988; **Med School:** Case West Res Univ 1979; **Resid:** Pathology, Barnes Jewish Hosp 1983; Internal Medicine, Barnes Jewish Hosp 1984; **Fellow:** Medical Oncology, Meml Sloan-Ketter Cancer Ctr 1988; **Fac Appt:** Prof Onc, Case West Res Univ

Stadler, Walter M MD [Onc] - **Spec Exp:** Kidney Cancer; Bladder Cancer; Prostate Cancer; Testicular Cancer; **Hospital:** Univ of Chicago Med; **Address:** Univ Chicago Med Ctr, 5841 S Maryland Ave, Chicago, IL 60637; **Phone:** 773-702-6149; **Board Cert:** Internal Medicine 2012; Medical Oncology 2003; **Med School:** Yale Univ 1988; **Resid:** Internal Medicine, Michael Reese Hosp 1991; **Fellow:** Medical Oncology, Univ Chicago Hosps 1994; **Fac Appt:** Prof Med, Univ Chicago-Pritzker Sch Med

Triozzi, Pierre L MD [Onc] - **Spec Exp:** Melanoma; Vaccine Therapy; Clinical Trials; **Hospital:** Cleveland Clin (page 55); **Address:** Cleveland Clinic Fdn, 9500 Euclid Ave, MC R40, Cleveland, OH 44195; **Phone:** 216-445-5141; **Board Cert:** Internal Medicine 1983; Medical Oncology 1987; Hematology 1988; **Med School:** Ohio State Univ 1980; **Resid:** Internal Medicine, Duke Univ Med Ctr 1983; **Fellow:** Hematology & Oncology, Duke Univ Med Ctr 1987; **Fac Appt:** Prof Med, Case West Res Univ

Urba, Susan G MD [Onc] - **Spec Exp:** Head & Neck Cancer; **Hospital:** Univ Michigan Med Ctr; **Address:** Univ Michigan Comprehensive Cancer Ctr, 1500 E Medical Center Drive Fl B1, Ann Arbor, MI 48109; **Phone:** 734-647-8902; **Board Cert:** Internal Medicine 1986; Medical Oncology 2012; Hospice & Palliative Medicine 2010; **Med School:** Univ Mich Med Sch 1983; **Resid:** Internal Medicine, Univ Mich Med Ctr 1986; **Fellow:** Hematology & Oncology, Univ Mich Med Ctr 1988; **Fac Appt:** Assoc Prof Med, Univ Mich Med Sch

Vokes, Everett E MD [Onc] - **Spec Exp:** Lung Cancer; Head & Neck Cancer; Esophageal Cancer; **Hospital:** Univ of Chicago Med; **Address:** Univ Chicago Hosp, 5841 S Maryland Ave, MC 2115, Chicago, IL 60637-1470; **Phone:** 773-834-3093; **Board Cert:** Internal Medicine 1983; Medical Oncology 1985; **Med School:** Germany 1980; **Resid:** Internal Medicine, Ravenswood Hosp-Univ Illinois 1982; Internal Medicine, USC Med Ctr 1983; **Fellow:** Medical Oncology, Univ Chicago 1986; **Fac Appt:** Prof Med, Univ Chicago-Pritzker Sch Med

Weiner, George J MD [Onc] - **Spec Exp:** Lymphoma; Leukemia; Immunotherapy; **Hospital:** Univ Iowa Hosp & Clins; **Address:** Holden Comprehensive Cancer Ctr, Med Onc, 200 Hawkins Drive, Ste 5970HJPP, Iowa City, IA 52242; **Phone:** 319-384-8442; **Board Cert:** Internal Medicine 1985; Hematology 1988; Medical Oncology 1987; **Med School:** Ohio State Univ 1981; **Resid:** Internal Medicine, Med Coll Ohio Affil Hosp 1985; **Fellow:** Hematology & Oncology, Univ Mich Med Ctr 1987; **Fac Appt:** Prof Med, Univ Iowa Coll Med

Wicha, Max S MD [Onc] - **Spec Exp:** Breast Cancer; Stem Cell Transplant; **Hospital:** Univ Michigan Med Ctr; **Address:** Univ Michigan Comprehensive Cancer Ctr, 1500 E Med Ctr Dr, rm SPC 5916, Ann Arbor, MI 48109-5942; **Phone:** 734-936-6000; **Board Cert:** Internal Medicine 1977; Medical Oncology 1983; **Med School:** Stanford Univ 1974; **Resid:** Internal Medicine, Univ Chicago Hosp 1977; **Fellow:** Medical Oncology, Natl Inst Hlth 1980; **Fac Appt:** Prof Med, Univ Mich Med Sch

Wilding, George MD [Onc] - **Spec Exp:** Prostate Cancer; Kidney Cancer; Genitourinary Cancer; Drug Discovery & Development; **Hospital:** Univ WI Hosp & Clins; **Address:** 1111 Highland Ave, Ste 7057WIMR, Madison, WI 53705; **Phone:** 608-263-8610; **Board Cert:** Internal Medicine 1983; Medical Oncology 1985; **Med School:** Univ Mass Sch Med 1980; **Resid:** Internal Medicine, Univ Mass Med Ctr 1983; **Fellow:** Medical Oncology, Natl Cancer Inst 1985; **Fac Appt:** Prof Med, Univ Wisc

Worden, Francis P MD [Onc] - **Spec Exp:** Head & Neck Cancer; Palliative Care; Clinical Trials; **Hospital:** Univ Michigan Med Ctr; **Address:** Univ Michigan Comprehensive Cancer Ctr, 1500 E Medical Center Drive Fl B1, Ann Arbor, MI 48109; **Phone:** 734-647-8902; **Board Cert:** Medical Oncology 2010; **Med School:** Indiana Univ 1993; **Resid:** Internal Medicine & Pediatrics, Detroit Med Ctr 1997; **Fellow:** Hematology & Oncology, Univ Michigan Med Ctr 2000; **Fac Appt:** Asst Clin Prof Med, Univ Mich Med Sch

Yee, Douglas MD [Onc] - **Spec Exp:** Breast Cancer; **Hospital:** Univ Minn Med Ctr, Fairview - West Bank Campus; **Address:** Masonic Cancer Ctr-Breast Ctr, 420 Delaware St SE, MMC 160, Minneapolis, MN 55455; **Phone:** 612-273-9685; **Board Cert:** Internal Medicine 1984; Medical Oncology 1987; **Med School:** Univ Chicago-Pritzker Sch Med 1981; **Resid:** Internal Medicine, Univ NC Med Ctr 1984; **Fellow:** Medical Oncology, NIH-Clin Ctr 1987; **Fac Appt:** Prof Med, Univ Minn

Great Plains and Mountains

Akerley III, Wallace L MD [Onc] - **Spec Exp:** Lung Cancer; Clinical Trials; **Hospital:** Univ Utah Hlth Care; **Address:** Huntsman Canc Inst, 1950 Circle of Hope, Salt Lake City, UT 84112; **Phone:** 801-587-4470; **Board Cert:** Internal Medicine 1984; Medical Oncology 1987; Hematology 1988; **Med School:** Brown Univ 1981; **Resid:** Internal Medicine, USC Med Ctr 1985; **Fellow:** Medical Oncology, USC Med Ctr 1986; Hematology, Dartmouth - Hitchcock Med Ctr 1988; **Fac Appt:** Prof Med, Univ Utah

Armitage, James MD [Onc] - **Spec Exp:** Lymphoma; Bone Marrow Transplant; Hematologic Malignancies; **Hospital:** Nebraska Med Ctr; **Address:** 987835 Nebraska Medical Center, Emile @ 42nd St, Omaha, NE 68198-7630; **Phone:** 402-559-5600; **Board Cert:** Internal Medicine 1976; Medical Oncology 1977; Hematology 1984; **Med School:** Univ Nebr Coll Med 1973; **Resid:** Internal Medicine, Univ Nebraska Med Ctr 1975; **Fellow:** Hematology & Oncology, Univ Iowa Hosp 1977; **Fac Appt:** Prof Med, Univ Nebr Coll Med

Beatty, Patrick G MD/PhD [Onc] - **Spec Exp:** Hematologic Malignancies; Lymphoma; **Hospital:** Community Med Ctr; **Address:** 2827 Fort Missoula Rd, Missoula, MT 59804; **Phone:** 406-327-3911; **Board Cert:** Internal Medicine 1980; Medical Oncology 1985; **Med School:** Univ Chicago-Pritzker Sch Med 1976; **Resid:** Internal Medicine, Vanderbilt Univ Med Ctr 1979; **Fellow:** Oncology, Univ WA Med Ctr 1982

Bierman, Philip J MD [Onc] - **Spec Exp:** Lymphoma; Bone Marrow Transplant; **Hospital:** Nebraska Med Ctr; **Address:** Nebraska Medical Ctr, Dept Hem/Oncology, 987835 Nebraska Medical Ctr, Emile @ 42nd St, Omaha, NE 68198-7630; **Phone:** 402-559-5600; **Board Cert:** Internal Medicine 1982; Medical Oncology 1985; Hematology 1986; **Med School:** Univ MO-Kansas City 1979; **Resid:** Internal Medicine, Univ Nebraska Med Ctr 1983; **Fellow:** Medical Oncology, Univ Nebraska Med Ctr 1985; Hematology, City of Hope Natl Med Ctr 1986; **Fac Appt:** Prof Med, Univ Nebr Coll Med

Bunn Jr, Paul A MD [Onc] - **Spec Exp:** Lung Cancer; Clinical Trials; Thymoma; Mesothelioma; **Hospital:** Univ Colorado Hosp; **Address:** Univ CO Hosp, Cancer Ctr, 12605 E 16th Ave, Ste 2004, Aurora, CO 80045; **Phone:** 720-848-0300; **Board Cert:** Internal Medicine 1974; Medical Oncology 1975; **Med School:** Cornell Univ-Weill Med Coll 1971; **Resid:** Internal Medicine, Moffitt Cancer Ctr 1973; **Fellow:** Medical Oncology, Natl Cancer Inst 1976; **Fac Appt:** Prof Med, Univ Colorado

Buys, Saundra S MD [Onc] - **Spec Exp:** Breast Cancer; Breast Cancer Risk Assessment; Breast Cancer Genetics; **Hospital:** Univ Utah Hlth Care; **Address:** Huntsman Canc Inst, 1950 Circle of Hope, Salt Lake City, UT 84112; **Phone:** 801-587-4241; **Board Cert:** Internal Medicine 1982; Hematology 1984; Medical Oncology 1985; **Med School:** Tufts Univ 1979; **Resid:** Internal Medicine, Univ Utah Affil Hosps 1982; **Fellow:** Hematology & Oncology, Univ Utah Affil Hosps 1985; **Fac Appt:** Prof Med, Univ Utah

Cowan, Kenneth H MD/PhD [Onc] - **Spec Exp:** Breast Cancer; **Hospital:** Nebraska Med Ctr; **Address:** 987835 Nebraska Medical Center, Emile @ 42nd St, Omaha, NE 68198-7630; **Phone:** 402-559-5600; **Board Cert:** Internal Medicine 1978; Medical Oncology 1981; **Med School:** Case West Res Univ 1975; **Resid:** Internal Medicine, Parkland Meml Hosp 1977

Dakhil, Shaker R MD [Onc] - **Spec Exp:** Leukemia; Mesothelioma; Lymphoma; **Hospital:** Univ of Kansas Hosp; **Address:** Cancer Ctr of Kansas, 818 N Emporia, Ste 403, Wichita, KS 67214; **Phone:** 316-262-4467; **Board Cert:** Internal Medicine 1978; Medical Oncology 1981; **Med School:** Lebanon 1976; **Resid:** Internal Medicine, Wayne State Univ Affil Hosps 1978; **Fellow:** Hematology & Oncology, Univ Michigan Med Sch 1981; **Fac Appt:** Assoc Clin Prof Med, Univ Kansas

Eckhardt, S Gail MD [Onc] - **Spec Exp:** Gastrointestinal Cancer; Colon & Rectal Cancer; Anal Cancer; Drug Discovery & Development; **Hospital:** Univ Colorado Hosp; **Address:** Anschutz Cancer Pavilion, 1665 Aurora Ct, MS F-704, Aurora, CO 80045; **Phone:** 720-848-0300; **Board Cert:** Internal Medicine 1988; Medical Oncology 2006; **Med School:** Univ Tex Med Br, Galveston 1985; **Resid:** Internal Medicine, Univ Virginia Med Ctr 1988; **Fellow:** Research, Scripps Clinic 1989; Medical Oncology, UCSD Med Ctr 1992; **Fac Appt:** Prof Med, Univ Colorado

Elias, Anthony D MD [Onc] - **Spec Exp:** Breast Cancer; Sarcoma; **Hospital:** Univ Colorado Hosp; **Address:** UCH Breast Ctr, Anschutz OPD Pavillion, MS-724, 1635 Aurora Ct, Aurora, CO 80045; **Phone:** 720-848-1030; **Board Cert:** Internal Medicine 1983; Medical Oncology 1985; **Med School:** NYU Sch Med 1980; **Resid:** Internal Medicine, Johns Hopkins Hsop 1983; **Fellow:** Medical Oncology, Dana-Farber Cancer Inst 1986; **Fac Appt:** Prof Onc, Univ Colorado

Fabian, Carol J MD [Onc] - **Spec Exp:** Breast Cancer; Breast Cancer Risk Assessment; **Hospital:** Univ of Kansas Hosp; **Address:** Univ of Kansas Hosp, Dept Hem/Onc, Westwood Med Pavilion, MS 5015, 2330 Shawnee Mission Pkwy, Ste 1102, Westwood, KS 66205; **Phone:** 913-588-6029; **Board Cert:** Internal Medicine 1976; Medical Oncology 1977; **Med School:** Univ Kansas 1972; **Resid:** Internal Medicine, Wesley Med Ctr 1975; **Fellow:** Medical Oncology, Univ Kansas Med Ctr 1977; **Fac Appt:** Prof Med, Univ Kansas

Glode, L. Michael MD [Onc] - **Spec Exp:** Prostate Cancer; Genitourinary Cancer; **Hospital:** Univ Colorado Hosp; **Address:** Univ CO Hosp, Urologic Oncology, 12605 E 16th Ave, Aurora, CO 80045; **Phone:** 720-848-0170; **Board Cert:** Internal Medicine 1975; Medical Oncology 1981; **Med School:** Washington Univ, St Louis 1972; **Resid:** Internal Medicine, UT SW Med Ctr 1973; Immunology, Natl Inst Hlth-Clin Ctr 1976; **Fellow:** Medical Oncology, Dana Farber Cancer Inst 1978; **Fac Appt:** Prof Med, Univ Colorado

Grem, Jean L MD [Onc] - **Spec Exp:** Colon & Rectal Cancer; Pancreatic Cancer; Stomach Cancer; Esophageal Cancer; **Hospital:** Nebraska Med Ctr; **Address:** 987835 Nebraska Medical Ctr, Emile @ 42nd St, Omaha, NE 68198-7630; **Phone:** 402-559-5600; **Board Cert:** Internal Medicine 1983; Medical Oncology 1985; **Med School:** Jefferson Med Coll 1980; **Resid:** Internal Medicine, Univ Iowa Hosps & Clinics 1983; **Fellow:** Medical Oncology, Univ Wisc Clin Cancer Ctr 1986; **Fac Appt:** Prof Med, Univ Nebr Coll Med

Hauke, Ralph J MD [Onc] - **Spec Exp:** Urologic Cancer; Clinical Trials; Testicular Cancer; Prostate Cancer; **Hospital:** Methodist Hosp - Omaha, Alegent Hlth - Bergan Mercy Med Ctr; **Address:** 8303 Dodge St, Ste 250, Omaha, NE 68114; **Phone:** 402-354-8124; **Board Cert:** Medical Oncology 2012; Hospice & Palliative Medicine 2012; **Med School:** Panama 1990; **Resid:** Internal Medicine, Univ Nebraska Med Ctr 1996; **Fellow:** Medical Oncology, Univ Nebraska Med Ctr 2001; **Fac Appt:** Assoc Prof Onc, Univ Nebr Coll Med

Kane, Madeleine A MD/PhD [Onc] - **Spec Exp:** Head & Neck Cancer; Gastrointestinal Cancer; Neuroendocrine Tumors; **Hospital:** Univ Colorado Hosp, VA Eastern CO Health Care Sys-Denver; **Address:** Anschutz Cancer Pavilion, 1665 Aurora Ct, MS F-703, Aurora, CO 80045; **Phone:** 720-848-0300; **Board Cert:** Internal Medicine 1981; Medical Oncology 1983; Hematology 1986; **Med School:** Univ Miami Sch Med 1978; **Resid:** Internal Medicine, Stanford Univ Med Ctr 1981; **Fellow:** Hematology & Oncology, Univ CO Hlth Sci Ctr 1984; **Fac Appt:** Prof Med, Univ Colorado

Messersmith, Wells A MD [Onc] - **Spec Exp:** Gastrointestinal Cancer; Colon & Rectal Cancer; **Hospital:** Univ Colorado Hosp; **Address:** Univ CO Hosp, Cancer Ctr, 12605 E 16th Ave, Ste 2004, Aurora, CO 80045; **Phone:** 720-848-0300; **Board Cert:** Medical Oncology 2003; **Med School:** Harvard Med Sch 1998; **Resid:** Medical Oncology, Mass Genl Hosp 2001; **Fellow:** Medical Oncology, Johns Hopkins Hosp 2004; **Fac Appt:** Asst Prof Onc, Univ Colorado

Samuels, Brian L MD [Onc] - **Spec Exp:** Sarcoma; **Hospital:** Kootenai Med Ctr; **Address:** 750 N Syringa St, Post Falls, ID 83854; **Phone:** 208-262-2381; **Board Cert:** Internal Medicine 1984; Medical Oncology 1987; **Med School:** Zimbabwe 1976; **Resid:** Internal Medicine, Albert Einstein Med Ctr 1981; Internal Medicine, Albert Einstein Med Ctr 1984; **Fellow:** Hematology & Oncology, Univ Chicago Hosps 1988

Steen, Preston D MD [Onc] - **Spec Exp:** Colon & Rectal Cancer; Lung Cancer; Palliative Care; **Hospital:** Sanford Med Ctr Fargo; **Address:** 820 N Fourth St, Fargo, ND 58122; **Phone:** 701-234-6161; **Board Cert:** Internal Medicine 1987; Medical Oncology 2011; Hospice & Palliative Medicine 2010; **Med School:** Univ Minn 1984; **Resid:** Internal Medicine, Maricopa Med Ctr 1987; **Fellow:** Hematology & Oncology, Univ Utah 1990; **Fac Appt:** Clin Prof Onc, Univ ND Sch Med

Sweetenham, John W MD [Onc] - **Spec Exp:** Lymphoma; Stem Cell Transplant; Castleman's Disease; **Hospital:** Univ Utah Hlth Care; **Address:** Huntsman Cancer Institute, 2000 Circle of Hope, Salt Lake City, UT 84112-5550; **Phone:** 801-585-0303; **Med School:** England, UK 1980; **Resid:** Internal Medicine, Royal United Hosp 1984; **Fellow:** Hematology & Oncology, Univ Southampton Hosp 1989; **Fac Appt:** Prof Onc, UCSD

Ward, John H MD [Onc] - **Spec Exp:** Breast Cancer; Gastrointestinal Cancer; Brain Tumors; Unknown Primary Cancer; **Hospital:** Univ Utah Hlth Care, St. John's Med Ctr; **Address:** Huntsman Cancer Inst, 2000 Circle of Hope, Ste 2100 - rm 2141, MS 84112, Salt Lake City, UT 84112-5550; **Phone:** 801-585-0255; **Board Cert:** Internal Medicine 1979; Medical Oncology 1981; Hematology 1982; **Med School:** Univ Utah 1976; **Resid:** Internal Medicine, Duke Univ Med Ctr 1979; **Fellow:** Hematology & Oncology, Univ Utah Med Ctr 1982; **Fac Appt:** Prof Onc, Univ Utah

Southwest

Abbruzzese, James L MD [Onc] - **Spec Exp:** Gastrointestinal Cancer; Pancreatic Cancer; Clinical Trials; **Hospital:** UT MD Anderson Canc Ctr; **Address:** Univ TX MD Anderson Canc Ctr, 1515 Holcombe Blvd, Unit 426, Houston, TX 77030; **Phone:** 713-792-2828; **Board Cert:** Internal Medicine 1981; Medical Oncology 1983; **Med School:** Univ Chicago-Pritzker Sch Med 1978; **Resid:** Internal Medicine, Johns Hopkins Hosp 1981; **Fellow:** Medical Oncology, Dana-Farber Canc Inst 1983; **Fac Appt:** Prof Med, Univ Tex, Houston

Ahmann, Frederick R MD [Onc] - **Spec Exp:** Prostate Cancer; Testicular Cancer; Bladder Cancer; **Hospital:** Univ Arizona Med Ctr-Univ Campus; **Address:** Arizona Cancer Ctr-UMC North, 3838 N Campbell Ave, Tucson, AZ 85719; **Phone:** 520-694-2873; **Board Cert:** Internal Medicine 1977; Medical Oncology 1981; **Med School:** Univ MO-Columbia Sch Med 1974; **Resid:** Internal Medicine, Georgetown Univ Med Ctr 1977; **Fellow:** Medical Oncology, Univ Arizona 1980; **Fac Appt:** Prof Med, Univ Ariz Coll Med

Ajani, Jaffer A MD [Onc] - **Spec Exp:** Gastrointestinal Cancer; Esophageal Cancer; Stomach Cancer; Neuroendocrine Tumors; **Hospital:** UT MD Anderson Canc Ctr; **Address:** UT MD Anderson Canc Ctr, 1515 Holcombe Blvd, Unit 426, Houston, TX 77230; **Phone:** 713-792-2828; **Board Cert:** Internal Medicine 1979; Medical Oncology 1983; **Med School:** India 1971; **Resid:** Family Medicine, Penn State Affil Hosp 1977; Internal Medicine, Tulane Affil Hosp 1980; **Fellow:** Medical Oncology, MD Anderson Canc Ctr 1983; **Fac Appt:** Prof Med, Univ Tex, Houston

Alberts, David S MD [Onc] - **Spec Exp:** Cancer Prevention; Ovarian Cancer; **Hospital:** Univ Arizona Med Ctr-Univ Campus; **Address:** 1515 N Campbell Ave, Tucson, AZ 85724; **Phone:** 520-626-7685; **Board Cert:** Internal Medicine 1973; Medical Oncology 1973; **Med School:** Univ VA Sch Med 1966; **Resid:** Medical Oncology, Natl Cancer Inst-NIH 1969; Internal Medicine, U Minn Hosps 1971; **Fellow:** Clinical Pharmacology, UCSF 1974; **Fac Appt:** Prof Med, Univ Ariz Coll Med

Argiris, Athanassios MD [Onc] - **Spec Exp:** Head & Neck Cancer; Lung Cancer; **Hospital:** Univ Hosp-San Antonio; **Address:** Cancer Therapy & Research Center, 7979 Wurzbach Rd, Fl 4th, rm Z418, San Antonio, TX 78229; **Phone:** 210-450-3838; **Board Cert:** Medical Oncology 2010; **Med School:** Greece 1990; **Resid:** Internal Medicine, Beth Israel Med Ctr 1997; **Fellow:** Medical Oncology, Yale-New Haven Hosp 2000; **Fac Appt:** Prof Onc, Univ Tex, San Antonio

Arun, Banu K MD [Onc] - **Spec Exp:** Breast Cancer; Cancer Prevention; Clinical Trials; **Hospital:** UT MD Anderson Canc Ctr; **Address:** 1515 Holcombe Blvd, Unit 1354, Houston, TX 77030; **Phone:** 713-792-2817; **Board Cert:** Internal Medicine 2010; Medical Oncology 2011; **Med School:** Turkey 1989; **Resid:** Internal Medicine, Univ Istanbul Affil Hosp 1994; **Fellow:** Hematology & Oncology, Lombardi Canc Ctr-Georgetown Univ 1997; **Fac Appt:** Assoc Prof Med, Univ Tex, Houston

Benjamin, Robert S MD [Onc] - **Spec Exp:** Sarcoma; **Hospital:** UT MD Anderson Canc Ctr; **Address:** UT MD Anderson Canc Ctr, 1515 Holcombe Blvd, Unit 450, Houston, TX 77030; **Phone:** 713-563-9701; **Board Cert:** Internal Medicine 1973; Medical Oncology 1973; **Med School:** NYU Sch Med 1968; **Resid:** Internal Medicine, Bellevue Hosp Ctr 1972; **Fellow:** Medical Oncology, Baltimore Canc Rsch Ctr 1973; **Fac Appt:** Prof Med, Univ Tex, Houston

Bergsagel, Peter Leif MD [Onc] - **Spec Exp:** Multiple Myeloma; Hematologic Malignancies; **Hospital:** Mayo Clinic - Scottsdale, Mayo Clinic - Phoenix; **Address:** Mayo Clinic-Hematology/Oncology, 13400 E Shea Blvd Fl 3, Scottsdale, AZ 85259; **Phone:** 480-301-8335; **Board Cert:** Internal Medicine 1987; Medical Oncology 1989; **Med School:** Univ Toronto 1984; **Resid:** Internal Medicine, Sunnybrook Medical Centre 1986; Internal Medicine, Stanford Univ Med Ctr 1987; **Fellow:** Medical Oncology, Natl Cancer Inst 1990; **Fac Appt:** Prof Med, Mayo Med Sch

Bruera, Eduardo MD [Onc] - **Spec Exp:** Palliative Care; **Hospital:** UT MD Anderson Canc Ctr; **Address:** 1515 Holcombe Blvd, MS 1414, Houston, TX 77030; **Phone:** 713-792-6085; **Board Cert:** Internal Medicine 2011; Hospice & Palliative Medicine 2012; **Med School:** Argentina 1979; **Resid:** Internal Medicine, Hospital Privado; **Fellow:** Medical Oncology, Cross Cancer Inst; **Fac Appt:** Prof Onc, Univ Tex, Houston

Buzdar, Aman U MD [Onc] - **Spec Exp:** Breast Cancer; **Hospital:** UT MD Anderson Canc Ctr; **Address:** UT MD Anderson Cancer Ctr, 1515 Holcome Blvd, Unit 1354, Houston, TX 77030; **Phone:** 713-792-2817; **Board Cert:** Internal Medicine 1975; Medical Oncology 1979; **Med School:** Pakistan 1967; **Resid:** Internal Medicine, Norwalk Hosp 1973; Internal Medicine, Lakewood Hosp 1971; **Fellow:** Hematology, Norwalk Hosp 1974; Oncology, MD Anderson Cancer Ctr 1975; **Fac Appt:** Prof Onc, Univ Tex, Houston

Camoriano, John K MD [Onc] - **Spec Exp:** Lymphoma; Breast Cancer; Bone Marrow Transplant; Castleman's Disease; **Hospital:** Mayo Clinic - Scottsdale, Mayo Clinic - Phoenix; **Address:** Mayo Clinic-Hematology/Oncology, 13400 E Shea Blvd Fl 3, Scottsdale, AZ 85259; **Phone:** 480-301-8335; **Board Cert:** Internal Medicine 1985; Hematology 1988; Medical Oncology 1989; **Med School:** Univ Nebr Coll Med 1982; **Resid:** Internal Medicine, Univ OK Affil Hosp 1985; Medical Oncology, Mayo Clinic 1989; **Fellow:** Hematology, Mayo Clinic 1988; **Fac Appt:** Asst Prof Med, Mayo Med Sch

Chang, Jenny C N MD [Onc] - **Spec Exp:** Breast Cancer; Clinical Trials; **Hospital:** Methodist Hosp - Houston; **Address:** Outpatient Ctr, 6445 Main St Fl 21, Houston, TX 77030; **Phone:** 713-441-9948; **Board Cert:** Internal Medicine 2004; **Med School:** England, UK 1989; **Resid:** Internal Medicine, Royal Marsden Hosp 1993; **Fellow:** Medical Oncology, Royal Marsden Hosp 1997

Edelman, Martin J MD [Onc] - **Spec Exp:** Thoracic Cancers; Lung Cancer; Drug Discovery & Development; **Hospital:** Univ Hosp - New Mexico; **Address:** Univ New Mexico Cancer Ctr, 1201 Camino de Salud NE, MS C074025, Albuquerque, NM 87131; **Phone:** 505-925-0411; **Board Cert:** Internal Medicine 1986; Medical Oncology 1989; **Med School:** Albany Med Coll 1982; **Resid:** Internal Medicine, Naval Hosp 1986; **Fellow:** Hematology & Oncology, Naval Hosp 1990; **Fac Appt:** Prof Med, Univ New Mexico

Fay, Joseph W MD [Onc] - **Spec Exp:** Bone Marrow Transplant; Melanoma; Leukemia & Lymphoma; Multiple Myeloma; **Hospital:** Baylor Univ Med Ctr-Dallas; **Address:** Sammons Canc Ctr, 3410 Worth St, Ste 300, Dallas, TX 75246; **Phone:** 214-370-1500; **Board Cert:** Internal Medicine 1975; Medical Oncology 1977; Hematology 1978; **Med School:** Ohio State Univ 1972; **Resid:** Internal Medicine, Duke Med Ctr 1974; Oncology, Natl Canc Inst 1976; **Fellow:** Hematology, Duke Med Ctr 1977

Fitch, Tom R MD [Onc] - **Spec Exp:** Breast Cancer; Palliative Care; Cancer Prevention; Sarcoma; **Hospital:** Mayo Clinic - Phoenix, Mayo Clinic - Scottsdale; **Address:** Mayo Clinic-Hematology/Oncology, 5777 E Mayo Blvd, Phoenix, AZ 85054; **Phone:** 480-301-8335; **Board Cert:** Internal Medicine 1985; Medical Oncology 1987; Hematology 1988; Hospice & Palliative Medicine 2008; **Med School:** Univ Kansas 1982; **Resid:** Internal Medicine, Univ Mich Med Ctr 1985; **Fellow:** Hematology & Oncology, Mayo Clinic 1988; **Fac Appt:** Asst Prof Med, Mayo Med Sch

Fossella, Frank V MD [Onc] - **Spec Exp:** Lung Cancer; **Hospital:** UT MD Anderson Canc Ctr; **Address:** Dept Thoracic Head/Neck Med Oncology, 1515 Holcombe Blvd, Unit 432, rm FC9.3064, Houston, TX 77030; **Phone:** 713-792-6363; **Board Cert:** Internal Medicine 1985; Medical Oncology 1987; **Med School:** Baylor Coll Med 1982; **Resid:** Internal Medicine, Baylor Coll Med Affil Hosp 1985; **Fellow:** Medical Oncology, Baylor Coll Med Affil Hosp 1987; **Fac Appt:** Prof Med, Univ Tex, Houston

Glisson, Bonnie S MD [Onc] - **Spec Exp:** Head & Neck Cancer; Lung Cancer; **Hospital:** UT MD Anderson Canc Ctr; **Address:** UT MD Anderson Canc Ctr, 1515 Holcombe Blvd, Unit 432, rm FC9.3065, Houston, TX 77230-1402; **Phone:** 713-792-6363; **Board Cert:** Internal Medicine 1982; Medical Oncology 1985; **Med School:** Ohio State Univ 1979; **Resid:** Internal Medicine, Univ Virginia Health Sys 1982; **Fellow:** Medical Oncology, Shands Univ FL 1985; **Fac Appt:** Prof Med, Univ Tex, Houston

Haley, Barbara B MD [Onc] - **Spec Exp:** Breast Cancer; **Hospital:** UT Southwestern Med Ctr at Dallas; **Address:** UT Southwestern Med Ctr, 5323 Harry Hines Blvd, Ste NB2102, Dallas, TX 75390-8852; **Phone:** 214-648-4180; **Board Cert:** Internal Medicine 1979; Hematology 1984; **Med School:** Univ Tex SW, Dallas 1976; **Resid:** Internal Medicine, Parkland Hlth & Hosp Sys 1979; **Fellow:** Hematology & Oncology, Parkland Hlth & Hosp Sys 1983; **Fac Appt:** Prof Med, Univ Tex SW, Dallas

Hong, Waun K MD [Onc] - **Spec Exp:** Lung Cancer; Head & Neck Cancer; Thoracic Cancers; **Hospital:** UT MD Anderson Canc Ctr; **Address:** Dept Thoracic Head/Neck Oncology, 1515 Holcombe Blvd, Unit 1101, Houston, TX 77030; **Phone:** 713-792-6110; **Board Cert:** Internal Medicine 1976; Medical Oncology 1979; **Med School:** South Korea 1967; **Resid:** Internal Medicine, VA Boston Hlthcare Sys-Jamaica Plain Div 1973; **Fellow:** Medical Oncology, Meml Sloan-Kettering Canc Ctr 1975; **Fac Appt:** Prof Med, Univ Tex, Houston

Hortobagyi, Gabriel N MD [Onc] - **Spec Exp:** Breast Cancer; Clinical Trials; Gene Therapy; Breast Cancer-Male; **Hospital:** UT MD Anderson Canc Ctr; **Address:** 1155 Pressler Blvd, CPB, Fl 5, Ste 3405, Houston, TX 77030-1439; **Phone:** 713-792-2817; **Board Cert:** Internal Medicine 1975; Medical Oncology 1977; **Med School:** Colombia 1970; **Resid:** Internal Medicine, St Lukes Hosp 1974; **Fellow:** Medical Oncology, MD Anderson Cancer Ctr 1976; **Fac Appt:** Prof Onc, Univ Tex, Houston

Hutchins, Laura F MD [Onc] - **Spec Exp:** Breast Cancer; Melanoma; **Hospital:** UAMS Med Ctr; **Address:** Univ Arkansas Med Scis, Dept Hem/Onc, 4301 W Markham St, Slot 508, Little Rock, AR 72205; **Phone:** 501-686-8511; **Board Cert:** Internal Medicine 1980; Hematology 1984; Medical Oncology 1987; Hospice & Palliative Medicine 2010; **Med School:** Univ Ark 1977; **Resid:** Internal Medicine, Univ Ark Affil Hosp 1980; **Fellow:** Hematology & Oncology, Univ Arkansas 1983; **Fac Appt:** Prof Med, Univ Ark

Hwu, Patrick MD [Onc] - **Spec Exp:** Melanoma; Immunotherapy; Clinical Trials; **Hospital:** UT MD Anderson Canc Ctr; **Address:** UT MD Anderson Canc Ctr, Melanoma & Skin Ctr, 1515 Holcombe Blvd, Unit 347, Houston, TX 77030; **Phone:** 713-792-6800; **Board Cert:** Medical Oncology 2008; **Med School:** Med Coll PA 1987; **Resid:** Internal Medicine, Johns Hopkins Hosp 1990; **Fellow:** Medical Oncology, Natl Canc Inst 1993

Jonasch, Eric MD [Onc] - **Spec Exp:** Kidney Cancer; Testicular Cancer; Bladder Cancer; Genitourinary Cancer; **Hospital:** UT MD Anderson Canc Ctr; **Address:** GU Medical Oncology, 1220 Holcombe Blvd, Unit 1374, Houston, TX 77030; **Phone:** 713-792-2830; **Board Cert:** Internal Medicine 2005; Hematology 2009; Medical Oncology 2010; **Med School:** Canada 1992; **Resid:** Internal Medicine, Royal Victoria Hosp 1995; **Fellow:** Hematology & Oncology, New England Med Ctr 1997; Research, Beth Israel Deaconess Med Ctr 1999; **Fac Appt:** Assoc Prof Onc, Univ Tex, Houston

Kies, Merrill S MD [Onc] - **Spec Exp:** Head & Neck Cancer; Lung Cancer; **Hospital:** UT MD Anderson Canc Ctr; **Address:** UT MD Anderson Canc Ctr, 1515 Holcombe Blvd, Unit 432, Houston, TX 77030; **Phone:** 713-792-6363; **Board Cert:** Internal Medicine 1976; Medical Oncology 1979; **Med School:** Loyola Univ-Stritch Sch Med 1973; **Resid:** Internal Medicine, Walter Reed Natl Military Med Ctr 1976; **Fellow:** Medical Oncology, Brooke Army Med Ctr 1979; **Fac Appt:** Prof Med, Univ Tex, Houston

Kwak, Larry W MD/PhD [Onc] - **Spec Exp:** Lymphoma; Multiple Myeloma; Vaccine Therapy; Immunotherapy; **Hospital:** UT MD Anderson Canc Ctr; **Address:** MD Anderson Canc Ctr, Dept Lymphoma/Myeloma, 1515 Holcombe Blvd, Unit 429, Houston, TX 77030; **Phone:** 713-794-4186; **Board Cert:** Internal Medicine 1987; Medical Oncology 1989; **Med School:** Northwestern Univ 1982; **Resid:** Internal Medicine, Stanford Univ Hosp & Clin 1987; **Fellow:** Medical Oncology, Stanford Univ Hosp & Clin 1989

Livingston, Robert B MD [Onc] - **Spec Exp:** Breast Cancer; **Hospital:** Univ Arizona Med Ctr-Univ Campus; **Address:** Arizona Cancer Ctr-UMC North, 3838 N Campbell Ave, Tucson, AZ 85719; **Phone:** 520-694-2873; **Board Cert:** Internal Medicine 1972; Medical Oncology 1973; **Med School:** Univ Okla Coll Med 1965; **Resid:** Internal Medicine, Univ Oklahoma Med Ctr 1971; **Fellow:** Medical Oncology, Univ Texas Cancer Ctr 1972; **Fac Appt:** Prof Med, Univ Wash

Logothetis, Christopher J MD [Onc] - **Spec Exp:** Prostate Cancer; Bladder Cancer; **Hospital:** UT MD Anderson Canc Ctr; **Address:** UT MD Anderson Canc Ctr, Unit 1374, Box 301439, Houston, TX 77230; **Phone:** 713-745-7020; **Board Cert:** Internal Medicine 1978; Medical Oncology 1981; **Med School:** Greece 1974; **Resid:** Internal Medicine, Stroger Hosp of Cook Co 1978; **Fellow:** Hematology & Oncology, MD Anderson Canc Ctr 1981; **Fac Appt:** Prof Med, Univ Tex, Houston

Makhoul, Issam MD [Onc] - **Spec Exp:** Gastrointestinal Cancer; Breast Cancer; Colon Cancer; **Hospital:** UAMS Med Ctr; **Address:** 4301 W Markham St, Slot# 721-5, Little Rock, AR 72205; **Phone:** 501-686-8530; **Board Cert:** Medical Oncology 2002; Hematology 2013; **Med School:** Syria 1980; **Resid:** Emergency Medicine, Genl Hosp 1986; Internal Medicine, Penn State Affil Hosp 1999; **Fellow:** Hematology & Oncology, Hershey Med Ctr 2002; **Fac Appt:** Asst Prof Med, Univ Ark

Miller, Thomas P MD [Onc] - **Spec Exp:** Lymphoma; Lymphoma, Non-Hodgkin's; **Hospital:** Univ Arizona Med Ctr-Univ Campus; **Address:** Univ of Arizona Cancer Ctr North Campus, 3838 N Campbell Ave, Tucson, AZ 85719; **Phone:** 520-694-2873; **Board Cert:** Internal Medicine 1977; Medical Oncology 1981; **Med School:** Univ IL Coll Med 1972; **Resid:** Internal Medicine, Univ Illinois Hosps 1977; **Fellow:** Hematology & Oncology, Arizona Univ Med Ctr 1980; **Fac Appt:** Prof Med, Univ Ariz Coll Med

Northfelt, Donald W MD [Onc] - **Spec Exp:** Breast Cancer; Lymphoma; Lymphoma; **Hospital:** Mayo Clinic - Scottsdale, Mayo Clinic - Phoenix; **Address:** Mayo Clinic-Hematology/Oncology, 13400 E Shea Blvd Fl 3, Scottsdale, AZ 85259; **Phone:** 480-301-8335; **Board Cert:** Internal Medicine 1988; Medical Oncology 2011; **Med School:** Univ Minn 1985; **Resid:** Internal Medicine, UCLA Med Ctr 1988; **Fellow:** Hematology & Oncology, UCSF Med Ctr 1991; **Fac Appt:** Assoc Prof Med, Mayo Med Sch

O'Brien, Susan M MD [Onc] - **Spec Exp:** Leukemia; Lymphoma; **Hospital:** UT MD Anderson Canc Ctr; **Address:** Dept Leukemia, 1515 Holcombe Blvd, Unit 428, Houston, TX 77230; **Phone:** 713-792-7305; **Board Cert:** Internal Medicine 1983; Medical Oncology 1987; **Med School:** UMDNJ-NJ Med Sch, Newark 1980; **Resid:** Internal Medicine, Univ Hosp-UMDNJ 1983; **Fellow:** Medical Oncology, Univ TX MD Anderson Med Canc Ctr 1987; **Fac Appt:** Prof Med, Univ Tex, Houston

O'Shaughnessy, Joyce A MD [Onc] - **Spec Exp:** Breast Cancer; **Hospital:** Baylor Univ Med Ctr-Dallas; **Address:** TX Oncology, 3410 Worth St, Ste 400, Dallas, TX 75246; **Phone:** 214-370-1000; **Board Cert:** Internal Medicine 1985; Medical Oncology 1987; **Med School:** Yale Univ 1982; **Resid:** Internal Medicine, Mass Genl Hosp 1985; **Fellow:** Medical Oncology, Natl Canc Inst 1988

Orlowski, Robert Z MD/PhD [Onc] - **Spec Exp:** Multiple Myeloma; Lymphoma, Non-Hodgkin's; Leukemia; Clinical Trials; **Hospital:** UT MD Anderson Canc Ctr; **Address:** MD Anderson Canc Ctr, Lymphoma & Myeloma Clin, 1515 Holcombe Blvd, Unit 429, Houston, TX 77030; **Phone:** 713-792-3510; **Med School:** Yale Univ 1991; **Resid:** Internal Medicine, Barnes-Jewish Hosp 1994; **Fellow:** Hematology & Oncology, Johns Hopkins Hosp 1997; **Fac Appt:** Prof Med, Univ Tex, Houston

Osborne, C. Kent MD [Onc] - **Spec Exp:** Breast Cancer; **Hospital:** Methodist Hosp - Houston; **Address:** 1 Baylor Plaza, MS BCM600, Houston, TX 77030; **Phone:** 713-798-1641; **Board Cert:** Internal Medicine 1975; Medical Oncology 1977; **Med School:** Univ MO-Columbia Sch Med 1972; **Resid:** Internal Medicine, Johns Hopkins Hosp 1975; **Fellow:** Medical Oncology, Natl Cancer Inst 1977; **Fac Appt:** Prof Med, Baylor Coll Med

Patel, Shreyaskumar MD [Onc] - **Spec Exp:** Sarcoma; **Hospital:** UT MD Anderson Canc Ctr; **Address:** UT MD Anderson Canc Ctr, 1515 Holcombe Blvd, Box 450, Houston, TX 77030; **Phone:** 713-563-9701; **Board Cert:** Internal Medicine 1987; Medical Oncology 2011; **Med School:** India 1983; **Resid:** Internal Medicine, Wayne State Affil Hosp 1987; **Fellow:** Medical Oncology, Mayo Clin 1990

Patt, Yehuda Z MD [Onc] - **Spec Exp:** Liver Cancer; Biliary Cancer; Colon & Rectal Cancer; Gastrointestinal Cancer; **Hospital:** Univ Hosp - New Mexico; **Address:** Univ New Mexico Hosp Cancer Ctr, 1201 Camino de Salud NE, Albuquerque, NM 87131; **Phone:** 505-272-4946; **Board Cert:** Internal Medicine 1982; Medical Oncology 1987; **Med School:** Israel 1967; **Resid:** Internal Medicine, Tel Aviv-Sheba Med Ctr 1974; **Fellow:** Medical Oncology, UT MD Anderson Cancer Ctr 1977; **Fac Appt:** Prof Med, Univ New Mexico

Pisters, Katherine M MD [Onc] - **Spec Exp:** Lung Cancer; **Hospital:** UT MD Anderson Canc Ctr; **Address:** UT MD Anderson Canc Ctr, 1515 Holcombe Blvd, Unit 432, Houston, TX 77230-1402; **Phone:** 713-792-6363; **Board Cert:** Internal Medicine 1988; **Med School:** Univ Western Ontario 1985; **Resid:** Internal Medicine, N Shore Univ Hosp 1988; **Fellow:** Medical Oncology, Meml Sloan Kettering Canc Ctr 1991; **Fac Appt:** Prof Med, Univ Tex, Houston

Romaguera, Jorge E MD [Onc] - **Spec Exp:** Lymphoma; **Hospital:** UT MD Anderson Canc Ctr; **Address:** Lymphoma & Myeloma Clin, 1515 Holcombe Blvd, Box 429, Houston, TX 77030; **Phone:** 713-792-3510; **Board Cert:** Internal Medicine 1988; Medical Oncology 1989; **Med School:** Univ Puerto Rico 1982; **Resid:** Internal Medicine, Univ District Hosp 1985; **Fellow:** Hematology & Oncology, Univ District Hosp 1987

Ross, Helen J MD [Onc] - **Spec Exp:** Lung Cancer; Mesothelioma; Esophageal Cancer; Thoracic Cancers; **Hospital:** Mayo Clinic - Scottsdale, Mayo Clinic - Phoenix; **Address:** Mayo Clinic-Hematology/Oncology, 13400 E Shea Blvd Fl 3, Scottsdale, AZ 85259; **Phone:** 480-301-8335; **Board Cert:** Internal Medicine 1987; Medical Oncology 1989; **Med School:** UCLA 1984; **Resid:** Internal Medicine, Cedars-Sinai Med Ctr 1987; **Fellow:** Hematology & Oncology, UCLA Med Ctr 1990; **Fac Appt:** Assoc Prof Med, Mayo Med Sch

Saiki, John H MD [Onc] - **Spec Exp:** Leukemia; Lymphoma; **Hospital:** Univ Hosp - New Mexico; **Address:** University of New Mexico Cancer Center, 1201 Camino de Salud NE, Albuquerque, NM 87106; **Phone:** 505-272-4946; **Board Cert:** Internal Medicine 1970; Medical Oncology 1973; **Med School:** McGill Univ 1961; **Resid:** Internal Medicine, Royal Victoria Hosp 1966; Internal Medicine, Univ New Mexico 1968; **Fellow:** Hematology, Univ New Mexico Affil Hosp 1969; Medical Oncology, MD Anderson Hosp 1970; **Fac Appt:** Prof Emeritus Med, Univ New Mexico

Schiller, Joan H MD [Onc] - **Spec Exp:** Lung Cancer; **Hospital:** UT Southwestern Med Ctr at Dallas; **Address:** UT Southwestern Med Ctr, 5323 Harry Hines Blvd, Ste NB2102, Dallas, TX 75390-8852; **Phone:** 214-648-4180; **Board Cert:** Internal Medicine 1983; Medical Oncology 1987; **Med School:** Univ IL Coll Med 1980; **Resid:** Internal Medicine, Northwestern Meml Hosp 1983; **Fellow:** Medical Oncology, Univ WI Hosp & Clins 1986; **Fac Appt:** Prof Med, Univ Wisc

Simon, George R MD [Onc] - **Spec Exp:** Mesothelioma; Lung Cancer; Thymoma; **Hospital:** UT MD Anderson Canc Ctr; **Address:** MD Anderson Canc Ctr, 1400 Holcombe Blvd, Unit 0432, Houston, TX 77030; **Phone:** 713-792-6363; **Board Cert:** Internal Medicine 2007; Medical Oncology 2007; **Med School:** India 1986; **Resid:** Internal Medicine, Exempla Saint Jos Hosp 1995; **Fellow:** Hematology & Oncology, Univ Colorado Hosp 1997

Stopeck, Alison T MD [Onc] - **Spec Exp:** Breast Cancer; Hemophilia; Thrombotic Disorders; **Hospital:** Univ Arizona Med Ctr-Univ Campus; **Address:** Univ AZ Cancer Ctr-N Campus, 3838 N Campbell Ave, Tucson, AZ 85719; **Phone:** 520-626-2816; **Board Cert:** Internal Medicine 1988; Medical Oncology 2012; Hematology 2012; **Med School:** Columbia P&S 1985; **Resid:** Internal Medicine, Columbia-Presby Med Ctr 1988; **Fellow:** Hematology & Oncology, New York Hosp 1991; **Fac Appt:** Assoc Prof Med, Univ Ariz Coll Med

Taetle, Raymond MD [Onc] - **Spec Exp:** Hematologic Malignancies; Gastrointestinal Cancer; Lung Cancer; Neuroendocrine Tumors; **Hospital:** St. Joseph's Hosp - Tucson, Tucson Med Ctr; **Address:** Arizona Oncology, 6565 E Carondolet Drive, Ste 155, Tucson, AZ 85710; **Phone:** 520-886-0206; **Board Cert:** Internal Medicine 1976; Hematology 1978; Medical Oncology 1979; **Med School:** Northwestern Univ 1973; **Resid:** Internal Medicine, UCSD Med Ctr 1976; **Fellow:** Hematology & Oncology, UCSD 1979; **Fac Appt:** Clin Prof Onc, Univ Ariz Coll Med

Valero, Vicente K MD [Onc] - **Spec Exp:** Breast Cancer; **Hospital:** UT MD Anderson Canc Ctr; **Address:** UT MD Anderson Canc Ctr, 1515 Holcombe Blvd, Unit 1354, Houston, TX 77030; **Phone:** 713-792-2817; **Board Cert:** Internal Medicine 1985; Medical Oncology 1987; Hematology 1988; **Med School:** Mexico 1980; **Resid:** Internal Medicine, Univ Cincinnati Med Ctr 1985; Hematology & Oncology, Univ Cincinnati Med Ctr 1987; **Fellow:** Hematology & Oncology, UT Med Br(John Sealy Hosp) 1988; **Fac Appt:** Prof Med, Univ Tex, Houston

Varadhachary, Gauri MD [Onc] - **Spec Exp:** Unknown Primary Cancer; Pancreatic Cancer; **Hospital:** UT MD Anderson Canc Ctr; **Address:** UT MD Anderson Canc Ctr, 1515 Holcombe Blvd, Box 426, Houston, TX 77030; **Phone:** 713-792-2828; **Board Cert:** Internal Medicine 2004; Medical Oncology 2008; **Med School:** India 1991; **Resid:** Internal Medicine, Greater Baltimore Med Ctr 1995; **Fellow:** Hematology & Oncology, Baylor Univ Affil Hosp 1998; **Fac Appt:** Prof Onc, Univ Tex SW, Dallas

Von Burton, Gary MD [Onc] - **Spec Exp:** Breast Cancer; Sarcoma; Brain Tumors; **Hospital:** Louisiana State Univ Hosp; **Address:** LSU Health Shreveport, Feist-Weiller Cancer Ctr, 1501 Kings Hwy, Box 33932, Shreveport, LA 71103; **Phone:** 318-813-1200; **Board Cert:** Internal Medicine 1981; Medical Oncology 1983; **Med School:** Univ Utah 1978; **Resid:** Internal Medicine, Duke Univ Med Ctr 1981; **Fellow:** Hematology & Oncology, Duke Univ Med Ctr 1983; **Fac Appt:** Prof Med, Louisiana State U, Shrevport

Von Hoff, Daniel D MD [Onc] - **Spec Exp:** Pancreatic Cancer; Breast Cancer; Drug Discovery; **Hospital:** Scottsdale Hlthcare - Shea; **Address:** 10510 N 92nd St Ste 200, Scottsdale, AZ 85258; **Phone:** 480-323-1350; **Board Cert:** Internal Medicine 1976; Medical Oncology 1979; **Med School:** Columbia P&S 1973; **Resid:** Internal Medicine, UCSF Med Ctr 1975; **Fellow:** Medical Oncology, Nat'l Cancer Inst 1979; **Fac Appt:** Clin Prof Med, Univ Ariz Coll Med

Willson, James KV MD [Onc] - **Spec Exp:** Colon & Rectal Cancer; Gastrointestinal Cancer; **Hospital:** UT Southwestern Med Ctr at Dallas; **Address:** UT Southwestern Simmons Cancer Center, 5323 Harry Hines Blvd, MS 8590, Dallas, TX 75390-8590; **Phone:** 214-648-1677; **Board Cert:** Internal Medicine 1980; Medical Oncology 1981; **Med School:** UAB Sch Med 1976; **Resid:** Internal Medicine, Johns Hopkins Hosp 1978; **Fellow:** Medical Oncology, Natl Cancer Inst-NIH 1980; **Fac Appt:** Prof Onc, Univ Tex SW, Dallas

Wolff, Robert A MD [Onc] - **Spec Exp:** Gastrointestinal Cancer; Pancreatic Cancer; Colon & Rectal Cancer; Clinical Trials; **Hospital:** UT MD Anderson Canc Ctr; **Address:** UT MD Anderson Canc Ctr, Dept Med Onc, 1515 Holcombe Blvd, Unit 421, Houston, TX 77030; **Phone:** 713-745-5476; **Board Cert:** Internal Medicine 1989; Medical Oncology 2008; **Med School:** Albany Med Coll 1986; **Resid:** Internal Medicine, Duke Univ Hosp 1989; **Fellow:** Hematology & Oncology, Duke Univ Hosp 1992

West Coast and Pacific

Aboulafia, David M MD [Onc] - **Spec Exp:** AIDS Related Cancers; Leukemia & Lymphoma; Myeloproliferative Disorders; Multiple Myeloma; **Hospital:** Virginia Mason Med Ctr; **Address:** Virginia Mason Med Ctr, Sect of Hematology/Oncology, 1100 Ninth Ave, MS C2-Hem, Seattle, WA 98101; **Phone:** 206-223-6193; **Board Cert:** Internal Medicine 1986; Medical Oncology 1989; Hematology 2003; **Med School:** Univ Mich Med Sch 1983; **Resid:** Internal Medicine, UCLA Ronald Reagan Med Ctr 1986; **Fellow:** Hematology & Oncology, UCLA Ronald Reagan Med Ctr 1989; **Fac Appt:** Clin Prof Med, Univ Wash

Abrams, Donald I MD [Onc] - **Spec Exp:** AIDS Related Cancers; Complementary Medicine; **Hospital:** San Francisco Genl Hosp; **Address:** Osher Center for Integrative Medicine, 1545 Divisadero St Fl 4, San Francisco, CA 94110; **Phone:** 415-353-7700; **Board Cert:** Internal Medicine 1980; Medical Oncology 1983; **Med School:** Stanford Univ 1977; **Resid:** Internal Medicine, Kaiser Fdn Hosp 1980; **Fellow:** Medical Oncology, UCSF Cancer Rsch 1982; **Fac Appt:** Clin Prof Med, UCSF

Advani, Ranjana H MD [Onc] - **Spec Exp:** Lymphoma; Hematologic Malignancies; Clinical Trials; **Hospital:** Stanford Univ Hosp & Clins; **Address:** Lymphoma Clinic, 875 Blake Wilbur Drive, Clinic C, Stanford, CA 94305; **Phone:** 650-498-6000; **Board Cert:** Medical Oncology 2009; **Med School:** India 1982; **Resid:** Internal Medicine, Santa Clara Vly Med Ctr 1987; Internal Medicine, Stanford Univ Med Ctr 1991; **Fellow:** Hematology, Stanford Univ Med Ctr 1990; **Fac Appt:** Asst Prof Med, Stanford Univ

Appelbaum, Frederick R MD [Onc] - **Spec Exp:** Bone Marrow Transplant; Leukemia-Myeloid; Graft vs Host Disease; **Hospital:** Univ Wash Med Ctr; **Address:** Seattle Cancer Care Alliance, 382 Eastlake Ave E, Seattle, WA 98109; **Phone:** 206-288-1024; **Board Cert:** Internal Medicine 1975; Medical Oncology 1977; **Med School:** Tufts Univ 1972; **Resid:** Internal Medicine, Univ Michigan Med Ctr 1974; **Fellow:** Medical Oncology, Natl Cancer Inst 1976; **Fac Appt:** Prof Med, Univ Wash

Audeh, M William MD [Onc] - **Spec Exp:** Breast Cancer; Ovarian Cancer; Clinical Trials; **Hospital:** Cedars-Sinai Med Ctr; **Address:** Cedars-Sinai, Samuel Oschin Cancer Inst, 8700 Beverly Blvd, Ste AC-1046, Los Angeles, CA 90048; **Phone:** 310-423-1188; **Board Cert:** Internal Medicine 1986; Medical Oncology 1989; **Med School:** Univ Iowa Coll Med 1982; **Resid:** Internal Medicine, Stanford Univ Hosp & Clinics 1986; **Fellow:** Hematology & Oncology, Stanford Univ Hosp & Clinics 1989

Back, Anthony L MD [Onc] - **Spec Exp:** Palliative Care; Gastrointestinal Cancer; **Hospital:** Univ Wash Med Ctr; **Address:** Seattle Cancer Care Alliance, 825 Eastlake Ave E, Box G4810, Seattle, WA 98109; **Phone:** 206-288-6797; **Board Cert:** Internal Medicine 1987; Hospice & Palliative Medicine 2008; Medical Oncology 2012; **Med School:** Harvard Med Sch 1984; **Resid:** Internal Medicine, Univ Wash Med Ctr 1988; **Fellow:** Oncology, Univ Wash Med Ctr 1991; **Fac Appt:** Prof Med, Univ Wash

Ball, Edward D MD [Onc] - **Spec Exp:** Bone Marrow & Stem Cell Transplant; Leukemia & Lymphoma; Multiple Myeloma; Immunotherapy; **Hospital:** UCSD Med Ctr; **Address:** 3855 Health Sciences Dr, Ste 0960, La Jolla, CA 92093-0960; **Phone:** 858-822-6600; **Board Cert:** Internal Medicine 1979; Medical Oncology 1983; Hematology 2011; **Med School:** Case West Res Univ 1976; **Resid:** Internal Medicine, Hartford Hosp 1979; **Fellow:** Hematology & Oncology, Univ Hosps Cleveland 1981; Hematology & Oncology, Dartmouth-Hitchcock Hosp 1982; **Fac Appt:** Prof Hem & Onc, UCSD

Beer, Tomasz M MD [Onc] - **Spec Exp:** Prostate Cancer; **Hospital:** OR Hlth & Sci Univ, VA Medical Center - Portland; **Address:** 3303 SW Bond Ave, CH14R, Portland, OR 97239; **Phone:** 503-494-6594; **Board Cert:** Medical Oncology 2010; **Med School:** Johns Hopkins Univ 1991; **Resid:** Internal Medicine, Oreg Hlth Sci Univ 1994; Internal Medicine, Oreg Hlth Sci Univ 1996; **Fellow:** Hematology & Oncology, Oreg Hlth Sci Univ 1999; **Fac Appt:** Prof Med, Oregon Hlth & Sci Univ

Bensinger, William I MD [Onc] - **Spec Exp:** Multiple Myeloma; Stem Cell Transplant; **Hospital:** Univ Wash Med Ctr; **Address:** Fred Hutchinson Cancer Rsch Ctr, 1100 Fairview Ave N, MS DS-390, Seattle, WA 98109-1024; **Phone:** 206-288-1024; **Board Cert:** Internal Medicine 1978; Medical Oncology 1979; **Med School:** Northwestern Univ 1973; **Resid:** Internal Medicine, Univ Wash Med Ctr 1978; **Fellow:** Medical Oncology, Univ Wash Med Ctr 1979; **Fac Appt:** Assoc Prof Med, Univ Wash

Berry, John Michael MD [Onc] - **Spec Exp:** Anal Cancer; HPV-Human Papilloma Virus; **Hospital:** UCSF - Mt Zion Med Ctr; **Address:** UCSF, Dysplasia Clinic, 1600 Divisadero St, 4th Floor, San Francisco, CA 94143; **Phone:** 415-353-7100; **Board Cert:** Internal Medicine 1985; Medical Oncology 1989; **Med School:** Univ Miami Sch Med 1982; **Resid:** Internal Medicine, UCSF Med Ctr 1985; **Fellow:** Medical Oncology, Stanford Univ 1989; **Fac Appt:** Asst Clin Prof Med, UCSF

Chang, Susan M MD [Onc] - **Spec Exp:** Brain Tumors; Spinal Cord Tumors; **Hospital:** UCSF Med Ctr; **Address:** UCSF, Dept Neurological Surgery, 400 Parnassus Ave, rm A808, San Francisco, CA 94143; **Phone:** 415-353-2184; **Med School:** Univ British Columbia Fac Med 1985; **Resid:** Internal Medicine, Plains Hlth Ctr 1987; Internal Medicine, Toronto Genl Hosp 1989; **Fellow:** Medical Oncology, Princess Margaret Hosp 1991; Neuro-Oncology, UCSF Med Ctr 1995; **Fac Appt:** Prof Med, UCSF

Chap, Linnea I MD [Onc] - **Spec Exp:** Breast Cancer; Gynecologic Cancer; Clinical Trials; **Hospital:** St. John's Hlth Ctr, Santa Monica; **Address:** Beverly Hills Cancer Center, 8900 Wilshire Blvd Fl 2, Beverly Hills, CA 90211; **Phone:** 310-432-8900; **Board Cert:** Medical Oncology 2005; **Med School:** Univ Chicago-Pritzker Sch Med 1988; **Resid:** Internal Medicine, Northwestern Meml Hosp 1991; **Fellow:** Hematology & Oncology, UCLA Med Ctr 1994; **Fac Appt:** Assoc Clin Prof Onc, UCLA-David Geffen Sch Med

Chew, Helen K MD [Onc] - **Spec Exp:** Breast Cancer; **Hospital:** UC Davis Med Ctr; **Address:** UC Davis Cancer Ctr, 4501 X St Fl 2, Sacramento, CA 95817; **Phone:** 916-734-5959; **Board Cert:** Medical Oncology 2007; **Med School:** Univ Tex, San Antonio 1991; **Resid:** Internal Medicine, U Tex Hlth Sci Ctr 1994; **Fellow:** Medical Oncology, U Tex Hlth Sci Ctr 1997

Chlebowski, Rowan T MD/PhD [Onc] - **Spec Exp:** Breast Cancer; Breast Cancer Risk Assessment; Women's Health; **Hospital:** LAC - Harbor - UCLA Med Ctr; **Address:** Harbor-UCLA Med Ctr, 1000 W Carson St J-3 Bldg, Torrance, CA 90509; **Phone:** 310-222-2217; **Board Cert:** Internal Medicine 1980; Medical Oncology 1981; **Med School:** Case West Res Univ 1974; **Resid:** Internal Medicine, Cleveland Metro Genl Hosp 1978; **Fellow:** Medical Oncology, LAC-USC Med Ctr 1981; **Fac Appt:** Prof Med, UCLA

Chow, Warren A MD [Onc] - **Spec Exp:** Sarcoma-Soft Tissue; Hematologic Malignancies; Melanoma; **Hospital:** City of Hope Natl Med Ctr; **Address:** City of Hope, Med Oncology Dept, 1500 E Duarte Rd, Duarte, CA 91010; **Phone:** 626-471-9200; **Board Cert:** Internal Medicine 1989; Medical Oncology 2003; Hematology 2004; **Med School:** Univ Hlth Scis, Chicago Med Sch 1986; **Resid:** Internal Medicine, Cedars-Sinai Med Ctr 1990; **Fellow:** Hematology & Oncology, City Hope Natl Med Ctr 1992; Molecular Genetics, City Hope Natl Med Ctr 1994; **Fac Appt:** Clin Prof Onc, Ros Franklin Univ/Chicago Med Sch

Crocenzi, Todd MD [Onc] - **Spec Exp:** Gastrointestinal Cancer; **Hospital:** Providence Portland Med Ctr; **Address:** Providence Cancer Ctr, 4805 NE Glisan St, Ste 6N40, Portland, OR 97213; **Phone:** 503-215-5696; **Board Cert:** Medical Oncology 2004; **Med School:** Jefferson Med Coll 1994; **Resid:** Internal Medicine, Univ MD Med Ctr 1997; **Fellow:** Hematology & Oncology, Dartmouth Hitchcock Med Ctr 2004; Immunology, Dartmouth Hitchcock Med Ctr 2005

Daud, Adil I MD [Onc] - **Spec Exp:** Melanoma; Skin Cancer; Drug Development; **Hospital:** UCSF Med Ctr; **Address:** 1600 Divisadero St Fl 4, San Francisco, CA 94115; **Phone:** 415-353-9900; **Med School:** India 1986; **Resid:** Internal Medicine, Indiana Univ Med Ctr 1997; **Fellow:** Hematology & Oncology, Meml Sloan Kettering Cancer Ctr 2000; **Fac Appt:** Clin Prof Med, UCSF

Deeg, H. Joachim MD [Onc] - **Spec Exp:** Myelodysplastic Syndromes; Myeloproliferative Disorders; Bone Marrow Failure Disorders; Graft vs Host Disease; **Hospital:** Univ Wash Med Ctr; **Address:** Fred Hutchinson Cancer Rsch Ctr, 1100 Fairview Avenue N, D1-100, Box 19024, Seattle, WA 98109-1024; **Phone:** 206-667-5985; **Board Cert:** Internal Medicine 1976; Medical Oncology 1979; **Med School:** Germany 1972; **Resid:** Internal Medicine, Genessee Hosp 1976; **Fellow:** Medical Oncology, Univ Wash Med Ctr 1978; **Fac Appt:** Prof Med, Univ Wash

Disis, Mary L MD [Onc] - **Spec Exp:** Breast Cancer; Ovarian Cancer; Clinical Trials; **Hospital:** Univ Wash Med Ctr; **Address:** Univ Washington, Tumor Vaccine Group, 815 Mercer St, Box 358050, Seattle, WA 98109; **Phone:** 206-616-1823; **Board Cert:** Internal Medicine 1989; Medical Oncology 2008; **Med School:** Univ Nebr Coll Med 1986; **Resid:** Internal Medicine, Univ IL Med Ctr 1990; **Fellow:** Medical Oncology, Fred Hutchinson Cancer Ctr 1993; **Fac Appt:** Assoc Prof Med, Univ Wash

Druker, Brian J MD [Onc] - **Spec Exp:** Leukemia; Leukemia-Chronic Myeloid; Hematologic Malignancies; **Hospital:** OR Hlth & Sci Univ; **Address:** OHSU Ctr Hematologic Malignancies, 3181 SW Sam Jackson Park Rd, Multnomah Pavilion, MC UHN73A, Portland, OR 97239-3098; **Phone:** 503-494-5058; **Board Cert:** Internal Medicine 1984; Medical Oncology 1987; **Med School:** UCSD 1981; **Resid:** Internal Medicine, Barnes-Jewish Hosp 1984; **Fellow:** Medical Oncology, Dana-Farber Cancer Inst 1987; **Fac Appt:** Prof Med, Oregon Hlth & Sci Univ

Ellis, Georgiana K MD [Onc] - **Spec Exp:** Breast Cancer; Clinical Trials; **Hospital:** Univ Wash Med Ctr; **Address:** Seattle Cancer Care Alliance, 825 Eastlake Ave E, Box 358081, MS G3-630, Seattle, WA 98103; **Phone:** 206-288-1000; **Board Cert:** Internal Medicine 1985; Medical Oncology 1987; **Med School:** Univ Wash 1982; **Resid:** Internal Medicine, Univ Washington Med Ctr 1985; **Fellow:** Medical Oncology, Univ Washington Med Ctr 1987; **Fac Appt:** Assoc Prof Med, Univ Wash

Estey, Elihu H MD [Onc] - **Spec Exp:** Leukemia; Leukemia-Myeloid; Clinical Trials; Myelodysplastic Syndromes; **Hospital:** Univ Wash Med Ctr; **Address:** Seattle Cancer Care Alliance, 825 Eastlake Ave E, MS G3-200, Seattle, WA 98109; **Phone:** 206-288-7222; **Board Cert:** Internal Medicine 1975; Medical Oncology 1981; **Med School:** Johns Hopkins Univ 1972; **Resid:** Internal Medicine, Bellevue Hosp Ctr 1975; **Fellow:** Medical Oncology, MD Anderson Cancer Ctr 1978

Fakih, Marwan G MD [Onc] - **Spec Exp:** Gastrointestinal Cancer; Colon & Rectal Cancer; **Hospital:** City of Hope Natl Med Ctr; **Address:** City of Hope, Med Oncology Dept, 1500 E Duarte Rd, Duarte, CA 91010; **Phone:** 626-471-9200; **Board Cert:** Medical Oncology 2011; **Med School:** Lebanon 1992; **Resid:** Internal Medicine, Detroit Med Ctr 1995; **Fellow:** Hematology & Oncology, UPMC 2001; **Fac Appt:** Prof Onc

Figlin, Robert A MD [Onc] - **Spec Exp:** Kidney Cancer; Urologic Cancer; Immunotherapy; Lung Cancer; **Hospital:** Cedars-Sinai Med Ctr; **Address:** Samuel Oschin Cancer Institute, Cedars-Sinai Med Ctr, Saperstein Tower, 8700 Beverly Blvd, Ste 1S30, Los Angeles, CA 90048; **Phone:** 310-423-1331; **Board Cert:** Internal Medicine 1979; Medical Oncology 1983; **Med School:** Med Coll PA Hahnemann 1976; **Resid:** Internal Medicine, Cedars Sinai Med Ctr 1980; **Fellow:** Hematology & Oncology, UCLA Hlth Sci Ctr 1983; **Fac Appt:** Prof Med, UCLA

Fisher Jr, George A MD/PhD [Onc] - **Spec Exp:** Gastrointestinal Cancer; Pancreatic Cancer; Neuroendocrine Tumors; **Hospital:** Stanford Univ Hosp & Clins; **Address:** Stanford Cancer Center, 875 Blake Wilbur Drive, Stanford, CA 94305; **Phone:** 650-498-6000; **Med School:** Stanford Univ 1987; **Resid:** Internal Medicine, Stanford Univ Med Ctr 1991; **Fellow:** Medical Oncology, Stanford Univ Med Ctr 1993; **Fac Appt:** Assoc Prof Med, Stanford Univ

Ford, James M MD [Onc] - **Spec Exp:** Gastrointestinal Cancer; Colon & Rectal Cancer; Cancer Genetics; Li-Fraumeni Syndrome; **Hospital:** Stanford Univ Hosp & Clins; **Address:** Stanford Comp Cancer Ctr, 875 Blake Wilbur Drive, Clinic F, Stanford, CA 94305; **Phone:** 650-723-7621; **Board Cert:** Medical Oncology 2005; **Med School:** Yale Univ 1989; **Resid:** Internal Medicine, Stanford Univ Med Ctr 1991; **Fellow:** Medical Oncology, Stanford Univ Med Ctr 1994; **Fac Appt:** Assoc Prof Onc, Stanford Univ

Forscher, Charles A MD [Onc] - **Spec Exp:** Sarcoma-Soft Tissue; **Hospital:** Cedars-Sinai Med Ctr, UCLA Ronald Reagan Med Ctr; **Address:** Cedars-Sinai, Samuel Oschin Cancer Inst, 8700 Beverly Blvd, Ste AC-1042D, Los Angeles, CA 90048; **Phone:** 310-423-8045; **Board Cert:** Internal Medicine 1981; Hematology 1986; Medical Oncology 1987; **Med School:** Albert Einstein Coll Med 1978; **Resid:** Internal Medicine, Montefiore Med Ctr 1981; **Fellow:** Hematology, Montefiore Med Ctr 1984; Medical Oncology, Mount Sinai Med Ctr 1986; **Fac Appt:** Clin Prof Med, UCLA

Gandara, David R MD [Onc] - **Spec Exp:** Lung Cancer; **Hospital:** UC Davis Med Ctr; **Address:** UC Davis Cancer Ctr, 4501 X St, Ste 3016, Sacramento, CA 95817; **Phone:** 916-734-3772; **Board Cert:** Internal Medicine 1976; Medical Oncology 1979; **Med School:** Univ Tex Med Br, Galveston 1973; **Resid:** Internal Medicine, Madigan Med Ctr 1976; **Fellow:** Hematology & Oncology, Letterman AMC 1978; **Fac Appt:** Prof Med, UC Davis

Ganz, Patricia A MD [Onc] - **Spec Exp:** Breast Cancer; Cancer Survivors-Late Effects of Therapy; Cancer Prevention; **Hospital:** UCLA Ronald Reagan Med Ctr; **Address:** 200 UCLA Med Plaza, Ste 120, Los Angeles, CA 90095-6900; **Phone:** 310-206-1404; **Board Cert:** Internal Medicine 1976; Medical Oncology 1979; **Med School:** UCLA 1973; **Resid:** Internal Medicine, UCLA Med Ctr 1976; **Fellow:** Hematology, UCLA Med Ctr 1978; **Fac Appt:** Prof Med, UCLA

Glaspy, John A MD [Onc] - **Spec Exp:** Breast Cancer; Melanoma; Lymphoma; Gastrointestinal Cancer; **Hospital:** UCLA Ronald Reagan Med Ctr, Santa Monica - UCLA Med Ctr & Ortho Hosp; **Address:** UCLA Med Ctr- Hematology Oncology Div, 100 UCLA Medical Plaza, Ste 550, Los Angeles, CA 90095; **Phone:** 310-794-4955; **Board Cert:** Internal Medicine 1982; Medical Oncology 1985; Hematology 1986; **Med School:** UCLA 1979; **Resid:** Internal Medicine, UCLA Med Ctr 1982; **Fellow:** Hematology & Oncology, UCLA Med Ctr 1985; **Fac Appt:** Prof Med, UCLA

Gold, Philip J MD [Onc] - **Spec Exp:** Gastrointestinal Cancer; Clinical Trials; **Hospital:** Swedish Med Ctr-First Hill-Seattle; **Address:** Swedish Cancer Inst, 1221 Madison St, Fl 2, Ste 200, Seattle, WA 98104; **Phone:** 206-386-2121; **Board Cert:** Internal Medicine 2005; Medical Oncology 2007; **Med School:** Univ Miami Sch Med 1991; **Resid:** Internal Medicine, Univ Wash Med Ctr 1994; **Fellow:** Medical Oncology, Fred Hutchinson Canc Rsch Ctr 1996

Gralow, Julie MD [Onc] - **Spec Exp:** Breast Cancer; **Hospital:** Univ Wash Med Ctr; **Address:** Seattle Cancer Care Alliance, 825 Eastlake Ave E, MS G3-630, Seattle, WA 98109; **Phone:** 206-288-7222; **Board Cert:** Medical Oncology 2005; **Med School:** USC Sch Med 1988; **Resid:** Internal Medicine, Brigham & Women's Hosp 1991; **Fellow:** Oncology, Univ Wash Med Ctr 1994; **Fac Appt:** Assoc Prof Med, Univ Wash

Gruber, Stephen B MD/PhD [Onc] - **Spec Exp:** Cancer Genetics; Colon & Rectal Cancer; Melanoma; **Hospital:** USC Norris Cancer Hosp; **Address:** USC Norris Cancer Ctr, 1441 Eastlake Ave, Los Angeles, CA 90089; **Phone:** 323-865-0816; **Board Cert:** Medical Oncology 2009; **Med School:** Univ Pennsylvania 1992; **Resid:** Internal Medicine, Hosp Univ Penn 1994; **Fellow:** Medical Oncology, Johns Hopkins Hosp 1997; Clinical Genetics, Univ Michigan Hlth Sys 1999; **Fac Appt:** Prof Med, USC-Keck School of Medicine

Higano, Celestia S MD [Onc] - **Spec Exp:** Genitourinary Cancer; Prostate Cancer; Testicular Cancer; **Hospital:** Univ Wash Med Ctr; **Address:** Seattle Cancer Care Alliance, 825 Eastlake Ave E, MS G4-830, Seattle, WA 98109; **Phone:** 206-288-7222; **Board Cert:** Internal Medicine 1982; Medical Oncology 1985; **Med School:** Univ Mass Sch Med 1979; **Resid:** Internal Medicine, Mayo Clin 1982; **Fellow:** Oncology, Univ Washington Med Ctr 1985; **Fac Appt:** Prof Med, Univ Wash

Jacobs, Charlotte D MD [Onc] - **Spec Exp:** Sarcoma; Unknown Primary Cancer; **Hospital:** VA Hlth Care Sys - Palo Alto; **Address:** 3801 Miranda Ave, Palo Alto, CA 94304; **Phone:** 650-493-5000; **Board Cert:** Internal Medicine 1975; Medical Oncology 1977; **Med School:** Washington Univ, St Louis 1972; **Resid:** Internal Medicine, Barnes Hosp 1974; Internal Medicine, UCSF Med Ctr 1975; **Fellow:** Medical Oncology, Stanford Univ 1977; **Fac Appt:** Prof Med, Stanford Univ

Kaplan, Lawrence D MD [Onc] - **Spec Exp:** Lymphoma; AIDS Related Lymphoma; Bone Marrow Transplant; **Hospital:** UCSF Med Ctr; **Address:** UCSF Medical Center, 400 Parnassus Ave, rm A-502, Box 0324, San Francisco, CA 94143-0324; **Phone:** 415-353-2421; **Board Cert:** Internal Medicine 1983; Medical Oncology 1985; **Med School:** UCLA 1980; **Resid:** Internal Medicine, Boston City Hosp 1983; **Fellow:** Hematology & Oncology, UCSF Med Ctr 1985; **Fac Appt:** Clin Prof Onc, UCSF

Kelly, Karen Lee MD [Onc] - **Spec Exp:** Lung Cancer; **Hospital:** UC Davis Med Ctr; **Address:** UC Davis Comprehensive Cancer Ctr, 4501 X St, Ste 3016, Sacramento, CA 95817; **Phone:** 917-734-5959; **Board Cert:** Internal Medicine 1987; Medical Oncology 2003; **Med School:** Univ Kansas 1984; **Resid:** Internal Medicine, Univ CO Hlth Sci Ctr 1987; **Fellow:** Medical Oncology, Univ CO Hlth Sci Ctr 1990; **Fac Appt:** Prof Med, UCSD

Koczywas, Marianna MD [Onc] - **Spec Exp:** Lung Cancer; Bone Marrow Transplant; Hematology; **Hospital:** City of Hope Natl Med Ctr; **Address:** City of Hope, Med Oncology Dept, 1500 E Duarte Rd, Duarte, CA 91010; **Phone:** 626-471-9200; **Board Cert:** Medical Oncology 2011; **Med School:** Poland 1984; **Resid:** Internal Medicine, Troczewski City Hosp 1988; Internal Medicine, St Francis Med Ctr 1997; **Fellow:** Hematology & Oncology, City Hope Natl Med Ctr 2000; **Fac Appt:** Assoc Clin Prof Onc, UCLA

Leong, Lucille Ann MD [Onc] - **Hospital:** City of Hope Natl Med Ctr; **Address:** City of Hope, Med Oncology Dept, 1500 E Duarte Rd, Duarte, CA 91010; **Phone:** 626-471-9200; **Board Cert:** Internal Medicine 1982; Hematology 1984; Medical Oncology 1985; Hospice & Palliative Medicine 2012; **Med School:** Stanford Univ 1979; **Resid:** Internal Medicine, Harbor-UCLA Med Ctr 1982; **Fellow:** Hematology, Harbor-UCLA Med Ctr 1983; Medical Oncology, City of Hope Natl Med Ctr 1985; **Fac Appt:** Clin Prof Onc

Lim, Dean W MD [Onc] - **Spec Exp:** Hematology; **Hospital:** City of Hope Natl Med Ctr; **Address:** City of Hope, Med Oncology Dept, 1500 E Duarte Rd, Duarte, CA 91010; **Phone:** 626-471-9200; **Board Cert:** Internal Medicine 1985; Medical Oncology 1989; **Med School:** Philippines 1980; **Resid:** Internal Medicine, Cabrini Med Ctr 1985; **Fellow:** Hematology & Oncology, St Lukes-Roosevelt Hosp Ctr 1987; **Fac Appt:** Assoc Clin Prof Onc

Maloney, David G MD/PhD [Onc] - **Spec Exp:** Lymphoma; Bone Marrow & Stem Cell Transplant; Vaccine Therapy; Immunotherapy; **Hospital:** Univ Wash Med Ctr; **Address:** Fred Hutchinson Cancer Rsch Ctr, 1100 Fairview Ave N, D1-100, Box 19024, Seattle, WA 98109-1024; **Phone:** 206-288-1024; **Board Cert:** Internal Medicine 1988; Medical Oncology 2005; **Med School:** Stanford Univ 1985; **Resid:** Internal Medicine, Brigham & Women's Hosp 1988; **Fellow:** Medical Oncology, Stanford Univ Med Ctr 1994; **Fac Appt:** Prof Med, Univ Wash

Margolin, Kim A MD [Onc] - **Spec Exp:** Melanoma; Kidney Cancer; Germ Cell Tumors; **Hospital:** Univ Wash Med Ctr; **Address:** Seattle Cancer Care Alliance, 825 Eastlake Ave E, MS G4-810, Seattle, WA 98109; **Phone:** 206-288-1062; **Board Cert:** Internal Medicine 1982; Medical Oncology 2006; Hematology 1986; **Med School:** Stanford Univ 1979; **Resid:** Internal Medicine, Yale-New Haven Hosp 1982; **Fellow:** Hematology & Oncology, UCSD Med Ctr 1983; Hematology & Oncology, City Hope Med Ctr 1985; **Fac Appt:** Prof Med, Univ Wash

Martins, Renato G MD [Onc] - **Spec Exp:** Lung Cancer; Mesothelioma; Salivary Gland Tumors; **Hospital:** Univ Wash Med Ctr; **Address:** Seattle Cancer Care Alliance, 825 Eastlake Ave E, MS G4-490, Seattle, WA 98109; **Phone:** 206-288-1135; **Board Cert:** Internal Medicine 2005; Medical Oncology 2008; **Med School:** Brazil 1992; **Resid:** Internal Medicine, Gunderson Lutheran Hlth Sys 1995; **Fellow:** Medical Oncology, Mass Genl Hosp 1998; **Fac Appt:** Assoc Prof Med, Univ Wash

McClay, Edward F MD [Onc] - **Spec Exp:** Melanoma; Brain Tumors; **Hospital:** UCSD Med Ctr, Scripps Green Hosp; **Address:** 477 N El Camino Real, Ste D-200, Encinitas, CA 92024; **Phone:** 760-452-3340; **Board Cert:** Internal Medicine 1983; Medical Oncology 1989; **Med School:** Temple Univ 1980; **Resid:** Internal Medicine, Thomas Jefferson Univ Hosp 1983; **Fellow:** Medical Oncology, Thomas Jefferson Univ Hosp 1986

Meyskens Jr, Frank L MD [Onc] - **Spec Exp:** Melanoma; Sarcoma; **Hospital:** UC Irvine Med Ctr; **Address:** 101 The City Drive S Bldg 56 - rm 215, Orange, CA 92868; **Phone:** 714-456-6310; **Board Cert:** Internal Medicine 1975; Medical Oncology 1981; **Med School:** UCSF 1972; **Resid:** Internal Medicine, Moffit-Calif Hosps 1974; **Fellow:** Hematology & Oncology, Natl Cancer Inst 1977; **Fac Appt:** Prof Med, UC Irvine

Mitsuyasu, Ronald T MD [Onc] - **Spec Exp:** AIDS Related Cancers; Hematologic Malignancies; Immunotherapy; Clinical Trials; **Hospital:** UCLA Ronald Reagan Med Ctr, Santa Monica - UCLA Med Ctr & Ortho Hosp; **Address:** UCLA CARE Ctr, 1399 S Roxbury Drive, Ste 100, Los Angeles, CA 90035; **Phone:** 310-557-2273; **Board Cert:** Internal Medicine 1981; **Med School:** UCLA 1978; **Resid:** Internal Medicine, Rush Presby St Lukes Hosp 1981; **Fellow:** Hematology & Oncology, UCLA Med Ctr 1984; **Fac Appt:** Prof Hem & Onc, UCLA

Morgan Jr, Robert J MD [Onc] - **Spec Exp:** Gynecologic Cancer; **Hospital:** City of Hope Natl Med Ctr; **Address:** City of Hope, Med Oncology Dept, 1500 E Duarte Rd, Duarte, CA 91010; **Phone:** 626-471-9200; **Board Cert:** Internal Medicine 1984; Hematology 1986; Medical Oncology 2010; Hospice & Palliative Medicine 2012; **Med School:** Univ IL Coll Med 1981; **Resid:** Internal Medicine, Mayo Clin 1984; **Fellow:** Hematology & Oncology, Mayo Clin 1987; Medical Oncology, City Hope Natl Med Ctr 1988; **Fac Appt:** Prof Onc

Mortimer, Joanne MD [Onc] - **Spec Exp:** Breast Cancer; Clinical Trials; **Hospital:** City of Hope Natl Med Ctr; **Address:** City of Hope, Med Oncology Dept, 1500 E Duarte Rd, Duarte, CA 91010; **Phone:** 626-471-9200; **Board Cert:** Internal Medicine 1980; Medical Oncology 1983; **Med School:** Loyola Univ-Stritch Sch Med 1977; **Resid:** Internal Medicine, Cleveland Clin 1980; **Fellow:** Medical Oncology, Cleveland Clin 1982; **Fac Appt:** Prof Onc

Natale, Ronald B MD [Onc] - **Spec Exp:** Lung Cancer; Bladder Cancer; Prostate Cancer; **Hospital:** Cedars-Sinai Med Ctr; **Address:** Cedars-Sinai, Samuel Oschin Cancer Ctr, 8700 Beverly Blvd, Ste MS-33, Los Angeles, CA 90048; **Phone:** 310-423-1101; **Board Cert:** Internal Medicine 1977; Medical Oncology 1979; **Med School:** Wayne State Univ 1974; **Resid:** Internal Medicine, Wayne State Univ 1977; **Fellow:** Hematology & Oncology, Meml Sloan-Kettering Cancer Ctr 1980

Parker, Barbara A MD [Onc] - **Spec Exp:** Breast Cancer; Nutrition in Cancer Therapy; **Hospital:** UCSD Med Ctr; **Address:** UCSD Moores Cancer Ctr, 3855 Health Sciences Drive, MC 0987, La Jolla, CA 92093; **Phone:** 858-822-6195; **Board Cert:** Internal Medicine 1984; Medical Oncology 1987; **Med School:** Stanford Univ 1981; **Resid:** Internal Medicine, UCSD Med Ctr 1985; **Fellow:** Medical Oncology, UCSD Med Ctr 1987; **Fac Appt:** Clin Prof Med, UCSD

Pegram, Mark D MD [Onc] - **Spec Exp:** Breast Cancer; Breast Cancer-Novel Therapies; **Hospital:** Stanford Univ Hosp & Clins; **Address:** Stanford Womens Cancer Ctr, 900 Blake Wilbur Drive, Stanford, CA 94305; **Phone:** 650-498-6004; **Board Cert:** Internal Medicine 1989; Medical Oncology 2003; **Med School:** Univ NC Sch Med 1986; **Resid:** Internal Medicine, Parkland Meml Hosp 1989; **Fellow:** Hematology & Oncology, UCLA Med Ctr 1993; **Fac Appt:** Prof Med, Stanford Univ

Picozzi Jr, Vincent J MD [Onc] - **Spec Exp:** Gastrointestinal Cancer; Pancreatic Cancer; Genitourinary Cancer; Hematologic Malignancies; **Hospital:** Virginia Mason Med Ctr; **Address:** Virginia Mason Med Ctr, Div Hem/Onc, 1100 Ninth Ave, MS C2-Hem, Seattle, WA 98111; **Phone:** 206-223-6193; **Board Cert:** Internal Medicine 1981; Hematology 1986; Medical Oncology 1987; **Med School:** Stanford Univ 1978; **Resid:** Internal Medicine, Brigham & Women's Hosp 1981; **Fellow:** Hematology & Oncology, Stanford Univ Hosp & Clin 1985; **Fac Appt:** Clin Prof Med, Univ Wash

Pinto, Harlan A MD [Onc] - **Spec Exp:** Head & Neck Cancer; Clinical Trials; **Hospital:** Stanford Univ Hosp & Clins, VA Hlth Care Sys - Palo Alto; **Address:** Stanford Comp Cancer Ctr, 875 Blake Wilbur Drive, Clinic C, Stanford, CA 94305; **Phone:** 650-498-6000; **Board Cert:** Internal Medicine 1986; Medical Oncology 2012; **Med School:** Yale Univ 1983; **Resid:** Internal Medicine, Mass Genl Hosp 1986; **Fellow:** Medical Oncology, Stanford Univ Med Sch 1991; **Fac Appt:** Assoc Prof Med, Stanford Univ

Prados, Michael MD [Onc] - **Spec Exp:** Neuro-Oncology; Brain Tumors; **Hospital:** UCSF Med Ctr; **Address:** UCSF Med Ctr, Div Neuro-Oncology, 400 Parnassus Ave Fl 8 - rm A-808, San Francisco, CA 94143; **Phone:** 415-353-2408; **Board Cert:** Internal Medicine 1977; **Med School:** Louisiana State U, New Orleans 1974; **Resid:** Internal Medicine, Earl K Long Hosp 1977; **Fac Appt:** Prof NS, UCSF

Press, Oliver W MD/PhD [Onc] - **Spec Exp:** Lymphoma; Bone Marrow Transplant; **Hospital:** Univ Wash Med Ctr; **Address:** Fred Hutchinson Cancer Rsch Ctr, 1100 Fairview Ave N, MS D3-190, Seattle, WA 98109; **Phone:** 206-288-6202; **Board Cert:** Internal Medicine 1982; Medical Oncology 1985; **Med School:** Univ Wash 1979; **Resid:** Internal Medicine, Mass Genl Hosp 1982; Internal Medicine, Univ Wash Med Ctr 1983; **Fellow:** Medical Oncology, Univ Wash Med Ctr 1985; **Fac Appt:** Prof Med, Univ Wash

Quinn, David I MD/PhD [Onc] - **Spec Exp:** Testicular Cancer; Bladder Cancer; Kidney Cancer; Prostate Cancer; **Hospital:** USC Norris Cancer Hosp, Keck Med Ctr of USC; **Address:** 1441 Eastlake Ave, Ste 3440, Los Angeles, CA 90033; **Phone:** 323-865-3105; **Med School:** Australia 1987; **Resid:** Internal Medicine, St Vincents Hosp 1992; **Fellow:** Medical Oncology, St Vincents Hosp 1995; Research, Garvan Institute 1996; **Fac Appt:** Assoc Prof Onc, USC-Keck School of Medicine

Reckamp, Karen MD [Onc] - **Spec Exp:** Lung Cancer; Hematology; Thoracic Cancers; **Hospital:** City of Hope Natl Med Ctr; **Address:** City of Hope, Med Oncology Dept, 1500 E Duarte Rd, Duarte, CA 91010; **Phone:** 626-471-9200; **Board Cert:** Medical Oncology 2004; Hematology 2004; **Med School:** Univ Chicago-Pritzker Sch Med 1998; **Resid:** Internal Medicine, Barnes-Jewish Hosp 2001; **Fellow:** Hematology & Oncology, UCLA Ronald Reagan Med Ctr 2004; **Fac Appt:** Assoc Prof Onc

Reid, Tony R MD/PhD [Onc] - **Spec Exp:** Gastrointestinal Cancer; Pancreatic Cancer; Esophageal Cancer; Liver Cancer; **Hospital:** UCSD Med Ctr; **Address:** UCSD Moores Cancer Center, 3855 Health Scienes Drive, Ste 1102, MC 0987, La Jolla, CA 92093; **Phone:** 858-822-6100; **Board Cert:** Medical Oncology 2009; **Med School:** Stanford Univ 1991; **Resid:** Internal Medicine, Stanford Univ Med Ctr 1997; **Fellow:** Oncology, Stanford Univ Med Ctr 1999; Cancer Research, Stanford Univ Med Ctr 2000; **Fac Appt:** Assoc Prof Med, UCSD

Rosove, Michael H MD [Onc] - **Spec Exp:** Bleeding/Coagulation Disorders; Myeloproliferative Disorders; Myelodysplastic Syndromes; Hematologic Malignancies; **Hospital:** UCLA Ronald Reagan Med Ctr; **Address:** UCLA Med Ctr-Hematology/Oncology Div, 100 UCLA Med Plaza, Ste 550, Los Angeles, CA 90024-6970; **Phone:** 310-794-4955; **Board Cert:** Internal Medicine 1976; Hematology 1982; Medical Oncology 1981; **Med School:** UCLA 1973; **Resid:** Internal Medicine, UCLA Med Ctr 1976; **Fellow:** Hematology & Oncology, UCLA Med Ctr 1979; Hematology & Oncology, Columbia Presby Med Ctr 1978; **Fac Appt:** Clin Prof Onc, UCLA-David Geffen Sch Med

Rugo, Hope S MD [Onc] - **Spec Exp:** Breast Cancer; Complementary Medicine; Breast Cancer-Novel Therapies; **Hospital:** UCSF Med Ctr; **Address:** UCSF, Helen Diller Family Comp Cancer Center, 1600 Divisadero St Fl 2, Box 1710, San Francisco, CA 94115; **Phone:** 415-353-7070; **Board Cert:** Internal Medicine 1987; Medical Oncology 1989; **Med School:** Univ Pennsylvania 1984; **Resid:** Internal Medicine, UCSF Med Ctr 1987; **Fellow:** Hematology & Oncology, UCSF Med Ctr 1989; **Fac Appt:** Clin Prof Med, UCSF

Russell, Christy A MD [Onc] - **Spec Exp:** Breast Cancer; **Hospital:** Keck Med Ctr of USC, USC Norris Cancer Hosp; **Address:** Norris Cancer Hosp-The Breast Ctr, 1441 Eastlake Ave, Ste 3448, Los Angeles, CA 90033; **Phone:** 323-865-3371; **Board Cert:** Internal Medicine 1983; Medical Oncology 1985; **Med School:** Med Coll PA Hahnemann 1980; **Resid:** Internal Medicine, Good Sam Med Ctr 1983; **Fellow:** Hematology & Oncology, LAC-USC Med Ctr 1986; **Fac Appt:** Assoc Prof Med, USC Sch Med

Samlowski, Wolfram E MD [Onc] - **Spec Exp:** Kidney Cancer; Melanoma; Sarcoma; Merkel Cell Carcinoma; **Hospital:** St. Rose Dom Hosp-San Martin, Southern Hills Hosp & Med Ctr; **Address:** 9280 W Sunset Rd, Ste 100, Las Vegas, NV 89148; **Phone:** 702-952-1251; **Board Cert:** Internal Medicine 1981; Medical Oncology 1985; **Med School:** Ohio State Univ 1978; **Resid:** Internal Medicine, Wayne State Univ Affil Hosp 1981; **Fellow:** Hematology & Oncology, Univ Utah Affil Hosp 1984; **Fac Appt:** Prof Onc, Univ Nevada

Scudder, Sidney A MD [Onc] - **Spec Exp:** Ovarian Cancer; Uterine Cancer; Cervical Cancer; **Hospital:** UC Davis Med Ctr; **Address:** 4501 X St Fl 2, Sacramento, CA 95817; **Phone:** 916-734-5959; **Board Cert:** Internal Medicine 1983; Medical Oncology 1985; **Med School:** Univ Fla Coll Med 1980; **Resid:** Internal Medicine, Barnes Hosp-Washington Univ 1983; **Fellow:** Medical Oncology, Stanford Univ 1987; **Fac Appt:** Prof Med, UC Davis

Slamon, Dennis J MD/PhD [Onc] - **Spec Exp:** Breast Cancer; Ovarian Cancer; **Hospital:** Santa Monica - UCLA Med Ctr & Ortho Hosp; **Address:** UCLA, Med Oncology Dept, 2020 Santa Monica Blvd, Ste 600, Santa Monica, CA 90404; **Phone:** 310-829-5471; **Board Cert:** Internal Medicine 1978; Medical Oncology 1981; **Med School:** Univ Chicago-Pritzker Sch Med 1975; **Resid:** Internal Medicine, Univ Chicago Med Ctr 1978; **Fellow:** Hematology & Oncology, UCLA Med Ctr 1981; **Fac Appt:** Prof Med, UCLA

Small, Eric J MD [Onc] - **Spec Exp:** Prostate Cancer; Vaccine Therapy; Urologic Cancer; **Hospital:** UCSF Med Ctr; **Address:** UCSF Urologic Oncology Practice, 1600 Divisadero St Fl 3, San Francisco, CA 94115; **Phone:** 415-353-7171; **Board Cert:** Internal Medicine 1988; **Med School:** Case West Res Univ 1985; **Resid:** Internal Medicine, Beth Israel Deaconess 1988; **Fellow:** Hematology & Oncology, Cancer Research Inst/UCSF 1990; **Fac Appt:** Prof Med, UCSF

Somlo, George MD [Onc] - **Spec Exp:** Breast Cancer; Multiple Myeloma; Hematologic Malignancies; **Hospital:** City of Hope Natl Med Ctr; **Address:** City of Hope, Med Oncology Dept, 1500 E Duarte Rd, Duarte, CA 91010; **Phone:** 626-471-9200; **Board Cert:** Hematology 1988; Medical Oncology 1987; **Med School:** Hungary 1978; **Resid:** Internal Medicine, VA Med Ctr 1985; **Fellow:** Hematology & Oncology, City Hope Natl Med Ctr 1988; **Fac Appt:** Prof Neuro-Onc

Stein, Cy A MD/PhD [Onc] - **Spec Exp:** Prostate Cancer; Bladder Cancer; Urologic Cancer; **Hospital:** City of Hope Natl Med Ctr; **Address:** City of Hope, Med Oncology Dept, 1500 E Duarte Rd, Duarte, CA 91010; **Phone:** 626-471-9200; **Board Cert:** Internal Medicine 1986; Medical Oncology 1987; **Med School:** Albert Einstein Coll Med 1982; **Resid:** Internal Medicine, NY-Presby/Weill Cornell Med Ctr 1985; **Fellow:** Medical Oncology, Natl Inst Hlth-Clin Ctr 1988; **Fac Appt:** Prof Onc

Stewart, F. Marc M MD [Onc] - **Spec Exp:** Unknown Primary Cancer; Sarcoma; **Hospital:** Univ Wash Med Ctr; **Address:** Seattle Cancer Care Alliance, 825 Eastlake Ave E, MS G3-630, Seattle, WA 98109; **Phone:** 206-288-1024; **Board Cert:** Internal Medicine 1980; Hematology 1982; Medical Oncology 1985; **Med School:** Indiana Univ 1977; **Resid:** Internal Medicine, Indiana Univ Med Ctr 1980; Medical Oncology, Indiana Univ Med Ctr 1985; **Fellow:** Hematology, Univ Virginia Med Ctr 1982; **Fac Appt:** Prof Med, Univ Wash

Stockdale, Frank E MD/PhD [Onc] - **Spec Exp:** Breast Cancer; **Hospital:** Stanford Univ Hosp & Clins; **Address:** Stanford Univ Medical Ctr, 875 Blake Wilbur Drive, Stanford, CA 94305-5826; **Phone:** 650-498-6000; **Med School:** Univ Pennsylvania 1963; **Resid:** Internal Medicine, Stanford Univ Med Ctr 1967; Medical Oncology, Stanford Univ Med Ctr; **Fac Appt:** Prof Emeritus Onc, Stanford Univ

Tempero, Margaret A MD [Onc] - **Spec Exp:** Pancreatic Cancer; Gastrointestinal Cancer; **Hospital:** UCSF Med Ctr, VA Med Ctr - San Francisco; **Address:** 1600 Divisadero St Fl 4, San Francisco, CA 94115; **Phone:** 415-353-9888; **Board Cert:** Internal Medicine 1980; Medical Oncology 1983; Hematology 1984; **Med School:** Univ Nebr Coll Med 1977; **Resid:** Internal Medicine, Univ Nebraska Hosp 1980; **Fellow:** Medical Oncology, Univ Nebraska Hosp 1983; **Fac Appt:** Prof Med, UCSF

Terpenning, Marilou MD [Onc] - **Spec Exp:** Breast Cancer; Gynecologic Cancer; Hematologic Malignancies; Hereditary Cancer; **Hospital:** St. John's Hlth Ctr, Santa Monica; **Address:** Santa Monica Hem-Onc Consultants, 2021 Santa Monica Blvd, Ste 400E, Santa Monica, CA 90404; **Phone:** 310-453-5654; **Board Cert:** Internal Medicine 1979; Medical Oncology 1981; **Med School:** Washington Univ, St Louis 1976; **Resid:** Internal Medicine, Univ Michigan Med Ctr 1979; **Fellow:** Hematology & Oncology, UCLA Med Ctr 1981; **Fac Appt:** Assoc Clin Prof Onc, UCLA

Thompson, John A MD [Onc] - **Spec Exp:** Melanoma; Kidney Cancer; **Hospital:** Univ Wash Med Ctr; **Address:** Seattle Cancer Care Alliance, 825 Eastlake Ave E, MS G4-200, Seattle, WA 98109-1023; **Phone:** 206-288-2015; **Board Cert:** Internal Medicine 1982; Medical Oncology 1985; **Med School:** UAB Sch Med 1979; **Resid:** Internal Medicine, Univ Wash Med Ctr 1982; **Fellow:** Medical Oncology, Univ Wash Med Ctr 1985

Tripathy, Debasish MD [Onc] - **Spec Exp:** Breast Cancer; Clinical Trials; **Hospital:** USC Norris Cancer Hosp; **Address:** 1441 Eastlake Ave, Ste 3440, Los Angeles, CA 90033; **Phone:** 323-865-3105; **Board Cert:** Internal Medicine 1988; Medical Oncology 2011; **Med School:** Duke Univ 1985; **Resid:** Internal Medicine, Duke Univ Med Ctr 1988; **Fellow:** Hematology & Oncology, USCF Med Ctr 1991; **Fac Appt:** Prof Med, Univ SC Sch Med

Twardowski, Przemyslaw W MD [Onc] - **Spec Exp:** Genitourinary Cancer; Hematology; **Hospital:** City of Hope Natl Med Ctr; **Address:** City of Hope, Med Oncology Dept, 1500 E Duarte Rd, Duarte, CA 91010; **Phone:** 626-471-9200; **Board Cert:** Medical Oncology 2009; **Med School:** Univ MO-Columbia Sch Med 1990; **Resid:** Internal Medicine, Northwestern Meml Hosp 1994; **Fellow:** Hematology & Oncology, Northwestern Meml Hosp 1996; **Fac Appt:** Clin Prof Onc

Urba, Walter J MD/PhD [Onc] - **Spec Exp:** Breast Cancer; **Hospital:** Providence Portland Med Ctr; **Address:** Providence Cancer Ctr, 4805 NE Glisan St, Ste 6N40, Portland, OR 97213; **Phone:** 503-215-5696; **Board Cert:** Internal Medicine 1985; Medical Oncology 1987; **Med School:** Univ Miami Sch Med 1981; **Resid:** Internal Medicine, Morristown Meml Hosp 1983; **Fellow:** Medical Oncology, Natl Cancer Inst 1986; **Fac Appt:** Assoc Clin Prof Med, Oregon Hlth & Sci Univ

Venook, Alan P MD [Onc] - **Spec Exp:** Gastrointestinal Cancer; Colon & Rectal Cancer; Liver Cancer; **Hospital:** UCSF Med Ctr; **Address:** Gastrointestinal Surg and Onc Clin, 1600 Divisadero St Fl 4, San Francisco, CA 94115; **Phone:** 415-353-9888; **Board Cert:** Internal Medicine 1985; Medical Oncology 1987; Hematology 1988; **Med School:** UCSF 1980; **Resid:** Internal Medicine, UC Davis Med Ctr 1985; **Fellow:** Hematology & Oncology, UCSF Med Ctr 1987; **Fac Appt:** Prof Med

Vescio, Robert A MD [Onc] - **Spec Exp:** Multiple Myeloma; Amyloidosis; **Hospital:** Cedars-Sinai Med Ctr; **Address:** Samuel Oschin Cancer Ctr, 8700 Beverly Blvd, Ste AC1049, North Tower, Lower Level, Los Angeles, CA 90048; **Phone:** 310-423-1825; **Board Cert:** Internal Medicine 1989; Medical Oncology 2003; Hematology 2004; **Med School:** UCSD 1986; **Resid:** Internal Medicine, UCSD Med Ctr 1989; **Fellow:** Hematology & Oncology, UCLA Med Ctr 1993; **Fac Appt:** Assoc Prof Med, UCLA-David Geffen Sch Med

Vogelzang, Nicholas J MD [Onc] - **Spec Exp:** Prostate Cancer; Mesothelioma; Kidney Cancer; Genitourinary Cancer; **Hospital:** Sunrise Hosp & Med Ctr, Desert Springs Hosp Med Ctr - Las Vegas; **Address:** Comprehensive Cancer Centers of Nevada, 3730 S Eastern Ave, Las Vegas, NV 89169; **Phone:** 702-952-3400; **Board Cert:** Internal Medicine 1977; Medical Oncology 1981; **Med School:** Univ IL Coll Med 1974; **Resid:** Internal Medicine, Rush-Presby St Lukes Med Ctr 1978; **Fellow:** Medical Oncology, Univ Minn Med Ctr 1980; **Fac Appt:** Prof Onc, Univ Nevada

Volberding, Paul Arthur MD [Onc] - **Spec Exp:** AIDS Related Cancers; **Hospital:** UCSF Med Ctr, VA Med Ctr - San Francisco; **Address:** UCSF AIDS Research Institute, 50 Beale St, Ste 1300, San Francisco, CA 94121; **Phone:** 415-221-4810; **Board Cert:** Internal Medicine 1978; Medical Oncology 1981; **Med School:** Univ Minn 1975; **Resid:** Internal Medicine, Univ Utah Med Ctr 1978; **Fellow:** Medical Oncology, UCSF Med Ctr 1981; **Fac Appt:** Prof Onc, UCSF

Wierman, Ann MD [Onc] - **Spec Exp:** Breast Cancer; Lymphoma; Lung Cancer; **Hospital:** Mountainview Hosp - Las Vegas, Summerlin Hosp Med Ctr; **Address:** Mountainview Med Office Bldg, 3150 N Tenaya Way, Las Vegas, NV 89128; **Phone:** 702-445-4075; **Board Cert:** Internal Medicine 2012; Medical Oncology 2007; **Med School:** Baylor Coll Med 1989; **Resid:** Internal Medicine, Baylor Hosps 1992; Internal Medicine, Ben Taub Genl Hosp 1993; **Fellow:** Hematology & Oncology, Univ CO Hlth Sci Ctr 1996; **Fac Appt:** Assoc Clin Prof Med, Univ Nevada

Wolin, Edward M MD [Onc] - **Spec Exp:** Neuroendocrine Tumors; Pancreatic Cancer; **Hospital:** Cedars-Sinai Med Ctr; **Address:** Cedars-Sinai, Samuel Oschin Cancer Inst, 8700 Beverly Blvd, Ste AC-1045, Los Angeles, CA 90048; **Phone:** 310-423-0709; **Board Cert:** Internal Medicine 1978; Medical Oncology 1979; **Med School:** Yale Univ 1974; **Resid:** Internal Medicine, Stanford Univ Hosp & Clins 1976; **Fellow:** Medical Oncology, Stanford Univ Hosp & Clins 1979

Yen, Yun MD/PhD [Onc] - **Spec Exp:** Liver Cancer; Biliary Cancer; **Hospital:** City of Hope Natl Med Ctr; **Address:** City of Hope Comprehensive Cancer Ctr, 1500 E Duarte Rd, Duarte, CA 91010; **Phone:** 626-471-9200 x62867; **Board Cert:** Medical Oncology 2003; **Med School:** Taiwan 1982; **Resid:** Internal Medicine, St Luke's Hosp 1990; **Fellow:** Hematology & Oncology, Yale-New Haven Hosp 1993; **Fac Appt:** Prof Med, USC Sch Med

NYU Langone MEDICAL CENTER

NYU Langone Medical Center
550 First Avenue, New York, NY 10016
www.NYULMC.org

Clinical Cancer Center
160 East 34th Street, New York, NY 10016
www.NYUCI.org

The Stephen D. Hassenfeld Children's Center for Cancer and Blood Disorders
160 East 32nd Street, New York, NY 10016
www.NYULMC.org/hassenfeld

NYU CANCER INSTITUTE

The NYU Cancer Institute is an NCI-designated cancer center providing personalized patient care that is compassionate and state-of-the-art. The Cancer Institute is world-renowned for excellence in cancer-focused research, personalized care, education and community outreach. Its mission is to discover the origins of human cancer and to use that knowledge to eradicate the personal and societal burden of cancer in our community, the nation and the world. For more information about our expert physicians, call 1.888.769.8633.

Patient-Focused Setting

The Clinical Cancer Center is the principal outpatient facility of The Cancer Institute. The Center and its multidisciplinary team of experts provide access to the latest treatment options and clinical trials, along with programs in cancer risk reduction/prevention, screening, diagnostics, genetic counseling and supportive services. In addition, the Center emphasizes the importance of a holistic approach involving integrative health, psychosocial support, survivorship and palliative care. Services are also available at our Ambulatory Care Center on 38th Street in Manhattan, Rego Park, NY, and Lake Success, NY.

Renowned Expertise

The NYU Cancer Institute brings together experts from a variety of disciplines to create collaborative research endeavors and clinical care teams. Our teams are highly skilled in minimally invasive techniques along with video-assisted and robotic surgery. We have created special programs to treat diseases such as breast cancer, brain cancer, melanoma, GI cancer, prostate cancer, hematologic malignancies and lung cancer, as well as translational programs in cancer healthcare disparities; molecularly targeted as well as immune- and stem-cell-based therapies; and the cell signaling pathways involved in cancer.

A Translational Approach

Our scientists and researchers excel in uncovering how cancer develops at the molecular level, and how we can harness that knowledge to reduce the risk of cancer and treat the disease.

Stephen D. Hassenfeld Children's Center for Cancer and Blood Disorders

As part of the Hassenfeld Children's Hospital, the center is a leading pediatric outpatient facility for the treatment of childhood cancers and blood diseases. Its interdisciplinary and family-centered approach combines the most advanced medical treatments with psychosocial and emotional support services.

Maimonides Cancer Center

6300 Eighth Avenue
Brooklyn, New York 11220
Phone: 718.765.2500 • Fax: 718.765.2574
www.maimonidesmed.org/cancer

The Maimonides Cancer Center offers a fully integrated, multimodal approach to cancer care that includes prevention, education, screening, diagnostics, treatment, palliative care and clinical research. The Lena Cymbrowitz Pavilion contains the following specialty divisions:

Radiation Oncology: equipped with state-of-the art imaging and treatment delivery technologies; offers patients the most precise treatments available, yet does so in an airy, life-affirming environment.

Medical Oncology: provides comprehensive diagnosis, oral drug therapies, intravenous chemotherapy infusions, and biological and hormonal therapies.

Pediatric Oncology: treats children with cancer and diseases of the blood in a child-friendly environment, and features special areas set aside for parent conferences.

Surgical Oncology: provides a convenient location for minor surgical procedures, as well as innovative surgical techniques, such as sentinel node mapping and biopsy, skin/tissue-sparing mastectomy, and nerve-sparing prostatectomy.

Research Center: conducts basic science and genetic research, as well as clinical trials that offer appropriately screened patients, who wish to volunteer, new therapies and medications.

Resource Center: offers access to integrative (complementary) oncology services, dietary advice, as well as psychological and social services.

Located around the block from the Lena Cymbrowitz Pavilion, the newly opened Gilbert Rivera Pavilion houses the **Maimonides Breast Cancer Center**. With a spa-like decor and life-affirming environment, the Center provides digital mammography, sonography, computerized interpretation, digital stereotactic biopsies, breast-specific gamma imaging, and treatment plans tailored to each patient. A genetic counselor is also on-site.

Clinicians at the Maimonides Cancer Center – Brooklyn's only dedicated cancer center – are talented specialists, recruited specifically for their expertise. Our doctors emphasize multimodal care, which means that multiple methods of treatment are available to patients, sometimes simultaneously. Every week, physicians from radiology, surgery, pathology, radiation oncology and medical oncology meet to discuss patient treatment at our case management meetings. The patient's needs, as well as the disease, are considered from many perspectives.

Maimonides Medical Center
The right care.
Right here.

www.maimonidesmed.org/cancer

MOFFITT CANCER CENTER

OVERVIEW

Moffitt is the only National Cancer Institute-designated Comprehensive Cancer Center based in Florida and the No. 1 cancer hospital in the state, according to the *U.S. News & World Report* "Best Hospitals" ranking. Moffitt is licensed for 206 beds, 36 of which are dedicated to the blood and marrow transplantation unit. Moffitt has an outpatient clinic with a complete digital imaging center, a radiation therapy department, infusion center, 14 operating rooms, two research buildings, and off-site locations including a screening center for high-risk patients and a 50,000-square-foot outpatient center.

Moffitt is accredited by the following: The Joint Commission, Foundation for the Accreditation of Cellular Therapy, College of American Pathologists, American College of Surgeons Commission on Cancer, American College of Radiology and the National Accreditation Program for Breast Centers.

ACADEMIC/CLINICAL AFFILIATIONS

Moffitt's numerous institutional collaborations include the University of South Florida, University of Florida, Florida Agricultural and Mechanical University, Florida State University, Scripps Florida, University of Central Florida, and the University of Louisville.

MEDICAL STAFF

Moffitt supports a staff of physicians, known as the Moffitt Medical Group. Most are fellowship trained and are among the best in their respective fields. Physicians, including residents and interns, total more than 300.

Moffitt Cancer Center trains more oncologists than any other institution in the state and has been designated a Statutory Teaching Hospital by the Florida Agency for Health Care Administration.

PERSONALIZED MEDICINE: KEY TO IMPROVING OUTCOMES

Moffitt's clinical services are organized into disease-oriented interdisciplinary programs with a full complement of services. Moffitt is at the forefront of personalized medicine with its commitment to Total Cancer Care® - a system designed to enable researchers and treatment teams to identify and meet all of the needs of patients and their families. Personalized treatments are a key element to improving cancer outcomes at Moffitt.

REFERRAL INFORMATION: To make an appointment, please call 1-888-MOFFITT or visit MOFFITT.org

MOFFITT CANCER CENTER
12902 MAGNOLIA DRIVE, TAMPA, FL

MOFFITT CANCER CENTER AT INTERNATIONAL PLAZA
4101 JIM WALTER BOULEVARD, TAMPA, FL

H. LEE MOFFITT CANCER CENTER & RESEARCH INSTITUTE
AN NCI COMPREHENSIVE CANCER CENTER

CLINICAL PATHWAYS: Improving Patient Care and Outcomes

Moffitt's Clinical Pathways Program provides a patient management tool that helps standardize and outline a patient's clinical course of care based on best practices specific to each patient's situation and treatment needs. Goals are to streamline related patient care processes, increase the use of generic drugs for both chemotherapy and supportive care and to assure that patients receive the most appropriate, personalized care to optimize their desired outcomes. Clinical pathways are continually updated to provide a basis for health care providers to evaluate best practices, outcomes information and cost of care. The program also includes information to assist Moffitt clinicians and partner practitioners in identifying relevant clinical trials.

MOFFITT CANCER CENTER®

CLOSER TO OUR PATIENTS.
CLOSER TO A CURE.®

THE MOUNT SINAI MEDICAL CENTER

The Tisch Cancer Institute

Mount Sinai

One Gustave L. Levy Place
Fifth Avenue and 100th Street
New York, NY 10029-6574

Physician Referral: 1-800-MD-SINAI (637-4624)
www.mountsinai.org

THE TISCH CANCER INSTITUTE is embedded within a renowned medical center that has world-class research facilities, one of the nation's top-ranked hospitals, and an outstanding medical school. Patients have access to the best possible cancer care across a variety of disciplines, including medical, surgical, and radiation treatments; palliative care; behavioral medicine; physical therapy; psychosocial services—and cutting-edge cancer research. For fully integrated, multidisciplinary care, our patients are also treated by the best specialists in every field at Mount Sinai and can receive seamless referrals.

Services and Programs — The Tisch Cancer Institute employs a multidisciplinary treatment approach, providing access to clinical breakthroughs, innovative techniques, leading-edge technologies, and a wide range of diagnostic, therapeutic, and support services for all types of cancer. The Institute treats: breast cancer; hematological malignancies (including multiple myeloma, myelodysplastic syndrome, and myeloproliferative disorders); genitourinary cancers (including prostate, bladder, and kidney); head and neck cancers; thoracic cancer (including lung and esophagus); gynecologic cancers; brain tumors; and other diagnoses. In addition to surgical treatment, the Institute provides radiation and medical oncology therapies, as well as bone marrow transplantation. The Dubin Breast Center, consisting of 15,000 square feet, is a state-of-the-art facility that opened in April 2011 and significantly expands the treatment space for breast cancer patients.

The Tisch Cancer Institute encourages collaboration with colleagues across the Medical Center, drawing upon the knowledge of a vast network of specialists who are outstanding in their fields. These experts consist of award-winning physicians and surgeons specializing in cardiac care, neurology, urology, pediatrics, digestive diseases, obstetrics and gynecology, and other therapeutic areas. Oncologists, surgeons, radiation oncologists, and specialists from across the medical spectrum work together to provide the highest quality care to all cancer patients. Furthermore, Mount Sinai's nursing staff is an important part of the Medical Center's focus on delivering exceptional patient care, and it has received the prestigious Magnet Award for nursing excellence. Mount Sinai is also renowned for its palliative care program, which provides the highest level of care, focusing on the relief of pain, symptoms, and stress in cancer patients in both an inpatient and outpatient setting.

A Heritage of Breakthroughs — Teams of physicians and scientists at The Tisch Cancer Institute at Mount Sinai work together to rapidly translate laboratory research into new patient treatments. Among the advances pioneered at Mount Sinai are the first successful treatment of tumors of the bladder by transurethral electrocoagulation, the first demonstration of how asbestos can cause cancerous changes in the DNA of cells, and the first development of an ultrasound-guided technique to insert radioactive seeds into the prostate to treat prostate cancer.

THE RUTTENBERG TREATMENT CENTER
The Derald H. Ruttenberg Treatment Center, home to the ambulatory cancer program of The Tisch Cancer Institute is now housed in the newly constructed Leon and Norma Hess Center for Science and Medicine.

THE DUBIN BREAST CENTER
The Dubin Breast Center offers the latest, most innovative approaches available for breast health and the treatment of breast cancer.

NorthShore
University HealthSystem

Kellogg Cancer Center

NorthShore Kellogg Cancer Center
2650 Ridge Avenue, Evanston, IL 60201
(847) 570-2112
northshore.org/cancer

NorthShore Kellogg Cancer Center, part of NorthShore University HealthSystem, combines advanced scientific knowledge and technology with a holistic, compassionate approach to create one of the region's leading programs for diagnosis, treatment and support for patients and their families.

A National Model for Multidisciplinary Care

Kellogg Cancer Center's highly specialized physicians have extensive experience in treating specific cancer types. The staff includes more than 20 Castle Connolly-recognized physicians.

Kellogg Cancer Center continues to break new ground in patient care and collaboration. Patients are cared for by teams of fellowship-trained medical and surgical oncologists with expertise in every type of cancer.

Together, the team explores every treatment option, including the latest technology and ground-breaking research. Disease-specific tumor boards meet to discuss diagnoses. Patients are also supported by NorthShore's integrated team of nationally certified oncology nurses, clinical oncology pharmacists, social workers, clinical nutritionists and psychologists.

Innovative Treatment and Research

At Kellogg Cancer Center, researchers are an integral part of the multidisciplinary care team, supporting a wide range of research designed to improve cancer prevention, detection and treatment. For instance, NorthShore was the only site in Illinois for the expanded access afatinib trial for metastatic lung cancer. Translational research being carried out at NorthShore University HealthSystem's Research Institute ensures that the most promising breakthroughs in the lab are translated into clinical studies.

Clinical trials allow patients to benefit from new diagnostic tools and new therapies that may identify cancers earlier, prevent recurrence or minimize side effects.

KELLOGG CANCER CENTER SPECIALTIES INCLUDE:

- Bladder Cancer
- Brain Cancer
- Breast Cancer
- Cervical Cancer
- Central Nervous System (CNS)
- Colon Cancer
- Endocrine Cancer
- Esophageal Cancer
- Gestational Trophoblastic Neoplasia
- Head and Neck Cancer
- Kidney Cancer
- Leukemia
- Liver Cancer
- Lung Cancer
- Lymphoma
- Myeloma
- Neuroendocrine Cancer
- Ovarian Cancer
- Pancreatic Cancer
- Penile Cancer
- Prostate Cancer
- Sarcoma
- Skin Cancer
- Stomach Cancer
- Thyroid Cancer
- Testicular Cancer
- Uterine (Endometrial Cancer)
- Vaginal Cancer

NYU Langone MEDICAL CENTER

NYU Langone Medical Center
550 First Avenue, New York, NY 10016
www.NYULMC.org

Clinical Cancer Center
160 East 34th Street, New York, NY 10016
www.NYUCI.org

The Stephen D. Hassenfeld Children's Center for Cancer and Blood Disorders
160 East 32nd Street, New York, NY 10016
www.NYULMC.org/hassenfeld

NYU CANCER INSTITUTE

The NYU Cancer Institute is an NCI-designated cancer center providing personalized patient care that is compassionate and state-of-the-art. The Cancer Institute is world-renowned for excellence in cancer-focused research, personalized care, education and community outreach. Its mission is to discover the origins of human cancer and to use that knowledge to eradicate the personal and societal burden of cancer in our community, the nation and the world. For more information about our expert physicians, call 1.888.769.8633.

Patient-Focused Setting

The Clinical Cancer Center is the principal outpatient facility of The Cancer Institute. The Center and its multidisciplinary team of experts provide access to the latest treatment options and clinical trials, along with programs in cancer risk reduction/prevention, screening, diagnostics, genetic counseling and supportive services. In addition, the Center emphasizes the importance of a holistic approach involving integrative health, psychosocial support, survivorship and palliative care. Services are also available at our Ambulatory Care Center on 38th Street in Manhattan, Rego Park, NY, and Lake Success, NY.

Renowned Expertise

The NYU Cancer Institute brings together experts from a variety of disciplines to create collaborative research endeavors and clinical care teams. Our teams are highly skilled in minimally invasive techniques along with video-assisted and robotic surgery. We have created special programs to treat diseases such as breast cancer, brain cancer, melanoma, GI cancer, prostate cancer, hematologic malignancies and lung cancer, as well as translational programs in cancer healthcare disparities; molecularly targeted as well as immune- and stem-cell-based therapies; and the cell signaling pathways involved in cancer.

A Translational Approach

Our scientists and researchers excel in uncovering how cancer develops at the molecular level, and how we can harness that knowledge to reduce the risk of cancer and treat the disease.

Stephen D. Hassenfeld Children's Center for Cancer and Blood Disorders

As part of the Hassenfeld Children's Hospital, the center is a leading pediatric outpatient facility for the treatment of childhood cancers and blood diseases. Its interdisciplinary and family-centered approach combines the most advanced medical treatments with psychosocial and emotional support services.

Hospice & Palliative Medicine

Hospice and Palliative Medicine is a subspecialty of family medicine, internal medicine, anesthesiology, emergency medicine, obstetrics and gynecology, neurology, pediatrics, physical medicine and rehabilitation, radiology and surgery.

Palliative care relieves the suffering and provides the best quality of life to people suffering from serious and severe chronic illness. Hospice care focuses on the palliation of a terminally ill patient's symptoms and also provides compassionate support to both the patient and their surrounding loved ones.

Training Required: Physicians must be board certified in one of the above ABMS specialties and complete an additional year of training in an ACGME approved Hospice and Palliative Medicine fellowship program and then pass the official examination to be board certified in this subspecialty.

Hospice & Palliative Medicine

New England

Abrahm, Janet L MD [H & PM] - **Spec Exp:** Palliative Care; Pain-Cancer; **Hospital:** Dana-Farber Cancer Inst, Brigham & Women's Hosp; **Address:** Dana-Farber Cancer Institute, 450 Brookline Ave, Boston, MA 02215; **Phone:** 617-632-6464; **Board Cert:** Internal Medicine 1976; Medical Oncology 2010; Hematology 1978; Hospice & Palliative Medicine 2008; **Med School:** UCSF 1973; **Resid:** Internal Medicine, Mass Genl Hosp 1975; Internal Medicine, Moffitt Hosp-UCSF 1977; **Fellow:** Hematology, Mass Genl Hosp 1976; Hematology & Oncology, Hosp Univ Penn 1980; **Fac Appt:** Prof H & PM, Harvard Med Sch

Block, Susan D MD [H & PM] - **Spec Exp:** Psychiatry in Cancer; Palliative Care; **Hospital:** Dana-Farber Cancer Inst, Brigham & Women's Hosp; **Address:** Dana Farber Cancer Inst, 450 Brookline Ave, Boston, MA 02115; **Phone:** 617-632-5788; **Board Cert:** Internal Medicine 1981; Psychiatry 1984; Hospice & Palliative Medicine 2003; **Med School:** Case West Res Univ 1977; **Resid:** Internal Medicine, Beth Israel Hosp 1980; Psychiatry, Beth Israel Hosp 1982; **Fac Appt:** Prof Psyc, Harvard Med Sch

Jackson, Vicki MD [H & PM] - **Spec Exp:** Palliative Care; **Hospital:** Mass Genl Hosp; **Address:** Palliative Care Service, 55 Fruit St, FND 600, Boston, MA 02114; **Phone:** 617-724-9197; **Board Cert:** Internal Medicine 2008; Hospice & Palliative Medicine 2010; **Med School:** Univ Wisc 1995; **Resid:** Internal Medicine, Cambridge Hlth Alliance 1998; **Fellow:** Pain & Palliative Care, Dana Farbar Cancer Inst 2002

Selvaggi, Kathy J MD [H & PM] - **Spec Exp:** Palliative Care; Pain-Cancer; **Hospital:** Dana-Farber Cancer Inst; **Address:** Dana Farber Cancer Inst, 450 Brookline Ave, Ste 411, Boston, MA 02215; **Phone:** 617-632-6464; **Board Cert:** Internal Medicine 1989; Medical Oncology 2005; Hospice & Palliative Medicine 2008; **Med School:** Penn State Coll Med 1985; **Resid:** Internal Medicine, UPMC Shadyside Hosp 1989; **Fellow:** Medical Oncology, UPMC Shadyside Hosp 1992; **Fac Appt:** Asst Prof Med, Harvard Med Sch

Mid Atlantic

Arnold, Robert M MD [H & PM] - **Spec Exp:** Palliative Care; Ethics; Pain-HIV patients; **Hospital:** UPMC Montefiore, UPMC Presby, Pittsburgh; **Address:** UPMC HIV/AIDS Program Falk Med Bldg, 3601 Fifth Ave Fl 7th, Pittsburgh, PA 15213; **Phone:** 412-647-7228; **Board Cert:** Internal Medicine 1986; Hospice & Palliative Medicine 2008; **Med School:** Univ MO-Kansas City 1983; **Resid:** Internal Medicine, Rhode Island Hosp 1986; Internal Medicine, Hosp Univ Penn 1988; **Fellow:** Public Health, Robert Wood Johnson Univ Affil Hosp 1998; **Fac Appt:** Prof Med, Univ Pittsburgh

Levy, Michael H MD/PhD [H & PM] - **Spec Exp:** Pain Management; Palliative Care; Pain-Cancer; Ethics; **Hospital:** Fox Chase Cancer Ctr (page 57); **Address:** Fox Chase Cancer Ctr, Pain & Palliative Care Program, 333 Cottman Ave, Ste C307, Philadelphia, PA 19111; **Phone:** 215-728-3637; **Board Cert:** Internal Medicine 1979; Medical Oncology 1981; Hospice & Palliative Medicine 2008; **Med School:** Jefferson Med Coll 1976; **Resid:** Internal Medicine, Mt Sinai Med Ctr 1978; Internal Medicine, Hosp Univ Penn 1979; **Fellow:** Hematology & Oncology, Hosp Univ Penn 1981; **Fac Appt:** Assoc Prof Onc, Temple Univ

Portenoy, Russell MD [H & PM] - **Spec Exp:** Pain Management; Palliative Care; **Hospital:** Beth Israel Med Ctr - Petrie Div (page 56); **Address:** Beth Israel Med Ctr, Dept Pain Medicine/Palliative Care, First Ave at 16th St, New York, NY 10003; **Phone:** 212-844-1505; **Board Cert:** Neurology 1985; Hospice & Palliative Medicine 2008; **Med School:** Univ MD Sch Med 1980; **Resid:** Neurology, Montefiore Med Ctr 1984; **Fellow:** Pain Medicine, Meml Sloan-Kettering Cancer Ctr 1985; **Fac Appt:** Prof N, Albert Einstein Coll Med

Quill, Timothy E MD [H & PM] - **Spec Exp:** Palliative Care; **Hospital:** Univ Rochester Strong Meml Hosp; **Address:** URMC-Palliative Care Program, 601 Elmwood Ave, Box 687, Rochester, NY 14642; **Phone:** 585-273-1154; **Board Cert:** Internal Medicine 1979; Hospice & Palliative Medicine 2008; **Med School:** Univ Rochester 1976; **Resid:** Internal Medicine, Univ Rochester/Strong Meml Hosp 1979; **Fellow:** Liaison Psychiatry, Univ Rochester Med Psych Liason Program 1981; **Fac Appt:** Prof Med, Univ Rochester

Southeast

Tucker, Rodney O MD [H & PM] - **Spec Exp:** Palliative Care; **Hospital:** UAB Hosp, Children's Hosp AL; **Address:** UAB Ctr, Palliative Care, CH19, Ste 219, 1720 2nd Ave S, Birmingham, AL 35294; **Phone:** 205-975-8197; **Board Cert:** Internal Medicine 2012; Hospice & Palliative Medicine 2010; **Med School:** UAB Sch Med 1989; **Resid:** Internal Medicine, Carraway Methodist Med Ctr 1993; **Fac Appt:** Assoc Prof Med, UAB Sch Med

Tulsky, James A MD [H & PM] - **Spec Exp:** Palliative Care; **Hospital:** Duke Univ Hosp; **Address:** DUMC, Box 2706, Durham, NC 27710; **Phone:** 919-668-7215; **Board Cert:** Hospice & Palliative Medicine 2012; Internal Medicine 2012; **Med School:** Univ IL Coll Med 1987; **Resid:** Internal Medicine, UCSF Med Ctr 1990; **Fellow:** Research, UCSF Med Ctr 1993; **Fac Appt:** Prof Med, Duke Univ

Midwest

Bricker, Leslie J MD [H & PM] - **Spec Exp:** Palliative Care; **Hospital:** Henry Ford Hosp; **Address:** Henry Ford Hospital, 2799 W Grand Blvd Fl K13, Detroit, MI 48202; **Phone:** 313-916-1859; **Board Cert:** Internal Medicine 1980; Hematology 1982; Medical Oncology 1983; Hospice & Palliative Medicine 2008; **Med School:** Wayne State Univ 1977; **Resid:** Internal Medicine, Sinai Hosp 1980; **Fellow:** Hematology & Oncology, Univ Mich Hosp 1983; **Fac Appt:** Assoc Prof Med, Wayne State Univ

Davis, Mellar P MD [H & PM] - **Spec Exp:** Palliative Care; Lung Cancer (advanced); Amyloidosis; **Hospital:** Cleveland Clin (page 55); **Address:** Cleveland Clin Fdn, 9500 Euclid Ave, Desk R35, Cleveland, OH 44195; **Phone:** 216-445-4622; **Board Cert:** Internal Medicine 1980; Hematology 1982; Medical Oncology 1983; Hospice & Palliative Medicine 2012; **Med School:** Ohio State Univ 1977; **Resid:** Internal Medicine, Riverside Methodist Hosp 1979; **Fellow:** Hematology, Mayo Clinic 1981; Medical Oncology, Mayo Clinic 1982; **Fac Appt:** Prof Med, Cleveland Cl Coll Med/Case West Res

Ferris, Frank D MD [H & PM] - **Spec Exp:** Palliative Care; **Address:** Ohio Health-Kobacker House, 800 McConnell Drive, Columbus, OH 43214; **Phone:** 614-533-6299; **Board Cert:** Hospice & Palliative Medicine 1998; **Med School:** Canada 1981; **Resid:** Internal Medicine, Univ Toronto Affil Hosp; Radiation Oncology, Univ Toronto Affil Hosp; **Fellow:** Pain Management, Toronto-Sunnybrook Reg Cancer Ctr

Friebert, Sarah E MD [H & PM] - **Spec Exp:** Palliative Care; Cancer Survivors-Late Effects of Therapy; **Hospital:** Akron Children's Hosp; **Address:** Children's Hosp Med Ctr of Akron, One Perkins Sq Fl 6, Akron, OH 44308; **Phone:** 330-543-3343; **Board Cert:** Pediatrics 2011; Pediatric Hematology-Oncology 2008; Hospice & Palliative Medicine 2008; **Med School:** Case West Res Univ 1993; **Resid:** Pediatrics, Chldns Hosp 1996; **Fellow:** Pediatric Hematology-Oncology, Rainbow Babies-Chldns Hosp 1999; **Fac Appt:** Assoc Prof Ped, NE Ohio Univ

Santa-Emma, Philip H MD [H & PM] - **Spec Exp:** Palliative Care; **Hospital:** Mt Carmel W Hosp; **Address:** 1144 Dublin Rd, Columbus, OH 43215; **Phone:** 614-234-5000; **Board Cert:** Family Medicine 2010; Hospice & Palliative Medicine 2008; **Med School:** Ohio State Univ 1988; **Resid:** Family Medicine, Mt Carmel Med Ctr 1991

Von Gunten, Charles MD/PhD [H & PM] - **Spec Exp:** Palliative Care; **Address:** Ohio Health-Kobacker House, 800 McConnell Drive, Columbus, OH 43214; **Phone:** 614-533-6299; **Board Cert:** Hospice & Palliative Medicine 2008; Medical Oncology 2003; **Med School:** Univ Colorado 1988; **Resid:** Internal Medicine, Northwestern Meml Hosp 1991; **Fellow:** Medical Oncology, Northwestern Meml Hosp 1993; **Fac Appt:** Assoc Clin Prof Med, UCSD

Great Plains and Mountains

Kutner, Jean S MD [H & PM] - **Spec Exp:** Palliative Care; **Hospital:** Univ Colorado Hosp; **Address:** Univ CO Hosp, Internal Med Dept, 8111 E Lowry Blvd, Ste 120, Denver, CO 80230; **Phone:** 720-848-9500; **Board Cert:** Internal Medicine 2004; Geriatric Medicine 2008; Hospice & Palliative Medicine 2008; **Med School:** UCSF 1991; **Resid:** Internal Medicine, UCSF Med Ctr 1994; **Fellow:** Geriatric Medicine, Univ Colorado Hosp 1997; **Fac Appt:** Prof Med, Univ Colorado

Weinstein, Sharon M MD [H & PM] - **Spec Exp:** Pain-Cancer; Palliative Care; **Hospital:** Univ Utah Hlth Care; **Address:** Huntsman Canc Inst, 1950 Circle of Hope, Salt Lake City, UT 84112; **Phone:** 801-585-0157; **Board Cert:** Neurology 1993; Pain Medicine 2010; Hospice & Palliative Medicine 2008; **Med School:** Albert Einstein Coll Med 1986; **Resid:** Neurology, Montefiore Med Ctr 1990; **Fellow:** Pain Medicine, Meml Sloan-Kettering Canc Ctr 1991; **Fac Appt:** Assoc Prof Anes, Univ Utah

Southwest

Fine, Robert L MD [H & PM] - **Spec Exp:** Palliative Care; **Hospital:** Baylor Univ Med Ctr-Dallas; **Address:** Supportive & Palliative Care Clin, 3600 Gaston Ave, Barnett Twr, Suite 605, Dallas, TX 75246; **Phone:** 214-820-9248; **Board Cert:** Internal Medicine 1981; Hospice & Palliative Medicine 2008; **Med School:** Univ Tex SW, Dallas 1978; **Resid:** Internal Medicine, Baylor Univ Med Ctr 1981

West Coast and Pacific

Pantilat, Steven MD [H & PM] - **Spec Exp:** Palliative Care; **Hospital:** UCSF Med Ctr; **Address:** 521 Parnassus Ave, San Francisco, CA 94143-0903; **Phone:** 415-476-9019; **Board Cert:** Internal Medicine 2003; Hospice & Palliative Medicine 2008; **Med School:** UCSF 1989; **Resid:** Internal Medicine, UCSF Med Ctr 1992; **Fac Appt:** Prof Med, UCSF

Ritchie, Christine S MD [H & PM] - **Spec Exp:** Palliative Care; **Hospital:** UCSF Med Ctr; **Address:** Dept of Medicine, Division of Geriatrics, 3333 California St, Ste 380, San Francisco, CA 94118; **Phone:** 415-502-0951; **Board Cert:** Internal Medicine 2012; Geriatric Medicine 2006; Hospice & Palliative Medicine 2010; **Med School:** Univ NC Sch Med 1988; **Resid:** Internal Medicine, UAB Med Ctr 1992; **Fellow:** Geriatric Medicine, UAB Med Ctr 1994; **Fac Appt:** Prof Med, UCSF

Top Doctors Make A Difference

Infectious Disease

a subspecialty of Internal Medicine

An internist who deals with infectious diseases of all types and in all organs. Conditions requiring selective use of antibiotics call for this special skill. This physician often diagnoses and treats AIDS patients and patients with fevers which have not been explained. Infectious disease specialists may also have expertise in preventive medicine and conditions associated with travel.

Training Required: Three years in internal medicine *plus* additional training and examination for certification in infectious disease.

Infectious Disease

New England

Flanigan, Timothy P MD [Inf] - **Spec Exp:** AIDS/HIV; **Hospital:** Miriam Hosp, Rhode Island Hosp; **Address:** 1125 N Main St, Providence, RI 02904; **Phone:** 401-793-2928; **Board Cert:** Internal Medicine 1986; Infectious Disease 1988; **Med School:** Cornell Univ-Weill Med Coll 1983; **Resid:** Internal Medicine, Hosp Univ Penn 1986; **Fellow:** Infectious Disease, Case West Res Univ 1987; **Fac Appt:** Prof Med, Brown Univ

Quagliarello, Vincent J MD [Inf] - **Spec Exp:** Meningitis; Pneumonia; Endocarditis; **Hospital:** Yale-New Haven Hosp; **Address:** Yale Univ Sch Med, 300 Cedar St, TAC S169A, New Haven, CT 06520-8022; **Phone:** 203-785-4140; **Board Cert:** Internal Medicine 1984; Infectious Disease 1988; **Med School:** Washington Univ, St Louis 1980; **Resid:** Internal Medicine, Yale-New Haven Hosp 1984; **Fellow:** Infectious Disease, Univ VA Hlth Sci Ctr 1987; **Fac Appt:** Prof Med, Yale Univ

Sax, Paul E MD [Inf] - **Spec Exp:** AIDS/HIV; **Hospital:** Brigham & Women's Hosp; **Address:** Brigham & Women's Hosp, Div Infectious Disease, 15 Francis St Fl 4, Boston, MA 02115; **Phone:** 617-732-8881; **Board Cert:** Internal Medicine 2010; Infectious Disease 2012; **Med School:** Harvard Med Sch 1987; **Resid:** Internal Medicine, Brigham & Womens Hosp 1990; **Fellow:** Infectious Disease, Mass Genl Hosp 1992

Mid Atlantic

Auwaerter, Paul G MD [Inf] - **Spec Exp:** Lyme Disease; Ehrlichiosis; Tick-borne Diseases; Fevers of Unknown Origin; **Hospital:** Johns Hopkins Hosp (page 59); **Address:** Rockland Physicians-Johns Hopkins, 10751 Falls Rd, Ste 412, Lutherville, MD 21093; **Phone:** 410-583-2900; **Board Cert:** Internal Medicine 2012; Infectious Disease 2004; **Med School:** Columbia P&S 1988; **Resid:** Internal Medicine, Johns Hopkins Med Ctr 1992; **Fellow:** Infectious Disease, Johns Hopkins Med Ctr 1994; **Fac Appt:** Assoc Prof Med, Johns Hopkins Univ

Bartlett, John G MD [Inf] - **Spec Exp:** AIDS/HIV; Antibiotic Resistance; Pneumonia; **Hospital:** Johns Hopkins Hosp (page 59); **Address:** 1830 E Monument St, Ste 447, Baltimore, MD 21287; **Phone:** 410-955-7634; **Board Cert:** Internal Medicine 1972; **Med School:** SUNY Upstate Med Univ 1963; **Resid:** Internal Medicine, Peter Bent Brigham Hosp 1965; Internal Medicine, Univ Alabama Med Ctr 1968; **Fellow:** Infectious Disease, UCLA Med Ctr 1970; **Fac Appt:** Prof Med, Johns Hopkins Univ

Berkowitz, Leonard B MD [Inf] - **Spec Exp:** AIDS/HIV; **Hospital:** Brooklyn Hosp Ctr; **Address:** 121 DeKalb Ave, Ste 5H, Brooklyn, NY 11201-5425; **Phone:** 718-250-6922; **Board Cert:** Internal Medicine 1980; Infectious Disease 1984; **Med School:** SUNY Downstate 1977; **Resid:** Internal Medicine, Kings Co Hosp Ctr 1981; **Fellow:** Infectious Disease, Kings Co Hosp Ctr 1983; **Fac Appt:** Asst Clin Prof Med, SUNY Hlth Sci Ctr

Brause, Barry MD [Inf] - **Spec Exp:** Bone/Joint Infections; Skin/Soft Tissue Infections; Infections in Prosthetic Devices; **Hospital:** Hosp For Special Surgery (page 58), NY-Presby/Weill Cornell Med Ctr, NY (page 65); **Address:** 535 E 70th St, Ste 657W, New York, NY 10021-5718; **Phone:** 212-774-7411; **Board Cert:** Internal Medicine 1973; Infectious Disease 1976; **Med School:** Univ Pittsburgh 1970; **Resid:** Internal Medicine, NY Presby/Weill Cornell Med Ctr 1973; **Fellow:** Infectious Disease, NY Presby/Weill Cornell Med Ctr 1975; **Fac Appt:** Clin Prof Med, Cornell Univ-Weill Med Coll

Cunha, Burke A MD [Inf] - **Spec Exp:** Infections in Immunocompromised Patients; Fevers of Unknown Origin; Pneumonia; Chronic Fatigue Syndrome; **Hospital:** Winthrop Univ Hosp; **Address:** 222 Station Plz N, Ste 432, Mineola, NY 11501; **Phone:** 516-663-2507; **Board Cert:** Internal Medicine 1977; Infectious Disease 1978; **Med School:** Penn State Coll Med 1972; **Resid:** Internal Medicine, Hartford Hosp 1975; **Fellow:** Infectious Disease, Hartford Hosp 1977; **Fac Appt:** Prof Med, SUNY Stony Brook

Frank, Ian MD [Inf] - **Spec Exp:** AIDS/HIV; **Hospital:** Hosp Univ Penn - UPHS (page 69); **Address:** Hosp Univ Penn, Div Infectious Disease, 3400 Spruce St, 3 Silverstein, Ste D, Philadelphia, PA 19104; **Phone:** 215-662-6932; **Board Cert:** Internal Medicine 1983; Infectious Disease 2006; **Med School:** Dartmouth Med Sch 1980; **Resid:** Internal Medicine, Graduate Hosp 1983; **Fellow:** Infectious Disease, Hosp Univ Penn 1984; **Fac Appt:** Prof Med, Univ Pennsylvania

Gumprecht, Jeffrey P MD [Inf] - **Spec Exp:** AIDS/HIV; Travel Medicine; Infections-Surgical; **Hospital:** Mt Sinai Med Ctr (page 62); **Address:** 1100 Park Ave, Ste 1C, New York, NY 10128; **Phone:** 212-427-9550; **Board Cert:** Internal Medicine 1987; Infectious Disease 2003; **Med School:** Albany Med Coll 1983; **Resid:** Internal Medicine, Mt Sinai Hosp 1987; **Fellow:** Infectious Disease, Montefiore Med Ctr 1990; **Fac Appt:** Asst Clin Prof Med, Mount Sinai Sch Med

Hammer, Glenn S MD [Inf] - **Spec Exp:** AIDS/HIV; Hospital Acquired Infections; Infections-Surgical; **Hospital:** Mt Sinai Med Ctr (page 62); **Address:** 1100 Park Ave, Ste 1C, New York, NY 10128-1202; **Phone:** 212-427-9550; **Board Cert:** Infectious Disease 1974; Internal Medicine 1973; **Med School:** NYU Sch Med 1969; **Resid:** Internal Medicine, Mount Sinai Hosp 1972; **Fellow:** Infectious Disease, Mount Sinai Hosp 1974; **Fac Appt:** Asst Clin Prof Med, Mount Sinai Sch Med

Hammer, Scott M MD [Inf] - **Spec Exp:** AIDS/HIV; **Hospital:** NY-Presby/Columbia Univ Med Ctr, NY (page 65); **Address:** 630 W 168th St, P&S Box 82, New York, NY 10032; **Phone:** 212-305-8039; **Board Cert:** Internal Medicine 1975; Infectious Disease 1980; **Med School:** Columbia P&S 1972; **Resid:** Internal Medicine, Columbia-Presby Hosp 1975; Internal Medicine, Stanford Univ Hosp 1975; **Fellow:** Infectious Disease, Mass Genl Hosp 1981; **Fac Appt:** Prof Med, Columbia P&S

Hartman, Barry J MD [Inf] - **Spec Exp:** Endocarditis; Infections-Surgical; Parasitic Infections; **Hospital:** NY-Presby/Weill Cornell Med Ctr, NY (page 65); **Address:** 407 E 70th St, Fl 4, New York, NY 10021-5302; **Phone:** 212-744-4882; **Board Cert:** Internal Medicine 1976; Infectious Disease 1980; **Med School:** Penn State Coll Med 1973; **Resid:** Internal Medicine, NY Hosp/Cornell Med Ctr 1976; **Fellow:** Infectious Disease, NY Hosp/Cornell Med Ctr 1981; **Fac Appt:** Clin Prof Med, Cornell Univ-Weill Med Coll

Kumar, Princy N MD [Inf] - **Spec Exp:** AIDS/HIV; Hepatitis C; Infections-Transplant; Infections-Surgical; **Hospital:** MedStar Georgetown Univ Hosp; **Address:** Georgetown Univ Hosp, Pasquerilla Healthcare Center 5th Fl, 3800 Reservoir Rd NW, Ste 110, Washington, DC 20007; **Phone:** 202-444-0086; **Board Cert:** Internal Medicine 1988; Infectious Disease 2010; **Med School:** India 1981; **Resid:** Internal Medicine, Englewood Hosp 1988; **Fellow:** Infectious Disease, Georgetown Univ Hosp 1990; **Fac Appt:** Prof Med, Georgetown Univ

Lorber, Bennett MD [Inf] - **Spec Exp:** Foodborne Illnesses; **Hospital:** Temple Univ Hosp; **Address:** Temple Univ Infectious Diseases, 3401 N Broad St, Parkinson Pavilion, Ste 501, Philadelphia, PA 19140; **Phone:** 215-707-3807; **Board Cert:** Internal Medicine 1974; Infectious Disease 1976; **Med School:** Univ Pennsylvania 1968; **Resid:** Internal Medicine, Temple Univ Hosp 1971; **Fellow:** Infectious Disease, Temple Univ Hosp 1973; **Fac Appt:** Prof Med, Temple Univ

Louie, Eddie MD [Inf] - **Spec Exp:** Lyme Disease; AIDS/HIV; Hospital Acquired Infections; **Hospital:** NYU Langone Med Ctr (page 68); **Address:** 5 31st Ave, Ste 7J, New York, NY 10016; **Phone:** 212-682-9202; **Board Cert:** Internal Medicine 1982; Infectious Disease 1986; **Med School:** NYU Sch Med 1979; **Resid:** Internal Medicine, Kings County Hosp 1983; **Fellow:** Infectious Disease, NYU Med Ctr 1985; **Fac Appt:** Assoc Clin Prof Med, NYU Sch Med

McGowan, Joseph MD [Inf] - **Spec Exp:** AIDS/HIV; HIV in Pregnancy; HIV & Hepatitis co-infection; AIDS/HIV in Elderly; **Hospital:** NS-LIJ Hlth Sys (page 66); **Address:** 400 Community Drive, Manhasset, NY 11030; **Phone:** 516-562-4280; **Board Cert:** Internal Medicine 2002; Infectious Disease 2002; **Med School:** Mount Sinai Sch Med 1987; **Resid:** Internal Medicine, Montefiore Med Ctr 1990; **Fellow:** Infectious Disease, Montefiore Med Ctr 1993

Mildvan, Donna MD [Inf] - **Spec Exp:** AIDS/HIV; Clinical Trials; **Hospital:** Beth Israel Med Ctr - Petrie Div (page 56); **Address:** Beth Israel Med Ctr, Div Infectious Dis, 1st Ave at 16th St, 19BH17, New York, NY 10003; **Phone:** 212-420-4005; **Board Cert:** Internal Medicine 1972; Infectious Disease 1972; **Med School:** Johns Hopkins Univ 1967; **Resid:** Internal Medicine, Mt Sinai Med Ctr 1970; **Fellow:** Infectious Disease, Mt Sinai Med Ctr 1972; **Fac Appt:** Prof Med, Albert Einstein Coll Med

Nahass, Ronald G MD [Inf] - **Spec Exp:** HIV; Hepatitis B & C; Diagnostic Problems; Bone Infections; **Hospital:** Robert Wood Johnson Univ Hosp - New Brunswick, Univ Med Ctr Princeton at Plainsboro; **Address:** Infectious Disease Care, 105 Raider Blvd, Ste 101, Hillsborough, NJ 08844-4254; **Phone:** 908-281-0221; **Board Cert:** Internal Medicine 1985; Infectious Disease 1988; **Med School:** UMDNJ-RW Johnson Med Sch 1982; **Resid:** Internal Medicine, RWJ Univ Hosp 1985; **Fellow:** Infectious Disease, RWJ Univ Hosp 1988; **Fac Appt:** Clin Prof Med, UMDNJ-RW Johnson Med Sch

Perlman, David MD [Inf] - **Spec Exp:** AIDS/HIV; Lyme Disease; Travel Medicine; Tuberculosis; **Hospital:** Beth Israel Med Ctr - Petrie Div (page 56), Lenox Hill Hosp (page 66); **Address:** Beth Israel Med Ctr, 120 E 16th St Fl 12, New York, NY 10003; **Phone:** 212-844-8549; **Board Cert:** Internal Medicine 1986; Infectious Disease 1988; **Med School:** Albert Einstein Coll Med 1983; **Resid:** Internal Medicine, New York Hosp/Meml-Sloan Kettering 1986; **Fellow:** Infectious Disease, Montefiore Hosp 1988; **Fac Appt:** Prof Med, Albert Einstein Coll Med

Polsky, Bruce W MD [Inf] - **Spec Exp:** AIDS/HIV; Viral Infections; Infections in Cancer Patients; AIDS Related Cancers; **Hospital:** St. Luke's - Roosevelt Hosp Ctr - Roosevelt Div (page 56), St. Luke's - Roosevelt Hosp Ctr - St Luke's Hosp (page 56); **Address:** University Medical Practice Associates, 425 W 59th St, Ste 8A, New York, NY 10019; **Phone:** 212-523-7335; **Board Cert:** Internal Medicine 1983; Infectious Disease 1986; **Med School:** Wayne State Univ 1980; **Resid:** Internal Medicine, Montefiore Hosp 1983; **Fellow:** Infectious Disease, Meml Sloan Kettering Cancer Ctr 1986; **Fac Appt:** Prof Med, Columbia P&S

Rao, Nalini G MD [Inf] - **Spec Exp:** Bone/Joint Infections; Tropical Diseases; Travel Medicine; **Hospital:** UPMC Presby, Pittsburgh, UPMC Shadyside; **Address:** Centre Commons, Suite 510, 5750 Centre Ave, Pittsburgh, PA 15206-3721; **Phone:** 412-661-1633; **Board Cert:** Internal Medicine 1975; Infectious Disease 1980; **Med School:** India 1970; **Resid:** Internal Medicine, Geo Wash Univ Hosp 1974; **Fellow:** Infectious Disease, Baylor Coll Med 1975; Infectious Disease, Univ Pittsburgh Sch Med 1977; **Fac Appt:** Clin Prof Med, Univ Pittsburgh

Romagnoli, Mario MD [Inf] - **Spec Exp:** AIDS/HIV; Bone/Joint Infections; **Hospital:** Lenox Hill Hosp (page 66); **Address:** 903 Park Ave, New York, NY 10075; **Phone:** 212-396-3390; **Board Cert:** Internal Medicine 1979; Infectious Disease 1982; **Med School:** Columbia P&S 1976; **Resid:** Internal Medicine, Columbia-Presby Med Ctr 1979; **Fellow:** Infectious Disease, Beth Israel Med Ctr 1981; **Fac Appt:** Assoc Prof Med, Columbia P&S

Segal, Brahm H MD [Inf] - **Spec Exp:** Infections in Cancer Patients; Immune Deficiencies-Primary; **Hospital:** Roswell Park Canc Inst; **Address:** Roswell Park Cancer Inst, Elm & Carlton Streets, Buffalo, NY 14263; **Phone:** 716-845-1642; **Board Cert:** Infectious Disease 2009; **Med School:** Albert Einstein Coll Med 1992; **Resid:** Internal Medicine, Tufts New England Med Ctr 1995; **Fellow:** Infectious Disease, Natl Inst Allergy/Inf Dis 1997; **Fac Appt:** Prof Med, SUNY Buffalo

Sepkowitz, Kent A MD [Inf] - **Spec Exp:** Hospital Acquired Infections; Tuberculosis; Infections in Cancer Patients; **Hospital:** Meml Sloan-Kettering Canc Ctr, NY-Presby/Weill Cornell Med Ctr, NY (page 65); **Address:** 1275 York Ave, New York, NY 10065; **Phone:** 212-639-2441; **Board Cert:** Internal Medicine 1983; Infectious Disease 2010; **Med School:** Univ Okla Coll Med 1980; **Resid:** Internal Medicine, St Luke's-Roosevelt Hosp 1983; **Fellow:** Infectious Disease, Meml Sloan Kettering Cancer Ctr 1990; **Fac Appt:** Prof Med, Cornell Univ-Weill Med Coll

Squires, Kathleen E MD [Inf] - **Spec Exp:** AIDS/HIV; AIDS/HIV in Women; **Hospital:** Thomas Jefferson Univ Hosp; **Address:** 1015 Chestnut St, Ste 1020, Philadelphia, PA 19107; **Phone:** 215-955-7785; **Board Cert:** Internal Medicine 1984; Infectious Disease 1988; **Med School:** Med Coll PA 1981; **Resid:** Internal Medicine, Med Coll Penn 1984; **Fellow:** Infectious Disease, NY Presby Hosp/Cornell Weill Med Ctr 1988; **Fac Appt:** Prof Med, Thomas Jefferson Univ

Wallach, Frances MD [Inf] - **Spec Exp:** AIDS/HIV; Infection Control; HIV & Blood Transfusions; **Hospital:** Mt Sinai Med Ctr (page 62); **Address:** 17 E 102nd St Fl 3rd, New York, NY 10029; **Phone:** 212-241-7968; **Board Cert:** Internal Medicine 1989; Infectious Disease 2002; **Med School:** Albany Med Coll 1985; **Resid:** Internal Medicine, Montefiore Med Ctr 1989; **Fellow:** Nuclear Medicine, Montefiore Med Ctr 1990; Infectious Disease, NY Hosp-Cornell Med Ctr 1992; **Fac Appt:** Asst Prof Med, Mount Sinai Sch Med

Wormser, Gary P MD [Inf] - **Spec Exp:** Lyme Disease; AIDS/HIV; Diagnostic Problems; **Hospital:** Westchester Med Ctr; **Address:** New York Med Coll, Div Infectious Disease, Munger Pavilion, rm 149, Valhalla, NY 10595; **Phone:** 914-493-8865; **Board Cert:** Internal Medicine 1978; Infectious Disease 1982; **Med School:** Johns Hopkins Univ 1972; **Resid:** Internal Medicine, Mt Sinai Hosp 1975; **Fellow:** Infectious Disease, Mt Sinai Hosp 1977; **Fac Appt:** Prof Med, NY Med Coll

Yancovitz, Stanley R MD [Inf] - **Spec Exp:** Lyme Disease; Endocarditis; Bone/Joint Infections; Tuberculosis; **Hospital:** Beth Israel Med Ctr - Petrie Div (page 56); **Address:** 10 Union Sq, Ste 3F, New York, NY 10003; **Phone:** 212-420-2600; **Board Cert:** Internal Medicine 1973; Infectious Disease 1976; **Med School:** SUNY Downstate 1967; **Resid:** Internal Medicine, Metropolitan Hosp 1969; Internal Medicine, Beth Israel Med Ctr 1972; **Fellow:** Infectious Disease, Mt Sinai Hosp 1975; **Fac Appt:** Prof Med, Albert Einstein Coll Med

Southeast

Alvarez-Elcoro, Salvador MD [Inf] - **Spec Exp:** Tuberculosis; Travel Medicine; Infections-Transplant; **Hospital:** Mayo - Jacksonville; **Address:** Mayo Clin, Infectious Disease Dept, 4500 San Pablo Rd, Jacksonville, FL 32224; **Phone:** 904-953-2272; **Board Cert:** Internal Medicine 1977; Infectious Disease 1982; **Med School:** Mexico 1972; **Resid:** Internal Medicine, Charity Hosp 1977; **Fellow:** Infectious Disease, Boston Med Ctr 1979; **Fac Appt:** Prof Med, Mayo Med Sch

Cancio, Margarita MD [Inf] - **Spec Exp:** AIDS/HIV; **Hospital:** Tampa Genl Hosp; **Address:** Infectious Disease Assocs, 4729 N Habana Ave, Tampa, FL 33614; **Phone:** 813-251-8444; **Board Cert:** Internal Medicine 1985; Infectious Disease 1988; **Med School:** Univ S Fla Coll Med 1982; **Resid:** Internal Medicine, Univ S FL Affil Hosp 1985; **Fellow:** Infectious Disease, Univ S FL Affil Hosp 1988; **Fac Appt:** Assoc Prof Med, Univ S Fla Coll Med

Corey, G Ralph MD [Inf] - **Spec Exp:** Tropical Diseases; Travel Medicine; Endocarditis; Staphylococcal Infections; **Hospital:** Duke Univ Hosp; **Address:** 310 Trent Drive, rm 235, Trent Box 90519, Durham, NC 27708; **Phone:** 919-668-7174; **Board Cert:** Internal Medicine 1977; Infectious Disease 1980; **Med School:** Baylor Coll Med 1973; **Resid:** Internal Medicine, Duke Univ Med Ctr 1978; **Fellow:** Infectious Disease, Duke Univ Med Ctr 1980; **Fac Appt:** Prof Med, Duke Univ

Edmond, Michael B MD [Inf] - **Spec Exp:** Bone/Joint Infections; Skin/Soft Tissue Infections; Antibiotic Resistance; Hospital Acquired Infections; **Hospital:** Med Coll of VA Hosp; **Address:** VCU Medical Center, Box 980019, Richmond, VA 23298-0019; **Phone:** 804-828-2121; **Board Cert:** Internal Medicine 1989; Infectious Disease 2012; **Med School:** W VA Univ 1986; **Resid:** Internal Medicine, W Virginia Univ Hosps 1989; **Fellow:** Infectious Disease, Univ Pittsburgh 1992; Epidemiology, Univ Iowa; **Fac Appt:** Prof Med, Med Coll VA

Gorensek, Margaret J MD [Inf] - **Spec Exp:** AIDS/HIV; Infections-Transplant; Chronic Fatigue Syndrome; Pediatric Infectious Disease; **Hospital:** Holy Cross Hosp - Fort Lauderdale, Broward Hlth Med Ctr; **Address:** Holy Cross Med Grp, Infectious Disease, 5601 N Dixie Hwy, Ste 107, Fort Lauderdale, FL 33334; **Phone:** 954-493-9752; **Board Cert:** Internal Medicine 1985; Pediatrics 1986; Infectious Disease 1988; Pediatric Infectious Disease 2009; **Med School:** Case West Res Univ 1981; **Resid:** Internal Medicine & Pediatrics, Cleveland Clin 1985; **Fellow:** Infectious Disease, Cleveland Clin 1987; Pediatric Infectious Disease, Chldns Med Ctr 1988; **Fac Appt:** Asst Clin Prof Med, Univ Miami Sch Med

Katner, Harold P MD [Inf] - **Spec Exp:** AIDS/HIV; **Hospital:** Med Ctr of Central GA; **Address:** Mercer Hlth Sys, Infectious Disease, 707 Pine St, Macon, GA 31201; **Phone:** 478-301-5801; **Board Cert:** Internal Medicine 1983; Infectious Disease 1986; **Med School:** Louisiana State U, New Orleans 1980; **Resid:** Internal Medicine, Univ Med Ctr 1983; **Fellow:** Infectious Disease, Ochsner Fdn Hosp 1986; **Fac Appt:** Prof Med, Mercer Univ Sch Med

Pearson, Richard D MD [Inf] - **Spec Exp:** Tropical Diseases; Travel Medicine; Parasitic Infections; **Hospital:** Univ of Virginia Hlth Sys; **Address:** Univ VA Sch Med, Dept Internal Med, 1 University Drive, Charlottesville, VA 22903; **Phone:** 434-982-1700; **Board Cert:** Internal Medicine 1976; Infectious Disease 1980; **Med School:** Univ Mich Med Sch 1973; **Resid:** Internal Medicine, Strong Meml Hosp 1976; **Fellow:** Infectious Disease, Strong Meml Hosp 1979; **Fac Appt:** Prof Med, Univ VA Sch Med

Ratzan, Kenneth MD [Inf] - **Spec Exp:** AIDS/HIV; **Hospital:** Mount Sinai Med Ctr - Miami, Miami Heart Inst; **Address:** Mount Sinai Med Ctr, Infectious Disease, 4300 Alton Rd, Ste 450, Miami Beach, FL 33140; **Phone:** 305-673-5490; **Board Cert:** Internal Medicine 1977; Infectious Disease 1974; **Med School:** Harvard Med Sch 1965; **Resid:** Internal Medicine, NY-Presby/Columbia Univ Med Ctr 1967; Infectious Disease, Tufts Med Ctr 1972; **Fellow:** Infectious Disease, Tufts Med Ctr 1971; **Fac Appt:** Prof Med, Univ Miami Sch Med

Saag, Michael S MD [Inf] - **Spec Exp:** AIDS/HIV; Clinical Trials; **Hospital:** UAB Hosp; **Address:** UAB Div Infectious Diseases, 845 19th St South, BBRB 256, Birmingham, AL 35294; **Phone:** 205-934-7349; **Board Cert:** Internal Medicine 1985; Infectious Disease 1988; **Med School:** Univ Louisville Sch Med 1981; **Resid:** Internal Medicine, Univ Ala Hosp 1984; **Fellow:** Infectious Disease, Univ Alabama 1987; **Fac Appt:** Prof, UAB Sch Med

Scheld, W Michael MD [Inf] - **Spec Exp:** Meningitis; Endocarditis; AIDS/HIV; Antibiotic Resistance; **Hospital:** Univ of Virginia Hlth Sys; **Address:** UVA-Infectious Disease, 1215 Lee St, Charlottesville, VA 22908; **Phone:** 434-924-5059; **Board Cert:** Internal Medicine 1976; Infectious Disease 1978; **Med School:** Cornell Univ-Weill Med Coll 1973; **Resid:** Internal Medicine, Univ VA Hosp 1976; **Fellow:** Infectious Disease, Univ VA Hosp 1979; **Fac Appt:** Prof Med, Univ VA Sch Med

Van Der Horst, Charles M MD [Inf] - **Spec Exp:** AIDS/HIV; Fungal Infections; Viral Infections; Immune Deficiency; **Hospital:** NC Memorial Hosp - UNC; **Address:** Univ NC-Dept Med, Box CB7030, Chapel Hill, NC 27599; **Phone:** 919-966-2536; **Board Cert:** Internal Medicine 1982; Infectious Disease 1986; **Med School:** Harvard Med Sch 1979; **Resid:** Internal Medicine, Montefiore Med Ctr 1982; **Fellow:** Infectious Disease, NC Meml Hosp 1985; **Fac Appt:** Prof Med, Univ NC Sch Med

Wallace, Mark R MD [Inf] - **Spec Exp:** Fever in Returning Travelers; Travel Medicine; Malaria; HIV; **Hospital:** Orlando Regl Med Ctr; **Address:** Orlando Hlth, Infectious Disease, 1012 Lucerne Terr, Orlando, FL 32806; **Phone:** 321-841-7750; **Board Cert:** Internal Medicine 1984; Infectious Disease 2010; **Med School:** St Louis Univ 1981; **Resid:** Internal Medicine, Univ Wash Med Ctr 1984; **Fellow:** Infectious Disease, Naval Hosp 1989; **Fac Appt:** Clin Prof Med, FSU College Medicine

Midwest

Bakken, Johan S MD/PhD [Inf] - **Spec Exp:** Human Granulocytic Anaplasmosis; Tick-borne Diseases; Diarrheal Diseases; Ehrlichiosis; **Hospital:** St. Luke's Hosp - Duluth, St. Mary's Med Ctr - Duluth; **Address:** 1001 E Superior St, Ste L201, Duluth, MN 55802; **Phone:** 218-249-7990; **Board Cert:** Internal Medicine 2009; **Med School:** Univ Wash 1972; **Resid:** Internal Medicine, Univ Wash Hosps 1978; Internal Medicine, Lillehammer Fylkessykehus 1981; **Fellow:** Infectious Disease, Ulleval Hosp 1985; Microbiology, Creighton Univ 1987; **Fac Appt:** Assoc Clin Prof FMed, Univ Minn

Campbell, J William MD [Inf] - **Spec Exp:** AIDS/HIV; **Hospital:** St. Luke's Hosp - Chesterfield, MO, Barnes-Jewish Hosp; **Address:** St Luke's Hosp, 222 S Woods Mill Rd, Ste 750 N, Chesterfield, MO 63017; **Phone:** 314-205-6600; **Board Cert:** Internal Medicine 1980; Infectious Disease 1982; **Med School:** Washington Univ, St Louis 1977; **Resid:** Internal Medicine, Barnes Hosp-Wash Univ 1980; **Fellow:** Infectious Disease, Univ Tex Hlth Sci Ctr 1981; Infectious Disease, Wash Univ 1982; **Fac Appt:** Clin Prof Med, Washington Univ, St Louis

Cohn, Susan E MD [Inf] - **Spec Exp:** AIDS/HIV; AIDS/HIV in Women; Women's Health; HIV in Pregnancy; **Hospital:** Northwestern Meml Hosp; **Address:** 676 N St Clair St, Ste 940, Chicago, IL 60611; **Phone:** 312-926-8358; **Board Cert:** Internal Medicine 1987; Infectious Disease 2005; **Med School:** Cornell Univ 1984; **Resid:** Internal Medicine, Boston City Hosp 1987; **Fellow:** Infectious Disease, Univ NC Affil Hosp 1992; **Fac Appt:** Prof Med, Northwestern Univ-Feinberg Sch Med

Fichtenbaum, Carl J MD [Inf] - **Spec Exp:** AIDS/HIV; **Hospital:** Univ Cincinnati Med Ctr; **Address:** UC Health-Holmes Hosp, 231 Albert Sabin Way, Cincinnati, OH 45267; **Phone:** 513-584-6977; **Board Cert:** Infectious Disease 2004; Internal Medicine 2004; **Med School:** Univ MO-Kansas City 1985; **Resid:** Internal Medicine & Pediatrics, Bridgeport Hosp 1990; **Fellow:** Infectious Disease, Yale-New Haven Hosp 1991; Infectious Disease, Washington Univ Med Ctr 1992; **Fac Appt:** Prof Med, Univ Cincinnati

Flaherty, John P MD [Inf] - **Spec Exp:** AIDS/HIV; Travel Medicine; Orthopaedic Infectious Disease; **Hospital:** Northwestern Meml Hosp; **Address:** 676 N St Clair St, Ste 940, Chicago, IL 60611; **Phone:** 312-926-8358; **Board Cert:** Internal Medicine 1986; Infectious Disease 1988; **Med School:** Univ IL Coll Med 1983; **Resid:** Internal Medicine, Univ Iowa Hosp 1986; **Fellow:** Infectious Disease, Univ Chicago Hosps 1988; **Fac Appt:** Prof Med, Northwestern Univ

Longworth, David L MD [Inf] - **Spec Exp:** HIV; **Hospital:** Cleveland Clin (page 55); **Address:** Cleveland Clinic, 9500 Euclid Ave, MC G10, Cleveland, OH 44195; **Phone:** 216-444-5665; **Board Cert:** Internal Medicine 1981; Infectious Disease 1984; **Med School:** Cornell Univ-Weill Med Coll 1978; **Resid:** Internal Medicine, UCSF-HC Moffitt Hosp 1981; **Fellow:** Infectious Disease, Brigham & Womens Hosp 1985; **Fac Appt:** Assoc Prof Med, Ohio State Univ

Maki, Dennis G MD [Inf] - **Spec Exp:** Urinary Tract Infections; Critical Care; **Hospital:** Univ WI Hosp & Clins; **Address:** Univ WI Hosp & Clins - Div Infect Dis, 600 Highland Ave, MC B6/2442, Madison, WI 53792-2442; **Phone:** 608-263-0946; **Board Cert:** Internal Medicine 1972; Infectious Disease 1974; Critical Care Medicine 2012; **Med School:** Univ Wisc 1967; **Resid:** Internal Medicine, Harvard-Boston City Hosp 1972; **Fellow:** Infectious Disease, Mass Genl Hosp 1974; **Fac Appt:** Prof Med, Univ Wisc

Novak, Richard M MD [Inf] - **Spec Exp:** AIDS/HIV; **Hospital:** Univ of IL Med Ctr at Chicago; **Address:** Univ IL Med Ctr-Infectious Disease, 808 S Wood St, Ste 888, MC 735, Chicago, IL 60612; **Phone:** 312-996-6763; **Board Cert:** Internal Medicine 1984; Infectious Disease 1988; **Med School:** Rush Med Coll 1981; **Resid:** Internal Medicine, Univ IL Med Ctr 1984; **Fellow:** Infectious Disease, Univ IL Coll of Med 1989; **Fac Appt:** Prof Med, Univ IL Coll Med

O'Keefe, J Paul MD [Inf] - **Spec Exp:** AIDS/HIV; Fungal Infections; Infections-Surgical; Travel Medicine; **Hospital:** Loyola Univ Med Ctr; **Address:** Loyola Univ Med Ctr, 2160 S 1st Ave Bldg 54, Maywood, IL 60153-3304; **Phone:** 708-216-0160; **Board Cert:** Internal Medicine 1974; Infectious Disease 1978; **Med School:** Loyola Univ-Stritch Sch Med 1971; **Resid:** Internal Medicine, Loyola Univ Med Ctr 1974; **Fellow:** Infectious Disease, VA Hosp 1975; Infectious Disease, Tufts New England Med Ctr 1977; **Fac Appt:** Prof Med, Loyola Univ-Stritch Sch Med

Pursell, Kenneth MD [Inf] - **Spec Exp:** Infections-Transplant; AIDS/HIV; Infections in Immunocompromised Patients; **Hospital:** Univ of Chicago Med; **Address:** Univ Chicago Med Ctr, 5841 S Maryland Ave, Chicago, IL 60637; **Phone:** 773-834-1443; **Board Cert:** Internal Medicine 1988; Infectious Disease 2011; **Med School:** Univ Conn 1985; **Resid:** Internal Medicine, N Shore Univ Hosp 1988; **Fellow:** Infectious Disease, Meml Sloan-Kettering Cancer Ctr 1990; **Fac Appt:** Prof Med, Univ Chicago-Pritzker Sch Med

Salata, Robert A MD [Inf] - **Spec Exp:** AIDS/HIV; **Hospital:** UH Case Med Ctr; **Address:** UH Case Medical Center, Infectious Disease-Foley Bldg 411, 11100 Euclid Ave, Cleveland, OH 44106; **Phone:** 216-844-1709; **Board Cert:** Internal Medicine 1982; Infectious Disease 1986; **Med School:** Case West Res Univ 1979; **Resid:** Internal Medicine, Case Med Ctr 1982; **Fellow:** Infectious Disease, Univ VA Med Ctr 1985; **Fac Appt:** Prof Med, Case West Res Univ

Schmitt, Steven K MD [Inf] - **Spec Exp:** Bone/Joint Infections; **Hospital:** Cleveland Clin (page 55); **Address:** Cleveland Clinic, 9500 Euclid Ave, Desk G21, Cleveland, OH 44195; **Phone:** 216-444-8845; **Board Cert:** Internal Medicine 2012; Infectious Disease 2004; **Med School:** Univ Cincinnati 1988; **Resid:** Internal Medicine, Cleveland Clinic 1991; **Fellow:** Infectious Disease, Cleveland Clinic 1994

Sha, Beverly E MD [Inf] - **Spec Exp:** AIDS/HIV in Women; **Hospital:** Rush Univ Med Ctr; **Address:** 600 S Paulina St, Ste 140-143, Chicago, IL 60612; **Phone:** 312-942-5865; **Board Cert:** Internal Medicine 1989; Infectious Disease 2012; **Med School:** Johns Hopkins Univ 1986; **Resid:** Internal Medicine, Rush-Presby St Lukes Med Ctr 1989; **Fellow:** Infectious Disease, Rush-Presby St Lukes Med Ctr 1991; **Fac Appt:** Prof Med, Rush Med Coll

Slama, Thomas G MD [Inf] - **Spec Exp:** Hematologic Infections; Bone Infections; Infections in Prosthetic Devices; Parasitic Infections; **Hospital:** St. Vincent Indianapolis Hosp; **Address:** Metro Infectious Disease Consultants, 8240 Naab Rd, Ste 300, Indianapolis, IN 46260; **Phone:** 317-870-1970; **Board Cert:** Internal Medicine 1976; Infectious Disease 1978; **Med School:** Indiana Univ 1973; **Resid:** Internal Medicine, Methodist Hosp 1976; **Fellow:** Infectious Disease, OSU Med Ctr 1978; **Fac Appt:** Clin Prof Med, Indiana Univ

Sobel, Jack MD [Inf] - **Spec Exp:** Vaginitis; Fungal Infections; Urinary Tract Infections; **Hospital:** Harper Univ Hosp, Detroit Receiving Hospital; **Address:** 3901 Chrysler Service Drive, Ste 4A, Detroit, MI 48201; **Phone:** 313-745-9035; **Board Cert:** Internal Medicine 1978; Infectious Disease 1982; **Med School:** South Africa 1965; **Resid:** Internal Medicine 1970; **Fellow:** Infectious Disease, Univ Penn Hosps 1977; Research, Natl Inst Hlth 1978; **Fac Appt:** Prof Med, Wayne State Univ

Tomford, J Walton MD [Inf] - **Hospital:** Cleveland Clin (page 55); **Address:** Cleveland Clinic, 9500 Euclid Ave, Desk G21, Cleveland, OH 44195; **Phone:** 216-444-5665; **Board Cert:** Internal Medicine 1978; Infectious Disease 1980; **Med School:** Johns Hopkins Univ 1975; **Resid:** Internal Medicine, Johns Hopkins Hosp 1977; Internal Medicine, Univ Hosps of Cleveland 1978; **Fellow:** Infectious Disease, Cleveland Univ Hosp 1980; **Fac Appt:** Assoc Prof Med, Cleveland Cl Coll Med/Case West Res

Trenholme, Gordon M MD [Inf] - **Spec Exp:** Fevers of Unknown Origin; Malaria; Tropical Diseases; **Hospital:** Rush Univ Med Ctr; **Address:** Rush Univ Med Ctr, Infectious Disease, 600 S Paulina St, Ste 140-143, Chicago, IL 60612-3809; **Phone:** 312-942-3665; **Board Cert:** Internal Medicine 1972; Infectious Disease 1976; **Med School:** Med Coll Wisc 1970; **Resid:** Internal Medicine, Univ Chicago Hosp 1973; **Fellow:** Infectious Disease, Rush/Presby-St Luke's Med Ctr 1975; **Fac Appt:** Prof Med, Rush Med Coll

Great Plains and Mountains

Freifeld, Alison G MD [Inf] - **Spec Exp:** Infectious Disease during Chemotherapy; Infections in Cancer Patients; **Hospital:** Nebraska Med Ctr; **Address:** Univ Nebraska Med Ctr, 985400 Nebraska Medical Center, Omaha, NE 68198-5400; **Phone:** 402-559-8650; **Board Cert:** Internal Medicine 1985; Infectious Disease 1988; **Med School:** Johns Hopkins Univ 1982; **Resid:** Internal Medicine, Johns Hopkins Univ Med Ctr 1985; **Fellow:** Infectious Disease, Natl Inst of Allergy & Infectious Disease 1988; **Fac Appt:** Prof Med, Johns Hopkins Univ

Huitt, Gwen A MD [Inf] - **Spec Exp:** Tuberculosis; Cystic Fibrosis; Mycobacterial Infections; **Hospital:** Natl Jewish Hlth; **Address:** National Jewish Health, 1400 Jackson St, rm J222, Denver, CO 80206; **Phone:** 303-398-1667; **Board Cert:** Internal Medicine 2003; Infectious Disease 2004; **Med School:** Univ Colorado 1988; **Resid:** Internal Medicine, Univ Colorado Hlth Sci Ctr 1991; **Fellow:** Infectious Disease, Univ Colorado Hlth Sci Ctr 1993; **Fac Appt:** Assoc Prof Med, Univ Colorado

Johnson, Steven C MD [Inf] - **Spec Exp:** AIDS/HIV; **Hospital:** Univ Colorado Hosp; **Address:** Univ Colorado Infectious Disease Group, 1635 Aurora Ct, MS B163, P O Box 6510, Aurora, CO 80045; **Phone:** 720-848-0191; **Board Cert:** Internal Medicine 1987; Infectious Disease 2010; **Med School:** Northwestern Univ 1984; **Resid:** Internal Medicine, Fitzsimons Army Med Ctr 1987; **Fellow:** Infectious Disease, Walter Reed Army Med Ctr 1989; **Fac Appt:** Prof Med, Univ Colorado

Southwest

DuPont, Herbert L MD [Inf] - **Spec Exp:** Tropical Diseases; Diarrheal Diseases; Travel Medicine; **Hospital:** St. Luke's Episcopal Hosp-Houston; **Address:** 6720 Bertner Ave, MC 1-164, Houston, TX 77030-1602; **Phone:** 832-355-4122; **Board Cert:** Internal Medicine 1972; **Med School:** Emory Univ 1965; **Resid:** Internal Medicine, Univ Minn Hosps 1967; **Fellow:** Infectious Disease, Univ Maryland Hosp 1969; **Fac Appt:** Clin Prof Med, Baylor Coll Med

Galgiani, John N MD [Inf] - **Spec Exp:** Valley Fever; Infection Control; Fungal Infections; **Hospital:** Univ Arizona Med Ctr-South Campus; **Address:** Valley Fever Ctr, 500 W Thomas Rd, Phoenix, AZ 85013; **Phone:** 602-406-8253; **Board Cert:** Internal Medicine 1978; **Med School:** Northwestern Univ 1972; **Resid:** Internal Medicine, Santa Clara Vly Med Ctr 1974; **Fellow:** Infectious Disease, Stanford Univ Hosp & Clins 1976; **Fac Appt:** Prof Med, Univ Ariz Coll Med

Keiser, Philip H MD [Inf] - **Spec Exp:** AIDS/HIV; International Health; **Hospital:** UT Med Br at Galveston(John Sealy Hosp); **Address:** 301 University Blvd, Galveston, TX 77555; **Phone:** 409-772-2222; **Board Cert:** Internal Medicine 1989; **Med School:** Univ MD Sch Med 1986; **Resid:** Internal Medicine, Francis Scott Key Med Ctr 1989; **Fellow:** Infectious Disease, Univ Maryland 1992; **Fac Appt:** Prof Med, Univ Tex Med Br, Galveston

Luby, James P MD [Inf] - **Spec Exp:** Viral Infections; **Hospital:** Parkland Hlth & Hosp Sys, UT Southwestern Med Ctr at Dallas; **Address:** Univ Tex SW Med Ctr, Div Internal Med, 5303 Harry Hines Blvd, Dallas, TX 75390-9113; **Phone:** 214-645-2800; **Board Cert:** Internal Medicine 1968; Infectious Disease 1972; **Med School:** Northwestern Univ 1961; **Resid:** Internal Medicine, Northwestern Univ 1964; **Fac Appt:** Prof Med, Univ Tex SW, Dallas

Wallace Jr, Richard James MD [Inf] - **Spec Exp:** Non Tuberculous Mycobacteria; Nocardia Infection; **Hospital:** Univ of Texas Hlth Sci Ctr at Tyler; **Address:** 11937 US Hwy 271, Tyler, TX 75708; **Phone:** 903-877-7916; **Board Cert:** Internal Medicine 1975; Infectious Disease 1976; **Med School:** Baylor Coll Med 1972; **Resid:** Internal Medicine, Boston City Hosp 1974; **Fellow:** Infectious Disease, Boston City Hosp 1975; Infectious Disease, Baylor Coll Med 1977

West Coast and Pacific

Ballon-Landa, Gonzalo MD [Inf] - **Spec Exp:** Hospital Acquired Infections; AIDS/HIV; Travel Medicine; **Hospital:** Scripps Mercy Hosp & Med Ctr; **Address:** 4136 Bachman Pl, San Diego, CA 92103; **Phone:** 619-298-1443; **Board Cert:** Internal Medicine 1980; Infectious Disease 1984; **Med School:** Northwestern Univ 1977; **Resid:** Internal Medicine, Evanston Hosp 1981; **Fellow:** Infectious Disease, UCSD Med Ctr 1983

Bayer, Arnold MD [Inf] - **Spec Exp:** Infective Endocarditis; Arthritis-Septic; Coccidioidomycosis; **Hospital:** LAC - Harbor - UCLA Med Ctr, UCLA Ronald Reagan Med Ctr; **Address:** 1124 W Carson St, Torrance, CA 90502; **Phone:** 310-222-6422; **Board Cert:** Internal Medicine 1973; Infectious Disease 1978; **Med School:** Temple Univ 1970; **Resid:** Internal Medicine, Thomas Jefferson Univ Hosp 1972; Internal Medicine, LAC-Harbor UCLA Med Ctr 1974; **Fellow:** Infectious Disease, VA Med Ctr 1976; Infectious Disease, LAC-Harbor UCLA Med Ctr 1977; **Fac Appt:** Prof Med, UCLA

Daar, Eric S MD [Inf] - **Spec Exp:** AIDS/HIV; **Hospital:** LAC - Harbor - UCLA Med Ctr; **Address:** Division of HIV Medicine, Harbor-UCLA Medical Center, 1124 W Carson St., CDCRC 205, Torrance, CA 90502; **Phone:** 424-201-3000 xx7317; **Board Cert:** Internal Medicine 1988; **Med School:** Georgetown Univ 1985; **Resid:** Internal Medicine, Cedars-Sinai Med Ctr 1988; **Fellow:** Infectious Disease, Cedars-Sinai Med Ctr 1991; **Fac Appt:** Prof Med, UCLA-David Geffen Sch Med

Palefsky, Joel M MD [Inf] - **Spec Exp:** AIDS Related Cancers; **Hospital:** UCSF - Mt Zion Med Ctr; **Address:** 1600 Divisadero St Fl 4, San Francisco, CA 94115; **Phone:** 415-353-7100; **Board Cert:** Internal Medicine 1984; Infectious Disease 1988; **Med School:** McGill Univ 1980; **Resid:** Internal Medicine, Royal Victoria Hosp 1984; **Fellow:** Infectious Disease, Stanford U 1988; **Fac Appt:** Prof Med, UCSF

Richman, Douglas D MD [Inf] - **Spec Exp:** AIDS/HIV; **Hospital:** VA San Diego Hlthcre Sys, UCSD Med Ctr; **Address:** UCSD-Stein Clin Rsch Bldg, 9500 Gilman Drive, MC 0679, La Jolla, CA 92093-0679; **Phone:** 858-552-8585 x7439; **Board Cert:** Internal Medicine 1973; Infectious Disease 1976; **Med School:** Stanford Univ 1970; **Resid:** Internal Medicine, Stanford Univ Hosp 1972; **Fellow:** Infectious Disease, NIAID/NIH 1975; Infectious Disease, Beth Israel/Chldns Hosp 1976; **Fac Appt:** Prof Med, UCSD

Schooley, Robert T MD [Inf] - **Spec Exp:** AIDS/HIV; HIV; **Hospital:** UCSD Med Ctr; **Address:** Hillcrest Medical Offices, 4168 Front St, San Diego, CA 92103; **Phone:** 858-822-0216; **Board Cert:** Internal Medicine 1977; **Med School:** Johns Hopkins Univ 1974; **Resid:** Internal Medicine, Johns Hopkins Hosp 1976; **Fellow:** Infectious Disease, Natl Inst Hlth 1979; Infectious Disease, Mass Genl Hosp 1981; **Fac Appt:** Prof Med, UCSD

Wiviott, Lory D MD [Inf] - **Spec Exp:** AIDS/HIV; **Hospital:** CA Pacific Med Ctr-Pacific Campus, CA Pacific Med Ctr - Davies Campus; **Address:** 2100 Webster St, Ste 400, San Francisco, CA 94115; **Phone:** 415-923-3883; **Board Cert:** Internal Medicine 1986; Infectious Disease 2010; **Med School:** Albert Einstein Coll Med 1982; **Resid:** Internal Medicine, Columbia Presby Med Ctr 1985; **Fellow:** Infectious Disease, UCSF Med Ctr 1989; **Fac Appt:** Asst Clin Prof Med, UCSF

THE MOUNT SINAI MEDICAL CENTER

Infectious Diseases

Mount Sinai

One Gustave L. Levy Place
Fifth Avenue and 100th Street
New York, NY 10029-6574

Physician Referral: 1-800-MD-SINAI (637-4624)
www.mountsinai.org

Infectious Diseases – The Mount Sinai Medical Center's **DIVISION OF INFECTIOUS DISEASES** boasts an impressive history of achievement, with our physicians treating conditions that are extremely rare or even unheard of in other parts of the country.

In addition to unrivaled inpatient care, we offer comprehensive outpatient services through our Infectious Disease Faculty Practice as well as two specialty clinics. Our physicians diagnose and treat all types of communicable diseases and deliver state-of-the-art care to patients with HIV and other sexually transmitted diseases (STDs), Lyme disease, influenza, hepatitis, human papillomavirus (HPV), as well as food-borne and diarrheal diseases encountered in the U.S. and abroad.

HIV/AIDS Prevention and Treatment – Mount Sinai Hospital was named a "Designated AIDS Center" by the NYSDOH/AIDS Institute in 1989; as such we provide comprehensive inpatient/outpatient primary medical and nursing care, specialty care, case management services, nutritional counseling, health professional education and training and access to clinical trials. In 2010 Mount Sinai Hospital added the Saint Vincent's Hospital HIV program (Chelsea) to its existing Jack Martin Clinic (East Harlem), creating one of the largest HIV service lines in the State. Together the programs provide HIV primary care and case management services to over 3,000 HIV+ individuals living throughout the five boroughs of New York City. Our locations track the current epidemiology of HIV/AIDS as both neighborhoods have the highest incidence/prevalence of HIV/AIDS in the City. Our patient population represents the current face of HIV/AIDS in the City: African American, Hispanic, undocumented, recently incarcerated, women, adolescents, MSM, and mental illness/substance abuse. The programs both have significant linkages to community based organizations that have solidified a bi-directional referral network for HIV primary care and supplemental support services to meet the needs of the client. Our program has a number of specialty projects now in operation, predominantly supported by City, State, and Federal grants. Some of these projects include:

- Prevention with Positives,
- Sexual/Behavioral Health,
- Non Occupational Post Exposure Prophylaxis
- Women, Infants, Children and Youth (WICY)
- HIV Mental Health Services
- Early Intervention Services
- Care Coordination

In addition to those listed above, we have initiatives in the developmental stages to address HIV transmission as it relates to sexually transmitted infections (STI's). STI's are surrogate markers for HIV infection, and NYC is experiencing an epidemic of such conditions.

Antimicrobial Stewardship Program – The Mount Sinai Antimicrobial Stewardship Program strives to improve patient outcomes, to reduce the burden of antimicrobial resistance, and to save healthcare dollars through a collaborative, multidisciplinary, educational and evidence-based approach. This includes ensuring patients receive appropriate antibiotics, at optimal doses, and for the appropriate duration.

Transplant ID Program – Our Transplant Infectious Diseases Program is dedicated to preventing and managing all infectious diseases in solid organ and bone marrow transplant recipients and works in collaboration with Mount Sinai's Recanati-Miller Transplant Institute and our Bone Marrow Transplant Program to produce excellent outcomes.

HIV Hepatitis C Co-Infection Program – As highly active anti-retroviral therapy has improved and extended the lives of people living with HIV/AIDS, the hepatitis C virus (HCV), and the liver disease it can cause, has become an increasing problem. As the only hospital in the state with a division devoted exclusively to the treatment of liver disease, we offer coordinated multidisciplinary care, and transplants when necessary, to patients co-infected with HIV and HCV.

NeuroAIDS Program – We provide compassionate, comprehensive care to HIV-positive patients with neurological disorders including dementia, neuropathy, brain infections, and disorders of the spinal cord and muscle. HIV can affect any part of the nervous system, such as the brain, spinal cord, nerves, or muscle. Symptoms of neurologic disease in HIV-infected individuals may include memory loss, headache, dizziness, weakness, numbness, pain, vision changes, or trouble walking.

Travel Program – The Mount Sinai Travel Medicine Program is a designated Yellow Fever Center and offers official yellow fever vaccine certificates to both adults and children. As an academic center for travel medicine, Mount Sinai serves as a referral center for patients working for the United Nations and Doctors Without Borders. We provide both pre-travel assessments, including all immunizations, health counseling and prescriptions for travel medications, such as anti-malaria medications, and post-travel care, including evaluation and treatment for any travel-acquired health problems. Customized services for business travelers, NGOs, and others are available. Please call us to discuss your particular travel health concerns and needs. We speak English and Spanish.

Top Doctors Make A Difference

Internal Medicine

A personal physician who provides long-term, comprehensive care in the office and the hospital, managing both common and complex illness of adolescents, adults and the elderly. Internists are trained in the diagnosis and treatment of cancer, infections and diseases affecting the heart, blood, kidneys, joints and digestive, respiratory and vascular systems. They are also trained in the essentials of primary care internal medicine which incorporates an understanding of disease prevention, wellness, substance abuse, mental health and effective treatment of common problems of the eyes, ears, skin, nervous system and reproductive organs.

Note: *Internal Medicine normally includes many primary care physicians. However, for purposes of this directory, no primary care physicians are included.*

Training Required: Three years

Internal Medicine

Mid Atlantic

Cirigliano, Michael D MD [IM] - **Spec Exp:** Complementary Medicine; Preventive Medicine; Women's Health; **Hospital:** Hosp Univ Penn - UPHS (page 69); **Address:** 3701 Market St, Ste 370, Philadelphia, PA 19104; **Phone:** 215-615-3232; **Board Cert:** Internal Medicine 2005; **Med School:** Univ Pennsylvania 1990; **Resid:** Internal Medicine, Hosp Univ Penn 1993; **Fac Appt:** Assoc Prof Med, Univ Pennsylvania

Galland, Leo MD [IM] - **Spec Exp:** Nutrition; Chronic Illness; Complementary Medicine; **Address:** Foundation for Integrated Medicine, 20 Fifth Ave, Ste 1E, New York, NY 10011; **Phone:** 212-989-6733; **Board Cert:** Internal Medicine 1972; **Med School:** NYU Sch Med 1968; **Resid:** Internal Medicine, Bellevue Hosp 1972; **Fellow:** Behavioral Medicine, Univ Conn Hlth Ctr 1981

Rader, Daniel J MD [IM] - **Spec Exp:** Cholesterol/Lipid Disorders; Preventive Cardiology; Metabolic Disorders; **Hospital:** Hosp Univ Penn - UPHS (page 69), Penn Presby Med Ctr - UPHS (page 69); **Address:** Penn Heart & Vascular Ctr, Perelman Ctr for Advanced Medicine, 3400 Civic Center Blvd 2 Fl E Pavilion, Philadelphia, PA 19104; **Phone:** 215-615-4949; **Board Cert:** Internal Medicine 1987; **Med School:** Med Coll PA 1984; **Resid:** Internal Medicine, Yale-New Haven Hosp 1987; **Fellow:** Research, Natl Inst Hlth 1992; **Fac Appt:** Prof Med, Univ Pennsylvania

Selwyn, Peter MD [IM] - **Spec Exp:** AIDS/HIV; Palliative Care; Addiction/Substance Abuse; **Hospital:** Montefiore Med Ctr-Moses Campus, NY; **Address:** Montfiore Family Hlth Ctr, 360 E 193rd St Fl 2, Bronx, NY 10458; **Phone:** 718-933-2400; **Board Cert:** Family Medicine 2005; Hospice & Palliative Medicine 2012; **Med School:** Harvard Med Sch 1981; **Resid:** Family Medicine, Montefiore Med Ctr 1984; **Fac Appt:** Prof Med, Albert Einstein Coll Med

Southeast

Braunstein, Seth N MD/PhD [IM] - **Spec Exp:** Diabetes; Preventive Medicine; **Hospital:** New Hanover Reg Med Ctr; **Address:** Wilmington Health Endocrinology Dept, 1500 Physicians Drive E Bldg, Wilmington, NC 28401; **Phone:** 910-763-6332; **Board Cert:** Internal Medicine 1975; **Med School:** NYU Sch Med 1972; **Resid:** Internal Medicine, Hosp Univ Penn 1975; **Fac Appt:** Clin Prof Med, Univ NC Sch Med

Cushman, William C MD [IM] - **Spec Exp:** Hypertension; Preventive Cardiology; Cholesterol/Lipid Disorders; **Hospital:** VA Med Ctr - Memphis; **Address:** VA Medical Ctr, 1030 Jefferson Ave, Memphis, TN 38104-2127; **Phone:** 901-523-8990 x7357; **Board Cert:** Internal Medicine 1977; **Med School:** Univ Miss 1974; **Resid:** Internal Medicine, Univ Mississippi Med Ctr 1977; **Fac Appt:** Prof Med, Univ Tenn Coll Med

Fischl, Margaret A MD [IM] - **Spec Exp:** Immunotherapy; Infectious Disease; AIDS/HIV; Clinical Trials; **Hospital:** Univ of Miami Hosp, Univ of Miami Hosp & Clins/Sylvester Comp Canc Ctr; **Address:** Univ Miami Hosp, Special Immunology, 1800 NW 10th Ave, Miami, FL 33136; **Phone:** 305-243-3838; **Board Cert:** Internal Medicine 1979; **Med School:** Univ Miami Sch Med 1976; **Resid:** Internal Medicine, Univ Miami Hosp 1979; **Fellow:** Infectious Disease, Univ Miami Hosp 1980; **Fac Appt:** Prof Med, Univ Miami Sch Med

Midwest

Burt, Richard K MD [IM] - **Spec Exp:** Stem Cell Transplant in Lupus/Crohn's; Stem Cell Transplant in MS; Autoimmune Disease; **Hospital:** Northwestern Meml Hosp; **Address:** Northwestern - Div Immunotherapy, 675 N St Clair, Chicago, IL 60611; **Phone:** 312-695-4960; **Board Cert:** Internal Medicine 1989; **Med School:** St Louis Univ 1984; **Resid:** Internal Medicine, Baylor Coll Med 1988; **Fellow:** Hematology & Oncology, Natl Inst of Hlth 1993; **Fac Appt:** Assoc Prof Med, Northwestern Univ

Fischbein, Lewis C MD [IM] - **Spec Exp:** Preventive Medicine; Hypertension; Rheumatology; **Hospital:** Barnes-Jewish Hosp; **Address:** 4921 Parkview Pl, Ste 5G, St Louis, MO 63110; **Phone:** 314-747-1970; **Board Cert:** Internal Medicine 1977; Rheumatology 1980; **Med School:** Washington Univ, St Louis 1974; **Resid:** Internal Medicine, Barnes Jewish Hosp 1977; **Fellow:** Rheumatology, Washington Univ 1979; **Fac Appt:** Assoc Prof Med, Washington Univ, St Louis

Wright Jr, Jackson T MD/PhD [IM] - **Spec Exp:** Hypertension; **Hospital:** UH Case Med Ctr; **Address:** CWRU Div Hypertension, 11100 Euclid Ave, Bolwell Bldg - rm 2200, Cleveland, OH 44106-6053; **Phone:** 216-844-5174; **Board Cert:** Internal Medicine 1980; **Med School:** Univ Pittsburgh 1976; **Resid:** Internal Medicine, Univ Michigan Hosps 1980; **Fac Appt:** Prof Med, Case West Res Univ

Great Plains and Mountains

Mehler, Philip S MD [IM] - **Spec Exp:** Eating Disorders; Substance Abuse; Hypertension; Anorexia Nervosa-Severe; **Hospital:** Denver Health Med Ctr; **Address:** Denver Health Med Ctr, 777 Bannock St, MC 0278, Denver, CO 80204; **Phone:** 303-602-4971; **Board Cert:** Internal Medicine 1989; **Med School:** Univ Colorado 1983; **Resid:** Internal Medicine, Univ Colorado Affil Hosp 1987; **Fac Appt:** Prof Med, Univ Colorado

West Coast and Pacific

Bissell Jr, Dwight M MD [IM] - **Spec Exp:** Porphyria; **Hospital:** UCSF Med Ctr; **Address:** UCSF Med Ctr, Dept Gastroenterology, 350 Parnassus Ave, Ste 300, San Francisco, CA 94117; **Phone:** 415-353-2318; **Board Cert:** Internal Medicine 1974; **Med School:** Harvard Med Sch 1967; **Resid:** Internal Medicine, Boston City Hosp-Harvard 1970; **Fellow:** Gastroenterology, UCSF Med Ctr 1973; **Fac Appt:** Prof Med, UCSF

Rabow, Michael W MD [IM] - **Spec Exp:** Palliative Care; **Hospital:** UCSF - Mt Zion Med Ctr; **Address:** 1545 Divisadero St, General Internal Med Practice, San Francisco, CA 94115; **Phone:** 415-353-7900; **Board Cert:** Internal Medicine 2006; Hospice & Palliative Medicine 2010; **Med School:** UCSF 1993; **Resid:** Internal Medicine, UCSF Med Ctr 1996; **Fellow:** Internal Medicine, UCSF Med Ctr 1997; **Fac Appt:** Clin Prof Med, UCSF

NYU Langone
MEDICAL CENTER

550 First Avenue *(at 31st Street)*
New York, NY 10016

www.NYULMC.org

Physician Referral: **888-7-NYU-MED** *(888-769-8633)*

INTERNAL MEDICINE

Internal medicine physicians at NYU Langone Medical Center are dedicated to treating the whole patient, and not just their disease. Our team addresses both the physical and psychological aspects of health and disease through clear communication and a fully integrated regimen of care. We specialize in the following areas:

Primary and Specialized Healthcare

General Internal Medicine offers a multidisciplinary medical approach to treating illnesses involving the heart, lungs, gastrointestinal tract, joints, bones, muscles, endocrine organs and kidneys. A wide range of laboratory, imaging and advanced diagnostic testing, ranging from throat cultures to the complex mapping of the electrical surface of the heart, is available on-site or by referral. Comprehensive women's healthcare, including cancer screening and osteoporosis prevention and treatment, is also available. We offer a variety of convenient office locations in Manhattan and the surrounding metropolitan area.

Geriatrics

Our geriatric specialists provide comprehensive and multidisciplinary care, consultation and follow-up for elderly patients ranging from prevention and healthy aging to the treatment and care of chronic conditions including dementia, functional impairment and degenerative disorders.

Top Doctors Make A Difference

Maternal & Fetal Medicine

a subspecialty of Obstetrics & Gynecology

An obstetrician/gynecologist possesses special knowledge, skills and professional capability in the medical and surgical care of the female reproductive system and associated disorders. This physician serves as a consultant to other physicians and as a primary physician for women.

Training Required: Four years *plus* two years in clinical practice before certification in obstetrics and gynecology is complete *plus* additional training and examination in maternal-fetal medicine.

MATERNAL & FETAL MEDICINE

New England

Baker, Emily R MD [MF] - **Spec Exp:** Ultrasound; Pregnancy-High Risk; **Hospital:** Dartmouth - Hitchcock Med Ctr; **Address:** Dartmouth-Hitchcock Med Ctr, Dept Ob/Gyn, 1 Medical Center Drive, Lebanon, NH 03756; **Phone:** 603-653-9306; **Board Cert:** Obstetrics & Gynecology 2012; Maternal & Fetal Medicine 2012; **Med School:** Stanford Univ 1986; **Resid:** Obstetrics & Gynecology, Univ Chicago Hosps 1990; Maternal & Fetal Medicine, Univ Washington Med Ctr 1991; **Fellow:** Maternal & Fetal Medicine, St Margaret's Hosp-Tufts Univ 1992; **Fac Appt:** Assoc Prof ObG, Dartmouth Med Sch

Carr, Stephen R MD [MF] - **Spec Exp:** Twin to Twin Transfusion Syndrome (TTTS); Multiple Gestation; Fetal Surgery; **Hospital:** Women & Infants Hosp of RI; **Address:** 101 Dudley St, Division of Maternal-Fetal Medicine, Providence, RI 02905; **Phone:** 401-274-1122 x7448; **Board Cert:** Obstetrics & Gynecology 2012; Maternal & Fetal Medicine 2012; **Med School:** Univ Hawaii JA Burns Sch Med 1982; **Resid:** Obstetrics & Gynecology, Univ Illinois Med Ctr 1986; **Fellow:** Maternal & Fetal Medicine, Brown Univ Affil Hosp 1988; **Fac Appt:** Prof ObG, Brown Univ

Copel, Joshua A MD [MF] - **Spec Exp:** Prenatal Diagnosis; Fetal Echocardiography; Pregnancy-High Risk; Fetal Diagnosis & Therapy; **Hospital:** Yale-New Haven Hosp; **Address:** Yale Maternal/Fetal Medicine, 150 Sargent Drive Fl 2, New Haven, CT 06511; **Phone:** 203-785-5682; **Board Cert:** Obstetrics & Gynecology 2012; Maternal & Fetal Medicine 2012; **Med School:** Tufts Univ 1979; **Resid:** Obstetrics & Gynecology, Hosp Univ Penn 1983; **Fellow:** Maternal & Fetal Medicine, Yale-New Haven Hosp 1986; **Fac Appt:** Prof ObG, Yale Univ

Greene, Michael F MD [MF] - **Spec Exp:** Pregnancy-High Risk; Multiple Gestation; Seizure Disorders & Pregnancy; **Hospital:** Mass Genl Hosp; **Address:** Mass Genl Hosp, Dept Ob/Gyn, 55 Fruit St Yawkey Bldg - Ste 4F, Boston, MA 02114; **Phone:** 617-724-2229; **Board Cert:** Obstetrics & Gynecology 2012; Maternal & Fetal Medicine 2012; **Med School:** SUNY Downstate 1976; **Resid:** Obstetrics & Gynecology, Brigham & Women's Hosp 1980; **Fellow:** Maternal & Fetal Medicine, Brigham & Women's Hosp 1982; **Fac Appt:** Prof ObG, Harvard Med Sch

Norwitz, Errol R MD/PhD [MF] - **Spec Exp:** Diabetes in Pregnancy; Critical Care; Prematurity Prevention; **Hospital:** Tufts Med Ctr; **Address:** Tufts Medical Center, 800 Washington St, Box 324, Boston, MA 02111; **Phone:** 617-636-2382; **Board Cert:** Obstetrics & Gynecology 2012; Maternal & Fetal Medicine 2012; **Med School:** South Africa 1986; **Resid:** Obstetrics & Gynecology, Brigham & Women's Hosp 1996; **Fellow:** Maternal & Fetal Medicine, Brigham & Women's Hosp 1998; **Fac Appt:** Prof ObG, Tufts Univ

Paidas, Michael J MD [MF] - **Spec Exp:** Pregnancy-High Risk; Clotting Disorders in Pregnancy; Miscarriage-Recurrent; **Hospital:** Yale-New Haven Hosp; **Address:** Yale Maternal/Fetal Medicine, 150 Sargent Drive Fl 2, New Haven, CT 06511; **Phone:** 203-785-5682; **Board Cert:** Obstetrics & Gynecology 2012; Maternal & Fetal Medicine 2012; **Med School:** Tufts Univ 1987; **Resid:** Obstetrics & Gynecology, Pennsylvania Hosp 1991; **Fellow:** Maternal & Fetal Medicine, Mount Sinai Med Ctr 1993; **Fac Appt:** Prof ObG, Yale Univ

Riley, Laura E MD [MF] - **Spec Exp:** AIDS/HIV in Pregnancy; Infectious Disease in Pregnancy; Pregnancy-High Risk; **Hospital:** Mass Genl Hosp; **Address:** Mass Genl Hosp, Yawkey Bldg, 32 Fruit St, Ste 4200, Boston, MA 02114; **Phone:** 617-724-2229; **Board Cert:** Obstetrics & Gynecology 2012; Maternal & Fetal Medicine 2012; **Med School:** Univ Pittsburgh 1985; **Resid:** Obstetrics & Gynecology, Univ Pittsburgh Med Ctr 1988; **Fellow:** Maternal & Fetal Medicine, Brigham & Womens Hosp 1991; Infectious Disease, Boston Univ Med Ctr 1993; **Fac Appt:** Assoc Prof ObG, Harvard Med Sch

Robinson, Julian N MD [MF] - **Spec Exp:** Prenatal Diagnosis; Fetal Echocardiography; Amniocentesis; Ultrasound; **Hospital:** Brigham & Women's Hosp; **Address:** Brigham & Women's Hosp, Div Maternal Fetal Medicine, 75 Francis St, Ste 305, Boston, MA 02115; **Phone:** 617-732-4840; **Board Cert:** Obstetrics & Gynecology 2012; Maternal & Fetal Medicine 2012; **Med School:** England, UK 1986; **Resid:** Obstetrics & Gynecology, Eastern VA Med Sch 1997; **Fellow:** Maternal & Fetal Medicine, Brigham & Women's Hosp 1998; **Fac Appt:** Assoc Prof ObG, Harvard Med Sch

Wenstrom, Katharine D MD [MF] - **Spec Exp:** Reproductive Genetics; Pregnancy-High Risk; **Hospital:** Women & Infants Hosp of RI; **Address:** Women's & Infants Hosp RI, Maternal Fetal Medicine Div, 101 Dudley St, Fl 3rd, Providence, RI 02905; **Phone:** 401-274-1122 x7452; **Board Cert:** Obstetrics & Gynecology 2012; Maternal & Fetal Medicine 2012; Clinical Genetics 1990; **Med School:** Case West Res Univ 1983; **Resid:** Obstetrics & Gynecology, Univ Illinois Hosp 1987; **Fellow:** Maternal & Fetal Medicine, Univ Illinois Hosp 1989; Clinical Genetics, Univ Iowa Med Ctr 1990; **Fac Appt:** Prof ObG, Brown Univ

Wilkins-Haug, Louise E MD/PhD [MF] - **Spec Exp:** Fetal Diagnosis & Therapy; Pregnancy-High Risk; Genetic Disorders; Fetal Surgery; **Hospital:** Brigham & Women's Hosp; **Address:** Brigham & Womens Hosp, Div Maternal Fetal Medicine, 75 Francis St, Ste 305, Boston, MA 02115; **Phone:** 617-732-4840; **Board Cert:** Obstetrics & Gynecology 2012; Maternal & Fetal Medicine 2012; **Med School:** Stanford Univ 1985; **Resid:** Obstetrics & Gynecology, Univ Colorado Med Ctr 1989; **Fellow:** Maternal & Fetal Medicine, Brigham & Women's Hosp 1992; **Fac Appt:** Assoc Prof ObG, Harvard Med Sch

Mid Atlantic

Berkowitz, Richard L MD [MF] - **Spec Exp:** Fetal Therapy; Multiple Gestation; Pregnancy & Hematologic Abnormalities; **Hospital:** NY-Presby/Columbia Univ Med Ctr, NY (page 65); **Address:** 5939 Broadway, New York, NY 10032; **Phone:** 212-326-8951; **Board Cert:** Obstetrics & Gynecology 2005; Maternal & Fetal Medicine 2005; **Med School:** NYU Sch Med 1965; **Resid:** Obstetrics & Gynecology, NY Hosp-Cornell Med Ctr 1972; **Fac Appt:** Prof ObG, Columbia P&S

Blakemore, Karin J MD [MF] - **Spec Exp:** Fetal Diagnosis & Therapy; Pregnancy-High Risk; Ultrasound; **Hospital:** Johns Hopkins Hosp (page 59); **Address:** Johns Hopkins Hosp, Dept Maternal/Fetal Med, 600 N Wolfe St Phipps Bldg - rm 228, Baltimore, MD 21287-1228; **Phone:** 410-502-3200; **Board Cert:** Clinical Genetics 1984; Obstetrics & Gynecology 2012; Maternal & Fetal Medicine 2012; **Med School:** Med Coll OH 1978; **Resid:** Obstetrics & Gynecology, NYU Med Ctr 1982; Clinical Genetics, Yale Univ Sch Med 1985; **Fellow:** Maternal & Fetal Medicine, Washington Univ Affil Hosp 1987; **Fac Appt:** Assoc Prof ObG, Johns Hopkins Univ

Caritis, Steve N MD [MF] - **Spec Exp:** Pregnancy-High Risk; **Hospital:** Magee-Womens Hosp - UPMC; **Address:** Magee-Womens Hosp, Dept Maternal/Fetal Med, 300 Halket St, Ste 0610, Pittsburgh, PA 15213-3180; **Phone:** 412-641-6361; **Board Cert:** Obstetrics & Gynecology 1999; Maternal & Fetal Medicine 1999; **Med School:** W VA Univ 1969; **Resid:** Obstetrics & Gynecology, Univ Pittsburgh Med Ctr 1973; **Fellow:** Maternal & Fetal Medicine, Columbia-Presby Med Ctr 1975; **Fac Appt:** Prof ObG, Univ Pittsburgh

Cohen, Arnold W MD [MF] - **Spec Exp:** Pregnancy-High Risk; Diabetes in Pregnancy; **Hospital:** Einstein Med Ctr; **Address:** AEMC 5501 Old York Rd, Klein Building, Ste. 410, Philadelphia, PA 19141; **Phone:** 215-456-6991; **Board Cert:** Obstetrics & Gynecology 1994; Maternal & Fetal Medicine 1982; **Med School:** Cornell Univ 1971; **Resid:** Obstetrics & Gynecology, Hosp Univ Penn 1976; **Fellow:** Maternal & Fetal Medicine, Hosp Univ Penn 1980; **Fac Appt:** Prof ObG, Thomas Jefferson Univ

D'Alton, Mary E MD [MF] - **Spec Exp:** Pregnancy-High Risk; Multiple Gestation; Prenatal Diagnosis; **Hospital:** NY-Presby/Columbia Univ Med Ctr, NY (page 65); **Address:** 51 W 51st St, Ste 320, New York, NY 10019; **Phone:** 212-326-8951; **Board Cert:** Obstetrics & Gynecology 2012; Maternal & Fetal Medicine 2012; **Med School:** Ireland 1976; **Resid:** Obstetrics & Gynecology, Ottowa Genl Hosp 1982; **Fellow:** Maternal & Fetal Medicine, Tufts-New Eng Med Ctr 1984; **Fac Appt:** Clin Prof ObG, Columbia P&S

Dugoff, Lorraine MD [MF] - **Spec Exp:** Pregnancy-High Risk; Prenatal Diagnosis; Ultrasound; Reproductive Genetics; **Hospital:** Hosp Univ Penn - UPHS (page 69); **Address:** 579 Dulles Building, 3400 Spruce St, Philadelphia, PA 19104; **Phone:** 215-615-3739; **Board Cert:** Obstetrics & Gynecology 2012; Maternal & Fetal Medicine 2012; Clinical Genetics 2010; **Med School:** Georgetown Univ 1989; **Resid:** Obstetrics & Gynecology, Philadelphia Hosp 1990; Obstetrics & Gynecology, Univ Colorado Hlth Sci Ctr 1993; **Fellow:** Maternal & Fetal Medicine, Univ Colorado Hlth Sci Ctr 1995; Clinical Genetics, Univ Colorado Hlth Sci Ctr 1996; **Fac Appt:** Assoc Prof ObG, Univ Pennsylvania

Eddleman, Keith A MD [MF] - **Spec Exp:** Obstetric Ultrasound; Pregnancy-High Risk; Fetal Therapy; Reproductive Genetics; **Hospital:** Mt Sinai Med Ctr (page 62); **Address:** 5 E 98th St, Box 1171, New York, NY 10029; **Phone:** 212-241-5681; **Board Cert:** Obstetrics & Gynecology 2012; Maternal & Fetal Medicine 2012; Clinical Genetics 2010; **Med School:** Wake Forest Univ 1985; **Resid:** Obstetrics & Gynecology, George Washington Univ Med Ctr 1989; **Fellow:** Maternal & Fetal Medicine, Mt Sinai Med Ctr 1991; Genetics, NY Presby Hosp/Weill Cornell 1996; **Fac Appt:** Prof ObG, Mount Sinai Sch Med

Fox, Harold E MD [MF] - **Spec Exp:** Pregnancy-High Risk; Prematurity Prevention; Multiple Gestation; **Hospital:** Johns Hopkins Hosp (page 59); **Address:** Johns Hopkins Hosp, Dept Maternal/Fetal Med, 600 N Wolfe St Phipps Bldg - rm 264, Baltimore, MD 21287; **Phone:** 410-614-0178; **Board Cert:** Obstetrics & Gynecology 2012; Maternal & Fetal Medicine 2012; **Med School:** Univ Rochester 1972; **Resid:** Obstetrics & Gynecology, Strong Meml Hosp 1975; **Fellow:** Maternal & Fetal Medicine, Univ Rochester Hosps 1977; **Fac Appt:** Prof ObG, Johns Hopkins Univ

Genc, Mehmet R MD/PhD [MF] - **Spec Exp:** Amniocentesis; Hypertension in Pregnancy; Pregnancy-High Risk; Fetal Abnormalities; **Hospital:** NY-Presby/Weill Cornell Med Ctr, NY (page 65); **Address:** 525 E 68th St, Ste J-130, New York, NY 10065; **Phone:** 212-746-1604; **Board Cert:** Obstetrics & Gynecology 2012; Maternal & Fetal Medicine 2012; **Med School:** Turkey 1994; **Resid:** Obstetrics & Gynecology, NY-Presby/Weill Cornell Med Ctr 2000; **Fellow:** Maternal & Fetal Medicine, NY-Presby/Weill Cornell Med Ctr 2001; Maternal & Fetal Medicine, Brigham & Women's Hosp 2003; **Fac Appt:** Asst Prof ObG, Cornell Univ-Weill Med Coll

Grunebaum, Amos MD [MF] - **Spec Exp:** Pregnancy-High Risk; Amniocentesis; **Hospital:** NY-Presby/Weill Cornell Med Ctr, NY (page 65); **Address:** Dept Obstetrics & Gynecology, 525 E 68th St, Ste J-130, New York, NY 10065; **Phone:** 212-746-0714; **Board Cert:** Obstetrics & Gynecology 2012; Maternal & Fetal Medicine 2012; **Med School:** Germany 1974; **Resid:** Anesthesiology, Maimonides Med Ctr 1978; Obstetrics & Gynecology, Downstate Med Ctr 1982; **Fellow:** Maternal & Fetal Medicine, Downstate Med Ctr 1984; **Fac Appt:** Assoc Prof ObG, Columbia P&S

Landy, Helain J MD [MF] - **Spec Exp:** Pregnancy-High Risk; Miscarriage-Recurrent; Diabetes in Pregnancy; **Hospital:** MedStar Georgetown Univ Hosp, Sibley Mem Hosp; **Address:** Pasquerilla Hlthcare Ctr, 3800 Reservoir Rd NW Fl 3, Washington, DC 20007-2113; **Phone:** 202-444-8801; **Board Cert:** Obstetrics & Gynecology 2012; Maternal & Fetal Medicine 2012; **Med School:** Northwestern Univ 1982; **Resid:** Obstetrics & Gynecology, Pennsylvania Hosp-UPHS 1986; **Fellow:** Maternal & Fetal Medicine, G Washington Univ Hosp 1988; **Fac Appt:** Prof ObG, Georgetown Univ

Parry, Samuel I MD [MF] - **Spec Exp:** Pregnancy-High Risk; Premature Labor; Infections in Pregnancy; Fetal Ultrasound; **Hospital:** Hosp Univ Penn - UPHS (page 69); **Address:** Univ Penn, Dept Maternal & Fetal Med, 3400 Spruce St, 2000 Courtyard Bldg, Philadelphia, PA 19104; **Phone:** 215-662-6913; **Board Cert:** Obstetrics & Gynecology 2012; Maternal & Fetal Medicine 2012; **Med School:** Columbia P&S 1990; **Resid:** Obstetrics & Gynecology, SUNY Buffalo Affil Hosp 1995; **Fellow:** Maternal & Fetal Medicine, Hosp Univ Penn 1997; **Fac Appt:** Assoc Prof ObG, Univ Pennsylvania

Pinckert, Thomas L MD [MF] - **Spec Exp:** Pregnancy-High Risk; Prenatal Diagnosis; **Hospital:** Shady Grove Adven Hosp, Holy Cross Hospital - Silver Spring; **Address:** Greater Washington Maternal-Fetal Med, 9707 Med Ctr Drive, Ste 230, Rockville, MD 20850; **Phone:** 301-279-6060; **Board Cert:** Obstetrics & Gynecology 2012; Clinical Genetics 1990; Maternal & Fetal Medicine 2012; **Med School:** Oregon Hlth & Sci Univ 1979; **Resid:** Obstetrics & Gynecology, David Grant Med Ctr 1983; **Fellow:** Maternal & Fetal Medicine, UCSF Med Ctr 1989; Clinical Genetics, UCSF Med Ctr 1990; **Fac Appt:** Clin Prof ObG, Geo Wash Univ

Plante, Lauren A MD [MF] - **Spec Exp:** Pregnancy-High Risk; Diabetes in Pregnancy; **Hospital:** Hahnemann Univ Hosp; **Address:** Drexel Med Ctr, Women's Care, Dept Genetics & Fetal Med, 1427 Vine St Fl 7, Philadelphia, PA 19102; **Phone:** 215-762-7824; **Board Cert:** Anesthesiology 2004; Critical Care Medicine 1993; Obstetrics & Gynecology 2011; Maternal & Fetal Medicine 2012; **Med School:** Albert Einstein Coll Med 1984; **Resid:** Anesthesiology, Montefiore Med Ctr 1989; Obstetrics & Gynecology, Hahnemann Univ Hosp 1996; **Fellow:** Critical Care Medicine, Montefiore Med Ctr 1991; Maternal & Fetal Medicine, Temple Univ Med Ctr 1998; **Fac Appt:** Assoc Prof ObG, Hahnemann Univ

Repke, John T MD [MF] - **Spec Exp:** Pregnancy-High Risk; Hypertension in Pregnancy; Women's Health; **Hospital:** Penn State Milton S Hershey Med Ctr; **Address:** MS Hershey Med Ctr Maternal Fetal Med, 500 University Drive, Hershey, PA 17033; **Phone:** 717-531-3503 x4; **Board Cert:** Obstetrics & Gynecology 2012; Maternal & Fetal Medicine 2012; **Med School:** NY Med Coll 1978; **Resid:** Obstetrics & Gynecology, Johns Hopkins Hosp 1982; **Fellow:** Maternal & Fetal Medicine, Johns Hopkins Hosp 1984; **Fac Appt:** Prof ObG, Penn State Coll Med

Thomas, Ronald L MD [MF] - **Spec Exp:** Pregnancy-High Risk; **Hospital:** West Penn Hosp; **Address:** Federal North Bldg, 1307 Federal St, Ste B100, Pittsburgh, PA 15212; **Phone:** 412-359-3437; **Board Cert:** Obstetrics & Gynecology 2012; Maternal & Fetal Medicine 2012; **Med School:** Univ Pittsburgh 1981; **Resid:** Obstetrics & Gynecology, Natl Naval Ctr 1985; **Fellow:** Maternal & Fetal Medicine, Johns Hopkins Hosp 1988; **Fac Appt:** Assoc Prof ObG, Drexel Univ Coll Med

Wapner, Ronald J MD [MF] - **Spec Exp:** Perinatal Medicine; Genetic Disorders; Multiple Gestation; Vomiting-Cyclic; **Hospital:** NY-Presby/Columbia Univ Med Ctr, NY (page 65); **Address:** Div Maternal/Fetal Medicine, 51 W 51st St, Ste 320, New York, NY 10019; **Phone:** 212-326-8951; **Board Cert:** Obstetrics & Gynecology 2000; Maternal & Fetal Medicine 2000; Clinical Genetics 2010; **Med School:** Jefferson Med Coll 1972; **Resid:** Obstetrics & Gynecology, Jefferson Univ Hosp 1976; **Fellow:** Maternal & Fetal Medicine, Jefferson Med Coll 1978; **Fac Appt:** Prof ObG, Columbia P&S

Witter, Frank R MD [MF] - **Spec Exp:** Pregnancy-High Risk; Multiple Gestation; Lupus/SLE in Pregnancy; **Hospital:** Johns Hopkins Hosp (page 59), Johns Hopkins Bayview Med Ctr (page 59); **Address:** 600 N Wolfe St, Nelson 2170, Baltimore, MD 21287; **Phone:** 410-502-3200; **Board Cert:** Obstetrics & Gynecology 2012; Maternal & Fetal Medicine 2012; **Med School:** Univ Chicago-Pritzker Sch Med 1976; **Resid:** Obstetrics & Gynecology, Johns Hopkins Hosp 1980; **Fellow:** Maternal & Fetal Medicine, Johns Hopkins Hosp 1982; Clinical Pharmacology, Johns Hopkins Hosp 1984; **Fac Appt:** Prof ObG, Johns Hopkins Univ

Southeast

Abuhamad, Alfred Z MD [MF] - **Spec Exp:** Twin to Twin Transfusion Syndrome (TTTS); Prenatal Diagnosis; Prenatal Ultrasound; Multiple Gestation; **Hospital:** Sentara Norfolk Genl Hosp; **Address:** E VA Med Sch, Div Mat Fetal Med, 825 Fairfax Ave, Ste 310, Norfolk, VA 23507; **Phone:** 757-446-7900; **Board Cert:** Obstetrics & Gynecology 2012; Maternal & Fetal Medicine 2012; **Med School:** Amer Univ Beirut 1985; **Resid:** Obstetrics & Gynecology, Jackson Meml Hosp 1989; **Fellow:** Maternal & Fetal Medicine, Jackson Meml Hosp-Univ Miami 1991; Ultrasound, Yale Univ 1991; **Fac Appt:** Prof ObG, Eastern VA Med Sch

Andrews, William W MD/PhD [MF] - **Spec Exp:** Infectious Disease; Prematurity/Low Birth Weight Infants; **Hospital:** UAB Hosp; **Address:** UAB Dept Obstetrics & Gynecology, 619 19th St S, 176F, rm 10360, Birmingham, AL 35233; **Phone:** 205-934-7330; **Board Cert:** Obstetrics & Gynecology 2012; Maternal & Fetal Medicine 2012; **Med School:** UAB Sch Med 1984; **Resid:** Obstetrics & Gynecology, UAB Hosp 1988; **Fellow:** Maternal & Fetal Medicine, Univ Texas SW Affil Hosp 1990

Duff, William P MD [MF] - **Spec Exp:** Pregnancy-High Risk; Infections in Pregnancy; **Hospital:** UF Hlth Shands Hosp; **Address:** UF Hlth, Womens Ctr, 4037 NW 86th Terr, Gainesville, FL 32606; **Phone:** 352-265-6200; **Board Cert:** Obstetrics & Gynecology 2003; Maternal & Fetal Medicine 2003; **Med School:** Georgetown Univ 1974; **Resid:** Obstetrics & Gynecology, Walter Reed Natl Military Med Ctr 1978; **Fellow:** Maternal & Fetal Medicine, Univ Hosp 1983; **Fac Appt:** Prof ObG, Univ S Fla Coll Med

Ferguson II, James E MD [MF] - **Spec Exp:** Pregnancy-High Risk; Ultrasound; Premature Labor; **Hospital:** Univ of Virginia Hlth Sys; **Address:** Dept Ob/Gyn, Univ Virginia Sch Med, Box 800712, Charlottesville, VA 22908-0712; **Phone:** 434-924-9937; **Board Cert:** Obstetrics & Gynecology 2012; Maternal & Fetal Medicine 2012; **Med School:** Wake Forest Univ 1977; **Resid:** Obstetrics & Gynecology, Stanford Univ Med Ctr 1980; Obstetrics & Gynecology, Wake Forest Univ Med Ctr 1981; **Fellow:** Maternal & Fetal Medicine, Stanford Univ Med Ctr 1984; **Fac Appt:** Prof ObG, Univ VA Sch Med

Grandis, Arnold MD/PhD [MF] - **Spec Exp:** Pregnancy-High Risk; **Hospital:** Wake Forest Baptist Med Ctr; **Address:** 500 Shepherd St, Ste 200, Winston-Salem, NC 27103; **Phone:** 336-716-6893; **Board Cert:** Obstetrics & Gynecology 1980; Maternal & Fetal Medicine 1982; **Med School:** Univ Pennsylvania 1974; **Resid:** Obstetrics & Gynecology, Duke Univ Med Ctr 1978; **Fellow:** Maternal & Fetal Medicine, Duke Univ Sch Med 1980; **Fac Appt:** Assoc Prof ObG, Wake Forest Univ

Heyl, Peter S MD [MF] - **Spec Exp:** Pregnancy-High Risk; **Hospital:** Univ of Louisville Hosp; **Address:** Louisville Outpatient Ctr, 401 E Chestnut St, Ste 410, Louisville, KY 40202; **Phone:** 502-271-5999; **Board Cert:** Obstetrics & Gynecology 2012; Maternal & Fetal Medicine 2012; **Med School:** Wake Forest Univ 1976; **Resid:** Obstetrics & Gynecology, Brigham & Women's Hosp 1981; **Fellow:** Maternal & Fetal Medicine, Brigham & Women's Hosp 1983; **Fac Appt:** Assoc Prof ObG, Univ Louisville Sch Med

Kuller, Jeffrey MD [MF] - **Spec Exp:** Prenatal Diagnosis; **Hospital:** Duke Univ Hosp; **Address:** 2406 Blue Ridge Rd, Ste 200, Raleigh, NC 27607; **Phone:** 919-783-4299; **Board Cert:** Obstetrics & Gynecology 2012; Clinical Genetics 2010; Maternal & Fetal Medicine 2012; **Med School:** Univ Cincinnati 1984; **Resid:** Obstetrics & Gynecology, Johns Hopkins Hosp 1988; **Fellow:** Maternal & Fetal Medicine, UPMC Affil Hosp 1990; Medical Genetics, UCSF Med Ctr 1992; **Fac Appt:** Prof ObG, Duke Univ

Mari, Giancarlo MD [MF] - **Spec Exp:** Fetal Therapy; Obstetric Ultrasound; Pregnancy-High Risk; **Hospital:** Le Bonheur Chldns Med Ctr; **Address:** Le Bonheur Children's Hospital, 51 N Dunlap St, Ste 305, Memphis, TN 38105; **Phone:** 901-287-6981; **Board Cert:** Obstetrics & Gynecology 2012; Maternal & Fetal Medicine 2012; **Med School:** Italy 1982; **Resid:** Obstetrics & Gynecology, Yale New Haven Hosp 1994; **Fellow:** Maternal & Fetal Medicine, Yale New Haven Hosp 1996; **Fac Appt:** Prof ObG, Univ Tenn Coll Med

McLaren, Rodney A MD [MF] - **Spec Exp:** Prenatal Diagnosis; Amniocentesis; Pregnancy-High Risk; **Address:** 4001 Fair Ridge Drive, Ste 304, Fairfax, VA 22033; **Phone:** 703-359-2466; **Board Cert:** Obstetrics & Gynecology 2012; Maternal & Fetal Medicine 2012; **Med School:** Tufts Univ 1983; **Resid:** Obstetrics & Gynecology, LI Coll Hosp 1987; **Fellow:** Maternal & Fetal Medicine, Georgetown Univ 1989; **Fac Appt:** Assoc Prof ObG, Georgetown Univ

Nies, Barbara MD [MF] - **Spec Exp:** Pregnancy-High Risk; Amniocentesis; **Hospital:** Inova Fairfax Hosp, Inova Fair Oaks Hosp; **Address:** 3020 Hamaker Ct, Ste 501, Fairfax, VA 22031; **Phone:** 703-698-5350; **Board Cert:** Obstetrics & Gynecology 2009; Maternal & Fetal Medicine 2009; **Med School:** Mich State Univ 1984; **Resid:** Obstetrics & Gynecology, Univ Conn Med Ctr 1988; **Fellow:** Maternal & Fetal Medicine, George Washington Univ Med Ctr 1990

Thorp Jr, John M MD [MF] - **Spec Exp:** Multiple Gestation; Premature Labor; **Hospital:** NC Memorial Hosp - UNC; **Address:** UNC School of Medicine, Obstetrics/Gynecology, 3027 Old Clinic Bldg, CB 7570, Chapel Hill, NC 27599; **Phone:** 919-966-2131; **Board Cert:** Obstetrics & Gynecology 2012; Maternal & Fetal Medicine 2012; **Med School:** E Carolina Univ 1983; **Resid:** Obstetrics & Gynecology, Univ NC Hosp 1987; **Fellow:** Maternal & Fetal Medicine, Univ NC Hosp 1989; **Fac Appt:** Prof ObG, Univ NC Sch Med

Van Dorsten, J Peter MD [MF] - **Spec Exp:** Pregnancy-High Risk; **Hospital:** MUSC Med Ctr, McLeod Reg Med Ctr; **Address:** MUSC Med Ctr, Dept Ob Gyn, 96 Jonathan Lucas St, Ste 634 MSC619, Charleston, SC 29425; **Phone:** 843-792-4509; **Board Cert:** Obstetrics & Gynecology 2008; Maternal & Fetal Medicine 2008; **Med School:** Univ NC Sch Med 1971; **Resid:** Obstetrics & Gynecology, Med Univ SC Hosp 1976; **Fellow:** Maternal & Fetal Medicine, USC-LAC Hosp 1981; **Fac Appt:** Prof ObG, Med Univ SC

Midwest

Bahado-Singh, Ray O MD [MF] - **Spec Exp:** Pregnancy-High Risk; Genetic Disorders; Obstetric Ultrasound; Twin to Twin Transfusion Syndrome (TTTS); **Hospital:** Beaumont Hosp-Royal Oak; **Address:** Beaumont Ob/Gyn, 3535 W 13 Mile Rd, Med Office Bldg - rm 233, Royal Oak, MI 48073; **Phone:** 248-551-1470; **Board Cert:** Obstetrics & Gynecology 2007; Maternal & Fetal Medicine 2007; Clinical Genetics 2010; **Med School:** Jamaica 1979; **Resid:** Obstetrics & Gynecology, Metropolitan Hosp 1985; **Fellow:** Perinatal Medicine, UC Irvine Med Ctr 1987; Clinical Genetics, Yale-New Haven Hosp 1993; **Fac Appt:** Prof ObG, Oakland Univ-William Beaumont Med Sch

Bartelsmeyer, James A MD [MF] - **Spec Exp:** Pregnancy-High Risk; Multiple Gestation; **Hospital:** Mercy Hosp - St Louis; **Address:** 621 S New Ballas Rd, Ste 2007B, St Louis, MO 63141; **Phone:** 314-991-5000; **Board Cert:** Obstetrics & Gynecology 2012; Maternal & Fetal Medicine 2012; **Med School:** Univ IL Coll Med 1985; **Resid:** Obstetrics & Gynecology, Univ Illinois Affil Hosps 1989; **Fellow:** Maternal & Fetal Medicine, Barnes Hosp-Univ Wash 1991; **Fac Appt:** Assoc Prof ObG, Washington Univ, St Louis

Dooley, Sharon L MD [MF] - **Spec Exp:** Fetal Abnormalities; Pregnancy-High Risk; Multiple Gestation; **Hospital:** Northwestern Meml Hosp; **Address:** 675 N St Clair Fl 14 - Ste 200, Chicago, IL 60611; **Phone:** 312-695-7542; **Board Cert:** Obstetrics & Gynecology 2005; Maternal & Fetal Medicine 2005; **Med School:** Univ VA Sch Med 1973; **Resid:** Obstetrics & Gynecology, Northwestern Meml Hosp 1977; **Fac Appt:** Prof ObG, Northwestern Univ

Gonik, Bernard MD [MF] - **Spec Exp:** Infectious Disease in Pregnancy; Prenatal Diagnosis; Vaccinations in Pregnancy; **Hospital:** Detroit Med Ctr, Sinai-Grace Hosp; **Address:** DMC Hutzel Women's Hosp, 3990 John R, MS 163, Detroit, MI 48201; **Phone:** 313-993-1375; **Board Cert:** Obstetrics & Gynecology 2012; Maternal & Fetal Medicine 2012; **Med School:** Mich State Univ 1978; **Resid:** Obstetrics & Gynecology, Univ Texas Affil Hosp 1982; **Fellow:** Maternal & Fetal Medicine, Univ Texas 1985; **Fac Appt:** Prof ObG, Wayne State Univ

Goodman, Jean R MD [MF] - **Spec Exp:** Diabetes in Pregnancy; Prenatal Diagnosis; Prenatal Ultrasound; Pregnancy-High Risk; **Hospital:** Loyola Univ Med Ctr; **Address:** Loyola Univ Med Ctr-Maternal/Fetal Med, 2160 S First Ave, Maywood, IL 60153; **Phone:** 708-216-4033; **Board Cert:** Obstetrics & Gynecology 2012; Maternal & Fetal Medicine 2012; **Med School:** Georgetown Univ 1983; **Resid:** Obstetrics & Gynecology, Univ Miami/Jackson Meml Hosp 1987; **Fellow:** Maternal & Fetal Medicine, Univ Miami/Jackson Meml Hosp 1989; **Fac Appt:** Prof ObG, Loyola Univ-Stritch Sch Med

Hibbard, Judith MD [MF] - **Spec Exp:** Pregnancy-High Risk; Heart Disease in Pregnancy; Prenatal Diagnosis; Ultrasound; **Hospital:** Univ of IL Med Ctr at Chicago; **Address:** 1801 W Taylor St, Ste 4C, Chicago, IL 60612; **Phone:** 312-413-7500; **Board Cert:** Obstetrics & Gynecology 2012; Maternal & Fetal Medicine 2012; **Med School:** Loyola Univ-Stritch Sch Med 1982; **Resid:** Obstetrics & Gynecology, Univ Chicago Hosps 1986; **Fellow:** Maternal & Fetal Medicine, Univ Chicago Hosps 1988; **Fac Appt:** Prof ObG, Univ IL Coll Med

Hussey, Michael J MD [MF] - **Spec Exp:** Prenatal Diagnosis; Multiple Gestation; **Hospital:** Central DuPage Hosp; **Address:** Cadence Physician Group, 25 N Winfield Rd, Winfield, IL 60190; **Phone:** 630-933-6091; **Board Cert:** Obstetrics & Gynecology 2012; Maternal & Fetal Medicine 2012; **Med School:** Univ IL Coll Med 1986; **Resid:** Obstetrics & Gynecology, Loyola Univ Med Ctr 1993; **Fellow:** Maternal & Fetal Medicine, Rush-Presby-St Lukes Hosp 1995; Ultrasound, Univ Col Hlth Sci Ctr 1996

Ismail, Mahmoud A MD [MF] - **Spec Exp:** Pregnancy-High Risk; Perinatal Medicine; Infections-Neonatal; Infections in Pregnancy; **Hospital:** Univ of Chicago Med; **Address:** Univ Chicago, Dept Ob/Gyn, 5841 S Maryland Ave, MC 2050, Chicago, IL 60637-1463; **Phone:** 773-702-5200; **Board Cert:** Obstetrics & Gynecology 2012; Maternal & Fetal Medicine 2012; **Med School:** Egypt 1970; **Resid:** Obstetrics & Gynecology, Wayne St Univ Affil Hosps 1977; **Fellow:** Maternal & Fetal Medicine, Univ Chicago Hosps 1982; **Fac Appt:** Prof ObG, Univ Chicago-Pritzker Sch Med

Johnson, Timothy R B MD [MF] - **Spec Exp:** Prenatal Diagnosis; **Hospital:** Univ Michigan Med Ctr; **Address:** Univ Mich, Dept Ob/Gyn, 1500 E Medical Ctr Drive, rm L4000, Ann Arbor, MI 48109; **Phone:** 734-764-8123; **Board Cert:** Obstetrics & Gynecology 2001; Maternal & Fetal Medicine 2001; **Med School:** Univ VA Sch Med 1975; **Resid:** Obstetrics & Gynecology, Univ Michigan Med Ctr 1979; **Fellow:** Maternal & Fetal Medicine, Johns Hopkins Hosp 1981; **Fac Appt:** Prof ObG, Univ Mich Med Sch

Landers, Daniel V MD [MF] - **Spec Exp:** Infectious Disease; **Hospital:** Univ Minn Med Ctr, Fairview - West Bank Campus; **Address:** Univ Minn Maternal & Fetal Med Ctr, 606 24th Ave S Prof Bldg Fl 4, Minneapolis, MN 55454; **Phone:** 612-273-2223; **Board Cert:** Obstetrics & Gynecology 2012; Maternal & Fetal Medicine 2012; **Med School:** UCSF 1980; **Resid:** Obstetrics & Gynecology, UCSF Med Ctr 1984; **Fellow:** Maternal & Fetal Medicine, UCSF Med Ctr 1986; Infectious Disease, UCSF Med Ctr 1988; **Fac Appt:** Prof ObG, Univ Minn

Landon, Mark B MD [MF] - **Spec Exp:** Diabetes in Pregnancy; **Hospital:** OSU Wexner Med Ctr; **Address:** 2050 Kenny Rd Fl 5, Columbus, OH 43221; **Phone:** 614-293-2222; **Board Cert:** Obstetrics & Gynecology 2012; Maternal & Fetal Medicine 2012; **Med School:** Cornell Univ-Weill Med Coll 1980; **Resid:** Obstetrics & Gynecology, Hosp Univ Penn 1984; **Fellow:** Maternal & Fetal Medicine, Hosp Univ Penn 1986; **Fac Appt:** Assoc Prof ObG, Ohio State Univ

Leslie, Kimberly K MD [MF] - **Spec Exp:** Uterine Cancer; **Hospital:** Univ Iowa Hosp & Clins; **Address:** Univ Iowa Hosp & Clins, 200 Hawkins Drive, Iowa City, IA 52242; **Phone:** 319-356-1976; **Board Cert:** Obstetrics & Gynecology 2012; Maternal & Fetal Medicine 2012; **Med School:** Univ Tex SW, Dallas 1981; **Resid:** Obstetrics & Gynecology, Georgetown Univ Med Ctr 1983; **Fellow:** Maternal & Fetal Medicine, Georgetown Univ Med Ctr 1987; **Fac Appt:** Prof ObG, Univ Iowa Coll Med

MacGregor, Scott N DO [MF] - **Spec Exp:** Pregnancy-High Risk; Prematurity Prevention; Fetal Diagnosis & Therapy; **Hospital:** Evanston Hosp/NorthShore Univ Hlth Sys (page 67); **Address:** NorthShore Medical Group, 2650 Ridge Ave, Evanston, IL 60201; **Phone:** 847-570-2280; **Med School:** Chicago Coll Osteo Med 1981; **Resid:** Obstetrics & Gynecology, Chicago Coll Of Osteopathic Med 1985; **Fellow:** Maternal & Fetal Medicine, Northwestern Meml Hosp 1987; **Fac Appt:** Assoc Prof ObG, Northwestern Univ

Macones, George A MD [MF] - **Spec Exp:** Pregnancy-High Risk; Premature Labor; **Hospital:** Barnes-Jewish Hosp, St. Louis Chldns Hosp; **Address:** 4921 Parkview Pl Fl 5th - Ste A, St Louis, MO 63110; **Phone:** 314-747-1336; **Board Cert:** Obstetrics & Gynecology 2013; Maternal & Fetal Medicine 2013; **Med School:** Jefferson Med Coll 1988; **Resid:** Obstetrics & Gynecology, Pennsylvania Hosp 1992; **Fellow:** Maternal & Fetal Medicine, Jefferson Univ Hosp 1994; **Fac Appt:** Prof ObG, Washington Univ, St Louis

Philipson, Elliot MD [MF] - **Spec Exp:** Pregnancy-High Risk; Amniocentesis; **Hospital:** Cleveland Clin (page 55), Hillcrest Hosp-Mayfield Hts; **Address:** Hillcrest Hosp, Dept OB/Gyn, 6770 Mayfield Rd, Ste 426, Mayfield Heights, OH 44124; **Phone:** 440-312-7774; **Board Cert:** Obstetrics & Gynecology 2012; Maternal & Fetal Medicine 2012; **Med School:** Italy 1975; **Resid:** Obstetrics & Gynecology, Albany Med Ctr 1980; **Fellow:** Maternal & Fetal Medicine, Metro Genl Hosp 1982; **Fac Appt:** Assoc Prof ObG, Cleveland Cl Coll Med/Case West Res

Samuels, Philip MD [MF] - **Spec Exp:** Epilepsy in Pregnancy; Hypertension in Pregnancy; Pregnancy & Hematologic Abnormalities; **Hospital:** OSU Wexner Med Ctr; **Address:** 2050 Kenny Rd Fl 5, Columbus, OH 43221; **Phone:** 614-293-2222; **Board Cert:** Obstetrics & Gynecology 2012; Maternal & Fetal Medicine 2012; **Med School:** Texas Tech Univ 1980; **Resid:** Obstetrics & Gynecology, E VA Grad Sch Med 1984; **Fellow:** Maternal & Fetal Medicine, Hosp Univ Penn 1986; **Fac Appt:** Assoc Prof ObG, Ohio State Univ

Silver, Richard K MD [MF] - **Spec Exp:** Pregnancy-High Risk; Fetal Diagnosis & Therapy; **Hospital:** Evanston Hosp/NorthShore Univ Hlth Sys (page 67); **Address:** Evanston Hospital - Northshore Med Grp, 2650 Ridge Ave, Walgreen Bldg - Ste 1507, Evanston, IL 60201; **Phone:** 847-570-2860; **Board Cert:** Obstetrics & Gynecology 2012; Maternal & Fetal Medicine 2012; **Med School:** Northwestern Univ 1981; **Resid:** Obstetrics & Gynecology, Univ Tex Hlth Scis Ctr 1986; **Fellow:** Maternal & Fetal Medicine, McGaw Med Ctr/Northwestern Univ 1988; **Fac Appt:** Clin Prof Med, Univ Chicago-Pritzker Sch Med

Socol, Michael MD [MF] - **Spec Exp:** Diabetes in Pregnancy; Multiple Gestation; Premature Labor; **Hospital:** Northwestern Meml Hosp; **Address:** 675 N St Clair St Fl 14 - Ste 200, Chicago, IL 60611-3056; **Phone:** 312-695-7542; **Board Cert:** Obstetrics & Gynecology 1989; Maternal & Fetal Medicine 1981; **Med School:** Univ IL Coll Med 1974; **Resid:** Obstetrics & Gynecology, Univ Illinois Med Ctr 1977; **Fellow:** Maternal & Fetal Medicine, USC Med Ctr 1979; **Fac Appt:** Prof ObG, Northwestern Univ

Strassner, Howard T MD [MF] - **Spec Exp:** Pregnancy-High Risk; Amniocentesis; Obstetric Ultrasound; **Hospital:** Rush Univ Med Ctr, Presence St Joseph Hosp; **Address:** Women's Hlth Consultants, 1725 W Harrison St, Ste 408, Chicago, IL 60612; **Phone:** 312-997-2229; **Board Cert:** Obstetrics & Gynecology 2012; Maternal & Fetal Medicine 2012; **Med School:** Univ Chicago-Pritzker Sch Med 1974; **Resid:** Obstetrics & Gynecology, Columbia Presby Med Ctr 1978; **Fellow:** Maternal & Fetal Medicine, LA Co-USC Med Ctr 1980; **Fac Appt:** Prof ObG, Rush Med Coll

Treadwell, Marjorie C MD [MF] - **Spec Exp:** Ultrasound; Pregnancy-High Risk; Fetal Diagnosis & Therapy; **Hospital:** Univ Michigan Med Ctr; **Address:** 1500 E Med Ctr Drive, F4806 MOTT Bldg, Ann Arbor, MI 48109-0264; **Phone:** 734-763-4264; **Board Cert:** Obstetrics & Gynecology 2012; Maternal & Fetal Medicine 2012; **Med School:** Univ Mich Med Sch 1984; **Resid:** Obstetrics & Gynecology, Wayne State Univ 1988; **Fellow:** Maternal & Fetal Medicine, Wayne State Univ 1990; **Fac Appt:** Prof ObG, Univ Mich Med Sch

Winn, Hung N MD [MF] - **Spec Exp:** Multiple Gestation; Pregnancy-High Risk; **Hospital:** Univ of Missouri Hlth Care; **Address:** 500 N Keene St, Ste 406, Columbia, MO 65201; **Phone:** 573-499-6041; **Board Cert:** Obstetrics & Gynecology 2012; Maternal & Fetal Medicine 2012; **Med School:** Univ IL Coll Med 1982; **Resid:** Obstetrics & Gynecology, Univ Ill Hosp 1986; **Fellow:** Maternal & Fetal Medicine, Yale-New Haven Hosp 1988; **Fac Appt:** Prof ObG, Univ MO-Columbia Sch Med

Great Plains and Mountains

Gibbs, Ronald S MD [MF] - **Spec Exp:** Pregnancy-High Risk; Women's Health; Infectious Disease in Pregnancy; **Hospital:** Univ Colorado Hosp; **Address:** Univ Colorado Womens Services, 1635 Aurora Court, MS F711, Aurora, CO 80045; **Phone:** 720-848-1060; **Board Cert:** Obstetrics & Gynecology 1989; Maternal & Fetal Medicine 1981; **Med School:** Univ Pennsylvania 1969; **Resid:** Obstetrics & Gynecology, Hosp Univ Penn 1974; **Fellow:** Maternal & Fetal Medicine, Univ Tex Hlth Sci Ctr 1978; **Fac Appt:** Prof ObG, Univ Colorado

Tomich, Paul G MD [MF] - **Spec Exp:** Pregnancy-High Risk; Prenatal Ultrasound; **Hospital:** Nebraska Med Ctr; **Address:** Olson Ctr for Women's Hlth, 4400 Emile St, Omaha, NE 68198-3255; **Phone:** 402-559-4500; **Board Cert:** Obstetrics & Gynecology 2012; Maternal & Fetal Medicine 2012; **Med School:** Loyola Univ-Stritch Sch Med 1973; **Resid:** Obstetrics & Gynecology, Mayo Clinic 1978; **Fellow:** Maternal & Fetal Medicine, Barnes Hosp-Wash Univ 1980; **Fac Appt:** Prof ObG, Univ Nebr Coll Med

Southwest

Adam, Karolina MD [MF] - **Spec Exp:** Pregnancy-High Risk; Heart Disease in Pregnancy; **Hospital:** Methodist Hosp - Houston, Texas Chldns Hosp; **Address:** Houston Perinatal Assocs, 7900 Fannin St, Ste 2600, Houston, TX 77054; **Phone:** 713-791-9700; **Board Cert:** Obstetrics & Gynecology 2012; Maternal & Fetal Medicine 2012; **Med School:** Med Coll PA 1983; **Resid:** Obstetrics & Gynecology, Baylor Affil Hosp 1987; **Fellow:** Maternal & Fetal Medicine, Baylor Affil Hosp 1989

Hankins, Gary DV MD [MF] - **Spec Exp:** Pregnancy-High Risk; Hypertension in Pregnancy; **Hospital:** UT Med Br at Galveston(John Sealy Hosp); **Address:** UTMB, Maternal & Fetal Med Dept, 301 University Blvd, rm 3.400, Galveston, TX 77555; **Phone:** 409-772-1957; **Board Cert:** Obstetrics & Gynecology 2000; Maternal & Fetal Medicine 2000; **Med School:** Med Coll VA 1977; **Resid:** Obstetrics & Gynecology, Wilford Hall Med Ctr 1981; **Fellow:** Critical Care Medicine, Wilford Hall Med Ctr 1982; Maternal & Fetal Medicine, Parkland Hosp 1984; **Fac Appt:** Prof ObG, Univ Tex Med Br, Galveston

Mastrobattista, Joan M MD [MF] - **Spec Exp:** Ultrasound; Prenatal Diagnosis; Pregnancy-High Risk; **Hospital:** Texas Chldns Hosp; **Address:** UT Hlth, Maternal & Fetal Ctr, 16605 Southwest Freeway, Ste 500, Sugarland, TX 77479; **Phone:** 832-828-3150; **Board Cert:** Obstetrics & Gynecology 2012; Maternal & Fetal Medicine 2012; **Med School:** UMDNJ-NJ Med Sch, Newark 1988; **Resid:** Obstetrics & Gynecology, NY-Presby/Weill Cornell Med Ctr 1992; **Fellow:** Maternal & Fetal Medicine, Univ Genl Hosp 1994; **Fac Appt:** Prof ObG, Baylor Coll Med

Pridjian, Gabriella C MD [MF] - **Spec Exp:** Pregnancy-High Risk; Prenatal Diagnosis; Genetic Disorders; Prenatal Ultrasound; **Hospital:** Tulane-Lakeside Hosp, Tulane Med Ctr; **Address:** Tulane Womens Hlth Ctr, 4720 S I-10 Service Road, Ste 302, Metairie, LA 70001; **Phone:** 504-988-8070; **Board Cert:** Obstetrics & Gynecology 2012; Maternal & Fetal Medicine 2012; Clinical Genetics 2010; **Med School:** Med Coll Wisc 1982; **Resid:** Obstetrics & Gynecology, Univ Chicago Affil Hosp 1986; **Fellow:** Maternal & Fetal Medicine, Univ Chicago Affil Hosp 1989; Clinical Genetics, Hayward Genetics Ctr/Tulane Univ 1994; **Fac Appt:** Prof ObG, Tulane Univ

Reed, Kathryn L MD [MF] - **Spec Exp:** Prenatal Diagnosis; Ultrasound; Fetal Echocardiography; **Hospital:** Univ Arizona Med Ctr-Univ Campus; **Address:** Univ AZ Dept Ob/Gyn-Womens Resource Ctr, 1501 N Campbell Ave Fl 8, Tucson, AZ 85724; **Phone:** 520-694-6010; **Board Cert:** Obstetrics & Gynecology 2012; Maternal & Fetal Medicine 2012; **Med School:** Univ Ariz Coll Med 1977; **Resid:** Obstetrics & Gynecology, Univ AZ Med Ctr 1981; **Fellow:** Maternal & Fetal Medicine, Univ AZ Med Ctr 1983; **Fac Appt:** Prof ObG, Univ Ariz Coll Med

Robichaux III, Alfred G MD [MF] - **Spec Exp:** Fetal Surgery; Fetal Abnormalities; Pregnancy-High Risk; **Hospital:** Ochsner Med Ctr-New Orleans; **Address:** Ochsner Med Ctr, Div Maternal-Fetal Med, 1514 Jefferson Hwy Fl 6, New Orleans, LA 70121; **Phone:** 504-842-4151; **Board Cert:** Obstetrics & Gynecology 2011; Maternal & Fetal Medicine 2012; **Med School:** Louisiana State U, New Orleans 1978; **Resid:** Obstetrics & Gynecology, Ochsner Med Ctr 1982; **Fellow:** Maternal & Fetal Medicine, G Washington Univ Hosp 1984

Saade, George R MD [MF] - **Spec Exp:** Pregnancy-High Risk; Hypertension in Pregnancy; Premature Labor; **Hospital:** UT Med Br at Galveston(John Sealy Hosp); **Address:** UTMB, Maternal & Fetal Med Dept, 301 University Blvd, rm 3.400, Galveston, TX 77555; **Phone:** 409-747-0482; **Board Cert:** Obstetrics & Gynecology 2010; Maternal & Fetal Medicine 2010; **Med School:** Amer Univ Beirut 1985; **Resid:** Obstetrics & Gynecology, Union Meml Hosp 1991; **Fellow:** Maternal & Fetal Medicine, Baylor Affil Hosp 1994; **Fac Appt:** Prof ObG, Univ Tex Med Br, Galveston

West Coast and Pacific

Adashek, Joseph MD [MF] - **Spec Exp:** Pregnancy-High Risk; Prematurity Prevention; Prenatal Diagnosis; **Hospital:** Southern Hills Hosp & Med Ctr, Summerlin Hosp Med Ctr; **Address:** Desert Perinatal Associates, 5761 S Fort Apache, Las Vegas, NV 89148; **Phone:** 702-341-6610; **Board Cert:** Obstetrics & Gynecology 2011; Maternal & Fetal Medicine 2011; **Med School:** Penn State Coll Med 1989; **Resid:** Obstetrics & Gynecology, Northwestern Meml Hosp 1993; **Fellow:** Maternal & Fetal Medicine, UC Irvine Med Ctr 1995

Benedetti, Thomas J MD [MF] - **Spec Exp:** Prematurity Prevention; Fetal Macrosomia; **Hospital:** Univ Wash Med Ctr, Yakima Valley Mem Hosp; **Address:** 1959 NE Pacific St, Box 356159, Seattle, WA 98195; **Phone:** 206-598-4070; **Board Cert:** Obstetrics & Gynecology 1980; Maternal & Fetal Medicine 1981; **Med School:** Univ Wash 1973; **Resid:** Obstetrics & Gynecology, LAC-USC Med Ctr 1977; **Fellow:** Maternal & Fetal Medicine, LAC-USC Med Ctr 1979; **Fac Appt:** Prof ObG, Univ Wash

Cheng, Edith Y MD [MF] - **Spec Exp:** Prenatal Diagnosis; Genetic Disorders; Fetal Therapy; **Hospital:** Univ Wash Med Ctr, Seattle Chldns Hosp; **Address:** Univ Washington- Dept of Ob/Gyn, 1959 NE Pacific St, Box 356460, Seattle, WA 98195; **Phone:** 206-598-4070; **Board Cert:** Clinical Genetics 2010; Obstetrics & Gynecology 2012; Maternal & Fetal Medicine 2012; **Med School:** Univ Wash 1987; **Resid:** Obstetrics & Gynecology, Univ Washington Med Ctr 1991; **Fellow:** Clinical Genetics, Univ Washington Med Ctr 1993; Maternal & Fetal Medicine, Univ Washington Med Ctr 1995; **Fac Appt:** Prof ObG, Univ Wash

Chmait, Ramen H MD [MF] - **Spec Exp:** Twin to Twin Transfusion Syndrome (TTTS); Fetal Surgery; **Hospital:** Hollywood Presby Med Ctr; **Address:** Inst for Maternal Fetal Health, 1300 N Vermont Ave, Ste 310, Doctors Tower at Hollywood Presby Med Ctr, Los Angles, CA 90027; **Phone:** 323-361-6074; **Board Cert:** Obstetrics & Gynecology 2007; Maternal & Fetal Medicine 2007; **Med School:** UCLA 1996; **Resid:** Obstetrics & Gynecology, LAC & USC Med Ctr 2001; **Fellow:** Maternal & Fetal Medicine, UCSD Med Ctr 2003

Druzin, Maurice L MD [MF] - **Spec Exp:** Lupus/SLE in Pregnancy; Miscarriage-Recurrent; **Hospital:** Lucile Packard Chldn's Hosp; **Address:** 770 Welch Rd, Ste 201, Palo Alto, CA 94304; **Phone:** 650-498-4069; **Board Cert:** Obstetrics & Gynecology 2012; Maternal & Fetal Medicine 2012; **Med School:** South Africa 1970; **Resid:** Obstetrics & Gynecology, Rose Med Ctr-Univ Colo 1977; **Fellow:** Maternal & Fetal Medicine, LAC-USC Med Ctr 1979; **Fac Appt:** Prof ObG, Stanford Univ

Goldberg, James D MD [MF] - **Spec Exp:** Prenatal Diagnosis; Fetal Diagnosis & Therapy; **Hospital:** CA Pacific Med Ctr-Pacific Campus; **Address:** San Francisco Perinatal Assoc, One Daniel Burnham Ct, Ste 230C, San Francisco, CA 94109; **Phone:** 415-202-1200; **Board Cert:** Obstetrics & Gynecology 2012; Clinical Genetics 1987; Maternal & Fetal Medicine 2012; **Med School:** Univ Minn 1979; **Resid:** Obstetrics & Gynecology, UCSF Med Ctr 1983; **Fellow:** Maternal & Fetal Medicine, Mt Sinai Hosp 1985; Clinical Genetics, Mt Sinai Hosp 1985

Gravett, Michael G MD [MF] - **Spec Exp:** Infectious Disease-Perinatal; Pregnancy-High Risk; Prematurity Prevention; Prematurity/Low Birth Weight Infants; **Hospital:** Univ Wash Med Ctr; **Address:** Univ Washington, Dept OB/GYN, 1959 NE Pacific St, Ste 350, Hlth Sci Bldg, Seattle, WA 98195-6460; **Phone:** 206-598-4070; **Board Cert:** Obstetrics & Gynecology 1985; Maternal & Fetal Medicine 1987; **Med School:** UCLA 1977; **Resid:** Obstetrics & Gynecology, Univ Wash Med Ctr 1981; **Fellow:** Maternal & Fetal Medicine, Univ Wash Med Ctr 1983; **Fac Appt:** Prof ObG, Univ Wash

Kelly, Thomas F MD [MF] - **Spec Exp:** Pregnancy-High Risk; **Hospital:** UCSD Med Ctr, Scripps Meml Hosp - La Jolla; **Address:** UCSD Med Ctr, Dept Reproductive Med, 200 W Arbor Drive, San Diego, CA 92103; **Phone:** 619-543-2384; **Board Cert:** Obstetrics & Gynecology 2012; Maternal & Fetal Medicine 2012; **Med School:** Univ Nevada 1986; **Resid:** Obstetrics & Gynecology, USCD Med Ctr 1990; **Fellow:** Maternal & Fetal Medicine, USCD Med Ctr 1992; **Fac Appt:** Prof Med, UCSD

Koos, Brian J MD [MF] - **Spec Exp:** High Risk Pregnancy; Fetal Diagnosis & Therapy; Miscarriage-Recurrent; **Hospital:** UCLA Ronald Reagan Med Ctr; **Address:** UCLA Rhonda Fleming Ob/Gyn, 200 UCLA Medical Plaza, Ste 430, Los Angeles, CA 90095; **Phone:** 310-794-7852; **Board Cert:** Obstetrics & Gynecology 1999; Maternal & Fetal Medicine 1999; **Med School:** Loma Linda Univ 1975; **Resid:** Obstetrics & Gynecology, Brigham & Womens Hosp 1979; **Fellow:** Maternal & Fetal Medicine, Nuffield Inst for Med Rsch 1982; Maternal & Fetal Medicine, LAC/USC Womens Hosp 1983; **Fac Appt:** Prof ObG, UCLA

Moore, Thomas R MD [MF] - **Spec Exp:** Diabetes in Pregnancy; Fetal Diagnosis & Therapy; **Hospital:** UCSD Med Ctr, Scripps Meml Hosp - La Jolla; **Address:** 200 W Arbor Drive, MPF Bldg, Ste 170, San Diego, CA 92103; **Phone:** 619-543-7900; **Board Cert:** Obstetrics & Gynecology 2012; Maternal & Fetal Medicine 2012; **Med School:** Yale Univ 1979; **Resid:** Obstetrics & Gynecology, Naval Hosp 1983; **Fellow:** Maternal & Fetal Medicine, UCSD Med Ctr 1985; **Fac Appt:** Prof ObG, UCSD

Platt, Lawrence D MD [MF] - **Spec Exp:** Obstetric Ultrasound; Prenatal Diagnosis; Pregnancy-High Risk; **Hospital:** Cedars-Sinai Med Ctr, St. John's Hlth Ctr, Santa Monica; **Address:** Ctr Fetal Medicine & Women's Ultrasound, 6310 San Vincente Blvd, Ste 520, Los Angeles, CA 90048; **Phone:** 323-857-1952; **Board Cert:** Obstetrics & Gynecology 1979; Maternal & Fetal Medicine 1981; **Med School:** Wayne State Univ 1972; **Resid:** Obstetrics & Gynecology, Sinai Hosp 1976; **Fellow:** Maternal & Fetal Medicine, LAC/USC Med Ctr 1978; **Fac Appt:** Prof ObG, UCLA-David Geffen Sch Med

Robertson, Patricia A MD [MF] - **Spec Exp:** Pregnancy-High Risk; **Hospital:** UCSF Med Ctr; **Address:** 400 Parnassus Ave, Box 0346, San Francisco, CA 94143; **Phone:** 415-353-2566; **Board Cert:** Obstetrics & Gynecology 2012; Maternal & Fetal Medicine 2012; **Med School:** Univ Tex, San Antonio 1976; **Resid:** Obstetrics & Gynecology, UCSF Med Ctr 1980; **Fellow:** Maternal & Fetal Medicine, UCSF Med Ctr 1990; **Fac Appt:** Prof ObG, UCSF

Tabsh, Khalil MA MD [MF] - **Spec Exp:** Pregnancy-High Risk; Fetal Diagnosis & Therapy; **Hospital:** Santa Monica - UCLA Med Ctr & Ortho Hosp, UCLA Ronald Reagan Med Ctr; **Address:** UCLA Perinatology Group, 200 UCLA Medical Plaza, Ste 430, Los Angeles, CA 90095; **Phone:** 310-208-4492; **Board Cert:** Obstetrics & Gynecology 1981; Maternal & Fetal Medicine 1982; **Med School:** Lebanon 1974; **Resid:** Obstetrics & Gynecology, American Univ Beirut Med Ctr 1976; Obstetrics & Gynecology, Yale-New Haven Hosp 1978; **Fellow:** Maternal & Fetal Medicine, UCLA Med Ctr 1979; **Fac Appt:** Clin Prof ObG, UCLA-David Geffen Sch Med

Zalud, Ivica MD/PhD [MF] - **Spec Exp:** Obstetric Ultrasound; Pregnancy-High Risk; **Hospital:** Kapiolani Med Ctr for Women & Chldn; **Address:** Fetal Diagnostic Center, 1319 Punahou St, Ste 540, Hololulu, HI 96826; **Phone:** 808-203-6546; **Board Cert:** Obstetrics & Gynecology 2012; Maternal & Fetal Medicine 2012; **Med School:** Croatia 1986; **Resid:** Obstetrics & Gynecology, Winthrop Univ Hosp 1997; **Fellow:** Maternal & Fetal Medicine, Georgetown Univ Med Ctr 2000; **Fac Appt:** Assoc Prof ObG, Univ Hawaii JA Burns Sch Med

Mount Sinai

THE MOUNT SINAI MEDICAL CENTER

Obstetrics Programs and Services

One Gustave L. Levy Place
Fifth Avenue and 100th Street
New York, NY 10029-6574

Physician Referral: 1-800-MD-SINAI (637-4624)
www.mountsinai.org

As an expectant mother, you want the very best medical care to ensure that your baby is born healthy and that you stay strong enough to care for your newborn. If prior pregnancies were difficult or you have an underlying medical condition that could impact your pregnancy, you want to rest assured that you are doing everything possible to keep you and your baby healthy. That's why more women come to Mount Sinai's **CENTER FOR MATERNAL AND FETAL MEDICINE** than anywhere else in the greater New York area.

We've welcomed tens of thousands of babies into the world since the first baby was born at Mount Sinai in 1856 and although much has changed in the field of obstetrics since then, one thing has stayed the same—our dedication to providing new families with a nurturing and comfortable environment in which to experience one of life's most precious moments—the birth of your child. Our integrated approach to labor and delivery involves multiple fields—from obstetrics, nursing, and anesthesiology to neonatal intensive care, pediatric surgery, and genetics. Mount Sinai's Jo Carole and Ronald S. Lauder Center for Maternity Care includes the new Alexandra and Steven Cohen Center for Labor and Birth—a state-of-the-art labor and delivery floor that provides safe, modern, and technically advanced care for mother and child in over 6,000 deliveries each year.

Our Jo Carole and Ronald S. Lauder Center for Maternity Care provides:

- 14 labor and delivery rooms
- Four designated ante partum beds
- Three operating rooms
- Mother-baby suites
- General care units
- Level III NICU

We're one of a select few obstetrics practices using progressive technology on our labor and delivery floor. Our doctors are trained in handling high risk births and birthing emergencies on the NOELLE® and newborn HAL® mother and infant simulators, which allows us to take our training and experience to new high-tech levels. NOELLE is a robot simulator that provides trainees a complete birthing experience before, during, and after delivery. With controls that smoothly transition between physiologic states in response to commands from a wireless PC, physicians and trainees can monitor maternal and neonatal vital signs, including blood pressure and oxygen saturation, using real equipment. NOELLE and baby HAL allow our teams to practice birthing drills and the handling of life-threatening complications.

Our obstetrics team includes "The Mount Sinai Midwives," a group of experts in low-risk women's health care, who attend over 500 deliveries per year on Mount Sinai's labor and delivery unit. They provide prenatal, postpartum and well-woman gynecology services to low-risk women at Mount Sinai Hospital in Manhattan, Mount Sinai of Queens, Settlement Health, in East Harlem, and Boriken Health Center in Manhattan. Our midwives offer a broad range of services to support new moms, including breastfeeding assistance, and support groups.

Neonatal-Perinatal Medicine

a subspecialty of Pediatrics

A subspecialist in neonatal-perinatal medicine is a pediatrician who is the principal care provider for sick newborn infants. Clinical expertise is used for direct patient care and for consulting with obstetrical colleagues to plan for the care of mothers who have high-risk pregnancies.

Training Required: Three years in pediatrics *plus* additional training and examination.

NEONATAL-PERINATAL MEDICINE

New England

Davis, Jonathan M MD [NP] - **Spec Exp:** Lung Disease in Newborns; Infections-Neonatal; **Hospital:** Tufts Med Ctr; **Address:** Tufts Medical Ctr, 800 Washington St, Box 44, Boston, MA 02111; **Phone:** 617-636-5322; **Board Cert:** Pediatrics 1985; Neonatal-Perinatal Medicine 1987; **Med School:** McGill Univ 1981; **Resid:** Pediatrics, Chldns Hosp 1984; **Fellow:** Neonatal-Perinatal Medicine, Chldns Hosp 1986; **Fac Appt:** Prof Ped, Tufts Univ

Ehrenkranz, Richard A MD [NP] - **Spec Exp:** Nutrition; Lung Disease in Newborns; Prematurity/Low Birth Weight Infants; **Hospital:** Yale-New Haven Hosp; **Address:** Yale-New Haven Chldn's Hosp, Div of Neonatology, 20 York St, New Haven, CT 06520; **Phone:** 203-688-2320; **Board Cert:** Pediatrics 1977; Neonatal-Perinatal Medicine 1979; **Med School:** SUNY Downstate 1972; **Resid:** Pediatrics, Yale-New Haven Hosp 1975; **Fellow:** Research, Natl Inst Child Hlth & Human Dev 1976; Neonatal-Perinatal Medicine, Yale-New Haven Hosp 1979; **Fac Appt:** Prof Ped, Yale Univ

Frantz III, Ivan D MD [NP] - **Spec Exp:** Lung Disease in Newborns; **Hospital:** Children's Hospital - Boston; **Address:** Boston Chldn's Hosp, 300 Longwood Ave, Boston, MA 02115; **Phone:** 617-919-3397; **Board Cert:** Pediatrics 1976; Neonatal-Perinatal Medicine 2009; **Med School:** Univ Minn 1971; **Resid:** Pediatrics, Univ Minn Hosp 1973; **Fellow:** Neonatal-Perinatal Medicine, McGill Royal Victoria Hosp 1974; Neonatal-Perinatal Medicine, Mass Genl Hosp 1975; **Fac Appt:** Prof Ped, Tufts Univ

Gross, Ian MD [NP] - **Spec Exp:** Breathing Disorders; Critical Care; **Hospital:** Yale-New Haven Hosp; **Address:** Yale Sch Med, Dept Pediatrics, 333 Cedar St, PO Box 208064, New Haven, CT 06520-8064; **Phone:** 203-688-2320; **Board Cert:** Pediatrics 1974; Neonatal-Perinatal Medicine 1977; **Med School:** South Africa 1967; **Resid:** Pediatrics, Univ Witwatersrand Affil Hosps 1971; Pediatrics, Chldns Hosp Med Ctr 1974; **Fellow:** Neonatal-Perinatal Medicine, Yale-New Haven Hosp 1977; **Fac Appt:** Prof Ped, Yale Univ

Van Marter, Linda J MD [NP] - **Spec Exp:** Neonatal Chronic Lung Disease (CLD); Lung Disease in Newborns; Pulmonary Hypertension of Newborn (PPHN); **Hospital:** Brigham & Women's Hosp, Children's Hospital - Boston; **Address:** Children's Hospital Boston, 300 Longwood Ave, Hunnewell 430 - Newborn Med, Boston, MA 02115; **Phone:** 617-355-6027; **Board Cert:** Pediatrics 1985; Neonatal-Perinatal Medicine 2009; **Med School:** Univ Pittsburgh 1980; **Resid:** Pediatrics, Childrens Hosp Med Ctr 1983; **Fellow:** Neonatology, Harvard Med Sch Affil Hosp 1986; **Fac Appt:** Assoc Prof Ped, Harvard Med Sch

Mid Atlantic

Anday, Endla K MD [NP] - **Spec Exp:** Brain Injury-Neonatal; **Hospital:** St. Christopher's Hosp for Chldn, Hahnemann Univ Hosp; **Address:** St Christophers Hosp for Children, 3601 A St, Neonatology, Philadelphia, PA 19134; **Phone:** 215-427-5202; **Board Cert:** Pediatrics 1978; Neonatal-Perinatal Medicine 1981; **Med School:** Med Coll PA 1973; **Resid:** Pediatrics, Childrens Hosp 1975; **Fellow:** Neonatology, Childrens Hosp 1978; Pulmonary Disease, Univ Penn Hosp 1979; **Fac Appt:** Prof Ped, Drexel Univ Coll Med

Davidson, Dennis MD [NP] - **Spec Exp:** Lung Disease in Newborns; **Hospital:** Stony Brook Univ Med Ctr; **Address:** Stony Brook Univ Med Ct, Dept Pediatrics, 101 Nicholls Rd, HSC T11-060, Stony Brook, NY 11794-8111; **Phone:** 631-444-7653; **Board Cert:** Pediatrics 1980; Neonatal-Perinatal Medicine 2009; **Med School:** Loyola Univ-Stritch Sch Med 1974; **Resid:** Pediatrics, Babies Hosp-Columbia Univ 1978; **Fellow:** Neonatal-Perinatal Medicine, Babies Hosp-Columbia Univ 1981; **Fac Appt:** Clin Prof Ped, Albert Einstein Coll Med

Delivoria-Papadopoulos, Maria MD [NP] - **Spec Exp:** Neonatology; Prematurity/Low Birth Weight Infants; Breathing Disorders; Brain Injury; **Hospital:** St. Christopher's Hosp for Chldn, Hahnemann Univ Hosp; **Address:** St Christopher's Hosp for Children, 3601 A St, Ste 2212, Neonatology, Philadelphia, PA 19134; **Phone:** 215-427-5202; **Board Cert:** Pediatrics 1971; Neonatal-Perinatal Medicine 1975; **Med School:** Greece 1957; **Resid:** Pediatrics, Chldns Hosp 1959; Psychiatry, Colo State Hosp 1962; **Fellow:** Neonatology, Hosp Sick Chldn 1964; **Fac Appt:** Prof Ped, Drexel Univ Coll Med

Dennery, Phyllis A MD [NP] - **Spec Exp:** Lung Disease in Newborns; **Hospital:** Chldns Hosp of Philadelphia; **Address:** Childrens Hosp Div Neonatology, 34th St and Civic Ctr Blvd Fl 2, Philadelphia, PA 19104; **Phone:** 215-590-1653; **Board Cert:** Neonatal-Perinatal Medicine 2011; **Med School:** Howard Univ 1984; **Resid:** Pediatrics, Chldns Hosp Natl Med Ctr 1988; **Fellow:** Neonatal-Perinatal Medicine, Case Western Reserve 1989; **Fac Appt:** Prof Ped, Univ Pennsylvania

Holzman, Ian R MD [NP] - **Spec Exp:** Neonatal Nutrition; Necrotizing Enterocolitis; Ethics; Prematurity/Low Birth Weight Infants; **Hospital:** Mt Sinai Med Ctr (page 62); **Address:** Newborn Assocs, 1 Gustave L Levy Pl, Box 1508, New York, NY 10029-6500; **Phone:** 212-241-5446; **Board Cert:** Pediatrics 1974; Neonatal-Perinatal Medicine 1977; **Med School:** Univ Pittsburgh 1971; **Resid:** Pediatrics, Chldns Hosp 1975; **Fellow:** Neonatal-Perinatal Medicine, Univ Colorado 1977; **Fac Appt:** Prof Ped, Mount Sinai Sch Med

Hurt, Hallam MD [NP] - **Spec Exp:** Neonatology; **Hospital:** Chldns Hosp of Philadelphia, Hosp Univ Penn - UPHS (page 69); **Address:** Special Babies Clinic, 3535 Market St Fl 14, Philadelphia, PA 19104; **Phone:** 215-590-0560; **Board Cert:** Pediatrics 1976; Neonatal-Perinatal Medicine 2002; **Med School:** Univ VA Sch Med 1971; **Resid:** Pediatrics, Univ Virginia Hosp 1974; **Fellow:** Neonatal-Perinatal Medicine, Univ Virginia 1976; **Fac Appt:** Prof Ped, Univ Pennsylvania

La Gamma, Edmund F MD [NP] - **Spec Exp:** Neonatal Infections; Prematurity/Low Birth Weight Infants; Necrotizing Enterocolitis; **Hospital:** Westchester Med Ctr, Children's & Women's Phys.of Westchester; **Address:** Maria Fareri Chldns Hosp, 100 Woods Rd, rm 2215, Valhalla, NY 10595; **Phone:** 914-493-8558; **Board Cert:** Pediatrics 1981; Neonatal-Perinatal Medicine 1981; **Med School:** NY Med Coll 1976; **Resid:** Pediatrics, NY Hosp-Cornell Med Ctr 1978; **Fellow:** Neonatal-Perinatal Medicine, NY Hosp-Cornell Med Ctr 1980; Cardiovascular Disease, UCSF Med Ctr 1981; **Fac Appt:** Prof Ped, NY Med Coll

Lawson, Edward E MD [NP] - **Spec Exp:** Prematurity/Low Birth Weight Infants; Respiratory Distress Syndrome (RDS); Neonatal Critical Care; Breathing Disorders; **Hospital:** Johns Hopkins Hosp (page 59), Johns Hopkins Bayview Med Ctr (page 59); **Address:** 1800 Orleans St, Ste 8513, Baltimore, MD 21287; **Phone:** 410-955-5259; **Board Cert:** Pediatrics 1990; Neonatal-Perinatal Medicine 1997; **Med School:** Northwestern Univ 1972; **Resid:** Pediatrics, Chldns Hosp Med Ctr 1975; **Fellow:** Neonatal-Perinatal Medicine, Harvard Med Sch 1977; **Fac Appt:** Prof Ped, Johns Hopkins Univ

Nogee, Lawrence M MD [NP] - **Spec Exp:** Lung Disease in Newborns-Genetic; **Hospital:** Johns Hopkins Hosp (page 59); **Address:** Johns Hopkins Hosp, Div Neonatolgy, 600 N Wolfe St, CMSC 6-104A, Baltimore, MD 21287-3200; **Phone:** 410-614-3355; **Board Cert:** Pediatrics 1986; Neonatal-Perinatal Medicine 1987; **Med School:** Johns Hopkins Univ 1981; **Resid:** Pediatrics, Johns Hopkins Hosp 1984; **Fellow:** Neonatal-Perinatal Medicine, Chldns Hosp Med Ctr 1986; **Fac Appt:** Prof Ped, Johns Hopkins Univ

Perlman, Jeffrey M MD [NP] - **Spec Exp:** Neonatal Critical Care; Prematurity/Low Birth Weight Infants; Neonatal Neurology; Lung Disease in Newborns; **Hospital:** NY-Presby/Weill Cornell Med Ctr, NY (page 65); **Address:** 525 E 68th St, Ste N 506, New York, NY 10065; **Phone:** 212-746-3530; **Board Cert:** Pediatrics 1983; Neonatal-Perinatal Medicine 1983; **Med School:** South Africa 1974; **Resid:** Pediatrics, Johannesburg Chldns Hosp 1979; Pediatrics, St Louis Chldns Hosp 1981; **Fellow:** Neonatology, St Louis Chldns Hosp 1983; **Fac Appt:** Prof Ped, Cornell Univ-Weill Med Coll

Polin, Richard A MD [NP] - **Spec Exp:** Neonatal Infections; **Hospital:** Morgan Stanley Children's Hosp of NY-Presby, NY (page 65); **Address:** 3959 Broadway CHN-1201, New York, NY 10032; **Phone:** 212-305-5827; **Board Cert:** Pediatrics 1975; Neonatal-Perinatal Medicine 2010; **Med School:** Temple Univ 1970; **Resid:** Pediatrics, Chldns Meml Hosp 1972; Pediatrics, Babies Hosp 1973; **Fellow:** Neonatal-Perinatal Medicine, Babies Hosp-Columbia 1974; **Fac Appt:** Prof Ped, Columbia P&S

Short, Billie L MD [NP] - **Hospital:** Chldns Natl Med Ctr; **Address:** Sheikh Zayed Campus-Neonatology, 111 Michigan Ave NW, Washington, DC 20010; **Phone:** 202-476-3314; **Board Cert:** Pediatrics 1979; Neonatal-Perinatal Medicine 1979; **Med School:** Univ Okla Coll Med 1974; **Resid:** Pediatrics, Chldns Hosp OU Med Ctr 1978; **Fellow:** Neonatal-Perinatal Medicine, Chldns Natl Med Ctr 1979; **Fac Appt:** Prof Ped, Geo Wash Univ

Silverman, Gary A MD/PhD [NP] - **Hospital:** Chldns Hosp of Pittsburgh - UPMC, Magee-Womens Hosp - UPMC; **Address:** Chldn's Hosp Pittsburgh, 1 Chldn's Hosp Drive, 4401 Penn Ave, rm 7130, Pittsburgh, PA 15224; **Phone:** 412-692-9448; **Board Cert:** Neonatal-Perinatal Medicine 2011; **Med School:** Univ Chicago-Pritzker Sch Med 1984; **Resid:** Pediatrics, Childns Hosp 1987; **Fellow:** Neonatology, St Louis Chldns Hosp 1989; Research, Washington Univ Phys 1991; **Fac Appt:** Prof Ped, Univ Pittsburgh

Watchko, Jon F MD [NP] - **Hospital:** Magee-Womens Hosp - UPMC, Chldns Hosp of Pittsburgh - UPMC; **Address:** Magee-Womens Hosp, Newborn Medicine, 300 Halket St, Pittsburgh, PA 15213; **Phone:** 412-641-1834; **Board Cert:** Pediatrics 1985; Neonatal-Perinatal Medicine 1985; **Med School:** Univ Pittsburgh 1980; **Resid:** Pediatrics, Upstate Med Ctr 1983; **Fellow:** Neonatology, Univ Washington Med Ctr 1986; **Fac Appt:** Prof Ped, Univ Pittsburgh

Zubrow, Alan B MD [NP] - **Spec Exp:** Neonatology; **Hospital:** St. Christopher's Hosp for Chldn, Hahnemann Univ Hosp; **Address:** St Christopher's Hosp for Chldn, 3601 A St, Philadelphia, PA 19134; **Phone:** 215-427-5252; **Board Cert:** Pediatrics 1980; Neonatal-Perinatal Medicine 2009; **Med School:** Univ Pennsylvania 1976; **Resid:** Pediatrics, Chldns Hosp 1979; **Fellow:** Neonatology, Columbia-Presby Med Ctr 1981; **Fac Appt:** Prof Ped, Drexel Univ Coll Med

Southeast

Boyle, Robert J MD [NP] - **Spec Exp:** Neonatology; Ethics; **Hospital:** Univ of Virginia Hlth Sys; **Address:** UVA Division of Neonatology, 1215 Lee St, Charlottesville, VA 22908; **Phone:** 434-924-5429; **Board Cert:** Pediatrics 1978; Neonatal-Perinatal Medicine 1979; **Med School:** Johns Hopkins Univ 1973; **Resid:** Pediatrics, Rainbow Babies Chldns Hosp 1976; **Fellow:** Neonatal-Perinatal Medicine, Women & Infants Hosp 1978; **Fac Appt:** Prof Ped, Univ VA Sch Med

Bucciarelli, Richard L MD [NP] - **Spec Exp:** Neonatal Cardiology; **Hospital:** UF Hlth Shands Hosp; **Address:** UF Hlth, Neonatalogy Dept, 1600 SW Archer Rd, Gainesville, FL 32608; **Phone:** 352-273-9004; **Board Cert:** Pediatrics 1977; Neonatal-Perinatal Medicine 1977; Pediatric Cardiology 1977; **Med School:** Univ Mich Med Sch 1972; **Resid:** Pediatrics, Shands at Univ FL 1975; **Fellow:** Neonatal-Perinatal Medicine, Shands at Univ FL 1977; Pediatric Cardiology, Shands at Univ FL 1977; **Fac Appt:** Prof Ped, Univ Fla Coll Med

Dhanireddy, Ramasubbareddy MD [NP] - **Spec Exp:** Neonatology; Prematurity/Low Birth Weight Infants; **Hospital:** Regional Med Ctr - Memphis, Le Bonheur Chldns Med Ctr; **Address:** Univ Tennessee, Div Neonatology, 853 Jefferson Ave, rm 201, Memphis, TN 38163; **Phone:** 901-448-5950; **Board Cert:** Pediatrics 1980; Neonatal-Perinatal Medicine 2009; **Med School:** India 1974; **Resid:** Pediatrics, Lousiana State Univ Med Ctr 1978; **Fellow:** Neonatology, Georgetown Univ Med Ctr 1980; **Fac Appt:** Prof Ped, Univ Tenn Coll Med

Hendricks-Munoz, Karen MD [NP] - **Spec Exp:** Breathing Disorders; Neonatal Neurology; Retinopathy of Prematurity; **Hospital:** VCU Med Ctr; **Address:** VCU Med Ctr, Div Neonatology, Critical Care Hosp, 6th Fl, Box 980276, Richmond, VA 23298; **Phone:** 804-828-9964; **Board Cert:** Pediatrics 1985; Neonatal-Perinatal Medicine 2009; **Med School:** Yale Univ 1978; **Resid:** Pediatrics, Yale-New Haven Hosp 1981; **Fellow:** Neonatology, Strong Meml Hosp 1984; **Fac Appt:** Prof Ped, Va Commonwealth Univ Sch Med

Holtzman, Ronald B MD [NP] - **Spec Exp:** Neonatology; Lung Disease in Newborns; **Hospital:** Gaston Meml Hosp; **Address:** Gaston Meml Hosp, NICU Office, 2525 Court Drive, Gastonia, NC 28056; **Phone:** 704-834-3390; **Board Cert:** Pediatrics 1987; Neonatal-Perinatal Medicine 2011; **Med School:** Rush Med Coll 1983; **Resid:** Pediatrics, Chldns Meml Hosp 1986; **Fellow:** Neonatal-Perinatal Medicine, Chldns Meml Hosp 1989

Stiles, Alan D MD [NP] - **Spec Exp:** Neonatology; **Hospital:** NC Memorial Hosp - UNC; **Address:** 260 MacNider Bldg, CB 7220, Chapel Hill, NC 27599-7220; **Phone:** 919-966-5570; **Board Cert:** Pediatrics 1984; Neonatal-Perinatal Medicine 1985; **Med School:** Univ NC Sch Med 1977; **Resid:** Pediatrics, North Carolina Meml Hosp 1982; **Fellow:** Neonatal-Perinatal Medicine, Chldns Hosp/Brigham Hosp 1985; **Fac Appt:** Prof Ped, Univ NC Sch Med

Midwest

Bell, Edward F MD [NP] - **Spec Exp:** Prematurity/Low Birth Weight Infants; Neonatal Critical Care; Neonatal Hemochromatosis; **Hospital:** Univ Iowa Hosp & Clins; **Address:** Dept of Pediatrics, Univ Iowa, 200 Hawkins Drive, rm 8811 JPP, Iowa City, IA 52242; **Phone:** 319-356-4006; **Board Cert:** Pediatrics 1978; Neonatal-Perinatal Medicine 1995; **Med School:** Columbia P&S 1973; **Resid:** Pediatrics, Babies Hosp-Columbia Presby 1976; **Fellow:** Neonatology, McMaster Univ Med Ctr 1977; Neonatology, Women & Infants Hosp-Brown Univ 1979; **Fac Appt:** Prof Ped, Univ Iowa Coll Med

Cole III, Francis Sessions MD [NP] - **Spec Exp:** Neonatal Chronic Lung Disease (CLD); Respiratory Distress Syndrome (RDS); Surfactant Biology; Prematurity/Low Birth Weight Infants; **Hospital:** St. Louis Chldns Hosp, Barnes-Jewish Hosp; **Address:** Wash Univ-Div Newborn Med, 660 S Euclid Ave, Box 8116, St Louis, MO 63110; **Phone:** 314-454-6148; **Board Cert:** Pediatrics 1980; Neonatal-Perinatal Medicine 1983; **Med School:** Yale Univ 1973; **Resid:** Pediatrics, Chldns Hosp Med Ctr 1978; **Fellow:** Neonatology, Brigham and Women's Hosp 1981; **Fac Appt:** Prof Ped, Washington Univ, St Louis

Donn, Steven M MD [NP] - **Spec Exp:** Breathing Disorders; Respiratory Distress Syndrome (RDS); Pulmonary Hypertension of Newborn (PPHN); Surfactant Biology; **Hospital:** Mott Chldns Hosp, Univ Michigan Med Ctr; **Address:** 1540 E Hospital Drive, MS 5254, Ann Arbor, MI 48109-5254; **Phone:** 734-763-4109; **Board Cert:** Pediatrics 1981; Neonatal-Perinatal Medicine 1981; **Med School:** Tulane Univ 1974; **Resid:** Pediatrics, Univ Vermont Med Ctr 1978; **Fellow:** Neonatology, Univ Michigan 1980; **Fac Appt:** Prof Ped, Univ Mich Med Sch

Gewolb, Ira H MD [NP] - **Spec Exp:** Breathing Disorders; Gastroesophageal Reflux Disease (GERD); **Hospital:** Mich State Univ-Sparrow Hos; **Address:** 1215 E Michigan Ave, Lansing, MI 48912; **Phone:** 517-364-2670; **Board Cert:** Pediatrics 1980; Neonatal-Perinatal Medicine 1981; **Med School:** Yale Univ 1976; **Resid:** Pediatrics, Chldns Hosp Med Ctr 1979; **Fellow:** Neonatology, Yale-New Haven Hosp 1982; **Fac Appt:** Prof Med, Mich State Univ

Hamvas, Aaron MD [NP] - **Spec Exp:** Lung Disease in Newborns-Genetic; **Hospital:** St. Louis Chldns Hosp, Barnes-Jewish Hosp; **Address:** Wash Univ-Div Newborn Med, 660 S Euclid Ave, Box 8116, St Louis, MO 63110; **Phone:** 314-454-6148; **Board Cert:** Neonatal-Perinatal Medicine 2013; **Med School:** Washington Univ, St Louis 1981; **Resid:** Pediatrics, St Louis Chldns Hosp 1984; **Fellow:** Neonatology, St Louis Chldns Hosp 1990; **Fac Appt:** Prof Ped, Washington Univ, St Louis

Martin, Richard John MD [NP] - **Spec Exp:** Breathing Disorders; **Hospital:** UH Rainbow Babies & Chldns Hosp; **Address:** 11100 Euclid Ave, Div Neonatology, Cleveland, OH 44106-6010; **Phone:** 216-844-3387; **Board Cert:** Pediatrics 1976; Neonatal-Perinatal Medicine 2005; **Med School:** Australia 1970; **Resid:** Pediatrics, Univ Missouri 1973; **Fellow:** Neonatal-Perinatal Medicine, Case West Res Univ 1975; **Fac Appt:** Prof Ped, Univ Cincinnati

Meadow, William Lee MD/PhD [NP] - **Spec Exp:** Neonatal Infections; Ethics; **Hospital:** Univ Chicago Med-Comer Chldn's Hosp; **Address:** 5841 S Maryland Ave, rm 657, MC 6060, Chicago, IL 60637; **Phone:** 773-702-6210; **Board Cert:** Pediatrics 1979; Neonatal-Perinatal Medicine 1981; **Med School:** Univ Pennsylvania 1974; **Resid:** Pediatrics, Chldns Meml Hosp 1978; **Fellow:** Neonatology, Wyler Chldns Hosp 1981; Infectious Disease, Wyler Chldns Hosp 1981; **Fac Appt:** Prof Ped, Univ Chicago-Pritzker Sch Med

Muraskas, Jonathan MD [NP] - **Spec Exp:** Prematurity/Low Birth Weight Infants; Multiple Gestation; Conjoined Twins; Ethics; **Hospital:** Loyola Univ - Ronald McDonald Children's Hosp; **Address:** Loyola Univ Med Ctr, Bldg 107, 2160 S First Ave, Russo Pavilion, Neo Unit, Rm 5811, Maywood, IL 60153-5500; **Phone:** 708-216-1067; **Board Cert:** Pediatrics 1987; Neonatal-Perinatal Medicine 1987; **Med School:** Loyola Univ-Stritch Sch Med 1982; **Resid:** Pediatrics, Loyola Univ Med Ctr 1985; **Fellow:** Neonatal-Perinatal Medicine, Loyola Univ Med Ctr 1987; **Fac Appt:** Prof Ped, Loyola Univ-Stritch Sch Med

Whitsett, Jeffrey A MD [NP] - **Spec Exp:** Lung Disease in Newborns-Genetic; **Hospital:** Cincinnati Chldns Hosp Med Ctr, Good Samaritan Hosp - Cincinnati; **Address:** Cincinnati Chldns Hosp, Div Neonatalogy, 3333 Burnet Ave, Cincinnati, OH 45229-3039; **Phone:** 513-636-4830; **Board Cert:** Pediatrics 1979; Neonatal-Perinatal Medicine 1979; **Med School:** Columbia P&S 1973; **Resid:** Pediatrics, Mt Sinai Hosp 1976; **Fellow:** Neonatology, Chldns Hosp Med Ctr 1977; **Fac Appt:** Prof Ped, Univ Cincinnati

Great Plains and Mountains

Milley, J Ross MD/PhD [NP] - **Spec Exp:** Nutrition; **Hospital:** Primary Children's Med Ctr, Univ Utah Hlth Care; **Address:** 100 N Mario Capecchi Drive, Salt Lake City, UT 84113; **Phone:** 801-662-4100; **Board Cert:** Pediatrics 1980; Neonatal-Perinatal Medicine 1981; **Med School:** Univ Chicago-Pritzker Sch Med 1975; **Resid:** Pediatrics, Johns Hopkins Hosp 1978; **Fellow:** Neonatology, Johns Hopkins Hosp 1980; **Fac Appt:** Prof Ped, Univ Utah

Zach, Terence MD [NP] - **Spec Exp:** Neonatal Critical Care; **Hospital:** Alegent Creighton Univ Med Ctr; **Address:** Creighton Univ, Neonatal-Perinatal Med, 601 N 30th St, Omaha, NE 68198-1205; **Phone:** 402-559-6750; **Board Cert:** Pediatrics 1987; Neonatal-Perinatal Medicine 2011; **Med School:** Univ Nebr Coll Med 1983; **Resid:** Pediatrics, Univ Nebr Med Ctr 1986; **Fellow:** Neonatology, Univ Minnesota Affil Hosp 1989; **Fac Appt:** Prof Ped, Creighton Univ

Southwest

Adams Jr, James M MD [NP] - **Spec Exp:** Lung Disease in Newborns; **Hospital:** Texas Chldns Hosp; **Address:** TX Chldns Hosp, Neonatology Dept, 6621 Fannin St, Ste W6104, Houston, TX 77030; **Phone:** 832-826-1380; **Board Cert:** Pediatrics 1975; Neonatal-Perinatal Medicine 1975; **Med School:** Baylor Coll Med 1970; **Resid:** Pediatrics, Baylor Affil Hosp 1973; **Fellow:** Neonatal-Perinatal Medicine, Baylor Affil Hosp 1975; **Fac Appt:** Prof Ped, Baylor Coll Med

Escobedo, Marilyn B MD [NP] - **Spec Exp:** Neonatology; Nutrition; **Hospital:** Chldns Hosp OU Med Ctr; **Address:** 1200 Everett Drive, North Pavilion Fl 7 - rm 7504, Oklahoma City, OK 73104; **Phone:** 405-271-5215; **Board Cert:** Pediatrics 1986; Neonatal-Perinatal Medicine 2004; **Med School:** Washington Univ, St Louis 1970; **Resid:** Pediatrics, Chldns Hosp 1972; Neonatal-Perinatal Medicine, Chldns Hosp 1973; **Fellow:** Neonatal-Perinatal Medicine, Vanderbilt Univ 1976; **Fac Appt:** Prof Ped, Univ Okla Coll Med

Garcia-Prats, Joseph MD [NP] - **Spec Exp:** Lung Disease in Newborns; **Hospital:** Texas Chldns Hosp, Ben Taub Genl Hosp; **Address:** TX Chldns Hosp, Neonatology Dept, 6621 Fannin St, Ste W6104, Houston, TX 77030; **Phone:** 713-873-3515; **Board Cert:** Pediatrics 1977; Neonatal-Perinatal Medicine 2009; **Med School:** Tulane Univ 1972; **Resid:** Pediatrics, Baylor Affil Hosp 1975; **Fellow:** Neonatal-Perinatal Medicine, Baylor Affil Hosp 1977; **Fac Appt:** Prof Ped, Baylor Coll Med

Odom, Michael W MD [NP] - **Spec Exp:** Neonatology; **Hospital:** Univ Hosp-San Antonio; **Address:** UTHSCSA, Neonatology Dept, 7703 Floyd Curl Drive, MC 7812, San Antonio, TX 78229; **Phone:** 210-567-5225; **Board Cert:** Pediatrics 1987; Neonatal-Perinatal Medicine 2011; **Med School:** Univ Tex SW, Dallas 1983; **Resid:** Pediatrics, Vanderbilt Univ Med Ctr 1986; **Fellow:** Neonatal-Perinatal Medicine, UCSF-Mt Zion Med Ctr 1989; Molecular Biology, Univ Hosp 1995; **Fac Appt:** Assoc Prof Ped, Univ Tex, San Antonio

Seidner, Steven R MD [NP] - **Spec Exp:** Neonatal Chronic Lung Disease (CLD); Respiratory Distress Syndrome (RDS); Pulmonary Hypertension of Newborn (PPHN); **Hospital:** Univ Hosp-San Antonio; **Address:** UTHSCSA, Neonatology Dept, 7703 Floyd Curl Drive, MC 7812, San Antonio, TX 78229; **Phone:** 210-567-5225; **Board Cert:** Pediatrics 1987; Neonatal-Perinatal Medicine 1987; **Med School:** Univ Ariz Coll Med 1982; **Resid:** Pediatrics, LAC-Harbor-UCLA Med Ctr 1985; **Fellow:** Neonatal-Perinatal Medicine, LAC-Harbor-UCLA Med Ctr 1988; **Fac Appt:** Prof Ped, Univ Tex, San Antonio

West Coast and Pacific

Gleason, Christine A MD [NP] - **Spec Exp:** Prematurity/Low Birth Weight Infants; Neonatal Critical Care; **Hospital:** Seattle Chldns Hosp; **Address:** UW Neonatal-Perinatal Medicine, 1959 NE Pacific St, Box 356320, Seattle, WA 98195; **Phone:** 206-543-3200; **Board Cert:** Pediatrics 1984; Neonatal-Perinatal Medicine 2002; **Med School:** Univ Rochester 1979; **Resid:** Pediatrics, Univ Hosps 1982; **Fellow:** Neonatal-Perinatal Medicine, UCSF Affil Hosps 1985; **Fac Appt:** Prof Ped, Univ Wash

Simmons Jr, Charles F MD [NP] - **Spec Exp:** Prematurity/Low Birth Weight Infants; Critical Care; Infections-Neonatal; **Hospital:** Cedars-Sinai Med Ctr; **Address:** Cedars-Sinai Medical Center, Maxine Dunitz Children's Health Center, 8700 Beverly Blvd, NT 4226, Los Angeles, CA 90048; **Phone:** 310-423-4416; **Board Cert:** Pediatrics 1986; Neonatal-Perinatal Medicine 1987; **Med School:** Harvard Med Sch 1980; **Resid:** Pediatrics, Children's Hosp 1983; **Fellow:** Neonatal-Perinatal Medicine, Children's Hosp 1986; **Fac Appt:** Prof Ped, UCLA-David Geffen Sch Med

Stevenson, David K MD [NP] - **Spec Exp:** Neonatology; **Hospital:** Lucile Packard Chldn's Hosp; **Address:** 750 Welch Rd, Ste 315, Palo Alto, CA 94304-1510; **Phone:** 650-723-5711; **Board Cert:** Pediatrics 1979; Neonatal-Perinatal Medicine 2004; **Med School:** Univ Wash 1975; **Resid:** Pediatrics, Univ Washington 1977; **Fellow:** Neonatal-Perinatal Medicine, Stanford Univ 1979; **Fac Appt:** Prof Ped, Stanford Univ

Top Doctors Make A Difference

Nephrology

a subspecialty of Internal Medicine

An internist who treats disorders of the kidney, high blood pressure, fluid and mineral balance and dialysis of body wastes when the kidneys do not function. This specialist consults with surgeons about kidney transplantation.

Training Required: Three years in internal medicine *plus* additional training and examination for certification in nephrology.

NEPHROLOGY

New England

Bazari, Hasan MD [Nep] - **Spec Exp:** Kidney Failure-Acute; Nephrotic Syndrome; Hypertension; **Hospital:** Mass Genl Hosp; **Address:** MGH, Renal Associates, 165 Cambridge St, Ste 302, Boston, MA 02114; **Phone:** 617-726-5050; **Board Cert:** Internal Medicine 1986; Nephrology 1988; **Med School:** Albert Einstein Coll Med 1983; **Resid:** Internal Medicine, Mass Genl Hosp 1986; **Fellow:** Nephrology, Mass Genl Hosp 1988; **Fac Appt:** Assoc Prof Med, Harvard Med Sch

Kliger, Alan S MD [Nep] - **Spec Exp:** Kidney Disease; Kidney Disease-Metabolic; **Hospital:** Yale-New Haven Hosp - St Raphael Campus; **Address:** Metabolism Assocs, 136 Sherman Ave, Ste 405, New Haven, CT 06511; **Phone:** 203-787-0117 x307; **Board Cert:** Internal Medicine 1973; Nephrology 1976; **Med School:** SUNY Upstate Med Univ 1970; **Resid:** Internal Medicine, SUNY Upstate Med Ctr 1973; **Fellow:** Nephrology, Georgetown Univ Med Ctr 1975; **Fac Appt:** Clin Prof Med, Yale Univ

Perrone, Ronald D MD [Nep] - **Spec Exp:** Kidney Disease-Chronic; Kidney Failure-Acute; Polycystic Kidney Disease; Hypertension; **Hospital:** Tufts Med Ctr; **Address:** Tufts Med Ctr, Div Nephrology, 800 Washington St, Box 391, Boston, MA 02111; **Phone:** 617-636-5866; **Board Cert:** Internal Medicine 1979; Nephrology 1982; **Med School:** Hahnemann Univ 1975; **Resid:** Internal Medicine, Grady Meml Hosp 1978; **Fellow:** Nephrology, Boston Med Ctr 1982; **Fac Appt:** Prof Med, Tufts Univ

Salant, David J MD [Nep] - **Spec Exp:** Kidney Disease-Glomerular; Kidney Disease-Autoimmune; Lupus Nephritis; Vasculitis; **Hospital:** Boston Med Ctr; **Address:** Boston Med Ctr, 650 Albany St, Ste X504, Boston, MA 02118; **Phone:** 617-638-7330; **Board Cert:** Internal Medicine 1978; Nephrology 1980; **Med School:** South Africa 1969; **Resid:** Internal Medicine, Johannesburg Genl Hosp 1973; **Fellow:** Nephrology, Boston Med Ctr 1978; **Fac Appt:** Prof Med, Boston Univ

Seifter, Julian L MD [Nep] - **Spec Exp:** Diabetic Kidney Disease; Kidney Failure-Chronic; Kidney Stones; **Hospital:** Brigham & Women's Hosp; **Address:** Brigham & Women's Hosp, Div Renal Med, 75 Francis St, Boston, MA 02115; **Phone:** 617-732-6383; **Board Cert:** Internal Medicine 1978; Nephrology 1980; **Med School:** Albert Einstein Coll Med 1975; **Resid:** Internal Medicine, Bronx Municipal Hosp Ctr 1981; **Fellow:** Nephrology, Yale-New Haven Hosp 1982; **Fac Appt:** Assoc Prof Med, Harvard Med Sch

Tolkoff-Rubin, Nina MD [Nep] - **Spec Exp:** Transplant Medicine-Kidney; Hypertension; Kidney Failure-Acute; Polycystic Kidney Disease; **Hospital:** Mass Genl Hosp; **Address:** MGH Renal Associates, 165 Cambridge St, Ste 302, Boston, MA 02114; **Phone:** 617-726-3706; **Board Cert:** Nephrology 1974; Internal Medicine 1972; **Med School:** Harvard Med Sch 1968; **Resid:** Internal Medicine, Mass Genl Hosp 1970; **Fellow:** Nephrology, Mass Genl Hosp 1972; **Fac Appt:** Assoc Prof Med, Harvard Med Sch

Mid Atlantic

Appel, Gerald B MD/PhD [Nep] - **Spec Exp:** Glomerulonephritis; Lupus Nephritis; Nephrotic Syndrome; **Hospital:** NY-Presby/Columbia Univ Med Ctr, NY (page 65); **Address:** 161 Fort Washington Ave Fl 2 - Ste 202, New York, NY 10032-3720; **Phone:** 212-305-0320 x3; **Board Cert:** Internal Medicine 1975; Nephrology 1978; **Med School:** Albert Einstein Coll Med 1972; **Resid:** Internal Medicine, Columbia Presby Hosp 1975; **Fellow:** Nephrology, Columbia Presby Hosp 1976; Nephrology, Yale-New Haven Hosp 1978; **Fac Appt:** Clin Prof Med, Columbia P&S

August, Phyllis MD [Nep] - **Spec Exp:** Hypertension; Hypertension in Pregnancy; Kidney Disease; **Hospital:** NY-Presby/Weill Cornell Med Ctr, NY (page 65); **Address:** NY Presby/Weill Cornell Med Ctr, Hypertension Center, 424 E 70th St, New York, NY 10021-4870; **Phone:** 646-962-2605; **Board Cert:** Internal Medicine 1980; Nephrology 1982; **Med School:** Yale Univ 1977; **Resid:** Internal Medicine, NY Hosp-Cornell Med Ctr 1980; **Fellow:** Nephrology, NY Hosp-Cornell Med Ctr 1983; **Fac Appt:** Prof Med, Cornell Univ-Weill Med Coll

Bernardo, Jose F MD [Nep] - **Spec Exp:** Kidney Disease; Dialysis Care; **Hospital:** UPMC Mercy, Pittsburgh; **Address:** UPMC Kidney Clin, 120 Lytton Ave, Ste 300, Pittsburgh, PA 15213; **Phone:** 412-802-3043; **Board Cert:** Internal Medicine 2009; Nephrology 2001; **Med School:** Peru 1984; **Resid:** Internal Medicine, Universidad Peruana 1989; Internal Medicine, UPMC 2000; **Fellow:** Nephrology, UPMC 2002; **Fac Appt:** Asst Prof Med, Univ Pittsburgh

Berns, Jeffrey S MD [Nep] - **Spec Exp:** Kidney Disease-Chronic; Glomerulonephritis; Hypertension; **Hospital:** Hosp Univ Penn - UPHS (page 69); **Address:** Univ Penn Nephrology, Perelman Ctr for Advanced Medicine, 3400 Civic Center Blvd, Ste 1-300 S, Philadelphia, PA 19104-2699; **Phone:** 215-662-2638; **Board Cert:** Internal Medicine 1984; Nephrology 2011; **Med School:** Case West Res Univ 1981; **Resid:** Internal Medicine, Univ Hosp 1984; **Fellow:** Nephrology, Yale Univ 1987; **Fac Appt:** Prof Med, Univ Pennsylvania

Blumenfeld, Jon D MD [Nep] - **Spec Exp:** Polycystic Kidney Disease; Hypertension; Adrenal Disorders; **Hospital:** NY-Presby/Weill Cornell Med Ctr, NY (page 65), Rockefeller Univ; **Address:** The Rogosin Institute, 505 E 70th St, Fl 2, New York, NY 10021; **Phone:** 212-746-1495; **Board Cert:** Internal Medicine 1984; Nephrology 1986; **Med School:** Yale Univ 1981; **Resid:** Internal Medicine, New York Hosp 1984; **Fellow:** Nephrology, Brigham & Womens Hosp 1988; **Fac Appt:** Prof Med, Cornell Univ-Weill Med Coll

Cohen, David J MD [Nep] - **Spec Exp:** Transplant Medicine-Kidney; Glomerulonephritis; **Hospital:** NY-Presby/Columbia Univ Med Ctr, NY (page 65); **Address:** Columbia Univ Med Ctr, 622 W 168th St, rm PH 4-124, New York, NY 10032-3720; **Phone:** 212-305-0320 x4; **Board Cert:** Internal Medicine 1980; Nephrology 1984; **Med School:** Albert Einstein Coll Med 1977; **Resid:** Internal Medicine, Mount Sinai Hosp 1980; **Fellow:** Nephrology, Columbia-Presby Hosp 1981; Transplant Immunobiology, Brigham & Womens Hosp 1983; **Fac Appt:** Clin Prof Med, Columbia P&S

Dember, Laura MD [Nep] - **Spec Exp:** Kidney Failure-Chronic; Nephrotic Syndrome; Amyloidosis; **Hospital:** Hosp Univ Penn - UPHS (page 69); **Address:** Perelman Center for Advanced Medicine, South Pavilion, 1st Fl, 3400 Civic Center Blvd, Ste 1-300S, Philadelphia, PA 19104; **Phone:** 215-662-2638; **Board Cert:** Nephrology 2000; **Med School:** Yale Univ 1988; **Resid:** Internal Medicine, Hosp Univ Penn 1991; **Fellow:** Nephrology, Hosp Univ Penn 1992; Nephrology, Brigham & Womens Hosp 1995; **Fac Appt:** Prof Med, Univ Pennsylvania

Holzman, Lawrence B MD [Nep] - **Spec Exp:** Glomerulonephritis; Lupus Nephritis; Vasculitis; **Hospital:** Hosp Univ Penn - UPHS (page 69), VA Med Ctr - Philadelphia; **Address:** Renal Electrolyte and Hypertension Div, 3400 Civic Center Blvd, 1st FL, Ste 300, Philadelphia, PA 19104; **Phone:** 215-662-2638; **Board Cert:** Internal Medicine 1987; **Med School:** UMDNJ-NJ Med Sch, Newark 1984; **Resid:** Internal Medicine, Med Coll Penn Affil Hosp 1987; **Fellow:** Nephrology, Univ Mich Med Ctr 1989; **Fac Appt:** Prof Med, Univ Pennsylvania

Johnston, James R MD [Nep] - **Spec Exp:** Diabetic Kidney Disease; Hypertension; **Hospital:** UPMC Presby, Pittsburgh; **Address:** UPMC Kidney Clinic, 120 Lytton Ave, Ste 300, Pittsburgh, PA 15213; **Phone:** 412-802-3043; **Board Cert:** Internal Medicine 1982; Nephrology 1984; **Med School:** Univ Pittsburgh 1979; **Resid:** Internal Medicine, Montefiore Hosp 1982; **Fellow:** Nephrology, Univ Pittsburgh Med Ctr 1983; Nephrology, Brigham & Women's Hosp 1986; **Fac Appt:** Prof Med, Univ Pittsburgh

Kelepouris, Ellie MD [Nep] - **Spec Exp:** Kidney Stones; Hypertension/Kidney Disease; Polycystic Kidney Disease; **Hospital:** Hahnemann Univ Hosp; **Address:** 219 N Broad St Fl 9, Philadelphia, PA 19107; **Phone:** 215-762-2688; **Board Cert:** Nephrology 2008; **Med School:** Greece 1976; **Resid:** Internal Medicine, Mercy Cath Med Ctr 1979; **Fellow:** Nephrology, Hosp Univ Penn 1982; **Fac Appt:** Prof Med, Drexel Univ Coll Med

Kobrin, Sidney M MD [Nep] - **Spec Exp:** Dialysis Care; Diabetic Kidney Disease; Kidney Failure; Hypertension; **Hospital:** Hosp Univ Penn - UPHS (page 69); **Address:** Univ Penn, Div Nephrology, Perelman Ctr for Advanced Medicine, 3400 Civic Center Blvd, Ste 1-300 S, Philadelphia, PA 19104-2699; **Phone:** 215-662-2638; **Board Cert:** Nephrology 2012; **Med School:** South Africa 1978; **Resid:** Internal Medicine, Johannesburg Tchg Hosp 1984; **Fellow:** Nephrology, Einstein Med Ctr 1988; **Fac Appt:** Assoc Prof Med, Univ Pennsylvania

Piraino, Beth M MD [Nep] - **Spec Exp:** Kidney Failure; Hypertension; **Hospital:** UPMC Presby, Pittsburgh; **Address:** 3504 Fifth Ave, Ste 200, Pittsburgh, PA 15213; **Phone:** 412-383-4899; **Board Cert:** Internal Medicine 1980; Nephrology 1982; **Med School:** Med Coll PA Hahnemann 1977; **Resid:** Internal Medicine, Presby Univ Hosp 1980; **Fellow:** Nephrology, Presby Univ Hosp 1982; **Fac Appt:** Prof Med, Univ Pittsburgh

Rudnick, Michael R MD [Nep] - **Spec Exp:** Hypertension; Kidney Disease; Kidney Failure-Acute; Kidney Stones; **Hospital:** Penn Presby Med Ctr - UPHS (page 69); **Address:** Penn Presbyterian Med Ctr, 51 N 39th St, 240 Medical Office Bldg, Philadelphia, PA 19104-2699; **Phone:** 215-662-8730; **Board Cert:** Internal Medicine 1975; Nephrology 1976; **Med School:** Hahnemann Univ 1972; **Resid:** Internal Medicine, Hahnemann Univ Med Ctr 1974; **Fellow:** Nephrology, Hosp Univ Penn 1976; **Fac Appt:** Assoc Prof Med, Hahnemann Univ

Stern, Leonard MD [Nep] - **Spec Exp:** Kidney Failure-Chronic; Transplant Medicine-Kidney; Bone Disorders-Metabolic; Dialysis Care; **Hospital:** NY-Presby/Columbia Univ Med Ctr, NY (page 65); **Address:** 622 W 168th St, Room PH4-4124, New York, NY 10032-3702; **Phone:** 212-305-3273; **Board Cert:** Internal Medicine 1978; Nephrology 1980; **Med School:** NY Med Coll 1975; **Resid:** Internal Medicine, Jacobi Med Ctr 1978; **Fellow:** Nephrology, Montefiore Med Ctr 1979; Nephrology, Yale-New Haven Hosp 1981; **Fac Appt:** Assoc Prof Med, Columbia P&S

Townsend, Raymond R MD [Nep] - **Spec Exp:** Hypertension-Complex; Renal Artery Stenosis; Kidney Disease-Chronic; **Hospital:** Hosp Univ Penn - UPHS (page 69); **Address:** Univ Penn, Div Nephrology, Perelman Ctr for Advanced Medicine, 3400 Civic Center Blvd, Ste 1-300 S, Philadelphia, PA 19104-2699; **Phone:** 215-662-2638; **Board Cert:** Internal Medicine 1982; Nephrology 1984; **Med School:** Hahnemann Univ 1979; **Resid:** Internal Medicine, Allegheny Genl Hosp 1982; **Fellow:** Nephrology, Temple Univ Hosp 1984; **Fac Appt:** Prof Med, Univ Pennsylvania

Wilcox, Christopher S MD/PhD [Nep] - **Spec Exp:** Hypertension-Renovascular; Hypertension-Drug Resistent; **Hospital:** MedStar Georgetown Univ Hosp; **Address:** Pasquerilla Hlth Ctr, 3800 Reservoir Rd NW, Fl 6 - rm F6003, Washington, DC 20007-2113; **Phone:** 202-444-9183; **Board Cert:** Internal Medicine 1983; Nephrology 1986; **Med School:** England, UK 1968; **Resid:** Internal Medicine, Middlesex Hosp 1971; **Fellow:** Nephrology, Middlesex Hosp 1974; **Fac Appt:** Prof Med, Georgetown Univ

Williams, Gail S MD [Nep] - **Spec Exp:** Kidney Failure-Chronic; Transplant Medicine-Kidney; Hypertension; **Hospital:** NY-Presby/Columbia Univ Med Ctr, NY (page 65); **Address:** NY-Presby, Neurology Dept, 161 Fort Washington Ave, Ste 351, New York, NY 10032; **Phone:** 212-305-5376; **Board Cert:** Internal Medicine 1972; Nephrology 1974; **Med School:** Columbia P&S 1968; **Resid:** Internal Medicine, NY-Presby/Columbia Univ Med Ctr 1973; **Fellow:** Nephrology, NY-Presby/Columbia Univ Med Ctr 1974; **Fac Appt:** Assoc Clin Prof Med, Columbia P&S

Winston, Jonathan MD [Nep] - **Spec Exp:** Kidney Disease-Chronic; Kidney Failure; HIV Related Kidney Disease; Glomerulonephritis; **Hospital:** Mt Sinai Med Ctr (page 62); **Address:** 5 E 98th St Fl 11, New York, NY 10029-6501; **Phone:** 212-241-4060; **Board Cert:** Internal Medicine 1980; Nephrology 1984; **Med School:** Geo Wash Univ 1977; **Resid:** Internal Medicine, LI Jewish Med Ctr 1980; **Fellow:** Nephrology, Mt Sinai Hosp 1982; **Fac Appt:** Assoc Prof Med, Mount Sinai Sch Med

Southeast

Allon, Michael MD [Nep] - **Hospital:** UAB Hosp; **Address:** UAB Nephrology, 1530 3rd Ave S, PB 226, Birmingham, AL 35294; **Phone:** 205-975-9676; **Board Cert:** Internal Medicine 1985; Nephrology 1988; **Med School:** Univ Mich Med Sch 1982; **Resid:** Internal Medicine, Emory Univ Affil Hosp 1985; **Fellow:** Nephrology, Emory Univ Affil Hosp 1987; **Fac Appt:** Prof Med, UAB Sch Med

Bolton, W Kline MD [Nep] - **Spec Exp:** Kidney Disease-Glomerular; Kidney Disease-Chronic; Glomerulonephritis; **Hospital:** Univ of Virginia Hlth Sys; **Address:** Univ VA Hlth Scis Ctr, Box 800 133, Charlottesville, VA 22908-0001; **Phone:** 434-924-5125; **Board Cert:** Internal Medicine 1972; Nephrology 1974; **Med School:** Univ VA Sch Med 1969; **Resid:** Internal Medicine, Boston City Hosp 1971; **Fellow:** Nephrology, Univ Chicago 1973; **Fac Appt:** Prof Med, Univ VA Sch Med

Butterly, David W MD [Nep] - **Spec Exp:** Transplant Medicine-Kidney; Kidney Disease; **Hospital:** Duke Univ Hosp; **Address:** Duke Box 2747, 200 Trent Drive, Ste 2B/2C, Durham, NC 27710; **Phone:** 919-668-7630; **Board Cert:** Internal Medicine 2010; Nephrology 2000; **Med School:** Duke Univ 1987; **Resid:** Internal Medicine, Duke Univ Med Ctr 1990; **Fellow:** Nephrology, Duke Univ Med Ctr 1992

Coffman, Thomas M MD [Nep] - **Spec Exp:** Transplant Medicine-Kidney; Hypertension; **Hospital:** Duke Univ Hosp, Durham VA Med Ctr; **Address:** Duke Box 103015, Room 2018/MSRB 2, 106 Research Drive, Durham, NC 27710; **Phone:** 919-684-9708; **Board Cert:** Internal Medicine 1983; Nephrology 1988; **Med School:** Ohio State Univ 1980; **Resid:** Internal Medicine, Duke Univ Med Ctr 1983; **Fellow:** Nephrology, Duke Univ Med Ctr 1985; **Fac Appt:** Prof Med, Duke Univ

Falk, Ronald J MD [Nep] - **Spec Exp:** Glomerulonephritis; Lupus Nephritis; Wegener's Granulomatosis; Vasculitis; **Hospital:** NC Memorial Hosp - UNC; **Address:** UNC Kidney Ctr, 7024 Burnett Womack Bldg CB #7155, Chapel Hill, NC 27599-7155; **Phone:** 919-966-2561; **Board Cert:** Internal Medicine 1980; Nephrology 1982; **Med School:** Univ NC Sch Med 1977; **Resid:** Internal Medicine, Univ North Carolina Hosps 1980; Nephrology, Univ NC 1981; **Fellow:** Research, Univ Minn 1983; **Fac Appt:** Prof Med, Univ NC Sch Med

Fulop, Tibor MD [Nep] - **Spec Exp:** Kidney Stones; Vasculitis; Renal Replacement Therapy; Hypertension; **Hospital:** Univ Mississippi Med Ctr; **Address:** 2500 N State St, Jackson, MS 39216; **Phone:** 601-984-5670; **Board Cert:** Internal Medicine 2005; Nephrology 2007; **Med School:** Hungary 1990; **Resid:** Internal Medicine, Henry Ford Hosp 1995; **Fellow:** Nephrology, Henry Ford Hosp 1997; Nephrology, Univ of Iowa Hosp & Clin 1998; **Fac Appt:** Assoc Prof Med, Univ Miss

Gaston, Robert S MD [Nep] - **Spec Exp:** Transplant Medicine-Kidney; Kidney Disease; Dialysis Care; **Hospital:** UAB Hosp; **Address:** UAB Hosp, Div Nephrology, 1720 2nd Ave S, THT 625, Birmingham, AL 35294; **Phone:** 205-934-7220; **Board Cert:** Internal Medicine 1982; Nephrology 1986; **Med School:** St Louis Univ 1979; **Resid:** Internal Medicine, UAMS Med Ctr 1982; **Fellow:** Nephrology, UAMS Med Ctr 1986; Transplant Medicine, UAB Hosp 1988; **Fac Appt:** Prof Med, UAB Sch Med

Helderman, J Harold MD [Nep] - **Spec Exp:** Transplant Medicine-Kidney; Kidney Disease-Glomerular; Kidney Disease-Autoimmune; **Hospital:** Vanderbilt Univ Med Ctr; **Address:** Vanderbilt Nephrology, 1161 21st Ave S, S-3223 Medical Center N, Nashville, TN 37232; **Phone:** 615-343-1064; **Board Cert:** Internal Medicine 1974; **Med School:** SUNY Downstate 1971; **Resid:** Internal Medicine, Johns Hopkins Hosp 1973; **Fellow:** Nephrology, Harvard Univ 1976; **Fac Appt:** Prof Med, Vanderbilt Univ

Lea, Janice I MD [Nep] - **Spec Exp:** Hypertension-Complex; Kidney Disease-Chronic; Diabetic Kidney Disease; Dialysis Care; **Hospital:** Emory Univ Hosp Midtown; **Address:** Emory Clin, Nephrology Dept, 550 Peachtree St NE Fl 7, Atlanta, GA 30308; **Phone:** 404-686-5038; **Board Cert:** Nephrology 2005; **Med School:** Univ Tex Med Br, Galveston 1988; **Resid:** Internal Medicine, Emory Univ Hosp 1991; **Fellow:** Nephrology, Emory Univ Hosp 1994; **Fac Appt:** Prof Med, Emory Univ

Okusa, Mark D MD [Nep] - **Spec Exp:** Kidney Failure-Chronic; Nephrotic Syndrome; Kidney Failure-Acute; **Hospital:** Univ of Virginia Hlth Sys; **Address:** Univ VA Hlth Sci Ctr, Div Nephrology, Box 800133, Charlottesville, VA 22908-0001; **Phone:** 434-924-2187; **Board Cert:** Internal Medicine 1985; Nephrology 1988; **Med School:** Med Coll VA 1982; **Resid:** Internal Medicine, Med Coll Virginia 1985; **Fellow:** Nephrology, Yale Univ Sch Med 1988; **Fac Appt:** Prof Med, Univ VA Sch Med

Rakowski, Thomas A MD [Nep] - **Spec Exp:** Polycystic Kidney Disease; Kidney Disease-Glomerular; **Hospital:** Virginia Hosp Ctr - Arlington; **Address:** Virginia Nephrology Grp, 1635 N George Mason Drive, Ste 215, Arlington, VA 22205; **Phone:** 703-841-0707; **Board Cert:** Internal Medicine 1972; Nephrology 1974; **Med School:** Hahnemann Univ 1969; **Resid:** Internal Medicine, Georgetown Univ 1971; **Fellow:** Nephrology, Georgetown Univ 1973; **Fac Appt:** Assoc Prof Med, Georgetown Univ

Roth, David MD [Nep] - **Spec Exp:** Transplant Medicine-Kidney; Kidney Failure-Chronic; **Hospital:** Jackson Meml Hosp, Univ of Miami Hosp; **Address:** Diabetes Research Inst, 1450 NW 10th Ave, Miami, FL 33136; **Phone:** 305-243-6251; **Board Cert:** Internal Medicine 1980; Nephrology 1982; **Med School:** SUNY Downstate 1977; **Resid:** Internal Medicine, Jackson Meml Hosp 1980; **Fellow:** Nephrology, Jackson Meml Hosp 1982; **Fac Appt:** Prof Med, Univ Miami Sch Med

Weiner, I David MD [Nep] - **Spec Exp:** Kidney Disease-Chronic; Hypertension; Fluid/Electrolyte Balance; **Hospital:** UF Hlth Shands Hosp; **Address:** 2000 SW Archer Rd, Gainesville, FL 32610; **Phone:** 352-265-0139; **Board Cert:** Internal Medicine 1987; Nephrology 2011; **Med School:** Vanderbilt Univ 1984; **Resid:** Internal Medicine, Univ TX Hlth Sci Ctr 1987; **Fellow:** Nephrology, Barnes-Jewish Hosp 1990; **Fac Appt:** Prof Med, Univ Fla Coll Med

Midwest

Bakris, George L MD [Nep] - **Spec Exp:** Hypertension; Kidney Disease; **Hospital:** Univ of Chicago Med; **Address:** ASH Comprehensive Hypertension Ctr, 5841 S Maryland Ave, MC 1027, Chicago, IL 60637; **Phone:** 773-702-7936; **Board Cert:** Internal Medicine 1986; **Med School:** Ros Franklin Univ/Chicago Med Sch 1981; **Resid:** Internal Medicine, Mayo Clinic 1983; Internal Medicine, Univ IL Med Ctr 1986; **Fellow:** Clinical Pharmacology, Univ Chicago Hosps 1987; Nephrology, Univ Chicago Hosps 1988; **Fac Appt:** Prof Med, Univ Chicago-Pritzker Sch Med

Brennan, Daniel C MD [Nep] - **Spec Exp:** Transplant Medicine-Kidney; **Hospital:** Barnes-Jewish Hosp; **Address:** Wash Univ Sch Med, Div Renal Diseases, 660 S Euclid Ave, Box 8126, St Louis, MO 63110; **Phone:** 314-362-7603; **Board Cert:** Internal Medicine 1988; Nephrology 2012; **Med School:** Univ Iowa Coll Med 1985; **Resid:** Internal Medicine, Univ Iowa Hosps 1988; **Fellow:** Nephrology, Brigham and Women's Hosp 1992; **Fac Appt:** Assoc Prof Med, Washington Univ, St Louis

Coe, Fredric MD [Nep] - **Spec Exp:** Kidney Stones; Fluid/Electrolyte Balance; **Hospital:** Univ of Chicago Med; **Address:** 5841 S Maryland Ave, MC 5100, Chicago, IL 60637; **Phone:** 773-702-1475; **Board Cert:** Internal Medicine 1968; **Med School:** Univ Chicago-Pritzker Sch Med 1961; **Resid:** Internal Medicine, Michael Reese Hosp 1965; **Fellow:** Renal Disease, Univ Texas SW 1969; **Fac Appt:** Prof Med, Univ Chicago-Pritzker Sch Med

Delmez, James A MD [Nep] - **Spec Exp:** Kidney Disease; **Hospital:** Barnes-Jewish Hosp, Washington Univ Phys; **Address:** Wash Univ Sch Med, Div Renal Diseases, 660 S Euclid Ave, Box 8126, St Louis, MO 63110; **Phone:** 314-362-7603; **Board Cert:** Internal Medicine 1976; Nephrology 1982; **Med School:** Univ Rochester 1973; **Resid:** Internal Medicine, Barnes Hosp 1976; **Fellow:** Nephrology, Barnes Hosp 1978; **Fac Appt:** Prof Med, Washington Univ, St Louis

Hruska, Keith A MD [Nep] - **Spec Exp:** Kidney Disease-Pediatric & Adult; Kidney Stones; Bone Disorders-Metabolic; Inherited Metabolic Disorders; **Hospital:** St. Louis Chldns Hosp, Barnes-Jewish Hosp; **Address:** 4921 Parkview Pl Fl 5 - Ste 5C, St Louis, MO 63110-1010; **Phone:** 314-362-9096; **Board Cert:** Internal Medicine 1972; Nephrology 1976; **Med School:** Creighton Univ 1969; **Resid:** Internal Medicine, New York Hosp-Cornell 1971; Internal Medicine, Barnes Hosp-Wash Univ 1972; **Fellow:** Nephrology, Barnes Hosp-Wash Univ 1974; **Fac Appt:** Prof Ped, Washington Univ, St Louis

Josephson, Michelle A MD [Nep] - **Spec Exp:** Transplant Medicine-Kidney; Hypertension; **Hospital:** Univ of Chicago Med; **Address:** 5841 S Maryland Ave, MC 5100, Chicago, IL 60637; **Phone:** 773-702-6134; **Board Cert:** Internal Medicine 1986; Nephrology 2010; **Med School:** Univ Pennsylvania 1983; **Resid:** Internal Medicine, Univ Chicago Hosps 1986; **Fellow:** Nephrology, Univ Chicago Hosps 1991; **Fac Appt:** Prof Med, Univ Chicago-Pritzker Sch Med

Kasiske, Bertram L MD [Nep] - **Spec Exp:** Transplant Medicine-Kidney; Kidney Disease-Geriatric; **Hospital:** Hennepin Cnty Med Ctr; **Address:** Hennepin Cnty Med Ctr, Div Nephrology, 701 Park Ave, Minneapolis, MN 55415; **Phone:** 612-347-6088; **Board Cert:** Internal Medicine 1980; Nephrology 1982; **Med School:** Univ Iowa Coll Med 1976; **Resid:** Internal Medicine, Hennepin Co Med Ctr 1980; **Fellow:** Nephrology, Hennepin Co Med Ctr 1983; **Fac Appt:** Prof Med, Univ Minn

Kraus, Michael A MD [Nep] - **Spec Exp:** Kidney Disease-Chronic; Kidney Failure-Acute; Dialysis Care; **Hospital:** IU Hlth Univ Hosp, IU Health North Hosp; **Address:** Northside Kidney Ctr, 8803 N Meridian St, Ste 150, Indianapolis, IN 46260; **Phone:** 317-963-6875; **Board Cert:** Internal Medicine 1988; Nephrology 2012; **Med School:** Indiana Univ 1985; **Resid:** Internal Medicine, IU Hlth Hosp 1988; **Fellow:** Nephrology, Univ Iowa Hosps & Clins 1991; **Fac Appt:** Prof Med, Indiana Univ

McCarthy, James T MD [Nep] - **Spec Exp:** Kidney Failure-Chronic; Dialysis Care; **Hospital:** Mayo Med Ctr & Clin - Rochester; **Address:** Mayo Clin, Div Nephrology/Hypertension, 200 First St SW, Rochester, MN 55905; **Phone:** 507-266-6711; **Board Cert:** Internal Medicine 1980; Nephrology 1982; **Med School:** Univ Kansas 1977; **Resid:** Internal Medicine, Mayo Clin 1980; **Fellow:** Nephrology, Mayo Clin 1983; **Fac Appt:** Prof Med, Mayo Med Sch

Miller, Brent W MD [Nep] - **Spec Exp:** Kidney Failure-Chronic; Transplant Medicine-Kidney; Dialysis Care; **Hospital:** Barnes-Jewish Hosp; **Address:** Wash Univ Sch Med, Div Renal Diseases, 660 S Euclid Ave, Box 8126, St Louis, MO 63110; **Phone:** 314-362-7603; **Board Cert:** Internal Medicine 2003; Nephrology 2007; **Med School:** Washington Univ, St Louis 1990; **Resid:** Internal Medicine, Washington Univ Sch Med 1993; **Fellow:** Nephrology, Washington Univ Sch Med 1998; **Fac Appt:** Assoc Prof Med, Univ Wash

Pohl, Marc MD [Nep] - **Spec Exp:** Hypertension; Kidney Disease; Diabetic Kidney Disease; **Hospital:** Cleveland Clin (page 55); **Address:** Dept Nephrology & Hypertension, 9500 Euclid Ave, Desk Q7, Cleveland, OH 44195; **Phone:** 216-444-6776; **Board Cert:** Internal Medicine 1972; Nephrology 1978; **Med School:** Case West Res Univ 1966; **Resid:** Internal Medicine, Univ Hosps of Cleveland 1968; Internal Medicine, Mass Genl Hosp 1971; **Fellow:** Nephrology, Boston City Hosp-Boston Univ 1972; Nephrology, Mass Genl Hosp 1973

Rodby, Roger A MD [Nep] - **Spec Exp:** Diabetic Kidney Disease; Glomerulonephritis; Lupus Nephritis; Dialysis Care; **Hospital:** Rush Univ Med Ctr; **Address:** 1426 W Washington Blvd, Chicago, IL 60607; **Phone:** 312-850-8434; **Board Cert:** Internal Medicine 1985; Nephrology 1988; **Med School:** Univ IL Coll Med 1982; **Resid:** Internal Medicine, Rutgers/UMDNJ-RWJ Med Ctr 1985; **Fellow:** Nephrology, Rush Univ Med Ctr 1987; **Fac Appt:** Prof Med, Rush Med Coll

Schreiber, Martin J MD [Nep] - **Spec Exp:** Dialysis Care; Diabetic Kidney Disease; Heart Failure in Kidney Disease; **Hospital:** Cleveland Clin (page 55); **Address:** Cleveland Clinic-Nephrology, 9500 Euclid Ave, Desk Q7, Cleveland, OH 44195; **Phone:** 216-444-6365; **Board Cert:** Internal Medicine 1984; Nephrology 2003; **Med School:** Wake Forest Univ 1976; **Resid:** Internal Medicine, Cleveland Clinic 1979; **Fellow:** Nephrology, Cleveland Clinic 1980; Nephrology, Mass Genl Hosp 1982

Schwartz, Gary Lee MD [Nep] - **Spec Exp:** Hypertension; Kidney Disease-Chronic; Diabetic Kidney Disease; **Hospital:** St. Mary's Hosp - Rochester MN (Mayo), Rochester Methodist Hosp; **Address:** Mayo Clinic, 200 1st St SW, Rochester, MN 55905-0002; **Phone:** 507-266-7093; **Board Cert:** Internal Medicine 1980; Nephrology 1982; **Med School:** Univ Wisc 1977; **Resid:** Internal Medicine, Mayo Clinic 1980; **Fellow:** Nephrology, Mayo Clinic 1982; **Fac Appt:** Clin Prof Med, Mayo Med Sch

Somerville, James H MD [Nep] - **Hospital:** Fairview Southdale Hosp, Fairview Ridges Hosp; **Address:** 6363 France Ave S, Ste 400, Edina, MN 55435; **Phone:** 952-920-2070; **Board Cert:** Internal Medicine 1978; Nephrology 1982; **Med School:** Univ MD Sch Med 1975; **Resid:** Internal Medicine, Hennepin Co Med Ctr 1978; **Fellow:** Nephrology, Hennepin Co Med Ctr 1980

Swartz, Richard D MD [Nep] - **Spec Exp:** Kidney Failure; Dialysis Care; **Hospital:** Univ Michigan Med Ctr; **Address:** Univ Michigan Med Ctr, Div Nephrology, 1500 E Med Ctr Drive, 3914 Taubman Ctr, Ann Arbor, MI 48109-0364; **Phone:** 734-647-9342; **Board Cert:** Internal Medicine 1975; Nephrology 1978; **Med School:** Univ Mich Med Sch 1970; **Resid:** Internal Medicine, Boston City Hosp 1975; Nephrology, Beth Israel Hosp-Harvard 1977; **Fac Appt:** Prof Med, Univ Mich Med Sch

Textor, Stephen C MD [Nep] - **Spec Exp:** Transplant Medicine-Kidney; Hypertension; Renal Artery Stenosis; **Hospital:** Mayo Med Ctr & Clin - Rochester; **Address:** Mayo Clin, Div Nephrology/Hypertension, 200 First St SW, rm MA 19-E, Rochester, MN 55905; **Phone:** 507-266-7093; **Board Cert:** Internal Medicine 1977; Nephrology 1980; **Med School:** UCLA 1973; **Resid:** Internal Medicine, Boston City Hosp 1977; **Fellow:** Nephrology, Boston Univ 1978; Hypertension, Fogarty Inst 1980; **Fac Appt:** Prof Med, Mayo Med Sch

Thomas, Christie P MD [Nep] - **Spec Exp:** Transplant Medicine-Kidney; Fabry's Disease; **Hospital:** Univ Iowa Hosp & Clins; **Address:** UIHC Nephrology Dept, 200 Hawkins Drive, Iowa City, IA 52242; **Phone:** 319-356-4216; **Board Cert:** Internal Medicine 2007; Nephrology 2008; **Med School:** India 1982; **Resid:** Internal Medicine, MMM Hosp Kolenchery 1983; Internal Medicine, Genl Hosp 1986; **Fellow:** Nephrology, Univ Sheffield Hosp 1988; Nephrology, Case Western Res Univ Hosp 1991; **Fac Appt:** Prof Med, Univ Iowa Coll Med

Torres, Vicente E MD [Nep] - **Spec Exp:** Polycystic Kidney Disease; Glomerulonephritis; **Hospital:** Mayo Med Ctr & Clin - Rochester; **Address:** Mayo Clin, Div Nephrology/Hypertension, 200 First St SW, Mayo E-19, Rochester, MN 55905; **Phone:** 507-266-7093; **Board Cert:** Internal Medicine 1977; Nephrology 1980; **Med School:** Spain 1969; **Resid:** Internal Medicine, Mayo Med Ctr & Clin 1977; **Fellow:** Nephrology, Mayo Med Sch 1979; **Fac Appt:** Prof Med, Mayo Med Sch

Venkat, K. K. MD [Nep] - **Spec Exp:** Transplant Medicine-Kidney; Kidney Disease; **Hospital:** Henry Ford Hosp; **Address:** Henry Ford Hosp, Div Nephrology, 2799 W Grand Blvd Fl K16, Detroit, MI 48202-2689; **Phone:** 313-916-2710; **Board Cert:** Internal Medicine 1977; Nephrology 1978; **Med School:** India 1970; **Resid:** Internal Medicine, Henry Ford Hosp 1976; **Fellow:** Nephrology, Henry Ford Hosp 1978

Yee, Jerry MD [Nep] - **Spec Exp:** Kidney Disease-Chronic; Hypertension; Diabetic Kidney Disease; **Hospital:** Henry Ford Hosp; **Address:** Henry Ford Hospital, 2799 W Grand Blvd, CFP-5, Detroit, MI 48202; **Phone:** 313-916-9405; **Board Cert:** Internal Medicine 1985; Nephrology 2012; **Med School:** Jefferson Med Coll 1982; **Resid:** Internal Medicine, Brooke AMC-Fort Sam 1985; **Fellow:** Nephrology, Temple Univ Hosp 1986; Hypertension, Hosp Univ Penn 1987; **Fac Appt:** Assoc Prof Med, Wayne State Univ

Southwest

Brennan, Stephen T MD [Nep] - **Spec Exp:** Transplant Medicine-Kidney; Kidney Stones; Kidney Failure-Chronic; **Hospital:** Methodist Hosp - Houston, St. Luke's Episcopal Hosp-Houston; **Address:** Kidney Inst, 1415 La Concha Ln, Houston, TX 77054; **Phone:** 713-790-9080; **Board Cert:** Internal Medicine 1983; Nephrology 1988; **Med School:** Loyola Univ-Stritch Sch Med 1979; **Resid:** Internal Medicine, Loyola Univ Med Ctr 1983; **Fellow:** Nephrology, Barnes-Jewish Hosp 1986; **Fac Appt:** Assoc Clin Prof Med, Baylor Coll Med

Fadem, Stephen Z MD [Nep] - **Spec Exp:** Kidney Disease-Chronic; Kidney Failure; Hypertension; Polycystic Kidney Disease; **Hospital:** Methodist Hosp - Houston, St. Luke's Episcopal Hosp-Houston; **Address:** Kidney Assocs, 6624 Fannin St, Ste 1400, Houston, TX 77030; **Phone:** 713-795-5511; **Board Cert:** Internal Medicine 1976; Nephrology 1978; **Med School:** Univ Okla Coll Med 1973; **Resid:** Internal Medicine, UT MD Anderson Hosp 1976; **Fellow:** Renal Disease, Audie L Murphy Meml Vets Hosp 1978; **Fac Appt:** Clin Prof Med, Baylor Coll Med

Kasinath, Balakuntalam S MD [Nep] - **Spec Exp:** Glomerulonephritis; Diabetic Kidney Disease; **Hospital:** Audie L Murphy Meml Vets Hosp - San Antonio, Univ Hosp-San Antonio; **Address:** STVHCS, Nephrology Dept, 7400 Merton Minter Blvd, San Antonio, TX 78229; **Phone:** 210-617-5300 x14740; **Board Cert:** Internal Medicine 1980; Nephrology 1982; **Med School:** India 1975; **Resid:** Internal Medicine, IL Masonic Med Ctr 1980; **Fellow:** Nephrology, Univ Chicago Med Ctr 1983; **Fac Appt:** Prof Med, Univ Tex, San Antonio

Nolan III, Charles Raymond MD [Nep] - **Spec Exp:** Transplant Medicine-Kidney; Transplant Medicine-Pancreas; Hypertension; **Hospital:** Univ Hosp-San Antonio; **Address:** UTHSCSA, Transplant Ctr, 7703 Floyd Curl Drive, Ste 313L, San Antonio, TX 78229; **Phone:** 210-567-5771; **Board Cert:** Internal Medicine 1983; Nephrology 1986; Hospice & Palliative Medicine 2012; **Med School:** Univ Colorado 1980; **Resid:** Internal Medicine, Wilford Hall Med Ctr 1983; **Fellow:** Nephrology, Univ CO Hosp 1985; **Fac Appt:** Prof Med, Univ Tex, San Antonio

Olivero, Juan Jose MD [Nep] - **Spec Exp:** Kidney Failure-Acute; Kidney Failure-Chronic; Fluid/Electrolyte Balance; Hypertension; **Hospital:** Methodist Hosp - Houston; **Address:** Nephrology, 6560 Fannin St, Ste 2206, Houston, TX 77030; **Phone:** 713-790-4615; **Board Cert:** Internal Medicine 1974; Nephrology 1976; **Med School:** Guatemala 1970; **Resid:** Internal Medicine, Baylor Affil Hosp 1973; Internal Medicine, Ben Taub Genl Hosp 1974; **Fellow:** Nephrology, Baylor Affil Hosp 1975; **Fac Appt:** Clin Prof Med, Baylor Coll Med

Toto, Robert D MD [Nep] - **Spec Exp:** Hypertension/Kidney Disease; Dialysis Care; Diabetic Kidney Disease; Kidney Failure-Acute; **Hospital:** UT Southwestern Med Ctr at Dallas; **Address:** Univ Hosp, Kidney & Liver Clin, 5939 Harry Hines Blvd, Ste 700, Dallas, TX 75390; **Phone:** 214-645-1919; **Board Cert:** Internal Medicine 1980; Nephrology 1982; **Med School:** Univ IL Coll Med 1977; **Resid:** Internal Medicine, Univ Michigan Med Ctr 1979; Internal Medicine, Baylor Med Ctr 1980; **Fellow:** Nephrology, US Public Hlth Svc Hosp 1981; Nephrology, UT Southwestern Med Ctr 1983; **Fac Appt:** Prof Med, Univ Tex SW, Dallas

West Coast and Pacific

Ahmad, Suhail MD [Nep] - **Spec Exp:** Hypertension; Kidney Failure-Chronic; Kidney Stones; **Hospital:** Univ Wash Med Ctr; **Address:** Scribner Kidney Ctr, 2150 N 107th St, Ste 160, Seattle, WA 98133; **Phone:** 206-363-5090; **Med School:** India 1968; **Resid:** Internal Medicine, Univ Allahabad 1971; **Fellow:** Nephrology, Univ Washington Med Ctr 1978; **Fac Appt:** Prof Med, Univ Wash

Bennett, William M MD [Nep] - **Spec Exp:** Transplant Medicine-Kidney; **Hospital:** Legacy Good Samaritan Med Ctr; **Address:** Legacy Good Samaritan Hosp, Transplant Svcs, 1040 NW 22nd Ave, Ste 480, Portland, OR 97210; **Phone:** 503-413-6555; **Board Cert:** Internal Medicine 2012; Nephrology 2012; **Med School:** Northwestern Univ 1963; **Resid:** Internal Medicine, Chicago VA Rsch Hosp 1966; Internal Medicine, OR Hlth Sci Univ 1967; **Fellow:** Nephrology, Mass Genl Hosp 1970; **Fac Appt:** Prof Emeritus Med, Oregon Hlth & Sci Univ

Cho, Kerry C MD [Nep] - **Spec Exp:** Kidney Disease; Glomerulonephritis; **Hospital:** UCSF Med Ctr; **Address:** UCSF, Dept Nephrology, 521 Parnassus Ave, Ste C443, Box 0532, San Francisco, CA 94143-0532; **Phone:** 415-476-2173; **Board Cert:** Nephrology 2003; **Med School:** Cornell Univ-Weill Med Coll 1996; **Resid:** Internal Medicine, Univ Michigan Med Ctr 1999; **Fellow:** Nephrology, USCF Med Ctr 2002; **Fac Appt:** Asst Prof Med, UCSF

Gluck, Stephen L MD [Nep] - **Spec Exp:** Kidney Disease; Fluid/Electrolyte Balance; Hypertension; Kidney Stones; **Hospital:** UCSF Med Ctr; **Address:** UCSF, Div Nephrology, 521 Parnassus Ave, rm C443, Box 0532, San Francisco, CA 94143-0532; **Phone:** 415-476-2173; **Board Cert:** Internal Medicine 1980; Nephrology 1984; **Med School:** UCLA 1977; **Resid:** Internal Medicine, Columbia Presby Med Ctr 1980; **Fellow:** Nephrology, Columbia Presby Med Ctr 1983; **Fac Appt:** Prof Med, UCSF

King, Andrew J MD [Nep] - **Spec Exp:** Kidney Disease-Chronic; Hypertension; Dialysis Care; **Hospital:** Scripps Green Hosp; **Address:** Scripps Clinic Torrey Pines, 10666 N Torrey Pines Rd, MC N239, La Jolla, CA 92037-1027; **Phone:** 858-554-9765; **Board Cert:** Internal Medicine 1986; Nephrology 1988; **Med School:** Northwestern Univ 1983; **Resid:** Internal Medicine, Northwestern Meml Hosp 1986; **Fellow:** Nephrology, Brigham & Womens Hosp 1990; **Fac Appt:** Clin Prof Med, UCSD

Ott, Susan M MD [Nep] - **Spec Exp:** Bone Disorders-Metabolic; Osteoporosis; **Hospital:** Univ Wash Med Ctr; **Address:** Bone & Joint Center, UWMC- Roosevelt, 4245 Roosevelt Way NE, Box 354740, Seattle, WA 98105; **Phone:** 206-598-4288; **Board Cert:** Internal Medicine 1978; Nephrology 1982; **Med School:** Univ Wash 1974; **Resid:** Family Medicine, UC Davis Med Ctr 1978; **Fellow:** Nephrology, Univ Wash Med Ctr 1982; **Fac Appt:** Prof Med, Univ Wash

Riordan, John W MD [Nep] - **Hospital:** CA Pacific Med Ctr-Pacific Campus; **Address:** 2100 Webster St, Ste 412, San Francisco, CA 94115; **Phone:** 415-923-3815; **Board Cert:** Nephrology 2005; **Med School:** Univ Tex Med Br, Galveston 1987; **Resid:** Internal Medicine, Univ Texas Hlth Sci Ctr 1990; **Fellow:** Nephrology, UCSF Med Ctr 1995

Scandling Jr, John D MD [Nep] - **Spec Exp:** Transplant Medicine-Kidney; Transplant Medicine-Pancreas; **Hospital:** Stanford Univ Hosp & Clins; **Address:** Stanford Nephrology/Transplant, 750 Welsh Rd, Ste 200, Palo Alto, CA 94304-1509; **Phone:** 650-725-9891; **Board Cert:** Internal Medicine 1981; Nephrology 1984; **Med School:** Med Coll VA 1978; **Resid:** Internal Medicine, West Virginia Univ Hosp 1981; **Fellow:** Nephrology, Univ Rochester 1983; **Fac Appt:** Prof Med, Stanford Univ

Ward, David M MD [Nep] - **Spec Exp:** Immunotherapy; Dialysis Care; Transplant Medicine-Kidney; **Hospital:** UCSD Med Ctr; **Address:** Hillcrest-Medical Offices South, 4168 Front St, San Diego, CA 92103; **Phone:** 619-543-6303; **Med School:** Scotland, UK 1970; **Resid:** Internal Medicine, Glasgow Royal Infirmary 1972; **Fellow:** Nephrology, Glasgow Royal Infirmary 1975; Immunopathology, Scripps Research Foundation 1977; **Fac Appt:** Prof Med, UCSD

Nephrology

The Glickman Urological & Kidney Institute's Department of Nephrology & Hypertension provides comprehensive diagnostic and therapeutic services for patients with kidney disease and hypertension. The department participates in an active kidney transplant program, all modalities of dialysis care and clinical research studies of diabetic and other glomerular diseases. The nephrology program has been named No. 2 in the nation in *U.S. News & World Report's* Best Hospitals survey, and is renowned for expertise in renovascular hypertension, primary aldosteronism and pheochromocytoma.

Intensive Care Nephrology Services

The Department of Nephrology & Hypertension is a major participant in the intensive care setting. Our nephrologists are leaders in research into the risk factors for acute renal failure after surgeries and in evaluations and diagnosis of different techniques for treatment of acute renal failure, such as slow continuous ultrafiltration, continuous arterio-venous hemofiltration and venovenous hemofiltration.

Hypertension

We utilize the latest technology for accurate measurement of blood pressure and detailed risk assessment. Specialists tailor treatment to the individual needs of each patient. Patients with severe or uncontrolled resistant hypertension are seen in our Resistant Hypertension Clinic.

Chronic Kidney Disease (CKD)

Our CKD clinic provides health evaluation, screenings and treatment for patients. This innovative model of health management focuses on educating and involving the patient in his or her care. We focus on care of the entire patient with assessment of cardiovascular risk factors as well as care of kidney related problems.

Polycystic Kidney Disease (PKD)

Polycystic kidney disease can cause other health problems such as high blood pressure, frequent urination, low back pain and fatigue. Our nephrologists can help PKD patients create a health management plan for dealing with the disease.

THE MOUNT SINAI MEDICAL CENTER

Nephrology

Mount Sinai

One Gustave L. Levy Place
Fifth Avenue and 100th Street
New York, NY 10029-6574

Physician Referral: 1-800-MD-SINAI (637-4624)
www.mountsinai.org

Mount Sinai's Department of Nephrology ranks among the best in the nation, according to the 2013-2014 issue of *U.S. News & World Report's* "Americas Best Hospitals."

We have been an international leader in the treatment of kidney disease since we performed the first hemodialysis in the United States in the 1950s. We established New York State's first dialysis center in 1957. We currently operate the largest home dialysis program in New York City, and our **Geriatric Nephrology Program** is the only one of its kind in the country. We have world renowned scientists and physicians to study and treat patients with kidney glomerular disease including diabetic kidney disease.

EXPERT PHYSICIANS

Building on the talent and expertise of our physicians, including Jonathan Winston, MD, Tonia Kim, MD, Mark Swidler, MD, Jaime Uribarri, MD, Joseph Vassalotti, MD, Brian Radbill, MD, and Richard Stein, MD, along with transplantation specialists, Bernd Schroppel, MD, and Vinay Nair, MD, we provide patients with the most advanced and appropriate approach to care. With so much research taking place, we can also offer patients access to experimental treatments often unavailable elsewhere.

Our expertise spans numerous kidney diseases and treatments, including:

- Chronic kidney disease
- Polycystic kidney disease
- Geriatric kidney disease
- Diabetes-related kidney disease
- Glomerular disease
- Hypertensive kidney disease
- HIV-associated nephropathy
- Kidney transplantation
- Hemodialysis
- Peritoneal Dialysis
- Kidney stone

Initiated in 1967, our **kidney transplant program** is now one of the largest and most successful in the country, with our physician-scientists actively investigating new and innovative ways to detect, prevent, and treat rejection.

Under the direction of Barbara Murphy, MD, Chair of Department of Medicine and John He, MD/PhD, the new Division Chief of Nephrology, we are continuing our leadership in patient care, research and education. Proof of our clinical excellence is evident daily in our practice and hospital. Our physicians care for patients referred to us by other nephrologists who recognize the need for our expertise in their most challenging and complex cases.

A Strong Focus on Research

With one of the largest National Institutes of Health research budgets of any nephrology division in the country, we conduct and support numerous clinical trials, and our faculty members have achieved international recognition as authorities on the causes and treatments of all forms of kidney diseases and disorders.

Mount Sinai *Recanati/Miller Transplantation Institute*

THE MOUNT SINAI MEDICAL CENTER

Transplantation

One Gustave L. Levy Place
Fifth Avenue and 100th Street
New York, NY 10029-6574

Physician Referral: 1-800-MD-SINAI (637-4624)
www.mountsinai.org

Scientific breakthroughs, technological advances, and improved clinical therapies make it possible to save more lives through organ transplantation than ever before. The Mount Sinai Medical Center's **RECANATI MILLER/ TRANSPLANTATION INSTITUTE** (RMTI) has been a world leader in these advances. The RMTI brings together clinical programs in adult and pediatric liver, kidney, pancreas, and intestinal transplantation. It is one of the largest transplant centers in the United States and performs more than 350 transplant procedures annually. In addition, RMTI surgeons also perform complex hepatobiliary surgical procedures.

History of Achievement – The kidney transplant program was instituted at Mount Sinai in 1967 and is now one of the largest adult and pediatric programs in the nation, having performed more than 3,000 transplants. The first liver transplant to be performed in New York State was in 1988 at Mount Sinai. There have been many other firsts in the program's history, including the first pediatric liver transplant and the first adult-to-adult living-donor liver transplant in New York State.

Tradition of Excellence – Mount Sinai is one of the few hospitals in the country that offers comprehensive, multi-organ transplant services for both children and adults. Our physicians are able to accept and care for the sickest and most complex patients.

INNOVATIVE PROGRAMS

- **Recipients with HIV** – Since 2001, the RMTI has been one of the only centers in the nation to transplant carefully selected kidney and liver patients with HIV.

- **Living Donor Program** – Mount Sinai has an active living-donor program. The newly endowed Zweig Family Center for Living Donation is the first multi-organ living donor center where dedicated resources ensure the well-being of these heroes who give one, or a part, of their own organs to save another person's life. We also participate in local and national paired-exchange and donor-chain initiatives. RMTI has performed over 1500 living donor kidney transplants and over 250 living donor liver transplants.

- **Multi-organ Transplantation and Intestinal Rehabilitation Program** – We have performed many combined transplant procedures. Our rehabilitation program offers patients with intestinal failure the opportunity, when possible, to avoid transplantation through medical and/or surgical interventions.

- **Translational Research** – Our scientists are actively investigating new and innovative ways to detect, prevent and treat rejection. We have nationally-recognized and well-funded transplant, genomic, and proteomic projects.

Neurological Surgery

A neurological surgeon provides the operative and non-operative management (i.e., prevention, diagnosis, evaluation, treatment, critical care and rehabilitation) of disorders of the central, peripheral and autonomic nervous systems, including their supporting structures and vascular supply; the evaluation and treatment of pathological processes which modify function or activity of the nervous system; and the operative and non-operative management of pain. A neurological surgeon treats patients with disorders of the nervous system; disorders of the brain, meninges, skull and their blood supply, including the extracranial carotid and vertebral arteries; disorders of the pituitary gland; disorders of the spinal cord, meninges and vertebral column, including those which may require treatment by spinal fusion or instrumentation; and disorders of the cranial and spinal nerves throughout their distribution.

Training Required: Seven years (including general surgery)

The American Board of Pediatric Neurological Surgery (ABPNS) is not a recognized ABMS subspecialty. However, this designation has been included because the certification process is meaningful and rigorous. It is awarded to those doctors who hold a current ABMS certification in Neurological Surgery, have completed a fully accredited one year, post-graduate fellowship in pediatric neurological surgery, and have submitted surgical logs indicating a practice of pediatric neurological surgery for one year, followed by a written examination.

Neurological Surgery

New England

Al-Mefty, Ossama MD [NS] - **Spec Exp:** Skull Base Surgery; Brain Tumors; Cerebrovascular Surgery; **Hospital:** Brigham & Women's Hosp, Children's Hospital - Boston; **Address:** Brigham & Women's Hosp, Neurosurgery, 75 Francis St, Boston, MA 02115; **Phone:** 617-525-9451; **Board Cert:** Neurological Surgery 1980; **Med School:** Syria 1972; **Resid:** Surgery, Med Coll Ohio Affil Hosp 1974; Neurological Surgery, West VA Med Ctr 1978

Borges, Lawrence F MD [NS] - **Spec Exp:** Spinal Surgery; Spinal Tumors; **Hospital:** Mass Genl Hosp; **Address:** Mass General Hosp, 55 Fruit St White Bldg - Ste 1205, Boston, MA 02114; **Phone:** 617-726-6156; **Board Cert:** Neurological Surgery 1986; **Med School:** Johns Hopkins Univ 1977; **Resid:** Neurological Surgery, Mass Genl Hosp 1983; **Fac Appt:** Assoc Prof S, Harvard Med Sch

Butler, William E MD [NS] - **Spec Exp:** Pediatric Neurosurgery; Brain Tumors-Adult & Pediatric; Cerebrovascular Surgery; Chiari's Deformity; **Hospital:** Mass Genl Hosp; **Address:** Mass General Hospital, 15 Parkman St, Wang Bldg - rm 331, Boston, MA 02114-3117; **Phone:** 617-726-3801; **Board Cert:** Neurological Surgery 2011; **Med School:** Harvard Med Sch 1987; **Resid:** Neurological Surgery, Mass Genl Hosp 1994; **Fac Appt:** Asst Prof NS, Harvard Med Sch

Chiocca, E. Antonio MD [NS] - **Spec Exp:** Brain Tumors; Spinal Cord Tumors; Peripheral Nerve Surgery; **Hospital:** Brigham & Women's Hosp; **Address:** Brigham & Women's Hosp, Div Neurol Surgery, PBB3, 75 Francis St, Boston, MA 02115; **Phone:** 617-525-9419; **Board Cert:** Neurological Surgery 2011; **Med School:** Univ Tex, Houston 1988; **Resid:** Neurological Surgery, Mass Genl Hosp 1995; **Fac Appt:** Prof NS, Harvard Med Sch

Cohen, Alan R MD [NS] - **Spec Exp:** Pediatric Neurosurgery; Brain & Spinal Tumors-Pediatric; Minimally Invasive Surgery; **Hospital:** Children's Hospital - Boston; **Address:** Boston Chldn's Hosp, Dept Neurosurgery, 300 Longwood Ave Hunnewell Bldg Fl 2, Boston, MA 02115; **Phone:** 617-355-1484; **Board Cert:** Neurological Surgery 1991; Pediatric Neurological Surgery 2007; **Med School:** Cornell Univ-Weill Med Coll 1978; **Resid:** Surgery, NYU Medical Ctr 1980; Neurological Surgery, NYU Medical Ctr 1987; **Fellow:** Neurology, Natl Hosp Queen's Square 1982; **Fac Appt:** Prof NS, Harvard Med Sch

Cosgrove, Garth Rees MD [NS] - **Spec Exp:** Epilepsy/Seizure Disorders; Brain Tumors; Spinal Surgery; Pain-Chronic; **Hospital:** Rhode Island Hosp, Miriam Hosp; **Address:** Rhode Island Hosp, Neurosurgery Dept, 593 Eddy St, APC Bldg - Fl 6, Providence, RI 02903; **Phone:** 401-793-9132; **Board Cert:** Neurological Surgery 1989; **Med School:** Queens Univ 1980; **Resid:** Neurological Surgery, Montreal Neuro Inst 1986; **Fac Appt:** Prof NS, Brown Univ

David, Carlos A MD [NS] - **Spec Exp:** Cerebrovascular Surgery; Brain Tumors; Pituitary Tumors; Carotid Artery Surgery; **Hospital:** Lahey Hosp & Med Ctr; **Address:** Lahey Clinic, Dept Neurosurgery, 41 Mall Rd Fl 7, Burlington, MA 01805; **Phone:** 781-744-8643; **Board Cert:** Neurological Surgery 2012; **Med School:** Univ Miami Sch Med 1990; **Resid:** Neurological Surgery, Jackson Memorial Hosp 1996; **Fellow:** Cerebrovascular & Skull Base Surgery, Barrow Neuro Inst 1997; **Fac Appt:** Asst Clin Prof NS, Tufts Univ

Duhaime, Ann Christine MD [NS] - **Spec Exp:** Pediatric Neurosurgery; Brain Tumors; Epilepsy; Craniofacial Surgery; **Hospital:** Mass Genl Hosp; **Address:** Mass Genl Hosp for Children, 15 Parkman St, Ste WAC 331, Boston, MA 02114; **Phone:** 617-643-9175; **Board Cert:** Neurological Surgery 1990; Pediatric Neurological Surgery 2005; **Med School:** Univ Pennsylvania 1981; **Resid:** Neurological Surgery, Hosp U Penn 1987; **Fellow:** Pediatric Neurological Surgery, Children's Hosp 1987; **Fac Appt:** Prof NS, Harvard Med Sch

Goumnerova, Liliana MD [NS] - **Spec Exp:** Pediatric Neurosurgery; Brain & Spinal Cord Tumors; Endoscopic Surgery/Ventriculoscopy; Intraoperative MRI; **Hospital:** Children's Hospital - Boston, Dana-Farber Cancer Inst; **Address:** Boston Chldn's Hosp, Dept of Neurosurgery, Hunnewell 2, 300 Longwood Ave, Boston, MA 02115; **Phone:** 617-355-6364; **Board Cert:** Neurological Surgery 1992; Pediatric Neurological Surgery 2006; **Med School:** Canada 1980; **Resid:** Neurological Surgery, Univ Ottawa 1986; **Fellow:** Pediatric Neurological Surgery, Hosp for Sick Chldn 1988; Neurological Science, Univ Hosp Penn 1990; **Fac Appt:** Assoc Prof S, Harvard Med Sch

Heilman, Carl B MD [NS] - **Spec Exp:** Skull Base Surgery; **Hospital:** Tufts Med Ctr; **Address:** Tufts Med Ctr, Dept Neurosurgery, 800 Washington St, Box 178, Boston, MA 02111; **Phone:** 617-636-5860; **Board Cert:** Neurological Surgery 1996; **Med School:** Univ Pennsylvania 1986; **Resid:** Neurological Surgery, Tufts New England Med Ctr 1993; **Fellow:** Skull Base Surgery, Baptist Meml Hosp 1993; **Fac Appt:** Assoc Prof NS, Tufts Univ

Madsen, Joseph R MD [NS] - **Spec Exp:** Pediatric Neurosurgery; Epilepsy/Seizure Disorders; **Hospital:** Children's Hospital - Boston; **Address:** Boston Chldn's Hosp, 300 Longwood Ave, Honeywell 2, Boston, MA 02115; **Phone:** 617-355-6005; **Board Cert:** Neurological Surgery 1994; Pediatric Neurological Surgery 1997; **Med School:** Harvard Med Sch 1981; **Resid:** Neurological Surgery, Mass Genl Hosp 1989; **Fellow:** Research, Beth Israel Hosp 1983; **Fac Appt:** Assoc Prof NS, Harvard Med Sch

Martuza, Robert L MD [NS] - **Spec Exp:** Brain Tumors; Acoustic Neuroma; Skull Base Surgery; **Hospital:** Mass Genl Hosp; **Address:** Mass General Hosp, Dept Neurosurgery, 55 Fruit St White Bldg - Ste 502, Boston, MA 02114; **Phone:** 617-726-8581; **Board Cert:** Neurological Surgery 1983; **Med School:** Harvard Med Sch 1973; **Resid:** Neurological Surgery, Mass Genl Hosp 1979; **Fac Appt:** Prof NS, Harvard Med Sch

Moser, Richard P MD [NS] - **Spec Exp:** Brain & Spinal Cord Tumors; Stereotactic Radiosurgery; **Hospital:** UMass Memorial Med Ctr, Wing Mem Hosp-UMass; **Address:** UMass Meml Med Ctr-Univ Campus, 55 Lake Ave N, Worcester, MA 01655; **Phone:** 508-334-0605; **Board Cert:** Neurological Surgery 1985; **Med School:** Loyola Univ-Stritch Sch Med 1974; **Resid:** Surgery, Univ MN Med Coll 1977; Neurological Surgery, Univ MN Med Coll 1982; **Fellow:** Neuro-Oncology, Karolinska Inst 1982; **Fac Appt:** Prof S, Univ Mass Sch Med

Penar, Paul L MD [NS] - **Spec Exp:** Brain & Spinal Cord Tumors; Epilepsy/Seizure Disorders; Movement Disorders; Stereotactic Radiosurgery; **Hospital:** FAHC - Med Ctr Campus; **Address:** Fletcher Allen Hlthcare, 111 Colchester Ave, East Pavilion, Fl 5, Burlington, VT 05401; **Phone:** 802-847-4590; **Board Cert:** Neurological Surgery 1989; **Med School:** Univ Mich Med Sch 1981; **Resid:** Neurological Surgery, Yale-New Haven Hosp 1987

Piepmeier, Joseph MD [NS] - **Spec Exp:** Neuro-Oncology; Brain & Spinal Cord Tumors; **Hospital:** Smilow Cancer Hosp at Yale-New Haven; **Address:** Smilow Cancer Hosp, Neuro-Oncology, 35 Park St Fl 8, New Haven, CT 06520; **Phone:** 203-785-2791; **Board Cert:** Neurological Surgery 1984; **Med School:** Univ Tenn Coll Med 1975; **Resid:** Neurological Surgery, Yale-New Haven Hosp 1982; **Fac Appt:** Prof NS, Yale Univ

Spencer, Dennis D MD [NS] - **Spec Exp:** Epilepsy/Seizure Disorders; Brain Tumors; **Hospital:** Yale-New Haven Hosp; **Address:** Surgical Specialties, 800 Howard Ave, Yale Physicians Bldg, Lower Level, New Haven, CT 06519; **Phone:** 203-785-4891; **Board Cert:** Neurological Surgery 1980; **Med School:** Washington Univ, St Louis 1971; **Resid:** Surgery, Barnes Hosp 1972; Neurological Surgery, Yale-New Haven Hosp 1977; **Fac Appt:** Prof NS, Yale Univ

Swearingen, Brooke MD [NS] - **Spec Exp:** Pituitary Tumors; Brain & Spinal Cord Tumors; Neuroendocrine Tumors; Spinal Surgery; **Hospital:** Mass Genl Hosp; **Address:** Mass Genl Hosp, Neurological Associates, 15 Parkman St, WACC 331, Boston, MA 02114-3117; **Phone:** 617-726-3910; **Board Cert:** Neurological Surgery 1993; **Med School:** Harvard Med Sch 1981; **Resid:** Neurological Surgery, Mass Genl Hosp 1987; **Fac Appt:** Assoc Prof NS, Harvard Med Sch

Mid Atlantic

Anderson, Richard CE MD [NS] - **Spec Exp:** Spinal Disorders; Spina Bifida; Peripheral Nerve Surgery; Pediatric Neurosurgery; **Hospital:** Morgan Stanley Children's Hosp of NY-Presby, NY (page 65), St. Joseph's Regl Med Ctr - Paterson; **Address:** Morgan Stanley Children's Hosp, The Neurological Institute, 710 W 168th St, rm 213, New York, NY 10032; **Phone:** 212-305-0219; **Board Cert:** Neurological Surgery 2007; Pediatric Neurological Surgery 2008; **Med School:** Johns Hopkins Univ 1997; **Resid:** Neurological Surgery, Columbia Neuro Inst 2004; **Fellow:** Pediatric Neurological Surgery, Univ Utah Med Ctr 2005; **Fac Appt:** Prof NS, Columbia P&S

Andrews, David W MD [NS] - **Spec Exp:** Brain Tumors; Stereotactic Radiosurgery; **Hospital:** Thomas Jefferson Univ Hosp; **Address:** Jefferson Neurosurgical Assocs, 909 Walnut St Fl 3, Philadelphia, PA 19107-5109; **Phone:** 215-503-7005; **Board Cert:** Neurological Surgery 1992; **Med School:** Univ Colorado 1983; **Resid:** Neurological Surgery, New York Hosp 1989; **Fellow:** Neuro-Oncology, Meml Sloan Kettering Cancer Ctr 1987; **Fac Appt:** Prof NS, Thomas Jefferson Univ

Baltuch, Gordon H MD/PhD [NS] - **Spec Exp:** Movement Disorders; Parkinson's Disease; Epilepsy/Seizure Disorders; Dystonia; **Hospital:** Hosp Univ Penn - UPHS (page 69), Pennsylvania Hosp-UPHS (page 69); **Address:** Penn Neurosurgery, 235 S 8th St, Philadelphia, PA 19106; **Phone:** 215-829-6700; **Board Cert:** Neurological Surgery 1998; **Med School:** McGill Univ 1986; **Resid:** Surgery, Montreal Genl Hosp 1988; Neurological Surgery, Montreal Neuro Inst 1994; **Fellow:** Neurological Surgery, Centre Hospitalier Univ Vaudois 1995; **Fac Appt:** Prof NS, Univ Pennsylvania

Bederson, Joshua B MD [NS] - **Spec Exp:** Brain & Spinal Cord Tumors; Aneurysm-Cerebral; Meningioma; Cerebrovascular Surgery; **Hospital:** Mt Sinai Med Ctr (page 62); **Address:** Mount Sinai Med Ctr, 1 Gustave Levy Pl, Box 1136, New York, NY 10029; **Phone:** 212-241-2377; **Board Cert:** Neurological Surgery 1993; **Med School:** UCSF 1984; **Resid:** Neurological Surgery, UCSF Med Ctr 1990; **Fellow:** Neurovascular Surgery, Barrow Neur Inst 1990; Neurovascular Surgery, Univ Hosp Zurich 1990; **Fac Appt:** Prof NS, Mount Sinai Sch Med

Belzberg, Allan J MD [NS] - **Spec Exp:** Peripheral Nerve Disorders; Nerve Surgery & Transplantation; Nerve Tumors; Spinal Surgery; **Hospital:** Johns Hopkins Hosp (page 59); **Address:** Johns Hopkins Dept Neurosurgery, 600 N Wolfe St, Meyer Bldg, rm 5-181, Baltimore, MD 21287; **Phone:** 410-955-5810; **Board Cert:** Neurological Surgery 1997; **Med School:** Univ Calgary 1982; **Resid:** Neurological Surgery, Univ Calgary Affil Hosps 1990; **Fellow:** Neurological Surgery, Johns Hopkins Hosp 1992; **Fac Appt:** Assoc Prof NS, Johns Hopkins Univ

Bilsky, Mark H MD [NS] - **Spec Exp:** Brain & Spinal Cord Tumors; Skull Base Tumors; Spinal Cord Tumors; Spinal Surgery; **Hospital:** Meml Sloan-Kettering Canc Ctr, NY-Presby/Weill Cornell Med Ctr, NY (page 65); **Address:** Meml Sloan Kettering Cancer Ctr-Neurosurgery, 1275 York Ave, Ste C705, New York, NY 10065; **Phone:** 212-639-8526; **Board Cert:** Neurological Surgery 2010; **Med School:** Emory Univ 1988; **Resid:** Neurological Surgery, NY Hosp-Cornell Med Ctr 1994; **Fellow:** Neurological Surgery, Louisville Univ Med Ctr 1995; Spine Surgery, Louisville Univ Med Ctr 1995; **Fac Appt:** Prof NS, Cornell Univ-Weill Med Coll

Brem, Henry MD [NS] - **Spec Exp:** Brain & Spinal Cord Tumors; Skull Base Tumors; Pituitary Tumors; **Hospital:** Johns Hopkins Hosp (page 59), Johns Hopkins Bayview Med Ctr (page 59); **Address:** Johns Hopkins Hosp, Div Neurosurgery, Sheikh Zayed Tower, Ste 6115A, 1800 Orleans St, Baltimore, MD 21287; **Phone:** 410-955-2248; **Board Cert:** Neurological Surgery 1986; **Med School:** Harvard Med Sch 1978; **Resid:** Neurological Surgery, Columbia-Presby Med Ctr 1984; **Fellow:** Neurological Surgery, Johns Hopkins Hosp 1980; **Fac Appt:** Prof NS, Johns Hopkins Univ

Brem, Steven MD [NS] - **Spec Exp:** Brain Tumors; Pituitary Tumors; Clinical Trials; Neuro-Oncology; **Hospital:** Hosp Univ Penn - UPHS (page 69); **Address:** Hosp of the Univ of Pennsylvania, 3 Silverstein, 3400 Spruce St, Philadelphia, PA 19104; **Phone:** 215-662-7854; **Board Cert:** Neurological Surgery 1983; **Med School:** Harvard Med Sch 1972; **Resid:** Neurological Surgery, Massachusetts Genl Hosp 1981; **Fellow:** Oncology, Natl Cancer Inst 1976; **Fac Appt:** Prof NS, Univ Pennsylvania

Bruce, Jeffrey N MD [NS] - **Spec Exp:** Brain Tumors-Complex; Pituitary Tumors; Skull Base Surgery; Meningioma; **Hospital:** NY-Presby/Columbia Univ Med Ctr, NY (page 65); **Address:** Neurological Inst, 710 W 168th St N1 Bldg Fl 4 - rm 434, New York, NY 10032; **Phone:** 212-305-7346; **Board Cert:** Neurological Surgery 1993; **Med School:** UMDNJ-RW Johnson Med Sch 1983; **Resid:** Neurological Surgery, Columbia-Presby Med Ctr 1990; **Fellow:** Neurological Surgery, Nat Inst Hlth 1985; **Fac Appt:** Prof NS, Columbia P&S

Caputy, Anthony J MD [NS] - **Spec Exp:** Epilepsy/Seizure Disorders; Spinal Surgery; Minimally Invasive Surgery; Brain & Spinal Cord Tumors; **Hospital:** G Washington Univ Hosp, Suburban Hosp; **Address:** Dept Neurosurgery, 2150 Pennsylvania Ave NW, Ste 7-420, Washington, DC 20037; **Phone:** 202-741-2735; **Board Cert:** Neurological Surgery 1989; **Med School:** Univ VA Sch Med 1980; **Resid:** Neurological Surgery, Georgetown Univ Hosp 1988; **Fac Appt:** Prof NS, Geo Wash Univ

Carson, Benjamin S MD [NS] - **Spec Exp:** Pediatric Neurosurgery; Trigeminal Neuralgia; Brain & Spinal Cord Tumors; Brain Injury; **Hospital:** Johns Hopkins Hosp (page 59); **Address:** Johns Hopkins Hosp, Div Pediatric Neurosurgery, 600 N Wolfe St, Harvey Bldg, Ste 811, Baltimore, MD 21287-8811; **Phone:** 410-955-7888; **Board Cert:** Neurological Surgery 1988; Pediatric Neurological Surgery 1997; **Med School:** Univ Mich Med Sch 1977; **Resid:** Neurological Surgery, Johns Hopkins Hosp 1983; **Fellow:** Pediatric Neurological Surgery, Queen Elizabeth II Med Ctr 1984; **Fac Appt:** Prof NS, Johns Hopkins Univ

Chen, Chun Siang MD [NS] - **Spec Exp:** Skull Base Tumors; Skull Base Surgery; Microsurgery; Brain & Spinal Cord Tumors; **Hospital:** Mt Sinai Med Ctr (page 62); **Address:** Mount Sinai Med Ctr, Annenberg Bldg, One Gustave L Levy Pl, Fl 8, rm 10, New York, NY 10029; **Phone:** 212-241-8480; **Med School:** Brazil 1978; **Resid:** Neurological Surgery, Santa Casa de Misericordia of Sao Paulo Med Sch 1983; Neurological Surgery, Mt Sinai Med Ctr 2005; **Fellow:** Skull Base Surgery, St Lukes Roosevelt Hosp 2006; **Fac Appt:** Asst Prof NS, Mount Sinai Sch Med

Di Giacinto, George V MD [NS] - **Spec Exp:** Spinal Surgery; Pain Management; **Hospital:** St. Luke's - Roosevelt Hosp Ctr - Roosevelt Div (page 56); **Address:** 425 W 59th St, Ste 4E, New York, NY 10019; **Phone:** 212-523-8500; **Board Cert:** Neurological Surgery 1981; **Med School:** Harvard Med Sch 1970; **Resid:** Surgery, St Luke's-Roosevelt Hosp Ctr 1972; Neurological Surgery, Columbia-Presby Hosp 1978

Dias, Mark S MD [NS] - **Spec Exp:** Pediatric Neurosurgery; Spina Bifida; Hydrocephalus; Craniosynostosis; **Hospital:** Penn State Milton S Hershey Med Ctr; **Address:** Penn State-Hersey Med Ctr, Dept Neurosurgery, 30 Hope Drive, Ste 2200, Hershey, PA 17033; **Phone:** 717-531-8807; **Board Cert:** Neurological Surgery 1995; Pediatric Neurological Surgery 2006; **Med School:** Johns Hopkins Univ 1982; **Resid:** Neurological Surgery, Univ Pittsburgh Med Ctr 1989; **Fellow:** Pediatric Neurological Surgery, Univ Utah-Primary Chldns Hosp 1991; **Fac Appt:** Prof NS, Penn State Coll Med

Eisenberg, Howard M MD [NS] - **Spec Exp:** Acoustic Neuroma; Skull Base Surgery; Deep Brain Stimulation; Epilepsy/Seizure Disorders; **Hospital:** Univ of MD Med Ctr; **Address:** UMMC-Dept of Neurosurgery, 22 S Greene St, Ste S12D, Baltimore, MD 21201-1544; **Phone:** 410-328-3514; **Board Cert:** Neurological Surgery 1973; **Med School:** SUNY Downstate 1964; **Resid:** Surgery, New York Hosp 1966; Neurological Surgery, Peter Bent Brigham Hosp/Chldns Hosp 1970; **Fellow:** Neurological Surgery, Harvard Univ Affil Hosp 1970; **Fac Appt:** Prof NS, Univ MD Sch Med

El-Kadi, Hikmat Abbas MD/PhD [NS] - **Spec Exp:** Spinal Surgery; Spinal Tumors; Minimally Invasive Spinal Surgery; Spinal Reconstructive Surgery; **Hospital:** UPMC Passavant-McCandless, UPMC Presby, Pittsburgh; **Address:** Tri-State Neurological Assocs, UPMC Passavant Hospital, 9100 Babcock Blvd, 2 Main, Ste 2096, Pittsburgh, PA 15237; **Phone:** 412-630-7640; **Board Cert:** Neurological Surgery 2002; **Med School:** Russia 1983; **Resid:** Neurological Surgery, Burdenko Neurosurgical Inst 1989; Neurological Surgery, WV Univ Med Ctr 1999; **Fellow:** Research, LAC-USC Med Ctr 1992; Neurological Surgery, Hartford Hosp 1994; **Fac Appt:** Prof NS, Univ Pittsburgh

Evans, James J MD [NS] - **Spec Exp:** Skull Base Surgery; Neuro-Oncology; Brain Tumors; Endoscopic Surgery; **Hospital:** Thomas Jefferson Univ Hosp; **Address:** Jefferson Neurosurgical Assocs, 909 Walnut St, Fl 3, Philadelphia, PA 19107; **Phone:** 215-503-7005; **Board Cert:** Neurological Surgery 2006; **Med School:** Univ Mass Sch Med 1995; **Resid:** Neurological Surgery, Cleveland Clinic 1999; **Fellow:** Cranial Base Surgery, Fairfax Hosp 2001; **Fac Appt:** Assoc Prof NS, Thomas Jefferson Univ

Feldstein, Neil A MD [NS] - **Spec Exp:** Brain & Spinal Tumors-Pediatric; MoyaMoya Disease; Chiari's Deformity; Hydrocephalus; **Hospital:** Morgan Stanley Children's Hosp of NY-Presby, NY (page 65), NY-Presby/Columbia Univ Med Ctr, NY (page 65); **Address:** Neurological Inst, 710 W 168th St, Fl 2, rm 213, New York, NY 10032; **Phone:** 212-305-1396; **Board Cert:** Neurological Surgery 1995; **Med School:** NYU Sch Med 1984; **Resid:** Neurological Surgery, Baylor Coll Med 1990; **Fellow:** Pediatric Neurological Surgery, NYU Med Ctr 1991; **Fac Appt:** Assoc Prof NS, Columbia P&S

Fenstermaker, Robert A MD [NS] - **Spec Exp:** Brain Tumors; Pituitary Tumors; Stereotactic Radiosurgery; Skull Base Surgery; **Hospital:** Roswell Park Canc Inst; **Address:** Roswell Park Cancer Inst, Elm and Carlton Streets, Buffalo, NY 14263; **Phone:** 716-845-3154; **Board Cert:** Neurological Surgery 1991; **Med School:** NE Ohio Univ 1981; **Resid:** Neurological Surgery, Univ Hosps Cleveland 1987; **Fellow:** Pharmacology, Case Western Reserve 1989; **Fac Appt:** Prof NS, SUNY Buffalo

Gokaslan, Ziya L MD [NS] - **Spec Exp:** Spinal Tumors; Spinal Surgery-Complex; Spinal Reconstructive Surgery; **Hospital:** Johns Hopkins Hosp (page 59), Johns Hopkins Bayview Med Ctr (page 59); **Address:** Johns Hopkins Hosp, Dept Neurosurgery Spine Ctr, 600 N Wolfe St, Meyer 7-109, Baltimore, MD 21287; **Phone:** 443-287-4934; **Board Cert:** Neurological Surgery 1997; **Med School:** Turkey 1983; **Resid:** Neurological Surgery, Baylor Coll Med Affil Hosp 1993; **Fellow:** Neurological Trauma, Baylor Coll Med 1988; Spine Surgery, NYU Med Ctr 1994; **Fac Appt:** Prof NS, Johns Hopkins Univ

Golfinos, John G MD [NS] - **Spec Exp:** Brain Tumors; Skull Base Tumors; **Hospital:** NYU Langone Med Ctr (page 68), Bellevue Hosp Ctr; **Address:** 530 First Ave, Ste 8R, New York, NY 10016; **Phone:** 212-263-2950; **Board Cert:** Neurological Surgery 1998; **Med School:** Columbia P&S 1988; **Resid:** Neurological Surgery, Barrow Neuro Inst 1995; **Fac Appt:** Assoc Prof NS, NYU Sch Med

Goodman, Robert R MD/PhD [NS] - **Spec Exp:** Parkinson's Disease/Movement Disorders; Epilepsy; Trigeminal Neuralgia; Hydrocephalus-Adult; **Hospital:** St. Luke's - Roosevelt Hosp Ctr - Roosevelt Div (page 56), Beth Israel Med Ctr - Petrie Div (page 56); **Address:** 1000 Tenth Ave, Ste 5G-80, New York, NY 10019; **Phone:** 212-636-3666; **Board Cert:** Neurological Surgery 1993; **Med School:** Johns Hopkins Univ 1982; **Resid:** Neurological Surgery, Columbia-Presby Med Ctr 1989; **Fac Appt:** Assoc Prof NS, Columbia P&S

Grady, M Sean MD [NS] - **Spec Exp:** Cerebrovascular Surgery; Aneurysm-Cerebral; Arteriovenous Malformations; Brain Injury-Traumatic; **Hospital:** Hosp Univ Penn - UPHS (page 69), Pennsylvania Hosp-UPHS (page 69); **Address:** Univ Penn, Dept Neurosurgery, 3400 Spruce St, Silverstein Bldg Fl 3, Philadelphia, PA 19104; **Phone:** 215-662-3483; **Board Cert:** Neurological Surgery 1990; **Med School:** Georgetown Univ 1981; **Resid:** Neurological Surgery, Univ Virginia Hosp 1987; **Fac Appt:** Prof NS, Univ Pennsylvania

Gutin, Philip H MD [NS] - **Spec Exp:** Brain Tumors; Meningioma; Acoustic Neuroma; **Hospital:** Meml Sloan-Kettering Canc Ctr, NY-Presby/Weill Cornell Med Ctr, NY (page 65); **Address:** 1275 York Ave, rm C703, New York, NY 10065; **Phone:** 212-639-8556; **Board Cert:** Neurological Surgery 1981; **Med School:** Univ Pennsylvania 1971; **Resid:** Neurological Surgery, UCSF Med Ctr 1979; **Fellow:** Neurological Surgery, Natl Cancer Inst 1976; **Fac Appt:** Prof NS, Cornell Univ-Weill Med Coll

Harbaugh, Robert E MD [NS] - **Spec Exp:** Carotid Artery Surgery; Aneurysm-Cerebral; MoyaMoya Disease; **Hospital:** Penn State Milton S Hershey Med Ctr; **Address:** Penn State Hershey Med Ctr, Dept Neurosurgery, 30 Hope Drive, Hershey, PA 17033-0850; **Phone:** 717-531-4383; **Board Cert:** Neurological Surgery 1989; **Med School:** Penn State Coll Med 1978; **Resid:** Surgery, Dartmouth-Hitchcock Med Ctr 1980; Neurological Surgery, Dartmouth-Hitchcock Med Ctr 1985; **Fac Appt:** Prof NS, Penn State Coll Med

Harrop, James S MD [NS] - **Spec Exp:** Spinal Cord Tumors; Spinal Tumors; Spinal Disorders; Spinal Cord Injury; **Hospital:** Thomas Jefferson Univ Hosp; **Address:** Department of Neurological Surgery, 909 Walnut St, COB Bldg Fl 3, Philadelphia, PA 19107; **Phone:** 215-955-7000; **Board Cert:** Neurological Surgery 2006; **Med School:** Jefferson Med Coll 1995; **Resid:** Neurological Surgery, Thomas Jefferson Univ Hosp 2002; **Fellow:** Neurological Surgery, Cleveland Clinic 2004; Spine Surgery, Cleveland Clinic 2004; **Fac Appt:** Assoc Prof NS, Jefferson Med Coll

Hartl, Roger MD [NS] - **Spec Exp:** Spinal Surgery-Complex; Minimally Invasive Spinal Surgery; Spinal Disc Replacement; Spinal Trauma; **Hospital:** NY-Presby/Weill Cornell Med Ctr, NY (page 65); **Address:** Cornell Neurosurgery, 520 E 70th St, Starr Pavillion Fl 6 - rm 651, New York, NY 10065; **Phone:** 212-746-2152; **Board Cert:** Neurological Surgery 2008; **Med School:** Germany 1993; **Resid:** Neurological Surgery, NY Presby-Cornell Med Ctr 2003; **Fellow:** Spine Surgery, Barrow Neurological Inst 2004; **Fac Appt:** Assoc Prof NS, Cornell Univ-Weill Med Coll

Hopkins, L. Nelson MD [NS] - **Spec Exp:** Cerebrovascular Disease; Endovascular Surgery; Stroke; **Hospital:** Buffalo Genl Hosp; **Address:** UB Neurosurgery, 100 High St, Ste B4, Buffalo, NY 14203; **Phone:** 716-218-1000; **Board Cert:** Neurological Surgery 1977; **Med School:** Albany Med Coll 1969; **Resid:** Neurological Surgery, SUNY Buffalo Affil Hosp 1975; **Fac Appt:** Prof NS, SUNY Buffalo

Huang, Judy MD [NS] - **Spec Exp:** Aneurysm-Cerebral; Cerebrovascular Surgery; Brain Tumors; Spinal Disorders; **Hospital:** Johns Hopkins Hosp (page 59), Johns Hopkins Bayview Med Ctr (page 59); **Address:** Johns Hopkins Hosp, Dept Neurosurgery, Sheikh Zayed Tower, Ste 6115F, 1800 Orleans St, Baltimore, MD 21287; **Phone:** 410-502-5767; **Board Cert:** Neurological Surgery 2006; **Med School:** Columbia P&S 1995; **Resid:** Neurological Surgery, NY-Presby/Columbia Univ Med Ctr 2002; **Fellow:** Research, NY-Presby/Columbia Univ Med Ctr 2000; **Fac Appt:** Assoc Prof NS, Johns Hopkins Univ

Jallo, George I MD [NS] - **Spec Exp:** Pediatric Neurosurgery; Chiari's Deformity; Brain & Spinal Cord Tumors; Epilepsy; **Hospital:** Johns Hopkins Hosp (page 59), Johns Hopkins Bayview Med Ctr (page 59); **Address:** Johns Hopkins Hosp, Dept Neurosurgery, 600 N Wolfe St, Phipps 556, Baltimore, MD 21287; **Phone:** 410-955-7851; **Board Cert:** Neurological Surgery 2013; Pediatric Neurological Surgery 2004; **Med School:** Univ VA Sch Med 1991; **Resid:** Neurological Surgery, NYU Med Ctr 1998; **Fellow:** Pediatric Neurological Surgery, Beth Israel Med Ctr 1999; **Fac Appt:** Prof NS, Johns Hopkins Univ

Jenkins III, Arthur L MD [NS] - **Spec Exp:** Spinal Surgery; Minimally Invasive Spinal Surgery; Scoliosis; Spinal Tumors; **Hospital:** Mt Sinai Med Ctr (page 62); **Address:** Faculty Practice Assocs, 5 E 98th St, Fl 7, Box 1136, New York, NY 10029; **Phone:** 212-241-8175; **Board Cert:** Neurological Surgery 2005; **Med School:** Univ Pennsylvania 1993; **Resid:** Neurological Surgery, Mtount Sinai Med Ctr 2000; **Fellow:** Spine Surgery, Brigham & Women's Hosp 2001; **Fac Appt:** Assoc Prof NS, Mount Sinai Sch Med

Jho, Hae-Dong MD/PhD [NS] - **Spec Exp:** Minimally Invasive Surgery; Spinal Surgery; Endoscopic Surgery; **Hospital:** Allegheny Genl Hosp; **Address:** Jho Inst for Min Invasive Neurosurgery, 320 E North Ave, Allegheny Genl Hosp, Pittsburgh, PA 15212-4746; **Phone:** 412-359-6110; **Board Cert:** Neurological Surgery 1991; **Med School:** Korea 1971; **Resid:** Neurological Surgery, Hanyang Univ Hosp 1979; Neurological Surgery, Univ Pittsburgh 1989; **Fellow:** Microsurgery, Univ Pittsburgh 1983; **Fac Appt:** Prof NS, Drexel Univ Coll Med

Judy, Kevin D MD [NS] - **Spec Exp:** Brain Tumors; Acoustic Neuroma; Skull Base Tumors; **Hospital:** Thomas Jefferson Univ Hosp; **Address:** Jefferson Neurosurgical Assocs, 909 Walnut St, 3rd Fl, Philadelphia, PA 19107; **Phone:** 215-503-7005; **Board Cert:** Neurological Surgery 1997; **Med School:** Univ Pittsburgh 1984; **Resid:** Surgery, Mercy Hosp 1986; Neurological Surgery, Johns Hopkins Hosp 1992; **Fellow:** Neurological Surgery, Johns Hopkins Hosp 1991; **Fac Appt:** Prof NS, Jefferson Med Coll

Kaiser, Michael G MD [NS] - **Spec Exp:** Spinal Surgery-Complex; Minimally Invasive Spinal Surgery; Spinal Disc Replacement; Spinal Cord Tumors; **Hospital:** NY-Presby/Columbia Univ Med Ctr, NY (page 65); **Address:** Neurological Institute, Dept Neurological Surgery, 710 W 168th St, New York, NY 10032; **Phone:** 212-305-0378; **Board Cert:** Neurological Surgery 2004; **Med School:** Yale Univ 1994; **Resid:** Neurological Surgery, Columbia Neuro Inst 2000; **Fellow:** Spine Surgery, Emory Univ 2001; **Fac Appt:** Assoc Prof NS, Columbia P&S

Khan, Agha S MD [NS] - **Spec Exp:** Skull Base Surgery; Spinal Surgery; Microsurgery; Stereotactic Radiosurgery; **Hospital:** Sinai Hosp - Baltimore, Maryland Genl Hosp; **Address:** Mid-Atlantic Neurosurgical Assocs, 2411 W Belvedere Ave, Ste 402, Baltimore, MD 21215; **Phone:** 410-601-8314; **Board Cert:** Neurological Surgery 1995; **Med School:** Pakistan 1979; **Resid:** Neurological Surgery, Univ Wisconsin Hosp 1990; **Fellow:** Neurological Surgery, Allegheny Genl Hosp 1991

Kobrine, Arthur I MD/PhD [NS] - **Spec Exp:** Spinal Cord Surgery; Brain & Spinal Cord Tumors; Spinal Surgery; **Hospital:** Sibley Mem Hosp, MedStar Georgetown Univ Hosp; **Address:** 2440 M St NW, Ste 315, Washington, DC 20037-1404; **Phone:** 202-293-7136; **Board Cert:** Neurological Surgery 1976; **Med School:** Northwestern Univ 1968; **Resid:** Neurological Surgery, Northwestern Meml Hosp 1970; Neurological Surgery, Walter Reed Natl Military Med Ctr 1975; **Fellow:** Physiology, G Washington Univ Hosp 1979; **Fac Appt:** Clin Prof NS, Georgetown Univ

Kondziolka, Douglas MD [NS] - **Spec Exp:** Brain Tumors-Adult & Pediatric; Brain Tumors-Metastatic; Stereotactic Radiosurgery; Movement Disorders; **Hospital:** NYU Langone Med Ctr (page 68); **Address:** 530 First Ave, Ste 8R, New York, NY 10016; **Phone:** 646-501-2360; **Board Cert:** Neurological Surgery 1994; **Med School:** Univ Toronto 1985; **Resid:** Neurological Surgery, Univ Toronto Affil Hosp 1989; **Fellow:** Stereotactic Neurological Surgery, Univ Pittsburgh Med Ctr 1991

Kotapka, Mark J MD [NS] - **Spec Exp:** Pituitary Tumors; Skull Base Surgery; Spinal Disorders-Degenerative; Trauma; **Hospital:** Einstein Med Ctr; **Address:** Einstein Medical Ctr, 5401 Old York Rd, Klein Bldg - Ste 400, Philadelphia, PA 19141; **Phone:** 215-456-6127; **Board Cert:** Neurological Surgery 1997; **Med School:** Univ MD Sch Med 1985; **Resid:** Neurological Surgery, Hosp Univ Penn 1991; **Fellow:** Pediatric Neurological Surgery, Children's Hosp 1992; Skull Base Surgery, Univ Pittsburgh 1992; **Fac Appt:** Prof NS, Albert Einstein Coll Med

Laske, Douglas W MD [NS] - **Spec Exp:** Brain & Spinal Cord Tumors; Stereotactic Radiosurgery; Brain Tumors-Metastatic; Pituitary Tumors; **Hospital:** Temple Univ Hosp, Fox Chase Cancer Ctr (page 57); **Address:** Temple Univ Dep Neurosurgery, 3401 N Broad St, Ste C540, Phildelphia, PA 19140; **Phone:** 215-707-7200; **Board Cert:** Neurological Surgery 1996; **Med School:** Columbia P&S 1985; **Resid:** Neurological Surgery, VCU Med Ctr 1991; **Fellow:** Neurosurgical Oncology, Natl Inst Hlth 1995; **Fac Appt:** Assoc Prof NS, Temple Univ

Lavyne, Michael H MD [NS] - **Spec Exp:** Spinal Cord Tumors; **Hospital:** NY-Presby/Weill Cornell Med Ctr, NY (page 65), Hosp For Special Surgery (page 58); **Address:** 110 E 55th St Fl 9, MS 10022, New York, NY 10022; **Phone:** 212-486-9100; **Board Cert:** Neurological Surgery 1982; **Med School:** Cornell Univ-Weill Med Coll 1972; **Resid:** Neurological Surgery, Mass Genl Hosp 1979; **Fellow:** Neurology, Beth Israel Hosp 1974; **Fac Appt:** Clin Prof NS, Cornell Univ-Weill Med Coll

Levy, Elad I MD [NS] - **Spec Exp:** Endovascular Surgery; Stroke; Clinical Trials; **Hospital:** Buffalo Genl Hosp; **Address:** UB Neurosurgery, 3980A Sheridan Drive, Amherst, NY 14226; **Phone:** 716-218-1000; **Board Cert:** Neurological Surgery 2007; **Med School:** Geo Wash Univ 1997; **Resid:** Neurological Surgery, Univ Pittsburgh Affil Hosp 2004; **Fellow:** SUNY Buffalo 2003; **Fac Appt:** Prof NS, SUNY Buffalo

Lunsford, L Dade MD [NS] - **Spec Exp:** Brain Tumors; Stereotactic Radiosurgery; Movement Disorders; Vascular Malformations; **Hospital:** UPMC Presby, Pittsburgh, Chldns Hosp of Pittsburgh - UPMC; **Address:** UPMC Presbyterian Hosp, 200 Lothrop St, Ste B400, Pittsburgh, PA 15213-2536; **Phone:** 412-647-0953; **Board Cert:** Neurological Surgery 1983; **Med School:** Columbia P&S 1974; **Resid:** Neurological Surgery, Univ Pittsburgh Med Ctr 1980; **Fellow:** Stereotactic Neurological Surgery, Karolinska Hospital 1981; **Fac Appt:** Prof NS, Univ Pittsburgh

Maroon, Joseph C MD [NS] - **Spec Exp:** Minimally Invasive Spinal Surgery; Microdiscectomy; Brain Injury-Traumatic; Pituitary Tumors; **Hospital:** UPMC Presby, Pittsburgh, UPMC Passavant-McCandless; **Address:** UPMC Presbyterian, Dept Neuro Surg, 200 Lothrop St, Ste 5-C, Pittsburgh, PA 15213; **Phone:** 412-647-3604; **Board Cert:** Neurological Surgery 1973; **Med School:** Indiana Univ 1965; **Resid:** Surgery, Georgetown Univ Hosp 1967; Neurological Surgery, Indiana Univ Med Ctr 1971; **Fellow:** Neurological Surgery, Radcliffe Infirmary 1969; Microsurgery, Univ Vermont Affil Hosp 1972; **Fac Appt:** Prof NS, Univ Pittsburgh

McCormick, Paul C MD [NS] - **Spec Exp:** Spinal Surgery; Spinal Tumors; Arteriovenous Malformations; **Hospital:** NY-Presby/Columbia Univ Med Ctr, NY (page 65); **Address:** 710 W 168th St, Ste 506, New York, NY 10032-2603; **Phone:** 212-305-7976; **Board Cert:** Neurological Surgery 1993; **Med School:** Columbia P&S 1982; **Resid:** Neurological Surgery, Columbia Presby Med Ctr 1989; **Fellow:** Neurological Surgery, Natl Inst Hlth 1984; Spine Surgery, John Doyne Hosp 1990; **Fac Appt:** Prof NS, Columbia P&S

Moore, Frank M MD [NS] - **Spec Exp:** Aneurysm-Cerebral; Brain Tumors; Spinal Cord Tumors; Spinal Surgery; **Hospital:** Englewood Hosp & Med Ctr, Mt Sinai Med Ctr (page 62); **Address:** Metropolitan Neurosurgery Assocs, 309 Engle St, Ste 6, Englewood, NJ 07631; **Phone:** 201-569-7737; **Board Cert:** Neurological Surgery 1992; **Med School:** France 1983; **Resid:** Neurological Surgery, Mt Sinai Hosp 1988; **Fac Appt:** Assoc Prof NS, Mount Sinai Sch Med

Myseros, John S MD [NS] - **Spec Exp:** Pediatric Neurosurgery; Brain Tumors; Congenital Nervous System Malformations; **Hospital:** Inova Fairfax Hosp for Chldn, Chldns Natl Med Ctr; **Address:** Children's National Medical Center, Department of Neurosurgery, 111 Michigan Ave NW, Ste 4W-100, Washington, DC 20010; **Phone:** 202-476-3020; **Board Cert:** Neurological Surgery 2011; **Med School:** Johns Hopkins Univ 1990; **Resid:** Neurological Surgery, Med Coll Virginia 1996; **Fellow:** Pediatric Neurological Surgery, Hosp for Sick Children 1997; **Fac Appt:** Assoc Prof NS, Geo Wash Univ

Naff, Neal J MD [NS] - **Spec Exp:** Brain Tumors; Cerebrovascular Surgery; Peripheral Nerve Surgery; **Hospital:** Univ of MD-St. Joseph Med Ctr, Sinai Hosp - Baltimore; **Address:** Chesapeake Neurosurgery, 2700 Quarry Lake Drive, Ste 360, Baltimore, MD 21209; **Phone:** 410-486-0090; **Board Cert:** Neurological Surgery 2011; **Med School:** Johns Hopkins Univ 1991; **Resid:** Neurological Surgery, Johns Hopkins Hosp 1998; **Fellow:** Endovascular Surgery, Johns Hopkins Hosp 2000; **Fac Appt:** Asst Prof NS, Johns Hopkins Univ

O'Rourke, Donald M MD [NS] - **Spec Exp:** Neuro-Oncology; Brain Tumors; Spinal Disorders; **Hospital:** Hosp Univ Penn - UPHS (page 69); **Address:** Hosp Univ Penn-Dept Neurosurgery, 3400 Spruce St, 3 Silverstein, Philadelphia, PA 19104; **Phone:** 215-662-3490; **Board Cert:** Neurological Surgery 1998; **Med School:** Univ Pennsylvania 1987; **Resid:** Neurological Surgery, Hosp Univ Penn 1994; **Fac Appt:** Assoc Prof NS, Univ Pennsylvania

Olivi, Alessandro MD [NS] - **Spec Exp:** Brain & Spinal Cord Tumors; Skull Base Tumors; Brain Tumors-Metastatic; Meningioma; **Hospital:** Johns Hopkins Hosp (page 59); **Address:** Johns Hopkins Hosp, Dept Neurosurgery, 600 N Wolfe St, Phipps 1-100, Baltimore, MD 21287-0001; **Phone:** 410-955-0703; **Board Cert:** Neurological Surgery 1994; **Med School:** Italy 1979; **Resid:** Neurological Surgery, Univ of Padova; Neurological Surgery, Mayfield Neur Inst 1998; **Fellow:** Neuro-Oncology, Johns Hopkins Hosp 1991; **Fac Appt:** Prof NS, Johns Hopkins Univ

Patel, Aman B MD [NS] - **Spec Exp:** Interventional Neuroradiology; Endovascular Neurosurgery; Aneurysm-Cerebral; Arteriovenous Malformations; **Hospital:** Mt Sinai Med Ctr (page 62); **Address:** 14668 Madison Ave Fl 8th - rm 40, New York, NY 10029; **Phone:** 212-241-3457; **Board Cert:** Neurological Surgery 2004; **Med School:** UCLA 1993; **Resid:** Neurological Surgery, UCLA Med Ctr 1999; **Fellow:** Interventional Neuroradiology, UCLA Med Ctr 2001; **Fac Appt:** Assoc Prof NS, Mount Sinai Sch Med

Piatt Jr, Joseph H MD [NS] - **Spec Exp:** Brachial Plexus Palsy-Pediatric; Spasticity & Movement Disorders; Chiari's Deformity; Syringomyelia & Spinal Cord Diseases; **Hospital:** Nemours/Alfred I. duPont Hosp for Chldn; **Address:** Nemours, Neurological Surgery Dept, 1600 Rockland Rd, Wilmington, DE 19803; **Phone:** 302-651-5993; **Board Cert:** Neurological Surgery 1989; Pediatric Neurological Surgery 2006; **Med School:** Univ Pennsylvania 1979; **Resid:** Neurological Surgery, Duke Univ Hosp 1986; **Fellow:** Pediatric Neurological Surgery, Hosp Sick Chldn 1987

Pollack, Ian F MD [NS] - **Spec Exp:** Pediatric Neurosurgery; Brain Tumors; Craniofacial Surgery; Neuro-Oncology; **Hospital:** Chldns Hosp of Pittsburgh - UPMC, UPMC Presby, Pittsburgh; **Address:** Chldns Hosp Pittsburgh, Div Neurosurgery, 4401 Penn Ave, Ste FP4129, Pittsburgh, PA 15224; **Phone:** 412-692-5881; **Board Cert:** Neurological Surgery 1996; Pediatric Neurological Surgery 2006; **Med School:** Johns Hopkins Univ 1984; **Resid:** Neurological Surgery, Univ Pittsburgh Med Ctr 1991; **Fellow:** Pediatric Neurological Surgery, Hosp Sick Chldn 1992; **Fac Appt:** Prof NS, Univ Pittsburgh

Quigley, Matthew R MD [NS] - **Spec Exp:** Brain Tumors; Spinal Cord Tumors; Neuro-Oncology; **Hospital:** Allegheny Genl Hosp; **Address:** Allegeny General Hosp, Neurosurgery, 420 E North Ave, Ste 302, Pittsburgh, PA 15212; **Phone:** 412-359-4764; **Board Cert:** Neurological Surgery 1991; **Med School:** Northwestern Univ-Feinberg Sch Med 1981; **Resid:** Neurological Surgery, Northwestern Meml Hosp 1987; **Fac Appt:** Assoc Prof NS, Drexel Univ Coll Med

Rigamonti, Daniele MD [NS] - **Spec Exp:** Hydrocephalus-Adult; Brain Tumors; Spinal Disorders; Vascular Neurosurgery; **Hospital:** Johns Hopkins Hosp (page 59); **Address:** Johns Hopkins Hosp, Dept Neurosurgery, 600 N Wolfe St, Phipps Bldg - Ste 126, Baltimore, MD 21287; **Phone:** 410-955-2259; **Board Cert:** Neurological Surgery 1988; **Med School:** Italy 1976; **Resid:** Neurological Surgery, Mt Sinai Hosp Med Ctr 1984; **Fellow:** Neurovascular Surgery, Barrow Neuro Inst 1987; **Fac Appt:** Prof NS, Johns Hopkins Univ

Riina, Howard A MD [NS] - **Spec Exp:** Neuroradiology; Aneurysm-Cerebral; Cerebrovascular Malformations; Stroke; **Hospital:** NYU Langone Med Ctr (page 68); **Address:** NYU Langone Med Ctr, 530 First Ave, SK1, Ste 8R, New York, NY 10016; **Phone:** 212-263-5382; **Board Cert:** Neurological Surgery 2004; **Med School:** Temple Univ 1993; **Resid:** Neurological Surgery, Hosp Univ Penn 2000; **Fellow:** Interventional Neuroradiology, Beth Israel Med Ctr 1997; Skull Base Surgery, Barrow Neuro Inst 2001; **Fac Appt:** Prof NS, NYU Sch Med

Rosenwasser, Robert H MD [NS] - **Spec Exp:** Aneurysm-Cerebral; Cerebrovascular Surgery; Arteriovenous Malformations; **Hospital:** Thomas Jefferson Univ Hosp; **Address:** Jefferson University Physicians, Dept Neurosurgery, 909 Walnut St Fl 3, Philadelphia, PA 19107; **Phone:** 215-955-7000; **Board Cert:** Neurological Surgery 1987; **Med School:** Louisiana State U, New Orleans 1979; **Resid:** Neurological Surgery, Temple Univ Hosp 1984; **Fellow:** Neurovascular Surgery, Univ West Ontarion 1985; Interventional Neuroradiology, NYU Med Ctr 1993; **Fac Appt:** Prof NS, Thomas Jefferson Univ

Schwartz, Theodore H MD [NS] - **Spec Exp:** Brain Tumors; Pituitary Tumors; Minimally Invasive Surgery; **Hospital:** NY-Presby/Weill Cornell Med Ctr, NY (page 65); **Address:** Weill Cornell Med Ctr-Neurosurgery Dept, 525 E 68th St, rm 651, Starr Pavilion, Box 99, New York, NY 10065; **Phone:** 212-746-5620; **Board Cert:** Neurological Surgery 2013; **Med School:** Harvard Med Sch 1993; **Resid:** Neurological Surgery, Columbia-Presby Med Ctr 1999; **Fellow:** Neurological Surgery, Yale-New Haven Med Ctr 2000; **Fac Appt:** Prof NS, Cornell Univ-Weill Med Coll

Sen, Chandranath MD [NS] - **Spec Exp:** Brain Tumors; Skull Base Tumors; Meningioma; **Hospital:** NYU Langone Med Ctr (page 68); **Address:** NYU Langone Med Ctr-Dept Neurosurgery, 530 First Ave, Ste 8R, New York, NY 10016; **Phone:** 212-263-5333; **Board Cert:** Neurological Surgery 1989; **Med School:** India 1976; **Resid:** Surgery, Univ Wisconsin Hosps 1980; Neurological Surgery, Univ Wisconsin Hosps 1985; **Fellow:** Neurological Surgery, Univ Pittsburgh Med Ctr 1986; **Fac Appt:** Prof NS, Mount Sinai Sch Med

Sisti, Michael B MD [NS] - **Spec Exp:** Brain Tumors-Complex; Meningioma; Arteriovenous Malformations; **Hospital:** NY-Presby/Columbia Univ Med Ctr, NY (page 65); **Address:** Neurological Inst, 710 W 168th St, Ste 413, New York, NY 10032-2603; **Phone:** 212-305-1728; **Board Cert:** Neurological Surgery 1991; **Med School:** Columbia P&S 1981; **Resid:** Neurological Surgery, NY-Presby/Columbia Med Ctr 1988; **Fellow:** Neurological Surgery, Natl Inst Hlth 1983; **Fac Appt:** Assoc Prof NS, Columbia P&S

Solomon, Robert A MD [NS] - **Spec Exp:** Aneurysm-Cerebral; Arteriovenous Malformations; **Hospital:** NY-Presby/Columbia Univ Med Ctr, NY (page 65); **Address:** 710 W 168th St, Ste 439, New York, NY 10032; **Phone:** 212-305-4118; **Board Cert:** Neurological Surgery 1988; **Med School:** Johns Hopkins Univ 1980; **Resid:** Neurological Surgery, Neuro Inst-Columbia 1986; **Fac Appt:** Prof NS, Columbia P&S

Souweidane, Mark M MD [NS] - **Spec Exp:** Pediatric Neurosurgery; Minimally Invasive Surgery; Endoscopic Surgery; Brain Tumors-Pediatric; **Hospital:** NY-Presby/Weill Cornell Med Ctr, NY (page 65), Meml Sloan-Kettering Canc Ctr; **Address:** Weill Cornell Med Ctr-Neurosurgery Dept, 525 E 68th St, Ste 651, Starr Pavilion, Box 99, New York, NY 10065-4870; **Phone:** 212-746-2363; **Board Cert:** Neurological Surgery 2010; **Med School:** Wayne State Univ 1988; **Resid:** Neurological Surgery, NYU Med Ctr 1994; **Fellow:** Pediatric Neurological Surgery, Hosp Sick Chldn 1995; **Fac Appt:** Prof NS, Cornell Univ-Weill Med Coll

Stieg, Philip E MD/PhD [NS] - **Spec Exp:** Aneurysm-Cerebral; Stroke; Meningioma; Arteriovenous Malformations; **Hospital:** NY-Presby/Weill Cornell Med Ctr, NY (page 65); **Address:** Weill Cornell Med Ctr-Neurosurgery Dept, 525 E 68th St, Ste 651, Starr Pavilion, Box 99, New York, NY 10065; **Phone:** 212-746-1349; **Board Cert:** Neurological Surgery 1992; **Med School:** Med Coll Wisc 1983; **Resid:** Neurological Surgery, Parkland Meml Hosp/Dallas Chldns Hosp 1989; **Fellow:** Neurological Biology, Karolinska Inst 1988; **Fac Appt:** Prof NS, Cornell Univ-Weill Med Coll

Sundaresan, Narayan MD [NS] - **Spec Exp:** Spinal Surgery; Brain Tumors; Neuro-Oncology; **Hospital:** Mt Sinai Med Ctr (page 62), Bronx Lebanon Hosp Ctr; **Address:** Central Park Neurosurgery, 1148 5th Ave, New York, NY 10128; **Phone:** 212-876-7575; **Board Cert:** Neurological Surgery 1980; **Med School:** India 1969; **Resid:** Neurological Surgery, Northwestern Meml Hosp 1976; **Fellow:** Neuro-Oncology, Meml Sloan Kettering Cancer Ctr 1977; **Fac Appt:** Prof NS, Mount Sinai Sch Med

Sutton, Leslie N MD [NS] - **Spec Exp:** Brain Tumors-Pediatric; Fetal Neurosurgery; Hydrocephalus; **Hospital:** Chldns Hosp of Philadelphia; **Address:** Childrens Hosp Phila-Neurosurgery, 34th St & Civic Center Blvd, Wood Bldg Fl 6, Philadelphia, PA 19104; **Phone:** 215-590-2780; **Board Cert:** Neurological Surgery 1984; Pediatric Neurological Surgery 1996; **Med School:** Univ Pennsylvania 1975; **Resid:** Neurological Surgery, Hosp Univ Penn 1981; **Fac Appt:** Prof NS, Univ Pennsylvania

Tamargo, Rafael J MD [NS] - **Spec Exp:** Neurovascular Surgery; Aneurysm-Cerebral; Arteriovenous Malformations; Skull Base Surgery; **Hospital:** Johns Hopkins Hosp (page 59), Johns Hopkins Bayview Med Ctr (page 59); **Address:** Johns Hopkins Hosp, Dept Neurosurgery, Zayed Tower, Ste 6115G, 1800 Orleans St, Baltimore, MD 21287; **Phone:** 410-614-1533; **Board Cert:** Neurological Surgery 1995; **Med School:** Columbia P&S 1984; **Resid:** Neurological Surgery, Johns Hopkins Hosp 1992; **Fac Appt:** Prof NS, Johns Hopkins Univ

Weiner, Howard L MD [NS] - **Spec Exp:** Pediatric Neurosurgery; Epilepsy; Tuberous Sclerosis; **Hospital:** NYU Langone Med Ctr (page 68); **Address:** NYU Med Ctr, Div Pediatric Neurosurgery, 317 E 34th St, Ste 1002, New York, NY 10016; **Phone:** 212-263-6419; **Board Cert:** Neurological Surgery 2012; **Med School:** Cornell Univ 1989; **Resid:** Neurological Surgery, NYU Med Ctr 1996; **Fellow:** Pediatric Neurological Surgery, NYU Med Ctr 1997; **Fac Appt:** Prof NS, NYU Sch Med

Weingart, Jon D MD [NS] - **Spec Exp:** Brain Tumors; Spinal Disorders; Gliomas; Chiari's Deformity; **Hospital:** Johns Hopkins Hosp (page 59); **Address:** Johns Hopkins Hosp, Dept Neurosurgery, Sheikh Zayed Tower, Ste 6115D, 1800 Orleans St, Baltimore, MD 21287; **Phone:** 410-614-3052; **Board Cert:** Neurological Surgery 1998; **Med School:** Duke Univ 1987; **Resid:** Neurological Surgery, Johns Hopkins Hosp 1993; **Fellow:** Neurosurgical Oncology, Johns Hopkins Hosp; **Fac Appt:** Prof NS, Johns Hopkins Univ

Welch, William C MD [NS] - **Spec Exp:** Spinal Surgery; **Hospital:** Pennsylvania Hosp-UPHS (page 69); **Address:** Penn Neurosurgery-Pennsylvania Hosp, Washington Square West Bldg, 235 S 8th St, Philadelphia, PA 19106; **Phone:** 215-829-6700; **Board Cert:** Neurological Surgery 1995; **Med School:** SUNY Downstate 1985; **Resid:** Neurological Surgery, Strong Meml Hosp 1991; **Fellow:** Neuro-Oncology, Montefiore Med Ctr 1992; Spine Surgery, Weiler-Einstein Hosp 1993; **Fac Appt:** Prof NS, Univ Pennsylvania

Whiting, Donald M MD [NS] - **Spec Exp:** Movement Disorders; Pain & Spasticity; Deep Brain Stimulation; Spinal Reconstructive Surgery; **Hospital:** Allegheny Genl Hosp, Washington Hosp, The; **Address:** 380 W Chestnut St, Washington, PA 15301-4657; **Phone:** 724-228-1414; **Board Cert:** Neurological Surgery 1995; **Med School:** Jefferson Med Coll 1985; **Resid:** Surgery, Geisinger Med Ctr 1986; Neurological Surgery, Cleveland Clinic 1991; **Fellow:** Neurological Trauma, Allegheny Genl Hosp 1990; **Fac Appt:** Prof NS, Drexel Univ Coll Med

Wilberger Jr, James E MD [NS] - **Spec Exp:** Epilepsy; Brain Injury; Brain Tumors-Benign; **Hospital:** Allegheny Genl Hosp; **Address:** Allegheny General Hosp, Neorosurgery, 420 E North Ave, Ste 208, Pittsburgh, PA 15212; **Phone:** 412-359-4764; **Board Cert:** Neurological Surgery 1986; **Med School:** Med Coll VA 1978; **Resid:** Neurological Surgery, Univ Pittsburgh Med Ctr 1984; **Fac Appt:** Prof NS, Drexel Univ Coll Med

Wisoff, Jeffrey H MD [NS] - **Spec Exp:** Pediatric Neurosurgery; Brain Tumors-Pediatric; Arteriovenous Malformations; **Hospital:** NYU Langone Med Ctr (page 68), Maimonides Med Ctr (page 60); **Address:** 317 E 34th St, Ste 1002, New York, NY 10016-4974; **Phone:** 212-263-6419; **Board Cert:** Neurological Surgery 1990; Pediatric Neurological Surgery 2008; **Med School:** Geo Wash Univ 1978; **Resid:** Neurological Surgery, NYU/Bellevue Hosp 1984; **Fellow:** Pediatric Neurological Surgery, NYU Med Ctr 1985; **Fac Appt:** Assoc Prof NS, NYU Sch Med

Zager, Eric L MD [NS] - **Spec Exp:** Peripheral Nerve Disorders; Carpal Tunnel Syndrome; Pediatric Neurosurgery; Cerebrovascular Surgery; **Hospital:** Hosp Univ Penn - UPHS (page 69), Chldns Hosp of Philadelphia; **Address:** Hosp Univ Penn, Neurosurgery, 3400 Spruce St, 3 Silverstein, Philadelphia, PA 19104; **Phone:** 215-662-3497; **Board Cert:** Neurological Surgery 1992; **Med School:** Stanford Univ 1982; **Resid:** Neurological Surgery, Mass Genl Hosp 1988; **Fellow:** Peripheral Nerve Surgery, Univ Toronto 1989; Peripheral Nerve Surgery, LSU Med Ctr 1989; **Fac Appt:** Prof NS, Univ Pennsylvania

Southeast

Asher, Anthony MD [NS] - **Spec Exp:** Brain Tumors; Stereotactic Radiosurgery; Epilepsy; **Hospital:** Carolinas Med Ctr, Presby Hosp - Charlotte; **Address:** 225 Baldwin Ave, Charlotte, NC 28204; **Phone:** 704-376-1605; **Board Cert:** Neurological Surgery 1998; **Med School:** Wayne State Univ 1987; **Resid:** Neurological Surgery, Univ Mich Med Ctr 1995; **Fellow:** Surgical Oncology, Natl Cancer Inst 1991

Barrow, Daniel L MD [NS] - **Spec Exp:** Cerebrovascular Disease; Stroke; Aneurysm-Cerebral; Carotid Artery Disease; **Hospital:** Emory Univ Hosp; **Address:** Emory Univ Hosp, Neurosurgery Dept, 1365B Clifton Rd NE, Ste 2200, Atlanta, GA 30322; **Phone:** 404-778-5770; **Board Cert:** Neurological Surgery 1988; **Med School:** Southern IL Univ 1979; **Resid:** Neurological Surgery, Emory Univ Hosp 1985; **Fellow:** Cerebrovascular Neurosurgery, Mayo Clin 1986; **Fac Appt:** Prof NS, Emory Univ

Boop, Frederick A MD [NS] - **Spec Exp:** Pediatric Neurosurgery; Epilepsy; Brain Tumors; **Hospital:** Le Bonheur Chldns Med Ctr, Methodist Univ Hosp - Memphis; **Address:** Semmes-Murphey Neurologic & Spine Inst, 6325 Humphreys Blvd, Memphis, TN 38120; **Phone:** 901-259-5340; **Board Cert:** Neurological Surgery 1993; Pediatric Neurological Surgery 2005; **Med School:** Univ Ark 1983; **Resid:** Neurological Surgery, Univ Tex Hlth Sci Ctr 1989; Neurological Surgery, Inst Neur/Hosp Sick Chldn 1987; **Fellow:** Epilepsy, Univ Minn Affil Hosp 1989; Pediatric Neurological Surgery, Ark Chldns Hosp 1990; **Fac Appt:** Assoc Prof NS, Univ Tenn Coll Med

Branch Jr, Charles L MD [NS] - **Spec Exp:** Spinal Reconstructive Surgery; Minimally Invasive Spinal Surgery; Stereotactic Radiosurgery; **Hospital:** Wake Forest Baptist Med Ctr; **Address:** Wake Forest Univ Baptist Med Ctr, Medical Center Blvd, Winston-Salem, NC 27157-1029; **Phone:** 336-716-4083; **Board Cert:** Neurological Surgery 1991; **Med School:** Univ Tex SW, Dallas 1981; **Resid:** Neurological Surgery, NC Baptist Hosp 1987; **Fellow:** Neurological Surgery, UCSF Med Ctr 1987; **Fac Appt:** Prof NS, Wake Forest Univ

Ewend, Matthew MD [NS] - **Spec Exp:** Brain Tumors; Pituitary Tumors; Pediatric Neurosurgery; Epilepsy; **Hospital:** NC Memorial Hosp - UNC; **Address:** UNC Neurosurgery, 170 Manning Drive, MC 7060, Physicians Office Bldg, Chapel Hill, NC 27599; **Phone:** 919-966-1374; **Board Cert:** Neurological Surgery 2012; **Med School:** Johns Hopkins Univ 1990; **Resid:** Neurological Surgery, Johns Hopkins Hosp 1994; **Fellow:** Neuro-Oncology, Natl Inst Hlth 1996; **Fac Appt:** Prof NS, Univ NC Sch Med

Foley, Kevin T MD [NS] - **Spec Exp:** Spinal Surgery; Minimally Invasive Spinal Surgery; **Hospital:** Methodist Univ Hosp - Memphis, Baptist Memorial Hospital-Memphis; **Address:** Semmes-Murphey Neurologic & Spine Inst, 6325 Humphreys Blvd, Memphis, TN 38120; **Phone:** 901-522-7700; **Board Cert:** Neurological Surgery 1987; **Med School:** UCLA 1979; **Resid:** Neurological Surgery, UCLA Med Ctr 1985; **Fac Appt:** Prof NS, Univ Tenn Coll Med

Freeman, Thomas B MD [NS] - **Spec Exp:** Parkinson's Disease; Nerve Surgery & Transplantation; Spinal Surgery; **Hospital:** Tampa Genl Hosp; **Address:** USF Hlth, Neurosurgery & Brain Repair, 2 Tampa General Cir Fl 3, Tampa, FL 33606; **Phone:** 813-259-0889; **Board Cert:** Neurological Surgery 1993; **Med School:** Johns Hopkins Univ 1981; **Resid:** Neurological Surgery, NYU Med Ctr 1988; **Fac Appt:** Prof NS, Univ S Fla Coll Med

Friedman, Allan H MD [NS] - **Spec Exp:** Brain Tumors; Skull Base Tumors; Gliomas; **Hospital:** Duke Univ Hosp; **Address:** Duke Univ Med Ctr, Box 3807, Durham, NC 27710; **Phone:** 919-681-6421; **Board Cert:** Neurological Surgery 1983; **Med School:** Univ IL Coll Med 1974; **Resid:** Neurological Surgery, Duke Univ Med Ctr 1980; **Fellow:** Vascular Surgery, Univ Western Ontario 1981; **Fac Appt:** Prof S, Duke Univ

Green, Barth A MD [NS] - **Spec Exp:** Spinal Surgery; Spinal Cord Injury; Spinal Tumors; **Hospital:** Univ of Miami Hosp, Jackson Meml Hosp; **Address:** UHlth, Neurosurgery Dept, 1095 NW 14th Terr, Miami, FL 33136; **Phone:** 305-243-6946; **Board Cert:** Neurological Surgery 1978; **Med School:** Indiana Univ 1969; **Resid:** Neurological Surgery, Northwestern Med Ctr 1975; **Fac Appt:** Prof NS, Univ Miami Sch Med

Guthrie, Barton L MD [NS] - **Spec Exp:** Brain Tumors; Stereotactic Radiosurgery; Parkinson's Disease/Movement Disorders; Neuro-Oncology; **Hospital:** UAB Hosp; **Address:** The Kirklin Clinic, 2000 6th Ave S, Birmingham, AL 35233; **Phone:** 205-934-8136; **Board Cert:** Neurological Surgery 1992; **Med School:** UAB Sch Med 1980; **Resid:** Neurological Surgery, Mayo Clinic 1988; **Fellow:** Neurological Surgery, Stanford Univ Med Ctr 1988; **Fac Appt:** Assoc Prof NS, UAB Sch Med

Hadley, Mark N MD [NS] - **Spec Exp:** Spinal Surgery-Complex; Spinal Disorders-Degenerative; **Hospital:** UAB Hosp; **Address:** UAB Hosp, Div Neurosurgery, 1530 3rd Ave S, FOT Bldg - Ste 1030, Birmingham, AL 35294-3410; **Phone:** 205-934-1439; **Board Cert:** Neurological Surgery 1992; **Med School:** Albany Med Coll 1982; **Resid:** Neurological Surgery, St. Joseph's Hosp & Med Ctr 1988; **Fac Appt:** Prof NS, UAB Sch Med

Haid Jr, Regis W MD [NS] - **Spec Exp:** Spinal Surgery; Minimally Invasive Spinal Surgery; Spinal Disc Replacement; Microdiscectomy; **Hospital:** Piedmont Hosp, Shepherd Ctr - Atlanta; **Address:** Atlanta Brain & Spine Care, 2001 Peachtree Rd NE, Ste 575, Atlanta, GA 30309; **Phone:** 404-350-0106; **Board Cert:** Neurological Surgery 2011; **Med School:** W VA Univ 1982; **Resid:** Neurological Surgery, W Va Univ Hosps 1988; **Fellow:** Spine Surgery, Univ Florida 1989; **Fac Appt:** Prof NS, Emory Univ

Heros, Roberto C MD [NS] - **Spec Exp:** Cerebrovascular Surgery; Skull Base Surgery; Brain Tumors; **Hospital:** Jackson Meml Hosp, Univ of Miami Hosp & Clins/Sylvester Comp Canc Ctr; **Address:** Univ Miami, Dept Neurosurgery, 1095 NW 14th Terrace, Miami, FL 33136; **Phone:** 305-243-4572; **Board Cert:** Neurological Surgery 1979; **Med School:** Univ Tenn Coll Med 1968; **Resid:** Surgery, Mass Genl Hosp 1970; Neurological Surgery, Mass Genl Hosp 1976; **Fac Appt:** Prof NS, Univ Miami Sch Med

Kim, Jhinho N MD [NS] - **Spec Exp:** Cancer Surgery; Spinal Cord Surgery; Cerebrovascular Malformations; **Hospital:** Meml Hosp; **Address:** 1340 Broad Ave, Ste 440, Gulfport, MS 39501; **Phone:** 228-867-4856; **Board Cert:** Neurological Surgery 1976; **Med School:** South Korea 1966; **Resid:** Neurological Surgery, Tufts-New Eng Med Ctr 1973; **Fellow:** Neurological Surgery, NYU Langone Med Ctr 1974

Landy, Howard J MD [NS] - **Spec Exp:** Stereotactic Radiosurgery; **Hospital:** Univ of Miami Hosp, Jackson Meml Hosp; **Address:** UHlth, Neurosurgery Dept, 1095 NW 14th Terr, Miami, FL 33136; **Phone:** 305-243-4675; **Board Cert:** Neurological Surgery 1991; **Med School:** Univ Miami Sch Med 1980; **Resid:** Neurological Surgery, Jackson Meml Hosp 1987; **Fac Appt:** Prof NS, Univ Miami Sch Med

Levi, Allan MD/PhD [NS] - **Spec Exp:** Spinal Surgery; Peripheral Nerve Disorders; Minimally Invasive Spinal Surgery; Spinal Cord Injury; **Hospital:** Univ of Miami Hosp, Jackson Meml Hosp; **Address:** UHlth, Neurosurgery Dept, 1095 NW 14th Terr, Miami, FL 33136; **Phone:** 305-243-2088; **Board Cert:** Neurological Surgery 2010; **Med School:** Univ Ottawa 1986; **Resid:** Neurological Surgery, Univ Toronto Affil Hosp 1991; **Fellow:** Spine Surgery, Barrow Neurological Inst 1995; **Fac Appt:** Prof NS, Univ Miami Sch Med

Markert Jr, James M MD [NS] - **Spec Exp:** Brain Tumors; Stereotactic Radiosurgery; Clinical Trials; Gliomas; **Hospital:** UAB Hosp; **Address:** Univ Alabama, Div Neurosurgery, 510 20th St S, FOT, rm 1060, Birmingham, AL 35294; **Phone:** 205-975-6985; **Board Cert:** Neurological Surgery 2010; **Med School:** Columbia P&S 1988; **Resid:** Neurological Surgery, Univ Mich Med Ctr 1995; **Fellow:** Neuro-Oncology, Mass Genl Hosp 1991; **Fac Appt:** Prof NS, UAB Sch Med

Morcos, Jacques J MD [NS] - **Spec Exp:** Cerebrovascular Surgery; Brain Tumors; Skull Base Tumors & Surgery; Arteriovenous Malformations; **Hospital:** Jackson Meml Hosp; **Address:** University of Miami, Dept Neurosurgery, 1095 NW 14th Terr, Fl 2, Miami, FL 33136; **Phone:** 305-243-4675; **Board Cert:** Neurological Surgery 2010; **Med School:** Lebanon 1985; **Resid:** Neurological Surgery, Natl Hosp for Nervous Diseases 1990; Neurological Surgery, Univ Minnesota 1993; **Fellow:** Cerebrovascular Neurosurgery, Univ Florida/Shands Med Ctr 1994; Skull Base Surgery, Barrow Neurolical Inst 1995; **Fac Appt:** Assoc Prof NS, Univ Miami Sch Med

Oakes, W. Jerry MD [NS] - **Spec Exp:** Pediatric Neurosurgery; Chiari's Deformity; Occult Spinal Dysraphism (OSD); **Hospital:** Children's Hosp AL; **Address:** 1600 7th Ave S Lowder Bldg - Ste 400, Birmingham, AL 35233; **Phone:** 205-638-9653; **Board Cert:** Neurological Surgery 1981; Pediatric Neurological Surgery 2005; **Med School:** Duke Univ 1972; **Resid:** Neurological Surgery, Duke Univ Hosp 1978; **Fellow:** Neurological Surgery, Hosp for Sick Chldn 1975; Neurological Surgery, Great Ormond St Hosp 1979; **Fac Appt:** Prof NS, UAB Sch Med

Olson, Jeffrey J MD [NS] - **Spec Exp:** Neuro-Oncology; Brain Tumors; Skull Base Tumors; Von Hippel-Lindau Disease; **Hospital:** Emory Univ Hosp; **Address:** Emory Univ Hosp, Neurosurgery Dept, 1365B Clifton Rd NE, Ste 2200, Atlanta, GA 30322; **Phone:** 404-778-5770; **Board Cert:** Neurological Surgery 1989; **Med School:** Univ Minn 1981; **Resid:** Neurological Surgery, Univ Iowa Hosps & Clins 1987; **Fellow:** Neurological Surgery, Natl Inst Hlth-Clin Ctr 1990; **Fac Appt:** Prof NS, Emory Univ

Parent, Andrew D MD [NS] - **Spec Exp:** Pediatric Neurosurgery; Neuroendocrine Tumors; Pituitary Tumors; **Hospital:** Univ Mississippi Med Ctr; **Address:** Univ Miss Med Ctr-Dept Neurosurgery, 2500 N State St, Jackson, MS 39216-4500; **Phone:** 601-984-5702; **Board Cert:** Neurological Surgery 1981; **Med School:** Univ VT Coll Med 1970; **Resid:** Neurological Surgery, Emory Univ 1978; **Fellow:** Neurological Surgery, Univ Tex Med Br 1974; **Fac Appt:** Prof NS, Univ Miss

Patel, Sunil J MD [NS] - **Spec Exp:** Brain Tumors; Skull Base Surgery; Pain-Facial; Trigeminal Neuralgia; **Hospital:** MUSC Med Ctr, R H Johnson VA Med Ctr - Charleston; **Address:** MUSC-Adult Neurological Surgery, CSB, Ste 428, Charleston, SC 29425; **Phone:** 843-792-7700; **Board Cert:** Neurological Surgery 1996; **Med School:** Med Univ SC 1985; **Resid:** Neurological Surgery, Univ South Carolina 1991; **Fellow:** Neurological Surgery, Nagoya Univ Med School 1991; Skull Base Surgery, Univ Pittsburgh 1993; **Fac Appt:** Prof NS, Med Univ SC

Ragheb, John MD [NS] - **Spec Exp:** Pediatric Neurosurgery; Spinal Cord Tumors-Pediatric; Brain Injury-Pediatric; Epilepsy; **Hospital:** Miami Children's Hosp; **Address:** Miami Chldns Hosp, Neurosurgery Dept, 3100 SW 62nd Ave, Ste 3109, Miami, FL 33155; **Phone:** 305-662-8386; **Board Cert:** Neurological Surgery 1996; Pediatric Neurological Surgery 1998; **Med School:** Univ Mich Med Sch 1985; **Resid:** Neurological Surgery, Univ MD Med Ctr 1991; **Fellow:** Pediatric Neurological Surgery, NYU Med Ctr 1992; **Fac Appt:** Prof NS, Univ Miami Sch Med

Reid, William S MD [NS] - **Spec Exp:** Minimally Invasive Spinal Surgery; Brain & Spinal Cord Tumors; Pituitary Tumors; Microsurgery; **Hospital:** Fort Sanders Reg Med Ctr; **Address:** Fort Sanders Regional Med Ctr, 501 19th St, Ste 600, Knoxville, TN 37916; **Phone:** 865-329-4003; **Board Cert:** Neurological Surgery 1980; **Med School:** Univ Ariz Coll Med 1971; **Resid:** Neurological Surgery, Univ Texas SW Med Ctr 1977; **Fac Appt:** Assoc Clin Prof NS, Univ Tenn Coll Med

Robertson, Jon H MD [NS] - **Spec Exp:** Brain & Spinal Cord Tumors; Skull Base Tumors; Stereotactic Radiosurgery; **Hospital:** Methodist Univ Hosp - Memphis; **Address:** Semmes-Murphey Neurologic & Spine Inst, 6325 Humphreys Blvd, Memphis, TN 38120; **Phone:** 901-522-7700; **Board Cert:** Neurological Surgery 1982; **Med School:** Univ Tenn Coll Med 1971; **Resid:** Surgery, City Memphis Hosp 1974; Neurological Surgery, Univ TN Med Ctr 1979; **Fac Appt:** Prof NS, Univ Tenn Coll Med

Rodts Jr, Gerald E MD [NS] - **Spec Exp:** Spinal Surgery; Spinal Trauma; Spinal Tumors; Minimally Invasive Spinal Surgery; **Hospital:** Emory Univ Hosp, Emory Univ Hosp Midtown; **Address:** Emory Spine Ctr, 59 Executive Park S, Ste 3000, Atlanta, GA 30329; **Phone:** 404-778-7000; **Board Cert:** Neurological Surgery 1998; **Med School:** Columbia P&S 1987; **Resid:** Neurological Surgery, UCLA Med Ctr 1994; **Fellow:** Spine Surgery, Emory Univ Hosp 1995; **Fac Appt:** Prof NS, Emory Univ

Sampson, John H MD/PhD [NS] - **Spec Exp:** Brain Tumors; Clinical Trials; **Hospital:** Duke Univ Hosp; **Address:** Duke Univ Med Ctr, Box 3050, Durham, NC 27710; **Phone:** 919-684-9041; **Board Cert:** Neurological Surgery 2013; **Med School:** Univ Manitoba 1990; **Resid:** Neurological Surgery, Duke Univ Med Ctr 1998; **Fellow:** Neurological Intensive Care, Duke Univ Med Ctr 1999; **Fac Appt:** Prof NS, Duke Univ

Shaffrey, Christopher I MD [NS] - **Spec Exp:** Spinal Surgery; Spinal Surgery-Pediatric; **Hospital:** Univ of Virginia Hlth Sys; **Address:** Univ Virg, Dept Neurosurgery, 2 Hospital Drive, West Complex-Barringer Wing Fl 3, Charlottesville, VA 22908; **Phone:** 434-243-7026; **Board Cert:** Neurological Surgery 1997; Orthopaedic Surgery 2008; **Med School:** Univ VA Sch Med 1986; **Resid:** Neurological Surgery, Univ Virginia Med Ctr 1992; Orthopaedic Surgery, Univ Virginia Med Ctr 1995; **Fellow:** Spine Surgery, Univ Virginia Med Ctr 1996; **Fac Appt:** Prof NS, Univ VA Sch Med

Shaffrey, Mark E MD [NS] - **Spec Exp:** Brain Tumors; Clinical Trials; Spinal Cord Tumors; Spinal Tumors; **Hospital:** Univ of Virginia Hlth Sys; **Address:** Univ VA Hlth Sys, Dept Neurosurgery, 1300 Jefferson Park Ave, Charlottesville, VA 22908; **Phone:** 434-924-1843; **Board Cert:** Neurological Surgery 2011; **Med School:** Univ VA Sch Med 1987; **Resid:** Neurological Surgery, Univ VA Hlth Sys 1991; **Fellow:** Microvascular Physiology, Natl Inst Hlth - Clin Ctr 1992; Neurological Pathology, Univ VA Hlth Sys 1993; **Fac Appt:** Prof NS, Univ VA Sch Med

Sills Jr, Allen MD [NS] - **Spec Exp:** Brain & Spinal Cord Tumors; Sports Injuries; Concussion; **Hospital:** Vanderbilt Univ Med Ctr, Williamson Med Ctr; **Address:** 2009 Malary Ln, Ste 230, Franklin, TN 37067; **Phone:** 615-875-7054; **Board Cert:** Neurological Surgery 2013; **Med School:** Johns Hopkins Univ 1990; **Resid:** Neurological Surgery, Johns Hopkins Hosp 1994; **Fellow:** Neuro-Oncology, Hunterian Neurosurg Lab/Johns Hopkins 1996; **Fac Appt:** Assoc Prof NS, Vanderbilt Univ

Swaid, Swaid N MD [NS] - **Spec Exp:** Stereotactic Radiosurgery; Brain Tumors; Pituitary Tumors; Acoustic Neuroma; **Hospital:** Brookwood Med Ctr; **Address:** Neurological Surgery Assocs, 513 Brookwood Blvd, Ste 372, Birmingham, AL 35209; **Phone:** 205-949-1800; **Board Cert:** Neurological Surgery 1983; **Med School:** UAB Sch Med 1976; **Resid:** Neurological Surgery, UAB Med Ctr 1981; **Fac Appt:** Assoc Prof NS, UAB Sch Med

Tatter, Stephen MD/PhD [NS] - **Spec Exp:** Brain Tumors; Pituitary Tumors; Stereotactic Radiosurgery; **Hospital:** Wake Forest Baptist Med Ctr; **Address:** Wake Forest Baptist Hlth, Dept Neurosurgery, One Medical Center Blvd, Winston-Salem, NC 27157-1029; **Phone:** 336-716-4047; **Board Cert:** Neurological Surgery 2004; **Med School:** Cornell Univ-Weill Med Coll 1990; **Resid:** Neurological Surgery, Mass Genl Hosp 1996; **Fellow:** Neurological Surgery, Mass Genl Hosp 1997; **Fac Appt:** Prof NS, Wake Forest Univ

Thompson, Reid C MD [NS] - **Spec Exp:** Neuro-Oncology; Brain & Spinal Cord Tumors; Neurovascular Surgery; Skull Base Tumors; **Hospital:** Vanderbilt Univ Med Ctr; **Address:** Vanderbilt Neurosurgery, 1500 21st Ave S, Ste 1506, Nashville, TN 37212; **Phone:** 615-322-7417; **Board Cert:** Neurological Surgery 2012; **Med School:** Johns Hopkins Univ 1989; **Resid:** Neurological Surgery, Johns Hopkins Hosp 1995; **Fellow:** Neuro-Oncology, Johns Hopkins Hosp 1996; Cerebrovascular Neurosurgery, Stanford Univ Med Ctr 1997; **Fac Appt:** Prof NS, Vanderbilt Univ

Van Loveren, Harry R MD [NS] - **Spec Exp:** Cerebrovascular Surgery; Skull Base Surgery; Trigeminal Neuralgia; Brain Tumors; **Hospital:** Tampa Genl Hosp; **Address:** 2 Tampa General Cir, Tampa, FL 33606; **Phone:** 813-259-0965; **Board Cert:** Neurological Surgery 1988; **Med School:** Univ Cincinnati 1979; **Resid:** Neurological Surgery, Univ of Cincinnati Med Ctr 1985; **Fellow:** Neurological Surgery, Universitatspital 1985; **Fac Appt:** Prof NS, Univ S Fla Coll Med

Wharen Jr, Robert E MD [NS] - **Spec Exp:** Parkinson's Disease; Brain Tumors; Epilepsy; **Hospital:** Mayo - Jacksonville; **Address:** Mayo Clin, Neurosurgery Dept, 4500 San Pablo Rd, Jacksonville, FL 32224; **Phone:** 904-953-2103; **Board Cert:** Neurological Surgery 1988; **Med School:** Penn State Coll Med 1979; **Resid:** Neurological Surgery, Mayo Clin 1985; **Fac Appt:** Prof NS, Mayo Med Sch

Wilson, John A MD [NS] - **Spec Exp:** Cerebrovascular Surgery; Skull Base Surgery; Spinal Surgery; MoyaMoya Disease; **Hospital:** Wake Forest Baptist Med Ctr; **Address:** Wake Forest Univ Baptist Medical Center, Medical Center Blvd, Winston-Salem, NC 27157-1029; **Phone:** 336-716-4020; **Board Cert:** Neurological Surgery 1996; **Med School:** Jefferson Med Coll 1982; **Resid:** Surgery, Allegheny Genl Hosp 1985; **Fellow:** Neurological Surgery, New England Med Ctr 1990; Neurological Surgery, Parcelsus Clinic 1990; **Fac Appt:** Prof NS, Wake Forest Univ

Midwest

Atkinson, John L MD [NS] - **Spec Exp:** Pituitary Surgery; Stroke; Cerebrovascular Disease; **Hospital:** Mayo Med Ctr & Clin - Rochester; **Address:** Mayo Clinic, Dept Neurosurgery, 200 First St SW, Gonda 8, Rochester, MN 55905; **Phone:** 507-284-5317; **Board Cert:** Neurological Surgery 1992; **Med School:** UAB Sch Med 1984; **Resid:** Neurological Surgery, Mayo Clinic 1990; **Fac Appt:** Assoc Prof NS, Mayo Med Sch

Bailes Jr, Julian E MD [NS] - **Spec Exp:** Spinal Disorders; Brain Injury; Cerebrovascular Disease; **Hospital:** Evanston Hosp/NorthShore Univ Hlth Sys (page 67); **Address:** Evanston Hospital - Northshore Med Grp, 1000 Central St, Ste 800, Evanston, IL 60201; **Phone:** 847-570-1440; **Board Cert:** Neurological Surgery 1992; **Med School:** Louisiana State U, New Orleans 1982; **Resid:** Surgery, Northwestern Meml Hosp 1987; **Fellow:** Neurological Surgery, Barrow Neurological Inst 1988; **Fac Appt:** Clin Prof NS, Univ Chicago-Pritzker Sch Med

Bakay, Roy AE MD [NS] - **Spec Exp:** Parkinson's Disease/Movement Disorders; Epilepsy; Stereotactic Radiosurgery; **Hospital:** Rush Univ Med Ctr; **Address:** University Neurosurgery, 1725 W Harrison St, Ste 855, Chicago, IL 60612; **Phone:** 312-942-6644; **Board Cert:** Neurological Surgery 1985; **Med School:** Northwestern Univ 1975; **Resid:** Neurological Surgery, Univ Washington Med Ctr 1981; **Fellow:** Neuronal Plasticity, Natl Inst Hlth 1982; **Fac Appt:** Prof NS, Rush Med Coll

Barnett, Gene H MD [NS] - **Spec Exp:** Brain Tumors; Stereotactic Radiosurgery; Von Hippel-Lindau Disease; **Hospital:** Cleveland Clin (page 55); **Address:** Cleveland Clinic, 9500 Euclid Ave, rm S73, Cleveland, OH 44195; **Phone:** 216-444-5381; **Board Cert:** Neurological Surgery 1990; **Med School:** Case West Res Univ 1980; **Resid:** Neurological Surgery, Cleveland Clin 1986; **Fellow:** Neurology, Cleveland Clin 1982; Research, Mass Genl Hosp-Harvard 1987; **Fac Appt:** Prof NS, Cleveland Cl Coll Med/Case West Res

Bauer, Jerry MD [NS] - **Spec Exp:** Pain-Back; Minimally Invasive Surgery; Spinal Surgery; **Hospital:** Adv Luth Genl Hosp; **Address:** 1875 Dempster, Ste 410, Park Ridge, IL 60068-1168; **Phone:** 847-698-1088; **Board Cert:** Neurological Surgery 1982; **Med School:** Univ IL Coll Med 1974; **Resid:** Neurological Surgery, Univ of Illinois Med Ctr 1979; **Fac Appt:** Asst Clin Prof NS, Univ IL Coll Med

Benzel, Edward C MD [NS] - **Spec Exp:** Spinal Surgery; **Hospital:** Cleveland Clin (page 55); **Address:** 9500 Euclid Ave, Desk S40, Cleveland, OH 44195; **Phone:** 216-445-5514; **Board Cert:** Neurological Surgery 1986; **Med School:** Univ Wisc 1975; **Resid:** Neurological Surgery, Med Coll Wisc Clins 1980; **Fellow:** Spinal Cord Injury Medicine, Wood VA Med Ctr 1981; **Fac Appt:** Prof NS, Case West Res Univ

Bierbrauer, Karin S MD [NS] - **Spec Exp:** Pediatric Neurosurgery; Spina Bifida; Hydrocephalus; Hydrocephalus; **Hospital:** Cincinnati Chldns Hosp Med Ctr; **Address:** Cincinnati Childrens Hospital, 3333 Burnet Ave, MC 2016, Cincinnati, OH 45229; **Phone:** 513-636-7124; **Board Cert:** Neurological Surgery 1994; Pediatric Neurological Surgery 2007; **Med School:** Med Univ SC 1984; **Resid:** Neurological Surgery, Emory Univ Hosp 1990; **Fellow:** Pediatric Neurological Surgery, Chldns Meml Hosp 1991; **Fac Appt:** Assoc Prof NS, Temple Univ

Bingaman, William MD [NS] - **Spec Exp:** Epilepsy; Spinal Surgery; **Hospital:** Cleveland Clin (page 55); **Address:** Cleveland Clinic, Neurological Clinic, 9500 Euclid Ave, Desk S60, Cleveland, OH 44195; **Phone:** 216-444-9058; **Board Cert:** Neurological Surgery 2011; **Med School:** Temple Univ 1990; **Resid:** Neurological Surgery, Cleveland Clinic Fdn 1996; **Fellow:** Spine Surgery, Cleveland Clinic Fdn 1997

Bucholz, Richard D MD [NS] - **Spec Exp:** Epilepsy/Seizure Disorders; Stereotactic Radiosurgery; **Hospital:** St. Louis Univ Hosp; **Address:** 1320 S Grand Ave, O'Donnell Hall Fl 1, St Louis, MO 63104; **Phone:** 314-977-4750; **Board Cert:** Neurological Surgery 1985; **Med School:** Yale Univ 1977; **Resid:** Neurological Surgery, Yale New Haven Hosp 1983; **Fac Appt:** Prof NS, St Louis Univ

Chandler, James P MD [NS] - **Spec Exp:** Skull Base Surgery; Neuro-Oncology; Brain Tumors; Spinal Disorders; **Hospital:** Northwestern Meml Hosp; **Address:** 675 N St Clair St, Galter Pavilion, Ste 20-250, Chicago, IL 60611; **Phone:** 312-695-8143; **Board Cert:** Neurological Surgery 2013; **Med School:** Univ MD Sch Med 1990; **Resid:** Neurological Surgery, Northwestern Meml Hosp 1996; **Fellow:** Microvascular Surgery, Inst Neurologico De Sao Paulo 1996; Cranial Base Surgery, George Washington Univ Hosp 1997; **Fac Appt:** Asst Prof NS, Northwestern Univ

Charbel, Fady T MD [NS] - **Spec Exp:** Aneurysm-Cerebral; Brain Tumors; Skull Base Tumors; Arteriovenous Malformations; **Hospital:** Univ of IL Med Ctr at Chicago; **Address:** Univ Illinois Med Ctr, Dept of Neurosurgery, 912 S Wood St, MS 799, Chicago, IL 60612; **Phone:** 312-996-4842; **Board Cert:** Neurological Surgery 1998; **Med School:** Lebanon 1984; **Resid:** Surgery, Henry Ford Hosp 1991; **Fellow:** Neurological Surgery, Montreal Neurological Inst 1986; Neurological Surgery, Univ IL Coll Med 1993; **Fac Appt:** Prof NS, Univ IL Coll Med

Dacey Jr, Ralph G MD [NS] - **Spec Exp:** Cerebrovascular Surgery; Aneurysm-Cerebral; Brain Tumors; **Hospital:** Barnes-Jewish Hosp, Barnes-Jewish West County Hosp; **Address:** 4921 Parkview Pl, Ste 6C, St. Louis, MO 63110; **Phone:** 314-362-3577; **Board Cert:** Internal Medicine 1978; Neurological Surgery 1985; **Med School:** Univ VA Sch Med 1974; **Resid:** Internal Medicine, Strong Meml Hosp 1977; Neurological Surgery, Univ Virginia Med Ctr 1983; **Fac Appt:** Prof NS, Washington Univ, St Louis

Dempsey, Robert J MD [NS] - **Spec Exp:** Vascular Neurosurgery; Aneurysm-Cerebral; Stroke; **Hospital:** Univ WI Hosp & Clins; **Address:** Univ Wisc Hosp & Clins - Neurosurgery, 600 Highland Ave, rm K4-822, Madison, WI 53792; **Phone:** 608-263-7502; **Board Cert:** Neurological Surgery 1985; **Med School:** Univ Chicago-Pritzker Sch Med 1977; **Resid:** Neurological Surgery, Univ Mich Affil Hosp 1985; **Fac Appt:** Prof NS, Univ Wisc

Diaz, Fernando G MD/PhD [NS] - **Spec Exp:** Arteriovenous Malformations; Spinal Surgery; **Hospital:** Providence Hosp - Southfield, Beaumont Hosp-Royal Oak; **Address:** Michigan Head & Spine Inst, 29275 Northwestern Hwy, Ste 100, Southfield, MI 48034; **Phone:** 877-784-3667; **Board Cert:** Neurological Surgery 1980; **Med School:** Mexico 1968; **Resid:** Surgery, Univ Kansas Med Ctr 1973; Neurological Surgery, Univ Minn Med Ctr 1978; **Fellow:** Cerebrovascular Disease, Univ Minn Med Ctr 1979; **Fac Appt:** Prof NS, Wayne State Univ

Fessler, Richard G MD/PhD [NS] - **Spec Exp:** Spinal Surgery; Minimally Invasive Spinal Surgery; Head & Neck Trauma; Pain-Back; **Hospital:** Rush Univ Med Ctr; **Address:** University Neurosurgery, 1725 W Harrison St, Ste 855, Chicago, IL 60612; **Phone:** 312-942-6644; **Board Cert:** Neurological Surgery 1992; **Med School:** Univ Chicago-Pritzker Sch Med 1983; **Resid:** Neurological Surgery, Univ Chicago Hosp 1989; **Fac Appt:** Prof NS, Rush Med Coll

Frim, David M MD/PhD [NS] - **Spec Exp:** Pediatric Neurosurgery; Hydrocephalus; Brain & Spinal Cord Tumors; Chiari's Deformity; **Hospital:** Univ of Chicago Med; **Address:** University of Chicago, Section of Neurosurgery, MC 3026, 5841 S Maryland Ave, Chicago, IL 60637-1463; **Phone:** 773-702-2123; **Board Cert:** Neurological Surgery 1998; Pediatric Neurological Surgery 2009; **Med School:** Harvard Med Sch 1988; **Resid:** Neurological Surgery, Mass Genl Hosp 1995; **Fellow:** Pediatric Neurological Surgery, Chldns Hosp 1996; **Fac Appt:** Prof NS, Univ Chicago-Pritzker Sch Med

Grubb Jr, Robert L MD [NS] - **Spec Exp:** Brain Tumors; Acoustic Neuroma; Trigeminal Neuralgia; Skull Base Tumors; **Hospital:** Barnes-Jewish Hosp, St. Louis Chldns Hosp; **Address:** 4921 Parkview Pl, Ste 6C, St Louis, MO 63110; **Phone:** 314-362-3577; **Board Cert:** Neurological Surgery 1976; **Med School:** Univ NC Sch Med 1965; **Resid:** Surgery, Barnes Jewish Hosp 1967; Neurological Surgery, Barnes Jewish Hosp 1973; **Fellow:** Neurological Surgery, National Inst Health 1969; **Fac Appt:** Prof NS, Washington Univ, St Louis

Guthikonda, Murali MD [NS] - **Spec Exp:** Skull Base Tumors; Pituitary Tumors; Aneurysm-Cerebral; Spinal Tumors; **Hospital:** Harper Univ Hosp, Beaumont Hosp-Royal Oak; **Address:** Wayne St U Physicians Grp-Neurosurgery, 4160 John R, Ste 925, Detroit, MI 48201; **Phone:** 313-831-0777; **Board Cert:** Neurological Surgery 1982; **Med School:** India 1971; **Resid:** Surgery, St Elizabeth Hosp 1976; Neurological Surgery, Med Ctr Hosp VT 1980; **Fellow:** Skull Base Surgery, Univ Cincinnati Affil Hosp 1993; **Fac Appt:** Prof NS, Wayne State Univ

Kaufman, Bruce A MD [NS] - **Spec Exp:** Pediatric Neurosurgery; Brain & Spinal Cord Tumors; Spasticity & Movement Disorders; **Hospital:** Chldns Hosp - Wisconsin; **Address:** Chldns Corporate Ctr, Dept Neurosurg, 999 N 92nd St, Ste 310, Milwaukee, WI 53226; **Phone:** 414-266-6435; **Board Cert:** Neurological Surgery 1992; Pediatric Neurological Surgery 2006; **Med School:** Case West Res Univ 1982; **Resid:** Neurological Surgery, Univ Hosp Cleveland/Case West Res 1988; **Fellow:** Pediatric Neurological Surgery, Chldns Meml Hosp/Northwestern Univ 1989; **Fac Appt:** Prof NS, Med Coll Wisc

Kuntz IV, Charles MD [NS] - **Spec Exp:** Spinal Surgery; Peripheral Nerve Surgery; Spinal Disorders; **Hospital:** Univ Cincinnati Med Ctr; **Address:** 222 Piedmont Ave, Ste 3100, Cincinnati, OH 45219; **Phone:** 513-569-5220; **Board Cert:** Neurological Surgery 2004; **Med School:** Case West Res Univ 1991; **Resid:** Surgery, Univ Wash Med Ctr 1993; Neurological Surgery, Univ Wash Med Ctr 1999; **Fellow:** Neurological Surgery, Atkinson Morley's Hosp 1996; Peripheral Nerve Surgery, Univ Wash Med Ctr 2000; **Fac Appt:** Prof NS, Univ Cincinnati

Link, Michael J MD [NS] - **Spec Exp:** Skull Base Tumors; Brain Tumors; Cerebrovascular Surgery; **Hospital:** Mayo Med Ctr & Clin - Rochester; **Address:** Mayo Clinic, Dept Neurosurgery, 200 First St SW, Rochester, MN 55905; **Phone:** 507-284-8008; **Board Cert:** Neurological Surgery 2011; **Med School:** Mayo Med Sch 1990; **Resid:** Neurological Surgery, Mayo Clinic 1996; **Fellow:** Cerebrovascular & Skull Base Surgery, Univ Cincinnati/Mayfield Clinic 1998; **Fac Appt:** Assoc Prof NS, Mayo Med Sch

Loftus, Christopher M MD [NS] - **Spec Exp:** Carotid Artery Surgery; Aneurysm-Cerebral; Arteriovenous Malformations; Cerebrovascular Surgery; **Hospital:** Loyola Univ Med Ctr; **Address:** Loyola Outpatient Center, 2160 S First Ave, Maywood, IL 60153; **Phone:** 708-216-8563; **Board Cert:** Neurological Surgery 1987; **Med School:** SUNY Downstate 1979; **Resid:** Neurological Surgery, Columbia-Presby Med Ctr 1985; **Fac Appt:** Prof NS, Temple Univ

Luken III, Martin G MD [NS] - **Spec Exp:** Brain Tumors; Spinal Surgery; Chiari's Deformity; **Hospital:** Ingalls Meml Hosp, Rush Univ Med Ctr; **Address:** 71 W 156th St, Ste 205, Harvey, IL 60426; **Phone:** 708-596-3344; **Board Cert:** Neurological Surgery 1983; **Med School:** Columbia P&S 1973; **Resid:** Surgery, Univ Illinois Med Ctr 1976; Neurological Surgery, Neurological Inst-Columbia Presby Hosp 1980; **Fac Appt:** Asst Prof NS, Rush Med Coll

Malik, Ghaus M MD [NS] - **Spec Exp:** Trigeminal Neuralgia; Cerebrovascular Surgery; Brain & Spinal Cord Tumors; **Hospital:** Henry Ford- W Bloomfield Hosp, Beaumont Hosp-Royal Oak; **Address:** Henry Ford W Bloomfield Hosp, Dept Neurosurgery, 6777 W Maple Rd Fl 2, West Bloomfield, MI 48322; **Phone:** 248-661-6417; **Board Cert:** Neurological Surgery 1978; **Med School:** Pakistan 1968; **Resid:** Surgery, Henry Ford Hosp 1971; Neurological Surgery, Henry Ford Hosp 1975

Menezes, Arnold H MD [NS] - **Spec Exp:** Pediatric Neurosurgery; Craniocervical Disorders; Spinal Surgery-Pediatric; **Hospital:** Univ Iowa Hosp & Clins; **Address:** Univ Iowa Hosp, Dept Neurosurgery, 200 Hawkins Drive, Iowa City, IA 52242; **Phone:** 319-356-2768; **Board Cert:** Neurological Surgery 1976; Pediatric Neurological Surgery 2009; **Med School:** India 1967; **Resid:** Surgery, Univ Iowa Hosps 1970; Neurological Surgery, Univ Iowa Hosps 1974; **Fellow:** Child Neurology, Univ Iowa Hosps; **Fac Appt:** Prof NS, Univ Iowa Coll Med

Meyer, Fredric B MD [NS] - **Spec Exp:** Cerebrovascular Disease; Brain Tumors; Epilepsy; Pituitary Tumors; **Hospital:** Mayo Med Ctr & Clin - Rochester; **Address:** Mayo Clinic, Dept Neurosurgery, 200 First St SW, Gonda 8, Rochester, MN 55905; **Phone:** 507-284-5317; **Board Cert:** Neurological Surgery 1990; **Med School:** Boston Univ 1981; **Resid:** Neurological Surgery, Mayo Clinic 1987; **Fellow:** Neurological Surgery, Mayo Clinic 1988; **Fac Appt:** Prof NS, Mayo Med Sch

Nagib, Mahmoud G MD [NS] - **Spec Exp:** Pediatric Neurosurgery; Skull Base Surgery; **Hospital:** Children's Hosps & Clinics of Minnesota, Abbott - Northwestern Hosp; **Address:** 800 E 28th St Piper Bldg - Ste 305, Minneapolis, MN 55407; **Phone:** 612-871-7278; **Board Cert:** Neurological Surgery 1985; Pediatric Neurological Surgery 2006; **Med School:** Egypt 1973; **Resid:** Neurological Surgery, Univ Minn Hosps 1982; **Fellow:** Neurophysiology, Univ Oslo 1976; **Fac Appt:** Clin Prof NS, Univ Minn

Park, Tae Sung MD [NS] - **Spec Exp:** Pediatric Neurosurgery; Cerebral Palsy-Select Dorsal Rhizotomy; Brachial Plexus Palsy-Pediatric; Neuro-Oncology; **Hospital:** St. Louis Chldns Hosp; **Address:** St Louis Children's Hospital, 1 Children's Place Fl 4 - Ste E, St Louis, MO 63110; **Phone:** 314-454-2810; **Board Cert:** Neurological Surgery 1985; **Med School:** Korea 1971; **Resid:** Neurological Surgery, Univ Virginia Hosp 1981; **Fellow:** Pediatric Neurological Surgery, Hosp for Sick Chldn 1983; **Fac Appt:** Prof NS, Washington Univ, St Louis

Parsa, Andrew T MD/PhD [NS] - **Spec Exp:** Brain & Spinal Cord Tumors; Skull Base Tumors; Acoustic Neuroma; Brain Mapping; **Hospital:** Northwestern Meml Hosp; **Address:** Northwestern-Dept of Neurosurgery, Galter Pavilion, 675 N St Clair St, Ste 20-250, Chicago, IL 60611; **Phone:** 312-695-8143; **Board Cert:** Neurological Surgery 2008; **Med School:** SUNY Downstate 1996; **Resid:** Neurological Surgery, NY Presby Hosp/Columbia 2002; **Fac Appt:** Prof NS, Northwestern Univ-Feinberg Sch Med

Rezai, Ali R MD [NS] - **Spec Exp:** Parkinson's Disease; Pain-Chronic; Deep Brain Stimulation; Alzheimer's Disease; **Hospital:** OSU Wexner Med Ctr; **Address:** OSU Med Ctr, 410 W 10th Ave, rm N1043, Doan Hall, Columbus, OH 43210; **Phone:** 614-366-2420; **Board Cert:** Neurological Surgery 2003; **Med School:** USC Sch Med 1990; **Resid:** Neurological Surgery, NYU Med Ctr 1997; **Fellow:** Stereotactic Neurological Surgery, Univ Toronto Med Ctr 1998; Neurological Surgery, Karolinska Inst; **Fac Appt:** Prof NS, Ohio State Univ

Rich, Keith M MD [NS] - **Spec Exp:** Brain Tumors; Neurovascular Surgery; Stereotactic Radiosurgery; **Hospital:** Barnes-Jewish Hosp; **Address:** 4921 Parkview Pl, Ste 6C, St Louis, MO 63110; **Phone:** 314-362-3577; **Board Cert:** Neurological Surgery 1987; **Med School:** Indiana Univ 1977; **Resid:** Neurological Surgery, Barnes Jewish Hosp 1982; **Fellow:** Neurological Pharmacology, Barnes Jewish Hosp 1984; **Fac Appt:** Assoc Prof NS, Washington Univ, St Louis

Rock, Jack P MD [NS] - **Spec Exp:** Neuro-Oncology; Pituitary Surgery; Skull Base Surgery; Brain Tumors; **Hospital:** Henry Ford Hosp; **Address:** Henry Ford Hosp, Dept Neurosurgery, 2799 W Grand Blvd Fl K11, Detroit, MI 48202; **Phone:** 313-916-2241; **Board Cert:** Neurological Surgery 1989; **Med School:** Univ Miami Sch Med 1979; **Resid:** Neurological Surgery, New York Hosp-Cornell 1985; **Fellow:** Trauma, Univ Maryland 1986

Rosenblatt, Szymon S MD [NS] - **Spec Exp:** Skull Base Surgery; Cerebrovascular Surgery; Brain Tumors; **Hospital:** Alexian Brothers Med Ctr; **Address:** Alexian Brothers Neuroscience Inst, 800 Biesterfield Rd, Ste 610, Elk Grove Village, IL 60007; **Phone:** 847-981-3630; **Board Cert:** Neurological Surgery 2010; **Med School:** Germany 1980; **Resid:** Neurological Surgery, Northwestern Meml Hosp 1988; **Fellow:** Cerebrovascular & Skull Base Surgery, Mayfield Neurological Inst 1992; Research, Mass Genl Hosp 1994; **Fac Appt:** Asst Prof NS, Rush Med Coll

Rosenblum, Mark L MD [NS] - **Spec Exp:** Brain Tumors; Spinal Surgery; Infections-Neurologic; Neuro-Oncology; **Hospital:** Henry Ford Hosp; **Address:** Henry Ford Hosp, 2799 W Grand Blvd Fl K11, Detroit, MI 48202; **Phone:** 313-916-1340; **Board Cert:** Neurological Surgery 1982; **Med School:** NY Med Coll 1969; **Resid:** Surgery, UCLA Med Ctr 1973; Neurological Surgery, UCSF Med Ctr 1979; **Fellow:** Neuro-Oncology, NIH/Natl Cancer Inst 1972

Ruge, John R MD [NS] - **Spec Exp:** Pediatric Neurosurgery; Brain Tumors; Hydrocephalus; **Hospital:** Adv Luth Genl Hosp; **Address:** Ctr Brain & Spine Surg-Parkside Ctr, 1875 Dempster St, Ste 415, Park Ridge, IL 60068; **Phone:** 847-698-1088; **Board Cert:** Neurological Surgery 1993; **Med School:** Northwestern Univ-Feinberg Sch Med 1983; **Resid:** Neurological Surgery, Northwestern Meml Hosp 1989; **Fellow:** Pediatric Neurological Surgery, Chldns Meml Hosp 1990; **Fac Appt:** Asst Prof S, Rush Med Coll

Ryken, Timothy C MD [NS] - **Spec Exp:** Brain Tumors; Spinal Surgery; **Hospital:** Covenant Med Ctr; **Address:** Iowa Spine & Brain Institute, 2710 St Francis Drive, Ste 110, Waterloo, IA 50702; **Phone:** 319-272-6700; **Board Cert:** Neurological Surgery 1998; **Med School:** Univ Iowa Coll Med 1988; **Resid:** Neurological Surgery, Univ Iowa 1995; **Fellow:** Research, Cambridge Univ/Ctr for Brain Repair 1996; **Fac Appt:** Assoc Prof NS, Univ Iowa Coll Med

Selman, Warren R MD [NS] - **Spec Exp:** Stroke; Pituitary Surgery; Aneurysm-Cerebral; Microsurgery; **Hospital:** UH Case Med Ctr; **Address:** Dept Neurosurgery, 11100 Euclid Ave, 5th Fl Bolwell Bldg, Cleveland, OH 44106; **Phone:** 216-844-5745; **Board Cert:** Neurological Surgery 1986; **Med School:** Case West Res Univ 1977; **Resid:** Neurological Surgery, Univ Hosps 1984; **Fellow:** Neurological Surgery, Mayo Clinic 1985; **Fac Appt:** Prof NS, Case West Res Univ

Shapiro, Scott A MD [NS] - **Spec Exp:** Brain Tumors; Aneurysm-Cerebral; Spinal Cord Injury; Pituitary Tumors; **Hospital:** IU Health Methodist Hosp, Wishard Hlth Srvs; **Address:** IU Hlth, Neuroscience Ctr, 355 W 16th St, Ste 5100, Indianapolis, IN 46202; **Phone:** 317-396-1300; **Board Cert:** Neurological Surgery 1990; **Med School:** Indiana Univ 1981; **Resid:** Neurological Surgery, Indiana Univ Med Ctr 1987; **Fac Appt:** Prof NS, Indiana Univ

Spinner, Robert J MD [NS] - **Spec Exp:** Peripheral Nerve Surgery; Brachial Plexus Palsy; Brain Tumors; **Hospital:** Mayo Med Ctr & Clin - Rochester; **Address:** Mayo Clinic, Dept Neurosurgery, 200 First St SW, Gonda 8, Rochester, MN 55905; **Phone:** 507-284-5317; **Board Cert:** Orthopaedic Surgery 2003; Neurological Surgery 2006; **Med School:** Mayo Med Sch 1989; **Resid:** Orthopaedic Surgery, Duke Univ Med Ctr 1996; Neurological Surgery, Mayo Clinic 2000; **Fellow:** Peripheral Nerve Surgery, LSU Med Ctr 2000; **Fac Appt:** Prof NS, Mayo Med Sch

Thompson Jr, B Gregory MD [NS] - **Spec Exp:** Acoustic Neuroma; Neurovascular Surgery; Skull Base Tumors & Surgery; Aneurysm-Cerebral; **Hospital:** Univ Michigan Med Ctr; **Address:** Univ Michigan, Dept Neurosurgery, 1500 E Medical Center Drive, Ann Arbor, MI 48109-5338; **Phone:** 734-936-7493; **Board Cert:** Neurological Surgery 1998; **Med School:** Univ Kansas 1986; **Resid:** Neurological Surgery, Univ Pittsburgh 1993; Research, Natl Inst Hlth 1992; **Fellow:** Neurological Surgery, Barrow Neuro Inst 1994; Interventional Radiology, Thomas Jefferson Univ 2005

Tomita, Tadanori MD [NS] - **Spec Exp:** Pediatric Neurosurgery; Brain Tumors-Pediatric; Hydrocephalus; **Hospital:** Lurie Chldn's Hosp-Chicago, Northwestern Meml Hosp; **Address:** Lurie Chldn's Hosp, Div Ped Neurosurg, 225 E Chicago Ave, Box 28, Chicago, IL 60611; **Phone:** 312-227-4220; **Board Cert:** Neurological Surgery 1984; Pediatric Neurological Surgery 1996; **Med School:** Japan 1970; **Resid:** Neurological Surgery, Kobe Univ 1974; Neurological Surgery, Northwestern Meml Hosp 1980; **Fellow:** Surgery, Meml Sloan Kettering Canc Ctr 1981; **Fac Appt:** Prof NS, Northwestern Univ

Traynelis, Vincent C MD [NS] - **Spec Exp:** Spinal Surgery; Minimally Invasive Spinal Surgery; Spinal Cord Injury; Spinal Tumors; **Hospital:** Rush Univ Med Ctr; **Address:** University Neurosurgery, 1725 W Harrison St, Ste 855, Chicago, IL 60612; **Phone:** 312-942-6644; **Board Cert:** Neurological Surgery 1992; **Med School:** W VA Univ 1983; **Resid:** Neurological Surgery, Univ West Virginia Med Ctr 1989; **Fac Appt:** Prof NS, Rush Med Coll

Warnick, Ronald E MD [NS] - **Spec Exp:** Neuro-Oncology; Brain Tumors; **Hospital:** Univ Cincinnati Med Ctr, Good Samaritan Hosp - Cincinnati; **Address:** 222 Piedmont Ave, Ste 3100, Cincinnati, OH 45219; **Phone:** 513-569-5286; **Board Cert:** Neurological Surgery 1995; **Med School:** Univ Rochester 1982; **Resid:** Neurological Surgery, NYU Med Ctr 1989; **Fellow:** Neuro-Oncology, UCSF Med Ctr 1991; **Fac Appt:** Prof NS, Univ Cincinnati

Great Plains and Mountains

Brockmeyer, Douglas L MD [NS] - **Spec Exp:** Pediatric Neurosurgery; Spinal Surgery-Pediatric; **Hospital:** Primary Children's Med Ctr, Univ Utah Hlth Care; **Address:** Primary Chldns Med Ctr, Dept Neurosurg, 100 N Mario Capecchi Drive, Ste 1475, Salt Lake City, UT 84113; **Phone:** 801-662-5340; **Board Cert:** Neurological Surgery 1988; Pediatric Neurological Surgery 2008; **Med School:** Case West Res Univ 1987; **Resid:** Neurological Surgery, Univ Utah Med Ctr 1993; **Fellow:** Pediatric Neurological Surgery, Univ Utah Med Ctr/Prim Chldns Hosp 1994; **Fac Appt:** Prof NS, Univ Utah

Cherny, W Bruce MD [NS] - **Spec Exp:** Pediatric Neurosurgery; Brain Tumors; Spina Bifida; **Hospital:** St. Luke's Boise Med Ctr; **Address:** Childrens Specialty Ctr, 100 E Idaho St, Ste 200, Boise, ID 83712; **Phone:** 208-381-7360; **Board Cert:** Neurological Surgery 2011; **Med School:** Univ Ariz Coll Med 1987; **Resid:** Neurological Surgery, Barrow Neuro Inst/St Joseph's Med Ctr 1994; **Fellow:** Pediatric Neurological Surgery, Primary Chldns Hosp 1995

Couldwell, William T MD/PhD [NS] - **Spec Exp:** Skull Base Surgery; Vascular Neurosurgery; Pituitary Tumors; Skull Base Tumors; **Hospital:** Univ Utah Hlth Care; **Address:** Univ Utah, Dept Neurological Surgery, 175 N Medical Drive E, Salt Lake City, UT 84132-2303; **Phone:** 801-581-6908; **Board Cert:** Neurological Surgery 1994; **Med School:** McGill Univ 1984; **Resid:** Neurological Surgery, LAC & USC Med Ctr 1989; **Fellow:** Neurological Immunology, Montreal Neur Inst/McGill Univ 1990; Neurological Surgery, CHUV 1991; **Fac Appt:** Prof Emeritus NS, Univ Utah

Johnson, Stephen D MD [NS] - **Spec Exp:** Skull Base Tumors & Surgery; Craniofacial Surgery; **Hospital:** Presby - St Luke's Med Ctr; **Address:** Western Neurological Grp, 1601 E 19th Ave, Ste 4400, Denver, CO 80218; **Phone:** 303-861-2266; **Board Cert:** Neurological Surgery 1988; **Med School:** Univ Tenn Coll Med 1974; **Resid:** Surgery, Virginia Mason Med Ctr 1978; Neurological Surgery, NY-Presby/Weill Cornell Med Ctr 1982; **Fellow:** Spine Surgery, Univ Tenn Coll Med 1983; **Fac Appt:** Assoc Prof NS, Univ Colorado

Lillehei, Kevin O MD [NS] - **Spec Exp:** Neuro-Oncology; Pituitary Tumors; Peripheral Nerve Surgery; Gliomas; **Hospital:** Univ Colorado Hosp; **Address:** Univ CO Hosp, Neurosurgery Dept, 12631 E 17th Ave, rm 5001, MS C307, Aurora, CO 80045; **Phone:** 303-724-2280; **Board Cert:** Neurological Surgery 1989; **Med School:** Univ Minn 1979; **Resid:** Neurological Surgery, Univ Michigan Med Ctr 1985; **Fac Appt:** Prof NS, Univ Colorado

Nazzaro, Jules M MD [NS] - **Spec Exp:** Parkinson's Disease; Movement Disorders; Stereotactic Radiosurgery; **Hospital:** Univ of Kansas Hosp; **Address:** Univ of Kansas Hosp, 3901 Rainbow Blvd, MS 3021, Kansas City, KS 66160; **Phone:** 913-588-6122; **Board Cert:** Neurological Surgery 1996; **Med School:** Albert Einstein Coll Med 1984; **Resid:** Neurological Surgery, NYU Langone Med Ctr 1991; **Fellow:** Neurosurgical Oncology, Meml Sloan-Kettering Canc Ctr 1992; **Fac Appt:** Assoc Prof NS, Univ Kansas

Origitano, Thomas C MD/PhD [NS] - **Spec Exp:** Skull Base Tumors & Surgery; Brain Tumors; Pituitary Tumors; Craniofacial Surgery; **Hospital:** Kalispell Regl Med Ctr; **Address:** Neuroscience & Spine Institute, Dept Neurological Surgery, 200 Commons Way, Kalispell, MT 59901; **Phone:** 406-752-5170; **Board Cert:** Neurological Surgery 1995; **Med School:** Loyola Univ-Stritch Sch Med 1984; **Resid:** Neurological Surgery, Loyola Univ Med Ctr 1990

Taylon, Charles MD [NS] - **Spec Exp:** Spinal Surgery-Cervical; Spinal Surgery-Low Back; Carpal Tunnel Syndrome; Trauma; **Hospital:** Alegent Creighton Univ Med Ctr; **Address:** Creighton Univ, Dept Surg, 601 N 30th St, Ste 3700, Omaha, NE 68131; **Phone:** 402-280-4497; **Board Cert:** Neurological Surgery 1984; **Med School:** Creighton Univ 1975; **Resid:** Neurological Surgery, Univ Wisc Hosps 1981; **Fac Appt:** Assoc Prof NS, Creighton Univ

Walker, Marion L MD [NS] - **Spec Exp:** Pediatric Neurosurgery; Spasticity & Movement Disorders; Hydrocephalus; Brain Tumors; **Hospital:** Primary Children's Med Ctr, Univ Utah Hlth Care; **Address:** Primary Chldns Med Ctr, Div Ped Neurosurgery, 100 N Mario Capecchi Drive, Ste 1475, Salt Lake City, UT 84113-1103; **Phone:** 801-662-5340; **Board Cert:** Neurological Surgery 1979; Pediatric Neurological Surgery 2006; **Med School:** Univ Tenn Coll Med 1969; **Resid:** Surgery, St Joseph's Hosp 1971; Neurological Surgery, St Joseph's Hosp-Barrow Neuro Inst 1976; **Fellow:** Pediatric Neurological Surgery, Hosp for Sick Chldn 1973; **Fac Appt:** Prof NS, Univ Utah

Zimmerman, Christian G MD [NS] - **Spec Exp:** Spinal Surgery-Complex; **Hospital:** St. Alphonsus Regl Med Ctr; **Address:** 901 N Curtis Rd, Ste 503, Boise, ID 83706; **Phone:** 208-367-4000; **Board Cert:** Neurological Surgery 1996; Pain Medicine 1998; **Med School:** Univ MD Sch Med 1985; **Resid:** Surgery, Univ Md Hosp-Prince Georges Med Ctr 1987; Neurological Surgery, Oreg Hlth Sci Univ 1992; **Fellow:** Spine Surgery, Barrow Neur Inst 1993

Southwest

Adelson, P David MD [NS] - **Spec Exp:** Pediatric Neurosurgery; Brain Injury; Epilepsy/Seizure Disorders; Spinal Cord Injury; **Hospital:** Phoenix Children's Hosp, Maricopa Med Ctr; **Address:** Barrow Neurological Inst, 1919 E Thomas Rd, Ambulatory Bldg Fl 4, Phoenix, AZ 85016; **Phone:** 602-933-0975; **Board Cert:** Neurological Surgery 1997; Pediatric Neurological Surgery 2009; **Med School:** Columbia P&S 1986; **Resid:** Neurological Surgery, UCLA Med Ctr 1992; **Fellow:** Pediatric Neurological Surgery, Children's Hosp 1994; **Fac Appt:** Prof NS, Univ Ariz Coll Med

De Monte, Franco MD [NS] - **Spec Exp:** Skull Base Tumors & Surgery; Neuro-Oncology; **Hospital:** UT MD Anderson Canc Ctr; **Address:** Dept Neurosurgery, 1515 Holcombe Blvd, Unit 442, Houston, TX 77030; **Phone:** 713-792-2400; **Board Cert:** Neurological Surgery 1995; **Med School:** Canada 1985; **Resid:** Neurological Surgery, Univ W Ontario Affil Hosp 1991; **Fellow:** Skull Base Surgery, Loyola Univ Med Ctr 1992; **Fac Appt:** Prof NS, Baylor Coll Med

Greene Jr, Clarence S MD [NS] - **Spec Exp:** Pediatric Neurosurgery; Congenital Nervous System Malformations; Brain Tumors; **Hospital:** Children's Hospital - New Orleans; **Address:** Children's Hosp, Dept Neurosurgery, 200 Henry Clay Ave, Ste 210, New Orleans, LA 70118; **Phone:** 504-896-9568; **Board Cert:** Neurological Surgery 1984; Pediatric Neurological Surgery 2007; **Med School:** Howard Univ 1974; **Resid:** Neurological Surgery, Chldns Hosp 1981; Neurological Surgery, Peter Bent Brigham Hosp 1981; **Fellow:** Pediatric Neurology, Chldns Hosp 1984; **Fac Appt:** Assoc Clin Prof NS, UC Irvine

Hankinson, Hal L MD [NS] - **Spec Exp:** Brain Tumors; **Hospital:** Christus St Vincent Reg Med Ctr-Santa Fe; **Address:** CSV Neurosurgical Assocs, 465 St Michael's Drive, Ste 107, Sante Fe, NM 87505; **Phone:** 505-988-3233; **Board Cert:** Neurological Surgery 1977; **Med School:** Tulane Univ 1967; **Resid:** Neurological Surgery, UCSF Med Ctr 1975; **Fac Appt:** Clin Prof NS, Univ New Mexico

Harper, Richard L MD [NS] - **Spec Exp:** Spinal Surgery; Brain Tumors & Hemifacial Spasms; **Hospital:** Methodist Hosp - Houston; **Address:** Neurosurgical Grp, 6565 Fannin St, Ste 1200, Scurlock Tower, Houston, TX 77030; **Phone:** 713-790-1211; **Board Cert:** Neurological Surgery 1983; **Med School:** Baylor Coll Med 1971; **Resid:** Neurological Surgery, Baylor Affil Hosp 1978; **Fac Appt:** Asst Clin Prof NS, Baylor Coll Med

Jimenez, David F MD [NS] - **Spec Exp:** Pediatric Neurosurgery; Craniosynostosis; Endoscopic Strip Craniectomy; Spinal Surgery; **Hospital:** Univ Hosp-San Antonio, St. Luke's Baptist Hosp; **Address:** Univ Hosp, Neurosurgery Dept, 4502 Medical Drive Fl 5, San Antonio, TX 78229; **Phone:** 210-358-8555; **Board Cert:** Neurological Surgery 1995; **Med School:** Temple Univ 1985; **Resid:** Neurological Surgery, Temple Univ Hosp 1991; **Fellow:** Pediatric Neurological Surgery, Montefiore Med Ctr 1992; **Fac Appt:** Prof NS, Univ Tex, San Antonio

Kim, Daniel H MD [NS] - **Spec Exp:** Spinal Surgery; Peripheral Nerve Surgery; **Hospital:** Meml Hermann Hosp - Texas Med Ctr; **Address:** Mischer Neuroscience Assocs, 6400 Fannin St, Ste 2800, Houston, TX 77030; **Phone:** 713-704-7100; **Board Cert:** Neurological Surgery 1998; **Med School:** Tulane Univ 1989; **Resid:** Neurological Surgery, LSU Med Ctr 1995; **Fellow:** Spine Surgery, Shands at Univ FL 1998; **Fac Appt:** Prof NS, Baylor Coll Med

Kim, Dong H MD [NS] - **Spec Exp:** Cerebrovascular Surgery; Aneurysm-Cerebral; Brain Tumors; Arteriovenous Malformations; **Hospital:** Meml Hermann Hosp - Texas Med Ctr; **Address:** Mischer Neuroscience Assocs, 6400 Fannin St, Ste 2800, Houston, TX 77030; **Phone:** 713-704-7100; **Board Cert:** Neurological Surgery 2012; **Med School:** UCSF 1990; **Resid:** Neurological Surgery, UCSF Med Ctr 1996; **Fellow:** Cerebrovascular & Skull Base Surgery, Shands at Univ FL 1997; **Fac Appt:** Prof NS, Univ Tex, Houston

Krisht, Ali F MD [NS] - **Spec Exp:** Skull Base Surgery; Meningioma; Vascular Neurosurgery; **Hospital:** St. Vincent Health System; **Address:** Arkansas Neuroscience Inst, 5 St. Vincent Circle, Ste 210, Little Rock, AR 72205; **Phone:** 501-552-6400; **Board Cert:** Neurological Surgery 2010; **Med School:** Amer Univ Beirut 1985; **Resid:** Neurological Surgery, Emory Univ Affil Hosp 1994; **Fac Appt:** Prof NS, Univ Ark

Lang Jr, Frederick F MD [NS] - **Spec Exp:** Brain & Spinal Cord Tumors; Gliomas; Brain Tumors-Complex; Pediatric Neurosurgery; **Hospital:** UT MD Anderson Canc Ctr; **Address:** UT MD Anderson Canc Ctr, 1515 Holcombe Blvd, Unit 442, Houston, TX 77030; **Phone:** 713-792-2400; **Board Cert:** Neurological Surgery 2011; **Med School:** Yale Univ 1988; **Resid:** Neurological Surgery, NYU Langone Med Ctr 1995; **Fellow:** Neurosurgical Oncology, UT MD Anderson Canc Ctr 1996; **Fac Appt:** Prof NS, Univ Tex, Houston

Lee, Mark R MD/PhD [NS] - **Spec Exp:** Pediatric Neurosurgery; Epilepsy-Adult & Pediatric; **Hospital:** Dell Children's Med Ctr of Central Texas, Seton Med Ctr; **Address:** Pediatric Neurosurgery, 1301 Barbara Jordan Blvd, Ste 307, Austin, TX 78723; **Phone:** 512-324-0907; **Board Cert:** Neurological Surgery 1997; Pediatric Neurological Surgery 2003; **Med School:** Univ Chicago-Pritzker Sch Med 1986; **Resid:** Neurological Surgery, NYU Med Ctr 1993; **Fellow:** Pediatric Neurological Surgery, NYU 1994; Epilepsy Surgery, Med College GA 1995

Lemole Jr, G Michael MD [NS] - **Spec Exp:** Skull Base Surgery; Stereotactic Radiosurgery; Cerebrovascular Surgery; Minimally Invasive Surgery; **Hospital:** Univ Arizona Med Ctr-Univ Campus; **Address:** University of Arizona, Division of Neurosurgery, 1501 N Campbell Ave, 4th Fl - Ste 4303, Box 245070, Tucson, AZ 85724-5070; **Phone:** 520-694-6144; **Board Cert:** Neurological Surgery 2007; **Med School:** Univ Pennsylvania 1995; **Resid:** Neurological Surgery, St Josephs Hosp Med Ctr/Barrow Neuro Inst 2002; **Fellow:** Cerebrovascular & Skull Base Surgery, Barrow Neuro Inst 2000; Spine Surgery, Barrow Neuro Inst 2000; **Fac Appt:** Prof NS, Univ Ariz Coll Med

Luerssen, Thomas G MD [NS] - **Spec Exp:** Pediatric Neurosurgery; Congenital Cranial Deformities; **Hospital:** Texas Chldns Hosp; **Address:** TX Chldns Hosp, Ped Neurosurgery, 6701 Fannin St, rm 1230.01, Houston, TX 77030; **Phone:** 832-822-3950; **Board Cert:** Neurological Surgery 1985; Pediatric Neurological Surgery 2005; **Med School:** Indiana Univ 1976; **Resid:** Neurological Surgery, IU Hlth Hosp 1981; **Fellow:** Pediatric Neurological Surgery, Chldns Hosp 1984; **Fac Appt:** Prof NS, Baylor Coll Med

Mapstone, Timothy B MD [NS] - **Spec Exp:** Brain Tumors-Adult & Pediatric; Pediatric Neurosurgery; Congenital Anomalies; **Hospital:** OU Med Ctr, Chldns Hosp OU Med Ctr; **Address:** Univ OK Hlth Sci Ctr, Dept Neurosurgery, 1000 N Lincoln Blvd, Ste 400, Oklahoma City, OK 73104; **Phone:** 405-271-4912; **Board Cert:** Neurological Surgery 1985; Pediatric Neurological Surgery 2005; **Med School:** Case West Res Univ 1977; **Resid:** Neurological Surgery, Univ Hosps 1983; **Fellow:** Research, Case West Reserve Univ; **Fac Appt:** Prof NS, Univ Okla Coll Med

Mickey, Bruce E MD [NS] - **Spec Exp:** Brain Tumors; Skull Base Surgery; Pituitary Tumors; **Hospital:** UT Southwestern Med Ctr at Dallas, Parkland Hlth & Hosp Sys; **Address:** UTSW Med Ctr, Dept Neurosurgery, 5323 Harry Hines Blvd, Dallas, TX 75390-8855; **Phone:** 214-645-2300; **Board Cert:** Neurological Surgery 1987; **Med School:** Univ Tex SW, Dallas 1978; **Resid:** Neurological Surgery, Parkland Meml Hosp 1984; **Fellow:** Research, Righospitalet 1983; **Fac Appt:** Prof NS, Univ Tex SW, Dallas

Samson, Duke S MD [NS] - **Spec Exp:** Vascular Neurosurgery; Cerebrovascular Disease; Arteriovenous Malformations; **Hospital:** UT Southwestern Med Ctr at Dallas, Parkland Hlth & Hosp Sys; **Address:** UT Southwestern Med Ctr, Neurosurgery, 5323 Harry Hines Blvd, Dallas, TX 75390; **Phone:** 214-645-2300; **Board Cert:** Neurological Surgery 1978; **Med School:** Washington Univ, St Louis 1969; **Resid:** Neurological Surgery, Univ Texas SW Med Ctr 1975; **Fellow:** Neurological Surgery, Ctr Medico-Chirurgical Fech 1973; Neurological Surgery, Univ Zurich 1973; **Fac Appt:** Prof NS, Univ Tex SW, Dallas

Sandberg, David I MD [NS] - **Spec Exp:** Pediatric Neurosurgery; Brain Tumors-Pediatric; Hydrocephalus; Minimally Invasive Surgery; **Hospital:** Meml Hermann Hosp - Texas Med Ctr; **Address:** UT Physicians, Pediatric Neurological Surgery, 6410 Fannin St Fl 9 - Ste 950, Houston, TX 77030; **Phone:** 832-325-7242; **Board Cert:** Neurological Surgery 2007; Pediatric Neurological Surgery 2007; **Med School:** Johns Hopkins Univ 1997; **Resid:** Surgery, NY Presby-Cornell Med Ctr 1998; Neurological Surgery, NY Presby-Cornell Med Ctr 2002; **Fellow:** Neurosurgical Oncology, Meml Sloan Kettering Cancer Ctr 2003; Pediatric Neurological Surgery, Children's Hosp 2004; **Fac Appt:** Assoc Prof NS, Univ Tex, Houston

Sawaya, Raymond MD [NS] - **Spec Exp:** Brain Tumors; **Hospital:** UT MD Anderson Canc Ctr; **Address:** UT MD Anderson Canc Ctr, 1400 Holcombe Blvd, Unit 442, Houston, TX 77030; **Phone:** 713-792-2400; **Board Cert:** Neurological Surgery 1985; **Med School:** Lebanon 1974; **Resid:** Neurological Surgery, Univ Cincinnati Med Ctr 1980; Neurological Surgery, Johns Hopkins Hosp 1981; **Fellow:** Neuro-Oncology, Natl Inst Hlth 1982; **Fac Appt:** Prof NS, Baylor Coll Med

Sklar, Frederick H MD [NS] - **Spec Exp:** Pediatric Neurosurgery; Craniofacial Surgery; Hydrocephalus; **Hospital:** Chldns Med Ctr of Dallas, Texas Scottish Rite Hosp for Chldn; **Address:** Neurosurgeons for Chldn, 1935 Medical District Drive, Ste B3200, Dallas, TX 75235; **Phone:** 214-456-6660; **Board Cert:** Neurological Surgery 1978; **Med School:** Johns Hopkins Univ 1970; **Resid:** Neurological Surgery, Johns Hopkins Hosp 1976; **Fac Appt:** Assoc Clin Prof NS, Univ Tex SW, Dallas

Spetzler, Robert F MD [NS] - **Spec Exp:** Skull Base Tumors & Surgery; Cerebrovascular Surgery; **Hospital:** St. Joseph's Hosp & Med Ctr - Phoenix; **Address:** Barrow Neurosurgical Assocs, 2910 N Third Ave, Phoenix, AZ 85013; **Phone:** 602-406-3489; **Board Cert:** Neurological Surgery 1979; **Med School:** Northwestern Univ 1971; **Resid:** Neurological Surgery, UCSF Med Ctr 1976; **Fac Appt:** Prof NS, Univ Ariz Coll Med

Theodore, Nicholas MD [NS] - **Spec Exp:** Brain & Spinal Surgery; Minimally Invasive Surgery; Robotic Surgery; **Hospital:** St. Joseph's Hosp & Med Ctr - Phoenix; **Address:** Barrow Neurosurgical Assocs, 2910 N Third Ave, Phoenix, AZ 85013; **Phone:** 602-406-3621; **Board Cert:** Neurological Surgery 2004; **Med School:** Georgetown Univ 1991; **Resid:** Neurological Surgery, Natl Naval Med Ctr 1997; **Fellow:** Neurological Surgery, St Josephs Hosp & Med Ctr 2001

Yonas, Howard MD [NS] - **Spec Exp:** Stroke; Vascular Neurosurgery; Skull Base Surgery; Trigeminal Neuralgia; **Hospital:** Univ Hosp - New Mexico; **Address:** 1 Univ of New Mexico, Dept Neurological Surgery, MSC10-5615, Albuquerque, NM 87131-0001; **Phone:** 505-272-9494; **Board Cert:** Neurological Surgery 1981; **Med School:** Ohio State Univ 1970; **Resid:** Neurological Surgery, Case West Res 1976; **Fellow:** Microsurgery, Univ Pittsburgh 1978; **Fac Appt:** Prof NS, Univ New Mexico

West Coast and Pacific

Amar, Arun P MD/PhD [NS] - **Spec Exp:** Interventional Neuroradiology; Cerebrovascular Disease; Vascular Malformations; Stroke; **Hospital:** Keck Med Ctr of USC; **Address:** USC Med Ctr-Dept of Neurosurgery, 1520 San Pablo St, Ste 3800, Los Angeles, CA 90033; **Phone:** 323-442-7512; **Board Cert:** Neurological Surgery 2005; **Med School:** UCSF 1993; **Resid:** Neurological Surgery, LAC-USC Univ Hosp 2000; **Fellow:** Interventional Neuroradiology, LAC-USC Univ Hosp 2003; **Fac Appt:** Assoc Prof NS, USC-Keck School of Medicine

Ames, Christopher P MD [NS] - **Spec Exp:** Spinal Trauma; Spinal Cord Tumors; Spinal Reconstructive Surgery; Skull Base Tumors & Surgery; **Hospital:** UCSF Med Ctr; **Address:** Spine Center, 400 Parnassus Ave, Fl 3, San Francisco, CA 94143-0332; **Phone:** 866-817-7463; **Board Cert:** Neurological Surgery 2006; **Med School:** UCLA-David Geffen Sch Med 1994; **Resid:** Neurological Surgery, UCSD Med Ctr 2000; **Fellow:** Spine Surgery, Barrow Neurological Inst 2002; **Fac Appt:** Prof NS, UCLA-David Geffen Sch Med

Apuzzo, Michael L J MD [NS] - **Spec Exp:** Brain Tumors; Movement Disorders; Stereotactic Radiosurgery; **Hospital:** Keck Med Ctr of USC, USC Norris Cancer Hosp; **Address:** 1520 San Pablo St, Ste 3800, Los Angeles, CA 90033; **Phone:** 323-442-5720; **Board Cert:** Neurological Surgery 1975; **Med School:** Boston Univ 1965; **Resid:** Neurological Surgery, Hartford Hosp 1973; **Fellow:** Neurophysiology, Yale Univ Hosp 1974; Neurological Pathology, Yale Univ Hosp 1975; **Fac Appt:** Prof NS, USC Sch Med

Badie, Behnam MD [NS] - **Spec Exp:** Brain Tumors; Spinal Tumors; **Hospital:** City of Hope Natl Med Ctr; **Address:** City of Hope-Division of Neurosurgery, 1500 E Duarte Rd, Duarte, CA 91010; **Phone:** 626-471-7100; **Board Cert:** Neurological Surgery 1998; **Med School:** UCLA 1989; **Resid:** Neurological Surgery, UCLA Med Ctr 1996; **Fac Appt:** Prof S, UCLA

Berger, Mitchel S MD [NS] - **Spec Exp:** Brain & Spinal Cord Tumors; Pituitary Tumors; Neuro-Oncology; Pain Management; **Hospital:** UCSF Med Ctr; **Address:** UCSF Med Ctr, Dept Neurosurgery, 505 Parnassus Avenue, M-786, San Francisco, CA 94143-0112; **Phone:** 415-353-3933; **Board Cert:** Neurological Surgery 1991; **Med School:** Univ Miami Sch Med 1979; **Resid:** Neurological Surgery, UCSF Med Ctr 1985; **Fellow:** Neuro-Oncology, UCSF Med Ctr 1985; Pediatric Neurological Surgery, Hosp Sick Chldn 1986; **Fac Appt:** Prof NS, UCSF

Black, Keith L MD [NS] - **Spec Exp:** Brain Tumors; Pineal Tumors; Microsurgery; **Hospital:** Cedars-Sinai Med Ctr; **Address:** Cedars-Sinai Med Ctr, Dept Neurosugery, 8631 W Third St, Ste 800 East, Los Angeles, CA 90048; **Phone:** 310-423-7900; **Board Cert:** Neurological Surgery 1990; **Med School:** Univ Mich Med Sch 1981; **Resid:** Neurological Surgery, Univ Michigan Med Ctr 1987; **Fac Appt:** Prof N, UCLA

Boggan, James E MD [NS] - **Spec Exp:** Skull Base Tumors & Surgery; Pediatric Neurosurgery; **Hospital:** UC Davis Med Ctr; **Address:** Dept Neurological Surgery, 4860 Y St, Ste 0100, Sacramento, CA 95817-2307; **Phone:** 916-734-4300; **Board Cert:** Neurological Surgery 1985; **Med School:** Univ Chicago-Pritzker Sch Med 1976; **Resid:** Neurological Surgery, UCSF Med Ctr 1982; **Fac Appt:** Prof NS, UC Davis

Bray Jr, Robert S MD [NS] - **Spec Exp:** Minimally Invasive Spinal Surgery; Spinal Disorders-Degenerative; Spinal Surgery-Complex; **Address:** DISC Sports & Spine Center, 13160 Mindanao Way, Ste 300, Marina del Rey, CA 90292; **Phone:** 310-574-0400; **Board Cert:** Neurological Surgery 1991; **Med School:** Baylor Coll Med 1980; **Resid:** Neurological Surgery, Baylor Affil Hosp 1986

Burchiel, Kim J MD [NS] - **Spec Exp:** Movement Disorders; Parkinson's Disease; Movement Disorders; **Hospital:** OR Hlth & Sci Univ; **Address:** OHSU, Dept Neurosurgery, 3303 SW Bond Ave Fl 8, Portland, OR 97239; **Phone:** 503-494-4314; **Board Cert:** Neurological Surgery 1984; **Med School:** UCSD 1976; **Resid:** Neurological Surgery, Univ Wash Med Ctr 1982; **Fac Appt:** Prof NS, Oregon Hlth & Sci Univ

Chen, Thomas C MD/PhD [NS] - **Spec Exp:** Brain & Spinal Cord Tumors; Brain Tumors-Metastatic; Gliomas; Spinal Tumors; **Hospital:** USC Norris Cancer Hosp, Keck Med Ctr of USC; **Address:** USC Health Consultation Clinic 2, 1520 San Pablo St, Ste 3800, MC 9197, Los Angeles, CA 90033; **Phone:** 323-442-5720; **Board Cert:** Neurological Surgery 2011; **Med School:** UCSF 1988; **Resid:** Neurological Surgery, USC Univ Hosp 1995; **Fellow:** Spine Surgery, Med Coll Wisconsin Affil Hosp 1997; **Fac Appt:** Assoc Prof NS, USC-Keck School of Medicine

Danielpour, Moise MD [NS] - **Spec Exp:** Pediatric Neurosurgery; Brain Tumors; Epilepsy; Craniofacial Surgery; **Hospital:** Cedars-Sinai Med Ctr; **Address:** 127 S San Vincente Blvd Fl 6th, Los Angeles, CA 90048; **Phone:** 310-423-7900; **Board Cert:** Neurological Surgery 2004; Pediatric Neurological Surgery ; **Med School:** Albert Einstein Coll Med 1992; **Resid:** Neurological Surgery, Northwestern Meml Med Ctr 1999; **Fellow:** Pediatric Neurological Surgery, UCSF Med Ctr 2000

Edwards, Michael S. B. MD [NS] - **Spec Exp:** Brain Tumors-Pediatric; Pediatric Neurosurgery; Stereotactic Radiosurgery; Spinal Cord Tumors; **Hospital:** Lucile Packard Chldn's Hosp, Stanford Univ Hosp & Clins; **Address:** Pediatric Neurosurgery, 300 Pasteur Drive, Ste R211, Stanford, CA 94305; **Phone:** 650-497-8775; **Board Cert:** Neurological Surgery 1980; Pediatric Neurological Surgery 2006; **Med School:** Tulane Univ 1970; **Resid:** Neurological Surgery, Oschner Fdn Hosp/Charity Hosp 1977; **Fellow:** Pediatric Neuro-Oncology, UCSF Med Ctr 1978; **Fac Appt:** Prof NS, Stanford Univ

Ellenbogen, Richard G MD [NS] - **Spec Exp:** Chiari's Deformity; Brain Tumors; Minimally Invasive Surgery; Congenital Nervous System Malformations; **Hospital:** Seattle Chldns Hosp, Univ Wash Med Ctr; **Address:** SCH, Dept Neurological Surgery, 4800 Sand Point Way NE, MS OA.9.321, Seattle, WA 98105; **Phone:** 206-987-2544; **Board Cert:** Neurological Surgery 1992; Pediatric Neurological Surgery 2009; **Med School:** Brown Univ 1983; **Resid:** Neurological Surgery, Brigham & Women's Hosp/Chldn's Hosp 1989; **Fac Appt:** Prof NS, Univ Wash

Giannotta, Steven L MD [NS] - **Spec Exp:** Cerebrovascular Surgery; Stereotactic Radiosurgery; Arteriovenous Malformations; Skull Base Surgery; **Hospital:** Keck Med Ctr of USC, LAC & USC Med Ctr; **Address:** USC Keck Med Ctr-Dept of Neurosurgery, 1520 San Pablo St, Ste 3800, Los Angeles, CA 90033; **Phone:** 323-442-5720; **Board Cert:** Neurological Surgery 1980; **Med School:** Univ Mich Med Sch 1972; **Resid:** Neurological Surgery, Univ Michigan Med Ctr 1979; **Fac Appt:** Prof NS, USC Sch Med

Gupta, Nalin MD/PhD [NS] - **Spec Exp:** Pediatric Neurosurgery; **Hospital:** UCSF Med Ctr; **Address:** 400 Parnassus Ave, Ste A808, San Francisco, CA 94143; **Phone:** 415-353-7500; **Board Cert:** Neurological Surgery 2013; Pediatric Neurological Surgery 2003; **Med School:** Univ Toronto 1987; **Resid:** Neurological Surgery, Univ Ottawa 1989; Neurological Surgery, Univ Toronto 1997; **Fellow:** Pediatric Neurological Surgery, Hosp for Sick Chldn 1998; **Fac Appt:** Asst Prof NS, UCSF

Harsh IV, Griffith R MD [NS] - **Spec Exp:** Brain & Spinal Cord Tumors; Skull Base Tumors; Pituitary Tumors; Acoustic Neuroma; **Hospital:** Stanford Univ Hosp & Clins; **Address:** Stanford Center for Advanced Medicine, 300 Pasteur Drive, Stanford, CA 94305; **Phone:** 650-723-7093; **Board Cert:** Neurological Surgery 1989; **Med School:** Harvard Med Sch 1980; **Resid:** Neurological Surgery, UCSF Med Ctr 1986; **Fellow:** Neuro-Oncology, UCSF Med Ctr 1987; **Fac Appt:** Prof NS, Stanford Univ

Levy, Michael L MD/PhD [NS] - **Spec Exp:** Pediatric Neurosurgery; **Hospital:** Rady Children's Hosp - San Diego, UCSD Med Ctr; **Address:** Rady Chldn's Specialists, 8010 Frost St, Ste 502, San Diego, CA 92123; **Phone:** 858-966-8574; **Board Cert:** Neurological Surgery 1997; Pediatric Neurological Surgery 1998; **Med School:** UCSF 1986; **Resid:** Neurological Surgery, USC Med Ctr 1993; **Fellow:** Pediatric Neurological Surgery, Chldns Hosp 1995; **Fac Appt:** Asst Prof NS, USC Sch Med

Liau, Linda M MD/PhD [NS] - **Spec Exp:** Brain Tumors; Neuro-Oncology; Gliomas; Meningioma; **Hospital:** UCLA Ronald Reagan Med Ctr; **Address:** UCLA Neurosurgical Associates, 300 UCLA Medical Plaza, Ste B200, Los Angeles, CA 90095-6901; **Phone:** 310-267-2621; **Board Cert:** Neurological Surgery 2013; **Med School:** Stanford Univ 1991; **Resid:** Neurological Surgery, UCLA Med Ctr 1998; **Fellow:** Neuro-Oncology, UCLA Med Ctr 1999; **Fac Appt:** Prof NS, UCLA

Liker, Mark A MD [NS] - **Spec Exp:** Spinal Surgery; Deep Brain Stimulation; Parkinson's Disease; Dystonia; **Hospital:** Henry Mayo Newhall Memorial Hosp, Keck Med Ctr of USC; **Address:** Brain & Spine Ctr, 25751 McBean Pkwy, Ste 305, Valencia, CA 91355; **Phone:** 661-799-2542; **Board Cert:** Neurological Surgery 2005; **Med School:** SUNY Downstate 1995; **Resid:** Neurological Surgery, USC Med Ctr 2001; **Fellow:** Spine Surgery, USC Med Ctr 2002; **Fac Appt:** Asst Prof NS, USC-Keck School of Medicine

Linskey, Mark E MD [NS] - **Spec Exp:** Brain Tumors; Stereotactic Radiosurgery; Skull Base Surgery; Trigeminal Neuralgia; **Hospital:** UC Irvine Med Ctr, Chldns Hosp Orange Co; **Address:** UC Irvine Med Ctr, Dept Neuro Surg, 101 The City Drive S, Orange, CA 92868; **Phone:** 714-456-6966; **Board Cert:** Neurological Surgery 1996; **Med School:** Columbia P&S 1986; **Resid:** Neurological Surgery, Univ Pittsburgh Med Ctr 1993; **Fellow:** Neuro-Oncology, Ludwig Inst Cancer Rsch/Univ Coll London 1994; Neuro-Oncology, Pittsburgh Cancer Inst/Univ Pittsburgh 1992; **Fac Appt:** Prof NS, UC Irvine

Liu, Charles Y MD [NS] - **Spec Exp:** Epilepsy; Skull Base Tumors & Surgery; Stereotactic Radiosurgery; Pituitary Surgery; **Hospital:** Keck Med Ctr of USC; **Address:** 1520 San Pablo St, Ste 3800, Los Angeles, CA 90033; **Phone:** 323-442-5720; **Board Cert:** Neurological Surgery 2007; **Med School:** Yale Univ 1996; **Resid:** Neurological Surgery, LAC/USC Med Ctr 2003; **Fellow:** Spine Surgery, LAC/USC Med Ctr 2005; **Fac Appt:** Assoc Prof NS, USC-Keck School of Medicine

Mamelak, Adam N MD [NS] - **Spec Exp:** Brain Tumors; Pituitary Surgery; Gliomas; **Hospital:** Cedars-Sinai Med Ctr; **Address:** Maxine Dunitz Neurosurgical Institute, 8631 W Third St, Ste 800-East, Los Angeles, CA 90048; **Phone:** 310-423-7900; **Board Cert:** Neurological Surgery 2011; **Med School:** Harvard Med Sch 1990; **Resid:** Neurological Surgery, UCSF Med Ctr 1995; **Fellow:** Epilepsy, UCSF Epilepsy Research Lab 1996; Research, CIT/ Huntington Med Rsch Inst 1997

Martin, Neil A MD [NS] - **Spec Exp:** Vascular Neurosurgery; Aneurysm-Cerebral; Endoscopic Surgery; Microvascular Surgery; **Hospital:** UCLA Ronald Reagan Med Ctr; **Address:** 300 Medical Plaza, Ste B200, Los Angeles, CA 90095; **Phone:** 310-825-5482; **Board Cert:** Neurological Surgery 1989; **Med School:** Med Coll VA 1978; **Resid:** Neurological Surgery, UCSF Med Ctr 1984; **Fellow:** Neurovascular Surgery, Barrow Neuro Inst/St. Joseph's Hosp 1985; **Fac Appt:** Prof NS, UCLA

Mayberg, Marc R MD [NS] - **Spec Exp:** Pituitary Surgery; Skull Base Tumors; Acoustic Neuroma; **Hospital:** Swedish Med Ctr-Cherry Hill Campus, Prov Reg Med Ctr -Colby Campus; **Address:** Seattle Neuroscience Inst, 550 17th Ave, Ste 500, James Tower, Seattle, WA 98122; **Phone:** 206-320-2800; **Board Cert:** Neurological Surgery 1988; **Med School:** Mayo Med Sch 1978; **Resid:** Neurological Surgery, Mass Genl Hosp 1984; **Fellow:** Neurological Surgery, Natl Hosp for Nervous Dis 1985

McDermott, Michael W MD [NS] - **Spec Exp:** Brain Tumors; Meningioma; Stereotactic Radiosurgery; Skull Base Tumors; **Hospital:** UCSF Med Ctr; **Address:** UCSF Dept Neurosurgery, 400 Parnassus Ave, rm A808, San Francisco, CA 94143; **Phone:** 415-353-2243; **Board Cert:** Neurological Surgery 2003; **Med School:** Univ Toronto 1982; **Resid:** Neurological Surgery, U British Columbia 1988; **Fellow:** Neuro-Oncology, UCSF Med Ctr 1990; **Fac Appt:** Prof NS, UCSF

Neuwelt, Edward A MD [NS] - **Spec Exp:** Neuro-Oncology; Brain Tumors; **Hospital:** OR Hlth & Sci Univ; **Address:** Oregon Hlth Sci Univ, Dept Neurosurgery, 3181 SW Sam Jackson Pk Rd, MC-L603, Portland, OR 97239; **Phone:** 503-494-5626; **Board Cert:** Neurological Surgery 1980; **Med School:** Univ Colorado 1972; **Resid:** Neurological Surgery, Univ Tex SW Affil Hosp 1978; **Fellow:** Neuro-Oncology, Natl Canc Inst/NIH 1976; **Fac Appt:** Prof NS, Oregon Hlth & Sci Univ

Ojemann, Jeffrey G MD [NS] - **Spec Exp:** Pediatric Neurosurgery; Brain Tumors; Hydrocephalus; Epilepsy; **Hospital:** Seattle Chldns Hosp, Univ Wash Med Ctr; **Address:** 4800 Sand Point Way NE, Box W7729, Seattle, WA 98105; **Phone:** 206-987-2544; **Board Cert:** Neurological Surgery 2013; **Med School:** Washington Univ, St Louis 1992; **Resid:** Neurological Surgery, Barnes Jewish Hosp 1998; **Fellow:** Pediatric Neurological Surgery, Chldn's Hosp 2000; Neurological Surgery, Univ Wash Med Ctr 2002; **Fac Appt:** Assoc Prof NS, Univ Wash

Ott, Kenneth H MD [NS] - **Spec Exp:** Brain Tumors; Stereotactic Radiosurgery; **Hospital:** Scripps Meml Hosp - La Jolla; **Address:** Neurosurgical Med Clinic, 2100 Fifth Ave, Ste 200, San Diego, CA 92101; **Phone:** 619-297-4481 x102; **Board Cert:** Neurological Surgery 1980; **Med School:** UCSF 1970; **Resid:** Surgery, Mass Genl Hosp 1972; Neurological Surgery, Mass Genl Hosp 1976

Raffel, Corey MD/PhD [NS] - **Spec Exp:** Pediatric Neurosurgery; Brain Tumors; Medulloblastoma; **Hospital:** UCSF Med Ctr, Good Samaritan Hosp - San Jose; **Address:** 2540 Samaritan Drive, Ste 2, San Jose, CA 94143-0112; **Phone:** 408-356-5554; **Board Cert:** Neurological Surgery 1990; Pediatric Neurological Surgery 2006; **Med School:** UCSD 1980; **Resid:** Neurological Surgery, UCSF Med Ctr 1986; **Fellow:** Pediatric Neurological Surgery, Hosp Sick Chldn 1988; **Fac Appt:** Clin Prof NS, UCSF

Sekhar, Laligam N MD [NS] - **Spec Exp:** Aneurysm-Cerebral; Arteriovenous Malformations; Brain Tumors; Skull Base Tumors; **Hospital:** Harborview Med Ctr, Univ Wash Med Ctr; **Address:** HMC-Neurosurgery, 908 Jefferson St, Ninth & Jefferson Bldg, Fl 5, Seattle, WA 98104-2499; **Phone:** 206-744-9340; **Board Cert:** Neurological Surgery 1986; **Med School:** India 1973; **Resid:** Neurology, Univ Cincinnati Med Ctr 1977; Neurology, UPMC 1982; **Fellow:** Skull Base Surgery, Norstadt Krankenhaus 1983; Cerebrovascular Neurosurgery, Univ Zurich Hosp 1985; **Fac Appt:** Prof NS, Univ Wash

Sekhon, Lali MD/PhD [NS] - **Spec Exp:** Spinal Surgery; Spinal Disorders-Degenerative; Spinal Disc Replacement; Minimally Invasive Spinal Surgery; **Hospital:** Renown Reg Med Ctr, St. Mary's Reg Med Ctr; **Address:** Sierra Neurosurgery Group, 75 Pringle Way, Ste 1007, Reno, NV 89502; **Phone:** 775-323-2080; **Med School:** Australia 1994; **Resid:** Neurological Surgery, Royal North Shore Hosp 1998; **Fellow:** Neurological Surgery, Mayo Clinic 1999; Neurological Orthopaedic Surgery, Toronto Western Hosp 2000; **Fac Appt:** Clin Prof S, Univ Nevada

Selden, Nathan R MD/PhD [NS] - **Spec Exp:** Pediatric Neurosurgery; Brain Tumors-Pediatric; Chiari's Deformity; Spina Bifida; **Hospital:** Doernbecher Chldns Hosp/OHSU, OR Hlth & Sci Univ; **Address:** 3303 SW Bond Ave, MC CH8N, Portland, OR 97239; **Phone:** 503-494-4314; **Board Cert:** Neurological Surgery 2004; **Med School:** Harvard Med Sch 1993; **Resid:** Neurological Surgery, Univ Michigan Med Ctr 1999; **Fellow:** Pediatric Neurological Surgery, Northwestern Meml Hosp 2000; **Fac Appt:** Prof NS, Oregon Hlth & Sci Univ

Shuer, Lawrence M MD [NS] - **Spec Exp:** Spinal Tumors; Brain Tumors; Epilepsy; Chiari's Deformity; **Hospital:** Stanford Univ Hosp & Clins, Lucile Packard Chldn's Hosp; **Address:** Stanford Univ Med Ctr, Dept Neurosurgery, 300 Pasteur Drive, rm R229, Stanford, CA 94305-5327; **Phone:** 650-723-6093; **Board Cert:** Neurological Surgery 1986; **Med School:** Univ Mich Med Sch 1978; **Resid:** Neurological Surgery, Stanford Univ Med Ctr 1984; **Fac Appt:** Prof NS, Stanford Univ

Silbergeld, Daniel L MD [NS] - **Spec Exp:** Brain Tumors; Brain Tumors-Metastatic; Brain Mapping; **Hospital:** Univ Wash Med Ctr; **Address:** 1959 NE Pacific St, Box 356470, Seattle, WA 98195; **Phone:** 206-598-5637; **Board Cert:** Neurological Surgery 1995; **Med School:** Univ Cincinnati 1984; **Resid:** Neurological Surgery, Univ Wash Med Ctr 1990; Research, Univ Wash Med Ctr 1988; **Fellow:** Neuro-Oncology, Univ Wash Med Ctr 1991; Epilepsy, Univ Wash Med Ctr 1991; **Fac Appt:** Assoc Prof NS, Univ Wash

Steinberg, Gary K MD/PhD [NS] - **Spec Exp:** Aneurysm-Cerebral; MoyaMoya Disease; Arteriovenous Malformations; Cerebrovascular Surgery; **Hospital:** Stanford Univ Hosp & Clins; **Address:** Stanford Univ Dept Neurosurgery, 300 Pasteur Drive, rm R281, Stanford, CA 94305-5327; **Phone:** 650-725-5562; **Board Cert:** Neurological Surgery 1989; **Med School:** Stanford Univ 1980; **Resid:** Neuropathology, Stanford Univ Med Ctr 1982; Neurological Surgery, Stanford Univ Med Ctr 1987; **Fellow:** Cerebrovascular Neurosurgery, Univ West Ontario 1985; **Fac Appt:** Prof NS, Stanford Univ

Sun, Peter P MD [NS] - **Spec Exp:** Pediatric Neurosurgery; Spinal Surgery; Spinal Tumors; **Hospital:** Chldns Hosp - Oakland; **Address:** Chldns Hosp, Neurological Surgery, 744 52nd St, Ste 5203, Oakland, CA 94609; **Phone:** 510-428-3319; **Board Cert:** Neurological Surgery 2013; Pediatric Neurological Surgery 2006; **Med School:** Columbia P&S 1991; **Resid:** Neurological Surgery, UC Davis Med Ctr 1994; Neurological Surgery, Yale-New Haven Hosp 1996; **Fellow:** Spine Surgery, NYU Med Ctr 1997; Pediatric Neurological Surgery, Chldns Hosp 1998; **Fac Appt:** NS, UCSF

Yu, John S MD [NS] - **Spec Exp:** Brain Tumors; Spinal Tumors; Clinical Trials; Spinal Surgery; **Hospital:** Cedars-Sinai Med Ctr; **Address:** Maxine Dunitz Neurosurgical Institute, Comprehensive Brain Tumor Program, 8631 W 3rd St, Ste 800 E, Los Angeles, CA 90048; **Phone:** 310-423-7900; **Board Cert:** Neurological Surgery 2013; **Med School:** Harvard Med Sch 1990; **Resid:** Neurological Surgery, Mass General Hosp 1997

THE MOUNT SINAI MEDICAL CENTER

Neurosurgery

Mount Sinai

One Gustave L. Levy Place
Fifth Avenue and 100th Street
New York, NY 10029-6574

Physician Referral: 1-800-MD-SINAI (637-4624)
www.mountsinai.org

THE DEPARTMENT OF NEUROSURGERY at Mount Sinai, established in 1914, has earned a distinguished international reputation. Since assuming the position of Chair five years ago, Joshua Bederson, MD, has expanded the department by more than 50 percent through a combination of strategic recruitments, new hospital affiliations, and numerous outreach programs. Neurosurgery is the fastest growing surgical subspecialty at Mount Sinai, performing more than 2,500 procedures a year at The Mount Sinai Hospital. Areas of clinical expertise include the treatment of meningiomas and other skull base tumors, primary and metastatic brain tumors, pituitary adenomas and acoustic neuromas, deep brain stimulation for movement disorders and minimally invasive treatment of spine and spinal cord disorders. The department is a regional leader in endovascular and microsurgical treatment of aneurysms, arteriovenous malformations and stroke, microvascular decompression for trigeminal neuralgia and hemifacial spasm. We are the first medical center in the nation to use the Neurotouch virtual reality brain surgery simulator, which will be used to train our residents, assess skill level and to rehearse upcoming cases.

The Meningioma Program has pioneered endoscopic, minimally invasive surgical approaches for the treatment of meningiomas. Transnasal endoscopic tumor resections and computer-aided navigation help our surgeons achieve even greater precision during surgery. Both tactics reduce risk to the patient and help us avoid critical vascular and intracranial structures. Working with the Minimally Invasive and Endoscopic Skull Base Surgery Program, we unite specialists in neurosurgery, otolaryngology, head and neck cancer, craniofacial surgery, oral and maxillofacial surgery, and microvascular and reconstructive procedures.

The Cerebrovascular Program is composed of an experienced team that provides a complete range of services for the diagnosis and treatment of patients with neurovascular disorders of the brain and spinal cord. Some current treatments include endovascular treatment of aneurysms with coils and/or stents, endovascular treatment of AVMs with liquid acrylics, stereotactic radiosurgical treatment of AVMs, endovascular treatment of stenoses with stents and angioplasty and microsurgical treatment of stenoses and occlusions with bypass. We also specialize in microsurgical treatment of aneurysms and AVMs with clipping and resection. We are the most experienced program in stent-assisted embolization of cerebral aneurysms and stent treatment of carotid artery disease amongst neurovascular centers in New York. The Comprehensive Brain Tumor Program collaborates with The Tisch Cancer Institute and the Departments of Neurology, Radiation Oncology, Radiology, and Pathology to provide comprehensive therapies for primary and metastatic malignant brain tumors. We have pioneered minimally invasive approaches using imaging technology, frameless stereotaxy, awake and asleep brain mapping, and advanced microneurosurgery. Stereotactic radiosurgery, a minimally invasive treatment that does not require open surgery, gene therapy, and clinical trials are also possible options.

The Neurosurgery Spinal Disorders Program offers treatment for all disorders of the spinal column and spinal cord, including degenerative disorders, trauma, infections, congenital disorders (including scoliosis), and tumors. Our neurosurgeons have pioneered endoscopic, minimally invasive approaches for tumor resection and treatment of degenerative diseases. These approaches reduce pain and hospital stays, and facilitate an early return to normal activity.

The Neuroendocrine Program sees more than 200 new pituitary tumor patients each year, more than 300 follow-up patients annually, and has performed more than 2,500 transphenoidal pituitary operations.

The Center for Neuromodulation, a collaboration between the Departments of Neurology and Neurosurgery, uses the latest technology to precisely target areas of abnormal activity in the brain and spinal cord. Our physicians are focused on developing minimally invasive neurosurgical techniques that either modulate neural function, replace lost neuronal populations, or halt the neurodegenerative process altogether. Currently, deep brain stimulation dominates this field, but many technologies with great potential are on the horizon. Our Center for Neuromodulation is currently the highest volume center of its kind in the Northeast.

NYU Langone
MEDICAL CENTER

550 First Avenue *(at 31st Street)*
New York, NY 10016
www.NYULMC.org/neurology
www.NYULMC.org/neurosurgery
Physician Referral: **888-7-NYU-MED** *(888-769-8633)*

NEUROLOGY & NEUROSURGERY

NYU Langone Medical Center's Departments of Neurology and Neurosurgery continue to be **ranked among the nation's top 10 in the 2013-2014 U.S. News & World Report's annual survey of "Best Hospitals" in America.**

Patients travel from around the world to consult our renowned specialists for their expertise in the care, treatment, and research of neurological diseases and disorders of the brain, spine and nervous system. These conditions range from migraine headaches, nerve and muscle problems, pain, autism, movement disorders and Alzheimer's disease to stroke, vascular disorders, epilepsy, multiple sclerosis and brain tumors. NYU Langone is home to one of the largest epilepsy centers in the United States, as well as the largest multiple sclerosis program in New York and the first primary stroke center established in New York City.

Neurological Expertise

Autonomic Diseases: Our specialized Center evaluates and treats children and adults with familial dysautonomia and other inherited or acquired autonomic nervous system diseases, including orthostatic hypotension and rare forms of hereditary sensory neuropathy.

Epilepsy: Our Level 4 Comprehensive Epilepsy Center offers the most advanced medical and surgical options. Complementary management approaches complete the comprehensive care plan.

Multiple Sclerosis: The Comprehensive MS Care Center provides state-of-the-art diagnostic evaluations and follow-up care and management.

Neurogenetics: We focus on inherited diseases of the nervous system. Services include diagnosis and management of inherited diseases, biochemical and molecular testing and genetic counseling.

Neuro-oncology: In partnership with the NYU Cancer Institute, our multidisciplinary Brain Tumor Center is one of the nation's leading brain and spinal cord tumor programs, including physicians highly experienced in neuro-oncology, neurosurgery and neuroradiology.

Neuromuscular Diseases: We offer multidisciplinary programs for neuromuscular diseases, including acquired peripheral neuropathy, Charcot Marie Tooth neuropathy, myasthenia gravis, amyotrophic lateral sclerosis, spinal muscular atrophy, post-polio syndrome, muscular dystrophy and Lyme neuroborreliosis.

Parkinson's Disease and Movement Disorders: Our specialized center helps individuals affected by Parkinson's or other movement disorders to achieve the highest possible quality of life. Experts are also available to offer functional neurosurgery for certain conditions that involve involuntary muscle contractions.

(continued)

Penn Medicine

PENN NEUROSURGERY

The Department of Neurosurgery at Penn provides comprehensive medical and surgical care for people with disorders of the brain, spinal cord and peripheral nervous system. One of the hallmarks of Penn's neurosurgery program is its integration of research and clinical practice, embracing new technologies and seeking the highest quality and best outcomes possible. More Penn neurosurgeons are listed in *The Best Doctors in America®* than are found at any other hospital or medical center in the Philadelphia region. Penn Neurology and Neurosurgery at the Hospital of the University of Pennsylvania (HUP) are ranked 12th in the nation by *U.S. News & World Report*, the top-ranked neuroscience program in the region

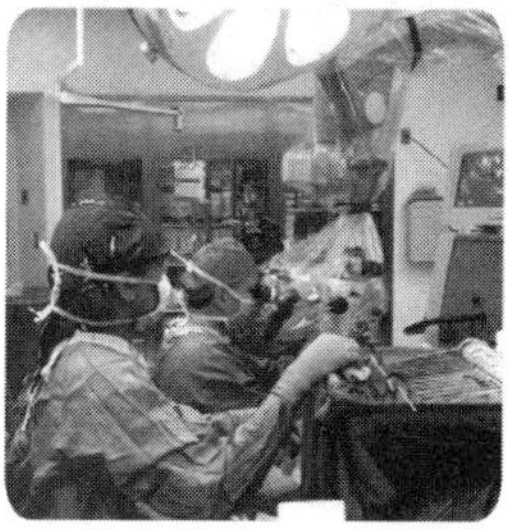

Penn's world-class neuroscience programs within the areas of clinical care, research and education. Penn's neurosurgical specialists backed by the most extensive neurodiagnostic and imaging facilities in the region, perform more than 4,500 operations each year. The neurosurgical faculty all have a particular subspecialty focus, covering the entire spectrum of surgically-treated disorders of the nervous system.

Excellence and Expertise

The Penn Brain Tumor Center provides evaluation, diagnosis and treatment to patients with brain and spinal tumors and other cancer-related neurological central nervous system and peripheral nervous system problems. The program utilizes a patient-oriented team approach bringing together some of the nation's leading experts in the field.

The Center for Cranial Base Surgery offers expert evaluation and treatment of tumors of the head, neck, face and other complex skull base disorders. With the development of innovative and endoscopic surgical procedures and state-of-the-art imaging, many of these tumors, previously inaccessible, can now be successfully treated.

The Penn Gamma Knife® Center at Pennsylvania Hospital offers power, precision and hope to patients suffering from brain tumors and other serious brain disorders. Gamma Knife® Perfexion™ radiosurgery is noninvasive, effective, and safe for treating conditions including benign or malignant brain tumors, blood vessel malformations and trigeminal neuralgia.

The Center for Functional and Restorative Neurosurgery at Pennsylvania Hospital performed more deep brain stimulation procedures for the treatment of Parkinson's disease and epilepsy in the past year than any other hospital or health system in the U.S.

The Comprehensive Spine Center provides medical and surgical care for the most complex disorders of the spinal cord. Penn is a regional and national leader in providing quality spine care. Utilizing a multidisciplinary team approach, the Center implements the latest advances in techniques and technology.

The Neurovascular Center offers minimally invasive (endovascular) coiling and stent treatments of brain aneurysms, vascular malformations and atherosclerotic narrowing of the blood vessels of the brain, combining the skill sets of neurosurgeons and interventional neuroradiologists to obtain the best possible outcomes.

For more information or to schedule an appointment, call 800.789.PENN (7366) or visit PennMedicine.org/neurosurgery

The Next Generation in Treatment Advances

Penn neurosurgeons are advancing minimally-invasive endoscopic surgery to the next level using three-dimensional (3D) endoscopy technology. Penn Medicine is one of only a few academic medical centers in the nation, and the first in the mid-Atlantic region, to utilize this groundbreaking technology.

Penn Neurosurgery patients have access to the Roberts Proton Therapy Center at Penn's Abramson Cancer Center, the world's largest proton therapy center associated with an academic medical center. It is the world's most comprehensive proton therapy center, offering the unique ability to fully integrate conventional radiation treatment with proton radiation.

Penn Neurosurgery Programs

- Center for Brain Injury and Repair
- Center for Cranial Base Surgery
- Center for Cranial Nerve
- Center for Functional and Restorative Neurosurgery
- Penn Brain Tumor Center
- Penn Gamma Knife® Center
- Neuro Intensive Care
- Neurovascular Center
- Neurosurgical Spine Center

Gamma Knife and Leksell Gamma Knife are U.S. federally registered trademarks of Elekta Instrument S.A., Geneva, Switzerland.

Locations

Hospital of the University of Pennsylvania
Pennsylvania Hospital
Penn Medicine Bucks County
Penn Medicine Cherry Hill
Penn Medicine Chestnut Hill
Penn Medicine Egg Harbor
Penn Medicine Valley Forge
Penn Medicine West Chester
Affiliate: Doylestown Hospital

Top Doctors Make A Difference

Neurology

A neurologist specializes in the diagnosis and treatment of all types of disease or impaired function of the brain, spinal cord, peripheral nerves, muscles and autonomic nervous system, as well as the blood vessels that relate to these structures. A child neurologist has special skills in the diagnosis and management of neurologic disorders of the neonatal period, infancy, early childhood and adolescence.

Training Required: Four years

Neurology

New England

Amato, Anthony A MD [N] - **Spec Exp:** Peripheral Neuropathy; Neuromuscular Disorders; Muscular Dystrophy; **Hospital:** Brigham & Women's Hosp; **Address:** Brigham & Women's Hosp, Dept Neurology, 75 Francis St, Boston, MA 02115; **Phone:** 617-732-8046; **Board Cert:** Neurology 1991; Neuromuscular Medicine 2008; **Med School:** Univ Cincinnati 1986; **Resid:** Neurology, Wilford Hall USAF Med Ctr 1990; **Fellow:** Neuromuscular Medicine, Ohio State Med Ctr 1992; **Fac Appt:** Prof N, Harvard Med Sch

Batchelor, Tracy T MD [N] - **Spec Exp:** Brain Tumors; Gliomas; **Hospital:** Mass Genl Hosp; **Address:** Mass Genl Hosp Cancer Ctr-Neuro-Oncology, 55 Fruit St, Ste YAW 9E, Boston, MA 02114; **Phone:** 617-724-8770; **Board Cert:** Neurology 2005; **Med School:** Emory Univ 1990; **Resid:** Neurology, Mass Genl Hosp 1994; **Fellow:** Neuro-Oncology, Meml Sloan Kettering Cancer Ctr 1995; **Fac Appt:** Prof N, Harvard Med Sch

Blum, Andrew S MD/PhD [N] - **Spec Exp:** Epilepsy; **Hospital:** Rhode Island Hosp; **Address:** Neurology Foundation Inc, 110 Lockwood St, Ste 342, Providence, RI 02905; **Phone:** 401-444-3032; **Board Cert:** Neurology 2005; Clinical Neurophysiology 2006; **Med School:** Cornell Univ 1989; **Resid:** Neurology, Johns Hopkins Hosp 1994; **Fellow:** Clinical Neurophysiology, Beth Israel Deaconess Med Ctr 1995

Caplan, Louis R MD [N] - **Spec Exp:** Stroke; **Hospital:** Beth Israel Deaconess Med Ctr - Boston; **Address:** Beth Israel Deaconess Med Ctr, 330 Brookline Ave, Boston, MA 02215; **Phone:** 617-632-8911; **Board Cert:** Internal Medicine 1969; Neurology 1972; Vascular Neurology 2005; **Med School:** Univ MD Sch Med 1962; **Resid:** Neurology, Boston City Hosp 1969; **Fellow:** Neurology, Mass Genl Hosp 1970; **Fac Appt:** Prof N, Harvard Med Sch

Cohen, Jeffrey Allen MD [N] - **Spec Exp:** Neuromuscular Disorders; Peripheral Neuropathy; **Hospital:** Dartmouth - Hitchcock Med Ctr; **Address:** Department of Neurology, 1 Medical Center Drive, Lebanon, NH 03756; **Phone:** 603-650-8589; **Board Cert:** Neurology 1982; Clinical Neurophysiology 2011; Neuromuscular Medicine 2008; **Med School:** Univ Okla Coll Med 1977; **Resid:** Neurology, Mt Sinai Hosp 1981; **Fellow:** Neuromuscular Disease, Mass Genl Hosp 1982; Peripheral Nerve Surgery, Mayo Clin 1986; **Fac Appt:** Prof Med, Dartmouth Med Sch

Cole, Andrew J MD [N] - **Spec Exp:** Epilepsy/Seizure Disorders; Rasmussen's Syndrome; **Hospital:** Mass Genl Hosp; **Address:** MGH Neurology Associates, 15 Parkman St, Boston, MA 02114; **Phone:** 617-726-3311; **Board Cert:** Neurology 1987; Clinical Neurophysiology 2009; **Med School:** Dartmouth Med Sch 1982; **Resid:** Neurology, Neuro Inst-McGill 1986; **Fellow:** Electroencephalography, Neuro Inst-McGill 1987; Neurology, Johns Hopkins Hosp 1988; **Fac Appt:** Asst Prof N, Harvard Med Sch

Cudkowicz, Merit MD [N] - **Spec Exp:** Amyotrophic Lateral Sclerosis (ALS); Neuromuscular Disorders; **Hospital:** Beth Israel Deaconess Med Ctr - Boston; **Address:** MGH Neurology Associates, 15 Parkman St, WAC 835, Boston, MA 02114; **Phone:** 617-724-3914; **Board Cert:** Neurology 2005; **Med School:** Harvard Med Sch 1990; **Resid:** Neurology, Mass Genl Hosp 1994; **Fellow:** Neurology, Mass Genl Hosp 1996; **Fac Appt:** Prof N, Harvard Med Sch

Flaherty, Alice W MD/PhD [N] - **Spec Exp:** Parkinson's Disease; Movement Disorders; Deep Brain Stimulation; Tourette's Syndrome; **Hospital:** Mass Genl Hosp; **Address:** MGH Neurology Assocs, 15 Parkman St, WACC 715, Boston, MA 02114; **Phone:** 617-724-9234; **Board Cert:** Neurology 2009; **Med School:** Harvard Med Sch 1994; **Resid:** Neurology, Mass Genl Hosp 1998; **Fellow:** Movement Disorders, Mass Genl Hosp 2000

Furie, Karen L MD [N] - **Spec Exp:** Stroke; Cerebrovascular Disease; **Hospital:** Rhode Island Hosp; **Address:** Rhode Island Hospital, 110 Lockwood St, Ste 324, Providence, RI 02903; **Phone:** 401-444-3032; **Board Cert:** Neurology 2006; Vascular Neurology 2008; **Med School:** Brown Univ 1990; **Resid:** Neurology, Rhode Island Hosp 1994; **Fellow:** Cerebrovascular Disease, Brown Univ Affil Hosp 1995

Greer, David M MD [N] - **Spec Exp:** Stroke; Cerebrovascular Disease; Neurological Imaging; Stroke Prevention; **Hospital:** Yale-New Haven Hosp; **Address:** Yale Neurology, 800 Howard Ave, Yale Physicians Bldg, Lower Level, New Haven, CT 06519; **Phone:** 203-785-5947; **Board Cert:** Neurology 2010; Vascular Neurology 2008; **Med School:** Univ Fla Coll Med 1995; **Resid:** Neurology, Mass Genl Hosp 1999; **Fellow:** Stroke, Mass Genl Hosp 2001; **Fac Appt:** Prof N, Yale Univ

Gross, Paul T MD [N] - **Spec Exp:** Epilepsy; Sleep Disorders; **Hospital:** Lahey Hosp & Med Ctr; **Address:** Lahey Hosp & Med Ctr, 41 Mall Rd, Burlington, MA 01805; **Phone:** 781-744-3263; **Board Cert:** Neurology 1981; Sleep Medicine 1992; **Med School:** Hahnemann Univ 1976; **Resid:** Neurology, Univ Wisc Hosp 1980; **Fellow:** Clinical Neurophysiology, Boston Chldn's Hosp 1981; **Fac Appt:** Clin Prof N, Tufts Univ

Jobst, Barbara C MD [N] - **Spec Exp:** Epilepsy/Seizure Disorders; Epilepsy in Women; **Hospital:** Dartmouth - Hitchcock Med Ctr; **Address:** Dartmouth-Hitchcock Medical Center, One Medical Center Drive, Lebanon, NH 03756-1000; **Phone:** 603-653-6118; **Board Cert:** Neurology 2012; **Med School:** Germany 1993; **Resid:** Neurology, Krankenhaus Barmherzigen Bruder 1996; Neurology, Dartmouth-Hitchcock Med Ctr 1999; **Fellow:** Epilepsy, Dartmouth-Hitchcock Med Ctr 2001; **Fac Appt:** Assoc Prof N, Dartmouth Med Sch

Kase, Carlos S MD [N] - **Spec Exp:** Stroke; **Hospital:** Boston Med Ctr; **Address:** Boston Med Ctr, Shapiro Ctr, 725 Albany St Fl 7th - Ste 7B, Boston, MA 02118; **Phone:** 617-638-8456; **Board Cert:** Neurology 1980; Vascular Neurology 2005; **Med School:** Chile 1967; **Resid:** Neurology, Mass Genl Hosp 1973; **Fellow:** Neurology, Mass Genl Hosp 1978; **Fac Appt:** Prof N, Boston Univ

Oaklander, Anne Louise MD/PhD [N] - **Spec Exp:** Nerve Injuries; Peripheral Neuropathy; Pain-Neuropathic; Complex Regional Pain Syndromes; **Hospital:** Mass Genl Hosp; **Address:** Mass General Hosp, Dept Neurology, 55 Fruit St, Wang Bldg Fl 8 - rm 835, Boston, MA 02114; **Phone:** 617-724-3992; **Board Cert:** Neurology 1992; Pain Medicine 2010; **Med School:** Albert Einstein Coll Med 1987; **Resid:** Neurology, UMDNJ Univ Med Ctr 1991; **Fellow:** Neuromuscular Medicine, Johns Hopkins Hosp 1994; Neurological Surgery, Johns Hopkins Hosp 1995; **Fac Appt:** Assoc Prof N, Harvard Med Sch

Pennell, Page B MD [N] - **Spec Exp:** Epilepsy in Women; Epilepsy in Pregnancy; Clinical Trials; **Hospital:** Brigham & Women's Hosp; **Address:** Brigham & Womens Hosp, Div Epilepsy, EEG & Sleep Neurology, 75 Francis St, Boston, MA 02115; **Phone:** 617-732-7547; **Board Cert:** Neurology 2004; **Med School:** Univ Fla Coll Med 1989; **Resid:** Neurology, Univ Michigan Med Ctr 1993; **Fellow:** Clinical Neurophysiology, Univ Michigan Med Ctr 1995; **Fac Appt:** Assoc Clin Prof N, Emory Univ

Ronan, Lara K MD [N] - **Spec Exp:** Neuro-Oncology; Brain Tumors; **Hospital:** Dartmouth - Hitchcock Med Ctr; **Address:** 1 Medical Center Drive, Dept Neurology, Lebanon, NH 03756; **Phone:** 603-650-7491; **Board Cert:** Neurology 2009; **Med School:** Univ Pittsburgh 1994; **Resid:** Neurology, Univ Michigan Med Ctr 1998; **Fellow:** Neuro-Oncology, MD Anderson Cancer Ctr 1999; **Fac Appt:** Asst Prof N, Dartmouth Med Sch

Ropper, Allan H MD [N] - **Spec Exp:** Guillain-Barre Syndrome; Parkinson's Disease; **Hospital:** Brigham & Women's Hosp; **Address:** Brigham & Women's Hosp, Dept Neurology, 75 Francis St, Boston, MA 02115; **Phone:** 617-732-8047; **Board Cert:** Internal Medicine 1977; Neurology 1980; **Med School:** Harvard Med Sch 1974; **Resid:** Internal Medicine, UCSF Med Ctr 1976; Neurology, Mass Genl Hosp 1979; **Fac Appt:** Prof N, Tufts Univ

Rutkove, Seward B MD [N] - **Spec Exp:** Neuromuscular Disorders; Amyotrophic Lateral Sclerosis (ALS); **Hospital:** Beth Israel Deaconess Med Ctr - Boston; **Address:** BIDMC - Dept Neurology, 330 Brookline Ave, Ste TCC-810, Boston, MA 02215; **Phone:** 617-667-8130; **Board Cert:** Neurology 2006; Clinical Neurophysiology 2007; **Med School:** Columbia P&S 1989; **Resid:** Internal Medicine, St Joseph Mercy Hosp 1991; Neurology, Harvard-Longwood Neuro Prgm 1994; **Fellow:** Clinical Neurophysiology, Brigham & Women's Hosp 1995; **Fac Appt:** Assoc Prof N, Harvard Med Sch

Samuels, Martin A MD [N] - **Spec Exp:** Neurological Aspects of Systemic Disease; **Hospital:** Brigham & Women's Hosp; **Address:** Brigham & Women's Hosp, Dept Neurology, 75 Francis St Fl 2, Boston, MA 02115; **Phone:** 617-732-7432; **Board Cert:** Internal Medicine 1974; Neurology 1978; **Med School:** Univ Cincinnati 1971; **Resid:** Internal Medicine, Boston City Hosp 1975; Neurology, Mass Genl Hosp 1977; **Fac Appt:** Prof N, Harvard Med Sch

Saper, Clifford MD/PhD [N] - **Spec Exp:** Sleep Disorders/Apnea; **Hospital:** Beth Israel Deaconess Med Ctr - Boston; **Address:** Beth Israel Deaconess Med Ctr, 330 Brookline Ave, Neurology, Kirstein 406, Boston, MA 02215; **Phone:** 617-667-2622; **Board Cert:** Neurology 1982; **Med School:** Washington Univ, St Louis 1977; **Resid:** Neurology, NY Hosp 1981; **Fac Appt:** Prof N, Harvard Med Sch

Taylor, Lynne P MD [N] - **Spec Exp:** Neuro-Oncology; Brain Tumors; Gliomas; Palliative Care; **Hospital:** Tufts Med Ctr; **Address:** Tufts Med Ctr, Neurology-Hem/Onc, 800 Washington St, South Bldg Fl 7 - rm 7119, Box 245, Boston, MA 02111; **Phone:** 617-636-2694; **Board Cert:** Neurology 1987; Hospice & Palliative Medicine 2010; **Med School:** Washington Univ, St Louis 1982; **Resid:** Neurology, Hosp Univ Penn 1986; **Fellow:** Neuro-Oncology, Meml Sloan Kettering Cancer Ctr 1988; **Fac Appt:** Assoc Prof N, Tufts Univ

Wen, Patrick Y MD [N] - **Spec Exp:** Neuro-Oncology; Brain Tumors; **Hospital:** Dana-Farber Cancer Inst, Brigham & Women's Hosp; **Address:** Dana-Farber Cancer Inst, 450 Brookline Ave, Ste DA2-124, Boston, MA 02115; **Phone:** 617-632-2166; **Board Cert:** Neurology 1989; **Med School:** England, UK 1981; **Resid:** Internal Medicine, Whittington Hosp 1983; Internal Medicine, Nat'l Hosp for Nervous Disease 1984; **Fellow:** Neurology, Harvard-Longwood Neurology 1988; **Fac Appt:** Prof N, Harvard Med Sch

Mid Atlantic

Apatoff, Brian R MD/PhD [N] - **Spec Exp:** Multiple Sclerosis; Neuro-Immunology; **Hospital:** NY-Presby/Weill Cornell Med Ctr, NY (page 65); **Address:** Multiple Sclerosis Institute, 401 E 55th St, New York, NY 10022; **Phone:** 212-593-6262; **Board Cert:** Neurology 1991; **Med School:** Univ Chicago-Pritzker Sch Med 1984; **Resid:** Neurology, Columbia Presby Med Ctr 1990; **Fellow:** Multiple Sclerosis, Neuro Inst-Columbia Univ 1992; **Fac Appt:** Assoc Prof N, Cornell Univ-Weill Med Coll

Azizi, S Ausim MD/PhD [N] - **Spec Exp:** Movement Disorders; Parkinson's Disease; Stroke; **Hospital:** Temple Univ Hosp, Hahnemann Univ Hosp; **Address:** Temple Univ Dept Neurology, 3509 N Broad St, Boyer Bldg Fl 5, Philadelphia, PA 19140; **Phone:** 215-707-5953; **Board Cert:** Neurology 2008; **Med School:** Univ Tex SW, Dallas 1990; **Resid:** Neurology, Yale-New Haven Hosp 1994; **Fac Appt:** Prof N, Temple Univ

Balcer, Laura J MD [N] - **Spec Exp:** Neuro-Ophthalmology; Multiple Sclerosis/Visual Disorders; Parkinson's Disease/Visual Disorders; **Hospital:** NYU Langone Med Ctr (page 68); **Address:** NYU Dept Neurology, 240 E 38th St Fl 15, New York, NY 10016; **Phone:** 646-501-7681; **Board Cert:** Neurology 2006; **Med School:** Johns Hopkins Univ 1991; **Resid:** Neurology, Hosp Univ Penn 1995; **Fellow:** Neuro-Ophthalmology, Hosp Univ Penn/Scheie Inst 1995; **Fac Appt:** Prof N, NYU Sch Med

Baser, Susan M MD [N] - **Spec Exp:** Parkinson's Disease; Huntington's Disease; Dystonia; Movement Disorders; **Hospital:** Allegheny Genl Hosp; **Address:** Allegheny Neurological Assocs, 490 E North Ave Prof Bldg - Ste 500, Pittsburgh, PA 15212; **Phone:** 412-359-8860; **Board Cert:** Neurology 1990; **Med School:** Loyola Univ-Stritch Sch Med 1983; **Resid:** Neurology, Univ Pittsburgh 1987; **Fellow:** Neuropharmacology, Natl Inst Hlth 1990; **Fac Appt:** Assoc Prof N, Thomas Jefferson Univ

Bell, Rodney D MD [N] - **Spec Exp:** Stroke; **Hospital:** Thomas Jefferson Univ Hosp; **Address:** Thomas Jefferson Univ Dept Neurology, 901 Walnut St, Philadelphia, PA 19107; **Phone:** 215-955-4087; **Board Cert:** Internal Medicine 1975; Neurotology 1981; Vascular Neurology 2005; **Med School:** Oregon Hlth & Sci Univ 1971; **Resid:** Internal Medicine, Parkland Meml Hosp 1975; Neurology, Parkland Meml Hosp 1978; **Fac Appt:** Prof N, Thomas Jefferson Univ

Bergey, Gregory K MD [N] - **Spec Exp:** Epilepsy/Seizure Disorders; Epilepsy in Women; Epilepsy in Pregnancy; **Hospital:** Johns Hopkins Hosp (page 59); **Address:** Johns Hopkins Epilepsy Ctr, 600 N Wolfe St Meyer Bldg - rm 2-147, Baltimore, MD 21287; **Phone:** 410-955-7338; **Board Cert:** Internal Medicine 1978; Neurology 1984; **Med School:** Univ Pennsylvania 1975; **Resid:** Internal Medicine, Yale-New Haven Hosp 1978; Neurology, Johns Hopkins Hosp 1982; **Fellow:** Neurophysiology, Natl Inst Health 1983; **Fac Appt:** Prof N, Johns Hopkins Univ

Bressman, Susan MD [N] - **Spec Exp:** Parkinson's Disease; Movement Disorders; Dystonia; **Hospital:** Beth Israel Med Ctr - Petrie Div (page 56); **Address:** 10 Union Square East, Ste 5H, New York, NY 10003-3314; **Phone:** 212-844-8379; **Board Cert:** Neurology 1983; **Med School:** Columbia P&S 1977; **Resid:** Neurology, Columbia-Presby Med Ctr 1981; **Fellow:** Movement Disorders, Columbia-Presby Med Ctr 1983; **Fac Appt:** Prof N, Albert Einstein Coll Med

Brick, John F MD [N] - **Spec Exp:** Epilepsy; **Hospital:** Ruby Memorial - WVU Hosp; **Address:** WVU Eye Inst - Dept Neurology, 1 Stadium Drive Fl 3, Morgantown, WV 26506; **Phone:** 304-598-6127; **Board Cert:** Neurology 1982; Vascular Neurology 2009; **Med School:** W VA Univ 1977; **Resid:** Neurology, W Va Univ Affil Hosp 1981; **Fellow:** Electroencephalography, Mayo Clin 1983; **Fac Appt:** Prof N, W VA Univ

Buchholz, David W MD [N] - **Spec Exp:** Migraine; Headache; **Hospital:** Johns Hopkins Hosp (page 59); **Address:** Johns Hopkins Hosp - Green Spring Sta, 10753 Falls Rd, Ste 315, Lutherville, MD 21093; **Phone:** 410-583-2830; **Board Cert:** Neurology 1984; **Med School:** Univ Pennsylvania 1979; **Resid:** Neurology, Johns Hopkins Hosp 1984; **Fac Appt:** Assoc Prof N, Johns Hopkins Univ

Busis, Neil A MD [N] - **Spec Exp:** Electromyography; Neuromuscular Disorders; Movement Disorders; Muscle Disorders; **Hospital:** UPMC Shadyside; **Address:** UPP Neurology-Shadyside, 532 S Aiken Ave, Ste 300, Pittsburgh, PA 15232-1326; **Phone:** 412-681-2000; **Board Cert:** Neurology 1985; **Med School:** Univ Pennsylvania 1977; **Resid:** Internal Medicine, Johns Hopkins Hosp 1979; Neurology, Mass Genl Hosp 1984; **Fellow:** Electromyography, Mass Genl Hosp 1985; **Fac Appt:** Asst Clin Prof N, Univ Pittsburgh

Calabresi, Peter A MD [N] - **Spec Exp:** Multiple Sclerosis; Clinical Trials; **Hospital:** Johns Hopkins Hosp (page 59); **Address:** Johns Hopkins Hosp- Dept Neurology, 600 N Wolfe St, Pathology Bldg - rm 627, Baltimore, MD 21287; **Phone:** 410-614-1522; **Board Cert:** Neurology 2005; **Med School:** Brown Univ 1988; **Resid:** Internal Medicine, Strong Meml Hosp 1993; **Fellow:** Neurological Immunology, Natl Inst Hlth 1995; **Fac Appt:** Prof N, Johns Hopkins Univ

Charney, Jonathan Z MD [N] - **Spec Exp:** Headache; Stroke; **Hospital:** Mt Sinai Med Ctr (page 62); **Address:** 1111 Park Ave, Ste 1H, New York, NY 10128-1234; **Phone:** 212-831-2886; **Board Cert:** Neurology 1977; **Med School:** NY Med Coll 1969; **Resid:** Neurology, Methodist Hosp-Baylor 1971; Neurology, Columbia-Presby Med Ctr 1973; **Fac Appt:** Asst Prof N, Mount Sinai Sch Med

Cook, Stuart D MD [N] - **Spec Exp:** Multiple Sclerosis; Infectious & Demyelinating Diseases; **Hospital:** Univ Hosp (Newark); **Address:** 65 Bergen St, rm 1435, Newark, NJ 07103; **Phone:** 973-972-9181; **Board Cert:** Neurology 1970; **Med School:** Univ VT Coll Med 1962; **Resid:** Neurology, Albert Einstein Coll Med 1968; **Fac Appt:** Prof N, UMDNJ-NJ Med Sch, Newark

Cornblath, David R MD [N] - **Spec Exp:** Peripheral Neuropathy; **Hospital:** Johns Hopkins Hosp (page 59); **Address:** Johns Hopkins Hosp-Dept of Neurology, 600 N Wolfe St Meyer Bldg - Ste 6-181-A, Baltimore, MD 21287-6965; **Phone:** 410-955-2229; **Board Cert:** Neurology 1982; **Med School:** Case West Res Univ 1977; **Resid:** Neurology, Hosp Univ Penn 1981; **Fellow:** Neuromuscular Medicine, Hosp Univ Penn 1982; **Fac Appt:** Prof N, Johns Hopkins Univ

Coyle, Patricia K MD [N] - **Spec Exp:** Multiple Sclerosis; Neuro-Immunology; Lyme Disease; Infections-Neurologic; **Hospital:** Stony Brook Univ Med Ctr; **Address:** Stony Brook Univ Med Ctr, 179 Belle Mead Rd, East Setauket, NY 11733; **Phone:** 631-444-2599; **Board Cert:** Neurology 2004; **Med School:** Johns Hopkins Univ 1974; **Resid:** Neurology, Johns Hopkins Hosp 1978; **Fellow:** Neurological Immunology, Johns Hopkins Hosp 1980; **Fac Appt:** Prof N, SUNY Stony Brook

DeAngelis, Lisa M MD [N] - **Spec Exp:** Neuro-Oncology; Brain Tumors; Clinical Trials; **Hospital:** Meml Sloan-Kettering Canc Ctr; **Address:** Meml Sloan Kettering Cancer Ctr, Neurology Dept, 1275 York Ave, New York, NY 10065; **Phone:** 212-639-7123; **Board Cert:** Neurology 1986; **Med School:** Columbia P&S 1980; **Resid:** Neurology, Neuro Inst-Presby Hosp 1984; **Fellow:** Neuro-Oncology, Neuro Inst-Presby Hosp 1985; Neuro-Oncology, Meml Sloan-Kettering Cancer Ctr 1986; **Fac Appt:** Prof N, Cornell Univ-Weill Med Coll

Devinsky, Orrin MD [N] - **Spec Exp:** Epilepsy; Tuberous Sclerosis; Behavioral Neurology; **Hospital:** NYU Langone Med Ctr (page 68), Saint Barnabas Med Ctr; **Address:** 223 E 34th St Fl Ground, New York, NY 10016-4972; **Phone:** 646-558-0803; **Board Cert:** Neurology 1987; **Med School:** Harvard Med Sch 1982; **Resid:** Neurology, NY Hosp-Cornell Med Ctr 1986; **Fellow:** Epilepsy, Natl Inst Health 1988; **Fac Appt:** Prof N, NYU Sch Med

Dewberry, Robert G MD [N] - **Hospital:** Maryland Genl Hosp; **Address:** Maryland Genl Hosp, Div Neurology, 827 Linden Ave, Ste 2A, Baltimore, MD 21201; **Phone:** 410-225-8290; **Board Cert:** Neurology 1992; **Med School:** Univ MD Sch Med 1987; **Resid:** Neurology, Barnes-Jewish Hosp 1991; **Fellow:** Neuromuscular Disease, Univ Virginia Hosp 1993

Elkind, Mitchell MD [N] - **Spec Exp:** Stroke; Cerebrovascular Disease; Dizziness/Vertigo; **Hospital:** NY-Presby/Columbia Univ Med Ctr, NY (page 65); **Address:** 710 W 168th St Neurologic Bldg Fl 2, Neurological Inst-Stroke Div, rm 640, New York, NY 10032; **Phone:** 212-305-1710; **Board Cert:** Neurotology 2007; Vascular Neurology 2008; **Med School:** Harvard Med Sch 1992; **Resid:** Internal Medicine, Brigham & Women's Hosp 1993; Neurology, Mass General Hosp 1996; **Fac Appt:** Asst Prof N, Columbia P&S

Fahn, Stanley MD [N] - **Spec Exp:** Movement Disorders; Parkinson's Disease; **Hospital:** NY-Presby/Columbia Univ Med Ctr, NY (page 65); **Address:** Neurological Institute, 710 W 168th St Fl 3 - rm 350, New York, NY 10032; **Phone:** 212-305-1303; **Board Cert:** Neurology 1968; **Med School:** UCSF 1958; **Resid:** Neurology, Neuro Inst-Columbia 1962; **Fellow:** Neurological Chemistry, Natl Inst Hlth 1968; **Fac Appt:** Prof N, Columbia P&S

Feinberg, Todd E MD [N] - **Spec Exp:** Alzheimer's Disease; Dementia; **Hospital:** Beth Israel Med Ctr - Petrie Div (page 56); **Address:** Yarmon Neurobehavior Ctr, 1st Ave at 16th St, Bernstein Pavilion Fl 10th, New York, NY 10003; **Phone:** 212-420-4111; **Board Cert:** Psychiatry 1984; Neurology 1987; **Med School:** Mount Sinai Sch Med 1978; **Resid:** Psychiatry, Mt Sinai Med Ctr 1982; Neurology, Mt Sinai Med Ctr 1984; **Fellow:** Behavioral Neurology, Univ Florida 1986; **Fac Appt:** Clin Prof N, Albert Einstein Coll Med

Fellus, Jonathan L MD [N] - **Spec Exp:** Brain Injury; Neuro-Rehabilitation; **Address:** Advanced Neurocare, 227 Route 206 N Bldg 2 - Ste 101, Flanders, NJ 07836; **Phone:** 732-494-7600; **Board Cert:** Neurology 2009; **Med School:** UMDNJ-RW Johnson Med Sch 1992; **Resid:** Neurology, Penn Hosp 1996; **Fellow:** Neurological Rehabilitation, Kernan Hosp/Univ MD Med Ctr 1997; **Fac Appt:** Asst Clin Prof N, UMDNJ-NJ Med Sch, Newark

Fink, Matthew E MD [N] - **Spec Exp:** Cerebrovascular Disease; Stroke; Critical Care; **Hospital:** NY-Presby/Weill Cornell Med Ctr, NY (page 65); **Address:** Presby/Weill Cornell, Neurology Dept, 525 E 68 St F Bldg - Ste 610, New York, NY 10065; **Phone:** 212-746-4564; **Board Cert:** Internal Medicine 1980; Neurology 1983; Vascular Neurology 2005; Neurocritical Care 2010; **Med School:** Univ Pittsburgh 1976; **Resid:** Internal Medicine, Boston Med Ctr 1978; Neurology, NY-Presby/Columbia Univ Med Ctr 1982; **Fac Appt:** Prof N, Cornell Univ

Foo, Sun-Hoo MD [N] - **Spec Exp:** Stroke; Headache; Parkinson's Disease; Dementia; **Hospital:** NYU Langone Med Ctr (page 68), NY-Presby/Lower Manhattan Hosp (page 65); **Address:** 650 1st Ave, Fl 4 Floor, New York, NY 10016-3240; **Phone:** 212-213-0270; **Board Cert:** Internal Medicine 1976; Neurology 1980; **Med School:** Taiwan 1972; **Resid:** Internal Medicine, St Vincent's Hosp 1976; Neurology, NYU Med Ctr 1979; **Fac Appt:** Prof N, NYU Sch Med

French, Jacqueline MD [N] - **Spec Exp:** Epilepsy/Seizure Disorders; **Hospital:** NYU Langone Med Ctr (page 68); **Address:** 223 E 34th St, New York, NY 10016; **Phone:** 646-558-0802; **Board Cert:** Neurology 1987; **Med School:** Brown Univ 1982; **Resid:** Neurology, Mount Sinai Hosp 1986; **Fellow:** Epilepsy, Mount Sinai Hosp 1988; Epilepsy, Yale-New Haven Hosp 1989; **Fac Appt:** Prof N, NYU Sch Med

Galetta, Steven MD [N] - **Spec Exp:** Neuro-Ophthalmology; Optic Nerve Disorders; Multiple Sclerosis; **Hospital:** NYU Langone Med Ctr (page 68); **Address:** NYU Med Ctr, Neurology Dept, 240 E 38 St, Fl 15, New York, NY 10016; **Phone:** 646-501-7680; **Board Cert:** Neurology 1988; **Med School:** Cornell Univ-Weill Med Coll 1983; **Resid:** Neurology, Hosp Univ Penn 1987; **Fellow:** Neuro-Ophthalmology, Bascom Palmer Eye Inst 1988; **Fac Appt:** Prof N, NYU Sch Med

Gendelman, Seymour MD [N] - **Spec Exp:** Parkinson's Disease; Dementia; Headache; **Hospital:** Mt Sinai Med Ctr (page 62); **Address:** 5 E 98th St, Fl 7, Box 1139, New York, NY 10029-6501; **Phone:** 212-241-8172; **Board Cert:** Neurology 1971; **Med School:** Geo Wash Univ 1964; **Resid:** Neurology, Mt Sinai Hosp 1968; **Fac Appt:** Clin Prof N, Mount Sinai Sch Med

Neurology

Gizzi, Martin S MD/PhD [N] - **Spec Exp:** Neuro-Ophthalmology; Stroke; Progressive Supranuclear Palsy (PSP); Stroke; **Hospital:** JFK Med Ctr - Edison; **Address:** NJ Neuroscience Institute, 65 James St, Edison, NJ 08820-3947; **Phone:** 732-321-7010; **Board Cert:** Neurology 1990; Vascular Neurology 2008; **Med School:** Univ Miami Sch Med 1985; **Resid:** Neurology, Mount Sinai Hosp 1989; **Fellow:** Neuro-Ophthalmology, Mount Sinai Hosp 1991; **Fac Appt:** Prof N, Seton Hall Univ Sch Hlth & Med Scis

Glass, Jon MD [N] - **Spec Exp:** Neuro-Oncology; Brain Tumors; Spinal Tumors; **Hospital:** Thomas Jefferson Univ Hosp; **Address:** Jefferson Neurosurgical Assocs, 909 Walnut St Fl 3, Philadelphia, PA 19107; **Phone:** 215-503-7005; **Board Cert:** Neurology 1993; **Med School:** SUNY Downstate 1986; **Resid:** Neurology, Boston Univ Med Ctr 1990; **Fellow:** Neuro-Oncology, Mass Genl Hosp 1992; **Fac Appt:** Assoc Prof N, Jefferson Med Coll

Golbe, Lawrence I MD [N] - **Spec Exp:** Parkinson's Disease; Progressive Supranuclear Palsy (PSP); Movement Disorders; **Hospital:** Robert Wood Johnson Univ Hosp - New Brunswick; **Address:** 125 Paterson St, Fl 6, rm 6100, New Brunswick, NJ 08901-2160; **Phone:** 732-235-7733; **Board Cert:** Neurology 1984; **Med School:** NYU Sch Med 1978; **Resid:** Internal Medicine, Hahnemann Univ Hosp 1980; Neurology, Bellevue Hosp 1983; **Fac Appt:** Prof N, UMDNJ-RW Johnson Med Sch

Hiesiger, Emile M MD [N] - **Spec Exp:** Pain-Spine; Pain-Cancer, Spine; Pain-Back; **Hospital:** NYU Langone Med Ctr (page 68), VA NY Harbor Hlthcare Sys-Manhattan Campus; **Address:** 345 E 37th St, Ste 320, New York, NY 10016; **Phone:** 212-263-6123; **Board Cert:** Neurology 1983; **Med School:** NY Med Coll 1978; **Resid:** Neurology, NYU Med Ctr 1982; **Fellow:** Neurology, Meml Sloan-Kettering Cancer Ctr 1983; **Fac Appt:** Assoc Clin Prof N, NYU Sch Med

Hurtig, Howard I MD [N] - **Spec Exp:** Parkinson's Disease; Movement Disorders; **Hospital:** Pennsylvania Hosp-UPHS (page 69); **Address:** Pennsylvania Hosp Neurological Inst, 330 S 9th St Fl 3, Philadelphia, PA 19107; **Phone:** 800-789-7366; **Board Cert:** Neurology 1976; **Med School:** Tulane Univ 1966; **Resid:** Internal Medicine, New York Hosp 1968; Neurology, Hosp Univ Penn 1973; **Fac Appt:** Prof N, Univ Pennsylvania

Jordan, Barry D MD [N] - **Spec Exp:** Brain Injury; Sports Neurology; Concussion; Memory Disorders; **Hospital:** Burke Rehab Hosp; **Address:** Burke Rehabilitation Hosp, 785 Mamaroneck Ave, White Plains, NY 10605; **Phone:** 914-597-2332; **Board Cert:** Neurology 1989; **Med School:** Harvard Med Sch 1981; **Resid:** Neurology, New York Hosp 1986; **Fellow:** Hosp Spec Surgery 1987; UCLA Med Ctr 1998; **Fac Appt:** Assoc Prof N, Cornell Univ-Weill Med Coll

Kasner, Scott E MD [N] - **Spec Exp:** Cerebrovascular Disease; Stroke; **Hospital:** Hosp Univ Penn - UPHS (page 69); **Address:** Univ Penn - Dept Neurology, 3400 Spruce St, 3W Gates Bldg, Philadelphia, PA 19104; **Phone:** 215-662-3606; **Board Cert:** Neurology 2007; Vascular Neurology 2006; **Med School:** Yale Univ 1992; **Resid:** Neurology, Hosp Univ Penn 1996; **Fellow:** Stroke, Univ Texas 1997; Neurocritical Care, Univ Texas 1997; **Fac Appt:** Prof N, Univ Pennsylvania

Kieburtz, Karl D MD [N] - **Spec Exp:** Huntington's Disease; Parkinson's Disease; Dementia; **Hospital:** Univ Rochester Strong Meml Hosp; **Address:** URMC, Neurology Dept, 919 Westfall Rd, Ste 220, Rochester, NY 14618; **Phone:** 585-273-2153; **Board Cert:** Neurology 1990; **Med School:** Univ Rochester 1985; **Resid:** Neurology, Univ Rochester Strong Meml Hosp 1989; **Fac Appt:** Prof N, Univ Rochester

Krauss, Gregory L MD [N] - **Spec Exp:** Epilepsy/Seizure Disorders; **Hospital:** Johns Hopkins Hosp (page 59); **Address:** Johns Hopkins Hosp-Dept Neurology, 600 N Wolfe St Meyer Bldg - rm 2-147, Baltimore, MD 21287; **Phone:** 410-955-2822; **Board Cert:** Neurology 1990; **Med School:** Oregon Hlth & Sci Univ 1985; **Resid:** Neurology, Johns Hopkins Hosp 1989; **Fellow:** Epilepsy, Johns Hopkins Hosp 1991; **Fac Appt:** Prof N, Johns Hopkins Univ

Krumholz, Allan MD [N] - **Spec Exp:** Epilepsy/Seizure Disorders; Sleep Disorders/Apnea; **Hospital:** Univ of MD Med Ctr; **Address:** Univ Maryland Med Ctr, Dept Neurology, 22 S Greene St, rm S12C09, Baltimore, MD 21201-1544; **Phone:** 410-328-6266; **Board Cert:** Neurology 1977; Clinical Neurophysiology 2006; **Med School:** Ros Franklin Univ/Chicago Med Sch 1970; **Resid:** Internal Medicine, Baltimore City Hosp 1972; Neurology, Johns Hopkins Hosp 1975; **Fellow:** Electroencephalography, Johns Hopkins Hosp 1980; **Fac Appt:** Prof N, Univ MD Sch Med

Kula, Roger W MD [N] - **Spec Exp:** Neuromuscular Disorders; Chiari's Deformity; Syringomyelia & Spinal Cord Diseases; Myasthenia Gravis; **Hospital:** N Shore Univ Hosp (page 66), Steven & Alexandra Cohen Chldn's Med Ctr of NY (page 66); **Address:** 611 Northern Blvd, Ste 150, Great Neck, NY 11021; **Phone:** 516-570-4400 x4; **Board Cert:** Internal Medicine 1975; Neurology 1977; Neuromuscular Medicine 2008; **Med School:** Johns Hopkins Univ 1970; **Resid:** Internal Medicine, New York Hosp 1972; Neurology, UCSF Med Ctr 1974; **Fellow:** Neuromuscular Medicine, Natl Inst Hlth 1977; **Fac Appt:** Assoc Prof N, Hofstra N Shore-LIJ Sch Med

Kuzniecky, Ruben MD [N] - **Spec Exp:** Epilepsy/Seizure Disorders; MRI; Developmental Disorders; Brain Malformations; **Hospital:** NYU Langone Med Ctr (page 68); **Address:** 223 E 34th St Fl Ground, New York, NY 10016; **Phone:** 646-558-0806; **Board Cert:** Neurology 1990; **Med School:** Argentina 1980; **Resid:** Neurology, McGill Univ 1986; **Fellow:** Epilepsy, McGill Univ 1988; **Fac Appt:** Prof N, NYU Sch Med

Labar, Douglas R MD/PhD [N] - **Spec Exp:** Epilepsy/Seizure Disorders; **Hospital:** NY-Presby/Weill Cornell Med Ctr, NY (page 65); **Address:** Weill Cornell Epilepsy Center, 525 E 68th St, rm K-619, New York, NY 10065; **Phone:** 212-746-2359; **Board Cert:** Neurology 1987; **Med School:** Med Coll PA 1982; **Resid:** Neurology, Columbia Presby Med Ctr 1986; **Fellow:** Epilepsy, Columbia Presby Med Ctr 1988; **Fac Appt:** Prof N, Cornell Univ-Weill Med Coll

Lacomis, David MD [N] - **Spec Exp:** Amyotrophic Lateral Sclerosis (ALS); Muscle Disorders; Myasthenia Gravis; Neuromuscular Disorders; **Hospital:** UPMC Presby, Pittsburgh; **Address:** Dept Neurology-Kaufmann Med Bldg, 3471 Fifth Ave, Ste 810, Pittsburgh, PA 15213; **Phone:** 412-692-4917; **Board Cert:** Neurology 1992; Clinical Neurophysiology 2004; Neuromuscular Medicine 2009; **Med School:** Penn State Coll Med 1987; **Resid:** Neurology, Harvard Affil Hosp 1991; **Fellow:** Neuromuscular Disease, Univ Mass Med Ctr 1993; **Fac Appt:** Prof N, Univ Pittsburgh

Lassman, Andrew B MD [N] - **Spec Exp:** Neuro-Oncology; Gliomas; Brain Tumors; Brain Tumors-Metastatic; **Hospital:** NY-Presby/Columbia Univ Med Ctr, NY (page 65); **Address:** NY Presbyterian-Columbia Medical Ctr, Div Neuro-Oncology, 622 W 168th St Fl 2, New York, NY 10032; **Phone:** 212-342-0571; **Board Cert:** Neurology 2012; **Med School:** Columbia P&S 1997; **Resid:** Neurology, NY-Presby/Columbia Univ Med Ctr 2001; **Fellow:** Neuro-Oncology, Meml Sloan-Kettering Cancer Ctr 2001; **Fac Appt:** Assoc Prof N, Columbia P&S

Laterra, John J MD/PhD [N] - **Spec Exp:** Neuro-Oncology; Brain Tumors; Gliomas; **Hospital:** Johns Hopkins Hosp (page 59), Kennedy Krieger Inst; **Address:** Johns Hopkins Hosp-Div Neurology, 600 N Wolfe St Phipps Bldg - Ste 119, Baltimore, MD 21287; **Phone:** 410-614-3853; **Board Cert:** Neurology 1990; **Med School:** Case West Res Univ 1984; **Resid:** Neurology, Univ Mich Hosps 1988; **Fellow:** Research, Johns Hopkins Hosp 1989; **Fac Appt:** Prof N, Johns Hopkins Univ

Latov, Norman MD/PhD [N] - **Spec Exp:** Peripheral Neuropathy; Neuro-Immunology; **Hospital:** NY-Presby/Weill Cornell Med Ctr, NY (page 65); **Address:** 1305 York Ave Fl 2 - Ste 217, New York, NY 10021; **Phone:** 646-962-3320; **Board Cert:** Neurology 1989; **Med School:** Univ Pennsylvania 1975; **Resid:** Internal Medicine, Boston City Hosp 1976; Neurology, Columbia-Presby Med Ctr 1979; **Fellow:** Immunology, Columbia-Presby Med Ctr 1981; **Fac Appt:** Prof N, Cornell Univ-Weill Med Coll

Levine, David N MD [N] - **Spec Exp:** Dementia; Stroke; Spinal Cord Disorders; Syringomyelia & Spinal Cord Diseases; **Hospital:** NYU Langone Med Ctr (page 68); **Address:** 240 E 38th St Fl 15th, New York, NY 10016-4901; **Phone:** 212-263-7744; **Board Cert:** Neurology 1976; **Med School:** Harvard Med Sch 1968; **Resid:** Neurology, Mass Genl Hosp 1974; **Fellow:** Neurology, Mass Genl Hosp 1976; **Fac Appt:** Prof N, NYU Sch Med

Levine, Steven R MD [N] - **Spec Exp:** Stroke; Cerebrovascular Disease; **Hospital:** SUNY Downstate Med Ctr (Univ Hosp Brooklyn); **Address:** SUNY Downstate Medical Center, 450 Clarkson Ave, rm B6-344, MS 1213, Brooklyn, NY 11203; **Phone:** 718-221-5188; **Board Cert:** Neurology 1986; Vascular Neurology 2005; **Med School:** Med Coll Wisc 1981; **Resid:** Neurology, Univ Mich Hosps 1985; **Fellow:** Cerebrovascular Disease, Henry Ford Hosp 1987; **Fac Appt:** Prof N, Mount Sinai Sch Med

Liporace, Joyce D MD [N] - **Spec Exp:** Epilepsy in Women; Women's Health; Epilepsy in Pregnancy; **Hospital:** Riddle Meml Hosp; **Address:** Center for Neuroscience, 1088 W Baltimore Pike, HCC II, Ste 2205, Media, PA 19063; **Phone:** 610-744-2960; **Board Cert:** Neurology 1993; **Med School:** Johns Hopkins Univ 1988; **Resid:** Neurology, Hosp Univ Penn 1992; **Fellow:** Clinical Neurophysiology, Graduate Hosp 1994; **Fac Appt:** Assoc Prof Med, Thomas Jefferson Univ

Lipton, Richard MD [N] - **Spec Exp:** Headache; Clinical Trials; **Hospital:** Montefiore Med Ctr-Einstein Campus, NY; **Address:** Montefiore at AECOM, 1300 Morris Park Ave, Bronx, NY 10461-1900; **Phone:** 718-430-3886; **Board Cert:** Neurology 1985; **Med School:** Univ Chicago-Pritzker Sch Med 1980; **Resid:** Neurology, Montefiore Med Ctr 1984; **Fellow:** Neurophysiology, Montefiore Med Ctr 1985; NeuroEpidemiology, Columbia Univ 1990; **Fac Appt:** Prof N, Albert Einstein Coll Med

Liu, Grant T MD [N] - **Spec Exp:** Pediatric Neuro-Ophthalmology; Neuro-Ophthalmology; **Hospital:** Hosp Univ Penn - UPHS (page 69), Chldns Hosp of Philadelphia; **Address:** Univ Penn, Dept Neurology, Div Neuro-Ophthalmology, 3400 Spruce St, 3W Gates, Philadelphia, PA 19104; **Phone:** 215-662-3606; **Board Cert:** Neurology 1993; **Med School:** Columbia P&S 1988; **Resid:** Neurology, Harvard-Longwood Neuro Program 1992; **Fellow:** Neuro-Ophthalmology, Bascom Palmer Eye Inst 1993; **Fac Appt:** Prof N, Univ Pennsylvania

Logigian, Eric L MD [N] - **Spec Exp:** Neuromuscular Disorders; Electromyography; Lyme Disease; Peripheral Neuropathy; **Hospital:** Univ Rochester Strong Meml Hosp, Highland Hosp of Rochester; **Address:** Strong Meml Hosp, Neurology Dept, 601 Elmwood Ave, Box 673, Rochester, NY 14618; **Phone:** 585-275-2559; **Board Cert:** Internal Medicine 1981; Neurology 1985; Clinical Neurophysiology 2009; **Med School:** Boston Univ 1978; **Resid:** Neurology, Mass Genl Hosp 1984; **Fellow:** Clinical Neurophysiology, Mass Genl Hosp 1985; **Fac Appt:** Prof N, Univ Rochester

Louis, Elan D MD [N] - **Spec Exp:** Tremor & Dystonia; Huntington's Disease; Parkinson's Disease/Movement Disorders; **Hospital:** NY-Presby/Columbia Univ Med Ctr, NY (page 65); **Address:** Neurological Inst of New York, 710 W 168th St, Ste 350, New York, NY 10032; **Phone:** 212-305-1303; **Board Cert:** Neurology 2004; **Med School:** Yale Univ 1989; **Resid:** Neurology, NY-Presby/Columbia Univ Med Ctr 1993; **Fellow:** Movement Disorders, Neurol Inst of New York 1995; Epidemiology, Neurol Inst of New York 1995; **Fac Appt:** Prof N, Columbia P&S

Lublin, Fred D MD [N] - **Spec Exp:** Multiple Sclerosis; **Hospital:** Mt Sinai Med Ctr (page 62); **Address:** Mount Sinai Med Ctr, Corinne Goldsmith Dickinson Ctr for MS, 5 E 98th St, Box 1138, New York, NY 10029-6574; **Phone:** 212-241-6854; **Board Cert:** Neurology 1977; **Med School:** Jefferson Med Coll 1972; **Resid:** Neurology, NY Hosp/Cornell Med Ctr 1976; **Fac Appt:** Prof N, Mount Sinai Sch Med

Marder, Karen S MD [N] - **Spec Exp:** Huntington's Disease; Alzheimer's Disease; Dementia; **Hospital:** NY-Presby/Columbia Univ Med Ctr, NY (page 65); **Address:** Neurological Institute, 710 W 168th St, Ste 104, New York, NY 10032-2603; **Phone:** 212-305-6939; **Board Cert:** Neurology 1989; **Med School:** Cornell Univ-Weill Med Coll 1983; **Resid:** Neurology, Columbia Presby Med Ctr 1987; **Fellow:** Behavioral Neurology, Columbia Presby Med Ctr 1989; **Fac Appt:** Assoc Prof N, Columbia P&S

Marshall, Randolph S MD [N] - **Spec Exp:** Stroke; Cerebrovascular Disease; Dizziness/Vertigo; Behavioral Neurology; **Hospital:** NY-Presby/Columbia Univ Med Ctr, NY (page 65); **Address:** CUMC/Neurological Inst-Stroke Div, 710 W 168th St Neurologic Bldg, Fl 2nd - rm 640, New York, NY 10032; **Phone:** 212-305-8389; **Board Cert:** Neurology 2004; Vascular Neurology 2008; **Med School:** UCSF 1988; **Resid:** Internal Medicine, NY Presby-Cornell Med Ctr 1989; Neurology, NY Presby-Columbia Med Ctr 1992; **Fellow:** Cerebrovascular Disease, Neurological Inst/Columbia Med Ctr 1994; **Fac Appt:** Prof N, Columbia P&S

Mayeux, Richard MD [N] - **Spec Exp:** Alzheimer's Disease; Dementia; **Hospital:** NY-Presby/Columbia Univ Med Ctr, NY (page 65); **Address:** 630 W 168th St, PH 19, New York, NY 10032; **Phone:** 212-305-6939; **Board Cert:** Neurology 1978; **Med School:** Univ Okla Coll Med 1972; **Resid:** Internal Medicine, Boston City Hosp 1974; Neurology, Columbia Presby Med Ctr 1977; **Fellow:** Neurology, Boston Univ 1978; **Fac Appt:** Prof N, Columbia P&S

McArthur, Justin C MD [N] - **Spec Exp:** AIDS/HIV; Multiple Sclerosis; Infections-Neurologic; **Hospital:** Johns Hopkins Hosp (page 59), Johns Hopkins Bayview Med Ctr (page 59); **Address:** Johns Hopkins Hosp-Dept Neurology, 600 N Wolfe St Meyer Bldg - Ste 6-113, Baltimore, MD 21287; **Phone:** 410-955-3730; **Board Cert:** Internal Medicine 1984; Neurology 1986; **Med School:** England, UK 1979; **Resid:** Internal Medicine, Johns Hopkins Hosp 1982; Neurology, Johns Hopkins Hosp 1985; **Fac Appt:** Prof N, Johns Hopkins Univ

McCluskey, Leo MD [N] - **Spec Exp:** Amyotrophic Lateral Sclerosis (ALS); **Hospital:** Pennsylvania Hosp-UPHS (page 69); **Address:** Pennsylvania Hosp, Dept Neurology, 330 S 9th St, Philadelphia, PA 19107; **Phone:** 800-789-7366; **Board Cert:** Neurology 1986; **Med School:** Columbia P&S 1980; **Resid:** Internal Medicine, Univ Mich Med Ctr 1982; Neurology, Hosp Univ Penn 1985; **Fellow:** Neuromuscular Disease, Hosp Univ Penn 1986; **Fac Appt:** Assoc Prof N, Univ Pennsylvania

Miller, Aaron E MD [N] - **Spec Exp:** Multiple Sclerosis; Autoimmune Disease; Optic Nerve Disorders; **Hospital:** Mt Sinai Med Ctr (page 62); **Address:** 5 E 98th St, Fl 1st, Box 1138, New York, NY 10029; **Phone:** 212-241-6854; **Board Cert:** Internal Medicine 1972; Neurology 1977; **Med School:** NYU Sch Med 1968; **Resid:** Internal Medicine, Jacobi Med Ctr 1970; Neurology, Montefiore Med Ctr 1975; **Fellow:** Neurovirology, Johns Hopkins Hosp 1977; **Fac Appt:** Prof N, Mount Sinai Sch Med

Mitsumoto, Hiroshi MD [N] - **Spec Exp:** Amyotrophic Lateral Sclerosis (ALS); Neuromuscular Disorders; Clinical Trials; **Hospital:** NY-Presby/Columbia Univ Med Ctr, NY (page 65); **Address:** Neurological Institute, 710 W 168th St Fl 9, New York, NY 10032; **Phone:** 212-305-1319; **Board Cert:** Neurology 1978; **Med School:** Japan 1968; **Resid:** Internal Medicine, Toho Univ Hosps 1972; Neurology, Univ Hosps 1976; **Fellow:** Neurological Pathology, Cleveland Clinic 1978; Neuromuscular Medicine, New England Med Ctr 1981; **Fac Appt:** Prof N, Columbia P&S

Mohr, JP MD [N] - **Spec Exp:** Stroke; Arteriovenous Malformations; Aphasia; MoyaMoya Disease; **Hospital:** NY-Presby/Columbia Univ Med Ctr, NY (page 65); **Address:** 710 W 168th St, Fl 6, rm 616, New York, NY 10032-2603; **Phone:** 212-305-8033; **Board Cert:** Neurology 1971; Vascular Neurology 2005; **Med School:** Univ VA Sch Med 1963; **Resid:** Neurology, Columbia Presby Med Ctr 1966; Neurology, Mass Genl Hosp 1968; **Fellow:** Neurology, Mass Genl Hosp 1969; **Fac Appt:** Prof N, Columbia P&S

Montgomery Jr, Erwin B MD [N] - **Spec Exp:** Parkinson's Disease; Movement Disorders; **Address:** Greenville Neuromodulation Ctr, 179 Main St, Greenville, PA 16125; **Phone:** 724-588-1324; **Board Cert:** Neurology 1982; **Med School:** SUNY Buffalo 1976; **Resid:** Neurology, Barnes-Jewish Hosp 1980; **Fellow:** Neurophysiology, Washington Univ Phys 1981

Newman, Lawrence C MD [N] - **Spec Exp:** Headache; Pain-Facial; **Hospital:** St. Luke's - Roosevelt Hosp Ctr - Roosevelt Div (page 56); **Address:** St Luke's-Roosevelt Hosp-Headache Inst, 425 W 59th St Fl 4 - Ste A, New York, NY 10019; **Phone:** 212-523-5869; **Board Cert:** Neurology 2005; Headache Medicine 2006; **Med School:** Mexico 1983; **Resid:** Internal Medicine, Elmhurst Hosp 1986; Neurology, Montefiore Med Ctr 1989; **Fellow:** Headache, Montefiore Med Ctr 1990; **Fac Appt:** Prof N, Albert Einstein Coll Med

Olanow, C Warren MD [N] - **Spec Exp:** Parkinson's Disease; Movement Disorders; **Hospital:** Mt Sinai Med Ctr (page 62); **Address:** 5 E 98 St, New York, NY 10029; **Phone:** 212-241-8435; **Med School:** Univ Toronto 1965; **Resid:** Neurology, Toronto Genl Hosp 1968; Neurology, Columbia Presby Hosp 1970; **Fellow:** Neurological Anatomy, Columbia Presby Hosp 1971; **Fac Appt:** Prof N, Mount Sinai Sch Med

Patchell, Roy A MD [N] - **Spec Exp:** Neuro-Oncology; Brain Tumors; Spinal Tumors; **Hospital:** Capital Health Med Ctr - Hopewell; **Address:** Capital Inst Neurosciences, 2 Capital Way, Ste 456, Pennington, NJ 08534; **Phone:** 609-537-7300; **Board Cert:** Neurology 1984; **Med School:** Univ KY Coll Med 1979; **Resid:** Neurology, Johns Hopkins Hosp 1983; **Fellow:** Neuro-Oncology, Meml Sloan-Kettering Cancer Ctr 1985

Petito, Frank A MD [N] - **Spec Exp:** Multiple Sclerosis; Headache; Lyme Disease; **Hospital:** NY-Presby/Weill Cornell Med Ctr, NY (page 65); **Address:** 525 E 68th St, Ste 607, New York, NY 10065; **Phone:** 212-746-2309; **Board Cert:** Neurology 1974; **Med School:** Columbia P&S 1967; **Resid:** Neurology, New York Hosp 1971; **Fac Appt:** Prof N, Cornell Univ-Weill Med Coll

Posner, Jerome B MD [N] - **Spec Exp:** Neuro-Oncology; Brain Tumors; Paraneoplastic Syndromes; **Hospital:** Meml Sloan-Kettering Canc Ctr; **Address:** 1275 York Ave, rm C731, New York, NY 10065; **Phone:** 212-639-7047; **Board Cert:** Neurology 1962; **Med School:** Univ Wash 1955; **Resid:** Neurology, Univ WA Affil Hosp 1959; **Fellow:** Biochemistry, Univ WA Affil Hosp 1963; **Fac Appt:** Prof N, Cornell Univ-Weill Med Coll

Pula, Thaddeus MD [N] - **Spec Exp:** Neurophysiology; Electromyography; **Hospital:** Maryland Genl Hosp; **Address:** Maryland Genl Hosp, Div Neurology, 827 Linden Ave, Ste 2A, Baltimore, MD 21201; **Phone:** 410-225-8290; **Board Cert:** Neurology 1981; **Med School:** Univ MD Sch Med 1976; **Resid:** Internal Medicine, Mercy Hosp Med Ctr; **Fellow:** Neurology, Univ Maryland

Reich, Stephen G MD [N] - **Spec Exp:** Movement Disorders; Parkinson's Disease; Ataxia; Dystonia-Botox Therapy; **Hospital:** Univ of MD Med Ctr; **Address:** Univ Maryland Med Ctr, Frenkil Bldg, 16 S Eutaw St Fl 3, Baltimore, MD 21201; **Phone:** 410-328-5858; **Board Cert:** Neurology 1989; **Med School:** Tulane Univ 1983; **Resid:** Neurology, Case West Res Univ Hosp 1987; **Fellow:** Movement Disorders, Johns Hopkins Hosp 1988; **Fac Appt:** Assoc Prof N, Univ MD Sch Med

Relkin, Norman R MD/PhD [N] - **Spec Exp:** Alzheimer's Disease; Dementia; Memory Disorders; **Hospital:** NY-Presby/Weill Cornell Med Ctr, NY (page 65); **Address:** Weill Cornell Memory Disorders Program, 428 E 72nd St, Ste 500, New York, NY 10021; **Phone:** 212-746-2441; **Board Cert:** Neurology 1992; **Med School:** Albert Einstein Coll Med 1987; **Resid:** Neurology, New York Hosp 1991; **Fellow:** Behavioral Neurology, New York Hosp-Cornell 1992; **Fac Appt:** Asst Prof N, Cornell Univ-Weill Med Coll

Sadiq, Saud MD [N] - **Spec Exp:** Multiple Sclerosis; **Hospital:** St. Luke's - Roosevelt Hosp Ctr - Roosevelt Div (page 56); **Address:** International MS Management Practice, 521 W 57th St Fl 4, New York, NY 10019; **Phone:** 212-265-8070; **Board Cert:** Neurology 2009; **Med School:** Africa 1979; **Resid:** Neurology, Univ TX Med Branch 1988; **Fellow:** Neurological Immunology, Ny Presby-Columbia Med Ctr 1991; **Fac Appt:** , Albert Einstein Coll Med

Sage, Jacob I MD [N] - **Spec Exp:** Parkinson's Disease; Dystonia; **Hospital:** Robert Wood Johnson Univ Hosp - New Brunswick; **Address:** Rutgers RWJ Med School-Dept Neurology, 125 Paterson St Fl 6 - Ste 6100, New Brunswick, NJ 08901-2160; **Phone:** 732-235-7733; **Board Cert:** Neurology 1979; **Med School:** Univ Pittsburgh 1972; **Resid:** Neurology, Univ Pittsburgh Hosps 1978; **Fellow:** Neurological Chemistry, NY Hosp-Cornell 1980; **Fac Appt:** Prof N, UMDNJ-RW Johnson Med Sch

Shefner, Jeremy M MD/PhD [N] - **Spec Exp:** Amyotrophic Lateral Sclerosis (ALS); Neuromuscular Disorders; **Hospital:** SUNY Upstate Med Univ Hosp; **Address:** Univ Hlth, Neuromuscular Clin, 90 Presidential Plaza Fl 4, Syracuse, NY 13202; **Phone:** 315-464-4243; **Board Cert:** Neurology 1989; Clinical Neurophysiology 2004; Neuromuscular Medicine 2012; **Med School:** Northwestern Univ 1983; **Resid:** Neurology, Beth Israel Deaconess Med Ctr 1988; **Fellow:** Neuromuscular Disease, Brigham & Womens Hosp 1990; **Fac Appt:** Prof N, SUNY Upstate Med Univ

Shulman, Lisa M MD [N] - **Spec Exp:** Movement Disorders; Movement Disorders-Botox Therapy; Parkinson's Disease; **Hospital:** Univ of MD Med Ctr; **Address:** 110 S Paca St Fl 3, Baltimore, MD 21201; **Phone:** 410-328-7809; **Board Cert:** Neurology 1994; **Med School:** Univ Miami Sch Med 1988; **Resid:** Neurology, Jackson Meml Hosp 1992; **Fellow:** Movement Disorders, Jackson Meml Hosp 1994; **Fac Appt:** Assoc Prof N, Univ MD Sch Med

Silberstein, Stephen D MD [N] - **Spec Exp:** Headache; Migraine; **Hospital:** Thomas Jefferson Univ Hosp; **Address:** Jefferson Headache Center, 900 Walnut St, rm 4200, Philadelphia, PA 19107; **Phone:** 215-955-2243; **Board Cert:** Neurology 1975; Headache Medicine 2006; **Med School:** Univ Pennsylvania 1967; **Resid:** Internal Medicine, Hosp Univ Penn 1969; Neurology, Hosp Univ Penn 1975; **Fac Appt:** Clin Prof N, Temple Univ

Simpson, David M MD [N] - **Spec Exp:** Infections-CNS; AIDS-Neurologic Complications; Peripheral Neuropathy; Neuromuscular Disorders; **Hospital:** Mt Sinai Med Ctr (page 62); **Address:** Mt Sinai Med Ctr, Dept Neurology, 1 Gustave L Levy Pl, Box 1052, Annenberg, 2nd Flr, New York, NY 10029; **Phone:** 212-241-8748; **Board Cert:** Neurology 1984; Clinical Neurophysiology 2005; Neuromuscular Medicine 2008; **Med School:** SUNY Buffalo 1979; **Resid:** Neurology, NY Hosp-Cornell Med Ctr 1983; **Fellow:** Clinical Neurophysiology, Mass Genl Hosp 1984; **Fac Appt:** Prof N, Mount Sinai Sch Med

Sirdofsky, Michael D MD [N] - **Spec Exp:** Peripheral Nerve Disorders; Neuromuscular Disorders; Electrodiagnosis; **Hospital:** MedStar Georgetown Univ Hosp; **Address:** Pasquerilla Hlthcare Ctr, 3800 Reservoir Rd NW, Washington, DC 20007; **Phone:** 202-444-8525; **Board Cert:** Neurology 1981; Neuromuscular Medicine 2012; **Med School:** Georgetown Univ 1976; **Resid:** Neurology, Georgetown Univ Hosp 1981; **Fac Appt:** Prof N, Georgetown Univ

Sperling, Michael R MD [N] - **Spec Exp:** Epilepsy; **Hospital:** Thomas Jefferson Univ Hosp; **Address:** Thomas Jefferson Univ Hosp, Dept Neurology, 909 Walnut St Fl 2nd, Philadelphia, PA 19107; **Phone:** 215-955-1222; **Board Cert:** Neurology 1984; Clinical Neurophysiology 2009; **Med School:** Temple Univ 1978; **Resid:** Neurology, Mt Sinai Hosp 1982; **Fellow:** Epilepsy, UCLA Med Ctr 1984; **Fac Appt:** Prof N, Thomas Jefferson Univ

Stern, Matthew B MD [N] - **Spec Exp:** Parkinson's Disease; Movement Disorders; Botox Therapy; **Hospital:** Pennsylvania Hosp-UPHS (page 69), Hosp Univ Penn - UPHS (page 69); **Address:** Pennsylvania Hosp, Dept Neurology, 330 S 9th St, Fl 3, Philadelphia, PA 19107; **Phone:** 215-829-6500; **Board Cert:** Neurology 1983; **Med School:** Duke Univ 1978; **Resid:** Neurology, Hosp Univ Penn 1982; **Fac Appt:** Prof N, Univ Pennsylvania

Swerdlow, Michael L MD [N] - **Spec Exp:** Myasthenia Gravis; Spinal Disorders; Multiple Sclerosis; **Hospital:** Montefiore Med Ctr-Moses Campus, NY; **Address:** 3400 Bainbridge Ave, Bronx, NY 10467-2401; **Phone:** 718-920-4178; **Board Cert:** Neurology 1975; **Med School:** Univ Pennsylvania 1967; **Resid:** Internal Medicine, Mount Sinai Hosp 1969; Neurology, Montefiore Med Ctr 1972; **Fellow:** Neurology, Natl Inst Hlth 1974; **Fac Appt:** Prof N, Albert Einstein Coll Med

Tayal, Ashis H MD [N] - **Spec Exp:** Stroke; Vascular Neurology; **Hospital:** Allegheny Genl Hosp; **Address:** Allegheny Neurology Assocs, 490 E North Ave, Ste 500, Professional Bldg, Pittsburgh, PA 15212; **Phone:** 412-359-8870; **Board Cert:** Internal Medicine 2007; Neurology 2006; Vascular Neurology 2008; **Med School:** Tufts Univ 1994; **Resid:** Internal Medicine, Mount Sinai Med Ctr 1997; Neurology, Univ Pittsburgh Med Ctr 2001; **Fellow:** Vascular Neurology, Univ Pittsburgh Med Ctr 2006

Vas, George A MD [N] - **Spec Exp:** Stroke; Multiple Sclerosis; **Hospital:** SUNY Downstate Med Ctr (Univ Hosp Brooklyn), Kings Co Hosp Ctr; **Address:** 450 Clarkson Ave N, Ste A, Brooklyn, NY 11203-2056; **Phone:** 718-270-2502; **Board Cert:** Internal Medicine 1973; Neurology 1977; Clinical Neurophysiology 2002; **Med School:** Univ Pittsburgh 1970; **Resid:** Internal Medicine, New York Hosp 1972; Neurology, New York Hosp 1975; **Fac Appt:** Prof N, SUNY Downstate

Waters, Cheryl H MD [N] - **Spec Exp:** Parkinson's Disease; Movement Disorders; **Hospital:** NY-Presby/Columbia Univ Med Ctr, NY (page 65); **Address:** NY-Presby, Neurological Inst, 710 W 168th St Fl 3, New York, NY 10032; **Phone:** 212-305-1303; **Board Cert:** Neurology 1986; **Med School:** Univ Toronto 1980; **Resid:** Internal Medicine, Univ Toronto Med Ctr 1982; Neurology, Univ Toronto Med Ctr 1985; **Fellow:** Clinical Pharmacology, Univ Toronto Med Ctr 1987; **Fac Appt:** Prof N, Columbia P&S

Wechsler, Lawrence R MD [N] - **Spec Exp:** Cerebrovascular Disease; Stroke; **Hospital:** UPMC Presby, Pittsburgh, UPMC Shadyside; **Address:** UPMC Stroke Institute, 3471 Fifth Ave, Ste 810, Pittsburgh, PA 15213; **Phone:** 412-647-3030; **Board Cert:** Internal Medicine 1983; Neurology 1984; Vascular Neurology 2005; **Med School:** Univ Pennsylvania 1978; **Resid:** Internal Medicine, Presby-Univ Hosp 1980; Neurology, Mass Genl Hosp 1983; **Fellow:** Clinical Neurophysiology, Mass Genl Hosp 1984; Cerebrovascular Disease, Mass Genl Hosp 1985; **Fac Appt:** Prof N, Univ Pittsburgh

Weinberg, Harold J MD [N] - **Spec Exp:** Headache; Spinal Disorders; Neuromuscular Disorders; Memory Disorders; **Hospital:** NYU Langone Med Ctr (page 68); **Address:** Neurology Consultants of NY, 650 1st Ave Fl 4, New York, NY 10016-3240; **Phone:** 212-213-9339; **Board Cert:** Neurology 1983; Electrodiagnostic Medicine 1989; **Med School:** Albert Einstein Coll Med 1978; **Resid:** Neurology, Columbia-Presby Med Ctr 1982; **Fellow:** Neuromuscular Medicine, Columbia-Presby Med Ctr 1982; **Fac Appt:** Clin Prof N, NYU Sch Med

Zimmerman, Earl A MD [N] - **Spec Exp:** Alzheimer's Disease; Dementia; **Hospital:** Albany Med Ctr; **Address:** AMC, Alzheimers Ctr, 47 New Scotland Ave, MC 65, Albany, NY 12208; **Phone:** 518-262-0800; **Board Cert:** Neurology 1970; Internal Medicine 1970; **Med School:** Univ Pennsylvania 1963; **Resid:** Internal Medicine, NY-Presby/Columbia Univ Med Ctr 1965; Neurology, NY-Presby/Columbia Univ Med Ctr 1968; **Fellow:** Neuroendocrinology, NY-Presby/Columbia Univ Med Ctr 1972; **Fac Appt:** Prof N, Albany Med Coll

Southeast

Abou-Khalil, Bassel MD [N] - **Spec Exp:** Epilepsy; Neurophysiology; **Hospital:** Vanderbilt Univ Med Ctr; **Address:** Vanderbilt Univ-Dept Neurology, 2220 Pierce Ave, Ste B1053, Nashville, TN 37232-2551; **Phone:** 615-936-0060; **Board Cert:** Neurology 1986; Clinical Neurophysiology 2012; **Med School:** Amer Univ Beirut 1978; **Resid:** Neurology, Strong Meml Hosp/Univ Rochester 1980; Neurology, Univ Mich Hosps 1982; **Fellow:** Epilepsy, Univ Mich Hosps 1985; Electroencephalography, Univ Mich Hosps 1985; **Fac Appt:** Prof N, Vanderbilt Univ

Adams, David J MD [N] - **Spec Exp:** Diagnostic Problems; Pseudotumor Cerebri; Autoimmune Disease; **Hospital:** Univ of Miami Hosp, Jackson Meml Hosp; **Address:** Univ Miami Hosp, Neurology Dept, 1150 NW 14th St, Ste 609, Miami, FL 33136; **Phone:** 305-243-1691; **Board Cert:** Neurology 1977; **Med School:** Columbia P&S 1969; **Resid:** Neurology, Neurological Inst 1975; **Fac Appt:** Prof N, Univ Miami Sch Med

Alexandrov, Andrei V MD [N] - **Spec Exp:** Stroke; Cerebrovascular Disease; **Hospital:** UAB Hosp; **Address:** 1813 6 Ave S RWUH Bldg - Ste M226, Birmingham, AL 35249; **Phone:** 205-934-2401; **Med School:** Russia 1989; **Resid:** Neurology, Inst of Neurology, Russian Acad Med Sciences 1991; **Fellow:** Vascular Neurology, Buffalo Genl Hosp 1995; Vascular Neurology, Univ Texas Affil Hosp 2004; **Fac Appt:** Prof N, UAB Sch Med

Ashizawa, Tetsuo MD [N] - **Spec Exp:** Movement Disorders; Myasthenia Gravis; Parkinson's Disease; Huntington's Disease; **Hospital:** UF Hlth Shands Hosp; **Address:** UF Hlth, Neurology Dept, 1600 SW Archer Rd, Box 100236, Gainesville, FL 32610; **Phone:** 352-265-8408; **Board Cert:** Neurology 1980; **Med School:** Japan 1973; **Resid:** Neurology, Baylor Med Ctr 1978; **Fellow:** Neuromuscular Disease, Baylor Med Ctr 1978; **Fac Appt:** Prof N, Univ Fla Coll Med

Bebin, E Martina MD [N] - **Spec Exp:** Epilepsy; Child Neurology; Tuberous Sclerosis; **Hospital:** UAB Hosp; **Address:** 1719 6th Ave S, Birmingham, AL 35294; **Phone:** 205-934-5567; **Board Cert:** Child Neurology 2012; **Med School:** Univ Miss 1986; **Resid:** Neurology, Mayo Clin 1991; **Fac Appt:** Assoc Prof N, UAB Sch Med

Berger, Joseph R MD [N] - **Spec Exp:** Multiple Sclerosis; AIDS/HIV; Infectious & Demyelinating Diseases; **Hospital:** Univ of Kentucky Albert B. Chandler Hosp; **Address:** Kentucky Neuroscience Clin, 740 S Limestone St, Lexington, KY 40536; **Phone:** 859-323-5661; **Board Cert:** Internal Medicine 1977; Neurology 1983; **Med School:** Jefferson Med Coll 1974; **Resid:** Internal Medicine, MedStar Georgetown Univ Hosp 1977; Neurology, Jackson Meml Hosp 1981; **Fac Appt:** Prof N, Univ KY Coll Med

Bertorini, Tulio E MD [N] - **Spec Exp:** Clinical Neurophysiology; Neuromuscular Disorders; Electromyography; **Hospital:** Methodist Univ Hosp - Memphis; **Address:** 1211 Union Ave, Ste 400, Memphis, TN 38104; **Phone:** 901-725-8920; **Board Cert:** Neurology 1977; Clinical Neurophysiology 2011; Neuromuscular Medicine 2012; **Med School:** Peru 1970; **Resid:** Neurology, Georgetown Univ Med Ctr 1973; Neurology, VA Hosp/Armed Forces Inst Path 1974; **Fellow:** Electrodiagnosis, Mass Genl Hosp 1975; Clinical Neurophysiology, Natl Inst Neuro Comm Dis & Stroke/NIH 1977; **Fac Appt:** Prof N, Univ Tenn Coll Med

Brooks, Benjamin R MD [N] - **Spec Exp:** Neuromuscular Disorders; Multiple Sclerosis; Neurotoxicology; **Hospital:** Carolinas Med Ctr, Levine Chldns Hosp; **Address:** CMC Dept Neurology, 1010 Edgehill Rd N, Charlotte, NC 28207-1885; **Phone:** 704-446-1900; **Board Cert:** Internal Medicine 1974; Neurology 1978; **Med School:** Harvard Med Sch 1970; **Resid:** Neurology, Mass Genl Hosp 1974; Neurology, Natl Inst Neuro Disorders & Stroke-NIH 1976; **Fellow:** Neurovirology, Johns Hopkins Hosp 1978

Corbett, James John MD [N] - **Spec Exp:** Neuro-Ophthalmology; Pseudotumor Cerebri; Neurosarcoidosis; Headache; **Hospital:** Univ Mississippi Med Ctr; **Address:** Univ Mississippi Med Ctr, Dept Neurology, 2500 N State St, Jackson, MS 39216-4505; **Phone:** 601-984-5501; **Board Cert:** Neurology 2004; **Med School:** Ros Franklin Univ/Chicago Med Sch 1966; **Resid:** Internal Medicine, Rhode Island Hosp 1968; Neurology, Univ Hosp-Case Western Reserve 1971; **Fac Appt:** Prof N, Univ Miss

DeLong, Mahlon R MD [N] - **Spec Exp:** Parkinson's Disease; Movement Disorders; Dystonia; **Hospital:** Emory Univ Hosp, Wesley Woods Ger Hosp; **Address:** Emory Clin, Neurology, 1841 Clifton Rd NE Fl 3, Atlanta, GA 30329; **Phone:** 404-778-3444; **Board Cert:** Neurology 1980; **Med School:** Harvard Med Sch 1966; **Resid:** Internal Medicine, Boston Med Ctr 1968; Neurology, Johns Hopkins Hosp 1976; **Fellow:** Neurology, Natl Inst Mental Hlth 1971; **Fac Appt:** Prof N, Emory Univ

Donofrio, Peter D MD [N] - **Spec Exp:** Amyotrophic Lateral Sclerosis (ALS); Muscular Dystrophy; Peripheral Neuropathy; Pain-Neuropathic; **Hospital:** Vanderbilt Univ Med Ctr; **Address:** Preston Reaearch Bldg, 2220 Pierce Ave, Ste B-1053, Nashville, TN 37232; **Phone:** 615-936-0060; **Board Cert:** Internal Medicine 1978; Neurology 1982; Neuromuscular Medicine 2012; **Med School:** Ohio State Univ 1975; **Resid:** Internal Medicine, Good Samaritan Hosp 1978; Neurology, Univ Michigan Med Ctr 1981; **Fellow:** Neuromuscular Medicine, Univ Michigan 1982; **Fac Appt:** Prof N, Vanderbilt Univ

Finkel, Alan G MD [N] - **Spec Exp:** Headache; Pain-Facial; Migraine; **Address:** Carolina Headache Inst, 103 Market St, Chapel Hill, NC 27516; **Phone:** 919-942-4424; **Board Cert:** Neurology 1991; Pain Medicine 2003; Headache Medicine 2006; **Med School:** SUNY Buffalo 1985; **Resid:** Neurology, NC Meml Hosp 1989; **Fellow:** Pain & Headache Medicine, Univ NC Hosp

Finkel, Michael F MD [N] - **Spec Exp:** Movement Disorders-Lower Limb; ADD/ADHD; Headache in Women; Trauma; **Hospital:** Physicians Regl Hlthcare Med Ctr-Pine Ridge; **Address:** Physicians Regl Med Grp, Neurology Dept, 6101 Pine Ridge Rd, Ste 2122, Naples, FL 34119; **Phone:** 239-348-4093; **Board Cert:** Neurology 1979; **Med School:** Washington Univ, St Louis 1973; **Resid:** Neurology, Univ Rochester Strong Meml Hosp 1977

Glass, Jonathan D MD [N] - **Spec Exp:** Amyotrophic Lateral Sclerosis (ALS); Peripheral Neuropathy; Neuromuscular Disorders; **Hospital:** Emory Univ Hosp, Grady Hlth Sys; **Address:** Emory Clin, Neurology, 1365B Clifton Rd NE, Ste 2200, Atlanta, GA 30322; **Phone:** 404-778-3444; **Board Cert:** Neurology 1990; Neuropathology 1997; **Med School:** Univ VT Coll Med 1985; **Resid:** Neurology, Johns Hopkins Hosp 1989; **Fellow:** Neuropathology, Johns Hopkins Hosp 1991; **Fac Appt:** Prof N, Emory Univ

Goldstein, Larry B MD [N] - **Spec Exp:** Stroke; Carotid Artery Disease; **Hospital:** Duke Univ Hosp, Durham VA Med Ctr; **Address:** DUMC, Box 3651, Durham, NC 27710; **Phone:** 919-684-3801; **Board Cert:** Neurology 1987; Vascular Neurology 2005; **Med School:** Mount Sinai Sch Med 1981; **Resid:** Neurology, Mt Sinai Hosp 1985; **Fellow:** Cerebrovascular Disease, Duke Univ Med Ctr 1986; **Fac Appt:** Prof N, Duke Univ

Gress, Daryl Ray MD [N] - **Spec Exp:** Critical Care; Stroke; **Hospital:** Univ of Virginia Hlth Sys; **Address:** Univ of VA Health Sys, Dept Neurology, Box 800394, Charlottesville, VA 22908; **Phone:** 434-924-8371; **Board Cert:** Neurology 1989; **Med School:** Washington Univ, St Louis 1982; **Resid:** Internal Medicine, Johns Hopkins Hosp 1984; Neurology, Mass Genl Hosp 1987; **Fellow:** Stroke, Mass Genl Hosp 1988

Haley Jr, Elliott C MD [N] - **Spec Exp:** Stroke; **Hospital:** Univ of Virginia Hlth Sys; **Address:** Univ VA Hlth Sys, Dept Neurology, 1215 Lee St, Charlottesville, VA 22908; **Phone:** 434-982-6952; **Board Cert:** Internal Medicine 1978; Neurology 1985; Vascular Neurology 2008; **Med School:** Tulane Univ 1974; **Resid:** Internal Medicine, Univ Va Hosp 1978; Neurology, Univ Va Hosp 1982; **Fellow:** Cerebrovascular Disease, Mass Genl Hosp 1984; **Fac Appt:** Prof N, Univ VA Sch Med

Hauser, Robert A MD [N] - **Spec Exp:** Movement Disorders; Parkinson's Disease; Tremor & Dystonia; **Hospital:** Tampa Genl Hosp; **Address:** USF Hlth, Movement Disorder Ctr, 4001 E Fletcher Ave, 6th Fl, Tampa, FL 33613; **Phone:** 813-396-0751; **Board Cert:** Neurology 1989; **Med School:** Temple Univ 1982; **Resid:** Neurological Surgery, Eastern VA Med Ctr 1985; Neurology, Eastern VA Med Ctr 1988; **Fellow:** Movement Disorders, Univ S FL Affil Hosp 1990; **Fac Appt:** Prof N, Univ S Fla Coll Med

Heilman, Kenneth M MD [N] - **Spec Exp:** Behavioral Neurology; Memory Disorders; Aphasia; Speech Disorders; **Hospital:** UF Hlth Shands Hosp, Malcom Randall VA Med Ctr; **Address:** UF Hlth, Neurology Dept, 1600 SW Archer Rd, Gainesville, FL 32610; **Phone:** 352-273-5550; **Board Cert:** Neurology 1973; **Med School:** Univ VA Sch Med 1963; **Resid:** Internal Medicine, Bellevue Hosp 1965; Neurology, Boston Med Ctr 1970; **Fac Appt:** Prof N, Univ Fla Coll Med

Hess, David C MD [N] - **Spec Exp:** Stroke; Antiphospholipid Syndrome (APS); Pediatric Neurology; **Hospital:** Georgia Regents Med Ctr-Augusta; **Address:** GA Regents, Neurology Dept, 1120 15th St, rm BI-3080, Augusta, GA 30912; **Phone:** 706-721-1691; **Board Cert:** Internal Medicine 1986; Neurology 1990; Vascular Neurology 2008; **Med School:** Univ MD Sch Med 1983; **Resid:** Internal Medicine, Allegheny Genl Hosp 1985; Neurology, Med Coll GA Affil Hosp 1989; **Fellow:** Cerebrovascular Disease, Med Coll GA Affil Hosp 1990; **Fac Appt:** Prof N, Med Coll GA

Janss, Anna J MD/PhD [N] - **Spec Exp:** Brain Tumors-Pediatric; Clinical Trials; Cancer Survivors-Late Effects of Therapy; **Hospital:** Chldns Hlthcare Atlanta @ Scottish Rite; **Address:** Aflac Cancer & Blood Disorders Ctr, 5455 Meridian Mark Rd NE, Ste 400, Atlanta, GA 30342; **Phone:** 404-785-3240; **Board Cert:** Neurology 1993; **Med School:** Univ Iowa Coll Med 1988; **Resid:** Neurology, Hosp Univ Penn 1992; **Fellow:** Pediatric Neuro-Oncology, Chldns Hosp 1996; **Fac Appt:** Assoc Prof N, Emory Univ

Kirshner, Howard S MD [N] - **Spec Exp:** Stroke; Aphasia; Alzheimer's Disease; Neuro-Rehabilitation; **Hospital:** Vanderbilt Univ Med Ctr, Vanderbilt Stallworth Rehab Hosp; **Address:** Vanderbilt Clinic, 1301 Medical Center Drive, Ste 3930, Nashville, TN 37232-2551; **Phone:** 615-936-0060; **Board Cert:** Neurology 1980; Vascular Neurology 2005; **Med School:** Harvard Med Sch 1972; **Resid:** Neurology, Mass Genl Hosp 1978; **Fellow:** Neurological Science, Natl Inst Hlth 1975; **Fac Appt:** Prof N, Vanderbilt Univ

Kurtzke, Robert N MD [N] - **Spec Exp:** Electromyography; Neuromuscular Disorders; **Hospital:** Inova Fairfax Hosp, Reston Hosp Ctr; **Address:** Neurology Ctr of Fairfax, 3020 Hamaker Ct, Ste 400, Fairfax, VA 22031-2220; **Phone:** 703-876-0800; **Board Cert:** Neurology 1990; Clinical Neurophysiology 2004; **Med School:** Georgetown Univ 1985; **Resid:** Neurology, Neurology Inst-Columbia Presby 1989; **Fellow:** Neuromuscular Disease, Duke Univ Med Ctr 1990

Lavin, Patrick J MD [N] - **Spec Exp:** Neuro-Ophthalmology; Eye Movement Disorders; Headache; Neuro-Otology; **Hospital:** Vanderbilt Univ Med Ctr; **Address:** Vanderbilt Eye Institute, 2311 Pierce Ave, Nashville, TN 37232-2551; **Phone:** 615-936-2020; **Board Cert:** Neurology 1985; **Med School:** Ireland 1970; **Resid:** Internal Medicine, St Vincent Hosp Elm Pk 1973; Internal Medicine, Genl Hosp-Royal Infirm 1976; **Fellow:** Neurology, Case Western Reserve Univ 1981; Neuro-Ophthalmology, Case Western Reserve Univ 1983; **Fac Appt:** Prof N, Vanderbilt Univ

Moots, Paul L MD [N] - **Spec Exp:** Neuro-Oncology; Brain Tumors; Neurological Complications of Cancer; Neurofibromatosis; **Hospital:** Vanderbilt Univ Med Ctr, VA Tennessee Valley Healthcare System-Alvin C. Yor; **Address:** Vanderbilt Clinic, 2220 Pierce Ave, Ste 1710, Nashville, TN 37232; **Phone:** 615-322-6053; **Board Cert:** Neurology 1989; **Med School:** Ohio State Univ 1980; **Resid:** Neurology, Univ Va Med Ctr 1984; **Fellow:** Neuropathology, Univ Virginia 1986; Neuro-Oncology, Meml Sloan Kettering Canc 1989; **Fac Appt:** Assoc Prof N, Vanderbilt Univ

Morgenlander, Joel C MD [N] - **Spec Exp:** Neuromuscular Disorders; Stroke; Multiple Sclerosis; **Hospital:** Duke Univ Hosp; **Address:** Duke Univ Med Ctr, 200 Trent Dr, Clinic 1-L, Durham, NC 27710; **Phone:** 919-684-6887; **Board Cert:** Neurology 1992; **Med School:** Univ Pittsburgh 1986; **Resid:** Neurology, Duke Univ Med Ctr 1990; **Fellow:** Neuromuscular Disease, Duke Univ Med Ctr 1991; **Fac Appt:** Prof N, Duke Univ

Nabors III, Louis Burt MD [N] - **Spec Exp:** Neuro-Oncology; Brain Tumors; **Hospital:** UAB Hosp; **Address:** 510 20th St S, FOT 1020, Birmingham, AL 35294-0001; **Phone:** 205-934-1432; **Board Cert:** Neurology 2009; **Med School:** Univ Tenn Coll Med 1991; **Resid:** Neurology, Univ Alabama Med Ctr 1998; **Fellow:** Neuro-Oncology, Univ Alabama 1999; **Fac Appt:** Prof N, UAB Sch Med

Newman, Nancy J MD [N] - **Spec Exp:** Neuro-Ophthalmology; Optic Nerve Disorders; **Hospital:** Emory Univ Hosp; **Address:** Emory Eye Ctr, Neuro-Ophthalmology, 1365 Clifton Rd NE, Clin B, Ste 4500, Atlanta, GA 30322; **Phone:** 404-778-5360; **Board Cert:** Neurology 1989; **Med School:** Harvard Med Sch 1984; **Resid:** Neurology, Mass Genl Hosp 1988; **Fellow:** Neuro-Ophthalmology, Mass Eye & Ear Infirm 1989; **Fac Appt:** Prof N, Emory Univ

Nolan, Bruce A MD [N] - **Spec Exp:** Sleep Disorders/Apnea; Sleep Medicine; **Hospital:** Jackson Meml Hosp; **Address:** UHlth, Sleep Disorders Dept, 900 NW 17th St, Ste 520, Miami, FL 33136; **Phone:** 305-243-9999; **Board Cert:** Neurology 1974; **Med School:** Wayne State Univ 1966; **Resid:** Neurology, Univ Miami Hosp 1970; **Fac Appt:** Assoc Prof N, Univ Miami Sch Med

Oh, Shin Joong MD [N] - **Spec Exp:** Neuromuscular Disorders; Electromyography; **Hospital:** UAB Hosp; **Address:** UAB Hosp, Dept Neurology, 1530 3rd Ave S, SC 200, Birmingham, AL 35294-0017; **Phone:** 205-934-2120; **Board Cert:** Neurology 1973; Clinical Neurophysiology 2011; Neuromuscular Medicine 2009; **Med School:** Korea 1960; **Resid:** Internal Medicine, Seoul Natl Univ Hosp 1964; Neurology, MedStar Georgetown Univ Hosp 1967; **Fellow:** NeuroEpidemiology, Univ Minnesota Affil Hosp 1969; **Fac Appt:** Prof N, UAB Sch Med

Sacco, Ralph L MD [N] - **Spec Exp:** Stroke; Stroke Prevention; **Hospital:** Jackson Meml Hosp, Univ of Miami Hosp & Clins/Sylvester Comp Canc Ctr; **Address:** UHlth, Neurology Dept, 1120 NW 14th St, Ste 1352, Miami, FL 33136; **Phone:** 305-243-7519; **Board Cert:** Neurology 1989; **Med School:** Boston Univ 1983; **Resid:** Neurology, NY-Presby/Columbia Univ Med Ctr 1987; **Fellow:** Cerebrovascular Disease, NY-Presby/Columbia Univ Med Ctr 1989; **Fac Appt:** Prof N, Univ Miami Sch Med

Sadowsky, Carl H MD [N] - **Spec Exp:** Memory Disorders; Alzheimer's Disease; **Hospital:** West Palm Hosp; **Address:** Palm Beach Neurology, 4631 Congress Ave, Ste 200, West Palm Beach, FL 33407-2234; **Phone:** 561-845-0500 x129; **Board Cert:** Neurology 1977; **Med School:** Cornell Univ 1971; **Resid:** Internal Medicine, Dartmouth-Hitchcock Med Ctr 1973; Neurology, Dartmouth-Hitchcock Med Ctr 1976; **Fac Appt:** Clin Prof N, Nova SE Univ, Coll Osteo Med

Schatz, Norman J MD [N] - **Spec Exp:** Neuro-Ophthalmology; Multiple Sclerosis/Visual Disorders; Vision-Unexplained Loss; **Hospital:** Bascom Palmer Eye Inst, Univ of Miami Hosp; **Address:** 4302 Alton Rd, Ste 845, Miami Beach, FL 33140; **Phone:** 305-532-2885; **Board Cert:** Neurology 1969; **Med School:** Hahnemann Univ 1961; **Resid:** Neurology, Thomas Jefferson Univ Hosp 1965; **Fellow:** Neuro-Ophthalmology, Bascom Palmer Eye Inst 1966

Schiff, David MD [N] - **Spec Exp:** Brain Tumors; Spinal Cord Tumors; Neurological Complications of Cancer; Neuro-Oncology; **Hospital:** Univ of Virginia Hlth Sys; **Address:** Univ VA Hlth Sys, Neuro-Oncology, 1215 Lee St, Box 800432, Charlottesville, VA 22908; **Phone:** 434-982-4415; **Board Cert:** Neurology 1994; **Med School:** Harvard Med Sch 1988; **Resid:** Neurology, Harvard Affil Hosps 1992; **Fellow:** Neuro-Oncology, Meml Sloan Kettering Canc Ctr 1993; Mayo Clin 1994; **Fac Appt:** Assoc Prof NS, Univ VA Sch Med

Sethi, Kapil D MD [N] - **Spec Exp:** Parkinson's Disease; Restless Legs Syndrome; Movement Disorders; Botox Therapy; **Hospital:** Georgia Regents Med Ctr-Augusta; **Address:** GA Regents, Neurology Dept, 1120 15th St, rm HF-1121A, Augusta, GA 30912; **Phone:** 706-721-2798; **Board Cert:** Neurology 1987; **Med School:** India 1976; **Resid:** Neurology, Pgimer 1981; Neurology, Med Coll GA Affil Hosp 1985; **Fac Appt:** Prof N, Med Coll GA

Singer, Carlos MD [N] - **Spec Exp:** Parkinson's Disease; Movement Disorders; Botox Therapy; **Hospital:** Jackson Meml Hosp; **Address:** UHlth, Neurology Dept, 1150 NW 14th St, Ste 609, Miami, FL 33136; **Phone:** 305-243-3100; **Board Cert:** Internal Medicine 1976; Neurology 1981; **Med School:** Venezuela 1972; **Resid:** Internal Medicine, Montefiore Hosp 1976; Neurology, Albert Einstein Coll Med Affil Hosp 1979; **Fellow:** Electromyography, Jackson Meml Hosp 1981; Movement Disorders, Univ Miami Hosp 1989; **Fac Appt:** Prof N, Univ Miami Sch Med

Watts, Ray L MD [N] - **Spec Exp:** Parkinson's Disease; Movement Disorders; **Hospital:** UAB Hosp; **Address:** 510 20th St S, FOT 1203, Birmingham, AL 35294; **Phone:** 205-996-7777; **Board Cert:** Neurology 1985; **Med School:** Washington Univ, St Louis 1980; **Resid:** Neurology, Mass Genl Hosp 1984; **Fellow:** Electromyography, Mass Genl Hosp 1985; **Fac Appt:** Prof N, UAB Sch Med

Wooten Jr, George F MD [N] - **Spec Exp:** Movement Disorders; Parkinson's Disease; Tremor & Dystonia; **Hospital:** Univ of Virginia Hlth Sys; **Address:** Univ VA Hlth Sys, Box 800394, Charlottesville, VA 22908; **Phone:** 434-924-8369; **Board Cert:** Neurology 1977; **Med School:** Cornell Univ-Weill Med Coll 1970; **Resid:** Neurology, NY Hosp-Cornell 1977; **Fellow:** Pharmacology, Natl Inst Hlth-NIMH 1974; **Fac Appt:** Prof N, Univ VA Sch Med

Midwest

Adams Jr, Harold P MD [N] - **Spec Exp:** Stroke; Cerebrovascular Disease; **Hospital:** Univ Iowa Hosp & Clins; **Address:** Univ Iowa Hosp, Dept Neurology, 200 Hawkins Drive, rm 2148-RCP, Iowa City, IA 52242; **Phone:** 319-356-4110; **Board Cert:** Neurology 2004; Vascular Neurology 2005; **Med School:** Northwestern Univ 1970; **Resid:** Neurology, Univ Iowa Hosp 1974; **Fac Appt:** Prof N, Univ Iowa Coll Med

Ahlskog, J Eric MD/PhD [N] - **Spec Exp:** Parkinson's Disease; Movement Disorders; **Hospital:** Mayo Med Ctr & Clin - Rochester, St. Mary's Hosp - Rochester MN (Mayo); **Address:** Mayo Clinic, Dept Neurology, 200 First St SW, Rochester, MN 55905; **Phone:** 507-266-5800; **Board Cert:** Neurology 1984; **Med School:** Dartmouth Med Sch 1976; **Resid:** Internal Medicine, Univ Chicago Med Ctr 1978; Neurology, Mayo Clin 1981; **Fac Appt:** Prof N, Mayo Med Sch

Aiken, Robert D MD [N] - **Spec Exp:** Neuro-Oncology; Brain Tumors; Clinical Trials; **Hospital:** Rush Univ Med Ctr; **Address:** 1725 W Harrison St, Ste 1106, Chicago, IL 60612-3824; **Phone:** 312-563-3452; **Board Cert:** Neurology 1983; Neuro-Oncology 2008; **Med School:** Wayne State Univ 1976; **Resid:** Internal Medicine, Baylor Affil Hosp 1978; Neurology, Columbia Presby Hosp 1981; **Fellow:** Neuro-Oncology, Meml Sloan Kettering Cancer Ctr 1983; **Fac Appt:** Prof N, Rush Med Coll

Arnason, Barry G W MD [N] - **Spec Exp:** Multiple Sclerosis; Guillain-Barre Syndrome; Myasthenia Gravis; **Hospital:** Univ of Chicago Med; **Address:** 5758 S Maryland Ave, Chicago, IL 60637; **Phone:** 773-702-6222; **Board Cert:** Neurology 1971; **Med School:** Univ Manitoba 1957; **Resid:** Neurology, Mass Genl Hosp 1959; Neurology, Mass Genl Hosp 1962; **Fac Appt:** Prof N, Univ Chicago-Pritzker Sch Med

Barger, Geoffrey R MD [N] - **Spec Exp:** Neuro-Oncology; Brain Tumors; **Hospital:** Detroit Med Ctr, Barbara Ann Karmanos Cancer Inst; **Address:** Detroit Medical Ctr, 4201 St Antoine, Ste 8A, Detroit, MI 48201; **Phone:** 313-745-4275; **Board Cert:** Neurology 1981; **Med School:** Jefferson Med Coll 1975; **Resid:** Neurology, Penn Hosp 1979; **Fellow:** Neuro-Oncology, Moffitt Hosp & Brain Tumor Ctr/UCSF 1982; **Fac Appt:** Assoc Prof N, Wayne State Univ

Barkley, Gregory L MD [N] - **Spec Exp:** Epilepsy/Seizure Disorders; **Hospital:** Henry Ford Hosp; **Address:** Henry Ford Hosp, Dept Neurology, 2799 W Grand Blvd, Detroit, MI 48202; **Phone:** 313-916-2585; **Board Cert:** Neurology 1988; Clinical Neurophysiology 2011; **Med School:** Mich State Univ 1981; **Resid:** Neurology, Henry Ford Hosp 1985; **Fellow:** Clinical Neurophysiology, Henry Ford Hosp 1986; **Fac Appt:** Assoc Prof N, Wayne State Univ

Bernstein, Richard A MD/PhD [N] - **Spec Exp:** Stroke/Cerebrovascular Disease; **Hospital:** Northwestern Meml Hosp; **Address:** 675 N St Claire St, Galter Bldg Fl 20 - Ste 100, Chicago, IL 60026; **Phone:** 312-695-7950; **Board Cert:** Neurology 2011; Vascular Neurology 2005; **Med School:** Cornell Univ-Weill Med Coll 1996; **Resid:** Neurology, Columbia-Presby Med Ctr 2000; **Fellow:** Vascular Neurology, UCSF Med Ctr 2001; Stroke, Stanford Med Ctr 2002; **Fac Appt:** Assoc Prof N, Northwestern Univ-Feinberg Sch Med

Biller, Jose MD [N] - **Spec Exp:** Stroke/Cerebrovascular Disease; Stroke in Children; Aneurysm; **Hospital:** Loyola Univ Med Ctr; **Address:** Loyola Univ Med Ctr, Dept Neurology, 2160 S First Ave, Maywood, IL 60153; **Phone:** 708-216-6006; **Board Cert:** Neurology 2005; Vascular Neurology 2005; **Med School:** Uruguay 1974; **Resid:** Neurology, Henry Ford Hosp 1978; Neurology, Loyola Univ/Hines VA Med Ctr 1980; **Fellow:** Cerebrovascular Disease, Bowman Gray Sch of Med 1981; **Fac Appt:** Prof N, Loyola Univ-Stritch Sch Med

Broderick, Joseph P MD [N] - **Spec Exp:** Stroke; **Hospital:** Univ Cincinnati Med Ctr; **Address:** Univ Cincinnati, Dept Neurology, 222 Piedmont Ave, Ste 3200, Cincinnati, OH 45219; **Phone:** 513-475-8730; **Board Cert:** Neurology 1988; Vascular Neurology 2005; **Med School:** Univ Cincinnati 1982; **Resid:** Neurology, Mayo Clinic 1986; **Fellow:** Cerebrovascular Disease, Mayo Clinic 1987; **Fac Appt:** Prof N, Univ Cincinnati

Brown Jr, Robert D MD [N] - **Spec Exp:** Stroke; Cerebrovascular Disease; **Hospital:** Mayo Med Ctr & Clin - Rochester; **Address:** Mayo Clinic, Dept Neurology, 200 First St SW, Rochester, MN 55905; **Phone:** 507-266-4143; **Board Cert:** Neurology 1994; Vascular Neurology 2008; **Med School:** Mayo Med Sch 1987; **Resid:** Neurology, Mayo Clin 1991; **Fellow:** Cerebrovascular Disease, Mayo Clin 1992; **Fac Appt:** Prof N, Mayo Med Sch

Burke, Allan M MD [N] - **Spec Exp:** Cerebrovascular Disease; Neurological Imaging; **Hospital:** Northwestern Meml Hosp; **Address:** 233 E Erie St, Ste 500, Chicago, IL 60611-2912; **Phone:** 312-944-0063; **Board Cert:** Neurology 1982; Neuroimaging 2002; **Med School:** Columbia P&S 1976; **Resid:** Internal Medicine, NY Hosp 1978; Neurology, Columbia-Presby Med Ctr 1981; **Fellow:** Cerebrovascular Disease, Hosp Univ Penn 1983; **Fac Appt:** Clin Prof N, Northwestern Univ

Cascino, Terrence L MD [N] - **Spec Exp:** Neuro-Oncology; **Hospital:** Mayo Med Ctr & Clin - Rochester; **Address:** Mayo Clinic, Dept Neurology, 200 1st St SW, Rochester, MN 55905; **Phone:** 507-284-2576; **Board Cert:** Neurology 1984; **Med School:** Loyola Univ-Stritch Sch Med 1972; **Resid:** Neurology, Mayo Clinic 1980; **Fellow:** Neuro-Oncology, Meml Sloan Kettering Cancer Ctr; **Fac Appt:** Assoc Prof N, Mayo Med Sch

Chelimsky, Thomas C MD [N] - **Hospital:** Froedtert & Med Coll WI; **Address:** Froedtert & Med Coll WI - Dept Neurology, 9200 W Wisconsin Ave, Milwaukee, WI 53226; **Phone:** 414-805-8710; **Board Cert:** Internal Medicine 1986; Neurology 1992; **Med School:** Washington Univ, St Louis 1983; **Resid:** Internal Medicine, Mayo Clin 1986; Neurology, Mayo Clin 1989; **Fellow:** Physiology, Mayo Clin 1987; **Fac Appt:** Prof N, Case West Res Univ

Cohen, Jeffrey Alan MD [N] - **Spec Exp:** Multiple Sclerosis; Neuro-Immunology; **Hospital:** Cleveland Clin (page 55); **Address:** Cleveland Clinic, 9500 Euclid Ave, Desk U10, Cleveland, OH 44195; **Phone:** 216-445-8110; **Board Cert:** Neurology 1985; **Med School:** Univ Chicago-Pritzker Sch Med 1980; **Resid:** Neurology, Hosp Univ Penn 1984; **Fellow:** Neurological Immunology, Hosp Univ Penn 1987

Corbetta, Maurizio MD [N] - **Spec Exp:** Stroke; Brain Injury Rehabilitation; Neuro-Rehabilitation; Neurological Imaging; **Hospital:** Washington Univ Phys, Barnes-Jewish Hosp; **Address:** 4921 Parkview Pl, Ste 6C, St Louis, MO 63110; **Phone:** 314-362-4503; **Board Cert:** Neurology 2008; **Med School:** Italy 1985; **Resid:** Neurology, Univ Verona Affil Hosp 1990; Neurology, Barnes Jewish Hosp 1996; **Fellow:** Neuroimaging, Barnes Jewish Hosp 1992; **Fac Appt:** Prof N, Washington Univ, St Louis

Cutrer, F Michael MD [N] - **Spec Exp:** Headache; Pain-Facial; Migraine; **Hospital:** Mayo Med Ctr & Clin - Rochester, Rochester Methodist Hosp; **Address:** Mayo Clinic, Dept Neurology, 200 First St SW, Rochester, MN 55905-0001; **Phone:** 507-266-5800; **Board Cert:** Neurology 1993; **Med School:** Univ Miss 1988; **Resid:** Neurology, UCLA Med Ctr 1992; **Fellow:** Neurology, Mass Genl Hosp-Harvard 1994; **Fac Appt:** Assoc Prof N, Mayo Med Sch

Elias, Stanton B MD [N] - **Spec Exp:** Multiple Sclerosis; Myasthenia Gravis; **Hospital:** Henry Ford Hosp; **Address:** Henry Ford Hosp, Dept Neurology, 2799 W Grand Blvd, rm K-11, Detroit, MI 48202-2689; **Phone:** 313-916-2585; **Board Cert:** Neurology 1979; **Med School:** Univ Pittsburgh 1972; **Resid:** Neurology, Duke Univ Med Ctr 1976; **Fellow:** Neurology, Duke Univ Med Ctr 1977

Farlow, Martin R MD [N] - **Spec Exp:** Alzheimer's Disease; Neurodegenerative Disorders; Prion Diseases; **Hospital:** IU Hlth Univ Hosp; **Address:** IU Health Physicians- Neurology, 355 W 16th St, Ste 3200, Indianapolis, IN 46202; **Phone:** 317-948-5450; **Board Cert:** Neurology 1988; **Med School:** Indiana Univ 1979; **Resid:** Neurology, Indiana Univ Hosp 1983; **Fac Appt:** Prof N, Indiana Univ

Feldman, Eva L MD/PhD [N] - **Spec Exp:** Neuromuscular Disorders; Amyotrophic Lateral Sclerosis (ALS); Peripheral Neuropathy; **Hospital:** Univ Michigan Med Ctr; **Address:** Univ Mich, Dept Neurology, 1500 E Med Ctr Drive, Taubman 1324 SPC 5322, Ann Arbor, MI 48109; **Phone:** 734-936-9020; **Board Cert:** Neurology 1988; **Med School:** Univ Mich Med Sch 1983; **Resid:** Neurology, Johns Hopkins Hosp 1987; **Fellow:** Neuromuscular Medicine, Univ Mich Hosps 1988; **Fac Appt:** Prof N, Univ Mich Med Sch

Furlan, Anthony J MD [N] - **Spec Exp:** Stroke; Thrombolytic Therapy; **Hospital:** UH Case Med Ctr; **Address:** Dept Neurology, 11100 Euclid Ave, Fl 5, Hanna House, Cleveland, OH 44106; **Phone:** 216-844-3192; **Board Cert:** Neurology 1979; Vascular Neurology 2005; **Med School:** Loyola Univ-Stritch Sch Med 1973; **Resid:** Neurology, Cleveland Clinic 1977; **Fellow:** Cerebrovascular Disease, Mayo Clinic 1978; **Fac Appt:** Prof N, Case West Res Univ

Goetz, Christopher G MD [N] - **Spec Exp:** Movement Disorders; Parkinson's Disease; Dyskinesias; **Hospital:** Rush Univ Med Ctr; **Address:** 1725 W Harrison St, Ste 755, Chicago, IL 60612-3835; **Phone:** 312-563-2030; **Board Cert:** Neurology 1982; **Med School:** Rush Med Coll 1975; **Resid:** Neurology, Michael Reese Med Ctr 1977; Neurology, Rush-Presby-St Luke's Med Ctr 1979; **Fac Appt:** Prof N, Rush Med Coll

Goodwin, James MD [N] - **Spec Exp:** Neuro-Ophthalmology; Optic Nerve Disorders; Neuromuscular Disorder & Vision Problems; **Hospital:** Univ of IL Med Ctr at Chicago; **Address:** Univ Illinois Eye & Ear Infirm, 1855 W Taylor St, rm 3.158, MC 64, Chicago, IL 60612; **Phone:** 312-996-9120; **Board Cert:** Neurology 1975; **Med School:** Univ IL Coll Med 1969; **Resid:** Neurology, Univ MN Hosps 1973; **Fellow:** Neuro-Ophthalmology, Bascom Palmer Eye Inst 1976; **Fac Appt:** Prof Oph, Univ IL Coll Med

Hain, Timothy C MD [N] - **Spec Exp:** Neuro-Otology; Balance Disorders; Motion Sickness; Meniere's Disease; **Hospital:** Northwestern Meml Hosp; **Address:** Chicago Dizziness & Hearing, 645 N Michigan Ave, Ste 410, Chicago, IL 60611; **Phone:** 312-274-0197; **Board Cert:** Neurology 1983; **Med School:** Univ IL Coll Med 1978; **Resid:** Neurology, Univ Illinois Affil Hosp 1982; **Fellow:** Neurology, Johns Hopkins Hosp 1984; Ophthalmology, Johns Hopkins Hosp 1984; **Fac Appt:** Prof N, Northwestern Univ

Hecox, Kurt E MD [N] - **Spec Exp:** Pediatric Neurology; Epilepsy/Seizure Disorders; Hearing Loss; **Hospital:** Chldns Hosp - Wisconsin; **Address:** Chlds Hosp of Wisconsin-Dept Neurology, 9000 W Wisconsin Ave, Ste 210, Milwaukee, WI 53226; **Phone:** 414-266-3464; **Board Cert:** Clinical Neurophysiology 1977; **Med School:** UCSD 1975; **Resid:** Pediatric Neurology, Parkland Meml Hosp 1979; **Fac Appt:** Prof N, Med Coll Wisc

Homer, Daniel MD [N] - **Spec Exp:** Stroke; **Hospital:** Evanston Hosp/NorthShore Univ Hlth Sys (page 67), Highland Park Hosp/NorthShore Univ Hlth Syst (page 67); **Address:** North Shore Med Grp, Neurology, 1000 Central St, Ste 615, Evanston, IL 60201; **Phone:** 847-570-2570; **Board Cert:** Neurology 1990; Vascular Neurology 2008; **Med School:** Northwestern Univ 1979; **Resid:** Neurology, Stanford Univ Hosp & Clins 1983; **Fellow:** Stroke, Mayo Clin 1984; **Fac Appt:** Asst Prof N, Univ Chicago-Pritzker Sch Med

Josephson, David A MD [N] - **Spec Exp:** Electromyography; Epilepsy; Stroke; **Hospital:** St. Vincent Indianapolis Hosp, Community Hosp N - Indianapolis; **Address:** JWM Neurology, 8402 Harcourt Rd, Ste 615, Indianapolis, IN 46260; **Phone:** 317-806-6991; **Board Cert:** Neurology 2004; **Med School:** Indiana Univ 1971; **Resid:** Neurology, Univ MI Med Ctr 1973; Neurology, Indiana Univ Med Ctr 1975

Katirji, Bashar MD [N] - **Spec Exp:** Neuromuscular Disorders; **Hospital:** UH Case Med Ctr; **Address:** UH Neurological Institute, 11100 Euclid Ave, Cleveland, OH 44106; **Phone:** 216-844-4854; **Board Cert:** Neurology 1985; Neuromuscular Medicine 2008; **Med School:** Syria 1977; **Resid:** Internal Medicine, King Faisal Spec Hosp 1980; Neurology, Univ Pittsburgh Med Ctr 1983; **Fellow:** Electromyography, Cleveland Clinic 1984; **Fac Appt:** Prof N, Case West Res Univ

Kincaid, John C MD [N] - **Spec Exp:** Neuromuscular Disorders; Electromyography; Pain-Facial; Peripheral Neuropathy; **Hospital:** IU Hlth Univ Hosp; **Address:** IU Health Physicians-Neurology, 355 W 16th St, Ste 3200, Indianapolis, IN 46202; **Phone:** 317-948-5450; **Board Cert:** Neurology 2010; Clinical Neurophysiology 2000; **Med School:** Indiana Univ 1975; **Resid:** Neurology, Indiana Univ Affil Hosp 1979; **Fellow:** Electromyography, Mayo Clinic 1980; **Fac Appt:** Prof N, Indiana Univ

Lisak, Robert P MD [N] - **Spec Exp:** Multiple Sclerosis; Myasthenia Gravis; Vasculitis; Demyelinating Neuropathy; **Hospital:** Harper Univ Hosp, Detroit Receiving Hospital; **Address:** 4201 St Antoine Blvd, UHC Bldg - Fl 8 - Ste A, Detroit, MI 48201; **Phone:** 313-745-4240; **Board Cert:** Neurology 1975; **Med School:** Columbia P&S 1965; **Resid:** Internal Medicine, Bronx Municipal Hosp-Einstein 1969; Neurology, Hosp Univ Penn 1972; **Fellow:** Allergy & Immunology, Hosp Univ Penn 1972; **Fac Appt:** Prof N, Wayne State Univ

Logan, William R MD [N] - **Spec Exp:** Stroke; Cerebrovascular Disease; **Hospital:** Mercy Hosp - St Louis; **Address:** St Johns Mercy Med Ctr, Div Neur, 621 S New Ballas Rd, Ste 5003-B, St Louis, MO 63141; **Phone:** 314-227-2020; **Board Cert:** Internal Medicine 1981; Neurology 1986; Vascular Neurology 2009; **Med School:** Univ Okla Coll Med 1978; **Resid:** Internal Medicine, Univ Missouri Hosps 1981; Neurology, Univ Texas Hlth Sci Ctr 1984

Luders, Hans MD/PhD [N] - **Spec Exp:** Epilepsy; **Hospital:** UH Case Med Ctr; **Address:** University Hosps-Case Med Ctr, 11100 Euclid Ave, Dept Neurology, Lakeside Bldg - Ste 3200, Cleveland, OH 44106; **Phone:** 216-844-3650; **Board Cert:** Neurology 1985; **Med School:** Chile 1965; **Resid:** Neurology, Neur Inst-Kyushu Univ 1971; **Fellow:** Neurophysiology, Mayo Grad Sch Med 1975; **Fac Appt:** Prof N, Cleveland Cl Coll Med/Case West Res

Maraganore, Demetrius MD [N] - **Spec Exp:** Movement Disorders; Parkinson's Disease; **Hospital:** Glenbrook Hosp/NorthShore Univ Hlth Syst (page 67); **Address:** Glenbrook Hosp, Neurology Dept, 2180 Pfingsten Rd, Ste 2000, Glenview, IL 60026; **Phone:** 847-570-2570; **Board Cert:** Neurology 1990; **Med School:** Northwestern Univ-Feinberg Sch Med 1985; **Resid:** Neurology, Mayo Clin 1989; **Fellow:** Movement Disorders, Natl Hosp Nervous Disorders 1990

Mesulam, Marsel MD [N] - **Spec Exp:** Alzheimer's Disease; Tourette's Syndrome; Dementia; **Hospital:** Northwestern Meml Hosp; **Address:** Cognitive Neurology & Alzheimer's Ctr, 320 E Superior St, Searle Bldg Fl 11 - rm 453, Chicago, IL 60611; **Phone:** 312-908-9339; **Board Cert:** Neurology 1977; **Med School:** Harvard Med Sch 1972; **Resid:** Neurology, Boston City Hosp 1976; **Fac Appt:** Prof N, Northwestern Univ

Mikkelsen, Tom MD [N] - **Spec Exp:** Brain Tumors; Gliomas; **Hospital:** Henry Ford Hosp; **Address:** Henry Ford Hospital, 2799 W Grand Blvd Fl K11, Detroit, MI 48202; **Phone:** 313-916-2241; **Board Cert:** Neurology 2008; **Med School:** Univ Calgary 1983; **Resid:** Internal Medicine, Calgary General Hosp 1985; Neurology, Montreal Neuro Inst 1988; **Fellow:** Neuro-Oncology, Royal Victoria Hosp 1990; Neuro-Oncology, Ludwig Inst for Cancer Rsch 1992; **Fac Appt:** Assoc Prof N, Case West Res Univ

Morris, John C MD [N] - **Spec Exp:** Alzheimer's Disease; **Hospital:** Barnes-Jewish Hosp; **Address:** Memory Diagnostic Ctr, 4921 Parkview Pl, Ste 6C, St Louis, MO 63110; **Phone:** 314-286-1967; **Board Cert:** Internal Medicine 1979; Neurology 1985; **Med School:** Univ Rochester 1974; **Resid:** Internal Medicine, Akron Genl Med Ctr 1979; Neurology, Cleveland Metro Genl Hosp 1982; **Fellow:** Neuropharmacology, Washington Univ 1985; **Fac Appt:** Prof N, Washington Univ, St Louis

Newman, Daniel S MD [N] - **Spec Exp:** Amyotrophic Lateral Sclerosis (ALS); Neuromuscular Disorders; **Hospital:** Henry Ford Hosp; **Address:** Henry Ford Hosp, 2799 W Grand Blvd Fl K11, Detroit, MI 48202; **Phone:** 313-916-2594; **Board Cert:** Neurology 1992; Neuromuscular Medicine 2008; **Med School:** Univ Mich Med Sch 1983; **Resid:** Neurology, Henry Ford Hosp 1988; **Fellow:** Electromyography, Mayo Clinic 1989; **Fac Appt:** Assoc Prof N, Wayne State Univ

Newton, Herbert B MD [N] - **Spec Exp:** Neuro-Oncology; Brain & Spinal Cord Tumors; Clinical Trials; **Hospital:** OSU Wexner Med Ctr, Arthur G James Cancer Hosp & Research Inst; **Address:** 320 W 10th Ave, Starling Loving Bldg, rm M410, Columbus, OH 43210; **Phone:** 614-293-4448; **Board Cert:** Neurology 1989; **Med School:** SUNY Buffalo 1984; **Resid:** Neurology, Univ Michigan Hosp 1988; **Fellow:** Neuro-Oncology, Meml Sloan-Kettering Cancer Ctr 1990; **Fac Appt:** Prof N, Ohio State Univ

Pascuzzi, Robert M MD [N] - **Spec Exp:** Neuromuscular Disorders; Amyotrophic Lateral Sclerosis (ALS); Myasthenia Gravis; Post Polio Syndrome; **Hospital:** IU Hlth Univ Hosp, Wishard Hlth Srvs; **Address:** IU Health Physicians- Neurology, 11725 Illinois St, Ste 275, Indianapolis, IN 46032; **Phone:** 317-948-5450; **Board Cert:** Neurology 2004; **Med School:** Indiana Univ 1979; **Resid:** Neurology, Univ Va Med Ctr 1983; **Fellow:** Neuromuscular Medicine, Univ Virginia 1985; **Fac Appt:** Prof N, Indiana Univ

Perlmutter, Joel S MD [N] - **Spec Exp:** Parkinson's Disease; Movement Disorders; Huntington's Disease; **Hospital:** Barnes-Jewish Hosp; **Address:** 660 S Euclid Ave, Box 8111, St Louis, MO 63110; **Phone:** 314-362-6908; **Board Cert:** Neurology 1985; **Med School:** Univ MO-Columbia Sch Med 1979; **Resid:** Neurology, Barnes Hosp-Wash Univ 1983; **Fellow:** Movement Disorders, Barnes Hosp-Wash Univ 1984; **Fac Appt:** Prof N, Washington Univ, St Louis

Pestronk, Alan MD [N] - **Spec Exp:** Neuromuscular Disorders; Peripheral Neuropathy; **Hospital:** Barnes-Jewish Hosp; **Address:** Washington Univ Sch Med, Dept Neurology, Div Neuromuscular Disorders, 660 S Euclid Ave, Box 8111, St Louis, MO 63110; **Phone:** 314-362-6981; **Board Cert:** Neurology 1978; Neuromuscular Medicine 2008; **Med School:** Johns Hopkins Univ 1970; **Resid:** Neurology, Johns Hopkins Hosp 1974; **Fellow:** Neuromuscular Medicine, Johns Hopkins Hosp 1977; **Fac Appt:** Prof NPath, Washington Univ, St Louis

Petersen, Ronald C MD/PhD [N] - **Spec Exp:** Alzheimer's Disease; Cognitive Impairment/Mild; **Hospital:** Mayo Med Ctr & Clin - Rochester; **Address:** Mayo Clinic, Dept Neurology, 200 First St SW, Rochester, MN 55905; **Phone:** 507-266-5800; **Board Cert:** Neurology 1986; **Med School:** Mayo Med Sch 1980; **Resid:** Neurology, Mayo Clinic 1984; **Fellow:** Behavioral Neurology, Beth Israel Med Ctr 1986; **Fac Appt:** Prof N, Mayo Med Sch

Puduvalli, Vinay K MD [N] - **Spec Exp:** Neuro-Oncology; Brain Tumors; Gliomas; **Hospital:** Ohio State U Hosp East; **Address:** OSU Arthur James Cancer Hosp, 320 W 10th Ave, Starling Loving Hall, Ste M410, Columbus, OH 43210; **Phone:** 614-293-4448; **Board Cert:** Neurology 2009; **Med School:** India 1989; **Resid:** Neurology, Univ Tex Affil Hosp 1996; **Fellow:** Neuro-Oncology, UT MD Anderson Cancer Ctr 1998; **Fac Appt:** Prof N, Ohio State Univ

Reder, Anthony T MD [N] - **Spec Exp:** Multiple Sclerosis; Tetanus; Myasthenia Gravis; Reflex Sympathetic Dystrophy (RSD); **Hospital:** Univ of Chicago Med; **Address:** Univ Chicago- Dept Neurology, 5758 S Maryland Ave, MC 9017, Chicago, IL 60637; **Phone:** 773-702-6222; **Board Cert:** Neurology 1984; **Med School:** Univ Mich Med Sch 1978; **Resid:** Neurology, Univ Minn Hosps 1982; **Fellow:** Neurological Immunology, Univ Chicago Med Ctr 1984; **Fac Appt:** Assoc Prof N, Univ Chicago-Pritzker Sch Med

Reed, Robert L MD [N] - **Spec Exp:** Multiple Sclerosis; Stroke; **Hospital:** Good Samaritan Hosp - Cincinnati; **Address:** 111 Wellington Pl, Cincinnati, OH 45219; **Phone:** 513-241-2370; **Board Cert:** Neurology 1975; **Med School:** Univ Cincinnati 1966; **Resid:** Internal Medicine, Mayo Grad Sch Med 1970; Neurology, Mayo Grad Sch Med 1973

Richerson, George B MD/PhD [N] - **Hospital:** Univ Iowa Hosp & Clins, Iowa City VA Hlth Care Sys; **Address:** UIHC Dept Neurology, 200 Hawkins Drive, Iowa City, IA 52242; **Phone:** 319-356-4296; **Board Cert:** Neurology 1993; **Med School:** Univ Iowa Coll Med 1984; **Resid:** Neurology, Yale-New Haven Hosp 1990; **Fac Appt:** Prof N, Univ Iowa Coll Med

Rogers, Lisa R DO [N] - **Spec Exp:** Neuro-Oncology; Brain Tumors; Brain Radiation Toxicity; **Hospital:** UH Case Med Ctr; **Address:** UH Case Med Ctr, Dept Neuro, 11100 Euclid Ave, Cleveland, OH 44106; **Phone:** 216-844-5160; **Board Cert:** Neurology 1982; **Med School:** Kirksville Coll Osteo Med 1976; **Resid:** Neurology, Cleveland Clinic 1980; **Fellow:** Neuro-Oncology, Meml-Sloan Kettering Cancer Ctr 1982; **Fac Appt:** Prof N, Case West Res Univ

Roos, Karen L MD [N] - **Spec Exp:** Infections-Neurologic; Encephalitis; Vascular Disease; Neurofibromatosis; **Hospital:** IU Hlth Univ Hosp, Wishard Hlth Srvs; **Address:** IU Health Physicians-Neurology, 355 W 16th St, Ste 3200, Indianapolis, IN 46202; **Phone:** 317-963-7441; **Board Cert:** Neurology 1986; **Med School:** Hahnemann Univ 1981; **Resid:** Neurology, Univ Virginia Med Ctr 1985; **Fac Appt:** Prof N, Indiana Univ

Roos, Raymond MD [N] - **Spec Exp:** Amyotrophic Lateral Sclerosis (ALS); Multiple Sclerosis; Neuromuscular Disorders; **Hospital:** Univ of Chicago Med; **Address:** Univ Chicago, Dept Neurology, 5841 S Maryland Ave, Chicago, IL 60637; **Phone:** 773-702-5659; **Board Cert:** Neurology 1976; **Med School:** SUNY Downstate 1968; **Resid:** Neurology, Johns Hopkins Hosp 1974; **Fellow:** Neurology, Natl Inst Neur Dis & Stroke 1971; Neurological Viral Immunology, Johns Hopkins Hosp 1976; **Fac Appt:** Prof N, Univ Chicago-Pritzker Sch Med

Rosenfeld, Steven S MD [N] - **Spec Exp:** Brain Tumors; Gliomas; Neuro-Oncology; **Hospital:** Cleveland Clin (page 55); **Address:** Cleveland Clinic, Burkhardt Brain Tumor Ctr, 9500 Euclid Ave, MC S73, Cleveland, OH 44195; **Phone:** 216-444-4461; **Board Cert:** Neurology 1994; **Med School:** Northwestern Univ 1985; **Resid:** Neurology, Duke Univ Med Ctr 1989; **Fellow:** Neuro-Oncology, Duke Univ Med Ctr 1990; **Fac Appt:** Prof N, Cleveland Cl Coll Med/Case West Res

Rubin, Susan M MD [N] - **Spec Exp:** Multiple Sclerosis in Women; Epilepsy in Pregnancy; Headache in Women; Migraine in Women; **Hospital:** Glenbrook Hosp/NorthShore Univ Hlth Syst (page 67); **Address:** Glenbrook Hosp, Neurology Dept, 2180 Pfingsten Rd, Ste 2000, Glenview, IL 60026; **Phone:** 847-503-2000; **Board Cert:** Neurology 2006; **Med School:** Univ IL Coll Med 1988; **Resid:** Neurology, Northwestern Meml Hosp 1993; **Fellow:** Neurophysiology, Northwestern Meml Hosp 1994; **Fac Appt:** Asst Clin Prof N, Univ Chicago-Pritzker Sch Med

Saper, Joel R MD [N] - **Spec Exp:** Headache; Pain-Chronic after Head Injury; Migraine; **Hospital:** Chelsea Comm Hosp; **Address:** Michigan Head Pain & Neurological Inst, 3120 Professional Drive, Ann Arbor, MI 48104; **Phone:** 734-677-6000; **Board Cert:** Neurology 1975; Headache Medicine ; **Med School:** Univ IL Coll Med 1969; **Resid:** Neurology, Univ Michigan Hosps 1973; **Fac Appt:** Clin Prof N, Mich State Univ

Siddique, Teepu MD [N] - **Spec Exp:** Amyotrophic Lateral Sclerosis (ALS); Muscular Dystrophy; Neurogenetics; Spasticity Management; **Hospital:** Northwestern Meml Hosp; **Address:** 675 N St Clair St, Galter Bldg Fl 20 - Ste 100, Chicago, IL 60611; **Phone:** 312-695-7950; **Board Cert:** Neurology 1980; **Med School:** Pakistan 1973; **Resid:** Neurology, UMDNJ Affil Hosp 1979; **Fellow:** Electromyography, Hosp Special Surg 1980; Neuromuscular Disease, Natl Inst Hlth 1981; **Fac Appt:** Prof N, Northwestern Univ

Sila, Cathy A MD [N] - **Spec Exp:** Cerebrovascular Disease; Stroke-Young Adults; **Hospital:** UH Case Med Ctr; **Address:** University Hospitals - Case Med Ctr, Dept of Neurology, 11100 Euclid Ave, Cleveland, OH 44106-5040; **Phone:** 216-844-3192; **Board Cert:** Neurology 1986; Vascular Neurology 2005; **Med School:** Case West Res Univ 1981; **Resid:** Neurology, Cleveland Clin 1983; Neurology, Mayo Clin 1985; **Fellow:** Vascular Neurology, Cleveland Clin 1986; Research, Cleveland Clin 1986; **Fac Appt:** Prof N, Case West Res Univ

Swanson, Jerry W MD [N] - **Spec Exp:** Headache; Migraine; **Hospital:** Mayo Med Ctr & Clin - Rochester; **Address:** Mayo Clinic, Dept Neurology, 200 First St SW, Rochester, MN 55905-0001; **Phone:** 507-538-1036; **Board Cert:** Neurology 1984; Headache Medicine 2006; **Med School:** Northwestern Univ 1977; **Resid:** Neurology, Mayo Clinic 1982; **Fellow:** Electroencephalography, Mayo Clinic 1983; **Fac Appt:** Prof N, Mayo Med Sch

Vick, Nicholas A MD [N] - **Spec Exp:** Brain Tumors; Neuro-Oncology; **Hospital:** Evanston Hosp/NorthShore Univ Hlth Sys (page 67); **Address:** Evanston Kellog Cancer Ctr, 2650 Ridge Ave, Evanston, IL 60201; **Phone:** 847-570-1808; **Board Cert:** Neurology 1971; **Med School:** Univ Chicago-Pritzker Sch Med 1965; **Resid:** Neurology, Univ Chicago Hosps 1968; **Fellow:** Neurology, Natl Inst Hlth 1970; **Fac Appt:** Prof N, Univ Chicago-Pritzker Sch Med

Vitek, Jerrold Lee MD/PhD [N] - **Spec Exp:** Parkinson's Disease/Movement Disorders; Tremor & Dystonia; Deep Brain Stimulation; **Hospital:** Univ Minn Med Ctr, Fairview - West Bank Campus; **Address:** Univ Minn, Dept Neurology, 516 Delaware St SE, First Floor, Clinic 1A, Minneapolis, MN 55455; **Phone:** 612-626-6688; **Board Cert:** Neurology 1992; **Med School:** Univ Minn 1984; **Resid:** Neurology, Johns Hopkins Hosp 1988; **Fac Appt:** Prof N, Univ Minn

Windebank, Anthony J MD [N] - **Spec Exp:** Peripheral Neuropathy; Amyotrophic Lateral Sclerosis (ALS); Multiple Sclerosis; **Hospital:** Mayo Med Ctr & Clin - Rochester; **Address:** Mayo Clinic, Dept Neurology, 200 First St SW, Rochester, MN 55905; **Phone:** 507-266-5800; **Board Cert:** Neurology 1982; **Med School:** England, UK 1974; **Resid:** Internal Medicine, Radcliffe Infirm 1977; Neurology, Mayo Clin 1981; **Fellow:** Neurology, Mayo Clin 1982; **Fac Appt:** Prof N, Mayo Med Sch

Wright, Robert B MD [N] - **Spec Exp:** Myasthenia Gravis; Migraine; **Hospital:** Rush Univ Med Ctr; **Address:** 1725 W Harrison St, Ste 1118, Chicago, IL 60612-3841; **Phone:** 312-942-5936; **Board Cert:** Neurology 1988; **Med School:** Univ IL Coll Med 1982; **Resid:** Neurology, Rush Presby-St Luke's Med Ctr 1986; **Fellow:** Neuromuscular Medicine, Rush Presby-St Luke's Med Ctr 1987; **Fac Appt:** Asst Prof N, Rush Med Coll

Zimnowodzki, Simon MD [N] - **Spec Exp:** Electromyography; Amyotrophic Lateral Sclerosis (ALS); Myasthenia Gravis; Nerve Injuries; **Hospital:** Rush Univ Med Ctr, Stroger Hosp of Cook Co; **Address:** 1901 W Harrison St, Chicago, IL 60612; **Phone:** 312-864-7280; **Board Cert:** Neurology 1984; Clinical Neurophysiology 2011; Neuromuscular Medicine 2008; **Med School:** Loyola Univ-Stritch Sch Med 1978; **Resid:** Neurology, Univ MI Hosp 1982; **Fellow:** Neuromuscular Disease, Univ WI Hosps & Clinics 1983; **Fac Appt:** Assoc Prof N, Rush Med Coll

Great Plains and Mountains

Barohn, Richard J MD [N] - **Spec Exp:** Peripheral Neuropathy; Myasthenia Gravis; Amyotrophic Lateral Sclerosis (ALS); Guillain-Barre Syndrome; **Hospital:** Univ of Kansas Hosp; **Address:** Univ Kansas Hosp, Dept Neurology, 3599 Rainbow Blvd, MS 2012, Kansas City, KS 66160; **Phone:** 913-588-6820; **Board Cert:** Neurology 1987; Clinical Neurophysiology 2004; Neuromuscular Medicine 2008; **Med School:** Univ MO-Kansas City 1980; **Resid:** Neurology, Lackland AFB 1985

Bromberg, Mark B MD/PhD [N] - **Spec Exp:** Peripheral Neuropathy; Neuromuscular Disorders; **Hospital:** Univ Utah Hlth Care; **Address:** 175 N Medical Drive, Clinical Neurosciences Ctr, Salt Lake City, UT 84132; **Phone:** 801-585-7575; **Board Cert:** Neurology 1988; Clinical Neurophysiology 2012; **Med School:** Univ Mich Med Sch 1982; **Resid:** Neurology, Univ Mich Med Ctr 1986; **Fellow:** Electromyography, Univ Mich Med Ctr 1987; Neuromuscular Disease, Univ Mich Med Ctr 1987; **Fac Appt:** Prof N, Univ Utah

Filley, Christopher M MD [N] - **Spec Exp:** White Matter Disorders; Behavioral Neurology; Neuro-Pathology; Alzheimer's Disease; **Hospital:** Univ Colorado Hosp, VA Eastern CO Health Care Sys-Denver; **Address:** Univ CO Hosp-Neurology Clinic, 12631 E 17th Ave, AO 1 Bldg, Box B185, Aurora, CO 80045; **Phone:** 720-848-2080; **Board Cert:** Neurology 1984; Behavioral Neurology & Neuropsychiatry 2006; **Med School:** Johns Hopkins Univ 1979; **Resid:** Neurology, Univ Colorado Hosp 1983; **Fellow:** Behavioral Neurology, Boston VA Hosp 1984; **Fac Appt:** Prof N, Univ Colorado

Gilden, Donald H MD [N] - **Spec Exp:** Multiple Sclerosis; Infections-CNS; **Hospital:** Univ Colorado Hosp; **Address:** UCH-Neurology Clinic, Anschutz Outpatient Pavilion, 1635 N Aurora Ct, Ste 4200, MS F727, Aurora, CO 80045; **Phone:** 720-848-2080; **Board Cert:** Neurology 1970; **Med School:** Univ MD Sch Med 1963; **Resid:** Neurology, Univ Chicago Med Ctr 1967; **Fellow:** Neurovirology, Johns Hopkins Hosp 1971; **Fac Appt:** Prof N, Univ Colorado

Lane, Judy C MD [N] - **Spec Exp:** Headache; Migraine; **Hospital:** Swedish Med Ctr - Denver; **Address:** Head Pain Ctr, 3601 S Clarkson St, Ste 210, Englewood, CO 80113; **Phone:** 303-781-5505; **Board Cert:** Neurology 1993; Headache Medicine ; **Med School:** Univ Colorado 1987; **Resid:** Neurology, Univ N Carolina Med Ctr 1991; **Fellow:** Neurological Rehabilitation, Rocky Mountain Mult Sclerosis Ctr 1992; **Fac Appt:** Assoc Prof FMed, Univ Colorado

Pulst, Stefan M MD [N] - **Spec Exp:** Parkinson's Disease; Multiple Sclerosis; **Hospital:** Univ Utah Hlth Care; **Address:** University of Utah, Clinical Neurosciences Ctr, 175 North Medical Drive E, Salt Lake City, UT 84132; **Phone:** 801-585-7575; **Board Cert:** Neurology 1990; **Med School:** Germany 1979; **Resid:** Neurology, Hannover Med Sch 1983; Neurology, Longwood/Harvard Program; **Fellow:** Neurological Biology, UCSF Med Ctr; **Fac Appt:** Prof Med, Univ Utah

Ringel, Steven P MD [N] - **Spec Exp:** Neuromuscular Disorders; **Hospital:** Univ Colorado Hosp; **Address:** Univ Colorado Hosp, Neuromuscular Dept, 12631 E 17th Ave, MS B185, Aurora, CO 80045; **Phone:** 303-724-2209; **Board Cert:** Neurology 1974; **Med School:** Univ Mich Med Sch 1968; **Resid:** Neurology, Rush-Presby-St Lukes Med Ctr 1972; **Fellow:** Neurology, Natl Inst Neuro Dis-NIH 1976; **Fac Appt:** Prof N, Univ Colorado

Sabo, Tonia M MD [N] - **Spec Exp:** Headache; Migraine; Concussion; Pediatric Neurology; **Address:** Vail Headache & Concussion, 105 Edwards Village Blvd, Ste 102A, Edwards, CO 81632; **Phone:** 303-439-7777; **Board Cert:** Child Neurology 2009; Headache Medicine ; **Med School:** Univ Colorado 1993; **Resid:** Child Neurology, Univ Colorado Hlth Sci Ctr 1997; **Fellow:** Headache, Univ Colorado Hlth Sci Ctr 1998

Strom, Laura A MD [N] - **Spec Exp:** Epilepsy/Seizure Disorders; **Hospital:** Univ Colorado Hosp; **Address:** UCH-Neurology Clinic, Anschutz Outpatient Pavilion, 1635 N Aurora Ct, Ste 4200, MS F727, Aurora, CO 80045; **Phone:** 720-848-2080; **Board Cert:** Neurology 2007; **Med School:** Penn State Coll Med 1997; **Resid:** Neurology, Univ CO Hlth Sci Ctr 2002; **Fellow:** Epilepsy, Univ CO Hlth Sci Ctr 2004; **Fac Appt:** Asst Prof N, Univ Colorado

Vollmer, Timothy L MD [N] - **Spec Exp:** Multiple Sclerosis; Myasthenia Gravis; Vasculitis of the Nervous System; Stroke; **Hospital:** Univ Colorado Hosp; **Address:** Univ Colorado Dept Neurology, 12631 E 17th Ave, Aurora, CO 80045; **Phone:** 720-848-2080; **Board Cert:** Neurology 1991; **Med School:** Stanford Univ 1983; **Resid:** Neurology, Stanford Univ Hosp 1987; **Fellow:** Neurological Immunology, Stanford Univ Hosp 1986; **Fac Appt:** Prof N, Univ Colorado

Southwest

Ahern, Geoffrey L MD/PhD [N] - **Spec Exp:** Behavioral Neurology; Dementia; Alzheimer's Disease; **Hospital:** Univ Arizona Med Ctr-Univ Campus; **Address:** Univ Arizona, Dept Neurology, 1501 N Campbell Ave, rm 7319, Tucson, AZ 85724; **Phone:** 520-626-6524; **Board Cert:** Neurology 1992; Behavioral Neurology & Neuropsychiatry 2006; **Med School:** Yale Univ 1984; **Resid:** Neurology, Boston Univ Affil Hosps 1988; **Fellow:** Behavioral Neurology, Beth Israel Deaconess Med Ctr 1990; **Fac Appt:** Prof N, Univ Ariz Coll Med

Alberts, Mark J MD [N] - **Spec Exp:** Stroke/Cerebrovascular Disease; **Hospital:** UT Southwestern Med Ctr at Dallas; **Address:** Neurology Clinic, 5303 Harry Hines Blvd, Dallas, TX 75390; **Phone:** 214-645-8800; **Board Cert:** Neurology 1987; Vascular Neurology 2005; **Med School:** Tufts Univ 1982; **Resid:** Neurology, Duke Univ Med Ctr 1986; **Fellow:** Cerebrovascular Disease, Duke Univ Med Ctr 1987; **Fac Appt:** Prof N, Univ Tex SW, Dallas

Coull, Bruce M MD [N] - **Spec Exp:** Stroke; **Hospital:** Univ Arizona Med Ctr-South Campus; **Address:** Univ of Arizona-Neurology, 2800 E Ajo Way UPH Clinic Bldg, Tucson, AZ 85713; **Phone:** 520-874-2700; **Board Cert:** Neurology 1979; Vascular Neurology 2005; **Med School:** Univ Pittsburgh 1972; **Resid:** Neurology, Stanford Univ Med Ctr 1976; **Fellow:** Vascular Neurology, Stanford Univ Med Ctr 1978; **Fac Appt:** Prof N, Univ Ariz Coll Med

Dodick, David W MD [N] - **Spec Exp:** Headache; Migraine; **Hospital:** Mayo Clinic - Phoenix, Mayo Clinic - Scottsdale; **Address:** Mayo Clin - Dept Neurology, 5777 E Mayo Blvd, 5e, Phoenix, AZ 85054; **Phone:** 480-301-8100; **Board Cert:** Neurology 2006; Vascular Neurology 2005; Headache Medicine 2006; **Med School:** Dalhousie Univ 1990; **Resid:** Neurology, Mayo Clin 1994; **Fellow:** Headache, Sunnybrook Hlth Sci Ctr 1996; **Fac Appt:** Prof N, Mayo Med Sch

Doody, Rachelle S MD/PhD [N] - **Spec Exp:** Alzheimer's Disease; Memory Disorders; **Hospital:** Methodist Hosp - Houston; **Address:** BCM, Alzheimer's Disease-Neurology, 1977 Butler Blvd, Ste E5.101, Houston, TX 77030; **Phone:** 713-798-4734; **Board Cert:** Neurology 1988; **Med School:** Baylor Coll Med 1983; **Resid:** Neurology, Baylor Affil Hosp 1987; **Fac Appt:** Prof N, Baylor Coll Med

Ferrendelli, James A MD [N] - **Spec Exp:** Epilepsy/Seizure Disorders; Dementia; **Hospital:** Meml Hermann Hosp - Texas Med Ctr; **Address:** UT Neurology Physician Practice, 6410 Fannin St, UTHSC Bldg, Ste 1014, Houston, TX 77030; **Phone:** 832-325-7080; **Board Cert:** Neurology 1973; **Med School:** Univ Colorado 1962; **Resid:** Neurology, Cleveland Metro Genl Hosp 1968; **Fellow:** Neuropharmacology, Washington Univ Med Sch 1971; **Fac Appt:** Prof N, Univ Tex, Houston

Frohman, Elliot M MD/PhD [N] - **Spec Exp:** Multiple Sclerosis; Neuro-Ophthalmology; **Hospital:** UT Southwestern Med Ctr at Dallas, Parkland Hlth & Hosp Sys; **Address:** UT Southwestern Med Ctr, Neurology Dept, 5323 Harry Hines Blvd, Dallas, TX 75390; **Phone:** 214-645-8800; **Board Cert:** Neurology 2005; **Med School:** UC Irvine 1990; **Resid:** Neurology, Johns Hopkins Hosp 1994; **Fellow:** Neuro-Ophthalmology, Johns Hopkins Hosp 1995; **Fac Appt:** Prof N, Univ Tex SW, Dallas

Gilbert, Mark R MD [N] - **Spec Exp:** Brain Tumors; Neuro-Oncology; **Hospital:** UT MD Anderson Canc Ctr; **Address:** UT MD Anderson Canc Ctr, 1515 Holcombe Blvd, Unit 431, Houston, TX 77030; **Phone:** 713-792-4008; **Board Cert:** Internal Medicine 1985; Neurology 1990; **Med School:** Johns Hopkins Univ 1982; **Resid:** Internal Medicine, Johns Hopkins Hosp 1985; Neurology, Johns Hopkins Hosp 1988; **Fellow:** Neuro-Oncology, Johns Hopkins Hosp 1988; **Fac Appt:** Prof N, Univ Tex, Houston

Grotta, James C MD [N] - **Spec Exp:** Stroke; **Hospital:** Meml Hermann Hosp - Texas Med Ctr; **Address:** UT Phys Neurology, 6410 Fannin St, Ste 1014, Houston, TX 77030; **Phone:** 832-325-7080; **Board Cert:** Neurology 1978; Vascular Neurology 2005; **Med School:** Univ VA Sch Med 1971; **Resid:** Neurology, Univ CO Hosp 1977; **Fellow:** Diagnostic Radiology, Mass Genl Hosp 1979; **Fac Appt:** Prof N, Univ Tex, Houston

Harati, Yadollah MD [N] - **Spec Exp:** Neuromuscular Disorders; Amyotrophic Lateral Sclerosis (ALS); Myasthenia Gravis; **Hospital:** St. Luke's Episcopal Hosp-Houston; **Address:** BCM, Neurology Dept, 6550 Fannin St, Smith Tower, Ste 1801, Houston, TX 77030; **Phone:** 713-798-7411; **Board Cert:** Neurology 1978; Neuromuscular Medicine 2011; **Med School:** Iran 1970; **Resid:** Neurology, Univ Nebraska Med Ctr 1974; Neurology, Baylor Affil Hosp 1975; **Fellow:** Neuromuscular Disease, Baylor Affil Hosp 1976; **Fac Appt:** Prof N, Baylor Coll Med

Jankovic, Joseph MD [N] - **Spec Exp:** Movement Disorders; Parkinson's Disease; Tourette's Syndrome; **Hospital:** Methodist Hosp - Houston; **Address:** BCM, Parkinson Disease Ctr, 6550 Fannin St, Smith Tower, Ste 1801, Houston, TX 77030; **Phone:** 713-798-5998; **Board Cert:** Neurology 1979; **Med School:** Univ Ariz Coll Med 1973; **Resid:** Neurology, NY-Presby/Columbia Univ Med Ctr 1977; **Fac Appt:** Prof N, Baylor Coll Med

Kent, Thomas A MD [N] - **Spec Exp:** Stroke; Neuro-Psychiatry; Cerebrovascular Disease; **Hospital:** DeBakey VA Med Ctr-Houston; **Address:** Debakey VA Med Ctr, Neurology Dept, 2002 Holcombe Blvd, MC 127, Houston, TX 77030; **Phone:** 713-794-7393; **Board Cert:** Psychiatry 1993; Neurology 2006; **Med School:** Univ Kansas 1979; **Resid:** Psychiatry, Univ Kansas Hosp 1983; Neurology, UT Med Branch 1985; **Fellow:** Psychopharmacology, Univ Kansas Hosp 1983; Cerebrovascular Disease, Univ Kansas Hosp 1983; **Fac Appt:** Prof N, Baylor Coll Med

Labiner, David M MD [N] - **Spec Exp:** Epilepsy; Seizure Disorders; **Hospital:** Univ Arizona Med Ctr-Univ Campus, Yuma Regl Med Ctr; **Address:** 707 N Alvernon Way, Tucson, AZ 85711; **Phone:** 520-694-8888; **Board Cert:** Neurology 1992; **Med School:** Med Coll GA 1984; **Resid:** Neurology, NY-Presby/Columbia Univ Med Ctr 1988; **Fellow:** Epilepsy, Duke Univ Hosp 1989; **Fac Appt:** Prof N, Univ Ariz Coll Med

Nicholl, Jeffrey S MD [N] - **Spec Exp:** Seizure Disorders; Epilepsy; **Hospital:** Tulane Med Ctr; **Address:** Tulane Med Ctr, Dept Neurology, 1430 Tulane Ave, Ste 8065, New Orleans, LA 70112; **Phone:** 504-988-5030; **Board Cert:** Neurology 2009; Psychiatry 2011; Clinical Neurophysiology 2011; Emergency Medicine 2004; **Med School:** Georgetown Univ 1974; **Resid:** Psychiatry, UCLA Neuro Psyc Inst 1979; Neurology, Tulane Univ Affil Hosp 1997; **Fellow:** Clinical Neurophysiology, Tulane Univ Affil Hosp 1998; Epilepsy, UCLA Ronald Reagan Med Ctr 2000; **Fac Appt:** Assoc Prof N, Tulane Univ

Oommen, Kalarickal J MD [N] - **Spec Exp:** Epilepsy; **Hospital:** Covenant Med Ctr; **Address:** Covenant Hlth, Neurology Dept, 3506 21st St, Ste 400, Lubbock, TX 79410; **Phone:** 806-725-4115; **Board Cert:** Neurology 1983; **Med School:** India 1973; **Resid:** Psychiatry, AZ Hlth Sci Ctr 1979; Neurology, AZ Hlth Sci Ctr 1982; **Fellow:** Electroencephalography, Med Coll GA Affil Hosp 1983; **Fac Appt:** Prof N, Texas Tech Univ

Shapiro, William R MD [N] - **Spec Exp:** Neuro-Oncology; **Hospital:** St. Joseph's Hosp & Med Ctr - Phoenix; **Address:** Barrow Neurological Institute, 500 W Thomas Rd, Ste 300, Phoenix, AZ 85013; **Phone:** 602-406-6262; **Board Cert:** Neurology 1969; **Med School:** UCSF 1961; **Resid:** Neurology, NY Hosp-Cornell Med Ctr 1966; **Fellow:** Neuro-Oncology, Natl Inst Health 1969; **Fac Appt:** Prof N, Univ Ariz Coll Med

Sheikh, Kazim A MD [N] - **Spec Exp:** Amyotrophic Lateral Sclerosis (ALS); Peripheral Nerve Disorders; Neuromuscular Disorders; **Hospital:** Meml Hermann Hosp - Texas Med Ctr; **Address:** UT Phys Neurology, 6410 Fannin St, Ste 1014, Houston, TX 77030; **Phone:** 832-325-7080; **Board Cert:** Neurology 1998; **Med School:** Pakistan 1987; **Resid:** Neurology, Mayo Hosp 1991; Neurology, Neurological Inst 1996; **Fellow:** Peripheral Nerve Disorders, Johns Hopkins Hosp 1997; **Fac Appt:** Prof N, Univ Tex, Houston

Suarez, Jose MD [N] - **Spec Exp:** Stroke; Critical Care; **Hospital:** St. Luke's Episcopal Hosp-Houston; **Address:** BCM, Neurology Dept, 6550 Fannin St, Smith Tower, Ste 1801, Houston, TX 77030; **Phone:** 713-798-7411; **Board Cert:** Neurology 2008; Vascular Neurology 2005; **Med School:** Colombia 1988; **Resid:** Neurology, Univ Hosp 1996; **Fellow:** Neurocritical Care, Johns Hopkins Hosp 1998; **Fac Appt:** Assoc Prof N, Baylor Coll Med

Wolinsky, Jerry S MD [N] - **Spec Exp:** Multiple Sclerosis; Clinical Trials; **Hospital:** Meml Hermann Hosp - Texas Med Ctr; **Address:** UT Phys Neurology, 6410 Fannin St, Ste 1014, Houston, TX 77030; **Phone:** 832-325-7080; **Board Cert:** Neurology 1975; **Med School:** Univ IL Coll Med 1969; **Resid:** Neurology, UCSF Med Ctr 1973; **Fellow:** Neuropathology, VA Hosp 1975; **Fac Appt:** Prof N, Univ Tex, Houston

Yung, W.K. Alfred MD [N] - **Spec Exp:** Neuro-Oncology; Brain Tumors; **Hospital:** UT MD Anderson Canc Ctr; **Address:** UT MD Anderson Canc Ctr, 1515 Holcombe Blvd, Unit 431, Houston, TX 77030-4017; **Phone:** 713-794-1285; **Board Cert:** Neurology 1980; **Med School:** Univ Chicago-Pritzker Sch Med 1975; **Resid:** Neurology, UCSD Med Ctr 1978; **Fellow:** Neuro-Oncology, Meml Sloan-Kettering Canc Ctr 1981; **Fac Appt:** Prof N, Univ Tex, Houston

West Coast and Pacific

Adornato, Bruce T MD [N] - **Spec Exp:** Stroke; Peripheral Neuropathy; Sleep Disorders/Apnea; **Hospital:** Stanford Univ Hosp & Clins, VA Hlth Care Sys - Palo Alto; **Address:** 326 Bryant St, Palo Alto, CA 94301; **Phone:** 650-324-4300; **Board Cert:** Internal Medicine 1975; Neurology 1978; **Med School:** UCSD 1972; **Resid:** Internal Medicine, UCSF-Moffitt Hosp 1974; Neurology, UCSF-Moffitt Hosp 1976; **Fellow:** Neurology, Natl Inst Hlth 1978; **Fac Appt:** Clin Prof N, Stanford Univ

Albers, Gregory W MD [N] - **Spec Exp:** Cerebrovascular Disease; Stroke; Clinical Trials; **Hospital:** Stanford Univ Hosp & Clins; **Address:** Stanford Univ Med Ctr, Dept Neurology, 300 Pasteur Drive, Ste A301, MC 5325, Stanford, CA 94305; **Phone:** 650-723-4448; **Board Cert:** Neurology 1990; Vascular Neurology 2008; **Med School:** UCSD 1984; **Resid:** Neurology, Stanford Univ Med Ctr 1988; **Fellow:** Stroke, Stanford Univ Med Ctr 1989; **Fac Appt:** Prof N, Stanford Univ

Aminoff, Michael J MD [N] - **Spec Exp:** Movement Disorders; Parkinson's Disease; **Hospital:** UCSF Med Ctr; **Address:** UCSF Med Ctr, Dept Neurology, 400 Parnassus Ave Fl 8 - rm M-795, San Francisco, CA 94143-0114; **Phone:** 415-353-2273; **Board Cert:** Neurology 2004; **Med School:** England, UK 1965; **Resid:** Internal Medicine, Univ London Hosps 1970; Neurology, Middlesex Hosp/Natl Hosp Queen Sq 1972; **Fac Appt:** Prof N, UCSF

Becker, Kyra J MD [N] - **Spec Exp:** Stroke/Cerebrovascular Disease; Neuro-Immunology; Stroke-Young Adults; Critical Care; **Hospital:** Harborview Med Ctr; **Address:** Harborview Med Ctr, 325 9th Ave, Box 359721, Seattle, WA 98104; **Phone:** 206-744-1712; **Board Cert:** Neurology 2006; Vascular Neurology 2005; **Med School:** Duke Univ 1989; **Resid:** Neurology, Johns Hopkins Hosp 1993; **Fellow:** Critical Care Neurology, Johns Hopkins Hosp 1995; Stroke, Natl Inst Neurol Disorders 1996; **Fac Appt:** Prof N, Univ Wash

Bruno, Michiko K MD [N] - **Spec Exp:** Movement Disorders; Parkinson's Disease; Tourette's Syndrome; **Hospital:** Queen's Med Ctr - Honolulu; **Address:** Queens Physicians Office, 1380 Lusitana St, Ste 705, Honolulu, HI 96813; **Phone:** 808-537-9105; **Board Cert:** Neurology 2013; **Med School:** Japan 1996; **Resid:** Neurology, NY Presby-Cornell Med Ctr 2002; **Fellow:** Movement Disorders, Natl Inst Hlth 2004

Chamberlain, Marc C MD [N] - **Spec Exp:** Brain Tumors; Neuro-Oncology; Clinical Trials; **Hospital:** Univ Wash Med Ctr; **Address:** Seattle Cancer Care Alliance, 825 Eastlake Ave E, Seattle, WA 98109; **Phone:** 206-288-8280; **Board Cert:** Pediatrics 1985; Child Neurology 1989; **Med School:** Columbia P&S 1977; **Resid:** Pediatrics, Montefiore Med Ctr 1981; **Fellow:** Neurology, UCLA Med Ctr 1983; Neuro-Oncology, UCSF Med Ctr 1986; **Fac Appt:** Prof N, Univ Wash

Charles, Andrew C MD [N] - **Spec Exp:** Headache; Migraine; **Hospital:** UCLA Ronald Reagan Med Ctr; **Address:** UCLA Neurological Services, 300 Medical Plaza, Ste B-200, Los Angeles, CA 90095; **Phone:** 310-794-1195; **Board Cert:** Neurology 1992; **Med School:** UCLA 1986; **Resid:** Neurology, UCLA Med Ctr 1990; **Fellow:** Neurology, UCLA Med Ctr 1992; **Fac Appt:** Prof N, UCLA

Chui, Helena C MD [N] - **Spec Exp:** Stroke; Dementia; Alzheimer's Disease; **Hospital:** Keck Med Ctr of USC, Rancho Los Amigos Natl Rehab Ctr; **Address:** USC Dept Neurology, 1520 San Pablo St, Ste 3000, Los Angeles, CA 90033; **Phone:** 323-442-5710; **Board Cert:** Neurology 1984; **Med School:** Johns Hopkins Univ 1977; **Resid:** Neurology, Univ Iowa Med Ctr 1982; **Fellow:** Behavioral Neurology, Univ Iowa Med Ctr 1984; **Fac Appt:** Prof N, USC Sch Med

Cloughesy, Timothy F MD [N] - **Spec Exp:** Neuro-Oncology; Seizure Disorders; Brain Tumors; **Hospital:** UCLA Ronald Reagan Med Ctr; **Address:** 710 Westwood Plaza, Ste 1230, Los Angeles, CA 90095; **Phone:** 310-825-9113; **Board Cert:** Neurology 1993; **Med School:** Tulane Univ 1987; **Resid:** Neurology, UCLA Med Ctr 1991; **Fellow:** Clinical Neurophysiology, UCLA Med Ctr 1992; Neuro-Oncology, Meml Sloan-Kettering Canc Ctr 1992; **Fac Appt:** Clin Prof N, UCLA

Corey-Bloom, Jody MD/PhD [N] - **Spec Exp:** Multiple Sclerosis; Huntington's Disease; **Hospital:** UCSD Med Ctr; **Address:** 8950 Villa La Jolla Drive, Ste C129, La Jolla, CA 92037-0948; **Phone:** 858-246-1288; **Board Cert:** Neurology 1993; **Med School:** UCSD 1986; **Resid:** Neurology, UCSD Med Ctr 1990; **Fellow:** Dementia & Aging, UCSD Med Ctr 1992; **Fac Appt:** Prof N, UCSD

Cummings, Jeffrey L MD [N] - **Spec Exp:** Alzheimer's Disease; Clinical Trials; Neuro-Psychiatry; **Hospital:** Cleveland Clin (page 55); **Address:** Cleveland Clinic Nevada, Lou Ruvo Ctr for Brain Health, 888 W Bonneville Ave, Las Vegas, NV 89106; **Phone:** 702-483-6000; **Board Cert:** Neurology 1979; **Med School:** Univ Wash 1974; **Resid:** Neurology, Boston Univ Sch Med 1978; **Fellow:** Behavioral Neurology and Psychiatry, Boston Univ Sch Med 1979; Neurological Pathology, The Natl Hosp 1980

DeGiorgio, Christopher M MD [N] - **Spec Exp:** Epilepsy; Seizure Disorders; **Hospital:** UCLA Ronald Reagan Med Ctr; **Address:** UCLA Neurological Services, 300 Medical Plaza, Ste B-200, Los Angeles, CA 90095; **Phone:** 310-794-1195; **Board Cert:** Neurology 1987; **Med School:** Loyola Univ-Stritch Sch Med 1981; **Resid:** Neurology, Wadsworth VA Hosp 1985; **Fellow:** Epilepsy, UCLA Mee Ctr 1987; **Fac Appt:** Assoc Prof N, UCLA

Engstrom, John W MD [N] - **Spec Exp:** Peripheral Neuropathy; Spinal Cord Disorders; **Hospital:** UCSF Med Ctr; **Address:** UCSF Med Ctr, Dept Neurology, 400 Parnassus Ave Fl 8 - rm M-795, San Francisco, CA 94143; **Phone:** 415-353-2273; **Board Cert:** Internal Medicine 1984; Neurology 1991; Clinical Neurophysiology 2013; **Med School:** Stanford Univ 1981; **Resid:** Internal Medicine, Johns Hopkins Hosp 1984; Neurology, UCSF Med Ctr 1988; **Fellow:** Neuromuscular Disease, UCSF Med Ctr 1989; **Fac Appt:** Prof N, UCSF

Fisher, Mark Jay MD [N] - **Spec Exp:** Stroke; Cerebrovascular Disease; **Hospital:** UC Irvine Med Ctr, VA Long Beach Hlthcare Sys; **Address:** UC Irvine Med Ctr, Dept Neurology, 101 The City Drive S, Shanbrom Hall, rm 121, Orange, CA 92868; **Phone:** 714-456-6856; **Board Cert:** Neurology 1981; Vascular Neurology 2005; **Med School:** Univ Cincinnati 1975; **Resid:** Neurology, UCLA-Wadsworth VA Hosp 1980; **Fac Appt:** Prof N, UC Irvine

Fisher, Robert S MD [N] - **Spec Exp:** Epilepsy/Seizure Disorders; **Hospital:** Stanford Univ Hosp & Clins; **Address:** Stanford Univ Dept Neurology, 300 Pasteur Drive, rm A-343, Stanford, CA 94305-5235; **Phone:** 650-498-3056; **Board Cert:** Neurology 1983; Clinical Neurophysiology 2011; **Med School:** Stanford Univ 1977; **Resid:** Internal Medicine, Stanford Univ 1979; **Fellow:** Neurology, Johns Hopkins Univ 1982; **Fac Appt:** Prof N, Stanford Univ

Goodin, Douglas S MD [N] - **Spec Exp:** Multiple Sclerosis; **Hospital:** UCSF Med Ctr, VA Med Ctr - San Francisco; **Address:** UCSF Multiple Sclerosis Ctr, 1500 Owens St, Ste 320, San Francisco, CA 94128; **Phone:** 415-353-2069; **Board Cert:** Neurology 1985; **Med School:** UC Irvine 1978; **Resid:** Neurology, UCSF Med Ctr 1981; **Fac Appt:** Assoc Clin Prof N, UCSF

Graves, Michael C MD [N] - **Spec Exp:** Amyotrophic Lateral Sclerosis (ALS); Electromyography; Guillain-Barre Syndrome; Muscular Dystrophy; **Hospital:** UCLA Ronald Reagan Med Ctr; **Address:** UCLA Neurological Services, 300 Medical Plaza, Ste B-200, Los Angeles, CA 90095-6975; **Phone:** 310-794-1195; **Board Cert:** Neurology 1977; **Med School:** Stanford Univ 1970; **Resid:** Internal Medicine, UCSD Med Ctr 1972; Neurology, Johns Hopkins Hosp 1975; **Fac Appt:** Assoc Prof N, UCLA

Guilleminault, Christian MD [N] - **Spec Exp:** Sleep Disorders/Apnea; **Hospital:** Stanford Univ Hosp & Clins; **Address:** Stanford Sleep Medicine Center, 450 Broadway St, Pavilion B, Redwood City, CA 94063-5704; **Phone:** 650-723-6601; **Med School:** France 1962; **Resid:** Neurology, Hospital Foch 1966; Hosp de la Salpetriere 1968; **Fellow:** Univ Geneva 1967; **Fac Appt:** Prof Psyc, Stanford Univ

Hauser, Stephen L MD [N] - **Spec Exp:** Multiple Sclerosis; **Hospital:** UCSF Med Ctr; **Address:** UCSF Multiple Sclerosis Center, 1500 Owens St, Ste 320, San Francisco, CA 94158; **Phone:** 415-353-2069; **Board Cert:** Internal Medicine 1978; Neurology 1981; **Med School:** Harvard Med Sch 1975; **Resid:** Internal Medicine, NY Presby-Cornell 1978; **Fellow:** Neurology, Mass Genl Hosp 1980

Heck, Christianne N MD [N] - **Spec Exp:** Epilepsy; **Hospital:** Keck Med Ctr of USC; **Address:** Neurologic Care & Research Ctr, 1520 San Pablo St, Ste 3000, Los Angeles, CA 90033; **Phone:** 323-442-5710; **Board Cert:** Neurology 2011; **Med School:** USC-Keck School of Medicine 1991; **Resid:** Neurology, LAC/USC Med Ctr 1996; **Fellow:** Epilepsy, USC Med Ctr 1997; **Fac Appt:** Assoc Prof N, USC-Keck School of Medicine

Henderson, Victor W MD [N] - **Spec Exp:** Alzheimer's Disease; Dementia; Memory Disorders; **Hospital:** Stanford Univ Hosp & Clins; **Address:** Stanford Univ Med Ctr, Neurology, 300 Pasteur Drive, Ste A301, MC 5325, Stanford, CA 94305-5405; **Phone:** 650-723-6469; **Board Cert:** Neurology 1981; **Med School:** Johns Hopkins Univ 1976; **Resid:** Internal Medicine, Duke Univ Med Ctr 1977; Neurology, Barnes Hosp- Wash Univ 1980; **Fellow:** Behavioral Neurology, Aphasia Rsch Ctr-Boston Univ 1981; **Fac Appt:** Prof N, Stanford Univ

Kesari, Santosh MD/PhD [N] - **Spec Exp:** Neuro-Oncology; Stem Cell Therapy; Leukoencephalopathy; **Hospital:** UCSD Thornton Hosp, UCSD Med Ctr; **Address:** UCSD Moores Cancer Center, 3855 Health Sciences Drive, La Jolla, CA 92093; **Phone:** 858-822-6346; **Board Cert:** Neurology 2005; **Med School:** Univ Pennsylvania 1999; **Resid:** Neurology, Mass Genl Hosp 2003; **Fellow:** Neuro-Oncology, Dana Farber Cancer Inst 2004; **Fac Appt:** Prof N, UCSD

Langston, J William MD [N] - **Spec Exp:** Parkinson's Disease; Movement Disorders; Tremor; **Hospital:** Parkinson's Inst/Movement Disorders Trmt Ctr, The; **Address:** The Parkinsons Inst, 675 Almanor Ave, Sunnyvale, CA 94085; **Phone:** 408-542-5633; **Board Cert:** Neurology 1986; **Med School:** Univ MO-Columbia Sch Med 1967; **Resid:** Neurology, Stanford Univ 1974; **Fellow:** Electroencephalography, Stanford Univ 1974

Lew, Mark F MD [N] - **Spec Exp:** Movement Disorders; Parkinson's Disease; Dystonia; **Hospital:** Keck Med Ctr of USC; **Address:** 1520 San Pablo St, Ste 3000, Los Angeles, CA 90033; **Phone:** 323-442-5817; **Board Cert:** Neurology 1993; **Med School:** Geo Wash Univ 1987; **Resid:** Neurology, USC-LAC Med Ctr 1991; **Fellow:** Movement Disorders, USC-LAC Med Ctr 1992; **Fac Appt:** Prof N, USC Sch Med

Lewis, Richard A MD [N] - **Spec Exp:** Neuromuscular Disorders; **Hospital:** Cedars-Sinai Med Ctr; **Address:** 127 S San Vicente Blvd, Los Angeles, CA 90048; **Phone:** 310-423-6472; **Board Cert:** Neurology 1980; **Med School:** Med Coll VA 1974; **Resid:** Neurology, Hosp Univ Penn 1978

Longo, Frank M MD/PhD [N] - **Spec Exp:** Alzheimer's Disease; Huntington's Disease; **Hospital:** Stanford Univ Hosp & Clins, UCSF Med Ctr; **Address:** Stanford Univ Med Ctr, Neurology, 300 Pasteur Drive, MC 5235, H3160, Stanford, CA 94305; **Phone:** 650-723-6469; **Board Cert:** Neurology 1981; **Med School:** UCSD 1981; **Resid:** Neurology, UCSF Med Ctr 1987; **Fellow:** Neurology, UCSF Med Ctr 1989; **Fac Appt:** Prof N, Stanford Univ

Lutsep, Helmi L MD [N] - **Spec Exp:** Stroke/Cerebrovascular Disease; Stroke Prevention; **Hospital:** OR Hlth & Sci Univ; **Address:** Oregon Stroke Ctr, OHSU, 3181 SW Sam Jackson Park Rd, Portland, OR 97239; **Phone:** 503-494-7225; **Board Cert:** Neurology 1994; Vascular Neurology 2005; **Med School:** Mayo Med Sch 1988; **Resid:** Neurology, Mayo Clin 1992; **Fellow:** Behavioral Neurology, UC Davis Med Ctr 1995; Stroke, Stanford Univ 1996; **Fac Appt:** Prof N, Oregon Hlth & Sci Univ

Morrell, Martha J MD [N] - **Spec Exp:** Epilepsy; Epilepsy in Women; **Hospital:** Stanford Univ Hosp & Clins; **Address:** Stanford Univ Dept Neurology, 300 Pasteur Drive, rm A-301, Stanford, CA 94305; **Phone:** 650-498-7551; **Board Cert:** Neurology 1989; Clinical Neurophysiology 2003; **Med School:** Stanford Univ 1984; **Resid:** Neurology, Hosp Univ Penn 1988; **Fellow:** Epilepsy, Graduate Hosp-Univ Penn 1990; **Fac Appt:** Clin Prof N, Stanford Univ

Nutt Jr, John G MD [N] - **Spec Exp:** Parkinson's Disease; Movement Disorders; **Hospital:** OR Hlth & Sci Univ; **Address:** Parkinson's Ctr of Oregon, 3181 SW Sam Jackson Park Rd, MC OP32, Portland, OR 97239; **Phone:** 503-494-7230; **Board Cert:** Neurology 1978; **Med School:** Baylor Coll Med 1970; **Resid:** Neurology, Univ Wash Med Ctr 1976; **Fellow:** Pharmacology, NIH 1978; **Fac Appt:** Prof N, Oregon Hlth & Sci Univ

Phuphanich, Surasak MD [N] - **Spec Exp:** Neuro-Oncology; Brain Tumors; Spinal Tumors; **Hospital:** Cedars-Sinai Med Ctr; **Address:** 8631 W 3rd St, Ste 410E, Los Angeles, CA 90048; **Phone:** 310-423-4413; **Board Cert:** Neurology 1983; **Med School:** Thailand 1975; **Resid:** Internal Medicine, St. Francis Hosp 1978; Neurology, Univ Illinois Med Ctr 1981; **Fellow:** Neuro-Oncology, UCSF Med Ctr 1984; **Fac Appt:** Prof N, UCLA-David Geffen Sch Med

Rosenbaum, Richard B MD [N] - **Spec Exp:** Neuromuscular Disorders; Parkinson's Disease; **Hospital:** OR Hlth & Sci Univ, Providence Portland Med Ctr; **Address:** Oregon Clin, Dept Neurology, 1600 NE Broadway, Portland, OR 97232; **Phone:** 503-963-3100; **Board Cert:** Internal Medicine 1975; Neurology 1979; **Med School:** Harvard Med Sch 1971; **Resid:** Internal Medicine, Stanford Univ Hosp & Clins 1975; Neurology, UCSF Med Ctr 1979; **Fac Appt:** Clin Prof N, Oregon Hlth & Sci Univ

Rothrock, John F MD [N] - **Spec Exp:** Headache; Migraine; Stroke; **Hospital:** Renown Reg Med Ctr; **Address:** 85 Kirman Ave, Ste 301, Reno, NV 89502; **Phone:** 775-982-2970; **Board Cert:** Neurology 1984; Vascular Neurology 2009; Headache Medicine 2009; **Med School:** Univ VA Sch Med 1977; **Resid:** Neurology, Univ Ariz Med Ctr 1981; **Fac Appt:** Prof N, UAB Sch Med

Samii, Ali MD [N] - **Spec Exp:** Movement Disorders; Parkinson's Disease; Tremor & Dystonia; **Hospital:** Univ Wash Med Ctr; **Address:** UW Medical Center, Dept Neurology, 1959 NE Pacific St, Box 356169, Seattle, WA 98195; **Phone:** 206-598-7688; **Board Cert:** Neurology 2007; **Med School:** McGill Univ 1989; **Resid:** Neurology, UC Davis Med Ctr 1993; **Fellow:** Movement Disorders, NIH/Motor Control Sect 1996; Movement Disorders, Univ BC 1997; **Fac Appt:** Prof N, Univ Wash

Saver, Jeffrey L MD [N] - **Spec Exp:** Stroke; Stroke Prevention; **Hospital:** UCLA Ronald Reagan Med Ctr; **Address:** UCLA Stroke Ctr, 300 Medical Plaza, Ste B-200, Los Angeles, CA 90095; **Phone:** 310-794-1195; **Board Cert:** Neurology 1991; Vascular Neurology 2005; **Med School:** Harvard Med Sch 1986; **Resid:** Neurology, Brigham & Womens Hosp 1990; **Fellow:** Behavioral Neurology, Univ Iowa Hosps 1991; Cerebrovascular Disease, Rhode Island Hosp 1992; **Fac Appt:** Prof N, UCLA-David Geffen Sch Med

Smith, Wade S MD/PhD [N] - **Spec Exp:** Stroke; Pain-Back & Shoulder; **Hospital:** UCSF Med Ctr; **Address:** UCSF Vascular Neurology, 400 Parnassus Ave Fl 8, Box 0114, San Francisco, CA 94143-0114; **Phone:** 415-353-1489; **Board Cert:** Neurology 2006; Vascular Neurology 2008; **Med School:** Univ Wash 1989; **Resid:** Neurology, UCSF-Moffitt Hosp 1993; **Fellow:** Critical Care Medicine, UCSF Med Ctr 1994; **Fac Appt:** Prof N, UCSF

Tanner, Caroline M MD/PhD [N] - **Spec Exp:** Parkinson's Disease; Movement Disorders; Dystonia; **Hospital:** Parkinson's Inst/Movement Disorders Trmt Ctr, The; **Address:** Parkinson's Institute and Clinical Ctr, 675 Almanor Ave, Sunnyvale, CA 94085; **Phone:** 408-734-2800; **Board Cert:** Neurology 1982; **Med School:** Loyola Univ-Stritch Sch Med 1976; **Resid:** Neurology, Rush-Presby-St Luke's Med Ctr 1980; **Fellow:** Neurological Pharmacology, Rush-Presby-St Luke's Med Ctr 1982

Tetrud, James W MD [N] - **Spec Exp:** Movement Disorders; Parkinson's Disease; Tremor; **Hospital:** Parkinson's Inst/Movement Disorders Trmt Ctr, The; **Address:** The Parkinson's Inst, 675 Almanor Ave, Sunnyvale, CA 94085; **Phone:** 408-734-2800; **Board Cert:** Neurology 1981; **Med School:** NYU Sch Med 1973; **Resid:** Internal Medicine, VA Med Ctr-West Los Angeles 1974; Neurology, VA Med Ctr-West Los Angeles 1978

Weiner, Leslie P MD [N] - **Spec Exp:** Multiple Sclerosis; **Hospital:** Keck Med Ctr of USC, LAC & USC Med Ctr; **Address:** USC Dept Neurology, 1520 San Pablo St, Ste 3000, Los Angeles, CA 90033; **Phone:** 323-442-5710; **Board Cert:** Neurology 1969; **Med School:** Univ Cincinnati 1961; **Resid:** Neurology, Mercy Med Ctr 1963; Neurology, Johns Hopkins Hosp 1965; **Fellow:** Neurology, Johns Hopkins Hosp 1968; Viral Immunology, NIH Laboratory 1969; **Fac Appt:** Prof N, USC Sch Med

Weiss, Michael D MD [N] - **Spec Exp:** Neuromuscular Disorders; Amyotrophic Lateral Sclerosis (ALS); Myasthenia Gravis; Peripheral Neuropathy; **Hospital:** Univ Wash Med Ctr; **Address:** Univ Wash Med Ctr SS 824, Box 356169, 1959 NE Pacific St, Seattle, WA 98195; **Phone:** 206-598-7688; **Board Cert:** Neurology 2006; Neuromuscular Medicine 2011; Electrodiagnostic Medicine 2011; **Med School:** Albert Einstein Coll Med 1991; **Resid:** Neurology, Georgetown Univ Hosp 1996; **Fellow:** Neurology, Univ Maryland 1997; Neuromuscular Disease, Natl Inst Hlth 1999; **Fac Appt:** Prof N, Univ Wash

Maimonides Medical Center

JAFFE STROKE CENTER

4802 Tenth Avenue
Brooklyn, New York 11219
Phone: 718.283.7670 • Fax: 718.635.7223
www.maimonidesmed.org/stroke

The Jaffe Stroke Center is ranked among the top 5% in the nation, and the top two in New York State. There are several other stroke centers in Brooklyn, but the services at Maimonides are far more advanced than at any other institution.

Steven Rudolph, MD, Director of Jaffe Stroke Center, has been selected as the investigator in two clinical trials for the newest medical stroke therapies. This distinction is bestowed only on the most respected clinicians in the field. These therapies, too, will be able to provide treatment up to nine hours after the onset of symptoms.

After the onset of stroke symptoms, there is a three-hour window of opportunity for the administration of a clot-busting drug. With highly specialized training, experts at certified stroke centers can administer this drug to appropriate patients. But there is a nine-hour window of opportunity for advanced treatment, and Maimonides is one of only a handful of hospitals in the New York metropolitan area with the capability of providing that treatment.

Razvan Buciuc, MD, Director of Interventional Neuroradiology, and his team utilize, where particularly indicated, procedures to access blood vesels in the brain and remove a stroke-causing blood clot. This procedure can greatly reduce stroke damage and, in some cases, has completely reversed all symptoms. Dr. Buciuc is among few in the nation with significant experience utilizing this procedure..

In addition, Maimonides has a multidisciplinary team of stroke experts that includes physicians and nurses from the Department of Emergency Medicine, providing the vital first line of defense in combating stroke. The ER at Maimonides is equipped with telemedicine, an interactive system which allows consultation with a stroke neurologist in real time, even when the doctor is at a remote location.

In our stroke unit and interventional neuroradiology suite, nurses are certified and experienced in these specialties, and they coordinate recovery plans that include numerous technicians and therapists.

The Jaffe Stroke Center at Maimonides Medical Center was awarded the Gold Plus Award for excellence in performance from the American Stroke Association's "Get With the Guidelines" Program. In addition, we have been named to the "Target: Stroke" Honor Roll – one of only 50 hospitals in the U.S. to achieve the recognition.

Maimonides Medical Center

**The right care.
Right here.**

www.maimonidesmed.org/stroke

Mount Sinai

THE MOUNT SINAI MEDICAL CENTER

Neurology

One Gustave L. Levy Place
Fifth Avenue and 100th Street
New York, NY 10029-6574

Physician Referral: 1-800-MD-SINAI (637-4624)
www.mountsinai.org

THE ESTELLE AND DANIEL MAGGIN DEPARTMENT OF NEUROLOGY at Mount Sinai provides compassionate, state-of-the-art, interdisciplinary care for disorders of the brain and nervous system. *US News World & Report* recently ranked Mount Sinai Neurology and Neurosurgery as a top program nationwide in recognition of our ability to care for patients with complex diseases of the nervous system.

THE ESTELLE AND DANIEL MAGGIN DEPARTMENT OF NEUROLOGY is renowned for its unique integration of outstanding patient care and cutting-edge research in neurological disease, and can bring the latest advances in treatment to our patients. Our physicians and neuroscientists have made enormous strides in basic and translational research, bringing medical breakthroughs that will change the course of neurological treatment. The department is led by some of the most prominent figures in American neurology, is #3 nationally in the number of academic neurologists trained in our residency program, and receives annual research grants of more than $20 million.

The Robert and John M. Bendheim Parkinson and Movement Disorders Center is one of the world's leading multidisciplinary centers for clinical care and translational research aimed at Parkinson's disease, dystonia, tremor, Huntington's disease, restless legs syndrome, and others. The Center incorporates a world-renowned deep brain stimulation (DBS) program, and is at the forefront in clinical trials and experimental therapeutics for movement disorders.

The Corinne Goldsmith Dickinson Center for Multiple Sclerosis is an internationally recognized comprehensive center, uniting the efforts of leading physicians and scientists from many disciplines to understand the causes and consequences of MS. The Center provides services in all aspects of diagnosis, disease management, rehabilitation, and patient support, and the opportunity for patients to participate in potentially groundbreaking clinical trials.

The Clinical Program for Cerebrovascular Disorders includes an outstanding team of medical experts who specialize in the most advanced approaches in the evaluation, treatment, and rehabilitation of patients with cerebrovascular diseases. Services include the early diagnosis of stroke, advanced endovascular therapies, a specialized Neurointensive Care Unit, and an advanced inpatient stroke unit. Physicians are available at all times for emergency consultation with referring physicians. The Stroke Center is the first Comprehensive Stroke Center designated by The Joint Commission in New York State.

The NeuroAIDS Program provides diagnosis and treatment for neurological disorders associated with HIV disease. This program is one of the few in the world to treat the various complications of the disease that affect the central and peripheral nervous systems in as many as 70 percent of patients.

The Epilepsy Center provides specific expertise in the diagnosis and treatment of epilepsy and related disorders. The Center encompasses outstanding epileptologists, a new modern inpatient epilepsy monitoring unit, and full outpatient EEG and diagnostic capabilities.

The Center for Headache and Pain Medicine is a multidisciplinary center for the diagnosis and treatment of chronic and acute headaches and other painful disorders of the skull, brain, or face in both adults and children. Specialists in neurology, pain medicine, ENT, ophthalmology, psychiatry, and rehabilitation medicine are available to evaluate and treat individuals with painful disorders.

The Division of Neuromuscular Diseases provides diagnosis, clinical research trials, and compassionate comprehensive care for patients with disorders in neuromuscular transmission, muscle diseases, peripheral nerve problems, and spasticity resulting from stroke or other insults to the central nervous system.

The Center for Cognitive Health provides state-of-the-art diagnosis and treatment for memory disorders, dementias, traumatic brain injury, and other cognitive disorders. Our multidisciplinary team of neurologists, psychiatrists, neuropsychiatrists, neuroscientists, neuropsychologists, and patient care managers bridge the brain-related specialties to provide individualized comprehensive care.

The Eye Movement and Vestibular Disorder Program provides outstanding diagnosis and treatment for visual problems, balance problems, and motion sickness. Our physicians participate in NASA programs, employing technology used to assess these disorders in space, and studying possible treatment applications on earth.

NorthShore
University HealthSystem
Neurological Institute

NorthShore Neurological Institute
2650 Ridge Avenue, Evanston, IL 60201
1-877-570-7020
northshore.org/neuro

NorthShore Neurological Institute is a preeminent provider of advanced care for difficult brain and spine conditions. With locations across the Chicago area, it provides the region's most accessible neurological and neurosurgical care.

Demetrius Maraganore, MD and Julian Bailes, MD

World-Class Neurological Experts

NorthShore Neurological Institute's multidisciplinary team is dedicated to putting patients and families at the center of a healthcare experience that delivers exceptional, compassionate care in a wide range of specialties.

More than 70 leading neurologists, neurosurgeons, researchers and rehabilitation specialists collaborate to provide patients with outstanding care. The program is led by two Castle Connolly-recognized physicians, world-renowned neurosurgeon Julian Bailes, MD and internationally noted Parkinson's expert Demetrius Maraganore, MD.

Through NorthShore's collaboration with Mayo Clinic, patients have access to the combined strength of two leading teams of neurologists. They work together on the most complex cases, collaborating on diagnoses and innovative treatment options.

A Destination for Neurological Research

NorthShore Neurological Institute actively pursues new discoveries to ensure that advanced clinical treatments, the latest technology and innovative surgical techniques are available for their patients today. Through the groundbreaking work of physician scientists, they dramatically enhance the ability to understand the causes of neurological diseases and predict future outcomes.

NORTHSHORE NEUROLOGICAL INSTITUTE SPECIALTIES:

- Alzheimer's Disease & Memory Disorders
- Brain Aneurysm
- Brain & Spine Tumors
- Carotid Disease
- Concussion & Head Injury
- Epilepsy
- Headache
- Parkinson's Disease & Movement Disorders
- Pituitary & Skull Base Surgery
- Multiple Sclerosis
- Neuromuscular
- Neurophysiology
- Neuroradiology
- Sleep
- Spine Surgery
- Stroke

NYU Langone
MEDICAL CENTER

550 First Avenue *(at 31st Street)*
New York, NY 10016
www.NYULMC.org/neurology
www.NYULMC.org/neurosurgery
Physician Referral: **888-7-NYU-MED** *(888-769-8633)*

NEUROLOGY & NEUROSURGERY

NYU Langone Medical Center's Departments of Neurology and Neurosurgery continue to be **ranked among the nation's top 10 in the 2013-2014 U.S. News & World Report's annual survey of "Best Hospitals" in America.**

Patients travel from around the world to consult our renowned specialists for their expertise in the care, treatment, and research of neurological diseases and disorders of the brain, spine and nervous system. These conditions range from migraine headaches, nerve and muscle problems, pain, autism, movement disorders and Alzheimer's disease to stroke, vascular disorders, epilepsy, multiple sclerosis and brain tumors. NYU Langone is home to one of the largest epilepsy centers in the United States, as well as the largest multiple sclerosis program in New York and the first primary stroke center established in New York City.

<u>Neurological Expertise</u>

Autonomic Diseases: Our specialized Center evaluates and treats children and adults with familial dysautonomia and other inherited or acquired autonomic nervous system diseases, including orthostatic hypotension and rare forms of hereditary sensory neuropathy.

Epilepsy: Our Level 4 Comprehensive Epilepsy Center offers the most advanced medical and surgical options. Complementary management approaches complete the comprehensive care plan.

Multiple Sclerosis: The Comprehensive MS Care Center provides state-of-the-art diagnostic evaluations and follow-up care and management.

Neurogenetics: We focus on inherited diseases of the nervous system. Services include diagnosis and management of inherited diseases, biochemical and molecular testing and genetic counseling.

Neuro-oncology: In partnership with the NYU Cancer Institute, our multidisciplinary Brain Tumor Center is one of the nation's leading brain and spinal cord tumor programs, including physicians highly experienced in neuro-oncology, neurosurgery and neuroradiology.

Neuromuscular Diseases: We offer multidisciplinary programs for neuromuscular diseases, including acquired peripheral neuropathy, Charcot Marie Tooth neuropathy, myasthenia gravis, amyotrophic lateral sclerosis, spinal muscular atrophy, post-polio syndrome, muscular dystrophy and Lyme neuroborreliosis.

Parkinson's Disease and Movement Disorders: Our specialized center helps individuals affected by Parkinson's or other movement disorders to achieve the highest possible quality of life. Experts are also available to offer functional neurosurgery for certain conditions that involve involuntary muscle contractions.

(continued)

Nuclear Medicine

A nuclear medicine specialist employs the properties of radioactive atoms and molecules in the diagnosis and treatment of disease, and in research. Radiation detection and imaging instrument systems are used to detect disease as it changes the function and metabolism of normal cells, tissues and organs. A wide variety of diseases can be found in this way, usually before the structure of the organ involved by the disease can be seen to be abnormal by any other techniques. Early detection of coronary artery disease (including acute heart attack); early cancer detection and evaluation of the effect of tumor treatment; diagnosis of infection and inflammation anywhere in the body; and early detection of blood clot in the lungs, are all possible with these techniques. Unique forms of radioactive molecules can attack and kill cancer cells (e.g., lymphoma, thyroid cancer) or can relieve the severe pain of cancer that has spread to bone.

The nuclear medicine specialist has special knowledge in the biologic effects of radiation exposure, the fundamentals of the physical sciences and the principles and operation of radiation detection and imaging instrumentation systems.

Training required: Three years

NUCLEAR MEDICINE

Mid Atlantic

Agress Jr, Harry MD [NuM] - **Spec Exp:** PET Imaging; Cancer Detection & Staging; Nuclear Oncology; CT Scan; **Hospital:** Hackensack Univ Med Ctr; **Address:** Hackensack University Medical Center, 30 Prospect Ave, Hackensack, NJ 07601; **Phone:** 201-996-2196; **Board Cert:** Nuclear Medicine 1976; Diagnostic Radiology 1978; **Med School:** Tufts Univ 1972; **Resid:** Radiology, Columbia- Presby Med Ctr 1978; **Fellow:** Nuclear Medicine, Natl Inst Hlth 1975; **Fac Appt:** Clin Prof Rad, Columbia P&S

Alavi, Abass MD [NuM] - **Spec Exp:** PET Imaging-Brain; **Hospital:** Hosp Univ Penn - UPHS (page 69), Chldns Hosp of Philadelphia; **Address:** Hosp Univ Penn, Div Nuclear Med, 3400 Spruce St, Donner Bldg rm 117, Philadelphia, PA 19104; **Phone:** 215-662-3069; **Board Cert:** Internal Medicine 1972; Nuclear Medicine 1973; **Med School:** Iran 1964; **Resid:** Internal Medicine, Albert Einstein Med Ctr/Phila VA Hosp 1969; Hematology, Hosp Univ Penn 1970; **Fellow:** Nuclear Medicine, Hosp Univ Penn 1973; **Fac Appt:** Prof Rad, Univ Pennsylvania

Carrasquillo, Jorge A MD [NuM] - **Spec Exp:** Radioimmunotherapy of Cancer; PET Imaging; Nuclear Endocrinology; **Hospital:** Meml Sloan-Kettering Canc Ctr; **Address:** 1275 York Ave, Nuclear Medicine Svc, Box 77, New York, NY 10065; **Phone:** 212-639-2459; **Board Cert:** Internal Medicine 1977; Nuclear Medicine 1982; **Med School:** Univ Puerto Rico 1974; **Resid:** Internal Medicine, Univ Dist Hosp 1977; Nuclear Medicine, Univ Wash Hosp 1982; **Fac Appt:** Prof NuM, SUNY Upstate Med Univ

Freeman, Leonard M MD [NuM] - **Spec Exp:** Nuclear Oncology; Gastrointestinal Disorders; PET Imaging; CT Scan; **Hospital:** Montefiore Med Ctr-Moses Campus, NY; **Address:** 111 E 210th St Foreman Bldg Fl 4, Bronx, NY 10467-2401; **Phone:** 718-920-6060; **Board Cert:** Diagnostic Radiology 1966; Nuclear Medicine 1972; Nuclear Radiology 1974; **Med School:** Ros Franklin Univ/Chicago Med Sch 1961; **Resid:** Diagnostic Radiology, Bronx Municipal Hosp 1965; **Fac Appt:** Prof NuM, Albert Einstein Coll Med

Goldsmith, Stanley J MD [NuM] - **Spec Exp:** Thyroid Cancer; Thyroid Disorders; Nuclear Cardiology; PET Imaging; **Hospital:** NY-Presby/Weill Cornell Med Ctr, NY (page 65); **Address:** 520 E 70th St Starr Bldg - rm 2-21, New York, NY 10021-9800; **Phone:** 212-746-4588; **Board Cert:** Internal Medicine 1969; Nuclear Medicine 1972; Endocrinology, Diabetes & Metabolism 1972; **Med School:** SUNY Downstate 1962; **Resid:** Internal Medicine, Kings Co Hosp 1968; **Fellow:** Endocrinology, Diabetes & Metabolism, Mt Sinai Hosp 1970; Nuclear Medicine, Bronx VA Hosp 1972; **Fac Appt:** Prof Rad, Cornell Univ-Weill Med Coll

Lamonica, Dominick M MD [NuM] - **Spec Exp:** Thyroid Cancer; Lymphoma, Non-Hodgkin's; Radioimmunotherapy of Cancer; PET Imaging; **Hospital:** Roswell Park Canc Inst; **Address:** Roswell Park Cancer Inst, Dept of Nuclear Medicine, Elm & Carlton St, Buffalo, NY 14263; **Phone:** 716-845-3282; **Board Cert:** Internal Medicine 2005; Nuclear Medicine 2006; **Med School:** Mount Sinai Sch Med 1987; **Resid:** Internal Medicine, Univ Hosp-SUNY Stony Brook 1991; Diagnostic Radiology, Nassau City Med Ctr 1992; **Fellow:** Nuclear Medicine, DVAMC North Port-SUNY Stony Brook 1994; Nuclear Medicine, SUNY Buffalo-RPCI 1995; **Fac Appt:** Asst Prof NuM, SUNY Buffalo

Neumann, Ronald D MD [NuM] - **Spec Exp:** Nuclear Oncology; **Hospital:** Natl Inst of Hlth - Clin Ctr; **Address:** NIH, Bldg 10, 1C-401, 9000 Rockville Drive, MSC 1180, Bethesda, MD 20892-1180; **Phone:** 301-496-6455; **Board Cert:** Nuclear Medicine 1979; **Med School:** Yale Univ 1974; **Resid:** Anatomic Pathology, Yale-New Haven Hosp 1977; Nuclear Medicine, Yale-New Haven Hosp 1979

Pandit-Taskar, Neeta MD [NuM] - **Spec Exp:** Radioimmunotherapy of Cancer; Thyroid Cancer; PET Imaging; **Hospital:** Meml Sloan-Kettering Canc Ctr; **Address:** Memorial Sloan Kettering Cancer Ctr, 1275 York Ave, New York, NY 10065; **Phone:** 212-639-7372; **Board Cert:** Nuclear Medicine 2008; **Med School:** India 1990; **Resid:** Nuclear Medicine, Mt Sinai Med Ctr 1995; **Fellow:** Nuclear Medicine, Meml Sloan Kettering Cancer Ctr 2001

Sanger, Joseph J MD [NuM] - **Spec Exp:** Nuclear Cardiology; Nuclear Oncology; **Hospital:** NYU Langone Med Ctr (page 68), Bellevue Hosp Ctr; **Address:** Department of Radiology, 560 First Ave Fl 2nd, New York, NY 10016-6402; **Phone:** 212-263-7410; **Board Cert:** Nuclear Medicine 1981; **Med School:** NYU Sch Med 1977; **Resid:** Diagnostic Radiology, NYU Med Ctr 1979; **Fellow:** Nuclear Medicine, NYU Med Ctr 1981; **Fac Appt:** Assoc Prof Rad, NYU Sch Med

Strashun, Arnold M MD [NuM] - **Spec Exp:** Neurological Imaging; Nuclear Cardiology; Thyroid Disorders; PET Imaging-Brain; **Hospital:** SUNY Downstate Med Ctr (Univ Hosp Brooklyn), Kings Co Hosp Ctr; **Address:** 450 Clarkson Ave, Box 1210, Dept Radiology, Brooklyn, NY 11203; **Phone:** 718-270-1603; **Board Cert:** Internal Medicine 1977; Nuclear Medicine 1979; **Med School:** Baylor Coll Med 1974; **Resid:** Internal Medicine, Texas Med Ctr 1977; **Fellow:** Nuclear Medicine, VA Med Ctr 1978; Nuclear Medicine, Mount Sinai Hosp 1979; **Fac Appt:** Prof Rad, SUNY Downstate

Wahl, Richard L MD [NuM] - **Spec Exp:** Radioimmunotherapy of Cancer; PET Imaging; PET Imaging-Breast; **Hospital:** Johns Hopkins Hosp (page 59); **Address:** Johns Hopkins Outpatient Ctr, 601 N Caroline St, Ste 3223-Nuclear Med, Baltimore, MD 21287; **Phone:** 410-614-3764; **Board Cert:** Diagnostic Radiology 1982; Nuclear Radiology 1983; Nuclear Medicine 1985; **Med School:** Washington Univ, St Louis 1978; **Resid:** Diagnostic Radiology, Mallinckrodt Inst 1982; **Fellow:** Nuclear Radiology, Mallinckrodt Inst 1983; **Fac Appt:** Prof Rad, Johns Hopkins Univ

Southeast

Alazraki, Naomi P MD [NuM] - **Spec Exp:** Nuclear Oncology; **Hospital:** Atlanta VA Med Ctr, Emory Univ Hosp; **Address:** VA Med Ctr, Nuclear Med Dept, 1670 Clairmont Rd, MC 115, Decatur, GA 30033; **Phone:** 404-321-6111 x6156; **Board Cert:** Nuclear Medicine 1972; Diagnostic Radiology 1972; **Med School:** Albert Einstein Coll Med 1966; **Resid:** Diagnostic Radiology, UCSD Med Ctr 1971; **Fac Appt:** Prof Rad, Emory Univ

Sandler, Martin P MD [NuM] - **Spec Exp:** Nuclear Endocrinology; Cardiac Imaging; PET Imaging; **Hospital:** Vanderbilt Univ Med Ctr; **Address:** Vanderbilt Univ Med Ctr, CCC 1121 MCN, 1161 21st Ave S, Nashville, TN 37232-2675; **Phone:** 615-322-0860; **Board Cert:** Nuclear Medicine 1983; **Med School:** South Africa 1972; **Resid:** Internal Medicine, Groote Schur Hosp; **Fellow:** Endocrinology, Diabetes & Metabolism, Vanderbilt Univ Med Ctr 1980; Nuclear Medicine, Vanderbilt Univ Med Ctr 1982; **Fac Appt:** Prof Rad, Vanderbilt Univ

Ziffer, Jack A MD/PhD [NuM] - **Spec Exp:** Nuclear Cardiology; Cardiac CT Angiography; Thyroid Disorders; Thyroid Cancer; **Hospital:** Baptist Hosp of Miami, Doctors' Hosp - Coral Gables (FL); **Address:** Baptist Hlth South FL/Med Group, 1500 San Remo Ave, Ste 360, Coral Gables, FL 33146; **Phone:** 786-527-9200; **Board Cert:** Diagnostic Radiology 1987; Nuclear Radiology 1988; Nuclear Medicine 1988; **Med School:** Univ Miami Sch Med 1983; **Resid:** Diagnostic Radiology, Emory Univ Hosps 1987; **Fellow:** Nuclear Medicine, Emory Univ Hosps 1988; **Fac Appt:** Clin Prof Rad, FIU Coll Med

Midwest

Appelbaum, Daniel MD [NuM] - **Spec Exp:** PET Imaging; Nuclear Cardiology; Nuclear Oncology; **Hospital:** Univ of Chicago Med; **Address:** Univ Chicago, Dept of Radiology, 5841 S Maryland Ave, MC 2026, Chicago, IL 60637-1463; **Phone:** 773-834-2012; **Board Cert:** Diagnostic Radiology 1999; Nuclear Medicine 2009; **Med School:** Mount Sinai Sch Med 1995; **Resid:** Diagnostic Radiology, Univ Chicago Hosp 1999; **Fellow:** Nuclear Medicine, Mallinckrodt Institute 2000; **Fac Appt:** Assoc Prof Rad, Univ Chicago-Pritzker Sch Med

Dillehay, Gary L MD [NuM] - **Spec Exp:** Thyroid Cancer; Nuclear Cardiology; **Hospital:** Northwestern Meml Hosp; **Address:** Northwestern Meml Hosp, Dept Nuclear Medicine, 675 N St Clair St, Galter 8-110, Chicago, IL 60611; **Phone:** 312-926-5119; **Board Cert:** Nuclear Medicine 1985; Nuclear Radiology 1987; Diagnostic Radiology 2010; **Med School:** Mayo Med Sch 1979; **Resid:** Diagnostic Radiology, Northwestern Meml Hosp 1983; Nuclear Medicine, Northwestern Meml Hosp 1984; **Fac Appt:** Prof Rad, Northwestern Univ-Feinberg Sch Med

Neumann, Donald R MD [NuM] - **Spec Exp:** Nuclear Oncology; Nuclear Cardiology; Parathyroid Disease; Pheochromocytoma; **Hospital:** Cleveland Clin (page 55); **Address:** Cleveland Clinic, Dept Nuclear Medicine, 9500 Euclid Ave, MS Jb3, Cleveland, OH 44195; **Phone:** 216-444-2193; **Board Cert:** Diagnostic Radiology 1987; Nuclear Radiology 1990; **Med School:** Wright State Univ 1980; **Resid:** Diagnostic Radiology, Mount Sinai Med Ctr 1987; **Fellow:** Magnetic Resonance Imaging, Mount Sinai Med Ctr 1988

Siegel, Barry A MD [NuM] - **Spec Exp:** Cancer Detection & Staging; PET Imaging; Thyroid Disorders; **Hospital:** Barnes-Jewish Hosp, St. Louis Chldns Hosp; **Address:** 510 S Kingshighway Blvd, St Louis, MO 63110-1016; **Phone:** 314-362-2809; **Board Cert:** Nuclear Medicine 1973; Diagnostic Radiology 1977; Nuclear Radiology 1981; **Med School:** Washington Univ, St Louis 1969; **Resid:** Diagnostic Radiology, Mallinckrodt Inst Radiology 1973; **Fellow:** Nuclear Medicine, Mallinckrodt Inst Radiology 1973; **Fac Appt:** Prof Rad, Washington Univ, St Louis

Wiseman, Gregory Alden MD [NuM] - **Spec Exp:** Lymphoma, Non-Hodgkin's; Multiple Myeloma; Radioimmunotherapy of Cancer; **Hospital:** Mayo Med Ctr & Clin - Rochester; **Address:** Mayo Clinic, Dept Nuc Med, 200 First St SW, Charlton Bldg, Rochester, MN 55905; **Phone:** 507-284-9599; **Board Cert:** Internal Medicine 1986; Hematology 1988; Nuclear Medicine 2002; **Med School:** Univ Utah 1983; **Resid:** Internal Medicine, Mayo Clinic 1986; Nuclear Medicine, Univ Washington Med Ctr 1992; **Fellow:** Hematology, Mayo Clinic 1989; Medical Oncology, Univ Washington 1991; **Fac Appt:** Asst Prof, Mayo Med Sch

Southwest

Podoloff, Donald A MD [NuM] - **Spec Exp:** Prostate Cancer; Breast Cancer; Lymphoma, Non-Hodgkin's; **Hospital:** UT MD Anderson Canc Ctr; **Address:** UT MD Anderson Cancer Ctr, 1515 Holcombe Blvd, SCRB III Bldg, rm SCR3.3930, Box 1905, Houston, TX 77030; **Phone:** 713-745-1160; **Board Cert:** Diagnostic Radiology 1973; Nuclear Medicine 1975; Nuclear Radiology 1975; **Med School:** SUNY Downstate 1964; **Resid:** Internal Medicine, Beth Israel Med Ctr 1968; Diagnostic Radiology, Wilford Hall USAF Med Ctr 1973; **Fac Appt:** Prof NuM, Univ Tex, Houston

West Coast and Pacific

Dae, Michael W MD [NuM] - **Spec Exp:** Nuclear Cardiology; Pediatric Nuclear Medicine; **Hospital:** UCSF Med Ctr; **Address:** UCSF Med Ctr, 505 Parnassus Ave, Box 0628, San Francisco, CA 94143; **Phone:** 415-353-1521; **Board Cert:** Pediatrics 1983; Nuclear Medicine 1984; **Med School:** Duke Univ 1976; **Resid:** Pediatrics, Chldns Hosp 1978; **Fellow:** Pediatric Cardiology, UCSF Med Ctr 1982; Nuclear Cardiology, UCSF Med Ctr 1983; **Fac Appt:** Prof Rad, UCSF

Klaas, Virginia E MD [NuM] - **Spec Exp:** Nuclear Radiology; **Hospital:** Valley Med Ctr-Renton, WA, Auburn Reg Med Ctr; **Address:** Vantage Radiology, 533 S 336th St, Ste C, Federal Way, WA 98003; **Phone:** 253-661-1700; **Board Cert:** Diagnostic Radiology 1994; Nuclear Radiology 1995; Nuclear Medicine 2004; **Med School:** UC Irvine 1989; **Resid:** Diagnostic Radiology, Stanford Univ Med Ctr 1994; **Fellow:** Nuclear Medicine, Mallinckrodt Inst of Radiology 1995

Schelbert, Heinrich R MD/PhD [NuM] - **Spec Exp:** Nuclear Cardiology; Coronary Artery Disease; **Hospital:** UCLA Ronald Reagan Med Ctr, Santa Monica - UCLA Med Ctr & Ortho Hosp; **Address:** UCLA Dept Molecular & Med Pharmacology, 650 Charles E Young Drive S, rm B2-085JCHS, Los Angeles, CA 90095-6948; **Phone:** 310-825-3076; **Board Cert:** Nuclear Medicine 1976; **Med School:** Germany 1964; **Resid:** Internal Medicine, Mercy Med Ctr 1971; Research, Univ Duesseldorf 1972; **Fellow:** Cardiovascular Research, UCSD Med Ctr 1975; Nuclear Radiology, UCSD Med Ctr 1976; **Fac Appt:** Prof Pharm, UCLA-David Geffen Sch Med

Waxman, Alan D MD [NuM] - **Spec Exp:** PET Imaging-Brain; Thyroid Cancer; Cancer Detection & Staging; **Hospital:** Cedars-Sinai Med Ctr, Keck Med Ctr of USC; **Address:** Cedars-Sinai Med Ctr, Taper Imaging, 8700 Beverly Blvd, rm 1258, Los Angeles, CA 90048-1804; **Phone:** 310-423-4216; **Board Cert:** Nuclear Medicine 1972; **Med School:** USC-Keck School of Medicine 1963; **Resid:** Nuclear Medicine, Wadsworth VA Hosp 1965; **Fellow:** Internal Medicine, Natl Inst Hlth 1967; **Fac Appt:** Clin Prof Rad, USC Sch Med

Nuclear Medicine

Cleveland Clinic Imaging Institute is one of the leading academic imaging centers in the world and one of the busiest clinical departments in the country. Each year, Cleveland Clinic imagers perform and interpret more than 2 million examinations, for which all images are acquired digitally.

Cleveland Clinic's Department of Nuclear Medicine's advanced imaging capabilities can identify both anatomic and physiologic changes in organ function. A Cyclotron enables on-site production of customized PET tracers for both clinical and research needs. Cleveland Clinic has 12 gamma cameras – three PET/CT scanners, three SPECT/CT scanners and six traditional gamma cameras. Our mobile PET/CT system brings main campus capabilities to Cleveland Clinic community hospitals.

Our unique expertise and unsurpassed technology are available to individualize patient diagnosis and management and treatment with the highest degree possible of accuracy and timeliness. Hybrid SPECT/CT and PET/CT fusion imaging is performed on specialized scanners that directly map the abnormal tissue depicted on the nuclear images to the affected area displayed on the high-resolution CT images.

The department possesses an abundant depth of expertise in both imaging and clinical medicine. Physicians are board-certified and clinically experienced in a broad array of specialties, including cardiology, neurology and radiology.

Patient therapy is a significant component of nuclear medicine. Treatments, and sometimes pain relief, are offered for conditions such as Graves' disease, thyroid cancer, liver cancer, cancer that has spread to the bone and refractory lymphomas. PET/CT scans also assist radiation oncologists in planning treatment with external sources of radiation.

Obstetrics & Gynecology

An obstetrician/gynecologist possesses special knowledge, skills and professional capability in the medical and surgical care of the female reproductive system and associated disorders. This physician serves as a consultant to other physicians and as a primary physician for women.

Training Required: Four years *plus* two years in clinical practice before certification is complete.

Obstetrics & Gynecology

New England

Cramer, Daniel W MD [ObG] - Spec Exp: Ovarian Cancer-High Risk Consult; **Hospital:** Dana-Farber Cancer Inst, Brigham & Women's Hosp; **Address:** Dana-Farber Cancer Inst, 450 Brookline Ave, Boston, MA 02215; **Phone:** 617-632-6431; **Board Cert:** Obstetrics & Gynecology 1979; **Med School:** Univ Colorado 1970; **Resid:** Obstetrics & Gynecology, Boston Womens Hosp 1976; **Fellow:** Public Health, Harvard Med Sch 1982; **Fac Appt:** Prof ObG, Harvard Med Sch

Eckler, Kristen P MD [ObG] - Spec Exp: Pelvic Reconstruction; Uro-Gynecology; **Hospital:** Mass Genl Hosp; **Address:** Vincent OB/GYN Service, 40 Second Ave, Ste 402, YAW 4, Boston, MA 02114; **Phone:** 781-487-3860; **Board Cert:** Obstetrics & Gynecology 2012; **Med School:** Tufts Univ 1994; **Resid:** Obstetrics & Gynecology, Brigham & Women's Hosp 1998

Einarsson, Jon I MD [ObG] - Spec Exp: Minimally Invasive Surgery; Endometriosis; Pelvic Organ Prolapse Repair; Incontinence-Female; **Hospital:** Brigham & Women's Hosp; **Address:** Brigham & Womens Hosp, Dept Obstetrics & Gynecology, 75 Francis St, Boston, MA 02115; **Phone:** 617-525-8582; **Board Cert:** Obstetrics & Gynecology 2012; **Med School:** Iceland 1995; **Resid:** Obstetrics & Gynecology, Baylor Affil Hosp 2002; **Fellow:** Minimally Invasive Surgery, Baylor Affil Hosp 2004; **Fac Appt:** Assoc Prof ObG, Harvard Med Sch

Laufer, Marc R MD [ObG] - Spec Exp: Endometriosis-Adolescent; Endometriosis; Congenital Anomalies-Gynecologic; **Hospital:** Children's Hospital - Boston, Brigham & Women's Hosp; **Address:** Boston Chldn's Hosp, Dept of Gynecology, 300 Longwood Ave, Boston, MA 02115; **Phone:** 617-355-5785; **Board Cert:** Obstetrics & Gynecology 2012; **Med School:** Univ Pennsylvania 1986; **Resid:** Obstetrics & Gynecology, Brigham & Womens Hosp/Mass Genl Hosp 1990; **Fellow:** Reproductive Endocrinology, Brigham & Womens Hosp/Chldns Hosp 1992; Gynecology, Chldns Hosp 1992; **Fac Appt:** Prof ObG, Harvard Med Sch

Myers, Deborah L MD [ObG] - Spec Exp: Uro-Gynecology; **Hospital:** Women & Infants Hosp of RI; **Address:** Women & Infants Hosp, 695 Eddy St, Providence, RI 02905; **Phone:** 401-453-7560; **Board Cert:** Obstetrics & Gynecology 2012; **Med School:** SUNY Stony Brook 1981; **Resid:** Obstetrics & Gynecology, Women & Infants Hosp 1985; **Fac Appt:** Asst Prof ObG, Brown Univ

Nour, Nawal M MD [ObG] - Spec Exp: Female Genital Cutting (FGC) Education; Gynecology-African women only; Pregnancy-African women only; **Hospital:** Brigham & Women's Hosp; **Address:** Brigham & Women's Hosp, Dept Ob/Gyn, 75 Francis St CWN-3 Bldg - Ste 340, Boston, MA 02115; **Phone:** 617-732-4740; **Board Cert:** Obstetrics & Gynecology 2012; **Med School:** Harvard Med Sch 1994; **Resid:** Obstetrics & Gynecology, Brgham & Women's Hosp 1998

Mid Atlantic

Brodman, Michael L MD [ObG] - Spec Exp: Incontinence; Laparoscopic Surgery; Pelvic Organ Prolapse Repair; Uro-Gynecology; **Hospital:** Mt Sinai Med Ctr (page 62); **Address:** Dept Gynecology/Urogynecology, 5 E 98th St Fl 2, New York, NY 10029; **Phone:** 212-241-7952; **Board Cert:** Obstetrics & Gynecology 2012; **Med School:** Mount Sinai Sch Med 1982; **Resid:** Obstetrics & Gynecology, Mt Sinai Hosp 1986; **Fellow:** Pelvic Surgery, Mt Sinai Hosp 1987; **Fac Appt:** Assoc Prof ObG, Mount Sinai Sch Med

Carson, Donald G MD [ObG] - **Spec Exp:** Gynecology Only; **Hospital:** Magee-Womens Hosp - UPMC; **Address:** Ob/Gyn Assocs, 3380 Boulevard of the Allies, Ste 1, Pittsburgh, PA 15213; **Phone:** 412-621-7575; **Board Cert:** Obstetrics & Gynecology 2012; **Med School:** Univ Pittsburgh 1977; **Resid:** Obstetrics & Gynecology, Magee-Womens Hosp 1981; **Fac Appt:** Assoc Clin Prof ObG, Univ Pittsburgh

Evans, Mark I MD [ObG] - **Spec Exp:** Reproductive Genetics; Fetal Diagnosis & Therapy; Multiple Gestation; Ultrasound; **Hospital:** Mt Sinai Med Ctr (page 62); **Address:** Comprehensive Genetics, 131 E 65th St, New York, NY 10065; **Phone:** 212-288-1422; **Board Cert:** Obstetrics & Gynecology 2012; Clinical Genetics 1984; **Med School:** SUNY Downstate 1978; **Resid:** Obstetrics & Gynecology, Lying-In Hosp 1982; **Fellow:** Clinical Genetics, Natl Inst Hlth 1984; **Fac Appt:** Prof ObG, Mount Sinai Sch Med

Goldstein, Martin S MD [ObG] - **Spec Exp:** Uterine Fibroids; Laparoscopic Surgery; Pelvic Organ Prolapse Repair; Endometriosis; **Hospital:** Mt Sinai Med Ctr (page 62); **Address:** 40 E 84th St, New York, NY 10028-1314; **Phone:** 212-472-6500; **Board Cert:** Obstetrics & Gynecology 1980; **Med School:** SUNY Hlth Sci Ctr 1966; **Resid:** Obstetrics & Gynecology, Mount Sinai Hosp 1971; **Fac Appt:** Assoc Clin Prof ObG, Mount Sinai Sch Med

Hockstein, Steven MD [ObG] - **Spec Exp:** Uterine Fibroids; **Hospital:** NY-Presby/Weill Cornell Med Ctr, NY (page 65); **Address:** 425 E 61st St Fl 11, New York, NY 10021; **Phone:** 212-821-0810; **Board Cert:** Obstetrics & Gynecology 2012; **Med School:** Univ MD Sch Med 1993; **Resid:** Obstetrics & Gynecology, McGaw Med Ctr 1997; **Fac Appt:** Asst Clin Prof ObG, Cornell Univ-Weill Med Coll

Iglesia, Cheryl B MD [ObG] - **Spec Exp:** Uro-Gynecology; **Hospital:** MedStar Washington Hosp Ctr; **Address:** 106 Irving St NW, Ste 405-S, Washington, DC 20010; **Phone:** 202-877-6526; **Board Cert:** Obstetrics & Gynecology 2012; **Med School:** Univ MD Sch Med 1991; **Resid:** Obstetrics & Gynecology, Shands Jacksonville Med Ctr 1996; **Fellow:** Uro-Gynecology, Rush Univ Med Ctr 1998; **Fac Appt:** Assoc Prof ObG, Georgetown Univ

Lucente, Vincent R MD [ObG] - **Spec Exp:** Uro-Gynecology; Pelvic Floor Reconstruction; Incontinence-Female; Pelvic Organ Prolapse Repair; **Hospital:** St. Luke's Hosp - Allentown; **Address:** Inst Female Pevlic Med, 3050 Hamilton Blvd, Ste 200, Allentown, PA 18103; **Phone:** 610-435-9575; **Board Cert:** Obstetrics & Gynecology 2012; **Med School:** SUNY Stony Brook 1985; **Resid:** Obstetrics & Gynecology, N Shore Univ Hosp 1989; **Fellow:** Uro-Gynecology, Methodist Hosp 1990; **Fac Appt:** Clin Prof ObG, Temple Univ

Maynard, Steven R MD [ObG] - **Spec Exp:** Minimally Invasive Surgery; Incontinence; **Hospital:** MedStar Georgetown Univ Hosp; **Address:** MedStar Georgetown Univ Hosp, 3800 Reservoir Rd NW, PHC Bldg Fl 3, Washington, DC 20007; **Phone:** 202-444-8531; **Board Cert:** Obstetrics & Gynecology 2012; **Med School:** McGill Univ 1986; **Resid:** Obstetrics & Gynecology, Women & Infants Hosp 1993; **Fac Appt:** Asst Prof ObG, Georgetown Univ

Ordorica, Steven Anthony MD [ObG] - **Spec Exp:** Pregnancy-High Risk; Miscarriage-Recurrent; Maternal & Fetal Medicine; **Hospital:** NYU Langone Med Ctr (page 68); **Address:** NYU Med Ctr, Dept OB/GYN, 530 1st Ave, Ste 10Q, New York, NY 10016-6402; **Phone:** 212-263-5982; **Board Cert:** Obstetrics & Gynecology 2013; Maternal & Fetal Medicine 2012; **Med School:** SUNY Stony Brook 1983; **Resid:** Obstetrics & Gynecology, NYU Med Ctr 1987; **Fellow:** Maternal & Fetal Medicine, NYU Med Ctr 1989; **Fac Appt:** Assoc Prof ObG, NYU Sch Med

Simon, James A MD [ObG] - **Spec Exp:** Infertility; Menopause Problems; Osteoporosis; Sexual Dysfunction; **Hospital:** G Washington Univ Hosp, Sibley Mem Hosp; **Address:** 1850 M St NW, Ste 450, Washington, DC 20036; **Phone:** 202-293-1000; **Board Cert:** Obstetrics & Gynecology 2012; Reproductive Endocrinology 2012; **Med School:** Rush Med Coll 1978; **Resid:** Obstetrics & Gynecology, G Washington Univ Hosp 1982; **Fellow:** Reproductive Endocrinology, LAC - Harbor - UCLA Med Ctr 1984; **Fac Appt:** Clin Prof ObG, Geo Wash Univ

Simpson, Joe Leigh MD [ObG] - **Spec Exp:** Prenatal Diagnosis; Ovarian Failure; Infertility/Genetics; **Address:** March of Dimes Foundation, 1275 Mamaroneck Ave, White Plains, NY 10605; **Phone:** 914-997-4555; **Board Cert:** Obstetrics & Gynecology 2012; Clinical Genetics 1982; **Med School:** Duke Univ 1968; **Resid:** Obstetrics & Gynecology, NY-Presby/Weill Cornell Med Ctr 1973

Wiesenfeld, Harold C MD [ObG] - **Spec Exp:** Infectious Diseases-Gynecologic; Sexually Transmitted Diseases; **Hospital:** Magee-Womens Hosp - UPMC; **Address:** Magee-Womens Hosp, Ob/Gyn Dept, 300 Halket St, Ste 0610, Pittsburgh, PA 15213; **Phone:** 412-641-6412; **Board Cert:** Obstetrics & Gynecology 2012; **Med School:** McGill Univ 1987; **Resid:** Obstetrics & Gynecology, McGill Univ 1990; **Fac Appt:** Assoc Prof ObG, Univ Pittsburgh

Young, Bruce Kenneth MD [ObG] - **Spec Exp:** Infertility; Minimally Invasive Surgery; Miscarriage-Recurrent; Pelvic Reconstruction; **Hospital:** NYU Langone Med Ctr (page 68), Bellevue Hosp Ctr; **Address:** 530 1st Ave, HCC-5th Fl, Ste 5G, NYU-Langone Medical Center, New York, NY 10016; **Phone:** 212-263-6359; **Board Cert:** Obstetrics & Gynecology 1970; Maternal & Fetal Medicine 1975; **Med School:** NYU Sch Med 1963; **Resid:** Obstetrics & Gynecology, NYU Med Ctr 1968; **Fellow:** Reproductive Endocrinology, NYU Med Ctr 1968; **Fac Appt:** Prof ObG, NYU Sch Med

Southeast

Amundsen, Cindy L MD [ObG] - **Spec Exp:** Uro-Gynecology; Pelvic Organ Prolapse Repair; Pelvic Reconstruction; **Hospital:** Duke Univ Hosp, Duke Raleigh Hosp; **Address:** Duke Univ Med Ctr, Dept Ob/Gyn, 5324 McFarlon Drive, Ste 310, Durham, NC 27707; **Phone:** 919-684-2471; **Board Cert:** Obstetrics & Gynecology 2012; **Med School:** Univ Tenn Coll Med 1991; **Resid:** Obstetrics & Gynecology, Hermann Hosp 1995; **Fellow:** Female Urology, Univ TX Med Ctr 1996; **Fac Appt:** Prof ObG, Duke Univ

Andersen, Glenna R MD [ObG] - **Hospital:** Inova Fairfax Hosp; **Address:** 8501 Arlington Blvd, Ste 300, Fairfax, VA 22031; **Phone:** 703-560-1611; **Board Cert:** Obstetrics & Gynecology 2012; **Med School:** Univ VA Sch Med 1981; **Resid:** Obstetrics & Gynecology, SUNY Buffalo Affil Hosps 1985

Berga, Sarah L MD [ObG] - **Spec Exp:** Infertility; Menopause Problems; Reproductive Endocrinology; Menstrual Disorders; **Hospital:** Wake Forest Baptist Med Ctr; **Address:** Wake Forest Baptist Medical Center, One Medical Ctr Blvd, Watlington Bldg - Fl 4, Winston-Salem, NC 27157-1066; **Phone:** 336-716-6476; **Board Cert:** Obstetrics & Gynecology 2012; Reproductive Endocrinology/Infertility 2012; **Med School:** Univ VA Sch Med 1980; **Resid:** Obstetrics & Gynecology, Mass Genl Hosp 1984; **Fellow:** Reproductive Endocrinology, UCSD Med Ctr 1986; **Fac Appt:** Prof ObG, Wake Forest Univ

Hullfish, Kathie L MD [ObG] - **Spec Exp:** Uro-Gynecology; Pelvic Reconstruction; Pelvic Organ Prolapse Repair; Incontinence; **Hospital:** Univ of Virginia Hlth Sys; **Address:** Univ Virginia Med Ctr, Div Urogynecology, Pelvic Reconst Med, 1215 Lee St, Charlottesville, VA 22908-0712; **Phone:** 434-924-2103; **Board Cert:** Obstetrics & Gynecology 2012; **Med School:** Univ VA Sch Med 1992; **Resid:** Obstetrics & Gynecology, Univ Virginia Med Ctr 1996; **Fellow:** Uro-Gynecology, Rush Med Ctr 1998; **Fac Appt:** Assoc Prof ObG, Univ VA Sch Med

Jenkins, Todd MD [ObG] - **Spec Exp:** Minimally Invasive Surgery; Hysteroscopic Surgery; Endometriosis; Uterine Fibroids; **Hospital:** UAB Hosp; **Address:** UAB Hosp, Dept Obstetrics/Gynecology, 1700 6th Ave S, Birmingham, AL 35249-7333; **Phone:** 205-996-3130; **Board Cert:** Obstetrics & Gynecology 2010; **Med School:** UAB Sch Med 1994; **Resid:** Obstetrics & Gynecology, UAB Hosp 1998; **Fac Appt:** Prof ObG, UAB Sch Med

Morgan, Linda S MD [ObG] - **Spec Exp:** Gynecologic Cancer; Women's Health; **Hospital:** UF Hlth Shands Hosp; **Address:** UF Hlth, Gynecologic Oncology Dept, 2000 SW Archer Rd, Ste 4101, Gainesville, FL 32608; **Phone:** 352-265-8200; **Board Cert:** Obstetrics & Gynecology 2012; Gynecologic Oncology 2012; **Med School:** Med Coll PA Hahnemann 1975; **Resid:** Obstetrics & Gynecology, Shands at Univ FL 1979; **Fellow:** Gynecologic Oncology, Mass Genl Hosp 1981; **Fac Appt:** Prof ObG, Univ Fla Coll Med

Sanz, Luis E MD [ObG] - **Spec Exp:** Uro-Gynecology; Robotic Surgery; Vaginal Reconstruction; Pelvic Reconstruction; **Hospital:** Virginia Hosp Ctr - Arlington; **Address:** 1625 N George Mason Drive, Ste 475, Arlington, VA 22205; **Phone:** 703-717-4000; **Board Cert:** Obstetrics & Gynecology 1982; **Med School:** Georgetown Univ 1976; **Resid:** Obstetrics & Gynecology, Georgetown Univ Hosp 1980; **Fellow:** Gynecologic Oncology, Georgetown Univ 1982; **Fac Appt:** Prof ObG, Georgetown Univ

Steege, John F MD [ObG] - **Spec Exp:** Laparoscopic Surgery; Endometriosis; Pain-Pelvic & Perineal; Gynecologic Surgery; **Hospital:** NC Memorial Hosp - UNC; **Address:** UNC-Dept OB/GYN, CB 7570, Chapel Hill, NC 27599-7570; **Phone:** 919-843-6727; **Board Cert:** Obstetrics & Gynecology 1978; **Med School:** Yale Univ 1972; **Resid:** Obstetrics & Gynecology, Yale - New Haven Hosp 1976; **Fac Appt:** Prof ObG, Univ NC Sch Med

Visco, Anthony G MD [ObG] - **Spec Exp:** Uro-Gynecology; Pelvic Organ Prolapse Repair; Robotic Hysterectomy; Minimally Invasive Surgery; **Hospital:** Duke Univ Hosp, Durham Regional Hosp; **Address:** 5324 McFarland Drive, Ste 310, Box 3192, Durham, NC 27617; **Phone:** 919-684-2471; **Board Cert:** Obstetrics & Gynecology 2012; **Med School:** SUNY Upstate Med Univ 1993; **Resid:** Obstetrics & Gynecology, Univ Rochester Med Ctr 1997; **Fellow:** Uro-Gynecology, Duke Univ Med Ctr 2000; Reconstructive Pelvic Surgery, Duke Univ Med Ctr 2000; **Fac Appt:** Assoc Prof ObG, Duke Univ

Midwest

Argenta, Peter A MD [ObG] - **Spec Exp:** Laparoscopic Surgery; Women's Health; Cervical Cancer; Ovarian Cancer; **Hospital:** Univ Minn Med Ctr, Fairview - West Bank Campus; **Address:** Womens Health Clin, 516 Delaware St SE, Clinic 1C Fl 1, Minneapolis, MN 55455; **Phone:** 612-626-3444; **Board Cert:** Obstetrics & Gynecology 2012; Gynecologic Oncology 2012; **Med School:** Duke Univ 1995; **Resid:** Obstetrics & Gynecology, Hosp U Penn 1999; **Fellow:** Gynecologic Oncology, Mt Sinai Med Ctr 2002; **Fac Appt:** Assoc Prof ObG, Univ Minn

Bartholomew, Deborah A MD [ObG] - **Spec Exp:** Gynecologic Pathology; Robotic Surgery; Minimally Invasive Surgery; **Hospital:** OSU Wexner Med Ctr; **Address:** 4053 W Dublin Granville Rd, Dublin, OH 43017; **Phone:** 614-764-2262; **Board Cert:** Anatomic Pathology 1990; Obstetrics & Gynecology 2012; **Med School:** Med Coll VA 1983; **Resid:** Obstetrics & Gynecology, David Grant USAF Med Ctr 1987; Anatomic Pathology, UC Davis Med Ctr 1987; **Fellow:** Gynecologic Pathology, UC Davis Med Ctr 1989; **Fac Appt:** Assoc Prof ObG, Ohio State Univ

Bradley, Linda D MD [ObG] - **Spec Exp:** Hysteroscopic Surgery; Menstrual Disorders; Endoscopy; Uterine Fibroids; **Hospital:** Cleveland Clin (page 55); **Address:** Cleveland Clinic Fdn, Dept Ob/Gyn, 9500 Euclid Ave, Desk A81, Cleveland, OH 44195; **Phone:** 216-444-6601; **Board Cert:** Obstetrics & Gynecology 2012; **Med School:** Univ Cincinnati 1981; **Resid:** Obstetrics & Gynecology, Cleveland Metro Genl Hosp 1985

Corteville, Jane E MD [ObG] - **Spec Exp:** Fetal Diagnosis & Therapy; Maternal & Fetal Medicine; Prenatal Genetic Diagnosis; Obstetric Ultrasound; **Hospital:** UH Case Med Ctr; **Address:** UH MacDonald Women's Hospital, 11100 Euclid Ave, Cleveland, OH 44106; **Phone:** 216-844-8545; **Board Cert:** Obstetrics & Gynecology 2012; Clinical Genetics 2010; **Med School:** Washington Univ, St Louis 1983; **Resid:** Obstetrics & Gynecology, Barnes-Jewish Hosp 1987; **Fellow:** Ultrasound/CT, Barnes-Jewish Hosp 1989; Medical Genetics, Chldns Hosp 1992; **Fac Appt:** Asst Prof ObG, Case West Res Univ

Culbertson, Sandra MD [ObG] - **Spec Exp:** Pelvic Reconstruction; Uro-Gynecology; Pelvic Organ Prolapse Repair; **Hospital:** Univ of Chicago Med; **Address:** Univ Chicago Med Ctr, 5758 S Maryland Ave Fl 3 - Ste H, Chicago, IL 60637; **Phone:** 773-702-6118; **Board Cert:** Obstetrics & Gynecology 2012; **Med School:** Univ VA Sch Med 1987; **Resid:** Obstetrics & Gynecology, Univ Chicago Med Ctr 1993; **Fellow:** Uro-Gynecology, Univ Chicago Med Ctr 1994; **Fac Appt:** Prof ObG, Univ Chicago-Pritzker Sch Med

De Lancey, John O MD [ObG] - **Spec Exp:** Uro-Gynecology; Incontinence; Pelvic Organ Prolapse Repair; **Hospital:** Univ Michigan Med Ctr; **Address:** Univ Mich Med Ctr, Dept ObGyn, 1500 E Med Ctr Drive, rm L4000, Box 5276, Ann Arbor, MI 48109; **Phone:** 734-764-8429; **Board Cert:** Obstetrics & Gynecology 1997; **Med School:** Univ Mich Med Sch 1977; **Resid:** Obstetrics & Gynecology, Univ Mich Med Ctr 1981; **Fac Appt:** Prof ObG, Univ Mich Med Sch

De Lia, Julian E MD [ObG] - **Spec Exp:** Fetal Surgery; Twin to Twin Transfusion Syndrome (TTTS); **Hospital:** Froedtert & Med Coll WI, Chldns Hosp - Wisconsin; **Address:** Froedtert & Med Coll WI - Dept OB/GYN, 9200 W Wisconsin Ave, Milwaukee, WI 53226; **Phone:** 414-805-6600; **Board Cert:** Obstetrics & Gynecology 1993; **Med School:** UMDNJ-NJ Med Sch, Newark 1972; **Resid:** Obstetrics & Gynecology, Saint Barnabas Med Ctr 1976; **Fac Appt:** Prof ObG, Med Coll Wisc

Famuyide, Abimbola O MD [ObG] - **Spec Exp:** Minimally Invasive Surgery; Uterine Fibroids; **Hospital:** Mayo Med Ctr & Clin - Rochester; **Address:** Mayo Clinic, Dept Ob/Gyn, 200 First St SW, 4A Eisenberg, Rochester, MN 55905; **Phone:** 507-284-2511; **Board Cert:** Obstetrics & Gynecology 2012; **Med School:** Nigeria 1985; **Resid:** Obstetrics & Gynecology, Barnsley District Hosp/Central Sheffield Hosp; Obstetrics & Gynecology, Mayo Grad Sch; **Fac Appt:** Asst Prof ObG, Mayo Med Sch

Gilliam, Melissa MD [ObG] - **Spec Exp:** Adolescent Gynecology; Menstrual Disorders; Pediatric Gynecology; Pap Smear Abnormalities; **Hospital:** Univ of Chicago Med; **Address:** Univ Chicago Med Ctr, 5841 S Maryland Ave, MC 2050, Chicago, IL 60637; **Phone:** 773-702-6118; **Board Cert:** Obstetrics & Gynecology 2009; **Med School:** Harvard Med Sch 1993; **Resid:** Obstetrics & Gynecology, Northwestern Meml Hosp 1998; **Fac Appt:** Prof ObG, Univ Chicago-Pritzker Sch Med

Greenfield, Marjorie MD [ObG] - **Spec Exp:** Adolescent Gynecology; **Hospital:** UH Case Med Ctr; **Address:** UH MacDonald Women's Hosp, Obstetrics & Gynecology, 11100 Euclid Ave, Ste 1200, Cleveland, OH 44106; **Phone:** 216-844-3941; **Board Cert:** Obstetrics & Gynecology 2012; **Med School:** Case West Res Univ 1983; **Resid:** Obstetrics & Gynecology, Univ Hosp 1987; **Fac Appt:** Prof ObG, Case West Res Univ

Hale, Douglass S MD [ObG] - **Spec Exp:** Uro-Gynecology; Pelvic Floor Reconstruction; Reconstructive Surgery; Robotic Surgery; **Hospital:** IU Health Methodist Hosp; **Address:** 1633 N Capitol Ave, Ste 436, Indianapolis, IN 46202; **Phone:** 317-962-6600; **Board Cert:** Obstetrics & Gynecology 2012; **Med School:** Med Coll OH 1989; **Resid:** Obstetrics & Gynecology, Thomas Jefferson Univ Hosp 1993; **Fellow:** Uro-Gynecology, IU Methodist Hosp 1995; Reconstructive Surgery, IU Methodist Hosp 1995; **Fac Appt:** Assoc Clin Prof ObG, Indiana Univ

Karram, Mickey M MD [ObG] - **Spec Exp:** Uro-Gynecology; Pelvic Floor Reconstruction; Incontinence-Female; **Hospital:** Christ Hosp, The - Cincinnati; **Address:** 7759 University Drive, Ste G, Westchester, OH 45069; **Phone:** 513-463-2500; **Board Cert:** Obstetrics & Gynecology 2012; **Med School:** Egypt 1982; **Resid:** Obstetrics & Gynecology, Good Samaritan Hosp 1985; **Fellow:** Gynecologic Urology, Harbor Hosp-UCLA 1988; **Fac Appt:** Prof ObG, Univ Cincinnati

Kenton, Kimberly S MD [ObG] - **Spec Exp:** Pelvic Reconstruction; Uro-Gynecology; Pelvic Organ Prolapse Repair; Minimally Invasive Gynecologic Surgery; **Hospital:** Northwestern Meml Hosp; **Address:** 676 N St Clair Fl 9 - Ste 950, Chicago, IL 60611; **Phone:** 312-926-4747; **Board Cert:** Obstetrics & Gynecology 2012; **Med School:** Rush Med Coll 1995; **Resid:** Obstetrics & Gynecology, Rush Univ Med Ctr 1999; **Fellow:** Uro-Gynecology, Rush-Presby St Luke's Med Ctr 2000; Reconstructive Pelvic Surgery, Loyola Univ Med Ctr 2002; **Fac Appt:** Prof ObG, Northwestern Univ

Levine, Elliot MD [ObG] - **Spec Exp:** Sexually Transmitted Diseases; Sexual Dysfunction; Vulvar & Vaginal Disorders; Vulvar Pain; **Hospital:** Adv Illinois Masonic Med Ctr; **Address:** 3000 N Halsted St, Ste 625, Chicago, IL 60657; **Phone:** 773-296-3450; **Board Cert:** Obstetrics & Gynecology 1984; **Med School:** Ros Franklin Univ/Chicago Med Sch 1978; **Resid:** Obstetrics & Gynecology, Illinois Masonic Med Ctr 1982; **Fac Appt:** Asst Prof ObG, Rush Med Coll

Merritt, Diane F MD [ObG] - **Spec Exp:** Adolescent Gynecology; Pediatric Gynecology; Endometriosis; Congenital Anomalies-Gynecologic; **Hospital:** Barnes-Jewish Hosp, St. Louis Chldns Hosp; **Address:** 4921 Park View Pl Fl 13th - Ste C, St Louis, MO 63110; **Phone:** 314-362-4211; **Board Cert:** Obstetrics & Gynecology 1984; **Med School:** NYU Sch Med 1975; **Resid:** Surgery, Barnes Hosp-Wash Univ 1977; Obstetrics & Gynecology, Barnes Hosp-Wash Univ 1980; **Fac Appt:** Prof ObG, Washington Univ, St Louis

Niebyl, Jennifer R MD [ObG] - **Spec Exp:** Premature Labor; Vomiting-Cyclic; **Hospital:** Univ Iowa Hosp & Clins; **Address:** Univ Iowa Hosps & Clins, 200 Hawkins Drive, Dept Ob/Gyn, Iowa City, IA 52242; **Phone:** 319-384-9247; **Board Cert:** Obstetrics & Gynecology 1998; Maternal & Fetal Medicine 1998; **Med School:** Yale Univ 1967; **Resid:** Obstetrics & Gynecology, NY Hosp-Cornell Med Ctr 1970; Obstetrics & Gynecology, Johns Hopkins Hosp 1973; **Fellow:** Maternal & Fetal Medicine, Johns Hopkins Hosp 1978; **Fac Appt:** Prof ObG, Univ Iowa Coll Med

Sand, Peter K MD [ObG] - **Spec Exp:** Uro-Gynecology; Incontinence; Pelvic Organ Prolapse Repair; Voiding Dysfunction; **Hospital:** Evanston Hosp/NorthShore Univ Hlth Sys (page 67), Skokie Hosp/NorthShore Univ Htlh Syst (page 67); **Address:** North Shore Med Grp, Ob/Gyn, 9650 Gross Point Rd, Ste 3900, Skokie, IL 60076; **Phone:** 224-251-2374; **Board Cert:** Obstetrics & Gynecology 2012; **Med School:** Northwestern Univ 1980; **Resid:** Obstetrics & Gynecology, Northwestern Meml Hosp 1984; **Fellow:** Uro-Gynecology, UC Irvine Med Ctr 1986; **Fac Appt:** Prof ObG, Univ Chicago-Pritzker Sch Med

Valaitis, Sandra MD [ObG] - **Spec Exp:** Uro-Gynecology; Pelvic Organ Prolapse Repair; Incontinence; **Hospital:** Univ of Chicago Med; **Address:** Univ Chicago Med Ctr, Dept Ob/Gyn, 5841 S Maryland Ave, MC 2050, Chicago, IL 60637; **Phone:** 773-834-8622; **Board Cert:** Obstetrics & Gynecology 2012; **Med School:** Univ Chicago-Pritzker Sch Med 1989; **Resid:** Obstetrics & Gynecology, Univ Chicago Med Ctr 1993; **Fellow:** Uro-Gynecology, St Georges Hosp; **Fac Appt:** Assoc Prof ObG, Univ Chicago-Pritzker Sch Med

Walters, Mark D MD [ObG] - **Spec Exp:** Uro-Gynecology; Vaginal Reconstruction; Incontinence-Female; Pelvic Organ Prolapse Repair; **Hospital:** Cleveland Clin (page 55); **Address:** Cleveland Clinic, Dept Ob/Gyn, 9500 Euclid Ave, Desk A81, Cleveland, OH 44195; **Phone:** 216-444-6601; **Board Cert:** Obstetrics & Gynecology 2012; **Med School:** Ohio State Univ 1980; **Resid:** Obstetrics & Gynecology, New England Med Ctr 1984

Great Plains and Mountains

Byrne, Janice LB MD [ObG] - **Spec Exp:** Prenatal Diagnosis; Ultrasound; Reproductive Genetics; **Hospital:** Univ Utah Hlth Care; **Address:** 50 N Medical Drive, Ste 2B200, Salt Lake City, UT 84132; **Phone:** 801-581-8425; **Board Cert:** Obstetrics & Gynecology 2012; Clinical Genetics 2010; Maternal & Fetal Medicine 2012; **Med School:** Univ Tex SW, Dallas 1987; **Resid:** Obstetrics & Gynecology, Univ Utah Hosps & Clins 1991; **Fellow:** Clinical Genetics, Univ Utah Hosps & Clins 1993; Maternal & Fetal Medicine, Univ Utah Hosps & Clins 1994; **Fac Appt:** Clin Prof ObG, Univ Utah

King, Aileen MD [ObG] - **Spec Exp:** Women's Health; **Hospital:** St. Luke's Boise Med Ctr; **Address:** Women's Health Assocs, 333 N First St, Ste 240, Boise, ID 83702; **Phone:** 208-338-8900; **Board Cert:** Obstetrics & Gynecology 2012; **Med School:** UC Irvine 1996; **Resid:** Obstetrics & Gynecology, Univ CO Hlth Sci Ctr 2000

Richardson, Marilyn R MD [ObG] - **Spec Exp:** Reproductive Endocrinology; Hormonal Disorders; Menopause Problems; Gynecology Only; **Address:** Hormone, Hair, & Vein Ctr, 12616 W 62nd Terr, Ste 112, Shawnee, KS 66216; **Phone:** 913-631-0277; **Board Cert:** Obstetrics & Gynecology 2012; **Med School:** Univ Kansas 1979; **Resid:** Obstetrics & Gynecology, Truman Med Ctr 1984; **Fellow:** Reproductive Endocrinology, Univ TX Hlth Scis Ctr 1987; **Fac Appt:** Asst Clin Prof ObG, Univ Kansas

Southwest

Bradshaw, Karen D MD [ObG] - **Spec Exp:** Women's Health; Preventive Medicine; Pediatric & Adolescent Gynecology; Menstrual Disorders; **Hospital:** UT Southwestern Med Ctr at Dallas; **Address:** Lowe Fdn Ctr Womens Preventive Hlth Care, 5939 Harry Hines Blvd Fl 5 - Ste 200, Dallas, TX 75390; **Phone:** 214-645-3888; **Board Cert:** Obstetrics & Gynecology 2012; Reproductive Endocrinology 2012; **Med School:** Univ Tex SW, Dallas 1981; **Resid:** Obstetrics & Gynecology, Parkland Meml Hosp 1985; **Fellow:** Reproductive Endocrinology, UT Southwestern Med Ctr 1987; **Fac Appt:** Prof ObG, Univ Tex SW, Dallas

Cornella, Jeffrey L MD [ObG] - **Spec Exp:** Pelvic Reconstruction; Robotic Surgery; Uro-Gynecology; Vaginal Reconstruction; **Hospital:** Mayo Clinic - Phoenix; **Address:** Mayo Clin - Dept Gynecology, 5779 E Mayo Blvd, Phoenix, AZ 85054; **Phone:** 480-301-8484; **Board Cert:** Obstetrics & Gynecology 2012; **Med School:** Washington Univ, St Louis 1981; **Resid:** Obstetrics & Gynecology, Mayo Clin 1986; **Fellow:** Uro-Gynecology, UC Irvine Med Ctr 1987; **Fac Appt:** Prof ObG, Mayo Med Sch

Snyder, Russell R MD [ObG] - **Spec Exp:** Gynecologic Surgery; Pap Smear Abnormalities; Vulvar & Vaginal Disorders; **Hospital:** UT Med Br at Galveston(John Sealy Hosp); **Address:** UTMB, Womens Hlth Ctr, 301 University Blvd, Rte 1386 Fl 3, Galveston, TX 77555; **Phone:** 409-772-9507; **Board Cert:** Obstetrics & Gynecology 2013; **Med School:** Univ Tex, Houston 1978; **Resid:** Obstetrics & Gynecology, Wilford Hall USAF Med Ctr 1982; **Fellow:** Gynecologic Pathology, Armed Forces Inst Path 1984; **Fac Appt:** Assoc Prof ObG, Univ Tex Med Br, Galveston

West Coast and Pacific

Eschenbach, David A MD [ObG] - **Spec Exp:** Gynecologic Surgery-Complex; Vulvar & Vaginal Disorders; **Hospital:** Univ Wash Med Ctr; **Address:** Univ Washington Women's Health Care, 4245 Roosevelt Way NE, Box 354765, Seattle, WA 98105; **Phone:** 206-598-5500; **Board Cert:** Obstetrics & Gynecology 1975; **Med School:** Univ Wisc 1968; **Resid:** Obstetrics & Gynecology, Univ Wash Hosp 1973; **Fellow:** Infectious Disease, Univ Wash Hosp 1974; **Fac Appt:** Prof ObG, Univ Wash

Goldman, Mindy E MD [ObG] - **Spec Exp:** Breast Cancer; **Hospital:** UCSF Med Ctr; **Address:** 2356 Sutter St, 5th Floor, San Francisco, CA 94115; **Phone:** 415-885-7788; **Board Cert:** Obstetrics & Gynecology 2007; **Med School:** Univ VT Coll Med 1989; **Resid:** Obstetrics & Gynecology, UCSF Med Ctr 1993; **Fac Appt:** Clin Prof ObG

Parker, William H MD [ObG] - **Spec Exp:** Uterine Fibroids; Gynecologic Surgery; Hysteroscopic Surgery; Uro-Gynecology; **Hospital:** Santa Monica - UCLA Med Ctr & Ortho Hosp, St. John's Hlth Ctr, Santa Monica; **Address:** 1450 10th St, Ste 404, Santa Monica, CA 90401-2804; **Phone:** 310-451-8144; **Board Cert:** Obstetrics & Gynecology 1981; **Med School:** SUNY Downstate 1974; **Resid:** Obstetrics & Gynecology, UCSD Med Ctr 1978; **Fac Appt:** Clin Prof ObG, UCLA

Ophthalmology

An ophthalmologist has the knowledge and professional skills needed to provide comprehensive eye and vision care. Ophthalmologists are medically trained to diagnose, monitor and medically or surgically treat all ocular and visual disorders. This includes problems affecting the eye and its component structures, the eyelids, the orbit and the visual pathways. In so doing, an ophthalmologist prescribes vision services, including glasses and contact lenses.

Training Required: Four years

OPHTHALMOLOGY

New England

Dana, Reza MD [Oph] - **Spec Exp:** Corneal Disease & Transplant; Dry Eye Syndrome; Uveitis; **Hospital:** Mass Eye & Ear Infirm; **Address:** Mass Eye & Ear Infirmary, 243 Charles St, Boston, MA 02114; **Phone:** 617-573-4331; **Board Cert:** Ophthalmology 2006; **Med School:** Johns Hopkins Univ 1989; **Resid:** Ophthalmology, Illinois Eye & Ear Infirm 1993; **Fellow:** Cornea & Ext Eye Disease, Wills Eye Hosp 1994; Uveitis, Mass Eye & Ear Infirm 1995; **Fac Appt:** Prof Oph, Harvard Med Sch

Duker, Jay S MD [Oph] - **Spec Exp:** Retinal Disorders; Retinal Disorders-Pediatric; Diabetic Eye Disease/Retinopathy; **Hospital:** Tufts Med Ctr; **Address:** New England Eye Center, 260 Tremont St Biewend Bldg, Boston, MA 02116; **Phone:** 617-636-4677; **Board Cert:** Ophthalmology 1989; **Med School:** Jefferson Med Coll 1984; **Resid:** Ophthalmology, Wills Eye Hosp 1988; **Fellow:** Vitreoretinal Surgery & Disease, Wills Eye Hosp 1990; **Fac Appt:** Assoc Prof Oph, Tufts Univ

Foster, C Stephen MD [Oph] - **Spec Exp:** Uveitis; Corneal Disease; Cataract Surgery; **Hospital:** Mass Eye & Ear Infirm, Mount Auburn Hosp; **Address:** Mass Eye Research & Surgery Inst, 5 Cambridge Center Fl 8, Cambridge, MA 02142; **Phone:** 617-621-6377; **Board Cert:** Ophthalmology 1976; **Med School:** Duke Univ 1969; **Resid:** Ophthalmology, Barnes Hosp 1975; **Fellow:** Cornea, Mass EE Infirm-Harvard 1976; Ocular Immunology, Mass EE Infirm-Harvard 1977; **Fac Appt:** Prof Oph, Harvard Med Sch

Hedges, Thomas R MD [Oph] - **Spec Exp:** Neuro-Ophthalmology; **Hospital:** Tufts Med Ctr; **Address:** New England Eye Center, 260 Tremont St Biewend Bldg, Boston, MA 02116; **Phone:** 617-636-5488; **Board Cert:** Ophthalmology 1980; **Med School:** Tufts Univ 1975; **Resid:** Ophthalmology, Mass EE Infirm 1980; **Fellow:** Neuro-Ophthalmology, UCSF Med Ctr 1981; **Fac Appt:** Prof Oph, Tufts Univ

Hunter, David G MD/PhD [Oph] - **Spec Exp:** Pediatric Ophthalmology; Eye Muscle Disorders; Strabismus; Congenital Fibrosis-Extraocular Muscles; **Hospital:** Children's Hospital - Boston; **Address:** Boston Chldn's Hosp, Dept Ophthalmology, 300 Longwood Ave, Fegan 4, Boston, MA 02115; **Phone:** 617-355-6401; **Board Cert:** Ophthalmology 2013; **Med School:** Baylor Coll Med 1987; **Resid:** Ophthalmology, Mass EE Infirm 1991; **Fellow:** Pediatric Ophthalmology, Wilmer Ophthalmic Inst/Johns Hopkins 1992; **Fac Appt:** Prof Oph, Harvard Med Sch

Kornmehl, Ernest W MD [Oph] - **Spec Exp:** LASIK-Refractive Surgery; PRK-Refractive Surgery; Dry Eye Syndrome; Keratoconus; **Hospital:** Mass Eye & Ear Infirm, Brigham & Women's Hosp; **Address:** Kornmehl Laser Eye Assoc, 54 Washington St, Wellesley, MA 02481; **Phone:** 877-870-2010; **Board Cert:** Ophthalmology 1989; **Med School:** SUNY Downstate 1984; **Resid:** Ophthalmology, Yale-New Haven Hosp 1988; **Fellow:** Cornea & Ext Eye Disease, Mass E&E Infirm 1990; **Fac Appt:** Assoc Clin Prof Oph, Harvard Med Sch

Miller, Joan W MD [Oph] - **Spec Exp:** Macular Degeneration; Retinal Disorders; **Hospital:** Mass Eye & Ear Infirm; **Address:** Mass Eye & Ear Infirm, Ophthalmology, 243 Charles St, Boston, MA 02114; **Phone:** 617-573-3915; **Board Cert:** Ophthalmology 1991; **Med School:** Harvard Med Sch 1985; **Resid:** Ophthalmology, Mass Eye & Ear Infirm 1989; **Fellow:** Retina, Mass Eye & Ear Infirm 1991; **Fac Appt:** Prof Oph, Harvard Med Sch

Mitchell, Paul R MD [Oph] - **Spec Exp:** Pediatric Ophthalmology; Nystagmus; Strabismus; **Hospital:** CT Chldns Med Ctr, Hartford Hosp; **Address:** Chldns Eye Care, 366 Colt Hwy, Rte 6 Bldg 2, Farmington, CT 06032; **Phone:** 860-409-0449; **Board Cert:** Ophthalmology 1977; **Med School:** Geo Wash Univ 1970; **Resid:** Ophthalmology, Wills Eye Hosp 1976; **Fellow:** Pediatric Ophthalmology, Chldns Hosp 1977; **Fac Appt:** Asst Clin Prof Oph, Univ Conn

Rizzo III, Joseph F MD [Oph] - **Spec Exp:** Neuro-Ophthalmology; Optic Nerve Disorders; **Hospital:** Mass Eye & Ear Infirm; **Address:** Mass Eye & Ear Infirmary, 243 Charles St Fl 9, Boston, MA 02114; **Phone:** 617-573-3412; **Board Cert:** Neurology 1984; Ophthalmology 1987; **Med School:** Louisiana State U, New Orleans 1978; **Resid:** Neurology, Tufts-New Engl Med Ctr 1982; Ophthalmology, Boston Univ Med Ctr 1985; **Fellow:** Neuro-Ophthalmology, Harvard Univ 1986; **Fac Appt:** Assoc Prof Oph, Harvard Med Sch

Rubin, Peter MD [Oph] - **Spec Exp:** Oculoplastic Surgery; Orbital & Eyelid Tumors/Cancer; Eyelid Cancer & Reconstruction; Eyelid Cosmetic & Reconstructive Surgery; **Hospital:** Beth Israel Deaconess Med Ctr - Boston; **Address:** Boston Eye Phys and Surgeons, 44 Washington St, Ste 103A, Brookline, MA 02445; **Phone:** 617-232-9600; **Board Cert:** Ophthalmology 1991; **Med School:** Yale Univ 1985; **Resid:** Ophthalmology, Lenox Hill Hosp 1989; **Fellow:** Oculoplastic Surgery, Mass Eye & Ear Infirmary 1991; **Fac Appt:** Assoc Prof Oph, Univ Tenn Coll Med

Shingleton, Bradford J MD [Oph] - **Spec Exp:** Cataract Surgery; Glaucoma; **Hospital:** Mass Eye & Ear Infirm; **Address:** Ophthalmic Consultants of Boston, 50 Stanford St, Ste 600, Boston, MA 02114; **Phone:** 617-314-2614; **Board Cert:** Ophthalmology 1982; **Med School:** Univ Mich Med Sch 1977; **Resid:** Ophthalmology, Mass E&E Infirm 1981; **Fellow:** Refractive Surgery, Mass E&E Infirm 1982; **Fac Appt:** Asst Clin Prof Oph, Harvard Med Sch

Tsai, James C MD [Oph] - **Spec Exp:** Glaucoma; **Hospital:** Yale-New Haven Hosp; **Address:** Yale Eye Ctr, 40 Temple St Fl 3, New Haven, CT 06520-8061; **Phone:** 203-785-2020; **Board Cert:** Ophthalmology 2006; **Med School:** Stanford Univ 1989; **Resid:** Internal Medicine, Cedars-Sinai Med Ctr 1990; Ophthalmology, Doheny Eye Inst/USC 1993; **Fellow:** Glaucoma, Bascom Palmer Eye Inst 1994; Glaucoma, Moorfields Eye Hosp 1995; **Fac Appt:** Prof Oph, Yale Univ

Walton, David S MD [Oph] - **Spec Exp:** Glaucoma-Pediatric; Cataract-Pediatric; Neuro-Ophthalmology; **Hospital:** Mass Eye & Ear Infirm, Mass Genl Hosp; **Address:** 2 Longfellow Pl, Ste 201, Boston, MA 02114; **Phone:** 617-227-3011; **Board Cert:** Ophthalmology 1969; Pediatrics 1983; **Med School:** Duke Univ 1961; **Resid:** Ophthalmology, Mass EE Infirm 1967; **Fellow:** Glaucoma, Mass EE Infirm 1968; **Fac Appt:** Prof Oph, Harvard Med Sch

Mid Atlantic

Abramson, David H MD [Oph] - **Spec Exp:** Eye Tumors/Cancer; Orbital Tumors/Cancer; Retinoblastoma; Melanoma-Choroidal (eye); **Hospital:** Meml Sloan-Kettering Canc Ctr, NY-Presby/Weill Cornell Med Ctr, NY (page 65); **Address:** 70 E 66th St, New York, NY 10065; **Phone:** 212-744-1700; **Board Cert:** Ophthalmology 1975; **Med School:** Albert Einstein Coll Med 1969; **Resid:** Ophthalmology, Harkness Eye Inst 1974; **Fellow:** Ocular Oncology, Columbia-Presby Med Ctr 1975; **Fac Appt:** Prof Oph, Cornell Univ-Weill Med Coll

Asbell, Penny A MD [Oph] - **Spec Exp:** Corneal Disease & Transplant; LASIK-Refractive Surgery; Cataract Surgery; Keratoconus; **Hospital:** Mt Sinai Med Ctr (page 62); **Address:** 17 E 102nd St Fl 8, New York, NY 10029; **Phone:** 212-241-7977; **Board Cert:** Ophthalmology 1980; **Med School:** SUNY Buffalo 1975; **Resid:** Ophthalmology, NYU Med Ctr 1979; **Fellow:** Immunology, NYU Med Ctr 1980; Cornea & Ext Eye Disease, LSU Eye Ctr 1982; **Fac Appt:** Prof Oph, Mount Sinai Sch Med

Barile, Gaetano R MD [Oph] - **Spec Exp:** Macular Disease/Degeneration; Retinal Disorders; Diabetic Eye Disease/Retinopathy; Retina/Vitreous Consultation; **Hospital:** Lenox Hill Hosp (Manh Eye, Ear & Throat Hosp) (page 66); **Address:** 210 E 64 St, Fl 7, New York, NY 10065; **Phone:** 212-702-7400; **Board Cert:** Ophthalmology 2008; **Med School:** Cornell Univ 1991; **Resid:** Ophthalmology, Manhattan EET Hosp 1995; **Fellow:** Retina/Vitreous Surgery, Roosevelt Hosp/Harkness Eye Inst 1997; Retina, Moorfields Eye Hosp 1997

Braunstein, Richard E MD [Oph] - **Spec Exp:** LASIK-Refractive Surgery; Corneal Disease & Transplant; Cataract Surgery; **Hospital:** Lenox Hill Hosp (Manh Eye, Ear & Throat Hosp) (page 66); **Address:** MEETH Ophthalmology, 210 E 64th St, New York, NY 10065; **Phone:** 212-702-7300; **Board Cert:** Ophthalmology 2006; **Med School:** Columbia P&S 1989; **Resid:** Ophthalmology, Harkness Eye Inst 1993; **Fellow:** Cornea & Ext Eye Disease, Wilmer Inst/Johns Hopkins Hosp 1994

Bressler, Neil M MD [Oph] - **Spec Exp:** Retinal Disorders; **Hospital:** Johns Hopkins Hosp (page 59); **Address:** Johns Hopkins Wilmer Eye Inst, 600 N Wolfe St, Maumenee Bldg 752, Baltimore, MD 21287; **Phone:** 410-955-8342; **Board Cert:** Ophthalmology 1987; **Med School:** Johns Hopkins Univ 1982; **Resid:** Internal Medicine, Johns Hopkins Hosp 1983; Ophthalmology, Mass Eye & Ear Infirm 1986; **Fellow:** Retina, Wilmer Eye Inst/Johns Hopkins Hosp 1987; **Fac Appt:** Assoc Prof Oph, Johns Hopkins Univ

Bressler, Susan B MD [Oph] - **Spec Exp:** Diabetic Eye Disease/Retinopathy; Retinal Disorders; Macular Degeneration; **Hospital:** Johns Hopkins Hosp (page 59); **Address:** Johns Hopkins Wilmer Eye Inst, 600 N Wolfe St, Maumenee 706, Baltimore, MD 21287; **Phone:** 410-955-3648; **Board Cert:** Ophthalmology 1987; **Med School:** Johns Hopkins Univ 1982; **Resid:** Ophthalmology, Mass Eye & Ear Infirmary 1986; **Fellow:** Ophthalmology, Wilmer Eye Inst 1987; Retinal Surgery, Mass Eye & Ear Infirmary 1988; **Fac Appt:** Prof Oph, Johns Hopkins Univ

Brown, Gary C MD [Oph] - **Spec Exp:** Retinal Disorders; Retinal Vascular Diseases; Macular Degeneration; Diabetic Eye Disease/Retinopathy; **Hospital:** Wills Eye Hosp (page 71), Thomas Jefferson Univ Hosp; **Address:** Mid-Atlantic Retina, 4060 Butler Pike, Ste 200, Plymouth Meeting, PA 19462; **Phone:** 800-331-6634; **Board Cert:** Ophthalmology 1980; **Med School:** SUNY Upstate Med Univ 1975; **Resid:** Ophthalmology, Wills Eye Hosp 1979; **Fellow:** Retina/Vitreous Surgery, Wills Eye Hosp 1981; **Fac Appt:** Prof Oph, Jefferson Med Coll

Brucker, Alexander J MD [Oph] - **Spec Exp:** Retinal Disorders; Retina/Vitreous Surgery; Macular Degeneration; **Hospital:** Penn Presby Med Ctr - UPHS (page 69), Hosp Univ Penn - UPHS (page 69); **Address:** Scheie Eye Inst, Penn Eye Care, 51 N 39th St, Ste 517, Philadelphia, PA 19104; **Phone:** 215-662-8100; **Board Cert:** Ophthalmology 1977; **Med School:** NY Med Coll 1972; **Resid:** Ophthalmology, Friedenwald Inst 1976; **Fellow:** Retina/Vitreous Surgery, Johns Hopkins Hosp 1977; **Fac Appt:** Prof Oph, Univ Pennsylvania

Campochiaro, Peter MD [Oph] - **Spec Exp:** Retina/Vitreous Surgery; **Hospital:** Johns Hopkins Hosp (page 59); **Address:** Johns Hopkins Wilmer Eye Inst, 600 N Wolfe St, Maumenee 205, Baltimore, MD 21287-9277; **Phone:** 410-955-3518; **Board Cert:** Ophthalmology 1983; **Med School:** Johns Hopkins Univ 1978; **Resid:** Ophthalmology, Univ Virginia Affil Hosp 1982; **Fellow:** Retina/Vitreous Surgery, Johns Hopkins Hosp 1984; **Fac Appt:** Prof Oph, Johns Hopkins Univ

Caputo, Anthony R MD [Oph] - **Spec Exp:** Pediatric Ophthalmology; Strabismus; **Hospital:** Clara Maass Med Ctr; **Address:** 556 Eagle Rock Ave, Ste 203, Roseland, NJ 07068-1500; **Phone:** 973-228-3111; **Board Cert:** Ophthalmology 1976; **Med School:** Italy 1969; **Resid:** Ophthalmology, UMDNJ-Univ Hosp 1974; **Fellow:** Ophthalmology, Wills Eye Hosp 1975; **Fac Appt:** Prof Oph, UMDNJ-NJ Med Sch, Newark

Chang, Stanley MD [Oph] - **Spec Exp:** Retina/Vitreous Surgery; Diabetic Eye Disease/Retinopathy; Macular Disease/Degeneration; Retinal Disorders; **Hospital:** NY-Presby/Columbia Univ Med Ctr, NY (page 65); **Address:** 635 W 165th St, Box 92, New York, NY 10032; **Phone:** 212-305-9535; **Board Cert:** Ophthalmology 1979; **Med School:** Columbia P&S 1974; **Resid:** Ophthalmology, Mass Eye & Ear Infirm 1978; **Fellow:** Vitreoretinal Surgery, Bascom Palmer Eye Inst 1979; **Fac Appt:** Prof Oph, Columbia P&S

Cioffi, George MD [Oph] - **Spec Exp:** Glaucoma; Cataract Surgery; Anterior Segment Surgery; **Hospital:** NY-Presby/Columbia Univ Med Ctr, NY (page 65); **Address:** 635 W 165th St, Columbia Ophthalmic Consultants, Flazner Ste, New York, NY 10032; **Phone:** 212-305-9535; **Board Cert:** Ophthalmology 2004; **Med School:** Univ SC Sch Med 1987; **Resid:** Ophthalmology, Univ Maryland Affil Hosp 1991; **Fellow:** Glaucoma, Devers Eye Inst 1992; **Fac Appt:** Prof Oph, Columbia P&S

Clinch, Thomas E MD [Oph] - **Spec Exp:** Laser Vision Surgery; LASIK-Refractive Surgery; Cataract Surgery; **Address:** Eye Doctors of Washington, 2 Wisconsin Cir, Ste 230, Chevy Chase, MD 20815; **Phone:** 301-215-7100; **Board Cert:** Ophthalmology 1989; **Med School:** Jefferson Med Coll 1983; **Resid:** Ophthalmology, Wills Eye Hosp 1988

Cykiert, Robert MD [Oph] - **Spec Exp:** LASIK-Refractive Surgery; Cataract Surgery; Corneal Disease & Transplant; Keratoconus; **Hospital:** NYU Langone Med Ctr (page 68), New York Eye & Ear Infirm (page 64); **Address:** 345 E 37th St, Ste 210, New York, NY 10016-3217; **Phone:** 212-922-1430; **Board Cert:** Ophthalmology 1981; **Med School:** NY Med Coll 1976; **Resid:** Ophthalmology, Montefiore Med Ctr 1980; **Fellow:** Cornea & Ext Eye Disease, Wills Eye Hosp 1981; **Fac Appt:** Assoc Clin Prof Oph, NYU Sch Med

D'Amico, Donald J MD [Oph] - **Spec Exp:** Diabetic Eye Disease/Retinopathy; Retinal Detachment; Retinal Disorders; **Hospital:** NY-Presby/Weill Cornell Med Ctr, NY (page 65); **Address:** Weill Cornell Eye Associates, Dept of Ophthalmology, 1305 York Ave, Fl 11th, New York, NY 10021; **Phone:** 646-962-2020; **Board Cert:** Ophthalmology 1982; **Med School:** Univ IL Coll Med 1977; **Resid:** Ophthalmology, Mass Eye & Ear Infirm 1981; **Fellow:** Vitreoretinal Surgery, Bascom Palmer Eye Inst 1982; **Fac Appt:** Prof Oph, Cornell Univ-Weill Med Coll

Della Rocca, Robert C MD [Oph] - **Spec Exp:** Orbital Tumors/Cancer; Eyelid Tumors/Cancer; Oculoplastic Surgery; Eyelid Cancer & Reconstruction; **Hospital:** New York Eye & Ear Infirm (page 64), Sound Shore Med Ctr - Westchester; **Address:** 310 E 14th St, South Bldg, rm 319, New York, NY 10003; **Phone:** 212-979-4575; **Board Cert:** Ophthalmology 1975; **Med School:** Creighton Univ 1967; **Resid:** Ophthalmology, NY Eye & Ear Infirm 1973; **Fellow:** Oculoplastic Surgery, Albany Med Coll/NY Eye & Ear Infirm 1975

Dhaliwal, Deepinder K MD [Oph] - **Spec Exp:** Corneal & External Eye Disease; Anterior Segment Surgery; LASIK-Refractive Surgery; **Hospital:** UPMC Presby, Pittsburgh; **Address:** UPMC Eye Ctr, 203 Lothrop St, Ste 718, Pittsburgh, PA 15213; **Phone:** 412-647-2200; **Board Cert:** Ophthalmology 2007; **Med School:** Northwestern Univ-Feinberg Sch Med 1990; **Resid:** Ophthalmology, Eye & Ear Inst-UPMC 1994; **Fellow:** Refractive Surgery, Univ Utah Hlth Care 1995; **Fac Appt:** Assoc Prof Oph, Univ Pittsburgh

Dodick, Jack M MD [Oph] - **Spec Exp:** Cataract Surgery-Lens Implant; Laser Vision Surgery; **Hospital:** NYU Langone Med Ctr (page 68), Lenox Hill Hosp (Manh Eye, Ear & Throat Hosp) (page 66); **Address:** 535 Park Ave, New York, NY 10065; **Phone:** 212-288-7638; **Board Cert:** Ophthalmology 1969; **Med School:** Univ Toronto 1963; **Resid:** Ophthalmology, Manhattan EE&T Hosp 1967; **Fellow:** Anterior Segment - External Disease, Westchester Co Med Ctr 1968; **Fac Appt:** Prof Oph, NYU Sch Med

Eagle, Ralph C MD [Oph] - **Spec Exp:** Ophthalmic Pathology; **Hospital:** Wills Eye Hosp (page 71); **Address:** Wills Eye Hosp, Pathology Dept, 840 Walnut St, Ste 1410, Philadelphia, PA 19107; **Phone:** 215-928-3280; **Board Cert:** Ophthalmology 1976; **Med School:** Univ Pennsylvania 1970; **Resid:** Ophthalmology, Scheie Eye Inst 1975; **Fellow:** Ophthalmic Pathology, Armed Forces Inst Path 1978; **Fac Appt:** Prof Oph, Jefferson Med Coll

Eggers, Howard M MD [Oph] - **Spec Exp:** Pediatric Ophthalmology; Strabismus-Adult & Pediatric; **Hospital:** NY-Presby/Columbia Univ Med Ctr, NY (page 65); **Address:** Harkness Eye Institute, 635 W 165th St, New York, NY 10032-3724; **Phone:** 212-305-5409; **Board Cert:** Ophthalmology 1978; **Med School:** Columbia P&S 1971; **Resid:** Ophthalmology, Harkness Inst-Presby Hosp 1975; **Fac Appt:** Prof Oph, Columbia P&S

Feldon, Steven E MD [Oph] - **Spec Exp:** Neuro-Ophthalmology; Orbital Surgery; Strabismus; Thyroid Eye Disease; **Hospital:** Univ Rochester Strong Meml Hosp; **Address:** Flaum Eye Institute, 210 Crittenden Blvd, Rochester, NY 14642; **Phone:** 585-273-3937; **Board Cert:** Ophthalmology 1979; **Med School:** Albert Einstein Coll Med 1973; **Resid:** Ophthalmology, Mass Eye & Ear Infirmary 1978; **Fellow:** Neurological Surgery, Mass Genl Hosp 1975; Neuro-Ophthalmology, UCSF Med Ctr 1979; **Fac Appt:** Prof Oph, Univ Rochester

Finger, Paul T MD [Oph] - **Spec Exp:** Eye Tumors/Cancer; Melanoma-Choroidal (eye); Retinoblastoma; Orbital Tumors/Cancer; **Hospital:** New York Eye & Ear Infirm (page 64), Lenox Hill Hosp (Manh Eye, Ear & Throat Hosp) (page 66); **Address:** 115 E 61st St, Fl 5, Ste B, New York, NY 10065; **Phone:** 212-832-8170; **Board Cert:** Ophthalmology 1990; **Med School:** Tulane Univ 1982; **Resid:** Ophthalmology, Manhattan EET Hosp 1986; **Fellow:** Ocular Oncology, N Shore Univ Hosp 1987; **Fac Appt:** Clin Prof Oph, NYU Sch Med

Florakis, George J MD [Oph] - **Spec Exp:** Cornea Transplant; Corneal Disease; Keratoconus; Anterior Segment Trauma/Reconstruction; **Hospital:** NY-Presby/Columbia Univ Med Ctr, NY (page 65), White Plains Hosp; **Address:** Edward S Harkness Eye Inst, Columbia Univ Med Ctr/NY Presby Hosp, 635 W 165th St, Ste 303, New York, NY 10032; **Phone:** 212-927-2394; **Board Cert:** Ophthalmology 1989; **Med School:** Columbia P&S 1983; **Resid:** Ophthalmology, Harkness Eye Inst 1987; **Fellow:** Cornea & Ext Eye Disease, Univ Iowa Hosps & Clins 1988; **Fac Appt:** Clin Prof Oph, Columbia P&S

Friberg, Thomas R MD [Oph] - **Spec Exp:** Retinal Disorders; Diabetic Eye Disease/Retinopathy; Macular Degeneration; **Hospital:** UPMC Presby, Pittsburgh; **Address:** UPMC Eye Ctr, 203 Lothrop St, Ste 718, Pittsburgh, PA 15213; **Phone:** 412-647-2200; **Board Cert:** Ophthalmology 1979; **Med School:** Univ Minn 1973; **Resid:** Ophthalmology, Stanford Univ Hosp & Clins 1977; **Fellow:** Retina, Mass Eye & Ear Infirm 1978; Vitreoretinal Surgery, Duke Univ Hosp 1979; **Fac Appt:** Prof Oph, Univ Pittsburgh

Fuchs, Wayne MD [Oph] - **Spec Exp:** Diabetic Eye Disease/Retinopathy; Macular Disease/Degeneration; Retinal Disorders; Pseudoxanthoma Elasticum; **Hospital:** Mt Sinai Med Ctr (page 62), Lenox Hill Hosp (Manh Eye, Ear & Throat Hosp) (page 66); **Address:** 121 E 60th St, Ste 5B, New York, NY 10022-1186; **Phone:** 212-319-8205; **Board Cert:** Ophthalmology 1985; **Med School:** Mount Sinai Sch Med 1979; **Resid:** Ophthalmology, Mt Sinai Hosp 1983; **Fellow:** Vitreoretinal Surgery & Disease, NY Hosp-Cornell Med Ctr 1984; **Fac Appt:** Clin Prof Oph, Mount Sinai Sch Med

Gallin, Pamela F MD [Oph] - **Spec Exp:** Pediatric Ophthalmology; Amblyopia; Strabismus; Lacrimal Gland Disorders; **Hospital:** NY-Presby/Columbia Univ Med Ctr, NY (page 65), Lenox Hill Hosp (Manh Eye, Ear & Throat Hosp) (page 66); **Address:** NY Presbyterian-Columbia Univ Med Ctr, 635 W 165th St, Ste 224, New York, NY 10032-3701; **Phone:** 212-305-5407; **Board Cert:** Ophthalmology 1983; **Med School:** Washington Univ, St Louis 1978; **Resid:** Ophthalmology, Mount Sinai Med Ctr 1982; **Fellow:** Pediatric Ophthalmology, Chldns Natl Med Ctr 1983; Strabismus, Columbia-Presby Med Ctr 1983; **Fac Appt:** Prof Oph, Columbia P&S

Gentile, Ronald C MD [Oph] - **Spec Exp:** Retina/Vitreous Surgery; Diabetic Eye Disease/Retinopathy; Macular Degeneration; Retinal Disorders; **Hospital:** New York Eye & Ear Infirm (page 64), Winthrop Univ Hosp; **Address:** 310 E 14th St, South Bldg, Ste 319S, New York, NY 10003-4201; **Phone:** 212-979-4120; **Board Cert:** Ophthalmology 2008; **Med School:** SUNY Downstate 1991; **Resid:** Ophthalmology, NY Eye & Ear Infirm 1995; **Fellow:** Ocular Pathology, NY Eye & Ear Infirm 1996; Retina/Vitreous Surgery, Kresge Eye Inst 1998; **Fac Appt:** Prof Oph, NY Med Coll

Gibralter, Richard P MD [Oph] - **Spec Exp:** Cataract Surgery; Laser Vision Surgery; Cornea Transplant; Corneal Disease & Surgery; **Hospital:** Lenox Hill Hosp (Manh Eye, Ear & Throat Hosp) (page 66), New York Eye & Ear Infirm (page 64); **Address:** 154 E 71st St, New York, NY 10021-5123; **Phone:** 212-628-2202; **Board Cert:** Ophthalmology 1981; **Med School:** Mount Sinai Sch Med 1976; **Resid:** Ophthalmology, Manhattan EE&T Hosp 1980; **Fellow:** Cornea, Manhattan EE&T Hosp 1981; **Fac Appt:** Assoc Clin Prof Oph, NYU Sch Med

Goldberg, Daniel B MD [Oph] - **Spec Exp:** LASIK-Refractive Surgery; Cornea Transplant; Cataract Surgery; Lens Implants; **Address:** Atlantic Eye Physicians, 180 White Rd, Ste 202, Little Silver, NJ 07739-1166; **Phone:** 732-219-9220; **Board Cert:** Ophthalmology 1979; **Med School:** SUNY Downstate 1974; **Resid:** Ophthalmology, SUNY Downstate 1978; **Fellow:** Cornea, Eye & Ear Hosp 1979; **Fac Appt:** Asst Clin Prof Oph, Drexel Univ Coll Med

Guyton, David L MD [Oph] - **Spec Exp:** Strabismus; Pediatric Ophthalmology; **Hospital:** Johns Hopkins Hosp (page 59); **Address:** Johns Hopkins Wilmer Eye Inst, 600 N Wolfe St, Wilmer 233, Baltimore, MD 21287; **Phone:** 410-955-8314; **Board Cert:** Ophthalmology 1977; **Med School:** Harvard Med Sch 1969; **Resid:** Ophthalmology, Johns Hopkins Hosp 1976; **Fellow:** Pediatric Ophthalmology, Baylor Coll Med 1977; **Fac Appt:** Prof Oph, Johns Hopkins Univ

Hall, Lisabeth S MD [Oph] - **Spec Exp:** Pediatric Ophthalmology; Strabismus-Adult & Pediatric; Eye Muscle Disorders; Cataract-Pediatric; **Hospital:** New York Eye & Ear Infirm (page 64); **Address:** 40 W 72nd St, New York, NY 10023; **Phone:** 212-979-4614; **Board Cert:** Ophthalmology 2009; **Med School:** SUNY Stony Brook 1992; **Resid:** Ophthalmology, Manhattan Eye & Ear Infirm 1996; **Fellow:** Pediatric Ophthalmology, Jules Stein Eye Inst 1997; **Fac Appt:** Assoc Prof Oph, NY Med Coll

Haller, Julia A MD [Oph] - **Spec Exp:** Retina/Vitreous Surgery; Retinal Disorders; Retinal Vascular Diseases; **Hospital:** Wills Eye Hosp (page 71), Thomas Jefferson Univ Hosp; **Address:** Wills Eye Hosp, Retina, 840 Walnut St, Ste 1510, Philadelphia, PA 19107; **Phone:** 215-928-3073; **Board Cert:** Ophthalmology 1987; **Med School:** Harvard Med Sch 1980; **Resid:** Ophthalmology, Wilmer Eye Inst 1985; **Fellow:** Retina/Vitreous Surgery, Wilmer Eye Inst/Johns Hopkins 1986; **Fac Appt:** Prof Oph, Jefferson Med Coll

Handa, James T MD [Oph] - **Spec Exp:** Macular Degeneration; Melanoma-Choroidal (eye); Retinoblastoma; **Hospital:** Johns Hopkins Hosp (page 59); **Address:** Wilmer Eye Inst Retina Div, 600 N Wolfe St, Ste 100, Baltimore, MD 21287; **Phone:** 410-955-3518; **Board Cert:** Ophthalmology 1991; **Med School:** Univ Pennsylvania 1986; **Resid:** Ophthalmology, Wills Eye Hosp 1990; **Fellow:** Retina/Vitreous Surgery, Duke Eye Ctr 1992; Ophthalmic Oncology, USC Sch Med 1993; **Fac Appt:** Assoc Prof Oph, Johns Hopkins Univ

Hersh, Peter S MD [Oph] - **Spec Exp:** LASIK-Refractive Surgery; Cornea Transplant; Keratoconus; **Hospital:** Univ Hosp (Newark); **Address:** The Cornea & Laser Eye Inst-Hersh Vision Grp, Glenpointe Center East, 300 Frank W Burr Blvd, Ste 71, Teaneck, NJ 07666-6704; **Phone:** 201-883-0505; **Board Cert:** Ophthalmology 1987; **Med School:** Johns Hopkins Univ 1982; **Resid:** Internal Medicine, Lenox Hill Hosp 1983; Ophthalmology, Mass Eye & Ear Infirm 1986; **Fellow:** Cornea & Ext Eye Disease, Mass Eye & Ear Infirm 1987; **Fac Appt:** Clin Prof Oph, UMDNJ-NJ Med Sch, Newark

Ho, Allen C MD [Oph] - **Spec Exp:** Retina/Vitreous Surgery; Macular Degeneration; Diabetic Eye Disease/Retinopathy; **Hospital:** Wills Eye Hosp (page 71); **Address:** Mid Atlantic Retina, 840 Walnut St, Ste 1020, Philadelphia, PA 19107; **Phone:** 800-331-6634; **Board Cert:** Ophthalmology 2004; **Med School:** Columbia P&S 1988; **Resid:** Ophthalmology, Wills Eye Hosp 1992; **Fellow:** Retina/Vitreous Surgery, Manhattan EET Hosp 1994; **Fac Appt:** Prof Oph, Jefferson Med Coll

Iliff, Nicholas T MD [Oph] - **Spec Exp:** Oculoplastic Surgery; Orbital & Eyelid Tumors/Cancer; **Hospital:** Johns Hopkins Hosp (page 59); **Address:** Wilmer Eye Inst, Bayview Med Ctr, 4940 Eastern Ave, Baltimore, MD 21224; **Phone:** 410-550-2360; **Board Cert:** Ophthalmology 1978; **Med School:** Johns Hopkins Univ 1972; **Resid:** Ophthalmology, Johns Hopkins-Wilmer Inst 1977; **Fellow:** Retinal Surgery, Johns Hopkins-Wilmer Inst 1978; Oculoplastic & Reconstructive Surgery, Johns Hopkins-Wilmer Inst 1980; **Fac Appt:** Prof Oph, Johns Hopkins Univ

Jabs, Douglas A MD [Oph] - **Spec Exp:** Uveitis; **Hospital:** Mt Sinai Med Ctr (page 62); **Address:** 17 E 102nd St, New York, NY 10029; **Phone:** 212-241-0939; **Board Cert:** Ophthalmology 1982; Internal Medicine 1983; **Med School:** Johns Hopkins Univ 1977; **Resid:** Ophthalmology, Wilmer Eye Inst 1981; Internal Medicine, Johns Hopkins Hosp 1983; **Fellow:** Rheumatology, Johns Hopkins Hosp 1984; **Fac Appt:** Prof Oph, Mount Sinai Sch Med

Katowitz, James A MD [Oph] - **Spec Exp:** Oculoplastic & Orbital Surgery; Pediatric Ophthalmology; Corneal Disease & Surgery; **Hospital:** Chldns Hosp of Philadelphia; **Address:** Chldns Hosp, Ophthalmology Dept, 3400 Civic Center Blvd Wood Bldg Fl 1, Philadelphia, PA 19104; **Phone:** 215-590-2791; **Board Cert:** Ophthalmology 1969; **Med School:** Univ Pennsylvania 1963; **Resid:** Ophthalmology, Hosp Univ Penn 1967; **Fellow:** Oculoplastic Surgery, Queen Victoria Hosp 1968; Oculoplastic Surgery, Moorfield Eye Hosp 1968; **Fac Appt:** Prof Emeritus Oph, Univ Pennsylvania

Katz, L. Jay MD [Oph] - **Spec Exp:** Glaucoma; **Hospital:** Wills Eye Hosp (page 71), Thomas Jefferson Univ Hosp; **Address:** Wills Eye Hosp, Glaucoma, 840 Walnut St, Ste 1110, Philadelphia, PA 19107; **Phone:** 215-928-3197; **Board Cert:** Ophthalmology 1985; **Med School:** Yale Univ 1979; **Resid:** Ophthalmology, Yale-New Haven Hosp 1983; **Fellow:** Glaucoma, Wills Eye Hosp 1985; **Fac Appt:** Prof Oph, Thomas Jefferson Univ

Kazim, Michael MD [Oph] - **Spec Exp:** Thyroid Eye Disease; Oculoplastic Surgery; Orbital Tumors/Cancer; Eyelid Tumors/Cancer; **Hospital:** NY-Presby/Columbia Univ Med Ctr, NY (page 65), New York Eye & Ear Infirm (page 64); **Address:** 635 W 165th St, Ste 207, New York, NY 10032-3701; **Phone:** 212-305-5477; **Board Cert:** Ophthalmology 1989; **Med School:** Columbia P&S 1984; **Resid:** Ophthalmology, Columbia-Presby Hosp 1988; **Fellow:** Oculoplastic Surgery, Univ Penn-Childrens Hosp 1989; Orbital Surgery, Allegheny Genl Hosp 1990; **Fac Appt:** Clin Prof Oph, Columbia P&S

Kidwell Jr, Earl R MD [Oph] - **Spec Exp:** Oculoplastic Surgery; **Hospital:** Howard Univ Hosp; **Address:** 2041 Georgia Ave NW, Towers Building 2100, Washington, DC 20060; **Phone:** 202-865-1258; **Board Cert:** Ophthalmology 1978; **Med School:** Johns Hopkins Univ 1973; **Resid:** Ophthalmology, Johns Hopkins Hosp 1978; **Fellow:** Oculoplastic Surgery, Univ Miami Affil Hosps 1980

Koller, Harold P MD [Oph] - **Spec Exp:** Pediatric Ophthalmology; Eye Muscle Surgery; Visual Perception & Learning Disorders; Strabismus; **Hospital:** Wills Eye Hosp (page 71); **Address:** Huntingdon Vly Eye Care Consultants, 1650 Huntington Pike, Ste 150, Meadowbrook, PA 19046; **Phone:** 215-947-6660; **Board Cert:** Ophthalmology 1971; **Med School:** Tulane Univ 1964; **Resid:** Ophthalmology, Tulane Med Ctr 1968; **Fellow:** Pediatric Ophthalmology, Chldns Hosp 1970; **Fac Appt:** Clin Prof Oph, Thomas Jefferson Univ

Kupersmith, Mark J MD [Oph] - **Spec Exp:** Neuro-Ophthalmology; **Hospital:** St. Luke's - Roosevelt Hosp Ctr - Roosevelt Div (page 56); **Address:** Roosevelt Hosp, 1000 10th Ave, 10 INN Bldg, New York, NY 10019; **Phone:** 212-636-3200 x1; **Board Cert:** Ophthalmology 1981; Neurology 1981; **Med School:** Northwestern Univ 1974; **Resid:** Neurology, NYU Med Ctr 1978; Ophthalmology, NYU Med Ctr 1980; **Fac Appt:** Prof Oph, Albert Einstein Coll Med

Levin, Alex V MD [Oph] - **Spec Exp:** Pediatric Ophthalmology; Strabismus; Ophthalmic Genetics; Glaucoma; **Hospital:** Wills Eye Hosp (page 71); **Address:** Wills Eye Hosp, Ped Ophthalmology, 840 Walnut St, Ste 1210, Philadelphia, PA 19107; **Phone:** 215-928-3240; **Board Cert:** Pediatrics 1986; Ophthalmology 1991; Child Abuse Pediatrics 2009; **Med School:** Jefferson Med Coll 1982; **Resid:** Pediatrics, Chldns Hosp 1985; Ophthalmology, Wills Eye Hosp 1989; **Fellow:** Pediatric Ophthalmology, Hosp Sick Chldn 1990

Liebmann, Jeffrey M MD [Oph] - **Spec Exp:** Glaucoma; Cataract Surgery; **Hospital:** New York Eye & Ear Infirm (page 64), Lenox Hill Hosp (Manh Eye, Ear & Throat Hosp) (page 66); **Address:** Glaucoma Associates of New York, 121 E 60th St Fl 8, New York, NY 10022; **Phone:** 212-477-7540; **Board Cert:** Ophthalmology 1989; **Med School:** Boston Univ 1983; **Resid:** Ophthalmology, SUNY Downstate Med Ctr 1987; **Fellow:** Glaucoma, New York EE Infirmary 1988; **Fac Appt:** Clin Prof Oph, NYU Sch Med

Lisman, Richard D MD [Oph] - **Spec Exp:** Oculoplastic Surgery; Eyelid/Tear Duct Reconstruction; Eyelid Cosmetic & Reconstructive Surgery; Orbital & Eyelid Tumors/Cancer; **Hospital:** NYU Langone Med Ctr (page 68), Lenox Hill Hosp (Manh Eye, Ear & Throat Hosp) (page 66); **Address:** 635 Park Ave, New York, NY 10065-6546; **Phone:** 212-585-1405; **Board Cert:** Ophthalmology 1981; **Med School:** NYU Sch Med 1976; **Resid:** Ophthalmology, Manhattan EE Hosp 1980; **Fellow:** Ophthalmic Plastic Surgery, NY Eye & Ear Infirmary 1981; Plastic Surgery, Manhattan EE&T Hosp 1982; **Fac Appt:** Prof Oph, NYU Sch Med

Mackool, Richard J MD [Oph] - **Spec Exp:** Cataract Surgery; LASIK-Refractive Surgery; Lens Implants-Multifocal; Corneal Disease & Surgery; **Hospital:** New York Eye & Ear Infirm (page 64), NYU Langone Med Ctr (page 68); **Address:** Mackool Eye Institute, 31-27 41st St, Astoria, NY 11103; **Phone:** 718-728-3400; **Board Cert:** Ophthalmology 1976; **Med School:** Boston Univ 1968; **Resid:** Ophthalmology, New York EE Infirm 1973; **Fac Appt:** Clin Prof Oph, NYU Sch Med

Magramm, Irene MD [Oph] - **Spec Exp:** Pediatric Ophthalmology; Strabismus; Cataract Surgery; Diplopia; **Hospital:** Lenox Hill Hosp (Manh Eye, Ear & Throat Hosp) (page 66); **Address:** 220 E 63rd St, Ste LM, New York, NY 10055; **Phone:** 212-644-5100; **Board Cert:** Ophthalmology 1987; **Med School:** Cornell Univ-Weill Med Coll 1981; **Resid:** Ophthalmology, North Shore Univ Hosp 1985; **Fellow:** Pediatric Ophthalmology, Manhattan EE&T Hosp 1986; **Fac Appt:** Asst Clin Prof Oph, Cornell Univ-Weill Med Coll

Maguire, Joseph I MD [Oph] - **Spec Exp:** Retinal Disorders; Macular Degeneration; Diabetic Eye Disease/Retinopathy; **Hospital:** Wills Eye Hosp (page 71), Lankenau Hosp; **Address:** Mid Atlantic Retina, 840 Walnut St, Ste 1020, Philadelphia, PA 19107; **Phone:** 800-331-6634; **Board Cert:** Ophthalmology 1989; **Med School:** Jefferson Med Coll 1983; **Resid:** Ophthalmology, Wills Eye Hosp 1987; **Fellow:** Retina/Vitreous Surgery, Wills Eye Hosp 1989; Retina, Moorfields Hosp 1990; **Fac Appt:** Assoc Prof Oph, Thomas Jefferson Univ

Mandel, Eric R MD [Oph] - **Spec Exp:** LASIK-Refractive Surgery; PRK-Refractive Surgery; Corneal Disease; **Hospital:** Lenox Hill Hosp (page 66); **Address:** 211 E 70th St, New York, NY 10021; **Phone:** 212-734-0111; **Board Cert:** Ophthalmology 1988; **Med School:** SUNY Stony Brook 1982; **Resid:** Ophthalmology, Lenox Hill Hosp 1986; **Fellow:** Cornea & Ext Eye Disease, Mass EE Infirm 1987

McDonnell, Peter J MD [Oph] - **Spec Exp:** Cornea Transplant; Corneal Disease; Refractive Surgery; **Hospital:** Johns Hopkins Hosp (page 59); **Address:** Johns Hopkins Hosp, Wilmer Eye Inst, 727 Maumenee, 600 N Wolfe St, Baltimore, MD 21287; **Phone:** 443-287-1511; **Board Cert:** Ophthalmology 1988; **Med School:** Johns Hopkins Univ 1982; **Resid:** Ophthalmology, Wilmer Eye Inst 1986; **Fellow:** Cornea & Ext Eye Disease, Doheny Eye Inst 1987; **Fac Appt:** Prof Oph, Johns Hopkins Univ

Medow, Norman B MD [Oph] - **Spec Exp:** Cataract-Pediatric; Glaucoma-Pediatric; Corneal Disease-Pediatric; **Hospital:** Montefiore Med Ctr-Moses Campus, NY; **Address:** Montefiore Hosp Ctr, Dept Ophthalmology, 3400 Bainbridge Ave, Bronx, NY 10467; **Phone:** 718-920-2020; **Board Cert:** Ophthalmology 1975; **Med School:** SUNY Hlth Sci Ctr 1966; **Resid:** Ophthalmology, Manhattan EE&T Hosp 1972; **Fellow:** Cataract/Lens Implant Surgery, Charles Kelman, MD 1973; **Fac Appt:** Clin Prof Oph, Cornell Univ-Weill Med Coll

Miller, Neil MD [Oph] - **Spec Exp:** Neuro-Ophthalmology; Orbital Diseases; Thyroid Eye Disease; **Hospital:** Johns Hopkins Hosp (page 59); **Address:** Johns Hopkins Wilmer Eye Inst, 600 N Wolfe St Wilmer Bldg - rm 233, Baltimore, MD 21287-0001; **Phone:** 410-955-8679; **Board Cert:** Ophthalmology 1976; **Med School:** Johns Hopkins Univ 1971; **Resid:** Ophthalmology, Johns Hopkins Hosp 1975; **Fellow:** Neuro-Ophthalmology, UCSF Med Ctr 1975; **Fac Appt:** Prof Oph, Johns Hopkins Univ

Mills, Monte D MD [Oph] - **Spec Exp:** Pediatric Ophthalmology; Eye Muscle Disorders; Strabismus; Glaucoma; **Hospital:** Chldns Hosp of Philadelphia; **Address:** Chldns Hosp, Ophthalmology Dept, 3400 Civic Ctr Blvd Wood Bldg Fl 1, Philadelphia, PA 19104; **Phone:** 215-590-2791; **Board Cert:** Ophthalmology 2004; **Med School:** Baylor Coll Med 1988; **Resid:** Ophthalmology, Mass Eye & Ear Infirm 1992; **Fellow:** Pediatric Ophthalmology, Chldns Hosp 1993; **Fac Appt:** Prof Oph, Univ Pennsylvania

Muldoon, Thomas O MD [Oph] - **Spec Exp:** Retina/Vitreous Surgery; Macular Disease/Degeneration; Diabetic Eye Disease/Retinopathy; **Hospital:** New York Eye & Ear Infirm (page 64); **Address:** 310 E 14th St, Ste 402, New York, NY 10003-4201; **Phone:** 212-979-4595; **Board Cert:** Ophthalmology 1971; **Med School:** Univ Rochester 1962; **Resid:** Surgery, St Lukes Hosp 1966; Ophthalmology, NY EE Infirm 1969; **Fellow:** Retinal Surgery, NY EE Infirm 1970; **Fac Appt:** Assoc Clin Prof Oph, NY Med Coll

Myers, Jonathan S MD [Oph] - **Spec Exp:** Glaucoma; **Hospital:** Wills Eye Hosp (page 71); **Address:** Wills Eye Hosp, Glaucoma, 840 Walnut St, Ste 1110, Philadelphia, PA 19107; **Phone:** 215-928-3197; **Board Cert:** Ophthalmology 2008; **Med School:** Univ Pennsylvania 1992; **Resid:** Ophthalmology, Wills Eye Hosp 1996; **Fellow:** Glaucoma, Duke Univ Hosp 1997; **Fac Appt:** Asst Prof Oph, Thomas Jefferson Univ

Nelson, Leonard B MD [Oph] - **Spec Exp:** Pediatric Ophthalmology; Strabismus; Eye Muscle Disorders; **Hospital:** Wills Eye Hosp (page 71); **Address:** Ophthalmic Partners, 100 Presidential Blvd, Ste 200, Bala Cynwyd, PA 19004; **Phone:** 484-434-2700; **Board Cert:** Ophthalmology 1981; **Med School:** Harvard Med Sch 1976; **Resid:** Ophthalmology, Bellevue Hosp Ctr 1980; **Fellow:** Pediatric Ophthalmology, Chldns Hosp Med Ctr 1981; Ocular Genetics, Johns Hopkins Hosp 1982; **Fac Appt:** Assoc Prof Oph, Jefferson Med Coll

O'Brien, Joan M MD [Oph] - **Spec Exp:** Eye Tumors/Cancer; Retinoblastoma; **Hospital:** Hosp Univ Penn - UPHS (page 69); **Address:** Penn Presbyterian Med Ctr, Scheie Eye Inst, 51 N 39th St, Philadelphia, PA 19104; **Phone:** 215-662-8100; **Board Cert:** Ophthalmology 2007; **Med School:** Dartmouth Med Sch 1986; **Resid:** Ophthalmology, Mass Eye & Ear Infirm 1992; **Fellow:** Ophthalmic Pathology, Mass Eye & Ear Infirm 1989; Ocular Oncology, UCSF Med Ctr 1993; **Fac Appt:** Prof Oph, Univ Pennsylvania

Odel, Jeffrey G MD [Oph] - **Spec Exp:** Neuro-Ophthalmology; Retinal Disorders; Optic Nerve Disorders; **Hospital:** NY-Presby/Columbia Univ Med Ctr, NY (page 65); **Address:** Harkness Eye Institute, 635 W 165th St, rm 316, New York, NY 10032-3701; **Phone:** 212-305-5415; **Board Cert:** Ophthalmology 1981; **Med School:** Univ Rochester 1975; **Resid:** Ophthalmology, Mt Sinai Hosp 1981; **Fellow:** Ophthalmology, Bascom-Palmer Eye Inst 1977; Ophthalmology, Columbia Presby Med Ctr 1982; **Fac Appt:** Assoc Clin Prof Oph, Columbia P&S

Orlin, Stephen E MD [Oph] - **Spec Exp:** Cataract Surgery; Corneal Disease & Surgery; Refractive Surgery; **Hospital:** Penn Presby Med Ctr - UPHS (page 69), Hosp Univ Penn - UPHS (page 69); **Address:** Scheie Eye Inst, Penn Eye Care, 51 N 39th St, Ste 517, Philadelphia, PA 19104; **Phone:** 215-662-8100; **Board Cert:** Ophthalmology 1987; **Med School:** South Africa 1977; **Resid:** Ophthalmology, Scheie Eye Inst 1985; **Fellow:** Cornea & Ext Eye Disease, Scheie Eye Inst 1986; **Fac Appt:** Assoc Prof Oph, Univ Pennsylvania

Prenner, Jonathan L MD [Oph] - **Spec Exp:** Retina/Vitreous Surgery; Macular Degeneration; Retinal Detachment; Diabetic Eye Disease/Retinopathy; **Hospital:** Robert Wood Johnson Univ Hosp - New Brunswick; **Address:** NJ Retina, 10 Plum St Fl 6, New Brunswick, NJ 08901; **Phone:** 732-220-1600; **Board Cert:** Ophthalmology 2003; **Med School:** SUNY Stony Brook 1998; **Resid:** Ophthalmology, Scheie Eye Inst 2002; **Fellow:** Vitreoretinal Surgery & Disease, William Beaumont Hosp 2004; **Fac Appt:** Asst Clin Prof Oph, UMDNJ-RW Johnson Med Sch

Quigley, Harry A MD [Oph] - **Spec Exp:** Glaucoma; **Hospital:** Johns Hopkins Hosp (page 59); **Address:** Johns Hopkins Hosp, 600 N Wolfe St, Maumenee B-110, Baltimore, MD 21287-9205; **Phone:** 410-955-6052; **Board Cert:** Ophthalmology 1976; **Med School:** Johns Hopkins Univ 1971; **Resid:** Ophthalmology, Wilmer Inst-Johns Hopkins Hosp 1975; **Fellow:** Ophthalmology, Bascom Palmer Eye Inst 1977; **Fac Appt:** Prof Oph, Johns Hopkins Univ

Quinn, Graham E MD [Oph] - **Spec Exp:** Pediatric Ophthalmology; Retinopathy of Prematurity; Eye Growth/Development; **Hospital:** Chldns Hosp of Philadelphia; **Address:** Chldns Hosp, Ophthalmology Dept, 3400 Civic Ctr Blvd Wood Bldg Fl 1, Philadelphia, PA 19104; **Phone:** 215-590-2791; **Board Cert:** Ophthalmology 1979; **Med School:** Duke Univ 1973; **Resid:** Pathology, Metro Genl Hosp 1975; Ophthalmology, Hosp Univ Penn 1978; **Fellow:** Pediatric Ophthalmology, Chldns Hosp 1979; **Fac Appt:** Prof Oph, Univ Pennsylvania

Rapuano, Christopher J MD [Oph] - **Spec Exp:** Corneal Disease; Refractive Surgery; **Hospital:** Wills Eye Hosp (page 71); **Address:** Corneal Assoc-Wills Eye Hosp, 840 Walnut St, Ste 920, Philadelphia, PA 19107; **Phone:** 215-928-3180; **Board Cert:** Ophthalmology 1991; **Med School:** Columbia P&S 1986; **Resid:** Ophthalmology, Wills Eye Hosp 1990; **Fellow:** Cornea & Ext Eye Disease, Univ Iowa 1991; **Fac Appt:** Prof Oph, Jefferson Med Coll

Regillo, Carl D MD [Oph] - **Spec Exp:** Retinal Disorders; Macular Degeneration; Diabetic Eye Disease/Retinopathy; **Hospital:** Wills Eye Hosp (page 71), Thomas Jefferson Univ Hosp; **Address:** Mid Atlantic Retina, 840 Walnut St, Ste 1020, Philadelphia, PA 19107; **Phone:** 800-331-6634; **Board Cert:** Ophthalmology 2004; **Med School:** Harvard Med Sch 1988; **Resid:** Ophthalmology, Wills Eye Hosp 1992; **Fellow:** Retinal Surgery, Wills Eye Hosp 1994; **Fac Appt:** Prof Oph, Jefferson Med Coll

Reynolds, James D MD [Oph] - **Spec Exp:** Pediatric Ophthalmology; Retinopathy of Prematurity; Strabismus; **Hospital:** Women & Chldn's Hosp of Buffalo, The; **Address:** 1176 Main St, Buffalo, NY 14209; **Phone:** 716-881-7900; **Board Cert:** Ophthalmology 1982; **Med School:** SUNY Buffalo 1978; **Resid:** Ophthalmology, Erie Co Med Ctr 1981; **Fellow:** Pediatric Ophthalmology, Univ Pittsburgh 1982; **Fac Appt:** Prof Oph, SUNY Buffalo

Ritch, Robert MD [Oph] - **Spec Exp:** Glaucoma; Complementary Medicine; **Hospital:** New York Eye & Ear Infirm (page 64); **Address:** 310 E 14th St, South Bldg - Fl 3, New York, NY 10003-4201; **Phone:** 212-477-7540; **Board Cert:** Ophthalmology 1977; **Med School:** Albert Einstein Coll Med 1972; **Resid:** Ophthalmology, Mt Sinai Med Ctr 1976; **Fellow:** Glaucoma, Mt Sinai Med Ctr 1978; **Fac Appt:** Prof Oph, NY Med Coll

Robin, Alan L MD [Oph] - **Spec Exp:** Glaucoma; Cataract Surgery; **Hospital:** Greater Baltimore Med Ctr; **Address:** Glaucoma Specialists, 6115 Falls Rd, Ste 333, Baltimore, MD 21209; **Phone:** 410-377-2422; **Board Cert:** Ophthalmology 1979; **Med School:** Tufts Univ 1974; **Resid:** Ophthalmology, Greater Baltimore Med Ctr 1978; **Fellow:** Glaucoma, Wilmer Eye Inst 1979; **Fac Appt:** Clin Prof Oph, Univ MD Sch Med

Schein, Oliver D MD [Oph] - **Spec Exp:** Cataract Surgery; Corneal Disease & Surgery; **Hospital:** Johns Hopkins Hosp (page 59); **Address:** Johns Hopkins Wilmer Eye Inst, 600 N Wolfe St, Maumenee 317, Baltimore, MD 21287; **Phone:** 410-955-7677; **Board Cert:** Internal Medicine 1984; Ophthalmology 1990; **Med School:** Johns Hopkins Univ 1981; **Resid:** Internal Medicine, Johns Hopkins Hosp 1984; Ophthalmology, Mass Eye & Ear Infirm 1987; **Fellow:** Cornea & Ext Eye Disease, Mass Eye & Ear Infirm 1988; **Fac Appt:** Prof Oph, Johns Hopkins Univ

Schiff, William M MD [Oph] - **Spec Exp:** Macular Disease/Degeneration; Diabetic Eye Disease/Retinopathy; Retinal Detachment; **Hospital:** Lenox Hill Hosp (Manh Eye, Ear & Throat Hosp) (page 66), St. Luke's - Roosevelt Hosp Ctr - Roosevelt Div (page 56); **Address:** 210 E 64th St, Fl 7, New York, NY 10068; **Phone:** 212-702-7400; **Board Cert:** Ophthalmology 2006; **Med School:** NYU Sch Med 1988; **Resid:** Ophthalmology, New York Eye & Ear Infirm 1994; **Fellow:** Retina/Vitreous Surgery, NY Hosp-Harkness Eye Inst 1996; **Fac Appt:** Prof Oph, Hofstra N Shore-LIJ Sch Med

Schuman, Joel S MD [Oph] - **Spec Exp:** Glaucoma; Cataract Surgery; **Hospital:** UPMC Presby, Pittsburgh, UPMC Shadyside; **Address:** UPMC Eye Center, Eye & Ear Institute, Ste 816, 203 Lothrop St, Pittsburgh, PA 15213; **Phone:** 412-647-2200; **Board Cert:** Ophthalmology 1990; **Med School:** Mount Sinai Sch Med 1984; **Resid:** Ophthalmology, Med Coll Virginia Hosps 1988; **Fellow:** Glaucoma, Harvard/Mass Eye & Ear Infirmary 1990; **Fac Appt:** Prof Oph, Univ Pittsburgh

Sergott, Robert C MD [Oph] - **Spec Exp:** Neuro-Ophthalmology; Optic Nerve Disorders; Glaucoma; Thyroid Eye Disease; **Hospital:** Wills Eye Hosp (page 71), Thomas Jefferson Univ Hosp; **Address:** Wills Eye Hosp, Neuro-Ophthalmology, 840 Walnut St, Ste 930, Philadelphia, PA 19107; **Phone:** 215-928-3130; **Board Cert:** Ophthalmology 1982; **Med School:** Johns Hopkins Univ 1975; **Resid:** Ophthalmology, Wills Eye Hosp 1979; **Fellow:** Neuro-Ophthalmology, Bascom Palmer Eye Inst 1980; Neurological Immunology, Hosp Univ Penn 1981; **Fac Appt:** Prof Oph, Thomas Jefferson Univ

Shabto, Uri MD [Oph] - **Spec Exp:** Retinopathy of Prematurity; Macular Disease/Degeneration; Diabetic Eye Disease/Retinopathy; Retinal Detachment; **Hospital:** New York Eye & Ear Infirm (page 64); **Address:** 310 E 14th St, South Bldg, Ste 419, New York, NY 10003-4201; **Phone:** 212-677-2000; **Board Cert:** Ophthalmology 1991; **Med School:** Harvard Med Sch 1986; **Resid:** Ophthalmology, NY Eye & Ear Infirm 1990; **Fellow:** Vitreoretinal Surgery, Montefiore Hosp 1991; **Fac Appt:** Asst Clin Prof Oph, NY Med Coll

Shields, Carol L MD [Oph] - **Spec Exp:** Orbital Tumors/Cancer; Melanoma-Choroidal (eye); Retinoblastoma; Pediatric Ophthalmology; **Hospital:** Wills Eye Hosp (page 71), Jefferson Reg Med Ctr - Pittsburgh; **Address:** Wills Eye Inst, Ocular Oncology Service, 840 Walnut St, Ste 1440, Phildelphia, PA 19107; **Phone:** 215-928-3105; **Board Cert:** Ophthalmology 1989; **Med School:** Univ Pittsburgh 1983; **Resid:** Ophthalmology, Willis Eye Hosp 1987; **Fellow:** Ophthalmic Pathology, Willis Eye Hosp 1988; Ophthalmic Oncology, Willis Eye Hosp 1989; **Fac Appt:** Prof Oph, Jefferson Med Coll

Shields, Jerry MD [Oph] - **Spec Exp:** Eye Tumors/Cancer; Pediatric Ophthalmology; Retinoblastoma; Melanoma-Choroidal (eye); **Hospital:** Wills Eye Hosp (page 71), Thomas Jefferson Univ Hosp; **Address:** Wills Eye Hosp, Ocular Oncology Svce, 840 Walnut St, Ste 1440, Philadelphia, PA 19107; **Phone:** 215-928-3105; **Board Cert:** Ophthalmology 1972; **Med School:** Univ Mich Med Sch 1964; **Resid:** Ophthalmology, Wills Eye Hosp 1970; **Fellow:** Ophthalmic Pathology, Armed Forces Inst Pathology 1971; Retinal Surgery, Wills Eye Hosp 1972; **Fac Appt:** Prof Oph, Thomas Jefferson Univ

Simon, John W MD [Oph] - **Spec Exp:** Pediatric Ophthalmology; Strabismus; **Hospital:** Albany Med Ctr; **Address:** Chldns Med Eye Consultants, 1220 New Scotland Rd, Ste 202, Slingerlands, NY 12159; **Phone:** 518-533-6502; **Board Cert:** Ophthalmology 1981; **Med School:** Mount Sinai Sch Med 1976; **Resid:** Ophthalmology, Mount Sinai Med Ctr 1980; **Fellow:** Pediatric Ophthalmology, Wills Eye Hosp 1981; **Fac Appt:** Prof Oph, Albany Med Coll

Spaeth, George L MD [Oph] - **Spec Exp:** Glaucoma; **Hospital:** Wills Eye Hosp (page 71), Thomas Jefferson Univ Hosp; **Address:** Wills Eye Hosp, Glaucoma Dept, 840 Walnut St, Ste 1110, Philadelphia, PA 19107; **Phone:** 215-928-3197; **Board Cert:** Ophthalmology 1965; **Med School:** Harvard Med Sch 1959; **Resid:** Ophthalmology, Wills Eye Hosp 1963; **Fellow:** Glaucoma, Natl Inst Neurological Dis & Blindness 1965; **Fac Appt:** Prof Oph, Thomas Jefferson Univ

Spaide, Richard F MD [Oph] - **Spec Exp:** Retinal Disorders; Macular Degeneration; Diabetic Eye Disease/Retinopathy; Retina/Vitreous Surgery; **Hospital:** Lenox Hill Hosp (Manh Eye, Ear & Throat Hosp) (page 66); **Address:** Vitreous-Retina-Macula Consultants of NY, 460 Park Ave Fl 5, New York, NY 10022; **Phone:** 212-861-9797; **Board Cert:** Ophthalmology 1987; **Med School:** Jefferson Med Coll 1981; **Resid:** Ophthalmology, St Vincent's Hosp & Med Ctr 1985; **Fellow:** Vitreoretinal Surgery & Disease, Manhattan EET Hosp 1990; **Fac Appt:** Assoc Clin Prof Oph, NY Med Coll

Sperber, Laurence TD MD [Oph] - **Spec Exp:** LASIK-Refractive Surgery; Cornea Transplant; Corneal Ring Implants; Cataract Surgery; **Hospital:** Lenox Hill Hosp (Manh Eye, Ear & Throat Hosp) (page 66); **Address:** Refractive Laser Specialists of NY, 166 E 63rd St, New York, NY 10021-7636; **Phone:** 212-753-8300; **Board Cert:** Ophthalmology 2013; **Med School:** Boston Univ 1987; **Resid:** Ophthalmology, Lenox Hill Hosp (Manh Eye, Ear & Throat Hosp) 1991; **Fellow:** Cornea & Ext Eye Disease, Wills Eye Inst 1992; **Fac Appt:** Clin Prof Oph, NYU Sch Med

Stark, Walter J MD [Oph] - **Spec Exp:** Corneal Disease & Transplant; Cataract Surgery; Refractive Surgery; **Hospital:** Johns Hopkins Hosp (page 59); **Address:** Johns Hopkins Wilmer Eye Inst, 600 N Wolfe St, Maumenee 327, Baltimore, MD 21287-9238; **Phone:** 410-955-5490; **Board Cert:** Ophthalmology 1973; **Med School:** Univ Okla Coll Med 1967; **Resid:** Ophthalmology, Wilmer Inst-Johns Hopkins 1971; **Fac Appt:** Prof Oph, Johns Hopkins Univ

Starr, Christopher E MD [Oph] - **Spec Exp:** Corneal Disease & Surgery; Cornea Transplant; Cataract Surgery-Lens Implant; LASIK-Refractive Surgery; **Hospital:** NY-Presby/Weill Cornell Med Ctr, NY (page 65); **Address:** Weill Cornell Eye Assocs, Weill Greenberg Ctr, 1305 York Ave, Fl 12, New York, NY 10021; **Phone:** 646-962-2020; **Board Cert:** Ophthalmology 2003; **Med School:** Cornell Univ-Weill Med Coll 1998; **Resid:** Ophthalmology, Harvard/Mass Eye & Ear Infirm 2002; **Fellow:** Cornea & Refractive Surgery, Johns Hopkins Hosp/Wilmer Eye Inst 2003; **Fac Appt:** Assoc Prof Oph, Cornell Univ-Weill Med Coll

Stefanyszyn, Mary MD [Oph] - **Spec Exp:** Cosmetic Surgery-Eyes; Oculoplastic & Orbital Surgery; Eyelid Surgery; **Hospital:** Wills Eye Hosp (page 71), Thomas Jefferson Univ Hosp; **Address:** Wills Eye Hosp, Cosmetic Eye, 840 Walnut St, Ste 912, Philadelphia, PA 19107; **Phone:** 215-928-3171; **Board Cert:** Ophthalmology 1983; **Med School:** Harvard Med Sch 1978; **Resid:** Ophthalmology, Wills Eye Hosp 1982; Ophthalmic Pathology, Armed Forces Inst of Pathology 1982; **Fellow:** Oculoplastic & Reconstructive Surgery, Wills Eye Hosp 1983; Orbital Surgery, Moorfields Eye Hosp 1985

Sterns, Gwen K MD [Oph] - **Spec Exp:** Geriatric Ophthalmology; Low Vision; **Hospital:** Rochester Genl Hosp, Univ Rochester Strong Meml Hosp; **Address:** 1425 Portland Ave, Rochester, NY 14621; **Phone:** 585-922-4794; **Board Cert:** Ophthalmology 1976; **Med School:** Med Coll PA 1970; **Resid:** Ophthalmology, Nassau Co Med Ctr 1974; **Fellow:** Ophthalmology, NY-Presby/Columbia Univ Med Ctr 1975; **Fac Appt:** Clin Prof Oph, Univ Rochester

Udell, Ira J MD [Oph] - **Spec Exp:** Cornea Transplant; Corneal Disease; Keratoconus; PROSE Contact Lens; **Hospital:** Long Is Jewish Med Ctr (page 66), N Shore Univ Hosp (page 66); **Address:** LI Jewish Med Ctr, Dept Ophthalmology, 600 Northern Blvd, Ste 214, Great Neck, NY 11021-5200; **Phone:** 516-470-2020; **Board Cert:** Ophthalmology 1980; **Med School:** Tulane Univ 1974; **Resid:** Ophthalmology, LI Jewish Med Ctr 1979; **Fellow:** Cornea, Mass Eye & Ear Infirm 1981; **Fac Appt:** Prof Oph, Hofstra N Shore-LIJ Sch Med

Vander, James F MD [Oph] - **Spec Exp:** Diabetic Eye Disease/Retinopathy; Retinal Disorders; Macular Degeneration; Retinopathy of Prematurity; **Hospital:** Wills Eye Hosp (page 71); **Address:** Mid Atlantic Retina, 840 Walnut St, Ste 1020, Philadelphia, PA 19107; **Phone:** 800-331-6634; **Board Cert:** Ophthalmology 1989; **Med School:** Univ Mich Med Sch 1984; **Resid:** Ophthalmology, Univ Michigan Med Ctr 1988; **Fellow:** Retina/Vitreous Surgery, Wills Eye Hosp 1990; **Fac Appt:** Clin Prof Oph, Thomas Jefferson Univ

Walsh, Joseph B MD [Oph] - **Spec Exp:** Diabetic Eye Disease/Retinopathy; Macular Degeneration; Retinal Disorders; **Hospital:** New York Eye & Ear Infirm (page 64); **Address:** 310 E 14th St, S Bldg Fl 3 - Ste 319, New York, NY 10003-4201; **Phone:** 212-979-4282; **Board Cert:** Ophthalmology 2005; **Med School:** Georgetown Univ 1966; **Resid:** Internal Medicine, Univ Hosp 1968; Ophthalmology, NY Eye & Ear Infirmary 1973; **Fellow:** Retina, Montefiore Med Ctr 1974; **Fac Appt:** Prof Oph, NY Med Coll

Wang, Frederick Mark MD [Oph] - **Spec Exp:** Pediatric Ophthalmology; Strabismus; Eye Muscle Disorders; **Hospital:** Lenox Hill Hosp (Manh Eye, Ear & Throat Hosp) (page 66), Montefiore Med Ctr-Moses Campus, NY; **Address:** 30 E 40th St, Ste 405, New York, NY 10016-1201; **Phone:** 212-684-3980; **Board Cert:** Pediatrics 1978; Ophthalmology 1980; **Med School:** Albert Einstein Coll Med 1972; **Resid:** Pediatrics, Jacobi Med Ctr 1974; Ophthalmology, Albert Einstein 1979; **Fellow:** Pediatric Ophthalmology, Children's Hosp Natl Med Ctr 1980; **Fac Appt:** Clin Prof Oph, Albert Einstein Coll Med

Yannuzzi, Lawrence A MD [Oph] - **Spec Exp:** Retina/Vitreous Surgery; Macular Disease/Degeneration; Diabetic Eye Disease/Retinopathy; **Hospital:** NY-Presby/Columbia Univ Med Ctr, NY (page 65), Lenox Hill Hosp (Manh Eye, Ear & Throat Hosp) (page 66); **Address:** Vitreous-Retina-Macula Consultants of NY, 460 Park Ave Fl 5, New York, NY 10022; **Phone:** 212-861-9797; **Board Cert:** Ophthalmology 1970; **Med School:** Boston Univ 1964; **Resid:** Ophthalmology, Manhattan EE&T Hosp 1968; **Fellow:** Ophthalmology, Manhattan EE&T Hosp 1971; **Fac Appt:** Clin Prof Oph, Columbia P&S

Southeast

Alfonso, Eduardo C MD [Oph] - **Spec Exp:** Corneal Disease & Surgery; Cornea Transplant & Artificial Cornea; Ophthalmic Pathology; **Hospital:** Bascom Palmer Eye Inst, Jackson Meml Hosp; **Address:** Bascom Palmer Eye Institute, 900 NW 17th St, Miami, FL 33136-1119; **Phone:** 305-243-2020; **Board Cert:** Ophthalmology 1985; **Med School:** Yale Univ 1980; **Resid:** Ophthalmology, Bascom Palmer Eye Inst 1984; **Fellow:** Cornea & Ext Eye Disease, Mass Eye & Ear Hosp 1986; Ophthalmological Pathology, Mass Eye & Ear Hosp 1986; **Fac Appt:** Prof Oph, Univ Miami Sch Med

Biousse, Valerie MD [Oph] - **Spec Exp:** Neuro-Ophthalmology; Optic Nerve Disorders; **Hospital:** Emory Univ Hosp; **Address:** Emory Eye Center, 1365B Clifton Rd NE, Ste 4500, Atlanta, GA 30322; **Phone:** 404-778-2020; **Board Cert:** Ophthalmology 2004; **Med School:** France 1988; **Resid:** Neurology, Univ Paris VI Affil Hosp 1994; Ophthalmology, Emory Univ Med Ctr 2002; **Fellow:** Stroke, Univ Paris VI 1996; Neuro-Ophthalmology, Emory Univ 1996; **Fac Appt:** Prof Oph, Emory Univ

Buckley, Edward G MD [Oph] - **Spec Exp:** Pediatric Ophthalmology; Strabismus; Cataract-Pediatric; Neuro-Ophthalmology; **Hospital:** Duke Univ Hosp; **Address:** Duke Eye Center, 2351 Erwin Rd, Box 3802, Durham, NC 27710; **Phone:** 919-681-3937; **Board Cert:** Ophthalmology 2007; **Med School:** Duke Univ 1977; **Resid:** Ophthalmology, Duke Univ Eye Ctr 1981; **Fellow:** Pediatric Ophthalmology, Bascom Palmer Eye Inst 1983; Neuro-Ophthalmology, Bascom Palmer Eye Inst 1983; **Fac Appt:** Prof Oph, Duke Univ

Budenz, Donald L MD [Oph] - **Spec Exp:** Glaucoma; Cataract Surgery; **Hospital:** NC Memorial Hosp - UNC, Person Meml Hosp; **Address:** 226 Nelson Hwy, Ste 200, Chapel Hill, NC 27517; **Phone:** 919-966-5296; **Board Cert:** Ophthalmology 2013; **Med School:** Harvard Med Sch 1987; **Resid:** Ophthalmology, Scheie Eye Inst/Univ of Penn 1991; **Fellow:** Glaucoma, Bascom Palmer Eye Inst/Univ of Miami 1992; **Fac Appt:** Prof Oph, Univ NC Sch Med

Capo, Hilda MD [Oph] - **Spec Exp:** Pediatric Ophthalmology; Strabismus; Neuro-Ophthalmology; Botox Therapy; **Hospital:** Bascom Palmer Eye Inst; **Address:** Bascom Palmer Eye Inst, 900 NW 17th St, Miami, FL 33136; **Phone:** 305-243-2020; **Board Cert:** Ophthalmology 1989; **Med School:** Puerto Rico 1982; **Resid:** Ophthalmology, Univ Puerto Rico Affil Hosp 1987; **Fellow:** Pediatric Ophthalmology, Wilmer Eye Inst 1988; Neuro-Ophthalmology, NYU Med Ctr 1989; **Fac Appt:** Prof Oph, Univ Miami Sch Med

Carlson, Alan N MD [Oph] - **Spec Exp:** Cornea & External Eye Disease; Cornea Transplant; LASIK-Refractive Surgery; **Hospital:** Duke Univ Hosp; **Address:** Duke Univ Eye Center, 2351 Erwin Rd, Durham, NC 27710; **Phone:** 919-684-5769; **Board Cert:** Ophthalmology 1988; **Med School:** Duke Univ 1982; **Resid:** Ophthalmology, Baylor Med Ctr 1986; **Fellow:** Cornea & Ext Eye Disease, Baylor Med Ctr 1987; Cornea & Ext Eye Disease, Duke Univ Med Ctr 1988; **Fac Appt:** Prof Oph, Duke Univ

Cheeseman Jr, Edward W MD [Oph] - **Spec Exp:** Pediatric Ophthalmology; Strabismus; Eye Movement Disorders; **Hospital:** MUSC Med Ctr; **Address:** MUSC Storm Eye Inst, 167 Ashley Ave, Charleston, SC 29425; **Phone:** 843-792-8100 x3; **Board Cert:** Ophthalmology 2005; **Med School:** Uniformed Srvs Univ, Bethesda 1987; **Resid:** Ophthalmology, Natl Naval Med Ctr 1993; **Fellow:** Pediatric Ophthalmology, Wilmer Eye Inst/Johns Hopkins Hosp 1997; **Fac Appt:** Assoc Prof Oph, Med Univ SC

Culbertson, William MD [Oph] - **Spec Exp:** Cataract Surgery-Lens Implant; Corneal & External Eye Disease; LASIK-Refractive Surgery; **Hospital:** Bascom Palmer Eye Inst; **Address:** Bascom Palmer Eye Inst, 900 NW 17th St, Miami, FL 33136; **Phone:** 305-243-2020; **Board Cert:** Ophthalmology 1976; **Med School:** Emory Univ 1970; **Resid:** Ophthalmology, Vanderbilt Univ Hosp 1974; **Fellow:** Cornea & Ext Eye Disease, Bascom Palmer Eye Inst 1979; **Fac Appt:** Prof Oph, Univ Miami Sch Med

Davis, Janet L MD [Oph] - **Spec Exp:** Uveitis; Retina/Vitreous Surgery; Macular Degeneration; Diabetic Eye Disease/Retinopathy; **Hospital:** Bascom Palmer Eye Inst; **Address:** Bascom Palmer Eye Inst, 900 NW 17th St, Miami, FL 33136; **Phone:** 305-243-2020; **Board Cert:** Ophthalmology 2006; **Med School:** Baylor Coll Med 1981; **Resid:** Ophthalmology, Baylor Med Ctr 1986; **Fellow:** Vitreoretinal Surgery, Bascom Palmer Eye Inst 1987; Ocular Immunology, Natl Eye Inst 1989; **Fac Appt:** Prof Oph, Univ Miami Sch Med

Del Priore, Luciano V MD/PhD [Oph] - **Spec Exp:** Diabetic Eye Disease/Retinopathy; Macular Degeneration; Retinal Detachment; Retina-Artificial; **Hospital:** MUSC Med Ctr, Ashley River Tower; **Address:** MUSC Department of Ophthalmology, 825 Storm Eye Institute MSC676, 167 Ashley Ave, Charleston, SC 29425; **Phone:** 843-792-2020; **Board Cert:** Ophthalmology 1989; **Med School:** Univ Rochester 1982; **Resid:** Ophthalmology, Wilmer Eye Inst/Johns HopkinsHosp 1987; **Fellow:** Glaucoma, Wilmer Eye Inst/Johns Hopkins Hosp 1988; Vitreoretinal Surgery, Wilmer Eye Inst/Johns Hopkins Hosp 1989; **Fac Appt:** Prof Oph, Med Univ SC

Dutton, Jonathan J MD/PhD [Oph] - **Spec Exp:** Oculoplastic Surgery; Eye Tumors/Cancer; Melanoma-Choroidal (eye); **Hospital:** NC Memorial Hosp - UNC; **Address:** Univ North Carolina, Dept Ophthalmology, 130 Mason Farm Rd, 5156 Bioinformatics, CB 7040, Chapel Hill, NC 27599; **Phone:** 919-966-5296; **Board Cert:** Ophthalmology 1983; **Med School:** Washington Univ, St Louis 1977; **Resid:** Ophthalmology, Washington Univ Med Ctr 1982; **Fellow:** Oculoplastic Surgery, Univ Iowa Med Ctr 1983; **Fac Appt:** Prof Oph, Univ NC Sch Med

Eiseman, Andrew S MD [Oph] - **Spec Exp:** Oculoplastic & Orbital Surgery; **Hospital:** MUSC Med Ctr; **Address:** MUSC Storm Eye Inst, 167 Ashley Ave, Charleston, SC 29425; **Phone:** 843-792-8100; **Board Cert:** Ophthalmology 2007; **Med School:** Uniformed Srvs Univ, Bethesda 1990; **Resid:** Ophthalmology, Walter Reed Army Med Ctr 1994; **Fellow:** Ophthalmic Plastic & Reconstructive Surgery, Wills Eye Hosp 1998; **Fac Appt:** Assoc Prof Oph, Med Univ SC

Flynn Jr, Harry W MD [Oph] - **Spec Exp:** Retina/Vitreous Surgery; Diabetic Eye Disease/Retinopathy; Macular Disease/Degeneration; **Hospital:** Bascom Palmer Eye Inst; **Address:** Bascom Palmer Eye Institute, 900 NW 17th St, Miami, FL 33136-1119; **Phone:** 305-243-2020; **Board Cert:** Ophthalmology 1976; **Med School:** Univ VA Sch Med 1971; **Resid:** Ophthalmology, Univ Virginia Hosp 1975; **Fellow:** Retina, Pacific Med Ctr 1976; **Fac Appt:** Prof Oph, Univ Miami Sch Med

Freedman, Sharon F MD [Oph] - **Spec Exp:** Pediatric Ophthalmology; Glaucoma-Pediatric; Strabismus; Retinopathy of Prematurity; **Hospital:** Duke Univ Hosp; **Address:** Duke Eye Center, 2351 Erwin Rd, Box 3802, Durham, NC 27710; **Phone:** 919-681-3937; **Board Cert:** Ophthalmology 1991; **Med School:** Harvard Med Sch 1985; **Resid:** Ophthalmology, Mass Eye & Ear Infirm 1989; **Fellow:** Pediatric Ophthalmology, Childns Hosp 1990; Glaucoma, Duke Eye Ctr 1992; **Fac Appt:** Prof Oph, Duke Univ

Gorovoy, Mark S MD [Oph] - **Spec Exp:** Corneal Disease & Transplant; Cataract Surgery; Glaucoma; LASIK-Refractive Surgery; **Hospital:** Lee Memorial Hlth Systems; **Address:** 12381 S Cleveland Ave, Ste 300, Fort Myers, FL 33907; **Phone:** 239-939-1444; **Board Cert:** Ophthalmology 1982; **Med School:** Geo Wash Univ 1973; **Resid:** Ophthalmology, Geo Washington Univ Hosp 1980; **Fellow:** Cornea & Ext Eye Disease, Univ Florida 1982

Greenfield, David S MD [Oph] - **Spec Exp:** Glaucoma; Cataract Surgery-Lens Implant; **Hospital:** Bascom Palmer Eye Inst; **Address:** Bascom Palmer Eye Inst, 7101 Fairway Drive, Palm Beach Gardens, FL 33418; **Phone:** 561-515-1500; **Board Cert:** Ophthalmology 2007; **Med School:** NYU Sch Med 1990; **Resid:** Ophthalmology, New England Eye Center 1994; **Fellow:** Glaucoma, Bascom Palmer Eye Inst 1995; Neuro-Ophthalmology, Bascom Palmer Eye Inst 1995; **Fac Appt:** Prof Oph, Univ Miami Sch Med

Grossniklaus, Hans E MD [Oph] - **Spec Exp:** Ophthalmic Pathology; Melanoma-Choroidal (eye); Macular Disease/Degeneration; Retinal Disorders; **Hospital:** Emory Univ Hosp; **Address:** Emory Clin, LF Montgomery Lab, 1365B Clifton Rd NE, rm BT428, Atlanta, GA 30322; **Phone:** 404-778-4611; **Board Cert:** Ophthalmology 1985; Anatomic Pathology 1987; **Med School:** Ohio State Univ 1980; **Resid:** Ophthalmology, Case West Res Univ Hosp 1984; Pathology, Case West Res Univ Hosp 1987; **Fellow:** Ophthalmological Pathology, Johns Hopkins Hosp 1985; **Fac Appt:** Prof Oph, Emory Univ

Guy, John R MD [Oph] - **Spec Exp:** Neuro-Ophthalmology; **Hospital:** Bascom Palmer Eye Inst; **Address:** Bascom Palmer Eye Inst, 900 NW 17th St, Miami, FL 33136; **Phone:** 305-243-2020; **Board Cert:** Ophthalmology 1983; **Med School:** Univ Miami Sch Med 1977; **Resid:** Neurology, Temple Univ Hosp 1979; Ophthalmology, Georgetown Univ Med Ctr 1988; **Fellow:** Neuro-Ophthalmology, Wills Eye Hosp 1983; **Fac Appt:** Assoc Prof Oph, Univ Miami Sch Med

Haik, Barrett MD [Oph] - **Spec Exp:** Eye Tumors/Cancer; Orbital Diseases; Pediatric Ophthalmology; **Hospital:** St. Jude Children's Research Hosp; **Address:** Hamilton Eye Institute, 930 Madison Ave, Ste 200, Memphis, TN 38135; **Phone:** 901-448-6650; **Board Cert:** Ophthalmology 1981; **Med School:** Louisiana State U, New Orleans 1976; **Resid:** Ophthalmology, Columbia-Presby/Harkness Eye Inst 1980; **Fac Appt:** Prof Oph, Univ Tenn Coll Med

Harbour, J William MD [Oph] - **Spec Exp:** Eye Tumors/Cancer; Melanoma-Choroidal (eye); Retinoblastoma; **Hospital:** Bascom Palmer Eye Inst, Univ of Miami Hosp & Clins/Sylvester Comp Canc Ctr; **Address:** Bascom Palmer Eye Inst, 900 NW 17th St, Ste 254, Miami, FL 33136; **Phone:** 305-326-6166; **Board Cert:** Ophthalmology 2007; **Med School:** Johns Hopkins Univ 1990; **Resid:** Ophthalmology, Wills Eye Hosp 1994; **Fellow:** Retina/Vitreous Surgery, Bascom Palmer Eye Inst 1995; Ocular Oncology, UCSF Med Ctr 1996; **Fac Appt:** Prof Oph, Univ Miami Sch Med

Hess, Jeffrey Bruce MD [Oph] - **Spec Exp:** Pediatric Ophthalmology; Strabismus; **Hospital:** All Children's Hosp, Bayfront Med Ctr; **Address:** 601 5th St S, Ste 601, St Petersburg, FL 33701; **Phone:** 727-767-4393; **Board Cert:** Ophthalmology 1978; **Med School:** Baylor Coll Med 1971; **Resid:** Ophthalmology, Geisinger Med Ctr 1977; **Fellow:** Ophthalmology, Wills Eye Inst 1978; **Fac Appt:** Assoc Prof Oph, Univ S Fla Coll Med

Hodapp, Elizabeth A MD [Oph] - **Spec Exp:** Glaucoma-Pediatric; **Hospital:** Bascom Palmer Eye Inst; **Address:** Bascom Palmer Eye Inst, 900 NW 17th St, Miami, FL 33136; **Phone:** 305-243-2020; **Board Cert:** Ophthalmology 1980; **Med School:** Harvard Med Sch 1975; **Resid:** Ophthalmology, Barnes-Jewish Hosp 1979; **Fellow:** Glaucoma, Barnes-Jewish Hosp 1981

Jaafar, Mohamad S MD [Oph] - **Spec Exp:** Pediatric Ophthalmology; Strabismus-Adult & Pediatric; Glaucoma-Pediatric; **Hospital:** Chldns Natl Med Ctr, G Washington Univ Hosp; **Address:** 3023 Hamaker Ct, Ste 500, Fairfax, VA 22031; **Phone:** 571-766-3100; **Board Cert:** Ophthalmology 2008; **Med School:** Amer Univ Beirut 1978; **Resid:** Ophthalmology, Am Univ Beirut Med Ctr 1981; Ophthalmology, Washington Hosp Ctr 1994; **Fellow:** Pediatric Ophthalmology, Chldn's Hosp 1982; Pediatric Ophthalmology, Baylor Coll Med 1983; **Fac Appt:** Prof Oph, Geo Wash Univ

Kerr, Natalie C MD [Oph] - **Spec Exp:** Pediatric Ophthalmology; Strabismus; Cataract-Pediatric; Genetic Disorders-Eye; **Hospital:** Le Bonheur Chldns Med Ctr, St. Jude Children's Research Hosp; **Address:** Hamilton Eye Inst, 930 Madison Ave, Ste 400, Memphis, TN 38103; **Phone:** 901-448-6650; **Board Cert:** Ophthalmology 2013; **Med School:** Univ Fla Coll Med 1987; **Resid:** Ophthalmology, Shands Hosp/Univ FL 1991; **Fellow:** Pediatric Ophthalmology, Univ TN Affil Hosp 1992; **Fac Appt:** Prof Oph, Univ Tenn Coll Med

Lambert, Scott R MD [Oph] - **Spec Exp:** Pediatric Ophthalmology; Strabismus; Cataract-Pediatric; **Hospital:** Chldns Hlthcare Atlanta @ Egleston, Emory Univ Hosp; **Address:** Emory Eye Ctr, Ped Ophthalmology, 1365B Clifton Rd NE, Ste 4513, Atlanta, GA 30322; **Phone:** 404-778-3431; **Board Cert:** Ophthalmology 1989; **Med School:** Yale Univ 1983; **Resid:** Ophthalmology, UCSF Med Ctr 1987; **Fellow:** Pediatric Ophthalmology, Hosp Sick Chldn 1988; Strabismus, Smith Kettlewell Eye Rsch 1988; **Fac Appt:** Prof Oph, Emory Univ

Mawn, Louise A MD [Oph] - **Spec Exp:** Orbital Surgery; Reconstructive Surgery; Neuro-Ophthalmology; Eyelid/Tear Duct Reconstruction; **Hospital:** Vanderbilt Univ Med Ctr; **Address:** Vanderbilt Eye Institute, 2311 Pierce Ave, Nashville, TN 37232; **Phone:** 615-936-2020; **Board Cert:** Ophthalmology 2008; **Med School:** Wake Forest Univ 1990; **Resid:** Ophthalmology, Univ Iowa Hosps & Clin 1995; **Fellow:** Neuro-Ophthalmology, New England Med Ctr 1996; Ophthalmic Plastic & Reconstructive Surgery, Univ Ottawa Eye Inst 1997; **Fac Appt:** Assoc Prof Oph, Vanderbilt Univ

McKeown, Craig A MD [Oph] - **Spec Exp:** Pediatric Ophthalmology; Strabismus-Adult & Pediatric; Eye Muscle Disorders; **Hospital:** Bascom Palmer Eye Inst; **Address:** Bascom Palmer Eye Inst, 900 NW 17th St, Miami, FL 33136; **Phone:** 305-243-2020; **Board Cert:** Ophthalmology 1982; **Med School:** Northwestern Univ 1971; **Resid:** Ophthalmology, Walter Reed Med Ctr 1980; **Fellow:** Pediatric Ophthalmology, Chldns Hosp Natl Med Ctr 1984; Pediatric Ophthalmology, Wilmer Inst-Johns Hopkins 1985; **Fac Appt:** Clin Prof Oph, Univ Miami Sch Med

Meredith, Travis A MD [Oph] - **Spec Exp:** Retina/Vitreous Surgery; Macular Degeneration; Diabetic Eye Disease/Retinopathy; **Hospital:** NC Memorial Hosp - UNC; **Address:** 5151 Bioinformatics, CB#7040, Chapel Hill, NC 27599-7040; **Phone:** 919-966-5296; **Board Cert:** Ophthalmology 1976; **Med School:** Johns Hopkins Univ 1969; **Resid:** Ophthalmology, Wilmer Inst-Johns Hopkins 1971; Ophthalmology, Wilmer Inst-Johns Hopkins 1975; **Fellow:** Vitreoretinal Surgery, Med Coll Wisconsin 1976; **Fac Appt:** Prof Oph, Univ NC Sch Med

Murray, Timothy G MD [Oph] - **Spec Exp:** Eye Tumors/Cancer; Retinal Disorders; Macular Degeneration; Diabetic Eye Disease/Retinopathy; **Hospital:** Baptist Hosp of Miami, Miami Children's Hosp; **Address:** Murray Ocular Oncology and Retina, 6705 Red Rd, Ste 412, Coral Gables, FL 33143; **Phone:** 305-487-7470; **Board Cert:** Ophthalmology 1990; **Med School:** Johns Hopkins Univ 1985; **Resid:** Ophthalmology, UCSF Med Ctr 1989; **Fellow:** Ophthalmology, UCSF Med Ctr 1990; Vitreoretinal Disease, Med Coll Wisconsin 1991; **Fac Appt:** Prof Emeritus Oph, Univ Miami Sch Med

Nunery, William R MD [Oph] - **Spec Exp:** Orbital Surgery; Oculoplastic Surgery; Thyroid Eye Disease; **Hospital:** Univ of Louisville Hosp; **Address:** Kentucky Lions Eye Ctr, 301 E Muhammad Ali Blvd, Louisville, KY 40202; **Phone:** 502-889-1000; **Board Cert:** Ophthalmology 1980; **Med School:** Case West Res Univ 1975; **Resid:** Ophthalmology, IU Hlth Univ Hosp 1979; **Fellow:** Ophthalmic Plastic Surgery, Emory Univ Hosp 1980

Nussbaum, Julian MD [Oph] - **Spec Exp:** Diabetic Eye Disease/Retinopathy; Macular Degeneration; Retinopathy of Prematurity; **Hospital:** Georgia Regents Med Ctr-Augusta; **Address:** 1120 15th St BA Bldg Fl 2 - rm 2331, Augusta, GA 30912; **Phone:** 706-721-1148; **Board Cert:** Ophthalmology 1981; **Med School:** Univ Miami Sch Med 1976; **Resid:** Internal Medicine, Jackson Memorial Hosp 1977; Ophthalmology, Med Coll Georgia 1980; **Fellow:** Vitreoretinal Surgery, Mass Eye & Ear Infirmary 1982; **Fac Appt:** Prof Oph, Med Coll GA

Olsen, Timothy W MD [Oph] - **Spec Exp:** Macular Degeneration; Diabetic Eye Disease/Retinopathy; Retinal Detachment; Retinal Disorders-Pediatric; **Hospital:** Emory Univ Hosp; **Address:** Emory Eye Center, 1365B Clifton Rd NE, Ste 3500, Atlanta, GA 30322; **Phone:** 404-778-2020; **Board Cert:** Ophthalmology 2007; **Med School:** Univ Kansas 1989; **Resid:** Ophthalmology, Univ Minn Affil Hosps 1993; **Fellow:** Vitreoretinal Surgery & Disease, Emory Univ 1996; **Fac Appt:** Prof Oph, Emory Univ

Parrish II, Richard K MD [Oph] - **Spec Exp:** Glaucoma; Cataract Surgery-Lens Implant; **Hospital:** Bascom Palmer Eye Inst, Jackson Meml Hosp; **Address:** Bascom Palmer Eye Inst, 900 NW 17th St, Miami, FL 33136; **Phone:** 305-243-2020; **Board Cert:** Ophthalmology 1981; **Med School:** Indiana Univ 1976; **Resid:** Ophthalmology, Wills Eye Hosp 1980; **Fellow:** Glaucoma, Bascom Palmer Eye Inst 1982; **Fac Appt:** Prof Oph, Univ Miami Sch Med

Patrinely, James R MD [Oph] - **Spec Exp:** Ophthalmic Plastic Surgery; Eyelid Surgery; Orbital Surgery; **Hospital:** Methodist Hosp - Houston, St. Luke's Episcopal Hosp-Houston; **Address:** 17 E Main St, Ste 100, Pensacola, FL 32502; **Phone:** 850-473-0990; **Board Cert:** Ophthalmology 1986; **Med School:** Vanderbilt Univ 1980; **Resid:** Ophthalmology, Baylor Med Ctr 1984; **Fellow:** Ophthalmological Pathology, Johns Hopkins Hosp 1985; Ophthalmic Plastic & Reconstructive Surgery, Univ Utah Med Ctr 1986; **Fac Appt:** Clin Prof Oph, Baylor Coll Med

Perez, Victor L MD [Oph] - **Spec Exp:** Cataract Surgery-Lens Implant; Uveitis; Cornea Transplant; Cornea & External Eye Disease; **Hospital:** Bascom Palmer Eye Inst; **Address:** Bascom Palmer Eye Inst, 900 NW 17th St, Miami, FL 33136; **Phone:** 305-243-2020; **Board Cert:** Ophthalmology 2012; **Med School:** Univ Puerto Rico 1991; **Resid:** Ophthalmology, Mass Eye & Ear Infirmary 2000; **Fellow:** Immunology, Schepens Eye Rsch Inst 1997; Cornea, Mass Eye & Ear Infirmary 2002; **Fac Appt:** Assoc Prof Oph, Univ Miami Sch Med

Pollard, Zane F MD [Oph] - **Spec Exp:** Pediatric Ophthalmology; Strabismus; Tear Duct Problems; **Hospital:** Chldns Hlthcare Atlanta @ Scottish Rite, Piedmont Hosp; **Address:** Eye Consultants of Atlanta, 5445 Meridian Mark Rd, Ste 220, Atlanta, GA 30342-4722; **Phone:** 404-255-2419; **Board Cert:** Ophthalmology 1975; **Med School:** Tulane Univ 1966; **Resid:** Surgery, UCSF Med Ctr 1968; Ophthalmology, USC Med Ctr 1973; **Fellow:** Pediatric Ophthalmology, Wills Eye Hosp 1975

Rosenfeld, Philip J MD/PhD [Oph] - **Spec Exp:** Macular Disease/Degeneration; Diabetic Eye Disease/Retinopathy; Retinal Detachment; Retina/Vitreous Surgery; **Hospital:** Bascom Palmer Eye Inst; **Address:** Bascom Palmer Eye Inst, 900 NW 17th St, Miami, FL 33136; **Phone:** 305-326-6148; **Board Cert:** Ophthalmology 2008; **Med School:** Johns Hopkins Univ 1988; **Resid:** Ophthalmology, Mass Eye & Ear Infirm 1995; **Fellow:** Retina, Bascom Palmer Eye Inst 1996; **Fac Appt:** Prof Oph, Univ Miami Sch Med

Sherwood, Mark B MD [Oph] - **Spec Exp:** Glaucoma; **Hospital:** UF Hlth Shands Hosp; **Address:** UF Hlth, Ophthalmology Dept, 1600 SW Archer Rd, Box 100383, Gainesville, FL 32610; **Phone:** 352-265-7080; **Med School:** England, UK 1976; **Resid:** Ophthalmology, Moorefields Eye Hosp 1980; **Fellow:** Glaucoma, Wills Eye Hosp 1982; Glaucoma, Moorefields Eye Hosp 1983; **Fac Appt:** Prof Oph, Univ Fla Coll Med

Solomon, Kerry D MD [Oph] - **Spec Exp:** Cataract Surgery; Corneal Disease; Refractive Surgery; Lens Implants-Multifocal; **Address:** 1101 Clarity Rd, Mt Pleasant, SC 29464; **Phone:** 843-881-3937; **Board Cert:** Ophthalmology 2004; **Med School:** Univ VT Coll Med 1987; **Resid:** Ophthalmology, Univ Kentucky Med Ctr 1992; **Fellow:** Ophthalmic Pathology, Univ Utah Hlth Sci Ctr 1988; Cornea & Ext Eye Disease, Wilmer Inst/Johns Hopkins Hosp 1993; **Fac Appt:** Clin Prof Oph, Univ SC Sch Med

Sternberg Jr, Paul MD [Oph] - **Spec Exp:** Macular Degeneration; Eye Tumors/Cancer; Diabetic Eye Disease/Retinopathy; Trauma; **Hospital:** Vanderbilt Univ Med Ctr, Vanderbilt Monroe Carrell Jr. Chldn's Hosp; **Address:** Vanderbilt Eye Institute, 2311 Pierce Ave, Nashville, TN 37232-8808; **Phone:** 615-936-2020; **Board Cert:** Ophthalmology 1985; **Med School:** Univ Chicago-Pritzker Sch Med 1979; **Resid:** Ophthalmology, Johns Hopkins Hosp 1983; **Fellow:** Vitreoretinal Surgery, Duke Univ Med Ctr 1984; **Fac Appt:** Prof Oph, Vanderbilt Univ

Stulting, R. Doyle MD/PhD [Oph] - **Spec Exp:** Corneal Disease & Transplant; Laser Vision Surgery; Cataract Surgery; Keratoconus; **Address:** Woolfson Eye Inst, 800 Mount Vernon Hwy NE, Ste 125, Atlanta, GA 30328; **Phone:** 404-256-1125; **Board Cert:** Ophthalmology 1982; **Med School:** Duke Univ 1976; **Resid:** Internal Medicine, Barnes-Jewish Hosp 1978; Ophthalmology, Bascom Palmer Eye Inst 1981; **Fellow:** Cornea, Emory Univ Hosp 1982

Tse, David T MD [Oph] - **Spec Exp:** Oculoplastic Surgery; Orbital Tumors/Cancer; Lacrimal Gland Disorders; Anophthalmia; **Hospital:** Bascom Palmer Eye Inst; **Address:** Bascom Palmer Eye Inst, 900 NW 17th St Fl 4, Miami, FL 33136; **Phone:** 305-326-6086; **Board Cert:** Ophthalmology 2013; **Med School:** Univ Miami Sch Med 1976; **Resid:** Ophthalmology, LAC & USC Med Ctr 1981; **Fellow:** Ophthalmic Plastic Surgery, Univ Iowa Hosps & Clins 1982; Ophthalmic Oncology, Univ Iowa Hosps & Clins 1982; **Fac Appt:** Prof Oph, Univ Miami Sch Med

Updegraff, Stephen A MD [Oph] - **Spec Exp:** LASIK-Refractive Surgery; Corneal Disease & Surgery; Refractive Surgery; **Address:** 1601 38th Ave N, St Petersburg, FL 33713; **Phone:** 727-822-4287; **Board Cert:** Ophthalmology 2008; **Med School:** Penn State Coll Med 1989; **Resid:** Ophthalmology, LSU Eye Ctr 1994; **Fellow:** Cornea, Univ Genl Hosp 1995

Wang, Ming X MD/PhD [Oph] - **Spec Exp:** LASIK-Refractive Surgery; Laser Surgery; Cataract Surgery; **Hospital:** Saint Thomas West Hosp - Nashville, University Med Ctr; **Address:** Wang Vision 3D Cataract & LASIK Ctr, 1801 West End Ave, Ste 1150, Nashville, TN 37203; **Phone:** 615-321-8881; **Board Cert:** Ophthalmology 2009; **Med School:** Harvard Med Sch 1991; **Resid:** Ophthalmology, Wills Eye Hosp 1996; **Fellow:** Refractive Surgery, Bascom Palmer Eye Inst 1997; **Fac Appt:** Assoc Clin Prof Oph, Univ Tenn Coll Med

Waring III, George O MD [Oph] - **Spec Exp:** LASIK-Refractive Surgery; Cataract Surgery; Lens Implants; **Hospital:** Northside Hosp; **Address:** 10080 Medlock Bridge Rd, Duluth, GA 30097; **Phone:** 404-442-9577; **Board Cert:** Ophthalmology 1975; **Med School:** Baylor Coll Med 1967; **Resid:** Ophthalmology, Wills Eye Hosp 1973; **Fellow:** Cornea & Ext Eye Disease, Wills Eye Hosp 1974

Warman, Roberto MD [Oph] - **Spec Exp:** Pediatric Ophthalmology; Strabismus-Adult & Pediatric; Amblyopia; Pediatric Neuro-Ophthalmology; **Hospital:** Miami Children's Hosp; **Address:** Miami Childrens Hosp, Pediatric Ophthalmology Consultants, 3200 SW 60th Court, Ste 103, Miami, FL 33155; **Phone:** 305-662-8390; **Board Cert:** Ophthalmology 1987; **Med School:** Mexico 1981; **Resid:** Ophthalmology, Oschner Med Fndn 1985; **Fellow:** Neuro-Ophthalmology, Bascom Palmer Eye Inst 1986; Pediatric Ophthalmology, Bascom Palmer Eye Inst 1987; **Fac Appt:** Clin Prof Oph, Univ Miami Sch Med

Wilson Jr, Marion E MD [Oph] - **Spec Exp:** Pediatric Ophthalmology; Cataract-Pediatric; Strabismus; Lens Implants-Pediatric; **Hospital:** MUSC Chldns Hosp; **Address:** MUSC Storm Eye Inst, 167 Ashley Ave, Box 250676, Charleston, SC 29425; **Phone:** 843-792-7622; **Board Cert:** Ophthalmology 1987; **Med School:** Med Univ SC 1980; **Resid:** Ophthalmology, Natl Naval Med Ctr 1986; **Fellow:** Pediatric Ophthalmology, Chldns Hosp - Naval Med Ctr 1987; **Fac Appt:** Prof Oph, Med Univ SC

Wilson, Matthew W MD [Oph] - **Spec Exp:** Eye Tumors/Cancer; Retinoblastoma; Melanoma-Choroidal (eye); **Hospital:** St. Jude Children's Research Hosp, Methodist Univ Hosp - Memphis; **Address:** Univ Tenn Med Grp, Ophthalmology, 930 Madison Ave, Ste 200, Memphis, TN 38103; **Phone:** 901-448-6650; **Board Cert:** Ophthalmology 2007; **Med School:** Emory Univ 1990; **Resid:** Ophthalmology, Emory Univ Med Ctr 1994; Ophthalmic Pathology, Emory Univ Med Ctr 1995; **Fellow:** Ocular Oncology, Moorfields Eye Hosp 1996; Ophthalmic Plastic & Reconstructive Surgery, Casey Eye Inst 1998; **Fac Appt:** Prof Oph, Univ Tenn Coll Med

Yeatts, R. Patrick MD [Oph] - **Spec Exp:** Oculoplastic Surgery; Orbital Tumors/Cancer; Eyelid Tumors/Cancer; Orbital Diseases; **Hospital:** Wake Forest Baptist Med Ctr; **Address:** Wake Forest Baptist Health Eye Ctr, Janeway Tower Fl 6, One Medical Ctr Blvd, Winston-Salem, NC 27157; **Phone:** 336-716-4091; **Board Cert:** Ophthalmology 1983; **Med School:** Wake Forest Univ 1978; **Resid:** Ophthalmology, Mayo Med Ctr & Clin 1982; **Fellow:** Oculoplastic & Reconstructive Surgery, Mass Eye & Ear Infirmary 1983; **Fac Appt:** Prof Oph, Wake Forest Univ

Midwest

Abrams, Gary W MD [Oph] - **Spec Exp:** Retina/Vitreous Surgery; Macular Disease/Degeneration; **Hospital:** Harper Univ Hosp; **Address:** Kresge Eye Inst, 4717 St Antoine St, Detroit, MI 48201; **Phone:** 313-577-8900; **Board Cert:** Ophthalmology 1977; **Med School:** Univ Okla Coll Med 1968; **Resid:** Ophthalmology, Med Coll Wisc Affil Hosps 1976; **Fellow:** Vitreoretinal Surgery, Bascom Palmer Eye Inst 1978; **Fac Appt:** Prof Oph, Wayne State Univ

Ahmad, Amjad Z MD [Oph] - **Spec Exp:** Oculoplastic & Orbital Surgery; Cosmetic & Reconstructive Surgery; Eyelid Cosmetic & Reconstructive Surgery; Tear Duct Problems; **Hospital:** Univ of IL Med Ctr at Chicago; **Address:** Univ Ill at Chicago, Dept Ophthalmology & Visual Scis, 1855 W Taylor St Fl 3 - rm 3.158, Chicago, IL 60612; **Phone:** 312-996-9120; **Board Cert:** Ophthalmology 2011; **Med School:** Univ Mich Med Sch 1994; **Resid:** Ophthalmology, Univ Michigan Affil Hosp 1998; **Fellow:** Oculoplastic & Reconstructive Surgery, Univ Michigan Affil Hosp 2000; **Fac Appt:** Asst Prof Oph, Univ IL Coll Med

Albert, Daniel M MD [Oph] - **Spec Exp:** Eye Tumors/Cancer; Ophthalmic Pathology; **Hospital:** Univ WI Hosp & Clins; **Address:** 600 Highland Ave CSC Bldg - rm K6/412, Madison, WI 53792-3284; **Phone:** 608-263-9798; **Board Cert:** Ophthalmology 1969; **Med School:** Univ Pennsylvania 1962; **Resid:** Ophthalmology, Hosp Univ Penn - UPHS 1966; **Fellow:** Neuro-Ophthalmology, Natl Inst Hlth 1968; Pathology, Armed Forces Inst Path 1969; **Fac Appt:** Prof Oph, Univ Wisc

Alward, Wallace LM MD [Oph] - **Spec Exp:** Glaucoma; Anterior Segment Surgery; Cataract Surgery; Eye Tumors/Cancer; **Hospital:** Univ Iowa Hosp & Clins; **Address:** UI Hospitals and Clinics, Department of Ophthalmology, 200 Hawkins Drive, Iowa City, IA 52242-1009; **Phone:** 319-356-3938; **Board Cert:** Ophthalmology 2006; **Med School:** Ohio State Univ 1976; **Resid:** Ophthalmology, Univ Louisville 1986; **Fellow:** Glaucoma, Univ Miami-Bascom Palmer Eye Inst 1987; **Fac Appt:** Prof Oph, Univ Iowa Coll Med

Archer, Steven M MD [Oph] - **Spec Exp:** Pediatric Ophthalmology; **Hospital:** Univ Michigan Med Ctr; **Address:** Kellogg Eye Ctr, 1000 Wall St, Ann Arbor, MI 48105; **Phone:** 734-764-7558; **Board Cert:** Ophthalmology 1986; **Med School:** Univ Chicago-Pritzker Sch Med 1978; **Resid:** Ophthalmology, Univ Chicago Med Ctr 1984; **Fellow:** Pediatric Ophthalmology, Indiana Univ 1986; **Fac Appt:** Asst Prof Oph, Univ Mich Med Sch

Augsburger, James J MD [Oph] - **Spec Exp:** Eye Tumors/Cancer; Melanoma-Choroidal (eye); Retinoblastoma; **Hospital:** Univ Cincinnati Med Ctr, Cincinnati Chldns Hosp Med Ctr; **Address:** 222 Piedmont Ave, MSB Bldg Fl 1 - Ste 1500, Cincinnati, OH 45219; **Phone:** 513-475-7300; **Board Cert:** Ophthalmology 1979; **Med School:** Univ Cincinnati 1974; **Resid:** Ophthalmology, Univ Hosp 1978; **Fellow:** Ocular Oncology, Wills Eye Hosp 1980; **Fac Appt:** Prof Oph, Univ Cincinnati

Azar, Dimitri T MD [Oph] - **Spec Exp:** LASIK-Refractive Surgery; **Hospital:** Univ of IL at Chicago Eye & Ear Infirm, Univ of IL Med Ctr at Chicago; **Address:** Millenium Park Eye Ctr, 30 N Michigan Ave, Ste 410, Chicago, IL 60602; **Phone:** 312-996-2020; **Board Cert:** Ophthalmology 1991; **Med School:** Lebanon 1983; **Resid:** Ophthalmology, American Univ Med Ctr 1986; Ophthalmology, Mass E&E Infirm 1991; **Fellow:** Cornea & Ext Eye Disease, Mass E&E Infirm 1988; Cornea Research, Harvard Med Sch 1991; **Fac Appt:** Prof Oph, Univ IL Coll Med

Azar, Nathalie F MD [Oph] - **Spec Exp:** Pediatric Ophthalmology; Strabismus; **Hospital:** Univ of IL at Chicago Eye & Ear Infirm; **Address:** Millenium Park Eye Ctr, 30 N Michigan Ave, Ste 410, Chicago, IL 60602; **Phone:** 312-996-2020; **Board Cert:** Ophthalmology 2007; **Med School:** Boston Univ 1990; **Resid:** Ophthalmology, George Washington U Med Ctr 1994; **Fellow:** Pediatric Ophthalmology, Wilmer Eye Inst 1995; **Fac Appt:** Assoc Clin Prof Oph, Univ IL Coll Med

Baker, John D MD [Oph] - **Spec Exp:** Pediatric Ophthalmology; **Hospital:** Chldns Hosp of Michigan; **Address:** 7001 Orchard Lake Rd, Ste 200, Ste 200, West Bloomfield, MI 48322-3009; **Phone:** 248-538-7400; **Board Cert:** Ophthalmology 1974; **Med School:** Wayne State Univ 1967; **Resid:** Ophthalmology, Detroit Genl Hosp 1971; **Fellow:** Pediatric Ophthalmology, Chldns Natl Med Ctr 1972; **Fac Appt:** Clin Prof Oph, Wayne State Univ

Bouchard, Charles MD [Oph] - **Spec Exp:** Cataract Surgery; Tearing Disorders; Cornea Transplant; **Hospital:** Loyola Univ Med Ctr; **Address:** Loyola Univ Med Ctr, Ophthalmology Dept, 2160 S First Ave, Maywood, IL 60153; **Phone:** 708-216-3833; **Board Cert:** Ophthalmology 1991; **Med School:** Northwestern Univ 1985; **Resid:** Ophthalmology, G Washington Univ Hosp 1989; **Fellow:** Cornea & Ext Eye Disease, Georgetown Univ Hosp 1990; **Fac Appt:** Prof Oph, Loyola Univ-Stritch Sch Med

Burke, Miles J MD [Oph] - **Spec Exp:** Pediatric Ophthalmology; Eye Muscle Surgery; Amblyopia & Vision Development; Strabismus; **Hospital:** Cincinnati Chldns Hosp Med Ctr, Jewish Hosp - Kenwood - Cincinnati; **Address:** 10475 Montgomery Rd, Ste 4F, MS 45242, Cincinnati, OH 45242-5200; **Phone:** 513-984-4949; **Board Cert:** Ophthalmology 1979; **Med School:** Univ Ariz Coll Med 1974; **Resid:** Ophthalmology, Univ Michigan Med Ctr 1978; **Fellow:** Pediatric Ophthalmology, Wills Eye Hosp 1979

Cahill, Kenneth V MD [Oph] - **Spec Exp:** Eyelid Surgery; Eyelid/Tear Duct Reconstruction; Orbital Surgery; Oculoplastic Surgery; **Hospital:** Nationwide Chldn's Hosp; **Address:** The Eye Center, 262 Neil Ave, Ste 430, Columbus, OH 43215; **Phone:** 614-221-7464; **Board Cert:** Ophthalmology 1984; **Med School:** Ohio State Univ 1979; **Resid:** Ophthalmology, Univ of Pittsburgh 1983; **Fellow:** Oculoplastic Surgery, OSU Med Ctr 1984; Oculoplastic Surgery, Chldns Hosp Philadelphia 1984; **Fac Appt:** Clin Prof Oph, Ohio State Univ

Carter, Keith D MD [Oph] - **Spec Exp:** Oculoplastic & Orbital Surgery; Eyelid Surgery; Botox Therapy; **Hospital:** Univ Iowa Hosp & Clins; **Address:** UIHC Dept Ophthalmology, 200 Hawkins Dr, PFP 11136-F, Iowa City, IA 52242; **Phone:** 319-356-2852; **Board Cert:** Ophthalmology 1988; **Med School:** Indiana Univ 1983; **Resid:** Ophthalmology, Univ Michigan Med Ctr 1987; **Fellow:** Oculoplastic Surgery, Univ Iowa 1988; **Fac Appt:** Prof Oph, Univ Iowa Coll Med

Del Monte, Monte A MD [Oph] - **Spec Exp:** Pediatric Ophthalmology; Strabismus-Adult & Pediatric; Cataract-Pediatric; Ophthalmic Genetics; **Hospital:** Univ Michigan Med Ctr; **Address:** Kellogg Eye Center, 1000 Wall St, Ann Arbor, MI 48105-1912; **Phone:** 734-764-7558; **Board Cert:** Ophthalmology 1982; **Med School:** Johns Hopkins Univ 1974; **Resid:** Pediatrics, Chldns Hosp Med Ctr 1977; Ophthalmology, Wilmer Eye Inst 1981; **Fellow:** Ophthalmology, Wilmer Eye Inst 1978; Pediatric Ophthalmology, Chldns Hosp Natl Med Ctr 1981; **Fac Appt:** Prof Oph, Univ Mich Med Sch

Drack, Arlene V MD [Oph] - **Spec Exp:** Eye Diseases-Hereditary; Eye Tumors/Cancer; Pediatric Ophthalmology; Strabismus; **Hospital:** Univ Iowa Hosp & Clins; **Address:** UIHC Dept Ophthalmology, 200 Hawkins Drive, Iowa City, IA 52242; **Phone:** 319-356-2852; **Board Cert:** Ophthalmology 1991; **Med School:** Penn State Coll Med 1986; **Resid:** Ophthalmology, Georgetown Univ Med Ctr 1990; **Fellow:** Pediatric Ophthalmology, Univ IA Hosps & Clin 1991; Molecular Genetics, Univ IA Hosps & Clin 1992; **Fac Appt:** Assoc Prof Oph, Univ Iowa Coll Med

Edwards, Paul A MD [Oph] - **Spec Exp:** Retinal Disorders; Macular Degeneration; Diabetic Eye Disease/Retinopathy; Ophthalmic Genetics; **Hospital:** Henry Ford Hosp, Henry Ford- W Bloomfield Hosp; **Address:** Henry Ford Hosp, Dept Ophthalmology, 2799 W Grand Blvd, K-10, Detroit, MI 48202; **Phone:** 313-916-3245; **Board Cert:** Ophthalmology 2005; **Med School:** West Indies 1979; **Resid:** Surgery, Washington Hosp Ctr 1984; Ophthalmology, Henry Ford Hosp 1989; **Fellow:** Research, Natl Eye Inst 1991; Retina/Vitreous Surgery, Henry Ford Hosp 1993; **Fac Appt:** Prof Oph, Wayne State Univ

Elner, Victor H MD/PhD [Oph] - **Spec Exp:** Eyelid Tumors/Cancer; Orbital Tumors/Cancer; **Hospital:** Univ Michigan Med Ctr; **Address:** Kellogg Eye Ctr, 1000 Wall St, Ann Arbor, MI 48105; **Phone:** 734-763-9142; **Board Cert:** Ophthalmology 1983; Pathology 1988; **Med School:** Univ Chicago-Pritzker Sch Med 1979; **Resid:** Ophthalmology, Univ Chicago Med Ctr 1982; Pathology, Univ Chicago Med Ctr 1984; **Fellow:** Ophthalmological Pathology, Armed Forces Inst 1985; Ophthalmic Plastic & Reconstructive Surgery, Univ Wisconsin Affil Hosp 1987; **Fac Appt:** Prof Oph, Univ Mich Med Sch

Feder, Robert S MD [Oph] - **Spec Exp:** Corneal Disease; LASIK-Refractive Surgery; Cataract Surgery; **Hospital:** Northwestern Meml Hosp; **Address:** 675 N St Clair St, Galter Bldg - Ste 15-150, Chicago, IL 60611-5975; **Phone:** 312-695-8150; **Board Cert:** Ophthalmology 1983; **Med School:** Northwestern Univ 1978; **Resid:** Ophthalmology, Barnes Hosp 1982; **Fellow:** Cornea & Ext Eye Disease, Univ Iowa Hosp & Clinics 1983; **Fac Appt:** Assoc Prof Oph, Northwestern Univ

Fishman, Gerald MD [Oph] - **Spec Exp:** Retinitis Pigmentosa; Retinal Disorders-Inherited; **Address:** Chicago Lighthouse, 1850 W Roosevelt Rd, Chicago, IL 60608; **Phone:** 312-997-3666; **Board Cert:** Ophthalmology 1975; **Med School:** Ohio State Univ 1969; **Resid:** Ophthalmology, Univ IL Eye & Ear Infirmary 1973; **Fellow:** Ocular Pathology, Univ IL Eye & Ear Infirmary 1974; **Fac Appt:** Prof Oph, Univ IL Coll Med

Greenwald, Mark MD [Oph] - **Spec Exp:** Pediatric Ophthalmology; Strabismus; **Hospital:** Univ of Chicago Med; **Address:** Univ Chicago Med Ctr, Dept Ophthalmology, 5758 S Maryland Ave, rm 1B, Chicago, IL 60637; **Phone:** 773-702-3937; **Board Cert:** Ophthalmology 1981; **Med School:** Harvard Med Sch 1976; **Resid:** Ophthalmology, Univ Illinois Hosp 1980; **Fellow:** Pediatric Ophthalmology, Chldns Hosp 1981; **Fac Appt:** Assoc Prof Oph, Univ Wash

Hariprasad, Seenu M MD [Oph] - **Spec Exp:** Retinal Disorders; Macular Degeneration; Diabetic Eye Disease/Retinopathy; Retinal Detachment; **Hospital:** Univ of Chicago Med, Weiss Meml Hosp; **Address:** Univ Chicago Med Ctr-Dept Ophthalmology, 5758 S Maryland Ave, rm 1B, Chicago, IL 60637; **Phone:** 773-702-3937; **Board Cert:** Ophthalmology 2004; **Med School:** Univ Pennsylvania 1999; **Resid:** Ophthalmology, Cullen Eye Inst/Baylor Coll of Med 2003; **Fellow:** Retina/Vitreous Surgery, Barnes Retina Inst/Wash Univ 2005; **Fac Appt:** Assoc Prof Oph, Univ Chicago-Pritzker Sch Med

Heckenlively, John R MD [Oph] - **Spec Exp:** Eye Diseases-Hereditary; Retinal Disorders; Retinal Dystrophies; Autoimmune Retinopathy; **Hospital:** Univ Michigan Med Ctr; **Address:** Univ Michigan Kellogg Eye Ctr, 1000 Wall St, Ann Arbor, MI 48105; **Phone:** 734-763-2280; **Board Cert:** Ophthalmology 1977; **Med School:** Univ Colorado 1972; **Resid:** Ophthalmology, Univ Kentucky Affil Hosps 1976; **Fellow:** Vitreoretinal Disease, Jules Stein Eye Inst 1977; Medical Genetics, Johns Hopkins Univ 1978; **Fac Appt:** Prof Oph, Univ Mich Med Sch

Heuer, Dale K MD [Oph] - **Spec Exp:** Glaucoma; **Hospital:** Froedtert & Med Coll WI; **Address:** The Eye Inst, 925 N 87th St, Milwaukee, WI 53226; **Phone:** 414-955-2020; **Board Cert:** Ophthalmology 2013; **Med School:** Northwestern Univ 1978; **Resid:** Ophthalmology, Med Coll Wisc Affil Hosp 1982; **Fellow:** Glaucoma, Bascom Palmer Eye Inst 1984; **Fac Appt:** Prof Oph, Med Coll Wisc

Holland, Edward J MD [Oph] - **Spec Exp:** Corneal Disease; Refractive Surgery; Cataract Surgery; **Hospital:** St. Elizabeth Hlthcare-Edgewood; **Address:** Cincinnati Eye Inst, 1945 CEI Drive, Cincinnati, OH 45242; **Phone:** 513-984-5133; **Board Cert:** Ophthalmology 1986; **Med School:** Loyola Univ-Stritch Sch Med 1981; **Resid:** Ophthalmology, Univ Minn Med Ctr 1985; **Fellow:** Cornea & Ext Eye Disease, Univ Iowa Affil Hosp 1986; Ocular Immunology, Natl Eye Inst 1987; **Fac Appt:** Clin Prof Oph, Univ Cincinnati

John, Thomas MD [Oph] - **Spec Exp:** Cornea Transplant & Artificial Cornea; Cataract Surgery; Refractive Surgery; Lens Implants; **Hospital:** Adv S Suburban Hosp; **Address:** 16532 S Oak Park Ave, Ste 201, Tinley Park, IL 60477; **Phone:** 708-429-2223; **Board Cert:** Ophthalmology 1987; **Med School:** India 1977; **Resid:** Ophthalmology, Hosp Univ Penn 1984; **Fellow:** Cornea & Ext Eye Disease, Univ Rochester Sch Med & Dentistry 1985; Cornea & Ext Eye Disease, Mass Eye & Ear Infirmary 1987; **Fac Appt:** Assoc Clin Prof Oph, Loyola Univ-Stritch Sch Med

Kaufman, Paul L MD [Oph] - **Spec Exp:** Glaucoma; **Hospital:** Univ WI Hosp & Clins; **Address:** Univ Wisc Hosp, Dept Ophthalmology, 2880 University Ave, Madison, WI 53705; **Phone:** 608-263-7171; **Board Cert:** Ophthalmology 1976; **Med School:** NYU Sch Med 1967; **Resid:** Ophthalmology, Barnes-Jewish Hosp 1973; **Fellow:** Ocular Pharmacology, Univ Uppsala Affil Hosp 1975; **Fac Appt:** Prof Oph, Univ Wisc

Krueger, Ronald R MD [Oph] - **Spec Exp:** Corneal Disease; Refractive Surgery; **Hospital:** Cleveland Clin (page 55); **Address:** Cleveland Clinic Fdn - Cole Eye Inst, 9500 Euclid Ave, Desk I30, Cleveland, OH 44195; **Phone:** 216-444-8158; **Board Cert:** Ophthalmology 2013; **Med School:** UMDNJ-NJ Med Sch, Newark 1987; **Resid:** Ophthalmology, Columbia Presby Med Ctr 1991; **Fellow:** Refractive Surgery, Univ Okla Hlth Sci Ctr-McGee Eye Inst 1992; Cornea, USC-Doheny Eye Inst 1993

Kushner, Burton J MD [Oph] - **Spec Exp:** Pediatric Ophthalmology; Strabismus-Adult & Pediatric; **Hospital:** Univ WI Hosp & Clins; **Address:** Pediatric Eye Clinic, 2880 University Ave, Madison, WI 53705; **Phone:** 608-263-6414; **Board Cert:** Ophthalmology 1975; **Med School:** Northwestern Univ 1969; **Resid:** Ophthalmology, Univ Wisc Hosp 1973; **Fellow:** Pediatric Ophthalmology, Bascom Palmer Eye Inst 1974; **Fac Appt:** Prof Oph, Univ Wisc

Kwon, Young H MD/PhD [Oph] - **Spec Exp:** Glaucoma; **Hospital:** Univ Iowa Hosp & Clins; **Address:** UIHC Dept of Ophthalmology, 200 Hawkins Drive, Iowa City, IA 52242; **Phone:** 319-356-2852; **Board Cert:** Ophthalmology 2008; **Med School:** Yale Univ 1991; **Resid:** Ophthalmology, Mass Eye & Ear Infirmary 1995; **Fellow:** Glaucoma, Yale Univ Affil Hosp 1996; **Fac Appt:** Prof Oph, Univ Iowa Coll Med

Lane, Stephen S MD [Oph] - **Spec Exp:** Cataract Surgery; Cornea & External Eye Disease; Anterior Segment Surgery; Refractive Surgery; **Hospital:** United Hosp; **Address:** Associated Eye Care, 2950 Curve Crest Blvd, Stillwater, MN 55082; **Phone:** 651-275-3000; **Board Cert:** Ophthalmology 1986; **Med School:** Univ Minn 1980; **Resid:** Ophthalmology, MS Hershey Med Ctr 1984; **Fellow:** Cornea & Ext Eye Disease, Univ Minn 1985; **Fac Appt:** Clin Prof Oph, Univ Minn

Lass, Jonathan H MD [Oph] - **Spec Exp:** Cataract Surgery-Lens Implant; Cornea & External Eye Disease; **Hospital:** UH Case Med Ctr; **Address:** UH Case Med Ctr, Dept Ophthalmology, 11100 Euclid Ave, Ste 4115, Cleveland, OH 44106; **Phone:** 216-844-8590; **Board Cert:** Ophthalmology 1978; **Med School:** Boston Univ 1973; **Resid:** Ophthalmology, Boston Univ Med Ctr 1977; **Fellow:** Ophthalmology, Mass Eye & Ear Infirm 1979; **Fac Appt:** Prof Oph, Case West Res Univ

Lee, Paul P MD [Oph] - **Spec Exp:** Glaucoma; **Hospital:** Univ Michigan Med Ctr; **Address:** Kellogg Eye Ctr, 1000 Wall St, Ann Arbor, MI 48105; **Phone:** 734-763-5874; **Board Cert:** Ophthalmology 2011; **Med School:** Univ Mich Med Sch 1986; **Resid:** Ophthalmology, Wilmer Eye Inst/Johns Hopkins 1990; **Fellow:** Glaucoma, Mass Eye & Ear Infirm 1991; **Fac Appt:** Prof Oph, Univ Mich Med Sch

Lichter, Paul R MD [Oph] - **Spec Exp:** Cataract Surgery; Glaucoma; **Hospital:** Univ Michigan Med Ctr; **Address:** Kellogg Eye Ctr, 1000 Wall St, Ann Arbor, MI 48105; **Phone:** 734-763-5874; **Board Cert:** Ophthalmology 1970; **Med School:** Univ Mich Med Sch 1964; **Resid:** Ophthalmology, Univ Mich Hosp 1968; **Fellow:** Ophthalmology, UCSF Med Ctr 1969; **Fac Appt:** Prof Oph, Univ Mich Med Sch

Lim, Jennifer MD [Oph] - **Spec Exp:** Retina/Vitreous Surgery; Macular Degeneration; Diabetic Eye Disease/Retinopathy; Retinal Detachment; **Hospital:** Univ of IL at Chicago Eye & Ear Infirm; **Address:** IL Eye & Ear Infirmary-Retina Service, 1901 W Taylor St, Chicago, IL 60612; **Phone:** 312-996-6660; **Board Cert:** Ophthalmology 1991; **Med School:** Northwestern Univ-Feinberg Sch Med 1986; **Resid:** Ophthalmology, IL Eye & Ear Infirmary 1990; **Fellow:** Retina/Vitreous Surgery, Johns Hopkins/Wilmer Eye Inst 1992; **Fac Appt:** Prof Oph, Univ IL Coll Med

Lindstrom, Richard L MD [Oph] - **Spec Exp:** Corneal Disease; Cataract Surgery; Refractive Surgery; **Hospital:** Abbott - Northwestern Hosp, Phillips Eye Inst; **Address:** 9801 DuPont Ave S, Ste 200, Bloomington, MN 55431; **Phone:** 612-813-3600; **Board Cert:** Ophthalmology 1978; **Med School:** Univ Minn 1972; **Resid:** Ophthalmology, Univ Minn Med Ctr 1978; Ophthalmology, Univ Minn Med Ctr 1980; **Fellow:** Anterior Segment - External Disease, Mary Shields Eye Hosp; Glaucoma, Univ Hosps; **Fac Appt:** Prof Oph, Univ Minn

Lucarelli, Mark J MD [Oph] - **Spec Exp:** Ophthalmic Plastic Surgery; Reconstructive Plastic Surgery; Oculoplastic & Orbital Surgery; Thyroid Eye Disease; **Hospital:** Univ WI Hosp & Clins; **Address:** Univ Wisc Hosp & Clins - Ophthalmology, 2880 University Ave, Madison, WI 53705; **Phone:** 608-263-7171; **Board Cert:** Ophthalmology 2008; **Med School:** Washington Univ, St Louis 1991; **Resid:** Ophthalmology, Mass Eye & Ear Infirm 1995; **Fellow:** Ophthalmic Plastic & Reconstructive Surgery, Univ Wisconsin Hosp & Clins 1997; **Fac Appt:** Prof Oph, Univ Wisc

Lueder, Gregg T MD [Oph] - **Spec Exp:** Strabismus; Lacrimal Gland Disorders; Cataract-Pediatric; Glaucoma-Pediatric; **Hospital:** St. Louis Chldns Hosp; **Address:** St Louis Children's Hospital, One Children's Pl, Ste 2 South 89, St Louis, MO 63110; **Phone:** 314-454-6026; **Board Cert:** Ophthalmology 2013; **Med School:** Univ Iowa Coll Med 1985; **Resid:** Pediatrics, St Louis Children's Hosp 1988; Ophthalmology, Univ Iowa Med Ctr 1991; **Fellow:** Pediatric Ophthalmology, Hosp for Sick Children 1993; **Fac Appt:** Prof Oph, Washington Univ, St Louis

Maguire, Leo J MD [Oph] - **Spec Exp:** Cornea Transplant; Refractive Surgery; **Hospital:** Mayo Med Ctr & Clin - Rochester; **Address:** Mayo Clinic-Ophthalmology, 200 First St SW, Rochester, MN 55905; **Phone:** 507-284-4152; **Board Cert:** Ophthalmology 1986; **Med School:** Jefferson Med Coll 1980; **Resid:** Ophthalmology, Univ Michigan Hosp 1984; **Fellow:** Cornea & Ext Eye Disease, LSU Eye Ctr 1986; **Fac Appt:** Assoc Prof Oph, Mayo Med Sch

McDonnell, James F MD [Oph] - **Spec Exp:** Pediatric Ophthalmology; Strabismus-Adult & Pediatric; Retinopathy of Prematurity; **Hospital:** Loyola Univ Med Ctr, Loyola Univ - Ronald McDonald Children's Hosp; **Address:** Loyola Univ Med Ctr, Dept Ophthalmology, 2160 S First Ave, Maywood, IL 60153; **Phone:** 708-216-6756; **Board Cert:** Ophthalmology 1991; **Med School:** Northwestern Univ 1985; **Resid:** Ophthalmology, The Eye Inst - Med Coll Wisc 1990; **Fellow:** Pediatric Ophthalmology, Univ Wisconsin Affil Hosp 1991; **Fac Appt:** Prof Oph, Loyola Univ-Stritch Sch Med

Mets, Marilyn B MD [Oph] - **Spec Exp:** Pediatric Ophthalmology; Ophthalmic Genetics; Strabismus; Retinal Disorders; **Hospital:** Lurie Chldn's Hosp-Chicago; **Address:** Lurie Children's Hosp, 225 E Chicago Ave, Box 70, Chicago, IL 60611; **Phone:** 312-227-6718; **Board Cert:** Ophthalmology 2005; **Med School:** Geo Wash Univ 1976; **Resid:** Ophthalmology, Cleveland Clinic 1980; **Fellow:** Pediatric Ophthalmology, Natl Chldns Hosp 1981; **Fac Appt:** Prof Oph, Northwestern Univ

Mieler, William F MD [Oph] - **Spec Exp:** Retina/Vitreous Surgery; Eye Tumors/Cancer; Macular Disease/Degeneration; Trauma; **Hospital:** Univ of IL at Chicago Eye & Ear Infirm, Weiss Meml Hosp; **Address:** Univ of IL Med Ctr, Dept Ophthalmology, 1905 W Taylor St, Chicago, IL 60612; **Phone:** 312-996-6660; **Board Cert:** Ophthalmology 2009; **Med School:** Univ Wisc 1979; **Resid:** Ophthalmology, Bascom-Palmer Eye Inst 1983; **Fellow:** Retina/Vitreous Surgery, Med Ctr Wisconsin Eye Inst 1984; Ocular Oncology, Wills Eye Hosp 1986; **Fac Appt:** Prof Oph, Univ IL Coll Med

Mizen, Thomas R MD [Oph] - **Spec Exp:** Neuro-Ophthalmology; Optic Nerve Disorders; **Hospital:** Rush Univ Med Ctr, MacNeal Hosp; **Address:** 6187 S Archer Ave, Ste 101, Chicago, IL 60638; **Phone:** 312-942-3500; **Board Cert:** Ophthalmology 1986; **Med School:** Finch/Chicago Med Sch 1980; **Resid:** Ophthalmology, Rush-Presby-St Lukes Med Ctr 1984; **Fellow:** Neuro-Ophthalmology, Barnes Hosp/Wash Univ 1985; **Fac Appt:** Asst Prof Oph, Rush Med Coll

Nerad, Jeffrey MD [Oph] - **Spec Exp:** Orbital Tumors/Cancer; Eyelid Cancer & Reconstruction; Oculoplastic Surgery; **Address:** Cincinnati Eye Inst, 1945 CEI Drive, Cincinnati, OH 45242; **Phone:** 513-984-5133; **Board Cert:** Ophthalmology 1984; **Med School:** St Louis Univ 1979; **Resid:** Ophthalmology, St Louis Univ Med Ctr 1983; **Fellow:** Oculoplastic & Reconstructive Surgery, Univ Iowa 1984; **Fac Appt:** Prof Oph, Univ Iowa Coll Med

Olitsky, Scott E MD [Oph] - **Spec Exp:** Pediatric Ophthalmology; Strabismus; **Hospital:** Chldns Mercy Hosps & Clinics; **Address:** Chldns Mercy Hosp, Dept Oph, 3101 Broadway, Kansas City, MO 64111; **Phone:** 816-234-3046; **Board Cert:** Ophthalmology 2004; **Med School:** Jefferson Med Coll 1988; **Resid:** Ophthalmology, SUNY Buffalo Med Ctr 1992; **Fellow:** Pediatric Ophthalmology, Wills Eye Inst 1993; **Fac Appt:** Prof Oph, Univ MO-Kansas City

Osher, Robert H MD [Oph] - **Spec Exp:** Cataract Surgery-Lens Implant; **Address:** 1945 CEI Drive, Cincinnati, OH 45242; **Phone:** 513-984-5133; **Board Cert:** Ophthalmology 1981; **Med School:** Univ Rochester 1976; **Resid:** Ophthalmology, Bascom Palmer Eye Inst 1980; **Fellow:** Ophthalmology, Bascom Palmer Eye Inst 1981; **Fac Appt:** Prof Oph, Univ Cincinnati

Page, Timothy MD [Oph] - **Spec Exp:** Cataract Surgery; Cataract Surgery-Lens Implant; Refractive Surgery; Anterior Segment Surgery; **Hospital:** Beaumont Hosp-Royal Oak; **Address:** Oakland Ophthalmic Surgery, 800 S Adams Rd, Ste 201, Birmingham, MI 48009; **Phone:** 248-644-8060; **Board Cert:** Ophthalmology 2011; **Med School:** Wayne State Univ 1994; **Resid:** Ophthalmology, William Beaumont Hosp 1998; **Fac Appt:** Prof Oph, Oakland Univ-William Beaumont Med Sch

Pepose, Jay MD/PhD [Oph] - **Spec Exp:** LASIK-Refractive Surgery; Cataract Surgery; Corneal & External Eye Disease; **Hospital:** Barnes-Jewish Hosp, Mercy Hosp - St Louis; **Address:** 1815 Clarkson Rd, Chesterfield, MO 63017; **Phone:** 636-728-0111; **Board Cert:** Ophthalmology 1989; **Med School:** UCLA 1982; **Resid:** Ophthalmology, Johns Hopkins Hosp 1987; **Fellow:** Cornea & Ext Eye Disease, Georgetown Univ Med Ctr 1988; **Fac Appt:** Prof Oph, Washington Univ, St Louis

Petersen, Michael R MD/PhD [Oph] - **Spec Exp:** Diabetic Eye Disease/Retinopathy; Macular Degeneration; Retinal Detachment; Uveitis; **Hospital:** Bethesda North Hosp; **Address:** Cincinnati Eye Institute, 1945 CEI Drive, Cincinnati, OH 45242-5664; **Phone:** 513-984-5133; **Board Cert:** Ophthalmology 1991; **Med School:** Univ Mich Med Sch 1986; **Resid:** Ophthalmology, Kellogg Eye Ctr 1990; **Fellow:** Vitreoretinal Surgery, Univ Wash Med Ctr 1992

Plager, David A MD [Oph] - **Spec Exp:** Pediatric Ophthalmology; Strabismus; Cataract-Pediatric; Glaucoma-Pediatric; **Hospital:** Riley Hosp for Children; **Address:** Ped Ophthalmology & Strabismus Clinic, 705 Riley Hosp Drive, rm 3340, Indianapolis, IN 46202; **Phone:** 317-944-8103; **Board Cert:** Ophthalmology 2006; **Med School:** Indiana Univ 1983; **Resid:** Ophthalmology, Indiana Univ Hosps 1987; **Fellow:** Pediatric Ophthalmology, Chldns Hosp Natl Med Ctr 1988; Strabismus, Chldns Hosp Natl Med Ctr 1988; **Fac Appt:** Prof Oph, Indiana Univ

Pulido, Jose S MD [Oph] - **Spec Exp:** Retina/Vitreous Surgery; Eye Tumors/Cancer; **Hospital:** Mayo Med Ctr & Clin - Rochester; **Address:** 200 1st St SW, Rochester, MN 55905; **Phone:** 507-284-3721; **Board Cert:** Ophthalmology 1986; **Med School:** Tulane Univ 1981; **Resid:** Ophthalmology, Illinois Eye & Ear Infirm 1986; **Fellow:** Vitreoretinal Surgery & Disease, Bascom-Palmer Eye Inst 1987; Ocular Oncology, Wills Eye Hosp; **Fac Appt:** Prof Oph, Mayo Med Sch

Putterman, Allen M MD [Oph] - **Spec Exp:** Oculoplastic & Orbital Surgery; Cosmetic Surgery-Face & Eyes; Thyroid Eye Disease; Eyelid Cosmetic & Reconstructive Surgery; **Hospital:** Presence St Joseph Hosp; **Address:** 111 N Wabash Ave, Ste 1722, Chicago, IL 60602-2002; **Phone:** 312-372-2256; **Board Cert:** Ophthalmology 1971; **Med School:** Univ Wisc 1963; **Resid:** Ophthalmology, Michael Reese Hosp 1969; **Fellow:** Oculoplastic Surgery, Manhattan Eye/Ear Infirm 1970; **Fac Appt:** Prof Oph, Univ IL Coll Med

Rogers, Gary L MD [Oph] - **Spec Exp:** Strabismus-Adult & Pediatric; **Hospital:** Nationwide Chldn's Hosp; **Address:** 555 S 18th St, Ste 4C, Columbus, OH 43205; **Phone:** 614-224-6222; **Board Cert:** Ophthalmology 1974; **Med School:** Ohio State Univ 1968; **Resid:** Ophthalmology, Mt Sinai Hosp 1972; **Fellow:** Pediatric Ophthalmology, Chldns Hosp Natl Med Ctr 1974; **Fac Appt:** Clin Prof Oph, Ohio State Univ

Rosenberg, Michael A MD [Oph] - **Spec Exp:** Refractive Surgery; Cataract Surgery; Eye Muscle Surgery; **Hospital:** Northwestern Meml Hosp; **Address:** 675 N St Clair St, Galter Bldg - Ste 15-150, Chicago, IL 60611-5967; **Phone:** 312-695-8150; **Board Cert:** Ophthalmology 1975; **Med School:** Northwestern Univ 1967; **Resid:** Ophthalmology, Bascom Palmer Eye Inst 1973; **Fellow:** Neuro-Ophthalmology, UCSF Med Ctr 1974; Refractive Surgery, Univ Monterrey 1998; **Fac Appt:** Assoc Clin Prof Oph, Northwestern Univ

Samuelson, Thomas W MD [Oph] - **Spec Exp:** Glaucoma; Cataract Surgery; Anterior Segment Surgery; Refractive Surgery; **Hospital:** Phillips Eye Inst; **Address:** Minnesota Eye Consultants, 710 E 24th St, Ste 100, Minneapolis, MN 55404-3810; **Phone:** 612-813-3600; **Board Cert:** Ophthalmology 1991; **Med School:** Univ Minn 1985; **Resid:** Ophthalmology, Univ S Florida 1990; **Fellow:** Glaucoma, Wills Eye Hosp 1991; **Fac Appt:** Assoc Clin Prof Oph, Univ Minn

Schachat, Andrew P MD [Oph] - **Spec Exp:** Retina/Vitreous Surgery; Diabetic Eye Disease/Retinopathy; Melanoma-Choroidal (eye); **Hospital:** Cleveland Clin (page 55); **Address:** The Cleveland Clinic Fdn, Cole Eye Inst, 9500 Euclid Ave, Desk I30, Cleveland, OH 44195; **Phone:** 216-444-7963; **Board Cert:** Ophthalmology 1983; **Med School:** Johns Hopkins Univ 1979; **Resid:** Ophthalmology, Wilmer Inst-John Hopkins Hosp 1982; **Fellow:** Vitreoretinal Surgery & Disease, Wilmer Eye Inst-Johns Hopkins Hosp 1983

Stone, Edwin M MD [Oph] - **Spec Exp:** Retinal Disorders; Eye Diseases-Hereditary; **Hospital:** Univ Iowa Hosp & Clins; **Address:** UIHC Dept Ophthalmology, 200 Hawkins Drive, Iowa City, IA 52242; **Phone:** 319-356-2852; **Board Cert:** Ophthalmology 1990; **Med School:** Baylor Coll Med 1985; **Resid:** Ophthalmology, Univ Iowa Hosps 1989; **Fellow:** Retina, Univ Iowa Hosps 1992; **Fac Appt:** Prof Oph, Univ Iowa Coll Med

Summers, C Gail MD [Oph] - **Spec Exp:** Eye Diseases-Hereditary; Albinism; **Address:** Park Plaza Bldg, 701 25th Ave S Fl 3, Minneapolis, MN 55455; **Phone:** 612-365-8350; **Board Cert:** Ophthalmology 1984; **Med School:** Univ Minn 1979; **Resid:** Ophthalmology, Univ Minnesota Med Ctr 1983; **Fellow:** Pediatric Ophthalmology, Unin Minnesota Med Ctr 1984; **Fac Appt:** Prof Oph, Univ Minn

Traboulsi, Elias Iskandar MD [Oph] - **Spec Exp:** Pediatric Ophthalmology; Glaucoma-Pediatric; **Hospital:** Cleveland Clin (page 55); **Address:** Cleveland Clinic Fdn, Cole Eye Inst, 9500 Euclid Ave, Desk I30, Cleveland, OH 44195; **Phone:** 216-444-4363; **Board Cert:** Clinical Genetics 1987; Ophthalmology 1991; **Med School:** Amer Univ Beirut 1982; **Resid:** Ophthalmology, American Univ Beirut Hosp 1985; Ophthalmology, Georgetown Univ Hosp 1989; **Fellow:** Ophthalmology, Johns Hopkins Hosp 1986; Pediatric Ophthalmology, Chldns Hosp 1990; **Fac Appt:** Prof Oph, Ohio State Univ

Trese, Michael T MD [Oph] - **Spec Exp:** Retina/Vitreous Surgery; Retinal Disorders-Pediatric; **Hospital:** Beaumont Hosp-Royal Oak, Chldns Hosp of Michigan; **Address:** Associated Retinal Consultants, 3535 W 13 Mile Rd, Ste 344, Royal Oak, MI 48073-6710; **Phone:** 248-288-2280; **Board Cert:** Ophthalmology 1981; **Med School:** Georgetown Univ 1976; **Resid:** Ophthalmology, Jules Stein Eye Inst-UCLA 1980; **Fellow:** Retina, Duke Univ Hosp 1981; **Fac Appt:** Assoc Clin Prof Oph, Wayne State Univ

Trobe, Jonathan D MD [Oph] - **Spec Exp:** Neuro-Ophthalmology; Optic Nerve Disorders; **Hospital:** Univ Michigan Med Ctr; **Address:** Kellogg Eye Ctr, 1000 Wall St, rm 8349, Ann Arbor, MI 48105; **Phone:** 734-763-9147; **Board Cert:** Ophthalmology 1974; Neurology 1988; **Med School:** Harvard Med Sch 1968; **Resid:** Ophthalmology, Wills Eye Hosp 1972; Neurology, Jackson Meml Hosp/U Miami 1986; **Fellow:** Neuro-Ophthalmology, Bascom Palmer Eye Inst 1977; **Fac Appt:** Prof Oph, Univ Mich Med Sch

Tychsen, Lawrence MD [Oph] - **Spec Exp:** Pediatric Ophthalmology; Strabismus; Amblyopia; **Hospital:** St. Louis Chldns Hosp, Barnes-Jewish Hosp; **Address:** Chldns Eye Ctr, 1 Children's Pl Fl 2 S-89, St Louis, MO 63110; **Phone:** 314-454-6026; **Board Cert:** Ophthalmology 1984; **Med School:** Georgetown Univ 1979; **Resid:** Ophthalmology, Univ Iowa Hosp 1983; **Fellow:** Pediatric Ophthalmology, UCSF Med Ctr 1985; **Fac Appt:** Assoc Prof Oph, Washington Univ, St Louis

Vajaranant, Thasarat S MD [Oph] - **Spec Exp:** Glaucoma; Women's Eye Health; **Hospital:** Univ of IL at Chicago Eye & Ear Infirm; **Address:** Univ Illinois Chicago Eye Ctr, Glaucoma Service, 1855 W Taylor St, rm 3171, Chicago, IL 60612; **Phone:** 312-996-7030; **Board Cert:** Ophthalmology 2008; **Med School:** Thailand 1996; **Resid:** Ophthalmology, Univ of Illinois 2006; **Fellow:** Glaucoma, Univ of Illinois 2007; Research, Univ of Illinois 2008; **Fac Appt:** Asst Prof Oph, Univ IL Coll Med

Varma, Rohit MD [Oph] - **Spec Exp:** Glaucoma; **Hospital:** Univ of IL at Chicago Eye & Ear Infirm; **Address:** Millenium Park Eye Ctr, 30 N Michigan Ave, Ste 410, Chicago, IL 60602; **Phone:** 312-996-2020; **Board Cert:** Ophthalmology 2007; **Med School:** India 1986; **Resid:** Ophthalmology, Johns Hopkins Hosp 1993; **Fellow:** Glaucoma, USC/Doheny Eye Inst 1994; **Fac Appt:** Prof Oph, Univ IL Coll Med

Volpe, Nicholas J MD [Oph] - **Spec Exp:** Neuro-Ophthalmology; Strabismus; **Hospital:** Northwestern Meml Hosp; **Address:** 675 N St Clair, Galter Pavilion, Ste 15-150, Chicago, IL 60611; **Phone:** 312-695-8150; **Board Cert:** Ophthalmology 2003; **Med School:** SUNY Downstate 1987; **Resid:** Ophthalmology, Mass E&E Infirmary 1993; **Fellow:** Neuro-Ophthalmology, Mass E&E Infirmary 1992; **Fac Appt:** Prof Oph, Northwestern Univ-Feinberg Sch Med

Williams, George A MD [Oph] - **Spec Exp:** Retinal Disorders; Macular Degeneration; **Hospital:** Beaumont Hosp-Royal Oak; **Address:** Associated Retinal Consultants, 3535 W 13 Mile Rd, Ste 344, Royal Oak, MI 48073-6710; **Phone:** 248-288-2280; **Board Cert:** Ophthalmology 2005; **Med School:** Northwestern Univ 1978; **Resid:** Ophthalmology, Med Coll Wisconsin 1982; **Fellow:** Retina/Vitreous Surgery, Med Coll Wisconsin 1984; **Fac Appt:** Clin Prof Oph, Univ Mich Med Sch

Wilson, Steven E MD [Oph] - **Spec Exp:** LASIK-Refractive Surgery; PRK-Refractive Surgery; Corneal Disease; **Hospital:** Cleveland Clin (page 55); **Address:** Cleveland Clinic Fdn - Cole Eye Inst, 9500 Euclid Ave, Ste I32, Cleveland, OH 44195; **Phone:** 216-444-5887; **Board Cert:** Ophthalmology 1990; **Med School:** UCSD 1984; **Resid:** Ophthalmology, Mayo Clinic 1988; **Fellow:** Cornea & Ext Eye Disease, Med Ctr Louisiana-LSU 1990; **Fac Appt:** Prof Oph, Cleveland Cl Coll Med/Case West Res

Great Plains and Mountains

Anderson, Richard L MD [Oph] - **Spec Exp:** Orbital & Eyelid Tumors/Cancer; Eyelid Problems/Ptosis/Blepharospasm; Cosmetic Surgery-Face & Eyes; **Hospital:** Salt Lake Regional Med Ctr, Intermountain Shriners Hosp; **Address:** 1002 E South Temple, Ste 308, Salt Lake City, UT 84102-1525; **Phone:** 801-363-3355; **Board Cert:** Ophthalmology 1976; **Med School:** Univ Iowa Coll Med 1971; **Resid:** Ophthalmology, Univ Iowa Affil Hosps 1975; **Fellow:** Oculoplastic & Reconstructive Surgery, Albany Med Ctr 1975; Oculoplastic & Reconstructive Surgery, UCSF Med Ctr 1976; **Fac Appt:** Prof PlS, Univ Utah

Cionni, Robert J MD [Oph] - **Spec Exp:** Cataract Surgery-Lens Implant; Refractive Surgery; **Hospital:** LDS Hosp, Univ Utah Hlth Care; **Address:** The Eye Institue of Utah, 755 E 3900 South, Salt Lake City, UT 84107; **Phone:** 801-266-2283; **Board Cert:** Ophthalmology 1991; **Med School:** Univ Cincinnati 1985; **Resid:** Ophthalmology, Univ Louisville Hosp 1987; **Fellow:** Cataract/Lens Implant Surgery, Cincinnati Eye Inst

Crandall, Alan S MD [Oph] - **Spec Exp:** Glaucoma; Cataract Surgery; **Hospital:** Univ Utah Hlth Care; **Address:** John A Moran Eye Center, 65 N Mario Capecchi Drive, Salt Lake City, UT 84132; **Phone:** 801-581-2352; **Board Cert:** Ophthalmology 1977; **Med School:** Univ Utah 1973; **Resid:** Ophthalmology, Hosp Univ Penn 1976; **Fellow:** Glaucoma, Scheie Eye Inst 1981; **Fac Appt:** Clin Prof Oph, Univ Utah

Durrie, Daniel S MD [Oph] - **Spec Exp:** LASIK-Refractive Surgery; Corneal Disease; **Hospital:** Univ of Kansas Hosp; **Address:** 5520 College Blvd, Ste 201, Overland Park, KS 66211; **Phone:** 913-491-3330; **Board Cert:** Ophthalmology 1979; **Med School:** Univ Nebr Coll Med 1975; **Resid:** Ophthalmology, Univ Nebr Med Coll Affil Hosp 1979; **Fellow:** Cornea, Filkins Eye Inst 1980; **Fac Appt:** Clin Prof Oph, Univ Kansas

Gigantelli, James W MD [Oph] - **Spec Exp:** Orbital Tumors/Cancer; Eyelid Cancer & Reconstruction; Lymphoma-Ocular (eye); **Hospital:** Nebraska Med Ctr; **Address:** 985540 Nebraska Medical Center, Omaha, NE 68198-5540; **Phone:** 402-559-4276; **Board Cert:** Ophthalmology 1991; **Med School:** Vanderbilt Univ 1985; **Resid:** Ophthalmology, Baylor Coll Med 1989; **Fellow:** Ophthalmic Plastic & Reconstructive Surgery, Duke Unv Med Ctr 1990; **Fac Appt:** Prof Oph, Univ Nebr Coll Med

McCann, John D MD/PhD [Oph] - **Spec Exp:** Oculoplastic Surgery; Cosmetic & Reconstructive Surgery; Orbital Diseases; Thyroid Eye Disease; **Hospital:** Intermountain Med Ctr; **Address:** Center For Facial Appearances, 9350 S 150 E, Ste 400, Sandy, UT 84070; **Phone:** 801-363-3355; **Board Cert:** Ophthalmology 2007; **Med School:** Univ Iowa Coll Med 1991; **Resid:** Ophthalmology, Univ CA Affil Hosp 1995; **Fellow:** Oculoplastic Surgery, Univ Utah Med Ctr 1996

Southwest

Ellis Jr, George S MD [Oph] - **Spec Exp:** Pediatric Ophthalmology; Eye Muscle Disorders; **Hospital:** Children's Hospital - New Orleans, E Jefferson Genl Hosp; **Address:** Chldns Hosp - New Orleans, 200 Henry Clay Ave, Ste 3106, New Orleans, LA 70118; **Phone:** 504-896-9426; **Board Cert:** Ophthalmology 1982; **Med School:** Tulane Univ 1977; **Resid:** Ophthalmology, LSU Interim Public Hosp-Eye Ctr 1979; Ophthalmology, Duke Univ Hosp 1982; **Fellow:** Pediatric Ophthalmology, Hall Eye Clin 1982; Pediatric Ophthalmology, Chldns Hosp 1983; **Fac Appt:** Assoc Clin Prof Oph, Tulane Univ

Esmaeli-Azad, Bita MD [Oph] - **Spec Exp:** Orbital & Eyelid Tumors/Cancer; Eyelid Cancer & Reconstruction; Oculoplastic Surgery; **Hospital:** UT MD Anderson Canc Ctr; **Address:** MD Anderson Cancer Ctr, Ophthalmology /Plastic Surgery, 1515 Holcombe Blvd, Unit 1445, Houston, TX 77030; **Phone:** 713-792-6523; **Board Cert:** Ophthalmology 2006; **Med School:** Univ Hlth Scis, Chicago Med Sch 1990; **Resid:** Ophthalmology, Univ Mich-Kellogg Eye Ctr 1994; **Fellow:** Ophthalmic Plastic & Reconstructive Surgery, Univ Toronto 1996; **Fac Appt:** Prof Oph, Univ Tex, Houston

Eustis Jr, H. 504Sprague MD [Oph] - **Spec Exp:** Pediatric Ophthalmology; Strabismus; **Hospital:** Ochsner Med Ctr-New Orleans, Children's Hospital - New Orleans; **Address:** Ochsner Clin, Dept Ophthalmology, 1514 Jefferson Hwy Fl 10, New Orleans, LA 70121; **Phone:** 504-842-3995; **Board Cert:** Ophthalmology 1985; **Med School:** Louisiana State U, New Orleans 1980; **Resid:** Ophthalmology, LSU Eye Ctr 1984; **Fellow:** Pediatric Ophthalmology, Hosp Sick Chldn 1985; Pediatric Ophthalmology, Natl Chldns Med Ctr 1985; **Fac Appt:** Clin Prof Oph, Louisiana State U, New Orleans

Koch, Douglas D MD [Oph] - **Spec Exp:** Cataract Surgery; Refractive Surgery; **Hospital:** Methodist Hosp - Houston, St. Luke's Episcopal Hosp-Houston; **Address:** BCM, Alkek Eye Ctr, 1977 Butler Blvd Fl 2, Houston, TX 77030; **Phone:** 713-798-6100; **Board Cert:** Ophthalmology 1982; **Med School:** Harvard Med Sch 1977; **Resid:** Ophthalmology, Baylor Affil Hosp 1981; **Fellow:** Cornea, Moorfields Eye Hosp 1982; Refractive Surgery, Baylor Affil Hosp 1982; **Fac Appt:** Prof Oph, Baylor Coll Med

Lee, Andrew G MD [Oph] - **Spec Exp:** Neuro-Ophthalmology; Optic Nerve Disorders; Optic Nerve Tumors; **Hospital:** Methodist Hosp - Houston; **Address:** Methodist Eye Assocs, 6560 Fannin St Scurlock Bldg - Ste 450, Houston, TX 77030; **Phone:** 713-441-8843; **Board Cert:** Ophthalmology 2006; **Med School:** Univ VA Sch Med 1989; **Resid:** Ophthalmology, Cullen Eye Inst-Baylor 1993; **Fellow:** Neuro-Ophthalmology, Wilmer Eye Inst-Johns Hopkins 1994; **Fac Appt:** Clin Prof Oph, Univ Tex Med Br, Galveston

Lewis, Richard Alan MD [Oph] - **Spec Exp:** Eye Diseases-Hereditary; Ophthalmic Genetics; Retinal Disorders; Macular Degeneration; **Hospital:** Methodist Hosp - Houston, Texas Chldns Hosp; **Address:** BCM, Alkek Eye Ctr, 1977 Butler Blvd Fl 2, Houston, TX 77030; **Phone:** 713-798-6100; **Board Cert:** Ophthalmology 1976; **Med School:** Univ Mich Med Sch 1969; **Resid:** Ophthalmology, Univ Michigan Hosp 1974; **Fellow:** Retina, Montefiore Hosp 1974; Macular Disease, Bascom Palmer Eye Inst 1975; **Fac Appt:** Prof Oph, Baylor Coll Med

McCulley, James P MD [Oph] - **Spec Exp:** Corneal & External Eye Disease; Laser Vision Surgery; Cataract Surgery; **Hospital:** UT Southwestern Med Ctr at Dallas; **Address:** UTSW Med Ctr, Laser Ctr Vision Care, 5323 Harry Hines Blvd, Dallas, TX 75390; **Phone:** 214-645-2020; **Board Cert:** Ophthalmology 1974; **Med School:** Washington Univ, St Louis 1968; **Resid:** Ophthalmology, Mass Eye & Ear Infirm 1973; **Fellow:** Cornea, Cornea Rsch-Retina Fdn 1974; Cornea, Mass Eye & Ear Infirm 1974; **Fac Appt:** Prof Oph, Univ Tex SW, Dallas

Miller, Joseph M MD [Oph] - **Spec Exp:** Pediatric Ophthalmology; Strabismus; Amblyopia; **Hospital:** Univ Arizona Med Ctr-Univ Campus, Yuma Regl Med Ctr; **Address:** Univ Ariz, Dept Ophthalmology, 707 N Alvernon Way, Ste 301, Tucson, AZ 85711; **Phone:** 520-694-1460; **Board Cert:** Ophthalmology 1991; **Med School:** NE Ohio Univ 1985; **Resid:** Ophthalmology, Yale New Haven Hosp 1990; **Fellow:** Pediatric Ophthalmology, Johns Hopkins Hosp 1991; Refractive Surgery, Univ Arizona Hosp 2001; **Fac Appt:** Prof Oph, Univ Ariz Coll Med

Mims III, James Luther MD [Oph] - **Spec Exp:** Pediatric Ophthalmology; Strabismus-Adult & Pediatric; **Hospital:** Baptist Med Ctr - San Antonio, Methodist Chldns Hosp of South Texas; **Address:** 311 Camden St, Ste 511, San Antonio, TX 78215; **Phone:** 210-225-0084; **Board Cert:** Ophthalmology 1977; **Med School:** Tulane Univ 1968; **Resid:** Ophthalmology, Wills Eye Hosp 1976; **Fellow:** Pediatric Ophthalmology, Wills Eye Hosp 1977; **Fac Appt:** Clin Prof Oph, Univ Tex, San Antonio

Pflugfelder, Stephen C MD [Oph] - **Spec Exp:** Corneal Disease; LASIK-Refractive Surgery; Cataract Surgery; Dry Eye Syndrome; **Hospital:** Methodist Hosp - Houston, St. Luke's Episcopal Hosp-Houston; **Address:** BCM, Alkek Eye Ctr, 1977 Butler Blvd Fl 2, Houston, TX 77030; **Phone:** 713-798-6100; **Board Cert:** Ophthalmology 1987; **Med School:** SUNY Upstate Med Univ 1981; **Resid:** Ophthalmology, Baylor Affil Hosp 1985; **Fellow:** Cornea & Ext Eye Disease, Bascom Palmer Eye Inst 1986; **Fac Appt:** Prof Oph, Baylor Coll Med

Richard, James M MD [Oph] - **Spec Exp:** Pediatric Ophthalmology; Eye Muscle Surgery; **Hospital:** Chldns Hosp OU Med Ctr, INTEGRIS Baptist Med Ctr - OK; **Address:** 11013 Hefner Pointe Drive, Oklahoma City, OK 73120-5050; **Phone:** 405-751-2020; **Board Cert:** Ophthalmology 1979; **Med School:** Univ Okla Coll Med 1974; **Resid:** Ophthalmology, Baylor Coll Med Affil Hosp 1978; **Fellow:** Pediatric Ophthalmology, Chldns Hosp 1979; Ophthalmology, Johns Hopkins Hosp 1980; **Fac Appt:** Clin Prof Oph, Univ Okla Coll Med

Schiffman, Jade S MD [Oph] - **Spec Exp:** Neuro-Ophthalmology; **Hospital:** UT MD Anderson Canc Ctr; **Address:** MD Anderson Canc Ctr, 1515 Holcombe Blvd, Unit 1445, Houston, TX 77035; **Phone:** 713-792-3798; **Board Cert:** Neurology 1983; Ophthalmology 1991; **Med School:** SUNY Upstate Med Univ 1975; **Resid:** Neurology, Univ Miami Affil Hosp 1980; Ophthalmology, UCSF Med Ctr 1989; **Fellow:** Neuro-Ophthalmology, UCSF Med Ctr 1981; **Fac Appt:** Prof Oph, Univ Tex, Houston

Siatkowski, R Michael MD [Oph] - **Spec Exp:** Pediatric Ophthalmology; Neuro-Ophthalmology; Retinopathy of Prematurity; Strabismus; **Hospital:** OU Med Ctr; **Address:** Dean McGee Eye Institute, 608 Stanton L. Young Blvd, rm 512, Oklahoma City, OK 73104; **Phone:** 405-271-1094; **Board Cert:** Ophthalmology 2009; **Med School:** Jefferson Med Coll 1987; **Resid:** Ophthalmology, St Francis Med Ctr 1991; **Fellow:** Neuro-Ophthalmology, Bascom Palmer Eye Inst 1992; Pediatric Ophthalmology, Bascom Palmer Eye Inst 1993; **Fac Appt:** Prof Oph, Univ Okla Coll Med

Soparkar, Charles MD [Oph] - **Spec Exp:** Eye Tumors/Cancer; Orbital & Eyelid Tumors/Cancer; Oculoplastic Surgery; **Hospital:** Methodist Hosp - Houston, Texas Chldns Hosp; **Address:** Plastic Eye Surg Assocs, 3730 Kirby Drive, Ste 900, Houston, TX 77098; **Phone:** 713-795-0705; **Board Cert:** Ophthalmology 2007; **Med School:** Univ Mass Sch Med 1990; **Resid:** Ophthalmology, Baylor Affil Hosps 1994; **Fellow:** Ophthalmic Oncology, Meml Hermann Hosp - Texas Med Ctr 1995; Ophthalmic Plastic Surgery, Meml Hermann Hosp - Texas Med Ctr 1995; **Fac Appt:** Asst Clin Prof Oph, Baylor Coll Med

Wallace III, Robert B MD [Oph] - **Spec Exp:** Refractive Surgery; Cataract Surgery; Glaucoma; **Hospital:** CHRISTUS St. Frances Cabrini Hosp; **Address:** 4110 Parliament Drive, Alexandria, LA 71303; **Phone:** 318-448-4488; **Board Cert:** Ophthalmology 1979; **Med School:** Tulane Univ 1974; **Resid:** Ophthalmology, Tulane Univ Affil Hosp 1978; **Fac Appt:** Clin Prof Oph, Louisiana State U, New Orleans

West Coast and Pacific

Abbott, Richard L MD [Oph] - **Spec Exp:** Cornea & External Eye Disease; **Hospital:** UCSF Med Ctr; **Address:** UCSF, Dept Ophthalmology, 8 Koret Way, Ste U545, San Francisco, CA 94143-0730; **Phone:** 415-514-8200; **Board Cert:** Ophthalmology 1978; **Med School:** Geo Wash Univ 1971; **Resid:** Ophthalmology, Presby-Pacific Med Ctr 1977; **Fellow:** Cornea & Ext Eye Disease, Bascom Palmer Eye Inst 1978; **Fac Appt:** Prof Oph, UCSF

Afshari, Natalie A MD [Oph] - **Spec Exp:** Cataract Surgery; Cornea Transplant; LASIK-Refractive Surgery; PRK-Refractive Surgery; **Hospital:** UCSD Med Ctr; **Address:** UC San Diego Shiley Eye Center, 9415 Campus Pointe Drive, La Jolla, CA 92093; **Phone:** 858-534-6290; **Board Cert:** Ophthalmology 2011; **Med School:** Stanford Univ 1995; **Resid:** Ophthalmology, Mass Eye & Ear Infirmary 1999; **Fellow:** Cornea & Refractive Surgery, Mass Eye & Ear Infirmary 2001; **Fac Appt:** Prof Oph, UCSD

Arnold, Anthony C MD [Oph] - **Spec Exp:** Neuro-Ophthalmology; **Hospital:** UCLA Ronald Reagan Med Ctr; **Address:** Jules Stein Eye Institute, 100 Stein Plaza, Fl 2, Los Angeles, CA 90095-7005; **Phone:** 310-825-4344; **Board Cert:** Ophthalmology 2008; **Med School:** UCLA 1975; **Resid:** Ophthalmology, Jules Stein Eye Inst-UCLA 1979; **Fellow:** Neuro-Ophthalmology, Jules Stein Eye Inst-UCLA 1983; **Fac Appt:** Clin Prof Oph, UCLA

Baerveldt, George MD [Oph] - **Spec Exp:** Glaucoma; **Hospital:** UC Irvine Med Ctr; **Address:** Nvision Laser Eye Center, 3501 Jamboree Rd, Ste 200 B, Newport Beach, CA 92660; **Phone:** 949-854-7400; **Med School:** South Africa 1967; **Resid:** Ophthalmology, Univ of Witwaterstrand 1975; **Fellow:** Neuro-Ophthalmology, SUNY Downstate Med Ctr 1976; **Fac Appt:** Prof Emeritus Oph, UC Irvine

Bernardino, Carlo R MD [Oph] - **Spec Exp:** Oculoplastic Surgery; Orbital Surgery; Thyroid Eye Disease; Anophthalmia; **Hospital:** Comm Hosp of Monterey Pen; **Address:** Vantage Eye Center, Medical Bldg B, Ste 130, 2 Upper Ragsdale Drive, Monterey, CA 93940; **Phone:** 831-647-3900; **Board Cert:** Ophthalmology 2003; **Med School:** Jefferson Med Coll 1997; **Resid:** Ophthalmology, Wills Eye Hosp 2001; **Fellow:** Oculoplastic Surgery, Mass Eye & Ear Infirm 2003

Blumenkranz, Mark S MD [Oph] - **Spec Exp:** Retinal Disorders; Macular Degeneration; **Hospital:** Stanford Univ Hosp & Clins; **Address:** Byers Eye Institute at Stanford, 2452 Watson Court Fl 2, Palo Alto, CA 94303-5353; **Phone:** 650-723-6995; **Board Cert:** Ophthalmology 1980; **Med School:** Brown Univ 1975; **Resid:** Ophthalmology, Stanford Univ Hosp 1979; **Fellow:** Vitreoretinal Surgery, Bascom Palmer Eye Inst 1980; **Fac Appt:** Prof Oph, Stanford Univ

Borchert, Mark S MD [Oph] - **Spec Exp:** Pediatric Neuro-Ophthalmology; Vision-Unexplained Loss; Optic Nerve Disorders; **Hospital:** Chldns Hosp - Los Angeles; **Address:** Chldns Hosp, Div Ophthalmology, 4650 Sunset Blvd, MS 88, Los Angeles, CA 90027-6062; **Phone:** 323-361-4510; **Board Cert:** Ophthalmology 1989; **Med School:** Baylor Coll Med 1983; **Resid:** Ophthalmology, LAC-USC Med Ctr 1987; **Fellow:** Neuro-Ophthalmology, Mass EE Infirm-Harvard 1988; **Fac Appt:** Assoc Prof Oph, USC Sch Med

Boxer Wachler, Brian S MD [Oph] - **Spec Exp:** Keratoconus; LASIK-Refractive Surgery; Corneal Disease & Surgery; Cataract Surgery; **Hospital:** Cedars-Sinai Med Ctr; **Address:** 465 N Roxbury Drive, Ste 902, Beverly Hills, CA 90210; **Phone:** 310-594-5209; **Board Cert:** Ophthalmology 2010; **Med School:** Dartmouth Med Sch 1993; **Resid:** Ophthalmology, St Louis Univ Eye Inst 1997; **Fellow:** Refractive Surgery, Univ Kansas Med Ctr 1998

Boxrud, Cynthia Ann MD [Oph] - **Spec Exp:** Oculoplastic Surgery; Eye Tumors/Cancer; Orbital Diseases; **Hospital:** UCLA Ronald Reagan Med Ctr, St. John's Hlth Ctr, Santa Monica; **Address:** 2021 Santa Monica Blvd, Ste 700E, Santa Monica, CA 90404-2208; **Phone:** 310-829-9060; **Board Cert:** Ophthalmology 2008; **Med School:** Case West Res Univ 1986; **Resid:** Ophthalmology, NYU-Bellevue Hosp Ctr 1990; **Fellow:** Ophthalmic Oncology, New York Hosp-Cornell Med Ctr 1992; Ophthalmic Plastic Surgery, UCLA-Jules Stein Eye Inst 1993; **Fac Appt:** Asst Prof Oph, UCLA

Caprioli, Joseph MD [Oph] - **Spec Exp:** Glaucoma; Cataract Surgery; Anterior Segment Surgery; **Hospital:** UCLA Ronald Reagan Med Ctr; **Address:** Jules Stein Eye Institute, 100 Stein Plaza Fl 2 - Ste 2-273, Los Angeles, CA 90095-7006; **Phone:** 310-794-9442; **Board Cert:** Ophthalmology 1985; **Med School:** SUNY Buffalo 1979; **Resid:** Ophthalmology, Yale-New Haven Hosp 1983; **Fellow:** Glaucoma, Wills Eye Hosp 1984; **Fac Appt:** Prof Oph, UCLA

Caster, Andrew I MD [Oph] - **Spec Exp:** LASIK-Refractive Surgery; Laser Vision Surgery; **Hospital:** Cedars-Sinai Med Ctr; **Address:** Caster Eye Center, 9100 Wilshire Blvd, Ste 265E, Beverly Hills, CA 90212; **Phone:** 310-274-1221; **Board Cert:** Ophthalmology 1986; **Med School:** Harvard Med Sch 1980; **Resid:** Ophthalmology, UCLA Jules Stein Eye Inst 1984

Char, Devron H MD [Oph] - **Spec Exp:** Eye Tumors/Cancer; Thyroid Eye Disease; Oculoplastic Surgery; **Hospital:** CA Pacific Med Ctr-Pacific Campus, UCSF Med Ctr; **Address:** 45 Castro St, Ste 309, San Francisco, CA 94114; **Phone:** 415-522-0700; **Board Cert:** Ophthalmology 1978; **Med School:** Univ Minn 1970; **Resid:** Internal Medicine, Mass Genl Hosp 1972; Ophthalmology, UCSF Med Ctr 1977; **Fellow:** Research, Natl Cancer Inst 1974; **Fac Appt:** Prof Oph, Stanford Univ

Choy, Andrew MD [Oph] - **Spec Exp:** Eye Muscle Disorders; Oculoplastic & Orbital Surgery; Orbital Tumors/Cancer; **Hospital:** Long Beach Meml Med Ctr, Los Alamitos Med Ctr; **Address:** 4100 Long Beach Blvd, Ste 108, Long Beach, CA 90807-2619; **Phone:** 562-426-3925; **Board Cert:** Ophthalmology 1976; **Med School:** USC-Keck School of Medicine 1969; **Resid:** Neurology, LAC-USC Med Ctr 1971; Ophthalmology, Bellevue Hosp Ctr-NYU 1974; **Fellow:** Strabismus, Columbia-Presby Med Ctr 1975; **Fac Appt:** Assoc Clin Prof Oph, UCLA

Cockerham, Kimberly P MD [Oph] - **Spec Exp:** Meningioma-Orbital (eye); Orbital Tumors/Cancer; Eyelid Cancer & Reconstruction; Neuro-Ophthalmology; **Hospital:** El Camino Hosp, Stanford Univ Hosp & Clins; **Address:** 1801 E March Ln, Ste A160, Stockton, CA 95210; **Phone:** 209-461-2160; **Board Cert:** Ophthalmology 2004; **Med School:** Geo Wash Univ 1987; **Resid:** Ophthalmology, Walter Reed Army Med Ctr 1992; **Fellow:** Neuro-Ophthalmology, Walter Reed Army Med Ctr 1993; Neuro-Ophthalmology, Allegheny General Hosp 1995

Day, Susan H MD [Oph] - **Spec Exp:** Pediatric Ophthalmology; Strabismus-Adult & Pediatric; **Hospital:** CA Pacific Med Ctr-Pacific Campus, Chldns Hosp - Oakland; **Address:** 2340 Clay St, Ste 100, San Francisco, CA 94115; **Phone:** 415-202-1500; **Board Cert:** Ophthalmology 2009; **Med School:** Louisiana State U, New Orleans 1975; **Resid:** Ophthalmology, California Pacific Med Ctr 1979; **Fellow:** Pediatric Ophthalmology, Hosp Sick Chldn 1980

De Juan Jr, Eugene MD [Oph] - **Spec Exp:** Retina/Vitreous Surgery; **Hospital:** UCSF Med Ctr; **Address:** UCSF Dept Ophthalmology, 400 Parnassus Ave Fl 7, San Francisco, CA 94143; **Phone:** 415-353-2084; **Board Cert:** Ophthalmology 1985; **Med School:** Univ S Ala Coll Med 1979; **Resid:** Ophthalmology, Johns Hopkins Hosp 1983; **Fellow:** Vitreoretinal Surgery, Duke Univ Eye Ctr 1984; **Fac Appt:** Prof Oph, UCSF

Demer, Joseph L MD/PhD [Oph] - **Spec Exp:** Pediatric Ophthalmology; Strabismus; Nystagmus; **Hospital:** UCLA Ronald Reagan Med Ctr; **Address:** Jules Stein Eye Institute, 200 Stein Plaza Fl 2, Los Angeles, CA 90095-7065; **Phone:** 310-825-5931; **Board Cert:** Ophthalmology 1988; **Med School:** Johns Hopkins Univ 1983; **Resid:** Ophthalmology, Baylor Coll Med Affil Hosp 1987; **Fellow:** Pediatric Ophthalmology, Texas Chldns Hosp 1988; **Fac Appt:** Prof Oph, UCLA

Freeman, William R MD [Oph] - **Spec Exp:** Retinal Disorders; **Hospital:** UCSD Med Ctr; **Address:** UCSD Shiley Eye Ctr, 9415 Campus Point Drive, La Jolla, CA 92037; **Phone:** 858-534-6290; **Board Cert:** Ophthalmology 1984; **Med School:** Mount Sinai Sch Med 1979; **Resid:** Ophthalmology, Lenox Hill Hosp 1983; **Fellow:** Uveitis, UCSF Francis Proctor Fdn 1985; Vitreoretinal Disease, USC Doheny Eye Inst 1986; **Fac Appt:** Prof Oph, UCSD

Gorin, Michael B MD/PhD [Oph] - **Spec Exp:** Retinal Disorders; Macular Degeneration; Eye Diseases-Hereditary; **Hospital:** UCLA Ronald Reagan Med Ctr; **Address:** Jules Stein Eye Institute, 100 Stein Plaza, Los Angeles, CA 90095-7000; **Phone:** 310-794-5400; **Board Cert:** Ophthalmology 1987; **Med School:** Univ Pennsylvania 1980; **Resid:** Ophthalmology, Jules Stein Eye Inst 1986; **Fellow:** Medical Retina, Moorfields Eye Hosp 1987; **Fac Appt:** Prof Oph, UCLA-David Geffen Sch Med

Granet, David B MD [Oph] - **Spec Exp:** Pediatric Ophthalmology; Eye Muscle Disorders; Strabismus; Nystagmus; **Hospital:** UCSD Med Ctr, Rady Children's Hosp - San Diego; **Address:** UCSD Ratner Children's Eye Center, 9415 Campus Point Drive, La Jolla, CA 92093; **Phone:** 858-534-2020; **Board Cert:** Ophthalmology 2005; **Med School:** Yale Univ 1987; **Resid:** Ophthalmology, NYU/Bellevue Hosp 1991; **Fellow:** Pediatric Ophthalmology, Chldns Hosp & UPenn Scheie Eye Inst 1993; Ocular Disease, UPenn Scheie Eye Inst 1993; **Fac Appt:** Prof Oph, UCSD

Humayun, Mark S MD/PhD [Oph] - **Spec Exp:** Retina/Vitreous Surgery; Retinal Disorders; Retinal Vascular Diseases; Diabetic Eye Disease/Retinopathy; **Hospital:** Keck Med Ctr of USC; **Address:** Doheny Eye Institute, 1450 San Pablo St Fl 4, Los Angeles, CA 90033; **Phone:** 323-442-6335; **Board Cert:** Ophthalmology 2006; **Med School:** Duke Univ 1989; **Resid:** Ophthalmology, Duke Eye Ctr 1993; **Fellow:** Vitreoretinal Surgery, Wilmer Inst-Johns Hopkins 1995

Irvine, John A MD [Oph] - **Spec Exp:** Corneal & External Eye Disease; **Hospital:** Keck Med Ctr of USC; **Address:** Doheny Eye Institute, 1450 San Pablo St Fl 4, Los Angeles, CA 90033; **Phone:** 323-442-6335; **Board Cert:** Ophthalmology 1989; **Med School:** USC-Keck School of Medicine 1982; **Resid:** Ophthalmology, Mass Eye & Ear Infirmary 1986; **Fellow:** Cornea & Ext Eye Disease, Mass Eye & Ear Infirmary 1987; **Fac Appt:** Prof Oph, USC Sch Med

Isenberg, Sherwin MD [Oph] - **Spec Exp:** Strabismus; Pediatric Ophthalmology; **Hospital:** LAC - Harbor - UCLA Med Ctr, UCLA Ronald Reagan Med Ctr; **Address:** Jules Stein Eye Inst, 200 Stein Plaza Fl 2, Los Angeles, CA 90095-7000; **Phone:** 310-825-8840; **Board Cert:** Ophthalmology 1978; **Med School:** UCLA-David Geffen Sch Med 1973; **Resid:** Ophthalmology, Illinois Ear & Eye Infirm 1977; **Fellow:** Pediatric Ophthalmology, Chldns Hosp Natl Med Ctr 1978; **Fac Appt:** Prof Oph, UCLA

Iwach, Andrew G MD [Oph] - **Spec Exp:** Glaucoma; **Hospital:** CA Pacific Med Ctr - CA Campus, UCSF Med Ctr; **Address:** Glaucoma Ctr of San Francisco, 55 Stevenson St, San Francisco, CA 94105; **Phone:** 415-981-2020; **Board Cert:** Ophthalmology 1991; **Med School:** UCLA 1984; **Resid:** Ophthalmology, Stanford Univ Med Ctr 1988; **Fellow:** Glaucoma, UCSF Med Ctr 1989; **Fac Appt:** Assoc Clin Prof Oph, UCSF

Kikkawa, Don MD [Oph] - **Spec Exp:** Ophthalmic Plastic Surgery; Oculoplastic & Orbital Surgery; Thyroid Eye Disease; Lacrimal Gland Disorders; **Hospital:** UCSD Med Ctr; **Address:** UCSD Shiley Eye Ctr, 9415 Campus Point Drive, rm 255, MC 0946, La Jolla, CA 92093; **Phone:** 858-534-6290; **Board Cert:** Ophthalmology 2013; **Med School:** St Louis Univ 1987; **Resid:** Ophthalmology, Jules Stein Eye Inst 1991; **Fellow:** Ophthalmic Plastic & Reconstructive Surgery, Univ WI Hosp & Clins 1992; **Fac Appt:** Clin Prof Oph, UCSD

Kim, Jonathan W MD [Oph] - **Spec Exp:** Oculoplastic Surgery; Orbital Tumors/Cancer; Retinoblastoma; **Hospital:** Chldns Hosp - Los Angeles; **Address:** CHLA, Vision Ctr, 4650 Sunset Blvd, Los Angeles, CA 90027; **Phone:** 323-361-2347; **Board Cert:** Ophthalmology 2012; **Med School:** Univ Iowa Coll Med 1994; **Resid:** Ophthalmology, CA Pacific Med Ctr 1998; **Fellow:** Oculoplastic Surgery, Jules Stein Eye Inst 2000; Neuro-Ophthalmology, Mass Eye & Ear Infirm 2004

Krauss, Howard R MD [Oph] - **Spec Exp:** Neuro-Ophthalmology; LASIK-Refractive Surgery; Oculoplastic Surgery; **Hospital:** UCLA Ronald Reagan Med Ctr; **Address:** Pacific Eye & Ear Specialists, 11645 Wilshire Blvd Fl 6, Los Angeles, CA 90025; **Phone:** 310-477-5558; **Board Cert:** Ophthalmology 1982; **Med School:** NY Med Coll 1977; **Resid:** Ophthalmology, Jules Stein Eye Inst 1981; **Fellow:** Neuro-Ophthalmology, UPMC 1982; **Fac Appt:** Clin Prof Oph, UCLA-David Geffen Sch Med

Maloney, Robert K MD [Oph] - **Spec Exp:** Refractive Surgery; LASIK-Refractive Surgery; Cataract Surgery; **Hospital:** UCLA Ronald Reagan Med Ctr; **Address:** Maloney Vision Inst, 10921 Wilshire Blvd, Ste 900, Los Angeles, CA 90024-4002; **Phone:** 310-208-3937; **Board Cert:** Ophthalmology 1991; **Med School:** UCSF 1985; **Resid:** Ophthalmology, Johns Hopkins Hosp 1989; **Fellow:** Refractive Surgery, Emory Univ Hosp 1991; **Fac Appt:** Clin Prof Oph, UCLA-David Geffen Sch Med

Manche, Edward E MD [Oph] - **Spec Exp:** LASIK-Refractive Surgery; Cornea Transplant; PRK-Refractive Surgery; **Hospital:** Stanford Univ Hosp & Clins; **Address:** Byers Eye Institute at Stanford, 2452 Watson Court, Palo Alto, CA 94303-5353; **Phone:** 650-723-6995; **Board Cert:** Ophthalmology 2007; **Med School:** Albert Einstein Coll Med 1990; **Resid:** Ophthalmology, UMDNJ Affil Hosp 1994; **Fellow:** Cornea & Ext Eye Disease, Jules Stein Eye Inst-UCLA 1996; **Fac Appt:** Assoc Prof Oph, Stanford Univ

Mannis, Mark J MD [Oph] - **Spec Exp:** Cornea Transplant & Artificial Cornea; Cornea & External Eye Disease; **Hospital:** UC Davis Med Ctr; **Address:** UC Davis Med Ctr, Dept Ophthalmology, 4860 Y St, Ste 2400, Sacramento, CA 95817; **Phone:** 916-734-6602; **Board Cert:** Ophthalmology 2009; **Med School:** Univ Fla Coll Med 1975; **Resid:** Ophthalmology, Washington Univ Med Ctr 1979; **Fellow:** Cornea & Ext Eye Disease, Univ IA Hosps & Clins 1980; **Fac Appt:** Prof Oph, UC Davis

Marmor, Michael F MD [Oph] - **Spec Exp:** Retinal Disorders; Retinal Dystrophies; Electroretinograms (ERG); Retinal Drug Toxicity; **Hospital:** Stanford Univ Hosp & Clins; **Address:** Byers Eye Institute at Stanford, 2452 Watson Court, Palo Alto, CA 94303-5353; **Phone:** 650-723-6995; **Board Cert:** Ophthalmology 1974; **Med School:** Harvard Med Sch 1966; **Resid:** Ophthalmology, Mass EE Infirm 1973; **Fellow:** Neurophysiology, Natl Inst Hlth 1970; **Fac Appt:** Prof Oph, Stanford Univ

Masket, Samuel MD [Oph] - **Spec Exp:** Cataract Surgery; Cataract Surgery Revision; Congenital Eye Disorders-Rare; **Address:** Advanced Vision Care, 2080 Century Park East, Ste 911, Los Angeles, CA 90067; **Phone:** 310-229-1220; **Board Cert:** Ophthalmology 1974; **Med School:** NY Med Coll 1968; **Resid:** Ophthalmology, Metro Hosp Ctr 1973; **Fac Appt:** Asst Clin Prof Oph, UCLA-David Geffen Sch Med

Miller, Kevin M MD [Oph] - **Spec Exp:** Cataract Surgery-Lens Implant; Refractive Surgery; Congenital Eye Disorders-Rare; **Hospital:** UCLA Ronald Reagan Med Ctr; **Address:** Jules Stein Eye Institute, 200 Stein Plaza Fl 1, Los Angeles, CA 90095-7000; **Phone:** 310-206-9951; **Board Cert:** Ophthalmology 2013; **Med School:** Johns Hopkins Univ 1985; **Resid:** Ophthalmology, Jules Stein Eye Inst 1991; **Fellow:** Ophthalmic Optics, Wilmer Inst/Johns Hopkins 1988; **Fac Appt:** Prof Oph, UCLA

Mondino, Bartly MD [Oph] - **Spec Exp:** Cornea & External Eye Disease; **Hospital:** UCLA Ronald Reagan Med Ctr; **Address:** Jules Stein Eye Institute, 200 Stein Plaza Fl 1, Los Angeles, CA 90095-7065; **Phone:** 310-825-5053; **Board Cert:** Ophthalmology 1976; **Med School:** Stanford Univ 1971; **Resid:** Ophthalmology, NY Hosp/Cornell Univ 1975; **Fellow:** Cornea & Ext Eye Disease, Univ Pittsburgh Eye & Ear Hosp 1976; **Fac Appt:** Prof Oph, UCLA

Murphree, A Linn MD [Oph] - **Spec Exp:** Retinoblastoma; Eye Tumors/Cancer; Ophthalmic Genetics; Pediatric Ophthalmology; **Hospital:** Chldns Hosp - Los Angeles, USC Norris Cancer Hosp; **Address:** Chldns Hosp, Dept Ophthalmology, 4650 Sunset Blvd, MS 88, Los Angeles, CA 90027-6016; **Phone:** 323-361-2347; **Board Cert:** Ophthalmology 1978; **Med School:** Baylor Coll Med 1972; **Resid:** Ophthalmology, Baylor Univ Med Ctr 1976; **Fellow:** Pediatric Ophthalmology, Wilmer Inst/Johns Hopkins 1977; **Fac Appt:** Prof Oph, USC-Keck School of Medicine

Ng, John MD [Oph] - **Spec Exp:** Oculoplastic & Orbital Surgery; Reconstructive Surgery; Trauma; **Hospital:** OR Hlth & Sci Univ; **Address:** Casey Eye Inst, 3375 SW Terwilliger Blvd, Portland, OR 97239; **Phone:** 503-494-3004; **Board Cert:** Ophthalmology 2007; **Med School:** Geo Wash Univ 1988; **Resid:** Ophthalmology, Letterman/Madigan Army Med Ctr 1994; **Fellow:** Oculoplastic & Reconstructive Surgery, Midwest Eye Inst 1997; **Fac Appt:** Assoc Prof Oph, Oregon Hlth & Sci Univ

Paul, T Otis MD [Oph] - **Spec Exp:** Pediatric Ophthalmology; Strabismus-Adult & Pediatric; **Hospital:** Chldns Hosp - Oakland, CA Pacific Med Ctr-Pacific Campus; **Address:** 5275 Claremont Ave Fl 1, Oakland, CA 94618; **Phone:** 510-428-3050; **Board Cert:** Ophthalmology 1974; **Med School:** UCLA 1967; **Resid:** Ophthalmology, Naval Hosp 1972; **Fellow:** Pediatric Ophthalmology, CA Pacific Med Ctr 1974

Puliafito, Carmen A MD [Oph] - **Spec Exp:** Retinal Disorders; Macular Degeneration; **Hospital:** Keck Med Ctr of USC; **Address:** Doheny Eye Institute, 1450 San Pablo St Fl 4, Los Angeles, CA 90033; **Phone:** 323-442-6335; **Board Cert:** Ophthalmology 2012; **Med School:** Harvard Med Sch 1978; **Resid:** Ophthalmology, Mass Eye & Ear Infirm 1982; **Fellow:** Vitreoretinal Surgery, Mass Eye & Ear Infirm 1983; **Fac Appt:** Prof Oph, USC-Keck School of Medicine

Rao, Narsing A MD [Oph] - **Spec Exp:** Uveitis/AIDS; Eye Pathology; **Hospital:** Keck Med Ctr of USC; **Address:** Doheny Eye Institute, 1450 San Pablo St Fl 4, Los Angeles, CA 90033-4697; **Phone:** 323-442-6335; **Board Cert:** Anatomic Pathology 1974; Ophthalmology 1977; **Med School:** India 1967; **Resid:** Pathology, Georgetown Univ Hosp 1972; Ophthalmology, Georgetown Univ Hosp 1975; **Fac Appt:** Prof Oph, USC Sch Med

Sadda, SriniVas R MD [Oph] - **Spec Exp:** Macular Degeneration; Diabetic Eye Disease/Retinopathy; Retinal Disorders-Inherited; Retinal Vascular Diseases; **Hospital:** Keck Med Ctr of USC; **Address:** Doheny Eye Institute, 1450 San Pablo St Fl 4, Beverly Hills, CA 90033; **Phone:** 323-442-6335; **Board Cert:** Ophthalmology 2010; **Med School:** Johns Hopkins Univ 1994; **Resid:** Ophthalmology, Wilmer Eye Inst 1997; **Fellow:** Neuro-Ophthalmology, Wilmer Eye Inst 1998; Retina, Wilmer Eye Inst 1998; **Fac Appt:** Assoc Prof Oph, USC-Keck School of Medicine

Salz, James J MD [Oph] - **Spec Exp:** LASIK-Refractive Surgery; Cataract Surgery; **Hospital:** Cedars-Sinai Med Ctr; **Address:** 11620 Wilshire Blvd, Ste 711, Los Angeles, CA 90025; **Phone:** 310-444-1134; **Board Cert:** Ophthalmology 1971; **Med School:** Duke Univ 1965; **Resid:** Ophthalmology, LAC-USC Med Ctr 1969; **Fac Appt:** Clin Prof Oph, USC Sch Med

Savino, Peter J MD [Oph] - **Spec Exp:** Neuro-Ophthalmology; **Hospital:** UCSD Med Ctr; **Address:** UCSD Shiley Eye Ctr, 9415 Campus Point Drive, MC 0946, La Jolla, CA 92093-0946; **Phone:** 858-534-6290; **Board Cert:** Ophthalmology 1975; **Med School:** Italy 1968; **Resid:** Ophthalmology, Georgetown Med Ctr 1973; **Fellow:** Neuro-Ophthalmology, Bascom Palmer Eye Inst 1974; **Fac Appt:** Clin Prof Oph, Thomas Jefferson Univ

Schwartz, Steven D MD [Oph] - **Spec Exp:** Diabetic Eye Disease/Retinopathy; Retinal Detachment; Retinal Disorders; Macular Degeneration; **Hospital:** UCLA Ronald Reagan Med Ctr; **Address:** Jules Stein Eye Institute, 200 Stein Plaza Fl 1, Los Angeles, CA 90095; **Phone:** 310-206-7474; **Board Cert:** Ophthalmology 2005; **Med School:** USC-Keck School of Medicine 1988; **Resid:** Ophthalmology, UCLA Med Ctr 1992; **Fellow:** Medical Retina, Moorfields Eye Hosp 1993; Vitreoretinal Surgery, Moorfields Eye Hosp 1994; **Fac Appt:** Asst Prof Oph, UCLA-David Geffen Sch Med

Seibel, Barry S MD [Oph] - **Spec Exp:** Cataract Surgery; **Hospital:** Cedars-Sinai Med Ctr; **Address:** 11620 Wilshire Blvd, Ste 711, Los Angeles, CA 90025; **Phone:** 310-444-1134; **Board Cert:** Ophthalmology 1991; **Med School:** Univ Tex, Houston 1985; **Resid:** Ophthalmology, Hollywood Presby Med Ctr 1987; Ophthalmology, USC-Doheny Eye Clin 1989; **Fac Appt:** Asst Clin Prof Oph, UCLA

Seiff, Stuart R MD [Oph] - **Spec Exp:** Oculoplastic Surgery; Orbital Tumors/Cancer; Facial Plastic Surgery; **Hospital:** UCSF Med Ctr, CA Pacific Med Ctr-Pacific Campus; **Address:** 2100 Webster St, Ste 214, San Francisco, CA 94115; **Phone:** 415-923-3007; **Board Cert:** Ophthalmology 1986; **Med School:** UCSF 1980; **Resid:** Ophthalmology, UCSF Med Ctr 1984; **Fellow:** Ophthalmic Plastic & Reconstructive Surgery, Jules Stein Eye Inst 1985; **Fac Appt:** Prof Emeritus Oph, UCSF

Serafano, Donald N MD [Oph] - **Spec Exp:** LASIK-Refractive Surgery; Cataract Surgery; Lens Implants; Glaucoma; **Hospital:** Los Alamitos Med Ctr; **Address:** Complete Eye Care Associates, 10861 Cherry St, Ste 204, Los Alamitos, CA 90720-5403; **Phone:** 562-598-3160; **Board Cert:** Ophthalmology 1978; **Med School:** Wayne State Univ 1971; **Resid:** Ophthalmology, Mayo Clinic 1978; **Fac Appt:** Assoc Clin Prof Oph, USC Sch Med

Shamie, Neda MD [Oph] - **Spec Exp:** Cornea Transplant; Cataract Surgery; Anterior Segment Surgery; Keratoconus; **Hospital:** Keck Med Ctr of USC; **Address:** Doheny Eye Ctr, 9033 Wilshire Blvd, Ste 360, Beverly Hills, CA 90211; **Phone:** 310-601-3366; **Board Cert:** Ophthalmology 2006; **Med School:** UCSF 1998; **Resid:** Ophthalmology, UC-Irvine Med Ctr 2002; **Fellow:** Cornea & Refractive Surgery, UC-Irvine Med Ctr 2003

Smith, Ronald Edward MD [Oph] - **Spec Exp:** Corneal Disease; Uveitis; **Hospital:** Keck Med Ctr of USC; **Address:** Doheny Eye Institute, 1450 San Pablo Rd Fl 4, Los Angeles, CA 90033; **Phone:** 323-442-6335; **Board Cert:** Ophthalmology 1974; **Med School:** Johns Hopkins Univ 1967; **Resid:** Ophthalmology, Johns Hopkins Hosp 1973; **Fellow:** Research, UCSF Med Ctr 1972; **Fac Appt:** Prof Oph, USC Sch Med

Steinert, Roger F MD [Oph] - **Spec Exp:** Refractive Surgery; Cataract Surgery; Cornea Transplant; Corneal Disease; **Hospital:** UC Irvine Med Ctr; **Address:** UC Irvine-Gavin Herbert Eye Institute, 850 Health Sciences Rd, Irvine, CA 92697-4375; **Phone:** 949-824-2020; **Board Cert:** Ophthalmology 1982; **Med School:** Harvard Med Sch 1977; **Resid:** Ophthalmology, Mass Eye & Ear Infirmary 1981; **Fac Appt:** Prof Oph, UC Irvine

Stout, J. Timothy MD/PhD [Oph] - **Spec Exp:** Retinal Disorders-Pediatric; Retinoblastoma; Retinopathy of Prematurity; **Hospital:** OR Hlth & Sci Univ, Providence St Vincent Med Ctr; **Address:** 3375 SW Terwilliger Blvd, Portland, OR 97239; **Phone:** 503-494-2435; **Board Cert:** Ophthalmology 2010; **Med School:** Baylor Coll Med 1989; **Resid:** Ophthalmology, Doheny Eye Inst 1993; **Fellow:** Ophthalmology, Moorfields Eye Hosp 1994; Retinal Surgery, Doheny Eye Inst 1995; **Fac Appt:** Assoc Prof Oph, Oregon Hlth & Sci Univ

Weinreb, Robert N MD [Oph] - **Spec Exp:** Glaucoma; **Hospital:** UCSD Med Ctr; **Address:** UCSD Shiley Eye Ctr, 9415 Campus Point Drive, La Jolla, CA 92093; **Phone:** 858-534-6290; **Board Cert:** Ophthalmology 1982; **Med School:** Harvard Med Sch 1975; **Resid:** Ophthalmology, UCSF Med Ctr 1981; **Fellow:** Glaucoma, UCSF Med Ctr 1982; **Fac Appt:** Prof Oph, UCSD

Weiss, Avery H MD [Oph] - **Spec Exp:** Pediatric Ophthalmology; Strabismus; Amblyopia; Glaucoma-Pediatric; **Hospital:** Seattle Chldns Hosp; **Address:** Seattle Chldns Hosp, Dept Ophthalmology, 4800 Sand Point Way NE, Seattle, WA 98105; **Phone:** 206-987-2177; **Board Cert:** Ophthalmology 1981; **Med School:** Univ Miami Sch Med 1974; **Resid:** Internal Medicine, Barnes-Jewish Hosp 1976; Ophthalmology, Barnes-Jewish Hosp 1980; **Fellow:** Research, Barnes-Jewish Hosp 1977; Pediatric Ophthalmology, Chldns Hosp Natl Med Ctr 1981; **Fac Appt:** Prof Oph, Univ Wash

Wilson, David Jean MD [Oph] - **Spec Exp:** Eye Tumors/Cancer; Ophthalmic Pathology; **Hospital:** OR Hlth & Sci Univ; **Address:** 3375 SW Terwilliger Blvd, Portland, OR 97239; **Phone:** 503-494-7881; **Board Cert:** Ophthalmology 2009; **Med School:** Baylor Coll Med 1981; **Resid:** Ophthalmology, Univ Oregon Affil Hosp 1985; **Fellow:** Ophthalmic Pathology, Johns Hopkins Hosp 1987; Retina/Vitreous Surgery, Mass Eye & Ear Infirmary 1988; **Fac Appt:** Prof Oph, Oregon Hlth & Sci Univ

Wright, Kenneth W MD [Oph] - **Spec Exp:** Pediatric Ophthalmology; Cataract-Pediatric; **Hospital:** Cedars-Sinai Med Ctr; **Address:** Wright Eye Center, 520 S San Vicente Blvd, Los Angeles, CA 90048; **Phone:** 310-652-6420; **Board Cert:** Ophthalmology 1983; **Med School:** Boston Univ 1977; **Resid:** Ophthalmology, LAC-USC Med Ctr 1981; **Fellow:** Pediatric Ophthalmology, Johns Hopkins Hosp 1981; Strabismus, Chldns Hosp Natl Med Ctr 1982; **Fac Appt:** Asst Prof Oph, USC Sch Med

THE MOUNT SINAI MEDICAL CENTER

Ophthalmology

Mount Sinai

One Gustave L. Levy Place
Fifth Avenue and 100th Street
New York, NY 10029-6574

Physician Referral: 1-800-MD-SINAI (637-4624)
www.mountsinai.org

Specializing in the prevention, diagnosis, and treatment of eye disorders, Mount Sinai's **DEPARTMENT OF OPHTHALMOLOGY** features faculty with wide experience in special eye problems, offers comprehensive eye care services, and houses a state-of-the-art optical shop.

Services include:

- Comprehensive ophthalmology, refractive errors, and cataract surgery
- Corneal and external diseases of the eye
- Refractive surgery
- Retinal disorders (diabetic retinopathy, macular degeneration, inherited retinal diseases, retinal detachment)
- Glaucoma
- Pediatric eye care and strabismus
- Uveitis (inflammation of the eye)
- Neuro-ophthalmic disorders
- Oculplastic surgery, including cosmetic surgery, orbital tumors, and thyroid-related eye problems

Specialized treatments and procedures include:

- LASIK and other refractive surgical procedures
- Cataract surgery, including premium intraocular lenses
- Specialists in dry eye management
- Cosmetic lid treatments, including Botox and Restalayne injections
- Laser surgery
- Management of macular degeneration, including Lucentis and Avastin injections
- Advanced management for severe uveitis, including immunosuppressive drug therapy

INTERNATIONAL LEADERS IN THE FIELD OF UVEITIS

Uveitis, a collection of 30 diseases characterized by inflammation inside the eye, is the 5th leading cause of blindness in the United States. Management of severe uveitis often requires the skilled use of systemically-administered, immunosuppressive drugs, resulting in superior outcomes. Mount Sinai ophthalmologists have been pioneers in these treatments and are internationally recognized for their leadership in the field. A team of three uveitis specialists, augmented by a uveitis training program, offer a comprehensive treatment approach to these diseases.

We offer the full range of sophisticated diagnostic tests for evaluating patient conditions, including spectral domain optical coherence tomography, fluorescein angiography, indocyanine green angiography, autofluorescence, diagnostic ultrasound, electroretinography, visually evoked potential measurements, electro-oculography, corneal topography, confocal microscopy, state-of-the-art perimetry, HRT II imaging, allowing for faster, more accurate diagnosis and help determining the best treatment plan for each patient.

We perform cataract surgery, corneal transplants, refractive, glaucoma, strabismus, laser, ophthalmic plastic and reconstructive surgery, and vitreoretinal surgery for complicated retinal problems. We also offer minimally invasive procedures to treat eye disease, including non-laser refractive surgeries, and small-incision cataract surgery.

LEADERS IN CLINICAL RESEARCH

Mount Sinai ophthalmologists helped pioneer and evaluate new treatments for eye diseases and problems, including glaucoma, uveitis, ocular infections and farsightedness.

Orthopaedic Surgery

An orthopaedic surgeon is trained in the preservation, investigation and restoration of the form and function of the extremities, spine and associated structures by medical, surgical and physical means.

An orthopaedic surgeon is involved with the care of patients whose musculoskeletal problems include congenital deformities, trauma, infections, tumors, metabolic disturbances of the musculoskeletal system, deformities, injuries and degenerative diseases of the spine, hands, feet, knee, hip, shoulder and elbow in children and adults. An orthopaedic surgeon is also concerned with primary and secondary muscular problems and the effects of central or peripheral nervous system lesions of the musculoskeletal system.

Note: *There are many Orthopaedic Surgeons who are trained in Sports Medicine and prefer to be listed under that heading; some trained in Sports Medicine prefer to be listed under Orthopaedics.*

Training Required: Five years (including general surgery training) *plus* two years in clinical practice before final certification is achieved.

Orthopaedic Surgery

New England

Abdu, William A MD [OrS] - **Spec Exp:** Spinal Surgery; Spinal Disorders; Spinal Cord Injury; **Hospital:** Dartmouth - Hitchcock Med Ctr; **Address:** Darthmouth-Hitchcock Med Ctr, Spine Ctr, 1 Med Ctr Drive, Lebanon, NH 03756; **Phone:** 603-650-2225; **Board Cert:** Orthopaedic Surgery 2004; **Med School:** Tufts Univ 1985; **Resid:** Surgery, Darthmouth-Hitchcock Med Ctr 1990; Orthopaedic Surgery, Newington Chldns Hosp 1989; **Fellow:** Spine Surgery, Case Western Reserve Univ Hosp 1991; **Fac Appt:** Assoc Prof OrS, Dalhousie Univ

Bono, James V MD [OrS] - **Spec Exp:** Hip Surgery; Knee Surgery; **Hospital:** New England Bapt Hosp (page 63); **Address:** New England Baptist Hosp, 125 Parker Hill Ave, Ste 573, Boston, MA 02120; **Phone:** 617-731-6337; **Board Cert:** Orthopaedic Surgery 2008; **Med School:** Albany Med Coll 1987; **Resid:** Orthopaedic Surgery, Albany Med Ctr 1993; **Fellow:** Hip & Knee Surgery, Hosp for Special Surgery 1994; **Fac Appt:** Clin Prof OrS, Tufts Univ

Brick, Gregory W MD [OrS] - **Spec Exp:** Hip Replacement; Knee Replacement; Spinal Surgery; **Hospital:** Brigham & Women's Hosp; **Address:** Brigham & Womens, Dept Orth Surg, 75 Francis St, Boston, MA 02115; **Phone:** 617-732-5386; **Med School:** New Zealand 1976; **Resid:** Surgery, Greenlane Hosp 1981; Orthopaedic Surgery, Middlemore Hosp 1984; **Fellow:** Joint Replacement Surgery, Brigham & Women's Hosp 1986; Spine Surgery, Vanderbilt Univ Med Ctr 1987; **Fac Appt:** Assoc Clin Prof OrS, Harvard Med Sch

Browner, Bruce D MD [OrS] - **Spec Exp:** Fractures-Complex; Osteomyelitis; Bone Infections; Fractures-Non Union; **Hospital:** Hartford Hosp; **Address:** Hartford Hosp, Orthopaedic Surgery, 80 Seymour St, Ste 3601, Hartford, CT 06102; **Phone:** 860-545-2245; **Board Cert:** Orthopaedic Surgery 1979; **Med School:** SUNY Downstate 1973; **Resid:** Orthopaedic Surgery, Albany Med Ctr 1978; **Fellow:** Trauma, Albany Med Ctr 1975; **Fac Appt:** Prof OrS, Univ Conn

Burke, Dennis MD [OrS] - **Spec Exp:** Knee Replacement; Hip Replacement; Reconstructive Surgery; **Hospital:** Mass Genl Hosp; **Address:** Mass General Hosp, Yawkey 3B, 55 Fruit St, Boston, MA 02114; **Phone:** 617-726-3411; **Board Cert:** Orthopaedic Surgery 2009; **Med School:** Loyola Univ-Stritch Sch Med 1978; **Resid:** Surgery, Beth Israel Deaconess Med Ctr 1980; Orthopaedic Surgery, Mass Genl Hosp 1984

DiGiovanni, Christopher W MD [OrS] - **Spec Exp:** Foot & Ankle Surgery; Sports Injuries-Foot & Ankle; **Hospital:** Rhode Island Hosp; **Address:** University Orthopedics Inc, 100 Butler Dr, Providence, RI 02906-4862; **Phone:** 401-330-1430; **Board Cert:** Orthopaedic Surgery 2012; **Med School:** Dartmouth Med Sch 1991; **Resid:** Orthopaedic Surgery, Rhode Island Hosp 1997; **Fellow:** Joint Replacement Surgery, Hosp Spec Surgery 1998; Foot & Ankle Surgery, Harborview Med Ctr 1999; **Fac Appt:** Prof OrS, Brown Univ

Einhorn, Thomas A MD [OrS] - **Spec Exp:** Hip & Knee Replacement; Bone Disorders-Metabolic; Hip & Knee Reconstruction; Osteonecrosis; **Hospital:** Boston Med Ctr; **Address:** Boston Univ Orthopaedic Surgical Assocs, 725 Albany St, Ste 4B, Boston, MA 02118; **Phone:** 617-638-8435; **Board Cert:** Orthopaedic Surgery 1998; **Med School:** Cornell Univ-Weill Med Coll 1976; **Resid:** Orthopaedic Surgery, St Lukes-Roosevelt Hosp 1981; Pediatric Orthopaedic Surgery, Alfred DuPont Inst 1981; **Fellow:** Orthopaedic Surgery, Hosp Special Surgery 1982; **Fac Appt:** Prof OrS, Boston Univ

Endrizzi, Donald P MD [OrS] - **Spec Exp:** Shoulder Surgery; Rotator Cuff Surgery; Elbow Surgery; Joint Replacement; **Hospital:** Maine Med Ctr; **Address:** Maine Med Partners Orthopedics, Div Joint Replacement, 5 Bucknam Rd, Ste 1D, Falmouth, ME 04105; **Phone:** 207-781-1551; **Board Cert:** Orthopaedic Surgery 2011; **Med School:** Columbia P&S 1982; **Resid:** Surgery, NY-Presby/Columbia Univ Med Ctr 1984; Orthopaedic Surgery, NY-Presby/Columbia Univ Med Ctr 1987; **Fac Appt:** Assoc Clin Prof S, Univ VT Coll Med

Friedlaender, Gary E MD [OrS] - **Spec Exp:** Bone & Soft Tissue Tumors; Limb Surgery/Reconstruction; Fractures-Complex & Non Union; Tissue Banking; **Hospital:** Yale-New Haven Hosp; **Address:** Yale Orthopaedics and Rehabilitation, 800 Howard Ave, Yale Physicians Building YPB 133, Fl 1, New Haven, CT 06519; **Phone:** 203-737-5660; **Board Cert:** Orthopaedic Surgery 1975; **Med School:** Univ Mich Med Sch 1969; **Resid:** Surgery, Michigan Med Ctr 1971; Orthopaedic Surgery, Yale-New Haven Hosp 1974; **Fellow:** Musculoskeletal Oncology, Mass Genl Hosp 1983; **Fac Appt:** Prof OrS, Yale Univ

Fulkerson, John P MD [OrS] - **Spec Exp:** Knee-Patella Problems; Arthroscopic Surgery-Knee; Sports Medicine; Shoulder Arthroscopic Surgery; **Hospital:** Hartford Hosp; **Address:** Orthopedic Assocs, 499 Farmington Ave, Ste 300, Farmington, CT 06032; **Phone:** 860-549-8269; **Board Cert:** Orthopaedic Surgery 1980; **Med School:** Yale Univ 1972; **Resid:** Orthopaedic Surgery, Yale-New Haven Hosp 1978; **Fellow:** Arthroscopic Surgery, Berg-Sloat Traveling 1979; **Fac Appt:** Clin Prof OrS, Univ Conn

Gebhardt, Mark MD [OrS] - **Spec Exp:** Musculoskeletal Tumors; Bone Tumors; **Hospital:** Beth Israel Deaconess Med Ctr - Boston, Children's Hospital - Boston; **Address:** BIDMC-Dept of Orthopedics, 330 Brookline Ave Shapiro Bldg Fl 2, Boston, MA 02215; **Phone:** 617-667-7675; **Board Cert:** Orthopaedic Surgery 2007; **Med School:** Univ Cincinnati 1975; **Resid:** Surgery, Univ Pittsburg Med Ctr 1977; Orthopaedic Surgery, Harvard Affil Hosps 1982; **Fellow:** Pediatric Orthopaedic Surgery, Boston Chldns Hosp 1983; Orthopaedic Oncology, Mass Genl Hosp 1983; **Fac Appt:** Prof OrS, Harvard Med Sch

Green, Andrew MD [OrS] - **Spec Exp:** Shoulder Surgery; Elbow Surgery; Rotator Cuff Surgery; Arthroscopic Surgery; **Hospital:** Rhode Island Hosp, Miriam Hosp; **Address:** Univ Orthopedics Inc, 2 Dudley St, Ste 200, Providence, RI 02905-3248; **Phone:** 401-457-1533; **Board Cert:** Orthopaedic Surgery 2006; Orthopaedic Sports Medicine 2011; **Med School:** Columbia P&S 1987; **Resid:** Orthopaedic Surgery, Rhode Island Hosp 1992; **Fellow:** Pacific Med Ctr 1993; **Fac Appt:** Assoc Prof OrS, Brown Univ

Hornicek, Francis J MD/PhD [OrS] - **Spec Exp:** Bone Tumors; Sarcoma; Bone Tumors-Metastatic; Soft Tissue Tumors; **Hospital:** Mass Genl Hosp; **Address:** MGH Orthpaedic Oncology, 55 Fruit St, Yawkey 3B, Boston, MA 02114; **Phone:** 617-724-3700; **Board Cert:** Orthopaedic Surgery 2010; **Med School:** Univ Pittsburgh 1991; **Resid:** Orthopaedic Surgery, Jackson Meml Hosp 1996; **Fellow:** Orthopaedic Oncology, Mass Genl Hosp/Chldns Hosp 1997; **Fac Appt:** Assoc Prof OrS, Harvard Med Sch

Jokl, Peter MD [OrS] - **Spec Exp:** Knee Surgery; Sports Medicine; Shoulder Surgery; **Hospital:** Yale-New Haven Hosp; **Address:** Yale Sports Med, Dept Orthopaedics, 800 Howard Ave, New Haven, CT 06519-1369; **Phone:** 203-785-2579; **Board Cert:** Orthopaedic Surgery 1974; **Med School:** Yale Univ 1968; **Resid:** Orthopaedic Surgery, Yale-New Haven Hosp 1972; **Fac Appt:** Prof OrS, Yale Univ

Kasser, James MD [OrS] - **Spec Exp:** Pediatric Orthopaedic Surgery; **Hospital:** Children's Hospital - Boston; **Address:** Boston Chldn's Hosp, Ortho Center, 300 Longwood Ave, Honeywell 221, Boston, MA 02115; **Phone:** 617-355-6617; **Board Cert:** Orthopaedic Surgery 2005; **Med School:** Tufts Univ 1976; **Resid:** Orthopaedic Surgery, Tufts Med Ctr 1981; **Fellow:** Pediatric Orthopaedic Surgery, Dupont Inst 1984; **Fac Appt:** Prof OrS, Harvard Med Sch

Kocher, Mininder S MD [OrS] - **Spec Exp:** Pediatric Orthopaedic Surgery; Pediatric Sports Medicine; Arthroscopic Surgery; Arthroscopic Surgery-Hip; **Hospital:** Children's Hospital - Boston, Beth Israel Deaconess Med Ctr - Boston; **Address:** Boston Chldn's Hosp, Dept Ortho Surg, 319 Longwood Ave Fl 6, Boston, MA 02115; **Phone:** 617-355-3501; **Board Cert:** Orthopaedic Surgery 2013; Orthopaedic Sports Medicine 2013; **Med School:** Duke Univ 1993; **Resid:** Orthopaedic Surgery, Beth Israel Deaconess Med Ctr 1999; **Fellow:** Pediatric Orthopaedic Surgery, Chldns Hosp 1999; Sports Medicine, Steadman Hawkins Clin 2000; **Fac Appt:** Asst Prof OrS, Harvard Med Sch

Laurencin, Cato T MD/PhD [OrS] - **Spec Exp:** Shoulder & Knee Surgery; Sports Medicine; **Hospital:** Univ of Conn Hlth Ctr, John Dempsey Hosp; **Address:** Univ Conn Hlth Ctr, Orthopaedic Surgery, 263 Farmington Ave, MRB 3, Farmington, CT 06030; **Phone:** 860-679-1495; **Board Cert:** Orthopaedic Surgery 2007; **Med School:** Harvard Med Sch 1987; **Resid:** Orthopaedic Surgery, Beth Israel Deaconess Med Ctr 1993; **Fellow:** Sports Medicine & Shoulder Surgery, Hosp Special Surgery 1994; **Fac Appt:** Prof OrS, Univ Conn

Marsh, James S MD [OrS] - **Spec Exp:** Pediatric Orthopaedic Surgery; **Hospital:** Yale-New Haven Hosp, Yale-New Haven Hosp - St Raphael Campus; **Address:** Family Orthopaedics, 34 York St, Ste 2, Guilford, CT 06437; **Phone:** 203-453-1088; **Med School:** Harvard Med Sch 1981; **Resid:** Orthopaedic Surgery, Stanford Univ Affil Hosp 1986; **Fellow:** Pediatric Orthopaedic Surgery, Mass Genl Hosp 1987; **Fac Appt:** Assoc Prof OrS, Yale Univ

Medvecky, Michael J MD [OrS] - **Spec Exp:** Sports Medicine; Shoulder Surgery; Rotator Cuff Surgery; **Hospital:** Yale-New Haven Hosp; **Address:** 800 Howard Ave Fl 1, New Haven, CT 06520; **Phone:** 203-785-3851; **Board Cert:** Orthopaedic Surgery 2003; Orthopaedic Sports Medicine 2007; **Med School:** NY Med Coll 1995; **Resid:** Surgery, NYU Med Ctr 1996; Orthopaedic Surgery, NYU (Hosp for Joint Diseases) 2000; **Fellow:** Sports Medicine, Cincinnati Sports Med & Ortho ctr 2001

Minas, Tom MD [OrS] - **Spec Exp:** Arthroscopic Surgery; Cartilage Damage & Transplant; Joint Replacement; **Hospital:** Brigham & Women's Hosp; **Address:** Brigham & Women's Hosp, Dept Orthopaedic Surgery, 850 Boylston St, Ste 112, Chestnut Hill, MA 02467; **Phone:** 617-732-9967; **Board Cert:** Orthopaedic Surgery 2008; **Med School:** Univ Toronto 1982; **Resid:** Orthopaedic Surgery, Univ Toronto Affil Hosp 1988; **Fellow:** Orthopaedic Surgery, Sunnybrook Univ Affil Hosp 1989; Joint Reconstruction, Brigham & Womens Hosp 1990; **Fac Appt:** Assoc Prof OrS, Harvard Med Sch

Parazin, Stephen J MD [OrS] - **Spec Exp:** Spinal Surgery; Scoliosis; Minimally Invasive Spinal Surgery; **Hospital:** New England Bapt Hosp (page 63); **Address:** New England Orthopaedic & Spine Surgery, 830 Boylston St, Ste 211, Chestnut Hill, MA 02467; **Phone:** 617-734-2450; **Board Cert:** Orthopaedic Surgery 2012; **Med School:** UC Irvine 1993; **Resid:** Orthopaedic Surgery, New England Med Ctr 1998

Ready, John E MD [OrS] - **Spec Exp:** Bone Cancer; Sarcoma-Soft Tissue; Hip & Knee Replacement in Bone Tumors; Hip & Knee Replacement; **Hospital:** Brigham & Women's Hosp, Dana-Farber Cancer Inst; **Address:** Brigham & Women's Hospital, Dept of Orthopedic Surgery, 75 Francis St, Boston, MA 02115; **Phone:** 617-732-5368; **Board Cert:** Orthopaedic Surgery 2012; **Med School:** Dalhousie Univ 1982; **Resid:** Orthopaedic Surgery, Dalhousie Univ Hosp 1987; **Fellow:** Orthopaedic Oncology, St Michael's Hosp 1988; Orthopaedic Oncology, Mass Genl Hosp/Childns Hosp 1989

Reilly, Donald T MD [OrS] - **Spec Exp:** Knee Replacement; Hip Replacement; **Hospital:** New England Bapt Hosp (page 63); **Address:** Pro Sports Orthopaedics, 20 Guest St, Ste 225, Brighton, MA 02135; **Phone:** 617-738-8642; **Board Cert:** Orthopaedic Surgery 1984; **Med School:** Case West Res Univ 1975; **Resid:** Orthopaedic Surgery, Harvard Combined Ortho 1981

Scott, Richard D MD [OrS] - **Spec Exp:** Knee Replacement; **Hospital:** New England Bapt Hosp (page 63); **Address:** New England Baptist Hosp, 125 Parker Hill Ave, Boston, MA 02120; **Phone:** 617-738-9151; **Board Cert:** Orthopaedic Surgery 1975; **Med School:** Temple Univ 1968; **Resid:** Orthopaedic Surgery, Mass Genl Hosp 1974; **Fellow:** Orthopaedic Surgery, Mass Genl Hosp 1974; Arthritis Surgery, Brigham & Women's Hosp 1975; **Fac Appt:** Prof OrS, Harvard Med Sch

Sethi, Paul MD [OrS] - **Spec Exp:** Sports Medicine; Knee Injuries; Shoulder Injuries; Fractures; **Hospital:** Greenwich Hosp; **Address:** Orthopaedic & Neurosurgery Specialists, 6 Greenwich Office Park, 10 Valley Drive, Greenwich, CT 06831; **Phone:** 203-869-1145; **Board Cert:** Orthopaedic Surgery 2005; Orthopaedic Sports Medicine 2007; **Med School:** Mount Sinai Sch Med 1997; **Resid:** Orthopaedic Surgery, Yale-New Haven Hosp 2002; **Fellow:** Sports Medicine, Kerlan Jobe Ortho Clin 2003; Arthroscopic Surgery, Kerlan Jobe Ortho Clin 2004

Smith, Eric L MD [OrS] - **Spec Exp:** Hip & Knee Reconstruction; Hip & Knee Replacement; Trauma; **Hospital:** Tufts Med Ctr, New England Bapt Hosp (page 63); **Address:** Tufts Medical Center, 800 Washington St, Box 306, Boston, MA 02111; **Phone:** 617-636-5160; **Board Cert:** Orthopaedic Surgery 2004; **Med School:** Tulane Univ 1996; **Resid:** Orthopaedic Surgery, Tripler Army Med Ctr 2002; **Fellow:** Adult Reconstructive Surgery, New England Baptist Hosp 2007; **Fac Appt:** Asst Prof OrS, Tufts Univ

Thornhill, Thomas S MD [OrS] - **Spec Exp:** Hip & Knee Replacement; Arthritis; Shoulder & Elbow Surgery; Joint Replacement; **Hospital:** Brigham & Women's Hosp; **Address:** Brigham & Women's Hosp, Dept Orthopaedic Surgery, 75 Francis St, Boston, MA 02115; **Phone:** 617-732-5383; **Board Cert:** Internal Medicine 1973; Orthopaedic Surgery 1979; **Med School:** Cornell Univ-Weill Med Coll 1970; **Resid:** Internal Medicine, Brigham & Women's Hosp 1972; Orthopaedic Surgery, Mass Genl Hosp 1978; **Fellow:** Joint Replacement Surgery, Brigham & Women's Hosp 1979; **Fac Appt:** Prof OrS, Harvard Med Sch

Tornetta III, Paul MD [OrS] - **Spec Exp:** Trauma; Fractures-Complex; Minimally Invasive Surgery; Fractures in the Elderly; **Hospital:** Boston Med Ctr; **Address:** Boston Univ Orthopaedic Surgical Assocs, 725 Albany St, Shapiro Bldg Fl 4 - Ste 4B, Boston, MA 02118; **Phone:** 617-414-4865; **Board Cert:** Orthopaedic Surgery 2006; **Med School:** SUNY Downstate 1987; **Resid:** Orthopaedic Surgery, Downstate Med Ctr 1992; **Fellow:** Trauma, Good Samaritan Hosp 1993; **Fac Appt:** Prof OrS, Boston Univ

Weinstein, James DO [OrS] - **Spec Exp:** Pain-Back; Spinal Tumors; **Hospital:** Dartmouth - Hitchcock Med Ctr; **Address:** DHMC, Dept Orthopaedic Surgery, One Medical Ctr Drive, Lebanon, NH 03756; **Phone:** 603-650-2225; **Board Cert:** Orthopaedic Surgery 2002; **Med School:** Chicago Coll Osteo Med 1973; **Resid:** Orthopaedic Surgery, Rush Presby-St Lukes Med Ctr 1983; **Fac Appt:** Prof OrS, Dartmouth Med Sch

Zarins, Bertram MD [OrS] - **Spec Exp:** Knee Injuries/ACL; Rotator Cuff Surgery; Cartilage Damage; Shoulder Injuries; **Hospital:** Mass Genl Hosp; **Address:** MGH Sports Medicine, 175 Cambridge St, Ste 400, Boston, MA 02114; **Phone:** 617-726-3421; **Board Cert:** Orthopaedic Surgery 1994; **Med School:** SUNY Upstate Med Univ 1967; **Resid:** Surgery, Johns Hopkins Hosp 1969; Orthopaedic Surgery, Harvard Ortho Prog 1973; **Fellow:** Sports Medicine, Mass Genl Hosp 1976; **Fac Appt:** Clin Prof OrS, Harvard Med Sch

Mid Atlantic

Aboulafia, Albert J MD [OrS] - **Spec Exp:** Soft Tissue Tumors; Limb Sparing Surgery; Bone Tumors; Sarcoma; **Hospital:** Sinai Hosp - Baltimore, Univ of MD Med Ctr; **Address:** Alvin & Lois Lapidus Cancer Inst, 2401 W Belvedere Ave, Baltimore, MD 21215; **Phone:** 410-601-9266; **Board Cert:** Orthopaedic Surgery 2004; **Med School:** Univ Mich Med Sch 1985; **Resid:** Orthopaedic Surgery, LAC/USC Sch Med Affil Hosp 1990; **Fellow:** Orthopaedic Oncology, Chldn's Natl Med Ctr/NIH 1991; **Fac Appt:** Asst Prof OrS, Univ MD Sch Med

Ahmad, Christopher S MD [OrS] - **Spec Exp:** Sports Medicine; Knee Injuries/ACL; Pediatric Orthopaedic Surgery; Shoulder and Elbow Surgery; **Hospital:** NY-Presby/Columbia Univ Med Ctr, NY (page 65); **Address:** 161 Fort Washington Ave, Fl 2, New York, NY 10032; **Phone:** 212-305-4565; **Board Cert:** Orthopaedic Surgery 2003; Orthopaedic Sports Medicine 2007; **Med School:** NYU Sch Med 1994; **Resid:** Orthopaedic Surgery, NY Orthopaedic Hosp/Columbia 2000; **Fellow:** Sports Medicine, Kerlan-Jobe Orthopaedic Clinic 2001; **Fac Appt:** Assoc Prof OrS, Columbia P&S

Albert, Todd J MD [OrS] - **Spec Exp:** Spinal Surgery; Spinal Surgery-Cervical; Spinal Deformity; **Hospital:** Thomas Jefferson Univ Hosp; **Address:** Rothman Inst, Spine Surgery, 925 Chesnut St, Fl 5, Philadelphia, PA 19107; **Phone:** 800-321-9999; **Board Cert:** Orthopaedic Surgery 2006; **Med School:** Univ VA Sch Med 1987; **Resid:** Orthopaedic Surgery, Thomas Jefferson Univ Hosp 1992; **Fellow:** Spine Surgery, Minnesota Spine Ctr 1993; **Fac Appt:** Prof OrS, Thomas Jefferson Univ

Balderston, Richard A MD [OrS] - **Spec Exp:** Spinal Disc Replacement; Spinal Disorders-Degenerative; Scoliosis; Spinal Microdiscectomy; **Hospital:** Aria Hlth - Bucks County; **Address:** Aria 3B Orthopedic Institute, Curtis Center, 6th & Walnut Streets, Philadelphia, PA 19106; **Phone:** 215-269-9306; **Board Cert:** Orthopaedic Surgery 1985; **Med School:** Univ Pennsylvania 1977; **Resid:** Orthopaedic Surgery, Pennsylvania Hosp 1983; **Fellow:** Spine Surgery, Univ Minn 1985

Bartolozzi, Arthur R MD [OrS] - **Spec Exp:** Knee Replacement & Revision; Arthroscopic Surgery-Knee; Knee Ligament Reconstruction; Sports Medicine; **Hospital:** Aria Hlth - Bucks County; **Address:** Aria 3B Orthopaedic Inst, Curtis Ctr, 601 Walnut St, Ste L44, Philadelphia, PA 19106; **Phone:** 215-409-9330; **Board Cert:** Orthopaedic Surgery 2010; **Med School:** UCSD 1981; **Resid:** Orthopaedic Surgery, Pennsylvania Hosp 1986; **Fellow:** Sports Medicine, UCLA Med Ctr 1987

Bauman, Phillip A MD [OrS] - **Spec Exp:** Foot & Ankle Surgery; Knee Surgery; Dance/Sports Medicine; Arthroscopic Surgery; **Hospital:** St. Luke's - Roosevelt Hosp Ctr - Roosevelt Div (page 56); **Address:** Orthopaedic Associates of NY, 343 W 58th St, Ste 1, New York, NY 10019; **Phone:** 212-506-0228; **Board Cert:** Orthopaedic Surgery 2011; **Med School:** Columbia P&S 1981; **Resid:** Surgery, St Lukes-Roosevelt Hosp Ctr 1983; Orthopaedic Surgery, Columbia-Presby Med Ctr 1987; **Fac Appt:** Asst Prof OrS, Columbia P&S

Benevenia, Joseph MD [OrS] - **Spec Exp:** Limb Sparing Surgery; Bone Cancer; Sarcoma-Soft Tissue; **Hospital:** Univ Hosp (Newark); **Address:** 140 Bergen St, Ste ACC1610, Newark, NJ 07103; **Phone:** 973-972-2153; **Board Cert:** Orthopaedic Surgery 2013; **Med School:** UMDNJ-NJ Med Sch, Newark 1984; **Resid:** Orthopaedic Surgery, UMDNJ-NJ Med Sch Hosp 1988; **Fellow:** Orthopaedic Oncology, Case Western Reserve Univ 1991; **Fac Appt:** Prof OrS, UMDNJ-NJ Med Sch, Newark

Betz, Randal R MD [OrS] - **Spec Exp:** Spinal Cord Injury-Pediatric; Praxis Functional Electrical Stim (FES); Scoliosis; Spinal Deformity-Pediatric; **Hospital:** Philadelphia Shriners Hosp; **Address:** Shriners Hosp for Chldn, Orthopaedics, 3551 N Broad St, Philadelphia, PA 19140; **Phone:** 215-430-4233; **Board Cert:** Orthopaedic Surgery 1985; Spinal Cord Injury Medicine 2008; **Med School:** Temple Univ 1977; **Resid:** Orthopaedic Surgery, Shriners Hosp 1980; Orthopaedic Surgery, Temple Univ Hosp 1982; **Fellow:** Pediatric Orthopaedic Surgery, duPont Hosp Chldn 1983; **Fac Appt:** Prof OrS, Temple Univ

Bigliani, Louis U MD [OrS] - **Spec Exp:** Shoulder Surgery; Sports Medicine; Arthroscopic Surgery; Rotator Cuff Surgery; **Hospital:** NY-Presby/Columbia Univ Med Ctr, NY (page 65); **Address:** Presby/Columbia Univ Med Ctr-Dept Ortho Surg, 622 W 168 St, rm 1130, New York, NY 10032-3720; **Phone:** 212-305-0998; **Board Cert:** Orthopaedic Surgery 1979; **Med School:** Loyola Univ-Stritch Sch Med 1973; **Resid:** Surgery, St Luke's-Roosevelt Hosp Ctr 1974; Orthopaedic Surgery, NY-Presby/Columbia Univ Med Ctr 1978; **Fac Appt:** Prof OrS, Columbia P&S

Bitan, Fabien D MD [OrS] - **Spec Exp:** Spinal Surgery-Pediatric & Adult; Spinal Disc Replacement; Spinal Deformity; Spinal Disorders-Degenerative; **Hospital:** Lenox Hill Hosp (page 66), Beth Israel Med Ctr - Petrie Div (page 56); **Address:** Manhattan Orthopaedics, 130 E 77th St Fl 7, New York, NY 10075; **Phone:** 212-744-8114; **Med School:** France 1981; **Resid:** Orthopaedic Surgery, Hospital Beaujon 1987; Pediatric Orthopaedic Surgery, Hosp des Enfants Malades 1996; **Fellow:** Pediatric Orthopaedic Surgery, Hosp Special Surgery 1997; Spine Surgery, Beth Israel Med Ctr 1998

Boachie-Adjei, Oheneba MD [OrS] - **Spec Exp:** Spinal Surgery; Scoliosis; Spinal Reconstructive Surgery; **Hospital:** Hosp For Special Surgery (page 58); **Address:** Hosp for Special Surgery, 535 E 70th St, New York, NY 10021; **Phone:** 212-606-1948; **Board Cert:** Orthopaedic Surgery 2010; **Med School:** Columbia P&S 1980; **Resid:** Surgery, St Vincents Hosp 1982; Orthopaedic Surgery, Hosp Spec Surg 1986; **Fellow:** Orthopaedic Pathology, Hosp Spec Surg 1983; Spine Surgery, Twin Cities Scoliosis Ctr/Minn Spine Ctr 1987; **Fac Appt:** Prof OrS, Cornell Univ-Weill Med Coll

Booth Jr, Robert E MD [OrS] - **Spec Exp:** Knee Replacement & Revision; Knee Ligament Reconstruction; **Hospital:** Aria Hlth - Bucks County; **Address:** Aria 3B Orthopaedic Inst, Curtis Ctr, 601 Walnut St, Ste L44, Philadelphia, PA 19106; **Phone:** 215-409-9330; **Board Cert:** Orthopaedic Surgery 1978; **Med School:** Univ Pennsylvania 1971; **Resid:** Orthopaedic Surgery, Pennsylvania Hosp 1977; **Fac Appt:** Assoc Clin Prof OrS, Univ Pennsylvania

Bostrom, Mathias P MD [OrS] - **Spec Exp:** Knee Replacement & Revision; Hip Replacement & Revision; Hip & Knee Reconstruction; Musculoskeletal Infections; **Hospital:** Hosp For Special Surgery (page 58), NY-Presby/Weill Cornell Med Ctr, NY (page 65); **Address:** 535 E 70th St Fl 3, New York, NY 10021; **Phone:** 212-606-1674; **Board Cert:** Orthopaedic Surgery 2009; **Med School:** Johns Hopkins Univ 1989; **Resid:** Orthopaedic Surgery, Hosp for Special Surg 1995; **Fellow:** Reconstructive Surgery, Hosp for Special Surg 1996; **Fac Appt:** Prof OrS, Cornell Univ-Weill Med Coll

Bronson, Michael J MD [OrS] - **Spec Exp:** Joint Replacement; Knee Replacement; Hip Replacement; Arthritis; **Hospital:** Mt Sinai Med Ctr (page 62); **Address:** Mt Sinai Med Ctr, Dept Orthopedic Surg, 5 E 98th St, Box 1188, New York, NY 10029; **Phone:** 212-241-1640; **Board Cert:** Orthopaedic Surgery 1984; **Med School:** NY Med Coll 1976; **Resid:** Orthopaedic Surgery, Lenox Hill Hosp 1980; **Fellow:** Joint Replacement Surgery, NY Presby/Columbia Med Ctr 1981; Hip & Knee Surgery, NY Presby/Columbia Med Ctr 1981; **Fac Appt:** Assoc Prof OrS, Mount Sinai Sch Med

Buly, Robert L MD [OrS] - **Spec Exp:** Hip Replacement & Revision; Arthroscopic Surgery-Hip; Knee Replacement; Arthritis; **Hospital:** Hosp For Special Surgery (page 58), NY-Presby/Weill Cornell Med Ctr, NY (page 65); **Address:** Hospital for Special Surgery, 535 E 70th St, New York, NY 10021; **Phone:** 212-606-1971; **Board Cert:** Orthopaedic Surgery 2004; **Med School:** Cornell Univ-Weill Med Coll 1985; **Resid:** Orthopaedic Surgery, Hosp for Special Surg 1990; **Fellow:** Hip Surgery, Mueller Fdn 1991; Joint Reconstruction, Case Western Res/Univ Hosp 1992; **Fac Appt:** Assoc Clin Prof OrS, Cornell Univ-Weill Med Coll

Cammisa Jr, Frank P MD [OrS] - **Spec Exp:** Spinal Surgery; Spinal Disc Replacement; Minimally Invasive Spinal Surgery; Scoliosis; **Hospital:** Hosp For Special Surgery (page 58); **Address:** 523 E 72nd St, Fl 3, New York, NY 10021; **Phone:** 212-606-1946; **Board Cert:** Orthopaedic Surgery 2011; **Med School:** Columbia P&S 1982; **Resid:** Surgery, Columbia-Presby Hosp 1983; Orthopaedic Surgery, Hosp for Special Surgery 1987; **Fellow:** Spine Surgery, Jackson Meml Hosp 1988; **Fac Appt:** Assoc Prof OrS, Cornell Univ-Weill Med Coll

Cappuccino, Andrew MD [OrS] - **Spec Exp:** Spinal Surgery; Spinal Disc Replacement; Minimally Invasive Spinal Surgery; **Hospital:** Eastern Niagara Hosp-Lockport; **Address:** Buffalo Spine Surgery, 46 Davison Ct, Lockport, NY 14094; **Phone:** 716-438-2973; **Board Cert:** Orthopaedic Surgery 2007; Spine Surgery 2013; **Med School:** SUNY Buffalo 1988; **Resid:** Orthopaedic Surgery, Monmouth Med Ctr 1993; Pediatric Orthopaedic Surgery, Chldns Hosp 1992; **Fellow:** Spine Surgery, Johns Hopkins Hosp 1994

Cornell, Charles N MD [OrS] - **Spec Exp:** Hip Replacement; Knee Replacement; **Hospital:** Hosp For Special Surgery (page 58); **Address:** 535 E 70th St, Ste 306, New York, NY 10021; **Phone:** 212-606-1414; **Board Cert:** Orthopaedic Surgery 2009; **Med School:** Cornell Univ-Weill Med Coll 1980; **Resid:** Surgery, Presby Hosp 1982; Orthopaedic Surgery, Hosp For Special Surgery 1985; **Fellow:** Orthopaedic Trauma Surgery, Univ Washington Med Ctr 1986; **Fac Appt:** Clin Prof OrS, Cornell Univ-Weill Med Coll

Craig, Edward V MD [OrS] - **Spec Exp:** Shoulder Arthroscopic Surgery; Shoulder Replacement; Sports Medicine; Elbow Surgery; **Hospital:** Hosp For Special Surgery (page 58), NY-Presby/Weill Cornell Med Ctr, NY (page 65); **Address:** 535 E 70th St, New York, NY 10021; **Phone:** 212-606-1966; **Board Cert:** Orthopaedic Surgery 1984; **Med School:** Columbia P&S 1972; **Resid:** Surgery, St Lukes-Roosevelt Hosp 1976; Orthopaedic Surgery, Columbia-Presby Hosp 1980; **Fellow:** Shoulder Surgery, Columbia-Presby Hosp 1981; Hand Surgery, Columbia-Presby Hosp 1982; **Fac Appt:** Clin Prof OrS, Cornell Univ-Weill Med Coll

Crossett, Lawrence MD [OrS] - **Spec Exp:** Hip Surgery; Knee Surgery; **Hospital:** UPMC Shadyside, UPMC Presby, Pittsburgh; **Address:** UPMC, Joint Reconstruction Ctr, 5200 Centre Ave, Ste 415, Pittsburgh, PA 15232; **Phone:** 412-802-4100; **Board Cert:** Orthopaedic Surgery 2010; **Med School:** Temple Univ 1981; **Resid:** Orthopaedic Surgery, Temple Univ Hosp 1986; Orthopaedic Surgery, Shriners Chldns Hosp 1984; **Fac Appt:** Asst Prof OrS, Univ Pittsburgh

Davidson, Richard S MD [OrS] - **Spec Exp:** Limb Lengthening (Ilizarov Procedure); Limb Deformities; Foot Deformities; Clubfoot; **Hospital:** Chldns Hosp of Philadelphia; **Address:** Chldns Hosp, Orthopaedic Surgery Dept, 34th St & Civic Ctr Blvd Wood Bldg Fl 2, Philadelphia, PA 19104; **Phone:** 215-590-1527; **Board Cert:** Orthopaedic Surgery 2007; **Med School:** NYU Sch Med 1976; **Resid:** Orthopaedic Surgery, Hosp Special Surgery 1981; **Fellow:** Pediatric Orthopaedic Surgery, Hosp Sick Chldn 1982; **Fac Appt:** Prof OrS, Univ Pennsylvania

Delahay, John N MD [OrS] - **Spec Exp:** Pediatric Orthopaedic Surgery; Trauma; **Hospital:** MedStar Georgetown Univ Hosp; **Address:** Pasquerilla Hlthcare Ctr, 3800 Reservoir Rd NW, Ground Fl, Washington, DC 20007; **Phone:** 202-444-1438; **Board Cert:** Orthopaedic Surgery 1975; **Med School:** Georgetown Univ 1969; **Resid:** Orthopaedic Surgery, MedStar Georgetown Univ Hosp 1975; **Fac Appt:** Prof OrS, Georgetown Univ

Deland, Jonathan T MD [OrS] - **Spec Exp:** Foot & Ankle Surgery; Sports Medicine; Arthritis; **Hospital:** Hosp For Special Surgery (page 58); **Address:** Hosp Spec Surg-Dept Foot & Ankle Service, 535 E 70th St, New York, NY 10021-4099; **Phone:** 212-606-1665; **Board Cert:** Orthopaedic Surgery 2013; **Med School:** Columbia P&S 1980; **Resid:** Surgery, St Luke's-Roosevelt Hosp Ctr 1982; Orthopaedic Surgery, Mass Genl Hosp 1987; **Fellow:** Foot & Ankle Surgery, St Luke's-Roosevelt Hosp 1988; Trauma, Mass Genl Hosp 1989; **Fac Appt:** Clin Prof S, Cornell Univ-Weill Med Coll

Dines, David M MD [OrS] - **Spec Exp:** Shoulder Arthroscopic Surgery; Shoulder Surgery; Shoulder Replacement; Sports Medicine; **Hospital:** Long Is Jewish Med Ctr (page 66), Hosp For Special Surgery (page 58); **Address:** 333 Earl Ovington Blvd, Ste 106, Uniondale, NY 11553; **Phone:** 516-482-1037; **Board Cert:** Orthopaedic Surgery 1980; **Med School:** UMDNJ-NJ Med Sch, Newark 1974; **Resid:** Surgery, NY Hosp-Cornell Med Ctr 1976; Orthopaedic Surgery, Hosp Special Surg 1979; **Fac Appt:** Clin Prof OrS, Albert Einstein Coll Med

Donaldson III, William F MD [OrS] - **Spec Exp:** Spinal Surgery; **Hospital:** UPMC Presby, Pittsburgh; **Address:** UPMC, Orthopaedic Surgery Dept, 3471 5th Ave, Ste 1010, Pittsburgh, PA 15213; **Phone:** 412-605-3218; **Board Cert:** Orthopaedic Surgery 2009; **Med School:** Rush Med Coll 1980; **Resid:** Surgery, Rush Presby-St Lukes Med Ctr 1981; Orthopaedic Surgery, Hosp Special Surgery 1985; **Fellow:** Spine Surgery, Hosp Special Surgery 1986; **Fac Appt:** Prof OrS, Univ Pittsburgh

Dormans, John P MD [OrS] - **Spec Exp:** Bone Cancer; Spinal Surgery-Pediatric; Pediatric Orthopaedic Surgery; Scoliosis; **Hospital:** Chldns Hosp of Philadelphia; **Address:** Childrens Hosp Phila-Orthopaedic Surg, 34th St & Civic Center Blvd, Wood Bldg Fl 2, Philadelphia, PA 19104-4399; **Phone:** 215-590-1527; **Board Cert:** Orthopaedic Surgery 2012; **Med School:** Indiana Univ 1983; **Resid:** Orthopaedic Surgery, Michigan State Univ Hosps 1988; **Fellow:** Pediatric Orthopaedic Surgery, Hosp for Sick Children 1989; **Fac Appt:** Prof OrS, Univ Pennsylvania

Errico, Thomas J MD [OrS] - **Spec Exp:** Spinal Surgery; Pediatric Orthopaedic Surgery; Scoliosis; **Hospital:** NYU Langone Med Ctr (page 68), NYU Hosp For Joint Dis; **Address:** Ctr for Musculoskeletal Care, 333 E 38th St Fl 6, MS 10016, New York, NY 10016-6402; **Phone:** 646-501-7200; **Board Cert:** Orthopaedic Surgery 2007; **Med School:** UMDNJ-NJ Med Sch, Newark 1978; **Resid:** Orthopaedic Surgery, NYU Med Ctr 1983; **Fellow:** Spine Surgery, Toronto Genl Hosp 1984; **Fac Appt:** Prof OrS, NYU Sch Med

Farmer, James C MD [OrS] - **Spec Exp:** Spinal Disorders-Degenerative; Trauma; Spinal Surgery; **Hospital:** Hosp For Special Surgery (page 58); **Address:** Hosp for Special Surgery, 523 E 72nd St Fl 3, East River Professional Bldg, New York, NY 10021; **Phone:** 212-606-1591; **Board Cert:** Orthopaedic Surgery 2007; **Med School:** Georgetown Univ 1988; **Resid:** Orthopaedic Surgery, Hosp Univ Penn 1993; **Fellow:** Spine Surgery, Thos Jefferson Univ Hosp 1994; **Fac Appt:** Assoc Prof OrS, Cornell Univ-Weill Med Coll

Feldman, David S MD [OrS] - **Spec Exp:** Limb Deformities; Spinal Surgery; Pediatric Orthopaedic Surgery; Scoliosis; **Hospital:** NYU Hosp For Joint Dis, NYU Langone Med Ctr (page 68); **Address:** 67 Irving Pl Fl 8, New York, NY 10003; **Phone:** 212-533-5310; **Board Cert:** Orthopaedic Surgery 2007; **Med School:** Albert Einstein Coll Med 1988; **Resid:** Surgery, NYU Med Ctr 1989; Orthopaedic Surgery, Hosp for Joint Diseases 1993; **Fellow:** Pediatric Surgery, Hosp For Sick Chldn 1994; **Fac Appt:** Prof OrS, NYU Sch Med

Flatow, Evan L MD [OrS] - **Spec Exp:** Rotator Cuff Surgery; Shoulder Injuries; Shoulder Replacement; Shoulder Arthroscopic Surgery; **Hospital:** Mt Sinai Med Ctr (page 62); **Address:** 5 E 98th St, Fl 9, Box 1188, New York, NY 10029; **Phone:** 212-241-1663; **Board Cert:** Orthopaedic Surgery 2010; **Med School:** Columbia P&S 1981; **Resid:** Surgery, Roosevelt Hosp 1983; Orthopaedic Surgery, Columbia-Presby Med Ctr 1986; **Fellow:** Shoulder Surgery, Columbia-Presby Med Ctr 1987; **Fac Appt:** Prof OrS, Mount Sinai Sch Med

Frassica, Frank J MD [OrS] - **Spec Exp:** Bone Cancer; Bone Tumors; Multiple Myeloma; Paget's Disease of Bone; **Hospital:** Johns Hopkins Hosp (page 59), Johns Hopkins Bayview Med Ctr (page 59); **Address:** Johns Hopkins Hosp-Ortho Dept., 601 N Caroline St, Ste 5253, Baltimore, MD 21287; **Phone:** 410-502-2698; **Board Cert:** Orthopaedic Surgery 2011; **Med School:** Univ SC Sch Med 1982; **Resid:** Orthopaedic Surgery, Mayo Clinic 1988; **Fellow:** Orthopaedic Oncology, Mayo Clinic 1989; **Fac Appt:** Prof OrS, Johns Hopkins Univ

Gladstone, James N MD [OrS] - **Spec Exp:** Shoulder & Knee Surgery; Cartilage Damage; Knee-Patella Problems; Arthritis; **Hospital:** Mt Sinai Med Ctr (page 62); **Address:** Mt Sinai Med Ctr, 5 E 98th St Fl 9, Box 1188, New York, NY 10029; **Phone:** 212-241-1645; **Board Cert:** Orthopaedic Surgery 2009; Orthopaedic Sports Medicine 2007; **Med School:** Tufts Univ 1990; **Resid:** Orthopaedic Surgery, Columbia-Presby Med Ctr 1995; **Fellow:** Sports Medicine, American Sports Med Inst 1996; **Fac Appt:** Assoc Prof OrS, Mount Sinai Sch Med

Glashow, Jonathan L MD [OrS] - **Spec Exp:** Sports Medicine; Shoulder Surgery; Knee Surgery; Arthroscopic Surgery; **Hospital:** Mt Sinai Med Ctr (page 62); **Address:** 737 Park Ave, Ste 1C, New York, NY 10021; **Phone:** 212-794-5096; **Board Cert:** Orthopaedic Surgery 2004; **Med School:** Cornell Univ-Weill Med Coll 1984; **Resid:** Surgery, Mt Sinai Hosp 1985; Orthopaedic Surgery, Lenox Hill Hosp 1989; **Fellow:** Arthroscopic Surgery, S CA Ortho Inst/UCLA Med Ctr 1990; Shoulder Surgery, Univ Texas Med Ctr 1990; **Fac Appt:** Assoc Clin Prof OrS, Mount Sinai Sch Med

Goldstein, Jeffrey A MD [OrS] - **Spec Exp:** Spinal Surgery; Minimally Invasive Spinal Surgery; Spinal Disc Replacement; Scoliosis; **Hospital:** NYU Hosp For Joint Dis, NYU Langone Med Ctr (page 68); **Address:** NYU Hospital for Joint Diseases, 19 Beekman St, New York, NY 10038; **Phone:** 212-513-7711; **Board Cert:** Orthopaedic Surgery 2009; **Med School:** SUNY Downstate 1990; **Resid:** Orthopaedic Surgery, Case West Univ Med Ctr 1995; **Fellow:** Spine Surgery, Maryland Spine Ctr 1996; **Fac Appt:** Clin Prof OrS, NYU Sch Med

Greisberg, Justin K MD [OrS] - **Spec Exp:** Foot & Ankle Surgery-Complex; Ankle Replacement & Revision; Reconstructive Surgery; Trauma; **Hospital:** NY-Presby/Columbia Univ Med Ctr, NY (page 65); **Address:** Presby/Columbia Univ Med Ctr-Dept Ortho Surg, 622 W 168 St Fl PH 11 - rm 1153, New York, NY 10032; **Phone:** 212-305-5604; **Board Cert:** Orthopaedic Surgery 2004; **Med School:** Albert Einstein Coll Med 1995; **Resid:** Surgery, Brown Univ Affil Hosp 1996; Orthopaedic Surgery, Rhode Island Hosp 2000; **Fellow:** Orthopaedic Trauma Surgery, Rhode Island Hosp 2001; Foot & Ankle Surgery, Harborview Med Ctr 2002; **Fac Appt:** Assoc Clin Prof OrS, Columbia P&S

Grelsamer, Ronald P MD [OrS] - **Spec Exp:** Knee-Patella Problems Consult; Arthritis-Hip & Knee; **Hospital:** Mt Sinai Med Ctr (page 62); **Address:** 303 2nd Ave, Ste 19, Ground Floor, New York, NY 10003; **Phone:** 646-704-4158; **Board Cert:** Orthopaedic Surgery 2008; **Med School:** Columbia P&S 1979; **Resid:** Orthopaedic Surgery, Columbia Presby Med Ctr 1984; **Fellow:** Hip & Knee Surgery, Columbia Presby Med Ctr 1985; **Fac Appt:** Assoc Prof OrS, Mount Sinai Sch Med

Haas, Steven B MD [OrS] - **Spec Exp:** Knee Surgery; Knee Replacement; Minimally Invasive Knee Replacement; **Hospital:** Hosp For Special Surgery (page 58); **Address:** Hosp for Special Surgery, 535 E 70th St, Fl 3, New York, NY 10021; **Phone:** 212-606-1852; **Board Cert:** Orthopaedic Surgery 2004; **Med School:** Univ Rochester 1985; **Resid:** Orthopaedic Surgery, Hosp Special Surgery 1990; **Fellow:** Knee Surgery, Hosp Special Surgery 1991; **Fac Appt:** Clin Prof OrS, Cornell Univ-Weill Med Coll

Hannafin, Jo Ann MD/PhD [OrS] - **Spec Exp:** Sports Medicine-Women; Shoulder Arthroscopic Surgery; Knee Injuries/Ligament Surgery; Ligament Reconstruction; **Hospital:** Hosp For Special Surgery (page 58), NY-Presby/Weill Cornell Med Ctr, NY (page 65); **Address:** 523 E 72nd St, Fl 6, New York, NY 10021-4872; **Phone:** 212-606-1469; **Board Cert:** Orthopaedic Surgery 2005; Orthopaedic Sports Medicine 2009; **Med School:** Albert Einstein Coll Med 1985; **Resid:** Orthopaedic Surgery, Montefiore Med Ctr 1990; **Fellow:** Sports Medicine, Hosp Special Surgery 1992; **Fac Appt:** Prof OrS, Cornell Univ-Weill Med Coll

Hausman, Michael R MD [OrS] - **Spec Exp:** Hand Reconstruction; Elbow Reconstruction; Reconstructive Microvascular Surgery; Arthroscopic Surgery; **Hospital:** Mt Sinai Med Ctr (page 62); **Address:** 5 E 98th St, Fl 9, Box 1188, New York, NY 10029-6501; **Phone:** 212-241-1658; **Board Cert:** Orthopaedic Surgery 2010; Hand Surgery 2010; **Med School:** Yale Univ 1979; **Resid:** Surgery, Yale-New Haven Hosp 1981; Orthopaedic Surgery, Yale-New Haven Hosp 1985; **Fellow:** Hand Surgery, Roosevelt Hosp 1987; **Fac Appt:** Assoc Clin Prof OrS, Mount Sinai Sch Med

Healey, John H MD [OrS] - **Spec Exp:** Bone Tumors; Hip & Knee Replacement in Bone Tumors; Sarcoma; Sarcoma-Soft Tissue; **Hospital:** Meml Sloan-Kettering Canc Ctr, Hosp For Special Surgery (page 58); **Address:** 1275 York Ave, Ste A342, New York, NY 10065; **Phone:** 212-639-7610; **Board Cert:** Orthopaedic Surgery 2007; **Med School:** Univ VT Coll Med 1978; **Resid:** Orthopaedic Surgery, Hosp Special Surg 1983; **Fellow:** Musculoskeletal Oncology, Meml Sloan Kettering Cancer Ctr 1984; Orthopaedic Surgery, Hosp Special Surgery 1984; **Fac Appt:** Prof OrS, Cornell Univ-Weill Med Coll

Hecht, Andrew MD [OrS] - **Spec Exp:** Spinal Surgery; Minimally Invasive Spinal Surgery; Spinal Surgery-Cervical; Spinal Cord Injury; **Hospital:** Mt Sinai Med Ctr (page 62); **Address:** Mount Sinai Med Ctr, Dept Orthopaedic Surg, 5 E 98th St, Fl 9, Box 1188, New York, NY 10029; **Phone:** 212-241-0735; **Board Cert:** Orthopaedic Surgery 2013; **Med School:** Harvard Med Sch 1994; **Resid:** Orthopaedic Surgery, Mass Genl Hosp 1999; **Fellow:** Spine Surgery, Emory Univ Spine Ctr 2001; **Fac Appt:** Assoc Prof OrS, Mount Sinai Sch Med

Helfet, David L MD [OrS] - **Spec Exp:** Fractures-Complex & Non Union; Deformity Reconstruction; Pelvic & Acetabular Fractures; Fractures-Stress; **Hospital:** Hosp For Special Surgery (page 58), NY-Presby/Weill Cornell Med Ctr, NY (page 65); **Address:** 525 E 71st St Belaire Bldg Fl 2, New York, NY 10021; **Phone:** 212-606-1888; **Board Cert:** Orthopaedic Surgery 1984; **Med School:** South Africa 1975; **Resid:** Surgery, Edendale Hosp 1977; Orthopaedic Surgery, Johns Hopkins Hosp 1981; **Fellow:** Orthopaedic Surgery, Insel Hosp 1981; Orthopaedic Sports Medicine, UCLA Med Ctr 1982; **Fac Appt:** Prof OrS, Cornell Univ-Weill Med Coll

Henshaw, Robert M MD [OrS] - **Spec Exp:** Musculoskeletal Tumors; Bone Tumors; **Hospital:** MedStar Washington Hosp Ctr, Chldns Natl Med Ctr; **Address:** 110 Irving St NW, Ste C2173, Washington, DC 20010; **Phone:** 202-877-3970; **Board Cert:** Orthopaedic Surgery 2010; **Med School:** Tufts Univ 1990; **Resid:** Orthopaedic Surgery, UCLA Ronald Reagan Med Ctr 1996; **Fellow:** Orthopaedic Oncology, MedStar Washington Hosp Ctr 1998; **Fac Appt:** Assoc Prof OrS, Georgetown Univ

Herman, Martin J MD [OrS] - **Spec Exp:** Pediatric Orthopaedic Surgery; Hip Disorders-Pediatric; Scoliosis; Trauma; **Hospital:** St. Christopher's Hosp for Chldn; **Address:** St Christophers Hosp, Orthopaedics, 3601 A St, rm 133-1, Philadelphia, PA 19134; **Phone:** 215-427-3131; **Board Cert:** Orthopaedic Surgery 2009; **Med School:** Columbia P&S 1990; **Resid:** Orthopaedic Surgery, RW Johnson Univ Hosp 1995; **Fellow:** Pediatric Orthopaedic Surgery, Campbell Clin/Univ Tenn 1996; **Fac Appt:** Assoc Prof OrS, Drexel Univ Coll Med

Herzenberg, John E MD [OrS] - **Spec Exp:** Limb Lengthening (Ilizarov Procedure); Limb Deformities; Pediatric Orthopaedic Surgery; Clubfoot; **Hospital:** Sinai Hosp - Baltimore; **Address:** Intl Ctr for Limb Lengthening, 2401 W Belvedere Ave, Sinai Hospital, Baltimore, MD 21215; **Phone:** 410-601-1724; **Board Cert:** Orthopaedic Surgery 2009; **Med School:** Boston Univ 1979; **Resid:** Orthopaedic Surgery, Duke Univ Med Ctr 1985; **Fellow:** Pediatric Orthopaedic Surgery, Hosp for Sick Children 1986; **Fac Appt:** Clin Prof OrS, Univ MD Sch Med

Hilibrand, Alan S MD [OrS] - **Spec Exp:** Spinal Surgery; Spinal Surgery-Cervical; Spinal Trauma; Minimally Invasive Spinal Surgery; **Hospital:** Thomas Jefferson Univ Hosp, Virtua West Jersey Hosp-Marlton; **Address:** Rothman Inst, Spine Surgery, 925 Chestnut St, Fl 5, Philadelphia, PA 19107; **Phone:** 800-321-9999; **Board Cert:** Orthopaedic Surgery 2009; **Med School:** Yale Univ 1990; **Resid:** Orthopaedic Surgery, Univ Michigan Med Ctr 1995; **Fellow:** Spine Surgery, Cleveland Spine Inst 1996; **Fac Appt:** Prof OrS, Jefferson Med Coll

Hozack, William J MD [OrS] - **Spec Exp:** Hip & Knee Replacement; Joint Replacement; **Hospital:** Thomas Jefferson Univ Hosp; **Address:** Rothman Inst, Hip/Knee Surgery, 925 Chesnut St Fl 5, Philadelphia, PA 19107; **Phone:** 800-321-9999; **Board Cert:** Orthopaedic Surgery 2010; **Med School:** McGill Univ 1981; **Resid:** Orthopaedic Surgery, Hosp Univ Penn 1986; **Fellow:** Joint Replacement Surgery, Thomas Jefferson Univ Hosp 1987; **Fac Appt:** Prof OrS, Jefferson Med Coll

Hume, Eric L MD [OrS] - **Spec Exp:** Hip Replacement; Knee Replacement; **Hospital:** Penn Presby Med Ctr - UPHS (page 69); **Address:** Penn Presbyterian Med Ctr, Orthopaedics, 51 N 39th St, 1 Cupp Pav, Philadelphia, PA 19104; **Phone:** 215-662-3340; **Board Cert:** Orthopaedic Surgery 2007; **Med School:** SUNY Upstate Med Univ 1978; **Resid:** Orthopaedic Surgery, Thomas Jefferson Univ Hosp 1983; **Fac Appt:** Assoc Prof OrS, Univ Pennsylvania

Hungerford, Marc W MD [OrS] - **Spec Exp:** Knee Replacement & Revision; Hip Replacement & Revision; Shoulder Arthroscopic Surgery; **Hospital:** Mercy Med Ctr - Baltimore, Johns Hopkins Hosp (page 59); **Address:** Mercy Orthopedics & Joint Replacement, 301 Saint Paul Pl, Baltimore, MD 21202; **Phone:** 410-539-2227; **Board Cert:** Orthopaedic Surgery 2012; **Med School:** Vanderbilt Univ 1992; **Resid:** Orthopaedic Surgery, Johns Hopkins Hosp 1997; **Fac Appt:** Asst Prof OrS, Johns Hopkins Univ

Hyman, Joshua E MD [OrS] - **Spec Exp:** Pediatric Orthopaedic Surgery; Fractures-Pediatric; Scoliosis; Clubfoot/Foot Deformities in Children; **Hospital:** Morgan Stanley Children's Hosp of NY-Presby, NY (page 65), NY-Presby/Columbia Univ Med Ctr, NY (page 65); **Address:** Columbia Orthopedics, 3959 Broadway, Ste 8 North, New York, NY 10032-3784; **Phone:** 212-305-5475; **Board Cert:** Orthopaedic Surgery 2013; **Med School:** Columbia P&S 1990; **Resid:** Surgery, Beth Israel Hosp 1993; Orthopaedic Surgery, Mass Genl Hosp/Beth Israel Hosp 1998; **Fellow:** Pediatric Orthopaedic Surgery, Hosp for Sick Children 1999; **Fac Appt:** Assoc Prof OrS, Columbia P&S

Johanson, Norman A MD [OrS] - **Spec Exp:** Hip Replacement & Revision; Knee Replacement & Revision; Juvenile Arthritis; **Hospital:** Hahnemann Univ Hosp, Abington Meml Hosp; **Address:** Univ Orthopaedic Inst, 216 N Broad St Feinstein Bldg Fl 2, Philadelphia, PA 19102; **Phone:** 215-762-2663; **Board Cert:** Orthopaedic Surgery 2007; **Med School:** Cornell Univ 1978; **Resid:** Orthopaedic Surgery, Hosp Special Surgery 1984; **Fellow:** Orthopaedic Pathology, Hosp Special Surgery 1984; **Fac Appt:** Prof OrS, Drexel Univ Coll Med

Kaplan, Frederick S MD [OrS] - **Spec Exp:** Bone Disorders-Metabolic; Fibrodysplasia Ossificans Progressiv FOP; Progressive Osseous Heteroplasia POH; **Hospital:** Hosp Univ Penn - UPHS (page 69); **Address:** Hosp Univ Penn, Orthopaedic Surgery Dept, 3400 Spruce St, 2 Silverstein Pav, Philadelphia, PA 19104; **Phone:** 215-349-8727; **Med School:** Johns Hopkins Univ 1976; **Resid:** Orthopaedic Surgery, Hosp Univ Penn 1981; **Fellow:** Orthopaedic Research, Hosp Univ Penn 1982; Musculoskeletal Disorders, Dr Michael Zasloff/Univ Penn 1991; **Fac Appt:** Prof OrS, Univ Pennsylvania

Kelly, Bryan T MD [OrS] - **Spec Exp:** Hip Surgery; Arthroscopic Surgery; Sports Medicine; **Hospital:** Hosp For Special Surgery (page 58); **Address:** Ctr for Hip Pain & Preservation, 541 E 71 St Caspary Bldg Fl Ground, New York, NY 10021; **Phone:** 212-606-1159; **Board Cert:** Orthopaedic Surgery 2006; **Med School:** Duke Univ 1996; **Resid:** Surgery, NY-Presby/ Weill Cornell Med Ctr 1997; Orthopaedic Surgery, Hosp Special Surg 2001; **Fellow:** Orthopaedic Sports Medicine, Hosp Special Surg 2003; Hip Sports Injuries/Arthroscopy, Univ Pittsburgh Med Ctr 2004; **Fac Appt:** Assoc Prof OrS, Cornell Univ-Weill Med Coll

Kenan, Samuel MD [OrS] - **Spec Exp:** Bone Tumors; Limb Sparing Surgery; Pediatric Orthopaedic Surgery; Reconstructive Surgery-Complex; **Hospital:** Lenox Hill Hosp (page 66), N Shore Univ Hosp (page 66); **Address:** 1001 Franklin Ave, Ste 110, Garden City, NY 11530; **Phone:** 212-684-5511; **Med School:** Israel 1976; **Resid:** Orthopaedic Surgery, Hadassah Univ Hosp 1984; **Fellow:** Orthopaedic Pathology, Hosp for Joint Diseases 1987; **Fac Appt:** Prof OrS, NYU Sch Med

Krackow, Kenneth A MD [OrS] - **Spec Exp:** Knee Replacement; Knee Reconstruction; Hip Replacement & Revision; Arthroscopic Surgery; **Hospital:** Buffalo Genl Hosp; **Address:** Buffalo Genl Hosp, Dept Orthopaedic Surg, 100 High St, Ste B276, Buffalo, NY 14203; **Phone:** 716-859-1256; **Board Cert:** Orthopaedic Surgery 1993; **Med School:** Duke Univ 1971; **Resid:** Surgery, Johns Hopkins Hosp 1973; Orthopaedic Surgery, Johns Hopkins Hosp 1976; **Fac Appt:** Prof OrS, SUNY Buffalo

Lane, Joseph M MD [OrS] - **Spec Exp:** Bone Tumors-Benign; Bone Tumors-Metastatic; Bone Tumors; Bone Disorders-Metabolic; **Hospital:** Hosp For Special Surgery (page 58), NY-Presby/Weill Cornell Med Ctr, NY (page 65); **Address:** Hosp for Special Surgery-Ortho Surg Dept, 535 E 70th St, New York, NY 10021; **Phone:** 212-606-1172; **Board Cert:** Orthopaedic Surgery 1998; **Med School:** Harvard Med Sch 1965; **Resid:** Surgery, Hosp Univ Penn 1967; Orthopaedic Surgery, Hosp Univ Penn 1973; **Fellow:** Research, NIH 1969; 1970; **Fac Appt:** Prof OrS, Cornell Univ-Weill Med Coll

Lauerman, William C MD [OrS] - **Spec Exp:** Spinal Deformity-Pediatric & Adult; Spinal Surgery; Pain-Back; Scoliosis; **Hospital:** MedStar Georgetown Univ Hosp; **Address:** Spine Surgery Clin, 3800 Reservoir Rd NW, Gorman Bldg, Fl 1, Washington, DC 20007; **Phone:** 202-444-8766 x2; **Board Cert:** Orthopaedic Surgery 2011; **Med School:** Georgetown Univ 1982; **Resid:** Orthopaedic Surgery, Georgetown Univ Med Ctr 1987; **Fellow:** Orthopaedic Surgery, Univ Minn-Twin Cities Scoliosis Ctr 1988; **Fac Appt:** Prof OrS, Georgetown Univ

Leadbetter, Wayne MD [OrS] - **Spec Exp:** Knee-Patella Problems; Arthritis-Knee; **Hospital:** Sinai Hosp - Baltimore; **Address:** Ctr Joint Surgery & Sports Med, 13 Western Maryland Pkwy, Ste 104, Hagerstown, MD 21740; **Phone:** 301-665-4575; **Board Cert:** Orthopaedic Surgery 1977; **Med School:** Creighton Univ 1970; **Resid:** Surgery, Johns Hopkins Hosp 1972; Orthopaedic Surgery, Johns Hopkins Hosp 1976

Lee, Francis Y MD/PhD [OrS] - **Spec Exp:** Bone & Soft Tissue Tumors; Pediatric Orthopaedic Surgery; Bone Tumors-Metastatic; Bone Tumors-Benign; **Hospital:** Morgan Stanley Children's Hosp of NY-Presby, NY (page 65), NY-Presby/Columbia Univ Med Ctr, NY (page 65); **Address:** Columbia Univ Med Ctr, 3959 Broadway, Ste 800 N, New York, NY 10032; **Phone:** 212-305-3293; **Board Cert:** Orthopaedic Surgery 2012; **Med School:** South Korea 1986; **Resid:** Orthopaedic Surgery, NJ Med Ctr 1997; **Fellow:** Orthopaedic Oncology, Mass Genl Hosp/Chldns Hosp 1998; Pediatric Orthopaedic Surgery, Hosp for Sick Chldn/Univ Toronto 1999; **Fac Appt:** Prof OrS, Columbia P&S

Levin, L. Scott MD [OrS] - **Spec Exp:** Toe-to-Hand Transfer; Reconstructive Microsurgery; Hand & Upper Extremity Surgery; **Hospital:** Hosp Univ Penn - UPHS (page 69), Pennsylvania Hosp-UPHS (page 69); **Address:** Hosp Univ Penn, Orthopaedic Surgery Dept, 3400 Spruce St, 2 Silverstein Pav, Philadelphia, PA 19104; **Phone:** 215-662-3340; **Board Cert:** Plastic Surgery 2010; Orthopaedic Surgery 2014; Hand Surgery 2014; **Med School:** Temple Univ 1982; **Resid:** Orthopaedic Surgery, Duke Univ Hosp 1988; Plastic Surgery, Duke Univ Hosp 1992; **Fellow:** Hand & Microvascular Surgery, Christine Kleinert Inst 1994; **Fac Appt:** Prof OrS, Univ Pennsylvania

Levine, David S MD [OrS] - **Spec Exp:** Foot & Ankle Surgery; Ankle Reconstruction; **Hospital:** Hosp For Special Surgery (page 58); **Address:** Hospital for Special Surgery, 523 E 72 St Fl 5, East River Professional Bldg, New York, NY 10021; **Phone:** 212-606-1940; **Board Cert:** Orthopaedic Surgery 2011; **Med School:** Cornell Univ-Weill Med Coll 1992; **Resid:** Surgery, UCSD Med Ctr 1993; Orthopaedic Surgery, Hosp for Special Surgery 1997; **Fellow:** Foot & Ankle Surgery, Harborview Med Ctr 1998; **Fac Appt:** Asst Prof OrS, Cornell Univ-Weill Med Coll

Macaulay, William B MD [OrS] - **Spec Exp:** Hip Replacement; Knee Replacement; Minimally Invasive Surgery; Reconstructive Surgery; **Hospital:** NY-Presby/Columbia Univ Med Ctr, NY (page 65); **Address:** Columbia-Orthopaedics Dept, 161 Fort Washington Ave, Irving Pavilion Fl 2, New York, NY 10032; **Phone:** 212-305-6959; **Board Cert:** Orthopaedic Surgery 2012; **Med School:** Columbia P&S 1992; **Resid:** Surgery, Univ Pittsburgh Med Ctr 1993; Orthopaedic Surgery, Univ Pittsburgh Med Ctr 1997; **Fellow:** Adult Reconstructive Surgery, Hosp for Special Surgery 1999; **Fac Appt:** Prof OrS, Columbia P&S

Malawer, Martin M MD [OrS] - **Spec Exp:** Bone Tumors; Limb Sparing Surgery; Pediatric Orthopaedic Surgery; Sarcoma; **Hospital:** MedStar Georgetown Univ Hosp, G Washington Univ Hosp; **Address:** Washington Musculoskeletal Tumor Ctr, 7830 Old Georgetown Rd, Ste C15, Bethesda, MD 20814; **Phone:** 301-215-7940; **Board Cert:** Orthopaedic Surgery 1976; **Med School:** NYU Sch Med 1969; **Resid:** Surgery, Bronx Muni Hosp 1972; Orthopaedic Surgery, Bellevue Hosp Ctr 1975; **Fellow:** Orthopaedic Oncology, Shands Hosp-Univ Florida 1978; **Fac Appt:** Prof OrS, Geo Wash Univ

Marx, Robert G MD [OrS] - **Spec Exp:** Shoulder Surgery; Knee Injuries/Ligament Surgery; Knee Replacement; Sports Medicine; **Hospital:** Hosp For Special Surgery (page 58); **Address:** 519 E 72nd St, Ste 206, New York, NY 10021; **Phone:** 212-606-1645; **Board Cert:** Orthopaedic Surgery 2003; **Med School:** McGill Univ 1991; **Resid:** Orthopaedic Surgery, Univ Toronto Affil Hosp 1996; **Fellow:** Sports Medicine, Hosp Special Surgery 1998; **Fac Appt:** Prof OrS, Cornell Univ-Weill Med Coll

McAfee, Paul C MD [OrS] - **Spec Exp:** Spinal Reconstructive Surgery; Spinal Surgery-Cervical; Scoliosis; Minimally Invasive Surgery; **Hospital:** Univ of MD-St. Joseph Med Ctr; **Address:** 7505 Osler Drive, Ste 104, Towson, MD 21204; **Phone:** 410-337-8888; **Board Cert:** Orthopaedic Surgery 2007; **Med School:** SUNY Upstate Med Univ 1979; **Resid:** Orthopaedic Surgery, SUNY Upstate Med Ctr 1984; **Fellow:** Spine Surgery, Case West Res Univ Hosp 1986; **Fac Appt:** Assoc Prof OrS, Johns Hopkins Univ

McCance, Sean E MD [OrS] - **Spec Exp:** Spinal Surgery; Scoliosis; **Hospital:** Mt Sinai Med Ctr (page 62), Lenox Hill Hosp (page 66); **Address:** Spine Assocs, 1155 Park Ave Fl Ground - Ste E, New York, NY 10128; **Phone:** 212-360-6500; **Board Cert:** Orthopaedic Surgery 2010; **Med School:** Columbia P&S 1991; **Resid:** Surgery, Strong Meml Hosp 1992; Orthopaedic Surgery, Strong Meml Hosp 1996; **Fellow:** Spine Surgery, Twin Cities Spine Ctr 1997; **Fac Appt:** Asst Clin Prof OrS, Mount Sinai Sch Med

McCann, Peter D MD [OrS] - **Spec Exp:** Shoulder Surgery; Elbow Surgery; **Hospital:** Beth Israel Med Ctr - Petrie Div (page 56); **Address:** Beth Israel Orthopedics & Sports Med, 10 Union Square E, Ste 3M, New York, NY 10003; **Phone:** 212-844-6735; **Board Cert:** Orthopaedic Surgery 2009; **Med School:** Columbia P&S 1980; **Resid:** Surgery, St Vincent's Hosp 1982; Orthopaedic Surgery, Columbia-Presby Med Ctr 1985; **Fellow:** Shoulder Surgery, Columbia-Presby Med Ctr 1986; **Fac Appt:** Clin Prof OrS, Albert Einstein Coll Med

McFarland, Edward G MD [OrS] - **Spec Exp:** Sports Medicine; Rotator Cuff Surgery; Shoulder Surgery; **Hospital:** Johns Hopkins Hosp (page 59); **Address:** Johns Hopkins Orthopaedics, 10753 Falls Rd, Ste 215, Pavilion II Bldg, Lutherville, MD 21093; **Phone:** 410-583-2851; **Board Cert:** Orthopaedic Surgery 2011; Orthopaedic Sports Medicine 2010; **Med School:** Univ Louisville Sch Med 1982; **Resid:** Surgery, Mayo Clin 1983; Orthopaedic Surgery, Mayo Clin 1987; **Fellow:** Sports Medicine, Kerlan-Jobe Ortho Clin 1989; **Fac Appt:** Prof OrS, Johns Hopkins Univ

Meere, Patrick MD [OrS] - **Spec Exp:** Hip Replacement & Revision; Knee Replacement & Revision; Knee Injuries/ACL/Meniscus Tears; Joint Infections; **Hospital:** NYU Hosp For Joint Dis, NYU Langone Med Ctr (page 68); **Address:** 530 1st Ave FPO Bldg - Ste 5J, New York, NY 10016; **Phone:** 212-263-2366; **Board Cert:** Orthopaedic Surgery 2008; **Med School:** McGill Univ 1988; **Resid:** Orthopaedic Surgery, McGill Univ Affil Hosp 1993; **Fellow:** Reconstructive Surgery, Hosp for Joint Diseases 1995; **Fac Appt:** Assoc Prof OrS, NYU Sch Med

Moucha, Calin Stefan MD [OrS] - **Spec Exp:** Hip Replacement & Revision; Knee Reconstruction & Revision; Knee Replacement & Revision; Infections in Prosthetic Devices; **Hospital:** Mt Sinai Med Ctr (page 62); **Address:** Mount Sinai Medical Center, 5 E 98th St, Fl 7, New York, NY 10029; **Phone:** 212-241-1461; **Board Cert:** Orthopaedic Surgery 2005; **Med School:** Mount Sinai Sch Med 1997; **Resid:** Orthopaedic Surgery, St Lukes-Roosevelt Hosp 2002; **Fellow:** Hip/Knee Reconstruction, Rush Univ Med Ctr 2003; **Fac Appt:** Asst Prof OrS, Mount Sinai Sch Med

Myerson, Mark S MD [OrS] - **Spec Exp:** Foot & Ankle Surgery; Foot & Ankle Surgery-Complex; Cartilage Damage & Transplant; **Hospital:** Mercy Med Ctr - Baltimore, MedStar Union Meml Hosp; **Address:** Mercy Inst Foot & Ankle Reconstruction, 301 Saint Paul Pl, Baltimore, MD 21202; **Phone:** 410-659-2800; **Board Cert:** Orthopaedic Surgery 2011; **Med School:** South Africa 1979; **Resid:** Orthopaedic Surgery, Johns Hopkins Hosp 1984; **Fellow:** Foot & Ankle Surgery, Hospital Joint Diseases 1985

Neuwirth, Michael G MD [OrS] - **Spec Exp:** Scoliosis; Spinal Deformity; Spinal Surgery; **Hospital:** Mt Sinai Med Ctr (page 62); **Address:** 17 E 102nd St Fl 5, New York, NY 10029; **Phone:** 212-241-1071; **Board Cert:** Orthopaedic Surgery 1980; **Med School:** SUNY Hlth Sci Ctr 1974; **Resid:** Orthopaedic Surgery, Hosp for Joint Diseases 1979; **Fellow:** Spine Surgery, Rush-Presby Med Ctr 1980; **Fac Appt:** Prof OrS, Mount Sinai Sch Med

Nicholas, Stephen J MD [OrS] - **Spec Exp:** Sports Medicine; Shoulder & Knee Surgery; Arthroscopic Surgery; **Hospital:** Lenox Hill Hosp (page 66); **Address:** NY Orthopedics, 130 E 77th St Fl 5, New York, NY 10075; **Phone:** 212-737-3301; **Board Cert:** Orthopaedic Surgery 2005; **Med School:** NY Med Coll 1986; **Resid:** Orthopaedic Surgery, Hosp for Special Surgery 1991; **Fellow:** Sports Medicine, Lenox Hill Hosp 1992

O'Keefe, Regis J MD/PhD [OrS] - **Spec Exp:** Bone Tumors; Reconstructive Surgery; Soft Tissue Tumors; **Hospital:** Highland Hosp of Rochester, Univ Rochester Strong Meml Hosp; **Address:** Univ Rochester Med Ctr-Ortho Dept, 601 Elmwood Ave, Box 665, Rochester, NY 14642; **Phone:** 585-275-3100; **Board Cert:** Orthopaedic Surgery 2007; **Med School:** Harvard Med Sch 1985; **Resid:** Orthopaedic Surgery, Univ Rochester Med Ctr 1992; **Fellow:** Orthopaedic Oncology, Mass Genl Hosp 1993; **Fac Appt:** Prof S, Univ Rochester

O'Leary, Patrick F MD [OrS] - **Spec Exp:** Spinal Surgery; **Hospital:** Hosp For Special Surgery (page 58); **Address:** 1015 Madison Ave, Fl 4, New York, NY 10075; **Phone:** 212-249-8100; **Board Cert:** Orthopaedic Surgery 1983; **Med School:** Ireland 1968; **Resid:** Surgery, Roosevelt Hosp 1972; Orthopaedic Surgery, Hosp Spec Surg 1975; **Fellow:** Spine Surgery, Univ Toronto Genl Ortho Hosp 1976; **Fac Appt:** Assoc Clin Prof OrS, Cornell Univ-Weill Med Coll

Otsuka, Norman Y MD [OrS] - **Spec Exp:** Pediatric Orthopaedic Surgery; Trauma; Neuromuscular Disorders; Cerebral Palsy; **Hospital:** NYU Hosp For Joint Dis; **Address:** NYU Hosp for Joint Diseases, Center for Children, 301 E 17th St, Ste 301/303, New York, NY 10003; **Phone:** 212-598-6286; **Board Cert:** Orthopaedic Surgery 2009; **Med School:** McMaster Univ 1988; **Resid:** Orthopaedic Surgery, Univ Toronto Affil Hosps 1994; **Fellow:** Pediatric Orthopaedic Surgery, Childrens Hosp 1995; **Fac Appt:** Prof OrS, NYU Sch Med

Padgett, Douglas E MD [OrS] - **Spec Exp:** Hip & Knee Replacement; Arthroscopic Surgery-Hip; Arthroscopic Surgery-Knee; Dance Medicine; **Hospital:** Hosp For Special Surgery (page 58); **Address:** Hosp for Special Surgery, 535 E 70 St Fl 3, New York, NY 10021; **Phone:** 212-606-1642; **Board Cert:** Orthopaedic Surgery 2013; **Med School:** NY Med Coll 1982; **Resid:** Surgery, St Luke's-Roosevelt Hosp Ctr 1983; Orthopaedic Surgery, Hosp Spec Surg 1989; **Fellow:** Hip & Knee Surgery, Rush Presby Med Ctr 1990; **Fac Appt:** Assoc Prof OrS, Cornell Univ-Weill Med Coll

Parvizi, Javad MD [OrS] - **Spec Exp:** Hip Replacement & Revision; Knee Replacement & Revision; Joint Reconstruction; **Hospital:** Thomas Jefferson Univ Hosp; **Address:** Rothman Inst, Hip/Knee Surgery, 925 Chestnut St, Fl 5, Philadelphia, PA 19107; **Phone:** 800-321-9999; **Board Cert:** Orthopaedic Surgery 2005; **Med School:** England, UK 1991; **Resid:** Cardiovascular Surgery, Univ Newcastle 2001; Orthopaedic Surgery, Mayo Clin 2005; **Fellow:** Joint Arthroplasty, Univ Berne 2006; **Fac Appt:** Prof OrS, Thomas Jefferson Univ

Pellicci, Paul M MD [OrS] - **Spec Exp:** Hip Replacement-Young Adults; Knee Replacement; Joint Replacement; Hip Replacement; **Hospital:** Hosp For Special Surgery (page 58), NY-Presby/Weill Cornell Med Ctr, NY (page 65); **Address:** Hosp for Spec Surgery, 535 E 70th St, New York, NY 10021-4872; **Phone:** 212-606-1010; **Board Cert:** Orthopaedic Surgery 1982; **Med School:** Cornell Univ-Weill Med Coll 1975; **Resid:** Surgery, NY Hosp 1977; Orthopaedic Surgery, Hosp Spec Surg 1981; **Fellow:** Adult Reconstructive Surgery, Brigham & Womens Hosp 1982; **Fac Appt:** Clin Prof OrS, Cornell Univ-Weill Med Coll

Pizzutillo, Peter D MD [OrS] - **Spec Exp:** Pediatric Orthopaedic Surgery; Sports Medicine; Congenital Anomalies-Orthopaedic; **Hospital:** St. Christopher's Hosp for Chldn; **Address:** St Christophers Hosp, Orthopaedics, 3601 A St, rm 133-1, Philadelphia, PA 19134; **Phone:** 215-427-3131; **Board Cert:** Orthopaedic Surgery 1976; **Med School:** Jefferson Med Coll 1970; **Resid:** Orthopaedic Surgery, Thomas Jefferson Univ Hosp 1975; Pediatric Orthopaedic Surgery, duPont Inst Chldn 1974; **Fac Appt:** Prof OrS, Jefferson Med Coll

Plancher, Kevin D MD [OrS] - **Spec Exp:** Shoulder Surgery; Elbow Surgery; Cartilage Damage & Transplant; Shoulder Replacement; **Hospital:** Beth Israel Med Ctr - Petrie Div (page 56), Lenox Hill Hosp (page 66); **Address:** Plancher Orthopaedics & Sports Medicine, 1160 Park Ave, New York, NY 10128; **Phone:** 212-876-5200; **Board Cert:** Orthopaedic Surgery 2007; Hand Surgery 2008; Orthopaedic Sports Medicine 2009; **Med School:** Georgetown Univ 1986; **Resid:** Orthopaedic Surgery, Mass Genl Hosp/Brigham & Womens Hosp 1991; **Fellow:** Hand Surgery, Indiana Hand Ctr 1993; Sports Medicine, Steadman-Hawkins Clinic 1994; **Fac Appt:** Assoc Clin Prof OrS, Albert Einstein Coll Med

Ramsey, Matthew L MD [OrS] - **Spec Exp:** Shoulder Surgery; Elbow Surgery; Sports Medicine; **Hospital:** Thomas Jefferson Univ Hosp; **Address:** Rothman Inst, Shoulder & Elbow Surgery, 925 Chestnut St, Fl 5, Philadelphia, PA 19107; **Phone:** 800-321-9999; **Board Cert:** Orthopaedic Surgery 2009; **Med School:** SUNY Hlth Sci Ctr 1990; **Resid:** Orthopaedic Surgery, Thomas Jefferson Univ Hosp 1995; **Fellow:** Shoulder Surgery, Hosp Univ Penn 1996; **Fac Appt:** Assoc Prof OrS, Thomas Jefferson Univ

Rodriguez, Jose A MD [OrS] - **Spec Exp:** Hip & Knee Replacement; Arthroscopic Surgery-Hip; Arthroscopic Surgery-Knee; Fractures-Complex; **Hospital:** Lenox Hill Hosp (page 66); **Address:** NY Orthopedics, 130 E 77th St Fl 11, New York, NY 10021; **Phone:** 212-434-4799; **Board Cert:** Orthopaedic Surgery 2009; **Med School:** Columbia P&S 1989; **Resid:** Surgery, NY Presby-Colombia Med Ctr 1990; Orthopaedic Surgery, Hosp fpr Special Surgery 1994; **Fellow:** Arthritis Surgery, Lenox Hill Hosp 1995

Rothman, Richard H MD/PhD [OrS] - **Spec Exp:** Hip Replacement; Knee Replacement; Joint Replacement; **Hospital:** Thomas Jefferson Univ Hosp; **Address:** Rothman Inst, Hip/Knee Surgery, 925 Chestnut St Fl 5, Philadelphia, PA 19107; **Phone:** 800-321-9999; **Board Cert:** Orthopaedic Surgery 1970; **Med School:** Univ Pennsylvania 1962; **Resid:** Orthopaedic Surgery, Thomas Jefferson Univ Hosp 1968; **Fac Appt:** Prof OrS, Jefferson Med Coll

Roye Jr, David P MD [OrS] - **Spec Exp:** Pediatric Orthopaedic Surgery; Scoliosis; Hip Disorders-Pediatric; Neuromuscular Disorders; **Hospital:** Morgan Stanley Children's Hosp of NY-Presby, NY (page 65), NY-Presby/Columbia Univ Med Ctr, NY (page 65); **Address:** Columbia Orthopaedics, 3959 Broadway, rm 800-North, New York, NY 10032-1559; **Phone:** 212-305-5475; **Board Cert:** Orthopaedic Surgery 1981; **Med School:** Columbia P&S 1975; **Resid:** Orthopaedic Surgery, Columbia-Presby Med Ctr 1980; **Fellow:** Pediatric Orthopaedic Surgery, Hosp for Sick Chldn 1981; **Fac Appt:** Prof OrS, Columbia P&S

Rozbruch, S Robert MD [OrS] - **Spec Exp:** Limb Lengthening; Limb Deformities; Limb Surgery/Reconstruction; Fractures-Complex & Non Union; **Hospital:** Hosp For Special Surgery (page 58), NY-Presby/Weill Cornell Med Ctr, NY (page 65); **Address:** Hospital for Special Surgery, 535 E 70th St, River Terr Bldg Fl 2 - Ste 204, New York, NY 10021; **Phone:** 212-606-1415; **Board Cert:** Orthopaedic Surgery 2009; **Med School:** Cornell Univ-Weill Med Coll 1990; **Resid:** Orthopaedic Surgery, Hosp Special Surgery 1995; **Fellow:** Trauma, Univ Bern Hosp 1997; Limb Lengthening, Intl Ctr Limb Length/Univ MD 1999; **Fac Appt:** Prof OrS, Cornell Univ-Weill Med Coll

Salvati, Eduardo A MD [OrS] - **Spec Exp:** Hip Replacement; Knee Replacement; **Hospital:** Hosp For Special Surgery (page 58); **Address:** 535 E 71st St Belaire Bldg, New York, NY 10021; **Phone:** 212-606-1472; **Board Cert:** Orthopaedic Surgery 1972; **Med School:** Argentina 1963; **Resid:** Orthopaedic Surgery, Univ Florence Ortho Clinic 1965; Orthopaedic Surgery, Hosp Buenos Aires 1969; **Fellow:** Hip & Knee Surgery, Hosp For Spec Surg 1972; **Fac Appt:** Clin Prof OrS, Cornell Univ-Weill Med Coll

Sandhu, Harvinder S MD [OrS] - **Spec Exp:** Minimally Invasive Spinal Surgery; Spinal Surgery; **Hospital:** Hosp For Special Surgery (page 58); **Address:** Hosp for Special Surgery, 523 E 72nd St, East River Professional Bldg, New York, NY 10021; **Phone:** 212-606-1798; **Board Cert:** Orthopaedic Surgery 2007; **Med School:** Northwestern Univ 1987; **Resid:** Orthopaedic Surgery, Univ Hosp-SUNY Hlth Sci Ctr 1992; **Fellow:** Spine Surgery, UCLA Med Ctr 1993; **Fac Appt:** Assoc Prof OrS, Cornell Univ-Weill Med Coll

Schlesinger, Iris E MD [OrS] - **Spec Exp:** Pediatric Orthopaedic Surgery; **Hospital:** Westchester Med Ctr, Phelps Meml Hosp Ctr; **Address:** 19 Bradhurst Ave, Ste 1300 N, Hawthorne, NY 10532; **Phone:** 914-789-2731; **Board Cert:** Orthopaedic Surgery 2012; **Med School:** Albany Med Coll 1983; **Resid:** Orthopaedic Surgery, NYU Med Ctr 1988; **Fellow:** Pediatric Orthopaedic Surgery, Hosp Sick Children 1989; **Fac Appt:** Assoc Prof OrS, NY Med Coll

Schmidt, Richard G MD [OrS] - **Spec Exp:** Bone Tumors; Sarcoma-Soft Tissue; Limb Sparing Surgery; Bone Tumors-Metastatic; **Hospital:** Lankenau Hosp, Fox Chase Cancer Ctr (page 57); **Address:** 15 N Presidential Blvd, Ste 300, Bala Cynwyd, PA 19004; **Phone:** 610-667-2663; **Board Cert:** Orthopaedic Surgery 2009; **Med School:** Penn State Coll Med 1980; **Resid:** Orthopaedic Surgery, Hosp Univ Penn 1985; **Fellow:** Orthopaedic Oncology, Shands Hosp 1986

Schwab, Frank J MD [OrS] - **Spec Exp:** Spinal Surgery; Pain-Back; Spinal Deformity; Scoliosis; **Hospital:** NYU Hosp For Joint Dis, New York Methodist Hosp; **Address:** 333 E 38th St, Fl 6th, New York, NY 10003; **Phone:** 212-598-2781; **Board Cert:** Orthopaedic Surgery 2010; **Med School:** Columbia P&S 1990; **Resid:** Surgery, NY Presby-Columbia Med Ctr 1992; Orthopaedic Surgery, NY Presby-Columbia Med Ctr 1996; **Fellow:** Orthopaedic Surgery, Hospital Lariboisiere 1991; Spine Surgery, Maimonides Med Ctr 1997; **Fac Appt:** Clin Prof OrS, NYU Sch Med

Scott, W Norman MD [OrS] - **Spec Exp:** Knee Injuries; Knee Replacement; Sports Medicine; Knee Surgery; **Hospital:** Lenox Hill Hosp (page 66); **Address:** ISK-Inst for Ortho & Sports Med, 210 E 64th St Fl 4, New York, NY 10065; **Phone:** 646-293-7501; **Board Cert:** Orthopaedic Surgery 1978; **Med School:** Cornell Univ-Weill Med Coll 1972; **Resid:** Surgery, St Lukes-Roosevelt Hosp Ctr 1974; Orthopaedic Surgery, Hosp Special Surg 1978; **Fac Appt:** Clin Prof OrS, Cornell Univ-Weill Med Coll

Sculco, Thomas P MD [OrS] - **Spec Exp:** Hip Replacement; Knee Replacement; Minimally Invasive Surgery; Joint Replacement; **Hospital:** Hosp For Special Surgery (page 58); **Address:** 535 E 70th St, New York, NY 10021-4872; **Phone:** 212-606-1475; **Board Cert:** Orthopaedic Surgery 1976; **Med School:** Columbia P&S 1969; **Resid:** Surgery, Roosevelt Hosp 1971; Orthopaedic Surgery, Hosp For Special Surgery 1974; **Fellow:** Orthopaedic Surgery, The London Hosp 1975; **Fac Appt:** Prof OrS, Cornell Univ-Weill Med Coll

Sharkey, Peter F MD [OrS] - **Spec Exp:** Hip Replacement; Knee Replacement; **Hospital:** Thomas Jefferson Univ Hosp, Riddle Meml Hosp; **Address:** Rothman Inst, Hip/Knee Surgery, 925 Chestnut St Fl 5, Philadelphia, PA 19107; **Phone:** 800-321-9999; **Board Cert:** Orthopaedic Surgery 2013; **Med School:** SUNY Upstate Med Univ 1984; **Resid:** Orthopaedic Surgery, Thomas Jefferson Univ Hosp 1990; **Fellow:** Hip/Knee Reconstruction, Rothman Inst 1992; **Fac Appt:** Prof OrS, Thomas Jefferson Univ

Spivak, Jeffrey M MD [OrS] - **Spec Exp:** Spinal Surgery; Scoliosis; Sports Medicine Back Injuries; **Hospital:** NYU Hosp For Joint Dis, NYU Langone Med Ctr (page 68); **Address:** Hosp for Joint Diseases, Spine Ctr, 301 E 17th St, Ste 400, New York, NY 10003-3804; **Phone:** 212-598-6696; **Board Cert:** Orthopaedic Surgery 2006; **Med School:** Cornell Univ-Weill Med Coll 1986; **Resid:** Orthopaedic Surgery, Hosp for Joint Diseases 1992; **Fellow:** Spine Surgery, Thos Jefferson Univ Hosp 1993; **Fac Appt:** Asst Prof OrS, NYU Sch Med

Sponseller, Paul D MD [OrS] - **Spec Exp:** Spinal Deformity-Pediatric; Scoliosis; Pediatric Orthopaedic Surgery; Hip Disorders & Dysplasia; **Hospital:** Johns Hopkins Hosp (page 59), Greater Baltimore Med Ctr; **Address:** 601 N Caroline St, Ste 5212, Baltimore, MD 21287-0882; **Phone:** 410-955-3136; **Board Cert:** Orthopaedic Surgery 2010; **Med School:** Univ Mich Med Sch 1980; **Resid:** Orthopaedic Surgery, Univ Wisconsin Hosp 1985; **Fellow:** Pediatric Orthopaedic Surgery, Children's Hosp 1986; **Fac Appt:** Prof OrS, Johns Hopkins Univ

Strongwater, Allan M MD [OrS] - **Spec Exp:** Pediatric Orthopaedic Surgery; Cerebral Palsy; Deformity Reconstruction; **Hospital:** St. Joseph's Regl Med Ctr - Paterson; **Address:** St Josephs Chldns Hosp-Dept Ped Ortho Surg, 703 Main St Xavier Bldg - Ste 702, Paterson, NJ 07503; **Phone:** 973-754-2414; **Board Cert:** Orthopaedic Surgery 2007; **Med School:** Rush Med Coll 1978; **Resid:** Orthopaedic Surgery, Yale-New Haven Hosp 1983; Pediatric Orthopaedic Surgery, Hosp Joint Diseases 1984; **Fac Appt:** Clin Prof OrS, NYU Sch Med

Stuchin, Steven A MD [OrS] - **Spec Exp:** Hand Surgery; Arthritis; Hip & Knee Replacement; Hip Resurfacing; **Hospital:** NYU Hosp For Joint Dis; **Address:** 333 E 38th St, New York, NY 10016; **Phone:** 212-598-6708; **Board Cert:** Orthopaedic Surgery 1984; **Med School:** Columbia P&S 1976; **Resid:** Surgery, St Luke's-Roosevelt Hosp 1978; Orthopaedic Surgery, Hosp for Special Surg 1982; **Fellow:** Hand Surgery, Thos Jefferson Univ Hosp 1983; **Fac Appt:** Assoc Prof OrS, NYU Sch Med

Vaccaro, Alexander R MD/PhD [OrS] - **Spec Exp:** Spinal Surgery; Spinal Trauma; Spinal Cord Injury; **Hospital:** Thomas Jefferson Univ Hosp; **Address:** Rothman Inst, Spine Surgery, 925 Chestnut St Fl 5, Philadelphia, PA 19107; **Phone:** 800-321-9999; **Board Cert:** Orthopaedic Surgery 2006; **Med School:** Georgetown Univ 1987; **Resid:** Orthopaedic Surgery, Thomas Jefferson Univ Hosp 1992; **Fellow:** Spine Surgery, UCSD Med Ctr 1993; **Fac Appt:** Prof OrS, Thomas Jefferson Univ

Wapner, Keith L MD [OrS] - **Spec Exp:** Foot & Ankle Surgery; Tendon Surgery; Arthritis; **Hospital:** Pennsylvania Hosp-UPHS (page 69); **Address:** Penn Orthopaedic Foot & Ankle Surgeons, 230 W Washington Sq Fl 5, Philadelphia, PA 19106; **Phone:** 215-829-3668; **Board Cert:** Orthopaedic Surgery 2009; **Med School:** Temple Univ 1980; **Resid:** Surgery, Hosp Univ Penn 1981; Orthopaedic Surgery, Hosp Univ Penn 1985; **Fellow:** Joint Reconstruction, OSU Med Ctr 1986; Foot & Ankle Surgery, UCSF Med Ctr 1987; **Fac Appt:** Clin Prof OrS, Univ Pennsylvania

Ward Sr, William G MD [OrS] - **Spec Exp:** Bone Tumors; Soft Tissue Tumors; Reconstructive Surgery; Hip & Knee Surgery; **Hospital:** Robert Packer Hosp; **Address:** Guthrie Clinic, One Guthrie Square, Sayre, PA 18840; **Phone:** 570-887-2841; **Board Cert:** Orthopaedic Surgery 2004; **Med School:** Duke Univ 1975; **Resid:** Surgery, Duke Univ Med Ctr 1985; Orthopaedic Surgery, Duke Univ Med Ctr 1989; **Fellow:** Sports Medicine, Cleveland Clinic 1990; Orthopaedic Oncology, UCLA Med Ctr 1991

Warren, Russell MD [OrS] - **Spec Exp:** Knee Injuries/Ligament Surgery; Shoulder Surgery; Shoulder Replacement; Rotator Cuff Surgery; **Hospital:** Hosp For Special Surgery (page 58); **Address:** 525 E 71st St Belaire Bldg, New York, NY 10021-4892; **Phone:** 212-606-1178; **Board Cert:** Orthopaedic Surgery 1974; **Med School:** SUNY Upstate Med Univ 1966; **Resid:** Surgery, St Lukes Hosp 1968; Orthopaedic Surgery, Hosp For Special Surgery 1973; **Fellow:** Shoulder Surgery, Columbia-Presby Med Ctr 1977; **Fac Appt:** Prof OrS, Cornell Univ-Weill Med Coll

Weiland, Andrew J MD [OrS] - **Spec Exp:** Hand Surgery; Hand Reconstruction; Wrist/Hand Injuries; **Hospital:** Hosp For Special Surgery (page 58), NY-Presby/Weill Cornell Med Ctr, NY (page 65); **Address:** Hosp for Special Surgery, 535 E 70th St, New York, NY 10021-4872; **Phone:** 212-606-1575; **Board Cert:** Orthopaedic Surgery 1977; **Med School:** Wake Forest Univ 1968; **Resid:** Surgery, Univ Michigan Med Ctr 1970; Orthopaedic Surgery, Johns Hopkins Hosp 1975; **Fellow:** Hand Surgery, Univ Louisville Hosp 1975; **Fac Appt:** Prof OrS, Cornell Univ-Weill Med Coll

Weinfeld, Steven B MD [OrS] - **Spec Exp:** Foot & Ankle Surgery; Diabetic Leg/Foot; Foot Deformities; **Hospital:** Mt Sinai Med Ctr (page 62), Hackensack Univ Med Ctr; **Address:** Mt Sinai Hosp-Dept Ortho Surgery, 5 E 98th St Fl 9, Box 1188, New York, NY 10029; **Phone:** 212-241-1634; **Board Cert:** Orthopaedic Surgery 2009; **Med School:** Albany Med Coll 1990; **Resid:** Orthopaedic Surgery, Albany Med Ctr 1995; **Fellow:** Ankle and Foot Surgery, Union Meml Hosp 1996; **Fac Appt:** Assoc Prof OrS, Mount Sinai Sch Med

Westrich, Geoffrey H MD [OrS] - **Spec Exp:** Hip Replacement & Revision; Knee Replacement & Revision; Arthroscopic Surgery-Hip; Arthroscopic Surgery-Knee; **Hospital:** Hosp For Special Surgery (page 58), NY-Presby/Weill Cornell Med Ctr, NY (page 65); **Address:** Hospital for Special Surgery, 535 E 70th St Fl 3, New York, NY 10021; **Phone:** 212-606-1510; **Board Cert:** Orthopaedic Surgery 2009; **Med School:** Tufts Univ 1990; **Resid:** Surgery, North Shore Hosp 1991; Orthopaedic Surgery, Hosp for Spec Surg 1995; **Fellow:** Orthopaedic Trauma Surgery, Inselspital 1996; Hip/Knee Reconstruction, Hosp for Special Surg 1998; **Fac Appt:** Assoc Prof OrS, Cornell Univ-Weill Med Coll

Wetzel, F. Todd MD [OrS] - **Spec Exp:** Spinal Surgery; Minimally Invasive Surgery; **Hospital:** Temple Univ Hosp, Jeanes Hosp; **Address:** Temple Univ, Orthopaedics Dept, 3509 N Broad St Fl 5, Philadelphia, PA 19140; **Phone:** 215-707-2111; **Board Cert:** Orthopaedic Surgery 2011; **Med School:** Univ Pennsylvania 1981; **Resid:** Surgery, Yale-New Haven Hosp 1984; Orthopaedic Surgery, Yale-New Haven Hosp 1987; **Fellow:** Spinal Reconstructive Surgery, Tulane Med Ctr 1988; **Fac Appt:** Prof OrS, Temple Univ

Wickiewicz, Thomas L MD [OrS] - **Spec Exp:** Knee Injuries/ACL; Sports Medicine; Shoulder Surgery; Rotator Cuff Surgery; **Hospital:** Hosp For Special Surgery (page 58), NY-Presby/Weill Cornell Med Ctr, NY (page 65); **Address:** Hosp for Spec Surg, 525 E 71st St Belaire Bldg Fl 1, New York, NY 10021; **Phone:** 212-606-1450; **Board Cert:** Orthopaedic Surgery 1984; **Med School:** UMDNJ-NJ Med Sch, Newark 1976; **Resid:** Orthopaedic Surgery, Hosp for Special Surg 1981; **Fellow:** Sports Medicine, UCLA Med Ctr 1982; **Fac Appt:** Clin Prof OrS, Cornell Univ-Weill Med Coll

Wiesel, Sam W MD [OrS] - **Spec Exp:** Spinal Surgery; **Hospital:** MedStar Georgetown Univ Hosp; **Address:** Pasquerilla Hlthcare Ctr, 3800 Reservoir Rd NW, Ground Fl, Washington, DC 20007-2113; **Phone:** 202-444-8766 x2; **Board Cert:** Orthopaedic Surgery 1977; **Med School:** Univ Pennsylvania 1971; **Resid:** Orthopaedic Surgery, Hosp Univ Penn - UPHS 1977; **Fac Appt:** Prof OrS, Georgetown Univ

Williams Jr, Gerald R MD [OrS] - **Spec Exp:** Shoulder Reconstruction; Shoulder Cartilage Implant; Shoulder Replacement; Rotator Cuff Surgery; **Hospital:** Thomas Jefferson Univ Hosp, Methodist Hosp; **Address:** Rothman Inst, Shoulder Surgery, 925 Chestnut St Fl 5, Philadelphia, PA 19107; **Phone:** 800-321-9999; **Board Cert:** Orthopaedic Surgery 2013; **Med School:** Temple Univ 1984; **Resid:** Orthopaedic Surgery, Univ Hosp 1989; **Fellow:** Shoulder Surgery, Univ Hosp 1990; **Fac Appt:** Prof OrS, Jefferson Med Coll

Wittig, James C MD [OrS] - **Spec Exp:** Bone Tumors; Sarcoma-Soft Tissue; Reconstructive Surgery; Pediatric Orthopaedic Cancers; **Hospital:** Mt Sinai Med Ctr (page 62), Hackensack Univ Med Ctr; **Address:** 5 E 98th St, Fl 9, New York, NY 10029; **Phone:** 212-241-1807; **Board Cert:** Orthopaedic Surgery 2003; **Med School:** NYU Sch Med 1994; **Resid:** Orthopaedic Surgery, Columbia Presby Med Ctr 1999; **Fellow:** Orthopaedic Oncology, Washington Cancer Inst 2001; Orthopaedic Oncology, NIH 2001; **Fac Appt:** Assoc Prof OrS, Mount Sinai Sch Med

Zuckerman, Joseph D MD [OrS] - **Spec Exp:** Shoulder Surgery; Hip Replacement; Knee Replacement; Rotator Cuff Surgery; **Hospital:** NYU Hosp For Joint Dis, NYU Langone Med Ctr (page 68); **Address:** NYU Hosp for Joint Diseases, Dept Ortho Surg, 301 E 17th St, Fl 14, Ste 1402, New York, NY 10003; **Phone:** 212-598-6674; **Board Cert:** Orthopaedic Surgery 2007; **Med School:** Med Coll Wisc 1978; **Resid:** Orthopaedic Surgery, Univ WA Med Ctr 1983; **Fellow:** Arthritis Surgery, Brigham & Womans Hosp 1984; Shoulder Surgery, Mayo Clinic 1984; **Fac Appt:** Prof OrS, NYU Sch Med

Southeast

Beaty, James H MD [OrS] - **Spec Exp:** Pediatric Orthopaedic Surgery; Fractures-Pediatric; Hip Disorders-Pediatric; Clubfoot; **Hospital:** Le Bonheur Chldns Med Ctr; **Address:** Campbell Clinic, 1211 Union Ave, Memphis, TN 38104; **Phone:** 901-759-3125; **Board Cert:** Orthopaedic Surgery 2007; **Med School:** Univ Tenn Coll Med 1976; **Resid:** Surgery, Baptist Meml Hosp 1979; Orthopaedic Surgery, Campbell Clin Fdn 1981; **Fellow:** Pediatric Orthopaedic Surgery, Alfred I Dupont Inst 1982; **Fac Appt:** Prof OrS, Univ Tenn Coll Med

Boden, Scott D MD [OrS] - **Spec Exp:** Spinal Disorders; Spinal Surgery; Spinal Disc Replacement; Microdiscectomy; **Hospital:** Emory Univ Hosp; **Address:** Emory Orthopaedics & Spine Center, 59 Executive Park South, Ste 3000, Atlanta, GA 30329; **Phone:** 404-778-7143; **Board Cert:** Orthopaedic Surgery 2005; **Med School:** Univ Pennsylvania 1986; **Resid:** Orthopaedic Surgery, Geo Washington Univ Hosp 1991; **Fellow:** Spine Surgery, Case Western Reserve Univ 1992; **Fac Appt:** Prof OrS, Emory Univ

Brigman, Brian E MD/PhD [OrS] - **Spec Exp:** Bone & Soft Tissue Tumors; Bone Cancer; Musculoskeletal Tumors; Pediatric Orthopaedic Surgery; **Hospital:** Duke Univ Hosp; **Address:** Duke Univ Med Ctr, 20 Duke Medicine Cir, Durham, NC 27710; **Phone:** 919-681-6982; **Board Cert:** Orthopaedic Surgery 2003; **Med School:** Univ NC Sch Med 1994; **Resid:** Orthopaedic Surgery, Creighton Univ Med Ctr 2000; **Fellow:** Orthopaedic Oncology, Mass Genl & Chldns Hosp 2001; **Fac Appt:** Asst Clin Prof OrS, Duke Univ

Busch, Michael T MD [OrS] - **Spec Exp:** Pediatric Orthopaedic Surgery; Pediatric Sports Medicine; Knee Injuries/ACL; Discoid Meniscus; **Hospital:** Chldns Hlthcare Atlanta @ Scottish Rite; **Address:** 5445 Meridian Mark Rd, Ste 250, Atlanta, GA 30342; **Phone:** 404-255-1933; **Board Cert:** Orthopaedic Surgery 2010; Orthopaedic Sports Medicine 2009; **Med School:** Northwestern Univ 1980; **Resid:** Orthopaedic Surgery, Northwestern Meml Hosp 1985; **Fellow:** Pediatric Orthopaedic Surgery, Scottish Rite Chldns Hosp 1986; Orthopaedic Sports Medicine, Chldns Healthcare Atlanta 1986

DeOrio, James K MD [OrS] - **Spec Exp:** Ankle Replacement & Revision; Foot & Ankle Surgery; Foot Deformities; **Hospital:** Duke Univ Hosp; **Address:** 4709 Creekstone Drive, Ste 200, Durham, NC 27703; **Phone:** 919-613-7797; **Board Cert:** Orthopaedic Surgery 1983; **Med School:** Geo Wash Univ 1977; **Resid:** Orthopaedic Surgery, Mayo Clinic 1982; **Fellow:** Orthopaedic Surgery, Chur Hosp 1983; **Fac Appt:** Assoc Prof OrS, Duke Univ

Diduch, David R MD [OrS] - **Spec Exp:** Sports Medicine; Knee Injuries/ACL; Shoulder Reconstruction; Rotator Cuff Surgery; **Hospital:** Univ of Virginia Hlth Sys; **Address:** Univ Virginia Dept Ortho Surg, 515 Ray C. Hunt Drive, Charlottesville, VA 22908; **Phone:** 434-243-7778; **Board Cert:** Orthopaedic Surgery 2008; Orthopaedic Sports Medicine 2008; **Med School:** Harvard Med Sch 1988; **Resid:** Orthopaedic Surgery, Univ Virginia Med Ctr 1994; **Fellow:** Sports Medicine, Insall-Scott-Kelly Inst 1995; **Fac Appt:** Prof OrS, Univ VA Sch Med

Eismont, Frank J MD [OrS] - **Spec Exp:** Spinal Surgery; Spinal Tumors; Spinal Trauma; Spinal Disorders; **Hospital:** Jackson Meml Hosp, Univ of Miami Hosp; **Address:** UHlth, Orthopaedic Surgery Dept, 1475 NW 12th Ave, Miami, FL 33136; **Phone:** 305-243-3000; **Board Cert:** Orthopaedic Surgery 2007; **Med School:** Univ Rochester 1973; **Resid:** Orthopaedic Surgery, Univ Hosp 1978; **Fellow:** Spine Surgery, Univ Hosp 1979; Spine Surgery, Pennsylvania Hosp-UPHS 1980; **Fac Appt:** Prof OrS, Univ Miami Sch Med

Estwanik, Joseph J MD [OrS] - **Spec Exp:** Knee Surgery; **Hospital:** Carolinas Specialty Hosp; **Address:** Metrolina Ortho & Sports Med Clinic, 335 Bellingsley Rd, Ste 201, Charlotte, NC 28211; **Phone:** 704-334-4663; **Board Cert:** Orthopaedic Surgery 1979; **Med School:** Wake Forest Univ 1973; **Resid:** Orthopaedic Surgery, Cleveland Clinic 1976; Orthopaedic Surgery, North Carolina Baptist Hosp 1978; **Fac Appt:** Asst Prof OrS, Wake Forest Univ

Garrett Jr, William E MD/PhD [OrS] - **Spec Exp:** Sports Medicine; Knee Surgery; Knee Reconstruction; Arthroscopic Surgery; **Hospital:** Duke Univ Hosp; **Address:** 280 Frank Bassett Drive, Durham, NC 27706; **Phone:** 919-684-5678; **Board Cert:** Orthopaedic Surgery 2007; Orthopaedic Sports Medicine 2007; **Med School:** Duke Univ 1976; **Resid:** Orthopaedic Surgery, Duke Univ Med Ctr 1982; **Fac Appt:** Prof OrS, Duke Univ

Goldner, Richard D MD [OrS] - **Spec Exp:** Hand & Wrist Surgery; Hand & Wrist Reconstrction; Arthroscopic Surgery-Wrist; **Hospital:** Duke Univ Hosp; **Address:** 4709 Creekstone Drive, Ste 300, Durham, NC 27703; **Phone:** 919-684-6461; **Board Cert:** Orthopaedic Surgery 1982; Hand Surgery 2010; **Med School:** Duke Univ 1974; **Resid:** Orthopaedic Surgery, Univ Virginia Med Ctr 1980; Surgery, Duke Univ Med Ctr 1976; **Fellow:** Hand Surgery, Duke Univ Med Ctr 1981; **Fac Appt:** Assoc Prof OrS, Duke Univ

Jiranek, William A MD [OrS] - **Spec Exp:** Knee Replacement; Arthritis; Minimally Invasive Surgery; Hip Replacement; **Hospital:** Med Coll of VA Hosp; **Address:** MCV Dept Orthopaedic Surgery, 9000 Stony Point Pkwy, Richmond, VA 23235; **Phone:** 804-228-4155; **Board Cert:** Orthopaedic Surgery 2005; **Med School:** Univ VA Sch Med 1985; **Resid:** Orthopaedic Surgery, Tufts Combined Program 1991; **Fellow:** Orthopaedic Surgery, Mass Genl Hosp/Harvard 1992; **Fac Appt:** Assoc Prof OrS, Med Coll VA

Johnson, Darren L MD [OrS] - **Spec Exp:** Knee Injuries; Sports Medicine; Knee Ligament Reconstruction; Arthroscopic Surgery; **Hospital:** Univ of Kentucky Albert B. Chandler Hosp; **Address:** Kentucky Clin-Dept Orthopedic Surgery, 740 S Limestone, Ste K-401, Lexington, KY 40536-0284; **Phone:** 859-257-4969; **Board Cert:** Orthopaedic Surgery 2006; Orthopaedic Sports Medicine 2007; **Med School:** UCLA 1987; **Resid:** Orthopaedic Surgery, LAC & USC Med Ctr 1992; **Fellow:** Sports Medicine, UPMC 1993; **Fac Appt:** Prof OrS, Univ KY Coll Med

Karas, Spero G MD [OrS] - **Spec Exp:** Sports Medicine; Shoulder Injuries; Knee Injuries/ACL/Meniscus Tears; Cartilage Damage; **Hospital:** Emory Univ Hosp; **Address:** Emory Orthopaedics & Sports Medicine, 59 Executive Park South, Ste 1000, Atlanta, GA 30329; **Phone:** 404-778-7204; **Board Cert:** Orthopaedic Surgery 2002; Orthopaedic Sports Medicine 2008; **Med School:** Indiana Univ 1993; **Resid:** Orthopaedic Surgery, Duke Univ Med Ctr 1999; **Fellow:** Orthopaedic Sports Medicine, Steadman Hawkins Clinic 2000; **Fac Appt:** Assoc Prof OrS, Emory Univ

Kneisl, Jeffrey S MD [OrS] - **Spec Exp:** Bone Cancer; Musculoskeletal Tumors; **Hospital:** Carolinas Med Ctr; **Address:** Levine Cancer Inst, 1021 Morehead Medical Drive, Ste 3200, Charlotte, NC 28204; **Phone:** 980-442-2000; **Board Cert:** Orthopaedic Surgery 2010; **Med School:** Northwestern Univ 1980; **Resid:** Orthopaedic Surgery, Northwestern Univ Med Ctr 1987; **Fellow:** Orthopaedic Oncology, Univ Chicago Med Ctr 1990

Kress, Kenneth J MD [OrS] - **Spec Exp:** Hip & Knee Replacement; Hip & Knee Reconstruction; Sports Medicine; Robotic Surgery; **Hospital:** St. Joseph's Hosp - Atlanta, Northside Hosp; **Address:** Resergens Orthopaedics, 5671 Peachtree Dunwoody Rd NE, Ste 700, Atlanta, GA 30342; **Phone:** 404-847-9999; **Board Cert:** Orthopaedic Surgery 2004; **Med School:** Cornell Univ 1985; **Resid:** Orthopaedic Surgery, Hosp for Special Surg 1990; **Fellow:** Knee Reconstruction, Dr John C Garrett 1991

Lebwohl, Nathan H MD [OrS] - **Spec Exp:** Spinal Surgery; Spinal Deformity; Scoliosis; **Hospital:** Jackson Meml Hosp, Univ of Miami Hosp; **Address:** Univ Miami Spine Inst, 1475 NW 12th Ave, Miami, FL 33136; **Phone:** 305-585-8225; **Board Cert:** Orthopaedic Surgery 2013; **Med School:** Harvard Med Sch 1983; **Resid:** Surgery, Mount Sinai Med Ctr 1985; Orthopaedic Surgery, New York Ortho Hosp 1988; **Fellow:** Spine Surgery, Univ Louisville 1989; **Fac Appt:** Assoc Prof OrS, Univ Miami Sch Med

Miller, Mark D MD [OrS] - **Spec Exp:** Sports Medicine; Knee Ligament Reconstruction; Knee Cartilage/Meniscus Transplants; Shoulder Arthroscopic Surgery; **Hospital:** Univ of Virginia Hlth Sys; **Address:** Univ Virginia Dept Ortho Surg, 515 Ray C. Hunt Drive, Ste 1100, Charlottesville, VA 22908; **Phone:** 434-243-7778; **Board Cert:** Orthopaedic Surgery 2006; Orthopaedic Sports Medicine 2007; **Med School:** Uniformed Srvs Univ, Bethesda 1987; **Resid:** Orthopaedic Surgery, Wilford Hall USAF Med Ctr 1992; **Fellow:** Shoulder Surgery, Univ Pittsburgh 1993; Sports Medicine, Univ Pittsburgh 1993; **Fac Appt:** Prof OrS, Univ VA Sch Med

Nunley II, James A MD [OrS] - **Spec Exp:** Foot & Ankle Surgery; Ankle Replacement & Revision; Arthritis; Sports Injuries-Foot & Ankle; **Hospital:** Duke Univ Hosp; **Address:** 4709 Creekstone Drive, Ste 300, Durham, NC 27703; **Phone:** 919-684-4033; **Board Cert:** Orthopaedic Surgery 1981; **Med School:** Tulane Univ 1973; **Resid:** Orthopaedic Surgery, Duke Univ Med Ctr 1979; **Fellow:** Hand Surgery, Duke Univ Med Ctr 1980; **Fac Appt:** Prof OrS, Duke Univ

Pettrone, Frank A MD [OrS] - **Spec Exp:** Sports Medicine; Shoulder & Knee Surgery; Joint Replacement; **Hospital:** Virginia Hosp Ctr - Arlington; **Address:** Commonwealth Orthopaedics, 1635 N George Mason Drive, Ste 310, Arlington, VA 22205-3616; **Phone:** 703-810-5215; **Board Cert:** Orthopaedic Surgery 1975; **Med School:** Georgetown Univ 1969; **Resid:** Orthopaedic Surgery, Georgetown Hosp 1974; **Fac Appt:** Clin Prof OrS, Georgetown Univ

Poehling, Gary G MD [OrS] - **Spec Exp:** Hand Surgery; Arthroscopic Surgery; Sports Medicine; **Hospital:** Wake Forest Baptist Med Ctr; **Address:** Wake Forest Medical Ctr, Comp Rehab Plaza, 131 Miller St, Winston-Salem, NC 27103; **Phone:** 336-716-8091; **Board Cert:** Orthopaedic Surgery 1977; **Med School:** Marquette Sch Med 1968; **Resid:** Surgery, Duke Univ Med Ctr 1970; Orthopaedic Surgery, Duke Univ Med Ctr 1976; **Fac Appt:** Prof OrS, Wake Forest Univ

Richardson, William J MD [OrS] - **Spec Exp:** Spinal Surgery; Spinal Deformity; Spinal Disc Replacement; Spinal Trauma; **Hospital:** Duke Univ Hosp; **Address:** Box 3077 Med Ctr, 5340 Duke South, Orange Zone, Durham, NC 27710; **Phone:** 919-684-5711; **Board Cert:** Orthopaedic Surgery 2010; **Med School:** Eastern VA Med Sch 1979; **Resid:** Orthopaedic Surgery, Duke Univ Med Ctr 1986; **Fellow:** Spine Surgery, Totonto General Hosp 1987; **Fac Appt:** Prof OrS, Duke Univ

Robinson, Raymond P MD [OrS] - **Spec Exp:** Hip Replacement; Knee Replacement; **Hospital:** Univ of Miami Hosp, Jackson Meml Hosp; **Address:** Univ Miami Hosp, 1400 NW 12th Ave, Ste 2, East Bldg - Ste 2, Miami, FL 33136; **Phone:** 305-689-4683 x5; **Board Cert:** Orthopaedic Surgery 1982; **Med School:** Columbia P&S 1975; **Resid:** Orthopaedic Surgery, Hosp for Special Surg 1980; **Fellow:** Research, Hosp for Special Surg 1981; **Fac Appt:** Clin Prof OrS, Univ Miami Sch Med

Scarborough, Mark T MD [OrS] - **Spec Exp:** Bone Tumors; Sarcoma; **Hospital:** UF Hlth Shands Hosp; **Address:** UF Orthopaedics & Sports Med Inst, 3450 Hull Rd, Gainesville, FL 32607; **Phone:** 352-273-7001; **Board Cert:** Orthopaedic Surgery 2004; **Med School:** Univ Fla Coll Med 1985; **Resid:** Orthopaedic Surgery, UT Med Branch 1990; **Fellow:** Orthopaedic Oncology, Mass Genl Hosp 1991; **Fac Appt:** Prof OrS, Univ Fla Coll Med

Schuler, Thomas C MD [OrS] - **Spec Exp:** Spinal Surgery-Cervical; Spinal Surgery-Low Back; Sports Medicine Back Injuries; **Hospital:** Reston Hosp Ctr; **Address:** Virginia Spine Inst, 1831 Wiehle Ave, rm 200, Reston, VA 20190; **Phone:** 703-709-1114; **Board Cert:** Orthopaedic Surgery 2005; **Med School:** Indiana Univ 1986; **Resid:** Surgery, William Beaumont Hosp 1987; **Fellow:** Orthopaedic Surgery, William Beaumont Hosp 1991; Spine Surgery, Kerlan-Jobe Orth Clinic

Schwartz, Herbert S MD [OrS] - **Spec Exp:** Bone Tumors-Metastatic; Bone Tumors; Sarcoma; Musculoskeletal Tumors; **Hospital:** Vanderbilt Univ Med Ctr; **Address:** Vanderbilt Orthopaedic Institute, 1215 21st Ave S, Medical Ctr East, South Tower, Ste 4200, Nashville, TN 37232-8774; **Phone:** 615-343-8612; **Board Cert:** Orthopaedic Surgery 2007; **Med School:** Univ Chicago-Pritzker Sch Med 1981; **Resid:** Orthopaedic Surgery, Univ Chicago Hosps 1986; **Fellow:** Orthopaedic Oncology, Mayo Clinic 1987; Molecular Biology, Vanderbilt Univ 1989; **Fac Appt:** Prof OrS, Vanderbilt Univ

Siegel, Herrick J MD [OrS] - **Spec Exp:** Hip & Knee Replacement; Bone & Soft Tissue Tumors; Shoulder Replacement; Bone Tumors-Metastatic; **Hospital:** UAB Hosp, UAB Highlands Hosp; **Address:** UAB Orthopaedic Specialty Bldg, 1313 13th St, Birmingham, AL 35205; **Phone:** 205-930-8339; **Board Cert:** Orthopaedic Surgery 2005; **Med School:** NYU Sch Med 1995; **Resid:** Orthopaedic Surgery, USC Univ Hosp 2000; **Fellow:** Orthopaedic Oncology, Mayo Clinic 2002; **Fac Appt:** Assoc Prof OrS, UAB Sch Med

Spengler, Dan M MD [OrS] - **Spec Exp:** Spinal Surgery; **Hospital:** Vanderbilt Univ Med Ctr; **Address:** Vanderbilt Orthopedic Inst, 1215 21st Ave S, MCE-South Tower, Ste 4300, Nashville, TN 37232-8774; **Phone:** 615-875-5100; **Board Cert:** Orthopaedic Surgery 1988; **Med School:** Univ Mich Med Sch 1966; **Resid:** Orthopaedic Surgery, Univ Mich Med Ctr 1968; Orthopaedic Surgery, Univ Mich Med Ctr 1973; **Fellow:** Orthopaedic Surgery, Case West Res Hosps 1974; **Fac Appt:** Prof OrS, Vanderbilt Univ

Spindler, Kurt P MD [OrS] - **Spec Exp:** Sports Medicine; Knee Ligament Reconstruction; Arthroscopic Surgery-Knee; **Hospital:** Vanderbilt Univ Med Ctr; **Address:** Vanderbilt Sports Medicine, 1215 21st Ave S, Medical Ctr East, Ste 3200, Nashville, TN 37232; **Phone:** 615-343-6364; **Board Cert:** Orthopaedic Surgery 2004; Orthopaedic Sports Medicine 2007; **Med School:** Univ Pennsylvania 1985; **Resid:** Orthopaedic Surgery, Hosp Univ Penn 1990; **Fellow:** Sports Medicine, Cleveland Clinic 1991; **Fac Appt:** Prof OrS, Vanderbilt Univ

Vo, Phuc MD [OrS] - **Spec Exp:** Sports Medicine; Arthroscopic Surgery; Minimally Invasive Surgery; Joint Replacement; **Hospital:** Lakeland Regl Med Ctr; **Address:** Watson Clin, 1600 Lakeland Hills Blvd, Lakeland, FL 33805; **Phone:** 863-680-7214; **Board Cert:** Orthopaedic Surgery 2007; Orthopaedic Sports Medicine 2007; **Med School:** Univ Fla Coll Med 1986; **Resid:** Pathology, Shands at Univ FL 1988; Orthopaedic Surgery, Shands at Univ FL 1993; **Fellow:** Adult Orthopedic Surgery, Shands at Univ FL 1993; Sports Medicine, Univ Penn Sports Med Ctr 1994; **Fac Appt:** Assoc Prof OrS, Univ S Fla Coll Med

Walling, Arthur K MD [OrS] - **Spec Exp:** Bone Tumors; Soft Tissue Tumors; Foot & Ankle Surgery; Musculoskeletal Tumors; **Hospital:** Tampa Genl Hosp; **Address:** FL Orthopaedic Inst, 13020 Telecom Pkwy N, Tampa, FL 33637; **Phone:** 813-978-9700; **Board Cert:** Orthopaedic Surgery 1982; **Med School:** Creighton Univ 1976; **Resid:** Orthopaedic Surgery, Univ S FL Affil Hosp 1980; **Fellow:** Musculoskeletal Oncology, Shands at Univ FL 1981; **Fac Appt:** Assoc Clin Prof OrS, Univ S Fla Coll Med

Webb, Lawrence X MD [OrS] - **Spec Exp:** Trauma; Pelvic & Acetabular Fractures; Fractures-Complex & Non Union; Musculoskeletal Infections; **Hospital:** Med Ctr of Central GA; **Address:** 840 Pine St, Ste 500, Macon, GA 31201; **Phone:** 478-633-8682; **Board Cert:** Orthopaedic Surgery 2007; **Med School:** Temple Univ 1978; **Resid:** Orthopaedic Surgery, Bowman Gray Affil Hosp 1983; **Fellow:** Trauma, Harborview Med Ctr 1984; **Fac Appt:** Prof OrS, Mercer Univ Sch Med

Weiner, Richard L MD [OrS] - **Spec Exp:** Trauma; Hip & Knee Reconstruction; Hip & Knee Replacement; **Hospital:** St. Mary's Med Ctr - W Palm Bch, Palm Beach Gardens Med Ctr; **Address:** Orthopaedic Care Specialists, 733 US Highway 1, North Palm Beach, FL 33408; **Phone:** 561-840-1090; **Board Cert:** Orthopaedic Surgery 2013; **Med School:** Univ Pennsylvania 1986; **Resid:** Orthopaedic Surgery, Univ Hosp-UMDNJ 1991

Midwest

Albright, John P MD [OrS] - **Spec Exp:** Sports Medicine; **Hospital:** Univ Iowa Hosp & Clins; **Address:** UI Inst Orthopaedics, Sports Med & Rehab, 2701 Prairie Meadow Drive, Iowa City, IA 52242; **Phone:** 319-384-7070; **Board Cert:** Orthopaedic Surgery 2007; **Med School:** Loyola Univ-Stritch Sch Med 1967; **Resid:** Orthopaedic Surgery, Yale-New Haven Hosp 1971; **Fellow:** Research, Yale-New Haven Hosp 1972; **Fac Appt:** Prof OrS, Univ Iowa Coll Med

An, Howard MD [OrS] - **Spec Exp:** Spinal Surgery; Scoliosis; Spinal Microdiscectomy; **Hospital:** Rush Univ Med Ctr; **Address:** Midwest Orthopaedics at Rush, 1611 W Harrison St, Ste 400, Chicago, IL 60612; **Phone:** 312-243-4244; **Board Cert:** Orthopaedic Surgery 2012; **Med School:** Med Coll OH 1982; **Resid:** Orthopaedic Surgery, Med College Ohio Hosps 1988; **Fellow:** Spine Surgery, Jefferson Med College 1989; **Fac Appt:** Prof OrS, Rush Med Coll

Anglen, Jeffrey O MD [OrS] - **Spec Exp:** Trauma; Fractures-Complex & Non Union; Bone Infections; **Hospital:** Wishard Hlth Srvs, IU Hlth Univ Hosp; **Address:** Indiana Univ Dept Ortho Surgery, 1050 Wishard Blvd, Indianapolis, IN 46202; **Phone:** 317-630-7318; **Board Cert:** Orthopaedic Surgery 2011; **Med School:** Johns Hopkins Univ 1983; **Resid:** Orthopaedic Surgery, Johns Hopkins Hosp 1988; **Fellow:** Orthopaedic Trauma Surgery, Tampa Genl Hosp 1989; **Fac Appt:** Prof OrS, Indiana Univ

Archdeacon, Michael T MD [OrS] - **Spec Exp:** Trauma; Pelvic & Acetabular Fractures; **Hospital:** Univ Cincinnati Med Ctr; **Address:** 222 Piedmont Ave, Ste 2200, Cincinnati, OH 45219; **Phone:** 513-475-8690; **Board Cert:** Orthopaedic Surgery 2003; **Med School:** Ohio State Univ 1993; **Resid:** Orthopaedic Surgery, Case West Res Univ Hosp 2000; **Fellow:** Orthopaedic Trauma Surgery, Florida Orth Inst/Tampa Genl Hosp 2001; **Fac Appt:** Prof OrS, Univ Cincinnati

Berry, Daniel John MD [OrS] - **Spec Exp:** Hip Replacement & Revision; Knee Replacement & Revision; **Hospital:** Mayo Med Ctr & Clin - Rochester; **Address:** Mayo Clin, Dept Orth Surg, 200 1st St SW, Rochester, MN 55905; **Phone:** 507-284-2511; **Board Cert:** Orthopaedic Surgery 2004; **Med School:** Harvard Med Sch 1984; **Resid:** Orthopaedic Surgery, Harvard Univ Affil Hosps 1989; **Fellow:** Adult Reconstructive Surgery, Mauric E Muller Foundation 1990; Hip Surgery, Mayo Clinic 1991; **Fac Appt:** Prof OrS, Mayo Med Sch

Biermann, J Sybil MD [OrS] - **Spec Exp:** Sarcoma; Bone Cancer; Multiple Myeloma; Limb Sparing Surgery; **Hospital:** Univ Michigan Med Ctr; **Address:** Univ Michigan Comprehensive Cancer Ctr, 1500 E Medical Ctr Drive, B1-363, Ann Arbor, MI 48109; **Phone:** 734-647-8902; **Board Cert:** Orthopaedic Surgery 2006; **Med School:** Stanford Univ 1987; **Resid:** Orthopaedic Surgery, Univ Iowa Hosp 1992; **Fellow:** Orthopaedic Oncology, Univ Chicago Hosps 1993; **Fac Appt:** Prof OrS, Univ Mich Med Sch

Blaha, John D MD [OrS] - **Spec Exp:** Knee Replacement; **Hospital:** Univ Michigan Med Ctr; **Address:** Univ Michigan, Dept Orthopaedic Surg, 1500 E Medical Ctr Dr, Taubman 2912, Ann Arbor, MI 48109; **Phone:** 734-647-9961; **Board Cert:** Orthopaedic Surgery 1979; **Med School:** Univ Mich Med Sch 1973; **Resid:** Surgery, Univ Mich Hosp 1975; Orthopaedic Surgery, Univ Mich Hosp 1978; **Fellow:** Joint Replacement Surgery, Univ London 1980; **Fac Appt:** Prof OrS, Univ Mich Med Sch

Bridwell, Keith Happ MD [OrS] - **Spec Exp:** Spinal Deformity; Scoliosis; Spinal Surgery; **Hospital:** Barnes-Jewish Hosp, St. Louis Chldns Hosp; **Address:** Washington Univ Sch Med, 660 S Euclid Ave, Campus Box 8233, St Louis, MO 63110; **Phone:** 314-747-2560; **Board Cert:** Orthopaedic Surgery 1985; **Med School:** Washington Univ, St Louis 1977; **Resid:** Orthopaedic Surgery, Barnes Hosp-Wash Univ 1981; **Fellow:** Spine Surgery, Rush Presby-St Lukes Med Ctr 1982; **Fac Appt:** Prof OrS, Washington Univ, St Louis

Buckwalter IV, Joseph A MD [OrS] - **Spec Exp:** Bone Cancer; Bone Tumors-Metastatic; Sarcoma-Soft Tissue; **Hospital:** Univ Iowa Hosp & Clins; **Address:** Univ Iowa Hosp & Clin, Orthopaedic Surgery Dept, 200 Hawkins Drive, Iowa City, IA 52242; **Phone:** 319-356-2595; **Board Cert:** Orthopaedic Surgery 1991; **Med School:** Univ Iowa Coll Med 1974; **Resid:** Orthopaedic Surgery, Univ Iowa Hosp & Clin 1980; **Fac Appt:** Prof OrS, Univ Iowa Coll Med

Callaghan, John J MD [OrS] - **Spec Exp:** Hip & Knee Replacement; Sports Medicine; **Hospital:** Univ Iowa Hosp & Clins; **Address:** Univ Iowa Hosp, Dept Orthopaedics, 200 Hawkins Drive, Iowa City, IA 52242; **Phone:** 319-356-2223; **Board Cert:** Orthopaedic Surgery 2011; **Med School:** Loyola Univ-Stritch Sch Med 1978; **Resid:** Orthopaedic Surgery, Univ Iowa Hosp 1983; **Fellow:** Orthopaedic Surgery, Hosp Special Surg 1984; **Fac Appt:** Prof OrS, Univ Iowa Coll Med

Cheng, Edward Y MD [OrS] - **Spec Exp:** Bone & Soft Tissue Tumors; Reconstructive Surgery; **Hospital:** Univ Minn Med Ctr, Fairview - West Bank Campus; **Address:** Univ Minnesota, Dept Orthopaedic Surgery, 2512 S Seventh St, Ste R-200, Minneapolis, MN 55454; **Phone:** 612-273-1177; **Board Cert:** Orthopaedic Surgery 2013; **Med School:** Northwestern Univ 1983; **Resid:** Surgery, Northwestern Univ 1985; Orthopaedic Surgery, Beth Israel Hosp 1989; **Fellow:** Surgical Oncology, Mass Genl Hosp 1990; **Fac Appt:** Prof OrS, Univ Minn

Clohisy, Denis MD [OrS] - **Spec Exp:** Bone Cancer; **Hospital:** Univ Minn Med Ctr, Fairview - West Bank Campus; **Address:** Univ Minn, Dept Orthopaedic Surgery, 2512 S Seventh St, Ste R200, Minneapolis, MN 55454; **Phone:** 612-273-1177; **Board Cert:** Orthopaedic Surgery 2004; **Med School:** Northwestern Univ 1983; **Resid:** Orthopaedic Surgery, Univ Minn 1990; **Fellow:** Pathology, Wash Univ Med Ctr 1987; Musculoskeletal Oncology, Mass Genl Hosp 1991; **Fac Appt:** Prof OrS, Univ Minn

Clohisy, John MD [OrS] - **Spec Exp:** Hip Replacement & Revision; Hip Replacement-Young Adults; Hip Resurfacing; Hip Disorders & Dysplasia; **Hospital:** Barnes-Jewish Hosp; **Address:** Washington Univ Orthopaedics, 4921 Parkview Pl Fl 6, St Louis, MO 63110; **Phone:** 314-747-2500; **Board Cert:** Orthopaedic Surgery 2010; **Med School:** Northwestern Univ 1989; **Resid:** Orthopaedic Surgery, Barnes Jewish Hosp 1996; **Fellow:** Adult Reconstructive Surgery, Mass Genl Hosp 1997; **Fac Appt:** Prof OrS, Washington Univ, St Louis

Dirschl, Douglas R MD [OrS] - **Spec Exp:** Musculoskeletal Injuries; Fractures; Trauma; **Hospital:** Univ of Chicago Med; **Address:** Univ Chicago Dept Orthopaedic Surgery, 5841 S Maryland Ave, Chicago, IL 60637; **Phone:** 773-834-3531; **Board Cert:** Orthopaedic Surgery 2006; **Med School:** Oregon Hlth & Sci Univ 1988; **Resid:** Orthopaedic Surgery, Univ NC Hosp 1993; **Fac Appt:** Prof OrS, Univ Chicago-Pritzker Sch Med

Ebraheim, Nabil A MD [OrS] - **Spec Exp:** Trauma; Fractures-Complex & Non Union; Bone Infections; Reconstructive Surgery; **Hospital:** Univ of Toledo Med Ctr; **Address:** Univ Toledo Med Ctr, Dept Orthopaedics, 3065 Arlington Ave, MS 1123, Toledo, OH 43614; **Phone:** 419-383-3761; **Board Cert:** Orthopaedic Surgery 2008; **Med School:** Egypt 1975; **Resid:** Surgery, St Clare's Hosp 1980; Orthopaedic Surgery, SUNY Downstate Med Ctr 1983; **Fellow:** Trauma, Univ Maryland Hosps 1984; Orthopaedic Surgery, Hanover Trauma Ctr 1985; **Fac Appt:** Prof OrS, Univ Toledo, Med Univ OH

Gitelis, Steven MD [OrS] - **Spec Exp:** Bone Cancer; Soft Tissue Tumors; Limb Sparing Surgery; Hip Replacement; **Hospital:** Rush Univ Med Ctr; **Address:** Midwest Orthopaedics at Rush, 1611 W Harrison St, Ste 300, Chicago, IL 60612; **Phone:** 312-432-2397; **Board Cert:** Orthopaedic Surgery 1982; **Med School:** Rush Med Coll 1975; **Resid:** Orthopaedic Surgery, Rush Presby-St Lukes Med Ctr 1980; **Fellow:** Orthopaedic Oncology, Rizzoli Inst 1980; Orthopaedic Oncology, Mayo Clinic 1981; **Fac Appt:** Prof OrS, Rush Med Coll

Goitz, Henry MD [OrS] - **Spec Exp:** Sports Medicine; Knee Injuries/ACL/Meniscus Tears; Rotator Cuff Surgery; Elbow Surgery; **Hospital:** DMC Surgery Hosp, Harper Univ Hosp; **Address:** DMC Sports Medicine, 28800 Ryan Rd, Ste 120, Warren, MI 48092; **Phone:** 586-558-2860; **Board Cert:** Orthopaedic Surgery 2006; **Med School:** UMDNJ-Rutgers Med Sch 1985; **Resid:** Orthopaedic Surgery, Univ Virginia Affil Hosp 1991; **Fellow:** Sports Medicine & Hand Surgery, Univ Virginia Affil Hosp 1991; Sports Medicine, American Sports Med Inst 1992

Goldstein, Wayne M MD [OrS] - **Spec Exp:** Hip Replacement; Knee Replacement; **Hospital:** Adv Luth Genl Hosp; **Address:** Illinois Bone & Joint Institute, 9000 Waukegan Rd, Ste 200, Morton Grove, IL 60053; **Phone:** 847-375-3000; **Board Cert:** Orthopaedic Surgery 2007; **Med School:** Univ IL Coll Med 1978; **Resid:** Orthopaedic Surgery, Univ Illinois Med Ctr 1983; **Fellow:** Arthritis Surgery, Brigham & Women's Hosp 1984; **Fac Appt:** Assoc Clin Prof OrS, Univ Chicago-Pritzker Sch Med

Graf, Ben K MD [OrS] - **Spec Exp:** Sports Medicine; **Hospital:** Univ WI Hosp & Clins; **Address:** UW Hosp - Sports Med Clin, 621 Science Drive, Madison, WI 53711; **Phone:** 608-263-8850; **Board Cert:** Orthopaedic Surgery 2008; Orthopaedic Sports Medicine 2007; **Med School:** Univ Wisc 1979; **Resid:** Orthopaedic Surgery, Univ Wisc Hosp & Clins 1985; **Fellow:** Sports Medicine, Long Beach Meml Med Ctr 1986; **Fac Appt:** Assoc Prof S, Univ Wisc

Hanssen, Arlen Dale MD [OrS] - **Spec Exp:** Hip Surgery; Knee Surgery; **Hospital:** Mayo Med Ctr & Clin - Rochester; **Address:** Mayo Clin, Dept Orth Surg, 200 First St SW, Rochester, MN 55905; **Phone:** 507-284-9218; **Board Cert:** Orthopaedic Surgery 2011; **Med School:** St Louis Univ 1983; **Resid:** Orthopaedic Surgery, Mayo Clin 1988; **Fac Appt:** Prof OrS, Mayo Med Sch

Iannotti, Joseph MD/PhD [OrS] - **Spec Exp:** Shoulder Surgery; Rotator Cuff Surgery; **Hospital:** Cleveland Clin (page 55); **Address:** Cleveland Clinic, Dept Orthopaedic Surg, 9500 Euclid Ave, Desk A40, Cleveland, OH 44195-5027; **Phone:** 216-445-5151; **Board Cert:** Orthopaedic Surgery 2007; **Med School:** Northwestern Univ 1979; **Resid:** Orthopaedic Surgery, Hosp Univ Penn 1984; **Fellow:** Orthopaedic Research, Hosp Univ Penn 1985; **Fac Appt:** Prof OrS, Cleveland Cl Coll Med/Case West Res

Irwin, Ronald B MD [OrS] - **Spec Exp:** Bone Cancer; Limb Sparing Surgery; Sarcoma-Soft Tissue; **Hospital:** McLaren Macomb; **Address:** 1080 Harrington Blvd, Ste 201, Mount Clemens, MI 48043; **Phone:** 586-493-7575; **Board Cert:** Orthopaedic Surgery 1979; **Med School:** Univ Mich Med Sch 1971; **Resid:** Orthopaedic Surgery, William Beaumont Hosp 1978; **Fellow:** Orthopaedic Oncology, Mayo Clinic 1978

Jacobs, Joshua J MD [OrS] - **Spec Exp:** Hip Replacement & Revision; Knee Replacement & Revision; **Hospital:** Rush Univ Med Ctr; **Address:** Midwest Orthopaedics at Rush, 1611 W Harrison St, Ste 400, Chicago, IL 60612; **Phone:** 312-243-4244; **Board Cert:** Orthopaedic Surgery 2011; **Med School:** Univ IL Coll Med 1981; **Resid:** Orthopaedic Surgery, Harvard Univ Affil Hosp 1987; **Fellow:** Joint Replacement Surgery, Rush Univ Med Ctr 1988; **Fac Appt:** Prof OrS, Rush Med Coll

Joyce, Michael J MD [OrS] - **Spec Exp:** Bone & Soft Tissue Tumors; Fractures-Complex & Non Union; Musculoskeletal Tissue Banking; Pelvic & Acetabular Fractures; **Hospital:** Cleveland Clin (page 55); **Address:** Cleveland Clin, Dept Orth Surgery, 9500 Euclid Ave, MS A41, Cleveland, OH 44195; **Phone:** 216-444-4282; **Board Cert:** Orthopaedic Surgery 1985; **Med School:** Univ Louisville Sch Med 1976; **Resid:** Surgery, Johns Hopkins Hosp 1978; Orthopaedic Surgery, Harvard Combined Program 1981; **Fellow:** Orthopaedic Oncology, Mass Genl Hosp 1982; Trauma, Univ Toronto-Sunnybrook Hosp 1983; **Fac Appt:** Assoc Clin Prof OrS, Case West Res Univ

Kaeding, Christopher C MD [OrS] - **Spec Exp:** Sports Medicine; Knee Injuries/ACL; Shoulder Injuries; Rotator Cuff Surgery; **Hospital:** OSU Wexner Med Ctr; **Address:** OSU Sports Med Ctr, 2050 Kenny Rd, Ste 3100, Columbus, OH 43221; **Phone:** 614-293-8813; **Board Cert:** Orthopaedic Surgery 2012; Orthopaedic Sports Medicine 2012; **Med School:** Northwestern Univ 1983; **Resid:** Orthopaedic Surgery, Northwestern Univ Affil Hosps 1988; **Fellow:** Sports Medicine, Cleveland Clin 1989; **Fac Appt:** Clin Prof OrS, Ohio State Univ

Kenter, Keith MD [OrS] - **Spec Exp:** Sports Medicine; Shoulder Reconstruction; Knee Surgery; **Hospital:** Univ Cincinnati Med Ctr; **Address:** Univ Cincinnati Physicians, 222 Piedmont Ave, Ste 2200, Cincinnati, OH 45219; **Phone:** 513-475-8690; **Board Cert:** Orthopaedic Surgery 2010; Orthopaedic Sports Medicine 2007; **Med School:** Univ MO-Columbia Sch Med 1990; **Resid:** Surgery, Duke Univ Med Ctr 1992; Orthopaedic Surgery, Duke Univ Med Ctr 1996; **Fellow:** Sports Medicine & Shoulder Surgery, Hosp Special Surg 1997; **Fac Appt:** Assoc Prof OrS, Univ Cincinnati

Kraay, Matthew J MD [OrS] - **Spec Exp:** Arthritis; Reconstructive Surgery; Joint Replacement; **Hospital:** UH Case Med Ctr; **Address:** UH Case Med Ctr, Dept Orthopaedic Surgery, 11100 Euclid Ave, Cleveland, OH 44106; **Phone:** 216-844-8372; **Board Cert:** Orthopaedic Surgery 2004; **Med School:** Wayne State Univ 1983; **Resid:** Orthopaedic Surgery, Univ Hosps 1989; **Fellow:** Adult Reconstructive Surgery, Univ Hosps 1990; Orthopaedic Surgery, Hosp Special Surgery 1991; **Fac Appt:** Prof OrS, Case West Res Univ

Lenke, Lawrence G MD [OrS] - **Spec Exp:** Spinal Surgery; Spinal Deformity; Scoliosis; Spinal Reconstructive Surgery; **Hospital:** Barnes-Jewish Hosp, St. Louis Chldns Hosp; **Address:** Washington Univ Sch Med, 660 S Euclid Ave, Campus Box 8233, St Louis, MO 63110; **Phone:** 314-747-2509; **Board Cert:** Orthopaedic Surgery 2005; **Med School:** Northwestern Univ 1986; **Resid:** Orthopaedic Surgery, Barnes-Jewish Hosp 1989; **Fellow:** Spine Surgery, Barnes-Jewish Hosp 1992; **Fac Appt:** Prof OrS, Washington Univ, St Louis

Les, Kimberly A MD [OrS] - **Spec Exp:** Bone Cancer; **Hospital:** Beaumont Hosp-Royal Oak; **Address:** Rose Cancer Treatment Ctr, 3577 W 13 Mile Rd, Ste 402, Royal Oak, MI 48073; **Phone:** 248-551-9910; **Board Cert:** Orthopaedic Surgery 2011; **Med School:** Geo Wash Univ 1992; **Resid:** Orthopaedic Surgery, Henry Ford Hosp 1997; **Fellow:** Orthopaedic Oncology, Univ Chicago Hosps 1998

Lock, Terrence Ralph MD [OrS] - **Spec Exp:** Sports Medicine; Arthroscopic Surgery; Shoulder & Knee Reconstruction; **Hospital:** Henry Ford Hosp, Henry Ford Med Ctr-Cottage; **Address:** Henry Ford Ctr for Athletic Med, 6525 Second Ave, Detroit, MI 48202; **Phone:** 313-972-4060; **Board Cert:** Orthopaedic Surgery 2012; Orthopaedic Sports Medicine 2007; **Med School:** Wayne State Univ 1983; **Resid:** Orthopaedic Surgery, Wayne State Univ Affil Hosp 1988; **Fellow:** Sports Medicine, Mass Genl Hosp 1989

Manoli II, Arthur MD [OrS] - **Spec Exp:** Foot & Ankle Surgery; Reconstructive Surgery; **Hospital:** St. Joseph Mercy Oakland Hosp; **Address:** 44555 Woodward Ave, Ste 503, Pontiac, MI 48341; **Phone:** 248-858-6773; **Board Cert:** Orthopaedic Surgery 2007; **Med School:** Univ Mich Med Sch 1970; **Resid:** Surgery, Oakwood Hosp 1972; Orthopaedic Surgery, Wayne State Univ Affil Hosps 1975; **Fellow:** Ankle and Foot Surgery, Univ Wash/Vanderbilt Univ 1990

Mayerson, Joel L MD [OrS] - **Spec Exp:** Bone Tumors; Sarcoma-Soft Tissue; Limb Surgery/Reconstruction; Musculoskeletal Tumors; **Hospital:** OSU Wexner Med Ctr; **Address:** Ohio State Univ, Div Musculoskeletal Onc, 300 W 10th Ave, Columbus, OH 43210; **Phone:** 614-293-4420; **Board Cert:** Orthopaedic Surgery 2003; **Med School:** Johns Hopkins Univ 1994; **Resid:** Orthopaedic Surgery, Cleveland Clinic 1999; **Fellow:** Orthopaedic Oncology, Univ Wash Med Ctr 2000; **Fac Appt:** Assoc Prof OrS, Ohio State Univ

McCarthy, James J MD [OrS] - **Spec Exp:** Lower Limb Surgery in Children; Arthroscopic Surgery-Hip; Pediatric Orthopaedic Surgery; Hip Disorders-Pediatric; **Hospital:** Cincinnati Chldns Hosp Med Ctr; **Address:** Cincinnati Chldns, Dept Ped Ortho Surg, 3333 Burnet Ave, ML 2017, Cincinnati, OH 45229; **Phone:** 513-636-4454; **Board Cert:** Orthopaedic Surgery 2010; **Med School:** Univ NC Sch Med 1991; **Resid:** Orthopaedic Surgery, Cleveland Clinic 1996; **Fellow:** Arthroscopic Surgery, Chldns Hosp 1997; **Fac Appt:** Prof OrS, Univ Wisc

McDonald, Douglas J MD [OrS] - **Spec Exp:** Bone & Soft Tissue Tumors; Ewing's Sarcoma; Sarcoma; Hip & Knee Reconstruction; **Hospital:** Barnes-Jewish Hosp, St. Louis Chldns Hosp; **Address:** Ctr Advanced Med, Orthopaedic Surg Ctr, 4921 Parkview Pl Fl 6 - Ste A, St Louis, MO 63110; **Phone:** 314-747-2500; **Board Cert:** Orthopaedic Surgery 2011; **Med School:** Univ Minn 1982; **Resid:** Orthopaedic Surgery, Mayo Clinic 1987; **Fellow:** Orthopaedic Oncology, Mayo Clinic 1988; Orthopaedic Surgery, Rizzoli Inst 1989; **Fac Appt:** Prof OrS, Washington Univ, St Louis

Morcuende, Jose A MD/PhD [OrS] - **Spec Exp:** Clubfoot; Pediatric Orthopaedic Surgery; **Hospital:** Univ Iowa Hosp & Clins; **Address:** UIHC Dept Orthopaedics & Rehab, 200 Hawkins Drive, Iowa City, IA 52242; **Phone:** 319-356-2223; **Board Cert:** Orthopaedic Surgery 2004; **Med School:** Spain 1981; **Resid:** Orthopaedic Surgery, Univ IA Hosp & Clin 2001; **Fellow:** Pediatric Orthopaedic Surgery, Univ IA Hosp & Clin 2002; **Fac Appt:** Assoc Prof OrS, Univ Iowa Coll Med

Mott, Michael P MD [OrS] - **Spec Exp:** Soft Tissue Tumors; Musculoskeletal Tumors; Bone Cancer; **Hospital:** Henry Ford Hosp, Henry Ford- W Bloomfield Hosp; **Address:** Henry Ford Hosp, Dept Ortho Surg, 2799 W Grand Blvd Fl 12, Detroit, MI 48202; **Phone:** 313-916-1961; **Board Cert:** Orthopaedic Surgery 2007; **Med School:** Univ Mich Med Sch 1989; **Resid:** Orthopaedic Surgery, Wayne State Univ Affil Hosp 1994; **Fellow:** Musculoskeletal Oncology, Mass Genl Hosp 1995; Orthopaedic Oncology, Wayne State Univ 1996; **Fac Appt:** Assoc Prof OrS, Wayne State Univ

Muschler, George F MD [OrS] - **Spec Exp:** Hip Replacement; Knee Replacement; Fractures-Complex & Non Union; **Hospital:** Cleveland Clin (page 55); **Address:** Cleveland Clinic, Orthopaedic and Rheumatologic Inst, 9500 Euclid Ave, Desk A40, Cleveland, OH 44195-0001; **Phone:** 216-444-2606; **Board Cert:** Orthopaedic Surgery 2011; **Med School:** Northwestern Univ 1981; **Resid:** Orthopaedic Surgery, Univ Texas SW Med Ctr 1986; **Fellow:** Metabolic Bone Research, Hosp Special Surg 1988; Musculoskeletal Oncology, Meml Sloan-Kettering Cancer Ctr 1988; **Fac Appt:** Prof OrS, Cleveland Cl Coll Med/Case West Res

Nepola, James V MD [OrS] - **Spec Exp:** Trauma; Shoulder Reconstruction; **Hospital:** Univ Iowa Hosp & Clins; **Address:** UIHC Dept Orthopaedics & Rehab, 200 Hawkins Drive, Iowa City, IA 52242; **Phone:** 319-356-2223; **Board Cert:** Orthopaedic Surgery 2009; **Med School:** Columbia P&S 1978; **Resid:** Surgery, Roosevelt Hosp 1980; Orthopaedic Surgery, NY-Presby Hosp/Columbia 1983; **Fellow:** Orthopaedic Trauma Surgery, NY-Presby Hosp/Columbia 1984; **Fac Appt:** Prof OrS, Univ Iowa Coll Med

O'Driscoll, Shawn W MD/PhD [OrS] - **Spec Exp:** Sports Medicine; Shoulder Surgery; Elbow Surgery; Cartilage Damage; **Hospital:** Mayo Med Ctr & Clin - Rochester; **Address:** Mayo Clin, Dept Orth Surg, 200 1st St SW, Rochester, MN 55905; **Phone:** 507-538-1953; **Board Cert:** Orthopaedic Surgery 2013; Orthopaedic Sports Medicine 2013; **Med School:** Univ Toronto 1980; **Resid:** Orthopaedic Surgery, Univ Toronto 1987; **Fellow:** Arthroscopic Surgery, Toronto Western Hosp; Elbow & Shoulder Surgery, Mayo Clinic 1988; **Fac Appt:** Prof OrS, Mayo Med Sch

Parsons III, Theodore W MD [OrS] - **Spec Exp:** Bone & Soft Tissue Tumors; Reconstructive Surgery; **Hospital:** Henry Ford Hosp, Henry Ford- W Bloomfield Hosp; **Address:** Henry Ford Hosp, Dept Orthopaedics, 2799 West Grand Blvd Fl 12, Detroit, MI 48202; **Phone:** 313-916-1964; **Board Cert:** Orthopaedic Surgery 2005; **Med School:** Uniformed Srvs Univ, Bethesda 1986; **Resid:** Orthopaedic Surgery, Wilford Hall USAF Med Ctr 1991; **Fellow:** Pediatric Oncology, Boston Chldns Hosp 1992; Orthopaedic Oncology, Mass Genl Hosp 1992; **Fac Appt:** Prof OrS, Wayne State Univ

Peabody, Terrance D MD [OrS] - **Spec Exp:** Soft Tissue Tumors; Bone Tumors; Pediatric Orthopaedic Cancers; Limb Sparing Surgery; **Hospital:** Northwestern Meml Hosp; **Address:** Northwestern Meml Hosp, Galter Pavilion, 675 N St Clair, rm 17-100, Chicago, IL 60611; **Phone:** 312-695-6800; **Board Cert:** Orthopaedic Surgery 2013; **Med School:** UC Irvine 1985; **Resid:** Orthopaedic Surgery, UC Irvine Med Ctr 1990; **Fellow:** Orthopaedic Oncology, Univ Chicago Med Ctr 1991; **Fac Appt:** Prof OrS, Univ Chicago-Pritzker Sch Med

Pinzur, Michael S MD [OrS] - **Spec Exp:** Diabetes-Amputation; Foot & Ankle Surgery; Amputation Surgery; Charcot Foot; **Hospital:** Loyola Univ Med Ctr; **Address:** Loyola University Medical Center, 2160 S 1st Ave, Maywood, IL 60153-3304; **Phone:** 708-216-4993; **Board Cert:** Orthopaedic Surgery 1980; **Med School:** Rush Med Coll 1974; **Resid:** Orthopaedic Surgery, Northwestern Meml Hosp 1979; **Fac Appt:** Prof OrS, Loyola Univ-Stritch Sch Med

Polly Jr, David W MD [OrS] - **Spec Exp:** Spinal Surgery; Scoliosis; **Hospital:** Shriners Hosps for Children-Twin Cities; **Address:** Univ Minn Orthopaedic Clin, 2512 S 7th St, rm R-102, Minneapolis, MN 55454; **Phone:** 612-273-9400; **Board Cert:** Orthopaedic Surgery 2005; **Med School:** Uniformed Srvs Univ, Bethesda 1985; **Resid:** Orthopaedic Surgery, Walter Reed Army Med Ctr 1991; **Fellow:** Spine Surgery, Univ Minn Affil Hosp 1992; **Fac Appt:** Prof S, Univ Minn

Riew, K Daniel MD [OrS] - **Spec Exp:** Spinal Surgery-Cervical; Minimally Invasive Spinal Surgery; Spinal Microdiscectomy; **Hospital:** Barnes-Jewish Hosp; **Address:** Ctr for Advanced Med-Spine Ctr, 4921 Parkview Pl, CAM Bldg Fl 12 - Ste A, St Louis, MO 63110; **Phone:** 314-514-3500; **Board Cert:** Internal Medicine 1987; Orthopaedic Surgery 2008; **Med School:** Case West Res Univ 1984; **Resid:** Internal Medicine, NY Hosp-Cornell Med Ctr 1987; Orthopaedic Surgery, G Washington Univ Hosp 1994; **Fellow:** Spine Surgery, Case West Res Univ 1995; **Fac Appt:** Prof OrS, Washington Univ, St Louis

Romeo, Anthony A MD [OrS] - **Spec Exp:** Shoulder Reconstruction; Shoulder Problems-Complex; Sports Medicine; Elbow Surgery; **Hospital:** Rush Univ Med Ctr, Rush Oak Park Hosp; **Address:** Midwest Orthopaedics at Rush, 1611 W Harrison St, Ste 400, Chicago, IL 60612; **Phone:** 312-432-2342; **Board Cert:** Orthopaedic Surgery 2008; Orthopaedic Sports Medicine 2010; **Med School:** St Louis Univ 1987; **Resid:** Orthopaedic Surgery, Cleveland Clinic 1992; **Fellow:** Shoulder Surgery, Univ Washington Med Ctr 1993; **Fac Appt:** Assoc Prof OrS, Rush Med Coll

Schafer, Michael F MD [OrS] - **Spec Exp:** Sports Medicine; Spinal Surgery; Scoliosis; **Hospital:** Northwestern Meml Hosp; **Address:** 675 N St Clair St, Galter Bldg Fl 17 - Ste 100, Chicago, IL 60611-5968; **Phone:** 312-695-6800; **Board Cert:** Orthopaedic Surgery 1983; **Med School:** Univ Iowa Coll Med 1967; **Resid:** Orthopaedic Surgery, Northwestern Univ Hosp 1972; **Fellow:** Spine Surgery, Natl Fdn Traveling Fellowship 1973; **Fac Appt:** Prof OrS, Northwestern Univ

Shelbourne, K Donald MD [OrS] - **Spec Exp:** Knee Surgery; Arthroscopic Surgery; Knee Rehabilitation (Non-Surgical); Knee Ligament Reconstruction; **Hospital:** IU Health Methodist Hosp; **Address:** 1815 N Capitol Ave, Ste 600, Indianapolis, IN 46202; **Phone:** 317-924-8636; **Board Cert:** Orthopaedic Surgery 1984; **Med School:** Indiana Univ 1976; **Resid:** Orthopaedic Surgery, Indiana Univ Hosp 1981; **Fellow:** Sports Medicine, Univ Wisconsin 1982; **Fac Appt:** Assoc Clin Prof OrS, Indiana Univ

Sim, Franklin H MD [OrS] - **Spec Exp:** Sarcoma; Bone Cancer; **Hospital:** Mayo Med Ctr & Clin - Rochester; **Address:** Mayo Clinic Dept. Orthopaedic Surg, 200 1st St SW, Rochester, MN 55905; **Phone:** 507-284-3661; **Board Cert:** Orthopaedic Surgery 1971; **Med School:** Dalhousie Univ 1965; **Resid:** Orthopaedic Surgery, Mayo Clinic 1970; **Fac Appt:** Prof OrS, Mayo Med Sch

Stulberg, S David MD [OrS] - **Spec Exp:** Hip & Knee Replacement; **Hospital:** Northwestern Meml Hosp; **Address:** 680 N Lake Shore Drive, Ste 924, Chicago, IL 60611; **Phone:** 312-664-6848; **Board Cert:** Orthopaedic Surgery 1977; **Med School:** Univ Mich Med Sch 1969; **Resid:** Orthopaedic Surgery, Mass Genl Hosp 1974; **Fellow:** Research, Toronto Hosp Sick Chldn 1976; **Fac Appt:** Prof OrS, Northwestern Univ

Swiontkowski, Marc F MD [OrS] - **Spec Exp:** Osteomyelitis; Fractures-Non Union; Trauma; Bone Infections; **Hospital:** Regions Hosp - St Paul; **Address:** Tria Orthopedic Ctr, 8100 Northland Drive, Bloomington, MN 55431; **Phone:** 952-831-8742; **Board Cert:** Orthopaedic Surgery 2008; **Med School:** USC Sch Med 1979; **Resid:** Orthopaedic Surgery, Univ Washington Med Ctr 1984; **Fac Appt:** Prof OrS, Univ Minn

Thompson, George H MD [OrS] - **Spec Exp:** Pediatric Orthopaedic Surgery; Scoliosis; Spinal Deformity-Pediatric; **Hospital:** UH Rainbow Babies & Chldns Hosp; **Address:** UH Rainbow Babies & Chldns Hosp, Div Ped Ortho Surg, 11100 Euclid Ave, MS RBC6081, Cleveland, OH 44106; **Phone:** 216-844-5416; **Board Cert:** Orthopaedic Surgery 1994; **Med School:** Univ Okla Coll Med 1970; **Resid:** Surgery, UCLA Med Ctr 1972; Orthopaedic Surgery, UCLA Med Ctr 1977; **Fellow:** Pediatric Orthopaedic Surgery, Hosp Sick Chldn 1978; **Fac Appt:** Prof OrS, Case West Res Univ

Weinstein, Stuart L MD [OrS] - **Spec Exp:** Scoliosis; Hip Disorders & Dysplasia; Hip Disorders-Pediatric; Spinal Deformity; **Hospital:** Univ Iowa Hosp & Clins; **Address:** 200 Hawkins Drive, Iowa City, IA 52242-1009; **Phone:** 319-356-1872; **Board Cert:** Orthopaedic Surgery 2007; **Med School:** Univ Iowa Coll Med 1972; **Resid:** Orthopaedic Surgery, Univ Iowa Hosps 1976; **Fac Appt:** Prof OrS, Univ Iowa Coll Med

Wixson, Richard L MD [OrS] - **Spec Exp:** Hip & Knee Replacement; **Hospital:** Northwestern Meml Hosp; **Address:** 680 N Lake Shore Drive, rm 924, Chicago, IL 60611; **Phone:** 312-664-6848; **Board Cert:** Orthopaedic Surgery 1979; **Med School:** Univ Wisc 1972; **Resid:** Orthopaedic Surgery, Henry Ford Hosp 1977; Orthopaedic Surgery, New Eng Baptist Hosp 1979; **Fellow:** Orthopaedic Surgery, Mass Genl Hosp 1978; **Fac Appt:** Clin Prof OrS, Northwestern Univ

Wurtz, L Daniel MD [OrS] - **Spec Exp:** Bone & Soft Tissue Tumors; Limb Sparing Surgery; Sarcoma; Pediatric Orthopaedic Cancers; **Hospital:** IU Hlth Univ Hosp, IU Health Methodist Hosp; **Address:** 1801 N Senate Blvd, Ste 535, Indianapolis, IN 46202; **Phone:** 317-963-1963; **Board Cert:** Orthopaedic Surgery 2004; **Med School:** Univ S Ala Coll Med 1985; **Resid:** Orthopaedic Surgery, Wilford Hall USAF Med Ctr 1990; **Fellow:** Musculoskeletal Oncology, Univ Chicago Hosp 1993; **Fac Appt:** Assoc Prof OrS, Indiana Univ

Yamaguchi, Ken MD [OrS] - **Spec Exp:** Shoulder Surgery; Elbow Surgery; Rotator Cuff Surgery; **Hospital:** Barnes-Jewish Hosp; **Address:** Washington Univ Sch Med, 660 S Euclid Ave, Campus Box 8233, St Louis, MO 63110; **Phone:** 314-747-2534; **Board Cert:** Orthopaedic Surgery 2008; **Med School:** Geo Wash Univ 1989; **Resid:** Orthopaedic Surgery, G Washington Univ Hosp 1994; **Fellow:** Shoulder Surgery, NY-Presby/Columbia Univ Med Ctr 1995; **Fac Appt:** Prof OrS, Washington Univ, St Louis

Zdeblick, Thomas MD [OrS] - **Spec Exp:** Spinal Surgery; **Hospital:** Univ WI Hosp & Clins; **Address:** UW Hosp - Sports Med Clin, 621 Science Drive, Madison, WI 53711; **Phone:** 608-265-3207; **Board Cert:** Orthopaedic Surgery 2012; **Med School:** Tufts Univ 1982; **Resid:** Orthopaedic Surgery, Case West Res Univ Affil Hosp 1988; **Fellow:** Spine Surgery, Johns Hopkins Hosp 1989; **Fac Appt:** Prof OrS, Univ Wisc

Great Plains and Mountains

Coughlin, Michael J MD [OrS] - **Spec Exp:** Foot & Ankle Surgery; **Hospital:** St. Alphonsus Regl Med Ctr; **Address:** 1075 N Curtis Rd, Ste 300, Boise, ID 83706; **Phone:** 208-367-3330; **Board Cert:** Orthopaedic Surgery 1980; **Med School:** Oregon Hlth & Sci Univ 1974; **Resid:** Orthopaedic Surgery, UCSF Med Ctr 1978; **Fellow:** Foot & Ankle Surgery, Samuel Merrit Hosp 1979; **Fac Appt:** Clin Prof OrS, Oregon Hlth & Sci Univ

Garvin, Kevin L MD [OrS] - **Spec Exp:** Hip & Knee Reconstruction; Musculoskeletal Infections; **Hospital:** Nebraska Med Ctr; **Address:** Durham Outpatient Center, 4400 Emile St Fl 2, Omaha, NE 68198; **Phone:** 402-559-8000; **Board Cert:** Orthopaedic Surgery 2011; **Med School:** Med Coll Wisc 1982; **Resid:** Orthopaedic Surgery, Univ Arkansas Hosp 1987; **Fellow:** Hip Surgery, Hosp for Special Surgery 1988; **Fac Appt:** Prof OrS, Univ Nebr Coll Med

Heiden, Eric A MD [OrS] - **Spec Exp:** Sports Medicine; Knee Surgery; **Hospital:** Ortho Spec Hosp, The (TOSH); **Address:** Heiden Davidson Orthopedics, 2200 Park Ave D Bldg - Ste 100, Park City, UT 84060; **Phone:** 435-615-8822; **Board Cert:** Orthopaedic Surgery 2011; **Med School:** Stanford Univ 1991; **Resid:** Orthopaedic Surgery, UC Davis Med Ctr 1996; **Fellow:** Sports Medicine, Amer Sports Med Inst 1997

Kelly, Cynthia M MD [OrS] - **Spec Exp:** Bone Cancer; Bone & Soft Tissue Tumors; Osteonecrosis; Pediatric Orthopaedic Cancers; **Hospital:** Presby - St Luke's Med Ctr, Rocky Mountain Hosp for Children; **Address:** Colorado Limb Consultants, 1601 E 19th Ave, Ste 3300, Denver, CO 80218; **Phone:** 303-837-0072; **Board Cert:** Orthopaedic Surgery 2011; **Med School:** UCLA 1989; **Resid:** Orthopaedic Surgery, LAC-Harbor-UCLA Med Ctr 1994; **Fellow:** Orthopaedic Oncology, UCLA Med Ctr 1995; **Fac Appt:** OrS

Millett, Peter J MD [OrS] - **Spec Exp:** Shoulder Surgery; Sports Medicine; Arthroscopic Surgery; Knee Surgery; **Hospital:** Vail Valley Med Ctr; **Address:** The Steadman Clinic, 181 W Meadow Drive, Ste 400, Vail, CO 81657; **Phone:** 970-476-1100; **Board Cert:** Orthopaedic Surgery 2003; **Med School:** Dartmouth Med Sch 1995; **Resid:** Orthopaedic Surgery, Hosp Special Surgery 2000; **Fellow:** Sports Medicine, Steadman Hawkins Clinic 2001

Philippon, Marc J MD [OrS] - **Spec Exp:** Arthroscopic Surgery-Hip; Sports Medicine; **Hospital:** Vail Valley Med Ctr; **Address:** The Steadman Clinic, 181 W Meadow Drive, Ste 400, Vail, CO 81657; **Phone:** 970-476-1100; **Board Cert:** Orthopaedic Surgery 2010; **Med School:** Canada 1990; **Resid:** Orthopaedic Surgery, Jackson Meml Hosp 1995; **Fac Appt:** , Univ Pittsburgh

Randall, R. Lor MD [OrS] - **Spec Exp:** Bone Tumors; Sarcoma-Soft Tissue; Pediatric Orthopaedic Surgery; **Hospital:** Univ Utah Hlth Care, Primary Children's Med Ctr; **Address:** 2000 Circle of Hope, Ste 4260, Salt Lake City, UT 84112; **Phone:** 801-585-0300; **Board Cert:** Orthopaedic Surgery 2012; **Med School:** Yale Univ 1992; **Resid:** Orthopaedic Surgery, UCSF Med Ctr 1997; **Fellow:** Musculoskeletal Oncology, Univ WA Med Ctr 1998; **Fac Appt:** Assoc Prof OrS, Univ Utah

Rosenberg, Thomas D MD [OrS] - **Spec Exp:** Knee Surgery; Sports Medicine; **Hospital:** Park City Med Ctr, Intermountain Med Ctr; **Address:** Park City Orthopedic Clinic, 900 Round Valley Drive, Ste 100, Park City, UT 84060; **Phone:** 435-655-6600; **Board Cert:** Orthopaedic Surgery 1979; **Med School:** Univ Utah 1973; **Resid:** Orthopaedic Surgery, Univ Utah Affil Hosps 1977; **Fellow:** Sports Medicine, Univ Wisconsin Hosp 1978

Saltzman, Charles L MD [OrS] - **Spec Exp:** Foot & Ankle Surgery; **Hospital:** Univ Utah Hlth Care; **Address:** University Orthopaedic Center, 590 Wakara Way, Salt Lake City, UT 84108; **Phone:** 801-213-3668; **Board Cert:** Orthopaedic Surgery 2004; **Med School:** Univ NC Sch Med 1985; **Resid:** Orthopaedic Surgery, Univ Michigan Med Ctr; **Fellow:** Orthopaedic Surgery, Mayo Clinic; **Fac Appt:** Prof OrS, Univ Utah

Schlegel, Theodore F MD [OrS] - **Spec Exp:** Shoulder & Knee Surgery; Shoulder & Knee Injuries; Sports Medicine; Arthroscopic Surgery; **Hospital:** Sky Ridge Med Ctr, Swedish Med Ctr - Denver; **Address:** Steadman Hawkins Clinic-Denver, 8200 E Belleview Ave, Ste 615, Greenwood Village, CO 80111; **Phone:** 303-694-3333; **Board Cert:** Orthopaedic Surgery 2006; Orthopaedic Sports Medicine 2010; **Med School:** Univ Cincinnati 1987; **Resid:** Orthopaedic Surgery, Univ Utah Affil Hosp 1992; **Fellow:** Sports Medicine, Steadman Hawkins Clinic 1995; **Fac Appt:** Assoc Clin Prof OrS, Univ Colorado

Steadman, J Richard MD [OrS] - **Spec Exp:** Knee-Microfracture Surgery; Sports Medicine; Arthroscopic Surgery-Knee; Knee Injuries/ACL/Meniscus Tears; **Hospital:** Vail Valley Med Ctr; **Address:** The Steadman Clinic, 181 W Meadow Drive, Ste 400, Vail, CO 81657; **Phone:** 970-476-1100; **Board Cert:** Orthopaedic Surgery 1972; **Med School:** Univ Tex SW, Dallas 1963; **Resid:** Orthopaedic Surgery, Charity Hosp 1965; Orthopaedic Surgery, Louisiana St Univ Hosp 1970

Wilkins, Ross M MD [OrS] - **Spec Exp:** Bone Tumors; Bone Infections; Fractures-Non Union; Limb Sparing Surgery; **Hospital:** Presby - St Luke's Med Ctr; **Address:** CO Limb Consultants, 1601 E 19th Ave, Ste 3300, Denver, CO 80218; **Phone:** 303-837-0072; **Board Cert:** Orthopaedic Surgery 2007; **Med School:** Wayne State Univ 1978; **Resid:** Orthopaedic Surgery, Univ Colorado Hosp 1983; **Fellow:** Orthopaedic Oncology, Mayo Clin 1984

Southwest

Agarwal, Animesh MD [OrS] - **Spec Exp:** Trauma; Reconstructive Surgery; **Hospital:** Univ Hosp-San Antonio; **Address:** UTHSCSA-Div Orthopaedics, 7703 Floyd Curl Drive, MC 7774, San Antonio, TX 78229-3900; **Phone:** 210-567-5154; **Board Cert:** Orthopaedic Surgery 2011; **Med School:** Univ Tex, San Antonio 1992; **Resid:** Orthopaedic Surgery, Unix TX Med Ctr 1997; **Fellow:** Trauma, Grant Med Ctr 1998; **Fac Appt:** Prof OrS, Univ Tex, San Antonio

Aronson, James MD [OrS] - **Spec Exp:** Limb Lengthening (Ilizarov Procedure); Hip Disorders & Dysplasia; Clubfoot; Limb Deformities; **Hospital:** Arkansas Chldns Hosp; **Address:** Arkansas Chldns Hosp, Dept Orthopaedics, 1 Children's Way, Slot 839, Little Rock, AR 72202; **Phone:** 501-364-1468; **Board Cert:** Orthopaedic Surgery 2007; **Med School:** Univ Pittsburgh 1975; **Resid:** Surgery, Maine Med Ctr 1977; Orthopaedic Surgery, Duke Univ Med Ctr 1982; **Fellow:** Pediatric Orthopaedic Surgery, Alfred I DuPont Inst 1983; **Fac Appt:** Prof OrS, Univ Ark

Brodsky, James W MD [OrS] - **Spec Exp:** Foot & Ankle Surgery; **Hospital:** Baylor Univ Med Ctr-Dallas; **Address:** Orthopaedic Assocs of Dallas, 3900 Junius St, Ste 500, Dallas, TX 75246; **Phone:** 469-800-7200; **Board Cert:** Orthopaedic Surgery 2008; **Med School:** Case West Res Univ 1979; **Resid:** Orthopaedic Surgery, Bellevue Hosp Ctr/NYU 1981; Orthopaedic Surgery, Baylor Coll Med 1984; **Fellow:** Foot & Ankle Surgery, Rancho Los Amigos/USC/LAC Hosp 1985; **Fac Appt:** Clin Prof OrS, Univ Tex SW, Dallas

Bucholz, Robert W MD [OrS] - **Spec Exp:** Hip & Knee Replacement; Joint Replacement; **Hospital:** UT Southwestern Med Ctr at Dallas; **Address:** Ortho Surg Clin, 1801 Inwood Rd, Dallas, TX 75390-8882; **Phone:** 214-645-3300; **Board Cert:** Orthopaedic Surgery 2005; **Med School:** Yale Univ 1973; **Resid:** Surgery, Univ Hosp 1974; Orthopaedic Surgery, Yale-New Haven Hosp 1978; **Fac Appt:** Prof OrS, Univ Tex SW, Dallas

Cooper, Daniel E MD [OrS] - **Spec Exp:** Sports Medicine; Knee Injuries/ACL; Arthroscopic Surgery; Reconstructive Surgery; **Hospital:** Baylor Univ Med Ctr-Dallas; **Address:** Carrell Clin Ctr, 9301 N Central Expwy, Ste 400, Tower 1, Dallas, TX 75231; **Phone:** 214-220-2468; **Board Cert:** Orthopaedic Surgery 2013; **Med School:** Univ Tex SW, Dallas 1984; **Resid:** Orthopaedic Surgery, Univ Texas Health Scis Ctr 1989; **Fellow:** Sports Medicine, Hosp for Special Surgery 1990

Gugenheim Jr, Joseph J MD [OrS] - **Spec Exp:** Limb Lengthening (Ilizarov Procedure); Limb Deformities; Pediatric Orthopaedic Surgery; **Hospital:** Texas Ortho Hosp, Methodist Hosp - Houston; **Address:** Fondren Orthopaedic Group, 7401 S Main St, Houston, TX 77030; **Phone:** 713-799-2300; **Board Cert:** Orthopaedic Surgery 1978; **Med School:** Northwestern Univ 1972; **Resid:** Surgery, Evanston Hosp 1973; Orthopaedic Surgery, Baylor Affil Hosp 1976; **Fellow:** Pediatric Orthopaedic Surgery, Boston Chldns Hosp 1977; **Fac Appt:** Assoc Prof OrS, Baylor Coll Med

Hochschuler, Stephen H MD [OrS] - **Spec Exp:** Spinal Surgery; Spinal Disorders; **Hospital:** TX Hlth Presby Hosp Plano, Baylor Med Ctr at Frisco; **Address:** Texas Back Institute, 6020 W Parker Rd, Ste 200, Plano, TX 75093-7916; **Phone:** 972-608-5000; **Board Cert:** Orthopaedic Surgery 1978; **Med School:** Harvard Med Sch 1968; **Resid:** Surgery, Boston City Hosp 1971; Orthopaedic Surgery, Univ Texas SW Med Ctr 1977

Lewis, Valerae O MD [OrS] - **Spec Exp:** Bone Tumors; Soft Tissue Tumors; **Hospital:** UT MD Anderson Canc Ctr; **Address:** 1400 Pressler St, FCT Bldg, Ste 10.5048, Houston, TX 77030; **Phone:** 713-792-5073; **Board Cert:** Orthopaedic Surgery 2013; **Med School:** Harvard Med Sch 1993; **Resid:** Orthopaedic Surgery, Harvard Comb Ortho Program 1999

Mabrey, Jay D MD [OrS] - **Spec Exp:** Knee Replacement & Revision; Hip Replacement & Revision; Arthroscopic Surgery-Hip; **Hospital:** Baylor Univ Med Ctr-Dallas, Baylor Med Ctr at Uptown; **Address:** North TX Ortho Specs, 3600 Gaston Ave, Ste 1101, Dallas, TX 75246; **Phone:** 214-820-7010; **Board Cert:** Orthopaedic Surgery 2010; **Med School:** Cornell Univ-Weill Med Coll 1981; **Resid:** Surgery, Duke Univ Med Ctr 1983; Orthopaedic Surgery, Duke Univ Med Ctr 1987; **Fellow:** Joint Replacement Surgery, Hosp Special Surg 1991; **Fac Appt:** Prof OrS, Univ Tex SW, Dallas

Seltzer, Dana G MD [OrS] - **Spec Exp:** Sports Medicine; Trauma; Arthroscopic Surgery; Shoulder Surgery-Complex; **Hospital:** St. Joseph's Hosp & Med Ctr - Phoenix; **Address:** 500 W Thomas Rd, Ste 850, Phoenix, AZ 85013; **Phone:** 602-406-2663; **Board Cert:** Orthopaedic Surgery 2007; **Med School:** USC-Keck School of Medicine 1986; **Resid:** Orthopaedic Surgery, Univ Miami-Jackson Meml Hosp 1991; **Fellow:** Sports Medicine, Kerlan-Jobe Orthopedic Clin 1992; Shoulder Surgery, UTSA 1993

Souryal, Tarek O MD [OrS] - **Spec Exp:** Sports Medicine; Knee Injuries/ACL; **Hospital:** TX Hlth Presby Hosp Dallas; **Address:** TX Sports Med & Ortho Grp, 6901 Snider Plaza, Ste 200, Dallas, TX 75205; **Phone:** 214-369-7733; **Board Cert:** Orthopaedic Surgery 2011; **Med School:** Univ Tex, San Antonio 1982; **Resid:** Orthopaedic Surgery, UTSW Med Ctr 1987; **Fellow:** Sports Medicine, Sports Med Clin N Tex 1987; Sports Medicine, Hughston Ortho Clinic 1988; **Fac Appt:** Clin Prof OrS, Univ Tex SW, Dallas

Williams, Ronald P MD [OrS] - **Spec Exp:** Bone Tumors; **Hospital:** Seton Med Ctr; **Address:** TX Oncology, 901 W 38th St, Ste 200, Austin, TX 78705; **Phone:** 512-421-4100; **Med School:** Univ Tex, San Antonio 1984; **Resid:** Orthopaedic Surgery, Univ Kans Sch Med Affil Hosp 1989; **Fellow:** Orthopaedic Oncology, Case West Res Univ Affil Hosp 1990

Wirth, Michael A MD [OrS] - **Spec Exp:** Shoulder Surgery; Shoulder Replacement; **Hospital:** Univ Hosp-San Antonio; **Address:** 8300 Floyd Curl Drive Fl 3 - Ste 3C, Med Arts & Research Ctr, San Antonio, TX 78229; **Phone:** 210-450-9300; **Board Cert:** Orthopaedic Surgery 2004; **Med School:** Oregon Hlth & Sci Univ 1985; **Resid:** Orthopaedic Surgery, Univ Texas Hlth Sci Ctr 1990; **Fellow:** Shoulder Surgery, Charles Rockwood Jr MD 1991; **Fac Appt:** Prof OrS, Univ Tex, San Antonio

West Coast and Pacific

Anderson, Lesley J MD [OrS] - **Spec Exp:** Knee Injuries/ACL; Knee Cartilage/Meniscus Transplants; Rotator Cuff Surgery; Stem Cells in Orthopedics; **Hospital:** CA Pacific Med Ctr-Pacific Campus, St. Francis Memorial Hosp; **Address:** 2100 Webster St, Ste 309, San Francisco, CA 94115; **Phone:** 415-923-3029; **Board Cert:** Orthopaedic Surgery 2007; **Med School:** Penn State Coll Med 1976; **Resid:** Orthopaedic Surgery, UCLA Med Ctr 1983; **Fellow:** Sports Medicine/Knee Surgery, Blazina Ortho Clinic 1984; **Fac Appt:** Asst Clin Prof OrS, UCSF

Bos, Gary D MD [OrS] - **Spec Exp:** Musculoskeletal Tumors; Sarcoma; Reconstructive Surgery; **Hospital:** Kittitas Valley Community Hosp, Kaiser Sunnyside Med Ctr; **Address:** 611 S Chestnut St, Ste D, Ellensburg, WA 98926; **Phone:** 509-933-8700; **Board Cert:** Orthopaedic Surgery 2008; **Med School:** Univ Chicago-Pritzker Sch Med 1978; **Resid:** Orthopaedic Surgery, Case West Reserve Univ 1984; **Fellow:** Orthopaedic Surgery, Case West Reserve Univ 1980; Orthopaedic Oncology, Mayo Clinic 1985; **Fac Appt:** Asst Clin Prof OrS

Bozic, Kevin J MD [OrS] - **Spec Exp:** Knee Repacement; Hip Replacement; Arthritis; **Hospital:** UCSF Med Ctr; **Address:** Orthopaedic Inst, 1500 Owens St, San Fransisco, CA 94158; **Phone:** 415-353-2808; **Board Cert:** Orthopaedic Surgery 2014; **Med School:** UCSF 1994; **Resid:** Orthopaedic Surgery, Mass General Hosp 1999; **Fellow:** Orthopaedic Trauma Surgery, Mass General Hosp 2001; Reconstructive Surgery, St Lukes Med Ctr 2002; **Fac Appt:** Prof OrS, UCSF

Brage, Michael E MD [OrS] - **Spec Exp:** Foot & Ankle Surgery-Complex; Ankle Replacement & Revision; Cartilage Damage; Fractures; **Hospital:** Harborview Med Ctr, Univ Wash Med Ctr; **Address:** 908 Jefferson St, Box 359799, Seattle, WA 98104; **Phone:** 206-744-4830; **Board Cert:** Orthopaedic Surgery 2005; **Med School:** Univ IL Coll Med 1986; **Resid:** Orthopaedic Surgery, Univ Chicago Hosps 1991; **Fellow:** Foot & Ankle Surgery, Univ Wash Med Ctr 1992; **Fac Appt:** Assoc Prof OrS, Univ Wash

Brien, Earl Warren MD [OrS] - **Spec Exp:** Bone & Soft Tissue Tumors; **Hospital:** Cedars-Sinai Med Ctr; **Address:** 8700 Beverly Blvd, rm AC1058, Los Angeles, CA 90048; **Phone:** 310-423-9887; **Board Cert:** Orthopaedic Surgery 2006; **Med School:** Howard Univ 1986; **Resid:** Orthopaedic Surgery, LAC-King Drew Med Ctr 1992; **Fellow:** Musculoskeletal Disorders, Memorial Sloan Kettering 1993; Metabolic Bone Research, Hosp for Special Surgery 1994

Bukata, Susan MD [OrS] - **Spec Exp:** Bone & Soft Tissue Tumors; Bone Cancer; Musculoskeletal Tumors; Paget's Disease of Bone; **Hospital:** UCLA Ronald Reagan Med Ctr; **Address:** UCLA Orthopaedic Inst, 1250 16th St, Ste 2100, Santa Monica, CA 90404; **Phone:** 310-319-1234; **Board Cert:** Orthopaedic Surgery 2006; **Med School:** Columbia P&S 1995; **Resid:** Orthopaedic Surgery, Univ Rochester Strong Meml Hosp 2002; **Fellow:** Orthopaedic Oncology, Meml Sloan-Kettering Cancer Ctr 2004; Metabolic Bone Research, Hosp Special Surgery 2004; **Fac Appt:** Assoc Prof OrS, Univ Rochester

Caillouette, James T MD [OrS] - **Spec Exp:** Joint Replacement; Hip & Knee Reconstruction; Minimally Invasive Surgery; **Hospital:** Hoag Meml Hosp Presby; **Address:** Newport Orthopedic Institute, 22 Corporate Plaza Drive, Newport Beach, CA 92660; **Phone:** 949-722-5000; **Board Cert:** Orthopaedic Surgery 2011; **Med School:** USC Sch Med 1983; **Resid:** Orthopaedic Surgery, UC Irvine Med Ctr 1988; **Fac Appt:** Assoc Clin Prof OrS, UC Irvine

Carragee, Eugene J MD [OrS] - **Spec Exp:** Spinal Surgery; Spinal Disc Replacement; **Hospital:** Stanford Univ Hosp & Clins; **Address:** Orthopaedic Spine Center, 450 Broadway St, Pavilion A, 1st Fl, Redwood City, CA 94063-6110; **Phone:** 650-725-5905; **Board Cert:** Orthopaedic Surgery 2005; **Med School:** Stanford Univ 1982; **Resid:** Internal Medicine, Stanford Univ Hosp 1984; Orthopaedic Surgery, Stanford Univ Hosp 1988; **Fac Appt:** Prof OrS, Stanford Univ

Chapman, Jens Robert MD [OrS] - **Spec Exp:** Spinal Disorders; Spinal Cord Injury; Spinal Surgery-Cervical; **Hospital:** Univ Wash Med Ctr, Harborview Med Ctr; **Address:** Roosevelt Bone & Joint Surgery Ctr, 4245 Roosevelt Way NE Fl 2, Box 354740, Seattle, WA 98105; **Phone:** 206-598-4288; **Board Cert:** Orthopaedic Surgery 2014; **Med School:** Germany 1983; **Resid:** Surgery, Klinkum F.D. Isar 1985; Orthopaedic Surgery, Univ Texas Southern Med Ctr 1990; **Fellow:** Trauma, Harborview Med Ctr 1990; Spine Surgery, Univ Washington Med School 1991; **Fac Appt:** Prof OrS, Univ Wash

Conrad III, Ernest U MD [OrS] - **Spec Exp:** Pediatric Orthopaedic Surgery; Bone Tumors; **Hospital:** Seattle Chldns Hosp, Univ Wash Med Ctr; **Address:** 4800 Sand Point Way NE, Box 359300, Seattle, WA 98105; **Phone:** 206-987-5678; **Board Cert:** Orthopaedic Surgery 2009; **Med School:** Univ VA Sch Med 1979; **Resid:** Orthopaedic Surgery, Hosp Special Surgery 1984; **Fellow:** Orthopaedic Oncology, Univ Fla Coll Med Affil Hosp 1985; Pediatric Orthopaedic Surgery, Hosp for Sick Chldn 1986; **Fac Appt:** Prof OrS, Univ Wash

Copp, Steven N MD [OrS] - **Spec Exp:** Hip & Knee Replacement; Reconstructive Surgery-Complex; **Hospital:** Scripps Green Hosp; **Address:** Scripps Clinic Torrey Pines, 10666 N Torrey Pines Rd, MS 116, La Jolla, CA 92037; **Phone:** 858-554-8519; **Board Cert:** Orthopaedic Surgery 2012; **Med School:** UCSD 1983; **Resid:** Orthopaedic Surgery, UCSD Med Ctr 1988

Delamarter, Rick B MD [OrS] - **Spec Exp:** Spinal Surgery; Minimally Invasive Spinal Surgery; Spinal Disc Replacement; Spinal Reconstructive Surgery; **Hospital:** Cedars-Sinai Med Ctr; **Address:** The Spine Institute, 444 S San Vincente Blvd, Ste 900, Los Angeles, CA 90048; **Phone:** 310-248-7300; **Board Cert:** Orthopaedic Surgery 2010; **Med School:** Oregon Hlth & Sci Univ 1981; **Resid:** Orthopaedic Surgery, UCLA Med Ctr 1986; **Fellow:** Spinal Cord Injury Medicine, Cleveland Vets Hosp 1987; **Fac Appt:** Assoc Prof S, UCLA

Dillingham, Michael F MD [OrS] - **Spec Exp:** Sports Medicine; **Hospital:** Sequoia Hosp; **Address:** 500 Arguello St, Ste 100, Redwood City, CA 94063; **Phone:** 650-851-4900; **Board Cert:** Orthopaedic Surgery 1977; Physical Medicine & Rehabilitation 1979; **Med School:** Stanford Univ 1971; **Resid:** Orthopaedic Surgery, Standford Univ Med Ctr 1975; Physical Medicine & Rehabilitation, Santa Clara Valley Med Ctr 1977; **Fellow:** Spine Surgery, Santa Clara Valley Med Ctr 1976; **Fac Appt:** Clin Prof OrS, Stanford Univ

Dorr, Lawrence D MD [OrS] - **Spec Exp:** Hip Replacement; **Hospital:** Keck Med Ctr of USC; **Address:** Dorr Arthritis Institute, 1520 San Pablo St, Ste 2000, Los Angeles, CA 90017; **Phone:** 323-442-5762; **Board Cert:** Orthopaedic Surgery 1978; **Med School:** Univ Iowa Coll Med 1967; **Resid:** Orthopaedic Surgery, LAC-USC Med Ctr 1976; **Fellow:** Joint Replacement Surgery, Hosp Special Surgery 1977; **Fac Appt:** Prof OrS, USC Sch Med

Elattrache, Neal S MD [OrS] - **Spec Exp:** Shoulder & Elbow Surgery; Knee Surgery; Sports Medicine; **Hospital:** Keck Med Ctr of USC; **Address:** Kerlan-Jobe Orthopaedic Clinic, 6801 Park Terrace Drive, Ste 500, Los Angeles, CA 90045; **Phone:** 310-665-7257; **Board Cert:** Orthopaedic Surgery 2004; Orthopaedic Sports Medicine 2007; **Med School:** Univ Pittsburgh 1985; **Resid:** Orthopaedic Surgery, Univ Pittsburgh Med Ctr 1990; **Fellow:** Sports Medicine, Kerlan-Jobe Orthpaedic Clin 1991; **Fac Appt:** Assoc Clin Prof OrS, USC-Keck School of Medicine

Finerman, Gerald A MD [OrS] - **Spec Exp:** Sports Medicine; Hip & Knee Replacement; Arthroscopic Surgery; **Hospital:** UCLA Ronald Reagan Med Ctr, Santa Monica - UCLA Med Ctr & Ortho Hosp; **Address:** 1250 16th St, rm 2100, Santa Monica, CA 90404; **Phone:** 310-825-6019; **Board Cert:** Orthopaedic Surgery 1971; **Med School:** Johns Hopkins Univ 1962; **Resid:** Surgery, Johns Hopkins Hosp 1964; Orthopaedic Surgery, Johns Hopkins Hosp 1969; **Fac Appt:** Prof Emeritus OrS, UCLA

Garfin, Steven R MD [OrS] - **Spec Exp:** Spinal Surgery; Minimally Invasive Spinal Surgery; Spinal Deformity; **Hospital:** UCSD Med Ctr; **Address:** UCSD, Dept Orthopedic Surgery, 9350 Campus Pointe Drive, Ste 1B, La Jolla, CA 92037; **Phone:** 858-657-8200; **Board Cert:** Orthopaedic Surgery 1982; **Med School:** Univ Minn 1972; **Resid:** Orthopaedic Surgery, UCSD Med Ctr 1980; **Fellow:** Spine Surgery, Pennsylvania Hosp 1981; **Fac Appt:** Prof OrS, UCSD

Goodman, Stuart B MD/PhD [OrS] - **Spec Exp:** Arthritis; Joint Replacement; Reconstructive Surgery; **Hospital:** Stanford Univ Hosp & Clins, Lucile Packard Chldn's Hosp; **Address:** 450 Broadway St, Pavilion A, Redwood City, CA 94063-6110; **Phone:** 650-723-5643; **Board Cert:** Orthopaedic Surgery 2008; **Med School:** Univ Toronto 1978; **Resid:** Orthopaedic Surgery, Univ Toronto Affil Hosp 1984; **Fellow:** Adult Orthopedic Surgery, Univ Toronto Affil Hosp 1985; **Fac Appt:** Prof OrS, Stanford Univ

Gorab II, Robert S MD [OrS] - **Spec Exp:** Hip & Knee Replacement; Arthritis; Minimally Invasive Surgery; **Hospital:** Hoag Hosp Irvine, St. Joseph's Hosp - Orange; **Address:** Orthopaedic Specialty Institute, 280 S Main St, Ste 200, Orange, CA 92868; **Phone:** 714-634-4567; **Board Cert:** Orthopaedic Surgery 2006; **Med School:** Univ Pittsburgh 1989; **Resid:** Orthopaedic Surgery, UC-Irvine Med Ctr 1995; **Fellow:** Joint Replacement Surgery, Cleveland Clinic 1996; **Fac Appt:** OrS

Howe, Kevin MD [OrS] - **Spec Exp:** Arthritis-Hip & Knee; Hip Replacement; **Hospital:** Santa Rosa Meml Hosp, Healdsburg Dist Hosp; **Address:** Redwood Orthopaedic Surgery Assocs, 208 Concourse Blvd, Ste 1, Santa Rosa, CA 95403; **Phone:** 707-544-3400; **Board Cert:** Orthopaedic Surgery 2013; **Med School:** UCLA 1994; **Resid:** Orthopaedic Surgery, UC Davis Med Ctr 1998; **Fellow:** Joint Replacement Surgery, New England Bapt Hosp 1999

Johnson, Eric E MD [OrS] - **Spec Exp:** Pelvic & Acetabular Fractures; Trauma; Hip Replacement; **Hospital:** UCLA Ronald Reagan Med Ctr, Santa Monica - UCLA Med Ctr & Ortho Hosp; **Address:** UCLA Med Ctr-Dept Orthopedic Surgery, 10833 Le Conte Ave, rm 76-143 CHF, Los Angeles, CA 90095-6902; **Phone:** 310-206-1169; **Board Cert:** Orthopaedic Surgery 1985; **Med School:** Univ Utah 1976; **Resid:** Surgery, Univ Utah Med Ctr 1978; Orthopaedic Surgery, UCLA Med Ctr 1981; **Fellow:** Orthopaedic Trauma Surgery, Univ Hanover Affil Hosp 1982; Hip Surgery, Hosp Porte De Choisy 1984; **Fac Appt:** Assoc Prof OrS, UCLA

Kim, Choll W MD/PhD [OrS] - **Spec Exp:** Minimally Invasive Spinal Surgery; Spinal Surgery; Scoliosis; Trauma; **Hospital:** Pomerado Hosp, Alvarado Hosp & Med Ctr; **Address:** Spine Institute of San Diego, 6719 Alvarado Rd, Ste 308, San Diego, CA 92120; **Phone:** 619-265-7912; **Board Cert:** Orthopaedic Surgery 2005; **Med School:** Harvard Med Sch 1996; **Resid:** Orthopaedic Surgery, UCSD Med Ctr 2001; **Fellow:** Spine Surgery, Mayo Clin 2002; **Fac Appt:** Assoc Clin Prof OrS, UCSD

Lieberman, Jay R MD [OrS] - **Spec Exp:** Joint Replacement; Hip Replacement; Knee Replacement; **Hospital:** Keck Med Ctr of USC, LAC & USC Med Ctr; **Address:** USC, Orthopaedic Surgery Dept, 1520 San Pablo St, Ste 2000, Los Angeles, CA 90033; **Phone:** 323-442-5860; **Board Cert:** Orthopaedic Surgery 2004; **Med School:** Albany Med Coll 1984; **Resid:** Orthopaedic Surgery, Albany Med Ctr 1990; **Fellow:** Hip Surgery, Hosp for Special Surgery 1991; Joint Arthroplasty, Hosp for Special Surgery 1991; **Fac Appt:** Prof OrS, USC-Keck School of Medicine

Lowenberg, David W MD [OrS] - **Spec Exp:** Osteomyelitis; Limb Lengthening (Ilizarov Procedure); Fractures-Complex & Non Union; Limb Deformities; **Hospital:** Stanford Univ Hosp & Clins; **Address:** 450 Broadway, Pavilion A, Redwood City, CA 94063; **Phone:** 650-723-5643; **Board Cert:** Orthopaedic Surgery 2013; **Med School:** UCLA 1985; **Resid:** Orthopaedic Surgery, UCSF Med Ctr 1990; **Fac Appt:** Clin Prof OrS, Stanford Univ

Luck Jr, James V MD [OrS] - **Spec Exp:** Reconstructive Surgery; **Hospital:** Santa Monica - UCLA Med Ctr & Ortho Hosp; **Address:** LA Orthopaedic Med Ctr-Downtown Campus, 2400 S Flower St, Los Angeles, CA 90007; **Phone:** 213-749-8255; **Board Cert:** Orthopaedic Surgery 2000; **Med School:** USC Sch Med 1967; **Resid:** Orthopaedic Surgery, Orthopaedic Hosp 1973; **Fellow:** Orthopaedic Oncology, Orthopaedic Hosp 1974; Reconstructive Surgery, Rancho Los Amigos 1974; **Fac Appt:** Prof OrS, UCLA

Mandelbaum, Bert R MD [OrS] - **Spec Exp:** Sports Medicine; Knee Injuries/ACL; Cartilage Damage; **Hospital:** St. John's Hlth Ctr, Santa Monica; **Address:** Santa Monica Ortho & Sports Med Grp, 2020 Santa Monica Blvd, Ste 400, Santa Monica, CA 90404; **Phone:** 310-829-2663; **Board Cert:** Orthopaedic Surgery 2009; Orthopaedic Sports Medicine 2010; **Med School:** Washington Univ, St Louis 1980; **Resid:** Orthopaedic Surgery, Johns Hopkins Hosp 1985; **Fellow:** Sports Medicine, UCLA Med Ctr 1986

Matsen III, Frederick A MD [OrS] - **Spec Exp:** Shoulder Replacement; Rotator Cuff Surgery; **Hospital:** Univ Wash Med Ctr; **Address:** Bone & Joint Ctr, 4245 Roosevelt Way NE, Box 354740, Seattle, WA 98105; **Phone:** 206-598-4288; **Board Cert:** Orthopaedic Surgery 1978; **Med School:** Baylor Coll Med 1968; **Resid:** Orthopaedic Surgery, Univ Washington Med Ctr 1974; **Fac Appt:** Prof OrS, Univ Wash

Menendez, Lawrence R MD [OrS] - **Spec Exp:** Musculoskeletal Tumors; Bone Tumors; Reconstructive Surgery; **Hospital:** Cedars-Sinai Med Ctr; **Address:** 444 S San Vicente Blvd, Ste 603, Los Angeles, CA 90048; **Phone:** 310-423-3502; **Board Cert:** Orthopaedic Surgery 2008; **Med School:** NYU Sch Med 1979; **Resid:** Orthopaedic Surgery, NYU Med Ctr 1984; **Fellow:** Orthopaedic Oncology, Univ Fla Affil Hosp 1985; **Fac Appt:** Clin Prof OrS, USC-Keck School of Medicine

O'Donnell, Richard John MD [OrS] - **Spec Exp:** Bone Cancer; Sarcoma-Soft Tissue; Pediatric Orthopaedic Cancers; **Hospital:** UCSF Med Ctr; **Address:** Orthopedic Surgical Oncology, 1600 Divisadero St Fl 4, San Francisco, CA 94115; **Phone:** 415-885-3800; **Board Cert:** Orthopaedic Surgery 2010; **Med School:** Harvard Med Sch 1989; **Resid:** Orthopaedic Surgery, Mass Genl Hosp 1995; **Fellow:** Musculoskeletal Oncology, U WA Med Ctr 1996; **Fac Appt:** Clin Prof OrS, UCSF

Oakes, Daniel A MD [OrS] - **Spec Exp:** Joint Replacement; Hip & Knee Replacement; Hip & Knee Reconstruction; Osteonecrosis; **Hospital:** Keck Med Ctr of USC; **Address:** USC Joint Replacement, 1520 San Pablo St, Ste 2000, Los Angeles, CA 90033; **Phone:** 323-442-6950; **Board Cert:** Orthopaedic Surgery 2006; **Med School:** Harvard Med Sch 1997; **Resid:** Orthopaedic Surgery, UCLA Med Ctr 2003; **Fellow:** Joint Reconstruction, Mayo Clinic 2004; **Fac Appt:** Assoc Prof OrS, USC-Keck School of Medicine

Oppenheim, William L MD [OrS] - **Spec Exp:** Cerebral Palsy; Pediatric Orthopaedic Surgery; **Hospital:** UCLA Ronald Reagan Med Ctr, Santa Monica - UCLA Med Ctr & Ortho Hosp; **Address:** UCLA Luskin Clinic, 1250 16th St, Ste G129, Santa Monica, CA 90404; **Phone:** 424-259-6593; **Board Cert:** Orthopaedic Surgery 1992; **Med School:** Georgetown Univ 1970; **Resid:** Orthopaedic Surgery, Univ Washington Hosp 1978; **Fellow:** Pediatric Orthopaedic Surgery, Orthopaedic Hosp UCLA 1979; Orthopaedic Surgery, Nuffield Orthopaedic Ctr 1977; **Fac Appt:** Prof OrS, Georgetown Univ

Peterson, Davis C MD [OrS] - **Spec Exp:** Spinal Surgery; **Hospital:** Providence Alaska Med Ctr, Alaska Regl Hosp; **Address:** Anchorage Fracture & Orthopedic Clin, 3831 Piper St, Ste S-220, Anchorage, AK 99508; **Phone:** 907-563-3145; **Board Cert:** Orthopaedic Surgery 2009; **Med School:** Baylor Coll Med 1980; **Resid:** Orthopaedic Surgery, Madigan Army Med Ctr 1986; **Fellow:** Spine Surgery, St. Luke's Episcopal Hosp 1990

Rajacich, Nicholas MD [OrS] - **Spec Exp:** Pediatric Orthopaedic Surgery; **Hospital:** Mary Bridge Chldns Hosp & Hlth Ctr, Tacoma Genl Hosp; **Address:** Mary Bridge Orthopaedic Clin, 311 S L St, Tacoma, WA 98405; **Phone:** 253-403-1507; **Board Cert:** Orthopaedic Surgery 2013; **Med School:** Johns Hopkins Univ 1982; **Resid:** Surgery, Rhode Island Hosp 1985; Orthopaedic Surgery, St Mary's Hosp 1989; **Fellow:** Pediatric Orthopaedic Surgery, Hosp Sick Chldn 1990

Sangeorzan, Bruce J MD [OrS] - **Spec Exp:** Foot & Ankle Surgery; Trauma; Ankle Replacement & Revision; **Hospital:** Harborview Med Ctr, Univ Wash Med Ctr; **Address:** 908 Jefferson St, MS 359799, Seattle, WA 98104; **Phone:** 206-744-4830; **Board Cert:** Orthopaedic Surgery 2010; **Med School:** Wayne State Univ 1981; **Resid:** Orthopaedic Surgery, Wayne State Univ Affil Hosp 1986; **Fellow:** Trauma, Univ Wash Med Ctr 1986; Foot & Ankle Reconstruction, Univ Wash Med Ctr 1987; **Fac Appt:** Prof OrS, Univ Wash

Schmalzried, Thomas P MD [OrS] - **Spec Exp:** Hip & Knee Replacement; **Hospital:** St. Vincent's Med Ctr - Los Angeles; **Address:** The Joint Replacement Inst, 2200 W 3rd St, Ste 400, Los Angeles, CA 90057; **Phone:** 213-484-7600; **Board Cert:** Orthopaedic Surgery 2004; **Med School:** UCLA-David Geffen Sch Med 1984; **Resid:** Orthopaedic Surgery, UCLA Med Ctr 1990; **Fellow:** Hip Surgery, Mass Genl Hosp 1991; **Fac Appt:** Asst Prof OrS, UCLA

Singer, Daniel I MD [OrS] - **Spec Exp:** Hand Surgery; Bone Cancer; Hand & Upper Extremity Tumors; **Hospital:** Queen's Med Ctr - Honolulu; **Address:** Queens Med Ctr, Orthopaedic Surgery Dept, 1380 Lusitana St, Ste 615, Honolulu, HI 96813; **Phone:** 808-521-8109; **Board Cert:** Orthopaedic Surgery 2010; Hand Surgery 2010; **Med School:** Boston Univ 1979; **Resid:** Surgery, Univ Conn Hlth Ctr 1981; Orthopaedic Surgery, Univ Hawaii Affil Hosp 1984; **Fellow:** Hand Surgery, Thomas Jefferson Univ Hosp 1985; Microvascular Surgery, St Vincents Hosp 1986; **Fac Appt:** Assoc Prof OrS, Univ Hawaii JA Burns Sch Med

Smith, Douglas George MD [OrS] - **Spec Exp:** Amputation Surgery; Foot & Ankle Surgery; Limb Sparing Surgery; **Hospital:** Harborview Med Ctr; **Address:** Harborview Med Ctr, 908 Jefferson St, Box 359859, Seattle, WA 98104; **Phone:** 206-744-3462; **Board Cert:** Orthopaedic Surgery 2013; **Med School:** Univ Chicago-Pritzker Sch Med 1984; **Resid:** Orthopaedic Surgery, Loyola Univ Hosp 1989; **Fellow:** Foot & Ankle Surgery, Harborview Med Ctr 1990; **Fac Appt:** Prof OrS, Univ Wash

Thomas, Bert J MD [OrS] - **Spec Exp:** Hip Replacement & Revision; Shoulder Replacement; Knee Replacement & Revision; Arthroscopic Surgery; **Hospital:** UCLA Ronald Reagan Med Ctr, Santa Monica - UCLA Med Ctr & Ortho Hosp; **Address:** UCLA Orthopaedic Ctr, 1250 16th St, Ste 2100, Santa Monica, CA 90404; **Phone:** 424-259-9882; **Board Cert:** Orthopaedic Surgery 2008; **Med School:** Univ Pennsylvania 1979; **Resid:** Orthopaedic Surgery, UCLA Med Ctr 1984; **Fellow:** Hip Replacement Surgery, Hosp Special Surg 1985; **Fac Appt:** Clin Prof OrS, UCLA-David Geffen Sch Med

Vail, Thomas P MD [OrS] - **Spec Exp:** Hip & Knee Replacement; Hip Resurfacing; Arthritis; Osteonecrosis; **Hospital:** UCSF Med Ctr; **Address:** 500 Parnassus Ave, West Bldg - Fl 3, Box 0728, San Francisco, CA 94143-0728; **Phone:** 415-502-5183; **Board Cert:** Orthopaedic Surgery 2005; **Med School:** Loyola Univ-Stritch Sch Med 1985; **Resid:** Thoracic Surgery, Duke Univ Med Ctr 1987; Orthopaedic Surgery, Duke Univ Med Ctr 1991; **Fellow:** Reconstructive Surgery, Duke Univ Med Ctr 1992; **Fac Appt:** Prof OrS, UCSF

Wang, Jeffrey C MD [OrS] - **Spec Exp:** Spinal Surgery; Spinal Cord Injury; Spinal Tumors; Spinal Trauma; **Hospital:** UCLA Ronald Reagan Med Ctr, Santa Monica - UCLA Med Ctr & Ortho Hosp; **Address:** USC Spine Center, 1520 San Pablo St, Ste 2000, Los Angeles, CA 90033; **Phone:** 424-259-9875; **Board Cert:** Orthopaedic Surgery 2010; **Med School:** Univ Pittsburgh 1991; **Resid:** Orthopaedic Surgery, Orthopaedic Hosp UCLA 1996; **Fellow:** Spine Surgery, Univ Hosp 1997; **Fac Appt:** Prof OrS, UCLA-David Geffen Sch Med

Watkins III, Robert G MD [OrS] - **Spec Exp:** Spinal Surgery; Spinal Disc Replacement; Sports Medicine; **Hospital:** Marina Del Rey Hosp; **Address:** Watkins Spine, 4640 Admiralty Way, Ste 600, Marina Del Rey, CA 90292; **Phone:** 310-448-7890; **Board Cert:** Orthopaedic Surgery 1982; **Med School:** Univ Tenn Coll Med 1969; **Resid:** Orthopaedic Surgery, LAC-USC Med Ctr 1978; **Fellow:** Spine Surgery, Jones-Hunt Orth Hosp 1979; **Fac Appt:** Assoc Prof OrS, USC Sch Med

Yoo, Jung U MD [OrS] - **Spec Exp:** Spinal Surgery; **Hospital:** OR Hlth & Sci Univ; **Address:** 3181 SW Sam Jackson Park Rd, MC OP31, Portland, OR 97239; **Phone:** 503-494-6400; **Board Cert:** Orthopaedic Surgery 2004; **Med School:** Univ Chicago-Pritzker Sch Med 1984; **Resid:** Orthopaedic Surgery, Case Western Reserve Univ Affil Hosps 1990; **Fellow:** Orthopaedic Surgery, SUNY Hlth Sci Ctr 1991; **Fac Appt:** Prof OrS, Oregon Hlth & Sci Univ

HOSPITAL FOR SPECIAL SURGERY

HOSPITAL FOR SPECIAL SURGERY
ORTHOPEDICS

535 East 70th Street • New York, NY 10021
Physician Referral: 800.854.0071 • www.HSS.edu
Facebook, Twitter and YouTube @ HSpecialSurgery

FIRST IN ITS FIELD
Founded in 1863, Hospital for Special Surgery is a leading tertiary care academic medical center for orthopedics, rheumatology, and rehabilitation.

PIONEERS IN ORTHOPEDIC SURGERY
HSS performs more joint replacements than any other hospital in the world, and more hip and knee procedures than any other hospital in the nation. Surgeries that are rare at other hospitals are routine procedures here. HSS pioneered designs and surgical techniques for the modern artificial knee replacement in the 1970's and has been leading total knee replacement ever since. HSS also pioneered minimally invasive spine surgery techniques that reduce the need for spinal fusion. Our surgeons are also innovators in hand, elbow, shoulder, and spine surgery techniques and are leading experts in arthroscopy and hip preservation.

WORLD'S MOST EXPERIENCED MUSCULOSKELETAL RADIOLOGISTS
HSS is the world's largest academic center dedicated to musculoskeletal imaging. Our experts developed novel MRI techniques that detect early failure of joint arthroplasty and implants. HSS innovations in ultrasound and MRI also allow earlier diagnosis of autoimmune conditions and arthritis.

RECOGNIZED FOR QUALITY
HSS has one of the lowest surgical complication rates in the country as well as top scores for patient safety. For the fourth consecutive year, HSS was recognized by the state for having an infection rate that is significantly lower than the New York State average for hip replacement. 95% of our hip and knee replacement patients receive regional anesthesia, shown to provide superior outcomes with less pain and complications, compared to 11% elsewhere. 92% of patients say they would recommend HSS to their friends and family, compared to 71% for other U.S. hospitals.

Conditions, Treatments, and Services:

- **Sports Medicine**
- **Back and Neck Pain**
- **Orthopedic Trauma**
- **Hip Replacements**
- **Knee Replacements**
- **Joint Replacements**
- **Sports Injuries**
- **Hip Pain and Preservation**
- **Hand & Upper Extremity Issues**
- **Hip & Knee Problems**
- **Foot & Ankle Conditions**
- **Shoulder Problems**
- **Physiatry – Non-operative Treatment of Pain & Musculoskeletal Disorders**
- **Arthroscopy**
- **Pediatric Orthopedics**
- **Pain Management**
- **Physical Therapy**
- **Spine Conditions**
- **Scoliosis**
- **Brachial Plexus and Traumatic Nerve Injury**
- **Musculoskeletal Nerve Damage**
- **Osteogenesis Imperfecta**
- **Osteoporosis**
- **Skeletal Dysplasia**
- **Spina Bifida**
- **Carpal Tunnel Syndrome**
- **Cerebral Palsy Mobility**

Ranked #1 in the Nation for Orthopedics in *U.S.News & World Report* "Best Hospitals" 2013-14 issue

First hospital in NY State to receive Magnet Recognition for Nursing Excellence by the American Nurses Credentialing Center three consecutive times

HSS.edu

Every Musculoskeletal Specialty.
One Comprehensive Web Site.

Official Hospital of the NY Mets, NY Giants, NY Knicks, NY Liberty, NY Red Bulls, The PGA of America, New York Road Runners for the ING New York City Marathon, St. John's Athletics, CUNY Athletic Conference, and other professional and college teams

Designated as the first National Medical Center of the United States Olympic Committee's National Medical Network

First Women's Sports Medicine Center, a model across the nation

NEW ENGLAND BAPTIST™
HOSPITAL

Expertise in *motion*

New England Baptist Hospital
125 Parker Hill Avenue
Boston, MA 02120
Physician Referral: **1-855-370-6324**
nebh.org

New England Baptist Hospital (NEBH) is one of the few hospitals across the country and the only hospital in New England to specialize exclusively in musculoskeletal care. NEBH offers nationally recognized expertise in orthopedic surgery, neurosurgery and non-surgical treatments with an exceptional blend of advanced medical knowledge and superb patient care.

Joint Replacement Program: Our reputation as a national leader in joint replacements was built by pioneering innovative surgical techniques and implants. Today, the program is one of the most comprehensive programs in the country equipped to perform replacements on all patients, including those with more unique issues such as deformities, failed implants and revisions, and tertiary problems.

Spine Care Center: The NEBH Spine Center physiatrists (medical specialists in Physical Medicine and Rehabilitation) are experts in the evaluation, treatment and management of spinal disorders. Following evaluation, our physiatrists provide extensive education and information so patients can make an informed decision about surgical and non-surgical treatment options.

Sports Medicine: We deliver the highest quality sports care tailored to each individual's needs and goals. We treat professional and elite athletes including the World Champion Boston Celtics, World Cup soccer players and Olympic athletes and offer this same high level of care to amateur and recreational athletes.

NEBH offers musculoskeletal specialty expertise in all fields of Medicine to support complex cases and high risk patients. Our Musculoskeletal Radiologists and Anesthesiologists are dedicated exclusively to the needs of the orthopedic patient, ensuring accurate diagnosis and protocols designed to reduce operative and post-operative pain.

Consistently ranked as a top hopital in the nation for orthopedics
US News and World Report

Six-time Guardian of Excellence /Summit Award Winner For Patient Satisfaction by *Press Ganey*

Recipient of the 2013 Patient Safety Excellence Award from *Healthgrades* (Top 5% in the nation for patient safety)

Recipient of the 2013 Outstanding Patient Experience Award from *Healthgrades* (Top 10% in the nation for patient experience)

Becker's Hospital Review 101 Top Hospitals wih Orthopedic Programs

---

Proud to be the Official Hospital of the Boston Celtics and to provide services to many student and professional athletes from across the country.

NYU Langone
MEDICAL CENTER

550 First Avenue *(at 31st Street)*
New York, NY 10016
www.NYULMC.org/orthosurgery
Physician Referral: **888-7-NYU-MED** *(888-769-8633)*

ORTHOPAEDIC SURGERY

The Department of Orthopaedic Surgery at NYU Langone Medical Center continues to be recognized as a national leader, **ranked #5 in the nation by *U.S. News & World Report's* 2013-2014 "Best Hospitals" survey**. Our physicians combine extensive experience with cutting-edge research and technology to address bone and joint problems that affect a patient's quality of life. The expertise of our world-class orthopaedists represents the full range of subspecialty areas including **Adult Reconstructive, Sports Medicine and Primary Care Sports Medicine, Spine, Shoulder & Elbow, Foot & Ankle, Hand Surgery, Trauma & Fracture, Orthopaedic Oncology, and Pediatric Orthopaedics**; additional areas of specialization include minimally-invasive surgery and robotic-assisted joint replacement.

Premier Areas of Expertise

Joint Replacement Center physicians evaluate degenerative joint conditions caused by arthritis, injuries, congenital problems and general wear-and-tear to determine the best course of treatment. Our surgeons are experts in knee, hip and shoulder replacements, complex joint revisions, and minimally invasive surgeries, conducting more than 3,000 procedures annually. The experts in our **Hip Center** also specialize in the cutting-edge, minimally invasive anterior total hip replacement technique.

The Spine Center provides conservative care for lower back and neck pain, scoliosis, osteoporosis, problems associated with failed previous surgery, idiopathic disorders, growth disorders, neuromuscular disease, degenerative and congenital conditions, and traumatic deformity. Our surgeons perform over 2,000 procedures a year, including minimally invasive spinal fusions.

Hand Center specialists diagnose and offer operative and non-operative care for a wide range of upper extremity conditions, including fractures, congenital anomalies, soft tissue and skeletal trauma, degenerative and rheumatoid arthritis, sports-related injuries, vascular disorders, tumors and occupational disorders.

Sports Medicine and Primary Care Sports Medicine physicians treat sports-related injuries or conditions of the knee, shoulder, elbow and ankle, using joint preservation techniques as well as surgical procedures. Our patients range from athletes playing at the high school, college and professional levels to recreational athletes/active individuals from every age group.

(continued)

Penn Medicine

Penn Orthopaedics

Penn Orthopaedics, a leader in treating patients with musculoskeletal injuries and disorders from the most common to the most complex, provides comprehensive, quality care that ranks among the very best in the nation. Our multidisciplinary team of surgeons and staff use the latest technology and techniques to get people – grandparents and professional athletes alike – back in motion.

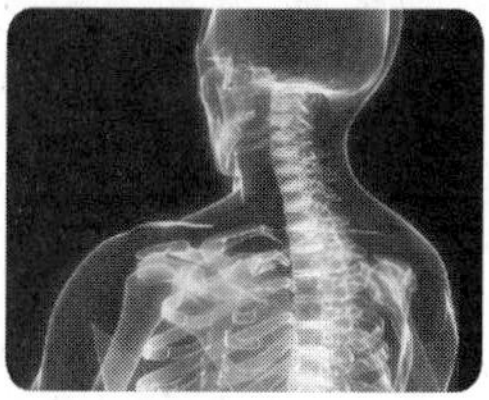

Programs

Penn Orthopaedics offers specialized services and programs to treat a wide range of orthopaedic problems, including:

- Foot and ankle
- General orthopaedics
- Hand and wrist
- Hip and knee replacement
- Neuro-orthopaedics
- Orthopaedic oncology
- Shoulder and elbow
- Spine
- Sports medicine
- Trauma and fracture

Leadership

As recognized clinical leaders, our doctors offer state-of-the-art treatment options, including:

- Advanced minimally invasive joint replacement procedures.
- Upper extremity services dedicated to the treatment of shoulder, elbow, wrist and hand disorders.
- Treatment for malignant and benign tumors of the bone and soft tissue.

Our physicians serve on the boards of the nation's premiere orthopaedic organizations and publish articles in many of the leading orthopaedic journals in the world.

Also a noted research group, Penn Orthopaedics is helping to create the next generation of orthopaedic care, in areas including tissue engineering, tendon healing and biomechanics of the shoulder and spine. Penn Orthopaedics is a top-ranked orthopaedic department in the country for orthopaedic grants from the National Institutes of Health.

Expertise

Penn Orthopaedics is consistently recognized as a national leader in outstanding care. *U.S. News & World Report* ranked the Hospital of the University of Pennsylvania among the best in Philadelphia region for outstanding orthopaedic care. Many of our surgeons are listed among the *Best Doctors in America®*, and a number of our physicians are listed annually in *Philadelphia* magazine's "*Top Docs*" issue.

Locations

Hospital of the University of Pennsylvania

Penn Presbyterian Medical Center

Pennsylvania Hospital

Penn Sports Medicine Center—Weightman Hall

Penn Medicine Cherry Hill

Penn Medicine Radnor

Penn Medicine Valley Forge

For more information or to schedule an appointment, call 800.789.PENN (7366) or visit PennMedicine.org/ortho

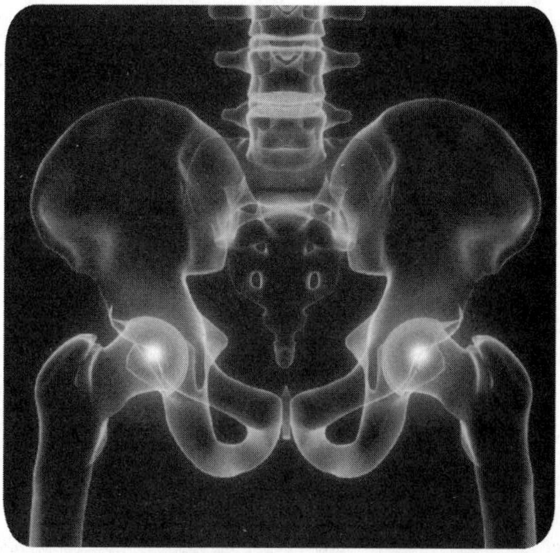

Hospital of the University of Pennsylvania | Penn Presbyterian Medical Center | Pennsylvania Hospital | The Chester County Hospital

800.789.PENN | PennMedicine.org

Top Doctors Make A Difference

Otolaryngology

An otolaryngologist-head and neck surgeon provides comprehensive medical and surgical care for patients with diseases and disorders that affect the ears, nose, throat, the respiratory and upper alimentary systems and related structures of the head and neck.

An otolaryngologist diagnoses and provides medical and/or surgical therapy or prevention of diseases, allergies, neoplasms, deformities, disorders and/or injuries of the ears, nose, sinuses, throat, respiratory and upper alimentary systems, face, jaws and the other head and neck systems. Head and neck oncology, facial plastic and reconstructive surgery and the treatment of disorders of hearing and voice are fundamental areas of expertise.

Training Required: Five years

Certification in the following subspecialty requires additional training and examination.

Plastic Surgery within the Head and Neck: An otolaryngologist with additional training in plastic and reconstructive procedures within the head, face, neck and associated structures, including cutaneous head and neck oncology and reconstruction, management of maxillofacial trauma, soft tissue repair and neural surgery.

Facial Plastic and Reconstructive Surgery is not a recognized ABMS subspecialty. However this designation has been included because the certification process is meaningful and rigorous. It is awarded to those doctors who hold a current ABMS certification in Otolaryngology, but those board certified in Plastic Surgery, Ophthalmology, or Dermatology are also eligible. Certification requires a post-graduate fellowship in Facial Plastic and Reconstructive Surgery followed by a written examination.

This field is diverse and involves a wide age range of patients, from the newborn to the aged. While both cosmetic and reconstructive surgeries are practiced, there are many additional procedures which interface with them.

Otolaryngology

New England

Bhattacharyya, Neil MD [Oto] - **Spec Exp:** Sinus Disorders; Endoscopic Sinus Surgery; Sleep Apnea; **Hospital:** Brigham & Women's Hosp; **Address:** Brigham & Women's Hospital, Div of Otolaryngology, 45 Francis St Fl 2, Boston, MA 02115; **Phone:** 617-525-6540; **Board Cert:** Otolaryngology 1998; **Med School:** Univ IL Coll Med 1992; **Resid:** Otolaryngology, Mass Eye & Ear Infirm 1997; **Fac Appt:** Prof Oto, Harvard Med Sch

Burns, James A MD [Oto] - **Spec Exp:** Laryngeal & Vocal Cord Surgery; Laryngeal & Tracheal Disorders; Voice Disorders; **Hospital:** Mass Genl Hosp; **Address:** Ctr for Laryngeal Surgery, One Bowdoin Square Fl 11, BS01-11, Boston, MA 02114; **Phone:** 617-726-1444; **Board Cert:** Otolaryngology 1997; **Med School:** Univ VA Sch Med 1991; **Resid:** Otolaryngology, Univ Virginia Affil Hosp 1996; **Fellow:** Laryngology, Mass Eye & Ear Infirmary 2003

Couch, Marion E MD [Oto] - **Spec Exp:** Head & Neck Cancer; Thyroid & Parathyroid Cancer & Surgery; Microvascular Surgery; Airway Reconstruction; **Hospital:** FAHC - Med Ctr Campus; **Address:** FAHC, Div Otolaryngology, 111 Colchester Ave, Burlington, VT 05401; **Phone:** 802-847-4537; **Board Cert:** Otolaryngology 1997; **Med School:** Rush Med Coll 1990; **Resid:** Surgery, Johns Hopkins Hosp 1991; Otolaryngology, Johns Hopkins Hosp 1996; **Fac Appt:** Prof Oto, Univ VT Coll Med

Deschler, Daniel G MD [Oto] - **Spec Exp:** Head & Neck Cancer; Head & Neck Reconstruction; Salivary Gland Tumors & Surgery; Voice after Laryngeal Cancer Surgery; **Hospital:** Mass Eye & Ear Infirm, Mass Genl Hosp; **Address:** Mass Eye & Ear Infirmary, Head & Neck Surgery Dept, 243 Charles St, Fl 11, Ste 1199, Boston, MA 02114; **Phone:** 617-573-4100; **Board Cert:** Otolaryngology 1996; **Med School:** Harvard Med Sch 1990; **Resid:** Otolaryngology, UCSF Med Ctr 1995; **Fellow:** Head & Neck Surgical Oncology, Hahnemann Univ Med Ctr 1996; **Fac Appt:** Prof Oto, Harvard Med Sch

Gliklich, Richard E MD [Oto] - **Spec Exp:** Cosmetic Surgery-Face & Neck; Rhinoplasty; Skin Laser Surgery-Resurfacing; **Hospital:** Mass Eye & Ear Infirm; **Address:** Mass Eye & Ear Infirmary, 243 Charles St Fl 9, Boston, MA 02114; **Phone:** 617-573-4105; **Board Cert:** Otolaryngology 1994; Facial Plastic & Reconstr Surgery 1996; **Med School:** Harvard Med Sch 1988; **Resid:** Otolaryngology, Mass Eye & Ear Infirmary 1993; **Fellow:** Facial Plastic Surgery, Mass Eye & Ear Infirmary 1994; **Fac Appt:** Prof Oto, Harvard Med Sch

Gosselin, Benoit J MD [Oto] - **Spec Exp:** Head & Neck Cancer; Facial Plastic & Reconstructive Surgery; Head & Neck Reconstruction; **Hospital:** Dartmouth - Hitchcock Med Ctr; **Address:** Dartmouth-Hitchcock Med Ctr, Dept Oto, 1 Med Ctr Drive, Lebanon, NH 03756; **Phone:** 603-650-8121; **Board Cert:** Otolaryngology 1994; **Med School:** Univ Ottawa 1988; **Resid:** Head and Neck Surgery, Univ Ottawa 1993; **Fellow:** Head and Neck Surgery, Univ Toronto 1994; Facial Plastic Surgery, Mercy Hosp 1995; **Fac Appt:** Assoc Clin Prof Oto, Dartmouth Med Sch

Grillone, Gregory A MD [Oto] - **Spec Exp:** Laryngeal Disorders; Laryngeal Cancer; Head & Neck Cancer; Voice Disorders; **Hospital:** Boston Med Ctr; **Address:** BMC-Dept Otolaryngology, 830 Harrison Ave, Moakley Bldg, Ste 1400, Boston, MA 02118; **Phone:** 617-638-8124; **Board Cert:** Otolaryngology 1988; **Med School:** Mount Sinai Sch Med 1983; **Resid:** Otolaryngology, Boston Med Ctr 1988; **Fac Appt:** Assoc Prof Oto, Boston Univ

Grundfast, Kenneth M MD [Oto] - **Spec Exp:** Hearing Loss; Pediatric Otolaryngology; **Hospital:** Boston Med Ctr, VA Boston Hlthcare Sys-Jamaica Plain Div; **Address:** BMC-Dept Otolaryngology, 830 Harrison Ave, Moakley Bldg - Ste 1400, Boston, MA 02118; **Phone:** 617-638-8124; **Board Cert:** Otolaryngology 1977; **Med School:** SUNY Upstate Med Univ 1969; **Resid:** Surgery, Sibley Meml Hosp 1974; Otolaryngology, Boston-Affil Hosps 1977; **Fellow:** Pediatric Otolaryngology, Chldns Hosp 1978; **Fac Appt:** Prof Oto, Boston Univ

Hadlock, Theresa MD [Oto] - **Spec Exp:** Facial Paralysis; **Hospital:** Mass Eye & Ear Infirm; **Address:** Mass Eye & Ear Infirm, Facial Plastic Surgery, 243 Charles St, Boston, MA 02114; **Phone:** 617-573-3641; **Board Cert:** Otolaryngology 2012; **Med School:** Harvard Med Sch 1994; **Resid:** Otolaryngology, Mass Eye & Ear Infirm 1998; **Fellow:** Facial Plastic Surgery, Mass Eye & Ear Infirm 1999; **Fac Appt:** Asst Prof Oto, Harvard Med Sch

Kim, Daniel Y MD [Oto] - **Spec Exp:** Head & Neck Surgery; Thyroid & Parathyroid Surgery; Skull Base Tumors & Surgery; Sinus Disorders/Surgery; **Hospital:** UMass Memorial Med Ctr, UMass Mem Med Ctr-Memorial Campus; **Address:** UMass Meml Med Ctr-Univ Campus, 55 Lake Ave N, Worcester, MA 01655; **Phone:** 508-856-4161; **Board Cert:** Otolaryngology 1986; **Med School:** UMDNJ-RW Johnson Med Sch 1980; **Resid:** Surgery, Boston Univ Med Ctr 1982; Otolaryngology, NYU Med Ctr 1985; **Fellow:** Head & Neck Surgical Oncology, Einstein Coll Med - Montefiore Med Ctr 1986; **Fac Appt:** Assoc Clin Prof Oto, Univ Mass Sch Med

Kveton, John F MD [Oto] - **Spec Exp:** Ear Disorders/Surgery; Cochlear Implants; Acoustic Neuroma; Hearing Loss; **Hospital:** Yale-New Haven Hosp, Yale-New Haven Hosp - St Raphael Campus; **Address:** ENT Med & Surgical Grp, 46 Prince St, Ste 601, New Haven, CT 06519-1634; **Phone:** 203-752-1726; **Board Cert:** Otolaryngology 1982; Neurotology 2004; **Med School:** St Louis Univ 1978; **Resid:** Otolaryngology, Yale-New Haven Hosp 1982; **Fellow:** Neurotology, The Otology Group 1983; **Fac Appt:** Clin Prof Oto, Yale Univ

McKenna, Michael J MD [Oto] - **Spec Exp:** Skull Base Surgery; Otology; Neuro-Otology; **Hospital:** Mass Eye & Ear Infirm; **Address:** Massachusetts Eye & Ear Infirm, 243 Charles St Fl 2, Boston, MA 02114; **Phone:** 617-573-3672; **Board Cert:** Otolaryngology 1988; Neurotology 2004; **Med School:** USC Sch Med 1982; **Resid:** Otolaryngology, Mass Eye & Ear Infirm 1988; **Fellow:** Neurotology, Otologic Med Grp 1989; **Fac Appt:** Prof Oto, Harvard Med Sch

Metson, Ralph MD [Oto] - **Spec Exp:** Sinus Disorders/Surgery; **Hospital:** Mass Eye & Ear Infirm; **Address:** Zero Emerson Pl, Ste 2D, Boston, MA 02114; **Phone:** 617-227-4366; **Board Cert:** Otolaryngology 1985; **Med School:** UCSD 1979; **Resid:** Otolaryngology, UCLA Med Ctr 1985; **Fac Appt:** Assoc Clin Prof Oto, Harvard Med Sch

Randolph, Gregory W MD [Oto] - **Spec Exp:** Thyroid Disorders; Thyroid Cancer; Parathyroid Disease; **Hospital:** Mass Eye & Ear Infirm; **Address:** Mass Eye & Ear Infirmary, 243 Charles St, Ste 271, Boston, MA 02114; **Phone:** 617-573-4115; **Board Cert:** Otolaryngology 1993; **Med School:** Cornell Univ-Weill Med Coll 1987; **Resid:** Otolaryngology, Mass Eye & Ear Infirmary 1992; **Fellow:** Thyroid Oncology, Mass Eye & Ear Infirmary 1993; **Fac Appt:** Asst Prof Oto, Harvard Med Sch

Rauch, Steven D MD [Oto] - **Spec Exp:** Hearing & Balance Disorders; Meniere's Disease; Neuro-Otology; **Hospital:** Mass Eye & Ear Infirm; **Address:** Mass Eye & Ear Infirm, Dept Otolaryngology, 243 Charles St, Boston, MA 02114; **Phone:** 617-573-3644; **Board Cert:** Otolaryngology 1984; **Med School:** Univ Cincinnati 1979; **Resid:** Surgery, U Mass Med Ctr 1981; Otolaryngology, Mass Eye & Ear Infirm 1984; **Fac Appt:** Prof Oto, Harvard Med Sch

Rebeiz, Elie E MD [Oto] - **Spec Exp:** Head & Neck Surgery; Sinus Disorders/Surgery; Skull Base Surgery; **Hospital:** Tufts Med Ctr; **Address:** Tufts Med Ctr, Dept Otolaryngology, 860 Washington St, Boston, MA 02111; **Phone:** 617-636-1664; **Board Cert:** Otolaryngology 2000; **Med School:** Lebanon 1984; **Resid:** Otolaryngology, Amer Univ Med Ctr 1988; **Fellow:** Otolaryngology, Mass E&E Infirm 1990; **Fac Appt:** Prof Oto, Tufts Univ

Sasaki, Clarence T MD [Oto] - **Spec Exp:** Head & Neck Cancer; Swallowing Disorders; Zenker Diverticulum; Voice Disorders; **Hospital:** Yale-New Haven Hosp; **Address:** Yale Sch Med, Dept Otolaryngology, 333 Cedar St, Box 208041, New Haven, CT 06520-8041; **Phone:** 203-785-2592; **Board Cert:** Otolaryngology 1973; **Med School:** Yale Univ 1966; **Resid:** Surgery, Mary Hitchcock Hosp 1968; Otolaryngology, Yale-New Haven Hosp 1973; **Fellow:** Head and Neck Surgery, Univ of Milan 1978; Skull Base Surgery, Univ Zurich 1982; **Fac Appt:** Prof Oto, Yale Univ

Silverman, Damon A MD [Oto] - **Spec Exp:** Head & Neck Cancer & Surgery; Voice Disorders; Throat Disorders; **Hospital:** FAHC - Med Ctr Campus; **Address:** Fletcher Allen Otolaryngology, 111 Colchester Ave, Medical Ctr West Pavilion 4, Burlington, VT 05401-1473; **Phone:** 802-847-4041; **Board Cert:** Otolaryngology 2004; **Med School:** UC Davis 1997; **Resid:** Otolaryngology, Cleveland Clinic 2003; **Fellow:** Laryngology, Vanderbilt Univ 2004; **Fac Appt:** Assoc Prof Oto, Univ VT Coll Med

Spiegel, Jeffrey H MD [Oto] - **Spec Exp:** Head & Neck Surgery; Reconstructive Surgery; Cosmetic Surgery-Face; **Hospital:** Boston Med Ctr; **Address:** Advanced Facial Aesthetics, 1200 Boylston St, Chestnut Hill, MA 02467; **Phone:** 617-566-3223; **Board Cert:** Otolaryngology 2000; Facial Plastic & Reconstr Surgery 2001; **Med School:** Univ Mich Med Sch 1994; **Resid:** Otolaryngology, UCSF Med Ctr 1999; **Fellow:** Facial Plastic & Reconstr Surgery, Mass Eye & Ear Infirmary 2000; **Fac Appt:** Assoc Prof Oto, Boston Univ

Vining, Eugenia M MD [Oto] - **Spec Exp:** Sinus Disorders/Surgery; Skull Base Tumors; Endoscopic Sinus Surgery; **Hospital:** Yale-New Haven Hosp, Yale-New Haven Hosp - St Raphael Campus; **Address:** ENT Medical & Surgical Grp, 46 Prince St, Ste 601, New Haven, CT 06519; **Phone:** 203-752-1726; **Board Cert:** Otolaryngology 1993; **Med School:** Yale Univ 1987; **Resid:** Otolaryngology, Yale-New Haven Hosp 1991; Otolaryngology, Yale-New Haven Hosp 1992; **Fellow:** Sinus Surgery, Univ Penn 1993

Yarbrough, Wendell G MD [Oto] - **Spec Exp:** Head & Neck Cancer; Salivary Gland Tumors; **Hospital:** Yale-New Haven Hosp; **Address:** 800 Howard Ave, Fl 4, New Haven, CT 06519; **Phone:** 203-785-4862; **Board Cert:** Otolaryngology 1995; **Med School:** Univ NC Sch Med 1989; **Resid:** Otolaryngology, Univ NC Hosps 1994; **Fellow:** Surgical Oncology, Univ NC Med Sch 1996

Zeitels, Steven M MD [Oto] - **Spec Exp:** Laryngeal Cancer; Voice Disorders; Head & Neck Cancer & Surgery; **Hospital:** Mass Genl Hosp; **Address:** MGH Center for Laryngeal Surgery, One Bowdoin Square Fl 11, Boston, MA 02114; **Phone:** 617-726-0218; **Board Cert:** Otolaryngology 1988; **Med School:** Boston Univ 1982; **Resid:** Surgery, Univ Hosp-Boston City Hosp 1983; Otolaryngology, Boston Univ-Tufts Univ Affil Hosps 1987; **Fellow:** Head and Neck Surgery, Boston VA Med Ctr 1988; **Fac Appt:** Prof Oto, Harvard Med Sch

Mid Atlantic

Aviv, Jonathan MD [Oto] - **Spec Exp:** Voice Disorders; Swallowing Disorders; Cough; Endoscopy; **Hospital:** Mt Sinai Med Ctr (page 62); **Address:** ENT & Allergy Assocs, 210 E 86th St Fl 9, New York, NY 10028; **Phone:** 212-722-5570; **Board Cert:** Otolaryngology 1990; **Med School:** Columbia P&S 1985; **Resid:** Surgery, Mt Sinai Med Ctr 1987; Otolaryngology, Mt Sinai Med Ctr 1990; **Fellow:** Head and Neck Surgery, Mt Sinai Med Ctr 1991; **Fac Appt:** Prof Oto, Mount Sinai Sch Med

Blitzer, Andrew MD/DDS [Oto] - **Spec Exp:** Voice Disorders; Swallowing Disorders; Nasal & Sinus Surgery; Botox Therapy; **Hospital:** St. Luke's - Roosevelt Hosp Ctr - Roosevelt Div (page 56); **Address:** 425 W 59th St Fl 10, New York, NY 10019-1104; **Phone:** 212-262-9500; **Board Cert:** Otolaryngology 1977; **Med School:** Mount Sinai Sch Med 1973; **Resid:** Surgery, Beth Israel Med Ctr 1974; Otolaryngology, Mt Sinai Hosp 1977; **Fac Appt:** Clin Prof Oto, Columbia P&S

Califano III, Joseph A MD [Oto] - **Spec Exp:** Head & Neck Cancer; Thyroid Cancer; Skull Base Tumors; Melanoma; **Hospital:** Johns Hopkins Hosp (page 59), Greater Baltimore Med Ctr; **Address:** Johns Hopkins Outpatient Clin, 601 N Caroline St Fl 6, Baltimore, MD 21287; **Phone:** 443-849-8940; **Board Cert:** Otolaryngology 2000; **Med School:** Harvard Med Sch 1993; **Resid:** Otolaryngology, Johns Hopkins Hosp 1999; **Fellow:** Head & Neck Surgical Oncology, Meml Sloan-Kettering Cancer Ctr 2000; **Fac Appt:** Prof Oto, Johns Hopkins Univ

Carey, John P MD [Oto] - **Spec Exp:** Skull Base Surgery; Hearing Disorders; Neuro-Otology; **Hospital:** Johns Hopkins Hosp (page 59); **Address:** Johns Hopkins Outpatient Ctr, 601 N Caroline St, rm 6255, Baltimore, MD 21287; **Phone:** 443-997-6467; **Board Cert:** Otolaryngology 1999; Neurotology 2008; **Med School:** Washington Univ, St Louis 1991; **Resid:** Surgery, Virginia Mason Hosp 1994; Otolaryngology, Univ Wash Med Ctr 1999; **Fellow:** Neurotology, Johns Hopkins Hosp 2007; **Fac Appt:** Prof Oto, Johns Hopkins Univ

Caruana, Salvatore M MD [Oto] - **Spec Exp:** Head & Neck Cancer; Thyroid & Parathyroid Cancer & Surgery; Laser Surgery; Robotic Surgery; **Hospital:** NY-Presby/Columbia Univ Med Ctr, NY (page 65); **Address:** 180 Fort Washington Ave, Harkness Bldg - Fl 7, New York, NY 10032; **Phone:** 212-305-5335; **Board Cert:** Otolaryngology 1996; **Med School:** Mount Sinai Sch Med 1989; **Resid:** Otolaryngology, NY EE Infirm 1995; **Fellow:** Head & Neck Surgical Oncology, Meml Sloan-Kettering Canc Ctr 1997; **Fac Appt:** Asst Prof Oto, Columbia P&S

Chalian, Ara A MD [Oto] - **Spec Exp:** Head & Neck Cancer; Head & Neck Reconstruction; Thyroid Cancer; Reconstructive Surgery-Face; **Hospital:** Hosp Univ Penn - UPHS (page 69); **Address:** Hosp Univ Penn, Dept Otolaryngology, 3400 Spruce St, 5 Silverstein, Philadelphia, PA 19104; **Phone:** 215-662-2777; **Board Cert:** Otolaryngology 1994; **Med School:** Indiana Univ 1988; **Resid:** Surgery, Indiana Univ Hosp 1990; Otolaryngology, Indiana Univ Hosp 1993; **Fellow:** Molecular Biology, Hosp Univ Penn 1994; Head and Neck Surgery, Hosp Univ Penn 1995; **Fac Appt:** Assoc Prof Oto, Univ Pennsylvania

Close, Lanny Garth MD [Oto] - **Spec Exp:** Sinus Disorders/Surgery; Endoscopic Sinus Surgery; **Hospital:** NY-Presby/Columbia Univ Med Ctr, NY (page 65); **Address:** 51 W 51st St, Fl 3rd, New York, NY 10022; **Phone:** 212-326-8475; **Board Cert:** Otolaryngology 1977; **Med School:** Baylor Coll Med 1972; **Resid:** Surgery, Johns Hopkins Hosp 1974; Otolaryngology, Baylor Affil Hosps 1977; **Fellow:** Head and Neck Surgery, MD Anderson Cancer Ctr 1979; **Fac Appt:** Prof Oto, Columbia P&S

Costantino, Peter D MD [Oto] - **Spec Exp:** Skull Base Tumors; Head & Neck Cancer; Craniofacial Surgery/Reconstruction; **Hospital:** Lenox Hill Hosp (page 66); **Address:** 130 E 77th St Fl 10, New York, NY 10075; **Phone:** 212-434-4500; **Board Cert:** Otolaryngology 1990; Facial Plastic & Reconstr Surgery 2000; **Med School:** Northwestern Univ 1984; **Resid:** Surgery, Northwestern Meml Hosp 1986; Otolaryngology, Northwestern Meml Hosp 1989; **Fellow:** Head and Neck Surgery, Northwestern Meml Hosp 1990; Skull Base Surgery, Univ Pittsburgh 1991; **Fac Appt:** Prof Oto, Columbia P&S

Davidson, Bruce J MD [Oto] - **Spec Exp:** Head & Neck Cancer; Thyroid Disorders; **Hospital:** MedStar Georgetown Univ Hosp; **Address:** Georgetown Univ Med Ctr, Dept Otolaryngology-Head & Neck Surgery, 3800 Reservoir Rd NW, Gorman Bldg - Fl 1, Washington, DC 20007; **Phone:** 202-444-8186; **Board Cert:** Otolaryngology 1993; **Med School:** W VA Univ 1987; **Resid:** Otolaryngology, Georgetown Univ Med Ctr 1992; **Fellow:** Head and Neck Surgery, Memorial Sloan-Kettering Cancer Ctr 1994; **Fac Appt:** Asst Prof Oto, Georgetown Univ

Edelstein, David R MD [Oto] - **Spec Exp:** Endoscopic Sinus Surgery; Nasal Reconstruction; Sleep Disorders/Apnea; Sleep Disorders/Apnea; **Hospital:** Lenox Hill Hosp (Manh Eye, Ear & Throat Hosp) (page 66), Mt Sinai Med Ctr (page 62); **Address:** Manhattan Otolaryngology Head & Neck Surg, 1421 3rd Ave Fl 4, New York, NY 10028; **Phone:** 212-452-1500; **Board Cert:** Otolaryngology 1985; **Med School:** Boston Univ 1980; **Resid:** Surgery, Mount Sinai Hosp 1981; Otolaryngology, Mount Sinai Hosp 1984; **Fac Appt:** Clin Prof Oto, Cornell Univ-Weill Med Coll

Eisele, David W MD [Oto] - **Spec Exp:** Salivary Gland Tumors & Surgery; Head & Neck Cancer; Thyroid Cancer; Neck Masses; **Hospital:** Johns Hopkins Hosp (page 59); **Address:** 601 N Caroline St Fl 6, Baltimore, MD 21287; **Phone:** 443-997-6467; **Board Cert:** Otolaryngology 1988; **Med School:** Cornell Univ-Weill Med Coll 1982; **Resid:** Surgery, Univ Wash Med Ctr 1984; Otolaryngology, Univ Wash Med Ctr 1988; **Fac Appt:** Prof Oto, Johns Hopkins Univ

Feghali, Joseph G MD [Oto] - **Spec Exp:** Ear Disorders/Surgery; Acoustic Neuroma; Hearing Disorders; Cholesteatoma; **Hospital:** Montefiore Med Ctr-Moses Campus, NY; **Address:** 182 E 210th St, Bronx, NY 10467; **Phone:** 718-881-3277; **Board Cert:** Otolaryngology 1990; **Med School:** Lebanon 1978; **Resid:** Surgery, meml Sloan Kettering Cancer Ctr 1986; Otolaryngology, Montefiore Med Ctr 1990; **Fellow:** Otology & Neurotology, House Ear Inst 1983; Neurological Surgery, Meml Sloan Kettering Cancer Ctr 1985; **Fac Appt:** Clin Prof Oto, Albert Einstein Coll Med

Ferris, Robert L MD/PhD [Oto] - **Spec Exp:** Head & Neck Cancer; Thyroid & Parathyroid Cancer & Surgery; Salivary Gland Tumors; Laryngeal Cancer; **Hospital:** UPMC Presby, Pittsburgh; **Address:** University ENT Specialists, Eye & Ear Institute, 203 Lothrop St, Ste 300, Pittsburgh, PA 15213; **Phone:** 412-647-2100; **Board Cert:** Otolaryngology 2012; **Med School:** Johns Hopkins Univ 1995; **Resid:** Otolaryngology, Johns Hopkins Hosp 2001; **Fac Appt:** Assoc Prof Oto, Univ Pittsburgh

Fried, Marvin P MD [Oto] - **Spec Exp:** Endoscopic Sinus Surgery; Head & Neck Tumors; Laryngeal & Voice Disorders; Sinus Disorders/Surgery; **Hospital:** Montefiore Med Ctr-Moses Campus, NY, Montefiore Med Ctr-Einstein Campus, NY; **Address:** 3400 Bainbridge Ave, Fl 3, Bronx, NY 10467; **Phone:** 718-920-4646; **Board Cert:** Otolaryngology 1975; **Med School:** Tufts Univ 1969; **Resid:** Surgery, Barnes-Jewish Hosp 1971; Otolaryngology, Barnes-Jewish Hosp 1975; **Fellow:** Washington Univ 1976; **Fac Appt:** Prof Oto, Albert Einstein Coll Med

Genden Sr, Eric M MD [Oto] - **Spec Exp:** Head & Neck Cancer & Surgery; Head & Neck Cancer Reconstruction; Airway Reconstruction; Thyroid & Parathyroid Cancer & Surgery; **Hospital:** Mt Sinai Med Ctr (page 62); **Address:** Mt Sinai Dept Otolaryngology, 1 Gustave L Levy Pl, Box 1191, New York, NY 10029; **Phone:** 212-241-9410; **Board Cert:** Otolaryngology 1999; Facial Plastic & Reconstr Surgery 2000; **Med School:** Mount Sinai Sch Med 1992; **Resid:** Otolaryngology, Barnes Jewish Hosp 1998; **Fellow:** Head and Neck Surgery, Mt Sinai Med Ctr 1999; **Fac Appt:** Prof Oto, Mount Sinai Sch Med

Gold, Scott D MD [Oto] - **Spec Exp:** Endoscopic Sinus Surgery; Sinus Disorders/Surgery; **Hospital:** Beth Israel Med Ctr - Petrie Div (page 56), Mt Sinai Med Ctr (page 62); **Address:** NY Otolaryngology Group, 36A E 36th St, Ste 200, New York, NY 10016-3401; **Phone:** 212-889-8575; **Board Cert:** Otolaryngology 1983; **Med School:** Mount Sinai Sch Med 1979; **Resid:** Surgery, Mt Sinai Med Ctr 1980; Otolaryngology, Mt Sinai Med Ctr 1983; **Fac Appt:** Asst Clin Prof Oto, Mount Sinai Sch Med

Goldenberg, David MD [Oto] - **Spec Exp:** Head & Neck Cancer & Surgery; Thyroid & Parathyroid Cancer & Surgery; Salivary Gland Tumors & Surgery; **Hospital:** Penn State Milton S Hershey Med Ctr; **Address:** Otolaryngology-Head and Neck Surgery, 500 University Drive, Hershey, PA 17033-0850; **Phone:** 717-531-8945; **Med School:** Israel 1995; **Resid:** Otolaryngology, Rambam Med Ctr 2002; **Fellow:** Head & Neck Surgical Oncology, Johns Hopkins Med Ctr 2005; **Fac Appt:** Prof S, Penn State Coll Med

Grandis, Jennifer R MD [Oto] - **Spec Exp:** Head & Neck Cancer; **Hospital:** UPMC Presby, Pittsburgh, Magee-Womens Hosp - UPMC; **Address:** University ENT Specialists, Eye & Ear Institute, 203 Lothrop St, Ste 300, Pittsburgh, PA 15213; **Phone:** 412-647-2100; **Board Cert:** Otolaryngology 1994; **Med School:** Univ Pittsburgh 1987; **Resid:** Otolaryngology, Univ Pittsburgh Med Ctr 1993; **Fellow:** Research, Univ Pittsburgh Med Ctr 1992; **Fac Appt:** Asst Prof Oto, Univ Pittsburgh

Hammerschlag, Paul E MD [Oto] - **Spec Exp:** Cochlear Implants; Hearing Loss; Meniere's Disease; Balance Disorders; **Hospital:** NYU Langone Med Ctr (page 68), New York Eye & Ear Infirm (page 64); **Address:** 650 First Ave, New York, NY 10016-3240; **Phone:** 212-889-2600; **Board Cert:** Otolaryngology 1978; **Med School:** Albert Einstein Coll Med 1972; **Resid:** Surgery, Virginia Mason Hosp 1974; Otolaryngology, Mass Eye & Ear Infirm 1978; **Fellow:** Otolaryngology, Mass Eye & Ear Infirm 1978; **Fac Appt:** Assoc Clin Prof Oto, NYU Sch Med

Har-El, Gady MD [Oto] - **Spec Exp:** Head & Neck Cancer; Thyroid & Parathyroid Surgery; Sinus Tumors; Skull Base Tumors; **Hospital:** Lenox Hill Hosp (page 66), Lenox Hill Hosp (Manh Eye, Ear & Throat Hosp) (page 66); **Address:** 186 E 76th St E, Fl 2, New York, NY 10021; **Phone:** 212-744-4368; **Board Cert:** Otolaryngology 1992; **Med School:** Israel 1982; **Resid:** Otolaryngology, SUNY Downstate Med Ctr 1991; **Fellow:** Head and Neck Surgery, Long Island Coll Hosp 1987; **Fac Appt:** Prof Oto, SUNY Hlth Sci Ctr

Hicks Jr, Wesley L MD/DDS [Oto] - **Spec Exp:** Head & Neck Cancer & Surgery; Reconstructive Surgery; **Hospital:** Roswell Park Canc Inst; **Address:** Roswell Park Cancer Inst, Dept Head & Neck Surgery, Elm & Carlton Sts, Buffalo, NY 14263; **Phone:** 716-845-3158; **Board Cert:** Otolaryngology 1993; **Med School:** SUNY Buffalo 1984; **Resid:** Otolaryngology, Manhattan Eye Ear & Throat Hosp 1988; Otolaryngology, New York Hosp/Meml Sloan Kettering Cancer Ctr 1990; **Fellow:** Head and Neck Surgery, Stanford Univ Med Ctr 1993; **Fac Appt:** Prof Oto, SUNY Buffalo

Hirsch, Barry E MD [Oto] - **Spec Exp:** Neuro-Otology; Skull Base Tumors; Hearing Disorders; Cochlear Implants; **Hospital:** UPMC Presby, Pittsburgh, UPMC Shadyside; **Address:** University ENT Specialists, Eye & Ear Institute, 203 Lothrop St, Ste 300, Pittsburgh, PA 15213; **Phone:** 412-647-2100; **Board Cert:** Otolaryngology 1982; Neurotology 2005; **Med School:** Univ Pennsylvania 1977; **Resid:** Otolaryngology, Univ Pittsburgh Med Ctr 1982; **Fellow:** Neurotology, Univ Pittsburgh 1985; Neurotology, Univ Zurich 1986; **Fac Appt:** Prof Oto, Univ Pittsburgh

Hoffman, Ronald A MD [Oto] - **Spec Exp:** Cochlear Implants; Balance Disorders; Ear Disorders/Surgery; **Hospital:** New York Eye & Ear Infirm (page 64), Beth Israel Med Ctr - Petrie Div (page 56); **Address:** 380 2nd Ave Fl 9, New York, NY 10010; **Phone:** 212-614-8388; **Board Cert:** Otolaryngology 1976; **Med School:** Jefferson Med Coll 1971; **Resid:** Surgery, Lenox Hill Hosp 1973; Otolaryngology, NYU Med Ctr 1976; **Fac Appt:** Prof Oto, Albert Einstein Coll Med

Holliday, Michael J MD [Oto] - **Spec Exp:** Neuro-Otology; Skull Base Surgery; Otology; **Hospital:** Johns Hopkins Hosp (page 59), Johns Hopkins Bayview Med Ctr (page 59); **Address:** Johns Hopkins Outpatient Clin, 601 N Caroline St Fl 6, Baltimore, MD 21287; **Phone:** 410-955-1686; **Board Cert:** Otolaryngology 1976; **Med School:** Marquette Sch Med 1969; **Resid:** Otolaryngology, Johns Hopkins Hosp 1976; **Fellow:** Neurotology, Univ Zurich 1979; **Fac Appt:** Assoc Prof Oto, Johns Hopkins Univ

Hopping, Steven B MD [Oto] - **Spec Exp:** Cosmetic Surgery-Face; Hair Restoration/Transplant; **Hospital:** G Washington Univ Hosp; **Address:** The Ctr for Cosmetic Surgery, 2311 M St NW, Ste 503, Washington, DC 20037; **Phone:** 202-785-3175; **Board Cert:** Otolaryngology 1980; Facial Plastic & Reconstr Surgery 1986; Hair Restoration Surgery 1990; **Med School:** Univ Cincinnati 1975; **Resid:** Surgery, G Washington Univ Hosp 1977; Otolaryngology, Mass Eye & Ear Infirmary 1980; **Fellow:** Plastic Surgery, Mass Eye & Ear Infirmary 1981; **Fac Appt:** Clin Prof S, Geo Wash Univ

Hurst, Michael K MD/DDS [Oto] - **Spec Exp:** Nasal Allergy; Sleep Disorders/Apnea; Thyroid Surgery; **Hospital:** Ruby Memorial - WVU Hosp, Monongalia Genl Hosp; **Address:** Morgantown ENT Clin, 1188 Pineview Drive, Morgantown, WV 26505; **Phone:** 304-599-3959; **Board Cert:** Otolaryngology 1994; **Med School:** Marshall Univ 1988; **Resid:** Otolaryngology, W VA Univ Affil Hosps 1993; **Fac Appt:** Assoc Prof Oto, W VA Univ

Jacobs, Joseph B MD [Oto] - **Spec Exp:** Endoscopic Sinus Surgery; Sinus Disorders/Surgery; Sinus Surgery-Revision; **Hospital:** NYU Langone Med Ctr (page 68); **Address:** 345 E 37 St, Ste 306, MS 10016, New York, NY 10016-6402; **Phone:** 646-754-1203; **Board Cert:** Otolaryngology 1978; **Med School:** Albert Einstein Coll Med 1974; **Resid:** Surgery, Montefiore Med Ctr 1975; Otolaryngology, NYU Med Ctr 1978; **Fellow:** Plastic/Reconstructive Surgery, UCLA Med Ctr 1979; **Fac Appt:** Prof Oto, NYU Sch Med

Johnson, Jonas T MD [Oto] - **Spec Exp:** Head & Neck Surgery; Head & Neck Cancer; Sleep Disorders/Apnea/Snoring; Parotid Gland Tumors; **Hospital:** UPMC Presby, Pittsburgh, Magee-Womens Hosp - UPMC; **Address:** University ENT Specialists, 203 Lothrop St, Ste 300, Pittsburgh, PA 15213; **Phone:** 412-647-2100; **Board Cert:** Otolaryngology 1977; **Med School:** SUNY Upstate Med Univ 1972; **Resid:** Surgery, Med Coll Virginia Hosps 1974; Otolaryngology, SUNY-Univ Hosp 1977; **Fac Appt:** Prof Oto, Univ Pittsburgh

Jones, Jacqueline E MD [Oto] - **Spec Exp:** Pediatric Otolaryngology; Sinus Disorders/Surgery; Ear Infections; **Hospital:** NY-Presby/Weill Cornell Med Ctr, NY (page 65), Lenox Hill Hosp (page 66); **Address:** 1175 Park Ave, Ste 1A, New York, NY 10128; **Phone:** 212-996-2559; **Board Cert:** Otolaryngology 1989; **Med School:** Cornell Univ 1984; **Resid:** Otolaryngology, Hosp Univ Penn 1989; **Fellow:** Pediatric Otolaryngology, Chldns Hosp 1990; **Fac Appt:** Assoc Prof Oto, Cornell Univ-Weill Med Coll

Josephson, Jordan S MD [Oto] - **Spec Exp:** Rhinoplasty Revision; Endoscopic Sinus Surgery; Nasal & Sinus Disorders; Sleep Apnea; **Hospital:** Lenox Hill Hosp (Manh Eye, Ear & Throat Hosp) (page 66); **Address:** 205 E 76th St, Ste M1, New York, NY 10021; **Phone:** 212-717-1773; **Board Cert:** Otolaryngology 1988; **Med School:** SUNY Downstate 1983; **Resid:** Surgery, LI Jewish Med Ctr 1984; Otolaryngology, LI Jewish Med Ctr 1988; **Fellow:** Sinus Surgery, Johns Hopkins Hosp 1989

Keane, William M MD [Oto] - **Spec Exp:** Head & Neck Cancer & Surgery; Thyroid Cancer; Parathyroid Surgery; **Hospital:** Thomas Jefferson Univ Hosp; **Address:** Jefferson Univ Physicians, Dept Otolaryngology, 925 Chestnut St Fl 6, Philadelphia, PA 19107; **Phone:** 215-955-6760; **Board Cert:** Otolaryngology 1978; **Med School:** Harvard Med Sch 1970; **Resid:** Surgery, Strong Meml Hosp 1972; Otolaryngology, Hosp Univ Penn 1977; **Fac Appt:** Prof Oto, Thomas Jefferson Univ

Kennedy, David W MD [Oto] - **Spec Exp:** Endoscopic Sinus Surgery; Skull Base Tumors & Surgery; Minimally Invasive Surgery; Esthesioneuroblastoma; **Hospital:** Hosp Univ Penn - UPHS (page 69), Pennsylvania Hosp-UPHS (page 69); **Address:** Hosp Univ Penn-Dept Otolaryngology, 3400 Spruce St, 5 Silverstein, Philadelphia, PA 19104-4229; **Phone:** 215-662-2777; **Board Cert:** Otolaryngology 1978; **Med School:** Ireland 1972; **Resid:** Surgery, Johns Hopkins Hosp 1974; Otolaryngology, Johns Hopkins Hosp 1978; **Fac Appt:** Prof Oto, Univ Pennsylvania

Koch, Wayne M MD [Oto] - **Spec Exp:** Head & Neck Cancer; Sinus Tumors; **Hospital:** Johns Hopkins Hosp (page 59); **Address:** Johns Hopkins Outpatient Clin, 601 N Caroline St Fl 6, Baltimore, MD 21287; **Phone:** 410-955-1686; **Board Cert:** Otolaryngology 1987; **Med School:** Univ Pittsburgh 1982; **Resid:** Otolaryngology, Tufts-Boston Univ Hosps 1987; **Fellow:** Surgical Oncology, Johns Hopkins Hosp 1989; **Fac Appt:** Assoc Prof Oto, Johns Hopkins Univ

Koufman, Jamie A MD [Oto] - **Spec Exp:** Voice Disorders; Laryngeal Disorders; **Hospital:** New York Eye & Ear Infirm (page 64); **Address:** 200 W 57th St, Ste 1203, New York, NY 10019; **Phone:** 212-463-8014; **Board Cert:** Otolaryngology 1978; **Med School:** Boston Univ 1973; **Resid:** Surgery, Hartford Hosp 1975; Otolaryngology, Boston Univ Med Ctr 1978

Kraus, Dennis H MD [Oto] - **Spec Exp:** Head & Neck Cancer; Skull Base Tumors; Thyroid & Parathyroid Surgery; Sarcoma; **Hospital:** Lenox Hill Hosp (page 66); **Address:** 130 E 77th St, Fl 10, New York, NY 10075-1851; **Phone:** 212-434-4500; **Board Cert:** Otolaryngology 1990; **Med School:** Univ Rochester 1985; **Resid:** Surgery, Cleveland Clinic 1987; Otolaryngology, Cleveland Clinic 1990; **Fellow:** Head and Neck Surgery, Meml Sloan Kettering Cancer Ctr 1991; **Fac Appt:** Prof Oto, Cornell Univ-Weill Med Coll

Krespi, Yosef P MD [Oto] - **Spec Exp:** Sleep Disorders/Apnea/Snoring; Nasal & Sinus Surgery; Head & Neck Cancer & Surgery; Thyroid Cancer; **Hospital:** Lenox Hill Hosp (Manh Eye, Ear & Throat Hosp) (page 66); **Address:** 110 E 59th St, Ste 10A, New York, NY 10022; **Phone:** 212-434-4500; **Board Cert:** Otolaryngology 1981; **Med School:** Israel 1973; **Resid:** Surgery, Mt Sinai Hosp 1976; Otolaryngology, Mt Sinai Hosp 1980; **Fellow:** Surgery, Northwestern Meml Hosp 1981; **Fac Appt:** Clin Prof Oto, Columbia P&S

Kuhel, William I MD [Oto] - **Spec Exp:** Head & Neck Cancer & Surgery; Thyroid Cancer; Parathyroid Cancer; **Hospital:** NY-Presby/Weill Cornell Med Ctr, NY (page 65); **Address:** 1305 York Ave Fl 5, Weill-Greenberg Ctr, New York, NY 10021; **Phone:** 646-962-6325; **Board Cert:** Otolaryngology 1988; **Med School:** Univ Mich Med Sch 1983; **Resid:** Surgery, St Vincent's Hosp 1985; Otolaryngology, Indiana Univ 1988; **Fellow:** Head and Neck Surgery, MD Anderson Cancer Ctr 1989; **Fac Appt:** Assoc Clin Prof Oto, Cornell Univ-Weill Med Coll

Lalwani, Anil K MD [Oto] - **Spec Exp:** Ear Disorders/Surgery; Facial Nerve Disorders; Cochlear Implants; Skull Base Surgery; **Hospital:** NY-Presby/Columbia Univ Med Ctr, NY (page 65), Morgan Stanley Children's Hosp of NY-Presby, NY (page 65); **Address:** 180 Fort Washington Ave, Harkness Pavilion Fl 7, New York, NY 10032; **Phone:** 212-305-1696; **Board Cert:** Otolaryngology 1992; Neurotology 2010; **Med School:** Univ Mich Med Sch 1985; **Resid:** Surgery, Duke Univ Med Ctr 1987; Otolaryngology, UCSF Med Ctr 1991; **Fellow:** Skull Base Surgery, UCSF Med Ctr 1992; Molecular Genetics, Natl Inst Hlth 1994; **Fac Appt:** Prof Oto, Columbia P&S

Lawson, William MD [Oto] - **Spec Exp:** Sinus Disorders/Surgery; Endoscopic Sinus Surgery; **Hospital:** Mt Sinai Med Ctr (page 62); **Address:** 5 E 98th St Fl 8, Box 1191, New York, NY 10029-6501; **Phone:** 212-241-9410; **Board Cert:** Otolaryngology 1974; **Med School:** NYU Sch Med 1965; **Resid:** Surgery, Bronx VA Hosp 1967; Otolaryngology, Mt Sinai Hosp 1974; **Fac Appt:** Prof Oto, Mount Sinai Sch Med

Lebovics, Robert S MD [Oto] - **Spec Exp:** Head & Neck Inflammatory Disorders; Head & Neck Autoimmune Disease; Head & Neck Infectious Disease; Wegener's Granulomatosis; **Hospital:** St. Luke's - Roosevelt Hosp Ctr - Roosevelt Div (page 56); **Address:** 425 W 59th St, Fl 10, New York, NY 10019; **Phone:** 212-262-2002; **Board Cert:** Otolaryngology 1988; **Med School:** SUNY Downstate 1982; **Resid:** Surgery, Montefiore-Weiler Einstein Div 1983; Otolaryngology, Montefiore-Weiler Einstein Div 1987

Linstrom, Christopher J MD [Oto] - **Spec Exp:** Cochlear Implants; Acoustic Neuroma; Encephalocele; Cholesteatoma; **Hospital:** New York Eye & Ear Infirm (page 64); **Address:** NY Eye & Ear Infirmary, Dept Otolaryngology, 310 E 14th St, New York, NY 10003-4201; **Phone:** 212-979-4200; **Board Cert:** Otolaryngology 1987; Neurotology 2004; **Med School:** McGill Univ 1982; **Resid:** Surgery, Geo Wash Med Ctr 1984; Otolaryngology, Cornell Univ Med Ctr 1987; **Fellow:** Otology & Neurotology, Michigan Ear Inst 1989; **Fac Appt:** Prof Oto, Albert Einstein Coll Med

McMenomey, Sean O'Leary MD [Oto] - **Spec Exp:** Otology & Neuro-Otology; Hearing Loss; Dizziness/Vertigo; Cochlear Implants; **Hospital:** NYU Langone Med Ctr (page 68), Bellevue Hosp Ctr; **Address:** NYU Otology Assocs, 550 First Ave, Ste 7Q, MC PV-01, New York, NY 10016; **Phone:** 212-263-5565; **Board Cert:** Otolaryngology 1993; Neurotology 2004; **Med School:** St Louis Univ 1987; **Resid:** Otolaryngology, Oregon Hlth Sci Ctr 1992; **Fellow:** Otology & Neurotology, Vanderbilt Univ Hosp 1993; **Fac Appt:** Prof Oto, NYU Sch Med

Mirza, Natasha MD [Oto] - **Spec Exp:** Vocal Cord Disorders; Voice Disorders; Laryngeal Disorders; Swallowing Disorders; **Hospital:** Hosp Univ Penn - UPHS (page 69); **Address:** Hosp Univ Penn, Otorhinolaryngology Dept, 3400 Spruce St, Silverstein Bldg Fl 5, Philadelphia, PA 19104; **Phone:** 215-662-2777; **Board Cert:** Otolaryngology 1993; **Med School:** Pakistan 1983; **Resid:** Surgery, OSU Hosp 1987; Otolaryngology, UC Irvine Med Ctr 1992; **Fac Appt:** Prof Oto, Univ Pennsylvania

Newkirk, Kenneth A MD [Oto] - **Spec Exp:** Sinus Disorders; Head & Neck Cancer; **Hospital:** MedStar Georgetown Univ Hosp; **Address:** MedStar Georgetown Univ Hosp - Dept Oto, 3800 Reservoir Rd NW, Gorman Bldg Fl 1 - rm G-104, Washington, DC 20007; **Phone:** 202-444-8186; **Board Cert:** Otolaryngology 2012; **Med School:** Mount Sinai Sch Med 1993; **Resid:** Otolaryngology, MedStar Georgetown Univ Hosp 2000; **Fellow:** Pediatric Otolaryngology, UT MD Anderson Canc Ctr 2003; **Fac Appt:** Asst Prof Oto, Georgetown Univ

O'Malley Jr, Bert W MD [Oto] - **Spec Exp:** Head & Neck Cancer; Sinus Tumors; Skull Base Tumors; **Hospital:** Hosp Univ Penn - UPHS (page 69); **Address:** Hosp Univ Penn, Dept Otolaryngology, 3400 Spruce St, 5 Silverstein, Philadelphia, PA 19104; **Phone:** 215-662-2777; **Board Cert:** Otolaryngology 1995; **Med School:** Univ Tex SW, Dallas 1988; **Resid:** Surgery, Parkland Meml Hosp 1989; Otolaryngology, Baylor Affil Hosp 1994; **Fellow:** Head & Neck Surgical Oncology, Univ Pittsburgh Med Ctr 1995; **Fac Appt:** Prof Oto, Univ Pennsylvania

Papel, Ira D MD [Oto] - **Spec Exp:** Rhinoplasty; Cosmetic Surgery-Face; Reconstructive Surgery-Face; Skin Cancer/Facial Reconstruction; **Hospital:** Greater Baltimore Med Ctr, Johns Hopkins Hosp (page 59); **Address:** 1838 Greene Tree Rd, Ste 370, Baltimore, MD 21208; **Phone:** 410-486-3400; **Board Cert:** Otolaryngology 1986; Facial Plastic & Reconstr Surgery 1991; **Med School:** Boston Univ 1981; **Resid:** Otolaryngology, Johns Hopkins Hosp 1986; **Fellow:** Facial Plastic Surgery, UCSF Med Ctr 1987; **Fac Appt:** Assoc Prof Oto, Johns Hopkins Univ

Persky, Mark S MD [Oto] - **Spec Exp:** Head & Neck Cancer; Skull Base Tumors; Thyroid Cancer; Vascular Lesions-Head & Neck; **Hospital:** Beth Israel Med Ctr - Petrie Div (page 56), New York Eye & Ear Infirm (page 64); **Address:** 10 Union Square East, Ste 4J, New York, NY 10003; **Phone:** 212-844-8648; **Board Cert:** Otolaryngology 1976; **Med School:** SUNY Upstate Med Univ 1972; **Resid:** Otolaryngology, Bellevue Hosp 1976; **Fellow:** Head and Neck Surgery, Beth Israel Med Ctr 1977; **Fac Appt:** Clin Prof Oto, Albert Einstein Coll Med

Picken, Catherine A MD [Oto] - **Spec Exp:** Head & Neck Reconstruction; Thyroid Disorders; Sinus Disorders/Surgery; **Hospital:** MedStar Georgetown Univ Hosp, Sibley Mem Hosp; **Address:** WA ENT Grp, 2440 M St NW, Ste 620, Washington, DC 20037; **Phone:** 202-785-5000; **Board Cert:** Otolaryngology 1989; **Med School:** Northwestern Univ 1979; **Resid:** Surgery, Natl Heart Lung Blood Inst 1983; Otolaryngology, MedStar Georgetown Univ Hosp 1989; **Fac Appt:** Assoc Prof Oto, Georgetown Univ

Pribitkin, Edmund A MD [Oto] - **Spec Exp:** Rhinoplasty; Thyroid Disorders; Facial Plastic Surgery; **Hospital:** Thomas Jefferson Univ Hosp; **Address:** Thomas Jefferson Univ, Otolaryngology, 925 Chestnut St Fl 6, Philadelphia, PA 19107; **Phone:** 215-955-6760; **Board Cert:** Otolaryngology 1992; Facial Plastic & Reconstr Surgery 1995; **Med School:** Univ Pennsylvania 1986; **Resid:** Otolaryngology, Hosp Univ Penn 1991; **Fellow:** Facial Plastic & Reconstr Surgery, Stanford Univ Hosp & Clin 1992; **Fac Appt:** Prof Oto, Thomas Jefferson Univ

Quatela, Vito C MD [Oto] - **Spec Exp:** Facial Plastic Surgery; Rhinoplasty; Reconstructive Surgery; Hair Restoration/Transplant; **Hospital:** Univ Rochester Strong Meml Hosp, Rochester Genl Hosp; **Address:** Quatela Ctr Plastic Surgery, 973 East Ave, Rochester, NY 14607; **Phone:** 585-244-1000; **Board Cert:** Otolaryngology 1985; Facial Plastic & Reconstr Surgery 1991; Hair Restoration Surgery 2008; **Med School:** Northwestern Univ 1979; **Resid:** Surgery, Med Ctr Hosp Vermont 1981; Otolaryngology, Northwestern Univ Hosp 1985; **Fellow:** Facial Plastic Surgery, Tulane Med Ctr 1986; Facial Plastic Surgery, OR Hlth Sci Univ 1987; **Fac Appt:** Assoc Clin Prof Oto, Univ Rochester

Rassekh, Christopher H MD [Oto] - **Spec Exp:** Head & Neck Cancer; Skull Base Surgery; Salivary Gland Tumors & Surgery; Airway Disorders; **Hospital:** Hosp Univ Penn - UPHS (page 69); **Address:** 3400 Spruce St, Silverstein Bldg Fl 5, Philadelphia, PA 19104; **Phone:** 215-662-2777; **Board Cert:** Otolaryngology 1993; **Med School:** Univ Iowa Coll Med 1986; **Resid:** Otolaryngology, Univ Iowa Med Ctr 1992; **Fellow:** Head and Neck Surgery, Univ Pittsburgh Med Ctr 1993; **Fac Appt:** Assoc Prof Oto, Univ Pennsylvania

Roland Jr, J Thomas MD [Oto] - **Spec Exp:** Acoustic Neuroma; Cochlear Implants; Neuro-Otology; Facial Nerve Disorders; **Hospital:** NYU Langone Med Ctr (page 68), Bellevue Hosp Ctr; **Address:** NYU Otology Assocs, 550 First Ave, Ste 7Q, New York, NY 10016; **Phone:** 212-263-5565; **Board Cert:** Otolaryngology 1993; Neurotology 2004; **Med School:** Temple Univ 1983; **Resid:** Otolaryngology, NYU Med Ctr 1992; **Fellow:** Neurotology, NYU Med Ctr 1993; **Fac Appt:** Prof Oto, NYU Sch Med

Rosen, Clark A MD [Oto] - **Spec Exp:** Voice Disorders; **Hospital:** UPMC Mercy, Pittsburgh; **Address:** UPMC, Voice Ctr, 1400 Locust St D Bldg - Ste 2100, Pittsburgh, PA 15219; **Phone:** 412-232-7464; **Board Cert:** Otolaryngology 1995; **Med School:** Rush Med Coll 1989; **Resid:** Otolaryngology, Oregon Hlth Sci Univ 1994; **Fellow:** Otolaryngology, Univ Tenn Med Ctr 1995; **Fac Appt:** Assoc Prof Oto, Univ Pittsburgh

Rosen, Marc R MD [Oto] - **Spec Exp:** Sinus Disorders/Surgery; Endoscopic Sinus Surgery; **Hospital:** Thomas Jefferson Univ Hosp; **Address:** 925 Chestnut St, Fl 6, Philadelphia, PA 19107; **Phone:** 215-955-6760; **Board Cert:** Otolaryngology 1988; **Med School:** SUNY Upstate Med Univ 1983; **Resid:** Surgery, Hosp U Penn 1985; Otolaryngology, Hosp U Penn 1988; **Fac Appt:** Prof Oto, Thomas Jefferson Univ

Sataloff, Robert T MD [Oto] - **Spec Exp:** Neuro-Otology; Voice Disorders; Laryngeal Disorders; Throat Disorders; **Hospital:** Hahnemann Univ Hosp, St. Christopher's Hosp for Chldn; **Address:** PA ENT Assocs, 1721 Pine St, Philadelphia, PA 19103; **Phone:** 215-545-3322; **Board Cert:** Otolaryngology 1980; **Med School:** Jefferson Med Coll 1975; **Resid:** Otolaryngology, Univ Michigan Med Ctr 1980; **Fellow:** Neurotology, Univ Michigan Med Ctr 1981; **Fac Appt:** Prof Oto, Drexel Univ Coll Med

Schaefer, Steven D MD [Oto] - **Spec Exp:** Sinus Disorders/Surgery; Head & Neck Surgery; Endoscopic Sinus Surgery; **Hospital:** Lenox Hill Hosp (Manh Eye, Ear & Throat Hosp) (page 66); **Address:** NY Head & Neck Inst, 110 W 59th St Fl 10 - Ste 10A, New York, NY 10022; **Phone:** 212-434-4500 x3; **Board Cert:** Otolaryngology 1978; **Med School:** UC Irvine 1972; **Resid:** Surgery, UCLA Med Ctr 1974; Otolaryngology, Stanford Med Ctr 1977; **Fac Appt:** Prof Oto, NY Med Coll

Schaitkin, Barry M MD [Oto] - **Spec Exp:** Sinus Disorders/Surgery; Endoscopic Sinus Surgery; Rhinosinusitis; Facial Nerve Disorders; **Hospital:** UPMC Shadyside; **Address:** UPMC, ENT Dept, 5200 Centre Ave, Ste 211, Pittsburgh, PA 15232; **Phone:** 412-621-0123; **Board Cert:** Otolaryngology 1990; **Med School:** Penn State Coll Med 1984; **Resid:** Otolaryngology, Hershey Med Ctr 1990; **Fac Appt:** Prof Oto, Univ Pittsburgh

Schantz, Stimson P MD [Oto] - **Spec Exp:** Head & Neck Surgery; Head & Neck Cancer; Thyroid Cancer; **Hospital:** New York Eye & Ear Infirm (page 64), Beth Israel Med Ctr - Petrie Div (page 56); **Address:** 310 E 14th St Fl 6, New York, NY 10003; **Phone:** 212-979-4535; **Board Cert:** Surgery 2005; **Med School:** Univ Cincinnati 1975; **Resid:** Surgery, Georgetown Univ Med Ctr 1982; Otolaryngology, Univ Illinois Eye & Ear Infirm 1980; **Fellow:** Surgical Oncology, MD Anderson Cancer Ctr 1984; **Fac Appt:** Prof Oto, NY Med Coll

Schley, W Shain MD [Oto] - **Spec Exp:** Nasal & Sinus Disorders; Throat Disorders; Voice Disorders; Gastroesophageal Reflux Disease (GERD); **Hospital:** NY-Presby/Weill Cornell Med Ctr, NY (page 65); **Address:** 1305 York Ave Fl 5, New York, NY 10021; **Phone:** 646-962-2221; **Board Cert:** Otolaryngology 1973; **Med School:** Emory Univ 1966; **Resid:** Surgery, St Lukes-Roosevelt Hosp 1968; Otolaryngology, New York Presby Hosp 1973; **Fac Appt:** Assoc Clin Prof Oto, Cornell Univ-Weill Med Coll

Setzen, Michael MD [Oto] - **Spec Exp:** Nasal & Sinus Surgery; Rhinoplasty; Sleep Disorders/Apnea; Snoring/Sleep Apnea; **Hospital:** N Shore Univ Hosp (page 66), St. Francis Hosp - The Heart Ctr (page 70); **Address:** 600 Northern Blvd, Ste 312, Great Neck, NY 11021-5200; **Phone:** 516-829-0045; **Board Cert:** Otolaryngology 1982; **Med School:** South Africa 1974; **Resid:** Surgery, Cleveland Clinic Fdn 1978; Otolaryngology, Barnes Jewish Hosp 1982; **Fac Appt:** Assoc Clin Prof Oto, NYU Sch Med

Shapshay, Stanley M MD [Oto] - **Spec Exp:** Laryngeal Cancer; Head & Neck Cancer; **Hospital:** Albany Med Ctr; **Address:** Albany Med Ctr-Otolaryngology Dept, 35 Hackett Blvd, Albany, NY 12208-3420; **Phone:** 518-262-5575; **Board Cert:** Otolaryngology 1975; **Med School:** Med Coll VA 1968; **Resid:** Surgery, Tufts Med Ctr 1972; Otolaryngology, Tufts Med Ctr 1975; **Fellow:** Surgery, Serafimer Hosp 1972; **Fac Appt:** Prof Oto, Albany Med Coll

Singh, Bhuvanesh MD/PhD [Oto] - **Spec Exp:** Head & Neck Cancer & Surgery; Thyroid Cancer; **Hospital:** Meml Sloan-Kettering Canc Ctr; **Address:** 1275 York Ave, MC C1073, New York, NY 10065; **Phone:** 212-639-2024; **Board Cert:** Otolaryngology 1998; **Med School:** SUNY Downstate 1991; **Resid:** Otolaryngology, SUNY Downstate Med Ctr 1997; **Fellow:** Head and Neck Surgery, Meml Sloan-Kettering Canc Ctr 1999; **Fac Appt:** Assoc Prof Oto, Cornell Univ-Weill Med Coll

Snyderman, Carl H MD [Oto] - **Spec Exp:** Skull Base Tumors & Surgery; Sinus Tumors; Head & Neck Cancer; Endoscopic Surgery; **Hospital:** UPMC Presby, Pittsburgh, Chldns Hosp of Pittsburgh - UPMC; **Address:** 200 Lothrop St, EEI Bldg - Fl 3 - Ste 300, Pittsburgh, PA 15213; **Phone:** 412-647-2100; **Board Cert:** Otolaryngology 1987; **Med School:** Univ Chicago-Pritzker Sch Med 1982; **Resid:** Otolaryngology, Eye-Ear Hosp/Univ Pittsburgh 1987; **Fellow:** Skull Base Surgery, Eye-Ear Hosp/Univ Pittsburgh 1989; **Fac Appt:** Prof Oto, Univ Pittsburgh

Stewart, Michael G MD [Oto] - **Spec Exp:** Nasal & Sinus Disorders; Sleep Disorders/Apnea; Head & Neck Surgery; Vocal Cord Disorders; **Hospital:** NY-Presby/Weill Cornell Med Ctr, NY (page 65); **Address:** Weill Greenberg Center, 1305 York Ave Fl 5, New York, NY 10021; **Phone:** 646-962-6673; **Board Cert:** Otolaryngology 1995; **Med School:** Johns Hopkins Univ 1988; **Resid:** Surgery, Baylor Coll Med Affil Hosp 1990; Otolaryngology, Baylor Coll Med Affil Hosp 1994; **Fac Appt:** Prof Oto, Cornell Univ-Weill Med Coll

Strome, Marshall MD [Oto] - **Spec Exp:** Voice Disorders; Swallowing Disorders; Head & Neck Cancer Reconstruction; Head & Neck Cancer & Surgery; **Hospital:** St. Luke's - Roosevelt Hosp Ctr - St Luke's Hosp (page 56), Mt Sinai Med Ctr (page 62); **Address:** 425 W 59th St, Fl 10, New York, NY 10019; **Phone:** 212-262-4444; **Board Cert:** Otolaryngology 1970; **Med School:** Univ Mich Med Sch 1964; **Resid:** Surgery, Harper Hosp 1966; Otolaryngology, Univ Michigan Hosp 1970; **Fac Appt:** Prof Oto, Univ Mich Med Sch

Strome, Scott E MD [Oto] - **Spec Exp:** Microsurgery; Head & Neck Cancer; Head & Neck Reconstruction; Laryngeal Cancer; **Hospital:** Univ of MD Med Ctr; **Address:** UMMC Dept Otorhinolaryngology, 16 S Eutaw St, Ste 500, Baltimore, MD 21201; **Phone:** 410-328-6467; **Board Cert:** Otolaryngology 1998; **Med School:** Harvard Med Sch 1991; **Resid:** Otolaryngology, Univ Michigan 1997; **Fellow:** Head and Neck Surgery, Allegheny Genl Hosp 1998; Microvascular Surgery, Allegheny Genl Hosp 1998; **Fac Appt:** Prof Oto, Univ MD Sch Med

Sulica, Radu Lucian MD [Oto] - **Spec Exp:** Laryngeal & Vocal Cord Surgery; Voice Disorders; Vocal Cord Disorders; Botox Therapy; **Hospital:** NY-Presby/Weill Cornell Med Ctr, NY (page 65); **Address:** 1305 York Ave, Fl 5th Floor, New York, NY 10021; **Phone:** 646-962-4734; **Board Cert:** Otolaryngology 2000; **Med School:** Georgetown Univ 1993; **Resid:** Surgery, Georgetown Univ Hosp 1995; Otolaryngology, Georgetown Univ Hosp 1999; **Fellow:** Laryngology, St Lukes Roosevelt Hosp 2000; **Fac Appt:** Assoc Prof Oto, Cornell Univ-Weill Med Coll

Thaler, Erica R MD [Oto] - **Spec Exp:** Apnea/Robotic Surgery; Thyroid Surgery; Sinus Disorders/Surgery; **Hospital:** Hosp Univ Penn - UPHS (page 69); **Address:** Hosp Univ Penn, Otorhinolaryngology Dept, 3400 Spruce St, Silverstein Bldg Fl 5, Philadelphia, PA 19104; **Phone:** 215-662-2777; **Board Cert:** Otolaryngology 1996; **Med School:** Harvard Med Sch 1990; **Resid:** Otolaryngology, Hosp Univ Penn 1995; **Fac Appt:** Prof Oto, Univ Pennsylvania

Tufano, Ralph P MD [Oto] - **Spec Exp:** Thyroid Disorders; Parathyroid Surgery; Head & Neck Cancer; **Hospital:** Johns Hopkins Hosp (page 59); **Address:** Johns Hopkins Outpatient Clin, 601 N Caroline St, Ste 6242, Baltimore, MD 21287; **Phone:** 410-955-3628; **Board Cert:** Otolaryngology 2001; **Med School:** SUNY Buffalo 1995; **Resid:** Otolaryngology, Univ Penn Affil Hosps 2000; **Fellow:** Head and Neck Surgery, Johns Hopkins Hosp 2001; **Fac Appt:** Prof Oto, Johns Hopkins Univ

Urken, Mark MD [Oto] - **Spec Exp:** Head & Neck Cancer & Surgery; Head & Neck Cancer Reconstruction; Thyroid & Parathyroid Cancer & Surgery; Salivary Gland Tumors; **Hospital:** Beth Israel Med Ctr - Petrie Div (page 56); **Address:** Inst for Head, Neck & Thyroid Cancer, 10 Union Square E, Ste 5B, New York, NY 10003-3314; **Phone:** 212-844-8775; **Board Cert:** Otolaryngology 1986; **Med School:** Univ VA Sch Med 1981; **Resid:** Otolaryngology, Mt Sinai Hosp 1986; **Fellow:** Microvascular Surgery, Mercy Hosp 1987; **Fac Appt:** Prof Oto, Albert Einstein Coll Med

Waner, Milton MD [Oto] - **Spec Exp:** Pediatric Facial Plastic Surgery; Birthmarks/Hemangiomas; Vascular Malformations; **Hospital:** Lenox Hill Hosp (Manh Eye, Ear & Throat Hosp) (page 66); **Address:** The Center for Vascular Birthmarks, 210 E 64th St Fl 7, New York, NY 10065; **Phone:** 212-434-4050; **Med School:** South Africa 1977; **Resid:** Surgery, Univ of Witwatersrand 1980; Otolaryngology, Univ of Witwatersrand 1984; **Fellow:** Otolaryngology, Univ Cincinnatti Med Ctr 1985

Weinstein, Gregory S MD [Oto] - **Spec Exp:** Head & Neck Cancer; Laryngeal Cancer; Robotic Surgery; **Hospital:** Hosp Univ Penn - UPHS (page 69); **Address:** Hosp Univ Penn, Dept Otolaryngology, 3400 Spruce St, 5 Silverstein, Philadelphia, PA 19104; **Phone:** 215-662-2777; **Board Cert:** Otolaryngology 1990; **Med School:** NY Med Coll 1985; **Resid:** Otolaryngology, Univ Iowa Hosp 1990; **Fellow:** Head & Neck Oncology, UC Davis 1991; **Fac Appt:** Prof Oto, Univ Pennsylvania

Wong, Richard J MD [Oto] - **Spec Exp:** Head & Neck Cancer; Thyroid Cancer; **Hospital:** Meml Sloan-Kettering Canc Ctr; **Address:** 1275 York Ave, C-1069, New York, NY 10065; **Phone:** 212-639-7638; **Board Cert:** Otolaryngology 2000; **Med School:** Harvard Med Sch 1994; **Resid:** Otolaryngology, Mass General Hosp 1999; **Fellow:** Head & Neck Surgical Oncology, Meml Sloan Kettering Cancer Ctr 2000

Woo, Peak MD [Oto] - **Spec Exp:** Voice Disorders; Laryngeal Disorders; Laryngeal Cancer; **Hospital:** Mt Sinai Med Ctr (page 62); **Address:** 300 Central Park West, Ste 1-H, New York, NY 10024; **Phone:** 212-580-1004; **Board Cert:** Otolaryngology 1983; **Med School:** Boston Univ 1978; **Resid:** Otolaryngology, Boston Univ Med Ctr 1983; **Fac Appt:** Clin Prof Oto, Mount Sinai Sch Med

Zalzal, George H MD [Oto] - **Spec Exp:** Airway Disorders; Laryngeal & Tracheal Disorders; Ear Disorders/Surgery; **Hospital:** Chldns Natl Med Ctr; **Address:** Childrens Outpatient Center, 9850 Key West Ave, Rockville, MD 20850; **Phone:** 301-765-5400; **Board Cert:** Otolaryngology 1996; **Med School:** Lebanon 1979; **Resid:** Otolaryngology, American Univ Hosp 1983; **Fellow:** Pediatric Otolaryngology, Univ Cincinnati 1985; **Fac Appt:** Prof Oto, Geo Wash Univ

Zwillenberg, Seth MD [Oto] - **Spec Exp:** Pediatric Otolaryngology; **Hospital:** Einstein Med Ctr, St. Christopher's Hosp for Chldn; **Address:** Einstein Med Ctr, ENT Dept, 5501 Old York Rd Fl 2, Philadelphia, PA 19141; **Phone:** 215-456-7140; **Board Cert:** Otolaryngology 1987; **Med School:** SUNY Downstate 1981; **Resid:** Surgical Pathology, St Vincents Hosp 1983; Otolaryngology, Hosp Univ Penn 1986; **Fellow:** Pediatric Otolaryngology, Med Coll Penn 1987

Southeast

Becker, Ferdinand F MD [Oto] - **Spec Exp:** Botox Therapy; **Hospital:** Indian River Med Ctr; **Address:** 5070 N A1A, Ste A, Vero Beach, FL 32963-1229; **Phone:** 772-234-3700; **Board Cert:** Otolaryngology 1972; **Med School:** Tulane Univ 1965; **Resid:** Surgery, Charity Hosp 1969; Otolaryngology, Charity Hosp 1972

Bolger, William E MD [Oto] - **Spec Exp:** Sinus Disorders/Surgery; Nasal Surgery; Sinus Tumors; **Hospital:** Mayo - Jacksonville; **Address:** Mayo Clinic, Otolaryngology Dept, 4500 San Pablo Rd, Davis E-3B, Jacksonville, FL 32224; **Phone:** 904-953-6674; **Board Cert:** Otolaryngology 1992; **Med School:** Uniformed Srvs Univ, Bethesda 1986; **Resid:** Otolaryngology, Willford Hall USAF Med Ctr 1991; **Fellow:** Rhinology, Hosp Univ Penn 1992; **Fac Appt:** Prof S, Mayo Med Sch

Browne, J. Dale MD [Oto] - **Spec Exp:** Head & Neck Cancer; Thyroid Cancer; Skull Base Surgery; Head & Neck Reconstruction; **Hospital:** Wake Forest Baptist Med Ctr; **Address:** Medical Ctr Blvd, Winston-Salem, NC 27103; **Phone:** 336-716-3854; **Board Cert:** Otolaryngology 1987; **Med School:** Med Coll GA 1982; **Resid:** Otolaryngology, NC Baptist Hosp 1987; **Fellow:** Otolaryngology, Univ Hosp 1991; **Fac Appt:** Prof Oto, Wake Forest Univ

Bumpous, Jeffrey M MD [Oto] - **Spec Exp:** Head & Neck Cancer; Head & Neck Reconstruction; Thyroid & Parathyroid Cancer & Surgery; **Hospital:** Univ of Louisville Hosp, Norton Hosp; **Address:** Univ Surgical Assocs, 401 E Chestnut St, Ste 710, Louisville, KY 40202-1845; **Phone:** 502-583-8303; **Board Cert:** Otolaryngology 1994; **Med School:** Univ Louisville Sch Med 1988; **Resid:** Otolaryngology, Univ Louisville Hosp 1993; **Fellow:** Head and Neck Surgery, Univ Pittsburgh Med Ctr 1994; **Fac Appt:** Prof Oto, Univ Louisville Sch Med

Civantos, Francisco J MD [Oto] - **Spec Exp:** Head & Neck Cancer; Skull Base Surgery; **Hospital:** Univ of Miami Hosp & Clins/Sylvester Comp Canc Ctr; **Address:** SCCC, Otolaryngology Dept, 1475 NW 12th Ave, Ste 3550, Miami, FL 33136; **Phone:** 305-243-5276; **Board Cert:** Otolaryngology 1992; **Med School:** Columbia P&S 1986; **Resid:** Otolaryngology, Univ IL Med Ctr 1991; **Fellow:** Head & Neck Oncology, Vanderbilt Univ Med Ctr 1992; **Fac Appt:** Assoc Prof Oto, Univ Miami Sch Med

Day, Terry A MD [Oto] - **Spec Exp:** Head & Neck Cancer; Reconstructive Microvascular Surgery; Skull Base Surgery; **Hospital:** MUSC Med Ctr; **Address:** 135 Rutledge Ave, MSC Bldg, Box 550, Charleston, SC 29425; **Phone:** 843-792-0719; **Board Cert:** Otolaryngology 1996; **Med School:** Univ Okla Coll Med 1989; **Resid:** Otolaryngology, LSU Med Ctr 1995; **Fellow:** Head & Neck Surgical Oncology, UC Davis Med Ctr 1996; Maxillofacial Surgery, Univ Hosp 1994; **Fac Appt:** Prof Oto, Med Univ SC

DiNardo, Laurence J MD [Oto] - **Spec Exp:** Head & Neck Cancer; Endoscopic Sinus Surgery; Skull Base Surgery; Sinus Disorders/Surgery; **Hospital:** Med Coll of VA Hosp; **Address:** VCU Dept Otolaryngology, 401 N 11th St Nelson Bldg, Richmond, VA 23298-0146; **Phone:** 804-628-4368; **Board Cert:** Otolaryngology 1992; **Med School:** Stanford Univ 1986; **Resid:** Otolaryngology, Hosp Univ Penn - UPHS 1991; **Fac Appt:** Prof Oto, Va Commonwealth Univ Sch Med

Epstein, Jeffrey S MD [Oto] - **Spec Exp:** Hair Restoration/Transplant; Facial Plastic Surgery; **Hospital:** South Miami Hosp; **Address:** 6280 Sunset Drive, Ste 504, Miami, FL 33143; **Phone:** 305-666-1774; **Board Cert:** Otolaryngology 1994; Facial Plastic & Reconstr Surgery 1995; Hair Restoration Surgery 1998; **Med School:** Univ VT Coll Med 1988; **Resid:** Otolaryngology, Jackson Meml Hosp 1993; **Fellow:** Facial Plastic Surgery, Sheldon S Kabaker MD 1994; **Fac Appt:** Clin Prof Oto, Univ Miami Sch Med

Farrior, Edward H MD [Oto] - **Spec Exp:** Rhinoplasty; Ear Reshaping (Otoplasty); Facial Plastic Surgery; **Hospital:** Tampa Genl Hosp, St. Joseph's Hosp - Tampa; **Address:** 2908 W Azeele St, Tampa, FL 33609; **Phone:** 813-875-3223; **Board Cert:** Otolaryngology 1987; Facial Plastic & Reconstr Surgery 2007; **Med School:** Univ VA Sch Med 1982; **Resid:** Otolaryngology, Univ Michigan Hosp 1987; **Fellow:** Facial Plastic & Reconstr Surgery, Tampa Genl Hosp 1988

Farrior III, Joseph Brown MD [Oto] - **Spec Exp:** Otosclerosis/Stapedectomy; Hearing Loss; Meniere's Disease; Otology; **Hospital:** St. Joseph's Hosp - Tampa, Tampa Genl Hosp; **Address:** Farrior Ear Clin, 2727 W Martin Luther King Jr Blvd, Ste 520, Tampa, FL 33607; **Phone:** 813-879-0810; **Board Cert:** Otolaryngology 1981; **Med School:** Emory Univ 1975; **Resid:** Surgery, Johns Hopkins Hosp 1977; Otolaryngology, Johns Hopkins Hosp 1981; **Fellow:** Otolaryngology, Farrior Clin/St Josephs Hosp 1980; **Fac Appt:** Assoc Clin Prof Oto, Univ S Fla Coll Med

Goodwin Jr, W. Jarrard MD [Oto] - **Spec Exp:** Head & Neck Cancer; **Hospital:** Univ of Miami Hosp & Clins/Sylvester Comp Canc Ctr; **Address:** SCCC, Otolaryngology Dept, 1475 NW 12th Ave, Ste 4037, Miami, FL 33136-1015; **Phone:** 305-243-4387; **Board Cert:** Otolaryngology 1978; **Med School:** Albany Med Coll 1972; **Resid:** Surgery, Jackson Meml Hosp 1974; Otolaryngology, Jackson Meml Hosp 1977; **Fellow:** Head & Neck Surgical Oncology, UT MD Anderson Cancer Ctr 1980; **Fac Appt:** Prof Oto, Univ Miami Sch Med

Haynes, David S MD [Oto] - **Spec Exp:** Otology; Neuro-Otology; Acoustic Neuroma; Skull Base Tumors; **Hospital:** Vanderbilt Univ Med Ctr, Saint Thomas West Hosp - Nashville; **Address:** Vanderbilt Otolaryngology Clinic, 1215 21st Ave S, Medical Ctr East-South Tower, Ste 7209, Nashville, TN 37232; **Phone:** 615-322-6180; **Board Cert:** Otolaryngology 1994; Neurotology 2004; **Med School:** Univ Tenn Coll Med 1987; **Resid:** Surgery, Vanderbilt Univ Med Ctr 1989; Otolaryngology, Vanderbilt Univ Med Ctr 1993; **Fellow:** Otology & Neurotology, Otology Grp/ Ear Fdn 1995; **Fac Appt:** Prof Oto, Vanderbilt Univ

Kesser, Bradley W MD [Oto] - **Spec Exp:** Aural Atresia Repair; Neuro-Otology; **Hospital:** Univ of Virginia Hlth Sys; **Address:** Dept. Oto-HNS, Unviersity of Virginia Health System, Box 800713, Charlottesville, VA 22908-0713; **Phone:** 434-924-2040; **Board Cert:** Otolaryngology 1999; Neurotology 2008; **Med School:** Univ VA Sch Med 1993; **Resid:** Otolaryngology, Univ Va Med Ctr 1998; **Fellow:** Otology & Neurotology, House Ear Clinic 2000; **Fac Appt:** Assoc Prof Oto, Univ VA Sch Med

Kuhn, Frederick A MD [Oto] - **Spec Exp:** Endoscopic Sinus Surgery; Allergic Fungal Sinusitis; Rhinoplasty Revision; **Hospital:** Meml Hlth Univ Med Ctr - Savannah, St. Joseph's-Candler Hosp; **Address:** Georgia Nasal & Sinus Inst, 4750 Waters Ave, Ste 112, Savannah, GA 31404; **Phone:** 912-355-1070; **Board Cert:** Otolaryngology 1972; **Med School:** Univ Okla Coll Med 1966; **Resid:** Surgery, St Lukes Hosp 1968; **Fellow:** Otolaryngology, Barnes Hosp/Wash Univ 1972

Lambert, Paul R MD [Oto] - **Spec Exp:** Neuro-Otology; Cochlear Implants; Cholesteatoma; **Hospital:** MUSC Med Ctr; **Address:** MUSC, Dept Otolaryngology, 135 Rutledge Ave, Box 550, Charleston, SC 29425; **Phone:** 843-792-3531; **Board Cert:** Otolaryngology 1981; Neurotology 2004; **Med School:** Duke Univ 1976; **Resid:** Surgery, UCLA Med Ctr 1978; Otolaryngology, UCLA Med Ctr 1981; **Fellow:** Neurotology, Otologic Med Group 1982; **Fac Appt:** Prof Oto, Med Univ SC

Lanza, Donald C MD [Oto] - **Spec Exp:** Skull Base Tumors; Sinus Disorders/Surgery; Rhinitis; Graves' Disease-Eye; **Hospital:** St. Anthony's Hosp - St Petersburg, All Children's Hosp; **Address:** Sinus & Nasal Inst, 550 94th Ave N, St Petersburg, FL 33702; **Phone:** 727-573-0074; **Board Cert:** Otolaryngology 1990; **Med School:** SUNY Hlth Sci Ctr 1985; **Resid:** Surgery, Albany Med Ctr 1987; Otolaryngology, Albany Med Ctr 1990; **Fellow:** Rhinology, Johns Hopkins Hosp 1990; Rhinology, Hosp Univ Penn 1991

Levine, Paul A MD [Oto] - **Spec Exp:** Head & Neck Cancer; Skull Base Tumors; **Hospital:** Univ of Virginia Hlth Sys; **Address:** UVA-Otolaryngology Dept, Hospital West, rm 2746, 1 Hospital Drive, Charlottesville, VA 22908; **Phone:** 434-924-5593; **Board Cert:** Otolaryngology 1978; **Med School:** Albany Med Coll 1973; **Resid:** Otolaryngology, Yale-New Haven Hosp 1977; **Fellow:** Head and Neck Surgery, Stanford Med Ctr 1978; **Fac Appt:** Prof Oto, Univ VA Sch Med

Mattox, Douglas E MD [Oto] - **Spec Exp:** Neuro-Otology; Meniere's Disease; Hearing Loss; Cochlear Implants; **Hospital:** Emory Univ Hosp, Chldns Hlthcare Atlanta @ Egleston; **Address:** Emory Univ Dept Otolaryngology, 550 Peachtree St, Ste 4400, Atlanta, GA 30322; **Phone:** 404-778-3381; **Board Cert:** Otolaryngology 1977; Neurotology 2004; **Med School:** Yale Univ 1973; **Resid:** Otolaryngology, Stanford Univ Hosp 1977; **Fellow:** Neurotology, Univ Hosp 1985; **Fac Appt:** Prof Oto, Emory Univ

Netterville, James L MD [Oto] - **Spec Exp:** Head & Neck Surgery; Head & Neck Cancer; Vocal Cord Disorders; Skull Base Tumors; **Hospital:** Vanderbilt Univ Med Ctr, Vanderbilt Monroe Carrell Jr. Chldn's Hosp; **Address:** Vanderbilt Otolaryngology Clinic, 1215 21st Ave S, 7209 Medical Ctr East-South Tower, Nashville, TN 37232; **Phone:** 615-322-6180; **Board Cert:** Otolaryngology 1985; **Med School:** Univ Tenn Coll Med 1980; **Resid:** Surgery, Methodist Hosp 1982; Otolaryngology, Univ Tenn Med Ctr 1985; **Fellow:** Head and Neck Surgery, Univ Iowa 1986; Facial Plastic & Reconstr Surgery, Univ Iowa 1986; **Fac Appt:** Prof Oto, Vanderbilt Univ

Ossoff, Robert H MD/DMD [Oto] - **Spec Exp:** Voice Disorders; Vocal Cord Disorders; **Hospital:** Vanderbilt Univ Med Ctr; **Address:** 1215 21st Ave S, Ste 7302, Nashville, TN 37212-8783; **Phone:** 615-343-7464; **Board Cert:** Otolaryngology 1982; **Med School:** Tufts Univ 1975; **Resid:** Otolaryngology, Northwestern Meml Hosp 1980; **Fellow:** Head and Neck Surgery, Northwestern Meml Hosp 1981; **Fac Appt:** Prof Oto, Vanderbilt Univ

Peters, Glenn E MD [Oto] - **Spec Exp:** Thyroid & Parathyroid Cancer & Surgery; Head & Neck Cancer; **Hospital:** UAB Hosp; **Address:** The Kirklin Clinic, 2000 6th Ave S, Birmingham, AL 35249; **Phone:** 205-934-9766; **Board Cert:** Otolaryngology 1985; **Med School:** Louisiana State U, New Orleans 1980; **Resid:** Surgery, Baptist Med Ctr 1982; Otolaryngology, Univ Alabama Hosp 1984; **Fellow:** Head & Neck Surgical Oncology, Johns Hopkins Hosp 1987; **Fac Appt:** Prof S, UAB Sch Med

Petruzzelli, Guy MD/PhD [Oto] - **Spec Exp:** Head & Neck Cancer & Surgery; Skull Base Tumors; Thyroid Cancer; Pituitary Tumors; **Hospital:** Meml Hlth Univ Med Ctr - Savannah; **Address:** 4700 Waters Ave, ACI Bldg, Savannah, GA 31404; **Phone:** 912-350-2299; **Board Cert:** Otolaryngology 1993; **Med School:** Rush Med Coll 1987; **Resid:** Otolaryngology, Univ Pittsburgh Med Ctr 1992; **Fellow:** Head & Neck Oncology, Univ Pittsburgh Med Ctr 1993; Skull Base Surgery, Univ Pittsburgh Ctr Cranial Base Surg 1993; **Fac Appt:** Prof Oto, Mercer Univ Sch Med

Pillsbury, Harold C MD [Oto] - **Spec Exp:** Cochlear Implants; Neuro-Otology; Ear Disorders/Surgery; **Hospital:** NC Memorial Hosp - UNC; **Address:** UNC Dept of Otolaryngology/HSN Drive, G125 Physicians Office Bldg, 170 Manning Drive, CB 7070, Chapel Hill, NC 27599-7070; **Phone:** 919-966-6483; **Board Cert:** Otolaryngology 1978; Neurotology 2004; **Med School:** Geo Wash Univ 1972; **Resid:** Surgery, Univ NC Hosp 1973; Otolaryngology, NC Meml Hosp 1976; **Fac Appt:** Prof Oto, Univ NC Sch Med

Poole, Michael D MD/PhD [Oto] - **Spec Exp:** Pediatric Otolaryngology; Ear Infections; Sleep Disorders/Apnea; Sinus Disorders; **Hospital:** Meml Hlth Univ Med Ctr - Savannah, St. Joseph's-Candler Hosp; **Address:** Georgia Ear Institute, 4700 Waters Ave, Savannah, GA 31404; **Phone:** 912-356-1515; **Board Cert:** Otolaryngology 1986; **Med School:** Univ NC Sch Med 1981; **Resid:** Otolaryngology, NC Meml Hosp 1986; **Fac Appt:** Prof Oto, Mercer Univ Sch Med

Postma, Gregory N MD [Oto] - **Spec Exp:** Voice Disorders; **Hospital:** Georgia Regents Med Ctr-Augusta; **Address:** Med Coll Georgia, Voice & Swallowing Center, 1447 Harper St, Augusta, GA 30912; **Phone:** 706-721-4400; **Board Cert:** Otolaryngology 1994; **Med School:** Hahnemann Univ 1984; **Resid:** Otolaryngology, Oakland Naval Hosp 1992; Otolaryngology, Univ N Carolina Hosps 1993; **Fellow:** Otolaryngology, Vanderbilt Univ 1996; **Fac Appt:** Prof Oto, Med Coll GA

Ries, W Russell MD [Oto] - **Spec Exp:** Reconstructive Surgery; Cosmetic Surgery-Face; Rhinoplasty; **Hospital:** Vanderbilt Univ Med Ctr; **Address:** Vanderbilt Otolaryngology Clinic, 1215 21st Ave S, Medical Ctr East-South Tower, Ste 7209, Nashville, TN 37232; **Phone:** 615-322-6180; **Board Cert:** Otolaryngology 1985; Facial Plastic & Reconstr Surgery 1992; **Med School:** Univ Tenn Coll Med 1978; **Resid:** Surgery, Baptist Meml Hosp 1981; Otolaryngology, Northwestern Meml Hosp 1984; **Fellow:** Facial Plastic Surgery, Tulane Univ 1985; **Fac Appt:** Assoc Prof Oto, Vanderbilt Univ

Rosenthal, Eben MD [Oto] - **Spec Exp:** Head & Neck Cancer; Microvascular Surgery; Reconstructive Surgery; Minimally Invasive Surgery; **Hospital:** UAB Hosp; **Address:** BDB 563, 1720 2nd Ave S, Birmingham, AL 35294; **Phone:** 205-934-9713; **Board Cert:** Otolaryngology 2001; **Med School:** Univ Mich Med Sch 1994; **Resid:** Otolaryngology, U MI Med Ctr 2000; **Fellow:** Head and Neck Surgery, OR Hlth Sci Univ 2001; **Fac Appt:** Prof S, UAB Sch Med

Samant, Sandeep MD [Oto] - **Spec Exp:** Head & Neck Cancer & Surgery; Skull Base Surgery; Endoscopic Surgery; Thyroid & Parathyroid Cancer & Surgery; **Hospital:** Methodist Univ Hosp - Memphis; **Address:** UT Med Group, ENT Dept, 7945 Wolf River Blvd, Ste 220, Germantown, TN 38138; **Phone:** 901-347-8220; **Board Cert:** Otolaryngology 2009; **Med School:** India 1986; **Resid:** Otolaryngology, ALL-Indian Inst 1989; Otolaryngology, Royal Coll Surgeons 1994; **Fellow:** Head and Neck Surgery, Univ Miami/Sylvester Comprehensive Cancer Ctr 1995; Head & Neck Oncology, Univ TN Med Ctr 1996

Senior, Brent A MD [Oto] - **Spec Exp:** Sinus Disorders/Surgery; Nasal Allergy; Sleep Disorders; **Hospital:** NC Memorial Hosp - UNC; **Address:** UNC, Otolaryngology Dept, Physicians Office Building, G-120, 170 Manning Drive, CB 7070, Chapel Hill, NC 27599-7070; **Phone:** 919-966-6483; **Board Cert:** Otolaryngology 1996; **Med School:** Univ Mich Med Sch 1990; **Resid:** Otolaryngology, Boston Univ/Tufts Univ Affil Hosp 1995; **Fellow:** Sinus Surgery, HOsp Univ Penn 1996; **Fac Appt:** Prof Oto, Univ NC Sch Med

Shockley, William W MD [Oto] - **Spec Exp:** Facial Plastic & Reconstructive Surgery; Rhinoplasty; Skin Cancer; Salivary Gland Tumors & Surgery; **Hospital:** NC Memorial Hosp - UNC; **Address:** 170 Manning Drive, Physicians Office Bldg, CB 7070, Chapel Hill, NC 27599-7070; **Phone:** 919-966-3342; **Board Cert:** Otolaryngology 1981; Facial Plastic & Reconstr Surgery ; **Med School:** Indiana Univ 1976; **Resid:** Otolaryngology, Univ Cincinnati Hosps 1981; **Fellow:** Head and Neck Surgery, H&N Surg Assoc 1982; **Fac Appt:** Prof Oto, Univ NC Sch Med

Sillers, Michael J MD [Oto] - **Spec Exp:** Nasal & Sinus Disorders; Sinus Disorders/Surgery; **Hospital:** St. Vincent's Hosp - Birmingham; **Address:** Alabama Nasal & Sinus Ctr, 7191 Cahaba Valley Rd, Ste 301, Birmingham, AL 35242; **Phone:** 205-980-2091; **Board Cert:** Otolaryngology 1994; **Med School:** UAB Sch Med 1988; **Resid:** Otolaryngology, Univ Alabama Hosp 1993; **Fellow:** Sinus Surgery, Med Coll Georgia 1994; **Fac Appt:** Asst Prof S, UAB Sch Med

Silverstein, Herbert MD [Oto] - **Spec Exp:** Ear Disorders/Surgery; Meniere's Disease; **Hospital:** Sarasota Meml Hosp; **Address:** Silverstein Inst, 1901 Floyd St, Sarasota, FL 34239; **Phone:** 941-366-9222; **Board Cert:** Otolaryngology 1967; **Med School:** Temple Univ 1961; **Resid:** Surgery, Hosp Univ Penn 1963; Otolaryngology, Mass Eye & Ear Infirm 1966; **Fac Appt:** Clin Prof S, Univ S Fla Coll Med

Stringer, Scott P MD [Oto] - **Spec Exp:** Rhinitis; Skull Base Surgery; **Hospital:** Univ Mississippi Med Ctr, G.V. (Sonny) Montgomery VA Med Ctr - Jackson; **Address:** Univ Miss Med Ctr, Dept Otolaryngology, 2500 N State St, Jackson, MS 39216-4505; **Phone:** 601-984-5160; **Board Cert:** Otolaryngology 1987; **Med School:** Univ Tex SW, Dallas 1982; **Resid:** Surgery, Univ Tex SW Med Ctr 1984; Otolaryngology, Univ Tex SW Med Ctr 1987; **Fac Appt:** Prof Oto, Univ Miss

Telischi, Fred F MD [Oto] - **Spec Exp:** Ear Disorders/Surgery; Hearing Loss; Cochlear Implants; Neuro-Otology; **Hospital:** Jackson Meml Hosp; **Address:** UHlth, Otolaryngology Dept, 1120 NW 14th St Fl 5, Miami, FL 33136; **Phone:** 305-243-2000; **Board Cert:** Otolaryngology 1990; Neurotology 2010; **Med School:** Univ Miami Sch Med 1985; **Resid:** Otolaryngology, Jackson Meml Hosp 1990; **Fellow:** Neurotology, House Ear Clin 1992; **Fac Appt:** Prof Oto, Univ Miami Sch Med

Terris, David J MD [Oto] - **Spec Exp:** Thyroid Surgery; Thyroid Cancer; Parathyroid Disease; **Hospital:** Georgia Regents Med Ctr-Augusta, Doctors Hosp; **Address:** Georgia Regents Univ-Otolaryngology, 1120 15th St, rm BP-4109, Augusta, GA 30912; **Phone:** 706-721-4400; **Board Cert:** Otolaryngology 1994; **Med School:** Duke Univ 1988; **Resid:** Surgery, Stanford Univ Med Ctr 1989; Otolaryngology, Stanford Univ Med Ctr 1993; **Fellow:** Head and Neck Surgery, Stanford Univ Med Ctr 1994; **Fac Appt:** Prof Oto, Med Coll GA

Tucci, Debara L MD [Oto] - **Spec Exp:** Skull Base Surgery; Otology; Cochlear Implants; Hearing & Balance Disorders; **Hospital:** Duke Univ Hosp; **Address:** Duke Clinic, Ste 1F, 40 Duke Med Cir, Durham, NC 27710; **Phone:** 919-684-6968; **Board Cert:** Otolaryngology 1990; Neurotology 2004; **Med School:** Univ VA Sch Med 1985; **Resid:** Otolaryngology, Univ Va Med ctr 1990; **Fellow:** Otology & Neurotology, Univ Mich Med Ctr 1992; **Fac Appt:** Prof S, Duke Univ

Valentino, Joseph MD [Oto] - **Spec Exp:** Head & Neck Cancer; Reconstructive Microvascular Surgery; Thyroid Cancer; **Hospital:** Univ of Kentucky Albert B. Chandler Hosp; **Address:** UK Albert B Chandler Hosp, Whitney-Henderickson Bldg, 800 Rose St, Lexington, KY 40536; **Phone:** 859-257-5405; **Board Cert:** Otolaryngology 1993; **Med School:** UMDNJ-RW Johnson Med Sch 1987; **Resid:** Otolaryngology, Univ Minn Med Ctr 1992; **Fellow:** Otolaryngology, Univ Iowa Hosps & Clin 1993; **Fac Appt:** Assoc Prof Oto, Univ KY Coll Med

Wazen, Jack J MD [Oto] - **Spec Exp:** Skull Base Surgery; Meniere's Disease; Acoustic Neuroma; Hearing & Balance Disorders; **Hospital:** Sarasota Meml Hosp; **Address:** Silverstein Inst, 1901 Floyd St, Sarasota, FL 34239; **Phone:** 941-366-9222; **Board Cert:** Otolaryngology 1983; Neurotology 2012; **Med School:** Lebanon 1978; **Resid:** Surgery, St Lukes Hosp 1980; Otolaryngology, NY-Presby/Columbia Univ Med Ctr 1983; **Fellow:** Neurotology, Ear Rsch Fdn 1984

Weissler, Mark C MD [Oto] - **Spec Exp:** Head & Neck Cancer; Laryngeal & Tracheal Disorders; Voice Disorders; Salivary Gland Tumors; **Hospital:** NC Memorial Hosp - UNC; **Address:** 170 Manning Drive, G106 Physician's Office Bldg, Campus Box 7070, Chapel Hill, NC 27599-7070; **Phone:** 919-843-4820; **Board Cert:** Otolaryngology 1985; **Med School:** Boston Univ 1980; **Resid:** Surgery, Mass Genl Hosp 1982; Otolaryngology, Mass Eye & Ear Infirm 1985; **Fellow:** Head & Neck Oncology, Univ Cincinnati 1986; **Fac Appt:** Prof Oto, Univ NC Sch Med

Midwest

Akervall, Jan A MD/PhD [Oto] - **Spec Exp:** Head & Neck Cancer; Head & Neck Reconstruction; Minimally Invasive Surgery; **Hospital:** Beaumont Hosp-Royal Oak, St. Joseph Mercy Hosp - Ann Arbor; **Address:** 28300 Orchard Lake Rd, Ste 100, Farmington Hills, MI 48334; **Phone:** 248-737-4030; **Med School:** Sweden 1990; **Resid:** Otolaryngology, Lund Univ Fac Med 1998; **Fellow:** Head & Neck Oncology, Univ MI Hosps 2002; **Fac Appt:** Prof Oto, Oakland Univ-William Beaumont Med Sch

Alam, Daniel Syed MD [Oto] - **Spec Exp:** Nasal Reconstruction; Head & Neck Reconstruction; Parotid Gland Tumors; Cancer Reconstruction; **Hospital:** Cleveland Clin (page 55); **Address:** Cleveland Clin Main Campus, 9500 Euclid Ave, MC A71, Cleveland, OH 44195; **Phone:** 216-445-6594; **Board Cert:** Otolaryngology 2012; **Med School:** Johns Hopkins Univ 1996; **Resid:** Otolaryngology, Mass Genl Hosp 2001; **Fellow:** Facial Plastic & Reconstr Surgery, UCLA Med Ctr 2002

Arts, H Alexander MD [Oto] - **Spec Exp:** Skull Base Tumors & Surgery; Neuro-Otology; Hearing Loss; Cochlear Implants; **Hospital:** Univ Michigan Med Ctr; **Address:** Univ Michigan Taubman Center, Dept Otolaryngology, 1500 E Medical Ctr Drive, Ste 1904, Ann Arbor, MI 48109; **Phone:** 734-936-8006; **Board Cert:** Otolaryngology 1992; Neurotology 2004; **Med School:** Baylor Coll Med 1983; **Resid:** Surgery, Univ Washington Med Ctr 1985; Otolaryngology, Univ Washington Med Ctr 1990; **Fellow:** Neurotology, Univ Virginia 1991; **Fac Appt:** Prof Oto, Univ Mich Med Sch

Baim, Howard M MD [Oto] - **Spec Exp:** Head & Neck Surgery; Sleep Disorders/Apnea; Sinus Disorders; **Hospital:** Adv Illinois Masonic Med Ctr, Highland Park Hosp/NorthShore Univ Hlth Syst (page 67); **Address:** 2532 N Lincoln Ave, Chicago, IL 60614-2468; **Phone:** 773-883-1177; **Board Cert:** Otolaryngology 1978; **Med School:** Univ IL Coll Med 1973; **Resid:** Surgery, IL Met Grp Hosps 1975; Otolaryngology, IL Eye & Ear Infirmary 1978; **Fac Appt:** Asst Clin Prof Oto, Univ IL Coll Med

Baker, Shan R MD [Oto] - **Spec Exp:** Cosmetic Surgery-Face & Neck; Reconstructive Surgery; **Hospital:** Univ Michigan Med Ctr; **Address:** Ctr for Facial Cosmetic Surgery, 19900 Haggerty Rd, Ste 103, Livonia, MI 48152-1054; **Phone:** 734-432-7634; **Board Cert:** Otolaryngology 1977; Facial Plastic & Reconstr Surgery 1990; **Med School:** Univ Iowa Coll Med 1971; **Resid:** Surgery, UCSD Med Ctr 1973; Otolaryngology, Univ Iowa Hosps 1977; **Fac Appt:** Prof Oto, Univ Mich Med Sch

Bastian, Robert W MD [Oto] - **Spec Exp:** Voice Disorders; Swallowing Disorders; Laryngeal Disorders; **Hospital:** Adv Good Samaritan Hosp; **Address:** Bastian Voice Inst, 3010 Highland Parkway, Ste 550, Downers Grove, IL 60515-5500; **Phone:** 630-724-1100; **Board Cert:** Otolaryngology 1983; **Med School:** Washington Univ, St Louis 1978; **Resid:** Surgery, Barnes Hosp 1979; Otolaryngology, Barnes Hosp 1983; **Fellow:** Otolaryngology, Hosp Foch 1983

Beatty, Charles W MD [Oto] - **Spec Exp:** Otology & Neuro-Otology; Acoustic Neuroma; Meniere's Disease; Cochlear Implants; **Hospital:** Mayo Med Ctr & Clin - Rochester; **Address:** Mayo Clin-Dept Ear, Nose and Throat, 200 First St SW, Gonda-12, Rochester, MN 55905; **Phone:** 507-284-8532; **Board Cert:** Otolaryngology 1982; **Med School:** Univ Iowa Coll Med 1977; **Resid:** Otolaryngology, Mayo Clinic 1982; **Fac Appt:** Prof Oto, Mayo Med Sch

Beeson, William H MD [Oto] - **Spec Exp:** Facial Plastic & Reconstructive Surgery; Cosmetic Surgery-Face; Eyelid Surgery; Ear Reshaping (Otoplasty); **Hospital:** IU Hlth Univ Hosp; **Address:** Beeson Cosmetic Surgery, 13590 N Meridian St, Carmel, IN 46032; **Phone:** 317-846-0846; **Board Cert:** Otolaryngology 1982; Facial Plastic & Reconstr Surgery 1991; **Med School:** Indiana Univ 1976; **Resid:** Otolaryngology, IU Hlth Affil Hosp 1981; **Fac Appt:** Clin Prof Oto, Indiana Univ

Benninger, Michael S MD [Oto] - **Spec Exp:** Nasal & Sinus Disorders; Nasal & Sinus Surgery; Laryngeal & Voice Disorders; Subglottic Stenosis; **Hospital:** Cleveland Clin (page 55); **Address:** Cleveland Clinic, 9500 Euclid Ave, Cleveland, OH 44195; **Phone:** 216-444-6686; **Board Cert:** Otolaryngology 1988; **Med School:** Case West Res Univ 1983; **Resid:** Surgery, Cleveland Clin 1985; Otolaryngology, Cleveland Clin 1988; **Fac Appt:** Prof S, Cleveland Cl Coll Med/Case West Res

Blair, Elizabeth MD [Oto] - **Spec Exp:** Head & Neck Cancer & Surgery; Thyroid & Parathyroid Surgery; Salivary Gland Tumors; Skull Base Tumors; **Hospital:** Univ of Chicago Med, Univ Chicago Med-Comer Chldn's Hosp; **Address:** Univ Chicago Medicine, Oto/ENT, DCAM Bldg Fl 4H, 5758 S Maryland Ave, Chicago, IL 60637; **Phone:** 773-702-1865; **Board Cert:** Otolaryngology 1994; **Med School:** Creighton Univ 1988; **Resid:** Otolaryngology, Univ Pittsburgh Med Ctr 1993; **Fellow:** Head & Neck Surgical Oncology, MD Anderson Cancer Ctr 1994; **Fac Appt:** Assoc Prof Oto, Univ Chicago-Pritzker Sch Med

Bojrab, Dennis I MD [Oto] - **Spec Exp:** Otology & Neuro-Otology; Facial Nerve Disorders; Skull Base Tumors; Ear Tumors; **Hospital:** Beaumont Hosp-Royal Oak; **Address:** Michigan Ear Inst, 30055 Northwestern Hwy, Ste 101, Farmington Hills, MI 48334; **Phone:** 248-865-4444; **Board Cert:** Otolaryngology 1985; Neurotology 2005; **Med School:** Indiana Univ 1979; **Resid:** Surgery, Butterworth Hosp 1981; Otolaryngology, Univ Indiana Sch Med 1984; **Fellow:** Skull Base Surgery, Vanderbilt Univ Med Ctr 1985; **Fac Appt:** Prof Oto, Oakland Univ-William Beaumont Med Sch

Bradford, Carol MD [Oto] - **Spec Exp:** Head & Neck Cancer; Melanoma-Head & Neck; Skin Cancer-Head & Neck; **Hospital:** Univ Michigan Med Ctr; **Address:** Univ of Michigan, Dept Otolaryngology, 1500 E Medical Ctr Drive, rm 1904-TC, Ann Arbor, MI 48109; **Phone:** 734-936-8029; **Board Cert:** Otolaryngology 1993; **Med School:** Univ Mich Med Sch 1986; **Resid:** Otolaryngology, Univ Michigan Med Ctr 1992; **Fellow:** Head and Neck Surgery, Univ Michigan Med Ctr 1988; **Fac Appt:** Prof Oto, Univ Mich Med Sch

Branham, Gregory H MD [Oto] - **Spec Exp:** Cosmetic & Reconstructive Surgery-Face; Nasal Surgery; Botox Therapy; Skin Laser Surgery-Resurfacing; **Hospital:** Barnes-Jewish West County Hosp, Barnes-Jewish Hosp; **Address:** 605 Old Ballas Rd, Ste 100, St Louis, MO 63141; **Phone:** 314-996-3880; **Board Cert:** Otolaryngology 1989; Facial Plastic & Reconstr Surgery 1993; **Med School:** Univ SC Sch Med 1983; **Resid:** Otolaryngology, St Louis Univ Hosp 1989; **Fellow:** Facial Plastic & Reconstr Surgery, Washington Univ Affil Hosp 1990; **Fac Appt:** Prof Oto, St Louis Univ

Burkey, Brian MD [Oto] - **Spec Exp:** Parotid Gland Tumors; Head & Neck Cancer; Reconstructive Surgery; Carotid Body Tumors; **Hospital:** Cleveland Clin (page 55); **Address:** Head & Neck Inst, Desk A71, The Cleveland Clinic, 9500 Euclid Ave, Cleveland, OH 44195; **Phone:** 216-445-8837; **Board Cert:** Otolaryngology 1992; **Med School:** Univ VA Sch Med 1986; **Resid:** Otolaryngology, Univ Mich Med Ctr 1991; **Fellow:** Microsurgery, Ohio State Univ 1991; **Fac Appt:** Prof Oto, Vanderbilt Univ

Campbell, Bruce H MD [Oto] - **Spec Exp:** Head & Neck Cancer; Thyroid Surgery; **Hospital:** Froedtert & Med Coll WI, Chldns Hosp - Wisconsin; **Address:** Med Coll Wisc-Dept Oto, 9200 W Wisconsin Ave, Milwaukee, WI 53226; **Phone:** 414-805-5583; **Board Cert:** Otolaryngology 1986; **Med School:** Rush Med Coll 1980; **Resid:** Otolaryngology, Med Coll Wisconsin 1985; **Fellow:** Head and Neck Surgery, MD Anderson Cancer Ctr 1987; **Fac Appt:** Prof Oto, Med Coll Wisc

Corey, Jacquelynne P MD [Oto] - **Spec Exp:** Nasal & Sinus Disorders; Allergy; Voice Disorders; Sleep Disorders; **Hospital:** Univ of Chicago Med; **Address:** University of Chicago, 5841 S Maryland Ave, Chicago, IL 60637; **Phone:** 773-702-1865; **Board Cert:** Otolaryngology 1985; **Med School:** Univ IL Coll Med 1979; **Resid:** Otolaryngology, Rush Presby-St Lukes Med Ctr 1984; **Fac Appt:** Prof S, Univ Chicago-Pritzker Sch Med

Driscoll, Colin L W MD [Oto] - **Spec Exp:** Acoustic Neuroma; Cochlear Implants; Skull Base Tumors; **Hospital:** Mayo Med Ctr & Clin - Rochester; **Address:** Mayo Clinic, Dept of Ear, Nose and Throat, 200 First St SW, Rochester, MN 55905; **Phone:** 507-284-4065; **Board Cert:** Otolaryngology 1998; Neurology 2006; **Med School:** Univ New Mexico 1992; **Resid:** Otolaryngology, Mayo Clinic 1997; **Fellow:** Neurotology, UCSF Med Ctr 1998; Skull Base Surgery, UCSF Med Ctr 1999; **Fac Appt:** Assoc Prof Oto, Mayo Med Sch

Friedman, Michael MD [Oto] - **Spec Exp:** Sleep Disorders/Apnea/Snoring; Thyroid & Parathyroid Surgery; Sinus Disorders/Surgery; **Hospital:** Adv Illinois Masonic Med Ctr, Rush Univ Med Ctr; **Address:** 30 N Michigan Ave, Ste 1107, Chicago, IL 60602; **Phone:** 312-236-3642; **Board Cert:** Otolaryngology 1977; **Med School:** Univ IL Coll Med 1972; **Resid:** Surgery, Illinois Masonic Hosp 1974; Otolaryngology, Univ Illinois Med Ctr 1977; **Fac Appt:** Prof Oto, Rush Med Coll

Funk, Gerry F MD [Oto] - **Spec Exp:** Head & Neck Cancer; Head & Neck Reconstruction; Parathyroid Surgery; **Hospital:** Univ Iowa Hosp & Clins; **Address:** Univ Iowa Hosp & Clinics, 200 Hawkins Drive, PFP-Otolaryngology, Iowa City, IA 52242; **Phone:** 319-356-2201; **Board Cert:** Otolaryngology 1992; **Med School:** Univ Chicago-Pritzker Sch Med 1986; **Resid:** Surgery, LAC-USC Med Ctr 1987; Otolaryngology, LAC-USC Med Ctr 1991; **Fellow:** Head and Neck Surgery, Univ Iowa Hosp 1992; **Fac Appt:** Prof Oto, Univ Iowa Coll Med

Gantz, Bruce J MD [Oto] - **Spec Exp:** Cochlear Implants; Neuro-Otology; Skull Base Surgery; **Hospital:** Univ Iowa Hosp & Clins; **Address:** Univ Hosp & Clins, Dept Otolaryngology, 200 Hawkins Drive, Iowa City, IA 52242-1078; **Phone:** 319-356-2173; **Board Cert:** Otolaryngology 1980; Neurotology 2004; **Med School:** Univ Iowa Coll Med 1974; **Resid:** Otolaryngology, Univ Iowa Hosps 1980; **Fellow:** Neurotology, Univ Zurich 1982; **Fac Appt:** Prof Oto, Univ Iowa Coll Med

Goebel, Joel Alan MD [Oto] - **Spec Exp:** Dizziness/Vertigo; Hearing Disorders; Otology & Neuro-Otology; **Hospital:** Barnes-Jewish Hosp, St. Louis Chldns Hosp; **Address:** Barnes Jewish Hosp South, 660 S Euclid Ave, Box 8115, St Louis, MO 63110; **Phone:** 314-362-7509; **Board Cert:** Otolaryngology 1985; **Med School:** Washington Univ, St Louis 1980; **Resid:** Otolaryngology, Barnes Hosp/Wash Univ 1985; **Fac Appt:** Prof Oto, Washington Univ, St Louis

Hartig, Gregory K MD [Oto] - **Spec Exp:** Head & Neck Cancer; Skull Base Tumors; **Hospital:** Univ WI Hosp & Clins; **Address:** 600 Highland Ave, rm K4/720, Madison, WI 53792-7375; **Phone:** 608-263-6190; **Board Cert:** Otolaryngology 1994; **Med School:** Univ Mich Med Sch 1988; **Resid:** Otolaryngology, Univ Mich Med Ctr 1993; **Fellow:** Otolaryngology, Univ Penn Med Ctr 1994; **Fac Appt:** Prof Oto, Univ Mich Med Sch

Haughey, Bruce H MD [Oto] - **Spec Exp:** Reconstructive Surgery-Face; Head & Neck Cancer; Head & Neck Reconstruction; **Hospital:** Barnes-Jewish Hosp, St. Louis Chldns Hosp; **Address:** 4921 Parkview Pl, Ste A11, St Louis, MO 63110; **Phone:** 314-362-7509; **Board Cert:** Otolaryngology 1984; **Med School:** New Zealand 1976; **Resid:** Surgery, Univ Auckland 1981; Otolaryngology, Univ Iowa Med Ctr 1984; **Fellow:** Otolaryngology, Univ Iowa Med Ctr 1985; **Fac Appt:** Prof Oto, Washington Univ, St Louis

Hilger, Peter Andrew MD [Oto] - **Spec Exp:** Head & Neck Surgery; Facial Plastic Surgery; **Hospital:** Regions Hosp - St Paul, Fairview Southdale Hosp; **Address:** Centennial Lakes Med Bldg, 7373 France Ave S, Ste 410, Edina, MN 55435; **Phone:** 952-844-0404; **Board Cert:** Otolaryngology 1979; **Med School:** Univ Minn 1974; **Resid:** Surgery, Univ Minn Hosp 1975; Otolaryngology, Univ Minn Hosp 1979; **Fellow:** Plastic Surgery, Mass Eye & Ear Infirm 1980; **Fac Appt:** Asst Prof Oto, Univ Minn

Hoffman, Henry T MD [Oto] - **Spec Exp:** Voice Disorders; Head & Neck Cancer; Salivary Gland Tumors & Surgery; **Hospital:** Univ Iowa Hosp & Clins; **Address:** UIHC-Otolaryngology Dept, 200 Hawkins Drive, Iowa City, IA 52242; **Phone:** 319-356-2201; **Board Cert:** Otolaryngology 1985; **Med School:** UCSD 1980; **Resid:** Otolaryngology, Univ Iowa Hosp & Clinics 1985; **Fellow:** Facial Plastic & Reconstr Surgery, Univ Michigan Hosp 1989; **Fac Appt:** Prof Oto, Univ Iowa Coll Med

Hogikyan, Norman D MD [Oto] - **Spec Exp:** Voice Disorders; Vocal Cord Disorders; Swallowing Disorders; Airway Disorders; **Hospital:** Univ Michigan Med Ctr; **Address:** 1500 E Medical Ctr Drive, 1904 Taubman Ctr, Ann Arbor, MI 48109-5312; **Phone:** 734-936-7633; **Board Cert:** Otolaryngology 1995; **Med School:** Univ Mich Med Sch 1988; **Resid:** Otolaryngology, Barnes-Jewish Hosp 1994; **Fellow:** Laryngology, Loyola Univ Med Ctr 1995; **Fac Appt:** Prof Oto, Univ Mich Med Sch

Hom, David B MD [Oto] - **Spec Exp:** Facial Plastic & Reconstructive Surgery; Cosmetic Surgery-Face; Facial Paralysis; Cancer Reconstruction; **Hospital:** Univ Cincinnati Med Ctr, West Chester Hosp; **Address:** UC Hlth Phys, 7675 Wellness Way, Ste 309, West Chester, OH 45069; **Phone:** 513-475-8400; **Board Cert:** Otolaryngology 1988; Facial Plastic & Reconstr Surgery 2009; **Med School:** UCLA 1982; **Resid:** Surgery, UC Irvine Hosp 1984; Otolaryngology, Univ Michigan Med Ctr 1988; **Fellow:** Facial Plastic & Reconstr Surgery, American Acad FPRS 1989; **Fac Appt:** Prof Oto, Univ Cincinnati

Hotaling, Andrew J MD [Oto] - **Spec Exp:** Pediatric Otolaryngology; Sleep Disorders/Apnea; Neck Masses; Ear Infections; **Hospital:** Loyola Univ Med Ctr; **Address:** Loyola Univ Med Ctr, 2160 S First Ave, Bldg 105, rm 1870, Maywood, IL 60153-5590; **Phone:** 708-216-9183; **Board Cert:** Otolaryngology 1985; **Med School:** Case West Res Univ 1979; **Resid:** Surgery, Case Western Reserve Univ Hosp 1981; Otolaryngology, Northwestern Meml Hosp 1984; **Fellow:** Pediatric Otolaryngology, Univ Pittsburgh Med Ctr 1985; **Fac Appt:** Prof Oto, Loyola Univ-Stritch Sch Med

Jones, Paul J MD [Oto] - **Spec Exp:** Pediatric Otolaryngology; **Hospital:** Rush Univ Med Ctr; **Address:** 1611 W Harrison St, Ste 550, Chicago, IL 60612; **Phone:** 312-942-6100; **Board Cert:** Otolaryngology 1989; **Med School:** Rush Med Coll 1983; **Resid:** Otolaryngology, Rush Presby-St Lukes Med Ctr 1988; **Fac Appt:** Asst Prof Oto, Rush Med Coll

Kern, Robert C MD [Oto] - **Spec Exp:** Sinus Disorders/Surgery; Nasal & Sinus Disorders; Snoring/Sleep Apnea; Taste & Smell Disorders; **Hospital:** Northwestern Meml Hosp; **Address:** Northwestern Medical Faculty Fdn, 675 N St Clair St Fl 15, Chicago, IL 60611; **Phone:** 312-695-8182; **Board Cert:** Otolaryngology 1990; **Med School:** Jefferson Med Coll 1985; **Resid:** Otolaryngology, Wayne State Affil Hosp 1990; **Fellow:** Research, Natl Inst Hlth 1991; **Fac Appt:** Prof Oto, Northwestern Univ

Lavertu, Pierre MD [Oto] - **Spec Exp:** Thyroid Cancer; Head & Neck Cancer; Skull Base Tumors; **Hospital:** UH Case Med Ctr; **Address:** 11100 Euclid Ave, Cleveland, OH 44106-5045; **Phone:** 216-844-4773; **Board Cert:** Otolaryngology 1981; **Med School:** Univ Montreal 1976; **Resid:** Otolaryngology, Univ Montreal Med Ctr 1981; **Fellow:** Head and Neck Surgery, Notre Dame Hosp 1982; Head and Neck Surgery, Cleveland Clinic 1983; **Fac Appt:** Prof Oto, Case West Res Univ

Leonetti, John P MD [Oto] - **Spec Exp:** Skull Base Tumors & Surgery; Neuro-Otology; Head & Neck Cancer; Facial Paralysis; **Hospital:** Loyola Univ Med Ctr; **Address:** Loyola Univ Med Ctr, Dept Otolaryngology, 2160 S First Ave Bldg 105 - rm 1870, Maywood, IL 60153; **Phone:** 708-216-4804; **Board Cert:** Otolaryngology 1987; **Med School:** Loyola Univ-Stritch Sch Med 1982; **Resid:** Otolaryngology, Loyola Univ Med Ctr 1987; Research, House Ear Inst 1987; **Fellow:** Neurotology, Barnes Jewish Hosp 1988; **Fac Appt:** Prof Oto, Loyola Univ-Stritch Sch Med

Marentette, Lawrence J MD [Oto] - **Spec Exp:** Skull Base Tumors & Surgery; Facial Plastic & Reconstructive Surgery; **Hospital:** Univ Michigan Med Ctr; **Address:** 1500 E Medical Ctr Drive, 1904 Taubman Ctr, Ann Arbor, MI 48109; **Phone:** 734-936-8051; **Board Cert:** Otolaryngology 1981; Facial Plastic & Reconstr Surgery 1995; **Med School:** Wayne State Univ 1976; **Resid:** Otolaryngology, Wayne State Univ Hosp 1980; **Fellow:** Maxillofacial Surgery, Univ of Zurich 1985; **Fac Appt:** Prof Oto, Univ Mich Med Sch

Miyamoto, Richard T MD [Oto] - **Spec Exp:** Neuro-Otology; Acoustic Neuroma; Ear Disorders/Surgery; Cochlear Implants; **Hospital:** Riley Hosp for Children, IU Hlth Univ Hosp; **Address:** 705 Riley Hosp Drive, Ste 0860, Indianapolis, IN 46202; **Phone:** 317-274-3556; **Board Cert:** Otolaryngology 1975; Neurotology 2004; **Med School:** Univ Mich Med Sch 1970; **Resid:** Surgery, Butterworth Hosp 1972; Otolaryngology, Indiana Univ Hosps 1975; **Fellow:** Otology & Neurotology, Otologic Med Grp 1978; **Fac Appt:** Prof Oto, Indiana Univ

Naclerio, Robert M MD [Oto] - **Spec Exp:** Sinus Disorders/Surgery; Pediatric Otolaryngology; Rhinitis; **Hospital:** Univ of Chicago Med; **Address:** Univ Chicago Med Ctr, 5758 S Maryland Ave, Chicago, IL 60637; **Phone:** 773-702-1865; **Board Cert:** Otolaryngology 1983; **Med School:** Baylor Coll Med 1976; **Resid:** Surgery, Johns Hopkins Hosp 1978; Otolaryngology, Baylor Coll Med 1983; **Fellow:** Clinical Immunology, Johns Hopkins Hosp 1982; **Fac Appt:** Prof Oto, Univ Chicago-Pritzker Sch Med

Olsen, Kerry D MD [Oto] - **Spec Exp:** Head & Neck Cancer & Surgery; Esthesioneuroblastoma; Salivary Gland Tumors & Surgery; Skull Base Tumors; **Hospital:** Mayo Med Ctr & Clin - Rochester; **Address:** Mayo Clinic, Dept Otolaryngology, 200 1st St SW, Rochester, MN 55905-0001; **Phone:** 507-284-3542; **Board Cert:** Otolaryngology 1981; **Med School:** Mayo Med Sch 1976; **Resid:** Otolaryngology, Mayo Clinic 1981; **Fac Appt:** Prof Oto, Mayo Med Sch

Ozer, Enver MD [Oto] - **Spec Exp:** Head & Neck Cancer; Head & Neck Surgery; **Hospital:** OSU Wexner Med Ctr; **Address:** 300 W 10th Ave Fl 1, Columbus, OH 43210; **Phone:** 614-293-8074; **Med School:** Turkey 1994; **Resid:** Otolaryngology, Marmara Univ Med Sch 1996; Head and Neck Surgery, Marmara Univ Med Sch 2000; **Fellow:** Head & Neck Oncology, Ohio St Univ Med Ctr 2005; **Fac Appt:** Asst Prof Oto, Ohio State Univ

Paparella, Michael M MD [Oto] - **Spec Exp:** Hearing Disorders; Neuro-Otology; Meniere's Disease; Ear Infections; **Hospital:** Univ Minn Med Ctr, Fairview - West Bank Campus, Maple Grove Hosp; **Address:** 701 25th Ave S, Ste 200, 9825 Hospital Drive, Fl LL, Ste 10, Minneapolis, MN 55454-1443; **Phone:** 612-339-2836; **Board Cert:** Otolaryngology 1963; **Med School:** Univ Mich Med Sch 1957; **Resid:** Otolaryngology, Henry Ford Hosp 1961; **Fac Appt:** Clin Prof Oto, Univ Minn

Patil, Yash J MD [Oto] - **Spec Exp:** Thyroid & Parathyroid Cancer & Surgery; Head & Neck Cancer & Surgery; Airway Disorders; **Hospital:** Univ Cincinnati Med Ctr; **Address:** UC Health Ear, Nose and Throat Spcs, 222 Piedmont Ave, Ste 5200, Cincinnati, OH 45219; **Phone:** 513-475-8400; **Board Cert:** Otolaryngology 2012; **Med School:** Vanderbilt Univ 1996; **Resid:** Otolaryngology, Univ IL Med Ctr 2000; **Fellow:** Microvascular Surgery, Washington Univ Affil Hosp 2002; **Fac Appt:** Assoc Clin Prof Oto, Univ Cincinnati

Pelzer, Harold J MD/DDS [Oto] - **Spec Exp:** Head & Neck Cancer; Swallowing Disorders; **Hospital:** Northwestern Meml Hosp; **Address:** Northwestern Dept Otolaryngology, 675 N St Clair St Fl 15, Chicago, IL 60611; **Phone:** 312-695-8182; **Board Cert:** Otolaryngology 1985; **Med School:** Northwestern Univ 1979; **Resid:** Surgery, Northwestern Meml Hosp 1983; **Fellow:** Head and Neck Surgery, Northwestern Meml Hosp 1985; **Fac Appt:** Asst Prof Oto, Northwestern Univ

Pensak, Myles L MD [Oto] - **Spec Exp:** Skull Base Tumors; Facial Paralysis; Hearing & Balance Disorders; **Hospital:** Univ Cincinnati Med Ctr, Good Samaritan Hosp - Cincinnati; **Address:** UC Health Ear, Nose and Throat Spcs, 222 Piedmont Ave, Ste 5200, Cincinnati, OH 45219; **Phone:** 513-475-8400; **Board Cert:** Otolaryngology 1983; Neurotology 2004; **Med School:** NY Med Coll 1978; **Resid:** Surgery, Upstate Med Ctr 1980; Otolaryngology, Yale Univ 1983; **Fellow:** Otology & Neurotology, The Otology Grp 1984; **Fac Appt:** Prof Oto, Univ Cincinnati

Piccirillo, Jay Francis MD [Oto] - **Spec Exp:** Sleep Disorders/Apnea; Sinus Disorders/Surgery; **Hospital:** Barnes-Jewish Hosp; **Address:** Barnes Jewish Hosp South, 660 S Euclid Ave, Box 8115, St Louis, MO 63110; **Phone:** 314-362-7509; **Board Cert:** Otolaryngology 1990; **Med School:** Univ VT Coll Med 1985; **Resid:** Otolaryngology, Albany Med Ctr 1990; **Fellow:** Yale Univ 1992; **Fac Appt:** Asst Prof Oto, Washington Univ, St Louis

Siegel, Gordon J MD [Oto] - **Spec Exp:** Head & Neck Cancer; Nasal & Sinus Disorders; **Hospital:** Northwestern Meml Hosp, Lurie Chldn's Hosp-Chicago; **Address:** Midwest Ear, Nose & Throat, 3 E Huron St, Fl 1, Chicago, IL 60611-2705; **Phone:** 312-988-7777; **Board Cert:** Otolaryngology 1984; **Med School:** Ros Franklin Univ/Chicago Med Sch 1978; **Resid:** Otolaryngology, Northwestern Univ Affil Hosp 1982; **Fac Appt:** Asst Clin Prof Oto, Northwestern Univ

Stankiewicz, James MD [Oto] - **Spec Exp:** Endoscopic Sinus Surgery; Rhinosinusitis; Nasal & Sinus Disorders; **Hospital:** Loyola Univ Med Ctr; **Address:** Loyola Univ Med Ctr, Dept Oto, 2160 S First Ave, Maywood, IL 60153-5590; **Phone:** 708-216-9183; **Board Cert:** Otolaryngology 1978; **Med School:** Univ Chicago-Pritzker Sch Med 1974; **Resid:** Otolaryngology, Univ Chicago Hosp 1978; **Fac Appt:** Prof Oto, Loyola Univ-Stritch Sch Med

Stenson, Kerstin M MD [Oto] - **Spec Exp:** Head & Neck Cancer & Surgery; Head & Neck Cancer Reconstruction; Trauma; Vocal Cord Disorders; **Hospital:** Univ of Chicago Med; **Address:** Univ Chicago Med Ctr, Otol/ENT Clin, 5841 S Maryland Ave, MC 1035, Chicago, IL 60637-1463; **Phone:** 773-702-1865; **Board Cert:** Otolaryngology 1994; **Med School:** Ros Franklin Univ/Chicago Med Sch 1988; **Resid:** Otolaryngology, Univ Illinois Med Ctr 1993; **Fellow:** Head & Neck Oncology, Univ Michigan Hosp 1994; **Fac Appt:** Asst Prof S, Univ Chicago-Pritzker Sch Med

Szachowicz II, Edward H MD [Oto] - **Spec Exp:** Cosmetic Surgery-Face; Rhinoplasty; **Hospital:** Abbott - Northwestern Hosp; **Address:** Centennial Lakes Med Bldg, 7373 France Ave S, Ste 508, Edina, MN 55435-4538; **Phone:** 952-835-5665; **Board Cert:** Otolaryngology 1984; **Med School:** Univ IL Coll Med 1979; **Resid:** Surgery, Fairview Univ Med Ctr 1980; Otolaryngology, Fairview Univ Med Ctr 1984; **Fellow:** Facial Plastic Surgery, Fairview Univ Med Ctr 1986; **Fac Appt:** Asst Clin Prof Oto, Univ Minn

Teknos, Theodoros N MD [Oto] - **Spec Exp:** Head & Neck Cancer; Thyroid Cancer; Facial Plastic & Reconstructive Surgery; Reconstructive Microvascular Surgery; **Hospital:** OSU Wexner Med Ctr; **Address:** 300 W 10th Ave Fl 1, Columbus, OH 43210; **Phone:** 614-293-8074; **Board Cert:** Otolaryngology 1997; **Med School:** Harvard Med Sch 1991; **Resid:** Otolaryngology, Mass Eye & Ear Hosp 1996; **Fellow:** Head and Neck Surgery, Vanderbilt Univ Med Ctr 1997; Microvascular Surgery, Vanderbilt Univ Med Ctr 1997; **Fac Appt:** Prof Oto, Ohio State Univ

Telian, Steven A MD [Oto] - **Spec Exp:** Cochlear Implants; Ear Disorders/Surgery; Acoustic Neuroma; **Hospital:** Univ Michigan Med Ctr; **Address:** Univ Mich Med Ctr, Dept Otolaryngology-Head & Neck Surgery, 1500 E Med Ctr Drive, 1904 Taubman Ctr, Ann Arbor, MI 48109-0312; **Phone:** 734-936-8006; **Board Cert:** Otolaryngology 1985; Neurotology 2004; **Med School:** Univ Pennsylvania 1981; **Resid:** Otolaryngology, Hosp Univ Penn 1985; **Fellow:** Neurotology, Univ Mich Med Ctr 1986; **Fac Appt:** Prof Oto, Univ Mich Med Sch

Toriumi, Dean MD [Oto] - **Spec Exp:** Rhinoplasty; Cosmetic Surgery-Face; Reconstructive Plastic Surgery; **Hospital:** Univ of IL Med Ctr at Chicago; **Address:** 60 E Delaware Pl Fl 14 - Ste 1460, Chicago, IL 60611; **Phone:** 312-255-8812; **Board Cert:** Otolaryngology 1988; **Med School:** Rush Med Coll 1981; **Resid:** Surgery, Univ Illinois Med Ctr 1985; Otolaryngology, Northwestern Univ Med Sch 1987; **Fellow:** Facial Plastic Surgery, Tulane Med Sch 1988; Facial Plastic Surgery, Virginia Mason Med Ctr 1989; **Fac Appt:** Assoc Prof Oto, Univ IL Coll Med

Wiet, Richard J MD [Oto] - **Spec Exp:** Acoustic Neuroma; Hearing Loss; Otosclerosis/Stapedectomy; Cochlear Implants; **Hospital:** Adventist Hinsdale Hosp, Northwestern Meml Hosp; **Address:** Ear Institute of Chicago, 11 Salt Creek Ln, Ste 101, Hinsdale, IL 60521; **Phone:** 630-789-3110; **Board Cert:** Otolaryngology 1976; Neurotology 2004; **Med School:** Loyola Univ-Stritch Sch Med 1971; **Resid:** Otolaryngology, Cincinnati Med Ctr 1976; **Fellow:** Neurotology, Univ Zurich/Ear Fdn 1979; **Fac Appt:** Clin Prof Oto, Northwestern Univ

Wilson, Keith M MD [Oto] - **Spec Exp:** Head & Neck Cancer & Surgery; Voice Disorders; **Hospital:** Univ Cincinnati Med Ctr; **Address:** UC Health Ear, Nose and Throat Spcs, 222 Piedmont Ave, Ste 5200, Cincinnati, OH 45219; **Phone:** 513-475-8400; **Board Cert:** Otolaryngology 1992; **Med School:** Cornell Univ-Weill Med Coll 1986; **Resid:** Otolaryngology, St Louis Univ Med Ctr 1991; **Fellow:** Head & Neck Surgical Oncology, Ohio State Med Ctr 1992; **Fac Appt:** Assoc Prof Oto, Univ Cincinnati

Woodson, B. Tucker MD [Oto] - **Spec Exp:** Sleep Disorders/Apnea; **Hospital:** Froedtert & Med Coll WI, Chldns Hosp - Wisconsin; **Address:** Froedtert West ENT Clin, 9200 W Wisconsin Ave, Milwaukee, WI 53226-3522; **Phone:** 414-805-7667; **Board Cert:** Otolaryngology 1988; **Med School:** Univ MO-Columbia Sch Med 1983; **Resid:** Surgery, Henry Ford Hosp 1984; Otolaryngology, Henry Ford Hosp 1988; **Fac Appt:** Assoc Prof Oto, Med Coll Wisc

Woodson, Gayle Ellen MD [Oto] - **Spec Exp:** Voice Disorders; Swallowing Disorders; **Hospital:** St. John's Hosp - Springfield, Memorial Med Ctr-Springfield; **Address:** Div Otolaryngology, 301 N 8 St Fl 5, Box 19662, Springfield, IL 62702; **Phone:** 217-545-6099; **Board Cert:** Otolaryngology 1981; **Med School:** Baylor Coll Med 1975; **Resid:** Surgery, Johns Hopkins Hosp 1978; Otolaryngology, Baylor Coll Med 1981; **Fellow:** Laryngology, Inst Laryngology and Otology 1982; **Fac Appt:** Prof Oto, Southern IL Univ

Yoo, George H MD [Oto] - **Spec Exp:** Laryngeal Cancer; Oral Cancer; Thyroid Cancer; Sinus Tumors; **Hospital:** Barbara Ann Karmanos Cancer Inst; **Address:** Barbara Ann Karmanos Cancer Inst, 4100 John R, Detroit, MI 48201; **Phone:** 800-527-6266; **Board Cert:** Otolaryngology 1996; **Med School:** Univ Kansas 1990; **Resid:** Otolaryngology, Johns Hopkins Hosp 1994; **Fellow:** Head and Neck Surgery, Johns Hopkins Hosp 1997; **Fac Appt:** Prof Oto, Wayne State Univ

Young, Nancy MD [Oto] - **Spec Exp:** Cochlear Implants; Cholesteatoma; Hearing Loss; Baha Implant; **Hospital:** Lurie Chldn's Hosp-Chicago, Glenbrook Hosp/NorthShore Univ Hlth Syst (page 67); **Address:** Lurie Chldn's Hosp, Div Otolaryngology, 225 E Chicago Ave, Box 25, Chicago, IL 60611; **Phone:** 312-227-6807; **Board Cert:** Otolaryngology 1987; **Med School:** NYU Sch Med 1982; **Resid:** Surgery, Montefiore Med Ctr 1984; Otolaryngology, Northwestern Univ Hosp 1987; **Fellow:** Neurotology, Hinsdale Hosp 1988; **Fac Appt:** Prof Oto, Northwestern Univ

Yueh, Bevan MD [Oto] - **Spec Exp:** Head & Neck Cancer; Hearing Loss; **Hospital:** Univ Minn Med Ctr, Fairview - West Bank Campus; **Address:** Univ Minnesota Med Ctr, 516 Delware St SE, Clinic 8A, Minneapolis, MN 55455-0932; **Phone:** 612-626-5900; **Board Cert:** Otolaryngology 1995; **Med School:** Stanford Univ 1989; **Resid:** Otolaryngology, Johns Hopkins Hosp 1994; **Fellow:** Otolaryngology, Johns Hopkins Hosp 1995; **Fac Appt:** Assoc Prof Oto, Univ Minn

Great Plains and Mountains

Abaza, Mona M MD [Oto] - **Spec Exp:** Voice Disorders; Swallowing Disorders; **Hospital:** Univ Colorado Hosp; **Address:** Univ Colorado, Dept Otolaryngology, 1635 Aurora Court Fl 6, Aurora, CO 80045; **Phone:** 720-848-2820; **Board Cert:** Otolaryngology 1999; **Med School:** Med Coll PA Hahnemann 1991; **Resid:** Surgery, UMDNJ Affil Hosp 1992; Otolaryngology, Univ Texas Hlth Sci Ctr 1998; **Fellow:** Research, Natl Insts of Deafness & Communicative Disorders 1994; Laryngology, Thos Jefferson Univ Hosp 1999; **Fac Appt:** Assoc Prof Oto, Univ Colorado

Chowdhury, Khalid MD [Oto] - **Spec Exp:** Skull Base Tumors & Surgery; Craniofacial Surgery; Maxillofacial Surgery; Head & Neck Cancer; **Hospital:** Porter Adventist Hosp, Rocky Mountain Hosp for Children; **Address:** Ctr Craniofacial Surgery, 1601 E 19th Ave, Ste 3000, Denver, CO 80218; **Phone:** 303-839-5155; **Board Cert:** Otolaryngology 1990; Facial Plastic & Reconstr Surgery 1995; **Med School:** Univ Saskatchewan 1982; **Resid:** Surgery, Univ Saskatchewan Hosp 1984; Otolaryngology, McGill Univ Hosps 1989; **Fellow:** Craniofacial Surgery, Univ Bern Hosp 1990; Facial Plastic & Reconstr Surgery, Univ Bern Hosp 1990; **Fac Appt:** Assoc Prof Oto, Univ Colorado

Denenberg, Steven M MD [Oto] - **Spec Exp:** Cosmetic Surgery-Face; Rhinoplasty; **Hospital:** Nebraska Meth Hosp, Alegent Hlth - Bergan Mercy Med Ctr; **Address:** 7640 Pacific St, Omaha, NE 68114-5421; **Phone:** 402-391-7640; **Board Cert:** Otolaryngology 1984; Facial Plastic & Reconstr Surgery 1992; **Med School:** Univ Nebr Coll Med 1980; **Resid:** Otolaryngology, Stanford Univ Med Ctr 1984; **Fellow:** Facial Plastic Surgery, Amer Acad Facial Pl & Reconstr Surg 1985; **Fac Appt:** Asst Clin Prof Oto, Univ Nebr Coll Med

Jenkins, Herman A MD [Oto] - **Spec Exp:** Ear Disorders/Surgery; Neuro-Otology; Acoustic Neuroma; Cochlear Implants; **Hospital:** Univ Colorado Hosp, Chldn's Hosp - Aurora (CO); **Address:** Univ Colorado Hosp, Dept Otolaryngology, 1635 Aurora Ct, Fl 6, Aurora, CO 80045; **Phone:** 720-848-2820; **Board Cert:** Otolaryngology 1977; Neurotology 2004; **Med School:** Vanderbilt Univ 1970; **Resid:** Surgery, UCLA Med Ctr 1972; Otolaryngology, UCLA Med Ctr 1977; **Fellow:** Neurotology, Univ Hosp 1980; **Fac Appt:** Prof Oto, Univ Colorado

Kang, Dong-Kyoo Richard MD [Oto] - **Spec Exp:** Cochlear Implants; Ear Disorders/Surgery; **Hospital:** Boys Town Natl Rsch Hosp, Children's Hosp - Omaha; **Address:** Boystown Medical Campus-Downtown Clinic, 555 N 30th St, Omaha, NE 68131; **Phone:** 402-498-6540; **Board Cert:** Otolaryngology 1986; **Med School:** Boston Univ 1980; **Resid:** Otolaryngology, Naval Med Ctr 1986; **Fellow:** Pediatric Otolaryngology, St. Louis Chldn's Hosp 1991; Pediatric Otolaryngology, San Diego Chldn's Hosp 1993

Kingdom, Todd T MD [Oto] - **Spec Exp:** Nasal & Sinus Disorders; Endoscopic Sinus Surgery; Skull Base Surgery; **Hospital:** Univ Colorado Hosp, Natl Jewish Hlth; **Address:** Univ Colorado Hosp-Dept Otolaryngology, 1635 Aurora Court Fl 6, MS F737, Aurora, CO 80045; **Phone:** 720-848-2820; **Board Cert:** Otolaryngology 1997; **Med School:** Emory Univ 1991; **Resid:** Surgery, UCSF Med Ctr 1992; Otolaryngology, UCSF Med Ctr 1996; **Fac Appt:** Prof Oto, Univ Colorado

Kriet, John David MD [Oto] - **Spec Exp:** Facial Plastic & Reconstructive Surgery; Cleft Palate/Lip; Cosmetic Surgery-Face; Rhinoplasty; **Hospital:** Univ of Kansas Hosp; **Address:** Univ KS Med Ctr, Head & Neck Surgery, 3901 Rainbow Blvd, MS 3010, Kansas City, KS 66160; **Phone:** 913-871-9785; **Board Cert:** Otolaryngology 1998; Facial Plastic & Reconstr Surgery 1998; **Med School:** Univ Okla Coll Med 1991; **Resid:** Otolaryngology, Univ WA Med Ctr 1997; **Fellow:** Facial Plastic & Reconstr Surgery, Oregon Health Sci Ctr 1998; **Fac Appt:** Assoc Prof Oto, Univ Kansas

Lydiatt, Daniel D MD/DDS [Oto] - **Spec Exp:** Head & Neck Cancer; **Hospital:** Nebraska Med Ctr, Methodist Hosp - Omaha; **Address:** Nebraska Med Ctr, Dept Otolaryngology, 981225 Nebraska Medical Ctr, Omaha, NE 68198-1225; **Phone:** 402-559-1700; **Board Cert:** Otolaryngology 1992; **Med School:** Univ Nebr Coll Med 1983; **Resid:** Otolaryngology, Univ Nebraska Med Ctr 1990; **Fellow:** Head and Neck Surgery, MD Anderson Med Ctr 1991; **Fac Appt:** Assoc Prof Oto, Univ Nebr Coll Med

Lydiatt, William M MD [Oto] - **Spec Exp:** Head & Neck Cancer; Thyroid Cancer; Salivary Gland Tumors & Surgery; **Hospital:** Nebraska Med Ctr, Nebraska Meth Hosp; **Address:** 981225 Nebraska Medical Ctr, Omaha, NE 68198-7630; **Phone:** 402-559-1700; **Board Cert:** Otolaryngology 1994; **Med School:** Univ Nebr Coll Med 1988; **Resid:** Otolaryngology, Univ Nebraska Med Ctr 1993; **Fellow:** Head and Neck Surgery, Meml Sloan Kettering Cancer Ctr 1995; **Fac Appt:** Prof Oto, Univ Nebr Coll Med

Shelton, Clough MD [Oto] - **Spec Exp:** Facial Nerve Disorders; Acoustic Neuroma; Hearing & Balance Disorders; Cochlear Implants; **Hospital:** Univ Utah Hlth Care, Intermountain Med Ctr; **Address:** UUMC Ped Otolaryngology Dept, 50 N Medical Drive, Salt Lake City, UT 84132; **Phone:** 801-581-8915; **Board Cert:** Otolaryngology 1986; Neurotology 2004; **Med School:** Univ Tex SW, Dallas 1981; **Resid:** Otolaryngology, Stanford Univ Med Ctr 1986; **Fellow:** Neurotology, Otologic Med Group 1987; **Fac Appt:** Prof S, Univ Utah

Smith, Russell B MD [Oto] - **Spec Exp:** Head & Neck Cancer; Thyroid Cancer; Skull Base Tumors; **Hospital:** Nebraska Med Ctr, Nebraska Meth Hosp; **Address:** 981225 Nebraska Medical Center, Omaha, NE 68198-1225; **Phone:** 402-559-1700; **Board Cert:** Otolaryngology 2001; **Med School:** Univ MO-Columbia Sch Med 1995; **Resid:** Otolaryngology, Univ Missouri Med Ctr 2000; **Fellow:** Head & Neck Surgical Oncology, Univ Iowa Hosps & Clins 2001; **Fac Appt:** Assoc Prof Oto, Univ Nebr Coll Med

Song, John I MD [Oto] - **Spec Exp:** Head & Neck Cancer; Skull Base Tumors; Thyroid Disorders; Parathyroid Disease; **Hospital:** Univ Colorado Hosp, Children's Hosp - Denver; **Address:** Univ Colorado Hospital- Otolaryngology, 1635 Aurora Ct, Fl 6, Aurora, CO 80045; **Phone:** 720-848-2820; **Board Cert:** Otolaryngology 1998; **Med School:** NYU Sch Med 1991; **Resid:** Otolaryngology, UCLA Med Ctr 1997; **Fellow:** Head and Neck Surgery, Univ Pittsburgh Med Ctr 2000; **Fac Appt:** Assoc Prof Oto, Univ Colorado

Southwest

Amedee, Ronald G MD [Oto] - **Spec Exp:** Otology & Neuro-Otology; Skull Base Surgery; Sinus Disorders/Surgery; Hearing & Balance Disorders; **Hospital:** Ochsner Med Ctr-New Orleans, Tulane Med Ctr; **Address:** 1514 Jefferson Hwy, Fl 4, Ste ENT Clinic, New Orleans, LA 70121; **Phone:** 504-842-3640; **Board Cert:** Otolaryngology 1987; **Med School:** Louisiana State U, New Orleans 1981; **Resid:** Surgery, Charity Hosp 1983; Otolaryngology, Charity Hosp 1986; **Fellow:** Skull Base Surgery, Klinikum der Albert Ludwigs 1988; **Fac Appt:** Prof Oto, Tulane Univ

Arriaga, Moises A MD [Oto] - **Spec Exp:** Meniere's Disease; Skull Base Surgery; Acoustic Neuroma; Cochlear Implants; **Hospital:** Our Lady of the Lake Regl Med Ctr, Children's Hospital - New Orleans; **Address:** Hearing & Balance Ctr, 7777 Hennessy Blvd, Ste 709, Baton Rouge, LA 70808; **Phone:** 225-765-7735; **Board Cert:** Otolaryngology 1990; Neurotology 2004; **Med School:** Brown Univ 1985; **Resid:** Otolaryngology, UPMC 1990; **Fellow:** Neurotology, House Ear Clin 1991; **Fac Appt:** Prof Oto, Louisiana State U, New Orleans

Clark, Keith F MD/PhD [Oto] - **Spec Exp:** Airway Reconstruction; Voice Disorders; Vocal Cord Disorders-Botox Therapy; Endoscopic Sinus Surgery; **Hospital:** St. Anthony Hosp -Oklahoma City; **Address:** 535 NW 9th St, Ste 300, Oklahoma City, OK 73012; **Phone:** 405-272-6027; **Board Cert:** Otolaryngology 1983; **Med School:** Univ Mich Med Sch 1978; **Resid:** Otolaryngology, Univ Iowa Hosp & Clin 1983

Clayman, Gary L MD/DMD [Oto] - **Spec Exp:** Thyroid Cancer & Surgery; Salivary Gland Tumors & Surgery; Head & Neck Cancer; Thyroid & Parathyroid Surgery; **Hospital:** UT MD Anderson Canc Ctr; **Address:** UT MD Anderson Canc Ctr, 1515 Holcombe Blvd, Unit 1445, Houston, TX 77030-4009; **Phone:** 713-792-8837; **Board Cert:** Otolaryngology 1992; **Med School:** NE Ohio Univ 1986; **Resid:** Surgery, Hennepin Cnty Med Ctr 1987; Otolaryngology, Univ Minn Med Ctr 1991; **Fellow:** Head and Neck Surgery, UT MD Anderson Canc Ctr 1993; **Fac Appt:** Prof Oto, Univ Tex, Houston

Diaz Jr, Eduardo M MD [Oto] - **Spec Exp:** Head & Neck Cancer; Laryngeal Cancer; Laryngeal Cancer-Organ Preservation; Tongue Cancer; **Hospital:** UT MD Anderson Canc Ctr; **Address:** UT MD Anderson Canc Ctr, Head & Neck Ctr, 7007 Bertner Ave, Unit 1667, Houston, TX 77030; **Phone:** 713-745-2231; **Board Cert:** Otolaryngology 1995; **Med School:** Baylor Coll Med 1989; **Resid:** Surgery, Univ TX Affil Hosp 1991; Ophthalmology, Univ TX Affil Hosp 1994; **Fellow:** Head & Neck Surgical Oncology, UT MD Anderson Canc Ctr 1995; **Fac Appt:** Prof Oto, Univ Tex, Houston

Donovan, Donald T MD [Oto] - **Spec Exp:** Head & Neck Cancer; Voice Disorders; Vocal Cord Disorders; Thyroid Disorders; **Hospital:** Methodist Hosp - Houston, St. Luke's Episcopal Hosp-Houston; **Address:** Baylor-Dept of Otolaryngology, Smith Tower, 6550 Fannin St, Ste 1701, Houston, TX 77030; **Phone:** 713-798-5900; **Board Cert:** Otolaryngology 1981; **Med School:** Baylor Coll Med 1976; **Resid:** Surgery, Baylor Affil Hosps 1978; Otolaryngology, Baylor Affil Hosps 1981; **Fellow:** Head and Neck Surgery, Presby/Columbia Univ Med Ctr 1982; **Fac Appt:** Prof Oto, Baylor Coll Med

Dornhoffer, John L MD [Oto] - **Spec Exp:** Hearing & Balance Disorders; Neuro-Otology; Hearing Loss; **Hospital:** UAMS Med Ctr; **Address:** UAMS, Dept Otolaryngology, Head & Neck Surgery, 4301 W Markham St, Little Rock, AR 72205; **Phone:** 501-686-5878; **Board Cert:** Otolaryngology 1994; **Med School:** Univ Kansas 1988; **Resid:** Otolaryngology, UAMS Med Ctr 1992; **Fellow:** Otology, Univ of Zurich Affil Hosp 1994; Otology, Univ of Wuzburg Affil Hosp 1994; **Fac Appt:** Prof Oto, Univ Ark

Gianoli, Gerard Joseph MD [Oto] - **Spec Exp:** Dizziness/Vertigo; Hearing Loss; Ear Disorders/Surgery; Balance Disorders; **Hospital:** North Oaks Med Ctr; **Address:** The Ear and Balance Institute, 1401 Ochsner Blvd, Ste A, Covington, LA 70433; **Phone:** 985-809-1111; **Board Cert:** Otolaryngology 1993; Neurotology 2004; **Med School:** Tulane Univ 1986; **Resid:** Pediatrics, Tulane Univ 1988; Otolaryngology, Tulane Univ 1992; **Fellow:** Otology & Neurotology, Michigan Ear Inst; **Fac Appt:** Assoc Clin Prof Oto, Tulane Univ

Graham III, H. Devon MD [Oto] - **Spec Exp:** Cosmetic & Reconstructive Surgery-Face; Snoring/Sleep Apnea; Nasal Reconstruction; Facial Rejuvenation; **Hospital:** Ochsner Med Ctr-New Orleans; **Address:** 1514 Jefferson Hwy Fl 4, New Orleans, LA 70121; **Phone:** 504-842-4080; **Board Cert:** Otolaryngology 1989; Facial Plastic & Reconstr Surgery 1993; **Med School:** Louisiana State U, New Orleans 1984; **Resid:** Surgery, Ochsner Med Ctr 1986; Otolaryngology, Tulane Med Ctr 1989; **Fellow:** Facial Plastic Surgery, Baptist Hosp 1990; Facial Plastic Surgery, St Joseph Hosp 1990; **Fac Appt:** Asst Clin Prof Oto, Tulane Univ

Hanna, Ehab YN MD [Oto] - **Spec Exp:** Skull Base Tumors & Surgery; Head & Neck Cancer & Surgery; Salivary Gland Tumors; **Hospital:** UT MD Anderson Canc Ctr; **Address:** Univ Tex MD Anderson Cancer Ctr, 1515 Holcolmbe Blvd, Unit 1445, Houston, TX 77030; **Phone:** 713-745-1815; **Board Cert:** Otolaryngology 1994; **Med School:** Egypt 1982; **Resid:** Otolaryngology, Cleveland Clinic 1989; Otolaryngology, Cleveland Clinic 1993; **Fellow:** Otolaryngology, Univ Pittsburgh Med Ctr 1994; **Fac Appt:** Prof Oto, Univ Tex, Houston

Hayden, Richard E MD [Oto] - **Spec Exp:** Head & Neck Surgery; Thyroid & Parathyroid Surgery; Facial Plastic & Reconstructive Surgery; Microvascular Surgery; **Hospital:** Mayo Clinic - Phoenix; **Address:** Mayo Clinic, Dept Otolaryngology, 5777 E Mayo Blvd, Phoenix, AZ 85054; **Phone:** 480-342-2912; **Board Cert:** Otolaryngology 1978; **Med School:** McGill Univ 1974; **Resid:** Otolaryngology, Univ Toronto Affil Hosp 1978; **Fellow:** Head & Neck Oncology, MD Anderson Hosp 1979; Radiation Oncology, Princess Margaret Hosp 1980; **Fac Appt:** Prof Oto, Mayo Med Sch

Johnson Jr, Calvin M MD [Oto] - **Spec Exp:** Ear Disorders/Surgery; Nasal Surgery; Cosmetic Surgery-Face; **Address:** Hedgewood Surgical Ctr, 2427 St Charles Ave, New Orleans, LA 70130; **Phone:** 504-895-7642; **Board Cert:** Otolaryngology 1974; Facial Plastic & Reconstr Surgery 1991; **Med School:** Tulane Univ 1967; **Resid:** Surgery, Tulane Univ Affil Hosp 1971; Otolaryngology, Tulane Univ Affil Hosp 1974; **Fellow:** Facial Plastic Surgery, Amer Academy Facial Plastic & Recon Surg 1975

Macias, John D MD [Oto] - **Spec Exp:** Otology; Neuro-Otology; Cochlear Implants; Hearing Loss; **Hospital:** Banner Good Samaritan Regl Med Ctr - Phoenix, Phoenix Children's Hosp; **Address:** 1515 N 9th St, Ste B, Phoenix, AZ 85006-2523; **Phone:** 602-257-4228; **Board Cert:** Otolaryngology 1994; Neurotology 2005; **Med School:** Stanford Univ 1988; **Resid:** Otolaryngology, Univ Iowa Hosps & Clins 1993; **Fellow:** Otology & Neurotology, Ear Fdn/Otology Grp 1994

Miller, Frank R MD [Oto] - **Spec Exp:** Head & Neck Surgery; Thyroid & Parathyroid Surgery; Sinus Disorders; Zenker Diverticulum; **Hospital:** Univ Hosp-San Antonio; **Address:** 8300 Floyd Curl Drive Fl 6 - Ste 6-B, MC 8300, MARC Bldg, San Antonio, TX 78229; **Phone:** 210-450-0719; **Board Cert:** Otolaryngology 1995; **Med School:** Brown Univ 1989; **Resid:** Surgery, Cleveland Clin 1990; Otolaryngology, Cleveland Clin 1994; **Fellow:** Head & Neck Oncology, Vancerbilt Univ Hosp 1998; **Fac Appt:** Prof Oto, Univ Tex, San Antonio

Myers, Jeffrey N MD/PhD [Oto] - **Spec Exp:** Head & Neck Cancer; Melanoma-Head & Neck; Tongue Cancer; **Hospital:** UT MD Anderson Canc Ctr; **Address:** UT MD Anderson Canc Ctr, 1515 Holcombe Blvd, Unit 1445, Houston, TX 77030; **Phone:** 713-745-2667; **Board Cert:** Otolaryngology 1997; **Med School:** Univ Pennsylvania 1991; **Resid:** Otolaryngology, UPMC 1996; **Fellow:** Head & Neck Surgical Oncology, MD Anderson Canc Ctr 1997; **Fac Appt:** Assoc Prof Oto, Univ Tex, Houston

Nuss, Daniel W MD [Oto] - **Spec Exp:** Head & Neck Cancer; Skull Base Tumors & Surgery; **Hospital:** Our Lady of the Lake Regl Med Ctr; **Address:** Our Lady of the Lake Regl Med Ctr, 4950 Essen Ln, Ste 400, Baton Rouge, LA 70809; **Phone:** 225-765-1765; **Board Cert:** Otolaryngology 1987; **Med School:** Louisiana State U, New Orleans 1981; **Resid:** Surgery, Charity Hosp 1983; Otolaryngology, LSU Med Ctr 1987; **Fellow:** Surgical Oncology, MD Anderson Hosp & Tumor Inst 1984; Head and Neck Surgery, Ctr Cranial Base Surg-Univ Pittsburgh 1991; **Fac Appt:** Prof Oto, Louisiana State U, New Orleans

Otto, Randal A MD [Oto] - **Spec Exp:** Head & Neck Cancer; Thyroid & Parathyroid Cancer & Surgery; Sinus Disorders/Surgery; **Hospital:** Univ Hosp-San Antonio; **Address:** Univ Texas Health Sci Ctr, 8300 Floyd Curl Drive, MSC 7777, San Antonio, TX 78229-3900; **Phone:** 210-450-0700; **Board Cert:** Otolaryngology 1987; **Med School:** Univ MO-Columbia Sch Med 1981; **Resid:** Pathology, Queens Med Ctr 1982; Otolaryngology, Univ of Missouri 1987; **Fac Appt:** Prof Emeritus Oto, Univ Tex, San Antonio

Pitman, Karen MD [Oto] - **Spec Exp:** Head & Neck Cancer & Surgery; Thyroid & Parathyroid Cancer & Surgery; Sentinel Node Surgery; **Hospital:** Banner Gateway Med Ctr; **Address:** 2946 E Banner Gateway Drive, Gilbert, AZ 85234; **Phone:** 480-256-6444; **Board Cert:** Otolaryngology 1995; **Med School:** Uniformed Srvs Univ, Bethesda 1987; **Resid:** Otolaryngology, Naval Med Ctr 1994; **Fellow:** Head & Neck Oncology, Univ Pittsburgh 1996; **Fac Appt:** Prof Oto, Univ Miss

Stasney, C Richard MD [Oto] - **Spec Exp:** Voice Disorders; Vocal Cord Disorders; Laryngeal Disorders; **Hospital:** Methodist Hosp - Houston; **Address:** Texas Voice Center, 6550 Fannin St, Ste 2025, Houston, TX 77030; **Phone:** 713-796-2181; **Board Cert:** Otolaryngology 1974; **Med School:** Baylor Coll Med 1969; **Resid:** Surgery, Baylor Affil Hosps 1971; Otolaryngology, Baylor Affil Hosps 1974; **Fac Appt:** Assoc Clin Prof Oto, Baylor Coll Med

Suen, James Y MD [Oto] - **Spec Exp:** Head & Neck Cancer; Vascular Lesions-Head & Neck; Laryngeal Disorders; Thyroid Cancer; **Hospital:** UAMS Med Ctr, Arkansas Chldns Hosp; **Address:** Univ Hosp Arkansas Med Scis, 4301 W Markham St, Slot 543, Little Rock, AR 72205; **Phone:** 501-686-7009; **Board Cert:** Otolaryngology 1973; **Med School:** Univ Ark 1966; **Resid:** Surgery, Univ Arkansas Med Ctr 1970; Otolaryngology, Univ Arkansas Med Ctr 1973; **Fellow:** Head and Neck Surgery, MD Anderson Cancer Ctr 1974; **Fac Appt:** Prof Oto, Univ Ark

Weber, Randal S MD [Oto] - **Spec Exp:** Skin Cancer; Thyroid & Parathyroid Cancer & Surgery; Salivary Gland Tumors & Surgery; Head & Neck Cancer; **Hospital:** UT MD Anderson Canc Ctr; **Address:** 1400 Pressler St, Unit 1445, Houston, TX 77030-4009; **Phone:** 713-745-0497; **Board Cert:** Otolaryngology 1985; **Med School:** Univ Tenn Coll Med 1976; **Resid:** Surgery, Baylor Affil Hosp 1982; Otolaryngology, Baylor Affil Hosp 1985; **Fellow:** Head and Neck Surgery, MD Anderson Cancer Ctr 1986; **Fac Appt:** Prof Oto, Univ Tex, Houston

Weber, Samuel C MD [Oto] - **Spec Exp:** Thyroid Cancer; Parathyroid Cancer; Nasal & Sinus Surgery; Head & Neck Surgery; **Hospital:** St. Luke's Episcopal Hosp-Houston, Methodist Hosp - Houston; **Address:** 6624 Fannin St, Ste 1480, Houston, TX 77030-2385; **Phone:** 713-795-5343; **Board Cert:** Otolaryngology 1972; **Med School:** Univ Tenn Coll Med 1965; **Resid:** Surgery, Baylor Affil Hosp 1971; Otolaryngology, Baylor Affil Hosp 1972; **Fac Appt:** Clin Prof Oto, Baylor Coll Med

West Coast and Pacific

Andersen, Peter MD [Oto] - **Spec Exp:** Laryngeal Cancer; Nasal & Sinus Cancer & Surgery; Head & Neck Cancer & Surgery; Neck Masses; **Hospital:** OR Hlth & Sci Univ; **Address:** OHSU Dept Otolaryngology, 3181 SW Sam Jackson Park Rd, MC PV-01, Portland, OR 97239; **Phone:** 503-494-5355; **Board Cert:** Otolaryngology 1994; **Med School:** Washington Univ, St Louis 1988; **Resid:** Otolaryngology, Oregon Hlth & Sci Univ 1993; **Fellow:** Head & Neck Surgical Oncology, Meml Sloan-Kettering Cancer Ctr 1995; **Fac Appt:** Prof Oto, Oregon Hlth & Sci Univ

Berke, Gerald S MD [Oto] - **Spec Exp:** Airway Disorders; Swallowing Disorders; Voice Disorders; Laryngeal Disorders; **Hospital:** UCLA Ronald Reagan Med Ctr; **Address:** UCLA Head & Neck Clinic, 200 UCLA Medical Plaza, Ste 550, Los Angeles, CA 90095; **Phone:** 310-794-8634; **Board Cert:** Otolaryngology 1984; **Med School:** USC Sch Med 1978; **Resid:** Surgery, LAC-USC Med Ctr 1980; **Fellow:** Otolaryngology, UCLA Med Ctr 1984; **Fac Appt:** Prof Oto, UCLA

Blackwell, Keith Edward MD [Oto] - **Spec Exp:** Head & Neck Reconstruction; Head & Neck Cancer & Surgery; **Hospital:** UCLA Ronald Reagan Med Ctr; **Address:** UCLA Head & Neck Clinic, 200 UCLA Med Plaza, Ste 550, Los Angeles, CA 90095; **Phone:** 310-206-6688; **Board Cert:** Otolaryngology 1995; **Med School:** Northwestern Univ 1988; **Resid:** Otolaryngology, UCLA Med Ctr 1994; **Fellow:** Otolaryngology, Mount Sinai Med Ctr 1995; **Fac Appt:** Prof Oto, UCLA

Brackmann, Derald E MD [Oto] - **Spec Exp:** Ear Disorders/Surgery; Facial Nerve Disorders; Acoustic Neuroma; Otosclerosis/Stapedectomy; **Hospital:** St. Vincent's Med Ctr - Los Angeles, Good Samaritan Hosp - LA; **Address:** House Ear Clinic, 2100 W 3rd St Fl 1st - Ste 111, Los Angeles, CA 90057-1902; **Phone:** 213-483-9930; **Board Cert:** Otolaryngology 1971; Neurotology 2005; **Med School:** Univ IL Coll Med 1962; **Resid:** Otolaryngology, LAC/USC Med Ctr 1970; **Fellow:** Otology & Neurotology, House Ear Clinic 1971; **Fac Appt:** Clin Prof Oto, USC-Keck School of Medicine

Courey, Mark S MD [Oto] - **Spec Exp:** Laryngeal Disorders; Swallowing Disorders; Laryngeal Cancer; **Hospital:** UCSF - Mt Zion Med Ctr, UCSF Med Ctr; **Address:** UCSF Voice & Swallowing Ctr, 2330 Post St Fl 5, San Francisco, CA 94115; **Phone:** 415-885-7700; **Board Cert:** Otolaryngology 1993; **Med School:** SUNY Buffalo 1987; **Resid:** Otolaryngology, SUNY-Buffalo Med Ctr 1992; **Fellow:** Laryngology, Vanderbilt Univ 1993; **Fac Appt:** Prof Oto, UCSF

Duckert, Larry G MD/PhD [Oto] - **Spec Exp:** Otology & Neuro-Otology; Otosclerosis/Stapedectomy; Acoustic Neuroma; Skull Base Surgery; **Hospital:** Univ Wash Med Ctr; **Address:** 1959 NE Pacific St, Box 356161, Seattle, WA 98195; **Phone:** 206-598-4022; **Board Cert:** Otolaryngology 1978; **Med School:** Univ Minn 1972; **Resid:** Otolaryngology, Univ Minnesota Hosp 1978; **Fellow:** Research, Ohio State Univ Coll of Med 1973; Otology & Neurotology, Univ Wuzburg Affil Hosp 1990; **Fac Appt:** Prof Oto, Univ Wash

Flint, Paul W MD [Oto] - **Spec Exp:** Voice Disorders; Laryngeal Disorders; **Hospital:** OR Hlth & Sci Univ; **Address:** Oregon Health & Science Univ, 3181 SW Sam Jackson Park Rd, MC PV01, Portland, OR 97239; **Phone:** 503-494-5947; **Board Cert:** Otolaryngology 1989; **Med School:** Baylor Coll Med 1983; **Resid:** Surgery, Univ Wash Med Ctr 1985; Otolaryngology, Univ Wash Med Ctr 1988; **Fellow:** Otolaryngology, Guys Hosp 1989; **Fac Appt:** Prof Oto, Oregon Hlth & Sci Univ

Futran, Neal D MD/DMD [Oto] - **Spec Exp:** Head & Neck Cancer & Surgery; Head & Neck Cancer Reconstruction; Skull Base Tumors & Surgery; **Hospital:** Univ Wash Med Ctr, Harborview Med Ctr; **Address:** UWMC, Otolaryngology, 1959 NE Pacific St, Box 356515, Seattle, WA 98195-6515; **Phone:** 206-598-4022; **Board Cert:** Otolaryngology 1993; **Med School:** SUNY Downstate 1987; **Resid:** Surgery, SUNY Downstate Med Ctr (Univ Hosp Brooklyn) 1985; Otolaryngology, Univ Rochester Strong Meml Hosp 1992; **Fellow:** Microvascular Surgery, Mt Sinai Med Ctr 1993; **Fac Appt:** Prof Oto, Univ Wash

Harris, Jeffrey P MD/PhD [Oto] - **Spec Exp:** Neuro-Otology; Hearing & Balance Disorders; Skull Base Surgery; Meniere's Disease; **Hospital:** UCSD Med Ctr, VA San Diego Hlthcre Sys; **Address:** UCSD Med Ctr-Div Otolaryngology, 200 W Arbor Drive, MC 8895, San Diego, CA 92103-9001; **Phone:** 619-543-7896; **Board Cert:** Otolaryngology 1979; Neurotology 2004; **Med School:** Univ Pennsylvania 1974; **Resid:** Otolaryngology, Mass EE Infirmary 1979; **Fellow:** Neurology, Univ Zurich Med Ctr 1983; **Fac Appt:** Prof S, UCSD

Jackler, Robert K MD [Oto] - **Spec Exp:** Neuro-Otology; Skull Base Surgery; Ear Tumors; **Hospital:** Stanford Univ Hosp & Clins; **Address:** Stanford Univ Med Ctr, Dept Oto - Head & Neck Surg, 801 Welch Rd, Stanford, CA 94305-5739; **Phone:** 650-723-5281; **Board Cert:** Otolaryngology 1984; Neurotology 2004; **Med School:** Boston Univ 1979; **Resid:** Otolaryngology, UCSF Med Ctr 1984; **Fellow:** Otolaryngology, Oto Med Grp 1985; **Fac Appt:** Prof Oto, Stanford Univ

Kaplan, Michael J MD [Oto] - **Spec Exp:** Head & Neck Surgery; Skull Base Surgery; Head & Neck Cancer; **Hospital:** Stanford Univ Hosp & Clins; **Address:** 875 Blake Wilbur Drive, Clinic B, Stanford, CA 94305-5739; **Phone:** 650-498-6000; **Board Cert:** Otolaryngology 1982; **Med School:** Harvard Med Sch 1977; **Resid:** Surgery, Beth Israel-Chldns Hosps 1979; Otolaryngology, Mass EE Infirm 1982; **Fellow:** Head and Neck Surgery, Univ Virginia 1984; **Fac Appt:** Prof Oto, Stanford Univ

Keller, Gregory S MD [Oto] - **Spec Exp:** Cosmetic Surgery-Face; **Hospital:** Santa Barbara Cottage Hosp, UCLA Ronald Reagan Med Ctr; **Address:** 221 W Pueblo St, Ste A, Santa Barbara, CA 93105; **Phone:** 805-687-6408; **Board Cert:** Otolaryngology 1976; Facial Plastic & Reconstr Surgery 1991; **Med School:** Univ IL Coll Med 1971; **Resid:** Surgery, Cottage Hosp 1973; Otolaryngology, Univ Illinois Hosp 1976; **Fac Appt:** Assoc Clin Prof S, UCLA

Larrabee Jr, Wayne F MD [Oto] - **Spec Exp:** Cosmetic Surgery-Face; Eyelid Surgery; Rhinoplasty; Nasal Surgery; **Hospital:** Swedish Med Ctr-First Hill-Seattle; **Address:** Facial Plastic Surgery Ctr, 600 Broadway Ste 280, Seattle, WA 98122-5371; **Phone:** 206-386-3550; **Board Cert:** Otolaryngology 1979; Facial Plastic & Reconstr Surgery 1999; **Med School:** Tulane Univ 1971; **Resid:** Surgery, Charity Hosp 1976; Otolaryngology, Tulane Univ Med Ctr 1979; **Fac Appt:** Clin Prof Oto, Univ Wash

Lustig, Lawrence R MD [Oto] - **Spec Exp:** Cochlear Implants; Hearing Loss; **Hospital:** UCSF Med Ctr; **Address:** Cochlear Implant Center, 2380 Sutter St Fl 1, San Francisco, CA 94115; **Phone:** 415-353-2464; **Board Cert:** Otolaryngology 1998; Neurotology 2006; **Med School:** UCSF 1992; **Resid:** Otolaryngology, UCSF Med Ctr 1997; **Fellow:** Neurotology, John Hopkins Hosp 1999

Moe, Kristen MD [Oto] - **Spec Exp:** Facial Plastic & Reconstructive Surgery; Skull Base Surgery; Cosmetic Surgery-Face; **Hospital:** Harborview Med Ctr, Univ Wash Med Ctr; **Address:** Head & Neck Surgery-4 West Clinic, 325 Ninth Ave, Seattle, WA 98104; **Phone:** 206-744-3231; **Board Cert:** Otolaryngology 1996; **Med School:** Univ Wash 1989; **Resid:** Surgery, Univ Washington Med Ctr 1991; Otolaryngology, Univ Michigan Med Ctr 1994; **Fellow:** Skull Base Surgery, Univ Bern Hosp; Facial Plastic & Reconstr Surgery, Univ Zurich Hosp; **Fac Appt:** Prof Oto, Univ Wash

Niparko, John K MD [Oto] - **Spec Exp:** Ear Disorders/Surgery; Neuro-Otology; Hearing Loss; Cochlear Implants; **Hospital:** Keck Med Ctr of USC; **Address:** USC Head & Neck Surgery, 1520 San Pablo St, Ste 4600, Los Angeles, CA 90033-1029; **Phone:** 323-442-5790; **Board Cert:** Otolaryngology 1986; Neurotology 2004; **Med School:** Univ Mich Med Sch 1980; **Resid:** Surgery, William Beaumont Hosp 1982; Otolaryngology, Univ Michigan Hosp 1986; **Fellow:** Skull Base Surgery, Univ Michigan Hosp 1986; **Fac Appt:** Prof Oto, USC-Keck School of Medicine

O'Leary, Michael J MD [Oto] - **Spec Exp:** Skull Base Tumors & Surgery; Pituitary Tumors; Neuro-Otology; Cochlear Implants; **Hospital:** Alvarado Hosp & Med Ctr, Scripps Hlth; **Address:** Senta Clinic, 6645 Alvarado Rd, Ste 4000, San Diego, CA 92120-5208; **Phone:** 619-229-4903; **Board Cert:** Otolaryngology 1987; Neurotology 2012; **Med School:** Georgetown Univ 1980; **Resid:** Otolaryngology, Naval Medical Ctr 1987; **Fellow:** Skull Base Surgery, House Ear Clinic 1990; Microvascular Surgery, Washington Univ Affil Hosp 1991

Oghalai, John S MD [Oto] - **Spec Exp:** Neuro-Otology; Acoustic Neuroma; Hearing Loss; **Hospital:** Stanford Univ Hosp & Clins, Lucile Packard Chldn's Hosp; **Address:** Stanford Univ, 801 Welch Rd, Stanford, CA 94305; **Phone:** 650-723-5281; **Board Cert:** Otolaryngology 2010; Neurotology 2010; **Med School:** Univ Wisc 1994; **Resid:** Otolaryngology, Baylor Coll Med Ctr 2001; **Fellow:** Otolaryngology, UCSF Med Ctr 2003; Neurological Surgery, UCSF Med Ctr 2003; **Fac Appt:** Assoc Prof Oto, Baylor Coll Med

Orloff, Lisa MD [Oto] - **Spec Exp:** Thyroid & Parathyroid Cancer & Surgery; Minimally Invasive Surgery; Head & Neck Surgery; **Hospital:** UCSF Med Ctr; **Address:** Head & Neck Surg Canc Clin, 2380 Sutter St Fl 2, San Francisco, CA 94115; **Phone:** 415-885-7528; **Board Cert:** Otolaryngology 1993; **Med School:** UCLA-David Geffen Sch Med 1986; **Resid:** Surgery, Univ Washington Med Ctr 1988; Otolaryngology, Univ Washington Med Ctr 1992; **Fellow:** Microvascular Surgery, Mt Sinai Med Ctr 1993; **Fac Appt:** Assoc Prof S, UCSD

Rice, Dale H MD [Oto] - **Spec Exp:** Head & Neck Cancer; Sinus Disorders/Surgery; Rhinitis; **Hospital:** Keck Med Ctr of USC; **Address:** USC Head & Neck Surgery, 1520 San Pablo St, Ste 4600, Los Angeles, CA 90033-1029; **Phone:** 323-442-5790; **Board Cert:** Otolaryngology 1976; **Med School:** Univ Mich Med Sch 1968; **Resid:** Surgery, Univ of Michigan Hosp 1970; Otolaryngology, Univ of Michigan Hosp 1976; **Fac Appt:** Prof Oto, USC Sch Med

Rubinstein, Jay T MD/PhD [Oto] - **Spec Exp:** Cochlear Implants; Acoustic Neuroma; Hearing Loss; Neuro-Otology; **Hospital:** Univ Wash Med Ctr, Seattle Chldns Hosp; **Address:** Univeristy of Washington Medical Center, 1959 NE Pacific St, Box 356161, Seattle, WA 98195; **Phone:** 206-598-4022; **Board Cert:** Otolaryngology 1995; Neurotology 2005; **Med School:** Univ Wash 1987; **Resid:** Otolaryngology, Mass Eye & Ear Infirmary 1994; **Fellow:** Research, Mass Eye & Ear Infirmary 1990; Otology & Neurotology, Univ Iowa Affil Hosp 1995; **Fac Appt:** Prof Oto, Univ Wash

Senders, Craig W MD [Oto] - **Spec Exp:** Pediatric Otolaryngology; Cleft Palate/Lip; Endoscopic Sinus Surgery; Sleep Disorders/Apnea; **Hospital:** UC Davis Med Ctr; **Address:** UC Davis, Dept Otolaryngology, 2521 Stockton Blvd, Ste 7200, Sacramento, CA 95817; **Phone:** 916-734-5400; **Board Cert:** Otolaryngology 1984; **Med School:** Oregon Hlth & Sci Univ 1979; **Resid:** Otolaryngology, Univ Iowa Hosps & Clins 1983; **Fellow:** Maxillofacial Surgery, Univ Iowa Hosps & Clins 1984; **Fac Appt:** Prof Oto, UC Davis

Shindo, Maisie L MD [Oto] - **Spec Exp:** Thyroid Cancer & Surgery; Parathyroid Surgery; Parathyroid Cancer; Head & Neck Surgery; **Hospital:** OR Hlth & Sci Univ, Providence St Vincent Med Ctr; **Address:** Thyroid & Parathyroid Clinic, 3181 SW Sam Jackson Park Rd, MC PV-01, Portland, OR 97239; **Phone:** 503-494-5355; **Board Cert:** Otolaryngology 1989; **Med School:** USC-Keck School of Medicine 1984; **Resid:** Otolaryngology, LAC-USC Med Ctr 1989; **Fellow:** Head and Neck Surgery, Northwestern Meml Hosp 1991; **Fac Appt:** Prof Oto, Oregon Hlth & Sci Univ

Singer, Mark I MD [Oto] - **Spec Exp:** Head & Neck Surgery; Head & Neck Cancer; Melanoma; **Hospital:** CA Pacific Med Ctr-Pacific Campus; **Address:** 2340 Clay St Fl 2, San Francisco, CA 94115; **Phone:** 415-600-3898; **Board Cert:** Otolaryngology 1976; **Med School:** Columbia P&S 1970; **Resid:** Surgery, Northwestern Meml Hosp 1973; Otolaryngology, Northwestern Meml Hosp 1976; **Fellow:** Oncology, Northwestern Meml Hosp 1976

Sinha, Uttam K MD [Oto] - **Spec Exp:** Head & Neck Cancer; Voice Disorders; Thyroid Disorders; Swallowing Disorders; **Hospital:** Keck Med Ctr of USC, House Ear Inst; **Address:** USC Head & Neck Surgery, 1520 San Pablo St, Ste 4600, Los Angeles, CA 90033; **Phone:** 323-442-5790; **Board Cert:** Otolaryngology 1998; **Med School:** India 1985; **Resid:** Otolaryngology, LAC-USC Med Ctr 1995; **Fellow:** Plastic/Reconstructive Surgery, Mount Sinai Med Ctr 1996; Laryngology 1997; **Fac Appt:** Assoc Prof Oto, USC Sch Med

Wackym, P Ashley MD [Oto] - **Spec Exp:** Cochlear Implants; Acoustic Neuroma; Head & Neck Surgery; **Hospital:** Legacy Good Samaritan Med Ctr, Randall Chldns Hosp at Legacy; **Address:** Ear and Skull Base Center, 1225 NE 2nd Ave, Ste 305, Portland, OR 97232; **Phone:** 503-233-6068; **Board Cert:** Otolaryngology 1992; Neurotology 2004; **Med School:** Vanderbilt Univ 1985; **Resid:** Neurological Surgery, UCLA Med Ctr 1987; Head and Neck Surgery, UCLA Med Ctr 1991; **Fellow:** Otology & Neurotology, Univ Iowa 1992; Neurological Science, UCLA Med Ctr 1989; **Fac Appt:** Prof Oto

Wang, Steven J MD [Oto] - **Spec Exp:** Head & Neck Cancer; Head & Neck Surgery; **Hospital:** UCSF Med Ctr; **Address:** 2380 Sutter St Fl 2, San Francisco, CA 94115; **Phone:** 415-885-7528; **Board Cert:** Otolaryngology 2002; **Med School:** Harvard Med Sch 1995; **Resid:** Otolaryngology, UCLA Med Ctr 2001; **Fellow:** Head & Neck Surgical Oncology, Univ Michigan 2003; **Fac Appt:** Assoc Prof Oto, UCSF

Wax, Mark K MD [Oto] - **Spec Exp:** Facial Nerve Disorders; Skull Base Tumors & Surgery; Facial Plastic & Reconstructive Surgery; Microvascular Surgery; **Hospital:** OR Hlth & Sci Univ; **Address:** Oregon Hlth & Sci Univ, Dept Ototlaryngology, 3181 SW Sam Jackson Park Rd, MC PV-01, Portland, OR 97239; **Phone:** 503-494-5355; **Board Cert:** Otolaryngology 1985; Facial Plastic & Reconstr Surgery 2000; **Med School:** Univ Toronto 1980; **Resid:** Otolaryngology, Univ Toronto 1985; Surgery, Cedars-Sinai Med Ctr 1983; **Fellow:** Head and Neck Surgery, St Michaels Hosp 1991; **Fac Appt:** Prof Oto, Oregon Hlth & Sci Univ

Weisman, Robert A MD [Oto] - **Spec Exp:** Head & Neck Cancer; Skull Base Surgery; Thyroid & Parathyroid Cancer & Surgery; Facial Plastic & Reconstructive Surgery; **Hospital:** UCSD Med Ctr; **Address:** UCSD Moores Cancer Center, 3855 Hlth Sci Drive, MC 0987, La Jolla, CA 92093-0987; **Phone:** 858-822-6197; **Board Cert:** Otolaryngology 1978; **Med School:** Washington Univ, St Louis 1973; **Resid:** Surgery, Cedars Sinai Med Ctr 1975; Head and Neck Surgery, UCLA Med Ctr 1978; **Fac Appt:** Prof S, UCSD

Weymuller Jr, Ernest A MD [Oto] - **Spec Exp:** Head & Neck Cancer; Sinus Disorders/Surgery; **Hospital:** Univ Wash Med Ctr; **Address:** UWMC, Dept Otolaryngology, 1959 NE Pacific St, Box 356161, Seattle, WA 98195; **Phone:** 206-598-4022; **Board Cert:** Otolaryngology 1973; **Med School:** Harvard Med Sch 1966; **Resid:** Surgery, Vanderbilt Univ Med Ctr 1968; Otolaryngology, Mass Eye & Ear Infirm 1973; **Fac Appt:** Prof Oto, Univ Wash

Wong, Brian JF MD [Oto] - **Spec Exp:** Facial Plastic & Reconstructive Surgery; Head & Neck Surgery; Vascular Malformations; **Hospital:** UC Irvine Med Ctr; **Address:** UC Irvine, Dept Head & Neck Surgery, 101 The City Drive S 30 A Bldg, Pavillion 2, Orange, CA 92868; **Phone:** 714-456-7017; **Board Cert:** Otolaryngology 1998; Facial Plastic & Reconstr Surgery 2007; **Med School:** Johns Hopkins Univ 1990; **Resid:** Otolaryngology, UC Irvine Med Ctr 1996; **Fellow:** Facial Plastic & Reconstr Surgery, UC Irvine Med Ctr 1998; **Fac Appt:** Prof Oto, UC Irvine

Otolaryngology

Cleveland Clinic's Head & Neck Institute is recognized nationally and internationally in this multidisciplinary field and is ranked #6 in the nation by *U.S. News & World Report*. The Institute is composed of extensively trained specialists in these areas:

Audiology: Comprehensive evaluation and treatment through assistive listening devices, hearing devices, bone anchored auditory implants and cochlear implants.

Facial Plastic and Reconstructive Surgery: Office-based injectables to rhinoplasty, facelifts and major facial reconstructive surgery, including the world's first near-total face transplant.

Head and Neck Surgery and Oncology: Evaluation and treatment of benign and malignant tumors.

Laryngotracheal Reconstruction: Laryngeal airway obstruction, esophageal reflux, tracheal aspiration and voice preservation/rehabilitation.

Rhinology, Sinus and Skull Base Disorders: Offering minimally invasive, computer-aided techniques for sinusitis, nasal obstructions, allergies and skull base surgery.

Otology-Neurotology: Middle and posterior cranial fossa surgery for cerebellopontine and skull base tumors, immune-mediated inner ear disease (deafness), Meniere's disease and cochlear implantation.

Pediatric Otolaryngology: Treatment of all forms of pediatric disorders.

Speech-Language Pathology: Evaluation and treatment for patients with speech, language, voice, cognitive and swallowing disorders.

Vestibular and Balance Disorders: Diagnosis and vestibular rehabilitation for dizziness and disequilibrium.

The Voice Center and Section of Laryngology: Multidisciplinary clinic comprised of laryngologists and speech language pathologists providing sub-specialty care for surgical and non-surgical voice disorders including: care of the performing/professional voice, vocal cord paralysis, vocal cord nodules/polyps/cysts, spasmodic dysphonia, vocal tremor, and other neurologic disorders of the larynx.

THE MOUNT SINAI MEDICAL CENTER

Otolaryngology – Ear, Nose and Throat

Mount Sinai

One Gustave L. Levy Place
Fifth Avenue and 100th Street
New York, NY 10029-6574

Physician Referral: 1-800-MD-SINAI (637-4624)
www.mountsinai.org

Mount Sinai's **DEPARTMENT OF OTOLARYNGOLOGY – HEAD AND NECK SURGERY –** ranks as one of the finest in the nation. In 2013, *U.S. News & World Report* ranked us at #10 in the United States, continuing our impressive history of achievement. Since the early nineteenth century, we have pioneered surgical advances in endoscopy, otology, skull-base surgery, laryngology, rhinology, facial plastic surgery, and head and neck oncology and reconstruction. More recently, we have incorporated advanced technology in robotic and endoscopic surgery, basic science research, and translational science programs.

Robotic Head and Neck Surgery – We are a world leader in robotic head and neck surgery. Our surgeons and researchers have published techniques that have changed the paradigm for management of head and neck cancer, allowing for endoscopic surgery without external incisions, shortening hospital stays, and improving outcomes.

THE MULTIDISCIPLINARY HEAD AND NECK ONCOLOGY TEAM— Acclaimed as one of the finest in the country, our multidisciplinary team includes 35 physicians, surgeons, and ancillary staff from 12 departments. We offer top-rated courses, training and research fellowships and enjoy national recognition for expertise in head, neck, and skull-base cancer. Our minimally invasive and endoscopic team includes surgeons and oncologists focused on treating tumors of the oral cavity, jaw, and larynx, while preserving each patient's quality of life. Speech and swallowing rehabilitation therapists work with patients to help them recover, all of which keeps Mount Sinai on the cutting edge of head and neck cancer therapy, reconstruction, and rehabilitation.

Thyroid and Parathyroid Surgery – We are nationally recognized for excellence in clinical care and clinical outcomes research. Our minimally invasive and robotic surgical techniques offer patients surgery through tiny incisions. Cure rates for thyroid cancer using these techniques are higher than 95 percent. Parathyroid surgery is performed using similar techniques and intraoperative parathyroid hormone monitoring.

Otology and Neurotology – Long recognized among the best in the nation, our otologic surgeons have pioneered surgical techniques to manage chronic ear disease and cochlear implantation that have resulted in excellent outcomes.

The Center for Comprehensive Management of Nasal and Sinus Disease – We deliver the most advanced care for patients suffering from allergic and invasive fungal sinusitis, acute and chronic sinusitis, benign and malignant tumors of the sinonasal cavity, cerebrospinal fluid leaks and encephalocele treatment and inflammatory polyp disease.

Endoscopic Laser Surgery of the Larynx and Trachea – Our surgeons and scientists have introduced techniques in laryngeal and tracheal surgery, including endoscopic laser surgery, tracheal transplantation, and reconstructive surgery, allowing removal of malignant disease while preserving voice and swallowing functions.

The Grabscheid Voice Center – Our multidisciplinary group provides professional singers and patients in need with cutting-edge treatments, using endoscopic laser and minimally invasive surgery. We pioneered office-based procedures that offer patients the opportunity to undergo therapy without the need for general anesthesia.

Cranial Base Surgery – Techniques in endoscopic trans-nasal surgery have revolutionized the management of skull base tumors and cerebrospinal leaks. We have developed procedures for accessing the cranial base and frontal lobes of the brain through the nose, delivering excellent outcomes with lower complications rates.

The Sleep Surgery Center – We offer comprehensive management and treatment of obstructive sleep apnea (OSA) and snoring. Collaboration with the divisions of pulmonary medicine, sleep medicine and endocrinology, provides the collective expertise of a multidisciplinary approach, which is necessary to address all conditions in sleep disordered breathing.

Center for Facial Plastic and Reconstructive Surgery – Our plastic surgeons provide expertise in the areas of facial plastic surgery and complex reconstructive surgery. Our team is expert in the areas of congenital and traumatic deformities, skin cancer, and facial nerve paralysis with reanimation. With expertise, they reverse the signs of aging, remove contour irregularities or deformities, and make the overall appearance of the face more natural and youthful.

THE NEW YORK EYE AND EAR INFIRMARY

310 East 14th Street
New York, New York 10003
Tel. 212.979.4000 Fax. 212.228.0664
http://www.nyee.edu

PROVIDING EXCEPTIONAL CARE OF THE EAR, NOSE, THROAT, AND HEAD & NECK

Established in 1820 the Department of Otolaryngology/Head & Neck Surgery is the first training program in this specialty in the Western Hemisphere. Over nearly two centuries the department has evolved to be an international referral center for the medical and surgical treatment of diseases of the ear, nose, throat and face.

OUTSTANDING SERVICES:

Ear Institute (Otology – Neuro-otology): Specializing in the care of acute and chronic ear disease including hearing loss, cochlear implantation, dizziness, tinnitus, intra cranial tumors and facial nerve disorders. Our advanced otologic and vestibular diagnostic labs assist physicians in treatment.

Facial Plastic Surgery: Highly specialized and renowned surgeons perform in-office or ambulatory procedures utilizing state-of-the-art technology and techniques to produce outstanding results with minimal incisions, rapid recovery and a natural, youthful appearance.

Facial Paralysis: Comprehensive center treating all causes and offering reconstruction of the paralyzed face.

Head & Neck Oncology: A multi-disciplinary team including board-certified surgeons, medical & radiation oncologists, nutritionists and rehabilitation specialists insure rapid recovery from complex, life-saving surgical procedures and return to daily activities.

Pediatric Otolaryngology: Treating children has long been a priority at the Infirmary. Pediatric care ranges from middle ear infection, tonsil and adenoid disease, and neck masses to complex sinus and airway diseases.

Rhinology and Sinus Surgery: Internationally known specialists utilize minimally invasive techniques to treat disorders from sinusitis to intra cranial tumors.

Thyroid Center: A comprehensive program to streamline the diagnosis and treatment of thyroid diseases and cancers. A highly skilled team of surgeons, endocrinologists and radiologists manage the patient's care.

Voice & Swallowing Institute: Combining the expertise of physicians, speech pathologists and a voice physiologist to diagnose and treat voice problems – not only for performing artists but also for teachers, stockbrokers, receptionists, salespeople – anyone for whom voice is an important part of life.

Otolaryngology Clinical Services

General Otolaryngology *plus*
Facial Plastic & Reconstructive Surgery
Cochlear Implantation
Voice & Vocal Dynamics
Head & Neck Oncology
Laryngology
Otology & Neuro-otology
Pediatric Otolaryngology
Rhinology & Sinus Surgery
Swallowing Disorders
Thyroid Center

Facilities

Academic Faculty Practice, *including multiple locations throughout metropolitan NY*
Hearing Aid Dispensary
Vestibular Rehabilitation
Ambulatory Care Services

About The New York Eye and Ear Infirmary

The New York Eye and Ear Infirmary is the nation's first specialty hospital and one of the most experienced in terms of the number of patients it treats and complexity of its cases. Each year the otolaryngology department performs more than 6,000 surgeries and sees more than 70,000 visits from outpatients.

Physician Referral
1.800.449.HOPE (4673)

NYU Langone
MEDICAL CENTER

550 First Avenue *(at 31st Street)*
New York, NY 10016

www.NYULMC.org

Physician Referral: **888-7-NYU-MED** *(888-769-8633)*

OTOLARYNGOLOGY

The Department of Otolaryngology at NYU Langone Medical Center provides the highest quality treatment for ear, nose, throat, head and neck disorders, including one of the premier head and neck surgery programs in the country. We specialize in the following areas:

Cochlear Implants
Patients are provided with extensive evaluation, surgical implantation, device mapping, and speech rehabilitation.

Facial Plastic and Reconstructive Surgery
Care is provided to patients requiring facial reconstructive surgery for a wide variety of facial deformities, and to those seeking facial cosmetic surgery. Specialties include functional and aesthetic rhinoplasty, facial rejuvenation surgery, injectable fillers, Botulinum Toxin (Botox) for facial spasm or wrinkles, and chemical peels and microdermabrasion.

General Otolaryngology and Sleep Surgery
Care is provided to adult patients with voice, sleep, allergy and nasal breathing disorders. Additionally, services for children are provided through our pediatric otolaryngologists.

Head and Neck Surgery and Oncology
Care is provided to patients with cancer of the head and neck, including cancer of the larynx, oral cavity, throat, nasal cavity and sinuses, salivary glands and lymph nodes in the neck.

Neurotology/Skull Base Surgery
The Otolaryngology team provides expert care to patients with hearing loss, facial nerve palsy, vertigo and tinnitus, and treats lesions such as acoustic neuromas and skull base meningiomas. Featured services include facial palsy rehabilitation, auditory brainstem implants, cochlear implants, laser surgery and endoscopic anterior and lateral skull base surgery.

Voice and Swallowing Disorders
We treat voice and swallowing disorders, including sore throat, chronic cough, hoarseness, voice loss, swallowing dysfunction, benign growths and cancerous tumors, vocal cord paralysis, the aging voice, recurrent or chronic laryngitis, gastroesophageal reflux, and injuries from overuse and misuse of the voice. Specialized services are available for vocal performers.

Specialized Expertise
Audiology treats patients suffering with hearing or balance disorders; Head and Neck Speech Pathology treats voice, speech or swallowing problems; Rhinology treats all diseases of the paranasal sinuses, nose and related structures; Skull Base Surgery offers a minimally invasive and advanced surgical approach to tumors of the anterior and posterior skull base.

Top Doctors Make A Difference

Pain Medicine

subspecialty of Anesthesiology, Neurology, and in Physical Medicine and Rehabilitation or Psychiatry

Some physicians who have their primary board certification in anesthesiology, neurology, physical medicine and rehabilitation, or psychiatry have completed additional training and passed an examination in the subspecialty called pain management. These doctors provide a high level of care, either as a primary physician or consultant, for patients experiencing problems with acute, chronic and/or cancer pain in both hospital and ambulatory settings.

For more information about the main specialties of these physicians, see **Anesthesiology, Neurology, Physical Medicine** and **Rehabilitation** or **Psychiatry** section(s).

Training Required: Number of years required for primary specialty *plus* additional training and examination

Pain Medicine

New England

Berde, Charles Benjamin MD/PhD [PM] - **Spec Exp:** Pain Management-Pediatric; Critical Care; Reflex Sympathetic Dystrophy (RSD); **Hospital:** Children's Hospital - Boston, Spaulding Rehab Hosp; **Address:** Chldns Hosp, PTS, 333 Longwood Ave Fl 5, Boston, MA 02115; **Phone:** 617-355-7040; **Board Cert:** Pediatrics 1988; Anesthesiology 2009; Pain Medicine 2004; Hospice & Palliative Medicine 2012; **Med School:** Stanford Univ 1980; **Resid:** Pediatrics, Chldns Hosp 1983; Anesthesiology, Mass Genl Hosp 1985; **Fellow:** Pediatric Anesthesiology, Chldns Hosp 1985; **Fac Appt:** Prof Ped, Harvard Med Sch

Loder, Elizabeth W MD [PM] - **Spec Exp:** Headache; Migraine; **Hospital:** Brigham & Women's Hosp, Brigham and Women's Faulkner Hosp; **Address:** Brigham and Women's Faulkner Hosp, 1153 Centre St, Ste 4970, Boston, MA 02130; **Phone:** 617-983-7580; **Board Cert:** Internal Medicine 2010; **Med School:** Univ ND Sch Med 1985; **Resid:** Internal Medicine, Faulkner Hosp 1989; **Fellow:** Headache, Graham Headache Ctr 1990; **Fac Appt:** Asst Prof Med, Harvard Med Sch

Peeters-Asdourian, Christine MD [PM] - **Hospital:** Beth Israel Deaconess Med Ctr - Boston; **Address:** Arnold Pain Management Ctr, One Brookline Pl, Ste 105, Brookline, MA 02445; **Phone:** 617-278-8000; **Board Cert:** Anesthesiology 1987; Pain Medicine 2004; **Med School:** Belgium 1978; **Resid:** Anesthesiology, Univ Mass Med Ctr 1981; **Fellow:** Pain Medicine, Univ Mass Med Ctr 1982; **Fac Appt:** Asst Prof Anes, Univ Mass Sch Med

Ross, Edgar L MD [PM] - **Spec Exp:** Pain-Cancer; Spinal Cord Stimulation; **Hospital:** Brigham & Women's Hosp; **Address:** Brigham & Women's Dept of Pain Medicine, 850 Boylston St Fl 3 - Ste 320, Chestnut Hill, MA 02467; **Phone:** 617-732-9056; **Board Cert:** Anesthesiology 1984; Pain Medicine 2004; **Med School:** Wayne State Univ 1980; **Resid:** Anesthesiology, Case West Univ Hosps 1983; **Fellow:** Pain Medicine, Case West Univ Hosps 1984; **Fac Appt:** Asst Prof Anes, Harvard Med Sch

Mid Atlantic

Argoff, Charles E MD [PM] - **Spec Exp:** Pain Management; Headache; Botox Therapy; Pain-Interventional Techniques; **Hospital:** Albany Med Ctr; **Address:** AMC, Neurology Grp, 47 New Scotland Ave, MC 70, Albany, NY 12208; **Phone:** 518-262-5226; **Board Cert:** Neurology 1990; Pain Medicine 2009; **Med School:** Northwestern Univ-Feinberg Sch Med 1984; **Resid:** Neurology, Stony Brook Univ Med Ctr 1988; **Fellow:** Neurology, Natl Inst of Hlth-Clin Ctr 1990; **Fac Appt:** Prof N, Albany Med Coll

Christo, Paul J MD [PM] - **Spec Exp:** Reflex Sympathetic Dystrophy (RSD); Spinal Cord Stimulation; Pain-Spine; Pain-Low Back; **Hospital:** Johns Hopkins Hosp (page 59); **Address:** Blaustein Pain Treatment Ctr, 601 N Caroline St, Ste 3062, Baltimore, MD 21287; **Phone:** 410-955-7246; **Board Cert:** Anesthesiology 2012; Pain Medicine 2013; **Med School:** Univ Louisville Sch Med 1995; **Resid:** Anesthesiology, Mass Genl Hosp 2000; **Fellow:** Pain Medicine, Johns Hopkins Hosp 2001; **Fac Appt:** Assoc Prof Anes, Johns Hopkins Univ

Cope, Doris K MD [PM] - **Spec Exp:** Pain-Spine; **Address:** KURE Pain, 116 Defense Hwy, Ste 403, Annapolis, MD 21401; **Phone:** 410-571-2946; **Board Cert:** Anesthesiology 1989; Pain Medicine 2007; **Med School:** Med Coll GA 1982; **Resid:** Anesthesiology, Univ S Alabama 1986

DeLeon, Oscar A MD [PM] - **Spec Exp:** Pain-Cancer; **Hospital:** Roswell Park Canc Inst; **Address:** Roswell Park Cancer Inst, Dept of Anesthesiology, Elm & Carlton Sts, Buffalo, NY 14263; **Phone:** 716-845-3240; **Board Cert:** Anesthesiology 1991; Critical Care Medicine 1993; Pain Medicine 2005; **Med School:** Guatemala 1982; **Resid:** Surgery, SUNY-Downstate Med Ctr 1987; Anesthesiology, Univ Buffalo Affil Hosps 1991; **Fac Appt:** Prof Anes, SUNY Buffalo

Diwan, Sudhir MD [PM] - **Spec Exp:** Pain-after Spinal Intervention; Pain-Musculoskeletal; Pain-Neuropathic; Pain-Cancer; **Hospital:** Lenox Hill Hosp (page 66); **Address:** Manhattan Spine & Pain Med, 115 E 57th St, Ste 610, New York, NY 10022; **Phone:** 212-535-3505; **Board Cert:** Anesthesiology 2012; Pain Medicine 2013; **Med School:** India 1983; **Resid:** Surgery, St Lukes-Roosevelt Hosp Ctr 1994; Anesthesiology, St Lukes-Roosevelt Hosp Ctr 1997; **Fellow:** Pain Medicine, NY-Presby/Weill Cornell Med Ctr 1998

Falco, Frank J.E. MD [PM] - **Spec Exp:** Spinal Disorders; Pain-Musculoskeletal-Spine; Pain-Chronic; **Hospital:** Union Hosp; **Address:** Mid Atlantic Spine & Pain Ctr, 100 Biddle Ave, Ste 101, Newark, DE 19702; **Phone:** 302-392-6501; **Board Cert:** Pain Medicine 2011; Physical Medicine & Rehabilitation 2013; Sports Medicine 2007; Electrodiagnostic Medicine 2004; **Med School:** Temple Univ 1988; **Resid:** Physical Medicine & Rehabilitation, Temple Univ Hosp 1992; **Fellow:** Pain Management, GA Spine & Sports Ctr 1994

Gharibo, Christopher G MD [PM] - **Spec Exp:** Pain-Back & Neck; Pain-Neuropathic; Pain-Chronic; Complex Regional Pain Syndromes; **Hospital:** NYU Langone Med Ctr (page 68), NYU Hosp For Joint Dis; **Address:** Ctr for Musculoskeletal Care, 333 E 38th St N Fl 6, New York, NY 10016; **Phone:** 646-501-7246; **Board Cert:** Anesthesiology 1997; Pain Medicine 2009; **Med School:** UMDNJ-NJ Med Sch, Newark 1992; **Resid:** Internal Medicine, UMDNJ-RW Johnson Univ Hosp 1993; Anesthesiology, NYU Med Ctr 1996; **Fellow:** Pain Medicine, Jefferson Univ Hosp 1997; **Fac Appt:** Assoc Prof Anes, NYU Sch Med

Jain, Subhash MD [PM] - **Spec Exp:** Pain-Cancer; Pain-Pelvic; Reflex Sympathetic Dystrophy (RSD); Complex Regional Pain Syndromes; **Hospital:** Beth Israel Med Ctr - Petrie Div (page 56); **Address:** 360 E 72nd St, Ste C, New York, NY 10021; **Phone:** 212-439-6100; **Board Cert:** Anesthesiology 1994; **Med School:** India 1968; **Resid:** Surgery, St Vincent Med Ctr 1977; Anesthesiology, New York Hosp 1979; **Fellow:** Pain Medicine, New York Hosp/Meml Sloan Kettering Cancer Ctr 1980; **Fac Appt:** Assoc Prof Anes, Cornell Univ-Weill Med Coll

Kreitzer, Joel M MD [PM] - **Spec Exp:** Pain-Back; Pain-Cancer; Pain-Neuropathic; **Hospital:** Mt Sinai Med Ctr (page 62), Mount Sinai Hosp of Queens (page 62); **Address:** Upper East Side Pain Medicine, 1540 York Ave, New York, NY 10028; **Phone:** 212-288-2180; **Board Cert:** Anesthesiology 1990; Pain Medicine 2004; **Med School:** Albert Einstein Coll Med 1985; **Resid:** Anesthesiology, Mt Sinai Hosp 1989; **Fellow:** Pain Medicine, Mt Sinai Hosp 1989; **Fac Appt:** Assoc Clin Prof Anes, Mount Sinai Sch Med

Ngeow, Jeffrey Y MD [PM] - **Spec Exp:** Pain-Musculoskeletal-Spine & Neck; Reflex Sympathetic Dystrophy (RSD); Acupuncture; Pain-Neuropathic; **Hospital:** Hosp For Special Surgery (page 58); **Address:** Hosp Spec Surg-Integrative Care Ctr, 635 Madison Ave Fl 5, New York, NY 10022; **Phone:** 212-224-7918; **Board Cert:** Anesthesiology 1980; Pain Medicine 2005; **Med School:** England, UK 1971; **Resid:** Anesthesiology, Peter Bent Brigham Hosp 1977; **Fellow:** Pain Medicine, Tufts New England Med Ctr 1978; **Fac Appt:** Assoc Clin Prof Anes, Cornell Univ-Weill Med Coll

Raja, Srinivasa N MD [PM] - **Spec Exp:** Pain-Neuropathic; Herpetic Neuralgia (Shingles); Reflex Sympathetic Dystrophy (RSD); **Hospital:** Johns Hopkins Hosp (page 59); **Address:** 601 N Caroline St, Ste 3062, Johns Hopkins Outpatient Center, Baltimore, MD 21287; **Phone:** 410-955-7246; **Board Cert:** Anesthesiology 1982; Pain Medicine 2004; **Med School:** India 1974; **Resid:** Anesthesiology, Univ Wash Med Ctr 1979; **Fellow:** Pain Medicine, Univ Virginia Hosp 1981; **Fac Appt:** Prof Anes, Johns Hopkins Univ

Richman, Daniel MD [PM] - **Spec Exp:** Pain-Back & Neck; Complex Regional Pain Syndromes; Reflex Sympathetic Dystrophy (RSD); Pain-Neuropathic; **Hospital:** Hosp For Special Surgery (page 58); **Address:** Hosp Special Surgery, Pain Mgmt Ctr, 429 E 75th St Fl 5, New York, NY 10021; **Phone:** 212-606-1768; **Board Cert:** Anesthesiology 1991; Pain Medicine 2005; **Med School:** UMDNJ-NJ Med Sch, Newark 1986; **Resid:** Anesthesiology, Hartford Hosp 1990; **Fellow:** Pain Medicine, Hosp Special Surgery 1991; **Fac Appt:** Asst Clin Prof Anes, Cornell Univ-Weill Med Coll

Staats, Peter MD [PM] - **Spec Exp:** Pain-Cancer; Pain-Back; **Hospital:** Riverview Med Ctr, CentraState Med Ctr; **Address:** Premier Pain Centers, 160 Avenue at the Commons, Ste 1, Shrewsbury, NJ 07702; **Phone:** 732-380-0200; **Board Cert:** Anesthesiology 1994; Pain Medicine 2005; **Med School:** Univ Mich Med Sch 1989; **Resid:** Anesthesiology, Johns Hopkins Hosp 1993; **Fellow:** Pain Medicine, Johns Hopkins Hosp 1994

Weinberger, Michael L MD [PM] - **Spec Exp:** Pain-Cancer; Pain-Back; Palliative Care; **Hospital:** NY-Presby/Columbia Univ Med Ctr, NY (page 65); **Address:** 630 W 168th St, PH5, rm 500, New York, NY 10032-3720; **Phone:** 212-305-7114; **Board Cert:** Internal Medicine 1986; Anesthesiology 1990; Pain Medicine 2004; Hospice & Palliative Medicine 2006; **Med School:** Columbia P&S 1983; **Resid:** Internal Medicine, St Vincent's Hosp 1986; Anesthesiology, Columbia-Presby Med Ctr 1989; **Fellow:** Pain Medicine, Meml Sloan Kettering Cancer Ctr 1990; **Fac Appt:** Assoc Prof Anes, Columbia P&S

Southeast

Anghelescu, Doralina L MD [PM] - **Spec Exp:** Pain Management-Pediatric; Pain-Cancer; **Hospital:** St. Jude Children's Research Hosp; **Address:** St Jude Chldn's Rsch Hosp, Dept Anesthesiology/Pain Management, 262 Danny Thomas Pl, MS 130, Memphis, TN 38105; **Phone:** 901-595-4032; **Board Cert:** Anesthesiology 1998; Pain Medicine 2012; **Med School:** Romania 1985; **Resid:** Anesthesiology, Univ N Mex Hosp 1997; **Fellow:** Pain Medicine, Chldns Natl Med Ctr 1998; Pain Medicine, Univ N Mex Hosp 1999

Baumann, Patricia L MD [PM] - **Spec Exp:** Pain-Back; Pain-Neuropathic; Spinal Disorders; Complex Regional Pain Syndromes; **Hospital:** Emory Univ Hosp Midtown, Emory Univ Hosp; **Address:** Emory Center for Pain Management, 550 Peachtree St NE, Ste 1950, Atlanta, GA 30308; **Phone:** 404-686-2410; **Board Cert:** Anesthesiology 1993; Pain Medicine 2005; **Med School:** Emory Univ 1988; **Resid:** Anesthesiology, Emory Univ Med Ctr 1992; **Fac Appt:** Asst Prof Anes, Emory Univ

Gobrial, Wagih W MD [PM] - **Spec Exp:** Pain-Interventional Techniques; Pain-Spine; **Hospital:** Cleveland Clin - Weston (page 55); **Address:** Cleveland Clin, Pain Med Dept, 2950 Cleveland Clinic Blvd, MC FLA, Weston, FL 33331; **Phone:** 954-659-5045; **Board Cert:** Anesthesiology 1997; Pain Medicine 2009; **Med School:** Egypt 1976; **Resid:** Anesthesiology, Cleveland Clin 1996; **Fellow:** Pain Management, Cleveland Clin 1997; **Fac Appt:** Asst Prof Anes, Nova SE Univ, Coll Osteo Med

Huntoon, Marc MD [PM] - **Spec Exp:** Pain-Cancer; Pain-after Spinal Intervention; Palliative Care; **Hospital:** Vanderbilt Univ Med Ctr; **Address:** 719 Thompson Ln, Nashville, TN 37204; **Phone:** 615-322-4311; **Board Cert:** Anesthesiology 2009; Pain Medicine 2004; Hospice & Palliative Medicine 2010; **Med School:** Wayne State Univ 1985; **Resid:** Anesthesiology, Naval Hosp Med Ctr 1991; **Fellow:** Pain Medicine, Naval Hosp Med Ctr 1992; **Fac Appt:** Prof Anes, Vanderbilt Univ

Mays, Kit S MD [PM] - **Spec Exp:** Pain-Interventional Techniques; Pain-Neuropathic; **Hospital:** Baptist Memorial Hospital-Memphis; **Address:** 55 Humphreys Ctr Drive, Ste 200, Memphis, TN 38120; **Phone:** 901-747-0040; **Med School:** Univ Tenn Coll Med 1972; **Resid:** Anesthesiology, City of Memphis Hosp 1977; **Fellow:** Pain Medicine, City of Memphis Hosp 1978

Rauck, Richard L MD [PM] - **Spec Exp:** Pain-Cancer; Spinal Cord Stimulation; Complex Regional Pain Syndromes; **Hospital:** Forsyth Med Ctr, Wake Forest Baptist Med Ctr; **Address:** Carolinas Pain Inst, 145 Kimel Park Drive, Ste 330, Winston-Salem, NC 27103; **Phone:** 336-765-6181; **Board Cert:** Anesthesiology 1987; Pain Medicine 2005; **Med School:** Bowman Gray 1982; **Resid:** Anesthesiology, Univ Cincinnati Hosp 1985; **Fellow:** Pain Medicine, Univ Cincinnati Hosp 1986; **Fac Appt:** Assoc Prof Anes, Wake Forest Univ

Schnapp, Moacir MD [PM] - **Spec Exp:** Pain-Interventional Techniques; Pain-Neuropathic; **Hospital:** Baptist Memorial Hospital-Memphis; **Address:** 55 Humphreys Ctr Drive, Ste 200, Memphis, TN 38120; **Phone:** 901-747-0040; **Med School:** Brazil 1975; **Resid:** Neurology, Hosp das Clinicas 1979; **Fellow:** Pain Management, Univ Tennessee Med Ctr 1981

Vetter, Thomas R MD [PM] - **Spec Exp:** Pain Management; Pain-Chronic; **Hospital:** UAB Hosp; **Address:** UAB Hosp, Anesthesiology/Pain Med, 619 19th St S, JT 865, Birmingham, AL 35249-6810; **Phone:** 205-934-6501; **Board Cert:** Anesthesiology 2009; Pain Medicine 2009; **Med School:** Ohio State Univ 1984; **Resid:** Anesthesiology, UPMC 1988; **Fellow:** Pain Management, Chldns Hosp 1989; **Fac Appt:** Prof Anes, UAB Sch Med

Midwest

Abram, Stephen E MD [PM] - **Hospital:** Froedtert & Med Coll WI; **Address:** Froedtert Med College WI-Pain Mngmt Clin, 959 N Mayfair Rd, Wauwatosa, WI 53226; **Phone:** 414-456-7600; **Board Cert:** Anesthesiology 2001; Pain Medicine 2004; **Med School:** Jefferson Med Coll 1970; **Resid:** Anesthesiology, Mary Hitchcock Mem Hosp 1975; **Fac Appt:** Prof Anes, Med Coll Wisc

Benzon, Honorio T MD [PM] - **Spec Exp:** Pain-Back; Complex Regional Pain Syndromes; Pain-Neuropathic; **Hospital:** Northwestern Meml Hosp; **Address:** 675 N Saint Clair St, Fl 17 - Ste 200, Chicago, IL 60611-3015; **Phone:** 312-695-2500; **Board Cert:** Anesthesiology 2009; Pain Medicine 2013; **Med School:** Philippines 1971; **Resid:** Anesthesiology, Univ Cincinnati Med Ctr 1975; Anesthesiology, Northwestern Meml Hosp 1976; **Fellow:** Research, Brigham & Womens Hosp 1986; **Fac Appt:** Prof Anes, Northwestern Univ

Covington, Edward C MD [PM] - **Spec Exp:** Pain-Chronic; **Hospital:** Cleveland Clin (page 55); **Address:** 10524 Stokes Blvd, C21, Cleveland, OH 44106; **Phone:** 216-636-5860; **Board Cert:** Psychiatry 1978; Addiction Psychiatry 2013; Pain Medicine 2012; **Med School:** Univ Tenn Coll Med 1970; **Resid:** Psychiatry, Mayo Clinic 1975

Freitag, Frederick G DO [PM] - **Spec Exp:** Headache; Migraine-Chronic; Botox Therapy; **Hospital:** Froedtert & Med Coll WI; **Address:** 9200 W Wisconsin Ave, Milwaukee, WI 53226; **Phone:** 414-805-5200; **Board Cert:** Family Medicine 1982; Headache Medicine 2007; **Med School:** Chicago Coll Osteo Med 1979; **Resid:** Family Medicine, Brentwood Hosp 1981; **Fellow:** Headache, Cleveland Clinic 1981; **Fac Appt:** Assoc Prof N, Med Coll Wisc

Green, Carmen R MD [PM] - **Hospital:** Univ Michigan Med Ctr; **Address:** 1301 Catherine St, 4120 Medical Science Bldg 1, Ann Arbor, MI 48109; **Phone:** 734-936-4240; **Board Cert:** Anesthesiology 1996; Pain Medicine 2009; **Med School:** Mich State Univ 1987; **Resid:** Anesthesiology, Univ Mich Med Ctr 1989; **Fellow:** Pain Medicine, Univ Mich Med Ctr 1992; **Fac Appt:** Prof Anes, Univ Mich Med Sch

Hooten, William Michael MD [PM] - **Spec Exp:** Pain-Interventional Techniques; **Hospital:** Mayo Med Ctr & Clin - Rochester, St. Mary's Hosp - Rochester MN (Mayo); **Address:** Mayo Clinic, Dept Anesthesia/Pain, 200 First St SW, Eisenberg Blgd 8G, Rochester, MN 55905; **Phone:** 507-266-9240; **Board Cert:** Anesthesiology 2004; Pain Medicine 2005; Psychiatry 2010; **Med School:** St Louis Univ 1993; **Resid:** Internal Medicine, Mayo Clinic 1998; Psychiatry, Johns Hopkins Hosp 1998; **Fellow:** Pain Medicine, Barnes Jewish Hosp 2005; Anesthesiology, Washington University School of Medicine; **Fac Appt:** Assoc Prof Anes, Mayo Med Sch

Lubenow, Timothy R MD [PM] - **Spec Exp:** Complex Regional Pain Syndromes; Spinal Cord Stimulation; **Hospital:** Rush Univ Med Ctr, Rush Oak Park Hosp; **Address:** Rush Pain Center, 610 S St, Ste 550, Chicago, IL 60612; **Phone:** 312-942-6631; **Board Cert:** Anesthesiology 1987; Pain Medicine 2005; **Med School:** Med Coll Wisc 1983; **Resid:** Anesthesiology, Rush-Presby-St Lukes Med Ctr 1986; **Fellow:** Pain Medicine, Rush-Presby-St Lukes Med Ctr 1987; **Fac Appt:** Prof Anes, Rush Med Coll

Macadaeg, Kevin E MD [PM] - **Spec Exp:** Spinal Disorders; Pain-Spine; Pain-Interventional Techniques; **Hospital:** St. Vincent Indianapolis Hosp; **Address:** Indiana Spine Group, 13225 N Meridian St, Carmel, IN 46032; **Phone:** 317-228-7000; **Board Cert:** Anesthesiology 1992; Pain Medicine 2004; **Med School:** Wayne State Univ 1988; **Resid:** Anesthesiology, SUNY Upstate Med Ctr 1992; **Fac Appt:** Asst Clin Prof Anes, Indiana Univ

Mekhail, Nagy A MD/PhD [PM] - **Spec Exp:** Pain-Back & Neck; Pain-Chronic; Pain-Neuropathic; Pain-Cancer; **Hospital:** Cleveland Clin (page 55); **Address:** Cleveland Clinic Pain Management, 10524 Euclid Ave, Desk C25, Cleveland, OH 44106; **Phone:** 216-444-7246; **Board Cert:** Anesthesiology 1993; Pain Medicine 2004; **Med School:** Egypt 1975; **Resid:** Anesthesiology, Cleveland Clinic 1991; **Fellow:** Pain Medicine, Cleveland Clinic 1992; **Fac Appt:** Prof Anes, Cleveland Cl Coll Med/Case West Res

Robbins, Larry D MD [PM] - **Spec Exp:** Headache; Migraine; Psychopharmacology; Pain Management; **Address:** 60 Revere Drive, Ste 330, Northbrook, IL 60062; **Phone:** 847-480-9399; **Board Cert:** Anesthesiology 2005; **Med School:** Univ IL Coll Med 1981; **Resid:** Neurology, Univ Illinois Med Ctr 1985; **Fellow:** Pain Medicine, Diamond Headache Clinic 1986

Rosenquist, Richard W MD [PM] - **Spec Exp:** Complex Regional Pain Syndromes; Pain-Back; Pain-Facial; Headache; **Hospital:** Cleveland Clin (page 55); **Address:** Cleveland Clinic Pain Management, 10524 Euclid Ave, Desk C25, Cleveland, OH 44106; **Phone:** 216-444-7246; **Board Cert:** Anesthesiology 1988; Pain Medicine 2004; **Med School:** Northwestern Univ 1984; **Resid:** Anesthesiology, Northwestern Univ Med Ctr 1987; **Fellow:** Anesthesiology & Pain Management, Emory Univ Hosp 1988

Suresh, Santhanam MD [PM] - **Hospital:** Lurie Chldn's Hosp-Chicago; **Address:** Lurie Chldn's Hosp, 225 E Chicago Ave, Box 19, Chicago, IL 60611; **Phone:** 312-227-5157; **Board Cert:** Pediatrics 2011; Anesthesiology 2012; Pain Medicine 2009; **Med School:** India 1983; **Resid:** Pediatrics, Cook Co Hosp 1988; Anesthesiology, Loyola Univ Med Ctr 1990; **Fellow:** Pediatric Anesthesiology, Northwestern Meml Hosp 1991; **Fac Appt:** Prof Anes, Northwestern Univ-Feinberg Sch Med

Swarm, Robert A MD [PM] - **Spec Exp:** Pain-Acute; Pain-Chronic; Pain-Cancer; **Hospital:** Barnes-Jewish Hosp; **Address:** Ctr for Advanced Med-Pain Mngmt Ctr, 4921 Parkview Pl, Ste 10A, St Louis, MO 63110; **Phone:** 314-362-8820; **Board Cert:** Anesthesiology 1990; Pain Medicine 2004; **Med School:** Washington Univ, St Louis 1983; **Resid:** Surgery, Barnes Hosp 1986; Anesthesiology, Barnes Hosp 1989; **Fellow:** Pain Medicine, Univ Sydney 1991; **Fac Appt:** Prof Anes, Washington Univ, St Louis

Weisman, Steven J MD [PM] - **Spec Exp:** Pain Management-Pediatric; Complex Regional Pain Syndromes; Pain-Cancer; **Hospital:** Chldns Hosp - Wisconsin; **Address:** Children's Hosp WI, 9000 W Wisconsin Ave, Box 1997, Milwaukee, WI 53201-1997; **Phone:** 414-266-2775; **Board Cert:** Pediatrics 1982; Pediatric Hematology-Oncology 1984; Anesthesiology 2009; **Med School:** Albert Einstein Coll Med 1978; **Resid:** Pediatrics, Chldns Hosp 1981; Anesthesiology, Univ of Conn Hlth Ctr, John Dempsey Hosp 1994; **Fellow:** Pediatric Hematology-Oncology, Indiana Univ Sch Med 1984; **Fac Appt:** Prof Anes, Med Coll Wisc

Wellington, Joshua R MD [PM] - **Spec Exp:** Pain-Spine; Pain-Cancer; Pain-Neuropathic; Pain-Pediatric; **Hospital:** IU Hlth Univ Hosp; **Address:** IU Pain Clinic, 550 N University Blvd, Ste 2007, Indianapolis, IN 46202; **Phone:** 317-944-2891; **Board Cert:** Physical Medicine & Rehabilitation 2004; Pain Medicine 2005; **Med School:** Med Coll OH 1999; **Resid:** Physical Medicine & Rehabilitation, Spaulding Rehab Hosp 2003; **Fellow:** Pain Management, Chldns Hosp/Brigham & Womens Hosp/Beth Israel 2004; **Fac Appt:** Asst Clin Prof PMR, Indiana Univ

Great Plains and Mountains

Fine, Perry G MD [PM] - **Spec Exp:** Pain-Cancer; Palliative Care; Pain-Chronic; **Hospital:** Univ Utah Hlth Care; **Address:** 546 S Chipeta Way, Ste 220, Salt Lake City, UT 84108; **Phone:** 801-581-7246; **Board Cert:** Anesthesiology 1985; Pain Medicine 2004; Hospice & Palliative Medicine 2012; **Med School:** Med Coll VA 1981; **Resid:** Anesthesiology, Univ Utah Hlth Sci Ctr 1985; **Fellow:** Pain Medicine, Univ Toronto Affil Hosp 1986; **Fac Appt:** Prof Anes, Univ Utah

Southwest

Burton, Allen W MD [PM] - **Spec Exp:** Pain-Cancer; Palliative Care; **Hospital:** St. Luke's Episcopal Hosp-Houston; **Address:** Houston Pain Ctr, 7700 Main St, Ste 400, Houston, TX 77030; **Phone:** 713-973-7246; **Board Cert:** Anesthesiology 1996; Pain Medicine 2009; **Med School:** Baylor Coll Med 1991; **Resid:** Anesthesiology, Brigham & Women's Hosp 1996; **Fellow:** Pain Medicine, UT Med Br (John Sealy Hosp) 1998; **Fac Appt:** Assoc Prof Anes, Univ Tex Med Br, Galveston

Driver, Larry C MD [PM] - **Spec Exp:** Pain-Cancer; Palliative Care; **Hospital:** UT MD Anderson Canc Ctr; **Address:** UT MD Anderson Canc Ctr, Dept Pain Med, 1400 Holcombe Blvd, Unit 409, Houston, TX 77030; **Phone:** 713-745-7246; **Board Cert:** Anesthesiology 1992; Hospice & Palliative Medicine 2012; Pain Medicine 2013; **Med School:** Univ Tex, San Antonio 1980; **Resid:** Anesthesiology, Univ CO Affil Hosp 1984; **Fellow:** Pain Medicine, UT MD Anderson Canc Ctr 1999; **Fac Appt:** Assoc Prof Anes, Univ Tex, Houston

Noe, Carl E MD [PM] - **Spec Exp:** Pain-Back & Neck; Pain Management; Spinal Cord Stimulation; **Hospital:** UT Southwestern Med Ctr at Dallas; **Address:** Eugene McDermott Ctr for Pain Management, 1801 Inwood Rd, Ste 502, Dallas, TX 75390-9189; **Phone:** 214-645-8450; **Board Cert:** Anesthesiology 1989; Pain Medicine 2004; Critical Care Medicine 1989; **Med School:** Univ Tex, San Antonio 1984; **Resid:** Anesthesiology, TX Tech Univ Hlth Sci Ctr 1987; Anesthesiology, Stanford Univ Med Ctr 1988; **Fellow:** Critical Care Medicine, Stanford Univ Med Ctr 1988; Pain Management, TX Tech Univ Hlth Sci Ctr 1989; **Fac Appt:** Prof Anes, Univ Tex SW, Dallas

Racz, Gabor MD [PM] - **Spec Exp:** Pain-after Spinal Intervention; Reflex Sympathetic Dystrophy (RSD); Pain-Back, Head & Neck; Headache/Facial Pain; **Hospital:** Univ Med Ctr-Lubbock, Grace Med Ctr; **Address:** 3601 4th St, MS 8182, Lubbock, TX 79430-0002; **Phone:** 806-743-3112; **Board Cert:** Anesthesiology 1993; Pain Medicine 2004; **Med School:** England, UK 1962; **Resid:** Anesthesiology, SUNY Upstate Med Ctr 1966; **Fac Appt:** Prof Anes, Texas Tech Univ

Ramamurthy, Somayaji MD [PM] - **Spec Exp:** Pain-Back; Pain-Chronic; **Hospital:** Univ Hosp-San Antonio; **Address:** UT Med Pain Consultants, 5282 Medical Drive, Ste 614, Westgate-Med Ctr, San Antonio, TX 78229; **Phone:** 210-450-9850; **Board Cert:** Anesthesiology 1972; Pain Medicine 2004; **Med School:** India 1965; **Resid:** Anesthesiology, Edgewater Hosp 1968; Anesthesiology, Cook Co Hosp 1972; **Fellow:** Pain Medicine, Cook Co Hosp 1973; **Fac Appt:** Prof Anes, Univ Tex, San Antonio

Walsh, Nicolas E MD [PM] - **Spec Exp:** Pain-Back; Trauma Rehabilitation; Post Polio Syndrome/Rehabilitation; **Hospital:** Univ Hosp-San Antonio, Audie L Murphy Meml Vets Hosp - San Antonio; **Address:** Univ Tex Hlth Sci Ctr, Rehab Med, 7703 Floyd Curl Drive, MC 7798, San Antonio, TX 78229-3901; **Phone:** 210-358-0770; **Board Cert:** Physical Medicine & Rehabilitation 2009; Pain Medicine 2011; **Med School:** Univ Colorado 1979; **Resid:** Physical Medicine & Rehabilitation, Univ Tex Hlth Sci Ctr 1983; **Fac Appt:** Prof PMR, Univ Tex, San Antonio

West Coast and Pacific

Audell, Laura G MD [PM] - **Spec Exp:** Complex Regional Pain Syndromes; Herpetic Neuralgia (Shingles); Spinal Cord Disorders; Reflex Sympathetic Dystrophy (RSD); **Hospital:** Cedars-Sinai Med Ctr; **Address:** 444 S San Vincente Blvd, Ste 1101, Los Angeles, CA 90048; **Phone:** 310-423-9600; **Board Cert:** Internal Medicine 1986; Anesthesiology 1988; Pain Medicine 2007; **Med School:** Univ Wash 1982; **Resid:** Internal Medicine, UCLA Med Ctr 1986; Anesthesiology, UCLA Med Ctr 1988; **Fellow:** Pain Medicine, UCLA Med Ctr 1990; **Fac Appt:** Asst Prof Anes, UCLA-David Geffen Sch Med

Ballantyne, Jane C MD [PM] - **Spec Exp:** Pain-Chronic; Pain-Cancer; **Hospital:** Harborview Med Ctr; **Address:** Univ Wash Pain Ctr, 4225 Roosevelt Way NE Fl 4 - Ste 401, Seattle, WA 98105; **Phone:** 206-598-4282; **Board Cert:** Anesthesiology 1997; **Med School:** England, UK 1978; **Resid:** Surgery, London & Oxford 1985; Anesthesiology, John Radcliffe Hosp 1990; **Fellow:** Anesthesiology, Mass Genl Hosp 1992; Pain Medicine, Mass Genl Hosp 1994; **Fac Appt:** Prof Anes, Univ Wash

Bedder, Marshall MD [PM] - **Spec Exp:** Pain-Spine; Pain-Neuropathic; Spinal Cord Stimulation; **Hospital:** Swedish Med Ctr-First Hill-Seattle; **Address:** Pacific Med Ctr-First Hill, 1101 Madison St, Ste 400, Seattle, WA 98104; **Phone:** 206-505-1300; **Board Cert:** Anesthesiology 1987; Pain Medicine 2004; **Med School:** Univ Manitoba 1982; **Resid:** Anesthesiology, Univ Manitoba Affil Hosp 1986; **Fellow:** Pain Management, Univ Washington/Univ Manitoba Affil Hosp 1986

Ferrante, F Michael MD [PM] - **Spec Exp:** Pain-Back & Neck; Reflex Sympathetic Dystrophy (RSD); Pain-Cancer; Spinal Cord Stimulation; **Hospital:** Santa Monica - UCLA Med Ctr & Ortho Hosp, UCLA Ronald Reagan Med Ctr; **Address:** UCLA Pain Program, 1245 16th St, Ste 225, Santa Monica, CA 90404; **Phone:** 310-319-2241; **Board Cert:** Internal Medicine 1985; Anesthesiology 1987; Pain Medicine 2004; **Med School:** NY Med Coll 1980; **Resid:** Internal Medicine, Emroy Univ Hosp 1983; Anesthesiology, Emroy Univ Hosp 1986; **Fellow:** Infectious Disease, Barnes Hosp-Wash Univ 1984; Pain Medicine, Brigham & Womens Hosp 1987; **Fac Appt:** Clin Prof Anes, UCLA

Fishman, Scott M MD [PM] - **Spec Exp:** Pain-Cancer; Pain-Chronic; **Hospital:** UC Davis Med Ctr; **Address:** UC Davis Med Ctr, Pain Management Clinic, 4860 Y St, Ste 2700, Sacramento, CA 95817; **Phone:** 916-734-6824; **Board Cert:** Psychiatry 1998; Pain Medicine 1995; **Med School:** Univ Mass Sch Med 1990; **Resid:** Internal Medicine, Greenwich Hosp 1993; Psychiatry, Mass Genl Hosp 1996; **Fellow:** Pain Medicine, Mass Genl Hosp 1995; **Fac Appt:** Prof Anes, UC Davis

Fitzgibbon, Dermot R MD [PM] - **Spec Exp:** Pain-Cancer; **Hospital:** Univ Wash Med Ctr; **Address:** Univ Wash Med Ctr, Dept Anesthesiology, 1959 NE Pacific St, Box 356540, Seattle, WA 98195; **Phone:** 206-598-4100; **Board Cert:** Anesthesiology 1996; Pain Medicine 2009; **Med School:** Ireland 1983; **Resid:** Anesthesiology, St Vincent's Hosp 1992; Anesthesiology, Univ Washington Med Ctr 1995; **Fellow:** Pain Medicine, Univ Wash-Pain Mngmt Clinic 1994; **Fac Appt:** Assoc Prof Anes, Univ Wash

Fuller, Nicholas S MD [PM] - **Spec Exp:** Pain Management; **Hospital:** Cedars-Sinai Med Ctr; **Address:** 8929 Wilshire Blvd, Ste 200, Beverly Hills, CA 90211; **Phone:** 310-883-3388; **Board Cert:** Anesthesiology 1996; **Med School:** SUNY Buffalo 1991; **Resid:** Anesthesiology, Brigham & Women's Hosp 1996; **Fellow:** Pain Medicine, Univ Washington Med Ctr 1997

Jasmin, Luc J MD/PhD [PM] - **Spec Exp:** Spinal Cord Stimulation; Spasticity & Movement Disorders; Stereotactic Radiosurgery; Pain-Cancer; **Hospital:** Ashland Community Hosp; **Address:** Ashland Neurosurgery, 521 N Main St, Ashland, OR 97520; **Phone:** 541-414-9814; **Board Cert:** Neurological Surgery 2012; **Med School:** Canada 1981; **Resid:** Neurological Surgery, Notre-Dame Hosp 1984; **Fellow:** Research, UCSF Med Ctr 1985; Neurosurgical Oncology, UCSF Med Ctr 1988

Koh, Jeffrey L MD [PM] - **Spec Exp:** Pain Management-Pediatric; **Hospital:** Doernbecher Chldns Hosp/OHSU, OR Hlth & Sci Univ; **Address:** OHSU - Dept Pain Med, 3181 SW Sam Jackson Park Rd, MC BTE-2, Portland, OR 97239; **Phone:** 503-418-5188; **Board Cert:** Pediatrics 2011; Anesthesiology 1993; Pain Medicine 2007; **Med School:** Wayne State Univ 1985; **Resid:** Pediatrics, Emory Univ Hosp 1988; Anesthesiology, Brigham & Women's Hosp 1991; **Fellow:** Pediatric Anesthesiology, Chldns Hosp 1992; Pediatric Pain Management, UCLA Ronald Reagan Med Ctr 1993; **Fac Appt:** Prof Ped, Oregon Hlth & Sci Univ

Mackey, Sean C MD/PhD [PM] - **Spec Exp:** Pain-Cancer; Pain-Chronic; **Hospital:** Stanford Univ Hosp & Clins; **Address:** Stanford Univ-Pain Mngment Clinic, 450 Broadway St, Redwood City, CA 94063; **Phone:** 650-723-6238; **Board Cert:** Anesthesiology 2009; Pain Medicine 2011; **Med School:** Univ Ariz Coll Med 1994; **Resid:** Anesthesiology, Stanford Univ Med Ctr 1998; **Fellow:** Pain Medicine, Stanford Univ Med Ctr 1999

Prager, Joshua P MD [PM] - **Spec Exp:** Complex Regional Pain Syndromes; Spinal Cord Stimulation; Pain Management; **Hospital:** UCLA Ronald Reagan Med Ctr; **Address:** California Pain Medicine Ctr, 100 UCLA Medical Plaza, Ste 760, Los Angeles, CA 90095; **Phone:** 310-794-7246 x100; **Board Cert:** Internal Medicine 1984; Anesthesiology 1987; Pain Medicine 2004; **Med School:** Stanford Univ 1981; **Resid:** Internal Medicine, UCLA Med Ctr 1983; Anesthesiology, Stanford Hosp 1986; **Fellow:** Anesthesiology, Mass Genl Hosp 1987; **Fac Appt:** Asst Clin Prof Anes, UCLA-David Geffen Sch Med

Rosner, Howard L MD [PM] - **Spec Exp:** Spinal Cord Stimulation; Pain-Back; Pain-Neuropathic; Pain Management; **Hospital:** Cedars-Sinai Med Ctr; **Address:** 444 S San Vincente Blvd, Ste 1101, Los Angeles, CA 90048; **Phone:** 310-423-9749; **Board Cert:** Anesthesiology 1989; Pain Medicine 2004; **Med School:** Univ Miami Sch Med 1980; **Resid:** Anesthesiology, Mass Genl Hosp 1984; **Fellow:** Pain Medicine, Columbia-Presby Med Ctr 1985

Slatkin, Neal E MD [PM] - **Spec Exp:** Pain-Cancer; Palliative Care; **Hospital:** El Camino Hosp, Good Samaritan Hosp - San Jose; **Address:** 4850 Union Ave, San Jose, CA 95124-5156; **Phone:** 408-559-5600; **Board Cert:** Neurology 1982; Pain Medicine 2000; **Med School:** SUNY Stony Brook 1976; **Resid:** Neurology, Bellevue Hosp Ctr-NYU 1978; Neurology, Med Coll Va Hosps 1981; **Fellow:** Neurology, Med Coll Va 1982; Neuro-Oncology, Meml Sloan-Kettering Cancer Ctr 1984

Wallace, Mark Steven MD [PM] - **Spec Exp:** Pain-Chronic; Pain-Cancer; Palliative Care; **Hospital:** UCSD Med Ctr; **Address:** 9350 Campus Point Drive, Ste 2C, La Jolla, CA 92037; **Phone:** 858-657-6035; **Board Cert:** Anesthesiology 1992; Pain Medicine 2005; **Med School:** Creighton Univ 1987; **Resid:** Anesthesiology, Univ Maryland Hosp 1992; **Fellow:** Pain Medicine, UCSD Med Ctr 1994; **Fac Appt:** Prof Anes

Mount Sinai

THE MOUNT SINAI MEDICAL CENTER

Pain Management and Integrative Pain

One Gustave L. Levy Place
Fifth Avenue and 100th Street
New York, NY 10029-6574

Physician Referral: 1-800-MD-SINAI (637-4624)
www.mountsinai.org

The Mount Sinai Medical Center's **DIVISION OF PAIN MANAGEMENT AND INTEGRATIVE PAIN** stands on the cutting edge of this vital and rapidly growing field. Our certified pain physicians deliver a blend of traditional and complementary treatment options to eliminate or reduce pain, restore mobility and enhance the quality of our patients' lives.

Committed to both easing pain and identifying and treating its underlying causes, we begin care by conducting diagnostic tests and a complete examination on all patients. This process helps us identify root conditions, determine optimal therapies, and tailor treatment plans to each patient's medical and personal needs. When our outpatients are admitted to Mount Sinai, we continue treating them inside the hospital, delivering uninterrupted care to achieve the best outcomes.

Offering a Range of Pain Management Treatments

Our team of experts range from specialists with decades of experience to those recently trained in the latest techniques at some of our country's top medical centers. All our physicians excel in core pain management, yet each has a different area of special interest, such as kyphoplasty, integrative medicine, and cancer pain management, permitting us to draw from a wide range of medical perspectives and specialties to provide the best possible course of treatment.

Incorporating Complementary Pain Management Techniques

We incorporate both Eastern and Western medicine within our service. We consider each patient's values and preferences to determine what therapies are most likely to succeed. Our resulting approach might incorporate evidence-based therapies, such as medical acupuncture, cupping (the use of suction to promote healing), and yoga, as well as Western treatments. We also incorporate physical therapy as well as dietary changes; for example, we help patients decrease inflammation by making nutritional changes instead of relying on Ibuprofen.

Delivering Successful Pain Management

There are few absolute cures in medicine, and we can't promise to make all patients pain free, but we do offer everyone the best chance at managing pain effectively. Whether it's helping a cancer patient sleep through the night unburdened by pain, or allowing an arthritic patient to participate in activities with grandchildren, our goal is to reduce pain so our patients can enjoy life to the fullest.

Pathology

A pathologist deals with the causes and nature of disease and contributes to diagnosis, prognosis and treatment through knowledge gained by the laboratory application of the biologic, chemical and physical sciences.

A pathologist uses information gathered from the microscopic examination of tissue specimens, cells and body fluids, and from clinical laboratory tests on body fluids and secretions for the diagnosis, exclusion and monitoring of disease.

Training Required: Five to seven years

Certification in the following subspecialty requires additional training and examination.

Dermatopathology: A dermatopathologist has the expertise to diagnose and monitor diseases of the skin including infectious, immunologic, degenerative and neoplastic diseases. This entails the examination and interpretation of specially prepared tissue sections, cellular scrapings and smears of skin lesions by means of routine and special (electron and flourescent) microscopes.

Pathology

New England

Bhan, Atul K MD [Path] - **Spec Exp:** Immunopathology; Liver Pathology; Liver Cancer; **Hospital:** Mass Genl Hosp; **Address:** Mass Genl Hosp, Dept Pathology, 55 Fruit St, Warren 501, Boston, MA 02114-2620; **Phone:** 617-726-2588; **Board Cert:** Anatomic Pathology 1976; Immunopathology 1985; **Med School:** India 1965; **Resid:** Pathology, Boston Univ Hosp 1971; Pathology, Chldns Univ Hosp 1974; **Fac Appt:** Prof Path, Harvard Med Sch

Chhieng, David Cheung MD [Path] - **Spec Exp:** Pancreatic Cancer; Thyroid Cancer; Cervical Cancer; **Hospital:** Yale-New Haven Hosp; **Address:** Yale, Pathology Dept, 20 York St, Ste CB510, New Haven, CT 06510; **Phone:** 203-737-2658; **Board Cert:** Pathology 1997; Cytopathology 1998; **Med School:** Hong Kong 1987; **Resid:** Pathology, Albany Meml Hosp 1996; **Fellow:** Surgical Pathology, Meml Sloan-Kettering Cancer Ctr 1997; Cytopathology, NYU Med Ctr 1998; **Fac Appt:** Prof Path, Yale Univ

Connolly, James L MD [Path] - **Spec Exp:** Breast Pathology; Breast Cancer; **Hospital:** Beth Israel Deaconess Med Ctr - Boston, Brigham & Women's Hosp; **Address:** BIDMC-Dept of Anatomic Pathology, 330 Brookline Ave, Ste E106, Boston, MA 02215; **Phone:** 617-667-5754; **Board Cert:** Anatomic Pathology 1980; **Med School:** Vanderbilt Univ 1974; **Resid:** Anatomic Pathology, Beth Israel Deaconess Med Ctr 1978; **Fac Appt:** Prof Path, Harvard Med Sch

De Las Morenas, Antonio MD [Path] - **Spec Exp:** Thyroid Disorders; Gynecologic Pathology; Breast Pathology; **Hospital:** Boston Med Ctr; **Address:** Boston Med Ctr, 670 Albany St Fl 3rd - Ste 307, Boston, MA 02118; **Phone:** 617-414-5059; **Board Cert:** Pathology 1989; Cytopathology 1990; **Med School:** Spain 1978; **Resid:** Anatomic Pathology, Boston Med Ctr 1987; **Fellow:** Cytopathology, Hosp Univ Penn 1988; **Fac Appt:** Prof Path, Boston Univ

Fletcher, Christopher DM MD [Path] - **Spec Exp:** Soft Tissue Tumors; Sarcoma; Surgical Pathology; **Hospital:** Brigham & Women's Hosp, Dana-Farber Cancer Inst; **Address:** Brigham & Women's Hosp, Dept Pathology, 75 Francis St, Boston, MA 02115-6110; **Phone:** 617-732-8558; **Med School:** England, UK 1981; **Resid:** Pathology, St Thomas Hosp 1985; **Fellow:** Pathology, St Thomas Hosp 1986; **Fac Appt:** Prof Path, Harvard Med Sch

Gottlieb, Geoffrey J MD [Path] - **Spec Exp:** Dermatopathology; Melanoma; **Address:** StrataDx & Strata Pathology Services, One Cranberry Hill, Ste 303, Lexington, MA 02421; **Phone:** 617-252-6880; **Board Cert:** Anatomic Pathology 1979; Dermatopathology 1982; **Med School:** Cornell Univ-Weill Med Coll 1976; **Resid:** Pathology, NY Hosp-Cornell Med Ctr 1979; **Fellow:** Dermatopathology, NYU Med Ctr 1982

Harris, Nancy L MD [Path] - **Spec Exp:** Lymphoma; Hematopathology; **Hospital:** Mass Genl Hosp; **Address:** Mass Genl Hosp, Dept Pathology, 55 Fruit St, Warren-2, Boston, MA 02114; **Phone:** 617-726-5155; **Board Cert:** Anatomic & Clinical Pathology 1978; **Med School:** Stanford Univ 1970; **Resid:** Pathology, Beth Israel Deaconess Hosp 1978; **Fellow:** Immunopathology, Mass Genl Hosp 1980; **Fac Appt:** Prof Path, Harvard Med Sch

Kaufman, Richard M MD [Path] - **Spec Exp:** Transfusion Medicine; **Hospital:** Brigham & Women's Hosp, Dana-Farber Cancer Inst; **Address:** Brigham & Women's Hosp, 75 Francis St, Boston, MA 02115; **Phone:** 617-732-4749; **Board Cert:** Clinical Pathology 2000; Blood Banking Transfusion Medicine 2002; **Med School:** Washington Univ, St Louis 1992; **Resid:** Pathology, Wash Univ Affi Hosp 2000; **Fellow:** Blood Banking Transfusion Medicine, Wash Univ Affil Hosp 2001; **Fac Appt:** Asst Prof Path, Harvard Med Sch

Mark, Eugene J MD [Path] - **Spec Exp:** Pulmonary Pathology; Forensic Pathology; Occupational Lung Disease; Lung Pathology-Rare Tumors; **Hospital:** Mass Genl Hosp; **Address:** Mass Genl Hosp, Dept Pathology, 55 Fruit St, Warren 246, Boston, MA 02114; **Phone:** 617-726-8891; **Board Cert:** Anatomic & Clinical Pathology 1973; Dermatopathology 1975; **Med School:** Harvard Med Sch 1967; **Resid:** Pathology, Mass Genl Hosp 1972; **Fellow:** Pathology, Kantonspital 1966; **Fac Appt:** Prof Path, Harvard Med Sch

Morrow, Jon S MD/PhD [Path] - **Spec Exp:** Kidney Cancer; Colon Cancer; Breast Cancer; Hematopathology; **Hospital:** Yale-New Haven Hosp; **Address:** Yale, Pathology, 310 Cedar St, BML 140, New Haven, CT 06510; **Phone:** 203-785-3624; **Board Cert:** Pathology 1980; **Med School:** Yale Univ 1976; **Resid:** Pathology, Yale-New Haven Hosp 1978; **Fellow:** Pathology, Yale-New Haven Hosp 1980; **Fac Appt:** Prof Path, Yale Univ

O'Brien, Michael J MD [Path] - **Hospital:** Boston Med Ctr; **Address:** Boston Med Ctr, Dept Anatomic Pathology, 670 Albany St Fl 3, Boston, MA 02118; **Phone:** 617-414-4988; **Board Cert:** Anatomic Pathology 1983; Cytopathology 1997; Cytopathology ; **Med School:** Ireland 1971; **Resid:** Pathology, Univ Hosp 1976; Pathology, Boston Med Ctr 1978; **Fellow:** Gastrointestinal Pathology, Boston Med Ctr 1979; **Fac Appt:** Prof Path, Boston Univ

Odze, Robert D MD [Path] - **Spec Exp:** Gastrointestinal Pathology; Liver Pathology; Esophageal Cancer; **Hospital:** Brigham & Women's Hosp; **Address:** Brigham & Women's Hosp, Dept Pathology, 75 Francis St, Boston, MA 02115; **Phone:** 617-732-7549; **Board Cert:** Anatomic Pathology 1990; **Med School:** McGill Univ 1984; **Resid:** Surgery, McGill Univ Affil Hosp 1987; Pathology, McGill Univ Affil Hosp 1990; **Fellow:** Gastrointestinal Pathology, New England Deaconess Med Ctr 1991; **Fac Appt:** Prof Path, Harvard Med Sch

Rennke, Helmut G MD [Path] - **Spec Exp:** Kidney Pathology; **Hospital:** Brigham & Women's Hosp; **Address:** Brigham & Womens Hosp, Dept Pathology, 75 Francis St Emory Bldg - rm AL 380, Boston, MA 02115; **Phone:** 617-732-6518; **Board Cert:** Anatomic Pathology 1980; **Med School:** Chile 1971; **Resid:** Pathology, Boston Med Ctr 1974; **Fellow:** Renal Pathology, Brigham & Women's Hosp 1977; **Fac Appt:** Prof Path, Harvard Med Sch

Rimm, David MD/PhD [Path] - **Spec Exp:** Gastrointestinal Pathology; Breast Cancer; Melanoma; **Hospital:** Yale-New Haven Hosp; **Address:** Yale, Pathology Dept, 310 Cedar St, Ste 116, New Haven, CT 06510; **Phone:** 203-737-4204; **Board Cert:** Anatomic Pathology 1995; Cytopathology 1996; **Med School:** Johns Hopkins Univ 1989; **Resid:** Pathology, Yale-New Haven Hosp 1993; **Fellow:** Cytopathology, Med Coll VA 1994; **Fac Appt:** Prof Path, Yale Univ

Schnitt, Stuart J MD [Path] - **Spec Exp:** Breast Pathology; Breast Cancer; **Hospital:** Beth Israel Deaconess Med Ctr - Boston; **Address:** BIDMC-Dept of Anatomic Pathology, 330 Brookline Ave, Ste 112, Boston, MA 02215; **Phone:** 617-667-4344; **Board Cert:** Anatomic & Clinical Pathology 1983; **Med School:** Albany Med Coll 1979; **Resid:** Anatomic Pathology, Beth Israel Deaconess Med Ctr 1983; **Fellow:** Surgical Pathology, Beth Israel Deaconess Med Ctr 1984; **Fac Appt:** Assoc Prof Path, Harvard Med Sch

Smith, Thomas W MD [Path] - **Spec Exp:** Neuro-Pathology; **Hospital:** UMass Memorial Med Ctr; **Address:** Univ Mass Dept Pathology, Div Neuropathology, 55 Lake Ave N, Worcester, MA 01655; **Phone:** 508-856-2331; **Board Cert:** Neuropathology 1976; **Med School:** Cornell Univ 1972; **Resid:** Neuropathology, Brigham & Women's Hosp 1976; Radiology, Mass General Hosp 1977; **Fellow:** Anatomic Pathology, Brigham & Women's Hosp 1978; **Fac Appt:** Prof Path, Univ Mass Sch Med

Tavassoli, Fattaneh MD [Path] - **Spec Exp:** Breast Pathology; Gynecologic Pathology; **Hospital:** Yale-New Haven Hosp; **Address:** Yale, Pathology Dept, 310 Cedar St, Ste LH222, New Haven, CT 06510; **Phone:** 203-785-5439; **Board Cert:** Anatomic Pathology 2010; **Med School:** St Louis Univ 1972; **Resid:** Pathology, Barnes-Jewish Hosp 1974; **Fellow:** Gynecologic Pathology, St Johns Mercy Hosp 1976; **Fac Appt:** Prof Path, Yale Univ

Young, Robert H MD [Path] - **Spec Exp:** Gynecologic Pathology; Gynecologic Cancer; **Hospital:** Mass Genl Hosp; **Address:** Mass General Hosp, Dept Pathology, 55 Fruit St Warren Bldg - Ste 215, Boston, MA 02114; **Phone:** 617-726-8892; **Board Cert:** Anatomic Pathology 1980; **Med School:** Ireland 1974; **Resid:** Pathology, Mass Genl Hosp 1979; Pathology, Dublin Univ 1977; **Fac Appt:** Prof Path, Harvard Med Sch

Mid Atlantic

Antonescu, Cristina R MD [Path] - **Spec Exp:** Bone Pathology; Sarcoma-Soft Tissue; Ewing's Sarcoma; **Hospital:** Meml Sloan-Kettering Canc Ctr; **Address:** Meml Sloan Kettering Cancer Ctr, Dept Pathology, 1275 York Ave, New York, NY 10021; **Phone:** 212-639-5905; **Board Cert:** Anatomic Pathology 1998; **Med School:** Romania 1992; **Resid:** Anatomic Pathology, Lenox Hill Hosp 1996; **Fellow:** Pathology-Oncology, Meml Sloan-Kettering Canc Ctr 1997; **Fac Appt:** Assoc Prof Path, Cornell Univ-Weill Med Coll

Bagg, Adam MD [Path] - **Spec Exp:** Hematopathology; Leukemia & Lymphoma; Myelodysplastic Syndromes; **Hospital:** Hosp Univ Penn - UPHS (page 69); **Address:** Hosp Univ Penn, Dept Pathology & Lab Medicine, 3400 Spruce St, 7-103 Founders, Phildelphia, PA 19104; **Phone:** 215-662-6550; **Board Cert:** Clinical Pathology 1992; Hematology 1999; **Med School:** South Africa 1981; **Resid:** Internal Medicine, Univ Witwatersrand Hosp 1992; Clinical Pathology, Georgetown Univ 1992; **Fellow:** Hematopathology, Georgetown Univ 1993; **Fac Appt:** Prof Path, Univ Pennsylvania

Baloch, Zubair W MD/PhD [Path] - **Spec Exp:** Endocrine Pathology; Thyroid Disorders; Thyroid Cancer; **Hospital:** Hosp Univ Penn - UPHS (page 69); **Address:** Hosp U Penn-Dept Path & Lab Medicine, 3400 Spruce St, Founders Bldg - Fl 6, Philadelphia, PA 19104; **Phone:** 215-662-6503; **Board Cert:** Anatomic & Clinical Pathology 1995; Cytopathology 1997; **Med School:** Pakistan 1985; **Resid:** Pathology, Hahnemann Univ Hosp 1995; **Fellow:** Surgical Oncology Pathology, Meml Sloan-Kettering Canc Ctr 1996; Cytopathology, Hosp U Penn 1997; **Fac Appt:** Prof Path, Univ Pennsylvania

Bleiweiss, Ira J MD [Path] - **Spec Exp:** Breast Pathology; Breast Cancer; **Hospital:** Mt Sinai Med Ctr (page 62); **Address:** Mt Sinai Med Ctr, Dept Pathology, 1 Gustave Levy Pl, Box 1194, New York, NY 10029-6504; **Phone:** 212-241-9159; **Board Cert:** Anatomic & Clinical Pathology 1988; **Med School:** West Indies 1984; **Resid:** Pathology, Mt Sinai Med Ctr 1988; **Fellow:** Surgical Pathology, Mt Sinai Med Ctr 1989; Surgical Pathology, Meml-Sloan Kettering Cancer Ctr 1990; **Fac Appt:** Prof Path, Mount Sinai Sch Med

Brooks, John S MD [Path] - **Spec Exp:** Bone & Soft Tissue Pathology; Sarcoma; **Hospital:** Pennsylvania Hosp-UPHS (page 69); **Address:** Pennsylvania Hospital, 800 Spruce St, Preston, 6th Fl, Philadelphia, PA 19107; **Phone:** 215-829-3541; **Board Cert:** Anatomic Pathology 1978; Immunopathology 1983; **Med School:** Thomas Jefferson Univ 1974; **Resid:** Pathology, Hosp Univ Penn 1978; **Fac Appt:** Prof Path, Univ Pennsylvania

Burger, Peter MD [Path] - **Spec Exp:** Brain Tumors; Neuro-Pathology; **Hospital:** Johns Hopkins Hosp (page 59); **Address:** Johns Hopkins Hosp, Div Pathology, 1800 Orleans St, Sheikh Zayed Tower, M-2101, Baltimore, MD 21231; **Phone:** 410-955-8378; **Board Cert:** Anatomic Pathology 1976; Neuropathology 1976; **Med School:** Northwestern Univ 1966; **Resid:** Anatomic Pathology, Duke Univ Med Ctr 1973; **Fellow:** Neuropathology, Duke Univ Med Ctr 1973

Crawford, James M MD/PhD [Path] - **Spec Exp:** Liver Pathology; Gastrointestinal Pathology; Gastrointestinal Cancer; **Hospital:** N Shore Univ Hosp (page 66), Long Is Jewish Med Ctr (page 66); **Address:** N Shore-LIJHS Laboratories, 10 Nevada Drive, Lake Success, NY 11042-1114; **Phone:** 516-719-1061; **Board Cert:** Anatomic Pathology 1987; **Med School:** Duke Univ 1982; **Resid:** Pathology, Duke Univ Med Ctr 1983; Pathology, Brigham & Women's Hosp 1987; **Fellow:** Gastrointestinal Pathology, Brigham & Women's Hosp 1987; Research, Royal Free hosp 1989; **Fac Appt:** Prof Path, Hofstra N Shore-LIJ Sch Med

Demetris, Anthony J MD [Path] - **Spec Exp:** Transplant Pathology; Liver Pathology; **Hospital:** UPMC Montefiore; **Address:** UPMC, Pathology Dept, 3459 5th Ave, rm E741, Pittsburgh, PA 15213; **Phone:** 412-647-2067; **Board Cert:** Anatomic & Clinical Pathology 1987; **Med School:** Univ Pittsburgh 1982; **Resid:** Anatomic & Clinical Pathology, UPMC 1986; **Fac Appt:** Prof Path, Univ Pittsburgh

Ehya, Hormoz MD [Path] - **Spec Exp:** Cytopathology; Breast Pathology; Lung Pathology; Fine Needle Aspiration Biopsy; **Hospital:** Fox Chase Cancer Ctr (page 57); **Address:** Fox Chase Cancer Center, 333 Cottman Ave, rm C427, Philadelphia, PA 19111-2497; **Phone:** 215-728-5389; **Board Cert:** Anatomic Pathology 1979; Cytopathology 1989; **Med School:** Iran 1974; **Resid:** Pathology, Univ Mississippi Med Ctr 1979; **Fellow:** Cytopathology, Meml Sloan-Kettering Cancer Ctr 1980; **Fac Appt:** Prof Path, Temple Univ

Epstein, Jonathan MD [Path] - **Spec Exp:** Bladder Cancer; Prostate Cancer; Urologic Pathology; **Hospital:** Johns Hopkins Hosp (page 59); **Address:** 401 N Broadway, Weinberg 2242, Baltimore, MD 21231; **Phone:** 410-955-5043; **Board Cert:** Anatomic Pathology 1986; **Med School:** Boston Univ 1981; **Resid:** Pathology, Johns Hopkins Hosp 1985; **Fellow:** Pathology, Meml Sloan-Kettering Cancer Ctr 1984; **Fac Appt:** Prof Path, Johns Hopkins Univ

Fogt, Franz MD/PhD [Path] - **Spec Exp:** Gastrointestinal Pathology; Ophthalmic Pathology; **Hospital:** Penn Presby Med Ctr - UPHS (page 69); **Address:** Penn Presbyterian-Dept Pathology, 51 N 39th St, W542 Wright Saunders Bldg, Philadelphia, PA 19104; **Phone:** 215-662-8077; **Board Cert:** Anatomic & Clinical Pathology 1995; **Med School:** Germany 1988; **Resid:** Anatomic & Clinical Pathology, New England Deaconess Hosp 1995; **Fellow:** Gastrointestinal Pathology, New England Deaconess Hosp 1996; **Fac Appt:** Prof Path, Univ Pennsylvania

Gupta, Prabodh K MD [Path] - **Spec Exp:** Lung Pathology; Cervical Cancer; Fine Needle Aspiration Biopsy; **Hospital:** Hosp Univ Penn - UPHS (page 69); **Address:** 3400 Spruce St, Philadelphia, PA 19104; **Phone:** 215-662-3238; **Board Cert:** Anatomic Pathology 1975; Cytopathology 1989; **Med School:** India 1960; **Resid:** Pathology, All India Inst Med Scis 1967; **Fellow:** Pathology, Mass Genl Hosp 1968; Cytopathology, Johns Hopkins Hosp 1969; **Fac Appt:** Prof Path, Univ Pennsylvania

Heller, Debra S MD [Path] - **Spec Exp:** Gynecologic Pathology; Pediatric Pathology; Perinatal Pathology; **Hospital:** Univ Hosp (Newark); **Address:** UMDNJ-NJ Med Sch Dept Pathology, 185 S Orange Ave, Newark, NJ 07101; **Phone:** 973-972-0751; **Board Cert:** Anatomic Pathology 1988; Obstetrics & Gynecology 2012; Pediatric Pathology 1999; **Med School:** NY Med Coll 1977; **Resid:** Obstetrics & Gynecology, Beth Israel Med Ctr 1981; Anatomic Pathology, Mt Sinai Med Ctr 1988; **Fellow:** Pediatric Pathology, Mt Sinai Med Ctr 1987; Gynecologic Pathology, Mt Sinai Med Ctr 1989; **Fac Appt:** Prof Path, UMDNJ-NJ Med Sch, Newark

Hoda, Syed A MD [Path] - **Spec Exp:** Breast Cancer; Surgical Pathology; **Hospital:** NY-Presby/Weill Cornell Med Ctr, NY (page 65); **Address:** 525 E 68th St, 1028 Starr, New York, NY 10021-4870; **Phone:** 212-746-2700; **Board Cert:** Anatomic & Clinical Pathology 2012; Cytopathology 1991; **Med School:** Pakistan 1984; **Resid:** Anatomic & Clinical Pathology, Tulane Univ Affil Hosps 1990; **Fellow:** Cytopathology, Meml Sloan Kettering Cancer Ctr 1991; Pathology, Meml Sloan Kettering Cancer Ctr 1992; **Fac Appt:** Clin Prof Path, Cornell Univ-Weill Med Coll

Hruban, Ralph H MD [Path] - **Spec Exp:** Gastrointestinal Pathology; Pancreatic Cancer; **Hospital:** Johns Hopkins Hosp (page 59); **Address:** Johns Hopkins Hosp, Dept Pathology, 401 N Broadway, Weinberg Bldg - rm 2242, Baltimore, MD 21231; **Phone:** 410-955-2163; **Board Cert:** Anatomic Pathology 1990; **Med School:** Johns Hopkins Univ 1985; **Resid:** Pathology, Johns Hopkins Hosp 1990; **Fellow:** Anatomic Pathology, Meml Sloan-Kettering Cancer Ctr 1989; **Fac Appt:** Prof Path, Johns Hopkins Univ

Kahn, Leonard B MD [Path] - **Spec Exp:** Bone Pathology; Head & Neck Pathology; Soft Tissue Tumors; Jaw Tumors; **Hospital:** Long Is Jewish Med Ctr (page 66), N Shore Univ Hosp (page 66); **Address:** 6 Ohio Drive, Ste 202 - rm 21, Lake Success, NY 10042; **Phone:** 516-304-7264; **Board Cert:** Anatomic Pathology 1980; **Med School:** South Africa 1960; **Resid:** Pathology, Univ Cape Town Affil Hosp 1966; **Fellow:** Surgical Pathology, Washington Univ Affil Hosp 1969; **Fac Appt:** Prof Path, Albert Einstein Coll Med

Katzenstein, Anna-Luise A MD [Path] - **Spec Exp:** Lung Cancer; Pulmonary Pathology; Interstitial Lung Disease; **Hospital:** SUNY Upstate Med Univ Hosp; **Address:** SUNY Upstate Medical Univ, 750 E Adams St, UH Bldg, rm 6709, Syracuse, NY 13210; **Phone:** 315-464-7125; **Board Cert:** Anatomic Pathology 1976; **Med School:** Johns Hopkins Univ 1971; **Resid:** Pathology, Univ Hosp 1975; **Fellow:** Surgical Pathology, Barnes Hosp-Wash Univ 1976; **Fac Appt:** Prof Path, SUNY Upstate Med Univ

Klimstra, David MD [Path] - **Spec Exp:** Gastrointestinal Pathology; Pulmonary Pathology; **Hospital:** Meml Sloan-Kettering Canc Ctr; **Address:** Meml Sloan Kettering Canc Ctr, Dept Pathology, 1275 York Ave, New York, NY 10065; **Phone:** 212-639-5905; **Board Cert:** Anatomic Pathology 1992; **Med School:** Yale Univ 1988; **Resid:** Pathology, Yale New Haven Hosp 1991; **Fellow:** Pathology, Meml Sloan Kettering Canc Ctr 1992; **Fac Appt:** Asst Prof Path, Cornell Univ

Kurman, Robert J MD [Path] - **Spec Exp:** Gynecologic Pathology; Ovarian Cancer; Uterine Cancer; **Hospital:** Johns Hopkins Hosp (page 59); **Address:** Johns Hopkins Hosp, Div Gyn Pathology, 401 N Broadway, Weinberg 2242, Baltimore, MD 21231; **Phone:** 443-287-4996; **Board Cert:** Anatomic Pathology 1972; Obstetrics & Gynecology 1980; **Med School:** SUNY Upstate Med Univ 1968; **Resid:** Pathology, Peter Bent Brigham Hosp/Mass Genl Hosp 1970; Obstetrics & Gynecology, LAC Hosp/USC 1978; **Fellow:** Gynecologic Pathology, Brigham & Women's Hosp 1973; **Fac Appt:** Prof Path, Johns Hopkins Univ

LiVolsi, Virginia A MD [Path] - **Spec Exp:** Endocrine Cancers; Thyroid Cancer; Gynecologic Cancer; **Hospital:** Hosp Univ Penn - UPHS (page 69); **Address:** Hosp Univ Penn - Pathology, 3400 Spruce St, Founders 6, rm 6009, Philadelphia, PA 19104; **Phone:** 215-662-6545; **Board Cert:** Anatomic Pathology 1974; **Med School:** Columbia P&S 1969; **Resid:** Anatomic Pathology, Presbyterian Hosp 1974; **Fac Appt:** Prof Path, Univ Pennsylvania

Melamed, Jonathan MD [Path] - **Spec Exp:** Prostate Cancer; Tumor Banking-Prostate; **Hospital:** NYU Langone Med Ctr (page 68); **Address:** NYU Medical Ctr, Dept Pathology, TH-461, 560 First Ave, New York, NY 10016; **Phone:** 212-263-8927; **Board Cert:** Anatomic & Clinical Pathology 1992; **Med School:** South Africa 1985; **Resid:** Pathology, Lenox Hill Hosp 1991; **Fellow:** Pathology, Meml Sloan Kettering Cancer Ctr 1992; Urologic Pathology, Meml Sloan Kettering Cancer Ctr 1993; **Fac Appt:** Prof Path, NYU Sch Med

Mies, Carolyn MD [Path] - **Spec Exp:** Breast Cancer; Breast Pathology; **Hospital:** Hosp Univ Penn - UPHS (page 69); **Address:** Hosp Univ Penn-Surgical Pathology, 3400 Spruce St, 6 Founders, Philadelphia, PA 19104; **Phone:** 215-662-6503; **Board Cert:** Anatomic Pathology 1984; **Med School:** Rush Med Coll 1980; **Resid:** Pathology, Tufts-New England Med Ctr 1982; Pathology, New England Deaconess Hosp 1984; **Fellow:** Surgical Pathology, Meml Sloan Kettering Cancer Ctr 1986; **Fac Appt:** Assoc Prof Path, Univ Pennsylvania

Montgomery, Elizabeth A MD [Path] - **Spec Exp:** Barrett's Esophagus; Gastrointestinal Pathology; Soft Tissue Pathology; **Hospital:** Johns Hopkins Hosp (page 59); **Address:** Johns Hopkins Univ, Dept Pathology, 401 N Broadway Weinberg Bldg - rm 2242, Baltimore, MD 21231; **Phone:** 410-614-2308; **Board Cert:** Anatomic Pathology 1988; Cytopathology 1994; **Med School:** Geo Wash Univ 1984; **Resid:** Pathology, Walter Reed AMC 1988; **Fac Appt:** Prof Path, Johns Hopkins Univ

Orazi, Attilio MD [Path] - **Spec Exp:** Hematopathology; Bone Marrow Pathology; Lymph Node Pathology; Spleen Pathology; **Hospital:** NY-Presby/Weill Cornell Med Ctr, NY (page 65); **Address:** NY Presby-Cornell Medical Ctr, 525 E 68th St, Starr Pavilion, rm 715, New York, NY 10065; **Phone:** 212-746-2050; **Board Cert:** Anatomic Pathology 1997; Hematology 1998; **Med School:** Italy 1979; **Resid:** Internal Medicine, Leicester Royal Infirmary 1982; Histopathology, Northampton Genl Hosp 1983; **Fellow:** Anatomic Pathology, Natl Cancer Inst 1985; **Fac Appt:** Prof Path, Cornell Univ-Weill Med Coll

Patchefsky, Arthur S MD [Path] - **Spec Exp:** Breast Cancer; Pulmonary Pathology; Sarcoma; **Hospital:** Fox Chase Cancer Ctr (page 57); **Address:** Fox Chase Cancer Center, 333 Cottman Ave, rm C433, Philadelphia, PA 19111; **Phone:** 215-728-5389; **Board Cert:** Anatomic Pathology 1969; **Med School:** Hahnemann Univ 1963; **Resid:** Pathology, Johns Hopkins Hosp 1966; Pathology, Hosp Univ Penn 1967; **Fellow:** Pathology, Meml Sloan Kettering Cancer Ctr 1968; **Fac Appt:** Prof Path, Thomas Jefferson Univ

Reuter, Victor E MD [Path] - **Spec Exp:** Prostate Cancer; Genitourinary Pathology; Bladder Cancer; Testicular Cancer; **Hospital:** Meml Sloan-Kettering Canc Ctr; **Address:** Memorial Sloan Kettering Cancer Ctr, Dept Pathology, 1275 York Ave, New York, NY 10021; **Phone:** 212-639-6780; **Board Cert:** Anatomic & Clinical Pathology 1983; **Med School:** Dominican Republic 1978; **Resid:** Anatomic Pathology, Thos Jefferson Univ Hosp 1981; Clinical Pathology, Thos Jefferson Univ Hosp 1983; **Fellow:** Surgical Pathology, Meml Sloan Kettering Cancer Ctr 1985; **Fac Appt:** Prof Path, Cornell Univ-Weill Med Coll

Ronnett, Brigitte M MD [Path] - **Spec Exp:** Gynecologic Pathology; Gynecologic Cancer; **Hospital:** Johns Hopkins Hosp (page 59); **Address:** Johns Hopkins Hosp, 401 N Broadway, Weinberg Bldg - rm 2242, Baltimore, MD 21231; **Phone:** 410-614-2971; **Board Cert:** Clinical Pathology 1993; Anatomic Pathology 1991; **Med School:** Univ Chicago-Pritzker Sch Med 1986; **Resid:** Pathology, Johns Hopkins Hosp 1989; Pathology, Johns Hopkins Hosp 1991; **Fellow:** Gynecologic Pathology, Johns Hopkins Hosp 1995; Surgical Pathology, Meml Sloan-Kettering Cancer Ctr 1990; **Fac Appt:** Prof Path, Johns Hopkins Univ

Rosenblum, Marc K MD [Path] - **Spec Exp:** Neuro-Pathology; Brain Tumors; **Hospital:** Meml Sloan-Kettering Canc Ctr; **Address:** Meml Sloan-Kettering Cancer Ctr, 1275 York Ave, New York, NY 10065; **Phone:** 212-639-3844; **Board Cert:** Anatomic Pathology 1984; Neuropathology 1988; **Med School:** Univ Miami Sch Med 1979; **Resid:** Anatomic Pathology, Mt Sinai Med Ctr 1984; **Fellow:** Pathology, Meml Sloan-Kettering Cancer Ctr 1985; Neurological Pathology, Bellevue-NYU Med Ctr 1987; **Fac Appt:** Prof Path, Cornell Univ-Weill Med Coll

Ross, Jeffrey S MD [Path] - **Spec Exp:** Urologic Cancer; Prostate Cancer; Breast Cancer; **Hospital:** Albany Med Ctr; **Address:** Affiliated Pathology Services, 47 New Scotland Ave, MC 80, Albany, NY 12208; **Phone:** 518-262-5471; **Board Cert:** Anatomic & Clinical Pathology 1974; **Med School:** SUNY Buffalo 1970; **Resid:** Anatomic & Clinical Pathology, Mass Genl Hosp 1974; **Fac Appt:** Prof Path, Albany Med Coll

Sanchez, Miguel A MD [Path] - **Spec Exp:** Breast Cancer; Thyroid Cancer; **Hospital:** Englewood Hosp & Med Ctr; **Address:** 350 Engle St, Dean Bldg - Fl LL1, Englewood, NJ 07631-1898; **Phone:** 201-894-3423; **Board Cert:** Anatomic Pathology 1975; Clinical Pathology 1979; Cytopathology 1991; **Med School:** Spain 1969; **Resid:** Pathology, Englewood Hosp 1972; Pathology, Temple Univ 1973; **Fellow:** Pathology, Meml Sloan Kettering Cancer Ctr 1974; Clinical Pathology, St Vincents Hosp 1975; **Fac Appt:** Assoc Prof Path, Mount Sinai Sch Med

Silverman, Jan F MD [Path] - **Spec Exp:** Fine Needle Aspiration Biopsy; Surgical Pathology; Gastrointestinal Pathology; Cytopathology; **Hospital:** Allegheny Genl Hosp, West Penn Hosp-Forbes Campus; **Address:** Allegheny Gen Hosp-Dept Lab Medicine, 320 E North Ave, Pittsburgh, PA 15212; **Phone:** 412-359-6886; **Board Cert:** Anatomic & Clinical Pathology 1975; Cytopathology 1989; **Med School:** Med Coll VA 1970; **Resid:** Pathology, Med Coll Virginia Hosps 1975; **Fellow:** Surgical Pathology, Med Coll Virginia Hosps 1975; **Fac Appt:** Prof Path, Drexel Univ Coll Med

Soslow, Robert A MD [Path] - **Spec Exp:** Gynecologic Pathology; **Hospital:** Meml Sloan-Kettering Canc Ctr; **Address:** 1275 York Avenue, Pathology Department, New York, NY 10065; **Phone:** 212-639-5905; **Board Cert:** Anatomic Pathology 1995; **Med School:** Univ Pennsylvania 1991; **Resid:** Anatomic Pathology, Stanford Univ Med Ctr 1994; **Fellow:** Immunopathology, Stanford Univ Med Ctr 1995; **Fac Appt:** Assoc Prof Path, Cornell Univ

Swerdlow, Steven H MD [Path] - **Spec Exp:** Lymphoma; Hematopathology; Transplant Pathology; **Hospital:** UPMC Presby, Pittsburgh; **Address:** University of Pittsburgh Physicians, Div Hematopathology, 200 Lothrop St, Ste G-300, Pittsburgh, PA 15213-2536; **Phone:** 412-647-5191; **Board Cert:** Anatomic & Clinical Pathology 2005; **Med School:** Harvard Med Sch 1975; **Resid:** Pathology, Beth Israel Hosp 1979; **Fellow:** Hematopathology, Vanderbilt Univ 1981; Hematopathology, St Bartholmew's Hosp 1983; **Fac Appt:** Prof Path, Univ Pittsburgh

Tomaszewski, John E MD [Path] - **Spec Exp:** Kidney Pathology; Genitourinary Pathology; Immunopathology; **Hospital:** Buffalo Genl Hosp, Women & Chldn's Hosp of Buffalo, The; **Address:** Pathology and Anatomical Sciences, 206 Farber Hall, South Campus, 3435 Main St, Buffalo, NY 14214; **Phone:** 716-352-7370; **Board Cert:** Anatomic Pathology 1982; Immunopathology 1983; **Med School:** Univ Pennsylvania 1977; **Resid:** Pathology, Hosp Univ Penn 1982; **Fellow:** Surgical Pathology, Hosp Univ Penn 1983; Renal Pathology, Columbia Univ Affil Hosp 1984; **Fac Appt:** Prof Path, SUNY Buffalo

Tornos, Carmen MD [Path] - **Spec Exp:** Gynecologic Cancer; Breast Cancer; Ovarian Cancer; **Hospital:** Stony Brook Univ Med Ctr; **Address:** Stony Brook Univ Hosp, Dept Pathology, 10 Nicolls Rd, HSC Level 2, rm 766, Stony Brook, NY 11794; **Phone:** 631-444-2222; **Board Cert:** Anatomic & Clinical Pathology 1989; **Med School:** Spain 1977; **Resid:** Hematology, Ciudad Sanitaria Valle de Hebron 1982; Anatomic & Clinical Pathology, Univ Texas HSC 1989; **Fellow:** Surgical Pathology, MD Anderson Cancer Ctr 1990; **Fac Appt:** Prof Path, SUNY Stony Brook

Travis, William D MD [Path] - **Spec Exp:** Pulmonary Pathology; Lung Cancer; **Hospital:** Meml Sloan-Kettering Canc Ctr; **Address:** Meml Sloan Kettering Cancer Ctr-Dept Path, 1275 York Ave, New York, NY 10065; **Phone:** 212-639-6364; **Board Cert:** Anatomic & Clinical Pathology 1985; **Med School:** Univ Fla Coll Med 1981; **Resid:** Anatomic Pathology, New England Deaconess Hosp 1983; Clinical Pathology, Mayo Clinic 1985; **Fellow:** Surgical Pathology, Mayo Clinic 1986

Wang, Beverly Y MD [Path] - **Spec Exp:** Head & Neck Pathology; **Hospital:** Beth Israel Med Ctr - Petrie Div (page 56); **Address:** Beth Israel Medical Ctr, Dept Pathology, First Avenue at 16th St, Silver Bldg Fl 11, New York, NY 10003; **Phone:** 212-844-1959; **Board Cert:** Anatomic Pathology 1998; Cytopathology 1999; **Med School:** China 1982; **Resid:** Pathology, Mount Sinai Med Ctr 1998; **Fellow:** Cytopathology, Mount Sinai Med Ctr 1999; **Fac Appt:** Prof Path, Albert Einstein Coll Med

Yousem, Samuel A MD [Path] - **Spec Exp:** Pulmonary Pathology; Transplant-Lung; Lung Cancer; **Hospital:** UPMC Presby, Pittsburgh; **Address:** UPMC Presbyterian Hosp, Dept Pathology, 200 Lothrop St, A-610, Pittsburgh, PA 15213; **Phone:** 412-647-6193; **Board Cert:** Anatomic Pathology 1985; Cytopathology 1997; **Med School:** Univ MD Sch Med 1981; **Resid:** Pathology, Stanford Univ Med Ctr 1983; **Fellow:** Surgical Pathology, Stanford Univ Med Ctr 1984; **Fac Appt:** Prof Path, Univ Pittsburgh

Zagzag, David MD/PhD [Path] - **Spec Exp:** Neuro-Pathology; Brain Tumors; Tumor Banking-Brain; **Hospital:** NYU Langone Med Ctr (page 68), Bellevue Hosp Ctr; **Address:** NYU Med Ctr, Dept Pathology, 550 First Ave, Div Neuropathology, NB-4N30, New York, NY 10016; **Phone:** 212-263-6449; **Board Cert:** Anatomic Pathology 1993; Neuropathology 1993; **Med School:** France 1984; **Resid:** Surgical Pathology, NYU Med Ctr 1990; **Fellow:** Neurological Pathology, NYU Med Ctr 1992; **Fac Appt:** Assoc Prof Path, NYU Sch Med

Southeast

Banks, Peter MD [Path] - **Spec Exp:** Hematopathology; Lymphoma; **Hospital:** Carolinas Med Ctr; **Address:** Dept Pathology, 1000 Blythe Blvd Fl 4, Charlotte, NC 28203; **Phone:** 704-355-2251; **Board Cert:** Anatomic Pathology 2008; **Med School:** Harvard Med Sch 1971; **Resid:** Pathology, Natl Cancer Inst 1974; Pathology, Duke Univ Med Ctr 1975; **Fellow:** Surgical Pathology, Univ Minn Med Ctr 1976; **Fac Appt:** Prof Path, Univ NC Sch Med

Bostwick, David MD [Path] - **Spec Exp:** Urologic Pathology; Prostate Cancer; Bladder Cancer; Gastrointestinal Pathology; **Address:** 4355 Innslake Drive, Glen Allen, VA 23060; **Phone:** 804-967-9225; **Board Cert:** Anatomic Pathology 2003; **Med School:** Univ MD Sch Med 1979; **Resid:** Pathology, Stanford Univ Hosp & Clin 1981; **Fellow:** Surgical Pathology, Stanford Univ Hosp & Clin 1984

Chesney, Carolyn M MD [Path] - **Spec Exp:** Hematopathology; Bleeding/Coagulation Disorders; **Hospital:** Univ of Tennesee Med Ctr; **Address:** Pathology Group of the MidSouth, 7550 Wolf River Blvd, Ste 200, Germantown, TN 38138; **Phone:** 901-542-6801; **Board Cert:** Internal Medicine 1972; Hematology 1999; **Med School:** Vanderbilt Univ 1968; **Resid:** Internal Medicine, Vanderbilt Univ Hosp 1970; **Fellow:** Hematology, Mass Genl Hosp 1972; **Fac Appt:** Prof Hem, Univ Tenn Coll Med

Cote, Richard J MD [Path] - **Spec Exp:** Lymph Node Pathology; Bladder Cancer; Breast Cancer; **Hospital:** Univ of Miami Hosp, Jackson Meml Hosp; **Address:** UHlth, Pathology Dept, 1120 NW 14th St CRB Bldg - Ste 1416, Miami, FL 33136; **Phone:** 305-243-2683; **Board Cert:** Anatomic Pathology 1987; **Med School:** Univ Chicago-Pritzker Sch Med 1980; **Resid:** Pathology, NY Hosp 1987; **Fellow:** Pathology, Meml Sloan-Kettering Cancer Ctr 1990; **Fac Appt:** Prof Path, Univ Miami Sch Med

Faye-Petersen, Ona MD [Path] - **Spec Exp:** Perinatal Pathology; Fetal Pathology; Neonatal Pathology; Pediatric Pathology; **Hospital:** UAB Hosp, UAB Highlands Hosp; **Address:** UAB Hosp, Dept Pathology, 619 19th St S, NP 3547, Birmingham, AL 35249; **Phone:** 205-975-8880; **Board Cert:** Anatomic & Clinical Pathology 1987; Pediatric Pathology 1991; **Med School:** Univ Colorado 1980; **Resid:** Pathology, Presby - St Luke's Med Ctr 1985; **Fellow:** Surgical Pathology, Meml Sloan-Kettering Canc Ctr 1986; Pediatric Pathology, Mt Sinai Med Ctr 1987; **Fac Appt:** Prof Path, UAB Sch Med

Lage, Janice M MD [Path] - **Spec Exp:** Obstetric Pathology; Gynecologic Pathology; Breast Pathology; **Hospital:** Univ Mississippi Med Ctr; **Address:** University of Mississippi Medical Center, 2500 N State St, Jackson, MS 39216; **Phone:** 601-984-1540; **Board Cert:** Anatomic Pathology 1985; **Med School:** Washington Univ, St Louis 1980; **Resid:** Pathology, Barnes Hosp/Wash Univ 1982; Obstetrics & Gynecology, Barnes Hosp/Wash Univ 1983; **Fellow:** Surgical Pathology, Barnes Hosp/Wash Univ 1984; **Fac Appt:** Prof Path, Univ Miss

Masood, Shahla MD [Path] - **Spec Exp:** Breast Cancer; Breast Pathology; **Hospital:** UF Hlth Jacksonville; **Address:** Univ of FL Coll of Med - Jacksonville, 655 W 8th St, Jacksonville, FL 32209-6511; **Phone:** 904-244-4387; **Board Cert:** Anatomic & Clinical Pathology 1977; Cytopathology 1990; **Med School:** Iran 1973; **Resid:** Anatomic Pathology, Univ Hosp 1977; **Fac Appt:** Prof Path, Univ Fla Coll Med

Mills, Stacey E MD [Path] - **Spec Exp:** Surgical Pathology; Cytopathology; Bone & Soft Tissue Pathology; **Hospital:** Univ of Virginia Hlth Sys; **Address:** UVA Dept of Pathology, 1215 Lee St, rm 3022, Charlottesville, VA 22908-0214; **Phone:** 434-982-4406; **Board Cert:** Anatomic Pathology 2009; **Med School:** Univ VA Sch Med 1977; **Resid:** Anatomic Pathology, Univ VA Hosp 1979; **Fellow:** Surgical Pathology, Univ VA Hosp 1980; **Fac Appt:** Prof Path, Univ VA Sch Med

Nicosia, Santo MD [Path] - **Spec Exp:** Ovarian Cancer; Cytopathology; **Hospital:** Moffitt Canc Ctr (page 61); **Address:** USF Hlth, Pathology Dept, 12901 Bruce B Downs Blvd, Tampa, FL 33612-4742; **Phone:** 813-974-0536; **Board Cert:** Anatomic Pathology 1978; Cytopathology 1990; **Med School:** Italy 1967; **Resid:** Anatomic Pathology, Michael Reese Hosp & Med Ctr 1972; **Fellow:** Reproductive Medicine, Hosp Univ Penn 1973; **Fac Appt:** Prof Path, Univ S Fla Coll Med

Petito, Carol K MD [Path] - **Spec Exp:** Neuro-Pathology; **Hospital:** Jackson Meml Hosp; **Address:** UHlth, Pathology Dept R-5, 1550 NW 10th Ave, Miami, FL 33136; **Phone:** 305-585-8970; **Board Cert:** Anatomic Pathology 1973; Neuropathology 1973; **Med School:** Columbia P&S 1967; **Resid:** Pathology, NY-Presby/Weill Cornell Med Ctr 1970; Neuropathology, Armed Forces Inst; **Fac Appt:** Prof Path, Univ Miami Sch Med

Rosenberg, Andrew E MD [Path] - **Spec Exp:** Bone & Joint Pathology; **Hospital:** Univ of Miami Hosp; **Address:** UHlth, Pathology Dept, 1400 NW 12th Ave, rm 4076, Miami, FL 33136; **Phone:** 305-243-8730; **Board Cert:** Anatomic Pathology 1985; **Med School:** Temple Univ 1981; **Resid:** Anatomic Pathology, Mass Genl Hosp 1984; **Fellow:** Immunopathology, Mass Genl Hosp 1985; **Fac Appt:** Prof Path, Univ Miami Sch Med

Sewell, C. Whitaker MD [Path] - **Spec Exp:** Breast Pathology; Surgical Pathology; **Hospital:** Emory Univ Hosp; **Address:** Emory Univ Hosp, Pathology Dept, 1364 Clifton Rd NE, rm H185C, Atlanta, GA 30322; **Phone:** 404-712-7003; **Board Cert:** Anatomic & Clinical Pathology 1974; **Med School:** Emory Univ 1969; **Resid:** Pathology, Emory Univ Hosp 1974; **Fac Appt:** Prof Path, Emory Univ

Weiss, Sharon A W MD [Path] - **Spec Exp:** Soft Tissue Pathology; Surgical Pathology; Sarcoma; **Hospital:** Emory Univ Hosp; **Address:** Emory Univ Hosp, Pathology Dept, 1364 Clifton Rd NE, rm H176, Atlanta, GA 30322; **Phone:** 404-712-0708; **Board Cert:** Anatomic Pathology 1974; **Med School:** Johns Hopkins Univ 1971; **Resid:** Pathology, Johns Hopkins Hosp 1975; **Fac Appt:** Prof Path, Emory Univ

Midwest

Allred, D. Craig MD [Path] - **Spec Exp:** Breast Cancer; Breast Pathology; Breast Cancer Risk Assessment; **Hospital:** Barnes-Jewish Hosp; **Address:** Washington Univ Sch Med, Dept Pathology, 660 S Euclid Ave, Box 8118, St Louis, MO 63110; **Phone:** 314-362-6313; **Board Cert:** Anatomic Pathology 1984; **Med School:** Univ Utah 1979; **Resid:** Anatomic Pathology, Univ Conn Hlth Ctr 1983; **Fellow:** Immunopathology, Univ Conn Hlth Ctr 1982; **Fac Appt:** Prof Path, Baylor Coll Med

Appelman, Henry MD [Path] - **Spec Exp:** Gastrointestinal Pathology; Liver Pathology; **Hospital:** Univ Michigan Med Ctr; **Address:** 1301 Catherine St, rm M5220, Box 5602, Ann Arbor, MI 48109-5602; **Phone:** 734-936-6770; **Board Cert:** Anatomic & Clinical Pathology 1966; **Med School:** Univ Mich Med Sch 1961; **Resid:** Pathology, Univ Mich Med Ctr 1966; **Fac Appt:** Prof Path, Univ Mich Med Sch

Balla, Andre K MD/PhD [Path] - **Spec Exp:** Prostate Cancer; Gynecologic Pathology; Tumor Banking; **Hospital:** Univ of IL Med Ctr at Chicago; **Address:** Univ Illinois Chicago, Dept Pathology, 840 S Wood St, 130 CSN Bldg, MC 847, Chicago, IL 60612; **Phone:** 312-996-3879; **Board Cert:** Anatomic & Clinical Pathology 1988; **Med School:** Brazil 1972; **Resid:** Pathology, Hahnemann Univ Hosp 1988; **Fellow:** Clinical Immunology, Scripps Clin Rsch Fdn 1981; **Fac Appt:** Prof Path, Univ IL Coll Med

Behm, Frederick G MD [Path] - **Spec Exp:** Hematopathology; **Hospital:** Univ of IL Med Ctr at Chicago; **Address:** Univ Illinois, Dept Pathology, 840 S Wood St, 130 CSN Bldg, MC 847, Chicago, IL 60612-7335; **Phone:** 312-996-3150; **Board Cert:** Anatomic & Clinical Pathology 1980; Hematology 1983; **Med School:** Med Coll Wisc 1974; **Resid:** Pathology, Med Coll of VA Hosp 1979; **Fac Appt:** Prof Path, Univ IL Coll Med

Bell, Debra A MD [Path] - **Spec Exp:** Gynecologic Pathology; Ovarian Cancer; **Hospital:** Mayo Med Ctr & Clin - Rochester; **Address:** Mayo Clinic-Pathology Dept, 200 First St SW, Rochester, MN 55905; **Phone:** 507-284-1800; **Board Cert:** Anatomic Pathology 1980; Cytopathology 1989; **Med School:** Albany Med Coll 1976; **Resid:** Pathology, NYU Med Ctr 1981; **Fellow:** Cytopathology, Meml Sloan Kettering Cancer Ctr 1982; **Fac Appt:** Assoc Prof Path, Mayo Med Sch

Cho, Kathleen R MD [Path] - **Spec Exp:** Gynecologic Pathology; Ovarian Cancer; Cervical Cancer; **Hospital:** Univ Michigan Med Ctr; **Address:** Univ Michigan Med Sch, 109 Zina Pitcher Pl, rm 1506, Ann Arbor, MI 48109; **Phone:** 734-764-1549; **Board Cert:** Anatomic Pathology 1990; **Med School:** Vanderbilt Univ 1984; **Resid:** Pathology, Johns Hopkins Hosp 1988; **Fellow:** Gynecologic Pathology, Johns Hopkins Hosp 1990; **Fac Appt:** Prof Path, Univ Mich Med Sch

Dahmoush, Laila MD [Path] - **Spec Exp:** Breast Pathology; Gynecologic Pathology; Urologic Pathology; **Hospital:** Univ Iowa Hosp & Clins; **Address:** UIHC - Dept Pathology, 200 Hawkins Dr, RCP Bldg - Ste 5216D, Iowa City, IA 52242; **Phone:** 319-356-4440; **Board Cert:** Anatomic & Clinical Pathology 1999; Cytopathology 2001; **Med School:** Egypt 1984; **Resid:** Anatomic & Clinical Pathology, G Washington Univ Hosp 1997; Anatomic & Clinical Pathology, Univ MD Med Sys 1999; **Fellow:** Surgical Pathology, Univ MD Med Sys 2000; Cytopathology, NIH/Natl Canc Inst 2001; **Fac Appt:** Assoc Clin Prof Path, Univ Iowa Coll Med

Gambetti, Pierluigi MD [Path] - **Spec Exp:** Neuro-Pathology; Neurodegenerative Disorders; Creutzfeldt-Jakob Disease (CJD); Huntington's Disease; **Hospital:** UH Case Med Ctr; **Address:** Case Western Res Univ, Inst Path, 2085 Adelbert Rd, rm 419, Cleveland, OH 44106; **Phone:** 216-368-0587; **Board Cert:** Neuropathology 1981; **Med School:** Italy 1960; **Resid:** Neurology, Univ Bologna Med Ctr 1963; **Fellow:** Neurological Pathology, Institut Bunge 1965; Neurological Pathology, Hosp Univ Penn 1968; **Fac Appt:** Prof Path, Case West Res Univ

Goldblum, John R MD [Path] - **Spec Exp:** Soft Tissue Pathology; Esophageal Cancer; Gastrointestinal Pathology; Sarcoma; **Hospital:** Cleveland Clin (page 55); **Address:** Cleveland Clinic, Anatomic Pathology, L25, 9500 Euclid Ave, Cleveland, OH 44195; **Phone:** 216-444-8238; **Board Cert:** Anatomic Pathology 1993; **Med School:** Univ Mich Med Sch 1989; **Resid:** Anatomic Pathology, Univ Michigan Hosps 1993; **Fac Appt:** Prof Path, Cleveland Cl Coll Med/Case West Res

Greenson, Joel K MD [Path] - **Spec Exp:** Liver Cancer; Gastrointestinal Pathology; Liver Pathology; **Hospital:** Univ Michigan Med Ctr; **Address:** Univ Michigan Hospitals, Dept Pathology, 1301 Catherine St, Med Sci 1 Bldg, rm 5218, Ann Arbor, MI 48109-5602; **Phone:** 734-936-6770; **Board Cert:** Anatomic & Clinical Pathology 1988; **Med School:** Univ Mich Med Sch 1984; **Resid:** Pathology, Cedars-Sinai Med Ctr 1988; **Fellow:** Gastrointestinal Pathology, Johns Hopkins Hosp 1990; **Fac Appt:** Prof Path, Univ Mich Med Sch

Kurtin, Paul J MD [Path] - **Spec Exp:** Lymph Node Pathology; Bone Marrow Pathology; Lymphoma; **Hospital:** Mayo Med Ctr & Clin - Rochester; **Address:** Mayo Clinic - Div Hematopathology, 200 First St SW, Rochester, MN 55905; **Phone:** 507-284-4939; **Board Cert:** Anatomic & Clinical Pathology 1983; Hematology 1988; **Med School:** Med Coll Wisc 1979; **Resid:** Anatomic & Clinical Pathology, Vanderbilt Univ Med Ctr 1983; **Fellow:** Hematopathology, Brigham & Women's Hosp 1984; Surgical Pathology, Brigham & Women's Hosp 1986; **Fac Appt:** Prof Path, Mayo Med Sch

Lowe, Lori MD [Path] - **Spec Exp:** Dermatopathology; Skin Cancer; **Hospital:** Univ Michigan Med Ctr; **Address:** Univ Michigan Dept Pathology, 1301 Catherine Rd, M3261-Med Sci I, Ann Arbor, MI 48109-5602; **Phone:** 734-764-4460; **Board Cert:** Dermatology 1990; Dermatopathology 1991; **Med School:** Univ Tex, Houston 1985; **Resid:** Dermatology, Univ Tex Hlth Sci Ctr 1990; **Fellow:** Dermatopathology, Univ Colo Hlth Sci Ctr 1991; **Fac Appt:** Prof D, Univ Mich Med Sch

Lucas, David R MD [Path] - **Spec Exp:** Bone Tumors; Soft Tissue Tumors; Surgical Pathology; **Hospital:** Univ Michigan Med Ctr; **Address:** 1500 E Med Ctr Drive, Ste 2G332 UH, Ann Arbor, MI 48109; **Phone:** 734-232-0022; **Board Cert:** Anatomic Pathology 1993; **Med School:** Wayne State Univ 1988; **Resid:** Pathology, Wayne State Univ Med Ctr 1991; **Fellow:** Surgical Pathology, Mayo Clinic 1993; **Fac Appt:** Prof Path, Univ Mich Med Sch

Moore, Steven A MD/PhD [Path] - **Spec Exp:** Muscular Dystrophy; Neuro-Pathology; **Hospital:** Univ Iowa Hosp & Clins; **Address:** UIHC, Dept Pathology, 200 Hawkins Dr, RCP Bldg - rm 5239B, Iowa City, IA 52242; **Phone:** 319-384-9084; **Board Cert:** Anatomic Pathology 1986; Neuropathology 1986; **Med School:** Indiana Univ 1982; **Resid:** Pathology, Univ IA Hosp & Clin 1984; **Fellow:** Neurological Pathology, Univ IA Hosp & Clin 1986; **Fac Appt:** Prof NPath, Univ Iowa Coll Med

Myers, Jeffrey L MD [Path] - **Spec Exp:** Lung Cancer; Lung Pathology; **Hospital:** Univ Michigan Med Ctr; **Address:** Univ Michigan, Dept Pathology, 1500 E Medical Center Drive, Ann Arbor, MI 48109-5912; **Phone:** 734-936-1888; **Board Cert:** Anatomic Pathology 1986; **Med School:** Washington Univ, St Louis 1981; **Resid:** Anatomic Pathology, Barnes Jewish Hosp 1984; **Fellow:** Surgical Pathology, Univ Alabama Med Ctr 1985; **Fac Appt:** Prof Path, Univ Mich Med Sch

Petras, Robert E MD [Path] - **Spec Exp:** Gastrointestinal Pathology; **Address:** Ameripath Cleveland, 7730 First Pl, Ste A, Oakwood Village, OH 44146; **Phone:** 440-703-2100; **Board Cert:** Anatomic & Clinical Pathology 2004; **Med School:** Ohio State Univ 1978; **Resid:** Anatomic & Clinical Pathology, Cleveland Clin 1982; **Fellow:** Gastrointestinal Pathology, St Marks Hosp; **Fac Appt:** Assoc Clin Prof Path, NE Ohio Univ

Rubin, Brian P MD [Path] - **Spec Exp:** Bone & Soft Tissue Pathology; Sarcoma; **Hospital:** Cleveland Clin (page 55); **Address:** Cleveland Clinic, Dept Anatomic Pathology, L25, 9500 Euclid Ave, Cleveland, OH 44195; **Phone:** 216-445-5551; **Board Cert:** Anatomic Pathology 1999; **Med School:** Cornell Univ-Weill Med Coll 1995; **Resid:** Pathology, Brigham & Womens Hosp 2000; **Fac Appt:** Asst Prof Path, Univ Wash

Suster, Saul M MD [Path] - **Spec Exp:** Surgical Pathology; Mediastinal Tumors; Thyroid Cancer; Thyroid Disorders; **Hospital:** Froedtert & Med Coll WI; **Address:** Med College WI, Dept Pathology, Dynacare Lab Bldg, rm 226, 9200 W Wisconsin Ave, Milwaukee, WI 53226; **Phone:** 414-805-6968; **Board Cert:** Anatomic & Clinical Pathology 1988; **Med School:** Ecuador 1976; **Resid:** Anatomic Pathology, Tel Aviv Univ Med Ctr 1984; Anatomic & Clinical Pathology, Mt Sinai Med Ctr 1988; **Fellow:** Surgical Pathology, Yale-New Haven Hosp 1990; **Fac Appt:** Prof Path, Med Coll Wisc

Ulbright, Thomas M MD [Path] - **Spec Exp:** Testicular Cancer; Gynecologic Pathology; **Hospital:** IU Hlth Univ Hosp; **Address:** IU Health Pathology Laboratory, 350 W 11th St, rm 4078, Indianapolis, IN 46202; **Phone:** 317-491-6498; **Board Cert:** Anatomic Pathology 1980; **Med School:** Washington Univ, St Louis 1975; **Resid:** Pathology, Barnes Jewish Hosp 1978; Surgical Pathology, Barnes Jewish Hosp 1979; **Fellow:** Gynecologic Pathology, St Johns Mercy Med Ctr 1980; **Fac Appt:** Prof Path, Indiana Univ

Great Plains and Mountains

Cohen, Michael B MD [Path] - **Spec Exp:** Urologic Cancer; Cytopathology; **Hospital:** Univ Utah Hlth Care, Huntsman Cancer Hosp; **Address:** Univ of Utah - Dept Pathology, 1950 Circle of Hope, Ste N3100, Salt Lake City, UT 84112; **Phone:** 801-587-4392; **Board Cert:** Anatomic Pathology 2008; Cytopathology 1996; **Med School:** Albany Med Coll 1982; **Resid:** Pathology, UCSF Med Ctr 1986; **Fellow:** Cytopathology, UCSF Med Ctr 1987; **Fac Appt:** Prof Path, Univ Utah

DeMasters, Bette K MD [Path] - **Spec Exp:** Neuro-Pathology; Brain Tumors; Central Nervous System Cancer; **Hospital:** Univ Colorado Hosp, Chldn's Hosp - Aurora (CO); **Address:** Univ CO Hosp, Neuropathology Dept, 12605 E 16th Ave, rm 3026, MS F-768, Aurora, CO 80045; **Phone:** 720-848-4421; **Board Cert:** Anatomic & Clinical Pathology 1982; Neuropathology 1985; **Med School:** Univ Wisc 1977; **Resid:** Internal Medicine, Presby Hosp 1979; Pathology, Univ Colorado Hosp 1980; **Fellow:** Neurological Pathology, Kansas Med Ctr 1984; **Fac Appt:** Prof NPath, Univ Colorado

Thor, Ann D MD [Path] - **Spec Exp:** Breast Cancer; Gynecologic Cancer; **Hospital:** Univ Colorado Hosp; **Address:** Univ CO Hosp, Pathology Dept, 12631 E 17th Ave, rm L15-2215, MS B216, Aurora, CO 80045; **Phone:** 303-724-3704; **Board Cert:** Anatomic Pathology 1987; Cytopathology 1989; **Med School:** Vanderbilt Univ 1981; **Resid:** Pathology, Vanderbilt Univ Med Ctr 1983; **Fellow:** Immunopathology, Natl Cancer Inst 1986; Gynecologic Pathology, Mass Genl Hosp 1990; **Fac Appt:** Prof Path, Univ Colorado

Southwest

Bruner, Janet M MD [Path] - **Spec Exp:** Brain Tumors; Neuro-Pathology; **Hospital:** UT MD Anderson Canc Ctr; **Address:** MD Anderson Canc Ctr, 1515 Holcombe, Unit 85 Blvd, Houston, TX 77030; **Phone:** 713-792-6127; **Board Cert:** Anatomic Pathology 1982; Neuropathology 1984; **Med School:** Med Coll OH 1979; **Resid:** Anatomic & Clinical Pathology, Med Coll Ohio Affil Hosp 1982; **Fellow:** Neurological Pathology, Baylor Coll Med Affil Hosp 1984; **Fac Appt:** Prof Path, Univ Tex, Houston

Cagle, Philip T MD [Path] - **Spec Exp:** Pulmonary Pathology; Lung Cancer; Mesothelioma; **Hospital:** Methodist Hosp - Houston; **Address:** Methodist Hosp, Dept Pathology, 6565 Fannin St, Ste 227, Houston, TX 77030; **Phone:** 713-441-6478; **Board Cert:** Anatomic & Clinical Pathology 1985; **Med School:** Univ Tenn Coll Med 1981; **Resid:** Pathology, Baylor Affil Hosp 1985; **Fellow:** Pulmonary Pathology, Univ British Columbia Affil Hosp 1987; **Fac Appt:** Prof Path, Baylor Coll Med

Foucar, M Kathryn MD [Path] - **Spec Exp:** Leukemia; Lymph Node Pathology; Bone Marrow Pathology; **Hospital:** Univ Hosp - New Mexico; **Address:** TriCore Reference Lab, Hematopathology, 1001 Woodward Pl NE, Albuquerque, NM 87102; **Phone:** 505-938-8122; **Board Cert:** Anatomic & Clinical Pathology 1978; **Med School:** Ohio State Univ 1974; **Resid:** Anatomic Pathology, Univ NM Health & Sci Ctr 1976; Anatomic Pathology, Univ Minn Med Ctr 1978; **Fellow:** Surgical Pathology, Univ Minn Med Ctr 1979; **Fac Appt:** Prof Path, Univ New Mexico

Hamilton, Stanley R MD [Path] - **Spec Exp:** Gastrointestinal Pathology; Liver Pathology; **Hospital:** UT MD Anderson Canc Ctr; **Address:** UT MD Anderson Canc Ctr, 1515 Holcombe Blvd, Unit 085, Houston, TX 77030-4009; **Phone:** 713-792-2040; **Board Cert:** Anatomic & Clinical Pathology 1978; **Med School:** Indiana Univ 1973; **Resid:** Pathology, Johns Hopkins Hosp 1978; **Fellow:** Gastrointestinal Pathology, St Marks Hosp 1980; **Fac Appt:** Prof Path, Univ Tex, Houston

Kinney, Marsha C MD [Path] - **Spec Exp:** Hematopathology; Lymphoma; Leukemia; **Hospital:** Univ Hosp-San Antonio; **Address:** Univ Texas Hlth & Sci Ctr, Dept Path, 7703 Floyd Curl Drive, San Antonio, TX 78229-3900; **Phone:** 210-567-4072; **Board Cert:** Anatomic & Clinical Pathology 1985; Hematology 1998; **Med School:** Univ Tex SW, Dallas 1981; **Resid:** Pathology, Vanderbilt Univ Med Ctr 1985; **Fellow:** Hematopathology, Vanderbilt Univ Med Ctr 1988; **Fac Appt:** Prof Path, Univ Tex, San Antonio

Leslie, Kevin O MD [Path] - **Spec Exp:** Pulmonary Pathology; Cytopathology; Surgical Pathology; **Hospital:** Mayo Clinic - Scottsdale, Mayo Clinic - Phoenix; **Address:** Mayo Clinic-Pathology Div, 13400 E Shea Blvd, Scottsdale, AZ 85259; **Phone:** 480-301-8021; **Board Cert:** Anatomic & Clinical Pathology 1982; **Med School:** Albert Einstein Coll Med 1978; **Resid:** Anatomic & Clinical Pathology, Univ Colorado Hlth Sci Ctr 1982; **Fellow:** Surgical Pathology, Stanford Univ Med Ctr 1983; **Fac Appt:** Prof Path, Mayo Med Sch

Moran, Cesar A MD [Path] - **Spec Exp:** Lung Cancer; Mediastinal Tumors; Mesothelioma; **Hospital:** UT MD Anderson Canc Ctr; **Address:** UT MD Anderson Canc Ctr, Dept Pathology, 1515 Holcombe Blvd, rm G1-3738, Houston, TX 77030; **Phone:** 713-792-8134; **Board Cert:** Anatomic Pathology 1992; **Med School:** Guatemala 1981; **Resid:** Anatomic Pathology, Mt Sinai Med Ctr 1988; **Fellow:** Surgical Pathology, Yale-New Haven Hosp 1989; **Fac Appt:** Prof Path, Univ Tex, Houston

Prieto, Victor G MD/PhD [Path] - **Spec Exp:** Dermatopathology; Melanoma; Skin Cancer; **Hospital:** UT MD Anderson Canc Ctr; **Address:** UT MD Anderson Canc Ctr, Dept Pathology, 1515 Holcombe Blvd, Box 85, Houston, TX 77030-4000; **Phone:** 713-792-0918; **Board Cert:** Anatomic Pathology 1995; Dermatopathology 1997; **Med School:** Spain 1986; **Resid:** Pathology, NY-Presby/Weill Cornell Med Ctr 1993; **Fellow:** Pathology, Meml Sloan Kettering Cancer Ctr 1995; Dermatopathology, New York Hosp-Cornell Med Ctr 1996; **Fac Appt:** Prof Path, Univ Tex, Houston

Rashid, Asif MD/PhD [Path] - **Spec Exp:** Gastrointestinal Pathology; Liver Pathology; **Hospital:** UT MD Anderson Canc Ctr; **Address:** Dept Pathology, UT MD Anderson Canc Ctr, 1515 Holcombe Blvd, Box 85, Houston, TX 77030; **Phone:** 713-745-1101; **Board Cert:** Anatomic Pathology 1994; **Med School:** Pakistan 1984; **Resid:** Anatomic Pathology, Mass Genl Hosp 1993; **Fellow:** Anatomic Pathology, Mass Genl Hosp 1994; Anatomic Pathology, Johns Hopkins 1996

Roberts, William C MD [Path] - **Spec Exp:** Cardiac Pathology; **Hospital:** Baylor Univ Med Ctr-Dallas; **Address:** Baylor Univ Med Ctr, Heart & Vascular Inst, 3500 Gaston Ave, Ste H-030, Dallas, TX 75246-2017; **Phone:** 214-820-7911; **Board Cert:** Anatomic Pathology 1965; **Med School:** Emory Univ 1958; **Resid:** Anatomic Pathology, Natl Heart Inst-NIH 1962; Internal Medicine, Johns Hopkins Hosp 1963; **Fellow:** Cardiovascular Disease, Natl Heart Inst-NIH 1964

Sahin, Aysegul MD [Path] - **Spec Exp:** Breast Cancer; **Hospital:** UT MD Anderson Canc Ctr; **Address:** UT MD Anderson Canc Ctr, 1515 Holcombe Blvd, Box 0085, Houston, TX 77030; **Phone:** 713-794-1500; **Board Cert:** Pathology 1987; **Med School:** Turkey 1980; **Resid:** Pathology, OR Hlth & Sci Univ 1986; **Fellow:** Surgical Pathology, Univ Iowa Hosps & Clins 1987; **Fac Appt:** Prof Path, Univ Tex, Houston

Silva, Elvio G MD [Path] - **Spec Exp:** Gynecologic Pathology; Gynecologic Cancer; **Hospital:** UT MD Anderson Canc Ctr, Cedars-Sinai Med Ctr; **Address:** UT MD Anderson Canc Ctr, Dept Pathology, 1515 Holcombe Blvd, Unit 85, Houston, TX 77030; **Phone:** 713-792-2143; **Board Cert:** Anatomic Pathology 2007; **Med School:** Argentina 1969; **Resid:** Pathology, Natl Univ Med Ctr 1975; Anatomic Pathology, Univ Toronto Affil Hosp 1978; **Fellow:** Surgical Pathology, UT MD Anderson Canc Ctr 1979

Walker, David H MD [Path] - **Spec Exp:** Infections-Emerging; Tropical Diseases; Bioterrorism Preparedness; **Hospital:** UT Med Br at Galveston(John Sealy Hosp); **Address:** UT Med Br Galveston, Dept Path, 301 University Blvd, Galveston, TX 77555-0609; **Phone:** 409-772-3989; **Board Cert:** Anatomic & Clinical Pathology 1974; **Med School:** Vanderbilt Univ 1969; **Resid:** Anatomic & Clinical Pathology, Peter Bent Brigham Hosp 1973; **Fellow:** Pathology, Harvard Univ Affil Hosp 1974; **Fac Appt:** Prof Path, Univ Tex Med Br, Galveston

Wheeler, Thomas M MD [Path] - **Spec Exp:** Thyroid Disorders; Thyroid Cancer; Genitourinary Cancer; **Hospital:** Ben Taub Genl Hosp; **Address:** Baylor Coll Med, Dept Pathology, One Baylor Plaza, rm T203, MS 315, Houston, TX 77030; **Phone:** 713-798-4664; **Board Cert:** Anatomic & Clinical Pathology 1981; Cytopathology 1990; **Med School:** Baylor Coll Med 1977; **Resid:** Pathology, Baylor Affil Hosps 1981; **Fac Appt:** Prof Path, Baylor Coll Med

West Coast and Pacific

Amin, Mahul B MD [Path] - **Spec Exp:** Genitourinary Pathology; Bladder Cancer; Urologic Pathology; Prostate Cancer; **Hospital:** Cedars-Sinai Med Ctr; **Address:** Cedars Sinai Med Ctr- Dept of Pathology, 8700 Beverly Blvd, Ste 8709, Los Angeles, CA 90048; **Phone:** 310-423-6631; **Board Cert:** Anatomic & Clinical Pathology 1996; **Med School:** India 1983; **Resid:** Pathology, Henry Ford Hosp 1992; **Fellow:** Surgical Pathology, MD Anderson Cancer Ctr 1993; **Fac Appt:** Prof Path, UCLA-David Geffen Sch Med

Arber, Daniel A MD [Path] - **Spec Exp:** Bone Marrow Pathology; Lymph Node Pathology; Spleen Pathology; **Hospital:** Stanford Univ Hosp & Clins, Lucile Packard Chldn's Hosp; **Address:** Clinic Laboratories, Stanford Univ Med Ctr, 300 Pasteur Drive, rm H1507, Stanford, CA 94305; **Phone:** 650-725-5604; **Board Cert:** Anatomic & Clinical Pathology 1991; Hematology 1993; **Med School:** Univ Tex, San Antonio 1986; **Resid:** Anatomic & Clinical Pathology, Scott & White Meml Hosp 1991; **Fellow:** Hematopathology, City of Hope Natl Med Ctr 1993; **Fac Appt:** Prof Path, Stanford Univ

Bastian, Boris C MD/PhD [Path] - **Spec Exp:** Melanoma; Skin Cancer; Dermatopathology; **Hospital:** UCSF Med Ctr; **Address:** 1701 Divisadero St, Fl 2, UCSF Dermatopathology Service, San Francisco, CA 94115; **Phone:** 415-502-0267; **Med School:** Germany 1988; **Resid:** Dermatology, University of Wurzburg 1994; **Fellow:** Hematology, Ludwig-Maximilian-University 1989; Genetics, UCSF Helen Diller Comprehensive Cancer Ctr 1999; **Fac Appt:** Prof D, UCSF

Bollen, Andrew Wesley MD [Path] - **Spec Exp:** Neuro-Pathology; Brain Tumors; Brain Infections; Neuromuscular Disorders; **Hospital:** UCSF Med Ctr, San Francisco Genl Hosp; **Address:** UCSF School of Medicine, Dept Pathology/Neuropathology, 505 Parnassus Ave, rm M553, Box 0102, San Francisco, CA 94143; **Phone:** 415-476-5236; **Board Cert:** Neuropathology 1992; Anatomic Pathology 1992; Clinical Pathology 1993; **Med School:** UCSD 1985; **Resid:** Anatomic Pathology, UCSF Med Ctr 1991; **Fellow:** Neuropathology, UCSF Med Ctr 1989; **Fac Appt:** Prof Path, UCSF

Chandrasoma, Parakrama T MD [Path] - **Spec Exp:** Gastrointestinal Pathology; Esophageal Cancer; Neuro-Pathology; Surgical Pathology; **Hospital:** LAC & USC Med Ctr; **Address:** LAC-USC Med Ctr, Dept Path, Clinic Tower Fl 7 - rm A7A127, 1100 N State St, Los Angeles, CA 90033; **Phone:** 323-226-2622; **Board Cert:** Anatomic & Clinical Pathology 1982; **Med School:** Sri Lanka 1971; **Resid:** Anatomic Pathology, Univ Sri Lanka Affil Hosp 1978; Anatomic Pathology, LAC-USC Med Ctr 1982; **Fac Appt:** Prof Path, USC Sch Med

Chang, Karen L MD [Path] - **Spec Exp:** Leukemia; Lymphoma; **Hospital:** Kaiser Permanente LA Med Ctr; **Address:** SCPMG Regional Reference Laboratories, 11668 Sherman Way, North Hollywood, CA 91605; **Phone:** 818-503-6769; **Board Cert:** Anatomic & Clinical Pathology 1992; **Med School:** Mount Sinai Sch Med 1985; **Resid:** Anatomic Pathology, Stanford Univ Med Ctr 1988; Clinical Pathology, Cedars-Sinai Med Ctr 1991; **Fellow:** Surgical Pathology, Stanford Univ Med Ctr 1989

Chen, Yunn-Yi MD/PhD [Path] - **Spec Exp:** Breast Pathology; Breast Cancer; **Hospital:** UCSF Med Ctr; **Address:** 505 Parnassus Ave, rm M559, San Francisco, CA 94143; **Phone:** 415-353-1613; **Board Cert:** Anatomic & Clinical Pathology 1998; **Med School:** China 1985; **Resid:** Pathology, Beth Israel Deaconess Med Ctr 1998; **Fellow:** Surgical Pathology, UCSF Med Ctr 1999; **Fac Appt:** Clin Prof Path, UCSF

Cochran, Alistair J MD [Path] - **Spec Exp:** Melanoma; Dermatopathology; **Hospital:** UCLA Ronald Reagan Med Ctr; **Address:** UCLA Med Ctr, Dept Path & Lab Med, 10833 Le Conte Ave, Ste A4-215CHS, Los Angeles, CA 90095-1732; **Phone:** 310-206-3563; **Med School:** Scotland, UK 1959; **Resid:** Dermatopathology, Western Infirmary 1968; Pathology, Western Infirmary 1968; **Fellow:** Immunology, Karolinska Inst 1970; **Fac Appt:** Prof Path, UCLA

Dubeau, Louis MD/PhD [Path] - **Spec Exp:** Ovarian Cancer; **Hospital:** USC Norris Cancer Hosp; **Address:** 1441 Eastlake Ave, Ezralow Bldg, Ste 6338, Los Angeles, CA 90033-1048; **Phone:** 323-865-0720; **Board Cert:** Anatomic Pathology 1984; **Med School:** McGill Univ 1979; **Resid:** Anatomic Pathology, McGill Univ Med Ctr 1984; **Fellow:** Cancer Research, USC/Norris Comprehensive Cancer Ctr 1987; **Fac Appt:** Prof Path, USC Sch Med

Ferrell, Linda MD [Path] - **Spec Exp:** Liver Pathology; **Hospital:** UCSF Med Ctr; **Address:** UCSF Med Ctr, Dept Pathology, 505 Parnassus Ave, rm M590, Box 0102, San Francisco, CA 94143-0102; **Phone:** 415-353-1090; **Board Cert:** Anatomic Pathology 1982; **Med School:** Univ Kansas 1977; **Resid:** Pathology, Univ Kansas Med Ctr 1979; Surgical Pathology, UCSF Med Ctr 1981; **Fac Appt:** Prof Path, UCSF

Fishbein, Michael C MD [Path] - **Spec Exp:** Cardiovascular Pathology; Pulmonary Pathology; Surgical Pathology; **Hospital:** UCLA Ronald Reagan Med Ctr, Santa Monica - UCLA Med Ctr & Ortho Hosp; **Address:** UCLA Pathology & Lab Medicine, 10833 Le Conte Ave, rm 13-145 CHS, Los Angeles, CA 90095-1732; **Phone:** 310-825-6470; **Board Cert:** Anatomic & Clinical Pathology 1975; **Med School:** Univ IL Coll Med 1971; **Resid:** Anatomic & Clinical Pathology, UCLA-Harbor General Hosp 1975; **Fellow:** Pathology, Heart Lung Inst-NIH 1975; **Fac Appt:** Prof Path, UCLA

Govindarajan, Sugantha MD [Path] - **Spec Exp:** Liver Pathology; **Hospital:** Rancho Los Amigos Natl Rehab Ctr; **Address:** Rancho Los Amigos Natl Rehab Ctr-Pathology, 7601 E Imperial Hwy JPI Bldg - rm B170, Downey, CA 90242; **Phone:** 562-401-8994; **Board Cert:** Anatomic & Clinical Pathology 1976; **Med School:** India 1969; **Resid:** Pathology, St Lukes Hosp 1976; **Fellow:** Immunopathology, Cleveland Clinic 1977; **Fac Appt:** Prof Path, USC Sch Med

Hammar, Samuel P MD [Path] - **Spec Exp:** Lung Cancer; Pulmonary Pathology; **Hospital:** Harrison Med Ctr; **Address:** Diagnostic Specialties Lab, 700 Lebo Blvd, Bremerton, WA 98310; **Phone:** 360-479-7707; **Board Cert:** Anatomic & Clinical Pathology 1975; **Med School:** Univ Wash 1970; **Resid:** Pathology, Univ Wash Med Ctr 1975

Kanel, Gary C MD [Path] - **Spec Exp:** Liver Pathology; **Hospital:** Keck Med Ctr of USC; **Address:** Keck Hosp of USC-Dept of Pathology, 1500 San Pablo St Fl 2, Los Angeles, CA 90033; **Phone:** 323-442-8591; **Board Cert:** Anatomic & Clinical Pathology 1979; **Med School:** Tufts Univ 1974; **Resid:** Pathology, Tufts-New England Med Ctr 1976; Pathology, Univ Chicago Hosp 1977; **Fellow:** Pathology, Tufts-New England Med Ctr 1979; **Fac Appt:** Clin Prof Path, USC-Keck School of Medicine

Koss, Michael N MD [Path] - **Spec Exp:** Pulmonary Pathology; Lung Cancer; Kidney Pathology; **Hospital:** USC Norris Cancer Hosp, Keck Med Ctr of USC; **Address:** 2222 Ocean View Ave, Ste 212, Los Angeles, CA 90057; **Phone:** 213-381-2260; **Board Cert:** Anatomic Pathology 1979; **Med School:** Stanford Univ 1970; **Resid:** Pathology, Columbia Presby Med Ctr 1974; **Fellow:** Renal Pathology, Columbia Presby Med Ctr 1975; Pulmonary Pathology, Armed Forces Inst Path 1978; **Fac Appt:** Prof Path, USC Sch Med

Le Boit, Philip E MD [Path] - **Spec Exp:** Cutaneous Lymphoma; Skin Cancer; Dermatopathology; **Hospital:** UCSF Med Ctr; **Address:** UCSF - Dermatopathology Section, 1701 Divisadero St, rm 280, San Francisco, CA 94115; **Phone:** 415-353-7546; **Board Cert:** Anatomic Pathology 1983; Dermatopathology 1983; Clinical Pathology 1986; **Med School:** Albany Med Coll 1979; **Resid:** Anatomic Pathology, UCSF Med Ctr 1981; Clinical Pathology, Mt Sinai Hosp 1982; **Fellow:** Dermatopathology, NY Presby Hosp 1983; **Fac Appt:** Prof Path, UCSF

Ljung, Britt-Marie E MD [Path] - **Spec Exp:** Breast Cancer; Fine Needle Aspiration Biopsy; **Hospital:** UCSF - Mt Zion Med Ctr; **Address:** UCSF - Dept Pathology, 1600 Divisadero St, rm R200, San Francisco, CA 94115; **Phone:** 415-353-7043; **Board Cert:** Anatomic Pathology 1985; Cytopathology 1989; **Med School:** Sweden 1975; **Resid:** Pathology, Karolinska Hosp 1979; Anatomic Pathology, UCLA Med Ctr 1983; **Fac Appt:** Prof Path, UCSF

Mischel, Paul S MD [Path] - **Spec Exp:** Neuro-Pathology; Brain Tumors; Surgical Pathology; **Hospital:** UCSD Med Ctr; **Address:** Ludwig Institute for Cancer Research and UCSD Med Ctr, Dept of Pathology, 9500 Gilman Drive, Ste 0753, La Jolla, CA 92093-0753; **Phone:** 858-534-6080; **Board Cert:** Anatomic Pathology 1997; Neuropathology 1997; **Med School:** Cornell Univ-Weill Med Coll 1991; **Resid:** Anatomic & Clinical Pathology, UCLA Med Ctr 1996; **Fellow:** Neurological Pathology, UCLA Med Ctr 1995; Research, Howard Hughes Med Inst/UCSF 1997; **Fac Appt:** Prof Path, UCSD

Nathwani, Bharat N MD [Path] - **Spec Exp:** Hematopathology; Leukemia; Lymphoma; **Hospital:** Cedars-Sinai Med Ctr; **Address:** Cedars-Sinai Med Ctr- Dept Pathology, 8700 Beverly Blvd, Ste 7706, Los Angeles, CA 90048; **Phone:** 310-248-6659; **Board Cert:** Anatomic Pathology 1977; **Med School:** India 1969; **Resid:** Pathology, JJ Group-Grant Med Ctr 1972; Pathology, Rush-Presby-St Lukes Med Ctr 1974; **Fellow:** Hematopathology, City Hope Natl Med Ctr 1977; **Fac Appt:** Prof Path, USC Sch Med

Perry, Arie MD [Path] - **Spec Exp:** Neuro-Pathology; Brain Tumors; **Hospital:** UCSF Med Ctr; **Address:** UCSF-Dept of Neuropathology, 505 Parnassus Ave, rm M-551, San Francisco, CA 94143; **Phone:** 415-476-5236; **Board Cert:** Anatomic & Clinical Pathology 1995; Neuropathology 1997; **Med School:** Univ Tex SW, Dallas 1990; **Resid:** Pathology, Univ Tex SW 1994; **Fellow:** Surgical Pathology, Mayo Clin 1995; Neurological Pathology, Mayo Clin 1998; **Fac Appt:** Prof Path, UCSF

Rutgers, Joanne K MD [Path] - **Spec Exp:** Gynecologic Pathology; Gastrointestinal Pathology; Cytopathology; **Hospital:** Long Beach Meml Med Ctr, Miller Children's Hosp; **Address:** Long Beach Meml Med Ctr-Pathology Dept, 2801 Atlantic Ave, Long Beach, CA 90806; **Phone:** 562-933-0726; **Board Cert:** Clinical Pathology 1992; Anatomic Pathology 1985; Cytopathology 1997; **Med School:** UCSD 1981; **Resid:** Pathology, Montefiore Med Ctr 1983; Pathology, NYU Med Ctr 1985; **Fellow:** Gynecologic Pathology, Mass Genl Hosp 1989; **Fac Appt:** Assoc Clin Prof Path, UC Irvine

Schiller, Alan L MD [Path] - **Spec Exp:** Bone & Joint Pathology; Soft Tissue Pathology; Bone Tumors; **Hospital:** Queen's Med Ctr - Honolulu, Kapiolani Med Ctr @ Pali Momi; **Address:** John A Burns Schl of Med, Univ of HI, Dept of Pathology, 651 Ilalo St, Honolulu, HI 96813; **Phone:** 808-692-1130; **Board Cert:** Anatomic Pathology 1973; **Med School:** Ros Franklin Univ/Chicago Med Sch 1967; **Resid:** Pathology, Mass Genl Hosp 1972; **Fac Appt:** Prof Path, Univ Hawaii JA Burns Sch Med

Sibley, Richard K MD [Path] - **Spec Exp:** Kidney Pathology; Breast Pathology; Liver Pathology; **Hospital:** Stanford Univ Hosp & Clins; **Address:** Stanford U Med Ctr, Dept of Pathology, 300 Pasteur Drive, Ste L235, MC 5324, Stanford, CA 94305; **Phone:** 650-723-7211; **Board Cert:** Anatomic Pathology 1975; **Med School:** Univ Tex SW, Dallas 1971; **Resid:** Anatomic Pathology, U Chicago Hosps 1974; **Fellow:** Pathology, Stanford U Med Ctr 1975; **Fac Appt:** Prof Path, Stanford Univ

Triche, Timothy J MD/PhD [Path] - **Spec Exp:** Pediatric Pathology; Pediatric Cancers; Sarcoma; **Hospital:** Chldns Hosp - Los Angeles; **Address:** 4650 W Sunset Blvd, Los Angeles, CA 90027; **Phone:** 323-361-8898; **Board Cert:** Anatomic Pathology 1975; **Med School:** Tulane Univ 1971; **Resid:** Anatomic Pathology, Barnes Hosp-Wash Univ 1973; Surgical Pathology, Barnes Hosp 1974; **Fellow:** Pathology, Natl Cancer Inst 1975; **Fac Appt:** Prof Path, USC Sch Med

True, Lawrence D MD [Path] - **Spec Exp:** Urologic Pathology; Prostate Cancer; Bladder Cancer; **Hospital:** Univ Wash Med Ctr; **Address:** Univ Wash Med Ctr, Dept Anatomic Path, Campus Box 356100, rm NE110, 1959 NE Pacific St, Seattle, WA 98195-6100; **Phone:** 206-598-6400; **Board Cert:** Anatomic Pathology 1981; **Med School:** Tulane Univ 1971; **Resid:** Pathology, Univ CO Hosp 1980; **Fac Appt:** Prof Path, Univ Wash

Warnke, Roger A MD [Path] - **Spec Exp:** Lymphoma; Hematopathology; **Hospital:** Stanford Univ Hosp & Clins; **Address:** Stanford Hosp, 1291 Welch Rd, Pathology, rm L235, Stanford, CA 94305-5324; **Phone:** 650-498-6458; **Board Cert:** Anatomic Pathology 1975; **Med School:** Washington Univ, St Louis 1971; **Resid:** Pathology, Stanford Univ Med Ctr 1974; **Fellow:** Surgical Pathology, Stanford Univ Med Ctr 1975; Immunology, Stanford Univ Med Ctr 1976; **Fac Appt:** Prof Emeritus Path, Stanford Univ

Weisenburger, Dennis D MD [Path] - **Spec Exp:** Hematopathology; Lymphoma; **Hospital:** City of Hope Natl Med Ctr; **Address:** City of Hope, Pathology Dept, 1500 E Duarte, rm 2245, Duarte, CA 91010; **Phone:** 626-256-4673 x63584; **Board Cert:** Anatomic & Clinical Pathology 1979; **Med School:** Univ Minn 1974; **Resid:** Anatomic Pathology, Univ Iowa Hosp & Clins 1978; **Fellow:** Hematopathology, City Hope Natl Med Ctr 1980

Weiss, Lawrence M MD [Path] - **Spec Exp:** Surgical Pathology; Hematopathology; Immunopathology; **Address:** Clarient, 31 Columbia, Aliso Viejo, CA 92656; **Phone:** 949-362-7357; **Board Cert:** Anatomic Pathology 1985; **Med School:** Univ MD Sch Med 1981; **Resid:** Pathology, Brigham & Women's Hosp 1985; **Fellow:** Surgical Pathology, Stanford Univ Hosp 1986

Wilczynski, Sharon P MD/PhD [Path] - **Spec Exp:** Gynecologic Cancer; Breast Cancer; Ovarian Cancer; Clinical Trials; **Hospital:** City of Hope Natl Med Ctr; **Address:** City of Hope Natl Med Ctr-Pathology Dept, 1500 E Duarte Rd, Duarte, CA 91010; **Phone:** 626-256-4673 x68375; **Board Cert:** Anatomic & Clinical Pathology 1985; Cytopathology 1991; **Med School:** Med Coll PA Hahnemann 1981; **Resid:** Pathology, Hosp Univ Penn 1983; Anatomic & Clinical Pathology, Long Beach Meml Hosp 1985; **Fellow:** Pathology-Oncology, Hosp Univ Penn 1986; **Fac Appt:** Prof Path, USC-Keck School of Medicine

Top Doctors Make A Difference

Pediatrics

A pediatrician is concerned with the physical, emotional and social health of children from birth to young adulthood. Care encompasses a broad spectrum of health services ranging from preventive health-care to the diagnosis and treatment of acute and chronic diseases.

A pediatrician deals with biological, social and environmental influences on the developing child, and with the impact of disease and dysfunction on development.

Note: *The majority of general pediatricians are primary care physicians. However,, for purposes of this directory, no primary care physicians are included.*

Training Required: Three years

Pediatric Allergy and Immunology: An allergist-immunologist is trained in evaluation, physical and laboratory diagnosis and management of disorders involving the immune system. Selected examples of such conditions include asthma, anaphylaxis, rhinitis, eczema and adverse reactions to drugs, foods and insect stings as well as immune deficiency diseases (both acquired and congenital), defects in host defense and problems related to autoimmune disease, organ transplantation or malignancies of the immune system. As our understanding of the immune system develops, the scope of this specialty is widening.

Training Required: Prior certification in pediatrics *plus* two years in allergy/immunology. (Training programs are available at some medical centers to provide individuals with expertise in both allergy/immunology and pediatric pulmonology. Such individuals are candidates for dual certification.)

Certification in one of the following subspecialties requires additional training and examination.

Pediatric Cardiology: A pediatric cardiologist provides comprehensive care to patients with cardiovascular problems. This specialist is skilled in selecting, performing and evaluating the structural and functional assessment of the heart and blood vessels and the clinical evaluation of cardiovascular disease.

Pediatric Critical Care Medicine: A pediatrician who cares for children who are victims of life threatening disorders such as severe accidents, shock and diabetic acidosis.

Pediatric Endocrinology: A pediatrician who provides expert care to infants, children and adolescents who have diseases that result from an abnormality in the endocrine glands (glands which secrete hormones). These diseases include diabetes mellitus, growth failure, unusual size for age, early or late pubertal development, birth defects, the genital anomalies and disorders of the thyroid, the adrenal and pituitary glands.

Pediatric Gastroenterology: A pediatrician who specializes in the diagnosis and treatment of diseases of the digestive systems of infants, children and adolescents. This specialist treats conditions such as abdominal pain, ulcers, diarrhea, cancer and jaundice and performs complex diagnostic and therapeutic procedures using lighted scopes to see internal organs.

Pediatric Hematology-Oncology: A pediatrician trained in the combination of pediatrics, hematology and oncology to recognize and manage pediatric blood disorders and cancerous diseases.

Pediatric Infectious Diseases: A pediatrician trained to care for children in the diagnosis, treatment and prevention of infectious diseases. This specialist can apply specific knowledge to effect a better outcome for pediatric infections with complicated courses, underlying diseases that predispose to unusual or severe infections, unclear diagnoses, uncommon diseases and complex or investigational treatments.

Pediatric Nephrology: A pediatrician who deals with the normal and abnormal development and maturation of the kidney and urinary tract, the mechanisms by which the kidney can be damaged, the evaluation and treatment of renal diseases, fluid and electrolyte abnormalities, hypertension and renal replacement therapy.

Pediatric Otolaryngology: A pediatric otolaryngologist has special expertise in the management of infants and children with disorders that include congenital and acquired conditions involving the aerodigestive tract, nose and paranasal sinuses, the ear and other areas of the head and neck. The pediatric otolaryngologist has special skills in the diagnosis, treatment and management of childhood disorders of voice, speech, language and hearing.

Pediatric Pulmonology: A pediatrician dedicated to the prevention and treatment of all respiratory diseases affecting infants, children and young adults. This specialist is knowledgeable about the growth and development of the lung, assessment of respiratory function in infants and children and experienced in a variety of invasive and noninvasive diagnostic techniques.

Pediatric Rheumatology: A pediatrician who treats diseases of joints, muscle, bones and tendons. A pediatric rheumatologist diagnoses and treats arthritis, back pain, muscle strains, common athletic injuries and "collagen" diseases.

Pediatric Surgery: A surgeon with expertise in the management of surgical conditions in premature and newborn infants, children and adolescents.

Pediatric Urology: A board certified urologist who specializes in all aspects of urologic congenital anomalies, and childhood and adolescent acquired urologic problems such as disease and trauma.

Pediatrics

New England

Miller, Karen J MD [Ped] - **Spec Exp:** Developmental & Behavioral Disorders; **Hospital:** Tufts Med Ctr, Floating Hosp for Children at Tufts Med Ce; **Address:** Tufts Med Ctr, 800 Washington St, rm 334, Boston, MA 02111; **Phone:** 617-636-7242; **Board Cert:** Internal Medicine 1982; Developmental-Behavioral Pediatrics 2010; **Med School:** Tulane Univ 1977; **Resid:** Pediatrics, Georgetown Univ Hosp 1980; **Fellow:** Developmental-Behavioral Pediatrics, Schneider's Chldns Hosp 1996; **Fac Appt:** Assoc Prof Ped, Tufts Univ

Rappaport, Leonard MD [Ped] - **Spec Exp:** Developmental & Behavioral Disorders; **Hospital:** Children's Hospital - Boston; **Address:** Boston Chldn Hosp, Developmental Med Ctr, 300 Longwood Ave, Fegan Bldg Fl 10, Boston, MA 02115; **Phone:** 617-355-4683; **Board Cert:** Pediatrics 1983; Developmental-Behavioral Pediatrics 2010; **Med School:** Yale Univ 1977; **Resid:** Pediatrics, Chldn's Hosp 1981; **Fellow:** Developmental-Behavioral Pediatrics, Chldn's Hosp 1983; **Fac Appt:** Prof Ped, Harvard Med Sch

Shaywitz, Sally E MD [Ped] - **Spec Exp:** Learning Disorders; Dyslexia; **Hospital:** Yale-New Haven Hosp; **Address:** Yale Univ Dept Pediatrics, 333 Cedar St, New Haven, CT 06520-8064; **Phone:** 203-785-4641; **Board Cert:** Pediatrics 1971; **Med School:** Albert Einstein Coll Med 1966; **Resid:** Pediatrics, Albert Einstein Coll Med 1970; **Fellow:** Pediatrics, Bronx Muni Hosp Ctr 1968; Behavioral Pediatrics, Albert Einstein Coll Med 1970; **Fac Appt:** Prof Ped, Yale Univ

Mid Atlantic

Berlin Jr, Cheston M MD [Ped] - **Spec Exp:** Phenylketonuria (PKU); Tourette's Syndrome; **Hospital:** Penn State Milton S Hershey Med Ctr; **Address:** PennState Hershey Chldns Hosp, 35 Hope Drive, Ste 102, Hershey, PA 17033; **Phone:** 717-531-7300; **Board Cert:** Pediatrics 1982; **Med School:** Harvard Med Sch 1962; **Resid:** Internal Medicine & Pediatrics, Chldns Hosp 1967; **Fac Appt:** Prof Ped, Penn State Coll Med

Burgess, David B MD [Ped] - **Spec Exp:** Developmental & Behavioral Disorders; ADD/ADHD; Autism; **Hospital:** Chldns Hosp of Philadelphia; **Address:** CHOP-Pediatric Specialty Care Center, 4009 Black Horse Pike, Mays Landing, NJ 08330; **Phone:** 609-677-7895; **Board Cert:** Pediatrics 1978; Developmental-Behavioral Pediatrics 2012; **Med School:** Univ Wisc 1973; **Resid:** Pediatrics, Charity Hosp of LA/Tulane 1977; **Fellow:** Child Development, JFK Child Development Ctr/Univ Colorado 1980; **Fac Appt:** Assoc Clin Prof Ped, Univ Pennsylvania

Gartner Jr, J. Carlton MD [Ped] - **Spec Exp:** Diagnostic Problems; Multisystem Disorders; **Hospital:** Nemours/Alfred I. duPont Hosp for Chldn; **Address:** Nemours, Specialty Care, 1600 Rockland Rd, rm 3B367, Wilmington, DE 19803; **Phone:** 302-651-5638; **Board Cert:** Pediatrics 2007; **Med School:** Johns Hopkins Univ 1971; **Resid:** Pediatrics, Chldns Hosp 1974; **Fac Appt:** Prof Ped, Jefferson Med Coll

Hofkosh, Dena MD [Ped] - **Spec Exp:** Developmental & Behavioral Disorders; **Hospital:** Chldns Hosp of Pittsburgh - UPMC; **Address:** Chldns Hosp, Child Development Unit, Chldn's Oakland Med Bldg, 3420 5th Ave Fl 2, Pittsburgh, PA 15213; **Phone:** 412-692-5560; **Board Cert:** Pediatrics 2009; Neurodevelopmental Disabilities 2012; **Med School:** NYU Sch Med 1979; **Resid:** Pediatrics, Univ Pittsburgh Med Ctr 1982; **Fellow:** Ambulatory Pediatrics, Univ Pittsburgh Med Ctr 1984; **Fac Appt:** Prof Ped, Univ Pittsburgh

Oeffinger, Kevin C MD [Ped] - **Spec Exp:** Cancer Survivors-Late Effects of Therapy; **Hospital:** Meml Sloan-Kettering Canc Ctr; **Address:** 300 E 66th St, New York, NY 10065; **Phone:** 646-888-4730; **Board Cert:** Family Medicine 2006; **Med School:** Univ Tex, San Antonio 1984; **Resid:** Family Medicine, Baylor Coll Med 1987; **Fellow:** Family Medicine, Fam Practice Faculty Dev Ctr 1999; Research, Natl Cancer Inst 2000

Zitelli, Basil MD [Ped] - **Spec Exp:** Complex Diagnosis; **Hospital:** Chldns Hosp of Pittsburgh - UPMC; **Address:** Chldns Hosp, Diagnostics, 4401 Penn Ave, Faculty Pav Fl 3, Pittsburgh, PA 15201; **Phone:** 412-692-5135; **Board Cert:** Pediatrics 1976; **Med School:** Univ Pittsburgh 1971; **Resid:** Pediatrics, Johns Hopkins Hosp 1974; **Fellow:** Pediatrics, Johns Hopkins Hosp 1978; **Fac Appt:** Prof Ped, Univ Pittsburgh

Southeast

Hershorin, Eugene R MD [Ped] - **Spec Exp:** ADD/ADHD; Developmental & Mood Disorders; Learning Disorders; **Hospital:** Jackson Meml Hosp, Baptist Hosp of Miami; **Address:** 8932 SW 97th Ave, Ste D, Miami, FL 33176; **Phone:** 305-270-5050; **Board Cert:** Pediatrics 1980; Developmental-Behavioral Pediatrics 2012; **Med School:** Penn State Coll Med 1976; **Resid:** Pediatrics, Chldn's Hosp 1979; **Fac Appt:** Assoc Prof Ped, Univ Miami Sch Med

Midwest

Berman, Brian W MD [Ped] - **Spec Exp:** Sickle Cell Disease; Thrombotic Disorders; Thalassemia; Fanconi Aplastic Anemia; **Hospital:** Beaumont Hosp-Royal Oak; **Address:** 3601 W 13 Mile Road, Med Office Bldg, Ste 709, Royal Oak, MI 48073; **Phone:** 248-551-1644; **Board Cert:** Pediatrics 2009; Pediatric Hematology-Oncology 1989; **Med School:** Temple Univ 1975; **Resid:** Pediatrics, St. Chris Hosp for Chldn 1978; **Fellow:** Pediatric Hematology-Oncology, Yale-New Haven Hosp 1980; **Fac Appt:** Prof Ped, Oakland Univ-William Beaumont Med Sch

Bull, Marilyn J MD [Ped] - **Spec Exp:** Developmental Disorders; Down Syndrome; Birth Defects; **Hospital:** Riley Hosp for Children; **Address:** 705 Riley Hospital Drive, rm 1601, Indianapolis, IN 46202; **Phone:** 317-944-4846; **Board Cert:** Pediatrics 2009; Clinical Genetics 1982; Neurodevelopmental Disabilities 2012; **Med School:** Univ Mich Med Sch 1968; **Resid:** Pediatrics, Chldns Meml Hosp 1972; **Fellow:** Genetics, Floating Hosp Chldn 1973; **Fac Appt:** Prof Ped, Indiana Univ

Fost, Norman C MD [Ped] - **Spec Exp:** Ethics; **Hospital:** Univ WI Hosp & Clins; **Address:** Univ WI Hosp - Dept Pediatrics, 600 Highland Ave, MC 4108, Madison, WI 53792-4108; **Phone:** 608-265-6050; **Board Cert:** Pediatrics 1970; **Med School:** Yale Univ 1964; **Resid:** Pediatrics, Johns Hopkins Hosp 1971; **Fellow:** Pediatrics, Harvard Sch Public Hlth 1973; **Fac Appt:** Prof Ped, Univ Wisc

Lantos, John D MD [Ped] - **Spec Exp:** Ethics; Ethics Issues in Neonatalogy; **Hospital:** Chldns Mercy Hosps & Clinics; **Address:** Children's Mercy Bioethics Ctr, 2401 Gillham Rd, Kansas City, MO 64108; **Phone:** 816-701-5284; **Board Cert:** Pediatrics 2009; **Med School:** Univ Pittsburgh 1981; **Resid:** Pediatrics, Chldns Natl Med Ctr 1984; **Fellow:** Clinical Ethics, Univ Chicago Hosps 1987; **Fac Appt:** Prof Ped, Univ MO-Kansas City

Roizen, Nancy Jean M MD [Ped] - **Spec Exp:** Down Syndrome; Autism; ADD/ADHD; **Hospital:** UH Rainbow Babies & Chldns Hosp, UH Case Med Ctr; **Address:** UH Rainbow Specialty Center - Westlake, 10524 Euclid Ave, rm 3150, Cleveland, OH 44106; **Phone:** 216-844-3230; **Board Cert:** Pediatrics 1987; Neurodevelopmental Disabilities 2012; Developmental-Behavioral Pediatrics 2010; **Med School:** Tufts Univ 1972; **Resid:** Pediatrics, Johns Hopkins Hosp 1974; **Fellow:** Neurodevelopmental Disabilities, Johns Hopkins Hosp 1975; Behavioral Pediatrics, UCSF 1976; **Fac Appt:** Prof Psyc, Case West Res Univ

Sheldon, Stephen H DO [Ped] - **Spec Exp:** Sleep Disorders/Apnea; **Hospital:** Lurie Chldn's Hosp-Chicago; **Address:** Lurie Chldn's Hosp, 225 E Chicago Ave, Box 43, Chicago, IL 60611; **Phone:** 312-227-6260; **Board Cert:** Pediatrics 1980; Sleep Medicine 2007; **Med School:** Chicago Coll Osteo Med 1975; **Resid:** Pediatrics, Rush-Presby St Luke's Med Ctr 1978; **Fellow:** Neurophysiology, Univ Chicago Hosps 1988; **Fac Appt:** Prof Ped, Northwestern Univ

Southwest

Infante, Anthony J MD/PhD [Ped] - **Spec Exp:** Immune Deficiencies-Primary; Autoimmune Disease; Fevers-Periodic; **Hospital:** Christus Santa Rosa Children's Hosp; **Address:** 333 N Santa Rosa St Fl 8th, San Antonio, TX 78207; **Phone:** 210-704-2187; **Board Cert:** Pediatrics 2011; **Med School:** Indiana Univ 1978; **Resid:** Pediatrics, Mayo Clinic 1980; **Fellow:** Pediatric Immunology, Mayo Clinic 1981; Immunology, Stanford Univ Hosp 1983; **Fac Appt:** Prof Ped, Univ Tex, San Antonio

Kleinerman, Eugenie S MD [Ped] - **Spec Exp:** Ewing's Sarcoma; Cancer Survivors-Late Effects of Therapy; **Hospital:** UT MD Anderson Canc Ctr; **Address:** MD Anderson Canc Ctr, Dept Pediatrics, 1515 Holcombe Blvd, Unit 87, Houston, TX 77030; **Phone:** 713-792-8110; **Board Cert:** Pediatrics 1980; **Med School:** Duke Univ 1975; **Resid:** Pediatrics, Chldns Hosp-Natl Med Ctr 1979; **Fellow:** Immunology, Natl Cancer Inst 1981; **Fac Appt:** Prof Ped, Univ Tex, Houston

West Coast and Pacific

Berkowitz, Carol D MD [Ped] - **Spec Exp:** Child Abuse; **Hospital:** LAC - Harbor - UCLA Med Ctr; **Address:** LAC-Harbor-UCLA Med Ctr, Dept Pediatrics, 1000 W Carson St, Torrance, CA 90509-2910; **Phone:** 310-222-3091; **Board Cert:** Pediatrics 2000; Pediatric Emergency Medicine 2013; Child Abuse Pediatrics 2009; **Med School:** Columbia P&S 1969; **Resid:** Pediatrics, Roosevelt Hosp 1972; **Fac Appt:** Clin Prof Ped, UCLA

Feldman, Kenneth W MD [Ped] - **Spec Exp:** Child Abuse; **Hospital:** Seattle Chldns Hosp; **Address:** Odessa Brown Chldns Clin, 2101 E Yesler Way, Ste 100, Seattle, WA 98122; **Phone:** 206-987-7225; **Board Cert:** Pediatrics 1975; Child Abuse Pediatrics 2009; **Med School:** Univ Wisc 1970; **Resid:** Pediatrics, Chldns Regl Med Ctr 1974; **Fac Appt:** Clin Prof Ped, Univ Wash

Jones Jr, Kenneth Lyons MD [Ped] - **Spec Exp:** Genetic Disorders; Dysmorphology; Metabolic Disorders; **Hospital:** Rady Children's Hosp - San Diego, UCSD Med Ctr; **Address:** Rady Chldns Hosp, Pediatrics, 7920 Frost St, Ste 200, San Diego, CA 92123; **Phone:** 858-246-0047; **Board Cert:** Pediatrics 1971; **Med School:** Hahnemann Univ 1966; **Resid:** Pediatrics, Seattle Chldns Hosp 1969; **Fac Appt:** Prof Ped, UCSD

Walker, William O MD [Ped] - **Spec Exp:** Developmental & Behavioral Disorders; Autism; Cerebral Palsy; Hydrocephalus; **Hospital:** Seattle Chldns Hosp; **Address:** 4800 Sand Point Way NE, MS O.C.9.840, Seattle, WA 98145-5005; **Phone:** 206-987-2210; **Board Cert:** Pediatrics 1984; Developmental-Behavioral Pediatrics 2010; **Med School:** Tulane Univ 1979; **Resid:** Pediatrics, W Beaumont Army Med Ctr 1982; **Fellow:** Behavioral Pediatrics, W Beaumont Army Med Ctr 1987; **Fac Appt:** Prof Ped, Univ Wash

Zeltzer, Lonnie K MD [Ped] - **Spec Exp:** Pain Management; Complementary Medicine; **Hospital:** Mattel Chldns Hosp at UCLA; **Address:** UCLA Pediatric Pain Prgm, 200 Med Plaza, Ste 265, Los Angeles, CA 90024; **Phone:** 310-825-0731; **Board Cert:** Pediatrics 1976; **Med School:** Univ Cincinnati 1970; **Resid:** Pediatrics, Univ Arizona Med Ctr-Univ Campus 1973; **Fellow:** Adolescent Medicine, Chldns Hosp 1976; **Fac Appt:** Prof Ped, UCLA

Pediatric Allergy & Immunology

New England

Klein, Robert B MD [PA&I] - **Spec Exp:** Asthma; **Hospital:** Rhode Island Hosp; **Address:** Rhode Island Hosp, Dept of Pediatrics, 593 Eddy St, Providence, RI 02903; **Phone:** 401-444-5648; **Board Cert:** Pediatrics 1976; Allergy & Immunology 1977; **Med School:** Switzerland 1971; **Resid:** Pediatrics, Dartmouth/Hitchcock Med Ctr 1974; **Fellow:** Allergy & Immunology, UCLA Med Ctr 1976; **Fac Appt:** Prof Ped, Brown Univ

Mid Atlantic

Ehrlich, Paul M MD [PA&I] - **Spec Exp:** Asthma; Food Allergy; **Hospital:** NYU Langone Med Ctr (page 68), New York Eye & Ear Infirm (page 64); **Address:** Allergy & Asthma Assocs of Murray Hill, 35 E 35th St, Ste 202, New York, NY 10016-3823; **Phone:** 212-685-4225; **Board Cert:** Pediatrics 1975; Allergy & Immunology 1977; **Med School:** NYU Sch Med 1970; **Resid:** Pediatrics, Bellevue Hosp Ctr 1973; **Fellow:** Allergy & Immunology, Walter Reed Army Med Ctr 1976; **Fac Appt:** Asst Clin Prof Ped, NYU Sch Med

Josephs, Shelby H MD [PA&I] - **Spec Exp:** Food Allergy; Asthma; **Hospital:** MedStar Georgetown Univ Hosp; **Address:** 6000 Executive Blvd, Ste 615, North Bethesda, MD 20852; **Phone:** 240-747-5750; **Board Cert:** Pediatrics 1979; Allergy & Immunology 1985; **Med School:** Duke Univ 1975; **Resid:** Pediatrics, Chldns Hosp 1977; **Fellow:** Allergy & Immunology, Duke Univ Med Ctr 1979; **Fac Appt:** Assoc Clin Prof Ped, Georgetown Univ

Kamani, Naynesh R MD [PA&I] - **Spec Exp:** Stem Cell Transplant; Immunotherapy; Bone Marrow Transplant; **Hospital:** Chldns Natl Med Ctr; **Address:** 111 Michigan Ave NW, East Twr, Fl 4, Ste 4043, Washington, DC 20010; **Phone:** 202-476-2140; **Board Cert:** Pediatrics 1983; Allergy & Immunology 1983; Diagnostic Lab Immunology 1986; **Med School:** Ethiopia 1975; **Resid:** Pediatrics, Kings County Hosp Ctr 1981; **Fellow:** Pediatric Allergy & Immunology, Chldns Hosp 1983; **Fac Appt:** Prof Ped, Geo Wash Univ

Sampson Jr, Hugh A MD [PA&I] - **Spec Exp:** Food Allergy; Eczema; Atopic Dermatitis; **Hospital:** Mt Sinai Med Ctr (page 62); **Address:** Faculty Practice Assocs, 5 E 98th St Fl 10, New York, NY 10029; **Phone:** 212-241-5548; **Board Cert:** Pediatrics 1980; Allergy & Immunology 1981; **Med School:** SUNY Buffalo 1975; **Resid:** Pediatrics, Chldns Meml Hosp 1979; **Fellow:** Allergy & Immunology, Duke Univ Med Ctr 1980; **Fac Appt:** Prof Ped, Mount Sinai Sch Med

Schuberth, Kenneth C MD [PA&I] - **Spec Exp:** Allergy; Asthma; Drug Sensitivity; Food Allergy; **Hospital:** Johns Hopkins Hosp (page 59), Greater Baltimore Med Ctr; **Address:** Maryland Pediatric Grp, 10807 Falls Rd, Ste 200, Lutherville, MD 21093; **Phone:** 410-321-9393; **Board Cert:** Pediatrics 1979; Allergy & Immunology 1983; **Med School:** Johns Hopkins Univ 1973; **Resid:** Pediatrics, Johns Hopkins Hosp 1978; **Fellow:** Allergy & Immunology, Johns Hopkins Hosp 1980; **Fac Appt:** Assoc Prof Ped, Johns Hopkins Univ

Sicherer, Scott H MD [PA&I] - **Spec Exp:** Food Allergy; Drug Sensitivity; Eczema; Asthma; **Hospital:** Mt Sinai Med Ctr (page 62); **Address:** Faculty Practice Assocs, 5 E 98th St Fl 10, New York, NY 10029-6500; **Phone:** 212-241-5548; **Board Cert:** Pediatrics 2008; Allergy & Immunology 2007; **Med School:** Johns Hopkins Univ 1990; **Resid:** Pediatrics, Mt Sinai Hosp 1994; **Fellow:** Allergy & Immunology, Johns Hopkins Hosp 1997; **Fac Appt:** Prof Ped, Mount Sinai Sch Med

Skoner, David Peter MD [PA&I] - **Spec Exp:** Asthma & Allergy; Rhinitis; **Hospital:** Allegheny Genl Hosp; **Address:** Allegheny Genl Hosp, Asthma Allergy, 490 E North Ave, Ste 207, Pittsburgh, PA 15212; **Phone:** 412-359-6640; **Board Cert:** Pediatrics 1985; Allergy & Immunology 1985; **Med School:** Temple Univ 1980; **Resid:** Pediatrics, Chldns Hosp Med Ctr 1983; **Fellow:** Allergy & Immunology, Chldns Hosp 1985; **Fac Appt:** Prof Ped, Temple Univ

Sly, R Michael MD [PA&I] - **Spec Exp:** Asthma; Allergy; Atopic Dermatitis; **Hospital:** Chldns Natl Med Ctr; **Address:** Chldns Natl Med Ctr, 9850 Key West Ave Fl 4, Rockville, MD 20850; **Phone:** 301-765-5400; **Board Cert:** Pediatric Allergy & Immunology 1967; Pediatrics 1980; Allergy & Immunology 1987; **Med School:** Washington Univ, St Louis 1960; **Resid:** Pediatrics, St Louis Chldns Hosp 1962; Pediatrics, Univ Kentucky Med Ctr 1963; **Fellow:** Pediatric Allergy & Immunology, UCLA Med Ctr 1967; **Fac Appt:** Prof Ped, Geo Wash Univ

Spergel, Jonathan M MD/PhD [PA&I] - **Spec Exp:** Atopic Dermatitis; Food Allergy; Asthma; Eosinophilic Esophagitis; **Hospital:** Chldns Hosp of Philadelphia; **Address:** Chldns Hosp, Allergy & Immunology, 3550 Market St Fl 3, Philadelphia, PA 19104; **Phone:** 215-590-2549; **Board Cert:** Allergy & Immunology 2006; **Med School:** Mount Sinai Sch Med 1992; **Resid:** Pediatrics, Yale-New Haven Hosp 1994; **Fellow:** Allergy & Immunology, Chldns Hosp 1997; **Fac Appt:** Assoc Prof Ped, Univ Pennsylvania

Sullivan, Kathleen E MD/PhD [PA&I] - **Spec Exp:** Immune Deficiency; Lupus/SLE; **Hospital:** Chldns Hosp of Philadelphia; **Address:** Chldns Hosp, Allergy & Immunology, 3550 Market St Fl 3, Philadelphia, PA 19104; **Phone:** 215-590-2549; **Board Cert:** Pediatrics 2008; Pediatric Rheumatology 2009; **Med School:** UCSF 1988; **Resid:** Pediatrics, UCSF Med Ctr 1990; **Fellow:** Pediatric Rheumatology, Jonhs Hopkins Hosp 1993; **Fac Appt:** Prof Ped, Univ Pennsylvania

Wood, Robert A MD [PA&I] - **Spec Exp:** Food Allergy; Asthma; **Hospital:** Johns Hopkins Hosp (page 59); **Address:** Johns Hopkins Children's Ctr, 600 N Wolfe St, CMSC-1102, Baltimore, MD 21287; **Phone:** 410-955-5883; **Board Cert:** Pediatrics 1987; Allergy & Immunology 2010; **Med School:** Univ Rochester 1982; **Resid:** Pediatrics, Johns Hopkins Hosp 1986; **Fellow:** Allergy & Immunology, Johns Hopkins Hosp 1988; **Fac Appt:** Prof Ped, Johns Hopkins Univ

Southeast

Burks Jr, A Wesley MD [PA&I] - **Spec Exp:** Asthma; Allergic Rhinitis; Food Allergy; Anaphylaxis; **Hospital:** NC Memorial Hosp - UNC; **Address:** 101 Manning Drive, Chapel Hill, NC 27599; **Phone:** 919-966-1505; **Board Cert:** Pediatrics 1985; Allergy & Immunology 1985; **Med School:** Univ Ark 1980; **Resid:** Pediatrics, Ark Chldns Hosp 1983; **Fellow:** Allergy & Immunology, Duke Univ Med Ctr 1985; **Fac Appt:** Prof Ped, Duke Univ

Kelly, Cynthia S MD [PA&I] - **Spec Exp:** Asthma; Rhinitis; Sinusitis; **Hospital:** Chldns Hosp of King's Daughters; **Address:** Chlds Hosp of The Kings Daughters, 601 Childrens Lane, Fl 4th, Norfolk, VA 23507; **Phone:** 757-668-8255; **Board Cert:** Allergy & Immunology 2007; **Med School:** Wayne State Univ 1985; **Resid:** Pediatrics, Univ Mich 1987; **Fellow:** Allergy & Immunology, UCLA Med Ctr 1988; Pediatric Infectious Disease, Vanderbilt Univ 1989; **Fac Appt:** Assoc Prof Ped, Eastern VA Med Sch

Midwest

Lemanske Jr, Robert F MD [PA&I] - **Spec Exp:** Asthma; Allergy; Immune Deficiency; **Hospital:** Univ WI Hosp & Clins; **Address:** Univ WI Hosp - West Clin - Div Ped A&I, 451 Junction Rd, Madison, WI 53717; **Phone:** 608-263-6180; **Board Cert:** Pediatrics 1980; Allergy & Immunology 1981; **Med School:** Univ Wisc 1975; **Resid:** Pediatrics, Univ WI Hosp & Clins 1979; **Fellow:** Allergy & Immunology, Univ WI Hosp & Clins 1980; Allergy & Immunology, Natl Inst Hlth 1983; **Fac Appt:** Prof Ped, Univ Wisc

Pongracic, Jacqueline MD [PA&I] - **Spec Exp:** Latex Allergy; Asthma; Food Allergy; **Hospital:** Lurie Chldn's Hosp-Chicago; **Address:** Lurie Chldn's Hosp, 225 E Chicago Ave, Box 60, Chicago, IL 60611; **Phone:** 312-227-6010; **Board Cert:** Internal Medicine 1988; Allergy & Immunology 2012; **Med School:** Northwestern Univ 1985; **Resid:** Internal Medicine, North Shore Univ Hosp 1988; **Fellow:** Allergy & Immunology, Johns Hopkins Hosp 1991; **Fac Appt:** Prof Ped, Northwestern Univ-Feinberg Sch Med

Strunk, Robert C MD [PA&I] - **Spec Exp:** Asthma; **Hospital:** St. Louis Chldns Hosp; **Address:** 660 S Euclid Ave, Campus Box 8116, St Louis, MO 63110; **Phone:** 314-454-2694; **Board Cert:** Pediatrics 1974; Allergy & Immunology 1987; **Med School:** Northwestern Univ 1968; **Resid:** Pediatrics, Cincinnati Chldns Hosp 1970; **Fellow:** Pediatric Allergy & Immunology, Boston Chldns Hosp 1974; **Fac Appt:** Prof Ped, Washington Univ, St Louis

Wolf, Raoul MD [PA&I] - **Spec Exp:** Asthma; Allergy; Immune Deficiency; **Hospital:** Univ Chicago Med-Comer Chldn's Hosp; **Address:** Univ Chicago-Comer Chldn's Hosp, 5721 S Maryland Ave Fl 2, Chicago, IL 60637; **Phone:** 773-834-4010; **Board Cert:** Pediatrics 1980; Allergy & Immunology 1983; **Med School:** South Africa 1969; **Resid:** Pediatrics, Baragwanath Hosp 1973; Pediatrics, Transvaal Meml Hosp Chldn 1976; **Fellow:** Allergy & Immunology, Chldns Hosp Med Ctr 1979; **Fac Appt:** Prof Ped, Univ Chicago-Pritzker Sch Med

Great Plains and Mountains

Bock, Samuel A MD [PA&I] - **Spec Exp:** Asthma up to age 50; Allergy up to age 50; Food Allergy; **Hospital:** Boulder Community Hospital, Avista Adventist Hosp; **Address:** Boulder Valley Asthma And Allergy, 3950 Broadway, Boulder, CO 80304; **Phone:** 303-444-5995; **Board Cert:** Pediatrics 1977; Allergy & Immunology 1977; **Med School:** Univ MD Sch Med 1972; **Resid:** Pediatrics, Colo Med Ctr/Natl Jewish Med Ctr 1975; **Fellow:** Allergy & Immunology, Colo Med Ctr/Natl Jewish Med Ctr 1977; **Fac Appt:** Clin Prof Ped, Univ Colorado

Gelfand, Erwin W MD [PA&I] - **Spec Exp:** Immune Deficiency; Asthma; Allergy; **Hospital:** Natl Jewish Hlth, Chldn's Hosp - Aurora (CO); **Address:** National Jewish Health, 1400 Jackson St, Denver, CO 80206; **Phone:** 303-398-1196; **Board Cert:** Pediatrics 1972; **Med School:** McGill Univ 1966; **Resid:** Pediatrics, Montreal Childrens Hosp 1968; Pediatrics, Childrens Hosp Med Ctr 1969; **Fellow:** Immunology, Childrens Hosp Med Ctr 1971; **Fac Appt:** Prof Ped, Univ Colorado

Leung, Donald YM MD/PhD [PA&I] - **Spec Exp:** Atopic Dermatitis; Asthma; Food Allergy; **Hospital:** Natl Jewish Hlth, Chldn's Hosp - Aurora (CO); **Address:** National Jewish Health, 1400 Jackson St, Goodman Bldg, Ste K926i, Denver, CO 80206; **Phone:** 303-398-1379; **Board Cert:** Pediatrics 1982; Allergy & Immunology 1983; Diagnostic Lab Immunology 1990; **Med School:** Univ Chicago-Pritzker Sch Med 1977; **Resid:** Pediatrics, Chldn's Hosp 1980; **Fellow:** Allergy & Immunology, Chldn's Hosp 1982; **Fac Appt:** Prof Ped, Univ Colorado

Southwest

Bahna, Sami L MD [PA&I] - **Spec Exp:** Food & Drug Allergy; Asthma; Eczema; Immune Deficiency; **Hospital:** Louisiana State Univ Hosp; **Address:** LSU Hlth Scis Ctr, 1501 Kings Hwy, rm 5-323, Department Peds, Sect A&I, Shreveport, LA 71103; **Phone:** 318-675-7625; **Board Cert:** Pediatrics 1980; Allergy & Immunology 1981; **Med School:** Egypt 1964; **Resid:** Pediatrics, Univ Maryland Hosp 1975; **Fellow:** Allergy & Immunology, Harbor-UCLA Med Ctr 1978; **Fac Appt:** Prof Ped, Louisiana State U, Shrevport

Orange, Jordan MD/PhD [PA&I] - **Spec Exp:** Immunodeficiency Disorders; **Hospital:** Texas Chldns Hosp; **Address:** Texas Children's Hospital, Dept Allergy & Immunology, 6621 Fannin St, Houston, TX 77030; **Phone:** 832-824-2030; **Board Cert:** Pediatrics 2008; Allergy & Immunology 2003; **Med School:** Brown Univ 1997; **Resid:** Pediatrics, Chldn's Hosp 2000; **Fellow:** Allergy & Immunology, Chldn's Hosp 2003; **Fac Appt:** Prof Ped, Baylor Coll Med

Shearer, William T MD/PhD [PA&I] - **Spec Exp:** AIDS/HIV; Immune Deficiency; Asthma; Allergy; **Hospital:** Texas Chldns Hosp; **Address:** TX Chldns Allergy & Immunology Clin, TX Chldns Clinical Care Ctr, 6701 Fannin St Fl 9th, Houston, TX 77030-2399; **Phone:** 832-824-1319; **Board Cert:** Pediatrics 1986; Allergy & Immunology 1989; Clinical & Laboratory Immunology 1986; **Med School:** Washington Univ, St Louis 1970; **Resid:** Pediatrics, St Louis Chldns Hosp 1973; **Fellow:** Allergy & Immunology, Barnes Hosp/St Louis Chldns Hosp 1975; **Fac Appt:** Prof Ped, Baylor Coll Med

Wasserman, Richard L MD/PhD [PA&I] - **Spec Exp:** Immunodeficiency Disorders; Food Allergy; Asthma; Allergy; **Hospital:** Med City Dallas Hosp, Chldns Med Ctr of Dallas; **Address:** Dallas Allergy and Immunology, 7777 Forest Ln, Bldg B, Ste 332, Dallas, TX 75230; **Phone:** 972-566-7788; **Board Cert:** Pediatrics 1982; Allergy & Immunology 1987; **Med School:** Univ Tex SW, Dallas 1977; **Resid:** Pediatrics, Chldns Hosp of Philadelphia 1979; **Fellow:** Immunology, Chldns Hosp of Philadelphia 1980; Rheumatology, Rockefeller Univ 1982; **Fac Appt:** Clin Prof A&I, Univ Tex SW, Dallas

West Coast and Pacific

Church, Joseph A MD [PA&I] - **Spec Exp:** Immunodeficiency Disorders; AIDS/HIV; **Hospital:** Chldns Hosp - Los Angeles; **Address:** 4650 W Sunset Blvd, Children's Hospital Los Angeles, MS #75, Los Angeles, CA 90027; **Phone:** 323-361-2501; **Board Cert:** Pediatrics 1977; Allergy & Immunology 1977; **Med School:** UMDNJ-NJ Med Sch, Newark 1972; **Resid:** Pediatrics, Chldns Hosp/Natl Med Ctr 1975; **Fellow:** Allergy & Immunology, Georgetown Med Ctr 1976; **Fac Appt:** Prof Ped, USC-Keck School of Medicine

Cowan, Morton J MD [PA&I] - **Spec Exp:** Immunodeficiency Disorders; Stem Cell Transplant-Fetal; Bone Marrow Transplant; **Hospital:** UCSF Med Ctr; **Address:** UCSF Med Ctr, Peds BMT Program, 505 Parnassus Ave, rm M659, San Francisco, CA 94143-1278; **Phone:** 415-476-2188; **Board Cert:** Pediatrics 1981; Allergy & Immunology 1983; **Med School:** Univ Pennsylvania 1970; **Resid:** Surgery, Duke Univ Med Ctr 1972; Pediatrics, UCSF Med Ctr 1977; **Fellow:** Research, Natl Inst Hlth 1975; Immunology, UCSF Med Ctr 1979; **Fac Appt:** Prof Ped, UCSF

Epstein, Stuart Z MD [PA&I] - **Spec Exp:** Asthma & Allergy; Food Allergy; **Hospital:** Cedars-Sinai Med Ctr, UCLA Ronald Reagan Med Ctr; **Address:** 9735 Wilshire Blvd, Ste 121, Beverly Hills, CA 90212-2101; **Phone:** 310-274-6853; **Board Cert:** Allergy & Immunology 1999; **Med School:** Univ IL Coll Med 1978; **Resid:** Pediatrics, Cedars Sinai Med Ctr 1980; **Fellow:** Allergy & Immunology, UC Irvine 1981; Allergy & Immunology, USC Med Ctr 1982; **Fac Appt:** Assoc Clin Prof Ped, UCLA

Fanous, Yvonne F MD [PA&I] - **Spec Exp:** Asthma & Allergy; Cystic Fibrosis; Immune Deficiency; **Hospital:** Loma Linda Univ Med Ctr; **Address:** Loma Linda Hlth Care Pediatrics, 250 E Caroline St, Ste J, San Bernardino, CA 92408; **Phone:** 909-651-1901; **Board Cert:** Pediatrics 1983; Allergy & Immunology 1985; **Med School:** Egypt 1973; **Resid:** Pediatrics, Texas Tech Univ Hosp 1980; Pediatrics, Loma Linda Univ Med Ctr 1981; **Fellow:** Allergy & Immunology, UC Irvine Med Ctr 1984

Pediatric Cardiology

New England

De Moor, Michael MD [PCd] - **Spec Exp:** Interventional Cardiology; **Hospital:** Floating Hosp for Children at Tufts Med Ce; **Address:** Floating Hosp for Chldn at Tufts Med Ctr, 800 Washington St, Box 313, Boston, MA 02111; **Phone:** 617-636-7435; **Med School:** South Africa 1976; **Resid:** Internal Medicine, Red Cross Chldns Hosp 1983; **Fellow:** Pediatric Cardiology, Red Cross Chldns Hosp 1985; **Fac Appt:** Assoc Prof Ped, Tufts Univ

Hellenbrand, William E MD [PCd] - **Spec Exp:** Interventional Cardiology; **Hospital:** Yale-New Haven Hosp; **Address:** Yale-New Haven Children's Hosp, Pediatric Cardiology, 1 Park St, New Haven, CT 06510; **Phone:** 203-785-2022; **Board Cert:** Pediatrics 1975; Pediatric Cardiology 1977; **Med School:** SUNY Downstate 1970; **Resid:** Pediatrics, Yale-New Haven Hosp 1972; **Fellow:** Pediatric Cardiology, Yale-New Haven Hosp 1976; **Fac Appt:** Prof Ped, Columbia P&S

Lang, Peter MD [PCd] - **Hospital:** Children's Hospital - Boston; **Address:** Boston Chldn's Hosp, Dept Cardiology, 300 Longwood Ave, Boston, MA 02114; **Phone:** 617-355-8539; **Board Cert:** Pediatrics 1977; Pediatric Cardiology 1979; **Med School:** Mount Sinai Sch Med 1972; **Resid:** Pediatrics, Babies Hosp-Presby Med Ctr 1975; **Fellow:** Pediatric Cardiology, Chldns Hosp Med Ctr 1978; **Fac Appt:** Assoc Prof Ped, Harvard Med Sch

Lock, James E MD [PCd] - **Spec Exp:** Cardiac Catheterization; **Hospital:** Children's Hospital - Boston; **Address:** Chldns Hosp, Dept Cardiology, 300 Longwood Ave, Boston, MA 02115; **Phone:** 617-355-7313; **Board Cert:** Pediatrics 1978; Pediatric Cardiology 1981; **Med School:** Stanford Univ 1973; **Resid:** Pediatrics, Univ Minn Hosp 1975; Pediatric Cardiology, Univ Minn Hosp 1977; **Fellow:** Research, Hosp Sick Chldn 1979; **Fac Appt:** Prof Ped, Harvard Med Sch

Newburger, Jane MD [PCd] - **Spec Exp:** Kawasaki Disease; Congenital Heart Disease; **Hospital:** Children's Hospital - Boston, Brigham & Women's Hosp; **Address:** Boston Chldn's Hosp, Dept Ped Cardiology, 300 Longwood Ave, Farley Bldg Fl 2, Boston, MA 02115; **Phone:** 617-355-5427; **Board Cert:** Pediatrics 1979; Pediatric Cardiology 1983; **Med School:** Harvard Med Sch 1974; **Resid:** Pediatrics, Chldns Hosp Med Ctr 1976; **Fellow:** Pediatric Cardiology, Chldns Hosp Med Ctr 1979; **Fac Appt:** Prof Ped, Harvard Med Sch

Walsh, Edward P MD [PCd] - **Spec Exp:** Arrhythmias; **Hospital:** Children's Hospital - Boston; **Address:** Boston Chldn's Hosp, Dept Cardiology, 300 Longwood Ave Bader Bldg Fl 2, Boston, MA 02115; **Phone:** 617-355-6328; **Board Cert:** Pediatrics 1985; Pediatric Cardiology 1985; **Med School:** Univ Pennsylvania 1979; **Resid:** Pediatrics, Chldns Hosp 1982; **Fellow:** Pediatric Cardiology, Chldns Hosp 1985; **Fac Appt:** Assoc Prof Ped, Harvard Med Sch

Mid Atlantic

Beerman, Lee B MD [PCd] - **Spec Exp:** Congenital Heart Disease-Adult & Child; Arrhythmias; **Hospital:** Chldns Hosp of Pittsburgh - UPMC; **Address:** Chldns Hosp, Heart Ctr, 4401 Penn Ave Fl 5, Pittsburgh, PA 15224; **Phone:** 412-692-5540; **Board Cert:** Pediatrics 1979; Pediatric Cardiology 1979; **Med School:** Univ Pittsburgh 1974; **Resid:** Pediatrics, Chldns Hosp 1977; **Fellow:** Pediatric Cardiology, Chldns Hosp 1979; **Fac Appt:** Prof Ped, Univ Pittsburgh

Biancaniello, Thomas MD [PCd] - **Spec Exp:** Congenital Heart Disease; Fetal Echocardiography; Interventional Cardiology; Cardiac Catheterization; **Hospital:** Morgan Stanley Children's Hosp of NY-Presby, NY (page 65); **Address:** 57 Southern Blvd, Ste 3, Nesconset, NY 11767; **Phone:** 631-265-3300; **Board Cert:** Pediatrics 1979; Pediatric Cardiology 1981; **Med School:** NY Med Coll 1975; **Resid:** Pediatrics, North Shore Univ Hosp 1977; **Fellow:** Pediatric Cardiology, Cincinnati Chldns Hosp 1980; **Fac Appt:** Prof Ped, Columbia P&S

Bierman, Fredrick Zachary MD [PCd] - **Spec Exp:** Fetal Echocardiography; Kawasaki Disease; Congenital Heart Disease; Echocardiography; **Hospital:** Westchester Med Ctr; **Address:** 19 Bradhurst Ave, Hawthorne, NY 10532; **Phone:** 914-594-4370; **Board Cert:** Pediatrics 1978; Pediatric Cardiology 1981; **Med School:** SUNY Downstate 1973; **Resid:** Pediatrics, Mount Sinai Med Ctr 1976; **Fellow:** Pediatric Cardiology, Harvard Chldns Hosp 1979; **Fac Appt:** Prof Ped, NY Med Coll

Brenner, Joel I MD [PCd] - **Spec Exp:** Congenital Heart Disease; **Hospital:** Johns Hopkins Hosp (page 59); **Address:** Johns Hopkins Hosp, Div Pediatric Cardiology, 1800 Orleans St, Baltimore, MD 21287; **Phone:** 410-955-5987; **Board Cert:** Pediatrics 1975; Pediatric Cardiology 1977; **Med School:** NY Med Coll 1970; **Resid:** Pediatrics, NY Hosp 1972; **Fellow:** Pediatric Cardiology, Yale-New Haven Hosp 1974; **Fac Appt:** Assoc Prof Ped, Johns Hopkins Univ

Cooper, Rubin MD [PCd] - **Spec Exp:** Congenital Heart Disease; Rheumatic Heart Disease; Kawasaki Disease; **Hospital:** Steven & Alexandra Cohen Chldn's Med Ctr of NY (page 66), Long Is Jewish Med Ctr (page 66); **Address:** Steven & Alexandra Cohen Chldns Med Ctr, 269-01 76th Ave, Ste 139, New Hyde Park, NY 11040; **Phone:** 718-470-3661; **Board Cert:** Pediatrics 1976; Pediatric Cardiology 1979; **Med School:** NY Med Coll 1971; **Resid:** Pediatrics, Strong Meml Hosp 1976; **Fellow:** Pediatric Cardiology, Strong Meml Hosp 1979; **Fac Appt:** Prof Ped, Cornell Univ-Weill Med Coll

Crosson, Jane MD [PCd] - **Spec Exp:** Congenital Heart Disease-Adult & Child; Pacemakers; Syncope; Fetal Echocardiography; **Hospital:** Johns Hopkins Hosp (page 59); **Address:** 1800 Orleans St, Baltimore, MD 21287; **Phone:** 410-955-5987; **Board Cert:** Pediatrics 1987; Pediatric Cardiology 2010; **Med School:** Med Coll GA 1982; **Resid:** Pediatrics, Univ MD Hosp 1986; **Fellow:** Pediatric Cardiology, Univ Minn Hosp 1990

Gelb, Bruce D MD [PCd] - **Spec Exp:** Noonan Syndrome; Marfan's Syndrome; **Hospital:** Mt Sinai Med Ctr (page 62); **Address:** 1 Gustave Levy Pl, Box 1201, New York, NY 10029; **Phone:** 212-241-8592; **Board Cert:** Pediatric Cardiology 2013; **Med School:** Univ Rochester 1984; **Resid:** Pediatrics, NYPresby-Columbia Univ Med Ctr 1987; **Fellow:** Pediatric Cardiology, Baylor College Med 1991; **Fac Appt:** Prof Ped, Mount Sinai Sch Med

Gewitz, Michael H MD [PCd] - **Spec Exp:** Neonatal Cardiology; Kawasaki Disease; Echocardiography; Heart Failure; **Hospital:** Westchester Med Ctr, Children's & Women's Phys.of Westchester; **Address:** Maria Fareri Children's Hospital, 100 Woods Rd, Munger Pavilion, Ste 618, Valhalla, NY 10595; **Phone:** 914-594-4370; **Board Cert:** Pediatrics 1979; Pediatric Cardiology 1981; **Med School:** Hahnemann Univ 1974; **Resid:** Pediatrics, Chldns Hosp 1976; Pediatrics, Hosp Sick Chldn 1977; **Fellow:** Pediatric Cardiology, Yale-New Haven Hosp 1980; **Fac Appt:** Prof Ped, NY Med Coll

Hanna, Brian D MD/PhD [PCd] - **Spec Exp:** Pulmonary Hypertension; Cardiac Catheterization; Autonomic Disorders; Congenital Heart Disease; **Hospital:** Chldns Hosp of Philadelphia; **Address:** Chldns Hosp, Ped Cardiology Dept, 34th St & Civic Center Blvd, Philadelphia, PA 19104; **Phone:** 215-590-5248; **Board Cert:** Pediatric Cardiology 2009; **Med School:** Canada 1983; **Resid:** Pediatrics, Montreal Chldns Hosp 1986; **Fellow:** Pediatric Cardiology, Montreal Chldns Hosp 1987; Pediatric Cardiology, Childrens Hosp 1989; **Fac Appt:** Clin Prof Ped, Univ Pennsylvania

Hsu, Daphne T MD [PCd] - **Spec Exp:** Interventional Cardiology; Heart Failure; Transplant Medicine-Heart; **Hospital:** Montefiore Med Ctr-Moses Campus, NY; **Address:** Children's Hosp at Montefiore, 3415 Bainbridge Ave, Bronx, NY 10467; **Phone:** 718-741-2343; **Board Cert:** Pediatrics 1988; Pediatric Cardiology 2010; **Med School:** Yale Univ 1982; **Resid:** Pediatrics, Columbia Babies & Chldn's Hosp 1985; **Fellow:** Pediatric Cardiology, Columbia Babies & Chldn's Hosp 1988; **Fac Appt:** Prof Ped, Albert Einstein Coll Med

Murphy, John D MD [PCd] - **Spec Exp:** Cardiac Catheterization; Interventional Cardiology; **Hospital:** St. Christopher's Hosp for Chldn; **Address:** St Christophers Hosp, Heart Ctr, 3601 A St Fl 2, Philadelphia, PA 19134; **Phone:** 215-427-4820; **Board Cert:** Pediatrics 1980; Pediatric Cardiology 1981; **Med School:** Univ VT Coll Med 1975; **Resid:** Pediatrics, Chldns Hosp 1977; **Fellow:** Pediatric Cardiology, Chldns Hosp 1980; **Fac Appt:** Prof Ped, Drexel Univ Coll Med

Parness, Ira A MD [PCd] - **Spec Exp:** Echocardiography; Congenital Heart Disease; Fetal Echocardiography; **Hospital:** Mt Sinai Med Ctr (page 62), Englewood Hosp & Med Ctr; **Address:** 1 Gustave L Levy Pl, Anbg Bldg, rm 3-40, Box 1201, New York, NY 10029-6574; **Phone:** 212-241-6640; **Board Cert:** Pediatrics 1984; Pediatric Cardiology 1985; **Med School:** SUNY Downstate 1979; **Resid:** Pediatrics, Brookdale Hosp 1982; **Fellow:** Pediatric Cardiology, Chldns Hosp 1985; **Fac Appt:** Prof Ped, Mount Sinai Sch Med

Radtke, Wolfgang MD [PCd] - **Spec Exp:** Interventional Cardiology; Cardiac Catheterization; Congenital Heart Disease-Adult & Child; **Hospital:** Nemours/Alfred I. duPont Hosp for Chldn; **Address:** Nemours, Cardiac Ctr, 1600 Rockland Rd, Wilmington, DE 19803; **Phone:** 302-651-6600; **Board Cert:** Pediatric Cardiology 2012; **Med School:** Germany 1980; **Resid:** Pediatrics, Kiel Univ Chldns Hosp 1985; **Fellow:** Pediatric Cardiology, Chldns Hosp 1988; **Fac Appt:** Prof Ped, Jefferson Med Coll

Rome, Jonathan J MD [PCd] - **Spec Exp:** Interventional Cardiology; Percutaneous ASD/PFO Closure; Congenital Heart Disease; **Hospital:** Chldns Hosp of Philadelphia; **Address:** Chldns Hosp, Ped Cardiology Dept, 3400 Civic Center Blvd, Ste 6NE40, Philadelphia, PA 19104; **Phone:** 215-590-1790; **Board Cert:** Pediatrics 1987; Pediatric Cardiology 2010; **Med School:** Stanford Univ 1982; **Resid:** Pediatrics, Chldns Hosp 1986; **Fellow:** Pediatric Cardiology, Chldns Hosp 1989; **Fac Appt:** Assoc Prof Ped, Univ Pennsylvania

Rychik, Jack MD [PCd] - **Spec Exp:** Echocardiography; Fetal Cardiology; Congenital Heart Disease; **Hospital:** Chldns Hosp of Philadelphia; **Address:** Chldns Hosp, Fetal Heart, 34th St & Civic Center Blvd, Ste 6W61, Philadelphia, PA 19104; **Phone:** 215-590-5647; **Board Cert:** Pediatric Cardiology 2013; **Med School:** SUNY Downstate 1985; **Resid:** Pediatrics, Albert Einstein Med Coll Affil Hosp 1988; **Fellow:** Pediatric Cardiology, Chldns Hosp 1991; **Fac Appt:** Prof Ped, Univ Pennsylvania

Shaddy, Robert E MD [PCd] - **Spec Exp:** Transplant Medicine-Heart; Heart Failure; **Hospital:** Chldns Hosp of Philadelphia; **Address:** CHOP - Division Cardiology, 34th St & Civic Center Blvd, Main Hosp Bldg - Fl 2, rm 220, Philadelphia, PA 19104; **Phone:** 215-590-4040 x1; **Board Cert:** Pediatrics 1984; Pediatric Cardiology 2000; **Med School:** Creighton Univ 1980; **Resid:** Pediatrics, Univ Iowa Hosp & Clinics 1984; **Fellow:** Pediatric Cardiology, UCSF Med Ctr 1986; **Fac Appt:** Prof Ped, Univ Pennsylvania

Sherman, Frederick S MD [PCd] - **Spec Exp:** Fetal Cardiology; **Hospital:** Chldns Hosp of Pittsburgh - UPMC, Magee-Womens Hosp - UPMC; **Address:** Chldns Hosp, Heart Ctr, 4401 Penn Ave Fl 3, Pittsburgh, PA 15224; **Phone:** 412-692-5540; **Board Cert:** Pediatrics 1980; Pediatric Cardiology 1985; **Med School:** Yale Univ 1975; **Resid:** Pediatrics, Univ Virginia Hosp 1978; **Fellow:** Pediatric Cardiology, Chldns Hosp 1984; **Fac Appt:** Prof Ped, Univ Pittsburgh

Sommer, Robert J MD [PCd] - **Spec Exp:** Congenital Heart Disease; Atrial Septal Defect; Cardiac Catheterization; **Hospital:** NY-Presby/Columbia Univ Med Ctr, NY (page 65), St. Joseph's Regl Med Ctr - Paterson; **Address:** 161 Fort Washington Ave Fl 6, Herbert Irving Pavilion, New York, NY 10032; **Phone:** 212-342-0886; **Board Cert:** Pediatric Cardiology 2013; **Med School:** NYU Sch Med 1985; **Resid:** Pediatrics, Mt Sinai Med Ctr 1988; **Fellow:** Pediatric Cardiology, Mt Sinai Med Ctr 1991; Interventional Cardiology, Childrens Hosp 1991; **Fac Appt:** Asst Clin Prof Ped, Columbia P&S

Steinherz, Laurel J MD [PCd] - **Spec Exp:** Cardiac Effects of Cancer/Cancer Therapy; **Hospital:** Meml Sloan-Kettering Canc Ctr, NY-Presby/Weill Cornell Med Ctr, NY (page 65); **Address:** 1275 York Ave, New York, NY 10021; **Phone:** 212-639-8103; **Board Cert:** Pediatrics 1976; Pediatric Cardiology 1978; **Med School:** Albert Einstein Coll Med 1970; **Resid:** Pediatrics, NY Hosp-Cornell Med Ctr 1971; Pediatrics, Chldns Hosp 1972; **Fellow:** Pediatric Cardiology, NY Hosp-Cornell Med Ctr 1975; **Fac Appt:** Prof Ped, Cornell Univ-Weill Med Coll

Velvis, Harmannus MD [PCd] - **Spec Exp:** Cardiac Catheterization; Congenital Heart Disease; Heart Disease in Down Syndrome; Interventional Cardiology; **Hospital:** Albany Med Ctr; **Address:** Capital District Pediatric Cardiology, 319 S Manning Blvd, Ste 203, Albany, NY 12208; **Phone:** 518-489-3292; **Board Cert:** Pediatric Cardiology 2009; **Med School:** Netherlands 1980; **Resid:** Pediatrics, Albany Med Ctr 1987; **Fellow:** Pediatric Cardiology, UCSF Med Ctr 1990; **Fac Appt:** Assoc Clin Prof Ped, Albany Med Coll

Walsh, Christine A MD [PCd] - **Spec Exp:** Arrhythmias; Congenital Heart Disease; Sudden Infant Death Syndrome (SIDS); Syncope; **Hospital:** Montefiore Med Ctr-Moses Campus, NY; **Address:** 3415 Bainbridge Ave Fl 5, Bronx, NY 10467-2401; **Phone:** 718-741-2343; **Board Cert:** Pediatrics 1978; Pediatric Cardiology 1983; **Med School:** Yale Univ 1973; **Resid:** Pediatrics, Columbia-Presby Med Ctr 1976; **Fellow:** Pediatric Cardiology, Columbia-Presby Med Ctr 1980; **Fac Appt:** Prof Ped, Albert Einstein Coll Med

Weinberg, Paul M MD [PCd] - **Spec Exp:** Cardiac MRI; Congenital Heart Disease; **Hospital:** Chldns Hosp of Philadelphia; **Address:** Chldns Hosp, Div Cardiology, 3400 Civic Center Blvd, Ste 8NW90, Philadelphia, PA 19104; **Phone:** 215-590-3274; **Board Cert:** Pediatrics 1974; Pediatric Cardiology 1975; **Med School:** Jefferson Med Coll 1969; **Resid:** Pediatrics, Chldns Hosp 1971; Cardiology & Pathology, Chldns Hosp 1977; **Fellow:** Pediatric Cardiology, Chldns Hosp 1973; **Fac Appt:** Prof Ped, Univ Pennsylvania

Southeast

Colvin, Edward V MD [PCd] - **Spec Exp:** Congenital Heart Disease-Adult & Child; Fetal Echocardiography; Transplant Medicine-Heart; **Hospital:** Children's Hosp AL, UAB Hosp; **Address:** UAB Pediatric Cardiology, 1700 6th Ave S, 176F, Ste 9100, Birmingham, AL 35249; **Phone:** 205-934-3460; **Board Cert:** Pediatrics 1982; Pediatric Cardiology 1985; **Med School:** UAB Sch Med 1977; **Resid:** Pediatrics, Chldns Hosp 1980; **Fellow:** Pediatric Cardiology, Baylor Coll Med Affil Hosp 1983; **Fac Appt:** Prof Ped, UAB Sch Med

Fish, Frank A MD [PCd] - **Spec Exp:** Arrhythmias-Pediatric & Adult; Congenital Heart Disease-Adult; Pacemakers; Catheter Ablation; **Hospital:** Vanderbilt Monroe Carrell Jr. Chldn's Hosp, Vanderbilt Univ Med Ctr; **Address:** Vanderbilt Chldns Hosp, Div Pediatric Cardiology, 2200 Children's Way, 5230 DOT, Nashville, TN 37232-9119; **Phone:** 615-322-7447; **Board Cert:** Pediatrics 1987; Pediatric Cardiology 2013; **Med School:** Indiana Univ 1983; **Resid:** Pediatrics, Indiana Univ Hosp 1986; **Fellow:** Pediatric Cardiology, Vanderbilt Univ Med Ctr 1989; Cardiac Electrophysiology, Chldns Meml Hosp 1990; **Fac Appt:** Prof Ped, Vanderbilt Univ

Fricker, F. Jay MD [PCd] - **Spec Exp:** Transplant Medicine-Heart; Congenital Heart Disease; Heart Failure; **Hospital:** UF Hlth Shands Hosp; **Address:** UF Hlth, Congenital Heart Ctr, 1600 SW Archer Rd, Box 100296, Gainesville, FL 32608; **Phone:** 352-273-7770; **Board Cert:** Pediatrics 1975; Pediatric Cardiology 1981; **Med School:** Loyola Univ-Stritch Sch Med 1970; **Resid:** Pediatrics, Chldns Hosp 1973; **Fellow:** Pediatric Cardiology, Chldns Hosp 1977; **Fac Appt:** Prof Ped, Univ Fla Coll Med

Gullquist, Scott D MD [PCd] - **Spec Exp:** Cardiac Electrophysiology; **Hospital:** VCU Med Ctr; **Address:** VCU Med Ctr, Pediatric Cardiology, 1200 E Broad St, Ste 5-101, Richmond, VA 23298; **Phone:** 804-828-9339; **Board Cert:** Pediatric Cardiology 2009; **Med School:** Georgetown Univ 1987; **Resid:** Pediatrics, Chldns Hosp 1990; **Fellow:** Pediatric Cardiology, Chldns Hosp 1993; **Fac Appt:** Assoc Prof Ped, Med Coll VA

Latson, Larry A MD [PCd] - **Spec Exp:** Congenital Heart Disease-Adult & Child; Interventional Cardiology; Cardiac Catheterization; **Hospital:** Joe DiMaggio Chldns Hosp, Meml Regl Hosp; **Address:** 1150 N 35th Ave, Ste 575, Hollywood, FL 33021; **Phone:** 954-265-3437; **Board Cert:** Pediatrics 1981; Pediatric Cardiology 1983; **Med School:** Baylor Coll Med 1976; **Resid:** Pediatrics, Baylor Affil Hosp 1978; **Fellow:** Pediatric Cardiology, Baylor Coll Med 1981; **Fac Appt:** Clin Prof Med, Lk Erie Coll Osteo Med, FL

Moskowitz, William B MD [PCd] - **Spec Exp:** Patent Foramen Ovale; Cardiac Catheterization; Coarctation of the Aorta; Congenital Heart Disease-Adult & Child; **Hospital:** Med Coll of VA Hosp; **Address:** Childrens Heart Ctr, Med Coll Virginia, 1200 E Broad St, Richmond, VA 23298; **Phone:** 804-828-9143; **Board Cert:** Pediatrics 1983; Pediatric Cardiology 1985; **Med School:** Univ S Fla Coll Med 1978; **Resid:** Pediatrics, Chldns Hosp 1981; **Fellow:** Pediatric Cardiology, Chldns Hosp 1984; **Fac Appt:** Prof Ped, Med Coll VA

Young, Ming-Lon MD [PCd] - **Spec Exp:** Cardiac Electrophysiology; Arrhythmias; Syncope; **Hospital:** Joe DiMaggio Chldns Hosp; **Address:** Joe DiMaggio Chldns Hosp, Ped Cardiology, 1150 N 35th Ave, Ste 575, Hollywood, FL 33021; **Phone:** 954-265-3437; **Board Cert:** Pediatrics 1985; Pediatric Cardiology 2009; **Med School:** Taiwan 1976; **Resid:** Preventive Medicine, Johns Hopkins Hosp 1979; Pediatrics, St Agnes Hosp 1981; **Fellow:** Pediatric Cardiology, Univ Miami Hosp 1985; Pediatric Cardiac Electrophysiology, Univ Miami Hosp 1985; **Fac Appt:** Prof Ped, Univ Miami Sch Med

Midwest

Ackerman, Michael J MD/PhD [PCd] - **Spec Exp:** Long QT Interval Syndrome; Sudden Infant Death Syndrome (SIDS); Hypertrophic Cardiomyopathy; Sudden Unexplained Death Syndrome (SUDS); **Hospital:** Mayo Med Ctr & Clin - Rochester; **Address:** Mayo Clin, Dept Ped Cardiology, 200 First St SW, Rochester, MN 55905; **Phone:** 507-284-0101; **Board Cert:** Pediatric Cardiology 2010; **Med School:** Mayo Med Sch 1995; **Resid:** Pediatric & Adolescent Medicine, Mayo Clin 1998; **Fellow:** Pediatric Cardiology, Mayo Clin 2000; **Fac Appt:** Prof Ped, Mayo Med Sch

Agarwala, Brojendra MD [PCd] - **Spec Exp:** Congenital Heart Disease; **Hospital:** Univ Chicago Med-Comer Chldn's Hosp; **Address:** 5841 S Maryland Ave, rm C-104, MC 4051, Chicago, IL 60637; **Phone:** 773-702-6172; **Board Cert:** Pediatrics 1970; Pediatric Cardiology 1978; **Med School:** India 1965; **Resid:** Pediatrics, St Vincent Hosp Med Ctr 1969; **Fellow:** Pediatric Cardiology, NYU Med Ctr 1972; **Fac Appt:** Prof Ped, Univ Chicago-Pritzker Sch Med

Beekman III, Robert H MD [PCd] - **Spec Exp:** Interventional Cardiology; Cardiac Catheterization; **Hospital:** Cincinnati Chldns Hosp Med Ctr; **Address:** Cincinnati Chldns Hosp Med Ctr, Heart Inst, 3333 Burnet Ave, Cincinnati, OH 45229-3026; **Phone:** 513-636-7072; **Board Cert:** Pediatrics 1981; Pediatric Cardiology 1983; **Med School:** Duke Univ 1976; **Resid:** Pediatrics, UCLA Med Ctr 1979; **Fellow:** Pediatric Cardiology, Univ Mich Hosp 1981; **Fac Appt:** Prof Ped, Univ Cincinnati

Caldwell, Randall L MD [PCd] - **Spec Exp:** Transplant Medicine-Heart; Echocardiography; Congenital Heart Disease; **Hospital:** Riley Hosp for Children; **Address:** Riley Hosp for Chldn-Ped Cardiology, 705 Riley Hospital Drive, rm 127, Indianapolis, IN 46202-5128; **Phone:** 317-274-8906; **Board Cert:** Pediatrics 1976; Pediatric Cardiology 1978; **Med School:** Indiana Univ 1971; **Resid:** Pediatrics, Indiana Univ Med Ctr 1974; **Fellow:** Pediatric Cardiology, Indiana Univ Med Ctr 1978; **Fac Appt:** Prof Ped, Indiana Univ

Cetta Jr, Frank MD [PCd] - **Spec Exp:** Congenital Heart Disease-Adult; Congenital Heart Disease; **Hospital:** Mayo Med Ctr & Clin - Rochester; **Address:** Mayo Clinic, 200 1st St SW, Gonda 6-138 SW, Rochester, MN 55905; **Phone:** 507-266-0676; **Board Cert:** Pediatric Cardiology 2011; **Med School:** Loyola Univ-Stritch Sch Med 1987; **Resid:** Internal Medicine & Pediatrics, Loyola Med Ctr 1991; **Fac Appt:** Assoc Prof Ped, Mayo Med Sch

Cheatham, John P MD [PCd] - **Spec Exp:** Congenital Heart Disease-Adult & Child; Cardiac Catheterization; Interventional Cardiology; **Hospital:** Nationwide Chldn's Hosp; **Address:** The Heart Center, 700 Children's Drive, Columbus, OH 43205; **Phone:** 614-722-2459; **Board Cert:** Pediatrics 1981; Pediatric Cardiology 1983; **Med School:** Univ Okla Coll Med 1976; **Resid:** Pediatrics, Chldns Hosp 1978; **Fellow:** Pediatric Cardiology, Texas Chldns Hosp 1981; **Fac Appt:** Prof Ped, Ohio State Univ

Dick II, Macdonald MD [PCd] - **Spec Exp:** Congenital Heart Disease; **Hospital:** Mott Chldns Hosp; **Address:** U of M Congenital Heart Ctr, Mott Chldns Hosp, 1540 E Hospital Drive, Ann Arbor, MI 48109-4204; **Phone:** 734-764-5176; **Board Cert:** Pediatrics 1989; Pediatric Cardiology 2007; **Med School:** Univ VA Sch Med 1967; **Resid:** Pediatrics, Univ VA Hosp 1971; **Fellow:** Pediatric Cardiology, Chldns Hosp Med Ctr 1974; **Fac Appt:** Prof Ped, Univ Mich Med Sch

Driscoll, David J MD [PCd] - **Spec Exp:** Exercise Physiology; Klippel-Trenaunay Syndrome; Cardiomyopathy; **Hospital:** Mayo Med Ctr & Clin - Rochester; **Address:** Mayo Clin, Div Ped Cardiology, 200 First St SW, Rochester, MN 55905; **Phone:** 507-266-0676; **Board Cert:** Pediatrics 1976; Pediatric Cardiology 2006; **Med School:** Marquette Sch Med 1970; **Resid:** Pediatrics, Milwaukee Chldns Hosp 1972; Pediatrics, Milwaukee Chldns Hosp 1975; **Fellow:** Pediatric Cardiology, Baylor Coll Med 1978; **Fac Appt:** Prof Ped, Mayo Med Sch

Feltes, Timothy F MD [PCd] - **Spec Exp:** Congenital Heart Disease; **Hospital:** Nationwide Chldn's Hosp; **Address:** Nationwide Chldns Hosp, 700 Children's Drive, rm ED619, Columbus, OH 43205; **Phone:** 614-722-2565; **Board Cert:** Pediatrics 1985; Pediatric Cardiology 2010; **Med School:** Univ Toledo, Med Univ OH 1980; **Resid:** Pediatrics, Emory Univ Med Ctr 1983; **Fellow:** Pediatric Cardiology, Texas Chldns Hosp 1986; **Fac Appt:** Clin Prof Ped, Ohio State Univ

Hardin, Joel T MD [PCd] - **Spec Exp:** Congenital Heart Disease-Adult; Marfan's Syndrome; Muscular Dystrophy; **Hospital:** Loyola Univ - Ronald McDonald Children's Hosp, Lurie Chldn's Hosp-Chicago; **Address:** Loyola Univ Med Ctr, 2160 S 1st Ave, Maguire Bldg, rm 3312, Maywood, IL 60153-3328; **Phone:** 708-327-9103; **Board Cert:** Pediatrics 2012; Pediatric Cardiology 2009; **Med School:** Univ Tenn Coll Med 1987; **Resid:** Pediatrics, St Louis Chldn's Hosp 1990; **Fellow:** Pediatric Cardiology, St Louis Chldn's Hosp 1993; **Fac Appt:** Assoc Prof Ped, Loyola Univ-Stritch Sch Med

Hijazi, Ziyad M MD [PCd] - **Spec Exp:** Interventional Cardiology; Congenital Heart Disease; Coarctation of the Aorta; **Hospital:** Rush Univ Med Ctr; **Address:** 1653 W Congress Pkwy, Ste 770 Jones, Chicago, IL 60612; **Phone:** 312-942-8941; **Board Cert:** Pediatric Cardiology 2007; **Med School:** Jordan 1982; **Resid:** Pediatrics, Yale-New Haven Hosp 1988; **Fellow:** Pediatric Cardiology, Yale-New Haven Hosp 1991; **Fac Appt:** Prof Ped, Rush Med Coll

Hoyer, Mark H MD [PCd] - **Spec Exp:** Cardiac Catheterization; Congenital Heart Disease-Adult; **Hospital:** Riley Hosp for Children; **Address:** Riley Hosp Div Cardiology, 705 Riley Hospital Drive, rm 127, Indianapolis, IN 46202; **Phone:** 317-274-8906; **Board Cert:** Pediatric Cardiology 2013; **Med School:** Ohio State Univ 1985; **Resid:** Pediatrics, Wright-Patterson AFB Med Ctr 1988; **Fellow:** Pediatric Cardiac Surgery, Chldns Hosp 1991; **Fac Appt:** Clin Prof Ped, Indiana Univ

Pahl, Elfriede MD [PCd] - **Spec Exp:** Transplant Medicine-Heart; Heart Failure; Congenital Heart Disease; Kawasaki Disease; **Hospital:** Lurie Chldn's Hosp-Chicago; **Address:** Lurie Chldn's Hosp, Ped Cardiology, 225 E Chicago Ave, Box 21, Chicago, IL 60611; **Phone:** 312-227-4100; **Board Cert:** Pediatrics 1987; Pediatric Cardiology 2010; **Med School:** Northwestern Univ 1983; **Resid:** Pediatrics, Chldns Meml Hosp 1986; **Fellow:** Pediatric Cardiology, Chldns Hosp 1988; **Fac Appt:** Prof Ped, Northwestern Univ

Rocchini, Albert P MD [PCd] - **Spec Exp:** Congenital Heart Disease; Interventional Cardiology; Hypertension in Obesity; **Hospital:** Univ Michigan Med Ctr, Mott Chldns Hosp; **Address:** U of M Pediatric Cardiology, 1540 E Hospital Drive, Level 11, Ann Arbor, MI 48109; **Phone:** 734-936-8993; **Board Cert:** Pediatrics 1989; Pediatric Cardiology 1989; **Med School:** Univ Pittsburgh 1972; **Resid:** Pediatrics, Univ Minn 1974; **Fellow:** Pediatric Cardiology, Chldns Hosp Med Ctr 1977; **Fac Appt:** Prof Ped, Univ Mich Med Sch

Great Plains and Mountains

Minich, Lois LuAnn MD [PCd] - **Spec Exp:** Echocardiography; **Hospital:** Primary Children's Med Ctr; **Address:** Dept Ped Cardiology, 100 N Mario Capecchi Drive, Ste 1500, Salt Lake City, UT 84113; **Phone:** 801-662-5400; **Board Cert:** Pediatric Cardiology 2007; **Med School:** W VA Univ 1986; **Resid:** Pediatrics, Medical Ctr Hosp 1989; **Fellow:** Pediatric Cardiology, Univ Michigan Hosps 1992; **Fac Appt:** Prof Ped, Univ Utah

Pediatric Cardiology

Southwest

Dreyer, William J MD [PCd] - **Spec Exp:** Congenital Heart Disease; Transplant Medicine-Heart; Heart Failure; **Hospital:** Texas Chldns Hosp, St. Luke's Episcopal Hosp-Houston; **Address:** 6621 Fannin St, West Tower Fl 20, MC 19345-C, Houston, TX 77030; **Phone:** 832-826-5659; **Board Cert:** Pediatrics 1987; Pediatric Cardiology 2013; **Med School:** Univ Fla Coll Med 1981; **Resid:** Pediatrics, UCSF Med Ctr 1984; **Fellow:** Pediatric Cardiology, Baylor Coll Med 1987; **Fac Appt:** Prof Ped, Baylor Coll Med

Mahony, Lynn MD [PCd] - **Spec Exp:** Congenital Heart Disease; Marfan's Syndrome; Congestive Heart Failure; Complex Diagnosis; **Hospital:** Chldns Med Ctr of Dallas; **Address:** Chldns Med Ctr of Dallas- Dept Ped Cardiology, 1935 Medical District Drive, Ste C-3210, Dallas, TX 75235; **Phone:** 214-456-2333; **Board Cert:** Pediatrics 1979; Pediatric Cardiology 1997; **Med School:** Stanford Univ 1975; **Resid:** Pediatrics, Stanford Univ Hosp 1978; **Fellow:** Pediatric Cardiology, UCSF Med Ctr 1981; **Fac Appt:** Prof Ped, Univ Tex SW, Dallas

Moodie, Douglas S MD [PCd] - **Spec Exp:** Marfan's Syndrome; Congenital Heart Disease-Adult & Child; **Hospital:** Texas Chldns Hosp; **Address:** 6621 Fannin St Fl 20, MC 19345-C, Houston, TX 77030; **Phone:** 832-826-5659; **Board Cert:** Pediatrics 1977; Pediatric Cardiology 1977; **Med School:** Med Coll Wisc 1972; **Resid:** Pediatrics, Mayo Clinic 1975; **Fellow:** Pediatric Cardiology, Mayo Clinic 1977; **Fac Appt:** Prof Ped, Baylor Coll Med

Rogers Jr, James H MD [PCd] - **Spec Exp:** Congenital Heart Disease; **Hospital:** Christus Santa Rosa Children's Hosp, Methodist Hosp-San Antonio; **Address:** Chldns Heart Network, 1901 Babcock Rd, Ste 301, San Antonio, TX 78229; **Phone:** 210-341-7722; **Board Cert:** Pediatrics 1976; Pediatric Cardiology 2009; **Med School:** Med Coll GA 1971; **Resid:** Pediatrics, Wilford Hall USAF Med Ctr 1974; **Fellow:** Pediatric Cardiology, Med Coll Georgia Affil Hosp 1977; **Fac Appt:** Clin Prof Ped, Univ Tex, San Antonio

West Coast and Pacific

Bernstein, Daniel MD [PCd] - **Spec Exp:** Transplant Medicine-Heart; Congenital Heart Disease; Heart Failure; **Hospital:** Lucile Packard Chldn's Hosp, Stanford Univ Hosp & Clins; **Address:** Lucile Packard Chldns Hosp, Div Ped Card, 750 Welch Rd, Ste 305, Palo Alto, CA 94304-5731; **Phone:** 650-721-2121; **Board Cert:** Pediatrics 1984; Pediatric Cardiology 1985; **Med School:** NYU Sch Med 1978; **Resid:** Pediatrics, Montefiore Hosp-Einstein 1982; **Fellow:** Pediatric Cardiology, UCSF Med Ctr 1986; **Fac Appt:** Prof Ped, Stanford Univ

Lewin, Mark MD [PCd] - **Spec Exp:** Echocardiography; Fetal Cardiology; **Hospital:** Seattle Chldns Hosp, Univ Wash Med Ctr; **Address:** Seattle Chldns Hosp, 4800 Sand Point Way NE, Seattle, WA 98144; **Phone:** 206-987-2015; **Board Cert:** Pediatric Cardiology 2013; **Med School:** USC-Keck School of Medicine 1991; **Resid:** Pediatrics, Chldns Hosp 1994; **Fellow:** Pediatric Cardiology, Texas Chldns Hosp 1998; **Fac Appt:** Prof Ped, Univ Wash

Perry, Stanton MD [PCd] - **Spec Exp:** Cardiac Catheterization; **Hospital:** Lucile Packard Chldn's Hosp; **Address:** Lucile Packard Chldns Hosp, Dept Ped Cardiology, 750 Welch Rd, Ste 305, Palo Alto, CA 94304; **Phone:** 650-721-2121; **Board Cert:** Pediatrics 1986; **Med School:** Iceland 1978; **Resid:** Pediatrics, St Louis Chldn's Hosp 1983; **Fellow:** Pediatric Cardiology, Chldns Hosp 1987; **Fac Appt:** Assoc Prof Ped, Stanford Univ

Teitel, David F MD [PCd] - **Spec Exp:** Cardiac Catheterization; Congenital Heart Disease; **Hospital:** UCSF Med Ctr; **Address:** UCSF, Pediatric Heart Center, 400 Parnassus Ave, 2nd Fl, San Francisco, CA 94143-0544; **Phone:** 415-353-2008; **Board Cert:** Pediatrics 1980; Pediatric Cardiology 2004; **Med School:** Univ Toronto 1975; **Resid:** Pediatrics, Chldns Hosp 1980; **Fellow:** Pediatric Cardiology, UCSF Med Ctr 1982; **Fac Appt:** Prof Ped, UCSF

Zahn, Evan M MD [PCd] - **Spec Exp:** Interventional Cardiology; Ventricular Septal Defect (Amplatzer R); Congenital Heart Disease; Minimally Invasive Surgery; **Hospital:** Cedars-Sinai Med Ctr; **Address:** Cedar-Sinai, Ped Cariology Dept, 127 S San Vicente Blvd, AHSP, A3600, Los Angeles, CA 90048; **Phone:** 310-423-1153; **Board Cert:** Pediatric Cardiology 2007; **Med School:** NY Med Coll 1986; **Resid:** Pediatrics, Univ CO Hosp 1989; **Fellow:** Pediatric Cardiology, Hosp Sick Chldn 1991; Interventional Cardiology, Hosp Sick Chldn 1992

Pediatric Critical Care Medicine

Mid Atlantic

Thompson, Ann Ellen MD [PCCM] - **Spec Exp:** Mechanical Ventilation; Critical Care; Respiratory Failure; **Hospital:** Chldns Hosp of Pittsburgh - UPMC; **Address:** Chldns Hosp, Dept Ped Crit Care, 4401 Penn Ave, Fl 2, Pittsburgh, PA 15224; **Phone:** 412-692-5164; **Board Cert:** Pediatrics 1992; Anesthesiology 1980; Pediatric Critical Care Medicine 2010; **Med School:** Tufts Univ 1974; **Resid:** Pediatrics, Chldns Hosp 1977; Anesthesiology, Hosp Univ Penn 1980; **Fellow:** Pediatric Critical Care Medicine, Chldns Hosp 1979; **Fac Appt:** Prof Ped, Univ Pittsburgh

Midwest

Sarnaik, Ashok P MD [PCCM] - **Spec Exp:** Critical Care; Perinatal Medicine; **Hospital:** Chldns Hosp of Michigan; **Address:** Chldns Hosp, Div Crit Care Med, 3901 Beaubien St, Carls Bldg - Ste 4134, Detroit, MI 48201-2119; **Phone:** 313-745-5629; **Board Cert:** Pediatrics 1975; Neonatal-Perinatal Medicine 1979; Pediatric Critical Care Medicine 2003; **Med School:** India 1969; **Resid:** Pediatrics, JJ Hosp-Bombay Univ 1971; Pediatrics, Chldns Hosp Mich 1974; **Fellow:** Neonatal-Perinatal Medicine, Chldns Hosp Mich 1975; **Fac Appt:** Prof Ped, Wayne State Univ

Great Plains and Mountains

Dean, J. Michael MD [PCCM] - **Hospital:** Primary Children's Med Ctr, Intermountain Med Ctr; **Address:** Pediatric Critical Care, Univ Utah, 100 N Mario Capecchi Drive, Salt Lake City, UT 84158; **Phone:** 801-662-2400; **Board Cert:** Pediatrics 1981; Pediatric Critical Care Medicine 2010; **Med School:** Northwestern Univ 1977; **Resid:** Pediatrics, Children's Hosp 1981; **Fellow:** Pediatric Critical Care Medicine, Johns Hopkins Hosp 1983; **Fac Appt:** Prof Ped, Univ Utah

Southwest

Easley, Ronald B MD [PCCM] - **Spec Exp:** Congenital Heart Disease; Mechanical Ventilation; **Hospital:** Texas Chldns Hosp; **Address:** TX Chldns Hosp-Dept Anesthesiology, 6621 Fannin St, MC WT17417, Houston, TX 77030; **Phone:** 832-824-5800; **Board Cert:** Pediatric Critical Care Medicine 2012; Pediatrics 2013; Anesthesiology 2003; **Med School:** Univ MO-Columbia Sch Med 1995; **Resid:** Pediatrics, Univ MO Hosp 1999; Anesthesiology, Johns Hopkins Hosp 2002; **Fellow:** Pediatric Critical Care Medicine, Johns Hopkins Hosp 2004; **Fac Appt:** Assoc Prof Ped, Baylor Coll Med

Fuhrman, Bradley P MD [PCCM] - **Spec Exp:** Disaster Preparedness; **Hospital:** El Paso Chldns Hosp; **Address:** Professor and Chair Department of Pediatrics, Paul L. Foster School of Medicine, 4800 Alberta Ave, El Paso, TX 79905-2799; **Phone:** 915-545-6921; **Board Cert:** Pediatrics 1992; Pediatric Critical Care Medicine 2010; Neonatal-Perinatal Medicine 1979; Pediatric Cardiology 1979; **Med School:** NYU Sch Med 1971; **Resid:** Pediatrics, Univ Minnesota Med Ctr 1973; **Fellow:** Pediatric Cardiology, Univ Minnesota 1979; Neonatal-Perinatal Medicine, Univ Minnesota 1979; **Fac Appt:** Prof Ped, Texas Tech Univ

Perez Fontan, Jose Julio MD [PCCM] - **Spec Exp:** Respiratory Failure; Mechanical Ventilation; **Hospital:** UT Southwestern Med Ctr at Dallas, Chldns Med Ctr of Dallas; **Address:** UT SW Med Ctr, Dept Peds, 5323 Harry Hines Blvd, Ste K4.500, Dallas, TX 75390-9063; **Phone:** 214-648-9618; **Board Cert:** Pediatrics 1987; Pediatric Critical Care Medicine 2010; **Med School:** Spain 1977; **Resid:** Pediatrics, Chldns Hosp/Univ Barcelona 1981; **Fellow:** Critical Care Medicine, UCSF Med Ctr 1984; **Fac Appt:** Prof Ped, Univ Tex SW, Dallas

Taylor, Richard P MD [PCCM] - **Hospital:** Christus Santa Rosa Children's Hosp, Univ Hosp-San Antonio; **Address:** Dept Ped Critical Care, 7703 Floyd Curl Drive, San Antonio, TX 78229; **Phone:** 210-562-5816; **Board Cert:** Internal Medicine 1988; Pediatric Critical Care Medicine 2011; **Med School:** Univ Tex Med Br, Galveston 1984; **Resid:** Internal Medicine, St Joseph Mercy Hosp 1988; Pediatrics, UNiv Michigan Med Ctr 1988; **Fellow:** Pediatric Critical Care Medicine, Univ Michigan Med Ctr 1995; **Fac Appt:** Prof Ped, Univ Tex, San Antonio

West Coast and Pacific

Schwarz, Adam J MD [PCCM] - **Spec Exp:** Septic Shock; Respiratory Failure; Critical Care; Sepsis; **Hospital:** Chldns Hosp Orange Co; **Address:** CHOC-Ped Critical Care Med, 1201 W La Veta Ave, Orange, CA 92868; **Phone:** 714-509-8620; **Board Cert:** Pediatric Critical Care Medicine 2011; Pediatrics 2009; **Med School:** Stanford Univ 1990; **Resid:** Pediatrics, Stanford Med Ctr 1993; **Fellow:** Pediatric Critical Care Medicine, Harbor-UCLA Med Ctr 1996

Zimmerman, Jerry John MD [PCCM] - **Spec Exp:** Inflammation in Critical Illness; Sepsis; Septic Shock; **Hospital:** Seattle Chldns Hosp, Harborview Med Ctr; **Address:** Seattle Chldn's Hosp, 4800 Sand Point Way NE, MS W8866, Seattle, WA 98145-5440; **Phone:** 206-987-3862; **Board Cert:** Pediatrics 1992; Pediatric Critical Care Medicine 2010; **Med School:** Univ Wisc 1979; **Resid:** Pediatrics, Univ Wisconsin Hosp 1982; **Fellow:** Pediatric Critical Care Medicine, Chldns Natl Med Ctr 1984; **Fac Appt:** Prof Ped, Univ Wash

Pediatric Endocrinology

New England

Casella, Samuel J MD [PEn] - **Spec Exp:** Thyroid Disorders; Growth/Development Disorders; Diabetes; **Hospital:** Dartmouth - Hitchcock Med Ctr; **Address:** Dartmouth-Hitchcock Med Ctr, Dept Ped Endo, 1 Med Ctr Drive Fl 6M, Lebanon, NH 03756; **Phone:** 603-653-9877; **Board Cert:** Pediatrics 1985; Pediatric Endocrinology 2009; **Med School:** SUNY Upstate Med Univ 1981; **Resid:** Pediatrics, Upstate Med Ctr 1984; **Fellow:** Pediatric Endocrinology, NC Meml Hosp-Univ NC 1986; **Fac Appt:** Assoc Prof Ped, Johns Hopkins Univ

Gordon, Catherine M MD [PEn] - **Spec Exp:** Bone Disorders-Metabolic; **Hospital:** Rhode Island Hosp; **Address:** Hasbro Children's Hospital, 593 Eddy St, Providence, RI 02903; **Phone:** 401-444-4712; **Board Cert:** Pediatric Endocrinology 2007; Adolescent Medicine 2009; **Med School:** Univ NC Sch Med 1991; **Resid:** Pediatrics, Chldns Hosp 1994; **Fellow:** Pediatric Endocrinology, Chldns Hosp 1996

Levitsky, Lynne L MD [PEn] - **Spec Exp:** Diabetes; Growth/Development Disorders; Cushing's Syndrome; **Hospital:** Mass Genl Hosp; **Address:** MGH Pediatric Endocrine Assocs, 55 Fruit St Yawkey Bldg Fl 6, Boston, MA 02114; **Phone:** 617-726-2909; **Board Cert:** Pediatrics 1971; Pediatric Endocrinology 1978; **Med School:** Yale Univ 1966; **Resid:** Pediatrics, Chldns Hosp 1968; **Fellow:** Pediatric Endocrinology, Univ Maryland Hosp 1970; **Fac Appt:** Assoc Prof Ped, Harvard Med Sch

Ludwig, David S MD/PhD [PEn] - **Spec Exp:** Obesity; Nutrition; **Hospital:** Children's Hospital - Boston; **Address:** Boston Chldn's Hosp, Div Endocrinology, 330 Longwood Ave, Boston, MA 02115; **Phone:** 617-355-7476; **Board Cert:** Pediatric Endocrinology 2010; **Med School:** Stanford Univ 1990; **Resid:** Pediatrics, Chldns Hosp 1993; **Fellow:** Pediatric Endocrinology, Chldns Hosp 1995; **Fac Appt:** Prof Ped, Harvard Med Sch

Spack, Norman P MD [PEn] - **Spec Exp:** Transgender Issues; **Hospital:** Children's Hospital - Boston; **Address:** Boston Chldn's Hosp, Div Endocrinology, 330 Longwood Ave, Boston, MA 02115; **Phone:** 857-218-5094; **Board Cert:** Pediatrics 1975; **Med School:** Univ Rochester 1969; **Resid:** Pediatrics, Boston City Hosp/Chldns Hosp 1972; **Fellow:** Adolescent Medicine, Chldns Hosp 1975; Pediatric Endocrinology, Chldns Hosp 1978; **Fac Appt:** Assoc Prof Ped, Harvard Med Sch

Tamborlane, William V MD [PEn] - **Spec Exp:** Diabetes; **Hospital:** Yale-New Haven Hosp; **Address:** Yale Pediatric Endocrinology, 333 Cedar St, rm 3091-LMP, New Haven, CT 06519; **Phone:** 203-764-6747; **Board Cert:** Pediatrics 1978; Pediatric Endocrinology 1986; **Med School:** Georgetown Univ 1972; **Resid:** Pediatrics, Georgetown Univ Hosp 1975; **Fellow:** Pediatric Endocrinology, Yale-New Haven Hosp 1977; **Fac Appt:** Prof Ped, Yale Univ

Mid Atlantic

Alter, Craig A MD [PEn] - **Spec Exp:** Diabetes; Growth Disorders; Thyroid Disorders; Pubertal Disorders; **Hospital:** Chldns Hosp of Philadelphia; **Address:** Chldns Hosp, Ped Endocrinology, 3400 Civic Center Blvd, Philadelphia, PA 19104; **Phone:** 215-590-3174; **Board Cert:** Pediatrics 2012; Pediatric Endocrinology 2010; **Med School:** Harvard Med Sch 1987; **Resid:** Pediatrics, Chldns Hosp 1990; **Fellow:** Pediatric Endocrinology, Chldns Hosp 1993; **Fac Appt:** Clin Prof Ped, Univ Pennsylvania

Arslanian, Silva A MD [PEn] - **Spec Exp:** Obesity; Diabetes; **Hospital:** Chldns Hosp of Pittsburgh - UPMC; **Address:** Chldns Hosp, Ped Endocrinology Dept, 4401 Penn Ave Fl 7, Pittsburgh, PA 15224; **Phone:** 412-692-6935; **Board Cert:** Pediatrics 1983; Pediatric Endocrinology 1983; **Med School:** Lebanon 1978; **Resid:** Pediatrics, American Univ Hosp 1980; **Fellow:** Pediatric Endocrinology, Chldns Hosp 1983; **Fac Appt:** Prof Ped, Univ Pittsburgh

Becker, Dorothy J MD [PEn] - **Spec Exp:** Diabetes; **Hospital:** Chldns Hosp of Pittsburgh - UPMC; **Address:** Chldns Hosp, Ped Endocrinology Dept, 4401 Penn Ave, Faculty Pav Fl 8, Pittsburgh, PA 15224; **Phone:** 412-692-5172; **Board Cert:** Pediatrics 1978; Pediatric Endocrinology 1978; **Med School:** South Africa 1964; **Resid:** Pediatrics, Univ Capetown 1972; **Fellow:** Endocrinology, Diabetes & Metabolism, Univ Capetown 1974; Pediatric Endocrinology, UPMC 1976; **Fac Appt:** Prof Ped, Univ Pittsburgh

DeLuca, Francesco MD [PEn] - **Spec Exp:** Growth Disorders; Metabolic Syndrome; Osteoporosis; **Hospital:** St. Christopher's Hosp for Chldn; **Address:** St Christophers Hosp, Ped Endocrinology, 3601 A St Fl 3, Philadelphia, PA 19134; **Phone:** 215-427-8100; **Board Cert:** Pediatric Endocrinology 2010; **Med School:** Italy 1983; **Resid:** Pediatrics, Cath Univ Sacred Heart Affil Hosp 1986; Pediatrics, Albert Einstein Med Ctr 1992; **Fellow:** Pediatric Endocrinology, St Christophers Hosp 1993; Pediatric Endocrinology, Natl Inst Hlth 1995; **Fac Appt:** Prof Ped, Drexel Univ Coll Med

Fennoy, Ilene MD [PEn] - **Spec Exp:** Growth/Development Disorders; Diabetes; Klinefelter's Syndrome; Obesity; **Hospital:** Morgan Stanley Children's Hosp of NY-Presby, NY (page 65), Harlem Hosp Ctr; **Address:** 3959 Broadway, rm 106, New York, NY 10032; **Phone:** 212-305-6559; **Board Cert:** Pediatrics 1979; Pediatric Endocrinology 1980; **Med School:** UCSF 1973; **Resid:** Pediatrics, Montefiore Med Ctr 1975; **Fellow:** Nutrition, Columbia-Presby Med Ctr 1977; Endocrinology, Natl Inst Hlth 1979; **Fac Appt:** Assoc Clin Prof Ped, Columbia P&S

Gallagher, Mary P MD [PEn] - **Spec Exp:** Diabetes; **Hospital:** Morgan Stanley Children's Hosp of NY-Presby, NY (page 65); **Address:** 1150 St Nicholas Ave Fl 2, New York, NY 10032; **Phone:** 212-851-5494; **Board Cert:** Pediatrics 2006; Pediatric Endocrinology 2011; **Med School:** UMDNJ-NJ Med Sch, Newark 1995; **Resid:** Pediatrics, NY Presby-Columbia Med Ctr 1998; **Fellow:** Pediatric Endocrinology, NY Presby-Columbia Med Ctr 2002; **Fac Appt:** Asst Prof Ped, Columbia P&S

Garibaldi, Luigi R MD [PEn] - **Spec Exp:** Pubertal Disorders; Growth Disorders; Prader-Willi Syndrome; **Hospital:** Chldns Hosp of Pittsburgh - UPMC; **Address:** Chldns Hosp, Ped Endocrinology Dept, 4401 Penn Ave, Faculty Pav Fl 8, Pittsburgh, PA 15224; **Phone:** 412-692-5170; **Board Cert:** Pediatrics 1986; Pediatric Endocrinology 1986; **Med School:** Italy 1973; **Resid:** Pediatrics, Gaslini Inst-Chldns Hosp 1978; Pediatrics, Univ Michigan Med Ctr 1985; **Fellow:** Pediatric Endocrinology, Temple Univ Hosp 1981; Pediatric Endocrinology, Univ Chicago Med Ctr 1986; **Fac Appt:** Prof Ped, Univ Pittsburgh

Kohn, Brenda MD [PEn] - **Spec Exp:** Growth Disorders; Pituitary Disorders; Thyroid Disorders; Adrenal Disorders; **Hospital:** NYU Langone Med Ctr (page 68); **Address:** 160 E 32nd St, Ste L3, New York, NY 10016-6402; **Phone:** 212-263-5940 x6; **Board Cert:** Pediatrics 1981; Pediatric Endocrinology 1983; **Med School:** Albert Einstein Coll Med 1976; **Resid:** Pediatrics, NYU Med Ctr 1979; **Fellow:** Endocrinology, Diabetes & Metabolism, NY-Cornell Med Ctr 1983; **Fac Appt:** Assoc Prof Ped, NYU Sch Med

Levine, Michael A MD [PEn] - **Spec Exp:** Bone Disorders-Metabolic; Osteoporosis; **Hospital:** Chldns Hosp of Philadelphia; **Address:** Chldns Hosp, Ped Endocrinology, 3400 Civic Center Blvd, Philadelphia, PA 19104; **Phone:** 215-590-3174; **Board Cert:** Internal Medicine 1979; Endocrinology, Diabetes & Metabolism 1981; **Med School:** Hahnemann Univ 1976; **Resid:** Internal Medicine, Johns Hopkins Hosp 1979; **Fellow:** Endocrinology, Natl Inst Hlth 1981; Genetics, Natl Inst Hlth 1981; **Fac Appt:** Prof Ped, Univ Pennsylvania

New, Maria I MD [PEn] - **Spec Exp:** Adrenal Disorders; Growth/Development Disorders; **Hospital:** Mt Sinai Med Ctr (page 62); **Address:** Mount Sinai Medical Ctr, Ped Adrenal Steroid Disorders Program, 5 E 98th St Fl 10, New York, NY 10029; **Phone:** 212-241-8210; **Board Cert:** Pediatrics 1960; **Med School:** Univ Pennsylvania 1954; **Resid:** Pediatrics, New York Hosp 1957; **Fellow:** Pediatric Endocrinology, New York Hosp 1958; Endocrinology, Diabetes & Metabolism, New York Hosp 1964; **Fac Appt:** Prof Ped, Cornell Univ-Weill Med Coll

Oberfield, Sharon E MD [PEn] - **Spec Exp:** Adrenal Disorders; Neuroendocrine Disorders; Growth Disorders; **Hospital:** Morgan Stanley Children's Hosp of NY-Presby, NY (page 65); **Address:** 630 W 168th St, PH East Bldg - Fl 5 East - Ste 522, New York, NY 10032; **Phone:** 212-305-6559; **Board Cert:** Pediatrics 1979; Pediatric Endocrinology 2000; **Med School:** Cornell Univ 1974; **Resid:** Pediatrics, New York Hosp 1976; **Fellow:** Pediatric Endocrinology, New York Hosp-Cornell 1979; **Fac Appt:** Prof Ped, Columbia P&S

Plotnick, Leslie P MD [PEn] - **Spec Exp:** Diabetes; Growth Disorders; Thyroid Disorders; Pubertal Disorders; **Hospital:** Johns Hopkins Hosp (page 59); **Address:** Johns Hopkins Hosp, Rubenstein Child Hlth Bldg, 200 N Wolfe St, Baltimore, MD 21287; **Phone:** 410-955-6463; **Board Cert:** Pediatrics 1975; Pediatric Endocrinology 2009; **Med School:** Univ MD Sch Med 1970; **Resid:** Pediatrics, Johns Hopkins Hosp 1972; **Fellow:** Pediatric Endocrinology, Johns Hopkins Hosp 1974; **Fac Appt:** Prof Ped, Univ MD Sch Med

Sklar, Charles A MD [PEn] - **Spec Exp:** Cancer Survivors-Late Effects of Therapy; Growth Disorders in Childhood Cancer; **Hospital:** Meml Sloan-Kettering Canc Ctr; **Address:** 1275 York Avenue, New York, NY 10065; **Phone:** 212-639-8138; **Board Cert:** Pediatrics 1979; Pediatric Endocrinology 1980; **Med School:** USC Sch Med 1974; **Resid:** Pediatrics, Childrens Hosp 1976; **Fellow:** Pediatric Endocrinology, UCSF Med Ctr 1979; **Fac Appt:** Assoc Prof Ped, Cornell Univ-Weill Med Coll

Sperling, Mark A MD [PEn] - **Spec Exp:** Diabetes; Growth/Development Disorders; Hypoglycemia; Neonatal Diabetes; **Hospital:** Chldns Hosp of Pittsburgh - UPMC, UPMC Presby, Pittsburgh; **Address:** Chldns Hosp, Ped Endocrinology Dept, 4401 Penn Ave, Faculty Pav Ave Fl 8, Pittsburgh, PA 15224; **Phone:** 412-692-5172; **Board Cert:** Pediatrics 1986; Pediatric Endocrinology 1986; **Med School:** Australia 1962; **Resid:** Pediatrics, Royal Chldns Hosp 1968; **Fellow:** Endocrinology, Chldns Hosp 1970; **Fac Appt:** Prof Ped, Univ Pittsburgh

Southeast

Diamond, Frank B MD [PEn] - **Spec Exp:** Growth Disorders; Obesity; Calcium Disorders in Newborn; **Hospital:** All Children's Hosp; **Address:** All Chldns Hosp, Ped Endocrinology Dept, 501 6th St S, St Petersburg, FL 33701; **Phone:** 727-767-3636; **Board Cert:** Pediatrics 1979; Pediatric Endocrinology 1980; **Med School:** Penn State Coll Med 1974; **Resid:** Pediatrics, Chldns Hosp 1976; **Fellow:** Pediatric Endocrinology, Chldns Hosp 1978; **Fac Appt:** Prof Ped, Univ S Fla Coll Med

Freemark, Michael S MD [PEn] - **Spec Exp:** Prader-Willi Syndrome; Growth Disorders; Pubertal Disorders; Diabetes; **Hospital:** Duke Univ Hosp, Durham Regional Hosp; **Address:** Lenox Baker Children's Hosp, 3000 Erwin Rd, Durham, NC 27705; **Phone:** 919-684-8350; **Board Cert:** Pediatrics 1980; Pediatric Endocrinology 2010; **Med School:** Duke Univ 1976; **Resid:** Pediatrics, Duke Univ Med Ctr 1979; **Fellow:** Pediatric Endocrinology, Duke Univ Med Ctr 1983; Pediatric Endocrinology, Hospital Necker Enfants Malades 1993; **Fac Appt:** Prof Ped, Duke Univ

Meacham, Lillian R MD [PEn] - **Spec Exp:** Growth Disorders in Childhood Cancer; Cancer Survivors-Late Effects of Therapy; **Hospital:** Chldns Hlthcare Atlanta @ Scottish Rite, Chldns Hlthcare Atlanta @ Egleston; **Address:** Aflac Outpatient Center, 5455 Meridian Mark Rd NE, Ste 400, Atlanta, GA 30342; **Phone:** 404-785-3240; **Board Cert:** Pediatrics 2013; Pediatric Endocrinology 2013; **Med School:** Emory Univ 1984; **Resid:** Pediatrics, Emory Univ Hosp 1987; **Fellow:** Pediatric Endocrinology, Emory Univ Hosp 1990; **Fac Appt:** Prof Ped, Emory Univ

Silverstein, Janet H MD [PEn] - **Spec Exp:** Diabetes; Growth/Development Disorders; Obesity; **Hospital:** UF Hlth Shands Chldns Hosp; **Address:** UF Hlth, Ped Endocrinology Dept, 1600 SW Archer Rd, Gainesville, FL 32610; **Phone:** 352-334-1390; **Board Cert:** Pediatrics 1975; Pediatric Endocrinology 2004; **Med School:** Univ Pennsylvania 1970; **Resid:** Pediatrics, Chldns Hosp 1972; Pediatrics, Chldns Hosp 1975; **Fellow:** Pediatric Endocrinology, Duke Univ Hosp 1977; **Fac Appt:** Prof Ped, Univ Fla Coll Med

Midwest

Allen, David B MD [PEn] - **Spec Exp:** Growth Disorders; Pubertal Disorders; Diabetes; **Hospital:** Univ WI Hosp & Clins; **Address:** Univ WI Hosp & Clins - Dep Ped Endo, 600 Highland Ave, H4/477, MC 4108, Madison, WI 53792-4108; **Phone:** 608-263-9059; **Board Cert:** Pediatrics 1986; Pediatric Endocrinology 2011; **Med School:** Duke Univ 1980; **Resid:** Pediatrics, Univ WI Hosp & Clins 1985; **Fellow:** Pediatric Endocrinology, Univ WI Hosp & Clins 1988; **Fac Appt:** Prof Ped, Univ Wisc

DiMeglio, Linda A MD [PEn] - **Spec Exp:** Diabetes; Bone Disorders-Metabolic; Clinical Trials; **Hospital:** Riley Hosp for Children; **Address:** Riley Hosp for Children, Div Endocrinology, 705 Riley Hospital Drive, rm 5960, Indianapolis, IN 46202; **Phone:** 317-944-3889; **Board Cert:** Pediatrics 2011; Pediatric Endocrinology 2007; **Med School:** Univ Pennsylvania 1993; **Resid:** Pediatrics, Chldns Meml Hosp 1996; **Fellow:** Pediatric Endocrinology, Indiana Univ Med Ctr 1999; **Fac Appt:** Assoc Prof Ped, Indiana Univ

Eugster, Erica A MD [PEn] - **Spec Exp:** Pubertal Disorders; Turner Syndrome; Growth/Development Disorders; Sex Development Disorders; **Hospital:** Riley Hosp for Children, Franciscan St. Francis Hlth-Indianapolis; **Address:** Pediatric Endocrinology, 705 Riley Hospital Drive, rm 5960, Indianapolis, IN 46202; **Phone:** 317-944-3889; **Board Cert:** Pediatric Endocrinology 2012; **Med School:** Med Coll PA 1990; **Resid:** Pediatrics, Marshfield Clin-St Josephs Hosp 1994; **Fellow:** Pediatric Endocrinology, Univ MN Hosp 1997; **Fac Appt:** Prof Ped, Indiana Univ

Gutai, James P MD [PEn] - **Hospital:** Chldns Hosp of Michigan, Marquette Genl Hosp; **Address:** Comprehensive Diabetes Ctr, 4201 St Antoine St, Univ Hlth Ctr, Ste 6G14, Detroit, MI 48201; **Phone:** 313-577-0133; **Board Cert:** Pediatrics 1977; Pediatric Endocrinology 1980; **Med School:** Temple Univ 1970; **Resid:** Pediatrics, Johns Hopkins Hosp 1977; **Fellow:** Pediatric Endocrinology, Johns Hopkins Hosp 1980; **Fac Appt:** Prof Ped, Wayne State Univ

Menon, Ram K MD [PEn] - **Spec Exp:** Growth/Development Disorders; Diabetes; **Hospital:** Univ Michigan Med Ctr, Mott Chldns Hosp; **Address:** U of M Pediatric Multispecialty Clin, Dept Endocrinology, SPC 4259, 1540 E Hospital Drive Fl 8, Ann Arbor, MI 48109; **Phone:** 734-936-4185; **Board Cert:** Pediatrics 2009; Pediatric Endocrinology 2010; **Med School:** India 1979; **Resid:** Pediatrics, India Inst Med Sci 1984; **Fellow:** Endocrinology & Metabolism, Royal Free Hosp & Med Coll 1986; Pediatric Endocrinology, Chldn's Hosp Med Ctr 1989; **Fac Appt:** Prof Ped, Univ Mich Med Sch

Mirmira, Raghu G MD/PhD [PEn] - **Spec Exp:** Diabetes; **Hospital:** Riley Hosp for Children; **Address:** Riley Hosp Chldn-Endocrinology, 705 Riley Hospital Drive, rm 5960, Indianapolis, IN 46202; **Phone:** 317-944-3889; **Board Cert:** Endocrinology, Diabetes & Metabolism 2008; **Med School:** Univ Chicago-Pritzker Sch Med 1993; **Resid:** Internal Medicine, UCSF Med Ctr 1995; **Fellow:** Endocrinology, Diabetes & Metabolism, UCSF Med Ctr 1998; **Fac Appt:** Assoc Prof Ped, Indiana Univ

Norris, Andrew W MD/PhD [PEn] - **Spec Exp:** Diabetes; **Hospital:** Univ Iowa Hosp & Clins; **Address:** UIHC - Dept Ped Endocrinology, 200 Hawkins Dr, JPP Bldg - Ste 2857, Iowa City, IA 52242; **Phone:** 319-356-2229; **Board Cert:** Pediatric Endocrinology 2011; **Med School:** Washington Univ, St Louis 1997; **Resid:** Pediatrics, Univ IA Hosp & Clin 2000; **Fellow:** Pediatric Endocrinology, Chldns Hosp 2003; **Fac Appt:** Assoc Prof Ped, Univ Iowa Coll Med

Rogers, Douglas G MD [PEn] - **Spec Exp:** Diabetes; Growth/Development Disorders; Thyroid Disorders; **Hospital:** Cleveland Clin (page 55); **Address:** Cleveland Clinic, Ctr for Pediatric Endocrinology, 9500 Euclid Ave, MC A120, Cleveland, OH 44195-0001; **Phone:** 216-444-5437; **Board Cert:** Pediatrics 1984; Pediatric Endocrinology 1986; **Med School:** Ros Franklin Univ/Chicago Med Sch 1978; **Resid:** Pediatrics, Cardinal Glennon Chldns Hosp 1981; **Fellow:** Pediatric Endocrinology, St Louis Chldns Hosp 1985

White, Neil H MD [PEn] - **Spec Exp:** Diabetes; **Hospital:** St. Louis Chldns Hosp; **Address:** St Louis Chldns Hosp, One Children's Pl, CB 8116, St Louis, MO 63110-1010; **Phone:** 314-454-6051; **Board Cert:** Pediatrics 1981; Pediatric Endocrinology 1983; **Med School:** Albert Einstein Coll Med 1975; **Resid:** Pediatrics, St Louis Chldns Hosp 1977; **Fellow:** Endocrinology, Diabetes & Metabolism, Washington Univ 1979; **Fac Appt:** Prof Ped, Washington Univ, St Louis

Zimmerman, Donald MD [PEn] - **Spec Exp:** Growth Disorders in Childhood Cancer; Thyroid Cancer; Thyroid Disorders; Growth/Development Disorders; **Hospital:** Lurie Chldn's Hosp-Chicago; **Address:** Lurie Chldn's Hosp-Div Endocrinology, 225 E Chicago Ave, Box 54, Chicago, IL 60611; **Phone:** 312-227-6090; **Board Cert:** Internal Medicine 1977; Endocrinology 1979; Pediatrics 1983; Pediatric Endocrinology 2001; **Med School:** Univ IL Coll Med 1974; **Resid:** Internal Medicine, Johns Hopkins Hosp 1977; Pediatrics, Mayo Clinic 1981; **Fellow:** Endocrinology, Diabetes & Metabolism, Mayo Clinic 1980; **Fac Appt:** Prof Ped, Northwestern Univ

Great Plains and Mountains

Foster, Carol M MD [PEn] - **Spec Exp:** Diabetes; Growth/Development Disorders; Pubertal Disorders; **Hospital:** Primary Children's Med Ctr, Univ Utah Hlth Care; **Address:** 615 Arapeen Drive, Ste 100, Salt Lake City, UT 84108; **Phone:** 801-587-3922; **Board Cert:** Pediatrics 1983; Pediatric Endocrinology 1983; **Med School:** Washington Univ, St Louis 1978; **Resid:** Pediatrics, Univ Utah Hlth Scis Ctr 1981; **Fellow:** Pediatric Endocrinology, Natl Inst Hlth 1984; **Fac Appt:** Prof Med, Univ Utah

Kappy, Michael S MD/PhD [PEn] - **Spec Exp:** Growth/Development Disorders; Thyroid Disorders; Pubertal Disorders; **Hospital:** Chldn's Hosp - Aurora (CO); **Address:** Chldns Hosp, Endocrinology Dept, 13123 E 16th Ave, Box B265, Aurora, CO 80045; **Phone:** 720-777-6128; **Board Cert:** Pediatrics 1972; Pediatric Endocrinology 1980; **Med School:** Univ Wisc 1967; **Resid:** Pediatrics, Univ CO Hosp 1972; **Fellow:** Pediatric Endocrinology, Johns Hopkins Hosp 1980; **Fac Appt:** Prof Ped, Univ Colorado

Klingensmith, Georgeanna J MD [PEn] - **Spec Exp:** Diabetes; **Hospital:** Chldn's Hosp - Aurora (CO), Univ Colorado Hosp; **Address:** Barbara Davis Center, 1775 Aurora Court, Aurora, CO 80045; **Phone:** 303-724-2323; **Board Cert:** Pediatrics 1976; Pediatric Endocrinology 2000; **Med School:** Duke Univ 1971; **Resid:** Pediatrics, Childrens Hosp 1974; **Fellow:** Pediatric Endocrinology, Johns Hopkins Univ 1976; **Fac Appt:** Prof Ped, Univ Colorado

West Coast and Pacific

Geffner, Mitchell E MD [PEn] - **Spec Exp:** Growth Disorders; Pubertal Disorders; Thyroid Disorders; Pituitary Disorders; **Hospital:** Chldns Hosp - Los Angeles; **Address:** Chlds Hosp LA, Div Endocrinology, 4650 W Sunset Blvd, MS 61, Los Angeles, CA 90027; **Phone:** 323-361-1826; **Board Cert:** Pediatrics 1980; Pediatric Endocrinology 2006; **Med School:** Albert Einstein Coll Med 1975; **Resid:** Pediatrics, LAC-USC Med Ctr 1979; **Fellow:** Pediatric Endocrinology, UCLA Med Ctr 1982; **Fac Appt:** Prof Ped, USC-Keck School of Medicine

Gitelman, Stephen E MD [PEn] - **Spec Exp:** Diabetes; **Hospital:** UCSF Med Ctr; **Address:** UCSF Madison Clinic-Pediatric Diabetes, 1500 Owens St, Ste 300, San Francisco, CA 94158; **Phone:** 415-514-8500; **Board Cert:** Pediatric Endocrinology 2013; **Med School:** Univ NC Sch Med 1984; **Resid:** Pediatrics, UCSF Med Ctr 1987; **Fellow:** Pediatric Endocrinology, UCSF Med Ctr 1990; **Fac Appt:** Clin Prof Ped, UCSF

Lustig, Robert H MD [PEn] - **Spec Exp:** Obesity; Metabolic Syndrome; Neuroendocrinology; Hyperinsulinism; **Hospital:** UCSF Med Ctr; **Address:** UCSF Medical Ctr, Div Pediatric Endocrinology, 400 Parnassus Ave Fl 2, San Francisco, CA 94143; **Phone:** 415-353-2813; **Board Cert:** Pediatrics 1984; Pediatric Endocrinology 1986; **Med School:** Cornell Univ-Weill Med Coll 1980; **Resid:** Pediatrics, St Louis Chldn's Hosp 1983; **Fellow:** Pediatric Endocrinology, UCSF Medical Ctr 1984; Neuroendocrinology, Rockefeller Univ Hosp 1986; **Fac Appt:** Prof Ped, UCSF

Rosenthal, Stephen M MD [PEn] - **Spec Exp:** Diabetes; **Hospital:** UCSF Med Ctr; **Address:** UCSF Pediatric Specialty Clin, 400 Parnassus Ave Fl 2, San Francisco, CA 94143; **Phone:** 415-353-7337; **Board Cert:** Pediatrics 1982; Pediatric Endocrinology 1983; **Med School:** Columbia P&S 1976; **Resid:** Pediatrics, NY Presby-Columbia Med Ctr 1979; **Fellow:** Pediatric Endocrinology, UCSF Med Ctr 1982; **Fac Appt:** Prof Ped, UCSF

Wilson, Darrell M MD [PEn] - **Spec Exp:** Diabetes; Growth Disorders; Weight Management; **Hospital:** Lucile Packard Chldn's Hosp, Stanford Univ Hosp & Clins; **Address:** Pediatric Diabetes & Endocrinology Clin, 730 Welch Rd Fl 2, Stanford, CA 94305-5208; **Phone:** 650-723-5791 x3; **Board Cert:** Pediatrics 1982; **Med School:** UCSD 1977; **Resid:** Pediatrics, Stanford Univ Med Ctr 1980; **Fellow:** Endocrinology, Diabetes & Metabolism, Stanford Univ Med Ctr 1984; **Fac Appt:** Prof Ped, Stanford Univ

Pediatric Gastroenterology

New England

Fasano, Alessio MD [PGe] - **Spec Exp:** Celiac Disease; Diarrheal Diseases; Nutrition; **Hospital:** Mass Genl Hosp; **Address:** MGH Center for Celiac Research, 55 Fruit St, Yawkey Center, Ste 6B, Boston, MA 02114; **Phone:** 617-726-8705; **Med School:** Italy 1981; **Resid:** Pediatrics, Univ Naples 1985; **Fac Appt:** Assoc Prof Ped, Harvard Med Sch

Jonas, Maureen M MD [PGe] - **Spec Exp:** Liver Disease; Transplant Medicine-Liver; Hepatitis; **Hospital:** Children's Hospital - Boston, Brigham & Women's Hosp; **Address:** Boston Chldn's Hosp, Dept Ped Gastroenterology, 300 Longwood Ave, Boston, MA 02115; **Phone:** 617-355-5837; **Board Cert:** Pediatrics 1982; Pediatric Gastroenterology 2005; Pediatric Transplant Hepatology 2006; **Med School:** Univ Miami Sch Med 1977; **Resid:** Pediatrics, Chldns Hosp 1980; **Fellow:** Pediatric Gastroenterology, Chldns Hosp 1982; **Fac Appt:** Assoc Prof Ped, Harvard Med Sch

Kleinman, Ronald E MD [PGe] - **Spec Exp:** Transplant Medicine-Liver; Nutrition; **Hospital:** Mass Genl Hosp; **Address:** Mass Genl Hosp, Div Ped GI/Nutrition, 55 Fruit St, Yawkey Center, Ste 6B, Boston, MA 02114; **Phone:** 617-726-8705; **Board Cert:** Pediatrics 1992; Pediatric Gastroenterology 2012; **Med School:** NY Med Coll 1972; **Resid:** Pediatrics, Montefiore Med Ctr 1976; **Fellow:** Pediatric Gastroenterology, Mass Genl Hosp 1980; **Fac Appt:** Prof Ped, Harvard Med Sch

Leichtner, Alan M MD [PGe] - **Spec Exp:** Celiac Disease; Nutrition; **Hospital:** Children's Hospital - Boston; **Address:** Boston Chldn's Hosp, Gastroenterology, 300 Longwood Ave, Hunnewell-Ground, Boston, MA 02115; **Phone:** 617-355-2946; **Board Cert:** Pediatrics 1982; Pediatric Gastroenterology 2010; **Med School:** Harvard Med Sch 1977; **Resid:** Pediatrics, Chldn's Hosp 1980; **Fellow:** Pediatric Gastroenterology, Chldn's Hosp 1983; **Fac Appt:** Assoc Prof Ped, Harvard Med Sch

Mid Atlantic

Baker Jr, Robert D MD/PhD [PGe] - **Spec Exp:** Gastroesophageal Reflux Disease (GERD); Cystic Fibrosis; Nutrition; Malabsorption Syndrome; **Hospital:** Women & Chldn's Hosp of Buffalo, The; **Address:** Digestive Disease & Nutrition Ctr, Women & Children's Hosp Buffalo, 239 Bryant St Fl 2, Buffalo, NY 14222-2006; **Phone:** 716-878-7793; **Board Cert:** Pediatrics 1978; Pediatric Gastroenterology 2010; **Med School:** Temple Univ 1972; **Resid:** Pediatrics, Buffalo Chldns Hosp 1975; **Fellow:** Gastroenterology, Mass Genl Hosp/Chldns Hosp Med Ctr 1978; Nutritional Biochemistry, MIT 1984; **Fac Appt:** Prof Ped, SUNY Buffalo

Baker, Susan S MD/PhD [PGe] - **Spec Exp:** Nutrition; Obesity; Liver Disease; Gastroesophageal Reflux Disease (GERD); **Hospital:** Women & Chldn's Hosp of Buffalo, The; **Address:** Digestive Disease & Nutrition Ctr, Women & Chldns Hosp Buffalo, 239 Bryant St Fl 2, Buffalo, NY 14222; **Phone:** 716-878-7793; **Board Cert:** Pediatrics 1978; Pediatric Gastroenterology 2010; **Med School:** Temple Univ 1972; **Resid:** Pediatrics, Buffalo Chldns Hosp 1975; **Fellow:** Nutrition, MIT 1981; Gastroenterology, Mass Genl Hosp/Harvard 1984; **Fac Appt:** Prof Ped, SUNY Buffalo

Baldassano, Robert N MD [PGe] - **Spec Exp:** Inflammatory Bowel Disease; Ulcerative Colitis; Crohn's Disease; **Hospital:** Chldns Hosp of Philadelphia; **Address:** Chldns Hosp, Ped Gastroenterology Dept, 3404 Civic Center Blvd, Philadelphia, PA 19104; **Phone:** 215-590-3630; **Board Cert:** Pediatric Gastroenterology 2007; **Med School:** SUNY Downstate 1984; **Resid:** Pediatrics, Chldns Hosp 1988; **Fellow:** Pediatric Gastroenterology, Chldns Hosp 1991; **Fac Appt:** Prof Ped, Univ Pennsylvania

Baldridge, Alan D MD [PGe] - **Spec Exp:** Inflammatory Bowel Disease; Celiac Disease; Liver Disease; **Hospital:** Cooper Univ Hosp; **Address:** 3 Cooper Plaza, Ste 200, Camden, NJ 08034; **Phone:** 856-342-2001; **Board Cert:** Pediatrics 2008; Pediatric Gastroenterology 2012; **Med School:** Med Coll VA 1988; **Resid:** Pediatrics, Boston City Hosp 1991; **Fellow:** Pediatric Gastroenterology, Mass Genl Hosp 1994; **Fac Appt:** Asst Prof Ped, UMDNJ-RW Johnson Med Sch

Benkov, Keith J MD [PGe] - **Spec Exp:** Inflammatory Bowel Disease/Crohn's; Liver Disease; Celiac Disease; **Hospital:** Mt Sinai Med Ctr (page 62), Englewood Hosp & Med Ctr; **Address:** Mt Sinai Div Ped Gastroenterology, 5 E 98th St, Fl 10, New York, NY 10029; **Phone:** 212-241-5415; **Board Cert:** Pediatrics 1984; Pediatric Gastroenterology 2012; **Med School:** Mount Sinai Sch Med 1979; **Resid:** Pediatrics, Mt Sinai Hosp 1982; **Fellow:** Pediatric Gastroenterology, Mt Sinai Hosp 1984; **Fac Appt:** Assoc Prof Ped, Mount Sinai Sch Med

Levy, Joseph MD [PGe] - **Spec Exp:** Celiac Disease; Gastroesophageal Reflux Disease (GERD); Nutrition in Autism; Inflammatory Bowel Disease/Crohn's; **Hospital:** NYU Langone Med Ctr (page 68); **Address:** 160 E 32nd St, Medical Suite L-3, New York, NY 10016; **Phone:** 212-263-5407; **Board Cert:** Pediatrics 1981; Pediatric Gastroenterology 2012; **Med School:** Israel 1973; **Resid:** Pediatrics, Beth Israel Med Ctr 1977; **Fellow:** Research, Columbia-Presby Med Ctr 1975; Pediatric Gastroenterology, Columbia-Presby Med Ctr 1979; **Fac Appt:** Prof Ped, NYU Sch Med

Oliva-Hemker, Maria M MD [PGe] - **Spec Exp:** Inflammatory Bowel Disease/Crohn's; Ulcerative Colitis; Malabsorption Syndrome; **Hospital:** Johns Hopkins Hosp (page 59), Greater Baltimore Med Ctr; **Address:** Johns Hopkins Hosp, Ped GI & Nutrition, 200 N Wolfe St, Baltimore, MD 21287; **Phone:** 410-955-8769; **Board Cert:** Pediatrics 2007; Pediatric Gastroenterology 2007; **Med School:** Johns Hopkins Univ 1986; **Resid:** Pediatrics, Johns Hopkins Hosp 1989; **Fellow:** Gastroenterology, Johns Hopkins Hosp 1992; **Fac Appt:** Prof Ped, Johns Hopkins Univ

Piccoli, David A MD [PGe] - **Spec Exp:** Liver Disease; Inflammatory Bowel Disease; Crohn's Disease; **Hospital:** Chldns Hosp of Philadelphia; **Address:** Chlds Hosp, Ped Gastroenterology Dept, 3404 Civic Center Blvd Wood Bldg Fl 3, Philadelphia, PA 19104; **Phone:** 215-590-3630; **Board Cert:** Pediatrics 1984; Pediatric Gastroenterology 2012; **Med School:** Harvard Med Sch 1979; **Resid:** Pediatrics, Chldns Hosp 1983; **Fellow:** Gastroenterology, Chldns Hosp 1986; **Fac Appt:** Prof Ped, Univ Pennsylvania

Schwarz, Kathleen B MD [PGe] - **Spec Exp:** Hepatitis B & C; Transplant Medicine-Liver; Liver Disease; **Hospital:** Johns Hopkins Hosp (page 59); **Address:** Johns Hopkins Hosp, Ped GI & Nutrition, 200 N Wolfe St, Baltimore, MD 21287; **Phone:** 410-955-8769; **Board Cert:** Pediatrics 1977; Pediatric Gastroenterology 2012; Pediatric Transplant Hepatology 2006; **Med School:** Washington Univ, St Louis 1972; **Resid:** Pediatrics, St Louis Chldns Hosp 1974; **Fellow:** Pediatric Gastroenterology, St Louis Chldns Hosp 1976; **Fac Appt:** Prof Ped, Johns Hopkins Univ

Schwarz, Steven M MD [PGe] - **Spec Exp:** Gastroesophageal Reflux Disease (GERD); Nutrition; Endoscopy; Inflammatory Bowel Disease; **Hospital:** SUNY Downstate Med Ctr (Univ Hosp Brooklyn), Beth Israel Med Ctr - Petrie Div (page 56); **Address:** Children's Hosp at SUNY Downstate, 445 Lenox Rd, Box 49, Brooklyn, NY 11203; **Phone:** 718-270-4714; **Board Cert:** Pediatrics 1979; Pediatric Gastroenterology 2012; **Med School:** Columbia P&S 1974; **Resid:** Pediatrics, Columbia-Presby Med Ctr 1977; **Fellow:** Pediatric Gastroenterology, Stanford Univ Med Ctr 1978; Pediatric Gastroenterology, Columbia-Presby Med Ctr 1980; **Fac Appt:** Prof Ped, SUNY Downstate

Snyder, John D MD [PGe] - **Spec Exp:** Celiac Disease; Gastroesophageal Reflux Disease (GERD); **Hospital:** Chldns Natl Med Ctr; **Address:** Children's National Med Ctr, 111 Michigan Ave NW, Ste 100, Washington, DC 20010; **Phone:** 202-476-3032; **Board Cert:** Pediatrics 1982; Pediatric Gastroenterology 2012; **Med School:** UCLA 1975; **Resid:** Pediatrics, Duke Univ Med Ctr 1978; **Fellow:** Pediatric Gastroenterology, Mass Genl Hosp 1984

Spivak, William MD [PGe] - **Spec Exp:** Ulcerative Colitis; Crohn's Disease; Nutrition; Esophageal Disorders; **Hospital:** NY-Presby/Weill Cornell Med Ctr, NY (page 65), Lenox Hill Hosp (page 66); **Address:** 177 E 87th St, Ste 305, New York, NY 10128; **Phone:** 212-369-7700; **Board Cert:** Pediatrics 1981; Pediatric Gastroenterology 2012; **Med School:** Albert Einstein Coll Med 1976; **Resid:** Pediatrics, Jacobi Med Ctr/Albert Einstein Med Sch 1979; **Fellow:** Gastroenterology, Childrens Hosp 1982; Research, Brigham & Womens Hosp 1982; **Fac Appt:** Clin Prof Ped, Cornell Univ-Weill Med Coll

Squires Jr, Robert H MD [PGe] - **Spec Exp:** Liver Disease; Intestinal Disorders; Hepatitis B & C; **Hospital:** Chldns Hosp of Pittsburgh - UPMC; **Address:** Chldns Hosp, Ped Gastroenterology Dept, 4401 Penn Ave Fl 3, Pittsburgh, PA 15201; **Phone:** 412-692-5180; **Board Cert:** Pediatrics 1981; Pediatric Gastroenterology 2012; Pediatric Transplant Hepatology 2006; **Med School:** Univ Tex Med Br, Galveston 1977; **Resid:** Pediatrics, Chldns Hosp 1979; **Fellow:** Pediatric Gastroenterology, Chldns Hosp 1982; **Fac Appt:** Prof Ped, Univ Pittsburgh

Southeast

Black, Dennis D MD [PGe] - **Spec Exp:** Nutrition; Obesity; **Hospital:** Le Bonheur Chldns Med Ctr; **Address:** UT Medical Group, 7945 Wolf River Rd, Ste 250, Germantown, TN 38138; **Phone:** 901-866-8821; **Board Cert:** Pediatrics 1983; Pediatric Gastroenterology 2012; **Med School:** Univ Tenn Coll Med 1978; **Resid:** Pediatrics, Le Bonheur Chldns Med Ctr 1981; **Fellow:** Pediatric Gastroenterology, Univ Tenn Hlth Sci Ctr 1984; **Fac Appt:** Prof Ped, Univ Tenn Coll Med

Novak, Donald A MD [PGe] - **Spec Exp:** Liver Disease; Nutrition; Obesity; **Hospital:** UF Hlth Shands Chldns Hosp; **Address:** UF Hlth, Pediatric GI Dept, 1600 SW Archer Rd, rm RG120, Gainesville, FL 32610; **Phone:** 352-273-9350; **Board Cert:** Pediatrics 1988; Pediatric Gastroenterology 2010; **Med School:** Univ S Fla Coll Med 1981; **Resid:** Pediatrics, Univ S FL Affil Hosp 1984; **Fellow:** Pediatric Gastroenterology, Chldns Hosp 1987; **Fac Appt:** Prof Ped, Univ Fla Coll Med

Ulshen, Martin H MD [PGe] - **Spec Exp:** Liver Disease; Inflammatory Bowel Disease; Irritable Bowel Syndrome; **Hospital:** Duke Univ Hosp; **Address:** 2301 Erwin Rd, Durham, NC 27710; **Phone:** 919-684-5068; **Board Cert:** Pediatrics 1993; Pediatric Gastroenterology 2012; **Med School:** Univ Rochester 1969; **Resid:** Pediatrics, Univ Colorado Med Ctr 1974; **Fellow:** Pediatric Gastroenterology, Univ Colorado Med Ctr 1975; Pediatric Gastroenterology, Chldns Hosp 1977; **Fac Appt:** Prof Ped, Duke Univ

Midwest

Berman, James MD [PGe] - **Spec Exp:** Inflammatory Bowel Disease/Crohn's; Nutrition; Ulcerative Colitis; **Hospital:** Loyola Univ - Ronald McDonald Children's Hosp, Adv Luth Genl Hosp; **Address:** Loyola Univ Med Ctr, Dept Ped Gastro, 2160 S 1st Ave Bldg 105 Fl 3, Outpatient Ctr, Maywood, IL 60153-3304; **Phone:** 708-327-9073; **Board Cert:** Pediatrics 1986; Pediatric Gastroenterology 2012; **Med School:** Univ Pittsburgh 1981; **Resid:** Pediatrics, Chldns Hosp 1984; **Fellow:** Pediatric Gastroenterology, Mass Genl Hosp/Chldns Hosp 1987; **Fac Appt:** Assoc Clin Prof Ped, Loyola Univ-Stritch Sch Med

Bishop, Warren P MD [PGe] - **Spec Exp:** Liver Disease; Constipation; Diarrheal Diseases; Inflammatory Bowel Disease; **Hospital:** Univ Iowa Hosp & Clins; **Address:** UICH - Div Ped Gastroenterology, 200 Hawkins Drive, JPP Bldg - Ste 2869, Iowa City, IA 52242; **Phone:** 319-356-2229; **Board Cert:** Pediatrics 1984; Pediatric Gastroenterology 2012; **Med School:** Univ Wisc 1979; **Resid:** Pediatrics, Univ Michigan Affil Hosps 1982; **Fellow:** Pediatric Gastroenterology, Univ NC Affil Hosps 1989; **Fac Appt:** Prof Ped, Univ Iowa Coll Med

Cohen, Mitchell B MD [PGe] - **Spec Exp:** Inflammatory Bowel Disease; Diarrheal Diseases; Celiac Disease; **Hospital:** Cincinnati Chldns Hosp Med Ctr; **Address:** Chldns Hosp Med Ctr, 3333 Burnet Ave, MLC 2010, Cincinnati, OH 45229; **Phone:** 513-636-4415; **Board Cert:** Pediatrics 1981; Pediatric Gastroenterology 2012; **Med School:** Mount Sinai Sch Med 1977; **Resid:** Pediatrics, Johns Hopkins Hosp 1980; **Fellow:** Pediatric Gastroenterology, Chldns Hosp Med Ctr 1986; **Fac Appt:** Prof Ped, Univ Cincinnati

Di Lorenzo, Carlo MD [PGe] - **Spec Exp:** Gastrointestinal Motility Disorders; Gastrointestinal Functional Disorders; **Hospital:** Nationwide Chldn's Hosp; **Address:** Nationwide Children's Hosp, Div Gastroenterology & Nutrition, 700 Children's Drive, Columbus, OH 43205; **Phone:** 614-722-3450; **Board Cert:** Pediatric Gastroenterology 2012; **Med School:** Italy 1984; **Resid:** Pediatrics, Univ Naples Med Ctr 1988; **Fellow:** Pediatric Gastroenterology, Harbor-UCLA Med Ctr 1990; **Fac Appt:** Prof Ped, Ohio State Univ

El-Youssef, Mounif MD [PGe] - **Spec Exp:** Liver Disease; **Hospital:** Mayo Med Ctr & Clin - Rochester; **Address:** Mayo Clin, Div Ped Gastroenterology, 200 First St SW, Rochester, MN 55905; **Phone:** 507-266-4950; **Board Cert:** Pediatric Gastroenterology 2012; Pediatric Transplant Hepatology 2012; **Med School:** Belgium 1982; **Resid:** Pediatrics, Cleveland Clin 1987; **Fellow:** Pediatric Gastroenterology, Harvard Med Sch 1990

Guandalini, Stefano MD [PGe] - **Spec Exp:** Celiac Disease; Digestive Disorders; Diarrheal Diseases; **Hospital:** Univ Chicago Med-Comer Chldn's Hosp; **Address:** Univ Chicago-Comer Chldn's Hosp, 5721 S Maryland Ave, Chicago, IL 60637; **Phone:** 773-702-6418; **Med School:** Italy 1971; **Resid:** Pediatrics, Univ Messina Affil Hosp 1974; **Fellow:** Pediatric Gastroenterology, Univ Naples Affil Hosp; **Fac Appt:** Prof Ped, Univ Chicago-Pritzker Sch Med

Gunasekaran, T S MD [PGe] - **Spec Exp:** Gastroesophageal Reflux Disease (GERD); Esophageal Disorders; Inflammatory Bowel Disease; Pain-Abdominal Recurrent; **Hospital:** Adv Luth Genl Hosp, Loyola Univ Med Ctr; **Address:** Lutheran Genl Chldns Hosp, Dept Ped GI, Dept Ped GI, 1675 Dempster St, Park Ridge, IL 60068; **Phone:** 847-723-7700; **Board Cert:** Pediatric Gastroenterology 2007; **Med School:** India 1977; **Resid:** Pediatrics, Univ Madras 1982; Pediatrics, Chldn's Hosp 1987; **Fellow:** Pediatric Gastroenterology, Chldn's Hosp 1992; **Fac Appt:** Assoc Clin Prof Ped, Loyola Univ-Stritch Sch Med

Gupta, Sandeep K MD [PGe] - **Spec Exp:** Eosinophilic Esophagitis; Gastroesophageal Reflux Disease (GERD); Nutrition; Obesity; **Hospital:** Riley Hosp for Children; **Address:** Riley Hosp for Chldn, Div Ped Gastroenterology, 705 Riley Hosp Drive, ROC 4210, Indianapolis, IN 46202; **Phone:** 317-944-3774; **Board Cert:** Pediatric Gastroenterology 2012; **Med School:** Nigeria 1986; **Resid:** Pediatrics, UConn Hlth Ctr; **Fellow:** Pediatric Gastroenterology, IU Health Univ Hosp; **Fac Appt:** Clin Prof Ped, Indiana Univ

Hill, Ivor D MD [PGe] - **Spec Exp:** Celiac Disease; Inflammatory Bowel Disease; Malabsorption Syndrome; Diarrheal Diseases; **Hospital:** Nationwide Chldn's Hosp; **Address:** Nationwide Chldns, Ped Gastroenterology, 700 Childrens Drive, Columbus, OH 43205; **Phone:** 614-722-3450; **Board Cert:** Pediatrics 2007; Pediatric Gastroenterology 2010; **Med School:** South Africa 1972; **Resid:** Pediatrics, Addington Hosp 1976; Pediatrics, Red Cross Chldns Hosp 1977; **Fellow:** Pediatric Gastroenterology, Red Cross Chldns Hosp 1980; **Fac Appt:** Prof Ped, Ohio State Univ

Kirschner, Barbara S MD [PGe] - **Spec Exp:** Ulcerative Colitis; Pain-Abdominal Recurrent; Inflammatory Bowel Disease/Crohn's; **Hospital:** Univ Chicago Med-Comer Chldn's Hosp; **Address:** Univ Chicago-Comer Chldn's Hosp, 5721 S Maryland Ave, Chicago, IL 60637; **Phone:** 773-702-6418; **Board Cert:** Pediatrics 1972; Pediatric Gastroenterology 2005; **Med School:** Med Coll PA 1967; **Resid:** Pediatrics, Univ Chicago Hosps 1970; **Fellow:** Pediatric Gastroenterology, Univ Chicago Hosps 1977; **Fac Appt:** Prof Ped, Univ Chicago-Pritzker Sch Med

Molleston, Jean P MD [PGe] - **Spec Exp:** Liver Disease; Hepatitis; Transplant Medicine-Liver; Graft vs Host Disease; **Hospital:** Riley Hosp for Children, IU Health North Hosp; **Address:** Riley Hosp for Chldn, Div Ped Gastroenterology, 705 Riley Hosp Drive, ROC 4210, Indianapolis, IN 46202-5225; **Phone:** 317-944-3774; **Board Cert:** Pediatrics 2009; Pediatric Gastroenterology 2010; Pediatric Transplant Hepatology 2006; **Med School:** Washington Univ, St Louis 1986; **Resid:** Pediatrics, Chldns Hosp 1988; **Fellow:** Pediatric Gastroenterology, Washington Univ 1991; **Fac Appt:** Clin Prof Ped, Indiana Univ

Mousa, Hayat M MD [PGe] - **Spec Exp:** Gastroesophageal Reflux Disease (GERD); Gastrointestinal Motility Disorders; Gastrointestinal Functional Disorders; **Hospital:** Nationwide Chldn's Hosp; **Address:** Nationwide Children's Hosp, Div Gastroenterology & Nutrition, 700 Children's Drive, Columbus, OH 43205; **Phone:** 614-722-3450; **Board Cert:** Pediatric Gastroenterology 2007; **Med School:** Syria 1982; **Resid:** Pediatrics, Henry Ford Hosp 1993; **Fellow:** Pediatric Gastroenterology, Chldns Hosp 1998; **Fac Appt:** Assoc Clin Prof Ped, Ohio State Univ

Rothbaum, Robert J MD [PGe] - **Spec Exp:** Inflammatory Bowel Disease; **Hospital:** St. Louis Chldns Hosp, Barnes-Jewish Hosp; **Address:** St Louis Chldns Hosp, 1 Chldns Pl, NW Tower, Fl 9, Box 8116, St Louis, MO 63110; **Phone:** 314-454-6173; **Board Cert:** Pediatrics 1981; Pediatric Gastroenterology 2012; **Med School:** Univ Chicago-Pritzker Sch Med 1976; **Resid:** Pediatrics, St Louis Chldns Hosp 1978; **Fellow:** Ambulatory Pediatrics, St Louis Chldns Hosp 1979; Pediatric Gastroenterology, Chldns Hosp Med Ctr 1982; **Fac Appt:** Prof Ped, Washington Univ, St Louis

Whitington, Peter F MD [PGe] - **Spec Exp:** Transplant Medicine-Liver; Liver Disease; **Hospital:** Lurie Chldn's Hosp-Chicago; **Address:** Lurie Chldn's Hosp, Div Ped Gastro, 225 E Chicago Ave, Box 65, Chicago, IL 60611; **Phone:** 312-227-4200; **Board Cert:** Pediatrics 1977; Pediatric Gastroenterology 2012; Pediatric Transplant Hepatology 2006; **Med School:** Univ Tenn Coll Med 1971; **Resid:** Pediatrics, Univ TN Med Ctr 1976; **Fellow:** Gastroenterology, Johns Hopkins Hosp 1979; Gastroenterology, Univ Wisconsin Affil Hosp 1980; **Fac Appt:** Prof Ped, Northwestern Univ

Wyllie, Robert MD [PGe] - **Spec Exp:** Inflammatory Bowel Disease/Crohn's; Ulcerative Colitis; **Hospital:** Cleveland Clin (page 55); **Address:** 9500 Euclid Ave, Crile Bldg Fl 11, Cleveland, OH 44195; **Phone:** 216-444-2237; **Board Cert:** Pediatrics 1982; Pediatric Gastroenterology 2010; **Med School:** Indiana Univ 1976; **Resid:** Pediatrics, Indiana Univ Med Ctr 1978; **Fellow:** Pediatric Gastroenterology, Indiana Univ Med Ctr 1980; **Fac Appt:** Prof Ped, Cleveland Cl Coll Med/Case West Res

Great Plains and Mountains

Hoffenberg, Edward J MD [PGe] - **Spec Exp:** Inflammatory Bowel Disease; Celiac Disease; Liver Disease; Pancreatic Disease; **Hospital:** Chldn's Hosp - Aurora (CO); **Address:** Chldns Hosp, Digestive Inst, 13123 E 16th Ave, Box B290, Aurora, CO 80045; **Phone:** 720-777-6669; **Board Cert:** Pediatric Gastroenterology 2007; **Med School:** Case West Res Univ 1986; **Resid:** Pediatrics, Rainbow Babies & Chldns Hosp 1989; **Fellow:** Pediatric Gastroenterology, Chldns Hosp 1992; **Fac Appt:** Prof Ped, Univ Colorado

Krebs, Nancy F MD [PGe] - **Spec Exp:** Obesity; Nutrition; Weight Management; **Hospital:** Chldn's Hosp - Aurora (CO); **Address:** Chldns Hosp, Gastroenterology Dept, 13123 E 16th Ave, Box B270, Aurora, CO 80045; **Phone:** 720-777-2691; **Board Cert:** Pediatrics 2009; **Med School:** Univ Colorado 1987; **Resid:** Pediatrics, Univ CO Hosp 1990; **Fellow:** Pediatric Gastroenterology, Univ CO Hosp 1992; Nutrition, Univ CO Hosp 1993; **Fac Appt:** Prof Ped, Univ Colorado

Narkewicz, Michael R MD [PGe] - **Spec Exp:** Transplant Medicine-Liver; Liver Disease; Cystic Fibrosis; **Hospital:** Chldn's Hosp - Aurora (CO); **Address:** Chldns Hosp, Digestive Inst, 13123 E 16th Ave, Box B290, Aurora, CO 80045; **Phone:** 720-777-6669; **Board Cert:** Pediatrics 1988; Pediatric Gastroenterology 2012; Pediatric Transplant Hepatology 2006; **Med School:** Univ VT Coll Med 1983; **Resid:** Pediatrics, Univ CO Hosp 1986; **Fellow:** Pediatric Gastroenterology, Univ CO Hosp 1989; **Fac Appt:** Prof Ped, Univ Colorado

Sokol, Ronald Jay MD [PGe] - **Spec Exp:** Liver Disease; Transplant Medicine-Liver; Nutrition; Cystic Fibrosis; **Hospital:** Chldn's Hosp - Aurora (CO); **Address:** Chldns Hosp, Digestive Inst, 13123 E 16th Ave, Box B290, Aurora, CO 80045; **Phone:** 720-777-6669; **Board Cert:** Pediatrics 1981; Pediatric Gastroenterology 2012; Pediatric Transplant Hepatology 2010; **Med School:** Univ Chicago-Pritzker Sch Med 1976; **Resid:** Pediatrics, Univ CO Hosp 1980; **Fellow:** Pediatric Gastroenterology, Chldns Hosp 1983; **Fac Appt:** Prof Ped, Univ Colorado

Suchy, Frederick J MD [PGe] - **Spec Exp:** Hepatitis; Liver Disease; Neonatal Cholestasis; **Hospital:** Chldn's Hosp - Aurora (CO); **Address:** Chldns Hosp, Digestive Inst, 13123 E 16th Ave, Box B290, Aurora, CO 80045; **Phone:** 720-777-6669; **Board Cert:** Pediatrics 1982; Pediatric Gastroenterology 2012; Pediatric Transplant Hepatology 2006; **Med School:** Univ Cincinnati 1974; **Resid:** Pediatrics, Chldns Hosp Med Ctr 1978; **Fellow:** Pediatric Gastroenterology, Chldns Hosp Med Ctr 1981; **Fac Appt:** Prof Ped, Univ Colorado

Vanderhoof, Jon A MD [PGe] - **Spec Exp:** Nutrition; Short Bowel Syndrome; **Hospital:** Boys Town Natl Rsch Hosp, Children's Hosp - Omaha; **Address:** Boystown Hosp & Clin, 14080 Hosp Rd, Boys Town, NE 68010; **Phone:** 402-778-6820; **Board Cert:** Pediatrics 1993; Pediatric Gastroenterology 2012; **Med School:** Univ Nebr Coll Med 1972; **Resid:** Pediatrics, Univ Nebr Coll Med 1974; **Fellow:** Pediatric Gastroenterology, UCLA Med Ctr 1976; **Fac Appt:** Prof Emeritus Ped, Univ Nebr Coll Med

Southwest

Mittal, Naveen K MD [PGe] - **Spec Exp:** Transplant Medicine-Liver; Liver Disease; Short Bowel Syndrome; **Hospital:** Christus Santa Rosa Children's Hosp, Univ Hosp-San Antonio; **Address:** 8210 Callaghan Rd, San Antonio, TX 78236; **Phone:** 210-562-5844; **Board Cert:** Pediatrics 2009; Pediatric Gastroenterology 2007; Pediatric Transplant Hepatology 2006; **Med School:** India 1988; **Resid:** Pediatrics, S Cleveland Hosp 1990; Pediatrics, Hahnemann Univ Hosp 1993; **Fellow:** Pediatric Gastroenterology, Bristol Royal Hosp 1991; Pediatric Gastroenterology, Univ Chicago Hosp 1996; **Fac Appt:** Prof Ped, Univ Tex, San Antonio

Rhoads, J Marc MD [PGe] - **Spec Exp:** Diarrheal Diseases; Inflammatory Bowel Disease; Intestinal Disorders; **Hospital:** Meml Hermann Hosp - Texas Med Ctr; **Address:** UT Physicians-Pediatric Gastroenterology, 6410 Fannin St, Ste 500, Houston, TX 77030; **Phone:** 832-325-6516; **Board Cert:** Pediatrics 1986; Pediatric Gastroenterology 2012; **Med School:** Johns Hopkins Univ 1980; **Resid:** Pediatrics, UCLA Med Ctr 1983; **Fellow:** Pediatric Gastroenterology, Hosp for Sick Chldn 1986; **Fac Appt:** Prof Ped, Univ Tex, Houston

West Coast and Pacific

Christie, Dennis L MD [PGe] - **Spec Exp:** Inflammatory Bowel Disease; **Hospital:** Seattle Chldns Hosp; **Address:** Chldns Hosp Med Ctr, Div Gastroenterology, 4800 Sand Point Way NE, MS A-5950, Seattle, WA 98105-3901; **Phone:** 206-987-2521; **Board Cert:** Pediatrics 1992; Pediatric Gastroenterology 2012; **Med School:** Northwestern Univ 1968; **Resid:** Pediatrics, Univ Wash Med Ctr 1971; **Fellow:** Pediatric Gastroenterology, UCLA Ctr Hlth Sci 1976; **Fac Appt:** Prof Ped, Univ Wash

Dubinsky, Marla C MD [PGe] - **Spec Exp:** Inflammatory Bowel Disease; Crohn's Disease; Ulcerative Colitis; Clinical Trials; **Hospital:** Cedars-Sinai Med Ctr; **Address:** 8635 W 3rd St, Ste 1165W, Los Angeles, CA 90048; **Phone:** 310-423-7100; **Board Cert:** Pediatric Gastroenterology 2009; **Med School:** Canada 1993; **Resid:** Pediatrics, Alberta Chldrn's Hosp 1996; **Fellow:** Pediatric Gastroenterology, Sainte Justine Hosp 1999; Research, Cedars-Sinai Med Ctr 2000; **Fac Appt:** Asst Prof Ped, UCLA

Heyman, Melvin B MD [PGe] - **Spec Exp:** Inflammatory Bowel Disease/Crohn's; Gastroesophageal Reflux Disease (GERD); Nutrition; **Hospital:** UCSF Med Ctr; **Address:** UCSF, Dept Ped Gastroenterology, 500 Parnassus Ave, Ste MU 4E, Box 0136, San Francisco, CA 94143-0136; **Phone:** 415-353-7337; **Board Cert:** Pediatrics 1981; Pediatric Gastroenterology 2012; **Med School:** UCLA 1976; **Resid:** Pediatrics, LAC & USC Med Ctr 1979; **Fellow:** Gastroenterology, UCLA Ronald Reagan Med Ctr 1981; Nutrition, Human Nutrition Res Ctr 1990; **Fac Appt:** Prof Ped, UCSF

McDiarmid, Suzanne V MD [PGe] - **Spec Exp:** Transplant Medicine-Liver; Transplant Medicine-Bowel; Transplant Immunology; Liver Disease; **Hospital:** UCLA Ronald Reagan Med Ctr, Santa Monica - UCLA Med Ctr & Ortho Hosp; **Address:** UCLA Chldren's Health Center, 200 UCLA Medical Plaza, Ste 265, Los Angeles, CA 90095; **Phone:** 310-206-6136; **Board Cert:** Pediatrics 1984; Pediatric Gastroenterology 2007; **Med School:** New Zealand 1976; **Resid:** Pediatrics, Chldns Hosp Kings Daughters 1982; Pediatrics, Valley Med Ctr 1983; **Fellow:** Pediatric Gastroenterology, UCLA Ronald Reagan Med Ctr 1988; **Fac Appt:** Prof Ped, UCLA

Murray, Karen MD [PGe] - **Spec Exp:** Liver Disease; Hepatitis B & C; **Hospital:** Seattle Chldns Hosp; **Address:** Dept of Gastroenterology, 4800 Sand Point Way NE, MS A-5950, Seattle, WA 98105; **Phone:** 206-987-2521; **Board Cert:** Pediatrics 2008; Pediatric Gastroenterology 2012; Pediatric Transplant Hepatology 2006; **Med School:** Johns Hopkins Univ 1990; **Resid:** Pediatrics, Chldn's Hosp & Med Ctr 1994; **Fellow:** Gastroenterology, Boston Chldn's Hosp 1997; **Fac Appt:** Prof Ped, Univ Wash

Thomas, Dan W MD [PGe] - **Spec Exp:** Gastrointestinal Disorders-Neonatal; Transplant Medicine-Liver; Inflammatory Bowel Disease; Nutrition in Bowel Disorders; **Hospital:** Chldns Hosp - Los Angeles; **Address:** Childrens Hosp LA-Peds Gastroenterology, 4650 Sunset Blvd, MS #78, Los Angeles, CA 90027; **Phone:** 323-361-2181; **Board Cert:** Pediatrics 1979; Pediatric Gastroenterology 2012; Pediatric Transplant Hepatology 2006; **Med School:** Univ Cincinnati 1974; **Resid:** Pediatrics, Chldns Hosp 1977; **Fellow:** Pediatric Gastroenterology, Chldns Hosp 1979; **Fac Appt:** Clin Prof Ped, USC Sch Med

Pediatric Hematology-Oncology

New England

Altman, Arnold MD [PHO] - **Spec Exp:** Leukemia; **Hospital:** CT Chldns Med Ctr; **Address:** CT Chldns Med Ctr, Hematology/Oncology, 282 Washington St, Ste 5A, Hartford, CT 06106; **Phone:** 860-545-9630; **Board Cert:** Pediatrics 1971; Pediatric Hematology-Oncology 1974; **Med School:** Johns Hopkins Univ 1965; **Resid:** Pediatrics, Chldns Hosp 1970; **Fellow:** Pediatric Hematology-Oncology, Chldns Hosp 1972; **Fac Appt:** Prof Ped, Univ Conn

Billett, Amy L MD [PHO] - **Spec Exp:** Hodgkin's Lymphoma; Lymphoma, Non-Hodgkin's; **Hospital:** Dana-Farber Cancer Inst, Children's Hospital - Boston; **Address:** Dana-Farber Cancer Inst, Div Hematology/Oncology, 450 Brookline Ave, Boston, MA 02215; **Phone:** 617-632-5640; **Board Cert:** Pediatric Hematology-Oncology 2009; **Med School:** Harvard Med Sch 1984; **Resid:** Pediatrics, Univ Wash Affil Hosps 1987; **Fellow:** Pediatric Hematology-Oncology, Children's Hosp 1990; **Fac Appt:** Assoc Prof Ped, Harvard Med Sch

Diller, Lisa R MD [PHO] - **Spec Exp:** Neuroblastoma; Cancer Survivors-Late Effects of Therapy; **Hospital:** Dana-Farber Cancer Inst, Children's Hospital - Boston; **Address:** Dana-Farber Cancer Inst, Dept Pediatric Oncology, 450 Brookline Ave, Boston, MA 02215; **Phone:** 617-632-5642; **Board Cert:** Pediatric Hematology-Oncology 2007; **Med School:** UCSD 1985; **Resid:** Pediatrics, Chldns Hosp 1988; **Fellow:** Pediatric Hematology-Oncology, Chldns Hosp-Dana Farber Cancer Inst 1991; **Fac Appt:** Assoc Prof Ped, Harvard Med Sch

Guinan, Eva C MD [PHO] - **Spec Exp:** Bone Marrow Transplant; Anemia-Aplastic; Bone Marrow Failure Disorders; **Hospital:** Dana-Farber Cancer Inst, Children's Hospital - Boston; **Address:** Dana Faber Cancer Inst, 450 Brookline Ave, Boston, MA 02215; **Phone:** 617-632-4932; **Board Cert:** Pediatrics 1986; Pediatric Hematology-Oncology 2012; **Med School:** Harvard Med Sch 1980; **Resid:** Pediatrics, Children's Hosp 1982; **Fellow:** Pediatric Hematology-Oncology, Dana Farber Cancer Inst 1985; **Fac Appt:** Assoc Prof Ped, Harvard Med Sch

Homans, Alan C MD [PHO] - **Spec Exp:** Leukemia; **Hospital:** FAHC - Med Ctr Campus; **Address:** Fletcher Allen Hlthcare, 111 Colchester Ave Smith Bldg - Ste 559A, Burlington, VT 05401; **Phone:** 802-847-2850; **Board Cert:** Pediatrics 1985; Pediatric Hematology-Oncology 1987; **Med School:** Ohio State Univ 1979; **Resid:** Pediatrics, FAHC - Med Ctr Campus 1981; Pediatrics, Univ Mass Med Ctr 1982; **Fellow:** Pediatric Hematology-Oncology, Rhode Is Hosp 1985; **Fac Appt:** Prof Ped, Univ VT Coll Med

Kadan-Lottick, Nina S MD [PHO] - **Spec Exp:** Cancer Survivors-Late Effects of Therapy; **Hospital:** Yale-New Haven Hosp; **Address:** Yale Pediatric Hematology/Oncology, 333 Cedar St, LMP 2073, New Haven, CT 06510; **Phone:** 203-785-4640; **Board Cert:** Pediatric Hematology-Oncology 2008; **Med School:** Johns Hopkins Univ 1993; **Resid:** Pediatrics, Johns Hopkins Hosp 1996; **Fellow:** Pediatric Hematology-Oncology, Chldns Hosp 1999; Cancer Epidemiology, Univ Minnesota 2000; **Fac Appt:** Assoc Prof Ped, Yale Univ

Kieran, Mark W MD/PhD [PHO] - **Spec Exp:** Brain Tumors; Neuro-Oncology; **Hospital:** Dana-Farber Cancer Inst, Children's Hospital - Boston; **Address:** Dana Farber Cancer Inst, 450 Brookline Ave, Ste D3154, Boston, MA 02115; **Phone:** 617-632-4386; **Board Cert:** Pediatric Hematology-Oncology 2011; **Med School:** Univ Calgary 1986; **Resid:** Pediatrics, Montreal Chldns Hosp 1992; **Fellow:** Pediatric Hematology-Oncology, Chldns Hosp 1995; **Fac Appt:** Assoc Prof Ped, Harvard Med Sch

Rodriguez-Galindo, Carlos MD [PHO] - **Spec Exp:** Retinoblastoma; Sarcoma; Melanoma; Rare Tumors; **Hospital:** Dana-Farber Cancer Inst, Children's Hospital - Boston; **Address:** Dana Farber Cancer Inst, 450 Brookline Ave, Yawkey Bldg Fl 5, Boston, MA 02215; **Phone:** 617-632-4580; **Board Cert:** Pediatrics 2006; Pediatric Hematology-Oncology 2009; **Med School:** Spain 1986; **Resid:** Pediatrics, Hosp Infantil Vall d'Hebron 1992; **Fellow:** Pediatric Hematology-Oncology, St. Jude Children's Research Hosp 1997; **Fac Appt:** Assoc Prof Ped, Harvard Med Sch

Sallan, Stephen E MD [PHO] - **Spec Exp:** Pediatric Cancers; Leukemia; **Hospital:** Dana-Farber Cancer Inst, Children's Hospital - Boston; **Address:** Dana Farber Cancer Inst, Dept Pediatric Oncology, 450 Brookline Ave Dana Bldg - Ste 1642, Boston, MA 02215; **Phone:** 617-632-3316; **Board Cert:** Pediatrics 1972; **Med School:** Wayne State Univ 1967; **Resid:** Pediatrics, Chldns Hosp 1969; Pediatrics, Hosp Sick Chldn 1970; **Fellow:** Pediatric Oncology, Chldns Hosp Med Ctr 1975; **Fac Appt:** Prof Ped, Harvard Med Sch

Schwartz, Cindy Lee MD [PHO] - **Spec Exp:** Hodgkin's Lymphoma; Bone Cancer; Cancer Survivors-Late Effects of Therapy; **Hospital:** Rhode Island Hosp; **Address:** Rhode Island Hospital, Div Pediatric Hematology/Oncology, 593 Eddy St, MPS rm 117, Providence, RI 02903-4923; **Phone:** 401-444-5171; **Board Cert:** Pediatrics 1985; Pediatric Hematology-Oncology 2009; **Med School:** Brown Univ 1979; **Resid:** Pediatrics, Johns Hopkins Hosp 1982; **Fellow:** Pediatric Hematology-Oncology, Johns Hopkins Hosp 1985; **Fac Appt:** Assoc Prof Ped, Brown Univ

van Hoff, Jack MD [PHO] - **Spec Exp:** Brain Tumors; Clinical Trials; **Hospital:** Dartmouth - Hitchcock Med Ctr; **Address:** DHMC, Dept Pediatric Hem/Onc, One Medical Center Drive, Lebanon, NH 03756; **Phone:** 603-650-5541; **Board Cert:** Pediatrics 1985; Pediatric Hematology-Oncology 2009; **Med School:** UMDNJ-NJ Med Sch, Newark 1981; **Resid:** Pediatrics, Yale New Haven Hosp 1984; **Fellow:** Pediatric Hematology-Oncology, Yale New Haven Hosp 1986

Weinstein, Howard J MD [PHO] - **Spec Exp:** Leukemia; Lymphoma, Non-Hodgkin's; Hodgkin's Lymphoma; Pediatric Cancers; **Hospital:** Mass Genl Hosp; **Address:** Mass General Hosp, 55 Fruit St, Yawkey 8B, Boston, MA 02114-2622; **Phone:** 617-726-2737; **Board Cert:** Pediatrics 1977; **Med School:** Univ MD Sch Med 1972; **Resid:** Pediatrics, Mass Genl Hosp 1974; **Fellow:** Pediatric Hematology-Oncology, Dana Farber Cancer Inst/Chldns Hosp 1977; **Fac Appt:** Prof Ped, Harvard Med Sch

Mid Atlantic

Adamson, Peter C MD [PHO] - **Spec Exp:** Drug Development; Clinical Trials; Rhabdomyosarcoma; Pediatric Cancers; **Hospital:** Chldns Hosp of Philadelphia; **Address:** Chldns Hosp Div Oncology, 34th St & Civic Center Blvd, Philadelphia, PA 19104; **Phone:** 215-590-3025; **Board Cert:** Pediatric Hematology-Oncology 2012; **Med School:** Cornell Univ 1984; **Resid:** Pediatrics, Chldns Hosp 1987; **Fellow:** Pediatric Hematology-Oncology, Natl Cancer Inst 1990; **Fac Appt:** Clin Prof Ped, Univ Pennsylvania

Aledo, Alexander MD [PHO] - **Spec Exp:** Leukemia; Lymphoma; Bone Tumors; **Hospital:** NY-Presby/Weill Cornell Med Ctr, NY (page 65), NY Hosp Queens; **Address:** 525 E 68th St, rm P695, New York, NY 10021-4870; **Phone:** 212-746-3400; **Board Cert:** Pediatric Hematology-Oncology 2004; **Med School:** NYU Sch Med 1984; **Resid:** Pediatrics, NYPresby/Weill Cornell Med Ctr 1987; **Fellow:** Pediatric Hematology-Oncology, Meml Sloan Kettering Cancer Ctr 1990; **Fac Appt:** Assoc Clin Prof Ped, Cornell Univ-Weill Med Coll

Angiolillo, Anne L MD [PHO] - **Spec Exp:** Leukemia; Lymphoma; **Hospital:** Chldns Natl Med Ctr; **Address:** Dept Oncology, 111 Michigan Ave NW Fl 4 - Ste 4043, Washington, DC 20010; **Phone:** 202-476-2140; **Board Cert:** Pediatric Hematology-Oncology 2011; **Med School:** NY Med Coll 1989; **Resid:** Pediatrics, Chldns Natl Med Ctr 1993; **Fellow:** Pediatric Hematology-Oncology, Chldns Natl Med Ctr 1996

Brecher, Martin L MD [PHO] - **Spec Exp:** Leukemia; Lymphoma; Hodgkin's Lymphoma; Clinical Trials; **Hospital:** Roswell Park Canc Inst, Women & Chldn's Hosp of Buffalo, The; **Address:** Roswell Park Cancer Inst, Dept Pediatrics, Elm & Carlton Sts, Buffalo, NY 14263; **Phone:** 716-845-2333; **Board Cert:** Pediatrics 1977; Pediatric Hematology-Oncology 1978; **Med School:** SUNY Buffalo 1972; **Resid:** Pediatrics, Buffalo Chldns Hosp 1975; **Fellow:** Hematology & Oncology, Buffalo Chldns Hosp/Roswell Park Cancer Inst 1977; **Fac Appt:** Assoc Prof Ped, SUNY Buffalo

Bussel, James MD [PHO] - **Spec Exp:** Bleeding/Coagulation Disorders; Platelet Disorders; Wiskott-Aldrich Syndrome; **Hospital:** NY-Presby/Weill Cornell Med Ctr, NY (page 65), Lenox Hill Hosp (page 66); **Address:** 525 E 68th St, rm P-695, New York, NY 10065; **Phone:** 212-746-3400; **Board Cert:** Pediatrics 1979; Pediatric Hematology-Oncology 1980; **Med School:** Columbia P&S 1975; **Resid:** Pediatrics, Chldns Hosp 1978; **Fellow:** Pediatric Hematology-Oncology, NY Presby Hosp/Cornell 1981; **Fac Appt:** Prof Ped, Cornell Univ-Weill Med Coll

Cairo, Mitchell S MD [PHO] - **Spec Exp:** Bone Marrow Transplant; Stem Cell Transplant; Leukemia; Lymphoma; **Hospital:** Westchester Med Ctr, Children's & Women's Phys.of Westchester; **Address:** CWPW, Pediatric Hematology/Oncology Dept, 19 Bradhurst Ave, Hawthorne, NY 10532; **Phone:** 914-493-7997; **Board Cert:** Pediatrics 1980; Pediatric Hematology-Oncology 1982; **Med School:** UCSF 1976; **Resid:** Pediatrics, UCLA Med Ctr 1979; **Fellow:** Pediatric Hematology-Oncology, IU Hlth Hosp 1981; **Fac Appt:** Prof Ped, NY Med Coll

Carroll, William L MD [PHO] - **Spec Exp:** Leukemia; Hematologic Malignancies; **Hospital:** NYU Langone Med Ctr (page 68); **Address:** NYU Med Ctr, Div Ped Hem/Onc, 160 E 32nd Level L3 St, New York, NY 10016; **Phone:** 212-263-8400; **Board Cert:** Pediatrics 1984; Pediatric Hematology-Oncology 1987; **Med School:** UC Irvine 1978; **Resid:** Pediatrics, Chldns Hosp Med Ctr 1981; **Fellow:** Pediatric Hematology-Oncology, Stanford Univ Med Ctr 1987; **Fac Appt:** Prof Ped, NYU Sch Med

Chen, Allen R MD/PhD [PHO] - **Spec Exp:** Bone Marrow Transplant; Hodgkin's Lymphoma; Immunotherapy; Graft vs Host Disease; **Hospital:** Johns Hopkins Hosp (page 59); **Address:** Johns Hopkins Hosp, Div Peds Oncology, 1650 Orleans St, CRB Bldg - Fl 2M, rm 53, Baltimore, MD 21287; **Phone:** 410-955-8751; **Board Cert:** Pediatric Hematology-Oncology 2006; **Med School:** Duke Univ 1986; **Resid:** Pediatrics, Chldns Hosp Med Ctr 1989; **Fellow:** Pediatric Hematology-Oncology, Fred Hutchinson Canc Ctr 1993; Bone Marrow Transplant, Fred Hutchinson Canc Ctr 1994; **Fac Appt:** Assoc Prof Ped, Johns Hopkins Univ

Cheung, Nai-Kong V MD/PhD [PHO] - **Spec Exp:** Neuroblastoma; Pediatric Cancers; Clinical Trials; **Hospital:** Meml Sloan-Kettering Canc Ctr; **Address:** 1275 York Ave, New York, NY 10065; **Phone:** 646-888-2313; **Board Cert:** Pediatrics 1987; Pediatric Hematology-Oncology 2012; **Med School:** Harvard Med Sch 1978; **Resid:** Pediatrics, Stanford Univ Hosp 1981; **Fellow:** Pediatric Hematology-Oncology, Stanford Univ Hosp 1984; **Fac Appt:** Assoc Prof Ped, Cornell Univ-Weill Med Coll

Cohen, Kenneth J MD [PHO] - **Spec Exp:** Brain Tumors; Spinal Tumors; **Hospital:** Johns Hopkins Hosp (page 59); **Address:** Johns Hopkins Hosp, 1800 Orleans St, Bloomberg Bldg, rm 11379, Baltimore, MD 21287; **Phone:** 410-614-5055; **Board Cert:** Pediatric Hematology-Oncology 2009; **Med School:** SUNY Upstate Med Univ 1987; **Resid:** Pediatrics, Univ Colo Hlth Sci Ctr 1990; **Fellow:** Pediatric Hematology-Oncology, Johns Hopkins Hospital 1994; **Fac Appt:** Assoc Prof Ped, Johns Hopkins Univ

Dome, Jeffrey S MD [PHO] - **Spec Exp:** Solid Tumors; Wilms' Tumor; Bone Cancer; **Hospital:** Chldns Natl Med Ctr; **Address:** Dept Oncology, 111 Michigan Ave NW, Washington, DC 20010; **Phone:** 202-476-2800; **Board Cert:** Pediatric Hematology-Oncology 2013; **Med School:** Univ Pennsylvania 1991; **Resid:** Pediatrics, Yale-New Haven Hosp 1994; **Fellow:** Hematology & Oncology, Johns Hopkins Hosp 1997

Drachtman, Richard A MD [PHO] - **Spec Exp:** Pediatric Cancers; Sickle Cell Disease; **Hospital:** Robert Wood Johnson Univ Hosp - New Brunswick, Jersey Shore Univ Med Ctr; **Address:** Cancer Inst of New Jersey, 195 Little Albany St, rm 3507, New Brunswick, NJ 08903; **Phone:** 732-235-5437; **Board Cert:** Pediatric Hematology-Oncology 2007; **Med School:** Ros Franklin Univ/Chicago Med Sch 1984; **Resid:** Pediatrics, N Shore Univ Hosp 1988; **Fellow:** Pediatric Hematology-Oncology, Mount Sinai Hosp 1991; **Fac Appt:** Prof Ped, UMDNJ-RW Johnson Med Sch

Dunkel, Ira J MD [PHO] - **Spec Exp:** Retinoblastoma; Brain & Spinal Cord Tumors; Brain Tumors; Pediatric Cancers; **Hospital:** Meml Sloan-Kettering Canc Ctr; **Address:** 1275 York Ave, New York, NY 10065; **Phone:** 212-639-2153; **Board Cert:** Pediatric Hematology-Oncology 2007; **Med School:** Duke Univ 1985; **Resid:** Pediatrics, Duke Univ Med Ctr 1988; **Fellow:** Pediatric Hematology-Oncology, Memorial-Sloan Kettering 1992; Pediatric Infectious Disease, Duke Univ Med Ctr 1989; **Fac Appt:** Assoc Prof Ped, Cornell Univ-Weill Med Coll

Felix, Carolyn A MD [PHO] - **Spec Exp:** Leukemia; Leukemia in Infants; **Hospital:** Chldns Hosp of Philadelphia; **Address:** Childrens Hosp Div Oncology, 34th St & Civic Center Blvd, Philadelphia, PA 19104; **Phone:** 215-590-2299; **Board Cert:** Pediatrics 1987; Pediatric Hematology-Oncology 1987; **Med School:** Boston Univ 1981; **Resid:** Pediatrics, Chldns Hosp 1984; **Fellow:** Pediatric Hematology-Oncology, Natl Cancer Inst 1987; **Fac Appt:** Prof Ped, Univ Pennsylvania

Frantz, Christopher N MD [PHO] - **Spec Exp:** Solid Tumors; Neuroblastoma; Leukemia; **Hospital:** Nemours/Alfred I. duPont Hosp for Chldn; **Address:** Nemours, Ped Hem/Onc Dept, 1600 Rockland Rd, Wilmington, DE 19803; **Phone:** 302-651-5500; **Board Cert:** Pediatrics 1977; Pediatric Hematology-Oncology 2012; **Med School:** Albert Einstein Coll Med 1971; **Resid:** Pediatrics, Chldns Hosp 1976; **Fellow:** Pediatric Hematology-Oncology, Chldns Hosp/Dana Farber Cancer Inst 1979

Friedman, Alan D MD [PHO] - **Spec Exp:** Leukemia; **Hospital:** Johns Hopkins Hosp (page 59); **Address:** Johns Hopkins Hosp, Ped Oncology, 1800 Orleans St, Bloomberg Bldg - Ste 11N, Baltimore, MD 21287; **Phone:** 410-955-8751; **Board Cert:** Pediatrics 1987; Pediatric Hematology-Oncology 2012; **Med School:** Harvard Med Sch 1983; **Resid:** Pediatrics, Chldns Hosp 1986; **Fellow:** Pediatric Hematology-Oncology, Johns Hopkins Hosp 1987; **Fac Appt:** Prof Ped, Johns Hopkins Univ

Garvin Jr, James H MD/PhD [PHO] - **Spec Exp:** Brain Tumors; Pediatric Cancers; Bone Marrow Transplant; **Hospital:** Morgan Stanley Children's Hosp of NY-Presby, NY (page 65); **Address:** 161 Fort Washington Ave, Fl 7, rm 708, New York, NY 10032-3729; **Phone:** 212-305-5808; **Board Cert:** Pediatrics 1982; Pediatric Hematology-Oncology 1984; **Med School:** Jefferson Med Coll 1976; **Resid:** Pediatrics, Chldns Hosp 1978; Pediatrics, Middlesex Hosp 1979; **Fellow:** Pediatric Hematology-Oncology, Dana Farber Cancer Inst/Childrens Hosp 1982; **Fac Appt:** Clin Prof Ped, Columbia P&S

Giardina, Patricia J V MD [PHO] - **Spec Exp:** Thalassemia; Sickle Cell Disease; Hemophilia; **Hospital:** NY-Presby/Weill Cornell Med Ctr, NY (page 65); **Address:** 525 E 68th St, Payson Pavilion, Ste 695, New York, NY 10065; **Phone:** 212-746-3400; **Board Cert:** Pediatrics 1973; Pediatric Hematology-Oncology 1974; **Med School:** NY Med Coll 1968; **Resid:** Pediatrics, New York Hosp-Cornell 1971; **Fellow:** Pediatric Hematology-Oncology, New York Hosp-Cornell 1974; **Fac Appt:** Clin Prof Ped, Cornell Univ-Weill Med Coll

Greenberg, Jay N MD [PHO] - **Hospital:** Chldns Natl Med Ctr, Inova Fairfax Hosp; **Address:** Dept Oncology, 111 Michigan Ave NW Fl 4 - Ste 4043, Washington, DC 20010; **Phone:** 202-476-2140; **Board Cert:** Pediatrics 1981; Pediatric Hematology-Oncology 1982; **Med School:** Univ Pennsylvania 1976; **Resid:** Pediatrics, Univ Michigan Med Ctr 1978; Pediatrics, Chldns Hosp 1980; **Fellow:** Pediatric Hematology-Oncology, Chldns Hosp 1982

Grupp, Stephan A MD/PhD [PHO] - **Spec Exp:** Stem Cell Transplant; Neuroblastoma; Bone Marrow Transplant; **Hospital:** Chldns Hosp of Philadelphia; **Address:** Childrens Hosp - Oncology, 34th St & Civic Ctr Blvd, Philadelphia, PA 19104; **Phone:** 215-590-2821; **Board Cert:** Pediatric Hematology-Oncology 2009; **Med School:** Univ Cincinnati 1987; **Resid:** Pediatrics, Chldns Hosp 1990; **Fellow:** Pediatric Hematology-Oncology, Dana Farber Cancer Inst/Chldns Hosp 1992; **Fac Appt:** Asst Prof Ped, Univ Pennsylvania

Guarini, Ludovico MD [PHO] - **Spec Exp:** Leukemia; Solid Tumors; **Hospital:** Maimonides Med Ctr (page 60); **Address:** Maimonides Med Ctr-Pediatrics Dept, 6300 Eighth Ave Fl 2, Brooklyn, NY 11220; **Phone:** 718-765-2671; **Board Cert:** Pediatrics 1984; Pediatric Hematology-Oncology 2007; **Med School:** Italy 1974; **Resid:** Pediatrics, Beth Israel Hosp 1981; **Fellow:** Pediatric Hematology-Oncology, Columbia-Presby Med Ctr 1984; **Fac Appt:** Assoc Prof Ped, SUNY Hlth Sci Ctr

Pediatric Hematology-Oncology

Halligan, Gregory E MD [PHO] - **Spec Exp:** Clinical Trials; Solid Tumors; **Hospital:** St. Christopher's Hosp for Chldn; **Address:** St Christophers Hosp for Children, Oncology Division, 3601 A St, Philadelphia, PA 19134; **Phone:** 215-427-4447; **Board Cert:** Pediatrics 1982; Pediatric Hematology-Oncology 1984; **Med School:** Belgium 1977; **Resid:** Pediatrics, St Christophers Hosp for Chldn 1981; **Fellow:** Pediatric Hematology-Oncology, St Christophers Hosp for Chldn 1984; **Fac Appt:** Assoc Prof Ped, Drexel Univ Coll Med

Halpern, Steven L MD [PHO] - **Spec Exp:** Leukemia & Lymphoma; Brain Tumors; Hodgkin's Lymphoma; Hemophilia; **Hospital:** Morristown Med Ctr, Overlook Med Ctr; **Address:** 100 Madison Ave, Morristown, NJ 07960; **Phone:** 973-971-6720; **Board Cert:** Pediatrics 1981; Pediatric Hematology-Oncology 1982; **Med School:** Ros Franklin Univ/Chicago Med Sch 1976; **Resid:** Pediatrics, St Christophers Hosp for Children 1979; **Fellow:** Pediatric Hematology-Oncology, Childrens Hosp 1982; **Fac Appt:** Asst Prof Ped, UMDNJ-NJ Med Sch, Newark

Harris, Michael B MD [PHO] - **Spec Exp:** Leukemia & Lymphoma; Bone Tumors; Cancer Survivors-Late Effects of Therapy; **Hospital:** Hackensack Univ Med Ctr; **Address:** Tomorrows Chldns Inst, JM Sanzari Chldns Hosp, 30 Prospect Ave, Imus 1-TCI, rm PC116, Hackensack, NJ 07601; **Phone:** 201-996-5437; **Board Cert:** Pediatrics 1974; Pediatric Hematology-Oncology 1974; **Med School:** Albert Einstein Coll Med 1969; **Resid:** Pediatrics, Chldns Hosp 1971; **Fellow:** Pediatric Hematology-Oncology, Chldns Hosp 1974; **Fac Appt:** Prof Ped, UMDNJ-NJ Med Sch, Newark

Helman, Lee Jay MD [PHO] - **Spec Exp:** Solid Tumors; **Hospital:** Natl Inst of Hlth - Clin Ctr; **Address:** National Cancer Inst, 31 Center Drive, rm 3A11, Bethesda, MD 20892; **Phone:** 301-496-4256; **Board Cert:** Internal Medicine 1983; Medical Oncology 1985; **Med School:** Univ MD Sch Med 1980; **Resid:** Internal Medicine, Barnes Hosp 1983; **Fellow:** Oncology, Natl Inst Hlth 1986

Hoots, William Keith MD [PHO] - **Spec Exp:** Hemophilia; **Hospital:** Natl Inst of Hlth - Clin Ctr; **Address:** Nat Inst Hlth-Clin Ctr, 6701 Rockledge Drive, Ste 9030, rm 9136, Bethesda, MD 20892; **Phone:** 301-435-0080; **Board Cert:** Pediatrics 1980; Pediatric Hematology-Oncology 1980; **Med School:** Univ NC Sch Med 1975; **Resid:** Pediatrics, Chldns Med Ctr 1978; **Fellow:** Pediatric Hematology-Oncology, Univ NC Med Ctr 1980; **Fac Appt:** Prof Ped, Univ Tex, Houston

Jakacki, Regina I MD [PHO] - **Spec Exp:** Neuro-Oncology; Clinical Trials; Palliative Care; **Hospital:** Chldns Hosp of Pittsburgh - UPMC; **Address:** Childrens Hosp-Div Hematology/Oncology, 4401 Penn Ave, Plaza Bldg, Ste 507, Pittsburgh, PA 15224; **Phone:** 412-692-5055; **Board Cert:** Pediatric Hematology-Oncology 2007; **Med School:** Univ Pennsylvania 1985; **Resid:** Pediatrics, Childrens Hosp 1988; **Fellow:** Pediatric Hematology-Oncology, Childrens Hosp 1991; **Fac Appt:** Prof Ped, Univ Pittsburgh

Korones, David N MD [PHO] - **Spec Exp:** Brain Tumors; Palliative Care; Pediatric Cancers; **Hospital:** Univ Rochester Strong Meml Hosp; **Address:** 601 Elmwood Ave, Rochester, NY 14642-8777; **Phone:** 585-275-2981; **Board Cert:** Pediatrics 1987; Pediatric Hematology-Oncology 2013; Hospice & Palliative Medicine 2012; **Med School:** Vanderbilt Univ 1983; **Resid:** Pediatrics, Strong Meml Hosp 1986; **Fellow:** Pediatrics, Yale Univ 1988; Pediatric Hematology-Oncology, Strong Meml Hosp 1991; **Fac Appt:** Prof Ped, Univ Rochester

Kramer, Kim MD [PHO] - **Spec Exp:** Neuroblastoma; Brain & Spinal Cord Tumors; **Hospital:** Meml Sloan-Kettering Canc Ctr; **Address:** 1275 York, Box 429, New York, NY 10021; **Phone:** 212-639-6410; **Board Cert:** Pediatric Hematology-Oncology 2011; **Med School:** SUNY Upstate Med Univ 1989; **Resid:** Pediatrics, Strong Meml Hosp 1992; **Fellow:** Pediatric Hematology-Oncology, Meml Sloan Kettering Cancer Ctr 1994

Kushner, Brian H MD [PHO] - **Spec Exp:** Neuroblastoma; Bone Marrow Transplant; Immunotherapy; **Hospital:** Meml Sloan-Kettering Canc Ctr; **Address:** 1275 York Avenue, New York, NY 10065; **Phone:** 212-639-6793; **Board Cert:** Pediatrics 1983; Pediatric Hematology-Oncology 1987; **Med School:** Johns Hopkins Univ 1976; **Resid:** Pediatrics, Columbia-Presby Med Ctr 1978; Pediatrics, NY Hosp 1979; **Fellow:** Pediatric Hematology-Oncology, Boston Chldns Hosp 1980; Pediatric Hematology-Oncology, Meml Sloan Kettering Cancer Ctr 1986; **Fac Appt:** Prof Ped, Cornell Univ-Weill Med Coll

Laver, Joseph H MD [PHO] - **Spec Exp:** Stem Cell Transplant; Lymphoma, Non-Hodgkin's; **Hospital:** Stony Brook Univ Med Ctr; **Address:** Stony Brook Univ Hosp, Health Sciences Tower, Level 4, Ste 205, Stony Brook, NY 11794-8410; **Phone:** 631-638-1000; **Board Cert:** Pediatrics 1985; Pediatric Hematology-Oncology 1987; **Med School:** Israel 1979; **Resid:** Pediatrics, Assaf Harofeh Med Ctr 1982; **Fellow:** Pediatric Hematology-Oncology, Meml Sloan Kettering Cancer Ctr 1985; **Fac Appt:** Prof Ped, SUNY Stony Brook

Lipton, Jeffrey M MD/PhD [PHO] - **Spec Exp:** Bone Marrow Failure Disorders; Stem Cell Transplant; Bone Marrow Transplant; **Hospital:** Steven & Alexandra Cohen Chldn's Med Ctr of NY (page 66), N Shore Univ Hosp (page 66); **Address:** Steven & Alexandra Chldns Med Ctr NY, Pediatric Hema/Onc Dept, 269-01 76th Ave, New Hyde Park, NY 11040-1433; **Phone:** 718-470-3460; **Board Cert:** Pediatrics 1981; **Med School:** St Louis Univ 1975; **Resid:** Pediatrics, Boston Chldns Hosp 1978; **Fellow:** Pediatric Hematology-Oncology, Boston Chldns Hosp/Dana Farber Cancer Inst 1981; **Fac Appt:** Prof Ped, Hofstra N Shore-LIJ Sch Med

Loeb, David M MD/PhD [PHO] - **Spec Exp:** Bone Marrow Transplant; Bone Cancer; **Hospital:** Johns Hopkins Hosp (page 59); **Address:** Charlotte R Bloomberg Chldns Ctr, Pediatric Onc Clin, Bloomberg 11-N, 1800 Orleans St, Baltimore, MD 21287; **Phone:** 410-502-4997; **Board Cert:** Pediatric Hematology-Oncology 2008; **Med School:** Columbia P&S 1994; **Resid:** Pediatrics, Johns Hopkins Hosp 1997; **Fellow:** Pediatric Oncology, Johns Hopkins Hosp 1997; **Fac Appt:** Asst Prof Ped, Johns Hopkins Univ

Luchtman-Jones, Lori MD [PHO] - **Spec Exp:** Leukemia; Bleeding/Coagulation Disorders; Hemophilia; Sickle Cell Disease; **Hospital:** Chldns Natl Med Ctr; **Address:** Chldn's Natl Med Ctr, 111 Michigan Ave NW, Fl 4 - Ste 4043, Washington, DC 20010; **Phone:** 202-476-2140; **Board Cert:** Pediatric Hematology-Oncology 2011; **Med School:** UCSD 1987; **Resid:** Pediatrics, UCSD Med Ctr 1990; **Fellow:** Pediatric Hematology-Oncology, Washington Univ Affil Hosp 1995; **Fac Appt:** Assoc Prof Ped, Geo Wash Univ

Marcus, Judith R MD [PHO] - **Spec Exp:** Leukemia; Lymphoma; Bleeding/Coagulation Disorders; Solid Tumors; **Hospital:** Morgan Stanley Children's Hosp of NY-Presby, NY (page 65), White Plains Hosp; **Address:** 161 Ft Wasthington Ave, Ste 7I, New York, NY 10032; **Phone:** 212-305-5808; **Board Cert:** Pediatrics 1997; Pediatric Hematology-Oncology 1997; **Med School:** NYU Sch Med 1971; **Resid:** Pediatrics, Bronx Muni Hosp-Albert Einstein 1974; **Fellow:** Pediatric Hematology-Oncology, Meml Sloan Kettering Cancer Ctr 1979; **Fac Appt:** Clin Prof Ped, Columbia P&S

Maris, John M MD [PHO] - **Spec Exp:** Neuroblastoma; Clinical Trials; **Hospital:** Chldns Hosp of Philadelphia; **Address:** Childrens Hosp Div Oncology, 34th St & Civic Center Blvd, Philadelphia, PA 19104; **Phone:** 215-590-5244; **Board Cert:** Pediatric Hematology-Oncology 2011; **Med School:** Univ Pennsylvania 1989; **Resid:** Pediatrics, Chldns Hosp 1992; **Fellow:** Pediatric Hematology-Oncology, Chldns Hosp 1996

Meyers, Paul A MD [PHO] - **Spec Exp:** Pediatric Cancers; Bone Tumors; Sarcoma; **Hospital:** Meml Sloan-Kettering Canc Ctr; **Address:** 1275 York Ave, New York, NY 10065; **Phone:** 212-639-5952; **Board Cert:** Pediatrics 1978; Pediatric Hematology-Oncology 1978; **Med School:** Mount Sinai Sch Med 1973; **Resid:** Pediatrics, Mt Sinai Hosp 1976; **Fellow:** Pediatric Hematology-Oncology, NY Hosp-Cornell Med Ctr 1979; **Fac Appt:** Prof Ped, Cornell Univ-Weill Med Coll

Pediatric Hematology-Oncology

O'Reilly, Richard MD [PHO] - **Spec Exp:** Bone Marrow Transplant; Stem Cell Transplant; Hematologic Disorders; Hematologic Malignancies; **Hospital:** Meml Sloan-Kettering Canc Ctr; **Address:** 1275 York Avenue, New York, NY 10065; **Phone:** 212-639-5957; **Board Cert:** Pediatrics 1974; **Med School:** Univ Rochester 1968; **Resid:** Pediatrics, Chldrns Hosp 1972; **Fellow:** Hematology, Chldrns Hosp 1973; **Fac Appt:** Prof Ped, Cornell Univ-Weill Med Coll

Parker, Robert I MD [PHO] - **Spec Exp:** Pediatric Cancers; Bleeding/Coagulation Disorders; Platelet Disorders; Lymphoma; **Hospital:** Stony Brook Univ Med Ctr; **Address:** Stony Brook Univ Med Ctr, Dept Pediatric Hematology-Oncology, 3 Edmund D Pellegrino Rd, Stony Brook, NY 11794-9448; **Phone:** 631-444-7720; **Board Cert:** Pediatrics 1983; Pediatric Hematology-Oncology 1984; **Med School:** Brown Univ 1976; **Resid:** Internal Medicine, Roger Williams Med Ctr 1977; Pediatrics, Rhode Island Hosp 1979; **Fellow:** Pediatric Hematology-Oncology, Natl Cancer Inst 1981; Hematology, Natl Cancer Inst 1984; **Fac Appt:** Prof Ped, SUNY Stony Brook

Rheingold, Susan R MD [PHO] - **Spec Exp:** Leukemia; Complementary Medicine; Clinical Trials; **Hospital:** Chldns Hosp of Philadelphia; **Address:** Chldns Hosp Phila - Div Oncology, 34th St & Civic Center Blvd, Philadelphia, PA 19104; **Phone:** 215-590-3025; **Board Cert:** Pediatrics 2010; Pediatric Hematology-Oncology 2008; **Med School:** Univ Pennsylvania 1992; **Resid:** Pediatrics, Johns Hopkins Hosp 1995; **Fellow:** Pediatric Hematology-Oncology, Chldns Hosp 1999; **Fac Appt:** Assoc Prof Ped, Univ Pennsylvania

Ritchey, A Kim MD [PHO] - **Spec Exp:** Leukemia; Bleeding/Coagulation Disorders; Hematologic Malignancies; Clinical Trials; **Hospital:** Chldns Hosp of Pittsburgh - UPMC; **Address:** Chldns Hosp, Div Hematology/Oncology, One Children's Hosp Drive, 4401 Penn Ave, Faculty Pavilion Fl 8, Pittsburgh, PA 15224; **Phone:** 412-692-5055; **Board Cert:** Pediatrics 1977; Pediatric Hematology-Oncology 2007; **Med School:** Univ Cincinnati 1972; **Resid:** Pediatrics, Johns Hopkins Hosp 1975; **Fellow:** Pediatric Hematology-Oncology, Yale-New Haven Hosp 1980; **Fac Appt:** Prof Ped, Univ Pittsburgh

Rood, Brian R MD [PHO] - **Spec Exp:** Brain Tumors; **Hospital:** Chldns Natl Med Ctr; **Address:** Div Oncology, 111 Michigan Ave NW, Fl 4, West Wing, Washington, DC 20010; **Phone:** 202-476-2140; **Board Cert:** Pediatrics 2006; Pediatric Hematology-Oncology 2010; **Med School:** Jefferson Med Coll 1995; **Resid:** Pediatrics, FAHC - Med Ctr Campus 1998; **Fellow:** Pediatric Hematology-Oncology, Chldns Natl Med Ctr 2001; Research, Chldns Natl Med Ctr 2002

Small, Donald MD [PHO] - **Spec Exp:** Leukemia; Lymphoma; **Hospital:** Johns Hopkins Hosp (page 59); **Address:** Johns Hopkins Children's Center, 1800 Orleans St, Baltimore, MD 21231; **Phone:** 410-955-8817; **Board Cert:** Pediatric Hematology-Oncology 2002; **Med School:** Johns Hopkins Univ 1985; **Resid:** Pediatrics, Johns Hopkins Hosp 1987; **Fellow:** Pediatric Hematology-Oncology, Johns Hopkins Hosp 1990; **Fac Appt:** Prof Ped, Johns Hopkins Univ

Steinherz, Peter G MD [PHO] - **Spec Exp:** Leukemia & Lymphoma; Pediatric Cancers; Wilms' Tumor; Kidney Cancer; **Hospital:** Meml Sloan-Kettering Canc Ctr; **Address:** 1275 York Avenue, New York, NY 10065; **Phone:** 212-639-7951; **Board Cert:** Pediatrics 1973; Pediatric Hematology-Oncology 1978; **Med School:** Albert Einstein Coll Med 1968; **Resid:** Pediatrics, NYPresby/Weill Cornell Med Ctr 1971; **Fellow:** Pediatric Hematology-Oncology, NYPresby/Weill Cornell Med Ctr 1975; **Fac Appt:** Prof Ped, Cornell Univ-Weill Med Coll

Weinblatt, Mark E MD [PHO] - **Spec Exp:** Leukemia & Lymphoma; Sickle Cell Disease; Bleeding/Coagulation Disorders; Thalassemia; **Hospital:** Winthrop Univ Hosp; **Address:** 120 Mineola Blvd, Ste 460, Mineola, NY 11501; **Phone:** 516-663-9400; **Board Cert:** Pediatrics 1980; Pediatric Hematology-Oncology 1982; **Med School:** Albert Einstein Coll Med 1976; **Resid:** Pediatrics, Jacobi Med Ctr 1979; **Fellow:** Pediatric Hematology-Oncology, Children's Hosp 1981; **Fac Appt:** Prof Ped, SUNY Stony Brook

Weiner, Michael A MD [PHO] - **Spec Exp:** Lymphoma; Lymphoma, Non-Hodgkin's; Leukemia; **Hospital:** Morgan Stanley Children's Hosp of NY-Presby, NY (page 65); **Address:** 161 Fort Washington Ave, Herbert Irving Pavilion, FL 7, New York, NY 10032-3710; **Phone:** 212-305-9770; **Board Cert:** Pediatrics 1980; Pediatric Hematology-Oncology 1980; **Med School:** SUNY Hlth Sci Ctr 1972; **Resid:** Pediatrics, Montefiore Hosp 1973; Pediatrics, Thos Jefferson Univ Hosp 1974; **Fellow:** Pediatric Hematology-Oncology, NYU Med Ctr 1976; Pediatric Hematology-Oncology, Johns Hopkins Hosp 1977; **Fac Appt:** Prof Ped, Columbia P&S

Wexler, Leonard MD [PHO] - **Spec Exp:** Rhabdomyosarcoma; Bone Cancer; Gastrointestinal Stromal Tumors; Sarcoma-Soft Tissue; **Hospital:** Meml Sloan-Kettering Canc Ctr; **Address:** 1275 York Avenue, New York, NY 10065; **Phone:** 212-639-7990; **Board Cert:** Pediatrics 2007; Pediatric Hematology-Oncology 2007; **Med School:** Boston Univ 1985; **Resid:** Pediatrics, Montefiore Med Ctr 1988; **Fellow:** Pediatric Hematology-Oncology, National Cancer Inst 1991; **Fac Appt:** Assoc Prof Ped, Columbia P&S

Wiley, Joseph M MD [PHO] - **Spec Exp:** Infections in Cancer Patients; **Hospital:** Sinai Hosp - Baltimore; **Address:** Sinai Hosp, Div Pediatric Hem/Onc, 2401 W Belvedere Ave, Baltimore, MD 21215; **Phone:** 410-601-5864; **Board Cert:** Pediatrics 1986; Pediatric Hematology-Oncology 2012; **Med School:** Univ MD Sch Med 1982; **Resid:** Pediatrics, Johns Hopkins Hosp 1985; **Fellow:** Pediatric Hematology-Oncology, Johns Hopkins Hosp 1988; **Fac Appt:** Assoc Prof Ped, Johns Hopkins Univ

Wolfe, Lawrence C MD [PHO] - **Spec Exp:** Palliative Care; Adrenal Cancer; Congenital Hemolytic Anemia; Hemochromatosis; **Hospital:** Steven & Alexandra Cohen Chldn's Med Ctr of NY (page 66); **Address:** Steven & Alexandra Cohen Chldn's Med Ctr, Div Pediatric Hematology/Oncology, 269-01 76th Ave, New Hyde Park, NY 11040; **Phone:** 718-470-3460; **Board Cert:** Pediatrics 1981; Pediatric Hematology-Oncology 1987; Hospice & Palliative Medicine 2010; **Med School:** Harvard Med Sch 1976; **Resid:** Pediatrics, Chldns Hosp 1978; **Fellow:** Pediatric Hematology-Oncology, Chldns Hosp 1991; **Fac Appt:** Prof Ped

York, Teresa A MD [PHO] - **Spec Exp:** Leukemia; **Hospital:** Univ of MD Med Ctr; **Address:** Greenebaum Cancer Center, 22 S Greene St, rm N5E16, Baltimore, MD 21201; **Phone:** 410-328-2808; **Board Cert:** Pediatric Hematology-Oncology 2012; **Med School:** W VA Univ 1997; **Resid:** Pediatrics, W VA Univ Chldns Hosp 2000; **Fellow:** Pediatric Hematology-Oncology, Med Univ SC Hosp 2001; **Fac Appt:** Asst Prof Ped, Univ MD Sch Med

Southeast

Barredo, Julio C MD [PHO] - **Spec Exp:** Leukemia; Bone Marrow Transplant; Cancer Survivors-Late Effects of Therapy; Stem Cell Transplant; **Hospital:** Univ of Miami Hosp & Clins/Sylvester Comp Canc Ctr; **Address:** Univ Miami-Ped Hem/Onc, 1475 NW 12th Ave, Alex Ctr, Miami, FL 33136; **Phone:** 305-689-7210; **Board Cert:** Pediatric Hematology-Oncology 2007; **Med School:** Peru 1982; **Resid:** Pediatrics, Kings Co Hosp 1987; **Fellow:** Pediatric Hematology-Oncology, Chldns Hosp/USC 1988; **Fac Appt:** Prof Ped, Univ Miami Sch Med

Bertolone, Salvatore J MD [PHO] - **Spec Exp:** Bone Marrow Transplant; Kasabach-Merritt Syndrome (KMS); Sickle Cell Disease; **Hospital:** Kosair Chldn's Hosp, Norton Hosp; **Address:** Kosair Children's Hosp, Pediatric Hematology/Oncology, 601 S Floyd St, Ste 403, Louisville, KY 40202; **Phone:** 502-629-7750; **Board Cert:** Pediatrics 1975; Pediatric Hematology-Oncology 1976; **Med School:** Univ Louisville Sch Med 1970; **Resid:** Pediatrics, Univ Louisville Affil Hosps 1972; **Fellow:** Pediatric Hematology-Oncology, Univ Colorado 1974; **Fac Appt:** Prof Ped, Univ Louisville Sch Med

Pediatric Hematology-Oncology

Blatt, Julie MD [PHO] - **Spec Exp:** Neuroblastoma; Cancer Survivors-Late Effects of Therapy; **Hospital:** NC Memorial Hosp - UNC; **Address:** UNC, Dept Ped Hem/Onc, 170 Manning Drive, Campus Box 7236, Chapel Hill, NC 27599; **Phone:** 919-966-1178; **Board Cert:** Pediatrics 1981; Pediatric Hematology-Oncology 1982; **Med School:** Johns Hopkins Univ 1976; **Resid:** Pediatrics, Columbia-Presby Hosp 1978; **Fellow:** Pediatric Oncology, Natl Cancer Inst 1982; **Fac Appt:** Prof Ped, Univ NC Sch Med

Castellino, Sharon M MD [PHO] - **Spec Exp:** Cancer Survivors-Late Effects of Therapy; Leukemia; Lymphoma; **Hospital:** Brenner Chldrn's Hosp, Wake Forest Baptist Med Ctr; **Address:** Wake Forest Baptist Med Ctr, Div Pediatric Hem/Onc, Medical Ctr Blvd, Winston-Salem, NC 27157; **Phone:** 336-716-4085; **Board Cert:** Pediatrics 2010; Pediatric Hematology-Oncology 2013; **Med School:** Duke Univ 1992; **Resid:** Pediatrics, Chldns Hosp 1994; Pediatrics, Duke Univ Med Ctr 1995; **Fellow:** Pediatric Hematology-Oncology, Duke Univ Med Ctr 1997; **Fac Appt:** Asst Prof Ped, Wake Forest Univ

Frangoul, Haydar A MD [PHO] - **Spec Exp:** Stem Cell Transplant; Pediatric Cancers; **Hospital:** Vanderbilt Monroe Carrell Jr. Chldn's Hosp; **Address:** Vanderbilt Childrens Hosp, Div Hematology/Oncology, 2200 Childrens Way, 6102 DOT, Nashville, TN 37232; **Phone:** 615-936-1762; **Board Cert:** Pediatric Hematology-Oncology 2008; **Med School:** Amer Univ Beirut 1990; **Resid:** Pediatrics, Duke Univ Med Ctr 1993; **Fellow:** Pediatric Hematology-Oncology, Duke Univ Med Ctr 1994; Pediatric Hematology-Oncology, Seattle Chldns/Fred Hutchinson Cancer Ctr 1996; **Fac Appt:** Prof Ped, Vanderbilt Univ

Friedman, Debra L MD [PHO] - **Spec Exp:** Cancer Survivors-Late Effects of Therapy; Hodgkin's Lymphoma; Retinoblastoma; Pediatric Cancers; **Hospital:** Vanderbilt Monroe Carrell Jr. Chldn's Hosp, Vanderbilt Univ Med Ctr; **Address:** Vanderbilt Childrens Hosp, Div Hematology/Oncology, 2200 Childrens Way, 6102 DOT, Nashville, TN 37232; **Phone:** 615-936-1762; **Board Cert:** Pediatric Hematology-Oncology 2013; **Med School:** UMDNJ-RW Johnson Med Sch 1991; **Resid:** Pediatrics, Chldns Hosp 1994; **Fellow:** Pediatric Hematology-Oncology, Chldns Hosp 1997; Cancer Epidemiology, Univ Penn; **Fac Appt:** Assoc Prof Ped, Vanderbilt Univ

Furman, Wayne L MD [PHO] - **Spec Exp:** Neuroblastoma; Liver Cancer; Drug Development; **Hospital:** St. Jude Children's Research Hosp; **Address:** St Jude Children's Research Hospital, 262 Danny Thomas Pl, Memphis, TN 38105; **Phone:** 901-595-2800; **Board Cert:** Pediatrics 1985; Pediatric Hematology-Oncology 1987; **Med School:** Ohio State Univ 1979; **Resid:** Pediatrics, Children's Hosp 1983; **Fellow:** Pediatric Hematology-Oncology, St Jude Chldn's Rsch Hosp 1985; **Fac Appt:** Prof Ped, Univ Tenn Coll Med

Gajjar, Amar J MD [PHO] - **Spec Exp:** Brain Tumors; Medulloblastoma; Neuro-Oncology; Drug Development; **Hospital:** St. Jude Children's Research Hosp; **Address:** St Jude Children's Research Hospital, Neuro-Oncology, 262 Danny Thomas Pl, Memphis, TN 38105-2794; **Phone:** 901-595-4599; **Board Cert:** Pediatric Hematology-Oncology 2007; **Med School:** India 1984; **Resid:** Pediatrics, All Chldns Hosp 1989; **Fellow:** Hematology & Oncology, St Jude Chldns Hosp 1992; **Fac Appt:** Prof Ped, Univ Tenn Coll Med

Godder, Kamar MD/PhD [PHO] - **Spec Exp:** Stem Cell Transplant; Leukemia; Palliative Care; **Hospital:** Med Coll of VA Hosp; **Address:** VCU, Div Ped Hematology, Nelson Clin, 40109 N 11th St, Richmond, VA 23298; **Phone:** 804-828-9300; **Board Cert:** Pediatric Hematology-Oncology 2013; **Med School:** Israel 1980; **Resid:** Pediatrics, Hadassah-Mt Scopus 1984; **Fellow:** Pediatric Hematology-Oncology, Meml Sloan Kettering Canc Ctr 1988; **Fac Appt:** Prof Ped, Va Commonwealth Univ Sch Med

Gold, Stuart H MD [PHO] - **Spec Exp:** Leukemia; Brain Tumors; Cancer Survivors-Late Effects of Therapy; **Hospital:** NC Memorial Hosp - UNC; **Address:** UNC, Dept Ped Hem-Onc, 1185A Physicians Office Bldg, 170 Manning Drive, Campus Box 7236, Chapel Hill, NC 27599; **Phone:** 919-966-1178; **Board Cert:** Pediatrics 1986; Pediatric Hematology-Oncology 1987; **Med School:** Vanderbilt Univ 1981; **Resid:** Pediatrics, Univ Colorado Hlth Sci Ctr 1984; **Fellow:** Pediatric Hematology-Oncology, Univ Colorado Hlth Sci Ctr 1989; **Fac Appt:** Prof Ped, Univ NC Sch Med

Green, Daniel M MD [PHO] - **Spec Exp:** Wilms' Tumor; Fertility in Cancer Survivors; Cancer Survivors-Late Effects of Therapy; **Hospital:** St. Jude Children's Research Hosp; **Address:** Dept of Epidemiology & Cancer Control, St Jude Children's Research Hospital, 262 Danny Thomas Pl, Memphis, TN 38105-2794; **Phone:** 901-595-5915; **Board Cert:** Pediatrics 1986; Pediatric Hematology-Oncology 1997; **Med School:** St Louis Univ 1973; **Resid:** Pediatrics, Boston City Hosp 1975; **Fellow:** Pediatric Hematology-Oncology, Chldns Hosp Med Ctr 1978

Gururangan, Sridharan MD [PHO] - **Spec Exp:** Brain Tumors; Spinal Cord Tumors; Neuro-Oncology; **Hospital:** Duke Univ Hosp; **Address:** Robert Tisch Brain Tumor Ctr at Duke, Hanes House, rm 307, Box 102382, 315 Trent Drive, Durham, NC 27710; **Phone:** 919-668-6288; **Med School:** India 1981; **Resid:** Pediatrics, Le Bonheur Chldns Med Ctr 1992; **Fellow:** Pediatric Hematology-Oncology, St Jude Chldns Hosp 1993; Pediatric Hematology-Oncology, Meml Sloan-Kettering Cancer Ctr 1996; **Fac Appt:** Prof Ped, Duke Univ

Hudson, Melissa M MD [PHO] - **Spec Exp:** Cancer Survivors-Late Effects of Therapy; Hodgkin's Lymphoma; **Hospital:** St. Jude Children's Research Hosp; **Address:** St Jude Children's Research Hosp, 262 Danny Thomas Pl, Memphis, TN 38105; **Phone:** 901-595-3445; **Board Cert:** Pediatrics 1988; Pediatric Hematology-Oncology 2013; **Med School:** Univ Tex SW, Dallas 1983; **Resid:** Pediatrics, Univ Texas Affil Hosps 1986; **Fellow:** Pediatric Hematology-Oncology, MD Anderson Cancer Ctr 1989; **Fac Appt:** Prof Ped, Univ Tenn Coll Med

Johnston, J Martin MD [PHO] - **Spec Exp:** Leukemia; Lymphoma; Hemophilia; **Hospital:** Meml Hlth Univ Med Ctr - Savannah; **Address:** Backus Children's Hosp Outpatient Ctr, 4700 Waters Ave, Savannah, GA 31403-3089; **Phone:** 912-350-8194; **Board Cert:** Pediatric Hematology-Oncology 2009; **Med School:** Duke Univ 1984; **Resid:** Pediatrics, Univ Utah Med Ctr 1988; **Fellow:** Pediatric Hematology-Oncology, Barnes Jewish Hosp 1991; **Fac Appt:** Assoc Prof Ped, Mercer Univ Sch Med

Keller Jr, Frank G MD [PHO] - **Spec Exp:** Leukemia; Hodgkin's Lymphoma; **Hospital:** Chldns Hlthcare Atlanta @ Egleston; **Address:** Aflac Cancer Ctr at Egleston, 1405 Clifton Rd NE, Tower 1, 4th Fl, Atlanta, GA 30322; **Phone:** 404-785-1200; **Board Cert:** Pediatric Hematology-Oncology 2009; **Med School:** Univ NC Sch Med 1986; **Resid:** Pediatrics, Vanderbilt Univ Med Ctr 1990; **Fellow:** Pediatric Hematology-Oncology, Duke Univ Med Ctr 1993; **Fac Appt:** Assoc Prof Ped, Emory Univ

Kreissman, Susan G MD [PHO] - **Spec Exp:** Neuroblastoma; Clinical Trials; **Hospital:** Duke Univ Hosp; **Address:** Duke Univ Med Ctr, Box 102382, Durham, NC 27710; **Phone:** 919-684-3401; **Board Cert:** Pediatric Hematology-Oncology 2011; **Med School:** Mount Sinai Sch Med 1985; **Resid:** Pediatrics, Chldns Hosp 1988; **Fellow:** Pediatric Hematology-Oncology, Chldns Hosp/Dana-Farber Cancer Inst 1991; **Fac Appt:** Clin Prof Ped, Duke Univ

Kurtzberg, Joanne MD [PHO] - **Spec Exp:** Stem Cell Transplant; Bone Marrow Transplant; **Hospital:** Duke Univ Hosp; **Address:** Duke Univ Med Ctr, Box 3850, Durham, NC 27710; **Phone:** 919-668-1102; **Board Cert:** Pediatrics 1982; Pediatric Hematology-Oncology 1982; **Med School:** NY Med Coll 1976; **Resid:** Pediatrics, Dartmouth Med Ctr 1977; Pediatrics, Upstate Med Ctr 1979; **Fellow:** Pediatric Hematology-Oncology, Upstate Med Ctr 1980; Pediatric Hematology-Oncology, Duke Med Ctr 1983; **Fac Appt:** Prof Ped, Duke Univ

Leung, Wing H MD/PhD [PHO] - **Spec Exp:** Bone Marrow & Stem Cell Transplant; **Hospital:** St. Jude Children's Research Hosp; **Address:** St. Jude Children's Research Hospital, 262 Danny Thomas Pl, Memphis, TN 38105-3678; **Phone:** 901-595-3300; **Board Cert:** Pediatrics 2008; Pediatric Hematology-Oncology 2013; **Med School:** Hong Kong 1988; **Resid:** Pediatrics, Univ Hosp Downstate Med Ctr 1994; **Fellow:** Pediatric Hematology-Oncology, Johns Hopkins Hosp 1997; **Fac Appt:** Prof Ped, Univ Tenn Coll Med

McLean, Thomas W MD [PHO] - **Hospital:** Brenner Chldrn's Hosp, Wake Forest Baptist Med Ctr; **Address:** Div Pediatric Hem/Onc, Medical Ctr Blvd, Winston-Salem, NC 27157; **Phone:** 336-716-4085; **Board Cert:** Pediatrics 2009; Pediatric Hematology-Oncology 2013; **Med School:** Med Univ SC 1990; **Resid:** Pediatrics, Chldns Hosp 1993; **Fellow:** Pediatric Hematology-Oncology, Great Ormond St Hosp for Chldn 1994; Pediatric Hematology-Oncology, Dana-Farber Chldns Hosp 1997; **Fac Appt:** Assoc Prof Ped, Wake Forest Univ

Neuberg, Ronnie W MD [PHO] - **Spec Exp:** Pediatric Cancers; Brain Tumors; Gene Therapy; Clinical Trials; **Hospital:** Palmetto Health Richland Mem Hosp; **Address:** Childrens Ctr-Cancer & Blood Disorders, 7 Richland Medical Park Drive, Ste 7215, Columbia, SC 29203; **Phone:** 803-434-3533; **Board Cert:** Pediatrics 1982; Pediatric Hematology-Oncology 1982; **Med School:** SUNY Buffalo 1977; **Resid:** Pediatrics, Chldns Hosp 1980; **Fellow:** Pediatric Hematology-Oncology, SUNY Upstate Med Ctr 1982; **Fac Appt:** Assoc Clin Prof Ped, Univ SC Sch Med

Olson, Thomas A MD [PHO] - **Spec Exp:** Germ Cell Tumors; Retinoblastoma; Sarcoma; **Hospital:** Chldns Hlthcare Atlanta @ Egleston; **Address:** Aflac Cancer Ctr at Egleston, 1405 Clifton Rd NE, Tower 1, 4th Fl, Atlanta, GA 30322; **Phone:** 404-785-1200; **Board Cert:** Pediatrics 1982; Pediatric Hematology-Oncology 1984; **Med School:** Loyola Univ-Stritch Sch Med 1978; **Resid:** Pediatrics, Walter Reed AMC 1981; **Fellow:** Pediatric Hematology-Oncology, Walter Reed AMC 1983; **Fac Appt:** Prof Ped, Emory Univ

Pui, Ching-Hon MD [PHO] - **Spec Exp:** Leukemia; Lymphoma; **Hospital:** St. Jude Children's Research Hosp; **Address:** St Jude Chldns Rsch Hosp, 262 Danny Thomas Pl, Memphis, TN 38105; **Phone:** 901-595-3606; **Board Cert:** Pediatrics 1980; Pediatric Hematology-Oncology 1982; **Med School:** Taiwan 1976; **Resid:** Pediatrics, St Jude Chldns Rsch Hosp 1979; **Fellow:** Hematology & Oncology, St Jude Chldns Rsch Hosp 1981; **Fac Appt:** Prof Ped, Univ Tenn Coll Med

Ribeiro, Raul C MD [PHO] - **Spec Exp:** Leukemia & Lymphoma; **Hospital:** St. Jude Children's Research Hosp; **Address:** St Jude's Chldns Rsch Hosp, 262 Danny Thomas Pl, Memphis, TN 38105; **Phone:** 901-595-3694; **Board Cert:** Pediatric Hematology-Oncology 2009; **Med School:** Brazil 1975; **Resid:** Pediatrics, Univ Parana Sch Med 1978; **Fellow:** Hematology & Oncology, St Jude's Chldns Rsch Hosp 1987; **Fac Appt:** Prof Ped, Univ Tenn Coll Med

Rosoff, Philip M MD [PHO] - **Spec Exp:** Cancer Survivors-Late Effects of Therapy; Down Syndrome; Leukemia; **Hospital:** Duke Univ Hosp; **Address:** DUMC-Trent Ctr for Bioethics, Seeley Mud Bldg - Ste 108, Box 3850, 10 Bryan-Searle Rd, Durham, NC 27710-0001; **Phone:** 919-668-9000; **Board Cert:** Pediatrics 1984; Pediatric Hematology-Oncology 2009; **Med School:** Case West Res Univ 1978; **Resid:** Pediatrics, Chldns Hosp 1980; **Fellow:** Pediatric Hematology-Oncology, Chldns Hosp/Dana Farber Cancer Inst 1984; **Fac Appt:** Prof Hem & Onc, Duke Univ

Russo, Carolyn MD [PHO] - **Spec Exp:** Brain Tumors; Cancer Survivors-Late Effects of Therapy; Palliative Care; **Hospital:** Huntsville Hosp, The; **Address:** St Jude Clinic at Huntsville Hosp, 910 Adams St, Ste 310, Huntsville, AL 35801; **Phone:** 256-265-5833; **Board Cert:** Pediatric Hematology-Oncology 2012; **Med School:** UCLA-David Geffen Sch Med 1984; **Resid:** Pediatrics, Harbor-UCLA Med Ctr 1987; **Fellow:** Pediatric Hematology-Oncology, Stanford Med Ctr 1990

Sandler, Eric MD [PHO] - **Spec Exp:** Bone Marrow Transplant; Leukemia; Bone Tumors; Sickle Cell Disease; **Hospital:** Wolfson Chldns Hosp; **Address:** Nemours Chldns Clin, Hem/Onc Dept, 807 Childrens Way, Jacksonville, FL 32207; **Phone:** 904-697-3789; **Board Cert:** Pediatrics 2008; Pediatric Hematology-Oncology 2007; **Med School:** Univ VT Coll Med 1985; **Resid:** Pediatrics, UCSF Med Ctr 1988; **Fellow:** Pediatric Hematology-Oncology, Shands at Univ FL 1991

Santana, Victor M MD [PHO] - **Spec Exp:** Solid Tumors; Clinical Trials; Ethics; **Hospital:** St. Jude Children's Research Hosp; **Address:** St Jude Chldns Rsch Hosp, Dept Oncology, 262 Danny Thomas Pl, MS 274, Memphis, TN 38105-2794; **Phone:** 901-595-2801; **Board Cert:** Pediatrics 1982; Pediatric Hematology-Oncology 1984; **Med School:** Puerto Rico 1978; **Resid:** Pediatrics, Johns Hopkins Hosp 1981; **Fellow:** Pediatric Hematology-Oncology, Johns Hopkins Hosp 1984; **Fac Appt:** Prof Ped, Univ Tenn Coll Med

Tebbi, Cameron MD [PHO] - **Spec Exp:** Hemophilia; Hodgkin's Lymphoma; Leukemia; Sickle Cell Disease; **Hospital:** Tampa Genl Hosp; **Address:** USF Hlth, Pediatric Hematology/Oncology, 2 Tampa General Cir, Tampa, FL 33607; **Phone:** 813-259-8700; **Board Cert:** Pediatrics 1974; Pediatric Hematology-Oncology 1980; **Med School:** Iran 1968; **Resid:** Pediatrics, Chldns Hosp Med Ctr 1972; Pediatric Hematology-Oncology, UT MD Anderson Cancer Ctr 1972; **Fellow:** Pediatric Hematology-Oncology, Chldns Hosp 1973; Medical Oncology, Ontario Cancer Inst 1974; **Fac Appt:** Prof Ped, Univ S Fla Coll Med

Wang, Winfred C MD [PHO] - **Spec Exp:** Sickle Cell Disease; Bone Marrow Failure Disorders; Anemia-Aplastic; **Hospital:** St. Jude Children's Research Hosp, Le Bonheur Chldns Med Ctr; **Address:** St Jude Chldn Rsch Hosp, 262 Danny Thomas Pl, MS 800, Memphis, TN 38105-2729; **Phone:** 901-595-2051; **Board Cert:** Pediatrics 1972; Pediatric Hematology-Oncology 1974; **Med School:** Univ Chicago-Pritzker Sch Med 1967; **Resid:** Pediatrics, Montefiore Med Ctr 1969; Pediatrics, Kauikeolani Chldns Hosp 1970; **Fellow:** Pediatric Hematology-Oncology, UCSF Med Ctr 1975; **Fac Appt:** Prof Ped, Univ Tenn Coll Med

Wechsler, Daniel S MD/PhD [PHO] - **Spec Exp:** Leukemia & Lymphoma; Neuroblastoma; **Hospital:** Duke Univ Hosp; **Address:** Duke Univ Med Ctr-Ped Hem/Onc, 397 Hanes House, Box 102382, Durham, NC 27710; **Phone:** 919-684-3401; **Board Cert:** Pediatric Hematology-Oncology 2009; **Med School:** Canada 1987; **Resid:** Pediatrics, Johns Hopkins Hosp 1990; **Fellow:** Pediatric Hematology-Oncology, Johns Hopkins Hosp 1994; **Fac Appt:** Assoc Prof Ped, Duke Univ

Midwest

Arndt, Carola A MD [PHO] - **Spec Exp:** Sarcoma; Brain Tumors; Stem Cell Transplant; **Hospital:** Mayo Med Ctr & Clin - Rochester; **Address:** Mayo Clinic, Dept Pediatrics, 200 1st St SW, Rochester, MN 55905; **Phone:** 507-284-2695; **Board Cert:** Pediatrics 1982; Pediatric Hematology-Oncology 1987; **Med School:** Boston Univ 1978; **Resid:** Pediatrics, Naval Reg Med Ctr 1981; **Fellow:** Pediatric Hematology-Oncology, Natl Inst Hlth 1984

Beyer, Eric C MD/PhD [PHO] - **Spec Exp:** Pediatric Cancers; Bleeding/Coagulation Disorders; Anemia; **Hospital:** Univ Chicago Med-Comer Chldn's Hosp, Univ of Chicago Med; **Address:** Univ Chicago Comer Children's Hosp, 5721 S Maryland Ave, Chicago, IL 60637; **Phone:** 773-702-6808; **Board Cert:** Pediatrics 1987; **Med School:** UCSD 1982; **Resid:** Pediatrics, Chldns Hosp 1984; **Fellow:** Hematology & Oncology, Dana Farber Cancer Inst 1987; **Fac Appt:** Prof Ped, Univ Chicago-Pritzker Sch Med

Boxer, Laurence Alan MD [PHO] - **Spec Exp:** Congenital Neutropenia-Severe; Anemias & Red Cell Disorders; Bone Marrow Failure Disorders; Anemia-Aplastic; **Hospital:** Univ Michigan Med Ctr; **Address:** MPB Bldg, rm D3251, Box 5718, 1500 E Medical Center Drive, Ann Arbor, MI 48109-5718; **Phone:** 734-764-7126; **Board Cert:** Pediatrics 1971; Pediatric Hematology-Oncology 1974; **Med School:** Stanford Univ 1966; **Resid:** Pediatrics, Yale-New Haven Hosp 1968; Pediatrics, Stanford Univ Hosp 1969; **Fellow:** Hematology & Oncology, Chldns Hosp-Harvard 1974; **Fac Appt:** Prof Ped, Univ Mich Med Sch

Camitta, Bruce M MD [PHO] - **Spec Exp:** Leukemia; Anemia-Aplastic; Bone Marrow Transplant; **Hospital:** Chldns Hosp - Wisconsin; **Address:** MACC Fund Ctr for Cancer/Blood Disorders, 8701 Watertown Plank Rd, Ste 3018, Milwaukee, WI 53226; **Phone:** 414-266-2421; **Board Cert:** Pediatrics 1971; Pediatric Hematology-Oncology 1976; **Med School:** Johns Hopkins Univ 1966; **Resid:** Pediatrics, Chldns Hosp 1968; Pediatrics, Johns Hopkins Hosp 1969; **Fellow:** Pediatric Hematology-Oncology, Chldns Hosp 1973; **Fac Appt:** Prof Ped, Med Coll Wisc

Castle, Valerie P MD [PHO] - **Spec Exp:** Neuroblastoma; Bleeding/Coagulation Disorders; Cancer Survivors-Late Effects of Therapy; **Hospital:** Univ Michigan Med Ctr; **Address:** Univ Mich Comp Cancer Ctr, 1540 E Hospital Drive, Ann Arbor, MI 48109; **Phone:** 734-936-9814; **Board Cert:** Pediatric Hematology-Oncology 2013; **Med School:** McMaster Univ 1983; **Resid:** Pediatrics, McMaster Univ Med Ctr 1986; **Fellow:** Pediatric Hematology-Oncology, Univ Mich Hosps 1989; **Fac Appt:** Prof Ped, Univ Mich Med Sch

Cohn, Susan L MD [PHO] - **Spec Exp:** Pediatric Cancers; Neuroblastoma; **Hospital:** Univ of Chicago Med; **Address:** 900 E 57th St KCBD Bldg - rm 5100, Chicago, IL 60637; **Phone:** 773-702-6808; **Board Cert:** Pediatrics 1985; Pediatric Hematology-Oncology 1987; **Med School:** Univ IL Coll Med 1980; **Resid:** Pediatrics, Michael Reese Hosp 1984; **Fellow:** Hematology & Oncology, Chldns Meml Hosp 1987; **Fac Appt:** Prof Ped, Univ Chicago-Pritzker Sch Med

Corey, Seth J MD [PHO] - **Spec Exp:** Bone Marrow Failure Disorders; Leukemia; Myelodysplastic Syndromes; Ataxia Telangiectasia; **Hospital:** Lurie Chldn's Hosp-Chicago; **Address:** Robert Lurie Comp Cancer Ctr, 303 E Superior St, Chicago, IL 60611; **Phone:** 312-227-4874; **Board Cert:** Pediatrics 1986; Pediatric Hematology-Oncology 2004; **Med School:** Tulane Univ 1982; **Resid:** Pediatrics, St Louis Chldns Hosp 1985; **Fellow:** Pediatric Hematology-Oncology, Chldn's Hosp 1989; **Fac Appt:** Prof Ped, Northwestern Univ-Feinberg Sch Med

Croop, James M MD/PhD [PHO] - **Spec Exp:** Solid Tumors; Clinical Trials; **Hospital:** Riley Hosp for Children; **Address:** Riley Hospital for Children, Pediatric Hematology/Oncology ROC 4340, 705 Riley Hospital Drive, Indianapolis, IN 46202; **Phone:** 317-944-2143; **Board Cert:** Pediatrics 1985; Pediatric Hematology-Oncology 2010; **Med School:** Univ Pennsylvania 1980; **Resid:** Pediatrics, Chldns Hosp of Philadelphia 1983; **Fellow:** Pediatric Hematology-Oncology, Boston Chldns Hosp 1985; **Fac Appt:** Prof Ped, Indiana Univ

Cunningham, John M MD [PHO] - **Spec Exp:** Stem Cell Transplant; Sickle Cell Disease; Thalassemia; Clinical Trials; **Hospital:** Univ of Chicago Med; **Address:** Univ of Chicago Med Ctr, 5841 S Maryland Ave, MC 4060, Chicago, IL 60637; **Phone:** 773-834-8198; **Med School:** Ireland 1982; **Resid:** Pediatrics, St Laurence's Hosp 1985; Pediatrics, Mater Misericordiae Hosp 1987; **Fellow:** Pediatric Hematology-Oncology, Royal Free Hosp 1991; Transplant Surgery, Natl Heart, Lung, & Blood Inst/NIH 1993; **Fac Appt:** Prof Ped, Univ Chicago-Pritzker Sch Med

Davies, Stella M MD/PhD [PHO] - **Spec Exp:** Leukemia; Bone Marrow Transplant; Stem Cell Transplant; **Hospital:** Cincinnati Chldns Hosp Med Ctr; **Address:** Cincinnati Chldns Hosp Med Ctr, 3333 Burnet Ave, MLC 7015, Cincinnati, OH 45229-3039; **Phone:** 513-636-2469; **Med School:** England, UK 1981; **Resid:** Pediatrics, Univ Newcastle Med Ctr 1985; **Fellow:** Pediatric Hematology-Oncology, Univ MN Med Ctr 1993; **Fac Appt:** Prof Ped, Univ Cincinnati

Fallon, Robert J MD/PhD [PHO] - **Spec Exp:** Lymphoma; Hodgkin's Lymphoma; Stem Cell Transplant; **Hospital:** Riley Hosp for Children; **Address:** Riley Hosp-Ped Hem/Onc ROC 4340, 705 Riley Hospital Drive, Indianapolis, IN 46202; **Phone:** 317-944-2143; **Board Cert:** Internal Medicine 1983; Medical Oncology 1985; **Med School:** NYU Sch Med 1980; **Resid:** Internal Medicine, Brigham & Womens Hosp 1983; **Fellow:** Hematology & Oncology, Brigham & Womens Hosp/Dana Farber Cancer Inst 1985; **Fac Appt:** Prof Ped, Indiana Univ

Ferrara, James MD [PHO] - **Spec Exp:** Bone Marrow Transplant; Graft vs Host Disease; Inflammatory Cytokines; **Hospital:** Univ Michigan Med Ctr; **Address:** Univ Michigan Comprehensive Cancer Ctr, 1500 E Medical Center Drive, Ste 6308, Ann Arbor, MI 48109-5942; **Phone:** 734-615-1340; **Board Cert:** Pediatric Hematology-Oncology 2006; **Med School:** Georgetown Univ 1980; **Resid:** Pediatrics, Children's Hosp 1982; **Fellow:** Pediatric Hematology-Oncology, Dana-Farber Cancer Inst 1985; **Fac Appt:** Prof Ped, Univ Mich Med Sch

Fouladi, Maryam MD [PHO] - **Spec Exp:** Neuro-Oncology; Brain Tumors; Neurofibromatosis; **Hospital:** Cincinnati Chldns Hosp Med Ctr; **Address:** Cincinnati Chldn's Hosp-Ped Hem/Onc, 3333 Burnet Ave, Cincinnati, OH 45229; **Phone:** 513-636-4266; **Board Cert:** Pediatric Hematology-Oncology 2010; **Med School:** Univ Toronto 1991; **Resid:** Pediatrics, Hosp for Sick Chldn 1994; **Fellow:** Hematology & Oncology, Hosp for Sick Chldn 1997; Neuro-Oncology, St Jude Chldn's Rsch Hosp 1998; **Fac Appt:** Prof Ped

Goldman, Stewart MD [PHO] - **Spec Exp:** Neuro-Oncology; Brain Tumors; Clinical Trials; **Hospital:** Lurie Chldn's Hosp-Chicago; **Address:** Lurie Chldn's Hosp Div Hem/Onc, 225 E Chicago Ave, Box 30, Chicago, IL 60611; **Phone:** 312-227-4874; **Board Cert:** Pediatric Hematology-Oncology 2011; **Med School:** Loyola Univ-Stritch Sch Med 1985; **Resid:** Pediatrics, Univ Chicago Hosps 1988; **Fellow:** Pediatric Hematology-Oncology, Univ Chicago Hosps 1991

Haut, Paul R MD [PHO] - **Spec Exp:** Stem Cell Transplant; Bone Marrow Transplant; Leukemia; **Hospital:** Riley Hosp for Children, IU Health North Hosp; **Address:** Riley Hospital for Children, 705 Riley Hospital Drive ROC Bldg Fl 3rd, Indianapolis, IN 46202; **Phone:** 317-948-3717; **Board Cert:** Pediatric Hematology-Oncology 2008; **Med School:** Univ Ark 1990; **Resid:** Pediatrics, Arkansas Chldn's Hosp 1994; **Fellow:** Pediatric Hematology-Oncology, Chldn's Meml Hosp 1997; **Fac Appt:** Assoc Prof Ped, Indiana Univ

Hayani, Ammar MD [PHO] - **Spec Exp:** Leukemia; Solid Tumors; Lymphoma; **Hospital:** Adv Christ Med Ctr, Adv Good Samaritan Hosp; **Address:** Advocate Children's Hospital, 4440 W 95th St, Oak Lawn, IL 60453-2600; **Phone:** 708-684-4094; **Board Cert:** Pediatric Hematology-Oncology 2012; **Med School:** Syria 1982; **Resid:** Pediatrics, LSU Hosp 1987; **Fellow:** Pediatric Hematology-Oncology, Baylor Affil Hosp 1991

Hayashi, Robert J MD [PHO] - **Spec Exp:** Bone Marrow Transplant; Cancer Survivors-Late Effects of Therapy; Leukemia; **Hospital:** St. Louis Chldns Hosp; **Address:** St Louis Chldns Hosp, Div Ped Hem Onc, One Children's Pl Fl 9, St Louis, MO 63110; **Phone:** 314-454-6018; **Board Cert:** Pediatrics 2007; Pediatric Hematology-Oncology 2007; **Med School:** Washington Univ, St Louis 1986; **Resid:** Pediatrics, St Louis Childrens Hosp 1989; **Fellow:** Pediatric Hematology-Oncology, Johns Hopkins Hosp 1992; **Fac Appt:** Assoc Prof Ped, Washington Univ, St Louis

Hetherington, Maxine MD [PHO] - **Spec Exp:** Brain Tumors; **Hospital:** Chldns Mercy Hosps & Clinics; **Address:** Childrens Mercy Hosptial, 2401 Gillham Rd, Kansas City, MO 64108; **Phone:** 816-234-3265; **Board Cert:** Pediatrics 1983; Pediatric Hematology-Oncology 1987; **Med School:** Univ Tenn Coll Med 1978; **Resid:** Pediatrics, Childrens Med Ctr 1981; **Fellow:** Pediatric Hematology-Oncology, Univ Texas Hlth Sci Ctr 1987; **Fac Appt:** Assoc Prof Ped, Univ MO-Kansas City

Hord, Jeffrey D MD [PHO] - **Spec Exp:** Hematologic Malignancies; Bone Marrow Failure Disorders; Sickle Cell Disease; Pediatric Cancers; **Hospital:** Akron Children's Hosp; **Address:** Akron Chldn's Hosp, Hematology/Oncology, One Perkins Square, Akron, OH 44308; **Phone:** 330-543-8580; **Board Cert:** Pediatric Hematology-Oncology 2011; **Med School:** Univ KY Coll Med 1989; **Resid:** Pediatrics, Childrens Hosp 1992; **Fellow:** Pediatric Hematology-Oncology, Vanderbilt Univ Med Ctr 1995; **Fac Appt:** Prof Ped, NE Ohio Univ

Hsu, Lewis MD/PhD [PHO] - **Spec Exp:** Sickle Cell Disease; **Hospital:** Univ of IL Med Ctr at Chicago; **Address:** Univ IL Med Ctr, 840 S Wood St, MC 856, Chicago, IL 60612; **Phone:** 312-996-6143; **Board Cert:** Pediatrics 2013; Pediatric Hematology-Oncology 2009; **Med School:** Univ Rochester 1988; **Resid:** Pediatrics, Yale-New Haven Hosp 1991; **Fellow:** Pediatric Hematology-Oncology, Chldn's Hosp 1994; **Fac Appt:** Prof Ped, Univ IL Coll Med

Hutchinson, Raymond MD [PHO] - **Spec Exp:** Leukemia; Hodgkin's Lymphoma; Neuroblastoma; Lymphoma; **Hospital:** Univ Michigan Med Ctr; **Address:** CS Mott Chldns Hosp, Dept Hematology/Onc, 1540 E Hospital Drive, Ann Arbor, MI 48109-4259; **Phone:** 734-647-1576; **Board Cert:** Pediatrics 1979; Pediatric Hematology-Oncology 1980; **Med School:** Harvard Med Sch 1973; **Resid:** Pediatrics, New England Med Ctr 1975; **Fellow:** Pediatric Hematology-Oncology, Childrens Hosp 1978; **Fac Appt:** Prof Ped, Univ Mich Med Sch

Manera, Ricarchito B MD [PHO] - **Spec Exp:** Leukemia & Lymphoma; Brain Tumors; **Hospital:** Loyola Univ - Ronald McDonald Children's Hosp; **Address:** Loyola University Med Ctr, Div Pediatric Hematology/Oncology, 2160 S First Ave, Maywood, IL 60153; **Phone:** 708-327-9136; **Board Cert:** Pediatrics 2010; Pediatric Hematology-Oncology 2011; **Med School:** Philippines 1984; **Resid:** Pediatrics, Bronx-Lebanon Hosp Ctr 1995; **Fellow:** Pediatric Hematology-Oncology, MD Anderson Cancer Ctr 1994; Pediatric Hematology-Oncology, Columbia-Presby Med Ctr 1996; **Fac Appt:** Assoc Prof Ped, Loyola Univ-Stritch Sch Med

Morgan, Elaine R MD [PHO] - **Spec Exp:** Leukemia; Palliative Care; Ethics; Hemophagocytic Syndrome; **Hospital:** Lurie Chldn's Hosp-Chicago; **Address:** Ann & Robert H. Lurie Chldn's Hosp, 225 E Chicago Ave, Box 30, Chicago, IL 60611; **Phone:** 312-227-4090; **Board Cert:** Pediatrics 1976; Pediatric Hematology-Oncology 2009; Hospice & Palliative Medicine 2008; **Med School:** Univ Pennsylvania 1971; **Resid:** Pediatrics, Chldns Hosp 1974; **Fellow:** Pediatric Hematology-Oncology, Chldns Hosp Med Ctr 1975; Pediatric Hematology-Oncology, Chldns Meml Med Ctr 1976; **Fac Appt:** Prof Ped, Northwestern Univ-Feinberg Sch Med

Neglia, Joseph MD [PHO] - **Spec Exp:** Cancer Survivors-Late Effects of Therapy; **Hospital:** Univ Minn Med Ctr, Fairview - West Bank Campus; **Address:** Univ Minnesota-Div Ped Hem/Oncology, 2450 Riverside Ave, Minneapolis, MN 55455; **Phone:** 612-624-3113; **Board Cert:** Pediatrics 1986; Pediatric Hematology-Oncology 1987; **Med School:** Loma Linda Univ 1981; **Resid:** Pediatrics, Baylor Coll Med 1984; **Fellow:** Pediatric Hematology-Oncology, Univ Minn Hosp 1987; **Fac Appt:** Prof Ped, Univ Minn

O'Dorisio, M Sue MD/PhD [PHO] - **Spec Exp:** Neuroblastoma; Medulloblastoma; Neuroendocrine Tumors; **Hospital:** Univ Iowa Hosp & Clins; **Address:** Univ Iowa Hosp & Clin, Dept Ped Hem/Onc, 200 Hawkins Drive JCP Bldg - rm 2519, Iowa City, IA 52242; **Phone:** 319-356-7873; **Board Cert:** Pediatrics 2007; Pediatric Hematology-Oncology 2009; **Med School:** Ohio State Univ 1985; **Resid:** Pediatrics, Chldns Hosp 1988; **Fellow:** Pediatric Hematology-Oncology, Chldns Hosp 1992; **Fac Appt:** Prof Ped, Univ Iowa Coll Med

Olshefski, Randal S MD [PHO] - **Spec Exp:** Brain Tumors; **Hospital:** Nationwide Chldn's Hosp; **Address:** Nationwide Chldn's Hosp, Div Hematology/Oncology, 700 Children's Drive, Columbus, OH 43205; **Phone:** 614-722-3552; **Board Cert:** Pediatric Hematology-Oncology 2011; **Med School:** Univ Pittsburgh 1988; **Resid:** Pediatrics, Nationwide Chldns Hosp 1991; **Fellow:** Hematology & Oncology, Chldns Natl Med Ctr 1995; **Fac Appt:** Clin Prof Ped, Ohio State Univ

Plautz, Gregory E MD [PHO] - **Spec Exp:** Brain Tumors; Leukemia & Lymphoma; Wilms' Tumor; Cancer Survivors-Late Effects of Therapy; **Hospital:** Cleveland Clin (page 55); **Address:** 9500 Euclid Ave S Bldg Fl 2, MS S20, Cleveland, OH 44195; **Phone:** 216-445-4044; **Board Cert:** Pediatric Hematology-Oncology 2012; **Med School:** Indiana Univ 1984; **Resid:** Pediatrics, Johns Hopkins Hosp 1987; **Fellow:** Pediatric Hematology-Oncology, Univ Michigan Affil Hosp 1990; **Fac Appt:** Prof Ped, Case West Res Univ

Puccetti, Diane M MD [PHO] - **Spec Exp:** Brain Tumors; Neuro-Oncology; Cancer Survivors-Late Effects of Therapy; **Hospital:** Univ WI Hosp & Clins; **Address:** Univ WI Chldn's Hosp, 1675 Highland Ave Fl 2, Madison, WI 53792; **Phone:** 608-263-6420; **Board Cert:** Pediatric Hematology-Oncology 2007; **Med School:** Med Coll OH 1985; **Resid:** Pediatrics, UC Irvine Med Ctr 1986; Pediatrics, Med Coll Ohio Affil Hosps 1988; **Fellow:** Pediatric Hematology-Oncology, Riley Hosp Chldn 1991; **Fac Appt:** Assoc Clin Prof Ped, Univ Wisc

Razzouk, Bassem I MD [PHO] - **Spec Exp:** Leukemia; Clinical Trials; Lymphoma; Langerhans Cell Histiocytosis (LCH); **Hospital:** Peyton Manning Children's Hosp at St. Vincent; **Address:** Peyton Manning Chldns Hosp, Center for Cancer & Blood Diseases, 2001 W 86th St, Indianapolis, IN 46260; **Phone:** 317-338-4673; **Board Cert:** Pediatrics 2008; Pediatric Hematology-Oncology 2011; **Med School:** Lebanon 1987; **Resid:** Pediatrics, American Univ Med Ctr 1990; Pediatrics, SUNY Hlth Sci Ctr 1992; **Fellow:** Hematology & Oncology, St Jude Chldns Rsch Hosp 1995

Rubin, Charles M MD [PHO] - **Spec Exp:** Brain Tumors; Retinoblastoma; Bone Marrow Transplant; **Hospital:** Univ Chicago Med-Comer Chldn's Hosp, Univ of Chicago Med; **Address:** Univ Chicago Med Ctr, 5841 S Maryland Ave, MC 4060, Chicago, IL 60637; **Phone:** 773-702-6808; **Board Cert:** Pediatrics 1984; Clinical Cytogenetics 1987; Pediatric Hematology-Oncology 1984; **Med School:** Tufts Univ 1979; **Resid:** Pediatrics, Chldn's Hosp 1982; **Fellow:** Pediatric Hematology-Oncology, Univ Minnesota Hosp 1985; Medical Genetics, Univ Chicago Med Ctr 1987; **Fac Appt:** Assoc Prof Ped, Univ Chicago-Pritzker Sch Med

Salvi, Sharad MD [PHO] - **Spec Exp:** Leukemia & Lymphoma; Bleeding/Coagulation Disorders; Anemia; Solid Tumors; **Hospital:** Adv Christ Med Ctr, Adv Good Samaritan Hosp; **Address:** Advocate Children's Hospital, 4440 W 95th St, Oak Lawn, IL 60453; **Phone:** 708-684-4094; **Board Cert:** Pediatrics 1982; Pediatric Hematology-Oncology 1982; **Med School:** India 1974; **Resid:** Pediatrics, Lincoln Meml Hosp 1979; **Fellow:** Pediatric Hematology-Oncology, Chldns Hosp/Roswell Park Meml Cancer Inst 1981

Sencer, Susan F MD [PHO] - **Spec Exp:** Pediatric Cancers; Complementary Medicine; **Hospital:** Children's Hosps & Clinics of Minnesota; **Address:** Chldns Specialty Clinic, Hem/Onc Clin, 2525 Chicago Ave S, Ste CSC-175, Minneapolis, MN 55404; **Phone:** 612-813-5940; **Board Cert:** Pediatric Hematology-Oncology 2007; **Med School:** Univ Minn 1984; **Resid:** Pediatrics, Univ Minnesota Affil Hosp 1988; **Fellow:** Pediatric Hematology-Oncology, Univ Minnesota Affil Hosp 1991

Shapiro, Amy D MD [PHO] - **Spec Exp:** Hemophilia; Bleeding/Coagulation Disorders; **Hospital:** Peyton Manning Children's Hosp at St. Vincent; **Address:** Indiana Hemophilia & Thrombosis Ctr, 8402 Harcourt Rd, Ste 500, Indianapolis, IN 46260; **Phone:** 317-871-0000; **Board Cert:** Pediatrics 1986; Pediatric Hematology-Oncology 1987; **Med School:** NYU Sch Med 1980; **Resid:** Pediatrics, Univ Colo Affil Hosp 1982; **Fellow:** Pediatric Hematology-Oncology, Univ Colo Hlth Sci Ctr 1983

Sondel, Paul M MD/PhD [PHO] - **Spec Exp:** Immunotherapy; Stem Cell Transplant; Pediatric Cancers; Neuroblastoma; **Hospital:** Univ WI Hosp & Clins; **Address:** 4159 WIMR, 1111 Highland Ave, Madison, WI 53705; **Phone:** 608-263-6200; **Board Cert:** Pediatrics 1981; **Med School:** Harvard Med Sch 1977; **Resid:** Pediatrics, Univ MN Hosp 1978; Pediatrics, Univ Wisconsin Hosp 1980; **Fellow:** Research, Sidney Farber Cancer Inst/Harvard 1977; **Fac Appt:** Prof Ped, Univ Wisc

Pediatric Hematology-Oncology

Valentino, Leonard Anthony MD [PHO] - **Spec Exp:** Bleeding/Coagulation Disorders; Thrombotic Disorders; Hemophilia; Hereditary Hemorrhagic Telangiectasia; **Hospital:** Rush Univ Med Ctr, Rush Copley Med Ctr; **Address:** 1725 W Harrison St, Ste 710, Chicago, IL 60612-3828; **Phone:** 312-942-5983; **Board Cert:** Pediatrics 2007; Pediatric Hematology-Oncology 2012; **Med School:** Creighton Univ 1984; **Resid:** Pediatrics, Univ Illinios Med Ctr 1987; **Fellow:** Pediatric Hematology-Oncology, UCLA Med Ctr 1990; **Fac Appt:** Prof Ped, Rush Med Coll

Vik, Terry A MD [PHO] - **Spec Exp:** Neuroblastoma; Cancer Survivors-Late Effects of Therapy; Leukemia; Drug Development; **Hospital:** Riley Hosp for Children; **Address:** Riley Hosp-Ped Hem/Onc ROC 4340, 705 Riley Hospital Drive, Indianapolis, IN 46202; **Phone:** 317-944-2143; **Board Cert:** Pediatrics 1987; Pediatric Hematology-Oncology 2011; **Med School:** Johns Hopkins Univ 1983; **Resid:** Pediatrics, UCLA Med Ctr 1986; **Fellow:** Pediatric Hematology-Oncology, Chldns Hosp/Dana Farber 1989; **Fac Appt:** Assoc Prof Ped, Indiana Univ

Yaddanapudi, Ravindranath MD [PHO] - **Spec Exp:** Leukemia; **Hospital:** Chldns Hosp of Michigan; **Address:** Children's Hospital Michigan, Div Hem/Onc, 3901 Beaubien Blvd Carls Bldg Fl 2, Detroit, MI 48201; **Phone:** 313-745-5515; **Board Cert:** Pediatrics 1970; Pediatric Hematology-Oncology 1974; **Med School:** India 1964; **Resid:** Pathology, Western Penn Hosp 1967; Pediatrics, Children's Hosp 1969; **Fellow:** Pediatric Hematology-Oncology, Children's Hosp Michigan 1971; **Fac Appt:** Prof Ped, Wayne State Univ

Great Plains and Mountains

Abromowitch, Minnie MD [PHO] - **Hospital:** Children's Hosp - Omaha; **Address:** Children's Hosp & Med Ctr, Dept Pediatric Hem Onc, 8200 Dodge St, Omaha, NE 68114; **Phone:** 402-955-3950; **Board Cert:** Pediatrics 1980; Pediatric Hematology-Oncology 1982; **Med School:** Univ Manitoba 1973; **Resid:** Pediatrics, Hospital for Sick Children 1976; Pediatric Hematology-Oncology, Univ Manitoba 1978; **Fellow:** Pediatric Hematology-Oncology, St Jude Chldns Research Hosp 1980; **Fac Appt:** Assoc Prof Ped, Univ Nebr Coll Med

Bruggers, Carol S MD [PHO] - **Spec Exp:** Brain Tumors; Clinical Trials; **Hospital:** Primary Children's Med Ctr, Univ Utah Hlth Care; **Address:** Primary Chldns Med Ctr, 100 Mario Capecchi Drive, Salt Lake City, UT 84113; **Phone:** 801-662-4700; **Board Cert:** Pediatrics 2008; Pediatric Hematology-Oncology 2008; **Med School:** Mich State Univ 1984; **Resid:** Pediatrics, Univ CO Hlth Sci Ctr 1987; **Fellow:** Pediatric Hematology-Oncology, Duke Univ Hosp 1991; **Fac Appt:** Prof Ped, Univ Utah

Coccia, Peter F MD [PHO] - **Spec Exp:** Bone Marrow Transplant; Leukemia & Lymphoma; Bone Marrow Failure Disorders; Osteopetrosis; **Hospital:** Nebraska Med Ctr, Children's Hosp - Omaha; **Address:** Univ Nebr Med Ctr, Dept Pediatrics, 982168 Nebraska Med Ctr, Omaha, NE 68198-2168; **Phone:** 402-559-7257; **Board Cert:** Clinical Pathology 1972; Hematology 1975; Pediatrics 1976; Pediatric Hematology-Oncology 1976; **Med School:** SUNY Upstate Med Univ 1968; **Resid:** Pathology, Upstate Med Ctr 1970; Pediatrics, Univ Minn 1973; **Fellow:** Pediatric Hematology-Oncology, Univ Minn 1974; **Fac Appt:** Prof Ped, Univ Nebr Coll Med

Hilden, Joanne M MD [PHO] - **Spec Exp:** Leukemia in Infants; Brain Tumors-Pediatric; Leukemia & Lymphoma; Leukemia in Down Syndrome; **Hospital:** Chldn's Hosp - Aurora (CO); **Address:** Chldns Hosp, Cancer & Blood Disorders, 13123 E 16th St, Ste B115, Aurora, CO 80045; **Phone:** 720-777-2843; **Board Cert:** Pediatrics 2013; Pediatric Hematology-Oncology 2009; Hospice & Palliative Medicine 2008; **Med School:** Univ Minn 1988; **Resid:** Pediatrics, Univ Minn Med Ctr 1991; **Fellow:** Pediatric Hematology-Oncology, Univ Minn Med Ctr 1994; **Fac Appt:** Prof Ped, Univ Colorado

Kobrinsky, Nathan L MD [PHO] - **Spec Exp:** Pediatric Cancers; Immunotherapy; Hemophilia; Bleeding/Coagulation Disorders; **Hospital:** Sanford Med Ctr Fargo; **Address:** Sanford Roger Maris Cancer Ctr, 820 4th St N, Fargo, ND 58122; **Phone:** 701-234-7544; **Board Cert:** Pediatrics 1981; Pediatric Hematology-Oncology 1982; **Med School:** Univ Manitoba 1976; **Resid:** Pediatrics, Chldns Hlth Sci Ctr 1978; **Fellow:** Pediatric Hematology-Oncology, Chldns Hlth Sci Ctr 1979; Pediatric Hematology-Oncology, Univ Minn 1981; **Fac Appt:** Prof Ped, Univ ND Sch Med

Manco-Johnson, Marilyn MD [PHO] - **Spec Exp:** Hemophilia; Thrombotic Disorders; **Hospital:** Chldn's Hosp - Aurora (CO), Univ Colorado Hosp; **Address:** Chdns Hosp, Hemophilia & Thrombosis Ctr, 13199 E Montview Blvd, Ste 100, Aurora, CO 80045; **Phone:** 303-724-0362; **Board Cert:** Pediatrics 1979; Pediatric Hematology-Oncology 1980; **Med School:** Jefferson Med Coll 1974; **Resid:** Pediatrics, Univ CO Hosp 1977; **Fellow:** Pediatric Hematology-Oncology, Chldns Hosp 1981; **Fac Appt:** Prof Ped, Univ Colorado

Southwest

Albritton, Karen H MD [PHO] - **Spec Exp:** Sarcoma; **Hospital:** Cook Chldns Med Ctr, Harris Methodist Hosp - Fort Worth; **Address:** 1500 Cooper St Fl 5, Fort Worth, TX 76104; **Phone:** 682-885-4007; **Board Cert:** Pediatric Hematology-Oncology 2010; **Med School:** Univ Tex, San Antonio 1992; **Resid:** Internal Medicine & Pediatrics, Univ NC Affil Hosps 1996; **Fellow:** Pediatric Hematology-Oncology, Univ NC Affil Hosps 2000; **Fac Appt:** Assoc Prof Ped, Univ N Tex Hlth Sci Ctr, Coll Osteo Med

Arceci, Robert J MD/PhD [PHO] - **Spec Exp:** Leukemia; Histiocytoma; Bone Marrow Transplant; **Hospital:** Phoenix Children's Hosp; **Address:** 445 N 5th St, Fl 3, rm 322, Phoenix, AZ 85004; **Phone:** 602-546-0290; **Board Cert:** Pediatrics 1987; Pediatric Hematology-Oncology 2005; **Med School:** Univ Rochester 1981; **Resid:** Pediatrics, Chldns Hosp 1983; **Fellow:** Pediatric Hematology-Oncology, Chldns Hosp/Dana Farber Cancer Ctr 1986; **Fac Appt:** Prof Ped, Johns Hopkins Univ

Berg, Stacey L MD [PHO] - **Spec Exp:** Drug Discovery & Development; Brain Tumors; Solid Tumors; **Hospital:** Texas Chldns Hosp; **Address:** Texas Chldns Canc Ctr, Dept Ped Hem-Onc, 6701 Fannin St Fl 14, MC CC1400, Houston, TX 77030; **Phone:** 832-822-4242; **Board Cert:** Pediatrics 2007; Pediatric Hematology-Oncology 2007; Hospice & Palliative Medicine 2010; **Med School:** Univ Pittsburgh 1985; **Resid:** Pediatrics, Chldns Hosp 1989; **Fellow:** Pediatric Hematology-Oncology, Natl Inst Hlth 1992; **Fac Appt:** Prof Ped, Baylor Coll Med

Blaney, Susan MD [PHO] - **Spec Exp:** Brain Tumors; Neuro-Oncology; Drug Development; Clinical Trials; **Hospital:** Texas Chldns Hosp; **Address:** TX Chldns Canc Ctr, Dept Ped Hem-Onc, 6701 Fannin St, Houston, TX 77030; **Phone:** 832-822-1482; **Board Cert:** Pediatric Hematology-Oncology 2012; **Med School:** Med Coll OH 1984; **Resid:** Pediatrics, Letterman Army Med Ctr 1988; **Fellow:** Pediatric Oncology, Walter Reed Natl Military Med Ctr 1990; **Fac Appt:** Prof Ped, Baylor Coll Med

Buchanan, George R MD [PHO] - **Spec Exp:** Sickle Cell Disease; Thrombotic Disorders; Hemophilia; Leukemia; **Hospital:** Chldns Med Ctr of Dallas, UT Southwestern Med Ctr at Dallas; **Address:** Univ Texas SW Med Ctr-Dept Ped Hem Onc, 5323 Harry Hines Blvd, MC 9063, Dallas, TX 75390-9063; **Phone:** 214-456-2382; **Board Cert:** Pediatrics 1975; Pediatric Hematology-Oncology 2000; **Med School:** Univ Chicago-Pritzker Sch Med 1970; **Resid:** Pediatrics, Chldns Meml Hosp 1973; **Fellow:** Hematology & Oncology, Chldns Meml Hosp 1975; **Fac Appt:** Prof Ped, Univ Tex SW, Dallas

Cooper, Laurence J N MD/PhD [PHO] - **Spec Exp:** Immunotherapy; **Hospital:** UT MD Anderson Canc Ctr; **Address:** UT MD Anderson Canc Ctr, Dep Ped Hem-Onc, 1515 Holcombe Blvd, Unit 0907, Houston, TX 77030; **Phone:** 713-792-9860; **Board Cert:** Pediatrics 2012; **Med School:** Case West Res Univ 1994; **Resid:** Pediatrics, Chldns Hosp 1996; **Fellow:** Pediatric Hematology-Oncology, Fred Hutchinson Canc Rsch Ctr 1999; **Fac Appt:** Prof Ped, Univ Tex, Houston

Dreyer, ZoAnn E MD [PHO] - **Spec Exp:** Cancer Survivors-Late Effects of Therapy; Leukemia in Infants; **Hospital:** Texas Chldns Hosp; **Address:** TX Chldns Canc Ctr, Dept Ped Hem-Onc, 6701 Fannin St, Fl 15 - Ste 1510, MC CC1400, Houston, TX 77030; **Phone:** 832-822-4242; **Board Cert:** Pediatrics 1988; Pediatric Hematology-Oncology 2012; **Med School:** UC Davis 1982; **Resid:** Pediatrics, Baylor Affil Hosps 1986; **Fellow:** Pediatric Hematology-Oncology, Baylor Affil Hosps 1990; **Fac Appt:** Assoc Prof Ped, Baylor Coll Med

Goldman, Stanton C MD [PHO] - **Spec Exp:** Leukemia; Lymphoma; Stem Cell Transplant; **Hospital:** Med City Dallas Hosp; **Address:** 7777 Forest Ln, D Bldg, Ste 400, Dallas, TX 75230; **Phone:** 972-566-6647; **Board Cert:** Pediatric Hematology-Oncology 2011; Pediatrics 2008; **Med School:** Boston Univ 1990; **Resid:** Pediatrics, Chldns Natl Med Ctr 1993; **Fellow:** Pediatric Hematology-Oncology, Johns Hopkins Hosp 1994

Graham, Michael L MD [PHO] - **Spec Exp:** Bone Marrow Transplant; Leukemia; Stem Cell Transplant; **Hospital:** Cardon Children's Med Ctr; **Address:** Banner Hlth Clin-Hem/Onc Dept, 1432 S Dobson Rd, Ste 107, Mesa, AZ 85202; **Phone:** 480-412-4100; **Board Cert:** Pediatrics 1980; Pediatric Hematology-Oncology 1984; **Med School:** Brown Univ 1975; **Resid:** Pediatrics, Johns Hopkins Hosp 1978; Pediatric Hematology-Oncology, Johns Hopkins Hosp 1980; **Fellow:** Medical Oncology, Yale-New Haven Hosp 1982; **Fac Appt:** Assoc Prof Ped, Univ Ariz Coll Med

Kane, Javier R MD [PHO] - **Spec Exp:** Palliative Care; Pediatric Cancers; **Hospital:** Scott & White Mem Hosp; **Address:** Temple Clin, Pediatric Hematology/Oncology, 2401 S 31st St, Temple, TX 76508; **Phone:** 254-724-2006; **Board Cert:** Pediatrics 2007; Pediatric Hematology-Oncology 2012; Hospice & Palliative Medicine 2008; **Med School:** Mexico 1986; **Resid:** Pediatrics, Chldns Hosp 1992; **Fellow:** Pediatric Hematology-Oncology, St Judes Chldns Rsch Hosp 1995; **Fac Appt:** Prof Ped, Texas A&M Univ

Kuttesch, John F MD/PhD [PHO] - **Spec Exp:** Brain Tumors; Brain Tumors-Recurrent; Solid Tumors; Leukemia; **Hospital:** UNM Chldns Hosp; **Address:** Univ Hosp, Pediatric Hem/Onc, 1 University Blvd SE, Albuquerque, NM 87131; **Phone:** 505-272-4461; **Board Cert:** Pediatrics 2008; Pediatric Hematology-Oncology 2007; **Med School:** Univ Tex, Houston 1985; **Resid:** Pediatrics, Vanderbilt Univ Med Ctr 1988; **Fellow:** Pediatric Hematology-Oncology, St Judes Chldns Hosp 1990; **Fac Appt:** Prof Ped, Univ New Mexico

Meyer, William H MD [PHO] - **Spec Exp:** Sarcoma; Pediatric Cancers; **Hospital:** Chldns Hosp OU Med Ctr; **Address:** 1200 Children's Ave, Fl 10, Ste 10000, Oklahoma City, OK 73104; **Phone:** 405-271-4412; **Board Cert:** Pediatrics 1980; Pediatric Hematology-Oncology 1980; **Med School:** Jefferson Med Coll 1974; **Resid:** Pediatrics, Wilmington Med Ctr 1977; **Fellow:** Pediatric Hematology-Oncology, Johns Hopkins Hosp 1980; **Fac Appt:** Prof Ped, Univ Okla Coll Med

Tomlinson, Gail E MD [PHO] - **Spec Exp:** Cancer Survivors-Late Effects of Therapy; Cancer Genetics; Liver Cancer; Kidney Cancer; **Hospital:** Christus Santa Rosa Children's Hosp, Univ Hosp-San Antonio; **Address:** UT HSC at San Antonio, 7703 Floyd Curl Drive, MC 7810, San Antonio, TX 78229; **Phone:** 210-704-3405; **Board Cert:** Pediatrics 2008; Pediatric Hematology-Oncology 2009; **Med School:** Geo Wash Univ 1984; **Resid:** Pediatrics, Chldns Natl Med Ctr 1988; **Fellow:** Pediatric Hematology-Oncology, UT MD Anderson Canc Ctr 1989; Pediatric Hematology-Oncology, UT Med Br (John Sealy Hosp) 1992; **Fac Appt:** Prof Ped, Univ Tex, San Antonio

Williams, James A MD [PHO] - **Spec Exp:** Solid Tumors; **Hospital:** Phoenix Children's Hosp; **Address:** Phoenix Childrens Hosp, 5131 E Southern Ave, Mesa, AZ 85206; **Phone:** 602-546-0920; **Board Cert:** Pediatric Hematology-Oncology 2008; **Med School:** Wayne State Univ 1993; **Resid:** Pediatrics, Wayne St Univ Med Ctr 1996; **Fellow:** Pediatric Hematology-Oncology, Wayne St Univ Med Ctr 1999

Winick, Naomi J MD [PHO] - **Spec Exp:** Leukemia; **Hospital:** Chldns Med Ctr of Dallas; **Address:** Ctr Canc & Blood Disorders, 1935 Medical District Drive Fl 3, Dallas, TX 75235-7794; **Phone:** 214-456-2382; **Board Cert:** Pediatrics 1984; Pediatric Hematology-Oncology 1987; Hospice & Palliative Medicine 2012; **Med School:** Northwestern Univ 1978; **Resid:** Pediatrics, Babies Hosp-Columbia Presbyterian Med Ctr 1982; **Fellow:** Pediatric Hematology-Oncology, Meml Sloan-Kettering Canc Ctr 1984; **Fac Appt:** Prof Ped, Univ Tex SW, Dallas

West Coast and Pacific

Andrews, Robert G MD [PHO] - **Spec Exp:** Bone Marrow Transplant; Leukemia; Lymphoma; **Hospital:** Seattle Chldns Hosp; **Address:** 1100 Fairview Ave N, MS D2-373, Seattle, WA 98109; **Phone:** 206-667-5000; **Board Cert:** Pediatrics 1984; Pediatric Hematology-Oncology 1984; **Med School:** Univ Minn 1976; **Resid:** Pediatrics, New England Bapt Hosp 1980; **Fellow:** Pediatric Hematology-Oncology, Chldn's Hosp 1983; **Fac Appt:** Assoc Prof Ped, Univ Wash

Banerjee, Anuradha MD [PHO] - **Spec Exp:** Brain Tumors; **Hospital:** UCSF Med Ctr; **Address:** UC San Francisco, Div Ped Oncology/Neuro Oncology, 400 Parnassus Ave, rm A101, San Francisco, CA 94107; **Phone:** 415-353-2986; **Board Cert:** Pediatrics 2011; Pediatric Hematology-Oncology 2012; **Med School:** Tulane Univ 1992; **Resid:** Pediatrics, UCSF Med Ctr 1996; **Fellow:** Pediatric Hematology-Oncology, UCSF Med Ctr 1997; **Fac Appt:** Assoc Clin Prof Ped, UCSF

Carpenter, Paul MD [PHO] - **Spec Exp:** Graft vs Host Disease; Bone Marrow Transplant; **Hospital:** Seattle Chldns Hosp; **Address:** Fred Hutchinson Cancer Rsch Ctr, 825 Eastlake Ave E, MS G-6100, Seattle, WA 98109; **Phone:** 800-804-8824; **Med School:** Australia 1988; **Resid:** Pediatrics, Chldns Hosp 1992; **Fellow:** Pediatric Hematology-Oncology, Chldns Hosp 1994; Pediatric Hematology-Oncology, Univ WA Med Ctr 1998

Ducore, Jonathan M MD [PHO] - **Spec Exp:** Brain Tumors; Bone & Soft Tissue Tumors; Bleeding/Coagulation Disorders; **Hospital:** UC Davis Med Ctr; **Address:** 2279 45th St, Sacramento, CA 95817; **Phone:** 916-703-5210; **Board Cert:** Pediatrics 1978; Pediatric Hematology-Oncology 1978; **Med School:** Duke Univ 1973; **Resid:** Pediatrics, Chldns Med Ctr 1975; **Fellow:** Pediatric Hematology-Oncology, Univ Colorado Med Ctr 1977; Cancer Research, Natl Cancer Inst 1980; **Fac Appt:** Clin Prof Ped, UC Davis

Finklestein, Jerry Z MD [PHO] - **Spec Exp:** Cancer Survivors-Late Effects of Therapy; Anemias & Red Cell Disorders; **Hospital:** Long Beach Meml Med Ctr, LAC - Harbor - UCLA Med Ctr; **Address:** 2653 Elm Ave, Ste 200, Long Beach, CA 90806-1652; **Phone:** 562-728-5000; **Board Cert:** Pediatrics 1980; Pediatric Hematology-Oncology 1974; **Med School:** McGill Univ 1963; **Resid:** Pediatrics, Montreal Chldns Hosp 1966; **Fellow:** Pediatric Hematology-Oncology, LA Chldns Hosp 1968; **Fac Appt:** Clin Prof Ped, UCLA

Finlay, Jonathan L MD [PHO] - **Spec Exp:** Brain Tumors; **Hospital:** Chldns Hosp - Los Angeles, Chldns Hosp - Oakland; **Address:** 4650 Sunset Blvd, MS 54, Los Angeles, CA 90027-6016; **Phone:** 323-361-8147; **Board Cert:** Pediatrics 1984; Pediatric Hematology-Oncology 1987; **Med School:** England, UK 1973; **Resid:** Pediatrics, Univ Birmingham 1975; Pediatrics, Christie Hosp 1976; **Fellow:** Pediatric Allergy & Immunology, Univ Wisconsin Hosp 1978; Pediatric Hematology-Oncology, Univ Wisconsin Hosp 1980; **Fac Appt:** Prof Ped, USC-Keck School of Medicine

Geyer, J. Russell MD [PHO] - **Spec Exp:** Pediatric Cancers; Neuro-Oncology; Brain Tumors; **Hospital:** Seattle Chldns Hosp, Univ Wash Med Ctr; **Address:** Seattle Chldns Hosp - Div Hem/Onc, 4800 Sand Point Way NE, MS M.B.8.501, Seattle, WA 98105; **Phone:** 206-987-2106; **Board Cert:** Pediatrics 1983; Pediatric Hematology-Oncology 1987; **Med School:** Wayne State Univ 1977; **Resid:** Pediatrics, Chldns Hosp 1981; **Fellow:** Pediatric Hematology-Oncology, Univ MI Med Ctr 1985; **Fac Appt:** Prof Ped, Univ Wash

Glader, Bertil E MD/PhD [PHO] - **Spec Exp:** Genetic Disorders-Blood; Hemophilia; **Hospital:** Lucile Packard Chldn's Hosp; **Address:** Pediatric Hematology/Oncology, 1000 Welch Rd, Ste 300, Box 5798, Palo Alto, CA 94304; **Phone:** 650-497-8953; **Board Cert:** Pediatrics 1982; Pediatric Hematology-Oncology 2005; Hematology 1983; **Med School:** Northwestern Univ 1968; **Resid:** Pediatrics, Chldns Hosp 1973; **Fellow:** Hematology, Chldns Hosp 1975; **Fac Appt:** Prof Ped, Stanford Univ

Hawkins, Douglas S MD [PHO] - **Spec Exp:** Bone Tumors; Ewing's Sarcoma; Leukemia; Rhabdomyosarcoma; **Hospital:** Seattle Chldns Hosp; **Address:** Seattle Chldns Hosp - Div Hem/Onc, 4800 Sand Point Way NE, MS M.B.8.501, Seattle, WA 98105; **Phone:** 206-987-2106; **Board Cert:** Pediatric Hematology-Oncology 2011; **Med School:** Harvard Med Sch 1990; **Resid:** Pediatrics, Univ Wash Med Ctr 1993; **Fellow:** Pediatric Hematology-Oncology, Fred Hutchinson Cancer Rsch Ctr 1996; **Fac Appt:** Assoc Prof Ped, Univ Wash

Horn, Biljana N MD [PHO] - **Spec Exp:** Bone Marrow Transplant; Brain Tumors; Stem Cell Transplant; Immunotherapy; **Hospital:** UCSF Med Ctr; **Address:** UCSF Med Ctr, Pediatric BMT Prgm, 505 Parnassus Ave, rm M-659, San Francisco, CA 94143; **Phone:** 415-476-2188; **Board Cert:** Pediatrics 2013; Pediatric Hematology-Oncology 2011; **Med School:** Croatia 1983; **Resid:** Pediatrics, Case West Res Med Ctr 1991; **Fellow:** Pediatric Hematology-Oncology, Natl Cancer Inst 1994; Pediatric Neuro-Oncology, UCSF Med Ctr 1998; **Fac Appt:** Asst Clin Prof Ped, UCSF

Kapoor, Neena MD [PHO] - **Spec Exp:** Bone Marrow Transplant; Immune Deficiency; **Hospital:** Chldns Hosp - Los Angeles; **Address:** Chlds Hosp LA-Rsch Immunology/BMT, 4650 Sunset Blvd, MS 62, Los Angeles, CA 90027; **Phone:** 323-361-2546; **Board Cert:** Pediatrics 1978; **Med School:** India 1972; **Resid:** Pediatrics, Rhode Island Hosp 1976; **Fellow:** Pediatric Hematology-Oncology, Meml Sloan-Kettering Cancer Ctr 1978; **Fac Appt:** Prof Ped, USC Sch Med

Kung, Faith H MD [PHO] - **Spec Exp:** Leukemia & Lymphoma; Bleeding/Coagulation Disorders; Sickle Cell Disease; **Hospital:** Rady Children's Hosp - San Diego; **Address:** UCSD Med Ctr, Div Ped Hem/Oncology, 200 W Arbor Drive, MC 8447, San Diego, CA 92103-8447; **Phone:** 858-246-0027; **Board Cert:** Pediatrics 1962; Pediatric Hematology-Oncology 1974; **Med School:** Univ VA Sch Med 1957; **Resid:** Pediatrics, NC Meml Hosp 1960; **Fellow:** Pediatric Hematology-Oncology, Chldns Hosp/Babies Hosp 1962; **Fac Appt:** Prof Emeritus Ped, UCSD

Link, Michael P MD [PHO] - **Spec Exp:** Stem Cell Transplant; Lymphoma; Sarcoma; **Hospital:** Lucile Packard Chldn's Hosp, Stanford Univ Hosp & Clins; **Address:** Lucile Packard Chldn's Hosp at Stanford, 725 Welch Rd, Palo Alto, CA 94304; **Phone:** 650-497-8953; **Board Cert:** Pediatrics 1979; Pediatric Hematology-Oncology 1980; **Med School:** Stanford Univ 1974; **Resid:** Pediatrics, Chldns Hosp Med Ctr 1976; **Fellow:** Hematology & Oncology, Dana Farber Cancer Inst 1979; **Fac Appt:** Prof Ped, Stanford Univ

Marina, Neyssa MD [PHO] - **Spec Exp:** Sarcoma; Cancer Survivors-Late Effects of Therapy; Germ Cell Tumors; **Hospital:** Lucile Packard Chldn's Hosp; **Address:** Pediatric Hematology & Oncology, 725 Welch Rd, MC 5798, Palo Alto, CA 94304; **Phone:** 650-497-8953; **Board Cert:** Pediatrics 1987; Pediatric Hematology-Oncology 2012; **Med School:** Puerto Rico 1983; **Resid:** Pediatrics, U Pediatric Hosp 1986; **Fellow:** Pediatric Hematology-Oncology, St Jude Hosp 1989; **Fac Appt:** Prof Ped, Stanford Univ

Matthay, Katherine K MD [PHO] - **Spec Exp:** Neuroblastoma; Bone Marrow & Stem Cell Transplant; **Hospital:** UCSF Med Ctr; **Address:** UCSF, Dept Ped Onc, 505 Parnassus Ave, Box 0106, San Francisco, CA 94143; **Phone:** 415-476-3831; **Board Cert:** Pediatrics 1979; Pediatric Hematology-Oncology 1980; **Med School:** Univ Pennsylvania 1973; **Resid:** Pediatrics, Univ Colorado 1976; **Fellow:** Pediatric Hematology-Oncology, UCSF 1979; **Fac Appt:** Prof Ped, UCSF

Nicholson, H. Stacy MD [PHO] - **Spec Exp:** Brain Tumors; Cancer Survivors-Late Effects of Therapy; Histiocytoma; **Hospital:** Doernbecher Chldns Hosp/OHSU, OR Hlth & Sci Univ; **Address:** OR Hlth Scis Univ, 707 SW Gaines Rd, CDRCP, Portland, OR 97239; **Phone:** 503-494-4265; **Board Cert:** Pediatrics 2008; Pediatric Hematology-Oncology 2007; **Med School:** Med Coll GA 1985; **Resid:** Pediatrics, Chldns National Med Ctr 1988; **Fellow:** Pediatric Hematology-Oncology, Chldns National Med Ctr 1991; **Fac Appt:** Prof Ped, Oregon Hlth & Sci Univ

Olson, Janice F MD [PHO] - **Spec Exp:** Hodgkin's Lymphoma; Neuro-Oncology; Bone Marrow Transplant; **Hospital:** Randall Chldns Hosp at Legacy; **Address:** Randall Chldns Hosp, Cancer & Blood Dis, 2801 N Gantenbein Ave Fl 3, Portland, OR 97227; **Phone:** 503-276-9300; **Board Cert:** Pediatrics 2012; Pediatric Hematology-Oncology 2009; **Med School:** Univ Utah 1985; **Resid:** Pediatrics, TX Chldns Hosp 1988; **Fellow:** Hematology & Oncology, Duke Univ Hosp 1992

Park, Julie R MD [PHO] - **Spec Exp:** Pediatric Cancers; Neuroblastoma; **Hospital:** Seattle Chldns Hosp; **Address:** Seattle Chldn's Hosp - Div Hem/Onc, 4800 Sandpoint Way NE, MS M.B.8.501, Seattle, WA 98105; **Phone:** 206-987-2106; **Board Cert:** Pediatric Hematology-Oncology 2011; **Med School:** Univ VT Coll Med 1988; **Resid:** Pediatrics, Univ Wash Affil Hosp 1991; **Fellow:** Pediatric Hematology-Oncology, Univ Wash/Fred Hutchinson Cancer Rsch Ctr 1994; Pediatric Hematology-Oncology, Leukemia Soc/Fred Hutchinson Cancer Rsch Ctr 1996; **Fac Appt:** Assoc Prof Ped, Univ Wash

Pendergrass, Thomas W MD [PHO] - **Spec Exp:** Pediatric Cancers; Hematologic Disorders; Retinoblastoma; **Hospital:** Seattle Chldns Hosp, Univ Wash Med Ctr; **Address:** Seattle Chldn's Hosp - Div Hem/Onc, 4800 Sandpoint Way NE, MS M.B.8.501, Seattle, WA 98105; **Phone:** 206-987-2106; **Board Cert:** Pediatrics 1978; **Med School:** Univ Tenn Coll Med 1971; **Resid:** Pediatrics, Lurie Chldn's Hosp 1975; **Fellow:** Pediatric Hematology-Oncology, Chldn's Hosp 1977; **Fac Appt:** Prof Ped, Univ Wash

Recht, Michael MD/PhD [PHO] - **Spec Exp:** Hemophilia; Bleeding/Coagulation Disorders; Hematologic Disorders; **Hospital:** Doernbecher Chldns Hosp/OHSU; **Address:** OHSU - Div Peds Hem/Onc, 3181 SW Sam Jackson Park Rd, MC CDRC, Portland, OR 97239; **Phone:** 503-494-8716; **Board Cert:** Pediatric Hematology-Oncology 2013; **Med School:** Univ Wisc 1992; **Resid:** Pediatrics, Yale-New Haven Hosp 1995; **Fellow:** Pediatric Hematology-Oncology, Yale-New Haven Hosp 1998

Rosenthal, Joseph MD [PHO] - **Spec Exp:** Bone Marrow Transplant; Clinical Trials; **Hospital:** City of Hope Natl Med Ctr; **Address:** City of Hope, Ped Hem/Onc, 1500 E Duarte Rd, Duarte, CA 91010; **Phone:** 626-301-8442; **Board Cert:** Pediatrics 2010; Pediatric Hematology-Oncology 2011; **Med School:** Israel 1984; **Resid:** Pediatrics, Soroka Med Ctr 1988; Pediatrics, Chldns Hosp 1995; **Fellow:** Pediatric Hematology-Oncology, Univ CO Hosp 1991; Pediatric Hematology-Oncology, Chldns Hosp 1994; **Fac Appt:** Prof Ped, USC-Keck School of Medicine

Sakamoto, Kathleen M MD/PhD [PHO] - **Spec Exp:** Leukemia; Pediatric Cancers; Bone Marrow Transplant; **Hospital:** Lucile Packard Chldn's Hosp; **Address:** 269 Campus Drive, CCSR 1215C, Stanford, CA 94305-5162; **Phone:** 650-725-7126; **Board Cert:** Pediatrics 2007; Pediatric Hematology-Oncology 2007; **Med School:** Univ Cincinnati 1985; **Resid:** Pediatrics, Chldn's Hosp 1988; **Fellow:** Pediatric Hematology-Oncology, Chldn's Hosp 1991; **Fac Appt:** Prof Hem & Onc, Stanford Univ

Siegel, Stuart E MD [PHO] - **Spec Exp:** Pediatric Cancers; Infections in Cancer Patients; Psychosocial Support in Childhood Cancer; **Hospital:** Chldns Hosp - Los Angeles, Ventura Cnty Med Ctr; **Address:** Chldns Hosp, 4650 Sunset Blvd, MS 54, Los Angeles, CA 90027-6062; **Phone:** 323-361-2205; **Board Cert:** Pediatrics 1973; Pediatric Hematology-Oncology 1976; **Med School:** Boston Univ 1967; **Resid:** Pediatrics, Univ Minnesota Hosps 1969; **Fellow:** Pediatric Hematology-Oncology, Natl Cancer Inst 1972; **Fac Appt:** Prof Ped, USC-Keck School of Medicine

Thomas, Gregory A MD [PHO] - **Spec Exp:** Palliative Care; Anemias & Red Cell Disorders; Bleeding/Coagulation Disorders; **Hospital:** Doernbecher Chldns Hosp/OHSU; **Address:** 707 SW Gaines Rd, MC 1104-CDRCP, Portland, OR 97239; **Phone:** 503-346-0644; **Board Cert:** Pediatrics 1986; Pediatric Hematology-Oncology 2005; **Med School:** Oregon Hlth & Sci Univ 1981; **Resid:** Pediatrics, Univ Utah Med Ctr 1984; **Fellow:** Pediatric Hematology-Oncology, Univ Utah Med Ctr 1987; **Fac Appt:** Assoc Prof Ped, Oregon Hlth & Sci Univ

Wayne, Alan S MD [PHO] - **Spec Exp:** Leukemia; Lymphoma; **Hospital:** Chldns Hosp - Los Angeles; **Address:** Cancer & Blood Diseases, Chldn's Hosp Los Angeles, 4650 W Sunset Blvd, MS 54, Los Angeles, CA 90027; **Phone:** 323-361-2121; **Board Cert:** Pediatric Hematology-Oncology 2008; **Med School:** Northwestern Univ-Feinberg Sch Med 1984; **Resid:** Pediatrics, Chldn's Hosp 1988; **Fellow:** Pediatric Hematology-Oncology, Dana Farber Cancer Inst/Chldn's Hosp 1991; **Fac Appt:** Prof Ped, USC Sch Med

Pediatric Infectious Disease

New England

Andiman, Warren A MD [PInf] - **Spec Exp:** AIDS/HIV; Viral Infections; Lyme Disease; Infectious Mononucleosis; **Hospital:** Yale-New Haven Hosp; **Address:** Yale Ped Infectious Disease, 20 York St Fl 2, New Haven, CT 06520-8064; **Phone:** 203-785-4730; **Board Cert:** Pediatrics 1975; **Med School:** Albert Einstein Coll Med 1969; **Resid:** Pediatrics, Babies Hosp-Columbia Presby 1971; **Fellow:** Pediatric Infectious Disease, Yale-New Haven Hosp 1973; **Fac Appt:** Prof Ped, Yale Univ

Baltimore, Robert Samuel MD [PInf] - **Spec Exp:** Neonatal Infections; Hospital Acquired Infections; Tuberculosis; **Hospital:** Yale-New Haven Hosp; **Address:** Yale Pediatric Infectious Diseases, 1 Park St, New Haven, CT 06510; **Phone:** 203-785-4730; **Board Cert:** Pediatrics 1975; Pediatric Infectious Disease 2009; **Med School:** SUNY Buffalo 1968; **Resid:** Pediatrics, Univ Chicago Hosps 1971; **Fellow:** Infectious Disease, Boston Univ Hosp 1976; **Fac Appt:** Prof Ped, Yale Univ

Durbin Jr, William J MD [PInf] - **Spec Exp:** AIDS/HIV; Lyme Disease; **Hospital:** UMass Memorial Med Ctr; **Address:** UMass Meml Med Ctr-Univ Campus, 55 Lake Ave N, Worcester, MA 01655; **Phone:** 774-442-3947; **Board Cert:** Pediatrics 1978; Pediatric Infectious Disease 2009; **Med School:** Columbia P&S 1972; **Resid:** Pediatrics, Chldns Hosp 1977; **Fellow:** Infectious Disease, Chldns Hosp/Beth Israel 1979; **Fac Appt:** Prof Ped, Univ Mass Sch Med

Meissner, H Cody MD [PInf] - **Spec Exp:** Infections-Respiratory; Kawasaki Disease; Vaccines; **Hospital:** Tufts Med Ctr; **Address:** Tufts Medical Center, 800 Washington St, Ste 321, Boston, MA 02111; **Phone:** 617-636-8100; **Board Cert:** Pediatrics 1981; Pediatric Infectious Disease 2009; **Med School:** Tufts Univ 1973; **Resid:** Pediatrics, New England Med Ctr 1975; Pediatrics, Natl Inst of Health 1977; **Fellow:** Infectious Disease, Chldns Hosp Med Ctr 1998; **Fac Appt:** Assoc Prof Ped, Tufts Univ

Raszka Jr, William V MD [PInf] - **Spec Exp:** Travel Medicine; **Hospital:** FAHC - Med Ctr Campus; **Address:** Chldns Specialty Clin, Dept Ped Infect Disease, 111 Colchester Avenue, Burlington, VT 05401; **Phone:** 802-847-8200; **Board Cert:** Pediatrics 2008; Pediatric Infectious Disease 2009; **Med School:** Boston Univ 1985; **Resid:** Pediatrics, Tripler Army Med Ctr 1988; **Fellow:** Pediatric Infectious Disease, Uniformed Servs Hlth Ctr 1993; **Fac Appt:** Prof Ped, Univ VT Coll Med

Shapiro, Eugene D MD [PInf] - **Spec Exp:** Lyme Disease; Vaccines; **Hospital:** Yale-New Haven Hosp; **Address:** Yale Univ Sch Med, Dept Pediatrics, 333 Cedar St, Box 208064, New Haven, CT 06520-8064; **Phone:** 203-688-4518; **Board Cert:** Pediatrics 1980; Pediatric Infectious Disease 2009; **Med School:** UCSF 1976; **Resid:** Pediatrics, Chldn's Hosp 1979; **Fellow:** Pediatric Infectious Disease, Chldn's Hosp 1981; Epidemiology, Yale Univ 1983; **Fac Appt:** Prof Ped, Yale Univ

Mid Atlantic

Bell Jr, Louis M MD [PInf] - **Hospital:** Chldns Hosp of Philadelphia; **Address:** Chldns Hosp, Ped Infectious Diseases, 34th and Civic Center Blvd Fl 12, Philadelphia, PA 19104; **Phone:** 215-590-2195; **Board Cert:** Pediatrics 1985; Pediatric Infectious Disease 2007; **Med School:** Univ MD Sch Med 1980; **Resid:** Pediatrics, Hahnemann Univ Med Ctr 1983; **Fellow:** Pediatric Infectious Disease, Chldns Hosp 1985; **Fac Appt:** Prof Ped, Univ Pennsylvania

Green, Michael D MD [PInf] - **Spec Exp:** Infections-Transplant; **Hospital:** Chldns Hosp of Pittsburgh - UPMC; **Address:** Chldns Hosp, Ped Infectious Diseases, 4401 Penn Ave Fl 3, Pittsburgh, PA 15224; **Phone:** 412-692-7885; **Board Cert:** Pediatrics 1987; Pediatric Infectious Disease 2009; **Med School:** Univ IL Coll Med 1983; **Resid:** Pediatrics, Chldns Hosp 1986; **Fellow:** Pediatric Infectious Disease, Chldns Hosp 1989; **Fac Appt:** Prof Ped, Univ Pittsburgh

Kotloff, Karen MD [PInf] - **Spec Exp:** Diarrheal Diseases; Infectious Disease; Sexually Transmitted Diseases; **Hospital:** Univ of MD Med Ctr; **Address:** Ctr for Vaccine Development, 685 W Baltimore St, HSF Bldg, Ste 480, Baltimore, MD 21201; **Phone:** 410-706-5328; **Board Cert:** Pediatrics 1985; Pediatric Infectious Disease 2009; **Med School:** Temple Univ 1979; **Resid:** Pediatrics, Chldns Hosp 1983; **Fellow:** Pediatric Infectious Disease, Univ Maryland Med Ctr 1986; **Fac Appt:** Prof Ped, Univ MD Sch Med

Krilov, Leonard R MD [PInf] - **Spec Exp:** Infections-Respiratory; Infections in Int'l Adopted Children; Chronic Fatigue Syndrome; Lyme Disease; **Hospital:** Winthrop Univ Hosp, Good Samaritan Hosp Med Ctr - West Islip; **Address:** 120 Mineola Blvd, Ste 210, Mineola, NY 11501; **Phone:** 516-663-9414; **Board Cert:** Pediatrics 1983; Pediatric Infectious Disease 2009; **Med School:** Columbia P&S 1978; **Resid:** Pediatrics, Johns Hopkins Hosp 1981; **Fellow:** Pediatric Infectious Disease, Children's Hosp 1984; **Fac Appt:** Prof Ped, SUNY Stony Brook

Long, Sarah S MD [PInf] - **Spec Exp:** Whooping Cough; Vaccines; Antibiotic Resistance; **Hospital:** St. Christopher's Hosp for Chldn; **Address:** St Christophers Hosp, Ped Infectious Dis, 3601 A St Fl 1, Philadelphia, PA 19134; **Phone:** 215-427-5201; **Board Cert:** Pediatrics 2002; Pediatric Infectious Disease 2009; **Med School:** Jefferson Med Coll 1970; **Resid:** Pediatrics, St Christophers Hosp Chldn 1973; **Fellow:** Pediatric Infectious Disease, Temple Univ Hosp 1975; **Fac Appt:** Prof Ped, Drexel Univ Coll Med

Michaels, Marian G MD [PInf] - **Spec Exp:** Infections in Immunocompromised Patients; Infectious Disease-Perinatal; AIDS/HIV; **Hospital:** Chldns Hosp of Pittsburgh - UPMC, Magee-Womens Hosp - UPMC; **Address:** Chldns Hosp, Ped Infectious Diseases, 4401 Penn Ave Fl 3, Pittsburgh, PA 15224; **Phone:** 412-692-7885; **Board Cert:** Pediatric Infectious Disease 2009; **Med School:** Univ Pennsylvania 1985; **Resid:** Pediatrics, Chldns Hosp 1988; Pediatrics, Hosp Sick Chldn 1989; **Fellow:** Pediatric Infectious Disease, UPMC 1992; **Fac Appt:** Prof Ped, Univ Pittsburgh

Saiman, Lisa R MD [PInf] - **Spec Exp:** Cystic Fibrosis Infection; Fungal Infections; Tick-borne Diseases; Tuberculosis; **Hospital:** Morgan Stanley Children's Hosp of NY-Presby, NY (page 65); **Address:** 3959 Broadway, rm 106, New York, NY 10032; **Phone:** 212-305-0635; **Board Cert:** Pediatrics 1987; Pediatric Infectious Disease 2009; **Med School:** Albert Einstein Coll Med 1983; **Resid:** Pediatrics, Babies Hosp/NY Presby 1986; **Fellow:** Infectious Disease, Babies Hosp/NY Presby 1989; **Fac Appt:** Clin Prof Ped, Columbia P&S

Singh, Nalini MD [PInf] - **Hospital:** Chldns Natl Med Ctr; **Address:** Div Infectious Dis, 111 Michigan Ave NW, Ste 3400, Washington, DC 20010; **Phone:** 202-476-5051; **Board Cert:** Pediatrics 1982; Pediatric Infectious Disease 2012; **Med School:** India 1973; **Resid:** Pediatrics, Univ Mass Med Ctr 1979; **Fellow:** Infectious Disease, Natl Inst Hlth 1981; **Fac Appt:** Assoc Prof Ped, Geo Wash Univ

Southeast

Edwards, Kathryn M MD [PInf] - **Spec Exp:** Vaccines; Clinical Trials; **Hospital:** Vanderbilt Univ Med Ctr; **Address:** Vanderbilt Childrens Hosp, Div Infectious Diseases, 2200 Childrens Way, DOT 6th Fl, Nashville, TN 37232; **Phone:** 615-322-2250; **Board Cert:** Pediatrics 1978; Pediatric Infectious Disease 2012; **Med School:** Univ Iowa Coll Med 1973; **Resid:** Pediatrics, Chldns Meml Hosp 1976; **Fellow:** Pediatric Infectious Disease, Chldns Meml Hosp 1980; Immunology, Rush-Presby St Luke's Hosp; **Fac Appt:** Prof Ped, Vanderbilt Univ

Flynn, Patricia M MD [PInf] - **Spec Exp:** AIDS/HIV; Infections in Immunocompromised Patients; Clinical Trials; **Hospital:** St. Jude Children's Research Hosp, Le Bonheur Chldns Med Ctr; **Address:** St. Jude Children's Research Hosp, 262 Danny Thomas Pl, rm Q1114, Memphis, TN 38105; **Phone:** 901-595-2338; **Board Cert:** Pediatrics 1986; Pediatric Infectious Disease 2009; **Med School:** Louisiana State U, New Orleans 1981; **Resid:** Pediatrics, LeBonheur Chldns Med Ctr 1984; **Fellow:** Pediatric Infectious Disease, St Jude Chldns Rsch Hosp 1987; **Fac Appt:** Prof Ped, Univ Tenn Coll Med

Givner, Laurence B MD [PInf] - **Spec Exp:** Streptococcal Infections; Rocky Mountain Spotted Fever; **Hospital:** Brenner Chldrn's Hosp, Wake Forest Baptist Med Ctr; **Address:** Medical Ctr Blvd, Winston-Salem, NC 27157-0001; **Phone:** 336-716-6568; **Board Cert:** Pediatrics 1984; Pediatric Infectious Disease 2009; **Med School:** Univ MD Sch Med 1978; **Resid:** Pediatrics, Univ Maryland Affil Hosp 1982; **Fellow:** Infectious Disease, Baylor Coll Med 1984; **Fac Appt:** Prof Ped, Wake Forest Univ

Ingram, David L MD [PInf] - **Hospital:** WakeMed-Raleigh Campus; **Address:** WakeMed Faculty Physicians, Pediatrics, 3024 New Bern Ave, Ste 307, Raleigh, NC 27610; **Phone:** 919-350-8009; **Board Cert:** Pediatrics 1980; Pediatric Infectious Disease 2009; **Med School:** Yale Univ 1967; **Resid:** Pediatrics, Yale-New Haven Hosp 1971; **Fellow:** Pediatric Infectious Disease, Chldns Hosp Med Ctr 1973; **Fac Appt:** Prof Ped, Univ NC Sch Med

McKinney Jr, Ross E MD [PInf] - **Spec Exp:** Infections in Immunocompromised Patients; Fevers of Unknown Origin; AIDS/HIV; **Hospital:** Duke Univ Hosp; **Address:** 1 Duke Medical Ctr, Box 3461, Durham, NC 27710; **Phone:** 919-684-6335; **Board Cert:** Pediatrics 1983; Pediatric Infectious Disease 2009; **Med School:** Univ Rochester 1979; **Resid:** Pediatrics, Duke Univ Med Ctr 1982; **Fellow:** Pediatric Infectious Disease, Duke Univ Med Ctr 1985; **Fac Appt:** Prof Ped, Duke Univ

Mitchell, Charles D MD [PInf] - **Spec Exp:** AIDS/HIV; Viral Infections; Tuberculosis; **Hospital:** Jackson Meml Hosp; **Address:** Batchelor Rsch Inst, 1580 NW 10th Ave, Ste 286, Miami, FL 33136; **Phone:** 305-243-2700; **Board Cert:** Pediatrics 1986; Pediatric Infectious Disease 2009; **Med School:** Univ Tex Med Br, Galveston 1977; **Resid:** Pediatrics, Univ Minn Med Ctr 1981; **Fellow:** Pediatric Infectious Disease, Univ Minn Med Ctr 1984; **Fac Appt:** Prof Ped, Univ Miami Sch Med

Scott, Gwendolyn B MD [PInf] - **Spec Exp:** AIDS/HIV; **Hospital:** Jackson Meml Hosp, Univ of Miami Hosp & Clins/Sylvester Comp Canc Ctr; **Address:** Batchelor Rsch Inst, 1580 NW 10th Ave, Ste 286, Miami, FL 33136; **Phone:** 305-243-2700; **Board Cert:** Pediatrics 1978; Pediatric Infectious Disease 2009; **Med School:** UCSF 1972; **Resid:** Pediatrics, San Francisco Genl Hosp 1973; Pediatrics, Univ MD Hosp 1975; **Fellow:** Pediatric Infectious Disease, Univ Miami Hosp 1978; **Fac Appt:** Prof Ped, Univ Miami Sch Med

Midwest

Alexander, Kenneth MD/PhD [PInf] - **Spec Exp:** HPV-Human Papilloma Virus; Infections in Immunocompromised Patients; Fevers of Unknown Origin; Antibiotic Resistance; **Hospital:** Univ of Chicago Med; **Address:** Univ Chicago-Ped Infectious Disease, 5841 S Maryland Ave, MC 3055, Chicago, IL 60637; **Phone:** 773-702-6176; **Med School:** Univ Wash 1989; **Resid:** Pediatrics, Chldn's Hosp 1992; **Fellow:** Pediatric Infectious Disease, Duke Univ Hosp 1995; **Fac Appt:** Assoc Prof Ped, Univ Chicago-Pritzker Sch Med

Belcher, Christopher E MD [PInf] - **Spec Exp:** Travel Medicine; Drug-Resistant Infections; Histoplasmosis; Fungal Infections; **Hospital:** Peyton Manning Children's Hosp at St. Vincent, St. Vincent Carmel Hosp; **Address:** Infectious Disease of Indiana, 11455 N Meridian St, Ste 200, Carmel, IN 46032; **Phone:** 317-582-8180; **Board Cert:** Pediatrics 2013; Pediatric Infectious Disease 2009; **Med School:** UCSD 1994; **Resid:** Pediatrics, Stanford Univ Hosp & Clins 1997; **Fellow:** Pediatric Infectious Disease, Barnes-Jewish Hosp 1998; Pediatric Infectious Disease, Stanford Univ Hosp & Clins 2000

Christenson, John C MD [PInf] - **Spec Exp:** Travel Medicine; Lyme Disease; Viral Infections; Histoplasmosis; **Hospital:** Riley Hosp for Children; **Address:** Div Infectious Disease, 705 Riley Hosp Drive, ROC 4380, Indianapolis, IN 46202; **Phone:** 317-944-7260; **Board Cert:** Pediatrics 1986; Pediatric Infectious Disease 2009; **Med School:** Univ Puerto Rico 1981; **Resid:** Pediatrics, Univ Pediatric Hosp 1984; **Fellow:** Pediatric Infectious Disease, OK Chldns Meml Hosp 1987; **Fac Appt:** Clin Prof Ped, Indiana Univ

Leonard, Ethan G MD [PInf] - **Hospital:** UH Rainbow Babies & Chldns Hosp; **Address:** UH Rainbow Babies & Children's Hospital, Pediatric Infectious Disease, 11100 Euclid Ave, Cleveland, OH 44106; **Phone:** 216-844-3645; **Board Cert:** Pediatrics 2007; Pediatric Infectious Disease 2011; **Med School:** Case West Res Univ 1996; **Resid:** Pediatrics, Univ Hosps 2000; **Fellow:** Pediatric Infectious Disease, Univ Hosps 2003; **Fac Appt:** Assoc Prof Ped, Case West Res Univ

McComsey, Grace A MD [PInf] - **Spec Exp:** AIDS/HIV; Infections in Immunocompromised Patients; **Hospital:** UH Rainbow Babies & Chldns Hosp; **Address:** Div Pediatric Infectious Disease, 11100 Euclid Ave, Cleveland, OH 44106; **Phone:** 216-844-3607; **Board Cert:** Internal Medicine 2005; Pediatric Infectious Disease 2012; Infectious Disease 2007; **Med School:** Lebanon 1989; **Resid:** Internal Medicine & Pediatrics, MetroHealth Med Ctr 1994; **Fellow:** Infectious Disease, Univ Hosps 1997; **Fac Appt:** Prof Med, Case West Res Univ

Shulman, Stanford MD [PInf] - **Spec Exp:** Kawasaki Disease; Streptococcal Infections; **Hospital:** Lurie Chldn's Hosp-Chicago, Northwestern Meml Hosp; **Address:** Lurie Chldn's Hosp, 225 E Chicago Ave, Box 20, Chicago, IL 60611; **Phone:** 312-227-4080; **Board Cert:** Pediatrics 1972; Pediatric Infectious Disease 2010; **Med School:** Univ Chicago-Pritzker Sch Med 1967; **Resid:** Pediatrics, Univ Chicago Hosps 1970; **Fellow:** Infectious Disease, Shands Hosp 1973; **Fac Appt:** Prof Ped, Northwestern Univ

Wald, Ellen Rashkow MD [PInf] - **Spec Exp:** Urinary Tract Infections; Infections-Respiratory; Meningitis; Ear Infections; **Hospital:** Univ WI Hosp & Clins; **Address:** American Family Childrens Hosp, Dept Pediatrics, Box 4108, 600 Highland Ave, Madison, WI 57392; **Phone:** 608-263-8558; **Board Cert:** Pediatrics 1973; Pediatric Infectious Disease 2009; **Med School:** SUNY Downstate 1968; **Resid:** Pediatrics, Kings Co Hosp 1971; **Fellow:** Infectious Disease, Univ Maryland Hosp 1973; **Fac Appt:** Prof Ped, Univ Wisc

Southwest

Baker, Carol J MD [PInf] - **Spec Exp:** Streptococcal Infections; Neonatal Infections; Vaccines; **Hospital:** Texas Chldns Hosp; **Address:** 1102 Bates St, Feigin Ctr Fl 11 - Ste 1120, Houston, TX 77030; **Phone:** 832-824-1780; **Board Cert:** Pediatrics 1973; Pediatric Infectious Disease 2009; **Med School:** Baylor Coll Med 1968; **Resid:** Pediatrics, Baylor Affil Hosp 1971; **Fellow:** Pediatric Infectious Disease, Baylor Coll Med 1973; Infectious Disease, Boston City Hosp/Harvard 1974; **Fac Appt:** Prof Ped, Baylor Coll Med

Demmler-Harrison, Gail J MD [PInf] - **Spec Exp:** Congenital Infections; Vaccines; **Hospital:** Texas Chldns Hosp; **Address:** 6701 Fannin St Fl 16, MC 3-2371, Feigin Ctr, Ste 1150, Houston, TX 77030; **Phone:** 832-824-4330; **Board Cert:** Pediatrics 1981; Pediatric Infectious Disease 2009; **Med School:** Texas Tech Univ 1977; **Resid:** Pediatrics, Baylor Univ Med Ctr 1980; **Fellow:** Pediatric Infectious Disease, Baylor Univ Med Ctr 1985; Virology, NY-Presby/Columbia Univ Med Ctr 1987; **Fac Appt:** Prof Ped, Baylor Coll Med

Jacobs, Richard F MD [PInf] - **Spec Exp:** Viral Infections; Drug Discovery & Development; Neonatal Infections; **Hospital:** Arkansas Chldns Hosp, UAMS Med Ctr; **Address:** 1 Childrens Way, Little Rock, AR 72202-3591; **Phone:** 501-364-5262; **Board Cert:** Pediatrics 1982; Pediatric Infectious Disease 2009; **Med School:** Univ Ark 1977; **Resid:** Pediatrics, Ark Chldns Hosp 1980; **Fellow:** Infectious Disease, Univ Washington 1982; **Fac Appt:** Prof Ped, Univ Ark

Kaplan, Sheldon L MD [PInf] - **Spec Exp:** Pneumococcal Infections; Meningitis; **Hospital:** Texas Chldns Hosp; **Address:** Div Infectious Disease, 1102 Bates St, Ste 1150, Feigin Ctr, Houston, TX 77030; **Phone:** 832-824-4330; **Board Cert:** Pediatrics 1978; Pediatric Infectious Disease 2009; **Med School:** Univ MO-Columbia Sch Med 1973; **Resid:** Pediatrics, St Louis Chldns Hosp 1976; **Fellow:** Pediatric Infectious Disease, St Louis Chldns Hosp 1978; **Fac Appt:** Prof Ped, Baylor Coll Med

Kline, Mark W MD [PInf] - **Spec Exp:** AIDS/HIV; **Hospital:** Texas Chldns Hosp; **Address:** Texas Children's Hosp, 6621 Fannin St, MC A1150, Houston, TX 77030; **Phone:** 832-824-2233; **Board Cert:** Pediatrics 1987; Pediatric Infectious Disease 2009; **Med School:** Baylor Coll Med 1981; **Resid:** Pediatrics, Baylor Affil Hosp 1985; **Fellow:** Pediatric Infectious Disease, Baylor Coll Med 1987; **Fac Appt:** Prof Ped, Baylor Coll Med

McCracken Jr, George H MD [PInf] - **Spec Exp:** Meningitis; Antibiotic Resistance; Pneumococcal Infections; **Hospital:** UT Southwestern Med Ctr at Dallas; **Address:** Dept Pediatric Infectious Disease, 1935 Med District Drive, Dallas, TX 75235; **Phone:** 214-648-3720; **Board Cert:** Pediatrics 1966; **Med School:** Cornell Univ-Weill Med Coll 1962; **Resid:** Pediatrics, NY-Cornell Med Ctr 1965; Pediatrics, Univ Texas SW Med Ctr 1966; **Fac Appt:** Prof Ped, Univ Tex SW, Dallas

Starke, Jeffrey MD [PInf] - **Spec Exp:** Tuberculosis; **Hospital:** Texas Chldns Hosp; **Address:** Texas Chldns Hosp, Pulm Med Clinic, 6701 Fannin St Fl 16, MC FC-1150, Houston, TX 77030; **Phone:** 832-824-4330; **Board Cert:** Pediatrics 1985; Pediatric Infectious Disease 2009; **Med School:** Univ Rochester 1980; **Resid:** Pediatrics, Baylor Coll Med Ctr 1983; **Fellow:** Pediatric Infectious Disease, Baylor Coll Med Ctr 1985; **Fac Appt:** Prof Med, Baylor Coll Med

West Coast and Pacific

Bradley, John S MD [PInf] - **Spec Exp:** Infections-Respiratory; Antibiotic Resistance; Clinical Trials; **Hospital:** Rady Children's Hosp - San Diego, UCSD Med Ctr; **Address:** 8110 Birmingham Way Bldg 28, San Diego, CA 92123; **Phone:** 858-966-7785; **Board Cert:** Pediatrics 1981; Pediatric Infectious Disease 2009; **Med School:** UC Davis 1976; **Resid:** Pediatrics, Kaiser Foundation Hosp 1980; **Fellow:** Pediatric Infectious Disease, Stanford Univ Med Ctr 1981; **Fac Appt:** Prof Ped, UCSD

Bryson, Yvonne J MD [PInf] - **Spec Exp:** AIDS/HIV; Toxoplasmosis; Clinical Trials; **Hospital:** UCLA Ronald Reagan Med Ctr; **Address:** 200 UCLA Medical Plaza, Peter Morton Med Bldg, Ste 265, Los Angeles, CA 90095-1752; **Phone:** 310-825-0867; **Board Cert:** Pediatrics 1976; **Med School:** Univ Tex SW, Dallas 1970; **Resid:** Pediatrics, UCSD Med Ctr 1974; **Fellow:** Pediatric Infectious Disease, UCSD Med Ctr 1976; **Fac Appt:** Prof Ped, UCLA

Petru, Ann M MD [PInf] - **Spec Exp:** AIDS/HIV; **Hospital:** Chldns Hosp - Oakland; **Address:** Chldns Hosp, Div Infectious Dis, 744 52nd St, Oakland, CA 94609; **Phone:** 510-428-3336; **Board Cert:** Pediatrics 1983; Pediatric Infectious Disease 2009; **Med School:** UCSF 1978; **Resid:** Pediatrics, Chldns Hosp 1982; **Fellow:** Pediatric Infectious Disease, Chldns Hosp 1983

Pediatric Nephrology

New England

Harmon, William E MD [PNep] - **Spec Exp:** Nephrotic Syndrome; **Hospital:** Children's Hospital - Boston; **Address:** Boston Chldn's Hosp, Div Nephrology, 300 Longwood Ave, Hunnewell 319, Boston, MA 02115; **Phone:** 617-355-6129; **Board Cert:** Pediatrics 1976; **Med School:** Case West Res Univ 1971; **Resid:** Pediatrics, Chldns Hosp 1976; **Fellow:** Pediatric Nephrology, Chldns Hosp 1979; **Fac Appt:** Prof Ped, Harvard Med Sch

Mid Atlantic

Conley, Susan B MD [PNep] - **Spec Exp:** Transplant Medicine-Kidney; Dialysis Care; Transfusion Medicine; **Hospital:** St. Christopher's Hosp for Chldn; **Address:** St Christophers Hosp for Chldn, Kidney Center for Children, Fl 3, 3601 A St, Philadelphia, PA 19134; **Phone:** 215-427-5190; **Board Cert:** Pediatrics 1978; Pediatric Nephrology 1979; **Med School:** Univ Mich Med Sch 1973; **Resid:** Pediatrics, St. Louis Chldns Hosp 1976; **Fellow:** Pediatric Nephrology, St. Louis Chldns Hosp 1979; **Fac Appt:** Prof Ped, Drexel Univ Coll Med

Ellis, Demetrius MD [PNep] - **Spec Exp:** Transplant Medicine-Kidney; Hypertension; **Hospital:** Chldns Hosp of Pittsburgh - UPMC; **Address:** Chldns Hosp, Ped Nephrology Dept, 4401 Penn Ave Fl 3, Pittsburgh, PA 15224; **Phone:** 412-692-5182; **Board Cert:** Pediatrics 1978; Pediatric Nephrology 1979; **Med School:** SUNY Buffalo 1973; **Resid:** Pediatrics, Chldns Hosp 1975; **Fellow:** Pediatric Nephrology, Chldns Natl Med Ctr 1977; **Fac Appt:** Prof Ped, Univ Pittsburgh

Fivush, Barbara A MD [PNep] - **Spec Exp:** Transplant Medicine-Kidney; **Hospital:** Johns Hopkins Hosp (page 59); **Address:** Johns Hopkins Hosp-Div Ped Nephrology, 200 N Wolfe St, rm 3055, Baltimore, MD 21287; **Phone:** 410-955-2467; **Board Cert:** Pediatrics 1984; Pediatric Nephrology 2010; **Med School:** Boston Univ 1978; **Resid:** Pediatrics, Johns Hopkins Hosp 1981; **Fellow:** Pediatric Nephrology, Johns Hopkins Hosp 1983; Pediatric Nephrology, Chldns Hosp Natl Med Ctr 1984; **Fac Appt:** Prof Ped, Johns Hopkins Univ

Kaplan, Bernard S MD [PNep] - **Spec Exp:** Hemolytic Uremic Syndrome; Polycystic Kidney Disease; Nephrotic Syndrome; **Hospital:** Chldns Hosp of Philadelphia; **Address:** Chldns Hosp, Ped Nephrology Dept, 3401 Civic Center Blvd, rm 1E15, Philadelphia, PA 19104; **Phone:** 215-590-2449; **Board Cert:** Pediatrics 1972; Pediatric Nephrology 1974; **Med School:** South Africa 1964; **Resid:** Pediatrics, Baragwanath Hosp/Transvaal Meml Hosp 1970; Nephrology, Royal Victoria Hosp 1973; **Fellow:** Nephrology, Montreal Chldns Hosp 1972; **Fac Appt:** Prof Ped, Univ Pennsylvania

Mendley, Susan MD [PNep] - **Spec Exp:** Transplant Medicine-Kidney; Hypertension; Dialysis Care; Glomerulonephritis; **Hospital:** Univ of MD Med Ctr; **Address:** Univ MD Med Ctr-Div Ped Nephrology, 22 S Greene St, Pediatric Nephrol N5W67, Baltimore, MD 21201; **Phone:** 410-328-5303; **Board Cert:** Internal Medicine 1988; Nephrology 2012; **Med School:** Boston Univ 1984; **Resid:** Internal Medicine, Univ Chicago Affil Hosp 1987; **Fellow:** Nephrology, Univ Chicago Affil Hosp 1990; Pediatric Nephrology, Chldns Meml Hosp/Northwestern Univ 1991; **Fac Appt:** Assoc Prof Ped, Univ MD Sch Med

Roskes, Saul D MD [PNep] - **Spec Exp:** Kidney Disease; Glomerulonephritis; **Hospital:** Greater Baltimore Med Ctr; **Address:** Maryland Pediatric Grp, 10807 Falls Rd, Ste 200, Lutherville, MD 21093; **Phone:** 410-321-9393; **Board Cert:** Pediatrics 1970; Pediatric Nephrology 1976; **Med School:** Johns Hopkins Univ 1963; **Resid:** Pediatrics, Bronx Muni Hosp Ctr 1965; Pediatrics, Johns Hopkins Hosp 1970; **Fac Appt:** Assoc Prof Ped, Johns Hopkins Univ

Southeast

Ault, Bettina H MD [PNep] - **Spec Exp:** Hemolytic Uremic Syndrome; Kidney Failure; Anemia; **Hospital:** Le Bonheur Chldns Med Ctr; **Address:** UT Le Bonheur Pediatric Specialists, 51 N Dunlap St, Ste 400, Memphis, TN 38105; **Phone:** 901-866-8822; **Board Cert:** Pediatrics 2006; Pediatric Nephrology 2006; **Med School:** Univ Tenn Coll Med 1984; **Resid:** Pediatrics, Johns Hopkins Hosp 1987; **Fellow:** Pediatric Nephrology, Univ Tn Med Ctr 1990; **Fac Appt:** Assoc Prof Ped, Univ Tenn Coll Med

Benfield, Mark R MD [PNep] - **Spec Exp:** Hypertension; Glomerulonephritis; Nephrotic Syndrome; Transplant Medicine-Kidney; **Hospital:** Children's Hosp AL; **Address:** 1425 Richard Arriington Jr Blvd S, Ste 206, Birmingham, AL 35205; **Phone:** 205-558-3200; **Board Cert:** Pediatric Nephrology 2013; **Med School:** Tulane Univ 1984; **Resid:** Pediatrics, Chldns Hosp 1987; **Fellow:** Pediatric Nephrology, Univ Minnesota Affil Hosp 1990; **Fac Appt:** Prof Ped, UAB Sch Med

Chandar, Jayanthi J MD [PNep] - **Spec Exp:** Kidney Disease; Transplant Medicine-Kidney; Renal Replacement Therapy; **Hospital:** Jackson Meml Hosp; **Address:** UHlth, Ped Nephrology Dept, 1601 NW 12th Ave, Miami, FL 33136; **Phone:** 305-585-6726; **Board Cert:** Pediatrics 2012; Pediatric Nephrology 2010; **Med School:** India 1983; **Resid:** Pediatrics, Jackson Meml Hosp 1987; **Fellow:** Pediatric Nephrology, Jackson Meml Hosp 1993; **Fac Appt:** Assoc Prof Ped, Univ Miami Sch Med

Jabs, Kathy L MD [PNep] - **Spec Exp:** Transplant Medicine-Kidney; Kidney Failure-Chronic; Cystinosis; Hypertension; **Hospital:** Vanderbilt Monroe Carrell Jr. Chldn's Hosp; **Address:** Vanderbilt Children Hosp, Div Nephrology/Hypertension, 2200 Childrens Way, 10111 DOT, Nashville, TN 37232-9560; **Phone:** 615-322-7416; **Board Cert:** Pediatrics 1987; Pediatric Nephrology 2010; **Med School:** Columbia P&S 1982; **Resid:** Pediatrics, Columbia-Presby Hosp 1985; **Fellow:** Pediatric Nephrology, Childrens Hosp 1988; **Fac Appt:** Assoc Prof Ped, Vanderbilt Univ

Neiberger, Richard E MD/PhD [PNep] - **Spec Exp:** Kidney Disease-Genetic; Hypertension; Kidney Failure; **Hospital:** UF Hlth Shands Hosp; **Address:** UF Pediatrics, Div Pediatric Nephrology, 1600 SW Archer Rd, HD Bldg - Fl 2, rm 214B, Gainesville, FL 32610; **Phone:** 352-273-9180; **Board Cert:** Pediatrics 2013; Nephrology 2013; **Med School:** Univ Louisville Sch Med 1982; **Resid:** Pediatrics, Montefiore Med Ctr 1985; **Fellow:** Pediatric Nephrology, Montefiore Med Ctr 1988; **Fac Appt:** Assoc Prof Ped, Univ Fla Coll Med

Wyatt, Robert J MD [PNep] - **Spec Exp:** Kidney Disease-Autoimmune; Berger's Disease (IgA Nephropathy); **Hospital:** Le Bonheur Chldns Med Ctr; **Address:** UT Le Bonheur Pediatric Specialists, 51 N Dunlap St, Ste 400, Memphis, TN 38105; **Phone:** 901-866-8822; **Board Cert:** Pediatrics 1978; Pediatric Nephrology 1979; **Med School:** Med Coll GA 1973; **Resid:** Pediatrics, Kentucky Med Ctr 1975; Pediatric Nephrology, Kentucky Med Ctr 1976; **Fellow:** Pediatric Nephrology, Cincinnati Chldns Hosp 1979; **Fac Appt:** Prof Ped, Univ Tenn Coll Med

Zilleruelo, Gaston E MD [PNep] - **Spec Exp:** Transplant Medicine-Kidney; Nephrotic Syndrome; Congenital Anomalies-Genitourinary; **Hospital:** Jackson Meml Hosp, Broward Hlth Med Ctr; **Address:** UHlth, Ped Nephrology Dept, 1601 NW 12th Ave, Miami, FL 33136; **Phone:** 305-585-6726; **Board Cert:** Pediatrics 1979; Pediatric Nephrology 1991; **Med School:** Chile 1969; **Resid:** Pediatrics, L Calvo-Mackenna Chldns Hosp 1972; Pediatrics, Jackson Meml Hosp 1977; **Fellow:** Pediatric Nephrology, Jackson Meml Hosp 1978; **Fac Appt:** Prof Ped, Univ Miami Sch Med

Midwest

Andreoli, Sharon P MD [PNep] - **Spec Exp:** Kidney Failure; Kidney Failure-Chronic; Osteodystrophy; Glomerulonephritis; **Hospital:** Riley Hosp for Children, IU Health Methodist Hosp; **Address:** Riley Hosp for Chldn-Ped Nephrology, 699 Riley Hosp Drive, rm RR230, Indianapolis, IN 46202; **Phone:** 317-274-2563; **Board Cert:** Pediatrics 1983; Pediatric Nephrology 1985; **Med School:** Indiana Univ 1978; **Resid:** Pediatrics, Riley Hosp Chldn 1981; **Fellow:** Pediatric Nephrology, Univ Minnesota Hosp 1981; Pediatric Nephrology, IU Health 1984; **Fac Appt:** Prof Ped, Indiana Univ

Brophy, Patrick D MD [PNep] - **Spec Exp:** Polycystic Kidney Disease; Transplant Medicine-Kidney; Dialysis Care; **Hospital:** Univ Iowa Hosp & Clins; **Address:** Univ Iowa Chldns Hosp, Ped Nephrology, 200 Hawkins Drive, Iowa City, IA 52242; **Phone:** 319-356-7249; **Board Cert:** Pediatrics 2012; Pediatric Nephrology 2009; **Med School:** Canada 1994; **Resid:** Pediatrics, Univ Manitoba Affil Hosp 1998; **Fellow:** Pediatric Nephrology, Univ Michigan Affil Hosps 2001; **Fac Appt:** Assoc Prof Ped, Univ Iowa Coll Med

Clardy, Christopher W MD [PNep] - **Spec Exp:** Nephrotic Syndrome; Transplant Medicine-Kidney; Glomerulonephritis; Congenital Anomalies-Genitourinary; **Hospital:** Univ Chicago Med-Comer Chldn's Hosp; **Address:** 5721 S Maryland Ave, Chicago, IL 60637; **Phone:** 773-702-6412; **Board Cert:** Pediatrics 1987; Pediatric Critical Care Medicine 2011; Pediatric Nephrology 2010; **Med School:** Univ VA Sch Med 1981; **Resid:** Pediatrics, Vanderbilt Univ Hosp 1984; **Fellow:** Pediatric Nephrology, Children's Hosp 1987; Pediatric Critical Care Medicine, Rush Medical Center 1996; **Fac Appt:** Assoc Prof Ped, Univ Chicago-Pritzker Sch Med

Cohn, Richard Allan MD [PNep] - **Spec Exp:** Transplant Medicine-Kidney; Nephrotic Syndrome; Kidney Disease-Chronic; **Hospital:** Lurie Chldn's Hosp-Chicago; **Address:** Lurie Chldn's Hosp, 225 E Chicago Ave, Box 37, Chicago, IL 60611; **Phone:** 312-227-6160; **Board Cert:** Pediatrics 1978; Pediatric Nephrology 1979; **Med School:** Albert Einstein Coll Med 1972; **Resid:** Pediatrics, Johns Hopkins Hosp 1975; **Fellow:** Pediatric Nephrology, Univ Minnesota Hosp 1978; **Fac Appt:** Prof Ped, Northwestern Univ

Kashtan, Clifford E MD [PNep] - **Spec Exp:** Transplant Medicine-Kidney; Kidney Disease-Genetic; **Hospital:** Univ Minn Med Ctr, Fairview - West Bank Campus; **Address:** Univ Minn Amplatz Chldns Hosp, Div Ped Nephrology, 2450 Riverside Ave Fl 6, Minneapolis, MN 55454; **Phone:** 612-626-2922; **Board Cert:** Pediatrics 1983; Pediatric Nephrology 2010; **Med School:** Wayne State Univ 1978; **Resid:** Pediatrics, Boston City Hosp 1981; **Fellow:** Pediatric Nephrology, Mass Genl Hosp 1987; **Fac Appt:** Prof Ped, Univ Minn

Langman, Craig MD [PNep] - **Spec Exp:** Kidney Stones; Osteoporosis-Juvenile; Oxalosis; **Hospital:** Lurie Chldn's Hosp-Chicago, Evanston Hosp/NorthShore Univ Hlth Sys (page 67); **Address:** Lurie Chldn's Hosp, 225 E Chicago Ave, Box 37, Chicago, IL 60611; **Phone:** 312-227-6160; **Board Cert:** Pediatrics 1982; Pediatric Nephrology 1992; **Med School:** Hahnemann Univ 1977; **Resid:** Pediatrics, Chldns Hosp 1979; **Fellow:** Pediatric Nephrology, Chldns Hosp 1981; **Fac Appt:** Prof Ped, Northwestern Univ

Warady, Bradley A MD [PNep] - **Spec Exp:** Dialysis Care; Transplant Medicine-Kidney; Kidney Disease-Chronic; Birth Defects; **Hospital:** Chldns Mercy Hosps & Clinics; **Address:** Children's Mercy Hospital, 2401 Gillham Rd, Kansas City, MO 64108; **Phone:** 816-234-3010; **Board Cert:** Pediatrics 1984; Pediatric Nephrology 1985; **Med School:** Univ IL Coll Med 1979; **Resid:** Pediatrics, Chldns Mercy Hosp 1982; **Fellow:** Pediatric Nephrology, Colorado Univ Med Ctr 1984; **Fac Appt:** Prof Ped, Univ MO-Kansas City

West Coast and Pacific

Alexander, Steven R MD [PNep] - **Spec Exp:** Kidney Failure; Transplant Medicine-Kidney; Nephrotic Syndrome; Dialysis Care; **Hospital:** Lucile Packard Chldn's Hosp; **Address:** Lucile Packard Chldn's Hosp, 770 Welch Rd, Ste 300, Palo Alto, CA 94304; **Phone:** 650-724-0353; **Board Cert:** Pediatrics 1986; Pediatric Nephrology 1986; **Med School:** Baylor Coll Med 1971; **Resid:** Pediatrics, Baylor Affil Hosps 1976; **Fellow:** Pediatric Nephrology, Baylor Affil Hosps 1978; **Fac Appt:** Prof Ped, Stanford Univ

Ettenger, Robert B MD [PNep] - **Spec Exp:** Transplant Medicine-Kidney; Hypertension in Children; Urinary Tract Infections; Kidney Disease; **Hospital:** UCLA Ronald Reagan Med Ctr, Mattel Chldns Hosp at UCLA; **Address:** UCLA Pediatric Nephrology, 200 UCLA Medical Plaza, Ste 265, Los Angeles, CA 90095; **Phone:** 310-206-6987; **Board Cert:** Pediatrics 1986; Pediatric Nephrology 1986; **Med School:** Univ Pennsylvania 1968; **Resid:** Pediatrics, St Christophers Hosp Chldn 1971; **Fellow:** Pediatric Nephrology, Chldns Hosp 1975; **Fac Appt:** Prof Ped, UCLA

Flynn, Joseph T MD [PNep] - **Spec Exp:** Hypertension; Dialysis Care; Kidney Disease; Obesity; **Hospital:** Seattle Chldns Hosp; **Address:** Children's Hospital, Ped Nephrology, 4800 Sand Point Way NE, MS A-7931, Seattle, WA 98105; **Phone:** 206-987-2524; **Board Cert:** Pediatric Nephrology 2008; **Med School:** SUNY Upstate Med Univ 1987; **Resid:** Pediatrics, St Christophers Hosp 1990; **Fellow:** Pediatric Nephrology, St Christophers Hosp 1993; **Fac Appt:** Prof Ped, Univ Wash

Fouser, Laurie S MD [PNep] - **Spec Exp:** Congenital Kidney Disease; Glomerulonephritis; Hypertension in Children; Kidney Failure; **Hospital:** Swedish Med Ctr-First Hill-Seattle; **Address:** Swedish Ped Spec Care, 1101 Madison St, Ste 800, Seattle, WA 98104; **Phone:** 206-215-2700; **Board Cert:** Pediatrics 1985; Pediatric Nephrology 2010; **Med School:** Univ Nebr Coll Med 1979; **Resid:** Pediatrics, Chldns Ortho Hosp-Univ WA 1982; **Fellow:** Pediatric Nephrology, Univ Minnesota Hosp 1987; Research, Univ Washington Med Ctr 1989

Jordan, Stanley C MD [PNep] - **Spec Exp:** Transplant Medicine-Kidney; **Hospital:** Cedars-Sinai Med Ctr; **Address:** Cedars Sinai Med Ctr, Div Ped Nephrology, 8635 W 3rd St, Ste 590W, Los Angeles, CA 90048; **Phone:** 310-423-2641; **Board Cert:** Pediatrics 1978; Pediatric Nephrology 1979; Clinical & Laboratory Immunology 1988; **Med School:** Univ NC Sch Med 1973; **Resid:** Pediatrics, UCLA Ronald Reagan Med Ctr 1976; Pediatric Nephrology, UCLA Ronald Reagan Med Ctr 1977; **Fellow:** Renal Immunology, Scripps Clin 1978; Dialysis & Tranplantation, Chldns Hosp 1980; **Fac Appt:** Prof Ped, UCLA

McDonald, Ruth A MD [PNep] - **Spec Exp:** Transplant Medicine-Kidney; Kidney Disease; **Hospital:** Seattle Chldns Hosp; **Address:** 4800 Sand Point Way NE, MS A-7931, Seattle, WA 98105; **Phone:** 206-987-2524; **Board Cert:** Pediatric Nephrology 2012; **Med School:** Univ Minn 1987; **Resid:** Pediatrics, Chldns Hosp & Med Ctr 1990; **Fellow:** Pediatric Nephrology, Chldns Hosp & Med Ctr 1993; **Fac Appt:** Asst Prof Ped, Univ Wash

Pediatric Otolaryngology

New England

Cunningham, Michael J MD [PO] - **Spec Exp:** Head & Neck Tumors; Sinus Disorders; Hemangiomas; Vascular Malformations; **Hospital:** Children's Hospital - Boston; **Address:** Boston Chldn's Hosp, Dept Otolaryngology, 333 Longwood Ave Fl 3, Boston, MA 02115; **Phone:** 617-355-6460; **Board Cert:** Otolaryngology 1988; **Med School:** Univ Rochester 1981; **Resid:** Pediatrics, Mass Genl Hosp 1983; Otolaryngology, Univ Pittsburgh Eye & Ear Hosp 1988; **Fellow:** Pediatric Otolaryngology, Mass Eye & Ear Infirm 1989; **Fac Appt:** Prof Oto, Harvard Med Sch

McGill, Trevor J MD [PO] - **Spec Exp:** Head & Neck Tumors; Cholesteatoma; Lymphatic Malformations-Head & Neck; Hemangiomas; **Hospital:** Children's Hospital - Boston; **Address:** Boston Chldn's Hosp, Dept Otolaryngology, 333 Longwood Ave Fl 3, Boston, MA 02115; **Phone:** 617-355-6460; **Board Cert:** Otolaryngology 1988; **Med School:** Ireland 1967; **Resid:** Otolaryngology, Royal Natl Throat Nose & Ear Hosp 1974; **Fellow:** Otolaryngology, Mass Eye & Ear Infirm 1976; **Fac Appt:** Prof Oto, Harvard Med Sch

Poe, Dennis S MD [PO] - **Spec Exp:** Cochlear Implants; Neuro-Otology; Ear Disorders/Surgery; **Hospital:** Children's Hospital - Boston; **Address:** Boston Chldn's Hosp, Dept Otolaryngology, 333 Longwood Ave Fl 3, Boston, MA 02115-5724; **Phone:** 617-355-3794; **Board Cert:** Otolaryngology 1987; Neurotology 2004; **Med School:** SUNY Upstate Med Univ 1982; **Resid:** Surgery, Univ Mass Med Ctr 1983; Otolaryngology, Univ Chicago Hosps 1987; **Fellow:** Otology & Neurotology, Otology Group 1988; **Fac Appt:** Assoc Prof Oto, Harvard Med Sch

Mid Atlantic

April, Max M MD [PO] - **Spec Exp:** Sinus Disorders; Neck Masses; Laryngeal Disorders; Sleep Apnea; **Hospital:** NYU Langone Med Ctr (page 68); **Address:** NYU ENT Center, 240 E 38th St, Fl 14, New York, NY 10016; **Phone:** 646-501-7890; **Board Cert:** Otolaryngology 1990; **Med School:** Boston Univ 1985; **Resid:** Otolaryngology, Boston Univ Med Ctr 1990; **Fellow:** Pediatric Otolaryngology, Johns Hopkins 1991; **Fac Appt:** Clin Prof Oto, NYU Sch Med

Casselbrant, Margaretha L MD/PhD [PO] - **Spec Exp:** Ear Infections; **Hospital:** Chldns Hosp of Pittsburgh - UPMC; **Address:** Chldns Hosp, Ped Otolaryngology Dept, 4401 Penn Ave Fl 3, Pittsburgh, PA 15224; **Phone:** 412-692-5460; **Board Cert:** Otolaryngology 1992; **Med School:** Sweden 1973; **Resid:** Otolaryngology, Malmo Genl Hosp-Univ Lund 1978; **Fellow:** Pediatric Otolaryngology, UPMC 1982; **Fac Appt:** Prof Oto, Univ Pittsburgh

Dolitsky, Jay N MD [PO] - **Spec Exp:** Ear Infections; Neck Masses; Tonsil/Adenoid Disorders; Sleep Disorders; **Hospital:** New York Eye & Ear Infirm (page 64); **Address:** ENT & Allergy Assocs, 261 Fifth Ave Fl 9 - Ste 901, MS 10016, New York, NY 10016; **Phone:** 212-679-3499; **Board Cert:** Otolaryngology 1990; **Med School:** SUNY Downstate 1984; **Resid:** Surgery, NYU/Bellevue Hosp 1987; Otolaryngology, Manhattan EET Hosp 1990; **Fellow:** Pediatric Otolaryngology, Children's Hosp 1992; **Fac Appt:** Assoc Clin Prof, NY Med Coll

Goldsmith, Ari J MD [PO] - **Spec Exp:** Voice Disorders; Airway Disorders; Hearing Loss; Sleep Apnea; **Hospital:** Maimonides Med Ctr (page 60); **Address:** 921 49th St, Brooklyn, NY 11219; **Phone:** 718-283-6260 x2; **Board Cert:** Otolaryngology 1994; **Med School:** Albert Einstein Coll Med 1988; **Resid:** Otolaryngology, LI Jewish Hosp 1993; **Fellow:** Pediatric Otolaryngology, Chldns Hosp 1994; **Fac Appt:** Assoc Prof Oto, SUNY Hlth Sci Ctr

Haddad Jr, Joseph MD [PO] - **Spec Exp:** Ear Infections; Sinus Disorders; Cleft Palate/Lip; **Hospital:** Morgan Stanley Children's Hosp of NY-Presby, NY (page 65); **Address:** Morgan Stanley Chldns Hosp of NY-Presby, 3959 Broadway, Ste 501N, New York, NY 10032-1559; **Phone:** 212-305-8933; **Board Cert:** Otolaryngology 1988; **Med School:** NYU Sch Med 1983; **Resid:** Surgery, Columbia-Presby Hosp 1985; Otolaryngology, Columbia-Presby Hosp 1988; **Fellow:** Pediatric Otolaryngology, Chldns Hosp 1990; **Fac Appt:** Prof Oto, Columbia P&S

Harley, Earl H MD [PO] - **Hospital:** MedStar Georgetown Univ Hosp; **Address:** Georgetown Univ Hosp, 3800 Reservoir Rd NW, Gorman Bldg Fl 1, Washington, DC 20007; **Phone:** 202-444-8186; **Board Cert:** Otolaryngology 1984; **Med School:** Howard Univ 1971; **Resid:** Pediatrics, Naval Med Ctr 1973; Otolaryngology, Oakland Naval Hosp 1984; **Fellow:** Pediatric Otolaryngology, Chldns Natl Med Ctr 1988; Pediatric Otolaryngology, Mass Eye & Ear Infirmary 1989; **Fac Appt:** Assoc Prof Oto, Georgetown Univ

Kazahaya, Ken MD [PO] - **Spec Exp:** Cochlear Implants; Skull Base Surgery; Otology; Thyroid Surgery; **Hospital:** Chldns Hosp of Philadelphia; **Address:** Chldns Hosp, Ped Otolaryngology Dept, 3400 Civic Center Blvd Wood Bldg Fl 1, Philadelphia, PA 19104; **Phone:** 215-590-3440; **Board Cert:** Otolaryngology 1999; **Med School:** Univ Pennsylvania 1993; **Resid:** Otolaryngology, Hosp Univ Penn 1998; **Fellow:** Pediatric Otolaryngology, Chldns Hosp 2000; **Fac Appt:** Assoc Clin Prof Oto, Univ Pennsylvania

O'Reilly, Robert C MD [PO] - **Spec Exp:** Cochlear Implants; Balance Disorders; Hearing Loss; Neuro-Otology; **Hospital:** Nemours/Alfred I. duPont Hosp for Chldn; **Address:** 1600 Rockland Rd, Wilmington, DE 19803; **Phone:** 302-651-4200; **Board Cert:** Otolaryngology 1996; **Med School:** Thomas Jefferson Univ 1990; **Resid:** Otolaryngology, Thomas Jefferson Univ Hosp 1994; **Fellow:** Neurotology, Univ Pittsburgh 1996; **Fac Appt:** Assoc Prof Oto, Thomas Jefferson Univ

Rosenfeld, Richard M MD [PO] - **Spec Exp:** Sinus Disorders/Surgery; Head & Neck Surgery; Ear Disorders/Surgery; **Hospital:** SUNY Downstate Med Ctr (Univ Hosp Brooklyn); **Address:** Univ Otolaryngologists, 134 Atlantic Ave, Brooklyn, NY 11201; **Phone:** 718-780-1498; **Board Cert:** Otolaryngology 1989; **Med School:** SUNY Buffalo 1984; **Resid:** Surgery, Mount Sinai Med Ctr 1986; Otolaryngology, Mount Sinai Med Ctr 1989; **Fellow:** Pediatric Otolaryngology, Chldn's Hosp 1991; **Fac Appt:** Prof Oto, SUNY Downstate

Tunkel, David E MD [PO] - **Spec Exp:** Laryngeal Disorders; Otology; Head & Neck Surgery; **Hospital:** Johns Hopkins Hosp (page 59), Greater Baltimore Med Ctr; **Address:** 601 N Caroline St, rm 6161, Baltimore, MD 21287; **Phone:** 410-955-1559; **Board Cert:** Otolaryngology 1990; **Med School:** Johns Hopkins Univ 1984; **Resid:** Surgery, Johns Hopkins Hosp 1986; Otolaryngology, Johns Hopkins Hosp 1990; **Fellow:** Pediatric Otolaryngology, Chldns Natl Med Ctr 1991; **Fac Appt:** Assoc Prof Oto, Johns Hopkins Univ

Ward, Robert F MD [PO] - **Spec Exp:** Airway Disorders; Sinus Disorders/Surgery; Choanal Atresia; Cleft Palate/Lip; **Hospital:** NYU Langone Med Ctr (page 68); **Address:** NYU Langone Med Ctr-Dept Ped Otolaryngology, 240 E 38th St Fl 14, New York, NY 10016; **Phone:** 646-501-7890; **Board Cert:** Otolaryngology 1986; **Med School:** Cornell Univ-Weill Med Coll 1981; **Resid:** Surgery, NY Hosp 1983; Otolaryngology, NY Hosp 1986; **Fellow:** Pediatric Otolaryngology, Chldns Hosp 1987; **Fac Appt:** Clin Prof Ped, NYU Sch Med

Southeast

Darrow, David H MD/DDS [PO] - **Spec Exp:** Airway Disorders; Sinus Disorders; Otology; Neck Masses; **Hospital:** Chldns Hosp of King's Daughters; **Address:** Chldns Hosp of Kings Daughters, Div Otolaryngology, 601 Childrens Lane, Norfolk, VA 23507; **Phone:** 757-668-9327; **Board Cert:** Otolaryngology 1994; **Med School:** Duke Univ 1987; **Resid:** Otolaryngology, UCSD Med Ctr 1993; **Fellow:** Pediatric Otolaryngology, Chldns Meml Hosp 1994; **Fac Appt:** Assoc Prof Oto, Eastern VA Med Sch

Drake, Amelia F MD [PO] - **Spec Exp:** Head & Neck Surgery; **Hospital:** NC Memorial Hosp - UNC; **Address:** 170 Manning Drive, Box 7070, Physicians Office Bldg, Rm G116, Chapel Hill, NC 27599-7070; **Phone:** 919-966-3342; **Board Cert:** Otolaryngology 1987; **Med School:** Univ NC Sch Med 1981; **Resid:** Otolaryngology, Univ Michigan Hosps 1986; **Fac Appt:** Prof Oto, Univ NC Sch Med

Eavey, Roland D MD [PO] - **Spec Exp:** Ear Reconstruction/Microtia; Ear Disorders/Surgery; Otology; Hearing Loss; **Hospital:** Vanderbilt Univ Med Ctr; **Address:** Vanderbilt Pediatric Otolaryngology, 2200 Childrens Way, Doctors Office Tower Fl 7, Nashville, TN 37232; **Phone:** 615-936-8176; **Board Cert:** Otolaryngology 1981; Pediatrics 1982; **Med School:** Univ Pennsylvania 1975; **Resid:** Pediatrics, Chldns Hosp 1977; Surgery, Kaiser Fdn Hosp 1978; **Fellow:** Otolaryngology, Mass EE Infirm 1981; **Fac Appt:** Prof Oto, Vanderbilt Univ

Midwest

Arjmand, Ellis M MD/PhD [PO] - **Spec Exp:** Hearing Loss; Cochlear Implants; Sinus Disorders; **Hospital:** Cincinnati Chldns Hosp Med Ctr; **Address:** Cinncinatti Chldns Hosp-Otolaryngology, 3333 Burnet Ave, Fl C3, ML 2018, Cincinnati, OH 45229; **Phone:** 513-636-4355; **Board Cert:** Otolaryngology 1994; **Med School:** Northwestern Univ 1986; **Resid:** Otolaryngology, Barnes-Jewish Hosp 1993; **Fellow:** Pediatric Otolaryngology, St Louis Chldns Hosp 1994; **Fac Appt:** Prof Oto, Univ Cincinnati

Arnold, James E MD [PO] - **Spec Exp:** Airway Disorders; Otology; Ear Tumors; **Hospital:** UH Rainbow Babies & Chldns Hosp, UH Case Med Ctr; **Address:** 11100 Euclid Ave, Lakeside Bldg Fl 4 - Ste 4500, Cleveland, OH 44106-5045; **Phone:** 216-844-5031; **Board Cert:** Otolaryngology 1982; **Med School:** Univ Tex, San Antonio 1977; **Resid:** Otolaryngology, Fitzsimons Army Med Ctr 1982; **Fellow:** Pediatric Otolaryngology, Chldns Hosp 1987; **Fac Appt:** Prof Oto, Case West Res Univ

Baroody, Fuad MD [PO] - **Spec Exp:** Ear Infections; Sinus Disorders; Airway Disorders; Sleep Disorders/Apnea; **Hospital:** Univ Chicago Med-Comer Chldn's Hosp, Univ of Chicago Med; **Address:** Univ Chicago Comer Chldns Hosp, Dept Oto, 5758 S Maryland Ave, MC 1035, Chicago, IL 60637; **Phone:** 773-702-4790; **Board Cert:** Otolaryngology 2005; **Med School:** Lebanon 1984; **Resid:** Otolaryngology, Amer Univ Beirut Med Ctr 1988; **Fellow:** Otolaryngology, Johns Hopkins Hosp 1991; Pediatric Otolaryngology, Johns Hopkins Hosp 1992; **Fac Appt:** Prof Oto, Univ Chicago-Pritzker Sch Med

Cotton, Robin MD [PO] - **Spec Exp:** Tracheal Surgery; Head & Neck Surgery; Airway Reconstruction; **Hospital:** Cincinnati Chldns Hosp Med Ctr; **Address:** Cincinnati Chldns Hosp-Otolaryngology, 3333 Burnet Ave Fl C3, ML 2018, Cincinnati, OH 45229; **Phone:** 513-636-4355; **Board Cert:** Otolaryngology 1972; **Med School:** England, UK 1965; **Resid:** Otolaryngology, Univ Birmingham 1968; Otolaryngology, Univ Toronto Med Ctr 1972; **Fellow:** Head and Neck Surgery, Univ Cincinnati Med Ctr 1973; **Fac Appt:** Prof Oto, Univ Cincinnati

Holinger, Lauren D MD [PO] - **Spec Exp:** Airway Disorders; Swallowing Disorders; Cough-Chronic; Voice Disorders; **Hospital:** Lurie Chldn's Hosp-Chicago; **Address:** Lurie Chldn's Hosp, Dept Otolaryngology, 225 E Chicago Ave, Box 25, Chicago, IL 60611; **Phone:** 312-227-6805; **Board Cert:** Otolaryngology 1975; **Med School:** Ros Franklin Univ/Chicago Med Sch 1971; **Resid:** Surgery, Univ Colorado Affil Hosp 1972; Otolaryngology, Univ Colorado Affil Hosp 1975; **Fellow:** Pediatric Otolaryngology, Chldns Meml Hosp 1976; **Fac Appt:** Prof Oto, Northwestern Univ

Katz, Robert L MD [PO] - **Spec Exp:** Ear Infections; Sinus Disorders/Surgery; Hearing Loss; **Hospital:** Cleveland Clin (page 55); **Address:** 2550 SOM Ctr Rd, North Bldg, Willoughby Hills, OH 44094; **Phone:** 440-943-2500; **Board Cert:** Otolaryngology 1968; **Med School:** Case West Res Univ 1963; **Resid:** Surgery, Mount Sinai Hosp 1965; Otolaryngology, Mass Eye & Ear Infirm/Chldns Hosp 1968; **Fac Appt:** Clin Prof Oto, Cleveland Cl Coll Med/Case West Res

Miller, Robert Paul MD [PO] - **Spec Exp:** Ear Disorders/Surgery; Airway Disorders; Sinus Disorders; Tonsil/Adenoid Disorders; **Hospital:** Adv Luth Genl Hosp, Lurie Chldn's Hosp-Chicago; **Address:** 8780 W Golf Rd, Ste 200, Niles, IL 60714; **Phone:** 847-674-5585; **Board Cert:** Otolaryngology 1978; **Med School:** Loyola Univ-Stritch Sch Med 1974; **Resid:** Otolaryngology, Univ Illinois Hosps 1978; **Fellow:** Pediatric Otolaryngology, Chldns Hosp Med Ctr 1987; **Fac Appt:** Asst Clin Prof Oto, Univ IL Coll Med

Myer III, Charles M MD [PO] - **Spec Exp:** Airway Disorders; Head & Neck Tumors; Neck Masses; **Hospital:** Cincinnati Chldns Hosp Med Ctr, Univ Cincinnati Med Ctr; **Address:** Cincinnati Chldn's Hosp-Otolaryngology, 3333 Burnet Ave, Fl C3, ML 2018, Cincinnati, OH 45229; **Phone:** 513-636-4355; **Board Cert:** Otolaryngology 1984; **Med School:** UAB Sch Med 1978; **Resid:** Otolaryngology, Univ Cincinnati Med Ctr 1984; **Fellow:** Pediatric Otolaryngology, Chldns Hosp 1985; **Fac Appt:** Prof Oto, Univ Cincinnati

Thompson, Dana M MD [PO] - **Spec Exp:** Swallowing Disorders; Tracheal Reconstruction; Laryngeal & Voice Disorders; **Hospital:** Lurie Chldn's Hosp-Chicago; **Address:** Lurie Chldn's Hosp-Otolaryngology, 225 E Chicago Ave, Box 25, Chicago, IL 60611; **Phone:** 312-227-6230; **Board Cert:** Otolaryngology 1997; **Med School:** Univ MO-Kansas City 1991; **Resid:** Otolaryngology, Mayo Clinic 1996; **Fellow:** Research, Mayo Clinic 1997; Pediatric Otolaryngology, Chldns Hosp Med Ctr 1999; **Fac Appt:** Prof Oto, Northwestern Univ-Feinberg Sch Med

Great Plains and Mountains

Chan, Kenny H MD [PO] - **Spec Exp:** Ear Infections; Sinusitis; Hearing Disorders; **Hospital:** Chldn's Hosp - Aurora (CO), Parker Adventist Hosp; **Address:** Chldns Hosp, ENT Dept, 13123 E 16th Ave, Box B455, Aurora, CO 80045; **Phone:** 720-777-8501; **Board Cert:** Otolaryngology 1984; **Med School:** Loma Linda Univ 1977; **Resid:** Otolaryngology, Loma Linda Univ Hosp 1983; **Fellow:** Pediatric Otolaryngology, Chldns Hosp 1987; **Fac Appt:** Prof Oto, Univ Colorado

Lusk, Rodney P MD [PO] - **Spec Exp:** Cochlear Implants; Sinusitis; Sinus Disorders/Surgery; Sleep Disorders/Apnea; **Hospital:** Boys Town Natl Rsch Hosp, Children's Hosp - Omaha; **Address:** Boystown National Research Hosp, 555 N 30th St, Omaha, NE 68131; **Phone:** 402-498-6502; **Board Cert:** Otolaryngology 1982; **Med School:** Univ MO-Columbia Sch Med 1977; **Resid:** Head and Neck Surgery, Univ Iowa Hosp & Clinics 1982; **Fellow:** Pediatric Otolaryngology, Chldn's Hosp 1983

Southwest

Bower, Charles MD [PO] - **Spec Exp:** Airway Disorders; Sleep Disorders/Apnea; Sinus Disorders/Surgery; **Hospital:** Arkansas Chldns Hosp; **Address:** Arkansas Chldns Hosp, Dept Ped Oto, 1 Children's Way, Little Rock, AR 72202-3510; **Phone:** 501-364-1047; **Board Cert:** Otolaryngology 1990; **Med School:** Univ Ark 1985; **Resid:** Otolaryngology, Univ Ark Med Ctr 1991; **Fellow:** Pediatric Otolaryngology, Chldns Hosp 1992; **Fac Appt:** Assoc Prof Oto, Univ Ark

Duncan III, Newton O MD [PO] - **Spec Exp:** Sinus Disorders; Airway Disorders; Head & Neck Surgery; Cleft Palate/Lip; **Hospital:** Texas Chldns Hosp, Methodist Hosp - Houston; **Address:** Chldns ENT of Houston, 6550 Fannin St, Ste 2001, Smith Tower Office, Houston, TX 77030-2709; **Phone:** 713-796-2001; **Board Cert:** Otolaryngology 1986; **Med School:** Baylor Coll Med 1978; **Resid:** Surgery, Baylor Affil Hosp 1983; Otolaryngology, Baylor Affil Hosp 1986; **Fellow:** Pediatric Otolaryngology, Chldns Hosp 1991; Pediatric Otolaryngology, Royal Alexandra Hosp Chld 1992; **Fac Appt:** Asst Prof Oto, Baylor Coll Med

Friedman, Ellen M MD [PO] - **Spec Exp:** Airway Disorders; Lymphatic Malformations-Head & Neck; Neuro-Otology; **Hospital:** Texas Chldns Hosp, Methodist Hosp - Houston; **Address:** 6701 Fannin St, Ste 540, MC CC6102, Houston, TX 77030; **Phone:** 832-822-3250; **Board Cert:** Otolaryngology 1981; **Med School:** Albert Einstein Coll Med 1975; **Resid:** Surgery, Montefiore Hosp 1976; Otolaryngology, Washington Hosp Ctr 1980; **Fellow:** Pediatric Otolaryngology, Boston Chldns Hosp 1981; **Fac Appt:** Prof Oto, Baylor Coll Med

West Coast and Pacific

Crockett, Dennis M MD [PO] - **Spec Exp:** Head & Neck Cancer; Airway Disorders; **Hospital:** Mission Hosp-Mission Viejo, Saddleback Meml Med Ctr-San Clemente; **Address:** 26726 Crown Valley Pkwy, Ste 200, Mission Viejo, CA 92691; **Phone:** 949-364-4361; **Board Cert:** Otolaryngology 1985; **Med School:** USC-Keck School of Medicine 1979; **Resid:** Otolaryngology, LAC & USC Med Ctr 1984; **Fellow:** Pediatrics, Boston Chldns Hosp 1985; **Fac Appt:** Assoc Prof Oto, USC Sch Med

Inglis, Andrew MD [PO] - **Spec Exp:** Airway Disorders; Voice Disorders; **Hospital:** Seattle Chldns Hosp; **Address:** Children's Hospital & Medical Ctr, 4800 Sand Point Way NE, MS W6640, Seattle, WA 98105-0371; **Phone:** 206-987-2105; **Board Cert:** Otolaryngology 1987; **Med School:** Med Coll PA Hahnemann 1981; **Resid:** Surgery, Virginia Mason Hosp 1983; Otolaryngology, Univ Washington Hosps 1987; **Fellow:** Pediatric Otolaryngology, Royal Alexandria Hosp Chldn 1987; **Fac Appt:** Assoc Prof Oto, Univ Wash

Parikh, Sanjay R MD [PO] - **Spec Exp:** Airway Reconstruction; Sinus Disorders/Surgery; Vocal Cord Disorders; Hearing Disorders; **Hospital:** Seattle Chldns Hosp; **Address:** Seattle Children's Hosp, Div Pediatric Otolaryngology, 4800 Sand Point Way, NE, W-7729, Seattle, WA 98105; **Phone:** 206-987-2105; **Board Cert:** Otolaryngology 2000; **Med School:** Rush Med Coll 1994; **Resid:** Surgery, Harbor UCLA Med Ctr 1996; Otolaryngology, Univ Toronto 1999; **Fellow:** Pediatric Otolaryngology, Chldns Hosp 2001

Richardson, Mark A MD [PO] - **Spec Exp:** Sinus Disorders; Airway Disorders; **Hospital:** Doernbecher Chldns Hosp/OHSU; **Address:** 3181 SW Sam Jackson Park Rd, MC PV01, Portland, OR 97239; **Phone:** 503-494-5350; **Board Cert:** Otolaryngology 1979; **Med School:** Med Univ SC 1975; **Resid:** Otolaryngology, MUSC Med Ctr 1979; **Fellow:** Pediatric Otolaryngology, Chldns Hosp Med Ctr 1980; **Fac Appt:** Prof Oto, Oregon Hlth & Sci Univ

Rosbe, Kristina W MD [PO] - **Spec Exp:** Airway Disorders; Sinus Disorders/Surgery; Cochlear Implants; Neck Masses; **Hospital:** UCSF Med Ctr; **Address:** UCSF Med Ctr, Dept Otolaryngology, 2380 Sutter St, San Francisco, CA 94115; **Phone:** 415-353-2757; **Board Cert:** Otolaryngology 1999; **Med School:** Dartmouth Med Sch 1993; **Resid:** Surgery, Univ NC Sch Med Affil Hosp 1994; Otolaryngology, Univ NC Sch Med Affil Hosp 1998; **Fellow:** Pediatric Otolaryngology, Chldns Hosp 2000; **Fac Appt:** Assoc Prof Ped, UCSF

PEDIATRIC PULMONOLOGY

New England

Dorkin, Henry L MD [PPul] - **Spec Exp:** Cystic Fibrosis; Asthma; **Hospital:** Children's Hospital - Boston; **Address:** Boston Chldn's Hosp, Div Respiratory Diseases, 300 Longwood Ave, Box 343, Boston, MA 02111-1854; **Phone:** 617-355-1900; **Board Cert:** Pediatrics 1993; Pediatric Pulmonology 2010; **Med School:** Johns Hopkins Univ 1974; **Resid:** Pediatrics, Johns Hopkins Hosp 1977; **Fellow:** Pulmonary Disease, Chldn's Hosp 1980; **Fac Appt:** Assoc Prof Ped, Harvard Med Sch

Lapey, Allen MD [PPul] - **Spec Exp:** Cystic Fibrosis; Asthma; Food Allergy; **Hospital:** Mass Genl Hosp; **Address:** Mass Genl Hosp Cystic Fibrosis Ctr, 275 Cambridge St, Ste 530, Professional Office Bldg, Boston, MA 02114; **Phone:** 617-726-8707; **Board Cert:** Pediatrics 1972; Allergy & Immunology 1979; **Med School:** Univ Rochester 1966; **Resid:** Pediatrics, Chldns Hosp 1968; **Fellow:** Pediatric Pulmonology, Mass Genl Hosp 1972; Allergy & Immunology, Mass Genl Hosp 1972; **Fac Appt:** Asst Clin Prof Ped, Harvard Med Sch

Mid Atlantic

Borowitz, Drucy S MD [PPul] - **Spec Exp:** Cystic Fibrosis; Nutrition; Clinical Trials; **Hospital:** Women & Chldn's Hosp of Buffalo, The; **Address:** Women & Childrens Hospital, The Lung Center, 140 Hodge Ave, Buffalo, NY 14222; **Phone:** 716-878-7554; **Board Cert:** Pediatrics 1984; Pediatric Gastroenterology 2007; **Med School:** Cornell Univ 1979; **Resid:** Pediatrics, UCSF Med Ctr 1982; **Fellow:** Nutrition, UCSF 1983; **Fac Appt:** Clin Prof Ped, SUNY Buffalo

Dovey, Mark E MD [PPul] - **Spec Exp:** Cystic Fibrosis; Asthma; Chronic Lung Disease; **Hospital:** St. Christopher's Hosp for Chldn; **Address:** St Christopher's Hosp for Children, Div Pediatric Pulmonology, 3601 A St, Ste 2215, Philadelphia, PA 19134; **Phone:** 215-427-5183; **Board Cert:** Pediatrics 2008; Pediatric Pulmonology 2013; **Med School:** Duke Univ 1989; **Resid:** Pediatrics, Johns Hopkins Hosp 1992; **Fellow:** Pediatric Pulmonology, Childrens Hosp 1995; **Fac Appt:** Assoc Prof Ped, Drexel Univ Coll Med

Dozor, Allen J MD [PPul] - **Spec Exp:** Asthma; Cystic Fibrosis; **Hospital:** Westchester Med Ctr, Children's & Women's Phys.of Westchester; **Address:** CWPW, Pediatric Pulmonology Dept, 19 Bradhurst Ave, Ste 1400, Hawthorne, NY 10532; **Phone:** 914-493-7585; **Board Cert:** Pediatrics 1981; Pediatric Pulmonology 2010; **Med School:** Penn State Coll Med 1977; **Resid:** Pediatrics, St Vincents Hosp & Med Ctr 1980; **Fellow:** Pediatric Pulmonology, Chldns Hosp 1982; **Fac Appt:** Prof Ped, NY Med Coll

Kattan, Meyer MD [PPul] - **Spec Exp:** Asthma; Cystic Fibrosis; Chronic Lung Disease; **Hospital:** Morgan Stanley Children's Hosp of NY-Presby, NY (page 65), Englewood Hosp & Med Ctr; **Address:** Morgan Stanley Chldns Hosp of NY-Presby, 3959 Broadway, CHC 7-701, New York, NY 10032; **Phone:** 212-305-5122; **Board Cert:** Pediatrics 1980; Pediatric Pulmonology 2010; **Med School:** McGill Univ 1973; **Resid:** Pediatrics, Chldns Hosp 1975; Pediatrics, Hosp for Sick Chldn 1976; **Fellow:** Pulmonary Disease, Hosp for Sick Chldn 1978; **Fac Appt:** Prof Ped, Columbia P&S

Kurland, Geoffrey MD [PPul] - **Spec Exp:** Transplant Medicine-Lung; **Hospital:** Chldns Hosp of Pittsburgh - UPMC; **Address:** Chldns Hosp, Ped Pulmonology Dept, 4401 Penn Ave, Pittsburgh, PA 15224; **Phone:** 412-692-5630; **Board Cert:** Pediatrics 1978; Allergy & Immunology 1979; Pediatric Pulmonology 2010; **Med School:** Stanford Univ 1973; **Resid:** Pediatrics, Stanford Univ Hosp & Clins 1976; **Fellow:** Allergy & Immunology, Stanford Univ Hosp & Clins 1978; **Fac Appt:** Prof Ped, Univ Pittsburgh

Loughlin, Gerald M MD [PPul] - **Spec Exp:** Sleep Disorders/Apnea; Swallowing Disorders; Asthma & Chronic Lung Disease; Breathing Disorders; **Hospital:** NY-Presby/Weill Cornell Med Ctr, NY (page 65); **Address:** Cornell Med Coll, Dept Peds, 525 E 68th St, rm M-622, New York, NY 10021-4870; **Phone:** 646-962-3410; **Board Cert:** Pediatrics 1993; Pediatric Pulmonology 2010; **Med School:** Univ Rochester 1973; **Resid:** Pediatrics, Univ Ariz Med Ctr 1976; **Fellow:** Pediatric Pulmonology, Univ Ariz Med Ctr 1979; **Fac Appt:** Prof Ped, Cornell Univ-Weill Med Coll

Marcus, Carole L MD [PPul] - **Spec Exp:** Sleep Disorders/Apnea; **Hospital:** Chldns Hosp of Philadelphia; **Address:** Chldns Hosp, Ped Pulmonolgy Dept, 3400 Civic Center Blvd, Ste 9NW50, Philadelphia, PA 19104; **Phone:** 215-590-3749; **Board Cert:** Pediatric Pulmonology 2007; Sleep Medicine 2007; **Med School:** South Africa 1982; **Resid:** Pediatrics, LIJ Hosp 1986; **Fellow:** Pediatric Pulmonology, Chldns Hosp 1991; **Fac Appt:** Prof Ped, Univ Pennsylvania

McGrath-Morrow, Sharon A MD [PPul] - **Spec Exp:** Lung Injury-Neonatal; Bronchopulmonary Dysplasia; Ataxia Telangiectasia; Swallowing Disorders; **Hospital:** Johns Hopkins Hosp (page 59); **Address:** Johns Hopkins, Div Ped Pulmonology, Rubenstein Chldns Hlth Bldg, 200 N Wolfe St, Ste 3029, Baltimore, MD 21287; **Phone:** 410-955-2795; **Board Cert:** Pediatrics 2007; Pediatric Pulmonology 2007; **Med School:** Univ VA Sch Med 1985; **Resid:** Pediatrics, Johns Hopkins Hosp 1988; **Fellow:** Pulmonary Critical Care Medicine, Johns Hopkins Hosp 1992; **Fac Appt:** Assoc Prof Ped, Johns Hopkins Univ

Orenstein, David M MD [PPul] - **Spec Exp:** Cystic Fibrosis; **Hospital:** Chldns Hosp of Pittsburgh - UPMC; **Address:** Chldns Hosp, Ped Pulmonology Dept, 4401 Penn Ave, Pittsburgh, PA 15224; **Phone:** 412-692-5630; **Board Cert:** Pediatrics 1979; **Med School:** Case West Res Univ 1973; **Resid:** Pediatrics, Rainbow Babies & Chldns Hosp 1975; **Fellow:** Pediatric Pulmonology, Rainbow Babies & Chldns Hosp 1977; **Fac Appt:** Prof Ped, Univ Pittsburgh

Panitch, Howard B MD [PPul] - **Spec Exp:** Chronic Obstructive Lung Disease (COPD); Cystic Fibrosis; **Hospital:** Chldns Hosp of Philadelphia; **Address:** Chldns Hosp, Ped Pulmonology Dept, 3400 Civic Center Blvd, Ste 9NW50, Philadelphia, PA 19104; **Phone:** 215-590-3749; **Board Cert:** Pediatrics 1987; Pediatric Pulmonology 2011; **Med School:** Univ Pittsburgh 1982; **Resid:** Pediatrics, Chldns Hosp 1985; **Fellow:** Pediatric Pulmonology, St Christophers Hosp 1988; **Fac Appt:** Prof Ped, Univ Pennsylvania

Quittell, Lynne M MD [PPul] - **Spec Exp:** Cystic Fibrosis; Asthma; **Hospital:** Morgan Stanley Children's Hosp of NY-Presby, NY (page 65), NY-Presby/Columbia Univ Med Ctr, NY (page 65); **Address:** Morgan Stanley Children's Hosp of NY, 3959 Broadway, CHONY Bldg - Fl 7, New York, NY 10032; **Phone:** 212-305-5122; **Board Cert:** Pediatrics 1986; Pediatric Pulmonology 2011; **Med School:** Israel 1981; **Resid:** Pediatrics, Schneider Chldns Hosp 1984; **Fellow:** Pediatric Pulmonology, St Christopher's Hosp 1988

Tauber, Danna MD [PPul] - **Spec Exp:** Sleep Disorders; Cystic Fibrosis; **Hospital:** St. Christopher's Hosp for Chldn; **Address:** St Christophers Hosp, Ped Pulmonology, 3601 A St, Ste 2215, Phildelphia, PA 19134; **Phone:** 215-427-5183; **Board Cert:** Pediatric Pulmonology 2012; Sleep Medicine 2009; **Med School:** Tulane Univ 1997; **Resid:** Pediatrics, Montefiore Med Ctr 2000; **Fellow:** Pediatric Pulmonology, Chldns Hosp 2003; **Fac Appt:** Asst Prof Ped, Drexel Univ Coll Med

Zeitlin, Pamela L MD [PPul] - **Spec Exp:** Cystic Fibrosis; **Hospital:** Johns Hopkins Hosp (page 59), Mt Washington Ped Hosp; **Address:** Johns Hopkins-Ped Pulmonology Div, 200 N Wolfe St, rm 3051, Rubenstein Child Hlth Bldg, Baltimore, MD 21287; **Phone:** 410-955-2795; **Board Cert:** Pediatrics 1988; Pediatric Pulmonology 2007; **Med School:** Yale Univ 1983; **Resid:** Pediatrics, Johns Hopkins Hosp 1986; **Fellow:** Pediatric Pulmonology, Johns Hopkins Hosp 1989; **Fac Appt:** Prof Ped, Johns Hopkins Univ

Southeast

Rubin, Bruce Kalman MD [PPul] - **Spec Exp:** Asthma; Cystic Fibrosis; Cough-Chronic; Plastic Bronchitis; **Hospital:** Children's Hosp, Med Coll of VA Hosp; **Address:** Children's Hospital of Richmond at VCU, 1001 E Marshall St, Fl 2, Richmond, VA 23298; **Phone:** 804-828-2980; **Board Cert:** Pediatrics 1984; Pediatric Pulmonology 2011; **Med School:** Tulane Univ 1979; **Resid:** Pediatrics, Tulane Univ 1981; Pediatric Pulmonology, Hosp for Sick Children 1983; **Fellow:** Pediatric Pulmonary & Critical Care, Hosp for Sick Children 1983; **Fac Appt:** Prof Ped, Va Commonwealth Univ Sch Med

Sallent, Jorge A MD [PPul] - **Spec Exp:** Chronic Lung Disease of Infancy; Asthma & Chronic Lung Disease; Lung Injuries-RSV related; **Hospital:** St. Mary's Med Ctr - W Palm Bch, Palms - West Hosp; **Address:** Pediatric Respiratory Ctr, 500 Federal Hwy, Lake Park, FL 33403; **Phone:** 561-863-0105; **Board Cert:** Pediatrics 1984; Pediatric Pulmonology 2010; **Med School:** Dominican Republic 1978; **Resid:** Pediatrics, Orlando Regl Med Ctr 1983; **Fellow:** Pediatric Pulmonology, Shands at Univ FL 1986; **Fac Appt:** Asst Clin Prof Ped, Univ Fla Coll Med

Sherman, James MD [PPul] - **Spec Exp:** Asthma; Airway Disorders; Cough-Chronic; **Hospital:** Carilion Roanoke Meml Hosp; **Address:** 1906 Bellview Ave, Roanoke, VA 24013; **Phone:** 540-266-6012; **Board Cert:** Pediatrics 1981; Pediatric Pulmonology 2010; **Med School:** Univ S Fla Coll Med 1975; **Resid:** Pediatrics, SUNY Upstate Med Ctr 1977; Pediatrics, Tampa Genl Hosp- Univ So Florida 1978; **Fellow:** Pediatric Pulmonology, Rainbow Babies & Children's Hosp 1981; **Fac Appt:** Prof Ped, Univ Fla Coll Med

Midwest

Givan, Deborah C MD [PPul] - **Spec Exp:** Sleep Disorders/Apnea; Apnea in Infants; Asthma; Pulmonary Complications-Neurodisability; **Hospital:** Riley Hosp for Children; **Address:** Riley Hosp for Chldn-Ped Pulmonology, 702 Riley Hosp Drive, Ste ROC 4270, Indianapolis, IN 46202; **Phone:** 317-274-7208; **Board Cert:** Pediatrics 1982; Pediatric Pulmonology 2010; Sleep Medicine 2011; **Med School:** Indiana Univ 1977; **Resid:** Pediatrics, Methodist Hosp 1980; **Fellow:** Pediatric Pulmonology, Riley Chldns Hosp 1981; Pediatric Pulmonology, Texas Chldns Hosp 1982; **Fac Appt:** Clin Prof Ped, Indiana Univ

Green, Thomas P MD [PPul] - **Spec Exp:** Respiratory Failure; Breathing Disorders; **Hospital:** Lurie Chldn's Hosp-Chicago, Northwestern Meml Hosp; **Address:** Lurie Chldn's Hosp, Dept Pulm/Crit Care, 225 E Chicago Ave, Box 43, Chicago, IL 60611; **Phone:** 312-227-6260; **Board Cert:** Pediatrics 1992; Pediatric Pulmonology 2009; Pediatric Critical Care Medicine 2010; **Med School:** Stanford Univ 1974; **Resid:** Pediatrics, Univ MN Med Ctr 1977; **Fellow:** Pharmacology, Univ MN Med Ctr 1979; Pediatric Pulmonology, Univ MN Med Ctr 1994; **Fac Appt:** Prof Ped, Northwestern Univ

Kemp, James S MD [PPul] - **Spec Exp:** Sudden Infant Death Syndrome (SIDS); Breathing Disorders; Sleep Disorders; **Hospital:** St. Louis Chldns Hosp; **Address:** Wash Univ, Div Pulm Med, 1 Childrens Pl, Ste 5S30, St Louis, MO 63110; **Phone:** 314-454-2694; **Board Cert:** Pediatrics 1981; Sleep Medicine 2007; Pediatric Pulmonology 2010; **Med School:** Creighton Univ 1976; **Resid:** Pediatrics, Cardinal Glennon Chldns Hosp 1978; Pediatrics, Baylor Univ 1979; **Fellow:** Pediatric Pulmonology, Texas Chldns Hosp 1988; **Fac Appt:** Assoc Prof Ped, Washington Univ, St Louis

Kim, Young-Jee MD [PPul] - **Spec Exp:** Asthma; Rare Lung Disease-Pediatric; Pulmonary Complications-Sickle Cell Dis; Pulmonary Complications-Cancer Therapy; **Hospital:** Riley Hosp for Children; **Address:** Riley Hosp for Chldn-Ped Pulmonology, 705 Riley Hospital Drive, Ste ROC 4270, Indianapolis, IN 46202-5128; **Phone:** 317-274-7208; **Board Cert:** Pediatric Pulmonology 2013; **Med School:** South Korea 1982; **Resid:** Pediatrics, Duke Univ Med Ctr 1995; **Fellow:** Pediatric Pulmonology, Yale Univ Med Sch 1991; Pediatric Pulmonology, Riley Hosp Chldn 1998; **Fac Appt:** Assoc Clin Prof Ped, Indiana Univ

Konstan, Michael W MD [PPul] - **Spec Exp:** Cystic Fibrosis; **Hospital:** UH Rainbow Babies & Chldns Hosp, UH Case Med Ctr; **Address:** Dept Pediatrics-Pulmonary, 11100 Euclid Ave, MS RBC6007, Cleveland, OH 44106; **Phone:** 216-844-1997; **Board Cert:** Pediatrics 1986; Pediatric Pulmonology 2011; **Med School:** Case West Res Univ 1982; **Resid:** Pediatrics, Chldns Hosp 1985; **Fellow:** Pediatric Pulmonology, Rainbow Babies & Chldns Hosp 1988; **Fac Appt:** Prof Ped, Case West Res Univ

Kurachek, Stephen C MD [PPul] - **Spec Exp:** Critical Care; Asthma; **Hospital:** Children's Hosps & Clinics of Minnesota; **Address:** 2530 Chicago Ave S, Ste 400, Minneapolis, MN 55404; **Phone:** 612-813-3300; **Board Cert:** Pediatrics 1985; Pediatric Critical Care Medicine 2010; Pediatric Pulmonology 2011; **Med School:** Univ Miami Sch Med 1978; **Resid:** Pediatrics, Univ Hosp 1981; **Fellow:** Pulmonary Disease, Boston Chldns Hosp 1984; **Fac Appt:** Asst Clin Prof Ped, Univ Minn

McColley, Susanna A MD [PPul] - **Spec Exp:** Cystic Fibrosis; Asthma; Cough-Chronic; **Hospital:** Lurie Chldn's Hosp-Chicago; **Address:** Lurie Chldn's Hosp, 225 E Chicago Ave, Box 43, Chicago, IL 60611; **Phone:** 312-227-6260; **Board Cert:** Pediatric Pulmonology 2007; **Med School:** Northwestern Univ 1985; **Resid:** Pediatrics, Johns Hopkins Hosp 1989; **Fellow:** Pediatric Pulmonology, Johns Hopkins Hosp 1992; **Fac Appt:** Prof Ped, Northwestern Univ

McCoy, Karen S MD [PPul] - **Spec Exp:** Cystic Fibrosis; Asthma; **Hospital:** Nationwide Chldn's Hosp; **Address:** Nationwide Chldn's Hosp, Section Pulmonary Med, 555 S 18th St, Columbus, OH 43205; **Phone:** 614-722-4766; **Board Cert:** Pediatrics 1991; Pediatric Pulmonology 2010; **Med School:** Univ NC Sch Med 1975; **Resid:** Pediatrics, NC Meml Hosp 1979; **Fellow:** Pulmonary Disease, Arizona Hlth Scis Ctr 1982; **Fac Appt:** Prof Ped, Ohio State Univ

Great Plains and Mountains

Fan, Leland Lane MD [PPul] - **Spec Exp:** Interstitial Lung Disease; Asthma; **Hospital:** Chldn's Hosp - Aurora (CO); **Address:** Chldns Hosp, Pulmonary Clin, 13123 E 16th Ave, Box B395, Aurora, CO 80045; **Phone:** 720-777-6181; **Board Cert:** Pediatrics 1978; Pediatric Pulmonology 2010; **Med School:** Baylor Coll Med 1973; **Resid:** Pediatrics, UCSF Med Ctr 1975; Pediatrics, Univ CO Hosp 1976; **Fellow:** Pediatric Pulmonary & Critical Care, Univ CO Hosp 1978; **Fac Appt:** Prof Ped, Univ Colorado

Southwest

Morgan, Wayne J MD [PPul] - **Spec Exp:** Cystic Fibrosis; Asthma; **Hospital:** Univ Arizona Med Ctr-Univ Campus, Tucson Med Ctr; **Address:** Univ Arizona Hlth Sci Ctr, Div Pediatric Pulmonology, 1501 N Campbell Ave, Tucson, AZ 85724; **Phone:** 520-626-7780; **Board Cert:** Pediatrics 1982; Pediatric Pulmonology 2010; **Med School:** McGill Univ 1976; **Resid:** Pediatrics, Montreal Chldns Hosp 1980; **Fellow:** Pediatric Pulmonology, Univ Ariz 1982; **Fac Appt:** Prof Ped, Univ Ariz Coll Med

Warren, Robert H MD [PPul] - **Spec Exp:** Pulmonary Complications-Neurodisability; Pulmonary Rehabilitation; Ventilation Management-Long Term; **Hospital:** Arkansas Chldns Hosp; **Address:** Arkansas Chldns Hosp, Pulmonary Med, 1 Children's Way, Slot 512-17, Little Rock, AR 72202; **Phone:** 501-364-1006; **Board Cert:** Pediatrics 1973; **Med School:** Univ Ark 1967; **Resid:** Pediatrics, LSU Med Ctr 1971; **Fellow:** Pediatric Pulmonology, Tulane Univ Sch Med 1974; Pediatric Pulmonary & Critical Care, Children's Meml Hosp 1974; **Fac Appt:** Assoc Prof Ped, Univ Ark

West Coast and Pacific

Cooper, Dan M MD [PPul] - **Hospital:** Chldns Hosp Orange Co; **Address:** CHOC Chldns Hosp, 1201 W La Veta Ave, Bldg C, Orange, CA 92868; **Phone:** 714-532-7983; **Board Cert:** Pediatrics 1980; Pediatric Pulmonology 2009; **Med School:** UCSF 1974; **Resid:** Internal Medicine, Hadassah Hosp; Pediatrics, Bellevue Hosp Ctr 1980; **Fellow:** Pediatric Pulmonology, NY-Presby/Columbia Univ Med Ctr 1994; **Fac Appt:** Prof Ped, UC Irvine

Gibson, Ronald MD/PhD [PPul] - **Spec Exp:** Pulmonary Infections; Sleep Disorders; Cystic Fibrosis; Asthma; **Hospital:** Seattle Chldns Hosp; **Address:** Seattle Children's Hosp, 4800 Sand Point Way NE, Ste A-5937, Seattle, WA 98105; **Phone:** 206-987-2174; **Board Cert:** Pediatrics 1988; Pediatric Pulmonology 2007; **Med School:** Washington Univ, St Louis 1982; **Resid:** Pediatrics, Univ Washington Med Ctr 1985; **Fellow:** Pediatric Pulmonology, Univ Washington Med Ctr 1988; **Fac Appt:** Assoc Prof Ped, Univ Wash

Keens, Thomas G MD [PPul] - **Spec Exp:** Sudden Infant Death Syndrome (SIDS); Breathing Disorders; **Hospital:** Chldns Hosp - Los Angeles; **Address:** Div Ped Pulmonology, 4650 W Sunset Blvd, Ste 83, Los Angeles, CA 90027-6062; **Phone:** 323-361-2101; **Board Cert:** Pediatrics 1978; Neonatal-Perinatal Medicine 1983; Pediatric Pulmonology 2010; **Med School:** UCSD 1972; **Resid:** Pediatrics, Chldns Hosp 1975; **Fellow:** Pediatric Pulmonology, Hosp Sick Chldn 1977; **Fac Appt:** Prof Ped, USC Sch Med

Nielson, Dennis W MD/PhD [PPul] - **Spec Exp:** Cystic Fibrosis; Bronchopulmonary Dysplasia; **Hospital:** UCSF Med Ctr; **Address:** Division of Pediatric Pulmonary Medicine, 521 Parnassus Ave, rm C344, San Francisco, CA 94143; **Phone:** 415-476-2072; **Board Cert:** Pediatrics 1986; Pediatric Pulmonology 2010; **Med School:** Univ Utah 1976; **Resid:** Pediatrics, UCSF Med Ctr 1978; **Fellow:** Pediatric Pulmonology, UCSF Med Ctr 1981; **Fac Appt:** Prof Ped, UCSF

Ramsey, Bonnie W MD [PPul] - **Spec Exp:** Cystic Fibrosis; **Hospital:** Seattle Chldns Hosp; **Address:** 4800 Sand Point Way NE, Ste A-5937, Seattle, WA 98105; **Phone:** 206-987-2174; **Board Cert:** Pediatrics 1981; Pediatric Pulmonology 2007; **Med School:** Harvard Med Sch 1976; **Resid:** Pediatrics, Chldns Hosp 1978; Pediatrics, Chldns Hosp 1979; **Fellow:** Pediatric Critical Care Medicine, Chldns Hosp 1981; **Fac Appt:** Prof Ped, Univ Wash

Redding, Gregory MD [PPul] - **Spec Exp:** Chest Wall Deformities; Interstitial Lung Disease; Thoracic Insufficiency Syndrome; Ventilation Management-Long Term; **Hospital:** Seattle Chldns Hosp; **Address:** Seattle Children's Hospital, 4800 Sand Point Way NE, rm O.C.7.721, Seattle, WA 98105; **Phone:** 206-987-2174; **Board Cert:** Pediatrics 1992; Pediatric Pulmonology 2010; **Med School:** Stanford Univ 1974; **Resid:** Pediatrics, Harbor-UCLA Affil Hosps 1977; **Fellow:** Pediatric Pulmonology, Univ Colo Affil Hosps 1979; **Fac Appt:** Prof Ped, Univ Wash

Wall, Michael A MD [PPul] - **Spec Exp:** Cystic Fibrosis; Asthma; Pneumonia; **Hospital:** Doernbecher Chldns Hosp/OHSU, OR Hlth & Sci Univ; **Address:** OHSU - Dept Ped Pulmonolgy, 707 SW Campus Drive, Portland, OR 97239; **Phone:** 503-494-8023; **Board Cert:** Pediatrics 1992; Pediatric Pulmonology 2010; **Med School:** Univ NC Sch Med 1973; **Resid:** Pediatrics, Mass Genl Hosp 1976; **Fellow:** Pulmonary Disease, Chldns Hosp 1978; **Fac Appt:** Prof Ped, Oregon Hlth & Sci Univ

Pediatric Rheumatology

New England

McCarthy, Paul L MD [PRhu] - **Spec Exp:** Lupus/SLE; Juvenile Arthritis; Dermatomyositis; Vasculitis; **Hospital:** Yale-New Haven Hosp; **Address:** Yale New Haven Hosp-Ped Primary Care Ctr, 789 Howard Ave, New Haven, CT 06519; **Phone:** 203-688-2475; **Board Cert:** Pediatrics 1974; Pediatric Rheumatology 2007; **Med School:** Georgetown Univ 1969; **Resid:** Pediatrics, Chldns Hosp 1972; **Fellow:** Ambulatory Pediatrics, Chldns Hosp 1974; **Fac Appt:** Prof Ped, Yale Univ

Mid Atlantic

Goldsmith, Donald P MD [PRhu] - **Spec Exp:** Juvenile Arthritis; Multisystem Inflammatory Disease; **Hospital:** St. Christopher's Hosp for Chldn; **Address:** St Christophers Hosp, Ped Rheumatology, 3601 A St, Philadelphia, PA 19134; **Phone:** 215-427-5051; **Board Cert:** Pediatrics 1974; Allergy & Immunology 1975; Pediatric Rheumatology 2007; **Med School:** Univ VT Coll Med 1967; **Resid:** Pediatrics, St Christophers Hosp for Chldn 1973; **Fellow:** Allergy Immunology & Rheumatology, St Christophers Hosp for Chldn 1975; **Fac Appt:** Prof Ped, Drexel Univ Coll Med

Haines, Kathleen A MD [PRhu] - **Spec Exp:** Juvenile Arthritis; Lupus/SLE; Immune Deficiency; Scleroderma; **Hospital:** Hackensack Univ Med Ctr, NYU Langone Med Ctr (page 68); **Address:** WFAN Imus Bldg, 30 Prospect Ave, Fl 3, Hackensack, NJ 07601; **Phone:** 551-996-5306; **Board Cert:** Pediatrics 1980; Allergy & Immunology 1981; Pediatric Rheumatology 2007; **Med School:** Albert Einstein Coll Med 1975; **Resid:** Pediatrics, New York Hosp 1977; **Fellow:** Allergy & Immunology, New York Hosp 1980; Rheumatology, NYU Med Ctr 1982; **Fac Appt:** Assoc Prof Ped, UMDNJ-NJ Med Sch, Newark

Ilowite, Norman T MD [PRhu] - **Spec Exp:** Juvenile Arthritis; Lyme Disease; Lupus/SLE; Dermatomyositis; **Hospital:** Montefiore Med Ctr-Moses Campus, NY, Jacobi Med Ctr; **Address:** Chldns Hosp-Montefiore-Dept Rheumatology, 3415 Bainbridge Ave Fl Rosenthal3, Bronx, NY 10467; **Phone:** 718-741-2450; **Board Cert:** Pediatrics 1985; Clinical & Laboratory Immunology 1990; Pediatric Rheumatology 2007; **Med School:** SUNY Downstate 1979; **Resid:** Pediatrics, Chldns Hosp Natl Med Ctr 1982; **Fellow:** Pediatric Rheumatology, Univ WA Med Ctr 1984; **Fac Appt:** Prof Ped, Albert Einstein Coll Med

Lehman, Thomas J A MD [PRhu] - **Spec Exp:** Arthritis; Scleroderma; Lupus/SLE; Rheumatoid Arthritis; **Hospital:** Hosp For Special Surgery (page 58), NY-Presby/Weill Cornell Med Ctr, NY (page 65); **Address:** Hospital for Special Surgery, 535 E 70 St, Ste 714, New York, NY 10021-4872; **Phone:** 212-606-1151; **Board Cert:** Pediatrics 1979; Pediatric Rheumatology 2007; **Med School:** Jefferson Med Coll 1974; **Resid:** Pediatrics, Chldns Hosp 1976; Pediatrics, UCSF Med Ctr 1977; **Fellow:** Pediatric Rheumatology, Chldns Hosp 1979; Rheumatology, Natl Inst Hlth 1983; **Fac Appt:** Prof Ped, Cornell Univ-Weill Med Coll

Sherry, David D MD [PRhu] - **Spec Exp:** Pain-Musculoskeletal; Reflex Sympathetic Dystrophy (RSD); Juvenile Arthritis; Lupus/SLE; **Hospital:** Chldns Hosp of Philadelphia; **Address:** Chldns Hosp, Ped Rheumatology Dept, 3400 Civic Center Blvd, Philadelphia, PA 19104; **Phone:** 215-590-7234; **Board Cert:** Pediatrics 1981; Pediatric Rheumatology 2007; **Med School:** Texas Tech Univ 1977; **Resid:** Pediatrics, Duke Univ Hosp 1980; **Fellow:** Pediatric Rheumatology, Univ British Columbia 1982; **Fac Appt:** Prof Ped, Univ Pennsylvania

Sills, Edward M MD [PRhu] - **Spec Exp:** Juvenile Arthritis; Lupus/SLE; Dermatomyositis; Vasculitis; **Hospital:** Johns Hopkins Hosp (page 59); **Address:** Johns Hopkins Hosp, 200 N Wolfe St, Ste 2-127, Baltimore, MD 21205; **Phone:** 410-955-6145; **Board Cert:** Pediatrics 1968; **Med School:** NYU Sch Med 1963; **Resid:** Pediatrics, Bronx Muni Hosp 1967; **Fac Appt:** Assoc Prof Ped, Johns Hopkins Univ

Southeast

Finkel, Terri H MD/PhD [PRhu] - **Spec Exp:** Juvenile Arthritis; Lupus/SLE; Vasculitis; **Hospital:** Nemours Chldns Hosp - Orlando; **Address:** Nemours Chdns Hosp, Ped Rheumatology, 13535 Nemours Pkwy Fl 4, Orlando, FL 32827; **Phone:** 407-650-7280; **Board Cert:** Pediatrics 1988; Pediatric Rheumatology 2009; **Med School:** Stanford Univ 1982; **Resid:** Pediatrics, Univ CO Hosp 1985; **Fellow:** Pediatric Rheumatology, Natl Jewish Med Ctr 1990; **Fac Appt:** Prof Ped, Univ Fla Coll Med

Passo, Murray H MD [PRhu] - **Spec Exp:** Pain-Musculoskeletal; **Hospital:** MUSC Med Ctr; **Address:** MUSC, Dept Pediatrics, Div Pediatric Rheumatology, 135 Rutledge Ave, MSC 561, Charleston, SC 29425-5610; **Phone:** 843-792-5696; **Board Cert:** Pediatrics 1979; Pediatric Rheumatology 2007; **Med School:** Indiana Univ 1974; **Resid:** Pediatrics, Riley Chldns Hosp 1977; **Fellow:** Rheumatology, Indiana Univ Hosps 1979; **Fac Appt:** Prof Ped, Med Univ SC

Schanberg, Laura E MD [PRhu] - **Spec Exp:** Lupus/SLE; Juvenile Arthritis; Dermatomyositis; Spondyloarthropathies; **Hospital:** Duke Univ Hosp; **Address:** Duke Univ Med Ctr, 2301 Erwin Rd, Durham, NC 27710; **Phone:** 919-684-6575; **Board Cert:** Pediatric Rheumatology 2007; **Med School:** Duke Univ 1984; **Resid:** Pediatrics, Duke Univ Med Ctr 1987; **Fellow:** Pediatric Rheumatology, Duke Univ Med Ctr 1991; **Fac Appt:** Asst Prof Ped, Duke Univ

Warren, Robert W MD/PhD [PRhu] - **Spec Exp:** Juvenile Arthritis; Lupus/SLE; **Hospital:** MUSC Med Ctr; **Address:** MUSC Rutledge Tower, 135 Rutledge Ave, Charleston, SC 29425; **Phone:** 843-876-1985; **Board Cert:** Pediatrics 1983; Allergy & Immunology 1983; Pediatric Rheumatology 2007; **Med School:** Washington Univ, St Louis 1978; **Resid:** Pediatrics, Duke Univ Med Ctr 1980; **Fellow:** Rheumatology, Duke Univ Med Ctr 1983; **Fac Appt:** Prof Ped, Med Univ SC

Midwest

Klein-Gitelman, Marisa MD [PRhu] - **Spec Exp:** Lupus/SLE; Juvenile Arthritis; **Hospital:** Lurie Chldn's Hosp-Chicago; **Address:** Lurie Chldns Hosp, 225 E Chicago Ave, Box 50, Chicago, IL 60611; **Phone:** 312-227-6270; **Board Cert:** Pediatrics 2013; Pediatric Rheumatology 2009; **Med School:** Washington Univ, St Louis 1985; **Resid:** Pediatrics, Columbia-Presby Med Ctr 1989; **Fellow:** Pediatric Rheumatology, Tufts/New England Med Ctr 1993; **Fac Appt:** Assoc Prof Ped, Northwestern Univ

Onel, Karen B MD [PRhu] - **Spec Exp:** Lupus/SLE; Uveitis; Vasculitis; Juvenile Arthritis; **Hospital:** Univ Chicago Med-Comer Chldn's Hosp; **Address:** Univ Chicago-Comer Chldn's Hosp-Rheum, 5721 S Maryland Ave, Chicago, IL 60637; **Phone:** 773-702-6169; **Board Cert:** Pediatrics 2008; Pediatric Rheumatology 2011; **Med School:** Cornell Univ-Weill Med Coll 1989; **Resid:** Pediatrics, NY Presby Hosp/Columbia 1992; **Fellow:** Pediatric Rheumatology, Hosp Special Surgery 1995; **Fac Appt:** Assoc Prof Ped, Univ Chicago-Pritzker Sch Med

Wagner-Weiner, Linda MD [PRhu] - **Spec Exp:** Lupus/SLE; Juvenile Arthritis; Vasculitis; Dermatomyositis; **Hospital:** Univ Chicago Med-Comer Chldn's Hosp, La Rabida Chlds Hosp; **Address:** Univ Chicago-Comer Chldn's Hosp-Rheum, 5721 S Maryland Ave, Chicago, IL 60637; **Phone:** 773-702-2406; **Board Cert:** Pediatrics 1984; Pediatric Rheumatology 2007; **Med School:** Rush Med Coll 1979; **Resid:** Pediatrics, Univ Chicago Hosps 1982; **Fellow:** Pediatric Rheumatology, Univ Chicago/La Rabida Chldns Hosp 1984; **Fac Appt:** Assoc Prof Ped, Univ Chicago-Pritzker Sch Med

Southwest

Myones, Barry Lee MD [PRhu] - **Spec Exp:** Vasculitis; Kawasaki Disease; Dermatomyositis; Scleroderma; **Hospital:** Texas Chldns Hosp; **Address:** Pediatric Rheumatology Ctr, 6701 Fannin St Fl 11, Houston, TX 77030; **Phone:** 832-824-3830; **Board Cert:** Pediatrics 1983; Pediatric Rheumatology 2007; **Med School:** Albany Med Coll 1977; **Resid:** Pediatrics, Duke Univ Med Ctr 1981; **Fellow:** Pediatric Rheumatology, Chldns Hosp-Stanford 1983; Rheumatology, Univ N Carolina Affil Hosp 1988; **Fac Appt:** Assoc Prof Ped, Baylor Coll Med

Pediatric Surgery

New England

Caty, Michael G MD [PS] - **Spec Exp:** Neonatal Surgery; Thoracic Surgery; Gastrointestinal Motility Disorders; Laparoscopic Surgery; **Hospital:** Yale-New Haven Hosp; **Address:** Yale Pediatric Surgery, 310 Cedar St, FMB-131, New Haven, CT 06510; **Phone:** 203-785-2701; **Board Cert:** Pediatric Surgery 2003; **Med School:** Univ Mass Sch Med 1985; **Resid:** Surgery, Univ MI Hosp 1991; **Fellow:** Pediatric Surgery, Boston Chldns Hosp 1993; **Fac Appt:** Prof S, Yale Univ

Chwals, Walter J MD [PS] - **Spec Exp:** Necrotizing Enterocolitis; Cancer Surgery; Endocrine Surgery; Congenital Anomalies; **Hospital:** Tufts Med Ctr; **Address:** Tufts Med Ctr, 800 Washington St, Ste 207, Boston, MA 02111; **Phone:** 617-636-5025; **Board Cert:** Pediatric Surgery 2007; **Med School:** Poland 1980; **Resid:** Surgery, Univ Mass Med Ctr 1985; **Fellow:** Nutrition, New England Deaconess Hosp 1986; Pediatric Surgery, Chldns Hosp 1988; **Fac Appt:** Prof S, Case West Res Univ

Doody, Daniel P MD [PS] - **Spec Exp:** Neonatal Surgery; Inflammatory Bowel Disease; Hirschsprung's Disease; Minimally Invasive Surgery; **Hospital:** Mass Genl Hosp, Newton - Wellesley Hosp; **Address:** MGH, Dept Pediatric Surgery, 55 Fruit St, Warren Bldg Fl 11, Boston, MA 02114; **Phone:** 617-726-2913; **Board Cert:** Surgery 2006; Pediatric Surgery 2007; **Med School:** Univ IL Coll Med 1977; **Resid:** Surgery, Univ Illinois Hosps 1984; Pediatric Surgery, Chldn's Hosp 1987; **Fellow:** Transplant Research, Mass Genl Hosp 1985; **Fac Appt:** Assoc Prof S, Harvard Med Sch

Jennings, Russell W MD [PS] - **Spec Exp:** Pediatric Cardiac Surgery; Robotic Surgery; Esophageal Surgery; **Hospital:** Children's Hospital - Boston, Brigham & Women's Hosp; **Address:** Boston Chldn's Hosp, Fegan 3, 300 Longwood Ave, Boston, MA 02115; **Phone:** 617-355-3038; **Board Cert:** Surgery 2005; Pediatric Surgery 2007; **Med School:** UCSF 1986; **Resid:** Surgery, UCSF Med Ctr 1991; **Fellow:** Fetal Surgery, Fetal Trmt Ctr/UCSF Med Ctr 1994; Pediatric Surgery, Chldns Hosp 1996; **Fac Appt:** Asst Prof S, Harvard Med Sch

Latchaw, Laurie A MD [PS] - **Spec Exp:** Pediatric Thoracic Surgery; Cancer Surgery; Neonatal Surgery; Lung Disease in Newborns; **Hospital:** Dartmouth - Hitchcock Med Ctr; **Address:** DHMC, Clinic 6M, One Medical Center Drive, Lebanon, NH 03756; **Phone:** 603-653-9883; **Board Cert:** Surgery 2001; Pediatric Surgery 2011; **Med School:** Rush Med Coll 1976; **Resid:** Surgery, Univ Texas 1981; **Fellow:** Pediatric Surgery, Montreal Chldns Hosp 1983; **Fac Appt:** Assoc Prof S, Dartmouth Med Sch

Shamberger, Robert C MD [PS] - **Spec Exp:** Wilms' Tumor; Neuroblastoma; Inflammatory Bowel Disease; Ewing's Sarcoma; **Hospital:** Children's Hospital - Boston; **Address:** Boston Chldn's Hosp, 300 Longwood Ave, Hunnewell Bldg - Fl 3 - Ste 304, Boston, MA 02115; **Phone:** 617-355-8326; **Board Cert:** Surgery 2012; Pediatric Surgery 2003; **Med School:** Harvard Med Sch 1975; **Resid:** Surgery, Massachusetts Genl Hosp 1978; Pediatric Surgery, Children's Hosp 1985; **Fellow:** Surgical Oncology, NCI-Surgical Branch 1980; **Fac Appt:** Prof S, Harvard Med Sch

Tracy Jr, Thomas F MD [PS] - **Spec Exp:** Hepatobiliary Surgery; Endoscopic Surgery; Fetal Surgery; Hirschsprung's Disease; **Hospital:** Rhode Island Hosp, Women & Infants Hosp of RI; **Address:** 2 Dudley St, Ste 190, Providence, RI 02905; **Phone:** 401-421-1939; **Board Cert:** Surgery 2006; Pediatric Surgery 2006; **Med School:** Israel 1981; **Resid:** Surgery, Med Coll Virginia 1986; **Fellow:** Pediatric Surgery, Columbia Presby Med Ctr 1988; **Fac Appt:** Prof S, Brown Univ

Mid Atlantic

Adzick, N. Scott MD [PS] - **Spec Exp:** Fetal Surgery; Congenital Hyperinsulinism; Neonatal Surgery; Twin to Twin Transfusion Syndrome (TTTS); **Hospital:** Chldns Hosp of Philadelphia; **Address:** Chldns Hosp, Ped Surgery Dept, 3400 Civic Ctr Blvd Wood Bldg - Ste 5113, Philadelphia, PA 19104; **Phone:** 215-590-2727; **Board Cert:** Surgery 2006; Pediatric Surgery 2007; **Med School:** Harvard Med Sch 1979; **Resid:** Surgery, Mass Genl Hosp 1986; Pediatric Surgery, Chldns Hosp 1988; **Fellow:** Surgical Research, UCSF Med Ctr 1985; **Fac Appt:** Prof S, Univ Pennsylvania

Alexander, Frederick MD [PS] - **Spec Exp:** Gastrointestinal Surgery; Thoracic Surgery; Solid Tumors; Congenital Anomalies-Gastrointestinal; **Hospital:** Hackensack Univ Med Ctr, Valley Hosp; **Address:** Pediatric Surgical Associates, 30 W Century Rd, Ste 235, Paramas, NJ 07652; **Phone:** 201-225-0029; **Board Cert:** Pediatric Surgery 2010; **Med School:** Columbia P&S 1977; **Resid:** Surgery, Brigham-Womens Hosp 1984; **Fellow:** Pediatric Surgery, Chldns Hosp 1986; **Fac Appt:** Clin Prof S, UMDNJ-NJ Med Sch, Newark

Colombani, Paul M MD [PS] - **Spec Exp:** Pediatric Cardiothoracic Surgery; Transplant-Kidney; Transplant-Liver; Cancer Surgery; **Hospital:** Johns Hopkins Hosp (page 59); **Address:** Johns Hopkins Hosp, Ped Surgery, 1800 Orleans St, Bloomberg 7310, Baltimore, MD 21287; **Phone:** 410-955-5210; **Board Cert:** Surgery 2003; Pediatric Surgery 2003; **Med School:** Univ KY Coll Med 1976; **Resid:** Surgery, Geo Wash Univ Hosp 1981; **Fellow:** Pediatric Surgery, Johns Hopkins Hosp 1983; **Fac Appt:** Prof S, Johns Hopkins Univ

Dolgin, Stephen E MD [PS] - **Spec Exp:** Neonatal Surgery; Ulcerative Colitis; Inflammatory Bowel Disease/Crohn's; Ovarian Masses in Children/Adolescents; **Hospital:** Steven & Alexandra Cohen Chldn's Med Ctr of NY (page 66), N Shore Univ Hosp (page 66); **Address:** Cohen Chldn's Med Ctr, Dept Ped Surg, 269-01 76th Ave, Ste 171, New Hyde Park, NY 11040; **Phone:** 718-470-3636; **Board Cert:** Surgery 2011; Pediatric Surgery 2003; **Med School:** NYU Sch Med 1977; **Resid:** Surgery, Peter Bent Brigham Hosp/Harvard Univ 1982; **Fellow:** Pediatric Surgery, Chldns Meml Hosp/Northwestern Univ 1984; **Fac Appt:** Prof S, Hofstra N Shore-LIJ Sch Med

Dunn, Stephen P MD [PS] - **Spec Exp:** Transplant-Liver; Transplant-Kidney; Liver & Biliary Surgery; **Hospital:** Nemours/Alfred I. duPont Hosp for Chldn; **Address:** 1600 Rockland Rd, Wilmington, DE 19803; **Phone:** 302-651-4200; **Board Cert:** Surgery 2006; Pediatric Surgery 2007; Surgical Critical Care 2012; **Med School:** Indiana Univ 1978; **Resid:** Surgery, Indiana Univ Affil Hosps 1983; **Fellow:** Pediatric Surgery, Sy Christophers Hosp Chldn 1985; **Fac Appt:** Prof S, Jefferson Med Coll

Flake, Alan W MD [PS] - **Spec Exp:** Fetal Surgery; Stem Cell Transplant-Fetal; Neonatal Surgery; Minimally Invasive Surgery; **Hospital:** Chldns Hosp of Philadelphia; **Address:** Chldns Hosp, Ped Surgery Dept, 3400 Civic Ctr Blvd Wood Bldg - Ste 5113, Philadelphia, PA 19104; **Phone:** 215-590-2727; **Board Cert:** Surgery 2010; Pediatric Surgery 2011; **Med School:** Univ Ark 1981; **Resid:** Surgery, UCSF Med Ctr 1988; **Fellow:** Pediatric Surgery, Chldns Hosp 1990; **Fac Appt:** Prof S, Univ Pennsylvania

Gaines, Barbara A MD [PS] - **Spec Exp:** Trauma; Critical Care; Minimally Invasive Surgery; **Hospital:** Chldns Hosp of Pittsburgh - UPMC; **Address:** Chldn's Hosp Pittsburgh, One Chldn's Hosp Drive, 4401 Penn Ave, Faculty Pavilion, Fl 7, Pittsburgh, PA 15224; **Phone:** 412-692-8288; **Board Cert:** Surgery 2006; Surgical Critical Care 2007; Pediatric Surgery 2009; **Med School:** Univ VA Sch Med 1990; **Resid:** Surgery, Vanderbilt Univ Hosp 1995; **Fellow:** Pediatric Surgery, Children's Hosp 1998; **Fac Appt:** Asst Prof S, Univ Pittsburgh

Ginsburg, Howard B MD [PS] - **Spec Exp:** Neonatal Surgery; Tumor Surgery; Pediatric Urology; Gastrointestinal Surgery; **Hospital:** NYU Langone Med Ctr (page 68), Bellevue Hosp Ctr; **Address:** 530 First Ave, Ste 10W, New York, NY 10016-6402; **Phone:** 212-263-7391; **Board Cert:** Pediatric Surgery 2012; **Med School:** Univ Cincinnati 1972; **Resid:** Surgery, NYU-Bellvue Hosp 1977; Pediatric Surgery, Columbia-Presby Med Ctr 1979; **Fellow:** Pediatric Surgery, Mass Genl Hosp 1980; **Fac Appt:** Assoc Prof PS, NYU Sch Med

Gittes, George K MD [PS] - **Spec Exp:** Gastrointestinal Surgery; **Hospital:** Chldns Hosp of Pittsburgh - UPMC; **Address:** Chldns Hosp, Ped Surgery Dept, 4401 Penn Ave Fl 7, Pittsburgh, PA 15224; **Phone:** 412-692-7291; **Board Cert:** Surgery 2003; Pediatric Surgery 2007; **Med School:** Harvard Med Sch 1987; **Resid:** Surgery, UCSF Med Ctr 1994; **Fellow:** Pediatric Surgery, Chldns Mercy Hosp 1995; **Fac Appt:** Prof S, Univ Pittsburgh

Glick, Philip L MD [PS] - **Spec Exp:** Neonatal Surgery; Fetal Surgery; Chest Wall Deformities; Pediatric Cancers; **Hospital:** Sisters of Charity Hosp, Buffalo, Erie County Med Ctr; **Address:** University Surgeons, 3850 Sheridan Drive, Amherst, NY 14226; **Phone:** 716-859-3371; **Board Cert:** Surgery 2006; Pediatric Surgery 2009; **Med School:** UCSF 1979; **Resid:** Surgery, UCSF Med Ctr 1985; **Fellow:** Fetal Surgery, UCSF Med Ctr 1984; Pediatric Surgery, Chldns Hosp Med Ctr 1988; **Fac Appt:** Prof S, SUNY Buffalo

Hicks, Barry A MD [PS] - **Spec Exp:** Neonatal Surgery; Trauma; Chest Wall Deformities; **Hospital:** Nemours/Alfred I. duPont Hosp for Chldn; **Address:** 1600 Rockland Rd, Wilmington, DE 19803; **Phone:** 302-651-5999; **Board Cert:** Surgery 2001; Pediatric Surgery 2003; **Med School:** Indiana Univ 1984; **Resid:** Surgery, Vanderbilt Univ Med Ctr 1991; **Fellow:** Pediatric Surgery, Babies Hosp 1993; **Fac Appt:** Prof S, Jefferson Med Coll

Jan, Dominique M MD/PhD [PS] - **Spec Exp:** Transplant-Bowel; Transplant-Liver; Transplant Surgery-Pediatric; **Hospital:** Montefiore Med Ctr-Moses Campus, NY; **Address:** 3415 Bainbridge Ave Fl 5, Bronx, NY 10467; **Phone:** 718-920-7200; **Med School:** France 1984; **Resid:** Surgery, Assistance Poblique Hosp 1989; **Fellow:** Pediatric Surgery, Necker Malades Hosp; **Fac Appt:** Prof S, Albert Einstein Coll Med

Kane, Timothy D MD [PS] - **Spec Exp:** Minimally Invasive Surgery; Neonatal Surgery; **Hospital:** Chldns Natl Med Ctr; **Address:** Chldn's Natl Med Ctr, Dept Surgery, 111 Michigan Ave NW, Fl 4, Ste 200, Washington, DC 20010; **Phone:** 202-476-2151; **Board Cert:** Surgery 2001; Pediatric Surgery 2004; **Med School:** SUNY Upstate Med Univ 1992; **Resid:** Surgery, Univ Cincinnati Med Ctr 1999; **Fellow:** Pediatric Surgery, Children's Hosp 2002; **Fac Appt:** Assoc Prof S, Univ Wash

La Quaglia, Michael MD [PS] - **Spec Exp:** Cancer Surgery; Neuroblastoma; Liver Cancer; Wilms' Tumor; **Hospital:** Meml Sloan-Kettering Canc Ctr, NY-Presby/Weill Cornell Med Ctr, NY (page 65); **Address:** 1275 York Ave, Ste H1315, New York, NY 10065; **Phone:** 212-639-7002; **Board Cert:** Surgery 2003; Pediatric Surgery 2007; **Med School:** UMDNJ-NJ Med Sch, Newark 1976; **Resid:** Surgery, Mass Genl Hosp 1983; **Fellow:** Cardiothoracic Surgery, Broadgreen Ctr 1984; Pediatric Surgery, Chldns Hosp 1985; **Fac Appt:** Prof S, Cornell Univ-Weill Med Coll

Midulla, Peter MD [PS] - **Spec Exp:** Hernia; Gastrointestinal Surgery; Minimally Invasive Surgery; Neonatal Surgery; **Hospital:** Mt Sinai Med Ctr (page 62); **Address:** Mount Sinai, Pediatric Surgery Dept, 5 E 98 St Fl 10, New York, NY 10029; **Phone:** 212-241-1608; **Board Cert:** Surgery 2007; Pediatric Surgery 2009; **Med School:** Albert Einstein Coll Med 1990; **Resid:** Surgery, Mount Sinai Med Ctr 1997; **Fellow:** Pediatric Surgery, Chldns Natl Med Ctr 1999; **Fac Appt:** Asst Prof Ped, Mount Sinai Sch Med

Nance, Michael L MD [PS] - **Spec Exp:** Trauma; Neonatal Surgery; Brain Injury; Congenital Anomalies; **Hospital:** Chldns Hosp of Philadelphia; **Address:** Chldns Hosp, Ped Surgery Dept, 3400 Civic Ctr Blvd Wood Bldg - Ste 5113, Philadelphia, PA 19104; **Phone:** 215-590-2727; **Board Cert:** Surgery 2005; Surgical Critical Care 2008; Pediatric Surgery 2007; **Med School:** Louisiana State U, New Orleans 1988; **Resid:** Surgery, Hosp Univ Penn 1995; **Fellow:** Surgical Critical Care, Hosp Univ Penn 1996; Pediatric Surgery, Chldns Hosp 1997; **Fac Appt:** Prof S, Univ Pennsylvania

Quaegebeur, Jan M MD/PhD [PS] - **Spec Exp:** Arterial Switch; Heart Valve Surgery; Pediatric Cardiac Surgery; **Hospital:** Morgan Stanley Children's Hosp of NY-Presby, NY (page 65); **Address:** Morgan Stanley Chldns Hosp of NY-Presby, 3959 Broadway, Ste BHN276, New York, NY 10032; **Phone:** 212-305-5975; **Med School:** Belgium 1969; **Resid:** Surgery, St Michel Clinic 1973; **Fellow:** Thoracic Surgery, Baylor Coll Med 1974; Cardiothoracic Surgery, Univ Hosp 1978; **Fac Appt:** Prof S, Columbia P&S

Schwartz, Marshall Z MD [PS] - **Spec Exp:** Gastrointestinal Surgery; Neonatal Surgery; Transplant-Kidney; Inflammatory Bowel Disease; **Hospital:** St. Christopher's Hosp for Chldn, St. Luke's Hosp - Bethlehem; **Address:** St Christopher's Hosp for Children Dept Surgery, 3601 A St, Ste 2204, Philadelphia, PA 19134; **Phone:** 215-427-5446; **Board Cert:** Surgery 2009; Pediatric Surgery 2012; **Med School:** Univ Minn 1970; **Resid:** Surgery, Univ Minnesota Hosp 1976; Pediatric Surgery, Chldns Hosp Med Ctr - Harvard Med Sch 1978; **Fellow:** Research, Univ Minnesota Hosp 1975; **Fac Appt:** Prof S, Drexel Univ Coll Med

Spigland, Nitsana A MD [PS] - **Spec Exp:** Pediatric Cancers; Minimally Invasive Surgery; Pediatric Thoracic Surgery; Neonatal Surgery; **Hospital:** NY-Presby/Weill Cornell Med Ctr, NY (page 65); **Address:** NY Hosp-Cornell Med Ctr, 520 E 70th St, Ste Starr-7, New York, NY 10065; **Phone:** 212-746-5648; **Board Cert:** Pediatric Surgery 2003; **Med School:** NY Med Coll 1982; **Resid:** Surgery, Lenox Hill Hosp 1987; **Fellow:** Pediatric Surgery, St Justine Chldn's Hosp 1989; **Fac Appt:** Prof S, Cornell Univ-Weill Med Coll

Strauch, Eric D MD [PS] - **Spec Exp:** Pediatric Cancers; Neonatal Surgery; Conjoined Twins; **Hospital:** Univ of MD Med Ctr; **Address:** 419 W Redwood St, Ste 300, Baltimore, MD 21201; **Phone:** 410-328-5730; **Board Cert:** Surgery 2003; Pediatric Surgery 2005; **Med School:** Univ MD Sch Med 1988; **Resid:** Surgery, Univ MD Med Ctr 1994; **Fellow:** Pediatric Surgery, Johns Hopkins Hosp 1996; **Fac Appt:** Assoc Prof S, Univ MD Sch Med

Stylianos, Steven MD [PS] - **Spec Exp:** Trauma; Neonatal Surgery; Chest Wall Deformities; Congenital Anomalies; **Hospital:** Steven & Alexandra Cohen Chldn's Med Ctr of NY (page 66); **Address:** Cohen Chldns Med Ctr-Dept Ped Surg, 269-01 76th Ave, New Hyde Park, NY 11040; **Phone:** 718-470-3636; **Board Cert:** Surgery 2002; Pediatric Surgery 2003; **Med School:** NYU Sch Med 1983; **Resid:** Surgery, Columbia-Presby Med Ctr 1988; Pediatric Surgery, Chldns Hosp 1992; **Fellow:** Pediatric Surgical Critical Care, New England Med Ctr 1990; **Fac Appt:** Prof S, FIU Coll Med

Velcek, Francisca T MD [PS] - **Spec Exp:** Anorectal Malformations; Pediatric Gynecology; Neonatal Surgery; Hernia; **Hospital:** Lenox Hill Hosp (page 66); **Address:** Ped Surg, 965 5th Ave, New York, NY 10075; **Phone:** 212-744-9396; **Board Cert:** Surgery 1974; Pediatric Surgery 2007; **Med School:** Philippines 1966; **Resid:** Surgery, St Clares Hosp 1971; Pediatric Surgery, SUNY Downstate Med Ctr 1975; **Fac Appt:** Clin Prof S, SUNY Hlth Sci Ctr

Voigt, Roger W MD [PS] - **Spec Exp:** Minimally Invasive Surgery; Neonatal Surgery; Pediatric Urology; **Hospital:** Univ of MD Med Ctr; **Address:** UMMC, Dept Pediatric Surgery, 22 S Greene St, N4E37, Baltimore, MD 21201; **Phone:** 410-328-5730; **Med School:** New Zealand 1980; **Resid:** Surgery, Univ Auckland 1984; **Fellow:** Pediatric Surgery, Royal Chldns Hosp; Pediatric Urology, Univ Maryland Med Ctr; **Fac Appt:** Asst Prof S, Univ MD Sch Med

Southeast

Bond, Sheldon J MD [PS] - **Spec Exp:** Pediatric Cancers; Fetal Surgery; Trauma; **Hospital:** Univ of Louisville Hosp, Kosair Chldn's Hosp; **Address:** Univ Pediatric Surgery Assocs, 234 E Gray St, Med Twr S, Ste 766, Louisville, KY 40202; **Phone:** 502-583-7337; **Board Cert:** Surgery 2008; Pediatric Surgery 2009; Surgical Critical Care 2001; **Med School:** Med Coll Wisc 1983; **Resid:** Surgery, Univ Louisville Hosp 1989; **Fellow:** Fetal Surgery, Chldns Natl Med Ctr 1991; Pediatric Surgery, UCSF Med Ctr 1992; **Fac Appt:** Prof S, Univ Louisville Sch Med

Chen, Mike K MD [PS] - **Spec Exp:** Gastrointestinal Surgery; Transplant Surgery-Pediatric; **Hospital:** Children's Hosp AL; **Address:** UAB Hosp, Pediatric Surgery, 1600 7th Ave S, ACC 300, Birmingham, AL 35233; **Phone:** 205-939-9688; **Board Cert:** Surgery 2003; Pediatric Surgery 2007; **Med School:** Univ Tex, Houston 1987; **Resid:** Surgery, Shands at Univ of FL 1993; **Fellow:** Transplant Surgery, Shands at Univ of FL 1994; Pediatric Surgery, Univ Tennessee Med Ctr 1996; **Fac Appt:** Prof S, UAB Sch Med

Davidoff, Andrew M MD [PS] - **Spec Exp:** Neuroblastoma; Cancer Surgery; **Hospital:** St. Jude Children's Research Hosp, Le Bonheur Chldns Med Ctr; **Address:** St Jude Chldns Rsch Hosp, Dept Surg, 262 Danny Thomas Pl, MS 133, Memphis, TN 38105; **Phone:** 901-595-4060; **Board Cert:** Surgery 2005; Pediatric Surgery 2007; **Med School:** Univ Pennsylvania 1987; **Resid:** Surgery, Duke Med Ctr 1994; **Fellow:** Pediatric Surgery, Chldns Hosp 1996; **Fac Appt:** Assoc Prof S, Univ Tenn Coll Med

Fallat, Mary E MD [PS] - **Spec Exp:** Trauma; Burn Care; **Hospital:** Kosair Chldn's Hosp, Univ of Louisville Hosp; **Address:** 234 E Gray St, Ste 766, MS 40202, University Pediatric Surgery Associates, Louisville, KY 40202; **Phone:** 502-583-7337; **Board Cert:** Surgery 2005; **Med School:** SUNY Upstate Med Univ 1979; **Resid:** Surgery, Univ Louisville Hosp 1985; **Fellow:** Research, Mass Genl Hosp 1983; Pediatric Surgery, Chldns Natl Med Ctr 1987; **Fac Appt:** Prof S, Univ Louisville Sch Med

Morgan III, Walter M MD [PS] - **Spec Exp:** Germ Cell Tumors; Neuroblastoma; Bone Cancer; Congenital Anomalies; **Hospital:** Vanderbilt Monroe Carrell Jr. Chldn's Hosp, Vanderbilt Univ Med Ctr; **Address:** Vanderbilt Dept Pediatric Surgery, 2200 Children's Way, 7100 Doctors Office Tower, Nashville, TN 37232-9780; **Phone:** 615-936-1050; **Board Cert:** Pediatric Surgery 2001; **Med School:** Vanderbilt Univ 1982; **Resid:** Surgery, Johns Hopkins Hosp 1988; **Fellow:** Pediatric Surgery, Johns Hopkins Hosp 1990; **Fac Appt:** Asst Prof S, Vanderbilt Univ

Paidas, Charles N MD [PS] - **Spec Exp:** Pediatric Cancers; Chest Wall Deformities; Transplant Surgery-Pediatric; Hernia; **Hospital:** Tampa Genl Hosp; **Address:** USF Hlth, Surgery Dept, 1 Tampa General Cir, Tampa, FL 33606; **Phone:** 813-259-0929; **Board Cert:** Surgery 2010; Pediatric Surgery 2011; Surgical Critical Care 2002; **Med School:** NY Med Coll 1981; **Resid:** Surgery, NY Med Coll Affil Hosps 1987; **Fellow:** Pediatric Surgery, Johns Hopkins Hosp 1991; **Fac Appt:** Prof S, Univ S Fla Coll Med

Rice, Henry MD [PS] - **Spec Exp:** Neonatal Surgery; Cancer Surgery; **Hospital:** Duke Univ Hosp; **Address:** Duke Univ Med Ctr, Dept Ped Surg, DUMC, Box 3815, Durham, NC 27710; **Phone:** 919-681-5077; **Board Cert:** Surgery 2006; Pediatric Surgery 2009; **Med School:** Yale Univ 1988; **Resid:** Surgery, Univ Wash Affil Hosps 1996; **Fellow:** Pediatric Surgery, Chldns Hosp 1998; **Fac Appt:** Prof S, Duke Univ

Ricketts, Richard R MD [PS] - **Spec Exp:** Neonatal Surgery; Cancer Surgery; Gastrointestinal Surgery; Hirschsprung's Disease; **Hospital:** Chldns Hlthcare Atlanta @ Egleston, Chldns Hlthcare Atlanta @ Scottish Rite; **Address:** Emory Univ-CHOA Div Pediatric Surgery, 1975 Century Blvd, Ste 6, Atlanta, GA 30345; **Phone:** 404-982-9938; **Board Cert:** Surgery 2004; **Med School:** Northwestern Univ 1973; **Resid:** Surgery, LAC-USC Med Ctr 1978; **Fellow:** Pediatric Surgery, Chldns Meml Hosp 1980; **Fac Appt:** Prof S, Emory Univ

Rodgers, Bradley M MD [PS] - **Spec Exp:** Pediatric Thoracic Surgery; Neonatal Surgery; Minimally Invasive Surgery; **Hospital:** Univ of Virginia Hlth Sys; **Address:** Box 800709, Charlottesville, VA 22908; **Phone:** 434-924-2673; **Board Cert:** Surgery 1997; Pediatric Surgery 2005; Thoracic Surgery 1975; **Med School:** Johns Hopkins Univ 1966; **Resid:** Surgery, Duke Univ Med Ctr 1968; Cardiothoracic Surgery, Duke Univ Med Ctr 1973; **Fellow:** Pediatric Surgery, Chldns Hosp 1974; **Fac Appt:** Prof S, Univ VA Sch Med

Shochat, Stephen J MD [PS] - **Spec Exp:** Cancer Surgery; Chest Wall Deformities; Pediatric Cancers; **Hospital:** St. Jude Children's Research Hosp; **Address:** St Jude Childrens Research Hosp, Dept Surgery, 262 Danny Thomas Pl, Memphis, TN 38105; **Phone:** 901-595-2911; **Board Cert:** Surgery 1969; Thoracic & Cardiac Surgery 1975; Pediatric Surgery 2005; **Med School:** Med Coll VA 1963; **Resid:** Surgery, Barnes Hosp 1968; Pediatric Surgery, Boston Chldns Hosp 1970; **Fellow:** Thoracic Surgery, George Washington Univ 1974; **Fac Appt:** Prof S, Univ Tenn Coll Med

Midwest

Aiken, John J MD [PS] - **Spec Exp:** Tumor Surgery; Chest Wall Deformities; Hernia; Solid Tumors; **Hospital:** Chldns Hosp - Wisconsin; **Address:** 999 N 92nd St, Ste C-320, Milwaukee, WI 53226; **Phone:** 414-266-6550; **Board Cert:** Surgery 2004; Pediatric Surgery 2010; **Med School:** Univ Cincinnati 1984; **Resid:** Surgery, Mass Genl Hosp 1991; **Fellow:** Pediatric Surgery, Chldns Hosp 1993; **Fac Appt:** Assoc Prof S, Med Coll Wisc

Andrews, Walter S MD [PS] - **Spec Exp:** Transplant-Liver; Transplant-Kidney; **Hospital:** Chldns Mercy Hosps & Clinics; **Address:** Chldns Mercy Hosp, Surg Clin, 2401 Gillham Rd, Kansas City, MO 64108; **Phone:** 816-234-3199; **Board Cert:** Surgery 2012; Pediatric Surgery 2003; **Med School:** Boston Univ 1975; **Resid:** Surgery, Univ CO Hlth Science Ctr 1981; Pediatric Surgery, Univ Pittsburgh Med Ctr 1983; **Fellow:** Transplant Surgery, Univ Pittsburgh Med Ctr 1984; **Fac Appt:** Prof S, Univ MO-Kansas City

Arensman, Robert MD [PS] - **Spec Exp:** Congenital Anomalies; **Hospital:** Alexian Brothers Med Ctr; **Address:** Alexian Brothers Pediatric Surgery, 1555 Barrington Rd, Ste 415, Hoffman Estates, IL 60169; **Phone:** 847-490-4222; **Board Cert:** Pediatric Surgery 2010; **Med School:** Univ IL Coll Med 1969; **Resid:** Surgery, Univ IL Med Ctr 1972; Surgery, Univ IL Med Ctr 1976; **Fellow:** Pediatric Surgery, Chldns Natl Med Ctr 1978; Surgical Research, Boston Chldn's Hosp

Barksdale Jr, Edward M MD [PS] - **Spec Exp:** Gastrointestinal Surgery; Nutrition in Bowel Disorders; Neuroblastoma; Minimally Invasive Surgery; **Hospital:** UH Rainbow Babies & Chldns Hosp; **Address:** UH Rainbow Babies & Chldns Hosp, 11100 Euclid Ave, rm 122, Cleveland, OH 44106; **Phone:** 216-844-8623; **Board Cert:** Surgery 2011; Pediatric Surgery 2003; **Med School:** Harvard Med Sch 1984; **Resid:** Surgery, Mass Genl Hosp 1992; Pediatric Surgery, Chldns Hosp 1994; **Fellow:** Surgical Research, Mass Genl Hosp 1989; **Fac Appt:** Prof S, Case West Res Univ

Bove, Edward L MD [PS] - **Spec Exp:** Pediatric Cardiothoracic Surgery; Hypoplastic Left Heart Syndrome; Congenital Heart Surgery; **Hospital:** Univ Michigan Med Ctr; **Address:** 1500 E Med Ctr Drive, 5144 CVC, Ann Arbor, MI 48109-5864; **Phone:** 734-936-4980; **Board Cert:** Thoracic & Cardiac Surgery 2009; Congenital Cardiac Surgery 2009; **Med School:** Albany Med Coll 1972; **Resid:** Surgery, Univ Mich Med Ctr 1976; Thoracic Surgery, Univ Mich Med Ctr 1979; **Fellow:** Pediatric Cardiac Surgery, Hosp Sick Chldn 1980; **Fac Appt:** Prof S, Univ Mich Med Sch

Dillon, Patrick A MD [PS] - **Spec Exp:** Pediatric Cancers; Trauma; Gastrointestinal Disorders; Congenital Anomalies; **Hospital:** St. Louis Chldns Hosp, Barnes-Jewish Hosp; **Address:** St Louis Chldns Hosp, 1 Chldns Pl, Ste 5 South 40, St Louis, MO 63110; **Phone:** 314-454-6022; **Board Cert:** Surgery 2004; Pediatric Surgery 2007; **Med School:** Georgetown Univ 1988; **Resid:** Surgery, Barnes Hosp 1995; **Fellow:** Pediatric Surgery, Johns Hopkins Hosp 1997; **Fac Appt:** Assoc Prof S, Washington Univ, St Louis

Ehrlich, Peter F MD [PS] - **Spec Exp:** Pediatric Cancers; Wilms' Tumor; Thyroid Cancer; **Hospital:** Mott Chldns Hosp; **Address:** Mott Children's Hospital, 1540 E Hospital Drive, rm SPC 4217, Ann Arbor, MI 48109; **Phone:** 734-764-4151; **Board Cert:** Surgery 2007; Pediatric Surgery 2009; **Med School:** Canada 1989; **Resid:** Surgery, Univ Toronto Med Ctr 1996; **Fellow:** Pediatric Surgery, Children's Natl Med Ctr 1998; **Fac Appt:** Assoc Prof S, Univ Mich Med Sch

Holcomb III, George W MD [PS] - **Spec Exp:** Minimally Invasive Surgery; Chest Wall Deformities; Gastroesophageal Reflux Disease (GERD); **Hospital:** Chldns Mercy Hosps & Clinics; **Address:** Childrens Mercy Hosp Dept Surgery, 2401 Gillham Rd, Kansas City, MO 64108-4698; **Phone:** 816-234-3199; **Board Cert:** Surgery 2007; Pediatric Surgery 2009; **Med School:** Vanderbilt Univ 1980; **Resid:** Surgery, Vanderbilt Univ Med Ctr 1986; **Fellow:** Pediatric Surgery, Childrens Hosp 1988; **Fac Appt:** Prof S, Univ MO-Kansas City

Holterman, Mark J MD/PhD [PS] - **Spec Exp:** Minimally Invasive Surgery; Neonatal Surgery; Head & Neck Surgery; Congenital Anomalies; **Hospital:** OSF Saint Francis Med Ctr; **Address:** Chdn's Hosp Illinois, 420 NE Glen Oak Ave, Hillcrest Bldg - Ste 210, Peoria, IL 61637; **Phone:** 309-655-2343; **Board Cert:** Surgery 2001; Pediatric Surgery 2007; **Med School:** Univ VA Sch Med 1988; **Resid:** Surgery, Univ Virginia Hosp 1993; **Fellow:** Pediatric Surgery, Chldns Hosp & Med Ctr 1993; **Fac Appt:** Assoc Prof S, Univ IL Coll Med

Kandel, Jessica J MD [PS] - **Spec Exp:** Neuroblastoma; Cancer Surgery; Neonatal Surgery; Wilms' Tumor; **Hospital:** Univ Chicago Med-Comer Chldn's Hosp, Univ of Chicago Med; **Address:** Comer Chldn's Hosp-Ped Surgery, 5841 S Maryland Ave, MC 4062, Chicago, IL 60637; **Phone:** 773-702-6175; **Board Cert:** Surgery 2003; Pediatric Surgery 2005; **Med School:** Columbia P&S 1985; **Resid:** Pediatrics, Mass Genl Hosp 1993; **Fellow:** Pediatric Surgery, Johns Hopkins Hosp 1995; **Fac Appt:** Prof Ped, Univ Chicago-Pritzker Sch Med

Moss, R Lawrence MD [PS] - **Spec Exp:** Congenital Anomalies; Cancer Surgery; Minimally Invasive Surgery; **Hospital:** Nationwide Chldn's Hosp; **Address:** 700 Children's Drive, OCC Bldg - Fl 7th, rm FMB132, Columbus, OH 43205; **Phone:** 614-722-5163; **Board Cert:** Surgery 2010; Pediatric Surgery 2003; Surgical Critical Care 2011; **Med School:** UCSD 1986; **Resid:** Surgery, Virginia Mason Med Ctr 1991; Surgical Critical Care, Chldns Meml Hosp 1992; **Fellow:** Pediatric Surgery, Chldns Meml Hosp 1994; **Fac Appt:** Prof S, Ohio State Univ

Oldham, Keith T MD [PS] - **Spec Exp:** Neonatal Surgery; Pediatric Thoracic Surgery; Gastrointestinal Surgery; **Hospital:** Chldns Hosp - Wisconsin; **Address:** Chldns Hosp Wisconsin - Dept Ped Surgery, 9000 W Wisconsin Ave, Milwaukee, WI 53201; **Phone:** 414-266-6550; **Board Cert:** Surgery 2012; Pediatric Surgery 2009; **Med School:** Med Coll VA 1976; **Resid:** Surgery, Univ Wash Med Ctr 1981; **Fellow:** Pediatric Surgery, Chldns Hosp 1983; **Fac Appt:** Prof S, Med Coll Wisc

Pena, Alberto MD [PS] - **Spec Exp:** Imperforate Anus; Anorectal Malformations; Colon & Rectal Surgery; **Hospital:** Cincinnati Chldns Hosp Med Ctr; **Address:** Cincinnati Chlds Hosp Med Ctr, 3333 Burnet Ave, ML 2023, Cincinnati, OH 45229; **Phone:** 513-636-3238; **Med School:** Mexico 1962; **Resid:** Surgery, Military Hosp 1966; **Fellow:** Pediatric Surgery, Chldns Hosp 1971; Cardiovascular Surgery, Chldns Hosp 1969; **Fac Appt:** Prof S, Univ Cincinnati

Rescorla, Frederick J MD [PS] - **Spec Exp:** Neonatal Surgery; Cancer Surgery; Head & Neck Surgery; Gastrointestinal Surgery; **Hospital:** Riley Hosp for Children; **Address:** Riley Hospital for Children, 705 Riley Hospital Drive, rm 2500, Indianapolis, IN 46202; **Phone:** 317-274-4681; **Board Cert:** Surgery 2004; Surgical Critical Care 2009; Pediatric Surgery 2007; **Med School:** Univ Wisc 1981; **Resid:** Surgery, IU Health Affil Hosp 1986; Pediatric Surgery, IU Health Affil Hosp 1988; **Fac Appt:** Prof S, Indiana Univ

Reynolds, Marleta MD [PS] - **Spec Exp:** Critical Care; Trauma; Congenital Anomalies; Pediatric Cancers; **Hospital:** Lurie Chldn's Hosp-Chicago, Northwest Comm Hosp; **Address:** Lurie Chldns Hosp, Dept Ped Surg, 225 E Chicago Ave, Box 63, Chicago, IL 60611; **Phone:** 312-227-4210; **Board Cert:** Thoracic Surgery 2006; Pediatric Surgery 2003; **Med School:** Tulane Univ 1976; **Resid:** Surgery, Tulane Univ Affil Hosp 1981; Pediatric Surgery, Chldns Meml Hosp 1983; **Fellow:** Cardiothoracic Surgery, Northwestern Univ 1985; **Fac Appt:** Prof S, Northwestern Univ

Sato, Thomas T MD [PS] - **Spec Exp:** Neonatal Surgery; Congenital Anomalies; **Hospital:** Chldns Hosp - Wisconsin; **Address:** 999 N 92nd St, Ste C320, Milwaukee, WI 53226; **Phone:** 414-266-6550; **Board Cert:** Surgery 2006; Pediatric Surgery 2007; **Med School:** USC Sch Med 1988; **Resid:** Surgery, Univ Wash Med Ctr 1995; Pediatric Surgery, Chldns Natl Med Ctr 1997; **Fellow:** Trauma, Harborview Med Ctr 1993; **Fac Appt:** Prof S, Med Coll Wisc

Superina, Riccardo MD [PS] - **Spec Exp:** Transplant Surgery-Pediatric; Transplant-Kidney; Transplant-Liver; Hepatobiliary Surgery; **Hospital:** Lurie Chldn's Hosp-Chicago; **Address:** Lurie Chldn's Hosp-Transplant Surgery, 225 E Chicago Ave, Box 57, Chicago, IL 60611; **Phone:** 312-227-4040; **Med School:** McGill Univ 1975; **Resid:** Surgery, Royal Victoria Hosp 1981; **Fellow:** Pediatric Surgery, Hosp for Sick Chldn 1983; Transplant Surgery, Univ of Oxford 1985; **Fac Appt:** Prof S, Northwestern Univ-Feinberg Sch Med

Warner, Brad MD [PS] - **Spec Exp:** Gastrointestinal Surgery; Neonatal Surgery; Pediatric Cancers; Short Bowel Syndrome; **Hospital:** St. Louis Chldns Hosp; **Address:** 1 Children's Pl, Ste 2A, St Louis, MO 63110; **Phone:** 314-454-6022; **Board Cert:** Surgery 2009; Pediatric Surgery 2011; **Med School:** Univ MO-Kansas City 1982; **Resid:** Surgery, Univ Cincinnati Med Ctr 1989; **Fellow:** Pediatric Surgery, Chldns Hosp Med Ctr 1991; **Fac Appt:** Prof S, Univ Cincinnati

Great Plains and Mountains

Crombleholme, Timothy M MD [PS] - **Spec Exp:** Fetal Surgery; Twin to Twin Transfusion Syndrome (TTTS); Hernia; **Hospital:** Chldn's Hosp - Aurora (CO); **Address:** Chldns Hosp, Surgery Dept, 13123 E 16th Ave, Box B323, Aurora, CO 80045; **Phone:** 720-777-6571; **Board Cert:** Surgery 2003; Pediatric Surgery 2007; **Med School:** Tufts Univ 1984; **Resid:** Surgery, UCSF Med Ctr 1991; **Fellow:** Pediatric Surgery, Tufts Med Ctr 1993; **Fac Appt:** Prof S, Univ Cincinnati

Karrer, Frederick M MD [PS] - **Spec Exp:** Liver Surgery; Transplant-Liver; Critical Care; Neonatal Surgery; **Hospital:** Chldn's Hosp - Aurora (CO); **Address:** Chldns Hosp, Surgery Dept, 13123 E 16th Ave, Box B323, Aurora, CO 80045; **Phone:** 720-777-6571; **Board Cert:** Surgery 2007; Pediatric Surgery 2009; Surgical Critical Care 2012; **Med School:** Univ Nebr Coll Med 1979; **Resid:** Surgery, Univ Arizona Med Ctr 1984; Pediatric Surgery, Chldns Meml Hosp 1986; **Fellow:** Transplant Surgery, UPMC 1988; **Fac Appt:** Prof S, Univ Colorado

Meyers, Rebecka L MD [PS] - **Spec Exp:** Transplant-Liver; Tumor Surgery; Biliary Surgery; Pancreatic Surgery; **Hospital:** Primary Children's Med Ctr, Univ Utah Hlth Care; **Address:** PCMC-Dept Surg, 100 N Mario Capecchi Drive, Ste 2600, Salt Lake City, UT 84113-1103; **Phone:** 801-662-2950; **Board Cert:** Surgery 2003; Pediatric Surgery 2005; **Med School:** Oregon Hlth & Sci Univ 1985; **Resid:** Surgery, UCSF Med Ctr 1990; **Fellow:** Research, Cardio Rsch Inst-UCSF 1992; Pediatric Surgery, St Christophers Hosp for Chldn 1994; **Fac Appt:** Assoc Prof S, Univ Utah

Southwest

Black, C Thomas MD [PS] - **Spec Exp:** Neonatal Surgery; Minimally Invasive Surgery; Chest Wall Deformities; **Hospital:** Cook Chldns Med Ctr; **Address:** 7000 W Plano Pkwy, Ste 200, Plano, TX 75093; **Phone:** 214-483-9300; **Board Cert:** Pediatric Surgery 2007; Surgery 2005; **Med School:** Baylor Coll Med 1979; **Resid:** Surgery, Baylor College Affil Hosp 1984; **Fellow:** Pediatric Surgery, Riley Childrens Hospital 1985; Pediatric Surgery-ECMO, Chldn's Meml Hosp 1987

Cass, Darrell L MD [PS] - **Spec Exp:** Fetal Surgery; Neonatal Surgery; Chest Wall Deformities; **Hospital:** Texas Chldns Hosp, St. Luke's Episcopal Hosp-Houston; **Address:** Clinical Care Ctr, 6701 Fannin St, Ste 1210, Houston, TX 77030-2303; **Phone:** 832-822-3135; **Board Cert:** Surgery 2010; Pediatric Surgery 2011; **Med School:** UCLA-David Geffen Sch Med 1991; **Resid:** Surgery, UCSF Med Ctr 1999; **Fellow:** Pediatric Surgery, Baylor Coll Med 2001; **Fac Appt:** Assoc Prof PS, Baylor Coll Med

Foglia, Robert P MD [PS] - **Hospital:** Chldns Med Ctr of Dallas; **Address:** 1935 Medical District Drive, Ste B3250, Dallas, TX 75235; **Phone:** 214-456-6040; **Board Cert:** Pediatric Surgery 2005; **Med School:** Georgetown Univ 1974; **Resid:** Surgery, UCLA Med Ctr 1981; **Fellow:** Pediatric Surgery, Chldns Hosp Natl Med Ctr 1983; **Fac Appt:** Prof S, Univ Tex SW, Dallas

Graziano, Kathleen D MD [PS] - **Spec Exp:** Congenital Reproductive Anomalies; Sexual Anomalies; **Hospital:** Phoenix Children's Hosp; **Address:** Pediatric Surgeons of Phoenix, 1920 E Cambridge Ave, Ste 201, Phoenix, AZ 85006; **Phone:** 602-254-5561; **Board Cert:** Surgery 2004; Pediatric Surgery 2006; **Med School:** Columbia P&S 1996; **Resid:** Surgery, Univ Michigan Med Ctr 2003; **Fellow:** Pediatric Surgery, Univ MI/CS Mott Chldns Hosp 2005

Jackson, Richard J MD [PS] - **Spec Exp:** Pediatric Cancers; Neonatal Surgery; Robotic Surgery; **Hospital:** Arkansas Chldns Hosp; **Address:** Arkansas Children's Hospital, 1 Children's Way, Slot 837, Little Rock, AR 72202-3591; **Phone:** 501-364-1446; **Board Cert:** Surgery 2008; Pediatric Surgery 2012; **Med School:** W VA Univ 1983; **Resid:** Surgery, W Va Univ Hosps 1988; Pediatric Surgery, Chldns Hosp 1989; **Fellow:** Surgical Critical Care, Chldns Hosp-Univ Pittsburgh 1990; Pediatric Surgery, Chldns Hosp-Univ Pittsburgh 1992

McGill, Leigh C MD [PS] - **Spec Exp:** Congenital Anomalies; **Hospital:** Phoenix Children's Hosp, St. Joseph's Hosp & Med Ctr - Phoenix; **Address:** 1920 E Cambridge Ave, Ste 201, Phoenix, AZ 85006; **Phone:** 602-254-5561; **Board Cert:** Pediatric Surgery 2011; **Med School:** Univ Colorado 1976; **Resid:** Surgery, Maricopa Co General Hosp 1981; **Fellow:** Pediatric Surgery, Denver Childrens Hosp 1983; Pediatric Urology, Royal Children's Hosp; **Fac Appt:** Asst Clin Prof S, Univ Ariz Coll Med

Notrica, David MD [PS] - **Spec Exp:** Biliary Surgery; Inflammatory Bowel Disease; Laparoscopic Surgery-Advanced; Hirschsprung's Disease; **Hospital:** Phoenix Children's Hosp, St. Joseph's Hosp & Med Ctr - Phoenix; **Address:** Pediatric Surgeons of Phoenix, 1920 E Cambridge Ave, Ste 201, Phoenix, AZ 85006; **Phone:** 602-254-5561; **Board Cert:** Surgery 2005; Pediatric Surgery 2007; **Med School:** Emory Univ 1992; **Resid:** Surgery, Emory Univ Hosps 1997; **Fellow:** Pediatric Surgery, Texas Chldns Hosp 1999; **Fac Appt:** Asst Clin Prof S, Univ Ariz Coll Med

Nuchtern, Jed G MD [PS] - **Spec Exp:** Pediatric Thoracic Surgery; Cancer Surgery; Laparoscopic Surgery; **Hospital:** Texas Chldns Hosp, Ben Taub Genl Hosp; **Address:** Texas Children's Hosp, 6701 Fannin St, MC CCC1210, Houston, TX 77030; **Phone:** 832-822-3135; **Board Cert:** Surgery 2003; Surgical Critical Care 2012; Pediatric Surgery 2007; **Med School:** Harvard Med Sch 1985; **Resid:** Surgery, Univ Wash Med Ctr 1988; Pediatric Surgery, Baylor Affil Hosp 1995; **Fellow:** Cellular Molecular Biology, Natl Inst Hlth 1990; **Fac Appt:** Prof S, Baylor Coll Med

Skinner, Michael A MD [PS] - **Spec Exp:** Endocrine Cancers; Thyroid Cancer; **Hospital:** UT Southwestern Med Ctr at Dallas; **Address:** UT Southwestern Med Ctr Dallas, 1935 Medical District Drive, MC B3.01, Dallas, TX 75235; **Phone:** 214-456-6040; **Board Cert:** Surgery 2010; Pediatric Surgery 2012; **Med School:** Rush Med Coll 1984; **Resid:** Surgery, Duke Univ Med Ctr 1991; **Fellow:** Pediatric Surgery, Indiana Univ Affil Hosps 1993; **Fac Appt:** Assoc Prof S, Univ Tex SW, Dallas

West Coast and Pacific

Albanese, Craig T MD [PS] - **Spec Exp:** Fetal Surgery; Laparoscopic Surgery; Twin to Twin Transfusion Syndrome (TTTS); **Hospital:** Lucile Packard Chldn's Hosp; **Address:** 700 Welch Rd, Ste 125, Palo Alto, CA 94304; **Phone:** 650-724-3664; **Board Cert:** Surgery 2000; Pediatric Surgery 2003; **Med School:** SUNY Hlth Sci Ctr 1986; **Resid:** Surgery, Mt Sinai Med Ctr 1991; **Fellow:** Pediatric Surgery, Chldns Hosp 1994; **Fac Appt:** Prof S, Stanford Univ

Farmer, Diana MD [PS] - **Spec Exp:** Pediatric Cancers; Fetal Surgery; Spina Bifida; Twin to Twin Transfusion Syndrome (TTTS); **Hospital:** UC Davis Med Ctr; **Address:** 2315 Stockton Blvd, Sacramento, CA 95817; **Phone:** 916-734-2011; **Board Cert:** Surgery 2001; Pediatric Surgery 2005; **Med School:** Univ Wash 1983; **Resid:** Surgery, UCSF Med Ctr 1993; **Fellow:** Pediatric Surgery, Childrens Hosp 1995; **Fac Appt:** Prof S, UC Davis

Ford, Henri R MD [PS] - **Spec Exp:** Minimally Invasive Surgery; Trauma; **Hospital:** Chldns Hosp - Los Angeles, Long Beach Meml Med Ctr; **Address:** 4650 Sunset Blvd, MS 72, Los Angeles, CA 90027; **Phone:** 323-361-2104; **Board Cert:** Surgery 2002; Pediatric Surgery 2005; **Med School:** Harvard Med Sch 1984; **Resid:** Surgery, New York Hosp 1991; **Fellow:** Pediatric Surgery, Chldns Hosp 1995

Grikscheit, Tracy C MD [PS] - **Spec Exp:** Congenital Anomalies; Short Bowel Syndrome; Necrotizing Enterocolitis; Neonatal Surgery; **Hospital:** Chldns Hosp - Los Angeles; **Address:** CHLA, Surgery Dept, 4650 Sunset Blvd, MS 106, Los Angeles, CA 90027; **Phone:** 323-361-2322; **Board Cert:** Surgery 2005; Pediatric Surgery 2008; **Med School:** Columbia P&S 1997; **Resid:** Surgery, Mass Genl Hosp 2002; **Fellow:** Pediatric Surgery, Seattle Chldns Hosp 2004; **Fac Appt:** Asst Prof S, UCLA

Healey, Patrick J MD [PS] - **Spec Exp:** Transplant Surgery-Pediatric; Transplant-Kidney; Transplant-Liver; Congenital Anomalies; **Hospital:** Seattle Chldns Hosp; **Address:** 4800 Sand Point Way NE, Dept Surgery, MS MB.9.420, Seattle, WA 98105; **Phone:** 206-987-1800; **Board Cert:** Surgery 2002; Pediatric Surgery 2009; **Med School:** Boston Univ 1987; **Resid:** Surgery, Hartford Hosp 1993; **Fellow:** Transplant Surgery, Univ Wash Med Ctr 1995; Pediatric Surgery, Chldn's Hosp 1997; **Fac Appt:** Asst Prof S, Univ Wash

Hilfiker, Mary L MD/PhD [PS] - **Spec Exp:** Trauma; Neonatal Surgery; Cancer Surgery; Thoracic Surgery; **Hospital:** Rady Children's Hosp - San Diego; **Address:** 3030 Children's Way, Ste 107, MC 5136, San Diego, CA 92123; **Phone:** 858-966-7711; **Board Cert:** Surgery 2004; Pediatric Surgery 2007; **Med School:** Wright State Univ 1988; **Resid:** Surgery, Univ Hosp 1993; **Fellow:** Pediatric Surgery, Women & Chldn's Hosp of Buffalo 1995; **Fac Appt:** Assoc Clin Prof S, UCSD

Krummel, Thomas M MD [PS] - **Spec Exp:** Minimally Invasive Surgery; Robotic Surgery; Fetal Surgery; **Hospital:** Lucile Packard Chldn's Hosp, Stanford Univ Hosp & Clins; **Address:** Neurosciences & Pediatric Surgery, 730 Welch Rd Fl 2, MC 5883, Palo Alto, CA 94304; **Phone:** 650-724-4270; **Board Cert:** Surgery 2004; Pediatric Surgery 2007; **Med School:** Univ Wisc 1977; **Resid:** Surgery, Med Coll Va Hosp 1983; Pediatric Surgery, Chldns Hosp 1985; **Fellow:** Fetal Surgery, UCSF Med Ctr 1986; **Fac Appt:** Prof S, Stanford Univ

Proctor, Monja L MD [PS] - **Spec Exp:** Fetal Surgery; Neonatal Surgery; Hirschsprung's Disease; **Hospital:** Swedish Med Ctr-First Hill-Seattle; **Address:** Swedish Med Ctr-Ped Spec Care, 1101 Madison St, Ste 800, Seattle, WA 98104; **Phone:** 206-215-2700; **Board Cert:** Pediatric Surgery 2004; **Med School:** Univ Tex SW, Dallas 1993; **Resid:** Pediatrics, Univ TX SW Meml Med Ctr 2000; **Fellow:** Pediatric Surgery, Hosp For Sick Chldn 2002

Sawin, Robert S MD [PS] - **Spec Exp:** Pediatric Cancers; Pediatric Thoracic Surgery; Neonatal Surgery-Gastrointestinal; Transplant-Liver; **Hospital:** Seattle Chldns Hosp; **Address:** Seattle Chldn's Hosp, 4800 Sand Point Way NE, MS OA.9.220, Seattle, WA 98145-5005; **Phone:** 206-987-2794; **Board Cert:** Pediatric Surgery 2009; **Med School:** Univ Pittsburgh 1982; **Resid:** Surgery, Brigham & Women's Hosp 1987; **Fellow:** Pediatric Surgery, Chldn's Hosp 1989; **Fac Appt:** Prof S, Univ Wash

Stein, James E MD [PS] - **Hospital:** Chldns Hosp - Los Angeles; **Address:** Dept Pediatric Surgery, 4650 Sunset Blvd, MS 100, Los Angeles, CA 90027; **Phone:** 323-361-2491; **Board Cert:** Surgery 2004; Pediatric Surgery 2005; **Med School:** Tufts Univ 1986; **Resid:** Surgery, Tufts Med Ctr 1993; **Fellow:** Pediatric Surgery, Royal Chldns Hosp 1994; Pediatric Surgery, NY-Presby/Columbia Univ Med Ctr 1996; **Fac Appt:** Assoc Prof S, USC Sch Med

Stolar, Charles J H MD [PS] - **Spec Exp:** Neonatal Surgery; Hernia; Pediatric Cancers; **Hospital:** Santa Barbara Cottage Hosp; **Address:** 2403 Castillo St, Ste 202, Santa Barbara, CA 93105; **Phone:** 805-563-6560; **Board Cert:** Surgery 2012; Pediatric Surgery 2007; **Med School:** Georgetown Univ 1974; **Resid:** Surgery, Univ Illinois Hosp 1980; **Fellow:** Pediatric Surgery, Chldns Hosp Natl Med Ctr 1982

Waldhausen, John HT MD [PS] - **Spec Exp:** Minimally Invasive Surgery; Laparoscopic Surgery; Neonatal Surgery; Congenital Anomalies; **Hospital:** Seattle Chldns Hosp; **Address:** 4800 Sand Point Way, Dept Surgery, Seattle, WA 98105; **Phone:** 206-987-2794; **Board Cert:** Surgery 2010; Pediatric Surgery 2005; **Med School:** Penn State Coll Med 1986; **Resid:** Surgery, Univ Virginia Med Ctr 1992; **Fellow:** Pediatric Surgery, Chldns Hosp Med Ctr - Washington Univ 1994; **Fac Appt:** Prof S, Univ Wash

Pediatric Urology

New England

Bauer, Stuart B MD [Ped Uro] - **Spec Exp:** Neuro-Urology; Neurogenic Bladder; **Hospital:** Children's Hospital - Boston; **Address:** Boston Chldn's Hosp, Dept Urology, 300 Longwood Ave, Hunnewell 390, Boston, MA 02115-6264; **Phone:** 617-355-7796; **Board Cert:** Urology 1977; **Med School:** Univ Rochester 1968; **Resid:** Urology, Tufts New Engl Med Ctr 1975; **Fac Appt:** Prof U, Harvard Med Sch

Caldamone, Anthony A MD [Ped Uro] - **Spec Exp:** Hypospadias; Varicocele; **Hospital:** Rhode Island Hosp; **Address:** 2 Dudley St, Ste 185, Providence, RI 02905; **Phone:** 401-421-0710; **Board Cert:** Urology 1983; Pediatric Urology 2008; **Med School:** Brown Univ 1975; **Resid:** Urology, Strong Meml Hosp/Univ Rochester 1981; **Fellow:** Pediatric Urology, Childrens Hosp 1982; **Fac Appt:** Prof U, Brown Univ

Mid Atlantic

Canning, Douglas A MD [Ped Uro] - **Spec Exp:** Hypospadias; Bladder Exstrophy; Bladder Reconstruction; Genitourinary Congenital Anomalies; **Hospital:** Chldns Hosp of Philadelphia; **Address:** Chldns Hosp, Ped Urology Dept, 3400 Civic Center Blvd Wood Bldg Fl 3, Philadelphia, PA 19104; **Phone:** 215-590-2754; **Board Cert:** Urology 2010; Pediatric Urology 2008; **Med School:** Dartmouth Med Sch 1982; **Resid:** Urology, Naval Hosp 1987; **Fellow:** Pediatric Urology, Johns Hopkins Hosp/Brady Urological Inst 1989; **Fac Appt:** Prof U, Univ Pennsylvania

Docimo, Steven G MD [Ped Uro] - **Spec Exp:** Minimally Invasive Surgery; Bladder Reconstruction; Voiding Dysfunction; Urinary Reflux; **Hospital:** Chldns Hosp of Pittsburgh - UPMC; **Address:** Chldns Hosp, Ped Urology Dept, 4401 Penn Ave Fl 3, Pittsburgh, PA 15224; **Phone:** 412-692-7932; **Board Cert:** Urology 2008; Pediatric Urology 2008; **Med School:** Johns Hopkins Univ 1984; **Resid:** Surgery, Georgetown Univ Hosp 1986; Urology, Brigham & Womens Hosp 1990; **Fellow:** Pediatric Urology, Johns Hopkins 1994; Research, Chldns Hosp 1988; **Fac Appt:** Prof U, Univ Pittsburgh

Greenfield, Saul P MD [Ped Uro] - **Spec Exp:** Urinary Tract Infections; Neurogenic Bladder; Reconstructive Urologic Surgery; Clinical Trials; **Hospital:** Women & Chldn's Hosp of Buffalo, The; **Address:** Pediatric Urology of Western NY, 219 Bryant St, Buffalo, NY 14222; **Phone:** 716-878-7393; **Board Cert:** Urology 1984; Pediatric Urology 2008; **Med School:** Univ Pennsylvania 1977; **Resid:** Surgery, NYU Med Ctr 1979; Urology, Columbia-Presby Med Ctr 1982; **Fellow:** Pediatric Urology, Chldns Hosp Buffalo 1984; **Fac Appt:** Clin Prof U, SUNY Buffalo

Kolon, Thomas F MD [Ped Uro] - **Spec Exp:** Hypospadias; Wilms' Tumor; Varicocele; Urologic Cancer-Pediatric; **Hospital:** Chldns Hosp of Philadelphia; **Address:** Children's Hosp Philadelphia, Urology, 34th St & Civic Ctr Blvd Wood Bldg Fl 3, Philadelphia, PA 19104; **Phone:** 215-590-2754; **Board Cert:** Urology 2010; Pediatric Urology 2008; **Med School:** Georgetown Univ 1995; **Resid:** Surgery, Univ CT Med Ctr 1997; Urology, Univ CT Med Ctr 2000; **Fellow:** Pediatric Urology, Texas Children'sHosp 2007; **Fac Appt:** Assoc Prof U, Univ Pennsylvania

Poppas, Dix P MD [Ped Uro] - **Spec Exp:** Genital Reconstruction-Pediatric; Robotic Surgery-Pediatric; Minimally Invasive Surgery-Pediatric; **Hospital:** NY-Presby/Weill Cornell Med Ctr, NY (page 65); **Address:** Inst for Pediatric Urology, NY Presby Hosp-Weill Cornell, 525 E 68th St, rm F931, Box 94, New York, NY 10065; **Phone:** 212-746-5337; **Board Cert:** Urology 2008; Pediatric Urology 2008; **Med School:** Eastern VA Med Sch 1988; **Resid:** Surgery, Eastern VA Med Schl Affil Hosp 1990; Urology, NY Hosp-Cornell Med Ctr 1994; **Fellow:** Pediatric Urology, Boston Children's Hosp 1996; **Fac Appt:** Prof U, Cornell Univ-Weill Med Coll

Rushton Jr, H Gil MD [Ped Uro] - **Spec Exp:** Fetal Urology; Hypospadias; Hydronephrosis; Genitalia Ambiguity; **Hospital:** Chldns Natl Med Ctr; **Address:** Chldn's National Med Ctr, Dept Urology, 111 Michigan Ave NW, Ste 400-W, Washington, DC 20010; **Phone:** 202-476-5042; **Board Cert:** Urology 2009; Pediatric Urology 2009; **Med School:** Univ SC Sch Med 1978; **Resid:** Urology, Univ SC Med Ctr 1983; **Fellow:** Pediatric Urology, Hosp Sick Chldn 1984; Pediatric Urology, Emory Chldns Hosp 1986; **Fac Appt:** Prof U, Geo Wash Univ

Southeast

Atala, Anthony MD [Ped Uro] - **Spec Exp:** Reconstructive Surgery; Hernia; Hypospadias; Microsurgery; **Hospital:** Wake Forest Baptist Med Ctr; **Address:** Wake Forest Univ Baptist Med Ctr, Dept Urology, 140 Charlois Blvd, Winston-Salem, NC 27103; **Phone:** 336-716-4131; **Board Cert:** Urology 2008; Pediatric Urology 2008; **Med School:** Univ Louisville Sch Med 1985; **Resid:** Surgery, Univ Louisville Hosp 1987; Urology, Univ Louisville Hosp 1990; **Fellow:** Research, Boston Children's Hosp 1991; Pediatric Urology, Boston Children's Hosp 1992; **Fac Appt:** Prof U, Wake Forest Univ

Brock III, John W MD [Ped Uro] - **Spec Exp:** Reconstructive Surgery; Bladder Exstrophy; Spina Bifida; **Hospital:** Vanderbilt Monroe Carrell Jr. Chldn's Hosp; **Address:** Vanderbilt Chldns Hosp, Div Ped Urology, 2200 Childrens Way, 4102 DOT, Nashville, TN 37232-9820; **Phone:** 615-936-1060; **Board Cert:** Urology 2008; Pediatric Urology 2008; **Med School:** Med Coll GA 1978; **Resid:** Urology, Vanderbilt Univ Med Ctr 1983; **Fac Appt:** Prof U, Vanderbilt Univ

Joseph, David B MD [Ped Uro] - **Spec Exp:** Urodynamics; Neuro-Urology; Urologic Cancer-Pediatric; **Hospital:** Children's Hosp AL, UAB Hosp; **Address:** Chldns Hosp AL, Dept Urology, 1600 7th Ave S, Ste ACC-318, Birmingham, AL 35233; **Phone:** 205-638-9840; **Board Cert:** Urology 2008; Pediatric Urology 2008; **Med School:** Univ Wisc 1980; **Resid:** Urology, Univ WI Hosp & Clins 1985; **Fellow:** Pediatric Urology, Chldns Hosp 1986; **Fac Appt:** Prof U, UAB Sch Med

Kirsch, Andrew J MD [Ped Uro] - **Spec Exp:** Urinary Reconstruction; Urinary Reflux; Bladder Exstrophy; Urologic Cancer-Pediatric; **Hospital:** Chldns Hlthcare Atlanta @ Egleston, Chldns Hlthcare Atlanta @ Scottish Rite; **Address:** Georgia Urology, 5445 Meridian Mark Rd NE, Ste 420, Atlanta, GA 30342; **Phone:** 404-252-5206; **Board Cert:** Urology 2010; Pediatric Urology 2008; **Med School:** SUNY Downstate 1990; **Resid:** Surgery, Columbia-Presby Hosp 1992; Urology, Columbia-Presby Hosp 1996; **Fellow:** Pediatric Urology, Chldns Hosp 1998; **Fac Appt:** Clin Prof U, Emory Univ

Pope IV, John C MD [Ped Uro] - **Spec Exp:** Varicocele; Hypospadias; Urologic Cancer-Pediatric; **Hospital:** Vanderbilt Monroe Carrell Jr. Chldn's Hosp; **Address:** Vanderbilt Chldns Hosp, Div Ped Urology, 2200 Children's Way, Ste 4102 DOT, Nashville, TN 37232; **Phone:** 615-936-1060; **Board Cert:** Urology 2008; Pediatric Urology 2008; **Med School:** Univ Tenn Coll Med 1989; **Resid:** Surgery, Vanderbilt Univ Med Ctr 1991; Urology, Vanderbilt Univ Med Ctr 1995; **Fellow:** Pediatric Urology, Indiana Univ Med Ctr 1997; **Fac Appt:** Prof U, Vanderbilt Univ

Sutherland, Richard W MD [Ped Uro] - **Spec Exp:** Hypospadias; Varicocele; **Hospital:** NC Memorial Hosp - UNC; **Address:** 101 Manning Drive, Chapel Hill, NC 27599; **Phone:** 919-966-1401; **Board Cert:** Urology 2008; Pediatric Urology 2008; **Med School:** Oregon Hlth & Sci Univ 1989; **Resid:** Urology, Albany Med Ctr 1994; **Fellow:** Pediatric Urology, Baylor Coll Med 1996; **Fac Appt:** Assoc Prof U, Univ NC Sch Med

Midwest

Bloom, David A MD [Ped Uro] - **Spec Exp:** Genitourinary Reconstruction; Neurogenic Bladder; Hypospadias; Urologic Cancer-Pediatric; **Hospital:** Mott Chldns Hosp; **Address:** 1500 E Medical Ctr Drive, 3875 Taubman, Ann Arbor, MI 48109-5330; **Phone:** 734-232-4943; **Board Cert:** Urology 1982; Pediatric Urology 2008; **Med School:** SUNY Buffalo 1971; **Resid:** Surgery, UCLA Med Ctr 1976; Urology, UCLA Med Ctr 1980; **Fellow:** Pediatric Urology, Inst Urol-St Peters Hosp 1978; **Fac Appt:** Prof U, Univ Mich Med Sch

Cain, Mark P MD [Ped Uro] - **Spec Exp:** Hydronephrosis-Prenatal; Genitourinary Reconstruction; Bladder Exstrophy; Urologic Cancer-Pediatric; **Hospital:** Riley Hosp for Children, Peyton Manning Children's Hosp at St. Vincent; **Address:** Riley Hospital for Children, 705 Riley Hospital Drive, Ste 4230, Indianapolis, IN 46202; **Phone:** 317-944-7446; **Board Cert:** Urology 2008; Pediatric Urology 2008; **Med School:** Oregon Hlth & Sci Univ 1987; **Resid:** Surgery, Albany Med Ctr 1989; Urology, Albany Med Ctr 1992; **Fellow:** Pediatric Urology, Mayo Clinic 1994; **Fac Appt:** Prof U, Indiana Univ

Cheng, Earl Y MD [Ped Uro] - **Spec Exp:** Genital Reconstruction-Pediatric; Hypospadias; Urinary Reconstruction; Neurogenic Bladder; **Hospital:** Lurie Chldn's Hosp-Chicago, Central DuPage Hosp; **Address:** Lurie Chldn's Hosp-Urology, 225 E Chicago Ave, Box 24, Chicago, IL 60611; **Phone:** 312-227-6340; **Board Cert:** Urology 2008; Pediatric Urology 2008; **Med School:** Northwestern Univ 1988; **Resid:** Urology, Northwestern Meml Hosp 1994; **Fellow:** Pediatric Urology, Chldn's Meml Hosp 1996; **Fac Appt:** Prof U, Northwestern Univ-Feinberg Sch Med

Coplen, Douglas E MD [Ped Uro] - **Spec Exp:** Urologic Cancer-Pediatric; Testicular Cancer-Pediatric; Genitourinary Reconstruction; **Hospital:** St. Louis Chldns Hosp; **Address:** St Louis Children's Hosp, One Children's Pl, Ste 2A, St Louis, MO 63110; **Phone:** 314-454-6034; **Board Cert:** Urology 2008; Pediatric Urology 2008; **Med School:** Indiana Univ 1985; **Resid:** Urology, Barnes Jewish Hosp 1992; **Fellow:** Pediatric Urology, Children's Hosp 1994; **Fac Appt:** Assoc Prof S, Washington Univ, St Louis

Elder, Jack S MD [Ped Uro] - **Spec Exp:** Hypospadias; Urinary Reconstruction; Robotic Surgery; Hydronephrosis; **Hospital:** Henry Ford- W Bloomfield Hosp, Chldns Hosp of Michigan; **Address:** Chldns Hosp Michigan, 3901 Beaubien Blvd, Detroit, MI 48201; **Phone:** 313-745-5588; **Board Cert:** Urology 1984; Pediatric Urology 2009; **Med School:** Univ Okla Coll Med 1976; **Resid:** Surgery, Yale-New Haven Hosp 1978; Urology, Johns Hopkins Hosp 1982; **Fellow:** Pediatric Urology, Johns Hopkins Hosp 1982; Pediatric Urology, Chldns Hosp 1986; **Fac Appt:** Prof U, Case West Res Univ

Gundeti, Mohan S MD [Ped Uro] - **Spec Exp:** Robotic Surgery-Pediatric; Laparoscopic Surgery; Bladder Reconstruction; Congenital Anomalies; **Hospital:** Univ Chicago Med-Comer Chldn's Hosp; **Address:** UC Comer Chldn's Hosp-Ped Urology, 5721 S Maryland Ave, Chicago, IL 60637; **Phone:** 773-702-6150; **Med School:** India 1991; **Resid:** Surgery, Shivaji Univ Affil Hosp; Urology, Univ Bombay Affil Hosp; **Fellow:** Pediatric Urology, Great Ormond Street Hosp; **Fac Appt:** Assoc Prof U, Univ Chicago-Pritzker Sch Med

Hatch, David A MD [Ped Uro] - **Spec Exp:** Transplant-Kidney; Genital Birth Defects; **Hospital:** Loyola Univ - Ronald McDonald Children's Hosp; **Address:** Loyola Univ, Sect Ped Urol, 2160 S 1st Ave, Bldg 54 - rm 237, Maywood, IL 60153-3304; **Phone:** 708-216-6266; **Board Cert:** Urology 2008; Pediatric Urology 2008; **Med School:** Univ Utah 1980; **Resid:** Urology, Univ Oreg/Hlth Scis Univ 1986; **Fellow:** Pediatric Urology, Chldns Meml Hosp 1987; **Fac Appt:** Prof U, Loyola Univ-Stritch Sch Med

Kaefer, Martin MD [Ped Uro] - **Spec Exp:** Reconstructive Surgery; Genitourinary Congenital Anomalies; Hydronephrosis-Prenatal; Incontinence; **Hospital:** Riley Hosp for Children, Franciscan St. Francis Hlth-Indianapolis; **Address:** IU Health - Pediatric Urology, 705 Riley Hospital Drive, rm 4230, Indianapolis, IN 46202; **Phone:** 317-944-8896; **Board Cert:** Urology 2010; Pediatric Urology 2008; **Med School:** Northwestern Univ 1989; **Resid:** Surgery, IU Health Affil Hosp 1991; Urology, IU Health Affil Hosp 1995; **Fellow:** Pediatric Urology, Chldns Hosp 1998; **Fac Appt:** Prof U, Indiana Univ

Kass, Evan J MD [Ped Uro] - **Spec Exp:** Hydronephrosis; Hypospadias; Varicocele in Adolescents; **Hospital:** Beaumont Hosp-Royal Oak; **Address:** 2221 Livernois Ave, Ste 103, Troy, MI 48083; **Phone:** 248-519-0305; **Board Cert:** Urology 1978; Pediatric Urology 2009; **Med School:** SUNY Downstate 1968; **Resid:** Urology, Univ Mich Hosp 1976; **Fellow:** Pediatric Urology, Hosp for Sick Chldn 1978; **Fac Appt:** Assoc Prof U, Wayne State Univ

Maizels, Max MD [Ped Uro] - **Spec Exp:** Fetal Urology; Hypospadias; Genital Reconstruction-Pediatric; Urinary Reconstruction; **Hospital:** Lurie Chldn's Hosp-Chicago; **Address:** Lurie Chldn's Hosp-Urology, 225 E Chicago Ave, Box 24, Chicago, IL 60614; **Phone:** 312-227-6340; **Board Cert:** Urology 1982; **Med School:** UCLA 1974; **Resid:** Surgery, Boston Univ Med Ctr 1976; Urology, Northwestern Meml Hosp 1980; **Fac Appt:** Prof U, Northwestern Univ-Feinberg Sch Med

Mesrobian, Hrair-George O MD [Ped Uro] - **Spec Exp:** Bladder Exstrophy; Epispadias; **Hospital:** Chldns Hosp - Wisconsin; **Address:** Children's Hospital of Wisconsin, 9000 W Wisconsin Ave, Milwaukee, WI 53226; **Phone:** 414-266-3769; **Board Cert:** Urology 2008; Pediatric Urology 2008; **Med School:** Lebanon 1978; **Resid:** Surgery, SUNY Upstate Med Ctr 1980; Urology, UCSF Med Ctr 1983; **Fellow:** Pediatric Urology, Mayo Clin 1984; **Fac Appt:** Prof U, Med Coll Wisc

Rink, Richard C MD [Ped Uro] - **Spec Exp:** Reconstructive Urologic Surgery; Genital Reconstruction; Neurogenic Bladder; Hydronephrosis-Prenatal; **Hospital:** Riley Hosp for Children, IU Hlth Univ Hosp; **Address:** IU Health - Pediatric Urology, 705 Riley Hospital Drive, ROC Bldg, Ste 4230, Indianapolis, IN 46202; **Phone:** 317-948-8554; **Board Cert:** Urology 2008; Pediatric Urology 2008; **Med School:** Indiana Univ 1978; **Resid:** Surgery, Emory Univ Med Ctr 1980; Urology, Indiana Univ Med Ctr 1984; **Fellow:** Pediatric Urology, Chldns Hosp-Harvard 1985; **Fac Appt:** Prof U, Indiana Univ

Great Plains and Mountains

Cartwright, Patrick C MD [Ped Uro] - **Spec Exp:** Hypospadias; Varicocele; Urologic Cancer-Pediatric; **Hospital:** Primary Children's Med Ctr, Intermountain Med Ctr; **Address:** Primary Childrens Med Ctr, 100 N Mario Capecchi Drive, Ste 2200, Salt Lake City, UT 84113-1100; **Phone:** 801-662-5555; **Board Cert:** Urology 2010; Pediatric Urology 2010; **Med School:** Univ Tex SW, Dallas 1984; **Resid:** Urology, Univ Utah Affil Hosp 1989; **Fellow:** Pediatric Urology, Chldns Hosp 1990; **Fac Appt:** Prof S, Univ Utah

Southwest

Ewalt, David H MD [Ped Uro] - **Spec Exp:** Hypospadias; Urinary Reconstruction; Neurogenic Bladder; Urologic Cancer-Pediatric; **Hospital:** Chldns Med Ctr of Dallas, Med City Dallas Hosp; **Address:** Urology Clinics of North Texas, 8315 Walnut Hill Ln, Ste 205, Dallas, TX 75231; **Phone:** 214-750-0808; **Board Cert:** Urology 2008; Pediatric Urology 2008; **Med School:** Univ Tex SW, Dallas 1984; **Resid:** Urology, Parkland Hosp 1990; **Fellow:** Pediatric Urology, Chldns Hosp 1992

Gonzales, Edmond T MD [Ped Uro] - **Hospital:** Texas Chldns Hosp; **Address:** Texas Children's Clinical Care Center, 6701 Fannin St, Ste 620, Houston, TX 77030; **Phone:** 832-822-3160; **Board Cert:** Urology 1975; Pediatric Urology 2008; **Med School:** Tulane Univ 1965; **Resid:** Urology, Duke Univ Med Ctr 1972; **Fac Appt:** Prof U, Baylor Coll Med

Strand, William R MD [Ped Uro] - **Spec Exp:** Laparoscopic Surgery; Hypospadias; Reconstructive Surgery; **Hospital:** Chldns Med Ctr of Dallas; **Address:** Urology Clinics of North Texas, 4001 W 15th St, Ste 300, Plano, TX 75093; **Phone:** 214-750-0808 x5400; **Board Cert:** Urology 2008; Pediatric Urology 2008; **Med School:** Mayo Med Sch 1983; **Resid:** Urology, Natl Naval Med Ctr 1988; **Fellow:** Pediatric Urology, Chldns Meml Hosp 1989

West Coast and Pacific

Baskin, Laurence S MD [Ped Uro] - **Spec Exp:** Hypospadias; **Hospital:** UCSF Med Ctr; **Address:** Urology Faculty Practice, 400 Parnassus Ave Fl 6, Ste A-610, Box 0330, San Francisco, CA 94143-0330; **Phone:** 415-353-2200; **Board Cert:** Urology 2008; Pediatric Urology 2008; **Med School:** UCLA 1986; **Resid:** Urology, UCSF Med Ctr 1991; **Fellow:** Pediatric Urology, Chldns Hosp 1993; **Fac Appt:** Prof U, UCSF

Merguerian, Paul A MD [Ped Uro] - **Spec Exp:** Bladder Exstrophy; Genital Reconstruction; Minimally Invasive Surgery; Urologic Cancer-Pediatric; **Hospital:** Seattle Chldns Hosp; **Address:** Seattle Children's Hosp, Division of Urology, 4800 Sand Point Way NE, Seattle, WA 98105; **Phone:** 206-987-2509; **Board Cert:** Urology 2008; Pediatric Urology 2008; **Med School:** Israel 1980; **Resid:** Surgery, Strong Meml Hosp 1984; Urology, Strong Meml Hosp 1988; **Fellow:** Pediatric Urology, Hosp for Sick Chldn 1990; **Fac Appt:** Prof S, Dartmouth Med Sch

Maimonides
Medical Center

Maimonides Infants & Children's Hospital

4802 Tenth Avenue
Brooklyn, New York 11219
Phone: 718.283.7500 • Fax: 718.635.6149
www.maimonidesmed.org/pediatrics

The Maimonides Infants & Children's Hospital is a NACHRI-certified children's hospital-within-a-hospital. Offering over 30 sub-specialty divisions as well as primary care, the Pediatrics program is unrivaled in the region and serves one of the largest pediatric populations in the nation.

Danielle Laraque, MD, Vice President of the Maimonides Infants & Children's Hospital, leads a family-centered pediatrics program in a state-of-the-art medical environment, where babies, children and adolescents receive the best and most appropriate care. For most children, this involves preventing illness and promoting healthy growth. For those whose problems are more complicated, Maimonides specialists can treat every manner of childhood disorder, no matter how rare or complex. The level and quality of critical care provided is evidenced by the demand for the Maimonides Pediatric Transport Program, through which critically ill children from other hospitals are transferred to Maimonides.

In recognition of its excellence in obstetrics and pediatrics, Maimonides was designated a Regional Perinatal Center by the New York State Department of Health.

Pediatric specialties include:

- Allergy
- Behavioral & Developmental Pediatrics
- Cardiology
- Critical Care Medicine
- Dentistry & Dental Surgery
- Emergency Medicine
- Endocrinology
- Gastroenterology
- Genetics
- Hematology/Oncology
- Immunology
- Infectious Disease
- Neonatology
- Nephrology
- Neurology
- Ophthalmology
- Orthopedic Surgery
- Otolaryngology
- Psychiatry/Psychology
- Pulmonology
- Rheumatology
- Surgery
- Urology

Relying heavily on evidence-based medicine, Maimonides Medical Center has been commended for outstanding services by a number of independent rating organizations. Earlier this year, Maimonides was named a Distinguished Hospital for Clinical Excellence by HealthGrades – one of only three hospitals in the metropolitan area; the American Stroke Association bestowed its Gold Plus Achievement Award on the hospital; and the American Hospital Association once again named it a Most Wired hospital.

Maimonides Medical Center

The right care.
Right here.

www.maimonidesmed.org/pediatrics

THE MOUNT SINAI MEDICAL CENTER

The Kravis Children's Hospital

Mount Sinai

One Gustave L. Levy Place
Fifth Avenue and 100th Street
New York, NY 10029-6574

Physician Referral: 1-800-MD-SINAI (637-4624)
www.kravischildrenshospital.org

The **KRAVIS CHILDREN'S HOSPITAL** at The Mount Sinai Medical Center offers the most advanced treatments and technologies available, supported by groundbreaking research, because the health and care of your child is our first priority.

This year the Kravis Children's Hospital saw significant gains in the *U.S. News & World Report* pediatric rankings, which placed it among the country's best children's hospitals in seven of the ten pediatric specialties, as noted in the 2013-2014 edition of the annual "Best Children's Hospitals" report. The seven specialties are: Diabetes and endocrinology (#25), gastroenterology & GI Surgery (#25), nephrology (#26), urology (#28), pulmonology (#36), cancer (#46) and cardiology & heart surgery (#50). Previously, we were ranked in six specialties. The rankings reflect not only double-digit gains within specialties, but also first-time rankings in two new areas GI Surgery and Heart Surgery placing these specialties among the best pediatric programs in the United States.

In all of our services, including 31 subspecialty areas of care, we offer advanced treatments, supported by research, community outreach, and advocacy programs. Our ongoing efforts to recruit the finest physicians and scientists have resulted in our ability to provide fundamental insights into the causes of childhood diseases and to deliver breakthrough treatments.

We have opened a new Pediatric Intensive Care unite (PICU), a 15-bed unit that weds state-of-the-art medical technology with a family-friendly facility for our most critically ill children. Construction is underway on a new 46-bed Neonatal Intensive Care Unit (NICU).

THE ZONE SPACE AT KRAVIS

An especially unique feature of the Kravis Children's Hospital at Mount Sinai is the Zone – a 3,000 square foot state-of-the-art therapeutic and educational play environment for pediatric patients and their families. **The Zone space at Kravis is the only one of its kind in the northeast region of the United States.**

The area is staffed by the Child Life and Creative Arts Therapy Department, a full-time pediatric medical librarian, and numerous consultants and volunteers who share their talents in art, music, cooking, knitting and more. The facility includes a lounge, theatre, family resource center, teen area, full kitchen and performing space. **The Zone features KidsZone TV (KZTV), the first live, interactive broadcast studio in a children's hospital.** The space is also used as a pediatric television programming training site for hospitals across the county and abroad.

NewYork-Presbyterian

Affiliated with Columbia University College of Physicians and Surgeons and Weill Cornell Medical College

NewYork-Presbyterian
Morgan Stanley Children's Hospital
Columbia University Medical Center
3959 Broadway
New York, NY 10032

NewYork-Presbyterian
Phyllis and David Komansky
Center for Children's Health
Weill Cornell Medical Center
525 East 68th Street
New York, NY 10065

1-800-245-KIDS (1-800-245-5437)   www.nyp.org/kids

Accreditation: The Joint Commission

Overview

The pediatric services of NewYork-Presbyterian Hospital are comprised of NewYork-Presbyterian Morgan Stanley Children's Hospital, which is affiliated with Columbia University College of Physicians and Surgeons, and the NewYork-Presbyterian Phyllis and David Komansky Center for Children's Health, which is affiliated with Weill Cornell Medical College. Together, they serve as one of the nation's premier centers for comprehensive pediatric care. Skilled and experienced physicians, surgeons, nurses and other pediatric healthcare professionals manage some of the most complex medical conditions of children at every stage of development. Their expertise includes general pediatric care and the full range of medical and surgical subspecialties:

- Adolescent Medicine
- Allergy and Immunology
- Anesthesiology
- Blood Disorders
- Blood and Marrow Transplantation
- Cancer
- Cardiology and Cardiac Surgery
- Craniofacial and Plastic Surgery
- Critical Care
- Dermatology
- Digestive Disease
- Ear, Nose and Throat
- Emergency Department, including specialized units for burns and trauma injuries
- Endocrinology, Diabetes and Metabolism
- Epilepsy
- Genetics
- Infectious Diseases
- Kidney Disease
- Liver Disease
- Lung Disease
- Neonatal Medicine
- Neurology and Neurological Surgery
- Nutrition
- Obesity and Bariatric Surgery
- Ophthalmology
- Oral and Maxillofacial Surgery and Pediatric Dentistry
- Organ Transplantation
- Orthopaedic Surgery
- Pain Medicine
- Pediatric Surgery
- Pregnancy and Newborn Services
- Primary Care/General Pediatrics
- Psychiatry
- Radiology
- Rheumatology
- Urology

Highlights at a Glance:

- A national leader in pediatric open-heart surgery with one of the largest pediatric heart transplant programs in the nation.
- A pediatric kidney transplant program, which includes a Living Donor Program and leading edge therapies to help reduce the side effects of anti-rejection drugs.
- Pediatric cardiac surgeons at the forefront of ventricular assist devices for infants and small children as a bridge to recovery or transplantation.
- One of three Level 1-designated Regional Pediatric Trauma Centers in New York State and the only one in New York City.
- A New York State Department of Health-designated Regional Perinatal Center of Expertise for the care of women with high-risk pregnancies.
- One of the largest Type 1 diabetes programs in New York State.
- Outstanding neonatal intensive care programs setting standards of care nationwide for extremely ill newborns.
- The only program in the New York tri-state area that has active programs in both liver and small bowel transplantation.

NYU Langone
MEDICAL CENTER

550 First Avenue *(at 31st Street)*
New York, NY 10016

www.NYULMC.org

Hassenfeld Children's Hospital Access Line: **855-NYU-KIDS**

HASSENFELD CHILDREN'S HOSPITAL

Hassenfeld Children's Hospital (HCH) is a full-service specialty children's hospital encompassing all children's health services at NYU Langone Medical Center. At HCH, newborns, children, adolescents and young adults receive the most comprehensive and advanced care possible from a team of pediatricians and pediatric specialists across more than 30 medical and surgical disciplines. With more than 150 full-time pediatric specialists, as well as pediatric nurses, child life specialists and social workers, Hassenfeld Children's Hospital is uniquely equipped to provide innovative pediatric subspecialty care in a highly personalized manner.

A Family-Centered Approach

Integral to the care we provide is a myriad of support services for children and their families. We recognize that the best outcomes are achieved when the child's family is actively involved in every step of care. For that reason, our trained specialists address the needs of not just the patient, but of parents and siblings through ongoing education and communication.

Our pediatric specialties include:

Anesthesia
Cardiology
Cardiothoracic Surgery
Child and Adolescent Psychiatry and Psychology/Child Study Center
Critical Care
Dermatology
Developmental and Behavioral Pediatrics
Emergency Medicine
Endocrinology
Epilepsy
Gastroenterology
Genetics
Hematology/Oncology
Infectious Diseases
Neonatology
Nephrology
Neurosurgery
Ophthalmology
Orthopaedic Surgery
Otolaryngology
Pathology
Pulmonology
Radiology
Reconstructive Plastic Surgery
Rehabilitation
Rheumatology
Surgery
Urology

NYU Langone
MEDICAL CENTER

550 First Avenue *(at 31st Street)*
New York, NY 10016

www.NYULMC.org

Hassenfeld Children's Hospital Access Line: **855-NYU-KIDS**

HASSENFELD CHILDREN'S HOSPITAL

Hassenfeld Children's Hospital (HCH) is a full-service specialty children's hospital encompassing all children's health services at NYU Langone Medical Center. At HCH, newborns, children, adolescents and young adults receive the most comprehensive and advanced care possible from a team of pediatricians and pediatric specialists across more than 30 medical and surgical disciplines. With more than 150 full-time pediatric specialists, as well as pediatric nurses, child life specialists and social workers, Hassenfeld Children's Hospital is uniquely equipped to provide innovative pediatric subspecialty care in a highly personalized manner.

A Family-Centered Approach

Integral to the care we provide is a myriad of support services for children and their families. We recognize that the best outcomes are achieved when the child's family is actively involved in every step of care. For that reason, our trained specialists address the needs of not just the patient, but of parents and siblings through ongoing education and communication.

Our pediatric specialties include:

Anesthesia
Cardiology
Cardiothoracic Surgery
Child and Adolescent Psychiatry
and Psychology/Child Study Center
Critical Care
Dermatology
Developmental and Behavioral Pediatrics
Emergency Medicine
Endocrinology
Epilepsy
Gastroenterology
Genetics
Hematology/Oncology
Infectious Diseases
Neonatology
Nephrology
Neurosurgery
Ophthalmology
Orthopaedic Surgery
Otolaryngology
Pathology
Pulmonology
Radiology
Reconstructive Plastic Surgery
Rehabilitation
Rheumatology
Surgery
Urology

THE MOUNT SINAI MEDICAL CENTER
KRAVIS CHILDREN'S HOSPITAL

Pediatric Critical Care

Mount Sinai

One Gustave L. Levy Place
Fifth Avenue and 100th Street
New York, NY 10029-6574

Physician Referral: 1-800-MD-SINAI (637-4624)
www.kravischildrenshospital.org

INNOVATIVE MEDICINE, FAMILY-CENTERED CARE

The **DIVISION OF CRITICAL CARE MEDICINE** at The Mount Sinai Medical Center's Kravis Children's Hospital delivers quaternary level intensive care to critically ill and injured infants, children, and adolescents. Working with the most advanced diagnostic and therapeutic equipment, the faculty and staff have the training and the tools necessary to achieve optimal outcomes when treating children with serious medical and surgical conditions.

Board certified critical care physicians, together with award-winning nurses and highly skilled ancillary staff, deliver 24-hour care in the newly renovated **Alice Gottesman Bayer Pediatric Intensive Care Unit (PICU)**. The PICU is a state-of-the-art, 14-bed unit that averages 700 admissions per year, approximately one tenth of which are transported from referring hospitals. The PICU is equipped with a treatment room, a designated space for medical procedures and pediatric procedural sedation. Pediatric intensivists work closely with members of the **Division of Pediatric Cardiology** to provide expert critical care for patients in the 6-bed pediatric cardiac/cardiothoracic intensive care unit.

The interdisciplinary critical care team is trained and equipped to provide renal replacement therapy, therapeutic hypothermia, and advanced ventilation support modes, including nitric oxide therapy and high frequency oscillatory ventilation. In conjunction with colleagues in the cardiac/cardiothoracic intensive care unit, extracorporeal membrane oxygenation (ECMO), and ventricular assist device (VAD) support are utilized for the treatment of severe cardiac failure.

Pediatric intensive care unit patients benefit from the contributing expertise of pediatric medical and surgical subspecialists and a multidisciplinary staff which includes pediatric pharmacists, social workers, respiratory therapists, nutritionists, Child Life specialists and rehabilitation specialists. Staff also participates in a pediatric palliative care and pain team consultation service for children being cared for in all areas of Kravis Children's Hospital.

The PICU faculty and staff are committed to improving the health of infants, children, adolescents, and young adults, and look forward to continuing the long and distinguished tradition of excellence in innovative patient care, community involvement, professional education, and research across the translational spectrum.

NYU Langone
MEDICAL CENTER

550 First Avenue *(at 31st Street)*
New York, NY 10016

www.NYULMC.org

Hassenfeld Children's Hospital Access Line: **855-NYU-KIDS**

HASSENFELD CHILDREN'S HOSPITAL

Hassenfeld Children's Hospital (HCH) is a full-service specialty children's hospital encompassing all children's health services at NYU Langone Medical Center. At HCH, newborns, children, adolescents and young adults receive the most comprehensive and advanced care possible from a team of pediatricians and pediatric specialists across more than 30 medical and surgical disciplines. With more than 150 full-time pediatric specialists, as well as pediatric nurses, child life specialists and social workers, Hassenfeld Children's Hospital is uniquely equipped to provide innovative pediatric subspecialty care in a highly personalized manner.

A Family-Centered Approach

Integral to the care we provide is a myriad of support services for children and their families. We recognize that the best outcomes are achieved when the child's family is actively involved in every step of care. For that reason, our trained specialists address the needs of not just the patient, but of parents and siblings through ongoing education and communication.

Our pediatric specialties include:

Anesthesia
Cardiology
Cardiothoracic Surgery
Child and Adolescent Psychiatry and Psychology/Child Study Center
Critical Care
Dermatology
Developmental and Behavioral Pediatrics
Emergency Medicine
Endocrinology
Epilepsy
Gastroenterology
Genetics
Hematology/Oncology
Infectious Diseases
Neonatology
Nephrology
Neurosurgery
Ophthalmology
Orthopaedic Surgery
Otolaryngology
Pathology
Pulmonology
Radiology
Reconstructive Plastic Surgery
Rehabilitation
Rheumatology
Surgery
Urology

THE MOUNT SINAI MEDICAL CENTER
KRAVIS CHILDREN'S HOSPITAL

Pediatric Emergency Medicine

One Gustave L. Levy Place
Fifth Avenue and 100th Street
New York, NY 10029-6574

Physician Referral: 1-800-MD-SINAI (637-4624)
www.kravischildrenshospital.org

INNOVATIVE MEDICINE, FAMILY-CENTERED CARE

As part of The Mount Sinai Medical Center's Kravis Children's Hospital, which *U.S. News & World Report* consistently ranks among the best in the nation, members of our **DIVISION OF PEDIATRIC EMERGENCY MEDICINE** are dedicated to providing sick and injured infants, children, adolescents, and young adults with the most appropriate care as quickly as possible.

Our physicians are board certified in pediatric emergency medicine and see patients 24-hours a day, seven days a week in our state-of-the-art facility, which is located separate and apart from our adult emergency department, is designed for children's comfort, and has its own access from the waiting room.

We offer the most advanced treatment and technology available for the full range of medical and surgical conditions. Children requiring admission receive the best possible care for even the most complex conditions, and we consult with each child's own pediatrician when appropriate.

Our physicians, award -winning nurses and specially trained staff, understand the special clinical and emotional needs of children and have the right mix of experience, compassion and commitment to provide superior, family-centered care and guidance to young patients and their families.

As part of a major academic medical center, we also provide didactic and bedside teaching of pediatric emergency medicine to both the pediatric and emergency medicine residents and participate in clinical trials to investigate the causes and cures of pediatric illnesses. Some of our current research projects include the treatment of pediatric anaphylaxis, the use of positive airway pressure for patients with asthma, and the use of simulation to augment resident education

Our faculty, staff and trainees are committed to improving the health of infants, children, adolescents and young adults. We look forward to continuing our long and distinguished tradition of excellence in innovative patient care, community involvement, professional education, and research across the translational spectrum.

NYU Langone
MEDICAL CENTER

550 First Avenue *(at 31st Street)*
New York, NY 10016

www.NYULMC.org

Hassenfeld Children's Hospital Access Line: **855-NYU-KIDS**

HASSENFELD CHILDREN'S HOSPITAL

Hassenfeld Children's Hospital (HCH) is a full-service specialty children's hospital encompassing all children's health services at NYU Langone Medical Center. At HCH, newborns, children, adolescents and young adults receive the most comprehensive and advanced care possible from a team of pediatricians and pediatric specialists across more than 30 medical and surgical disciplines. With more than 150 full-time pediatric specialists, as well as pediatric nurses, child life specialists and social workers, Hassenfeld Children's Hospital is uniquely equipped to provide innovative pediatric subspecialty care in a highly personalized manner.

A Family-Centered Approach

Integral to the care we provide is a myriad of support services for children and their families. We recognize that the best outcomes are achieved when the child's family is actively involved in every step of care. For that reason, our trained specialists address the needs of not just the patient, but of parents and siblings through ongoing education and communication.

Our pediatric specialties include:

Anesthesia
Cardiology
Cardiothoracic Surgery
Child and Adolescent Psychiatry
  and Psychology/Child Study Center
Critical Care
Dermatology
Developmental and Behavioral Pediatrics
Emergency Medicine
Endocrinology
Epilepsy
Gastroenterology
Genetics
Hematology/Oncology
Infectious Diseases
Neonatology
Nephrology
Neurosurgery
Ophthalmology
Orthopaedic Surgery
Otolaryngology
Pathology
Pulmonology
Radiology
Reconstructive Plastic Surgery
Rehabilitation
Rheumatology
Surgery
Urology

Mount Sinai

THE MOUNT SINAI MEDICAL CENTER
KRAVIS CHILDREN'S HOSPITAL

Pediatric Diabetes and Endocrinology

One Gustave L. Levy Place
Fifth Avenue and 100th Street
New York, NY 10029-6574

Physician Referral: 1-800-MD-SINAI (637-4624)
www.kravischildrenshospital.org

INNOVATIVE MEDICINE, FAMILY-CENTERED CARE

THE HALL FAMILY CENTER FOR PEDIATRIC ENDOCRINOLOGY AND DIABETES at Kravis Children's Hospital at Mount Sinai is dedicated to excellence in clinical care, education and research – a fact that has led to our being named among the top 25 pediatric diabetes and endocrinology services in America, according to ***The U.S. News & World Report's*** **2013-2014 ranking of "Best Children's Hospitals."**

Under the direction of Robert Rapaport, MD, Division Chief, we use a team approach, which is patient and family centered, to manage:

- Diabetes (type 1 and type 2, medication-related, monogenic and pre-diabetes)
- Short stature
- Growth disorders, including growth hormone deficiency, growth in children born small for gestational age, and early and late puberty
- Genetic disorders, including Turner Syndrome and Noonan Syndrome
- Congenital and acquired hypothyroidism and hyperthyroidism
- Hyperparathyroidism
- Congenital adrenal hyperplasia/hypoplasia
- Obesity and other nutritional disorders, including Vitamin D deficiency

ANNUAL SYMPOSIUM

Our physician-scientists conduct investigations into the causes and treatments of childhood endocrine conditions, and we are committed to translating research into better methods of clinical care. To that end, we hold an annual symposium each November to update pediatricians practicing within the community on the latest advances in pediatric endocrinology and diabetes.

Diabetes – We offer the complete spectrum of high level diagnostic and treatment services, including simulation testing, for children and adolescents and bring families into their circle of care. Since education and support are vital to managing diabetes, we offer a variety of programs for patients and their families, including "Toddlers and Grandparents," "College Prep," for teens entering college, and a free one-week day camp in Central Park in conjunction with the Barton Center for Diabetes Education.

We collaborated with four other medical centers on the **R.O.A.D. (Reduce Obesity and Diabetes) project**, to study and educate middle school children in Harlem. By identifying the metabolic factors that lead from obesity to diabetes, we will develop a protocol for detecting which children will most likely develop diabetes, allowing us to streamline interventions and identify where best to allocate resources.

Endocrine Disorders and Growth – With our faculty leading investigations into both international and multi-center trials, we enjoy a stellar reputation for identifying and treating a host of common and complex endocrine disorders, including growth hormone deficiency, growth in children born small for gestational age, and other disorders caused by Turner or Noonan Syndrome, and congenital hypothyroidism. In addition to offering expert consultations, we employ early screening methods and breakthrough growth hormone therapy that enables children to grow and develop normally.

We also excel at diagnosing and treating children with precocious or delayed puberty and have developed methods to identify and manage these conditions before they appear clinically obvious.

HASSENFELD CHILDREN'S HOSPITAL

Hassenfeld Children's Hospital (HCH) is a full-service specialty children's hospital encompassing all children's health services at NYU Langone Medical Center. At HCH, newborns, children, adolescents and young adults receive the most comprehensive and advanced care possible from a team of pediatricians and pediatric specialists across more than 30 medical and surgical disciplines. With more than 150 full-time pediatric specialists, as well as pediatric nurses, child life specialists and social workers, Hassenfeld Children's Hospital is uniquely equipped to provide innovative pediatric subspecialty care in a highly personalized manner.

A Family-Centered Approach

Integral to the care we provide is a myriad of support services for children and their families. We recognize that the best outcomes are achieved when the child's family is actively involved in every step of care. For that reason, our trained specialists address the needs of not just the patient, but of parents and siblings through ongoing education and communication.

Our pediatric specialties include:

Anesthesia
Cardiology
Cardiothoracic Surgery
Child and Adolescent Psychiatry and Psychology/Child Study Center
Critical Care
Dermatology
Developmental and Behavioral Pediatrics
Emergency Medicine
Endocrinology
Epilepsy
Gastroenterology
Genetics
Hematology/Oncology
Infectious Diseases
Neonatology
Nephrology
Neurosurgery
Ophthalmology
Orthopaedic Surgery
Otolaryngology
Pathology
Pulmonology
Radiology
Reconstructive Plastic Surgery
Rehabilitation
Rheumatology
Surgery
Urology

NYU Langone
MEDICAL CENTER

550 First Avenue *(at 31st Street)*
New York, NY 10016

www.NYULMC.org

Hassenfeld Children's Hospital Access Line: **855-NYU-KIDS**

HASSENFELD CHILDREN'S HOSPITAL

Hassenfeld Children's Hospital (HCH) is a full-service specialty children's hospital encompassing all children's health services at NYU Langone Medical Center. At HCH, newborns, children, adolescents and young adults receive the most comprehensive and advanced care possible from a team of pediatricians and pediatric specialists across more than 30 medical and surgical disciplines. With more than 150 full-time pediatric specialists, as well as pediatric nurses, child life specialists and social workers, Hassenfeld Children's Hospital is uniquely equipped to provide innovative pediatric subspecialty care in a highly personalized manner.

A Family-Centered Approach

Integral to the care we provide is a myriad of support services for children and their families. We recognize that the best outcomes are achieved when the child's family is actively involved in every step of care. For that reason, our trained specialists address the needs of not just the patient, but of parents and siblings through ongoing education and communication.

Our pediatric specialties include:

Anesthesia
Cardiology
Cardiothoracic Surgery
Child and Adolescent Psychiatry
and Psychology/Child Study Center
Critical Care
Dermatology
Developmental and Behavioral Pediatrics
Emergency Medicine
Endocrinology
Epilepsy
Gastroenterology
Genetics
Hematology/Oncology
Infectious Diseases
Neonatology
Nephrology
Neurosurgery
Ophthalmology
Orthopaedic Surgery
Otolaryngology
Pathology
Pulmonology
Radiology
Reconstructive Plastic Surgery
Rehabilitation
Rheumatology
Surgery
Urology

NYU Langone
MEDICAL CENTER

550 First Avenue *(at 31st Street)*
New York, NY 10016

www.NYULMC.org

Hassenfeld Children's Hospital Access Line: **855-NYU-KIDS**

HASSENFELD CHILDREN'S HOSPITAL

Hassenfeld Children's Hospital (HCH) is a full-service specialty children's hospital encompassing all children's health services at NYU Langone Medical Center. At HCH, newborns, children, adolescents and young adults receive the most comprehensive and advanced care possible from a team of pediatricians and pediatric specialists across more than 30 medical and surgical disciplines. With more than 150 full-time pediatric specialists, as well as pediatric nurses, child life specialists and social workers, Hassenfeld Children's Hospital is uniquely equipped to provide innovative pediatric subspecialty care in a highly personalized manner.

A Family-Centered Approach

Integral to the care we provide is a myriad of support services for children and their families. We recognize that the best outcomes are achieved when the child's family is actively involved in every step of care. For that reason, our trained specialists address the needs of not just the patient, but of parents and siblings through ongoing education and communication.

Our pediatric specialties include:

Anesthesia
Cardiology
Cardiothoracic Surgery
Child and Adolescent Psychiatry and Psychology/Child Study Center
Critical Care
Dermatology
Developmental and Behavioral Pediatrics
Emergency Medicine
Endocrinology
Epilepsy
Gastroenterology
Genetics
Hematology/Oncology
Infectious Diseases
Neonatology
Nephrology
Neurosurgery
Ophthalmology
Orthopaedic Surgery
Otolaryngology
Pathology
Pulmonology
Radiology
Reconstructive Plastic Surgery
Rehabilitation
Rheumatology
Surgery
Urology

NYU Langone
MEDICAL CENTER

550 First Avenue *(at 31st Street)*
New York, NY 10016

www.NYULMC.org

Hassenfeld Children's Hospital Access Line: **855-NYU-KIDS**

HASSENFELD CHILDREN'S HOSPITAL

Hassenfeld Children's Hospital (HCH) is a full-service specialty children's hospital encompassing all children's health services at NYU Langone Medical Center. At HCH, newborns, children, adolescents and young adults receive the most comprehensive and advanced care possible from a team of pediatricians and pediatric specialists across more than 30 medical and surgical disciplines. With more than 150 full-time pediatric specialists, as well as pediatric nurses, child life specialists and social workers, Hassenfeld Children's Hospital is uniquely equipped to provide innovative pediatric subspecialty care in a highly personalized manner.

A Family-Centered Approach

Integral to the care we provide is a myriad of support services for children and their families. We recognize that the best outcomes are achieved when the child's family is actively involved in every step of care. For that reason, our trained specialists address the needs of not just the patient, but of parents and siblings through ongoing education and communication.

Our pediatric specialties include:

Anesthesia
Cardiology
Cardiothoracic Surgery
Child and Adolescent Psychiatry and Psychology/Child Study Center
Critical Care
Dermatology
Developmental and Behavioral Pediatrics
Emergency Medicine
Endocrinology
Epilepsy
Gastroenterology
Genetics
Hematology/Oncology
Infectious Diseases
Neonatology
Nephrology
Neurosurgery
Ophthalmology
Orthopaedic Surgery
Otolaryngology
Pathology
Pulmonology
Radiology
Reconstructive Plastic Surgery
Rehabilitation
Rheumatology
Surgery
Urology

NYU Langone
MEDICAL CENTER

550 First Avenue *(at 31st Street)*
New York, NY 10016

www.NYULMC.org

Hassenfeld Children's Hospital Access Line: **855-NYU-KIDS**

HASSENFELD CHILDREN'S HOSPITAL

Hassenfeld Children's Hospital (HCH) is a full-service specialty children's hospital encompassing all children's health services at NYU Langone Medical Center. At HCH, newborns, children, adolescents and young adults receive the most comprehensive and advanced care possible from a team of pediatricians and pediatric specialists across more than 30 medical and surgical disciplines. With more than 150 full-time pediatric specialists, as well as pediatric nurses, child life specialists and social workers, Hassenfeld Children's Hospital is uniquely equipped to provide innovative pediatric subspecialty care in a highly personalized manner.

A Family-Centered Approach

Integral to the care we provide is a myriad of support services for children and their families. We recognize that the best outcomes are achieved when the child's family is actively involved in every step of care. For that reason, our trained specialists address the needs of not just the patient, but of parents and siblings through ongoing education and communication.

Our pediatric specialties include:

Anesthesia
Cardiology
Cardiothoracic Surgery
Child and Adolescent Psychiatry and Psychology/Child Study Center
Critical Care
Dermatology
Developmental and Behavioral Pediatrics
Emergency Medicine
Endocrinology
Epilepsy
Gastroenterology
Genetics
Hematology/Oncology
Infectious Diseases
Neonatology
Nephrology
Neurosurgery
Ophthalmology
Orthopaedic Surgery
Otolaryngology
Pathology
Pulmonology
Radiology
Reconstructive Plastic Surgery
Rehabilitation
Rheumatology
Surgery
Urology

THE MOUNT SINAI MEDICAL CENTER
KRAVIS CHILDREN'S HOSPITAL

Pediatric Pulmonology

One Gustave L. Levy Place
Fifth Avenue and 100th Street
New York, NY 10029-6574

Physician Referral: 1-800-MD-SINAI (637-4624)
www.kravischildrenshospital.org

INNOVATIVE MEDICINE, FAMILY-CENTERED CARE

At Mount Sinai's **DIVISION OF PEDIATRIC PULMONOLOGY**, we are dedicated to treating the full spectrum of children's respiratory illnesses, both common and complex, with a high level of skill and compassion. This dedication has led to our being named among the top pediatric pulmonary services in America, according to ***U.S. News & World Report's*** **2013-2014 ranking of "Best Children's Hospitals."**

Under the direction of Alfin Vicencio, MD, Division Chief, our team of award winning pediatric pulmonologists, nurse practitioners, nurse educators, nutritionists, social workers and respiratory therapists deliver evidence-based care to children with asthma, cystic fibrosis, chronic respiratory failure, bronchopulmonary dysplasia and other respiratory conditions.

Offering medical support and guidance, our **Children's Asthma Center** offers advanced diagnostic and treatment protocols for refractory asthma along with advanced pulmonary function testing, allergy testing, environmental assessment, nutritional evaluation, education, and family services. We teach patients and their parents or guardians to identify asthma triggers and offer a personalized asthma action plan for each patient—a process that has our patients experiencing fewer emergency department visits and hospitalizations, missing less school and enjoying more active lives. In addition, through outreach efforts and care delivered to children from East Harlem—an area with one of the highest asthma rates in the country—we have succeeded in empowering these patients to manage their disease and face the future with confidence.

FROM BENCH TO BEDSIDE

We have recently recruited Rosalind Wright, MD, MPH, to serve as Vice Chair for Transitional Research and as a member of the Division of Pediatric Pulmonology.
Dr. Wright is recognized both nationally and internationally for her investigations into early life events in relation to the development of pediatric asthma and is a welcome addition to our team of physician-scientists.

To significantly enhance our pediatric flexible bronchoscopy service, we recently opened a new **Bronchoscopy Suite** that houses the most advanced technology for both diagnostic capabilities and interventional procedures.

As an accredited **Cystic Fibrosis Foundation Care Center**, we offer the latest therapies and participate in multi-center trials. With our team specially trained in caring for cystic fibrosis patients, we treat all aspects of the disease, ranging from the latest antimicrobial strategies to nutritional optimization. We offer services that include pediatric spirometry, plethysmography, and comprehensive psychosocial support and evaluation.

Our **Chronic Ventilator Program** provides the most advanced and compassionate management of children with chronic respiratory failure as well as those with muscular dystrophies and other conditions that require mechanical ventilation.

Our **Bronchopulmonary Dysplasia Program** offers the highest level of care for premature infants while they are in the hospital and, as outpatients, once they are discharged

NYU Langone
MEDICAL CENTER

550 First Avenue *(at 31st Street)*
New York, NY 10016

www.NYULMC.org

Hassenfeld Children's Hospital Access Line: **855-NYU-KIDS**

HASSENFELD CHILDREN'S HOSPITAL

Hassenfeld Children's Hospital (HCH) is a full-service specialty children's hospital encompassing all children's health services at NYU Langone Medical Center. At HCH, newborns, children, adolescents and young adults receive the most comprehensive and advanced care possible from a team of pediatricians and pediatric specialists across more than 30 medical and surgical disciplines. With more than 150 full-time pediatric specialists, as well as pediatric nurses, child life specialists and social workers, Hassenfeld Children's Hospital is uniquely equipped to provide innovative pediatric subspecialty care in a highly personalized manner.

A Family-Centered Approach

Integral to the care we provide is a myriad of support services for children and their families. We recognize that the best outcomes are achieved when the child's family is actively involved in every step of care. For that reason, our trained specialists address the needs of not just the patient, but of parents and siblings through ongoing education and communication.

Our pediatric specialties include:

Anesthesia
Cardiology
Cardiothoracic Surgery
Child and Adolescent Psychiatry and Psychology/Child Study Center
Critical Care
Dermatology
Developmental and Behavioral Pediatrics
Emergency Medicine
Endocrinology
Epilepsy
Gastroenterology
Genetics
Hematology/Oncology
Infectious Diseases
Neonatology
Nephrology
Neurosurgery
Ophthalmology
Orthopaedic Surgery
Otolaryngology
Pathology
Pulmonology
Radiology
Reconstructive Plastic Surgery
Rehabilitation
Rheumatology
Surgery
Urology

NYU Langone
MEDICAL CENTER

550 First Avenue *(at 31st Street)*
New York, NY 10016

www.NYULMC.org

Hassenfeld Children's Hospital Access Line: **855-NYU-KIDS**

HASSENFELD CHILDREN'S HOSPITAL

Hassenfeld Children's Hospital (HCH) is a full-service specialty children's hospital encompassing all children's health services at NYU Langone Medical Center. At HCH, newborns, children, adolescents and young adults receive the most comprehensive and advanced care possible from a team of pediatricians and pediatric specialists across more than 30 medical and surgical disciplines. With more than 150 full-time pediatric specialists, as well as pediatric nurses, child life specialists and social workers, Hassenfeld Children's Hospital is uniquely equipped to provide innovative pediatric subspecialty care in a highly personalized manner.

A Family-Centered Approach

Integral to the care we provide is a myriad of support services for children and their families. We recognize that the best outcomes are achieved when the child's family is actively involved in every step of care. For that reason, our trained specialists address the needs of not just the patient, but of parents and siblings through ongoing education and communication.

Our pediatric specialties include:

Anesthesia
Cardiology
Cardiothoracic Surgery
Child and Adolescent Psychiatry
and Psychology/Child Study Center
Critical Care
Dermatology
Developmental and Behavioral Pediatrics
Emergency Medicine
Endocrinology
Epilepsy
Gastroenterology
Genetics
Hematology/Oncology
Infectious Diseases
Neonatology
Nephrology
Neurosurgery
Ophthalmology
Orthopaedic Surgery
Otolaryngology
Pathology
Pulmonology
Radiology
Reconstructive Plastic Surgery
Rehabilitation
Rheumatology
Surgery
Urology

HASSENFELD CHILDREN'S HOSPITAL

Hassenfeld Children's Hospital (HCH) is a full-service specialty children's hospital encompassing all children's health services at NYU Langone Medical Center. At HCH, newborns, children, adolescents and young adults receive the most comprehensive and advanced care possible from a team of pediatricians and pediatric specialists across more than 30 medical and surgical disciplines. With more than 150 full-time pediatric specialists, as well as pediatric nurses, child life specialists and social workers, Hassenfeld Children's Hospital is uniquely equipped to provide innovative pediatric subspecialty care in a highly personalized manner.

A Family-Centered Approach

Integral to the care we provide is a myriad of support services for children and their families. We recognize that the best outcomes are achieved when the child's family is actively involved in every step of care. For that reason, our trained specialists address the needs of not just the patient, but of parents and siblings through ongoing education and communication.

Our pediatric specialties include:

Anesthesia
Cardiology
Cardiothoracic Surgery
Child and Adolescent Psychiatry
  and Psychology/Child Study Center
Critical Care
Dermatology
Developmental and Behavioral Pediatrics
Emergency Medicine
Endocrinology
Epilepsy
Gastroenterology
Genetics
Hematology/Oncology
Infectious Diseases
Neonatology
Nephrology
Neurosurgery
Ophthalmology
Orthopaedic Surgery
Otolaryngology
Pathology
Pulmonology
Radiology
Reconstructive Plastic Surgery
Rehabilitation
Rheumatology
Surgery
Urology

Mount Sinai

THE MOUNT SINAI MEDICAL CENTER
KRAVIS CHILDREN'S HOSPITAL

Pediatric Surgery

One Gustave L. Levy Place
Fifth Avenue and 100th Street
New York, NY 10029-6574

Physician Referral: 1-800-MD-SINAI (637-4624)
www.kravischildrenshospital.org

INNOVATIVE MEDICINE, FAMILY-CENTERED CARE

The Kravis Children's Hospital at Mount Sinai is dedicated to excellence in pediatric surgery. To achieve that goal we have assembled a care team with the right mix of experience, compassion and commitment to provide superior, family-centered care and guidance to young patients and their families.

We offer comprehensive surgical care for children with both common and complex conditions. Our highly skilled surgeons, board certified in pediatric surgery, are adept at performing the most advanced minimally invasive pediatric surgery techniques. We specialize in neonatal surgery and have extensive experience in the operative management of common conditions such as:

- Anal atresia
- Appendicitis
- Congenital diaphragmatic hernia
- Kidney tumors (Wilms' tumor)
- Pediatric inflammatory bowel disease (IBD)
- Pyloric stenosis

Our care team includes neonatologists, pediatricians, pediatric gastroenterologists, pediatric oncologists, and other skilled professionals. We understand the intense stress that parents experience when their child faces surgery. Our physicians and nurse practitioner work with child life specialists and others to make all procedures, big and small, as comfortable for the child and the family as possible. Our goal is to offer the most advanced care in the most sensitive way possible.

NYU Langone
MEDICAL CENTER

550 First Avenue *(at 31st Street)*
New York, NY 10016

www.NYULMC.org

Hassenfeld Children's Hospital Access Line: **855-NYU-KIDS**

HASSENFELD CHILDREN'S HOSPITAL

Hassenfeld Children's Hospital (HCH) is a full-service specialty children's hospital encompassing all children's health services at NYU Langone Medical Center. At HCH, newborns, children, adolescents and young adults receive the most comprehensive and advanced care possible from a team of pediatricians and pediatric specialists across more than 30 medical and surgical disciplines. With more than 150 full-time pediatric specialists, as well as pediatric nurses, child life specialists and social workers, Hassenfeld Children's Hospital is uniquely equipped to provide innovative pediatric subspecialty care in a highly personalized manner.

A Family-Centered Approach

Integral to the care we provide is a myriad of support services for children and their families. We recognize that the best outcomes are achieved when the child's family is actively involved in every step of care. For that reason, our trained specialists address the needs of not just the patient, but of parents and siblings through ongoing education and communication.

Our pediatric specialties include:

Anesthesia
Cardiology
Cardiothoracic Surgery
Child and Adolescent Psychiatry and Psychology/Child Study Center
Critical Care
Dermatology
Developmental and Behavioral Pediatrics
Emergency Medicine
Endocrinology
Epilepsy
Gastroenterology
Genetics
Hematology/Oncology
Infectious Diseases
Neonatology
Nephrology
Neurosurgery
Ophthalmology
Orthopaedic Surgery
Otolaryngology
Pathology
Pulmonology
Radiology
Reconstructive Plastic Surgery
Rehabilitation
Rheumatology
Surgery
Urology

Top Doctors Make A Difference

Physical Medicine & Rehabilitation

Physical medicine and rehabilitation, also referred to as rehabilitation medicine, is the medical specialty concerned with diagnosing, evaluating and treating patients with physical disabilities. These disabilities may arise from conditions affecting the musculoskeletal system such as neck and back pain, sports injuries, or other painful conditions affecting the limbs, for example carpal tunnel syndrome. Alternatively, the disabilities may result from neurological trauma or disease such as spinal cord injury, head injury or stroke.

A physician certified in physical medicine and rehabilitation is often called a physiatrist. The primary goal of the physiatrist is to achieve maximal restoration of physical, psychological, social and vocational function through comprehensive rehabilitation. Pain management is often an important part of the role of the physiatrist. For diagnosis and evaluation, a physiatrist may include the techniques of electromyography to supplement the standard history, physical, X-ray and laboratory examinations. The physiatrist has expertise in the appropriate use of therapeutic exercise, prosthetics (artificial limbs), orthotics and mechanical and electrical devices.

Training Required: Four years *plus* one year clinical practice.

Certification in the following subspecialty requires additional training and examination.

Spinal Cord Injury Medicine: A physician who addresses the prevention, diagnosis, treatment and management of traumatic spinal cord injury and non-traumatic etiologies of spinal cord dysfunction by working in an interdisciplinary manner. Care is provided to patients of all ages on a lifelong basis and covers related medical, physical, psychological and vocational disabilities and complications.

Physical Medicine & Rehabilitation

New England

Bloch, Rina M MD [PMR] - **Spec Exp:** Spinal Cord Injury; Brain Injury Rehabilitation; Geriatric Rehabilitation; Musculoskeletal Disorders; **Hospital:** Tufts Med Ctr; **Address:** Tufts Med Ctr, Rehab Medicine, 260 Tremont St Fl 14, Boston, MA 02116; **Phone:** 617-636-3003; **Board Cert:** Physical Medicine & Rehabilitation 1989; Spinal Cord Injury Medicine 2008; Electrodiagnostic Medicine 1997; **Med School:** Univ Louisville Sch Med 1983; **Resid:** Physical Medicine & Rehabilitation, Rehab Inst of Chicago 1987

Borg-Stein, Joanne MD [PMR] - **Spec Exp:** Pain Management; Sports Medicine; Acupuncture; Spinal Rehabilitation; **Hospital:** Spaulding Rehab Hosp, Newton - Wellesley Hosp; **Address:** Spaulding-Wellesley Outpatient Center, 65 Walnut St, Wellesley, MA 02481; **Phone:** 781-431-9144; **Board Cert:** Physical Medicine & Rehabilitation 1990; Pain Medicine 2011; Sports Medicine 2008; **Med School:** Albert Einstein Coll Med 1984; **Resid:** Physical Medicine & Rehabilitation, NY Presby/Columbia Univ Med Ctr 1988; **Fac Appt:** Asst Prof PMR, Harvard Med Sch

Glenn, Mel B MD [PMR] - **Spec Exp:** Brain Injury Rehabilitation; Spasticity Management; **Hospital:** Spaulding Rehab Hosp, Mass Genl Hosp; **Address:** Spaulding Rehab Hosp, 300 First Ave, Charlestown, MA 02129; **Phone:** 617-573-2200; **Board Cert:** Physical Medicine & Rehabilitation 1982; **Med School:** NYU Sch Med 1978; **Resid:** Physical Medicine & Rehabilitation, NYU Med Ctr 1981; **Fellow:** Spinal Cord Injury Medicine, NYU Med Ctr 1982; **Fac Appt:** Assoc Prof PMR, Harvard Med Sch

Richter, Edwin MD [PMR] - **Spec Exp:** Neuro-Rehabilitation; Brain Injury Rehabilitation; Amputee Rehabilitation; Lymphedema; **Hospital:** Stamford Hosp; **Address:** 166 W Broad St, Ste 305, Stamford, CT 06902; **Phone:** 203-316-0610; **Board Cert:** Physical Medicine & Rehabilitation 1992; **Med School:** NYU Sch Med 1987; **Resid:** Physical Medicine & Rehabilitation, NYU Med Ctr 1991; **Fac Appt:** Asst Clin Prof PMR, NYU Sch Med

Webster, Harry C MD [PMR] - **Spec Exp:** Pediatric Rehabilitation; Cerebral Palsy; Muscular Dystrophy; Spasticity Management; **Hospital:** Tufts Med Ctr; **Address:** Tufts Med Ctr, 800 Washington St, Ste 415, Boston, MA 02111; **Phone:** 617-636-5626; **Board Cert:** Pediatrics 1983; Physical Medicine & Rehabilitation 1988; **Med School:** UCSF 1977; **Resid:** Pediatrics, Chldns Hosp 1980; Physical Medicine & Rehabilitation, Tufts Med Ctr 1987; **Fac Appt:** Asst Prof PMR, Tufts Univ

Zafonte, Ross D DO [PMR] - **Spec Exp:** Brain Injury Rehabilitation; Spinal Cord Injury; **Hospital:** Spaulding Rehab Hosp; **Address:** Spaulding Rehab Hosp, 300 First Ave, Charlestown, MA 02129; **Phone:** 617-573-2200; **Board Cert:** Physical Medicine & Rehabilitation 1990; **Med School:** Nova SE Univ, Coll Osteo Med 1985; **Resid:** Physical Medicine & Rehabilitation, Mt Sinai Med Ctr 1989; **Fac Appt:** Clin Prof PMR, Boston Univ

Mid Atlantic

Ahn, Jung Hwan MD [PMR] - **Spec Exp:** Spinal Cord Injury; Stroke Rehabilitation; Neurologic Rehabilitation; **Hospital:** NYU Langone Med Ctr (page 68); **Address:** Ambulatory Care Ctr, 240 E 38th St Fl 15, New York, NY 10016; **Phone:** 212-263-6122; **Board Cert:** Physical Medicine & Rehabilitation 1980; Spinal Cord Injury Medicine 2008; **Med School:** South Korea 1970; **Resid:** Obstetrics & Gynecology, Elmhurst City Hosp 1976; Physical Medicine & Rehabilitation, NYU Med Ctr 1979; **Fellow:** Spinal Cord Injury Medicine, NYU Med Ctr 1980; **Fac Appt:** Clin Prof PMR, NYU Sch Med

Aseff, John N MD [PMR] - **Spec Exp:** Electrodiagnosis; Pain-Soft Tissue; **Hospital:** MedStar Natl Rehab Hosp, MedStar Washington Hosp Ctr; **Address:** MedStar National Rehab Hosp, 102 Irving St NW, Washington, DC 20010; **Phone:** 202-877-1916; **Board Cert:** Physical Medicine & Rehabilitation 1978; **Med School:** Ohio State Univ 1973; **Resid:** Surgery, Univ Affil Hosps Cleveland 1975; Physical Medicine & Rehabilitation, Ohio State Univ Hosp 1978; **Fac Appt:** Assoc Clin Prof PMR, Georgetown Univ

Bach, John R MD [PMR] - **Spec Exp:** Neuromuscular Disorders; Amyotrophic Lateral Sclerosis (ALS); Post Polio Syndrome/Rehabilitation; **Hospital:** Univ Hosp (Newark); **Address:** 90 Bergen St Fl 3 - Ste 3100, Newark, NJ 07103; **Phone:** 973-972-2850; **Board Cert:** Physical Medicine & Rehabilitation 1986; **Med School:** UMDNJ-NJ Med Sch, Newark 1976; **Resid:** Physical Medicine & Rehabilitation, NYU Med Ctr 1980; **Fellow:** Neuromuscular Disease, Univ Hosp 1983; **Fac Appt:** Prof PMR, UMDNJ-NJ Med Sch, Newark

Ballard, Pamela H MD [PMR] - **Spec Exp:** Spinal Cord Injury; Spasticity Management; Neuromuscular Disorders; **Hospital:** MedStar Natl Rehab Hosp; **Address:** MedStar Natl Rehab Hosp, 102 Irving St NW, Washington, DC 20010; **Phone:** 202-877-1621; **Board Cert:** Physical Medicine & Rehabilitation 1991; Spinal Cord Injury Medicine 2009; **Med School:** Howard Univ 1986; **Resid:** Physical Medicine & Rehabilitation, Sinai Hosp 1991

Braddom, Randall L MD [PMR] - **Spec Exp:** Electromyography; Pain-Neck; Pain-Low Back; Musculoskeletal Disorders; **Address:** Penn Diagnostics, 1801 Market St, Ste 200, Philadelphia, PA 19103; **Phone:** 215-569-9500; **Board Cert:** Physical Medicine & Rehabilitation 1974; **Med School:** Ohio State Univ 1968; **Resid:** Physical Medicine & Rehabilitation, OSU Hosp 1973

De Lateur, Barbara J MD [PMR] - **Spec Exp:** Geriatric Rehabilitation; Gait Disorders; Musculoskeletal Disorders; **Hospital:** Johns Hopkins Bayview Med Ctr (page 59), MedStar Good Samaritan Hosp; **Address:** Johns Hopkins Bayview Med Ctr, Dept Phys Med & Rehab, 4940 Eastern Ave, Baltimore, MD 21224; **Phone:** 410-550-5299; **Board Cert:** Physical Medicine & Rehabilitation 1970; **Med School:** Univ Wash 1963; **Resid:** Physical Medicine & Rehabilitation, Univ Wash Affil Hosp 1968; **Fac Appt:** Prof PMR, Johns Hopkins Univ

Dillard, James N MD [PMR] - **Spec Exp:** Pain Management; Acupuncture; Complementary Medicine; Nutrition; **Address:** 161 Madison Ave, Ste 11E, New York, NY 10016; **Phone:** 212-265-4038; **Board Cert:** Physical Medicine & Rehabilitation 2005; **Med School:** Rush Med Coll 1990; **Resid:** Physical Medicine & Rehabilitation, Columbia-Presby Med Ctr 1994; **Fac Appt:** Asst Clin Prof PMR, Columbia P&S

Esquenazi, Alberto M MD [PMR] - **Spec Exp:** Amputee Rehabilitation; Mobility Evaluation & Treatment; Spasticity Management; **Hospital:** Moss Rehab Hosp; **Address:** Moss Rehab Hosp, 60 Township Line Rd, Elkins Park, PA 19027; **Phone:** 215-663-6676; **Board Cert:** Physical Medicine & Rehabilitation 1986; **Med School:** Mexico 1981; **Resid:** Physical Medicine & Rehabilitation, Temple Univ Hosp 1985; **Fellow:** Gait and Prosthetics, Moss Rehab Hosp 1986; **Fac Appt:** Prof PMR, Temple Univ

Evans, Sarah H MD [PMR] - **Spec Exp:** Pediatric Rehabilitation; White Matter Disorders; Spina Bifida; Cerebral Palsy; **Hospital:** Chldns Natl Med Ctr, MedStar Natl Rehab Hosp; **Address:** Chldn's Natl Med Ctr, Pediatric Rehab, 111 Michigan Ave NW, Ste 1090, Washington, DC 20010; **Phone:** 202-476-3082; **Board Cert:** Physical Medicine & Rehabilitation 1992; Pediatric Rehabilitation Medicine 2003; **Med School:** Univ MD Sch Med 1984; **Resid:** Pediatrics, Univ Colorado Hlth Sci Ctr 1987; Physical Medicine & Rehabilitation, Univ Colorado Hlth Sci Ctr 1991; **Fellow:** Pediatric Rehabilitation Medicine, Chldns Hosp 1993

Feinberg, Joseph H MD [PMR] - **Spec Exp:** Peripheral Neuropathy; Spinal Rehabilitation; Electrodiagnosis; Sports Medicine; **Hospital:** Hosp For Special Surgery (page 58), Kessler Inst for Rehab - W Orange; **Address:** 429 E 75th St Fl 3, New York, NY 10021; **Phone:** 212-606-1568; **Board Cert:** Physical Medicine & Rehabilitation 1991; Sports Medicine 2009; **Med School:** Albany Med Coll 1983; **Resid:** Surgery, Mt Sinai Hosp 1985; Physical Medicine & Rehabilitation, Rusk Inst Rehab 1990; **Fellow:** Orthopaedic Pathology, Hosp Spec Surg 1986; Orthopaedic Biomechanics, Univ Iowa Hosp & Clins 1987; **Fac Appt:** Assoc Prof PMR, Cornell Univ-Weill Med Coll

Flanagan, Steven R MD [PMR] - **Spec Exp:** Brain Injury Rehabilitation; Stroke Rehabilitation; **Hospital:** NYU Langone Med Ctr (page 68), NYU Rusk Inst; **Address:** Ambulatory Care Ctr, 240 E 38th St Fl 15, New York, NY 10016; **Phone:** 212-263-6037; **Board Cert:** Physical Medicine & Rehabilitation 2013; **Med School:** UMDNJ-NJ Med Sch, Newark 1988; **Resid:** Physical Medicine & Rehabilitation, Mt Sinai Hosp 1992; **Fac Appt:** Prof PMR, NYU Sch Med

Francis, Kathleen D MD [PMR] - **Spec Exp:** Lymphedema; **Address:** Lymphedema Physician Services, 200 S Orange Ave, Ste 111, Livingston, NJ 07039; **Phone:** 973-322-7366; **Board Cert:** Physical Medicine & Rehabilitation 2004; **Med School:** UMDNJ-NJ Med Sch, Newark 1989; **Resid:** Physical Medicine & Rehabilitation, UMDNJ-Kessler Inst Rehab 1993; **Fac Appt:** Asst Clin Prof PMR, UMDNJ-NJ Med Sch, Newark

Fried, Guy W MD [PMR] - **Spec Exp:** Brain Injury Rehabilitation; Spinal Cord Injury; Neurogenic Bladder; **Hospital:** Magee Rehab Hosp; **Address:** Magee Rehab Hosp, Out Patient, 1513 Race St Fl 1, Philadelphia, PA 19102; **Phone:** 215-587-3394; **Board Cert:** Physical Medicine & Rehabilitation 1990; Spinal Cord Injury Medicine 2009; Pain Medicine 2011; **Med School:** Yale Univ 1985; **Resid:** Physical Medicine & Rehabilitation, Thomas Jefferson Univ Hosp 1988; Preventive Medicine, Thomas Jefferson Univ Hosp 1989; **Fac Appt:** Assoc Prof PMR, Thomas Jefferson Univ

Gater Jr, David R MD/PhD [PMR] - **Spec Exp:** Spinal Cord Injury; Electrodiagnosis; **Hospital:** Penn State Milton S Hershey Med Ctr, Penn State Hershey Rehabilitation Hosp; **Address:** Penn State Hershey Rehab Hospital, 1135 Old West Chocolate Ave, Hummelstown, PA 17036; **Phone:** 717-531-7010 x6583; **Board Cert:** Physical Medicine & Rehabilitation 2007; Spinal Cord Injury Medicine 2009; Electrodiagnostic Medicine 1998; **Med School:** Univ Ariz Coll Med 1992; **Resid:** Physical Medicine & Rehabilitation, UC Davis Med Ctr 1996; **Fac Appt:** Prof PMR, Penn State Coll Med

Kirshblum, Steven C MD [PMR] - **Spec Exp:** Spinal Cord Injury; Spasticity Management; **Hospital:** Kessler Inst for Rehab - W Orange, Saint Barnabas Med Ctr; **Address:** Kessler Institute, 1199 Pleasant Valley Way, West Orange, NJ 07052-1424; **Phone:** 973-731-3600 x2258; **Board Cert:** Physical Medicine & Rehabilitation 1991; Spinal Cord Injury Medicine 2008; **Med School:** Univ Hlth Scis, Chicago Med Sch 1986; **Resid:** Physical Medicine & Rehabilitation, Mount Sinai Med Ctr 1990; **Fac Appt:** Prof PMR, UMDNJ-NJ Med Sch, Newark

Lutz, Christopher MD [PMR] - **Spec Exp:** Pain-Spine; Pain-Low Back; Sports Medicine; **Hospital:** Hosp For Special Surgery (page 58); **Address:** Hosp for Special Surgery, 75th Street Campus, 429 E 75th St Fl 3, New York, NY 10021; **Phone:** 212-606-1494; **Board Cert:** Physical Medicine & Rehabilitation 2012; **Med School:** Georgetown Univ 1996; **Resid:** Physical Medicine & Rehabilitation, UMDNJ-Kessler Inst for Rehab 2000; **Fellow:** Sports Medicine, Hosp for Special Surgery 2001

Lutz, Gregory MD [PMR] - **Spec Exp:** Spinal Rehabilitation; Sports Medicine; Pain-Low Back; **Hospital:** Hosp For Special Surgery (page 58), Univ Med Ctr Princeton at Plainsboro; **Address:** 429 E 75 St Fl 3, New York, NY 10021; **Phone:** 212-606-1648; **Board Cert:** Physical Medicine & Rehabilitation 2013; **Med School:** Georgetown Univ 1988; **Resid:** Physical Medicine & Rehabilitation, Mayo Clinic 1992; **Fellow:** Sports Medicine, Hosp For Spec Surg 1993; **Fac Appt:** Assoc Prof PMR, Cornell Univ-Weill Med Coll

Ma, Dong M MD [PMR] - **Spec Exp:** Electromyography; Musculoskeletal Disorders; **Hospital:** NYU Rusk Inst, NYU Langone Med Ctr (page 68); **Address:** NYU Ctr for Musculoskeletal Care, 333 E 38th St Fl 5, New York, NY 10016; **Phone:** 646-501-7277; **Board Cert:** Physical Medicine & Rehabilitation 1979; **Med School:** South Korea 1968; **Resid:** Physical Medicine & Rehabilitation, NYU Med Ctr 1976; **Fellow:** Neuromuscular Disease, NYU Med Ctr 1977; **Fac Appt:** Clin Prof PMR, NYU Sch Med

Marino, Ralph J MD [PMR] - **Spec Exp:** Spinal Cord Injury; Spasticity Management; **Hospital:** Thomas Jefferson Univ Hosp; **Address:** 25 S 9th St, Philadelphia, PA 19107; **Phone:** 215-955-1200; **Board Cert:** Physical Medicine & Rehabilitation 1988; Spinal Cord Injury Medicine 2010; **Med School:** Jefferson Med Coll 1982; **Resid:** Physical Medicine & Rehabilitation, Thos Jefferson Univ Hosp 1987; **Fac Appt:** Prof PMR, Jefferson Med Coll

Mayer, Nathaniel H MD [PMR] - **Spec Exp:** Motor Control Analysis; Spasticity Management; Brain Injury Rehabilitation; **Hospital:** Moss Rehab Hosp; **Address:** Moss Rehab, Phys Med Dept, 60 Township Line Rd, Elkins Park, PA 19027; **Phone:** 215-663-6677; **Board Cert:** Physical Medicine & Rehabilitation 1976; **Med School:** Albert Einstein Coll Med 1968; **Resid:** Physical Medicine & Rehabilitation, Temple Univ Hosp 1973; **Fac Appt:** Prof Emeritus PMR, Temple Univ

Miknevich, Mary Ann MD [PMR] - **Spec Exp:** Amputee Rehabilitation; Electrodiagnosis; Spasticity Management; Geriatric Rehabilitation; **Hospital:** UPMC Mercy, Pittsburgh, UPMC McKeesport; **Address:** Mercy Professional Bldg C, 1350 Locust St, Ste 409, Pittsburgh, PA 15219; **Phone:** 412-232-7608; **Board Cert:** Physical Medicine & Rehabilitation 1985; **Med School:** Univ Pittsburgh 1980; **Resid:** Physical Medicine & Rehabilitation, St Francis Med Ctr 1983; **Fac Appt:** Asst Clin Prof PMR, Univ Pittsburgh

Munin, Michael C MD [PMR] - **Spec Exp:** Spasticity Management; Amputee Rehabilitation; Electrodiagnosis; Electrodiagnosis; **Hospital:** UPMC Presby, Pittsburgh, UPMC Mercy, Pittsburgh; **Address:** 3471 5th Ave, Ste 1103, Pittsburgh, PA 15213; **Phone:** 412-692-4400; **Board Cert:** Physical Medicine & Rehabilitation 2013; **Med School:** Jefferson Med Coll 1988; **Resid:** Physical Medicine & Rehabilitation, Thomas Jefferson Univ Hosp 1992; **Fac Appt:** Assoc Prof PMR, Univ Pittsburgh

Palmer, Jeffrey B MD [PMR] - **Spec Exp:** Neuro-Rehabilitation; Stroke Rehabilitation; Swallowing Disorders; Muscular Dystrophy; **Hospital:** Johns Hopkins Hosp (page 59), MedStar Good Samaritan Hosp; **Address:** Johns Hopkins Physical Med & Rehab, 600 N Wolfe St, Phipps Bldg, Ste 160, Baltimore, MD 21287; **Phone:** 410-502-2446; **Board Cert:** Physical Medicine & Rehabilitation 1984; Electrodiagnostic Medicine 1998; **Med School:** NYU Sch Med 1980; **Resid:** Physical Medicine & Rehabilitation, Univ Wash Med Ctr 1983; **Fac Appt:** Prof PMR, Johns Hopkins Univ

Ragnarsson, Kristjan T MD [PMR] - **Spec Exp:** Spinal Cord Injury; Brain Injury Rehabilitation; Pain-Back & Neck; **Hospital:** Mt Sinai Med Ctr (page 62); **Address:** Faculty Practice Assocs, 5 E 98th St Fl 6, New York, NY 10029-6501; **Phone:** 212-824-8380; **Board Cert:** Physical Medicine & Rehabilitation 1976; **Med School:** Iceland 1969; **Resid:** Physical Medicine & Rehabilitation, NYU Med Ctr 1974; **Fellow:** Spinal Cord & Brain Injury Rehab, NYU Med Ctr 1975; **Fac Appt:** Prof PMR, Mount Sinai Sch Med

Schwartz, Linden M MD [PMR] - **Spec Exp:** Pain-Musculoskeletal; Cancer Rehabilitation; Lymphedema; Head & Neck Cancer; **Hospital:** Chestnut Hill Hosp; **Address:** Montgomery Rehab Assocs, 8601 Stenton Ave, Wyndmoor, PA 19038; **Phone:** 215-233-6226; **Board Cert:** Physical Medicine & Rehabilitation 1992; Pain Medicine 2003; **Med School:** UMDNJ-NJ Med Sch, Newark 1987; **Resid:** Physical Medicine & Rehabilitation, Hosp Univ Penn 1989; Physical Medicine & Rehabilitation, Thos Jefferson Univ Hosp 1991; **Fac Appt:** Asst Clin Prof PMR, Univ Pennsylvania

Stubblefield, Michael Dean MD [PMR] - **Spec Exp:** Cancer Rehabilitation; Pain-Cancer; Pain-Neuropathic; Spasticity Management; **Hospital:** Meml Sloan-Kettering Canc Ctr; **Address:** Meml Sloan Kettering Cancer Ctr, Sillerman Ctr for Rehabilitation, 515 Madison Ave Fl 5, New York, NY 10022; **Phone:** 646-888-1936; **Board Cert:** Internal Medicine 2011; Physical Medicine & Rehabilitation 2012; Electrodiagnostic Medicine 2003; **Med School:** Columbia P&S 1996; **Resid:** Internal Medicine, Columbia Presby Med Ctr 1999; **Fellow:** Physical Medicine & Rehabilitation, Columbia Presby Med Ctr 2002; **Fac Appt:** Assoc Prof PMR, Cornell Univ-Weill Med Coll

Southeast

Alexander, Joshua MD [PMR] - **Spec Exp:** Pediatric Rehabilitation; Cerebral Palsy; Spina Bifida; **Hospital:** NC Memorial Hosp - UNC, Rex HlthCare; **Address:** UNC- Physical Med & Rehab, 101 Manning Drive, Campus Box 7200, Chapel Hill, NC 27599-7200; **Phone:** 919-966-5165; **Board Cert:** Physical Medicine & Rehabilitation 2006; Pediatric Rehabilitation Medicine 2005; **Med School:** Temple Univ 1990; **Resid:** Pediatrics, Baylor Coll of Med 1995; Physical Medicine & Rehabilitation, Baylor Coll of Med 1995; **Fac Appt:** Assoc Prof PMR, Univ NC Sch Med

Cardenas, Diana D MD [PMR] - **Spec Exp:** Spinal Cord Injury; Spina Bifida; Neurogenic Bladder; Urinary Tract Infections; **Hospital:** Univ of Miami Hosp & Clins/Sylvester Comp Canc Ctr, Jackson Meml Hosp; **Address:** UHlth, Phys Med & Rehab Dept, 1475 NW 12th Ave Fl 3, Miami, FL 33136; **Phone:** 305-243-3887; **Board Cert:** Physical Medicine & Rehabilitation 1977; Electrodiagnostic Medicine 1989; **Med School:** Univ Tex SW, Dallas 1973; **Resid:** Physical Medicine & Rehabilitation, Univ Wash Med Ctr 1976; **Fac Appt:** Prof PMR, Univ Miami Sch Med

Creamer, Michael J DO [PMR] - **Spec Exp:** Spinal Cord Injury; Pain Management; Electrodiagnosis; **Hospital:** Florida Hosp - Orlando, Orlando Regl Med Ctr; **Address:** Rehab Medical Grp, 100 W Gore St, Ste 500, Orlando, FL 32806; **Phone:** 407-649-8707; **Board Cert:** Physical Medicine & Rehabilitation 1992; Spinal Cord Injury Medicine 2008; Pain Medicine 2011; **Med School:** Chicago Coll Osteo Med 1987; **Resid:** Physical Medicine & Rehabilitation, Rehab Inst 1991; **Fac Appt:** Asst Clin Prof Med, Univ Fla Coll Med

Diamond, Paul T MD [PMR] - **Spec Exp:** Neuro-Rehabilitation; Geriatric Rehabilitation; **Hospital:** Univ of Virginia Hlth Sys; **Address:** Univ of Virginia Hlth Sci Ctr, Dept Rehabilitation, Box 801004, Charlottesville, VA 22908-1004; **Phone:** 434-243-5622; **Board Cert:** Internal Medicine 1989; Physical Medicine & Rehabilitation 2013; **Med School:** Univ VA Sch Med 1986; **Resid:** Internal Medicine, Johns Hospkins Bayview Hosp 1989; Physical Medicine & Rehabilitation, Sinai/Johns Hopkins Hosp 1992; **Fac Appt:** Assoc Prof PMR, Univ VA Sch Med

Kezar, Laura B MD [PMR] - **Spec Exp:** Pain-Back; Pain-Spine; **Hospital:** UAB Spain Rehab Ctr; **Address:** Spain Rehab Ctr, 1717 6th Ave S, rm 190, Birmingham, AL 35233; **Phone:** 205-934-4179; **Board Cert:** Physical Medicine & Rehabilitation 2006; **Med School:** Emory Univ 1985; **Resid:** Physical Medicine & Rehabilitation, UAB Hosp 1994; **Fac Appt:** Prof PMR, UAB Sch Med

King Jr, Richard W MD [PMR] - **Spec Exp:** Cancer Rehabilitation; Lymphedema; Soft Tissue Radiation Necrosis; Soft Tissue Radiation Necrosis-Breast; **Hospital:** WellStar Windy Hill Hosp, WellStar Cobb Hosp; **Address:** HyOx Medical Treatment Ctr, 2550 Windy Hill Rd, Ste 110, Marietta, GA 30067; **Phone:** 678-303-3200; **Board Cert:** Physical Medicine & Rehabilitation 1988; Undersea & Hyperbaric Medicine 2012; **Med School:** Emory Univ 1979; **Resid:** Physical Medicine & Rehabilitation, Emory Univ Hosp 1987; **Fac Appt:** Asst Clin Prof PMR, Emory Univ

Leslie, Donald P MD [PMR] - **Spec Exp:** Brain/Spinal Cord Injury; **Hospital:** Shepherd Ctr - Atlanta; **Address:** Shepherd Center, 2020 Peachtree Rd NW, Atlanta, GA 30309; **Phone:** 404-352-2020; **Board Cert:** Physical Medicine & Rehabilitation 1989; **Med School:** Univ Tenn Coll Med 1972; **Resid:** Internal Medicine, Mayo Clinic 1975; Physical Medicine & Rehabilitation, Emory Univ Hosp 1986

McKinley, William O MD [PMR] - **Spec Exp:** Spinal Cord Injury; **Hospital:** VCU Med Ctr; **Address:** VCU Med Ctr, Div Physical Med & Rehabilitation, 417 N 11th St, Richmond, VA 23298; **Phone:** 804-828-4097; **Board Cert:** Physical Medicine & Rehabilitation 1990; Spinal Cord Injury Medicine 2008; **Med School:** Albany Med Coll 1985; **Resid:** Physical Medicine & Rehabilitation, VA Commonwealth Univ Med Ctr 1989; **Fac Appt:** Prof PMR, Va Commonwealth Univ Sch Med

McLain, Amie B MD [PMR] - **Spec Exp:** Spinal Cord Injury; **Hospital:** UAB Spain Rehab Ctr, UAB Hosp; **Address:** Spain Rehab Ctr, 1717 6th Ave S, rm 190, Birmingham, AL 35249-7330; **Phone:** 205-934-3330; **Board Cert:** Physical Medicine & Rehabilitation 1990; **Med School:** UAB Sch Med 1984; **Resid:** Physical Medicine & Rehabilitation, UAB Hosp 1987; **Fac Appt:** Prof PMR, UAB Sch Med

Stewart, Paula JB MD [PMR] - **Spec Exp:** Lymphedema; Brain Tumors; Spinal Cord Tumors; Cancer Rehabilitation; **Hospital:** Healthsouth Lakeshore Rehab Hosp; **Address:** Healthsouth Lakeshore Rehab Hosp, 3800 Ridgeway Drive, Birmingham, AL 35209; **Phone:** 205-868-2347; **Board Cert:** Physical Medicine & Rehabilitation 2006; Spinal Cord Injury Medicine 2010; **Med School:** Univ Minn 1987; **Resid:** Physical Medicine & Rehabilitation, Mayo Clinic 1991

Midwest

Brown, Allen W MD [PMR] - **Spec Exp:** Brain Injury; Stroke; **Hospital:** St. Mary's Hosp - Rochester MN (Mayo), Rochester Methodist Hosp; **Address:** Mayo Clinic PM&R, 200 1st St SW, Rochester, MN 55905; **Phone:** 507-255-3116; **Board Cert:** Physical Medicine & Rehabilitation 2004; **Med School:** Univ Minn 1998; **Resid:** Physical Medicine & Rehabilitation, Mayo Med Ctr & Clin 1992; **Fac Appt:** Asst Prof PMR, Mayo Med Sch

Chen, David MD [PMR] - **Spec Exp:** Spinal Cord Injury; **Hospital:** Rehab Inst of Chicago; **Address:** 345 E Superior St, Ste 1146, Chicago, IL 60611; **Phone:** 312-238-1000; **Board Cert:** Physical Medicine & Rehabilitation 1992; Spinal Cord Injury Medicine 2008; **Med School:** Univ IL Coll Med 1987; **Resid:** Physical Medicine & Rehabilitation, Northwestern Med Sch 1991; **Fac Appt:** Asst Prof PMR, Northwestern Univ

Cheville, Andrea L MD [PMR] - **Spec Exp:** Lymphedema; Cancer Rehabilitation; Pain-Cancer; **Hospital:** Mayo Med Ctr & Clin - Rochester; **Address:** Mayo Clinic, Dept Physical Med & Rehab, 200 1st St SW, Rochester, MN 55905; **Phone:** 507-284-2747; **Board Cert:** Physical Medicine & Rehabilitation 2008; Pain Medicine 2004; Hospice & Palliative Medicine 2008; **Med School:** Harvard Med Sch 1993; **Resid:** Physical Medicine & Rehabilitation, UMDNJ Med Ctr 1997; **Fellow:** Pain & Palliative Care, Meml Sloan Kettering Cancer Ctr 1999; **Fac Appt:** Assoc Prof PMR, Mayo Med Sch

Clairmont, Albert C MD [PMR] - **Spec Exp:** Spasticity Management; Electrodiagnosis; **Hospital:** OSU Wexner Med Ctr; **Address:** 480 Medical Center Drive, Columbus, OH 43210; **Phone:** 614-293-7604; **Board Cert:** Physical Medicine & Rehabilitation 1985; Pediatrics 1985; **Med School:** Jamaica 1974; **Resid:** Pediatrics, Columbus Chldns Hosp 1981; Physical Medicine & Rehabilitation, Ohio St Univ Hosps 1983; **Fac Appt:** Assoc Clin Prof PMR, Ohio State Univ

Colachis III, Samuel C MD [PMR] - **Spec Exp:** Spinal Cord Injury; Electrodiagnosis; **Hospital:** OSU Wexner Med Ctr; **Address:** 2050 Kenny Rd, Columbus, OH 43221; **Phone:** 614-293-7604; **Board Cert:** Physical Medicine & Rehabilitation 1988; Spinal Cord Injury Medicine 2003; **Med School:** USC Sch Med 1984; **Resid:** Physical Medicine & Rehabilitation, Ohio State Univ Hosps 1987; **Fellow:** Electrodiagnosis, Ohio State Univ Hosps 1988; **Fac Appt:** Assoc Prof PMR, Ohio State Univ

DePompolo, Robert W MD [PMR] - **Spec Exp:** Cancer Rehabilitation; Lymphedema; **Hospital:** St. Mary's Hosp - Rochester MN (Mayo), Mayo Med Ctr & Clin - Rochester; **Address:** Mayo Clinic, Dept Phys Med & Rehab, 200 1st St SW, Rochester, MN 55905; **Phone:** 507-255-3116; **Board Cert:** Physical Medicine & Rehabilitation 1981; **Med School:** Wayne State Univ 1977; **Resid:** Physical Medicine & Rehabilitation, Univ Minnesota Affil Hosp 1980

Feldman, Joseph L MD [PMR] - **Spec Exp:** Lymphedema; Electromyography; **Hospital:** Evanston Hosp/NorthShore Univ Hlth Sys (page 67); **Address:** Northshore Medical Group, 1000 Central St, Ste 800, Evanston, IL 60201; **Phone:** 847-570-2066; **Board Cert:** Physical Medicine & Rehabilitation 1971; **Med School:** Univ IL Coll Med 1965; **Resid:** Physical Medicine & Rehabilitation, Univ Illinois Med Ctr 1969

Frost, Frederick S MD [PMR] - **Spec Exp:** Spinal Cord Injury; Stroke Rehabilitation; Geriatric Rehabilitation; **Hospital:** Cleveland Clin (page 55); **Address:** Cleveland Clinic Fdn, 9500 Euclid Ave, Desk S-31, Cleveland, OH 44195; **Phone:** 216-445-2006; **Board Cert:** Physical Medicine & Rehabilitation 1988; Spinal Cord Injury Medicine 2008; **Med School:** Northwestern Univ 1983; **Resid:** Physical Medicine & Rehabilitation, Northwestern Meml Hosp 1987; **Fellow:** Spinal Cord Injury Medicine, Rehab Inst Chicago; **Fac Appt:** Asst Prof PMR, Cleveland Cl Coll Med/Case West Res

Gittler, Michelle S MD [PMR] - **Spec Exp:** Spinal Cord Injury; Amputee Rehabilitation; **Hospital:** Schwab Rehab Hosp, Univ of Chicago Med; **Address:** Schwab Rehab Hosp, 1401 S California Blvd, Chicago, IL 60608; **Phone:** 773-522-6617; **Board Cert:** Physical Medicine & Rehabilitation 2013; Spinal Cord Injury Medicine 2008; **Med School:** Univ IL Coll Med 1988; **Resid:** Physical Medicine & Rehabilitation, Rehab Inst Chicago 1992; **Fac Appt:** Assoc Clin Prof S, Univ Chicago-Pritzker Sch Med

Haig, Andrew John MD [PMR] - **Spec Exp:** International Health; Pain-Back & Neck; Electrodiagnosis; **Hospital:** Univ Michigan Med Ctr; **Address:** 325 E Eisenhower, Burlington Bldg - Ste 100, Ann Arbor, MI 48108-3346; **Phone:** 734-763-4200; **Board Cert:** Physical Medicine & Rehabilitation 1987; Pain Medicine 2013; **Med School:** Med Coll Wisc 1983; **Resid:** Physical Medicine & Rehabilitation, Northwestern Univ 1986; **Fac Appt:** Prof PMR, Univ Mich Med Sch

Hammond, Flora MD [PMR] - **Spec Exp:** Brain Injury Rehabilitation; **Hospital:** Rehab Hosp of Indiana, IU Hlth Univ Hosp; **Address:** Rehabilitation Hosp Indiana, 4141 Shore Drive, Indianapolis, IN 46254; **Phone:** 317-329-2000; **Board Cert:** Physical Medicine & Rehabilitation 2005; **Med School:** Tulane Univ 1990; **Resid:** Physical Medicine & Rehabilitation, Baylor Coll Med Affil Hosp 1994; **Fellow:** Brain Injury, Rehab Inst Michigan 1995; **Fac Appt:** Prof PMR, Indiana Univ

Keen, Mary MD [PMR] - **Spec Exp:** Pediatric Rehabilitation; Spasticity Management; Neurodevelopmental Disabilities; Autism; **Hospital:** Marianjoy Rehab Hosp, Central DuPage Hosp; **Address:** Marianjoy Rehab Medical Clinic, 26 W 171 Roosevelt Rd, Wheaton, IL 60187; **Phone:** 630-909-7000 x2; **Board Cert:** Physical Medicine & Rehabilitation 1984; Pediatrics 2012; Neurodevelopmental Disabilities 2012; Pediatric Rehabilitation Medicine 2003; **Med School:** Northwestern Univ 1979; **Resid:** Physical Medicine & Rehabilitation, Univ Wash Med Ctr 1983; Pediatrics, Loyola Univ Med Ctr 1990; **Fac Appt:** Assoc Clin Prof Ped, Loyola Univ-Stritch Sch Med

Kirschner, Kristi MD [PMR] - **Spec Exp:** Spina Bifida-Adult; Neuromuscular Disorders; Women's Health/Disabilities; **Hospital:** Schwab Rehab Hosp, Northwestern Meml Hosp; **Address:** Schwab Rehab Hosp, 1401 S California Ave, Chicago, IL 60608; **Phone:** 773-522-6617; **Board Cert:** Physical Medicine & Rehabilitation 1991; **Med School:** Northwestern Univ-Feinberg Sch Med 1986; **Resid:** Physical Medicine & Rehabilitation, Rehab Inst of Chicago/Northwestern Univ 1990; **Fellow:** Clinical Ethics, Maclean Ctr/Univ Chicago 1995; **Fac Appt:** Prof PMR, Northwestern Univ-Feinberg Sch Med

Kuiken, Todd A MD/PhD [PMR] - **Spec Exp:** Amputee Rehabilitation; Prosthesis Control; Gait Disorders; **Hospital:** Rehab Inst of Chicago; **Address:** Rehabilitation Institute of Chicago, 345 E Superior St, rm 1309, Chicago, IL 60611; **Phone:** 312-238-8072; **Board Cert:** Physical Medicine & Rehabilitation 2006; **Med School:** Northwestern Univ 1990; **Resid:** Physical Medicine & Rehabilitation, Rehab Inst Chicago 1995; **Fac Appt:** Prof PMR, Northwestern Univ

LaBan, Myron M MD [PMR] - **Spec Exp:** Pain-Back; Electromyography; Neuromuscular Disorders; **Hospital:** Beaumont Hosp-Royal Oak; **Address:** 3535 W 13 Mile Rd, Ste 437, Royal Oak, MI 48073; **Phone:** 248-288-2237; **Board Cert:** Physical Medicine & Rehabilitation 1967; **Med School:** Univ Mich Med Sch 1961; **Resid:** Physical Medicine & Rehabilitation, Ohio State Univ Hosp 1965; **Fac Appt:** Clin Prof PMR, Ohio State Univ

Leonard Jr, James A MD [PMR] - **Spec Exp:** Amputee Rehabilitation; Electrodiagnosis; **Hospital:** Univ Michigan Med Ctr; **Address:** Eisenhower Corporate Park, 2850 S Industrial Hwy, Ste 400, Ann Arbor, MI 48104-5758; **Phone:** 734-973-2400; **Board Cert:** Physical Medicine & Rehabilitation 1977; **Med School:** Univ Mich Med Sch 1972; **Resid:** Physical Medicine & Rehabilitation, Univ Michigan Hosp 1975; **Fac Appt:** Clin Prof PMR, Univ Mich Med Sch

Mysiw, W. Jerry MD [PMR] - **Spec Exp:** Brain Injury Rehabilitation; **Hospital:** OSU Wexner Med Ctr; **Address:** 2050 Kenny Rd, Columbus, OH 43221; **Phone:** 614-293-7604; **Board Cert:** Physical Medicine & Rehabilitation 1985; **Med School:** Ohio State Univ 1981; **Resid:** Physical Medicine & Rehabilitation, Ohio State Univ Med Ctr 1984; **Fac Appt:** Assoc Prof PMR, Ohio State Univ

Nobunaga, Austin MD [PMR] - **Spec Exp:** Spinal Cord Injury; Electrodiagnosis; **Hospital:** Univ Cincinnati Med Ctr; **Address:** Drake Ctr, 151 W Galbraith Rd, S Pavillion, Cincinnati, OH 45216; **Phone:** 513-418-2707; **Board Cert:** Physical Medicine & Rehabilitation 1990; Spinal Cord Injury Medicine 2009; **Med School:** Univ Mich Med Sch 1985; **Resid:** Physical Medicine & Rehabilitation, Rehab Inst Chicago 1989

Press, Joel MD [PMR] - **Spec Exp:** Sports Medicine; Pain-Back; Musculoskeletal Injuries; **Hospital:** Rehab Inst of Chicago; **Address:** RIC-Spine & Sports Rehab Ctr, 1030 N Clark St, Ste 500, Chicago, IL 60610; **Phone:** 312-238-7767; **Board Cert:** Physical Medicine & Rehabilitation 1989; Sports Medicine 2009; **Med School:** Univ IL Coll Med 1984; **Resid:** Physical Medicine & Rehabilitation, Northwestern Meml Hosp 1988; **Fac Appt:** Prof PMR, Northwestern Univ

Roth, Elliot MD [PMR] - **Spec Exp:** Stroke Rehabilitation; Neurologic Rehabilitation; Geriatric Rehabilitation; **Hospital:** Rehab Inst of Chicago, Northwestern Meml Hosp; **Address:** Rehab Inst Chicago, 345 E Superior St Fl 3, Chicago, IL 60611-2654; **Phone:** 312-238-1000; **Board Cert:** Physical Medicine & Rehabilitation 1987; **Med School:** Northwestern Univ 1982; **Resid:** Physical Medicine & Rehabilitation, Northwestern Univ 1985; **Fellow:** Stroke Rehabilitation, Rehab Inst Chicago 1986; **Fac Appt:** Prof PMR, Northwestern Univ

Sisung, Charles MD [PMR] - **Spec Exp:** Rheumatic Diseases of Childhood; Trauma Rehabilitation; Burn Care; **Hospital:** Rehab Inst of Chicago; **Address:** 345 E Superior St Fl 3, Chicago, IL 60611; **Phone:** 312-238-1246; **Board Cert:** Pediatrics 2011; Physical Medicine & Rehabilitation 1991; Pediatric Rehabilitation Medicine 2003; **Med School:** Univ Mich Med Sch 1981; **Resid:** Pediatrics, Mott Chldns Hosp/Univ Mich 1984; Physical Medicine & Rehabilitation, Schwab Rehab Hosp 1989; **Fellow:** Pediatric Rheumatology, Univ Chicago Hosps 1991; **Fac Appt:** Asst Prof PMR, Northwestern Univ-Feinberg Sch Med

Sliwa, James A DO [PMR] - **Spec Exp:** Post Polio Syndrome/Rehabilitation; Multiple Sclerosis; Pain-Back; **Hospital:** Rehab Inst of Chicago; **Address:** Rehab Inst Chicago, 345 E Superior St Fl 3, Chicago, IL 60611; **Phone:** 312-238-4093; **Board Cert:** Physical Medicine & Rehabilitation 2005; **Med School:** Chicago Coll Osteo Med 1980; **Resid:** Physical Medicine & Rehabilitation, Rehab Institute Chicago 1984; **Fac Appt:** Prof PMR, Northwestern Univ

Volshteyn, Oksana MD [PMR] - **Spec Exp:** Spinal Cord Injury; Amputee Rehabilitation; **Hospital:** Rehab Inst St. Louis, Barnes-Jewish Hosp; **Address:** 4444 Forest Park Blvd, Ste 8518, St Louis, MO 63108; **Phone:** 314-362-4503; **Board Cert:** Physical Medicine & Rehabilitation 1986; Spinal Cord Injury Medicine 2009; **Med School:** Russia 1976; **Resid:** Physical Medicine & Rehabilitation, Barnes-Jewish Hosp 1985; **Fac Appt:** Prof N, Washington Univ, St Louis

Great Plains and Mountains

Mason, Kristin D MD [PMR] - **Spec Exp:** Neurologic Rehabilitation; Electrodiagnosis; Musculoskeletal Injuries; Stroke Rehabilitation; **Hospital:** Swedish Med Ctr - Denver; **Address:** Rehab Assocs, 9025 Grant St, Ste 103, Thornton, CO 80229; **Phone:** 303-286-2888; **Board Cert:** Physical Medicine & Rehabilitation 2013; **Med School:** Baylor Coll Med 1988; **Resid:** Physical Medicine & Rehabilitation, Rehab Inst 1992

Matthews, Dennis J MD [PMR] - **Spec Exp:** Brain Injury-Pediatric; Cerebral Palsy; Muscular Dystrophy; Neuromuscular Disorders; **Hospital:** Chldn's Hosp - Aurora (CO); **Address:** Chldns Hosp, Rehabilitation Dept, 13123 E 16th Ave, Box B285, Aurora, CO 80045; **Phone:** 720-777-3907; **Board Cert:** Physical Medicine & Rehabilitation 2009; Pediatric Rehabilitation Medicine 2003; Neuromuscular Medicine 2008; **Med School:** Univ Colorado 1975; **Resid:** Physical Medicine & Rehabilitation, Univ Minnesota Hosps 1978; **Fellow:** Research, Univ Minnesota Hosps 1978; **Fac Appt:** Prof PMR, Univ Colorado

Southwest

Currie, Donald M MD [PMR] - **Spec Exp:** Pediatric Rehabilitation; Neuro-Rehabilitation; **Hospital:** Univ Hosp-San Antonio, Christus Santa Rosa Med Ctr Hosp; **Address:** Univ Hospital, 4502 Medical Drive, MS 64-1, San Antonio, TX 78229; **Phone:** 210-358-0500; **Board Cert:** Physical Medicine & Rehabilitation 1978; **Med School:** Univ Tex SW, Dallas 1972; **Resid:** Physical Medicine & Rehabilitation, Baylor Univ Med Ctr 1975; Physical Medicine & Rehabilitation, Univ Washington Med Ctr 1977; **Fac Appt:** Prof PMR, Univ Tex, San Antonio

Dumitru, Daniel MD/PhD [PMR] - **Spec Exp:** Electrodiagnosis; **Hospital:** Univ Hosp-San Antonio; **Address:** 4502 Med Drive, MS 33-1, San Antonio, TX 78229-3900; **Phone:** 210-358-0770; **Board Cert:** Physical Medicine & Rehabilitation 1984; **Med School:** Univ Cincinnati 1980; **Resid:** Physical Medicine & Rehabilitation, VA Hosp 1983; **Fac Appt:** Prof PMR, Univ Tex, San Antonio

Francisco, Gerard E MD [PMR] - **Spec Exp:** Spasticity Management; Brain Injury Rehabilitation; Stroke Rehabilitation; **Hospital:** TIRR Meml Hermann, Meml Hermann Hosp - Texas Med Ctr; **Address:** 1333 Moursund Ave, Houston, TX 77030; **Phone:** 713-797-5246; **Board Cert:** Physical Medicine & Rehabilitation 2005; **Med School:** Philippines 1989; **Resid:** Physical Medicine & Rehabilitation, UMDNJ-Univ Hosp 1994; **Fellow:** Brain Injury, Baylor Coll Med 1995; **Fac Appt:** Clin Prof PMR, Univ Tex, Houston

Harris, David K MD [PMR] - **Spec Exp:** Spinal Rehabilitation; Spinal Cord Injury; Pain-Back; Pain-Spine; **Address:** Ctr for Healing & Regenerative Med, 7307 Creekbluff Drive, Austin, TX 78750; **Phone:** 512-614-3300; **Board Cert:** Physical Medicine & Rehabilitation 2004; Pain Medicine 2004; **Med School:** Univ Tex SW, Dallas 1988; **Resid:** Physical Medicine & Rehabilitation, Univ Colorado Hlth Sci Ctr 1992

Ivanhoe, Cindy MD [PMR] - **Spec Exp:** Brain Injury Rehabilitation; Spasticity Management; Movement Disorders; **Hospital:** TIRR Meml Hermann, Meml Hermann Hosp - Texas Med Ctr; **Address:** 1213 Hermann Drive, Ste 740, Houston, TX 77004; **Phone:** 713-942-7300; **Board Cert:** Physical Medicine & Rehabilitation 2013; **Med School:** Mexico 1984; **Resid:** Physical Medicine & Rehabilitation, Univ Illinois Affil Hosp 1992; **Fellow:** Brain Injury, Baylor Coll Med 1993; **Fac Appt:** Asst Prof PMR, Baylor Coll Med

Kevorkian, Charles G MD [PMR] - **Spec Exp:** Stroke Rehabilitation; Neuromuscular Disorders; Electrodiagnosis; **Hospital:** St. Luke's Episcopal Hosp-Houston; **Address:** Dept Physical Med & Rehab, 6624 Fannin St, Ste 1665, Houston, TX 77030-2335; **Phone:** 713-798-4061; **Board Cert:** Physical Medicine & Rehabilitation 1980; **Med School:** Australia 1972; **Resid:** Physical Medicine & Rehabilitation, Prince Henry Hosp 1976; Physical Medicine & Rehabilitation, Mayo Clinic 1979; **Fac Appt:** Assoc Prof PMR, Baylor Coll Med

King, John C MD [PMR] - **Spec Exp:** Stroke Rehabilitation; Pain-Chronic; Spinal Cord Injury; Electrodiagnosis; **Hospital:** Univ Hosp-San Antonio; **Address:** 4502 Medical Drive, San Antonio, TX 78229; **Phone:** 210-358-0770; **Board Cert:** Physical Medicine & Rehabilitation 1987; Spinal Cord Injury Medicine 2010; Pain Medicine 2013; **Med School:** Oral Roberts Sch Med 1983; **Resid:** Physical Medicine & Rehabilitation, Baylor Coll Med 1986; **Fac Appt:** Prof PMR, Univ Tex, San Antonio

Nelson, Maureen R MD [PMR] - **Spec Exp:** Pediatric Rehabilitation; Brachial Plexus Palsy; Electrodiagnosis; **Hospital:** Dell Children's Med Ctr of Central Texas; **Address:** 1301 Barbara Jordan Blvd, Ste 200, Austin, TX 78723; **Phone:** 512-628-1896; **Board Cert:** Physical Medicine & Rehabilitation 1990; Pediatric Rehabilitation Medicine 2003; **Med School:** Univ IL Coll Med 1985; **Resid:** Physical Medicine & Rehabilitation, Univ Tex Hlth Scis Ctr 1989; **Fellow:** Pediatric Rehabilitation Medicine, Alfred I Dupont Inst 1990

Wilson, Amy J MD [PMR] - **Spec Exp:** Amputee Rehabilitation; Stroke Rehabilitation; **Hospital:** Baylor Inst for Rehabilitation; **Address:** Baylor Institute for Rehabilitation, 909 N Washington Ave, Dallas, TX 75246; **Phone:** 214-820-9300; **Board Cert:** Physical Medicine & Rehabilitation 2007; **Med School:** Univ Tex, Houston 1992; **Resid:** Physical Medicine & Rehabilitation, Baylor Univ Med Ctr 1996

West Coast and Pacific

Apkon, Susan MD [PMR] - **Spec Exp:** Cerebral Palsy; Brain Injury Rehabilitation; Neuromuscular Disorders; **Hospital:** Seattle Chldns Hosp, Univ Wash Med Ctr; **Address:** Seattle Chldn's-Physical Med & Rehab, 4800 Sand Point Way NE, Seattle, WA 98105; **Phone:** 206-987-2114; **Board Cert:** Pediatrics 2007; Physical Medicine & Rehabilitation 2010; Pediatric Rehabilitation Medicine 2003; **Med School:** Univ VT Coll Med 1994; **Resid:** Pediatrics, Chldn's Hosp 1998; Physical Medicine & Rehabilitation, Chldn's Hosp 2000; **Fac Appt:** Assoc Prof PMR, Univ Wash

Friedman, Andrew S MD [PMR] - **Spec Exp:** Spinal Rehabilitation; Pain Management; Brain Injury Rehabilitation; Neuromuscular Disorders; **Hospital:** Virginia Mason Med Ctr; **Address:** 909 University St, MS G2-PMR, Seattle, WA 98111; **Phone:** 206-223-6746; **Board Cert:** Physical Medicine & Rehabilitation 2006; Pain Medicine 2003; **Med School:** Univ Mich Med Sch 1990; **Resid:** Physical Medicine & Rehabilitation, Univ Wash Med Ctr 1995; **Fac Appt:** Asst Clin Prof PMR, Univ Wash

Herring, Stanley A MD [PMR] - **Spec Exp:** Musculoskeletal Disorders; Spinal Rehabilitation; Concussion; Sports Medicine; **Hospital:** Harborview Med Ctr; **Address:** 908 Jefferson St, Box 359721, Seattle, WA 98104; **Phone:** 206-744-0401; **Board Cert:** Physical Medicine & Rehabilitation 1983; **Med School:** Univ Tex SW, Dallas 1979; **Resid:** Physical Medicine & Rehabilitation, Univ Wash Med Ctr 1982; **Fac Appt:** Clin Prof PMR, Univ Wash

Massagli, Teresa L MD [PMR] - **Spec Exp:** Spinal Cord Injury-Pediatric; Brain Injury Rehabilitation-Pediatric; Neuromuscular Disorders; Pediatric Rehabilitation; **Hospital:** Seattle Chldns Hosp, Harborview Med Ctr; **Address:** Seattle Chldn's-Physical Med & Rehab, 4800 Sand Point Way NE, Seattle, WA 98105; **Phone:** 206-987-2114; **Board Cert:** Pediatrics 1987; Physical Medicine & Rehabilitation 2009; Spinal Cord Injury Medicine 2008; Pediatric Rehabilitation Medicine 2009; **Med School:** Yale Univ 1982; **Resid:** Pediatrics, Yale-New Haven Hosp 1985; Physical Medicine & Rehabilitation, Univ Washington Med Ctr 1988; **Fac Appt:** Prof PMR, Univ Wash

Robinson, Lawrence R MD [PMR] - **Spec Exp:** Electrodiagnosis; Electromyography; Botox Therapy; Peripheral Nerve Disorders; **Hospital:** Harborview Med Ctr, Univ Wash Med Ctr; **Address:** Harborview Medical Ctr, 325 Ninth Ave, Box 356490, Seattle, WA 98104; **Phone:** 206-744-5862; **Board Cert:** Physical Medicine & Rehabilitation 1987; Neuromuscular Medicine 2011; **Med School:** Baylor Coll Med 1982; **Resid:** Physical Medicine & Rehabilitation, Rehab Inst Chicago 1985; **Fac Appt:** Prof PMR, Univ Wash

Saal, Jeffrey A MD [PMR] - **Spec Exp:** Pain-Lower Back (IDET procedure); Spinal Rehabilitation; Sports Medicine; **Address:** 500 Arguello St, Ste 100, Redwood City, CA 94063; **Phone:** 650-851-4900; **Board Cert:** Internal Medicine 1978; Physical Medicine & Rehabilitation 1982; **Med School:** Tulane Univ 1975; **Resid:** Internal Medicine, VA Boston Hlthcare Sys-Jamaica Plain Div 1978; Physical Medicine & Rehabilitation, Stanford Univ Hosp & Clins 1981; **Fac Appt:** Assoc Clin Prof PMR, UC Irvine

THE MOUNT SINAI MEDICAL CENTER

Rehabilitation Medicine

One Gustave L. Levy Place
Fifth Avenue and 100th Street
New York, NY 10029-6574

Physician Referral: 1-800-MD-SINAI (637-4624)
www.mountsinai.org

The **DEPARTMENT OF REHABILITATION MEDICINE** at Mount Sinai is a Center of Excellence in the delivery of complete care for people with disabilities. A wide range of comprehensive patient care services is available for individuals with spinal cord injuries, brain injuries, and a variety of neuromuscular, musculoskeletal, and chronic conditions. We are accredited by the Commission on Accreditation of Rehabilitation Facilities (CARF) for our inpatient spinal cord injury, amputation and brain injury programs—the only such accredited programs at non-VA hospitals in New York City—as well as for our comprehensive rehabilitation medicine program. Our Amputation Specialty Program was the first such CARF-accredited program in New York State.

Pivotal to successful rehabilitation, the multidisciplinary team approach at Mount Sinai takes advantage of all areas of expertise to provide the highest quality of coordinated care. Our experienced professionals evaluate each patient and meet regularly to develop and implement individualized treatment plans in partnership with patients and their families. Our goal is to make each individual with a disability maximally self-sufficient and mobile, and able to return to community life.

MODEL SYSTEMS OF CARE

The Department of Rehabilitation Medicine provides comprehensive services that serve as national models of care.

- Consistently ranked among the top rehabilitation centers by *U.S. News & World Report*, currently # 14.
- One of 16 programs designated by NIDRR as a Model System of Care for Traumatic Brain Injury, the only such designated program in New York State.
- The first CDC Injury Control Research Center focusing on traumatic brain injury research.

The Mount Sinai Rehabilitation Center team is led by Kristjan T. Ragnarsson, MD, whose leadership and innovative approach to patient care has had a major impact in the field of rehabilitation medicine. The Center includes physicians, primary rehabilitation nurses, nurse practitioners, and professional staff in physical therapy, occupational therapy, speech therapy, nutrition, social work, psychology, therapeutic recreation, and vocational counseling. Special rehabilitation medicine programs include the following:

- **The Spinal Cord Injury Rehabilitation Program** provides comprehensive care to individuals with spinal cord injuries. This includes a full range of innovative medical and rehabilitation services. For example, our "Do It" program is a unique outpatient program that facilitates community integration.
- **The Brain Injury Rehabilitation Program** provides comprehensive care to individuals with brain injuries. It is well recognized that the treatment of individuals with cognitive and behavioral challenges is critical to community integration. Our program contains specialists uniquely qualified to meet these challenges.
- **The Interventional Spine and Sports Medicine Program** provides the highest quality, evidence-based care for spine and musculoskeletal disorders. Our physiatrists combine a thorough examination with the latest high-tech diagnostic procedures to precisely identify and treat each patient. Our treatment options include physical and occupational therapy, medications, bracing, as well as ultrasound and fluoroscopic guided injections.
- **The Amputation Specialty Program** is designed to anticipate and meet the needs of persons with limb loss, as well as to prevent secondary complications and further amputations. Our interdisciplinary team works closely with other departments throughout the Medical Center to provide an integrated approach to our patients' healthcare.

NYU Langone
MEDICAL CENTER

550 First Avenue *(at 31st Street)*
New York, NY 10016
www.NYULMC.org/rusk
Physician Referral: **888-7-NYU-MED** *(888-769-8633)*

RUSK REHABILITATION

Rusk Rehabilitation at NYU Langone Medical Center (Rusk) has been ranked the best rehabilitation program in New York State and among the top ten in the country by *U.S. News & World Report* since 1989. Rusk is internationally renowned for the treatment of adults and children with injuries and disabilities, offering the full continuum of inpatient and outpatient care—physical, occupational, speech/swallowing and vocational therapy, psychology, music and recreational therapy, nutrition, nursing, and social work—for a wide range of conditions. Specialty programs and services include:

The **CARF-Accredited Brain Injury Rehabilitation Program** is tailored for patients who have medical, physical, cognitive, and behavioral changes as a result of a brain injury or neurological illness.

The **CARF-Accredited Stroke Program** offers an interdisciplinary team with specialized training in the medical, nursing or therapeutic care and treatment of stroke patients.

The Concussion Center is a collaborative effort between Rusk Rehabilitation and the Departments of Orthopaedic Surgery and Neurology, providing expert, multidisciplinary evaluation and treatment of individuals who have or are suspected of having a concussion.

Our **Amputee Program** provides specialized limb loss rehabilitation to patients who have undergone amputations.

The Joan and Joel Smilow Cardiac and Pulmonary Rehabilitation & Prevention Center offers a model of transitional care for patients with cardiac and lung conditions.

Orthopaedic/Musculoskeletal Rehabilitation is offered for patients with back, neck, hip, elbow and shoulder disorders, arthritis-related joint pain, conditions affecting the bones, tendon, ligaments and muscles, and for pre- and post-surgical patients.

Sports Injury Rehabilitation addresses the needs of patients with sports-related conditions, including post-operative rehabilitation for patients who require orthopaedic surgery.

Our **Spinal Cord Injury** program offers a comprehensive, patient-centered array of specialized and innovative clinical and educational programs to optimize quality of life.

(continued)

Top Doctors Make A Difference

Plastic Surgery

A plastic surgeon deals with the repair, reconstruction or replacement of physical defects of form or function involving the skin, musculoskeletal system, craniomaxillofacial structures, hand, extremities, breast and trunk and external genitalia. He/she uses aesthetic surgical principles not only to improve undesirable qualities of normal structures (commonly called "cosmetic surgery") but in all reconstructive procedures as well.

A plastic surgeon possesses special knowledge and skill in the design and surgery of grafts, flaps, free tissue transfer and replantation. Competence in the management of complex wounds, the use of implantable materials, and in tumor surgery is required.

Training Required: Five to seven years

Certification in one of the following subspecialties requires additional training and examination.

Plastic Surgery within the Head and Neck: A plastic surgeon with additional training in plastic and reconstructive procedures within the head, face, neck and associated structures, including cutaneous head and neck oncology and reconstruction, management of maxillofacial trauma, soft tissue repair and neural surgery.

The field is diverse and involves a wide age range of patients, from the newborn to the aged. While both cosmetic and reconstructive surgery are practiced, there are many additional procedures which interface with them.

Surgery of the Hand (see Hand Surgery)

Plastic Surgery

New England

Constantian, Mark B MD [PlS] - **Spec Exp:** Rhinoplasty; Cosmetic Surgery-Face; Breast Surgery; Hand Surgery; **Hospital:** St. Joseph Hosp & Trauma Ctr, Southern NH Med Ctr; **Address:** 19 Tyler St, Ste 302, Nashua, NH 03060-2951; **Phone:** 603-880-7700; **Board Cert:** Plastic Surgery 2009; **Med School:** Univ VA Sch Med 1972; **Resid:** Surgery, Boston Univ Med Ctr 1976; **Fellow:** Plastic/Reconstructive Surgery, Medical Coll VA 1978

Eriksson, Elof K MD [PlS] - **Spec Exp:** Abdominoplasty; Cosmetic Surgery-Breast; Facial Plastic & Reconstructive Surgery; **Hospital:** Brigham & Women's Hosp, Children's Hospital - Boston; **Address:** Brigham & Women's Hosp, Div Plas Surg, 75 Francis St, Boston, MA 02115; **Phone:** 617-732-5093; **Board Cert:** Plastic Surgery 2007; **Med School:** Sweden 1969; **Resid:** Surgery, Chicago Affil Hosps 1977; **Fellow:** Plastic Surgery, Med Coll VA Affil Hosp 1979; **Fac Appt:** Prof PlS, Harvard Med Sch

Feldman, Joel J MD [PlS] - **Spec Exp:** Cosmetic Surgery-Face & Neck; Burns-Reconstructive Plastic Surgery; Reconstructive Surgery; **Hospital:** Mount Auburn Hosp; **Address:** Doctors Office Bldg, 300 Mt Auburn St, Ste 304, Cambridge, MA 02138; **Phone:** 617-661-5998; **Board Cert:** Surgery 1975; Plastic Surgery 1977; **Med School:** Harvard Med Sch 1969; **Resid:** Surgery, Mass Genl Hosp 1974; Plastic Surgery, Johns Hopkins Hosp 1976; **Fac Appt:** Assoc Clin Prof PlS, Harvard Med Sch

Gallico III, G Gregory MD [PlS] - **Spec Exp:** Liposuction & Body Contouring; Rhinoplasty; Cosmetic Surgery-Face & Eyes; **Hospital:** Mass Eye & Ear Infirm; **Address:** Boston Ctr for Ambulatory Surgery, 170 Commonwealth Ave, Boston, MA 02116; **Phone:** 617-267-5553; **Board Cert:** Plastic Surgery 1982; **Med School:** Harvard Med Sch 1973; **Resid:** Surgery, Mass Genl Hosp 1980; Plastic Surgery, Mass Genl Hosp 1981; **Fac Appt:** Assoc Clin Prof S, Harvard Med Sch

Meara, John G MD/DMD [PlS] - **Spec Exp:** Cleft Palate/Lip; Craniofacial Surgery-Pediatric; **Hospital:** Children's Hospital - Boston; **Address:** Boston Chldn's Hosp, Dept Plastic Surg, 300 Longwood Ave, Boston, MA 02115; **Phone:** 617-355-4401; **Board Cert:** Plastic Surgery 2011; Otolaryngology 1998; **Med School:** Univ Mich Med Sch 1990; **Resid:** Plastic Surgery, Brigham & Womens & The Chldns Hosps 1999; Otolaryngology, Mass Eye & Ear Infirmary 1997; **Fellow:** Craniofacial Surgery, Royal Chldns Hosp 2000; **Fac Appt:** Assoc Prof PlS, Harvard Med Sch

Mulliken, John B MD [PlS] - **Spec Exp:** Pediatric Plastic Surgery; Cleft Palate/Lip; Vascular Malformations; **Hospital:** Children's Hospital - Boston; **Address:** Chldns Hosp, Div Plastic Surgery, 300 Longwood Ave, Hunnewell-1, Boston, MA 02115-5724; **Phone:** 617-355-7686; **Board Cert:** Surgery 1972; Plastic Surgery 1975; **Med School:** Columbia P&S 1964; **Resid:** Surgery, Mass Genl Hosp 1970; Plastic Surgery, Johns Hopkins Hosp 1974; **Fac Appt:** Prof S, Harvard Med Sch

Orgill, Dennis MD [PlS] - **Spec Exp:** Wound Healing/Care; Burns-Reconstructive Plastic Surgery; Liposuction & Body Contouring; Rhinoplasty; **Hospital:** Brigham & Women's Hosp; **Address:** Brigham & Women's Hosp, Dept Plas Surg, 75 Francis St, Boston, MA 02115; **Phone:** 617-732-5456; **Board Cert:** Surgery 2011; Plastic Surgery 2007; **Med School:** Harvard Med Sch 1985; **Resid:** Surgery, Brigham & Women's Hosp 1990; **Fellow:** Plastic Surgery, Brigham & Women's Hosp 1992; **Fac Appt:** Prof S, Harvard Med Sch

Persing, John A MD [PlS] - **Spec Exp:** Craniofacial Surgery; Vascular Malformations; Cosmetic & Reconstructive Surgery; **Hospital:** Yale-New Haven Hosp; **Address:** Yale Plastic Surgery, 800 Howard Ave Fl 4, New Haven, CT 06520; **Phone:** 203-785-2570; **Board Cert:** Plastic Surgery 2007; Neurological Surgery 1986; **Med School:** Univ VT Coll Med 1974; **Resid:** Surgery, Univ Arizona Med Ctr 1976; Neurological Surgery, Univ Virginia Med Ctr 1982; **Fellow:** Plastic Surgery, Univ Virginia Med Ctr 1984; **Fac Appt:** Prof PlS, Yale Univ

Pomahac, Bohdan MD [PlS] - **Spec Exp:** Facial Plastic & Reconstructive Surgery; Burns-Reconstructive Plastic Surgery; Breast Reconstruction; Body Contouring; **Hospital:** Brigham & Women's Hosp, Brigham and Women's Faulkner Hosp; **Address:** Brigham & Women's Hosp, Dept Plas Surg, 75 Francis St, Boston, MA 02115; **Phone:** 617-732-7796; **Board Cert:** Plastic Surgery 2005; **Med School:** Czech Republic 1996; **Resid:** Surgery, Brigham & Womens Hosp 2001; **Fellow:** Plastic Surgery, Brigham & Womens Hosp 2003

Slavin, Sumner A MD [PlS] - **Spec Exp:** Breast Reconstruction; Cosmetic Surgery-Face; Liposuction & Body Contouring; **Hospital:** Beth Israel Deaconess Med Ctr - Boston; **Address:** 1101 Beacon St, Ste 7E, Brookline, MA 02446; **Phone:** 617-277-7010; **Board Cert:** Plastic Surgery 1983; **Med School:** Univ VT Coll Med 1973; **Resid:** Surgery, Beth Israel Hosp 1978; Plastic Surgery, NYU Med Ctr 1980; **Fellow:** Hand & Microvascular Surgery, Bellevue Hosp-NYU Med Ctr 1981; **Fac Appt:** Assoc Clin Prof S, Harvard Med Sch

Stadelmann, Wayne K MD [PlS] - **Spec Exp:** Melanoma-Head & Neck; Breast Reconstruction; Breast Augmentation; **Hospital:** Concord Hospital, New London Hosp; **Address:** 246 Pleasant St, Ste 210, Concord, NH 03301; **Phone:** 603-224-5200; **Board Cert:** Plastic Surgery 2009; **Med School:** Univ Chicago-Pritzker Sch Med 1990; **Resid:** Surgery, Univ Chicago Hosps 1994; Plastic Surgery, Univ S Florida/H Lee Moffit Cancer Ctr 1997

Stahl, Richard S MD [PlS] - **Spec Exp:** Abdominal Wall Reconstruction; Chest Wall Reconstruction; Breast Reconstruction; Chest Wall Deformities; **Hospital:** Yale-New Haven Hosp, Yale-New Haven Hosp - St Raphael Campus; **Address:** 5 Durham Rd, Guilford, CT 06437; **Phone:** 203-458-4440; **Board Cert:** Surgery 2010; Plastic Surgery 1984; **Med School:** Vanderbilt Univ 1976; **Resid:** Surgery, Yale-New Haven Hosp 1981; **Fellow:** Plastic Surgery, Emory Univ Hosp 1983; **Fac Appt:** Clin Prof S, Yale Univ

Stotland, Mitchell A MD [PlS] - **Spec Exp:** Craniofacial Surgery-Pediatric; Cleft Palate/Lip; Pediatric Plastic Surgery; **Hospital:** Dartmouth - Hitchcock Med Ctr; **Address:** DHMC, Dept Plastic Surgery, 1 Medical Center Drive, Lebanon, NH 03756-1000; **Phone:** 603-650-8068; **Board Cert:** Plastic Surgery 2010; **Med School:** McGill Univ 1989; **Resid:** Surgery, McGill Univ Med Ctr 1994; Plastic Surgery, UCLA Med Ctr 1996; **Fellow:** Pediatric Craniofacial Surgery, UCLA Med Ctr 1997; **Fac Appt:** Assoc Prof S, Dartmouth Med Sch

Sullivan, Patrick K MD [PlS] - **Spec Exp:** Cosmetic Surgery-Face; Cosmetic Surgery-Breast; Rhinoplasty; Eyelid Surgery; **Hospital:** Rhode Island Hosp; **Address:** 235 Plain St, Ste 502, Providence, RI 02905; **Phone:** 401-831-8300; **Board Cert:** Otolaryngology 1985; Plastic Surgery 1989; **Med School:** Mayo Med Sch 1979; **Resid:** Otolaryngology, Univ Colo Hlth Scis Ctr 1984; Plastic Surgery, Rhode Island Hosp 1986; **Fellow:** Craniofacial Surgery, Dr Paul Tessier & Dr Hugo Obwegeser 1987; **Fac Appt:** Assoc Prof PlS, Brown Univ

Vidal, Dale C MD [PlS] - **Spec Exp:** Breast Cancer; Breast Reconstruction; **Hospital:** Dartmouth - Hitchcock Med Ctr; **Address:** Div Plastic Surgery, 1 Medical Center Drive, Lebanon, NH 03756; **Phone:** 603-650-5148; **Board Cert:** Plastic Surgery 2007; **Med School:** Emory Univ 1989; **Resid:** Plastic Surgery, Washington Univ Med Ctr 1994; **Fellow:** Microsurgery, Washington Univ Med Ctr 1995; **Fac Appt:** Prof S, Dartmouth Med Sch

Mid Atlantic

Allen, Robert J MD [PlS] - **Spec Exp:** Breast Reconstruction; Microsurgery; **Hospital:** NYU Langone Med Ctr (page 68), New York Eye & Ear Infirm (page 64); **Address:** The Ctr for Microsurgical Breast Recon, 630 3rd Ave, Ste 601, New York, NY 10017; **Phone:** 888-890-3437; **Board Cert:** Plastic Surgery 1985; **Med School:** Med Univ SC 1976; **Resid:** Surgery, LSU Med Ctr 1982; Plastic Surgery, LSU Med Ctr 1981; **Fellow:** Microsurgery, NYU Med Ctr 1983

Ascherman, Jeffrey MD [PlS] - **Spec Exp:** Breast Cosmetic & Reconstructive Surgery; Craniofacial Surgery; Cleft Palate/Lip; Cosmetic Surgery; **Hospital:** NY-Presby/Columbia Univ Med Ctr, NY (page 65), New York Eye & Ear Infirm (page 64); **Address:** 161 Ft Washington Ave, Ste 509, New York, NY 10032-3713; **Phone:** 212-305-9612; **Board Cert:** Plastic Surgery 2007; **Med School:** Columbia P&S 1988; **Resid:** Surgery, Columbia-Presby Med Ctr 1991; Plastic Surgery, Columbia-Presby Med Ctr 1994; **Fellow:** Craniofacial Surgery, Hosp Necke-Enfants Malades 1995; **Fac Appt:** Prof S, Columbia P&S

Aston, Sherrell MD [PlS] - **Spec Exp:** Cosmetic Surgery-Face & Body; Rhinoplasty; Cosmetic Surgery-Breast; Liposuction & Body Contouring; **Hospital:** Lenox Hill Hosp (page 66), NYU Langone Med Ctr (page 68); **Address:** 728 Park Ave, New York, NY 10021; **Phone:** 212-249-6000; **Board Cert:** Surgery 1974; Plastic Surgery 1978; **Med School:** Univ VA Sch Med 1968; **Resid:** Surgery, UCLA Med Ctr 1973; Plastic Surgery, NY Hosp 1975; **Fellow:** Surgery, Johns Hopkins Hosp 1970; **Fac Appt:** Prof PlS, NYU Sch Med

Attinger, Christopher E MD [PlS] - **Spec Exp:** Limb Surgery/Reconstruction; Diabetic Leg/Foot; Wound Healing/Care; Lower Limb Reconstruction; **Hospital:** MedStar Georgetown Univ Hosp; **Address:** Georgetown Univ Hosp-Wound Healing Ctr, 3800 Reservoir Rd NW, Bles Bldg Fl 1, Washington, DC 20007; **Phone:** 202-444-6161; **Board Cert:** Plastic Surgery 1992; **Med School:** Yale Univ 1981; **Resid:** Surgery, Brigham & Women's Hosp 1986; Plastic Surgery, NYU Langone Med Ctr 1989; **Fellow:** Vascular Surgery, Brigham & Women's Hosp 1987; Hand Surgery, NYU Langone Med Ctr 1990; **Fac Appt:** Prof PlS, Georgetown Univ

Baker III, Daniel C MD [PlS] - **Spec Exp:** Cosmetic Surgery-Face; Reconstructive Surgery-Face; Cancer Reconstruction; Facial Paralysis Reconstruction; **Hospital:** Lenox Hill Hosp (Manh Eye, Ear & Throat Hosp) (page 66); **Address:** 65 E 66th St, New York, NY 10065; **Phone:** 212-734-9695; **Board Cert:** Plastic Surgery 1978; **Med School:** Columbia P&S 1968; **Resid:** Surgery, UCSF Med Ctr 1975; Plastic Surgery, NYU Med Ctr 1977; **Fellow:** Head and Neck Surgery, Columbia Presby Med Ctr 1978; **Fac Appt:** Prof PlS, NYU Sch Med

Baker, Stephen B MD/DDS [PlS] - **Spec Exp:** Craniofacial Surgery/Reconstruction; Facial Trauma/Fractures; Cosmetic Surgery-Face; Cleft Palate/Lip; **Hospital:** MedStar Georgetown Univ Hosp, Inova Fairfax Hosp; **Address:** Pasquerilla Hlthcare Ctr, 3800 Reservoir Rd NW, Fl 1, MS 2210, Washington, DC 20007; **Phone:** 202-444-9302; **Board Cert:** Plastic Surgery 2012; **Med School:** Univ Pennsylvania 1993; **Resid:** Plastic Surgery, Hosp Univ Penn - UPHS 2001; **Fellow:** Craniofacial Surgery, Chldn's Hosp 2002; **Fac Appt:** Prof PlS, Georgetown Univ

Bartlett, Scott P MD [PlS] - **Spec Exp:** Craniofacial Surgery/Reconstruction; Cosmetic Surgery-Face; Reconstructive Surgery-Face; Pediatric Plastic Surgery; **Hospital:** Chldns Hosp of Philadelphia, Hosp Univ Penn - UPHS (page 69); **Address:** Childrens Hospital Phila, 34th St and Civic Center Blvd, Wood Bldg, 1st Fl, Philadelphia, PA 19104-4227; **Phone:** 215-590-2208; **Board Cert:** Plastic Surgery 2007; **Med School:** Washington Univ, St Louis 1975; **Resid:** Surgery, Mass Genl Hosp 1983; Plastic Surgery, Mass Genl Hosp 1985; **Fellow:** Craniofacial Surgery, Hosp Univ Penn 1986; **Fac Appt:** Prof PlS, Univ Pennsylvania

Boyajian, Michael J MD [PlS] - **Spec Exp:** Pediatric Plastic Surgery; Craniofacial Surgery; Cleft Palate/Lip; Vascular Malformations; **Hospital:** Chldns Natl Med Ctr; **Address:** Dept Plastic Surgery, 111 Michigan Ave NW, West Wing, Fl 4, Ste 100, Washington, DC 20010-2978; **Phone:** 202-476-2157; **Board Cert:** Plastic Surgery 1984; **Med School:** NYU Sch Med 1976; **Resid:** Surgery, Univ Colorado Hlth Sci Ctr 1979; Surgery, Univ Cincinnati Med Ctr 1981; **Fellow:** Plastic Surgery, Brigham & Women's Hosp 1983; Craniofacial Surgery, Chldn's Hosp 1984; **Fac Appt:** Asst Prof S, Geo Wash Univ

Bucky, Louis P MD [PlS] - **Spec Exp:** Cosmetic Surgery-Face; Cosmetic Surgery-Breast; Liposuction & Body Contouring; Breast Reconstruction; **Hospital:** Pennsylvania Hosp-UPHS (page 69); **Address:** 230 W Washington Square, Ste 101, Philadelphia, PA 19106; **Phone:** 215-829-6320; **Board Cert:** Plastic Surgery 2006; **Med School:** Harvard Med Sch 1986; **Resid:** Surgery, Mass Genl Hosp 1992; Plastic Surgery, Mass Genl Hosp 1994; **Fellow:** Microsurgery, Meml Sloan Kettering Cancer Ctr 1995; Craniofacial Surgery, Miami Chldns Hosp 1996; **Fac Appt:** Clin Prof S, Univ Pennsylvania

Chang, Benjamin MD [PlS] - **Spec Exp:** Hand Surgery; Melanoma; Microsurgery; Pediatric Plastic Surgery; **Hospital:** Hosp Univ Penn - UPHS (page 69), Chldns Hosp of Philadelphia; **Address:** Center for Human Appearance, Perelman Ctr for Advanced Medicine, 3400 Civic Center Blvd, Ste 1-150E, Philadelphia, PA 19104; **Phone:** 215-662-4283; **Board Cert:** Plastic Surgery 2006; Hand Surgery 2006; **Med School:** Harvard Med Sch 1986; **Resid:** Surgery, NYU Med Ctr 1992; Plastic Surgery, NYU Med Ctr 1994; **Fellow:** Hand Surgery, NYU Med Ctr 1995; **Fac Appt:** Assoc Clin Prof S, Univ Pennsylvania

Chiu, David T.W. MD [PlS] - **Spec Exp:** Hand & Microvascular Surgery; Reconstructive Surgery; Peripheral Nerve Surgery; **Hospital:** NYU Langone Med Ctr (page 68), Lenox Hill Hosp (page 66); **Address:** 900 Park Ave, New York, NY 10075; **Phone:** 212-879-8880; **Board Cert:** Plastic Surgery 1982; Hand Surgery 2010; **Med School:** Columbia P&S 1973; **Resid:** Surgery, Barnes-Jewish Hosp 1977; Plastic Surgery, NY-Presby/Columbia Univ Med Ctr 1979; **Fellow:** Hand Surgery, NYU Med Ctr 1980; **Fac Appt:** Prof PlS, NYU Sch Med

Cordeiro, Peter G MD [PlS] - **Spec Exp:** Reconstructive Surgery; Breast Reconstruction; Facial Plastic & Reconstructive Surgery; **Hospital:** Meml Sloan-Kettering Canc Ctr, Lenox Hill Hosp (Manh Eye, Ear & Throat Hosp) (page 66); **Address:** 1275 York Ave, New York, NY 10065; **Phone:** 212-639-2521; **Board Cert:** Surgery 2008; Plastic Surgery 2007; **Med School:** Harvard Med Sch 1983; **Resid:** Surgery, New Engl Deaconess Hosp-Harvard 1989; Plastic Surgery, NYU Med Ctr 1991; **Fellow:** Microsurgery, Meml Sloan-Kettering Cancer Ctr. 1992; Craniofacial Surgery, Univ Miami Affil Hosp 1992; **Fac Appt:** Prof S, Cornell Univ-Weill Med Coll

Dagum, Alexander B MD [PlS] - **Spec Exp:** Reconstructive Plastic Surgery; Cleft Palate/Lip; Hand Surgery; Microsurgery; **Hospital:** Stony Brook Univ Med Ctr; **Address:** Plastic & Cosmetic Surgery Center, 24 Research Way, Ste 100, East Setauket, NY 11733; **Phone:** 631-444-4666; **Board Cert:** Plastic Surgery 2013; Hand Surgery 2012; **Med School:** Canada 1987; **Resid:** Surgery, Univ Ottawa Civic Hosp 1988; Plastic Surgery, Univ Toronto Med Ctr 1993; **Fellow:** Microsurgery, Univ Toronto Med Ctr 1984; Hand Surgery, Stony Brook Univ Hosp 1995; **Fac Appt:** Prof S, SUNY Stony Brook

Disa, Joseph J MD [PlS] - **Spec Exp:** Cancer Reconstruction; Breast Reconstruction; Head & Neck Reconstruction; Microsurgery; **Hospital:** Meml Sloan-Kettering Canc Ctr; **Address:** 1275 York Ave, New York, NY 10065; **Phone:** 212-639-5022; **Board Cert:** Surgery 2005; Plastic Surgery 2009; **Med School:** Univ Mass Sch Med 1988; **Resid:** Surgery, Univ Md Med Ctr 1994; Plastic Surgery, Johns Hopkins Univ 1996; **Fellow:** Reconstructive Microsurgery, Meml Sloan-Kettering Cancer Ctr.; **Fac Appt:** Prof PlS, Cornell Univ-Weill Med Coll

Ducic, Ivica MD/PhD [PlS] - **Spec Exp:** Peripheral Nerve Surgery; Cosmetic Surgery-Face & Body; **Hospital:** MedStar Georgetown Univ Hosp; **Address:** Dept Plastic Surgery, 3800 Reservoir Rd NW, Washington, DC 20007; **Phone:** 202-444-8929; **Board Cert:** Plastic Surgery 2014; **Med School:** Croatia 1991; **Resid:** Plastic Surgery, MedStar Georgetown Univ Hosp 2002; **Fellow:** Peripheral Nerve Surgery, Inst Peripheral Nerve Surg 2003; **Fac Appt:** Prof PlS, Georgetown Univ

Dufresne, Craig R MD [PlS] - **Spec Exp:** Craniofacial Surgery; Reconstructive Surgery; Cosmetic Surgery-Face; Liposuction & Body Contouring; **Hospital:** Inova Fairfax Hosp, Sibley Mem Hosp; **Address:** Aesthetic, Plastic & Reconstructive Surg, 5530 Wisconsin Ave, Ste 1208, Chevy Chase, MD 20815; **Phone:** 301-654-9151; **Board Cert:** Plastic Surgery 1986; **Med School:** Columbia P&S 1977; **Resid:** Surgery, Johns Hopkins Hosp 1982; Plastic Surgery, NYU Langone Med Ctr 1984; **Fellow:** Craniofacial Surgery, NYU Langone Med Ctr 1985; **Fac Appt:** Clin Prof PlS, Georgetown Univ

Fox IV, James W MD [PlS] - **Spec Exp:** Breast Cancer & Surgery; Breast Cosmetic & Reconstructive Surgery; Cosmetic Surgery-Face; Facial Rejuvenation; **Hospital:** Thomas Jefferson Univ Hosp; **Address:** Jefferson Plastic Surgery, 840 Walnut St Fl 15, Philadelphia, PA 19107; **Phone:** 215-625-6630; **Board Cert:** Plastic Surgery 1978; **Med School:** Jefferson Med Coll 1970; **Resid:** Surgery, Jefferson Hosp 1974; Plastic Surgery, Univ VA Med Ctr 1976; **Fac Appt:** Prof S, Jefferson Med Coll

Glat, Paul M MD [PlS] - **Spec Exp:** Pediatric & Adult Plastic Surgery; Burns-Reconstructive Plastic Surgery; Craniofacial Surgery; Cleft Palate/Lip; **Hospital:** St. Christopher's Hosp for Chldn, Bryn Mawr Hosp; **Address:** 191 Presidential Blvd, Ste 101, Bala Cynwyd, PA 19004; **Phone:** 610-980-4000; **Board Cert:** Plastic Surgery 2009; **Med School:** NYU Sch Med 1988; **Resid:** Surgery, NYU Med Ctr 1994; Plastic Surgery, NYU Med Ctr 1996; **Fellow:** Craniofacial Surgery, Chldn's Hosp 1997; **Fac Appt:** Prof S, Drexel Univ Coll Med

Grant, Robert T MD [PlS] - **Spec Exp:** Cosmetic Surgery-Face & Eyes; Cosmetic Surgery-Breast; Breast Reconstruction; Reconstructive Plastic Surgery; **Hospital:** NY-Presby/Columbia Univ Med Ctr, NY (page 65), NY-Presby/Weill Cornell Med Ctr, NY (page 65); **Address:** 161 Fort Washington Ave, rm 511, 50 E 69th St, New York, NY 10032; **Phone:** 212-305-3103; **Board Cert:** Surgery 2011; Plastic Surgery 2013; **Med School:** Albany Med Coll 1983; **Resid:** Surgery, New York Hosp 1988; Plastic Surgery, NY-Presby/Weill Cornell Med Ctr 1990; **Fellow:** Microvascular Surgery, NYU Med Ctr/Bellevue Hosp 1991; **Fac Appt:** Prof PlS, Columbia P&S

Herman, Charles K MD [PlS] - **Spec Exp:** Cosmetic Surgery-Breast; Cosmetic Surgery-Face; Rhinoplasty; **Hospital:** Pocono Med Ctr; **Address:** 100 Plaza Ct, Ste C, E. Stroudsburg, PA 18301; **Phone:** 570-420-6220; **Board Cert:** Plastic Surgery 2006; **Med School:** Albany Med Coll 2000; **Resid:** Surgery, Montefiore Med Ctr 2003; Plastic/Reconstructive Surgery, Montefiore Med Ctr 2005; **Fac Appt:** Asst Clin Prof PlS, Albert Einstein Coll Med

Hidalgo, David A MD [PlS] - **Spec Exp:** Cosmetic Surgery-Face; Cosmetic Surgery-Breast; Rhinoplasty; **Hospital:** NY-Presby/Weill Cornell Med Ctr, NY (page 65), Lenox Hill Hosp (page 66); **Address:** 655 Park Ave, New York, NY 10065; **Phone:** 212-517-9777; **Board Cert:** Plastic Surgery 1987; **Med School:** Georgetown Univ 1978; **Resid:** Surgery, NYU Med Ctr 1983; Plastic Surgery, NYU Med Ctr 1985; **Fellow:** Microsurgery, NYU Med Ctr 1986; **Fac Appt:** Clin Prof S, Cornell Univ-Weill Med Coll

Hoffman, Lloyd A MD [PlS] - **Spec Exp:** Cosmetic Surgery-Face; Liposuction & Body Contouring; Breast Reconstruction; Facial Rejuvenation; **Hospital:** NY-Presby/Weill Cornell Med Ctr, NY (page 65), Lenox Hill Hosp (page 66); **Address:** 12 E 68th St, New York, NY 10021; **Phone:** 212-861-1640; **Board Cert:** Plastic Surgery 1989; **Med School:** Northwestern Univ 1978; **Resid:** Surgery, New York Hosp 1983; Plastic Surgery, NYU Med Ctr 1986; **Fellow:** Hand Surgery, NYU Med Ctr 1987; **Fac Appt:** Assoc Prof PlS, Cornell Univ-Weill Med Coll

Hurwitz, Dennis J MD [PlS] - **Spec Exp:** Body Contouring; Cosmetic Surgery-Face; Rhinoplasty; Breast Cosmetic & Reconstructive Surgery; **Hospital:** Magee-Womens Hosp - UPMC; **Address:** 3109 Forbes Ave, Ste 500, Pittsburgh, PA 15213; **Phone:** 412-802-6100; **Board Cert:** Plastic Surgery 2005; **Med School:** Univ MD Sch Med 1970; **Resid:** Surgery, Dartmouth Med Ctr 1975; Plastic Surgery, Univ Pittsburgh Med Ctr 1977; **Fac Appt:** Prof S, Univ Pittsburgh

Imber, Gerald MD [PlS] - **Spec Exp:** Cosmetic Surgery-Breast; Eyelid Surgery; Mohs' Surgery; Cosmetic Surgery-Face; **Hospital:** NY-Presby/Weill Cornell Med Ctr, NY (page 65); **Address:** 121A E 83rd St, New York, NY 10028; **Phone:** 212-472-1800; **Board Cert:** Plastic Surgery 1976; **Med School:** SUNY Downstate 1966; **Resid:** Surgery, LIJ Med Ctr 1972; Plastic Surgery, NY Hosp 1974; **Fac Appt:** Asst Clin Prof S, Cornell Univ-Weill Med Coll

Kolker, Adam R MD [PlS] - **Spec Exp:** Cosmetic Surgery-Breast; Breast Reconstruction; Abdominoplasty; Body Contouring after Weight Loss; **Hospital:** Mt Sinai Med Ctr (page 62), Lenox Hill Hosp (page 66); **Address:** 710 Park Ave, New York, NY 10021; **Phone:** 212-744-6500; **Board Cert:** Plastic Surgery 2011; Surgery 2005; **Med School:** Albany Med Coll 1990; **Resid:** Surgery, St Vincent's Hosp 1995; Plastic/Reconstructive Surgery, Beth Israel Deaconess Med Ctr 1998; **Fellow:** Microsurgery, NYU Med Ctr 1996; Craniofacial Surgery, Univ Melbourne Chldns Hosp 2000; **Fac Appt:** Assoc Clin Prof S, Mount Sinai Sch Med

LaBruna, Anthony N MD [PlS] - **Spec Exp:** Cosmetic Surgery-Face; Facial Plastic & Reconstructive Surgery; Rhinoplasty Revision; Facial Deformities/Reconstruction; **Hospital:** NY-Presby/Weill Cornell Med Ctr, NY (page 65), Mt Sinai Med Ctr (page 62); **Address:** 45 E 85th St, rm 1A, New York, NY 10028; **Phone:** 212-584-7001; **Board Cert:** Otolaryngology 1997; Plastic Surgery 2012; **Med School:** Cornell Univ-Weill Med Coll 1990; **Resid:** Surgery, Lenox Hill Hosp 1992; Otolaryngology, Manhattan EE&T Hosp 1996; **Fellow:** Plastic Surgery, Mt Sinai Med Ctr 2000; **Fac Appt:** Assoc Clin Prof PlS, Cornell Univ-Weill Med Coll

Leipziger, Lyle S MD [PlS] - **Spec Exp:** Cosmetic Surgery-Face & Eyes; Cosmetic Surgery-Breast; Breast Reconstruction; Liposuction & Body Contouring; **Hospital:** N Shore Univ Hosp (page 66), Long Is Jewish Med Ctr (page 66); **Address:** 825 Northern Blvd Fl 3, Great Neck, NY 11021; **Phone:** 516-465-8787; **Board Cert:** Plastic Surgery 1994; **Med School:** Cornell Univ-Weill Med Coll 1985; **Resid:** Plastic Surgery, NY Hosp 1990; **Fellow:** Craniofacial Surgery, Johns Hopkins Hosp 1991

Levine, Joshua L MD [PlS] - **Spec Exp:** Breast Reconstruction; Microsurgery; **Hospital:** New York Eye & Ear Infirm (page 64), Montefiore Med Ctr-Einstein Campus, NY; **Address:** 3 Columbus Cir, Ste 1410, New York, NY 10019; **Phone:** 212-245-8140; **Board Cert:** Plastic Surgery 2005; **Med School:** Med Coll GA 1994; **Resid:** Plastic Surgery, Montefiore Med Ctr 2001; Plastic Surgery, Montefiore Med Ctr 2003; **Fellow:** Cosmetic Plastic Surgery, NY Eye & Ear Infirm 2003; Reconstructive Microsurgery, Louisiana State Univ Affil Hosp 2004

Little III, John W MD [PlS] - **Spec Exp:** Cosmetic Surgery-Face; **Hospital:** MedStar Georgetown Univ Hosp, G Washington Univ Hosp; **Address:** 1145 19th St NW, Ste 802, Washington, DC 20036; **Phone:** 202-467-6700; **Board Cert:** Surgery 1975; Plastic Surgery 1977; **Med School:** Harvard Med Sch 1969; **Resid:** Surgery, Case Western Reserve Affil Hosps 1974; Plastic Surgery, Case Western Reserve Affil Hosps 1975; **Fellow:** Plastic Surgery, Jackson Meml Hosp 1977; **Fac Appt:** Clin Prof PlS, Georgetown Univ

Loree, Thom R MD [PlS] - **Spec Exp:** Head & Neck Cancer; Thyroid Cancer; Reconstructive Plastic Surgery; Breast Reconstruction; **Hospital:** Erie County Med Ctr; **Address:** Erie County Med Ctr, Dept Head & Neck/Plastic & Recon Surg, 462 Grider St, Main Bldg-Ground Fl, Buffalo, NY 14215; **Phone:** 716-898-3073; **Board Cert:** Surgery 2010; Plastic Surgery 2004; **Med School:** Geo Wash Univ 1982; **Resid:** Surgery, St Lukes-Roosevelt Hosp 1987; Plastic Surgery, St Lukes-Roosevelt Hosp 1988; **Fellow:** Head & Neck Surgical Oncology, Meml Sloan-Kettering Cancer Ctr 1989; **Fac Appt:** Assoc Prof S, SUNY Buffalo

Losee, Joseph E MD [PlS] - **Spec Exp:** Pediatric Plastic Surgery; Cleft Palate/Lip; Craniofacial Surgery/Reconstruction; **Hospital:** Chldns Hosp of Pittsburgh - UPMC; **Address:** Dept of Pediatric Surgery, 1 Chldn's Hosp Drive, 4401 Penn Ave Fl 3, Pittsburgh, PA 15224; **Phone:** 412-692-7949; **Board Cert:** Plastic Surgery 2011; **Med School:** Univ Rochester 1994; **Resid:** Plastic Surgery, Strong Meml Hosp 1999; **Fellow:** Craniofacial Surgery, Chldns Hosp 2000; **Fac Appt:** Prof S, Univ Pittsburgh

Low, David W MD [PlS] - **Spec Exp:** Microsurgery; Cosmetic & Reconstructive Surgery; Vascular Malformations; Cleft Palate/Lip; **Hospital:** Hosp Univ Penn - UPHS (page 69), Chldns Hosp of Philadelphia; **Address:** Center for Human Appearance, Perelman Ctr for Advanced Medicine, 3400 Civic Center Blvd, Ste 1-150E, Philadelphia, PA 19104; **Phone:** 215-662-4283; **Board Cert:** Plastic Surgery 1991; **Med School:** Harvard Med Sch 1980; **Resid:** Surgery, Hosp Univ Penn 1986; **Fellow:** Plastic/Reconstructive Surgery, Hosp Univ Penn 1989; **Fac Appt:** Prof S, Univ Pennsylvania

Mackay, Donald R MD/DDS [PlS] - **Spec Exp:** Pediatric Plastic Surgery; Craniofacial Surgery; Cleft Palate/Lip; Cosmetic Surgery-Face; **Hospital:** Penn State Milton S Hershey Med Ctr; **Address:** Hershey Med Ctr, Div Plastic Surg, 500 University Drive, Hershey, PA 17033-0850; **Phone:** 717-531-8952; **Board Cert:** Plastic Surgery 2006; **Med School:** South Africa 1980; **Resid:** Plastic Surgery, Johannesburg Teaching Hosps 1984; Plastic Surgery, MS Hershey Med Ctr 1995; **Fac Appt:** Prof PlS, Penn State Coll Med

Manders, Ernest K MD [PlS] - **Spec Exp:** Facial Nerve Disorders; **Hospital:** UPMC Presby, Pittsburgh, Magee-Womens Hosp - UPMC; **Address:** UPMC Presbyterian, 3601 Fifth Ave Falk Med Bldg - Ste 6B, Pittsburgh, PA 15213; **Phone:** 412-648-9670; **Board Cert:** Surgery 2009; Plastic Surgery 1982; **Med School:** Harvard Med Sch 1972; **Resid:** Surgery, Univ Michigan Med Ctr 1979; Plastic Surgery, Univ Michigan Med Ctr 1981; **Fellow:** Viral Oncology, Natl Insts of Allergy-Infectious Disease 1975; **Fac Appt:** Prof S, Univ Pittsburgh

Manson, Paul MD [PlS] - **Spec Exp:** Facial Trauma/Fractures; Skin Cancer; Reconstructive Surgery; Cosmetic Surgery-Face; **Hospital:** Johns Hopkins Hosp (page 59), Univ of MD Med Ctr; **Address:** 601 N Caroline St, McElderry-8152F, Baltimore, MD 21287; **Phone:** 443-997-9466; **Board Cert:** Plastic Surgery 1979; **Med School:** Northwestern Univ 1968; **Resid:** Surgery, New England Deaconess Hosp 1971; Plastic Surgery, Johns Hopkins Hosp 1978; **Fellow:** Surgery, Lahey Clinic 1974; **Fac Appt:** Prof PlS, Johns Hopkins Univ

Matarasso, Alan MD [PlS] - **Spec Exp:** Cosmetic Surgery-Face & Eyes; Rhinoplasty; Liposuction; Abdominoplasty; **Hospital:** Lenox Hill Hosp (Manh Eye, Ear & Throat Hosp) (page 66); **Address:** 1009 Park Ave, New York, NY 10028-0936; **Phone:** 212-249-7500; **Board Cert:** Plastic Surgery 1986; **Med School:** Univ Miami Sch Med 1979; **Resid:** Surgery, Montefiore Med Ctr 1983; Plastic Surgery, Montefiore Med Ctr 1985; **Fellow:** Plastic Surgery, Manhattan EET Hosp/NYU 1985; **Fac Appt:** Clin Prof PlS, Albert Einstein Coll Med

Mehrara, Babak J MD [PlS] - **Spec Exp:** Breast Reconstruction; Cancer Reconstruction; Microsurgery; Reconstructive Surgery-Face; **Hospital:** Meml Sloan-Kettering Canc Ctr; **Address:** 160 E 63rd St Fl 10, New York, NY 10022; **Phone:** 212-639-8639; **Board Cert:** Plastic Surgery 2003; **Med School:** Columbia P&S 1993; **Resid:** Surgery, NYU Med Ctr 1996; Plastic Surgery, NYU Med Ctr 2001; **Fellow:** Microsurgery, UCLA Med Ctr 2002; **Fac Appt:** Assoc Prof S, Cornell Univ-Weill Med Coll

Nahabedian, Maurice Y MD [PlS] - **Spec Exp:** Breast Reconstruction & Augmentation; Cosmetic Surgery-Face; Abdominoplasty; Liposuction; **Hospital:** MedStar Georgetown Univ Hosp, Inova Fairfax Hosp; **Address:** Pasquerilla Hlthcare Ctr, Dept Plastic Surgery, 3800 Reservoir Rd NW, Fl 1, Washington, DC 20007; **Phone:** 202-444-6576; **Board Cert:** Plastic Surgery 2005; **Med School:** UC Irvine 1987; **Resid:** Surgery, UC Irvine Med Ctr 1992; Plastic Surgery, Johns Hopkins Univ Hosp 1995; **Fac Appt:** Prof PlS, Georgetown Univ

Napoli, Joseph A MD/DDS [PlS] - **Spec Exp:** Cleft Palate/Lip; Maxillofacial Surgery; Craniofacial Surgery-Pediatric; Beckwith-Wiedemann Syndrome; **Hospital:** Nemours/Alfred I. duPont Hosp for Chldn, Wilmington Hosp-Christiana Care; **Address:** Nemours, Plastic Surgery, 1600 Rockland Rd, Wilmington, DE 19803; **Phone:** 302-651-6301; **Board Cert:** Plastic Surgery 2004; **Med School:** Columbia P&S 1987; **Resid:** Surgery, NY-Presby/Columbia Univ Med Ctr 1985; Plastic/Reconstructive Surgery, Dartmouth-Hitchcock Med Ctr 2001; **Fellow:** Craniofacial Surgery, Royal Chldns Hosp 2002; Pediatric Plastic Surgery, Royal Chldns Hosp 2002; **Fac Appt:** Asst Prof S, Jefferson Med Coll

Noone, R Barrett MD [PlS] - **Spec Exp:** Breast Cosmetic & Reconstructive Surgery; Cosmetic Surgery-Face; Liposuction & Body Contouring; **Hospital:** Bryn Mawr Hosp; **Address:** 888 Glenbrook Ave, Bryn Mawr, PA 19010-2506; **Phone:** 610-527-4833; **Board Cert:** Surgery 1972; Plastic Surgery 2007; **Med School:** Univ Pennsylvania 1965; **Resid:** Surgery, Hosp Univ Penn 1971; Plastic Surgery, Hosp Univ Penn 1973; **Fac Appt:** Clin Prof S, Univ Pennsylvania

Olding, Michael J MD [PlS] - **Spec Exp:** Liposuction & Body Contouring; Cosmetic Surgery-Face & Breast; **Hospital:** G Washington Univ Hosp; **Address:** GW Med Faculty Assocs, 2150 Pennslyvania Ave NW, Fl 9, Washington, DC 20037; **Phone:** 202-741-3241; **Board Cert:** Plastic Surgery 1986; **Med School:** Univ KY Coll Med 1980; **Resid:** Surgery, NY-Presby/Weill Cornell Med Ctr 1982; Plastic Surgery, Mcgill Univ Affil Hosps 1986; **Fac Appt:** Prof PlS, Geo Wash Univ

Patel, Sameer A MD [PlS] - **Spec Exp:** Breast Reconstruction; Head & Neck Reconstruction; **Hospital:** Fox Chase Cancer Ctr (page 57), Jeanes Hosp; **Address:** Fox Chase Cancer Ctr, 333 Cottman Ave, Philadelphia, PA 19111; **Phone:** 215-728-3559; **Board Cert:** Surgery 2005; Plastic Surgery 2008; **Med School:** UMDNJ-NJ Med Sch, Newark 1998; **Resid:** Surgery, Montefiore Med Ctr 2003; Plastic/Reconstructive Surgery, Montefiore Med Ctr 2004; **Fellow:** Reconstructive Microsurgery, MD Anderson Cancer Ctr 2005

Pitman, Gerald H MD [PlS] - **Spec Exp:** Cosmetic Surgery-Face; Liposuction & Body Contouring; Abdominoplasty; Cosmetic Surgery-Breast; **Hospital:** Lenox Hill Hosp (Manh Eye, Ear & Throat Hosp) (page 66); **Address:** Ctr Specialty Care, Plastic Surgery, 50 E 69th St Fl 5, New York, NY 10021; **Phone:** 212-517-2600; **Board Cert:** Plastic Surgery 1978; **Med School:** Univ Pennsylvania 1968; **Resid:** Surgery, NY-Presby/Columbia Univ Med Ctr 1975; Plastic Surgery, NYU Med Ctr 1977; **Fellow:** Microsurgery, NYU Med Ctr 1981; **Fac Appt:** Clin Prof PlS, NYU Sch Med

Posnick, Jeffrey C MD/DMD [PlS] - **Spec Exp:** Cosmetic Surgery-Face; Craniofacial Surgery/Reconstruction; Maxillofacial Surgery; **Hospital:** MedStar Georgetown Univ Hosp; **Address:** 5530 Wisconsin Ave, Ste 1250, Chevy Chase, MD 20815; **Phone:** 301-986-9475; **Board Cert:** Plastic Surgery 1988; **Med School:** Vanderbilt Univ 1979; **Resid:** Surgery, Mass Genl Hosp 1983; Plastic Surgery, Eastern Va Affil Hosp 1986; **Fellow:** Craniofacial Surgery, Hosp Univ Penn/Chldns Hosp 1983; **Fac Appt:** Clin Prof PlS, Georgetown Univ

Price, G Wesley MD [PlS] - **Spec Exp:** Cosmetic Surgery-Face & Breast; Liposuction & Body Contouring; **Hospital:** Sibley Mem Hosp; **Address:** Center for Plastic Surgery, 5550 Friendship Blvd, Ste 130, Chevy Chase, MD 20815; **Phone:** 301-652-7700; **Board Cert:** Plastic Surgery 1987; **Med School:** Bowman Gray 1977; **Resid:** Surgery, George Wash Univ Hosp 1982; Plastic Surgery, NYU Med Ctr 1984; **Fellow:** Facial Plastic & Reconstr Surgery, Univ Miami Affil Hosp 1985

Rodriguez, Eduardo De Jesus MD/DDS [PlS] - **Spec Exp:** Facial Plastic & Reconstructive Surgery; Transplant-Face; Craniofacial Surgery/Reconstruction; Microsurgery; **Hospital:** Univ of MD Med Ctr; **Address:** Univ MD Med Ctr, 22 S Greene St, Ste P1G01, Baltimore, MD 21201; **Phone:** 410-328-2999; **Board Cert:** Plastic Surgery 2005; **Med School:** Va Commonwealth Univ Sch Med 1999; **Resid:** Surgery, Johns Hopkins Hosp 2003; Plastic Surgery, Johns Hopkins Hosp 2005; **Fellow:** Reconstructive Microsurgery, Chang Gung Meml Hosp; **Fac Appt:** Prof PlS, Univ MD Sch Med

Rose, Elliott H MD [PlS] - **Spec Exp:** Facial Plastic & Reconstructive Surgery; Cosmetic Surgery-Face & Body; Facial Paralysis Reconstruction; Burns-Reconstructive Plastic Surgery; **Hospital:** Mt Sinai Med Ctr (page 62); **Address:** The Aesthetic Surgery Center, 895 Park Ave, New York, NY 10029; **Phone:** 212-639-1346; **Board Cert:** Plastic Surgery 1979; **Med School:** Univ Tex Med Br, Galveston 1970; **Resid:** Surgery, Johns Hopkins Hosp 1973; Plastic Surgery, Stanford Univ Med Ctr 1977; **Fellow:** Hand & Microvascular Surgery, UCSF Med Ctr 1978; **Fac Appt:** Assoc Clin Prof PlS, Mount Sinai Sch Med

Serletti, Joseph M MD [PlS] - **Spec Exp:** Breast Reconstruction; Head & Neck Reconstruction; Cosmetic Surgery; Reconstructive Surgery; **Hospital:** Hosp Univ Penn - UPHS (page 69); **Address:** Center for Human Appeaarance, Perelman Ctr for Advanced Medicine, 3400 Civic Center Blvd, Ste 1-150E, Philadelphia, PA 19104; **Phone:** 215-662-4283; **Board Cert:** Plastic Surgery 2003; **Med School:** Univ Rochester 1982; **Resid:** Surgery, Strong Meml Hosp 1986; Plastic Surgery, Strong Meml Hosp 1988; **Fellow:** Reconstructive Surgery, Johns Hopkins Hosp 1990; **Fac Appt:** Prof S, Univ Pennsylvania

Seyfer, Alan MD [PlS] - **Spec Exp:** Chest Wall Reconstruction; Cleft Palate/Lip; Reconstructive Surgery; Abdominal Wall Reconstruction; **Hospital:** Walter Reed Natl Military Med Ctr; **Address:** USUHS-School of Medicine, 4301 Jones Bridge Rd, Bethesda, MD 20814; **Phone:** 301-295-0441; **Board Cert:** Hand Surgery 1999; Plastic Surgery 1982; **Med School:** Louisiana State U, New Orleans 1973; **Resid:** Surgery, Fitzsimons AMC 1978; Plastic Surgery, Walter Reed AMC 1981; **Fellow:** Hand Surgery, Duke Univ Med Ctr 1980; **Fac Appt:** Prof S, Uniformed Srvs Univ, Bethesda

Singh, Navin MD [PlS] - **Spec Exp:** Cosmetic Surgery-Face & Breast; Liposuction & Body Contouring; Abdominoplasty; Facial Rejuvenation; **Hospital:** Sibley Mem Hosp; **Address:** Ivy Plastic Surgery Associates, 5454 Wisconsin Ave, Ste 1710, Chevy Chase, MD 20815; **Phone:** 301-244-0277; **Board Cert:** Plastic Surgery 2011; **Med School:** Brown Univ 1993; **Resid:** Surgery, Johns Hopkins Hosp 1997; Plastic/Reconstructive Surgery, Johns Hopkins Hosp 1999; **Fellow:** Craniofacial Surgery, Johns Hopkins Hosp 2000; **Fac Appt:** Asst Prof PlS, Johns Hopkins Univ

Slezak, Sheri MD [PlS] - **Spec Exp:** Breast Reconstruction; Cosmetic Surgery-Breast; **Hospital:** Univ of MD Med Ctr, Greater Baltimore Med Ctr; **Address:** Univ Maryland, Dept Plastic Surgery, 22 S Greene St, rm S8D18, Baltimore, MD 21201; **Phone:** 410-328-2360; **Board Cert:** Plastic Surgery 2008; **Med School:** Harvard Med Sch 1980; **Resid:** Surgery, NY-Presby/Columbia Univ Med Ctr 1986; Plastic Surgery, Johns Hopkins Hosp 1989; **Fellow:** Immunology, Johns Hopkins Hosp 1986; **Fac Appt:** Prof PlS, Univ MD Sch Med

Spence, Robert J MD [PlS] - **Spec Exp:** Burns-Reconstructive Plastic Surgery; Burn Care; Tissue Banking; **Hospital:** MedStar Good Samaritan Hosp; **Address:** 5601 Loch Raven Blvd, Baltimore, MD 21239; **Phone:** 443-444-2876; **Board Cert:** Plastic Surgery 1981; **Med School:** Johns Hopkins Univ 1972; **Resid:** Surgery, Johns Hopkins Hosp 1974; Surgery, Hershey Med Ctr 1978; **Fellow:** Plastic Surgery, Johns Hopkins Hosp 1980; **Fac Appt:** Assoc Prof S, Johns Hopkins Univ

Spinelli, Henry M MD [PlS] - **Spec Exp:** Cosmetic Surgery-Face; Craniofacial Surgery/Reconstruction; Oculoplastic & Orbital Surgery; Eyelid Surgery/Blepharoplasty; **Hospital:** NY-Presby/Weill Cornell Med Ctr, NY (page 65), Lenox Hill Hosp (Manh Eye, Ear & Throat Hosp) (page 66); **Address:** 875 5th Ave, New York, NY 10021; **Phone:** 212-570-6235; **Board Cert:** Ophthalmology 1987; Plastic Surgery 1993; **Med School:** NYU Sch Med 1981; **Resid:** Ophthalmology, Manhattan EE&T Hosp 1985; Plastic/Reconstructive Surgery, NYU Med Ctr 1990; **Fellow:** Craniofacial Surgery, NYU Med Ctr 1991; **Fac Appt:** Clin Prof S, Cornell Univ-Weill Med Coll

Staffenberg, David A MD [PlS] - **Spec Exp:** Maxillofacial & Craniofacial Surgery; Pediatric Plastic Surgery; Cleft Palate/Lip; Cosmetic & Reconstructive Surgery; **Hospital:** NYU Langone Med Ctr (page 68); **Address:** NYU Plastic Surgery Assocs, 305 E 33rd St, New York, NY 10016; **Phone:** 212-263-8065; **Board Cert:** Plastic Surgery 2009; **Med School:** NY Med Coll 1989; **Resid:** Surgery, Maimonides Med Ctr 1995; Plastic Surgery, Emory Univ Hosp 1997; **Fellow:** Craniofacial & Maxillofacial Surgery, UCLA Med Ctr 1998; **Fac Appt:** Clin Prof PlS, NYU Sch Med

Sultan, Mark R MD [PlS] - **Spec Exp:** Cosmetic Surgery-Face; Cosmetic Surgery-Breast; Breast Reconstruction; Liposuction & Body Contouring; **Hospital:** St. Luke's - Roosevelt Hosp Ctr - Roosevelt Div (page 56), Beth Israel Med Ctr - Petrie Div (page 56); **Address:** 1100 Park Ave, New York, NY 10128; **Phone:** 212-360-0700; **Board Cert:** Plastic Surgery 1992; **Med School:** Columbia P&S 1982; **Resid:** Surgery, Columbia-Presby Hosp 1987; Plastic Surgery, Columbia-Presby Hosp 1990; **Fellow:** Head and Neck Surgery, Emory Univ Hosp 1989; **Fac Appt:** Prof S, Columbia P&S

Tabbal, Nicolas MD [PlS] - **Spec Exp:** Rhinoplasty; Cosmetic Surgery-Face; Eyelid Surgery; **Hospital:** Lenox Hill Hosp (Manh Eye, Ear & Throat Hosp) (page 66), NYU Langone Med Ctr (page 68); **Address:** 521 Park Ave, New York, NY 10065; **Phone:** 212-644-5800; **Board Cert:** Plastic Surgery 1980; **Med School:** Lebanon 1972; **Resid:** Surgery, Ameri Univ Med Ctr 1976; Plastic Surgery, Akron City Hosp 1979; **Fellow:** Surgery, SUNY Upstate Med Univ Hosp 1977; Plastic/Reconstructive Surgery, NYU Med Ctr 1980; **Fac Appt:** Assoc Clin Prof PlS, NYU Sch Med

Talmor, Mia MD [PlS] - **Spec Exp:** Breast Reconstruction; Reconstructive Surgery; Cosmetic Surgery-Breast; Nipple Sparing Mastectomy; **Hospital:** NY-Presby/Weill Cornell Med Ctr, NY (page 65); **Address:** 425 E 61st St Fl 10, New York, NY 10065; **Phone:** 212-821-0933; **Board Cert:** Plastic Surgery 2012; Surgery 2011; **Med School:** Cornell Univ 1993; **Resid:** Surgery, NY Hosp-Cornell Med Ctr 1999; Plastic Surgery, NY Hosp-Cornell Med Ctr 2001; **Fac Appt:** Assoc Clin Prof PlS, Cornell Univ-Weill Med Coll

Taub, Peter J MD [PlS] - **Spec Exp:** Pediatric Plastic Surgery; Craniofacial Surgery; Maxillofacial Surgery; Cleft Palate/Lip; **Hospital:** Mt Sinai Med Ctr (page 62), Westchester Med Ctr; **Address:** 5 E 98th St Fl 14 - Ste B, New York, NY 10029-6574; **Phone:** 212-241-4178; **Board Cert:** Surgery 2009; Plastic Surgery 2013; **Med School:** Albert Einstein Coll Med 1993; **Resid:** Surgery, Mt Sinai Med Ctr 1999; Plastic Surgery, UCLA Med Ctr 2001; **Fellow:** Craniofacial Surgery, UCLA Med Ctr 2002; **Fac Appt:** Prof S, Mount Sinai Sch Med

Thorne, Charles H MD [PlS] - **Spec Exp:** Cosmetic Surgery-Face; Ear Reconstruction/Microtia; Ear Reshaping (Otoplasty); Craniofacial Surgery; **Hospital:** NYU Langone Med Ctr (page 68); **Address:** 812 Park Ave, New York, NY 10021; **Phone:** 212-794-0044; **Board Cert:** Plastic Surgery 2007; **Med School:** UCLA 1981; **Resid:** Surgery, Mass Genl Hosp 1986; Plastic Surgery, NYU Med Ctr 1988; **Fellow:** Craniofacial Surgery, NYU Med Ctr 1989; **Fac Appt:** Assoc Prof PlS, NYU Sch Med

Ting, Jess MD [PlS] - **Spec Exp:** Breast Reconstruction; Cosmetic Surgery; **Hospital:** Mt Sinai Med Ctr (page 62), Mount Sinai Hosp of Queens (page 62); **Address:** 5 E 98th St, Fl 14, Ste B, Box 1259, New York, NY 10029; **Phone:** 212-241-4410; **Board Cert:** Plastic Surgery 2012; Hand Surgery 2012; **Med School:** Columbia P&S 1995; **Resid:** Surgery, Columbia Presby Med Ctr 1998; Plastic Surgery, Univ Pittsburgh Med Ctr 2000; **Fellow:** Hand Surgery, Hosp Special Surgery 2001; **Fac Appt:** Asst Prof S, Mount Sinai Sch Med

Topham, Neal MD [PlS] - **Spec Exp:** Breast Reconstruction; Head & Neck Reconstruction; Microsurgery; **Hospital:** Fox Chase Cancer Ctr (page 57), Jeanes Hosp; **Address:** Fox Chase Cancer Center, Dept Surgical Oncology, 333 Cottman Ave, C308, Philadelphia, PA 19111; **Phone:** 215-728-2662; **Board Cert:** Plastic Surgery 2005; **Med School:** Case West Res Univ 1994; **Resid:** Surgery, Akron Med Ctr 1998; Plastic Surgery, Case Western Reserve Univ 2000; **Fellow:** Microvascular Surgery, MD Anderson Cancer Ctr 2003; **Fac Appt:** Asst Clin Prof S, Univ Pennsylvania

Tufaro, Anthony P MD/DDS [PlS] - **Spec Exp:** Head & Neck Cancer; Skin Cancer-Head & Neck; Merkel Cell Carcinoma; Craniofacial Surgery/Reconstruction; **Hospital:** Johns Hopkins Hosp (page 59); **Address:** 601 N Caroline St McElderry Bldg Fl 8, Baltimore, MD 21287; **Phone:** 410-955-9846; **Board Cert:** Plastic Surgery 2010; **Med School:** Hahnemann Univ 1993; **Resid:** Surgery, Johns Hopkins Hosp 1995; **Fellow:** Plastic Surgery, Johns Hopkins Hosp 1997; Head and Neck Surgery, Meml Sloan-Kettering Cancer Ctr 1998; **Fac Appt:** Assoc Prof S, Johns Hopkins Univ

Vander Kolk, Craig A MD [PlS] - **Spec Exp:** Cosmetic Surgery-Face; Cleft Palate/Lip; Craniofacial Surgery/Reconstruction; Cosmetic Surgery-Breast; **Hospital:** Mercy Med Ctr - Baltimore; **Address:** Cosmetic Medicine at Mercy, 227 St Paul Place Fl 6, Baltimore, MD 21202; **Phone:** 410-332-9700; **Board Cert:** Plastic Surgery 1989; **Med School:** Univ Mich Med Sch 1980; **Resid:** Surgery, Univ Mich Med Ctr 1983; Plastic Surgery, Univ Mich Med Ctr 1986; **Fellow:** Hand Surgery, St Vincents Hosp 1985; Craniofacial Surgery, Chldns Hosp 1987; **Fac Appt:** Prof PlS, Johns Hopkins Univ

Winters, Richard M MD [PlS] - **Spec Exp:** Cosmetic & Reconstructive Surgery; Rhinoplasty; Cosmetic Surgery-Face & Breast; Breast Reconstruction; **Hospital:** Hackensack Univ Med Ctr; **Address:** Aesthetic & Reconstructive Surgeons, 20 Prospect Ave, Ste 501, Hackensack, NJ 07601; **Phone:** 201-487-3400; **Board Cert:** Plastic Surgery 2009; **Med School:** Univ Conn 1990; **Resid:** Surgery, Univ Conn Affil Hosp 1995; **Fellow:** Plastic/Reconstructive Surgery, NY-Presby/Weill Cornell Med Ctr 1997; Microsurgery, CA Pacific Med Ctr - Davies Campus 1998

Zide, Barry M MD/DMD [PlS] - **Spec Exp:** Facial Surgery-Chin & Lip; Birthmarks/Hemangiomas; Reconstructive Plastic Surgery; Melanoma; **Hospital:** NYU Langone Med Ctr (page 68), Lenox Hill Hosp (page 66); **Address:** 420 E 55th St, Ste 1D, New York, NY 10022; **Phone:** 212-421-2424; **Board Cert:** Plastic Surgery 1981; **Med School:** Tufts Univ 1973; **Resid:** Surgery, Stanford Univ Hosp & Clins 1976; Plastic Surgery, Univ NC Hosp 1978; **Fellow:** Head & Neck Oncology, Roswell Park Cancer Inst 1979; Craniofacial Surgery, NYU Med Ctr 1980; **Fac Appt:** Prof PlS, NYU Sch Med

Southeast

Beasley, Michael E MD [PlS] - **Spec Exp:** Breast Reconstruction & Augmentation; Liposuction & Body Contouring; Facial Rejuvenation; **Address:** Charlotte Plastic Surgery, 2215 Randolph Rd, Charlotte, NC 28207-1523; **Phone:** 704-372-6846; **Board Cert:** Plastic Surgery 1989; **Med School:** Univ NC Sch Med 1980; **Resid:** Surgery, NC Meml Hosp 1985; Plastic Surgery, Emory Univ Hosp 1987; **Fellow:** Plastic Surgery, St Joseph's Hosp 1987; **Fac Appt:** Clin Prof PlS, Univ NC Sch Med

Burstein, Fernando D MD [PlS] - **Spec Exp:** Craniofacial Surgery-Pediatric; Cosmetic Surgery-Face; Maxillofacial Surgery; Rhinoplasty; **Hospital:** Northside Hosp, Chldns Hlthcare Atlanta @ Scottish Rite; **Address:** Ped Plastic Surg & Craniofacial Assocs, 975 Johnson Ferry Rd NE, Ste 100, Atlanta, GA 30342; **Phone:** 404-256-1311; **Board Cert:** Otolaryngology 1986; Plastic Surgery 1991; **Med School:** Univ Kansas 1980; **Resid:** Otolaryngology, UCLA Med Ctr 1986; Plastic Surgery, Yale-New Haven Hosp 1988; **Fellow:** Craniofacial Surgery, UCLA Med Ctr 1989; **Fac Appt:** Clin Prof PlS, Emory Univ

Carraway, James Howard MD [PlS] - **Spec Exp:** Oculoplastic Surgery; Cosmetic Surgery-Face; Eyelid Surgery; Body Contouring; **Hospital:** Sentara Leigh Hosp; **Address:** 5589 Greenwich Rd, Ste 100, Virginia Beach, VA 23462; **Phone:** 757-557-0300; **Board Cert:** Surgery 1972; Plastic Surgery 1974; **Med School:** Univ VA Sch Med 1962; **Resid:** Surgery, Norfolk Med Ctr 1970; Plastic Surgery, Eastern VA Med Ctr 1973; **Fellow:** Plastic Surgery, Glasgow Royal Infirmary 1970; **Fac Appt:** Prof PlS, Eastern VA Med Sch

Colen, Lawrence B MD [PlS] - **Spec Exp:** Cosmetic Surgery-Face; Cosmetic Surgery-Breast; Breast Reconstruction; **Hospital:** Sentara Norfolk Genl Hosp; **Address:** Norfolk Plastic Surgery, 6261 E Virginia Beach Blvd, Ste 100, Norfolk, VA 23502; **Phone:** 757-466-1000; **Board Cert:** Plastic Surgery 2007; **Med School:** Dartmouth Med Sch 1975; **Resid:** Surgery, UCSF Med Ctr 1979; **Fellow:** Plastic Surgery, UCSF Med Ctr 1983; **Fac Appt:** Assoc Prof PlS, Eastern VA Med Sch

Cruse, C. Wayne MD [PlS] - **Spec Exp:** Burns-Reconstructive Plastic Surgery; Cancer Reconstruction; Burn Care; Wound Healing/Care; **Hospital:** Moffitt Canc Ctr (page 61), Tampa Genl Hosp; **Address:** Moffitt Cancer Ctr, Plastic Surgery, 12902 Magnolia Drive, Ste 4035, Tampa, FL 33612; **Phone:** 813-745-8482; **Board Cert:** Plastic Surgery 2006; **Med School:** Univ Louisville Sch Med 1972; **Resid:** Surgery, Univ S FL Affil Hosp 1977; Plastic Surgery, Univ KY Hosp 1979; **Fac Appt:** Prof S, Univ S Fla Coll Med

Davis, Glenn M MD [PlS] - **Spec Exp:** Cosmetic Surgery-Breast; Abdominoplasty; Liposuction & Body Contouring; Facial Rejuvenation; **Hospital:** Rex HlthCare, WakeMed-Raleigh Campus; **Address:** 2304 Wesvill Ct, Ste 360, Raleigh, NC 27607-2981; **Phone:** 919-785-1220; **Board Cert:** Plastic Surgery 1986; **Med School:** Med Univ SC 1974; **Resid:** Surgery, National Naval Med Ctr 1982; Plastic Surgery, Eastern Va Affil Hosp 1985; **Fac Appt:** Assoc Clin Prof PlS, Univ NC Sch Med

Erdmann, Detlev MD/PhD [PlS] - **Spec Exp:** Body Contouring after Weight Loss; Abdominoplasty; Cosmetic Surgery-Breast; Hand Surgery; **Hospital:** Duke Univ Hosp; **Address:** Box 3181 Med Ctr, 131 Baker House, Brown Zone, Durham, NC 27710; **Phone:** 919-684-3320; **Board Cert:** Plastic Surgery 2000; Hand Surgery 2003; **Med School:** Germany 1990; **Resid:** Surgery, Univ Heidelberg Affil Hosp 1998; **Fellow:** Plastic Surgery, Univ Heidelberg 2000; Hand Surgery, Univ Heidelberg 2003; **Fac Appt:** Assoc Prof S, Duke Univ

Fix, Richard Jobe MD [PlS] - **Spec Exp:** Breast Reconstruction; Hand Surgery; Microsurgery; **Hospital:** UAB Hosp, Children's Hosp AL; **Address:** The Kirklin Clinic, 2000 6th Ave S, Birmingham, AL 35233; **Phone:** 205-801-8500; **Board Cert:** Surgery 2009; Plastic Surgery 2007; Hand Surgery 2010; **Med School:** Univ Nebr Coll Med 1982; **Resid:** Surgery, Valley Med Ctr 1987; Plastic Surgery, Univ Ala Hosp 1989; **Fac Appt:** Prof PlS, UAB Sch Med

Georgiade, Gregory S MD [PlS] - **Spec Exp:** Breast Reconstruction; Cleft Palate/Lip; **Hospital:** Duke Univ Hosp; **Address:** Duke Univ Med Ctr, Box 3960, Durham, NC 27710; **Phone:** 919-684-3039; **Board Cert:** Surgery 2011; Plastic Surgery 1981; **Med School:** Duke Univ 1973; **Resid:** Surgery, Duke Univ Med Ctr 1978; Plastic Surgery, Duke Univ Med Ctr 1980; **Fac Appt:** Prof S, Duke Univ

Gregory, Richard O MD [PlS] - **Spec Exp:** Skin Laser Surgery; Cosmetic Surgery-Face; Facial Rejuvenation; Liposuction & Body Contouring; **Hospital:** Florida Hosp Celebration Hlth, Florida Hosp - Orlando; **Address:** Inst of Aesthetic Surgery, 400 Celebration Pl, Ste A320, Kissimmee, FL 34747; **Phone:** 407-303-4250; **Board Cert:** Plastic Surgery 1981; **Med School:** Indiana Univ 1971; **Resid:** Surgery, Duke Univ Hosp 1977; Plastic Surgery, Duke Univ Hosp 1979; **Fellow:** Hand Surgery, Univ Louisville Hosp 1979

Grotting, James C MD [PlS] - **Spec Exp:** Cosmetic Surgery-Face & Body; Breast Reconstruction; Liposuction & Body Contouring; Rhinoplasty; **Hospital:** UAB Highlands Hosp, St. Vincent's Hosp - Birmingham; **Address:** One Inverness Ctr Pkwy, Ste 100, Birmingham, AL 35242-4865; **Phone:** 205-930-1600; **Board Cert:** Plastic Surgery 2007; **Med School:** Univ Minn 1978; **Resid:** Surgery, Univ Wash Affil Hosps 1983; Plastic Surgery, UCSF Med Ctr 1985; **Fac Appt:** Clin Prof PlS, UAB Sch Med

Hagan, Kevin F MD [PlS] - **Spec Exp:** Reconstructive Surgery; Cosmetic Surgery-Breast; Cosmetic Surgery; **Hospital:** Vanderbilt Univ Med Ctr; **Address:** 1301 Med Ctr Drive, Nashville, TN 37232-2345; **Phone:** 615-322-2350; **Board Cert:** Plastic Surgery 1983; **Med School:** Johns Hopkins Univ 1974; **Resid:** Surgery, Med Coll VA Hosps 1979; Plastic Surgery, UCSF Med Ctr 1982; **Fellow:** Microsurgery, Dr Harry Buncke Med Clinic 1980; **Fac Appt:** Assoc Prof PlS, Vanderbilt Univ

Hultman, C Scott MD [PlS] - **Spec Exp:** Breast Reconstruction; Burns-Reconstructive Plastic Surgery; Reconstructive Plastic Surgery; Cosmetic Surgery; **Hospital:** NC Memorial Hosp - UNC; **Address:** UNC Div Plastic & Reconstructive Surgery, CB 7195, Chapel Hill, NC 27599-7195; **Phone:** 919-966-2300; **Board Cert:** Surgery 1999; Plastic Surgery 2001; Surgical Critical Care 2002; **Med School:** Univ Pittsburgh 1990; **Resid:** Surgery, Univ NC Hosps 1996; Plastic Surgery, Emory Univ Med Ctr 2000; **Fellow:** Surgical Critical Care, Univ N Carolina 1998; **Fac Appt:** Assoc Prof S, Univ NC Sch Med

Hunstad, Joseph P MD [PlS] - **Spec Exp:** Facial Plastic & Reconstructive Surgery; Body Contouring after Weight Loss; Abdominoplasty; **Hospital:** Carolinas Med Ctr-Univ, Presby Hosp - Charlotte; **Address:** The Hunstad Center, 11208 Statesville Rd, Ste 300, Huntersville, NC 28078; **Phone:** 704-659-9000; **Board Cert:** Plastic Surgery 1989; **Med School:** Mich State Univ 1981; **Resid:** Surgery, Butterworth Hosp 1984; Plastic Surgery, Grand Rapids Area Med Ed Ct 1986; **Fellow:** Reconstructive Microsurgery, MECOM MicSurg Inst 1987

Kelly, Kevin J MD/DDS [PlS] - **Spec Exp:** Craniofacial Surgery; Pediatric Plastic Surgery; Cleft Palate/Lip; Ear Reshaping (Otoplasty); **Hospital:** Vanderbilt Univ Med Ctr, Vanderbilt Monroe Carrell Jr. Chldn's Hosp; **Address:** The Vanderbilt Clinic, 1301 Medical Center Drive, Nashville, TN 37232; **Phone:** 615-936-2350; **Board Cert:** Plastic Surgery 1991; **Med School:** SUNY Downstate 1982; **Resid:** Surgery, Albany Med Ctr 1986; Plastic Surgery, Albany Med Ctr 1988; **Fellow:** Craniofacial Surgery, Johns Hopkins Med Ctr 1989; **Fac Appt:** Assoc Prof PlS, Vanderbilt Univ

Magee Jr, William P MD/DDS [PlS] - **Spec Exp:** Cleft Palate/Lip; Craniofacial Surgery; **Hospital:** Chldns Hosp of King's Daughters; **Address:** Institute for Craniofacial/Plastic Surg, 400 W Brambleton Ave, Ste 301, Norfolk, VA 23510; **Phone:** 757-627-6700; **Board Cert:** Plastic Surgery 1979; **Med School:** Geo Wash Univ 1972; **Resid:** Surgery, Univ Va Med Ctr 1974; Plastic Surgery, Univ Va Med Ctr 1974; **Fellow:** Craniofacial Surgery, Hosp Foch 1978

Mast, Bruce A MD [PlS] - **Spec Exp:** Breast Cosmetic & Reconstructive Surgery; Body Contouring; Cosmetic Surgery-Face; Skin Cancer Reconstruction; **Hospital:** UF Hlth Shands Hosp, UF Hlth Shands Chldns Hosp; **Address:** 4037 NW 86th Terr, Springhill Bldg, Gainesville, FL 32607; **Phone:** 352-271-5367; **Board Cert:** Plastic Surgery 2008; **Med School:** UMDNJ-RW Johnson Med Sch 1987; **Resid:** Surgery, Med Coll Virginia Hosp 1993; **Fellow:** Plastic Surgery, Univ Pittsburgh Med Ctr 1995; **Fac Appt:** Assoc Prof PlS, Univ Fla Coll Med

Matthews, David C MD [PlS] - **Spec Exp:** Craniofacial Surgery/Reconstruction; Facial Trauma/Fractures; Cosmetic Surgery-Face; Cleft Palate/Lip; **Hospital:** Carolinas Med Ctr; **Address:** 1719 South Blvd, Ste B, Charlotte, NC 28203-2747; **Phone:** 704-375-2955; **Board Cert:** Plastic Surgery 1983; **Med School:** Univ Cincinnati 1974; **Resid:** Surgery, Hosp Univ Penn 1980; Plastic Surgery, Hosp Univ Penn 1982; **Fellow:** Craniofacial Surgery, Royal Melbourne Hosp 1982; **Fac Appt:** Clin Prof PlS, Univ NC Sch Med

Maxwell, G Patrick MD [PlS] - **Spec Exp:** Cosmetic Surgery-Breast; Cosmetic Surgery-Face; Breast Reconstruction; Liposuction & Body Contouring; **Hospital:** Saint Thomas Hosp-Midtown, Centennial Med Ctr; **Address:** 2020 21st Ave S, Nashville, TN 37212; **Phone:** 615-932-7700; **Board Cert:** Plastic Surgery 1981; **Med School:** Vanderbilt Univ 1972; **Resid:** Surgery, Johns Hopkins Hosp 1976; Plastic Surgery, Johns Hopkins Hosp 1979; **Fellow:** Microsurgery, Davies Med Ctr 1975; **Fac Appt:** Asst Clin Prof PlS, Vanderbilt Univ

Molnar, Joseph MD/PhD [PlS] - **Spec Exp:** Burns-Reconstructive Plastic Surgery; Reconstructive Microvascular Surgery; Hand Surgery; Wound Healing/Care; **Hospital:** Wake Forest Baptist Med Ctr, Moses H Cone Mem Hosp; **Address:** Wake Forest Univ Sch Med, Dept Plastic Surgery, Medical Center Blvd, Winston-Salem, NC 27157-1075; **Phone:** 336-716-4171; **Board Cert:** Plastic Surgery 2005; Hand Surgery 2010; **Med School:** Ohio State Univ 1977; **Resid:** Surgery, Univ Wash Med Ctr 1989; Plastic Surgery, Med Coll VA 1992; **Fellow:** Microsurgery, Med Coll Wisc 1199; Hand Surgery, Med Coll Wisc 1994; **Fac Appt:** Assoc Prof PlS, Wake Forest Univ

Morgan, Raymond F MD [PlS] - **Spec Exp:** Hand Surgery; Cosmetic Surgery; **Hospital:** Univ of Virginia Hlth Sys; **Address:** UVA Hand Center, Fontaine Research Park, 415 Ray C. Hunt Drive Fl 3, Charlottesville, VA 22908; **Phone:** 434-924-2413; **Board Cert:** Plastic Surgery 2007; Hand Surgery 2005; **Med School:** W VA Univ 1976; **Resid:** Surgery, Johns Hopkins Hosp 1980; Plastic Surgery, Johns Hopkins Hosp 1982; **Fellow:** Hand Surgery, Raymond M. Curtis Natl Hand Ctr; **Fac Appt:** Prof OrS, Univ VA Sch Med

Smith Jr, David J MD [PlS] - **Spec Exp:** Breast Reconstruction; Burns-Reconstructive Plastic Surgery; Reconstructive Surgery; Body Contouring after Weight Loss; **Hospital:** Tampa Genl Hosp; **Address:** USF Hlth, Plastic Surgery Dept, 2 Tampa General Cir Fl 7, Tampa, FL 33606; **Phone:** 813-844-8783; **Board Cert:** Plastic Surgery 2006; **Med School:** Indiana Univ 1973; **Resid:** Surgery, Grady Hosp 1988; Plastic Surgery, IU Hlth Hosp 1980; **Fellow:** Hand Surgery, Univ Louisville Hosp 1979; **Fac Appt:** Prof S, Univ S Fla Coll Med

Smith, Paul D MD [PlS] - **Spec Exp:** Facial Plastic Surgery; Reconstructive Surgery-Face; Breast Reconstruction; **Hospital:** Moffitt Canc Ctr (page 61); **Address:** USF Hlth, Plastic Surgery Dept, 2 Tampa General Cir Fl 7, Tampa, FL 33606-3589; **Phone:** 813-844-8783; **Board Cert:** Plastic Surgery 2012; **Med School:** Univ IL Coll Med 1994; **Resid:** Surgery, Univ IL Med Ctr 1999; Plastic Surgery, UT Southwestern Med Ctr 2001; **Fac Appt:** Prof PlS, Univ S Fla Coll Med

Stuzin, James M MD [PlS] - **Spec Exp:** Facial Rejuvenation; Skin Laser Surgery-Resurfacing; Cosmetic Surgery-Face & Neck; Rhinoplasty; **Hospital:** Mercy Hosp; **Address:** 3225 Aviation Ave, Ste 100, Coconut Grove, FL 33133; **Phone:** 305-854-8828; **Board Cert:** Plastic Surgery 2007; **Med School:** Univ Fla Coll Med 1978; **Resid:** Surgery, Univ Wash Med Ctr 1983; Plastic Surgery, NYU Med Ctr 1986; **Fellow:** Craniofacial Surgery, UCLA Med Ctr 1987

Thaller, Seth R MD/DMD [PlS] - **Spec Exp:** Cosmetic Surgery-Face; Rhinoplasty; Pediatric Plastic Surgery; Reconstructive Plastic Surgery; **Hospital:** Jackson Meml Hosp, Univ of Miami Hosp; **Address:** UHlth, Plastic Surgery Dept, 1321 NW 14th St, Ste 402, Miami, FL 33136; **Phone:** 305-243-4500; **Board Cert:** Otolaryngology 1985; Plastic Surgery 2007; **Med School:** Univ Louisville Sch Med 1975; **Resid:** Otolaryngology, Mass Eye & Ear Infirm 1983; Plastic Surgery, Montefiore Med Ctr 1985; **Fellow:** Craniofacial Surgery, UCLA Med Ctr 1986; **Fac Appt:** Prof PlS, Univ Miami Sch Med

Tobin II, Gordon R MD [PlS] - **Spec Exp:** Reconstructive Plastic Surgery; Transplant-Hand; Cosmetic Surgery; Pelvic Reconstruction After Cancer; **Hospital:** Univ of Louisville Hosp, Jewish Hosp (KY); **Address:** Univ Surgical Assocs, 401 E Chestnut St, Ste 790, Louisville, KY 40202; **Phone:** 502-583-8303; **Board Cert:** Plastic Surgery 1978; **Med School:** UCSF 1969; **Resid:** Surgery, Univ Ariz Coll Med Affil Hosps 1975; Plastic Surgery, Univ Ariz Coll Med Affil Hosps 1976; **Fellow:** Pediatric Plastic Surgery, Univ Miami Sch Med Affil Hosps 1973; Cosmetic Plastic Surgery, Univ Miami Sch Med Affil Hosps 1973; **Fac Appt:** Prof PlS, Univ Louisville Sch Med

Vasconez, Henry C MD [PlS] - **Spec Exp:** Craniofacial Surgery/Reconstruction; Pediatric Plastic Surgery; Breast Reconstruction; Cosmetic Surgery; **Hospital:** Univ of Kentucky Albert B. Chandler Hosp; **Address:** 740 S Limestone St, Ste K454, Lexington, KY 40536; **Phone:** 859-257-7171; **Board Cert:** Plastic Surgery 2007; **Med School:** Ecuador 1978; **Resid:** Surgery, Stroger Hosp of Cook Co 1984; Plastic Surgery, Emory Hosp 1986; **Fellow:** Craniofacial Surgery, Baylor Med Ctr/International Craniofacial Inst 1987; **Fac Appt:** Prof S, Univ KY Coll Med

Wilhelmi, Bradon J MD [PlS] - **Spec Exp:** Cosmetic Surgery; Hand Surgery; Reconstructive Plastic Surgery; **Hospital:** Norton Hosp, Univ of Louisville Hosp; **Address:** Univ Surgical Assocs, 401 E Chestnut St, Ste 790, Louisville, KY 40202; **Phone:** 502-583-8303; **Board Cert:** Plastic Surgery 2011; Hand Surgery 2011; **Med School:** Rush Med Coll 1992; **Resid:** Surgery, Northwestern Meml Hosp 1996; Plastic Surgery, Univ Tex Med Br 1998; **Fellow:** Hand & Microvascular Surgery, Mass Genl Hosp 1999; **Fac Appt:** Prof PlS, Univ Louisville Sch Med

Wolfe, S. Anthony MD [PlS] - **Spec Exp:** Craniofacial Surgery/Reconstruction; Maxillofacial Surgery; Cosmetic Surgery; **Hospital:** Miami Children's Hosp; **Address:** Miami Chldns Hosp, Plastic Surgery Dept, 3100 SW 62nd Ave, Ste 2230, Miami, FL 33155; **Phone:** 305-662-4111; **Board Cert:** Surgery 2013; Plastic Surgery 1973; **Med School:** Harvard Med Sch 1965; **Resid:** Surgery, Peter Bent Brigham Hosp 1972; Plastic Surgery, Jackson Meml Hosp 1974; **Fac Appt:** Assoc Clin Prof PlS, Univ Miami Sch Med

Yu, Jack C MD/DMD [PlS] - **Spec Exp:** Craniofacial Surgery-Pediatric; Facial Plastic & Reconstructive Surgery; Facial Tumors; Cleft Palate/Lip; **Hospital:** Georgia Regents Med Ctr-Augusta; **Address:** Med College of Georgia Health, 1447 Harper St Fl 3, Augusta, GA 30912; **Phone:** 706-721-4147; **Board Cert:** Surgery 2003; Plastic Surgery 2004; **Med School:** Univ Pennsylvania 1985; **Resid:** Surgery, Hosp Univ Penn 1991; Plastic Surgery, Hosp Univ Penn 1993; **Fellow:** Craniofacial Surgery, Chldn's Hosp 1994; **Fac Appt:** Prof PlS, Med Coll GA

Midwest

Bauer, Bruce S MD [PlS] - **Spec Exp:** Cleft Palate/Lip; Reconstructive Plastic Surgery; **Hospital:** Highland Park Hosp/NorthShore Univ Hlth Syst (page 67), Lurie Chldn's Hosp-Chicago; **Address:** NorthShore University Health System, 501 Skokie Blvd, Northbrook, IL 60062; **Phone:** 847-504-2300; **Board Cert:** Plastic Surgery 1980; **Med School:** Northwestern Univ 1974; **Resid:** Surgery, Northwestern Meml Hosp 1977; Plastic Surgery, Northwestern Meml Hosp 1979; **Fac Appt:** Clin Prof S, Univ Chicago-Pritzker Sch Med

Bentz, Michael L MD [PlS] - **Spec Exp:** Pediatric Plastic Surgery; Facial Deformities/Reconstruction; Pediatric Hand Surgery; Reconstructive Surgery; **Hospital:** Univ WI Hosp & Clins, Meriter Hosp; **Address:** UW Hosp & Clins - Dept Plastic Surgery, 600 Highland Ave CSC Bldg - rm G5-361, Madison, WI 53792-3236; **Phone:** 608-263-1367; **Board Cert:** Surgery 2009; Plastic Surgery 2007; **Med School:** Temple Univ 1984; **Resid:** Surgery, Temple Univ Hosp 1989; Plastic Surgery, Univ Pittsburgh Med Ctr 1992; **Fellow:** Research, Univ Pittsburgh Med Ctr 1990; **Fac Appt:** Prof S, Univ Wisc

Billmire, David A MD [PlS] - **Spec Exp:** Cleft Palate/Lip; Reconstructive Plastic Surgery; **Hospital:** Cincinnati Chldns Hosp Med Ctr, Univ Cincinnati Med Ctr; **Address:** 3333 Burnet Ave, MC 2020, Cincinnati, OH 45229; **Phone:** 513-636-7181; **Board Cert:** Plastic Surgery 1985; **Med School:** Ohio State Univ 1975; **Resid:** Surgery, Univ Hosp 1982; Plastic Surgery, Univ Hosp 1984; **Fellow:** Craniofacial Surgery, Texas Craniofacial Fdn 1985; **Fac Appt:** Clin Prof S, Univ Cincinnati

Brandt, Keith E MD [PlS] - **Spec Exp:** Breast Reconstruction; Cancer Reconstruction; Microsurgery; Reconstructive Surgery-Complex; **Hospital:** Barnes-Jewish Hosp, Barnes-Jewish West County Hosp; **Address:** 4921 Parkview Pl, Ste 6G, St Louis, MO 63110-1010; **Phone:** 314-362-7388; **Board Cert:** Hand Surgery 2005; Plastic Surgery 2003; **Med School:** Univ Tex, Houston 1983; **Resid:** Surgery, Univ Nebraska Med Ctr 1989; Plastic Surgery, Univ Tennessee 1991; **Fellow:** Hand & Microvascular Surgery, Wash Univ 1993; **Fac Appt:** Prof S, Washington Univ, St Louis

Buchman, Steven R MD [PlS] - **Spec Exp:** Pediatric Plastic Surgery; Craniofacial Surgery-Pediatric; Craniofacial Surgery; **Hospital:** Mott Chldns Hosp, Univ Michigan Med Ctr; **Address:** Mott Chldns Hosp, 1500 E Med Ctr Drive, rm 7859, Ann Arbor, MI 48109-5219; **Phone:** 734-763-8063; **Board Cert:** Plastic Surgery 2005; **Med School:** Univ VA Sch Med 1985; **Resid:** Surgery, Hosp Univ Penn 1990; Plastic Surgery, Hosp Univ Penn 1992; **Fellow:** Craniofacial Surgery, UCLA Med Ctr 1993; **Fac Appt:** Prof PlS, Univ Mich Med Sch

Cederna, Paul S MD [PlS] - **Spec Exp:** Burns-Reconstructive Plastic Surgery; Cosmetic Surgery-Face; Facial Rejuvenation; Body Contouring; **Hospital:** Univ Michigan Med Ctr; **Address:** 1500 E Med Ctr Drive, 2130 Taubman Ctr, Ann Arbor, MI 48109-0340; **Phone:** 734-998-6022; **Board Cert:** Plastic Surgery 2009; **Med School:** Univ Mich Med Sch 1989; **Resid:** Surgery, Univ Iowa Hosp & Clin 1994; **Fellow:** Microsurgery, Univ Iowa Hosp & Clin 1995; Plastic Surgery, Univ Michigan Hosps 1997; **Fac Appt:** Prof PlS, Univ Mich Med Sch

Coleman III, John J MD [PlS] - **Spec Exp:** Cancer Reconstruction; Breast Reconstruction; Head & Neck Surgery; Pediatric Plastic Surgery; **Hospital:** IU Hlth Univ Hosp, Riley Hosp for Children; **Address:** IU Plastic Surgery Assocs, 545 Barnhill Dr, Emerson Hall, Ste 232, Indianapolis, IN 46202-5120; **Phone:** 317-274-8106; **Board Cert:** Plastic Surgery 2007; **Med School:** Harvard Med Sch 1973; **Resid:** Surgery, Emory Univ Affil Hosp 1978; Plastic Surgery, Emory Univ Affil Hosp 1979; **Fellow:** Surgical Oncology, Univ Maryland Med Ctr 1981; **Fac Appt:** Prof S, Indiana Univ

Derman, Gordon H MD [PlS] - **Spec Exp:** Cosmetic & Reconstructive Surgery; Hand Surgery; Carpal Tunnel Syndrome; **Hospital:** Rush Univ Med Ctr, Evanston Hosp/NorthShore Univ Hlth Sys (page 67); **Address:** 1725 W Harrison St, Ste 740, Chicago, IL 60612; **Phone:** 312-432-9200; **Board Cert:** Plastic Surgery 1984; Hand Surgery 2009; **Med School:** Rush Med Coll 1975; **Resid:** Surgery, Loyola Univ Med Ctr 1981; Plastic Surgery, Univ MI Hosp 1983; **Fellow:** Microsurgery, Rush/Presby St Luke's Med Ctr 1976; **Fac Appt:** Asst Prof S, Rush Med Coll

Dumanian, Gregory MD [PlS] - **Spec Exp:** Abdominal Wall Reconstruction; Microsurgery; Peripheral Nerve Surgery; Cosmetic Surgery; **Hospital:** Northwestern Meml Hosp; **Address:** Northwestern Plastic Surgery, 675 N St Clair St, Ste 19-250, Chicago, IL 60611-5975; **Phone:** 312-695-6022; **Board Cert:** Surgery 2003; Plastic Surgery 2008; Hand Surgery 2008; **Med School:** Univ Chicago-Pritzker Sch Med 1987; **Resid:** Surgery, Mass Genl Hosp 1992; **Fellow:** Plastic Surgery, Univ Pittsburgh 1995; Hand Surgery, Curtis Hand Ctr 1996; **Fac Appt:** Prof S, Northwestern Univ

Gottlieb, Lawrence Jay MD [PlS] - **Spec Exp:** Burn Care; Reconstructive Plastic Surgery; Burns-Reconstructive Plastic Surgery; **Hospital:** Univ of Chicago Med; **Address:** Univ Chicago Med Ctr, 5758 S Maryland Ave, Chicago, IL 60637; **Phone:** 773-702-6302; **Board Cert:** Plastic Surgery 2007; **Med School:** Penn State Coll Med 1977; **Resid:** Surgery, Yale-New Haven Hosp 1982; Plastic Surgery, LA Co-USC Med Ctr 1984; **Fac Appt:** Prof S, Univ Chicago-Pritzker Sch Med

Hammond, Dennis C MD [PlS] - **Spec Exp:** Cosmetic Surgery-Breast; Breast Reconstruction; Body Contouring after Weight Loss; **Hospital:** Spectrum Hlth Blodgett Campus; **Address:** Partners in Plastic Surgery, 4070 Lake Drive SE, Ste 202, Grand Rapids, MI 49546; **Phone:** 616-464-4420; **Board Cert:** Plastic Surgery 1994; **Med School:** Univ Mich Med Sch 1985; **Resid:** Surgery, Blodgett Meml Med Ctr 1988; Plastic/Reconstructive Surgery, Grand Rapids Area Med Educ Ctr 1990; **Fellow:** Plastic Surgery, Baptist Hosp 1991; Hand & Microvascular Surgery, Med Coll Wisconsin 1992; **Fac Appt:** Prof PlS, Univ Mich Med Sch

Kirschner, Richard Eugene MD [PlS] - **Spec Exp:** Cleft Palate/Lip; Craniofacial Surgery; **Hospital:** Nationwide Chldn's Hosp; **Address:** Nationwide Chldn's Hosp, Div Plastic & Reconstructive Surg, 700 Children's Drive, Ste 260, Columbus, OH 43205; **Phone:** 614-722-6692; **Board Cert:** Plastic Surgery 2009; Surgery 2006; **Med School:** Univ Miami Sch Med 1989; **Resid:** Surgery, NY-Presby/Weill Cornell Med Ctr 1995; Plastic Surgery, Hosp Univ Penn 1997; **Fellow:** Plastic Surgery, Chldns Hosp 1998; **Fac Appt:** Clin Prof S, Ohio State Univ

Kuzon Jr, William M MD/PhD [PlS] - **Spec Exp:** Facial Paralysis Reconstruction; Abdominal Wall Reconstruction; Gender Reassignment Surgery; **Hospital:** Univ Michigan Med Ctr, John D. Dingell VA Med Ctr, Detroit; **Address:** 1500 E Med Ctr Drive, 2130 Taubman Ctr, Ann Arbor, MI 48109-0340; **Phone:** 734-998-6022; **Board Cert:** Plastic Surgery 2006; **Med School:** Univ Rochester 1981; **Resid:** Plastic Surgery, Univ Toronto Med Ctr 1990; **Fellow:** Microvascular Surgery, Univ Toronto Med Ctr 1991; Hand & Microvascular Surgery, Univ Pittsburgh Med Ctr 1992; **Fac Appt:** Prof PlS, Univ Mich Med Sch

Lee, Raphael MD [PlS] - **Spec Exp:** Reconstructive Surgery; Trauma-Reconstructive Plastic Surgery; Burns-Reconstructive Plastic Surgery; Nerve Injuries/Surgery; **Hospital:** Univ of Chicago Med; **Address:** Univ Chicago Med Ctr, 5758 S Maryland Ave, Chicago, IL 60637; **Phone:** 773-702-6302; **Board Cert:** Plastic Surgery 1989; **Med School:** Temple Univ 1975; **Resid:** Surgery, Univ Chicago Hosp 1981; Plastic Surgery, Mass Genl Hosp 1983; **Fellow:** Research, Harvard Med School 1979; **Fac Appt:** Prof PlS, Univ Chicago-Pritzker Sch Med

MacKinnon, Susan E MD [PlS] - **Spec Exp:** Nerve Surgery & Transplantation; Hand Surgery; Reconstructive Surgery; Peripheral Nerve Surgery; **Hospital:** Barnes-Jewish Hosp; **Address:** Washington Univ Sch Med, 660 S Euclid Ave, Box 8238, St Louis, MO 63110; **Phone:** 314-362-4586; **Med School:** Canada 1975; **Resid:** Surgery, Queens Univ-Kingston 1978; Plastic Surgery, Univ Toronto Med Ctr 1980; **Fellow:** Neurological Surgery, Univ Toronto Med Ctr 1981; Hand Surgery, Union Meml Hosp 1982; **Fac Appt:** Prof S, Washington Univ, St Louis

Marsh, Jeffrey L MD [PlS] - **Spec Exp:** Cleft Palate/Lip; Craniofacial Surgery/Reconstruction; Pediatric Plastic Surgery; **Hospital:** Mercy Hosp - St Louis; **Address:** 621 S New Ballas Rd, Ste 260A, St Louis, MO 63141; **Phone:** 314-251-4772; **Board Cert:** Plastic Surgery 1979; **Med School:** Johns Hopkins Univ 1970; **Resid:** Surgery, UCLA Med Ctr 1975; Plastic Surgery, Univ Virginia Hosp 1977; **Fellow:** Craniofacial Surgery, Cannisburn Hosp; Craniofacial Surgery, Clinic Belvedere; **Fac Appt:** Clin Prof PlS, St Louis Univ

Medalie, Daniel A MD [PlS] - **Spec Exp:** Cosmetic Surgery-Breast; Gynecomastia; Genital Enhancement; Gender Reassignment Surgery; **Hospital:** MetroHealth Med Ctr; **Address:** MetroHealth Med Ctr, 2500 MetroHealth Drive, Ste H953, Cleveland, OH 44109; **Phone:** 216-778-4450; **Board Cert:** Plastic Surgery 2010; **Med School:** Cornell Univ 1990; **Resid:** Surgery, Univ Pittsburgh Med Ctr 1995; **Fellow:** Research, Mass Genl Hosp 1996; Plastic Surgery, Univ Pittsburgh Med Ctr 1999; **Fac Appt:** Asst Prof PlS, Case West Res Univ

Miller, Michael John MD [PlS] - **Spec Exp:** Cancer Reconstruction; Breast Reconstruction; Head & Neck Reconstruction; **Hospital:** OSU Wexner Med Ctr; **Address:** Ohio State Univ Plastic Surgery, 915 Olentangy River Rd, Ste 2100, Columbus, OH 43212; **Phone:** 614-293-8566; **Board Cert:** Plastic Surgery 2003; **Med School:** Univ Mass Sch Med 1983; **Resid:** Surgery, Berkshire Med Ctr 1987; **Fellow:** Plastic Surgery, Ohio State Univ Med Ctr 1989; **Fac Appt:** Prof S, Ohio State Univ

Mixter, Roger C MD [PlS] - **Spec Exp:** Craniofacial Surgery; Tattoo Removal; **Hospital:** Columbia St Mary's Hosp-Milwaukee; **Address:** Clinic of Cosmetic Surgery, 5201 N Port Washington Rd, Milwaukee, WI 53217-4902; **Phone:** 414-963-0500; **Board Cert:** Plastic Surgery 2006; **Med School:** Columbia P&S 1976; **Resid:** Surgery, Mayo Clinic 1981; **Fellow:** Plastic Surgery, Mayo Clinic 1984; **Fac Appt:** Clin Prof PlS, Univ Wisc

Mustoe, Thomas A MD [PlS] - **Spec Exp:** Cosmetic Surgery-Face; Cosmetic Surgery-Breast; Rhinoplasty; Body Contouring; **Hospital:** Northwestern Meml Hosp; **Address:** Northwestern Plastic Surgery, 675 N St Clair St Fl 19 - Ste 250, Chicago, IL 60611-5975; **Phone:** 312-695-6022; **Board Cert:** Otolaryngology 1983; Plastic Surgery 2007; **Med School:** Harvard Med Sch 1978; **Resid:** Surgery, Brigham & Womens Hosp 1980; Otolaryngology, Mass Eye & Ear Infirm 1983; **Fellow:** Plastic Surgery, Brigham & Womens Hosp 1985; **Fac Appt:** Prof S, Northwestern Univ

Ness, John A MD [PlS] - **Spec Exp:** Cosmetic Surgery-Breast; Facial Plastic Surgery; Abdominoplasty; Cosmetic Surgery-Face; **Hospital:** Maple Grove Hosp; **Address:** 13911 Ridgedale Drive, Ste 300, Minnetonka, MN 55305; **Phone:** 763-559-4500; **Board Cert:** Otolaryngology 1992; Plastic Surgery 2009; Facial Plastic & Reconstr Surgery 1996; **Med School:** Univ Minn 1986; **Resid:** Otolaryngology, Loyola Univ Med Ctr 1991; Plastic Surgery, UC Davis Med Ctr 1998; **Fellow:** Facial Plastic & Reconstr Surgery, UC Davis 1993; Craniofacial Surgery, Australian Craniofacial Inst 1996; **Fac Appt:** Asst Clin Prof PlS, Univ Minn

Neumeister, Michael W MD [PlS] - **Spec Exp:** Hand Surgery; Microsurgery; Breast Reconstruction & Augmentation; Cleft Palate/Lip; **Hospital:** Memorial Med Ctr-Springfield; **Address:** SIU Div Plastic Surgery, Baylis Med Bldg, 747 N Rutledge St Fl 3, Springfield, IL 62702; **Phone:** 217-545-6314; **Board Cert:** Plastic Surgery 2005; Hand Surgery 2006; **Med School:** Univ Toronto 1988; **Resid:** Surgery, Dalhousie Univ Affil Hosp 1991; Plastic Surgery, Univ Manitoba Affil Hosp 1994; **Fellow:** Microsurgery, Brigham & Womens Hosp 1996; Hand & Microvascular Surgery, Southern Illinois Univ 1997; **Fac Appt:** Prof S, Southern IL Univ

Papay, Francis A MD [PlS] - **Spec Exp:** Craniofacial Surgery/Reconstruction; Maxillofacial Surgery; Cosmetic Surgery-Face; Pediatric Plastic Surgery; **Hospital:** Cleveland Clin (page 55); **Address:** Cleveland Clinic, 9500 Euclid Ave, Desk A60, Cleveland, OH 44195; **Phone:** 216-444-6906; **Board Cert:** Otolaryngology 1989; Plastic Surgery 2007; **Med School:** NE Ohio Univ 1984; **Resid:** Otolaryngology, Cleveland Clin 1989; Plastic/Reconstructive Surgery, Cleveland Clin 1991; **Fellow:** Craniofacial & Maxillofacial Surgery, Primary Chldns Med Ctr 1992; **Fac Appt:** Prof S, Cleveland Cl Coll Med/Case West Res

Patel, Pravin K MD [PlS] - **Spec Exp:** Pediatric Plastic Surgery; Craniofacial Surgery; Cleft Palate/Lip; Reconstructive Surgery-Complex; **Hospital:** Univ of IL Med Ctr at Chicago; **Address:** The Craniofacial Ctr, 811 S Paulina, rm 161, Chicago, IL 60612; **Phone:** 312-996-7546; **Board Cert:** Plastic Surgery 2009; **Med School:** Hahnemann Univ 1985; **Resid:** Surgery, Mayo Clinic 1989; Plastic Surgery, Northwestern Meml Hosp 1993; **Fellow:** Craniofacial Surgery, UCLA Med Ctr 1994; **Fac Appt:** Prof S, Univ IL Coll Med

Polley, John W MD [PlS] - **Spec Exp:** Craniofacial Surgery; Pediatric Plastic Surgery; Maxillofacial Surgery; **Hospital:** Rush Univ Med Ctr; **Address:** Rush Craniofacial Ctr, 1725 W Harrison St, Ste 425, Chicago, IL 60612; **Phone:** 312-563-3000; **Board Cert:** Plastic Surgery 1992; **Med School:** Northwestern Univ 1983; **Resid:** Surgery, MI State Univ Med Ctr 1986; Plastic Surgery, MI State Univ Med Ctr 1988; **Fellow:** Craniofacial & Maxillofacial Surgery, Chang Gung Meml Hosp 1989; Pediatric Craniofacial Surgery, Hosp for Sick Chldn 1990; **Fac Appt:** Prof PlS, Rush Med Coll

Puckett, Charles L MD [PlS] - **Spec Exp:** Cosmetic & Reconstructive Surgery; Breast Surgery; **Hospital:** Univ of Missouri Hlth Care, Columbia Regional Hosp; **Address:** 1 Hospital Drive, Ste M349, Columbia, MO 65212; **Phone:** 573-882-2275; **Board Cert:** Surgery 1972; Plastic Surgery 2006; **Med School:** Wake Forest Univ 1966; **Resid:** Surgery, Duke Univ Med Ctr 1971; Plastic Surgery, Duke Univ Med Ctr 1976; **Fellow:** Hand Surgery, Kleinert Hand Fellowship; **Fac Appt:** Prof S, Univ MO-Columbia Sch Med

Sanger, James R MD [PlS] - **Spec Exp:** Hand Surgery; Microsurgery; Reconstructive Surgery; **Hospital:** Froedtert & Med Coll WI, Chldns Hosp - Wisconsin; **Address:** Med Coll WI, Dept Plastic Surg, 8700 Watertown Plank Rd, Milwaukee, WI 53226; **Phone:** 414-805-5451; **Board Cert:** Plastic Surgery 2008; Hand Surgery 2009; **Med School:** Univ Wisc 1974; **Resid:** Surgery, LAC - Harbor - UCLA Med Ctr 1979; Plastic Surgery, Med Coll Wisc Affil Hosps 1981; **Fellow:** Hand Surgery, Med Coll Wisc Affil Hosps 1982; **Fac Appt:** Prof PlS, Med Coll Wisc

Siebert, John W MD [PlS] - **Spec Exp:** Facial Plastic & Reconstructive Surgery; Microsurgery; Cosmetic Surgery-Face; **Hospital:** Univ WI Hosp & Clins, New York Eye & Ear Infirm (page 64); **Address:** UW Hosp & Clins, Div Plastic & Reconstructive Surgery, 600 Highland Ave, Madison, WI 53792; **Phone:** 212-737-8300; **Board Cert:** Plastic Surgery 1991; **Med School:** Univ Wisc 1981; **Resid:** Surgery, Mass Genl Hosp 1986; Plastic Surgery, NYU Langone Med Ctr 1988; **Fellow:** Microsurgery, NYU Langone Med Ctr 1989; **Fac Appt:** Assoc Prof S, Univ Wisc

Siemionow, Maria MD/PhD [PlS] - **Spec Exp:** Microsurgery; Peripheral Nerve Surgery; Reconstructive Plastic Surgery; Transplant-Face; **Hospital:** Cleveland Clin (page 55); **Address:** Cleveland Clin Fdn, 9500 Euclid Ave, Desk A60, Cleveland, OH 44195; **Phone:** 216-445-2405; **Med School:** Poland 1974; **Resid:** Surgery, Inst Orth & Rehab Med; **Fellow:** Plastic Surgery, Univ Hosp; Microsurgery, Univ Louisville Hosp

Song, David H MD [PlS] - **Spec Exp:** Cosmetic & Reconstructive Surgery; Breast Reconstruction; Cancer Reconstruction; **Hospital:** Univ of Chicago Med; **Address:** University of Chicago Plastic Surgery, 5841 S Maryland Ave, rm J641, MS 6035, Chicago, IL 60637; **Phone:** 773-702-6302; **Board Cert:** Plastic Surgery 2012; **Med School:** UCLA-David Geffen Sch Med 1995; **Resid:** Surgery, Univ Chicago Med Ctr 2000; **Fellow:** Plastic Surgery, Univ Chicago Med Ctr 2001; **Fac Appt:** Prof S, Univ Chicago-Pritzker Sch Med

Sood, Rajiv MD [PlS] - **Spec Exp:** Burns-Reconstructive Plastic Surgery; Pediatric Hand Surgery; Breast Cosmetic & Reconstructive Surgery; Body Contouring after Weight Loss; **Hospital:** IU Hlth Univ Hosp, Riley Hosp for Children; **Address:** Richard Fairbanks Burn Ctr, 1001 W 10th St, Dunlap Bldg Fl 4, Indianapolis, IN 46202; **Phone:** 317-278-1022; **Board Cert:** Plastic Surgery 2007; Hand Surgery 2006; **Med School:** Albany Med Coll 1984; **Resid:** Surgery, Temple Univ Hosp 1989; **Fellow:** Plastic Surgery, Cleveland Clinic 1991; Hand Surgery, Union Meml Hosp 1992; **Fac Appt:** Prof S, Indiana Univ

Vogt, Peter A MD [PlS] - **Spec Exp:** Cosmetic Surgery; **Hospital:** Mercy Hosp - Coon Rapids, Unity Hosp - Fridley; **Address:** 319 Barry Ave S, Ste 300, Wayzata, MN 55391; **Phone:** 952-473-1111; **Board Cert:** Plastic Surgery 1974; **Med School:** Univ Manitoba 1965; **Resid:** Surgery, Montreal Genl Hosp 1970; Plastic Surgery, Winnipeg Hlth Scis Ctr 1973

Walton Jr, Robert L MD [PlS] - **Spec Exp:** Nasal Reconstruction; Breast Reconstruction; Ear Reconstruction/Microtia; Cosmetic Surgery-Face; **Hospital:** Presence St Joseph Hosp, Lurie Chldn's Hosp-Chicago; **Address:** 60 E Delaware Pl, Ste 1430, Chicago, IL 60611-1495; **Phone:** 312-337-7795; **Board Cert:** Plastic Surgery 2007; **Med School:** Univ Kansas 1972; **Resid:** Surgery, Johns Hopkins Hosp 1974; Plastic Surgery, Yale-New Haven Hosp 1978; **Fellow:** Hand Surgery, Hartford Hosp 1978; **Fac Appt:** Prof PlS, Northwestern Univ-Feinberg Sch Med

Wilkins, Edwin G MD [PlS] - **Spec Exp:** Breast Reconstruction; Lower Limb Reconstruction; Microsurgery; **Hospital:** Univ Michigan Med Ctr; **Address:** Univ Mich, Plastic Surgery Clinic, 24 Frank Lloyd Wright Drive, Ste A1200, Ann Arbor, MI 48105; **Phone:** 734-998-6022; **Board Cert:** Plastic Surgery 1991; **Med School:** Wake Forest Univ 1981; **Resid:** Surgery, Charlotte Meml Hosp 1986; Plastic Surgery, Vanderbilt Univ Med Ctr 1988; **Fellow:** Reconstructive Microsurgery, Univ Louisville Sch Med Affil Hosp 1989; **Fac Appt:** Assoc Prof PlS, Univ Mich Med Sch

Yetman, Randall MD [PlS] - **Spec Exp:** Breast Reconstruction; Melanoma; Microsurgery; **Hospital:** Cleveland Clin (page 55); **Address:** 9500 Euclid Ave, Desk A60, Cleveland, OH 44195; **Phone:** 216-444-6908; **Board Cert:** Plastic Surgery 1984; **Med School:** Univ Miami Sch Med 1975; **Resid:** Surgery, Montefiore Med Ctr 1979; Plastic Surgery, NY Cornell Med Ctr 1981; **Fellow:** Plastic Surgery, Cleveland Clin Fdn 1982

Young, V Leroy MD [PlS] - **Spec Exp:** Breast Augmentation; Skin Laser Surgery-Resurfacing; Body Contouring after Weight Loss; **Hospital:** Barnes-Jewish West County Hosp; **Address:** 969 N Mason Rd, Ste 170, St Louis, MO 63141; **Phone:** 314-628-8200; **Board Cert:** Plastic Surgery 1981; **Med School:** Univ KY Coll Med 1970; **Resid:** Surgery, Univ KY Med Ctr 1977; Plastic Surgery, Barnes Hosp-Wash Univ 1979; **Fac Appt:** Prof S, Washington Univ, St Louis

Zins, James E MD [PlS] - **Spec Exp:** Cosmetic Surgery-Face; Rhinoplasty; Facial Rejuvenation; Maxillofacial Surgery; **Hospital:** Cleveland Clin (page 55); **Address:** Dept Plastic Surgery, 9500 Euclid Ave, Desk A60, Cleveland, OH 44195; **Phone:** 216-444-6901; **Board Cert:** Plastic Surgery 2007; **Med School:** Univ Pennsylvania 1974; **Resid:** Surgery, Hosp Univ Penn 1980; Plastic Surgery, Hosp Univ Penn 1982; **Fellow:** Craniofacial Surgery, Hosp Univ Penn 1978; Maxillofacial Surgery, Hosp Sick Chldn 1983

Great Plains and Mountains

Deleyiannis, Frederic W.B. MD [PlS] - **Spec Exp:** Head & Neck Reconstruction; Maxillofacial Surgery; Craniofacial Surgery; Pediatric Plastic Surgery; **Hospital:** Chldn's Hosp - Aurora (CO), Univ Colorado Hosp; **Address:** Chldns Hosp, Plastic Surgery Dept, 13123 E 16th Ave, Box B467, Aurora, CO 80045; **Phone:** 720-777-3880; **Board Cert:** Otolaryngology 2000; Plastic Surgery 2013; **Med School:** Yale Univ 1992; **Resid:** Otolaryngology, Univ Washington Med Ctr 1999; Plastic Surgery, UPMC 2002; **Fellow:** Head and Neck Surgery, Univ Oviedo Med Ctr 2000; **Fac Appt:** Prof PlS, Univ Colorado

Grossman, John A MD [PlS] - **Spec Exp:** Cosmetic Surgery; Cosmetic Surgery-Breast; Facial Rejuvenation; Liposuction & Body Contouring; **Hospital:** Rose Med Ctr; **Address:** Grossman Plastic Surgery, 4600 E Hale Pkwy, Ste 100, Denver, CO 80220; **Phone:** 303-320-5566; **Board Cert:** Surgery 1974; Plastic Surgery 1976; **Med School:** Cornell Univ-Weill Med Coll 1967; **Resid:** Surgery, Boston Med Ctr 1973; Plastic Surgery, Univ CO Hosp 1975; **Fellow:** Surgery, Harvard Med Sch 1973; **Fac Appt:** Clin Prof S, Univ Colorado

Rockwell, William B MD [PlS] - **Spec Exp:** Microsurgery; Sarcoma; Breast Reconstruction; Hand Surgery; **Hospital:** Univ Utah Hlth Care; **Address:** 30 N 1900 E, Ste 3B400, Salt Lake City, UT 84132; **Phone:** 801-585-3253; **Board Cert:** Plastic Surgery 2007; Hand Surgery 2006; **Med School:** Washington Univ, St Louis 1984; **Resid:** Surgery, Washington Univ Phys 1987; Plastic Surgery, Univ Rochester Affil Hosps 1991; **Fellow:** Hand Surgery, Univ Rochester Affil Hosps 1993; **Fac Appt:** Assoc Prof PlS, Univ Utah

Southwest

Barone, Constance M MD [PlS] - **Spec Exp:** Cosmetic Surgery-Breast; Rhinoplasty; Craniofacial Surgery; Liposuction & Body Contouring; **Hospital:** Christus Santa Rosa Med Ctr Hosp, Univ Hosp-San Antonio; **Address:** 2829 Babcock Rd Tower 1 Bldg, Fl 6 - Ste 615, San Antonio, TX 78229; **Phone:** 210-614-0400; **Board Cert:** Plastic Surgery 1991; **Med School:** Mount Sinai Sch Med 1982; **Resid:** Surgery, Temple Univ Hosp 1987; Plastic Surgery, NYU Med Ctr 1989; **Fellow:** Craniofacial Surgery, Montefiore-Weiler Einstein Div 1992; **Fac Appt:** Prof NS, Univ Tex, San Antonio

Barton Jr, Fritz E MD [PlS] - **Spec Exp:** Cosmetic Surgery-Face; Liposuction & Body Contouring; Cosmetic Surgery-Breast; Facial Rejuvenation; **Hospital:** Baylor Univ Med Ctr-Dallas; **Address:** 4311 Oak Lawn Ave, Ste 380, Dallas, TX 75219; **Phone:** 214-821-9355; **Board Cert:** Surgery 1975; Plastic Surgery 1977; **Med School:** Univ Tex SW, Dallas 1967; **Resid:** Surgery, Parkland Meml Hosp 1974; Plastic/Reconstructive Surgery, NYU Med Ctr 1976; **Fac Appt:** Prof PlS, Univ Tex SW, Dallas

Beals, Stephen P MD [PlS] - **Spec Exp:** Craniofacial Surgery; Pediatric Plastic Surgery; Cosmetic Surgery-Face & Breast; Liposuction & Body Contouring; **Hospital:** St. Joseph's Hosp & Med Ctr - Phoenix, Phoenix Children's Hosp; **Address:** 500 W Thomas Rd, Ste 960, Phoenix, AZ 85013-4223; **Phone:** 602-266-9066; **Board Cert:** Plastic Surgery 1986; **Med School:** Wayne State Univ 1978; **Resid:** Surgery, William Beaumont Hosp 1983; Plastic Surgery, Phoenix Plastic Surgery Inst 1985; **Fellow:** Craniofacial Surgery, Hospital for Sick Chldn 1985; **Fac Appt:** Assoc Prof PlS, Mayo Med Sch

Burns, A Jay MD [PlS] - **Spec Exp:** Cosmetic Surgery-Face; Cosmetic Surgery-Breast; Facial Rejuvenation; Vascular Birthmarks; **Hospital:** Med City Dallas Hosp; **Address:** 9101 N Central Expresswy St, Ste 600, Dallas, TX 75231; **Phone:** 214-823-1978; **Board Cert:** Plastic Surgery 1990; **Med School:** Univ Tex SW, Dallas 1981; **Resid:** Surgery, Univ Utah Med Ctr 1986; Plastic Surgery, Univ Tex SW Med Ctr 1988; **Fellow:** Vascular Anomalies, Boston Chldns Hosp 1988; **Fac Appt:** Asst Prof PlS, Univ Tex SW, Dallas

Butler, Charles E MD [PlS] - **Spec Exp:** Breast Reconstruction; **Hospital:** UT MD Anderson Canc Ctr; **Address:** UT MD Anderson Cancer Ctr, 1515 Holcombe Blvd, Ste 1488, Houston, TX 77030; **Phone:** 713-794-1247; **Board Cert:** Plastic Surgery 2010; Surgery 2008; **Med School:** Univ Pennsylvania 1990; **Resid:** Surgery, Mass Genl Hosp 1993; Plastic Surgery, Harvard Affil Hosps 1999; **Fellow:** Research, Brigham & Women's Hosp 1995; **Fac Appt:** Prof PlS, Case West Res Univ

Byrd, H Stephenson MD [PlS] - **Spec Exp:** Rhinoplasty; Cosmetic Surgery-Face; Cosmetic Surgery-Breast; Liposuction & Body Contouring; **Hospital:** Forest Park Med Ctr; **Address:** 9101 N Central Expressway, Ste 600, Dallas, TX 75231; **Phone:** 214-821-9662; **Board Cert:** Plastic Surgery 1980; **Med School:** Univ Tex Med Br, Galveston 1972; **Resid:** Surgery, Univ Utah Med Ctr 1977; Plastic Surgery, Dallas Co Hosp-Parkland Meml 1978; **Fac Appt:** Clin Prof PlS, Univ Tex SW, Dallas

Chang, David W MD [PlS] - **Spec Exp:** Breast Reconstruction; Microsurgery; Cancer Reconstruction; **Hospital:** UT MD Anderson Canc Ctr; **Address:** MD Anderson Cancer Ctr, 1515 Holcombe Blvd, Unit 1488, Houston, TX 77030-4017; **Phone:** 713-794-1247; **Board Cert:** Plastic Surgery 2004; **Med School:** Univ Wisc 1987; **Resid:** Surgery, Metropolitan Group Hosps 1991; Plastic/Reconstructive Surgery, Montefiore Med Ctr 1993; **Fellow:** Hand Surgery, Buncke Clinic 1994; **Fac Appt:** Prof PlS, Univ Tex, Houston

Hamra, Sameer T MD [PlS] - **Spec Exp:** Cosmetic Surgery-Face; Rhinoplasty; **Hospital:** Baylor Med Ctr at Uptown; **Address:** 9301 N Central Expressway, Tower II, Ste 551, Dallas, TX 75231; **Phone:** 214-754-9001; **Board Cert:** Surgery 1970; Plastic Surgery 1977; **Med School:** Univ Okla Coll Med 1963; **Resid:** Surgery, OU Med Ctr 1968; Plastic Surgery, NYU Med Ctr 1973; **Fellow:** Surgery, Univ Lausanne 1966; **Fac Appt:** Clin Prof S, Univ Tex SW, Dallas

Kane, Alex A MD [PlS] - **Spec Exp:** Pediatric Plastic Surgery; Craniofacial Surgery; Cleft Palate/Lip; Hemangiomas/Birthmarks; **Hospital:** Chldns Med Ctr of Dallas; **Address:** 2350 N Stemmons Freeway, Ambulatory Care Pavilion Fl 4, Dallas, TX 75207; **Phone:** 214-456-2240; **Board Cert:** Plastic Surgery 2011; **Med School:** Dartmouth Med Sch 1991; **Resid:** Surgery, Barnes Jewish Hosp 1994; Plastic Surgery, Barnes Jewish Hosp 1998; **Fellow:** Craniofacial Surgery, Chang-Gung Meml Hosp 1999; Craniofacial Imaging, Nat'l Lab for Diagnostic Rsch 2000; **Fac Appt:** Prof S, Univ Tex SW, Dallas

Kenkel, Jeffrey M MD [PlS] - **Spec Exp:** Cosmetic Surgery-Face; Laser Surgery; Cosmetic Surgery-Breast; Body Contouring after Weight Loss; **Hospital:** UT Southwestern Med Ctr at Dallas; **Address:** UTSW Plastic Surgery, 1801 Inwood Rd Fl 5, Dallas, TX 75390; **Phone:** 214-645-2353; **Board Cert:** Plastic Surgery 2008; **Med School:** Georgetown Univ 1989; **Resid:** Surgery, Georgetown Univ Med Ctr 1994; Plastic Surgery, UT Southwestern Med Ctr 1996; **Fac Appt:** Assoc Prof PlS, Univ Tex SW, Dallas

Kronowitz, Steven J MD [PlS] - **Spec Exp:** Reconstructive Surgery; **Hospital:** UT MD Anderson Canc Ctr; **Address:** UT MD Anderson Canc Ctr, 1400 Pressler ST, Unit 1488, Houston, TX 77030; **Phone:** 713-794-1247; **Board Cert:** Surgery 2007; Plastic Surgery 2012; **Med School:** Univ Miami Sch Med 1992; **Resid:** Surgery, Mt Sinai Med Ctr 1998; Plastic Surgery, Mt Sinai Med Ctr 2002; **Fellow:** Microsurgery, UT MD Anderson Canc Ctr 2001; **Fac Appt:** Prof S, Univ Tex, Houston

Leighton, William D MD [PlS] - **Spec Exp:** Burns-Reconstructive Plastic Surgery; Cosmetic & Reconstructive Surgery; Cleft Palate/Lip; **Hospital:** Scottsdale Hlthcare - Shea, Scottsdale Hlthcare - Osborn; **Address:** 7425 E Shea Blvd, Ste 103, Scottsdale, AZ 85260; **Phone:** 480-948-3250; **Board Cert:** Plastic Surgery 2008; **Med School:** Univ IL Coll Med 1978; **Resid:** Surgery, Phoenix Integrated Surgery Residency 1983; Plastic Surgery, Phoenix Integrated Surgery Residency 1985; **Fellow:** Microvascular Surgery, S Illinois Univ Med Ctr 1986; **Fac Appt:** Assoc Prof S, Mayo Med Sch

Meltzer, Toby R MD [PlS] - **Spec Exp:** Gender Reassignment Surgery; Penile Inversion Technique; Breast Augmentation; Cosmetic Surgery-Face & Breast; **Hospital:** Scottsdale Hlthcare - Osborn; **Address:** 7025 N Scottsdale Rd, Ste 302, Scottsdale, AZ 85253; **Phone:** 480-657-7006; **Board Cert:** Plastic Surgery 1992; **Med School:** Louisiana State U, New Orleans 1983; **Resid:** Surgery, Charity Hosp Louisiana 1988; Plastic Surgery, Univ Michigan Med Ctr 1990; **Fellow:** Burn Surgery, Wayne State Univ 1987; **Fac Appt:** Asst Clin Prof S, Univ Ariz Coll Med

Menick, Frederick J MD [PlS] - **Spec Exp:** Reconstructive Surgery-Face; Nasal Reconstruction; Cancer Reconstruction; Rhinoplasty; **Hospital:** St. Joseph's Hosp - Tucson; **Address:** 1102 N Eldorado Pl, Tucson, AZ 85715; **Phone:** 520-881-4525; **Board Cert:** Plastic Surgery 1983; **Med School:** Yale Univ 1970; **Resid:** Surgery, Stanford Med Ctr 1974; Surgery, Univ Ariz Med Ctr 1979; **Fellow:** Plastic Surgery, UC Irvine 1981; Plastic Surgery, Univ Miami 1982; **Fac Appt:** Assoc Clin Prof S, Univ Ariz Coll Med

Metzinger, Stephen E MD [PlS] - **Spec Exp:** Rhinoplasty; Eyelid Surgery/Blepharoplasty; Cosmetic Surgery-Face; Cosmetic Surgery-Breast; **Hospital:** E Jefferson Genl Hosp; **Address:** Aesthetic Surgery Assocs, 3223 8th St, Ste 200, Metairie, LA 70002; **Phone:** 504-309-7061; **Board Cert:** Otolaryngology 1994; Plastic Surgery 2008; Facial Plastic & Reconstr Surgery 1998; **Med School:** Louisiana State U, New Orleans 1987; **Resid:** Otolaryngology, LSU Interim Public Hosp 1993; Plastic Surgery, Johns Hopkins Hosp 1996; **Fellow:** Facial Plastic & Reconstr Surgery, McCollough Aesthetic Med Ctr 1994; Craniofacial Surgery, Univ of MD Med Ctr 1996; **Fac Appt:** Assoc Prof PlS, Louisiana State U, New Orleans

Moses, Michael H MD [PlS] - **Spec Exp:** Cosmetic Surgery-Face; Cosmetic Surgery-Breast; Liposuction & Body Contouring; Rhinoplasty; **Hospital:** Touro Infirm, Children's Hospital - New Orleans; **Address:** 1603 2nd St, New Orleans, LA 70130; **Phone:** 504-895-7200; **Board Cert:** Plastic Surgery 1985; **Med School:** Tulane Univ 1977; **Resid:** Surgery, Yale-New Haven Hosp 1982; Plastic Surgery, Mass Genl Hosp 1984; **Fellow:** Craniofacial Surgery, Chldns Hosp 1985; **Fac Appt:** Assoc Clin Prof PlS, Tulane Univ

Rappaport, Norman H MD/DDS [PlS] - **Spec Exp:** Cosmetic Surgery-Face; Breast Cosmetic & Reconstructive Surgery; Body Contouring after Weight Loss; Facial Rejuvenation; **Hospital:** Methodist Hosp - Houston, St. Luke's Episcopal Hosp-Houston; **Address:** Houston Center for Plastic Surgey, 6560 Fannin St, Ste 1812 Scurlock Tower, Houston, TX 77030-2775; **Phone:** 713-790-4500; **Board Cert:** Plastic Surgery 2007; **Med School:** Hahnemann Univ 1975; **Resid:** Surgery, Abingdon Meml Hosp 1978; Plastic Surgery, Baylor Coll Med 1980; **Fellow:** Hand Surgery, Hosp Univ Penn 1978; **Fac Appt:** Assoc Clin Prof S, Baylor Coll Med

Robb, Geoffrey L MD [PlS] - **Spec Exp:** Breast Reconstruction; **Hospital:** UT MD Anderson Canc Ctr, St. Luke's Sugar Land Hosp; **Address:** UT MD Anderson Cancer Ctr, 1515 Holcombe Blvd, Ste 1488, Houston, TX 77030; **Phone:** 713-794-1247; **Board Cert:** Otolaryngology 1979; Plastic Surgery 2008; **Med School:** Univ Miami Sch Med 1974; **Resid:** Otolaryngology, Naval Reg Med Ctr 1979; Plastic Surgery, Univ Pittsburgh Med Ctr 1985; **Fellow:** Microvascular Surgery, Univ Pittsburgh 1986; **Fac Appt:** Prof PlS, Univ Tex, Houston

Rohrich, Rod J MD [PlS] - **Spec Exp:** Rhinoplasty; Cosmetic Surgery-Face; Facial Rejuvenation; Liposuction & Body Contouring; **Hospital:** UT Southwestern Med Ctr at Dallas, Baylor Univ Med Ctr-Dallas; **Address:** Univ Tex SW Med Ctr, Plastic Surgery, 1801 Inwood Rd, MS 9132, Dallas, TX 75390-9132; **Phone:** 214-645-2353; **Board Cert:** Plastic Surgery 2007; **Med School:** Baylor Coll Med 1979; **Resid:** Plastic Surgery, Univ Mich Hosp 1985; **Fellow:** Hand Surgery, Mass Genl Hosp 1987; **Fac Appt:** Prof PlS, Univ Tex SW, Dallas

Schusterman, Mark A MD [PlS] - **Spec Exp:** Breast Reconstruction; Cancer Reconstruction; Cosmetic Surgery-Face & Breast; Liposuction & Body Contouring; **Hospital:** Methodist Hosp - Houston, St. Luke's Episcopal Hosp-Houston; **Address:** MD Aesthetic Plastic Surgery, 1200 Binz St, Ste 1200, Houston, TX 77004; **Phone:** 713-794-0368; **Board Cert:** Plastic Surgery 1989; **Med School:** Univ Louisville Sch Med 1980; **Resid:** Surgery, Ohio State U Hosp East 1985; Plastic Surgery, Univ Pittsburgh Affil Hosps 1987; **Fellow:** Microsurgery, Univ Pittsburgh Affil Hosps 1988; **Fac Appt:** Clin Prof PlS, Baylor Coll Med

Tebbetts, John B MD [PlS] - **Spec Exp:** Cosmetic Surgery-Breast; Rhinoplasty; Liposuction; **Hospital:** Baylor Med Ctr at Uptown, Baylor Univ Med Ctr-Dallas; **Address:** 2801 Lemmon Ave W, Ste 300, Dallas, TX 75204; **Phone:** 214-220-2712; **Board Cert:** Plastic Surgery 1980; **Med School:** Univ Tex Med Br, Galveston 1972; **Resid:** Surgery, Univ Utah Med Ctr 1977; Plastic Surgery, Dallas Co Hosp-Parkland Meml Hosp 1979; **Fac Appt:** Asst Clin Prof PlS, Univ Tex SW, Dallas

Wilcox, Robert D MD [PlS] - **Spec Exp:** Cosmetic Surgery-Face; Cosmetic Surgery-Breast; Liposuction & Body Contouring; **Hospital:** Columbia Med Ctr - Plano; **Address:** Plastic & Cosmetic Surgery Ctr of Texas, 5316 W Plano Pkwy, Plano, TX 75093; **Phone:** 972-620-1700; **Board Cert:** Plastic Surgery 1994; Hand Surgery 2003; **Med School:** Univ Tex SW, Dallas 1984; **Resid:** Surgery, Univ Florida Hlth Sci Ctr 1989; Plastic/Reconstructive Surgery, Univ Texas-SW Med Sch Affil Hosp 1991; **Fellow:** Hand Surgery, Univ Texas-SW Med Sch Affil Hosp 1992

Yuen, James C MD [PlS] - **Spec Exp:** Hand Reconstruction; Breast Reconstruction; Head & Neck Cancer Reconstruction; Chest Wall Reconstruction; **Hospital:** UAMS Med Ctr; **Address:** 4301 W Markham, Ste 720, Little Rock, AR 72205; **Phone:** 501-686-8711; **Board Cert:** Surgery 2012; Plastic Surgery 2004; **Med School:** Med Coll VA 1985; **Resid:** Surgery, West Va U Hosp 1990; Plastic/Reconstructive Surgery, Duke Univ Med Ctr 1993; **Fellow:** Hand & Microvascular Surgery, Kleinert Inst of Hand & Microsurgery 1991; **Fac Appt:** Prof PlS, Univ Ark

West Coast and Pacific

Alter, Gary J MD [PlS] - **Spec Exp:** Genitourinary Reconstruction; Gender Reassignment Surgery; Genital Enhancement; **Hospital:** Cedars-Sinai Med Ctr, UCLA Ronald Reagan Med Ctr; **Address:** 416 N Bedford Drive, Ste 400, Beverly Hills, CA 90210-4318; **Phone:** 310-275-5566; **Board Cert:** Urology 1981; Plastic Surgery 2007; **Med School:** UCLA 1973; **Resid:** Urology, Baylor Med Ctr 1979; Plastic Surgery, Mayo Clin 1992; **Fellow:** Genitourinary Surgery, Eastern Va Med Sch 1992; **Fac Appt:** Clin Prof PlS, UCLA

Aly, Al S MD [PlS] - **Spec Exp:** Abdominoplasty; Body Contouring after Weight Loss; **Hospital:** UC Irvine Med Ctr; **Address:** UCI, Dept Plastic Surgery, 200 S Manchester Ave, Ste 650, Orange, CA 92868; **Phone:** 714-456-5471; **Board Cert:** Otolaryngology 1993; Plastic Surgery 2009; **Med School:** Georgetown Univ 1983; **Resid:** Otolaryngology, Vanderbilt Univ Med Ctr 1992; Plastic Surgery, Jackson Meml Hosp 1997; **Fellow:** Facial Plastic & Reconstr Surgery, UC Irvine Med Ctr 1993; **Fac Appt:** Prof PlS, UC Irvine

Andersen, James S MD [PlS] - **Spec Exp:** Breast Reconstruction; Head & Neck Reconstruction; Microsurgery; **Hospital:** City of Hope Natl Med Ctr, Huntington Memorial Hosp; **Address:** 1500 E Duarte Rd, Duarte, CA 91010; **Phone:** 626-471-7100; **Board Cert:** Plastic Surgery 1994; **Med School:** Jefferson Med Coll 1983; **Resid:** Surgery, Hosp Univ Penn 1989; Plastic Surgery, Hosp Univ Penn 1991; **Fellow:** Microsurgery, USC Med Ctr 1992; **Fac Appt:** Assoc Clin Prof S, USC Sch Med

Bradley, James P MD [PlS] - **Spec Exp:** Facial Plastic & Reconstructive Surgery; Cosmetic Surgery-Face; Pediatric Plastic Surgery; Cleft Palate/Lip; **Hospital:** UCLA Ronald Reagan Med Ctr; **Address:** UCLA, Dept Plastic Surgery, 200 UCLA Med Plaza, Ste 465, Los Angeles, CA 90095; **Phone:** 310-794-7616; **Board Cert:** Plastic Surgery 2011; Surgery 2010; **Med School:** Thomas Jefferson Univ 1991; **Resid:** Surgery, Pennsylvania Hosp-UPHS 1996; Plastic Surgery, NYU Langone Med Ctr 1998; **Fellow:** Craniofacial Surgery, UCLA Ronald Reagan Med Ctr 1999; **Fac Appt:** Prof PlS, UCLA-David Geffen Sch Med

Cohen, Steven Roy MD [PlS] - **Spec Exp:** Craniofacial Surgery-Pediatric; Craniofacial Surgery/Reconstruction; Cosmetic Surgery-Face; Rhinoplasty; **Hospital:** Rady Children's Hosp - San Diego, UCSD Med Ctr; **Address:** 4510 Executive Drive, Ste 200, San Diego, CA 92121; **Phone:** 858-453-7224; **Board Cert:** Plastic Surgery 1992; **Med School:** Geo Wash Univ 1980; **Resid:** Surgery, Dartmouth-Hitchcock Med Ctr 1987; Plastic Surgery, Hosp Univ Penn - UPHS 1989; **Fellow:** Craniofacial Surgery, UCLA Ronald Reagan Med Ctr 1990; **Fac Appt:** Clin Prof PlS, UCSD

Da Lio, Andrew L MD [PlS] - **Spec Exp:** Cosmetic Surgery-Face; Cosmetic Surgery-Breast; Breast Reconstruction; Liposuction & Body Contouring; **Hospital:** UCLA Ronald Reagan Med Ctr; **Address:** UCLA, Plastic & Reconstructive Surgery, 200 UCLA Med Plaza, Ste 465, Los Angeles, CA 90095; **Phone:** 310-206-7521; **Board Cert:** Plastic Surgery 2010; **Med School:** Univ Mich Med Sch 1989; **Resid:** Surgery, Dartmouth-Hitchcock Med Ctr 1994; Plastic Surgery, LAC & USC Med Ctr 1996; **Fellow:** Microsurgery, UCLA Med Ctr 1997; **Fac Appt:** Clin Prof PlS, UCLA-David Geffen Sch Med

Daniel, Rollin K MD [PlS] - **Spec Exp:** Rhinoplasty; **Hospital:** Hoag Meml Hosp Presby; **Address:** 1441 Avocado Ave, Ste 308, Newport Beach, CA 92660; **Phone:** 949-721-0494; **Board Cert:** Plastic Surgery 1977; **Med School:** Columbia P&S 1972; **Resid:** Plastic Surgery, McGill Univ Affil Hosps 1975; Hand Surgery, Univ Louisville Hosp 1976; **Fellow:** Craniofacial Surgery, Univ Toronto Affil Hosp 1984; **Fac Appt:** Clin Prof PlS, UC Irvine

Edwards, Michael C MD [PlS] - **Spec Exp:** Breast Cosmetic & Reconstructive Surgery; Liposuction & Body Contouring; Body Contouring after Weight Loss; **Hospital:** Summerlin Hosp Med Ctr; **Address:** 653 N Town Center Drive, Ste 214, Las Vegas, NV 89144; **Phone:** 702-248-8989; **Board Cert:** Surgery 2006; Plastic Surgery 2008; **Med School:** Uniformed Srvs Univ, Bethesda 1988; **Resid:** Surgery, David Grant Med Ctr 1993; **Fellow:** Plastic Surgery, Wilford Hall Med Ctr 1996

Evans, Gregory R MD [PlS] - **Spec Exp:** Cosmetic Surgery-Face; Cosmetic Surgery-Breast; Liposuction & Body Contouring; Breast Reconstruction; **Hospital:** UC Irvine Med Ctr; **Address:** Aesthetic & Plastic Surgery Inst, 200 S Manchester Ave, Ste 650, Orange, CA 92868; **Phone:** 714-456-3077; **Board Cert:** Surgery 2012; Plastic Surgery 2008; **Med School:** USC Sch Med 1985; **Resid:** Surgery, LAC & USC Med Ctr 1990; Plastic Surgery, Johns Hopkins Hosp 1993; **Fac Appt:** Prof S, UC Irvine

Fisher, Garth MD [PlS] - **Spec Exp:** Cosmetic Surgery-Face; Cosmetic Surgery-Breast; Rhinoplasty; Body Contouring; **Address:** 120 S Spalding Drive, Ste 222, Beverly Hills, CA 90212; **Phone:** 310-273-5995; **Board Cert:** Plastic Surgery 1993; **Med School:** Univ Miss 1984; **Resid:** Surgery, UC Irvine Med Ctr 1989; Plastic Surgery, UC Irvine Med Ctr 1991

Fodor, Peter B MD [PlS] - **Spec Exp:** Facial Rejuvenation; Liposuction & Body Contouring; Cosmetic Surgery-Breast; **Hospital:** Olympia Med Ctr; **Address:** 2080 Century Park E, Ste 710, Los Angeles, CA 90067; **Phone:** 310-402-0322; **Board Cert:** Plastic Surgery 1977; **Med School:** Univ Wisc 1966; **Resid:** Surgery, NY-Presby/Columbia Univ Med Ctr 1968; Plastic Surgery, St. Luke's - Roosevelt Hosp Ctr - St Luke's Hosp 1976; **Fac Appt:** Assoc Clin Prof S, UCLA

Garner, Warren L MD [PlS] - **Spec Exp:** Burns-Reconstructive Plastic Surgery; Wound Healing/Care; Skin Healing; **Hospital:** LAC & USC Med Ctr, Keck Med Ctr of USC; **Address:** 1510 San Pablo St, Ste 415, Los Angeles, CA 90033; **Phone:** 323-442-7920; **Board Cert:** Plastic Surgery 2008; Surgical Critical Care 2010; **Med School:** Univ Kansas 1978; **Resid:** Surgery, Ohio State Univ Hosp 1985; Plastic Surgery, Washington Univ Phys 1989; **Fellow:** Critical Care Medicine, Ohio State Univ Hosp 1986; **Fac Appt:** Assoc Prof PlS, USC Sch Med

Gruss, Joseph MD [PlS] - **Spec Exp:** Maxillofacial & Craniofacial Surgery; Facial Trauma/Fractures; Cleft Palate/Lip; Pediatric Plastic Surgery; **Hospital:** Seattle Chldns Hosp, Harborview Med Ctr; **Address:** Seattle Children's, 4800 Sand Point Way NE, MS W7847, Seattle, WA 98105; **Phone:** 206-987-2759; **Board Cert:** Plastic Surgery 1977; **Med School:** South Africa 1969; **Resid:** Plastic Surgery, Toronto Western Hosp 1976; Plastic Surgery, Hosp for Sick Children 1976; **Fellow:** Surgical Oncology, Princess Margaret Hosp 1977; Head and Neck Surgery, Princess Margaret Hosp 1977; **Fac Appt:** Prof PlS, Univ Wash

Hansen, Juliana MD [PlS] - **Spec Exp:** Breast Reconstruction; Cancer Reconstruction; **Hospital:** OR Hlth & Sci Univ; **Address:** 3303 SW Bond Ave, MC CH5P, Portland, OR 97239; **Phone:** 503-494-6687; **Board Cert:** Plastic Surgery 2008; **Med School:** Univ Wash 1988; **Resid:** Surgery, UCSF Med Ctr 1994; Plastic Surgery, UCSF Med Ctr 1996; **Fac Appt:** Assoc Prof S, Oregon Hlth & Sci Univ

Hardesty, Robert A MD [PlS] - **Spec Exp:** Cosmetic Surgery-Face & Body; Laser Surgery; Body Contouring; Cosmetic Surgery-Breast; **Hospital:** Riverside Comm Hosp, Redlands Comm Hosp; **Address:** Imagine Plastic Surgery, 4646 Brockton Ave, Ste 302, Riverside, CA 92506; **Phone:** 951-686-7600; **Board Cert:** Plastic Surgery 1989; **Med School:** Loma Linda Univ 1978; **Resid:** Surgery, Loma Linda Univ Med Ctr 1983; Plastic Surgery, Univ Pittsburgh Med Ctr 1986; **Fellow:** Pediatric Plastic Surgery, Washington Univ-Chldns Hosp 1987; **Fac Appt:** Clin Prof PlS, Loma Linda Univ

Hoffman, William Y MD [PlS] - **Spec Exp:** Pediatric Plastic Surgery; Cleft Palate/Lip; Craniofacial Surgery; Reconstructive Surgery; **Hospital:** UCSF Med Ctr, UCSF - Mt Zion Med Ctr; **Address:** UCSF Plastic Surgery, 350 Parnassus Ave, Ste 509, Box 0932, San Francisco, CA 94143-0932; **Phone:** 415-353-4287; **Board Cert:** Plastic Surgery 1987; **Med School:** Univ Rochester 1977; **Resid:** Surgery, UCSF Med Ctr 1983; Plastic Surgery, UCSF Med Ctr 1985; **Fellow:** Craniofacial Surgery, NYU Langone Med Ctr 1986; **Fac Appt:** Prof PlS, UCSF

Horowitz, Jed H MD [PlS] - **Spec Exp:** Cosmetic Surgery-Breast; Cosmetic Surgery-Face; Transumbilical Breast Augmentation(TUBA); **Hospital:** Hoag Meml Hosp Presby, Orange Coast Memorial Med Ctr; **Address:** Pacific Ctr for Plastic Surgery, 7677 Center Ave, Ste 401, Huntington Beach, CA 92647-3098; **Phone:** 714-902-1100; **Board Cert:** Plastic Surgery 1986; **Med School:** SUNY Buffalo 1977; **Resid:** Surgery, Grady Hlth Sys 1983; **Fellow:** Plastic Surgery, Univ VA Sch Med Affil Hosp 1985; **Fac Appt:** Asst Clin Prof PlS, USC Sch Med

Isik, F. Frank MD [PlS] - **Spec Exp:** Cosmetic Surgery; Breast Reconstruction; Cosmetic Surgery-Breast; Cosmetic Surgery-Face; **Hospital:** Swedish Med Ctr-First Hill-Seattle; **Address:** The Polyclinic, 1145 Broadway, Ste 1T, Seattle, WA 98122; **Phone:** 206-860-4566; **Board Cert:** Plastic Surgery 2007; **Med School:** Mount Sinai Sch Med 1985; **Resid:** Surgery, Boston Univ Hosps 1990; Plastic Surgery, Univ Wash Affil Hosp 1995; **Fellow:** Research, NIH / Univ Washington 1992

Jewell, Mark L MD [PlS] - **Spec Exp:** Liposuction & Body Contouring; Cosmetic Surgery-Face; Breast Reconstruction; Cosmetic Surgery-Breast; **Hospital:** McKenzie-Willamette Med Ctr; **Address:** 10 Coburg Rd, Ste 300, Eugene, OR 97401; **Phone:** 541-683-3234; **Board Cert:** Plastic Surgery 1981; **Med School:** Univ Kansas 1973; **Resid:** Surgery, LAC-Harbor Med Ctr 1976; Plastic Surgery, Erlanger Hosp 1979; **Fellow:** Burn Surgery, LAC-USC Med Ctr 1977; **Fac Appt:** Asst Clin Prof PlS, Oregon Hlth & Sci Univ

Koplin, Lawrence M MD [PlS] - **Spec Exp:** Cosmetic Surgery-Face; Breast Cosmetic & Reconstructive Surgery; Facial Rejuvenation; Liposuction & Body Contouring; **Hospital:** Cedars-Sinai Med Ctr; **Address:** 465 N Roxbury Drive, Ste 800, Beverly Hills, CA 90210; **Phone:** 310-277-3223; **Board Cert:** Plastic Surgery 1985; **Med School:** Baylor Coll Med 1976; **Resid:** Surgery, Kaiser Fdn Hosp 1981; Plastic Surgery, St Joseph Hosp 1983

Leaf, Norman MD [PlS] - **Spec Exp:** Cosmetic Surgery-Face & Neck; Cosmetic Surgery-Breast; Eyelid Surgery/Blepharoplasty; **Hospital:** Cedars-Sinai Med Ctr, UCLA Ronald Reagan Med Ctr; **Address:** 436 N Bedford Drive, Ste 104, Beverly Hills, CA 90210-4310; **Phone:** 310-274-8001; **Board Cert:** Surgery 1973; Plastic Surgery 1974; **Med School:** Univ Chicago-Pritzker Sch Med 1966; **Resid:** Surgery, Univ Chicago Hosps 1972; Plastic Surgery, Univ Chicago Hosps 1973; **Fellow:** Research, Univ Chicago Hosps 1969; **Fac Appt:** Assoc Clin Prof PlS, UCLA

Lesavoy, Malcolm A MD [PlS] - **Spec Exp:** Cosmetic Surgery-Face & Neck; Cosmetic Surgery-Breast; Abdominoplasty; Reconstructive Surgery; **Hospital:** UCLA Ronald Reagan Med Ctr; **Address:** 16311 Ventura Blvd, Ste 555, Encino, CA 91436-4314; **Phone:** 818-986-8270; **Board Cert:** Plastic Surgery 1977; **Med School:** Ros Franklin Univ/Chicago Med Sch 1969; **Resid:** Surgery, Univ Chicago Affil Hosps 1974; Plastic Surgery, Univ Miami Hosp & Clins 1976; **Fac Appt:** Prof Emeritus PlS, UCLA

Markowitz, Bernard L MD [PlS] - **Spec Exp:** Cosmetic Surgery-Face & Body; Abdominoplasty; Facial Rejuvenation; Craniofacial Surgery/Reconstruction; **Hospital:** UCLA Ronald Reagan Med Ctr, Cedars-Sinai Med Ctr; **Address:** 9675 Brighton Way, Ste 350, Beverly Hills, CA 90210; **Phone:** 310-205-5557; **Board Cert:** Plastic Surgery 1989; **Med School:** NYU Sch Med 1979; **Resid:** Surgery, NYU Langone Med Ctr 1984; Plastic Surgery, NYU Langone Med Ctr 1986; **Fellow:** Maxillofacial Surgery, Johns Hopkins Hosp 1987; Microvascular Surgery, Johns Hopkins Hosp 1987; **Fac Appt:** Clin Prof PlS, UCLA

Marten, Timothy J MD [PlS] - **Spec Exp:** Cosmetic Surgery-Face & Neck; Facial Rejuvenation; **Hospital:** CA Pacific Med Ctr-Pacific Campus, St. Mary's Med Ctr - San Fran; **Address:** 450 Sutter St, Ste 2222, San Francisco, CA 94108-4207; **Phone:** 415-677-9937; **Board Cert:** Plastic Surgery 1993; **Med School:** UC Davis 1982; **Resid:** Surgery, Kaiser Fdn Hosp 1987; Plastic Surgery, Univ IL Coll Med Affil Hosp 1989; **Fellow:** Cosmetic Plastic Surgery, UC Irvine Med Ctr 1991

Miller, Timothy A MD [PlS] - **Spec Exp:** Cosmetic Surgery-Face; Eyelid Surgery; Nasal Reconstruction; Burns-Reconstructive Plastic Surgery; **Hospital:** UCLA Ronald Reagan Med Ctr; **Address:** 200 UCLA Med Plaza, Ste 465, Los Angeles, CA 90095-8344; **Phone:** 310-825-5644; **Board Cert:** Surgery 1971; Plastic Surgery 1973; **Med School:** UCLA 1963; **Resid:** Surgery, UCLA Ronald Reagan Med Ctr 1969; **Fellow:** Plastic Surgery, UPMC 1971; **Fac Appt:** Prof S, UCLA

Nichter, Larry S MD [PlS] - **Spec Exp:** Cosmetic Surgery-Face & Body; Cosmetic Surgery-Breast; Liposuction & Body Contouring; Congenital Breast Anomalies; **Hospital:** Hoag Meml Hosp Presby, Orange Coast Memorial Med Ctr; **Address:** Pacific Ctr for Plastic Surgery, 3991 MacArthur Blvd, Ste 320, Newport Beach, CA 92660; **Phone:** 949-720-3888; **Board Cert:** Plastic Surgery 1986; **Med School:** Boston Univ 1978; **Resid:** Surgery, UCLA Ronald Reagan Med Ctr 1982; Plastic Surgery, Univ Virginia Sch Med Affil Hosp 1985; **Fellow:** Hand & Microvascular Surgery, Univ Virginia Sch Med Affil Hosp 1983; **Fac Appt:** Clin Prof PlS, USC-Keck School of Medicine

Ousterhout, Douglas K MD/DDS [PlS] - **Spec Exp:** Cosmetic Surgery-Face; Gender Reassignment Surgery; Craniofacial Surgery; Facial Feminization Surgery (FFS); **Hospital:** CA Pacific Med Ctr - Davies Campus; **Address:** 45 Castro St, Ste 150, San Francisco, CA 94114; **Phone:** 415-626-2888; **Board Cert:** Plastic Surgery 1974; **Med School:** Univ Mich Med Sch 1965; **Resid:** Surgery, Univ Mich Med Sch Affil Hosp 1969; Plastic Surgery, Stanford Univ Hosp & Clins 1972; **Fellow:** Craniofacial Surgery, Clin Belvedere 1973; **Fac Appt:** Clin Prof PlS, UCSF

Paul, Malcolm D MD [PlS] - **Spec Exp:** Cosmetic Surgery-Face & Neck; Cosmetic Surgery-Breast; Liposuction & Body Contouring; **Hospital:** Hoag Meml Hosp Presby; **Address:** 1401 Avocado Ave, Ste 610, Newport Beach, CA 92660-8708; **Phone:** 949-760-5047; **Board Cert:** Plastic Surgery 1976; **Med School:** Univ MD Sch Med 1969; **Resid:** Surgery, G Washington Univ Hosp 1973; Plastic Surgery, G Washington Univ Hosp 1975; **Fac Appt:** Clin Prof S, UC Irvine

Rand, Richard P MD [PlS] - **Spec Exp:** Cosmetic Surgery-Face; Cosmetic Surgery-Breast; Liposuction & Body Contouring; Facial Rejuvenation; **Hospital:** Overlake Hosp Med Ctr; **Address:** 1135 116th Ave NE, Ste 630, Bellevue, WA 98004; **Phone:** 425-688-8828; **Board Cert:** Plastic Surgery 1991; **Med School:** Univ Mich Med Sch 1981; **Resid:** Surgery, Tufts-New England Med Ctr 1986; Plastic Surgery, Emory Univ Hosp 1989; **Fellow:** Craniofacial Surgery, Univ Miami Hosp 1989; **Fac Appt:** Assoc Prof S, Univ Wash

Reinisch, John F MD [PlS] - **Spec Exp:** Birthmarks/Hemangiomas; Ear Reconstruction/Microtia; Pediatric Plastic Surgery; **Hospital:** Cedars-Sinai Med Ctr; **Address:** 250 N Robertson Blvd, Ste 506, Beverly Hills, CA 90211; **Phone:** 310-385-6090; **Board Cert:** Plastic Surgery 1980; **Med School:** Harvard Med Sch 1970; **Resid:** Surgery, Univ Michigan Med Ctr 1975; Plastic Surgery, Univ VA Sch Med Affil Hosp 1978; **Fac Appt:** Prof S, USC Sch Med

Romano, James John MD [PlS] - **Spec Exp:** Body Contouring; Cosmetic Surgery-Breast; Tuberous Breasts; Facial Rejuvenation; **Hospital:** CA Pacific Med Ctr - CA Campus, Seton Med Ctr; **Address:** 1650 Jackson St, Ste 101, San Francisco, CA 94109; **Phone:** 415-981-3911; **Board Cert:** Plastic Surgery 1990; **Med School:** Eastern VA Med Sch 1980; **Resid:** Surgery, Georgetown Univ Hosp 1985; Plastic Surgery, Johns Hopkins Hosp 1988; **Fac Appt:** Asst Prof PlS, USC Sch Med

Rosenberg, Howard L MD [PlS] - **Spec Exp:** Cosmetic Surgery-Face; Cosmetic Surgery-Breast; Liposuction & Body Contouring; Facial Rejuvenation; **Hospital:** El Camino Hosp; **Address:** Accent on Aesthetics, 2204 Grant Rd, Ste 201, Mountain View, CA 94040; **Phone:** 650-961-2652; **Board Cert:** Surgery 1975; Plastic Surgery 1977; **Med School:** Johns Hopkins Univ 1969; **Resid:** Surgery, UCLA Ronald Reagan Med Ctr 1974; Plastic Surgery, Stanford Univ Hosp & Clins 1976; **Fac Appt:** Asst Clin Prof PlS, Stanford Univ

Sanders III, George H MD [PlS] - **Spec Exp:** Eyelid Surgery; Liposuction; **Address:** 16633 Ventura Blvd, Ste 110, Encino, CA 91436-1834; **Phone:** 818-981-3333; **Board Cert:** Plastic Surgery 1986; **Med School:** Harvard Med Sch 1978; **Resid:** Surgery, UCLA Ronald Reagan Med Ctr 1980; Surgery, Cedars-Sinai Med Ctr 1983; **Fellow:** Plastic Surgery, UCLA Ronald Reagan Med Ctr 1985

Sherman, Randolph MD [PlS] - **Spec Exp:** Facial Paralysis; Breast Reconstruction; Limb Surgery/Reconstruction; **Hospital:** Cedars-Sinai Med Ctr; **Address:** 8635 W 3rd St, Ste 770-W, Los Angeles, CA 90048; **Phone:** 310-423-2129; **Board Cert:** Surgery 2004; Plastic Surgery 1986; **Med School:** Univ MO-Columbia Sch Med 1977; **Resid:** Surgery, UCSF Hosps 1981; Surgery, State Univ of New York 1983; **Fellow:** Plastic Surgery, USC Med Ctr 1985

Singer, Robert MD [PlS] - **Spec Exp:** Cosmetic Surgery-Face; Facial Rejuvenation; Liposuction & Body Contouring; Breast Surgery; **Hospital:** Scripps Meml Hosp - La Jolla; **Address:** 9834 Genesee Ave, Ste 100, La Jolla, CA 92037-1214; **Phone:** 858-455-0290; **Board Cert:** Plastic Surgery 1977; **Med School:** SUNY Buffalo 1967; **Resid:** Surgery, Stanford Univ Hosp & Clins 1969; Plastic Surgery, Vanderbilt Univ Med Ctr 1976; **Fellow:** Neurological Surgery, Rigs Hosp-Kommunes Hosp 1976; **Fac Appt:** Clin Prof PS, UCSD

Stevens, W. Grant MD [PlS] - **Spec Exp:** Cosmetic Surgery-Breast; Liposuction & Body Contouring; Cosmetic Surgery-Face; **Hospital:** Marina Del Rey Hosp; **Address:** Marina Plastic Surgery Assocs, 4644 Lincoln Blvd, Ste 552, Marina Del Rey, CA 90292-6391; **Phone:** 310-827-2653; **Board Cert:** Plastic Surgery 1989; **Med School:** Washington Univ, St Louis 1980; **Resid:** Surgery, LAC - Harbor - UCLA Med Ctr 1983; **Fellow:** Hand Surgery, Washington Univ Phys 1984; Plastic Surgery, Washington Univ Phys 1986; **Fac Appt:** Clin Prof PlS, USC Sch Med

Urata, Mark M MD/DDS [PlS] - **Spec Exp:** Craniofacial Surgery-Pediatric; Maxillofacial Surgery; Cosmetic Surgery-Head & Neck; **Hospital:** Chldns Hosp - Los Angeles, Keck Med Ctr of USC; **Address:** Division of Plastic and Reconstructive Surgery, 4650 W Sunset Blvd, MS 96, Los Angeles, CA 90027; **Phone:** 323-361-4544; **Board Cert:** Plastic Surgery 2005; **Med School:** USC-Keck School of Medicine 1996; **Resid:** USC Med Ctr 1993; Plastic Surgery, USC Med Ctr 2002; **Fellow:** Craniofacial Surgery, UCLA Med Ctr 2003; **Fac Appt:** Prof PlS, USC-Keck School of Medicine

Wells, James H MD [PlS] - **Spec Exp:** Cleft Palate/Lip; Breast Surgery; **Hospital:** Long Beach Meml Med Ctr; **Address:** 2880 Atlantic Ave, Ste 290, Long Beach, CA 90806; **Phone:** 562-595-6543; **Board Cert:** Plastic Surgery 2009; **Med School:** Univ Tex Med Br, Galveston 1966; **Resid:** Surgery, Ochsner Med Ctr 1971; Plastic Surgery, Univ Virginia Sch Med Affil Hosp 1975

Cleveland Clinic

Every life deserves world class care.

Plastic Surgery

Cleveland Clinic's Department of Plastic Surgery, part of the Cleveland Clinic Dermatology & Plastic Surgery Institute, offers a full array of subspecialized care for adult and pediatric patients. The department includes a team of surgeons extremely adept at handling all types of traumatic, congenital and work-related hand, peripheral nerve and upper extremity problems. Pediatric surgery and craniofacial surgery are strong specialties in the department. Among the department's major advancements is the successful completion of the first near-total face transplant in the United States. This achievement has progressed into our Reconstructive Transplant Center, which provides an alternative for patients seeking new avenues in reconstruction of difficult facial, abdominal, laryngeal and hand deformities and dysfunction.

Cleveland Clinic plastic surgeons offer numerous methods of breast reconstruction that can be performed either at the time of mastectomy or as a secondary procedure. These techniques include breast implants and expanders; pedicled transverse rectus abdominis myocutaneous flaps (using abdominal skin and muscle); and free-tissue transfers such as deep inferior epigastric perforator (or DIEP) flap.

The Department of Plastic Surgery focuses on minimally invasive techniques in facial cosmetic surgery. This includes alternatives to facelift and neck lift surgery, short-scar facelifts and minimally invasive facelift techniques. In addition to standard body contouring procedures including abdominoplasty and a wide variety of liposuction techniques, the department is particularly interested in plastic surgery after significant weight loss.

NY Eye & Ear Infirmary

THE NEW YORK EYE AND EAR INFIRMARY

310 East 14th Street
New York, New York 10003
Tel. 212.979.4000 Fax. 212.228.0664
http://www.nyee.edu

PROVIDING EXCEPTIONAL CARE

The Department of Plastic & Reconstructive Surgery is one of the region's most comprehensive centers for surgery which restores the body and spirit. More than 1,500 procedures a year are performed here, and 50 of the most noted board-certified plastic surgeons located throughout New York City and tri-state area comprise the attending medical staff.

IN A HIGHLY SPECIALIZED SETTING

As a specialty hospital, the Infirmary is uniquely qualified to handle the most complicated cases. It serves as a nationwide referral center with a commitment to teaching, research, and high-technology based patient care. Highly experienced staff using state-of-the-art instrumentation have made the Infirmary's 19 operating rooms a national benchmark in efficiency. In addition, private premium patient accommodations are available to assure that the hospital experience is as comfortable and convenient as possible.

FOR PATIENTS OF ALL AGES

The Department treats more than 1,500 patients a year who seek reconstructive surgery of the body as well as facial area as a result of accident, birth defect or cancer, and those who elect cosmetic surgery. It is one of the few hospitals in the region to perform breast reconstruction after mastectomy with microvascular surgery to harvest tissue from patients' lower body to create living, natural, and normal looking breasts, often preferred to artificial implants. State-of-the-art lymph node transfer to cure post-mastectomy lymphedema is also available.

Childhood problems, such as cleft lip and palate and ear deformities also fall under the care of our surgeons.

Innovative cosmetic surgery procedures such as endoscopic and other minimally invasive operations are offered. The Center for Nasal Plastic specializes in closed (no scar) nasal plastic techniques as well as repair of previous nasal surgeries, the secondary nasal plasty. Liposuction using the latest instrumentation and fat grafting by the latest technology is also available as are the latest variants of the abdominoplasty (tummy tuck) operation.

The latest version of a skin tightening Fraxel Re:pair laser enables many patients to avoid a surgical face and eyelid plastic operation.

The hospital has a Post Graduate Cosmetic Surgery Program which offers a year of intensive cosmetic surgery training to surgeons who have completed a formal plastic surgery residency. The program is the largest and most sought-after in the US and also provides a source for affordable cosmetic surgery for the community.

Plastic Surgery Clinical Services

Facial plasty

Eyelid plastic operations

Nasal plastic operations

Breast augmentation
Breast reduction procedures and suspension

Breast reconstruction using patient's own tissue (DIEP, S-GAP, I-GAP and SIEA flap procedures)

Liposuction

Abdominoplasty

Facial resurfacing and dermabrasion

Fraxel laser

Botox

About The New York Eye and Ear Infirmary

Founded in 1820, it is the nation's oldest, continuously operating specialty hospital. Throughout its history, The New York Eye and Ear Infirmary has led clinical advances and research in vision, hearing, speech and restoration of the physical appearance.

Physician Referral
1.800.449.HOPE (4673)

Preventive & Occupational Medicine

A preventive medicine specialist focuses on the health of individuals and defined populations in order to protect, promote and maintain health and well-being, and to prevent disease, disability and premature death. A preventive medicine physician may be a specialist in general preventive medicine, public health, occupational medicine, or aerospace medicine. This specialist works with large population groups as well as with individual patients to promote health and understand the risks of disease, injury, disability, and death, seeking to modify and eliminate these risks.

Training Required: Three years

Occupational Medicine

Mid Atlantic

Gochfeld, Michael MD/PhD [OM] - **Spec Exp:** Environmental Medicine; Mercury Toxic Exposure; Chemical Exposure; **Hospital:** Robert Wood Johnson Univ Hosp - New Brunswick; **Address:** EOHSI Clin Ctr, 170 Frelinghuysen Rd, Ste 200, Piscataway, NJ 08854; **Phone:** 848-445-0123; **Board Cert:** Occupational Medicine 1983; **Med School:** Albert Einstein Coll Med 1965; **Resid:** Behavioral Medicine, Rockefeller Univ Affil Hosp 1977; **Fac Appt:** Prof OM, UMDNJ-RW Johnson Med Sch

Kipen, Howard M MD [OM] - **Spec Exp:** Environmental Medicine; Occupational Lung Disease; **Hospital:** Robert Wood Johnson Univ Hosp - New Brunswick; **Address:** EOHSI Clin Ctr, 170 Frelinghuysen Rd, Ste 200, Piscataway, NJ 08854; **Phone:** 848-445-0123; **Board Cert:** Internal Medicine 1982; Occupational Medicine 1986; **Med School:** UCSF 1979; **Resid:** Internal Medicine, Columbia Presby Med Ctr 1982; Occupational Medicine, Mt Sinai Hosp 1984; **Fac Appt:** Prof Med, UMDNJ-RW Johnson Med Sch

Landrigan, Philip MD [OM] - **Spec Exp:** Environmental Health in Children; **Hospital:** Mt Sinai Med Ctr (page 62); **Address:** Dept Preventive Med, One Gustave L Levy Pl, Box 1057, New York, NY 10029-6500; **Phone:** 212-824-7018; **Board Cert:** Pediatrics 1973; Public Health & Genl Preventive Med 1979; Occupational Medicine 1983; **Med School:** Harvard Med Sch 1967; **Resid:** Internal Medicine, Metro Genl Hosp 1968; Pediatrics, Chldns Hosp 1970; **Fellow:** Epidemiology, Ctrs for Disease Control 1973; Occupational Medicine, Univ London 1977; **Fac Appt:** Prof Ped, Mount Sinai Sch Med

Southwest

Harber, Philip I MD [OM] - **Spec Exp:** Occupational Lung Disease; Occupational Asthma; Beryllium-induced Lung Disease; Asbestos-related Lung Disease; **Address:** College of Public Health, Univ Arizona, Community, Environment & Policy Div, 1656 E Mabel St, MRB rm 112, Tucson, AZ 85724; **Phone:** 310-433-5342; **Board Cert:** Internal Medicine 1979; Pulmonary Disease 1980; Occupational Medicine 1982; **Med School:** Univ Pennsylvania 1972; **Resid:** Internal Medicine, Georgetown Univ Med Ctr 1978; Occupational Medicine, Johns Hopkins Hosp 1980; **Fellow:** Pulmonary Disease, Johns Hopkins Hosp 1980; **Fac Appt:** Prof PrM, Univ Ariz Coll Med

Preventive Medicine

Mid Atlantic

Cahill, John MD [PrM] - **Spec Exp:** Tropical Diseases; Travel Medicine; Parasitic Infections; International Health; **Hospital:** St. Luke's - Roosevelt Hosp Ctr - Roosevelt Div (page 56); **Address:** Univ Med Practice Assocs, 36 W 60th St, New York, NY 10023; **Phone:** 212-523-8672; **Board Cert:** Emergency Medicine 2011; **Med School:** Mount Sinai Sch Med 1996; **Resid:** Emergency Medicine, Rhode Island Hosp 1997; Emergency Medicine, Rhode Island Hosp 2000; **Fellow:** Tropical Medicine, Royal Coll Surgeons 1998; **Fac Appt:** Asst Clin Prof Med, Columbia P&S

Hoffman, Robert S MD [PrM] - **Spec Exp:** Poison Control; Disaster Preparedness; **Hospital:** NYU Langone Med Ctr (page 68), Bellevue Hosp Ctr; **Address:** NY Poison Control Ctr, 455 1st Ave, rm 123, New York, NY 10016; **Phone:** 212-340-4494; **Board Cert:** Internal Medicine 1987; Emergency Medicine 2005; Medical Toxicology 2008; **Med School:** NYU Sch Med 1984; **Resid:** Internal Medicine, NYU Med Ctr 1987; **Fellow:** Medical Toxicology, NYU Med Ctr 1989; **Fac Appt:** Prof EM, NYU Sch Med

Southeast

Pearson, Thomas A MD/PhD [PrM] - **Spec Exp:** Preventive Cardiology; Cholesterol/Lipid Disorders; **Hospital:** Largo Med Ctr; **Address:** Diagnostic Clinic Med Grp, 1301 2nd Ave SW, Largo, FL 33770; **Phone:** 727-584-7706; **Board Cert:** Internal Medicine 1983; Public Health & Genl Preventive Med 1986; **Med School:** Johns Hopkins Univ 1976; **Resid:** Anatomic & Clinical Pathology, Johns Hopkins Hosp 1979; Internal Medicine, Johns Hopkins Hosp 1981; **Fellow:** Pulmonary Disease, Johns Hopkins Hosp 1983

Mount Sinai

THE MOUNT SINAI MEDICAL CENTER
Preventive Medicine

One Gustave L. Levy Place
Fifth Avenue and 100th Street
New York, NY 10029-6574

Physician Referral: 1-800-MD-SINAI (637-4624)
www.mountsinai.org

Mount Sinai's **DEPARTMENT OF PREVENTIVE MEDICINE** is internationally renowned for excellence in preventive medicine, occupational medicine, and environmental health, community health, and environmental pediatrics. The department is among the largest medical school departments of its kind in the United States. Our mission is to prevent disease, protect the environment, and promote health throughout the communities we serve.

Interdisciplinary research

The Department of Preventive Medicine undertakes interdisciplinary research in:

- Preventive medicine
- Public health
- Epidemiology
- Environmental and occupational medicine
- Social sciences

The department has 7 divisions:

- Behavioral Science and Social Work
- Biostatistics and Data Management
- Environmental Health
- Epidemiology
- International Health
- Occupational Medicine
- Mount Sinai Selikoff Centers for Occupational Health
- Preventive Medicine Residency

Under the direction of Chairman Philip J. Landrigan, MD, the department has strengthened its research base, training programs, and clinical services in environmental, occupational, and preventive medicine, by:

- Being the principal architect of New York's statewide network of Clinical Centers of Excellence in Occupational Medicine – the nation's only state-based network of occupational health clinics.
- Overseeing the creation of the Mount Sinai Irving J. Selikoff Centers for Occupational Health, providing the services of specialized physicians and other health and social service professionals to workers, labor and community organizations, employers and agencies.
- Guiding the development of Mount Sinai's World Trade Center Health Program, established to care for the men and women who responded to the 9/11 attacks and continuing to treat mental and health conditions related to their WTC service.
- Leading development of the Mount Sinai Children's Environmental Health Center to protect children from environmental threats through research, education, and clinical care.

Top Doctors Make A Difference

Psychiatry

A psychiatrist specializes in the prevention, diagnosis and treatment of mental, addictive and emotional disorders such as schizophrenia and other psychotic disorders, mood disorders, anxiety disorders, substance-related disorders, sexual and gender identity disorders and adjustment disorders. The psychiatrist is able to understand the biologic, psychologic and social components of illness, and therefore is uniquely prepared to treat the whole person. A psychiatrist is qualified to order diagnostic laboratory tests and to prescribe medications, evaluate and treat psychologic and interpersonal problems and to intervene with families who are coping with stress, crises and other problems in living.

Training Required: Four years

Certification in one of the following subspecialties requires additional training and examination.

Addiction Psychiatry: A psychiatrist who focuses on the evaluation and treatment of individuals with alcohol, drug, or other substance-related disorders and of individuals with the dual diagnosis of substance-related and other psychiatric disorders.

Child and Adolescent Psychiatry: A psychiatrist with additional training in the diagnosis and treatment of developmental, behavioral, emotional and mental disorders of childhood and adolescence.

Geriatric Psychiatry: A psychiatrist with expertise in the prevention, evaluation, diagnosis and treatment of mental and emotional disorders in the elderly. The geriatric psychiatrist seeks to improve the psychiatric care of the elderly both in health and in disease.

Psychiatry

New England

Adler, David A MD [Psyc] - **Spec Exp:** Depression; Personality Disorders; Schizophrenia; **Hospital:** Tufts Med Ctr; **Address:** Tufts Med Ctr, Dept Psyc, 800 Washington St, Ste 1007, Boston, MA 02111; **Phone:** 617-636-8755; **Board Cert:** Psychiatry 1977; **Med School:** Yale Univ 1973; **Resid:** Psychiatry, Mass Mental Hlth Ctr 1976; **Fac Appt:** Prof Psyc, Tufts Univ

Alpert, Jonathan E MD/PhD [Psyc] - **Spec Exp:** Depression; Psychopharmacology; **Hospital:** Mass Genl Hosp; **Address:** Mass Genl Hosp, Dept Psychiatry, 15 Parkman St, Boston, MA 02114; **Phone:** 617-726-5948; **Board Cert:** Psychiatry 1993; **Med School:** Yale Univ 1986; **Resid:** Pediatrics, Chldn's Hosp 1989; Psychiatry, McLean Hosp 1992; **Fac Appt:** Assoc Prof Psyc, Harvard Med Sch

Ellison, James M MD [Psyc] - **Spec Exp:** Geriatric Psychiatry; **Hospital:** McLean Hosp; **Address:** McLean Hospital, 115 Mill St, Belmont, MA 02478; **Phone:** 617-855-2532; **Board Cert:** Psychiatry 1984; Geriatric Psychiatry 2007; **Med School:** UCSF 1978; **Resid:** Psychiatry, Mass Genl Hosp 1982; **Fac Appt:** Assoc Prof Psyc, Harvard Med Sch

Friedman, Matthew J MD/PhD [Psyc] - **Spec Exp:** Post Traumatic Stress Disorder; Psychopharmacology; Anxiety & Mood Disorders; **Hospital:** White River Junction VA Med Ctr, Dartmouth - Hitchcock Med Ctr; **Address:** National Ctr for PTSD, VA Med Ctr, 215 N Main St, White River Junction, VT 05009; **Phone:** 802-296-5132; **Board Cert:** Psychiatry 1976; **Med School:** Univ KY Coll Med 1976; **Resid:** Psychiatry, Mass Genl Hosp 1972; Psychiatry, Dartmouth Hitchcock Med Ctr 1973; **Fac Appt:** Prof Psyc, Dartmouth Med Sch

Goldberg, Joseph F MD [Psyc] - **Spec Exp:** Bipolar/Mood Disorders; Psychopharmacology; Anxiety & Depression; Cognitive Psychotherapy; **Hospital:** Mt Sinai Med Ctr (page 62); **Address:** 128 East Avenue, Norwalk, CT 06851; **Phone:** 203-854-9607; **Board Cert:** Psychiatry 2009; **Med School:** Northwestern Univ 1992; **Resid:** Psychiatry, Payne Whitney Clinic 1995; **Fellow:** Psychopharmacology, Payne Whitney Clinic 1998; **Fac Appt:** Clin Prof Psyc, Mount Sinai Sch Med

Greenberg, Benjamin D MD/PhD [Psyc] - **Spec Exp:** Obsessive-Compulsive Disorder; **Hospital:** Butler Hosp; **Address:** 345 Blackstone Blvd, Providence, RI 02906; **Phone:** 401-455-6602; **Board Cert:** Psychiatry 1994; **Med School:** Univ Miami Sch Med 1987; **Resid:** Neurology, Columbian Univ/Presbyterian Hosp 1989; Psychiatry, Johns Hopkins Hosp 1992; **Fac Appt:** Assoc Prof Psyc, Brown Univ

Greenberg, Donna B MD [Psyc] - **Spec Exp:** Psychiatry in Cancer; **Hospital:** Mass Genl Hosp; **Address:** Mass Genl Hosp, Psychiatry Assocs, 55 Fruit St Warren Bldg Fl 6, Boston, MA 02114-2696; **Phone:** 617-726-2984; **Board Cert:** Internal Medicine 1978; Psychiatry 1990; **Med School:** Univ Rochester 1975; **Resid:** Internal Medicine, Boston City Hosp 1978; Psychiatry, Mass Genl Hosp 1989; **Fellow:** Psychiatry, Mass Genl Hosp 1979; **Fac Appt:** Assoc Prof Psyc, Harvard Med Sch

Greenberg, William E MD [Psyc] - **Hospital:** Beth Israel Deaconess Med Ctr - Boston; **Address:** Beth Israel Deaconess Med Ctr, Dept Psychiatry, 330 Brookline Ave, Boston, MA 02215; **Phone:** 617-667-4766; **Board Cert:** Psychiatry 1981; **Med School:** Univ Pennsylvania 1976; **Resid:** Psychiatry, Beth Israel Deaconess Med Ctr 1981; **Fac Appt:** Asst Prof Psyc, Harvard Med Sch

Gunderson, John G MD [Psyc] - **Spec Exp:** Personality Disorders, Consults; **Hospital:** McLean Hosp; **Address:** McLean Hospital, 115 Mill St, Belmont, MA 02478; **Phone:** 617-855-2293; **Board Cert:** Psychiatry 1974; **Med School:** Harvard Med Sch 1967; **Resid:** Psychiatry, Mass Mental Hlth Ctr 1971; **Fac Appt:** Prof Psyc, Harvard Med Sch

Henderson, David C MD [Psyc] - **Spec Exp:** Schizophrenia; Psychopharmacology; **Hospital:** Mass Genl Hosp; **Address:** Freedom Trail Clinic, 25 Staniford St Fl 2, Boston, MA 02114; **Phone:** 617-912-7800; **Board Cert:** Psychiatry 2007; **Med School:** Univ Mass Sch Med 1988; **Resid:** Psychiatry, Mass Genl Hosp 1992; **Fac Appt:** Assoc Prof Psyc, Harvard Med Sch

Jenike, Michael A MD [Psyc] - **Spec Exp:** Obsessive-Compulsive Disorder; **Hospital:** Mass Genl Hosp; **Address:** Obsessive Compulsive Disorders Unit, 185 Cambridge St, Ste 2000, Boston, MA 02114; **Phone:** 617-726-6766; **Board Cert:** Psychiatry 1984; **Med School:** Univ Okla Coll Med 1978; **Resid:** Psychiatry, Mass Genl Hosp 1982; **Fellow:** Research, Mass Genl Hosp 1983; **Fac Appt:** Prof Psyc, Harvard Med Sch

Jimerson, David C MD [Psyc] - **Spec Exp:** Eating Disorders; **Hospital:** Beth Israel Deaconess Med Ctr - Boston; **Address:** Beth Israel Deaconess Med Ctr, Dept Psyc, 330 Brookline Ave, Boston, MA 02215-5400; **Phone:** 617-667-4667; **Board Cert:** Psychiatry 1977; **Med School:** Cornell Univ-Weill Med Coll 1972; **Resid:** Psychiatry, UCSD Med Ctr 1974; Psychiatry, Natl Inst Hlth 1975; **Fac Appt:** Prof Psyc, Harvard Med Sch

Joffe, Hadine MD [Psyc] - **Spec Exp:** Women's Health-Mental Health; Menopause Problems; Psychiatry in Pregnancy; **Hospital:** Brigham & Women's Hosp; **Address:** Brigham & Women's Hosp, Dept of Psych, 75 Francis St, Boston, MA 02115; **Phone:** 617-732-6701; **Board Cert:** Psychiatry 2009; **Med School:** Cornell Univ-Weill Med Coll 1994; **Resid:** Psychiatry, Mc Lean Hosp 1998; **Fellow:** Psychiatry, Mass Genl Hosp 1999; **Fac Appt:** Assoc Prof Psyc, Harvard Med Sch

Kafka, Martin P MD [Psyc] - **Spec Exp:** Sexual Addiction; Sexual Behavior-Compulsive; Psychopharmacology; **Hospital:** McLean Hosp; **Address:** New England Forensic Associates, 22 Mill St, Ste 306, Arlington, MA 02476; **Phone:** 781-643-0610 x12; **Board Cert:** Psychiatry 1980; **Med School:** SUNY Downstate 1973; **Resid:** Psychiatry, Univ MI Hosp 1977; **Fac Appt:** Assoc Clin Prof Psyc, Harvard Med Sch

Phillips, Katharine A MD [Psyc] - **Spec Exp:** Body Dysmorphic Disorder (BDD); Obsessive-Compulsive Disorder; **Hospital:** Rhode Island Hosp; **Address:** BDD Program, Coro Center West, 1 Hoppin St, Ste 2.030, Providence, RI 02903; **Phone:** 401-444-1646; **Board Cert:** Psychiatry 1992; **Med School:** Dartmouth Med Sch 1987; **Resid:** Psychiatry, McLean Hosp 1991; **Fellow:** Research, McLean Hosp 1994; **Fac Appt:** Prof Psyc, Brown Univ

Price, Lawrence H MD [Psyc] - **Spec Exp:** Anxiety & Mood Disorders; Depression; Bipolar/Mood Disorders; Obsessive-Compulsive Disorder; **Hospital:** Butler Hosp, Kent Hosp; **Address:** Butler Hospital, Dept Psychiatry, 345 Blackstone Blvd, Providence, RI 02906; **Phone:** 401-455-6533; **Board Cert:** Psychiatry 1983; **Med School:** Univ Mich Med Sch 1978; **Resid:** Psychiatry, Yale-New Haven Hosp 1982; **Fellow:** Psychiatry, Yale-New Haven Hosp 1983; **Fac Appt:** Prof Psyc, Brown Univ

Rasmussen, Steven A MD [Psyc] - **Spec Exp:** Obsessive-Compulsive Disorder; **Hospital:** Butler Hosp; **Address:** Butler Hosp, 345 Blackstone Blvd, Providence, RI 02906; **Phone:** 401-455-6209; **Board Cert:** Psychiatry 1983; **Med School:** Brown Univ 1977; **Resid:** Psychiatry, Yale Univ 1981; **Fac Appt:** Assoc Prof Psyc, Brown Univ

Rauch, Paula K MD [Psyc] - **Spec Exp:** Parent Guidance in Parental Cancer; Psychiatry in Physical Illness; **Hospital:** Mass Genl Hosp; **Address:** Mass General Hosp, Dept Child Psychiatry, 55 Fruit St, Yawkey 6A, Boston, MA 02114; **Phone:** 617-724-3923; **Board Cert:** Psychiatry 1990; Child & Adolescent Psychiatry 1991; **Med School:** Univ Cincinnati 1981; **Resid:** Psychiatry, Mass Genl Hosp 1984; **Fellow:** Child Psychiatry, Cambridge Hosp 1986; **Fac Appt:** Assoc Prof Psyc, Harvard Med Sch

Salzman, Carl MD [Psyc] - **Spec Exp:** Psychopharmacology; Psychotherapy; **Hospital:** MA Mental Hlth Ctr, Beth Israel Deaconess Med Ctr - Boston; **Address:** 1330 Beacon St, Brookline, MA 02446; **Phone:** 617-754-1264; **Board Cert:** Psychiatry 1970; **Med School:** SUNY Upstate Med Univ 1963; **Resid:** Psychiatry, Mass Mental Hlth Ctr 1967; Psychiatry, Natl Inst Mental Hlth 1969; **Fac Appt:** Prof Psyc, Harvard Med Sch

Sanacora, Gerard MD/PhD [Psyc] - **Spec Exp:** Depression; Anxiety & Mood Disorders; Stress Management; **Hospital:** Yale New Haven Psychiatric Hosp; **Address:** Yale, Clin Neuroscience, 34 Park St, New Haven, CT 06519; **Phone:** 203-974-7560; **Board Cert:** Psychiatry 2010; **Med School:** SUNY Stony Brook 1994; **Resid:** Psychiatry, Yale-New Haven Hosp 1998; **Fellow:** Neuropsychiatry, Yale-New Haven Hosp 1999; **Fac Appt:** Prof Psyc, Yale Univ

Shapiro, Edward R MD [Psyc] - **Spec Exp:** Psychoanalysis; Family Therapy; **Hospital:** Austen Riggs Ctr, McLean Hosp; **Address:** Austen Riggs Ctr, 25 Main St, Stockbridge, MA 01262; **Phone:** 413-298-5511; **Board Cert:** Psychiatry 1974; **Med School:** Harvard Med Sch 1968; **Resid:** Psychiatry, Mass Mental Hlth Ctr 1972; **Fellow:** Psychiatry, Natl Inst Mental Hlth 1974; **Fac Appt:** Assoc Clin Prof Psyc, Harvard Med Sch

Summergrad, Paul MD [Psyc] - **Hospital:** Tufts Med Ctr; **Address:** Tufts Med Ctr, 800 Washington St, Ste 1007, Boston, MA 02111; **Phone:** 617-636-5773; **Board Cert:** Internal Medicine 1981; Psychiatry 1986; Geriatric Psychiatry 2007; Psychosomatic Medicine 2005; **Med School:** SUNY Buffalo 1978; **Resid:** Internal Medicine, Boston City Hosp 1981; **Fellow:** Psychiatry, Mass Genl Hosp 1985; **Fac Appt:** Prof Psyc, Tufts Univ

Mid Atlantic

Akhtar, Salman MD [Psyc] - **Spec Exp:** Psychoanalysis; **Hospital:** Thomas Jefferson Univ Hosp; **Address:** Jefferson Med College, Dept Psychiatry, 833 Chestnut St, Ste 210, Philadelphia, PA 19107; **Phone:** 215-955-2547; **Board Cert:** Psychiatry 1977; **Med School:** India 1968; **Resid:** Psychiatry, UMDNJ Univ Hosp 1974; Psychiatry, Univ Virginia Med Ctr 1976; **Fellow:** Psychoanalysis, Philadelphia Psych Inst 1986; **Fac Appt:** Prof Psyc, Thomas Jefferson Univ

Appelbaum, Paul S MD [Psyc] - **Spec Exp:** Forensic Psychiatry; Depression; Anxiety & Mood Disorders; **Hospital:** NY-Presby/Columbia Univ Med Ctr, NY (page 65); **Address:** Columbia University Medical Center, 1051 Riverside Drive, Unit 122, New York, NY 10032; **Phone:** 212-543-4184; **Board Cert:** Psychiatry 1981; Forensic Psychiatry 2013; **Med School:** Harvard Med Sch 1976; **Resid:** Psychiatry, Mass Mental Health Ctr 1980; **Fac Appt:** Prof Psyc, Columbia P&S

Arnold, Steven E MD [Psyc] - **Spec Exp:** Alzheimer's Disease; Memory Disorders; Dementia; Cognitive Impairment-Mild; **Hospital:** Hosp Univ Penn - UPHS (page 69); **Address:** Ralston House, 3615 Chestnut St, Philadelphia, PA 19104; **Phone:** 215-349-8226; **Board Cert:** Psychiatry 1988; Neurology 1991; **Med School:** Boston Univ 1983; **Resid:** Psychiatry, NYS Psychiatric Inst 1987; Neurology, Univ IA Hosps & Clins 1990; **Fellow:** Behavioral Neurology, Univ IA Hosps & Clins 1990; **Fac Appt:** Prof Psyc, Univ Pennsylvania

Basch, Samuel H MD [Psyc] - **Spec Exp:** Psychotherapy; Psychopharmacology; Psychoanalysis; Psychiatry in Cancer; **Hospital:** Mt Sinai Med Ctr (page 62); **Address:** 10 E 85th St, Ste 1B, New York, NY 10028; **Phone:** 212-427-0344; **Board Cert:** Psychiatry 1970; **Med School:** Hahnemann Univ 1961; **Resid:** Psychiatry, Mount Sinai Hosp 1965; **Fellow:** Psychoanalysis, Columbia Presby Hosp 1976; **Fac Appt:** Prof Psyc, Mount Sinai Sch Med

Bialer, Philip MD [Psyc] - **Spec Exp:** Psychiatry in Physical Illness; Psychiatry in Head & Neck Cancer; **Hospital:** Meml Sloan-Kettering Canc Ctr; **Address:** 641 Lexington Ave, at E 54th St, Fl 7, New York, NY 10022; **Phone:** 646-888-0009; **Board Cert:** Psychiatry 1989; Psychosomatic Medicine 2005; **Med School:** Ohio State Univ 1977; **Resid:** Internal Medicine, Mt Sinai Med Ctr 1978; Psychiatry, SUNY Hlth Sci Ctr 1988; **Fellow:** Psychosomatic Medicine, Beth Israel Med Ctr 1989; **Fac Appt:** Assoc Clin Prof Psyc, Cornell Univ-Weill Med Coll

Brandt, Harry A MD [Psyc] - **Spec Exp:** Eating Disorders; **Hospital:** Sheppard Pratt Hlth Sys, Univ of MD-St. Joseph Med Ctr; **Address:** Ctr for Eating Disorders, 6535 N Charles St, Ste 300, Towson, MD 21204; **Phone:** 410-938-5252; **Board Cert:** Psychiatry 1989; **Med School:** Univ MD Sch Med 1983; **Resid:** Psychiatry, Univ Maryland Hosp 1986; **Fac Appt:** Assoc Clin Prof Psyc, Univ MD Sch Med

Breitbart, William S MD [Psyc] - **Spec Exp:** Psychiatry in Cancer; AIDS Related Cancers; Pain-Cancer; Palliative Care; **Hospital:** Meml Sloan-Kettering Canc Ctr; **Address:** 1275 York Ave, New York, NY 10065; **Phone:** 646-888-0020; **Board Cert:** Internal Medicine 1982; Psychiatry 1986; Psychosomatic Medicine 2005; **Med School:** Albert Einstein Coll Med 1978; **Resid:** Internal Medicine, Bronx Muni Hosp Ctr 1982; Internal Medicine, Bronx Muni Hosp Ctr 1984; **Fellow:** Psychiatric Oncology, Meml Sloan Kettering Cancer Ctr 1986; **Fac Appt:** Prof Psyc, Cornell Univ-Weill Med Coll

Brodkin, Edward S MD [Psyc] - **Spec Exp:** Autism Spectrum Disorders-Adult; **Hospital:** Hosp Univ Penn - UPHS (page 69); **Address:** Penn Behavioral Health, 3535 Market St, Fl Mezzanine, Philadelphia, PA 19104; **Phone:** 215-746-4100; **Board Cert:** Psychiatry 2006; **Med School:** Harvard Med Sch 1992; **Resid:** Psychiatry, Yale Affil Hosp 1996; **Fellow:** Neurological Science, Yale Univ Sch Med 1998; Genetics, Princeton Univ 2002; **Fac Appt:** Assoc Prof Psyc, Univ Pennsylvania

Bronheim, Harold E MD [Psyc] - **Spec Exp:** Body Image Issues; Relationship Problems; Psychiatry in Physical Illness; Anxiety & Depression; **Hospital:** Mt Sinai Med Ctr (page 62); **Address:** 1155 Park Ave, New York, NY 10128; **Phone:** 212-996-5777; **Board Cert:** Psychiatry 1985; Internal Medicine 1986; Psychosomatic Medicine 2005; Geriatric Psychiatry 2011; **Med School:** SUNY Downstate 1980; **Resid:** Psychiatry, Mount Sinai Med Ctr 1986; Internal Medicine, Beth Israel Med Ctr 1985; **Fac Appt:** Clin Prof Psyc, Mount Sinai Sch Med

Buysse, Daniel J MD [Psyc] - **Spec Exp:** Sleep Disorders; **Hospital:** UPMC Presby, Pittsburgh; **Address:** 3811 O'Hara St, rm E-1127, Pittsburgh, PA 15213; **Phone:** 412-246-6413; **Board Cert:** Psychiatry 1988; Sleep Medicine 2007; **Med School:** Univ Mich Med Sch 1983; **Resid:** Psychiatry, Western Psych Inst 1987; **Fellow:** Sleep Medicine, Western Psych Inst 1989; **Fac Appt:** Asst Prof Psyc, Univ Pittsburgh

Cohen, Mitchell J MD [Psyc] - **Spec Exp:** Pain-Chronic; Psychiatry in Physical Illness; Anxiety Disorders; **Hospital:** Thomas Jefferson Univ Hosp; **Address:** 833 Chestnut St, Ste 230, Philadelphia, PA 19107; **Phone:** 215-955-6592; **Board Cert:** Psychiatry 1989; **Med School:** Med Coll PA 1984; **Resid:** Psychiatry, Johns Hopkins Hosp 1988; **Fac Appt:** Assoc Clin Prof Psyc, Thomas Jefferson Univ

DePaulo Jr, J Raymond MD [Psyc] - **Spec Exp:** Bipolar/Mood Disorders; Depression; **Hospital:** Johns Hopkins Hosp (page 59); **Address:** Johns Hopkins Hosp, Dept Psychiatry, 600 N Wolfe St, Meyer 4-113, Baltimore, MD 21287-7413; **Phone:** 410-955-3130; **Board Cert:** Psychiatry 1977; **Med School:** Johns Hopkins Univ 1972; **Resid:** Psychiatry, Johns Hopkins Hosp 1977; **Fac Appt:** Prof Psyc, Johns Hopkins Univ

Doghramji, Karl MD [Psyc] - **Spec Exp:** Sleep Disorders/Apnea; Narcolepsy; Restless Legs Syndrome; **Hospital:** Thomas Jefferson Univ Hosp; **Address:** 211 S Ninth St, Ste 500, Philadelphia, PA 19107; **Phone:** 215-955-6175; **Board Cert:** Psychiatry 1986; Sleep Medicine 2011; **Med School:** Thomas Jefferson Univ 1980; **Resid:** Psychiatry, Thomas Jefferson Univ Hosp 1984; **Fellow:** Sleep Medicine, Montefiore Med Ctr 1984; **Fac Appt:** Prof Psyc, Thomas Jefferson Univ

Eaton Jr, James S MD [Psyc] - **Spec Exp:** Anxiety Disorders; Sexual Identity Issues; Depression; Diagnostic Second Opinions; **Hospital:** MedStar Georgetown Univ Hosp, G Washington Univ Hosp; **Address:** 4214 50th St NW, Washington, DC 20016; **Phone:** 202-333-5796; **Board Cert:** Psychiatry 1976; **Med School:** Tulane Univ 1962; **Resid:** Internal Medicine, Tulane Univ Med Ctr 1966; Psychiatry, Tulane Univ Med Ctr 1968; **Fellow:** Psychoanalysis, Tulane Univ Med Ctr 1973; **Fac Appt:** Clin Prof Psyc, Georgetown Univ

Fallon, Brian A MD [Psyc] - **Spec Exp:** Lyme Disease-Neuro Complications; Psychosomatic Disorders; Obsessive-Compulsive Disorder; Psychiatry in Physical Illness; **Hospital:** NY State Psychiatric Inst, NY-Presby/Columbia Univ Med Ctr, NY (page 65); **Address:** NY State Psychiatric Inst, 1051 Riverside Drive, rm 3724, Box 69, New York, NY 10032; **Phone:** 212-543-5487; **Board Cert:** Psychiatry 1991; **Med School:** Columbia P&S 1985; **Resid:** Psychiatry, NYS Psychiatric Inst 1989; **Fellow:** Psychiatric Research, NYS Psychiatric Inst 1992; Psychodynamic Psychotherapy, NYS Psychiatric Inst 1990; **Fac Appt:** Prof Psyc, Columbia P&S

First, Michael B MD [Psyc] - **Spec Exp:** Psychotherapy; Psychopharmacology; Sexual Addiction; Sexual Behavior-Compulsive; **Hospital:** NY State Psychiatric Inst, NY-Presby/Columbia Univ Med Ctr, NY (page 65); **Address:** NY State Psychiatric Inst, 1051 Riverside Drive, Box 60, New York, NY 10032; **Phone:** 212-543-5531; **Board Cert:** Psychiatry 1989; **Med School:** Univ Pittsburgh 1983; **Resid:** Psychiatry, NYS Psychiatric Inst 1987; **Fellow:** Psychiatric Research, NYS Psychiatric Inst 1988; **Fac Appt:** Prof Psyc, Columbia P&S

Fyer, Abby J MD [Psyc] - **Spec Exp:** Anxiety Disorders; Panic Disorder; **Hospital:** NY State Psychiatric Inst, NY-Presby/Columbia Univ Med Ctr, NY (page 65); **Address:** NY State Psychiatric Inst, 1051 Riverside Drive, Ste 5814, New York, NY 10032; **Phone:** 212-543-5372; **Board Cert:** Psychiatry 1980; **Med School:** NYU Sch Med 1973; **Resid:** Psychiatry, Montefiore Med Ctr 1978; **Fac Appt:** Prof Psyc, Columbia P&S

Goff, Donald C MD [Psyc] - **Spec Exp:** Schizophrenia; Psychopharmacology; **Hospital:** NYU Langone Med Ctr (page 68); **Address:** 1 Park Ave Fl 8 - rm 8-212, New York, NY 10016; **Phone:** 646-754-4843; **Board Cert:** Psychiatry 1986; **Med School:** UCLA 1980; **Resid:** Psychiatry, Mass Genl Hosp 1984; **Fellow:** Psychopharmacology, Tufts-New England Med Ctr 1985; **Fac Appt:** Prof Psyc, NYU Sch Med

Guarda, Angela S MD [Psyc] - **Spec Exp:** Eating Disorders; **Hospital:** Johns Hopkins Hosp (page 59); **Address:** Johns Hopkins Hosp, Eating Disorder Program, 600 N Wolfe St Meyer Bldg - Ste 101, Baltimore, MD 21287; **Phone:** 410-614-4624; **Board Cert:** Psychiatry 2006; **Med School:** Univ MD Sch Med 1991; **Resid:** Psychiatry, Johns Hopkins Hosp 1995; **Fac Appt:** Assoc Prof Psyc, Johns Hopkins Univ

Hollander, Eric MD [Psyc] - **Spec Exp:** Obsessive-Compulsive Disorder; Anxiety Disorders; Autism; Body Dysmorphic Disorder (BDD); **Hospital:** Montefiore Med Ctr-Moses Campus, NY, Lenox Hill Hosp (page 66); **Address:** 901 5th Ave, New York, NY 10021; **Phone:** 212-873-4051; **Board Cert:** Psychiatry 1987; **Med School:** SUNY Hlth Sci Ctr 1982; **Resid:** Internal Medicine, Mount Sinai Med Ctr 1983; Psychiatry, Mount Sinai Med Ctr 1986; **Fellow:** Psychopharmacology, Columbia Univ-Psych Inst 1988; **Fac Appt:** Prof Psyc, Albert Einstein Coll Med

Karasu, T Byram MD [Psyc] - **Spec Exp:** Depression; Personality Disorders; Psychotherapy; **Hospital:** Montefiore Med Ctr-Moses Campus, NY, Montefiore Med Ctr-Einstein Campus, NY; **Address:** 2 E 88th St, New York, NY 10128-0555; **Phone:** 212-426-5208; **Board Cert:** Psychiatry 1972; **Med School:** Turkey 1959; **Resid:** Psychiatry, Yale Univ Affil Hosp 1969; **Fac Appt:** Prof Psyc, Albert Einstein Coll Med

Klagsbrun, Samuel C MD [Psyc] - **Spec Exp:** Psychiatry in Cancer; Psychiatry in Terminal Illness; **Hospital:** Four Winds Hosp; **Address:** 800 Cross River Rd, Katonah, NY 10536; **Phone:** 914-763-8151 x2222; **Board Cert:** Psychiatry 1977; **Med School:** Ros Franklin Univ/Chicago Med Sch 1962; **Resid:** Psychiatry, Yale-New Haven Hosp 1966; **Fac Appt:** Clin Prof Psyc, Albert Einstein Coll Med

Krueger, Richard B MD [Psyc] - **Spec Exp:** Sexual Behavior-Compulsive; **Hospital:** NY State Psychiatric Inst, NY-Presby/Columbia Univ Med Ctr, NY (page 65); **Address:** NY State Psychiatric Inst, 1051 Riverside Drive, Box 45, New York, NY 10032; **Phone:** 212-740-7330; **Board Cert:** Psychiatry 1984; Internal Medicine 1980; Addiction Psychiatry 2007; Forensic Psychiatry 2006; **Med School:** Harvard Med Sch 1977; **Resid:** Internal Medicine, Boston VA Hosp 1980; **Fellow:** Psychiatry, Boston Med Ctr 1983; **Fac Appt:** Assoc Clin Prof Psyc, Columbia P&S

Kunkel, Elisabeth J MD [Psyc] - **Spec Exp:** Psychiatry in Cancer; Psychiatry in Physical Illness; **Hospital:** Thomas Jefferson Univ Hosp, Methodist Hosp; **Address:** Thomas Jefferson Univ, Dept Psychiatry, 1020 Samson St, Thompson Bldg, Ste 1652, Philadelphia, PA 19107; **Phone:** 215-955-9545; **Board Cert:** Psychiatry 1989; Psychosomatic Medicine 2005; **Med School:** McGill Univ 1983; **Resid:** Psychiatry, NYU Med Ctr 1987; **Fellow:** Psychosomatic Medicine, Meml Sloan Kettering Cancer Ctr 1989; Consultation Psychiatry, Meml Sloan Kettering Cancer Ctr 1989; **Fac Appt:** Prof Psyc, Jefferson Med Coll

Kupfer, David J MD [Psyc] - **Spec Exp:** Bipolar/Mood Disorders; **Hospital:** Western Psych Inst & Clin-UPMC; **Address:** Univ of Pittsburgh School of Med, Psychiatry Dept, 3811 O'Hara St, Pittsburgh, PA 15213-2593; **Phone:** 412-246-6777; **Board Cert:** Psychiatry 1978; **Med School:** Yale Univ 1965; **Resid:** Psychiatry, Yale-New Haven Hosp 1970; Psychiatry, Natl Inst Mental Hlth 1969; **Fellow:** Psychiatry, Yale-New Haven Hosp 1967; **Fac Appt:** Prof Psyc, Univ Pittsburgh

Loewenstein, Richard J MD [Psyc] - **Spec Exp:** Trauma Psychiatry; Dissociative Disorders; Post Traumatic Stress Disorder; Psychopharmacology; **Hospital:** Sheppard Pratt Hlth Sys; **Address:** 6501 N Charles St, PJ 106, Baltimore, MD 21204; **Phone:** 410-938-5075; **Board Cert:** Psychiatry 1980; **Med School:** Yale Univ 1975; **Resid:** Psychiatry, Yale Affil Hosps 1979; **Fellow:** Biological Psychiatry, NIH,NIMH-Biol Psych Br 1982; **Fac Appt:** Clin Prof Psyc, Univ MD Sch Med

Manevitz, Alan MD [Psyc] - **Spec Exp:** Marital/Family/Sex Therapy; Depression-TMS Therapy; ADD/PTSD; Frbromyalgia Syndrome (FMS); **Hospital:** NY-Presby/Weill Cornell Med Ctr, NY (page 65), Lenox Hill Hosp (page 66); **Address:** 60 Sutton Place South, Ste 1CN, New York, NY 10022; **Phone:** 212-751-5072; **Board Cert:** Psychiatry 1987; **Med School:** Columbia P&S 1980; **Resid:** Psychiatry, NY Hosp 1984; **Fellow:** Psychopharmacology, NY Hosp 1985; **Fac Appt:** Assoc Clin Prof Psyc, Cornell Univ-Weill Med Coll

Mann, J. John MD/PhD [Psyc] - **Spec Exp:** Mood Disorders; Clinical Trials; Suicidal Behavior; **Hospital:** NY-Presby/Columbia Univ Med Ctr, NY (page 65); **Address:** 161 Fort Washington Ave, Irving Bldg, Fl 2 - Ste 209, New York, NY 10032; **Phone:** 212-543-5571; **Board Cert:** Psychiatry 1980; **Med School:** Australia 1971; **Resid:** Internal Medicine, Royal Melbourne Hosp 1974; Psychiatry, Royal Melbourne Hosp 1976; **Fac Appt:** Prof Psyc, Columbia P&S

Marin, Deborah B MD [Psyc] - **Spec Exp:** Memory Disorders; Depression; Depression in the Elderly; Geriatric Psychiatry; **Hospital:** Mt Sinai Med Ctr (page 62); **Address:** Mount Sinai Med Ctr, Psychiatry Dept, 1425 Madison Ave Fl 5, New York, NY 10029; **Phone:** 212-659-8092; **Board Cert:** Psychiatry 1990; **Med School:** Mount Sinai Sch Med 1984; **Resid:** Psychiatry, Mount Sinai Med Ctr 1988; **Fellow:** Psychiatry, NY-Presby/Weill Cornell Med Ctr 1991; **Fac Appt:** Prof Psyc, Mount Sinai Sch Med

McCann, Merle C MD [Psyc] - **Hospital:** Sheppard Pratt Hlth Sys; **Address:** Sheppard & Enoch Pratt Hosp, 6501 N Charles St, rm PJ-111, Tow, MD 21204; **Phone:** 410-938-3000; **Board Cert:** Psychiatry 1986; **Med School:** Med Coll VA 1981; **Resid:** Psychiatry, Geo Wash Univ Hosp 1985; **Fac Appt:** Asst Clin Prof Psyc, Univ MD Sch Med

Nunes, Edward MD [Psyc] - **Spec Exp:** Depression; Substance Abuse; **Hospital:** NY State Psychiatric Inst, NY-Presby/Columbia Univ Med Ctr, NY (page 65); **Address:** 617 West End Ave, Ste 1B, New York, NY 10032; **Phone:** 212-579-0339; **Board Cert:** Psychiatry 1986; Addiction Psychiatry 2002; **Med School:** Univ Conn 1981; **Resid:** Psychiatry, Columbia-Presby/NYS Psyc Inst 1985; **Fellow:** Psychopharmacology, Columbia-Presby/NYS Psyc Inst 1988; **Fac Appt:** Prof Psyc, Columbia P&S

Roose, Steven MD [Psyc] - **Spec Exp:** Depression in the Elderly; Psychoanalysis; **Hospital:** NY State Psychiatric Inst; **Address:** NY State Psychiatric Inst, 1051 Riverside Drive, rm 2211, Box 98, New York, NY 10032; **Phone:** 212-831-8644; **Board Cert:** Psychiatry 1979; **Med School:** Mount Sinai Sch Med 1974; **Resid:** Psychiatry, NY State Psych Inst 1978; **Fellow:** Research, NY-Presby/Columbia Univ Med Ctr 1981; **Fac Appt:** Prof Psyc, Columbia P&S

Rosenthal, Norman E MD [Psyc] - ; **Address:** 11110 Stephalee Ln, Rockville, MD 20852; **Phone:** 301-770-3843; **Board Cert:** Psychiatry 1980; **Med School:** South Africa 1973; **Resid:** Psychiatry, NY State Psych Inst 1979; **Fellow:** Psychiatry, Natl Inst Mental Health 1981; **Fac Appt:** Clin Prof Psyc, Georgetown Univ

Rosenthal, Richard N MD [Psyc] - **Spec Exp:** Anxiety & Mood Disorders; Addiction/Substance Abuse; **Hospital:** St. Luke's - Roosevelt Hosp Ctr - Roosevelt Div (page 56), Beth Israel Med Ctr - Petrie Div (page 56); **Address:** 1090 Amerstdam Ave, Ste 16G, New York, NY 10025; **Phone:** 212-523-5366; **Board Cert:** Psychiatry 1985; Addiction Psychiatry 2012; **Med School:** SUNY Hlth Sci Ctr 1980; **Resid:** Psychiatry, Mount Sinai Med Ctr 1984; **Fac Appt:** Prof Psyc, Columbia P&S

Rosse, Richard B MD [Psyc] - **Hospital:** VA Med Ctr - Washington; **Address:** VA Med Ctr, 50 Irving St NW, Washington, DC 20422-0001; **Phone:** 202-745-8156; **Board Cert:** Psychiatry 1986; **Med School:** Univ MD Sch Med 1980; **Resid:** Psychiatry, Georgetown Univ Med Ctr 1984; **Fac Appt:** Assoc Prof Psyc, Howard Univ

Roth, Andrew J MD [Psyc] - **Spec Exp:** Psychiatry of Prostate Cancer; Geriatric Psychiatry; **Hospital:** Meml Sloan-Kettering Canc Ctr; **Address:** 641 Lexington Ave, Fl 7, New York, NY 10022; **Phone:** 646-888-0024; **Board Cert:** Psychiatry 1993; Geriatric Psychiatry 2007; Psychosomatic Medicine 2005; **Med School:** NY Med Coll 1988; **Resid:** Psychiatry, Mt Sinai Med Ctr 1992; **Fellow:** Liaison Psychiatry, Meml Sloan-Kettering Canc Ctr 1994; **Fac Appt:** Clin Prof Psyc, Cornell Univ-Weill Med Coll

Sadock, Virginia MD [Psyc] - **Spec Exp:** Psychotherapy; Sexual Dysfunction; Anxiety & Depression; Marital/Family/Sex Therapy; **Hospital:** NYU Langone Med Ctr (page 68); **Address:** 4 E 89th St, Ste 1E, New York, NY 10128; **Phone:** 212-427-0885; **Board Cert:** Psychiatry 1975; **Med School:** NY Med Coll 1970; **Resid:** Psychiatry, Metropolitan Hosp Ctr 1973; **Fac Appt:** Clin Prof Psyc, NYU Sch Med

Samberg, Eslee MD [Psyc] - **Spec Exp:** Psychoanalysis; Personality Disorders; Psychotherapy; **Hospital:** NY-Presby/Weill Cornell Med Ctr, NY (page 65); **Address:** 165 W End Ave, Ste 1M, New York, NY 10024; **Phone:** 212-874-7725; **Board Cert:** Psychiatry 1983; **Med School:** Cornell Univ-Weill Med Coll 1978; **Resid:** Psychiatry, NY-Presby/Weill Cornell Med Ctr 1982; **Fac Appt:** Assoc Clin Prof Psyc, Cornell Univ-Weill Med Coll

Scott, C Paul MD [Psyc] - **Spec Exp:** Anxiety & Mood Disorders; Psychoanalysis; **Hospital:** UPMC Presby, Pittsburgh; **Address:** 401 Shady Ave, Ste C202, Pittsburgh, PA 15206; **Phone:** 412-661-2354; **Board Cert:** Psychiatry 1976; **Med School:** Case West Res Univ 1968; **Resid:** Internal Medicine, Mt. Sinai Hosp/Univ Hosp 1970; Psychiatry, Western Psych Inst 1975; **Fellow:** Psychoanalysis, Western Psych Inst 1982; **Fac Appt:** Clin Prof Psyc, Univ Pittsburgh

Sussman, Norman MD [Psyc] - **Spec Exp:** Psychopharmacology; Anxiety & Mood Disorders; Bipolar/Mood Disorders; **Hospital:** NYU Langone Med Ctr (page 68); **Address:** 150 E 58th St,, Fl 27, New York, NY 10155; **Phone:** 212-588-9722; **Board Cert:** Psychiatry 1980; **Med School:** NY Med Coll 1975; **Resid:** Psychiatry, Metropolitan Hosp Ctr 1977; Psychiatry, Westchester Med Ctr 1978; **Fac Appt:** Prof Psyc, NYU Sch Med

Thase, Michael E MD [Psyc] - **Spec Exp:** Anxiety & Mood Disorders; Psychopharmacology; Depression; **Hospital:** Hosp Univ Penn - UPHS (page 69); **Address:** Univ Penn, Dept Psychiatry, 3535 Market St, Ste 670, Philadelphia, PA 19104; **Phone:** 215-746-6680; **Board Cert:** Psychiatry 1984; **Med School:** Ohio State Univ 1979; **Resid:** Psychiatry, Western Psych Inst 1983; **Fellow:** Research, Univ Pittsburgh 1984; **Fac Appt:** Prof Psyc, Univ Pennsylvania

Wait, Susan B MD [Psyc] - **Spec Exp:** Post Traumatic Stress Disorder; Dissociative Disorders; Anxiety & Mood Disorders; Dialectical Behavioral Therapy; **Hospital:** Sheppard Pratt Hlth Sys; **Address:** Sheppard Pratt Hlth Sys, 6501 N Charles St, Baltimore, MD 21285; **Phone:** 410-938-5076; **Board Cert:** Psychiatry 1993; **Med School:** Med Coll PA Hahnemann 1987; **Resid:** Psychiatry, Sheppard Pratt Hosp 1991; **Fac Appt:** Assoc Clin Prof Psyc, Univ MD Sch Med

Walsh, B. Timothy MD [Psyc] - **Spec Exp:** Eating Disorders; Obesity; **Hospital:** NY State Psychiatric Inst, NY-Presby/Columbia Univ Med Ctr, NY (page 65); **Address:** NY State Psychiatric Inst, 1051 Riverside Drive, rm 2306, Box 98, New York, NY 10032; **Phone:** 212-543-5739; **Board Cert:** Psychiatry 1978; **Med School:** Harvard Med Sch 1972; **Resid:** Psychiatry, Bronx Muni Hosp Ctr 1977; **Fac Appt:** Prof Psyc, Columbia P&S

Southeast

Blazer II, Dan G MD/PhD [Psyc] - **Spec Exp:** Geriatric Psychiatry; Mood Disorders; **Hospital:** Duke Univ Hosp; **Address:** Duke Univ Med Ctr, Dept Psychiatary, 3521 Hospital South, Box 3003, Durham, NC 27710-3003; **Phone:** 919-684-4128; **Board Cert:** Psychiatry 1977; **Med School:** Univ Tenn Coll Med 1969; **Resid:** Psychiatry, Duke Univ Med Ctr 1975; **Fellow:** Liaison Psychiatry, Montefiore Hosp 1976; **Fac Appt:** Prof Psyc, Duke Univ

Canterbury II, Randolph J MD [Psyc] - **Spec Exp:** Panic Disorder; Depression; Substance Abuse; **Hospital:** Univ of Virginia Hlth Sys; **Address:** Univ Virginia Dept Psychiatry, Div Outpatient Psychiatry, Box 800623, Charlottesville, VA 22908-0623; **Phone:** 434-924-2241; **Board Cert:** Internal Medicine 1983; Psychiatry 1985; Psychosomatic Medicine 2005; **Med School:** W VA Univ 1979; **Resid:** Internal Medicine, Univ Va Hosp 1983; Psychiatry, Univ Va Hosp 1985; **Fac Appt:** Prof Psyc, Univ VA Sch Med

Eth, Spencer MD [Psyc] - **Spec Exp:** Forensic Psychiatry; Post Traumatic Stress Disorder; Geriatric Psychiatry; **Hospital:** VA Med Ctr - Miami, Univ of Miami Hosp; **Address:** VA Med Ctr, Psychiatry Dept, 1201 NW 16th St, Miami, FL 33125; **Phone:** 305-575-3301; **Board Cert:** Child & Adolescent Psychiatry 1982; Geriatric Psychiatry 2010; Forensic Psychiatry 2013; Addiction Psychiatry 2009; **Med School:** UCLA 1976; **Resid:** Psychiatry, NY-Presby/Weill Cornell Med Ctr 1979; **Fellow:** Child & Adolescent Psychiatry, Cedars-Sinai Med Ctr 1981; **Fac Appt:** Prof Psyc, Univ Miami Sch Med

Giustra Jr, Lawrence J MD [Psyc] - **Spec Exp:** Psychotherapy; Marital/Family/Sex Therapy; **Hospital:** Emory Univ Hosp; **Address:** 1945 Cliff Valley Way NE, Ste 202, Atlanta, GA 30329; **Phone:** 404-325-2139; **Board Cert:** Psychiatry 1982; **Med School:** Johns Hopkins Univ 1976; **Resid:** Psychiatry, Mass Genl Hosp 1980; **Fac Appt:** Asst Prof Psyc, Emory Univ

Klapheke, Martin M MD [Psyc] - **Spec Exp:** Transplantation Psychiatry; Psychoanalysis; **Address:** Univ Central FL, Psychiatry Dept, 6850 Lake Nona Blvd, rm 409K, Orlando, FL 32827; **Phone:** 407-266-1183; **Board Cert:** Psychiatry 1985; **Med School:** Univ KY Coll Med 1979; **Resid:** Psychiatry, Mayo Clin 1982; **Fellow:** Child & Adolescent Psychiatry, Mayo Clin 1984; Psychoanalysis, Menninger Clin 1994; **Fac Appt:** Prof Psyc, Univ C Fla Coll Med

Levy, Steven T MD [Psyc] - **Spec Exp:** Psychoanalysis; Depression; Anxiety & Mood Disorders; **Hospital:** Emory Univ Hosp, Grady Hlth Sys; **Address:** Emory Univ Psychoanalytic Inst, 2004 Ridgewood Drive, Ste 300, Tufts House, Atlanta, GA 30322; **Phone:** 404-727-5886; **Board Cert:** Psychiatry 1976; **Med School:** Duke Univ 1969; **Resid:** Psychiatry, Yale Affil Hosp 1973; **Fellow:** NIH 1974; Psychoanalysis, Columbia Univ 1980; **Fac Appt:** Prof Psyc, Emory Univ

Powers, Pauline MD [Psyc] - **Spec Exp:** Eating Disorders; Obesity; **Hospital:** Tampa Genl Hosp; **Address:** Powers Ctr of Hope, 7401A Temple Terrace Hwy, Tampa, FL 33637; **Phone:** 813-985-8888; **Board Cert:** Psychiatry 1977; **Med School:** Univ Iowa Coll Med 1971; **Resid:** Psychiatry, Univ Iowa Hosps & Clins 1974; Psychiatry, UC Davis Med Ctr 1975; **Fac Appt:** Prof Psyc, Univ S Fla Coll Med

Salloum, Ihsan M MD [Psyc] - **Spec Exp:** Bipolar/Mood Disorders; Addiction/Substance Abuse; Depression; **Hospital:** Univ of Miami Hosp; **Address:** UHlth, Psychiatry Dept, 1120 NW 14th St, Ste 1450, Miami, FL 33136; **Phone:** 305-243-7931; **Board Cert:** Psychiatry 1994; Addiction Psychiatry 2007; **Med School:** Italy 1980; **Resid:** Psychiatry, Univ Hlth Sci Ctr 1988; **Fellow:** Research, UPMC 1989; **Fac Appt:** Prof Psyc, Univ Miami Sch Med

Weiner, Richard D MD/PhD [Psyc] - **Spec Exp:** Bipolar/Mood Disorders; Electroconvulsive Therapy (ECT); Depression; Schizophrenia; **Hospital:** Duke Univ Hosp, Durham VA Med Ctr; **Address:** Duke Univ Medical Ctr, Box 3309, Durham, NC 27710; **Phone:** 919-681-8742; **Board Cert:** Psychiatry 1979; Clinical Neurophysiology 2003; **Med School:** Duke Univ 1973; **Resid:** Psychiatry, Duke Univ Med Ctr 1976; **Fellow:** Electroencephalography, Duke Univ Med Ctr 1977; **Fac Appt:** Prof Psyc, Duke Univ

Weisler, Richard H MD [Psyc] - **Spec Exp:** Depression; Bipolar/Mood Disorders; Clinical Trials; **Hospital:** NC Memorial Hosp - UNC; **Address:** 700 Spring Forest Rd, Ste 125, Raleigh, NC 27609; **Phone:** 919-872-5900; **Board Cert:** Psychiatry 1982; **Med School:** Univ NC Sch Med 1977; **Resid:** Psychiatry, Duke Univ Med Ctr 1982; **Fac Appt:** Assoc Prof Psyc, Duke Univ

Wilson, Daniel R MD/PhD [Psyc] - **Spec Exp:** Forensic Psychiatry; Psychopharmacology; Neuro-Psychiatry; **Hospital:** UF Hlth Jacksonville; **Address:** University of Florida HSC, Office of the VP & Dean, 653-1 W 8th St, LRC Bldg - Fl 4, Jacksonville, FL 32209; **Phone:** 904-244-3131; **Board Cert:** Psychiatry 1989; Forensic Psychiatry 2009; **Med School:** Univ Iowa Coll Med 1983; **Resid:** Psychiatry, McLean Hosp 1986; **Fellow:** Geriatric Psychiatry, McLean Hosp 1987; Genetics, Cambridge Univ 1993; **Fac Appt:** Prof Psyc, Univ Fla Coll Med

Midwest

Black, Donald W MD [Psyc] - **Spec Exp:** Obsessive-Compulsive Disorder; Personality Disorders; Bipolar/Mood Disorders; Psychotic Disorders; **Hospital:** Univ Iowa Hosp & Clins; **Address:** UIHC - Dept Psychiatry, 500 Newton Rd, MEB Bldg - rm 2-126B, Iowa City, IA 52242; **Phone:** 319-353-4431; **Board Cert:** Psychiatry 1988; **Med School:** Univ Utah 1982; **Resid:** Psychiatry, Univ Iowa Hosp & Clincs 1988; **Fellow:** Epidemiology, Univ Iowa Hosp & Clincs 1989; **Fac Appt:** Prof Psyc, Univ Iowa Coll Med

Black, Kevin J MD [Psyc] - **Spec Exp:** Neuro-Psychiatry; **Hospital:** Barnes-Jewish Hosp; **Address:** Washington Univ Sch Med, Dept Neurology, 660 S Euclid Ave, Box 8111, St Louis, MO 63110; **Phone:** 314-362-6908; **Board Cert:** Psychiatry 2005; **Med School:** Duke Univ 1990; **Resid:** Psychiatry, Barnes Hosp-Washington Univ 1994; **Fellow:** Movement Disorders, Barnes Hosp-Washington Univ 1996; **Fac Appt:** Assoc Prof Psyc, Washington Univ, St Louis

Calabrese, Joseph R MD [Psyc] - **Spec Exp:** Bipolar/Mood Disorders; **Hospital:** UH Case Med Ctr; **Address:** UH Case Med Ctr, Dept Psy-Adult, 10524 Euclid Ave, Ste 12-135, Cleveland, OH 44106; **Phone:** 216-844-2865; **Board Cert:** Psychiatry 1989; **Med School:** Ohio State Univ 1980; **Resid:** Psychiatry, Cleveland Clin 1984; **Fellow:** Biological Psychiatry, Natl Inst Mental Hlth 1986; **Fac Appt:** Prof Psyc, Case West Res Univ

Cloninger, C Robert MD [Psyc] - **Spec Exp:** Personality Disorders; **Hospital:** Barnes-Jewish Hosp; **Address:** Wash Univ Sch Med, Dept Psyc, 660 S Euclid Ave, Box 8134, St Louis, MO 63110; **Phone:** 314-362-7005; **Board Cert:** Psychiatry 1975; **Med School:** Washington Univ, St Louis 1970; **Resid:** Psychiatry, Barnes Hosp 1973; Psychiatry, Renard Hosp-Wash Univ 1973; **Fac Appt:** Prof Psyc, Washington Univ, St Louis

Crow, Scott J MD [Psyc] - **Spec Exp:** Eating Disorders; Obesity; **Address:** The Emily Program, 2265 Como Ave, St Paul, MN 55108; **Phone:** 651-645-5323; **Board Cert:** Psychiatry 1994; **Med School:** Univ Minn 1988; **Resid:** Psychiatry, Univ Minn Med Ctr 1992; **Fellow:** Psychiatry, Univ Minn 1992; **Fac Appt:** Prof Psyc, Univ Minn

Fox, Geraldine MD [Psyc] - **Spec Exp:** Child & Adolescent Psychiatry; Marital/Family/Sex Therapy; **Hospital:** Univ of IL Med Ctr at Chicago; **Address:** Inst for Juvenile Research, 1747 W Roosevelt Rd, rm 155, Chicago, IL 60608; **Phone:** 312-996-9506; **Board Cert:** Psychiatry 1988; Child & Adolescent Psychiatry 1989; **Med School:** Univ IL Coll Med 1983; **Resid:** Psychiatry, Northwestern Meml Hosp 1986; **Fellow:** Child & Adolescent Psychiatry, Univ IL Inst for Juvenile Rsch 1988; **Fac Appt:** Prof Psyc, Univ IL Coll Med

Grant, Jon E MD [Psyc] - **Spec Exp:** Impulse-Control Disorders; Gay & Lesbian Issues; Sexual Dysfunction; Addictive Disorders; **Hospital:** Univ of Chicago Med; **Address:** 5841 S Maryland Ave, MC 3077, Chicago, IL 60637; **Phone:** 773-702-6199; **Board Cert:** Psychiatry 2004; **Med School:** Brown Univ 1999; **Resid:** Psychiatry, Univ Minnesota Med Ctr 2003; **Fac Appt:** Prof Psyc, Univ Chicago-Pritzker Sch Med

Greden, John F MD [Psyc] - **Spec Exp:** Depression; **Hospital:** Univ Michigan Med Ctr; **Address:** Univ Michigan Comp Depression Ctr, Rachel Upjohn Bldg, 4250 Plymouth Rd, Ann Arbor, MI 48109-2700; **Phone:** 734-763-9629; **Board Cert:** Psychiatry 1975; **Med School:** Univ Minn 1967; **Resid:** Psychiatry, Univ Minn Med Ctr 1969; Psychiatry, Walter Reed Army Med Ctr 1972; **Fac Appt:** Prof Psyc, Univ Mich Med Sch

Janicak, Philip G MD [Psyc] - **Spec Exp:** Psychopharmacology; Mood Disorders; Psychotic Disorders; Depression-TMS Therapy; **Hospital:** Rush Univ Med Ctr; **Address:** Rush Univ Med Ctr, Dept Psych, 2150 W Harrison St, rm 253, Chicago, IL 60612; **Phone:** 312-942-7287; **Board Cert:** Psychiatry 1978; **Med School:** Loyola Univ-Stritch Sch Med 1973; **Resid:** Psychiatry, McGaw Hosp/Loyola Med Ctr 1976; **Fac Appt:** Prof Psyc, Rush Med Coll

Kumar, Anand MD [Psyc] - **Spec Exp:** Geriatric Psychiatry; Depression in the Elderly; Alzheimer's Disease; Dementia; **Hospital:** Univ of IL Med Ctr at Chicago; **Address:** Univ IL- Dept of Psychiatry, 1601 W Taylor St, MC 912, Chicago, IL 60612; **Phone:** 312-996-7383; **Board Cert:** Psychiatry 1989; **Med School:** India 1980; **Resid:** Psychiatry, Univ MI Hosp 1986; **Fac Appt:** Prof Psyc, Univ IL Coll Med

Levine, Stephen B MD [Psyc] - **Spec Exp:** Sexual Dysfunction; Relationship Problems; Sexual Identity Issues; **Hospital:** UH Case Med Ctr; **Address:** 23425 Commerce Park Rd, Ste 104, Beachwood, OH 44122-5446; **Phone:** 216-831-2900; **Board Cert:** Psychiatry 1976; **Med School:** Case West Res Univ 1967; **Resid:** Psychiatry, Univ Hosps 1973; **Fac Appt:** Clin Prof Psyc, Case West Res Univ

Locala, Joseph MD [Psyc] - **Spec Exp:** Psychiatry in Transplant Patients; Psychiatry in Physical Illness; Anxiety & Mood Disorders; Neuro-Psychiatry; **Hospital:** UH Case Med Ctr; **Address:** UH Case Med Ctr, W.O. Walker Ctr, 10524 Euclid Ave Fl 13, Cleveland, OH 44106; **Phone:** 216-844-2400; **Board Cert:** Psychiatry 2006; Psychosomatic Medicine 2006; **Med School:** Temple Univ 1990; **Resid:** Psychiatry, Medical Ctr Hosp 1994; **Fellow:** Psychosomatic Medicine, Cleveland Clin 1995; **Fac Appt:** Assoc Prof Psyc, Case West Res Univ

McCallum, Kimberli E MD [Psyc] - **Spec Exp:** Eating Disorders; **Hospital:** St. Louis Univ Hosp; **Address:** McCallum Place, 231 W Lockwood Ave, Ste 201, Webster Groves, MO 63119; **Phone:** 314-968-1900; **Board Cert:** Psychiatry 1993; Child & Adolescent Psychiatry 1994; **Med School:** Yale Univ 1986; **Resid:** Psychiatry, UCLA Neuropsyc Inst 1991; **Fellow:** Child Psychiatry, Washington Univ 1993; **Fac Appt:** Assoc Clin Prof Psyc, Washington Univ, St Louis

Nurnberger Jr, John I MD/PhD [Psyc] - **Spec Exp:** Bipolar/Mood Disorders; Depression; Psychiatric Genetics; **Hospital:** IU Hlth Univ Hosp, Wishard Hlth Srvs; **Address:** Inst Psychiatric Rsch-IUMC, 791 Union Drive, Indianapolis, IN 46202-4887; **Phone:** 317-944-7422; **Board Cert:** Psychiatry 1981; **Med School:** Indiana Univ 1975; **Resid:** Psychiatry, Columbia-Presby Med Ctr 1978; **Fellow:** Psychiatry & Genetics, NIMH Clinical Ctr 1983; **Fac Appt:** Prof Psyc, Indiana Univ

Pollack, Mark H MD [Psyc] - **Spec Exp:** Anxiety & Mood Disorders; Panic Disorder; Post Traumatic Stress Disorder; Psychopharmacology; **Hospital:** Rush Univ Med Ctr; **Address:** 1645 W Jackson Blvd, Westgate Bldg - Ste 600, Chicago, IL 60612; **Phone:** 312-942-5372; **Board Cert:** Psychiatry 1987; **Med School:** UMDNJ Sch Osteo Med 1982; **Resid:** Psychiatry, Mass Genl Hosp 1986; **Fellow:** Psychopharmacology, Mass Genl Hosp 1987; **Fac Appt:** Prof Psyc, Rush Med Coll

Riba, Michelle B MD [Psyc] - **Spec Exp:** Psychiatry in Cancer; **Hospital:** Univ Michigan Med Ctr; **Address:** Mott Chldns Hosp, MCHC F6236, 1500 E Medical Ctr Drive, Ste SPC 5295, Ann Arbor, MI 48109-0295; **Phone:** 734-764-6879; **Board Cert:** Psychiatry 1991; Psychosomatic Medicine 2005; **Med School:** Univ Conn 1985; **Resid:** Psychiatry, Univ Connecticut Affil Hosp 1988; **Fac Appt:** Clin Prof Psyc, Univ Mich Med Sch

Strakowski, Stephen M MD [Psyc] - Spec Exp: Bipolar/Mood Disorders; Psychotic Disorders; Dual Diagnosis; **Hospital:** Univ Cincinnati Med Ctr, Cincinnati Chldns Hosp Med Ctr; **Address:** Univ Cincinnati Dept Psychiatry, Campus Box 670559, Cincinnati, OH 45267-0559; **Phone:** 513-558-4274; **Board Cert:** Psychiatry 1993; **Med School:** Vanderbilt Univ 1988; **Resid:** Psychiatry, McLean Hosp-Harvard Med Sch 1992; **Fac Appt:** Prof Psyc, Univ Cincinnati

Wooten, Virgil D MD [Psyc] - Spec Exp: Sleep Disorders; **Hospital:** Univ Cincinnati Med Ctr, West Chester Hosp; **Address:** 200 Albert Sabin Way, Holms Bldg - Fl 3, Cincinnati, OH 45219; **Phone:** 513-584-1238; **Board Cert:** Psychiatry 1985; Sleep Medicine 2007; **Med School:** Univ Ark 1980; **Resid:** Psychiatry, Univ Hosp-VA Hosp 1984; **Fellow:** Sleep Medicine, Univ Hosp 1984; **Fac Appt:** Prof Med, Univ Cincinnati

Great Plains and Mountains

Greiner, Carl B MD [Psyc] - Spec Exp: Psychiatry in Cancer; Psychiatry in Physical Illness; Forensic Psychiatry; Post Traumatic Stress Disorder; **Hospital:** Nebraska Med Ctr; **Address:** UNMC, Dept Psychiatry, 985575 Nebraska Medical Ctr, Omaha, NE 68198-5575; **Phone:** 402-552-6002; **Board Cert:** Psychiatry 1984; Forensic Psychiatry 2008; **Med School:** Univ Cincinnati 1978; **Resid:** Psychiatry, Univ Cincinnati Med Ctr 1982; **Fac Appt:** Prof Psyc, Univ Nebr Coll Med

McIntosh, J Michael MD [Psyc] - Spec Exp: Depression; Schizophrenia; Anxiety Disorders; Bipolar/Mood Disorders; **Hospital:** Univ Utah Hlth Care; **Address:** 501 Chipeta Way, Salt Lake City, UT 84108; **Phone:** 801-581-7951; **Board Cert:** Psychiatry 1994; **Med School:** UCLA 1987; **Resid:** Psychiatry, Univ Colo Hlth Sci Ctr 1991; Psychiatry, Univ Utah Hosps 1992; **Fac Appt:** Clin Prof Psyc, Univ Utah

Mitchell III, James E MD [Psyc] - Spec Exp: Eating Disorders; Clinical Trials; **Hospital:** Sanford Med Ctr Fargo; **Address:** NeuroPsychiatric Research Inst, 700 First Ave S, Fargo, ND 58103; **Phone:** 701-293-1335; **Board Cert:** Psychiatry 1979; **Med School:** Northwestern Univ 1972; **Resid:** Psychiatry, Fairview-Univ Med Ctr 1976; **Fac Appt:** Prof Psyc, Univ ND Sch Med

Moench, Louis A MD [Psyc] - Hospital: LDS Hosp; **Address:** 324 Tenth Ave, Ste 178, Salt Lake City, UT 84103; **Phone:** 801-408-8500; **Board Cert:** Psychiatry 1978; Forensic Psychiatry 2004; **Med School:** Univ Utah 1970; **Resid:** Psychiatry, Hosp Univ Penn 1976; **Fellow:** Forensic Psychiatry, Hosp Univ Penn 1976; **Fac Appt:** Clin Prof Psyc, Univ Utah

Weiner, Kenneth L MD [Psyc] - Spec Exp: Eating Disorders; **Hospital:** Univ Colorado Hosp; **Address:** Eating Recovery Ctr, 1830 Franklin St, Ste 500, Denver, CO 80218; **Phone:** 303-825-8584; **Board Cert:** Psychiatry 1983; **Med School:** Tufts Univ 1977; **Resid:** Psychiatry, Univ CO Hosp 1981; **Fac Appt:** Asst Clin Prof Psyc, Univ Colorado

Southwest

Baile, Walter F MD [Psyc] - Spec Exp: Psychiatry in Cancer; **Hospital:** UT MD Anderson Canc Ctr; **Address:** UT MD Anderson Cancer Ctr, 1220 Holcombe Blvd, Texas, TX 77030; **Phone:** 713-563-1484; **Board Cert:** Psychiatry 1980; **Med School:** Italy 1973; **Resid:** Psychiatry, Johns Hopkins Hosp 1976; **Fellow:** Behavioral Medicine, Natl Inst Aging 1978; **Fac Appt:** Prof Psyc, Univ Tex, Houston

Bowden, Charles L MD [Psyc] - **Spec Exp:** Bipolar/Mood Disorders; **Hospital:** Univ Hosp-San Antonio; **Address:** Univ Tex Hlth Sci Ctr, Dept Psychiatry, 7526 Louis Pasteur Drive, Ste 318, San Antonio, TX 78229-3900; **Phone:** 210-567-5555; **Board Cert:** Psychiatry 1970; **Med School:** Baylor Coll Med 1964; **Resid:** Psychiatry, NY State Psyc Inst/Columbia-Presby Med Ctr 1968; **Fac Appt:** Prof Psyc, Univ Tex, San Antonio

Davidson, Joyce E MD [Psyc] - **Spec Exp:** Obsessive-Compulsive Disorder; Bipolar/Mood Disorders; Schizophrenia; **Hospital:** Menninger Clinic; **Address:** The Menninger Clinic, 12301 Main St, Houston, TX 77035; **Phone:** 713-275-5000; **Board Cert:** Psychiatry 1988; **Med School:** Univ MO-Kansas City 1979; **Resid:** Psychiatry, Menninger Clinic 1982; **Fellow:** Child & Adolescent Psychiatry, Karl Menninger Sch Psyc 1984; **Fac Appt:** Asst Prof Psyc, Baylor Coll Med

Gabbard, Glen O MD [Psyc] - **Spec Exp:** Personality Disorders-Borderline; Cognitive Psychotherapy; Psychoanalysis; **Address:** 6750 W Loop S, Ste 460, Bellaire, TX 77401; **Phone:** 713-665-1607; **Board Cert:** Psychiatry 1979; **Med School:** Rush Med Coll 1975; **Resid:** Psychiatry, Menninger Clinic 1978; **Fellow:** Psychoanalysis, Topeka Inst Psychoanalysis 1984; **Fac Appt:** Prof Psyc, Baylor Coll Med

Haque, Waheedul MD [Psyc] - **Spec Exp:** Depression; Panic Disorder; **Hospital:** UT Med Br at Galveston(John Sealy Hosp); **Address:** Dept Psychiatry, 301 University Blvd, Route 0190, Galveston, TX 77555; **Phone:** 409-747-9722; **Board Cert:** Psychiatry 1970; **Med School:** Pakistan 1962; **Resid:** Psychiatry, Barnes Jewish Med Ctr 1969; **Fac Appt:** Prof Psyc, Univ Tex Med Br, Galveston

Hirschfeld, Robert M A MD [Psyc] - **Spec Exp:** Bipolar/Mood Disorders; Schizophrenia; Depression; Suicide; **Hospital:** UT Med Br at Galveston(John Sealy Hosp); **Address:** Dept Psychiatry, 301 University Blvd, Route 0188, Galveston, TX 77555-0188; **Phone:** 409-747-9791; **Board Cert:** Psychiatry 1975; **Med School:** Univ Mich Med Sch 1968; **Resid:** Psychiatry, Stanford Univ Med Ctr 1972; **Fac Appt:** Prof Psyc, Univ Tex Med Br, Galveston

Mohl, Paul C MD [Psyc] - **Spec Exp:** Psychopharmacology; Psychotherapy; **Hospital:** UT Southwestern Med Ctr at Dallas; **Address:** 5323 Harry Hines Blvd, Dallas, TX 75390-9070; **Phone:** 214-645-8500; **Board Cert:** Psychiatry 1977; **Med School:** Duke Univ 1971; **Resid:** Psychiatry, Duke Univ Hosp 1974; **Fac Appt:** Prof Psyc, Univ Tex SW, Dallas

Valentine, Alan D MD [Psyc] - **Spec Exp:** Psychiatry in Cancer; Palliative Care; **Hospital:** UT MD Anderson Canc Ctr; **Address:** MD Anderson Cancer Center, Dept Psychiatry, 1515 Holcombe Blvd, Ste 1454, Houston, TX 77030-1402; **Phone:** 713-745-3344; **Board Cert:** Psychiatry 1992; Geriatric Psychiatry 2006; Psychosomatic Medicine 2005; **Med School:** Univ Tex, Houston 1986; **Resid:** Psychiatry, Univ Texas Affil Hosps 2000; **Fac Appt:** Clin Prof Psyc, Univ Tex, Houston

West Coast and Pacific

Blumenfield, Michael MD [Psyc] - **Spec Exp:** Psychotherapy; Psychopharmacology; Psychosomatic Disorders; Disaster Psychiatry; **Address:** 5901 Nita Ave, Woodland Hills, CA 91367; **Phone:** 818-564-4207; **Board Cert:** Psychiatry 1970; Psychosomatic Medicine 2005; **Med School:** SUNY Downstate 1964; **Resid:** Psychiatry, Kings County Hosp 1968; **Fellow:** Psychosomatic Medicine, Kings County Hosp 1971; **Fac Appt:** Prof Emeritus Psyc, NY Med Coll

Burt, Vivien K MD/PhD [Psyc] - **Spec Exp:** Women's Health-Mental Health; Impulse-Control Disorders; Psychiatry in Pregnancy; Postpartum Depression; **Hospital:** Resnick Neuropsychiatric Hosp at UCLA; **Address:** 300 UCLA Med Plaza, Ste 2337, Los Angeles, CA 90095; **Phone:** 310-562-4942; **Board Cert:** Psychiatry 1990; **Med School:** McGill Univ 1984; **Resid:** Psychiatry, UCLA Ronald Reagan Med Ctr 1989; **Fac Appt:** Assoc Clin Prof Psyc, UCLA

Bystritsky, Alexander MD/PhD [Psyc] - **Spec Exp:** Obsessive-Compulsive Disorder; Anxiety Disorders; Psychopharmacology; **Hospital:** Resnick Neuropsychiatric Hosp at UCLA; **Address:** UCLA Anxiety Disorders Clin, 300 UCLA Med Plaza, Ste 2335, Los Angeles, CA 90095-6968; **Phone:** 310-206-5133; **Board Cert:** Psychiatry 1988; **Med School:** Russia 1977; **Resid:** Psychiatry, NYU Langone Med Ctr 1985; **Fellow:** Psychiatry, UCLA Ronald Reagan Med Ctr 1987; **Fac Appt:** Prof Psyc, UCLA

Eisendrath, Stuart J MD [Psyc] - **Spec Exp:** Depression; Munchausen Syndrome; Cognitive Psychotherapy; **Hospital:** UCSF Med Ctr; **Address:** UCSF Med Ctr, 401 Parnassus Ave, Ste 278, San Francisco, CA 94143-0984; **Phone:** 415-476-7868; **Board Cert:** Psychiatry 1980; Psychosomatic Medicine 2008; **Med School:** Med Coll Wisc 1974; **Resid:** Psychiatry, Langley Porter Neuropsych Inst 1978; **Fellow:** Liaison Psychiatry, Langley Porter Neuropsych Inst 1979; **Fac Appt:** Prof Psyc, UCSF

Fann, Jesse R MD [Psyc] - **Spec Exp:** Psychiatry in Physical Illness; Psychiatry in Cancer; Neuro-Psychiatry; **Hospital:** Univ Wash Med Ctr, Seattle Cancer Care Alliance; **Address:** 1959 NE Pacific St, Box 356560, Seattle, WA 98195-6560; **Phone:** 206-685-4280; **Board Cert:** Psychiatry 2005; **Med School:** Northwestern Univ 1989; **Resid:** Psychiatry, Univ Washington Med Ctr 1993; **Fellow:** Liaison Psychiatry, Univ Washington Med Ctr 1995; Epidemiology, Univ Washington Med Ctr 1996; **Fac Appt:** Prof Psyc, Univ Wash

Friedman, Barry MD [Psyc] - **Spec Exp:** Psychopharmacology; Psychoanalysis; **Address:** Behavioral Hlth Med Grp of Beverly Hills, 9171 Wilshire Blvd, Ste 310, Beverly Hills, CA 90210; **Phone:** 310-274-4372; **Board Cert:** Psychiatry 1974; **Med School:** UCSF 1965; **Resid:** Psychiatry, UCLA Ronald Reagan Med Ctr 1971; **Fellow:** Psychoanalysis, Los Angeles Psychoanalytic Inst 1974; **Fac Appt:** Assoc Clin Prof Psyc, UCLA

Gitlin, Michael MD [Psyc] - **Spec Exp:** Mood Disorders; **Hospital:** Resnick Neuropsychiatric Hosp at UCLA; **Address:** UCLA NPI-Mood Disorders Clin, 300 Med Plaza, Ste 2200, Los Angeles, CA 90095-6968; **Phone:** 310-206-3654; **Board Cert:** Psychiatry 1981; **Med School:** Univ Pennsylvania 1975; **Resid:** Psychiatry, UCLA Neuropsychiatric Inst 1979; **Fac Appt:** Prof Psyc, UCLA

Keepers, George A MD [Psyc] - **Spec Exp:** Neuro-Psychiatry; ADD/ADHD; **Hospital:** OR Hlth & Sci Univ; **Address:** OHSU - Dept Psychiatry, 3181 SW Sam Jackson Park Rd, MC UHN80, Multnomah Pavilion, rm 2316, Portland, OR 97239; **Phone:** 503-494-8144; **Board Cert:** Psychiatry 1984; **Med School:** Baylor Coll Med 1977; **Resid:** Psychiatry, OR Hlth & Sci Univ 1984; **Fac Appt:** Prof Psyc, Oregon Hlth & Sci Univ

Leuchter, Andrew F MD [Psyc] - **Spec Exp:** Depression; **Hospital:** Resnick Neuropsychiatric Hosp at UCLA; **Address:** UCLA Neuropsychiatric Inst, 760 Westwood Pl, rm 57-456, Los Angeles, CA 90024; **Phone:** 310-825-0207; **Board Cert:** Psychiatry 1986; **Med School:** Baylor Coll Med 1980; **Resid:** Psychiatry, UCLA-Neuro Psyc Inst & Hosp 1984; **Fellow:** Geriatric Psychiatry, UCLA Ronald Reagan Med Ctr 1986; **Fac Appt:** Prof Psyc, UCLA

Marder, Stephen R MD [Psyc] - **Spec Exp:** Schizophrenia; Psychopharmacology; **Hospital:** VA Greater Los Angeles Hlthcare Sys, UCLA Ronald Reagan Med Ctr; **Address:** West Los Angeles VA - Gr LA Hlth Svcs, 11301 Wilshire Blvd, Bldg MIRECC 210A, Los Angeles, CA 90073; **Phone:** 310-268-3647; **Board Cert:** Psychiatry 1977; **Med School:** SUNY Buffalo 1971; **Resid:** Psychiatry, LAC & USC Med Ctr 1975; **Fac Appt:** Prof Psyc, UCLA

Nelson, J Craig MD [Psyc] - **Spec Exp:** Geriatric Psychiatry; Dementia; Depression; Psychopharmacology; **Hospital:** UCSF Med Ctr; **Address:** UCSF-Langley Porter Psychiatric Inst, 401 Parnassus Ave, Box 0984, San Francisco, CA 94143-0984; **Phone:** 415-476-7405; **Board Cert:** Psychiatry 1974; Geriatric Psychiatry 2012; **Med School:** Univ Wisc 1968; **Resid:** Psychiatry, Yale-New Haven Hosp 1973; **Fac Appt:** Prof Psyc, UCSF

Neppe, Vernon M MD/PhD [Psyc] - **Spec Exp:** Behavioral Neurology; Neuro-Psychiatry; Psychopharmacology; Forensic Psychiatry; **Hospital:** Overlake Hosp Med Ctr; **Address:** Pacific Neuropsychiatric Inst, 6300 Ninth Ave NE, Ste 353, Seattle, WA 98115; **Phone:** 206-527-6289; **Board Cert:** Psychiatry 1988; Behavioral Neurology & Neuropsychiatry 2006; **Med School:** South Africa 1973; **Resid:** Neurology, Univ Witwatersrand 1979; Psychiatry, Univ Witwatersrand 1980; **Fellow:** Psychopharmacology, Cornell Univ Med Ctr 1983; Neuropsychiatry, Cornell Univ Med Ctr 1983

Norman, Kim P MD [Psyc] - **Spec Exp:** Eating Disorders/Obesity; Personality Disorders; Dual Diagnosis; **Hospital:** UCSF Med Ctr; **Address:** UCSF-Langley Porter Psychiatric Inst, 401 Parnassus Ave, Box CAF-0984, San Francisco, CA 94143-0984; **Phone:** 415-476-7402; **Board Cert:** Psychiatry 1983; **Med School:** Albert Einstein Coll Med 1977; **Resid:** Psychiatry, Langley Porter Psych Inst 1981; **Fac Appt:** Clin Prof Psyc, UCSF

Pi, Edmond H MD [Psyc] - **Spec Exp:** Psychopharmacology; Cross Cultural Psychiatry; Anxiety Disorders; Mood Disorders; **Hospital:** LAC & USC Med Ctr; **Address:** LAC & USC Med Ctr, Dept Psyc, 1200 N State St, Los Angeles, CA 90033-1029; **Phone:** 310-668-8165; **Board Cert:** Psychiatry 1980; Psychosomatic Medicine 2008; **Med School:** South Korea 1972; **Resid:** Psychiatry, SUNY Affil Hosps 1977; Psychiatry, Univ Kentucky Hosp-Chandler Med Ctr 1978; **Fac Appt:** Prof Emeritus Psyc, USC-Keck School of Medicine

Pynoos, Robert S MD [Psyc] - **Spec Exp:** Post Traumatic Stress Disorder; Disaster Psychiatry; **Hospital:** Resnick Neuropsychiatric Hosp at UCLA; **Address:** Natl Ctr for Chld Traumatic Stress-UCLA, 11150 W Olympic Blvd, Ste 650, Los Angeles, CA 90064; **Phone:** 310-235-2633; **Board Cert:** Psychiatry 1980; **Med School:** Columbia P&S 1973; **Resid:** Pediatrics, Mt Sinai Hosp 1976; Psychiatry, NY-Presby/Weill Cornell Med Ctr 1979; **Fac Appt:** Prof Psyc, UCLA

Raskind, Murray A MD [Psyc] - **Spec Exp:** Geriatric Psychiatry; Alzheimer's Disease; Post Traumatic Stress Disorder; **Hospital:** VA Puget Sound Hlth Care Sys, Univ Wash Med Ctr; **Address:** VA Puget Sound Health Care System, 1660 S Columbian Way, Box 358280, Seattle, WA 98108; **Phone:** 206-764-2702; **Board Cert:** Psychiatry 1976; **Med School:** Columbia P&S 1968; **Resid:** Internal Medicine, Harlem Hosp Ctr 1970; Psychiatry, Univ Wash Affil Hosps 1973; **Fac Appt:** Prof Psyc, Univ Wash

Reus, Victor I MD [Psyc] - **Spec Exp:** Psychopharmacology; Bipolar/Mood Disorders; Behavioral Disorders; Depression; **Hospital:** UCSF Med Ctr; **Address:** Langley Porter Inst, 401 Parnassus Ave, San Francisco, CA 94143-0984; **Phone:** 415-476-7478; **Board Cert:** Psychiatry 1977; Geriatric Psychiatry 2010; **Med School:** Univ MD Sch Med 1973; **Resid:** Psychiatry, Univ Wisc Med Ctr 1976; **Fellow:** Biological Psychiatry, Natl Inst Mntl Hlth 1978; **Fac Appt:** Prof Psyc, UCSF

Roy-Byrne, Peter P MD [Psyc] - **Spec Exp:** Anxiety & Mood Disorders; Panic Disorder; Bipolar/Mood Disorders; Post Traumatic Stress Disorder; **Address:** Psychiatric Medicine Assocs, 1505 Westlake Ave N, Ste 920, Seattle, WA 98109; **Phone:** 206-386-3103; **Board Cert:** Psychiatry 1983; **Med School:** Tufts Univ 1978; **Resid:** Psychiatry, UCLA Neuropsych Inst 1982; **Fellow:** Biological Psychiatry, Natl Inst Hlth-NIMH 1984; **Fac Appt:** Prof Emeritus Psyc, Univ Wash

Saxena, Sanjaya MD [Psyc] - **Spec Exp:** Obsessive-Compulsive Disorder; Hoarding-Compulsive; Body Dysmorphic Disorder (BDD); Anxiety Disorders; **Hospital:** UCSD Med Ctr, VA San Diego Hlthcre Sys; **Address:** UCSD Obsessive-Compulsive Disorders Clin, 5060 Shoreham Pl, Ste 200, San Diego, CA 92122; **Phone:** 858-334-4640; **Board Cert:** Psychiatry 2006; **Med School:** Univ Minn 1990; **Resid:** Psychiatry, UCLA Neuropsychiatric Hosp 1994; **Fellow:** Neuroimaging, UCLA Ctr for Hlth Scis 1996; **Fac Appt:** Prof Psyc, UCSD

Schatzberg, Alan F MD [Psyc] - **Spec Exp:** Psychopharmacology; Anxiety & Mood Disorders; Depression; **Hospital:** Stanford Univ Hosp & Clins; **Address:** Stanford Univ-Dept Psychiatry, 401 Quarry Rd, Stanford, CA 94305-5797; **Phone:** 650-723-6811; **Board Cert:** Psychiatry 1975; **Med School:** NYU Sch Med 1968; **Resid:** Psychiatry, Mass Mental Hlth Ctr 1973; **Fellow:** Psychiatry, Harvard Med Sch Affil Hosp; **Fac Appt:** Prof Psyc, Stanford Univ

Spiegel, David MD [Psyc] - **Spec Exp:** Hypnosis; Psychiatry in Cancer; Post Traumatic Stress Disorder; **Hospital:** Stanford Univ Hosp & Clins, Lucile Packard Chldn's Hosp; **Address:** 401 Quarry Rd, Ste 2325, MC 5718, Stanford, CA 94305-5718; **Phone:** 650-723-2423; **Board Cert:** Psychiatry 1976; **Med School:** Harvard Med Sch 1971; **Resid:** Psychiatry, Mass Mental Hlth Ctr 1974; Psychiatry, Cambridge Hosp 1974; **Fellow:** Community Psychiatry, Lab of Comm Psych 1974; **Fac Appt:** Prof Psyc, Stanford Univ

Stein, Murray B MD [Psyc] - **Spec Exp:** Anxiety Disorders; Panic Disorder; Post Traumatic Stress Disorder; **Hospital:** UCSD Med Ctr, VA San Diego Hlthcre Sys; **Address:** UCSD Dept Psychiatry, 8939 Villa La Jolla Drive, Ste 200, MS 0855, La Jolla, CA 92037; **Phone:** 858-534-6400; **Board Cert:** Psychiatry 1989; **Med School:** Univ Manitoba 1983; **Resid:** Psychiatry, Univ Toronto Affil Hosp 1986; Psychiatry, Natl Inst Mental Hlth-NIH 1987; **Fellow:** Anxiety Disorder, Natl Inst Mental Hlth-NIH 1990; **Fac Appt:** Prof Psyc, UCSD

Strouse, Thomas B MD [Psyc] - **Spec Exp:** Psychiatry in Cancer; Pain-Cancer; Psychiatry in Physical Illness; Palliative Care; **Hospital:** UCLA Ronald Reagan Med Ctr, Cedars-Sinai Med Ctr; **Address:** UCLA Resnick Neuropsychiatric Hosp, 757 Westwood Plaza, Ste 4230B, Los Angeles, CA 90095; **Phone:** 310-267-9159; **Board Cert:** Psychiatry 1993; Hospice & Palliative Medicine 2008; Psychosomatic Medicine 2009; **Med School:** Case West Res Univ 1987; **Resid:** Psychiatry, UCLA Med Ctr 1991; **Fac Appt:** Clin Prof Psyc, UCLA

Walker, R. Dale MD [Psyc] - **Spec Exp:** Alcohol Abuse-Consultation; Drug Abuse-Consultation; Substance Abuse-Consultation; **Hospital:** OR Hlth & Sci Univ; **Address:** OHSU/One Sky Ctr, 3181 SW Sam Jackson Pk Rd, GH Bldg - Ste 151, Portland, OR 97239; **Phone:** 503-494-3703; **Board Cert:** Psychiatry 1982; **Med School:** Univ Okla Coll Med 1972; **Resid:** Psychiatry, Univ Oklahoma Med Ctr 1973; Psychiatry, UCSD Med Ctr 1977; **Fellow:** Public Health & Genl Preventive Med, Andriga Stampur; **Fac Appt:** Prof Psyc, Oregon Hlth & Sci Univ

Weinstock, Robert MD [Psyc] - **Spec Exp:** Adolescent Psychiatry; Addiction/Substance Abuse; **Hospital:** Cedars-Sinai Med Ctr; **Address:** 1823 Sawtelle Blvd, Los Angeles, CA 90025; **Phone:** 310-477-9933; **Board Cert:** Psychiatry 1975; Forensic Psychiatry 2004; **Med School:** NYU Sch Med 1966; **Resid:** Psychiatry, McLean Hosp 1970; Adolescent Medicine, McLean Hosp 1972; **Fellow:** Psychiatric Research, Boston Med Ctr 1974; **Fac Appt:** Clin Prof Psyc, UCLA

Zerbe, Kathryn J MD [Psyc] - **Spec Exp:** Eating Disorders; Women's Health-Mental Health; Psychoanalysis; **Address:** 4800 SW Macadam Ave, Ste 340, Portland, OR 97239; **Phone:** 503-295-9909; **Board Cert:** Psychiatry 1984; **Med School:** Temple Univ 1978; **Resid:** Psychiatry, Menninger Clin 1982; Psychoanalysis, Topeka Inst for Psychoanalysis 1992; **Fac Appt:** Prof Psyc, Oregon Hlth & Sci Univ

Addiction Psychiatry

New England

Ciraulo, Domenic A MD [AdP] - **Spec Exp:** Alcohol Abuse; Psychopharmacology; Anxiety & Depression; **Hospital:** Boston Med Ctr; **Address:** Boston Univ, Div Psychiatry, 720 Harrison Ave, Ste 914, Boston, MA 02118; **Phone:** 617-414-1995; **Board Cert:** Psychiatry 1980; Addiction Psychiatry 2013; **Med School:** Georgetown Univ 1975; **Resid:** Psychiatry, Inst Living 1977; **Fellow:** Psychopharmacology, Mass Mental Hlth Ctr 1978; **Fac Appt:** Prof Psyc, Boston Univ

Greenfield, Shelly F MD [AdP] - **Spec Exp:** Addiction/Substance Abuse; Alcohol Abuse; Women & Addiction; **Hospital:** McLean Hosp; **Address:** McLean Hospital, 115 Mill St, Belmont, MA 02478; **Phone:** 617-855-2241; **Board Cert:** Psychiatry 1992; Addiction Psychiatry 2006; **Med School:** Harvard Med Sch 1986; **Resid:** Psychiatry, McLean Hosp 1990; **Fellow:** Epidemiology, Univ North Carolina 1992; Research, NIH-Natl Inst Drug Abuse 1993; **Fac Appt:** Prof Psyc, Harvard Med Sch

Nitenson, Nancy C MD [AdP] - **Spec Exp:** Alcohol Abuse; Addiction/Substance Abuse; **Address:** 1577 Beacon St, Brookline, MA 02446; **Phone:** 617-608-3724; **Board Cert:** Psychiatry 1992; Addiction Psychiatry 2006; **Med School:** Univ Mass Sch Med 1986; **Resid:** Psychiatry, U Mass Med Ctr 1990; **Fellow:** Psychopharmacology, McLean Hosp 1991

Weiss, Roger D MD [AdP] - **Spec Exp:** Alcohol Abuse-Consultation; Drug Abuse-Consultation; Dual Diagnosis-Consultation; **Hospital:** McLean Hosp; **Address:** McLean Hospital, 115 Mill St, Belmont, MA 02478; **Phone:** 617-855-2242; **Board Cert:** Psychiatry 1980; Addiction Psychiatry 2013; **Med School:** Tufts Univ 1976; **Resid:** Psychiatry, McLean Hosp 1979; **Fac Appt:** Prof Psyc, Harvard Med Sch

Mid Atlantic

Collins, Eric D MD [AdP] - **Spec Exp:** Addiction/Substance Abuse; Opiate Addiction; Dual Diagnosis; Alcohol Abuse; **Hospital:** NY-Presby/Columbia Univ Med Ctr, NY (page 65), Silver Hill Hosp; **Address:** 180 Ft Washington Ave, Box HP-260, New York, NY 10032; **Phone:** 212-305-8732; **Board Cert:** Psychiatry 2005; Addiction Psychiatry 2007; Psychosomatic Medicine 2008; **Med School:** Columbia P&S 1990; **Resid:** Psychiatry, NY State Psyc Inst 1995; **Fellow:** Psychosomatic Medicine, NY-Presby/Columbia Univ Med Ctr 1996; Addiction Psychiatry, NY State Psyc Inst 1997; **Fac Appt:** Assoc Clin Prof Psyc, Columbia P&S

Frances, Richard J MD [AdP] - **Spec Exp:** Addiction/Substance Abuse; Anxiety & Mood Disorders; Forensic Psychiatry; **Hospital:** Silver Hill Hosp, NYU Langone Med Ctr (page 68); **Address:** 510 E 86th St, Ste 1D, New York, NY 10028; **Phone:** 212-861-0570; **Board Cert:** Psychiatry 1976; Addiction Psychiatry 2012; **Med School:** NYU Sch Med 1971; **Resid:** Psychiatry, Jacobi Med Ctr 1974; **Fellow:** Psychoanalysis, NY Psychoanalytic Inst 1983; **Fac Appt:** Clin Prof Psyc, NYU Sch Med

Galanter, I Marc MD [AdP] - **Spec Exp:** Alcohol Abuse; Drug Abuse; Anxiety & Depression; **Hospital:** NYU Langone Med Ctr (page 68); **Address:** 285 Central Park West, New York, NY 10024-3006; **Phone:** 212-877-4093; **Board Cert:** Psychiatry 1974; Addiction Psychiatry 2011; **Med School:** Albert Einstein Coll Med 1967; **Resid:** Pediatrics, UCLA Med Ctr 1978; Psychiatry, Bronx Muni Hosp-Einstein 1971; **Fac Appt:** Prof Psyc, NYU Sch Med

Kampman, Kyle M MD [AdP] - **Spec Exp:** Addiction/Substance Abuse; Cocaine Addiction; Opiate Addiction; Alcohol Abuse; **Hospital:** Hosp Univ Penn - UPHS (page 69); **Address:** Charles O'Brien Treatment Center, 3900 Chestnut St, Philadelphia, PA 19104; **Phone:** 215-222-3200 x109; **Board Cert:** Psychiatry 2004; Addiction Psychiatry 2006; **Med School:** Tulane Univ 1985; **Resid:** Psychiatry, Hosp Univ Penn 1993; **Fellow:** Substance Abuse, Hosp Univ Penn 1994; **Fac Appt:** Assoc Prof Psyc, Univ Pennsylvania

Kleber, Herbert D MD [AdP] - **Spec Exp:** Opiate Addiction; Cocaine Addiction; Drug Abuse; **Hospital:** NY-Presby/Columbia Univ Med Ctr, NY (page 65), NY State Psychiatric Inst; **Address:** NY State Psychiatric Inst, 1051 Riverside Drive, Rm 3713, Unit 66, New York, NY 10032-1007; **Phone:** 732-235-7729; **Med School:** Jefferson Med Coll 1960; **Resid:** Psychiatry, Yale-New Haven Hosp 1964; **Fac Appt:** Prof Psyc, Columbia P&S

Lawson, William B MD/PhD [AdP] - **Spec Exp:** Bipolar/Mood Disorders; Addiction/Substance Abuse; Dual Diagnosis; **Hospital:** Howard Univ Hosp; **Address:** Dept of Psychiatry, Howard Univ Hlth Sciences, 2041 Georgia Ave NW, Fl 5th, Ste 5B02, Washington, DC 20060; **Phone:** 202-865-6611; **Board Cert:** Psychiatry 1984; Addiction Psychiatry 2006; **Med School:** Univ Chicago-Pritzker Sch Med 1978; **Resid:** Psychiatry, Stanford Univ Med Ctr 1981; Psychiatry, Natl Inst Mental Hlth 1982; **Fellow:** Neuropsychiatry, Natl Inst Mental Hlth 1984; **Fac Appt:** Prof Psyc, Howard Univ

Serota, Ronald D MD [AdP] - **Spec Exp:** Addiction/Substance Abuse; Drug Abuse; Opiate Addiction; Cocaine Addiction; **Hospital:** Thomas Jefferson Univ Hosp; **Address:** Jefferson Univ Phys, Dept of Psych & Human Behavior, 833 Chestnut St, Ste 210, Philadelphia, PA 19107; **Phone:** 215-955-4834; **Board Cert:** Internal Medicine 1974; Psychiatry 1990; **Med School:** Thomas Jefferson Univ 1968; **Resid:** Internal Medicine, Mt Zion Hosp 1972; Psychiatry, Thomas Jefferson Univ Hosp 1981; **Fac Appt:** Asst Prof Psyc, Thomas Jefferson Univ

Strain, Eric C MD [AdP] - **Spec Exp:** Addiction/Substance Abuse; Dual Diagnosis; Opiate Addiction; **Hospital:** Johns Hopkins Bayview Med Ctr (page 59); **Address:** 5510 Mathen Shock Drive Fl 3 - Ste 3046, Baltimore, MD 21224; **Phone:** 410-550-1191; **Board Cert:** Psychiatry 1989; Addiction Psychiatry 2013; **Med School:** Ohio State Univ 1984; **Resid:** Psychiatry, Johns Hopkins Hosp 1989; **Fellow:** Addiction Psychiatry, Johns Hopkins Hosp 1990; **Fac Appt:** Prof Psyc, Johns Hopkins Univ

Midwest

Stine, Susan M MD/PhD [AdP] - **Spec Exp:** Addiction/Substance Abuse; Opiate Addiction; **Hospital:** John D. Dingell VA Med Ctr, Detroit; **Address:** Wayne State Univ Sch Med, Dept Psychiatry, 2761 E Jefferson Ave, Detroit, MI 48207; **Phone:** 313-993-9879; **Board Cert:** Psychiatry 1993; Addiction Psychiatry 2002; **Med School:** Univ Miami Sch Med 1983; **Resid:** Psychiatry, Yale-New Haven Hosp 1987; **Fac Appt:** Assoc Prof Psyc, Wayne State Univ

Great Plains and Mountains

Howell, Elizabeth F MD [AdP] - **Spec Exp:** Opiate Addiction; Alcohol Abuse; Addiction/Substance Abuse; Mood Disorders; **Hospital:** Univ Utah Hlth Care, Lakeview Hosp; **Address:** Univ Utah Neuropsychiatric Inst, 501 Chipeta Way, Salt Lake City, UT 84108; **Phone:** 801-583-2500; **Board Cert:** Psychiatry 1985; Addiction Psychiatry 2013; **Med School:** Med Univ SC 1980; **Resid:** Pediatrics, MUSC Med Ctr 1981; Psychiatry, MUSC Med Ctr 1984; **Fellow:** Psychiatric Research, MUSC Med Ctr 1985; **Fac Appt:** Assoc Clin Prof Psyc, Univ Utah

Southwest

Kosten, Thomas R MD [AdP] - **Spec Exp:** Cocaine Addiction; Alcohol Abuse; Psychopharmacology; Opiate Addiction; **Hospital:** DeBakey VA Med Ctr-Houston, UT MD Anderson Canc Ctr; **Address:** Michael DeBakey VA Medical Ctr, 2002 Holcombe Blvd, Research - Building 110, Houston, TX 77030; **Phone:** 713-794-7032; **Board Cert:** Psychiatry 1984; Addiction Psychiatry 2002; **Med School:** Cornell Univ-Weill Med Coll 1977; **Resid:** Psychiatry, Yale-New Haven Hosp 1981; **Fellow:** Epidemiology, Yale-New Haven Hosp 1983; **Fac Appt:** Prof Psyc, Baylor Coll Med

Child & Adolescent Psychiatry

New England

Biederman, Joseph MD [ChAP] - **Spec Exp:** ADD/ADHD; Anxiety & Mood Disorders; Psychopharmacology; **Hospital:** Mass Genl Hosp; **Address:** Mass Genl Hosp, Dept Psychiatry, 55 Fruit St Yawkey Bldg, Boston, MA 02114; **Phone:** 617-726-1743; **Board Cert:** Psychiatry 1983; Child & Adolescent Psychiatry 1984; **Med School:** Argentina 1971; **Resid:** Psychiatry, Hadassah Univ Hosp 1977; Psychiatry, Mass Genl Hosp 1981; **Fellow:** Child Psychiatry, Childrens Hosp 1979; **Fac Appt:** Prof Psyc, Harvard Med Sch

Hudziak, James J MD [ChAP] - **Spec Exp:** ADD/ADHD; Obsessive-Compulsive Disorder; Psychopharmacology; **Hospital:** FAHC - Med Ctr Campus; **Address:** VT Ctr for Chldn, Youth and Families, 1 S Prospect St, Burlington, VT 05401-5505; **Phone:** 802-847-4563; **Board Cert:** Psychiatry 2005; Child & Adolescent Psychiatry 2005; **Med School:** Univ Minn 1988; **Resid:** Psychiatry, Univ Wash Med Ctr 1993; **Fellow:** Child & Adolescent Psychiatry, St Louis Chldns Hosp 1995; **Fac Appt:** Prof Psyc, Univ VT Coll Med

Leckman, James F MD [ChAP] - **Spec Exp:** Tourette's Syndrome; Obsessive-Compulsive Disorder; Autism; **Hospital:** Yale-New Haven Hosp; **Address:** Yale Child Study Ctr, 230 S Frontage Rd, New Haven, CT 06520; **Phone:** 203-785-7971; **Board Cert:** Psychiatry 1980; Child & Adolescent Psychiatry 1982; **Med School:** Univ New Mexico 1973; **Resid:** Psychiatry, Yale-New Haven Hosp 1979; Child Psychiatry, Yale Chld Stdy Ctr 1980; **Fellow:** Psychiatry, Natl Inst Mental Hlth 1976; **Fac Appt:** Prof Psyc, Yale Univ

McDougle, Christopher J MD [ChAP] - **Spec Exp:** Autism & Developmental Disorders; Obsessive-Compulsive Disorder; Mental Retardation; **Hospital:** Mass Genl Hosp; **Address:** Lurie Center for Autism, 1 Maguire Rd, Lexington, MA 02421; **Phone:** 781-860-1700; **Board Cert:** Psychiatry 1992; Child & Adolescent Psychiatry 2006; **Med School:** Indiana Univ 1986; **Resid:** Psychiatry, Yale New Haven Hosp 1990; **Fellow:** Child & Adolescent Psychiatry, Yale Child Study Ctr 1995; **Fac Appt:** Prof Psyc, Harvard Med Sch

Sargent II, Albert J MD [ChAP] - **Spec Exp:** Eating Disorders; Suicide; Family Therapy; Trauma Psychiatry; **Hospital:** Tufts Med Ctr; **Address:** Tufts Med Ctr, 800 Washington St, Box 1007, Boston, MA 02111; **Phone:** 617-636-8768; **Board Cert:** Pediatrics 1979; Psychiatry 1988; Child & Adolescent Psychiatry 1989; **Med School:** Univ Rochester 1973; **Resid:** Pediatrics, Univ Wisc Hosp 1977; Psychiatry, Hosp Univ Penn 1987; **Fellow:** Ambulatory Pediatrics, Univ Wisconsin Hosp 1976; Child & Adolescent Psychiatry, Philadelphia Child Guidance Ctr 1980; **Fac Appt:** Prof Psyc, Tufts Univ

Spencer, Thomas MD [ChAP] - **Spec Exp:** ADD/ADHD; **Hospital:** Mass Genl Hosp; **Address:** Mass Gen Hosp, 55 Fruit St, Ste YAW 6A, Boston, MA 02114; **Phone:** 617-724-5600; **Board Cert:** Psychiatry 1983; Child & Adolescent Psychiatry 1992; **Med School:** Univ Wisc 1978; **Resid:** Psychiatry, New England Med Ctr 1984; **Fellow:** Child & Adolescent Psychiatry, Mass Genl Hosp 1992; **Fac Appt:** Assoc Prof Psyc, Harvard Med Sch

Wilens, Timothy E MD [ChAP] - **Spec Exp:** ADD/ADHD; Bipolar/Mood Disorders; Addiction/Substance Abuse; **Hospital:** Mass Genl Hosp; **Address:** Mass Genl Hosp, Dept Psyc, 55 Fruit St Yawkey Bldg - Ste 6A, Boston, MA 02114; **Phone:** 617-724-5600; **Board Cert:** Psychiatry 1990; Child & Adolescent Psychiatry 1991; Addiction Psychiatry 2004; **Med School:** Univ Mich Med Sch 1985; **Resid:** Psychiatry, Mass Genl Hosp 1988; **Fellow:** Child & Adolescent Psychiatry, Mass Genl Hosp 1990; **Fac Appt:** Assoc Prof Psyc, Harvard Med Sch

Mid Atlantic

Abright, A. Reese MD [ChAP] - **Spec Exp:** Mood Disorders; ADD/ADHD; Anxiety Disorders; **Hospital:** Elmhurst Hosp Ctr; **Address:** 140 E 40th St, Ste 1B, New York, NY 10016; **Phone:** 212-867-3131; **Board Cert:** Psychiatry 1978; Child & Adolescent Psychiatry 1981; **Med School:** Univ Tex SW, Dallas 1973; **Resid:** Psychiatry, St Vincent's Hosp 1974; Psychiatry, Presby/Weill Cornell Med Ctr 1977; **Fellow:** Child & Adolescent Psychiatry, Presby/Weill Cornell Med Ctr 1979; **Fac Appt:** Clin Prof Psyc, NY Med Coll

Birmaher, Boris MD [ChAP] - **Spec Exp:** Bipolar/Mood Disorders; Anxiety Disorders; **Hospital:** Western Psych Inst & Clin-UPMC; **Address:** Western Psych Inst & Clin-UPMC, 3811 O'Hara St, Pittsburgh, PA 15213; **Phone:** 412-246-5788; **Board Cert:** Psychiatry 1989; Child & Adolescent Psychiatry 1990; **Med School:** Colombia 1975; **Resid:** Psychiatry, Haddassah Med Coll-Hebrew U 1983; Psychiatry, Montefiore Med Ctr 1984; **Fellow:** Child Psychiatry, NY Presby-Columbia Med Ctr 1986; Child Psychiatry, NY Psych Inst-Columbia U 1987; **Fac Appt:** Prof Psyc, Univ Pittsburgh

Bogrov, Michael A MD [ChAP] - **Spec Exp:** ADD/ADHD; Bipolar/Mood Disorders; **Hospital:** Sheppard Pratt Hlth Sys; **Address:** Sheppard & Enoch Pratt Hosp, 6501 N Charles St, Baltimore, MD 21204-6819; **Phone:** 410-938-4913; **Board Cert:** Psychiatry 1993; Child & Adolescent Psychiatry 1994; **Med School:** Emory Univ 1987; **Resid:** Psychiatry, Univ Maryland Hosp 1990; **Fellow:** Child & Adolescent Psychiatry, Johns Hopkins Hosp 1992; **Fac Appt:** Asst Clin Prof ChAP, Univ MD Sch Med

Brent, David A MD [ChAP] - **Spec Exp:** Suicide; **Hospital:** Western Psych Inst & Clin-UPMC; **Address:** Western Psych Inst & Clin, 3811 O'Hara St, Ste 315 BFT, Pittsburgh, PA 15213-2593; **Phone:** 412-246-5619; **Board Cert:** Pediatrics 1981; Psychiatry 1982; Child & Adolescent Psychiatry 1983; **Med School:** Jefferson Med Coll 1974; **Resid:** Pediatrics, Univ Colorado Affil Hosp 1978; Psychiatry, Western Psych Inst 1982; **Fellow:** Child & Adolescent Psychiatry, Western Psych Inst 1983; **Fac Appt:** Prof Psyc, Univ Pittsburgh

Coffey, Barbara J MD [ChAP] - **Spec Exp:** Tourette's Syndrome; ADD/ADHD; Obsessive-Compulsive Disorder; Psychopharmacology; **Hospital:** Mt Sinai Med Ctr (page 62); **Address:** Tics & Tourette's Clin & Rsch Program, 1240 Park Ave, New York, NY 10029; **Phone:** 212-659-1663; **Board Cert:** Psychiatry 1981; Child & Adolescent Psychiatry 1986; **Med School:** Tufts Univ 1975; **Resid:** Psychiatry, Boston Med Ctr 1978; **Fellow:** Child & Adolescent Psychiatry, Tufts Med Ctr 1980; **Fac Appt:** Prof Psyc, Mount Sinai Sch Med

Foley, Carmel A MD [ChAP] - **Spec Exp:** Mood Disorders; **Hospital:** Steven & Alexandra Cohen Chldn's Med Ctr of NY (page 66); **Address:** 420 Lakeville Rd, 1st Floor, Ste 110, New Hyde Park, NY 11040; **Phone:** 718-470-3550; **Board Cert:** Psychiatry 1979; Child & Adolescent Psychiatry 1981; Psychosomatic Medicine 2009; **Med School:** Ireland 1972; **Resid:** Psychiatry, St Patricks Hosp 1976; Psychiatry, Lafayette Clin 1977; **Fellow:** Child & Adolescent Psychiatry, Lafayette Clin 1979

Fornari, Victor M MD [ChAP] - **Spec Exp:** Eating Disorders; Trauma Psychiatry; Post Traumatic Stress Disorder; **Hospital:** Zucker Hillside Hosp (page 66); **Address:** Zucker Hillside Hosp, Ambulatory Care Pav Lower Level, 75-59 263rd St, Glen Oaks, NY 11004; **Phone:** 718-470-3510; **Board Cert:** Psychiatry 1984; Child & Adolescent Psychiatry 1985; **Med School:** SUNY Downstate 1979; **Resid:** Psychiatry, Hosp Univ Penn - UPHS 1982; **Fellow:** Child & Adolescent Psychiatry, NS-LIJ Hlth Sys 1984; **Fac Appt:** Prof Psyc, NYU Sch Med

Hirsch, Glenn S MD [ChAP] - **Spec Exp:** Anxiety & Mood Disorders; Tourette's Syndrome; Bipolar/Mood Disorders; ADD/ADHD; **Hospital:** NYU Langone Med Ctr (page 68), Bellevue Hosp Ctr; **Address:** NYU Child Study Center, 1 Park Ave, Fl 7, New York, NY 10016; **Phone:** 212-263-8704; **Board Cert:** Psychiatry 1984; Child & Adolescent Psychiatry 1985; **Med School:** Albert Einstein Coll Med 1979; **Resid:** Psychiatry, New York Hosp-Cornell 1982; **Fellow:** Child & Adolescent Psychiatry, Columbia-Presby Med Ctr 1984; **Fac Appt:** Asst Prof ChAP, NYU Sch Med

Koplewicz, Harold S MD [ChAP] - **Spec Exp:** Anxiety & Mood Disorders; Psychopharmacology; ADD/ADHD; **Address:** Child Mind Inst, 445 Park Ave at 56th St, New York, NY 10022; **Phone:** 212-308-3118; **Board Cert:** Psychiatry 1983; Child & Adolescent Psychiatry 1984; **Med School:** Albert Einstein Coll Med 1978; **Resid:** Psychiatry, Presby/Westchester Div 1981; Psychiatry, NY State Psych Inst 1983; **Fellow:** Psychiatric Research, NY State Psych Inst 1985

Leventhal, Bennett L MD [ChAP] - **Spec Exp:** Autism; ADD/ADHD; Psychopharmacology; **Hospital:** NYU Langone Med Ctr (page 68); **Address:** 140 Old Orangeburg Rd, Bldg 35, Orangeburg, NY 10962; **Phone:** 845-398-5502; **Board Cert:** Psychiatry 1979; Child & Adolescent Psychiatry 1980; **Med School:** Louisiana State U, New Orleans 1974; **Resid:** Psychiatry, Duke Univ Med Ctr 1978; **Fellow:** Child & Adolescent Psychiatry, Duke Univ Med Ctr 1977; **Fac Appt:** Prof Psyc, NYU Sch Med

Pomeroy, John C MD [ChAP] - **Spec Exp:** Autism; Mental Retardation; Developmental Disorders; **Hospital:** Stony Brook Univ Med Ctr; **Address:** The Cody Center for Autism, 37 Research Way, East Setauket, NY 11733; **Phone:** 631-444-3070; **Board Cert:** Psychiatry 1984; Child & Adolescent Psychiatry 1988; **Med School:** England, UK 1973; **Resid:** Psychiatry, St Mary's Hosp 1979; **Fellow:** Child & Adolescent Psychiatry, Univ Iowa Hosps 1981; **Fac Appt:** Assoc Prof Psyc, SUNY Stony Brook

Riddle, Mark A MD [ChAP] - **Spec Exp:** Psychopharmacology; Anxiety Disorders; Mood Disorders; **Hospital:** Johns Hopkins Hosp (page 59); **Address:** Johns Hopkins, Psychiatry Dept, 1800 Orleans St Fl 12, Baltimore, MD 21287; **Phone:** 410-955-2321; **Board Cert:** Psychiatry 1982; Child & Adolescent Psychiatry 1986; **Med School:** Indiana Univ 1977; **Resid:** Psychiatry, Yale-New Haven Hosp 1981; **Fellow:** Child & Adolescent Psychiatry, Yale Child Study Ctr 1983; **Fac Appt:** Prof Psyc, Johns Hopkins Univ

Rostain, Anthony L MD [ChAP] - **Spec Exp:** ADD/ADHD; Autism; Tourette's Syndrome; Asperger's Syndrome; **Hospital:** Hosp Univ Penn - UPHS (page 69), Chldns Hosp of Philadelphia; **Address:** Hosp Univ Penn - Dept Psychiatry, 3535 Market St Fl 2 - rm 2007, Philadelphia, PA 19104; **Phone:** 215-746-7210; **Board Cert:** Pediatrics 1985; Psychiatry 1988; Child & Adolescent Psychiatry 1989; **Med School:** NYU Sch Med 1980; **Resid:** Pediatrics, Chldns Hosp 1983; Psychiatry, Hosp Univ Penn - UPHS 1987; **Fellow:** Child Psychiatry, Philadelphia Child Guidance Clin 1985; **Fac Appt:** Prof Psyc, Univ Pennsylvania

Turecki, Stanley K MD [ChAP] - **Spec Exp:** Temperamentally Difficult Child; ADD/ADHD; Parenting Issues; **Hospital:** Lenox Hill Hosp (page 66); **Address:** 136 E 64th St, Ste 1B, New York, NY 10065; **Phone:** 212-355-2535; **Board Cert:** Psychiatry 1978; Child & Adolescent Psychiatry 1981; **Med School:** South Africa 1961; **Resid:** Psychiatry, Tara Hospital 1969; Psychiatry, Mt Sinai Hosp 1971

Walkup, John T MD [ChAP] - **Spec Exp:** Anxiety Disorders; **Hospital:** NY-Presby/Weill Cornell Med Ctr, NY (page 65); **Address:** NY Presby/Weill Cornell Med Ctr, Div Child and Adolescent Psychiatry, 525 E 68th St, rm F-1109, New York, NY 10065; **Phone:** 212-746-1891; **Board Cert:** Psychiatry 1987; Child & Adolescent Psychiatry 1992; **Med School:** Univ Minn 1982; **Resid:** Psychiatry, Yale Univ Med Sch 1985; **Fellow:** Child Psychiatry, Yale Chld Study Ctr 1988; **Fac Appt:** Prof Psyc, Cornell Univ-Weill Med Coll

Southeast

Deas, Deborah V MD [ChAP] - **Spec Exp:** Addiction/Substance Abuse; Dual Diagnosis; Substance Abuse in ADHD Patients; **Hospital:** MUSC Med Ctr; **Address:** MUSC, Ctr for Drug & Alcohol Programs, 67 President St, Charleston, SC 29425; **Phone:** 843-792-5214; **Board Cert:** Psychiatry 2005; Child & Adolescent Psychiatry 2007; **Med School:** Med Univ SC 1989; **Resid:** Psychiatry, MUSC Med Ctr 1992; **Fellow:** Child & Adolescent Psychiatry, MUSC Med Ctr 1994; Addiction Psychiatry, MUSC/Natl Inst Alcohol Abuse & Alcoholism 1994; **Fac Appt:** Prof Psyc, Med Univ SC

Heston, Jerry D MD [ChAP] - **Spec Exp:** ADD/ADHD; Depression; Asperger's Syndrome; **Hospital:** Le Bonheur Chldns Med Ctr, St. Jude Children's Research Hosp; **Address:** Child & Adolescent Psychiatric Assocs, 1135 Cully Rd, Ste 100, Cordova, TN 38016; **Phone:** 901-752-1980; **Board Cert:** Psychiatry 1988; Child & Adolescent Psychiatry 1989; **Med School:** Univ S Fla Coll Med 1981; **Resid:** Pediatrics, LeBonheur Chldns Hosp 1984; Psychiatry, Univ Tenn Affil Hosp 1986; **Fellow:** Child & Adolescent Psychiatry, Univ Tenn Affil Hosp 1988; **Fac Appt:** Clin Prof Psyc, Univ Tenn Coll Med

Sexson, Sandra G.B. MD [ChAP] - **Spec Exp:** Psychiatry in Transplant Patients; Death & Dying; Autism; **Hospital:** Georgia Regents Med Ctr-Augusta; **Address:** GA Regents, Psychiatry Dept, 977 St Sebastian Way, Augusta, GA 30912; **Phone:** 706-721-6699; **Board Cert:** Psychiatry 1980; Child & Adolescent Psychiatry 1981; **Med School:** Univ Miss 1971; **Resid:** Psychiatry, TX Hlth Sci Ctr 1974; Child Psychiatry, Washington Univ Phys 1978; **Fac Appt:** Prof Psyc, Med Coll GA

Midwest

Alessi, Norman E MD [ChAP] - **Spec Exp:** Mood Disorders; Autism; Cognitive Psychotherapy; ADD/ADHD; **Hospital:** Univ Michigan Med Ctr; **Address:** 2311 E Stadium Blvd, Ste 216, Ann Arbor, MI 48104; **Phone:** 734-222-6222; **Board Cert:** Psychiatry 1982; Child & Adolescent Psychiatry 1985; **Med School:** Emory Univ 1976; **Resid:** Psychiatry, Univ Mich Med Ctr 1980; Child Psychiatry, Univ Mich Med Ctr 1981; **Fellow:** Child & Adolescent Psychiatry, Univ Mich Med Ctr 1983; **Fac Appt:** Prof Emeritus Psyc, Univ Mich Med Sch

Campo, John V MD [ChAP] - **Spec Exp:** Psychosomatic Disorders; Psychiatry in Physical Illness; **Hospital:** OSU Wexner Med Ctr, Nationwide Chldn's Hosp; **Address:** OSU Wexner Med Ctr, 1670 Upham Drive, Ste 130, Columbus, OH 43210; **Phone:** 614-685-5602; **Board Cert:** Pediatrics 1986; Psychiatry 1989; Child & Adolescent Psychiatry 1993; **Med School:** Univ Pennsylvania 1982; **Resid:** Pediatrics, Chldns Hosp 1985; Psychiatry, West Psych Inst Clin 1989; **Fac Appt:** Clin Prof Ped, Ohio State Univ

Dulcan, Mina K MD [ChAP] - **Spec Exp:** ADD/ADHD; **Hospital:** Lurie Chldn's Hosp-Chicago, Northwestern Meml Hosp; **Address:** Lurie Chldn's Hosp, Dept Psych, 225 E Chicago Ave, Box 10, Chicago, IL 60611; **Phone:** 312-227-3413; **Board Cert:** Psychiatry 1978; Child & Adolescent Psychiatry 1979; **Med School:** Penn State Coll Med 1974; **Resid:** Psychiatry, Western Psych Inst/Clinic 1977; **Fellow:** Child Psychiatry, Western Psych Inst 1978; **Fac Appt:** Prof Psyc, Northwestern Univ

Hirsch, Sharon MD [ChAP] - **Spec Exp:** Anxiety Disorders; Mood Disorders; ADD/ADHD; Psychopharmacology; **Hospital:** Univ of Chicago Med, Univ Chicago Med-Comer Chldn's Hosp; **Address:** Univ Chicago-Child & Adolescent Psych, 5841 S Maryland Ave, MC 3077, Chicago, IL 60637; **Phone:** 773-834-4093; **Board Cert:** Psychiatry 1992; Child & Adolescent Psychiatry 2005; **Med School:** Univ Tex Med Br, Galveston 1986; **Resid:** Psychiatry, UCSD Med Ctr 1990; **Fellow:** Psychopharmacology, UCSD Med Ctr 1991; Child & Adolescent Psychiatry, UCLA Med Ctr 1994; **Fac Appt:** Assoc Prof Psyc, Univ Chicago-Pritzker Sch Med

Luby, Joan L MD [ChAP] - **Spec Exp:** Mood Disorders; **Hospital:** Barnes-Jewish Hosp; **Address:** Wash Univ Sch Med, Dept Psyc, 660 S Euclid Ave, Box 8134, St Louis, MO 63110; **Phone:** 314-286-1700; **Board Cert:** Psychiatry 1993; Child & Adolescent Psychiatry 1993; **Med School:** Wayne State Univ 1985; **Resid:** Psychiatry, Stanford Univ Sch Med 1989; **Fellow:** Child & Adolescent Psychiatry, Stanford Univ Sch Med 1991; **Fac Appt:** Assoc Prof Psyc, Washington Univ, St Louis

Slomowitz, Marcia MD [ChAP] - **Spec Exp:** ADD/ADHD; Bipolar/Mood Disorders; Anxiety & Depression; **Hospital:** Northwestern Meml Hosp; **Address:** 333 N Michigan Ave, Ste 1125, Chicago, IL 60601; **Phone:** 312-726-1083; **Board Cert:** Psychiatry 1982; Child & Adolescent Psychiatry 1983; **Med School:** Univ Wisc 1977; **Resid:** Psychiatry, Univ Cincinnati Affil Hosp 1980; **Fellow:** Child & Adolescent Psychiatry, Univ Cincinnati Affil Hosp 1982; **Fac Appt:** Asst Prof Psyc, Northwestern Univ

Great Plains and Mountains

Hagman, Jennifer O MD [ChAP] - **Spec Exp:** Eating Disorders; Depression; Anxiety Disorders; **Hospital:** Chldn's Hosp - Aurora (CO); **Address:** Chldns Hosp, Dept Psychiatry, 13123 E 16th Ave, Ste B130, Aurora, CO 80045; **Phone:** 720-777-2539; **Board Cert:** Psychiatry 1992; Child & Adolescent Psychiatry 1992; **Med School:** Univ Kansas 1986; **Resid:** Psychiatry, UC Irvine Med Ctr 1990; **Fellow:** Child & Adolescent Psychiatry, UC Irvine Med Ctr 1992; **Fac Appt:** Assoc Prof Psyc, Univ Colorado

Martini, D Richard MD [ChAP] - **Spec Exp:** Psychiatry in Physical Illness; Post Traumatic Stress Disorder; ADD/ADHD; Brain Injury; **Hospital:** Primary Children's Med Ctr; **Address:** Primary Chldns Med Ctr, 100 N Mario Capecchi Drive, Salt Lake City, UT 84113; **Phone:** 801-313-7711; **Board Cert:** Psychiatry 1987; Child & Adolescent Psychiatry 1990; **Med School:** Univ Nebr Coll Med 1982; **Resid:** Psychiatry, Univ Pittsburgh Med Ctr 1985; Child Psychiatry, Univ Pittsburgh Med Ctr 1987; **Fac Appt:** Clin Prof Psyc, Univ Utah

Wamboldt, Marianne Z MD [ChAP] - **Spec Exp:** Psychosomatic Disorders; Anxiety Disorders; Family Therapy; **Hospital:** Chldn's Hosp - Aurora (CO); **Address:** Children's Hosp, Dept Psychiatry, 13123 E 16th Ave, Ste B130, Aurora, CO 80045; **Phone:** 720-777-8903; **Board Cert:** Psychiatry 1986; Child & Adolescent Psychiatry 1991; **Med School:** Univ Wisc 1981; **Resid:** Psychiatry, Univ Wisconsin Hosp 1986; **Fellow:** Research, Natl Inst of Hlth - Clin Ctr 1987; Child Psychiatry, Univ Colorado Hlth Sci Ctr 1991; **Fac Appt:** Assoc Prof Psyc, Univ Colorado

Southwest

Bleiberg, Efrain MD [ChAP] - **Spec Exp:** Trauma Psychiatry; Personality Disorders; **Hospital:** Menninger Clinic, Texas Chldns Hosp; **Address:** Texas Children's Hospital, 6701 Fannin, Ste 1740, Houston, TX 77280-9045; **Phone:** 832-822-1900; **Board Cert:** Psychiatry 1985; Child & Adolescent Psychiatry 1986; **Med School:** Mexico 1976; **Resid:** Psychiatry, Menninger Fdn 1980; **Fellow:** Child & Adolescent Psychiatry, Menninger Fdn 1981

Emslie, Graham J MD [ChAP] - **Spec Exp:** Depression; **Hospital:** Chldns Med Ctr of Dallas; **Address:** UT SW Med Ctr at Dallas, 6300 Harry Hines Blvd, Dallas, TX 75235; **Phone:** 214-456-5900; **Board Cert:** Psychiatry 1981; **Med School:** Scotland, UK 1974; **Resid:** Psychiatry, Univ Rochester 1978; Child Psychiatry, Stanford Med Ctr 1981; **Fac Appt:** Prof Psyc, Univ Tex SW, Dallas

Zeanah Jr, Charles H MD [ChAP] - **Spec Exp:** Attachment Disorders; Abuse/Neglect; Post Traumatic Stress Disorder; Infant-Toddler Psychiatry; **Hospital:** Tulane Med Ctr; **Address:** Tulane University School of Med, 1430 Tulane Ave, Box 8055, New Orleans, LA 70112; **Phone:** 504-988-5402; **Board Cert:** Psychiatry 1983; Child & Adolescent Psychiatry 1983; **Med School:** Tulane Univ 1977; **Resid:** Psychiatry, Duke Univ Med Ctr 1980; Child Psychiatry, Stanford Univ Med Ctr 1982; **Fellow:** Research, Stanford Univ 1984; **Fac Appt:** Prof Psyc, Tulane Univ

West Coast and Pacific

King, Bryan H MD [ChAP] - **Spec Exp:** Autism; Developmental Disorders; Behavioral Disorders; **Hospital:** Seattle Chldns Hosp; **Address:** 4800 Sand Point Way NE, MS 0A5154, Seattle, WA 98105; **Phone:** 206-987-2847; **Board Cert:** Psychiatry 1991; Child & Adolescent Psychiatry 2004; **Med School:** Med Coll Wisc 1983; **Resid:** Psychiatry, UCLA Neuropsych Inst 1987; **Fellow:** Child & Adolescent Psychiatry, UCLA Neuropsych Inst 1990; **Fac Appt:** Prof Psyc, Univ Wash

Kwon, Hower MD [ChAP] - **Spec Exp:** Autism; Developmental Disorders; Anxiety & Mood Disorders; ADD/ADHD; **Hospital:** Univ Wash Med Ctr, Seattle Chldns Hosp; **Address:** Bellevue Child Behavior Ctr, 365 118th Ave SE, Ste 118, Bellevue, WA 98005; **Phone:** 425-454-2911; **Board Cert:** Psychiatry 2009; Child & Adolescent Psychiatry 2009; **Med School:** NYU Sch Med 1993; **Resid:** Psychiatry, UCLA Neuropsychiatric Hosp 1996; **Fellow:** Child & Adolescent Psychiatry, UCLA Neuropsychiatric Hosp 1999; **Fac Appt:** Assoc Clin Prof Psyc, Univ Wash

McCracken, James T MD [ChAP] - **Spec Exp:** Obsessive-Compulsive Disorder; Autism; ADD/ADHD; Anxiety Disorders; **Hospital:** Resnick Neuropsychiatric Hosp at UCLA, UCLA Ronald Reagan Med Ctr; **Address:** UCLA Neuropsychiatric Inst, 760 Westwood Plaza, Ste 48-270, Los Angeles, CA 90024; **Phone:** 310-825-0470; **Board Cert:** Psychiatry 1986; Child & Adolescent Psychiatry 1988; **Med School:** Baylor Coll Med 1980; **Resid:** Psychiatry, Duke Univ Med Ctr 1984; **Fellow:** Child & Adolescent Psychiatry, UCLA Neuropsych Inst 1987; **Fac Appt:** Prof Psyc, UCLA

McKelvey, Robert S MD [ChAP] - **Spec Exp:** Suicide; Depression; Cross Cultural Psychiatry; Anxiety Disorders; **Hospital:** Doernbecher Chldns Hosp/OHSU; **Address:** 5520 SW Macadam Ave, Ste 265, Portland, OR 97239; **Phone:** 971-219-8363; **Board Cert:** Psychiatry 1980; Child & Adolescent Psychiatry 1982; **Med School:** Dartmouth Med Sch 1974; **Resid:** Psychiatry, Cambridge Hosp 1977; **Fellow:** Child Psychiatry, McLean Hosp 1979; **Fac Appt:** Prof Psyc, Oregon Hlth & Sci Univ

Ponton, Lynn Elisabeth MD [ChAP] - **Spec Exp:** Behavioral Disorders; Eating Disorders; **Hospital:** UCSF Med Ctr; **Address:** 201 Edgewood Ave, San Francisco, CA 94117; **Phone:** 415-664-3039; **Board Cert:** Psychiatry 1985; Child & Adolescent Psychiatry 1985; **Med School:** Univ Wisc 1978; **Resid:** Psychiatry, Hosp Univ Penn 1980; Psychiatry, UCSF Med Ctr 1981; **Fellow:** Child & Adolescent Psychiatry, UCSF Med Ctr 1983; **Fac Appt:** Prof Psyc, UCSF

Steiner, Hans MD [ChAP] - **Spec Exp:** Aggression Disorders; Eating Disorders; Trauma Psychiatry; Psychosomatic Disorders; **Hospital:** Stanford Univ Hosp & Clins, Lucile Packard Chldn's Hosp; **Address:** 401 Quarry Rd, rm 2237, Stanford, CA 94305-5719; **Phone:** 650-723-5511; **Board Cert:** Psychiatry 1979; Child & Adolescent Psychiatry 1981; **Med School:** Austria 1972; **Resid:** Psychiatry, SUNY Syracuse Med Ctr 1976; **Fellow:** Child & Adolescent Psychiatry, Univ Mich Hosps 1978; **Fac Appt:** Prof Emeritus Psyc, Stanford Univ

Geriatric Psychiatry

Mid Atlantic

Greenwald, Blaine MD [GerPsy] - **Spec Exp:** Depression; Dementia; **Hospital:** Zucker Hillside Hosp (page 66), N Shore Univ Hosp (page 66); **Address:** Zucker Hillside Hosp - ACP 2102, N Shore-Long Is Jewish Hlth Sys, 75-59 263rd St, Glen Oaks, NY 11004; **Phone:** 718-470-8159; **Board Cert:** Psychiatry 1983; Geriatric Psychiatry 2011; **Med School:** NY Med Coll 1978; **Resid:** Psychiatry, Mt Sinai Med Ctr 1982; **Fellow:** Geriatric Psychiatry, Mt Sinai Med Ctr/Bronx VA Hosp 1983; **Fac Appt:** Assoc Prof Psyc, Hofstra N Shore-LIJ Sch Med

Kennedy, Gary J MD [GerPsy] - **Spec Exp:** Alzheimer's Disease; Dementia; Depression; **Hospital:** Montefiore Med Ctr-Moses Campus, NY; **Address:** Dept of Psychiatry & Behavioral Sciences, Montefiore Medical Center, 111 E 210th St, Bronx, NY 10467-2490; **Phone:** 718-920-6270; **Board Cert:** Psychiatry 1980; Geriatric Psychiatry 2010; Psychosomatic Medicine 2005; **Med School:** Univ Tex, San Antonio 1975; **Resid:** Psychiatry, VA Hosp-Univ Texas 1979; **Fellow:** Geriatric Psychiatry, Montefiore Med Ctr 1981; Psychosomatic Medicine, Montefiore Med Ctr 1983; **Fac Appt:** Prof Psyc, Albert Einstein Coll Med

Lyketsos, Constantine G MD [GerPsy] - **Spec Exp:** Alzheimer's Disease; Neuro-Psychiatry; Depression; Dementia; **Hospital:** Johns Hopkins Bayview Med Ctr (page 59), Johns Hopkins Hosp (page 59); **Address:** Johns Hopkins, Psychiatry Dept, 5300 Alpha Commons Drive Fl 4, Baltimore, MD 21224; **Phone:** 410-550-0062; **Board Cert:** Psychiatry 1994; Psychosomatic Medicine 2005; **Med School:** Washington Univ, St Louis 1988; **Resid:** Psychiatry, Johns Hopkins Hosp 1992; **Fellow:** Neuropsychiatry, Johns Hopkins Hosp 1994; **Fac Appt:** Prof Psyc, Johns Hopkins Univ

Reisberg, Barry MD [GerPsy] - **Spec Exp:** Alzheimer's Disease; Dementia; Cognitive Loss in Aging; Depression; **Hospital:** NYU Langone Med Ctr (page 68); **Address:** NYU Med Ctr, Dept Psychiatry, 145 E 32nd St, Ste 508, New York, NY 10016; **Phone:** 212-263-8550; **Board Cert:** Psychiatry 1976; Geriatric Psychiatry 2012; **Med School:** NY Med Coll 1972; **Resid:** Psychiatry, Metropolitan Hosp 1975; **Fellow:** Psychiatric Research, Univ London 1975; **Fac Appt:** Prof Psyc, NYU Sch Med

Rovner, Barry W MD [GerPsy] - **Spec Exp:** Alzheimer's Disease; Behavioral Problems & Dementia; Memory Loss; **Hospital:** Thomas Jefferson Univ Hosp; **Address:** Jefferson Hosp Neuroscience, 900 Walnut St, Ste 200, Philadelphia, PA 19107; **Phone:** 215-503-1254; **Board Cert:** Psychiatry 1985; Geriatric Psychiatry 2011; **Med School:** Jefferson Med Coll 1980; **Resid:** Psychiatry, Johns Hopkins Hosp 1984; **Fellow:** Neuropsychiatry, Johns Hopkins Univ; **Fac Appt:** Prof Psyc, Jefferson Med Coll

Streim, Joel E MD [GerPsy] - **Spec Exp:** Psychiatry in Physical Illness; Psychiatric Barriers to Physical Rehab; Alzheimer's Disease; Behavioral Problems in Dementia; **Hospital:** Hosp Univ Penn - UPHS (page 69), VA Med Ctr - Philadelphia; **Address:** Univ Penn Geriatric Psychiatry, 3615 Chestnut St, rm 328, Philadelphia, PA 19104; **Phone:** 215-615-3086; **Board Cert:** Psychiatry 1988; Geriatric Psychiatry 2009; **Med School:** Univ Rochester 1978; **Resid:** Internal Medicine, Rochester Genl Hosp 1981; Psychiatry, Univ Wisconsin Hosp 1985; **Fellow:** Liaison Psychiatry, Univ Rochester/Strong Mem 1982; Geriatric Psychiatry, VA Med Ctr 1988; **Fac Appt:** Prof Psyc, Univ Pennsylvania

Southeast

Holroyd, Suzanne MD [GerPsy] - **Spec Exp:** Dementia; Psychoses-Late Onset; Mood Disorders; **Hospital:** Univ of Virginia Hlth Sys; **Address:** Univ of Virginia Health Sys, Dept Psych, 1300 Jefferson Park Ave, Charlottesville, VA 22908; **Phone:** 434-924-2241; **Board Cert:** Psychiatry 1992; Geriatric Psychiatry 2004; **Med School:** Univ VA Sch Med 1986; **Resid:** Psychiatry, Johns Hopkins Hosp 1990; **Fellow:** Geriatric Psychiatry, Johns Hopkins Hosp 1991; **Fac Appt:** Prof Psyc, Univ VA Sch Med

Tune, Larry E MD [GerPsy] - **Spec Exp:** Alzheimer's Disease; Dementia; Psychopharmacology; **Hospital:** Wesley Woods Ger Hosp, Emory Univ Hosp; **Address:** Wesley Woods Ctr, Psychiatry Dept, 1841 Clifton Rd NE, Atlanta, GA 30329; **Phone:** 404-728-6690; **Board Cert:** Psychiatry 1991; Geriatric Psychiatry 2004; **Med School:** Univ VA Sch Med 1975; **Resid:** Psychiatry, Johns Hopkins Hosp 1979; Neurology, Johns Hopkins Hosp 1983; **Fellow:** Psychopharmacology, Johns Hopkins Hosp 1981; **Fac Appt:** Prof Psyc, Emory Univ

Midwest

Grossberg, George MD [GerPsy] - **Spec Exp:** Alzheimer's Disease; Depression; Behavioral Problems & Dementia; **Hospital:** St. Louis Univ Hosp; **Address:** St Louis Univ Sch Med, Dept Neurology and Psychiatry, 1438 S Grand Blvd, St Louis, MO 63104; **Phone:** 314-977-4850; **Board Cert:** Psychiatry 1982; Geriatric Psychiatry 2011; **Med School:** St Louis Univ 1975; **Resid:** Psychiatry, St Louis Univ Med Ctr 1979; **Fac Appt:** Prof Psyc, St Louis Univ

Manepalli, Jothika M MD [GerPsy] - **Spec Exp:** Mood Disorders; Dementia; Depression; Palliative Care; **Hospital:** St. Louis Univ Hosp; **Address:** St Louis Univ Sch Med, Dept Neurology and Psychiatry, 1438 S Grand Blvd, St Louis, MO 63104; **Phone:** 314-977-4850; **Board Cert:** Psychiatry 1994; Geriatric Psychiatry 2007; **Med School:** India 1977; **Resid:** Psychiatry, Duke Univ Med Ctr 1987; Psychiatry, Barnes Hosp 1989; **Fellow:** Geriatric Psychiatry, St Louis Univ Hosp 1990; **Fac Appt:** Prof Psyc, St Louis Univ

Mellow, Alan M MD/PhD [GerPsy] - **Spec Exp:** Dementia; Depression; **Hospital:** VA Ann Arbor Healthcare Sys, Univ Michigan Med Ctr; **Address:** Dept VA Affairs, VISN 11 Office, Box 134002, 10N11, Ann Arbor, MI 48113; **Phone:** 734-222-4350; **Board Cert:** Psychiatry 1988; Geriatric Psychiatry 2002; **Med School:** Northwestern Univ 1981; **Resid:** Internal Medicine, Univ Chicago Hosp 1982; Psychiatry, McLean Hosp-Harvard 1985; **Fellow:** Psychiatry, Natl Inst Mental Hlth 1988; **Fac Appt:** Prof Psyc, Univ Mich Med Sch

Great Plains and Mountains

Burke, William J MD [GerPsy] - **Spec Exp:** Alzheimer's Disease; Dementia; Depression; Panic Disorder; **Hospital:** Nebraska Med Ctr; **Address:** Home Instead Ctr for Successful Aging, 730 S 38th Ave, Omaha, NE 68198-6150; **Phone:** 402-552-6007; **Board Cert:** Psychiatry 1986; Geriatric Psychiatry 2011; **Med School:** Univ Nebr Coll Med 1980; **Resid:** Internal Medicine, Univ Nebraska Med Ctr 1981; Psychiatry, Wash Univ Barnes Hosp 1984; **Fac Appt:** Prof Psyc, Univ Nebr Coll Med

West Coast and Pacific

Kramer, Barry A MD [GerPsy] - **Spec Exp:** Electroconvulsive Therapy (ECT); Depression; **Hospital:** Olympia Med Ctr, Cedars-Sinai Med Ctr; **Address:** Olympia Medical Center, 5900 W Olympic Blvd, Los Angeles, CA 90036; **Phone:** 323-932-5475; **Board Cert:** Psychiatry 1978; **Med School:** Hahnemann Univ 1974; **Resid:** Psychiatry, Montefiore Hosp Med Ctr 1977; **Fellow:** Geriatric Psychiatry, UCLA-USC Long Term Gero Ctr 1986

Stein, Elliott M MD [GerPsy] - **Spec Exp:** Anxiety & Depression; Memory Disorders; Dementia; Stress Management; **Address:** Jewish Home of San Francisco, 302 Silver Ave, San Francisco, CA 94112; **Phone:** 415-406-1516; **Board Cert:** Psychiatry 1979; Geriatric Psychiatry 2011; **Med School:** Univ Miami Sch Med 1973; **Resid:** Psychiatry, Herrick Meml Hosp 1976; **Fac Appt:** Assoc Clin Prof Psyc, Univ Miami Sch Med

Veith, Richard C MD [GerPsy] - **Spec Exp:** Depression in Cardiovascular Disease; **Hospital:** Univ Wash Med Ctr; **Address:** Univ Washington Med Ctr, 1959 NE Pacific St, BB 1644, Box 356560, Seattle, WA 98195; **Phone:** 206-543-3752; **Board Cert:** Psychiatry 1979; Geriatric Psychiatry 2000; **Med School:** Univ Wash 1973; **Resid:** Psychiatry, Univ Wash Med Ctr 1977; **Fac Appt:** Prof Psyc, Univ Wash

THE MOUNT SINAI MEDICAL CENTER

Psychiatry

Mount Sinai

One Gustave L. Levy Place
Fifth Avenue and 100th Street
New York, NY 10029-6574

Physician Referral: 1-800-MD-SINAI (637-4624)
www.mountsinai.org

THE DEPARTMENT OF PSYCHIATRY at Mount Sinai strives to bring breakthrough discoveries from neuroscience research to clinical care today. We provide services for children, adolescents, adults, and seniors, offering mental health evaluation and treatment for autism, attention-deficit hyperactivity disorder (ADHD), behavioral disorders, schizophrenia, Alzheimer's disease, mood and anxiety disorders, obsessive-compulsive disorder (OCD), tics and Tourette's Disorder (TD), substance abuse, post-traumatic stress disorder (PTSD), eating disorders, and personality disorders.

Clinical Services – The Department of Psychiatry is organized around key Centers of Excellence that integrate our three missions of clinical care, education and research. We offer a full range of diagnostic and treatment services, including psychotherapy, psychopharmacology, emergency services, electroconvulsive therapy, neuropsychological testing, and management of difficult clinical cases. We also provide mental health services in the Mount Sinai's World Trade Center Medical Monitoring and Treatment Program.

Specialty Programs – The Seaver Autism Center of Excellence offers a comprehensive assessment and treatment program that provides the finest patient care informed by the latest research. Our expert clinical staff is experienced in autism spectrum disorders, specializing in personalized and evidence-based treatment for very young children and high-functioning adults, as well as those individuals considered most difficult to assess and treat. The ADHD Center serves children and adults providing state-of-the-art psychiatric evaluation, psychological testing, behavioral and cognitive-behavioral treatments, and medication management. Our Center for Eating and Weight Disorders serves adults and children, offering innovative and evidence-based treatment for anorexia nervosa, bulimia nervosa, binge eating disorder, and obesity.

TRANSLATING KNOWLEDGE INTO NEW SOLUTIONS

Mount Sinai is at the forefront of unlocking the interactions between biological processes and the myriad states of the human mind. Among our major research programs in psychiatry are the Alzheimer's Disease Research Center, which conducts both basic science and clinical research, and The Seaver Autism Center for Research and Treatment, which is dedicated to unraveling the biological causes of this disorder and to developing innovative treatment strategies. In shedding important new light on mental illness, psychiatrists at Mount Sinai are frequently able to offer experimental interventions for treatment-resistant cases of depression, OCD, and other disorders.

The Mood and Anxiety Disorders Program (MAP) is devoted to understanding the causes of mood and anxiety disorders and aims to advance the latest integrative treatment strategies for patients who suffer from major depression, bipolar disorder, PTSD, panic attacks, generalized anxiety disorder, and social phobia. MAP at Mount Sinai uses state-of-the-art brain imaging, and genetic, and clinical trials methods to enhance our understanding of brain processes associated with these disorders.

The OCD and Tourette's Center of Excellence provides state-of-the-art diagnostic evaluation for children, adolescents and adults with OCD, tics and related disorders. The Center offers comprehensive evaluations, expert consultations, outpatient services, novel and evidence-based treatments, and research studies. We specialize in both behavioral therapy and biological interventions for patients who have not responded to conventional therapies. For adult patients with severe and intractable OCD, we offer Deep Brain Stimulation (DBS).

NYU Langone
MEDICAL CENTER

550 First Avenue *(at 31st Street)*
New York, NY 10016

www.NYULMC.org

Physician Referral: **888-7-NYU-MED** *(888-769-8633)*

PSYCHIATRY

NYU Langone's psychiatry team is dedicated to improving the health and well-being of patients by delivering peerless psychiatric services and care. NYU Langone is home to some of the nation's most respected clinical psychiatrists and psychologists, with specialties in psychoanalysis, psychopharmacology, behavioral therapy, child psychiatry, geriatric psychiatry and neuropsychiatry. We specialize in the following areas:

Child and Adolescent Psychiatry

Since 1997, the Child Study Center has treated thousands of children from around the world at its Faculty Group Practices in Manhattan and satellite clinical campuses in New Jersey and Long Island. Through its website, www.AboutOurKids.org, and through professional education programs, parents and practitioners are provided with the tools and knowledge needed to promote children's mental health. We specialize in Anxiety and Mood Disorders, Attention Deficit Hyperactivity and Behavior Disorders, Autism, Asperger's Syndrome and Communication Disorders, Learning Disorders, Tics and Tourette Disorder and more.

Adult Inpatient Services

The inpatient services unit combines comprehensive diagnostic assessment and treatment, including psychopharmacology, neuropsychology, psychotherapies and electroconvulsive therapy.

Adult Outpatient Psychiatry

The outpatient psychiatry program provides expert treatment to individuals suffering from a broad range of mental disorders and emotional problems, including anxiety, depression (including medicine resistant depression), insomnia, manic-depression, reproductive psychiatry, attention-deficit hyperactivity disorder and schizophrenia.

Post-Traumatic Stress Disorder

We offer assessment and treatment of PTSD for victims of sexual and physical assault, natural disasters, terrorism and combat trauma. Treatment includes cognitive behavioral therapy and strategies for the prevention of insomnia, stress, anxiety and depression. Our Military Family Clinic provides compassionate mental healthcare for veterans and their extended family members. The Steven and Alexandra Cohen Veterans Center is dedicated to improving diagnosis and treatment of PTSD and TBI through research.

Memory Impairment

The Pearl Barlow Center for Memory Evaluation and Treatment specializes in treating patients with memory impairments caused by neurological, psychological and physical ailments, as well as memory issues resulting from medication side effects, anxiety, depression and the effects of normal aging from illnesses like Alzheimer's disease.

PSYCHIATRY

NYU Langone's psychiatry team is dedicated to improving the health and well-being of patients by delivering peerless psychiatric services and care. NYU Langone is home to some of the nation's most respected clinical psychiatrists and psychologists, with specialties in psychoanalysis, psychopharmacology, behavioral therapy, child psychiatry, geriatric psychiatry and neuropsychiatry. We specialize in the following areas:

Child and Adolescent Psychiatry

Since 1997, the Child Study Center has treated thousands of children from around the world at its Faculty Group Practices in Manhattan and satellite clinical campuses in New Jersey and Long Island. Through its website, www.AboutOurKids.org, and through professional education programs, parents and practitioners are provided with the tools and knowledge needed to promote children's mental health. We specialize in Anxiety and Mood Disorders, Attention Deficit Hyperactivity and Behavior Disorders, Autism, Asperger's Syndrome and Communication Disorders, Learning Disorders, Tics and Tourette Disorder and more.

Adult Inpatient Services

The inpatient services unit combines comprehensive diagnostic assessment and treatment, including psychopharmacology, neuropsychology, psychotherapies and electroconvulsive therapy.

Adult Outpatient Psychiatry

The outpatient psychiatry program provides expert treatment to individuals suffering from a broad range of mental disorders and emotional problems, including anxiety, depression (including medicine resistant depression), insomnia, manic-depression, reproductive psychiatry, attention-deficit hyperactivity disorder and schizophrenia.

Post-Traumatic Stress Disorder

We offer assessment and treatment of PTSD for victims of sexual and physical assault, natural disasters, terrorism and combat trauma. Treatment includes cognitive behavioral therapy and strategies for the prevention of insomnia, stress, anxiety and depression. Our Military Family Clinic provides compassionate mental healthcare for veterans and their extended family members. The Steven and Alexandra Cohen Veterans Center is dedicated to improving diagnosis and treatment of PTSD and TBI through research.

Memory Impairment

The Pearl Barlow Center for Memory Evaluation and Treatment specializes in treating patients with memory impairments caused by neurological, psychological and physical ailments, as well as memory issues resulting from medication side effects, anxiety, depression and the effects of normal aging from illnesses like Alzheimer's disease.

Mount Sinai

THE MOUNT SINAI MEDICAL CENTER

Geriatric Psychiatry

One Gustave L. Levy Place
Fifth Avenue and 100th Street
New York, NY 10029-6574

Physician Referral: 1-800-MD-SINAI (637-4624)
www.mountsinai.org

THE DIVISION OF GERIATRIC PSYCHIATRY at The Mount Sinai Medical Center delivers effective, compassionate and individualized care to older adults with neuropsychiatric illness and provides therapy, support and guidance to families and caretakers, thereby enhancing the quality of life for all concerned.

Our program includes both an inpatient geriatric psychiatry unit and an outpatient geriatric psychiatry clinic, the latter of which is housed in our beautiful **Martha Stewart Center for Living**. Our staff includes physicians, psychiatric nurses, and licensed clinical social workers, among other professionals, all trained to care for the psychiatric needs of older adults through hands-on, evidence-based care. We also offer participation in clinical research protocols that offer state-of-the-art therapies.

Outpatient Geriatric Psychiatry Clinic

Physicians practicing in our outpatient clinic specialize in treating patients with psychiatric illness and memory problems. Our interdisciplinary team provides psychopharmacology; comprehensive cognitive evaluations for the diagnosis and treatment of memory disorders, including Alzheimer's disease; group therapy for depression and anxiety; and support groups for those suffering from dementia.

Research

Opportunities to participate in research abound. The Division of Geriatric Psychiatry is closely allied with Mount Sinai's **Alzheimer's Disease Research Center**, where physician-scientists study memory problems, such as Alzheimer's disease, and its Brain Stimulation Center of Excellence, where they investigate the treatment of psychiatric disorders with electroconvulsive therapy and deep brain stimulation.

Workshops

We encourage older adults and their caregivers who are interested in learning more about their disease process and other aspects of aging to attend our workshops. We run them in conjunction with staff and patients from Mount Sinai's Martha Stewart Center for Living and Alzheimer's disease Research Center.

Pulmonary Disease

a subspecialty of Internal Medicine

An internist who treats diseases of the lungs and airways. The pulmonologist diagnoses and treats cancer, pneumonia, pleurisy, asthma, occupational diseases, bronchitis, sleep disorders, emphysema and other complex disorders of the lungs.

Training Required: Three years in internal medicine *plus* additional training and examination for certification in pulmonary disease.

Pulmonary Disease

New England

Berk, John L MD [Pul] - **Spec Exp:** Amyloidosis; Interstitial Lung Disease; Pulmonary Fibrosis; **Hospital:** Boston Med Ctr; **Address:** Amyloid Treatment & Research Program, 72 E Concord St, Boston, MA 02118; **Phone:** 617-638-4317; **Board Cert:** Internal Medicine 1986; Pulmonary Disease 2011; **Med School:** Case West Res Univ 1983; **Resid:** Internal Medicine, Univ Hosp/VAMC 1986; **Fellow:** Pulmonary Critical Care Medicine, Boston Med Ctr 1991; **Fac Appt:** Assoc Prof Med, Boston Univ

Celli, Bartolome R MD [Pul] - **Spec Exp:** Chronic Obstructive Lung Disease (COPD); Mechanical Ventilation; Respiratory Failure; **Hospital:** Brigham & Women's Hosp; **Address:** Brigham & Women's Hosp, Pulmonary Div, 15 Francis St, Boston, MA 02115; **Phone:** 617-732-6770; **Board Cert:** Internal Medicine 1975; Pulmonary Disease 1978; **Med School:** Venezuela 1971; **Resid:** Internal Medicine, St Vincent Hosp 1973; Internal Medicine, Boston Med Hosp 1976; **Fellow:** Pulmonary Disease, Boston Med Ctr 1977; **Fac Appt:** Prof Med, Tufts Univ

Christiani, David MD [Pul] - **Spec Exp:** Occupational Lung Disease; **Hospital:** Mass Genl Hosp; **Address:** MGH, Pulmonary Assocs, 55 Fruit St Cox 201B, Boston, MA 02114; **Phone:** 617-726-1721; **Board Cert:** Internal Medicine 1979; Occupational Medicine 1984; Pulmonary Disease 1988; **Med School:** Tufts Univ 1976; **Resid:** Internal Medicine, Boston City Hosp 1979; Occupational Medicine, Harvard Sch Public Hlth 1981; **Fellow:** Pulmonary Disease, Mass Genl Hosp 1987; **Fac Appt:** Prof Med, Harvard Med Sch

Enelow, Richard I MD [Pul] - **Spec Exp:** Interstitial Lung Disease; Lung Disease; **Hospital:** Dartmouth - Hitchcock Med Ctr; **Address:** Dartmouth-Hitchcock Medical Ctr, Dept Pulmonary & Critical Care Med, 1 Medical Center Drive, Lebanon, NH 03756; **Phone:** 603-650-5533; **Board Cert:** Internal Medicine 1986; Pulmonary Disease 2002; **Med School:** Boston Univ 1983; **Resid:** Internal Medicine, New Engl Deaconess Med Ctr 1986; **Fellow:** Pulmonary Disease, Univ VA Hlth Scis Ctr 1992; **Fac Appt:** Prof Med, Dartmouth Med Sch

Fanta, Christopher MD [Pul] - **Spec Exp:** Asthma; Chronic Obstructive Lung Disease (COPD); Bronchiectasis; **Hospital:** Brigham & Women's Hosp, Brigham and Women's Faulkner Hosp; **Address:** Brigham & Women's Hosp, Center for Chest Diseases, 15 Francis St, Boston, MA 02115; **Phone:** 617-732-6770; **Board Cert:** Internal Medicine 1978; Pulmonary Disease 1980; **Med School:** Harvard Med Sch 1975; **Resid:** Internal Medicine, Peter Bent Brigham Hosp 1978; **Fellow:** Pulmonary Disease, Peter Bent Brigham Hosp 1980; **Fac Appt:** Assoc Prof Med, Harvard Med Sch

Friedman, Lloyd Neal MD [Pul] - **Spec Exp:** Tuberculosis; Mycobacterial Infections; Critical Care; **Hospital:** Milford Hosp, Yale-New Haven Hosp; **Address:** Milford Hospital, 300 Seaside Ave, Milford, CT 06460; **Phone:** 203-876-4070; **Board Cert:** Internal Medicine 1983; Pulmonary Disease 1988; Critical Care Medicine 2009; **Med School:** Yale Univ 1979; **Resid:** Internal Medicine, Beth Israel Med Ctr 1980; Internal Medicine, Oregon Hlth Scis Univ 1983; **Fellow:** Pulmonary Intensive Care, Yale-New Haven Hosp 1988; **Fac Appt:** Clin Prof Med, Yale Univ

Hill, Nicholas S MD [Pul] - **Spec Exp:** Pulmonary Hypertension; **Hospital:** Tufts Med Ctr; **Address:** Tufts Med Ctr, 800 Washington St, Box 257, Boston, MA 02111; **Phone:** 617-636-6377; **Board Cert:** Internal Medicine 1978; Pulmonary Disease 1982; Critical Care Medicine 2009; **Med School:** Dartmouth Med Sch 1975; **Resid:** Internal Medicine, New England Med Ctr 1977; Cardiovascular Disease, Boston VA Med Ctr 1978; **Fellow:** Pulmonary Disease, Univ Mass Med Ctr 1979; Critical Care Medicine, Boston Univ Med Ctr 1982; **Fac Appt:** Prof Med, Tufts Univ

Irwin, Richard S MD [Pul] - **Spec Exp:** Cough; Asthma; Critical Care; Chronic Obstructive Lung Disease (COPD); **Hospital:** UMass Memorial Med Ctr; **Address:** UMass Meml Med Ctr-Univ Campus, 55 Lake Ave N, rm F6-842, Worcester, MA 01655-0002; **Phone:** 508-856-1919; **Board Cert:** Internal Medicine 1972; Pulmonary Disease 1974; Critical Care Medicine 2007; **Med School:** Tufts Univ 1968; **Resid:** Internal Medicine, Tufts-New England Med Ctr 1970; **Fellow:** Pulmonary Disease, Columbia-Presby Hosp 1972; **Fac Appt:** Prof Med, Univ Mass Sch Med

Mahler, Donald A MD [Pul] - **Spec Exp:** Chronic Obstructive Lung Disease (COPD); Asthma; Breathing Disorders; **Hospital:** Dartmouth - Hitchcock Med Ctr; **Address:** Dartmouth-Hitchcock Med Ctr, Div Pulmonary Med, 1 Medical Center Drive, Lebanon, NH 03756-0001; **Phone:** 603-650-5533; **Board Cert:** Internal Medicine 1978; Pulmonary Disease 1980; **Med School:** Loyola Univ-Stritch Sch Med 1972; **Resid:** Internal Medicine, Dartmouth-Hitchcock Med Ctr 1977; **Fellow:** Pulmonary Disease, Yale-New Haven Hosp 1980; **Fac Appt:** Prof Med, Dartmouth Med Sch

Metersky, Mark L MD [Pul] - **Spec Exp:** Pulmonary Infections; Asthma; Bronchiectasis; **Hospital:** Univ of Conn Hlth Ctr, John Dempsey Hosp; **Address:** Univ Conn Hlth Ctr, Pulmonary Svcs, 263 Farmington Ave, Farmington, CT 06030; **Phone:** 860-679-8300; **Board Cert:** Internal Medicine 1988; Pulmonary Disease 2003; Critical Care Medicine 2003; Sleep Medicine 2009; **Med School:** NYU Sch Med 1985; **Resid:** Internal Medicine, Boston Med Ctr 1988; **Fellow:** Pulmonary Critical Care Medicine, UCSD Med Ctr 1992; **Fac Appt:** Prof Med, Univ Conn

Millman, Richard P MD [Pul] - **Spec Exp:** Sleep Disorders/Apnea; **Hospital:** Rhode Island Hosp, Miriam Hosp; **Address:** 1 James P Murphy Hwy, West Warwick, RI 02893; **Phone:** 401-615-5878; **Board Cert:** Internal Medicine 1979; Pulmonary Disease 1982; Sleep Medicine 2009; **Med School:** Univ Pennsylvania 1976; **Resid:** Internal Medicine, Univ Mich Hosp 1979; **Fellow:** Pulmonary Disease, Univ Penn Hosp 1981; **Fac Appt:** Prof Med, Brown Univ

Nardell, Edward MD [Pul] - **Spec Exp:** Tuberculosis; Mycobacterial Infections; **Hospital:** Brigham & Women's Hosp; **Address:** Brigham & Women's Hosp, Pulmonary Div, 15 Francis St, Boston, MA 02115; **Phone:** 617-732-6770; **Board Cert:** Internal Medicine 1975; Pulmonary Disease 1982; **Med School:** Hahnemann Univ 1972; **Resid:** Internal Medicine, Hahnemann Univ Hosp 1975; **Fellow:** Pulmonary Disease, Mass Genl Hosp 1977; **Fac Appt:** Assoc Prof Med, Harvard Med Sch

Redlich, Carrie MD [Pul] - **Spec Exp:** Occupational Lung Disease; Lung Disease; **Hospital:** Yale-New Haven Hosp; **Address:** Yale Occupational & Environmental Med, 135 College St Fl 3 - Ste 392, New Haven, CT 06510; **Phone:** 203-785-4197; **Board Cert:** Internal Medicine 1986; Occupational Medicine 1990; **Med School:** Yale Univ 1982; **Resid:** Internal Medicine, Yale-New Haven Hosp 1986; Occupational Medicine, Yale-New Haven Hosp 1987; **Fellow:** Pulmonary Disease, Univ Washington Affil Hosp 1989; **Fac Appt:** Assoc Prof Med, Yale Univ

Rochester, Carolyn L MD [Pul] - **Spec Exp:** Chronic Obstructive Lung Disease (COPD); Emphysema; **Hospital:** VA Conn Hlthcre Sys-W Haven Campus, Yale-New Haven Hosp; **Address:** Winchester Chest Clin, 789 Howard Ave, Fitkin Meml Pavilion, New Haven, CT 06519; **Phone:** 203-785-4163; **Board Cert:** Internal Medicine 1986; Critical Care Medicine 2006; **Med School:** Columbia P&S 1983; **Resid:** Internal Medicine, Columbia Presby Med Ctr 1986; **Fellow:** Pulmonary Disease, Columbia Presby Med Ctr 1988; Critical Care Medicine, Yale New Haven Hosp 1991; **Fac Appt:** Assoc Prof Med, Yale Univ

Villanueva, Andrew G MD [Pul] - **Spec Exp:** Asthma; Chronic Obstructive Lung Disease (COPD); Pleural Disease; **Hospital:** Lahey Hosp & Med Ctr; **Address:** Lahey Hosp & Med Ctr, Dept Pulmonary & Critical Care Med, 41 Mall Rd, Burlington, MA 01805; **Phone:** 781-744-8481; **Board Cert:** Internal Medicine 1983; Pulmonary Disease 1986; Critical Care Medicine 2007; **Med School:** UCSD 1980; **Resid:** Internal Medicine, Boston Univ Med Ctr 1984; **Fellow:** Pulmonary Disease, Boston Univ Med Ctr 1988; **Fac Appt:** Asst Clin Prof Med, Tufts Univ

White, David P MD [Pul] - **Spec Exp:** Sleep Disorders/Apnea; **Hospital:** Brigham & Women's Hosp; **Address:** Brigham & Women's Sleep Ctr, 1153 Centre St, Ste 4930, Jamaica Plains, MA 02130; **Phone:** 617-983-7420; **Board Cert:** Internal Medicine 1978; Pulmonary Disease 1982; Sleep Medicine 2007; **Med School:** Emory Univ 1975; **Resid:** Internal Medicine, Univ CO Med Ctr 1978; **Fellow:** Pulmonary Disease, Univ CO Med Ctr 1982; **Fac Appt:** Prof Med, Harvard Med Sch

Mid Atlantic

Ahya, Vivek N MD [Pul] - **Spec Exp:** Transplant Medicine-Lung; Lymphangioleiomyomatosis(LAM); **Hospital:** Hosp Univ Penn - UPHS (page 69); **Address:** Penn Lung Center, Lung Transplantation Program, Perelman Ctr for Advanced Medicine, 3400 Civic Center Blvd, 1st Fl W, Philadelphia, PA 19104; **Phone:** 215-662-2366; **Board Cert:** Pulmonary Disease 2010; Critical Care Medicine 2011; **Med School:** Boston Univ 1994; **Resid:** Internal Medicine, Barnes Jewish Hosp 1997; **Fellow:** Pulmonary Critical Care Medicine, Univ Penn 1998; **Fac Appt:** Assoc Prof Med, Univ Pennsylvania

Arcasoy, Selim M MD [Pul] - **Spec Exp:** Transplant Medicine-Lung; Interstitial Lung Disease; Chronic Obstructive Lung Disease (COPD); Pulmonary Embolism; **Hospital:** NY-Presby/Columbia Univ Med Ctr, NY (page 65); **Address:** Ctr for Advanced Lung Dis/Transp, 622 W 168th St, PH Bldg - Fl 14E, rm 104, New York, NY 10032-3720; **Phone:** 212-305-6589; **Board Cert:** Internal Medicine 2003; Pulmonary Disease 2006; Critical Care Medicine 2007; **Med School:** Turkey 1990; **Resid:** Internal Medicine, SUNY Downstate Med Ctr 1994; **Fellow:** Pulmonary Critical Care Medicine, Univ Pittsburgh Med Ctr 1998; **Fac Appt:** Prof Med, Columbia P&S

Bascom, Rebecca MD [Pul] - **Spec Exp:** Environmental Medicine; Chemical Exposure; Occupational Lung Disease; Pulmonary Fibrosis; **Hospital:** Penn State Milton S Hershey Med Ctr; **Address:** Hershey Med Ctr, Pulmonary Div, 500 University Drive, MC HO41, Hershey, PA 17033-0850; **Phone:** 717-531-6525 x7; **Board Cert:** Internal Medicine 1982; Occupational Medicine 1987; Pulmonary Disease 1988; **Med School:** Oregon Hlth & Sci Univ 1979; **Resid:** Internal Medicine, Johns Hopkins Hosp 1982; **Fellow:** Pulmonary Disease, Johns Hopkins 1985; **Fac Appt:** Prof Med, Penn State Coll Med

Burschtin, Omar E MD [Pul] - **Spec Exp:** Sleep Medicine; Sleep Disorders/Apnea; **Hospital:** NYU Langone Med Ctr (page 68); **Address:** Sleep Med Assocs, 11 E 26th St Fl 13, New York, NY 10010; **Phone:** 212-481-1818; **Board Cert:** Pulmonary Disease 2008; Sleep Medicine 2009; **Med School:** Uruguay 1988; **Resid:** Internal Medicine, NYU Med Ctr 1994; **Fellow:** Pulmonary Critical Care Medicine, NYU Med Ctr 1997; Sleep Medicine, Bellevue Hosp 1998; **Fac Appt:** Asst Clin Prof Med, NYU Sch Med

Christie, Jason D MD [Pul] - **Spec Exp:** Transplant Medicine-Lung; Lung Disease; Critical Care; **Hospital:** Hosp Univ Penn - UPHS (page 69); **Address:** Penn Lung Ctr, Pearlman Ctr, West Pavilion Fl 1, 3400 Civic Ctr Blvd, Philadelphia, PA 19104; **Phone:** 215-615-5864; **Board Cert:** Internal Medicine 2006; Pulmonary Disease 2009; Critical Care Medicine 2010; **Med School:** Columbia P&S 1993; **Resid:** Internal Medicine, Hosp Univ Penn 1996; **Fellow:** Pulmonary Disease, Hosp Univ Penn 1998; **Fac Appt:** Assoc Prof Med, Univ Pennsylvania

Criner, Gerard J MD [Pul] - **Spec Exp:** Chronic Obstructive Lung Disease (COPD); Pulmonary Fibrosis; Pulmonary Hypertension; Critical Care; **Hospital:** Temple Univ Hosp; **Address:** Temple Univ Hosp, Pulmonary Med, 3401 N Broad St Fl 5, Philadelphia, PA 19140; **Phone:** 215-707-5864; **Board Cert:** Internal Medicine 1982; Pulmonary Disease 1986; Critical Care Medicine 2007; **Med School:** Temple Univ 1979; **Resid:** Internal Medicine, Temple Univ Hosp 1983; **Fellow:** Pulmonary Critical Care Medicine, Boston Med Ctr 1986; **Fac Appt:** Prof Med, Temple Univ

Deitz, Joel L MD [Pul] - **Spec Exp:** Respiratory Failure; Chronic Obstructive Lung Disease (COPD); Cough; Critical Care; **Hospital:** Penn Presby Med Ctr - UPHS (page 69), Hosp Univ Penn - UPHS (page 69); **Address:** Penn Lung Center, Penn-Presbyterian Med Ctr, 51 N 39th St, PHI, 1st Fl Rear, Philadelphia, PA 19104; **Phone:** 215-662-8766; **Board Cert:** Internal Medicine 1980; Pulmonary Disease 1984; Critical Care Medicine 2007; **Med School:** Tufts Univ 1977; **Resid:** Internal Medicine, Med Coll Va Med Ctr 1980; **Fellow:** Pulmonary Disease, Duke Univ Med Ctr 1984; **Fac Appt:** Assoc Clin Prof Med, Univ Pennsylvania

Donahoe, Michael MD [Pul] - **Spec Exp:** Critical Care; Respiratory Distress Syndrome (ARDS); Chronic Obstructive Lung Disease (COPD); **Hospital:** UPMC Montefiore; **Address:** UPMC Montefiore Hosp, NW628, 3601 Fifth Ave Fl 4, Pittsburgh, PA 15213; **Phone:** 412-648-6161; **Board Cert:** Internal Medicine 1986; Pulmonary Disease 1988; Critical Care Medicine 2010; **Med School:** Hahnemann Univ 1983; **Resid:** Internal Medicine, UPMC Presbyterian 1987; **Fellow:** Pulmonary Critical Care Medicine, UPMC Presbyterian 1989; **Fac Appt:** Assoc Prof Med, Univ Pittsburgh

Greenberg, Harly MD [Pul] - **Spec Exp:** Sleep Disorders/Apnea; Lung Disease; Critical Care; **Hospital:** Long Is Jewish Med Ctr (page 66), N Shore Univ Hosp (page 66); **Address:** N Shore-LIJ Sleep Disorders Ctr, 410 Lakeville Rd, Ste 107, New Hyde Park, NY 11042; **Phone:** 516-465-3899; **Board Cert:** Internal Medicine 1985; Pulmonary Disease 1988; Sleep Medicine 2011; **Med School:** NYU Sch Med 1982; **Resid:** Internal Medicine, North Shore Univ Hosp 1985; **Fellow:** Pulmonary Disease, Bellevue Hosp Ctr 1987; **Fac Appt:** Prof Med, Hofstra N Shore-LIJ Sch Med

Hansen-Flaschen, John MD [Pul] - **Spec Exp:** Diagnostic Problems; Interstitial Lung Disease; Chronic Obstructive Lung Disease (COPD); Bronchiectasis; **Hospital:** Hosp Univ Penn - UPHS (page 69); **Address:** Penn Lung Center, Perelman Center for Advanced Medicine, 3400 Civic Center Blvd, 1st Fl W, Philadelphia, PA 19104; **Phone:** 215-662-3202; **Board Cert:** Internal Medicine 1979; Pulmonary Disease 2012; **Med School:** NYU Sch Med 1976; **Resid:** Internal Medicine, Hosp Univ Penn 1981; **Fellow:** Pulmonary Critical Care Medicine, Hosp Univ Penn 1982; **Fac Appt:** Prof Med, Univ Pennsylvania

King, Earl D MD [Pul] - **Spec Exp:** Lung Cancer; Critical Care; Sleep Disorders/Apnea; **Hospital:** Fox Chase Cancer Ctr (page 57); **Address:** Fox Chase Cancer Center, 333 Cottman Ave, Philadelphia, PA 19111; **Phone:** 215-728-5703; **Board Cert:** Internal Medicine 1989; Pulmonary Disease 2012; Critical Care Medicine 2003; Sleep Medicine 1997; **Med School:** Penn State Coll Med 1986; **Resid:** Internal Medicine, Temple Univ Med Ctr 1989; **Fellow:** Pulmonary Critical Care Medicine, Johns Hopkins Hosp 1993

Kotloff, Robert M MD [Pul] - **Spec Exp:** Transplant Medicine-Lung; Lung Disease-Complex; Interstitial Lung Disease; Lymphangioleiomyomatosis(LAM); **Hospital:** Hosp Univ Penn - UPHS (page 69); **Address:** Penn Lung Center, Perelman Ctr for Advanced Medicine, 3400 Civic Center Blvd, 1 West, Philadelphia, PA 19104; **Phone:** 215-662-3202; **Board Cert:** Internal Medicine 1986; Pulmonary Disease 2005; Critical Care Medicine 2005; **Med School:** Yale Univ 1983; **Resid:** Internal Medicine, Temple Univ Hosp 1986; **Fellow:** Pulmonary Disease, Hosp Univ Penn 1990; **Fac Appt:** Prof Med, Univ Pennsylvania

Libby, Daniel M MD [Pul] - **Spec Exp:** Asthma; Lung Cancer; Interstitial Lung Disease; Chronic Obstructive Lung Disease (COPD); **Hospital:** NY-Presby/Weill Cornell Med Ctr, NY (page 65); **Address:** 635 Madison Ave, Ste 1101, New York, NY 10022; **Phone:** 212-628-6611; **Board Cert:** Internal Medicine 1977; Pulmonary Disease 1980; **Med School:** Baylor Coll Med 1974; **Resid:** Internal Medicine, NY Hosp 1977; **Fellow:** Pulmonary Disease, NY Hosp 1979; **Fac Appt:** Clin Prof Med, Cornell Univ-Weill Med Coll

Maxfield, Roger A MD [Pul] - **Spec Exp:** Emphysema & Asthma; Occupational Lung Disease; Lung Cancer; Bronchoscopy; **Hospital:** NY-Presby/Columbia Univ Med Ctr, NY (page 65); **Address:** 51 W 51st St, Ste 360, New York, NY 10019; **Phone:** 212-326-8415; **Board Cert:** Internal Medicine 1980; Pulmonary Disease 1986; **Med School:** Brown Univ 1977; **Resid:** Internal Medicine, Georgetown Univ Hosp 1980; **Fellow:** Pulmonary Disease, Bellevue Hosp 1985; **Fac Appt:** Clin Prof Med, Columbia P&S

Nash, Thomas MD [Pul] - **Spec Exp:** Asthma; Cough; Pneumonia; **Hospital:** NY-Presby/Weill Cornell Med Ctr, NY (page 65), Hosp For Special Surgery (page 58); **Address:** 310 E 72nd St, New York, NY 10021; **Phone:** 212-734-6612; **Board Cert:** Internal Medicine 1981; Infectious Disease 1984; Pulmonary Disease 1988; **Med School:** NYU Sch Med 1978; **Resid:** Internal Medicine, NY-Presby/Weill Cornell Med Ctr 1981; **Fellow:** Infectious Disease, NY-Presby/Weill Cornell Med Ctr 1983; Pulmonary Disease, Meml Sloan-Kettering Cancer Ctr 1985; **Fac Appt:** Assoc Clin Prof Med, NYU Sch Med

Nelson, Judith E MD [Pul] - **Spec Exp:** Palliative Care; **Hospital:** Mt Sinai Med Ctr (page 62); **Address:** Mt Sinai Medical Ctr, One Gustave Levy Pl, Box 1232, New York, NY 10029; **Phone:** 212-241-2587; **Board Cert:** Internal Medicine 1989; Pulmonary Disease 2012; Critical Care Medicine 2003; Hospice & Palliative Medicine 2012; **Med School:** NYU Sch Med 1986; **Resid:** Internal Medicine, Mt Sinai Med Ctr 1989; **Fellow:** Pulmonary Critical Care Medicine, Mt Sinai Med Ctr 1992; **Fac Appt:** Prof Med, Mount Sinai Sch Med

Niederman, Michael S MD [Pul] - **Spec Exp:** Infections-Respiratory; Emphysema; Respiratory Failure; Pneumonia; **Hospital:** Winthrop Univ Hosp; **Address:** 222 Station Plaza N, Ste 400, Mineola, NY 11501-3893; **Phone:** 516-663-2834; **Board Cert:** Internal Medicine 1980; Pulmonary Disease 1982; Critical Care Medicine 2007; **Med School:** Boston Univ 1977; **Resid:** Internal Medicine, Northwestern Univ Med Ctr 1980; **Fellow:** Pulmonary Disease, Yale-New Haven Hosp 1983; **Fac Appt:** Prof Med, SUNY Stony Brook

O'Donnell, Anne E MD [Pul] - **Spec Exp:** Bronchiectasis; Critical Care; Sleep Medicine; **Hospital:** MedStar Georgetown Univ Hosp; **Address:** Georgetown Univ Hosp-Pulm CCM, 3800 Reservoir Rd NW PHC Bldg Fl 5, Washington, DC 20007; **Phone:** 202-444-8830; **Board Cert:** Internal Medicine 1985; Pulmonary Disease 1988; Sleep Medicine 2007; Critical Care Medicine 2009; **Med School:** Georgetown Univ 1982; **Resid:** Internal Medicine, MedStar Georgetown Univ Hosp 1985; **Fellow:** Pulmonary Disease, MedStar Georgetown Univ Hosp 1988; **Fac Appt:** Prof Med, Georgetown Univ

Pack, Allan I MD/PhD [Pul] - **Spec Exp:** Sleep Disorders/Apnea; **Hospital:** Hosp Univ Penn - UPHS (page 69); **Address:** Penn Sleep Ctr, 3624 Market St, Ste 201, Philadelphia, PA 19104; **Phone:** 215-662-7772; **Med School:** Scotland, UK 1967; **Resid:** Internal Medicine, Univ Glasgow Med Ctr 1972; **Fellow:** Pulmonary Disease, Univ Glasgow 1975; **Fac Appt:** Prof Med, Univ Pennsylvania

Padilla, Maria L MD [Pul] - **Spec Exp:** Transplant Medicine-Lung; Sarcoidosis; Pulmonary Hypertension; Cystic Fibrosis; **Hospital:** Mt Sinai Med Ctr (page 62); **Address:** Mount Sinai Med Ctr, Pulmonary Assocs, 5 E 98th St Fl 8, New York, NY 10029; **Phone:** 212-241-5656; **Board Cert:** Internal Medicine 1978; Pulmonary Disease 1980; **Med School:** Mount Sinai Sch Med 1975; **Resid:** Internal Medicine, Mount Sinai Med Ctr 1978; **Fellow:** Pulmonary Disease, Mount Sinai Med Ctr 1980; Critical Care Medicine, Mount Sinai Med Ctr 1991; **Fac Appt:** Prof Med, Mount Sinai Sch Med

Palevsky, Harold I MD [Pul] - **Spec Exp:** Pulmonary Hypertension; Pulmonary Vascular Disease; Thromboembolic Disorders; **Hospital:** Penn Presby Med Ctr - UPHS (page 69), Hosp Univ Penn - UPHS (page 69); **Address:** Penn Lung Ctr at Penn Presby Med Ctr, 51 N 39th St, 1st Fl Rear, PHI Buildi Bldg, Philadelphia, PA 19104; **Phone:** 215-662-8766; **Board Cert:** Internal Medicine 2007; Pulmonary Disease 2007; Critical Care Medicine 2007; **Med School:** Med Coll VA 1978; **Resid:** Internal Medicine, Hosp Univ Penn 1981; **Fellow:** Pulmonary Critical Care Medicine, Hosp Univ Penn 1984; **Fac Appt:** Prof Med, Univ Pennsylvania

Rossman, Milton D MD [Pul] - **Spec Exp:** Beryllium-induced Lung Disease; Sarcoidosis; Interstitial Lung Disease; Pulmonary Fibrosis; **Hospital:** Hosp Univ Penn - UPHS (page 69); **Address:** Penn Lung Center, Perelman Ctr for Advanced Medicine, 3400 Civic Center Blvd, 1st Fl W, Philadelphia, PA 19104-4283; **Phone:** 215-662-3202; **Board Cert:** Internal Medicine 1975; Pulmonary Disease 1978; **Med School:** Jefferson Med Coll 1970; **Resid:** Internal Medicine, Univ Hosps 1975; **Fellow:** Pulmonary Disease, Hosp Univ Penn 1977; **Fac Appt:** Prof Med, Univ Pennsylvania

Schluger, Neil MD [Pul] - **Spec Exp:** Tuberculosis; **Hospital:** NY-Presby/Columbia Univ Med Ctr, NY (page 65); **Address:** NY-Presby, Pulmonology Dept, 161 Fort Washington Ave, rm 338, New York, NY 10032; **Phone:** 212-305-1544; **Board Cert:** Internal Medicine 1988; Pulmonary Disease 2003; **Med School:** Univ Pennsylvania 1985; **Resid:** Internal Medicine, St Lukes Hosp 1989; **Fellow:** Pulmonary Critical Care Medicine, NY-Presby/Weill Cornell Med Ctr 1992; **Fac Appt:** Prof Med, Columbia P&S

Schwab, Richard MD [Pul] - **Spec Exp:** Sleep Disorders/Apnea; **Hospital:** Hosp Univ Penn - UPHS (page 69); **Address:** Penn Sleep Center, 3624 Market St, Ste 201, Philadelphia, PA 19104; **Phone:** 215-662-7772; **Board Cert:** Internal Medicine 1986; Sleep Medicine 2009; **Med School:** Univ Pennsylvania 1983; **Resid:** Internal Medicine, Hosp Univ Penn 1986; **Fellow:** Pulmonary Critical Care Medicine, Hosp Univ Penn 1991; **Fac Appt:** Asst Prof Med, Univ Pennsylvania

Steiger, David MD [Pul] - **Spec Exp:** Rheumatologic Diseases of the Lung; Thromboembolic Disorders; Pulmonary Hypertension; Critical Care; **Hospital:** NYU Hosp For Joint Dis, NYU Langone Med Ctr (page 68); **Address:** 305 2nd Ave, Ste 16, New York, NY 10003; **Phone:** 212-598-6422; **Board Cert:** Internal Medicine 1987; Critical Care Medicine 2005; **Med School:** England, UK 1981; **Resid:** Internal Medicine, St Thomas's Hosp 1984; Internal Medicine, St Lukes Hosp 1989; **Fellow:** Pulmonary Disease, UCSF Med Ctr 1994; **Fac Appt:** Asst Prof Med, NYU Sch Med

Steinberg, Harry MD [Pul] - **Spec Exp:** Asthma; Emphysema; Lung Cancer; Pulmonary Hypertension; **Hospital:** Long Is Jewish Med Ctr (page 66), N Shore Univ Hosp (page 66); **Address:** 410 Lakeville Rd, Ste 107, New Hyde Park, NY 11042; **Phone:** 516-465-5400; **Med School:** Temple Univ 1966; **Resid:** Internal Medicine, LI Jewish Med Ctr 1969; Pulmonary Critical Care Medicine, LI Jewish Med Ctr 1970; **Fellow:** Pulmonary Disease, Hosp Univ Penn 1974; **Fac Appt:** Prof Med, Hofstra N Shore-LIJ Sch Med

Sterman, Daniel H MD [Pul] - **Spec Exp:** Interventional Pulmonology; Lung Cancer; Mesothelioma; Gene Therapy; **Hospital:** Hosp Univ Penn - UPHS (page 69); **Address:** Penn Lung Center, Perelman Ctr for Advanced Medicine, 3400 Civic Ctr Blvd, 1st Fl W, Philadelphia, PA 19104-4283; **Phone:** 215-662-3202; **Board Cert:** Internal Medicine 2007; Pulmonary Disease 2007; Critical Care Medicine 2007; **Med School:** Cornell Univ 1989; **Resid:** Internal Medicine, Hosp Univ Penn 1992; **Fellow:** Pulmonary Critical Care Medicine, Hosp Univ Penn 1997; **Fac Appt:** Assoc Prof Med, Univ Pennsylvania

Stover-Pepe, Diane E MD [Pul] - **Spec Exp:** Interstitial Lung Disease; Pulmonary Infections; Pulmonary Disease/Immunocompromised; Bronchiolitis Obliterans; **Hospital:** Meml Sloan-Kettering Canc Ctr; **Address:** 1275 York Ave, New York, NY 10065; **Phone:** 212-639-8380; **Board Cert:** Internal Medicine 1975; Pulmonary Disease 1978; **Med School:** Albert Einstein Coll Med 1970; **Resid:** Internal Medicine, Harlem Hosp Ctr 1972; Internal Medicine, NY Hosp-Cornell Med Ctr 1975; **Fellow:** Pulmonary Disease, Montefiore Med Ctr 1977; **Fac Appt:** Prof Med, Cornell Univ-Weill Med Coll

Strollo, Patrick J MD [Pul] - **Spec Exp:** Sleep Disorders/Apnea; Respiratory Failure; **Hospital:** UPMC Montefiore, UPMC Presby, Pittsburgh; **Address:** Montefiore Univ Hosp, 3459 5th Ave, Ste F639, Pittsburgh, PA 15213; **Phone:** 412-692-2880; **Board Cert:** Internal Medicine 1984; Pulmonary Disease 2009; Sleep Medicine 2007; **Med School:** Uniformed Srvs Univ, Bethesda 1981; **Resid:** Internal Medicine, Wilford Hall Med Ctr 1984; **Fellow:** Pulmonary Disease, Wilford Hall Med Ctr 1987; **Fac Appt:** Prof Med, Univ Pittsburgh

Thomashow, Byron MD [Pul] - **Spec Exp:** Emphysema & Asthma; Respiratory Failure; Chronic Obstructive Lung Disease (COPD); Interstitial Lung Disease; **Hospital:** NY-Presby/Columbia Univ Med Ctr, NY (page 65); **Address:** NY-Presby, Pulmonology Dept, 161 Fort Washington Ave, Ste 311, New York, NY 10032; **Phone:** 212-305-5261; **Board Cert:** Internal Medicine 1977; Pulmonary Disease 1980; **Med School:** Columbia P&S 1974; **Resid:** Internal Medicine, St Lukes Hosp 1977; Pulmonary Disease, St Lukes Hosp 1978; **Fellow:** Pulmonary Disease, Harlem Hosp Ctr 1979; **Fac Appt:** Clin Prof Med, Columbia P&S

Tino, Gregory MD [Pul] - **Spec Exp:** Interstitial Lung Disease; Bronchiectasis; Chronic Obstructive Lung Disease (COPD); Pulmonary Fibrosis; **Hospital:** Hosp Univ Penn - UPHS (page 69); **Address:** Dvi Pulmonary & Critical Care, Perelman Ctr for Advanced Medicine, 3400 Civic Ctr Blvd, Fl 1 West, Philadelphia, PA 19104; **Phone:** 215-662-3202; **Board Cert:** Internal Medicine 1989; Pulmonary Disease 2009; Critical Care Medicine 2009; **Med School:** Mount Sinai Sch Med 1986; **Resid:** Internal Medicine, Hosp Univ Penn 1989; **Fellow:** Pulmonary Disease, Hosp Univ Penn 1992; **Fac Appt:** Assoc Prof Med, Univ Pennsylvania

Unger, Michael MD [Pul] - **Spec Exp:** Lung Cancer; Lung Cancer in Women; Cancer Prevention; Interventional Pulmonology; **Hospital:** Fox Chase Cancer Ctr (page 57); **Address:** Fox Chase Cancer Center, 333 Cottman Ave, Philadelphia, PA 19111; **Phone:** 215-728-5703; **Board Cert:** Internal Medicine 1977; Pulmonary Disease 1978; **Med School:** France 1971; **Resid:** Internal Medicine, Mt Sinai Hosp 1974; **Fellow:** Pulmonary Disease, NY Hosp-Cornell 1976; **Fac Appt:** Clin Prof Med, Thomas Jefferson Univ

Wenzel, Sally E MD [Pul] - **Spec Exp:** Asthma & Allergy; Bronchiectasis; Autoimmune Lung Disease; Inflammatory Pulmonary Diseases; **Hospital:** UPMC Montefiore; **Address:** UPMC Montefiore, 3459 5th Ave Montefiore Bldg - Ste NW931, Falk Medical Bldg, Fl 4, Pittsburgh, PA 15213; **Phone:** 412-802-6859; **Board Cert:** Internal Medicine 1984; Pulmonary Disease 1986; **Med School:** Univ Fla Coll Med 1981; **Resid:** Internal Medicine, Wake Forest Baptist Med Ctr 1984; **Fellow:** Pulmonary Critical Care Medicine, VA Commonwealth Univ Med Ctr 1986; **Fac Appt:** Prof Med, Univ Pittsburgh

Young Jr, K Randall MD [Pul] - **Spec Exp:** Transplant Medicine-Lung; Cystic Fibrosis; **Hospital:** Einstein Med Ctr; **Address:** Albert Einstein Med Ctr, 5401 Old York Rd, Ste 363, Philadelphia, PA 19141; **Phone:** 215-456-6950; **Board Cert:** Internal Medicine 1982; Pulmonary Disease 2009; Allergy & Immunology 1987; **Med School:** Jefferson Med Coll 1978; **Resid:** Internal Medicine, Yale-New Haven Hosp 1982; Pulmonary Critical Care Medicine, Yale-New Haven Hosp 1985; **Fellow:** Allergy & Immunology, Nat Inst Hlth 1988

Southeast

Alberts, W. Michael MD [Pul] - **Spec Exp:** Lung Cancer; **Hospital:** Moffitt Canc Ctr (page 61); **Address:** H Lee Moffitt Cancer Ctr, Thoracic Onc, 12902 Magnolia Drive, Tampa, FL 33612; **Phone:** 813-745-3980; **Board Cert:** Internal Medicine 1980; Pulmonary Disease 1982; **Med School:** Univ IL Coll Med 1977; **Resid:** Internal Medicine, OSU Hosp 1980; **Fellow:** Pulmonary Critical Care Medicine, UCSD Med Ctr 1983; **Fac Appt:** Prof Med, Univ S Fla Coll Med

Antony, Veena B MD [Pul] - **Hospital:** UAB Med West; **Address:** UAB Med West, The Kirklin Clin, 2000 6th Ave S, Birmingham, AL 35233; **Phone:** 205-975-3258; **Board Cert:** Internal Medicine 1979; Pulmonary Disease 1982; **Med School:** India 1974; **Resid:** Internal Medicine, Kingsbrook Jewish Med Ctr 1978; **Fellow:** Pulmonary Disease, Univ Colorado Affil Hosp 1981; Pulmonary Disease, Natl Jewish Med & Rsch Ctr 1982; **Fac Appt:** Prof Med, UAB Sch Med

Campbell Jr, Guy Douglas MD [Pul] - **Spec Exp:** Infectious Disease-Lung; **Hospital:** Univ Mississippi Med Ctr, G.V. (Sonny) Montgomery VA Med Ctr - Jackson; **Address:** Univ Mississippi Med Ctr, Div Pulmonology, 2500 N State St, Jackson, MS 39216; **Phone:** 601-362-4471; **Board Cert:** Internal Medicine 1979; Pulmonary Disease 1986; **Med School:** Univ Miss 1976; **Resid:** Internal Medicine, Univ Miss Hosp 1979; **Fellow:** Pulmonary Disease, Univ Tex Hlth Sci Ctr 1983; Infectious Disease, Univ Calgary HSC 1985; **Fac Appt:** Prof Med, Univ Miss

Christman, Brian W MD [Pul] - **Spec Exp:** Chronic Obstructive Lung Disease (COPD); Sepsis; Critical Care; Respiratory Distress Syndrome (ARDS); **Hospital:** TN Valley Healthcare Sys-Nashville, Vanderbilt Univ Med Ctr; **Address:** VA Tennessee Valley Hlth Care Sys, 1310 24th Ave So (111), Nashville, TN 37212; **Phone:** 615-873-6979; **Board Cert:** Internal Medicine 1984; Pulmonary Disease 1986; Critical Care Medicine 2010; **Med School:** Univ Okla Coll Med 1981; **Resid:** Internal Medicine, Vanderbilt Univ Med Ctr 1984; **Fellow:** Pulmonary Disease, Vanderbilt Univ Med Ctr 1987; Critical Care Medicine, Vanderbilt Univ Med Ctr 1987; **Fac Appt:** Prof Med, Vanderbilt Univ

Cooper, J Allen D MD [Pul] - **Spec Exp:** Occupational Lung Disease; Chronic Obstructive Lung Disease (COPD); Drug Induced Lung Disease; **Hospital:** UAB Hosp, Birmingham VA Med Ctr; **Address:** UAB Pulmonary Medicine, 1530 3rd Ave S, TNT 422, Birmingham, AL 35294; **Phone:** 205-934-5400; **Board Cert:** Internal Medicine 1981; Pulmonary Disease 1984; **Med School:** Duke Univ 1978; **Resid:** Internal Medicine, Univ Washington Med Ctr 1979; Internal Medicine, Univ of Virginia Hosp 1981; **Fellow:** Pulmonary Disease, Yale Univ 1985; **Fac Appt:** Prof Med, UAB Sch Med

Cooper, William R MD [Pul] - **Spec Exp:** Lung Cancer; Asthma; Chronic Obstructive Lung Disease (COPD); **Hospital:** Sentara VA Beach Genl Hosp; **Address:** 1008 First Colonial Rd, Virginia Beach, VA 23454-3071; **Phone:** 757-481-2515; **Board Cert:** Internal Medicine 1972; Pulmonary Disease 1974; Critical Care Medicine 2009; **Med School:** Univ VA Sch Med 1969; **Resid:** Internal Medicine, Cleveland Metro Genl Hosp 1971; Pulmonary Disease, Univ Va Hosp 1973; **Fellow:** Pulmonary Disease, Mt Sinai Med Ctr 1974

Doherty, Dennis E MD [Pul] - **Spec Exp:** Asthma; Chronic Obstructive Lung Disease (COPD); Interstitial Lung Disease; **Hospital:** Univ of Kentucky Albert B. Chandler Hosp, Lexington VA Med Ctr-Leestown Div; **Address:** Univ Kentucky Med Ctr, Div Pulm & Crit Care, 740 S Limestone St, rm L-543, Lexington, KY 40536; **Phone:** 859-323-5045; **Board Cert:** Internal Medicine 1985; Pulmonary Disease 1988; **Med School:** Ohio State Univ 1980; **Resid:** Internal Medicine, Ohio State Univ Affil Hosps 1983; **Fellow:** Pulmonary Disease, Univ Colorado Affil Hosps 1986; **Fac Appt:** Prof Med, Univ KY Coll Med

Donohue, James F MD [Pul] - **Spec Exp:** Asthma; Chronic Obstructive Lung Disease (COPD); Sarcoidosis; Pulmonary Fibrosis; **Hospital:** NC Memorial Hosp - UNC; **Address:** UNC, Div Pulmonary Disease, 102 Mason Farm Rd, CB 7020, Chapel Hill, NC 27599-7020; **Phone:** 919-966-2531; **Board Cert:** Internal Medicine 1975; Pulmonary Disease 1976; **Med School:** UMDNJ-NJ Med Sch, Newark 1969; **Resid:** Internal Medicine, UMDNJ-Newark 1971; Internal Medicine, NC Meml Hosp 1974; **Fellow:** Pulmonary Disease, Univ North Carolina 1976; **Fac Appt:** Prof Med, Univ NC Sch Med

Fulkerson Jr, William J MD [Pul] - **Spec Exp:** Asthma; Chronic Obstructive Lung Disease (COPD); Pulmonary Fibrosis; **Hospital:** Duke Univ Hosp; **Address:** Duke Univ Med Ctr, Box 3708, Durham, NC 27710; **Phone:** 919-684-1860; **Board Cert:** Internal Medicine 1981; Pulmonary Disease 1984; **Med School:** Univ NC Sch Med 1977; **Resid:** Internal Medicine, Vanderbilt Univ Med Ctr 1980; **Fellow:** Pulmonary Disease, Vanderbilt Univ Med Ctr 1983; **Fac Appt:** Prof Med, Duke Univ

Garver Jr, Robert MD [Pul] - **Spec Exp:** Lung Cancer; Lung Disease; **Hospital:** Andalusia Regl Hosp; **Address:** 822 S Three Notch St, Andalusia, AL 36420; **Phone:** 888-681-5864; **Board Cert:** Internal Medicine 1984; Pulmonary Disease 1986; Critical Care Medicine 2008; **Med School:** Johns Hopkins Univ 1981; **Resid:** Internal Medicine, Johns Hopkins Hosp 1984; **Fellow:** Pulmonary Disease, NHLBI 1985; **Fac Appt:** Prof Med, UAB Sch Med

Goldman, Allan L MD [Pul] - **Spec Exp:** Occupational Lung Disease; Airway Disorders; Lung Cancer; **Hospital:** Tampa Genl Hosp, James A. Haley Veterans's Hosp-Tampa; **Address:** USF Coll Med, Dept Internal Medicine, 12901 Bruce B Downs Blvd, Box MDC19, Tampa, FL 33612-4742; **Phone:** 813-974-3558; **Board Cert:** Internal Medicine 1972; Pulmonary Disease 1972; **Med School:** Univ Minn 1968; **Resid:** Internal Medicine, Brooke Army Hosp 1970; **Fellow:** Pulmonary Disease, Walter Reed Army Hosp 1972; **Fac Appt:** Prof Med, Univ S Fla Coll Med

Harman, Eloise M MD [Pul] - **Spec Exp:** Critical Care; Diagnostic Problems; Mechanical Ventilation; **Hospital:** Malcom Randall VA Med Ctr; **Address:** VAMC, Pulmonary Disease Dept, 1601 SW Archer Rd, rm E39, Gainesville, FL 32608; **Phone:** 352-376-1611; **Board Cert:** Internal Medicine 1973; Pulmonary Disease 1976; Critical Care Medicine 2007; **Med School:** Johns Hopkins Univ 1970; **Resid:** Internal Medicine, Johns Hopkins Hosp 1972; **Fellow:** Pulmonary Disease, NY-Presby/Weill Cornell Med Ctr 1974; **Fac Appt:** Prof Med, Univ Fla Coll Med

Haynes Jr, Johnson MD [Pul] - **Spec Exp:** Sickle Cell Disease-Lung; Chronic Obstructive Lung Disease (COPD); **Hospital:** Univ of S AL Med Ctr; **Address:** 2451 Fillingim St, Moore Clin Bldg - rm 1505, MS 36617, Mobile, AL 36617; **Phone:** 251-470-5893; **Board Cert:** Internal Medicine 1983; Pulmonary Disease 1986; **Med School:** Univ S Ala Coll Med 1980; **Resid:** Internal Medicine, Univ of S AL Med Ctr 1983; **Fellow:** Pulmonary Disease, Univ of S AL Med Ctr 1986; Pulmonary Disease, Univ Colorado Affil Hosp 1988; **Fac Appt:** Prof Med, Univ S Ala Coll Med

Henke, David C MD [Pul] - **Spec Exp:** Asthma; Chronic Obstructive Lung Disease (COPD); Vasculitis; **Hospital:** NC Memorial Hosp - UNC; **Address:** UNC Pulmonary Clinic, 102 Mason Farm Rd, Chapel Hill, NC 27599-7020; **Phone:** 919-966-7933; **Board Cert:** Internal Medicine 1980; Dermatology 1983; Pulmonary Disease 1988; **Med School:** Univ NC Sch Med 1977; **Resid:** Internal Medicine, NC Memorial Hosp 1980; Dermatology, NC Meml NIEHS 1984; **Fellow:** Pulmonary Disease, NC Memorial Hosp 1987; **Fac Appt:** Assoc Prof Med, Univ NC Sch Med

Johnson, Bruce Ellsworth MD [Pul] - **Spec Exp:** Sleep Disorders/Apnea; **Hospital:** Sentara VA Beach Genl Hosp; **Address:** 1008 First Colonial Rd, Virginia Beach, VA 23454-3002; **Phone:** 757-481-2515; **Board Cert:** Internal Medicine 1981; Pulmonary Disease 1986; Critical Care Medicine 2012; Sleep Medicine 2009; **Med School:** Med Coll GA 1978; **Resid:** Internal Medicine, Univ VA Med Ctr 1981; **Fellow:** Pulmonary Disease, Univ VA Med Ctr 1983

Light, Richard W MD [Pul] - **Spec Exp:** Pleural Disease; **Hospital:** Vanderbilt Univ Med Ctr; **Address:** Vanderbilt Univ Med Ctr-Pulmonary Medicine, 1161 21st Ave S, T1218 MCN, Nashville, TN 37232-2650; **Phone:** 615-322-3412; **Board Cert:** Internal Medicine 1972; Pulmonary Disease 1974; **Med School:** Johns Hopkins Univ 1968; **Resid:** Internal Medicine, Johns Hopkins Hosp 1970; **Fellow:** Pulmonary Disease, Johns Hopkins Hosp 1972; **Fac Appt:** Prof Med, Vanderbilt Univ

LoRusso, Thomas J MD [Pul] - **Spec Exp:** Critical Care; Sleep Disorders/Apnea; **Hospital:** Inova Fairfax Hosp; **Address:** 1800 Town Ctr Drive, Ste 419, Reston, VA 20190; **Phone:** 703-620-3926; **Board Cert:** Pulmonary Disease 2012; Sleep Medicine 2009; Critical Care Medicine 2003; **Med School:** SUNY Upstate Med Univ 1987; **Resid:** Internal Medicine, Univ Hosp-SUNY 1990; **Fellow:** Pulmonary Disease, Cedars Sinai Med Ctr 1993

Loyd, James E MD [Pul] - **Spec Exp:** Pulmonary Fibrosis; Interstitial Lung Disease; Transplant Medicine-Lung; Mediastinal Fibrosis; **Hospital:** Vanderbilt Univ Med Ctr; **Address:** Vanderbilt Universtiy Medical Center, 1161 21st Ave S, Ste T-1218, Nashville, TN 37232-2650; **Phone:** 615-322-3412; **Board Cert:** Internal Medicine 1978; Pulmonary Disease 1984; **Med School:** W VA Univ 1973; **Resid:** Internal Medicine, Vanderbilt Univ Hosp 1978; **Fellow:** Pulmonary Disease, Vanderbilt Univ Hosp 1981; **Fac Appt:** Prof Med, Vanderbilt Univ

Sahn, Steven A MD [Pul] - **Spec Exp:** Pleural Disease; Interstitial Lung Disease; Chronic Obstructive Lung Disease (COPD); Pulmonary Fibrosis; **Hospital:** MUSC Med Ctr, R H Johnson VA Med Ctr - Charleston; **Address:** MUSC, Div Pulm & Crit Care Med, 96 Jonathan Lucas St, Box 250630, Charleston, SC 29425-8900; **Phone:** 843-792-3167; **Board Cert:** Internal Medicine 1974; Pulmonary Disease 1974; **Med School:** Univ Louisville Sch Med 1968; **Resid:** Internal Medicine, Univ Iowa Hosp 1971; **Fellow:** Pulmonary Disease, Univ CO Hlth Sci Ctr 1973; **Fac Appt:** Prof Med, Med Univ SC

Staton Jr, Gerald W MD [Pul] - **Spec Exp:** Interstitial Lung Disease; Chronic Obstructive Lung Disease (COPD); Pulmonary Fibrosis; Sarcoidosis; **Hospital:** Emory Univ Hosp Midtown, Wesley Woods Ger Hosp; **Address:** Emory Pulmonary Medicine, 1365A Clifton Rd NE Fl 4, Atlanta, GA 30322; **Phone:** 404-686-2505; **Board Cert:** Internal Medicine 1979; Pulmonary Disease 1982; Critical Care Medicine 2007; **Med School:** Med Coll GA 1976; **Resid:** Internal Medicine, Stanford Univ Med Ctr 1979; **Fellow:** Pulmonary Disease, Mass Genl Hosp 1981; **Fac Appt:** Prof Med, Emory Univ

Vaughey, Ellen MD [Pul] - **Spec Exp:** Critical Care; Sleep Disorders/Apnea; Asthma; **Hospital:** Inova Fairfax Hosp, Virginia Hosp Ctr - Arlington; **Address:** 3289 Woodburn Rd, Ste 350, Annandale, VA 22003; **Phone:** 703-641-8616; **Board Cert:** Internal Medicine 2011; Pulmonary Disease 2012; Critical Care Medicine 2003; **Med School:** Georgetown Univ 1987; **Resid:** Internal Medicine, Thomas Jefferson Univ Hosp 1990; **Fellow:** Pulmonary Disease, Roger Williams Hosp-Brown Univ 1993

Voelkel, Norbert F MD [Pul] - **Spec Exp:** Pulmonary Hypertension; Asthma; Emphysema; **Hospital:** Med Coll of VA Hosp; **Address:** 417 N 11th St, Richmond, VA 23298; **Phone:** 804-828-7929; **Med School:** Germany 1972; **Resid:** Internal Medicine, Univ Hamburg 1977; **Fellow:** Research, Univ Colorado 1978; Pulmonary Disease, Univ Colorado 1981; **Fac Appt:** Prof Med, Univ Colorado

Wanner, Adam MD [Pul] - **Spec Exp:** Asthma; **Hospital:** Jackson Meml Hosp, Univ of Miami Hosp; **Address:** UHlth, Pulmonary & Critical Care Dept, 1600 NW 10th Ave, Ste 7056, Miami, FL 33136; **Phone:** 305-243-3045; **Board Cert:** Internal Medicine 1973; Pulmonary Disease 1974; **Med School:** Switzerland 1966; **Resid:** Internal Medicine, Kantonsspital Aarau 1970; **Fellow:** Pulmonary Disease, Mount Sinai Med Ctr 1972; **Fac Appt:** Prof Med, Univ Miami Sch Med

Wheeler, Arthur P MD [Pul] - **Spec Exp:** Critical Care; Sepsis; Respiratory Distress Syndrome (ARDS); Thromboembolic Disorders; **Hospital:** Vanderbilt Univ Med Ctr; **Address:** Vanderbilt Univ Medical Ctr, 1161 21st Ave S, Ste T-1218, Nashville, TN 37232-2650; **Phone:** 615-322-3412; **Board Cert:** Internal Medicine 1985; Pulmonary Disease 1988; **Med School:** Univ MD Sch Med 1982; **Resid:** Internal Medicine, Vanderbilt Univ Med Ctr 1985; **Fellow:** Pulmonary Disease, Vanderbilt Univ Med Ctr 1986; **Fac Appt:** Assoc Prof Med, Vanderbilt Univ

Midwest

Balk, Robert A MD [Pul] - **Spec Exp:** Asthma; Cystic Fibrosis; Respiratory Failure; Lung Injury/ARDS; **Hospital:** Rush Univ Med Ctr; **Address:** 1725 W Harrison St, Ste 054, Chicago, IL 60612; **Phone:** 312-942-6744; **Board Cert:** Internal Medicine 1981; Pulmonary Disease 1986; Critical Care Medicine 2008; **Med School:** Univ MO-Kansas City 1978; **Resid:** Internal Medicine, Univ MO-Kansas City Affil Hosps 1981; **Fellow:** Pulmonary Critical Care Medicine, Univ Ark Hosp 1983; **Fac Appt:** Prof Med, Rush Med Coll

Bijwadia, Jagdeep S MD [Pul] - **Spec Exp:** Sleep Medicine; **Hospital:** Regions Hosp - St Paul; **Address:** HealthPartners Spec Ctr, Lung & Sleep Hlth, 401 Phalen Blvd, St Paul, MN 55130; **Phone:** 651-254-7670 x3; **Board Cert:** Pulmonary Disease 2004; Sleep Medicine 2007; **Med School:** India 1986; **Resid:** Internal Medicine, Nassau Co MC 1992; **Fellow:** Pulmonary Critical Care Medicine, USC Univ Hosp 1992; **Fac Appt:** Asst Prof Med, Univ Minn

Fahey, Patrick J MD [Pul] - **Spec Exp:** Asthma; Interstitial Lung Disease; Chronic Obstructive Lung Disease (COPD); **Hospital:** Loyola Univ Med Ctr, Edward Hines, Jr. VA Hosp; **Address:** Loyola Univ Med Ctr-Pulmonary Disease, 2160 S 1st Ave, Maywood, IL 60153-3304; **Phone:** 708-216-6850; **Board Cert:** Internal Medicine 1976; Pulmonary Disease 1978; **Med School:** Univ Wisc 1973; **Resid:** Internal Medicine, St Elizabeth's Hosp 1976; **Fellow:** Pulmonary Disease, Strong Meml Hosp 1980; **Fac Appt:** Prof Med, Loyola Univ-Stritch Sch Med

Fletcher, Eugene MD [Pul] - **Spec Exp:** Chronic Obstructive Lung Disease (COPD); Sleep Disorders/Apnea; **Hospital:** Reid Hosp & Hlth Care Servs; **Address:** 1100 Reid Pkwy, Richmond, IN 47374; **Phone:** 768-983-3000; **Board Cert:** Internal Medicine 1974; Pulmonary Disease 1980; Critical Care Medicine 2010; **Med School:** Temple Univ 1971; **Resid:** Internal Medicine, Univ Colo Affil Hosps 1973; Internal Medicine, Fitzsimons Army Med Ctr 1974; **Fellow:** Pulmonary Disease, Univ Okla Hlth Scis Ctr 1974; **Fac Appt:** Clin Prof Med, Univ Louisville Sch Med

Garrity Jr, Edward R MD [Pul] - **Spec Exp:** Transplant Medicine-Lung; Pulmonary Vascular Disease; Asthma; Cystic Fibrosis; **Hospital:** Univ of Chicago Med; **Address:** Lung Transplant Prgrm, 5841 S Maryland Ave, MS 0999, Chicago, IL 60637; **Phone:** 773-834-7235 x1655; **Board Cert:** Internal Medicine 2003; Pulmonary Disease 1984; **Med School:** Loyola Univ-Stritch Sch Med 1976; **Resid:** Internal Medicine, Loyola Univ Med Ctr 1979; **Fellow:** Pulmonary Disease, Univ Chicago Hosps 1983; **Fac Appt:** Prof Med, Univ Chicago-Pritzker Sch Med

Grum, Cyril M MD [Pul] - **Spec Exp:** Asthma; Cystic Fibrosis; **Hospital:** Univ Michigan Med Ctr; **Address:** Univ Michigan Med Ctr-Div Pulm Med, 1500 E Med Ctr Drive, 3916 TC, Ann Arbor, MI 48109; **Phone:** 734-647-9342; **Board Cert:** Internal Medicine 1980; Pulmonary Disease 1982; **Med School:** Med Coll Wisc 1977; **Resid:** Internal Medicine, Cleveland Clin 1980; **Fellow:** Pulmonary Disease, Univ Michigan Hosp 1982; **Fac Appt:** Prof Med, Univ Mich Med Sch

Hall, Jesse MD [Pul] - **Spec Exp:** Respiratory Failure; Critical Care; **Hospital:** Univ of Chicago Med; **Address:** Univ Chicago Med Ctr-Pulmonary Medicine, 5841 S Maryland Ave, rm W656, MC 6076, Chicago, IL 60637; **Phone:** 773-702-9660; **Board Cert:** Internal Medicine 1980; Critical Care Medicine 2011; **Med School:** Univ Chicago-Pritzker Sch Med 1977; **Resid:** Internal Medicine, Univ Chicago Hosps 1982; **Fac Appt:** Prof Med, Univ Chicago-Pritzker Sch Med

Hertz, Marshall I MD [Pul] - **Spec Exp:** Transplant Medicine-Lung; Transplant Medicine-Heart & Lung; Pulmonary Hypertension; **Hospital:** Univ Minn Med Ctr, Fairview - West Bank Campus; **Address:** Pulmonary, Allergy & Critical Care Med, 420 Delaware St SE, MMC 276, Minneapolis, MN 55455; **Phone:** 612-624-6100; **Board Cert:** Internal Medicine 1981; Pulmonary Disease 1984; **Med School:** Univ Mich Med Sch 1978; **Resid:** Internal Medicine, Univ Minn Med Ctr 1982; **Fellow:** Pulmonary Critical Care Medicine, Univ Minn Med Ctr 1984; **Fac Appt:** Prof Med, Univ Minn

Hyers, Thomas M MD [Pul] - **Spec Exp:** Thromboembolic Disorders; Chronic Obstructive Lung Disease (COPD); Occupational Lung Disease; Respiratory Distress Syndrome (ARDS); **Hospital:** SSM St. Clare Hlth Ctr, Mercy Hosp - St Louis; **Address:** CARE Clin Research, 522 N New Ballas Rd, Ste 350, St Louis, MO 63141; **Phone:** 314-699-9383; **Board Cert:** Internal Medicine 1974; Pulmonary Disease 1980; **Med School:** Duke Univ 1968; **Resid:** Internal Medicine, Univ Wash Med Ctr 1975; Pulmonary Disease, Univ Colorado Hosp 1977; **Fellow:** Pulmonary Disease, Natl Inst Hlth 1972; **Fac Appt:** Clin Prof Med, St Louis Univ

Ingbar, David H MD [Pul] - **Spec Exp:** Critical Care; Pulmonary Infections; Respiratory Failure; **Hospital:** Univ Minn Med Ctr, Fairview - West Bank Campus, Fairview Southdale Hosp; **Address:** Univ Minn Med Ctr, Div Pulm & Crit Care, 420 Delaware St SE, MMC 276, Minneapolis, MN 55455; **Phone:** 612-626-6100; **Board Cert:** Internal Medicine 1981; Critical Care Medicine 2007; Pulmonary Disease 1984; **Med School:** Harvard Med Sch 1978; **Resid:** Internal Medicine, Univ Wash Med Ctr 1982; **Fellow:** Pulmonary Disease, Yale Univ-New Haven Hosp 1985; **Fac Appt:** Prof Med, Univ Minn

Kaye, Mitchell G MD [Pul] - **Spec Exp:** Chronic Obstructive Lung Disease (COPD); Asthma; **Hospital:** Abbott - Northwestern Hosp; **Address:** Minnesota Lung Ctr, 920 E 28th St, Ste 700, Minneapolis, MN 55407; **Phone:** 952-567-7400; **Board Cert:** Internal Medicine 1987; Pulmonary Disease 2010; **Med School:** Univ Minn 1984; **Resid:** Internal Medicine, Univ IL Med Ctr 1987; **Fellow:** Pulmonary Disease, Northwestern Univ 1989

Kovitz, Kevin L MD [Pul] - **Spec Exp:** Interventional Pulmonology; **Hospital:** Univ of IL Med Ctr at Chicago, Central DuPage Hosp; **Address:** Chicago Chest Ctr, 800 Biesterfield Rd, Ste 510, Elk Grove Village, IL 60007; **Phone:** 847-498-5864; **Board Cert:** Internal Medicine 1988; Pulmonary Disease 2012; Critical Care Medicine 2005; **Med School:** Israel 1985; **Resid:** Internal Medicine, Univ Maryland Hosps 1988; **Fellow:** Pulmonary Intensive Care, Johns Hopkins Hosp 1992; Interventional Pulmonology, Sainte Marguerite Hosp 1993; **Fac Appt:** Prof Med, Univ IL Coll Med

Krowka, Michael J MD [Pul] - **Spec Exp:** Hepatopulmonary Syndrome; Pulmonary Hypertension; **Hospital:** Mayo Med Ctr & Clin - Rochester; **Address:** Mayo Clin, Div Pulm & Crit Care Med, 200 First St SW, Gonda-18 S, Rochester, MN 55905; **Phone:** 507-284-2158; **Board Cert:** Internal Medicine 1983; Pulmonary Disease 1986; **Med School:** Univ Nevada 1980; **Resid:** Internal Medicine, Evanston Hosp 1983; **Fellow:** Pulmonary Disease, Mayo Clinic 1986; **Fac Appt:** Prof Med, Mayo Med Sch

Lem, Vincent M MD [Pul] - **Spec Exp:** Asthma; **Hospital:** St. Luke's Hosp of Kansas City; **Address:** 4321 Washington St, Ste 6000, Kansas City, MO 64111; **Phone:** 816-756-2255; **Board Cert:** Internal Medicine 1982; Pulmonary Disease 1984; Critical Care Medicine 2004; **Med School:** Univ Kansas 1978; **Resid:** Internal Medicine, St Luke's Hosp 1982; **Fellow:** Pulmonary Disease, Univ Texas Hlth Sci Ctr 1984; **Fac Appt:** Assoc Clin Prof Med, Univ MO-Kansas City

Marini, John Joseph MD [Pul] - **Spec Exp:** Critical Care; Mechanical Ventilation; Chronic Obstructive Lung Disease (COPD); **Hospital:** Regions Hosp - St Paul; **Address:** 640 Jackson St, Box MS11203B, MS 11203B, St Paul, MN 55130; **Phone:** 651-254-7670; **Board Cert:** Internal Medicine 2003; Pulmonary Disease 2003; Critical Care Medicine 2012; **Med School:** Johns Hopkins Univ 1973; **Resid:** Internal Medicine, Univ Wash Med Ctr 1976; **Fellow:** Pulmonary Disease, Univ Wash Med Ctr 1978; **Fac Appt:** Prof Med, Univ Minn

Martinez, Fernando J MD [Pul] - **Spec Exp:** Lung Disease; Critical Care; **Hospital:** Univ Michigan Med Ctr; **Address:** Univ Michigan Med Ctr-Div Pulm Med, 1500 E Med Ctr Drive, 3916 TC, Ann Arbor, MI 48109; **Phone:** 734-647-9342; **Board Cert:** Internal Medicine 1986; Pulmonary Disease 1988; Critical Care Medicine 2010; **Med School:** Univ Fla Coll Med 1983; **Resid:** Internal Medicine, Beth Israel Deaconess Med Ctr 1986; **Fellow:** Pulmonary Disease, Boston Medical Ctr 1989; **Fac Appt:** Prof Med, Univ Mich Med Sch

Matuschak, George M MD [Pul] - **Spec Exp:** Chronic Obstructive Lung Disease (COPD); Asthma; **Hospital:** Mercy Hosp - St Louis; **Address:** 621 S New Ballas Rd, Ste 228A, St Louis, MO 63141; **Phone:** 314-251-4966; **Board Cert:** Internal Medicine 1980; Critical Care Medicine 2008; Pulmonary Disease 2008; **Med School:** Temple Univ 1977; **Resid:** Internal Medicine, Strong Meml Hosp 1980; **Fellow:** Critical Care Medicine, Univ Htlh Ctr 1981; Pulmonary Disease, Univ Hlth Ctr 1984; **Fac Appt:** Prof Med, St Louis Univ

Mazzone, Peter J MD [Pul] - **Spec Exp:** Lung Cancer-Early Detection; **Hospital:** Cleveland Clin (page 55); **Address:** Cleveland Clinic, 9500 Euclid Ave, Cleveland, OH 44195; **Phone:** 216-445-4812; **Board Cert:** Internal Medicine 2007; Pulmonary Disease 2010; Critical Care Medicine 2011; **Med School:** Canada 1994; **Resid:** Internal Medicine, Cleveland Clinici 1998; **Fellow:** Pulmonary Disease, Cleveland Clinic 2000; Pulmonary Critical Care Medicine, Cleveland Clinic 2001

Popovich Jr, John MD [Pul] - **Spec Exp:** Lung Disease; Pulmonary Embolism; Interstitial Lung Disease; Critical Care; **Hospital:** Henry Ford Hosp; **Address:** Henry Ford Hosp, 2799 W Grand Blvd, Detroit, MI 48202; **Phone:** 313-916-8058; **Board Cert:** Internal Medicine 1978; Pulmonary Disease 1980; **Med School:** Univ Mich Med Sch 1975; **Resid:** Internal Medicine, Henry Ford Hosp 1978; **Fellow:** Pulmonary Disease, Henry Ford Hosp 1980; **Fac Appt:** Prof Med, Wayne State Univ

Prakash, Udaya MD [Pul] - **Spec Exp:** Bronchoscopy; **Hospital:** Mayo Med Ctr & Clin - Rochester; **Address:** Mayo Clin, Div Pulm & Crit Care Med, 200 First St SW, Gonda-18 S, Rochester, MN 55905; **Phone:** 507-284-2158; **Board Cert:** Internal Medicine 1987; Pulmonary Disease 1976; **Med School:** India 1970; **Resid:** Internal Medicine, Mayo Clin 1973; **Fellow:** Pulmonary Disease, Mayo Clin 1976; **Fac Appt:** Prof Med, Mayo Med Sch

Rosenbluth, Daniel B MD [Pul] - **Spec Exp:** Cystic Fibrosis; **Hospital:** Barnes-Jewish Hosp; **Address:** Washington Univ Sch Med, 660 S Euclid Ave, Box 8052, St Louis, MO 63110; **Phone:** 314-454-8762; **Board Cert:** Internal Medicine 2002; Pulmonary Disease 2004; Critical Care Medicine 2005; **Med School:** Mount Sinai Sch Med 1989; **Resid:** Internal Medicine, Northwestern Meml Hosp 1992; **Fellow:** Pulmonary Critical Care Medicine, Barnes Hosp 1995; **Fac Appt:** Prof Med, Washington Univ, St Louis

Schraufnagel, Dean E MD [Pul] - **Spec Exp:** Pulmonary Infections; Tuberculosis; Pulmonary Vascular Disease; Sickle Cell Disease-Lung; **Hospital:** Univ of IL Med Ctr at Chicago; **Address:** Univ IL Outpatient Care Ctr, 1801 W Taylor St, Ste 3C, Chicago, IL 60612; **Phone:** 312-996-3300; **Board Cert:** Internal Medicine 1987; Pulmonary Disease 1980; **Med School:** Univ Wisc 1974; **Resid:** Internal Medicine, Univ IL Med Ctr 1977; **Fellow:** Pulmonary Disease, McGill Univ Affil Hosp 1981; **Fac Appt:** Prof Med, Univ IL Coll Med

Silver, Michael R MD [Pul] - **Spec Exp:** Chronic Obstructive Lung Disease (COPD); Lung Cancer; Asthma; **Hospital:** Rush Univ Med Ctr, Rush Oak Park Hosp; **Address:** Rush Univ Med Ctr, Professional Office Bldg 3, 1725 W Harrison St, Ste 054, Chicago, IL 60612; **Phone:** 312-942-6744; **Board Cert:** Internal Medicine 1984; Pulmonary Disease 1988; Critical Care Medicine 2009; **Med School:** Albany Med Coll 1981; **Resid:** Internal Medicine, Rush-Presby-St Lukes Med Ctr 1985; **Fellow:** Pulmonary Critical Care Medicine, Rush-Presby-St Lukes Med Ctr 1987; **Fac Appt:** Assoc Prof Med, Rush Med Coll

Simon, Richard H MD [Pul] - **Spec Exp:** Cystic Fibrosis; **Hospital:** Univ Michigan Med Ctr; **Address:** Univ Michigan Med Ctr-Div Pulm Med, 1500 E Med Ctr Drive, 3916 TC, Ann Arbor, MI 48109; **Phone:** 734-647-9342; **Board Cert:** Internal Medicine 1976; Pulmonary Disease 1980; **Med School:** Duke Univ 1972; **Resid:** Internal Medicine, UCSF Med Ctr 1975; Internal Medicine, Univ Colorado Affil Hosps 1976; **Fellow:** Pulmonary Disease, Univ Colorado 1981; **Fac Appt:** Prof Med, Univ Mich Med Sch

Stoller, James MD [Pul] - **Spec Exp:** Emphysema/Alpha-1 Antitrypsin Deficiency; **Hospital:** Cleveland Clin (page 55); **Address:** Cleveland Clinic Respiratory Therapy, 9500 Euclid Ave, Desk NA22, Cleveland, OH 44195; **Phone:** 216-444-1960; **Board Cert:** Internal Medicine 1982; Pulmonary Disease 1984; Critical Care Medicine 2007; **Med School:** Yale Univ 1979; **Resid:** Internal Medicine, Peter Bent Brigham Hosp 1982; **Fellow:** Pulmonary Disease, Brigham & Women's Hosp 1983; Pulmonary Critical Care Medicine, Yale-New Haven Hosp 1985; **Fac Appt:** Prof Med, Cleveland Cl Coll Med/Case West Res

Tobin, Martin J MD [Pul] - **Spec Exp:** Mechanical Ventilation; Chronic Obstructive Lung Disease (COPD); **Hospital:** Edward Hines, Jr. VA Hosp, Loyola Univ Med Ctr; **Address:** Hines VA Hosp (111N), Fifth Ave and Roosevelt Rd, Bldg 1 - rm E438, Hines, IL 60141; **Phone:** 708-202-2705; **Board Cert:** Internal Medicine 1983; Pulmonary Disease 1984; **Med School:** Ireland 1975; **Resid:** Internal Medicine, Trinity Coll Hosps 1979; Pulmonary Disease, Kings Coll Hosp 1980; **Fellow:** Pulmonary Critical Care Medicine, Mt Sinai Hosp 1983; Pulmonary Critical Care Medicine, Univ Pittsburgh 1983; **Fac Appt:** Prof Med, Loyola Univ-Stritch Sch Med

Trulock III, Elbert P MD [Pul] - **Spec Exp:** Transplant Medicine-Lung; Emphysema-Lung Volume Reduction; Pulmonary Hypertension; Cystic Fibrosis; **Hospital:** Barnes-Jewish Hosp; **Address:** 4901 Forrest Park Ave, MS 90-75-549, St Louis, MO 63108; **Phone:** 314-362-5378; **Board Cert:** Internal Medicine 1981; Pulmonary Disease 1984; **Med School:** Emory Univ 1978; **Resid:** Internal Medicine, Barnes Hosp 1981; **Fellow:** Pulmonary Disease, Wash Univ Med Ctr 1983; **Fac Appt:** Prof Med, Washington Univ, St Louis

Wiedemann, Herbert P MD [Pul] - **Spec Exp:** Respiratory Distress Syndrome (ARDS); Asthma; Emphysema; **Hospital:** Cleveland Clin (page 55); **Address:** Cleveland Clinic-Pulmonary & Allergy, 9500 Euclid Ave, Desk A90, Cleveland, OH 44195; **Phone:** 216-444-8335; **Board Cert:** Internal Medicine 1980; Pulmonary Disease 1984; **Med School:** Cornell Univ 1977; **Resid:** Internal Medicine, Univ Wash Hosps 1980; Internal Medicine, Harborview Hosp 1981; **Fellow:** Pulmonary Disease, Yale Univ 1984

Great Plains and Mountains

Brown, Kevin K MD [Pul] - **Spec Exp:** Pulmonary Fibrosis; Interstitial Lung Disease; Autoimmune Lung Disease; Clinical Trials; **Hospital:** Natl Jewish Hlth, Univ Colorado Hosp; **Address:** Natl Jewish Health, 1400 Jackson St, Denver, CO 80206-2762; **Phone:** 303-398-1621; **Board Cert:** Internal Medicine 1989; Pulmonary Disease 2005; **Med School:** Univ Minn 1984; **Resid:** Internal Medicine, Providence Med Ctr 1989; **Fellow:** Pulmonary Disease, Maine Med Ctr 1992; Pulmonary Disease, Univ Colo Hlth Scis Ctr 1994; **Fac Appt:** Prof Med, Univ Colorado

Elliott, C. Gregory MD [Pul] - **Spec Exp:** Pulmonary Hypertension; Thromboembolic Disorders; **Hospital:** Intermountain Med Ctr, Univ Utah Hlth Care; **Address:** Intermountain Med Ctr, Dept Medicine, 5121 S Cottonwood St, Ste 307, Murray, UT 84107; **Phone:** 801-507-3373; **Board Cert:** Internal Medicine 1976; Pulmonary Disease 1978; **Med School:** Univ MD Sch Med 1973; **Resid:** Internal Medicine, Univ Maryland Hosp 1976; **Fellow:** Pulmonary Disease, Univ Utah 1978; **Fac Appt:** Prof Med, Univ Utah

Kaplan, James D MD [Pul] - **Spec Exp:** Critical Care; Sleep Disorders/Apnea; **Hospital:** Overland Pk Regl Med Ctr; **Address:** 10550 Quivira Rd, Ste 335, Overland Park, KS 66215-2304; **Phone:** 913-599-3800; **Board Cert:** Internal Medicine 1987; Pulmonary Disease 2010; Critical Care Medicine 2003; **Med School:** Univ MO-Kansas City 1984; **Resid:** Internal Medicine, Barnes-Jewish Hosp 1987; **Fellow:** Pulmonary Disease, Barnes-Jewish Hosp 1989

Kern, Jeffrey A MD [Pul] - **Spec Exp:** Lung Cancer; **Hospital:** Natl Jewish Hlth; **Address:** Natl Jewish Hlth, Lung Cancer Ctr, 1400 Jackson St, Denver, CO 80206; **Phone:** 877-225-5654; **Board Cert:** Internal Medicine 1982; Pulmonary Disease 1986; **Med School:** Univ Wisc 1979; **Resid:** Internal Medicine, Parkland Meml Hosp 1982; **Fellow:** Pulmonary Critical Care Medicine, Hosp Univ Penn 1984

Martin, Richard J MD [Pul] - **Spec Exp:** Asthma; Vocal Cord Disorders; Chronic Obstructive Lung Disease (COPD); Airway Disorders; **Hospital:** Natl Jewish Hlth, Univ Colorado Hosp; **Address:** Natl Jewish Hlth, Pulmonary Disease, 1400 Jackson St, rm J206, Denver, CO 80206; **Phone:** 303-398-1847; **Board Cert:** Internal Medicine 1976; Pulmonary Disease 1978; **Med School:** Univ Mich Med Sch 1971; **Resid:** Internal Medicine, Tulane Med Ctr 1976; **Fellow:** Pulmonary Disease, Univ Oklahoma Coll Med Affil Hosp 1978; **Fac Appt:** Prof Med, Univ Colorado

Rennard, Stephen I MD [Pul] - **Spec Exp:** Chronic Obstructive Lung Disease (COPD); Emphysema; **Hospital:** Nebraska Med Ctr; **Address:** Univ Nebraska Med Ctr, 985910 Nebraska Med Ctr, Omaha, NE 68198-5910; **Phone:** 402-559-7313; **Board Cert:** Internal Medicine 1978; Pulmonary Disease 1982; **Med School:** Baylor Coll Med 1975; **Resid:** Internal Medicine, Barnes Hosp-Washington Univ 1977; **Fac Appt:** Prof Med, Univ Nebr Coll Med

Rose, Cecile MD [Pul] - **Spec Exp:** Occupational Lung Disease; Sarcoidosis; Pneumoconiosis; Asbestos-related Lung Disease; **Hospital:** Natl Jewish Hlth, Univ Colorado Hosp; **Address:** Natl Jewish Hosp, Occupational Med, 1400 Jackson St, rm G211, Denver, CO 80206; **Phone:** 303-398-1867; **Board Cert:** Internal Medicine 1983; Pulmonary Disease 1986; Occupational Medicine 1987; **Med School:** Univ IL Coll Med 1980; **Resid:** Internal Medicine, Med Coll Virginia Hosp 1983; **Fellow:** Pulmonary Disease, Med Coll Virginia Hosp 1985; **Fac Appt:** Assoc Prof Med, Univ Colorado

Sutherland, Everett Rand MD [Pul] - **Spec Exp:** Allergy; Occupational Asthma; Chronic Obstructive Lung Disease (COPD); Emphysema; **Hospital:** Natl Jewish Hlth; **Address:** Natl Jewish Hlth, Pulmonary Disease, 1400 Jackson St, rm J201, Denver, CO 80206; **Phone:** 303-398-1655; **Board Cert:** Internal Medicine 2007; Pulmonary Disease 2010; **Med School:** Univ Chicago-Pritzker Sch Med 1994; **Resid:** Internal Medicine, UCSF Med Ctr 1997; **Fellow:** Pulmonary Critical Care Medicine, Univ CO Hosp 2001; **Fac Appt:** Prof Med, Univ Colorado

Southwest

Arroliga, Alejandro C MD [Pul] - **Spec Exp:** Pulmonary Hypertension; Respiratory Distress Syndrome (ARDS); Critical Care; **Hospital:** Scott & White Mem Hosp; **Address:** 2401 S 31st St, Temple, TX 76508; **Phone:** 254-724-9887; **Board Cert:** Internal Medicine 2010; Pulmonary Disease 2012; Critical Care Medicine 2003; **Med School:** Mexico 1984; **Resid:** Internal Medicine, Coney Island Hosp 1990; **Fellow:** Pulmonary Critical Care Medicine, Yale-New Haven Hosp 1993; **Fac Appt:** Prof Med, Cleveland Cl Coll Med/Case West Res

Guidry, George G MD [Pul] - **Spec Exp:** Chronic Obstructive Lung Disease (COPD); Asthma; Pneumonia; Lung Cancer; **Hospital:** Lafayette Genl Med Ctr; **Address:** 155 Hospital Drive, Ste 206, Lafayette, LA 70503-2852; **Phone:** 337-234-3204; **Board Cert:** Internal Medicine 1988; Pulmonary Disease 2010; **Med School:** Louisiana State U, New Orleans 1985; **Resid:** Internal Medicine, LSU Hosp 1988; **Fellow:** Pulmonary Disease, LSU Hosp 1991; **Fac Appt:** Assoc Clin Prof Med, Louisiana State U, New Orleans

Levin, David C MD [Pul] - **Spec Exp:** Asthma; Chronic Obstructive Lung Disease (COPD); Smoking Cessation; **Hospital:** OU Med Ctr; **Address:** OU Physicians Bldg, 825 NE 10th St, Ste 2500, Oklahoma City, OK 73104; **Phone:** 405-271-7001; **Board Cert:** Internal Medicine 1973; Pulmonary Disease 1976; **Med School:** Case West Res Univ 1970; **Resid:** Internal Medicine, Univ Colorado Affil Hosp 1973; **Fellow:** Pulmonary Disease, Univ Colorado Affil Hosp 1975; **Fac Appt:** Prof Med, Univ Okla Coll Med

Nader, Daniel A DO [Pul] - **Spec Exp:** Lung Cancer; Interventional Pulmonology; **Hospital:** CTCA at Southwestern Regl Med Ctr; **Address:** Cancer Treatment Centers of America, 10109 E 79th St, Tulsa, OK 74133; **Phone:** 800-515-9610; **Board Cert:** Internal Medicine 1980; Pulmonary Disease 1982; **Med School:** Univ Hlth Sci, Coll Osteo Med 1977; **Resid:** Internal Medicine, Naval Regl Med Ctr 1980; **Fellow:** Pulmonary Disease, Naval Regl Med Ctr 1982; **Fac Appt:** Assoc Clin Prof Med, Okla State Univ, Coll Osteo Med

Perret, Philip S MD [Pul] - **Spec Exp:** Chronic Obstructive Lung Disease (COPD); **Hospital:** Our Lady of Lourdes Reg Med Ctr - Lafayette, Lafayette Genl Med Ctr; **Address:** 614 W St Mary Blvd, Lafayette, LA 70506; **Phone:** 337-232-6435; **Board Cert:** Internal Medicine 1978; Pulmonary Disease 1980; **Med School:** Emory Univ 1974; **Resid:** Internal Medicine, Emory Univ Hosp 1978; **Fellow:** Pulmonary Disease, Emory Univ Hosp 1980

Shellito, Judd E MD [Pul] - **Spec Exp:** Pulmonary Infections; Occupational Lung Disease; **Hospital:** Ochsner Med Ctr-Kenner; **Address:** LSU Pulmonary Med, 1901 Perdido St, Ste 3205, New Orleans, LA 70112; **Phone:** 504-412-1705; **Board Cert:** Internal Medicine 1977; Pulmonary Disease 1980; **Med School:** Tulane Univ 1974; **Resid:** Internal Medicine, Evanston Hosp/NorthShore Univ Hlth Sys 1978; **Fellow:** Pulmonary Critical Care Medicine, Univ Hosp 1980; **Fac Appt:** Prof Med, Louisiana State U, New Orleans

Weissler, Jonathan C MD [Pul] - **Spec Exp:** Interstitial Lung Disease; Asthma; **Hospital:** UT Southwestern Med Ctr at Dallas, Parkland Hlth & Hosp Sys; **Address:** 5909 Harry Hines Blvd, Dallas, TX 75390-8225; **Phone:** 214-645-1825; **Board Cert:** Internal Medicine 1982; Pulmonary Disease 1984; Critical Care Medicine 2007; **Med School:** NYU Sch Med 1979; **Resid:** Internal Medicine, UT Hlth Sci Ctr 1982; **Fellow:** Pulmonary Disease, UT Hlth Sci Ctr 1985; **Fac Appt:** Prof Med, Univ Tex SW, Dallas

West Coast and Pacific

Albertson, Timothy MD/PhD [Pul] - **Spec Exp:** Critical Care; Toxicology; **Hospital:** UC Davis Med Ctr; **Address:** UC Davis Med Grp - Dept Pulmonology, 2825 J St, Ste 400, Sacramento, CA 95816; **Phone:** 916-734-2737 x2; **Board Cert:** Pulmonary Disease 1984; Critical Care Medicine 2007; Emergency Medicine 2007; Medical Toxicology 2005; **Med School:** UC Davis 1977; **Resid:** Internal Medicine, Univ Arizona Coll Med Affil Hosps 1980; Internal Medicine, UC Davis Med Ctr 1981; **Fellow:** Pulmonary Critical Care Medicine, UC Davis Med Ctr 1983; **Fac Appt:** Prof Med, UC Davis

Auger, William R MD [Pul] - **Spec Exp:** Thromboembolic Disorders; Pulmonary Hypertension; **Hospital:** UCSD Med Ctr; **Address:** Thornton Hosp, UCSD, 9300 Campus Pt Drive, La Jolla, CA 92037; **Phone:** 858-657-7140; **Board Cert:** Internal Medicine 1986; Pulmonary Disease 1988; **Med School:** Univ Rochester 1982; **Resid:** Internal Medicine, Univ Rochester Strong Meml Hosp 1985; **Fellow:** Critical Care Medicine, Ellis Hosp 1986; Pulmonary Disease, UCSD Med Ctr 1989; **Fac Appt:** Prof Med, UCSD

Balmes, John R MD [Pul] - **Spec Exp:** Beryllium-induced Lung Disease; **Hospital:** San Francisco Genl Hosp, UCSF Med Ctr; **Address:** UCSF, Div Occup & Envr Med, 1001 Potrero Ave, rm 5K1, San Francisco, CA 94110; **Phone:** 415-206-8314; **Board Cert:** Internal Medicine 1979; Pulmonary Disease 1984; **Med School:** Mount Sinai Sch Med 1976; **Resid:** Internal Medicine, Mount Sinai Hosp 1979; **Fellow:** Pulmonary Disease, Yale-New Haven Hosp 1981; **Fac Appt:** Prof Med, UCSF

Bellamy, Paul E MD [Pul] - **Spec Exp:** Critical Care; **Hospital:** Kaiser Permanente Woodland Hills Med Ctr; **Address:** Kaiser Woodland Hills Med Ctr, Pulm Div, 5601 De Soto Ave, Med Office Twr,, Fl 4, Woodland Hills, CA 91367; **Phone:** 818-719-3530; **Board Cert:** Internal Medicine 1978; Pulmonary Disease 1980; Critical Care Medicine 2007; **Med School:** SUNY Buffalo 1975; **Resid:** Internal Medicine, Univ Hosps-Case West Res 1978; **Fellow:** Pulmonary Disease, UCLA Med Ctr 1980; **Fac Appt:** Clin Prof Med, UCLA

Boushey Jr, Homer A MD [Pul] - **Spec Exp:** Asthma; Lung Injuries-Inhalation Induced; **Hospital:** UCSF Med Ctr; **Address:** UCSF Med Ctr, Div Pulmonary Med, 505 Parnassus Ave, Box 0130, Room M1292, San Francisco, CA 94143; **Phone:** 415-476-8019; **Board Cert:** Internal Medicine 1972; Pulmonary Disease 1974; **Med School:** UCSF 1968; **Resid:** Internal Medicine, UCSF Med Ctr 1970; Internal Medicine, Beth Israel Deaconess Med Ctr 1971; **Fellow:** Pulmonary Disease, Oxford Univ 1972; Pulmonary Disease, UCSF Hosp 1974; **Fac Appt:** Prof Med, UCSF

Catanzaro, Antonino MD [Pul] - **Spec Exp:** Tuberculosis; Coccidioidomycosis; Mycobacterial Infections; **Hospital:** UCSD Med Ctr; **Address:** 9500 Gilman Drive, La Jolla, CA 92093; **Phone:** 619-543-5550; **Board Cert:** Internal Medicine 1972; Pulmonary Disease 1976; **Med School:** SUNY Buffalo 1965; **Resid:** Internal Medicine, MedStar Georgetown Univ Hosp 1970; **Fellow:** Pulmonary Critical Care Medicine, UCSD Med Ctr 1972; Research, Scripps Clin Rsch Fdn 1972; **Fac Appt:** Prof Med, UCSD

Gerboth, Gregory D MD [Pul] - **Spec Exp:** Asthma; Critical Care; **Hospital:** Providence Alaska Med Ctr; **Address:** Internal Med Assocs, 2841 De Barr Rd, Ste 50, Anchorage, AK 99508; **Phone:** 907-276-2811; **Board Cert:** Pulmonary Disease 2012; Critical Care Medicine 2000; **Med School:** Med Coll Wisc 1987; **Resid:** Internal Medicine, Med Coll Wisc Affil Hosp 1990; **Fellow:** Pulmonary Critical Care Medicine, Med Coll Wisc Affil Hosp 1991

Heffner, John E MD [Pul] - **Spec Exp:** Critical Care; Respiratory Failure; **Hospital:** Providence Portland Med Ctr; **Address:** 5050 NE Hoyt St, Ste 540, Portland, OR 97213; **Phone:** 503-215-6258; **Board Cert:** Internal Medicine 1977; Pulmonary Disease 1982; Critical Care Medicine 2005; **Med School:** UCLA 1974; **Resid:** Internal Medicine, Univ Colorado Med Ctr 1978; **Fac Appt:** Prof Med, Med Univ SC

Hopewell, Philip C MD [Pul] - **Spec Exp:** AIDS/HIV; Tuberculosis; Infectious Disease-Lung; **Hospital:** San Francisco Genl Hosp; **Address:** San Francisco Genl Hosp, 1001 Potrero Ave, 5K1, San Francisco, CA 94110; **Phone:** 415-206-8314; **Board Cert:** Internal Medicine 1973; Pulmonary Disease 1974; **Med School:** W VA Univ 1965; **Resid:** Internal Medicine, UCSF Med Ctr 1971; **Fellow:** Pulmonary Disease, UCSF Med Ctr 1973; **Fac Appt:** Prof Med, UCSF

Huang, Laurence MD [Pul] - **Spec Exp:** AIDS/HIV; Pneumocystis Carinii Pneumonia (PCP); **Hospital:** San Francisco Genl Hosp; **Address:** Positive Hlth Prgm-SFGH, HIV/AIDS Div, 995 Potrero Ave, Bldg 80-Ward 84, San Francisco, CA 94110; **Phone:** 415-206-2484; **Board Cert:** Internal Medicine 2003; Pulmonary Disease 2006; Critical Care Medicine 2007; **Med School:** Columbia P&S 1989; **Resid:** Internal Medicine, NY-Presby/Columbia Univ Med Ctr 1993; Pulmonary Critical Care Medicine, UCSF Med Ctr 1995; **Fac Appt:** Prof Med, UCSF

Jacoby, David B MD [Pul] - **Spec Exp:** Viral Infections; Infections-Respiratory; Asthma; **Hospital:** OR Hlth & Sci Univ; **Address:** OHSU-Dept Pulmonary/Crit Care, 3181 SW Sam Jackson Park Rd, MC UHN67, Portland, OR 97239; **Phone:** 503-494-6158; **Board Cert:** Internal Medicine 1983; Pulmonary Disease 1986; **Med School:** NY Med Coll 1980; **Resid:** Internal Medicine, Temple Univ Hosp 1984; **Fellow:** Pulmonary Critical Care Medicine, UCSF Hosp 1987; **Fac Appt:** Prof Med, Oregon Hlth & Sci Univ

King Jr, Talmadge E MD [Pul] - **Spec Exp:** Interstitial Lung Disease; Sarcoidosis; Asthma; Pulmonary Fibrosis; **Hospital:** UCSF Med Ctr; **Address:** UCSF, Dept Med, 505 Parnassus Ave Fl 9, Rm M994, Box 0120, San Francisco, CA 94143-0120; **Phone:** 415-476-0909; **Board Cert:** Internal Medicine 1977; Pulmonary Disease 2009; **Med School:** Harvard Med Sch 1974; **Resid:** Internal Medicine, Emory Univ Affil Hosps 1977; **Fellow:** Pulmonary Critical Care Medicine, Univ Colorado Affil Hosps 1980; **Fac Appt:** Prof Med, UCSF

Lynch III, Joseph P MD [Pul] - **Spec Exp:** Transplant Medicine-Lung; Interstitial Lung Disease; Pulmonary Fibrosis; Lymphangioleiomyomatosis(LAM); **Hospital:** UCLA Ronald Reagan Med Ctr; **Address:** UCLA - Div Pulmonary Med, 200 Med Plaza Ave, Ste 365B, Los Angeles, CA 90095; **Phone:** 310-825-7921; **Board Cert:** Internal Medicine 1976; Pulmonary Disease 1980; **Med School:** Harvard Med Sch 1973; **Resid:** Internal Medicine, Univ Michigan Med Ctr 1976; **Fellow:** Pulmonary Disease, Univ Michigan Med Ctr 1978; **Fac Appt:** Clin Prof Med, UCLA-David Geffen Sch Med

Mosenifar, Zab MD [Pul] - **Spec Exp:** Chronic Obstructive Lung Disease (COPD); Interstitial Lung Disease; Asthma; Pulmonary Hypertension; **Hospital:** Cedars-Sinai Med Ctr; **Address:** Cedars-Sinai Med Ctr, Div Pulmonary Med, 8700 Beverly Blvd, rm 6732 South Twr, Los Angeles, CA 90048-1804; **Phone:** 310-423-1835; **Board Cert:** Internal Medicine 1978; Pulmonary Disease 1980; **Med School:** Iran 1973; **Resid:** Internal Medicine, Thomas Jefferson Univ Hosp 1975; Internal Medicine, UCLA Ronald Reagan Med Ctr 1977; **Fellow:** Pulmonary Disease, UCLA Ronald Reagan Med Ctr 1980; **Fac Appt:** Prof Med, UCLA

Raghu, Ganesh MD [Pul] - **Spec Exp:** Interstitial Lung Disease; Pulmonary Fibrosis; Sarcoidosis; Transplant-Lung; **Hospital:** Univ Wash Med Ctr; **Address:** 1959 NE Pacific St, Box 356175, Seattle, WA 98195-6166; **Phone:** 206-598-4615; **Board Cert:** Internal Medicine 1982; **Med School:** India 1974; **Resid:** Internal Medicine, Univ Rochester-Strong Meml Hosp 1978; Internal Medicine, SUNY Buffalo Med Ctr 1981; **Fellow:** Pulmonary Critical Care Medicine, Univ Washington Med Ctr 1984; **Fac Appt:** Prof Med, Univ Wash

Rizk, Norman W MD [Pul] - **Spec Exp:** Critical Care; Asthma; Pulmonary Infections; **Hospital:** Stanford Univ Hosp & Clins; **Address:** 300 Pasteur Drive, rm A175, MC 5319, Stanford, CA 94305; **Phone:** 650-725-7061; **Board Cert:** Internal Medicine 1979; Pulmonary Disease 1984; Critical Care Medicine 2007; **Med School:** Yale Univ 1976; **Resid:** Internal Medicine, San Francisco Genl Hosp 1980; **Fellow:** Pulmonary Disease, H Lee Moffitt Canc Ctr & Resch Inst 1983; **Fac Appt:** Prof Med, Stanford Univ

Wallace, Jeanne M MD [Pul] - **Spec Exp:** Pulmonary Infections; Sleep Disorders/Apnea; Asthma; **Hospital:** Olive View-UCLA Med Ctr; **Address:** Olive View UCLA Med Ctr, 14445 Olive View Drive, Dept Medicine 2B 182, Sylmar, CA 91342-1437; **Phone:** 818-364-3205; **Board Cert:** Internal Medicine 1977; Pulmonary Disease 1980; Sleep Medicine 2007; **Med School:** UCLA 1974; **Resid:** Internal Medicine, UCSF Med Ctr 1977; **Fellow:** Pulmonary Disease, UCSD Med Ctr 1978; **Fac Appt:** Clin Prof Med, UCLA

Wolfe, Robert N MD [Pul] - **Hospital:** Cedars-Sinai Med Ctr; **Address:** Twr Sleep Med, 8635 W 3rd St, West Tower, Ste 965, Los Angeles, CA 90048-6101; **Phone:** 310-657-3792; **Board Cert:** Internal Medicine 1978; Pulmonary Disease 1980; **Med School:** UCLA 1975; **Resid:** Internal Medicine, UCLA Ronald Reagan Med Ctr 1978; **Fellow:** Pulmonary Disease, Wadsworth VA Med Ctr 1979; **Fac Appt:** Assoc Clin Prof Med, UCLA

Cleveland Clinic

Every life deserves world class care.

Pulmonary Disease

Individuals with all types of acute or chronic lung diseases, as well as sleep disordered breathing (sleep apnea) can access specialty care at Cleveland Clinic. In 2012, physicians in the Department of Pulmonary, Allergy and Critical Care Medicine provided more than 107,000 outpatient visits.

Lung Transplantation

Cleveland Clinic's Lung Transplant Program is the largest in Ohio and among the largest in the United States. In 2012 our program performed 104 lung transplants. The average wait time for a lung transplantation at Cleveland Clinic is significantly lower than the national average.

Sarcoidosis Center of Excellence

Cleveland Clinic established a Sarcoidosis Center of Excellence in 2003. The only such center in Northeast Ohio, the center aims to raise awareness of pulmonary sarcoidosis, improve the quality of sarcoidosis care and minimize the degree to which it can affect quality of life.

Areas of Expertise

Cleveland Clinic specializes in diagnosing and curing acute respiratory distress syndrome, allergic rhinitis and allergies (drug and food; latex) We have doctors and specialists in the field of aspirin desensitization, asthma and Beryllium-induced lung disease.

In collaboration with Cleveland Clinic thoracic surgeons, patients are evaluated for:

- Invasive diagnostic procedures
- Pulmonary rejections
- Lung transplantation
- Lung volume reduction surgery (LVRS) for emphysema
- Pulmonary thromboendarterectomy (for chronic pulmonary hypertension secondary to thromboemboli)

Cleveland Clinic
Pulmonary, Allergy and
Critical Care Medicine
9500 Euclid Ave.
Cleveland, OH 44195

Offering Same-Day Appointments
Call 866.320.4573

Treatment Guides
Cleveland Clinic has developed comprehensive treatment guides for many diseases and conditions. To download our free treatment guides, visit clevelandclinic.org/treatmentguides.

Online Medical Second Opinion
Call 216.444.3223 or
800.223.2273 ext. 43223 or
email eclevelandclinic@ccf.org

Out-of-State Patients Assistance
Call 800.223.2273, ext. 55580 or
email medicalconcierge@ccf.org

Visit Us At:
clevelandclinic.org

Follow Us On:

Facebook
facebook.com/clevelandclinic

Twitter
@ClevelandClinic

You Tube
youtube.com/clevelandclinic

Health Hub
clevelandclinic.org/HealthHub

Radiation Oncology

a subspecialty of Radiology

A radiation oncologist deals with the therapeutic applications of radiant energy and its modifiers and the study and management of disease, especially malignant tumors.

Training Required: Four years in radiology *plus* additional training and examination.

Radiation Oncology

New England

Choi, Noah C MD [RadRO] - **Spec Exp:** Lung Cancer; Esophageal Cancer; Mesothelioma; **Hospital:** Mass Genl Hosp; **Address:** Mass Genl Hosp, Dept Rad Oncology, 100 Blossom St, Cox 3, Boston, MA 02114; **Phone:** 617-726-5184; **Board Cert:** Therapeutic Radiology 1970; **Med School:** South Korea 1963; **Resid:** Radiation Oncology, Princess Margaret Hosp 1970; **Fac Appt:** Prof RadRO, Harvard Med Sch

D'Amico, Anthony V MD/PhD [RadRO] - **Spec Exp:** Prostate Cancer; Brachytherapy; Urologic Cancer; **Hospital:** Dana-Farber Cancer Inst, Brigham & Women's Hosp; **Address:** Brigham & Women's Hosp, Radiation Oncology, 75 Francis St, Ste ASB1-L2, Boston, MA 02115; **Phone:** 617-732-8821; **Board Cert:** Radiation Oncology 2010; **Med School:** Univ Pennsylvania 1990; **Resid:** Radiation Oncology, Hosp Univ Penn 1994; **Fac Appt:** Prof RadRO, Harvard Med Sch

DeLaney, Thomas F MD [RadRO] - **Spec Exp:** Sarcoma; Proton Beam Therapy; **Hospital:** Mass Genl Hosp; **Address:** Francis H. Burr Proton Therapy Ctr, MGH Radiation Oncology, 30 Fruit St, Boston, MA 02114; **Phone:** 617-726-6876; **Board Cert:** Therapeutic Radiology 1986; **Med School:** Harvard Med Sch 1982; **Resid:** Therapeutic Radiology, Mass Genl Hosp 1986; **Fac Appt:** Assoc Prof RadRO, Harvard Med Sch

Harris, Jay R MD [RadRO] - **Spec Exp:** Breast Cancer; **Hospital:** Brigham & Women's Hosp, Dana-Farber Cancer Inst; **Address:** Dana-Farber Cancer Institute, 450 Brookline Ave, Boston, MA 02215; **Phone:** 617-632-3591; **Board Cert:** Therapeutic Radiology 1976; **Med School:** Stanford Univ 1970; **Resid:** Radiation Therapy, Harvard Joint Ctr Rad Therapy 1977; **Fac Appt:** Prof RadRO, Harvard Med Sch

Hartford, Alan C MD/PhD [RadRO] - **Spec Exp:** Prostate Cancer; Brain & Spinal Cord Tumors; **Hospital:** Dartmouth - Hitchcock Med Ctr; **Address:** Darthmouth-Hitchcock Med Ctr, 1 Med Ctr Drive, Lebanon, NH 03756; **Phone:** 603-650-6600; **Board Cert:** Radiation Oncology 2010; **Med School:** Harvard Med Sch 1992; **Resid:** Radiation Oncology, Mass Genl Hosp 1998; **Fellow:** Radiation Oncology, Mass Genl Hosp 1999; **Fac Appt:** Assoc Prof RadRO, Dartmouth Med Sch

Heimann, Ruth MD [RadRO] - **Spec Exp:** Breast Cancer; Gastrointestinal Cancer; Lung Cancer; **Hospital:** FAHC - Med Ctr Campus; **Address:** Fletcher Allen Radiation Med, 111 Colchester Ave, Garden Pavilion, Fl 2, Burlington, VT 05401; **Phone:** 802-847-3506; **Board Cert:** Radiation Oncology 1995; **Med School:** UMDNJ-NJ Med Sch, Newark 1989; **Resid:** Radiation Oncology, Meml Sloan-Kettering Canc Ctr 1995; **Fac Appt:** Prof Med, Univ VT Coll Med

Kachnic, Lisa A MD [RadRO] - **Spec Exp:** Breast Cancer; Gastrointestinal Cancer; Thoracic Cancers; **Hospital:** Boston Med Ctr; **Address:** Boston Med Ctr, Dept Radiation Oncology, 830 Harrison Ave, Ste LL-100, Boston, MA 02118; **Phone:** 617-638-7070; **Board Cert:** Radiation Oncology 2006; **Med School:** Tufts Univ 1991; **Resid:** Radiation Oncology, Mass Genl Hosp 1996; **Fac Appt:** Prof RadRO, Boston Univ

Kaplan, Irving D MD [RadRO] - **Spec Exp:** Prostate Cancer; Brachytherapy; **Hospital:** Beth Israel Deaconess Med Ctr - Boston; **Address:** BIDMC, Dept of Rad Oncology, 330 Brookline Ave, Finard Basement, Boston, MA 02215; **Phone:** 617-667-2345; **Board Cert:** Radiation Oncology 1989; **Med School:** Stanford Univ 1985; **Resid:** Radiation Oncology, Stanford Univ Med Ctr 1989; **Fac Appt:** Asst Prof RadRO, Harvard Med Sch

Loeffler, Jay S MD [RadRO] - **Spec Exp:** Brain Tumors; Brain Tumors-Benign; Meningioma; Acoustic Neuroma; **Hospital:** Mass Genl Hosp; **Address:** Mass Genl Hosp, Radiation Oncology, 100 Blossom St, Boston, MA 02114; **Phone:** 617-724-1548; **Board Cert:** Therapeutic Radiology 1986; **Med School:** Brown Univ 1982; **Resid:** Radiation Oncology, Harvard Joint Ctr for Rad Ther 1986; **Fellow:** Cancer Biology, Harvard Sch Pub Hlth 1985; **Fac Appt:** Prof RadRO, Harvard Med Sch

Peschel, Richard E MD [RadRO] - **Spec Exp:** Prostate Cancer; Testicular Cancer; **Hospital:** Yale-New Haven Hosp; **Address:** 35 Park St, rm LL-510, MS 06510, New Haven, CT 06510; **Phone:** 203-785-2958; **Board Cert:** Therapeutic Radiology 1982; **Med School:** Yale Univ 1977; **Resid:** Radiation Oncology, Yale-New Haven Hosp 1981; **Fac Appt:** Prof RadRO, Yale Univ

Recht, Abram MD [RadRO] - **Spec Exp:** Breast Cancer; Gynecologic Cancer; **Hospital:** Beth Israel Deaconess Med Ctr - Boston; **Address:** Beth Israel Deaconess Med Ctr, 330 Brookline Ave, Finard Bldg, rm B25, Boston, MA 02215; **Phone:** 617-667-2345; **Board Cert:** Therapeutic Radiology 1984; **Med School:** Johns Hopkins Univ 1980; **Resid:** Radiation Oncology, Joint Ctr Radiation Therapy 1984; **Fac Appt:** Prof RadRO, Harvard Med Sch

Roberts, Kenneth MD [RadRO] - **Spec Exp:** Pediatric Cancers; Lymphoma; Hodgkin's Lymphoma; **Hospital:** Yale-New Haven Hosp; **Address:** Smilow Cancer Ctr, Radiation Therapy, 15 York St, New Haven, CT 06520-8040; **Phone:** 203-785-2957; **Board Cert:** Internal Medicine 1987; Medical Oncology 1989; Radiation Oncology 1995; **Med School:** Duke Univ 1984; **Resid:** Internal Medicine, Ohio State Univ Hosps 1987; Radiation Oncology, Duke Univ Med Ctr 1992; **Fellow:** Hematology & Oncology, Duke Univ Med Ctr 1989; **Fac Appt:** Assoc Prof Rad, Yale Univ

Russell, Anthony H MD [RadRO] - **Spec Exp:** Gynecologic Cancer; Intensity Modulated Radiotherapy (IMRT); Proton Beam Therapy; **Hospital:** Mass Genl Hosp; **Address:** MGH Dept Radiation Oncology, 55 Fruit St, Boston, MA 02114; **Phone:** 617-726-5184; **Board Cert:** Therapeutic Radiology 1978; **Med School:** Harvard Med Sch 1974; **Resid:** Radiation Oncology, Mass Genl Hosp 1978

Taghian, Alphonse G MD/PhD [RadRO] - **Spec Exp:** Breast Cancer; **Hospital:** Mass Genl Hosp; **Address:** MGH Dept Radiation Oncology, 100 Blossom St, COX 3, Boston, MA 02114; **Phone:** 617-726-7559; **Board Cert:** Radiation Oncology 2006; **Med School:** Egypt 1980; **Resid:** Radiation Oncology, Vautrin Cancer Ctr 1987; Radiation Oncology, Inst Gustave Roussy 1989; **Fellow:** Radiation Oncology, Mass Genl Hosp 1993; **Fac Appt:** Assoc Prof RadRO, Harvard Med Sch

Tarbell, Nancy J MD [RadRO] - **Spec Exp:** Brain Tumors-Pediatric; Proton Beam Therapy; **Hospital:** Mass Genl Hosp; **Address:** Mass Genl Hosp, Proton Therapy Ctr, 55 Fruit St, Ste 107, Boston, MA 02114; **Phone:** 617-724-1836; **Board Cert:** Therapeutic Radiology 1983; **Med School:** SUNY Upstate Med Univ 1979; **Resid:** Therapeutic Radiology, Beth Israel Deaconess Med Ctr 1983; **Fac Appt:** Prof RadRO, Harvard Med Sch

Wazer, David E MD [RadRO] - **Spec Exp:** Breast Cancer; Melanoma; Gastrointestinal Cancer; **Hospital:** Rhode Island Hosp, Tufts Med Ctr; **Address:** Rhode Island Hospital, Dept Radiation Oncology, 593 Eddy St, Providence, RI 02903; **Phone:** 401-444-8311; **Board Cert:** Radiation Oncology 1988; **Med School:** NYU Sch Med 1982; **Resid:** Radiation Oncology, Tufts New Eng Med Ctr 1988; **Fellow:** Neurological Chemistry, NYU Med Ctr 1984; **Fac Appt:** Asst Prof RadRO, Tufts Univ

Wilson, Lynn D MD [RadRO] - **Spec Exp:** Cutaneous T-cell Lymphoma; Lung Cancer; Head & Neck Cancer; **Hospital:** Yale-New Haven Hosp, Yale Med Group; **Address:** Yale Univ Sch Med, Dept Therapeutic Rad, 35 Park St, New Haven, CT 06513; **Phone:** 203-737-1202; **Board Cert:** Radiation Oncology 2004; **Med School:** Geo Wash Univ 1990; **Resid:** Therapeutic Radiology, Yale-New Haven Hosp 1994; **Fac Appt:** Prof RadRO, Yale Univ

Zietman, Anthony L MD [RadRO] - **Spec Exp:** Prostate Cancer; Urologic Cancer; Proton Beam Therapy; **Hospital:** Mass Genl Hosp; **Address:** Mass General Hosp Cancer Center, 55 Fruit St, Ste YAW 7E, Boston, MA 02114; **Phone:** 617-724-1158; **Board Cert:** Radiation Oncology 1994; **Med School:** England, UK 1983; **Resid:** Internal Medicine, St Stephens & Westminster Hosp 1986; Radiation Oncology, Mass Genl Hosp 1989; **Fellow:** Radiation Oncology, Middlesex Hosp 1991; Radiation Oncology, Mass Genl Hosp 1994; **Fac Appt:** Prof RadRO, Harvard Med Sch

Mid Atlantic

Bogart, Jeffrey A MD [RadRO] - **Spec Exp:** Lung Cancer; Thoracic Cancers; Prostate Cancer; Clinical Trials; **Hospital:** SUNY Upstate Med Univ Hosp, Crouse Hosp; **Address:** SUNY Upstate Medical Ctr, Dept Radiation Oncology, 750 E Adams St, rm 222, Syracuse, NY 13210; **Phone:** 315-464-5276; **Board Cert:** Radiation Oncology 1994; **Med School:** SUNY Upstate Med Univ 1989; **Resid:** Internal Medicine, Univ MD Affil Hosp 1990; Radiation Oncology, SUNY Hlth Sci Ctr 1993; **Fac Appt:** Prof U, SUNY Upstate Med Univ

Chadha, Manjeet MD [RadRO] - **Spec Exp:** Breast Cancer; Gynecologic Cancer; **Hospital:** Beth Israel Med Ctr - Petrie Div (page 56), St. Luke's - Roosevelt Hosp Ctr - St Luke's Hosp (page 56); **Address:** Charles & Bernice Blitman Dept, Div of Radiation Oncology, 10 Union Square E, Ste 4G, New York, NY 10003; **Phone:** 212-844-8022; **Board Cert:** Therapeutic Radiology 1985; **Med School:** India 1980; **Resid:** Radiation Oncology, Columbia Presby Med Ctr 1983; Radiation Oncology, Meml Sloan Kettering Cancer Ctr 1985; **Fac Appt:** Assoc Prof RadRO, Albert Einstein Coll Med

Chao, K.S. Clifford MD [RadRO] - **Spec Exp:** Intensity Modulated Radiotherapy (IMRT); **Hospital:** NY-Presby/Weill Cornell Med Ctr, NY (page 65); **Address:** 622 W 168th St, New York, NY 10032; **Phone:** 212-305-9987; **Board Cert:** Radiation Oncology 2010; **Med School:** Taiwan 1982; **Resid:** Radiation Oncology, Mallinckrodt Inst Rad-Wash Med Ctr 1993; **Fellow:** Radiation Oncology, Mallinckrodt Inst Rad-Wash Med Ctr 1994; **Fac Appt:** Prof RadRO, Cornell Univ-Weill Med Coll

Constine III, Louis Sanders MD [RadRO] - **Spec Exp:** Pediatric Cancers; Lymphoma; Cancer Survivors-Late Effects of Therapy; Sarcoma; **Hospital:** Univ Rochester Strong Meml Hosp; **Address:** 601 Elmwood Ave, Ste 647, Rochester, NY 14642; **Phone:** 585-275-5622; **Board Cert:** Pediatrics 1978; Pediatric Hematology-Oncology 1978; Therapeutic Radiology 1981; **Med School:** Johns Hopkins Univ 1973; **Resid:** Pediatrics, Stanford Univ Med Ctr 1976; Radiation Oncology, Stanford Hosp Med Ctr 1981; **Fellow:** Pediatric Hematology-Oncology, Univ Wash/Chldns Ortho Hosp 1978; **Fac Appt:** Prof RadRO, Univ Rochester

Cooper, Jay S MD [RadRO] - **Spec Exp:** Head & Neck Cancer; Skin Cancer; Chemo-Radiation Combined Therapy; Intensity Modulated Radiotherapy (IMRT); **Hospital:** Maimonides Med Ctr (page 60); **Address:** Maimonides Cancer Center, 6300 8th Ave, Brooklyn, NY 11220; **Phone:** 718-765-2700; **Board Cert:** Therapeutic Radiology 1977; **Med School:** NYU Sch Med 1973; **Resid:** Radiation Oncology, NYU Med Ctr 1977; **Fac Appt:** Prof RadRO, Albert Einstein Coll Med

DeWeese, Theodore L MD [RadRO] - **Spec Exp:** Urologic Cancer; Prostate Cancer; Testicular Cancer; **Hospital:** Johns Hopkins Hosp (page 59); **Address:** Sidney Kimmel Comprehensive Cancer Ctr, 401 N Broadway, Weinberg Bldg - rm 1343, Baltimore, MD 21231; **Phone:** 410-955-8964; **Board Cert:** Radiation Oncology 2005; **Med School:** Univ Colorado 1990; **Resid:** Radiation Oncology, Johns Hopkins Hosp 1994; **Fellow:** Urologic Oncology, Johns Hopkins Hosp 1995; **Fac Appt:** Prof RadRO, Johns Hopkins Univ

Dicker, Adam P MD/PhD [RadRO] - **Spec Exp:** Prostate Cancer; Urologic Cancer; **Hospital:** Thomas Jefferson Univ Hosp; **Address:** Jefferson Radiation Oncology, 111 South 11th St, Ste G-301, Philadelphia, PA 19107-5097; **Phone:** 215-955-6702; **Board Cert:** Radiation Oncology 2000; **Med School:** Cornell Univ 1992; **Resid:** Radiation Oncology, Meml Sloan Kettering Cancer Ctr 1997; **Fellow:** Radiation Oncology, Meml Sloan Kettering Cancer Ctr 1998; **Fac Appt:** Prof RadRO, Thomas Jefferson Univ

Dritschilo, Anatoly MD [RadRO] - **Spec Exp:** Prostate Cancer; Breast Cancer; Pediatric Cancers; **Hospital:** MedStar Georgetown Univ Hosp; **Address:** Georgetown Univ Hosp, Dept Radiation Medicine, LL-Bles, 3800 Reservoir Rd NW, Washington, DC 20007; **Phone:** 202-444-3320; **Board Cert:** Therapeutic Radiology 1977; **Med School:** UMDNJ-NJ Med Sch, Newark 1973; **Resid:** Radiation Therapy, Harvard Joint Rad Ther Ctr 1977; **Fac Appt:** Prof RadRO, Georgetown Univ

Ennis, Ronald D MD [RadRO] - **Spec Exp:** Prostate Cancer; Brachytherapy; Breast Cancer; Stereotactic Radiosurgery; **Hospital:** St. Luke's - Roosevelt Hosp Ctr - Roosevelt Div (page 56), Beth Israel Med Ctr - Petrie Div (page 56); **Address:** 1000 10th Ave, Lower Level, Dept Radiation Oncology, Roosevelt Hospital, New York, NY 10019; **Phone:** 212-523-7165; **Board Cert:** Radiation Oncology 2004; **Med School:** Yale Univ 1990; **Resid:** Therapeutic Radiology, Yale-New Haven Hosp 1994; **Fac Appt:** Assoc Prof RadRO, Albert Einstein Coll Med

Flickinger, John C MD [RadRO] - **Spec Exp:** Neuro-Oncology; Brain & Spinal Cord Tumors; **Hospital:** UPMC Shadyside, UPMC Presby, Pittsburgh; **Address:** UPMC Shadyside, Dept Radiation Oncology, 5230 Centre Ave, Pittsburgh, PA 15213; **Phone:** 412-623-6720; **Board Cert:** Therapeutic Radiology 1985; **Med School:** Univ Chicago-Pritzker Sch Med 1981; **Resid:** Radiation Therapy, Mass Genl Hosp 1985; **Fac Appt:** Prof RadRO, Univ Pittsburgh

Formenti, Silvia C MD [RadRO] - **Spec Exp:** Breast Cancer; Chemo-Radiation Combined Therapy; **Hospital:** NYU Langone Med Ctr (page 68); **Address:** NYU Med Ctr, Dept Radiation Oncology, 160 E 34th St, New York, NY 10016; **Phone:** 212-263-2601; **Board Cert:** Radiation Oncology 1991; **Med School:** Italy 1980; **Resid:** Internal Medicine, San Carlo Borromeo Hosp 1983; Medical Oncology, Univ of Pavia Med Ctr 1985; **Fellow:** Radiation Oncology, USC Med Ctr 1990; **Fac Appt:** Prof RadRO, NYU Sch Med

Freedman, Gary M MD [RadRO] - **Spec Exp:** Breast Cancer; **Hospital:** Hosp Univ Penn - UPHS (page 69); **Address:** Penn Radiation Oncology, PCAM-Abramson Cancer Ctr, Fl 3, 3400 Civic Ctr Blvd, Philadelphia, PA 19104; **Phone:** 215-615-0756; **Board Cert:** Radiation Oncology 2011; **Med School:** Temple Univ 1993; **Resid:** Radiation Oncology, Fox Chase Cancer Ctr 1998; **Fac Appt:** Assoc Prof RadRO, Univ Pennsylvania

Gejerman, Glen MD [RadRO] - **Spec Exp:** Prostate Cancer; Intensity Modulated Radiotherapy (IMRT); Brachytherapy; Urologic Cancer; **Hospital:** Hackensack Univ Med Ctr; **Address:** Hackensack University Medical Center, 92 Second St, Hackensack, NJ 07601; **Phone:** 201-996-2464; **Board Cert:** Radiation Oncology 2006; **Med School:** UMDNJ-NJ Med Sch, Newark 1990; **Resid:** Radiation Oncology, Montefiore Med Ctr 1995; **Fac Appt:** Asst Clin Prof RadRO, Albert Einstein Coll Med

Goodman, Robert L MD [RadRO] - **Spec Exp:** Breast Cancer; Lymphoma; Prostate Cancer; Brain Tumors; **Hospital:** Saint Barnabas Med Ctr; **Address:** Jersey City Radiation Oncology, 631 Grand St, Jersey City, NJ 07304; **Phone:** 201-942-3999; **Board Cert:** Internal Medicine 1971; Therapeutic Radiology 1974; Medical Oncology 1975; **Med School:** Columbia P&S 1966; **Resid:** Internal Medicine, Beth Israel Hosp 1971; Therapeutic Radiology, Harvard Joint Ctr Rad Therapy 1974; **Fellow:** Hematology, NY-Presby Hosp 1975; **Fac Appt:** Prof RadRO, Univ Pennsylvania

Greenberger, Joel S MD [RadRO] - **Spec Exp:** Lung Cancer; Esophageal Cancer; **Hospital:** UPMC Shadyside, UPMC Presby, Pittsburgh; **Address:** UPMC Shadyside, Dept Radiation Oncology, 5230 Centre Ave, Pittsburgh, PA 15232; **Phone:** 412-623-6720; **Board Cert:** Therapeutic Radiology 1977; **Med School:** Harvard Med Sch 1971; **Resid:** Radiation Therapy, Joint Ctr Radiation Therapy 1977; **Fac Appt:** Prof RadRO, Univ Pittsburgh

Haffty, Bruce G MD [RadRO] - **Spec Exp:** Breast Cancer; Head & Neck Cancer; **Hospital:** Robert Wood Johnson Univ Hosp - New Brunswick; **Address:** The Cancer Institute of New Jersey, 195 Little Albany St, rm 2038, New Brunswick, NJ 08903; **Phone:** 732-253-3939; **Board Cert:** Radiation Oncology 1988; **Med School:** Yale Univ 1984; **Resid:** Therapeutic Radiology, Yale-New Haven Hosp 1985; Radiation Oncology, Yale-New Haven Hosp 1988; **Fac Appt:** Prof RadRO, UMDNJ-RW Johnson Med Sch

Hahn, Stephen M MD [RadRO] - **Spec Exp:** Lung Cancer; Prostate Cancer; Sarcoma; Photodynamic Therapy; **Hospital:** Hosp Univ Penn - UPHS (page 69), Penn Presby Med Ctr - UPHS (page 69); **Address:** Penn Radiation Oncology, PCAM-Abramson Cancer Ctr,Concourse Level, 3400 Civic Center Blvd, Philadelphia, PA 19104; **Phone:** 215-662-7296; **Board Cert:** Internal Medicine 1987; Radiation Oncology 2004; **Med School:** Temple Univ 1984; **Resid:** Internal Medicine, UCSF Med Ctr 1988; Radiation Oncology, Natl Inst Hlth 1995; **Fellow:** Medical Oncology, Natl Inst Hlth 1991; **Fac Appt:** Prof RadRO, Univ Pennsylvania

Harrison, Louis B MD [RadRO] - **Spec Exp:** Brachytherapy; Head & Neck Cancer; Radiation Therapy-Intraoperative; **Hospital:** Beth Israel Med Ctr - Petrie Div (page 56); **Address:** Beth Israel Med Ctr, Dept Rad Onc, 10 Union Square East, Ste 4G, New York, NY 10003-3314; **Phone:** 212-844-8087; **Board Cert:** Therapeutic Radiology 1986; **Med School:** SUNY Downstate 1982; **Resid:** Therapeutic Radiology, Yale-New Haven Hosp 1986; **Fac Appt:** Prof RadRO, Albert Einstein Coll Med

Horwitz, Eric M MD [RadRO] - **Spec Exp:** Prostate Cancer; Intensity Modulated Radiotherapy (IMRT); Brachytherapy; **Hospital:** Fox Chase Cancer Ctr (page 57); **Address:** Fox Chase Cancer Ctr, Dept Radiation Oncology, 333 Cottman Ave, rm P0111, Philadelphia, PA 19111; **Phone:** 215-728-3540; **Board Cert:** Radiation Oncology 2010; **Med School:** Albany Med Coll 1992; **Resid:** Radiation Oncology, William Beaumont Hosp 1997

Isaacson, Steven R MD [RadRO] - **Spec Exp:** Brain Tumors; Neuro-Oncology; Stereotactic Radiosurgery; Gliomas; **Hospital:** NY-Presby/Columbia Univ Med Ctr, NY (page 65); **Address:** NY Presbyterian-Columbia Med Ctr, Dept Radiation Oncology, 622 W 168th St BHN Bldg - rm B-11, New York, NY 10032-3720; **Phone:** 212-305-2611; **Board Cert:** Radiation Oncology 1988; Otolaryngology 1978; **Med School:** Jefferson Med Coll 1973; **Resid:** Otolaryngology, Hosp Univ Penn 1978; Radiation Oncology, SUNY Hlth Sci Ctr 1988; **Fac Appt:** Clin Prof RadRO, Columbia P&S

Kalnicki, Shalom MD [RadRO] - **Spec Exp:** Lung Cancer; Head & Neck Cancer; Breast Cancer; Prostate Cancer; **Hospital:** Montefiore Med Ctr-Moses Campus, NY, Montefiore Med Ctr-Einstein Campus, NY; **Address:** Montefiore Medical Group, 1625 Poplar St Fl 2, Bronx, NY 10461; **Phone:** 718-920-5280; **Board Cert:** Therapeutic Radiology 1979; **Med School:** Brazil 1974; **Resid:** Radiation Oncology, Montefiore Med Ctr 1979; **Fac Appt:** Prof Rad, Albert Einstein Coll Med

Kleinberg, Lawrence MD [RadRO] - **Spec Exp:** Brain & Spinal Cord Tumors; Brain Tumors-Metastatic; Stereotactic Radiosurgery; Esophageal Cancer; **Hospital:** Johns Hopkins Hosp (page 59); **Address:** Johns Hopkins Oncology Ctr, 401 N Broadway, Weinberg Bldg - Ste 1440, Baltimore, MD 21231; **Phone:** 410-614-2597; **Board Cert:** Radiation Oncology 1994; **Med School:** Yale Univ 1989; **Resid:** Radiation Oncology, Meml Sloan-Kettering Canc Ctr 1993; **Fac Appt:** Assoc Prof RadRO, Johns Hopkins Univ

Knisely, Jonathan P S MD [RadRO] - **Spec Exp:** Brain Tumors; Stereotactic Radiosurgery; Skull Base Tumors; **Hospital:** NS-LIJ Hlth Sys (page 66), Glen Cove Hosp (page 66); **Address:** North Shore University Hospital, 300 Community Drive, Manhasset, NY 11030; **Phone:** 516-470-7190; **Board Cert:** Internal Medicine 1989; Radiation Oncology 1993; **Med School:** Univ Pennsylvania 1986; **Resid:** Internal Medicine, Michael Reese Hosp 1989; Radiation Oncology, Univ Toronto Med Ctr 1992; **Fac Appt:** Assoc Prof RadRO, Hofstra N Shore-LIJ Sch Med

Kuettel, Michael R MD/PhD [RadRO] - **Spec Exp:** Prostate Cancer; **Hospital:** Roswell Park Canc Inst, Buffalo Genl Hosp; **Address:** Roswell Park Cancer Inst-Radiation Med, Elm and Carlton Sts, Buffalo, NY 14263; **Phone:** 716-845-1562; **Board Cert:** Radiation Oncology 1992; **Med School:** Northwestern Univ 1985; **Resid:** Internal Medicine, Northwestern Hosp 1986; Radiation Oncology, Johns Hopkins Hosp 1990; **Fac Appt:** Prof RadRO, SUNY Buffalo

Lepanto, Philip B MD [RadRO] - **Hospital:** St. Mary's Med Ctr - Huntington, Cabell Huntington Hosp; **Address:** St Mary's Med Ctr, Dept Rad/Onc, 2900 First Ave, Huntington, WV 25702; **Phone:** 304-526-1143; **Board Cert:** Therapeutic Radiology 1975; **Med School:** Univ Louisville Sch Med 1970; **Resid:** Diagnostic Radiology, Hosp Univ Penn - UPHS 1972; Radiation Therapy, Hosp Univ Penn - UPHS 1975; **Fac Appt:** Clin Prof Rad, Marshall Univ

McCormick, Beryl MD [RadRO] - **Spec Exp:** Breast Cancer; Eye Tumors/Cancer; **Hospital:** Meml Sloan-Kettering Canc Ctr; **Address:** 1275 York Avenue, New York, NY 10065; **Phone:** 212-639-6828; **Board Cert:** Therapeutic Radiology 1977; **Med School:** UMDNJ-NJ Med Sch, Newark 1973; **Resid:** Therapeutic Radiology, Meml Sloan Kettering Cancer Ctr 1977; **Fac Appt:** Prof RadRO, Cornell Univ-Weill Med Coll

Mehta, Minesh P MD [RadRO] - **Spec Exp:** Brain Tumors; Neuro-Oncology; Lung Cancer; **Hospital:** Univ of MD Med Ctr; **Address:** Univ MD, Dept Rad Oncology, 22 S Greene St, Baltimore, MD 21201; **Phone:** 410-328-6911; **Board Cert:** Radiation Oncology 1988; **Med School:** Zambia 1981; **Resid:** Internal Medicine, Ndola Central Hosp 1983; Radiation Oncology, Univ WI Hosps 1988; **Fac Appt:** Prof RadRO, Univ MD Sch Med

Nicolaou, Nicos MD [RadRO] - **Spec Exp:** Lymphoma; Hodgkin's Lymphoma; Urologic Cancer; Breast Cancer; **Address:** Philadelphia Cancer Treatment, 1 Presidential Blvd, Ste 100, Bala Cynwyd, PA 19004; **Phone:** 610-632-4100; **Board Cert:** Radiation Oncology 2010; **Med School:** South Africa 1984; **Resid:** Radiation Oncology, Univ British Columbia Cancer Ctr 1994; **Fellow:** Radiation Oncology, Fox Chase Cancer Ctr 1995

Nori, Dattatreyudu MD [RadRO] - **Spec Exp:** Prostate Cancer; Brachytherapy; Lung Cancer; Breast Cancer; **Hospital:** NY-Presby/Weill Cornell Med Ctr, NY (page 65), NY Hosp Queens; **Address:** 525 E 68th St, Box 575, New York, NY 10065; **Phone:** 212-746-3679; **Board Cert:** Therapeutic Radiology 1979; **Med School:** India 1970; **Resid:** Radiation Oncology, Meml Sloan Kettering Cancer Ctr 1975; **Fellow:** Radiation Oncology, Meml Sloan Kettering Cancer Ctr 1978; **Fac Appt:** Prof RadRO, Cornell Univ-Weill Med Coll

Porrazzo, Michael S MD [RadRO] - **Spec Exp:** Prostate Cancer; Central Nervous System Cancer; Breast Cancer; Stereotactic Radiosurgery; **Hospital:** MedStar Washington Hosp Ctr; **Address:** Wash Hosp Ctr-Dept Radiation Onc, 110 Irving St NW, Ste CG-116, Washington, DC 20010; **Phone:** 202-877-3925; **Board Cert:** Radiation Oncology 1990; **Med School:** Meharry Med Coll 1985; **Resid:** Radiation Oncology, SUNY Hlth Sci Ctr 1989

Potters, Louis MD [RadRO] - **Spec Exp:** Prostate Cancer; Intensity Modulated Radiotherapy (IMRT); Brachytherapy; **Hospital:** Long Is Jewish Med Ctr (page 66), N Shore Univ Hosp (page 66); **Address:** LIJ Medical Ctr, 270-05 76th Ave, New Hyde Park, NY 11040; **Phone:** 718-470-7190; **Board Cert:** Internal Medicine 1988; Radiation Oncology 1999; **Med School:** UMDNJ-NJ Med Sch, Newark 1985; **Resid:** Internal Medicine, Beth Israel Med Ctr 1988; Radiation Oncology, SUNY Downstate Med Ctr 1991; **Fac Appt:** Prof RadRO, Hofstra N Shore-LIJ Sch Med

Randolph-Jackson, Pamela D MD [RadRO] - **Spec Exp:** Breast Cancer; Lung Cancer; Gastrointestinal Cancer; **Hospital:** MedStar Washington Hosp Ctr; **Address:** 110 Irving St NW, Ste CG-116, Washington, DC 20010; **Phone:** 202-877-3925; **Board Cert:** Radiation Oncology 2004; **Med School:** E Tenn State Univ 1988; **Resid:** Radiology, Howard Univ Hosp 1992; **Fellow:** Radiation Oncology, Jefferson Med Coll 1993

Regine, William F MD [RadRO] - **Spec Exp:** Stereotactic Radiosurgery; Brain & Spinal Cord Tumors; Gastrointestinal Cancer; **Hospital:** Univ of MD Med Ctr; **Address:** Univ MD Med System-Greenbaum Cancer Ctr, 22 S Green St, Baltimore, MD 21201; **Phone:** 410-328-6080; **Board Cert:** Radiation Oncology 1992; **Med School:** SUNY Upstate Med Univ 1987; **Resid:** Radiation Oncology, Thomas Jefferson Univ Hosp 1991; **Fellow:** Radiation Oncology, Thomas Jefferson Univ Hosp 1992; **Fac Appt:** Prof RadRO, Univ MD Sch Med

Rotman, Marvin Z MD [RadRO] - **Spec Exp:** Bladder Cancer; Gynecologic Cancer; Eye Tumors/Cancer; Prostate Cancer; **Hospital:** SUNY Downstate Med Ctr (Univ Hosp Brooklyn), VA NY Harbor Hlthcr Sys-Brooklyn Campus; **Address:** 450 Clarkson Ave, Box 1211, Brooklyn, NY 11203-2056; **Phone:** 718-270-2181; **Board Cert:** Diagnostic Radiology 1966; **Med School:** Jefferson Med Coll 1958; **Resid:** Internal Medicine, Albert Einstein Med Ctr 1962; Radiation Oncology, Montefiore Hosp Med Ctr 1966; **Fac Appt:** Prof RadRO, SUNY Downstate

Schiff, Peter B MD/PhD [RadRO] - **Spec Exp:** Prostate Cancer; Gynecologic Cancer; Lung Cancer; **Hospital:** NYU Langone Med Ctr (page 68); **Address:** NYU Clinical Cancer Ctr, 160 E 34th St Fl 1, New York, NY 10016; **Phone:** 212-731-5003; **Board Cert:** Radiation Oncology 1990; **Med School:** Albert Einstein Coll Med 1984; **Resid:** Radiation Oncology, Meml Sloan Kettering Cancer Ctr 1988; **Fac Appt:** Prof RadRO, NYU Sch Med

Solin, Lawrence J MD [RadRO] - **Spec Exp:** Breast Cancer; **Hospital:** Einstein Med Ctr; **Address:** AEMC, Radiation Oncology Dept, 5501 Old York Rd, Philadelphia, PA 19141; **Phone:** 215-456-6280; **Board Cert:** Therapeutic Radiology 1984; **Med School:** Brown Univ 1978; **Resid:** Surgery, Thomas Jefferson Univ Hosp 1981; Radiation Oncology, Thomas Jefferson Univ Hosp 1982; **Fellow:** Radiation Oncology, Hosp Univ Penn 1984; **Fac Appt:** Prof Emeritus RadRO, Univ Pennsylvania

Stock, Richard MD [RadRO] - **Spec Exp:** Prostate Cancer; Urologic Cancer; **Hospital:** Mt Sinai Med Ctr (page 62); **Address:** 61 E 77th St, level C, New York, NY 10075; **Phone:** 212-772-2130; **Board Cert:** Radiation Oncology 1993; **Med School:** Mount Sinai Sch Med 1988; **Resid:** Radiation Oncology, Meml Sloan Kettering Cancer Ctr 1992; **Fac Appt:** Prof RadRO, Mount Sinai Sch Med

Suntharalingam, Mohan MD [RadRO] - **Spec Exp:** Head & Neck Cancer; Lung Cancer; Esophageal Cancer; **Hospital:** Univ of MD Med Ctr; **Address:** 22 S Greene St, Ste GGK-0101, Baltimore, MD 21201; **Phone:** 410-328-2331; **Board Cert:** Radiation Oncology 2005; **Med School:** Thomas Jefferson Univ 1990; **Resid:** Radiation Oncology, Univ of MD Med Ctr 1993; **Fellow:** Radiation Oncology, Univ of MD Med Ctr 1994; **Fac Appt:** Prof RadRO, Univ MD Sch Med

Weiss, Marisa C MD [RadRO] - **Spec Exp:** Breast Cancer; **Hospital:** Lankenau Hosp; **Address:** Lankenau Radiation Oncology, 100 E Lancaster Ave, Wynnewood, PA 19096; **Phone:** 484-476-2433; **Board Cert:** Radiation Oncology 1988; **Med School:** Univ Pennsylvania 1984; **Resid:** Radiation Oncology, Hosp Univ Penn 1988; **Fellow:** Radiological Biology, Hosp Univ Penn 1990

Werner-Wasik, Maria MD [RadRO] - **Spec Exp:** Brain Tumors; Lung Cancer; Melanoma; Breast Cancer; **Hospital:** Thomas Jefferson Univ Hosp; **Address:** Jefferson Radiation Oncology, 111 S 11th St, Ste G-301, Bodine Center, Philadelphia, PA 19107; **Phone:** 215-955-6702; **Board Cert:** Radiation Oncology 1994; **Med School:** Poland 1979; **Resid:** Internal Medicine, Framingham Union Hosp 1990; Radiation Oncology, Tufts/New England Med Ctr 1993; **Fellow:** Radiation Oncology, Hosp Univ Penn 1994; **Fac Appt:** Prof RadRO, Thomas Jefferson Univ

Yahalom, Joachim MD [RadRO] - **Spec Exp:** Lymphoma; Hodgkin's Lymphoma; Multiple Myeloma; **Hospital:** Meml Sloan-Kettering Canc Ctr; **Address:** 1275 York Ave, SM03, Dept Radiation Onc, New York, NY 10065; **Phone:** 212-639-5999; **Board Cert:** Radiation Oncology 1988; **Med School:** Israel 1976; **Resid:** Internal Medicine, Hadassah Hosp 1979; Radiation Oncology, Hadassah Hosp 1984; **Fellow:** Radiation Oncology, Meml Sloan Kettering Canc Ctr 1986; **Fac Appt:** Prof RadRO, Cornell Univ-Weill Med Coll

Zelefsky, Michael J MD [RadRO] - **Spec Exp:** Prostate Cancer; Brachytherapy; Head & Neck Cancer; **Hospital:** Meml Sloan-Kettering Canc Ctr; **Address:** 1275 York Ave, New York, NY 10065; **Phone:** 212-639-6802; **Board Cert:** Radiation Oncology 1991; **Med School:** Albert Einstein Coll Med 1986; **Resid:** Radiation Oncology, Meml Sloan Kettering Cancer Ctr 1990; **Fac Appt:** Prof RadRO, Cornell Univ-Weill Med Coll

Southeast

Anscher, Mitchell S MD [RadRO] - **Spec Exp:** Prostate Cancer; Brachytherapy; Penile Cancer; Testicular Cancer; **Hospital:** Med Coll of VA Hosp, Hunter Holmes McGuire VA Med Ctr - Richmond; **Address:** Med Coll VA Hosp, Dept Radiation Onc, 401 College St, Box 980058, Richmond, VA 23298-0058; **Phone:** 804-828-7232; **Board Cert:** Internal Medicine 1984; Radiation Oncology 1987; **Med School:** Med Coll VA 1981; **Resid:** Internal Medicine, St Marys Hosp 1984; Radiation Oncology, Duke Univ Hosp 1987; **Fac Appt:** Prof RadRO, Va Commonwealth Univ Sch Med

Beitler, Jonathan J MD [RadRO] - **Spec Exp:** Head & Neck Cancer; Breast Cancer; Lung Cancer; Brachytherapy; **Hospital:** Emory Univ Hosp; **Address:** Emory Univ Hosp, Radiation Oncology Dept, 1365C Clifton Rd NE, Ste CT-104, Atlanta, GA 30322; **Phone:** 404-778-3473; **Board Cert:** Radiation Oncology 1990; **Med School:** Med Coll PA Hahnemann 1982; **Resid:** Surgery, SUNY Downstate Med Ctr 1985; Radiation Oncology, Meml Sloan-Kettering Cancer Ctr 1988; **Fac Appt:** Prof RadRO, Emory Univ

Blackstock Jr, A. William MD [RadRO] - **Spec Exp:** Lung Cancer; Gastrointestinal Cancer; Clinical Trials; **Hospital:** Wake Forest Baptist Med Ctr; **Address:** Wake Forest, Comprehensive Cancer Ctr, Dept Radiation Oncology, Medical Center Blvd, Winston-Salem, NC 27157; **Phone:** 336-713-3600; **Board Cert:** Radiation Oncology 2006; **Med School:** E Carolina Univ 1989; **Resid:** Radiation Oncology, Univ NC Hosps 1994; **Fac Appt:** Prof RadRO, Wake Forest Univ

Brizel, David M MD [RadRO] - **Spec Exp:** Head & Neck Cancer; Sarcoma; **Hospital:** Duke Univ Hosp; **Address:** Duke Univ Med Ctr, Dept Rad Onc, Box 3085, Durham, NC 27710-0001; **Phone:** 919-668-5637; **Board Cert:** Radiation Oncology 1987; **Med School:** Northwestern Univ 1983; **Resid:** Radiation Oncology, Harvard Joint Ctr Radiation Ther 1987; **Fac Appt:** Prof RadRO, Duke Univ

Chakravarthy, Anuradha (Bapsi) MD [RadRO] - **Spec Exp:** Breast Cancer; Gastrointestinal Cancer; **Hospital:** Vanderbilt Univ Med Ctr; **Address:** Vanderbilt Radiation Oncology, 2220 Pierce Ave, B-1003 TVC, Nashville, TN 37232; **Phone:** 615-322-2555; **Board Cert:** Radiation Oncology 1994; Internal Medicine 1986; Medical Oncology 1989; **Med School:** Geo Wash Univ 1983; **Resid:** Internal Medicine, Mayo Clinic 1986; Hematology & Oncology, Univ Maryland Cancer Ctr 1990; **Fellow:** Radiation Oncology, Johns Hopkins Univ 1993; **Fac Appt:** Assoc Prof RadRO, Vanderbilt Univ

Cmelak, Anthony J MD [RadRO] - **Spec Exp:** Brain Tumors; Stereotactic Radiosurgery; **Hospital:** Vanderbilt Univ Med Ctr; **Address:** 2220 Pierce Ave, PRB Bldg, rm B-1003, Nashville, TN 37232-5671; **Phone:** 615-322-2555; **Board Cert:** Radiation Oncology 2008; **Med School:** Northwestern Univ 1992; **Resid:** Radiation Oncology, Stanford Univ Med Ctr 1996; **Fac Appt:** Prof RadRO, Vanderbilt Univ

Crocker, Ian R MD [RadRO] - **Spec Exp:** Brain Tumors; Eye Tumors/Cancer; Melanoma-Choroidal (eye); **Hospital:** Emory Univ Hosp, Emory Univ Hosp Midtown; **Address:** Emory Univ Hosp, Radiation Oncology Dept, 1365C Clifton Rd NE, CT-104, Atlanta, GA 30322; **Phone:** 404-778-3473; **Board Cert:** Therapeutic Radiology 1983; Internal Medicine 1980; **Med School:** Univ Saskatchewan 1976; **Resid:** Internal Medicine, Univ Hosp 1980; Radiation Oncology, Princess Margaret Hosp 1983; **Fac Appt:** Prof RadRO, Emory Univ

Fiveash, John MD [RadRO] - **Spec Exp:** Brain Tumors; Pediatric Cancers; Prostate Cancer; **Hospital:** UAB Hosp; **Address:** Hazelrig-Salter Radiation-Oncology Ctr, 1700 6th Ave S, Birmingham, AL 35249; **Phone:** 205-975-0224; **Board Cert:** Radiation Oncology 2009; **Med School:** Med Coll GA 1993; **Resid:** Radiation Oncology, Med Col Georgia Hosps 1997; **Fac Appt:** Assoc Prof Med, UAB Sch Med

Henderson, Randal H MD [RadRO] - **Spec Exp:** Gynecologic Cancer; Prostate Cancer; Brachytherapy; Proton Beam Therapy; **Hospital:** UF Hlth Shands Hosp; **Address:** UF Proton Therapy Inst, 2015 N Jefferson St, Jacksonville, FL 32206; **Phone:** 904-588-1800; **Board Cert:** Therapeutic Radiology 1984; **Med School:** Texas Tech Univ 1979; **Resid:** Radiation Oncology, Shands at Univ FL 1983; **Fac Appt:** Prof RadRO, Univ Fla Coll Med

Kudrimoti, Mahesh R MD [RadRO] - **Spec Exp:** Lung Cancer; Head & Neck Cancer; Brachytherapy; **Hospital:** Univ of Kentucky Albert B. Chandler Hosp; **Address:** Chandler Medical Center, 800 Rose St, UKMC Bldg, C113, Lexington, KY 40536; **Phone:** 859-323-0283; **Board Cert:** Radiation Oncology 2003; **Med School:** India 1992; **Resid:** Radiation Oncology, Univ KY Chandler Med Ctr 2001; **Fac Appt:** Assoc Prof RadRO, Univ KY Coll Med

Kun, Larry E MD [RadRO] - **Spec Exp:** Brain Tumors; Pediatric Cancers; **Hospital:** St. Jude Children's Research Hosp, Le Bonheur Chldns Med Ctr; **Address:** St Jude Chldns Research Hosp, 262 Danny Thomas Pl, MS 220, Memphis, TN 38105; **Phone:** 901-595-3565; **Board Cert:** Therapeutic Radiology 1973; **Med School:** Jefferson Med Coll 1968; **Resid:** Therapeutic Radiology, Penrose Cancer Hosp 1972; **Fellow:** Radiation Oncology, Natl Cancer Inst 1974; Radiation Oncology, Rotterdam Radiotherapy Inst 1975; **Fac Appt:** Prof, Univ Tenn Coll Med

Landry, Jerome C MD [RadRO] - **Spec Exp:** Gastrointestinal Cancer; Sarcoma-Soft Tissue; **Hospital:** Emory Univ Hosp, Grady Hlth Sys; **Address:** Emory Univ Hosp, Radiation Oncology Dept, 1365C Clifton Rd NE, Ste CT-104, Atlanta, GA 30322; **Phone:** 404-778-3473; **Board Cert:** Radiation Oncology 1988; **Med School:** Harvard Med Sch 1983; **Resid:** Radiation Oncology, Mass Genl Hosp 1987; **Fac Appt:** Prof RadRO, Emory Univ

Larner, James M MD [RadRO] - **Spec Exp:** Neuro-Oncology; Brain Tumors; **Hospital:** Univ of Virginia Hlth Sys; **Address:** Univ VA Med Ctr, Dept Radiation Oncology, 1240 Lee St, Charlottesville, VA 22908; **Phone:** 434-924-5191; **Board Cert:** Internal Medicine 1983; Medical Oncology 1987; Hematology 1988; Radiation Oncology 1989; **Med School:** Univ VA Sch Med 1980; **Resid:** Internal Medicine, Thomas Jefferson Univ Hosp 1983; Radiation Oncology, Montefiore Med Ctr-Einstein Campus 1989; **Fellow:** Hematology & Oncology, Thomas Jefferson Univ Hosp 1986; **Fac Appt:** Assoc Prof Med, Univ VA Sch Med

Lee, W. Robert MD [RadRO] - **Spec Exp:** Prostate Cancer; Brachytherapy; Intensity Modulated Radiotherapy (IMRT); **Hospital:** Duke Univ Hosp; **Address:** Duke Univ Med Ctr, Div Radiation Oncology, Box 3085, Durham, NC 27710; **Phone:** 919-668-5640; **Board Cert:** Radiation Oncology 1994; **Med School:** Univ VA Sch Med 1989; **Resid:** Radiation Oncology, Univ Fl Affil Hosp 1993; **Fac Appt:** Prof RadRO, Duke Univ

Lewin, Alan A MD [RadRO] - **Spec Exp:** Breast Cancer; Lung Cancer; Brain & Spinal Cord Tumors; **Hospital:** Baptist Hosp of Miami; **Address:** Baptist Hosp, Radiation Oncology Dept, 8900 N Kendall Drive, Miami, FL 33176; **Phone:** 786-596-6566; **Board Cert:** Internal Medicine 1976; Hematology 1978; Medical Oncology 1981; Therapeutic Radiology 1982; **Med School:** Geo Wash Univ 1973; **Resid:** Internal Medicine, Mount Sinai Med Ctr 1976; **Fellow:** Hematology & Oncology, Beth Israel Deaconess Med Ctr 1978; Radiation Oncology, Joint Ctr Radiation Therapy 1980; **Fac Appt:** Clin Prof RadRO, Univ Miami Sch Med

Malcolm, Arnold W MD [RadRO] - **Spec Exp:** Prostate Cancer; Gynecologic Cancer; Brachytherapy; **Hospital:** Vanderbilt Univ Med Ctr; **Address:** Vanderbilt Radiation Oncology, 2220 Pierce Ave, B-1003 TVC, Nashville, TN 37232; **Phone:** 615-322-2555; **Board Cert:** Radiation Oncology 1977; **Med School:** Meharry Med Coll 1973; **Resid:** Radiation Oncology, Joint Ctr Radiation Therapy 1977; **Fac Appt:** Prof RadRO, Vanderbilt Univ

Marcus Jr, Robert B MD [RadRO] - **Spec Exp:** Pediatric Cancers; Proton Beam Therapy; Bone Cancer; Brain & Spinal Cord Tumors; **Hospital:** West FL Hosp, Sacred Heart Hosp - Pensacola; **Address:** Gulf Region Radiation Oncology Ctr, 8333 N Davis Hwy, Pensacola, FL 32514; **Phone:** 850-474-8264; **Board Cert:** Therapeutic Radiology 1980; **Med School:** Univ Fla Coll Med 1975; **Resid:** Radiation Oncology, Shands at Univ FL 1979

Markoe, Arnold M MD [RadRO] - **Spec Exp:** Eye Tumors/Cancer; Orbital Tumors/Cancer; Central Nervous System Cancer; Lymphoma; **Hospital:** Univ of Miami Hosp & Clins/Sylvester Comp Canc Ctr, Jackson Meml Hosp; **Address:** Univ of Miami Sylvester Comp Cancer Ctr, 1475 NW 12th Ave Ave NW, rm 1508, Miami, FL 33136; **Phone:** 305-243-4319; **Board Cert:** Therapeutic Radiology 1983; **Med School:** Hahnemann Univ 1977; **Resid:** Radiation Oncology, Hahnemann Hosp 1981; **Fac Appt:** Prof RadRO, Univ Miami Sch Med

Marks, Lawrence B MD [RadRO] - **Spec Exp:** Breast Cancer; Lung Cancer; **Hospital:** NC Memorial Hosp - UNC, Rex HlthCare; **Address:** UNC Cancer Ctr, Dept Rad Onc, 101 Manning Drive, rm CB 295, Level B, Campus Box 7512, Chapel Hill, NC 27599; **Phone:** 919-966-0400; **Board Cert:** Radiation Oncology 1989; **Med School:** Univ Rochester 1985; **Resid:** Radiation Oncology, Mass Genl Hosp 1989; **Fac Appt:** Prof RadRO, Univ NC Sch Med

McGarry, Ronald C MD/PhD [RadRO] - **Spec Exp:** Lung Cancer; Lymphoma; Clinical Trials; Stereotactic Radiosurgery; **Hospital:** Univ of Kentucky Albert B. Chandler Hosp; **Address:** UK Albert B Chandler Hosp, Radiation Medicine Ctr, 800 Rose St, rm C114C, Lexington, KY 40536; **Phone:** 859-323-6486; **Board Cert:** Radiation Oncology 2010; **Med School:** Canada 1992; **Resid:** Radiation Oncology, Univ W Ontario Regl Cancer Ctr 1997; **Fac Appt:** Prof RadRO, Univ KY Coll Med

Mendenhall, Nancy P MD [RadRO] - **Spec Exp:** Breast Cancer; Lymphoma; Hodgkin's Lymphoma; Prostate Cancer; **Hospital:** UF Hlth Shands Hosp; **Address:** UF Proton Therapy Inst, 2015 N Jefferson St, Jacksonville, FL 32206; **Phone:** 904-588-1800; **Board Cert:** Therapeutic Radiology 1985; **Med School:** Univ Fla Coll Med 1980; **Resid:** Diagnostic Radiology, Shands at Univ FL 1984; **Fac Appt:** Prof RadRO, Univ Fla Coll Med

Mendenhall, William M MD [RadRO] - **Spec Exp:** Head & Neck Cancer; Stereotactic Radiosurgery; Gastrointestinal Cancer; Gynecologic Cancer; **Hospital:** UF Hlth Shands Hosp; **Address:** UF Proton Therapy Inst, 2015 N Jefferson St, Jacksonville, FL 32209; **Phone:** 904-588-1800; **Board Cert:** Therapeutic Radiology 1983; **Med School:** Univ S Fla Coll Med 1978; **Resid:** Radiation Oncology, Shands at Univ FL 1983; **Fac Appt:** Prof RadRO, Univ Fla Coll Med

Merchant, Thomas E DO/PhD [RadRO] - **Spec Exp:** Brain Tumors-Pediatric; **Hospital:** St. Jude Children's Research Hosp; **Address:** St Jude Chldns Rsch Hosp, 262 Danny Thomas Pl, MS 220, Memphis, TN 38105; **Phone:** 901-595-3604; **Board Cert:** Radiation Oncology 2004; **Med School:** Chicago Coll Osteo Med 1989; **Resid:** Radiation Oncology, Meml Sloan Kettering Cancer Ctr 1994

Meredith, Ruby F MD/PhD [RadRO] - **Spec Exp:** Multiple Myeloma; Breast Cancer; Radionuclide Therapy; Bone Tumors-Metastatic; **Hospital:** UAB Hosp; **Address:** 1700 6th Ave S, Birmingham, AL 35249; **Phone:** 205-934-2763; **Board Cert:** Radiation Oncology 1987; **Med School:** Ohio State Univ 1983; **Resid:** Radiation Oncology, Med College Va Hosps 1987; **Fac Appt:** Prof RadRO, UAB Sch Med

Morris, Monica M MD [RadRO] - **Spec Exp:** Breast Cancer; **Hospital:** Univ of Virginia Hlth Sys; **Address:** UVA Radiation Oncology, 2871 Ivy Rd, Charlottesville, VA 22908; **Phone:** 434-982-0777; **Board Cert:** Radiation Oncology 2009; **Med School:** Baylor Coll Med 1993; **Resid:** Radiation Oncology, Mass Genl Hosp 1998; **Fac Appt:** Assoc Prof RadRO, Univ VA Sch Med

Pollack, Alan MD/PhD [RadRO] - **Spec Exp:** Prostate Cancer; Genitourinary Cancer; Sarcoma; **Hospital:** Univ of Miami Hosp & Clins/Sylvester Comp Canc Ctr; **Address:** SCCC, Radiation Oncology Dept, 1475 NW 12th Ave, Ste 1501, Miami, FL 33136; **Phone:** 305-243-4916; **Board Cert:** Radiation Oncology 1993; **Med School:** Univ Miami Sch Med 1987; **Resid:** Radiation Oncology, UT MD Anderson Cancer Ctr 1992; **Fac Appt:** Prof RadRO, Univ Miami Sch Med

Prosnitz, Leonard MD [RadRO] - **Spec Exp:** Lymphoma; Breast Cancer; Hyperthermia Treatment of Cancer; Sarcoma; **Hospital:** Duke Univ Hosp; **Address:** Duke Univ Med Ctr, Dept Rad Onc, Box 3085, Durham, NC 27710; **Phone:** 919-668-5637; **Board Cert:** Therapeutic Radiology 1970; **Med School:** SUNY Downstate 1961; **Resid:** Internal Medicine, Dartmouth Affil Hosps 1963; Radiation Oncology, Yale-New Haven Hosp 1969; **Fellow:** Hematology & Oncology, Yale-New Haven Hosp 1967; **Fac Appt:** Prof RadRO, Duke Univ

Randall, Marcus E MD [RadRO] - **Spec Exp:** Gynecologic Cancer; Stereotactic Radiosurgery; Vulvar & Vaginal Cancer; **Hospital:** Univ of Kentucky Albert B. Chandler Hosp; **Address:** Univ Kentucky Medical Ctr, 800 Rose St, rm C 114D, Office of Radiation Medicine, Lexington, KY 40536-0001; **Phone:** 859-257-7618; **Board Cert:** Therapeutic Radiology 1986; **Med School:** Univ NC Sch Med 1982; **Resid:** Radiation Oncology, Univ Va Med Ctr 1986; **Fellow:** Radiation Oncology, Univ Va Med Ctr 1986; **Fac Appt:** Prof RadRO, Univ KY Coll Med

Rosenman, Julian MD/PhD [RadRO] - **Spec Exp:** Lung Cancer; Breast Cancer; Prostate Cancer; **Hospital:** NC Memorial Hosp - UNC; **Address:** UNC Cancer Ctr, Dept Rad Onc, 101 Manning Drive, Level B, Campus Box 7512, Chapel Hill, NC 27599; **Phone:** 919-966-0400; **Board Cert:** Therapeutic Radiology 1981; **Med School:** Univ Tex SW, Dallas 1977; **Resid:** Therapeutic Radiology, Mass Genl Hosp 1981; **Fac Appt:** Prof RadRO, Univ NC Sch Med

Sailer, Scott MD [RadRO] - **Spec Exp:** Breast Cancer; Genitourinary Cancer; Head & Neck Cancer; **Hospital:** WakeMed Cary, WakeMed-Raleigh Campus; **Address:** Cancer Centers of North Carolina, 300 Ashville Ave, Ste 110, Cary, NC 27518; **Phone:** 919-854-4588; **Board Cert:** Radiation Oncology 1988; **Med School:** Harvard Med Sch 1984; **Resid:** Radiation Therapy, Mass Genl Hosp 1988

Shaw, Edward G MD [RadRO] - **Spec Exp:** Stereotactic Radiosurgery; Brain Tumors; **Hospital:** Wake Forest Baptist Med Ctr; **Address:** Wake Forest Baptist Health, Dept Radiation Oncology, Medical Ctr Blvd, Winston-Salem, NC 27157; **Phone:** 336-716-0891; **Board Cert:** Radiation Oncology 1987; **Med School:** Rush Med Coll 1983; **Resid:** Radiation Oncology, Mayo Grad Sch Med 1987; **Fac Appt:** Prof RadRO, Wake Forest Univ

Song, Shiyu MD/PhD [RadRO] - **Spec Exp:** Head & Neck Cancer; Lymphoma; **Hospital:** VCU Med Ctr; **Address:** Massey Canc Ctr, N Hosp, 1300 E Marshall St, Richmond, VA 23298-0037; **Phone:** 804-828-7232; **Board Cert:** Radiation Oncology 2006; **Med School:** China 1983; **Resid:** Radiation Oncology, Univ WI Hosp & Clins 2004; **Fellow:** Research, Johns Hopkins Hosp 1994; **Fac Appt:** Assoc Prof RadRO, Va Commonwealth Univ Sch Med

St Clair, William H MD/PhD [RadRO] - **Spec Exp:** Brain Tumors; Urologic Cancer; Intensity Modulated Radiotherapy (IMRT); **Hospital:** Univ of Kentucky Albert B. Chandler Hosp; **Address:** UK Albert B Chandler Hosp, Radiation Medicine Ctr, 800 Rose St, Ste CC112A, Lexington, KY 40536; **Phone:** 859-323-6486; **Board Cert:** Radiation Oncology 2000; **Med School:** Univ KY Coll Med 1995; **Resid:** Radiation Oncology, Mass Genl Hosp 2000; **Fellow:** Radiation Oncology, Mass Genl Hosp 2000; **Fac Appt:** Assoc Prof RadRO, Univ KY Coll Med

Stevens, Craig W MD/PhD [RadRO] - **Spec Exp:** Lung Cancer; **Hospital:** Moffitt Canc Ctr (page 61); **Address:** Moffitt Cancer Ctr, Radiation Oncology, 12902 Magnolia Drive Fl 1, Blue Valet Side, Tampa, FL 33612; **Phone:** 813-745-8424; **Board Cert:** Radiation Oncology 1994; **Med School:** Northwestern Univ 1988; **Resid:** Radiation Oncology, Georgetown Univ Hosp 1993; **Fac Appt:** Prof RadRO, Univ S Fla Coll Med

Tepper, Joel E MD/PhD [RadRO] - **Spec Exp:** Gastrointestinal Cancer; Sarcoma; Rectal Cancer; **Hospital:** NC Memorial Hosp - UNC; **Address:** UNC Cancer Ctr, Dept Rad Onc, 101 Manning Drive, Level B, Campus Box 7512, Chapel Hill, NC 27599; **Phone:** 919-445-5216; **Board Cert:** Therapeutic Radiology 1976; **Med School:** Washington Univ, St Louis 1972; **Resid:** Therapeutic Radiology, Mass Genl Hosp 1976; **Fellow:** Therapeutic Radiology, Mass Genl Hosp 1977; **Fac Appt:** Prof RadRO, Univ NC Sch Med

Vijayakumar, Srinivasan MD [RadRO] - **Spec Exp:** Brachytherapy; Prostate Cancer; **Hospital:** Univ Mississippi Med Ctr; **Address:** 350 Woodrow Wilson Drive, Jackson, MS 39213; **Phone:** 601-984-2550; **Board Cert:** Therapeutic Radiology 1986; **Med School:** India 1978; **Resid:** Radiation Oncology, Madras Univ Med Ctr 1981; Radiation Oncology, Michael Reese Hosp 1984; **Fellow:** Brachytherapy, Univ Chicago Hosps 1985; **Fac Appt:** Prof RadRO, Univ Miss

Willett, Christopher MD [RadRO] - **Spec Exp:** Gastrointestinal Cancer; Clinical Trials; **Hospital:** Duke Univ Hosp; **Address:** Duke Univ Med Ctr, Box 3085, Durham, NC 27710; **Phone:** 919-668-5640; **Board Cert:** Therapeutic Radiology 1985; **Med School:** Tufts Univ 1981; **Resid:** Radiation Oncology, Mass Genl Hosp 1986; **Fac Appt:** Prof RadRO, Duke Univ

Wolfson, Aaron H MD [RadRO] - **Spec Exp:** Gynecologic Cancer; Sarcoma; Skin Cancer; Lymphoma; **Hospital:** Univ of Miami Hosp & Clins/Sylvester Comp Canc Ctr, Jackson Meml Hosp; **Address:** UMHC Sylvester Comp Cancer Ctr, 1475 NW 12th Ave, Ste D31, Miami, FL 33136; **Phone:** 305-243-4210; **Board Cert:** Radiation Oncology 1999; **Med School:** Univ Fla Coll Med 1982; **Resid:** Radiation Oncology, Med Coll of Virginia 1989; **Fac Appt:** Prof RadRO, Univ Miami Sch Med

Woo, Shiao Y MD [RadRO] - **Spec Exp:** Brain Tumors-Adult & Pediatric; Proton Beam Therapy; Stereotactic Radiosurgery; Pediatric Cancers; **Hospital:** Univ of Louisville Hosp; **Address:** James Graham Brown Cancer Ctr, 529 S Jackson St, Lower Level, Louisville, KY 40202; **Phone:** 502-562-4759; **Board Cert:** Pediatrics 1980; Pediatric Hematology-Oncology 1980; Radiation Oncology 1988; **Med School:** Malaysia 1972; **Resid:** Pediatrics, Georgetown Univ Hosp 1978; Radiation Therapy, Stanford Univ Med Ctr 1988; **Fellow:** Pediatric Hematology-Oncology, Georgetown Univ Hosp 1980; **Fac Appt:** Prof RadRO, Univ Louisville Sch Med

Midwest

Abrams, Ross A MD [RadRO] - **Spec Exp:** Gastrointestinal Cancer; Lymphoma; **Hospital:** Rush Univ Med Ctr; **Address:** Women's Board Ctr for Radiation Therapy, 500 S Paulina, Ground Floor Atrium, Chicago, IL 60612; **Phone:** 312-942-5751; **Board Cert:** Internal Medicine 1976; Medical Oncology 1979; Hematology 1982; Radiation Oncology 1987; **Med School:** Univ Pennsylvania 1973; **Resid:** Internal Medicine, Pennsylvania Hosp 1975; Hematology & Oncology, Hosp Univ Penn 1976; **Fellow:** Hematology & Oncology, Natl Cancer Inst 1978; Radiation Oncology, Med Coll Wisconsin 1987; **Fac Appt:** Prof RadRO, Rush Med Coll

Awan, Azhar M MD [RadRO] - **Spec Exp:** Sarcoma-Soft Tissue; Prostate Cancer; Breast Cancer; **Hospital:** Adv Sherman Hosp, Univ of Chicago Med; **Address:** Advocate Sherman Hosp, 1425 N Randall Rd, Elgin, IL 60123; **Phone:** 224-783-8746; **Board Cert:** Therapeutic Radiology 1985; **Med School:** Loyola Univ-Stritch Sch Med 1981; **Resid:** Therapeutic Radiology, Rush Med Ctr 1985; **Fac Appt:** Assoc Prof RadRO, Univ Chicago-Pritzker Sch Med

Bradley, Jeffrey D MD [RadRO] - **Spec Exp:** Lung Cancer; Thoracic Cancers; Esophageal Cancer; Clinical Trials; **Hospital:** Barnes-Jewish Hosp; **Address:** Ctr for Advanced Medicine, Rad Oncology, 4921 Parkview Pl Fl LL, St Louis, MO 63110; **Phone:** 314-747-7236; **Board Cert:** Radiation Oncology 2009; **Med School:** Univ Ark 1993; **Resid:** Radiation Oncology, Univ Chicago 1998; **Fac Appt:** Assoc Prof RadRO, Washington Univ, St Louis

Buatti, John M MD [RadRO] - **Spec Exp:** Central Nervous System Cancer; Pediatric Cancers; **Hospital:** Univ Iowa Hosp & Clins; **Address:** Univ Iowa Hosp & Clin, Dept Rad Onc, 200 Hawkins Drive, PFP Bldg, rm 01626, Iowa City, IA 52242; **Phone:** 319-356-2699; **Board Cert:** Radiation Oncology 1994; **Med School:** Georgetown Univ 1986; **Resid:** Internal Medicine, Georgetown Univ 1989; **Fellow:** Radiation Oncology, Univ Arizona 1993; **Fac Appt:** Prof RadRO, Univ Iowa Coll Med

Chakravarti, Arnab MD [RadRO] - **Spec Exp:** Brain Tumors; **Hospital:** Arthur G James Cancer Hosp & Research Inst, OSU Wexner Med Ctr; **Address:** Arthur G James Comp Cancer Ctr, Ohio State Univ Medical School, 300 W 10th Ave, rm 080B, Columbus, OH 43210; **Phone:** 614-293-9437; **Board Cert:** Radiation Oncology 2010; **Med School:** Univ VA Sch Med 1995; **Resid:** Radiation Oncology, Mass Genl Hosp 2000; **Fac Appt:** Prof RadRO, Ohio State Univ

Ciezki, Jay P MD [RadRO] - **Spec Exp:** Brachytherapy; Prostate Cancer; Genitourinary Cancer; **Hospital:** Cleveland Clin (page 55); **Address:** Cleveland Clinic, 9500 Euclid Ave, MC T28, Cleveland, OH 44195; **Phone:** 216-445-9465; **Board Cert:** Radiation Oncology 2005; **Med School:** Med Coll Wisc 1991; **Resid:** Radiation Oncology, Cleveland Clinic 1995; **Fellow:** Brachytherapy, Cleveland Clinic 1996

Eisbruch, Avraham MD [RadRO] - **Spec Exp:** Head & Neck Cancer; **Hospital:** Univ Michigan Med Ctr; **Address:** Univ MI Hlth Sys, 1500 E Med Ctr Drive, UHB2C490, Ann Arbor, MI 48109; **Phone:** 734-936-4300; **Board Cert:** Radiation Oncology 1992; **Med School:** Israel 1979; **Resid:** Radiology, Washington Univ 1992; **Fellow:** Medical Oncology, Univ TX MD Anderson Cancer Ctr 1996; **Fac Appt:** Assoc Clin Prof RadRO, Univ Mich Med Sch

Emami, Bahman MD [RadRO] - **Spec Exp:** Head & Neck Cancer; Lung Cancer; **Hospital:** Loyola Univ Med Ctr, Edward Hines, Jr. VA Hosp; **Address:** Loyola Univ Med Ctr, Dept Rad Onc, 2160 S First Ave Bldg 150 - rm 0300, Maywood, IL 60153-3328; **Phone:** 708-216-2729; **Board Cert:** Therapeutic Radiology 1976; **Med School:** Iran 1968; **Resid:** Pathology, St Vincents Hosp 1973; Radiation Oncology, New England Med Ctr 1977; **Fac Appt:** Prof RadRO, Loyola Univ-Stritch Sch Med

Forman, Jeffrey D MD [RadRO] - **Spec Exp:** Neutron Therapy for Advanced Cancer; Genitourinary Cancer; Prostate Cancer; **Hospital:** Botsford Hosp; **Address:** 70 Fulton St, Pontiac, MI 48341; **Phone:** 248-338-0300; **Board Cert:** Radiation Oncology 1986; **Med School:** NYU Sch Med 1982; **Resid:** Radiation Oncology, Johns Hopkins Hosp 1986; **Fellow:** Therapeutic Radiology, Johns Hopkins Hosp 1987; **Fac Appt:** Prof RadRO, Wayne State Univ

Grigsby, Perry W MD [RadRO] - **Spec Exp:** Gynecologic Cancer; Thyroid Cancer; **Hospital:** Barnes-Jewish Hosp, St. Louis Chldns Hosp; **Address:** Ctr for Advanced Medicine, Rad Oncology, 4921 Parkview Pl Fl LL, St Louis, MO 63110; **Phone:** 314-747-7236; **Board Cert:** Radiation Oncology 1987; **Med School:** Univ KY Coll Med 1982; **Resid:** Radiation Oncology, Barnes Jewish Hosp 1985; **Fac Appt:** Prof RadRO, Washington Univ, St Louis

Halpern, Howard J MD/PhD [RadRO] - **Spec Exp:** Breast Cancer; Esophageal Cancer; Gynecologic Cancer; **Hospital:** Univ of IL Med Ctr at Chicago, Univ of Chicago Med; **Address:** Univ IL Med Ctr, Dept Radiation Oncology, 1800 W Taylor St, Chicago, IL 60612; **Phone:** 312-996-3630; **Board Cert:** Therapeutic Radiology 1984; **Med School:** Univ Miami Sch Med 1980; **Resid:** Therapeutic Radiology, Harvard Jnt Ctr Rad Ther 1984; **Fellow:** Therapeutic Radiology, Harvard Jnt Ctr Rad Ther 1985; **Fac Appt:** Prof RadRO, Univ Chicago-Pritzker Sch Med

Haraf, Daniel J MD [RadRO] - **Spec Exp:** Head & Neck Cancer; Lung Cancer; Prostate Cancer; **Hospital:** Univ of Chicago Med; **Address:** Univ Chicago Med Ctr, Dept Radiation Onc, 5758 S Maryland Ave, rm 1D, MC 9006, Chicago, IL 60637; **Phone:** 773-702-6870; **Board Cert:** Internal Medicine 1985; Radiation Oncology 1990; **Med School:** Ros Franklin Univ/Chicago Med Sch 1982; **Resid:** Internal Medicine, Michael Reese Hosp 1985; **Fellow:** Radiation Oncology, Univ Chicago Affil Hosp 1988; **Fac Appt:** Prof RadRO, Univ Chicago-Pritzker Sch Med

Harari, Paul M MD [RadRO] - **Spec Exp:** Head & Neck Cancer; **Hospital:** Univ WI Hosp & Clins; **Address:** Dept of Human Oncology, 600 Highland Ave, Ste K4/B100, Madison, WI 53792; **Phone:** 608-263-8500; **Board Cert:** Radiation Oncology 1990; **Med School:** Univ VA Sch Med 1984; **Resid:** Radiation Oncology, Univ Arizona Med Ctr 1990; **Fac Appt:** Prof RadRO, Univ Wisc

Hayman, James A MD [RadRO] - **Spec Exp:** Breast Cancer; Stomach Cancer; Lung Cancer; Brain Tumors; **Hospital:** Univ Michigan Med Ctr; **Address:** Univ Michigan Hosp, 1500 E Medical Ctr Drive, rm UH B2C490, Ann Arbor, MI 48109-0010; **Phone:** 734-936-4300; **Board Cert:** Radiation Oncology 2004; Hospice & Palliative Medicine 2012; **Med School:** Univ Chicago-Pritzker Sch Med 1991; **Resid:** Radiation Therapy, Joint Ctr for Radiation Therapy 1996; **Fac Appt:** Assoc Prof RadRO, Univ Mich Med Sch

Johnstone, Peter Anthony MD [RadRO] - **Spec Exp:** Prostate Cancer; Proton Beam Therapy; Head & Neck Cancer; **Hospital:** IU Hlth Univ Hosp; **Address:** IU Health Univ Hosp-Radiation Oncology, 535 Barnhill Drive, Indianapolis, IN 46202; **Phone:** 317-944-2524; **Board Cert:** Radiation Oncology 2010; **Med School:** Uniformed Srvs Univ, Bethesda 1989; **Resid:** Radiation Oncology, Natl Cancer Inst 1993; **Fac Appt:** Prof RadRO, Indiana Univ

Jose, Baby Oliapuram MD [RadRO] - **Spec Exp:** Head & Neck Cancer; Lung Cancer; Gynecologic Cancer; Prostate Cancer; **Hospital:** Floyd Meml Hosp & Hlth Svcs; **Address:** Univ Radiotherapy Assocs, Cancer Ctr of Indiana, 2210 Green Valley Rd, New Albany, IN 47150; **Phone:** 812-945-4000; **Board Cert:** Therapeutic Radiology 1978; **Med School:** India 1971; **Resid:** Surgery, Christian Med Coll Hosp 1974; Radiation Oncology, Christian Med Coll Hosp 1976; **Fellow:** Radiation Oncology, Brown Univ-RI Hosp 1979; **Fac Appt:** Prof RadRO, Univ Louisville Sch Med

Kestin, Larry L MD [RadRO] - **Spec Exp:** Lung Cancer; Thoracic Cancers; Genitourinary Cancer; Stereotactic Body Radiation Therapy; **Hospital:** Botsford Hosp, St. Joseph Mercy Oakland Hosp; **Address:** 21st Century Oncology, 28595 Orchard Lake Rd, Ste 110, Farmington Hills, MI 48334; **Phone:** 248-553-0606; **Board Cert:** Radiation Oncology 2011; **Med School:** Univ Kansas 1995; **Resid:** Radiation Oncology, William Beaumont Hosp 2000; **Fac Appt:** Prof RadRO, Oakland Univ-William Beaumont Med Sch

Konski, Andre MD [RadRO] - **Spec Exp:** Esophageal Cancer; Rectal Cancer; Pancreatic Cancer; Gastrointestinal Cancer; **Hospital:** Barbara Ann Karmanos Cancer Inst; **Address:** Karmanos Cancer Center, Dept Radiation Oncology, 4100 John R St, Detroit, MI 48201; **Phone:** 313-576-9620; **Board Cert:** Radiation Oncology 2000; **Med School:** NY Med Coll 1984; **Resid:** Radiation Oncology, Strong Meml Hosp 1988; **Fac Appt:** Prof RadRO, Wayne State Univ

Lawrence, Theodore S MD/PhD [RadRO] - **Spec Exp:** Gastrointestinal Cancer; Liver Cancer; Pancreatic Cancer; **Hospital:** Univ Michigan Med Ctr; **Address:** Univ of Mich Hosp, Dept Rad Onc, 1500 E Medical Center Drive, UHB2C490, Ann Arbor, MI 48109-5010; **Phone:** 734-936-4300; **Board Cert:** Internal Medicine 1983; Medical Oncology 1985; Radiation Oncology 1987; **Med School:** Cornell Univ-Weill Med Coll 1980; **Resid:** Internal Medicine, Stanford Univ Hosp 1983; Radiation Oncology, Natl Cancer Inst 1987; **Fellow:** Medical Oncology, Natl Cancer Inst 1986; **Fac Appt:** Prof RadRO, Univ Mich Med Sch

Lee, Chung K MD [RadRO] - **Spec Exp:** Head & Neck Cancer; Breast Cancer; Lymphoma; Gastrointestinal Cancer; **Hospital:** Univ Minn Med Ctr, Fairview - West Bank Campus; **Address:** Univ Minn, Dept Radiation Oncology, 420 Delaware St SE, Minneapolis, MN 55455; **Phone:** 612-273-6700; **Board Cert:** Therapeutic Radiology 1976; **Med School:** Korea 1965; **Resid:** Radiation Oncology, Yonsei Univ Hosp 1971; Therapeutic Radiology, Univ of Minn Hosp 1976; **Fellow:** Yonsei Univ Hosp; **Fac Appt:** Prof RadRO, Univ Minn

Machtay, Mitchell MD [RadRO] - **Spec Exp:** Head & Neck Cancer; Skin Cancer; Skull Base Tumors; **Hospital:** UH Case Med Ctr; **Address:** UH Case Med Ctr, Dept Rad Onc, 11100 Euclid Ave, Cleveland, OH 44106; **Phone:** 216-844-2530; **Board Cert:** Radiation Oncology 1994; **Med School:** NYU Sch Med 1989; **Resid:** Radiation Oncology, Hosp Univ Penn 1993; **Fac Appt:** Prof RadRO, Case West Res Univ

Macklis, Roger M MD [RadRO] - **Spec Exp:** Radioimmunotherapy of Cancer; Breast Cancer; Lymphoma; **Hospital:** Cleveland Clin (page 55); **Address:** Cleveland Cin Fdn, Dept Rad Onc, 9500 Euclid Ave, Desk T28, Cleveland, OH 44195; **Phone:** 216-444-5576; **Board Cert:** Radiation Oncology 1989; **Med School:** Harvard Med Sch 1983; **Resid:** Radiation Oncology, Joint Ctr Radiotherapy Inst 1987; **Fellow:** Research, Dana Farber Cancer Inst 1987; **Fac Appt:** Prof RadRO, Case West Res Univ

Martenson Jr, James A MD [RadRO] - **Spec Exp:** Mucositis; Esophageal Cancer; Gastrointestinal Cancer; **Hospital:** Mayo Med Ctr & Clin - Rochester; **Address:** Mayo Clinic, Dept Rad/Onc, 200 First St SW, Rochester, MN 55905; **Phone:** 507-284-4561; **Board Cert:** Therapeutic Radiology 1985; **Med School:** Univ Wash 1981; **Resid:** Radiation Oncology, Mayo Clinic 1985; **Fac Appt:** Prof RadRO, Mayo Med Sch

Michalski, Jeff M MD [RadRO] - **Spec Exp:** Prostate Cancer; Sarcoma; Pediatric Cancers; **Hospital:** Barnes-Jewish Hosp, St. Louis Chldns Hosp; **Address:** Ctr for Advanced Medicine, Rad Oncology, 4921 Parkview Pl Fl LL, St Louis, MO 63110; **Phone:** 314-747-7236; **Board Cert:** Radiation Oncology 1991; **Med School:** Med Coll Wisc 1986; **Resid:** Radiation Oncology, Columbia Presby Med Ctr 1988; Radiation Oncology, Mallinckrodt Inst of Radiology 1990; **Fellow:** Radiation Oncology, Mallinckrodt Inst of Radiology 1991; **Fac Appt:** Prof RadRO, Washington Univ, St Louis

Mittal, Bharat B MD [RadRO] - **Spec Exp:** Head & Neck Cancer; Lymphoma; Skin Cancer; **Hospital:** Northwestern Meml Hosp; **Address:** Northwestern Meml Hosp, 251 E Huron St, Chicago, IL 60611; **Phone:** 312-926-2520; **Board Cert:** Therapeutic Radiology 1981; **Med School:** India 1975; **Resid:** Internal Medicine, Christian Med Coll 1976; Radiation Oncology, Northwestern Meml Hosp 1980; **Fellow:** Radiation Oncology, Mallinckrodt Inst 1981; **Fac Appt:** Prof RadRO, Northwestern Univ

Movsas, Benjamin MD [RadRO] - **Spec Exp:** Lung Cancer; Brain Tumors; Prostate Cancer; Stereotactic Radiosurgery; **Hospital:** Henry Ford Hosp; **Address:** Henry Ford Health Sys, Dept Rad Oncology, 2799 W Grand Blvd, Detroit, MI 48202-2608; **Phone:** 313-916-1021; **Board Cert:** Radiation Oncology 2010; **Med School:** Washington Univ, St Louis 1990; **Resid:** Radiation Oncology, National Cancer Inst 1995

Pierce, Lori J MD [RadRO] - **Spec Exp:** Breast Cancer; **Hospital:** Univ Michigan Med Ctr; **Address:** Univ of Michigan Hosp, Dept Rad Onc, 1500 E Medical Center Drive, UHB2C490, Ann Arbor, MI 48109-5099; **Phone:** 734-936-4300; **Board Cert:** Radiation Oncology 1989; **Med School:** Duke Univ 1985; **Resid:** Radiation Oncology, Hosp Univ Penn 1989; **Fac Appt:** Prof RadRO, Univ Mich Med Sch

Simpson, Joseph R MD/PhD [RadRO] - **Spec Exp:** Brain Tumors; Gliomas; Central Nervous System Cancer; Stereotactic Radiosurgery; **Hospital:** Barnes-Jewish Hosp, St. Louis Chldns Hosp; **Address:** Ctr for Advanced Medicine, Siteman Cancer Ctr, 4921 Parview Pl, Lower Level, St Louis, MO 63110-1001; **Phone:** 314-747-7236; **Board Cert:** Internal Medicine 1977; Therapeutic Radiology 1978; **Med School:** Harvard Med Sch 1983; **Resid:** Internal Medicine, Michael Reese Hosp 1975; Radiation Oncology, Univ Wisconsin Hosp 1978; **Fac Appt:** Prof Rad, Univ Wash

Small Jr, William MD [RadRO] - **Spec Exp:** Gynecologic Cancer; Gastrointestinal Cancer; Breast Cancer; Pancreatic Cancer; **Hospital:** Loyola Univ Med Ctr; **Address:** Loyola Univ Med Ctr, Dept Radiation Oncology, 2160 S 1st Ave, Maguire Ctr, rm 2932, Maywood, IL 60153; **Phone:** 708-216-2559; **Board Cert:** Radiation Oncology 2004; **Med School:** Northwestern Univ 1990; **Resid:** Radiation Oncology, Northwestern Univ 1994; **Fac Appt:** Prof RadRO

Suh, John H MD [RadRO] - **Spec Exp:** Brain Tumors-Adult & Pediatric; Stereotactic Radiosurgery; Stereotactic Body Radiation Therapy; **Hospital:** Cleveland Clin (page 55); **Address:** Cleveland Clinic, Dept Rad/Onc, 9500 Euclid Ave, Desk T28, Cleveland, OH 44195-0001; **Phone:** 216-444-5574; **Board Cert:** Radiation Oncology 2011; **Med School:** Univ Miami Sch Med 1990; **Resid:** Radiation Oncology, Cleveland Clinic 1994; **Fellow:** Radiation Oncology, Cleveland Clinic 1995; **Fac Appt:** Prof RadRO, Cleveland Cl Coll Med/Case West Res

Vicini, Frank A MD [RadRO] - **Spec Exp:** Breast Cancer; Prostate Cancer; Brachytherapy; **Hospital:** Botsford Hosp; **Address:** Botsford Radiation Oncology Ctr, 28595 Orchard Lake Rd, Ste 110, Farmington Hills, MI 48334; **Phone:** 248-553-0606; **Board Cert:** Radiation Oncology 1990; **Med School:** Wayne State Univ 1985; **Resid:** Radiation Oncology, Beaumont Hosp 1989; **Fellow:** Radiation Oncology, Harvard Med Sch/Joint Ctr for Rad Ther 1990; **Fac Appt:** Clin Prof RadRO, Oakland Univ-William Beaumont Med Sch

Videtic, Gregory M MD [RadRO] - **Spec Exp:** Lung Cancer; Mesothelioma; Esophageal Cancer; Thymoma; **Hospital:** Cleveland Clin (page 55); **Address:** Cleveland Clinic, Radiation Oncology, 9500 Euclid Ave, MC T28, Cleveland, OH 44195; **Phone:** 216-444-9797; **Board Cert:** Radiation Oncology 2009; **Med School:** McGill Univ 1986; **Resid:** Radiation Oncology, Dalhousie Univ 1988; Radiation Oncology, London Regl Cancer Ctr 1997; **Fellow:** Radiation Oncology, Wayne State Univ 1998; **Fac Appt:** Assoc Prof Rad, Cleveland Cl Coll Med/Case West Res

Wilson, J. Frank MD [RadRO] - **Spec Exp:** Breast Cancer; Skin Cancer; **Hospital:** Froedtert & Med Coll WI; **Address:** Dept Radiation Oncology, 9200 W Wisconsin Ave, Milwaukee, WI 53226; **Phone:** 414-805-4400; **Board Cert:** Therapeutic Radiology 1971; **Med School:** Univ MO-Columbia Sch Med 1965; **Resid:** Radiation Therapy, Penrose Hosp 1969; **Fellow:** Radiation Therapy, Natl Cancer Inst/NIH 1971; **Fac Appt:** Prof RadRO, Med Coll Wisc

Great Plains and Mountains

Gaffney, David K MD/PhD [RadRO] - **Spec Exp:** Breast Cancer; Gynecologic Cancer; **Hospital:** Univ Utah Hlth Care; **Address:** Huntsman Canc Hosp, Dept Rad Oncology, 1950 Circle of Hope, rm 1440, Salt Lake City, UT 84112-5560; **Phone:** 801-581-2396; **Board Cert:** Radiation Oncology 2008; **Med School:** Med Coll Wisc 1992; **Resid:** Radiation Oncology, Univ UT Affil Hosps 1996; **Fac Appt:** Assoc Prof, Univ Utah

Rabinovitch, Rachel A MD [RadRO] - **Spec Exp:** Breast Cancer; Hodgkin's Lymphoma; **Hospital:** Univ Colorado Hosp; **Address:** Univ CO Hosp, Radiation Oncology, 1665 Aurora Ct, Ste 1032, MS F-706, Aurora, CO 80045; **Phone:** 720-848-0156; **Board Cert:** Radiation Oncology 1994; **Med School:** Albert Einstein Coll Med 1989; **Resid:** Radiation Oncology, Meml Sloan-Kettering Cancer Ctr 1993; **Fac Appt:** Prof RadRO, Univ Colorado

Shrieve, Dennis C MD/PhD [RadRO] - **Spec Exp:** Brain Tumors-Adult & Pediatric; Genitourinary Cancer; Gastrointestinal Cancer; **Hospital:** Univ Utah Hlth Care, Primary Children's Med Ctr; **Address:** Huntsman Canc Inst, Dept Rad Oncology, 1950 Circle of Hope, rm 1440, Salt Lake City, UT 84112; **Phone:** 801-581-2396; **Board Cert:** Radiation Oncology 1993; **Med School:** Univ Miami Sch Med 1989; **Resid:** Radiation Oncology, UCSF Med Ctr 1993; **Fac Appt:** Prof RadRO, Univ Utah

Smalley, Stephen R MD [RadRO] - **Spec Exp:** Colon Cancer; Gastrointestinal Cancer; **Hospital:** Olathe Med Ctr; **Address:** Olathe Medical Center, 20375 W 151st St, Doctors Bldg, Ste 180, Olathe, KS 66061-4575; **Phone:** 913-768-7200; **Board Cert:** Internal Medicine 1982; Radiation Oncology 1987; Medical Oncology 1985; **Med School:** Univ MO-Kansas City 1979; **Resid:** Internal Medicine, Mayo Clinic 1982; Medical Oncology, Mayo Clinic 1984; **Fellow:** Radiation Oncology, Mayo Clinic 1986; **Fac Appt:** Prof RadRO, Univ Kansas

Southwest

Buchholz, Thomas A MD [RadRO] - **Spec Exp:** Breast Cancer; **Hospital:** UT MD Anderson Canc Ctr; **Address:** Univ Texas MD Anderson Cancer Ctr, 1515 Holcombe Blvd, Unit 97, Houston, TX 77030; **Phone:** 713-794-4892; **Board Cert:** Radiation Oncology 1993; **Med School:** Tufts Univ 1988; **Resid:** Radiation Oncology, Univ Washington Med Ctr 1993; **Fellow:** Research, Univ Washington 1994; **Fac Appt:** Prof RadRO, Univ Tex, Houston

Choy, Hak MD [RadRO] - **Spec Exp:** Lung Cancer; **Hospital:** UT Southwestern Med Ctr at Dallas; **Address:** UT SW Med Ctr - Dallas, Dept Rad-Onc, 5801 Forest Park Rd, Dallas, TX 75390-9183; **Phone:** 214-645-7600; **Board Cert:** Radiation Oncology 1993; **Med School:** Univ Tex Med Br, Galveston 1987; **Resid:** Radiation Oncology, Ohio State U Hosp East 1989; Radiation Oncology, UT Med Br (John Sealy Hosp) 1992; **Fac Appt:** Prof RadRO, Univ Tex SW, Dallas

Cox, James D MD [RadRO] - **Spec Exp:** Lung Cancer; Esophageal Cancer; Thymoma; Thoracic Cancers; **Hospital:** UT MD Anderson Canc Ctr; **Address:** UT MD Anderson Canc Ctr, 1515 Holcombe Blvd, Unit 97, Houston, TX 77030; **Phone:** 713-563-2317; **Board Cert:** Therapeutic Radiology 1971; **Med School:** Univ Rochester 1965; **Resid:** Diagnostic Radiology, Penrose Hosp 1969; **Fellow:** Therapeutic Radiology, Inst Gustave-Roussy 1970; **Fac Appt:** Prof RadRO, Univ Tex, Houston

Crane, Christopher H MD [RadRO] - **Spec Exp:** Gastrointestinal Cancer; **Hospital:** UT MD Anderson Canc Ctr; **Address:** UT MD Anderson Canc Ctr, Dept Rad Onc, 1515 Holcombe Blvd, Unit 97, Houston, TX 77030; **Phone:** 713-563-6830; **Board Cert:** Radiation Oncology 2009; **Med School:** Univ VA Sch Med 1993; **Resid:** Radiation Oncology, Univ VA Health Sys 1998; **Fac Appt:** Prof RadRO, Univ Tex, Houston

Eifel, Patricia J MD [RadRO] - **Spec Exp:** Cervical Cancer; Uterine Cancer; Vulvar Disease/Cancer; Vaginal Cancer; **Hospital:** UT MD Anderson Canc Ctr; **Address:** MD Anderson Canc Ctr, Dept Rad Onc, 1515 Holcombe Blvd, Unit 1202, Houston, TX 77030-4009; **Phone:** 713-563-6830; **Board Cert:** Therapeutic Radiology 1982; **Med School:** Stanford Univ 1977; **Resid:** Radiation Oncology, Stanford Univ Med Ctr 1981; **Fellow:** Therapeutic Radiology, Stanford Univ Med Ctr 1982; **Fac Appt:** Prof RadRO, Univ Tex, Houston

Grado, Gordon L MD [RadRO] - **Spec Exp:** Prostate Cancer; Brachytherapy; **Hospital:** Scottsdale Hlthcare - Shea; **Address:** Southwest Oncology Centers, 2926 N Civic Center Plaza, Scottsdale, AZ 85251; **Phone:** 480-614-6300; **Board Cert:** Therapeutic Radiology 1981; **Med School:** Southern IL Univ 1977; **Resid:** Therapeutic Radiology, Mayo Clinic 1981; **Fac Appt:** Assoc Prof RadRO, Univ Minn

Halyard, Michele Y MD [RadRO] - **Spec Exp:** Breast Cancer; Head & Neck Cancer; **Hospital:** Mayo Clinic - Scottsdale; **Address:** Mayo Clinic-Radiation Oncology, 13400 E Shea Blvd, Scottsdale, AZ 85259-5404; **Phone:** 480-301-8000; **Board Cert:** Radiation Oncology 1989; **Med School:** Howard Univ 1984; **Resid:** Radiation Therapy, Howard Univ Hosp 1987; **Fellow:** Radiation Oncology, Mayo Clinic 1989; **Fac Appt:** Assoc Prof RadRO, Mayo Med Sch

Herman, Terence S MD [RadRO] - **Spec Exp:** Breast Cancer; Sarcoma; Brain Tumors; **Hospital:** OU Med Ctr; **Address:** Oklahoma Univ Health Sci Ctr, 800 NE 10th St, Ste L-100, Oklahoma City, OK 73104-5417; **Phone:** 405-271-5641; **Board Cert:** Internal Medicine 1975; Medical Oncology 1977; Therapeutic Radiology 1985; **Med School:** Univ Conn 1972; **Resid:** Internal Medicine, Univ Arizona Med Ctr 1975; Radiation Oncology, Stanford Univ Med Ctr 1985; **Fellow:** Medical Oncology, Univ Arizona Med Ctr 1977; **Fac Appt:** Prof RadRO, Univ Okla Coll Med

Jhingran, Anuja MD [RadRO] - **Spec Exp:** Gynecologic Cancer; Brachytherapy; **Hospital:** UT MD Anderson Canc Ctr; **Address:** UT MD Anderson Canc Ctr, Dept Rad Onc, 1515 Holcombe Blvd, Unit 1202, Houston, TX 77030; **Phone:** 713-563-6830; **Board Cert:** Radiation Oncology 1993; **Med School:** Texas Tech Univ 1988; **Resid:** Radiation Oncology, Baylor Affil Hosp 1993; **Fac Appt:** Assoc Prof RadRO, Univ Tex, Houston

Komaki, Ritsuko U MD [RadRO] - **Spec Exp:** Lung Cancer; Thymoma; Esophageal Cancer; **Hospital:** UT MD Anderson Canc Ctr; **Address:** UT MD Anderson Canc Ctr, Dept Rad Onc, 1515 Holcombe Blvd, Unit 97, Houston, TX 77030; **Phone:** 713-563-2300; **Board Cert:** Therapeutic Radiology 1977; **Med School:** Japan 1969; **Resid:** Radiation Oncology, Med Coll WI Affil Hosp 1978; **Fellow:** Radiation Oncology, UT MD Anderson Canc Ctr 1980; **Fac Appt:** Prof RadRO, Univ Tex, Houston

Kuban, Deborah A MD [RadRO] - **Spec Exp:** Genitourinary Cancer; **Hospital:** UT MD Anderson Canc Ctr; **Address:** UT MD Anderson Canc Ctr, Dept Rad Onc, 1515 Holcombe Blvd, Unit 1202, Houston, TX 77030-9904; **Phone:** 713-792-5905; **Board Cert:** Therapeutic Radiology 1986; **Med School:** Med Coll GA 1981; **Resid:** Radiation Oncology, Eastern VA Med Sch Affil Hosp 1985; **Fac Appt:** Prof RadRO, Univ Tex, Houston

Kuske, Robert R MD [RadRO] - **Spec Exp:** Breast Cancer; **Hospital:** Scottsdale Hlthcare - Shea; **Address:** Arizona Breast Cancer Specialists, 10460 N 92nd St, Ste 101, Scottsdale, AZ 85258; **Phone:** 480-922-4600; **Board Cert:** Therapeutic Radiology 1985; **Med School:** Univ Cincinnati 1980; **Resid:** Radiation Oncology, Univ Cincinnati Med Ctr 1984

Lee, Andrew K MD [RadRO] - **Spec Exp:** Prostate Cancer; Proton Beam Therapy; Genitourinary Cancer; **Hospital:** UT MD Anderson Canc Ctr; **Address:** UT MD Anderson Canc Ctr, Dept Rad Onc, 1515 Holcombe Blvd, Unit 97, Houston, TX 77030; **Phone:** 713-563-2300; **Board Cert:** Radiation Oncology 2011; **Med School:** Univ Minn 1996; **Resid:** Radiation Oncology, Harvard Med Sch 2001; **Fac Appt:** Assoc Prof RadRO, Univ Tex, Houston

Medbery III, Clinton A MD [RadRO] - **Spec Exp:** Stereotactic Radiosurgery; Prostate Cancer; Brachytherapy; Breast Cancer; **Hospital:** St. Anthony Hosp -Oklahoma City; **Address:** Southwest Radiation Oncology, 1011 N Dewey Ave, Ste 101, Oklahoma City, OK 73102; **Phone:** 405-272-7311; **Board Cert:** Internal Medicine 1980; Medical Oncology 1983; Radiation Oncology 1987; **Med School:** Med Univ SC 1976; **Resid:** Internal Medicine, Naval Hosp 1980; Radiation Oncology, Natl Cancer Inst 1987; **Fellow:** Medical Oncology, Naval Hosp 1982

Minsky, Bruce D MD [RadRO] - **Spec Exp:** Gastrointestinal Cancer; Esophageal Cancer; Colon & Rectal Cancer; Pancreatic Cancer; **Hospital:** UT MD Anderson Canc Ctr; **Address:** MD Anderson Cancer Center, 1515 Holcombe Blvd, Box 97, Houston, TX 77030; **Phone:** 713-563-2304; **Board Cert:** Radiation Oncology 1987; **Med School:** Univ Mass Sch Med 1982; **Resid:** Radiation Oncology, Harvard Jt Ctr Rad Ther 1986; **Fac Appt:** Prof RadRO, Univ Tex, Houston

Morrison, William H MD [RadRO] - **Spec Exp:** Head & Neck Cancer; Skin Cancer; Merkel Cell Carcinoma; **Hospital:** UT MD Anderson Canc Ctr; **Address:** 1515 Holcombe Blvd, #97, Houston, TX 77030-4000; **Phone:** 713-563-2322; **Board Cert:** Internal Medicine 1981; Therapeutic Radiology 1985; **Med School:** Johns Hopkins Univ 1978; **Resid:** Internal Medicine, Rush Presby/St Lukes Med Ctr 1981; Therapeutic Radiology, Stanford Univ Hosp 1985; **Fac Appt:** Prof RadRO, Univ Tex, Houston

Schild, Steven E MD [RadRO] - **Spec Exp:** Lung Cancer; Prostate Cancer; Genitourinary Cancer; Brain Tumors; **Hospital:** Mayo Clinic - Scottsdale; **Address:** Mayo Clinic-Radiation Oncology, 13400 E Shea Blvd, Scottsdale, AZ 85259; **Phone:** 480-301-8000; **Board Cert:** Radiation Oncology 1989; **Med School:** Creighton Univ 1985; **Resid:** Radiation Oncology, Mayo Clinic 1989; **Fac Appt:** Prof RadRO, Mayo Med Sch

Shina, Donald C MD [RadRO] - **Spec Exp:** Breast Cancer; **Hospital:** Christus St Vincent Reg Med Ctr-Santa Fe; **Address:** Christus St Vincent Cancer Ctr, 490 W Zia Rd, Santa Fe, NM 87505; **Phone:** 505-820-5233; **Board Cert:** Internal Medicine 1977; Medical Oncology 1979; Therapeutic Radiology 1981; **Med School:** Case West Res Univ 1974; **Resid:** Internal Medicine, Univ Hosps 1977; **Fellow:** Radiation Oncology, Univ Hosps 1980; Medical Oncology, Univ Hosps 1980

Stea, Baldassarre MD/PhD [RadRO] - **Spec Exp:** Brain Tumors; Stereotactic Radiosurgery; Pediatric Cancers; Lymphoma; **Hospital:** Univ Arizona Med Ctr-Univ Campus, St. Joseph's Hosp - Tucson; **Address:** 1501 N Campbell Ave, Tucson, AZ 85724-0001; **Phone:** 520-626-6724; **Board Cert:** Radiation Oncology 1987; **Med School:** Geo Wash Univ 1983; **Resid:** Radiation Oncology, Natl Cancer Inst 1987; **Fac Appt:** Prof RadRO, Univ Ariz Coll Med

West Coast and Pacific

Chang, Eric L MD [RadRO] - **Spec Exp:** Central Nervous System Cancer; **Hospital:** USC Norris Cancer Hosp; **Address:** USC Norris Cancer Hosp, Dept of Radiation Oncology, 1441 Eastlake Ave, Los Angeles, CA 90033; **Phone:** 323-865-3050; **Board Cert:** Radiation Oncology 2010; **Med School:** Harvard Med Sch 1994; **Resid:** Radiation Oncology, Harvard Univ Hosp 1999; **Fac Appt:** Prof RadRO, USC-Keck School of Medicine

Donaldson, Sarah S MD [RadRO] - **Spec Exp:** Pediatric Cancers; Hodgkin's Lymphoma; Sarcoma; Breast Cancer; **Hospital:** Stanford Univ Hosp & Clins; **Address:** 875 Blake Wilbur Drive, Clinic D, Stanford, CA 94305-5847; **Phone:** 650-736-0845; **Board Cert:** Therapeutic Radiology 1974; **Med School:** Harvard Med Sch 1968; **Resid:** Radiation Oncology, Stanford Univ Med Ctr 1972; **Fellow:** Pediatric Hematology-Oncology, Inst Gustave-Roussy 1973; Pediatric Hematology-Oncology, MD Anderson Cancer Ctr 1971; **Fac Appt:** Prof RadRO, Stanford Univ

Fowble, Barbara MD [RadRO] - **Spec Exp:** Breast Cancer; **Hospital:** UCSF Med Ctr; **Address:** 505 Parnassus Ave, rm L-75, San Francisco, CA 94115; **Phone:** 415-353-7175; **Board Cert:** Therapeutic Radiology 1976; **Med School:** Jefferson Med Coll 1972; **Resid:** Therapeutic Radiology, Bellevue Hosp Ctr-NYU 1975; Therapeutic Radiology, Hahnemann 1976; **Fellow:** Radiation Therapy, Jefferson Hosp 1977; **Fac Appt:** Prof RadRO, UCSF

Halberg, Francine MD [RadRO] - **Spec Exp:** Breast Cancer; **Hospital:** Marin Genl Hosp; **Address:** Marin Cancer Inst-Dept of Rad.Oncology, 1350 S Eliseo Drive, Ste 100, Greenbrae, CA 94904; **Phone:** 415-925-7326; **Board Cert:** Internal Medicine 1981; Therapeutic Radiology 1984; **Med School:** Cornell Univ-Weill Med Coll 1978; **Resid:** Internal Medicine, USPHS Hosp 1981; **Fellow:** Radiation Oncology, Stanford Univ Med Ctr 1984

Hancock, Steven MD [RadRO] - **Spec Exp:** Prostate Cancer; Breast Cancer; Cancer Survivors-Late Effects of Therapy; **Hospital:** Stanford Univ Hosp & Clins; **Address:** Stanford Cancer Center-Dept Rad Onc, 875 Blake Wilbur Drive, Clinic D, Stanford, CA 94305; **Phone:** 650-723-6171; **Board Cert:** Internal Medicine 1980; Therapeutic Radiology 1982; **Med School:** Stanford Univ 1976; **Resid:** Radiation Therapy, Stanford Univ Med Ctr 1981; Internal Medicine, Stanford Univ Med Ctr 1979; **Fac Appt:** Prof RadRO, Stanford Univ

Hoppe, Richard T MD [RadRO] - **Spec Exp:** Lymphoma; Hodgkin's Lymphoma; Cutaneous Lymphoma; **Hospital:** Stanford Univ Hosp & Clins; **Address:** 875 Blake Wilbur Drive, Clinic D, 875 Blake Wilbur Drive, rm CC-G228, Stanford, CA 94305-5847; **Phone:** 650-723-5510; **Board Cert:** Therapeutic Radiology 1976; **Med School:** Cornell Univ-Weill Med Coll 1971; **Resid:** Radiation Therapy, Stanford Univ Med Ctr 1976; **Fac Appt:** Prof, Stanford Univ

Koh, Wui-Jin MD [RadRO] - **Spec Exp:** Gynecologic Cancer; Brachytherapy; Gastrointestinal Cancer; **Hospital:** Univ Wash Med Ctr; **Address:** Seattle Canc Care Alliance, Dept Radiation Oncology, 825 Eastlake Ave E, MS G1-101, Seattle, WA 98109; **Phone:** 206-288-7318; **Board Cert:** Radiation Oncology 1988; **Med School:** Loma Linda Univ 1984; **Resid:** Radiation Oncology, Univ Wash Med Ctr 1988; **Fellow:** Tumor Imaging, Univ Wash Med Ctr 1988; **Fac Appt:** Prof RadRO, Univ Wash

Kupelian, Patrick A MD [RadRO] - **Spec Exp:** Genitourinary Cancer; Clinical Trials; Stereotactic Body Radiation Therapy; Stereotactic Radiosurgery; **Hospital:** UCLA Ronald Reagan Med Ctr; **Address:** UCLA Jonsson Comprehensive Cancer Center, 200 UCLA Medical Plaza, Ste B265, Los Angeles, CA 90095-6951; **Phone:** 310-825-9771; **Board Cert:** Radiation Oncology 2004; **Med School:** Lebanon 1989; **Resid:** Radiation Oncology, MD Anderson Cancer Ctr 1994; **Fellow:** Radiation Oncology, Cleveland Clinic 1995

Laramore, George E MD/PhD [RadRO] - **Spec Exp:** Neutron Therapy for Advanced Cancer; Salivary Gland Tumors; Head & Neck Cancer; Skin Cancer; **Hospital:** Univ Wash Med Ctr, Harborview Med Ctr; **Address:** Univ Washington Med Ctr, Dept Rad Onc Box 356043, 1959 NE Pacific St, Seattle, WA 98195; **Phone:** 206-598-4121; **Board Cert:** Therapeutic Radiology 1980; Radiation Oncology 2010; **Med School:** Univ Miami Sch Med 1976; **Resid:** Radiation Oncology, Univ Wash Med Ctr 1980; **Fac Appt:** Prof RadRO, Univ Wash

Larson, David A MD/PhD [RadRO] - **Spec Exp:** Neuro-Oncology; Brain Tumors; Stereotactic Radiosurgery; **Hospital:** UCSF Med Ctr, Washington Hosp; **Address:** UCSF Med Ctr, Dept Rad Onc, 505 Parnassus Ave, rm L-75, San Francisco, CA 94143-0226; **Phone:** 415-353-8900; **Board Cert:** Therapeutic Radiology 1986; **Med School:** Univ Miami Sch Med 1981; **Resid:** Radiation Therapy, Joint Ctr RadTh 1985; **Fac Appt:** Prof RadRO, UCSF

Le, Quynh-Thu Xuan MD [RadRO] - **Spec Exp:** Head & Neck Cancer; Lung Cancer; Thoracic Cancers; Clinical Trials; **Hospital:** Stanford Univ Hosp & Clins; **Address:** Stanford Univ, Dept Rad Oncology, 875 Blake Wilbur Drive, Clinic D, Stanford, CA 94305; **Phone:** 650-723-6171; **Board Cert:** Radiation Oncology 2009; **Med School:** UCSF 1993; **Resid:** Radiation Oncology, UCSF Med Ctr 1997; **Fac Appt:** Prof RadRO, Stanford Univ

Mundt III, Arno James MD [RadRO] - **Spec Exp:** Gynecologic Cancer; Intensity Modulated Radiotherapy (IMRT); Stereotactic Body Radiation Therapy; **Hospital:** UCSD Med Ctr; **Address:** UCSD Moores Cancer Center, 3855 Health Sciences Drive, MS 0843, La Jolla, CA 92093-0843; **Phone:** 858-822-6046; **Board Cert:** Radiation Oncology 1994; **Med School:** Univ Mich Med Sch 1987; **Resid:** Physical Medicine & Rehabilitation, George Washington Univ Hosp 1990; Radiation Oncology, Univ Chicago Hosps 1993; **Fellow:** Physical Medicine & Rehabilitation, Univ Chicago Hosps 1994; **Fac Appt:** Prof RadRO, UCSD

Park, Catherine C MD [RadRO] - **Spec Exp:** Breast Cancer; Lymphoma; **Hospital:** UCSF Med Ctr; **Address:** UCSF Helen Diller Comp Cancer Ctr, Department of Radiation Oncology, 1600 Divisadero St, Ste H1031, San Francisco, CA 94115; **Phone:** 415-353-7175; **Board Cert:** Radiation Oncology 2000; **Med School:** UCLA 1995; **Resid:** Radiation Oncology, Mass Genl Hosp 2000; **Fac Appt:** Assoc Prof RadRO, UCSF

Pezner, Richard D MD [RadRO] - **Spec Exp:** Sarcoma-Soft Tissue; Breast Cancer; Stereotactic Radiosurgery; **Hospital:** City of Hope Natl Med Ctr; **Address:** City of Hope Med Ctr-Div Radiation Onc, 1500 E Duarte Rd, Duarte, CA 91010-3000; **Phone:** 626-301-8247; **Board Cert:** Therapeutic Radiology 1979; **Med School:** Northwestern Univ 1975; **Resid:** Therapeutic Radiology, Oregon Health Sci Ctr 1979; **Fac Appt:** Clin Prof RadRO, UC Irvine

Quivey, Jeanne M MD [RadRO] - **Spec Exp:** Head & Neck Cancer; Breast Cancer; Eye Tumors/Cancer; Intensity Modulated Radiotherapy (IMRT); **Hospital:** UCSF Med Ctr; **Address:** Radiation Onc Dept, 1600 Divisadero St, Bsmt, San Francisco, CA 94143-1708; **Phone:** 415-353-7175; **Board Cert:** Therapeutic Radiology 1974; **Med School:** UCSF 1970; **Resid:** Radiation Therapy, UCSF Med Ctr 1974; **Fac Appt:** Prof RadRO, UCSF

Roach III, Mack MD [RadRO] - **Spec Exp:** Prostate Cancer; Genitourinary Cancer; Lung Cancer; **Hospital:** UCSF - Mt Zion Med Ctr, UCSF Med Ctr; **Address:** UCSF Radiation Oncology, 1600 Divisadero St Fl 3, San Francisco, CA 94143-1708; **Phone:** 415-353-9807; **Board Cert:** Internal Medicine 1984; Medical Oncology 1985; Radiation Oncology 1987; **Med School:** Stanford Univ 1979; **Resid:** Internal Medicine, Highland Genl Hosp 1984; Radiation Oncology, Stanford Univ Med Ctr 1987; **Fellow:** Medical Oncology, UCSF Med Ctr 1983; **Fac Appt:** Prof RadRO, UCSF

Rose, Christopher M MD [RadRO] - **Spec Exp:** Prostate Cancer; Breast Cancer; Intensity Modulated Radiotherapy (IMRT); **Hospital:** Providence St Joseph Med Ctr, Providence Tarzana Med Ctr; **Address:** Valley Radiotherapy Assocs Med Grp, 9229 Wilshire Blvd, Beverly Hills, CA 90210; **Phone:** 310-651-9292; **Board Cert:** Therapeutic Radiology 1979; **Med School:** Harvard Med Sch 1974; **Resid:** Internal Medicine, Beth Israel Deaconess 1976; Therapeutic Radiology, Joint Ctr Rad Therapy 1979; **Fellow:** Cancer Research, British Inst Cancer Rsch 1979; **Fac Appt:** Clin Prof RadRO, USC Sch Med

Rossi, Carl John MD [RadRO] - **Spec Exp:** Prostate Cancer; Proton Beam Therapy; **Hospital:** Scripps Green Hosp; **Address:** 10670 John J Hopkins Drive, San Diego, CA 92121; **Phone:** 858-554-4100; **Board Cert:** Radiation Oncology 1994; **Med School:** Loyola Univ-Stritch Sch Med 1988; **Resid:** Radiation Oncology, Loma Linda Univ Med Ctr 1992; **Fac Appt:** Asst Prof RadRO, Loma Linda Univ

Russell, Kenneth J MD [RadRO] - **Spec Exp:** Genitourinary Cancer; Prostate Cancer; Lymphoma; **Hospital:** Univ Wash Med Ctr; **Address:** Seattle Cancer Care Alliance, 825 Eastlake Ave E, Box 19023, MS G1-101, Seattle, WA 98109; **Phone:** 206-288-7318; **Board Cert:** Therapeutic Radiology 1984; **Med School:** Harvard Med Sch 1979; **Resid:** Radiation Oncology, Stanford Univ Med Ctr 1983; **Fellow:** Radiological Biology, Stanford Univ Med Ctr 1985; **Fac Appt:** Prof Rad, Univ Wash

Sandler, Howard M MD [RadRO] - **Spec Exp:** Prostate Cancer; Genitourinary Cancer; Brain Tumors; **Hospital:** Cedars-Sinai Med Ctr; **Address:** S Oschin Comprehensive Cancer Inst, Cedars-Sinai Med Ctr, 8700 Beverly Blvd, Ste AC1022, Los Angeles, CA 90048; **Phone:** 310-423-4234; **Board Cert:** Radiation Oncology 1989; **Med School:** Univ Conn 1985; **Resid:** Radiation Oncology, Hosp Univ Penn 1989

Schomberg, Paula J MD [RadRO] - **Spec Exp:** Brain Tumors; Pediatric Cancers; **Hospital:** Providence St. Joseph's Hosp; **Address:** 601 S Sherman St, Spokane, WA 99202; **Phone:** 509-228-1000; **Board Cert:** Therapeutic Radiology 1984; **Med School:** Med Coll Wisc 1979; **Resid:** Radiation Therapy, Mayo Clinic 1983

Seung, Steven K MD/PhD [RadRO] - **Spec Exp:** Stereotactic Radiosurgery; Brain Tumors; Esophageal Cancer; Lung Cancer; **Hospital:** Providence Portland Med Ctr; **Address:** 4805 NE Glisan St, Garden Level, Portland, OR 97213; **Phone:** 503-215-6029; **Board Cert:** Radiation Oncology 2010; **Med School:** Univ Chicago-Pritzker Sch Med 1994; **Resid:** Radiation Oncology, UCSF Med Ctr 1998

Streeter Jr, Oscar E MD [RadRO] - **Spec Exp:** Lung Cancer; Head & Neck Cancer; **Hospital:** San Joaquin Community Hosp, UC Davis Med Ctr; **Address:** AIS Cancer Center, 2620 Chester Ave, Bakersfield, CA 93301; **Phone:** 661-323-4673; **Board Cert:** Radiation Oncology 1989; **Med School:** Howard Univ 1982; **Resid:** Radiation Oncology, Howard Univ 1986; Radiation Oncology, USC Sch Med 1994; **Fac Appt:** Assoc Prof RadRO, USC Sch Med

Thomas Jr, Charles R MD [RadRO] - **Spec Exp:** Gastrointestinal Cancer; Esophageal Cancer; Colon & Rectal Cancer; **Hospital:** OR Hlth & Sci Univ; **Address:** 3181 SW Sam Jackson Park Rd, MC KPV4, Portland, OR 97239; **Phone:** 503-494-8756; **Board Cert:** Internal Medicine 1989; Radiation Oncology 2010; **Med School:** Univ IL Coll Med 1985; **Resid:** Internal Medicine, Baylor Coll Med 1988; Radiation Oncology, Univ Wash Med Ctr 1997; **Fellow:** Medical Oncology, Rush Univ Med Ctr 1999; **Fac Appt:** Prof RadRO, Oregon Hlth & Sci Univ

Tripuraneni, Prabhakar MD [RadRO] - **Spec Exp:** Prostate Cancer; Head & Neck Cancer; Lymphoma; **Hospital:** Scripps Green Hosp, Scripps Meml Hosp - La Jolla; **Address:** Scripps Clinic, 10670 John J Hopkins Drive, San Diego, CA 92121; **Phone:** 858-554-4100; **Board Cert:** Therapeutic Radiology 1983; **Med School:** India 1976; **Resid:** Radiation Oncology, Univ Alberta 1981; Radiation Oncology, UCSF Med Ctr 1983; **Fac Appt:** Clin Prof RadRO, UCSD

Wara, William M MD [RadRO] - **Spec Exp:** Brain & Spinal Cord Tumors; Sarcoma; Pediatric Cancers; **Hospital:** Kaiser Permanente S San Francisco Med Ctr; **Address:** Cancer Treatment Ctr, 220 Oyster Pt Blvd, South San Francisco, CA 94080; **Phone:** 650-827-6500; **Board Cert:** Therapeutic Radiology 1974; **Med School:** UC Irvine 1969; **Resid:** Therapeutic Radiology, UCSF Medical Ctr 1973; **Fac Appt:** Prof Emeritus RadRO, UCSF

Wong, Jeffrey Y C MD [RadRO] - **Spec Exp:** Radioimmunotherapy of Cancer; Prostate Cancer; Intensity Modulated Radiotherapy (IMRT); Bone Marrow Transplant; **Hospital:** City of Hope Natl Med Ctr; **Address:** City of Hope Med Ctr-Dept Radiation Onc, 1500 E Duarte Rd, Duarte, CA 91010-3012; **Phone:** 626-301-8247 x62969; **Board Cert:** Therapeutic Radiology 1985; **Med School:** Johns Hopkins Univ 1981; **Resid:** Radiation Oncology, UCSF Med Ctr 1985; **Fac Appt:** Prof RadRO

Mount Sinai

THE MOUNT SINAI MEDICAL CENTER
Radiology

One Gustave L. Levy Place
Fifth Avenue and 100th Street
New York, NY 10029-6574

Physician Referral: 1-800-MD-SINAI (637-4624)
www.mountsinai.org

The **DEPARTMENT OF RADIOLOGY** at Mount Sinai offers patients one of the world's most comprehensive and sophisticated arrays of diagnostic and interventional radiology services. The department uses filmless digital technology that spans high field magnetic resonance imaging (MRI), multi-slice computed tomography (CT), positron emission tomography CT (PET-CT), PET-MRI, single photon emission computed tomography CT (SPECT-CT), advanced ultrasound, conventional radiography, angiography, digital mammography, and state-of-the-art Picture Archiving Communication System (PACS) technology.

Comprehensive Diagnostic Services – Mount Sinai provides the entire range of diagnostic radiology services in a patient-friendly environment. Its nationally renowned radiologic physicians specialize in every area of disease diagnosis, as well as disease prevention and innovative therapeutic approaches. The combination of state-of-the-art imaging equipment with the finest imaging physicians makes Mount Sinai Radiology the place to go for all your imaging needs.

Early Detection Programs – We are committed to special screening approaches for early disease detection. We provide radiological screenings for colon, breast, and lung cancer and atherosclerosis. The early detection programs use a variety of imaging techniques, such as CT and MRI for atherosclerosis, CT for lung and colon cancer, PET for oncology, digital and 3D mammography, MRI, Ultrasound, and computer-aided diagnosis for breast cancer.

Minimally Invasive Procedures – Radiology at Mount Sinai has moved beyond diagnosis to the most sophisticated therapeutic interventions. Interventional radiologists at Mount Sinai perform biopsies, vascular therapies, and uterine artery embolization for fibroids-an alternative to hysterectomy-as well as treatments for aneurysms, atherosclerosis, and many types of cancer. In addition, advanced CT and MR angiography techniques are widely utilized to diagnose vascular diseases in a minimally invasive yet highly accurate manner.

DEVELOPING NEW DIAGNOSTIC TOOLS

Radiology at Mount Sinai is an active center of imaging research and development. Mount Sinai physicians and scientists developed a special form of MRI to diagnose heart disease and atherosclerosis noninvasively and thereby identify patients at greatest risk for stroke and heart attack. We actively collaborate with other disciplines to develop and refine imaging tools that will make prevention and diagnosis increasingly effective. That is the case, for example in neuroscience, where imaging innovations impact our understanding of neurodegenerative conditions, such as Parkinson's disease, multiple sclerosis, stroke, brain tumors, and various psychiatric disorders; cardiovascular disease, assess new therapies for aortic and cerebral artery aneurysms; lung and breast cancer screening; and liver disease, where radiologists, transplant surgeons, and hepatologists collaborate closely to develop optimal therapeutic strategies.

Oncology Imaging – Radiologists work closely with surgeons, oncologists, and other caregivers to optimize the diagnosis and treatment of patients with head and neck, liver, lung, breast, and gastrointestinal cancers. State-of-the-art CT, MRI, ultrasound, SPECT and PET CT are utilized to make the most accurate, least invasive and lowest dose diagnosis.

Penn Medicine

PENN RADIATION ONCOLOGY

Advancing Cancer Care

At Penn Medicine, the Department of Radiation Oncology is a national leader in clinical care, research, and education and is one of the largest and most respected clinical services in the region.

Excellence and Expertise

At Penn, patient care is backed by a nationally recognized research and teaching program. The department offers a wide range of services, including many that combine radiation therapy with chemotherapy and/or surgery.

Penn provides complete evaluation, treatment and follow-up care for patients whose cancer can be effectively treated with radiation and also sees patients with benign (non-cancerous) diseases that can be treated with radiation. In addition, Penn Radiation Oncology's advanced treatment options offer the possibility of retreatment when other radiation therapy treatments have failed. Understanding the emotional implications of cancer, support services are available for patients and their loved ones.

Imaging procedures for treatment planning include X-ray filming and fluoroscopy, and CT linkage with computerized dosimetry. Treatment options include Intensity-Modulated Radiation Therapy (IMRT), Image-Guided Radiation Therapy (IGRT), Conformal Radiation Therapy, CyberKnife®, Gamma Knife®, and Proton Therapy. Symptom management and access to innovative treatments, such as photodynamic therapy, further differentiates Penn Radiation Oncology from other radiation oncology centers.

Leaders in Research

Penn radiation oncologists are experts in cancer treatment and research, and have contributed many important advances in the field. The department conducts basic research to better understand tumor response to radiation and to increase that response, enabling the development of new treatment approaches. In its ongoing efforts to lead the advancement of proton therapy treatment, in 2012, Penn partnered to lead a 5-year study to better understand the efficacy of proton therapy for prostate cancer patients.

Penn Radiation Oncology also conducts a wide range of clinical trials involving the innovative use of radiation therapy in combination with other therapies to find better ways to treat patients with different types of cancer.

Penn Radiation Oncology Network

The Penn Radiation Oncology Network offers convenient locations throughout Southeastern Pennsylvania and New Jersey. At each facility, full-time, board-certified Penn radiation oncologists provide outstanding clinical and patient-focused care. Patients can be evaluated for proton therapy, CyberKnife and Gamma Knife at all network sites.

The Roberts Proton Therapy Center

The Roberts Proton Therapy Center is the world's largest proton therapy center and one of only 10 currently in the United States. It offers the unique ability to fully integrate conventional radiation treatment with proton radiation for certain types of cancer.

Because of its proximity to the Abramson Cancer Center, all cancer diagnostic and treatment services are available in one location. This allows patients to easily navigate from one department to the next, ensuring exceptional and timely care.

Stereotactic Radiosurgery at Pennsylvania Hospital

Pennsylvania Hospital, located in the Society Hill section of Philadelphia, offers both CyberKnife® and Gamma Knife®.

These non-invasive radiosurgery therapy treatment options provide extremely accurate, high-dose radiation for many types of tumors. CyberKnife treats tumors throughout the body including spine, lung, liver, pancreas and prostate. Gamma Knife provides powerful treatment for brain and head and neck tumors.

For more information or to schedule an appointment, call 800.789.PENN (7366) or visit PennMedicine.org/radiation-oncology.

Hospital of the University of Pennsylvania | Penn Presbyterian Medical Center | Pennsylvania Hospital | The Chester County Hospital

800.789.PENN | PennMedicine.org

Radiology

A radiologist utilizes radiologic methodologies to diagnose and treat disease. Physicians practicing in the field of radiology most often specialize in radiology, diagnostic radiology, radiation oncology or radiological physics.

Diagnostic Radiology: A radiologist who utilizes X-ray, radionuclides, ultrasound and electromagnetic radiation to diagnose and treat disease.

Training Required: Four years

Radiation Oncology: A radiologist who deals with the therapeutic applications of radiant energy and its modifiers and the study and management of disease, especially malignant tumors.

Certification in one of the following subspecialties requires additional training and examination.

Neuroradiology: A radiologist who diagnoses and treats diseases utilizing imaging procedures as they relate to the brain, spine and spinal cord, head, neck and organs of special sense in adults and children.

Pediatric Radiology: A radiologist who is proficient in all forms of diagnostic imaging as it pertains to the treatment of diseases in the newborn, infant, child and adolescent. This specialist has knowledge of both imaging and interventional procedures related to the care and management of diseases of children. A pediatric radiologist must be highly knowledgeable of all organ systems as they relate to growth and development, congenital malformations, diseases peculiar to infants and children and diseases that begin in childhood but cause substantial residual impairment in adulthood.

Vascular and Interventional Radiology: A radiologist who diagnoses and treats diseases by various radiologic imaging modalities. These include fluoroscopy, digital radiography, computed tomography, sonography and magnetic resonance imaging.

Diagnostic Radiology

New England

Benson, Carol B MD [DR] - **Spec Exp:** Obstetric Ultrasound; Thyroid Ultrasound; Fetal Surgical Imaging; Gynecologic Imaging; **Hospital:** Brigham & Women's Hosp; **Address:** Brigham & Women's Hospital, Dept Radiology, 75 Francis St, Boston, MA 02115; **Phone:** 617-732-6280; **Board Cert:** Diagnostic Radiology 1984; **Med School:** Univ Pennsylvania 1980; **Resid:** Diagnostic Radiology, NY Presby/Weill Cornell Med Ctr 1984; **Fellow:** Ultrasound, Brigham & Womens Hosp 1985; **Fac Appt:** Prof Rad, Harvard Med Sch

Black, William C MD [DR] - **Spec Exp:** Chest Radiology; Lung Cancer; CT Chest Scan; **Hospital:** Dartmouth - Hitchcock Med Ctr; **Address:** Dartmouth Hitchcock Med Ctr, Dept Radiology, 1 Medical Center Drive, Lebanon, NH 03756; **Phone:** 603-650-7443; **Board Cert:** Diagnostic Radiology 1983; **Med School:** Med Coll VA 1979; **Resid:** Diagnostic Radiology, Univ Virginia Hosp 1983; **Fellow:** Ultrasound/CT, Univ Virginia Hosp 1984; **Fac Appt:** Prof Rad, Dartmouth Med Sch

Doubilet, Peter M MD [DR] - **Spec Exp:** Ultrasound; Obstetric Ultrasound; **Hospital:** Brigham & Women's Hosp; **Address:** Brigham & Women's Hosp, Dept Radiology, 75 Francis St, Boston, MA 02115; **Phone:** 617-732-6757; **Board Cert:** Diagnostic Radiology 1981; **Med School:** Columbia P&S 1977; **Resid:** Diagnostic Radiology, Brigham & Women's Hosp 1981; **Fac Appt:** Prof Rad, Harvard Med Sch

Kruskal, Jonathan MD/PhD [DR] - **Spec Exp:** Liver Tumors; Abdominal Imaging; **Hospital:** Beth Israel Deaconess Med Ctr - Boston; **Address:** Beth Israel Deaconess Med Ctr-Radiology, One Deaconess Rd, W CC 302, Boston, MA 02215; **Phone:** 617-754-2519; **Board Cert:** Diagnostic Radiology 1994; **Med School:** South Africa 1982; **Resid:** Diagnostic Radiology, Beth Israel Deaconess Med Ctr 1994; **Fac Appt:** Prof Rad, Harvard Med Sch

Newman, Joel S MD [DR] - **Spec Exp:** Musculoskeletal Imaging; **Hospital:** New England Bapt Hosp (page 63); **Address:** New England Baptist Hosp, Dept Radiology, 125 Parker Hill Ave, Converse 2, Boston, MA 02120; **Phone:** 617-754-6687; **Board Cert:** Diagnostic Radiology 1992; **Med School:** Northwestern Univ-Feinberg Sch Med 1987; **Resid:** Diagnostic Radiology, Tufts Med Ctr 1992; **Fellow:** Cross Sectional Imaging, Michigan Hosp & Med Ctr 1993; Musculoskeletal Imaging, Michigan Hosp & Med Ctr 1994; **Fac Appt:** Clin Prof Rad, Tufts Univ

Palmer, William E MD [DR] - **Spec Exp:** Musculoskeletal Imaging; Sports Medicine Radiology; Pain Management; **Hospital:** Mass Genl Hosp; **Address:** Mass General Hospital, 55 Fruit St, YAW Bldg, rm 6033, Boston, MA 02114; **Phone:** 617-726-7717; **Board Cert:** Internal Medicine 1987; Diagnostic Radiology 1991; **Med School:** Yale Univ 1984; **Resid:** Internal Medicine, Hosp Univ Penn 1987; Diagnostic Radiology, Mass Genl Hosp 1991; **Fac Appt:** Asst Prof Rad, Harvard Med Sch

Weinreb, Jeffrey C MD [DR] - **Spec Exp:** MRI; Breast Cancer; Abdominal Imaging; CT Body Scan; **Hospital:** Yale-New Haven Hosp; **Address:** Yale, Diagnostic Radiology Dept, 333 Cedar St, rm MRC165, Box 208042, New Haven, CT 06520-8042; **Phone:** 203-785-5913; **Board Cert:** Diagnostic Radiology 1983; **Med School:** Mount Sinai Sch Med 1978; **Resid:** Diagnostic Radiology, Long Island Jewish Med Ctr 1982; **Fellow:** Ultrasound/CT, Hosp Univ Penn 1983; **Fac Appt:** Prof Rad, Yale Univ

Mid Atlantic

Adler, Ronald S MD/PhD [DR] - **Spec Exp:** Musculoskeletal Imaging; Ultrasound; Power Doppler Imaging; **Hospital:** NYU Langone Med Ctr (page 68), NYU Hosp For Joint Dis; **Address:** Ctr for Musculoskeletal Care-Radiology Dept, 333 E 38th St Fl 6, New York, NY 10016; **Phone:** 646-501-7440; **Board Cert:** Diagnostic Radiology 1988; **Med School:** Wayne State Univ 1984; **Resid:** Diagnostic Radiology, Univ Mich Med Ctr 1988; **Fellow:** Ultrasound/CT/MRI, Univ Mich Med Ctr 1989; **Fac Appt:** Prof Rad, Cornell Univ-Weill Med Coll

Austin, John H. M. MD [DR] - **Spec Exp:** Lung Cancer; Thoracic Radiology; **Hospital:** NY-Presby/Columbia Univ Med Ctr, NY (page 65); **Address:** 177 Fort Washington Ave, Milstein Hosp Bldg 3-202C, New York, NY 10032-3784; **Phone:** 212-305-2639; **Board Cert:** Diagnostic Radiology 1970; **Med School:** Yale Univ 1965; **Resid:** Diagnostic Radiology, UCSF Med Ctr 1968; **Fellow:** Diagnostic Radiology, UCSF Med Ctr 1970; **Fac Appt:** Prof Emeritus Rad, Columbia P&S

Bluemke, David MD/PhD [DR] - **Spec Exp:** Cardiac Imaging; MRI; **Hospital:** Natl Inst of Hlth - Clin Ctr; **Address:** NIH Clin Ctr, Radiology Dept, 10 Center Drive Bldg 10 - Ste 1C351, Betheseda, MD 20892; **Phone:** 301-402-1854; **Board Cert:** Diagnostic Radiology 1993; **Med School:** Univ Chicago-Pritzker Sch Med 1989; **Resid:** Diagnostic Radiology, Johns Hopkins Hosp 1993; **Fellow:** Diagnostic Imaging, Johns Hopkins Hosp 1994; **Fac Appt:** Prof Rad, Johns Hopkins Univ

Brem, Rachel F MD [DR] - **Spec Exp:** Breast Imaging; Breast Cancer; **Hospital:** G Washington Univ Hosp; **Address:** GWU Med Faculty Assocs, Mammography Clin, 2150 Pennsylvania Ave NW, DC Level, Washington, DC 20037; **Phone:** 202-741-3036; **Board Cert:** Diagnostic Radiology 1990; **Med School:** Columbia P&S 1984; **Resid:** Diagnostic Radiology, Johns Hopkins Hosp 1989; **Fellow:** Mammography, Johns Hopkins Hosp 1990; **Fac Appt:** Prof Rad, Geo Wash Univ

Cohen, Burton A MD [DR] - **Spec Exp:** CT Scan; MRI; PET Imaging; **Hospital:** Mt Sinai Med Ctr (page 62); **Address:** New York Medical Imaging Associates, 165 E 84th St, New York, NY 10028; **Phone:** 212-535-9770; **Board Cert:** Diagnostic Radiology 1979; **Med School:** NY Med Coll 1975; **Resid:** Diagnostic Radiology, Mt Sinai Hosp 1979; **Fac Appt:** Assoc Clin Prof Rad, Mount Sinai Sch Med

Coleman, Beverly G MD [DR] - **Spec Exp:** Abdominal Imaging; Ultrasound; **Hospital:** Hosp Univ Penn - UPHS (page 69); **Address:** Univ Penn Radiology, Ground Dulles, 3400 Spruce St, Philadelphia, PA 19104; **Phone:** 215-662-3046; **Board Cert:** Diagnostic Radiology 1978; **Med School:** Harvard Med Sch 1974; **Resid:** Diagnostic Radiology, Univ Penn Hosp 1975; Diagnostic Radiology, Univ Michigan Med Ctr 1978; **Fellow:** Ultrasound, Univ Penn Hosp 1979; **Fac Appt:** Prof Rad, Univ Pennsylvania

Conant, Emily F MD [DR] - **Spec Exp:** Breast Cancer; Breast Imaging; Interventional Radiology; **Hospital:** Hosp Univ Penn - UPHS (page 69); **Address:** Univ Penn- Radiology, 3400 Spruce St, 1 Silverstein, Philadelphia, PA 19104; **Phone:** 215-662-4032; **Board Cert:** Diagnostic Radiology 1989; **Med School:** Univ Pennsylvania 1984; **Resid:** Diagnostic Radiology, Hosp Univ Penn 1988; **Fellow:** Breast Imaging, Hosp Univ Penn 1989; **Fac Appt:** Prof Rad, Univ Pennsylvania

Copit, Debra Somers MD [DR] - **Spec Exp:** Mammography; Breast Imaging; Breast Cancer; **Hospital:** Einstein Med Ctr; **Address:** Marion L Salzman Women's Ctr, Einstein Medical Ctr, 5501 Old York Rd, Philadelphia, PA 19141; **Phone:** 215-254-2700; **Board Cert:** Diagnostic Radiology 1994; **Med School:** Jefferson Med Coll 1989; **Resid:** Diagnostic Radiology, Albert Einstein Med Ctr 1993; Diagnostic Radiology, Univ of Texas SW Med Ctr 1994; **Fellow:** Breast Imaging, Baylor Koman Breast Ctr 1995; **Fac Appt:** Asst Prof Rad, Jefferson Med Coll

Dalinka, Murray MD [DR] - **Spec Exp:** Bone Disorders-Metabolic; Musculoskeletal Imaging; MRI; **Hospital:** Hosp Univ Penn - UPHS (page 69); **Address:** Univ Penn Radiology, Ground Dulles, 3400 Spruce St, Philadelphia, PA 19104; **Phone:** 215-662-3019; **Board Cert:** Diagnostic Radiology 1969; **Med School:** Univ Mich Med Sch 1964; **Resid:** Diagnostic Radiology, Montefiore Med Ctr 1968; **Fac Appt:** Prof Emeritus Rad, Univ Pennsylvania

Dershaw, D David MD [DR] - **Spec Exp:** Breast Imaging; Breast Cancer; Mammography; **Hospital:** Meml Sloan-Kettering Canc Ctr; **Address:** 300 E 66th St, rm 727, New York, NY 10065; **Phone:** 646-888-4505; **Board Cert:** Diagnostic Radiology 1978; Radiology 1974; **Med School:** Jefferson Med Coll 1974; **Resid:** Diagnostic Radiology, New York Hosp 1978; **Fellow:** Ultrasound, Thos Jefferson Univ Hosp 1979; **Fac Appt:** Prof Rad, Cornell Univ-Weill Med Coll

Edelstein, Barbara A MD [DR] - **Spec Exp:** Breast Cancer; Women's Imaging; **Address:** 1045 Park Ave, New York, NY 10028; **Phone:** 212-860-7700; **Board Cert:** Diagnostic Radiology 1983; **Med School:** NY Med Coll 1977; **Resid:** Diagnostic Radiology, Montefiore Hosp 1982

Evers, Kathryn A MD [DR] - **Spec Exp:** Breast Cancer; Mammography; MRI-Breast; **Hospital:** Fox Chase Cancer Ctr (page 57); **Address:** Fox Chase Cancer Ctr, Diagnostic Imaging, 333 Cottman Ave, Philadelphia, PA 19111; **Phone:** 215-728-2646; **Board Cert:** Diagnostic Radiology 1980; **Med School:** NYU Sch Med 1975; **Resid:** Diagnostic Radiology, Hosp Univ Penn 1980; **Fellow:** Diagnostic Radiology, Hosp Univ Penn 1981; **Fac Appt:** Assoc Clin Prof Rad, Temple Univ

Fishman, Elliot Keith MD [DR] - **Spec Exp:** CT Body Scan; Abdominal Imaging; Cardiac Imaging; **Hospital:** Johns Hopkins Hosp (page 59); **Address:** Johns Hopkins, Radiology Dept, 601 N Caroline St, JHOC 3254, Baltimore, MD 21287-0006; **Phone:** 410-955-5173; **Board Cert:** Diagnostic Radiology 1981; **Med School:** Univ MD Sch Med 1977; **Resid:** Diagnostic Radiology, Sinai Hosp 1980; **Fellow:** Computerized Tomography, Johns Hopkins Hosp 1981; **Fac Appt:** Prof Rad, Johns Hopkins Univ

Fuhrman, Carl R MD [DR] - **Spec Exp:** Thoracic Imaging; **Hospital:** UPMC Presby, Pittsburgh; **Address:** UPMC-Dept Radiology, 200 Lothrop St, rm 2825, Presbyterian South Tower, Pittsburgh, PA 15213; **Phone:** 412-647-7288; **Board Cert:** Diagnostic Radiology 1983; **Med School:** Univ Pittsburgh 1979; **Resid:** Diagnostic Radiology, Presby Univ Hosp 1983; **Fac Appt:** Prof Rad, Univ Pittsburgh

Gefter, Warren B MD [DR] - **Spec Exp:** Thoracic Imaging; **Hospital:** Hosp Univ Penn - UPHS (page 69); **Address:** Univ Penn Radiology, Ground Dulles, 3400 Spruce St, Philadelphia, PA 19104; **Phone:** 215-662-6724; **Board Cert:** Diagnostic Radiology 1978; **Med School:** Univ Pennsylvania 1974; **Resid:** Diagnostic Radiology, Hosp Univ Penn 1978; **Fac Appt:** Prof Rad, Univ Pennsylvania

Henschke, Claudia L MD/PhD [DR] - **Spec Exp:** Lung Cancer; Lung Disease; Thoracic Radiology; **Hospital:** Mt Sinai Med Ctr (page 62); **Address:** Mt Sinai Med Ctr, Radiology Dept, 1 Gustave Levy Pl, Box 1234, New York, NY 10029; **Phone:** 212-241-2420; **Board Cert:** Diagnostic Radiology 1981; **Med School:** Howard Univ 1977; **Resid:** Diagnostic Radiology, Brigham & Womens Hosp 1982; **Fac Appt:** Prof Rad, Mount Sinai Sch Med

Holliday, Roy A MD [DR] - **Spec Exp:** Head & Neck Imaging; **Hospital:** New York Eye & Ear Infirm (page 64), Beth Israel Med Ctr - Petrie Div (page 56); **Address:** New York Eye & Ear Infirmary, Dept Radiology, 310 E 14th St, North Bldg - Ground Fl, New York, NY 10003; **Phone:** 212-979-4397; **Board Cert:** Diagnostic Radiology 1986; **Med School:** NYU Sch Med 1982; **Resid:** Diagnostic Radiology, NYU Med Ctr 1986; **Fellow:** Neuroradiology, NYU Med Ctr 1987; **Fac Appt:** Prof Rad, Albert Einstein Coll Med

Hricak, Hedvig MD/PhD [DR] - **Spec Exp:** Prostate Cancer-MR Spectroscopy (MRSI); Breast Imaging; Breast Cancer; Gynecologic Cancer; **Hospital:** Meml Sloan-Kettering Canc Ctr; **Address:** 1275 York Ave, Ste C278, New York, NY 10065; **Phone:** 800-525-2225; **Board Cert:** Diagnostic Radiology 1978; **Med School:** Yugoslavia 1970; **Resid:** Diagnostic Radiology, St Joseph Mercy Hosp 1977; **Fellow:** Ultrasound/CT, Henry Ford Hosp 1978; **Fac Appt:** Prof Rad, Cornell Univ-Weill Med Coll

Jaramillo, Diego MD [DR] - **Spec Exp:** Pediatric Radiology; **Hospital:** Chldns Hosp of Philadelphia; **Address:** CHOP-Radiology Dept, 34th & Civic Ctr Blvd Fl 3 - rm 3NW-17, Philadelphia, PA 19104; **Phone:** 267-425-7110; **Board Cert:** Diagnostic Radiology 1987; Pediatric Radiology 2005; **Med School:** Colombia 1981; **Resid:** Diagnostic Radiology, Univ Texas 1987; **Fellow:** Pediatric Radiology, Children's Hosp 1989; **Fac Appt:** Prof Rad, Univ Pennsylvania

Kanal, Emanuel MD [DR] - **Spec Exp:** Neuroradiology; MRI; **Hospital:** UPMC Presby, Pittsburgh; **Address:** Univ Pittsburgh Med Ctr, Dept Radiology, Presbyterian South Tower, rm 4776, Pittsburgh, PA 15213-2582; **Phone:** 412-647-7288; **Board Cert:** Diagnostic Radiology 1985; Neuroradiology 2009; **Med School:** Univ Pittsburgh 1981; **Resid:** Diagnostic Radiology, Univ Pittsburgh Med Ctr 1985; **Fellow:** Magnetic Resonance Imaging, Pittsburgh NMR Inst 1986; Neurological Radiology, Univ Pittsburgh Med Ctr 1993; **Fac Appt:** Prof Rad, Univ Pittsburgh

Kurtz, Alfred B MD [DR] - **Spec Exp:** Ultrasound; Obstetric Ultrasound; **Hospital:** Thomas Jefferson Univ Hosp; **Address:** 132 S 10th St, Main Bldg - Ste 763C, Philadelphia, PA 19107; **Phone:** 215-955-6226; **Board Cert:** Diagnostic Radiology 1977; **Med School:** Stanford Univ 1972; **Resid:** Diagnostic Radiology, Montefiore Med Ctr 1977; **Fellow:** Ultrasound/CT, Thomas Jefferson Univ Hosp 1978; **Fac Appt:** Prof Rad, Jefferson Med Coll

Levy, Angela D MD [DR] - **Spec Exp:** Gastrointestinal Imaging; Abdominal Imaging; **Hospital:** MedStar Georgetown Univ Hosp; **Address:** Georgetown University Hospital, 3800 Reservoir Rd NW, CCC Bldg Fl Ground, Washington, DC 20007; **Phone:** 202-444-3380; **Board Cert:** Diagnostic Radiology 1993; **Med School:** Uniformed Srvs Univ, Bethesda 1988; **Resid:** Diagnostic Radiology, Walter Reed Army Hosp 1993; **Fac Appt:** Prof Rad, Georgetown Univ

Megibow, Alec J MD [DR] - **Spec Exp:** Abdominal Imaging; Gastrointestinal Imaging; CT Body Scan; **Hospital:** NYU Langone Med Ctr (page 68), Bellevue Hosp Ctr; **Address:** 550 1st Ave, HHC 232, New York, NY 10016; **Phone:** 212-263-5222; **Board Cert:** Diagnostic Radiology 1978; **Med School:** SUNY Upstate Med Univ 1974; **Resid:** Diagnostic Radiology, Bellevue/NYU Langone Med Ctr 1978; **Fellow:** Abdominal Imaging, NYU Langone Med Ctr 1978; **Fac Appt:** Prof Rad, NYU Sch Med

Mirvis, Stuart E MD [DR] - **Spec Exp:** Trauma Radiology; MRI Angiography; Interventional Radiology; **Hospital:** Univ of MD Med Ctr; **Address:** Univ MD Med Ctr, Radiology Dept, 22 S Greene St, Baltimore, MD 21201; **Phone:** 410-328-8845; **Board Cert:** Diagnostic Radiology 1984; **Med School:** Johns Hopkins Univ 1979; **Resid:** Diagnostic Radiology, Univ MD Med Ctr 1984; **Fellow:** Trauma Radiology, Univ MD Med Ctr 1985; **Fac Appt:** Prof Rad, Univ MD Sch Med

Mitnick, Julie S MD [DR] - **Spec Exp:** Mammography; Breast Cancer; **Address:** Murray Hill Radiology & Mammography, 650 First Ave Fl 2, New York, NY 10016; **Phone:** 212-686-4440; **Board Cert:** Diagnostic Radiology 1977; **Med School:** NYU Sch Med 1972; **Resid:** Diagnostic Radiology, NYU Med Ctr 1977; **Fellow:** Pediatric Radiology, NYU Med Ctr 1978; **Fac Appt:** Assoc Clin Prof Rad, NYU Sch Med

Mountz, James M MD/PhD [DR] - **Spec Exp:** Neurological Imaging; Brain Imaging; **Hospital:** UPMC Presby, Pittsburgh; **Address:** UPMC Hlth Sys, Presby Univ Hosp, 200 Lothrop St, PET Facility, rm B932, Pittsburgh, PA 15213; **Phone:** 412-647-0104; **Board Cert:** Diagnostic Radiology 1985; Nuclear Medicine 1986; **Med School:** Case West Res Univ 1981; **Resid:** Diagnostic Radiology, Univ Michigan Hosps 1985; **Fellow:** Nuclear Medicine, Univ Michigan Hosps 1986; **Fac Appt:** Prof Rad, Univ Pittsburgh

Panicek, David M MD [DR] - **Spec Exp:** Bone Cancer; Soft Tissue Tumors; Musculoskeletal Tumors; **Hospital:** Meml Sloan-Kettering Canc Ctr; **Address:** Meml Sloan Kettering Cancer Ctr, Dept of Radiology, 1276 York Ave, Ste C276G, New York, NY 10065; **Phone:** 800-525-2225; **Board Cert:** Diagnostic Radiology 1984; **Med School:** Cornell Univ-Weill Med Coll 1980; **Resid:** Diagnostic Radiology, NY Hosp-Cornell Med Ctr 1984; **Fac Appt:** Prof Rad, Cornell Univ-Weill Med Coll

Parsons, Rosaleen B MD [DR] - **Spec Exp:** CT Body Scan; Genitourinary Cancer; Genitourinary Radiology; **Hospital:** Fox Chase Cancer Ctr (page 57); **Address:** Fox Chase Cancer Ctr, Diagnostic Imaging Dept, 333 Cottman Ave, Philadelphia, PA 19111; **Phone:** 215-728-3024; **Board Cert:** Diagnostic Radiology 1991; **Med School:** Med Coll PA Hahnemann 1986; **Resid:** Diagnostic Radiology, Med Coll Penn Affil Hosp 1991; **Fac Appt:** Prof Rad, Med Coll PA

Pavlov, Helene MD [DR] - **Spec Exp:** Sports Medicine Radiology; Musculoskeletal Imaging; Orthopaedic Imaging; **Hospital:** Hosp For Special Surgery (page 58), NY-Presby/Weill Cornell Med Ctr, NY (page 65); **Address:** Hosp for Special Surgery, 535 E 70th St Fl 3, New York, NY 10021-4892; **Phone:** 212-606-1132; **Board Cert:** Diagnostic Radiology 1976; **Med School:** Temple Univ 1972; **Resid:** Diagnostic Radiology, Germantown Hosp 1976; **Fellow:** Musculoskeletal Imaging, Hosp For Special Surg 1977; **Fac Appt:** Prof Rad, Cornell Univ-Weill Med Coll

Potter, Hollis G MD [DR] - **Spec Exp:** Musculoskeletal Imaging; Cartilage Damage; Arthroplasty Imaging; **Hospital:** Hosp For Special Surgery (page 58); **Address:** Hosp for Special Surgery, MRI-basement, 535 E 70th St, Ste MRI, New York, NY 10021-4892; **Phone:** 212-606-1023; **Board Cert:** Diagnostic Radiology 1990; **Med School:** NY Med Coll 1985; **Resid:** Diagnostic Radiology, N Shore Univ Hosp 1990; **Fellow:** Diagnostic Radiology, Hosp for Special Surgery 1991; **Fac Appt:** Prof Rad, Cornell Univ-Weill Med Coll

Prince, Martin R MD/PhD [DR] - **Spec Exp:** MRI Angiography; Abdominal Imaging; **Hospital:** NY-Presby/Weill Cornell Med Ctr, NY (page 65), NY-Presby/Columbia Univ Med Ctr, NY (page 65); **Address:** 416 E 55th St, New York, NY 10022; **Phone:** 212-746-6880; **Board Cert:** Diagnostic Radiology 1993; **Med School:** Harvard Med Sch 1985; **Resid:** Radiology, Mass Genl Hosp 1988; **Fellow:** Magnetic Resonance Imaging, Mass Genl Hosp 1989; Angiography, Mass Genl Hosp 1993; **Fac Appt:** Prof Rad, Cornell Univ-Weill Med Coll

Rao, Vijay M MD [DR] - **Spec Exp:** Head & Neck Tumors Imaging; TMJ Imaging; Ear Nose & Throat Imaging; **Hospital:** Thomas Jefferson Univ Hosp; **Address:** Jefferson Univ, Dept Radiology, 132 S 10th St, Main Bldg, Ste 1087, Philadelphia, PA 19107-4824; **Phone:** 215-955-7264; **Board Cert:** Diagnostic Radiology 1978; **Med School:** India 1973; **Resid:** Diagnostic Radiology, Thomas Jefferson Univ Hosp 1978; **Fac Appt:** Prof Rad, Thomas Jefferson Univ

Reinus, William R MD [DR] - **Spec Exp:** Musculoskeletal Imaging; MRI; **Hospital:** Temple Univ Hosp, Jeanes Hosp; **Address:** Radiology Dept, 3401 N Broad St, Philadelphia, PA 19140; **Phone:** 215-707-9745; **Board Cert:** Diagnostic Radiology 1983; **Med School:** NYU Sch Med 1979; **Resid:** Radiology, Mallinkradt Inst Rad 1983; **Fellow:** Musculoskeletal Imaging, Mallinkradt Inst Rad 1984; **Fac Appt:** Prof Rad, Temple Univ

Roth, Susan Orel MD [DR] - **Spec Exp:** Breast Imaging; Breast Cancer; **Hospital:** Hosp Univ Penn - UPHS (page 69); **Address:** Penn Radiology, 3400 Spruce St, 1 Silverstein, Philadelphia, PA 19104; **Phone:** 215-614-0124; **Board Cert:** Diagnostic Radiology 1989; **Med School:** Univ Pennsylvania 1984; **Resid:** Diagnostic Radiology, Johns Hopkins Hosp 1989; **Fac Appt:** Prof Rad, Univ Pennsylvania

Schwartz, Lawrence H MD [DR] - **Spec Exp:** Prostate Cancer; MRI; **Hospital:** NY-Presby/Columbia Univ Med Ctr, NY (page 65); **Address:** 180 Ft Washington Ave, Harkness Pav, rm 320, New York, NY 10032; **Phone:** 212-305-8994; **Board Cert:** Diagnostic Radiology 1991; **Med School:** Boston Univ 1986; **Resid:** Diagnostic Radiology, NY-Presby/Weill Cornell Med Ctr 1991; **Fellow:** Ultrasound/CT/MRI, Brigham & Women's Hosp 1991; **Fac Appt:** Prof Rad, Columbia P&S

Teal, James S MD [DR] - **Spec Exp:** Interventional Radiology; Neuroradiology; **Hospital:** Howard Univ Hosp; **Address:** 2041 Georgia Ave NW, Washington, DC 20060; **Phone:** 202-865-1571; **Board Cert:** Diagnostic Radiology 1970; **Med School:** Univ Tex Med Br, Galveston 1964; **Resid:** Diagnostic Radiology, Mt Zion Hosp 1969; **Fellow:** Neuroradiology, LAC-USC Med Ctr 1970; **Fac Appt:** Prof Rad, Howard Univ

White, Charles S MD [DR] - **Spec Exp:** Thoracic Imaging; Lung Cancer; Cardiac Imaging; **Hospital:** Univ of MD Med Ctr; **Address:** Univ MD Med Ctr, Radiology Dept, 22 S Greene St, Ste N2E23, Baltimore, MD 21201; **Phone:** 410-328-3477; **Board Cert:** Diagnostic Radiology 1991; Internal Medicine 1987; **Med School:** SUNY Buffalo 1984; **Resid:** Internal Medicine, NY-Presby/Columbia Univ Med Ctr 1987; Diagnostic Radiology, NY-Presby/Columbia Univ Med Ctr 1991; **Fac Appt:** Prof, Univ MD Sch Med

Yankelevitz, David F MD [DR] - **Spec Exp:** Lung Cancer; Thoracic Radiology; **Hospital:** Mt Sinai Med Ctr (page 62); **Address:** Mt Sinai Med Ctr, Radiology Dept, 1 Gustave Levy Pl, Box 1234, New York, NY 10029; **Phone:** 212-241-2420; **Board Cert:** Diagnostic Radiology 1987; Nuclear Medicine 1987; **Med School:** SUNY Hlth Sci Ctr 1981; **Resid:** Diagnostic Radiology, Long Island Coll Hosp 1984; Nuclear Medicine, NY-Cornell Med Ctr 1986; **Fellow:** Diagnostic Radiology, NY-Cornell Med Ctr 1987; **Fac Appt:** Prof Rad, Cornell Univ-Weill Med Coll

Yoon, Sydney S MD [DR] - **Spec Exp:** MRI; CT Scan; Neuroradiology; Interventional Radiology; **Hospital:** South Nassau Comm Hosp; **Address:** South Nassau Comm Hosp, Dept Radiology, 1 Healthy Way, Oceanside, NY 11572; **Phone:** 516-632-4660; **Board Cert:** Internal Medicine 1989; Diagnostic Radiology 1993; Vascular & Interventional Radiology 2011; Neuroradiology 2006; **Med School:** Univ Chicago-Pritzker Sch Med 1986; **Resid:** Internal Medicine, Johns Hopkins Hosp 1989; Diagnostic Radiology, UCLA Ronald Reagan Med Ctr 1993; **Fellow:** Neuroradiology, NY-Presby/Columbia Univ Med Ctr 1995; Vascular & Interventional Radiology, UCLA Ronald Reagan Med Ctr 1997

Zeman, Robert K MD [DR] - **Spec Exp:** Cardiovascular Imaging; Cardiac CT Angiography; **Hospital:** G Washington Univ Hosp; **Address:** GWU Hospital Diagnostic Radiology, 900 23rd St NW, Washington, DC 20037; **Phone:** 202-715-5154; **Board Cert:** Diagnostic Radiology 1980; **Med School:** Northwestern Univ 1976; **Resid:** Diagnostic Radiology, Yale-New Haven Hosp 1980; **Fellow:** Nuclear Medicine, Yale-New Haven Hosp 1980; **Fac Appt:** Prof Rad, Geo Wash Univ

Southeast

Abbitt, Patricia L MD [DR] - **Spec Exp:** Ultrasound; Interventional Radiology; Breast Imaging; Breast Cancer; **Hospital:** UF Hlth Shands Hosp; **Address:** UFHlth, Radiology Dept, 1600 SW Archer Rd, Box 100374, Gainesville, FL 32610; **Phone:** 352-265-0291; **Board Cert:** Diagnostic Radiology 1986; **Med School:** Tufts Univ 1981; **Resid:** Diagnostic Radiology, Univ VA Med Ctr 1986; **Fellow:** Breast Imaging, Univ VA Med Ctr 1987; **Fac Appt:** Prof Rad, Univ Fla Coll Med

Baker, Jay A MD [DR] - **Spec Exp:** Mammography; Breast Imaging; Breast Cancer; **Hospital:** Duke Univ Hosp; **Address:** Duke Univ Cancer Ctr, Breast Imaging, 2301 Erwin Rd, Durham, NC 27710; **Phone:** 919-684-7645; **Board Cert:** Diagnostic Radiology 1997; **Med School:** Duke Univ 1992; **Resid:** Diagnostic Radiology, Duke Univ Med Ctr 1997; **Fellow:** Breast Imaging, Duke Univ Med Ctr 1998

Berland, Lincoln L MD [DR] - **Spec Exp:** Abdominal Imaging; Gastrointestinal Imaging; **Hospital:** UAB Hosp; **Address:** UAB Hosp - Dept Radiology, 619 19th St S, N348 Jefferson Tower Bldg, Birmingham, AL 35249-6830; **Phone:** 205-996-4442; **Board Cert:** Diagnostic Radiology 1980; **Med School:** Washington Univ, St Louis 1975; **Resid:** Diagnostic Radiology, Med Coll Wisconsin Affil Hosps 1979; **Fellow:** Ultrasound/CT, Med Coll Wisconsin Affil Hosps 1980; **Fac Appt:** Prof Rad, UAB Sch Med

Cardenosa, Gilda MD [DR] - **Spec Exp:** Breast Imaging; **Hospital:** Med Coll of VA Hosp; **Address:** VCU Med Ctr Stony Pt, Dept Radiology, 9000 Stony Point Pkwy Fl 2, Richmond, VA 23235; **Phone:** 804-560-8906 x7862; **Board Cert:** Diagnostic Radiology 1989; **Med School:** Columbia P&S 1984; **Resid:** Diagnostic Radiology, Mass Genl Hosp 1989; **Fac Appt:** Prof Rad, Med Coll VA

Chiles, Caroline MD [DR] - **Spec Exp:** Thoracic Radiology; Lung Cancer; **Hospital:** Wake Forest Baptist Med Ctr; **Address:** Wake Forest Baptist Med Ctr, Medical Ctr Blvd, Winston-Salem, NC 27157; **Phone:** 336-716-4316; **Board Cert:** Diagnostic Radiology 1984; **Med School:** Duke Univ 1979; **Resid:** Diagnostic Radiology, Stanford Univ Hosp 1984; **Fellow:** Thoracic Radiology, Duke Univ Med Ctr 1985; **Fac Appt:** Clin Prof Rad, Wake Forest Univ

Cohen, Harris L MD [DR] - **Spec Exp:** Pediatric Radiology; Fetal Ultrasound/Obstetrical Imaging; Ultrasound; **Hospital:** Le Bonheur Chldns Med Ctr; **Address:** Le Bonheur Children's Hosp, Dept Radiology Fl Ground, 50 N Dunlap St, Memphis, TN 38103-2807; **Phone:** 901-287-7041; **Board Cert:** Diagnostic Radiology 1980; Pediatric Radiology 2005; **Med School:** SUNY Downstate 1976; **Resid:** Diagnostic Radiology, Univ Hosp 1980; **Fellow:** Pediatric Radiology, Chldns Hosp 1981; **Fac Appt:** Prof Rad, Univ Tenn Coll Med

Elster, Allen D MD [DR] - **Spec Exp:** MRI; Neurological Imaging; Brain Tumors; Spinal Tumor Imaging; **Hospital:** Wake Forest Baptist Med Ctr; **Address:** Wake Forest Baptist Med Ctr, Medical Center Blvd, Winston Salem, NC 27157-1088; **Phone:** 336-716-7095; **Board Cert:** Diagnostic Radiology 1987; Neuroradiology 2005; **Med School:** Baylor Coll Med 1980; **Resid:** Surgery, Mass Genl Hosp 1983; Diagnostic Radiology, Univ Texas Hlth Sci Ctr 1986; **Fellow:** Neuroradiology, Bowman Gray Sch Med 1987; **Fac Appt:** Prof Rad, Wake Forest Univ

Freimanis, Rita I MD [DR] - **Spec Exp:** Breast Cancer; Breast Imaging; **Hospital:** Wake Forest Baptist Med Ctr; **Address:** Wake Forest Baptist Med Ctr, One Medical Center Blvd, Winston-Salem, NC 27157; **Phone:** 336-713-4019; **Board Cert:** Diagnostic Radiology 1990; **Med School:** Bowman Gray 1985; **Resid:** Diagnostic Radiology, NC Bapt Hosp 1990; **Fac Appt:** Prof Rad, Wake Forest Univ

Mancuso, Anthony A MD [DR] - **Spec Exp:** Head & Neck Radiology; Neuroradiology; **Hospital:** UF Hlth Shands Hosp; **Address:** UF Hlth, Radiology Dept, 1600 SW Archer Rd, Ste G393, Gainesville, FL 32610; **Phone:** 352-265-0296; **Board Cert:** Diagnostic Radiology 1978; **Med School:** Univ Miami Sch Med 1973; **Resid:** Diagnostic Radiology, UCLA Med Ctr 1977; **Fellow:** Neuroradiology, UCLA Med Ctr 1978; **Fac Appt:** Prof Rad, Univ Fla Coll Med

Diagnostic Radiology

Partain, Clarence L MD/PhD [DR] - **Spec Exp:** MRI; Nuclear Radiology; Chest Radiology; **Hospital:** Vanderbilt Univ Med Ctr; **Address:** Vanderbilt Univ Med Ctr, Dept Radiology, 1161 21st Ave S, rm RR1223 MCN, Nashville, TN 37232-2675; **Phone:** 615-343-3588; **Board Cert:** Nuclear Medicine 1979; Diagnostic Radiology 1980; Nuclear Radiology 1981; **Med School:** Washington Univ, St Louis 1975; **Resid:** Diagnostic Radiology, Univ North Carolina 1979; Nuclear Medicine, Univ North Carolina 1979; **Fac Appt:** Prof Rad, Vanderbilt Univ

Patz Jr, Edward F MD [DR] - **Spec Exp:** Thoracic Radiology; PET Imaging; Lung Cancer; **Hospital:** Duke Univ Hosp; **Address:** Duke Univ Med Ctr, Dept Radiology, Box 3808, Durham, NC 27710; **Phone:** 919-684-2711; **Board Cert:** Diagnostic Radiology 1990; **Med School:** Univ MD Sch Med 1985; **Resid:** Diagnostic Radiology, Brigham & Womens Hosp 1990; **Fellow:** Thoracic Radiology, Brigham & Womens Hosp 1990; **Fac Appt:** Prof, Duke Univ

Rubin, Geoffrey D MD [DR] - **Spec Exp:** Cardiovascular Imaging; Cardiac Imaging; Thoracic Radiology; **Hospital:** Duke Univ Hosp; **Address:** Duke Clinical Research Institute, Box 17989, 2400 Pratt St, Durham, NC 27715; **Phone:** 919-684-7286; **Board Cert:** Diagnostic Radiology 1992; **Med School:** UCSD 1987; **Resid:** Diagnostic Radiology, Stanford Univ Med Ctr 1992; **Fellow:** Body Imaging, Stanford Univ Med Ctr 1993; **Fac Appt:** Prof Rad, Duke Univ

Midwest

Charboneau, J William MD [DR] - **Spec Exp:** Radiofrequency Tumor Ablation; Liver Cancer; Thyroid Cancer; **Hospital:** Mayo Med Ctr & Clin - Rochester; **Address:** Mayo Clinic Dept of Radiology, 200 First St SW, Rochester, MN 55905-0002; **Phone:** 507-284-2097; **Board Cert:** Diagnostic Radiology 1980; **Med School:** Univ Wisc 1976; **Resid:** Diagnostic Radiology, Mayo Clin 1980; **Fac Appt:** Prof, Mayo Med Sch

Dachman, Abraham H MD [DR] - **Spec Exp:** Gastrointestinal Imaging; Abdominal Imaging; Pancreatic Cancer; Colon Cancer; **Hospital:** Univ of Chicago Med; **Address:** Univ Chicago, Dept Radiology, 5841 S Maryland Ave, MC 2026, Chicago, IL 60637-1470; **Phone:** 773-702-6200; **Board Cert:** Diagnostic Radiology 1981; **Med School:** Albert Einstein Coll Med 1977; **Resid:** Diagnostic Radiology, Montefiore Med Ctr 1981; **Fellow:** Gastrointestinal Radiology, Armed Forces Inst of Pathology 1982; **Fac Appt:** Prof Rad, Univ Chicago-Pritzker Sch Med

Edelman, Robert R MD [DR] - **Spec Exp:** MRI; Cardiac CT Angiography; Cardiac MRI; **Hospital:** Evanston Hosp/NorthShore Univ Hlth Sys (page 67); **Address:** NorthShore Medical Group, Evanston Hosp, 2650 Ridge Ave Walgreen Bldg - rm G534, Evanston, IL 60201; **Phone:** 847-570-2553; **Board Cert:** Diagnostic Radiology 1984; **Med School:** Boston Univ 1980; **Resid:** Diagnostic Radiology, Beth Israel Deaconess Med Ctr 1984; **Fellow:** Radiology, Mass Genl Hosp 1985; **Fac Appt:** Prof Rad, Northwestern Univ

Fidler, Jeff L MD [DR] - **Spec Exp:** Gastrointestinal Imaging; CT Colonography; MRI; **Hospital:** Mayo Med Ctr & Clin - Rochester; **Address:** Mayo Clinic, Div Radiology, 200 First St SW, Rochester, MN 55905-0002; **Phone:** 507-284-2311; **Board Cert:** Diagnostic Radiology 1993; **Med School:** Univ Nebr Coll Med 1988; **Resid:** Radiology, Duke Univ Hosp 1993; **Fellow:** Abdominal Imaging, Duke Univ 1994; **Fac Appt:** Prof Rad, Mayo Med Sch

Flamm, Scott D MD [DR] - **Spec Exp:** Cardiac MRI; Cardiovascular Imaging; Congenital Heart Disease; **Hospital:** Cleveland Clin (page 55); **Address:** 9500 Euclid Ave, MS J1-4, Cleveland, OH 44195; **Phone:** 216-444-2740; **Board Cert:** Diagnostic Radiology 1993; **Med School:** Geo Wash Univ 1988; **Resid:** Diagnostic Radiology, UCLA Med Ctr 1993; **Fellow:** Cardiovascular Disease, UCSF Med Ctr 1994

Goodman, Lawrence R MD [DR] - **Spec Exp:** Thoracic Imaging; Pulmonary Embolism; Lung Disease; **Hospital:** Froedtert & Med Coll WI; **Address:** Froedtert & Med Coll - Dept Radiology, 9200 W Wisconsin Ave Fl 2, Milwaukee, WI 53226; **Phone:** 414-805-2060; **Board Cert:** Diagnostic Radiology 1973; **Med School:** SUNY Downstate 1968; **Resid:** Diagnostic Radiology, Boston Med Ctr 1972; **Fellow:** Thoracic Radiology, UCSF Med Ctr 1973; **Fac Appt:** Prof Rad, Med Coll Wisc

Helvie, Mark A MD [DR] - **Spec Exp:** Breast Imaging; Breast Cancer; Mammography; **Hospital:** Univ Michigan Med Ctr; **Address:** Univ MI Health Ctr, Taubman Center, 1500 E Medical Center Drive, rm 2910N, Ann Arbor, MI 48109-0326; **Phone:** 734-936-4367; **Board Cert:** Internal Medicine 1983; Diagnostic Radiology 1986; **Med School:** Univ NC Sch Med 1980; **Resid:** Internal Medicine, Univ Michigan Hosps 1983; Diagnostic Radiology, Univ Michigan Hosps 1986; **Fellow:** Breast Imaging, Univ Michigan Hosps 1987; **Fac Appt:** Prof Rad, Univ Mich Med Sch

Jackson, Valerie P MD [DR] - **Spec Exp:** Breast Imaging; Mammography; **Hospital:** IU Hlth Univ Hosp, Wishard Hlth Srvs; **Address:** Indiana Radiology Partners, 1001 W 10th St, Indianapolis, IN 46202; **Phone:** 317-944-1866; **Board Cert:** Diagnostic Radiology 1982; **Med School:** Indiana Univ 1978; **Resid:** Diagnostic Radiology, IU Health Univ Hosp 1982; **Fac Appt:** Prof Rad, Indiana Univ

Macmahon, Heber MD [DR] - **Spec Exp:** Thoracic Radiology; Lung Cancer; Thoracic Imaging; **Hospital:** Univ of Chicago Med; **Address:** 5841 S Maryland Ave, MC 2026, Univ of Chicago, Chicago, IL 60637-1463; **Phone:** 773-702-1604; **Board Cert:** Diagnostic Radiology 1975; **Med School:** Ireland 1970; **Resid:** Diagnostic Radiology, Mallinckrodt Institute 1975; **Fac Appt:** Prof Rad, Univ Chicago-Pritzker Sch Med

Miller, Frank H MD [DR] - **Spec Exp:** Abdominal Imaging; Gastrointestinal Imaging; Genitourinary Imaging; MRI; **Hospital:** Northwestern Meml Hosp; **Address:** 676 N St Clair, Ste 800, Chicago, IL 60611; **Phone:** 312-695-3775; **Board Cert:** Diagnostic Radiology 1993; **Med School:** Northwestern Univ 1988; **Resid:** Diagnostic Radiology, Northwestern Meml Hosp 1993; **Fellow:** Ultrasound/CT/MRI, Brigham & Women's Hosp 1994; Gastrointestinal Radiology, Hosp Univ Penn 1994; **Fac Appt:** Prof Rad, Northwestern Univ

Monsees, Barbara MD [DR] - **Spec Exp:** Mammography; Breast Cancer; **Hospital:** Barnes-Jewish Hosp; **Address:** 4921 Parkview Pl, St Louis, MO 63110; **Phone:** 314-454-7500; **Board Cert:** Diagnostic Radiology 1980; **Med School:** Washington Univ, St Louis 1975; **Resid:** Pediatrics, St Louis Chldns Hosp 1977; Diagnostic Radiology, Mallinckrodt Inst Radiology 1980; **Fac Appt:** Prof, Washington Univ, St Louis

Sivit, Carlos J MD [DR] - **Spec Exp:** Pediatric Radiology; Abdominal Imaging; Trauma Radiology; **Hospital:** UH Rainbow Babies & Chldns Hosp; **Address:** Dept Radiology, 11100 Euclid Ave, Cleveland, OH 44106-1736; **Phone:** 216-844-1172; **Board Cert:** Pediatrics 1987; Diagnostic Radiology 1987; **Med School:** Univ VA Sch Med 1981; **Resid:** Pediatrics, Vanderbilt Univ Hosp 1984; Diagnostic Radiology, George Washington Univ Hosp 1987; **Fellow:** Pediatric Radiology, Chldns Natl Med Ctr 1989

Swensen, Stephen J MD [DR] - **Spec Exp:** Lung Cancer; Lung Disease; **Hospital:** Mayo Med Ctr & Clin - Rochester; **Address:** Mayo Clinic - Diagnostic Radiology, 200 1st St SW, Rochester, MN 55905; **Phone:** 507-284-8550; **Board Cert:** Diagnostic Radiology 1986; **Med School:** Univ Wisc 1981; **Resid:** Diagnostic Radiology, Mayo Clinic 1986; **Fellow:** Pulmonary Radiology, Brigham & Womens Hosp 1987; **Fac Appt:** Prof Rad, Mayo Med Sch

Diagnostic Radiology

Thompson, Brad H MD [DR] - **Spec Exp:** Cardiovascular Imaging; **Hospital:** Univ Iowa Hosp & Clins; **Address:** UIHC, Dept Radiology, 200 Hawkins Drive, Iowa City, IA 52242; **Phone:** 319-356-3444; **Board Cert:** Diagnostic Radiology 1990; **Med School:** Univ Iowa Coll Med 1986; **Resid:** Diagnostic Radiology, Univ Iowa Hosp & Clins 1990; **Fac Appt:** Assoc Prof Rad, Univ Iowa Coll Med

Wells, Robert G MD [DR] - **Spec Exp:** Pediatric Radiology; **Hospital:** Chldns Hosp - Wisconsin; **Address:** Pediatric Diagnostic Imaging, 8522 W Capitol Drive, Milwaukee, WI 53222; **Phone:** 414-847-1800; **Board Cert:** Diagnostic Radiology 1984; Pediatric Radiology 2004; Vascular & Interventional Radiology 2004; **Med School:** Med Coll Wisc 1980; **Resid:** Diagnostic Radiology, Aurora St Luke's Med Ctr 1984; **Fellow:** Pediatric Radiology, Chldns Hosp 1985; **Fac Appt:** Prof Rad, Med Coll Wisc

White, Richard D MD [DR] - **Spec Exp:** Cardiovascular Imaging; Congenital Heart Disease-Adult & Child; **Hospital:** OSU Wexner Med Ctr; **Address:** 395 W 12th Ave, Ste 452A, Columbus, OH 43210; **Phone:** 614-293-4456; **Board Cert:** Diagnostic Radiology 1986; **Med School:** Duke Univ 1981; **Resid:** Diagnostic Radiology, UCSF Med Ctr 1985; **Fellow:** Cardiovascular Radiology, UCSF Med Ctr 1987; **Fac Appt:** Prof Med, Ohio State Univ

Great Plains and Mountains

Dodd III, Gerald Dewey MD [DR] - **Spec Exp:** Abdominal Imaging; Liver Cancer; **Hospital:** Univ Colorado Hosp; **Address:** Univ Co Hosp, Dept Radiology, 12605 E 16th Ave, Leprino Bldg, MS L954, P O Box 6511, Aurora, CO 80045; **Phone:** 720-848-6608; **Board Cert:** Diagnostic Radiology 1987; **Med School:** Univ Tex, Houston 1983; **Resid:** Diagnostic Radiology, Univ Hosp 1987; **Fellow:** Abdominal Imaging & Angio-Interventional, Univ Hosp 1988; **Fac Appt:** Prof Rad, Univ Colorado

Hubbard, Anne M MD [DR] - **Spec Exp:** Pediatric Radiology; Fetal MRI; Fetal Imaging; **Hospital:** Nebraska Med Ctr; **Address:** 981045 Nebraska Medical Ctr, Omaha, NE 68198-1045; **Phone:** 402-559-1010; **Board Cert:** Diagnostic Radiology 1983; Pediatric Radiology 2005; **Med School:** Univ Nebr Coll Med 1977; **Resid:** Internal Medicine, Mayo Clinic 1980; Diagnostic Radiology, Med Coll Wisc Affil Hosp 1983; **Fellow:** Pediatric Radiology, Milwaukee Chldns Hosp 1984; **Fac Appt:** Prof Rad, Univ Nebr Coll Med

Southwest

Erasmus, Jeremy J MD [DR] - **Spec Exp:** Lung Cancer; CT Body Scan; PET Imaging; Esophageal Cancer; **Hospital:** UT MD Anderson Canc Ctr; **Address:** MD Anderson Canc Ctr, Dept of Rad, 1515 Holcombe Blvd, Unit 1478, Houston, TX 77030; **Phone:** 713-792-3942; **Board Cert:** Diagnostic Radiology 1993; **Med School:** South Africa 1982; **Resid:** Diagnostic Radiology, Queens Univ Affil Hosp 1993; **Fac Appt:** Prof Rad, Univ Tex, Houston

Huynh, Phan T MD [DR] - **Spec Exp:** Mammography; Breast Cancer; **Hospital:** St. Luke's Episcopal Hosp-Houston; **Address:** 6624 Fannin St, St Luke's Medical Towers, Women's Center, Fl 10, Houston, TX 77030; **Phone:** 832-355-8130; **Board Cert:** Diagnostic Radiology 1994; **Med School:** Univ VA Sch Med 1989; **Resid:** Diagnostic Radiology, Univ Virginia Med Ctr 1994; **Fellow:** Breast Imaging, Univ Virginia Med Ctr 1995; **Fac Appt:** Assoc Clin Prof Rad, Baylor Coll Med

Otto, Pamela M MD [DR] - **Spec Exp:** Breast Imaging; Breast Cancer; **Hospital:** Univ Hosp-San Antonio, Audie L Murphy Meml Vets Hosp - San Antonio; **Address:** UTHSC-Dept Radiology, 7703 Floyd Curl Drive, MC 7800, San Antonio, TX 78229-7800; **Phone:** 210-567-3448; **Board Cert:** Diagnostic Radiology 1993; **Med School:** Univ MO-Columbia Sch Med 1988; **Resid:** Diagnostic Radiology, Univ TX Hlth Sci Ctr 1993; **Fellow:** Breast Imaging, Univ TX Hlth Sci Ctr 1994; **Fac Appt:** Assoc Prof Rad, Univ Tex, San Antonio

Stough, Rebecca G MD [DR] - **Spec Exp:** MRI-Breast; Breast Cancer; Breast Imaging; **Hospital:** Mercy Hlth Ctr - Oklahoma City; **Address:** Breast MRI of OK, 4300 McAuley Blvd, Oklahoma City, OK 73120; **Phone:** 405-749-7077; **Board Cert:** Diagnostic Radiology 1981; **Med School:** Univ Okla Coll Med 1975; **Resid:** Diagnostic Radiology, Univ OK Hlth Science Ctr 1980

West Coast and Pacific

Bahn, Duke K MD [DR] - **Spec Exp:** Prostate Cancer-Cryosurgery; Ultrasound; Immunotherapy; **Hospital:** Comm Meml Hosp - Ventura; **Address:** Prostate Inst of America, 168 N Brent St, Ste 402, Ventura, CA 93003; **Phone:** 805-585-3082; **Board Cert:** Diagnostic Radiology 1978; **Med School:** Korea 1970; **Resid:** Diagnostic Radiology, Wayne State Univ Med Ctr 1978; **Fac Appt:** Clin Prof Rad, Korea

Bassett, Lawrence W MD [DR] - **Spec Exp:** Breast Imaging; **Hospital:** UCLA Ronald Reagan Med Ctr; **Address:** 200 UCLA Med Plaza, rm 165-47, Los Angeles, CA 90095; **Phone:** 310-206-9608; **Board Cert:** Diagnostic Radiology 1975; **Med School:** UC Irvine 1968; **Resid:** Diagnostic Radiology, UCLA Med Ctr 1972; **Fac Appt:** Prof Rad, UCLA

Coakley, Fergus V MD [DR] - **Spec Exp:** Abdominal Imaging; Anal Cancer; Liver Cancer; Esophageal Cancer; **Hospital:** OR Hlth & Sci Univ; **Address:** Oregon Health & Science University, 3181 SW Sam Jackson Park Road, Mail Code: L340, Portland, OR 97239; **Phone:** 503-494-4511; **Board Cert:** Diagnostic Radiology 2001; **Med School:** Ireland 1988; **Resid:** Internal Medicine, Mater & St. Vincents Hosp 1991; Radiology, Leicester Univ Hosp 1996; **Fellow:** Body Imaging, Meml Sloan-Kettering Cancer Ctr 1997; **Fac Appt:** Prof Rad, UCSF

Federle, Michael P MD [DR] - **Spec Exp:** Abdominal Imaging; Gastrointestinal Imaging; **Hospital:** Stanford Univ Hosp & Clins; **Address:** Stanford Diagnostic Radiology, 300 Pasteur Drive, SO92, MC 5105, Stanford, CA 94305; **Phone:** 650-721-6411; **Board Cert:** Diagnostic Radiology 1978; **Med School:** Georgetown Univ 1974; **Resid:** Diagnostic Radiology, Univ Cincinnati Hosp 1978; **Fellow:** Body Imaging, UCSF Med Ctr 1979; **Fac Appt:** Prof Rad, Stanford Univ

Feig, Stephen A MD [DR] - **Spec Exp:** Breast Imaging; Breast Cancer; **Hospital:** UC Irvine Med Ctr; **Address:** UC Irvine Med Ctr, 101 The City Drive S, Rte 140, Orange, CA 92868-3298; **Phone:** 714-456-6905; **Board Cert:** Diagnostic Radiology 1972; **Med School:** NYU Sch Med 1967; **Resid:** Radiology, Bronx Muni Hosp-Einstein 1971; **Fac Appt:** Prof Rad, UC Irvine

Filly, Roy A MD [DR] - **Spec Exp:** Obstetric Ultrasound; **Hospital:** UCSF Med Ctr; **Address:** UCSF Med Ctr, Dept Diagnostic Radiology, 505 Parnassus Ave, Box 0628, San Francisco, CA 94143-0628; **Phone:** 415-353-1628; **Board Cert:** Diagnostic Radiology 1974; **Med School:** Ohio State Univ 1970; **Resid:** Diagnostic Radiology, Stanford Univ Med Ctr 1974; **Fac Appt:** Prof Emeritus Rad, UCSF

Gilsanz, Vicente MD [DR] - **Spec Exp:** Pediatric Radiology; Bone Disorders-Metabolic; **Hospital:** Chldns Hosp - Los Angeles; **Address:** Chdns Hosp LA, 4650 Sunset Blvd, MS 81, Los Angeles, CA 90027; **Phone:** 323-361-4571; **Board Cert:** Internal Medicine 1973; Diagnostic Radiology 1976; Pediatric Radiology 2004; **Med School:** Spain 1969; **Resid:** Internal Medicine, Mayo Clin 1973; Diagnostic Radiology, Mt Sinai Hosp 1976; **Fellow:** Pediatric Radiology, Chldns Hosp 1978; **Fac Appt:** Prof Rad, USC Sch Med

Grant, Edward G MD [DR] - **Spec Exp:** Ultrasound; Thyroid Ultrasound; Liver & Biliary Imaging; Abdominal Imaging; **Hospital:** Keck Med Ctr of USC, USC Norris Cancer Hosp; **Address:** Dept Rad, 1500 San Pablo St, Los Angeles, CA 90024-1301; **Phone:** 323-442-7450; **Board Cert:** Diagnostic Radiology 1978; **Med School:** Temple Univ 1974; **Resid:** Diagnostic Radiology, Georgetown Univ Med Ctr 1978; **Fellow:** Ultrasound, Herlev Hosp 1979; **Fac Appt:** Prof Rad, USC-Keck School of Medicine

Lehman, Constance D MD/PhD [DR] - **Spec Exp:** Breast Imaging; Breast Cancer; MRI-Breast; Mammography; **Hospital:** Univ Wash Med Ctr; **Address:** Seattle Cancer Care Alliance, 825 Eastlake Ave E, MS G2600, Seattle, WA 98109-1023; **Phone:** 206-288-2046; **Board Cert:** Diagnostic Radiology 1995; **Med School:** Yale Univ 1990; **Resid:** Diagnostic Radiology, Univ Wash Med Ctr 1995; **Fellow:** Breast Imaging, Univ Wash Med Ctr 1996; **Fac Appt:** Prof Rad, Univ Wash

McDonald, Dennis N MD [DR] - **Spec Exp:** Breast Imaging; Breast Cancer; **Hospital:** Sutter Mem Hospital-Sacramento, Sutter Gen Hosp; **Address:** Sutter Health Diagnostic Imaging, 2801 K St, Ste 502, Sacramento, CA 95816; **Phone:** 916-733-4401; **Board Cert:** Urology 1984; Diagnostic Radiology 1988; **Med School:** Loma Linda Univ 1977; **Resid:** Urology, White Meml Med Ctr 1982; Diagnostic Radiology, Loma Linda Univ Med Ctr 1988

Parikh, Jay Rajendra MD [DR] - **Spec Exp:** Breast Imaging; Breast Cancer; Mammography; **Hospital:** Swedish Med Ctr-First Hill-Seattle; **Address:** The Swedish Breast Imaging Ctr, 1101 Madison St, Ste 310, Seattle, WA 98104; **Phone:** 206-215-8100; **Board Cert:** Diagnostic Radiology 1996; **Med School:** Univ Ottawa 1990; **Resid:** Diagnostic Radiology, Queens Univ Faculty Hlth Scics 1996; **Fellow:** Breast Imaging, Univ of IL Med Ctr 1997; **Fac Appt:** Asst Clin Prof Rad, Univ Wash

Pathria, Mini N MD [DR] - **Spec Exp:** Musculoskeletal Imaging; Ultrasound; **Hospital:** UCSD Med Ctr; **Address:** UCSD Med Ctr, Dept Radiology, 200 W Arbor Drive, MC 8756, San Diego, CA 92103-8756; **Phone:** 619-543-6607; **Board Cert:** Diagnostic Radiology 1986; **Med School:** McMaster Univ 1982; **Resid:** Diagnostic Radiology, Mcmaster Univ 1986; **Fellow:** Musculoskeletal Imaging, UCSD Med Ctr 1987; **Fac Appt:** Clin Prof Rad, UCSD

Shaw, Dennis MD [DR] - **Spec Exp:** Pediatric Neuroradiology; Interventional Radiology; **Hospital:** Seattle Chldns Hosp; **Address:** 4800 Sand Point Way NE, R-5417 Radiology, Seattle, WA 98105; **Phone:** 206-987-2133; **Board Cert:** Diagnostic Radiology 1990; Pediatric Radiology 2006; **Med School:** Univ Wash 1983; **Resid:** Neurological Surgery, Univ Wash Med Ctr 1985; Diagnostic Radiology, Univ Wash Med Ctr 1990; **Fellow:** Pediatric Radiology, Chldns Hosp & Med Ctr 1991; Neuroradiology, Univ Wash Med Ctr; **Fac Appt:** Prof Rad, Univ Wash

Thurmond, Amy S MD [DR] - **Spec Exp:** Women's Imaging; Gynecologic Imaging; **Hospital:** OR Hlth & Sci Univ; **Address:** Siker Med Imaging, 1800 NE 2nd Ave, Portland, OR 97212; **Phone:** 503-595-3967; **Board Cert:** Diagnostic Radiology 1987; **Med School:** UCLA 1982; **Resid:** Cardiovascular Disease, St Vincent Hosp Med CtrProvidence St Vincent Med C 1984; Diagnostic Radiology, OR Hlth & Sci Univ 1987; **Fellow:** Interventional Radiology, OR Hlth & Sci Univ 1988; **Fac Appt:** Assoc Prof Rad, Oregon Hlth & Sci Univ

Ulissey, Michael J MD [DR] - **Spec Exp:** Breast Imaging; Breast Cancer; Mammography; **Hospital:** UT Southwestern Med Ctr at Dallas; **Address:** Breast Diagnostic Ctr, 1268 E Main St, Ste 1, Auburn, WA 98002; **Phone:** 253-735-1991; **Board Cert:** Diagnostic Radiology 1998; **Med School:** Texas A&M Univ 1991; **Resid:** Diagnostic Radiology, Univ OK Hlth Ctr 1998; **Fellow:** Radiology, Univ TX SW Clin Breast Radiology 1999; Magnetic Resonance Imaging, UT Southwestern Med Ctr 2004

Wood, Beverly P MD/PhD [DR] - **Spec Exp:** Pediatric Radiology; **Hospital:** LAC & USC Med Ctr, Loma Linda Chldns Hosp; **Address:** Loma Linda Univ Chldns Hosp, Div Pediatric Radiology, 11234 Anderson St, Ste 2841, Loma Linda, CA 92354; **Phone:** 909-558-4013; **Board Cert:** Diagnostic Radiology 1972; Pediatric Radiology 2003; **Med School:** Univ Rochester 1965; **Resid:** Diagnostic Radiology, Strong Meml Hosp 1971; **Fellow:** Pediatric Radiology, Strong Meml Hosp 1972; **Fac Appt:** Prof Rad, USC Sch Med

Zagoria, Ronald J MD [DR] - **Spec Exp:** Abdominal Imaging; Genitourinary Radiology; Interventional Radiology; MRI; **Hospital:** UCSF Med Ctr, UCSF - Mt Zion Med Ctr; **Address:** UCSF, Dept Radiology & Biomed Imaging, 505 Parnassus Ave, rm M372, San Francisco, CA 94143; **Phone:** 415-353-1786; **Board Cert:** Diagnostic Radiology 1987; Vascular & Interventional Radiology 2004; **Med School:** Univ MD Sch Med 1983; **Resid:** Radiology, Bowman Gray Med Ctr 1987; **Fellow:** Abdominal Imaging & Angio-Interventional, Bowman Gray Med Ctr 1987; **Fac Appt:** Prof Rad, UCSF

Neuroradiology

New England

Curtin, Hugh D MD [NRad] - **Spec Exp:** Head & Neck Radiology; **Hospital:** Mass Eye & Ear Infirm; **Address:** Mass Eye & Ear Infirmary, Dept Radiology, 243 Charles St, Boston, MA 02114; **Phone:** 617-573-3563 x4; **Board Cert:** Diagnostic Radiology 1976; Neuroradiology 2011; **Med School:** SUNY Upstate Med Univ 1972; **Resid:** Diagnostic Radiology, Presby Univ Hosp 1976; **Fellow:** Neuroradiology, Foundation Rothschild 1979; **Fac Appt:** Prof Rad, Harvard Med Sch

Hackney, David B MD [NRad] - **Hospital:** Beth Israel Deaconess Med Ctr - Boston; **Address:** BIDMC, Dept Radiology, 330 Brookline Ave, Boston, MA 02215; **Phone:** 617-754-2009; **Board Cert:** Diagnostic Radiology 1984; Neuroradiology 2005; **Med School:** Cornell Univ 1980; **Resid:** Diagnostic Radiology, UCSD Med Ctr 1983; **Fellow:** Neurological Radiology, Mass Genl Hosp 1985; **Fac Appt:** Prof Rad, Harvard Med Sch

Hirsch, Joshua A MD [NRad] - **Spec Exp:** Interventional Neuroradiology; Endovascular Surgery; Minimally Invasive Spinal Surgery; Osteoporosis Spine-Vertebroplasty; **Hospital:** Mass Genl Hosp; **Address:** Mass General Hosp, Interventional Neuroradiology GRB-241, 55 Fruit St, Boston, MA 02114; **Phone:** 617-726-1767; **Board Cert:** Diagnostic Radiology 1996; **Med School:** Univ Pennsylvania 1991; **Resid:** Diagnostic Radiology, Hosp Univ Penn 1996; **Fellow:** Neuroradiology, Hosp Univ Penn 1995; Interventional Neuroradiology, Lahey Clinic 1998; **Fac Appt:** Asst Prof Rad, Harvard Med Sch

Norbash, Alexander M MD [NRad] - **Spec Exp:** Interventional Neuroradiology; Aneurysm-Cerebral; Osteoporosis Spine-Kyphoplasty; Arteriovenous Malformations; **Hospital:** Boston Med Ctr; **Address:** BMC, Dept Radiology, 820 Harrison Ave, Boston, MA 02118; **Phone:** 617-638-6610; **Board Cert:** Diagnostic Radiology 1991; Neuroradiology 2004; **Med School:** Univ MO-Kansas City 1986; **Resid:** Diagnostic Radiology, St Francis Hosp 1990; Diagnostic Radiology, Presby Univ Hosp 1991; **Fellow:** Neurological Radiology, Stanford Univ Hosp 1993; Interventional Radiology, Stanford Univ Hosp 1994; **Fac Appt:** Prof Rad, Boston Univ

Neuroradiology

Orbach, Darren B MD/PhD [NRad] - **Spec Exp:** Stroke in Children; Vascular Malformations; Interventional Neuroradiology; **Hospital:** Children's Hospital - Boston; **Address:** Boston Chldn's Hosp, Interventional Radiology Dept, 300 Longwood Ave, Boston, MA 02115; **Phone:** 617-355-6579; **Board Cert:** Diagnostic Radiology 2004; Neurology 2004; Neuroradiology 2005; **Med School:** Cornell Univ 1998; **Resid:** Diagnostic Radiology, NYU Med Ctr 2002; Neurology, NYU Med Ctr 2004; **Fellow:** Neuroradiology, NYU Med Ctr 2005; **Fac Appt:** Asst Prof Rad, Harvard Med Sch

Sze, Gordon K MD [NRad] - **Spec Exp:** Brain Tumors; Spinal Cord Tumors; Head & Neck Cancer; MRI; **Hospital:** Yale-New Haven Hosp, Yale Med Group; **Address:** Yale, Diagnostic Radiology, 20 York St, New Haven, CT 06510; **Phone:** 203-785-5102; **Board Cert:** Diagnostic Radiology 1985; Neuroradiology 2008; **Med School:** Harvard Med Sch 1981; **Resid:** Diagnostic Radiology, UCSF Med Ctr 1985; **Fellow:** Neuroradiology, UCSF Med Ctr 1986; **Fac Appt:** Prof Rad, Yale Univ

Mid Atlantic

Berenstein, Alejandro MD [NRad] - **Spec Exp:** Interventional Neuroradiology; Aneurysm-Cerebral; Endovascular Surgery; Vascular Malformations; **Hospital:** St. Luke's - Roosevelt Hosp Ctr - Roosevelt Div (page 56); **Address:** Center for Endovascular Surgery, 1000 10th Ave, 10th Fl, Ste 10G - INN, New York, NY 10019; **Phone:** 212-636-3400; **Board Cert:** Diagnostic Radiology 1976; **Med School:** Mexico 1970; **Resid:** Diagnostic Radiology, Mt Sinai Med Ctr 1976; **Fellow:** Neuroradiology, NYU Med Ctr 1978; **Fac Appt:** Prof Rad, Albert Einstein Coll Med

Drayer, Burton P MD [NRad] - **Spec Exp:** Parkinson's Disease/Aging Brain; Alzheimer's Disease; Vascular Neurology; MRI & CT of Brain & Spine; **Hospital:** Mt Sinai Med Ctr (page 62); **Address:** 1176 Fifth Ave, New York, NY 10029; **Phone:** 212-241-8333; **Board Cert:** Neurology 1976; Diagnostic Radiology 1978; Neuroradiology 2006; **Med School:** Ros Franklin Univ/Chicago Med Sch 1971; **Resid:** Neurology, Univ Vt Med Ctr 1975; Diagnostic Radiology, Univ Pitt Hlth Ctr 1978; **Fellow:** Neuroradiology, Univ Pitt Hlth Ctr 1978; **Fac Appt:** Prof Rad, Mount Sinai Sch Med

Faro, Scott H MD [NRad] - **Spec Exp:** Brain Mapping; Brain Tumors; Epilepsy; Spinal Cord Injury; **Hospital:** Temple Univ Hosp; **Address:** Temple Univ Hosp- Div Neuroradiology, 3401 N Broad St, Philadelphia, PA 19140; **Phone:** 215-707-5003; **Board Cert:** Diagnostic Radiology 1993; Neuroradiology 2006; **Med School:** UMDNJ-Rutgers Med Sch 1986; **Resid:** Diagnostic Radiology, Med Ctr Delaware 1991; **Fellow:** Neuroradiology, Thomas Jefferson Univ Hosp 1992; Pediatric Neuroradiology, Childrens Hosp 1993; **Fac Appt:** Prof Rad, Temple Univ

Hurst, Robert W MD [NRad] - **Spec Exp:** Interventional Neuroradiology; Aneurysm; Carotid Artery Stent Placement; Intracranial Angioplasty & Stent; **Hospital:** Hosp Univ Penn - UPHS (page 69); **Address:** Hosp Univ Penn, Neuroradiology, 3400 Spruce St, Ground Dulles Bldg Fl 1, Philadelphia, PA 19104; **Phone:** 215-662-3064; **Board Cert:** Neurology 1986; Diagnostic Radiology 1989; Neuroradiology 2005; Vascular Neurology 2009; **Med School:** Univ Tex, Houston 1981; **Resid:** Neurology, Univ Virginia Hosp 1985; Diagnostic Radiology, Univ Virginia Hosp 1989; **Fellow:** Neurological Radiology, Hosp Univ Penn 1990; Interventional Radiology, NYU Langone Med Ctr 1991; **Fac Appt:** Prof Rad, Univ Pennsylvania

Khandji, Alexander G MD [NRad] - **Spec Exp:** Pituitary Disorders; Spine Imaging & Intervention; MRI; Headache; **Hospital:** NY-Presby/Columbia Univ Med Ctr, NY (page 65); **Address:** 177 Ft Washington Ave, Ste 3-113, New York, NY 10032-3173; **Phone:** 212-305-7669; **Board Cert:** Diagnostic Radiology 1985; Neuroradiology 2006; **Med School:** SUNY Downstate 1980; **Resid:** Surgery, MS Hershey Med Ctr 1982; Diagnostic Radiology, Columbia-Presby Med Ctr 1985; **Fellow:** Neuroradiology, Columbia-Presby Med Ctr 1987; **Fac Appt:** Prof Rad, Columbia P&S

Lis, Eric MD [NRad] - **Spec Exp:** Spinal Cord Tumors; Brain Tumors; Pain-Spine; MRI; **Hospital:** Meml Sloan-Kettering Canc Ctr; **Address:** Meml Sloan Kettering Cancer Ctr, 1275 York Ave, Ste MRI 1158, New York, NY 10065; **Phone:** 212-639-8330; **Board Cert:** Diagnostic Radiology 1995; Neuroradiology 2008; **Med School:** UMDNJ-NJ Med Sch, Newark 1990; **Resid:** Internal Medicine, Mountainside Hosp 1991; Diagnostic Radiology, UMDNJ-RW Johnson Med Sch 1995; **Fellow:** Neuroradiology, NY-Presby-Weill Cornell Med Ctr 1997

Loevner, Laurie A MD [NRad] - **Spec Exp:** Head & Neck Cancer; Thyroid Cancer; Brain Tumor Imaging; Spinal Tumor Imaging; **Hospital:** Hosp Univ Penn - UPHS (page 69); **Address:** Hosp Univ Penn, Neuroradiology, 3400 Spruce St, Ground Dulles Bldg, Philadelphia, PA 19104; **Phone:** 215-662-3020; **Board Cert:** Diagnostic Radiology 1993; Neuroradiology 2006; **Med School:** Univ Pennsylvania 1988; **Resid:** Diagnostic Radiology, Univ Michigan Med Ctr 1993; **Fellow:** Neuroradiology, Hosp Univ Penn 1995; **Fac Appt:** Prof Rad, Univ Pennsylvania

Pile-Spellman, John M MD [NRad] - **Spec Exp:** Interventional Neuroradiology; Cerebrovascular Disease; Aneurysm; Arteriovenous Malformations; **Hospital:** Winthrop Univ Hosp; **Address:** Neurological Surgery, 1991 Marcus Ave, Ste 108, Lake Success, NY 11042; **Phone:** 516-442-2250; **Board Cert:** Diagnostic Radiology 1984; **Med School:** Tufts Univ 1978; **Resid:** Neurological Surgery, New England Med Ctr 1981; Neurological Radiology, Mass Genl Hosp 1984; **Fellow:** Interventional Neuroradiology, NYU Med Ctr 1986; **Fac Appt:** Prof Rad, Columbia P&S

Vezina, Louis G MD [NRad] - **Spec Exp:** Pediatric Neuroradiology; Brain Tumors; Neurofibromatosis; **Hospital:** Chldns Natl Med Ctr; **Address:** Dept Radiology, 111 Michigan Ave NW, Washington, DC 20010-2970; **Phone:** 202-476-3651; **Board Cert:** Diagnostic Radiology 1987; Neuroradiology 2008; **Med School:** McGill Univ 1983; **Resid:** Diagnostic Radiology, Mass Genl Hosp 1987; **Fellow:** Neurological Radiology, Mass Genl Hosp 1989; Pediatric Neuroradiology, Chldns Natl Med Ctr 1991; **Fac Appt:** Prof Rad, Geo Wash Univ

Yousem, David M MD [NRad] - **Hospital:** Johns Hopkins Hosp (page 59); **Address:** Johns Hopkins Hosp, Div Neuroradiology, 600 N Wolfe St Phipps Bldg - rm B-100, Baltimore, MD 21287; **Phone:** 410-955-2353; **Board Cert:** Diagnostic Radiology 1987; Neuroradiology 2005; **Med School:** Univ Mich Med Sch 1983; **Resid:** Diagnostic Radiology, Johns Hopkins Hosp 1987; **Fellow:** Neuroradiology, Hosp Univ Penn 1990; **Fac Appt:** Prof Rad, Johns Hopkins Univ

Zimmerman, Robert A MD [NRad] - **Spec Exp:** Pediatric Neuroradiology; **Hospital:** Chldns Hosp of Philadelphia; **Address:** Childrens Hosp Philadelphia, Radiology, 324 S 34th St Wood Bldg - rm 2115, Philadelphia, PA 19104; **Phone:** 215-590-2569; **Board Cert:** Diagnostic Radiology 1970; Neuroradiology 2005; **Med School:** Georgetown Univ 1964; **Resid:** Diagnostic Radiology, Hosp Univ Penn 1969; **Fellow:** Neurological Radiology, Hosp Univ Penn 1995; **Fac Appt:** Prof Rad, Univ Pennsylvania

Zinreich, S. James MD [NRad] - **Spec Exp:** Head & Neck Radiology; **Hospital:** Johns Hopkins Hosp (page 59); **Address:** Johns Hopkins Hosp, 600 N Wolfe St Phipps Bldg - rm B-100, Baltimore, MD 21287; **Phone:** 410-614-3020; **Board Cert:** Diagnostic Radiology 1982; Neuroradiology 2006; **Med School:** Belgium 1976; **Resid:** Diagnostic Radiology, Sinai Hosp; **Fac Appt:** Prof Oto, Johns Hopkins Univ

Southeast

Burdette, Jonathan Hill MD [NRad] - **Spec Exp:** Brain Injury; MRI; **Hospital:** Wake Forest Baptist Med Ctr; **Address:** Medical Center Blvd, Winston-Salem, NC 27157; **Phone:** 336-716-1286; **Board Cert:** Diagnostic Radiology 1997; Neuroradiology 2011; **Med School:** Univ Tenn Coll Med 1993; **Resid:** Diagnostic Radiology, Univ Mich Affil Hosps 1997; **Fellow:** Neurological Radiology, Wake Forest Baptist Med Ctr 1999; **Fac Appt:** Prof Rad

Dion, Jacques E MD [NRad] - **Spec Exp:** Interventional Neuroradiology; Aneurysm-Cerebral; Intracranial Angioplasty & Stent; **Hospital:** Emory Univ Hosp; **Address:** Emory Interventional Neuroradiology, 1364 Clifton Rd NE, rm AG21, Atlanta, GA 30322; **Phone:** 404-712-4991; **Board Cert:** Diagnostic Radiology 1982; Neuroradiology 2009; **Med School:** Univ Ottawa 1978; **Resid:** Diagnostic Radiology, Harbor-UCLA Med Ctr 1981; Diagnostic Radiology, Notre Dame Hosp 1983; **Fellow:** Neuroradiology, Univ Hosp 1985; **Fac Appt:** Prof Rad, Emory Univ

Jensen, Mary E MD [NRad] - **Spec Exp:** Interventional Neuroradiology; Osteoporosis Spine-Vertebroplasty; Aneurysm-Cerebral; **Hospital:** Univ of Virginia Hlth Sys; **Address:** Univ of Virginia Med Ctr, Dept Radiology, 1215 Lee St, Charlottsville, VA 22908; **Phone:** 434-924-9719; **Board Cert:** Diagnostic Radiology 1987; **Med School:** Med Coll VA 1982; **Resid:** Diagnostic Radiology, Univ Virginia Med Ctr 1991; **Fellow:** Interventional Neuroradiology, UCLA Med Ctr 1992; **Fac Appt:** Prof Rad, Univ VA Sch Med

Johnson, Annette MD [NRad] - **Spec Exp:** Brain Tumors; MRI; **Hospital:** Wake Forest Baptist Med Ctr; **Address:** Wake Forest Baptist Hlth, Dept Radiology, One Medical Ctr Blvd, Winston-Salem, NC 27157; **Phone:** 336-716-2872; **Board Cert:** Diagnostic Radiology 1996; Neuroradiology 2009; **Med School:** Med Coll VA 1992; **Resid:** Diagnostic Radiology, Geisinger Med Ctr 1996; **Fellow:** Diagnostic Radiology, Mallinckrodt Inst Radiology/Washington Univ 1998; **Fac Appt:** Assoc Prof Rad, Wake Forest Univ

Joseph, Gregory J MD [NRad] - **Spec Exp:** Stroke; Aneurysm-Cerebral; Intracranial Angioplasty & Stent; **Hospital:** Presby Hosp - Charlotte; **Address:** Presbyterian Hosp, Dept Radiology, 200 Hawthorne Ln, Charlotte, NC 28204; **Phone:** 704-384-4057; **Board Cert:** Diagnostic Radiology 1989; Neuroradiology 2010; **Med School:** Georgetown Univ 1984; **Resid:** Diagnostic Radiology, Georgetown Univ Hosp 1989; Vascular & Interventional Radiology, Emory Univ Hosp 1990; **Fellow:** Neuroradiology, Emory Univ Hosp 1991

Maldjian, Joseph MD [NRad] - **Spec Exp:** Brain Tumors; Stroke; **Hospital:** Wake Forest Baptist Med Ctr; **Address:** Wake Forest Baptist Hlth, Dept Radiology, One Medical Ctr Blvd, MRI Bldg, Fl 3, Winston-Salem, NC 27157; **Phone:** 336-716-2872; **Board Cert:** Diagnostic Radiology 1993; Neuroradiology 2005; **Med School:** UMDNJ-NJ Med Sch, Newark 1988; **Resid:** Diagnostic Radiology, Mount Sinai Med Ctr 1993; **Fellow:** Neuroradiology, Hosp Univ Penn 1995

Morris, P. Pearse MD [NRad] - **Spec Exp:** Interventional Neuroradiology; Endovascular Neurosurgery; Aneurysm-Cerebral; Arteriovenous Malformations; **Hospital:** Wake Forest Baptist Med Ctr; **Address:** Medical Ctr Blvd, MRI Bldg Fl 3, Winston-Salem, NC 27157; **Phone:** 336-716-7849; **Board Cert:** Psychiatry 1989; Diagnostic Radiology 1994; Neuroradiology 2008; **Med School:** Ireland 1983; **Resid:** Psychiatry, Johns Hopkins Hosp 1987; Diagnostic Radiology, Mass Genl Hosp 1994; **Fellow:** Geriatric Psychiatry, Cornell Univ 1988; Neuroradiology, Mass Genl Hosp 1995; **Fac Appt:** Prof Rad, Wake Forest Univ

Murtagh, F. Reed MD [NRad] - **Spec Exp:** Neuro-Oncology; Brain Tumor Imaging; Spinal Tumor Imaging; Memory Disorders; **Hospital:** Moffitt Canc Ctr (page 61), James A. Haley Veterans's Hosp-Tampa; **Address:** USF Hlth, Diagnostic Inst, 3301 USF Alumni Drive, Tampa, FL 33612; **Phone:** 813-972-3351; **Board Cert:** Diagnostic Radiology 1978; Neuroradiology 2004; **Med School:** Temple Univ 1971; **Resid:** Diagnostic Radiology, Jackson Meml Hosp 1978; **Fellow:** Neurological Radiology, Univ Miami Hosp 1979; **Fac Appt:** Prof Rad, Univ S Fla Coll Med

Provenzale, James M MD [NRad] - **Spec Exp:** Brain Tumor Imaging; Multiple Sclerosis Imaging; Brain Imaging-Pediatric; **Hospital:** Duke Univ Hosp, Durham VA Med Ctr; **Address:** Duke Univ Med Ctr, Dept Radiology, Box 3808, Durham, NC 27710; **Phone:** 919-684-7218; **Board Cert:** Neurology 1988; Diagnostic Radiology 1991; **Med School:** Albany Med Coll 1983; **Resid:** Neurology, NC Meml Hosp 1987; Diagnostic Radiology, Mass Genl Hosp 1991; **Fellow:** Neuroradiology, Mass Genl Hosp 1992; **Fac Appt:** Prof Rad, Duke Univ

Quencer, Robert MD [NRad] - **Spec Exp:** Spinal Cord Injury; MRI; **Hospital:** Jackson Meml Hosp; **Address:** UHlth, Radiology Dept, 1611 NW 12th St, Miami, FL 33136; **Phone:** 305-243-4701; **Board Cert:** Diagnostic Radiology 1972; Neuroradiology 2006; **Med School:** SUNY Upstate Med Univ 1967; **Resid:** Diagnostic Radiology, NY-Presby/Columbia Univ Med Ctr 1971; **Fellow:** Neuroradiology, Neurological Inst 1972; **Fac Appt:** Prof Rad, Univ Miami Sch Med

Midwest

Christoforidis, Gregory MD [NRad] - **Spec Exp:** Interventional Neuroradiology; Stroke; Aneurysm; **Hospital:** Univ of Chicago Med; **Address:** Univ Chicago Med Ctr-Radiology, 5841 S Maryland Ave, MC 2026, Chicago, IL 60637; **Phone:** 773-702-3654; **Board Cert:** Diagnostic Radiology 1995; Neuroradiology 2009; **Med School:** Ohio State Univ 1990; **Resid:** Diagnostic Radiology, OH State Univ Hosp 1995; **Fellow:** Neuroradiology, Henry Ford Hosp 1997; Interventional Neuroradiology, -UniversitaetsSpital Zurich 1998; **Fac Appt:** Prof Rad, Univ Chicago-Pritzker Sch Med

Cross III, Dewitte T MD [NRad] - **Spec Exp:** Interventional Neuroradiology; Aneurysm-Cerebral; Stroke; **Hospital:** Barnes-Jewish Hosp, St. Louis Chldns Hosp; **Address:** Wash Univ, Dept Radiology, 510 S Kingshighway Blvd, Box 8131, St Louis, MO 63110-1016; **Phone:** 314-362-5949; **Board Cert:** Diagnostic Radiology 1985; Neuroradiology 2006; **Med School:** UAB Sch Med 1980; **Resid:** Diagnostic Radiology, Naval Hosp 1985; **Fellow:** Neuroradiology, NY Med Coll 1988; Neuroradiology, Columbia Univ 1989; **Fac Appt:** Prof Rad, Washington Univ, St Louis

Grobelny, Thomas MD [NRad] - **Spec Exp:** Interventional Neuroradiology; Aneurysm-Cerebral; Stroke; Arteriovenous Malformations; **Hospital:** Adv Christ Med Ctr, Adv Luth Genl Hosp; **Address:** 4400 W 95th St, Ste 301, Oak Lawn, IL 60453; **Phone:** 847-430-6108; **Board Cert:** Diagnostic Radiology 1996; Neuroradiology 2010; **Med School:** Poland 1986; **Resid:** Diagnostic Radiology, Harlem Hospital 1995; **Fellow:** Neurocritical Care, Thomas Jefferson Univ Hosp 1998; Interventional Neuroradiology, UCLA Med Ctr 1989

Haughton III, Victor M MD [NRad] - **Spec Exp:** Spinal Imaging; **Hospital:** Univ WI Hosp & Clins; **Address:** Univ WI Hosps & Clins, Dept Radiology, 600 Highland Ave, MC 3252, Madison, WI 53792; **Phone:** 608-263-9179; **Board Cert:** Diagnostic Radiology 1974; **Med School:** Yale Univ 1967; **Resid:** Diagnostic Radiology, Brigham & Women's Hosp 1973; **Fellow:** Neurological Radiology, Brigham & Women's Hosp 1974; **Fac Appt:** Prof Emeritus Rad, Univ Wisc

Kallmes, David F MD [NRad] - **Spec Exp:** Aneurysm-Cerebral; Stroke; Osteoporosis Spine-Vertebroplasty; **Hospital:** Mayo Med Ctr & Clin - Rochester; **Address:** Mayo Clinic, 200 First St SW, OL 1-115, Rochester, MN 55905; **Phone:** 507-266-3350; **Board Cert:** Diagnostic Radiology 1994; Neuroradiology 2009; **Med School:** Univ Mass Sch Med 1989; **Resid:** Diagnostic Radiology, Duke Univ Med Ctr 1993; **Fellow:** Neuroradiology, Univ Virginia Med Ctr 1995; **Fac Appt:** Assoc Prof Rad, Mayo Med Sch

Koeller, Kelly K MD [NRad] - **Spec Exp:** Brain Tumor Imaging; Head & Neck Tumors Imaging; Spinal Tumor Imaging; **Hospital:** Mayo Med Ctr & Clin - Rochester, St. Mary's Hosp - Rochester MN (Mayo); **Address:** Mayo Clinic, 200 First St SW, Charlton Bldg, rm 2-290, Rochester, MN 55905; **Phone:** 507-266-3412; **Board Cert:** Diagnostic Radiology 1990; Neuroradiology 2004; **Med School:** Univ Tenn Coll Med 1982; **Resid:** Diagnostic Radiology, Naval Hosp 1990; **Fellow:** Neuroradiology, UCSF Med Ctr 1992; **Fac Appt:** Assoc Prof Rad, Mayo Med Sch

Lee, Seon Kyu DO/PhD [NRad] - **Spec Exp:** Interventional Neuroradiology; Neurovascular Surgery; Stroke; Aneurysm; **Hospital:** Univ of Chicago Med; **Address:** Univ Chicago Med Ctr-Radiology, 5841 S Maryland Ave, MC 2026, Chicago, IL 60637; **Phone:** 773-702-3654; **Board Cert:** Diagnostic Radiology 2012; **Med School:** South Korea 1989; **Resid:** Diagnostic Radiology, Seoul Natl Univ Hosp 1994; **Fellow:** Interventional Neuroradiology, Univ Toronto Affil Hosp 2002; **Fac Appt:** Assoc Prof Rad, Univ Chicago-Pritzker Sch Med

Masaryk, Thomas MD [NRad] - **Spec Exp:** Cerebrovascular Disease; Aneurysm-Cerebral; Vascular Lesions of the CNS; Carotid Artery Stent Placement; **Hospital:** Cleveland Clin (page 55); **Address:** Cleveland Clinic, Dept Radiology, 9500 Euclid Ave, MC P34, Cleveland, OH 44195; **Phone:** 216-444-6653; **Board Cert:** Diagnostic Radiology 1985; Neuroradiology 2005; **Med School:** Med Coll OH 1981; **Resid:** Diagnostic Radiology, Cleveland Clinic 1984; **Fellow:** Neurological Radiology, Cleveland Clinic 1985

Modic, Michael MD [NRad] - **Spec Exp:** MRI; Spinal Imaging; **Hospital:** Cleveland Clin (page 55); **Address:** Cleveland Clinic, Dept Radiology, 9500 Euclid Ave, MC T13, Cleveland, OH 44195; **Phone:** 216-444-9308; **Board Cert:** Diagnostic Radiology 1979; Neuroradiology 2003; **Med School:** Case West Res Univ 1975; **Resid:** Diagnostic Radiology, Cleveland Clin Fdn 1978; **Fellow:** Neuroradiology, Cleveland Clin Fdn 1979; **Fac Appt:** Prof Rad, Ohio State Univ

Moran, Christopher J MD [NRad] - **Spec Exp:** Aneurysm-Cerebral; Cerebrovascular Disease/Stroke; Carotid Artery Stent Placement; Interventional Neuroradiology; **Hospital:** Barnes-Jewish Hosp; **Address:** Mallinckrodt Inst Radiology, Wash Univ Sch Med, Campus Box 8131, 510 S Kingshighway Blvd, St Louis, MO 63110; **Phone:** 314-362-5949; **Board Cert:** Diagnostic Radiology 1978; Neuroradiology 2004; **Med School:** St Louis Univ 1974; **Resid:** Diagnostic Radiology, Mallinckrodt Inst Rad/Wash U 1978; **Fellow:** Neuroradiology, Mallinckrodt Inst Rad/Wash U 1979; **Fac Appt:** Prof Rad, Washington Univ, St Louis

Mukherji, Suresh K MD [NRad] - **Spec Exp:** Head & Neck Radiology; Head & Neck Tumors Imaging; **Hospital:** Univ Michigan Med Ctr; **Address:** Univ of Michigan-Dept Radiology, 1500 E Med Ctr Drive Fl UH-B2 - rm A209B, Ann Arbor, MI 48109-0030; **Phone:** 734-936-8865; **Board Cert:** Diagnostic Radiology 1992; Neuroradiology 2006; **Med School:** Georgetown Univ 1987; **Resid:** Diagnostic Radiology, Brigham & Women's Hosp 1992; **Fellow:** Neuroradiology, Univ Florida Affil Hosp 1994; **Fac Appt:** Prof Rad, Univ Mich Med Sch

Rowley, Howard A MD [NRad] - **Spec Exp:** Epilepsy; Cerebrovascular Disease/Stroke; **Hospital:** Univ WI Hosp & Clins; **Address:** Univ WI Hosps & Clins - Dept Radiology, 600 Highland Ave, MC 3252, Madison, WI 53792; **Phone:** 608-263-9179; **Board Cert:** Neurology 1991; Diagnostic Radiology 1993; Neuroradiology 2008; **Med School:** Washington Univ, St Louis 1985; **Resid:** Neurology, UCSF Med Ctr 1990; Diagnostic Radiology, UCSF Med Ctr 1993; **Fellow:** Neurological Radiology, UCSF Med Ctr 1996; **Fac Appt:** Prof Rad, Univ Wisc

Russell, Eric MD [NRad] - **Spec Exp:** Head & Neck Imaging; Cerebrovascular Malformations; Spinal Imaging; Aneurysm-Cerebral; **Hospital:** Northwestern Meml Hosp; **Address:** 676 N St Clair St, Ste 800, Chicago, IL 60611; **Phone:** 312-695-5103; **Board Cert:** Diagnostic Radiology 1978; Neuroradiology 2005; **Med School:** SUNY Buffalo 1974; **Resid:** Diagnostic Radiology, Montefiore Med Ctr 1978; **Fellow:** Neuroradiology, NYU Med Ctr 1980; **Fac Appt:** Prof Rad, Northwestern Univ

Thulborn, Keith R MD/PhD [NRad] - **Spec Exp:** MRI; **Hospital:** Univ of IL Med Ctr at Chicago; **Address:** Univ Illinois Med Ctr, 1801 W Taylor St, Ste 1A, Chicago, IL 60612; **Phone:** 312-413-4900; **Board Cert:** Diagnostic Radiology 1989; **Med School:** Washington Univ, St Louis 1984; **Resid:** Diagnostic Radiology, Mass Genl Hosp 1989; **Fellow:** Neuroradiology, Mass Genl Hosp 1991; **Fac Appt:** Prof Rad, Univ IL Coll Med

Great Plains and Mountains

Frei, Donald F MD [NRad] - **Spec Exp:** Interventional Neuroradiology; Aneurysm-Cerebral; Cerebrovascular Disease/Stroke; **Hospital:** Swedish Med Ctr - Denver, Exempla Lutheran Med Ctr; **Address:** Radiology Imaging Assocs, 8200 E Belleview Ave, Ste 600E, Englewood, CO 80112; **Phone:** 303-761-9190; **Board Cert:** Diagnostic Radiology 1994; Neuroradiology 2008; **Med School:** Univ Cincinnati 1989; **Resid:** Diagnostic Radiology, Tulane Univ Med Ctr 1994; **Fellow:** Neurological Radiology, Mallinckrodt Inst Rad-Barnes Hosp 1996; Interventional Neuroradiology, Mallinckrodt Inst Rad-Barnes Hosp 1996

Osborn, Anne G MD [NRad] - **Spec Exp:** Spinal Imaging; Brain Imaging; Head & Neck Radiology; **Hospital:** Univ Utah Hlth Care; **Address:** Dept Radiology, 30 N 1900 E, rm 1A71, Salt Lake City, UT 84132-2140; **Phone:** 801-581-7553; **Board Cert:** Diagnostic Radiology 1974; Neuroradiology 2004; **Med School:** Stanford Univ 1970; **Resid:** Diagnostic Radiology, Stanford Univ Hosp 1974; **Fellow:** Diagnostic Radiology, Univ Utah Hosp 1977; **Fac Appt:** Prof Rad, Univ Utah

Southwest

Hunter, Jill V MD [NRad] - **Spec Exp:** Pediatric Neuroradiology; Brain Injury-Pediatric; Autism; Neurogenetics; **Hospital:** Texas Chldns Hosp, St. Luke's Episcopal Hosp-Houston; **Address:** 6621 Fannin St, MC W-1120, Houston, TX 77030; **Phone:** 832-822-5324; **Board Cert:** Diagnostic Radiology 1997; Neuroradiology 2009; **Med School:** England, UK 1975; **Resid:** Diagnostic Radiology, Baylor Affil Hosp 1978; **Fellow:** Neuroradiology, Queen Square Hosp 1992; **Fac Appt:** Prof Rad, Baylor Coll Med

Mawad, Michel E MD [NRad] - **Spec Exp:** Interventional Neuroradiology; **Hospital:** St. Luke's Episcopal Hosp-Houston; **Address:** BCM, Diagnostic Svcs, 6720 Bertner Ave, Box 4-267, Houston, TX 77030; **Phone:** 713-798-2200; **Board Cert:** Diagnostic Radiology 1980; Neuroradiology 2006; **Med School:** Lebanon 1976; **Resid:** Diagnostic Radiology, St Lukes-Roosevelt Hosp 1979; **Fellow:** Neurological Radiology, NY-Presby/Columbia Univ Med Ctr 1980; **Fac Appt:** Prof N, Baylor Coll Med

West Coast and Pacific

Atlas, Scott W MD [NRad] - **Spec Exp:** MRI-Brain & Spine; Brain Tumors; **Hospital:** Stanford Univ Hosp & Clins; **Address:** Stanford Univ Med Ctr, Dept Rad, 300 Pasteur Drive, Stanford, CA 94305-5105; **Phone:** 650-723-0340; **Board Cert:** Diagnostic Radiology 1985; Neuroradiology 2005; **Med School:** Univ Chicago-Pritzker Sch Med 1981; **Resid:** Diagnostic Radiology, Northwestern Univ Med Ctr 1985; **Fellow:** Neuroradiology, Hosp Univ Penn 1987; **Fac Appt:** Prof Rad, Stanford Univ

Barkovich, A James MD [NRad] - **Spec Exp:** Pediatric Neuroradiology; MRI; Brain Development Abnormalities; Stroke-Neonatal; **Hospital:** UCSF Med Ctr; **Address:** UCSF Med Ctr, Div Neuroradiology, 505 Parnassus Ave, rm L371, Box 0628, San Francisco, CA 94143-0628; **Phone:** 415-353-1655; **Board Cert:** Diagnostic Radiology 1984; Neuroradiology 2006; **Med School:** Geo Wash Univ 1980; **Resid:** Diagnostic Radiology, Letterman AMC 1984; **Fellow:** Neuroradiology, Walter Reed AMC 1986; **Fac Appt:** Prof Rad, UCSF

Barnes, Patrick D MD [NRad] - **Spec Exp:** Pediatric Neuroradiology; Brain Injury-Pediatric; Brain Development Abnormalities; Fetal Neuroradiology; **Hospital:** Lucile Packard Chldn's Hosp; **Address:** Lucile Packard Chldns Hosp, Pediatric Radiology, 725 Welch Rd, rm 0511, Palo Alto, CA 94304; **Phone:** 650-497-8376; **Board Cert:** Diagnostic Radiology 1977; Neuroradiology 2008; **Med School:** Univ Okla Coll Med 1973; **Resid:** Diagnostic Radiology, OK Univ Hlth Sci Ctr 1978; **Fellow:** Pediatric Neuroradiology, Chldns Hosp 1977; **Fac Appt:** Prof Rad, Stanford Univ

Cha, Soonmee MD [NRad] - **Spec Exp:** Brain Tumors; **Hospital:** UCSF Med Ctr; **Address:** 350 Parnassus Ave, Ste 307, San Francisco, CA 94143; **Phone:** 415-353-8913; **Board Cert:** Diagnostic Radiology 1996; Neuroradiology 2009; **Med School:** Georgetown Univ 1991; **Resid:** Diagnostic Radiology, North Shore U Hosp 1996; **Fellow:** Neuroradiology, NYU Med Ctr 1998; **Fac Appt:** Assoc Prof Rad, UCSF

Dillon, William P MD [NRad] - **Spec Exp:** Brain Tumors; Spinal Cord Injury; **Hospital:** UCSF Med Ctr; **Address:** 505 Parnassus Ave, rm L 371, San Francisco, CA 94143-0628; **Phone:** 415-353-1687; **Board Cert:** Diagnostic Radiology 1982; Neuroradiology 2006; **Med School:** UCLA 1978; **Resid:** Diagnostic Radiology, U Utah Hosp 1982; **Fellow:** Neuroradiology, UCSF Med Ctr 1983; **Fac Appt:** Prof Rad, UCSF

Hesselink, John R MD [NRad] - **Spec Exp:** MRI & CT of Brain & Spine; Stroke; Brain Tumor Imaging; **Hospital:** UCSD Med Ctr; **Address:** UCSD Med Ctr, Div Neuroradiology, 200 W Arbor Drive, MC 8749, San Diego, CA 92013; **Phone:** 619-543-6766; **Board Cert:** Diagnostic Radiology 1975; Neuroradiology 2005; **Med School:** Univ Wisc 1971; **Resid:** Diagnostic Radiology, U Wisconsin Med Ctr 1975; **Fellow:** Neuroradiology, Mass Genl Hosp 1979; **Fac Appt:** Prof Rad, UCSD

Higashida, Randall T MD [NRad] - **Spec Exp:** Aneurysm-Cerebral; Stroke; Intracranial Angioplasty & Stent; **Hospital:** UCSF Med Ctr; **Address:** UCSF Med Ctr, Dept Interven Neurorad, 505 Parnassus Ave, rm L352, San Francisco, CA 94143-0628; **Phone:** 415-353-1863; **Board Cert:** Diagnostic Radiology 1984; **Med School:** Tulane Univ 1980; **Resid:** Diagnostic Radiology, UCLA Med Ctr 1984; **Fellow:** Neuroradiology, UCLA Med Ctr 1985; **Fac Appt:** Clin Prof Rad, UCSF

Jarvik, Jeffrey G MD [NRad] - **Spec Exp:** Spinal Imaging; Brain Imaging; **Hospital:** Harborview Med Ctr, Univ Wash Med Ctr; **Address:** Harborview Med Ctr, Dept of Radiology, 325 Ninth Ave, Box 359728, Seattle, WA 98104; **Phone:** 206-744-3561; **Board Cert:** Diagnostic Radiology 1992; Neuroradiology 2005; **Med School:** UCSD 1987; **Resid:** Diagnostic Radiology, Hosp Univ Penn 1992; **Fellow:** Neuroradiology, Hosp Univ Penn 1993; **Fac Appt:** Prof Rad, Univ Wash

Larsen, Donald W MD [NRad] - **Spec Exp:** Interventional Neuroradiology; Stroke; Stroke Prevention; Aneurysm-Cerebral; **Hospital:** Keck Med Ctr of USC; **Address:** 1812 Verdugo Blvd, Glendale, CA 91208; **Phone:** 818-952-2236; **Board Cert:** Diagnostic Radiology 1990; **Med School:** Ros Franklin Univ/Chicago Med Sch 1985; **Resid:** Diagnostic Radiology, USC Med Ctr 1990; **Fellow:** Vascular & Interventional Radiology, USC Med Ctr 1991; Neuroradiology, USF Med Ctr 1995; **Fac Appt:** Assoc Prof Rad, USC-Keck School of Medicine

Teitelbaum, George P MD [NRad] - **Spec Exp:** Interventional Neuroradiology; Aneurysm-Cerebral; Carotid Artery Stent Placement; Vascular Lesions of the CNS; **Hospital:** Providence St Joseph Med Ctr; **Address:** Providence Med Inst-Neurosciences Ctr, 501 S Buena Vista St, Burbank, CA 91505; **Phone:** 818-847-4835; **Board Cert:** Diagnostic Radiology 1984; Neuroradiology 2008; **Med School:** UCSD 1980; **Resid:** Radiology, UC Irvine Med Ctr 1984; **Fellow:** Interventional Radiology, George Washington Univ Hosp 1985; Magnetic Resonance Imaging, Huntington Med Rsch Insts 1988; **Fac Appt:** Assoc Prof NS, USC Sch Med

Vascular & Interventional Radiology

New England

Aruny, John E MD [VIR] - **Spec Exp:** Thrombolytic Therapy; Dialysis Access; Vascular Disease; Vein Disorders; **Hospital:** Yale-New Haven Hosp; **Address:** Yale Interventional Radiology, 800 Howard Ave Fl 2, Yale Physicians Bldg, New Haven, CT 06519; **Phone:** 203-785-7026; **Board Cert:** Diag Rad with Spec Comp in Nuc Rad 1989; Vascular & Interventional Radiology 2009; **Med School:** Mexico 1983; **Resid:** Diagnostic Radiology, Westchester Co Med Ctr 1989; **Fellow:** Interventional Radiology, Brigham & Women's Hosp 1992; **Fac Appt:** Assoc Prof Rad, Yale Univ

Hallisey, Michael J MD [VIR] - **Spec Exp:** Uterine Fibroid Embolization; Liver Cancer/Chemoembolization; Peripheral Vascular Disease; Aneurysm-Aortic; **Hospital:** Hartford Hosp; **Address:** Jefferson Radiology, 399 Farmington Ave, Farmington, CT 06032; **Phone:** 860-289-3375; **Board Cert:** Diagnostic Radiology 1991; Vascular & Interventional Radiology 2009; **Med School:** Univ Conn 1986; **Resid:** Diagnostic Radiology, Hosp St Raphael 1991; **Fellow:** Cardiovascular Radiology, Alexandria Hosp 1992; **Fac Appt:** Assoc Clin Prof Rad, Univ Conn

Murphy, Timothy P MD [VIR] - **Spec Exp:** Uterine Fibroid Embolization; Aneurysm-Aortic; Hypertension-Renovascular; **Hospital:** Rhode Island Hosp; **Address:** RI Hosp, Diagnostic Imaging, 593 Eddy St Fl 3, Providence, RI 02903-4970; **Phone:** 401-444-5184; **Board Cert:** Diagnostic Radiology 1992; Vascular & Interventional Radiology 2005; **Med School:** Boston Univ 1987; **Resid:** Diagnostic Radiology, Rhode Island Hosp 1992; **Fellow:** Vascular & Interventional Radiology, Rhode Island Hosp 1993; **Fac Appt:** Prof Rad, Brown Univ

Mid Atlantic

Brown, Karen T MD [VIR] - **Spec Exp:** Liver Cancer; Radiofrequency Tumor Ablation; **Hospital:** Meml Sloan-Kettering Canc Ctr; **Address:** 1275 York Ave, New York, NY 10065; **Phone:** 212-639-5882; **Board Cert:** Diagnostic Radiology 1984; Vascular & Interventional Radiology 2004; **Med School:** Boston Univ 1979; **Resid:** Diagnostic Radiology, Mass Genl Hosp 1984; **Fellow:** Vascular & Interventional Radiology, Mass Genl Hosp 1985; **Fac Appt:** Clin Prof Rad, Cornell Univ-Weill Med Coll

Cohen, Gary S MD [VIR] - **Spec Exp:** Uterine Fibroid Embolization; Cancer Chemoembolization; Portal Hypertension; **Hospital:** Temple Univ Hosp, Jeanes Hosp; **Address:** Temple Univ-Interventional Radiology, 3401 N Broad St, Park Ave Pavilion, Fl 1, Ste C, Philadelphia, PA 19140; **Phone:** 215-707-7002; **Board Cert:** Diagnostic Radiology 1992; Vascular & Interventional Radiology 2006; **Med School:** Mount Sinai Sch Med 1988; **Resid:** Diagnostic Radiology, Temple Univ Hosp 1992; **Fellow:** Vascular & Interventional Radiology, Temple Univ Hosp 1993; **Fac Appt:** Prof Rad, Temple Univ

Denny, Donald F MD [VIR] - **Spec Exp:** Dialysis Access; Uterine Fibroids; **Hospital:** Univ Med Ctr Princeton at Plainsboro; **Address:** Princeton Radiology Assocs, 1 Plainsboro Rd, Plainsboro, NJ 08536; **Phone:** 609-497-4310; **Board Cert:** Diagnostic Radiology 1982; Vascular & Interventional Radiology 2005; **Med School:** Hahnemann Univ 1978; **Resid:** Diagnostic Radiology, Yale-New Haven Hosp 1982; **Fellow:** Cardiovascular Radiology, Brigham & Womens Hosp 1983; **Fac Appt:** Assoc Clin Prof Rad, Yale Univ

Geschwind, Jean-Francois H MD [VIR] - **Spec Exp:** Liver Cancer/Chemoembolization; Cancer Chemoembolization; Cancer Radiotherapy; **Hospital:** Johns Hopkins Hosp (page 59); **Address:** Johns Hopkins Hosp, Int Radiology, 1800 Orleans St, Ste 3287, Baltimore, MD 21287; **Phone:** 410-614-2227; **Board Cert:** Diagnostic Radiology 1998; **Med School:** Boston Univ 1991; **Resid:** Diagnostic Radiology, UCSF Med Ctr 1995; **Fellow:** Interventional Radiology, Johns Hopkins Hosp 1998; **Fac Appt:** Prof Rad, Johns Hopkins Univ

Haskal, Ziv MD [VIR] - **Spec Exp:** Uterine Fibroid Embolization; Vascular Malformations; Liver Cancer/Chemoembolization; **Hospital:** Univ of MD Med Ctr; **Address:** 419 W Redwood St, Ste 110, Baltimore, MD 21201; **Phone:** 410-328-0000; **Board Cert:** Diagnostic Radiology 1991; Vascular & Interventional Radiology 2010; **Med School:** Boston Univ 1986; **Resid:** Diagnostic Radiology, UCSF Med Ctr 1991; **Fellow:** Vascular & Interventional Radiology, UCSF Med Ctr 1992; **Fac Appt:** Prof Rad, Univ MD Sch Med

Khilnani, Neil M MD [VIR] - **Spec Exp:** Varicose Veins; Vein Disorders; Iliac Vein Obstruction; **Hospital:** NY-Presby/Weill Cornell Med Ctr, NY (page 65); **Address:** Weill Cornell Vascular Assocs, 2315 Broadway at 84th ST, Fl 4, New York, NY 10024; **Phone:** 646-962-9179; **Board Cert:** Diagnostic Radiology 1991; Vascular & Interventional Radiology 2008; **Med School:** Mount Sinai Sch Med 1986; **Resid:** Diagnostic Radiology, Columbia Presby Med Ctr 1991; **Fellow:** Vascular & Interventional Radiology, Columbia Presby Med Ctr 1992; **Fac Appt:** Assoc Prof Rad, Cornell Univ-Weill Med Coll

McLean, Gordon K MD [VIR] - **Spec Exp:** Uterine Fibroid Embolization; Angioplasty & Stent Placement; **Hospital:** St. Clair Hosp; **Address:** St Clair Hosp-Med Imaging, 1000 Bower Hill Rd, Pittsburgh, PA 15241; **Phone:** 412-942-2628; **Board Cert:** Diagnostic Radiology 1979; Vascular & Interventional Radiology 2005; **Med School:** Dartmouth Med Sch 1975; **Resid:** Diagnostic Radiology, Hosp Univ Penn 1979; **Fellow:** Angiography, Hosp Univ Penn 1980; **Fac Appt:** Prof Rad, Univ Pennsylvania

Shlansky-Goldberg, Richard D MD [VIR] - **Spec Exp:** Uterine Fibroid Embolization; Varicocele Embolization; Pelvic Congestion Syndrome; **Hospital:** Hosp Univ Penn - UPHS (page 69); **Address:** Hosp Univ Penn, Dept Radiology, 3400 Spruce St, Ground Dulles Bldg Fl 1, Philadelphia, PA 19104; **Phone:** 215-662-6839; **Board Cert:** Diagnostic Radiology 1989; Vascular & Interventional Radiology 2008; **Med School:** Univ Rochester 1984; **Resid:** Diagnostic Radiology, Thomas Jefferson Univ Hosp 1990; **Fellow:** Interventional Radiology, Hosp Univ Penn 1991; **Fac Appt:** Assoc Prof Rad, Univ Pennsylvania

Solomon, Stephen B MD [VIR] - **Spec Exp:** Radiofrequency Tumor Ablation; Kidney Cancer; Liver Cancer; Lung Cancer; **Hospital:** Meml Sloan-Kettering Canc Ctr; **Address:** Meml Sloan-Kettering Cancer Ctr, Ctr for Image Guided Intervention, 1275 York Ave, rm H118, New York, NY 10021; **Phone:** 212-639-5012; **Board Cert:** Diagnostic Radiology 1998; **Med School:** Yale Univ 1993; **Resid:** Diagnostic Radiology, Johns Hopkins Hosp 1998

Soulen, Michael C MD [VIR] - **Spec Exp:** Liver Cancer/Chemoembolization; Kidney Cancer; Radiofrequency Tumor Ablation; **Hospital:** Hosp Univ Penn - UPHS (page 69); **Address:** Hosp Univ Penn, Interventional Radiology, 3400 Spruce St, 1 Silverstein Bldg, Philadelphia, PA 19104; **Phone:** 215-615-4135; **Board Cert:** Diagnostic Radiology 1989; Vascular & Interventional Radiology 2006; **Med School:** Univ Pennsylvania 1984; **Resid:** Diagnostic Radiology, Johns Hopkins Hosp 1989; **Fellow:** Vascular & Interventional Radiology, Thomas Jefferson Univ Hosp 1991; **Fac Appt:** Prof Rad, Univ Pennsylvania

Trerotola, Scott O MD [VIR] - **Spec Exp:** Uterine Fibroid Embolization; Hereditary Hemorrhagic Telangiectasia; Arteriovenous Malformations; **Hospital:** Hosp Univ Penn - UPHS (page 69), Penn Presby Med Ctr - UPHS (page 69); **Address:** Hosp Univ Penn, Interventional Radiology, 3400 Spruce St, Ground Dulles, Fl 1, Philadelphia, PA 19104; **Phone:** 215-615-3540; **Board Cert:** Diagnostic Radiology 1991; Vascular & Interventional Radiology 2005; **Med School:** Univ Pennsylvania 1986; **Resid:** Diagnostic Radiology, Johns Hopkins Hosp 1991; **Fellow:** Vascular & Interventional Radiology, Johns Hopkins Hosp 1992; **Fac Appt:** Prof Rad, Univ Pennsylvania

Weintraub, Joshua L MD [VIR] - **Spec Exp:** Gastrointestinal Cancer; Chemoembolization & Tumor Ablation; Uterine Fibroid Embolization; Vascular Malformations; **Hospital:** NY-Presby/Columbia Univ Med Ctr, NY (page 65); **Address:** NY Presbyterian-Columbia Med Ctr, Dept Radiology, 622 W 168th St, New York, NY 10032; **Phone:** 212-305-7094; **Board Cert:** Diagnostic Radiology 1996; Vascular & Interventional Radiology 2009; **Med School:** Wayne State Univ 1991; **Resid:** Diagnostic Radiology, Beth Israel Hosp 1996; **Fellow:** Vascular & Interventional Radiology, Hosp Univ Penn 1997; **Fac Appt:** Assoc Prof Rad, Columbia P&S

Wood, Bradford J MD [VIR] - **Spec Exp:** Radiofrequency Tumor Ablation; Prostate Cancer; Clinical Trials; Gene Therapy Delivery Systems; **Hospital:** Natl Inst of Hlth - Clin Ctr; **Address:** NIH, Ctr for Interventional Oncology, 10 Center Drive Bldg 10 - rm 1C-341, MS 1182, Bethesda, MD 20892; **Phone:** 301-443-8191; **Board Cert:** Diagnostic Radiology 1996; Vascular & Interventional Radiology 2011; **Med School:** Univ VA Sch Med 1991; **Resid:** Diagnostic Radiology, Georgetown Univ Med Ctr 1996; **Fellow:** Abdominal/Interventional Radiology, Mass Genl Hosp-Harvard Med Sch 1997; Interventional Radiology, Mass Genl Hosp-Harvard Med Sch 1998

Southeast

Benenati, James F MD [VIR] - **Spec Exp:** Uterine Fibroid Embolization; Aneurysm-Abdominal Aortic; Peripheral Vascular Disease; **Hospital:** Baptist Hosp of Miami; **Address:** Baptist Hosp, Cardiac & Vascular Inst, 8900 N Kendall Drive, Miami, FL 33176; **Phone:** 786-596-5990; **Board Cert:** Diagnostic Radiology 1988; Vascular & Interventional Radiology 2005; **Med School:** Univ S Fla Coll Med 1984; **Resid:** Diagnostic Radiology, IU Hlth Hosp 1988; **Fellow:** Vascular & Interventional Radiology, Johns Hopkins Hosp 1989; **Fac Appt:** Assoc Clin Prof Rad, Univ S Fla Coll Med

Brown, Daniel B MD [VIR] - **Spec Exp:** Liver Cancer/Radioembolization; Radiofrequency Tumor Ablation; Kidney Cancer; **Hospital:** Vanderbilt Univ Med Ctr; **Address:** Vanderbilt Univ, Interventional Oncology, 1161 21st Ave S, MCN Bldg, Ste CCC-1106, Nashville, TN 37232; **Phone:** 615-343-1187; **Board Cert:** Diagnostic Radiology 2012; Vascular & Interventional Radiology 2012; **Med School:** Hahnemann Univ 1993; **Resid:** Diagnostic Radiology, Bryn Mawr Hosp 1998; **Fellow:** Vascular & Interventional Radiology, Penn State Univ 2001; **Fac Appt:** Prof Rad, Thomas Jefferson Univ

Coldwell, Douglas M MD [VIR] - **Spec Exp:** Palliative Care; Brachytherapy; Radiofrequency Tumor Ablation; Arteriovenous Malformations; **Hospital:** Univ of Louisville Hosp; **Address:** 530 S Jackson St, Louisville, KY 40202; **Phone:** 502-852-5875; **Board Cert:** Diagnostic Radiology 1986; Vascular & Interventional Radiology 1995; **Med School:** Univ Tex Med Br, Galveston 1980; **Resid:** Diagnostic Radiology, Hershey Med Ctr-Penn St Univ 1983; **Fellow:** Vascular & Interventional Radiology, MD Anderson Hosp-Tumor Inst 1984; **Fac Appt:** Prof Rad, Univ Louisville Sch Med

Katzen, Barry T MD [VIR] - **Spec Exp:** Peripheral Vascular Disease; Aneurysm-Aortic; Carotid Artery Disease; **Hospital:** Baptist Hosp of Miami; **Address:** Baptist Hosp, Cardiac & Vascular Inst, 8900 N Kendall Drive, Miami, FL 33176; **Phone:** 786-596-5990; **Board Cert:** Diagnostic Radiology 1974; Vascular & Interventional Radiology 2004; **Med School:** Univ Miami Sch Med 1970; **Resid:** Diagnostic Radiology, NY-Presby/Weill Cornell Med Ctr 1974; **Fellow:** Cardiovascular Radiology, St Vincent Med Ctr 1975; **Fac Appt:** Clin Prof Rad, Univ Miami Sch Med

Lewis, Curtis A MD [VIR] - **Spec Exp:** Interventional Radiology; Vein Disorders; **Hospital:** Grady Hlth Sys, Emory Univ Hosp; **Address:** Grady Meml Hosp, Dept Radiology, 80 Jesse Hill Jr Drive, Atlanta, GA 30303; **Phone:** 404-616-4261; **Board Cert:** Diagnostic Radiology 1991; Vascular & Interventional Radiology 2007; **Med School:** Emory Univ 1986; **Resid:** Diagnostic Radiology, Emory Univ Hosp 1991; **Fellow:** Vascular & Interventional Radiology, Emory Univ Hosp 1992; **Fac Appt:** Asst Prof Rad, Emory Univ

Matsumoto, Alan H MD [VIR] - **Spec Exp:** Aneurysm-Abdominal Aortic; Carotid Artery Disease; Vascular Disease; Endovascular Stent Grafts; **Hospital:** Univ of Virginia Hlth Sys; **Address:** Univ VA Hlth Systems Radiology, 1215 Lee St, Charlottesville, VA 22908; **Phone:** 434-243-4961; **Board Cert:** Internal Medicine 1983; Diagnostic Radiology 1987; Vascular & Interventional Radiology 2005; **Med School:** Wake Forest Univ 1980; **Resid:** Internal Medicine, U Mass Med Ctr 1983; Diagnostic Radiology, Univ NC Med Ctr 1987; **Fellow:** Interventional Radiology, Georgetown Univ Hosp 1988; **Fac Appt:** Prof Med, Univ VA Sch Med

Mauro, Matthew A MD [VIR] - **Spec Exp:** Cancer Chemoembolization; Cancer Radiotherapy; Gastrointestinal Cancer; **Hospital:** NC Memorial Hosp - UNC; **Address:** Univ NC Hosps, Dept Radiology, CB 7510, 2006 Old Clinic Bldg, 101 Manning Drive, Chapel Hill, NC 27599; **Phone:** 919-966-4238; **Board Cert:** Diagnostic Radiology 1981; Vascular & Interventional Radiology 2003; **Med School:** Cornell Univ-Weill Med Coll 1977; **Resid:** Diagnostic Radiology, Univ NC Hosps 1980; **Fellow:** Interventional Radiology, Univ NC Hosp 1981; Abdominal/Interventional Radiology, Mallinckrodt Inst 1982; **Fac Appt:** Prof Rad, Univ NC Sch Med

Midwest

Cho, Kyung J MD [VIR] - **Spec Exp:** Chemoembolization & Tumor Ablation; Vascular Malformations; Peripheral Vascular Disease; **Hospital:** Univ Michigan Med Ctr; **Address:** Univ Michigan Med Ctr, Dept Radiology, 1500 E Med Ctr Drive, CVC 5582, Ann Arbor, MI 48109-5868; **Phone:** 734-936-4466; **Board Cert:** Diagnostic Radiology 1974; Vascular & Interventional Radiology 2005; **Med School:** Korea 1966; **Resid:** Diagnostic Radiology, Wayne Med Ctr 1973; **Fellow:** Cardiovascular Radiology, Univ Michigan 1975; **Fac Appt:** Prof Rad, Univ Mich Med Sch

Darcy, Michael D MD [VIR] - **Spec Exp:** Portal Hypertension; Chemoembolization & Tumor Ablation; **Hospital:** Barnes-Jewish Hosp; **Address:** Washington Univ, Mallinckrodt Inst Radiology, 510 S Kingshighway Blvd, St Louis, MO 63110; **Phone:** 314-362-2900; **Board Cert:** Diagnostic Radiology 1985; Vascular & Interventional Radiology 2004; **Med School:** Ohio State Univ 1979; **Resid:** Surgery, Univ Minn Hosps 1982; Diagnostic Radiology, Univ Minn Hosps 1985; **Fellow:** Interventional Radiology, Univ Minn 1987; **Fac Appt:** Prof Rad, Washington Univ, St Louis

Funaki, Brian MD [VIR] - **Hospital:** Univ of Chicago Med; **Address:** Univ Chicago, Dept Radiology, 5841 S Maryland Ave, MC 2026, Chicago, IL 60637; **Phone:** 773-702-1607; **Board Cert:** Diagnostic Radiology 2010; Vascular & Interventional Radiology 2010; **Med School:** Geo Wash Univ 1992; **Resid:** Diagnostic Radiology, Univ Chicago Hosp 1996; **Fellow:** Angiography, Univ Chicago Hosp 1997; Interventional Radiology, Univ Chicago Hosp 1997; **Fac Appt:** Prof Rad, Univ Chicago-Pritzker Sch Med

Johnson, Matthew S MD [VIR] - **Spec Exp:** Liver Tumors; Uterine Fibroid Embolization; Portal Hypertension; Varicocele Embolization; **Hospital:** IU Hlth Univ Hosp, IU Health Methodist Hosp; **Address:** IU Health Univ Hosp, Interventional Radiology, 550 N University Blvd, rm 0290, Indianapolis, IN 46202-5253; **Phone:** 317-944-1828; **Board Cert:** Diagnostic Radiology 1992; Vascular & Interventional Radiology 2006; **Med School:** Univ Mich Med Sch 1986; **Resid:** Surgery, Loyola Univ Med Ctr 1988; Diagnostic Radiology, Loyola Univ Med Ctr 1992; **Fellow:** Interventional Radiology, Johns Hopkins Univ 1994; **Fac Appt:** Prof Rad, Indiana Univ

Nemcek Jr, Albert A MD [VIR] - **Spec Exp:** Radiofrequency Tumor Ablation; Vascular Disease; Liver Tumors; **Hospital:** Northwestern Meml Hosp; **Address:** Northwestern Meml Hosp, 251 E Huron St Feinberg Bldg Fl 4, Interventional Radiology Dept, Chicago, IL 60611; **Phone:** 312-926-5200; **Board Cert:** Diagnostic Radiology 1986; Vascular & Interventional Radiology 2005; **Med School:** UCSD 1982; **Resid:** Diagnostic Radiology, UCSD Med Ctr 1986; **Fellow:** Interventional Radiology, Northwestern Meml Hosp 1987; **Fac Appt:** Assoc Prof Rad, Northwestern Univ

Rilling, William S MD [VIR] - **Spec Exp:** Liver Cancer/Chemoembolization; Vascular Malformations; **Hospital:** Froedtert & Med Coll WI; **Address:** Froedtert Hosp, Dept Radiology, Div Vascular & Interventional Radiology, 9200 W Wisconsin Ave, rm 2803, Milwaukee, WI 53226; **Phone:** 414-805-3028; **Board Cert:** Diagnostic Radiology 1995; Vascular & Interventional Radiology 2008; **Med School:** Univ Wisc 1990; **Resid:** Diagnostic Radiology, Univ Wisc Affil Hosps 1995; **Fellow:** Vascular & Interventional Radiology, Northwestern Meml Hosp 1996; **Fac Appt:** Prof Rad, Univ Wisc

Salem, Riad MD [VIR] - **Spec Exp:** Cancer Radiotherapy; Cancer Chemoembolization; Liver Cancer/Chemoembolization; **Hospital:** Northwestern Meml Hosp; **Address:** Northwestern Univ Dept Radiology, 676 N St Clair St, Ste 800, Chicago, IL 60611; **Phone:** 312-695-1791; **Board Cert:** Diagnostic Radiology 1997; Vascular & Interventional Radiology 2010; **Med School:** McGill Univ 1993; **Resid:** Diagnostic Radiology, Geo Washington Univ Hosp 1997; **Fellow:** Interventional Radiology, Hosp Univ Penn 1998; **Fac Appt:** Assoc Prof Rad, Northwestern Univ

Smith, Steven J MD [VIR] - **Spec Exp:** Angioplasty-Peripheral; Uterine Fibroid Embolization; Varicocele Embolization; Arteriovenous Malformations; **Hospital:** Adventist La Grange Meml Hosp, Adventist Hinsdale Hosp; **Address:** VIRChicago, 911 N Elm St, Ste 327, Hinsdale, IL 60521; **Phone:** 630-856-7460; **Board Cert:** Diagnostic Radiology 1983; Vascular & Interventional Radiology 2006; **Med School:** Wayne State Univ 1979; **Resid:** Diagnostic Radiology, Henry Ford Hosp 1983; **Fellow:** Vascular & Interventional Radiology, Northwestern Meml Hosp 1984

Vogelzang, Robert MD [VIR] - **Spec Exp:** Uterine Fibroid Embolization; Varicocele Embolization; Vascular Malformations; **Hospital:** Northwestern Meml Hosp; **Address:** Northwestern Meml Hosp, 251 E Huron St Feinberg Bldg Fl 4, Interventional Radiology Dept, Chicago, IL 60611; **Phone:** 312-926-5200; **Board Cert:** Diagnostic Radiology 1981; Vascular & Interventional Radiology 2005; **Med School:** Ros Franklin Univ/Chicago Med Sch 1977; **Resid:** Diagnostic Radiology, Northwestern Meml Hosp 1981; **Fellow:** Vascular & Interventional Radiology, Northwestern Meml Hosp 1982; **Fac Appt:** Prof Rad, Northwestern Univ

Great Plains and Mountains

Durham, Janette D MD [VIR] - **Spec Exp:** Uterine Fibroid Embolization; Peripheral Vascular Disease; Liver Cancer; **Hospital:** Univ Colorado Hosp; **Address:** Univ CO Hosp, Interventional Radiology, 12605 E 16th Ave, MS B120, Aurora, CO 80045; **Phone:** 720-848-7440; **Board Cert:** Diagnostic Radiology 1987; Vascular & Interventional Radiology 2006; **Med School:** Indiana Univ 1983; **Resid:** Diagnostic Radiology, IU Hlth Hosp 1987; **Fellow:** Vascular & Interventional Radiology, Mass Genl Hosp 1988; **Fac Appt:** Prof Rad, Univ Colorado

Kumpe, David A MD [VIR] - **Spec Exp:** Aneurysm-Cerebral; Stroke; Interventional Neuroradiology; Cerebrovascular Disease; **Hospital:** Univ Colorado Hosp, Chldn's Hosp - Aurora (CO); **Address:** Univ CO Hosp, Interventional Radiology, 12605 E 16th Ave, MS B120, Aurora, CO 80045; **Phone:** 720-848-7440; **Board Cert:** Diagnostic Radiology 1972; Vascular & Interventional Radiology 2005; **Med School:** Harvard Med Sch 1967; **Resid:** Diagnostic Radiology, Mass Genl Hosp 1971; **Fellow:** Neurological Radiology, Kantonsspital 1976; Angiography, Kantonsspital 1976; **Fac Appt:** Prof Rad, Univ Colorado

Yakes, Wayne F MD [VIR] - **Spec Exp:** Vascular Malformations; Interventional Neuroradiology; **Hospital:** Swedish Med Ctr - Denver; **Address:** Vasacular Malformation Ctr, 501 E Hampden Ave, Ste 4600, Englewood, CO 80113; **Phone:** 303-788-4280; **Board Cert:** Diagnostic Radiology 1983; **Med School:** Creighton Univ 1979; **Resid:** Diagnostic Radiology, Fitzsimons Med Ctr 1983; **Fellow:** Angiography, Walter Reed Med Ctr 1984; Interventional Neuroradiology, Baptist Hosp 1992

Southwest

Hicks, Marshall E MD [VIR] - **Spec Exp:** Liver Cancer; Lung Cancer; **Hospital:** UT MD Anderson Canc Ctr; **Address:** UT MD Anderson Canc Ctr, Diagnostic Imaging, 1515 Holcombe Blvd, Unit 1479, Houston, TX 77030; **Phone:** 713-745-4794; **Board Cert:** Diagnostic Radiology 1987; Vascular & Interventional Radiology 2004; **Med School:** Univ KY Coll Med 1982; **Resid:** Diagnostic Radiology, IU Hlth Univ Hosp 1987; **Fellow:** Interventional Radiology, Univ CO Hosp 1988; **Fac Appt:** Prof Rad, Univ Tex, Houston

Kay, Dennis MD [VIR] - **Spec Exp:** Radiofrequency Tumor Ablation; **Hospital:** Ochsner Med Ctr-New Orleans; **Address:** Ochsner Clin, Dept Radiology, 1514 Jefferson Hwy, New Orleans, LA 70121-2429; **Phone:** 504-842-3470; **Board Cert:** Diagnostic Radiology 1986; Vascular & Interventional Radiology 2004; **Med School:** Tulane Univ 1981; **Resid:** Diagnostic Radiology, Ochsner Med Ctr 1985; **Fellow:** Vascular & Interventional Radiology, Beth Israel Deaconess Med Ctr 1986; **Fac Appt:** Assoc Clin Prof Rad, Tulane Univ

West Coast and Pacific

Dake, Michael D MD [VIR] - **Spec Exp:** Aortic Stent Grafts; Endovascular Stent Grafts; Vascular Disease; Aneurysm; **Hospital:** Stanford Univ Hosp & Clins; **Address:** Stanford Dept Cardiothoracic Surgery, 300 Pasteur Drive Fl 2nd, Falk Research Bldg, CVRB, MC5407, Stanford, CA 94305-5407; **Phone:** 650-724-0831; **Board Cert:** Internal Medicine 1981; Pulmonary Disease 1986; Diagnostic Radiology 1986; Vascular & Interventional Radiology 2006; **Med School:** Baylor Coll Med 1978; **Resid:** Internal Medicine, Baylor Affil Hosp 1982; Diagnostic Radiology, UCSF Med Ctr 1986; **Fellow:** Pulmonary Disease, UCSF Med Ctr 1983; Interventional Radiology, UCSF Med Ctr 1987; **Fac Appt:** Prof TS, Stanford Univ

Gomes, Antoinette S MD [VIR] - **Spec Exp:** Uterine Fibroid Embolization; Vascular Malformations; Chemoembolization & Tumor Ablation; Angioplasty & Stent Placement; **Hospital:** UCLA Ronald Reagan Med Ctr, Santa Monica - UCLA Med Ctr & Ortho Hosp; **Address:** UCLA Ronald Reagan Med Ctr-Dept Rad Sci, 757 Westwood Plaza, Ste 2125, Los Angeles, CA 90095; **Phone:** 310-267-8769; **Board Cert:** Diagnostic Radiology 1975; Vascular & Interventional Radiology 2004; **Med School:** Med Coll PA Hahnemann 1969; **Resid:** Internal Medicine, LAC-USC Med Ctr 1972; Diagnostic Radiology, Stanford Univ Med Ctr 1975; **Fellow:** Cardiovascular Radiology, UCLA Med Ctr 1976; Cardiovascular Radiology, Univ Minn 1978; **Fac Appt:** Prof Rad, UCLA

Goodwin, Scott C MD [VIR] - **Spec Exp:** Uterine Fibroids; Liver Cancer; **Hospital:** UC Irvine Med Ctr; **Address:** UC Irvine Med Ctr, 101 The City Drive S, MS 140, Orange, CA 92868; **Phone:** 714-456-7517; **Board Cert:** Diagnostic Radiology 1989; Vascular & Interventional Radiology 2007; **Med School:** Harvard Med Sch 1984; **Resid:** Diagnostic Radiology, UCLA Med Ctr 1988; **Fellow:** Vascular & Interventional Radiology, UCLA Med Ctr 1989; **Fac Appt:** Prof Rad, UC Irvine

Hovsepian, David M MD [VIR] - **Spec Exp:** Uterine Fibroid Embolization; Aneurysm-Aortic; Vascular Malformations; **Hospital:** Stanford Univ Hosp & Clins, Lucile Packard Chldn's Hosp; **Address:** Dept Interventional Radiology, 300 Pasteur Drive, rm H3630, MC 5642, Stanford, CA 94305-5642; **Phone:** 650-724-7362; **Board Cert:** Diagnostic Radiology 1991; Vascular & Interventional Radiology 2006; **Med School:** Columbia P&S 1986; **Resid:** Diagnostic Radiology, Columbia Presby Hosp 1991; **Fellow:** Interventional Radiology, Thomas Jefferson Univ Hosp 1993; **Fac Appt:** Prof Rad, Stanford Univ

Kaufman, John A MD [VIR] - **Spec Exp:** Uterine Fibroid Embolization; Angioplasty & Stent Placement; **Hospital:** OR Hlth & Sci Univ; **Address:** Dotter Interventional Inst, 3181 SW Sam Jackson Park Rd, Portland, OR 97239; **Phone:** 503-494-7660; **Board Cert:** Diagnostic Radiology 1990; Vascular & Interventional Radiology 2005; **Med School:** Boston Univ 1982; **Resid:** Obstetrics & Gynecology, Women & Infants Hosp 1986; Diagnostic Radiology, Boston Med Ctr 1990; **Fellow:** Vascular & Interventional Radiology, Boston Med Ctr 1991; **Fac Appt:** Prof Rad, Oregon Hlth & Sci Univ

Keller, Frederick S MD [VIR] - **Spec Exp:** Uterine Fibroid Embolization; Arterial & Venous Stents; Urinary Tract Interventions; **Hospital:** OR Hlth & Sci Univ; **Address:** Dotter Interventional Inst, 3181 SW Sam Jackson Park Rd, rm L605, Portland, OR 97239; **Phone:** 503-494-7660; **Board Cert:** Diagnostic Radiology 1977; Vascular & Interventional Radiology 2003; **Med School:** Univ Pennsylvania 1968; **Resid:** Diagnostic Radiology, OR Hlth & Sci Univ 1977; **Fac Appt:** Prof, Oregon Hlth & Sci Univ

McGahan, John P MD [VIR] - **Spec Exp:** Radiofrequency Tumor Ablation; Liver Cancer; Kidney Cancer; **Hospital:** UC Davis Med Ctr; **Address:** UC Davis Med Ctr, Radiology Dept, 4860 Y St, Ste ACC3100, Sacramento, CA 95817; **Phone:** 916-734-0655; **Board Cert:** Diagnostic Radiology 1979; **Med School:** Oregon Hlth & Sci Univ 1974; **Resid:** Surgery, UC Davis Med Ctr 1976; Diagnostic Radiology, UC Davis Med Ctr 1979; **Fac Appt:** Prof Rad, UC Davis

Roberts, Anne C MD [VIR] - **Spec Exp:** Uterine Fibroids; Pelvic Congestion Syndrome; Peripheral Vascular Disease; **Hospital:** UCSD Med Ctr, VA San Diego Hlthcre Sys; **Address:** UCSD Thornton Hosp- Dept of Rad, 9300 Campus Point Drive, La Jolla, CA 92037; **Phone:** 858-657-6698; **Board Cert:** Diagnostic Radiology 1986; Vascular & Interventional Radiology 2004; **Med School:** UCSD 1982; **Resid:** Diagnostic Radiology, Mass Genl Hospital 1986; **Fellow:** Vascular & Interventional Radiology, Mass Genl Hospital 1987; **Fac Appt:** Prof Rad, UCSD

Valji, Karim MD [VIR] - **Spec Exp:** Thrombolytic Therapy; **Hospital:** Univ Wash Med Ctr; **Address:** Univ of WA Med Ctr-Dept Rad, 1959 NE Pacific St, Box 357115, Seattle, WA 98195-7115; **Phone:** 206-598-7200; **Board Cert:** Diagnostic Radiology 1989; Vascular & Interventional Radiology 2009; **Med School:** Harvard Med Sch 1982; **Resid:** Internal Medicine, UCSF Med Ctr 1984; Diagnostic Radiology, UCSD Med Ctr 1988; **Fellow:** Angiography, UCSD Med Ctr 1989; **Fac Appt:** Prof Rad, Univ Wash

NYU Langone
MEDICAL CENTER

550 First Avenue *(at 31st Street)*
New York, NY 10016

www.NYULMC.org

Physician Referral: **888-7-NYU-MED** *(888-769-8633)*

RADIOLOGY

NYU Langone Radiology is committed to capturing the best images possible with the lowest dose of radiation. As an academic medical center, our radiologists are in a unique position to take the lead in helping to define and advance radiology in today's rapidly evolving technological environment.

Expertise

NYU Langone Medical Center's board certified radiologists and licensed technologists specialize in imaging and are involved in a variety of innovative collaborations and research initiatives. The Department consists of more than 100 sub-specialized academic radiologists, many of them acknowledged leaders and innovators in their fields.

Advanced Technology

NYU Langone uses some of the most advanced imaging equipment in the world, including high and ultra high-field MRI imaging systems (known as 1.5T and 3T magnets). MRI scanners are shorter and wider than ever, making for a more patient-friendly experience. The Center for Biomedical Imaging, an advanced research facility, features a powerful 7T magnet.

Recognition for Safety and Quality

We continually follow a rigorous set of quality standards and maintain accreditation by the American College of Radiology (ACR). Designated by the ACR as a "Breast Imaging Center of Excellence", our team maintains high practice standards in image quality, personnel qualifications, facility equipment, quality control procedures and quality assurance programs.

Patient Focused Approach

We are located in Manhattan, Brooklyn, Queens, and Long Island and participate in many insurance plans. Timely delivery of reports and images allow physicians to view patient exam status, reports and images online. In addition to our convenient hours, weekend, evening and often same-day appointments are available. Language interpretation services are available as needed.

Our Areas of Specialization

Diagnostic services include MRI, CT, ultrasound, PET/CT, X-ray, interventional radiology and nuclear medicine. Sub-specialized radiologists provide diagnostic interpretation in abdominal, biomedical, breast, cardiac, chest, emergency, general, musculoskeletal, neuroradiology, neuro interventional, nuclear medicine, pediatric, vascular interventional, and women's imaging. Specialty procedures include coronary artery disease and virtual colonoscopy screening, stereotactic biopsy capability, minimally invasive techniques including radiofrequency ablation, chemoembolization, radioimmunotherapy, and bone densitometry.

Top Doctors Make A Difference

Reproductive Endocrinology

a subspecialty of Obstetrics & Gynecology

An obstetrician/gynecologist who is capable of managing complex problems relating to reproductive endocrinology and infertility.

Training Required: Four years *plus* two years in clinical practice before certification in obstetrics and gynecology is complete *plus* additional training and examination in reproductive endocrinology.

REPRODUCTIVE ENDOCRINOLOGY

New England

Buster, John E MD [RE] - **Spec Exp:** Infertility-IVF; **Hospital:** Tufts Med Ctr; **Address:** Tufts Med Ctr, Repro Endocrinology, 800 Washington St, Box 36, Boston, MA 02111; **Phone:** 617-636-0053; **Board Cert:** Obstetrics & Gynecology 2012; Reproductive Endocrinology 2012; **Med School:** UCLA 1966; **Resid:** Obstetrics & Gynecology, Harbor-UCLA Med Ctr 1971; **Fellow:** Reproductive Endocrinology, Harbor-UCLA Med Ctr 1973; **Fac Appt:** Prof ObG, Tufts Univ

Crowley Jr, William F MD [RE] - **Spec Exp:** Pituitary Disorders; Kallmann's Syndrome; Fertility Preservation in Cancer; **Hospital:** Mass Genl Hosp; **Address:** MGH, Reproductive Endocrinology, 55 Fruit St, Ste BHX 511, Boston, MA 02114; **Phone:** 617-726-8433; **Board Cert:** Internal Medicine 1974; Endocrinology 1977; **Med School:** Tufts Univ 1969; **Resid:** Internal Medicine, Naval Hosp 1973; Internal Medicine, Mass Genl Hosp 1974; **Fellow:** Reproductive Endocrinology, Mass Genl Hosp 1976; **Fac Appt:** Prof Med, Harvard Med Sch

Ginsburg, Elizabeth S MD [RE] - **Spec Exp:** Infertility-IVF; Fertility Preservation in Cancer; **Hospital:** Brigham & Women's Hosp; **Address:** Brigham & Women's Hosp, Reproductive Med, 75 Francis St ASB1 Bldg - Ste 3300, Boston, MA 02115; **Phone:** 617-732-4222; **Board Cert:** Obstetrics & Gynecology 2012; Reproductive Endocrinology 2012; **Med School:** Mount Sinai Sch Med 1985; **Resid:** Obstetrics & Gynecology, Brigham & Womens Hosp 1989; **Fellow:** Reproductive Endocrinology, Brigham & Womens Hosp 1991; **Fac Appt:** Assoc Prof ObG, Harvard Med Sch

Hill III, Joseph A MD [RE] - **Spec Exp:** Miscarriage-Recurrent; Infertility-Female; Infertility-IVF; **Hospital:** Portsmouth Regl Hosp, Winchester Hosp; **Address:** Fertility Ctr of New England, 875 Greenland Rd, Orchard Park C Bldg, Portsmouth, NH 03801; **Phone:** 781-942-7000 x601; **Board Cert:** Obstetrics & Gynecology 2012; Reproductive Endocrinology 2012; **Med School:** Med Coll GA 1981; **Resid:** Obstetrics & Gynecology, Med Coll Ga Hosp 1985; **Fellow:** Reproductive Endocrinology, Brigham-Womens Hosp/Harvard 1987; Reproductive Immunology, Brigham-Womens Hosp/Harvard 1988

Hornstein, Mark D MD [RE] - **Spec Exp:** Infertility-IVF; Endometriosis; Laparoscopic Surgery; Hysteroscopic Surgery; **Hospital:** Brigham & Women's Hosp, Newton - Wellesley Hosp; **Address:** Brigham & Women's Hosp, 75 Francis St, Boston, MA 02115; **Phone:** 617-732-4648; **Board Cert:** Obstetrics & Gynecology 2012; Reproductive Endocrinology 2012; **Med School:** Univ Cincinnati 1982; **Resid:** Obstetrics & Gynecology, Brigham & Women's Hosp 1986; **Fellow:** Reproductive Endocrinology, Brigham & Women's Hosp 1988; **Fac Appt:** Assoc Prof ObG, Harvard Med Sch

Isaacson, Keith B MD [RE] - **Spec Exp:** Infertility; Endometriosis; Minimally Invasive Surgery; **Hospital:** Newton - Wellesley Hosp, Mass Genl Hosp; **Address:** 2014 Washington St Fl 2 West, Newton, MA 02462; **Phone:** 617-243-5205; **Board Cert:** Obstetrics & Gynecology 2012; Reproductive Endocrinology 2012; **Med School:** Med Coll GA 1983; **Resid:** Obstetrics & Gynecology, Ochsner Med Ctr 1987; **Fellow:** Reproductive Endocrinology, Hosp Univ Penn - UPHS 1989; **Fac Appt:** Assoc Prof ObG, Harvard Med Sch

Johnson, Julia V MD [RE] - **Spec Exp:** Infertility-IVF; Endometriosis; Menopause Problems; **Hospital:** UMass Mem Med Ctr-Memorial Campus; **Address:** U Mass Medical Ctr-Memorial Campus, 119 Belmont St, Worcester, MA 01605; **Phone:** 508-334-1345; **Board Cert:** Obstetrics & Gynecology 2012; Reproductive Endocrinology/Infertility 2012; **Med School:** Med Coll GA 1984; **Resid:** Obstetrics & Gynecology, Med Coll of Georgia 1988; **Fellow:** Reproductive Endocrinology, Univ Texas Hlth Sci Ctr 1990; **Fac Appt:** Prof ObG, Univ Mass Sch Med

Luciano, Anthony A MD [RE] - **Spec Exp:** Infertility; Endometriosis; Menopause Problems; Osteoporosis; **Hospital:** Hosp of Central CT at New Britain, Hartford Hosp; **Address:** Ctr Fertility & Womens Hlth, 100 Grand St, Ste E3, New Britain, CT 06050; **Phone:** 860-224-5467; **Board Cert:** Obstetrics & Gynecology 1980; Reproductive Endocrinology 1981; **Med School:** Univ Conn 1973; **Resid:** Obstetrics & Gynecology, Univ of Conn Hlth Ctr, John Dempsey Hosp 1978; **Fellow:** Reproductive Endocrinology, Univ of Conn Hlth Ctr, John Dempsey Hosp 1981; **Fac Appt:** Prof ObG, Univ Conn

Oskowitz, Selwyn P MD [RE] - **Spec Exp:** Infertility-IVF; **Hospital:** Beth Israel Deaconess Med Ctr - Boston; **Address:** Boston IVF, 1 Brookline Pl, Ste 302, Brookline, MA 02445; **Phone:** 617-735-9000; **Board Cert:** Obstetrics & Gynecology 1981; **Med School:** South Africa 1970; **Resid:** Obstetrics & Gynecology, Univ Colorado Med Ctr 1977; **Fellow:** Reproductive Endocrinology, Beth Israel Deaconess Med Ctr 1984; **Fac Appt:** Asst Prof ObG, Harvard Med Sch

Patrizio, Pasquale MD [RE] - **Spec Exp:** Infertility-IVF; Fertility Preservation in Cancer; **Hospital:** Yale-New Haven Hosp; **Address:** Yale Fertility Ctr, Dept OB/GYN, 150 Sargent Drive, New Haven, CT 06511; **Phone:** 203-785-4708; **Board Cert:** Obstetrics & Gynecology 2007; Reproductive Endocrinology 2010; **Med School:** Italy 1983; **Resid:** Obstetrics & Gynecology, Univ Naples 1987; Reproductive Endocrinology, Univ Pisa 1990; **Fellow:** Infertility, UC Irvine Med Ctr 1995; **Fac Appt:** Prof ObG, Yale Univ

Petrozza, John C MD [RE] - **Spec Exp:** Pain-Chronic Pelvic; Endometriosis; Minimally Invasive Surgery; Infertility-IVF; **Hospital:** Mass Genl Hosp; **Address:** Mass Genl Hosp, Fertility Ctr, 55 Fruit St Yawkey Bldg - Ste 10A, Boston, MA 02114; **Phone:** 617-726-8868; **Board Cert:** Obstetrics & Gynecology 2012; Reproductive Endocrinology/Infertility 2012; **Med School:** Univ Tex Med Br, Galveston 1990; **Resid:** Obstetrics & Gynecology, Univ Texas Affil Hosp 1994; **Fellow:** Reproductive Endocrinology, Tufts New England Med Ctr 1996; **Fac Appt:** Asst Prof ObG, Harvard Med Sch

Toth, Thomas L MD [RE] - **Spec Exp:** Infertility-IVF; Fertility Preservation; Infertility; **Hospital:** Mass Genl Hosp; **Address:** Mass Genl Hosp, Fertility Ctr, 55 Fruit St, Yawkey Bldg, Ste 10A, Boston, MA 02114-2621; **Phone:** 617-726-8868; **Board Cert:** Obstetrics & Gynecology 2012; Reproductive Endocrinology/Infertility 2012; **Med School:** Univ MO-Kansas City 1986; **Resid:** Obstetrics & Gynecology, Mass Genl Hosp/Brigham & Womens Hosp 1990; **Fellow:** Reproductive Endocrinology, Jones Inst for Reproductive Med 1992; **Fac Appt:** Assoc Prof ObG, Harvard Med Sch

Zinaman, Michael J MD [RE] - **Spec Exp:** Endometriosis; Infertility; Uterine Fibroids; **Hospital:** Steward St Elizabeth's Med Ctr-Boston; **Address:** St Elizabeth's Med Ctr, 736 Cambridge St, Fl 5, Boston, MA 02135; **Phone:** 617-562-7060; **Board Cert:** Obstetrics & Gynecology 2012; Reproductive Endocrinology 2012; **Med School:** SUNY Downstate 1981; **Resid:** Obstetrics & Gynecology, Univ Chicago Affil Hosps 1986; **Fellow:** Reproductive Endocrinology, Georgetown Univ Affil Hosps 1989; **Fac Appt:** Prof ObG, Tufts Univ

Mid Atlantic

Copperman, Alan B MD [RE] - **Spec Exp:** Infertility-IVF; Fertility Preservation in Cancer; Hysteroscopic Surgery; **Hospital:** Mt Sinai Med Ctr (page 62); **Address:** Reproductive Med Assocs, 635 Madison Ave Fl 10, New York, NY 10022; **Phone:** 212-756-5777; **Board Cert:** Obstetrics & Gynecology 2012; Reproductive Endocrinology 2012; **Med School:** NY Med Coll 1989; **Resid:** Obstetrics & Gynecology, Yale-New Haven Hosp 1993; **Fellow:** Reproductive Endocrinology, Mount Sinai Med Ctr 1995; **Fac Appt:** Clin Prof ObG, Mount Sinai Sch Med

De Cherney, Alan H MD [RE] - **Spec Exp:** Infertility; Gynecologic Surgery; **Hospital:** Natl Inst of Hlth - Clin Ctr, Unif Serv Univ of the Hlth Sci; **Address:** NIH-Reproductive Endocrinology, 10 Center Drive, rm 1-3140, MS 1109, Bethesda, MD 20814; **Phone:** 301-496-5800; **Board Cert:** Obstetrics & Gynecology 1989; Reproductive Endocrinology 1979; **Med School:** Temple Univ 1967; **Resid:** Obstetrics & Gynecology, Hosp Univ Penn 1972; **Fac Appt:** Prof ObG, Uniformed Srvs Univ, Bethesda

Gracia, Clarisa R MD [RE] - **Spec Exp:** Fertility Preservation in Cancer; **Hospital:** Hosp Univ Penn - UPHS (page 69); **Address:** Penn Fertility Care, 3701 Market St, Ste 800, Philadelphia, PA 19104; **Phone:** 215-662-6100; **Board Cert:** Obstetrics & Gynecology 2007; Reproductive Endocrinology 2007; **Med School:** SUNY Buffalo 1997; **Resid:** Obstetrics & Gynecology, Hosp Univ Penn 2001; **Fellow:** Reproductive Endocrinology, Hosp Univ Penn 2003; **Fac Appt:** Asst Prof ObG, Univ Pennsylvania

Grazi, Richard MD [RE] - **Spec Exp:** Infertility-IVF; Preimplantation Genetic Diagnosis; Fertility Preservation in Cancer; **Hospital:** Maimonides Med Ctr (page 60), Richmond Univ Med Ctr; **Address:** 1355 84th St, Brooklyn, NY 11228-3030; **Phone:** 718-283-8600; **Board Cert:** Obstetrics & Gynecology 2006; Reproductive Endocrinology/Infertility 2006; **Med School:** SUNY Buffalo 1981; **Resid:** Obstetrics & Gynecology, NYU Med Ctr 1985; **Fellow:** Reproductive Endocrinology, UMDNJ Med Ctr 1987; **Fac Appt:** Assoc Clin Prof ObG, Mount Sinai Sch Med

Grifo, James A MD/PhD [RE] - **Spec Exp:** Preimplantation Genetic Diagnosis; Fertility Preservation in Cancer; Hysteroscopic Surgery; Laparoscopic Surgery; **Hospital:** NYU Langone Med Ctr (page 68); **Address:** NYU Med Ctr, Reproductive Endocrinology, 660 1st Ave Fl 5, New York, NY 10016; **Phone:** 212-263-7978; **Board Cert:** Obstetrics & Gynecology 2012; Reproductive Endocrinology 2012; **Med School:** Case West Res Univ 1984; **Resid:** Obstetrics & Gynecology, NY-Presby/Weill Cornell Med Ctr 1988; **Fellow:** Reproductive Endocrinology, Yale-New Haven Hosp 1990; **Fac Appt:** Prof ObG, NYU Sch Med

Grunfeld, Lawrence MD [RE] - **Spec Exp:** Infertility-IVF; Hysteroscopic Surgery; **Hospital:** Mt Sinai Med Ctr (page 62); **Address:** Reproductive Medicine Associates of NY, 635 Madison Ave, Fl 10th, New York, NY 10022-1009; **Phone:** 212-756-5777; **Board Cert:** Obstetrics & Gynecology 2011; Reproductive Endocrinology 2011; **Med School:** Mount Sinai Sch Med 1979; **Resid:** Obstetrics & Gynecology, Montefiore Med Ctr 1984; **Fellow:** Reproductive Endocrinology, Montefiore Med Ctr 1987; **Fac Appt:** Assoc Clin Prof ObG, Mount Sinai Sch Med

Keefe, David L MD [RE] - **Spec Exp:** Infertility-IVF; Infertility-Advanced Maternal Age; **Hospital:** NYU Langone Med Ctr (page 68); **Address:** NYU Fertility Center, 660 First Ave Fl 5, New York, NY 10016; **Phone:** 212-263-3360; **Board Cert:** Obstetrics & Gynecology 2012; Reproductive Endocrinology 2012; **Med School:** Georgetown Univ 1980; **Resid:** Psychiatry, Cambridge Hosp 1983; Obstetrics & Gynecology, Yale New Haven Hosp 1989; **Fellow:** Neuroendocrinology, Northwestern Univ 1985; Reproductive Endocrinology, Yale New Haven Hosp 1992; **Fac Appt:** Prof ObG, NYU Sch Med

Keltz, Martin D MD [RE] - **Spec Exp:** Infertility-IVF; Pregnancy Loss-Recurrent; **Hospital:** St. Luke's - Roosevelt Hosp Ctr - Roosevelt Div (page 56); **Address:** 425 W 59th St, Ste 5A, New York, NY 10019; **Phone:** 212-523-7751; **Board Cert:** Obstetrics & Gynecology 2012; Reproductive Endocrinology 2012; **Med School:** NYU Sch Med 1989; **Resid:** Obstetrics & Gynecology, Bellevue Hosp 1993; **Fellow:** Reproductive Endocrinology, Yale-New Haven Hosp 1996; **Fac Appt:** Assoc Clin Prof ObG, Columbia P&S

Legro, Richard S MD [RE] - **Spec Exp:** Polycystic Ovarian Syndrome; Menstrual Disorders; Ovarian Failure; Infertility-IVF; **Hospital:** Penn State Milton S Hershey Med Ctr; **Address:** Hershey Med Ctr, 500 University Drive, Box 850, MC H103, Hershey, PA 17033-0850; **Phone:** 717-531-8478; **Board Cert:** Obstetrics & Gynecology 2012; Reproductive Endocrinology 2012; **Med School:** Mount Sinai Sch Med 1987; **Resid:** Obstetrics & Gynecology, Magee-Womens Hosp 1991; **Fellow:** Reproductive Endocrinology, USC Women's Hosp 1993; **Fac Appt:** Prof ObG, Penn State Coll Med

Licciardi, Frederick L MD [RE] - **Spec Exp:** Fertility Preservation in Cancer; Reproductive Surgery; Infertility; Infertility-IVF; **Hospital:** NYU Langone Med Ctr (page 68); **Address:** NYU Fertility Ctr, 660 First Ave, 5th Fl, New York, NY 10016; **Phone:** 212-263-7754; **Board Cert:** Obstetrics & Gynecology 2012; Reproductive Endocrinology 2012; **Med School:** UMDNJ-Rutgers Med Sch 1986; **Resid:** Obstetrics & Gynecology, St Barnabas Med Ctr 1990; **Fellow:** Reproductive Endocrinology, NY Hosp-Cornell Med Ctr 1992; **Fac Appt:** Assoc Prof ObG, NYU Sch Med

McClamrock, Howard D MD [RE] - **Spec Exp:** Infertility-IVF; Prenatal Genetic Diagnosis; **Hospital:** Univ of MD Med Ctr, Univ of MD-St. Joseph Med Ctr; **Address:** 720 Aliceanna St, Ste 300, Baltimore, MD 21202; **Phone:** 443-825-3340; **Board Cert:** Obstetrics & Gynecology 2012; Reproductive Endocrinology 2012; **Med School:** Univ NC Sch Med 1981; **Resid:** Obstetrics & Gynecology, Univ Maryland Affil Hosp 1986; **Fellow:** Reproductive Endocrinology, Univ Maryland 1988; **Fac Appt:** Assoc Prof ObG, Univ MD Sch Med

McGovern, Peter G MD [RE] - **Spec Exp:** Infertility-IVF; Fertility Preservation in Cancer; **Hospital:** Univ Hosp (Newark), Hackensack Univ Med Ctr; **Address:** University Reproductive Assocs, 214 Terrace Ave, Hasbrouck Heights, NJ 07604; **Phone:** 201-288-6330; **Board Cert:** Obstetrics & Gynecology 2012; Reproductive Endocrinology/Infertility 2012; **Med School:** NYU Sch Med 1986; **Resid:** Obstetrics & Gynecology, NYU-Bellevue Hosp Ctr 1990; **Fellow:** Reproductive Endocrinology, UMDNJ-Newark 1992; **Fac Appt:** Prof ObG, UMDNJ-NJ Med Sch, Newark

Mukherjee, Tanmoy MD [RE] - **Spec Exp:** Infertility-IVF; Endometriosis; Uterine Fibroids; **Hospital:** Mt Sinai Med Ctr (page 62); **Address:** Reproductive Medicine Assocs, 635 Madison Ave, Fl 10, New York, NY 10022; **Phone:** 212-756-5777; **Board Cert:** Obstetrics & Gynecology 2012; Reproductive Endocrinology 2012; **Med School:** Albert Einstein Coll Med 1990; **Resid:** Obstetrics & Gynecology, Montefiore Med Ctr 1994; **Fellow:** Reproductive Endocrinology, Mount Sinai Med Ctr 1996; **Fac Appt:** Clin Prof ObG, Mount Sinai Sch Med

Noyes, Nicole MD [RE] - **Spec Exp:** Fertility Preservation in Cancer; Infertility-IVF; Infertility; **Hospital:** NYU Langone Med Ctr (page 68), Bellevue Hosp Ctr; **Address:** NYU Fertility Ctr, 660 First Ave, 5th FL, New York, NY 10016; **Phone:** 212-263-7981; **Board Cert:** Obstetrics & Gynecology 2012; Reproductive Endocrinology 2012; **Med School:** Univ VT Coll Med 1986; **Resid:** Obstetrics & Gynecology, NY Hosp-Cornell Med Ctr 1990; **Fellow:** Reproductive Endocrinology, NY Hosp-Cornell Med Ctr 1992; **Fac Appt:** Assoc Prof ObG, NYU Sch Med

Pfeifer, Samantha M MD [RE] - **Spec Exp:** Infertility-Female; Endometriosis; Laparoscopic Surgery; Congenital Anomalies-Gynecologic; **Hospital:** Hosp Univ Penn - UPHS (page 69); **Address:** Penn Health for Women at Radnor, 250 King of Prussia Rd, Ste 2A, Radnor, PA 19087; **Phone:** 610-902-2500; **Board Cert:** Obstetrics & Gynecology 2012; Reproductive Endocrinology 2012; **Med School:** Univ Pennsylvania 1986; **Resid:** Obstetrics & Gynecology, Hosp Univ Penn 1990; **Fellow:** Reproductive Endocrinology, Hosp Univ Penn 1993; **Fac Appt:** Assoc Prof ObG, Univ Pennsylvania

Rosenwaks, Zev MD [RE] - **Spec Exp:** Infertility-IVF; Genetic Disorders; Fertility Preservation in Cancer; **Hospital:** NY-Presby/Weill Cornell Med Ctr, NY (page 65); **Address:** Ctr For Reproductive Medicine & Infertility, 1305 York Ave Fl 6, New York, NY 10021-4872; **Phone:** 646-962-3743; **Board Cert:** Obstetrics & Gynecology 1978; Reproductive Endocrinology 1981; **Med School:** SUNY Downstate 1972; **Resid:** Obstetrics & Gynecology, LI Jewish Med Ctr 1976; **Fellow:** Reproductive Endocrinology, Johns Hopkins Hosp 1978; **Fac Appt:** Prof ObG, Cornell Univ-Weill Med Coll

Sanfilippo, Joseph S MD [RE] - **Spec Exp:** Adolescent Gynecology; Pediatric Gynecology; Minimally Invasive Surgery; Infertility; **Hospital:** Magee-Womens Hosp - UPMC, Chldns Hosp of Pittsburgh - UPMC; **Address:** Ctr for Fertility & Repro Endocrinology, Magee-Womens Hosp, 300 Halket St, rm 2309, Pittsburgh, PA 15213; **Phone:** 412-641-1204; **Board Cert:** Obstetrics & Gynecology 2007; Reproductive Endocrinology 2007; **Med School:** Univ Hlth Scis, Chicago Med Sch 1973; **Resid:** Obstetrics & Gynecology, SUNY Upstate Med Ctr 1977; **Fellow:** Reproductive Endocrinology, Univ Louisville Hosp 1979; **Fac Appt:** Prof ObG, Univ Pittsburgh

Sauer, Mark V MD [RE] - **Spec Exp:** Infertility-IVF; Fertility Preservation in Cancer; **Hospital:** NY-Presby/Columbia Univ Med Ctr, NY (page 65); **Address:** 1790 Broadway, Fl 2, New York, NY 10019; **Phone:** 646-756-8282; **Board Cert:** Obstetrics & Gynecology 2012; Reproductive Endocrinology 2012; **Med School:** Univ IL Coll Med 1980; **Resid:** Obstetrics & Gynecology, Univ Illinois Med Ctr 1984; **Fellow:** Reproductive Endocrinology, Harbor-UCLA Med Ctr 1986; **Fac Appt:** Prof ObG, Columbia P&S

Schlaff, William D MD [RE] - **Spec Exp:** Infertility; Endometriosis; Vaginal/Uterine Abnormalities; **Hospital:** Thomas Jefferson Univ Hosp; **Address:** Jefferson Univ Dept OB&Gyn, 834 Chestnut St, Ste 300, Philadelphia, PA 19107; **Phone:** 215-955-5000; **Board Cert:** Obstetrics & Gynecology 2012; Reproductive Endocrinology 2012; **Med School:** Univ Mich Med Sch 1977; **Resid:** Obstetrics & Gynecology, Univ Mich Hosps 1981; **Fellow:** Reproductive Endocrinology, Johns Hopkins Hosp 1985; **Fac Appt:** Prof ObG, Jefferson Med Coll

Seifer, David B MD [RE] - **Spec Exp:** Infertility-IVF; Infertility-Advanced Maternal Age; Fertility Preservation in Cancer; **Hospital:** Maimonides Med Ctr (page 60); **Address:** Genesis Fertility & Reproductive Med, 1355 84th St, Brooklyn, NY 11228; **Phone:** 718-283-8600; **Board Cert:** Obstetrics & Gynecology 2012; Reproductive Endocrinology/Infertility 2012; **Med School:** Univ IL Coll Med 1981; **Resid:** Obstetrics & Gynecology, Stanford Univ Hosp & Clins 1985; **Fellow:** Reproductive Endocrinology, Yale-New Haven Hosp 1991; **Fac Appt:** Prof ObG, Mount Sinai Sch Med

Sondheimer, Steven J MD [RE] - **Spec Exp:** Infertility-Female; Infertility-IVF; Endometriosis; **Hospital:** Hosp Univ Penn - UPHS (page 69); **Address:** Penn Fertility Care, 3701 Market St, Ste 800, Philadelphia, PA 19104; **Phone:** 215-662-6100; **Board Cert:** Obstetrics & Gynecology 2005; Reproductive Endocrinology 2005; **Med School:** Univ Pennsylvania 1974; **Resid:** Obstetrics & Gynecology, Hosp Univ Penn 1978; **Fellow:** Reproductive Endocrinology, Hosp Univ Penn 1980; **Fac Appt:** Prof ObG, Univ Pennsylvania

Weiss, Gerson MD [RE] - **Spec Exp:** Infertility; Menopause Problems; **Hospital:** Hackensack Univ Med Ctr, Univ Hosp (Newark); **Address:** 214 Terrace Ave, Hasbrouck Heights, NJ 07604-1815; **Phone:** 201-288-6330; **Board Cert:** Obstetrics & Gynecology 2012; Reproductive Endocrinology 2012; **Med School:** NYU Sch Med 1964; **Resid:** Obstetrics & Gynecology, Bellevue Hosp Ctr 1969; **Fellow:** Reproductive Endocrinology, Univ Pittsburgh Affil Hosp 1973; **Fac Appt:** Prof ObG, UMDNJ-NJ Med Sch, Newark

Widra, Eric A MD [RE] - **Spec Exp:** Infertility-IVF; **Hospital:** MedStar Georgetown Univ Hosp; **Address:** Shady Grove Fertility, 2021 K St NW, Ste 701, Washington, DC 20006; **Phone:** 202-296-2595; **Board Cert:** Obstetrics & Gynecology 2012; Reproductive Endocrinology/Infertility 2012; **Med School:** UMDNJ-RW Johnson Med Sch 1990; **Resid:** Obstetrics & Gynecology, Thomas Jefferson Univ Hosp 1994; **Fellow:** Reproductive Endocrinology, George Washington Univ Hosp 1996; **Fac Appt:** Prof ObG, Georgetown Univ

Zacur, Howard A MD/PhD [RE] - **Spec Exp:** Prolactin Disorders; Uterine Fibroids; Hormonal Disorders; Infertility-IVF; **Hospital:** Johns Hopkins Hosp (page 59); **Address:** 10753 Falls Rd, Ste 335, Lutherville, MD 21093; **Phone:** 410-583-2794; **Board Cert:** Obstetrics & Gynecology 1994; Reproductive Endocrinology 1984; **Med School:** Univ Miami Sch Med 1973; **Resid:** Obstetrics & Gynecology, Johns Hopkins Hosp 1980; **Fellow:** Reproductive Endocrinology, Johns Hopkins Hosp 1982; **Fac Appt:** Prof ObG, Johns Hopkins Univ

Southeast

Azziz, Ricardo MD [RE] - **Spec Exp:** Infertility-Female; Reproductive Surgery; Polycystic Ovarian Syndrome; **Hospital:** Georgia Regents Med Ctr-Augusta; **Address:** Med Coll GA, Kelly Admin Bldg, rm 311, 1120 15th St, Augusta, GA 30912; **Phone:** 706-722-4434; **Board Cert:** Obstetrics & Gynecology 2007; Reproductive Endocrinology 2007; **Med School:** Penn State Coll Med 1981; **Resid:** Obstetrics & Gynecology, Georgetown Univ Hosp 1985; **Fellow:** Reproductive Endocrinology, Johns Hopkins Hosp 1987; **Fac Appt:** Prof ObG, UCLA

Bateman, Bruce MD [RE] - **Spec Exp:** Infertility-IVF; **Hospital:** Univ of Virginia Hlth Sys; **Address:** 595 Martha Jefferson Drive, Ste 390, Charlottesville, VA 22911; **Phone:** 434-654-8520; **Board Cert:** Obstetrics & Gynecology 1977; Reproductive Endocrinology/Infertility 1984; **Med School:** Med Coll GA 1970; **Resid:** Obstetrics & Gynecology, Univ Va Med Ctr 1975; **Fellow:** Reproductive Endocrinology, Univ Va Med Ctr 1975

Blackwell, Richard E MD/PhD [RE] - **Spec Exp:** Infertility-Female; Women's Health; Menopause Problems; **Hospital:** UAB Hosp; **Address:** Women & Infants Ctr, 1700 6 Ave S, rm 9103, Birmingham, AL 35249; **Phone:** 205-996-3130; **Board Cert:** Obstetrics & Gynecology 1982; Reproductive Endocrinology 1987; **Med School:** Baylor Coll Med 1975; **Resid:** Obstetrics & Gynecology, UAB Hosp 1980; **Fellow:** Reproductive Endocrinology, UAB Hosp 1983; **Fac Appt:** Prof Emeritus ObG, UAB Sch Med

DeVane, Gary W MD [RE] - **Spec Exp:** Infertility-IVF; Miscarriage-Recurrent; Endometriosis; Vaginal/Uterine Abnormalities; **Hospital:** Florida Hosp - Orlando, Winnie Palmer Hosp for Women & Babies; **Address:** Ctr Reproductive Med, 3435 Pinehurst Ave, Orlando, FL 32804-4049; **Phone:** 407-740-0909; **Board Cert:** Obstetrics & Gynecology 1977; Reproductive Endocrinology 1982; **Med School:** Baylor Coll Med 1971; **Resid:** Obstetrics & Gynecology, UCSD Med Ctr 1975; **Fellow:** Reproductive Endocrinology, UT Southwestern Med Ctr 1980; **Fac Appt:** Assoc Clin Prof ObG, Univ Fla Coll Med

Durso, Nancy MD [RE] - **Spec Exp:** Infertility-IVF; Uterine Fibroids; Endometriosis; **Hospital:** Inova Fairfax Hosp; **Address:** 8501 Arlington Blvd, Ste 500, Fairfax, VA 22031; **Phone:** 703-876-6311; **Board Cert:** Obstetrics & Gynecology 2012; Reproductive Endocrinology/Infertility 2012; **Med School:** Univ VA Sch Med 1983; **Resid:** Obstetrics & Gynecology, St Louis/Washington Univ 1987; **Fellow:** Reproductive Endocrinology, Washington Univ Sch Med 1989

Fritz, Marc A MD [RE] - **Spec Exp:** Infertility-IVF; Menopause Problems; **Hospital:** NC Memorial Hosp - UNC; **Address:** 7920 ACC Blvd, Ste 300, Releigh, NC 27617; **Phone:** 919-908-0000; **Board Cert:** Obstetrics & Gynecology 2012; Reproductive Endocrinology 2012; **Med School:** Tulane Univ 1977; **Resid:** Obstetrics & Gynecology, Wright-Patterson USAF Med Ctr 1981; **Fellow:** Reproductive Endocrinology, Oregon Hlth Sci Univ Hosp 1983; **Fac Appt:** Prof ObG, Univ NC Sch Med

Kutteh, William H MD/PhD [RE] - **Spec Exp:** Miscarriage-Recurrent; Infertility; **Hospital:** Baptist Memorial Hospital-Memphis; **Address:** Fertility Assocs of Memphis, 80 Humphrey's Center, Ste 307, Memphis, TN 38120-2363; **Phone:** 901-747-2229; **Board Cert:** Obstetrics & Gynecology 2012; Reproductive Endocrinology/Infertility 2012; **Med School:** Wake Forest Univ 1985; **Resid:** Obstetrics & Gynecology, UAB Med Ctr 1989; **Fellow:** Reproductive Endocrinology, Univ Tennessee Affil Hosp 1991

Ory, Steven J MD [RE] - **Spec Exp:** Infertility-IVF; Hormonal Disorders; Endometriosis; Uterine Fibroids; **Hospital:** Northwest Med Ctr, Meml Regl Hosp; **Address:** IVF Fl Reproductive Assocs, 2960 N State Road 7, Ste 300, Margate, FL 33063-5737; **Phone:** 954-247-6200; **Board Cert:** Obstetrics & Gynecology 2012; Reproductive Endocrinology 2012; **Med School:** Baylor Coll Med 1976; **Resid:** Obstetrics & Gynecology, Mayo Clin 1981; **Fellow:** Reproductive Endocrinology, Duke Univ Hosp 1984; **Fac Appt:** Prof ObG, FIU Coll Med

Session, Donna R MD [RE] - **Spec Exp:** Infertility-IVF; Reproductive Surgery; Polycystic Ovarian Syndrome; Ultrasound; **Hospital:** Emory Univ Hosp, Emory Univ Hosp Midtown; **Address:** Emory Reproductive Center, 550 Peachtree St NE, 18th Fl MOT, Atlanta, GA 30308; **Phone:** 404-778-3401; **Board Cert:** Obstetrics & Gynecology 2012; Reproductive Endocrinology 2012; **Med School:** Eastern VA Med Sch 1986; **Resid:** Obstetrics & Gynecology, Winthrop Hosp 1990; **Fellow:** Reproductive Endocrinology, Columbia-Presby Med Ctr 1993; **Fac Appt:** Assoc Prof ObG, Emory Univ

Steinkampf, Michael P MD [RE] - **Spec Exp:** Infertility-IVF; **Hospital:** Brookwood Med Ctr, St. Vincent's Hosp - Birmingham; **Address:** AL Fertility Specialists, 2700 Highway 280 South, Ste 370 East, Birmingham, AL 35223; **Phone:** 205-874-0000; **Board Cert:** Obstetrics & Gynecology 2012; Reproductive Endocrinology 2012; **Med School:** Louisiana State U, New Orleans 1981; **Resid:** Obstetrics & Gynecology, Parkland Hlth & Hosp Sys 1986; **Fellow:** Reproductive Endocrinology, Univ Texas SW Med Ctr 1989; **Fac Appt:** Prof ObG, UAB Sch Med

Walmer, David K MD/PhD [RE] - **Spec Exp:** Infertility-IVF; Miscarriage-Recurrent; Polycystic Ovarian Syndrome; Asherman's Syndrome; **Hospital:** Durham Regional Hosp; **Address:** Atlantic Reproductive Med Specialists, 10208 Cerny St, Ste 306, Raleigh, NC 27617; **Phone:** 919-248-8777; **Board Cert:** Obstetrics & Gynecology 2012; Reproductive Endocrinology 2012; **Med School:** Univ NC Sch Med 1983; **Resid:** Obstetrics & Gynecology, Univ Texas Affil Hosp 1987; **Fellow:** Reproductive Endocrinology, Duke Univ Hosp 1989; **Fac Appt:** Assoc Clin Prof ObG, Duke Univ

Midwest

Barnes, Randall B MD [RE] - **Spec Exp:** Infertility-IVF; Polycystic Ovarian Syndrome; Miscarriage-Recurrent; **Hospital:** Northwestern Meml Hosp; **Address:** Northwestern Meml Hosp, 675 N St Clair St, Galter Pavilion Fl 14 - Ste 200, Chicago, IL 60611; **Phone:** 312-695-7269; **Board Cert:** Obstetrics & Gynecology 2012; Reproductive Endocrinology 2012; **Med School:** Johns Hopkins Univ 1979; **Resid:** Obstetrics & Gynecology, LAC-USC Med Ctr 1984; **Fellow:** Reproductive Endocrinology, LAC-USC Med Ctr 1987; **Fac Appt:** Assoc Prof ObG, Northwestern Univ

Coddington III, Charles C MD [RE] - **Spec Exp:** Reproductive Surgery; Endometriosis; Infertility-IVF; **Hospital:** Mayo Med Ctr & Clin - Rochester; **Address:** Mayo Clin, Dept Reproductive Med, 200 First St SW, rm 3127, Rochester, MN 55905; **Phone:** 507-284-9792; **Board Cert:** Obstetrics & Gynecology 2006; Reproductive Endocrinology 2006; **Med School:** Med Univ SC 1977; **Resid:** Obstetrics & Gynecology, Natl Naval Med Ctr 1981; **Fellow:** Reproductive Endocrinology, Natl Inst Hlth 1985; **Fac Appt:** Prof ObG, Mayo Med Sch

Cohen, David Philip MD [RE] - **Spec Exp:** Fertility Preservation in Cancer; Infertility; Laparoscopic Surgery; **Hospital:** Univ of Chicago Med; **Address:** Univ Chicago, Ctr for Reproductive Med & Fertility, 333 S Desplaines St, Ste 201, Chicago, IL 60661; **Phone:** 773-702-6642; **Board Cert:** Obstetrics & Gynecology 2012; Reproductive Endocrinology/Infertility 2012; **Med School:** NY Med Coll 1988; **Resid:** Obstetrics & Gynecology, SUNY Hlth Sci Ctr 1992; **Fellow:** Reproductive Endocrinology, Med Coll GA Affil Hosp 1994; Reproductive Surgery, Cornell Univ Med Ctr 1996; **Fac Appt:** Prof ObG, Univ Chicago-Pritzker Sch Med

Dodds III, William G MD [RE] - **Spec Exp:** Infertility; Endometriosis; **Hospital:** Spectrum Hlth Butterworth Campus; **Address:** Fertility Ctr, 3230 Eagle Park Drive NE, Ste 100, Grand Rapids, MI 49525; **Phone:** 616-988-2229; **Board Cert:** Obstetrics & Gynecology 2012; Reproductive Endocrinology 2012; **Med School:** Ohio State Univ 1982; **Resid:** Obstetrics & Gynecology, OSU Wexner Med Ctr 1986; **Fellow:** Reproductive Endocrinology, OSU Wexner Med Ctr 1988; **Fac Appt:** Assoc Prof ObG, Univ Mich Med Sch

Falcone, Tommaso MD [RE] - **Spec Exp:** Minimally Invasive Surgery; Infertility-IVF; Endometriosis; Hysteroscopic Surgery; **Hospital:** Cleveland Clin (page 55); **Address:** Cleveland Clin, Dept Ob/Gyn, 9500 Euclid Ave, Desk A81, Cleveland, OH 44195-0001; **Phone:** 216-444-1758; **Board Cert:** Obstetrics & Gynecology 2012; Reproductive Endocrinology 2012; **Med School:** McGill Univ 1981; **Resid:** Obstetrics & Gynecology, McGill Univ Hlth Ctr 1986; **Fellow:** Reproductive Endocrinology, McGill Univ Hlth Ctr 1989; **Fac Appt:** Prof ObG, Cleveland Cl Coll Med/Case West Res

Friedman, Chad MD [RE] - **Spec Exp:** Infertility-IVF; Polycystic Ovarian Syndrome; **Hospital:** OSU Wexner Med Ctr; **Address:** 4830 Knightsbridge Blvd, Ste E, Columbus, OH 43214; **Phone:** 614-451-2280; **Board Cert:** Obstetrics & Gynecology 1982; Reproductive Endocrinology/Infertility 1983; **Med School:** Univ Chicago-Pritzker Sch Med 1975; **Resid:** Obstetrics & Gynecology, Ohio State Univ Hosp 1979; **Fellow:** Reproductive Endocrinology, Ohio State Univ Hosp 1981; **Fac Appt:** Assoc Prof ObG, Ohio State Univ

Goldberg, Jeffrey M MD [RE] - **Spec Exp:** Infertility-IVF; Endoscopic Surgery; Microsurgery; **Hospital:** Cleveland Clin (page 55); **Address:** Beachwood Family Health Ctr, 26900 Cedar Rd, MC BD20, Beechwood, OH 44122; **Phone:** 216-839-3150; **Board Cert:** Obstetrics & Gynecology 2012; Reproductive Endocrinology 2012; **Med School:** UMDNJ-NJ Med Sch, Newark 1983; **Resid:** Obstetrics & Gynecology, Emory Univ Med Ctr 1987; **Fellow:** Reproductive Endocrinology, Ohio State Univ 1989; **Fac Appt:** Prof ObG, Cleveland Cl Coll Med/Case West Res

Haney, Arthur F MD [RE] - **Spec Exp:** Infertility-Female; DES-Exposed Females; Minimally Invasive Gynecologic Surgery; **Hospital:** Univ of Chicago Med; **Address:** Univ Chicago Med Ctr, Dept Reproductive Endocrinology, 5841 S Maryland Ave, MC 2050, Chicago, IL 60637; **Phone:** 773-702-6642; **Board Cert:** Obstetrics & Gynecology 2010; Reproductive Endocrinology 2010; **Med School:** Univ Ariz Coll Med 1972; **Resid:** Obstetrics & Gynecology, Duke Univ Hosp 1977; **Fellow:** Reproductive Endocrinology, Duke Univ Hosp 1980; **Fac Appt:** Prof ObG, Univ Chicago-Pritzker Sch Med

Jacobs, Laurence A MD [RE] - **Spec Exp:** Infertility-IVF; Polycystic Ovarian Syndrome; Endometriosis; Obesity; **Hospital:** Adv Luth Genl Hosp, Northwest Comm Hosp; **Address:** 135 N Arlington Hts Rd, Ste 195, Buffalo Grove, IL 60089; **Phone:** 847-215-8899; **Board Cert:** Obstetrics & Gynecology 1981; **Med School:** Northwestern Univ 1975; **Resid:** Obstetrics & Gynecology, Northwestern Meml Hosp 1979; **Fellow:** Reproductive Endocrinology, Mayo Clinic 1988; **Fac Appt:** Assoc Prof ObG, Northwestern Univ-Feinberg Sch Med

Kazer, Ralph R MD [RE] - **Spec Exp:** Polycystic Ovarian Syndrome; Infertility-IVF; **Hospital:** Northwestern Meml Hosp; **Address:** Northwestern Meml Hosp, 675 N St Clair St Fl 14 - Ste 200, Galter Pavillion, Chicago, IL 60611; **Phone:** 312-695-7269; **Board Cert:** Obstetrics & Gynecology 2012; Reproductive Endocrinology 2012; **Med School:** Tufts Univ 1979; **Resid:** Obstetrics & Gynecology, Tufts Med Ctr 1984; **Fellow:** Reproductive Endocrinology, UCSD Med Ctr 1987; **Fac Appt:** Prof ObG, Northwestern Univ

Marut, Edward L MD [RE] - **Spec Exp:** Infertility-IVF; Miscarriage-Recurrent; Polycystic Ovarian Syndrome; Menstrual Disorders; **Hospital:** Highland Park Hosp/NorthShore Univ Hlth Syst (page 67); **Address:** FCI-Highland Park IVF Ctr, 767 Park Ave W, Highland Park, IL 60035; **Phone:** 847-433-4400; **Board Cert:** Obstetrics & Gynecology 1980; Reproductive Endocrinology 1983; **Med School:** Yale Univ 1974; **Resid:** Obstetrics & Gynecology, UCSF Med Ctr 1979; **Fellow:** Reproductive Endocrinology, Natl Inst Hlth 1982

Milad, Magdy P MD [RE] - **Spec Exp:** Reproductive Surgery; Infertility; Uterine Fibroids; **Hospital:** Northwestern Meml Hosp; **Address:** Northwestern Meml Hosp, 675 N St Clair St, Galter Pavilion Fl 14 - Ste 200, Chicago, IL 60611-5975; **Phone:** 312-695-7269; **Board Cert:** Obstetrics & Gynecology 2012; Reproductive Endocrinology 2012; **Med School:** Wayne State Univ 1987; **Resid:** Obstetrics & Gynecology, Beaumont Hosp 1993; **Fellow:** Reproductive Endocrinology, Mayo Clinic 1996; **Fac Appt:** Prof ObG, Northwestern Univ

Molo, Mary W MD [RE] - **Spec Exp:** Infertility-IVF; Uterine Fibroids; Fertility Preservation in Cancer; **Hospital:** Rush Univ Med Ctr; **Address:** 1725 W Harrison St, Ste 408 East, Chicago, IL 60612; **Phone:** 312-997-2229; **Board Cert:** Obstetrics & Gynecology 2012; Reproductive Endocrinology 2012; **Med School:** Southern IL Univ 1982; **Resid:** Obstetrics & Gynecology, Southern Illinois Affil Hosps 1984; Obstetrics & Gynecology, Rush Presby St Lukes Hosp 1987; **Fellow:** Reproductive Endocrinology, Rush Presby St Lukes Hosp 1989; **Fac Appt:** Asst Prof ObG, Rush Med Coll

Odem, Randall R MD [RE] - **Spec Exp:** Infertility; Reproductive Surgery; Miscarriage-Recurrent; Asherman's Syndrome; **Hospital:** Barnes-Jewish Hosp; **Address:** Ctr for Reproductive Med, 4444 Forest Park Ave, Ste 3100, St Louis, MO 63108-2212; **Phone:** 314-286-2400; **Board Cert:** Obstetrics & Gynecology 2011; Reproductive Endocrinology 2011; **Med School:** Univ Iowa Coll Med 1981; **Resid:** Obstetrics & Gynecology, Univ IL Hosps 1985; **Fellow:** Reproductive Endocrinology, Wash Univ Affil Hosp 1987; **Fac Appt:** Prof ObG, Washington Univ, St Louis

Ratts, Valerie S MD [RE] - **Spec Exp:** Infertility-IVF; Miscarriage-Recurrent; Endometriosis; Adolescent Gynecology; **Hospital:** Barnes-Jewish Hosp; **Address:** Ctr for Reproductive Med, 4444 Forest Park Ave, Ste 3100, St Louis, MO 63108-2212; **Phone:** 314-286-2400; **Board Cert:** Obstetrics & Gynecology 2012; Reproductive Endocrinology 2012; **Med School:** Johns Hopkins Univ 1987; **Resid:** Obstetrics & Gynecology, Johns Hopkins Hosp 1991; **Fellow:** Reproductive Endocrinology, Johns Hopkins Hosp 1993; **Fac Appt:** Assoc Prof ObG, Washington Univ, St Louis

Scoccia, Humberto MD [RE] - **Spec Exp:** Infertility-IVF; Polycystic Ovarian Syndrome; Hysteroscopic Surgery; Miscarriage-Recurrent; **Hospital:** Univ of IL Med Ctr at Chicago, Adv Christ Med Ctr; **Address:** Univ IL Fertility Ctr, 1801 W Taylor St, Ste 4A, Chicago, IL 60612; **Phone:** 312-355-4205; **Board Cert:** Obstetrics & Gynecology 2013; Reproductive Endocrinology 2013; **Med School:** Indiana Univ 1981; **Resid:** Obstetrics & Gynecology, Methodist Hosp 1985; **Fellow:** Reproductive Endocrinology, Michael Reese Hosp 1987; **Fac Appt:** Prof ObG, Univ IL Coll Med

Smith, Yolanda R MD [RE] - **Spec Exp:** Infertility-IVF; Pediatric & Adolescent Gynecology; Polycystic Ovarian Syndrome; Menopause Problems; **Hospital:** Univ Michigan Med Ctr; **Address:** UofM Ctr for Reproductive Med, 475 Market Pl, Ste B, Ann Arbor, MI 48108; **Phone:** 734-763-4323; **Board Cert:** Obstetrics & Gynecology 2012; Reproductive Endocrinology 2012; **Med School:** Wake Forest Univ 1989; **Resid:** Obstetrics & Gynecology, Univ Mich Affil Hosps 1994; **Fellow:** Reproductive Endocrinology, Johns Hopkins Hosp 1997; **Fac Appt:** Prof ObG, Univ Mich Med Sch

Stephenson, Mary D MD [RE] - **Spec Exp:** Pregnancy Loss-Recurrent; **Hospital:** Univ of IL Med Ctr at Chicago; **Address:** Univ IL Med Ctr, 1801 W Taylor St, Chicago, IL 60612; **Phone:** 312-996-4322; **Med School:** Univ British Columbia Fac Med 1981; **Resid:** Obstetrics & Gynecology, Univ British Columbia Affil Hosp 1991; **Fellow:** Reproductive Endocrinology, Univ British Columbia 1994; **Fac Appt:** Prof ObG, Univ IL Coll Med

Stewart, Elizabeth A MD [RE] - **Spec Exp:** Uterine Fibroids; Hysteroscopic Surgery; Infertility-IVF; **Hospital:** Mayo Med Ctr & Clin - Rochester; **Address:** Mayo Clin, Dept Reproductive Med, 200 First St SW, rm 3127, Rochester, MN 55905; **Phone:** 507-284-9792; **Board Cert:** Obstetrics & Gynecology 2012; Reproductive Endocrinology 2012; **Med School:** Harvard Med Sch 1985; **Resid:** Obstetrics & Gynecology, Brigham & Womens Hosp 1989; **Fellow:** Reproductive Endocrinology, Brigham & Womens Hosp 1992; **Fac Appt:** Prof ObG, Mayo Med Sch

Thomas, Michael A MD [RE] - **Spec Exp:** Infertility; Infertility-IVF; **Hospital:** Univ Cincinnati Med Ctr, Christ Hosp, The - Cincinnati; **Address:** UC Center for Reproductive Health, 2123 Auburn Ave, Ste A-44, Cincinnati, OH 45219; **Phone:** 513-585-2355; **Board Cert:** Obstetrics & Gynecology 2012; Reproductive Endocrinology/Infertility 2012; **Med School:** Univ IL Coll Med 1984; **Resid:** Obstetrics & Gynecology, Wayne State Univ Hosp 1988; **Fellow:** Endocrinology, Univ Cincinnati Med Ctr 1990; **Fac Appt:** Prof ObG, Univ Cincinnati

Van Voorhis, Bradley J MD [RE] - **Spec Exp:** Infertility-IVF; Endometriosis; Uterine Fibroids; **Hospital:** Univ Iowa Hosp & Clins; **Address:** UIHC, Reproductive Endocrinology Dept, 200 Hawkins Drive, Ste 31335 PFP, Iowa City, IA 52242; **Phone:** 319-356-1767; **Board Cert:** Obstetrics & Gynecology 2012; Reproductive Endocrinology 2012; **Med School:** Univ Iowa Coll Med 1984; **Resid:** Obstetrics & Gynecology, Med Coll Virginia Hosps 1988; **Fellow:** Reproductive Endocrinology, Brigham & Womens Hosp 1991; **Fac Appt:** Prof ObG, Univ Iowa Coll Med

Great Plains and Mountains

Surrey, Eric S MD [RE] - **Spec Exp:** Infertility-IVF; Endometriosis; **Hospital:** Sky Ridge Med Ctr, Swedish Med Ctr - Denver; **Address:** CO Ctr Reproductive Med, 10290 RidgeGate Cir, Lone Tree, CO 80124; **Phone:** 303-788-8300; **Board Cert:** Obstetrics & Gynecology 2012; Reproductive Endocrinology 2012; **Med School:** Univ Pennsylvania 1981; **Resid:** Obstetrics & Gynecology, UCLA Ronald Reagan Med Ctr 1986; **Fellow:** Reproductive Endocrinology, UCLA Ronald Reagan Med Ctr 1989

Southwest

Carr, Bruce R MD [RE] - **Spec Exp:** Infertility-Female; **Hospital:** UT Southwestern Med Ctr at Dallas, Parkland Hlth & Hosp Sys; **Address:** 1801 Inwood Rd Fl 6 - Ste 616, Dallas, TX 75390; **Phone:** 214-645-3858; **Board Cert:** Obstetrics & Gynecology 2000; Reproductive Endocrinology 2000; **Med School:** Univ Mich Med Sch 1971; **Resid:** Obstetrics & Gynecology, Parkland Meml Hosp 1975; **Fellow:** Reproductive Endocrinology, Univ Texas SW Med Ctr 1980; **Fac Appt:** Prof ObG, Univ Tex SW, Dallas

Clisham, P. Ronald MD [RE] - **Spec Exp:** Infertility-IVF; Endometriosis; Uterine Fibroids; Laparoscopic Surgery; **Hospital:** Tulane Med Ctr; **Address:** Audubon Fertility & Reproductive Med, 4321 Magnolia St, New Orleans, LA 70115; **Phone:** 504-891-1390; **Board Cert:** Obstetrics & Gynecology 2012; Reproductive Endocrinology 2012; **Med School:** Louisiana State U, New Orleans 1982; **Resid:** Obstetrics & Gynecology, Charity Hosp 1986; **Fellow:** Reproductive Endocrinology, UCLA Ronald Reagan Med Ctr 1988; **Fac Appt:** Prof ObG, Tulane Univ

Dickey, Richard P MD/PhD [RE] - **Spec Exp:** Infertility-IVF; **Hospital:** Tulane-Lakeside Hosp; **Address:** 800 N Causeway Blvd, Ste 2C, Mandeville, LA 70448; **Phone:** 985-892-7621; **Board Cert:** Obstetrics & Gynecology 1967; Reproductive Endocrinology/Infertility 1976; **Med School:** Case West Res Univ 1960; **Resid:** Obstetrics & Gynecology, Ohio State Univ Hosp 1965; **Fellow:** Reproductive Endocrinology, Ohio State Univ Hosp 1966; **Fac Appt:** Clin Prof ObG, Louisiana State U, New Orleans

Huang, Jaou-Chen MD [RE] - **Spec Exp:** Infertility-IVF; Endometriosis; Hysteroscopic Surgery; Uterine Fibroids; **Hospital:** Covenant Med Ctr; **Address:** TTU Center of Fertility & Reproduction, 3502 9th St, Ste G10, Lubbock, TX 79415; **Phone:** 806-743-4256; **Board Cert:** Obstetrics & Gynecology 2012; Reproductive Endocrinology/Infertility 2012; **Med School:** Taiwan 1980; **Resid:** Obstetrics & Gynecology, Natl Taiwan Univ Hosp 1985; Obstetrics & Gynecology, Harlem Hosp 1991; **Fellow:** Reproductive Endocrinology, Brigham & Women's Hosp 1993; **Fac Appt:** Assoc Prof ObG, Univ Tex, Houston

Moffitt, Drew MD [RE] - **Spec Exp:** Infertility-IVF; Reproductive Surgery; **Hospital:** Banner Good Samaritan Regl Med Ctr - Phoenix; **Address:** Arizona Reproductive Medicine, 1701 E Thomas Rd Bldg 1 - Ste 101, Phoenix, AZ 85016; **Phone:** 602-343-2767; **Board Cert:** Obstetrics & Gynecology 2012; Reproductive Endocrinology/Infertility 2012; **Med School:** UCLA 1988; **Resid:** Obstetrics & Gynecology, UCLA Med Ctr 1992; **Fellow:** Reproductive Endocrinology, Jones Inst/Eastern Va Med Sch 1994; **Fac Appt:** Assoc Prof ObG, Univ Ariz Coll Med

Putman, John M MD [RE] - **Spec Exp:** Infertility-IVF; Uterine Fibroids; Endometriosis; Minimally Invasive Surgery; **Hospital:** Baylor Univ Med Ctr-Dallas; **Address:** Fertility Center of Dallas, 3900 Junius St, Ste 610, Dallas, TX 75246; **Phone:** 214-823-2692; **Board Cert:** Obstetrics & Gynecology 1980; **Med School:** Med Coll GA 1973; **Resid:** Obstetrics & Gynecology, Baylor Univ Med Ctr 1977; **Fac Appt:** Assoc Clin Prof ObG, Univ Tex SW, Dallas

Schenken, Robert S MD [RE] - **Spec Exp:** Infertility; Endometriosis; **Hospital:** Univ Hosp-San Antonio, Baptist Hlth Sys; **Address:** Dept OB/GYN, 7703 Floyd Curl Dr, MSC 7836, San Antonio, TX 78229-3900; **Phone:** 210-567-4950; **Board Cert:** Obstetrics & Gynecology 2012; Reproductive Endocrinology 2012; **Med School:** Baylor Coll Med 1977; **Resid:** Obstetrics & Gynecology, Bexar Co Hosp 1981; **Fellow:** Reproductive Endocrinology, Natl Inst Hlth 1982; Reproductive Endocrinology, Univ Tex Hlth Sci Ctr 1983; **Fac Appt:** Prof ObG, Univ Tex, San Antonio

Wilson, Ellen E MD [RE] - **Spec Exp:** Infertility; Uterine Fibroids; Polycystic Ovarian Syndrome; Pediatric & Adolescent Gynecology; **Hospital:** UT Southwestern Med Ctr at Dallas; **Address:** 1801 Inwood Rd Fl 6 - Ste 616, Dallas, TX 75390-8539; **Phone:** 214-645-3858; **Board Cert:** Obstetrics & Gynecology 2012; Reproductive Endocrinology/Infertility 2012; **Med School:** Baylor Coll Med 1984; **Resid:** Obstetrics & Gynecology, George Washington Univ Hosp 1989; **Fellow:** Reproductive Endocrinology, UTSW Southwestern 1991; Laparoscopic Surgery, Womens Hosp 1992; **Fac Appt:** Asst Clin Prof ObG, Univ Tex SW, Dallas

West Coast and Pacific

Adamson, G. David MD [RE] - **Spec Exp:** Infertility; Endometriosis; Laparoscopic Surgery; **Hospital:** Stanford Univ Hosp & Clins, Good Samaritan Hosp - San Jose; **Address:** Fertility Phys N California, 2581 Samaritan Drive, Ste 302, San Jose, CA 95124; **Phone:** 408-356-5000; **Board Cert:** Obstetrics & Gynecology 1980; Reproductive Endocrinology 1982; **Med School:** Univ Toronto 1973; **Resid:** Obstetrics & Gynecology, Toronto Genl Hosp 1978; **Fellow:** Reproductive Endocrinology, Stanford Univ Hosp & Clins 1980; **Fac Appt:** Clin Prof ObG, Stanford Univ

Agarwal, Sanjay K MD [RE] - **Spec Exp:** Infertility-IVF; Endometriosis; **Hospital:** UCSD Med Ctr; **Address:** Univ California-San Diego Medical Ctr, 9350 Campus Point Drive, Ste LL-C, La Jolla, CA 92037-1300; **Phone:** 858-657-8745; **Board Cert:** Obstetrics & Gynecology 2012; Reproductive Endocrinology/Infertility 2012; **Med School:** England, UK 1986; **Resid:** Obstetrics & Gynecology, Duke Univ Med Ctr 1993; **Fellow:** Reproductive Endocrinology, UCLA Med Ctr 1995; **Fac Appt:** Clin Prof ObG, UCSD

Baker, Valerie L MD [RE] - **Spec Exp:** Infertility-IVF; **Hospital:** Stanford Univ Hosp & Clins; **Address:** Stanford Infertility Ctr, 900 Welch Rd, Ste 350, Palo Alto, CA 94303; **Phone:** 650-498-7911; **Board Cert:** Obstetrics & Gynecology 2012; Reproductive Endocrinology 2012; **Med School:** Harvard Med Sch 1988; **Resid:** Obstetrics & Gynecology, UCSF Med Ctr 1993; **Fellow:** Reproductive Endocrinology, UCSF Med Ctr 1995; **Fac Appt:** Assoc Prof ObG, Stanford Univ

Cedars, Marcelle I MD [RE] - **Spec Exp:** Infertility-IVF; Polycystic Ovarian Syndrome; **Hospital:** UCSF Med Ctr; **Address:** UCSF Ctr for Reproductive Hlth, 2356 Sutter St Fl 7, San Francisco, CA 94115; **Phone:** 415-353-7475; **Board Cert:** Obstetrics & Gynecology 2012; Reproductive Endocrinology 2012; **Med School:** Univ Tex SW, Dallas 1981; **Resid:** Obstetrics & Gynecology, Parkland Meml Hosp 1985; **Fellow:** Reproductive Endocrinology, UCLA Ronald Reagan Med Ctr 1987; **Fac Appt:** Prof ObG, UCSF

Chang, R Jeffrey MD [RE] - **Spec Exp:** Polycystic Ovarian Syndrome; Hormonal Disorders; Menstrual Disorders; Pituitary Tumors; **Hospital:** UCSD Med Ctr; **Address:** UCSD - Div Reproductive Med, 9350 Campus Pt Drive, Ste LL-C, La Jolla, CA 92037; **Phone:** 858-657-8745; **Board Cert:** Obstetrics & Gynecology 2002; Reproductive Endocrinology/Infertility 2002; **Med School:** Oregon Hlth & Sci Univ 1969; **Resid:** Obstetrics & Gynecology, LAC - Harbor - UCLA Med Ctr 1974; **Fellow:** Reproductive Endocrinology, LAC - Harbor - UCLA Med Ctr 1975; Reproductive Endocrinology, UCSF Med Ctr 1977; **Fac Appt:** Prof ObG, UCSD

Chenette, Philip E MD [RE] - **Spec Exp:** Infertility-IVF; **Hospital:** CA Pacific Med Ctr - CA Campus; **Address:** Pacific Fertility Ctr, 55 Francisco St Fl 5, San Francisco, CA 94133; **Phone:** 415-834-3000; **Board Cert:** Obstetrics & Gynecology 2011; Reproductive Endocrinology 2011; **Med School:** Indiana Univ 1983; **Resid:** Obstetrics & Gynecology, Magee-Womens Hosp - UPMC 1987; **Fellow:** Reproductive Endocrinology, USC Med Ctr 1989; **Fac Appt:** Asst Clin Prof ObG, UCSF

Dumesic, Daniel A MD [RE] - **Spec Exp:** Infertility-Female; Hormonal Disorders; Polycystic Ovarian Syndrome; Hysteroscopic Surgery; **Hospital:** UCLA Ronald Reagan Med Ctr; **Address:** UCLA - Dept OB/GYN, 200 UCLA Med Plaza, Peter Morton Med Bldg, Ste 220, Los Angeles, CA 90095; **Phone:** 310-794-7274; **Board Cert:** Obstetrics & Gynecology 2012; Reproductive Endocrinology 2012; **Med School:** Univ Wisc 1978; **Resid:** Obstetrics & Gynecology, UCSF Med Ctr 1984; **Fellow:** Reproductive Endocrinology, UCSF Med Ctr 1987; **Fac Appt:** Prof Med, UCLA

Giudice, Linda C MD/PhD [RE] - **Spec Exp:** Infertility-IVF; Endometriosis; **Hospital:** UCSF Med Ctr; **Address:** UCSF Ctr for Reproductive Hlth, 2356 Sutter St Fl 7, San Francisco, CA 94115; **Phone:** 415-353-7475; **Board Cert:** Obstetrics & Gynecology 2012; Reproductive Endocrinology 2012; **Med School:** Stanford Univ 1982; **Resid:** Obstetrics & Gynecology, Stanford Univ Hosp & Clins 1984; Obstetrics & Gynecology, Barnes Hosp-Washington Univ Phys 1986; **Fellow:** Reproductive Endocrinology, Stanford Univ Hosp & Clins 1987; **Fac Appt:** Prof ObG, UCSF

Hickok, Lee R MD [RE] - **Spec Exp:** Infertility-IVF; Hysteroscopic Surgery; **Hospital:** Swedish Med Ctr-First Hill-Seattle; **Address:** Pacific NW Fertility & IVF Specialists, 1101 Madison Ave, Ste 1050, Seattle, WA 98104; **Phone:** 206-515-0000; **Board Cert:** Obstetrics & Gynecology 2011; **Med School:** Univ Wash 1984; **Resid:** Obstetrics & Gynecology, Univ Washington Med Ctr 1988; **Fellow:** Reproductive Endocrinology, Oregan Hlth Science Ctr 1991; **Fac Appt:** Clin Prof ObG, Univ Wash

Kuo, John MD/PhD [RE] - **Spec Exp:** Infertility-IVF; Fertility Preservation in Cancer; Preimplantation Genetic Diagnosis; **Hospital:** UCLA Ronald Reagan Med Ctr; **Address:** UCLA, Ob/Gyn Dept, 200 UCLA Med Plaza, Ste 220, Los Angeles, CA 90095; **Phone:** 310-794-7274; **Board Cert:** Obstetrics & Gynecology 2012; Reproductive Endocrinology/Infertility 2012; **Med School:** USC Sch Med 2000; **Resid:** Obstetrics & Gynecology, UCLA Med Ctr 2004; **Fellow:** Reproductive Endocrinology/Infertility, UCLA Med Ctr/Cedars Sinai Med Ctr 2007; **Fac Appt:** Asst Prof ObG, UCLA-David Geffen Sch Med

Marrs, Richard P MD [RE] - **Spec Exp:** Infertility-Female; Endometriosis; Uterine Fibroids; **Address:** California Fertility Partners, 11818 Wilshire Blvd, Ste 300, Los Angeles, CA 90025; **Phone:** 310-828-4008; **Board Cert:** Obstetrics & Gynecology 1980; Reproductive Endocrinology 1983; **Med School:** Univ Tex Med Br, Galveston 1974; **Resid:** Obstetrics & Gynecology, Univ Tex Med Br Affil Hosps 1977; **Fellow:** Reproductive Endocrinology, LAC & USC Med Ctr 1979

Marshall, Lorna A MD [RE] - **Spec Exp:** Infertility-IVF; Fertility Preservation in Cancer; **Hospital:** Swedish Med Ctr-First Hill-Seattle; **Address:** Pacific Northwest Fertility & IVF, 1101 Madison St, Ste 1050, Seattle, WA 98104; **Phone:** 206-515-0000; **Board Cert:** Obstetrics & Gynecology 2011; Reproductive Endocrinology/Infertility 2011; **Med School:** Northwestern Univ 1979; **Resid:** Obstetrics & Gynecology, UCSD Med Ctr 1983; **Fellow:** Reproductive Endocrinology, UCSF Med Ctr 1986

Paulson, Richard J MD [RE] - **Spec Exp:** Infertility-IVF; Infertility-Advanced Maternal Age; **Hospital:** LAC & USC Med Ctr, Good Samaritan Hosp - LA; **Address:** USC Fertility, 1127 Wilshire Blvd, Ste 1400, Los Angeles, CA 90017; **Phone:** 213-975-9990; **Board Cert:** Obstetrics & Gynecology 2012; Reproductive Endocrinology 2012; **Med School:** UCLA 1980; **Resid:** Obstetrics & Gynecology, LAC - Harbor - UCLA Med Ctr 1984; **Fellow:** Reproductive Endocrinology, LAC & USC Med Ctr 1986; **Fac Appt:** Prof ObG, USC Sch Med

Schriock, Eldon D MD [RE] - **Spec Exp:** Infertility-IVF; **Hospital:** CA Pacific Med Ctr-Pacific Campus; **Address:** Pacific Fertility Ctr, 55 Francisco St Fl 5, San Francisco, CA 94133; **Phone:** 415-834-3000; **Board Cert:** Obstetrics & Gynecology 1984; Reproductive Endocrinology 1985; **Med School:** Northwestern Univ 1977; **Resid:** Obstetrics & Gynecology, Northwestern Meml Hosp 1981; **Fellow:** Reproductive Endocrinology, UCSF Med Ctr 1983

Smikle, Collin B MD [RE] - **Spec Exp:** Infertility-IVF; Laparoscopic Surgery; Fertility Preservation in Cancer; **Hospital:** CA Pacific Med Ctr-Pacific Campus; **Address:** Laurel Fertility Care, 1700 California St, Ste 570, San Francisco, CA 94109; **Phone:** 415-673-9199; **Board Cert:** Obstetrics & Gynecology 2012; Reproductive Endocrinology/Infertility 2012; **Med School:** Yale Univ 1985; **Resid:** Obstetrics & Gynecology, Brigham & Women's Hosp 1989; **Fellow:** Reproductive Endocrinology, UCSF Med Ctr 1991

Soules, Michael R MD [RE] - **Spec Exp:** Infertility-IVF; Polycystic Ovarian Syndrome; Endometriosis; **Hospital:** Northwest Hosp - Seattle; **Address:** 1505 Westlake Ave N, Ste 400, Seattle, WA 98109; **Phone:** 206-301-5000; **Board Cert:** Obstetrics & Gynecology 2002; Reproductive Endocrinology 2002; **Med School:** UCLA-David Geffen Sch Med 1972; **Resid:** Obstetrics & Gynecology, Univ Colorado Med Ctr 1976; **Fellow:** Reproductive Endocrinology, Duke Univ Hosp 1978; **Fac Appt:** Prof ObG, Univ Wash

Winer, Sharon A MD [RE] - **Spec Exp:** Hormonal Disorders; Infertility-IVF; Vaginitis; **Hospital:** Cedars-Sinai Med Ctr, Keck Med Ctr of USC; **Address:** 9400 Brighton Way, Ste 206, Beverly Hills, CA 90210-4709; **Phone:** 310-274-9100; **Board Cert:** Obstetrics & Gynecology 2012; Reproductive Endocrinology 2012; **Med School:** USC Sch Med 1978; **Resid:** Obstetrics & Gynecology, LAC & USC Med Ctr 1982; **Fellow:** Microsurgery, Hammersmith Hosp 1983; Reproductive Endocrinology, Univ MD Med Ctr 1985; **Fac Appt:** Clin Prof ObG, USC Sch Med

Yee, Billy MD [RE] - **Spec Exp:** Infertility-IVF; Microsurgery; Laparoscopic Surgery; Hysteroscopic Surgery; **Hospital:** Long Beach Meml Med Ctr; **Address:** Reproductive Partners Med Grp, 13950 Milton Ave, Ste 100, Westminster, CA 92683; **Phone:** 714-702-3001; **Board Cert:** Obstetrics & Gynecology 2012; Reproductive Endocrinology 2012; **Med School:** UC Davis 1978; **Resid:** Obstetrics & Gynecology, LAC & USC Med Ctr 1982; **Fellow:** Reproductive Endocrinology, LAC & USC Med Ctr 1985; **Fac Appt:** Assoc Clin Prof ObG, UC Irvine

Top Doctors Make A Difference

Rheumatology

a subspecialty of Internal Medicine

An internist who treats diseases of joints, muscle, bones and tendons. This specialist diagnoses and treats arthritis, back pain, muscle strains, common athletic injuries and "collagen" diseases.

Training Required: Three years in internal medicine *plus* additional training and examination for certification in rheumatology.

Rheumatology

New England

Albert, Daniel A MD [Rhu] - **Spec Exp:** Pediatric Rheumatology; Rheumatoid Arthritis; Vasculitis; **Hospital:** Dartmouth - Hitchcock Med Ctr; **Address:** Dartmouth-Hitchcock Med Ctr, Dept Rheumatology, One Medical Center Drive, Lebanon, NH 03756; **Phone:** 603-650-8622; **Board Cert:** Internal Medicine 1977; Rheumatology 1980; **Med School:** NYU Sch Med 1974; **Resid:** Internal Medicine, NC Meml Hosp 1977; **Fellow:** Rheumatology, UCSD Med Ctr 1981; Pharmacology, Dana-Farber/Harvard Cancer Inst 1982; **Fac Appt:** Prof Med, Dartmouth Med Sch

Coblyn, Jonathan S MD [Rhu] - **Spec Exp:** Rheumatoid Arthritis; Lupus/SLE; Vasculitis; Musculoskeletal Disorders; **Hospital:** Brigham & Women's Hosp; **Address:** Brigham & Women's Hosp, Div Rheumatology, 75 Francis St, PBB-B3, Boston, MA 02115; **Phone:** 617-732-5347; **Board Cert:** Internal Medicine 1977; Rheumatology 1980; **Med School:** Johns Hopkins Univ 1974; **Resid:** Internal Medicine, Brigham & Women's Hosp 1976; Internal Medicine, Stanford Univ Hosps 1977; **Fellow:** Rheumatology, Brigham & Women's Hosp 1979; **Fac Appt:** Assoc Prof Med, Harvard Med Sch

Kay, Jonathan MD [Rhu] - **Spec Exp:** Rheumatoid Arthritis; Psoriatic Arthritis; Ankylosing Spondylitis; Nephrogenic Systemic Fibrosis; **Hospital:** UMass Mem Med Ctr-Memorial Campus; **Address:** Rheumatology Ctr, UMass Meml Med Ctr-Meml Campus, 119 Belmont St, Worcester, MA 01605; **Phone:** 508-334-6273; **Board Cert:** Internal Medicine 1986; Rheumatology 1988; **Med School:** UCSF 1983; **Resid:** Internal Medicine, Hosp Univ Penn 1986; **Fellow:** Rheumatology/Immunology, Brigham & Womens Hosp 1989; **Fac Appt:** Prof Med, Univ Mass Sch Med

Massarotti, Elena M MD [Rhu] - **Spec Exp:** Lupus/SLE; Rheumatoid Arthritis; Psoriatic Arthritis; Gout; **Hospital:** Brigham & Women's Hosp; **Address:** Brigham & Women's Hosp, Div Rheumatology, 75 Francis St, PBB-B3, Boston, MA 02115; **Phone:** 617-732-5325; **Board Cert:** Internal Medicine 1987; Rheumatology 2010; **Med School:** Tufts Univ 1984; **Resid:** Internal Medicine, Tufts-New England Med Ctr 1987; **Fellow:** Rheumatology, Tufts-New England Med Ctr 1989; **Fac Appt:** Assoc Prof Med, Tufts Univ

McAlindon, Timothy E MD [Rhu] - **Spec Exp:** Arthritis; Autoimmune Rheumatic Disorders; **Hospital:** Tufts Med Ctr; **Address:** Tufts Med Ctr, Div Rheumatology, 800 Washington St, Ste 599, Boston, MA 02111; **Phone:** 617-636-5990; **Board Cert:** Internal Medicine 2003; **Med School:** England, UK 1982; **Resid:** Internal Medicine, Torbay Hosp 1985; Internal Medicine, Southmead Hosp 1988; **Fellow:** Rheumatology, Bristol Royal Infirmary 1990; Rheumatology, St Thomas Hosp 1995; **Fac Appt:** Prof Med, Tufts Univ

Schoen, Robert T MD [Rhu] - **Spec Exp:** Rheumatoid Arthritis; Lyme Disease; Osteoporosis; **Hospital:** Yale-New Haven Hosp; **Address:** New Haven Rheumatology, 60 Temple St, Ste 6A, New Haven, CT 06510-2716; **Phone:** 203-789-2255; **Board Cert:** Internal Medicine 1979; Rheumatology 1982; **Med School:** Columbia P&S 1976; **Resid:** Internal Medicine, Yale New Haven Hosp 1979; **Fellow:** Rheumatology, Brigham & Womens Hosp 1981; **Fac Appt:** Clin Prof Med, Yale Univ

Seton, Margaret P MD [Rhu] - **Spec Exp:** Paget's Disease of Bone; **Hospital:** Brigham & Women's Hosp; **Address:** Brigham & Women's Hosp, Rheumatology, 75 Francis St, Boston, MA 02115; **Phone:** 617-732-9500; **Board Cert:** Internal Medicine 1986; Rheumatology 2012; **Med School:** Med Coll VA 1980; **Resid:** Internal Medicine, Univ Hosp 1984; **Fellow:** Immunology, Mass Genl Hosp 1986; Rheumatology, Mass Genl Hosp 1991; **Fac Appt:** Asst Prof Med, Harvard Med Sch

Shadick, Nancy A MD [Rhu] - **Spec Exp:** Lyme Disease; Rheumatoid Arthritis; Osteoarthritis; **Hospital:** Brigham & Women's Hosp; **Address:** Brigham & Women's Hosp, Div Rheumatology, 75 Francis St, PBB-B3, Boston, MA 02115; **Phone:** 617-732-5325; **Board Cert:** Internal Medicine 1989; Rheumatology 2012; **Med School:** NYU Sch Med 1986; **Resid:** Internal Medicine, NY Presby/Columbia Univ Med Ctr 1989; **Fellow:** Rheumatology, Brigham & Womens Hosp 1992; **Fac Appt:** Asst Prof Med, Harvard Med Sch

Simms, Robert W MD [Rhu] - **Spec Exp:** Scleroderma; Rheumatoid Arthritis; Lyme Disease; **Hospital:** Boston Med Ctr; **Address:** Boston Med Ctr, Dept Rheumatology, 725 Albany St Shapiro Bldg - Ste 7B, Boston, MA 02118; **Phone:** 617-638-4312; **Board Cert:** Internal Medicine 1985; Rheumatology 1988; **Med School:** Univ Rochester 1980; **Resid:** Internal Medicine, N Shore Hosp 1982; Internal Medicine, Brigham & Women's Hosp 1985; **Fellow:** Rheumatology, Boston Univ Med Ctr 1987; **Fac Appt:** Prof Med, Boston Univ

Tsokos, George C MD [Rhu] - **Spec Exp:** Lupus/SLE; **Hospital:** Beth Israel Deaconess Med Ctr - Boston; **Address:** Beth Israel Deaconess Med Ctr, Dept Rheumatology, 110 Francis St, Ste 4B, Boston, MA 02215; **Phone:** 617-632-8658; **Board Cert:** Internal Medicine 1983; Diagnostic Lab Immunology 1986; Rheumatology 1984; **Med School:** Greece 1975; **Resid:** Internal Medicine, Natl Univ 1979; Immunology, Natl Inst of Hlth 1981; **Fellow:** Rheumatology, Natl Inst of Hlth 1983

Weinblatt, Michael E MD [Rhu] - **Spec Exp:** Rheumatoid Arthritis; **Hospital:** Brigham & Women's Hosp; **Address:** Brigham & Womens Hosp, Arthritis Ctr, 75 Francis St, Boston, MA 02115; **Phone:** 617-732-5331; **Board Cert:** Internal Medicine 1978; Rheumatology 1980; **Med School:** Univ MD Sch Med 1975; **Resid:** Internal Medicine, Univ Maryland Hosp 1978; **Fellow:** Rheumatology, Brigham & Women's Hosp 1980; **Fac Appt:** Prof Med, Harvard Med Sch

Mid Atlantic

Allman, Richard L MD [Rhu] - **Spec Exp:** Arthritis; **Hospital:** Einstein Med Ctr; **Address:** 5401 Old York Rd, Klein Bldg Fl 3 - Ste 331, Philadelphia, PA 19141; **Phone:** 215-456-8220; **Board Cert:** Internal Medicine 1987; Rheumatology 1974; **Med School:** Jefferson Med Coll 1969; **Resid:** Internal Medicine, Allentown State Hosp 1972; **Fellow:** Rheumatology, Temple Univ Hosp 1974; **Fac Appt:** Assoc Prof Med, Jefferson Med Coll

Belmont, H. Michael MD [Rhu] - **Spec Exp:** Lupus/SLE; Antiphospholipid Syndrome (APS); Wegener's Granulomatosis; Rheumatoid Arthritis; **Hospital:** NYU Hosp For Joint Dis, NYU Langone Med Ctr (page 68); **Address:** NYU, Ctr Musculoskeletal Care, 333 E 38th St Fl 4, New York, NY 10016; **Phone:** 646-501-7400; **Board Cert:** Internal Medicine 1983; Rheumatology 1986; **Med School:** Univ Pittsburgh 1980; **Resid:** Internal Medicine, Mount Sinai Med Ctr 1983; **Fellow:** Rheumatology, Bellevue Hosp Ctr 1985; **Fac Appt:** Assoc Prof Med, NYU Sch Med

Blume, Ralph S MD [Rhu] - **Spec Exp:** Vasculitis; Lupus/SLE; Rheumatoid Arthritis; **Hospital:** NY-Presby/Columbia Univ Med Ctr, NY (page 65); **Address:** NY-Presby, Rheumatology Dept, 161 Fort Washington Ave, Ste 638, New York, NY 10032; **Phone:** 212-305-5512; **Board Cert:** Internal Medicine 1972; Rheumatology 1974; **Med School:** Columbia P&S 1964; **Resid:** Internal Medicine, NY-Presby/Columbia Univ Med Ctr 1968; **Fellow:** Rheumatology, NY-Presby/Columbia Univ Med Ctr 1970; **Fac Appt:** Prof Med, Columbia P&S

Bunning, Robert D MD [Rhu] - **Spec Exp:** Exercise Physiology; Rheumatoid Arthritis; Musculoskeletal Disorders; **Hospital:** MedStar Natl Rehab Hosp; **Address:** MedStar Natl Rehab Hosp, 102 Irving St NW, Washington, DC 20010; **Phone:** 202-877-1660; **Board Cert:** Internal Medicine 1984; Rheumatology 1986; **Med School:** Univ Cincinnati 1979; **Resid:** Internal Medicine, Wash Hosp Ctr 1981; **Fellow:** Rheumatology, Wash Hosp Ctr 1983; **Fac Appt:** Asst Clin Prof Med, Geo Wash Univ

Buyon, Jill P MD [Rhu] - **Spec Exp:** Lupus/SLE in Pregnancy; Lupus/SLE in Menopause; **Hospital:** NYU Hosp For Joint Dis, NYU Langone Med Ctr (page 68); **Address:** NYU, Ctr Musculoskeletal Care, 333 E 38th St Fl 4, New York, NY 10016; **Phone:** 646-501-7400; **Board Cert:** Internal Medicine 1981; Rheumatology 1984; **Med School:** Albert Einstein Coll Med 1978; **Resid:** Internal Medicine, Montefiore Med Ctr 1981; **Fellow:** Rheumatology, NYU Med Ctr 1983; **Fac Appt:** Prof Med, NYU Sch Med

Cupps, Thomas R MD [Rhu] - **Spec Exp:** Vasculitis; Hepatitis B-Immune Response; **Hospital:** MedStar Georgetown Univ Hosp; **Address:** 3800 Resevoir Rd NW, George Univ Hosp, Dept of Med, Pasquerilla Bldg, Ste 3004, Washington, DC 20007; **Phone:** 202-444-6200; **Board Cert:** Internal Medicine 1978; Allergy & Immunology 1981; **Med School:** Stanford Univ 1975; **Resid:** Internal Medicine, Strong Meml Hosp 1978; **Fellow:** Allergy & Immunology, Natl Inst Allergy & Inf Dis 1981; **Fac Appt:** Assoc Prof Med, Georgetown Univ

Farber, Martin S MD/PhD [Rhu] - **Hospital:** Sunnyview Hosp & Rehab Ctr, Ellis Hosp; **Address:** 124 Rosa Rd, Ste 381, Schenectady, NY 12308-2198; **Phone:** 518-386-3644; **Board Cert:** Internal Medicine 1982; Rheumatology 1984; **Med School:** Albert Einstein Coll Med 1979; **Resid:** Internal Medicine, Boston City Hosp 1982; **Fellow:** Rheumatology, Boston Univ Sch Med 1984; **Fac Appt:** Asst Clin Prof Med, Albany Med Coll

Fields, Theodore R MD [Rhu] - **Spec Exp:** Gout; Rheumatoid Arthritis; Osteoarthritis; **Hospital:** Hosp For Special Surgery (page 58), NY-Presby/Weill Cornell Med Ctr, NY (page 65); **Address:** 535 E 70th St, Fl 8, Ste 848F, New York, NY 10021-4872; **Phone:** 212-606-1286; **Board Cert:** Internal Medicine 1979; Rheumatology 1982; **Med School:** SUNY Downstate 1976; **Resid:** Internal Medicine, Nassau Co Med Ctr 1979; **Fellow:** Rheumatology, Univ Hosp 1982; **Fac Appt:** Clin Prof Med, Cornell Univ-Weill Med Coll

Gorevic, Peter D MD [Rhu] - **Spec Exp:** Autoimmune Disease; Amyloidosis/Joint Disease; Cryoglobulinemia; **Hospital:** Mt Sinai Med Ctr (page 62); **Address:** Mount Sinai Med Ctr, Rheumatology Dept, 5 E 98th St Fl 11, New York, NY 10029; **Phone:** 212-241-1671; **Board Cert:** Internal Medicine 1973; Rheumatology 1976; Allergy & Immunology 1977; Diagnostic Lab Immunology 1986; **Med School:** NYU Sch Med 1970; **Resid:** Internal Medicine, NYU Med Ctr 1973; **Fellow:** Rheumatology, NYU Med Ctr 1975; Allergy & Immunology, NYU Med Ctr 1977; **Fac Appt:** Prof Med, Mount Sinai Sch Med

Gourley, Mark F MD [Rhu] - **Spec Exp:** Autoimmune Disease; Lupus/SLE; **Hospital:** Natl Inst of Hlth - Clin Ctr; **Address:** Natl Inst Hlth, 10 Center Drive Bldg 10 - rm 6N216F, Bethesda, MD 20892-1616; **Phone:** 301-451-6807; **Board Cert:** Internal Medicine 1988; **Med School:** Tulane Univ 1985; **Resid:** Internal Medicine, Univ Wisconsin Hosps 1988; **Fellow:** Rheumatology, Natl Inst Hlth 1991

Hochberg, Marc C MD [Rhu] - **Spec Exp:** Osteoporosis; Osteoarthritis; Rheumatoid Arthritis; **Hospital:** Univ of MD Med Ctr, Kernan Hosp; **Address:** Univ MD Sch Med, Div Rheum, 10 S Pine St, MSTF 8-34, Baltimore, MD 21201; **Phone:** 410-706-6474; **Board Cert:** Internal Medicine 1976; Rheumatology 1978; **Med School:** Johns Hopkins Univ 1973; **Resid:** Internal Medicine, Johns Hopkins Hosp 1975; **Fellow:** Rheumatology, Johns Hopkins Hosp 1977; **Fac Appt:** Prof Med, Univ MD Sch Med

Lahita, Robert G MD/PhD [Rhu] - **Spec Exp:** Lupus/SLE; Endocrinology & Joint Disorders; Immunodeficiency Disorders; Vasculitis; **Hospital:** Newark Beth Israel Med Ctr; **Address:** Newark Beth Israel Med Ctr, Rheumatology, 201 Lyons Ave, Fl 4, Newark, NJ 07112; **Phone:** 973-926-7472; **Board Cert:** Internal Medicine 2004; Rheumatology 2007; **Med School:** Jefferson Med Coll 1973; **Resid:** Internal Medicine, New York Hosp-Cornell 1976; **Fellow:** Rheumatology, Rockefeller Hosp 1978; **Fac Appt:** Prof Med, Mount Sinai Sch Med

Magid, Steven K MD [Rhu] - **Spec Exp:** Rheumatoid Arthritis; Osteoarthritis; Lyme Disease; Polymyalgia Rheumatica; **Hospital:** Hosp For Special Surgery (page 58); **Address:** HSS, Rheumatology Dept, 535 E 70th St, Fl 7, New York, NY 10021; **Phone:** 212-606-1060; **Board Cert:** Internal Medicine 1979; Rheumatology 1984; **Med School:** Cornell Univ 1976; **Resid:** Internal Medicine, New York Hosp 1979; **Fellow:** Rheumatology, Hosp For Special Surgery 1981; **Fac Appt:** Clin Prof Med, Cornell Univ-Weill Med Coll

Manzi, Susan MD [Rhu] - **Spec Exp:** Lupus/SLE; Lupus/SLE in Women; **Hospital:** West Penn Hosp, Allegheny Genl Hosp; **Address:** WPAHS-Lupus Ctr Excellence, 4815 Liberty Ave, Ste 222, Pittsburgh, PA 15224; **Phone:** 412-578-1152; **Board Cert:** Internal Medicine 1988; Rheumatology 2010; **Med School:** Univ Pittsburgh 1985; **Resid:** Internal Medicine, Duke Univ Med Ctr 1988; **Fellow:** Rheumatology, UPMC-Presby 1991; **Fac Appt:** Assoc Prof Med, Univ Pittsburgh

Medsger Jr, Thomas A MD [Rhu] - **Spec Exp:** Scleroderma; Raynaud's Disease; Polymyositis; Dermatomyositis; **Hospital:** UPMC Presby, Pittsburgh; **Address:** Arthritis & Autoimmunity Ctr, 3601 Fifth Ave Falk Med Bldg - Ste 2B, Pittsburgh, PA 15213; **Phone:** 412-647-6700; **Board Cert:** Internal Medicine 1972; Rheumatology 1972; **Med School:** Univ Pennsylvania 1962; **Resid:** Internal Medicine, UPMC Presby 1968; **Fellow:** Rheumatology, UPMC Presby 1966; Rheumatology, Univ Tenn Hlth Sci Ctr 1969; **Fac Appt:** Prof Med, Univ Pittsburgh

Merkel, Peter A MD [Rhu] - **Spec Exp:** Vasculitis; Scleroderma; Temporal Arteritis; **Hospital:** Hosp Univ Penn - UPHS (page 69); **Address:** Penn Rheumatology, Perelman Ctr for Advanced Medicine, 3400 Civic Center Blvd, Ste 300 S, Philadelphia, PA 19104; **Phone:** 215-615-4693; **Board Cert:** Rheumatology 2000; **Med School:** Yale Univ 1988; **Resid:** Internal Medicine, Hosp Univ Penn 1991; **Fellow:** Rheumatology, Harvard/Mass Genl Hosp 1994; **Fac Appt:** Prof Med, Univ Pennsylvania

Mitnick, Hal J MD [Rhu] - **Spec Exp:** Rheumatoid Arthritis; Psoriatic Arthritis; Osteoporosis; Dermatomyositis; **Hospital:** NYU Langone Med Ctr (page 68); **Address:** 333 E 34th St, Ste 1C, New York, NY 10016-4977; **Phone:** 212-889-7217; **Board Cert:** Internal Medicine 1976; Rheumatology 1978; **Med School:** NYU Sch Med 1972; **Resid:** Internal Medicine, Bellevue Hosp 1976; **Fellow:** Rheumatology, NYU Med Ctr 1978; **Fac Appt:** Clin Prof Med, NYU Sch Med

Oddis, Chester V MD [Rhu] - **Spec Exp:** Polymyositis; Dermatomyositis; Connective Tissue Disorders; **Hospital:** UPMC Presby, Pittsburgh; **Address:** UPMC-Div Rheumatology, 3601 Fifth Ave Falk Med Bldg - Ste 2B, Pittsburgh, PA 15213; **Phone:** 412-647-6700; **Board Cert:** Internal Medicine 1983; Rheumatology 1986; **Med School:** Penn State Coll Med 1980; **Resid:** Internal Medicine, Hershey Med Ctr 1984; **Fellow:** Rheumatology, UPMC Presby 1987; **Fac Appt:** Prof Med, Univ Pittsburgh

Paget, Stephen MD [Rhu] - **Spec Exp:** Rheumatoid Arthritis; Lupus/SLE; Vasculitis; Connective Tissue Disorders; **Hospital:** Hosp For Special Surgery (page 58); **Address:** HSS, Rheumatology Dept, 535 E 70th St Fl 7, New York, NY 10021; **Phone:** 212-606-1845; **Board Cert:** Internal Medicine 1974; Rheumatology 2009; **Med School:** SUNY Downstate 1971; **Resid:** Internal Medicine, Johns Hopkins Hosp 1973; **Fellow:** Rheumatology, Hosp Special Surgery 1975; **Fac Appt:** Prof Med, Cornell Univ-Weill Med Coll

Petri, Michelle A MD [Rhu] - **Spec Exp:** Lupus/SLE; Antiphospholipid Syndrome (APS); Autoimmune Disease; **Hospital:** Johns Hopkins Hosp (page 59); **Address:** Johns Hopkins Lupus Ctr, Div Rheumatology, 1830 E Monument St, Ste 7500, Baltimore, MD 21205-2100; **Phone:** 410-955-9114; **Board Cert:** Internal Medicine 1983; Allergy & Immunology 1985; Rheumatology 1986; **Med School:** Harvard Med Sch 1980; **Resid:** Internal Medicine, Mass Genl Hosp 1983; **Fellow:** Allergy & Immunology, UCSF Med Ctr 1985; Rheumatology, UCSF Med Ctr 1986; **Fac Appt:** Prof Med, Johns Hopkins Univ

Rothenberg, Russell R MD [Rhu] - **Spec Exp:** Fibromyalgia; Lupus/SLE; Rheumatoid Arthritis; Preventive Medicine; **Hospital:** G Washington Univ Hosp; **Address:** 10215 Fernwood Rd, Ste 401, Bethesda, MD 20817; **Phone:** 301-571-2273; **Board Cert:** Internal Medicine 1980; Rheumatology 1982; **Med School:** Albany Med Coll 1977; **Resid:** Internal Medicine, LIJ Med Ctr 1980; **Fellow:** Rheumatology, Mt Sinai Med Ctr 1982; **Fac Appt:** Assoc Prof Med, Geo Wash Univ

Salmon, Jane E MD [Rhu] - **Spec Exp:** Lupus/SLE; Antiphospholipid Syndrome (APS); Rheumatoid Arthritis; **Hospital:** Hosp For Special Surgery (page 58); **Address:** 535 E 70th St, New York, NY 10021-4872; **Phone:** 212-606-1728; **Board Cert:** Internal Medicine 1981; Rheumatology 1984; **Med School:** Columbia P&S 1978; **Resid:** Internal Medicine, New York Hosp 1981; **Fellow:** Rheumatology, Hosp Special Surgery 1983; **Fac Appt:** Prof Med, Cornell Univ-Weill Med Coll

Schubert, Richard D MD [Rhu] - **Spec Exp:** Arthritis; **Hospital:** Sibley Mem Hosp, MedStar Georgetown Univ Hosp; **Address:** 3301 New Mexico Ave NW, Ste 348, Washington, DC 20016; **Phone:** 202-362-4467; **Board Cert:** Rheumatology 1978; Internal Medicine 1975; **Med School:** SUNY Downstate 1972; **Resid:** Internal Medicine, Brigham & Women's Hosp 1975; **Fellow:** Rheumatology, Brigham & Women's Hosp 1978; **Fac Appt:** Assoc Clin Prof Med, Georgetown Univ

Solitar, Bruce M MD [Rhu] - **Spec Exp:** Arthritis; Fibromyalgia; Reiter's Syndrome; Retroperitoneal Fibrosis; **Hospital:** NYU Langone Med Ctr (page 68), NYU Hosp For Joint Dis; **Address:** NYU Med Ctr, Rheumatology Dept, 333 E 34th St, Ste 1C, New York, NY 10016; **Phone:** 212-889-7217; **Board Cert:** Internal Medicine 2012; Rheumatology 2004; **Med School:** NYU Sch Med 1988; **Resid:** Internal Medicine, Bellevue Hosp 1992; **Fellow:** Rheumatology, Bellevue Hosp 1994; **Fac Appt:** Assoc Clin Prof Med, NYU Sch Med

Solomon, Gary MD [Rhu] - **Spec Exp:** Psoriatic Arthritis; Rheumatoid Arthritis; Autoimmune Disease; **Hospital:** NYU Hosp For Joint Dis, NYU Langone Med Ctr (page 68); **Address:** Ctr for Musculoskeletal Care, 333 E 38th St, New York, NY 10016; **Phone:** 646-501-7400; **Board Cert:** Internal Medicine 1980; Rheumatology 1982; **Med School:** Mount Sinai Sch Med 1977; **Resid:** Internal Medicine, Mt Sinai Med Ctr 1980; **Fellow:** Rheumatology, Montefiore Med Ctr 1982; **Fac Appt:** Assoc Clin Prof Med, NYU Sch Med

Spiera, Harry MD [Rhu] - **Spec Exp:** Lupus/SLE; Scleroderma; Vasculitis; Behcet's Syndrome; **Hospital:** Mt Sinai Med Ctr (page 62); **Address:** Rheumatology Assocs, 1088 Park Ave, New York, NY 10128-1132; **Phone:** 212-860-4000 x2; **Board Cert:** Internal Medicine 1965; Rheumatology 1972; **Med School:** NYU Sch Med 1958; **Resid:** Internal Medicine, VA Med Ctr 1960; Internal Medicine, Mt Sinai Hosp 1961; **Fellow:** Rheumatology, Columbia-Presby Med Ctr 1963; **Fac Appt:** Clin Prof Med, Mount Sinai Sch Med

Starz, Terence W MD [Rhu] - **Spec Exp:** Arthritis; **Hospital:** UPMC Shadyside, UPMC St Margaret; **Address:** Arthritis & Int Medicine Assocs-UPMC, 3500 Fifth Ave Hieber Bldg Fl 4, Pittsburgh, PA 15213; **Phone:** 412-682-2434; **Board Cert:** Internal Medicine 1975; Rheumatology 1978; **Med School:** Jefferson Med Coll 1971; **Resid:** Internal Medicine, UPMC-Presby 1975; **Fellow:** Rheumatology, UPMC-Presby 1977; **Fac Appt:** Asst Clin Prof Med, Univ Pittsburgh

Steen, Virginia MD [Rhu] - **Spec Exp:** Scleroderma; Lupus/SLE; Polymyositis; **Hospital:** MedStar Georgetown Univ Hosp; **Address:** 3800 Reservoir Rd NW, Pasquerilla Bldg, Ste 3004, Washington, DC 20007; **Phone:** 202-444-6200; **Board Cert:** Internal Medicine 1978; Rheumatology 1980; **Med School:** Univ Pittsburgh 1975; **Resid:** Internal Medicine, Hosp Univ Penn 1978; **Fellow:** Rheumatology, Presby Hosp 1980; **Fac Appt:** Prof Med, Georgetown Univ

Vivino, Frederick B MD [Rhu] - **Spec Exp:** Sjogren's Syndrome; **Hospital:** Penn Presby Med Ctr - UPHS (page 69); **Address:** Penn Rheumatology Assocs & Sjogren's Ctr, 3910 Powelton Ave Fl 2, Philadelphia, PA 19104; **Phone:** 215-662-4333; **Board Cert:** Internal Medicine 1986; Rheumatology 1988; **Med School:** Temple Univ 1983; **Resid:** Internal Medicine, Med Coll Penn Hosp 1986; **Fellow:** Rheumatology, Hosp Univ Penn 1989; **Fac Appt:** Assoc Clin Prof Med, Univ Pennsylvania

Weinstein, Arthur MD [Rhu] - **Spec Exp:** Lupus/SLE; Lyme Disease; Rheumatoid Arthritis; Gout; **Hospital:** MedStar Washington Hosp Ctr; **Address:** MedStar Washington Hospital Center, rm 2A-66, 110 Irving St NW, Washington, DC 20010; **Phone:** 202-877-0333; **Board Cert:** Rheumatology 1976; Diagnostic Lab Immunology 1986; **Med School:** Univ Toronto 1967; **Resid:** Internal Medicine, Toronto Genl Hosp 1972; Rheumatology, Hammersmith Hosp 1971; **Fellow:** Rheumatology, Toronto Wellesley Hosp 1973; **Fac Appt:** Prof Med, Georgetown Univ

Wigley, Frederick M MD [Rhu] - **Spec Exp:** Scleroderma; Raynaud's Disease; **Hospital:** Johns Hopkins Bayview Med Ctr (page 59), Johns Hopkins Hosp (page 59); **Address:** 5501 Hopkins Bayview Cir, Ste 1B32, Baltimore, MD 21224; **Phone:** 410-550-7715; **Board Cert:** Internal Medicine 1975; Rheumatology 1980; **Med School:** Univ Fla Coll Med 1972; **Resid:** Internal Medicine, Johns Hopkins Hosp 1975; **Fellow:** Rheumatology, Johns Hopkins Hosp 1979; **Fac Appt:** Prof Med, Johns Hopkins Univ

Southeast

Allen, Nancy B MD [Rhu] - **Spec Exp:** Vasculitis; Wegener's Granulomatosis; Lupus/SLE; Temporal Arteritis; **Hospital:** Duke Univ Hosp; **Address:** Duke Box 3440, 4140 Purple Zone Hosp South, 201 Trent Drive, Durham, NC 27710; **Phone:** 919-684-2965; **Board Cert:** Internal Medicine 1981; Rheumatology 1984; **Med School:** Tufts Univ 1978; **Resid:** Internal Medicine, Duke Univ Med Ctr 1981; **Fellow:** Rheumatology, Duke Univ Med Ctr 1983; **Fac Appt:** Prof Med, Duke Univ

Chatham, W. Winn MD [Rhu] - **Spec Exp:** Lupus/SLE; Connective Tissue Disorders; Rheumatoid Arthritis; **Hospital:** UAB Hosp; **Address:** UAB Hosp, Div Rheumatology, 1530 3rd Ave S FOT Bldg - Ste 802, Birmingham, AL 35294-3408; **Phone:** 205-801-8191; **Board Cert:** Internal Medicine 1983; Rheumatology 1988; **Med School:** Vanderbilt Univ 1980; **Resid:** Internal Medicine, NC Memorial Hosp - UNC 1983; **Fellow:** Rheumatology, UAB Hosp 1988; **Fac Appt:** Prof Med, UAB Sch Med

Crofford, Leslie J MD [Rhu] - **Spec Exp:** Fibromyalgia; Rheumatoid Arthritis; Lupus/SLE; **Hospital:** Vanderbilt Univ Med Ctr; **Address:** 1301 Medical Center Drive, Ste 2501, Nashville, TN 37232; **Phone:** 615-322-4746; **Board Cert:** Internal Medicine 1987; Rheumatology 2003; **Med School:** Univ Tenn Coll Med 1984; **Resid:** Internal Medicine, Barnes/Wash Univ 1987; **Fellow:** Rheumatology, Natl Inst Hlth Clin Ctr 1992; **Fac Appt:** Prof Med, Vanderbilt Univ

Hadler, Nortin M MD [Rhu] - **Spec Exp:** Musculoskeletal Disorders; Occupational Musculoskeletal Disorders; Spondylitis; Pain-Back; **Hospital:** NC Memorial Hosp - UNC; **Address:** UNC,Div Rheumatology, 3330 Thurston Building, Box 7280, Chapel Hill, NC 27599-7280; **Phone:** 919-957-6786; **Board Cert:** Rheumatology 1974; Allergy & Immunology 1975; Internal Medicine 1987; **Med School:** Harvard Med Sch 1968; **Resid:** Internal Medicine, Mass Genl Hosp 1973; **Fellow:** Rheumatology, Natl Inst Hlth 1972; Allergy & Immunology, Clin Res Ctr 1974; **Fac Appt:** Prof Med, Univ NC Sch Med

Kimberly, Robert P MD [Rhu] - **Spec Exp:** Lupus/SLE; Rheumatoid Arthritis; Vasculitis; Autoimmune Disease; **Hospital:** UAB Hosp; **Address:** Kirklin Clin, 2000 6th Ave S, Birmingham, AL 35205; **Phone:** 205-930-8244; **Board Cert:** Internal Medicine 1976; Rheumatology 1978; **Med School:** Harvard Med Sch 1973; **Resid:** Internal Medicine, Hosp Univ Penn - UPHS 1975; **Fellow:** Rheumatology, NIAMS, NIH 1977; Rheumatology, Hosp Special Surgery 1979; **Fac Appt:** Prof Med, UAB Sch Med

Moore, Walter J MD [Rhu] - **Spec Exp:** Rheumatoid Arthritis; Lupus/SLE; **Hospital:** Georgia Regents Med Ctr-Augusta; **Address:** 1120 15th St, Ste BI 5083, Augusta, GA 30912; **Phone:** 706-721-1450; **Board Cert:** Internal Medicine 1980; Rheumatology 1984; **Med School:** Georgetown Univ 1977; **Resid:** Internal Medicine, Walter Reed AMC 1980; **Fellow:** Rheumatology, Walter Reed AMC 1983; **Fac Appt:** Assoc Prof Med, Med Coll GA

Sergent, John S MD [Rhu] - **Spec Exp:** Vasculitis; **Hospital:** Vanderbilt Univ Med Ctr; **Address:** Vanderbilt Rheumatology, 1301 Medical Center Drive, Ste 2501, Nashville, TN 37232; **Phone:** 615-322-1900; **Board Cert:** Internal Medicine 1972; Rheumatology 1974; **Med School:** Vanderbilt Univ 1966; **Resid:** Internal Medicine, Johns Hopkins Hosp 1968; Internal Medicine, Vanderbilt Univ Hosp 1972; **Fellow:** Rheumatology, Hosp Special Surgery 1974; **Fac Appt:** Prof Med, Vanderbilt Univ

Silver, Richard M MD [Rhu] - **Spec Exp:** Scleroderma & Lung Disease; Pediatric Rheumatology; Connective Tissue Disorders; **Hospital:** MUSC Med Ctr; **Address:** MUSC Med Ctr, 96 Jonathan Lucas St, Ste 912, Charleston, SC 29425; **Phone:** 843-792-9200; **Board Cert:** Internal Medicine 1978; Rheumatology 1982; **Med School:** Vanderbilt Univ 1975; **Resid:** Internal Medicine, Univ NC Hosps 1978; **Fellow:** Rheumatology, UCSD Med Ctr 1981; **Fac Appt:** Prof Med, Med Univ SC

Wise, Christopher M MD [Rhu] - **Spec Exp:** Gout; Sjogren's Syndrome; Rheumatoid Arthritis; **Hospital:** Med Coll of VA Hosp; **Address:** Virginia Commonwealth Univ/MCV Campus, 417 N 11th St, Richmond, VA 23219; **Phone:** 804-828-9341; **Board Cert:** Internal Medicine 1980; Rheumatology 1982; **Med School:** Univ NC Sch Med 1977; **Resid:** Internal Medicine, Med Coll Virginia Hosp 1980; **Fellow:** Rheumatology, Med Coll Virginia Hosp 1982; **Fac Appt:** Prof Med, Va Commonwealth Univ Sch Med

Midwest

Adams, Elaine MD [Rhu] - **Spec Exp:** Rheumatoid Arthritis; Lupus/SLE; Spondyloarthropathies; **Hospital:** Loyola Univ Med Ctr; **Address:** Loyola Univ Med Ctr, Dept Rheumatology, 2160 S 1st Ave, Bldg 150, Maywood, IL 60153-5590; **Phone:** 708-216-8563; **Board Cert:** Internal Medicine 1981; Rheumatology 1984; **Med School:** Loyola Univ-Stritch Sch Med 1978; **Resid:** Internal Medicine, Loyola Univ Med Ctr 1981; **Fellow:** Rheumatology, Univ Wisconsin Med Ctr 1983; **Fac Appt:** Prof Med, Loyola Univ-Stritch Sch Med

Brasington, Richard D MD [Rhu] - **Hospital:** Barnes-Jewish Hosp; **Address:** 660 S Euclid Ave, Box 8602, St Louis, MO 63110; **Phone:** 314-286-2635; **Board Cert:** Internal Medicine 1985; Rheumatology 1986; **Med School:** Duke Univ 1980; **Resid:** Internal Medicine, Univ Iowa Med Ctr 1982; Internal Medicine, Univ Iowa Med Ctr 1985; **Fellow:** Rheumatology, Univ Iowa 1986; **Fac Appt:** Assoc Prof Med, Washington Univ, St Louis

Chang, Rowland W MD [Rhu] - **Spec Exp:** Rheumatoid Arthritis; Arthritis; Ankylosing Spondylitis; **Hospital:** Rehab Inst of Chicago, Northwestern Meml Hosp; **Address:** Rehab Inst of Chicago Arthritis Ctr, 345 E Superior St, Fl 3, Chicago, IL 60611-2654; **Phone:** 312-238-0843; **Board Cert:** Internal Medicine 1979; Rheumatology 1982; **Med School:** Tufts Univ 1976; **Resid:** Internal Medicine, Mt Auburn Hosp 1979; **Fellow:** Rheumatology, Hammersmith Hosp 1980; Rheumatology, Brigham & Womens Hosp 1982; **Fac Appt:** Prof Med, Northwestern Univ

Curran, James J MD [Rhu] - **Spec Exp:** Rheumatoid Arthritis; Polymyositis; Sjogren's Syndrome; Lupus/SLE; **Hospital:** Univ of Chicago Med; **Address:** 5758 S Maryland Ave, Chicago, IL 60637; **Phone:** 773-702-6119; **Board Cert:** Internal Medicine 1980; Rheumatology 1982; **Med School:** Univ IL Coll Med 1976; **Resid:** Internal Medicine, Bethesda Naval Hosp 1980; **Fellow:** Rheumatology, Univ Chicago Hosps 1982; **Fac Appt:** Prof Med, Univ Chicago-Pritzker Sch Med

Fife, Rose S MD [Rhu] - **Spec Exp:** Women's Health; Arthritis; Osteoarthritis; **Hospital:** IU Hlth Univ Hosp; **Address:** IU Health Physicians Rheumatology, 550 N University Blvd, Ste 2180, Indianapolis, IN 46202; **Phone:** 317-944-7718; **Board Cert:** Internal Medicine 1978; Rheumatology 1982; **Med School:** Johns Hopkins Univ 1975; **Resid:** Internal Medicine, Johns Hopkins Hosp 1978; **Fellow:** Rheumatology, Univ Washington Med Ctr 1981; **Fac Appt:** Prof Med, Indiana Univ

Hugenberg, Steven T MD [Rhu] - **Spec Exp:** Rheumatoid Arthritis; Osteoarthritis; Psoriatic Arthritis; Ankylosing Spondylitis; **Hospital:** IU Hlth Univ Hosp; **Address:** IU Health Physicians Rheumatology, 550 N University Blvd, Ste 2180, Indianapolis, IN 46202; **Phone:** 317-944-7718; **Board Cert:** Internal Medicine 1985; Rheumatology 1988; **Med School:** Ohio State Univ 1982; **Resid:** Internal Medicine, Indiana Univ Med Ctr 1985; **Fellow:** Rheumatology, Indiana Univ Med Ctr 1987; **Fac Appt:** Assoc Prof Med, Indiana Univ

Katz, Robert S MD [Rhu] - **Spec Exp:** Rheumatoid Arthritis; Lupus/SLE; Fibromyalgia; Vasculitis; **Hospital:** Rush Univ Med Ctr, Northwestern Meml Hosp; **Address:** 1725 W Harrison St, Ste 365, Chicago, IL 60612-3841; **Phone:** 312-226-8228; **Board Cert:** Internal Medicine 1975; Rheumatology 1976; **Med School:** Univ MD Sch Med 1970; **Resid:** Internal Medicine, Washington Univ Med Ctr 1972; **Fellow:** Rheumatology, Johns Hopkins Hosp 1976; **Fac Appt:** Prof Med, Rush Med Coll

Langford, Carol MD [Rhu] - **Spec Exp:** Vasculitis; **Hospital:** Cleveland Clin (page 55); **Address:** Cleveland Clinic, 9500 Euclid Ave, Ste A50, Cleveland, OH 44195; **Phone:** 216-445-6056; **Board Cert:** Rheumatology 2000; **Med School:** UCLA 1987; **Resid:** Internal Medicine, Univ Mich Hosps & Med Ctr 1990; **Fellow:** Rheumatology, Duke Univ Med Ctr 1991

Luggen, Michael MD [Rhu] - **Hospital:** Univ Cincinnati Med Ctr, Deaconess Hosp - Cincinnati; **Address:** 2123 Auburn Ave, Ste 630, Cincinnati, OH 45219; **Phone:** 513-585-1970; **Board Cert:** Internal Medicine 1978; Rheumatology 1982; **Med School:** Columbia P&S 1974; **Resid:** Internal Medicine, Cincinnati Genl Hosp 1977; **Fellow:** Rheumatology, Univ Hosp 1982; **Fac Appt:** Prof Med, Univ Cincinnati

Luthra, Harvinder Singh MD [Rhu] - **Spec Exp:** Rheumatoid Arthritis; Ankylosing Spondylitis; Relapsing Polychondritis; **Hospital:** St. Mary's Hosp - Rochester MN (Mayo), Rochester Methodist Hosp; **Address:** Mayo Clin, 200 First St SW, Rochester, MN 55905-0002; **Phone:** 507-266-4439; **Board Cert:** Internal Medicine 1973; Rheumatology 2002; **Med School:** India 1967; **Resid:** Ophthalmology, Christian Med Coll; Internal Medicine, Mount Sinai Hosp 1972; **Fellow:** Rheumatology, Mayo Grad Sch Affil Hosp 1974; **Fac Appt:** Prof Med, Mayo Med Sch

McCune, W. Joseph MD [Rhu] - **Spec Exp:** Lupus/SLE; Rheumatoid Arthritis; **Hospital:** Univ Michigan Med Ctr; **Address:** U of M Taubman Hlth Care Ctr, 1500 E Medical Ctr Drive, Lobby A Fl 3, Ann Arbor, MI 48109-5358; **Phone:** 734-647-5900; **Board Cert:** Internal Medicine 1978; Rheumatology 2011; **Med School:** Univ Cincinnati 1975; **Resid:** Internal Medicine, Univ Mich Hosps 1978; **Fellow:** Rheumatology, Brigham and Women's Hosp 1981; **Fac Appt:** Prof Med, Univ Mich Med Sch

Moder, Kevin G MD [Rhu] - **Spec Exp:** Rheumatoid Arthritis; Lupus/SLE; **Hospital:** Mayo Med Ctr & Clin - Rochester; **Address:** Mayo Clin, Div Rheumatology, 200 First St SW, Rochester, MN 55905-0002; **Phone:** 507-284-4550; **Board Cert:** Rheumatology 2000; **Med School:** Univ MO-Columbia Sch Med 1987; **Resid:** Internal Medicine, Mayo Clinic 1990; **Fellow:** Rheumatology, Mayo Clinic 1994; **Fac Appt:** Asst Prof Med, Mayo Med Sch

Pope, Richard M MD [Rhu] - **Spec Exp:** Rheumatoid Arthritis; Sjogren's Syndrome; Psoriatic Arthritis; **Hospital:** Northwestern Meml Hosp; **Address:** 675 N St Clair Fl 14 - Ste 100, Chicago, IL 60611-5966; **Phone:** 312-695-8628; **Board Cert:** Internal Medicine 1973; Rheumatology 1976; Clinical & Laboratory Immunology 1986; **Med School:** Loyola Univ-Stritch Sch Med 1970; **Resid:** Internal Medicine, Michael Reese Hosp 1972; **Fellow:** Rheumatology, Univ Wash Med Ctr 1974; **Fac Appt:** Prof Med, Northwestern Univ

Varga, John MD [Rhu] - **Spec Exp:** Scleroderma; **Hospital:** Northwestern Meml Hosp; **Address:** 675 N St Clair, Galter Bldg - Ste 14-100, Chicago, IL 60611; **Phone:** 312-695-8628; **Board Cert:** Internal Medicine 1983; Rheumatology 1986; **Med School:** NYU Sch Med 1980; **Resid:** Internal Medicine, Rhode Island Hosp 1983; **Fellow:** Rheumatology, Boston Med Ctr 1985; **Fac Appt:** Prof Med, Northwestern Univ-Feinberg Sch Med

Warner, Ann E MD [Rhu] - **Hospital:** St. Luke's Hosp of Kansas City; **Address:** 4330 Wornall St, Ste 40, Kansas City, MO 64111-3210; **Phone:** 816-531-0930; **Board Cert:** Internal Medicine 1986; Rheumatology 1988; **Med School:** Univ Kansas 1983; **Resid:** Internal Medicine, St Luke's Hosp 1986; **Fellow:** Rheumatology, Univ Kansas Med Ctr 1989; **Fac Appt:** Asst Clin Prof Med, Univ MO-Kansas City

Great Plains and Mountains

O'Dell, James R MD [Rhu] - **Spec Exp:** Osteoarthritis; Rheumatoid Arthritis; **Hospital:** Nebraska Med Ctr; **Address:** Durham Outpatient Center, 42nd & Emile St, Omaha, NE 68198-9500; **Phone:** 402-559-4015; **Board Cert:** Internal Medicine 1980; Rheumatology 1984; **Med School:** Univ Nebr Coll Med 1977; **Resid:** Internal Medicine, Univ Nebraska Med Ctr 1981; **Fellow:** Rheumatology, Univ Colorado 1984; **Fac Appt:** Prof Med, Univ Nebr Coll Med

Southwest

Chang-Miller, April MD [Rhu] - **Spec Exp:** Spondyloarthritis-Consult; Inflammatory Arthritis-Consult; **Hospital:** Mayo Clinic - Scottsdale; **Address:** 13400 E Shea Blvd, Scottsdale, AZ 85259; **Phone:** 480-301-4342; **Board Cert:** Internal Medicine 1986; Rheumatology 2012; **Med School:** Yale Univ 1983; **Resid:** Internal Medicine, Mayo Clinic 1985; **Fellow:** Rheumatology, Mayo Clinic 1989; Biochemical and Molecular Biology, Mayo Clinic 1990; **Fac Appt:** Asst Prof Med, Mayo Med Sch

Davis, William E MD [Rhu] - **Spec Exp:** Lupus/SLE; Rheumatoid Arthritis; Gout; **Hospital:** Ochsner Med Ctr-New Orleans; **Address:** Ochsner Clin - Div Rheumatology, 1514 Jefferson Hwy Fl 5, New Orleans, LA 70121-2483; **Phone:** 504-842-3920; **Board Cert:** Internal Medicine 1987; Rheumatology 1988; **Med School:** Louisiana State U, New Orleans 1983; **Resid:** Internal Medicine, Ochsner Med Ctr 1986; **Fellow:** Rheumatology, Univ Michigan Med Sch Affil Hosps 1988

Lindsey, Stephen M MD [Rhu] - **Spec Exp:** Osteoporosis; Rheumatoid Arthritis; **Hospital:** Ochsner Med Ctr-Baton Rouge; **Address:** Ochsner Hlth Ctr, 9001 Summa Ave, Baton Rouge, LA 70809; **Phone:** 225-761-5481; **Board Cert:** Internal Medicine 1975; Rheumatology 1980; **Med School:** Louisiana State U, New Orleans 1972; **Resid:** Internal Medicine, Letterman AMC 1975; **Fellow:** Rheumatology, Walter Reed AMC 1979; **Fac Appt:** Clin Prof Med, Louisiana State U, New Orleans

Lipstate, James M MD [Rhu] - **Spec Exp:** Arthritis; Osteoporosis; **Hospital:** Our Lady of Lourdes Reg Med Ctr - Lafayette, Lafayette Genl Med Ctr; **Address:** Lafayette Arthritis & Endocrine Clin, 401 Audubon Blvd, Ste 102B, Lafayette, LA 70503; **Phone:** 337-237-7801; **Board Cert:** Internal Medicine 1983; Rheumatology 1986; **Med School:** Tulane Univ 1980; **Resid:** Internal Medicine, UAB Hosp 1983; **Fellow:** Rheumatology, UAB Hosp 1986; **Fac Appt:** Asst Clin Prof Med, Louisiana State U, New Orleans

Mayes, Maureen D MD [Rhu] - **Spec Exp:** Scleroderma; **Hospital:** Meml Hermann Hosp - Texas Med Ctr, LBJ General Hosp; **Address:** UT Physicians, Rheumatology, 6410 Fannin St, Ste 450, Houston, TX 77030-1501; **Phone:** 713-486-3100; **Board Cert:** Internal Medicine 1980; Rheumatology 1982; **Med School:** Eastern VA Med Sch 1976; **Resid:** Internal Medicine, Cleveland Clinic 1979; **Fellow:** Rheumatology, Cleveland Clinic 1981; **Fac Appt:** Prof Med, Univ Tex, Houston

Sessoms, Sandra L MD [Rhu] - **Spec Exp:** Arthritis; Lupus/SLE; Autoimmune Disease; **Hospital:** Methodist Hosp - Houston; **Address:** 7501 Fannin St, Univ General Hosp Bldg, Ste 730, Houston, TX 77054; **Phone:** 713-790-0102; **Board Cert:** Internal Medicine 1981; Rheumatology 1984; **Med School:** Baylor Coll Med 1978; **Resid:** Internal Medicine, Baylor Affil Hosp 1981; **Fellow:** Rheumatology, Baylor Affil Hosp 1983; **Fac Appt:** Assoc Prof Med, Baylor Coll Med

West Coast and Pacific

Bobrove, Arthur M MD [Rhu] - **Spec Exp:** Psoriatic Arthritis; Ankylosing Spondylitis; Rheumatoid Arthritis; Lupus/SLE; **Hospital:** Stanford Univ Hosp & Clins; **Address:** 795 El Camino Real, Palo Alto, CA 94301; **Phone:** 650-853-2083; **Board Cert:** Internal Medicine 1972; Rheumatology 1976; **Med School:** Temple Univ 1967; **Resid:** Internal Medicine, Univ Mich Affil Hosp 1972; **Fellow:** Immunology, Stanford Univ Hosp & Clins 1974; **Fac Appt:** Clin Prof Med, Stanford Univ

Clements, Philip J MD [Rhu] - **Spec Exp:** Scleroderma; Raynaud's Disease; **Hospital:** UCLA Ronald Reagan Med Ctr; **Address:** 200 UCLA Med Plaza, Ste 365B, Los Angeles, CA 90095-1670; **Phone:** 310-825-2448; **Board Cert:** Internal Medicine 1972; Rheumatology 1974; **Med School:** Indiana Univ 1965; **Resid:** Internal Medicine, Cedars-Sinai Med Ctr 1971; **Fellow:** Rheumatology, UCLA Ronald Reagan Med Ctr 1974; **Fac Appt:** Prof Med, UCLA

Ehresmann, Glenn R MD [Rhu] - **Spec Exp:** Rheumatoid Arthritis; Scleroderma; Rehabilitation for Rheumatic Diseases; Lupus/SLE; **Hospital:** Keck Med Ctr of USC; **Address:** Keck Med Ctr, 1520 San Pablo St, Ste 1000, Los Angeles, CA 90033; **Phone:** 323-442-5100; **Board Cert:** Internal Medicine 1977; Rheumatology 1978; **Med School:** UC Irvine 1973; **Resid:** Internal Medicine, LAC & USC Med Ctr 1976; **Fellow:** Rheumatology, LAC & USC Med Ctr 1978; **Fac Appt:** Assoc Prof Med, USC-Keck School of Medicine

Gershwin, Merrill E MD [Rhu] - **Spec Exp:** Allergy; Rheumatoid Arthritis; **Hospital:** UC Davis Med Ctr; **Address:** UC Davis Sch Med, Div Rheum, 451 Hlth Scis Drive, Ste 6510, Davis, CA 95616; **Phone:** 530-752-2884; **Board Cert:** Internal Medicine 1974; Rheumatology 1976; Allergy & Immunology 1979; **Med School:** Stanford Univ 1971; **Resid:** Internal Medicine, Tufts-New Eng Med Ctr 1973; **Fellow:** Rheumatology, Natl Inst Hlth 1975; Allergy & Immunology, Natl Inst Hlth 1977; **Fac Appt:** Prof Med, UC Davis

Lawry II, George V MD [Rhu] - **Spec Exp:** Gout; Rheumatoid Arthritis; Vasculitis; **Hospital:** UC Irvine Med Ctr; **Address:** UC Irvine Med Ctr, 101 The City Drive S Fl 4, South Orange, CA 92868; **Phone:** 714-456-7662; **Board Cert:** Internal Medicine 1978; Rheumatology 1982; **Med School:** Johns Hopkins Univ 1975; **Resid:** Internal Medicine, Mass Genl Hosp 1977; Internal Medicine, Stanford Hosp 1978; **Fellow:** Rheumatology, Wadsworth VA-UCLA Ronald Reagan Med Ctr 1981; **Fac Appt:** Clin Prof Med, UC Irvine

Mease, Philip J MD [Rhu] - **Spec Exp:** Arthritis; Autoimmune Disease; Osteoporosis; **Hospital:** Swedish Med Ctr-First Hill-Seattle, Swedish Med Ctr-Cherry Hill Campus; **Address:** 601 Broadway St, Ste 600, Seattle, WA 98122; **Phone:** 206-386-2000; **Board Cert:** Internal Medicine 1980; Rheumatology 1982; **Med School:** Stanford Univ 1977; **Resid:** Internal Medicine, Univ Wash Med Ctr 1981; **Fellow:** Rheumatology, Univ Wash Med Ctr 1982; **Fac Appt:** Assoc Clin Prof Med, Univ Wash

Peng, Stanford L MD [Rhu] - **Spec Exp:** Lupus/SLE; Inflammatory Arthritis; Scleroderma; Vasculitis; **Hospital:** Virginia Mason Med Ctr; **Address:** Virginia Mason, 1100 9th Ave, Ste X6-RHE, Seattle, WA 98101; **Phone:** 206-223-6824; **Board Cert:** Rheumatology 2012; Internal Medicine 2010; **Med School:** Yale Univ 1997; **Resid:** Internal Medicine, Univ Penn Hosp 1999; **Fellow:** Rheumatology, Brigham & Women's Hosp 2002; **Fac Appt:** Asst Clin Prof Med, Univ Wash

Wallace, Daniel J MD [Rhu] - **Spec Exp:** Lupus/SLE; Rheumatoid Arthritis; Scleroderma; **Hospital:** Cedars-Sinai Med Ctr, UCLA Ronald Reagan Med Ctr; **Address:** 8737 Beverly Blvd, Ste 302, Los Angeles, CA 90048-1828; **Phone:** 310-652-0920; **Board Cert:** Internal Medicine 1978; Rheumatology 1982; **Med School:** USC-Keck School of Medicine 1974; **Resid:** Internal Medicine, Cedars-Sinai Med Ctr 1977; **Fellow:** Rheumatology, UCLA Ronald Reagan Med Ctr 1979; **Fac Appt:** Clin Prof Med, UCLA-David Geffen Sch Med

Wener, Mark H MD [Rhu] - **Spec Exp:** Lupus/SLE; Vasculitis; Autoimmune Disease; **Hospital:** Univ Wash Med Ctr, Harborview Med Ctr; **Address:** Univ Washington Med Ctr, Medical Specialties, 1959 NE Pacific St, Box 356166, Seattle, WA 98195; **Phone:** 206-598-4615; **Board Cert:** Internal Medicine 1978; Rheumatology 1980; Clinical & Laboratory Immunology 1986; **Med School:** Washington Univ, St Louis 1974; **Resid:** Internal Medicine, Univ Iowa Hosps 1978; **Fellow:** Rheumatology, Univ Iowa Hosp 1980; Immunology, Univ Washington Med Ctr 1981; **Fac Appt:** Prof Med, Univ Wash

Wofsy, David MD [Rhu] - **Spec Exp:** Rheumatoid Arthritis; Lupus/SLE; Autoimmune Disease; Clinical Trials; **Hospital:** VA Med Ctr - San Francisco, UCSF Med Ctr; **Address:** 533 Parnassus Ave, Box 0633, San Francisco, CA 94143-0633; **Phone:** 415-750-2104; **Board Cert:** Internal Medicine 1977; Rheumatology 1980; **Med School:** UCSD 1974; **Resid:** Internal Medicine, UCSF Med Ctr 1977; **Fellow:** Rheumatology, UCSF Med Ctr 1979; **Fac Appt:** Prof Med, UCSF

Cleveland Clinic

Every life deserves world class care.

Rheumatology

Cleveland Clinic's Department of Rheumatic and Immunologic Diseases has a long-standing commitment to excellence and innovation in the research and care of patients with illnesses such as arthritis, osteoporosis and vasculitis. Since 1993, *U.S. News & World Report* has consistently ranked it among the nation's top 10 rheumatology programs.

Arthritis: Our department's Arthritis & Musculoskeletal Center is a multidisciplinary clinic combining the expertise of medical orthopaedists, physiatrist and rheumatologists in one location for patients with joint pain. Our doctors have a specific interest in joint pain problems, including rheumatoid arthritis and osteoarthritis, and work together to provide patients with the highest level of care so that they can return to their usual level of activity.

Osteoporosis: Our Center for Osteoporosis and Metabolic Bone Diseases is devoted to the evaluation and treatment of patients with osteoporosis and other diseases that affect bones. The Center's goal is to evaluate patients at an early stage to prevent the complications and additional disease manifestations of osteoporosis and other treatable diseases.

Vasculitis: Cleveland Clinic's Center for Vasculitis Care and Research aims to ensure the best possible care for patients with vasculitis, discover the causes of these diseases, identify improved therapies and alleviate discomfort. The department has established extensive collaborations with other Cleveland Clinic departments to bring complementary skills to both patient care and research.

Autoimmune Disease: Our Department of Rheumatic and Immunologic Diseases also provides expert care for autoimmune diseases, such as systemic lupus, scleroderma, myositis and polychondritis.

Cleveland Clinic
Rheumatic and Immunologic Diseases
9500 Euclid Ave.
Cleveland, OH 44195

Offering Same-Day Appointments
Call 866.320.4573

Treatment Guides
Cleveland Clinic has developed comprehensive treatment guides for many diseases and conditions. To download our free treatment guides, visit clevelandclinic.org/treatmentguides.

Online Medical Second Opinion
Call 216.444.3223 or
800.223.2273 ext. 43223 or
email eclevelandclinic@ccf.org

Out-of-State Patients Assistance
Call 800.223.2273, ext. 55580 or
email medicalconcierge@ccf.org

Visit Us At:
clevelandclinic.org

Follow Us On:
Facebook
facebook.com/clevelandclinic

Twitter
@ClevelandClinic

You Tube
youtube.com/clevelandclinic

Health Hub
clevelandclinic.org/HealthHub

NYU Langone
MEDICAL CENTER

550 First Avenue *(at 31st Street)*
New York, NY 10016
www.NYULMC.org/rheumatology
Physician Referral: **888-7-NYU-MED** *(888-769-8633)*

RHEUMATOLOGY

Rheumatologists at NYU Langone Medical Center are dedicated to the diagnosis and treatment of patients with rheumatic illnesses, particularly autoimmune diseases. *U.S. News & World Report* has repeatedly recognized the Division of Rheumatology as one of the best in the country, ranking #7 nationwide in the 2013-2014 "Best Hospitals" survey. The division provides care at NYU Langone's premier outpatient facility, The Center for Musculoskeletal Care (CMC); the internationally-renowned, inpatient Hospital for Joint Diseases; at NYU Langone's main campus; and at multiple locations in NYU Langone's growing network of community practices throughout the metro New York area.

Arthritis and Autoimmunity: We offer a comprehensive program for the prevention, diagnosis and treatment of all rheumatologic conditions. Patients also have access to complete rheumatologic evaluations, orthopaedic and neurological consultative services, and participation in clinical trials using the most advanced interventional therapies, highly sophisticated diagnostic testing, and complementary medicine.

Behçet's Syndrome: We have the largest North American Behçet's Center for research and the evaluation and treatment of patients with Behçet's Syndrome, a disease that involves inflammation of the blood vessels.

Biological Treatment: Biological treatments for inflammatory arthritis, rheumatoid arthritis, lupus, psoriatic arthritis, vasculitis, and osteoporosis are administered in our comfortable, state-of-the-art infusion center at CMC.

Lupus: The Center for Lupus Care and Research is devoted to the treatment and research of patients with this autoimmune disease. Patients have access to world renowned specialists in lupus, lupus and pregnancy, and related subspecialties.

Osteoporosis: We offer comprehensive care for the prevention, evaluation and treatment of osteoporosis, including state-of-the art bone densitometers, a range of advanced drug therapies, and programs in balance training and exercise.

Psoriatic Arthritis: Patients of our Psoriatic Arthritis Center, a collaborative effort with the Department of Dermatology, are seen by both a rheumatologist and dermatologist who specialize in psoriasis and psoriatic arthritis.

We are also leaders in the research of inflammatory diseases, focusing on the study of drugs, drug delivery systems and protocols, and the roles genes play in the development and treatment of rheumatic diseases, positioning us at the forefront of basic science and translational research, personalized medicine and the genetics of rheumatic diseases. **The Peter D. Seligman Center for Advanced Therapeutics**, renowned for breakthrough research in arthritis and Systematic Lupus Erythematosus, conducts clinical studies using a wide variety of newly developed therapies.

Top Doctors Make A Difference

Sports Medicine

a subspecialty of Internal Medicine, Family Practice, Pediatrics, Physical Medicine & Rehabilitation, or Orthopaedics

A specialist trained to be responsible for continuous care in the field of sports medicine, not only for the enhancement of health and fitness, but also for the prevention of injury and illness. A sports medicine physician must have knowledge and experience in the promotion of wellness and the prevention of injury. Knowledge about special areas of medicine such as exercise physiology, biomechanics, nutrition, psychology, physical rehabilitation, epidemiology, physical evaluation, injuries (treatment and prevention and referral practice) and the role of exercise in promoting a healthy life style are essential to the practice of sports medicine. The sports medicine physician requires special education to provide the knowledge to improve the healthcare of the individual engaged in physical exercise (sports) whether as an individual or in team participation.

Training Required: Three years in internal medicine, family practice, or pediatrics or seven years in orthopaedics *plus* additional training and examination for certification in sports medicine.

For more information about the main specialties of these physicians, see **Internal Medicine, Family Practice, Pediatrics, Physical Medicine & Rehabilitation, Orthopaedics** section(s).

Sports Medicine

New England

Gill IV, Thomas J MD [SM] - **Spec Exp:** Knee Injuries; Shoulder Injuries; Arthroscopic Surgery; **Hospital:** Mass Genl Hosp; **Address:** MGH Sports Medicine Ctr, 175 Cambridge St Fl 4, Boston, MA 02114; **Phone:** 617-726-7797; **Board Cert:** Orthopaedic Surgery 2011; **Med School:** Harvard Med Sch 1990; **Resid:** Orthopaedic Surgery, Hosp Special Surgery 1992; Orthopaedic Surgery, Brigham & Women's Hosp 1996; **Fellow:** Sports Medicine, Steadman Hawkins Clinic 1998; **Fac Appt:** Assoc Prof OrS, Harvard Med Sch

Micheli, Lyle J MD [SM] - **Spec Exp:** Pediatric Sports Medicine; Dance/Ballet Injuries; Knee Injuries/ACL; Ankle Surgery; **Hospital:** Children's Hospital - Boston, Beth Israel Deaconess Med Ctr - Boston; **Address:** Boston Chldn's Hosp, Div Sports Medicine, 319 Longwood Ave, Boston, MA 02115; **Phone:** 617-355-3501; **Board Cert:** Orthopaedic Surgery 1973; Orthopaedic Sports Medicine 2011; **Med School:** Harvard Med Sch 1966; **Resid:** Surgery, Univ Hosps 1968; Orthopaedic Surgery, Mass Genl Hosp/Chldns Hosp 1972; **Fellow:** Pediatric Orthopaedic Surgery, Orth Rsch Soc-Traveling 1973; **Fac Appt:** Clin Prof OrS, Harvard Med Sch

Richmond, John C MD [SM] - **Spec Exp:** Shoulder Injuries; Rotator Cuff Surgery; Knee Surgery; Arthroscopic Surgery; **Hospital:** New England Bapt Hosp (page 63); **Address:** Boston Sports & Shoulder Ctr, 830 Boylston St, Ste 107, Chestnut Hill, MA 02467; **Phone:** 617-264-1100; **Board Cert:** Orthopaedic Surgery 1984; Orthopaedic Sports Medicine 2011; **Med School:** Tufts Univ 1976; **Resid:** Surgery, Hosp Univ Penn 1978; Orthopaedic Surgery, New England Med Ctr 1981; **Fac Appt:** Prof OrS, Tufts Univ

Scheller, Arnold D MD [SM] - **Spec Exp:** Sports Injuries; Ankle Surgery; Shoulder Surgery; Knee Surgery; **Hospital:** New England Bapt Hosp (page 63); **Address:** Pro Sports Orthopaedics, 840 Winter St, Waltham, MA 02451; **Phone:** 781-487-9444; **Board Cert:** Orthopaedic Surgery 1980; **Med School:** Rush Med Coll 1973; **Resid:** Orthopaedic Surgery, Tufts Med Ctr 1979; **Fac Appt:** Asst Clin Prof OrS, Tufts Univ

Steiner, Mark E MD [SM] - **Spec Exp:** Shoulder Injuries; Knee Injuries; Arthroscopic Surgery; **Hospital:** New England Bapt Hosp (page 63); **Address:** Sports Medicine Associates, 830 Boylston St, Ste 205, Chestnut Hill, MA 02467; **Phone:** 617-739-2003; **Board Cert:** Orthopaedic Surgery 2008; Orthopaedic Sports Medicine 2011; **Med School:** Columbia P&S 1978; **Resid:** Surgery, Mass General Hosp 1980; Orthopaedic Surgery, Mass General Hosp 1984; **Fellow:** Sports Medicine, Univ Oklahoma Med Ctr 1985

Mid Atlantic

Altchek, David MD [SM] - **Spec Exp:** Shoulder Surgery; Elbow Surgery; Knee Surgery; Arthroscopic Surgery; **Hospital:** Hosp For Special Surgery (page 58); **Address:** HSS, Sports Med Dept, 535 E 70th St, New York, NY 10021; **Phone:** 212-606-1909; **Board Cert:** Orthopaedic Surgery 2011; **Med School:** Cornell Univ-Weill Med Coll 1982; **Resid:** Orthopaedic Surgery, Hosp Special Surgery 1987; **Fellow:** Sports Medicine, Hosp Special Surgery 1988; **Fac Appt:** Prof OrS, Cornell Univ-Weill Med Coll

Bradley, James P MD [SM] - **Spec Exp:** Reconstructive Surgery; Shoulder Surgery; Knee Surgery; **Hospital:** UPMC St Margaret, UPMC Shadyside; **Address:** 200 Delafield Rd, Suite 4010, Pittsburgh, PA 15215; **Phone:** 412-784-5770; **Board Cert:** Orthopaedic Surgery 2011; **Med School:** Georgetown Univ 1982; **Resid:** Surgery, Univ Tennessee Affil Hosp 1984; Orthopaedic Surgery, Univ Hlth Ctr 1987; **Fellow:** Sports Medicine, Kerlan-Jobe Ortho Clinic 1988; **Fac Appt:** Clin Prof OrS, Univ Pittsburgh

Burke, Charles J MD [SM] - **Spec Exp:** Knee Injuries; Shoulder Injuries; **Hospital:** UPMC St Margaret, UPMC Shadyside; **Address:** 200 Delafield Rd, Ste 4010, Pittsburgh, PA 15215; **Phone:** 412-784-5770; **Board Cert:** Orthopaedic Surgery 2009; Orthopaedic Sports Medicine 2011; **Med School:** Univ Cincinnati 1981; **Resid:** Orthopaedic Surgery, UPMC 1988; **Fellow:** Trauma, AO International Inst; **Fac Appt:** Asst Clin Prof OrS, Univ Pittsburgh

Ciccotti, Michael G MD [SM] - **Spec Exp:** Knee Reconstruction; Elbow Reconstruction; Shoulder Reconstruction; Arthroscopic Surgery; **Hospital:** Thomas Jefferson Univ Hosp, Bryn Mawr Hosp; **Address:** Rothman Institute, 925 Chestnut St Fl 5, Philadelphia, PA 19107; **Phone:** 800-321-9999; **Board Cert:** Orthopaedic Surgery 2005; **Med School:** Georgetown Univ 1986; **Resid:** Orthopaedic Surgery, Thos Jefferson Univ Med Ctr 1991; **Fellow:** Sports Medicine, Kerlan-Jobe Clinic/USC 1992; **Fac Appt:** Asst Clin Prof OrS, Jefferson Med Coll

Fu, Freddie H MD [SM] - **Spec Exp:** Sports Medicine; Knee Injuries/ACL; Shoulder Injuries; **Hospital:** UPMC Presby, Pittsburgh, UPMC South Side-Out Pt Ctr; **Address:** UPMC, Sports Med Dept, 3200 S Water St, Pittsburgh, PA 15213; **Phone:** 412-432-3611; **Board Cert:** Orthopaedic Surgery 1994; Orthopaedic Sports Medicine 2008; **Med School:** Univ Pittsburgh 1977; **Resid:** Orthopaedic Surgery, UPMC 1982; **Fellow:** Orthopaedic Sports Medicine, UPMC 1979; **Fac Appt:** Prof OrS, Univ Pittsburgh

Harner, Christopher D MD [SM] - **Spec Exp:** Knee Injuries; **Hospital:** UPMC South Side-Out Pt Ctr; **Address:** UPMC Ctr for Sports Med, 3200 S Water St, Pittsburgh, PA 15203; **Phone:** 412-432-3661; **Board Cert:** Orthopaedic Surgery 2010; Orthopaedic Sports Medicine 2007; **Med School:** Univ Mich Med Sch 1981; **Resid:** Orthopaedic Surgery, UPMC-Presby 1986; **Fellow:** Sports Medicine/Knee Surgery, Salt Lake City Knee & Sport 1987; **Fac Appt:** Prof OrS, Univ Pittsburgh

Hershman, Elliott B MD [SM] - **Spec Exp:** Knee Injuries; Knee Surgery; Arthroscopic Surgery; Ligament Reconstruction; **Hospital:** Lenox Hill Hosp (page 66); **Address:** 130 E 77th St, Fl 7, New York, NY 10075; **Phone:** 212-744-8114; **Board Cert:** Orthopaedic Surgery 2008; **Med School:** Univ Rochester 1979; **Resid:** Orthopaedic Surgery, Lenox Hill Hosp 1984; **Fellow:** Sports Medicine, Cleveland Clinic 1985; **Fac Appt:** Asst Clin Prof OrS, Mount Sinai Sch Med

Levine, William N MD [SM] - **Spec Exp:** Arthroscopic Surgery; Shoulder & Elbow Surgery; Knee Injuries; **Hospital:** NY-Presby/Columbia Univ Med Ctr, NY (page 65); **Address:** 622 W 168th St, PH-11, rm 1117, New York, NY 10032; **Phone:** 212-305-0762; **Board Cert:** Orthopaedic Surgery 2010; Orthopaedic Sports Medicine 2008; **Med School:** Case West Res Univ 1990; **Resid:** Surgery, Beth Israel Hosp 1991; Orthopaedic Surgery, New Eng Med Ctr Hosps 1995; **Fellow:** Shoulder Surgery, Columbia-Presby Med Ctr 1996; Sports Medicine, Univ MD Med Ctr 1998; **Fac Appt:** Clin Prof OrS, Columbia P&S

Metzl, Jordan D MD [SM] - **Spec Exp:** Adolescent Sports Medicine; Running Injuries; Dance/Ballet Injuries; **Hospital:** Hosp For Special Surgery (page 58); **Address:** 519 E 72nd St, Ste 206, New York, NY 10021; **Phone:** 212-606-1678; **Board Cert:** Sports Medicine 2012; **Med School:** Univ MO-Columbia Sch Med 1993; **Resid:** Pediatrics, Tufts-New Engl Med Ctr 1996; **Fellow:** Sports Medicine, Vanderbilt Univ Med Ctr 1997; Sports Medicine, Harvard Med Sch 1998; **Fac Appt:** Assoc Prof Ped, Cornell Univ-Weill Med Coll

Nisonson, Barton MD [SM] - **Spec Exp:** Shoulder & Knee Surgery; Arthroscopic Surgery; Knee Replacement; **Hospital:** Lenox Hill Hosp (page 66); **Address:** Lenox Hill Hosp, Orthopaedics, 130 E 77th St Fl 8, New York, NY 10021; **Phone:** 212-570-9120; **Board Cert:** Orthopaedic Surgery 1974; **Med School:** Columbia P&S 1966; **Resid:** Surgery, NY-Presby/Columbia Univ Med Ctr 1968; Orthopaedic Surgery, NY-Presby/Columbia Univ Med Ctr 1973

Rodeo, Scott A MD [SM] - **Spec Exp:** Knee Injuries; Cartilage Damage; Shoulder Surgery; **Hospital:** Hosp For Special Surgery (page 58); **Address:** HSS, Sports Med Dept, 535 E 70th St, New York, NY 10021; **Phone:** 212-606-1513; **Board Cert:** Orthopaedic Surgery 2009; Orthopaedic Sports Medicine 2007; **Med School:** Cornell Univ-Weill Med Coll 1989; **Resid:** Orthopaedic Surgery, Hosp Special Surgery 1994; **Fellow:** Sports Medicine, Hosp Special Surgery 1996; **Fac Appt:** Prof OrS, Cornell Univ-Weill Med Coll

Rodosky, Mark W MD [SM] - **Spec Exp:** Sports Medicine; Shoulder Arthroscopic Surgery; Rotator Cuff Surgery; **Hospital:** UPMC South Side-Out Pt Ctr; **Address:** UPMC, Sports Med Dept, 3200 S Water St, Pittsburgh, PA 15203; **Phone:** 412-432-3621; **Board Cert:** Orthopaedic Surgery 2008; Orthopaedic Sports Medicine 2011; **Med School:** Mount Sinai Sch Med 1987; **Resid:** Surgery, UPMC 1993; **Fellow:** Orthopaedic Surgery, NY-Presby/Columbia Univ Med Ctr 1994; **Fac Appt:** Asst Prof OrS, Univ Pittsburgh

Sennett, Brian J MD [SM] - **Spec Exp:** Arthroscopic Surgery; Cartilage Damage; Sports Injuries; Upper Extremity Trauma; **Hospital:** Hosp Univ Penn - UPHS (page 69); **Address:** Penn Sports Medicine Center, Weightman Hall, Fl 1, 235 S 33rd St, Philadelphia, PA 19104; **Phone:** 215-662-3340; **Board Cert:** Orthopaedic Surgery 2009; Orthopaedic Sports Medicine 2008; **Med School:** Univ Pennsylvania 1988; **Resid:** Orthopaedic Surgery, Hosp Univ Penn 1993; **Fellow:** Sports Medicine, Univ Penn Sports Med Ctr 1994; Hand Surgery, Hosp Univ Penn 1994; **Fac Appt:** Assoc Prof OrS, Univ Pennsylvania

Williams III, Riley J MD [SM] - **Spec Exp:** Cartilage Damage & Transplant; Shoulder Arthroscopic Surgery; Knee Injuries/ACL; Knee Surgery; **Hospital:** Hosp For Special Surgery (page 58), NY-Presby/Weill Cornell Med Ctr, NY (page 65); **Address:** HSS, Rheumatology Dept, 535 E 70th St, New York, NY 10021; **Phone:** 212-606-1855; **Board Cert:** Orthopaedic Sports Medicine 2012; Orthopaedic Surgery 2012; **Med School:** Stanford Univ 1992; **Resid:** Orthopaedic Surgery, Hosp Special Surgery 1997; **Fellow:** Sports Medicine & Shoulder Surgery, Hosp Special Surgery 1998; **Fac Appt:** Assoc Prof OrS, Cornell Univ-Weill Med Coll

Southeast

Andrews, James R MD [SM] - **Spec Exp:** Shoulder Surgery; Elbow Surgery; Knee Surgery; **Hospital:** Baptist Hosp - Pensacola, St. Vincent's Hosp - Birmingham; **Address:** Andrews Inst Orthopaedics & Sports Med, 1040 Gulf Breeze Pkwy, Ste 203, Gulf Breeze, FL 32561; **Phone:** 850-916-8700; **Board Cert:** Orthopaedic Surgery 1974; **Med School:** Louisiana State U, New Orleans 1967; **Resid:** Orthopaedic Surgery, USPHS Hosp 1969; Orthopaedic Surgery, Touro Infrim-Tulane 1970; **Fellow:** Orthopaedic Sports Medicine, Univ Virgina Med Ctr 1972; **Fac Appt:** Clin Prof OrS, UAB Sch Med

Byrd, J.W. Thomas MD [SM] - **Spec Exp:** Arthroscopic Surgery; Hip Surgery; **Hospital:** Saint Thomas Hosp-Midtown; **Address:** Nashville Sports Med & Ortho Ctr, 2011 Church St, Ste 100, Nashville, TN 37203; **Phone:** 615-284-5800; **Board Cert:** Orthopaedic Surgery 2011; Orthopaedic Sports Medicine 2007; **Med School:** Vanderbilt Univ 1982; **Resid:** Orthopaedic Surgery, Univ Louisville Hosp 1987; **Fellow:** Sports Medicine, Amer Sprts Inst 1988; Joint Replacement Surgery, New England Baptist Hosp 1989

Garth Jr, William P MD [SM] - **Spec Exp:** Knee Ligament Reconstruction; Shoulder Reconstruction; **Hospital:** UAB Hosp, Children's Hosp AL; **Address:** UAB Sports Med, 1600 7th Ave S, Ste 402, Birmingham, AL 35233-1711; **Phone:** 205-934-1041; **Board Cert:** Orthopaedic Surgery 1980; Orthopaedic Sports Medicine 2007; **Med School:** Tulane Univ 1973; **Resid:** Surgery, Duke Univ Hosp 1975; Orthopaedic Surgery, Campbell Clin 1979; **Fellow:** Sports Medicine, Sports Med Clin 1981; **Fac Appt:** Prof OrS, UAB Sch Med

Kaplan, Lee David MD [SM] - **Spec Exp:** Sports Injuries; Cartilage Damage; Shoulder Surgery; Ligament Reconstruction; **Hospital:** Univ of Miami Hosp, UHealth - Univ of Miami Hlth Sys; **Address:** Univ Miami Hosp, Sports Med-Orthopaedics, 1400 NW 12 Ave South Bldg - Ste 2, Miami, FL 33136; **Phone:** 305-243-3887; **Board Cert:** Orthopaedic Surgery 2004; Sports Medicine 2008; **Med School:** Geo Wash Univ 1995; **Resid:** Orthopaedic Surgery, Univ Miami Hosp 2000; **Fellow:** Sports Medicine, UPMC 2001; **Fac Appt:** Assoc Prof OrS, Univ Miami Sch Med

Taft, Timothy N MD [SM] - **Spec Exp:** Sports Medicine; Knee Injuries/ACL; Shoulder Surgery; **Hospital:** NC Memorial Hosp - UNC; **Address:** 3154 Bioinformatics Bldg, 130 Mason Farm Rd, UNC, Chapel Hill, NC 27599; **Phone:** 919-962-6637; **Board Cert:** Orthopaedic Surgery 1976; **Med School:** Univ MO-Columbia Sch Med 1969; **Resid:** Orthopaedic Surgery, UNC Hosps 1974; Orthopaedic Surgery, N Carolina Ortho Hosp 1972; **Fac Appt:** Prof OrS, Univ NC Sch Med

Xerogeanes, John W MD [SM] - **Spec Exp:** Knee Surgery; Shoulder Surgery; Knee Injuries/ACL; Arthroscopic Surgery; **Hospital:** Emory Univ Hosp; **Address:** Emory Sports Medicine Ctr, 59 Executive Park S, Ste 1000, Atlanta, GA 30329; **Phone:** 404-778-3350; **Board Cert:** Orthopaedic Surgery 2012; Orthopaedic Sports Medicine 2008; **Med School:** Emory Univ 1992; **Resid:** Orthopaedic Surgery, Univ Pittsburgh Med Ctr 1997; **Fellow:** Sports Medicine, Steadman-Hawkins Clinic 1998; **Fac Appt:** Assoc Prof OrS, Emory Univ

Midwest

Arendt, Elizabeth A MD [SM] - **Spec Exp:** Sports Medicine; Knee Ligament Reconstruction; Knee Injuries; **Hospital:** Univ Minn Med Ctr, Fairview - West Bank Campus; **Address:** 2512 7th St S, rm 102, Minneapolis, MN 55454; **Phone:** 612-273-9400; **Board Cert:** Orthopaedic Surgery 2008; Orthopaedic Sports Medicine 2007; **Med School:** Univ Rochester 1979; **Resid:** Surgery, Univ Rochester Med Ctr 1981; Orthopaedic Surgery, Univ Rochester Med Ctr 1984; **Fellow:** Sports Medicine, Univ Minn Med Ctr 1985; **Fac Appt:** Prof OrS, Univ Miss

Bach Jr, Bernard R MD [SM] - **Spec Exp:** Sports Medicine; Knee Surgery; Knee Injuries/ACL; Shoulder Surgery; **Hospital:** Rush Univ Med Ctr; **Address:** Midwest Orthopaedics at Rush, 1611 W Harrison St, Ste 400, Chicago, IL 60612; **Phone:** 312-243-4244; **Board Cert:** Orthopaedic Surgery 2010; Orthopaedic Sports Medicine 2010; **Med School:** Univ Cincinnati 1979; **Resid:** Surgery, New Eng Deaconess Hosp 1981; Orthopaedic Surgery, Mass Genl Hosp 1984; **Fellow:** Sports Medicine, Hosp Special Surgery 1986; **Fac Appt:** Prof OrS, Rush Med Coll

Bush-Joseph, Charles MD [SM] - **Spec Exp:** Knee Reconstruction; Cartilage Damage; Rotator Cuff Surgery; Arthroscopic Surgery; **Hospital:** Rush Univ Med Ctr, Rush Oak Park Hosp; **Address:** Midwest Orthopaedics at Rush, 1611 W Harrison St, Ste 400, Chicago, IL 60612; **Phone:** 312-243-4244; **Board Cert:** Orthopaedic Surgery 2013; Orthopaedic Sports Medicine 2007; **Med School:** Univ Mich Med Sch 1983; **Resid:** Orthopaedic Surgery, Rush Med Ctr 1988; **Fellow:** Sports Medicine, Cincinnati Sports Med Ctr 1989; **Fac Appt:** Prof OrS, Rush Med Coll

Ho, Sherwin S W MD [SM] - **Spec Exp:** Shoulder & Knee Surgery; Arthroscopic Surgery; Cartilage Damage; **Hospital:** Univ of Chicago Med; **Address:** Univ Chicago Dept Surgery, 5841 S Maryland Ave, MC 3079, Chicago, IL 60637-3079; **Phone:** 773-702-5978; **Board Cert:** Orthopaedic Surgery 2005; Orthopaedic Sports Medicine 2008; **Med School:** Univ Hawaii JA Burns Sch Med 1985; **Resid:** Orthopaedic Surgery, Univ Hawaii Med Ctr 1991; **Fellow:** Sports Medicine, Univ Chicago 1992; **Fac Appt:** Assoc Prof S, Univ Chicago-Pritzker Sch Med

Miniaci, Anthony MD [SM] - **Spec Exp:** Shoulder Reconstruction; Shoulder Arthroscopic Surgery; Knee Reconstruction; Cartilage Damage; **Hospital:** Cleveland Clin (page 55); **Address:** Cleveland Clinic, Sports Hlth Ctr, 5555 Transportation Blvd, Garfield Heights, OH 44125; **Phone:** 216-518-3444; **Med School:** Univ Western Ontario 1982; **Resid:** Orthopaedic Surgery, Univ Western Ontario 1987; **Fellow:** Sports Medicine, Kerlan-Jobe Orthopaedic Clin 1989; Orthopaedic Research, Univ Calgary 1990; **Fac Appt:** Prof S, Case West Res Univ

Paletta Jr, George A MD [SM] - **Spec Exp:** Ankle Surgery; Knee Surgery; Shoulder & Elbow Surgery; **Address:** The Orthopedic Ctr of St Louis, 14825 N Outer Forty Rd, Ste 200, Chesterfield, MO 63017; **Phone:** 314-336-2555; **Board Cert:** Orthopaedic Surgery 2009; **Med School:** Johns Hopkins Univ 1988; **Resid:** Orthopaedic Surgery, Cornell Univ Med Ctr 1994; **Fellow:** Sports Medicine, Cleveland Clin Fnd 1995; Pediatric Sports Medicine, Chldns Hosp Michigan; **Fac Appt:** Assoc Prof OrS, Washington Univ, St Louis

Great Plains and Mountains

Saint-Phard, Deborah MD [SM] - **Spec Exp:** Sports Medicine-Women; Spinal Rehabilitation; **Hospital:** Univ Colorado Hosp; **Address:** CU Sports Med, 2000 S Colorado Blvd, Tower 1, Ste 4500, Denver, CO 80222; **Phone:** 720-848-8200; **Board Cert:** Physical Medicine & Rehabilitation 2007; Pain Medicine 2004; Sports Medicine 2008; **Med School:** Temple Univ 1992; **Resid:** Physical Medicine & Rehabilitation, Univ CO Hosp 1996; **Fellow:** Sports Medicine, Mayo Clin 1997; **Fac Appt:** Assoc Prof PMR, Univ Colorado

Southwest

Jones, Deryk G MD [SM] - **Spec Exp:** Arthroscopic Surgery; Cartilage Damage & Transplant; **Hospital:** Ochsner Med Ctr-Kenner; **Address:** Ochsner Sports Med, 1201 S Clearview Pkwy, Ste 104, Jefferson, LA 70121; **Phone:** 504-736-4800; **Board Cert:** Orthopaedic Surgery 2011; Orthopaedic Sports Medicine 2009; **Med School:** Stanford Univ 1991; **Resid:** Orthopaedic Surgery, Harvard Combined Orthopaedic Prgm 1997; **Fellow:** Sports Medicine, UPMC 1998; **Fac Appt:** Asst Clin Prof OrS, Tulane Univ

Veitch, Andrew J MD [SM] - **Spec Exp:** Sports Medicine; Knee Injuries/ACL/Meniscus Tears; Shoulder Injuries; Fractures; **Hospital:** Univ Hosp - New Mexico; **Address:** UNM Orthopaedics, 2211 Lomas Blvd NE, Ste 1, Albuquerque, NM 87106; **Phone:** 505-272-2231; **Board Cert:** Orthopaedic Surgery 2006; Orthopaedic Sports Medicine 2010; **Med School:** Univ New Mexico 1996; **Resid:** Orthopaedic Surgery, Univ NM Med Ctr 2001; **Fellow:** Orthopaedic Sports Medicine, UCLA Med Ctr 2003; **Fac Appt:** Asst Prof OrS, Univ New Mexico

West Coast and Pacific

Fronek, Jan MD [SM] - **Spec Exp:** Knee Injuries; Shoulder Injuries; Arthroscopic Surgery; Rotator Cuff Surgery; **Hospital:** Scripps Green Hosp; **Address:** Scripps Clinic, 10666 N Torrey Pines Rd, MS B-4, La Jolla, CA 92037; **Phone:** 858-554-9753; **Board Cert:** Orthopaedic Surgery 2009; Orthopaedic Sports Medicine 2011; **Med School:** Univ Rochester 1978; **Resid:** Orthopaedic Surgery, UCSD Med Ctr 1984; **Fellow:** Sports Medicine, Hosp Special Surgery 1985

Gambardella, Ralph A MD [SM] - **Spec Exp:** Cartilage Damage; Shoulder & Elbow Surgery; Knee Surgery; **Hospital:** Marina Del Rey Hosp, White Memorial Med Ctr; **Address:** Kerlan-Jobe Clinic, 6801 Park Terr, Ste 400, Los Angeles, CA 90045; **Phone:** 310-665-7200; **Board Cert:** Orthopaedic Surgery 1985; **Med School:** USC-Keck School of Medicine 1977; **Resid:** Orthopaedic Surgery, USC Med Ctr 1982; **Fellow:** Sports Medicine, Southwestern Ortho Grp 1983; **Fac Appt:** Assoc Clin Prof S, USC Sch Med

Ma, C Benjamin MD [SM] - **Spec Exp:** Shoulder Surgery; Knee Surgery; Arthroscopic Surgery; Elbow Surgery; **Hospital:** UCSF Med Ctr; **Address:** Mission Bay Orthopaedic Inst, 1500 Owens St, San Francisco, CA 94158; **Phone:** 415-353-2808; **Board Cert:** Orthopaedic Surgery 2005; Orthopaedic Sports Medicine 2008; **Med School:** Johns Hopkins Univ 1996; **Resid:** Orthopaedic Surgery, Univ Pittsburgh Med Ctr 2002; **Fellow:** Shoulder Surgery, Hosp for Special Surg 2003; Orthopaedic Sports Medicine, Hosp for Special Surg 2004

Mirzayan, Raffy MD [SM] - **Spec Exp:** Arthroscopic Surgery; Shoulder & Elbow Surgery; Ligament Reconstruction; Knee Injuries; **Hospital:** Kaiser Permanente Baldwin Pk Med Ctr; **Address:** Kaiser Permanente Med Ctr, Orthopaedics, 1011 Baldwin Park Blvd, Baldwin Park, CA 91706; **Phone:** 626-851-5256; **Board Cert:** Orthopaedic Surgery 2003; Sports Medicine 2007; **Med School:** USC Sch Med 1995; **Resid:** Orthopaedic Surgery, LAC & USC Med Ctr 2000; **Fellow:** Sports Medicine, Kerlan Jobe Ortho Clin 2001

Schechter, David L MD [SM] - **Spec Exp:** Pain-Back; Sports Injuries; Muscle Pain-Stress Related; **Hospital:** Cedars-Sinai Med Ctr; **Address:** 8500 Wilshire Blvd, Ste 705, Beverly Hills, CA 90211; **Phone:** 310-657-1022; **Board Cert:** Family Medicine 2008; Sports Medicine 2003; **Med School:** NYU Sch Med 1984; **Resid:** Family Medicine, UCLA/Santa Monica Hosp 1987; **Fac Appt:** Assoc Clin Prof FMed, USC Sch Med

Teitz, Carol C MD [SM] - **Spec Exp:** Sports Injuries; Musculoskeletal Injuries in Dancers; Foot & Ankle Surgery; Knee Surgery; **Hospital:** Univ Wash Med Ctr; **Address:** University of Washington, Box 354060, Seattle, WA 98195; **Phone:** 206-543-1552; **Board Cert:** Orthopaedic Surgery 1981; Orthopaedic Sports Medicine 2007; **Med School:** Yale Univ 1974; **Resid:** Orthopaedic Surgery, Univ Wash Affil Hosps 1980; **Fellow:** Arthroscopic Surgery, J McGinty MD, Newton-Wellesley Hosp 1983; **Fac Appt:** Prof OrS, Univ Wash

Top Doctors Make A Difference

Surgery

A surgeon manages a broad spectrum of surgical conditions affecting almost any area of the body. The surgeon establishes the diagnosis and provides the preoperative, operative and postoperative care to surgical patients and is usually responsible for the comprehensive management of the trauma victim and the critically ill surgical patient.

The surgeon uses a variety of diagnostic techniques, including endoscopy, for observing internal structures and may use specialized instruments during operative procedures. A general surgeon is expected to be familiar with the salient features of other surgical specialties in order to recognize problems in those areas and to know when to refer a patient to another specialist.

Training Required: Five years

For a description of the subspecialty **Hand Surgery**, **Pediatric Surgery** and **Vascular Surgery** see the corresponding section(s).

Surgery

New England

Ashley, Stanley W MD [S] - **Spec Exp:** Gastrointestinal Cancer & Surgery; **Hospital:** Brigham & Women's Hosp, Dana-Farber Cancer Inst; **Address:** Brigham & Womens Hosp, Dept Surgery, 75 Francis St, ASBII Bldg - Fl 3, Boston, MA 02115; **Phone:** 617-732-6730; **Board Cert:** Surgery 2004; **Med School:** Cornell Univ-Weill Med Coll 1981; **Resid:** Surgery, Barnes Jewish Med Ctr 1989; **Fac Appt:** Prof S, Harvard Med Sch

Becker, James M MD [S] - **Spec Exp:** Inflammatory Bowel Disease; Gastrointestinal Cancer; Gastrointestinal Surgery; **Hospital:** Newton - Wellesley Hosp, Mass Genl Hosp; **Address:** Newton Wellesley Hospital, 2014 Washington St Green Bldg - Ste 563, Newton, MA 02462; **Phone:** 617-219-1285; **Board Cert:** Surgery 2010; **Med School:** Case West Res Univ 1975; **Resid:** Surgery, Univ Utah Med Ctr 1980; **Fellow:** Research, Mayo Clinic 1982; **Fac Appt:** Prof S, Boston Univ

Brooks, David C MD [S] - **Spec Exp:** Gastrointestinal Surgery; **Hospital:** Brigham & Women's Hosp; **Address:** Brigham & Women's Hosp, Dept Surgery, 75 Francis St, ASB II Fl 3, Boston, MA 02115; **Phone:** 617-732-6337; **Board Cert:** Surgery 2003; **Med School:** Brown Univ 1976; **Resid:** Surgery, Brigham & Women's Hosp 1983; **Fac Appt:** Assoc Prof S, Harvard Med Sch

Burke, Peter A MD [S] - **Spec Exp:** Trauma; Critical Care; **Hospital:** Boston Med Ctr; **Address:** Boston Med Ctr, 725 Albany St Fl 3, Shapiro Bldg, Boston, MA 02118; **Phone:** 617-414-8056; **Board Cert:** Surgery 2011; Surgical Critical Care 2001; **Med School:** Tufts Univ 1983; **Resid:** Surgery, New England Deaconess Med Ctr 1990; **Fac Appt:** Prof S, Boston Univ

Callery, Mark P MD [S] - **Spec Exp:** Pancreatic Cancer; Liver Cancer; Laparoscopic Surgery; **Hospital:** Beth Israel Deaconess Med Ctr - Boston; **Address:** Beth Israel Deaconess Med Ctr, 330 Brookline Ave Shapiro Bldg Fl 3, Boston, MA 02215; **Phone:** 617-667-3798; **Board Cert:** Surgery 2004; **Med School:** Albany Med Coll 1985; **Resid:** Surgery, Albany Med Coll Hosp 1987; Surgery, Barnes Jewish Med Ctr 1992; **Fellow:** Research, Wash Univ Sch Med 1990; **Fac Appt:** Assoc Prof S, Harvard Med Sch

Cioffi, William G MD [S] - **Spec Exp:** Liver & Biliary Cancer; Trauma; Critical Care; Esophageal Cancer; **Hospital:** Rhode Island Hosp, Miriam Hosp; **Address:** Rhode Island Hosp, Dept Surg, 2 Dudley St, Ste 470, Providence, RI 02905; **Phone:** 401-553-8348; **Board Cert:** Surgery 2007; Surgical Critical Care 2008; **Med School:** Univ VT Coll Med 1981; **Resid:** Surgery, Medical Ctr Hosp 1986; **Fac Appt:** Prof S, Brown Univ

Cusack Jr, James C MD [S] - **Spec Exp:** Gastrointestinal Cancer; Colon & Rectal Cancer; Melanoma; Merkel Cell Carcinoma; **Hospital:** Mass Genl Hosp; **Address:** MGH, Surgical Oncology Associates, 55 Fruit St, Yawkey Bldg - Fl 7, Boston, MA 02114; **Phone:** 617-724-4093; **Board Cert:** Surgery 2011; **Med School:** Emory Univ 1986; **Resid:** Surgery, Tufts-New England Med Ctr 1991; **Fellow:** Surgery, Brigham & Women's Hosp 1992; Surgical Oncology, MD Anderson Cancer Ctr 1992; **Fac Appt:** Assoc Prof S, Harvard Med Sch

Cushing, Brad M MD [S] - **Spec Exp:** Trauma; Critical Care; **Hospital:** Maine Med Ctr; **Address:** Maine Med Partners Surgical Assocs, 22 Bram Hall, Portland, ME 04102-3113; **Phone:** 207-774-2381; **Board Cert:** Surgery 2005; Surgical Critical Care 2003; **Med School:** Univ Rochester 1980; **Resid:** Surgery, St. Francis Hosp & Med Ctr 1985; **Fellow:** Trauma/Critical Care, Univ MD Sch Med Affil Hosp 1987; **Fac Appt:** Clin Prof S, Univ VT Coll Med

Doherty, Gerard M MD [S] - **Spec Exp:** Endocrine Surgery; Adrenal Surgery; Laparoscopic Surgery; Thyroid Surgery; **Hospital:** Boston Med Ctr; **Address:** Boston Med Ctr, 830 Harrison Ave Moakley Bldg Fl 3, Boston, MA 02118; **Phone:** 617-414-3558; **Board Cert:** Surgery 2003; **Med School:** Yale Univ 1986; **Resid:** Surgery, UCSF Med Ctr 1993; **Fellow:** Surgical Oncology, Natl Cancer Inst 1991; **Fac Appt:** Prof S, Boston Univ

Eisenberg, Burton L MD [S] - **Spec Exp:** Breast Cancer; Melanoma; Sarcoma; **Hospital:** Dartmouth - Hitchcock Med Ctr; **Address:** DHMC, Dept General Surgery, One Medical Center Drive, Lebanon, NH 03756; **Phone:** 603-650-9479; **Board Cert:** Surgery 2010; **Med School:** Univ Tenn Coll Med 1974; **Resid:** Surgery, Wilford Hall USAF Med Ctr 1979; **Fellow:** Surgical Oncology, Meml Sloan-Kettering Cancer Ctr 1981; **Fac Appt:** Prof S, Dartmouth Med Sch

Emre, Sukru MD [S] - **Spec Exp:** Transplant-Liver-Adult & Pediatric; Hepatobiliary Surgery; Liver Cancer; Portal Hypertension; **Hospital:** Yale-New Haven Hosp; **Address:** 330 Cedar St, FMB121 Bldg - Fl 1, FMB 121, New Haven, CT 07520-8062; **Phone:** 203-737-2804; **Med School:** Turkey 1977; **Resid:** Surgery, Univ Istanbul 1982; **Fellow:** Hepatobiliary Surgery, Univ Istanbul 1988; Transplant Surgery, Mount Sinai Med Ctr 1994; **Fac Appt:** Prof S, Yale Univ

Espat, N. Joseph MD [S] - **Spec Exp:** Liver Cancer; Gallbladder & Biliary Cancer; Hepatobiliary Cancer; **Hospital:** Roger Williams Med Ctr; **Address:** Roger Williams Med Ctr, Dept Surgery, 825 Chalkstone Ave, Providence, RI 02908; **Phone:** 401-456-2077; **Board Cert:** Surgery 2006; **Med School:** Univ Fla Coll Med 1990; **Resid:** Surgery, Shands Univ FL 1997; **Fellow:** Surgical Oncology, Meml Sloan-Kettering Canc Ctr 1999; **Fac Appt:** Prof S, Boston Univ

Gawande, Atul A MD [S] - **Spec Exp:** Endocrine Surgery; Thyroid Cancer; Adrenal Tumors; **Hospital:** Brigham & Women's Hosp, Dana-Farber Cancer Inst; **Address:** Brigham & Womens Hosp, 75 Francis St ASB2 Bldg Fl 3, Boston, MA 02115; **Phone:** 617-732-6830; **Board Cert:** Surgery 2004; **Med School:** Harvard Med Sch 1995; **Resid:** Surgery, Brigham & Womens Hosp 2003; **Fac Appt:** Assoc Prof S, Harvard Med Sch

Goodman, Martin D MD [S] - **Spec Exp:** Gastrointestinal Cancer; Peritoneal Carcinomatosis; **Hospital:** Tufts Med Ctr; **Address:** Tufts Med Ctr, Surgical Oncology, 800 Washington St, Box 9248, Boston, MA 02111; **Phone:** 617-636-9248; **Board Cert:** Surgery 2010; **Med School:** UMDNJ-RW Johnson Med Sch 1994; **Resid:** Surgery, Cooper Hosp 2000; **Fellow:** Surgical Oncology, Univ Pittsburgh Med Ctr 2002; **Fac Appt:** Asst Prof S, Tufts Univ

Graham, Roger A MD [S] - **Spec Exp:** Thyroid Cancer; Breast Cancer & Surgery; Gastrointestinal Cancer; Melanoma; **Hospital:** Tufts Med Ctr; **Address:** Tufts Med Ctr, Div Surgical Oncology, 800 Washington St, Box 1043, Boston, MA 02111; **Phone:** 617-636-8270; **Board Cert:** Surgery 2006; **Med School:** Johns Hopkins Univ 1982; **Resid:** Surgery, Tufts Med Ctr 1987; **Fellow:** Surgical Oncology, MD Anderson Cancer Ctr 1989; **Fac Appt:** Assoc Prof S, Tufts Univ

Gupta, Rajan MD [S] - **Spec Exp:** Trauma; Critical Care; **Hospital:** Dartmouth - Hitchcock Med Ctr; **Address:** Dartmouth Hitchcock Med Ctr, Dept Surgery, One Medical Center Drive, Lebanon, NH 03756; **Phone:** 603-650-8022; **Board Cert:** Surgery 2010; Surgical Critical Care 2012; **Med School:** Boston Univ 1991; **Resid:** Surgery, Dartmouth-Hitchcock Med Ctr 1997; **Fellow:** Trauma/Critical Care, Hosp Univ Penn 1999; **Fac Appt:** Asst Prof S, Dartmouth Med Sch

Hebert, James C MD [S] - **Spec Exp:** Gastrointestinal Surgery; Pancreatic & Biliary Surgery; Colon & Rectal Surgery; Hernia; **Hospital:** FAHC - Med Ctr Campus; **Address:** Fletcher Allen Hlth Care, 111 Colchester Ave, Burlington, VT 05401; **Phone:** 802-847-3344; **Board Cert:** Surgery 2012; **Med School:** Univ VT Coll Med 1977; **Resid:** Surgery, Med Ctr Hosp 1982; **Fac Appt:** Prof S, Univ VT Coll Med

Hodin, Richard A MD [S] - **Spec Exp:** Thyroid Cancer; Inflammatory Bowel Disease; Adrenal Tumors; Endocrine Surgery; **Hospital:** Mass Genl Hosp; **Address:** Mass General Hospital, 15 Parkman St Wang Bldg Fl 3 - Ste 460, Boston, MA 02114; **Phone:** 617-724-2570; **Board Cert:** Surgery 2010; **Med School:** Tulane Univ 1984; **Resid:** Surgery, Beth Israel Deaconess Med Ctr 1990; **Fellow:** Research, Brigham & Women's Hosp 1989; **Fac Appt:** Prof S, Harvard Med Sch

Hughes, Kevin S MD [S] - **Spec Exp:** Breast Cancer; Hereditary Cancer; Breast Disease; **Hospital:** Mass Genl Hosp, Newton - Wellesley Hosp; **Address:** Mass Genl Hosp, Dept Surgery, 55 Fruit St, YAW Bldg - Fl 9A, Boston, MA 02114; **Phone:** 617-724-4800; **Board Cert:** Surgery 2006; **Med School:** Dartmouth Med Sch 1979; **Resid:** Surgery, Mercy Hosp 1984; **Fellow:** Surgical Oncology, National Cancer Inst 1986; **Fac Appt:** Assoc Prof S, Harvard Med Sch

Iglehart, James Dirk MD [S] - **Spec Exp:** Breast Cancer; **Hospital:** Dana-Farber Cancer Inst, Brigham & Women's Hosp; **Address:** Dana-Farber Cancer Institute, 450 Brookline Ave, Boston, MA 02215; **Phone:** 617-632-5178 x1; **Board Cert:** Surgery 2005; **Med School:** Harvard Med Sch 1975; **Resid:** Surgery, Duke Univ Med Ctr 1981; **Fellow:** Research, Duke Univ Med Ctr 1984; **Fac Appt:** Prof S, Harvard Med Sch

Jenkins, Roger L MD [S] - **Spec Exp:** Transplant-Liver; Liver & Biliary Cancer; Pancreatic Cancer; **Hospital:** Lahey Hosp & Med Ctr, Children's Hospital - Boston; **Address:** Lahey Clinic, 41 Mall Rd, Ste 4 West, Burlington, MA 01805; **Phone:** 781-744-2500; **Board Cert:** Surgery 2005; **Med School:** Univ VT Coll Med 1977; **Resid:** Surgery, New Eng Deaconess Hosp 1982; **Fellow:** Cardiac Surgery, New Eng Deaconess Hosp 1983; Transplant Surgery, Univ Pittsburgh Hosp 1983; **Fac Appt:** Prof S, Tufts Univ

Jones, Daniel B MD [S] - **Spec Exp:** Minimally Invasive Surgery; Obesity/Bariatric Surgery; Laparoscopic Surgery; **Hospital:** Beth Israel Deaconess Med Ctr - Boston; **Address:** Beth Israel Deaconess Med Ctr, 330 Brookline Ave, TCC 350, Boston, MA 02215; **Phone:** 617-667-5101; **Board Cert:** Surgery 2008; **Med School:** Cornell Univ 1990; **Resid:** Surgery, Barnes Jewish Hosp 1997; **Fellow:** Minimally Invasive Surgery, Washington Univ 1995; **Fac Appt:** Prof S, Harvard Med Sch

Kavanah, Maureen MD [S] - **Spec Exp:** Breast Cancer; Gynecologic Cancer; Melanoma; **Hospital:** Boston Med Ctr; **Address:** BMC-Dept Surgical Onc & Endocrinology, 820 Harrison Ave, Ste 1200, Boston, MA 02118; **Phone:** 617-638-2778; **Board Cert:** Surgery 2009; **Med School:** Tufts Univ 1975; **Resid:** Surgery, Steward St Elizabeth's Med Ctr 1979; **Fellow:** Surgical Oncology, Boston Med Ctr 1981; **Fac Appt:** Assoc Prof S, Boston Univ

Krag, David N MD [S] - **Spec Exp:** Sentinel Node Surgery; Breast Cancer; Cancer Surgery; Melanoma; **Hospital:** FAHC - Med Ctr Campus; **Address:** Univ Vermont Coll Med, Dept Surgery, 89 Beaumont Ave, Given Bldg - E309C, Burlington, VT 05405; **Phone:** 802-656-5830; **Board Cert:** Surgery 2006; **Med School:** Loyola Univ-Stritch Sch Med 1980; **Resid:** Surgery, UC Davis Med Ctr 1986; **Fellow:** Surgical Oncology, UCLA Ronald Reagan Med Ctr 1987; **Fac Appt:** Assoc Prof S, Univ VT Coll Med

Lannin, Donald R MD [S] - **Spec Exp:** Breast Cancer; Breast Surgery; **Hospital:** Smilow Cancer Hosp at Yale-New Haven; **Address:** Smilow Cancer Hosp, Breast Surgery, 20 York St, New Haven, CT 06510; **Phone:** 203-785-2328; **Board Cert:** Surgery 2012; **Med School:** Univ Minn 1974; **Resid:** Surgery, Univ Minn Med Ctr 1982; **Fac Appt:** Prof S, Yale Univ

Lillemoe, Keith D MD [S] - **Spec Exp:** Pancreatic Cancer; Colon Cancer; Pancreatic & Biliary Surgery; Gastrointestinal Cancer; **Hospital:** Mass Genl Hosp; **Address:** Mass General Hosp, Dept Surgery, 15 Parkman St, Boston, MA 02114; **Phone:** 617-643-1010; **Board Cert:** Surgery 2007; **Med School:** Johns Hopkins Univ 1978; **Resid:** Surgery, Johns Hopkins Hosp 1985; **Fac Appt:** Prof S, Harvard Med Sch

Lipkowitz, George S MD [S] - **Spec Exp:** Transplant-Kidney; Dialysis Access; **Hospital:** Baystate Med Ctr, Mercy Med Ctr - Springfield, MA; **Address:** 208 Ashley Ave, West Springfield, MA 01089; **Phone:** 413-747-4170; **Board Cert:** Surgery 2006; **Med School:** SUNY Downstate 1980; **Resid:** Surgery, SUNY Kings Co Hosp 1985; **Fellow:** Transplant Surgery, SUNY Hlth Scis Ctr 1986; **Fac Appt:** Assoc Prof S, Tufts Univ

Markmann, James F MD/PhD [S] - **Spec Exp:** Transplant-Liver; Transplant-Kidney; Transplant-Pancreas; Pancreatic Islet Cell Transplant; **Hospital:** Mass Genl Hosp; **Address:** MGH Transplantation Clinic, 165 Cambridge St, Ste 301, Boston, MA 02114; **Phone:** 617-643-4533; **Board Cert:** Surgery 2006; **Med School:** Univ Pennsylvania 1986; **Resid:** Surgery, Hosp UPenn 1992; **Fellow:** Transplant Surgery, UCLA Med Ctr 1994; **Fac Appt:** Prof S, Harvard Med Sch

McAneny, David MD [S] - **Spec Exp:** Gastrointestinal Cancer & Surgery; Endocrine Tumors; Pancreatic Cancer; Biliary Surgery; **Hospital:** Boston Med Ctr; **Address:** Boston Medical Center, 830 Harrison Ave, Ste 3400, Moakley Bldg, Boston, MA 02118; **Phone:** 617-638-8446; **Board Cert:** Surgery 2008; **Med School:** Georgetown Univ 1983; **Resid:** Surgery, Boston Med Ctr 1988; **Fellow:** Gastrointestinal Surgery, Lahey Clinic 1989; **Fac Appt:** Assoc Prof S, Boston Univ

McFadden, David W MD [S] - **Spec Exp:** Pancreatic Cancer; Minimally Invasive Surgery; Esophageal Disorders; **Hospital:** Univ of Conn Hlth Ctr, John Dempsey Hosp; **Address:** UConn Health Center, Dept Surgery, 263 Farmington Ave, Farmington, CT 06030; **Phone:** 860-679-4801; **Board Cert:** Surgery 2007; Surgical Critical Care 2003; **Med School:** Univ VA Sch Med 1980; **Resid:** Surgery, Johns Hopkins Hosp 1986; **Fellow:** Surgery, Johns Hopkins Hosp 1988; **Fac Appt:** Prof S, Univ Conn

Moore Jr, Francis D MD [S] - **Spec Exp:** Endocrine Surgery; Thyroid Cancer; **Hospital:** Brigham & Women's Hosp, Dana-Farber Cancer Inst; **Address:** Brigham & Womens Hosp, 75 Francis St ASB2 Bldg Fl 3, Boston, MA 02115; **Phone:** 617-732-6830; **Board Cert:** Surgery 2004; **Med School:** Harvard Med Sch 1976; **Resid:** Surgery, Brigham & Womens Hosp 1984; **Fellow:** Immunology, Brigham & Womens Hosp 1981; **Fac Appt:** Prof S, Harvard Med Sch

Ponn, Teresa MD [S] - **Spec Exp:** Breast Cancer; **Hospital:** Elliot Hosp; **Address:** Elliot Breast Health Center, 185 Queen city Ave, Ste 1, MS 03109, Manchester, NH 03109; **Phone:** 603-668-3067; **Board Cert:** Surgery 2012; **Med School:** Univ Fla Coll Med 1976; **Resid:** Surgery, Stanford Univ Med Ctr 1982

Rattner, David W MD [S] - **Spec Exp:** Gastrointestinal Cancer & Surgery; Minimally Invasive Surgery; Gastroesophageal Reflux Disease (GERD); Natural Orifice Surgery (NOTES); **Hospital:** Mass Genl Hosp; **Address:** Mass General Hosp, Dept Surgery, 15 Parkman St, WACC 460, Boston, MA 02114; **Phone:** 617-726-1893; **Board Cert:** Surgery 2004; **Med School:** Johns Hopkins Univ 1978; **Resid:** Surgery, Mass General Hosp 1985; **Fac Appt:** Prof S, Harvard Med Sch

Ryan, Colleen M MD [S] - **Spec Exp:** Burn Care; Toxic Epidermal Necrolysis; Wound Healing/Care; **Hospital:** Mass Genl Hosp, Shriners Hosp for Chldn-Boston; **Address:** MGH Burn Assocs, 55 Fruit St GRB Bldg - Ste 1303, Boston, MA 02114-2621; **Phone:** 617-726-3712; **Board Cert:** Surgery 2009; Surgical Critical Care 2003; **Med School:** Georgetown Univ 1982; **Resid:** Surgery, Beth Israel Deaconess Med Ctr 1988; **Fellow:** Hepatology, Hammersmith Hosp 1986; Burn Surgery, Mass Genl Hosp 1989; **Fac Appt:** Assoc Prof S, Harvard Med Sch

Salem, Ronald R MD [S] - **Spec Exp:** Cancer Surgery; Pancreatic Cancer; Gastrointestinal Cancer; Liver Cancer; **Hospital:** Yale-New Haven Hosp; **Address:** Smilow Cancer Hosp, 35 Park St Fl 8, New Haven, CT 06520; **Phone:** 203-785-3577; **Board Cert:** Surgery 2011; **Med School:** Zimbabwe 1978; **Resid:** Surgery, Hammersmith Hosp 1985; Surgery, New England Deaconess Hosp 1989; **Fac Appt:** Prof S, Yale Univ

Shikora, Scott A MD [S] - **Spec Exp:** Obesity/Bariatric Surgery; Laparoscopic Abdominal Surgery; **Hospital:** Brigham & Women's Hosp; **Address:** Brigham & Women's Hosp, Dept Surgery, ASBII- 3rd Fl, 75 Francis St, Boston, MA 02115; **Phone:** 617-525-8570; **Board Cert:** Surgery 2011; **Med School:** Columbia P&S 1985; **Resid:** Surgery, New England Deaconess Hosp 1991; **Fellow:** Nutrition & Metabolism, New England Deaconess Hos 1989; **Fac Appt:** Prof S, Tufts Univ

Smith, Barbara L MD/PhD [S] - **Spec Exp:** Breast Cancer; Breast Cancer-High Risk Women; **Hospital:** Mass Genl Hosp; **Address:** MGH Cancer Center, 55 Fruit St, Ste YAW 9A, Boston, MA 02114; **Phone:** 617-724-1074; **Board Cert:** Surgery 2009; **Med School:** Harvard Med Sch 1983; **Resid:** Surgery, Brigham & Women's Hosp 1989; **Fac Appt:** Asst Prof S, Harvard Med Sch

Tanabe, Kenneth K MD [S] - **Spec Exp:** Liver Cancer; Colon & Rectal Cancer; Melanoma; **Hospital:** Mass Genl Hosp; **Address:** MGH, Surgical Oncology Associates, 55 Fruit St, YAW 7B, Boston, MA 02114; **Phone:** 617-724-3868; **Board Cert:** Surgery 2010; **Med School:** UCSD 1985; **Resid:** Surgery, New York Hosp-Cornell 1990; **Fellow:** Surgical Oncology, MD Anderson Cancer Ctr 1993; **Fac Appt:** Prof S, Harvard Med Sch

Thayer, Sarah P MD/PhD [S] - **Spec Exp:** Pancreatic Cancer; Gastrointestinal Cancer & Surgery; Hepatobiliary Surgery; Breast Cancer & Surgery; **Hospital:** Mass Genl Hosp; **Address:** Mass Genl Hosp, 15 Parkman St, WAC 460, Boston, MA 02114; **Phone:** 617-726-0624; **Board Cert:** Surgery 2010; **Med School:** Univ VA Sch Med 1991; **Resid:** Surgery, Mass Genl Hosp 1994; Surgery, Mass Genl Hosp 2001; **Fellow:** Research, Meml Sloan Kettering Cancer Ctr 1998; **Fac Appt:** Assoc Prof Surg & Onc, Harvard Med Sch

Tsangaris, Theodore N MD [S] - **Spec Exp:** Nipple Sparing Mastectomy; Breast Cancer & Surgery; **Hospital:** Yale-New Haven Hosp, Yale Med Group; **Address:** Smilow Cancer Hosp, Yale Breat Ctr, 35 Park St, New Haven, CT 06510; **Phone:** 203-200-2328; **Board Cert:** Surgery 2005; **Med School:** Geo Wash Univ 1983; **Resid:** Surgery, Geo Washington Univ Med Ctr 1989; **Fellow:** Surgical Oncology, Baylor Univ Med Ctr 1990; **Fac Appt:** Assoc Prof S, Yale Univ

Udelsman, Robert MD [S] - **Spec Exp:** Parathyroid Cancer; Adrenal Tumors; Thyroid Cancer; Endocrine Surgery; **Hospital:** Yale-New Haven Hosp; **Address:** Yale-New Haven Hosp, Dept Surgery, 330 Cedar St, Box 208062, New Haven, CT 06520-8062; **Phone:** 203-785-2697; **Board Cert:** Surgery 2009; **Med School:** Geo Wash Univ 1981; **Resid:** Surgery, Natl Inst Hlth 1986; Surgery, Johns Hopkins Hosp 1989; **Fellow:** Gastrointestinal Surgery, Johns Hopkins Hosp 1990; Surgical Oncology, Natl Cancer Inst 1985; **Fac Appt:** Prof S, Yale Univ

Ward, Barbara A MD [S] - **Spec Exp:** Breast Cancer; Breast Surgery; Breast Disease; **Hospital:** Greenwich Hosp; **Address:** 77 Lafayette Pl, Ste 302, Greenwich, CT 06830-5426; **Phone:** 203-863-4250; **Board Cert:** Surgery 2011; **Med School:** Temple Univ 1983; **Resid:** Surgery, Yale-New Haven Hosp 1990; **Fellow:** Surgical Oncology, Natl Cancer Inst 1987

Winchell, Robert J MD [S] - **Spec Exp:** Critical Care; Trauma; Burn Care; **Hospital:** Maine Med Ctr; **Address:** Maine Med Partners Surgical Assocs, 22 Bram Hall, Portland, ME 04102-3113; **Phone:** 207-774-2381; **Board Cert:** Surgery 2010; Surgical Critical Care 2012; **Med School:** Yale Univ 1984; **Resid:** Surgery, UCSD Med Ctr 1990; **Fellow:** Trauma/Critical Care, UCSD Med Ctr 1991

Zinner, Michael MD [S] - **Spec Exp:** Colon & Rectal Cancer & Surgery; Pancreatic Cancer; Stomach Cancer; Gastrointestinal Stromal Tumors; **Hospital:** Brigham & Women's Hosp, Dana-Farber Cancer Inst; **Address:** Brigham & Women's Hosp, Dept Surgery, 75 Francis St, Boston, MA 02115; **Phone:** 617-732-8181; **Board Cert:** Surgery 2010; **Med School:** Univ Fla Coll Med 1971; **Resid:** Surgery, Johns Hopkins Hosp 1974; Surgery, Johns Hopkins Hosp 1980; **Fac Appt:** Prof S, Harvard Med Sch

Mid Atlantic

Alexander Jr, H. Richard MD [S] - **Spec Exp:** Gastrointestinal Cancer & Surgery; Liver Cancer-Metastatic; Pancreatic Cancer; **Hospital:** Univ of MD Med Ctr; **Address:** UMMC, Dept Surgical Oncology, 22 S Greene St, rm S4B12, Baltimore, MD 21201; **Phone:** 410-328-7321; **Board Cert:** Surgery 2004; **Med School:** Georgetown Univ 1979; **Resid:** Surgery, Bethesda Naval Hosp 1985; **Fellow:** Surgical Oncology, Meml Sloan-Kettering Cancer Ctr 1989; **Fac Appt:** Prof S, Univ MD Sch Med

Alfonso II, Antonio E MD [S] - **Spec Exp:** Thyroid Cancer; Head & Neck Surgery; Breast Cancer; **Hospital:** SUNY Downstate Med Ctr (Univ Hosp Brooklyn); **Address:** 100 Amity St, Brooklyn, NY 11201; **Phone:** 718-875-3244; **Board Cert:** Surgery 1973; **Med School:** Philippines 1968; **Resid:** Surgery, Temple Univ Hosp 1972; **Fellow:** Surgical Oncology, Meml Sloan Kettering Cancer Ctr 1974; **Fac Appt:** Prof Emeritus S, SUNY Downstate

August, David A MD [S] - **Spec Exp:** Pancreatic Cancer; Esophageal Cancer; Stomach Cancer; Sarcoma-Soft Tissue; **Hospital:** Robert Wood Johnson Univ Hosp - New Brunswick; **Address:** Cancer Inst of New Jersey, 195 Little Albany St, New Brunswick, NJ 08903; **Phone:** 732-235-7701; **Board Cert:** Surgery 2005; **Med School:** Yale Univ 1980; **Resid:** Surgery, Yale-New Haven Hosp 1986; **Fellow:** Surgical Oncology, Natl Cancer Inst 1984; **Fac Appt:** Prof S, UMDNJ-RW Johnson Med Sch

Barie, Philip MD [S] - **Spec Exp:** Trauma; Critical Care; Hernia; Gastrointestinal Surgery; **Hospital:** NY-Presby/Weill Cornell Med Ctr, NY (page 65); **Address:** NY-Presby, Surgery Dept, 525 E 68th St, Box 116, New York, NY 10065; **Phone:** 212-746-5401; **Board Cert:** Surgery 2004; Surgical Critical Care 2005; **Med School:** Boston Univ 1977; **Resid:** Surgery, NY-Presby/Weill Cornell Med Ctr 1984; **Fellow:** Trauma, Albany Med Coll Affil Hosp 1981; **Fac Appt:** Prof S, Cornell Univ-Weill Med Coll

Bartlett, David L MD [S] - **Spec Exp:** Peritoneal Carcinomatosis; Pancreatic Cancer; Liver Cancer; Appendix Cancer; **Hospital:** UPMC Shadyside; **Address:** UPMC Cancer Pavilion-Surgical Oncology, 5150 Centre Ave, Ste 4E, Pittsburgh, PA 15232; **Phone:** 412-692-2852; **Board Cert:** Surgery 2004; **Med School:** Univ Tex, Houston 1987; **Resid:** Surgery, Hosp Univ Penn 1993; **Fellow:** Surgical Oncology, Meml Sloan-Kettering Cancer Ctr 1994; **Fac Appt:** Prof S, Univ Pittsburgh

Bartlett, Stephen T MD [S] - **Spec Exp:** Transplant-Pancreas; Transplant-Kidney; Vascular Surgery; **Hospital:** Univ of MD Med Ctr, Maryland Genl Hosp; **Address:** 22 S Greene St, Ste N4E40, Baltimore, MD 21201; **Phone:** 410-328-8407; **Board Cert:** Surgery 2004; Vascular Surgery 2007; **Med School:** Univ Chicago-Pritzker Sch Med 1979; **Resid:** Surgery, Hosp Univ Penn 1985; **Fellow:** Vascular Surgery, Northwestern Univ Affil Hosp 1986; **Fac Appt:** Prof S, Univ MD Sch Med

Bessey, Palmer Q MD [S] - **Spec Exp:** Burn Care; Wound Healing/Care; Trauma; **Hospital:** NY-Presby/Weill Cornell Med Ctr, NY (page 65); **Address:** NY-Presby, Burn Ctr, 525 E 68th St Fl 7, New York, NY 10065; **Phone:** 212-746-0242; **Board Cert:** Surgery 2011; Surgical Critical Care 2005; **Med School:** Univ VT Coll Med 1975; **Resid:** Surgery, UAB Hosp 1981; **Fellow:** Nutrition & Metabolism, Brigham & Womens Hosp 1983; **Fac Appt:** Prof S, Cornell Univ-Weill Med Coll

Bessler, Marc MD [S] - **Spec Exp:** Obesity/Bariatric Surgery; Laparoscopic Surgery; Gastrointestinal Metabolic Surgery; Natural Orifice Surgery (NOTES); **Hospital:** NY-Presby/Columbia Univ Med Ctr, NY (page 65), Valley Hosp; **Address:** NY-Presby, Surgery Dept, 161 Fort Washington Ave, rm 524, New York, NY 10032; **Phone:** 212-305-9506; **Board Cert:** Surgery 2007; **Med School:** NYU Sch Med 1989; **Resid:** Surgery, NY-Presby/Columbia Univ Med Ctr 1995; **Fac Appt:** Clin Prof S, Columbia P&S

Boraas, Marcia C MD [S] - **Spec Exp:** Breast Cancer; Breast Disease; **Hospital:** Fox Chase Cancer Ctr (page 57), Jeanes Hosp; **Address:** Fox Chase Cancer Center, 333 Cottman Ave, Philadelphia, PA 19111; **Phone:** 215-728-2570; **Board Cert:** Surgery 2005; **Med School:** Univ Pennsylvania 1977; **Resid:** Surgery, Hosp Univ Penn 1983

Borgen, Patrick I MD [S] - **Spec Exp:** Breast Cancer; Breast Cancer & Surgery; **Hospital:** Maimonides Med Ctr (page 60); **Address:** Maimonides Breast Ctr, 745 64th St, Brooklyn, NY 11220; **Phone:** 718-765-2570; **Board Cert:** Surgery 2002; **Med School:** Louisiana State U, New Orleans 1984; **Resid:** Surgery, Ochsner Fdn Hosp 1989; **Fellow:** Surgical Oncology, Meml Sloan Kettering Canc Ctr 1990; **Fac Appt:** Prof S, Cornell Univ-Weill Med Coll

Brady, Mary Sue MD [S] - **Spec Exp:** Melanoma; Merkel Cell Carcinoma; Sarcoma-Soft Tissue; **Hospital:** Meml Sloan-Kettering Canc Ctr; **Address:** 1275 York Ave, rm H1211, New York, NY 10065; **Phone:** 212-639-8347; **Board Cert:** Surgery 2009; **Med School:** Univ Miami Sch Med 1983; **Resid:** Surgery, NY Hosp-Cornell Med Ctr 1988; **Fellow:** Surgical Oncology, Meml Sloan-Kettering Cancer Ctr 1990; Immunology, Meml Sloan-Kettering Cancer Ctr 1992; **Fac Appt:** Assoc Prof S, Cornell Univ-Weill Med Coll

Brodsky, Jeffrey T MD [S] - **Spec Exp:** Esophageal Cancer; Gastrointestinal Cancer; Pancreatic Cancer; Minimally Invasive Surgery; **Hospital:** Lehigh Valley Hosp; **Address:** 1240 S Cedar Crest Blvd, Ste 205, Allentown, PA 18103; **Phone:** 610-402-7884; **Board Cert:** Surgery 2009; **Med School:** Univ Pennsylvania 1984; **Resid:** Surgery, NYU Langone Med Ctr 1989; **Fellow:** Surgical Oncology, Meml Sloan-Kettering Cancer Ctr 1991

Brody, Fred J MD [S] - **Spec Exp:** Gastrointestinal Surgery; Laparoscopic Surgery; Hernia; **Hospital:** G Washington Univ Hosp; **Address:** George Washington Univ Dept Surgery, 2150 Pennsylvania Ave NW, Ste 6B, Washington, DC 20037; **Phone:** 202-741-2587; **Board Cert:** Surgery 2008; **Med School:** Univ NC Sch Med 1991; **Resid:** Surgery, George Washington Univ Med Ctr 1997; **Fellow:** Laparoscopic Surgery, Duke Univ Med Ctr 1998; **Fac Appt:** Assoc Prof S, Geo Wash Univ

Bromberg, Jonathan S MD/PhD [S] - **Spec Exp:** Transplant-Kidney; Transplant-Pancreas; **Hospital:** Univ of MD Med Ctr; **Address:** Univ Maryland Med Ctr, 29 S Greene St, Ste 200, Baltimore, MD 21201; **Phone:** 410-328-5408; **Board Cert:** Surgery 2009; **Med School:** Harvard Med Sch 1983; **Resid:** Surgery, Univ Washington Med Ctr 1988; **Fellow:** Transplant Surgery, Hosp Univ Penn 1990; **Fac Appt:** Prof S, Univ MD Sch Med

Brooks, Ari D MD [S] - **Spec Exp:** Breast Cancer; Minimally Invasive Surgery; Gastrointestinal Cancer; **Hospital:** Pennsylvania Hosp-UPHS (page 69); **Address:** 800 Walnut St, Fl 20, Philadelphia, PA 19107; **Phone:** 215-829-8461; **Board Cert:** Surgery 2010; **Med School:** Hahnemann Univ 1992; **Resid:** Surgery, NYU Med Ctr 2000; **Fellow:** Surgical Oncology, Meml Sloan-Kettering Cancer Ctr 2001

Cameron, John L MD [S] - **Spec Exp:** Pancreatic Cancer; Pancreatic Surgery; Biliary Cancer; Liver Cancer; **Hospital:** Johns Hopkins Hosp (page 59); **Address:** Johns Hopkins Hosp, 600 N Wolfe St Blalock Bldg - Ste 679, Baltimore, MD 21287; **Phone:** 410-955-5166; **Board Cert:** Surgery 1970; Thoracic Surgery 1971; **Med School:** Johns Hopkins Univ 1962; **Resid:** Surgery, Johns Hopkins Hosp 1970; **Fellow:** Thoracic Surgery, Johns Hopkins Hosp 1971; **Fac Appt:** Prof S, Johns Hopkins Univ

Cance, William G MD [S] - **Spec Exp:** Pancreatic Cancer; Endocrine Cancers; Colon & Rectal Cancer; **Hospital:** Roswell Park Canc Inst; **Address:** Roswell Park Cancer Inst, Elm and Carlton Streets, Buffalo, NY 14263; **Phone:** 716-845-4010; **Board Cert:** Surgery 2009; **Med School:** Duke Univ 1982; **Resid:** Surgery, Barnes Jewish Hosp 1988; **Fellow:** Surgical Oncology, Meml Sloan Kettering Canc Ctr 1990; **Fac Appt:** Prof S, SUNY Buffalo

Carty, Sally E MD [S] - **Spec Exp:** Endocrine Surgery; Endocrine Tumors; Parathyroid Surgery; Von Hippel-Lindau Disease; **Hospital:** UPMC Montefiore, UPMC Presby, Pittsburgh; **Address:** 3471 Fifth Ave, Kaufmann Bldg, Ste 101, Pittsburgh, PA 15213; **Phone:** 412-647-0467; **Board Cert:** Surgery 2010; **Med School:** Penn State Coll Med 1984; **Resid:** Surgery, Penn State Hershey Med Ctr 1989; **Fellow:** Surgical Oncology, Natl Cancer Inst 1991; **Fac Appt:** Prof S, Univ Pittsburgh

Chabot, John A MD [S] - **Spec Exp:** Liver & Biliary Surgery; Pancreatic Cancer; Pancreatic Surgery; Thyroid & Parathyroid Surgery; **Hospital:** NY-Presby/Columbia Univ Med Ctr, NY (page 65); **Address:** NY Presby-Columbia Medical Ctr, 161 Ft Washington Ave Fl 8 - Ste 819, New York, NY 10032; **Phone:** 212-305-9468; **Board Cert:** Surgery 2010; **Med School:** Dartmouth Med Sch 1983; **Resid:** Surgery, Columbia-Presby Med Ctr 1990; **Fac Appt:** Prof S, Columbia P&S

Choti, Michael A MD [S] - **Spec Exp:** Pancreatic Cancer; Liver Cancer-Metastatic; Carcinoid Tumors; **Hospital:** Johns Hopkins Hosp (page 59); **Address:** Johns Hopkins Hosp, 600 N Wolfe St Blalock Bldg - rm 665, Baltimore, MD 21287; **Phone:** 410-955-7113; **Board Cert:** Surgery 2012; **Med School:** Yale Univ 1983; **Resid:** Surgery, Hosp Univ Penn 1990; **Fellow:** Surgical Oncology, Meml Sloan-Kettering Cancer Ctr 1992; **Fac Appt:** Prof S, Johns Hopkins Univ

Cohen, Murray J MD [S] - **Spec Exp:** Trauma; Critical Care; **Hospital:** Thomas Jefferson Univ Hosp, Paoli Hosp; **Address:** 1100 Walnut St, Ste 702, Philadelphia, PA 19107; **Phone:** 215-955-2165; **Board Cert:** Surgery 2006; Surgical Critical Care 2008; **Med School:** Temple Univ 1981; **Resid:** Surgery, Albert Einstein Med Ctr 1986; **Fellow:** Trauma, Hartford Hosp 1987; **Fac Appt:** Assoc Prof S, Thomas Jefferson Univ

Coit, Daniel G MD [S] - **Spec Exp:** Melanoma; Pancreatic Cancer; Stomach Cancer; **Hospital:** Meml Sloan-Kettering Canc Ctr; **Address:** 1275 York Avenue, Dept Surgery, New York, NY 10065; **Phone:** 212-639-8411; **Board Cert:** Surgery 2004; **Med School:** Univ Cincinnati 1976; **Resid:** Internal Medicine, New Eng Deaconess Hosp 1978; Surgery, New Eng Deaconess Hosp 1983; **Fellow:** Surgical Oncology, Meml Sloan Kettering Canc Ctr 1985; **Fac Appt:** Prof S, Cornell Univ-Weill Med Coll

Conti, David J MD [S] - **Spec Exp:** Transplant-Pancreas; Dialysis Access; Transplant-Kidney; **Hospital:** Albany Med Ctr; **Address:** AMC, Surgery-Transplant Dept, 47 New Scotland Ave, Ste 212, Albany, NY 12208; **Phone:** 518-262-5614; **Board Cert:** Surgery 2008; **Med School:** Northwestern Univ 1981; **Resid:** Surgery, Northwestern Meml Hosp 1987; **Fellow:** Transplant Surgery, Mass Genl Hosp 1989; **Fac Appt:** Prof S, Albany Med Coll

Cornwell III, Edward E MD [S] - **Spec Exp:** Trauma; **Hospital:** Howard Univ Hosp; **Address:** Howard Univ Hospital, 2041 Georgia Ave NW, Ste 4B02, Washington, DC 20060; **Phone:** 202-865-1441; **Board Cert:** Surgery 2006; **Med School:** Howard Univ 1982; **Resid:** Surgery, LAC-USC Med Ctr 1987; **Fellow:** Trauma, Emer/Med Svcs System 1989; **Fac Appt:** Assoc Prof S, Johns Hopkins Univ

Courcoulas, Anita P MD [S] - **Spec Exp:** Obesity/Bariatric Surgery; Minimally Invasive Surgery; **Hospital:** Magee-Womens Hosp - UPMC, UPMC Shadyside; **Address:** Magee-Womens Hosp, 3380 Boulevard of the Allies, Ste 390, Pittsburgh, PA 15213; **Phone:** 412-641-3632; **Board Cert:** Surgery 2005; **Med School:** Boston Univ 1988; **Resid:** Surgery, Univ Pitts Med Ctr 1996; **Fac Appt:** Prof S, Univ Pittsburgh

Curcillo II, Paul G MD [S] - **Spec Exp:** Minimally Invasive Surgery; Single Port Surgery; Gastrointestinal Cancer; **Hospital:** Fox Chase Cancer Ctr (page 57), Jeanes Hosp; **Address:** Fox Chase Cancer Ctr-Surgical Oncology, 333 Cottman Ave, Philadelphia, PA 19111; **Phone:** 215-728-5363; **Board Cert:** Surgery 2007; **Med School:** Univ Pennsylvania 1989; **Resid:** Surgery, T Jefferson Univ Hosp 1996; **Fellow:** Clinical Nutrition, Hosp Univ Penn 1991; **Fac Appt:** Assoc Prof S, Univ Pennsylvania

Czerniecki, Brian J MD/PhD [S] - **Spec Exp:** Breast Cancer & Surgery; Sentinel Node Surgery; Immunotherapy; **Hospital:** Hosp Univ Penn - UPHS (page 69); **Address:** Rena Rowan Breast Ctr, Perelman Ctr for Advanced Medicine, 3400 Civic Ctr Blvd, 3 West, Philadelphia, PA 19104; **Phone:** 215-662-4392; **Board Cert:** Surgery 2004; **Med School:** UMDNJ-RW Johnson Med Sch 1988; **Resid:** Surgery, Ohio State Univ Hosp 1993; **Fellow:** Surgical Oncology, Natl Inst Hlth 1995; **Fac Appt:** Prof S, Univ Pennsylvania

Dallal, Ramsey M MD [S] - **Spec Exp:** Obesity/Bariatric Surgery; **Hospital:** Einstein Med Ctr; **Address:** Einstein Medical Ctr, Bariatric Surgery, 60 Township Line Rd Fl 2, Elkins Park, PA 19027; **Phone:** 215-663-6422; **Board Cert:** Surgery 2003; **Med School:** Univ VA Sch Med 1996; **Resid:** Surgery, Univ Pittsburgh Med Ctr 2002; **Fellow:** Bariatric Surgery, Univ Pittsburgh Med Ctr 2003

Deitch, Edwin A MD [S] - **Spec Exp:** Burn Care; Abdominal Wall Reconstruction; Critical Care; **Hospital:** Univ Hosp (Newark); **Address:** 185 S Orange Ave, MSB, rm G506, Newark, NJ 07103; **Phone:** 973-972-6639; **Board Cert:** Surgery 2009; Surgical Critical Care 2006; **Med School:** Univ MD Sch Med 1973; **Resid:** Surgery, US Public Hlth Svc Hosp 1976; Surgery, US Public Hlth Svc Hosp 1978; **Fac Appt:** Prof S, UMDNJ-NJ Med Sch, Newark

DeMatteo, Ronald P MD [S] - **Spec Exp:** Liver Cancer; Gallbladder & Biliary Cancer; Pancreatic Cancer; Pancreatic Surgery; **Hospital:** Meml Sloan-Kettering Canc Ctr; **Address:** MSKCC, Surgery Dept, 1275 York Ave, rm C896, New York, NY 10065; **Phone:** 212-639-5726; **Board Cert:** Surgery 2008; **Med School:** Cornell Univ-Weill Med Coll 1990; **Resid:** Surgery, Hosp U Penn 1997; **Fellow:** Surgical Oncology, Meml Sloan-Kettering Cancer Ctr 1999; **Fac Appt:** Prof S, Cornell Univ-Weill Med Coll

Dempsey, Daniel T MD [S] - **Spec Exp:** Gastrointestinal Surgery; Laparoscopic Surgery; Obesity/Bariatric Surgery; Esophageal Surgery; **Hospital:** Hosp Univ Penn - UPHS (page 69); **Address:** Perelman Ctr for Advanced Medicine, Div Gastrointestinal Surgery, 3400 Civic Center Blvd, 4 West, Philadelphia, PA 19104; **Phone:** 215-614-0092; **Board Cert:** Surgery 2006; **Med School:** Univ Rochester 1979; **Resid:** Surgery, Hosp Univ Penn 1986; **Fac Appt:** Prof S, Univ Pennsylvania

Drebin, Jeffrey A MD/PhD [S] - **Spec Exp:** Pancreatic Cancer; Liver Cancer; Gallbladder & Biliary Disease; Cancer Genetics; **Hospital:** Hosp Univ Penn - UPHS (page 69); **Address:** Perelman Ctr for Advanced Medicine, Gastrointestinal Surgery, 3400 Civic Center Blvd, 4 West, Philadelphia, PA 19104; **Phone:** 215-662-2626; **Board Cert:** Surgery 2004; **Med School:** Harvard Med Sch 1987; **Resid:** Surgery, Johns Hopkins Hosp 1994; **Fellow:** Surgical Oncology, Johns Hopkins Hosp 1991; Surgical Oncology, Johns Hopkins Hosp 1995; **Fac Appt:** Prof S, Univ Pennsylvania

Duncan, Mark D MD [S] - **Spec Exp:** Gastrointestinal Cancer & Surgery; Minimally Invasive Surgery; **Hospital:** Johns Hopkins Bayview Med Ctr (page 59); **Address:** Johns Hopkins Bayview Med Ctr, Genl Surgery Clinic, 4940 Eastern Ave, Bldg A Fl 5, Baltimore, MD 21224; **Phone:** 410-550-1226; **Board Cert:** Surgery 2006; **Med School:** Mayo Med Sch 1987; **Resid:** Surgery, Georgetown Univ Hosp 1994; **Fellow:** Surgery, VA Medical Ctr 1991

Edington, Howard D MD [S] - **Spec Exp:** Melanoma; Breast Reconstruction; Reconstructive Surgery; Wound Healing/Care; **Hospital:** Allegheny Genl Hosp; **Address:** 4727 Friendship Ave, Ste 340, Pittsburgh, PA 15224; **Phone:** 412-359-3117; **Board Cert:** Surgery 2008; Plastic Surgery 1993; **Med School:** Temple Univ 1981; **Resid:** Surgery, Univ Pittsburgh Med Ctr 1989; Plastic Surgery, Univ Pittsburgh Med Ctr 1990; **Fellow:** Hand Surgery, Univ Pittsburgh 1991; Surgical Oncology, National Cancer Inst 1993; **Fac Appt:** Assoc Prof S, Univ Pittsburgh

Emond, Jean C MD [S] - **Spec Exp:** Transplant-Liver; Liver Cancer; Liver & Biliary Cancer; Hepatobiliary Surgery; **Hospital:** NY-Presby/Columbia Univ Med Ctr, NY (page 65); **Address:** 622 W 168th St, PH - Fl 14, New York, NY 10032; **Phone:** 212-305-9691; **Board Cert:** Surgery 2006; **Med School:** Univ Chicago-Pritzker Sch Med 1979; **Resid:** Surgery, Cook Cty Hosp 1984; **Fellow:** Surgery, Hopital P Brousse/Univ de Paris Sud 1985; Transplant Surgery, Univ Chicago Hosps 1987; **Fac Appt:** Prof S, Columbia P&S

Estabrook, Alison MD [S] - **Spec Exp:** Breast Cancer; Breast Surgery; Breast Cancer-High Risk Women; **Hospital:** St. Luke's - Roosevelt Hosp Ctr - Roosevelt Div (page 56); **Address:** Comprehensive Breast Center, 425 W 59th St Fl 7 - Ste 7A, New York, NY 10019-1104; **Phone:** 212-523-7500; **Board Cert:** Surgery 2004; **Med School:** NYU Sch Med 1978; **Resid:** Surgery, Columbia Presby Med Ctr 1984; **Fellow:** Surgical Oncology, Columbia Presby Med Ctr 1982; **Fac Appt:** Prof S, Columbia P&S

Fahey III, Thomas J MD [S] - **Spec Exp:** Endocrine Surgery; Pheochromocytoma; Pancreatic Cancer; Minimally Invasive Surgery; **Hospital:** NY-Presby/Weill Cornell Med Ctr, NY (page 65); **Address:** NY Presby Cornell Med Ctr, Dept Surgery, 525 E 68 St, rm Starr 8, Box 249, New York, NY 10065; **Phone:** 212-746-5130; **Board Cert:** Surgery 2002; **Med School:** Cornell Univ-Weill Med Coll 1986; **Resid:** Surgery, New York Hosp 1992; **Fellow:** Endocrine Surgery, Royal North Shore Hosp 1993; **Fac Appt:** Prof S, Cornell Univ-Weill Med Coll

Fong, Yuman MD [S] - **Spec Exp:** Pancreatic Cancer; Liver & Biliary Cancer; Stomach Cancer; **Hospital:** Meml Sloan-Kettering Canc Ctr; **Address:** 1275 York Ave, rm C887, New York, NY 10065; **Phone:** 212-639-2016; **Board Cert:** Surgery 2002; **Med School:** Cornell Univ-Weill Med Coll 1984; **Resid:** Surgery, NY Hosp-Cornell Med Ctr 1992; **Fellow:** Surgical Oncology, Meml Sloan-Kettering Cancer Ctr 1994; **Fac Appt:** Prof S, Cornell Univ-Weill Med Coll

Fraker, Douglas L MD [S] - **Spec Exp:** Endocrine Cancers; Liver Cancer; Sarcoma; **Hospital:** Hosp Univ Penn - UPHS (page 69); **Address:** Perelman Ctr for Advanced Medicine, 3400 Civic Center Blvd, 4 West, Philadelphia, PA 19104; **Phone:** 215-662-7866; **Board Cert:** Surgery 2012; **Med School:** Harvard Med Sch 1983; **Resid:** Surgery, UCSF Med Ctr 1986; Surgery, UCSF Med Ctr 1991; **Fellow:** Surgical Oncology, National Cancer Inst 1989; **Fac Appt:** Prof S, Univ Pennsylvania

Frazier, Thomas G MD [S] - **Spec Exp:** Breast Cancer; Breast Disease; **Hospital:** Bryn Mawr Hosp; **Address:** 101 S Bryn Mawr Ave, Ste 201, Bryn Mawr, PA 19010; **Phone:** 610-520-0700; **Board Cert:** Surgery 2004; **Med School:** Univ Pennsylvania 1968; **Resid:** Surgery, Hosp Univ Penn 1975; **Fellow:** Surgical Oncology, MD Anderson Cancer Ctr 1976; **Fac Appt:** Clin Prof S, Drexel Univ Coll Med

Geller, David A MD [S] - **Spec Exp:** Liver Cancer; Laparoscopic Surgery; Clinical Trials; **Hospital:** UPMC Presby, Pittsburgh, UPMC Passavant-McCandless; **Address:** UPMC Liver Cancer Center, 3459 5th Ave, Pittsburgh, PA 15213-2582; **Phone:** 412-692-2001; **Board Cert:** Surgery 2005; **Med School:** Northwestern Univ 1988; **Resid:** Surgery, UPMC-Presbyterian Hosp 1996; **Fellow:** Hepatobiliary Surgery, Univ Pittsburgh 1998; Transplant Surgery, Univ Pittsburgh 1998; **Fac Appt:** Prof S, Northwestern Univ-Feinberg Sch Med

Gibbs, John F MD [S] - **Spec Exp:** Gastrointestinal Cancer; Stomach Cancer; Pancreatic Cancer; Liver Cancer; **Hospital:** Buffalo Genl Hosp; **Address:** University Surgeons, 100 High St, C319, Buffalo, NY 14203; **Phone:** 716-859-2268; **Board Cert:** Surgery 2009; **Med School:** UCSD 1985; **Resid:** Surgery, Rush Presby-St Lukes Med Ctr 1990; **Fellow:** Transplant Surgery, Baylor Univ Med Ctr 1992; Surgical Oncology, Roswell Park Cancer Inst 1996; **Fac Appt:** Prof S, SUNY Buffalo

Haith Jr, Linwood R MD [S] - **Spec Exp:** Burn Care; Cancer Surgery; **Hospital:** Crozer - Chester Med Ctr; **Address:** One Medical Center Blvd, Ste 241, Upland, PA 19013; **Phone:** 610-619-7400; **Board Cert:** Surgery 2002; Surgical Critical Care 2007; **Med School:** Harvard Med Sch 1976; **Resid:** Surgery, Yale-New Haven Hosp 1982; **Fellow:** Surgical Critical Care, Thomas Jefferson Univ Hosp 1987; **Fac Appt:** Assoc Prof S, Temple Univ

Hanna, Nader N MD [S] - **Spec Exp:** Pancreatic Cancer; Adrenal Tumors; Peritoneal Carcinomatosis; Sarcoma-Soft Tissue; **Hospital:** Univ of MD Med Ctr; **Address:** 22 S Greene St, Ste S4B12, Baltimore, MD 21201; **Phone:** 410-328-7320; **Board Cert:** Surgery 2005; **Med School:** Egypt 1985; **Resid:** Surgery, St Elizabeth's Med Ctr-Tufts Univ 1994; **Fellow:** Surgical Oncology, Univ Chicago Med Ctr 1997; **Fac Appt:** Assoc Prof S, Univ MD Sch Med

Herron, Daniel M MD [S] - **Spec Exp:** Obesity/Bariatric Surgery; Laparoscopic Surgery; Endoscopic Surgery; **Hospital:** Mt Sinai Med Ctr (page 62); **Address:** 17 E 102nd St, CAM Bldg - Fl 5, New York, NY 10029; **Phone:** 212-824-7891; **Board Cert:** Surgery 2008; **Med School:** Univ Pennsylvania 1992; **Resid:** Surgery, New England Med Ctr 1998; **Fellow:** Laparoscopic Surgery, Oregon Univ Hlth Sci Ctr 1999; **Fac Appt:** Prof S, Mount Sinai Sch Med

Hiotis, Spiros P MD/PhD [S] - **Spec Exp:** Liver Cancer; Gallbladder & Biliary Cancer; Pancreatic Cancer; Stomach Cancer; **Hospital:** Mt Sinai Med Ctr (page 62); **Address:** Surgical Oncology Assocs, 1470 Madison Ave Fl 3rd, New York, NY 10029; **Phone:** 212-241-2891; **Board Cert:** Surgery 2010; **Med School:** Univ MD Sch Med 1992; **Resid:** Surgery, USF Med Ctr 1998; **Fellow:** Surgical Oncology, Meml Sloan Kettering Cancer Ctr 2000; **Fac Appt:** Assoc Prof S, Mount Sinai Sch Med

Hoffman, John P MD [S] - **Spec Exp:** Pancreatic Cancer; Gastrointestinal Cancer; Hepatobiliary Surgery; Liver Cancer; **Hospital:** Fox Chase Cancer Ctr (page 57), Jeanes Hosp; **Address:** Fox Chase Cancer Ctr, 333 Cottman Ave, Philadelphia, PA 19111-2497; **Phone:** 215-728-2570; **Board Cert:** Surgery 2010; **Med School:** Case West Res Univ 1970; **Resid:** Surgery, Virginia Mason Hosp 1977; **Fellow:** Surgical Oncology, Meml Sloan Kettering Cancer Ctr 1980; **Fac Appt:** Prof S, Temple Univ

Jarnagin, William MD [S] - **Spec Exp:** Hepatobiliary Surgery; Liver Cancer; Pancreatic Cancer; Gallbladder & Biliary Cancer; **Hospital:** Meml Sloan-Kettering Canc Ctr; **Address:** 1275 York Ave, Dept Surgery, New York, NY 10065; **Phone:** 212-639-7601; **Board Cert:** Surgery 2006; **Med School:** Rush Med Coll 1988; **Resid:** Surgery, UCSF Med Ctr 1996; **Fellow:** Hepatopancreatobiliary Surgery, Meml Sloan-Kettering Cancer Ctr 1997; **Fac Appt:** Prof S, Cornell Univ

Johnson, Lynt B MD [S] - **Spec Exp:** Transplant Surgery; Liver Surgery; Pancreatic Surgery; **Hospital:** MedStar Georgetown Univ Hosp; **Address:** 3800 Reservoir Rd NW PHC Bldg Fl 4, Washington, DC 20007; **Phone:** 202-444-4557; **Board Cert:** Surgery 1992; **Med School:** Harvard Med Sch 1985; **Resid:** Surgery, Mass Genl Hosp 1991; **Fellow:** Transplant Hepatology, Beth Israel Deaconess Med Ctr 1992; **Fac Appt:** Prof S, Georgetown Univ

Johnson, Ronald R MD [S] - **Spec Exp:** Breast Cancer; Breast Disease; **Hospital:** Magee-Womens Hosp - UPMC, UPMC Presby, Pittsburgh; **Address:** Magee-Womens Surgical Assocs, 300 Halket St, Ste 2601, Pittsburgh, PA 15213; **Phone:** 412-641-1225; **Board Cert:** Surgery 2010; **Med School:** Univ Pittsburgh 1983; **Resid:** Surgery, Univ Pittsburgh Med Ctr 1990; **Fac Appt:** Assoc Prof S, Univ Pittsburgh

Johnson Miller, Denise L MD [S] - **Spec Exp:** Breast Cancer; Breast Cancer-High Risk Women; Melanoma; Neuroendocrine Tumors; **Hospital:** Jersey Shore Univ Med Ctr, Ocean Med Ctr; **Address:** Meridian Hlth Breast Surgery Assocs, 1945 Hwy 33, Ackerman 5, Neptune, NJ 07753; **Phone:** 732-776-4594; **Board Cert:** Surgery 2012; **Med School:** Washington Univ, St Louis 1978; **Resid:** Immunology, Univ Texas SW Med Ctr 1982; Surgery, Univ IL Med Ctr 1986; **Fellow:** Surgical Oncology, City of Hope Med Ctr 1988

Julian, Thomas B MD [S] - **Spec Exp:** Breast Cancer & Surgery; Clinical Trials; **Hospital:** Allegheny Genl Hosp; **Address:** Allegheny Cancer Ctr, 320 E North Ave, Fl 5, Pittsburgh, PA 15212; **Phone:** 412-359-8229; **Board Cert:** Surgery 2012; **Med School:** Univ Pittsburgh 1976; **Resid:** Surgery, Univ Pittsburgh Med Ctr 1982; **Fac Appt:** Assoc Prof Med, Drexel Univ Coll Med

Kapur, Sandip MD [S] - **Spec Exp:** Transplant-Kidney; Transplant-Pancreas; **Hospital:** NY-Presby/Weill Cornell Med Ctr, NY (page 65); **Address:** 525 E 68th St, Baker Bldg Fl 19 - Ste F1919, Box 98, New York, NY 10065; **Phone:** 212-746-5330; **Board Cert:** Surgery 2007; **Med School:** Cornell Univ-Weill Med Coll 1990; **Resid:** Surgery, Cornell Univ Med Ctr 1996; **Fellow:** Research, The Rogosin Inst 1994; Transplant Surgery, Thomas E Starzl Transplant Inst 1998; **Fac Appt:** Assoc Prof S, Cornell Univ-Weill Med Coll

Karpeh Jr, Martin S MD [S] - **Spec Exp:** Gastrointestinal Cancer; Esophageal Cancer; Pancreatic Cancer; Liver Cancer; **Hospital:** Beth Israel Med Ctr - Petrie Div (page 56); **Address:** Beth Israel Medical Center, Philips Ambulatory Care Center, 10 Union Square E, Ste 4D, New York, NY 10003; **Phone:** 212-420-4041; **Board Cert:** Surgery 2006; **Med School:** Penn State Coll Med 1983; **Resid:** Surgery, Hosp Univ Penn 1989; **Fellow:** Surgical Oncology, Meml Sloan Kettering Cancer Ctr 1991; **Fac Appt:** Prof S, Mount Sinai Sch Med

Kato, Tomoaki MD [S] - **Spec Exp:** Transplant-Liver; Transplant Surgery-Pediatric; Transplant-Multi Organ; Transplant-Auto Transplantation; **Hospital:** NY-Presby/Columbia Univ Med Ctr, NY (page 65); **Address:** Columbia Univ Med Ctr, 622 W 168th St PH 14 Bldg - rm 105, New York, NY 10032; **Phone:** 212-305-5101; **Med School:** Japan 1991; **Resid:** Surgery, Itami City Hospital 1995; **Fellow:** Transplant Surgery, Jackson Meml Hosp 1997; **Fac Appt:** Prof S, Columbia P&S

Kinkhabwala, Milan M MD [S] - **Spec Exp:** Transplant-Liver; Hepatobiliary Surgery; Liver & Biliary Surgery; Liver & Biliary Cancer; **Hospital:** Montefiore Med Ctr-Moses Campus, NY, Montefiore Med Ctr-Einstein Campus, NY; **Address:** 111 E 210th St, Bronx, NY 10467; **Phone:** 718-920-6659; **Board Cert:** Surgery 2004; **Med School:** Cornell Univ-Weill Med Coll 1989; **Resid:** Surgery, NY-Presby/Weil Cornell Med Ctr 1994; **Fellow:** Hepatobiliary Surgery, UCLA Med Ctr 1996; **Fac Appt:** Prof S, Albert Einstein Coll Med

Leach, Steven D MD [S] - **Spec Exp:** Pancreatic Cancer; **Hospital:** Johns Hopkins Hosp (page 59); **Address:** Johns Hopkins Med Outpatient Ctr, 601 N Caroline St Fl 8, Baltimore, MD 21287; **Phone:** 410-933-1233; **Board Cert:** Surgery 2004; **Med School:** Emory Univ 1986; **Resid:** Surgery, Yale-New Haven Hosp 1993; **Fellow:** Surgical Oncology, MD Anderson Cancer Ctr 1995; **Fac Appt:** Prof S, Johns Hopkins Univ

Lee, James A MD [S] - **Spec Exp:** Adrenal Surgery; Endocrine Cancers; Thyroid & Parathyroid Cancer & Surgery; Pancreatic Surgery; **Hospital:** NY-Presby/Columbia Univ Med Ctr, NY (page 65); **Address:** Columbia Univ Med Ctr, Irving Pavilion, 161 Fort Washington Ave, rm 808, New York, NY 10032; **Phone:** 212-305-0444; **Board Cert:** Surgery 2005; **Med School:** Columbia P&S 1999; **Resid:** Surgery, NY Presby Hosp 2005; Research, NY Presby Hosp 2003; **Fellow:** Endocrine Surgery, UCSF Med Ctr 2006; **Fac Appt:** Assoc Prof S, Columbia P&S

Lee, Kenneth Kwock MD [S] - **Spec Exp:** Pancreatic Cancer; Gastrointestinal Cancer & Surgery; Minimally Invasive Surgery; **Hospital:** UPMC Presby, Pittsburgh, UPMC Shadyside; **Address:** 3550 Terrace St, Ste 497, Scaife Hall, Pittsburgh, PA 15261; **Phone:** 412-647-0457; **Board Cert:** Surgery 2008; **Med School:** Univ Chicago-Pritzker Sch Med 1981; **Resid:** Surgery, Univ Chicago Hosps 1988; **Fac Appt:** Assoc Prof S, Univ Pittsburgh

Libutti, Steven K MD [S] - **Spec Exp:** Neuroendocrine Tumors; Gastrointestinal Cancer; **Hospital:** Montefiore Med Ctr-Einstein Campus, NY, Montefiore Med Ctr-Moses Campus, NY; **Address:** Montefiore-Einstein Ctr for Cancer Care, 1521 Jarret Pl, Bronx, NY 10461; **Phone:** 718-862-8840; **Board Cert:** Surgery 2004; **Med School:** Columbia P&S 1990; **Resid:** Surgery, Columbia Presby Med Ctr 1995; **Fellow:** Surgical Oncology, Natl Cancer Inst 1996; **Fac Appt:** Prof S, Albert Einstein Coll Med

Lieberman, Michael D MD [S] - **Spec Exp:** Gastrointestinal Cancer; Colon & Rectal Cancer & Surgery; Hepatobiliary Surgery; Pancreatic Cancer; **Hospital:** NY-Presby/Weill Cornell Med Ctr, NY (page 65); **Address:** 1315 York Ave, Box 216, New York, NY 10021; **Phone:** 212-746-5434; **Board Cert:** Surgery 2003; **Med School:** UMDNJ-NJ Med Sch, Newark 1985; **Resid:** Surgery, Hosp Univ Penn 1992; **Fellow:** Surgical Oncology, Hosp Univ Penn 1990; Surgical Oncology, Meml Sloan-Kettering Cancer Ctr 1994; **Fac Appt:** Assoc Prof S, Cornell Univ-Weill Med Coll

Lind, D Scott MD [S] - **Spec Exp:** Breast Cancer; Melanoma; **Hospital:** Hahnemann Univ Hosp; **Address:** Drexel Surgery, 219 N Broad St, Berman Bldg Fl 8, Philadelphia, PA 19107; **Phone:** 215-762-4157; **Board Cert:** Surgery 2011; **Med School:** Eastern VA Med Sch 1984; **Resid:** Surgery, Univ Texas Affil Hosp 1989; **Fellow:** Surgical Oncology, Med Coll Virginia 1992; **Fac Appt:** Prof S, Drexel Univ Coll Med

Mannella Jr, William J MD [S] - **Spec Exp:** Vascular Surgery; Peripheral Vascular Disease; Wound Healing/Care; **Hospital:** Crozer - Chester Med Ctr; **Address:** One Medical Ctr Blvd, ACP Bldg - Ste 233, Upland, PA 19013; **Phone:** 610-499-0400; **Board Cert:** Surgery 2009; **Med School:** Hahnemann Univ 1973; **Resid:** Surgery, Hahnemann Univ Hosp 1978; **Fellow:** Vascular Surgery, Hahnemann Univ Hosp 1980; **Fac Appt:** Clin Prof S, Temple Univ

Marsh Jr, James W MD [S] - **Spec Exp:** Transplant-Liver; Liver Cancer; Pancreatic Cancer; **Hospital:** UPMC Presby, Pittsburgh, Monongahela Valley Hosp; **Address:** Starzl Transplantation Inst, UPMC Montefiore 7 South, 3459 Fifth Ave, Pittsburgh, PA 15213-2582; **Phone:** 412-647-5800; **Board Cert:** Surgery 2003; **Med School:** Univ Ark 1979; **Resid:** Surgery, St Paul Hosp 1984; **Fellow:** Transplant Surgery, Mayo Clinic 1985; Transplant Surgery, Univ Pittsburgh Hosps 1986; **Fac Appt:** Asst Prof S, Univ Pittsburgh

Meyers, William C MD [S] - **Spec Exp:** Hernia; Liver & Biliary Surgery; **Hospital:** Abington Meml Hosp; **Address:** 1200 Constitution Ave, Philadelphia, PA 19112; **Phone:** 215-334-1274; **Board Cert:** Surgery 2004; **Med School:** Columbia P&S 1975; **Resid:** Surgery, Duke Univ Med Ctr 1982; **Fellow:** Vascular Surgery, Duke Univ Med Ctr 1983; Gastroenterology, Duke Univ Med CTr 1983; **Fac Appt:** Prof S, Drexel Univ Coll Med

Michelassi, Fabrizio MD [S] - **Spec Exp:** Gastrointestinal Cancer; Crohn's Disease; Ulcerative Colitis; Colon Cancer; **Hospital:** NY-Presby/Weill Cornell Med Ctr, NY (page 65); **Address:** 525 E 68th St, Fl 7, rm F-739, Box 129, New York, NY 10065; **Phone:** 212-746-6006; **Board Cert:** Surgery 2002; **Med School:** Italy 1975; **Resid:** Surgery, NYU Med Ctr 1981; **Fellow:** Research, Mass Genl Hosp 1983; **Fac Appt:** Prof S, Cornell Univ-Weill Med Coll

Montgomery, Robert A MD/PhD [S] - **Spec Exp:** Transplant-Kidney; **Hospital:** Johns Hopkins Hosp (page 59); **Address:** Johns Hopkins Hosp, Transplant Surgery, 720 Rutland Ave Ross Bldg - Ste 765, Baltimore, MD 21205; **Phone:** 410-614-8297; **Board Cert:** Surgery 2006; **Med School:** Univ Rochester 1987; **Resid:** Surgery, Johns Hopkins Hosp 1995; **Fellow:** Transplant Surgery, Johns Hopkins Hosp 1997; **Fac Appt:** Prof S, Johns Hopkins Univ

Morrow, Monica MD [S] - **Spec Exp:** Breast Cancer; **Hospital:** Meml Sloan-Kettering Canc Ctr; **Address:** 300 E 66th St, Fl 4, New York, NY 10065; **Phone:** 646-888-5354; **Board Cert:** Surgery 2011; **Med School:** Jefferson Med Coll 1976; **Resid:** Surgery, Med Ctr Hosp Vermont 1981; **Fellow:** Surgical Oncology, Meml Sloan Kettering Cancer Ctr 1983; **Fac Appt:** Prof S, Cornell Univ-Weill Med Coll

Newman, Elliot MD [S] - **Spec Exp:** Gastrointestinal Cancer; Robotic Surgery; Liver & Biliary Cancer; Colon & Rectal Cancer; **Hospital:** NYU Langone Med Ctr (page 68); **Address:** NYU Clinical Cancer Ctr, 160 E 34th St Fl 9, New York, NY 10016; **Phone:** 212-731-5466; **Board Cert:** Surgery 2004; **Med School:** NYU Sch Med 1986; **Resid:** Surgery, NYU Langone Med Ctr 1993; **Fellow:** Research, Meml Sloan-Kettering Cancer Ctr 1991; Surgical Oncology, Meml Sloan-Kettering Cancer Ctr 1995; **Fac Appt:** Assoc Prof S, NYU Sch Med

Nowak, Eugene J MD [S] - **Spec Exp:** Breast Cancer; Hernia; Sentinel Node Surgery; Gastrointestinal Surgery; **Hospital:** NY-Presby/Weill Cornell Med Ctr, NY (page 65); **Address:** 325 E 79th St, Ground Fl, New York, NY 10075-0954; **Phone:** 212-517-6693; **Board Cert:** Surgery 2012; **Med School:** UMDNJ-NJ Med Sch, Newark 1975; **Resid:** Surgery, New York Hosp 1980; **Fac Appt:** Asst Clin Prof S, Cornell Univ-Weill Med Coll

O'Hea, Brian J MD [S] - **Spec Exp:** Breast Cancer; Sentinel Node Surgery; **Hospital:** Stony Brook Univ Med Ctr; **Address:** Stony Brook Univ Med Ctr, Breast Cancer Ctr, 3 Edmund D Pellegrino Rd, Stony Brook, NY 11794; **Phone:** 631-444-1795; **Board Cert:** Surgery 2012; **Med School:** Georgetown Univ 1986; **Resid:** Surgery, St Vincent's Hosp 1991; **Fellow:** Breast Disease, Meml Sloan-Kettering Cancer Ctr 1996; **Fac Appt:** Asst Prof S, SUNY Stony Brook

Olson Jr, John A MD/PhD [S] - **Spec Exp:** Endocrine Cancers; Breast Cancer; Melanoma; Clinical Trials; **Hospital:** Univ of MD Med Ctr; **Address:** 22 Greene St, S4B10, Baltimore, MD 21201; **Phone:** 410-328-6187; **Board Cert:** Surgery 2009; **Med School:** Univ Fla Coll Med 1992; **Resid:** Surgery, Barnes Hospital/Wash Univ 1998; Surgery, Royal Infirm of Edingurgh 1997; **Fellow:** Surgical Oncology, Meml Sloan-Kettering Cancer Ctr 2000; **Fac Appt:** Prof S, Univ MD Sch Med

Olthoff, Kim M MD [S] - **Spec Exp:** Transplant-Liver-Adult & Pediatric; Liver & Biliary Surgery; Liver Cancer; Transplant-Pancreas; **Hospital:** Hosp Univ Penn - UPHS (page 69), Chldns Hosp of Philadelphia; **Address:** Penn Transplant Institute, Perelman Ctr for Advanced Medicine, 3400 Civic Center Blvd, 2 West, Philadelphia, PA 19104; **Phone:** 215-662-6136; **Board Cert:** Surgery 2003; **Med School:** Univ Chicago-Pritzker Sch Med 1986; **Resid:** Surgery, UCLA Med Ctr 1993; **Fellow:** Transplant Surgery, The Dumont-UCLA Tranplant Ctr 1995; **Fac Appt:** Prof S, Univ Pennsylvania

Pachter, H Leon MD [S] - **Spec Exp:** Gastrointestinal Surgery; Pancreatic Cancer; Colon Cancer; Minimally Invasive Surgery; **Hospital:** NYU Langone Med Ctr (page 68); **Address:** 530 1st Ave, Ste 6C, New York, NY 10016; **Phone:** 212-263-7302; **Board Cert:** Surgery 2009; **Med School:** NYU Sch Med 1971; **Resid:** Surgery, NYU Med Ctr 1976; **Fac Appt:** Prof S, NYU Sch Med

Park, Adrian E MD [S] - **Spec Exp:** Minimally Invasive Surgery; Laparoscopic Surgery; Hernia-Complex; Gastroesophageal Reflux Disease (GERD); **Hospital:** Anne Arundel Med Ctr; **Address:** Ann Arundel Medical Ctr, Health Sciences Pavilion, Ste 600, 2000 Medical Pkwy, Annapolis, MD 21401; **Phone:** 443-481-6699; **Board Cert:** Surgery 2005; **Med School:** McMaster Univ 1987; **Resid:** Surgery, MCcMaster Univ Affil Hosp 1992; **Fellow:** Laparoscopic Surgery, Hotel Dieu de Montreal 1993

Paty, Philip B MD [S] - **Spec Exp:** Colon & Rectal Cancer; Gastrointestinal Cancer; Pelvic Tumors; **Hospital:** Meml Sloan-Kettering Canc Ctr; **Address:** 1275 York Avenue, Dept Surgery, New York, NY 10065; **Phone:** 212-639-6703; **Board Cert:** Surgery 2011; **Med School:** Stanford Univ 1983; **Resid:** Surgery, UCSF Med Ctr 1990; **Fellow:** Surgical Oncology, Meml Sloan Kettering Cancer Ctr 1992; **Fac Appt:** Prof S, Cornell Univ-Weill Med Coll

Pawlik, Timothy M MD [S] - **Spec Exp:** Liver Cancer; Pancreatic Cancer; Gastrointestinal Cancer; Gallbladder & Biliary Cancer; **Hospital:** Johns Hopkins Hosp (page 59); **Address:** Johns Hopkins Hosp, 600 N Wolfe St, Harvey Bldg - rm 611, Baltimore, MD 21287; **Phone:** 410-933-1233; **Board Cert:** Surgery 2004; **Med School:** Tufts Univ 1995; **Resid:** Surgery, Univ Michigan Hosp 2002; **Fellow:** Research, Mass Genl Hosp 2004; Surgical Oncology, Univ Tex-MD Anderson Cancer Ctr 2006; **Fac Appt:** Assoc Prof S, Johns Hopkins Univ

Peitzman, Andrew B MD [S] - **Spec Exp:** Trauma; **Hospital:** UPMC Presby, Pittsburgh; **Address:** UPMC, Dept Surg, 200 Lothrop St, Ste F1281, Pittsburgh, PA 15213; **Phone:** 412-647-0635; **Board Cert:** Surgery 2003; **Med School:** Univ Pittsburgh 1976; **Resid:** Surgery, Univ Pittsburgh Med Ctr 1979; **Fellow:** Surgery, NY Hosp-Cornell Med Ctr 1981; **Fac Appt:** Prof S, Univ Pittsburgh

Peters, Jeffrey H MD [S] - **Spec Exp:** Esophageal Surgery; Gastroesophageal Reflux Disease (GERD); **Hospital:** Univ Rochester Strong Meml Hosp; **Address:** 601 Elmwood Ave, Rochester, NY 14642-8410; **Phone:** 585-275-2725; **Board Cert:** Surgery 2007; **Med School:** Ohio State Univ 1981; **Resid:** Surgery, Johns Hopkins Hosp 1988; **Fellow:** Immunology, Johns Hopkins Hosp 1985; Esophageal Surgery, Creighton Univ Med Ctr 1990; **Fac Appt:** Prof S, Univ Rochester

Philosophe, Benjamin MD [S] - **Spec Exp:** Transplant-Liver; Transplant-Pancreas; Hepatobiliary Surgery; Liver Cancer; **Hospital:** Johns Hopkins Hosp (page 59); **Address:** 600 N Wolfe St, Blalock 654, Baltimore, MD 21287; **Phone:** 410-287-3062; **Board Cert:** Surgery 2010; **Med School:** Boston Univ 1990; **Resid:** Surgery, Barnes-Jewish Hosp 1995; **Fellow:** Hepatopancreatobiliary Surgery, Toronto Hosp 1996; Transplant Surgery, Toronto Hosp 1997; **Fac Appt:** Prof S, Johns Hopkins Univ

Pomp, Alfons MD [S] - **Spec Exp:** Obesity/Bariatric Surgery; Laparoscopic Abdominal Surgery; Hernia; **Hospital:** NY-Presby/Weill Cornell Med Ctr, NY (page 65); **Address:** NY-Presby, Surgery Dept, 525 E 68th St, Box 294, New York, NY 10065; **Phone:** 212-746-5294; **Board Cert:** Surgery 2010; **Med School:** Univ Sherbrooke 1980; **Resid:** Surgery, Univ Montreal Med Ctr 1985; **Fellow:** Nutrition, Rhode Island Hosp 1988; **Fac Appt:** Prof S, Cornell Univ-Weill Med Coll

Pryor, Aurora D MD [S] - **Spec Exp:** Laparoscopic Surgery-Advanced; Obesity/Bariatric Surgery; Gastroesophageal Reflux Disease (GERD); Achalasia; **Hospital:** Stony Brook Univ Med Ctr; **Address:** Stony Brook Univ Med Ctr, Surg Care Ctr, 37 Research Way, East Setauket, NY 11733-3465; **Phone:** 631-444-4545; **Board Cert:** Surgery 2012; **Med School:** Duke Univ 1995; **Resid:** Surgery, Duke Univ Med Ctr 2002; **Fellow:** Laparoscopic Surgery, Duke Univ 2003; **Fac Appt:** Prof S, SUNY Stony Brook

Ramanathan, Ramesh Chandran MD [S] - **Spec Exp:** Obesity/Bariatric Surgery; Minimally Invasive Surgery; Colon Cancer; Clinical Trials; **Hospital:** Magee-Womens Hosp - UPMC; **Address:** Magee-Womens Hosp, 300 Halket St, Ste 5600, Pittsburgh, PA 15213; **Phone:** 412-641-3632; **Board Cert:** Surgery 2004; **Med School:** India 1988; **Resid:** Surgery, Univ Pitts Med Ctr 2003; **Fellow:** Surgical Oncology, Univ Pitts Med Ctr 1999; Minimally Invasive Surgery, Univ Pitts Med Ctr 2000; **Fac Appt:** Asst Prof S, Univ Pittsburgh

Reich, David J MD [S] - **Spec Exp:** Transplant-Liver; Hepatobiliary Surgery; Liver Cancer; Liver Surgery-Complex; **Hospital:** Hahnemann Univ Hosp, Abington Meml Hosp; **Address:** Transplant Center, 216 N Broad St, Feinstein Bldg - Fl 5, Philadelphia, PA 19102; **Phone:** 215-762-8153; **Board Cert:** Surgery 2003; **Med School:** McGill Univ 1989; **Resid:** Surgery, Beth Israel Med Ctr 1994; **Fellow:** Transplant Surgery, Mt Sinai Med Ctr 1996; **Fac Appt:** Prof S, Drexel Univ Coll Med

Reiner, Mark A MD [S] - **Spec Exp:** Laparoscopic Surgery; Hernia; Esophageal Surgery; Pancreatic Surgery; **Hospital:** Mt Sinai Med Ctr (page 62); **Address:** Laparoscopic Surgical Ctr, 1010 5th Ave, New York, NY 10028; **Phone:** 212-879-6677; **Board Cert:** Surgery 2011; **Med School:** SUNY Downstate 1974; **Resid:** Surgery, Mount Sinai Med Ctr 1979; **Fac Appt:** Assoc Clin Prof S, Mount Sinai Sch Med

Ridge, John A MD/PhD [S] - **Spec Exp:** Head & Neck Cancer & Surgery; Thyroid Cancer & Surgery; Laryngeal Cancer; Robotic Surgery; **Hospital:** Fox Chase Cancer Ctr (page 57), Jeanes Hosp; **Address:** Fox Chase Cancer Ctr, 333 Cottman Ave, Philadelphia, PA 19111; **Phone:** 215-728-2570; **Board Cert:** Surgery 2006; **Med School:** Stanford Univ 1981; **Resid:** Surgery, Univ Colorado Med Ctr 1987; **Fellow:** Cancer Research, Meml Sloan-Kettering Cancer Ctr 1985; Surgical Oncology, Meml Sloan-Kettering Cancer Ctr 1989; **Fac Appt:** Prof S, Temple Univ

Rosenberg, Steven A MD/PhD [S] - **Spec Exp:** Melanoma; Kidney Cancer; **Hospital:** Natl Inst of Hlth - Clin Ctr; **Address:** National Cancer Inst, Surgery Branch, 9000 Rockville Pike, Bldg 10 - rm 3-3940, Bethesda, MD 20892; **Phone:** 301-496-4164; **Board Cert:** Surgery 1975; **Med School:** Johns Hopkins Univ 1964; **Resid:** Surgery, Peter Bent Brigham Hosp 1974; **Fac Appt:** Prof S, Uniformed Srvs Univ, Bethesda

Roses, Daniel F MD [S] - **Spec Exp:** Breast Cancer; Melanoma; Thyroid & Parathyroid Surgery; **Hospital:** NYU Langone Med Ctr (page 68); **Address:** NYU, Surgery Dept, 530 1 Ave, Ste 6B, New York, NY 10016; **Phone:** 212-263-7329; **Board Cert:** Surgery 1975; **Med School:** NYU Sch Med 1969; **Resid:** Surgery, NYU-Bellevue Hosp 1974; **Fellow:** Surgical Oncology, NYU-Bellevue Hosp 1978; **Fac Appt:** Prof S, NYU Sch Med

Salky, Barry A MD [S] - **Spec Exp:** Laparoscopic Abdominal Surgery; Gastroesophageal Reflux Disease (GERD); Colon Cancer; Ulcerative Colitis; **Hospital:** Mt Sinai Med Ctr (page 62); **Address:** Mount Sinai Med Ctr, Surgery Dept, 5 E 98th St Fl 14 - Ste C, Box 1259, New York, NY 10029; **Phone:** 212-241-6156; **Board Cert:** Surgery 2010; **Med School:** Univ Tenn Coll Med 1970; **Resid:** Surgery, Mount Sinai Med Ctr 1973; Surgery, Mount Sinai Med Ctr 1978; **Fac Appt:** Prof S, Mount Sinai Sch Med

Sataloff, Dahlia M MD [S] - **Spec Exp:** Breast Cancer; Breast Disease; **Hospital:** Pennsylvania Hosp-UPHS (page 69); **Address:** 800 Walnut St, Fl 20, Philadelphia, PA 19107; **Phone:** 215-829-8461; **Board Cert:** Surgery 2005; **Med School:** Univ Mich Med Sch 1978; **Resid:** Surgery, St Joseph Mercy Hosp 1980; Surgery, Pennsylvania Hosp 1985; **Fac Appt:** Clin Prof S, Univ Pennsylvania

Scantlebury, Velma P MD [S] - **Spec Exp:** Transplant-Kidney; **Hospital:** Wilmington Hosp-Christiana Care, Christiana Hosp; **Address:** Christiana Care, Surgery Dept, 4735 Ogletown-Stanton Rd, Ste 2224, Newark, DE 19713; **Phone:** 302-623-3866; **Board Cert:** Surgery 2012; **Med School:** Columbia P&S 1981; **Resid:** Surgery, Harlem Hosp 1986; **Fellow:** Transplant Surgery, UPMC 1988

Schnabel, Freya MD [S] - **Spec Exp:** Breast Cancer; Breast Cancer-High Risk Women; **Hospital:** NYU Langone Med Ctr (page 68); **Address:** 160 E 34th St Fl 3, NYU Clinical Cancer Ctr, New York, NY 10016; **Phone:** 212-731-5367; **Board Cert:** Surgery 2008; **Med School:** NYU Sch Med 1982; **Resid:** Surgery, NYU Med Ctr 1987; **Fellow:** Research, SUNY Hlth Sci Ctr 1988; **Fac Appt:** Prof S, NYU Sch Med

Schraut, Wolfgang H MD [S] - **Spec Exp:** Gastrointestinal Cancer & Surgery; Colon & Rectal Cancer & Surgery; Minimally Invasive Surgery; **Hospital:** UPMC Presby, Pittsburgh, UPMC Shadyside; **Address:** Digestive Disorders Ctr, 200 Lothrop St, Pittsburgh, PA 15213; **Phone:** 888-847-8836; **Board Cert:** Surgery 2009; **Med School:** Germany 1970; **Resid:** Surgery, Univ Chicago Hosps 1978; **Fellow:** Cardiovascular Surgery, Univ Chicago Hosps 1979; **Fac Appt:** Prof S, Univ Pittsburgh

Schwartz, Myron E MD [S] - **Spec Exp:** Gastrointestinal Cancer; Liver Cancer; Hepatobiliary Surgery; Transplant-Liver; **Hospital:** Mt Sinai Med Ctr (page 62); **Address:** Mount Sinai Med Ctr, 5 E 98th St Fl 12, Box 1104, New York, NY 10029; **Phone:** 212-659-8084; **Board Cert:** Surgery 2009; **Med School:** Jefferson Med Coll 1976; **Resid:** Surgery, Mt Sinai Hosp 1986; Vascular Surgery, Mt Sinai Hosp 1987; **Fac Appt:** Prof S, Mount Sinai Sch Med

Shah, Jatin P MD/PhD [S] - **Spec Exp:** Head & Neck Cancer & Surgery; Thyroid Cancer; Skull Base Tumors; Salivary Gland Tumors & Surgery; **Hospital:** Meml Sloan-Kettering Canc Ctr; **Address:** 1275 York Ave, New York, NY 10065; **Phone:** 646-497-9161; **Board Cert:** Surgery 1975; **Med School:** India 1964; **Resid:** Surgery, SSG Hosp 1967; Surgery, NY Eye & Ear Infirm 1974; **Fellow:** Head & Neck Surgical Oncology, Meml Sloan-Kettering Hosp 1972; **Fac Appt:** Prof S, Cornell Univ-Weill Med Coll

Shaked, Abraham MD/PhD [S] - **Spec Exp:** Transplant Surgery; Transplant-Liver; Hepatobiliary Surgery; **Hospital:** Hosp Univ Penn - UPHS (page 69); **Address:** Penn Transplant Institute, Perelman Ctr for Advanced Medicine, 3400 Civic Center Blvd, 2 West, Philadelphia, PA 19104; **Phone:** 215-662-6723; **Board Cert:** Surgery 2010; **Med School:** Israel 1982; **Resid:** Surgery, Mt Sinai Hosp 1989; **Fellow:** Transplant Surgery, UCLA Med Ctr 1990; **Fac Appt:** Prof S, Univ Pennsylvania

Shapiro, Richard L MD [S] - **Spec Exp:** Breast Cancer; Melanoma; Thyroid & Parathyroid Surgery; Cancer Surgery; **Hospital:** NYU Langone Med Ctr (page 68); **Address:** NYU Medical Clinical Cancer Center, 160 E 34th St Fl 4, New York, NY 10016; **Phone:** 212-731-5347; **Board Cert:** Surgery 2004; **Med School:** NYU Sch Med 1988; **Resid:** Surgery, NYU Langone Med Ctr 1993; **Fellow:** Surgical Oncology, NYU Langone Med Ctr 1995; **Fac Appt:** Assoc Prof S, NYU Sch Med

Shapiro, Ron MD [S] - **Spec Exp:** Transplant-Kidney; Transplant-Pancreas; Pancreatic Islet Cell Transplant; **Hospital:** UPMC Presby, Pittsburgh, Chldns Hosp of Pittsburgh - UPMC; **Address:** Starzl Transplantation Inst, UPMC Montefiore - 7 South, 3459 Fifth Ave, Pittsburgh, PA 15213-2582; **Phone:** 412-647-5800; **Board Cert:** Surgery 2005; **Med School:** Stanford Univ 1980; **Resid:** Surgery, Mt Sinai Hosp 1986; **Fellow:** Transplant Surgery, Univ Pittsburgh 1988; **Fac Appt:** Prof S, Univ Pittsburgh

Sigurdson, Elin R MD/PhD [S] - **Spec Exp:** Breast Cancer; Colon & Rectal Cancer; Melanoma; Liver Cancer; **Hospital:** Fox Chase Cancer Ctr (page 57), Jeanes Hosp; **Address:** Fox Chase Cancer Ctr, 333 Cottman Ave, Philadelphia, PA 19111-2412; **Phone:** 215-728-2570; **Board Cert:** Surgery 2006; **Med School:** Univ Toronto 1980; **Resid:** Surgery, Univ Toronto Affil Hosp 1986; **Fellow:** Surgical Oncology, Meml Sloan-Kettering Cancer Ctr 1987

Simmons, Rache M MD [S] - **Spec Exp:** Breast Cancer; Breast Surgery; **Hospital:** NY-Presby/Weill Cornell Med Ctr, NY (page 65); **Address:** Weill Cornell Breast Ctr, 425 E 61st St Fl 10, New York, NY 10065; **Phone:** 212-821-0853; **Board Cert:** Surgery 2005; **Med School:** Duke Univ 1988; **Resid:** Surgery, Univ NC Hosp 1993; **Fellow:** Surgical Oncology, NY Hosp-Cornell Hosp 1994; **Fac Appt:** Assoc Prof S, Cornell Univ-Weill Med Coll

Singer, Samuel MD [S] - **Spec Exp:** Sarcoma-Soft Tissue; Gastrointestinal Stromal Tumor; **Hospital:** Meml Sloan-Kettering Canc Ctr; **Address:** MSCC, GMT Surgery Dept, 1275 York Ave, Ste H1210, New York, NY 10065; **Phone:** 646-497-9072; **Board Cert:** Surgery 2010; **Med School:** Harvard Med Sch 1982; **Resid:** Surgery, Brigham & Womens Hosp 1988; **Fellow:** Surgical Oncology, Dana Farber Cancer Inst 1990; **Fac Appt:** Assoc Prof S, Cornell Univ-Weill Med Coll

Skinner, Kristin A MD [S] - **Spec Exp:** Breast Cancer; **Hospital:** Univ Rochester Strong Meml Hosp; **Address:** URMC Comprehensive Breast Care Ctr, 601 Elmwood Ave, Rochester, NY 14642; **Phone:** 585-276-4504; **Board Cert:** Surgery 2005; **Med School:** Johns Hopkins Univ 1988; **Resid:** Surgery, UCLA Med Ctr 1995; **Fellow:** Surgical Oncology, UCLA Med Ctr 1992; **Fac Appt:** Assoc Prof S, Univ Rochester

Sugarbaker, Paul H MD [S] - **Spec Exp:** Appendix Cancer; Peritoneal Carcinomatosis; Cystadenocarcinoma; Ovarian Cancer; **Hospital:** MedStar Washington Hosp Ctr; **Address:** Sugarbaker Oncology Associates, Washington Hosp Ctr, 106 Irving St NW, Ste 3900N, Washington, DC 20010; **Phone:** 202-877-3908; **Board Cert:** Surgery 1973; **Med School:** Cornell Univ-Weill Med Coll 1967; **Resid:** Surgery, Peter Bent Brigham Hosp 1973; **Fellow:** Surgical Oncology, Mass Genl Hosp 1976; **Fac Appt:** Prof S, Univ Wash

Swistel, Alexander J MD [S] - **Spec Exp:** Breast Cancer & Surgery; Cancer Reconstruction; Nipple Sparing Mastectomy; **Hospital:** NY-Presby/Weill Cornell Med Ctr, NY (page 65), St. Luke's - Roosevelt Hosp Ctr - Roosevelt Div (page 56); **Address:** 425 E 61st St, Fl 10, New York, NY 10065; **Phone:** 212-821-0602; **Board Cert:** Surgery 2005; **Med School:** Brown Univ 1975; **Resid:** Surgery, St Luke's Roosevelt Hosp Ctr 1981; **Fellow:** Surgical Oncology, Meml Sloan Kettering Canc Ctr 1983; **Fac Appt:** Assoc Clin Prof S, Cornell Univ-Weill Med Coll

Tafra, Lorraine MD [S] - **Spec Exp:** Breast Cancer; **Hospital:** Anne Arundel Med Ctr; **Address:** AAMC Breast Ctr, 2000 Medical Pkwy, Ste 200, Annapolis, MD 21401; **Phone:** 443-481-5300; **Board Cert:** Surgery 2005; **Med School:** Case West Res Univ 1986; **Resid:** Surgery, Rhode Island Hosp 1988; Surgery, Hosp Univ Penn 1992; **Fellow:** Surgical Oncology, John Wayne Cancer Inst 1994

Tartter, Paul I MD [S] - **Spec Exp:** Breast Cancer; Breast Cancer in Elderly; Sentinel Node Surgery; **Hospital:** St. Luke's - Roosevelt Hosp Ctr - Roosevelt Div (page 56); **Address:** Comprehensive Breast Center, 425 W 59th St, Ste 7A, New York, NY 10019-1104; **Phone:** 212-523-7500; **Board Cert:** Surgery 2011; **Med School:** Brown Univ 1977; **Resid:** Surgery, Mt Sinai Hosp 1982; **Fac Appt:** Assoc Prof S, Columbia P&S

Tchou, Julia C MD/PhD [S] - **Spec Exp:** Breast Cancer; Breast Disease; Breast Cancer Risk Assessment; **Hospital:** Hosp Univ Penn - UPHS (page 69); **Address:** Rowan Breast Center, Perelman Ctr for Advanced Medicine, 3400 Civic Center Blvd, 3 West, Philadelphia, PA 19104; **Phone:** 215-615-7575; **Board Cert:** Surgery 2010; **Med School:** SUNY Stony Brook 1995; **Resid:** Surgery, Johns Hopkins Hosp 2001; **Fellow:** Gastrointestinal Surgery, Johns Hopkins Hosp 2002; Breast Surgery, Northwestern Meml Hosp 2003; **Fac Appt:** Asst Prof S, Univ Pennsylvania

Teperman, Lewis W MD [S] - **Spec Exp:** Transplant-Liver; Transplant-Kidney; Liver Cancer; Hepatobiliary Surgery; **Hospital:** NYU Langone Med Ctr (page 68); **Address:** NYU Transplant Associates, 403 E 34th St Fl 3, New York, NY 10016; **Phone:** 212-263-8134; **Board Cert:** Surgery 2007; **Med School:** Mount Sinai Sch Med 1981; **Resid:** Surgery, Columbia Presby Med Ctr 1984; Surgery, LI Jewish Med Ctr 1986; **Fellow:** Transplant Surgery, Univ Pittsburgh Med Ctr 1988; **Fac Appt:** Assoc Prof S, NYU Sch Med

Tousimis, Eleni MD [S] - **Spec Exp:** Breast Cancer & Surgery; Breast Disease; Minimally Invasive Surgery; **Hospital:** MedStar Georgetown Univ Hosp; **Address:** MedStar Georgetown Univ Hosp, 3800 Reservoir Rd NW, Washington, DC 20007; **Phone:** 202-444-8595; **Board Cert:** Surgery 2012; **Med School:** Albany Med Coll 1996; **Resid:** Surgery, Guthrie Clin-Robert Packer Hosp 2001; **Fellow:** Surgery, Meml Sloan Kettering Canc Ctr 2002

Van Zee, Kimberly J MD [S] - **Spec Exp:** Breast Cancer; **Hospital:** Meml Sloan-Kettering Canc Ctr; **Address:** Meml Sloan Kettering Cancer Ctr, Evelyn H Lauder Breast Center, 300 E 66th St, New York, NY 10065; **Phone:** 646-888-5241; **Board Cert:** Surgery 2003; **Med School:** Harvard Med Sch 1987; **Resid:** Surgery, NY Hosp-Cornell Univ Med Ctr 1990; Surgery, NY Hosp-Cornell Univ Med Ctr 1994; **Fellow:** Research, NY Hosp-Cornell Univ Med Ctr 1993; **Fac Appt:** Prof S, Cornell Univ-Weill Med Coll

Willey, Shawna C MD [S] - **Spec Exp:** Breast Cancer; Clinical Trials; Breast Surgery; **Hospital:** MedStar Georgetown Univ Hosp; **Address:** 3800 Reservoir Rd NW, PHC Bldg Fl 4, Washington, DC 20007; **Phone:** 202-444-0241; **Board Cert:** Surgery 2009; **Med School:** Univ Iowa Coll Med 1982; **Resid:** Surgery, George Washington Univ Med Ctr 1988; **Fac Appt:** Assoc Prof S, Georgetown Univ

Yang, James C MD [S] - **Spec Exp:** Kidney Cancer; Clinical Trials; Immunotherapy; Melanoma; **Hospital:** Natl Inst of Hlth - Clin Ctr; **Address:** Surgery Branch, 9000 Rockville Pike, Bldg 10 CRC-rm 3-5952, Bethesda, MD 20892; **Phone:** 301-496-1574; **Board Cert:** Surgery 2005; **Med School:** UCSD 1978; **Resid:** Surgery, UCSD Med Ctr 1984; **Fellow:** Surgical Oncology, Natl Cancer Inst 1986

Yeo, Charles J MD [S] - **Spec Exp:** Pancreatic Cancer; Biliary Cancer; Gastrointestinal Surgery; Pancreatic Endocrine Tumors; **Hospital:** Thomas Jefferson Univ Hosp; **Address:** 1015 Walnut St, Ste 620, Philadelphia, PA 19107; **Phone:** 215-955-9402; **Board Cert:** Surgery 2005; **Med School:** Johns Hopkins Univ 1979; **Resid:** Surgery, Johns Hopkins Hosp 1985; **Fellow:** Research, SUNY Downstate 1982; **Fac Appt:** Prof S, Thomas Jefferson Univ

Yurt, Roger W MD [S] - **Spec Exp:** Burn Care; Wound Healing/Care; Hyperbaric Medicine; Critical Care; **Hospital:** NY-Presby/Weill Cornell Med Ctr, NY (page 65); **Address:** NY-Presby, Burn Ctr, 525 E 68th St, rm L706, New York, NY 10021; **Phone:** 212-746-5410; **Board Cert:** Surgery 2008; **Med School:** Univ Miami Sch Med 1972; **Resid:** Surgery, Parkland Meml Hosp 1974; Surgery, NY-Presby/Weill Cornell Med Ctr 1980; **Fellow:** Internal Medicine, Brigham & Womens Hosp 1978; **Fac Appt:** Prof S, Cornell Univ-Weill Med Coll

Southeast

Adams, Reid B MD [S] - **Spec Exp:** Hepatobiliary Surgery; Liver Cancer; Pancreatic & Biliary Surgery; **Hospital:** Univ of Virginia Hlth Sys; **Address:** UVA Health System, Dept Surgery, 1300 Jefferson Park Ave, Charlottesville, VA 22903; **Phone:** 434-924-2839; **Board Cert:** Surgery 2003; **Med School:** Univ VA Sch Med 1987; **Resid:** Surgery, Univ Va Hlth Sci Ctr 1994; **Fellow:** Hepatopancreatobiliary Surgery, Univ Toronto Med Ctr 1995; **Fac Appt:** Prof S, Univ VA Sch Med

Andreoni, Kenneth A MD [S] - **Spec Exp:** Transplant-Kidney-Adult & Pediatric; Transplant-Liver-Adult & Pediatric; Transplant-Pancreas; **Hospital:** UF Hlth Shands Hosp; **Address:** UF Hlth, Surgery Transplant Ctr, 1600 SW Archer Rd, Ste 6142, Gainsville, FL 32608; **Phone:** 352-265-0111 x44082; **Board Cert:** Surgery 2004; **Med School:** Yale Univ 1988; **Resid:** Surgery, Johns Hopkins Hosp 1993; **Fellow:** Transplant Surgery, OSU Med Ctr 1998; **Fac Appt:** Assoc Prof S, Univ Fla Coll Med

Baker, Christopher C MD [S] - **Spec Exp:** Trauma/Critical Care; Colon & Rectal Surgery; Hernia; Incontinence-Fecal; **Hospital:** Carilion Roanoke Meml Hosp; **Address:** Carillion Clinic, General Surgery, 3 Riverside Cir, Roanoke, VA 24016; **Phone:** 540-224-5170; **Board Cert:** Surgery 2011; Surgical Critical Care 2007; **Med School:** Harvard Med Sch 1974; **Resid:** Surgery, UCSF Med Ctr 1981; **Fellow:** Trauma, San Francisco Genl Hosp 1979; **Fac Appt:** Prof S, Louisiana State U, New Orleans

Bear, Harry D MD/PhD [S] - **Spec Exp:** Breast Cancer; Melanoma; Gastrointestinal Cancer; **Hospital:** Med Coll of VA Hosp; **Address:** 401 College St, Richmond, VA 23298; **Phone:** 804-828-9325; **Board Cert:** Surgery 2003; **Med School:** Med Coll VA 1975; **Resid:** Surgery, Brigham & Women's Hosp 1983; **Fellow:** Surgical Oncology, VCU Med Ctr 1984; **Fac Appt:** Prof Surg & Onc, Med Coll VA

Beauchamp, R Daniel MD [S] - **Spec Exp:** Gastrointestinal Cancer; Esophageal Cancer; Breast Cancer; Melanoma; **Hospital:** Vanderbilt Univ Med Ctr, TN Valley Healthcare Sys-Nashville; **Address:** Vanderbilt Surgery One Hundred Oaks, 719 Thompson Lane, Ste 25000, Nashville, TN 37232-2730; **Phone:** 615-322-2064; **Board Cert:** Surgery 2007; **Med School:** Univ Tex Med Br, Galveston 1982; **Resid:** Surgery, UTMB Affil Hosp 1987; **Fellow:** Cellular Molecular Biology, Vanderbilt Univ 1989; **Fac Appt:** Prof S, Vanderbilt Univ

Behrns, Kevin E MD [S] - **Spec Exp:** Pancreatic Cancer; Gastrointestinal Cancer & Surgery; **Hospital:** UF Hlth Shands Hosp; **Address:** UF Hlth, Surgery Dept, 1600 SW Archer Rd, Gainesville, FL 32610; **Phone:** 352-265-0604; **Board Cert:** Surgery 2011; **Med School:** Mayo Med Sch 1988; **Resid:** Surgery, Mayo Clin 1995; **Fac Appt:** Prof S, Univ Fla Coll Med

Bland, Kirby MD [S] - **Spec Exp:** Breast Cancer; Melanoma; Thyroid & Parathyroid Cancer & Surgery; Cancer Surgery; **Hospital:** UAB Hosp; **Address:** The Kirklin Clinic, 2000 6th Ave S, Birmingham, AL 35233; **Phone:** 205-934-9999; **Board Cert:** Surgery 2011; **Med School:** UAB Sch Med 1968; **Resid:** Surgery, Univ Fla Hosp 1976; Immunology, Univ Fla Hosp 1974; **Fellow:** Surgical Oncology, MD Anderson Cancer Ctr 1977; Cancer Research, MD Anderson Cancer Ctr 1978; **Fac Appt:** Prof S, UAB Sch Med

Britt, L D MD [S] - **Spec Exp:** Trauma; Head Injury; Thyroid Surgery; **Hospital:** Sentara Norfolk Genl Hosp; **Address:** Eastern Virginia Med Sch, Dept Surgery, 825 Fairfax Ave, Ste 610, Norfolk, VA 23507; **Phone:** 757-446-8950; **Board Cert:** Surgery 2003; Surgical Critical Care 2006; **Med School:** Harvard Med Sch 1977; **Resid:** Surgery, Barnes Hosp-Wash Univ 1979; Surgery, Univ Illinois Chicago Med Ctr 1984; **Fellow:** Trauma, Md Inst Emer Med Serv Sys 1986; **Fac Appt:** Prof S, Eastern VA Med Sch

Buchman, Timothy G MD/PhD [S] - **Spec Exp:** Critical Care; Pilonidal Disease; Burn Care; Trauma; **Hospital:** Emory Univ Hosp, Emory Univ Hosp Midtown; **Address:** 1440 Clifton Rd NE, Ste 313A, Atlanta, GA 30322; **Phone:** 404-712-2602; **Board Cert:** Surgery 2004; Surgical Critical Care 2005; **Med School:** Univ Chicago-Pritzker Sch Med 1980; **Resid:** Surgery, Johns Hopkins Hosp 1985; **Fellow:** Trauma, Maryland Inst for Emergency Med 1987; **Fac Appt:** Prof S, Emory Univ

Cairns, Bruce A MD [S] - **Spec Exp:** Burn Care; Wound Healing/Care; Electrical Injury; **Hospital:** NC Memorial Hosp - UNC; **Address:** Univ N Carolina Dept Surgery, NC Jaycee Burn Ctr, 101 Manning Drive, CB # 7600, Chapel Hill, NC 27599-7600; **Phone:** 919-966-3693; **Board Cert:** Surgery 2005; Surgical Critical Care 2010; **Med School:** Univ Pennsylvania 1989; **Resid:** Surgery, Univ NC Hosps 1994; **Fellow:** Surgical Critical Care, Univ NC Hosps 1996; **Fac Appt:** Assoc Prof S, Univ NC Sch Med

Calvo, Benjamin F MD [S] - **Spec Exp:** Liver & Biliary Cancer; Rectal Cancer; Colon Cancer; Endocrine Tumors; **Hospital:** NC Memorial Hosp - UNC; **Address:** UNC, Dept of Surgery, 170 Manning Drive, 1150 POB, CB #7213, Chapel Hill, NC 27599; **Phone:** 919-966-5221; **Board Cert:** Surgery 2010; **Med School:** Univ MD Sch Med 1981; **Resid:** Surgery, George Washington Univ Hosp 1988; Surgery, Natl Inst of Hlth - NCI 1991; **Fellow:** Surgery, Meml Sloan Kettering Cancer Ctr 1993; **Fac Appt:** Assoc Prof S, Univ NC Sch Med

Cole, David J MD [S] - **Spec Exp:** Breast Cancer; Gastrointestinal Cancer; Vaccine Therapy; **Hospital:** MUSC Med Ctr; **Address:** MUSC Surgery Dept, 96 Jonathan Lucas St, MSC 613 /CSB 420, Charleston, SC 29425; **Phone:** 843-792-4638; **Board Cert:** Surgery 2010; **Med School:** Cornell Univ 1986; **Resid:** Surgery, Emory Univ Affil Hosp 1991; **Fellow:** Surgical Oncology, Natl Cancer Inst 1994; **Fac Appt:** Prof S, Med Univ SC

Daneker Jr, George W MD [S] - **Spec Exp:** Gastrointestinal Cancer; Breast Cancer; Laparoscopic Surgery; **Hospital:** CTCA at Southeastern Regl Med Ctr; **Address:** CTCA at Southeastern Regional Med Ctr, 600 Parkway North, Newnan, GA 30265; **Phone:** 770-400-6000; **Board Cert:** Surgery 2002; **Med School:** Univ MD Sch Med 1983; **Resid:** Surgery, Univ Cincinnati Med Ctr 1990; **Fellow:** Cancer Research, New Engl Deaconess Med Ctr 1988; Surgical Oncology, UT MD Anderson Cancer Ctr 1992

Eason, James D MD [S] - **Spec Exp:** Transplant-Kidney; Transplant-Pancreas & Liver; Liver Cancer; **Hospital:** Methodist Univ Hosp - Memphis; **Address:** Methodist Univ Hosp, 1265 Union Ave, Memphis, TN 38104; **Phone:** 901-516-7469; **Board Cert:** Surgery 2002; **Med School:** Univ Tenn Coll Med 1987; **Resid:** Surgery, Wilford Hall USAF Med Ctr 1992; **Fellow:** Transplant Surgery, Mass Genl Hosp 1994; **Fac Appt:** Prof S, Univ Tenn Coll Med

Eckhoff, Devin E MD [S] - **Spec Exp:** Transplant-Liver; Hepatobiliary Surgery; Transplant-Kidney; Pancreatic Islet Cell Transplant; **Hospital:** UAB Hosp; **Address:** UAB Transplant Surgery, 1530 3rd Ave S, Lyons-Harrison Rsch Bldg, rm 710, Birmingham, AL 35294-0007; **Phone:** 205-975-7622; **Board Cert:** Surgery 2010; Surgical Critical Care 2012; **Med School:** Univ Minn 1986; **Resid:** Surgery, Univ Wisc Affil Hosp 1992; **Fellow:** Transplant Surgery, Univ Wisc Affil Hosp 1994; **Fac Appt:** Prof S, UAB Sch Med

Edge, Stephen B MD [S] - **Spec Exp:** Breast Cancer; Breast Disease; Cancer Surgery; **Hospital:** Baptist Memorial Hospital-Memphis; **Address:** 50 Humphreys Blvd, Memphis, TN 38120; **Phone:** 901-226-1472; **Board Cert:** Surgery 2006; **Med School:** Case West Res Univ 1979; **Resid:** Surgery, Univ Hosp 1986; **Fellow:** Surgical Oncology, Natl Cancer Inst 1984

Eubanks, W Stephen MD [S] - **Spec Exp:** Minimally Invasive Surgery-Advanced; Gastrointestinal Surgery; **Hospital:** Florida Hosp - Orlando; **Address:** 2415 N Orange Ave, Ste 400, Orlando, FL 32804; **Phone:** 407-303-7399; **Board Cert:** Surgery 2006; **Med School:** UAB Sch Med 1987; **Resid:** Surgery, Georgia Baptist Med Ctr 1993; **Fellow:** Laparoscopic Surgery, Duke Univ Med Ctr 1994

Flynn, Michael B MD [S] - **Spec Exp:** Head & Neck Cancer; Head & Neck Surgery; Thyroid & Parathyroid Surgery; **Hospital:** Univ of Louisville Hosp, Norton Hosp; **Address:** Univ Surgical Assocs, 410 E Chestnut St, Ste 710, Louisville, KY 40202; **Phone:** 502-583-8303; **Board Cert:** Surgery 1972; **Med School:** Ireland 1962; **Resid:** Surgery, Univ Maryland Hosp 1969; **Fellow:** Surgical Oncology, MD Anderson Hosp 1970; Head and Neck Surgery, MD Anderson Hosp 1971; **Fac Appt:** Prof S, Univ Louisville Sch Med

Gabram, Sheryl G A MD [S] - **Spec Exp:** Breast Cancer; Breast Cancer-High Risk Women; Breast Disease; **Hospital:** Grady Hlth Sys, Emory Univ Hosp; **Address:** Grady Surgery Clinic, 80 Jesse Hill Jr Drive SE Fl 9, Atlanta, GA 30303; **Phone:** 404-251-8914; **Board Cert:** Surgery 2006; **Med School:** Georgetown Univ 1982; **Resid:** Surgery, Washington Hosp Ctr 1987; **Fellow:** Trauma, Hartford Hosp 1988; **Fac Appt:** Prof S, Emory Univ

Galloway, John R MD [S] - **Spec Exp:** Gastrointestinal Surgery; Pancreatic Surgery; Pancreatic Islet Cell Transplant; Hepatobiliary Surgery; **Hospital:** Emory Univ Hosp; **Address:** Emory Univ Hosp, Dept Surgery, 1365A Clifton Rd NE, Ste A 3300, Atlanta, GA 30322; **Phone:** 404-778-3712; **Board Cert:** Surgery 2008; **Med School:** Emory Univ 1981; **Resid:** Surgery, Emory Affil Hosps 1986; **Fellow:** Portal Hypertension, Emory Univ 1987; **Fac Appt:** Prof S, Emory Univ

Hanks, John B MD [S] - **Spec Exp:** Endocrine Surgery; Thyroid & Parathyroid Surgery; Adrenal Surgery; **Hospital:** Univ of Virginia Hlth Sys; **Address:** Univ VA Hlth Sys, Dept Surgery, 1300 Jefferson Park Ave, PO Box 800709, Charlottesville, VA 22903; **Phone:** 434-924-0376; **Board Cert:** Surgery 2012; **Med School:** Univ Rochester 1973; **Resid:** Surgery, Duke Univ Med Ctr 1982; **Fac Appt:** Prof S, Univ VA Sch Med

Hawn, Mary T MD [S] - **Spec Exp:** Gastrointestinal Surgery; Hernia; Laparoscopic Surgery; Gastroesophageal Reflux Disease (GERD); **Hospital:** UAB Hosp; **Address:** 2000 6th Ave S, Birmingham, AL 35233; **Phone:** 205-975-3000; **Board Cert:** Surgery 2008; **Med School:** Univ Mich Med Sch 1991; **Resid:** Surgery, Univ Michigan Affil Hosp 1998; **Fellow:** Gastrointestinal Surgery, Oregon Hlth Science Univ 2001

Herrmann, Virginia M MD [S] - **Spec Exp:** Breast Cancer; Breast Cancer Genetics; Breast Surgery; Nutrition & Cancer Prevention/Control; **Hospital:** Hilton Head Reg Med Ctr, MUSC Med Ctr; **Address:** Hilton Head Regional Med Ctr, 25 Hospital Center Blvd, Breast Health Ctr, Ste 300, Hilton Head, SC 29926; **Phone:** 843-682-7377; **Board Cert:** Surgery 2009; **Med School:** St Louis Univ 1974; **Resid:** Surgery, St Louis Univ Hosps 1979; **Fellow:** Surgical Research, Brigham & Women's Hosp 1980; **Fac Appt:** Prof S, Med Univ SC

Heslin, Martin J MD [S] - **Spec Exp:** Gastrointestinal Cancer; Pancreatic Cancer; Biliary Cancer; Sarcoma-Soft Tissue; **Hospital:** UAB Hosp; **Address:** Univ Alabama, 1922 7th Ave S, Ste 321, Birmingham, AL 35294-0016; **Phone:** 205-934-3064; **Board Cert:** Surgery 2006; **Med School:** SUNY Upstate Med Univ 1987; **Resid:** Surgery, NYU Med Ctr 1994; Surgery, Meml Sloan-Kettering 1991; **Fellow:** Surgical Oncology, Meml Sloan-Kettering 1996; **Fac Appt:** Prof S, UAB Sch Med

Holzman, Michael D MD [S] - **Spec Exp:** Minimally Invasive Surgery; Gastrointestinal Cancer; Swallowing Disorders; Gastroesophageal Reflux Disease(GERD); **Hospital:** Vanderbilt Univ Med Ctr; **Address:** The Vanderbilt Clinic, 1301 Medical Center Drive, Nashville, TN 37232; **Phone:** 615-322-2063; **Board Cert:** Surgery 2005; **Med School:** Wake Forest Univ 1988; **Resid:** Surgery, Vanderbilt Univ Med Ctr 1995; **Fellow:** Minimally Invasive Surgery, Duke Univ Med Ctr 1996; **Fac Appt:** Assoc Prof S, Vanderbilt Univ

Howerton, Russell M MD [S] - **Spec Exp:** Hepatobiliary Surgery; Pancreatic Surgery; Colon & Rectal Surgery; Laparoscopic Surgery; **Hospital:** Wake Forest Baptist Med Ctr; **Address:** Medical Ctr Blvd, Winston-Salem, NC 27157; **Phone:** 336-716-0664; **Board Cert:** Surgery 2008; **Med School:** Vanderbilt Univ 1983; **Resid:** Surgery, Tufts/New England Med Ctr 1989; **Fellow:** Hepatobiliary Surgery, Hammersmith Hosp 1992; **Fac Appt:** Assoc Prof S, Wake Forest Univ

Kelley, Mark C MD [S] - **Spec Exp:** Breast Cancer; Melanoma; **Hospital:** Vanderbilt Univ Med Ctr, TN Valley Healthcare Sys-Nashville; **Address:** Vanderbilt Bareast Ctr One Hundred Oaks, 719 Thompson Lane, Ste 25000, Nashville, TN 37204; **Phone:** 615-322-2064; **Board Cert:** Surgery 2005; **Med School:** Univ Fla Coll Med 1989; **Resid:** Surgery, Shands Hosp 1995; **Fellow:** Surgical Oncology, John Wayne Cancer Inst 1997; **Fac Appt:** Assoc Prof S, Vanderbilt Univ

Knechtle, Stuart J MD [S] - **Spec Exp:** Transplant-Liver; Transplant-Kidney; Transplant Immunology; **Hospital:** Emory Univ Hosp; **Address:** Emory Transplant Surgery Program, 1365B Clifton Rd NE, Ste 6400, Atlanta, GA 30322; **Phone:** 404-712-5676; **Board Cert:** Surgery 2009; **Med School:** Cornell Univ 1982; **Resid:** Surgery, Duke Univ Med Ctr 1989; **Fellow:** Transplant Surgery, Univ Wisconsin 1991; **Fac Appt:** Prof S, Emory Univ

Koruda, Mark J MD [S] - **Spec Exp:** Gastrointestinal Surgery; Minimally Invasive Surgery; Inflammatory Bowel Disease; **Hospital:** NC Memorial Hosp - UNC; **Address:** Div Gastorintestinal Surgery, 4035 Burnett-Womack Bldg, Campus Box 7081, Chapel Hill, NC 27599-7081; **Phone:** 919-966-8436; **Board Cert:** Surgery 2009; **Med School:** Yale Univ 1981; **Resid:** Surgery, Hosp Univ Penn 1988; **Fac Appt:** Prof S, Univ NC Sch Med

Krontiras, Helen MD [S] - **Spec Exp:** Breast Cancer; **Hospital:** UAB Hosp; **Address:** The Kirklin Clinic, 2000 6th Ave S, Birmingham, AL 35233; **Phone:** 205-801-8266; **Board Cert:** Surgery 2010; **Med School:** UAB Sch Med 1994; **Resid:** Surgery, Univ AL Hosp 2000; **Fellow:** Surgical Oncology, Northwestern U Med Ctr 2001; **Fac Appt:** Assoc Prof S, UAB Sch Med

Levi, Joe U MD [S] - **Spec Exp:** Pancreatic Cancer; Liver Disease; Liver Cancer; Biliary Surgery; **Hospital:** Univ of Miami Hosp & Clins/Sylvester Comp Canc Ctr; **Address:** SCCC, Surgery Dept, 1475 NW 12th St, Miami, FL 33136; **Phone:** 305-243-4211; **Board Cert:** Surgery 1975; **Med School:** Univ Fla Coll Med 1967; **Resid:** Surgery, Johns Hopkins Hosp 1969; Surgery, Jackson Meml Hosp 1974; **Fac Appt:** Prof S, Univ Miami Sch Med

Levine, Edward A MD [S] - **Spec Exp:** Breast Cancer; Esophageal Cancer; Peritoneal Carcinomatosis; Sarcoma; **Hospital:** Wake Forest Baptist Med Ctr; **Address:** Wake Forest Univ Baptist Med Ctr, Dept Surgery, Med Ctr Blvd, Fl 5, Winston-Salem, NC 27157; **Phone:** 336-716-4276; **Board Cert:** Surgery 2010; **Med School:** Ros Franklin Univ/Chicago Med Sch 1985; **Resid:** Surgery, Michael Reese Hosp 1990; **Fellow:** Surgical Oncology, Univ Illinois 1992; **Fac Appt:** Prof S, Wake Forest Univ

Luterman, Arnold MD [S] - **Spec Exp:** Burn Care; Wound Healing/Care; Critical Care; **Hospital:** Univ of S AL Med Ctr; **Address:** Univ S Alabama Med Ctr, Dept Surgery, 2451 Fillingim St Mastin Bldg - Ste 101, Mobile, AL 36617; **Phone:** 251-445-8282; **Board Cert:** Surgery 2006; **Med School:** McGill Univ 1970; **Resid:** Surgery, Jewish Genl Hosp 1976; Surgery, Sinai Hospital 1973; **Fellow:** Burn Surgery, Univ Wash Affil Hosp 1976; **Fac Appt:** Prof S, Univ S Ala Coll Med

MacDonald Jr, Kenneth G MD [S] - **Spec Exp:** Gastrointestinal Surgery; Obesity/Bariatric Surgery; Pancreatic Surgery; **Hospital:** Univ Hlth Sys-Vidant Med Ctr, Nash Genl Hosp; **Address:** Physicians East, 1850 W Arlington Blvd, Greenville, NC 27834; **Phone:** 252-413-6735; **Board Cert:** Surgery 2009; **Med School:** W VA Univ 1981; **Resid:** Surgery, NC Baptist Hosp 1984; Surgery, Univ Med Ctr E Carolina 1987; **Fac Appt:** Prof S, E Carolina Univ

McGrath, Patrick C MD [S] - **Spec Exp:** Breast Cancer; Cancer Surgery; **Hospital:** Univ of Kentucky Albert B. Chandler Hosp; **Address:** 800 Rose St UKMC Bldg - rm C-224, Dept General Surgery, Lexington, KY 40536-0293; **Phone:** 859-323-6346 x240; **Board Cert:** Surgery 2008; **Med School:** Univ IL Coll Med 1980; **Resid:** Surgery, Med Coll Virginia Hosp 1986; **Fellow:** Surgical Oncology, Med Coll Virginia Hosp 1988; **Fac Appt:** Prof S, Univ KY Coll Med

McMasters, Kelly M MD [S] - **Spec Exp:** Melanoma; Breast Cancer; Liver Cancer; **Hospital:** Univ of Louisville Hosp; **Address:** Univ Surgical Assocs, 401 E Chestnut St, Ste 710, Louisville, KY 40202; **Phone:** 502-583-8303; **Board Cert:** Surgery 2005; **Med School:** UMDNJ-RW Johnson Med Sch 1989; **Resid:** Surgery, Univ Louisville Hosp 1994; **Fellow:** Surgical Oncology, MD Anderson Cancere Ctr 1996; **Fac Appt:** Prof S, Univ Louisville Sch Med

Mesko, Thomas W MD [S] - **Spec Exp:** Melanoma; Breast Cancer & Surgery; Thyroid & Parathyroid Cancer & Surgery; Minimally Invasive Surgery; **Hospital:** Mount Sinai Med Ctr - Miami; **Address:** Mt Sinai Comp Cancer Ctr, 4306 Alton Rd Fl 2, Miami, FL 33140; **Phone:** 305-535-2397; **Board Cert:** Surgery 2008; **Med School:** Albert Einstein Coll Med 1984; **Resid:** Surgery, Lenox Hill Hosp 1989; **Fellow:** Surgical Oncology, Tulane Med Ctr 1990; Surgical Oncology, Roswell Park Cancer Inst 1992; **Fac Appt:** Asst Clin Prof S, Univ Miami Sch Med

Meyer, Anthony A MD/PhD [S] - **Spec Exp:** Trauma; Burn Care; **Hospital:** NC Memorial Hosp - UNC; **Address:** UNC-Sch Med, Dept Surgery, 4041 Burnett-Womack Bldg, CB 7050, Chapel Hill, NC 27599-7050; **Phone:** 919-966-4320; **Board Cert:** Surgery 2001; Surgical Critical Care 2005; **Med School:** Univ Chicago-Pritzker Sch Med 1977; **Resid:** Surgery, UCSF Med Ctr 1982; **Fac Appt:** Prof S, Univ NC Sch Med

Neifeld, James P MD [S] - **Spec Exp:** Melanoma; Head & Neck Cancer; Gastrointestinal Cancer; Cancers-Rare & Unusual; **Hospital:** Med Coll of VA Hosp; **Address:** Medical College Virginia Hosp, Box 980645, Richmond, VA 23298-0645; **Phone:** 804-828-9324; **Board Cert:** Surgery 2008; **Med School:** Med Coll VA 1972; **Resid:** Surgery, Med Coll Va Hosps 1978; **Fac Appt:** Prof S, Va Commonwealth Univ Sch Med

Newell, Kenneth A MD/PhD [S] - **Spec Exp:** Transplant-Kidney; Transplant-Pancreas; **Hospital:** Emory Univ Hosp; **Address:** Emory Kidney/Pancreas Transplant Prgm, 1365B Clifton Rd NE, Ste 6400, Atlanta, GA 30322; **Phone:** 404-727-0717; **Board Cert:** Surgery 2008; **Med School:** Univ Mich Med Sch 1984; **Resid:** Surgery, Loyola Univ Med Ctr 1989; **Fellow:** Transplant Surgery, Univ Chicago 1994; **Fac Appt:** Prof S, Emory Univ

Norman Jr, James G MD [S] - **Spec Exp:** Parathyroid Surgery; **Hospital:** Tampa Genl Hosp; **Address:** Norman Parathyroid Ctr, 2400 Cypress Glen Drive, Wesley Chapel, FL 33544; **Phone:** 813-972-0000; **Board Cert:** Surgery 2011; **Med School:** Oral Roberts Sch Med 1986; **Resid:** Surgery, Univ S Fl/Tampa Genl Hosp 1991; **Fellow:** Endocrinology, Univ S FL 1992

Pappas, Theodore N MD [S] - **Spec Exp:** Pancreatic Surgery; Laparoscopic Surgery; **Hospital:** Duke Univ Hosp; **Address:** Duke Univ Med Ctr, Dept Surgery, DUMC Box 3479, Durham, NC 27710; **Phone:** 919-681-3442; **Board Cert:** Surgery 2009; **Med School:** Ohio State Univ 1981; **Resid:** Surgery, Brigham & Womens Hosp 1988; **Fellow:** Research, Wadworth VA Med Ctr 1985; **Fac Appt:** Prof S, Duke Univ

Paramo, Juan C MD [S] - **Spec Exp:** Head & Neck Cancer; Melanoma; **Hospital:** Mount Sinai Med Ctr - Miami; **Address:** Mt Sinai Comp Cancer Ctr, 4306 Alton Rd Fl 2, Miami, FL 33140; **Phone:** 305-674-2397; **Board Cert:** Surgery 2012; **Med School:** Colombia 1991; **Resid:** Surgery, Mount Sinai Med Ctr 2000; **Fellow:** Surgical Oncology, Mount Sinai Med Ctr 2003; **Fac Appt:** Assoc Clin Prof S, FIU Coll Med

Pinson, C Wright MD [S] - **Spec Exp:** Transplant-Liver; Liver & Biliary Cancer; Pancreatic Cancer; Liver & Biliary Surgery; **Hospital:** Vanderbilt Univ Med Ctr; **Address:** 1161 21st Ave S, Ste D3300MCN, Nashville, TN 37232-5545; **Phone:** 615-343-9324; **Board Cert:** Surgery 2007; Surgical Critical Care 2007; **Med School:** Vanderbilt Univ 1980; **Resid:** Surgery, Oregon Hlth Sci Ctr 1986; **Fellow:** Gastrointestinal Surgery, Lahey Clinic 1987; Transplant Surgery, Deaconess Hosp 1988; **Fac Appt:** Prof S, Vanderbilt Univ

Richards, William O MD [S] - **Spec Exp:** Laparoscopic Surgery; Obesity/Bariatric Surgery; Esophageal Disorders; Gastrointestinal Surgery; **Hospital:** Univ of S AL Med Ctr; **Address:** Univ S Alabama, Dept Surgery, 2451 Fillingim St Mastin Bldg - Ste 101, Mobile, AL 36617; **Phone:** 251-445-8282; **Board Cert:** Surgery 2004; **Med School:** Univ MD Sch Med 1979; **Resid:** Surgery, Univ of MD Med Ctr 1984; **Fellow:** Gastrointestinal Surgery, Emory Univ Hosp 1985; Gastrointestinal Surgery, Vanderbilt Univ Med Ctr 1987; **Fac Appt:** Prof S, Univ S Ala Coll Med

Roh, Mark S MD [S] - **Spec Exp:** Liver Cancer; Cancer Surgery; **Hospital:** MD Anderson Cancer Ctr-Orlando; **Address:** MD Anderson Cancer Ctr, Surgery Dept, 1400 S Orange Ave, Orlando, FL 32806; **Phone:** 321-841-5134; **Board Cert:** Surgery 2006; **Med School:** Ohio State Univ 1979; **Resid:** Surgery, UPMC 1982; Surgery, UPMC 1986; **Fellow:** Surgical Oncology, Meml Sloan-Kettering Cancer Ctr 1984; Surgical Oncology, Meml Sloan-Kettering Cancer Ctr 1987

Rosemurgy II, Alexander S MD [S] - **Spec Exp:** Pancreatic Cancer; Gastrointestinal Surgery; Minimally Invasive Surgery; Portal Hypertension; **Hospital:** Florida Hosp - Tampa; **Address:** FL Hosp, Surgery Dept, 3000 Medical Park Drive, Ste 310, Tampa, FL 33613; **Phone:** 813-615-7030; **Board Cert:** Surgery 2005; **Med School:** Univ Mich Med Sch 1979; **Resid:** Surgery, Univ Chicago Med Ctr 1984

Salo, Jonathan C MD [S] - **Spec Exp:** Gastrointestinal Cancer; Esophageal Cancer; **Hospital:** Carolinas Med Ctr; **Address:** Carolinas Med Ctr, 1021 Morehead Medical Drive, Ste 6100, Charlotte, NC 28204; **Phone:** 704-355-2884; **Board Cert:** Surgery 2005; **Med School:** UCSF 1981; **Resid:** Surgery, UCSF Med Ctr 1993; **Fellow:** Surgical Oncology, Natl Cancer Inst 1991; Surgical Oncology, Meml Sloan-Kettering Cancer Ctr 1998; **Fac Appt:** Asst Prof S, Univ NC Sch Med

Sarosi Jr, George A MD [S] - **Spec Exp:** Gastrointestinal Surgery; Laparoscopic Surgery; **Hospital:** Malcom Randall VA Med Ctr, UF Hlth Shands Hosp; **Address:** Malcom Randall VA Med Ctr, Dept Surgery, 1601 Archer St, Gainesville, FL 32608; **Phone:** 352-374-6078 x6078; **Board Cert:** Surgery 2009; **Med School:** Harvard Med Sch 1992; **Resid:** Surgery, Univ Michigan Med Ctr 1999; **Fellow:** Gastrointestinal Surgery, Univ Michigan Med Ctr 1997; **Fac Appt:** Prof S, Univ Fla Coll Med

Schirmer, Bruce D MD [S] - **Spec Exp:** Laparoscopic Surgery; Gastrointestinal Surgery; Colon Cancer; Obesity/Bariatric Surgery; **Hospital:** Univ of Virginia Hlth Sys; **Address:** Univ VA Hlth Sys, Dept Surgery, 1300 Jefferson Park Ave, Charlottesville, VA 22903; **Phone:** 434-924-2104; **Board Cert:** Surgery 2005; **Med School:** Duke Univ 1978; **Resid:** Surgery, Duke Univ Med Ctr 1985; **Fac Appt:** Prof S, Univ VA Sch Med

Sharp, Kenneth W MD [S] - **Spec Exp:** Gastrointestinal Surgery; Esophageal Disorders; Laparoscopic Surgery; Pancreatic Surgery; **Hospital:** Vanderbilt Univ Med Ctr; **Address:** 1301 Medical Center Drive, Ste 3501, Nashville, TN 37232-5780; **Phone:** 615-322-2063; **Board Cert:** Surgery 2003; **Med School:** Johns Hopkins Univ 1977; **Resid:** Surgery, Johns Hopkins Univ Med Ctr 1984; **Fellow:** Hepatobiliary Surgery, Loch Raven VA Hosp 1981; Surgery, John Radcliffe Hosp 1982; **Fac Appt:** Prof S, Vanderbilt Univ

Shen, Perry MD [S] - **Spec Exp:** Liver & Biliary Cancer; Pancreatic Cancer; Gastrointestinal Cancer; Melanoma; **Hospital:** Wake Forest Baptist Med Ctr; **Address:** Wake Forest Baptist Med Ctr, Dept Genl Surgery, One Medical Ctr Blvd Fl 5, Winston-Salem, NC 27157; **Phone:** 336-716-0545; **Board Cert:** Surgery 2008; **Med School:** USC Sch Med 1992; **Resid:** Surgery, LAC & USC Med Ctr 1998; **Fellow:** Surgical Oncology, John Wayne Cancer Inst 2000; **Fac Appt:** Prof S, Wake Forest Univ

Shibata, David MD [S] - **Spec Exp:** Colon & Rectal Cancer; Minimally Invasive Surgery; Laparoscopic Surgery; **Hospital:** Moffitt Canc Ctr (page 61); **Address:** Moffitt Cancer Ctr, Surgery Dept, 12902 Magnolia Drive FOB Bldg Fl 2, Tampa, FL 33612; **Phone:** 813-745-6898; **Board Cert:** Surgery 2008; **Med School:** McGill Univ 1991; **Resid:** Surgery, Beth Israel Deaconess Med Ctr 1994; Surgery, Beth Israel Deaconess Med Ctr 1998; **Fellow:** Cancer Biology, Beth Israel Deaconess Med Ctr 1996; Surgical Oncology, Meml Sloan-Kettering Cancer Ctr 2000; **Fac Appt:** Prof S, Univ S Fla Coll Med

Slingluff Jr, Craig L MD [S] - **Spec Exp:** Melanoma; Immunotherapy; **Hospital:** Univ of Virginia Hlth Sys; **Address:** UVA Health System, Dept Surgery, 1300 Jefferson Park Ave, Charlottesville, VA 22903; **Phone:** 434-924-1730; **Board Cert:** Surgery 2011; **Med School:** Univ VA Sch Med 1984; **Resid:** Surgery, Duke Univ Med Ctr 1991; **Fellow:** Surgical Research, Duke Univ Med Ctr 1988; **Fac Appt:** Prof S, Univ VA Sch Med

Solorzano, Carmen C MD [S] - **Spec Exp:** Endocrine Cancers; Neuroendocrine Tumors; Thyroid & Parathyroid Cancer & Surgery; Adrenal Cancer; **Hospital:** Vanderbilt Univ Med Ctr, VA Tennessee Valley Healthcare System-Alvin C. Yor; **Address:** Eskind Diabetes Clinic, 1215 21st Ave S, rm 8210, Nashville, TN 37232; **Phone:** 615-322-8761; **Board Cert:** Surgery 2009; **Med School:** Univ Fla Coll Med 1993; **Resid:** Surgery, Shands Hosp 1999; **Fellow:** Surgical Oncology, UT MD Anderson Cancer Ctr 2002; **Fac Appt:** Prof S, Vanderbilt Univ

Sondak, Vernon K MD [S] - **Spec Exp:** Cancer Surgery; Melanoma; Sarcoma; **Hospital:** Moffitt Canc Ctr (page 61); **Address:** H Lee Moffitt Cancer Ctr, Cutaneous Onc, 12902 Magnolia Drive, Tampa, FL 33612; **Phone:** 813-745-8482; **Board Cert:** Surgery 2008; **Med School:** Boston Univ 1980; **Resid:** Surgery, UCLA Med Ctr 1987; **Fellow:** Surgical Oncology, UCLA Med Ctr 1984; **Fac Appt:** Prof S, Univ S Fla Coll Med

Sosa, Julie A MD [S] - **Spec Exp:** Thyroid Cancer; Parathyroid Cancer; Endocrine Cancers; Head & Neck Surgery; **Hospital:** Duke Univ Hosp; **Address:** Duke Cancer Clin, Endocrine Surgery, 200 Trent Drive, 2-2, Durham, NC 27710; **Phone:** 919-668-1767; **Board Cert:** Surgery 2004; **Med School:** Johns Hopkins Univ 1994; **Resid:** Surgery, Johns Hopkins Hosp 2001; **Fellow:** Surgical Oncology, Johns Hopkins Hosp 2002; **Fac Appt:** Assoc Prof S, Yale Univ

Staley, Charles A MD [S] - **Spec Exp:** Gastrointestinal Cancer & Rare Tumors; Pancreatic Cancer; Liver & Biliary Cancer; **Hospital:** Emory Univ Hosp; **Address:** Emory - Winship Cancer Inst, 1365 Clifton Rd NE, C Bldg Fl 2, Atlanta, GA 30322; **Phone:** 404-778-3307; **Board Cert:** Surgery 2010; **Med School:** Dartmouth Med Sch 1987; **Resid:** Surgery, Univ Pittsburgh Med Ctr 1992; **Fellow:** Surgical Oncology, MD Anderson Cancer Ctr 1995; **Fac Appt:** Prof S, Emory Univ

Stratta, Robert J MD [S] - **Spec Exp:** Transplant-Pancreas; Transplant-Kidney; Dialysis Access; **Hospital:** Wake Forest Baptist Med Ctr; **Address:** Department of General Surgery, Watlington Hall Fl 5th, Medical Ctr Blvd, Winston-Salem, NC 27157-1095; **Phone:** 336-716-0548; **Board Cert:** Surgery 2006; **Med School:** Univ Chicago-Pritzker Sch Med 1980; **Resid:** Surgery, Univ Utah Med Ctr 1986; **Fellow:** Transplant Surgery, Univ Wisc Hosps & Clins 1988; **Fac Appt:** Prof S, Wake Forest Univ

Sweeney, John F MD [S] - **Spec Exp:** Obesity/Bariatric Surgery; Laparoscopic Surgery; Gastroesophageal Reflux Disease (GERD); Minimally Invasive Surgery; **Hospital:** Emory Univ Hosp; **Address:** Emory Univ Dept Surgery, 1365A Clifton Rd NE, Ste 3300, Atlanta, GA 30322; **Phone:** 404-778-3712; **Board Cert:** Surgery 2004; **Med School:** Rush Med Coll 1988; **Resid:** Surgery, Univ S Florida Affil Hosps 1995; **Fellow:** Surgical Research, Univ S Florida 1993; **Fac Appt:** Prof S, Emory Univ

Tyler, Douglas S MD [S] - **Spec Exp:** Melanoma; Pancreatic Cancer; Gastrointestinal Cancer; Melanoma; **Hospital:** Duke Univ Hosp, Durham VA Med Ctr; **Address:** Duke Univ Med Ctr, Box 3118, Durham, NC 27710; **Phone:** 919-684-6858; **Board Cert:** Surgery 2010; **Med School:** Dartmouth Med Sch 1985; **Resid:** Surgery, Duke Univ Med Ctr 1992; **Fellow:** Surgical Oncology, MD Anderson Cancer Ctr 1994; **Fac Appt:** Prof S, Duke Univ

Unger, Stephen W MD [S] - **Spec Exp:** Laparoscopic Surgery; Esophageal Surgery; **Hospital:** Mount Sinai Med Ctr - Miami; **Address:** Mount Sinai Med Ctr, Surgery Dept, 4302 Alton Rd, Ste 720, Miami Beach, FL 33140; **Phone:** 305-532-4835; **Board Cert:** Surgery 2010; **Med School:** Duke Univ 1975; **Resid:** Surgery, Univ Virginia Hlth Sys 1982; **Fellow:** Surgical Oncology, Univ Virginia Hlth Sys 1979

Urist, Marshall M MD [S] - **Spec Exp:** Cancer Surgery; Breast Cancer; Melanoma; Sarcoma; **Hospital:** UAB Hosp; **Address:** The Kirklin Clinic, 2000 6th Ave S, Birmingham, AL 35233; **Phone:** 205-934-3028; **Board Cert:** Surgery 2010; **Med School:** Univ Chicago-Pritzker Sch Med 1971; **Resid:** Surgery, Johns Hopkins Hosp 1974; Surgery, Johns Hopkins Hosp 1978; **Fellow:** Surgical Oncology, UCLA Med Ctr 1976; **Fac Appt:** Prof S, UAB Sch Med

Vitale, Gary C MD [S] - **Spec Exp:** Pancreatic Cancer; Pancreatic & Biliary Surgery; Gallbladder Surgery; Endoscopy; **Hospital:** Univ of Louisville Hosp, Jewish Hosp (KY); **Address:** University Surgical Assocs, 401 E Chestnut St, Ste 710, Louisville, KY 40202; **Phone:** 502-583-8303; **Board Cert:** Surgery 2007; **Med School:** Yale Univ 1979; **Resid:** Surgery, Univ Louisville Med Ctr 1986; **Fellow:** Research, Univ Dundee 1984; **Fac Appt:** Prof S, Univ Louisville Sch Med

Weber, Collin J MD [S] - **Spec Exp:** Endocrine Surgery; Thyroid & Parathyroid Surgery; Adrenal Surgery; Pancreatic Islet Cell Transplant; **Hospital:** Emory Univ Hosp; **Address:** Emory Clinic, Dept Surgery, 1365A Clifton Rd NE, Atlanta, GA 30322; **Phone:** 404-778-3322; **Board Cert:** Surgery 2008; **Med School:** Columbia P&S 1971; **Resid:** Surgery, Columbia Presby Med Ctr 1978; **Fellow:** Research, Natl Inst Hlth 1975; **Fac Appt:** Prof S, Emory Univ

White Jr, Richard L MD [S] - **Spec Exp:** Breast Cancer; Melanoma; Sarcoma; Immunotherapy; **Hospital:** Carolinas Med Ctr; **Address:** Carolinas Med Ctr, 1021 Morehead Medical Drive, Ste 6200, Charlotte, NC 28204; **Phone:** 704-355-2884; **Board Cert:** Surgery 2012; **Med School:** Columbia P&S 1986; **Resid:** Surgery, Georgetown Univ Hosp 1992; **Fellow:** Surgical Oncology, NIH-Natl Cancer Inst 1995; **Fac Appt:** Clin Prof S, Univ NC Sch Med

Whitworth, Pat W MD [S] - **Spec Exp:** Breast Cancer; **Hospital:** Saint Thomas Hosp-Midtown, Centennial Med Ctr; **Address:** Nashville Breast Center, 300 20th Ave N, Ste 401, Nashville, TN 37203; **Phone:** 615-620-5535; **Board Cert:** Surgery 2009; **Med School:** Univ Tenn Coll Med 1983; **Resid:** Surgery, Univ Louisville Med Ctr 1988; **Fellow:** Surgical Oncology, MD Anderson Cancer Ctr 1991; **Fac Appt:** Assoc Clin Prof S, Vanderbilt Univ

Yeatman, Timothy J MD [S] - **Spec Exp:** Liver Cancer; **Hospital:** Spartanburg Reg Med Ctr; **Address:** Spartanburg Regl, Surgical Oncology Dept, 380 Serpentine Drive Fl 3, Spartanburg, SC 29303; **Phone:** 864-560-1900; **Board Cert:** Surgery 2010; **Med School:** Emory Univ 1984; **Resid:** Surgery, Shands at Univ FL 1990; **Fellow:** Surgical Oncology, UT MD Anderson Cancer Ctr 1992; **Fac Appt:** Prof S, Univ S Fla Coll Med

Midwest

Abecassis, Michael MD [S] - **Spec Exp:** Transplant-Liver; Transplant-Kidney; Pancreatic & Biliary Surgery; Liver Cancer; **Hospital:** Northwestern Meml Hosp; **Address:** Northwestern Med Faculty Fdn, 676 N St Clair St, Galter Pavilion Fl 19 - Ste 1900, Chicago, IL 60611; **Phone:** 312-695-8900; **Board Cert:** Surgery 2009; **Med School:** Univ Toronto 1983; **Resid:** Surgery, Toronto Genl Hosp 1989; **Fellow:** Hepatopancreatobiliary Surgery, Toronto Genl Hosp 1990; Transplant Surgery, Univ Iowa Hosp 1991; **Fac Appt:** Prof S, Northwestern Univ-Feinberg Sch Med

Abouljoud, Marwan S MD [S] - **Spec Exp:** Transplant-Liver; Liver Cancer; Liver Surgery; **Hospital:** Henry Ford Hosp; **Address:** Henry Ford Hospital, 2799 W Grand Blvd Fl K16, Detroit, MI 48202; **Phone:** 313-916-2941; **Board Cert:** Surgery 2012; **Med School:** Lebanon 1985; **Resid:** Surgery, Univ of Mich igan Med Ctr 1988; Surgery, Henry Ford Hosp 1992; **Fellow:** Transplant Surgery, Univ Alabama 1994; Transplant Surgery, Baylor Univ Med Ctr 1996; **Fac Appt:** Prof S, Wayne State Univ

Angelos, Peter MD/PhD [S] - **Spec Exp:** Thyroid & Parathyroid Cancer & Surgery; Pheochromocytoma; Adrenal Tumors; Ethics; **Hospital:** Univ of Chicago Med; **Address:** Univ Chicago Med Ctr, Dept Surg, 5841 S Maryland Ave, MC 4052, Chicago, IL 60637; **Phone:** 773-702-4429; **Board Cert:** Surgery 2004; **Med School:** Boston Univ 1989; **Resid:** Surgery, Northwestern Univ 1995; **Fellow:** Medical Ethics, Univ of Chicago Hosps 1992; Endocrine Surgery, Univ of Michigan Med Ctr 1996; **Fac Appt:** Prof S, Univ Chicago-Pritzker Sch Med

Aranha, Gerard V MD [S] - **Spec Exp:** Pancreatic & Biliary Surgery; Stomach Cancer; Esophageal Cancer; **Hospital:** Loyola Univ Med Ctr, Edward Hines, Jr. VA Hosp; **Address:** Loyola Univ Med Ctr, 2160 S First Ave Bldg 110 - rm 3236, Maywood, IL 60153; **Phone:** 708-327-2391; **Board Cert:** Surgery 2006; **Med School:** India 1969; **Resid:** Surgery, Loyola Univ Med Ctr 1975; **Fellow:** Surgical Oncology, Univ Minn Hosp 1977; **Fac Appt:** Prof S, Loyola Univ-Stritch Sch Med

Averbook, Bruce J MD [S] - **Spec Exp:** Melanoma; Cancer Surgery; Clinical Trials; **Hospital:** MetroHealth Med Ctr; **Address:** MetroHealth Medical Center, Cancer Care Pavilion, 2500 MetroHealth Drive, rm C2110, Cleveland, OH 44109; **Phone:** 216-778-4795; **Board Cert:** Surgery 2010; **Med School:** Geo Wash Univ 1983; **Resid:** Surgery, UC Irvine Med Ctr 1990; **Fellow:** Surgical Oncology, Natl Cancer Inst 1993; **Fac Appt:** Assoc Prof S, Case West Res Univ

Basson, Marc D MD/PhD [S] - **Spec Exp:** Gastrointestinal Surgery; Colon & Rectal Surgery; **Hospital:** Mich State Univ-Sparrow Hos; **Address:** 1200 E Michigan Ave, Professional Bldg, Ste 655, Lansing, MI 48912; **Phone:** 517-267-2460; **Board Cert:** Surgery 2008; **Med School:** Univ Mich Med Sch 1981; **Resid:** Surgery, NY Presby-Columbia Med Ctr 1983; Surgery, SUNY Downstate Med Ctr 1985; **Fellow:** Research, Yale-New Haven Hosp 1987; Surgery, St Mary's Hosp 1989; **Fac Appt:** Prof S, Univ Mich Med Sch

Becker, Yolanda T MD [S] - **Spec Exp:** Transplant Surgery; Transplant-Kidney; Transplant-Pancreas; Dialysis Access; **Hospital:** Univ of Chicago Med; **Address:** Univ Chicago Med Ctr-Surgery Dept, 5841 S Maryland Ave, MC 5026, Chicago, IL 60637; **Phone:** 773-702-6319; **Board Cert:** Surgery 2006; **Med School:** Johns Hopkins Univ 1990; **Resid:** Surgery, Vanderbilt Univ Med Ctr 1997; **Fellow:** Transplant Surgery, Univ Wisconsin Hosp 1999; **Fac Appt:** Prof S, Univ Chicago-Pritzker Sch Med

Benedetti, Enrico MD [S] - **Spec Exp:** Transplant-Liver; Transplant-Pancreas; Transplant-Kidney; Transplant-Bowel; **Hospital:** Univ of IL Med Ctr at Chicago; **Address:** Univ Illinois, Dept Surg/Transplant, 840 S Wood St, rm 402, MS 958, Chicago, IL 60612; **Phone:** 312-996-6771; **Board Cert:** Surgery 2003; **Med School:** Italy 1985; **Resid:** Surgery, Univ IL Med Ctr 1993; **Fellow:** Transplant Surgery, Univ MN Med Ctr 1994; **Fac Appt:** Prof S, Univ IL Coll Med

Bentrem, David J MD [S] - **Spec Exp:** Gastrointestinal Cancer & Surgery; **Hospital:** Northwestern Meml Hosp; **Address:** Robert H Lurie Comprehensive Cancer Ctr, 675 N St Clair St, Galter Pavilion Fl 21, Chicago, IL 60611; **Phone:** 312-695-1130; **Board Cert:** Surgery 2004; **Med School:** Univ VA Sch Med 1996; **Resid:** Surgery, Northwestern Meml Hosp 2003; **Fellow:** Surgical Oncology, Meml Sloan-Kettering Cancer Ctr 2005; **Fac Appt:** Assoc Prof Surg & Onc, Northwestern Univ-Feinberg Sch Med

Brems, John J MD [S] - **Spec Exp:** Pancreatic Cancer; Liver Cancer; Transplant-Liver; Hepatobiliary Surgery; **Hospital:** Adv Sherman Hosp, Presence St Joseph Hosp-Elgin; **Address:** 1435 N Randall Rd, Ste 107, Elgin, IL 60123; **Phone:** 224-359-0100; **Board Cert:** Surgery 2004; **Med School:** St Louis Univ 1981; **Resid:** Surgery, St Louis Univ 1986; **Fellow:** Transplant Surgery, UCLA Med Ctr 1987; **Fac Appt:** Prof S, Loyola Univ-Stritch Sch Med

Brown, Charles K MD [S] - **Spec Exp:** Peritoneal Carcinomatosis; Gastrointestinal Cancer & Surgery; Melanoma; Sarcoma; **Hospital:** CTCA at Midwestern Reg Med Ctr; **Address:** Cancer Treatments Ctrs America, 2520 Elisha Ave, Zion, IL 60099; **Phone:** 800-322-9183; **Board Cert:** Surgery 2010; **Med School:** Univ Fla Coll Med 1992; **Resid:** Surgery, Univ Arizona Med Ctr 1999; **Fellow:** Immunotherapy, UPMC Med Ctr 2000; Surgical Oncology, Univ Chicago Med Ctr 2003

Brown, Eric A MD [S] - **Spec Exp:** Breast Cancer & Surgery; **Hospital:** Beaumont Hosp-Troy; **Address:** Beaumont Comprehensive Breast Care Ctr, 44199 Dequindre Rd, Ste 612, Troy, MI 48085; **Phone:** 248-687-7300; **Board Cert:** Surgery 2004; **Med School:** Univ Hlth Scis, Chicago Med Sch 1989; **Resid:** Surgery, St John Hosp & Med Ctr 1994

Brunt, L Michael MD [S] - **Spec Exp:** Minimally Invasive Surgery; Adrenal Tumors; Hernia; Hernia-Sports; **Hospital:** Barnes-Jewish Hosp; **Address:** 4921 Parkview Pl, Ste 8C, St Louis, MO 63110; **Phone:** 314-454-8877 x2; **Board Cert:** Surgery 2006; **Med School:** Johns Hopkins Univ 1980; **Resid:** Surgery, Barnes Jewish Hosp 1987; **Fellow:** Surgery, Barnes Jewish Hosp 1984; **Fac Appt:** Prof S, Washington Univ, St Louis

Chand, Bipan MD [S] - **Spec Exp:** Obesity/Bariatric Surgery; Gastroesophageal Reflux Disease (GERD); Barrett's Esophagus; Hernia; **Hospital:** Loyola Univ Med Ctr; **Address:** 2160 S First Ave Bldg 110 - rm 3224, Maywood, IL 60153; **Phone:** 708-327-2845; **Board Cert:** Surgery 2012; **Med School:** Univ MO-Kansas City 1996; **Resid:** Surgery, Cleveland Clinic 2002; **Fellow:** Laparoscopic Surgery, Cleveland Clinic 2003; **Fac Appt:** Assoc Prof S, Loyola Univ-Stritch Sch Med

Chang, Alfred E MD [S] - **Spec Exp:** Cancer Surgery; Breast Cancer; Gastrointestinal Cancer; Melanoma; **Hospital:** Univ Michigan Med Ctr; **Address:** 1500 E Medical Center Drive, SPC 5932, Ann Arbor, MI 48109-5932; **Phone:** 734-936-6000; **Board Cert:** Surgery 2011; **Med School:** Harvard Med Sch 1974; **Resid:** Surgery, Duke Univ Med Ctr 1976; Surgery, Hosp Univ Penn 1982; **Fellow:** Surgical Oncology, Natl Cancer Inst 1979; **Fac Appt:** Prof S, Univ Mich Med Sch

Chapman, William C MD [S] - **Spec Exp:** Transplant-Liver-Adult & Pediatric; Liver Cancer; Liver & Biliary Surgery; **Hospital:** Barnes-Jewish Hosp, St. Louis Chldns Hosp; **Address:** 4921 Parkview Pl, Ste 8C, St Louis, MO 63110; **Phone:** 314-362-7792; **Board Cert:** Surgery 2011; Surgical Critical Care 2001; **Med School:** Med Univ SC 1984; **Resid:** Surgery, Vanderbilt Univ Med Ctr 1991; **Fellow:** Hepatobiliary Surgery, Kings College Hosp 1992; **Fac Appt:** Prof S, Washington Univ, St Louis

Cronin II, David C MD/PhD [S] - **Spec Exp:** Transplant-Liver; Transplant Surgery-Pediatric; Liver & Biliary Surgery; Pancreatic Surgery; **Hospital:** Froedtert & Med Coll WI, Chldns Hosp - Wisconsin; **Address:** Froedtert Hosp - Div Transplant Surgery, 9200 W Wisconsin Ave, Ste E5700, Milwaukee, WI 53226; **Phone:** 414-955-6920; **Board Cert:** Surgery 2005; **Med School:** Mount Sinai Sch Med 1987; **Resid:** Surgery, Univ Chicago Affil Hosps 1995; **Fellow:** Transplant Surgery, Univ Chicago Affil Hosps 1997; Medical Ethics, Univ Chicago Affil Hosps 2002; **Fac Appt:** Prof S, Univ Wisc

Crowe Jr, Joseph P MD [S] - **Spec Exp:** Breast Cancer; Tumor Surgery; **Hospital:** Cleveland Clin (page 55); **Address:** Cleveland Clinic Fdn, Dept Surg, 9500 Euclid Ave, Desk A80, Cleveland, OH 44195; **Phone:** 216-444-3024; **Board Cert:** Surgery 2004; **Med School:** Case West Res Univ 1978; **Resid:** Surgery, Univ Hosp-Case Western Res 1983; **Fellow:** Surgical Oncology, Meml Sloan-Kettering Cancer Ctr 1985

Deziel, Daniel J MD [S] - **Spec Exp:** Hepatobiliary Surgery; Pancreatic Surgery; Laparoscopic Surgery; **Hospital:** Rush Univ Med Ctr; **Address:** 1725 W Harrison St, Ste 810, Chicago, IL 60612; **Phone:** 312-942-6500; **Board Cert:** Surgery 2003; **Med School:** Univ Minn 1979; **Resid:** Surgery, Rush-Presby-St Luke's Med Ctr 1984; **Fellow:** Gastrointestinal Surgery, Lahey Clinic 1985; **Fac Appt:** Prof S, Rush Med Coll

Dulchavsky, Scott A MD/PhD [S] - **Spec Exp:** Trauma; **Hospital:** Henry Ford Hosp; **Address:** Henry Ford Hosp, 2799 W Grand Blvd, CFP1, Detroit, MI 48202; **Phone:** 313-916-3152; **Board Cert:** Surgery 2007; **Med School:** Wayne State Univ 1983; **Resid:** Surgery, Wayne State Univ Affil Hosp 1989; **Fac Appt:** Prof S, Wayne State Univ

Dunnington, Gary L MD [S] - **Spec Exp:** Cancer Surgery; Breast Cancer & Surgery; **Hospital:** IU Hlth Univ Hosp; **Address:** 545 Barnhill Drive, EH 203, Indianapolis, IN 46202; **Phone:** 317-274-5707; **Board Cert:** Surgery 2007; **Med School:** Indiana Univ 1980; **Resid:** Surgery, Univ AZ Hlth Science Ctr 1986; **Fac Appt:** Prof S, Indiana Univ

Eberlein, Timothy J MD [S] - **Spec Exp:** Breast Cancer; Melanoma; Immunotherapy; **Hospital:** Barnes-Jewish Hosp, St. Louis Chldns Hosp; **Address:** 4921 Parkview Pl, Ste 5F, St Louis, MO 63110-1093; **Phone:** 314-362-2280; **Board Cert:** Surgery 2006; **Med School:** Univ Pittsburgh 1977; **Resid:** Surgery, Peter Bent Brigham Hosp 1979; Surgery, Brigham-Womens Hosp 1985; **Fellow:** Immunology, Natl Inst Hlth 1982; **Fac Appt:** Prof S, Washington Univ, St Louis

Edwards, Michael J MD [S] - **Spec Exp:** Breast Cancer; Melanoma; **Hospital:** Univ Cincinnati Med Ctr; **Address:** 234 Goodman St, ML 0772, Cincinnati, OH 45219; **Phone:** 513-584-8900; **Board Cert:** Surgery 2005; **Med School:** Emory Univ 1981; **Resid:** Surgery, Univ Louisville Hosp 1986; **Fellow:** Surgical Oncology, MD Anderson Cancer Ctr 1987; **Fac Appt:** Prof S, Univ Cincinnati

Ellison, E. Christopher MD [S] - **Spec Exp:** Biliary Surgery; Biliary Cancer; Pancreatic Cancer; **Hospital:** OSU Wexner Med Ctr; **Address:** 700 Ackerman Rd, Ste 600, Columbus, OH 43202; **Phone:** 614-293-4499; **Board Cert:** Surgery 2011; **Med School:** Univ Wisc 1976; **Resid:** Surgery, Ohio State Univ 1981; **Fac Appt:** Prof S, Ohio State Univ

Evans, Douglas B MD [S] - **Spec Exp:** Pancreatic Cancer; Thyroid Cancer; Endocrine Cancers; **Hospital:** Froedtert & Med Coll WI; **Address:** Med Coll WI, Dept Surgery, 9200 W Wisconsin Ave, Ste 3510, Milwaukee, WI 53226-6533; **Phone:** 414-805-5706; **Board Cert:** Surgery 2008; **Med School:** Boston Univ 1983; **Resid:** Surgery, Dartmouth-Hitchcock Med Ctr 1988; **Fellow:** Surgical Oncology, MD Anderson Cancer Ctr 1990; **Fac Appt:** Prof S, Med Coll Wisc

Farley, David R MD [S] - **Spec Exp:** Endocrine Surgery; Hepatobiliary Surgery; Laparoscopic Surgery; Hernia; **Hospital:** Mayo Med Ctr & Clin - Rochester; **Address:** Mayo Clin, Dept Surg, 200 1st St SW, Mayo West, Fl 12, Rochester, MN 55905; **Phone:** 507-284-2644; **Board Cert:** Surgery 2002; **Med School:** Univ Wisc 1988; **Resid:** Surgery, Mayo Clin 1994; **Fellow:** Endocrinology, Mayo Clin 1995; **Fac Appt:** Assoc Prof S, Mayo Med Sch

Farrar, William B MD [S] - **Spec Exp:** Breast Cancer; Thyroid Cancer; **Hospital:** Arthur G James Cancer Hosp & Research Inst, OSU Wexner Med Ctr; **Address:** 410 W 10th Ave, N924 Doan Hall, Columbus, OH 43210; **Phone:** 614-293-8890; **Board Cert:** Surgery 2010; **Med School:** Univ VA Sch Med 1975; **Resid:** Surgery, Ohio State Univ Hosps 1980; **Fellow:** Surgical Oncology, Meml Sloan-Kettering Cancer Ctr 1982; **Fac Appt:** Prof S, Ohio State Univ

Frantzides, Constantine T MD/PhD [S] - **Spec Exp:** Minimally Invasive Surgery; Laparoscopic Surgery; Obesity/Bariatric Surgery; Laparoscopic Abdominal Surgery; **Hospital:** Presence St Francis Hosp - Evanston, Evanston Hosp/NorthShore Univ Hlth Sys (page 67); **Address:** Chicago Inst of Minimally Invasive Surg, 4905 Old Orchard Ctr, Ste 409, Skokie, IL 60077; **Phone:** 847-676-2200; **Med School:** Greece 1976; **Resid:** Surgery, Athens Univ Affil Hosp 1982; **Fellow:** Surgery, Queen Mary's Hosp 1978; Surgery, Med Coll Wisc 1985; **Fac Appt:** Prof S, Univ IL Coll Med

Fung, John J MD/PhD [S] - **Spec Exp:** Transplant-Liver; Transplant-Kidney; Liver & Biliary Cancer; Laparoscopic Surgery; **Hospital:** Cleveland Clin (page 55), Hillcrest Hosp-Mayfield Hts; **Address:** 9500 Euclid Ave, MS A100, Cleveland, OH 44195; **Phone:** 216-444-3776; **Board Cert:** Surgery 2008; **Med School:** Univ Chicago-Pritzker Sch Med 1982; **Resid:** Surgery, Strong Meml Hosp 1988; **Fellow:** Transplant Surgery, Univ Pittsburgh Med Ctr 1986; **Fac Appt:** Prof S, Cleveland Cl Coll Med/Case West Res

Gamelli, Richard L MD [S] - **Spec Exp:** Burn Care; Trauma/Critical Care; **Hospital:** Loyola Univ Med Ctr; **Address:** 2160 S First Ave Bldg 103 - rm 1175, Maywood, IL 60153; **Phone:** 708-216-4444; **Board Cert:** Surgery 2009; **Med School:** Univ VT Coll Med 1974; **Resid:** Surgery, Vermont Med Ctr Hosp 1979; **Fac Appt:** Prof S, Loyola Univ-Stritch Sch Med

Goulet Jr, Robert J MD [S] - **Spec Exp:** Breast Cancer; Breast Surgery; **Hospital:** Community Hosp E - Indianapolis; **Address:** Community Hospital Breast Care, 1400 N Ritter Ave, Ste 485, Indianapolis, IN 46219; **Phone:** 317-355-2727; **Board Cert:** Surgery 2006; **Med School:** SUNY Downstate 1979; **Resid:** Surgery, SUNY-Downstate Med Ctr 1986; **Fellow:** Surgical Research, SUNY-Downstate Med Ctr 1983

Grant, Clive S MD [S] - **Spec Exp:** Thyroid & Parathyroid Cancer & Surgery; Adrenal Tumors; Breast Cancer; **Hospital:** Mayo Med Ctr & Clin - Rochester; **Address:** Mayo Clinic, Dept Surgery, 200 First St SW, Rochester, MN 55905-0001; **Phone:** 507-284-2644; **Board Cert:** Surgery 2010; **Med School:** Univ Colorado 1975; **Resid:** Surgery, Mayo Clinic 1980; **Fac Appt:** Prof S, Mayo Med Sch

Hansen, Nora M MD [S] - **Spec Exp:** Sentinel Node Surgery; Breast Cancer-High Risk Women; Breast Cancer Risk Assessment; **Hospital:** Northwestern Meml Hosp, Prentice Women's Hosp; **Address:** Lynn Sage Breast Surgery Ctr, 250 E Superior St, Fl 4, Ste 420, Chicago, IL 60611; **Phone:** 312-695-0990; **Board Cert:** Surgery 2006; **Med School:** NY Med Coll 1988; **Resid:** Surgery, Univ Chicago Hosps 1995; **Fellow:** Surgical Oncology, Univ Chicago Hosps 1996; **Fac Appt:** Assoc Prof S, Northwestern Univ

Hinshaw, Daniel B MD [S] - **Spec Exp:** Palliative Care; **Hospital:** VA Ann Arbor Healthcare Sys, Univ Michigan Med Ctr; **Address:** VA Medical Ctr, 2215 Fuller Rd, rm 530, MS 112, Ann Arbor, MI 48105; **Phone:** 734-769-7100 x5939; **Board Cert:** Surgery 2003; Hospice & Palliative Medicine 2008; **Med School:** Loma Linda Univ 1978; **Resid:** Surgery, Loma Linda U Med Ctr 1983; **Fellow:** Immunology, Scripps Clinic Rsch Fdn 1985; Cleveland Clin 2001; **Fac Appt:** Clin Prof S, Univ Mich Med Sch

Howe, James R MD [S] - **Spec Exp:** Endocrine Surgery; Gastrointestinal Cancer; Colon & Rectal Cancer; **Hospital:** Univ Iowa Hosp & Clins; **Address:** Univ Iowa Hosp & Clinics, Dept Surg, 200 Hawkins Drive, JCP Bldg, rm 4644, Iowa City, IA 52242-1086; **Phone:** 319-356-1727; **Board Cert:** Surgery 2006; **Med School:** Univ VT Coll Med 1987; **Resid:** Surgery, Barnes Hosp-Wash Univ 1994; **Fellow:** Research, Wash Univ-NCI 1991; Surgical Oncology, Meml Sloan-Kettering Cancer Ctr 1996; **Fac Appt:** Prof S, Univ Iowa Coll Med

Hurst, Roger D MD [S] - **Spec Exp:** Gastrointestinal Surgery; Inflammatory Bowel Disease/Crohn's; Gastrointestinal Cancer; Ulcerative Colitis; **Hospital:** Univ of Chicago Med; **Address:** Univ Chicago Med Ctr, Dept Surg, 5841 S Maryland Ave, rm G201, MC 5093, Chicago, IL 60637; **Phone:** 773-834-3524; **Board Cert:** Surgery 2007; **Med School:** Univ Chicago-Pritzker Sch Med 1983; **Resid:** Surgery, Univ Chicago Med Ctr 1989; **Fac Appt:** Prof S, Univ Chicago-Pritzker Sch Med

Ikramuddin, Sayeed MD [S] - **Spec Exp:** Minimally Invasive Surgery; Obesity/Bariatric Surgery; **Hospital:** Univ Minn Med Ctr, Fairview - West Bank Campus; **Address:** Univ Minn Med Ctr, Fairview, P Wagenstein Bldg, Fl 1, Clin 1E-MMC88, 516 Delaware St SE, Minneapolis, MN 55454; **Phone:** 612-625-8446; **Board Cert:** Surgery 2007; **Med School:** Albany Med Coll 1990; **Resid:** Surgery, SUNY Hlth Sci Ctr 1992; Surgery, SUNY Hlth Sci Ctr 1996; **Fellow:** Research, SUNY Hlth Sci Ctr 1993; Laparoscopic Surgery, Ohio State Univ Affil Hosp 1997; **Fac Appt:** Assoc Prof S, Univ Minn

Kagan, Richard J MD [S] - **Spec Exp:** Burn Care; **Hospital:** Cincinnati Shriners Hosp, Univ Cincinnati Med Ctr; **Address:** Cincinnati Shriners Hosp, 3229 Burnet Ave, Cincinnati, OH 45229; **Phone:** 513-872-6210; **Board Cert:** Surgery 2007; **Med School:** St Louis Univ 1974; **Resid:** Surgery, Univ IL Hosp 1980; **Fac Appt:** Prof S, Univ Cincinnati

Kaufman, Dixon MD/PhD [S] - **Spec Exp:** Transplant Surgery; Transplant-Kidney; Transplant-Pancreas; **Hospital:** Univ WI Hosp & Clins; **Address:** Univ WI Hosps & Clinics-Transplant Surg, 600 Highland Ave, Madison, WI 53792; **Phone:** 608-263-1385; **Board Cert:** Surgery 2010; **Med School:** Univ Minn 1983; **Resid:** Surgery, Univ MN Hosp 1991; **Fellow:** Transplant Surgery, Univ MN Hosp 1992; **Fac Appt:** Prof S, Univ Wisc

Kaufman, Howard L MD [S] - **Spec Exp:** Cancer Surgery; Melanoma; Immunotherapy; Vaccine Therapy; **Hospital:** Rush Univ Med Ctr; **Address:** 1725 W Harrison St, Ste 845, Chicago, IL 60612-3244; **Phone:** 312-942-0600; **Board Cert:** Surgery 2007; **Med School:** Loyola Univ-Stritch Sch Med 1986; **Resid:** Surgery, Boston Univ Hosp 1995; **Fellow:** Surgical Oncology, Natl Cancer Inst 1996; **Fac Appt:** Prof S, Loyola Univ-Stritch Sch Med

Kendrick, Michael L MD [S] - **Spec Exp:** Pancreatic Cancer; Liver Cancer; Hepatobiliary Surgery; Laparoscopic Surgery; **Hospital:** Mayo Med Ctr & Clin - Rochester; **Address:** Mayo Clinic Atten: Dept of Surgery, 200 First St SW, Rochester, MN 55905; **Phone:** 507-284-0362; **Board Cert:** Surgery 2004; **Med School:** Geo Wash Univ 1997; **Resid:** Surgery, Mayo Clinic 2003; **Fellow:** Hepatopancreatobiliary Surgery, Mayo Clinic 2004; Laparoscopic Surgery, Mt Sinai Med Ctr 2005; **Fac Appt:** Assoc Prof S, Mayo Med Sch

Kim, Julian A MD [S] - **Spec Exp:** Melanoma; Breast Cancer; Gastrointestinal Cancer; Immunotherapy; **Hospital:** UH Case Med Ctr; **Address:** 11100 Euclid Ave, Cleveland, OH 44106; **Phone:** 216-844-8247; **Board Cert:** Surgery 2012; **Med School:** Med Univ Ohio at Toledo 1986; **Resid:** Surgery, Univ Maryland Hosps 1991; **Fellow:** Surgical Oncology, Arthur James Cancer Hosp & Rsch Inst 1993; Immunotherapy, Ohio State Univ Comp Cancer Ctr 1994; **Fac Appt:** Prof S, Case West Res Univ

Kuo, Paul C MD [S] - **Spec Exp:** Transplant Surgery; Hepatobiliary Surgery; Cancer Surgery; Transplant-Kidney; **Hospital:** Loyola Univ Med Ctr; **Address:** Loyola Univ Med Ctr, 2160 S 1st Ave, Maywood, IL 60153; **Phone:** 708-216-3581; **Board Cert:** Surgery 2010; Surgical Critical Care 2012; **Med School:** Johns Hopkins Univ 1985; **Resid:** Surgery, Brigham & Women's Hosp 1991; **Fellow:** Transplant Surgery, Beth Israel/Deaconess Med Ctr; Hepatobiliary Surgery, Beth Israel/Deaconess Med Ctr; **Fac Appt:** Prof S, Loyola Univ-Stritch Sch Med

Leeming, Rosemary A MD [S] - **Spec Exp:** Breast Cancer & Surgery; Breast Disease; Clinical Trials; **Hospital:** UH Case Med Ctr; **Address:** 3909 Orange Pl, Ste 4400, Orange Village, OH 44122; **Phone:** 216-591-1909; **Board Cert:** Surgery 2009; **Med School:** Hahnemann Univ 1983; **Resid:** Surgery, Mt Sinai Med Ctr 1989; **Fellow:** Breast Disease, Univ Pitts-Shadyside Hosp 1989; **Fac Appt:** Asst Prof S, Case West Res Univ

Mahvi, David M MD [S] - **Spec Exp:** Gastrointestinal Cancer & Surgery; Liver Cancer; Pancreatic Cancer; **Hospital:** Northwestern Meml Hosp; **Address:** Northwestern Memorial Hospital, 675 N St Clair, Galter 21-100, Chicago, IL 60611; **Phone:** 312-695-0990; **Board Cert:** Surgery 2007; **Med School:** Med Univ SC 1981; **Resid:** Surgery, Duke Univ Med Ctr 1989; **Fac Appt:** Prof S, Northwestern Univ

Marks, Jeffrey M MD [S] - **Spec Exp:** Gastrointestinal Surgery; Endoscopy; Laparoscopic Surgery; Natural Orifice Surgery (NOTES); **Hospital:** UH Case Med Ctr; **Address:** Univ Hosp Case Medical Ctr, Dept Surgery, 11100 Euclid Ave, Cleveland, OH 44106; **Phone:** 216-844-7874; **Board Cert:** Surgery 2012; **Med School:** Tufts Univ 1987; **Resid:** Surgery, Mt Sinai Hosp 1992; **Fellow:** Advanced Endoscopy, Mt Sinai Hosp 1992; **Fac Appt:** Prof S, Case West Res Univ

Matas, Arthur J MD [S] - **Spec Exp:** Transplant-Kidney; **Hospital:** Univ Minn Med Ctr, Fairview - West Bank Campus; **Address:** Univ Minn Med Ctr, Dept Surg, 420 Delaware St SE, MMC 328, Minneapolis, MN 55455; **Phone:** 612-624-1927; **Board Cert:** Surgery 2010; **Med School:** Univ Manitoba 1972; **Resid:** Surgery, Univ Minn Hosps 1979; **Fellow:** Transplant Surgery, Univ Minn Hosps 1980; **Fac Appt:** Prof S, Univ Minn

Matthews, Jeffrey B MD [S] - **Spec Exp:** Gastrointestinal Surgery; Pancreatic Surgery; Liver & Biliary Surgery; **Hospital:** Univ of Chicago Med; **Address:** 5841 S Maryland Ave, Ste 0220, Chicago, IL 60637; **Phone:** 773-702-0881; **Board Cert:** Surgery 2012; **Med School:** Harvard Med Sch 1985; **Resid:** Surgery, Beth Israel Hosp 1990; **Fellow:** Hepatobiliary Surgery, Univ Bern 1989; **Fac Appt:** Prof S, Univ Chicago-Pritzker Sch Med

McHenry, Christopher R MD [S] - **Spec Exp:** Adrenal Surgery; Thyroid Surgery; Parathyroid Surgery; **Hospital:** MetroHealth Med Ctr; **Address:** MetroHealth Med Ctr, Dept Surgery, 2500 MetroHealth Drive, Cleveland, OH 44109; **Phone:** 216-778-4753; **Board Cert:** Surgery 2009; **Med School:** NE Ohio Univ 1984; **Resid:** Surgery, Loyola Univ Med Ctr 1989; **Fellow:** Endocrinology, Univ Toronto Med Ctr 1990; Head and Neck Surgery, Univ Toronto Med Ctr 1990; **Fac Appt:** Prof S, Case West Res Univ

Mellinger, John D MD [S] - **Spec Exp:** Gastrointestinal Surgery; Laparoscopic Surgery; Endoscopy; Pancreatic/Biliary Endoscopy (ERCP); **Hospital:** Memorial Med Ctr-Springfield; **Address:** Memorial Baylis Bldg, 747 N Rutledge St Fl 5, Springfield, IL 62702; **Phone:** 217-545-8000; **Board Cert:** Surgery 2009; **Med School:** Case West Res Univ 1984; **Resid:** Surgery, Blodgett-St Marys Hosp 1989; **Fellow:** Surgical Endoscopy, Mt Sinai/Case West Res 1990; **Fac Appt:** Prof S, Southern IL Univ

Melvin, W. Scott MD [S] - **Spec Exp:** Liver & Biliary Surgery; Pancreatic Cancer; Laparoscopic Surgery; **Hospital:** OSU Wexner Med Ctr; **Address:** 410 W 10th Ave, rm N729, North Doan Hall, Columbus, OH 43210; **Phone:** 614-293-4499; **Board Cert:** Surgery 2012; **Med School:** Med Coll OH 1987; **Resid:** Surgery, Univ Maryland 1992; **Fellow:** Gastrointestinal Surgery, Grant Med Ctr 1993; **Fac Appt:** Prof S, Ohio State Univ

Millis, J Michael MD [S] - **Spec Exp:** Transplant-Liver-Adult & Pediatric; Liver Cancer; Transplant-Pancreas; Liver Disease; **Hospital:** Univ of Chicago Med; **Address:** Univ Chicago Med Ctr, Dept Surg, 5841 S Maryland Ave, Chicago, IL 60637; **Phone:** 773-702-6319; **Board Cert:** Surgery 2011; Surgical Critical Care 2011; **Med School:** Univ Tenn Coll Med 1985; **Resid:** Surgery, UCLA Med Ctr 1991; **Fellow:** Transplant Surgery, UCLA Med Ctr 1994; **Fac Appt:** Prof S, Univ Chicago-Pritzker Sch Med

Moley, Jeffrey F MD [S] - **Spec Exp:** Thyroid Cancer & Surgery; Endocrine Cancers; Melanoma; **Hospital:** Barnes-Jewish Hosp; **Address:** 4921 Parkview Pl, St Louis, MO 63110; **Phone:** 314-362-2280; **Board Cert:** Surgery 2005; **Med School:** Columbia P&S 1980; **Resid:** Surgery, Yale-New Haven Hosp 1985; **Fellow:** Surgical Oncology, National Cancer Inst 1987; **Fac Appt:** Prof S, Washington Univ, St Louis

Nagorney, David M MD [S] - **Spec Exp:** Pancreatic Cancer; Hepatobiliary Surgery; Gastrointestinal Cancer; **Hospital:** Mayo Med Ctr & Clin - Rochester; **Address:** Mayo Clin, Dept Surgery, 200 1st St SW, Rochester, MN 55905; **Phone:** 507-284-0362; **Board Cert:** Surgery 2011; **Med School:** Univ Kansas 1975; **Resid:** Surgery, Mayo Clin 1982; **Fellow:** Hepatobiliary Surgery, Hammersmith Hosp 1985; **Fac Appt:** Prof S, Mayo Med Sch

Nathanson, S David MD [S] - **Spec Exp:** Breast Cancer; Breast Cancer Risk Assessment; Melanoma; Sarcoma; **Hospital:** Henry Ford- W Bloomfield Hosp, Henry Ford Hosp; **Address:** 6777 W Maple Rd, West Bloomfield, MI 48322; **Phone:** 248-661-6592; **Board Cert:** Surgery 2002; **Med School:** South Africa 1966; **Resid:** Surgery, Univ Witwaterstrand 1974; Surgical Oncology, UCLA Med Ctr 1980; **Fellow:** Surgery, UC Davis Med Ctr 1982; **Fac Appt:** Prof S, Wayne State Univ

Newman, Lisa A MD [S] - **Spec Exp:** Breast Cancer; **Hospital:** Univ Michigan Med Ctr; **Address:** Univ Michigan Cancer Center, 1500 E Medical Center Drive, SPC 5932, Ann Arbor, MI 48109-5932; **Phone:** 734-936-6000; **Board Cert:** Surgery 2011; **Med School:** SUNY Downstate 1985; **Resid:** Surgery, Downstate Med Ctr 1990; **Fac Appt:** Assoc Prof S, Univ Mich Med Sch

Oberholzer, Jose MD [S] - **Spec Exp:** Diabetes; Transplant-Pancreas; Pancreatic Islet Cell Transplant; Hepatobiliary Surgery; **Hospital:** Univ of IL Med Ctr at Chicago, Adv Luth Genl Hosp; **Address:** University of Illinois at Chicago, Div Transplant Surgery, 840 S Wood St CSB Bldg - Ste 402, MS 958, Chicago, IL 60612; **Phone:** 312-996-6771; **Med School:** Switzerland 1992; **Resid:** Surgery, Triemli Hosp 1996; Surgery, Univ Geneva Hosp 1998; **Fellow:** Transplant Surgery, Univ Geneva Hosp 2002; Hepatopancreatobiliary Surgery, Univ Alberta Hosp 2003; **Fac Appt:** Prof S, Univ IL Coll Med

Onders, Raymond P MD [S] - **Spec Exp:** Laparoscopic Surgery; Diaphragm Pacing via Laparoscopy; Gastrointestinal Cancer; **Hospital:** UH Case Med Ctr; **Address:** 11100 Euclid Ave, Cleveland, OH 44106; **Phone:** 216-844-5797; **Board Cert:** Surgery 2001; **Med School:** NE Ohio Univ 1988; **Resid:** Surgery, Case Western Res Univ Hosp 1993; **Fac Appt:** Assoc Prof S, NE Ohio Univ

Pollock, Raphael E MD/PhD [S] - **Spec Exp:** Sarcoma; **Hospital:** OSU Wexner Med Ctr; **Address:** OH State Univ Hosp, 410 W 10th Ave, Doan Hall, N924, Columbus, OH 43210; **Phone:** 614-293-7171; **Board Cert:** Surgery 2003; **Med School:** St Louis Univ 1977; **Resid:** Surgery, Univ Chicago Affil Hosps 1979; Surgery, Rush Univ Med Ctr 1982; **Fellow:** Surgical Oncology, UT MD Anderson Canc Ctr 1984; **Fac Appt:** Prof S, Ohio State Univ

Ponsky, Jeffrey L MD [S] - **Spec Exp:** Minimally Invasive Surgery; Gastrointestinal Surgery; Endoscopy; **Hospital:** UH Case Med Ctr; **Address:** Univ Hosp Case Med Ctr, Dept Surgery, 11100 Euclid Ave, Cleveland, OH 44106; **Phone:** 216-844-3209; **Board Cert:** Surgery 2007; **Med School:** Case West Res Univ 1971; **Resid:** Surgery, Univ Hosps 1976; **Fac Appt:** Prof S, Case West Res Univ

Posner, Mitchell C MD [S] - **Spec Exp:** Pancreatic Cancer; Gastrointestinal Cancer; Esophageal Cancer; **Hospital:** Univ of Chicago Med; **Address:** Univ Chicago Med Ctr, Dept Surg, 5841 S Maryland Ave, Ste G209, Chicago, IL 60637-1447; **Phone:** 773-834-4007; **Board Cert:** Surgery 2006; **Med School:** SUNY Buffalo 1981; **Resid:** Surgery, Univ Colorado Med Ctr 1986; **Fellow:** Surgical Oncology, Meml Sloan-Kettering Cancer Ctr 1988; **Fac Appt:** Prof S, Univ Chicago-Pritzker Sch Med

Reed, Alan I MD [S] - **Spec Exp:** Hepatobiliary Surgery; Transplant-Liver; Transplant-Kidney; Transplant-Pancreas; **Hospital:** Univ Iowa Hosp & Clins; **Address:** UIHC - Organ Transplant Ctr, 200 Hawkins Drive GH Bldg - Ste SE427, Iowa City, IA 52242-1009; **Phone:** 319-356-4778; **Board Cert:** Surgery 2010; **Med School:** Cornell Univ-Weill Med Coll 1984; **Resid:** Surgery, NY-Presby/Weill Cornell Med Ctr 1989; **Fellow:** Transplant Surgery, Univ Wisc Affil Hosp 1991; **Fac Appt:** Prof S, Univ Iowa Coll Med

Renz, John MD/PhD [S] - **Spec Exp:** Transplant-Liver; Transplant-Liver-Adult & Pediatric; Transplant Surgery; **Hospital:** Univ of Chicago Med, Univ Chicago Med-Comer Chldn's Hosp; **Address:** Univ Chicago Med Ctr-Surgery Dept, 5841 S Maryland Ave, MC 5027, Chicago, IL 60637; **Phone:** 773-702-4500; **Board Cert:** Surgery 2003; **Med School:** Jefferson Med Coll 1992; **Resid:** Surgery, UCSF Med Ctr 1999; **Fellow:** Transplant Surgery, UCLA Med Ctr 2002; **Fac Appt:** Prof S, Univ Chicago-Pritzker Sch Med

Rosen, Charles B MD [S] - **Spec Exp:** Transplant-Liver; Transplant-Bile Duct; Biliary Cancer; **Hospital:** Mayo Med Ctr & Clin - Rochester; **Address:** Mayo Clin, Dept Surg-Div Transplantation, 200 First St SW, Charlton 10A, Rochester, MN 55905-0001; **Phone:** 507-266-6640; **Board Cert:** Surgery 2009; **Med School:** Mayo Med Sch 1984; **Resid:** Surgery, Mayo Clin 1989; **Fellow:** Transplant Surgery, Mayo Clin 1991; **Fac Appt:** Prof S, Mayo Med Sch

Rosen, Michael J MD [S] - **Spec Exp:** Hernia; Gastrointestinal Surgery; Minimally Invasive Surgery; **Hospital:** UH Case Med Ctr; **Address:** Univ Hosp Case Med Ctr, 11100 Euclid Ave, LKS5047, Cleveland, OH 44106; **Phone:** 216-844-2763; **Board Cert:** Surgery 2005; **Med School:** USC-Keck School of Medicine 1997; **Resid:** Surgery, Mass Genl Hosp 2004; **Fellow:** Minimally Invasive Surgery, Cleveland Clin 2002; Laparoscopic Surgery, Carolinas Med Ctr 2005; **Fac Appt:** Asst Prof S, Case West Res Univ

Saha, Sukamal MD [S] - **Spec Exp:** Sentinel Node Surgery; Colon Cancer; Head & Neck Cancer & Surgery; **Hospital:** McLaren Flint, Genesys Reg Med Ctr - St Joseph Campus; **Address:** 3500 Calkins Rd, Ste A, Flint, MI 48532; **Phone:** 810-230-9600; **Board Cert:** Surgery 2010; **Med School:** India 1977; **Resid:** Surgery, Hahnemann Univ Hosp 1985; Surgery, Easton Hosp 1987; **Fellow:** Surgical Oncology, Tulane Univ Med Ctr 1989; Head and Neck Surgery, Roswell Park Meml Hosp 1990; **Fac Appt:** Asst Prof S, Mich State Univ

Sarr, Michael G MD [S] - **Spec Exp:** Pancreatic Cancer; Gastrointestinal Cancer; Obesity/Bariatric Surgery; Gastrointestinal Motility Disorders; **Hospital:** Mayo Med Ctr & Clin - Rochester; **Address:** Mayo Clinic, 200 First St SW, Rochester, MN 55905; **Phone:** 507-284-0362; **Board Cert:** Surgery 2001; **Med School:** Johns Hopkins Univ 1976; **Resid:** Surgery, Johns Hopkins Hosp 1982; **Fellow:** Surgery, Mayo Clinic 1984; Surgery, Johns Hopkins Hosp 1985; **Fac Appt:** Prof S, Mayo Med Sch

Schauer, Philip MD [S] - **Spec Exp:** Obesity/Bariatric Surgery; Minimally Invasive Surgery; **Hospital:** Cleveland Clin (page 55); **Address:** Cleveland Clinic, 9500 Euclid Ave, MC M61, Cleveland, OH 44195; **Phone:** 216-444-4794; **Board Cert:** Surgery 2004; **Med School:** Baylor Coll Med 1986; **Resid:** Surgery, Univ Texas Hlth Sci Ctr 1993; **Fellow:** Laparoscopic Surgery, Duke Univ Med Ctr 1995; **Fac Appt:** Prof S, Cleveland Cl Coll Med/Case West Res

Schwartzentruber, Douglas J MD [S] - **Spec Exp:** Cancer Surgery; Melanoma; Kidney Cancer; **Hospital:** IU Health Methodist Hosp, IU Hlth Univ Hosp; **Address:** Indiana Univ Hlth Cancer Services, 550 N University Blvd, AOC Bldg Fl 6 - Ste 6237, Indianapolis, IN 46202; **Phone:** 317-948-7449; **Board Cert:** Surgery 2008; **Med School:** Indiana Univ 1982; **Resid:** Surgery, Indiana Univ Med Ctr 1987; **Fellow:** Surgical Oncology, Natl Cancer Inst 1990; **Fac Appt:** Assoc Clin Prof S, Indiana Univ

Scott-Conner, Carol E H MD/PhD [S] - **Spec Exp:** Breast Cancer; Cancer Surgery; Laparoscopic Surgery; **Hospital:** Univ Iowa Hosp & Clins; **Address:** Univ Iowa Hosp & Clinics, Dept Surg, 200 Hawkins Drive JCP Bldg - rm 4622, Iowa City, IA 52242-1086; **Phone:** 319-356-0330; **Board Cert:** Surgery 2010; **Med School:** NYU Sch Med 1976; **Resid:** Surgery, NYU Med Ctr 1982; **Fac Appt:** Prof S, Univ Iowa Coll Med

Shenk, Robert R MD [S] - **Spec Exp:** Breast Cancer; Melanoma; Pancreatic Cancer; Stomach Cancer; **Hospital:** UH Case Med Ctr; **Address:** Univ Hosp Case Med Ctr, Dept Surgery, 11100 Euclid Ave, Cleveland, OH 44106; **Phone:** 216-844-3026; **Board Cert:** Surgery 2004; **Med School:** Case West Res Univ 1978; **Resid:** Surgery, Univ Hosp 1985; Immunology, Natl Cancer Inst 1982; **Fellow:** Surgical Oncology, MD Anderson Cancer Ctr 1987; **Fac Appt:** Assoc Prof S, Case West Res Univ

Sielaff, Timothy D MD/PhD [S] - **Spec Exp:** Liver Cancer; Pancreatic Cancer; Gallbladder & Biliary Cancer; **Hospital:** Abbott - Northwestern Hosp; **Address:** Virginia Piper Cancer Inst, Liver and Pancreas Clinic, 800 E 28th St, Minneapolis, MN 55407; **Phone:** 612-863-7553; **Board Cert:** Surgery 2008; **Med School:** Med Coll VA 1989; **Resid:** Surgery, Univ Minn Hosps 1997; **Fellow:** Transplant Surgery, Univ Toronto Affil Hosp 1998; **Fac Appt:** Assoc Prof S, Univ Minn

Simeone, Diane M MD [S] - **Spec Exp:** Pancreatic Cancer; Cancer Surgery; **Hospital:** Univ Michigan Med Ctr; **Address:** Univ Michigan Hlth Sys, 1500 E Med Ctr Drive, SPC 5343, Ann Arbor, MI 48109-5343; **Phone:** 734-936-5738; **Board Cert:** Surgery 2005; **Med School:** Duke Univ 1988; **Resid:** Surgery, Univ Mich Med Ctr 1995; **Fac Appt:** Prof S, Univ Mich Med Sch

Siperstein, Allan E MD [S] - **Spec Exp:** Laparoscopic Surgery; Endocrine Tumors; Thyroid & Parathyroid Cancer & Surgery; **Hospital:** Cleveland Clin (page 55); **Address:** Cleveland Clin, Dept Endocrine Surg F-20, 9500 Euclid Ave, Cleveland, OH 44195; **Phone:** 216-444-5664; **Board Cert:** Surgery 2007; **Med School:** Univ Tex SW, Dallas 1983; **Resid:** Surgery, UCSF Med Ctr 1990; **Fellow:** Research, UCSF Med Ctr 1988; **Fac Appt:** Prof S, Cleveland Cl Coll Med/Case West Res

Soper, Nathaniel MD [S] - **Spec Exp:** Laparoscopic Surgery; Gastroesophageal Reflux Disease (GERD); Biliary Surgery; Minimally Invasive Surgery; **Hospital:** Northwestern Meml Hosp; **Address:** Northwestern Med Faculty Fdn, 675 N St Clair St, Galter Bldg Fl 17 - Ste 1700, Chicago, IL 60611; **Phone:** 312-695-8918; **Board Cert:** Surgery 2005; **Med School:** Univ Iowa Coll Med 1980; **Resid:** Surgery, Univ Utah Hosps 1986; **Fellow:** Digestive Diseases, Mayo Clinic 1988; **Fac Appt:** Prof S, Northwestern Univ

Sundaram, Magesh MD [S] - **Spec Exp:** Gastrointestinal Cancer & Surgery; Pancreatic Cancer; Stomach Cancer; Liver & Biliary Cancer; **Hospital:** Carle Foundation Hosp; **Address:** Carle Cancer Ctr, 611 W Park St, Urbana, IL 61801; **Phone:** 217-383-3010; **Board Cert:** Surgery 2006; **Med School:** Univ MD Sch Med 1990; **Resid:** Surgery, Delaware Med Ctr 1995; **Fellow:** Surgical Oncology, Jackson Meml Hosp 1997; **Fac Appt:** Assoc Prof S, Univ IL Coll Med

Talamonti, Mark S MD [S] - **Spec Exp:** Pancreatic Cancer; Liver Cancer; Gastrointestinal Cancer & Surgery; Sarcoma; **Hospital:** Evanston Hosp/NorthShore Univ Hlth Sys (page 67), Glenbrook Hosp/NorthShore Univ Hlth Syst (page 67); **Address:** Northshore Medical Group, Kellog Cancer Ctr, 2560 Ridge Ave, Evanston, IL 60201; **Phone:** 847-570-1700; **Board Cert:** Surgery 2009; **Med School:** Northwestern Univ 1983; **Resid:** Surgery, Northwestern Meml Hosp 1989; **Fellow:** Surgical Oncology, MD Anderson Cancer Ctr 1991; **Fac Appt:** Clin Prof S, Univ Chicago-Pritzker Sch Med

Thistlethwaite, J Richard MD/PhD [S] - **Spec Exp:** Transplant-Kidney; Transplant-Pancreas; Transplant-Liver; Transplant Surgery-Pediatric; **Hospital:** Univ of Chicago Med; **Address:** 5841 S Maryland Ave, rm J-517, MC 5026, Chicago, IL 60637; **Phone:** 773-702-6319; **Board Cert:** Surgery 2008; **Med School:** Duke Univ 1977; **Resid:** Surgery, Mass Genl Hosp 1983; **Fellow:** Surgical Oncology, Natl Inst Hlth 1981; Transplant Surgery, Mass Genl Hosp 1984; **Fac Appt:** Prof S, Univ Chicago-Pritzker Sch Med

Tuttle, Todd M MD [S] - **Spec Exp:** Breast Cancer; Minimally Invasive Surgery; Cancer Surgery; **Hospital:** Univ Minn Med Ctr, Fairview - West Bank Campus; **Address:** Univ Minn, Dept Surgery, 420 Delaware St SE, MMC 195, Minneapolis, MN 55455; **Phone:** 612-273-5700; **Board Cert:** Surgery 2004; **Med School:** Johns Hopkins Univ 1988; **Resid:** Surgery, Med Coll Virginia Hosps 1994; **Fellow:** Surgical Oncology, MD Anderson Cancer Ctr 1996; **Fac Appt:** Assoc Prof S

Tzakis, Andreas G MD [S] - **Spec Exp:** Transplant-Liver; Transplant-Bowel; **Hospital:** Cleveland Clin (page 55); **Address:** Cleveland Clinic Transplant Ctr, 9500 Euclid Ave, Bldg A, Fl 10, Cleveland, OH 44195; **Phone:** 216-445-4793; **Board Cert:** Surgery 2012; **Med School:** Greece 1974; **Resid:** Surgery, Mount Sinai Hosp 1979; Surgery, SUNY Stony Brook 1983; **Fellow:** Transplant Surgery, Univ Pittsburgh 1985

Vickers, Selwyn M MD [S] - **Spec Exp:** Pancreatic Cancer; Liver Cancer; Gastrointestinal Surgery; **Hospital:** Univ Minn Med Ctr, Fairview - West Bank Campus; **Address:** University of Minnesota, 420 Delaware St SE, Phillips Wangensteen Bldg, MMC 195, Minneapolis, MN 55455; **Phone:** 612-626-1999; **Board Cert:** Surgery 2003; **Med School:** Johns Hopkins Univ 1986; **Resid:** Surgery, Johns Hopkins Hosp 1992; **Fellow:** NIH-Dept Aging 1987; **Fac Appt:** Prof S, Johns Hopkins Univ

Wakefield, Thomas MD [S] - **Spec Exp:** Thrombotic Disorders; Bleeding/Coagulation Disorders; Pulmonary Embolism; **Hospital:** Univ Michigan Med Ctr, VA Ann Arbor Healthcare Sys; **Address:** U of M Vascular Surg, Cardiovascular Ctr, Fl 5, 1500 E Med Ctr Drive, SPC5867, Ann Arbor, MI 48109; **Phone:** 734-936-5820; **Board Cert:** Surgery 2002; Vascular Surgery 2005; **Med School:** Med Coll OH 1978; **Resid:** Surgery, Univ Mich Med Ctr 1984; **Fellow:** Peripheral Vascular Surgery, Univ Mich Med Ctr 1986; **Fac Appt:** Prof S, Univ Mich Med Sch

Walker, Alonzo P MD [S] - **Spec Exp:** Breast Cancer; **Hospital:** Froedtert & Med Coll WI; **Address:** Clin Canc Ctr-Surgery Dept, 9200 W Wisconsin Ave, Milwaukee, WI 53226-3522; **Phone:** 414-805-5737; **Board Cert:** Surgery 2004; **Med School:** Univ Fla Coll Med 1976; **Resid:** Surgery, Univ Maryland Affil Hosps 1983; **Fac Appt:** Prof S, Med Coll Wisc

Walsh, R. Matthew MD [S] - **Spec Exp:** Pancreatic Cancer; Gastrointestinal Surgery; Hepatobiliary Surgery; **Hospital:** Cleveland Clin (page 55); **Address:** Cleveland Clin, Dept Surgery, 9500 Euclid Ave, Desk A100, Cleveland, OH 44195; **Phone:** 216-445-7576; **Board Cert:** Surgery 2009; **Med School:** Med Coll Wisc 1985; **Resid:** Surgery, Loyola Univ Hosp 1990; **Fellow:** Endoscopy, Mass Genl Hosp 1991; Hepatopancreatobiliary Surgery, Cleveland Clin 1991; **Fac Appt:** Assoc Prof S, Cleveland Cl Coll Med/Case West Res

Weber, Sharon M MD [S] - **Spec Exp:** Liver Cancer; Pancreatic Cancer; Gastrointestinal Cancer; Sarcoma; **Hospital:** Univ WI Hosp & Clins, Wm S Middleton Mem Vet Hosp-Madison; **Address:** 600 Highland Ave, Madison, WI 53792; **Phone:** 608-265-0500; **Board Cert:** Surgery 2009; **Med School:** Med Coll Wisc 1993; **Resid:** Surgery, UW Hosp & Clin 1999; **Fellow:** Surgical Oncology, Meml Sloan Kettering Cancer Ctr 2001; Hepatobiliary Surgery, Meml Sloan Kettering Cancer Ctr 2001; **Fac Appt:** Prof S, Univ Wisc

Weigel, Ronald J MD/PhD [S] - **Spec Exp:** Breast Cancer; Endocrine Surgery; **Hospital:** Univ Iowa Hosp & Clins; **Address:** University of IA, Carver College of Med, 200 Hawkins Drive, JCP Bldg, rm 1509, Iowa City, IA 52242; **Phone:** 319-353-7474; **Board Cert:** Surgery 2012; **Med School:** Yale Univ 1986; **Resid:** Surgery, Duke Univ Med Ctr 1988; Surgery, Duke Univ Med Ctr 1992; **Fellow:** Immunology, Duke Univ Med Ctr 1989; **Fac Appt:** Prof S, Univ Iowa Coll Med

Weigelt, John A MD [S] - **Spec Exp:** Trauma; Critical Care; **Hospital:** Froedtert & Med Coll WI; **Address:** Froedtert Hosp, Dept Surgery, 9200 W Wisconsin Ave, rm 295B, Milwaukee, WI 53226; **Phone:** 414-805-8636; **Board Cert:** Surgery 2010; Surgical Critical Care 2006; **Med School:** Med Coll Wisc 1974; **Resid:** Surgery, Univ Tex SW Affil Hosps 1980; **Fac Appt:** Prof S, Med Coll Wisc

Winchester, David J MD [S] - **Spec Exp:** Breast Cancer; **Hospital:** Evanston Hosp/NorthShore Univ Hlth Sys (page 67); **Address:** Northshore Medical Group, 1000 Central St, Ste 800, Evanston, IL 60201; **Phone:** 847-570-1700; **Board Cert:** Surgery 2011; **Med School:** Northwestern Univ 1986; **Resid:** Surgery, Northwestern Meml Hosp 1992; **Fellow:** Surgical Oncology, MD Anderson Cancer Ctr 1994; **Fac Appt:** Clin Prof S, Univ Chicago-Pritzker Sch Med

Witt, Thomas R MD [S] - **Spec Exp:** Breast Cancer; Breast Disease; **Hospital:** Rush Univ Med Ctr; **Address:** Surgical Oncology Group, 1725 W Harrison St, Ste 409, Chicago, IL 60612-3828; **Phone:** 312-942-2302; **Board Cert:** Surgery 2010; **Med School:** Northwestern Univ 1975; **Resid:** Surgery, Rush Presby-St Lukes Med Ctr 1980; **Fellow:** Surgical Oncology, Meml Sloan Kettering Cancer Ctr 1982; **Fac Appt:** Assoc Prof S, Rush Med Coll

Great Plains and Mountains

Edney, James A MD [S] - **Spec Exp:** Breast Cancer; Thyroid & Parathyroid Cancer & Surgery; Cancer Surgery; Melanoma; **Hospital:** Nebraska Med Ctr; **Address:** Univ Nebraska Med Ctr, Dept Surgery, 986345 Nebraska Medical Ctr, Omaha, NE 68198-4030; **Phone:** 402-559-7272; **Board Cert:** Surgery 2010; **Med School:** Univ Nebr Coll Med 1975; **Resid:** Surgery, Univ Nebraska Med Ctr 1980; **Fellow:** Surgical Oncology, Univ Colorado Med Ctr 1981; **Fac Appt:** Prof S, Univ Nebr Coll Med

Finlayson, Christina A MD [S] - **Spec Exp:** Breast Cancer & Surgery; Breast Disease; Gastrointestinal Cancer; Endocrine Surgery; **Hospital:** Univ Colorado Hosp; **Address:** Univ CO Hosp, GI Tumor & Endocrine Surg, 12631 E 17th Ave, Box C313, Aurora, CO 80045; **Phone:** 303-724-2728; **Board Cert:** Surgery 2004; **Med School:** Univ Utah 1989; **Resid:** Surgery, Univ Colorado Hosp 1994; **Fellow:** Surgical Oncology, Fox Chase Cancer Ctr 1996; **Fac Appt:** Prof S, Univ Colorado

Fitzgibbons Jr, Robert J MD [S] - **Spec Exp:** Abdominal Wall Reconstruction; Minimally Invasive Surgery; Gastrointestinal Surgery; Hernia; **Hospital:** Alegent Creighton Univ Med Ctr, Bergan Mercy Med Ctr-Alegant Hlth; **Address:** Creighton Univ, Dept Surgery, 601 N 30th St, Ste 3700, Omaha, NE 68131-2100; **Phone:** 402-280-4503; **Board Cert:** Surgery 2011; **Med School:** Creighton Univ 1974; **Resid:** Surgery, Charity Hosp/LA State Univ 1979; **Fellow:** Surgical Oncology, Lahey Clinic 1980; **Fac Appt:** Prof S, Creighton Univ

Loggie, Brian W MD [S] - **Spec Exp:** Mesothelioma; Solid Tumors; Melanoma; Pseudomyxoma Peritonei; **Hospital:** Alegent Creighton Univ Med Ctr; **Address:** 601 N 30th St, Ste 2803, Omaha, NE 68131; **Phone:** 402-280-5200; **Board Cert:** Surgery 2010; **Med School:** McGill Univ 1979; **Resid:** Surgery, Montreal Genl Hosp 1986; **Fellow:** Surgical Oncology, Univ Illinois 1988; **Fac Appt:** Prof S, Creighton Univ

McIntyre Jr, Robert C MD [S] - **Spec Exp:** Endocrine Surgery; Thyroid Cancer & Surgery; Critical Care; Gastrointestinal Cancer & Surgery; **Hospital:** Univ Colorado Hosp, Chldn's Hosp - Aurora (CO); **Address:** Univ CO, GI Tumor & Endocrine Surgery, 1635 Aurora Ct, Aurora, CO 80045; **Phone:** 303-724-2724; **Board Cert:** Surgery 2002; Surgical Critical Care 2003; **Med School:** Tulane Univ 1987; **Resid:** Surgery, Univ CO Hosp 1992; **Fac Appt:** Prof S, Univ Colorado

Mistry, Bhargav M MD [S] - **Spec Exp:** Transplant-Kidney; Transplant-Liver; Transplant-Pancreas; Trauma/Critical Care; **Hospital:** Sanford Med Ctr Fargo; **Address:** Sanford Health, Transplantation Surgery, 736 Broadway N, Fargo, ND 58122; **Phone:** 701-234-3400; **Board Cert:** Surgery 2009; Surgical Critical Care 2009; **Med School:** India 1984; **Resid:** Surgery, St Louis Univ Med Ctr 2000; **Fellow:** Surgical Critical Care, St Louis Univ 1995; Transplant Surgery, St Louis Univ 1998; **Fac Appt:** Assoc Clin Prof S, Univ ND Sch Med

Moore Jr, Ernest E MD [S] - **Spec Exp:** Liver Trauma; Aortic Injuries; Thoracic Aortic Surgery; Pelvic Surgery; **Hospital:** Denver Health Med Ctr, Yampa Valley Med Ctr; **Address:** Denver Hlth Med Ctr, Surgery Dept, 655 Broadway St, Ste 365, Denver, CO 80204; **Phone:** 303-602-7600; **Board Cert:** Surgery 2006; Surgical Critical Care 2006; **Med School:** Univ Pittsburgh 1972; **Resid:** Surgery, Univ VT Med Ctr 1976; **Fac Appt:** Prof S, Univ Colorado

Mulvihill, Sean J MD [S] - **Spec Exp:** Gastrointestinal Cancer; Liver & Biliary Cancer; Gastrointestinal Surgery; **Hospital:** Univ Utah Hlth Care; **Address:** University of Utah, Clinical Neurosciences Center, rm 5201, 175 N Medical Drive E, Salt Lake City, UT 84132; **Phone:** 801-581-4896; **Board Cert:** Surgery 2008; **Med School:** USC Sch Med 1981; **Resid:** Surgery, UCLA Med Ctr 1987; **Fac Appt:** Prof S, Univ Utah

Nelson, Edward W MD [S] - **Spec Exp:** Breast Cancer; **Hospital:** Univ Utah Hlth Care; **Address:** Univ Utah Med Ctr, Div Genl Surgery, 30 N 1900 E, rm 3B322, Salt Lake City, UT 84132; **Phone:** 801-581-7738; **Board Cert:** Surgery 2008; **Med School:** Univ Utah 1974; **Resid:** Surgery, Univ Utah Affil Hosps 1979; **Fac Appt:** Prof S, Univ Utah

Petelin, Joseph B MD [S] - **Spec Exp:** Laparoscopic Abdominal Surgery; **Hospital:** Shawnee Mission Med Ctr; **Address:** 9119 W 74th St, Ste 255, Shawnee Mission, KS 66204; **Phone:** 913-432-5420; **Board Cert:** Surgery 2010; **Med School:** Univ Kansas 1976; **Resid:** Surgery, Univ Kansas Hosp 1981; **Fac Appt:** Assoc Clin Prof S, Univ Kansas

Sasson, Aaron R MD [S] - **Spec Exp:** Gastrointestinal Cancer; Pancreatic Cancer; Liver Cancer; Neuroendocrine Tumors; **Hospital:** Nebraska Med Ctr; **Address:** 986345 Univ Nebraska Med Ctr, Omaha, NE 68198-4030; **Phone:** 402-559-8941; **Board Cert:** Surgery 2010; **Med School:** UMDNJ-NJ Med Sch, Newark 1993; **Resid:** Surgery, UCSD Med Ctr 1999; **Fellow:** Surgical Oncology, Fox Chase Cancer Ctr 2001; **Fac Appt:** Assoc Prof S, Univ Nebr Coll Med

Schulick, Richard D MD [S] - **Spec Exp:** Liver & Biliary Cancer; Pancreatic Cancer; Adrenal Tumors; Vaccine Therapy; **Hospital:** Univ Colorado Hosp; **Address:** Univ CO Hosp, Surgical Oncology Dept, 1665 Aurora Ct, rm 3337, Aurora, CO 80045; **Phone:** 720-848-3532; **Board Cert:** Surgery 2007; **Med School:** Johns Hopkins Univ 1989; **Resid:** Surgery, Johns Hopkins Hosp 1994; **Fellow:** Gastrointestinal Surgery, Johns Hopkins Hosp 1997; Surgical Oncology, Meml Sloan-Kettering Cancer Ctr 1999

Stiegmann, Gregory V MD [S] - **Spec Exp:** Gastrointestinal Surgery; Endoscopy; Pancreatic & Biliary Surgery; Liver Disease; **Hospital:** Univ Colorado Hosp; **Address:** Multi-Specialty Clinics, 1635 Aurora Court Fl 6, Aurora, CO 80045; **Phone:** 303-724-2728; **Board Cert:** Surgery 2003; **Med School:** Univ IL Coll Med 1975; **Resid:** Surgery, University Hosp 1982; **Fellow:** Gastrointestinal Surgery, Groote Schuur Hosp 1983; **Fac Appt:** Prof S, Univ Colorado

Traynor, Michael D MD [S] - **Spec Exp:** Endocrine Surgery; Thyroid & Parathyroid Surgery; Vascular Surgery; **Hospital:** Sanford Med Ctr Fargo; **Address:** MeritCare Broadway Health Ctr, 737 Broadway, Fargo, ND 58122; **Phone:** 701-234-2251; **Board Cert:** Surgery 2009; **Med School:** Univ ND Sch Med 1986; **Resid:** Surgery, Mayo Clinic 1991; **Fac Appt:** Clin Prof S, Univ ND Sch Med

Southwest

Ames, Frederick C MD [S] - **Spec Exp:** Breast Cancer; **Hospital:** UT MD Anderson Canc Ctr; **Address:** UT MD Anderson Canc Ctr, Dept Surgery, 1400 Pressler St Unit 1484, Houston, TX 77030-4009; **Phone:** 713-792-6929; **Board Cert:** Surgery 1975; **Med School:** Univ Tex Med Br, Galveston 1969; **Resid:** Surgery, UT Med Br(John Sealy Hosp) 1971; Surgery, St Joseph Hosp 1974; **Fellow:** Surgical Oncology, UT MD Anderson Canc Ctr 1975; **Fac Appt:** Prof S, Univ Tex, Houston

Babiera, Gildy V MD [S] - **Spec Exp:** Breast Cancer; **Hospital:** UT MD Anderson Canc Ctr; **Address:** UT MD Anderson Canc Ctr, Dept Surgical Oncology, 1515 Holcombe Blvd, Houston, TX 77030; **Phone:** 713-792-2121; **Board Cert:** Surgery 2007; **Med School:** NY Med Coll 1991; **Resid:** Surgery, NYU Langone Med Ctr 1995; Surgery, NYU Langone Med Ctr 1997; **Fellow:** Surgical Oncology, UT MD Anderson Canc Ctr 1996; **Fac Appt:** Prof Surg & Onc, Univ Tex, Houston

Beitsch, Peter D MD [S] - **Spec Exp:** Breast Cancer; **Hospital:** Med City Dallas Hosp; **Address:** Dallas Surgical Grp, 7777 Forrest Ln C Bldg - Ste 760, Dallas, TX 75230; **Phone:** 972-566-8039; **Board Cert:** Surgery 2012; **Med School:** Univ Tex SW, Dallas 1986; **Resid:** Surgery, UT Southwestern Med Ctr 1993; **Fellow:** Surgical Oncology, UT MD Anderson Canc Ctr 1990; Surgical Oncology, John Wayne Canc Inst 1994

Bentley, Frederick R MD [S] - **Spec Exp:** Transplant-Kidney; Colon Cancer; **Hospital:** UAMS Med Ctr; **Address:** 4301 W Markham St, Slot 520, Little Rock, AR 72205; **Phone:** 501-526-7053; **Board Cert:** Surgery 2006; **Med School:** Louisiana State U, New Orleans 1977; **Resid:** Surgery, LSU Med Ctr 1983; **Fellow:** Research, Univ Minnesota Affil Hosp 1982; Transplant Surgery, Univ Minnesota Affil Hosp 1984; **Fac Appt:** Assoc Prof S, Univ Louisville Sch Med

Blackstone, Robin S MD [S] - **Spec Exp:** Obesity/Bariatric Surgery; Laparoscopic Surgery; **Hospital:** Scottsdale Hlthcare - Shea; **Address:** Scottsdale Healthcare Bariatric Ctr, 10200 N 92nd St, Ste 101, Scottsdale, AZ 85258; **Phone:** 480-391-3885; **Board Cert:** Surgery 2005; **Med School:** Univ Tex, San Antonio 1988; **Resid:** Surgery, Univ Colorado Med Ctr 1993

Bolton, John S MD [S] - **Spec Exp:** Cancer Surgery; Esophageal Cancer; Pancreatic Cancer; Liver Cancer; **Hospital:** Ochsner Med Ctr-New Orleans; **Address:** Ochsner Clin, Dept Surg, 1514 Jefferson Hwy Fl 8, New Orleans, LA 70121; **Phone:** 504-842-4072; **Board Cert:** Surgery 2012; **Med School:** Louisiana State U, New Orleans 1976; **Resid:** Surgery, Charity Hosp 1981; **Fellow:** Hepatopancreatobiliary Surgery, Lahey Clinic 1980; Surgical Oncology, Meml Sloan Kettering Cancer Ctr 1982; **Fac Appt:** Asst Clin Prof S, Louisiana State U, New Orleans

Curley, Steven A MD [S] - **Spec Exp:** Colon & Rectal Cancer; Liver Cancer; Hepatobiliary Cancer; **Hospital:** UT MD Anderson Canc Ctr; **Address:** UT MD Anderson Canc Ctr, Dept Surg, 1515 Holcome Blvd, Unit 1484, Houston, TX 77230-1402; **Phone:** 713-792-2022; **Board Cert:** Surgery 2008; **Med School:** Univ Tex, Houston 1982; **Resid:** Surgery, Univ NM Affil Hosps 1988; **Fellow:** Surgical Oncology, UT MD Anderson Canc Ctr 1990; **Fac Appt:** Prof S, Univ Tex, Houston

Demarest III, Gerald B MD [S] - **Spec Exp:** Trauma; Burn Care; **Hospital:** Univ Hosp - New Mexico; **Address:** Univ New Mexico Surgical Clin, 2211 Lomas Blvd NE, Albuquerque, NM 87106; **Phone:** 505-272-2336; **Board Cert:** Surgery 2008; Surgical Critical Care 2005; **Med School:** Columbia P&S 1973; **Resid:** Surgery, Univ Washington Med Ctr 1976; **Fellow:** Burn Surgery, Harborview Med Ctr 1978; **Fac Appt:** Prof S, Univ New Mexico

Dooley, William C MD [S] - **Spec Exp:** Breast Cancer; Tumors-Rare & Multiple; Sarcoma; Melanoma; **Hospital:** OU Med Ctr, St. Anthony Hosp -Oklahoma City; **Address:** 825 NE 10th St, Ste 4500, Oklahoma City, OK 73104; **Phone:** 405-271-7867; **Board Cert:** Surgery 2010; **Med School:** Vanderbilt Univ 1982; **Resid:** Surgery, Johns Hopkins Hosp 1987; Surgical Oncology, Oxford Univ 1986; **Fellow:** Surgical Oncology, Johns Hopkins 1988; **Fac Appt:** Prof S, Univ Okla Coll Med

Dunkin, Brian J MD [S] - **Spec Exp:** Laparoscopic Surgery-Advanced; Gastroesophageal Reflux Disease (GERD); Hernia; Pancreatic/Biliary Endoscopy (ERCP); **Hospital:** Methodist Hosp - Houston; **Address:** 6550 Fannin St, SM 1601, Smith Tower Fl 16, Houston, TX 77030; **Phone:** 713-441-5141; **Board Cert:** Surgery 2008; **Med School:** Univ Nevada 1989; **Resid:** Surgery, George Washington Univ Hosp 1995; **Fellow:** Research, VA Admin Hosp 1996; Laparoscopic Surgery, Cleveland Clinic 1997; **Fac Appt:** Prof S, Univ Tex, Houston

Ellis, Lee M MD [S] - **Spec Exp:** Colon & Rectal Cancer; Metastatic Cancer; Peritoneal Carcinomatosis; **Hospital:** UT MD Anderson Canc Ctr; **Address:** MD Anderson Canc Ctr, Dept Surgery & Canc Bio, 1515 Holcombe Blvd, Unit 1484, Houston, TX 77030; **Phone:** 713-792-6926; **Board Cert:** Surgery 2009; **Med School:** Univ VA Sch Med 1983; **Resid:** Surgery, Shands Univ FL 1989; **Fellow:** Surgical Oncology, UT MD Anderson Canc Ctr 1991; **Fac Appt:** Prof S, Univ Tex, Houston

Euhus, David M MD [S] - **Spec Exp:** Breast Cancer; **Hospital:** UT Southwestern Med Ctr at Dallas; **Address:** Univ Hosp Ctr Breast Care, 2201 Inwood Rd Fl 3 - Ste 200, Dallas, TX 75390-9155; **Phone:** 214-645-4673; **Board Cert:** Surgery 2010; **Med School:** St Louis Univ 1984; **Resid:** Surgery, UCLA Ronald Reagan Med Ctr 1990; **Fellow:** Surgical Oncology, UCLA Ronald Reagan Med Ctr 1992; **Fac Appt:** Prof S, Univ Tex SW, Dallas

Feig, Barry W MD [S] - **Spec Exp:** Gastrointestinal Cancer; Sarcoma; Breast Cancer; **Hospital:** UT MD Anderson Canc Ctr; **Address:** UT MD Anderson Canc Ctr, Dept Surg Onc, 1515 Holcombe Blvd, Unit 1484, Houston, TX 77030; **Phone:** 713-792-2022; **Board Cert:** Surgery 2008; **Med School:** SUNY Upstate Med Univ 1984; **Resid:** Surgery, Northwestern Meml Hosp 1990; **Fellow:** Trauma, Univ Minn Affil Hosp 1991; Surgical Oncology, UT MD Anderson Canc Ctr 1994; **Fac Appt:** Prof S, Univ Tex, Houston

Fisher, William E MD [S] - **Spec Exp:** Pancreatic Cancer; **Hospital:** St. Luke's Episcopal Hosp-Houston; **Address:** 6620 Main St, Ste 1475, Houston, TX 77030; **Phone:** 832-355-1400; **Board Cert:** Surgery 2006; **Med School:** Univ Cincinnati 1990; **Resid:** Surgery, Ohio State Univ Affil Hosps 1997; **Fellow:** Cancer Research, Ohio State Univ Affil Hosps 1999; **Fac Appt:** Prof S, Baylor Coll Med

Franklin Jr, Morris E MD [S] - **Spec Exp:** Laparoscopic Surgery; Colon & Rectal Surgery; **Hospital:** Baptist Hlth Sys, Baptist Med Ctr - San Antonio; **Address:** TX Endosurgery Inst, 4242 E Southcross Blvd, Ste 1, San Antonio, TX 78222; **Phone:** 210-333-7510; **Board Cert:** Surgery 1973; **Med School:** Univ Tex SW, Dallas 1967; **Resid:** Surgery, Univ Hosp 1972; **Fac Appt:** Clin Prof S, Univ Tex, San Antonio

Friese, Randall S MD [S] - **Spec Exp:** Trauma; Critical Care; **Hospital:** Univ Arizona Med Ctr-Univ Campus; **Address:** University Med Ctr - Trauma, 1501 N Campbell Ave Fl 5, Tucson, AZ 85724; **Phone:** 520-694-6144; **Board Cert:** Surgery 2005; Surgical Critical Care 2012; **Med School:** Univ MD Sch Med 1990; **Resid:** Surgery, Univ Colorado Affil Hosp 1997; **Fellow:** Trauma/Critical Care, Univ Texas SW Med Ctr 2002; **Fac Appt:** Assoc Prof S, Univ Ariz Coll Med

Grant, Michael D MD [S] - **Spec Exp:** Breast Cancer; Breast Surgery; **Hospital:** Baylor Univ Med Ctr-Dallas; **Address:** Baylor Med Pavillion, 3900 Junius St, Ste 220, Dallas, TX 75246; **Phone:** 214-826-7300; **Board Cert:** Surgery 2001; **Med School:** Univ Tex, Houston 1987; **Resid:** Surgery, Baylor Univ Med Ctr 1992; **Fellow:** Breast Cancer, Baylor Univ Med Ctr 1993

Gray, Richard J MD [S] - **Spec Exp:** Cancer Surgery; Breast Cancer; Melanoma; Sarcoma; **Hospital:** Mayo Clinic - Phoenix, Mayo Clinic - Scottsdale; **Address:** Mayo Clinic-Surgical Oncology, 5777 E Mayo Blvd, Phoenix, AZ 85054; **Phone:** 480-342-2849; **Board Cert:** Surgery 2010; **Med School:** Mich State Univ 1995; **Resid:** Surgery, Mayo Clinic 2000; **Fellow:** Surgical Oncology, H Lee Moffitt Cancer Ctr 2002; **Fac Appt:** Assoc Prof S, Mayo Med Sch

Griswold Jr, John A MD [S] - **Spec Exp:** Burn Care; **Hospital:** Univ Med Ctr-Lubbock; **Address:** TX Tech Phys, Surgery, 3601 4th St Fl 4, MS 9905, Lubbock, TX 79414; **Phone:** 806-743-2373; **Board Cert:** Surgery 2009; Surgical Critical Care 2011; **Med School:** Creighton Univ 1981; **Resid:** Surgery, TX Tech Univ Hlth Scis Ctr 1986; **Fellow:** Burn Surgery, Univ Wash Med Ctr 1988

Halff, Glenn A MD [S] - **Spec Exp:** Transplant-Liver; Liver Surgery; Pancreatic Surgery; **Hospital:** Univ Hosp-San Antonio, Christus Santa Rosa Children's Hosp; **Address:** UT Transplant Ctr, 7703 Floyd Curl Drive, MC 7858, San Antonio, TX 78229; **Phone:** 210-567-5771; **Board Cert:** Surgery 2007; Surgical Critical Care 2011; **Med School:** Univ Tex, Houston 1983; **Resid:** Surgery, NYU Med Ctr 1987; **Fellow:** Transplant Surgery, UPMC 1989; **Fac Appt:** Prof S, Univ Tex, San Antonio

Holcomb, John B MD [S] - **Spec Exp:** Trauma; **Hospital:** Meml Hermann Hosp - Texas Med Ctr; **Address:** UT Hlth, Surgery Dept, 6431 Fannin St, MSB 4.170, Houston, TX 77030; **Phone:** 713-500-7218; **Board Cert:** Surgery 2012; Surgical Critical Care 2004; **Med School:** Univ Ark 1985; **Resid:** Surgery, William Beaumont AMC 1991; **Fellow:** Surgical Critical Care, Univ Hosp 2002; **Fac Appt:** Prof S, Univ Tex, Houston

Hollingsworth, Alan B MD [S] - **Spec Exp:** Breast Cancer Risk Assessment; Breast Cancer Genetics; **Hospital:** Mercy Hlth Ctr - Oklahoma City; **Address:** 4300 McAuley Blvd, Oklahoma City, OK 73120; **Phone:** 405-936-5455; **Board Cert:** Surgery 2009; **Med School:** Univ Okla Coll Med 1975; **Resid:** Surgery, Univ Oklahoma Hlth Sci Ctr 1980; **Fellow:** Anatomic Pathology, UCLA Med Ctr 1978; **Fac Appt:** Prof S, Univ Okla Coll Med

Hunt, Kelly K MD [S] - **Spec Exp:** Breast Cancer; Sarcoma-Soft Tissue; **Hospital:** UT MD Anderson Canc Ctr; **Address:** UT MD Anderson Canc Ctr, 1400 Pressler St, Unit 1484, Houston, TX 77030-4000; **Phone:** 713-792-7216; **Board Cert:** Surgery 2001; **Med School:** Univ Tenn Coll Med 1986; **Resid:** Surgery, UCLA Ronald Reagan Med Ctr 1993; **Fellow:** Surgical Oncology, UT MD Anderson Canc Ctr 1996; **Fac Appt:** Prof S, Univ Tex, Houston

Huth, James F MD [S] - **Spec Exp:** Melanoma; Skin Cancer; Vaccine Therapy; Sarcoma-Soft Tissue; **Hospital:** UT Southwestern Med Ctr at Dallas; **Address:** Univ Hosp Ctr Breast Care, 2201 Inwood Rd Fl 3 - Ste 200, Dallas, TX 75390-9125; **Phone:** 214-645-4673; **Board Cert:** Surgery 2010; **Med School:** Univ Rochester 1975; **Resid:** Surgery, Univ Wash Med Ctr 1980; **Fellow:** Surgical Oncology, UCLA Ronald Reagan Med Ctr 1981; **Fac Appt:** Prof S, Univ Tex SW, Dallas

Jackson, Gilchrist L MD [S] - **Spec Exp:** Thyroid & Parathyroid Surgery; Head & Neck Cancer & Surgery; Laparoscopic Surgery; Gastrointestinal Cancer; **Hospital:** St. Luke's Episcopal Hosp-Houston, Woman's Hosp TX; **Address:** Kelsey-Seybold Clin, 2727 W Holcombe Blvd Fl 3-A, Houston, TX 77025; **Phone:** 713-442-1132; **Board Cert:** Surgery 2008; **Med School:** Univ Louisville Sch Med 1974; **Resid:** Surgery, Parkland Hosp 1979; **Fellow:** Surgical Oncology, UT MD Anderson Canc Ctr 1980; **Fac Appt:** Assoc Clin Prof S, Baylor Coll Med

Jayaseelan, Nirmal S MD [S] - **Spec Exp:** Obesity/Bariatric Surgery; **Hospital:** Med City Dallas Hosp; **Address:** 11970 N Central Expy, Ste 670, Dallas, TX 75243; **Phone:** 972-331-1111; **Board Cert:** Surgery 2011; **Med School:** Texas Tech Univ 1994; **Resid:** Surgery, Emanuel Hosp 1999

Kim, Lawrence Thomas MD [S] - **Spec Exp:** Endocrine Surgery; Thyroid Cancer; Parathyroid Surgery; **Hospital:** UAMS Med Ctr; **Address:** 4301 W Markham, Slot 725, Little Rock, AR 72205; **Phone:** 501-296-5547; **Board Cert:** Surgery 2005; **Med School:** Univ Tex SW, Dallas 1987; **Resid:** Surgery, South Western Med Ctr 1994; **Fellow:** Research, South Western Med Ctr 1991; Research, Natl Inst Health 1996; **Fac Appt:** Prof S, Univ Ark

Klimberg, Vicki Suzanne MD [S] - **Spec Exp:** Breast Cancer; Radiofrequency Tumor Ablation; Sentinel Node Surgery; **Hospital:** UAMS Med Ctr; **Address:** Univ Arkansas Medical Sciences, 4301 W Markham, Slot 725, Little Rock, AR 72205-7199; **Phone:** 501-686-5669; **Board Cert:** Surgery 2007; **Med School:** Univ Fla Coll Med 1984; **Resid:** Surgery, Univ Fla Med Ctr 1989; **Fellow:** Clinical Oncology, Univ Fla 1990; Breast Disease, Univ Arkansas for Med Scis 1991; **Fac Appt:** Prof S, Univ Ark

Krouse, Robert S MD [S] - **Spec Exp:** Cancer Surgery; Gastrointestinal Cancer; **Hospital:** Southern AZ VA Health Care Sys - Tucson; **Address:** Southern AZ VA Health Care System, 3601 S 6th Ave, Tucson, AZ 85723-0001; **Phone:** 520-792-1450 x6145; **Board Cert:** Surgery 2007; Hospice & Palliative Medicine 2012; **Med School:** Hahnemann Univ 1991; **Resid:** Surgery, U HI Integrated Surg Prog 1993; Surgery, W Virginia Univ Sch Med 1997; **Fellow:** Immunotherapy, Natl Cancer Inst 1993; Surgical Oncology, City of Hope Natl Med Ctr 2000; **Fac Appt:** Prof S, Univ Ariz Coll Med

Kuhn, Joseph A MD [S] - **Spec Exp:** Liver Cancer; Peritoneal Carcinomatosis; Melanoma; Thyroid Cancer; **Hospital:** Baylor Univ Med Ctr-Dallas; **Address:** WLS Surgical Assocs, 7777 Forest Ln, Ste C-400, Dallas, TX 75230; **Phone:** 214-823-5000; **Board Cert:** Surgery 2009; Surgical Critical Care 2003; **Med School:** Univ Tex Med Br, Galveston 1984; **Resid:** Surgery, Baylor Univ Med Ctr 1989; **Fellow:** Surgical Oncology, City of Hope Natl Med Ctr 1992

Lee, Jeffrey E MD [S] - **Spec Exp:** Melanoma; Pancreatic Cancer; Endocrine Tumors; Adrenal Cancer; **Hospital:** UT MD Anderson Canc Ctr; **Address:** UT MD Anderson Cancer Ctr, 1400 Pressler St, FCT Bldg, rm 17.6000, Unit 1484, Houston, TX 77030-4009; **Phone:** 713-792-7218; **Board Cert:** Surgery 2010; **Med School:** Stanford Univ 1984; **Resid:** Surgery, Stanford Univ Hosp 1987; Surgery, Stanford Univ Hosp 1991; **Fellow:** Immunology, Stanford Univ 1989; Surgical Oncology, UT-MD Anderson Cancer Ctr 1993; **Fac Appt:** Prof S, Univ Tex, Houston

Leitch, A. Marilyn MD [S] - **Spec Exp:** Breast Cancer & Surgery; Melanoma; Sarcoma; **Hospital:** UT Southwestern Med Ctr at Dallas; **Address:** Univ Hosp Ctr Breast Care, 2201 Inwood Rd Fl 3 - Ste 200, Dallas, TX 75390-9125; **Phone:** 214-645-4673; **Board Cert:** Surgery 2003; **Med School:** Univ Tex SW, Dallas 1978; **Resid:** Surgery, UCLA Ronald Reagan Med Ctr 1984; **Fellow:** Surgical Oncology, UT MD Anderson Canc Ctr 1985; **Fac Appt:** Prof S, Univ Tex SW, Dallas

Lentz, Christopher W MD [S] - **Spec Exp:** Burn Care; Trauma; Critical Care; Wound Healing/Care; **Hospital:** Univ Hosp - New Mexico; **Address:** Univ New Mexico Surgical Clin, 2211 Lomas Blvd NE, Albuquerque, NM 87131-0001; **Phone:** 505-272-2336; **Board Cert:** Surgery 2005; Surgical Critical Care 2006; **Med School:** Wayne State Univ 1988; **Resid:** Surgery, Med Coll Wisc 1994; **Fellow:** Surgical Critical Care, Univ N Carolina Med Ctr 1995; Burn Surgery, Univ N Carolina Med Ctr 1996; **Fac Appt:** Assoc Prof S, Univ Rochester

Li, Benjamin D L MD [S] - **Spec Exp:** Gastrointestinal Cancer; Sarcoma; Breast Cancer; **Hospital:** Willis-Knighton Med Ctr; **Address:** LSU Hlth Scis Ctr, Dept Surgery, 1501 Kings Hwy, Shreveport, LA 71103; **Phone:** 318-675-6100; **Board Cert:** Surgery 2012; **Med School:** Yale Univ 1986; **Resid:** Surgery, Northwestern Univ-McGraw Med Ctr 1992; **Fellow:** Surgical Oncology, Roswell Park Cancer Inst 1995; **Fac Appt:** Prof S, Louisiana State U, New Orleans

Mansfield, Paul F MD [S] - **Spec Exp:** Appendix Cancer; Stomach Cancer; Colon Cancer; Melanoma; **Hospital:** UT MD Anderson Canc Ctr; **Address:** UT MD Anderson Canc Ctr, 1400 Pressler St, Unit 1485, Houston, TX 77030; **Phone:** 713-794-5499; **Board Cert:** Surgery 2006; **Med School:** Jefferson Med Coll 1983; **Resid:** Surgery, Pennsylvania Hosp-UPHS 1988; **Fellow:** Surgical Oncology, UT MD Anderson Canc Ctr 1991; **Fac Appt:** Prof Surg & Onc, Univ Tex, Houston

McCabe, Daniel P MD [S] - **Spec Exp:** Cancer Surgery; Melanoma; Gastrointestinal Cancer; **Hospital:** Tucson Med Ctr; **Address:** Southwestern Surgical Assocs, 1951 N Wilmot Rd, Tucson, AZ 85712; **Phone:** 520-795-5845; **Board Cert:** Surgery 2002; **Med School:** Creighton Univ 1979; **Resid:** Surgery, St Joseph Hosp 1982; Surgery, Baystate Med Ctr 1984; **Fellow:** Surgical Oncology, James Cancer Ctr 1986; **Fac Appt:** Asst Clin Prof S, Univ Ariz Coll Med

Meric-Bernstam, Funda MD [S] - **Spec Exp:** Breast Cancer & Surgery; Clinical Trials; **Hospital:** UT MD Anderson Canc Ctr; **Address:** UT MD Anderson Canc Ctr, 1400 Holcombe Blvd, FC8.3044, Houston, TX 77030; **Phone:** 713-745-4453; **Board Cert:** Surgery 2007; **Med School:** Yale Univ 1991; **Resid:** Surgery, Univ MI Med Ctr 1998; **Fellow:** Surgical Oncology, UT MD Anderson Canc Ctr 2001; **Fac Appt:** Prof Surg & Onc, Univ Tex, Houston

Pisters, Peter MD [S] - **Spec Exp:** Pancreatic Cancer; Sarcoma-Soft Tissue; Gastrointestinal Cancer; **Hospital:** UT MD Anderson Canc Ctr; **Address:** UT MD Anderson Canc Ctr, 1515 Holcombe Blvd, Unit 1484, Houston, TX 77230-1402; **Phone:** 713-792-2022; **Board Cert:** Surgery 2001; **Med School:** Univ Western Ontario 1985; **Resid:** Surgery, Bellevue Hosp Ctr 1992; **Fellow:** Surgical Research, Meml Sloan-Kettering Canc Ctr 1989; Surgical Oncology, Meml Sloan-Kettering Canc Ctr 1994; **Fac Appt:** Prof S, Univ Tex, Houston

Pockaj, Barbara A MD [S] - **Spec Exp:** Cancer Surgery; Breast Cancer; Melanoma; Stomach Cancer; **Hospital:** Mayo Clinic - Phoenix, Mayo Clinic - Scottsdale; **Address:** Mayo Clinic-Surgery, 5777 E Mayo Blvd, Phoenix, AZ 85054; **Phone:** 480-342-2849; **Board Cert:** Surgery 2005; **Med School:** Vanderbilt Univ 1987; **Resid:** Surgery, Univ Hosps 1995; **Fellow:** Surgical Oncology, Natl Inst Hlth 1992; **Fac Appt:** Assoc Prof S, Mayo Med Sch

Postier, Russell G MD [S] - **Spec Exp:** Pancreatic Cancer; Pancreatic Cancer-Early Detection; Pancreatic Surgery; **Hospital:** OU Med Ctr; **Address:** OU Physicians, Dept Surgery, OU Physicians Bldg, 825 NE 10th St, Ste 4500, Oklahoma City, OK 73104; **Phone:** 405-271-1400; **Board Cert:** Surgery 2011; **Med School:** Univ Okla Coll Med 1975; **Resid:** Surgery, Johns Hopkins Hosp 1981; **Fac Appt:** Prof S, Univ Okla Coll Med

Rege, Robert V MD [S] - **Spec Exp:** Gastrointestinal Surgery; Laparoscopic Surgery; Hernia; **Hospital:** UT Southwestern Med Ctr at Dallas; **Address:** Multidisciplinary Surgery Clin, 1801 Inwood Rd Fl 7 - Ste 100, Dallas, TX 75390; **Phone:** 214-645-2900; **Board Cert:** Surgery 2010; **Med School:** Penn State Coll Med 1975; **Resid:** Surgery, Penn State Hershey Med Ctr 1976; Surgery, Penn State Hershey Med Ctr 1982; **Fac Appt:** Prof S, Univ Tex SW, Dallas

Rhee, Peter M MD [S] - **Spec Exp:** Trauma; Critical Care; **Hospital:** Univ Arizona Med Ctr-Univ Campus; **Address:** 1501 N Campbell Ave, Tucson, AZ 85274; **Phone:** 520-694-6144; **Board Cert:** Surgery 2012; Surgical Critical Care 2006; **Med School:** Uniformed Srvs Univ, Bethesda 1987; **Resid:** Surgery, UC Irvine Med Ctr 1992; **Fellow:** Trauma, Harborview Med Ctr 1995; **Fac Appt:** Prof S, Univ Ariz Coll Med

Ross, Merrick I MD [S] - **Spec Exp:** Sentinel Node Surgery; Breast Cancer; Melanoma; **Hospital:** UT MD Anderson Canc Ctr; **Address:** UT MD Anderson Canc Ctr, Dept Surgery, 1515 Holcombe Blvd, Unit 1484, Houston, TX 77030; **Phone:** 713-792-2022; **Board Cert:** Surgery 2007; **Med School:** Univ IL Coll Med 1980; **Resid:** Surgery, Univ IL Affil Hosps 1982; Surgery, Univ IL Affil Hosps 1987; **Fellow:** Research, Scripps Meml Hosp 1984; Surgical Oncology, UT MD Anderson Canc Ctr 1989; **Fac Appt:** Prof S, Univ Tex, Houston

Sauter, Edward R MD/PhD [S] - **Spec Exp:** Breast Cancer; Breast Cancer Risk Assessment; Clinical Trials; **Hospital:** Univ of Texas Hlth Sci Ctr at Tyler; **Address:** UTHSCT Cancer Treatment & Prevention Ctr, 11937 US Highway 271, Tyler, TX 75708-3154; **Phone:** 903-877-7826; **Board Cert:** Surgery 2010; **Med School:** Louisiana State U, New Orleans 1986; **Resid:** Surgery, Ochsner Fdn Hosp 1991; **Fellow:** Surgical Oncology, Fox Chase Cancer Ctr 1993; **Fac Appt:** Prof S, Univ ND Sch Med

Schlinkert, Richard T MD [S] - **Spec Exp:** Endocrine Surgery; Laparoscopic Surgery; Gastrointestinal Surgery; Adrenal Surgery; **Hospital:** Mayo Clinic - Phoenix; **Address:** Mayo Clin, Dept Surgery, 5779 E Mayo Blvd, Phoenix, AZ 85054; **Phone:** 480-342-1051; **Board Cert:** Surgery 2006; **Med School:** Med Coll OH 1981; **Resid:** Surgery, Mayo Clinic 1986; **Fellow:** Hepatobiliary Surgery, Royal Infirmary 1987; **Fac Appt:** Prof S, Mayo Med Sch

Scott, Daniel J MD [S] - **Spec Exp:** Laparoscopic Surgery-Advanced; Obesity/Bariatric Surgery; **Hospital:** UT Southwestern Med Ctr at Dallas; **Address:** Multidisciplinary Surgery Clinic, 1801 Inwood Rd, Fl 7 - Ste 100, Dallas, TX 75390-9971; **Phone:** 214-645-2900; **Board Cert:** Surgery 2012; **Med School:** Louisiana State U, New Orleans 1995; **Resid:** Surgery, UTSW Med Ctr 2000; **Fellow:** Laparoscopic Surgery, Univ Texas SW 2002; **Fac Appt:** Prof S, Univ Tex SW, Dallas

Skibber, John M MD [S] - **Spec Exp:** Rectal Cancer/Sphincter Preservation; Colon & Rectal Cancer-Familial Polyposis; **Hospital:** UT MD Anderson Canc Ctr; **Address:** UT MD Anderson Canc Ctr, Dept Surgical Oncology, 1515 Holcombe, Unit 1484, Houston, TX 77230-1402; **Phone:** 713-792-5165; **Board Cert:** Surgery 2009; **Med School:** Jefferson Med Coll 1981; **Resid:** Surgery, NYU Langone Med Ctr 1989; **Fellow:** Surgical Oncology, UT MD Anderson Canc Ctr 1991; **Fac Appt:** Prof S, Univ Tex, Houston

Staren, Edgar D MD/PhD [S] - **Spec Exp:** Breast Cancer; Endocrine Cancers; Liver Cancer; **Hospital:** CTCA at Western Regl Med Ctr; **Address:** Cancer Treatment Ctrs America, 14200 W Fillmore St, MS 85338, Goodyear, AZ 85338; **Phone:** 623-207-3007; **Board Cert:** Surgery 2006; **Med School:** Loyola Univ-Stritch Sch Med 1982; **Resid:** Surgery, Rush-Presby-St Lukes Med Ctr 1987; **Fellow:** Surgical Oncology, Rush-Presby-St Lukes Med Ctr 1988; **Fac Appt:** Clin Prof S, Rush Med Coll

Stewart, Ronald M MD [S] - **Spec Exp:** Trauma; **Hospital:** Univ Hosp-San Antonio; **Address:** UTHSCSA, Trauma Ctr, 7703 Floyd Curl Drive, MC 7740, San Antonio, TX 78229; **Phone:** 210-567-3623; **Board Cert:** Surgery 2009; Surgical Critical Care 2002; **Med School:** Univ Tex, San Antonio 1985; **Resid:** Surgery, UT Hlth Sci Ctr 1991; **Fellow:** Trauma, Univ Tenn Coll Med Affil Hosp 1993; **Fac Appt:** Prof S, Univ Tex, San Antonio

Stolier, Alan J MD [S] - **Spec Exp:** Breast Cancer; **Hospital:** St. Charles Surgical Hosp; **Address:** St Charles Surgical Hosp, 1717 St Charles Ave, New Orleans, LA 70130; **Phone:** 504-529-6600; **Board Cert:** Surgery 2006; **Med School:** Louisiana State U, New Orleans 1970; **Resid:** Surgery, Charity Hosp 1973; Surgery, Charity Hosp 1976; **Fellow:** Surgical Oncology, MD Anderson Inst 1974; Surgical Oncology, Hammersmith Hosp 1975; **Fac Appt:** Clin Prof S, Tulane Univ

Vauthey, Jean-Nicholas MD [S] - **Spec Exp:** Hepatobiliary Surgery; Liver Cancer; Gallbladder & Biliary Cancer; **Hospital:** UT MD Anderson Canc Ctr; **Address:** UT MD Anderson Cancer Ctr - Surg Oncology, 1515 Holcombe Blvd, Unit 1484, Houston, TX 77030; **Phone:** 713-792-2022; **Board Cert:** Surgery 2008; **Med School:** Switzerland 1979; **Resid:** Surgery, Ochsner Med Fdn 1989; **Fellow:** Hepatobiliary Surgery, Med Fac Univ Bern 1991; Surgical Oncology, Meml Sloan-Kettering Cancer Ctr 1993; **Fac Appt:** Prof S, Univ Tex, Houston

Woltering, Eugene MD [S] - **Spec Exp:** Neuroendocrine Tumors; **Hospital:** Ochsner Med Ctr-New Orleans; **Address:** Ochsner Med Ctr, 200 W Esplanade, Ste 200, Kenner, LA 70065; **Phone:** 504-464-8500; **Board Cert:** Surgery 2002; **Med School:** Ohio State Univ 1975; **Resid:** Surgery, Vanderbilt Med Ctr 1982; Surgical Oncology, Natl Inst Hlth 1979; **Fellow:** Surgical Oncology, Ohio State Univ 1984; **Fac Appt:** Prof S, Louisiana State U, New Orleans

Wood, R. Patrick MD [S] - **Spec Exp:** Liver Cancer; Biliary Surgery; Laparoscopic Surgery; **Hospital:** St. Luke's Episcopal Hosp-Houston; **Address:** Transplantation/Genl Surgery Assocs, 6624 Fannin St, Ste 1200, Houston, TX 77030; **Phone:** 713-795-8994; **Board Cert:** Surgery 2004; **Med School:** Univ Rochester 1979; **Resid:** Surgery, Bellevue Hosp Ctr 1985; **Fellow:** Transplant Surgery, UPMC 1986; **Fac Appt:** Clin Prof S, Univ Tex, Houston

Zannis, Victor J MD [S] - **Spec Exp:** Breast Cancer; Breast Surgery; **Hospital:** Phoenix Baptist Hosp & Med Ctr, J C Lincoln Hosp - North Mountain; **Address:** Breast Care Ctr, 2525 W Greenway Rd, Ste 130, Phoenix, AZ 85023; **Phone:** 602-942-8000; **Board Cert:** Surgery 2010; **Med School:** UCLA 1976; **Resid:** Surgery, Maricopa Med Ctr 1981

West Coast and Pacific

Anderson, Benjamin O MD [S] - **Spec Exp:** Breast Cancer & Surgery; **Hospital:** Univ Wash Med Ctr; **Address:** Seattle Canc Care Alliance, 825 Eastlake Ave E, Seattle, WA 98109; **Phone:** 206-288-2166; **Board Cert:** Surgery 2002; **Med School:** Albert Einstein Coll Med 1985; **Resid:** Surgery, Univ CO Affil Hosps 1992; **Fellow:** Surgical Oncology, Meml Sloan-Kettering Canc Ctr 1994; **Fac Appt:** Prof S, Univ Wash

Ascher, Nancy L MD/PhD [S] - **Spec Exp:** Transplant-Liver-Adult & Pediatric; Transplant-Kidney; Portal Hypertension; Liver Cancer; **Hospital:** UCSF Med Ctr; **Address:** 513 Parnassus Ave, Box 0104, San Francisco, CA 94143-0104; **Phone:** 415-476-1236; **Board Cert:** Surgery 2002; **Med School:** Univ Mich Med Sch 1974; **Resid:** Surgery, Univ Minn Hosp 1981; **Fellow:** Transplant Surgery, Univ Minn Hosp 1982; **Fac Appt:** Prof S, UCSF

Attai, Deanna J MD [S] - **Spec Exp:** Breast Cancer & Surgery; Breast Cancer Risk Assessment; **Hospital:** Providence St Joseph Med Ctr, Providence Tarzana Med Ctr; **Address:** Ctr for Breast Care, 191 S Buena Vista St, Ste 415, Burbank, CA 91505; **Phone:** 818-333-2555; **Board Cert:** Surgery 2004; **Med School:** Georgetown Univ 1990; **Resid:** Surgery, Georgetown Univ Hosp 1995

Bilchik, Anton J MD/PhD [S] - **Spec Exp:** Gastrointestinal Cancer; Laparoscopic Surgery; Cancer Surgery; **Hospital:** St. John's Hlth Ctr, Santa Monica, Cedars-Sinai Med Ctr; **Address:** 2200 Santa Monica Blvd, Ste 113, Santa Monica, CA 90404; **Phone:** 310-449-5206; **Board Cert:** Surgery 2004; **Med School:** South Africa 1985; **Resid:** Surgery, UCLA Med Ctr 1996; **Fellow:** John Wayne Cancer Inst. 1998; **Fac Appt:** Asst Clin Prof S, UCLA

Billingsley, Kevin MD [S] - **Spec Exp:** Cancer Surgery; Liver Tumors; Hepatobiliary Surgery; Pancreatic Surgery; **Hospital:** OR Hlth & Sci Univ; **Address:** Surgical Oncology Div, 3181 SW Sam Jackson Park Rd, MC L619, Portland, OR 97239; **Phone:** 503-494-5501; **Board Cert:** Surgery 2007; **Med School:** Johns Hopkins Univ 1989; **Resid:** Surgery, OR Hlth & Sci Univ 1996; **Fellow:** Surgical Oncology, Natl Canc Inst 1994; Surgical Oncology, Meml Sloan Kettering Canc Ctr 1998; **Fac Appt:** Prof S, Oregon Hlth & Sci Univ

Bouvet, Michael MD [S] - **Spec Exp:** Endocrine Surgery; Pancreatic Cancer; Biliary Cancer; Robotic Surgery; **Hospital:** UCSD Med Ctr, UCSD Thornton Hosp; **Address:** UCSD Moores Cancer Ctr, 3855 Health Science Drive, La Jolla, CA 92093-0987; **Phone:** 858-822-6191; **Board Cert:** Surgery 2004; **Med School:** Univ Wash 1989; **Resid:** Surgery, UCSD Med Ctr 1995; **Fellow:** Surgical Oncology, MD Anderson Cancer Ctr 1998; **Fac Appt:** Prof S, UCSD

Brunicardi, F Charles MD/PhD [S] - **Spec Exp:** Pancreatic Islet Cell Transplant; Pancreatic Cancer; Endocrine Surgery; **Hospital:** Santa Monica - UCLA Med Ctr & Ortho Hosp; **Address:** UCLA, Surgery Dept, 1304 15 St, Ste 102, Santa Monica, CA 90404; **Phone:** 310-394-7069; **Board Cert:** Surgery 2009; **Med School:** UMDNJ-Rutgers Med Sch 1980; **Resid:** Surgery, SUNY Downstate Med Ctr 1989; **Fellow:** Pancreatic Physiology, SUNY Downstate Med Ctr 1986; **Fac Appt:** Prof S, UCLA-David Geffen Sch Med

Busuttil, Ronald W MD/PhD [S] - **Spec Exp:** Transplant-Liver; Liver Cancer; Hepatobiliary Surgery; **Hospital:** UCLA Ronald Reagan Med Ctr; **Address:** 200 UCLA Medical Plaza, Ste 214, Los Angeles, CA 90095-7430; **Phone:** 310-825-5318; **Board Cert:** Surgery 2007; **Med School:** Tulane Univ 1971; **Resid:** Surgery, UCLA Med Ctr 1976; **Fellow:** Surgery, UCLA Med Ctr 1975; **Fac Appt:** Prof S, UCLA

Butler, John A MD [S] - **Spec Exp:** Breast Cancer; Thyroid Cancer; Adrenal Tumors; Small Bowel Cancer; **Hospital:** UC Irvine Med Ctr; **Address:** UC Irvine Med Ctr, 101 The City Drive S, Ste 203, Bldg 56, Rte 81, ZOT 5376, Orange, CA 92868-3298; **Phone:** 714-456-8030; **Board Cert:** Surgery 2003; **Med School:** Loyola Univ-Stritch Sch Med 1976; **Resid:** Surgery, LAC-USC Med Ctr 1982; Surgery, Harbor-UCLA Med Ctr 1982; **Fellow:** Surgical Oncology, Meml Sloan-Kettering Cancer Ctr 1984; **Fac Appt:** Prof S, UC Irvine

Byrd, David R MD [S] - **Spec Exp:** Cancer Surgery; Thyroid Cancer; Melanoma; Breast Cancer & Surgery; **Hospital:** Univ Wash Med Ctr; **Address:** Univ Washington Med Ctr, Dept Surgical Specialites Ctr, 1959 NE Pacific St, Box 356165, Seattle, WA 98195; **Phone:** 206-543-7512; **Board Cert:** Surgery 2008; **Med School:** Tulane Univ 1982; **Resid:** Surgery, Univ Wash Med Ctr 1988; **Fellow:** Surgical Oncology, UT MD Anderson Canc Ctr 1992; **Fac Appt:** Prof S, Univ Wash

Chang, Helena MD [S] - **Spec Exp:** Breast Cancer; Cancer Surgery; **Hospital:** UCLA Ronald Reagan Med Ctr; **Address:** 200 UCLA Medical Plaza, Ste B265-1, Los Angeles, CA 90024; **Phone:** 310-825-2144; **Med School:** Temple Univ 1981; **Resid:** Surgery, Episcopal Hosp 1986; **Fellow:** Cellular Molecular Biology, Temple Univ 1977; Surgical Oncology, Meml Sloan-Kettering Cancer Ctr 1988; **Fac Appt:** Prof S, UCLA

Clark, Orlo H MD [S] - **Spec Exp:** Thyroid Cancer & Surgery; Neuroendocrine Tumors; Parathyroid Cancer; **Hospital:** UCSF - Mt Zion Med Ctr, UCSF Med Ctr; **Address:** UCSF Mt Zion Med Ctr, 1600 Divisadero St, Fl 3, Box 1926, San Francisco, CA 94115-1926; **Phone:** 415-353-7687; **Board Cert:** Surgery 1974; **Med School:** Cornell Univ-Weill Med Coll 1967; **Resid:** Surgery, UCSF Med Ctr 1973; **Fellow:** Surgery, Royal Med Sch London 1971; **Fac Appt:** Prof S, UCSF

Colquhoun, Steven D MD [S] - **Spec Exp:** Liver Cancer; Transplant-Liver; Pancreatic Cancer; Hepatobiliary Surgery; **Hospital:** Cedars-Sinai Med Ctr; **Address:** Cedars-Sinai Med Center, 8635 W 3rd St, Ste 590-W, Los Angeles, CA 90048; **Phone:** 310-423-2641; **Board Cert:** Surgery 2003; Surgical Critical Care 2008; **Med School:** Loyola Univ-Stritch Sch Med 1984; **Resid:** Surgery, UCLA Med Ctr 1990; **Fellow:** Surgical Oncology, UCLA Med Ctr 1993; Transplant Surgery, UCLA Med Ctr 1994; **Fac Appt:** Assoc Clin Prof S, UCLA

Crookes, Peter F MD [S] - **Spec Exp:** Obesity/Bariatric Surgery; Laparoscopic Surgery; Gastroesophageal Reflux Disease (GERD); Esophageal Surgery; **Hospital:** Keck Med Ctr of USC; **Address:** USC Upper G.I. and General Surgery, 1510 San Pablo St, Ste 514, Los Angeles, CA 90033-4612; **Phone:** 323-442-6868; **Med School:** Ireland 1978; **Resid:** Surgery, Royal Victoria Hosp 1989; Surgery, St Vincent's Hosp 1990; **Fellow:** Esophageal Surgery, Univ SC Affil Hosp 1992; **Fac Appt:** Assoc Prof S, Univ SC Sch Med

Dawson, Patricia MD/PhD [S] - **Spec Exp:** Breast Surgery; Breast Cancer & Surgery; **Hospital:** Swedish Med Ctr-First Hill-Seattle; **Address:** Swedish Cancer Inst, True Family Women's Cancer Ctr, 1221 Madison St, Ste 600, Seattle, WA 98104; **Phone:** 206-320-6400; **Board Cert:** Surgery 2011; **Med School:** UMDNJ-NJ Med Sch, Newark 1977; **Resid:** Surgery, UMDNJ Affil Hosp 1979; Surgery, Virginia Mason Med Ctr 1982; **Fac Appt:** Asst Clin Prof S, Univ Wash

Dixon, Sherwood M MD [S] - **Spec Exp:** Wound Healing/Care; **Hospital:** Northern Nevada Med Ctr, Renown Reg Med Ctr; **Address:** Genl & Vascular Assocs, 1500 E 2nd St, Ste 206, Reno, NV 89502; **Phone:** 775-789-7000; **Board Cert:** Surgery 2009; **Med School:** UAB Sch Med 1976; **Resid:** Surgery, UC Davis Med Ctr 1981; **Fellow:** Vascular Surgery, UCLA Med Ctr 1982

Duh, Quan-Yang MD [S] - **Spec Exp:** Endocrine Surgery; Thyroid & Parathyroid Cancer & Surgery; Adrenal Tumors; Minimally Invasive Surgery; **Hospital:** UCSF Med Ctr, VA Med Ctr - San Francisco; **Address:** UCSF, Endocrine Surgl & Oncology Clin, 1600 Divisadero St Fl 3, Box 1926, San Francisco, CA 94115; **Phone:** 415-353-7687; **Board Cert:** Surgery 2007; **Med School:** UCSF 1981; **Resid:** Surgery, UCSF Med Ctr 1988; **Fellow:** Endocrine Surgery, UCSF Med Ctr 1987; **Fac Appt:** Prof S, UCSF

Easter, David W MD [S] - **Spec Exp:** Breast Cancer; Gastrointestinal Cancer; Minimally Invasive Surgery; **Hospital:** VA San Diego Hlthcre Sys; **Address:** VA San Diego Healthcare Sys, 3350 La Jolla Village Drive, San Diego, CA 92161; **Phone:** 858-552-8585 x3320; **Board Cert:** Surgery 2010; **Med School:** Yale Univ 1983; **Resid:** Surgery, UCSD Med Ctr 1989; **Fellow:** Surgical Oncology, Ninewells Hosp, Dundee 1990; **Fac Appt:** Clin Prof S, UCSD

Eilber, Frederick R MD [S] - **Spec Exp:** Sarcoma; **Hospital:** UCLA Ronald Reagan Med Ctr; **Address:** 200 UCLA Medical Plaza, Ste 120, Los Angeles, CA 90095; **Phone:** 310-825-7086; **Board Cert:** Surgery 1973; **Med School:** Univ Mich Med Sch 1965; **Resid:** Surgery, Univ Maryland Hosp 1972; **Fellow:** Surgery, Univ Tex-MD Anderson Hosp 1973; **Fac Appt:** Prof S, UCLA

Ellenhorn, Joshua D MD [S] - **Spec Exp:** Gastrointestinal Cancer; Breast Cancer; Cancer Surgery; **Hospital:** Cedars-Sinai Med Ctr, St. John's Hlth Ctr, Santa Monica; **Address:** 8635 W 3rd St, Ste 1090W, Los Angeles, CA 90048; **Phone:** 310-659-9011; **Board Cert:** Surgery 2010; **Med School:** Boston Univ 1984; **Resid:** Surgery, Univ Cincinnati Hosp 1991; **Fellow:** Surgical Oncology, Meml Sloan-Kettering Cancer Ctr 1993; **Fac Appt:** Prof S

Esquivel, Carlos O MD/PhD [S] - **Spec Exp:** Transplant-Liver-Adult & Pediatric; **Hospital:** Stanford Univ Hosp & Clins, Lucile Packard Chldn's Hosp; **Address:** Surg Spec Clin, 300 Pasteur Drive, Ste A160, MC 5313, Stanford, CA 94305; **Phone:** 650-498-5689; **Board Cert:** Surgery 2003; **Med School:** Costa Rica 1975; **Resid:** Surgery, UC- Davis Med Ctr 1984; **Fellow:** Transplant Surgery, Univ Pittsburgh Med Ctr 1986; **Fac Appt:** Prof S, Stanford Univ

Esserman, Laura J MD [S] - **Spec Exp:** Breast Cancer; **Hospital:** UCSF - Mt Zion Med Ctr, UCSF Med Ctr; **Address:** UCSF-Helen Diller Family Comp Cancer Ctr, 1600 Divisadero St Fl 2, San Francisco, CA 94115; **Phone:** 415-353-7111; **Board Cert:** Surgery 2001; **Med School:** Stanford Univ 1983; **Resid:** Surgery, Stanford Univ Med Ctr 1991; **Fellow:** Oncology, Stanford Univ Med Ctr 1988; **Fac Appt:** Prof S, UCSF

Essner, Richard MD [S] - **Spec Exp:** Sentinel Node Surgery; Melanoma; Gastrointestinal Surgery; **Hospital:** Cedars-Sinai Med Ctr; **Address:** 8700 Beverly Blvd, Ste AC-1050, Los Angeles, CA 90048; **Phone:** 310-423-0301; **Board Cert:** Surgery 2002; **Med School:** Emory Univ 1985; **Resid:** Surgery, Univ NC Hosps 1992; **Fac Appt:** Asst Clin Prof S, USC Sch Med

Fisher, Jonathan S MD [S] - **Spec Exp:** Transplant-Kidney; Transplant-Liver; Transplant-Pancreas; Pancreatic Islet Cell Transplant; **Hospital:** Scripps Green Hosp; **Address:** Scripps Clinic Torrey Pines, 10666 N Torrey Pines Rd, MC 200N, La Jolla, CA 92037; **Phone:** 858-554-4310; **Board Cert:** Surgery 2012; **Med School:** Columbia P&S 1994; **Resid:** Surgery, Univ Chicago Hosps 2001; **Fellow:** Transplant Surgery, Univ Tennessee 2003

Giuliano, Armando E MD [S] - **Spec Exp:** Breast Cancer; Sentinel Node Surgery; Thyroid Cancer; **Hospital:** Cedars-Sinai Med Ctr; **Address:** Saul & Joyce Brandman Breast Ctr, 310 N San Vincente Blvd, Fl 3, Los Angeles, CA 90048; **Phone:** 310-423-9331 x0; **Board Cert:** Surgery 2009; **Med School:** Univ Chicago-Pritzker Sch Med 1973; **Resid:** Surgery, UCSF Med Ctr 1980; **Fellow:** Surgical Oncology, UCLA Med Ctr 1978; **Fac Appt:** Prof S, UCLA

Goodson III, William H MD [S] - **Spec Exp:** Breast Cancer; **Hospital:** CA Pacific Med Ctr-Pacific Campus, UCSF - Mt Zion Med Ctr; **Address:** 2100 Webster St, Ste 401, San Francisco, CA 94115-2378; **Phone:** 415-923-3925; **Board Cert:** Surgery 2006; **Med School:** Harvard Med Sch 1971; **Resid:** Surgery, Univ Hosps 1976; Surgery, Childrens Hosp 1977

Gosnell, Jessica E MD [S] - **Spec Exp:** Thyroid Cancer & Surgery; Parathyroid Surgery; **Hospital:** UCSF - Mt Zion Med Ctr; **Address:** 1600 Divisardero St Fl 3, San Francisco, CA 94115; **Phone:** 415-353-7687; **Board Cert:** Surgery 2004; **Med School:** UCSF 1995; **Resid:** Surgery, UCSF Med Ctr 2002; **Fellow:** Research, San Francisco Genl Hosp 2000; Endocrine Surgery, Univ Sydney 2003; **Fac Appt:** Asst Prof S, UCSF

Gower, Roland E MD [S] - **Spec Exp:** Breast Surgery; Biliary Surgery; Thyroid Surgery; **Hospital:** Providence Alaska Med Ctr, Alaska Regl Hosp; **Address:** 2841 De Barr Rd, Ste 41, Anchorage, AK 99508-2973; **Phone:** 907-279-3564; **Board Cert:** Surgery 2008; **Med School:** Vanderbilt Univ 1971; **Resid:** Surgery, Kansas Med Ctr 1975

Greenhalgh, David G MD [S] - **Spec Exp:** Burn Care; Wound Healing/Care; **Hospital:** Northern CA Shriners Hosp, UC Davis Med Ctr; **Address:** Shriners Hosp Chldn, 2425 Stockton Blvd, Sacramento, CA 95817; **Phone:** 916-453-2050; **Board Cert:** Surgery 2005; Surgical Critical Care 2008; **Med School:** SUNY Upstate Med Univ 1981; **Resid:** Surgery, MC Hosp of VT 1986; **Fellow:** Research, MC Hosp of VT 1987; Burn Surgery, Univ Wash Hosp 1989; **Fac Appt:** Prof S, UC Davis

Hemming, Alan W MD [S] - **Spec Exp:** Liver Cancer; Transplant-Liver; Hepatobiliary Surgery; Pancreatic Cancer; **Hospital:** UCSD Med Ctr, Rady Children's Hosp - San Diego; **Address:** UCSD Med Ctr-Hepatobiliary Dis & Trans Ctr, 200 W Arbor Drive, MS 8401, San Diego, CA 92103-8401; **Phone:** 619-543-5870; **Board Cert:** Surgery 2004; **Med School:** Univ British Columbia Fac Med 1987; **Resid:** Surgery, Univ British Columbia Med Ctr 1994; **Fellow:** Transplant Surgery, Univ of Toronto Hosp 1995; Hepatobiliary Surgery, Univ of Toronto Hosp 1996; **Fac Appt:** Prof S, UCSD

Horvath, Karen MD [S] - **Spec Exp:** Colon & Rectal Surgery; Gastrointestinal Surgery; Minimally Invasive Surgery; Pancreatic Surgery; **Hospital:** Univ Wash Med Ctr, Seattle Cancer Care Alliance; **Address:** 1959 NE Pacific St, Box 356165, Seattle, WA 98195; **Phone:** 206-598-4477; **Board Cert:** Surgery 2007; **Med School:** NY Med Coll 1990; **Resid:** Surgery, NY Presby Hosp/Columbia 1997; **Fellow:** Surgical Critical Care, Mt Sinai Hosp 1995; Laparoscopic Surgery, Oregon Hlth Sci Ctr 1998; **Fac Appt:** Prof S, Univ Wash

Hunter, John G MD [S] - **Spec Exp:** Gastrointestinal Surgery; Laparoscopic Abdominal Surgery; Gastroesophageal Reflux Disease (GERD); Esophageal Surgery; **Hospital:** OR Hlth & Sci Univ; **Address:** Digestive Hlth Ctr, 3303 SW Bond Ave Fl 6, MC CH6D, Portland, OR 97239; **Phone:** 503-494-4373; **Board Cert:** Surgery 2006; **Med School:** Univ Pennsylvania 1981; **Resid:** Surgery, Univ Utah Hlth Care 1987; **Fellow:** Gastrointestinal Surgery, Mass Genl Hosp 1988; Endoscopy, Univ West Ontario Affil Hosps 1989; **Fac Appt:** Assoc Prof S, Oregon Hlth & Sci Univ

Karlan, Scott R MD [S] - **Spec Exp:** Breast Cancer & Surgery; **Hospital:** Cedars-Sinai Med Ctr; **Address:** 310 N San Vicente Blvd Fl 3, Los Angeles, CA 90048; **Phone:** 310-423-9331; **Board Cert:** Surgery 2005; **Med School:** Harvard Med Sch 1982; **Resid:** Surgery, Yale-New Haven Hosp 1987; **Fac Appt:** Clin Prof S, UCLA

Katkhouda, Namir MD [S] - **Spec Exp:** Laparoscopic Surgery; Obesity/Bariatric Surgery; Gastrointestinal Surgery; **Hospital:** Keck Med Ctr of USC; **Address:** USC Healthcare Consultation Ctr, Dept Surgery, 1510 San Pablo St, Ste 514, Los Angeles, CA 90033; **Phone:** 323-442-6868; **Med School:** France 1984; **Resid:** Surgery, Univ Nice Affil Hosp 1987; **Fac Appt:** Prof S, USC-Keck School of Medicine

Kaufman, Cary S MD [S] - **Spec Exp:** Breast Cancer & Surgery; Breast Disease; **Hospital:** St. Joseph Hosp - Bellingham; **Address:** Bellingham Regl Breast Ctr, 2940 Squalicam Pkwy, Ste 101, Bellingham, WA 98225; **Phone:** 360-671-9877; **Board Cert:** Surgery 2010; **Med School:** UCLA 1973; **Resid:** Surgery, Univ Wash Med Ctr 1975; Surgery, LAC-Harbor-UCLA Med Ctr 1979; **Fac Appt:** Assoc Clin Prof S, Univ Wash

Kirgan, Daniel MD [S] - **Spec Exp:** Cancer Surgery; Breast Cancer & Surgery; **Hospital:** Univ Med Ctr - Las Vegas, Mountainview Hosp - Las Vegas; **Address:** 1707 W Charleston Blvd, Ste 160, Las Vegas, NV 89102; **Phone:** 702-671-2339; **Board Cert:** Surgery 2004; **Med School:** Geo Wash Univ 1986; **Resid:** Surgery, Univ Med Ctr 1992; **Fellow:** Surgical Oncology, John Wayne Cancer Inst 1994; **Fac Appt:** Assoc Prof S, Univ Nevada

Klein, Andrew S MD [S] - **Spec Exp:** Transplant-Liver; Liver Cancer; Liver Failure; **Hospital:** Cedars-Sinai Med Ctr; **Address:** Liver & Transplant Ctr at Cedars-Sinai, 8635 W Third St, Ste 590W, Los Angeles, CA 90048; **Phone:** 310-423-2641; **Board Cert:** Surgery 2007; **Med School:** Johns Hopkins Univ 1979; **Resid:** Surgery, Johns Hopkins Hosp 1982; Surgery, Johns Hopkins Hosp 1986; **Fellow:** Transplant Surgery, UCLA-CHS 1988; **Fac Appt:** Clin Prof S, UCLA

Knudson, Mary Margaret MD [S] - **Spec Exp:** Breast Cancer; Trauma; **Hospital:** San Francisco Genl Hosp; **Address:** 1001 Potrero Ave, Ste 3A, San Francisco, CA 94110; **Phone:** 415-206-4623; **Board Cert:** Surgery 2011; Surgical Critical Care 2008; **Med School:** Univ Mich Med Sch 1976; **Resid:** Surgery, Beth Israel Hosp 1979; Surgery, Univ Mich Med Ctr 1982; **Fellow:** Pediatric Surgery, Stanford Univ Hosps 1983; **Fac Appt:** Prof S, UCSF

Lowy, Andrew M MD [S] - **Spec Exp:** Pancreatic Cancer; Gastrointestinal Cancer; Peritoneal Carcinomatosis; Clinical Trials; **Hospital:** UCSD Med Ctr; **Address:** UCSD Moores Cancer Ctr, 3855 Health Sciences Drive Fl 2, MS 0987, La Jolla, CA 92093-0987; **Phone:** 858-822-2124; **Board Cert:** Surgery 2012; **Med School:** Cornell Univ-Weill Med Coll 1988; **Resid:** Surgery, NY-Cornell Med Ctr 1993; **Fellow:** Surgical Oncology, MD Anderson Cancer Ctr 1996; **Fac Appt:** Prof S, UCSD

Morton, John M MD [S] - **Spec Exp:** Obesity/Bariatric Surgery; Minimally Invasive Surgery; Natural Orifice Surgery (NOTES); **Hospital:** Stanford Univ Hosp & Clins, Lucile Packard Chldn's Hosp; **Address:** Surgical Specialties Clinic, 300 Pasteur Drive, rm H3680, Stanford, CA 94305-5655; **Phone:** 650-725-9777; **Board Cert:** Surgery 2011; **Med School:** Tulane Univ 1993; **Resid:** Surgery, Tulane Univ Hosp 1999; Surgery, Swedish Med Ctr 2001; **Fellow:** Laparoscopic Surgery, Univ N Carolina Affil Hosp 2003; **Fac Appt:** Assoc Prof S, Stanford Univ

Nakakura, Eric MD/PhD [S] - **Spec Exp:** Pancreatic Cancer; Liver Cancer; Gastrointestinal Cancer; Sarcoma; **Hospital:** UCSF Med Ctr; **Address:** UCSF, GI Cancer Surgery Dept, 1600 Divisadero St, Ste A723, San Francisco, CA 94115; **Phone:** 415-353-9888; **Board Cert:** Surgery 2004; **Med School:** Stanford Univ 1995; **Resid:** Surgery, Johns Hopkins Hosp 2003; **Fellow:** Surgical Oncology, Johns Hopkins Hosp 2004; **Fac Appt:** Assoc Prof S, UCSF

Nguyen, Ninh T MD [S] - **Spec Exp:** Laparoscopic Surgery; Obesity/Bariatric Surgery; Gastrointestinal Cancer & Surgery; **Hospital:** UC Irvine Med Ctr; **Address:** UC Irvine Med Ctr, Div Gastrointestinal Surgery, 333 City Blvd W, Ste 850, Orange, CA 92868; **Phone:** 714-456-8598; **Board Cert:** Surgery 2006; **Med School:** Univ Tex, San Antonio 1990; **Resid:** Surgery, Mt Sinai Med Ctr 1995; **Fellow:** Surgical Oncology, Univ Pittsburgh Med Ctr 1997; Laparoscopic Surgery, Univ Pittsburgh Med Ctr 1998; **Fac Appt:** Clin Prof S, UC Irvine

Nissen, Nicholas N MD [S] - **Spec Exp:** Liver Cancer; Transplant-Liver; Pancreatic Cancer; Minimally Invasive Surgery; **Hospital:** Cedars-Sinai Med Ctr; **Address:** Cedars-Sinai Medical Center, 8635 W 3rd St, Ste 590-W, Los Angeles, CA 90048; **Phone:** 310-423-2641; **Board Cert:** Surgery 2008; Surgical Critical Care 2009; **Med School:** Univ Minn 1991; **Resid:** Surgery, Loyola Univ Med Ctr 1998; **Fellow:** Surgical Critical Care, Univ Pittsburgh Med Ctr 1999; Transplant Surgery, UCLA Med Ctr 2001

Norton, Jeffrey A MD [S] - **Spec Exp:** Pancreatic Cancer; Gastrointestinal Cancer & Surgery; Endocrine Surgery; **Hospital:** Stanford Univ Hosp & Clins; **Address:** 875 Blake Wilbur Drive, Clin F, Stanford, CA 94305; **Phone:** 650-723-5461; **Board Cert:** Surgery 2011; **Med School:** SUNY Upstate Med Univ 1973; **Resid:** Surgery, Duke Univ Med Ctr 1982; **Fellow:** Research, Natl Cancer Inst 1979; **Fac Appt:** Prof S, Stanford Univ

Oelschlager, Brant K MD [S] - **Spec Exp:** Esophageal Surgery; Gastrointestinal Surgery; Minimally Invasive Surgery; Esophageal Cancer; **Hospital:** Univ Wash Med Ctr; **Address:** UWMC-Surgical Specialties, Fl 3, Box 356165, 1959 NE Pacific St, Seattle, WA 98195; **Phone:** 206-598-4547; **Board Cert:** Surgery 2009; **Med School:** Univ NC Sch Med 1995; **Resid:** Surgery, Univ Washington Med Ctr 2000; **Fellow:** Minimally Invasive Surgery, Univ Washington 2001; **Fac Appt:** Prof S, Univ Wash

Paz, Isaac Benjamin MD [S] - **Spec Exp:** Breast Cancer; Esophageal Cancer; **Hospital:** City of Hope Natl Med Ctr; **Address:** 209 Fair Oaks, South Pasadena, CA 91030; **Phone:** 626-396-2900; **Board Cert:** Surgery 2010; **Med School:** Chile 1981; **Resid:** Surgery, Univ Catolica de Chile 1985; Surgery, Univ Arizona 1990; **Fellow:** Surgical Oncology, City of Hope Med Ctr 1993

Pellegrini, Carlos A MD [S] - **Spec Exp:** Esophageal Cancer; Esophageal Surgery; Barrett's Esophagus; Gastrointestinal Cancer & Surgery; **Hospital:** Univ Wash Med Ctr; **Address:** Univ Washington Medical Ctr, Dept Surgery, Ctr Esophageal & Gastric Surgery, 1959 NE Pacific St, Box 356165, Seattle, WA 98195; **Phone:** 206-598-4547; **Board Cert:** Surgery 2010; **Med School:** Argentina 1971; **Resid:** Surgery, Granadero Hosp 1975; Surgery, Univ Chicago Affil Hosps 1979; **Fac Appt:** Prof S, Univ Wash

Perkins, James D MD [S] - **Spec Exp:** Transplant-Pancreas; Transplant-Liver; Transplant-Kidney; **Hospital:** Univ Wash Med Ctr, Seattle Chldns Hosp; **Address:** Univ Wash Med Ctr, Dept Surg, 1959 NE Pacific St, Box 356410, Seattle, WA 98195; **Phone:** 206-543-3825; **Board Cert:** Surgery 2004; **Med School:** Univ Ark 1979; **Resid:** Surgery, St Francis Regl Med Ctr 1984; **Fellow:** Transplant Surgery, Utah Univ Hosp 1985; Transplant Surgery, Mayo Clinic 1985; **Fac Appt:** Prof S, Univ Wash

Peterson, Laura D MD [S] - **Spec Exp:** Breast Cancer; Breast Surgery; **Hospital:** Kapiolani Med Ctr for Women & Chldn, Straub Clinic & Hosp; **Address:** Kapi'olani Womens Ctr, 1907 S Beretania St, Ste 501, Honolulu, HI 96826; **Phone:** 808-949-3444; **Board Cert:** Surgery 2004; **Med School:** UCSD 1998; **Resid:** Surgery, Univ Hawaii Affil Hosp 2004; **Fellow:** Minimally Invasive Surgery, Kaiser Permanente 2005; Surgical Oncology, Kaiser Permanente 2005

Phillips, Edward H MD [S] - **Spec Exp:** Laparoscopic Surgery; Obesity/Bariatric Surgery; Breast Cancer & Surgery; **Hospital:** Cedars-Sinai Med Ctr; **Address:** Ctr for Weight Loss, 8635 W 3rd St, Ste 795 West, Los Angeles, CA 90048-6101; **Phone:** 310-423-8350; **Board Cert:** Surgery 2008; **Med School:** USC-Keck School of Medicine 1973; **Resid:** Surgery, USC Med Ctr 1978; Vascular Surgery, USC Med Ctr 1979; **Fac Appt:** Assoc Clin Prof S, USC Sch Med

Posselt, Andrew M MD/PhD [S] - **Spec Exp:** Obesity/Bariatric Surgery; Pancreatic Islet Cell Transplant; Transplant-Liver-Adult & Pediatric; Transplant-Pancreas; **Hospital:** UCSF Med Ctr; **Address:** UCSF Medical Ctr, Dept Surgery, 505 Parnassus Ave, M884, San Francisco, CA 94143; **Phone:** 415-353-2161; **Board Cert:** Surgery 2011; **Med School:** Univ Pennsylvania 1993; **Resid:** Internal Medicine, UCSF Med Ctr 1996; Surgery, UCSF Med Ctr 2000; **Fellow:** Transplant Surgery, UCSF Med Ctr 2002; **Fac Appt:** Assoc Prof S, UCSF

Potenza, Bruce M MD [S] - **Spec Exp:** Burn Care; Critical Care; **Hospital:** UCSD Med Ctr; **Address:** UCSD Med Ctr, 200 W Arbor Drive, MC 8896, San Diego, CA 92103-8896; **Phone:** 619-543-6001; **Board Cert:** Surgery 2004; Internal Medicine 1988; Surgical Critical Care 2007; Critical Care Medicine 2006; **Med School:** Loyola Univ-Stritch Sch Med 1983; **Resid:** Internal Medicine, Good Samaritan Med Ctr 1987; Surgery, SUNY Syracuse Med Ctr 1993; **Fellow:** Surgical Critical Care, UCSD Med Ctr 1995; **Fac Appt:** Prof S, UCSD

Rassman, William R MD [S] - **Spec Exp:** Hair Restoration/Transplant; **Address:** New Hair Inst, 5757 Wilshire Blvd, Promenade 2, Los Angeles, CA 90036; **Phone:** 310-553-9113; **Board Cert:** Surgery 1975; **Med School:** Med Coll VA 1966; **Resid:** Surgery, NY Hosp-Weill Cornell Med Ctr 1969; Surgery, Dartmouth Med Ctr 1973

Reber, Howard A MD [S] - **Spec Exp:** Pancreatic Cancer; Pancreatic Surgery; Gastrointestinal Cancer; **Hospital:** UCLA Ronald Reagan Med Ctr; **Address:** UCLA General Surgery, 200 UCLA Medical Plaza, Ste 214, Los Angeles, CA 90095; **Phone:** 310-794-7788; **Board Cert:** Surgery 1971; **Med School:** Univ Pennsylvania 1963; **Resid:** Surgery, Hosp Univ Penn 1970; **Fac Appt:** Prof S, UCLA

Reyes, Jorge D MD [S] - **Spec Exp:** Transplant Surgery; Transplant Surgery-Pediatric; Transplant-Liver; Hepatobiliary Surgery; **Hospital:** Seattle Chldns Hosp, Univ Wash Med Ctr; **Address:** 4800 Sand Point Way NE, MS MB.9.420, Seattle, WA 98105; **Phone:** 206-987-1800; **Board Cert:** Surgery 2011; **Med School:** Brazil 1979; **Resid:** Surgical Pathology, New Eng Deaconess Hosp 1983; Surgery, Lincoln Hosp/NY Med Coll 1988; **Fellow:** Transplant Surgery, Presby Univ Hosp 1989; **Fac Appt:** Prof S, Univ Wash

Roberts, John Paul MD [S] - **Spec Exp:** Transplant-Liver; Transplant-Kidney; Transplant Surgery-Pediatric; **Hospital:** UCSF Med Ctr; **Address:** UCSF Medical Ctr, Div Transplant Surgery, 505 Parnassus Ave, rm M896, Box 0780, San Francisco, CA 94143-0780; **Phone:** 415-353-1888; **Board Cert:** Surgery 2006; **Med School:** UCSD 1980; **Resid:** Surgery, Univ Wash 1983; Surgery, Univ Wash 1986; **Fellow:** Research, Cornell-New York Hosp 1985; Transplant Surgery, Univ Minn Med Ctr 1987; **Fac Appt:** Prof S, UCSF

Rogers, Stanley J MD [S] - **Spec Exp:** Minimally Invasive Surgery; Gastrointestinal Surgery; Obesity/Bariatric Surgery; **Hospital:** UCSF Med Ctr, San Francisco Genl Hosp; **Address:** UCSF Med Ctr, Dept Surgery, 400 Parnassus Ave, Ste 665, Campus Box 0338, San Francisco, CA 94143; **Phone:** 415-353-2161; **Board Cert:** Surgery 2006; **Med School:** Univ Utah 1991; **Resid:** Surgery, UCSF Med Ctr 1996; **Fellow:** Laparoscopic Surgery, UCSF Med Ctr 1997; **Fac Appt:** Assoc Prof S, UCSF

Satava, Richard M MD [S] - **Spec Exp:** Laparoscopic Abdominal Surgery; Gastrointestinal Surgery; **Hospital:** Univ Wash Med Ctr; **Address:** Univ Washington Med Ctr, Dept Surgery, 1959 NE Pacific St, Box 356165, Seattle, WA 98195; **Phone:** 206-598-4477; **Board Cert:** Surgery 2000; **Med School:** Hahnemann Univ 1968; **Resid:** Surgery, Mayo Clinic 1974; **Fellow:** Research, Mayo Clinic 1972; **Fac Appt:** Prof S, Univ Wash

Schaffer III, Randolph L MD [S] - **Spec Exp:** Transplant-Liver; Transplant-Kidney; Transplant-Pancreas; Laparoscopic Surgery; **Hospital:** Scripps Green Hosp; **Address:** Scripps Clinic Torrey Pines, 10666 N Torrey Pines Rd, MC 200N, La Jolla, CA 92037; **Phone:** 858-544-4310; **Board Cert:** Surgery 2011; **Med School:** Baylor Coll Med 1995; **Resid:** Surgery, Baylor Affil Hosp 2001; **Fellow:** Transplant Surgery, Univ Chicago Hosp & Clins 2003

Selby, Robert R MD [S] - **Spec Exp:** Liver & Biliary Surgery; Liver Cancer; **Hospital:** Keck Med Ctr of USC; **Address:** USC Hepatobiliary, Pancreas & Abdominal Organ Transplant, 1510 San Pablo St HCC 1 Bldg - Ste 514, Los Angeles, CA 90033-4612; **Phone:** 323-442-7172; **Board Cert:** Surgery 2008; Surgical Critical Care 2011; **Med School:** Univ MO-Columbia Sch Med 1979; **Resid:** Internal Medicine, Good Samaritan Hosp 1981; Surgery, Good Samaritan Hosp 1986; **Fellow:** Transplant Surgery, Presby Univ Hosp 1989; **Fac Appt:** Prof S, USC Sch Med

Sener, Stephen F MD [S] - **Spec Exp:** Breast Cancer; Lymphedema; Thyroid Cancer; Melanoma; **Hospital:** Keck Med Ctr of USC; **Address:** USC Norris Comprehensive Cancer Ctr, 1510 San Pablo, Ste 412, Los Angeles, CA 90033; **Phone:** 323-865-3535; **Board Cert:** Surgery 2001; **Med School:** Northwestern Univ 1977; **Resid:** Surgery, Northwestern Mem Hosp 1982; **Fellow:** Surgery, Sloan Kettering Can Ctr 1984; **Fac Appt:** Prof S, USC-Keck School of Medicine

Silverstein, Melvin J MD [S] - **Spec Exp:** Breast Cancer & Surgery; **Hospital:** Hoag Meml Hosp Presby; **Address:** Hoag Breast Care Ctr, 1 Hoag Drive, Newport Beach, CA 92658; **Phone:** 949-764-8281; **Board Cert:** Surgery 1971; **Med School:** Albany Med Coll 1965; **Resid:** Surgery, Boston City Hosp-Tufts Univ 1970; **Fellow:** Surgical Oncology, UCLA Med Ctr 1975

Sinanan, Mika N MD/PhD [S] - **Spec Exp:** Gastrointestinal Surgery; Gastrointestinal Cancer; Liver & Biliary Cancer; Colon & Rectal Cancer; **Hospital:** Univ Wash Med Ctr; **Address:** Univ Wash, Dept Surgery, 1959 NE Pacific St, Box 356165, Seattle, WA 98195-6410; **Phone:** 206-598-4477; **Board Cert:** Surgery 2008; **Med School:** Johns Hopkins Univ 1980; **Resid:** Surgery, Univ Wash Hosp 1988; **Fac Appt:** Prof S, Univ Wash

Swanstrom, Lee L MD [S] - **Spec Exp:** Esophageal Surgery; Esophageal Disorders; Minimally Invasive Surgery; Gastrointestinal Motility Disorders; **Hospital:** Providence Portland Med Ctr; **Address:** 4805 NE Glisan St, Ste 6N60, Portland, OR 97213; **Phone:** 503-281-0561; **Board Cert:** Surgery 2009; **Med School:** Creighton Univ 1983; **Resid:** Surgery, Legacy Emanuel Hosp 1988; **Fac Appt:** Clin Prof S, Oregon Hlth & Sci Univ

Talamini, Mark A MD [S] - **Spec Exp:** Robotic Surgery; Minimally Invasive Surgery; Gastrointestinal Cancer; Cancer Surgery; **Hospital:** UCSD Med Ctr; **Address:** UCSD Med Ctr-Dept Surgery, 200 W Arbor Drive, Ste 8201, MC 8400, San Diego, CA 92103-8400; **Phone:** 619-543-6453; **Board Cert:** Surgery 2008; **Med School:** Johns Hopkins Univ 1981; **Resid:** Surgery, Johns Hopkins Hosp 1987; **Fellow:** Surgery, Univ Cincinnati 1985; **Fac Appt:** Prof S, UCSD

Trisal, Vijay MD [S] - **Spec Exp:** Skin Cancer; **Hospital:** City of Hope Natl Med Ctr; **Address:** City of Hope Med Ctr, Dept Surgery, 1500 E Duarte Rd, Duarte, CA 91010; **Phone:** 626-256-4673 x67100; **Board Cert:** Surgery 2003; **Med School:** India 1993; **Resid:** Surgery, Providence Hosp & Med Ctrs 2002; **Fellow:** Surgical Oncology, City of Hope Natl Med Ctr 2004

Vetto, John MD [S] - **Spec Exp:** Cancer Surgery; **Hospital:** OR Hlth & Sci Univ; **Address:** 3181 SW Sam Jackson Park Rd, MC L619, Portland, OR 97239; **Phone:** 503-494-5501; **Board Cert:** Surgery 2009; **Med School:** Oregon Hlth & Sci Univ 1982; **Resid:** Surgery, Brigham & Women's Hosp 1984; Surgery, UCLA Med Ctr 1989; **Fellow:** Surgical Oncology, Natl Cancer Inst 1986; Surgical Oncology, Meml Sloan-Kettering Cancer Ctr 1991; **Fac Appt:** Assoc Prof S, Oregon Hlth & Sci Univ

Wagman, Lawrence D MD [S] - **Spec Exp:** Liver Cancer; Gastrointestinal Cancer; Carcinoid Tumors; **Hospital:** St. Joseph's Hosp - Orange, City of Hope Natl Med Ctr; **Address:** 1010 W La Veta Ave, Ste 470, Orange, CA 92868; **Phone:** 714-835-8300; **Board Cert:** Surgery 2004; **Med School:** Columbia P&S 1978; **Resid:** Surgery, Med Coll Virginia Hosp 1985; **Fellow:** Surgical Oncology, Natl Inst Hlth 1982; **Fac Appt:** Assoc Clin Prof S, UCSD

Wallace, Anne Marie MD [S] - **Spec Exp:** Cancer Surgery; Reconstructive Surgery; Melanoma; Breast Cancer; **Hospital:** UCSD Med Ctr; **Address:** UCSD Moores Cancer Ctr, 3855 Health Sciences Drive #0987, La Jolla, CA 92093; **Phone:** 858-822-6193; **Board Cert:** Surgery 2011; Plastic Surgery 2005; **Med School:** Creighton Univ 1987; **Resid:** Surgery, Washington Hosp Ctr 1992; Plastic Surgery, UCSD Med Ctr 1994; **Fellow:** Surgical Breast Oncology, MD Anderson Cancer Ctr 1995; **Fac Appt:** Prof S, UCSD

Wapnir, Irene L MD [S] - **Spec Exp:** Breast Surgery; Breast Cancer; **Hospital:** Stanford Univ Hosp & Clins; **Address:** Stanford Univ Medical Ctr, 900 Blake Wilbur Drive, Stanford, CA 94305; **Phone:** 650-721-5705; **Board Cert:** Surgery 2008; **Med School:** Mexico 1980; **Resid:** Surgery, Lincoln Hosp 1985; **Fellow:** Breast Disease, RW Johnson Univ Med Ctr 1986; **Fac Appt:** Prof S, Stanford Univ

Warren, Robert S MD [S] - **Spec Exp:** Gastrointestinal Cancer; Liver Cancer; Biliary Cancer; **Hospital:** UCSF Med Ctr; **Address:** UCSF Comprehensive Cancer Center, GI Surgery & Oncology Clinic, 1600 Divisadero St, rm A-723, San Francisco, CA 94143; **Phone:** 415-353-9297; **Med School:** Univ Minn 1980; **Resid:** Surgery, Univ Minn Hosps 1988; **Fellow:** Surgical Oncology, Meml Sloan-Kettering Cancer Ctr 1986; **Fac Appt:** Prof S, UCSF

Yeung, Raymond S W MD [S] - **Spec Exp:** Liver & Biliary Cancer; Liver Cancer; Melanoma; Breast Cancer; **Hospital:** Univ Wash Med Ctr; **Address:** Univ Washington, Dept Surgery, 1959 NE Pacific St, Box 356165, Seattle, WA 98195; **Phone:** 206-598-4477; **Board Cert:** Surgery 2009; **Med School:** Univ Toronto 1982; **Resid:** Surgery, Univ Toronto 1987; **Fellow:** Surgical Oncology, Fox Chase Canc Ctr 1992; **Fac Appt:** Prof S, Univ Wash

Cleveland Clinic

Every life deserves world class care.

Cleveland Clinic
Digestive Disease Institute
9500 Euclid Ave.
Cleveland, OH 44195

General Surgery

Cleveland Clinic's Digestive Disease Institute (DDI) is one of the largest digestive programs in the country and is ranked No. 2 in the nation by *U.S. News & World Report*. DDI was one of the first to fully integrate its departments of Bariatric Surgery, Colorectal Surgery, Gastroenterology & Hepatology, General Surgery and Nutrition. Combining these disciplines in one location facilitates unprecedented patient care, multidisciplinary education and collaborative research. In 2012, DDI physicians performed more than 18,000 surgical cases and close to 60,000 endoscopic cases. Transplant surgeons completed more than 150 digestive disease-related organ transplants, including liver, pancreas and intestinal transplantation, achieving outstanding outcomes.

Highlights of the Department of General Surgery:

- Our general surgeons performed the nation's first robotic single-port gallbladder removal surgery.
- Cleveland Clinic is one of only a few programs in the country to offer Hyperthermic (or Heated) Intraoperative Peritoneal Chemotherapy to treat cancers that have spread to the lining of the abdominal cavity.
- Our Hernia Center performs more than 2,100 hernia repairs annually at 16 locations, from the routine to the most complex cases.
- The Acute Care Surgery program has a dedicated operating room 24/7 for emergent cases.
- Our Liver Tumor Clinic cares for patients with benign and cancerous liver tumors with treatment aimed at preserving liver function and quality of life.
- Our Pancreas Clinic is one of the few centers in the nation specializing in multidisciplinary, patient-centered treatments and frontline research for complicated acute pancreatitis, chronic pancreatitis, pancreatic cancer and pancreatic-biliary disorders.

Offering Same-Day Appointments
Call 866.320.4573

Treatment Guides
Cleveland Clinic has developed comprehensive treatment guides for many diseases and conditions. To download our free treatment guides, visit clevelandclinic.org/treatmentguides.

Online Medical Second Opinion
Call 216.444.3223 or
800.223.2273 ext. 43223 or
email eclevelandclinic@ccf.org

Out-of-State Patients Assistance
Call 800.223.2273, ext. 55580 or
email medicalconcierge@ccf.org

Visit Us At:
clevelandclinic.org

Follow Us On:

Facebook
facebook.com/clevelandclinic

Twitter
@ClevelandClinic

You Tube
youtube.com/clevelandclinic

Health Hub
clevelandclinic.org/HealthHub

SURGICAL ONCOLOGY

Studies show that experienced surgeons provide better surgical outcomes. At Fox Chase, our surgeons are fellowship-trained, meaning they have up to four years of additional training in the highly complex techniques of cancer surgery. They have extensive experience, focused entirely on cancer care and treat nearly all types of cancers with minimally invasive techniques. In addition, our plastic and reconstructive surgeons specialize in restoring form and function with excellent results for patients needing reconstructive surgery after cancer treatment.

Breast Cancer: Through our Women's Cancer Center—the first of its kind in the Philadelphia region—we offer advanced diagnostic techniques, including digital mammography, stereotactic breast biopsy and sentinel lymph-node surgery. Treatment options include breast-preserving surgery with radiation therapy as well as skin-sparing mastectomy with cosmetic reconstructive surgery.

Gastrointestinal Cancers: Our gastrointestinal surgeons have extensive expertise with colorectal, pancreatic, stomach, liver and other bowel cancers and are experienced in performing both laparoscopic and robotic procedures. We also offer the most advanced endoscopic and minimally invasive techniques to avoid major surgery. In addition, Fox Chase offers personalized care for patients with Barrett's esophagus—a condition that increases the risk of gastrointestinal cancer—to prevent the need for surgery and the development of cancer.

Genitourinary Cancers: Our urologic surgical oncologists have extensive expertise in the treatment of prostate, bladder, kidney, ureteral, adrenal, testicular and penile cancers. Our urologists emphasize organ preservation, quality of life and minimally invasive/robotic approaches to cancer surgery.

Gynecologic Cancers: Gynecologic surgeons in our Women's Cancer Center offer the most advanced laparoscopic and robotic techniques as well as complex open surgery for women with cancers of the uterus, ovary and cervix.

Head and Neck Cancers: Fox Chase provides patients with one-stop consultations with surgical, radiation and medical oncologists. Expertise includes otolaryngology, transoral laser surgery, plastic and microvascular reconstruction as well as robotic surgery.

Lung and Esophageal Cancers: Our thoracic surgeons offer a variety of minimally invasive techniques for patients with lung and esophageal cancers, including video-assisted thoracic surgery (VATS) and laparoscopic esophageal surgery. Fox Chase was one of the first centers in the country to offer these options.

Minimally Invasive Surgery

At Fox Chase, we offer the broadest range of minimally invasive treatment options for your cancer. Minimally invasive procedures allow the surgeon to reach the tumor through tiny incisions with pinpoint accuracy. This benefits patients because it means less scarring, reduced pain, less bleeding, fewer complications, and a faster recovery.

Fox Chase was one of the first institutions worldwide to use robot-assisted surgery to treat nearly all types of cancers, including prostate, gynecologic, kidney, bladder, colon, lung, and head and neck cancers. In addition, Fox Chase's highly skilled surgeons have extensive experience performing laparoscopic surgery for cancers of the liver, pancreas, bile ducts, and gallbladder; video-assisted thoracic surgery (VATS) for lung and other thoracic cancers; and transoral laser surgery for cancers of the head and neck.

For more about Fox Chase physicians and services, visit our website, www.foxchase.org, or call 1-888-FOX CHASE.

THE MOUNT SINAI MEDICAL CENTER

Surgery

One Gustave L. Levy Place
Fifth Avenue and 100th Street
New York, NY 10029-6574

Physician Referral: 1-800-MD-SINAI (637-4624)
www.mountsinai.org

The **DEPARTMENT OF SURGERY** continues to build upon the legacy of those who have gone before, caring for the very sickest of patients while developing new therapies and training tomorrow's physicians to save and enhance lives. Patients today are experiencing less pain, shorter hospital stays, and faster recovery times than was ever imaginable just 20 years ago.

TOP-RANKING MINIMALLY INVASIVE SURGEONS

In surveys of leading minimally invasive surgeons in a variety of specialties, Mount Sinai's physicians are consistently at the top of the list in surgery of the colon and rectum, liver and bile ducts, thyroid, hernia, chest, and blood vessels.

Colon and Rectal Surgery – Leaders in the treatment of gastrointestinal disorders, our surgeons care for a wide range of diseases, including: inflammatory bowel disease (Crohn's disease and ulcerative colitis), diverticulitis, colon and rectal cancer, and fecal incontinence. We offer many important procedures not commonly available.

General Surgery – The Division of General Surgery specializes in the treatment of abdominal surgical conditions. These include benign and malignant diseases of the gallbladder and gastrointestinal track (stomach, intestine, and colon). Our Comprehensive Hernia Center offers state-of-the-art repair of inguinal, ventral and hiatal hernias. We use minimally invasive and evidence-based surgery to deliver the highest standard of care to our patients.

Laparoscopic and Minimally Invasive Surgery – Mount Sinai surgeons rank as some of the world's most respected and innovative surgeons, performing more laparoscopic procedures than surgeons at any other hospital in New York.

Metabolic, Endocrine and Minimally Invasive Surgery – This division was formed to serve as the backbone for several disease-specific multidisciplinary programs. Ours is a truly novel metabolic surgery program that brings together traditional endocrine, bariatric and laparoscopic techniques to treat diseases of metabolism and the endocrine system.

Bariatric Surgery – The latest minimally invasive techniques are used to perform laparoscopic gastric bypass, lap band placement, duodenal switch, and sleeve gastrectomy.

Pediatric Surgery – Surgeries involving children can be met with even more apprehension than those for adults. Fortunately, Mount Sinai surgeons offer a full range of pediatric surgical procedures in a family-focused, child-sensitive environment.

Plastic and Reconstructive Surgery – Surgical care from aesthetic to complex reconstruction is offered for benign and malignant disease, as well as for deformities that are either congenital or acquired. The aim is to restore function and correct deformities caused by birth defects, aging, accident, or illness.

Surgical Oncology – Our surgeons provide expert care for both minimally invasive and open complex malignancies. Patients are seen promptly and are cared for by a multidisciplinary team of medical and surgical experts, enabling them to benefit from the opinions of dozens of nationally renowned doctors.

Vascular Surgery – Mount Sinai is a recognized world leader in the development of new minimally invasive techniques for the treatment of aortic aneurysms, carotid stenosis for the prevention of stroke and lower extremity ischemia. Mount Sinai performs research in areas ranging from stem cell therapy to specialized vascular devices. Our research serves to advance the field of vascular surgery. A wide array of advanced patient services is available, ensuring that conditions are managed successfully.

Thoracic & Cardiac Surgery

A thoracic and cardiac surgeon provides the operative, perioperative care and critical care of patients with pathologic conditions within the chest. Included is the surgical care of coronary artery disease, cancers of the lung, esophagus and chest wall, abnormalities of the trachea, abnormalities of the great vessels and heart valves, congenital anomalies, tumors of the mediastinum and diseases of the diaphragm. The management of the airway and injuries of the chest is within the scope of the specialty.

Thoracic and cardiac surgeons have the knowledge, experience and technical skills to accurately diagnose, operate upon safely and effectively manage patients with thoracic diseases of the chest. This requires substantial knowledge of cardiorespiratory physiology and oncology, as well as capability in the use of heart assist devices, management of abnormal heart rhythms and drainage of the chest cavity, respiratory support systems, endoscopy and invasive and noninvasive diagnostic techniques.

Training Required: Seven to eight years

THORACIC & CARDIAC SURGERY

New England

Bolman III, Ralph Morton MD [T&CS] - **Spec Exp:** Heart Failure & Ventricular Containment; Ventricular Assist Device (LVAD); Mitral Valve Surgery; Aneurysm; **Hospital:** Brigham & Women's Hosp; **Address:** Brigham & Womens Hosp, Dept Cardiac Surg, 75 Francis St, rm CA211, Boston, MA 02115; **Phone:** 617-732-7678; **Board Cert:** Thoracic & Cardiac Surgery 2004; **Med School:** St Louis Univ 1973; **Resid:** Surgery, Duke Univ Med Ctr 1980; **Fellow:** Thoracic Surgery, Univ Minn Hosp 1982; **Fac Appt:** Prof S, Harvard Med Sch

Brinckerhoff, Laurence H MD [T&CS] - **Spec Exp:** Lung Cancer; Esophageal Cancer; Minimally Invasive Thoracic Surgery; **Hospital:** Tufts Med Ctr; **Address:** Tufts Medical Center, 750 Washington St, Boston, MA 02111; **Phone:** 617-636-5589; **Board Cert:** Thoracic & Cardiac Surgery 2006; **Med School:** Dartmouth Med Sch 1994; **Resid:** Surgery, Univ Virginia Med Ctr 2001; **Fellow:** Cardiothoracic Surgery, Univ Colorado Hlth Sci Ctr 2004; **Fac Appt:** Asst Prof S, Tufts Univ

Bueno, Raphael MD [T&CS] - **Spec Exp:** Lung Cancer; Minimally Invasive Thoracic Surgery; Minimally Invasive Esophageal Surgery; Mesothelioma; **Hospital:** Brigham & Women's Hosp, Dana-Farber Cancer Inst; **Address:** Brigham and Women's Hospital, Div of Thoracic Surgery, 75 Francis St, Boston, MA 02115; **Phone:** 617-732-6824; **Board Cert:** Thoracic Surgery 2006; Surgery 2012; Surgical Critical Care 2003; **Med School:** Harvard Med Sch 1985; **Resid:** Surgery, Brigham & Women's Hosp 1992; **Fellow:** Surgical Critical Care, Brigham & Women's Hosp 1993; Thoracic Surgery, Mass Genl Hosp 1995; **Fac Appt:** Assoc Prof S, Harvard Med Sch

Byrne, John G MD [T&CS] - **Spec Exp:** Cardiothoracic Surgery; Heart Failure; Heart Valve Surgery; Transplant-Heart; **Hospital:** Brigham & Women's Hosp; **Address:** Brigham and Women's Hosp, Division of Cardiac Surgery, 75 Francis St, Boston, MA 02115; **Phone:** 617-732-7678; **Board Cert:** Thoracic Surgery 2008; **Med School:** Boston Univ 1987; **Resid:** Surgery, Univ Illinois Affil Hosp 1995; Thoracic Surgery, Brigham & Women's Hosp 1997; **Fellow:** Cardiothoracic Research, Harvard Med School 1992; **Fac Appt:** Prof S, Harvard Med Sch

Colson, Yolonda L MD/PhD [T&CS] - **Spec Exp:** Lung Cancer; Mesothelioma; Thoracic Cancers; **Hospital:** Brigham & Women's Hosp, Dana-Farber Cancer Inst; **Address:** Brigham & Women's Hosp, Div Thoracic Surgery, 75 Francis St Fl 2, Boston, MA 02115; **Phone:** 617-732-6824; **Board Cert:** Surgery 2010; Thoracic Surgery 2010; **Med School:** Mayo Med Sch 1989; **Resid:** Surgery, Univ Pittsburg Med Ctr 1995; **Fellow:** Research, Univ Pittsburg Med Ctr 1996; Cardiothoracic Surgery, Brigham & Women's Hosp 2001; **Fac Appt:** Assoc Prof S, Harvard Med Sch

Del-Nido, Pedro J MD [T&CS] - **Spec Exp:** Heart Valve Surgery-Pediatric; Congenital Heart Disease; Minimally Invasive Surgery; Robotic Surgery; **Hospital:** Children's Hospital - Boston; **Address:** Boston Chldn's Hosp, Dept Cardiac Surg, 300 Longwood Ave, Bader 273, Boston, MA 02115; **Phone:** 617-355-8290; **Board Cert:** Surgery 2006; Thoracic Surgery 2004; Congenital Cardiac Surgery 2011; **Med School:** Univ Wisc 1977; **Resid:** Surgery, Boston Med Ctr 1982; Thoracic Surgery, Toronto Genl Hosp 1985; **Fellow:** Pediatric Cardiothoracic Surgery, Hosp Sick Children 1986; **Fac Appt:** Prof S, Harvard Med Sch

Elefteriades, John A MD [T&CS] - **Spec Exp:** Aneurysm-Thoracic Aortic; Ventricular Assist Device (LVAD); **Hospital:** Yale-New Haven Hosp; **Address:** Yale Cardiothoracic Surgery, 330 Cedar St, rm BB 204, New Haven, CT 06520; **Phone:** 203-785-2705; **Board Cert:** Thoracic & Cardiac Surgery 2004; **Med School:** Yale Univ 1976; **Resid:** Surgery, Yale-New Haven Hosp 1981; **Fellow:** Cardiothoracic Surgery, Yale-New Haven Hosp 1983; **Fac Appt:** Prof T&CS, Yale Univ

Fernando, Hiran C MD [T&CS] - **Spec Exp:** Esophageal Cancer; Lung Cancer; Esophageal Disorders; Minimally Invasive Thoracic Surgery; **Hospital:** Boston Med Ctr; **Address:** Boston Med Ctr, Ctr for Thoracic Oncology, 830 Harrison Ave Fl 3 - Ste 3400, Boston, MA 02118; **Phone:** 617-638-5600; **Board Cert:** Surgery 2005; Thoracic Surgery 2009; **Med School:** England, UK 1986; **Resid:** Surgery, Harbor/UCLA Med Ctr 1993; Thoracic Surgery, UC Davis Med Ctr 1998; **Fellow:** Minimally Invasive Surgery, UPMC 2001; **Fac Appt:** Assoc Prof TS, Boston Univ

Gaissert, Henning A MD [T&CS] - **Spec Exp:** Esophageal Cancer; Tracheal Surgery; Lung Cancer; Thymoma; **Hospital:** Mass Genl Hosp, Newton - Wellesley Hosp; **Address:** Mass Genl Hosp, Div Thoracic Surgery, 55 Fruit St, BLK 1570, Boston, MA 02114; **Phone:** 617-726-5341; **Board Cert:** Surgery 2010; Thoracic & Cardiac Surgery 2004; **Med School:** Germany 1984; **Resid:** Surgery, Mass Genl Hosp 1989; Surgery, Barnes Jewish Hosp 1991; **Fellow:** Research, Harvard Med Sch 1993; Cardiothoracic Surgery, Barnes Jewish Hosp 1996; **Fac Appt:** Assoc Prof S, Harvard Med Sch

Hashim, Sabet W MD [T&CS] - **Spec Exp:** Mitral Valve Surgery; Heart Valve Surgery; Maze Procedure for Atrial Fibrillation; **Hospital:** Yale-New Haven Hosp; **Address:** Yale Surgical Specialties, 800 Howard Ave Fl 3, Yale Physician's Bldg, New Haven, CT 06520; **Phone:** 203-785-6214; **Board Cert:** Thoracic & Cardiac Surgery 2013; **Med School:** Lebanon 1975; **Resid:** Surgery, St Lukes Roosevelt Hosp 1979; Cardiothoracic Surgery, Yale-New Haven Hosp 1981; **Fac Appt:** Assoc Prof S, Yale Univ

Kirshbom, Paul M MD [T&CS] - **Spec Exp:** Pediatric Cardiothoracic Surgery; Cardiac Surgery-Neonatal; Congenital Heart Surgery; **Hospital:** Yale-New Haven Hosp, CT Chldns Med Ctr; **Address:** Yale-New Haven Childrens Hosp, 1 Park St Fl 2, New Haven, CT 06510; **Phone:** 203-785-2702; **Board Cert:** Thoracic & Cardiac Surgery 2010; Congenital Cardiac Surgery 2009; **Med School:** Johns Hopkins Univ 1991; **Resid:** Surgery, Duke Univ Med Ctr 1998; Cardiothoracic Surgery, Duke Univ Med Ctr 2000; **Fellow:** Pediatric Cardiac Surgery, Childrens Hosp 2002; **Fac Appt:** Prof S, Yale Univ

Kopf, Gary S MD [T&CS] - **Spec Exp:** Cardiac Surgery; Pediatric Cardiothoracic Surgery; Congenital Heart Disease; **Hospital:** Yale-New Haven Hosp; **Address:** Yale Surgical Specialties, 800 Howard Ave Fl 3, Yale Physicians Bldg, New Haven, CT 06520-8039; **Phone:** 203-785-2702; **Board Cert:** Thoracic Surgery 2011; **Med School:** Harvard Med Sch 1970; **Resid:** Surgery, Peter Bent Brigham Hosp 1977; **Fellow:** Cardiothoracic Surgery, Peter Bent Brigham Hosp 1980; **Fac Appt:** Prof S, Yale Univ

Lazar, Harold L MD [T&CS] - **Spec Exp:** Aortic Surgery; Coronary Artery Surgery; Heart Valve Surgery; Esophageal Surgery; **Hospital:** Boston Med Ctr; **Address:** Boston Med Ctr, 88 E Newton St Robinson Bldg - Ste B-402, Boston, MA 02118; **Phone:** 617-638-7350; **Board Cert:** Thoracic & Cardiac Surgery 2003; **Med School:** Boston Univ 1974; **Resid:** Surgery, Univ Michigan Med Ctr 1981; Cardiothoracic Surgery, NY Presby/Columbia Med Ctr 1983; **Fellow:** Cardiovascular Research, UCLA Med Ctr 1979; **Fac Appt:** Prof TS, Boston Univ

Mathisen, Douglas J MD [T&CS] - **Spec Exp:** Tracheal Surgery; Lung Cancer; Esophageal Cancer; **Hospital:** Mass Genl Hosp, Newton - Wellesley Hosp; **Address:** Mass Genl Hosp, Thoracic Surgery, 55 Fruit St, Blake 1570, Boston, MA 02114; **Phone:** 617-726-6826; **Board Cert:** Thoracic Surgery 2002; **Med School:** Univ IL Coll Med 1974; **Resid:** Surgery, Mass Genl Hosp 1981; Thoracic Surgery, Mass Genl Hosp 1982; **Fellow:** Surgical Oncology, Natl Cancer Inst 1979; **Fac Appt:** Prof S, Harvard Med Sch

Mayer Jr, John E MD [T&CS] - **Spec Exp:** Pediatric Cardiac Surgery; Cardiovascular Surgery; Transplant-Heart; Congenital Heart Surgery; **Hospital:** Children's Hospital - Boston; **Address:** Boston Chldn's Hosp, Dept Cardiac Surg, 300 Longwood Ave, Bader 273, Boston, MA 02115; **Phone:** 617-355-8258; **Board Cert:** Thoracic & Cardiac Surgery 2010; Congenital Cardiac Surgery 2009; **Med School:** Yale Univ 1972; **Resid:** Surgery, Univ Minn Med Ctr 1979; **Fellow:** Cardiothoracic Surgery, Univ Minn Med Ctr 1981; **Fac Appt:** Prof S, Harvard Med Sch

Nugent, William C MD [T&CS] - **Spec Exp:** Thoracic Cancers; Hyperhidrosis-Palmar; **Hospital:** Dartmouth - Hitchcock Med Ctr; **Address:** Dartmouth-Hitchcock Med Ctr, Dept Cardiothoracic Surgery, 1 Medical Center Drive, Lebanon, NH 03756; **Phone:** 603-650-8537; **Board Cert:** Thoracic Surgery 2013; **Med School:** Albany Med Coll 1975; **Resid:** Surgery, Beth Israel Hosp 1980; Thoracic Surgery, Univ Michigan Med Ctr 1983; **Fellow:** Cardiothoracic Surgery, Mass Genl Hosp 1981; **Fac Appt:** Prof S, Dartmouth Med Sch

Rastegar, Hassan MD [T&CS] - **Spec Exp:** Cardiac Surgery-Adult; Heart Valve Surgery; Minimally Invasive Cardiac Surgery; **Hospital:** Tufts Med Ctr; **Address:** Tufts Medical Center, 800 Washington St, Box 266, Boston, MA 02111; **Phone:** 617-636-5528; **Board Cert:** Thoracic Surgery 2003; **Med School:** Iran 1974; **Resid:** Surgery, Hosp Univ Penn 1980; Cardiothoracic Surgery, Northwestern Univ 1982; **Fac Appt:** Prof S, Tufts Univ

Sellke, Frank W MD [T&CS] - **Spec Exp:** Heart Valve Surgery; Aortic Surgery; Coronary Artery Surgery; Cardiac Tumors/Cancer; **Hospital:** Rhode Island Hosp, Miriam Hosp; **Address:** 2 Dudley St, MOC Bldg - Fl 3 - Ste 360, Providence, RI 02905; **Phone:** 401-274-7546; **Board Cert:** Surgery 2005; Thoracic Surgery 2009; **Med School:** Indiana Univ 1981; **Resid:** Surgery, Akron City Hosp 1987; Cardiothoracic Surgery, Univ Iowa Hosps & Clinics 1990; **Fac Appt:** Prof T&CS, Brown Univ

Singh, Arun K MD [T&CS] - **Spec Exp:** Cardiac Surgery; **Hospital:** Rhode Island Hosp; **Address:** University Cardiovascular Surgical, 2 Dudley St, Ste 360, Providence, RI 02905-3248; **Phone:** 401-274-7546; **Board Cert:** Surgery 1973; Thoracic Surgery 1975; **Med School:** India 1967; **Resid:** Surgery, Columbia Presby Med Ctr 1972; Cardiothoracic Surgery, Rhode Island Hosp 1974; **Fellow:** Cardiac Surgery, Hosp Sick Chldn 1975; **Fac Appt:** Clin Prof S, Brown Univ

Sugarbaker, David J MD [T&CS] - **Spec Exp:** Mesothelioma; Transplant-Lung; Esophageal Cancer; **Hospital:** Brigham & Women's Hosp, Dana-Farber Cancer Inst; **Address:** Brigham & Women's Hosp, Div Thoracic Surgery, 75 Francis St Fl 2, Boston, MA 02115-6110; **Phone:** 617-732-6824; **Board Cert:** Thoracic & Cardiac Surgery 2009; **Med School:** Cornell Univ-Weill Med Coll 1979; **Resid:** Surgery, Brigham & Women's Hosp 1982; Surgery, Toronto Genl Hosp 1986; **Fellow:** Thoracic Surgery, Toronto Genl Hosp 1988; **Fac Appt:** Assoc Prof S, Harvard Med Sch

Swanson, Scott J MD [T&CS] - **Spec Exp:** Lung Cancer; Video Assisted Thoracic Surgery (VATS); Esophageal Cancer; **Hospital:** Brigham & Women's Hosp, Dana-Farber Cancer Inst; **Address:** Brigham & Women's Hosp, Div Thoracic Surgery, 75 Francis St Fl 2, Boston, MA 02115; **Phone:** 617-732-6824; **Board Cert:** Surgery 2003; Thoracic Surgery 2006; **Med School:** Harvard Med Sch 1985; **Resid:** Surgery, Brigham & Womens Hosp 1990; **Fellow:** Thoracic Surgery, Brigham & Womens Hosp 1994; **Fac Appt:** Prof S, Harvard Med Sch

Vlahakes, Gus J MD [T&CS] - **Spec Exp:** Cardiac Surgery; Transplant-Heart; Maze Procedure for Atrial Fibrillation; **Hospital:** Mass Genl Hosp; **Address:** Mass Genl Hosp, 55 Fruit St, Ste COX 652, Boston, MA 02114; **Phone:** 617-726-1861; **Board Cert:** Surgery 2002; Surgical Critical Care 2012; Thoracic Surgery 2005; **Med School:** Harvard Med Sch 1975; **Resid:** Surgery, Mass Genl Hosp 1983; Cardiothoracic Surgery, Mass Genl Hosp 1985; **Fellow:** Pediatric Cardiac Surgery, Chldns Hosp 1985; **Fac Appt:** Prof S, Harvard Med Sch

Wain, John MD [T&CS] - **Spec Exp:** Transplant-Lung; Lung Cancer; Esophageal Cancer; **Hospital:** Mass Genl Hosp; **Address:** Mass Genl Hosp, Div Thoracic Surgery, 55 Fruit St, Blake 1570B, Boston, MA 02114; **Phone:** 617-726-5200; **Board Cert:** Thoracic & Cardiac Surgery 2010; **Med School:** Jefferson Med Coll 1980; **Resid:** Surgery, Mass Genl Hosp 1985; **Fellow:** Cardiothoracic Surgery, Mass Genl Hosp 1988; **Fac Appt:** Asst Prof TS, Harvard Med Sch

Warner, Kenneth G MD [T&CS] - **Spec Exp:** Cardiac Surgery-Adult & Pediatric; Congenital Heart Surgery; Heart Valve Surgery; Aortic Surgery; **Hospital:** Tufts Med Ctr; **Address:** Tufts Medical Center, 800 Washington St, Box 266, Boston, MA 02111-1526; **Phone:** 617-636-0033; **Board Cert:** Surgery 2007; Thoracic Surgery 2009; Surgical Critical Care 2001; **Med School:** Univ Mich Med Sch 1982; **Resid:** Surgery, Brigham & Women's Hosp 1988; Cardiothoracic Surgery, Brigham & Women's Hosp 1990; **Fellow:** Research, West Roxbury VA Hosp 1986; **Fac Appt:** Assoc Prof S, Tufts Univ

Weigel, Tracey L MD [T&CS] - **Spec Exp:** Esophageal Cancer; Lung Cancer; Mesothelioma; Graves' Disease; **Hospital:** Maine Med Ctr; **Address:** Dept Thoracic Surgery, 818 Congress St, Portland, ME 04102; **Phone:** 207-773-8161; **Board Cert:** Surgery 2003; Thoracic Surgery 2006; **Med School:** Univ Rochester 1986; **Resid:** Surgery, Rhode Is Hosp 1993; **Fellow:** Surgical Oncology, Meml Sloan Kettering Canc Ctr 1995; Cardiothoracic Surgery, Univ WI Hosp & Clins 1996; **Fac Appt:** Assoc Prof S, Univ Wisc

Whyte, Richard MD [T&CS] - **Spec Exp:** Lung Cancer; Esophageal Cancer; Chest Wall Tumors; **Hospital:** Beth Israel Deaconess Med Ctr - Boston; **Address:** Beth Israel Deaconess Med Ctr, 330 Brookline Ave Shapiro Bldg Fl 9, Boston, MA 02215; **Phone:** 617-632-8252; **Board Cert:** Surgery 2011; Thoracic & Cardiac Surgery 2013; **Med School:** Univ Pittsburgh 1983; **Resid:** Surgery, Mass Genl Hosp 1990; Thoracic Surgery, Univ Michigan Med Ctr 1992

Wright, Cameron D MD [T&CS] - **Spec Exp:** Lung Cancer; Esophageal Cancer; Tracheal Surgery; **Hospital:** Mass Genl Hosp; **Address:** Mass Genl Hosp, Div Thoracic Surgery, 55 Fruit St, Blake 1570, Boston, MA 02114; **Phone:** 617-726-5801; **Board Cert:** Surgery 2006; Thoracic & Cardiac Surgery 2007; **Med School:** Univ Mich Med Sch 1980; **Resid:** Surgery, Mass Genl Hosp 1986; Thoracic Surgery, Mass Genl Hosp 1988; **Fac Appt:** Assoc Prof S, Harvard Med Sch

Yuh, David D MD [T&CS] - **Spec Exp:** Heart Valve Surgery; Minimally Invasive Cardiac Surgery; RoboticSurgery; **Hospital:** Yale-New Haven Hosp; **Address:** Yale Cardiac Surgery, Yale Physicians Bldg Fl 3, 800 Howard Ave, New Haven, CT 06519; **Phone:** 203-785-3000; **Board Cert:** Thoracic & Cardiac Surgery 2011; **Med School:** Stanford Univ 1991; **Resid:** Surgery, Univ Minn Hosp & Clins 1994; Surgery, Stanford Univ Med Ctr 1996; **Fellow:** Cardiac Surgery, Stanford Univ Med Ctr 1998; **Fac Appt:** Prof S, Yale Univ

Mid Atlantic

Acker, Michael A MD [T&CS] - **Spec Exp:** Transplant-Heart; Ventricular Assist Device (LVAD); Coronary Artery Surgery; Heart Valve Surgery; **Hospital:** Hosp Univ Penn - UPHS (page 69); **Address:** Penn Heart & Vascular Center, Perelman Ctr for Advanced Medicine, 3400 Civic Center Blvd, 2 East, Philadelphia, PA 19104; **Phone:** 215-349-8305; **Board Cert:** Thoracic & Cardiac Surgery 2013; **Med School:** Brown Univ 1981; **Resid:** Surgery, Hosp Univ Penn 1988; **Fellow:** Cardiothoracic Surgery, Johns Hopkins Hosp 1991; **Fac Appt:** Prof S, Univ Pennsylvania

Adams, David H MD [T&CS] - **Spec Exp:** Mitral Valve Surgery; Heart Valve Surgery; Minimally Invasive Cardiac Surgery; Aortic Surgery; **Hospital:** Mt Sinai Med Ctr (page 62); **Address:** Mount Sinai, Cardiothoracic Surgery, 1190 5th Ave, New York, NY 10029; **Phone:** 212-659-6820; **Board Cert:** Thoracic & Cardiac Surgery 2003; **Med School:** Duke Univ 1983; **Resid:** Surgery, Brigham & Women's Hosp 1990; Thoracic & Cardiac Surgery, Brigham & Women's Hosp/Chldn's Hosp 1992; **Fellow:** Research, Harvard Med Sch 1988; Surgery, Brigham & Women's Hosp 1992; **Fac Appt:** Prof T&CS, Mount Sinai Sch Med

Altorki, Nasser K MD [T&CS] - **Spec Exp:** Esophageal Cancer; Lung Cancer; Thoracic Cancers; **Hospital:** NY-Presby/Weill Cornell Med Ctr, NY (page 65); **Address:** 525 E 68th St, M-404, New York, NY 10065; **Phone:** 212-746-5156; **Board Cert:** Surgery 2006; Thoracic Surgery 2007; **Med School:** Egypt 1978; **Resid:** Surgery, Univ Chicago Hosps 1985; **Fellow:** Cardiothoracic Surgery, Univ Chicago Hosps 1987; **Fac Appt:** Prof S, Cornell Univ-Weill Med Coll

Argenziano, Michael MD [T&CS] - **Spec Exp:** Robotic Cardiac Surgery; Coronary Artery Surgery; Maze Procedure for Atrial Fibrillation; **Hospital:** NY-Presby/Columbia Univ Med Ctr, NY (page 65); **Address:** NY Presby Med Ctr, Milstein Bldg, 177 Fort Washington Ave, rm 7-435, New York, NY 10032; **Phone:** 212-305-5888; **Board Cert:** Thoracic & Cardiac Surgery 2013; **Med School:** Columbia P&S 1992; **Resid:** Surgery, Columbia Presby Med Ctr 1998; **Fellow:** Cardiothoracic Surgery, Columbia Presby Med Ctr 1999; **Fac Appt:** Asst Prof S, Columbia P&S

Bacha, Emile A MD [T&CS] - **Spec Exp:** Pediatric Cardiac Surgery; Congenital Heart Surgery; Neonatal & Infant Cardiac Surgery; Minimally Invasive Cardiac Surgery; **Hospital:** NY-Presby/Columbia Univ Med Ctr, NY (page 65), Morgan Stanley Children's Hosp of NY-Presby, NY (page 65); **Address:** NY-Presby, Ped Cardiothoracic Surgery, 3959 Broadway, rm 276, New York, NY 10032; **Phone:** 212-305-2688; **Board Cert:** Thoracic & Cardiac Surgery 2009; Congenital Cardiac Surgery 2009; **Med School:** Germany 1989; **Resid:** Thoracic Surgery, Mass Genl Hosp 1993; Surgery, Emory Univ Med Ctr 1995; **Fellow:** Pediatric Cardiac Surgery, Hosp Marie Lanne Longe 1996; Pediatric Cardiac Surgery, Mass Genl Hosp 1998; **Fac Appt:** Prof S, Columbia P&S

Bains, Manjit MD [T&CS] - **Spec Exp:** Cardiothoracic Surgery; Esophageal Cancer; Lung Cancer; **Hospital:** Meml Sloan-Kettering Canc Ctr; **Address:** 1275 York Ave, rm C861, New York, NY 10065; **Phone:** 212-639-7450; **Board Cert:** Surgery 1971; Thoracic Surgery 1972; **Med School:** India 1963; **Resid:** Surgery, Rochester Genl Hosp 1970; **Fellow:** Thoracic Surgery, Sloan Kettering Cancer Ctr 1972; **Fac Appt:** Clin Prof S, Cornell Univ-Weill Med Coll

Battafarano, Richard J MD [T&CS] - **Spec Exp:** Lung Cancer; Barrett's Esophagus; Esophageal Surgery; Mesothelioma; **Hospital:** Univ of MD Med Ctr; **Address:** Univ Maryland Greenebaum Cancer Ctr, Div Thoracic Surgery, 22 S Greene St, N4E35, Baltimore, MD 21201; **Phone:** 410-328-6366; **Board Cert:** Surgery 2008; Thoracic Surgery 2009; **Med School:** Hahnemann Univ 1988; **Resid:** Surgery, Univ Minn Hosp & Clin 1997; **Fellow:** Thoracic Surgery, Meml Sloan-Kettering Cancer Ctr 1999; **Fac Appt:** Assoc Prof S, Univ MD Sch Med

Bavaria, Joseph E MD [T&CS] - **Spec Exp:** Aortic Surgery-Complex; Transplant-Heart & Lung; Heart Valve Surgery; Aortic Thoracic Reconstruction; **Hospital:** Hosp Univ Penn - UPHS (page 69); **Address:** Penn Heart & Vascular Ctr, Perelman Ctr for Advanced Medicine, 3400 Civic Center Blvd, 2 East, Philadelphia, PA 19104; **Phone:** 215-662-2017; **Board Cert:** Thoracic Surgery 2001; **Med School:** Tulane Univ 1983; **Resid:** Surgery, Hosp Univ Penn 1990; **Fellow:** Thoracic & Cardiac Surgery, Hosp Univ Penn/Chldns Hosp of PA 1992; **Fac Appt:** Assoc Prof S, Univ Pennsylvania

Bhora, Faiz Y MD [T&CS] - **Spec Exp:** Lung Cancer; Esophageal Cancer; Thoracic Cancers; Robotic Surgery; **Hospital:** St. Luke's - Roosevelt Hosp Ctr - Roosevelt Div (page 56); **Address:** 325 W 15th St, New York, NY 10011; **Phone:** 212-523-7475; **Board Cert:** Thoracic Surgery 2004; **Med School:** Pakistan 1992; **Resid:** Surgery, George Washington Univ Med Ctr 2000; Cardiothoracic Surgery, UCLA Med Ctr 2002; **Fellow:** Transplant Surgery, UCLA Med Ctr 2004; Thoracic Oncology, Hosp U Penn 2005; **Fac Appt:** Assoc Clin Prof S, Columbia P&S

Chen, Jonathan M MD [T&CS] - **Spec Exp:** Pediatric Cardiothoracic Surgery; Arrhythmias; Congenital Heart Disease-Adult & Child; **Hospital:** Morgan Stanley Children's Hosp of NY-Presby, NY (page 65), NY-Presby/Weill Cornell Med Ctr, NY (page 65); **Address:** NY-Presby, Cardiothoracic Surgery, 525 E 68th St, Ste M404, New York, NY 10065; **Phone:** 212-746-5014; **Board Cert:** Thoracic & Cardiac Surgery 2011; Congenital Cardiac Surgery 2010; **Med School:** Columbia P&S 1994; **Resid:** Surgery, NY-Presby/Columbia Univ Med Ctr 2000; **Fellow:** Cardiothoracic Surgery, NY-Presby/Columbia Univ Med Ctr 2001; **Fac Appt:** Prof Ped, Columbia P&S

Cohen, Neri M MD/PhD [T&CS] - **Spec Exp:** Minimally Invasive Thoracic Surgery; Hyperhydrosis-Palmar; Video Assisted Thoracic Surgery (VATS); **Hospital:** Greater Baltimore Med Ctr; **Address:** Greater Baltimore Thoracic Surgery, 6569 N Charles St, Ste 701, Baltimore, MD 21204; **Phone:** 443-849-3470; **Board Cert:** Surgery 2009; Thoracic Surgery 2008; **Med School:** Univ MD Sch Med 1989; **Resid:** Surgery, Med Coll Virginia Hosp 1996; **Fellow:** Cardiothoracic Surgery, Med Coll Virginia Hosp 1998; Thoracic Surgery, Cleveland Clinic 1998

Conte Jr, John V MD [T&CS] - **Spec Exp:** Transplant-Heart; Transplant-Lung; Cardiac Surgery-Adult; Coronary Artery Surgery; **Hospital:** Johns Hopkins Hosp (page 59); **Address:** 1800 Orleans St, Ste 7107, Baltimore, MD 21287-4618; **Phone:** 410-955-1753; **Board Cert:** Thoracic Surgery 2007; **Med School:** Georgetown Univ 1986; **Resid:** Surgery, Georgetown Univ Med Ctr 1992; Thoracic Surgery, Stanford Univ Med Ctr 1995; **Fac Appt:** Prof S, Johns Hopkins Univ

Cooper, Joel D MD [T&CS] - **Spec Exp:** Transplant-Lung; Emphysema-Lung Volume Reduction; Lung Surgery; **Hospital:** Hosp Univ Penn - UPHS (page 69); **Address:** Univ Penn Dept Surgery, 3400 Spruce St, 4 Silverstein, Philadelphia, PA 19104; **Phone:** 215-662-2022; **Board Cert:** Surgery 1971; Thoracic & Cardiac Surgery 1972; **Med School:** Harvard Med Sch 1964; **Resid:** Surgery, Mass Genl Hosp 1968; Thoracic Surgery, Frenchay Hosp 1968; **Fellow:** Research, Hammersmith Hosp 1969; Thoracic Surgery, Mass Genl Hosp 1971; **Fac Appt:** Prof S, Univ Pennsylvania

Demmy, Todd L MD [T&CS] - **Spec Exp:** Lung Cancer; Thoracic Cancers; Esophageal Cancer; Minimally Invasive Thoracic Surgery; **Hospital:** Roswell Park Canc Inst, Buffalo Genl Hosp; **Address:** Roswell Park Cancer Inst, Thoracic Surgery Dept, Elm & Carlton Sts, Buffalo, NY 14263; **Phone:** 716-845-1229; **Board Cert:** Surgery 2008; Thoracic Surgery 2010; Surgical Critical Care 2010; **Med School:** Jefferson Med Coll 1983; **Resid:** Surgery, Baylor Affil Hosp 1988; **Fellow:** Thoracic Surgery, Allegheny Genl Hosp 1991; **Fac Appt:** Assoc Prof S, SUNY Buffalo

DeRose Jr, Joseph J MD [T&CS] - **Spec Exp:** Robotic Cardiac Surgery; Aortic Valve Replacement; Mitral Valve Surgery; Minimally Invasive Heart Valve Surgery; **Hospital:** Montefiore Med Ctr-Einstein Campus, NY, Montefiore Med Ctr-Moses Campus, NY; **Address:** Montefiore-Weiler Medical Ctr, Dept Cardiothoracic Surgery, 1575 Blondell Ave, Ste 125, Bronx, NY 10461; **Phone:** 718-405-8371; **Board Cert:** Thoracic & Cardiac Surgery 2011; **Med School:** Columbia P&S 1993; **Resid:** Surgery, Columbia Presby Med Ctr 1999; **Fellow:** Cardiothoracic Surgery, Columbia Presby Med Ctr 2001; **Fac Appt:** Assoc Prof TS, Albert Einstein Coll Med

Diehl, James T MD [T&CS] - **Spec Exp:** Cardiac Surgery-Adult; Aortic Surgery; Heart Valve Surgery-Aortic; Heart Valve Surgery-Mitral; **Hospital:** Thomas Jefferson Univ Hosp; **Address:** 1100 Walnut St Fl 5, Philadelphia, PA 19107; **Phone:** 215-955-6996; **Board Cert:** Thoracic Surgery 2004; **Med School:** Albert Einstein Coll Med 1978; **Resid:** Surgery, Cleveland Clinic 1984; **Fellow:** Cardiothoracic Surgery, Toronto Genl Hosp 1986; **Fac Appt:** Prof S, Thomas Jefferson Univ

Downey, Robert J MD [T&CS] - **Spec Exp:** Lung Cancer; Thoracic Cancers; **Hospital:** Meml Sloan-Kettering Canc Ctr; **Address:** 1275 York Avenue, New York, NY 10065; **Phone:** 212-639-8124; **Board Cert:** Surgery 2002; Surgical Critical Care 2006; Thoracic & Cardiac Surgery 2005; **Med School:** Columbia P&S 1985; **Resid:** Surgery, Columbia-Presby Med Ctr 1991; **Fellow:** Thoracic Surgery, Mayo Clinic 1992; Thoracic Surgery, Columbia-Presby Med Ctr 1994

Edwards, Niloo M MD [T&CS] - **Spec Exp:** Transplant-Heart; Cardiac Surgery-Geriatric; **Hospital:** St. Peter's Hosp - Albany; **Address:** Albany Cardiothoracic Surgeons, 319 S Manning Blvd, Ste 110, Albany, NY 12208; **Phone:** 518-525-2525; **Board Cert:** Surgery 2004; Thoracic & Cardiac Surgery 2006; **Med School:** Columbia P&S 1986; **Resid:** Surgery, Strong Meml Hosp 1992; **Fellow:** Cardiothoracic Surgery, Columbia Presby Med Ctr 1996

Filsoufi, Farzan MD [T&CS] - **Spec Exp:** Mitral Valve Surgery; Minimally Invasive Heart Valve Surgery; Heart Valve Surgery; Robotic Cardiac Surgery; **Hospital:** Mt Sinai Med Ctr (page 62); **Address:** Mount Sinai, Cardiothoracic Surgery, 1190 5th Ave Fl 2, Box 1028, New York, NY 10029; **Phone:** 212-659-6813; **Med School:** France 1991; **Resid:** Surgery, Univ Paris Hosps 1994; Thoracic Surgery, Hosp Broussais/Univ Paris 1995; **Fellow:** Cardiothoracic Surgery, Hosp Broussais/Univ Paris 1996; Heart Valve Surgery, Brigham & Womens Hosp 2000; **Fac Appt:** Prof TS, Mount Sinai Sch Med

Flores, Raja M MD [T&CS] - **Spec Exp:** Mesothelioma; Lung Cancer; Video Assisted Thoracic Surgery (VATS); Esophageal Cancer; **Hospital:** Mt Sinai Med Ctr (page 62); **Address:** Mt Sinai Medical Ctr, 1190 Fifth Ave, Box 1028, New York, NY 10029; **Phone:** 212-241-9466; **Board Cert:** Surgery 2009; Thoracic & Cardiac Surgery 2010; **Med School:** Albert Einstein Coll Med 1992; **Resid:** Surgery, Columbia Presby Med Ctr 1997; **Fellow:** Thoracic Surgery, Brigham & Womens Hosp/Dana Faber Cancer Inst 2000; **Fac Appt:** Assoc Prof TS, Cornell Univ-Weill Med Coll

Fontana, Gregory MD [T&CS] - **Spec Exp:** Minimally Invasive Surgery; Cardiac Surgery-Pediatric; Mitral Valve Surgery; Coronary Artery Surgery; **Hospital:** Lenox Hill Hosp (page 66); **Address:** Lenox Hill Hosp, Cardiothoracic Dept, 130 E 77th St Fl 4, New York, NY 10075; **Phone:** 212-434-3792; **Board Cert:** Thoracic & Cardiac Surgery 2004; **Med School:** UCLA 1984; **Resid:** Surgery, Duke Univ Med Ctr 1989; Thoracic Surgery, Duke Univ Med Ctr 1993; **Fellow:** Pediatric Cardiac Surgery, UCLA Med Ctr 1994; Pediatric Cardiac Surgery, Chldns Hosp 1994

Friedberg, Joseph MD [T&CS] - **Spec Exp:** Mesothelioma; Pleural Disease; Lung Cancer; Video Assisted Thoracic Surgery (VATS); **Hospital:** Penn Presby Med Ctr - UPHS (page 69), Hosp Univ Penn - UPHS (page 69); **Address:** Penn-Presbyterian Medical Ctr, 51 N 39th St, Wright Saunders, Ste 266, Philadelphia, PA 19104; **Phone:** 215-662-9194; **Board Cert:** Surgery 2006; Thoracic Surgery 2006; **Med School:** Harvard Med Sch 1986; **Resid:** Surgery, Mass General Hosp 1994; **Fellow:** Cardiothoracic Surgery, Brigham & Womens Hosp 1996; **Fac Appt:** Assoc Prof TS, Univ Pennsylvania

Furukawa, Satoshi MD [T&CS] - **Spec Exp:** Cardiac Surgery-High Risk; Heart Valve Surgery; Minimally Invasive Cardiac Surgery; Heart Failure & Ventricular Containment; **Hospital:** Reading Hosp; **Address:** Cardiothoracic Surgical Assocs, 301 S Seventh Ave, Ste 1120, Reading, PA 19611; **Phone:** 484-628-0580; **Board Cert:** Surgery 2003; Thoracic Surgery 2005; **Med School:** Univ Pennsylvania 1984; **Resid:** Surgery, Hosp Univ Penn 1991; Thoracic & Cardiac Surgery, Hosp Univ Penn 1993

Galloway, Aubrey MD [T&CS] - **Spec Exp:** Minimally Invasive Heart Valve Surgery; Mitral Valve Surgery; Coronary Artery Surgery; Robotic Surgery; **Hospital:** NYU Langone Med Ctr (page 68); **Address:** NYU Med Ctr, Cardiothoracic Surgery, 560 1st Ave, Ste 9V, New York, NY 10016; **Phone:** 212-263-7185; **Board Cert:** Thoracic Surgery 2006; **Med School:** Tulane Univ 1978; **Resid:** Surgery, Univ CO Hlth Sci Ctr 1983; Cardiovascular Surgery, NYU Med Ctr 1985; **Fellow:** Research, Chldns Hosp 1981; Cardiothoracic Surgery, NYU Med Ctr 1985; **Fac Appt:** Prof TS, NYU Sch Med

Gaynor, J William MD [T&CS] - **Spec Exp:** Pediatric Cardiothoracic Surgery; Congenital Heart Surgery; Transplant-Heart & Lung; **Hospital:** Chldns Hosp of Philadelphia; **Address:** CHOP, Div of Cardiothoracic Surgery, 34th St & Civic Center Blvd, Ste 12NW10 Main, Philadelphia, PA 19104; **Phone:** 215-590-2708; **Board Cert:** Thoracic Surgery 2004; Congenital Cardiac Surgery 2009; **Med School:** Med Univ SC 1982; **Resid:** Surgery, Parkland Meml Hosp 1984; Surgery, Duke Univ Med Ctr 1991; **Fellow:** Cardiothoracic Surgery, Duke Univ Med Ctr 1992; Congenital Heart Surgery, Hosp for Sick Chldn 1993; **Fac Appt:** Assoc Prof S, Univ Pennsylvania

Ginsburg, Mark E MD [T&CS] - **Spec Exp:** Lung Cancer; Transplant-Lung; Emphysema-Lung Volume Reduction; **Hospital:** NY-Presby/Columbia Univ Med Ctr, NY (page 65), Good Samaritan Hosp - Suffern; **Address:** NY-Presby, Cardiothoracic Surgery, 161 Fort Washington Ave, Ste 301, New York, NY 10032; **Phone:** 212-305-3408; **Board Cert:** Surgery 2005; Thoracic & Cardiac Surgery 2006; **Med School:** Tufts Univ 1980; **Resid:** Surgery, Univ Rochester-Strong Meml Hosp 1985; **Fellow:** Thoracic & Cardiac Surgery, Univ Rochester-Strong Meml Hosp 1987; **Fac Appt:** Assoc Clin Prof S, Columbia P&S

Girardi, Leonard N MD [T&CS] - **Spec Exp:** Aneurysm-Aortic; Cardiac Surgery; Marfan's Syndrome; Aneurysm; **Hospital:** NY-Presby/Weill Cornell Med Ctr, NY (page 65); **Address:** NY-Presby, Cardiothoracic Surgery, 525 E 68th St, Ste M404, New York, NY 10065; **Phone:** 212-746-5194; **Board Cert:** Surgery 2005; Thoracic & Cardiac Surgery 2007; **Med School:** Cornell Univ-Weill Med Coll 1989; **Resid:** Surgery, NY-Presby/Weill Cornell Med Ctr 1994; **Fellow:** Cardiothoracic Surgery, NY-Presby/Weill Cornell Med Ctr 1996; Cardiothoracic Surgery, Baylor Med Ctr 1997; **Fac Appt:** Prof TS, Cornell Univ-Weill Med Coll

Graver, L. Michael MD [T&CS] - **Spec Exp:** Minimally Invasive Cardiac Surgery; Coronary Artery Surgery; Aortic Surgery; Heart Valve Surgery; **Hospital:** Long Is Jewish Med Ctr (page 66); **Address:** LIJ Med Ctr, Cardiothoracic Surgery, 270-05 76th Ave, Ste O-4000, New Hyde Park, NY 11040; **Phone:** 718-470-7460; **Board Cert:** Surgery 2003; Thoracic Surgery 2004; **Med School:** Albany Med Coll 1977; **Resid:** Surgery, St Lukes-Roosevelt Hosp Ctr 1982; Cardiovascular Surgery, Beth Israel Deaconess Hosp 1983; **Fellow:** Cardiovascular Pathology, NY-Presby/Weill Cornell Med Ctr 1985; **Fac Appt:** Prof TS, Hofstra N Shore-LIJ Sch Med

Griffith, Bartley MD [T&CS] - **Spec Exp:** Transplant-Heart & Lung; Aneurysm-Aortic; Heart Valve Surgery; **Hospital:** Univ of MD Med Ctr; **Address:** UMMC-Div Cardiothoracic Surg, 110 S Paca St Fl 7, Baltimore, MD 21201; **Phone:** 410-328-3822; **Board Cert:** Thoracic Surgery 2013; **Med School:** Jefferson Med Coll 1974; **Resid:** Surgery, Univ Hlth Ctr Hosps 1979; Thoracic Surgery, Univ Hlth Ctr Hosps 1981; **Fellow:** Research, Univ Hlth Ctr Hosps 1978; **Fac Appt:** Prof S, Univ MD Sch Med

Grossi, Eugene A MD [T&CS] - **Spec Exp:** Minimally Invasive Cardiac Surgery; Mitral Valve Surgery; Cardiac Tumors, Myxomas; **Hospital:** NYU Langone Med Ctr (page 68); **Address:** NYU Med Ctr, Cardiothoracic Surgery, 530 1st Ave, Ste 9V, New York, NY 10016; **Phone:** 212-263-7452; **Board Cert:** Thoracic & Cardiac Surgery 2011; **Med School:** Columbia P&S 1981; **Resid:** Surgery, NYU Med Ctr 1987; Thoracic Surgery, NYU Med Ctr 1991; **Fac Appt:** Prof S, NYU Sch Med

Guy, T Sloane MD [T&CS] - **Spec Exp:** Robotic Cardiac Surgery; Minimally Invasive Heart Valve Surgery; **Hospital:** Temple Univ Hosp; **Address:** Temple Cardiovascular Surgery, 3401 N Broad St, Green Zone - 3rd Fl, Philadelphia, PA 19140; **Phone:** 215-707-3601; **Board Cert:** Surgery 2011; Thoracic & Cardiac Surgery 2005; **Med School:** Univ Pennsylvania 1994; **Resid:** Surgery, Hosp Univ Penn 2002; **Fellow:** Thoracic & Cardiac Surgery, Hosp Univ Penn 2004; **Fac Appt:** Assoc Prof S, Temple Univ

Hargrove III, W Clark MD [T&CS] - **Spec Exp:** Mitral Valve Robotic Surgery; Heart Valve Surgery; Minimally Invasive Cardiac Surgery; **Hospital:** Penn Presby Med Ctr - UPHS (page 69); **Address:** Philadelphia Heart Inst, 51 N 39th St, Ste 2A, Philadelphia, PA 19104; **Phone:** 215-662-9595; **Board Cert:** Thoracic Surgery 2004; **Med School:** Wake Forest Univ 1973; **Resid:** Surgery, Hosp Univ Penn 1979; **Fellow:** Vascular Surgery, Hosp Univ Penn 1981; Thoracic & Cardiac Surgery, Hosp Univ Penn 1984; **Fac Appt:** Clin Prof S, Univ Pennsylvania

Heitmiller, Richard F MD [T&CS] - **Spec Exp:** Esophageal Cancer; Lung Cancer; **Hospital:** MedStar Union Meml Hosp; **Address:** Union Memorial Hosp, 3333 N Calvert St, Ste 610, Baltimore, MD 21218-2867; **Phone:** 410-554-2063; **Board Cert:** Thoracic & Cardiac Surgery 2008; **Med School:** Johns Hopkins Univ 1979; **Resid:** Surgery, Mass Genl Hosp 1985; **Fellow:** Thoracic Surgery, Mass Genl Hosp 1987; **Fac Appt:** Assoc Prof Surg & Onc, Johns Hopkins Univ

Horvath, Keith A MD [T&CS] - **Spec Exp:** Minimally Invasive Cardiac Surgery; Heart Valve Surgery; Heart Laser Revascularization; **Hospital:** Suburban Hosp, Johns Hopkins Hosp (page 59); **Address:** 8600 Old Georgetown Rd, Bethesda, MD 20814; **Phone:** 301-896-7610; **Board Cert:** Thoracic Surgery 2005; **Med School:** Univ Chicago-Pritzker Sch Med 1987; **Resid:** Surgery, Brigham & Women's Hosp 1994; **Fellow:** Thoracic & Cardiac Surgery, Brigham & Women's Hosp 1997; **Fac Appt:** Assoc Prof S, Northwestern Univ

Isom, O. Wayne MD [T&CS] - **Spec Exp:** Cardiac Surgery; Coronary Artery Surgery; Heart Valve Surgery; **Hospital:** NY-Presby/Weill Cornell Med Ctr, NY (page 65), NY Hosp Queens; **Address:** NY-Presby, Cardiothoracic Surgery, 525 E 68th St, Ste M404, New York, NY 10065; **Phone:** 212-746-5151; **Board Cert:** Surgery 1971; Thoracic Surgery 1972; **Med School:** Univ Tex, Houston 1965; **Resid:** Surgery, Parkland Meml Hosp 1970; **Fellow:** Thoracic Surgery, NYU Med Ctr 1972; **Fac Appt:** Prof TS, Cornell Univ-Weill Med Coll

Jonas, Richard A MD [T&CS] - **Spec Exp:** Pediatric Cardiothoracic Surgery; Congenital Heart Disease; **Hospital:** Chldns Natl Med Ctr, MedStar Georgetown Univ Hosp; **Address:** 111 Michigan Ave NW, Washington, DC 20010; **Phone:** 202-476-2811; **Med School:** Australia 1974; **Resid:** Surgery, Royal Melbourne Hosp 1979; Thoracic Surgery, Green Lane Hosp 1982; **Fellow:** Thoracic Surgery, Brigham & Women's Hosp 1984; **Fac Appt:** Prof S, Geo Wash Univ

Jones, David R MD [T&CS] - **Spec Exp:** Lung Cancer; Esophageal Cancer; Minimally Invasive Thoracic Surgery; **Hospital:** Meml Sloan-Kettering Canc Ctr; **Address:** Meml Sloan-Kettering Canc Ctr, 1275 York Ave, Box 7, New York, NY 10065; **Phone:** 646-497-9163; **Board Cert:** Surgery 2005; Thoracic Surgery 2007; **Med School:** W VA Univ 1989; **Resid:** Surgery, W VA Univ Affil Hosp 1995; **Fellow:** Thoracic Surgery, Univ NC Affil Hosp 1998; **Fac Appt:** Prof S, Cornell Univ-Weill Med Coll

Kaiser, Larry R MD [T&CS] - **Spec Exp:** Lung Cancer; Esophageal Cancer; Mediastinal Tumors; Myasthenia Gravis; **Hospital:** Temple Univ Hosp; **Address:** Temple Univ Sch Medicine, 3401 N Broad St, Philadelphia, PA 19140; **Phone:** 215-707-8773; **Board Cert:** Surgery 2005; Thoracic Surgery 2006; **Med School:** Tulane Univ 1977; **Resid:** Surgery, UCLA Med Ctr 1983; Cardiothoracic Surgery, Univ Toronto Hosps 1985; **Fellow:** Surgical Oncology, UCLA 1981; **Fac Appt:** Prof TS, Temple Univ

Keenan, Robert J MD [T&CS] - **Spec Exp:** Lung Cancer; Esophageal Cancer; Mediastinal Tumors; Emphysema-Lung Volume Reduction; **Hospital:** Allegheny Genl Hosp, West Penn Hosp-Forbes Campus; **Address:** Center for Thoracic Surgery, Allegheny Cancer Ctr, 320 E North Ave, Ste 363, Pittsburgh, PA 15212; **Phone:** 412-359-6137; **Board Cert:** Surgery 2009; **Med School:** Univ Alberta 1984; **Resid:** Surgery, Univ Toronto Affil Hosp 1989; **Fellow:** Thoracic Surgery, Univ Pittsburgh 1990; Thoracic Surgery, Univ Toronto 1992; **Fac Appt:** Prof S, Drexel Univ Coll Med

Keller, Steven M MD [T&CS] - **Spec Exp:** Lung Cancer; Esophageal Cancer; Mediastinal Tumors; Hyperhidrosis-Palmar; **Hospital:** Montefiore Med Ctr-Einstein Campus, NY; **Address:** Montefiore-Einstein Medical Ctr, 1575 Blondell Ave, Ste 125, Bronx, NY 10461; **Phone:** 718-405-8378; **Board Cert:** Thoracic Surgery 2007; **Med School:** Albany Med Coll 1977; **Resid:** Surgery, Mount Sinai Hosp 1985; Thoracic Surgery, Mem Sloan Kettering Cancer Ctr 1987; **Fellow:** Surgical Oncology, NIH/National Cancer Inst 1983; **Fac Appt:** Prof TS, Albert Einstein Coll Med

Kiev, Jonathan MD [T&CS] - **Spec Exp:** Chest Wall Tumors; Esophageal Cancer; Lung Cancer; **Hospital:** Cabell Huntington Hosp; **Address:** Cabell Huntington Hosp, Thoracic Surg, 1600 Medical Ctr Drive, Ste 2500, Huntington, WV 25701; **Phone:** 304-691-1200; **Board Cert:** Surgery 2005; Thoracic Surgery 2010; **Med School:** Tulane Univ 1989; **Resid:** Surgery, Hahnemann Univ Hosp 1996; Cardiothoracic Surgery, Loma Linda Univ 2000; **Fellow:** Thoracic Surgery, Univ Pittsburgh 2001; Thoracic Surgery, Mayo Clinic 2001

Kormos, Robert MD [T&CS] - **Spec Exp:** Transplant-Heart; Artificial Heart Devices; **Hospital:** UPMC Presby, Pittsburgh; **Address:** UPMC Presby Hosp, 200 Lothrop St, Ste C714, Pittsburgh, PA 15213; **Phone:** 412-648-6259; **Med School:** Univ Western Ontario 1976; **Resid:** Surgery, Toronto Western Hosp 1980; Cardiothoracic Surgery, Toronto Genl Hosp/Hosp for Sick Chldn 1983; **Fellow:** Transplant Surgery, Univ Pittsburgh Med Ctr 1987; **Fac Appt:** Prof S, Univ Pittsburgh

Krellenstein, Daniel J MD/PhD [T&CS] - **Spec Exp:** Lung Cancer; Minimally Invasive Thoracic Surgery; Asbestos-related Lung Disease; **Hospital:** Mt Sinai Med Ctr (page 62), Lenox Hill Hosp (page 66); **Address:** 16 E 98th St, Ste 1F, New York, NY 10029-6545; **Phone:** 212-423-9311; **Board Cert:** Surgery 1974; Thoracic & Cardiac Surgery 2006; **Med School:** SUNY Buffalo 1964; **Resid:** Surgery, SUNY Downstate Med Ctr 1971; **Fellow:** Thoracic & Cardiac Surgery, Kings County Hosp Ctr 1972; **Fac Appt:** Assoc Clin Prof TS, Mount Sinai Sch Med

Krieger, Karl H MD [T&CS] - **Spec Exp:** Heart Valve Surgery; Coronary Artery Surgery; Cardiac Surgery-Adult; **Hospital:** NY-Presby/Weill Cornell Med Ctr, NY (page 65); **Address:** NY-Presby, Cardiothoracic Surgery, 525 E 68th St, Ste M404, New York, NY 10065; **Phone:** 212-746-5152; **Board Cert:** Thoracic & Cardiac Surgery 2004; **Med School:** Johns Hopkins Univ 1975; **Resid:** Surgery, Johns Hopkins Hosp 1976; Bellevue Hosp 1979; **Fellow:** Thoracic Surgery, NYU Med Ctr 1981; **Fac Appt:** Prof S, Cornell Univ-Weill Med Coll

Kucharczuk, John C MD [T&CS] - **Spec Exp:** Lung Cancer; Esophageal Cancer; Chest Wall Tumors; Mediastinal Tumors; **Hospital:** Hosp Univ Penn - UPHS (page 69); **Address:** Penn Lung Center, Perelman Ctr for Advanced Medicine, 3400 Civic Center Blvd, 1 West, Philadelphia, PA 19104; **Phone:** 215-662-4988; **Board Cert:** Surgery 2008; Thoracic Surgery 2010; **Med School:** Univ Pennsylvania 1992; **Resid:** Surgery, Hosp Univ Penn 1999; **Fellow:** Cardiothoracic Surgery, Hosp Univ Penn 2001; **Fac Appt:** Assoc Prof S, Univ Pennsylvania

Lang, Samuel J MD [T&CS] - **Spec Exp:** Minimally Invasive Cardiac Surgery; Heart Valve Surgery; Cardiothoracic Surgery; **Hospital:** NY Hosp Queens, NY-Presby/Weill Cornell Med Ctr, NY (page 65); **Address:** NY Hosp, Cardiothoracic Surgery Dept, 56-45 Main St, rm 387, Flushing, NY 11355; **Phone:** 718-670-1137; **Board Cert:** Thoracic & Cardiac Surgery 2006; **Med School:** UAB Sch Med 1978; **Resid:** Surgery, UCLA Med Ctr 1982; Thoracic Surgery, NYU Med Ctr 1983; **Fellow:** Cardiothoracic Surgery, UCLA Med Ctr 1985; Pediatric Cardiac Surgery, Hosp Sick Chldn 1986; **Fac Appt:** Prof S, Cornell Univ-Weill Med Coll

Lansman, Steven L MD/PhD [T&CS] - **Spec Exp:** Coronary Artery Surgery; Heart Valve Surgery; Ventricular Assist Device (LVAD); Transplant-Heart; **Hospital:** Westchester Med Ctr; **Address:** Westchester Med Ctr, Heart Inst, 95 Grasslands Rd, Valhalla, NY 10595; **Phone:** 914-493-8793; **Board Cert:** Thoracic Surgery 2004; **Med School:** SUNY Hlth Sci Ctr 1977; **Resid:** Surgery, Montefiore Med Ctr 1982; **Fellow:** Thoracic Surgery, Univ Hosp 1984; **Fac Appt:** Prof S, NY Med Coll

Lazzaro, Richard S MD [T&CS] - **Spec Exp:** Thoracic Surgery; Robotic Surgery; Minimally Invasive Surgery; Thoracic Surgery; **Hospital:** Lenox Hill Hosp (page 66), N Shore Univ Hosp (page 66); **Address:** Lenox Hill Hosp, Cardiothoracic Surgery, 130 E 77th St Fl 4, New York, NY 10075; **Phone:** 212-434-3000; **Board Cert:** Surgery 2006; Thoracic & Cardiac Surgery 2007; **Med School:** Albany Med Coll 1988; **Resid:** Surgery, N Shore Univ Hosp 1994; **Fellow:** Cardiothoracic Surgery, Maimonides Med Ctr 1997; Thoracic Surgery, UPMC 1998

Loulmet, Didier F MD [T&CS] - **Spec Exp:** Heart Valve Surgery; Robotic Cardiac Surgery; Minimally Invasive Cardiac Surgery; Aneurysm-Aortic; **Hospital:** NYU Langone Med Ctr (page 68); **Address:** NYU Med Ctr, Cardiothoracic Surgery, 530 1st Ave, Ste 9V, New York, NY 10016; **Phone:** 212-263-2329; **Med School:** France 1984; **Resid:** Cardiothoracic Surgery, Paris Univ Hosp 1990; Cardiothoracic Surgery, Brigham & Womens Hosp 1991; **Fellow:** Pediatric Cardiac Surgery, Chdns Hosp 1992; **Fac Appt:** Assoc Prof TS, NYU Sch Med

Magovern Jr, George J MD [T&CS] - **Spec Exp:** Cardiac Surgery; Ventricular Assist Device (LVAD); **Hospital:** Allegheny Genl Hosp; **Address:** Cardiovascular Surgery Ctr, CVI-1, 320 E North Ave, NW Wing-Snyder Pavilion, Allegheny Genl Hosp, Pittsburgh, PA 15212; **Phone:** 412-359-8820; **Board Cert:** Thoracic Surgery 2005; **Med School:** Univ Pittsburgh 1978; **Resid:** Surgery, Johns Hopkins Hosp 1983; **Fellow:** Cardiovascular Surgery, Johns Hopkins Hosp 1985; **Fac Appt:** Prof S, Drexel Univ Coll Med

Marshall, M. Blair MD [T&CS] - **Spec Exp:** Lung Cancer; Esophageal Cancer; Thymoma; Chest Wall Tumors; **Hospital:** MedStar Georgetown Univ Hosp, Sibley Mem Hosp; **Address:** Georgetown Univ Hosp, Dept Thoracic Surg, 3800 Reservoir Rd NW, 4PHC, Washington, DC 20007; **Phone:** 202-444-5045; **Board Cert:** Surgery 2009; Thoracic Surgery 2012; **Med School:** Georgetown Univ 1991; **Resid:** Surgery, Georgetown Univ Med Ctr 1995; **Fellow:** Research, Chldn's Hosp 1998; Cardiothoracic Surgery, Hosp Univ Penn 2001; **Fac Appt:** Assoc Prof S, Georgetown Univ

Michler, Robert E MD [T&CS] - **Spec Exp:** Heart Valve Surgery; Coronary Artery Surgery; Atrial Fibrillation; Aneurysm-Aortic; **Hospital:** Montefiore Med Ctr-Moses Campus, NY, Montefiore Med Ctr-Einstein Campus, NY; **Address:** Montefiore, Dept Cardio/Thoracic Surgery, Green Medical Arts Pavilion, 3400 Bainbridge Ave, Ste 5, New York, NY 10467; **Phone:** 718-920-2100; **Board Cert:** Thoracic & Cardiac Surgery 2010; **Med School:** Dartmouth Med Sch 1981; **Resid:** Surgery, Columbia Presby Med Ctr 1987; **Fellow:** Cardiothoracic Surgery, Columbia Presby Med Ctr 1989; Congenital Heart Surgery, Boston Children's Hosp 1990; **Fac Appt:** Prof T&CS, Albert Einstein Coll Med

Morris, Rohinton J MD [T&CS] - **Spec Exp:** Transplant-Heart; Ventricular Assist Device (LVAD); Coronary Artery Surgery; **Hospital:** Abington Meml Hosp; **Address:** AMH-Cardiac Surgery, 1200 Old York Rd, Toll Bldg Fl 5, Abington, PA 19001; **Phone:** 215-481-4200; **Board Cert:** Thoracic Surgery 2013; **Med School:** Hahnemann Univ 1984; **Resid:** Surgery, Hahnemann Univ Hosp 1989; **Fellow:** Thoracic Surgery, Hahnemann Univ Hosp 1992; **Fac Appt:** Assoc Clin Prof S, Univ Pennsylvania

Mosca, Ralph S MD [T&CS] - **Spec Exp:** Congenital Heart Disease-Adult & Child; Pediatric Cardiac Surgery; **Hospital:** NYU Langone Med Ctr (page 68); **Address:** 530 1st Ave, Ste 9V, New York, NY 10016; **Phone:** 212-263-5989; **Board Cert:** Thoracic Surgery 2011; **Med School:** SUNY Upstate Med Univ 1985; **Resid:** Surgery, SUNY Hlth Sci Ctr 1990; **Fellow:** Cardiothoracic Surgery, Columbia-Presby Med Ctr 1992; Pediatric Cardiac Surgery, Univ Mich Med Ctr 1993; **Fac Appt:** Prof TS, NYU Sch Med

Naka, Yoshifumi MD/PhD [T&CS] - **Spec Exp:** Transplant-Heart; Ventricular Assist Device (LVAD); Heart Failure & Ventricular Containment; Mitral Valve Surgery; **Hospital:** NY-Presby/Columbia Univ Med Ctr, NY (page 65); **Address:** NY-Presby, Cardiothoracic Surgery, 177 Fort Washington Ave, Ste 7-435, New York, NY 10032; **Phone:** 212-305-0828; **Med School:** Japan 1984; **Resid:** Surgery, Osaka Police Hosp 1991; **Fellow:** Cardiovascular Surgery, Osaka Police Hosp 1993; Cardiothoracic Surgery, NY-Presby/Columbia Univ Med Ctr 1998; **Fac Appt:** Prof S, Columbia P&S

Oz, Mehmet C MD [T&CS] - **Spec Exp:** Transplant-Heart; Heart Valve Surgery; Minimally Invasive Cardiac Surgery; **Hospital:** NY-Presby/Columbia Univ Med Ctr, NY (page 65); **Address:** NY-Presby, Cardiothoracic Surgery, 177 Fort Washington Ave, Ste 7-435, New York, NY 10032; **Phone:** 212-305-4434; **Board Cert:** Thoracic Surgery 2003; **Med School:** Univ Pennsylvania 1986; **Resid:** Surgery, NY-Presby/Columbia Univ Med Ctr 1991; **Fellow:** Cardiothoracic Surgery, NY-Presby/Columbia Univ Med Ctr 1993; **Fac Appt:** Prof S, Columbia P&S

Park, Bernard J MD [T&CS] - **Spec Exp:** Lung Cancer; Esophageal Cancer; Mediastinal Tumors; Robotic Surgery; **Hospital:** Hackensack Univ Med Ctr, Hackensack UMC-Pascack Valley; **Address:** 30 Prospect Ave, Ste 5640, Hackensack, NJ 07601; **Phone:** 551-996-4218; **Board Cert:** Surgery 2011; Thoracic Surgery 2013; **Med School:** Univ Pennsylvania 1993; **Resid:** Surgery, New York Hosp 1996; Surgery, Meml Sloan Kettering Cancer Ctr 2000; **Fellow:** Cardiothoracic Surgery, Meml Sloan Kettering Cancer Ctr 2002; **Fac Appt:** Asst Clin Prof TS, UMDNJ-NJ Med Sch, Newark

Pass, Harvey I MD [T&CS] - **Spec Exp:** Lung Cancer; Mesothelioma; Clinical Trials; Robotic Surgery; **Hospital:** NYU Langone Med Ctr (page 68); **Address:** NYU Cancer Ctr, 160 E 34th St, Fl 8, New York, NY 10016; **Phone:** 212-731-5414; **Board Cert:** Thoracic & Cardiac Surgery 2001; **Med School:** Duke Univ 1973; **Resid:** Surgery, Duke Univ Med Ctr 1975; Surgery, Univ Miss Med Ctr 1980; **Fellow:** Cardiothoracic Surgery, MUSC Med Ctr 1982; Thoracic Oncology, Natl Cancer Inst 1985; **Fac Appt:** Prof T&CS, NYU Sch Med

Pechet, Taine T.V. MD [T&CS] - **Spec Exp:** Lung Cancer; Esophageal Cancer; Video Assisted Thoracic Surgery (VATS); Interventional Bronchoscopy; **Hospital:** Penn Presby Med Ctr - UPHS (page 69); **Address:** Penn Presby Med Ctr, 51 N 39th St, Wright Saunders, Ste 266, Philadelphia, PA 19104; **Phone:** 215-662-9194; **Board Cert:** Surgery 2009; Thoracic & Cardiac Surgery 2010; **Med School:** Harvard Med Sch 1992; **Resid:** Surgery, Brigham & Women's Hosp 2000; **Fellow:** Thoracic Surgery, Barnes-Jewish Hosp 2002; **Fac Appt:** Assoc Clin Prof S, Univ Pennsylvania

Pierson III, Richard N MD [T&CS] - **Spec Exp:** Transplant-Lung; Lung Cancer; Transplant-Heart; **Hospital:** Univ of MD Med Ctr, VA Med Ctr - Washington; **Address:** UMMC-Div Cardiothoracic Surg, 110 S Paca St Fl 7, Baltimore, MD 21201; **Phone:** 410-328-5842; **Board Cert:** Surgery 2011; Thoracic Surgery 2013; **Med School:** Columbia P&S 1983; **Resid:** Surgery, Univ Mich Med Ctr 1990; **Fellow:** Cardiothoracic Surgery, Mass Genl Hosp 1992; **Fac Appt:** Assoc Prof TS, Univ MD Sch Med

Port, Jeffrey L MD [T&CS] - **Spec Exp:** Lung Cancer; Esophageal Cancer; **Hospital:** NY-Presby/Weill Cornell Med Ctr, NY (page 65); **Address:** 525 E 68th St, Ste M404, New York, NY 10065; **Phone:** 212-746-5197; **Board Cert:** Surgery 2009; Thoracic & Cardiac Surgery 2009; **Med School:** NYU Sch Med 1991; **Resid:** Surgery, NYU Med Ctr 1998; **Fellow:** Thoracic Surgery, NY Presby Hosp 2000; **Fac Appt:** Assoc Prof TS, Cornell Univ-Weill Med Coll

Rusch, Valerie MD [T&CS] - **Spec Exp:** Mesothelioma; Lung Cancer; Esophageal Cancer; Thoracic Cancers; **Hospital:** Meml Sloan-Kettering Canc Ctr; **Address:** 1275 York Ave, New York, NY 10021-6094; **Phone:** 212-639-5873; **Board Cert:** Surgery 2011; Thoracic Surgery 2003; **Med School:** Columbia P&S 1975; **Resid:** Surgery, Univ Washington Med Ctr 1980; Cardiothoracic Surgery, Univ Washington Med Ctr 1982; **Fac Appt:** Prof TS, Cornell Univ-Weill Med Coll

Samuels, Louis E MD [T&CS] - **Spec Exp:** Transplant-Heart; Artificial Heart Devices; Ventricular Assist Device (LVAD); **Hospital:** Bryn Mawr Hosp, Paoli Hosp; **Address:** Main Line Cardiothoracic Surgery, 830 Old Lancaster Rd, MOB North, Ste 210, Bryn Mawr, PA 19010; **Phone:** 610-527-1600; **Board Cert:** Thoracic & Cardiac Surgery 2005; **Med School:** Hahnemann Univ 1987; **Resid:** Surgery, Hahnemann Univ Hosp 1992; **Fellow:** Thoracic & Cardiac Surgery, Hahnemann Univ Hosp 1995; **Fac Appt:** Asst Prof S, Hahnemann Univ

Sanchez, Juan A MD [T&CS] - **Spec Exp:** Lung Surgery; Esophageal Surgery; Cardiac Surgery; Thymoma; **Hospital:** St. Agnes Hosp; **Address:** St Agnes Hosp, Surgery Dept, 900 Caton Ave Fl 7, Box 207, Baltimore, MD 21229; **Phone:** 410-368-2730; **Board Cert:** Thoracic Surgery 2004; Surgery 2008; **Med School:** Univ Fla Coll Med 1984; **Resid:** Surgery, Georgetown Univ Hosp 1989; Thoracic Surgery, Yale-New Haven Hosp 1993; **Fellow:** Research, NY-Presby/Columbia Univ Med Ctr 1990; Transplant Surgery, Yale-New Haven Hosp 1991; **Fac Appt:** Prof S, Univ Conn

Scott, Walter J MD [T&CS] - **Spec Exp:** Lung Cancer; Esophageal Cancer; Mediastinal Tumors; Video Assisted Thoracic Surgery (VATS); **Hospital:** Fox Chase Cancer Ctr (page 57), Jeanes Hosp; **Address:** Fox Chase Cancer Ctr, 333 Cottman Ave, rm C308, Philadelphia, PA 19111; **Phone:** 215-214-1427; **Board Cert:** Thoracic & Cardiac Surgery 2010; **Med School:** Univ Chicago-Pritzker Sch Med 1981; **Resid:** Surgery, Univ Chicago Med Ctr 1987; **Fellow:** Cardiothoracic Surgery, Univ Chicago Med Ctr 1989

Smith Jr, Craig R MD [T&CS] - **Spec Exp:** Mitral Valve Surgery; Minimally Invasive Cardiac Surgery; Robotic Cardiac Surgery; Coronary Artery Surgery; **Hospital:** NY-Presby/Columbia Univ Med Ctr, NY (page 65); **Address:** NY-Presby, Cardiothoracic Surgery, 177 Fort Washington Ave, Ste 7-435, New York, NY 10032; **Phone:** 212-305-8312; **Board Cert:** Thoracic Surgery 2004; **Med School:** Case West Res Univ 1977; **Resid:** Surgery, Univ Rochester-Strong Meml Hosp 1982; **Fellow:** Cardiothoracic Surgery, NY-Presby/Columbia Univ Med Ctr 1984; **Fac Appt:** Prof S, Columbia P&S

Soberman, Mark S MD [T&CS] - **Spec Exp:** Thoracic Cancers; Lung Cancer; Esophageal Cancer; Esophageal Surgery; **Hospital:** Frederick Mem Hospital; **Address:** 501 W 7th St, Ste D, Frederick, MD 21701; **Phone:** 301-694-5861; **Board Cert:** Thoracic & Cardiac Surgery 2013; **Med School:** Emory Univ 1983; **Resid:** Surgery, Emory Univ Hosp 1990; Cardiothoracic Surgery, George Wash Univ Hosp 1992; **Fellow:** Thoracic & Cardiac Surgery, Cleveland Clinic 1992; 1993; **Fac Appt:** Assoc Clin Prof T&CS, Georgetown Univ

Sonett, Joshua R MD [T&CS] - **Spec Exp:** Minimally Invasive Thoracic Surgery; Transplant-Lung; Thoracic Cancers; Emphysema-Lung Volume Reduction; **Hospital:** NY-Presby/Columbia Univ Med Ctr, NY (page 65); **Address:** 161 Fort Washington Ave, Ste 301, New York, NY 10032; **Phone:** 212-305-8086; **Board Cert:** Surgery 2004; Thoracic Surgery 2007; **Med School:** E Carolina Univ 1988; **Resid:** Surgery, Univ Mass Med Ctr 1993; **Fellow:** Cardiothoracic Surgery, Univ Pittsburgh Med Ctr 1994; Thoracic Surgery, Meml Sloan Kettering Cancer Ctr; **Fac Appt:** Prof S, Columbia P&S

Spray, Thomas L MD [T&CS] - **Spec Exp:** Cardiac Surgery-Adult & Pediatric; Transplant-Heart & Lung; Neonatal & Infant Cardiac Surgery; Congenital Heart Surgery; **Hospital:** Chldns Hosp of Philadelphia, Hosp Univ Penn - UPHS (page 69); **Address:** Childrens Hosp, Div Cardiothoracic Surg, 34th St & Civic Ctr Blvd, Ste 12NW10 Main, Philadelphia, PA 19104; **Phone:** 215-590-2708; **Board Cert:** Thoracic Surgery 2004; Congenital Cardiac Surgery 2009; **Med School:** Duke Univ 1973; **Resid:** Surgery, Duke Univ Med Ctr 1975; Cardiothoracic Surgery, Duke Univ Med Ctr 1983; **Fac Appt:** Prof S, Univ Pennsylvania

Stewart, Allan MD [T&CS] - **Spec Exp:** Heart Valve Surgery-Aortic; Aneurysm-Aortic; Aortic Surgery; **Hospital:** Mt Sinai Med Ctr (page 62); **Address:** Mt Sinai Med Ctr, Guggenheim Pavilion, 1190 5th Ave Fl 2, Cardiothoracic Surgery, New York, NY 10029; **Phone:** 212-659-6820; **Board Cert:** Surgery 2003; Thoracic Surgery 2006; **Med School:** UMDNJ-NJ Med Sch, Newark 1995; **Resid:** Surgery, Hosp Univ Penn 2002; **Fellow:** Thoracic Surgery, NY-Presby/Columbia Univ Med Ctr 2004; **Fac Appt:** Asst Prof TS, Mount Sinai Sch Med

Swistel, Daniel MD [T&CS] - **Spec Exp:** Coronary Artery Surgery; Minimally Invasive Surgery; Heart Valve Surgery; Hypertrophic Cardiomyopathy; **Hospital:** St. Luke's - Roosevelt Hosp Ctr - St Luke's Hosp (page 56); **Address:** St Lukes Hosp, Cardiothoracic Surgery, 111 Amsterdam Ave, Ste A, New York, NY 10025; **Phone:** 212-523-4088; **Board Cert:** Thoracic & Cardiac Surgery 2006; **Med School:** UMDNJ-RW Johnson Med Sch 1979; **Resid:** Surgery, St Lukes Hosp 1984; Cardiothoracic Surgery, Montefiore Med Ctr 1986; **Fac Appt:** Assoc Clin Prof TS, Columbia P&S

Szeto, Wilson Y MD [T&CS] - **Spec Exp:** Thoracic Aortic Surgery; Heart Valve Disease; Ventricular Assist Device (LVAD); Endovascular Stent Grafts; **Hospital:** Penn Presby Med Ctr - UPHS (page 69), Hosp Univ Penn - UPHS (page 69); **Address:** Philadelphia Heart Inst, 51 N 39th St, Ste 2A, Philadelphia, PA 19104; **Phone:** 215-662-9595; **Board Cert:** Surgery 2004; Thoracic Surgery 2006; **Med School:** Med Coll VA 1996; **Resid:** Surgery, Hosp Univ Penn 2003; **Fellow:** Cardiothoracic Surgery, Hosp Univ Penn 2005; Endovascular Surgery, Hosp Univ Penn 2006; **Fac Appt:** Assoc Prof S, Univ Pennsylvania

Toyoda, Yoshiya MD/PhD [T&CS] - **Spec Exp:** Cardiothoracic Surgery; Transplant-Heart; Heart Valve Surgery; Coronary Artery Surgery; **Hospital:** Temple University Hosp-Episcopal Campus; **Address:** Parkinson Pavilion, Zone C, 3401 N Broad St, Ste 301, Philadelphia, PA 19140; **Phone:** 215-707-3601; **Med School:** Japan 1990; **Resid:** Surgery, Kobe Univ Hosp 1994; Cardiothoracic Surgery, Kobe Univ Hosp 1997; **Fellow:** Cardiothoracic Research, Harvard Med School 2001; Cardiovascular Surgery, Mass Genl Hosp 2004; **Fac Appt:** Prof S, Univ Pittsburgh

Tranbaugh, Robert F MD [T&CS] - **Spec Exp:** Coronary Artery Surgery; Heart Valve Surgery; Aneurysm-Thoracic Aortic; **Hospital:** Beth Israel Med Ctr - Petrie Div (page 56), St. Luke's - Roosevelt Hosp Ctr - Roosevelt Div (page 56); **Address:** Beth Israel Med Ctr, Division of Cardiac Surgery, 317 E 17th St, Fl 11, New York, NY 10003; **Phone:** 212-420-2584; **Board Cert:** Thoracic & Cardiac Surgery 2004; **Med School:** Univ Pennsylvania 1976; **Resid:** Surgery, UCSF Med Ctr 1983; Cardiothoracic Surgery, UCSF Med Ctr 1985; **Fac Appt:** Assoc Clin Prof T&CS, Albert Einstein Coll Med

Watson, Thomas J MD [T&CS] - **Spec Exp:** Esophageal Cancer; Gastroesophageal Reflux Disease (GERD); Lung Cancer; **Hospital:** Univ Rochester Strong Meml Hosp, Highland Hosp of Rochester; **Address:** 601 Elmwood Ave, Box SURG, Rochester, NY 14642; **Phone:** 585-275-1509; **Board Cert:** Surgery 2003; Thoracic Surgery 2007; **Med School:** USC-Keck School of Medicine 1988; **Resid:** Surgery, LAC-USC Med Ctr 1993; Cardiothoracic Surgery, LAC-USC Med Ctr 1996; **Fellow:** Esophageal Surgery, LAC-USC Med Ctr 1994; **Fac Appt:** Assoc Prof S, Univ Rochester

Weksler, Benny MD [T&CS] - **Spec Exp:** Minimally Invasive Thoracic Surgery; Lung Cancer; Esophageal Cancer; Thymoma; **Hospital:** UPMC Presby, Pittsburgh, VA Pittsburgh Hlth Care Sys-Univ Dr; **Address:** Univ of Pittsburgh Med Ctr, 200 Lothrop St, PUH Bldg - Fl C800, Pittsburgh, PA 15213; **Phone:** 412-648-6271; **Board Cert:** Surgery 2007; Thoracic & Cardiac Surgery 2007; **Med School:** Brazil 1987; **Resid:** Surgery, Lincoln Med Ctr 1995; Research, Meml Sloan Kettering Cancer Ctr 1993; **Fellow:** Cardiothoracic Surgery, New York Hosp/MSK Cancer Ctr 1997; Minimally Invasive Surgery, Univ Pittsburgh 2008; **Fac Appt:** Assoc Prof TS, Univ Pittsburgh

Williams, Mathew R MD [T&CS] - **Spec Exp:** Interventional Cardiology; Heart Valve Surgery; **Hospital:** NY-Presby/Columbia Univ Med Ctr, NY (page 65); **Address:** NY-Presby, Thoracic & Cardiac Surgery, 177 Fort Washington Ave, 5C-501, New York, NY 10032; **Phone:** 212-342-0444; **Board Cert:** Thoracic Surgery 2007; **Med School:** Columbia P&S 1996; **Resid:** Surgery, Columbia Univ Med Ctr 2003; Cardiothoracic Surgery, Columbia Univ Med Ctr 2005; **Fellow:** Research, Columbia Univ 2001; Interventional Cardiology, Columbia Univ 2006; **Fac Appt:** Asst Prof S, Columbia P&S

Woo, Y Joseph MD [T&CS] - **Spec Exp:** Minimally Invasive Cardiac Surgery; Robotic Cardiac Surgery; Aneurysm-Abdominal & Thoracic Aortic; Mitral Valve Robotic Surgery; **Hospital:** Hosp Univ Penn - UPHS (page 69); **Address:** Penn Heart & Vascular Ctr, Perelman Ctr for Advanced Medicine, 3400 Civic Center Blvd, 2 East, Philadelphia, PA 19104; **Phone:** 215-662-2956; **Board Cert:** Surgery 2009; Thoracic & Cardiac Surgery 2010; **Med School:** Univ Pennsylvania 1992; **Resid:** Surgery, Hosp Univ Penn 1999; **Fellow:** Cardiothoracic Surgery, Hosp Univ Penn 2001; **Fac Appt:** Prof S, Univ Pennsylvania

Yang, Stephen C MD [T&CS] - **Spec Exp:** Mesothelioma; Lung Cancer; Esophageal Cancer; Robotic Surgery; **Hospital:** Johns Hopkins Hosp (page 59), Johns Hopkins Bayview Med Ctr (page 59); **Address:** Johns Hopkins Hosp, 600 N Wolfe St Blalock Bldg - rm 240, Baltimore, MD 21287; **Phone:** 410-933-1233; **Board Cert:** Surgery 2003; Thoracic Surgery 2005; **Med School:** Med Coll VA 1984; **Resid:** Surgery, Univ Tex Hlth Sci Ctr 1990; **Fellow:** Thoracic Surgery, MD Anderson Cancer Ctr 1992; Cardiothoracic Surgery, Med Coll Virginia 1994; **Fac Appt:** Assoc Prof TS, Johns Hopkins Univ

Southeast

Athanasuleas, Constantine L MD [T&CS] - **Spec Exp:** Cardiac Surgery; Heart Failure; **Hospital:** UAB Hosp; **Address:** 1900 Univ Blvd, Tinsley Harrison Twr 720, Birmingham, AL 35294; **Phone:** 205-934-2536; **Board Cert:** Thoracic & Cardiac Surgery 2006; **Med School:** Univ Chicago-Pritzker Sch Med 1975; **Resid:** Surgery, Stanford Univ Med Ctr 1980; **Fellow:** Thoracic & Cardiac Surgery, Stanford Univ Med Ctr 1982; **Fac Appt:** Prof S, UAB Sch Med

Bichell, David P MD [T&CS] - **Spec Exp:** Cardiac Surgery-Neonatal; Cardiac Surgery-Pediatric; Congenital Heart Surgery; Minimally Invasive Cardiac Surgery; **Hospital:** Vanderbilt Monroe Carrell Jr. Chldn's Hosp, Vanderbilt Univ Med Ctr; **Address:** Vanderbilt Childrens Hosp, Div Pediatric Cardiac Surgery, 2200 Childrens Way, 5247 DOT, Nashville, TN 37232-9292; **Phone:** 615-343-5500; **Board Cert:** Thoracic & Cardiac Surgery 2006; **Med School:** Columbia P&S 1987; **Resid:** Surgery, Barnes Jewish Hosp 1994; Cardiothoracic Surgery, Brigham & Womens Hosp/Chldns Hosp 1997; **Fellow:** Cardiac Surgery, Brigham & Womens Hosp 1995; **Fac Appt:** Prof TS, Vanderbilt Univ

Bridges, Charles R MD [T&CS] - **Spec Exp:** Minimally Invasive Cardiac Surgery; Maze Procedure for Atrial Fibrillation; Aneurysm-Aortic; Heart Valve Surgery; **Hospital:** Carolinas Med Ctr-Univ, Carolinas Med Ctr-Pineville; **Address:** Sanger Heart & Vascular Inst, 1001 Blythe Blvd Fl 3 - Ste 300, Charlotte, NC 28203; **Phone:** 704-373-0212; **Board Cert:** Surgery 2003; Thoracic Surgery 2004; **Med School:** Harvard Med Sch 1981; **Resid:** Internal Medicine, Brigham & Women's Hosp 1984; Surgery, Hosp Univ Penn 1991; **Fellow:** Cardiothoracic Surgery, Hosp Univ Penn 1993; **Fac Appt:** Clin Prof T&CS, Univ NC Sch Med

Brunsting III, Louis A MD [T&CS] - **Spec Exp:** Robotic Cardiac Surgery; **Hospital:** UAB Hosp; **Address:** Kirklin Clin, 2000 6th Ave S, Birmingham, AL 35233; **Phone:** 205-934-6580; **Board Cert:** Thoracic Surgery 2011; **Med School:** UCSD 1983; **Resid:** Surgery, Univ Rochester Strong Meml Hosp 1985; **Fellow:** Surgery, Duke Univ Hosp 1987; Thoracic Surgery, Duke Univ Hosp 1991; **Fac Appt:** Assoc Prof T&CS, UAB Sch Med

Burke, Redmond P MD [T&CS] - **Spec Exp:** Pediatric Cardiac Surgery; Congenital Heart Surgery; Minimally Invasive Surgery; **Hospital:** Miami Children's Hosp; **Address:** MCH, Cardiac Surgery Dept, 3100 SW 62nd Ave Fl 2, Miami, FL 33155; **Phone:** 305-663-8401; **Board Cert:** Thoracic Surgery 2013; Surgery 2002; **Med School:** Harvard Med Sch 1984; **Resid:** Surgery, Brigham & Womens Hosp 1989; **Fellow:** Cardiovascular Surgery, Brigham & Womens Hosp 1990; Thoracic Surgery, Brigham & Womens Hosp 1992

Cerfolio, Robert J MD [T&CS] - **Spec Exp:** Lung Cancer; Tracheal Surgery; Chest Wall Tumors; Esophageal Cancer; **Hospital:** UAB Hosp; **Address:** The Kirklin Clinic, 2000 6th Ave S Fl 5, Birmingham, AL 35233; **Phone:** 205-934-5937; **Board Cert:** Surgery 2003; Thoracic Surgery 2006; **Med School:** Univ Rochester 1988; **Resid:** Surgery, Cornell-NY Hosp 1990; Surgery, Mayo Clinic 1993; **Fellow:** Cardiothoracic Surgery, Mayo Clinic 1996; **Fac Appt:** Prof TS, UAB Sch Med

Chitwood Jr, W Randolph MD [T&CS] - **Spec Exp:** Robotic Cardiac Surgery; Minimally Invasive Cardiac Surgery; Heart Valve Surgery; Mitral Valve Surgery; **Hospital:** Univ Hlth Sys-Vidant Med Ctr; **Address:** East Carolina Heart Inst, 115 Heart Drive, rm 3107, Greenville, NC 27834; **Phone:** 252-744-4536; **Board Cert:** Thoracic & Cardiac Surgery 2005; **Med School:** Univ VA Sch Med 1974; **Resid:** Surgery, Duke Univ Med Ctr 1983; **Fellow:** Cardiovascular Surgery, Duke Univ Med Ctr 1984; **Fac Appt:** Prof S, E Carolina Univ

Christian, Karla G MD [T&CS] - **Spec Exp:** Congenital Heart Surgery-Complex; Transplant-Heart; Cardiac Surgery-Adult & Pediatric; **Hospital:** Vanderbilt Monroe Carrell Jr. Chldn's Hosp, Vanderbilt Univ Med Ctr; **Address:** Vanderbilt Childrens Hosp, Div Pediatric Cardiac Surgery, 2200 Childrens Way, 5247 DOT, Nashville, TN 37232-9292; **Phone:** 615-343-5500; **Board Cert:** Surgery 2001; Thoracic & Cardiac Surgery 2003; Congenital Cardiac Surgery 2012; **Med School:** Univ Wash 1985; **Resid:** Surgery, Univ Washington Med Ctr 1988; Surgery, Vanderbilt Univ Med Ctr 1991; **Fellow:** Cardiothoracic Surgery, Vanderbilt Univ Med Ctr 1994; **Fac Appt:** Assoc Prof TS, Vanderbilt Univ

D'Amico, Thomas MD [T&CS] - **Spec Exp:** Lung Cancer; Esophageal Cancer; **Hospital:** Duke Univ Hosp; **Address:** Duke Univ Med Ctr, Dept Thoracic Surg, Box 3496, Durham, NC 27710; **Phone:** 919-684-4891; **Board Cert:** Surgery 2004; Thoracic Surgery 2006; **Med School:** Columbia P&S 1987; **Resid:** Surgery, Duke Univ Med Ctr 1989; Cardiothoracic Surgery, Duke Univ Med Ctr 1996; **Fellow:** Thoracic Oncology, Meml Sloan-Kettering Cancer Ctr; **Fac Appt:** Assoc Prof S, Duke Univ

Dabal, Robert J MD [T&CS] - **Spec Exp:** Pediatric Cardiac Surgery; Neonatal & Infant Cardiac Surgery; **Hospital:** UAB Hosp, Children's Hosp AL; **Address:** 619 19th St S, 176F Bldg - Ste 9100, Birmingham, AL 35294; **Phone:** 205-934-2419; **Board Cert:** Thoracic & Cardiac Surgery 2013; **Med School:** Duke Univ 1995; **Resid:** Surgery, NY-Presby/Columbia Univ Med Ctr 2000; Thoracic Surgery, Univ Wash Med Ctr 2003; **Fellow:** Pediatric Cardiothoracic Surgery, Chldns Hosp 2004; Pediatric Cardiothoracic Surgery, Chldns Hosp 2005; **Fac Appt:** Asst Prof S, UAB Sch Med

Drinkwater Jr, Davis C MD [T&CS] - **Spec Exp:** Cardiac Surgery-Adult & Pediatric; Heart Valve Surgery; Congenital Heart Surgery; **Hospital:** Centennial Med Ctr, Vanderbilt Monroe Carrell Jr. Chldn's Hosp; **Address:** 2400 Patterson St, Ste 307, Nashville, TN 37203; **Phone:** 615-342-6900; **Board Cert:** Thoracic & Cardiac Surgery 2005; **Med School:** Univ VT Coll Med 1976; **Resid:** Surgery, McGill Affil Hosp 1981; Cardiothoracic Surgery, McGill Affil Hosp 1983; **Fellow:** Cardiothoracic Surgery, Great Ormond Hosp 1983; Cardiothoracic Surgery, Childrens Hosp 1984; **Fac Appt:** Prof S, Vanderbilt Univ

Feins, Richard H MD [T&CS] - **Spec Exp:** Thoracic Cancers; Lung Cancer; Robotic Surgery; Esophageal Surgery; **Hospital:** NC Memorial Hosp - UNC; **Address:** UNC Dept Surgery, Div Cardiothoracic Surgery, 3040 Burnett-Womack Bldg, CB#7065, Chapel Hill, NC 27599-7065; **Phone:** 919-966-3383; **Board Cert:** Thoracic Surgery 2003; **Med School:** Univ VT Coll Med 1973; **Resid:** Surgery, Strong Meml Hosp 1980; Cardiothoracic Surgery, Univ Rochester Affil Hosp 1982; **Fac Appt:** Prof S, Univ NC Sch Med

Glassford Jr, David M MD [T&CS] - **Spec Exp:** Cardiothoracic Surgery; **Hospital:** Saint Thomas West Hosp - Nashville; **Address:** Cardiovascular Surgery Assocs, 4230 Harding Rd, Ste 430, Nashville, TN 37205; **Phone:** 615-385-4781; **Board Cert:** Thoracic Surgery 2007; **Med School:** Univ Tex Med Br, Galveston 1970; **Resid:** Surgery, Univ Texas Med Br 1975; Thoracic Surgery, Ochsner Clinic 1977

Guyton, Robert A MD [T&CS] - **Spec Exp:** Coronary Artery Surgery; Minimally Invasive Cardiac Surgery; Heart Valve Surgery-Percutaneous; Congenital Heart Surgery; **Hospital:** Emory Univ Hosp Midtown, Emory Univ Hosp; **Address:** Emory Dept Cardiothoracic Surgery, 550 Peachtree St NE Fl 6 MOT, Atlanta, GA 30308; **Phone:** 404-686-2513; **Board Cert:** Thoracic & Cardiac Surgery 2010; **Med School:** Harvard Med Sch 1971; **Resid:** Surgery, Mass Genl Hosp 1978; **Fellow:** Thoracic Surgery, National Heart Lung Inst 1975; Cardiothoracic Surgery, Mass Genl/Childrens Hosp 1979; **Fac Appt:** Prof S, Emory Univ

Harpole Jr, David H MD [T&CS] - **Spec Exp:** Lung Cancer; Mesothelioma; Esophageal Cancer; **Hospital:** Duke Univ Hosp; **Address:** 3627 DUMC, rm 3589, Durham, NC 27710; **Phone:** 919-668-8413; **Board Cert:** Surgery 2011; Thoracic Surgery 2013; **Med School:** Univ VA Sch Med 1984; **Resid:** Surgery, Duke Univ Med Ctr 1991; **Fellow:** Thoracic Surgery, Duke Univ Med Ctr 1993; **Fac Appt:** Prof S, Duke Univ

Kanter, Kirk R MD [T&CS] - **Spec Exp:** Pediatric Cardiac Surgery; Transplant-Heart-Pediatric; Transplant-Lung-Pediatric; **Hospital:** Chldns Hlthcare Atlanta @ Egleston, Emory Univ Hosp; **Address:** Childrens Hlthcare Atlanta at Egleston, Pediatric Cardiothoracic Surgery, 1405 Clifton Rd NE Fl 2, Atlanta, GA 30322; **Phone:** 404-785-6330; **Board Cert:** Thoracic & Cardiac Surgery 2008; Congenital Cardiac Surgery 2009; **Med School:** Albany Med Coll 1976; **Resid:** Surgery, Johns Hopkins Hosp 1982; Thoracic Surgery, Johns Hopkins Hosp 1984; **Fellow:** Pediatric Cardiac Surgery, Brompton/Harefield Hosps 1985; **Fac Appt:** Prof S, Emory Univ

Kirklin, James K MD [T&CS] - **Spec Exp:** Cardiac Surgery; Congenital Heart Surgery; Transplant-Heart & Lung; **Hospital:** UAB Hosp, Children's Hosp AL; **Address:** UAB Cardiothoracic Surgery, 1900 University Blvd, THT 760, Birmingham, AL 35294; **Phone:** 205-934-3368; **Board Cert:** Thoracic Surgery 2011; **Med School:** Harvard Med Sch 1973; **Resid:** Surgery, Mass Genl Hosp 1977; Cardiothoracic Surgery, Mass Genl Hosp 1979; **Fellow:** Cardiothoracic Surgery, Chidren's Hosp Med Ctr 1979; **Fac Appt:** Prof S, UAB Sch Med

Kron, Irving L MD [T&CS] - **Spec Exp:** Coronary Artery Surgery; Transplant-Heart; **Hospital:** Univ of Virginia Hlth Sys; **Address:** Univ VA Hlth Sys, Div Cardiovascular Surg, 1215 Lee St, Charlottesville, VA 22908; **Phone:** 434-924-2158; **Board Cert:** Vascular Surgery 2006; **Med School:** Med Coll Wisc 1975; **Resid:** Surgery, Maine Med Ctr 1980; **Fellow:** Cardiothoracic Surgery, Univ Virginia Med Ctr 1982; **Fac Appt:** Prof S, Univ VA Sch Med

Lau, Christine L MD [T&CS] - **Spec Exp:** Lung Cancer; Transplant-Lung; Esophageal Cancer; **Hospital:** Univ of Virginia Hlth Sys; **Address:** Univ VA Hlth System, Div Thoracic & Cardiovascular Surg, 1215 Lee St, Box 800679, Charlottesville, VA 22908; **Phone:** 434-924-8016; **Board Cert:** Surgery 2003; Thoracic Surgery 2007; **Med School:** Dartmouth Med Sch 1995; **Resid:** Surgery, Duke Univ Hosp 2003; **Fellow:** Cardiothoracic Surgery, Washington Univ Phys 2005; **Fac Appt:** Assoc Prof S, Univ VA Sch Med

Martin, Tomas D MD [T&CS] - **Spec Exp:** Vascular Surgery; Aortic Surgery; Aneurysm-Abdominal Aortic; **Hospital:** UF Hlth Shands Hosp; **Address:** UF Hlth, Thoracic & Cardiac Surgery, 1600 SW Archer Rd, Box 100129, Gainesville, FL 32608; **Phone:** 352-265-5470; **Board Cert:** Thoracic & Cardiac Surgery 2008; **Med School:** Univ Tex, Houston 1981; **Resid:** Surgery, Baylor Med Ctr 1986; Vascular Surgery, Baylor Med Ctr 1987; **Fellow:** Cardiothoracic Surgery, Shands at Univ FL 1989; **Fac Appt:** Prof T&CS, Univ Fla Coll Med

Mavroudis, Constantine MD [T&CS] - **Spec Exp:** Pediatric Cardiac Surgery; Congenital Heart Disease; Transplant-Heart & Lung; **Hospital:** Florida Hosp - Orlando; **Address:** FL Hosp for Chldn, Ped Cardiac Surgery, 2501 N Orange Ave, Ste 540, Orlando, FL 32804; **Phone:** 407-303-3697; **Board Cert:** Thoracic & Cardiac Surgery 2010; Congenital Cardiac Surgery 2009; **Med School:** Univ VA Sch Med 1973; **Resid:** Surgery, UCSF Med Ctr 1979; **Fellow:** Thoracic Surgery, UCSF Med Ctr 1977

Mill, Michael R MD [T&CS] - **Spec Exp:** Pediatric Cardiac Surgery; Transplant-Heart-Adult & Pediatric; Transplant-Heart & Lung; Heart Valve Surgery; **Hospital:** NC Memorial Hosp - UNC; **Address:** UNC Sch Med, Cardiothoracic Surgery, 3040 Burnett Womack Bldg, CB.7065, Chapel Hill, NC 27599-7965; **Phone:** 919-966-3381; **Board Cert:** Thoracic Surgery 2009; Congenital Cardiac Surgery 2009; **Med School:** Univ Colorado 1980; **Resid:** Surgery, Univ Colorado Hlth Sci Ctr 1985; **Fellow:** Cardiothoracic Surgery, Stanford Univ Med Ctr 1987; Transplant Surgery, Stanford Univ Med Ctr 1988; **Fac Appt:** Prof S, Univ NC Sch Med

Miller, Daniel L MD [T&CS] - **Spec Exp:** Lung Cancer; Esophageal Cancer; Mesothelioma; Emphysema-Lung Volume Reduction; **Hospital:** Emory Univ Hosp, Emory Univ Hosp Midtown; **Address:** The Emory Clinic, 1365A Clifton Rd NE, Ste 2219, Atlanta, GA 30322; **Phone:** 404-778-3755; **Board Cert:** Thoracic & Cardiac Surgery 2005; **Med School:** Univ KY Coll Med 1985; **Resid:** Surgery, Georgetown Univ Hosp 1991; **Fellow:** Cardiothoracic Surgery, Mayo Clinic 1994; **Fac Appt:** Prof TS, Emory Univ

Moore, John E MD [T&CS] - **Spec Exp:** Lung Cancer; Esophageal Cancer; Thoracic Cancers; Robotic Surgery; **Hospital:** Northside Hosp, St. Joseph's Hosp - Atlanta; **Address:** Atlanta Cardiac & Thoracic Surg Assocs, 960 Johnson Ferry Rd, Ste 100, Atlanta, GA 30342; **Phone:** 404-252-9063; **Board Cert:** Thoracic & Cardiac Surgery 2005; **Med School:** Univ Louisville Sch Med 1975; **Resid:** Surgery, Emory Univ Affil Hosps 1980; Cardiothoracic Surgery, Emory Univ Affil Hosps 1983

Mullett, Timothy W MD [T&CS] - **Spec Exp:** Lung Cancer; Transplant-Heart & Lung; Cardiac Surgery-Adult & Pediatric; Esophageal Surgery; **Hospital:** Univ of Kentucky Albert B. Chandler Hosp; **Address:** Markey Cancer Ctr, Whitney-Henderickson Bldg, 800 Rose St, Lexington, KY 40536; **Phone:** 859-323-6494; **Board Cert:** Surgery 2005; Thoracic Surgery 2007; **Med School:** Univ Fla Coll Med 1987; **Resid:** Surgery, Shands/Univ of FL 1990; **Fellow:** Pediatric Surgery, Shands/Univ of FL 1994; Cardiothoracic Surgery, Shands/Univ of FL 1995; **Fac Appt:** Assoc Prof S, Univ KY Coll Med

Murphy, Douglas A MD [T&CS] - **Spec Exp:** Robotic Surgery; Minimally Invasive Cardiac Surgery; Heart Valve Surgery; Mitral Valve Robotic Surgery; **Hospital:** St. Joseph's Hosp - Atlanta; **Address:** Peachtree Cardiovascular Surgeons, 5665 Peachtree Dunwoody Rd NE, Ste 200, Atlanta, GA 30342; **Phone:** 404-252-6104; **Board Cert:** Internal Medicine 1978; Thoracic & Cardiac Surgery 2004; **Med School:** Univ Pennsylvania 1975; **Resid:** Internal Medicine, Mass Genl Hosp 1977; Surgery, Mass Genl Hosp 1981; **Fellow:** Thoracic Surgery, Emory Univ Affil Hosp 1983; **Fac Appt:** Prof TS, Emory Univ

Nesbitt, Jonathan C MD [T&CS] - **Spec Exp:** Lung Cancer; Esophageal Cancer; Chest Diseases-Benign; Minimally Invasive Thoracic Surgery; **Hospital:** Vanderbilt Univ Med Ctr, Williamson Med Ctr; **Address:** The Vanderbilt Clinic, 1301 Medical Center Drive, Ste 1710, Nashville, TN 37232; **Phone:** 615-322-0064; **Board Cert:** Thoracic & Cardiac Surgery 2009; **Med School:** Georgetown Univ 1981; **Resid:** Surgery, Vanderbilt Univ Med Ctr 1987; Cardiothoracic Surgery, Albany Med Ctr 1989; **Fac Appt:** Assoc Prof TS, Vanderbilt Univ

Nguyen, Dao M MD [T&CS] - **Spec Exp:** Thoracic Cancers; Lung Cancer; Minimally Invasive Thoracic Surgery; **Hospital:** Univ of Miami Hosp & Clins/Sylvester Comp Canc Ctr, Jackson Meml Hosp; **Address:** UHlth, Thoracic & Cardiac Surgery, 1475 NW 12th Ave Fl 2, Miami, FL 33136; **Phone:** 305-243-2363; **Board Cert:** Thoracic & Cardiac Surgery 2005; **Med School:** McGill Univ 1986; **Resid:** Surgery, McGill Univ Affil Hosp 1992; Cardiothoracic Surgery, McGill Univ Affil Hosp 1994; **Fellow:** Thoracic Oncology, MD Anderson Cancer Ctr 1996; **Fac Appt:** Prof S, Univ Miami Sch Med

Oaks, Timothy E MD [T&CS] - **Spec Exp:** Cardiothoracic Surgery; Lung Cancer; Lung Surgery; **Hospital:** Alamance Regl Med Ctr; **Address:** 3940 Arrowhead Blvd, Ste 230, Mebane, NC 27302; **Phone:** 919-304-1081; **Board Cert:** Thoracic Surgery 2011; **Med School:** Penn State Coll Med 1984; **Resid:** Surgery, Penn State-Hershey Med Ctr 1990; **Fellow:** Cardiothoracic Surgery, Penn State-Hershey Med Ctr 1992; Cardiothoracic Surgery, Papworth Hosp 1993

Panos, Anthony MD [T&CS] - **Spec Exp:** Cardiac Surgery-Adult; Transplant-Heart; Minimally Invasive Cardiac Surgery; **Hospital:** Jackson Meml Hosp; **Address:** UHlth, Thoracic & Cardiac Surgery, 1611 NW 12th Ave, Ste ET3072, Miami, FL 33136; **Phone:** 305-585-5271; **Board Cert:** Thoracic & Cardiac Surgery 2004; Surgery 2012; **Med School:** Univ Toronto 1980; **Resid:** Surgery, Univ Toronto Affil Hosp 1987; **Fellow:** Cardiovascular Surgery, Univ Western Ontario Affil Hosp 1988; Thoracic Surgery, Univ Toronto Affil Hosp 1993; **Fac Appt:** Prof S, Univ Miami Sch Med

Philpott, Jonathan M MD [T&CS] - **Spec Exp:** Cardiac Surgery; Atrial Fibrillation; Clinical Trials; **Hospital:** Sentara Norfolk Genl Hosp; **Address:** Mid-Atlantic Cardiothoracic Surgeons, Sentara Heart Hospital Fl 6, 600 Gresham Drive, Ste 8600, Norfolk, VA 23507; **Phone:** 757-388-6005; **Board Cert:** Thoracic Surgery 2005; **Med School:** Eastern VA Med Sch 1994; **Resid:** Surgery, E Carolina Univ Affil Hosp 2000; **Fellow:** Thoracic Surgery, Hosp Univ Penn 2002; Med Coll VA-West Hosp 2004

Putnam Jr, Joe B MD [T&CS] - **Spec Exp:** Lung Cancer; Esophageal Cancer; Sarcoma-Soft Tissue; **Hospital:** Vanderbilt Univ Med Ctr, TN Valley Healthcare Sys-Nashville; **Address:** Vanderbilt Univ Med Ctr - Thoracic Surgery, 609 Oxford House, 1313 21st Ave S, Nashville, TN 37232-4682; **Phone:** 615-343-9202; **Board Cert:** Thoracic Surgery 2007; **Med School:** Univ NC Sch Med 1979; **Resid:** Surgery, Univ Rochester Med Ctr 1986; Thoracic Surgery, Univ Mich Med Ctr 1988; **Fellow:** Surgical Oncology, NCI/NIH-Surg Branch 1984; **Fac Appt:** Prof TS, Vanderbilt Univ

Quintessenza, James A MD [T&CS] - **Spec Exp:** Transplant-Heart; Coronary Artery Surgery; Cardiovascular Surgery; Congenital Heart Surgery; **Hospital:** All Children's Hosp; **Address:** All Chldns Hosp, Cardiovascular Surgery, 601 5th St S, Ste 475, St Petersburg, FL 33701; **Phone:** 727-767-6666; **Board Cert:** Thoracic & Cardiac Surgery 2007; **Med School:** Univ Fla Coll Med 1981; **Resid:** Surgery, Shands at Univ FL 1986; **Fellow:** Cardiothoracic Surgery, UCSD Med Ctr 1988; **Fac Appt:** Assoc Clin Prof S, Univ S Fla Coll Med

Robinson, Lary A MD [T&CS] - **Spec Exp:** Lung Cancer; Mesothelioma; **Hospital:** Moffitt Canc Ctr (page 61), Tampa Genl Hosp; **Address:** H Lee Moffitt Cancer Ctr, Div Thoracic Oncology, 12902 Magnolia Drive, Tampa, FL 33612-9497; **Phone:** 813-745-6895; **Board Cert:** Thoracic Surgery 2003; Surgery 2002; Surgical Critical Care 2011; **Med School:** Washington Univ, St Louis 1972; **Resid:** Surgery, Duke Univ Med Ctr 1974; Thoracic Surgery, Duke Univ Med Ctr 1981; **Fellow:** Cardiothoracic Surgery, St Thomas Hosp 1982; Cardiothoracic Surgery, Duke Univ Med Ctr 1983; **Fac Appt:** Prof S, Univ S Fla Coll Med

Rosenkranz, Eliot R MD [T&CS] - **Spec Exp:** Pediatric Cardiac Surgery; Transplant-Heart-Pediatric; Cardiac Surgery-Neonatal; Congenital Heart Surgery; **Hospital:** Jackson Meml Hosp, Univ of Miami Hosp; **Address:** UHlth, Thoracic & Cardiac Surgery, 1611 NW 12th Ave, Ste ET3072, Miami, FL 33136; **Phone:** 305-585-5271; **Board Cert:** Thoracic & Cardiac Surgery 2008; **Med School:** UCSD 1979; **Resid:** Surgery, UCLA Med Ctr 1985; **Fellow:** Cardiothoracic Surgery, UCLA Med Ctr 1987; **Fac Appt:** Prof S, Univ Miami Sch Med

Salerno, Tomas A MD [T&CS] - **Spec Exp:** Cardiothoracic Surgery; Heart Valve Surgery; Aortic Surgery; Coronary Artery Surgery; **Hospital:** Jackson Meml Hosp, Univ of Miami Hosp; **Address:** UHlth, Thoracic & Cardiac Surgery, 1611 NW 12th Ave, Ste ET3072, Miami, FL 33136; **Phone:** 305-585-5271; **Board Cert:** Thoracic Surgery 2008; **Med School:** McGill Univ 1971; **Resid:** Surgery, Royal Victoria Hosp 1975; Cardiothoracic Surgery, Royal Victoria Hosp 1977; **Fac Appt:** Prof S, Univ Miami Sch Med

Savage, Edward B MD [T&CS] - **Spec Exp:** Cardiac Surgery-Complex; Heart Failure; Minimally Invasive Heart Valve Surgery; Mitral Valve Surgery; **Hospital:** Cleveland Clin - Weston (page 55); **Address:** Cleveland Clin, Cardiothoracic Dept, 2950 Cleveland Clinic Blvd, Desk 23, Weston, FL 33331; **Phone:** 954-659-5320; **Board Cert:** Surgery 2004; Thoracic & Cardiac Surgery 2004; **Med School:** Yale Univ 1985; **Resid:** Surgery, Hosp Univ Penn 1992; Cardiothoracic Surgery, Brigham & Womens Hosp 1994

Slaughter, Mark S MD [T&CS] - **Spec Exp:** Ventricular Assist Device (LVAD); Mitral Valve Surgery; Transplant-Heart; **Hospital:** Jewish Hosp (KY); **Address:** 201 Abraham Flexner Way, Ste 1200, Louisville, KY 40202; **Phone:** 502-583-8383; **Board Cert:** Surgery 2002; Thoracic & Cardiac Surgery 2003; **Med School:** Indiana Univ 1986; **Resid:** Surgery, Northwestern Meml Hosp 1992; **Fellow:** Thoracic Surgery, Univ Minnesota Affil Hosp 1994; **Fac Appt:** Prof T&CS, Univ Louisville Sch Med

Smith, Peter K MD [T&CS] - **Spec Exp:** Coronary Artery Surgery; Heart Valve Surgery; **Hospital:** Duke Univ Hosp, Durham VA Med Ctr; **Address:** Box 3442 Med Ctr, 8660 HAFS Bldg, Durham, NC 27710; **Phone:** 919-684-2890; **Board Cert:** Thoracic Surgery 2007; **Med School:** Duke Univ 1977; **Resid:** Surgery, Duke Univ Med Ctr 1984; Thoracic Surgery, Duke Univ Med Ctr 1987; **Fac Appt:** Prof S, Duke Univ

Staples, Edward D MD [T&CS] - **Spec Exp:** Transplant-Heart & Lung; Ventricular Assist Device (LVAD); **Hospital:** Malcom Randall VA Med Ctr, UF Hlth Shands Hosp; **Address:** Malcom Randall VA Med Ctr, 1601 SW Archer Rd, Gainesville, FL 32610; **Phone:** 352-273-5501; **Board Cert:** Thoracic Surgery 2004; Surgical Critical Care 2002; **Med School:** Univ S Fla Coll Med 1977; **Resid:** Surgery, Med Coll VA Affil Hosp 1979; Surgery, Univ Hosp 1982; **Fellow:** Cardiothoracic Surgery, Univ Florida Affil Hosp 1984; **Fac Appt:** Assoc Prof S, Univ Fla Coll Med

Stowe, Cary MD [T&CS] - **Spec Exp:** Aortic Surgery; **Hospital:** Indian River Med Ctr; **Address:** IRMC, Cardiovascular Surgery, 1040 37th Pl, Ste 101, Vero Beach, FL 32960; **Phone:** 772-563-4580; **Board Cert:** Thoracic & Cardiac Surgery 2008; Vascular Surgery 2008; **Med School:** UAB Sch Med 1978; **Resid:** Surgery, Barnes-Jewish Hosp 1982; **Fellow:** Vascular Surgery, Baylor Med Ctr 1983; Cardiothoracic Surgery, Emory Univ Hosp 1994

Tedder, Mark MD [T&CS] - **Spec Exp:** Ventricular Assist Device (LVAD); Congenital Heart Disease; Heart Valve Surgery; **Hospital:** Saint Thomas West Hosp - Nashville; **Address:** St Thomas Heart Cardiovascular Surgery, 4230 Harding Rd, Ste 430, Nashville, TN 37205; **Phone:** 615-385-4781; **Board Cert:** Thoracic & Cardiac Surgery 2007; **Med School:** Duke Univ 1988; **Resid:** Surgery, Duke Univ Med Ctr 1995; Cardiothoracic Surgery, Duke Univ Med Ctr 1997

Ungerleider, Ross M MD [T&CS] - **Spec Exp:** Pediatric Cardiac Surgery; Cardiac Surgery; Congenital Heart Surgery; **Hospital:** Wake Forest Baptist Med Ctr; **Address:** Dept of Cardiothoracic Surgery, Medical Ctr Blvd, Winston-Salem, NC 27157-1096; **Phone:** 336-716-2124; **Board Cert:** Thoracic Surgery 2007; Congenital Cardiac Surgery 2009; **Med School:** Rush Med Coll 1977; **Resid:** Surgery, Duke Univ Med Ctr 1987; **Fellow:** Cardiothoracic Surgery, Duke Univ Med Ctr 1989; Pediatric Cardiac Surgery, UCSF Med Ctr; **Fac Appt:** Prof

Weiman, Darryl S MD [T&CS] - **Spec Exp:** Cardiothoracic Surgery; Lung Cancer; Esophageal Surgery; **Hospital:** VA Med Ctr - Memphis; **Address:** VA Medical Ctr, Dept Surgery, 1030 Jefferson Ave, Fl 3, rm CW353, Memphis, TN 38104; **Phone:** 901-577-7352; **Board Cert:** Surgery 2012; Thoracic & Cardiac Surgery 2010; **Med School:** St Louis Univ 1978; **Resid:** Surgery, Univ Chicago Pritzker Sch Med 1983; Thoracic Surgery, Univ Chicago Pritzker Sch Med 1984; **Fellow:** Cardiothoracic Surgery, Long Island Jewish Hosp 1991; **Fac Appt:** Prof S, Univ Tenn Coll Med

Zwischenberger, Joseph B MD [T&CS] - **Spec Exp:** Thoracic Cancers; Lung Cancer; Esophageal Cancer; Respiratory Failure; **Hospital:** Univ of Kentucky Albert B. Chandler Hosp; **Address:** Markey Cancer Ctr, Whitney-Henderickson Bldg, 800 Rose St, Lexington, KY 40536; **Phone:** 859-323-6013; **Board Cert:** Surgery 2002; Thoracic & Cardiac Surgery 2005; Surgical Critical Care 2008; **Med School:** Univ KY Coll Med 1977; **Resid:** Surgery, Univ Michigan Med Ctr 1983; Cardiothoracic Surgery, Univ Michigan Med Ctr 1986; **Fellow:** Research, Natl Inst Hlth 1981; Critical Care Medicine, Univ Michigan Med Ctr 1984; **Fac Appt:** Prof S, Univ KY Coll Med

Midwest

Abraham, V. Simon MD [T&CS] - **Spec Exp:** Pediatric Cardiothoracic Surgery; Neonatal Surgery; Congenital Heart Disease; **Hospital:** Peyton Manning Children's Hosp at St. Vincent, St. Vincent Indianapolis Hosp; **Address:** Childrens Heart Ctr at St Vincent, 8333 Naab Rd, Ste 320, Indianapolis, IN 46260; **Phone:** 317-338-3000; **Board Cert:** Thoracic Surgery 2006; Congenital Cardiac Surgery 2009; **Med School:** Univ Chicago-Pritzker Sch Med 1986; **Resid:** Surgery, Johns Hopkins Hosp 1993; Thoracic Surgery, Univ MI Hosp 1996; **Fellow:** Research, Natl Inst Hlth 1991; Pediatric Cardiothoracic Surgery, CHOP 1997

Baciewicz Jr, Frank A MD [T&CS] - **Spec Exp:** Esophageal Cancer; Lung Cancer; Minimally Invasive Thoracic Surgery; **Hospital:** Barbara Ann Karmanos Cancer Inst, Detroit Med Ctr; **Address:** Barbara Ann Karmanos Cancer Inst, 4100 John R, Ste 615, Detroit, MI 48201; **Phone:** 800-527-6266; **Board Cert:** Thoracic & Cardiac Surgery 2005; Surgical Critical Care 2011; **Med School:** Univ VA Sch Med 1978; **Resid:** Surgery, Northwestern Univ Affil Hosps 1983; **Fellow:** Cardiothoracic Surgery, Univ Penn Med Ctr 1985; **Fac Appt:** Prof S, Wayne State Univ

Backer, Carl L MD [T&CS] - **Spec Exp:** Pediatric Cardiothoracic Surgery; Transplant-Heart; Tracheal Surgery; Congenital Heart Disease-Adult; **Hospital:** Lurie Chldn's Hosp-Chicago, Northwestern Meml Hosp; **Address:** Lurie Chldn's Hosp, 225 E Chicago Ave, Box 22, Chicago, IL 60611; **Phone:** 312-227-4240; **Board Cert:** Thoracic Surgery 2007; Congenital Cardiac Surgery 2009; **Med School:** Mayo Med Sch 1980; **Resid:** Surgery, Northwestern Meml Hosp 1985; **Fellow:** Cardiothoracic Surgery, Northwestern Meml Hosp 1987; Pediatric Cardiac Surgery, Chldns Meml Hosp 1988; **Fac Appt:** Prof S, Northwestern Univ

Bakhos, Mamdouh MD [T&CS] - **Spec Exp:** Mitral Valve Surgery; Minimally Invasive Cardiac Surgery; Arrhythmias; Transplant-Heart & Lung; **Hospital:** Loyola Univ Med Ctr; **Address:** Loyola Univ, Dept Cardiothoracic Surgery, 2160 S First Ave, Bldg 110 - rm 6240, Maywood, IL 60153; **Phone:** 708-327-2503; **Board Cert:** Thoracic Surgery 2007; **Med School:** Syria 1971; **Resid:** Surgery, Huron Road Hosp 1976; **Fellow:** Thoracic Surgery, Loyola Univ Med Ctr 1978; **Fac Appt:** Prof TS, Loyola Univ-Stritch Sch Med

Brown, John W MD [T&CS] - **Spec Exp:** Cardiac Surgery-Neonatal & Pediatric; Transplant-Heart; Heart Valve Surgery; Congenital Heart Disease; **Hospital:** Riley Hosp for Children, IU Hlth Univ Hosp; **Address:** Indiana Univ Dept Surgery, 545 Barnhill Drive, Ste 215, Indianapolis, IN 46202; **Phone:** 317-274-7150; **Board Cert:** Thoracic Surgery 2007; Congenital Cardiac Surgery 2011; **Med School:** Indiana Univ 1970; **Resid:** Surgery, Univ MI Hosp 1976; Cardiothoracic Surgery, Univ MI Hosp 1978; **Fellow:** Cardiovascular Surgery, Natl Heart, Lung, Blood Inst 1974; **Fac Appt:** Prof S, Indiana Univ

Cassivi, Stephen D MD [T&CS] - **Spec Exp:** Thoracic Surgery; Minimally Invasive Surgery; Myasthenia Gravis; Esophageal Surgery; **Hospital:** Mayo Med Ctr & Clin - Rochester, St. Mary's Hosp - Rochester MN (Mayo); **Address:** Mayo Clinic, 200 First St SW, Mayo Bldg - Fl 12, rm 12-55W, Rochester, MN 55905; **Phone:** 507-266-0911; **Board Cert:** Thoracic & Cardiac Surgery 2011; **Med School:** Univ Ottawa 1994; **Resid:** Surgery, Univ Toronto Hosps 2000; **Fellow:** Cardiothoracic Surgery, Barnes-Jewish Hosp 2002; **Fac Appt:** Assoc Prof TS, Mayo Med Sch

Damiano Jr, Ralph J MD [T&CS] - **Spec Exp:** Minimally Invasive Cardiac Surgery; Coronary Artery Surgery; Endoscopic Surgery; **Hospital:** Barnes-Jewish Hosp; **Address:** 660 S Euclid Ave, Campus Box 8234, St Louis, MO 63110; **Phone:** 314-362-7327; **Board Cert:** Thoracic Surgery 2011; **Med School:** Duke Univ 1980; **Resid:** Surgery, Duke Univ Med Ctr 1988; **Fellow:** Cardiothoracic Surgery, Duke Univ Med Ctr 1989; **Fac Appt:** Prof S, Washington Univ, St Louis

DeCamp Jr, Malcolm M MD [T&CS] - **Spec Exp:** Lung Surgery; Esophageal Surgery; Emphysema-Lung Volume Reduction; **Hospital:** Northwestern Meml Hosp; **Address:** Northwestern Meml Hosp-Thoracic Surgery, 676 N St Clair St, Ste 600, Chicago, IL 60611; **Phone:** 312-695-3800; **Board Cert:** Thoracic & Cardiac Surgery 2013; **Med School:** Univ Louisville Sch Med 1983; **Resid:** Surgery, Brighams & Womens Hosp 1986; Surgery, Brighams & Womens Hosp 1990; **Fellow:** Cardiac Surgery, Brighams & Womens Hosp 1993; **Fac Appt:** Prof S, Northwestern Univ

Deeb, G. Michael MD [T&CS] - **Spec Exp:** Aortic Valve Disease; Aneurysm-Aortic; **Hospital:** Univ Michigan Med Ctr; **Address:** U of M Cardiovascular Ctr, Fl 3, Recept C, 1500 E Med Ctr Drive, SPC 5864, Ann Arbor, MI 48109; **Phone:** 734-647-7321; **Board Cert:** Thoracic Surgery 2013; **Med School:** Univ Pittsburgh 1975; **Resid:** Surgery, Univ Pitts Hosp 1979; **Fellow:** Thoracic & Cardiac Surgery, Univ Pitts Hosp 1979; **Fac Appt:** Prof T&CS, Univ Mich Med Sch

Delius, Ralph MD [T&CS] - **Spec Exp:** Pediatric Cardiac Surgery; Congenital Heart Surgery; **Hospital:** Chldns Hosp of Michigan; **Address:** Chldns Hosp Michigan, 3901 Beaubien Blvd, Detroit, MI 48201; **Phone:** 313-745-5538; **Board Cert:** Thoracic & Cardiac Surgery 2005; Congenital Cardiac Surgery 2011; **Med School:** UC Davis 1984; **Resid:** Surgery, Univ Michigan Hosp 1989; Cardiothoracic Surgery, Univ Iowa Hosp 1994; **Fellow:** Cardiothoracic Surgery, Univ Michigan Hosp 1990; Cardiac Surgery, Mass Genl Hosp 1992; **Fac Appt:** Assoc Prof S, Wayne State Univ

Deschamps, Claude MD [T&CS] - **Spec Exp:** Gastroesophageal Reflux Disease (GERD); Esophageal Cancer; Lung Cancer; **Hospital:** St. Mary's Hosp - Rochester MN (Mayo); **Address:** Mayo Clinic, Div Thoracic Surgery, 200 First St SW, Rochester, MN 55905; **Phone:** 507-284-8462; **Board Cert:** Surgery 2004; **Med School:** Univ Montreal 1979; **Resid:** Surgery, Univ Montreal Hosps 1984; Thoracic Surgery, Univ Montreal Hosps 1985; **Fellow:** Thoracic Surgery, Mayo Clinic 1987; **Fac Appt:** Prof S, Mayo Med Sch

Durham, Samuel J MD [T&CS] - **Spec Exp:** Cardiothoracic Surgery; **Hospital:** Lakeland Specialty Hosp; **Address:** Lakeshore Cardiothoracic Surgery, 2500 Niles Rd, Ste 6, St Joseph, MI 49085; **Phone:** 269-408-1660; **Board Cert:** Surgery 2011; Thoracic & Cardiac Surgery 2003; **Med School:** Harvard Med Sch 1983; **Resid:** Surgery, Univ Pittsburgh Hosp 1987; Thoracic Surgery, Univ Pittsburgh Hosp 1988; **Fellow:** Pediatric Surgery, Chldns Hosp 1993; **Fac Appt:** Prof S, Ohio State Univ

Ferguson, Mark K MD [T&CS] - **Spec Exp:** Lung Cancer; Esophageal Cancer; Barrett's Esophagus; Minimally Invasive Surgery; **Hospital:** Univ of Chicago Med; **Address:** Univ Chicago Medical Ctr, 5841 S Maryland Ave, MC 5035, Chicago, IL 60637; **Phone:** 773-702-3551; **Board Cert:** Thoracic & Cardiac Surgery 2003; **Med School:** Univ Chicago-Pritzker Sch Med 1977; **Resid:** Surgery, Univ Chicago Hosps 1981; **Fellow:** Cardiothoracic Surgery, Univ Chicago Hosps 1984; **Fac Appt:** Prof S, Univ Chicago-Pritzker Sch Med

Galantowicz, Mark E MD [T&CS] - **Spec Exp:** Cardiothoracic Surgery; **Hospital:** Nationwide Chldn's Hosp; **Address:** Nationwide Chldns Hosp, 700 Children's Drive, Columbus, OH 43205; **Phone:** 614-722-3101; **Board Cert:** Thoracic & Cardiac Surgery 2004; Congenital Cardiac Surgery 2011; **Med School:** Cornell Univ 1987; **Resid:** Surgery, NY-Presby/Columbia Univ Med Ctr 1993; **Fellow:** Cardiothoracic Surgery, NY-Presby/Columbia Univ Med Ctr 1995; **Fac Appt:** Clin Prof S, Ohio State Univ

Howington, John A MD [T&CS] - **Spec Exp:** Lung Cancer; Esophageal Cancer; Thymoma; Minimally Invasive Thoracic Surgery; **Hospital:** Evanston Hosp/NorthShore Univ Hlth Sys (page 67), Highland Park Hosp/NorthShore Univ Hlth Syst (page 67); **Address:** Northshore Medical Group, Walgreen Building, 2650 Ridge Ave, Evanston, IL 60201; **Phone:** 847-570-2868; **Board Cert:** Thoracic & Cardiac Surgery 2006; Surgery 2004; **Med School:** Univ Tenn Coll Med 1989; **Resid:** Surgery, Truman Med Ctr 1994; **Fellow:** Cardiothoracic Surgery, Vanderbilt Univ Med Ctr 1997; **Fac Appt:** Assoc Clin Prof S, Univ Chicago-Pritzker Sch Med

Huddleston, Charles B MD [T&CS] - **Spec Exp:** Transplant-Lung-Pediatric; Transplant-Heart-Pediatric; Hypoplastic Left Heart Syndrome; **Hospital:** SSM Cardinal Glennon Chldn's Hosp, St. Louis Univ Hosp; **Address:** 1465 S Grand Blvd Fl 5 - rm 5730, St Louis, MO 63104; **Phone:** 314-268-4183; **Board Cert:** Thoracic Surgery 2007; **Med School:** Vanderbilt Univ 1978; **Resid:** Surgery, Vanderbilt Univ Hosp 1986; Cardiothoracic Surgery, Vanderbilt Univ Hosp 1988; **Fellow:** Pediatric Cardiothoracic Surgery, Hosp for Sick Chldn 1989; **Fac Appt:** Prof S, St Louis Univ

Iannettoni, Mark D MD [T&CS] - **Spec Exp:** Transplant-Lung; Lung Cancer; Esophageal Surgery; **Hospital:** Univ Iowa Hosp & Clins; **Address:** UIHC-Dept Cardiothoracic Surgery, 200 Hawkins Drive, rm SE517GH, Iowa City, IA 52242; **Phone:** 319-356-1133; **Board Cert:** Surgery 2002; Thoracic Surgery 2002; **Med School:** SUNY Upstate Med Univ 1985; **Resid:** Surgery, SUNY Upstate Med Ctr 1991; **Fellow:** Thoracic & Cardiac Surgery, Univ Mich Med Ctr 1994; **Fac Appt:** Prof T&CS, Univ Iowa Coll Med

Ilbawi, Michel N MD [T&CS] - **Spec Exp:** Pediatric Cardiac Surgery; Congenital Anomalies; Congenital Heart Disease; Congenital Heart Disease-Adult; **Hospital:** Adv Christ Med Ctr, Univ of IL Med Ctr at Chicago; **Address:** Hope Chldns Hosp at Adv Christ Med Ctr, 4440 W 95th St, Oak Lawn, IL 60453; **Phone:** 708-684-3029; **Board Cert:** Thoracic Surgery 2007; Congenital Cardiac Surgery 2009; **Med School:** Amer Univ Beirut 1971; **Resid:** Surgery, American Univ Hosp 1975; Thoracic Surgery, Univ Hosps 1977; **Fellow:** Thoracic Surgery, Chldns Meml Hosp 1978; **Fac Appt:** Clin Prof S, Univ IL Coll Med

Jeevanandam, Valluvan MD [T&CS] - **Spec Exp:** Minimally Invasive Heart Valve Surgery; Transplant-Heart; Artificial Heart Devices; **Hospital:** Univ of Chicago Med; **Address:** 5841 S Maryland Ave, MC 5040, Chicago, IL 60637; **Phone:** 773-702-2500; **Board Cert:** Thoracic Surgery 2011; **Med School:** Columbia P&S 1984; **Resid:** Surgery, Columbia-Presby Med Ctr 1989; **Fellow:** Cardiothoracic Surgery, Columbia-Presby Med Ctr 1991; **Fac Appt:** Prof S, Univ Chicago-Pritzker Sch Med

Johnstone, David W MD [T&CS] - **Spec Exp:** Thoracic Cancers; Lung Cancer; **Hospital:** Froedtert & Med Coll WI; **Address:** MCW/Froedtert Hosp, Thoracic Surgery, 9200 W Wisconsin Ave, Milwaukee, WI 53226; **Phone:** 414-955-6902; **Board Cert:** Thoracic & Cardiac Surgery 2013; **Med School:** Northwestern Univ-Feinberg Sch Med 1984; **Resid:** Surgery, NY-Presby/Weill Cornell Med Ctr 1989; **Fellow:** Cardiothoracic Surgery, NY-Presby/Weill Cornell Med Ctr 1992; **Fac Appt:** Assoc Prof T&CS, Med Coll Wisc

Joyce, Lyle D MD [T&CS] - **Spec Exp:** Cardiac Surgery-Adult; Minimally Invasive Cardiac Surgery; Heart Valve Surgery; **Hospital:** Mayo Med Ctr & Clin - Rochester; **Address:** Mayo Clin, Dept Cardiac Surg, 200 1st St SW, Rochester, MN 55905; **Phone:** 507-255-2000; **Board Cert:** Thoracic & Cardiac Surgery 2013; **Med School:** Baylor Coll Med 1973; **Resid:** Surgery, Univ Minn Hosp 1980; Cardiothoracic Surgery, Univ Utah Affil Hosps 1982; **Fac Appt:** Prof S, Mayo Med Sch

Liao, Kenneth K MD [T&CS] - **Spec Exp:** Minimally Invasive Surgery; Transplant-Heart; Transplant-Lung; Aneurysm-Thoracic Aortic; **Hospital:** Univ Minn Med Ctr, Fairview - West Bank Campus; **Address:** Univ Minn Med Ctr, Dept Surg, 420 Delaware St SE, MMC 207, Minneapolis, MN 55455; **Phone:** 612-625-3904; **Board Cert:** Thoracic Surgery 2013; **Med School:** China 1989; **Resid:** Surgery, Brookdale Univ Hosp 1999; Cardiothoracic Surgery, Univ Minn Hosp 2002; **Fellow:** Research, Albert Einstein Coll Med 1994; **Fac Appt:** Assoc Prof S, Univ Minn

Love, Robert B MD [T&CS] - **Spec Exp:** Transplant-Heart & Lung; Cardiothoracic Surgery; Heart Valve Surgery; **Hospital:** Froedtert & Med Coll WI; **Address:** Froedtert Hosp - Dept Surgery, 9200 W Wisconsin Ave, Milwaukee, WI 53226; **Phone:** 414-955-6900; **Board Cert:** Surgery 2007; Thoracic & Cardiac Surgery 2010; Surgical Critical Care 2001; **Med School:** Rush Med Coll 1982; **Resid:** Surgery, Univ WI Hosps & Clins 1988; Thoracic Surgery, Gloucestershire Royal Hosp 1989; **Fellow:** Cardiothoracic Surgery, Univ WI Hosps & Clins 1991; **Fac Appt:** Prof TS, Med Coll Wisc

Lytle, Bruce W MD [T&CS] - **Spec Exp:** Heart Valve Surgery; Coronary Artery Surgery; Aortic Surgery; **Hospital:** Cleveland Clin (page 55); **Address:** Cleveland Clin, Dept Thoracic Surg, 9500 Euclid Ave, Desk J1-227, Cleveland, OH 44195; **Phone:** 216-444-6962; **Board Cert:** Thoracic & Cardiac Surgery 2007; **Med School:** Harvard Med Sch 1971; **Resid:** Surgery, Mass Genl Hsop 1975; Cardiothoracic Surgery, Shotley Bridge Hosp 1977; **Fellow:** Cardiovascular Surgery, Mass Genl Hosp 1979; **Fac Appt:** Prof TS, Cleveland Cl Coll Med/Case West Res

Mason, David P MD [T&CS] - **Spec Exp:** Minimally Invasive Thoracic Surgery; Lung Cancer; Mesothelioma; Transplant-Lung; **Hospital:** Cleveland Clin (page 55); **Address:** Cleveland Clinic, 9500 Euclid Ave, MC J4-1, Cleveland, OH 44195; **Phone:** 216-444-4053; **Board Cert:** Surgery 2011; Thoracic Surgery 2013; **Med School:** Columbia P&S 1994; **Resid:** Surgery, Brigham & Womens Hosp 2001; **Fellow:** Vascular Surgery, Univ Washington Med Ctr 1999; Thoracic Surgery, Brigham & Womens Hosp 2003

McCarthy, Patrick M MD [T&CS] - **Spec Exp:** Heart Valve Surgery; Coronary Artery Surgery; Ventricular Assist Device (LVAD); **Hospital:** Northwestern Meml Hosp; **Address:** Bluhm Cardiovascular Inst, 675 N St Clair St, Galter Bldg Fl 19 - Ste 100, Chicago, IL 60611-2968; **Phone:** 312-695-4965; **Board Cert:** Thoracic & Cardiac Surgery 2008; **Med School:** Loyola Univ-Stritch Sch Med 1980; **Resid:** Surgery, Mayo Clinic 1985; Thoracic Surgery, Mayo Clinic 1988; **Fellow:** Cardiopulmonary Transplant Surgery, Stanford Univ Med Ctr 1989; **Fac Appt:** Prof S, Northwestern Univ

Meyers, Bryan F MD [T&CS] - **Spec Exp:** Lung Cancer; Esophageal Cancer; Transplant-Lung; Emphysema-Lung Volume Reduction; **Hospital:** Barnes-Jewish Hosp, Barnes-Jewish West County Hosp; **Address:** 4921 Parkview Pl, Ste 8B, St Louis, MO 63110; **Phone:** 314-362-8598; **Board Cert:** Thoracic Surgery 2007; **Med School:** Univ Chicago-Pritzker Sch Med 1986; **Resid:** Surgery, Mass Genl Hosp 1996; **Fellow:** Cardiothoracic Surgery, Barnes Hosp-Wash Univ 1998; **Fac Appt:** Assoc Prof S, Washington Univ, St Louis

Moon, Marc R MD [T&CS] - **Spec Exp:** Aneurysm-Thoracic Aortic; Cardiothoracic Surgery; Mitral Valve Surgery; **Hospital:** Barnes-Jewish Hosp; **Address:** 660 S Euclid Ave, Box 8234, St Louis, MO 63110; **Phone:** 314-362-0993; **Board Cert:** Surgery 2005; Thoracic Surgery 2008; **Med School:** Wayne State Univ 1988; **Resid:** Surgery, Med Coll Wisc Affil Hosps 1995; Thoracic Surgery, Stanford Univ Hosp 1996; **Fac Appt:** Prof S, Washington Univ, St Louis

Morales, David L MD [T&CS] - **Spec Exp:** Pediatric Cardiothoracic Surgery; Congenital Heart Surgery; Transplant-Heart-Pediatric; Transplant-Lung-Pediatric; **Hospital:** Cincinnati Chldns Hosp Med Ctr; **Address:** Cincinnati Chldn's Hosp-Cardiac Surgery, 3333 Burnet Ave, MC 2013, Cincinnati, OH 45229; **Phone:** 513-803-9150; **Board Cert:** Surgery 2002; Thoracic & Cardiac Surgery 2004; Congenital Cardiac Surgery 2010; **Med School:** Yale Univ 1995; **Resid:** Surgery, Columbia Univ Med Ctr 1998; **Fellow:** Cardiothoracic Surgery, Columbia Univ Med Ctr 2003; Cardiac Surgery, Texas Chldns Hosp 2004

Naunheim, Keith S MD [T&CS] - **Spec Exp:** Lung Cancer; Esophageal Cancer; Chest Wall Tumors; Video Assisted Thoracic Surgery (VATS); **Hospital:** St. Louis Univ Hosp, SSM St Mary's Hlth Ctr - St Louis; **Address:** 3655 Vista Ave Fl 1, St Louis, MO 63110; **Phone:** 314-577-8360; **Board Cert:** Thoracic Surgery 2004; **Med School:** Univ Chicago-Pritzker Sch Med 1978; **Resid:** Surgery, Univ Chicago Hosp 1983; **Fellow:** Cardiothoracic Surgery, Univ Chicago Hosp 1985; **Fac Appt:** Prof TS, St Louis Univ

Orringer, Mark B MD [T&CS] - **Spec Exp:** Esophageal Cancer; Lung Cancer; Mediastinal Tumors; Lung Cancer; **Hospital:** Univ Michigan Med Ctr; **Address:** Univ Mich, Taubman Ctr, 1500 E Med Ctr Drive, rm TC 2120, Box 5344, Ann Arbor, MI 48109; **Phone:** 734-936-4975; **Board Cert:** Surgery 1973; Thoracic Surgery 1974; **Med School:** Univ Pittsburgh 1967; **Resid:** Thoracic Surgery, Johns Hopkins Hosp 1973; **Fac Appt:** Prof TS, Univ Mich Med Sch

Pagani, Francis D MD/PhD [T&CS] - **Spec Exp:** Transplant-Heart; Coronary Artery Surgery; Left Ventricular Assist Device (LVAD); **Hospital:** Univ Michigan Med Ctr; **Address:** Univ Mich Med Ctr, 5144 Cardiovascular Ctr, 1500 E Medical Ctr Drive, SPC 5864, Ann Arbor, MI 48109; **Phone:** 734-647-2894; **Board Cert:** Surgery 2002; Thoracic Surgery 2004; **Med School:** Georgetown Univ 1986; **Resid:** Surgery, Georgetown Univ Med Ctr 1993; Thoracic Surgery, Univ Mich Hosp 1995; **Fellow:** Research, Univ Mass Med Ctr 1990; **Fac Appt:** Prof S, Univ Mich Med Sch

Patterson, G Alexander MD [T&CS] - **Spec Exp:** Lung Cancer; Esophageal Cancer; Transplant-Lung; Transplant-Heart & Lung; **Hospital:** Barnes-Jewish Hosp; **Address:** 4921 Parkview Pl, Ste 8B, St Louis, MO 63110; **Phone:** 314-362-6025; **Board Cert:** Surgery 1978; Thoracic Surgery 1981; Vascular Surgery 1982; **Med School:** Canada 1974; **Resid:** Surgery, Queens Univ Med Ctr 1978; Vascular Surgery, Univ Toronto Med Ctr 1979; **Fellow:** Research, Toronto Genl Hosp 1981; Surgical Critical Care, Johns Hopkins Hosp 1982; **Fac Appt:** Prof S, Washington Univ, St Louis

Pochettino, Alberto B MD [T&CS] - **Spec Exp:** Aneurysm-Thoracic Aortic; Transplant-Lung; Left Ventricular Assist Device (LVAD); Heart Valve Surgery; **Hospital:** St. Mary's Hosp - Rochester MN (Mayo); **Address:** Mayo Clinic, 200 1st St SW, Rochester, MN 55905; **Phone:** 507-255-7066; **Board Cert:** Surgery 2005; Thoracic Surgery 2005; **Med School:** Northwestern Univ 1987; **Resid:** Surgery, SUNY-Upstate Med Ctr 1993; **Fellow:** Thoracic Surgery, Hosp Univ Penn 1995; Cardiopulmonary Transplant Surgery, Hosp Univ Penn 1997

Schaff, Hartzell V MD [T&CS] - **Spec Exp:** Heart Valve Surgery; Congenital Heart Disease; Maze Procedure for Atrial Fibrillation; **Hospital:** St. Mary's Hosp - Rochester MN (Mayo); **Address:** Mayo Clin, Div Cardiovasc Surg, 200 First St SW, Rochester, MN 55905; **Phone:** 507-255-7068; **Board Cert:** Thoracic Surgery 2010; **Med School:** Univ Okla Coll Med 1973; **Resid:** Surgery, Johns Hopkins Hosp 1978; **Fellow:** Thoracic Surgery, Johns Hopkins Hosp 1980; **Fac Appt:** Prof S, Mayo Med Sch

Smedira, Nicholas MD [T&CS] - **Spec Exp:** Transplant-Heart; Ventricular Assist Device (LVAD); Aortic Surgery; Heart Valve Surgery; **Hospital:** Cleveland Clin (page 55); **Address:** Cleveland Clin, Dept Cardiothoracic Surg, 9500 Euclid Ave, Desk J4-1, Cleveland, OH 44195; **Phone:** 216-445-7052; **Board Cert:** Thoracic & Cardiac Surgery 2003; **Med School:** Univ Rochester 1984; **Resid:** Surgery, UCSF Med Ctr 1991; Thoracic Surgery, UCSF Med Ctr 1994; **Fellow:** Cardiothoracic Surgery, UCSF Med Ctr 1994; Cardiothoracic Surgery, Cleveland Clin 1995; **Fac Appt:** Prof S, Cleveland Cl Coll Med/Case West Res

Smith, John Michael MD [T&CS] - **Spec Exp:** Mitral Valve Robotic Surgery; **Hospital:** Good Samaritan Hosp - Cincinnati, Bethesda North Hosp; **Address:** TriHealth Heart Inst, 10506 Montgomery Ln, Ste 302, Cincinnati, OH 45242; **Phone:** 513-865-5120; **Board Cert:** Surgery 2003; Thoracic & Cardiac Surgery 2006; **Med School:** Univ Louisville Sch Med 1989; **Resid:** Surgery, Good Samaritan Hosp 1994; **Fellow:** Cardiothoracic Surgery, Yale Univ Hosp 1996

Stuart, Richard S MD [T&CS] - **Spec Exp:** Cardiac Surgery; Cardiothoracic Surgery; Robotic Cardiac Surgery; **Hospital:** St. Luke's Hosp of Kansas City, N Kansas City Hosp; **Address:** St Luke's Hosp, MidAmerica Heart and Lung Inst, 4320 Wornall Rd Bldg 2 - Ste 50-11, Kansas City, MO 64111; **Phone:** 816-931-3312; **Board Cert:** Thoracic Surgery 2010; Surgical Critical Care 2003; **Med School:** Johns Hopkins Univ 1981; **Resid:** Surgery, Johns Hopkins Hosp 1986; **Fellow:** Cardiothoracic Surgery, Johns Hopkins Hosp 1989; **Fac Appt:** Clin Prof TS, Univ MO-Kansas City

Svensson, Lars G MD/PhD [T&CS] - **Spec Exp:** Aortic Surgery; Heart Valve Surgery-Percutaneous; Marfan's Syndrome; **Hospital:** Cleveland Clin (page 55); **Address:** Cleveland Clinic, 9500 Euclid Ave, Desk J4-1, Cleveland, OH 44195; **Phone:** 216-445-4813; **Med School:** South Africa 1978; **Resid:** Surgery, Johannesburg Hosp 1986; Cardiothoracic Surgery, Baylor Coll Med Affil Hosp 1991; **Fellow:** Cardiovascular Surgery, Cleveland Clin 1987; Cardiovascular Surgery, Baylor Coll Med 1989; **Fac Appt:** Prof S, Cleveland Cl Coll Med/Case West Res

Turrentine, Mark W MD [T&CS] - **Spec Exp:** Cardiac Surgery-Pediatric; Transplant-Heart; Transplant-Lung; Congenital Heart Disease; **Hospital:** Riley Hosp for Children, IU Hlth Univ Hosp; **Address:** Indiana Univ Dept Surgery, 545 Barnhill Drive, Ste 215, Indianapolis, IN 46202; **Phone:** 317-274-7150; **Board Cert:** Thoracic & Cardiac Surgery 2013; Congenital Cardiac Surgery 2011; **Med School:** Univ Kansas 1983; **Resid:** Surgery, Univ Kansas Med Ctr 1988; Cardiothoracic Surgery, Indiana Univ Med Ctr 1991; **Fellow:** Cardiothoracic Surgery, Texas Heart Inst 1986; Transplant Surgery, Indiana Univ Med Ctr 1989; **Fac Appt:** Prof S, Indiana Univ

Vigneswaran, Wickii MD [T&CS] - **Spec Exp:** Transplant-Lung; Thoracic Cancers; Mesothelioma; Hyperhidrosis-Palmar; **Hospital:** Univ of Chicago Med; **Address:** Univ Chicago Hosps, Lung Transplant Div, 5841 S Maryland Ave, MC 5040, Chicago, IL 60637; **Phone:** 773-795-1267; **Med School:** Sri Lanka 1978; **Resid:** Surgery, Royal Coll Surgeons 1983; Cardiothoracic Surgery, Royal Coll Surgeons 1990; **Fellow:** Cardiothoracic Transplant Surg, Mayo Clinic 1994; **Fac Appt:** Prof S, Univ Chicago-Pritzker Sch Med

Walters, Henry L MD [T&CS] - **Spec Exp:** Pediatric Cardiac Surgery; Transplant-Heart-Pediatric; Cardiac Surgery-Neonatal; **Hospital:** Chldns Hosp of Michigan; **Address:** Chldns Hosp Michigan, 3901 Beaubien Blvd, Detroit, MI 48201; **Phone:** 313-745-5538; **Board Cert:** Thoracic & Cardiac Surgery 2010; Congenital Cardiac Surgery 2009; **Med School:** Baylor Coll Med 1982; **Resid:** Surgery, Mass Genl Hosp 1988; **Fellow:** Pediatric Cardiothoracic Surgery, UAB Med Ctr 1992; **Fac Appt:** Prof S, Wayne State Univ

Ziemer, Gerhard MD/PhD [T&CS] - **Spec Exp:** Pediatric Cardiac Surgery; Neonatal & Infant Cardiac Surgery; Congenital Heart Disease; **Hospital:** Univ of Chicago Med; **Address:** Univ Chicago-Pediatric Cardiac Surgery, 5841 S Maryland Ave, MC 4050, Chicago, IL 60637; **Phone:** 773-702-6172; **Med School:** Germany 1978; **Resid:** Surgery, Hannover Med School Affil Hosp 1984; Cardiothoracic Surgery, Chldn's Hosp 1986; **Fellow:** Cardiothoracic Surgery, Hannover Med School Affil Hosp 1988; **Fac Appt:** Prof S, Univ Chicago-Pritzker Sch Med

Great Plains and Mountains

Bull, David A MD [T&CS] - **Spec Exp:** Cardiothoracic Surgery; Esophageal Cancer; **Hospital:** Univ Utah Hlth Care; **Address:** Univ Utah, Dept Cardiothoracic Surgery, 30 N 1900 East, Ste 3C127, Salt Lake City, UT 84132; **Phone:** 801-581-5311; **Board Cert:** Surgery 2008; Surgical Critical Care 2009; Vascular Surgery 2011; Thoracic Surgery 2004; **Med School:** UCSF 1985; **Resid:** Surgery, UCSF Med Ctr 1987; Surgery, Univ Arizona Affil Hosps 1990; **Fellow:** Vascular Surgery, Univ Arizona Affil Hosps 1992; Cardiothoracic Surgery, Univ Arizona Affil Hosps 1994; **Fac Appt:** Assoc Prof TS, Univ Utah

Campbell, David N MD [T&CS] - **Spec Exp:** Pediatric Cardiothoracic Surgery; Transplant-Heart-Pediatric; Transplant-Lung; Congenital Heart Surgery; **Hospital:** Chldn's Hosp - Aurora (CO), Univ Colorado Hosp; **Address:** Chldns Hosp, Cardiothoracic Surgery, 13123 E 16th Ave, Box B200, Aurora, CO 80045; **Phone:** 720-777-6624; **Board Cert:** Thoracic & Cardiac Surgery 2010; Congenital Cardiac Surgery 2009; **Med School:** Rush Med Coll 1974; **Resid:** Surgery, Univ CO Hosp 1980; Cardiothoracic Surgery, Univ CO Hosp 1979; **Fellow:** Cardiothoracic Surgery, Chldns Hosp 1981; **Fac Appt:** Prof S, Univ Colorado

Fullerton, David A MD [T&CS] - **Spec Exp:** Maze Procedure for Atrial Fibrillation; Ross Procedure for Aortic Valve Disease; Mitral Valve Surgery; Transplant-Heart & Lung; **Hospital:** Univ Colorado Hosp, VA Eastern CO Health Care Sys-Denver; **Address:** Univ CO Hosp, Cardiothoracic Surgery, 12631 E 17th Ave, rm 6602, MS C310, Aurora, CO 80045; **Phone:** 303-724-2798; **Board Cert:** Surgery 2007; Surgical Critical Care 2011; Thoracic Surgery 2011; **Med School:** Univ MO-Columbia Sch Med 1981; **Resid:** Surgery, Univ Wash Med Ctr 1987; Thoracic Surgery, Univ CO Hosp 1990; **Fac Appt:** Prof S, Univ Colorado

Guber, Myles S MD [T&CS] - **Spec Exp:** Minimally Invasive Heart Valve Surgery; Robotic Cardiac Surgery; Thoracic Surgery; **Hospital:** Porter Adventist Hosp; **Address:** CO Cardiovascular Surgical Assocs, 950 E Harvard Ave, Ste 550, Denver, CO 80210; **Phone:** 303-778-6527; **Board Cert:** Thoracic & Cardiac Surgery 2006; **Med School:** Northwestern Univ-Feinberg Sch Med 1980; **Resid:** Surgery, LSU Hosp 1985; **Fellow:** Thoracic & Cardiac Surgery, Good Samaritan Hosp 1987

Karwande, Shreekanth V MD [T&CS] - **Spec Exp:** Thoracic Cancers; Lung Cancer; Cardiac Surgery; **Hospital:** St. Mark's Hosp - Salt Lake City; **Address:** MountainStar Cardiovascular Surgery, 1160 E 3900 St S, Ste 3500, Salt Lake City, UT 84124; **Phone:** 801-743-4750; **Board Cert:** Thoracic Surgery 2003; **Med School:** India 1973; **Resid:** Surgery, Erie Co Med Ctr 1981; Cardiothoracic Surgery, Presby/Weill Cornell Med Ctr 1985

Mitchell, John D MD [T&CS] - **Spec Exp:** Lung Cancer; Esophageal Surgery; Transplant-Lung; Infections-Surgical; **Hospital:** Univ Colorado Hosp, Natl Jewish Hlth; **Address:** Univ Colorado, Dept Cardiothoracic Surg, 12631 E 17th Ave, C-310, Aurora, CO 80045; **Phone:** 303-724-2800; **Board Cert:** Surgery 2005; Thoracic Surgery 2007; **Med School:** Univ Mich Med Sch 1987; **Resid:** Surgery, Mass Genl Hosp 1994; Cardiothoracic Surgery, Mass Genl Hosp 1996; **Fac Appt:** Prof TS, Univ Colorado

Mitchell, Max B MD [T&CS] - **Spec Exp:** Congenital Heart Surgery; Heart Valve Surgery; Pediatric Cardiac Surgery; Transplant-Lung; **Hospital:** Chldn's Hosp - Aurora (CO), Univ Colorado Hosp; **Address:** Chldns Hosp, Cardiothoracic Surgery, 13123 E 16th Ave, Box B200, Aurora, CO 80045; **Phone:** 720-777-6624; **Board Cert:** Surgery 2004; Thoracic Surgery 2007; Congenital Cardiac Surgery 2009; **Med School:** Geo Wash Univ 1988; **Resid:** Surgery, Univ CO Hosp 1995; Cardiovascular Surgery, Univ CO Hosp 1998; **Fellow:** Pediatric Cardiac Surgery, Royal Chldns Hosp 1999; **Fac Appt:** Prof S, Univ Colorado

Southwest

Calhoon, John H MD [T&CS] - **Spec Exp:** Transplant-Heart & Lung; Congenital Heart Surgery; Cardiac Surgery-Adult & Pediatric; **Hospital:** Univ Hosp-San Antonio, Christus Santa Rosa Children's Hosp; **Address:** UTHSCSA, Cardiothoracic Surgery Dept, 7703 Floyd Curl Drive, Ste 211L, San Antonio, TX 78229; **Phone:** 210-567-2878; **Board Cert:** Surgery 2004; Thoracic Surgery 2007; Congenital Cardiac Surgery 2009; **Med School:** Baylor Coll Med 1981; **Resid:** Surgery, Univ Hosp 1986; Cardiothoracic Surgery, Univ Hosp 1988; **Fellow:** Pediatric Cardiac Surgery, Chldns Hosp 1989; **Fac Appt:** Prof TS, Univ Tex, San Antonio

Caskey, Michael P MD [T&CS] - **Spec Exp:** Coronary Artery Surgery; Heart Valve Surgery; Maze Procedure for Atrial Fibrillation; Carotid Artery Surgery; **Hospital:** Banner Good Samaritan Regl Med Ctr - Phoenix; **Address:** Southwest Heart & Lung, 10930 N Tatum Blvd, Ste 103, Phoenix, AZ 85028; **Phone:** 602-263-7600; **Board Cert:** Thoracic & Cardiac Surgery 2013; **Med School:** Univ Tex Med Br, Galveston 1983; **Resid:** Surgery, Good Samaritan/VA Hosp 1988; Cardiovascular Surgery, Rush Presby-St Lukes Med Ctr 1990

Coselli, Joseph S MD [T&CS] - **Spec Exp:** Aneurysm-Abdominal & Thoracic Aortic; Marfan's Syndrome; Aortic Surgery; **Hospital:** St. Luke's Episcopal Hosp-Houston; **Address:** BCM, Adult Cardiac Surgery, 6770 Bertner St, Ste C350, Houston, TX 77030; **Phone:** 832-355-9910; **Board Cert:** Thoracic Surgery 2004; **Med School:** Univ Tex Med Br, Galveston 1977; **Resid:** Surgery, Baylor Affil Hosp 1982; Thoracic Surgery, Baylor Affil Hosp 1984; **Fac Appt:** Prof T&CS, Baylor Coll Med

Echeverri, Luis G MD [T&CS] - **Spec Exp:** Cardiac Surgery; Aortic Surgery; Transplant-Heart; **Hospital:** Meml Hermann SW Hosp, Methodist Sugar Land Hosp; **Address:** Meml Hermann SW Hosp, Cardiothoracic, 7737 Southwest Freeway, Ste 201, Houston, TX 77074; **Phone:** 713-776-3402; **Board Cert:** Surgery 2007; Thoracic Surgery 2010; **Med School:** Colombia 1982; **Resid:** Surgery, UT Med Branch 1996; Cardiothoracic Surgery, Univ AZ Med Ctr 2001; **Fellow:** Transplant Surgery, UPMC 1993; Cardiovascular Surgery, TX Heart Inst 1997

Forbess, Joseph M MD [T&CS] - **Spec Exp:** Pediatric Cardiothoracic Surgery; Heart Valve Surgery-Pediatric; **Hospital:** Chldns Med Ctr of Dallas, UT Southwestern Med Ctr at Dallas; **Address:** Chldns Med Ctr, Cardiothoracic Surgery, 1935 Med District Drive, Ste E03.350.Z, Dallas, TX 75235; **Phone:** 214-456-5000; **Board Cert:** Thoracic & Cardiac Surgery 2008; Congenital Cardiac Surgery 2010; **Med School:** Harvard Med Sch 1990; **Resid:** Surgery, Duke Univ Hosp 1997; Cardiothoracic Surgery, Duke Univ Hosp 1999; **Fellow:** Cardiac Surgery, Chldns Hosp 1994; **Fac Appt:** Prof TS, Univ Tex SW, Dallas

Fraser Jr, Charles D MD [T&CS] - **Spec Exp:** Pediatric Cardiothoracic Surgery; Congenital Heart Surgery; **Hospital:** Texas Chldns Hosp; **Address:** TX Chldns Hosp, Congential Heart Ctr, 6621 Fannin St Fl 20, Houston, TX 77030; **Phone:** 832-826-5730; **Board Cert:** Surgery 2010; Thoracic & Cardiac Surgery 2002; Congenital Cardiac Surgery 2009; **Med School:** Univ Tex Med Br, Galveston 1984; **Resid:** Surgery, Johns Hopkins Hosp 1990; Cardiothoracic Surgery, Johns Hopkins Hosp 1993; **Fellow:** Pediatric Cardiothoracic Surgery, Royal Chldns Hosp 1994; **Fac Appt:** Prof S, Baylor Coll Med

Frazier Jr, O. Howard MD [T&CS] - **Spec Exp:** Transplant-Heart; Lung Surgery; Artificial Heart Devices; **Hospital:** St. Luke's Episcopal Hosp-Houston, Texas Chldns Hosp; **Address:** TX Heart Inst, Transplant Ctr, 6720 Bertner Ave, Ste C355, Houston, TX 77030; **Phone:** 832-355-3000; **Board Cert:** Surgery 1975; Thoracic & Cardiac Surgery 2005; **Med School:** Baylor Coll Med 1967; **Resid:** Surgery, Baylor Affil Hosp 1974; Thoracic Surgery, St Lukes Episcopal Hosp 1976; **Fac Appt:** Prof S, Univ Tex, Houston

Gharagozloo, Farid MD [T&CS] - **Spec Exp:** Video Assisted Thoracic Surgery (VATS); Lung Cancer; Robotic Surgery; **Hospital:** Univ Arizona Med Ctr-Univ Campus; **Address:** Univ Arizona Medical Ctr, Dept Cardiac & Thoracic Surgery, 1501 N Campbell Ave, Tucson, AZ 85724; **Phone:** 520-626-6668; **Board Cert:** Thoracic Surgery 2013; **Med School:** Johns Hopkins Univ 1983; **Resid:** Surgery, Mayo Clinic 1989; Surgery, Harvard Med Sch 1986; **Fellow:** Thoracic Surgery, Mayo Clinic 1992; **Fac Appt:** Prof S, Univ Ariz Coll Med

Harrell Jr, James E MD [T&CS] - **Spec Exp:** Transplant-Heart; Cardiac Surgery-Pediatric; Congenital Heart Disease; **Hospital:** Covenant Children's Hosp; **Address:** Covenant Hlth, Cardiothoracic Surgery, 3606 21st St, Ste 103, Lubbock, TX 79410; **Phone:** 806-725-4425; **Board Cert:** Surgery 2006; Thoracic Surgery 2006; **Med School:** Baylor Coll Med 1978; **Resid:** Surgery, UT Hlth Sci Ctr 1984; Thoracic Surgery, Baylor Affil Hosp 1986; **Fellow:** Pediatric Cardiac Surgery, Hosp Sick Chldn 1987

Jessen, Michael Erik MD [T&CS] - **Spec Exp:** Cardiac Surgery; Transplant-Heart; Aneurysm-Aortic; Heart Valve Surgery; **Hospital:** UT Southwestern Med Ctr at Dallas, Parkland Hlth & Hosp Sys; **Address:** UT Southwestern Med Ctr, Dept of Cardiovascular & Thoracic Surg, 5323 Harry Hines Rd, MS 8879, Dallas, TX 75390-8879; **Phone:** 214-645-7721; **Board Cert:** Surgery 2007; Thoracic Surgery 2011; **Med School:** Univ Manitoba 1981; **Resid:** Surgery, Univ Manitoba 1986; Thoracic Surgery, Duke Univ Med Ctr 1990; **Fellow:** Research, Duke Univ Med Ctr 1988; **Fac Appt:** Prof TS, Univ Tex SW, Dallas

Johnson, Scott B MD [T&CS] - **Spec Exp:** Thoracic Cancers; Esophageal Surgery; Transplant-Lung; **Hospital:** Baptist Med Ctr - San Antonio, Univ Hosp-San Antonio; **Address:** UT Health Science Center San Antonio, 7703 Floyd Curl Drive, MSC7841, San Antonio, TX 78229; **Phone:** 210-567-5615; **Board Cert:** Surgery 2010; Surgical Critical Care 2012; Thoracic Surgery 2004; **Med School:** Univ New Mexico 1987; **Resid:** Surgery, LAC-USC Hosp 1992; Surgery, UTHSC V Hosp 1995; **Fellow:** Cardiothoracic Surgery, LAC-USC Hosp 1993; **Fac Appt:** Assoc Prof TS, Univ Tex, San Antonio

Kernstine Sr, Kemp H MD/PhD [T&CS] - **Spec Exp:** Lung Cancer; Esophageal Cancer; Tracheal Surgery; Esophageal Surgery; **Hospital:** UT Southwestern Med Ctr at Dallas; **Address:** UT SW Med Ctr, Cardiothoracic Surgery, 5323 Harry Hines Blvd, Dallas, TX 75390-8879; **Phone:** 214-645-7748; **Board Cert:** Thoracic Surgery 2004; Surgery 2001; **Med School:** Duke Univ 1982; **Resid:** Surgery, Univ Minn Med Ctr 1988; **Fellow:** Cardiothoracic Surgery, Brigham & Women's Hosp 1994; **Fac Appt:** Prof TS, Univ Tex SW, Dallas

Landreneau, Rodney J MD [T&CS] - **Spec Exp:** Lung Cancer; Esophageal Cancer; Mesothelioma; Video Assisted Thoracic Surgery (VATS); **Hospital:** Ochsner Med Ctr-New Orleans; **Address:** Ochsner Med Ctr Dept of Thoracic Surgery, 1514 Jefferson Hwy, New Orleans, LA 70121; **Phone:** 504-842-3708; **Board Cert:** Thoracic & Cardiac Surgery 2005; **Med School:** Louisiana State U, New Orleans 1978; **Resid:** Surgery, Parkland Meml Hosp 1983; **Fellow:** Cardiothoracic Surgery, Univ Mich 1985; **Fac Appt:** Prof S, Univ Pittsburgh

Lanza, Louis MD [T&CS] - **Spec Exp:** Lung Cancer; Cardiothoracic Surgery; **Hospital:** Mayo Clinic - Phoenix; **Address:** Mayo Clinic Cardiothoracic Surgery, 5777 E Mayo Blvd, Phoenix, AZ 85054; **Phone:** 480-342-2270; **Board Cert:** Thoracic & Cardiac Surgery 2010; **Med School:** Loyola Univ-Stritch Sch Med 1981; **Resid:** Surgery, Univ Michigan Med Ctr 1988; Cardiovascular Surgery, Texas Heart Inst 1991; **Fellow:** Surgical Oncology, Natl Cancer Inst 1986; Thoracic Oncology, MD Anderson Cancer Ctr 1989

Mack, Michael J MD [T&CS] - **Spec Exp:** Transplant-Heart & Lung; Cardiac Surgery; Minimally Invasive Surgery; **Hospital:** Med City Dallas Hosp, Med Ctr of Plano; **Address:** Cardiac Surgery Specialists, 4716 Alliance Blvd, Ste 310, Plano, TX 75093; **Phone:** 972-596-6676; **Board Cert:** Internal Medicine 1976; Thoracic Surgery 2001; **Med School:** St Louis Univ 1973; **Resid:** Internal Medicine, Univ Minn Med Ctr 1976; Surgery, Parkland Meml Hosp 1980; **Fellow:** Thoracic Surgery, Parkland Meml Hosp 1982

Ott, David A MD [T&CS] - **Spec Exp:** Heart Valve Surgery; Coronary Artery Surgery; Aneurysm-Abdominal Aortic; Carotid Artery Surgery; **Hospital:** St. Luke's Episcopal Hosp-Houston; **Address:** 1101 Bates Ave, Ste P-514, Houston, TX 77030-2607; **Phone:** 832-355-4900; **Board Cert:** Thoracic & Cardiac Surgery 2008; **Med School:** Baylor Coll Med 1972; **Resid:** Surgery, Baylor Coll Med 1976; Cardiothoracic Surgery, Tex Heart Inst 1978; **Fac Appt:** Clin Prof S, Baylor Coll Med

Reardon, Michael J MD [T&CS] - **Spec Exp:** Cardiac Tumors/Cancer; Heart Valve Surgery-Aortic; **Hospital:** Methodist Hosp - Houston, UT MD Anderson Canc Ctr; **Address:** Methodist DeBakey Heart & Vascular Ctr, 6550 Fannin St, Ste 1401, Houston, TX 77030; **Phone:** 713-441-5200; **Board Cert:** Thoracic Surgery 2006; **Med School:** Baylor Coll Med 1978; **Resid:** Surgery, Baylor Affil Hosps 1983; Thoracic Surgery, Texas Heart Inst 1985; **Fac Appt:** Prof T&CS, Cornell Univ-Weill Med Coll

Rice, David C MD [T&CS] - **Spec Exp:** Mesothelioma; Thoracic Cancers; Minimally Invasive Surgery; **Hospital:** UT MD Anderson Canc Ctr; **Address:** MD Anderson Canc Ctr, 1515 Holcombe Blvd, Box 1489, Houston, TX 77030; **Phone:** 713-794-1477; **Board Cert:** Thoracic & Cardiac Surgery 2004; **Med School:** Ireland 1991; **Resid:** Surgery, Mayo Clin 1998; Cardiothoracic Surgery, Baylor Affil Hosps 2001; **Fellow:** Thoracic Surgery, Mayo Clin 1999; **Fac Appt:** Prof T&CS, Univ Tex, Houston

Rosengart, Todd K MD [T&CS] - **Spec Exp:** Transfusion Free Surgery; Gene Therapy-Cardiac Angiogenesis; Minimally Invasive Surgery; Cardiac Surgery; **Hospital:** St. Luke's Episcopal Hosp-Houston; **Address:** 6620 Main St, Baylor Clinic, Houston, TX 77030; **Phone:** 713-798-1317; **Board Cert:** Surgery 2010; Thoracic & Cardiac Surgery 2013; **Med School:** Northwestern Univ 1983; **Resid:** Surgery, NYU Med Ctr 1985; Surgery, NYU Med Ctr 1989; **Fellow:** Thoracic Surgery, Natl Inst Hlth 1987; Cardiothoracic Surgery, NY-Cornell Med Ctr 1991; **Fac Appt:** Prof S, Baylor Coll Med

Roth, Jack A MD [T&CS] - **Spec Exp:** Esophageal Cancer; Lung Cancer; Gene Therapy; **Hospital:** UT MD Anderson Canc Ctr; **Address:** UT MD Anderson Cancer Ctr, Dept Thoracic & Cardiovasc Surg, 1515 Holcombe Blvd, Uni 1489, Houston, TX 77030-4000; **Phone:** 713-792-7664; **Board Cert:** Thoracic & Cardiac Surgery 2011; **Med School:** Johns Hopkins Univ 1971; **Resid:** Surgery, Johns Hopkins Hosp 1973; Thoracic Surgery, UCLA Med Ctr 1979; **Fellow:** Surgical Oncology, UCLA 1975; **Fac Appt:** Prof TS, Univ Tex, Houston

Safi, Hazim J MD [T&CS] - **Spec Exp:** Aneurysm-Abdominal Aortic; Aortic Surgery; Vascular Surgery; **Hospital:** Meml Hermann Hosp - Texas Med Ctr; **Address:** UT Hlth, Cardiothoracic & Vascular Surg, 6400 Fannin St, Ste 2850, Houston, TX 77030; **Phone:** 713-486-5100; **Board Cert:** Vascular Surgery 2005; Thoracic Surgery 2007; **Med School:** Iraq 1970; **Resid:** Surgery, Baylor Affil Hosp 1980; Radiation Oncology, Baylor Affil Hosp 1981; **Fellow:** Thoracic Surgery, Baylor Affil Hosp 1983; **Fac Appt:** Prof S, Univ Tex, Houston

Smythe, W. Roy MD [T&CS] - **Spec Exp:** Lung Cancer; Mesothelioma; **Hospital:** Scott & White Mem Hosp; **Address:** Scott & White Meml Hosp, Vasicek Canc Ctr, 2401 S 31st St, Temple, TX 76508; **Phone:** 254-724-5918; **Board Cert:** Surgery 2009; Thoracic & Cardiac Surgery 2010; **Med School:** Texas A&M Univ 1989; **Resid:** Surgery, Hosp Univ Penn 1996; **Fellow:** Cardiothoracic Surgery, Hosp Univ Penn 1998; Surgical Oncology, Amer Canc Society 1996; **Fac Appt:** Asst Prof S, Univ Tex, Houston

Swisher, Stephen G MD [T&CS] - **Spec Exp:** Esophageal Cancer; Lung Cancer; Mesothelioma; Thoracic Cancers; **Hospital:** UT MD Anderson Canc Ctr; **Address:** UT MD Anderson Canc Ctr, Dept of Thoracic & Cardiovasc Surg, 1515 Holcombe Blvd, Unit 1489, Houston, TX 77030; **Phone:** 713-792-8659; **Board Cert:** Surgery 2002; Thoracic & Cardiac Surgery 2006; **Med School:** UCSD 1986; **Resid:** Surgery, UCLA Ronald Reagan Med Ctr 1993; **Fellow:** Surgical Oncology, UCLA Ronald Reagan Med Ctr 1990; Cardiothoracic Surgery, UT MD Anderson Canc Ctr 1996; **Fac Appt:** Prof TS, Univ Tex, Houston

Turner, William F MD [T&CS] - **Spec Exp:** Coronary Artery Surgery; Cardiac Surgery; **Hospital:** Trinity Mother Frances Hosp; **Address:** Trinity Clin, Cardiothoracic Surgery, 703 S Fleishel St, Ste 5000, Tyler, TX 75701; **Phone:** 903-593-0900; **Board Cert:** Thoracic Surgery 2008; **Med School:** Baylor Coll Med 1981; **Resid:** Surgery, Baylor Affil Hosp 1987; Thoracic Surgery, Baylor Affil Hosp 1989

Walsh, Garrett L MD [T&CS] - **Spec Exp:** Esophageal Cancer; **Hospital:** UT MD Anderson Canc Ctr; **Address:** UT MD Anderson Canc Ctr, Dept of Thoracic & Cardiovasc Surg, 1515 Holcombe Blvd, Unit 1489, Houston, TX 77030; **Phone:** 713-792-6849; **Board Cert:** Surgery 2009; Thoracic & Cardiac Surgery 2009; **Med School:** Queens Univ 1983; **Resid:** Surgery, Royal Victoria Hosp-McGill 1988; Cardiovascular Surgery, McGill Univ Affil Hosp 1990; **Fac Appt:** Prof S, Univ Tex, Houston

West Coast and Pacific

Aldea, Gabriel S MD [T&CS] - **Spec Exp:** Minimally Invasive Cardiac Surgery; Vascular Surgery; Thoracic Aortic Surgery; Heart Valve Surgery; **Hospital:** Univ Wash Med Ctr; **Address:** Univ Washington-Cardiothoracic Surgery, 1959 NE Pacific St, Box 356310, Seattle, WA 98195-6310; **Phone:** 206-598-3636; **Board Cert:** Thoracic Surgery 2010; **Med School:** Columbia P&S 1981; **Resid:** Surgery, NY Presby Hosp/Cornell 1986; Cardiothoracic Surgery, NY Presby Hosp/Cornell 1990; **Fellow:** Research, UCSF Affil Rsch Inst 1988; **Fac Appt:** Prof TS, Univ Wash

Bailey, Leonard L MD [T&CS] - **Spec Exp:** Cardiac Surgery-Pediatric; Congenital Heart Surgery; Transplant-Heart-Pediatric; **Hospital:** Loma Linda Chldns Hosp, Loma Linda Univ Med Ctr; **Address:** Loma Linda Intl Heart Inst, 11234 Anderson St, rm 1617, Loma Linda, CA 92354; **Phone:** 909-558-4200; **Board Cert:** Surgery 1975; Thoracic Surgery 2006; **Med School:** Loma Linda Univ 1969; **Resid:** Surgery, Loma Linda Univ Med Ctr 1973; Thoracic Surgery, Loma Linda Univ Med Ctr 1976; **Fellow:** Cardiovascular Surgery, Hosp Sick Chldn 1977; **Fac Appt:** Prof S, Loma Linda Univ

Bowdish, Michael E MD [T&CS] - **Spec Exp:** Thoracic Aortic Surgery; Aneurysm-Aortic; Left Ventricular Assist Device (LVAD); **Hospital:** Keck Med Ctr of USC; **Address:** USC Cardiothoracic Surgery, 1520 San Pablo St, Ste 4300, Los Angeles, CA 90033; **Phone:** 323-442-5849; **Board Cert:** Surgery 2005; Thoracic & Cardiac Surgery 2009; **Med School:** Washington Univ, St Louis 1998; **Resid:** Surgery, USC Med Ctr 2005; **Fellow:** Cardiothoracic Surgery, NY Presby-Columbia Hosp 2008; **Fac Appt:** Asst Prof S, USC-Keck School of Medicine

Boyd, Walter Douglas MD [T&CS] - **Spec Exp:** Robotic Cardiac Surgery; Minimally Invasive Cardiac Surgery; Stem Cell Therapy & Biosurgery; Coronary Artery Surgery; **Hospital:** UC Davis Med Ctr; **Address:** 2221 Stockton Blvd, Cypress Bldg - Ste 2112, Sacramento, CA 95817; **Phone:** 916-734-3861; **Med School:** Univ Ottawa 1984; **Resid:** Surgery, Ottawa Civic Hospital 1990; Cardiothoracic Surgery, Ottowa Civic Hospital 1993; **Fellow:** Transplantation/Mechanical Assist Devices, Ottawa Heart Inst 1995; **Fac Appt:** Prof S, UC Davis

Cameron, Robert B MD [T&CS] - **Spec Exp:** Lung Cancer; Mesothelioma; **Hospital:** UCLA Ronald Reagan Med Ctr; **Address:** 10780 Santa Monica Blvd, Ste 100, Los Angeles, CA 90025; **Phone:** 310-470-8980; **Board Cert:** Surgery 2011; Thoracic Surgery 2005; **Med School:** UCLA 1984; **Resid:** Surgery, UCLA Med Ctr 1992; **Fellow:** Surgical Oncology, Natl Inst Hlth 1989; Thoracic Surgery, NY Hosp/Cornell 1994

Cohen, Gordon A MD/PhD [T&CS] - **Spec Exp:** Pediatric Cardiothoracic Surgery; Neonatal Surgery; Transplant-Heart-Pediatric; Heart Failure; **Hospital:** UCSF Med Ctr; **Address:** 513 Parnassus Ave, Ste S549, Box 0117, San Francisco, CA 94143; **Phone:** 415-476-3501; **Board Cert:** Thoracic & Cardiac Surgery 2010; **Med School:** Tulane Univ 1989; **Resid:** Surgery, UCLA Med Ctr 1996; Cardiothoracic Surgery, Univ Wash Med Ctr 1998; **Fellow:** Pediatric Cardiac Surgery, Great Ormond St Hosp for Chldn 1999; **Fac Appt:** Prof TS, UCSF

Cohen, Robbin G MD [T&CS] - **Spec Exp:** Minimally Invasive Surgery; Heart Valve Surgery; Thoracic Aortic Surgery; Transplant-Heart; **Hospital:** Keck Med Ctr of USC, Huntington Memorial Hosp; **Address:** 1520 San Pablo St, Ste 4300, Los Angeles, CA 90033; **Phone:** 323-442-5849; **Board Cert:** Thoracic Surgery 2008; **Med School:** Univ Colorado 1980; **Resid:** Surgery, Stanford Univ Med Ctr 1986; **Fellow:** Cardiothoracic Surgery, Stanford Univ Med Ctr 1989; **Fac Appt:** Assoc Prof TS, USC Sch Med

Dang, Michael H MD [T&CS] - **Spec Exp:** Cardiac Surgery; Peripheral Vascular Disease; Transplant-Heart; **Hospital:** Maui Meml Med Ctr; **Address:** Maui Heart and Vascular Clinic, 1849 Wili Pa Loop, Wailuku, HI 96793; **Phone:** 808-442-5667; **Board Cert:** Thoracic Surgery 2002; **Med School:** Univ Colorado 1968; **Resid:** Surgery, Baylor Univ Med Ctr 1976; Thoracic Surgery, Baylor Univ Med Ctr 1978

DeFilippi, Vincent J MD [T&CS] - **Spec Exp:** Minimally Invasive Cardiac Surgery; Mitral Valve Surgery; Maze Procedure for Atrial Fibrillation; Robotic Cardiac Surgery; **Hospital:** Salinas Valley Meml Hlthcare Systs, Stanford Univ Hosp & Clins; **Address:** Stanford Univ at Salinas Valley, Cardiac Surgery Program, 212 San Jose St, Ste 301, Salinas, CA 93901; **Phone:** 831-759-3289; **Board Cert:** Thoracic Surgery 2005; **Med School:** Columbia P&S 1988; **Resid:** Surgery, Univ Chicago Hosps 1994; **Fellow:** Cardiothoracic Surgery, New York Hosp/Meml Sloan Kettering Cancer Ctr 1996; **Fac Appt:** Assoc Clin Prof TS, Stanford Univ

Grannis Jr, Frederic W MD [T&CS] - **Spec Exp:** Lung Cancer; Tobacco Abuse; Thoracic Cancers; Palliative Care; **Hospital:** City of Hope Natl Med Ctr, Methodist Hosp - Southern California; **Address:** City of Hope Natl Med Ctr Surg Div, 1500 E Duarte Rd, Duarte, CA 91010; **Phone:** 626-359-8111 x62669; **Board Cert:** Surgery 1975; Thoracic Surgery 2010; **Med School:** NY Med Coll 1969; **Resid:** Surgery, Mayo Clinic 1974; Thoracic Surgery, Mayo Clinic 1977; **Fac Appt:** Asst Clin Prof TS, UCSD

Gundry, Steven R MD [T&CS] - **Spec Exp:** Cardiac Surgery-Adult & Pediatric; Cardiac Surgery-High Risk; **Hospital:** Desert Regl Med Ctr; **Address:** Intl Heart & Lung Inst, 555 E Tachevah Drive 3West Bldg - Ste 103, Palm Springs, CA 92262; **Phone:** 760-323-5553; **Board Cert:** Thoracic Surgery 2005; **Med School:** Med Coll GA 1977; **Resid:** Surgery, Univ Michigan Hosps 1983; Thoracic Surgery, Univ Michigan Hosps 1985; **Fellow:** Pediatric Cardiac Surgery, Hosp Sick Chldn 1986; **Fac Appt:** Clin Prof S, Loma Linda Univ

Handy Jr, John R MD [T&CS] - **Spec Exp:** Lung Cancer; Esophageal Cancer; Mesothelioma; Chest Wall Tumors; **Hospital:** Providence Portland Med Ctr; **Address:** 4805 NE Glisan St, Ste 6N50, Portland, OR 97213; **Phone:** 503-215-2300; **Board Cert:** Surgery 2011; Thoracic Surgery 2001; **Med School:** Duke Univ 1983; **Resid:** Surgery, Brown Univ Hosp 1989; **Fellow:** Cardiothoracic Surgery, MUSC Med Ctr 1992

Hanley Jr, Frank L MD [T&CS] - **Spec Exp:** Pediatric Cardiothoracic Surgery; **Hospital:** Lucile Packard Chldn's Hosp, Chldns Hosp - Oakland; **Address:** Lucille Packard Chldns Hosp, Dept Cardiothoracic Surgery, 300 Pasteur Drive, FALK CVRB, MC 5407, Stanford, CA 94305-5407; **Phone:** 650-723-0190; **Board Cert:** Thoracic Surgery 2010; **Med School:** Tufts Univ 1978; **Resid:** Surgery, UCSF Med Ctr 1986; **Fellow:** Cardiothoracic Surgery, UCSF Med Ctr 1988; Cardiothoracic Research, UCSF Cardiovascular Rsch Inst 1989; **Fac Appt:** Prof S, UCSF

Harken, Alden H MD [T&CS] - **Spec Exp:** Arrhythmias; Cardiac Surgery; Coronary Artery Surgery; **Hospital:** Alameda County Med Ctr-Highland Campus, UCSF Med Ctr; **Address:** UCSF East Bay Surgery, 1411 E 31st St, QIC 22134, Oakland, CA 94602; **Phone:** 510-437-4091; **Board Cert:** Surgery 1990; Thoracic Surgery 2006; **Med School:** Case West Res Univ 1967; **Resid:** Surgery, Peter Bent Brigham Hosp 1970; Thoracic Surgery, Chldns Hosp 1973; **Fellow:** Cardiovascular Surgery, Boston Chldns Hosp 1971; **Fac Appt:** Prof S, UCSF

Herrington, Cynthia MD [T&CS] - **Spec Exp:** Pediatric Cardiac Surgery; Congenital Heart Surgery; Transplant-Heart-Pediatric; **Hospital:** Chldns Hosp - Los Angeles; **Address:** 4650 Sunset Blvd, MS 66, Los Angeles, CA 90027; **Phone:** 323-361-4148; **Board Cert:** Surgery 2006; Thoracic & Cardiac Surgery 2009; Congenital Cardiac Surgery 2010; **Med School:** NE Ohio Univ 1990; **Resid:** Surgery, St Luke's Med Ctr 1995; **Fellow:** Thoracic & Cardiac Surgery, Univ MN Hosps 1998; Congenital Heart Surgery, Chldn's Hosp 1999; **Fac Appt:** Assoc Prof S, USC-Keck School of Medicine

Hill, Mark MD [T&CS] - **Spec Exp:** Cardiac Surgery-Adult; Mitral Valve Surgery; Thoracic Surgery; Coronary Artery Surgery; **Hospital:** Virginia Mason Med Ctr; **Address:** Virgina Mason Heart Inst, 1201 Terry Ave, Seattle, WA 98111; **Phone:** 206-223-6198; **Board Cert:** Surgery 2004; Thoracic Surgery 2005; **Med School:** Univ Utah 1989; **Resid:** Surgery, Virginia Mason Med Ctr 1994; **Fellow:** Cardiothoracic Surgery, Univ Utah Hosp 1996

Jablons, David M MD [T&CS] - **Spec Exp:** Lung Cancer; Mesothelioma; Esophageal Surgery; **Hospital:** UCSF - Mt Zion Med Ctr; **Address:** UCSF, Thoracic Surgery Dept, 1600 Divisadero St Fl 4, San Francisco, CA 94115; **Phone:** 415-885-3882; **Board Cert:** Thoracic Surgery 2013; **Med School:** Albany Med Coll 1984; **Resid:** Surgery, Tufts Med Ctr 1986; Surgery, Tufts Med Ctr 1991; **Fellow:** Surgical Oncology, Natl Cancer Inst 1989; Cardiothoracic Surgery, NY-Presby/Weill Cornell Med Ctr 1993; **Fac Appt:** Prof S, UCSF

Jamieson, Stuart W MD [T&CS] - **Spec Exp:** Congenital Heart Surgery; Transplant-Heart & Lung; Coronary Artery Surgery; Mitral Valve Surgery; **Hospital:** UCSD Med Ctr; **Address:** UCSD Med Ctr-Cardiothoracic Surgery Div, 9300 Campus Point Drive, La Jolla, CA 92037; **Phone:** 858-657-7777; **Med School:** England, UK 1971; **Resid:** Surgery 1975; **Fellow:** Cardiothoracic Surgery 1977; Cardiothoracic Surgery, Stanford Univ/American Heart Assoc 1980; **Fac Appt:** Prof S, UCSD

Laks, Hillel MD [T&CS] - **Spec Exp:** Aneurysm-Aortic; Transplant-Heart-Pediatric; Transplant-Lung-Pediatric; Transplant-Heart & Lung; **Hospital:** UCLA Ronald Reagan Med Ctr; **Address:** Cardiology Clinic, 100 Medical Plaza, rm 630E, Los Angeles, CA 90095-1741; **Phone:** 310-206-1837; **Board Cert:** Surgery 1975; Thoracic Surgery 2006; **Med School:** Africa 1965; **Resid:** Surgery, Peter Bent Brigham Hosp 1969; Cardiothoracic Surgery, Brigham & Women's Hosp 1974; **Fac Appt:** Prof S, UCLA-David Geffen Sch Med

Lamberti Jr, John J MD [T&CS] - **Spec Exp:** Pediatric Cardiac Surgery; Heart Valve Surgery; Congenital Heart Surgery; **Hospital:** Rady Children's Hosp - San Diego; **Address:** 3030 Children's Way, Ste 202, MC 5078, San Diego, CA 92123-4227; **Phone:** 858-966-8030; **Board Cert:** Surgery 1973; Thoracic & Cardiac Surgery 1975; **Med School:** Univ Pittsburgh 1967; **Resid:** Surgery, Chldns Hosp Med Ctr 1969; Surgery, Peter Bent Brigham Hosp 1972; **Fellow:** Thoracic & Cardiac Surgery, Chldns Hosp/P B Brigham Hosp 1974; **Fac Appt:** Prof S, UCSD

Louie, Brian MD [T&CS] - **Spec Exp:** Esophageal Cancer; Lung Cancer; Gastroesophageal Reflux Disease (GERD); Gastroesophageal Reflux-LINX device; **Hospital:** Swedish Med Ctr-First Hill-Seattle; **Address:** Swedish Thoracic Surgery, 1101 Madison St, Ste 850, Seattle, WA 98104; **Phone:** 206-215-6800; **Board Cert:** Surgery 2003; **Med School:** Univ Toronto 1996; **Resid:** Surgery, Univ Alberta Hosp 2002; **Fellow:** Thoracic Surgery, McMaster University 2003

Merrick, Scot H MD [T&CS] - **Spec Exp:** Aortic Surgery; Heart Valve Disease; Minimally Invasive Cardiac Surgery; Mitral Valve Surgery; **Hospital:** UCSF Med Ctr; **Address:** UCSF Med Ctr, Div Cardiothoracic Surg, 500 Parnassus Ave, Ste MU425, San Francisco, CA 94143-0118; **Phone:** 415-353-1606; **Board Cert:** Thoracic Surgery 2008; **Med School:** Univ Wash 1980; **Resid:** Surgery, UCSF Med Ctr 1985; **Fellow:** Cardiothoracic Surgery, UCSF Med Ctr 1987; **Fac Appt:** Prof S, UCSF

Miller, D Craig MD [T&CS] - **Spec Exp:** Thoracic Aortic Surgery; Mitral Valve Surgery; Aortic Surgery; Endovascular Surgery; **Hospital:** Stanford Univ Hosp & Clins; **Address:** Stanford Univ Medical School, Dept Cardiovascular Surgery, 300 Pasteur Drive, Falk CVR Bldg, Stanford, CA 94305-5407; **Phone:** 650-725-3826; **Board Cert:** Thoracic Surgery 2008; **Med School:** Stanford Univ 1972; **Resid:** Thoracic & Cardiac Surgery, Standford Univ Med Ctr 1977; **Fac Appt:** Prof T&CS, Stanford Univ

Mulligan, Michael Scott MD [T&CS] - **Spec Exp:** Transplant-Lung; Lung Cancer; Esophageal Cancer; Emphysema-Lung Volume Reduction; **Hospital:** Univ Wash Med Ctr; **Address:** UWMC-Lung Transplantation Services, 1959 NE Pacific St, Seattle, WA 98195; **Phone:** 206-598-4477; **Board Cert:** Surgery 2005; Thoracic Surgery 2008; **Med School:** Univ Conn 1989; **Resid:** Surgery, NY Presby Hosp/Columbia 1995; **Fellow:** Cardiothoracic Surgery, Univ Michigan Med Ctr 1998; Thoracic Surgery, Univ Michigan Med Ctr 1999; **Fac Appt:** Prof TS, Univ Wash

Shemin, Richard J MD [T&CS] - **Spec Exp:** Congenital Heart Surgery; Heart Valve Surgery; Aneurysm-Aortic; Coronary Artery Surgery; **Hospital:** UCLA Ronald Reagan Med Ctr; **Address:** UCLA Cardiothoracic Surgery, 757 Westwood Plaza, rm 8501E, Los Angeles, CA 90095; **Phone:** 310-206-8232; **Board Cert:** Thoracic Surgery 2013; **Med School:** Boston Univ 1974; **Resid:** Surgery, Brigham & Women's Hosp 1976; Surgery, Brigham & Women's Hosp 1980; **Fellow:** Cardiothoracic Surgery, NYU Med Ctr 1982; Surgery, Natl Inst Hlth 1978; **Fac Appt:** Prof TS, UCLA-David Geffen Sch Med

Shrager, Joseph B MD [T&CS] - **Spec Exp:** Lung Cancer; Thymoma; Emphysema-Lung Volume Reduction; Chest Wall Tumors; **Hospital:** Stanford Univ Hosp & Clins, VA Hlth Care Sys - Palo Alto; **Address:** Stanford Univ, Cardiothoracic Oncology, 875 Blake Wilbur Drive, Clin E, Stanford, CA 94305; **Phone:** 650-498-6000; **Board Cert:** Thoracic Surgery 2008; Surgery 2009; **Med School:** Harvard Med Sch 1988; **Resid:** Surgery, Hosp Univ Penn 1995; Thoracic Surgery, Mass Genl Hosp 1997; **Fac Appt:** Prof TS, Stanford Univ

Starnes, Vaughn A MD [T&CS] - **Spec Exp:** Transplant-Heart & Lung; Heart Valve Surgery; Ross Procedure for Aortic Valve Disease; Transplant-Heart-Pediatric; **Hospital:** Keck Med Ctr of USC, Huntington Memorial Hosp; **Address:** USC Cardiothoracic Surgery, 1520 San Pablo St, Ste 4300, Los Angeles, CA 90033; **Phone:** 323-442-5849; **Board Cert:** Thoracic Surgery 2007; Congenital Cardiac Surgery 2010; **Med School:** Univ NC Sch Med 1977; **Resid:** Surgery, Vanderbilt Univ Hosp 1984; Cardiovascular Surgery, Stanford Unv Hosp 1986; **Fellow:** Cardiothoracic Transplant Surg, Stanford Unv Hosp 1987; Pediatric Cardiac Surgery, Hosp for Sick Chldn 1988; **Fac Appt:** Prof TS, USC Sch Med

Thistlethwaite, Patricia A MD/PhD [T&CS] - **Spec Exp:** Cardiac Surgery; Transplant-Heart & Lung; Lung Surgery; Minimally Invasive Thoracic Surgery; **Hospital:** UCSD Med Ctr, Rady Children's Hosp - San Diego; **Address:** UCSD Sulpizio Cardiovascular Ctr, 9434 Medical Ctr Drive, San Diego, CA 92103; **Phone:** 619-543-7777; **Board Cert:** Surgery 2005; Thoracic & Cardiac Surgery 2007; **Med School:** Harvard Med Sch 1989; **Resid:** Surgery, Mass Genl Hosp 1995; **Fellow:** Cardiothoracic Surgery, Univ Pittsburgh Med Ctr 1998; **Fac Appt:** Prof S, UCSD

Trento, Alfredo MD [T&CS] - **Spec Exp:** Transplant-Heart; Cardiac Surgery; Pediatric Cardiac Surgery; Coronary Artery Surgery; **Hospital:** Cedars-Sinai Med Ctr; **Address:** Cedars-Sinai Med Ctr, Dept Thoracic Surg, 127 S San Vicente Blvd, Ste A3600, Los Angeles, CA 90048; **Phone:** 310-423-3851; **Board Cert:** Thoracic Surgery 2005; **Med School:** Italy 1975; **Resid:** Surgery, Univ Mass Med Ctr 1982; **Fellow:** Thoracic Surgery, Univ Pittsburgh Med Ctr 1985; Cardiothoracic Surgery, Univ Mass Med Ctr 1987; **Fac Appt:** Prof S, UCLA

Vallieres, Eric MD [T&CS] - **Spec Exp:** Lung Cancer; Mesothelioma; Mediastinal Tumors; Thoracic Cancers; **Hospital:** Swedish Med Ctr-First Hill-Seattle; **Address:** Swedish Canc Inst-Surgical Prac, 1101 Madison St, Ste 850, Seattle, WA 98104; **Phone:** 206-215-6800; **Board Cert:** Surgery 1988; Thoracic Surgery 1990; **Med School:** Canada 1982; **Resid:** Surgery, Univ Toronto Affil Hosps 1988; Thoracic Surgery, Univ Toronto Affil Hosps 1989; **Fellow:** Thoracic Surgery, Univ Bordeaux Affil Hosps 1990

Verrier, Edward D MD [T&CS] - **Spec Exp:** Congenital Heart Disease-Adult; Heart Valve Surgery; Aortic Surgery; **Hospital:** Univ Wash Med Ctr, Northwest Hosp - Seattle; **Address:** University Washington Medical Ctr, 1959 NE Pacific St, Box 356310, Seattle, WA 98195-6310; **Phone:** 206-598-3636; **Board Cert:** Thoracic Surgery 2003; **Med School:** Tufts Univ 1974; **Resid:** Surgery, UCSF Med Ctr 1977; Thoracic Surgery, UCSF Med Ctr 1984; **Fellow:** Cardiac Surgery, UCSF Med Ctr 1980; **Fac Appt:** Prof TS, Univ Wash

Wells, Winfield J MD [T&CS] - **Spec Exp:** Tracheal Surgery-Pediatric; Congenital Heart Surgery; **Hospital:** Chldns Hosp - Los Angeles; **Address:** Chlds Hosp, Div Cardiothoracic Surgery, 4650 Sunset Blvd, MS 66, Los Angeles, CA 90027; **Phone:** 323-361-4148; **Board Cert:** Thoracic Surgery 2007; **Med School:** USC Sch Med 1970; **Resid:** Surgery, Columbia-Presby Med Ctr 1976; **Fac Appt:** Assoc Prof S, USC Sch Med

Wood, Douglas E MD [T&CS] - **Spec Exp:** Lung Cancer; Esophageal Cancer; Tracheal Surgery; Mesothelioma; **Hospital:** Univ Wash Med Ctr, Northwest Hosp - Seattle; **Address:** Univ Wash Med Ctr, 1959 NE Pacific St, AA Bldg - Ste 115, Seattle, WA 98195-6310; **Phone:** 206-598-0917; **Board Cert:** Surgery 2009; Thoracic Surgery 2011; **Med School:** Harvard Med Sch 1983; **Resid:** Surgery, Mass Genl Hosp 1989; **Fellow:** Surgical Critical Care, Mass Genl Hosp 1991; Cardiothoracic Surgery, Mass Genl Hosp 1993; **Fac Appt:** Prof TS, Univ Wash

NYU Langone
MEDICAL CENTER

CARDIAC AND VASCULAR INSTITUTE
550 First Avenue *(at 31st Street)*
New York, NY 10016
www.NYULMC.org
Physician Referral: **888-7-NYU-MED** *(888-769-8633)*

CARDIAC AND VASCULAR INSTITUTE

The Cardiac and Vascular Institute (CVI) at NYU Langone Medical Center continues to advance new techniques for repairing heart valves, curing heart rhythm disorders, and treating aortic diseases and congestive heart failure. We care for both adults and children. CVI is consistently ranked among the leading heart and heart surgery centers in *U.S. News & World Report's annual 'Best Hospitals'* rankings.

Cardiac Catheterization CVI offers superior catheter-based diagnosis and evaluation of cardiac health. Our laboratory provides a full range of procedures to evaluate, diagnose, and provide treatment options.

Cardiac Rehabilitation and Prevention The Joan and Joel Smilow Cardiopulmonary Rehabilitation and Prevention Center provides individualized treatment plans through NYU Langone's Rusk Rehabilitation, in a state-of-the-art and comfortable facility.

Cardiac Surgery NYU Langone is a nationally recognized leader in advanced surgical treatments for adult and congenital heart disease. We have world-renowned expertise in mitral valve repair, aortic valve replacement and aortic aneurysm repair, as well as specializing in high-risk and elderly patients.

Cardiology The Leon H. Charney Division of Cardiology is a leader in cardiovascular patient care, biomedical research, and education. We are advancing the field of cardiovascular medicine through a variety of innovative collaborations.

Congenital Heart Disease The pediatric and adult congenital cardiac program treats patients of all ages with inherited and acquired cardiac defects. We have a highly experienced team of specialists in pediatric and adult cardiology, pediatric interventional cardiology, congenital cardiac surgery, neonatal and pediatric cardiac intensive care, pediatric cardiac anesthesiology, nursing, and extracorporeal perfusion.

Heart Failure A multidisciplinary team offers the most advanced care for heart failure including echocardiograms, pacemaker and defibrillator implantations, open heart surgeries, and left ventricular assist devices.

Nuclear Cardiology/Stress The Nuclear Cardiology/Stress Laboratory performs a range of tests that assist cardiologists in the assessment and diagnosis of heart disease.

Vascular Surgery We offer diagnostic and treatment for patients with conditions ranging from arterial aneurysms to deep vein thrombosis, as well as carotid stenosis and limb salvage including minimally invasive vein surgery, endovascular aortic surgery, thoracic aneurysm correction and abdominal aneurysm interventions.

Urology

A urologist manages benign and malignant medical and surgical disorders of the genitourinary system and the adrenal gland. This specialist has comprehensive knowledge of, and skills in, endoscopic, percutaneous and open surgery of congenital and acquired conditions of the urinary and reproductive systems and their contiguous structures.

Training Required: Five years

UROLOGY

New England

Albertsen, Peter C MD [U] - **Spec Exp:** Prostate Cancer; **Hospital:** Univ of Conn Hlth Ctr, John Dempsey Hosp; **Address:** UConn Hlth Ctr, Urology, 263 Farmington Ave, Ste 220, Farmington, CT 06030; **Phone:** 860-679-4100; **Board Cert:** Urology 2004; **Med School:** Columbia P&S 1978; **Resid:** Surgery, New England Deaconess Hosp 1980; Urology, Johns Hopkins Hosp 1984; **Fellow:** Preventive Medicine, Univ WI Hosp & Clins 1990; **Fac Appt:** Prof U, Univ Conn

Babayan, Richard MD [U] - **Spec Exp:** Kidney Cancer; Prostate Cancer; **Hospital:** Boston Med Ctr; **Address:** Boston Med Ctr, Dept Urology, Shapiro Ctr Fl 3, 725 Albany St, Ste 3B, Boston, MA 02118; **Phone:** 617-638-8485; **Board Cert:** Urology 1982; **Med School:** Indiana Univ 1975; **Resid:** Surgery, Yale-New Haven Hosp 1977; Urology, Boston Univ Med Ctr 1980; **Fellow:** Urologic Oncology, Boston Univ Med Ctr 1982; **Fac Appt:** Prof U, Boston Univ

Carpinito, Gennaro A MD [U] - **Spec Exp:** Kidney Cancer; Prostate Cancer; Minimally Invasive Urologic Surgery; **Hospital:** Tufts Med Ctr; **Address:** Tufts Med Ctr, Dept of Urology, 800 Washington St, Box 142, Boston, MA 02111; **Phone:** 617-636-6317; **Board Cert:** Urology 1984; **Med School:** Boston Univ 1977; **Resid:** Urology, Boston Univ Affil Hosps 1982; **Fellow:** Urologic Oncology, Boston Univ 1984; **Fac Appt:** Prof U, Tufts Univ

Colberg, John W MD [U] - **Spec Exp:** Prostate Cancer; Bladder Cancer; Kidney Cancer; Testicular Cancer; **Hospital:** Yale-New Haven Hosp; **Address:** Smilow Cancer Hosp, 20 York St, N Pavilion Fl 4, New Haven, CT 06504; **Phone:** 203-785-2815; **Board Cert:** Urology 2001; **Med School:** Washington Univ, St Louis 1985; **Resid:** Surgery, Yale-New Haven Hosp 1987; Urology, Yale-New Haven Hosp 1990; **Fac Appt:** Assoc Prof U, Yale Univ

Foster Jr, Harris E MD [U] - **Spec Exp:** Incontinence; Urodynamics; Voiding Dysfunction; Urology-Female; **Hospital:** Yale-New Haven Hosp; **Address:** Smilow Cancer Hosp at Yale New Haven, South Frontage Rd & Park St, 4th Fl, Multispecialty Care Ctr, New Haven, CT 06510; **Phone:** 203-200-4822; **Board Cert:** Urology 2012; **Med School:** Univ Miami Sch Med 1987; **Resid:** Surgery, Univ Michigan Med Ctr 1989; Urology, Univ Michigan Med Ctr 1992; **Fac Appt:** Prof U, Yale Univ

Gomery, Pablo MD [U] - **Spec Exp:** Neuro-Urology; Erectile Dysfunction; Voiding Dysfunction; **Hospital:** Mass Genl Hosp, Spaulding Rehab Hosp; **Address:** Mass Genl Hosp-Dept Urology, 55 Fruit St, GRB 1102, Boston, MA 02114; **Phone:** 617-726-8482; **Board Cert:** Urology 2010; **Med School:** Albert Einstein Coll Med 1974; **Resid:** Surgery, New England Deaconess Hosp 1977; Urology, Mass General Hosp 1980

Heney, Niall M MD [U] - **Spec Exp:** Urologic Cancer; Prostate Cancer; **Hospital:** Mass Genl Hosp; **Address:** Mass General Urology Associates, 55 Fruit St, GRB 1102, Boston, MA 02114; **Phone:** 617-726-3011; **Board Cert:** Urology 1977; **Med School:** Ireland 1965; **Resid:** Urology, Regional Hosp 1972; Urology, Mass Genl Hosp 1976; **Fac Appt:** Prof U, Harvard Med Sch

Janeiro Jr, John J MD [U] - **Spec Exp:** Urologic Cancer; Kidney Stones; Vasectomy Reversal; **Hospital:** Southern NH Med Ctr, St. Joseph Hosp & Trauma Ctr; **Address:** Urology Center Southern New Hampshire, 17 Riverside St, Ste 201, Nashua, NH 03062; **Phone:** 603-883-1550; **Board Cert:** Urology 2008; **Med School:** Univ Mass Sch Med 1982; **Resid:** Urology, Lahey Clinic 1987; **Fellow:** Pediatric Urology, Childrens Hosp 1989

Kibel, Adam S MD [U] - **Spec Exp:** Prostate Cancer; Bladder Cancer; Kidney Cancer; Minimally Invasive Surgery; **Hospital:** Brigham & Women's Hosp, Dana-Farber Cancer Inst; **Address:** Brigham & Women's Hosp, Div Urology, 45 Francis St, Boston, MA 02115; **Phone:** 617-525-7697; **Board Cert:** Urology 2009; **Med School:** Cornell Univ-Weill Med Coll 1991; **Resid:** Urology, Brigham & Women's Hosp 1997; **Fellow:** Urologic Oncology, Johns Hopkins Hosp 1999; **Fac Appt:** Prof U, Harvard Med Sch

Libertino, John A MD [U] - **Spec Exp:** Kidney Cancer; Prostate Cancer; Adrenal Tumors; **Hospital:** Lahey Hosp & Med Ctr; **Address:** Lahey Clinic, Dept Urology, 41 Mall Rd, Burlington, MA 01805-0001; **Phone:** 781-744-2511; **Board Cert:** Urology 1973; **Med School:** Georgetown Univ 1965; **Resid:** Surgery, Strong Meml Hosp 1967; Urology, Yale-New Haven Hosp 1970; **Fellow:** Urology, Yale-New Haven Hosp 1969; **Fac Appt:** Prof S, Harvard Med Sch

Loughlin, Kevin R MD [U] - **Spec Exp:** Prostate Cancer; Bladder Cancer; Penile Cancer; Incontinence-Female; **Hospital:** Brigham & Women's Hosp, Dana-Farber Cancer Inst; **Address:** Brigham & Women's Hosp, Div Urology, 45 Francis St, ASBII-3, Boston, MA 02115; **Phone:** 617-732-6325; **Board Cert:** Urology 2004; **Med School:** NY Med Coll 1975; **Resid:** Pediatrics, NY Presby/Cornell Med Ctr 1978; Surgery, Bellevue Hosp Ctr 1979; **Fellow:** Urology, Brigham & Women's Hosp 1983; Urologic Oncology, Meml Sloan Kettering Cancer Ctr 1983; **Fac Appt:** Prof S, Harvard Med Sch

McDougal, W Scott MD [U] - **Spec Exp:** Penile Cancer; Prostate Cancer; Bladder Cancer; Urologic Cancer; **Hospital:** Mass Genl Hosp; **Address:** MGH Urology Associates, 55 Fruit St, GRB Bldg, rm 1102, Boston, MA 02114; **Phone:** 617-726-3010; **Board Cert:** Surgery 1975; Urology 1992; **Med School:** Cornell Univ-Weill Med Coll 1968; **Resid:** Surgery, Univ Hosps Cleveland 1975; Urology, Univ Hosps Cleveland 1975; **Fellow:** Physiology, Yale New Haven Hosp 1972; **Fac Appt:** Prof U, Harvard Med Sch

McGovern, Francis J MD [U] - **Spec Exp:** Prostate Cancer; Urologic Cancer; **Hospital:** Mass Genl Hosp; **Address:** 1 Hawthorne Pl, Ste 109, Boston, MA 02114; **Phone:** 617-726-3560; **Board Cert:** Urology 2009; **Med School:** Case West Res Univ 1983; **Resid:** Urology, Mass Genl Hosp 1989

O'Leary, Michael P MD [U] - **Spec Exp:** Sexual Dysfunction; Prostate Disease; Pelvic Pain Syndrome; Interstitial Cystitis; **Hospital:** Brigham & Women's Hosp; **Address:** Brigham & Women's Hosp, Div Urology, 45 Francis St, ASBII-3, Boston, MA 02115; **Phone:** 617-732-6398; **Board Cert:** Urology 2010; **Med School:** Geo Wash Univ 1980; **Resid:** Urology, Tufts New Eng Med Ctr 1982; Urology, Mass Genl Hosp 1986; **Fellow:** Urology, UCSF Med Ctr 1989; **Fac Appt:** Assoc Prof S, Harvard Med Sch

Oates, Robert D MD [U] - **Spec Exp:** Infertility-Male; Vasectomy Reversal; Reproductive Genetics; Congenital Absence of Vas Deferens; **Hospital:** Boston Med Ctr; **Address:** Boston Med Ctr, Dept Urology, 725 Albany St Shapiro Bldg - Ste 3B, Boston, MA 02118-2334; **Phone:** 617-638-8485; **Board Cert:** Urology 2010; **Med School:** Boston Univ 1982; **Resid:** Surgery, Boston Univ Hosp 1984; Urology, Boston Univ Hosp 1987; **Fellow:** Reproductive Medicine, Baylor Coll Med Affil Hosp 1988; **Fac Appt:** Prof U, Boston Univ

Olumi, Aria F MD [U] - **Spec Exp:** Prostate Cancer; Testicular Cancer; Kidney Cancer; Bladder Cancer; **Hospital:** Mass Genl Hosp; **Address:** Mass General Urology Associates, 55 Fruit St, Ste YAW 7E, Boston, MA 02114; **Phone:** 617-643-0237; **Board Cert:** Urology 2012; **Med School:** Univ SC Sch Med 1992; **Resid:** Surgery, Brigham & Women's Hosp 1994; Urology, Brigham & Women's Hosp 2000; **Fellow:** Research, UCSF Affil Hosp 1998; **Fac Appt:** Assoc Prof S, Harvard Med Sch

Richie, Jerome P MD [U] - **Spec Exp:** Prostate Cancer; Testicular Cancer; Kidney Cancer; **Hospital:** Brigham & Women's Hosp, Dana-Farber Cancer Inst; **Address:** Brigham & Women's Hosp, 45 Francis St, Fl 3, Ste ASB2, Boston, MA 02115; **Phone:** 617-732-6325; **Board Cert:** Urology 2002; **Med School:** Univ Tex Med Br, Galveston 1969; **Resid:** Surgery, UCLA Med Ctr 1971; Urology, UCLA Med Ctr 1975; **Fac Appt:** Prof S, Harvard Med Sch

Schulam, Peter G MD/PhD [U] - **Spec Exp:** Prostate Cancer; Kidney Cancer; Kidney Stones; Minimally Invasive Surgery; **Hospital:** Yale-New Haven Hosp; **Address:** Smilow Cancer Hosp, 20 York St, N Pavilion Fl 4 - rm 202B, New Haven, CT 06504; **Phone:** 203-200-4822; **Board Cert:** Urology 2009; **Med School:** Baylor Coll Med 1992; **Resid:** Surgery, Johns Hopkins Hosp 1994; Urology, Johns Hopkins Hosp 1998

Sigman, Mark MD [U] - **Spec Exp:** Infertility-Male; Vasectomy Reversal; Erectile Dysfunction; **Hospital:** Rhode Island Hosp; **Address:** 2 Dudley St, Ste 175, Providence, RI 02905-3247; **Phone:** 401-421-0710; **Board Cert:** Urology 2010; **Med School:** Univ Conn 1981; **Resid:** Surgery, Univ VA Med Ctr 1983; Urology, Univ VA Med Ctr 1987; **Fellow:** Male Reproduction, Baylor Coll Med 1989; **Fac Appt:** Assoc Prof U, Brown Univ

Singh, Dinesh MD [U] - **Spec Exp:** Laparoscopic Surgery; Robotic Surgery; Kidney Cancer; Prostate Cancer; **Hospital:** Smilow Cancer Hosp at Yale-New Haven; **Address:** Smilow Hosp, Prostate Urologic Cancer, 35 Park St Fl 4, New Haven, CT 06519; **Phone:** 203-785-2815; **Board Cert:** Urology 2006; **Med School:** Columbia P&S 1997; **Resid:** Surgery, Brigham & Womens Hosp 1999; Urology, Harvard Med Sch 2003; **Fellow:** Research, Dana Farber Cancer Inst 2001; Laparoscopic Surgery, Cleveland Clin 2004; **Fac Appt:** Asst Prof U, Yale Univ

Weiss, Robert M MD [U] - **Spec Exp:** Pediatric Urology; Testicular Cancer; Penile Cancer; Bladder Cancer; **Hospital:** Smilow Cancer Hosp at Yale-New Haven; **Address:** Smilow Hosp, Prostate & Urologic Cancer, 20 York St Fl 3, New Haven, CT 06510; **Phone:** 203-785-2815; **Board Cert:** Urology 1970; **Med School:** SUNY Downstate 1960; **Resid:** Surgery, Beth Israel Hosp 1962; Urology, NY-Presby/Columbia Univ Med Ctr 1967; **Fellow:** Pharmacology, NY-Presby/Columbia Univ Med Ctr 1965; **Fac Appt:** Prof U, Yale Univ

Mid Atlantic

Albala, David M MD [U] - **Spec Exp:** Prostate Cancer/Robotic Surgery; Kidney Stones; Laparoscopic Surgery; **Hospital:** Crouse Hosp, St. Joseph's Hosp Hlth Ctr; **Address:** Associated Medical Professionals, 1226 E Water St, Syracuse, NY 13210; **Phone:** 315-478-4185; **Board Cert:** Urology 2012; **Med School:** Mich State Univ 1983; **Resid:** Surgery, Dartmouth-Hitchcock Med Ctr 1985; Urology, Dartmouth-Hitchcock Med Ctr 1990; **Fellow:** Endourology, Wash Univ Med Ctr 1991

Alexander, Richard B MD [U] - **Spec Exp:** Prostate Disease; Prostate Cancer; **Hospital:** Univ of MD Med Ctr, Baltimore VA Med Ctr; **Address:** 29 S Greene St, Ste 500, Baltimore, MD 21201; **Phone:** 410-328-5109; **Board Cert:** Urology 2011; **Med School:** Johns Hopkins Univ 1981; **Resid:** Surgery, Vanderbilt Univ Affil Hosps 1983; Urology, Johns Hopkins Hosp 1988; **Fellow:** Cancer Immunology, Natl Cancer Inst 1989; **Fac Appt:** Prof U, Univ MD Sch Med

Bar-Chama, Natan MD [U] - **Spec Exp:** Infertility-Male; Erectile Dysfunction; Vasectomy Reversal; Varicocele Microsurgery; **Hospital:** Mt Sinai Med Ctr (page 62); **Address:** RMA, Ctr Male Reproductive Hlth, 635 Madison Ave Fl 10, New York, NY 10022; **Phone:** 212-756-5777; **Board Cert:** Urology 2006; **Med School:** Albert Einstein Coll Med 1987; **Resid:** Urology, Montefiore Med Ctr 1993; **Fellow:** Male Infertility, Baylor Med Ctr 1994; **Fac Appt:** Assoc Prof U, Mount Sinai Sch Med

Benson, Mitchell C MD [U] - **Spec Exp:** Prostate Cancer/Robotic Surgery; Bladder Cancer; Kidney Cancer; Continent Urinary Diversions; **Hospital:** NY-Presby/Columbia Univ Med Ctr, NY (page 65); **Address:** 161 Fort Washington Ave, Ste 1102, New York, NY 10032-3713; **Phone:** 212-305-5201; **Board Cert:** Urology 1984; **Med School:** Columbia P&S 1977; **Resid:** Surgery, Mount Sinai Med Ctr 1979; Urology, Columbia-Presby Hosp 1982; **Fellow:** Oncology, Johns Hopkins Hosp 1984; **Fac Appt:** Prof U, Columbia P&S

Blaivas, Jerry G MD [U] - **Spec Exp:** Uro-Gynecology; Urology-Female; Neurogenic Bladder; Incontinence after Prostate Cancer; **Hospital:** NY-Presby/Weill Cornell Med Ctr, NY (page 65), Lenox Hill Hosp (page 66); **Address:** UroCenter, 445 E 77th St, New York, NY 10075; **Phone:** 212-772-3900; **Board Cert:** Urology 1978; **Med School:** Tufts Univ 1968; **Resid:** Surgery, Boston Med Ctr 1971; Urology, Tufts Med Ctr 1976; **Fac Appt:** Clin Prof U, Cornell Univ-Weill Med Coll

Burnett II, Arthur L MD [U] - **Spec Exp:** Prostate Cancer; Erectile Dysfunction; Genitourinary Reconstruction; **Hospital:** Johns Hopkins Hosp (page 59); **Address:** Brady Urological Inst, 601 N Caroline St Fl 4, Baltimore, MD 21287; **Phone:** 410-955-6100; **Board Cert:** Urology 2007; **Med School:** Johns Hopkins Univ 1988; **Resid:** Surgery, Johns Hopkins Hosp 1990; Urology, Johns Hopkins Hosp 1994; **Fac Appt:** Prof U, Johns Hopkins Univ

Carter, H. Ballentine MD [U] - **Spec Exp:** Prostate Cancer; **Hospital:** Johns Hopkins Hosp (page 59); **Address:** Brady Urological Inst, 601 N Caroline St Fl 4, Baltimore, MD 21287; **Phone:** 410-955-6100; **Board Cert:** Urology 2010; **Med School:** Med Univ SC 1981; **Resid:** Surgery, New York Hosp 1983; Urology, New York Hosp 1987; **Fellow:** Research, Johns Hopkins Hosp 1989; **Fac Appt:** Prof U, Johns Hopkins Univ

Chen, David YT MD [U] - **Spec Exp:** Urologic Cancer; Robotic Surgery; Laparoscopic Surgery; **Hospital:** Fox Chase Cancer Ctr (page 57), Jeanes Hosp; **Address:** Fox Chase Cancer Ctr-Dept Urology, 333 Cottman Ave, Philadelphia, PA 19111; **Phone:** 215-728-2548; **Board Cert:** Urology 2006; **Med School:** Cornell Univ 1997; **Resid:** Urology, NY-Presby/Weill Cornell Med Ctr 2003; **Fellow:** Urologic Oncology, NY-Presby/Weill Cornell Med Ctr 2004; **Fac Appt:** Assoc Prof U, Temple Univ

Chun, Thomas MD [U] - **Spec Exp:** Prostate Cancer; Kidney Stones; Erectile Dysfunction; **Hospital:** Englewood Hosp & Med Ctr, Holy Name Med Ctr; **Address:** Urology Ctr, 300 Grand Ave, Ste 202, Englewood, NJ 07631; **Phone:** 201-816-1900; **Board Cert:** Urology 2008; **Med School:** Geo Wash Univ 1991; **Resid:** Surgery, NYU Med Ctr 1993; **Fellow:** Urology, NYU Med Ctr 1997

Cohen, Jeffrey K MD [U] - **Spec Exp:** Urologic Cancer; Prostate Cancer; **Hospital:** Allegheny Genl Hosp, Canonsburg General Hospital; **Address:** Triangle Urological Group, 1307 Federal St, Ste 300, Pittsburgh, PA 15212-1757; **Phone:** 412-281-1757; **Board Cert:** Urology 2005; **Med School:** SUNY Upstate Med Univ 1979; **Resid:** Surgery, Univ Hosp 1981; Urology, Univ Hosp 1984; **Fellow:** Urologic Oncology, MD Anderson Cancer Ctr 1985; **Fac Appt:** Assoc Prof S, Drexel Univ Coll Med

Coleman, Jonathan A MD [U] - **Spec Exp:** Prostate Cancer; Kidney Cancer; Adrenal Cancer; Minimally Invasive Surgery; **Hospital:** Meml Sloan-Kettering Canc Ctr; **Address:** 1275 York Ave, New York, NY 10065; **Phone:** 646-422-4432; **Board Cert:** Urology 2006; **Med School:** Cornell Univ-Weill Med Coll 1996; **Resid:** Surgery, NY Presby-Cornell Med Ctr 1998; **Fellow:** Urology, NY Presby-Cornell Med Ctr 2002; Urology, NIH/Natl Cancer Inst 2003

Droller, Michael J MD [U] - **Spec Exp:** Urologic Cancer; Bladder Cancer; Prostate Cancer; Kidney Cancer; **Hospital:** Mt Sinai Med Ctr (page 62); **Address:** 5 E 98th St, Fl 6, Box 1272, New York, NY 10029-6501; **Phone:** 212-241-3868; **Board Cert:** Urology 2001; **Med School:** Harvard Med Sch 1968; **Resid:** Surgery, Peter Bent Brigham Hosp 1970; Urology, Stanford Univ Med Ctr 1976; **Fellow:** Research, Univ Stockholm 1977; **Fac Appt:** Prof U, Mount Sinai Sch Med

Fisch, Harry MD [U] - **Spec Exp:** Infertility-Male; Microsurgery; Vasectomy Reversal; **Hospital:** NY-Presby/Weill Cornell Med Ctr, NY (page 65), Lenox Hill Hosp (page 66); **Address:** 944 Park Ave, Ste 1C, New York, NY 10028; **Phone:** 212-879-0800; **Board Cert:** Urology 2010; **Med School:** Mount Sinai Sch Med 1983; **Resid:** Surgery, Montefiore Med Ctr 1985; Urology, Montefiore Med Ctr 1989; **Fac Appt:** Prof U, Columbia P&S

Gearhart, John P MD [U] - **Spec Exp:** Pediatric Urology; **Hospital:** Johns Hopkins Hosp (page 59); **Address:** Johns Hopkins Hosp, Brady Urological Inst, 1800 Orleans St, Ste 7304, Baltimore, MD 21287; **Phone:** 410-955-5358; **Board Cert:** Urology 1982; **Med School:** Univ Louisville Sch Med 1975; **Resid:** Urology, Med Coll Georgia Hosp 1980; **Fellow:** Pediatric Urology, Alder Hey Chldns Hosp 1981; Pediatric Urology, Johns Hopkins Hosp 1985; **Fac Appt:** Prof U, Johns Hopkins Univ

Goldstein, Marc MD [U] - **Spec Exp:** Infertility-Male; Varicocele Microsurgery; Vasectomy & Vasectomy Reversal; Erectile Dysfunction; **Hospital:** NY-Presby/Weill Cornell Med Ctr, NY (page 65); **Address:** NY-Presby, Reproductive Med, 525 E 68th St, Box 269, New York, NY 10065; **Phone:** 212-746-5470; **Board Cert:** Urology 1982; **Med School:** SUNY Downstate 1972; **Resid:** Surgery, NY-Presby/Columbus Univ Med Ctr 1974; Urology, SUNY Downstate Med Ctr 1980; **Fellow:** Microsurgery, Rockefeller Univ 1982; Reproductive Medicine, Rockefeller Univ 1982; **Fac Appt:** Prof U, Cornell Univ-Weill Med Coll

Gomella, Leonard G MD [U] - **Spec Exp:** Prostate Cancer; Minimally Invasive Urologic Surgery; Urologic Cancer; **Hospital:** Thomas Jefferson Univ Hosp; **Address:** Thomas Jefferson Univ Hosp-Urology Dept, 833 Chestnut St Fl 7 - Ste 703, Philadelphia, PA 19107-5001; **Phone:** 215-955-1000; **Board Cert:** Urology 2008; **Med School:** Univ KY Coll Med 1980; **Resid:** Surgery, Univ Kentucky Med Ctr 1982; Urology, Univ Kentucky Med Ctr 1986; **Fellow:** Urologic Oncology, Natl Cancer Inst 1988; **Fac Appt:** Prof U, Jefferson Med Coll

Grasso III, Michael MD [U] - **Spec Exp:** Urologic Cancer; Laparoscopic Surgery; Kidney Stones; Testicular Cancer; **Hospital:** Lenox Hill Hosp (page 66), Westchester Med Ctr; **Address:** 100 E 77 th St, East Bldg - Fl 4th, New York, NY 10075; **Phone:** 212-434-6300; **Board Cert:** Urology 2013; **Med School:** Jefferson Med Coll 1986; **Resid:** Surgery, Jefferson Univ Hosp 1988; Urology, Jefferson Univ Hosp 1992; **Fac Appt:** Prof U, NY Med Coll

Greenberg, Richard E MD [U] - **Spec Exp:** Prostate Cancer; Bladder Cancer; Kidney Cancer; Prostate Cancer/Robotic Surgery; **Hospital:** Fox Chase Cancer Ctr (page 57), Jeanes Hosp; **Address:** Fox Chase Cancer Ctr-Urology Dept, 333 Cottman Ave, Philadelphia, PA 19111-2497; **Phone:** 215-728-5341; **Board Cert:** Urology 2004; **Med School:** Cornell Univ-Weill Med Coll 1976; **Resid:** Surgery, New York Hosp 1978; Urology, New York Hosp 1983; **Fac Appt:** Prof U, Temple Univ

Gribetz, Michael Elliot MD [U] - **Spec Exp:** Prostate Disease; Urology-Female; Sexual Dysfunction; Bladder Cancer; **Hospital:** Mt Sinai Med Ctr (page 62); **Address:** 1155 Park Ave, New York, NY 10128-1209; **Phone:** 212-831-1300; **Board Cert:** Urology 1980; **Med School:** Albert Einstein Coll Med 1973; **Resid:** Surgery, Montefiore Med Ctr 1975; Urology, Mt Sinai Hosp 1978; **Fac Appt:** Asst Clin Prof U, Mount Sinai Sch Med

Hall, Simon J MD [U] - **Spec Exp:** Urologic Cancer; Minimally Invasive Urologic Surgery; Continent Urinary Diversions; Prostate Cancer; **Hospital:** Mt Sinai Med Ctr (page 62); **Address:** 5 E 98th St, Box 1272, New York, NY 10029; **Phone:** 212-241-4812; **Board Cert:** Urology 2009; **Med School:** Columbia P&S 1988; **Resid:** Surgery, Mt Sinai Med Ctr 1990; Urology, Boston Univ 1994; **Fellow:** Urology, Baylor Coll Med 1996; **Fac Appt:** Assoc Prof U, Mount Sinai Sch Med

Hensle, Terry W MD [U] - **Spec Exp:** Pediatric Urology; Hypospadias; Urinary Reconstruction; Wilms' Tumor; **Hospital:** Hackensack Univ Med Ctr; **Address:** 699 Teaneck Rd, Ste 103, Teaneck, NJ 07666; **Phone:** 201-645-3362; **Board Cert:** Urology 1978; **Med School:** Cornell Univ-Weill Med Coll 1968; **Resid:** Surgery, Boston City Hosp 1973; Urology, Mass Genl Hosp 1976; **Fellow:** Pediatric Urology, Mass Genl Hosp 1977; Pediatric Urology, Great Ormond St Hosp 1978; **Fac Appt:** Prof U, Columbia P&S

Herr, Harry W MD [U] - **Spec Exp:** Bladder Cancer; Prostate Cancer; Testicular Cancer; **Hospital:** Meml Sloan-Kettering Canc Ctr, NY-Presby/Weill Cornell Med Ctr, NY (page 65); **Address:** 1275 York Avenue, New York, NY 10021; **Phone:** 646-422-4411; **Board Cert:** Urology 1976; **Med School:** UCSF 1969; **Resid:** Urology, UC Irvine Med Ctr 1974; **Fellow:** Urology, Meml Sloan Kettering Cancer Ctr 1976; **Fac Appt:** Assoc Prof S, Cornell Univ-Weill Med Coll

Hrebinko Jr, Ronald L MD [U] - **Spec Exp:** Kidney Cancer; Prostate Cancer; Bladder Cancer; Testicular Cancer; **Hospital:** UPMC Shadyside; **Address:** Univ Pittsburgh Dept of Urology, Shadyside Medical Bldg, Ste 209, 5200 Centre Ave, Pittsburgh, PA 15232; **Phone:** 412-605-3022; **Board Cert:** Urology 2013; **Med School:** Univ Pittsburgh 1986; **Resid:** Urology, Univ Pittsburgh Med Ctr 1992; **Fellow:** Urologic Oncology, Roswell Park Cancer Ctr 1993; **Fac Appt:** Assoc Prof U, Univ Pittsburgh

Jackman, Stephen V MD [U] - **Spec Exp:** Prostate Cancer/Robotic Surgery; Kidney Cancer; Kidney Stones; Laparoscopic Surgery; **Hospital:** UPMC Shadyside, UPMC Presby, Pittsburgh; **Address:** 3471 Fifth Ave, Ste 700, Univ Pittsburgh Med Ctr,Urology Dept, Pittsburgh, PA 15213; **Phone:** 412-692-4095; **Board Cert:** Urology 2011; **Med School:** Yale Univ 1994; **Resid:** Urology, Johns Hopkins Hosp 2000; **Fac Appt:** Prof U, Univ Pittsburgh

Kane, Michael H MD [U] - **Spec Exp:** Brachytherapy; Prostate Cancer; Minimally Invasive Surgery; Incontinence after Prostate Cancer; **Hospital:** Sinai Hosp - Baltimore; **Address:** 688 Poole Rd, Ste A, Westminister, MD 21157; **Phone:** 443-821-3674; **Board Cert:** Urology 2005; **Med School:** Cornell Univ 1989; **Resid:** Urology, Mt Sinai Hosp 1995

Kaplan, Steven A MD [U] - **Spec Exp:** Prostate Disease; Voiding Dysfunction; Incontinence after Prostate Cancer; Incontinence; **Hospital:** NY-Presby/Weill Cornell Med Ctr, NY (page 65); **Address:** 425 E 61 St, Fl 12, New York, NY 10065; **Phone:** 646-962-4811; **Board Cert:** Urology 2011; **Med School:** Mount Sinai Sch Med 1982; **Resid:** Surgery, Mount Sinai Hosp 1984; Urology, Columbia Presby Med Ctr 1988; **Fellow:** Urology, Columbia Presby Med Ctr 1990; **Fac Appt:** Prof U, Cornell Univ-Weill Med Coll

Katz, Aaron E MD [U] - **Spec Exp:** Prostate Cancer-Cryosurgery; Kidney Cancer-Cryosurgery; Complementary Medicine; Nutrition & Cancer Prevention; **Hospital:** Winthrop Univ Hosp; **Address:** Winthrop Urology, 1401 Franklin Ave, Garden City, NY 11530; **Phone:** 516-535-1900; **Board Cert:** Urology 2006; **Med School:** NY Med Coll 1986; **Resid:** Urology, Maimonides Med Ctr 1992; **Fellow:** Urologic Oncology, Columbia Presby Med Ctr 1993; **Fac Appt:** Assoc Clin Prof U, Columbia P&S

Kavoussi, Louis R MD [U] - **Spec Exp:** Robotic Surgery; Urologic Cancer; Prostate Cancer; Kidney Cancer; **Hospital:** Long Is Jewish Med Ctr (page 66), N Shore Univ Hosp (page 66); **Address:** Arthur Smith Institute for Urology, 450 Lakeville Rd, Ste M-41, New Hyde Park, NY 11042; **Phone:** 516-734-8558; **Board Cert:** Urology 2009; **Med School:** SUNY Buffalo 1983; **Resid:** Surgery, Barnes Jewish Hosp 1985; Urology, Barnes Jewish Hosp 1989; **Fac Appt:** Prof U, Hofstra N Shore-LIJ Sch Med

Kirschenbaum, Alexander M MD [U] - **Spec Exp:** Prostate Cancer; Bladder Cancer; Kidney Cancer; **Hospital:** Mt Sinai Med Ctr (page 62); **Address:** 229 E 79th St, Ste 1A, New York, NY 10075; **Phone:** 646-422-0926; **Board Cert:** Urology 2006; **Med School:** Mount Sinai Sch Med 1980; **Resid:** Surgery, Mt Sinai Hosp 1982; Urology, Mt Sinai Hosp 1985; **Fellow:** Urologic Oncology, Mt Sinai Hosp 1987; **Fac Appt:** Assoc Prof U, Mount Sinai Sch Med

Lanteri, Vincent J MD [U] - **Spec Exp:** Prostate Cancer/Robotic Surgery; Urologic Cancer; **Hospital:** Hackensack Univ Med Ctr, Holy Name Med Ctr; **Address:** NJ Ctr for Prostate Cancer & Urology, 255 W Spring Valley Ave, Ste 101, Maywood, NJ 07607; **Phone:** 201-487-8866; **Board Cert:** Urology 1982; **Med School:** Mexico 1974; **Resid:** Surgery, UMDNJ Med Ctr 1977; Urology, UMDNJ Med Ctr 1980; **Fellow:** Urologic Oncology, Roswell Park Cancer Inst 1982

Lepor, Herbert MD [U] - **Spec Exp:** Prostate Cancer; **Hospital:** NYU Langone Med Ctr (page 68); **Address:** 150 E 32nd St, Fl 2, NYU Urology Assocaites, New York, NY 10016; **Phone:** 646-825-6327; **Board Cert:** Urology 2006; **Med School:** Johns Hopkins Univ 1975; **Resid:** Urology, Johns Hopkins Hosp 1986; **Fac Appt:** Prof U, NYU Sch Med

Linsenmeyer, Todd A MD [U] - **Spec Exp:** Infertility-Male in Spinal Cord Injury; Voiding Dysfunction/Spinal Cord Injury; Urodynamics in Spinal Cord Injury; **Hospital:** Kessler Inst for Rehab - W Orange; **Address:** Kessler Inst Rehab, 1199 Pleasant Valley Way, West Orange, NJ 07052; **Phone:** 973-731-3600 x2274; **Board Cert:** Urology 2005; Physical Medicine & Rehabilitation 1990; **Med School:** Univ Hawaii JA Burns Sch Med 1979; **Resid:** Urology, Tripler AMC 1984; **Fellow:** Physical Medicine & Rehabilitation, Stanford Univ Hosp 1989; **Fac Appt:** Prof S, UMDNJ-NJ Med Sch, Newark

Loo, Marcus Hsieu-Hong MD [U] - **Spec Exp:** Prostate Disease; Kidney Stones; Voiding Dysfunction; Prostate Cancer; **Hospital:** NY-Presby/Weill Cornell Med Ctr, NY (page 65); **Address:** 254 Canal St, Ste 3001, New York, NY 10013-3501; **Phone:** 212-925-8388; **Board Cert:** Urology 2008; **Med School:** Cornell Univ-Weill Med Coll 1981; **Resid:** Surgery, NY Hosp-Cornell Med Ctr 1983; Urology, NY Hosp-Cornell Med Ctr 1988; **Fellow:** Urology, NY Hosp-Cornell Med Ctr 1984; **Fac Appt:** Clin Prof U, Cornell Univ-Weill Med Coll

Lowe, Franklin Charles MD [U] - **Spec Exp:** Prostate Disease; Complementary Medicine; Prostate Cancer; Kidney Stones; **Hospital:** St. Luke's - Roosevelt Hosp Ctr - Roosevelt Div (page 56), NY-Presby/Columbia Univ Med Ctr, NY (page 65); **Address:** 425 W 59th St, Ste 3A, New York, NY 10019-1104; **Phone:** 212-523-7790; **Board Cert:** Urology 2006; **Med School:** Columbia P&S 1979; **Resid:** Surgery, Johns Hopkins Hosp 1981; Urology, Johns Hopkins Hosp 1984; **Fac Appt:** Clin Prof U, Columbia P&S

Malkowicz, S. Bruce MD [U] - **Spec Exp:** Prostate Cancer; Bladder Cancer; Kidney Cancer; Gene Therapy; **Hospital:** Hosp Univ Penn - UPHS (page 69); **Address:** Penn Urology, Perelman Center, 3400 Civic Center Blvd, 3 West, Philadelphia, PA 19104; **Phone:** 215-662-2891 x7330; **Board Cert:** Urology 2009; **Med School:** Univ Pennsylvania 1981; **Resid:** Surgery, Hosp Univ Penn 1983; Urology, Hosp Univ Penn 1987; **Fellow:** Urologic Oncology, USC Med Ctr 1998; Urologic Oncology, Hosp Univ Penn/Wistar Inst 1990; **Fac Appt:** Prof U, Univ Pennsylvania

McCullough, Andrew R MD [U] - **Spec Exp:** Erectile Dysfunction; Infertility-Male; Prostate Cancer; **Hospital:** Albany Med Ctr; **Address:** Urological Inst NENY, 23 Hackett Blvd, MC 208, Albany, NY 12208; **Phone:** 518-262-3341; **Board Cert:** Urology 2005; **Med School:** Univ MD Sch Med 1978; **Resid:** Urology, Johns Hopkins Hosp 1983; **Fellow:** Urologic Oncology, Johns Hopkins Hosp 1984; **Fac Appt:** Assoc Prof U, Albany Med Coll

Mohler, James L MD [U] - **Spec Exp:** Prostate Cancer; Robotic Surgery; **Hospital:** Roswell Park Canc Inst; **Address:** Roswell Park Cancer Inst, Elm & Carlton Streets, Department of Urology, Buffalo, NY 14263; **Phone:** 716-845-3159; **Board Cert:** Urology 2007; **Med School:** Med Coll GA 1980; **Resid:** Surgery, Univ Kentucky Med Ctr 1982; Urology, Univ Kentucky Med Ctr 1985; **Fellow:** Urologic Oncology, Johns Hopkins Hosp 1987; **Fac Appt:** Prof U, SUNY Buffalo

Mostwin, Jacek L MD/PhD [U] - **Spec Exp:** Prostate Cancer; **Hospital:** Johns Hopkins Hosp (page 59); **Address:** Brady Urological Inst, 601 N Caroline St Fl 4, Baltimore, MD 21287; **Phone:** 410-955-6100; **Board Cert:** Urology 2007; **Med School:** Univ MD Sch Med 1975; **Resid:** Surgery, Univ Michigan Med Ctr 1978; Urology, Johns Hopkins Hosp 1983; **Fac Appt:** Prof U, Johns Hopkins Univ

Mulhall, John P MD [U] - **Spec Exp:** Erectile Dysfunction; Peyronie's Disease; Penile Prostheses; Infertility-Male; **Hospital:** Meml Sloan-Kettering Canc Ctr; **Address:** MSKCC, Urology Dept, 353 E 68th St, Fl 5, New York, NY 10021; **Phone:** 646-422-4359; **Board Cert:** Urology 2008; **Med School:** Ireland 1985; **Resid:** Urology, Univ Conn Hlth Ctr 1995; **Fellow:** Urology, Boston Med Ctr 1996; **Fac Appt:** Assoc Prof U, Cornell Univ-Weill Med Coll

Nagler, Harris M MD [U] - **Spec Exp:** Vasectomy Reversal; Infertility-Male; Varicocele Microsurgery; Erectile Dysfunction; **Hospital:** Beth Israel Med Ctr - Petrie Div (page 56); **Address:** Beth Israel Med Ctr, Dept Urology, 10 Union Square E, Ste 3A, New York, NY 10003-3314; **Phone:** 212-844-8700; **Board Cert:** Urology 1982; **Med School:** Temple Univ 1975; **Resid:** Urology, Columbia Presby Med Ctr 1980; **Fellow:** Reproductive Medicine, Columbia Presby Med Ctr 1981; **Fac Appt:** Prof U, Albert Einstein Coll Med

Naslund, Michael MD [U] - **Spec Exp:** Prostate Cancer; Prostate Disease; **Hospital:** Univ of MD Med Ctr; **Address:** UMMC-Maryland Prostate Ctr, 419 W Redwood St, Ste 320, Baltimore, MD 21201; **Phone:** 410-328-0800; **Board Cert:** Urology 2008; **Med School:** Johns Hopkins Univ 1981; **Resid:** Surgery, Johns Hopkins Hosp 1983; Urology, Johns Hopkins Hosp 1987; **Fac Appt:** Prof U, Univ MD Sch Med

Nelson, Joel B MD [U] - **Spec Exp:** Prostate Cancer; **Hospital:** UPMC Shadyside; **Address:** UPMC Shadyside Med Ctr, 5200 Centre Ave, Ste 209, Pittsburgh, PA 15232-1312; **Phone:** 412-605-3013; **Board Cert:** Urology 2008; **Med School:** Northwestern Univ 1988; **Resid:** Surgery, Northwestern MemL Hosp 1990; Urology, Northwestern Meml Hosp 1994; **Fellow:** Urology, Johns Hopkins Hosp 1995; **Fac Appt:** Prof U, Univ Pittsburgh

Nitti, Victor MD [U] - **Spec Exp:** Urology-Female; Incontinence-Male & Female; Urodynamics; Voiding Dysfunction; **Hospital:** NYU Langone Med Ctr (page 68); **Address:** NYU Urology Assocs, 150 E 32nd St Fl 2, New York, NY 10016; **Phone:** 646-825-6324; **Board Cert:** Urology 2002; **Med School:** UMDNJ-NJ Med Sch, Newark 1985; **Resid:** Surgery, Univ Hosp 1987; Urology, Univ Hosp 1991; **Fellow:** Female Urology, UCLA Med Ctr 1992; **Fac Appt:** Prof U, NYU Sch Med

Palese, Michael A MD [U] - **Spec Exp:** Kidney Cancer; Laparoscopic Surgery; Robotic Surgery; Kidney Stones; **Hospital:** Mt Sinai Med Ctr (page 62); **Address:** 5 E 98th St Fl 6, New York, NY 10029; **Phone:** 212-241-3868; **Board Cert:** Urology 2006; **Med School:** Mount Sinai Sch Med 1997; **Resid:** Surgery, Univ MD Med Ctr 1999; Urology, Univ MD Med Ctr 2003; **Fellow:** Urologic Oncology, NY Presby-Cornell Med Ctr 2004; Robotic Surgery, NY Presby-Cornell Med Ctr 2004; **Fac Appt:** Assoc Prof U, Mount Sinai Sch Med

Partin, Alan W MD/PhD [U] - **Spec Exp:** Prostate Cancer; Prostate Disease; **Hospital:** Johns Hopkins Hosp (page 59); **Address:** Brady Urological Inst, 601 N Caroline St Fl 4, Baltimore, MD 21287; **Phone:** 410-955-6100; **Board Cert:** Urology 2007; **Med School:** Johns Hopkins Univ 1989; **Resid:** Surgery, Johns Hopkins Hosp 1991; Urology, Johns Hopkins Hosp 1996; **Fac Appt:** Prof U, Johns Hopkins Univ

Sadeghi-Nejad, Hossein MD [U] - **Spec Exp:** Erectile Dysfunction; Peyronie's Disease; Prostate Disease; Infertility-Male; **Hospital:** Hackensack Univ Med Ctr, Univ Hosp (Newark); **Address:** 20 Prospect Ave, rm 711, Hackensack, NJ 07601; **Phone:** 201-342-7977 x214; **Board Cert:** Urology 2009; **Med School:** McGill Univ 1989; **Resid:** Surgery, UCSF Med Ctr 1991; Urology, Boston Univ Med Ctr 1996; **Fellow:** Microsurgery, Boston Univ Med Ctr 1997; Reproductive Medicine, Boston Univ Med Ctr 1997; **Fac Appt:** Prof U, UMDNJ-Rutgers Med Sch

Samadi, David B MD [U] - **Spec Exp:** Prostate Cancer/Robotic Surgery; Kidney Cancer; Bladder Cancer; Urologic Cancer; **Hospital:** Lenox Hill Hosp (page 66); **Address:** 485 Madison Ave Fl 21, New York, NY 10022; **Phone:** 212-365-5000; **Board Cert:** Urology 2013; **Med School:** SUNY Stony Brook 1994; **Resid:** Surgery, Montefiore Med Ctr 1996; Urology, Montefiore Med Ctr 2000; **Fellow:** Urologic Oncology, Meml Sloan Kettering Cancer Ctr 2001; Laparoscopic Surgery, Henri Mondor Hosp 2003; **Fac Appt:** Prof U, Hofstra N Shore-LIJ Sch Med

Sawczuk, Ihor S MD [U] - **Spec Exp:** Bladder Cancer; Kidney Cancer; Prostate Cancer/Robotic Surgery; **Hospital:** Hackensack Univ Med Ctr, NY-Presby/Columbia Univ Med Ctr, NY (page 65); **Address:** Hackensack Univ Med Ctr, Dept Urology, 360 Essex St, Ste 403, Hackensack, NJ 07601; **Phone:** 551-996-8090; **Board Cert:** Urology 2005; **Med School:** Med Coll PA Hahnemann 1979; **Resid:** Surgery, St Vincents Hosp 1981; Urology, Columbia-Presby Med Ctr 1984; **Fellow:** Urologic Oncology, Columbia-Presby Med Ctr 1986; **Fac Appt:** Prof U, UMDNJ-NJ Med Sch, Newark

Scardino, Peter T MD [U] - **Spec Exp:** Prostate Cancer; Bladder Cancer; Urologic Cancer; Urinary Reconstruction; **Hospital:** Meml Sloan-Kettering Canc Ctr; **Address:** 1275 York Avenue, New York, NY 10065; **Phone:** 646-422-4329; **Board Cert:** Urology 1981; **Med School:** Duke Univ 1971; **Resid:** Surgery, Mass Genl Hosp 1973; Urology, UCLA Med Ctr 1979; **Fellow:** Urology, Natl Cancer Inst 1976; **Fac Appt:** Prof U, Cornell Univ-Weill Med Coll

Scherr, Douglas S MD [U] - **Spec Exp:** Prostate Cancer/Robotic Surgery; Bladder Cancer; Robotic Surgery; Testicular Cancer; **Hospital:** NY-Presby/Weill Cornell Med Ctr, NY (page 65); **Address:** Brady Urologic Health Ctr, 525 E 68th St Starr 900, New York, NY 10021; **Phone:** 212-746-5788; **Board Cert:** Urology 2013; **Med School:** Geo Wash Univ 1994; **Resid:** Urology, NY Hosp-Cornell Med Ctr 2000; **Fellow:** Urologic Oncology, Meml Sloan-Kettering Canc Ctr 2002; **Fac Appt:** Asst Prof U, Cornell Univ-Weill Med Coll

Schlegel, Peter N MD [U] - **Spec Exp:** Prostate Cancer; Fertility Preservation in Cancer; Infertility-Male; Testicular Cancer; **Hospital:** NY-Presby/Weill Cornell Med Ctr, NY (page 65), Hosp For Special Surgery (page 58); **Address:** Brady Urologic Health Ctr, 525 E 68th St, Starr Bldg - Fl 9 - Ste 900, New York, NY 10065-4870; **Phone:** 212-746-5491; **Board Cert:** Urology 2011; **Med School:** Univ Mass Sch Med 1983; **Resid:** Surgery, Johns Hopkins Hosp 1985; Urology, Johns Hopkins Hosp 1989; **Fellow:** Medical Oncology, Johns Hopkins Hosp 1987; Male Reproduction, NY Hosp-Cornell Med Ctr 1991; **Fac Appt:** Prof U, Cornell Univ-Weill Med Coll

Schoenberg, Mark P MD [U] - **Spec Exp:** Bladder Cancer; Urinary Reconstruction; **Hospital:** Johns Hopkins Hosp (page 59); **Address:** Brady Urological Inst, 601 N Caroline St Fl 4, Baltimore, MD 21287; **Phone:** 410-955-1039; **Board Cert:** Urology 2005; **Med School:** Univ Tex, Houston 1986; **Resid:** Surgery, Hosp Univ Penn 1988; Urologic Surgery, Hosp Univ Penn 1992; **Fellow:** Urologic Oncology, Brady Inst/Johns Hopkins 1994; **Fac Appt:** Prof U, Johns Hopkins Univ

Seftel, Allen D MD [U] - **Spec Exp:** Sexual Dysfunction; Infertility-Male; Prostate Disease; Peyronie's Disease; **Hospital:** Cooper Univ Hosp; **Address:** Cooper Univ Hosp-Urology Div, 3 Cooper Plaza, Ste 403, Camden, NJ 08103; **Phone:** 856-963-3577; **Board Cert:** Urology 2003; **Med School:** SUNY Downstate 1984; **Resid:** Urology, SUNY Downstate Med Ctr 1987; Urology, Univ Hosps-Case West Res 1990; **Fellow:** Reproductive Medicine, Boston Univ Med Ctr 1992; **Fac Appt:** Prof U, UMDNJ-RW Johnson Med Sch

Shabsigh, Ridwan MD [U] - **Spec Exp:** Erectile Dysfunction; Hypogonadism; Clinical Trials; Incontinence; **Hospital:** Maimonides Med Ctr (page 60); **Address:** 6300 8th Ave, Brooklyn, NY 11220; **Phone:** 718-283-7746; **Board Cert:** Urology 2011; **Med School:** Syria 1976; **Resid:** Urology, Seepark Hosp 1983; Urology, Baylor Med Ctr 1990; **Fellow:** Urology, Baylor Med Ctr 1987; **Fac Appt:** Clin Prof U, Columbia P&S

Sheinfeld, Joel MD [U] - **Spec Exp:** Testicular Cancer; Fertility Preservation in Cancer; **Hospital:** Meml Sloan-Kettering Canc Ctr; **Address:** 353 E 68th St, New York, NY 10065; **Phone:** 646-422-4311; **Board Cert:** Urology 2009; **Med School:** Univ Fla Coll Med 1981; **Resid:** Urology, Strong Meml Hosp 1986; **Fellow:** Urologic Oncology, Meml Sloan Kettering Cancer Ctr 1989; **Fac Appt:** Assoc Prof U, Cornell Univ-Weill Med Coll

Shenot, Patrick J MD [U] - **Spec Exp:** Voiding Dysfunction/Spinal Cord Injury; Voiding Dysfunction; Reconstructive Urologic Surgery; Incontinence; **Hospital:** Thomas Jefferson Univ Hosp, Magee Rehab Hosp; **Address:** Thom Jefferson Univ Hosp-Urology Dept, 833 Chestnut St, Fl 7, Ste 703, Philadelphia, PA 19107; **Phone:** 215-955-1000; **Board Cert:** Urology 2010; **Med School:** SUNY Stony Brook 1991; **Resid:** Surgery, Thomas Jefferson Univ Hosp 1993; Urology, Thomas Jefferson Univ Hosp 1997; **Fellow:** Neurourology, Thomas Jefferson Univ Hosp 1999; **Fac Appt:** Assoc Prof U, Thomas Jefferson Univ

Siegelbaum, Marc H MD [U] - **Spec Exp:** Prostate Cancer; Laparoscopic Surgery; Kidney Cancer; Pediatric Urology; **Hospital:** Univ of MD-St. Joseph Med Ctr; **Address:** Chesapeake Urology Assocs, 7505 Osler Drive, Ste 506, Towson, MD 21204; **Phone:** 410-296-0167; **Board Cert:** Urology 2009; **Med School:** Univ MD Sch Med 1982; **Resid:** Surgery, Sinai Hosp 1989; Urology, Temple Univ Hlth Sci Ctr 1991

Taneja, Samir S MD [U] - **Spec Exp:** Prostate Cancer; Kidney Cancer; Bladder Cancer; **Hospital:** NYU Langone Med Ctr (page 68); **Address:** NYU Urology Associates, 150 E 32nd St, Fl 2, New York, NY 10016-6024; **Phone:** 646-825-6321; **Board Cert:** Urology 2009; **Med School:** Northwestern Univ 1990; **Resid:** Urology, UCLA Med Ctr 1996; **Fac Appt:** Prof U, NYU Sch Med

Tewari, Ashutosh K MD [U] - **Spec Exp:** Prostate Cancer/Robotic Surgery; **Hospital:** Mt Sinai Med Ctr (page 62); **Address:** 625 Madison Ave Fl 2, New York, NY 10019; **Phone:** 212-241-9955; **Board Cert:** Urology 2006; **Med School:** India 1984; **Resid:** Surgery, GSVM Medical College 1990; Urology, Henry Ford Hosp 2003; **Fellow:** Transplant Surgery, Liverpool Univ Med Ctr 1993; Urologic Oncology, Shands Healthcare 1995; **Fac Appt:** Assoc Prof U, Mount Sinai Sch Med

Trabulsi, Edouard J MD [U] - **Spec Exp:** Minimally Invasive Urologic Surgery; Urologic Cancer; Prostate Cancer/Robotic Surgery; Laparoscopic Surgery; **Hospital:** Thomas Jefferson Univ Hosp; **Address:** Jefferson Urology Associates, 833 Chestnut St, Fl 7, Ste 703, Philadelphia, PA 19107; **Phone:** 215-955-1000; **Board Cert:** Urology 2005; **Med School:** SUNY Buffalo 1995; **Resid:** Surgery, Thomas Jefferson Univ Hosp 1997; Urology, Thomas Jefferson Univ Hosp 2001; **Fellow:** Urologic Oncology, Meml Sloan-Kettering Cancer Ctr 2003; **Fac Appt:** Assoc Prof U, Thomas Jefferson Univ

Uzzo, Robert G MD [U] - **Spec Exp:** Urologic Cancer; Kidney Cancer; Robotic Surgery; Urinary Reconstruction; **Hospital:** Fox Chase Cancer Ctr (page 57), Jeanes Hosp; **Address:** Fox Chase Cancer Ctr-Urology Dept, 333 Cottman Ave, Philadelphia, PA 19111; **Phone:** 215-728-3501; **Board Cert:** Urology 2009; **Med School:** Cornell Univ-Weill Med Coll 1991; **Resid:** Surgery, NY-Presby/Weill Cornell Med Ctr 1993; Urology, NY-Presby/Weill Cornell Med Ctr 1997; **Fellow:** Urologic Oncology, Cleveland Clinic 1999; Renal Transplant, Cleveland Clinic 2000; **Fac Appt:** Prof S, Temple Univ

Van Arsdalen, Keith N MD [U] - **Spec Exp:** Infertility-Male; Varicocele Microsurgery; Urologic Cancer; Vasectomy Reversal; **Hospital:** Hosp Univ Penn - UPHS (page 69), Chldns Hosp of Philadelphia; **Address:** Penn Urology, 3400 Civic Center Blvd, Perelman Center, 3 West, Philadelphia, PA 19104-4283; **Phone:** 215-662-2891; **Board Cert:** Urology 1984; **Med School:** Med Coll VA 1977; **Resid:** Surgery, Univ Maryland Hosp 1979; Urology, Med Coll Virginia 1982; **Fellow:** Urodynamics, Hosp Univ Penn 1983; **Fac Appt:** Prof U, Univ Pennsylvania

Vapnek, Jonathan M MD [U] - **Spec Exp:** Incontinence; Urology-Female; Neurogenic Bladder; Urodynamics; **Hospital:** Mt Sinai Med Ctr (page 62); **Address:** 229 E 79th St, Ste 1A, New York, NY 10075; **Phone:** 212-717-9500; **Board Cert:** Urology 2005; **Med School:** UCSD 1986; **Resid:** Surgery, UCSD Med Ctr 1988; Urology, UCSF Med Ctr 1992; **Fellow:** Neurourology, UC Davis Med Ctr 1993; **Fac Appt:** Assoc Clin Prof U, Mount Sinai Sch Med

Verghese, Mohan MD [U] - **Spec Exp:** Urologic Cancer; **Hospital:** MedStar Washington Hosp Ctr; **Address:** 110 Irving St NW, Ste 3B19, Washington, DC 20010; **Phone:** 202-877-3968; **Board Cert:** Urology 2005; **Med School:** India 1976; **Resid:** Surgery, Bay State Med Ctr 1980; Urology, Washington Hosp Ctr 1984; **Fellow:** Urologic Oncology, Roswell Park Meml Inst 1992

Walsh, Patrick MD [U] - **Spec Exp:** Prostate Cancer; **Hospital:** Johns Hopkins Hosp (page 59); **Address:** Brady Urological Inst, 601 N Caroline St Fl 4, Baltimore, MD 21287; **Phone:** 410-955-6100; **Board Cert:** Urology 1975; **Med School:** Case West Res Univ 1964; **Resid:** Surgery, Peter Bent Brigham Hosp/Chldns Hosp 1967; Urology, UCLA Med Ctr 1971; **Fellow:** Endocrinology, Harbor Genl Hosp 1970; **Fac Appt:** Prof U, Johns Hopkins Univ

Wein, Alan J MD/PhD [U] - **Spec Exp:** Prostate Cancer; Neuro-Urology; Urologic Cancer; Urodynamics; **Hospital:** Hosp Univ Penn - UPHS (page 69), Pennsylvania Hosp-UPHS (page 69); **Address:** Univ Penn Hlth Sys, Div Urology, 34th & Civic Ctr Blvd, Perelman Ctr, W Pavilion, Fl 3, Philadelphia, PA 19104-4283; **Phone:** 215-662-2891; **Board Cert:** Urology 1995; **Med School:** Univ Pennsylvania 1966; **Resid:** Surgery, Hosp Univ Penn 1968; Urology, Hosp Univ Penn 1972; **Fellow:** Urology, Hosp Univ Penn 1969; **Fac Appt:** Prof U, Univ Pennsylvania

Weiss, Robert E MD [U] - **Spec Exp:** Bladder Cancer; Kidney Cancer; Testicular Cancer; Robotic Surgery; **Hospital:** Robert Wood Johnson Univ Hosp - New Brunswick; **Address:** 1 Robert Wood Johnson Pl Ste MB588, Dept Urology, New Brunswick, NJ 08901-1928; **Phone:** 732-235-7960; **Board Cert:** Urology 2004; **Med School:** NYU Sch Med 1985; **Resid:** Surgery, Mount Sinai Med Ctr 1987; Urology, Mount Sinai Med Ctr 1991; **Fellow:** Urologic Oncology, Meml Sloan Kettering Cancer Ctr 1994; **Fac Appt:** Assoc Prof U, UMDNJ-RW Johnson Med Sch

Yu, George W MD [U] - **Hospital:** G Washington Univ Hosp, Anne Arundel Med Ctr; **Address:** 122 Defense Hwy, Ste 224, Annapolis, MD 21401; **Phone:** 410-897-0540; **Board Cert:** Urology 1981; **Med School:** Tufts Univ 1973; **Resid:** Surgery, Brigham & Women's Hosp 1976; Urology, Johns Hopkins Hosp 1981; **Fac Appt:** Prof U, Geo Wash Univ

Southeast

Badlani, Gopal H MD [U] - **Spec Exp:** Incontinence; Pelvic Organ Prolapse Repair; **Hospital:** Wake Forest Baptist Med Ctr; **Address:** Dept Urology-Reynolds Tower, Medical Ctr Blvd, Winston-Salem, NC 27157; **Phone:** 336-716-4131; **Board Cert:** Urology 1982; **Med School:** India 1973; **Resid:** Surgery, St Agnes Hosp 1977; Urology, LI Jewish Hosp 1980; **Fellow:** Urology, Baylor Med Ctr 1983; **Fac Appt:** Prof U, Wake Forest Univ

Balaji, K. C. MD [U] - **Spec Exp:** Prostate Cancer; Urologic Cancer; Robotic Surgery; Minimally Invasive Surgery; **Hospital:** Wake Forest Baptist Med Ctr; **Address:** Wake Forest Baptist Med Ctr, Urology Clinic, 140 Charlois Blvd, Winston-Salem, NC 27103; **Phone:** 336-716-4131; **Board Cert:** Urology 2009; **Med School:** India 1986; **Resid:** Surgery, Lebanon Hosp Ctr 1993; Urology, Univ Mass Med Ctr 1997; **Fellow:** Urologic Oncology, Meml Sloan-Kettering Cancer Ctr 1999; **Fac Appt:** Prof U, Wake Forest Univ

Beall, Michael E MD [U] - **Spec Exp:** Prostate Cancer; Testicular Cancer; Vasectomy Reversal; **Hospital:** Inova Fairfax Hosp, Reston Hosp Ctr; **Address:** Northern Virginia Urology, 8503 Arlington Blvd, Ste 310, Fairfax, VA 22031; **Phone:** 703-208-4200; **Board Cert:** Urology 1979; **Med School:** Geo Wash Univ 1972; **Resid:** Urology, Geo Wash Univ Hosp 1977; **Fac Appt:** Assoc Clin Prof U, Geo Wash Univ

Broderick, Gregory MD [U] - **Spec Exp:** Erectile Dysfunction; Voiding Dysfunction; Peyronie's Disease; **Hospital:** Mayo - Jacksonville; **Address:** Mayo Clin, Urology Dept, 4500 San Pablo Rd, Jacksonville, FL 32224; **Phone:** 904-953-7330; **Board Cert:** Urology 2012; **Med School:** UCSF 1983; **Resid:** Surgery, UCSF Med Ctr 1985; Urology, UCSF Med Ctr 1988; **Fellow:** Neurourology, UC Davis Med Ctr 1990; **Fac Appt:** Prof U, Mayo Med Sch

Busby, Joseph Erik MD [U] - **Spec Exp:** Prostate Cancer; Robotic Surgery; **Hospital:** Greenville Meml Hosp; **Address:** 15 Park Creek Drive, Greenville, SC 29605; **Phone:** 864-797-7450; **Board Cert:** Urology 2009; **Med School:** Med Univ SC 1998; **Resid:** Urology, UC Davis Hlth Ctr 2004; **Fellow:** Urologic Oncology, UT MD Anderson Cancer Ctr 2007

Carson III, Culley C MD [U] - **Spec Exp:** Erectile Dysfunction; Kidney Stones; Peyronie's Disease; **Hospital:** NC Memorial Hosp - UNC, Durham Regional Hosp; **Address:** UNC, Urology Dept, 2113 Physicians Office Bldg, CB 7235, Chapel Hill, NC 27599-7235; **Phone:** 919-966-1315; **Board Cert:** Urology 1980; **Med School:** Geo Wash Univ 1971; **Resid:** Surgery, Dartmouth-Hitchcock Med Ctr 1973; Urology, Mayo Clinic 1978; **Fac Appt:** Prof U, Univ NC Sch Med

Chang, Sam S MD [U] - **Spec Exp:** Prostate Cancer; Bladder Cancer; Kidney Cancer; Testicular Cancer; **Hospital:** Vanderbilt Univ Med Ctr; **Address:** A1302 Vanderbilt Univ Med Ctr N, Nashville, TN 37232-2765; **Phone:** 615-322-2101; **Board Cert:** Urology 2010; **Med School:** Vanderbilt Univ 1992; **Resid:** Urology, Vanderbilt Univ Med Ctr 1998; **Fellow:** Urologic Oncology, Meml Sloan Kettering Cancer Ctr 2000; **Fac Appt:** Prof U, Vanderbilt Univ

Ciancio, Gaetano MD [U] - **Spec Exp:** Transplant-Kidney; Transplant-Pancreas; Kidney Cancer; **Hospital:** Jackson Meml Hosp, Univ of Miami Hosp; **Address:** UHlth, Transplant Dept, 1801 NW 9th Ave, Ste 519, Miami, FL 33136; **Phone:** 305-355-5111; **Board Cert:** Urology 2005; **Med School:** Venezuela 1982; **Resid:** Surgery, Jackson Meml Hosp 1989; Urology, Jackson Meml Hosp 1993; **Fellow:** Transplant Surgery, Jackson Meml Hosp 1995; **Fac Appt:** Prof U, Univ Miami Sch Med

Fraser Jr, Lionel B MD [U] - **Spec Exp:** Prostate Cancer; Incontinence after Prostate Cancer; Erectile Dysfunction; **Hospital:** Baptist Med Ctr-Jackson; **Address:** Metropolitan Urology, St Dominics West Med Tower, 971 Lakeland Drive, Ste 360, Jackson, MS 39216; **Phone:** 601-982-0982; **Board Cert:** Urology 2005; **Med School:** Univ Mich Med Sch 1977; **Resid:** Surgery, New England Deaconess Hosp 1979; **Fellow:** Urology, Brigham & Womens Hosp 1983

Greene, Graham MD [U] - **Spec Exp:** Urologic Cancer; Bladder Cancer; Reconstructive Urologic Surgery; **Hospital:** Lakeland Regl Med Ctr; **Address:** Lakeland Regl Cancer Ctr, 3525 Lakeland Hills Blvd, Lakeland, FL 33805; **Phone:** 863-603-6565; **Board Cert:** Urology 2007; **Med School:** Dalhousie Univ 1989; **Resid:** Urology, Victoria Genl Hosp 1994; **Fellow:** Urologic Oncology, UT MD Anderson Cancer Ctr 1997; **Fac Appt:** Assoc Prof

Hemal, Ashok K MD [U] - **Spec Exp:** Urologic Cancer; Robotic Surgery; Reconstructive Urologic Surgery; Laparoscopic Surgery; **Hospital:** Wake Forest Baptist Med Ctr; **Address:** Department of Urology, Medical Center Blvd, Winston-Salem, NC 27157; **Phone:** 336-716-5702; **Med School:** India 1981; **Resid:** Surgery, G R Med College 1985; Urology, Post Grad Inst Med Ed & Rsch 1988; **Fellow:** Robotic Surgery, Henry Ford Hosp; **Fac Appt:** Prof U, Wake Forest Univ

Irby III, Pierce B MD [U] - **Spec Exp:** Kidney Stones; Minimally Invasive Surgery; Vasectomy; **Hospital:** Carolinas Med Ctr, Presby Hosp - Charlotte; **Address:** McKay Urology, 1023 Edgehill Rd S, Charlotte, NC 28207; **Phone:** 704-355-8686; **Board Cert:** Urology 2013; **Med School:** Uniformed Srvs Univ, Bethesda 1983; **Resid:** Urology, Letterman Army Med Ctr 1990; **Fellow:** Endourology, UCSF Med Ctr 1992; **Fac Appt:** Assoc Clin Prof U, Univ NC Sch Med

Keane, Thomas E MD [U] - **Spec Exp:** Urologic Cancer; Genitourinary Cancer; Prostate Cancer; Clinical Trials; **Hospital:** MUSC Med Ctr; **Address:** MUSC-Urology Dept, 96 Jonathan Lucas St, Ste CSB644, MS 620, Charleston, SC 29425; **Phone:** 843-792-1666; **Board Cert:** Urology 2013; **Med School:** Ireland 1981; **Resid:** Urology, St Vincents Hosp 1986; Urology, N Tees Gen Hosp 1988; **Fellow:** Urology, Duke Univ Med Ctr 1993; **Fac Appt:** Prof U, Univ SC Sch Med

Kennelly, Michael J MD [U] - **Spec Exp:** Incontinence; Voiding Dysfunction; Pelvic Organ Prolapse Repair; Neurogenic Bladder; **Hospital:** Carolinas Med Ctr, Presby Hosp - Charlotte; **Address:** McKay Urology, 1023 Edgehill Rd S, Charlotte, NC 28207; **Phone:** 704-355-8686; **Board Cert:** Urology 2005; **Med School:** Univ Cincinnati 1989; **Resid:** Urology, Univ Mich Med Ctr 1994; **Fellow:** Neurology, UT Hlth Sci Ctr 1995; **Fac Appt:** Clin Prof U, Univ NC Sch Med

Kim, Edward D MD [U] - **Spec Exp:** Infertility-Male; Prostate Cancer; Bladder Cancer; **Hospital:** Univ of Tennesee Med Ctr; **Address:** University Urology, 1928 Alcoa Hwy, Ste 222, MS 37920, Med Office, B Bldg, Ste 222, Knoxville, TN 37920; **Phone:** 865-305-9254; **Board Cert:** Urology 2007; **Med School:** Northwestern Univ 1989; **Resid:** Urology, Northwestern Meml Hosp 1995; **Fellow:** Male Reproduction, Baylor Coll Med Affil Hosp 1996; **Fac Appt:** Prof U, Univ Tenn Coll Med

Lloyd, L. Keith MD [U] - **Spec Exp:** Erectile Dysfunction; Incontinence; Interstitial Cystitis; Neurogenic Bladder; **Hospital:** UAB Hosp; **Address:** UAB Hosp - Dept Urology, 1530 3rd Ave S FOT Bldg - Ste 1105, Birmingham, AL 35294-3400; **Phone:** 205-996-8765; **Board Cert:** Urology 1976; **Med School:** Tulane Univ 1966; **Resid:** Urology, Tulane Univ Med Ctr 1974; **Fac Appt:** Prof U, UAB Sch Med

Lockhart, Jorge L MD [U] - **Spec Exp:** Voiding Dysfunction; Bladder Cancer; Incontinence; Urinary Reconstruction; **Hospital:** Moffitt Canc Ctr (page 61); **Address:** USF Hlth, Urology Dept, 2 Tampa General Cir Fl 4, Tampa, FL 33606; **Phone:** 813-250-2213; **Board Cert:** Urology 1980; **Med School:** Uruguay 1973; **Resid:** Urology, Duke Univ Hosp 1977; **Fellow:** Urodynamics, Duke Univ Hosp 1978; **Fac Appt:** Prof S, Univ S Fla Coll Med

McConnell, John D MD [U] - **Spec Exp:** Prostate Cancer; **Hospital:** Wake Forest Baptist Med Ctr; **Address:** Wake Forest Baptist Med Ctr, Medical Center Blvd, Winston-Salem, NC 27157; **Phone:** 336-716-3408; **Board Cert:** Urology 2004; **Med School:** Loyola Univ-Stritch Sch Med 1978; **Resid:** Surgery, Parkland Hosp 1980; Urology, Parkland Hosp 1984; **Fac Appt:** Prof U, Wake Forest Univ

Milam, Douglas F MD [U] - **Spec Exp:** Urodynamics; Voiding Dysfunction; Sexual Dysfunction; Urinary Reconstruction; **Hospital:** Vanderbilt Univ Med Ctr; **Address:** Vanderbilt Dept Urologic Surgery, 1301 Medical Center Drive, Ste 3823, Nashville, TN 37232-2765; **Phone:** 615-322-2880; **Board Cert:** Urology 2013; **Med School:** W VA Univ 1986; **Resid:** Surgery, Univ Utah Hosps 1988; Urology, Univ Utah Hosps 1991; **Fac Appt:** Assoc Prof U, Vanderbilt Univ

Miller, Scott D MD [U] - **Spec Exp:** Robotic Surgery; Prostate Cancer/Robotic Surgery; Minimally Invasive Urologic Surgery; Reconstructive Surgery; **Hospital:** Northside Hosp; **Address:** Georgia Urology, 5670 Peachtree Dunwoody Rd, Ste 1250, Atlanta, GA 30342; **Phone:** 404-705-5201; **Board Cert:** Urology 2005; **Med School:** Med Coll GA 1990; **Resid:** Urology, Univ Kentucky Med Ctr 1995

Moul, Judd W MD [U] - **Spec Exp:** Prostate Cancer; Prostate Disease; Minimally Invasive Urologic Surgery; Clinical Trials; **Hospital:** Duke Univ Hosp, Durham VA Med Ctr; **Address:** Duke Univ Med Ctr, Duke South Bldg, rm 1573, Box 3707, Blue Zone, Durham, NC 27710; **Phone:** 919-684-5057; **Board Cert:** Urology 2008; **Med School:** Jefferson Med Coll 1982; **Resid:** Urology, Walter Reed Army Med Ctr 1987; **Fellow:** Urologic Oncology, Duke Univ Med Ctr 1989; **Fac Appt:** Prof S, Duke Univ

Nieder, Alan M MD [U] - **Spec Exp:** Bladder Cancer; Prostate Cancer; Prostate Disease; Laparoscopic Surgery; **Hospital:** Mount Sinai Med Ctr - Miami; **Address:** 4302 Alton Rd, Ste 540, Dept Urology, Miami Beach, FL 33140-2800; **Phone:** 305-674-2499; **Board Cert:** Urology 2007; **Med School:** NYU Sch Med 1997; **Resid:** Surgery, NYU Med Ctr 1999; Urology, NYU Med Ctr 2003; **Fellow:** Urologic Oncology, Univ Miami/Jackson Memorial Hosp 2004; **Fac Appt:** Asst Prof U, Univ Miami Sch Med

Parekh, Dipen J MD [U] - **Spec Exp:** Robotic Surgery; Prostate Cancer; Kidney Cancer; Bladder Cancer; **Hospital:** Univ of Miami Hosp & Clins/Sylvester Comp Canc Ctr, Univ of Miami Hosp; **Address:** Professional Arts Ctr, 1150 NW 14th, Miami, FL 33136; **Phone:** 305-243-6090; **Board Cert:** Urology 2008; **Med School:** India 1993; **Resid:** Urology, Mumbai Univ Med Ctr; Urology, Vanderbilt Univ Med Ctr 2008; **Fellow:** Urologic Oncology, Meml Sloan Kettering Cancer Ctr 2009; **Fac Appt:** Prof U, Univ Miami Sch Med

Patel, Vipul R MD [U] - **Spec Exp:** Prostate Cancer/Robotic Surgery; Kidney Cancer; **Hospital:** Florida Hosp Celebration Hlth; **Address:** Center for Urologic Surgery, 410 Celebration Pl, Ste 200, Celebration, FL 34747; **Phone:** 407-303-4673; **Board Cert:** Urology 2013; **Med School:** Baylor Coll Med 1995; **Resid:** Urology, Univ Miami; **Fellow:** Urologic Laparoscopic Surg-Endourology, Univ Miami; **Fac Appt:** Prof U, Univ C Fla Coll Med

Patterson, Anthony L MD [U] - **Spec Exp:** Laparoscopic Surgery; Kidney Stones; **Hospital:** Univ of Tennesee Med Ctr; **Address:** UT Medical Group, 7945 Wolf River Blvd, Ste 350, Germantown, TN 38138; **Phone:** 901-448-1924; **Board Cert:** Urology 2007; **Med School:** Univ Tenn Coll Med 1982; **Resid:** Surgery, Univ Tenn Med Ctr 1984; Urology, Univ Tenn Med Ctr 1987; **Fac Appt:** Assoc Prof U, Univ Tenn Coll Med

Penson, David F MD [U] - **Spec Exp:** Prostate Cancer; Urologic Cancer; Bladder Cancer; Prostate Disease; **Hospital:** Vanderbilt Univ Med Ctr, TN Valley Healthcare Sys-Nashville; **Address:** 2525 Westend Ave, Ste 1200, Nashville, TN 37203; **Phone:** 615-343-1529; **Board Cert:** Urology 2009; **Med School:** Boston Univ 1991; **Resid:** Urology, UCLA Med Ctr 1997; **Fellow:** Urologic Oncology, Yale-New Haven Hosp 1999; **Fac Appt:** Prof U, Vanderbilt Univ

Pow-Sang, Julio M MD [U] - **Spec Exp:** Prostate Cancer; **Hospital:** Moffitt Canc Ctr (page 61); **Address:** H Lee Moffitt Cancer Ctr, GU Clin, 12902 Magnolia Drive, Tampa, FL 33612; **Phone:** 813-745-8418; **Board Cert:** Urology 2011; **Med School:** Mexico 1978; **Resid:** Surgery, Univ Miami Hosp 1983; Urology, Univ Miami Hosp 1986; **Fellow:** Urologic Oncology, Shands at Univ FL 1987; **Fac Appt:** Prof S, Univ S Fla Coll Med

Preminger, Glenn M MD [U] - **Spec Exp:** Kidney Stones; **Hospital:** Duke Univ Hosp; **Address:** Box 3167 Med Ctr, Rm 1572D Duke South, White Zone, Durham, NC 27710; **Phone:** 919-684-2446; **Board Cert:** Urology 2013; **Med School:** NY Med Coll 1977; **Resid:** Surgery, N Carolina Meml Hosp 1979; Urology, N Carolina Meml Hosp 1983; **Fellow:** Urology, Univ Texas SW Med Ctr 1985; **Fac Appt:** Prof U, Duke Univ

Pruthi, Raj S MD [U] - **Spec Exp:** Urologic Cancer; Robotic Surgery; **Hospital:** NC Memorial Hosp - UNC; **Address:** UNC Div Urologic Surgery, 101 Manning Drive, Chapel Hill, NC 27599; **Phone:** 919-966-2571; **Board Cert:** Urology 2010; **Med School:** Duke Univ 1992; **Resid:** Surgery, Stanford Univ Hosp 1993; Urology, Stanford Univ Hosp 1998; **Fac Appt:** Prof U, Univ NC Sch Med

Robertson, Cary N MD [U] - **Spec Exp:** Prostate Cancer; Kidney Cancer; High Intensity Focused Ultrasound(HIFU); Testicular Cancer; **Hospital:** Duke Univ Hosp; **Address:** Duke Raleigh Hosp, 3480 Wake Forest Rd, Ste 506, Raleigh, NC 27609; **Phone:** 919-862-5600; **Board Cert:** Urology 2006; **Med School:** Tulane Univ 1977; **Resid:** Urology, Duke Univ Med Ctr 1985; **Fellow:** Urologic Oncology, Natl Inst Hlth 1987; **Fac Appt:** Assoc Prof U, Duke Univ

Sanda, Martin G MD [U] - **Spec Exp:** Prostate Cancer; Bladder Cancer; Kidney Cancer; Urologic Cancer; **Hospital:** Emory Univ Hosp, St. Joseph's Hosp - Atlanta; **Address:** Emory Univ Hosp, 1365 Clifton Rd NE B Bldg - Ste 1400, Atlanta, GA 30322; **Phone:** 404-778-6874; **Board Cert:** Urology 2007; **Med School:** Columbia P&S 1987; **Resid:** Surgery, Med Coll Virginia 1989; Urology, Johns Hopkins Hosp 1994; **Fellow:** Surgical Oncology, Natl Cancer Inst 1991; **Fac Appt:** Prof U, Emory Univ

Sanders, William Holt MD [U] - **Spec Exp:** Prostate Cancer; Urologic Cancer; Vasectomy; Kidney Stones; **Hospital:** Northside Hosp; **Address:** 980 Johnson Ferry Rd NE, Ste 490, Atlanta, GA 30342-1767; **Phone:** 404-257-0133; **Board Cert:** Urology 2006; **Med School:** Emory Univ 1988; **Resid:** Surgery, Emory Affil Hosp 1990; Urology, Yale-New Haven Hosp 1993; **Fellow:** Urologic Oncology, Emory Univ Hosp 1994

Sexton, Wade J MD [U] - **Spec Exp:** Urologic Cancer; Laparoscopic Surgery; Bladder Cancer; Kidney Cancer; **Hospital:** Moffitt Canc Ctr (page 61); **Address:** H Lee Moffitt Cancer Ctr-GU Clinic, 12902 Magnolia Drive, Tampa, FL 33612; **Phone:** 813-745-8418; **Board Cert:** Urology 2003; **Med School:** Emory Univ 1993; **Resid:** Surgery, Wake Forest Univ Hosp 1995; Urology, Wake Forest Univ Hosp 1999; **Fellow:** Urologic Oncology, MD Anderson Cancer Ctr 2001; **Fac Appt:** Assoc Prof U, Univ S Fla Coll Med

Shaban, Stephen F MD [U] - **Spec Exp:** Infertility-Male; Congenital Absence of Vas Deferens; **Hospital:** Rex HlthCare, WakeMed-Raleigh Campus; **Address:** 3821 Ed Drive, Raleigh, NC 27612; **Phone:** 919-851-5482; **Board Cert:** Urology 2013; **Med School:** Mount Sinai Sch Med 1982; **Resid:** Urology, Univ S Fla 1987; **Fellow:** Male Reproduction, Baylor Coll Med 1988; **Fac Appt:** Prof U, Univ NC Sch Med

Smith, Joseph A MD [U] - **Spec Exp:** Prostate Cancer/Robotic Surgery; Bladder Cancer; Kidney Cancer; **Hospital:** Vanderbilt Univ Med Ctr; **Address:** Vanderbilt Urology, 1301 Medical Center Drive, Ste 3823, Nashville, TN 37232; **Phone:** 615-322-2880; **Board Cert:** Urology 2000; **Med School:** Univ Tenn Coll Med 1974; **Resid:** Surgery, Parkland Meml Hosp 1976; Urology, Univ Utah Med Ctr 1979; **Fellow:** Urologic Oncology, Meml Sloan Kettering Cancer Ctr 1980; **Fac Appt:** Prof U, Vanderbilt Univ

Soloway, Mark S MD [U] - **Spec Exp:** Bladder Cancer; Kidney Cancer; Prostate Cancer; Urologic Pathology; **Hospital:** Univ of Miami Hosp & Clins/Sylvester Comp Canc Ctr, Jackson Meml Hosp; **Address:** 1150 NW 14th St, Ste 309, Miami, FL 33136; **Phone:** 305-243-6596; **Board Cert:** Urology 1977; **Med School:** Case West Res Univ 1968; **Resid:** Surgery, Univ Hosps 1970; Urology, Univ Hosps 1975; **Fellow:** Surgery, Natl Cancer Inst 1972; **Fac Appt:** Prof U, Univ Miami Sch Med

Steers, William D MD [U] - **Spec Exp:** Incontinence; Erectile Dysfunction; Prostate Cancer/Robotic Surgery; **Hospital:** Univ of Virginia Hlth Sys; **Address:** Dept of Urology, Univ VA Hlth Science Ctr, Hospital Drive, Charlottesville, VA 22908-0422; **Phone:** 434-924-9107; **Board Cert:** Urology 2009; **Med School:** Med Coll OH 1980; **Resid:** Urology, Univ Tex Hlth Sci Ctr 1986; **Fellow:** Neurology, Univ Pittsburgh Med Ctr 1988; **Fac Appt:** Prof U, Univ VA Sch Med

Strup, Stephen E MD [U] - **Spec Exp:** Urologic Cancer; Minimally Invasive Urologic Surgery; Robotic Surgery; **Hospital:** Univ of Kentucky Albert B. Chandler Hosp; **Address:** UK Albert B Chandler Hosp, 800 Rose St, Lexington, KY 40536-0001; **Phone:** 859-323-6677; **Board Cert:** Urology 2007; **Med School:** Indiana Univ 1988; **Resid:** Urology, Thomas Jefferson Univ Hosp 1994; **Fellow:** Urologic Oncology, Natl Inst of Hlth - Clin Ctr 1996; **Fac Appt:** Prof S, Univ KY Coll Med

Su, Li-Ming MD [U] - **Spec Exp:** Prostate Cancer; Kidney Cancer; Robotic Surgery; Laparoscopic Surgery; **Hospital:** UF Hlth Shands Hosp; **Address:** UF Hlth, Urology Dept, 1600 SW Archer Rd, Box 100247, Gainesville, FL 32610; **Phone:** 352-265-8282; **Board Cert:** Urology 2012; **Med School:** Cornell Univ-Weill Med Coll 1994; **Resid:** Surgery, NY-Presby/Weill Cornell Med Ctr 1996; Urology, NY-Presby/Weill Cornell Med Ctr 2000; **Fellow:** Robotic Surgery, Johns Hopkins Hosp 2001; **Fac Appt:** Prof U, Univ Fla Coll Med

Teigland, Chris M MD [U] - **Spec Exp:** Prostate Cancer/Robotic Surgery; Kidney Cancer; Laparoscopic Surgery; **Hospital:** Carolinas Med Ctr; **Address:** McKay Urology, 1023 Edgehill Rd S, Charlotte, NC 28207; **Phone:** 704-355-8686; **Board Cert:** Urology 2007; **Med School:** Duke Univ 1980; **Resid:** Surgery, Univ Utah Affil Hosps 1982; Urology, Univ Texas SW Med Ctr 1987; **Fac Appt:** Clin Prof U, Univ NC Sch Med

Terris, Martha K MD [U] - **Spec Exp:** Prostate Cancer; Brachytherapy; Urologic Cancer; Bladder Cancer; **Hospital:** Georgia Regents Med Ctr-Augusta, Charlie Norwood VA Med Ctr - Augusta; **Address:** Georgia Regents, Urology Dept, 1447 Harper St Fl 4, Augusta, GA 30912; **Phone:** 706-721-3042; **Board Cert:** Urology 2007; **Med School:** Univ Miss 1986; **Resid:** Surgery, Duke Univ Hosp 1988; Urology, Stanford Univ Hosp & Clins 1995; **Fellow:** Ultrasound, Stanford Univ Hosp & Clins 1991; **Fac Appt:** Prof S, Med Coll GA

Wallen, Eric M MD [U] - **Spec Exp:** Laparoscopic Surgery; Prostate Cancer; Urologic Cancer; Robotic Surgery; **Hospital:** NC Memorial Hosp - UNC; **Address:** Div Urologic Surgery, 2113 Physicians Office Bldg, 170 Manning Drive, Box 7235, Chapel Hill, NC 27599; **Phone:** 919-966-8802; **Board Cert:** Urology 2010; **Med School:** UCLA 1994; **Resid:** Surgery, Stanford Univ Med Ctr 1996; Urology, Stanford Univ Med Ctr 2000; **Fac Appt:** Clin Prof S, Univ NC Sch Med

Winfield, Howard N MD [U] - **Spec Exp:** Kidney Stones; Laparoscopic Surgery; Robotic Surgery; **Hospital:** DCH Reg Med Ctr; **Address:** W Alabama Urology Assoc, 701 University Blvd E, Ste 908, DCH Medical Tower 1, Tuscaloosa, AL 35401; **Phone:** 205-759-7878; **Board Cert:** Urology 2008; **Med School:** McGill Univ 1978; **Resid:** Urology, McGill Univ Tchg Hosp 1984; **Fellow:** Endourology, Washington Univ Phys 1985; Endourology, UCLA Ronald Reagan Med Ctr 1986; **Fac Appt:** , Univ Iowa Coll Med

Midwest

Andriole Jr, Gerald L MD [U] - **Spec Exp:** Urologic Cancer; Prostate Cancer; Laparoscopic Surgery; **Hospital:** Barnes-Jewish Hosp, Barnes-Jewish West County Hosp; **Address:** Washington Univ School of Medicine, 4921 Parkview Pl, Ste 11C, St Louis, MO 63110; **Phone:** 314-362-8200; **Board Cert:** Urology 2013; **Med School:** Jefferson Med Coll 1978; **Resid:** Surgery, Strong Meml Hosp 1980; Urology, Brigham & Womens Hosp 1983; **Fellow:** Urologic Oncology, NCI/NIH 1985; **Fac Appt:** Prof U, Washington Univ, St Louis

Bahnson, Robert Roy MD [U] - **Spec Exp:** Prostate Cancer; Bladder Cancer; Continent Urinary Diversions; **Hospital:** OSU Wexner Med Ctr; **Address:** 915 Olentangy River Rd, Ste 3100, Columbus, OH 43212; **Phone:** 614-293-3646; **Board Cert:** Urology 2006; **Med School:** Tufts Univ 1979; **Resid:** Surgery, Northwestern Meml Hosp 1981; Urology, Northwestern Meml Hosp 1985; **Fellow:** Urology, Northwestern Meml Hosp 1984; Research, Univ Pittsburgh 1991; **Fac Appt:** Prof U, Ohio State Univ

Bales, Gregory T MD [U] - **Spec Exp:** Incontinence-Male & Female; Pelvic Organ Prolapse Repair; Reconstructive Urologic Surgery; Urology-Female; **Hospital:** Univ of Chicago Med; **Address:** Univ Chicago Med Ctr, Urology Section, 5841 S Maryland Ave, MC 6038, Chicago, IL 60637-6038; **Phone:** 773-702-6325; **Board Cert:** Urology 2013; Female Pelvic Medicine & Reconstuctive Surgery 2013; **Med School:** Tufts Univ 1990; **Resid:** Urology, Univ Chicago Med Ctr 1995; **Fellow:** Female Urology, Univ Hosp Wales 1996; **Fac Appt:** Assoc Prof S, Univ Chicago-Pritzker Sch Med

Bodner, Donald MD [U] - **Spec Exp:** Neuro-Urology; Urologic Cancer; **Hospital:** UH Case Med Ctr; **Address:** Univ Hosps Urology Inst, 11100 Euclid Ave, MS LKS5046, Cleveland, OH 44106; **Phone:** 216-844-3009; **Board Cert:** Urology 2004; **Med School:** Indiana Univ 1979; **Resid:** Surgery, Case West Res Univ Affil Hosp 1981; Urology, Case West Res Univ Affil Hosp 1984

Brendler, Charles B MD [U] - **Spec Exp:** Prostate Cancer; **Hospital:** Evanston Hosp/NorthShore Univ Hlth Sys (page 67); **Address:** North Shore Medical Group, 2180 Pfingsten Rd, Ste 3000, Glenview, IL 60026; **Phone:** 847-503-3000; **Board Cert:** Urology 2003; **Med School:** Univ VA Sch Med 1974; **Resid:** Surgery, Duke Univ Med Ctr 1976; Urology, Duke Univ Med Ctr 1979; **Fellow:** Urologic Oncology, Univ Hosp Wales 1980; Urologic Oncology, Johns Hopkins Hosp 1982; **Fac Appt:** Clin Prof U, Univ Chicago-Pritzker Sch Med

Bushman, Wade MD [U] - **Spec Exp:** Neuro-Urology; Urodynamics; Urology-Female; **Hospital:** Univ WI Hosp & Clins; **Address:** UW Hosp & Clins - Dept Urology, 600 Highland Ave, rm C52, MC 2451, Madison, WI 53792-3236; **Phone:** 608-263-4757; **Board Cert:** Urology 2006; **Med School:** Univ Chicago-Pritzker Sch Med 1986; **Resid:** Surgery, Rhode Is Hosp 1989; Urology, Univ VA Hlth Sys 1993; **Fac Appt:** Prof U, Univ Wisc

Campbell, Steven C MD/PhD [U] - **Spec Exp:** Kidney Cancer; Prostate Cancer; Bladder Cancer; **Hospital:** Cleveland Clin (page 55); **Address:** Glickman Urological & Kidney Inst, 9500 Euclid Ave, MS Q10-1, Cleveland, OH 44195; **Phone:** 216-444-5595; **Board Cert:** Urology 2008; **Med School:** Univ Chicago-Pritzker Sch Med 1989; **Resid:** Urology, Cleveland Clinic 1995; **Fellow:** Urology, Meml Sloan-Kettering Cancer Ctr 1996; **Fac Appt:** Prof S, Cleveland Cl Coll Med/Case West Res

Catalona, William J MD [U] - **Spec Exp:** Prostate Cancer; Prostate Disease; **Hospital:** Northwestern Meml Hosp; **Address:** Northwestern Med Faculty Foundation, 675 N St Clair St, Ste 20-150, Chicago, IL 60611; **Phone:** 312-695-6126; **Board Cert:** Urology 1978; **Med School:** Yale Univ 1968; **Resid:** Surgery, UCSF Med Ctr 1970; Urology, Johns Hopkins Hosp 1976; **Fellow:** Surgical Oncology, Natl Cancer Inst 1972; **Fac Appt:** Prof U, Northwestern Univ

Chancellor, Michael B MD [U] - **Spec Exp:** Incontinence-Female; Urology-Female; Neuro-Urology; **Hospital:** Beaumont Hosp-Royal Oak; **Address:** William Beaumont Hosp, Urology, 3535 W 13 Mile Rd, Ste 404, Royal Oak, MI 48073; **Phone:** 248-551-3519; **Board Cert:** Urology 2010; **Med School:** Med Coll Wisc 1983; **Resid:** Surgery, Univ Michigan Hosp 1985; Urology, Univ Michigan Hosp 1988; **Fellow:** Neurourology, NY-Presby/Columbia Univ Med Ctr 1990; **Fac Appt:** Prof U, Univ Mich Med Sch

Donovan Jr, James F MD [U] - **Spec Exp:** Prostate Cancer/Robotic Surgery; Infertility-Male; Erectile Dysfunction; Kidney Cancer; **Hospital:** Univ Cincinnati Med Ctr, Christ Hosp, The - Cincinnati; **Address:** Univ Cincinnati Med Ctr, Medical Arts Bldg, 222 Piedmont Ave, Ste 7000, Cincinnati, OH 45219; **Phone:** 513-475-8787; **Board Cert:** Urology 2009; **Med School:** Northwestern Univ 1978; **Resid:** Surgery, Northwestern Meml Hosp 1982; Urology, Northwestern Meml Hosp 1986; **Fellow:** Male Infertility, Baylor Coll Med 1986; **Fac Appt:** Prof U, Univ Cincinnati

Flanigan, Robert C MD [U] - **Spec Exp:** Urologic Cancer; Prostate Cancer; Kidney Cancer; Bladder Cancer; **Hospital:** Loyola Univ Med Ctr; **Address:** Loyola Univ Med-Fahey Bldg, 2160 S First Ave, rm 267, Maywood, IL 60153; **Phone:** 708-216-5100; **Board Cert:** Urology 2001; **Med School:** Case West Res Univ 1972; **Resid:** Surgery, Case West Univ Med Ctr 1978; Urology, Case West Univ Med Ctr 1978; **Fellow:** Urologic Oncology, Univ KY Med Ctr 1982; **Fac Appt:** Prof U, Loyola Univ-Stritch Sch Med

Foster, Richard S MD [U] - **Spec Exp:** Testicular Cancer; Reconstructive Surgery; **Hospital:** IU Hlth Univ Hosp; **Address:** IU Health, Indiana Cancer Pavilion, 535 N Barnhill Drive, Ste 420, Indianapolis, IN 46202; **Phone:** 317-944-3458; **Board Cert:** Urology 2008; **Med School:** Indiana Univ 1980; **Resid:** Urology, Indiana Univ Hosp 1986; **Fac Appt:** Prof U, Indiana Univ

Gluckman, Gordon R MD [U] - **Spec Exp:** Prostate Cancer; Kidney Cancer; Minimally Invasive Urologic Surgery; Robotic Surgery; **Hospital:** Adv Luth Genl Hosp, Northwest Comm Hosp; **Address:** Northwest Suburban Urologists, 900 Rand Rd, Ste 120, Des Plaines, IL 60016; **Phone:** 847-823-3185; **Board Cert:** Urology 2006; **Med School:** Northwestern Univ 1989; **Resid:** Surgery, UCSF Med Ctr 1991; Urology, UCSF Med Ctr 1995; **Fac Appt:** Asst Clin Prof S, Ros Franklin Univ/Chicago Med Sch

Gujral, Saroj MD [U] - **Hospital:** Albert Lea Med Ctr-Mayo Hlth Sys; **Address:** 404 W Fountain St, Albert Lea, MN 56007; **Phone:** 507-379-2130; **Board Cert:** Urology 1979; **Med School:** India 1970; **Resid:** Urology, Suburban Hosp 1978; Urology, Dalhousie Univ Med Ctrs 1979

Jones, J Stephen MD [U] - **Spec Exp:** Prostate Cancer; **Hospital:** Cleveland Clin (page 55), Fairview Hosp; **Address:** Glickman Urological & Kidney Inst, 9500 Euclid Ave, Q10-1, Cleveland, OH 44195; **Phone:** 216-476-0757; **Board Cert:** Urology 2012; **Med School:** Univ Ark 1986; **Resid:** Urology, Vanderbilt Univ Med Ctr 1993; **Fac Appt:** Prof S, Cleveland Cl Coll Med/Case West Res

Klein, Eric A MD [U] - **Spec Exp:** Urologic Cancer; Testicular Cancer; Kidney Cancer; Prostate Cancer; **Hospital:** Cleveland Clin (page 55); **Address:** Glickman Urologic and Kidney Inst, 9500 Euclid Ave, MS Q10-1, Cleveland, OH 44195-0001; **Phone:** 216-444-5591; **Board Cert:** Urology 2008; **Med School:** Univ Pittsburgh 1981; **Resid:** Urology, Cleveland Clinic Fdn 1986; **Fellow:** Urologic Oncology, Meml Sloan-Kettering Canc Ctr 1989; **Fac Appt:** Prof S, Cleveland Cl Coll Med/Case West Res

Klutke, Carl G MD [U] - **Spec Exp:** Urology-Female; Incontinence; Urodynamics; **Hospital:** Barnes-Jewish Hosp; **Address:** 1040 N Mason Rd Bldg 1 - Ste 122, St Louis, MO 63141; **Phone:** 314-996-8060; **Board Cert:** Urology 2009; **Med School:** Univ Mich Med Sch 1983; **Resid:** Surgery, Henry Ford Hosp 1985; Urology, Henry Ford Hosp 1988; **Fellow:** Female Urology, UCLA Med Ctr 1989; **Fac Appt:** Assoc Prof S, Washington Univ, St Louis

Koch, Michael O MD [U] - **Spec Exp:** Prostate Cancer; Bladder Cancer; Robotic Surgery; Reconstructive Urologic Surgery; **Hospital:** IU Hlth Univ Hosp; **Address:** IU Health, Indiana Cancer Pavilion, 535 Barnhill Drive, Ste 420, Indianapolis, IN 46202; **Phone:** 317-944-7338; **Board Cert:** Urology 2007; **Med School:** Dartmouth Med Sch 1981; **Resid:** Surgery, Dartmouth-Hitchcock Med Ctr 1983; Urology, Vanderbilt Univ Med Ctr 1987; **Fellow:** Surgical Research, Dartmouth Med Sch 1984; **Fac Appt:** Prof U, Indiana Univ

Kozlowski, James M MD [U] - **Spec Exp:** Urologic Cancer; Continent Urinary Diversions; Laparoscopic Surgery; Robotic Surgery; **Hospital:** Northwestern Meml Hosp; **Address:** Northwestern Medical Faculty Foundation, 675 N St Clair St Fl 20 - rm 241, Chicago, IL 60611; **Phone:** 312-695-8146; **Board Cert:** Surgery 2004; Urology 1983; **Med School:** Northwestern Univ 1975; **Resid:** Surgery, McGaw Med Ctr 1979; Urology, McGaw Med Ctr 1982; **Fellow:** Research, NCI-Frederick Cancer Rsch 1984; **Fac Appt:** Prof U, Northwestern Univ

Lee, Cheryl T MD [U] - **Spec Exp:** Urologic Cancer; Bladder Cancer; **Hospital:** Univ Michigan Med Ctr; **Address:** Univ of Michigan Cancer Ctr, 1500 E Medical Ctr Drive, SPC 5913, Ann Arbor, MI 48109; **Phone:** 734-647-8903; **Board Cert:** Urology 2011; **Med School:** Albany Med Coll 1991; **Resid:** Urology, Albany Med Ctr; **Fellow:** Urologic Oncology, Meml Sloan Kettering Cancer Ctr 2000; **Fac Appt:** Assoc Prof U, Univ Mich Med Sch

Levine, Laurence A MD [U] - **Spec Exp:** Erectile Dysfunction; Infertility-Male; Peyronie's Disease; Prostate Cancer; **Hospital:** Rush Univ Med Ctr; **Address:** Uropartners-Urology Specialists, 1725 W Harrison St, Ste 352, Chicago, IL 60612; **Phone:** 312-563-5000; **Board Cert:** Urology 2009; **Med School:** Univ Colorado 1980; **Resid:** Surgery, Tufts-New Eng Med Ctr 1982; Urology, Brigham & Women's Hosp 1987; **Fac Appt:** Prof U, Rush Med Coll

McVary, Kevin T MD [U] - **Spec Exp:** Prostate Cancer; Erectile Dysfunction; Prostate Disease; Minimally Invasive Surgery; **Hospital:** St. John's Hosp - Springfield, Memorial Med Ctr-Springfield; **Address:** SIU, Urology Dept, 301 N 8th St, Box 19665, Springfield, IL 62794; **Phone:** 217-545-8860; **Board Cert:** Urology 2010; **Med School:** Northwestern Univ 1983; **Resid:** Surgery, Northwestern Meml Hosp 1985; Urology, Northwestern Meml Hosp 1990; **Fac Appt:** Prof U, Southern IL Univ

Menon, Mani MD [U] - **Spec Exp:** Prostate Cancer/Robotic Surgery; Transplant-Kidney; Urologic Cancer; **Hospital:** Henry Ford Hosp; **Address:** Henry Ford Hosp - Vattikuti Urology Inst, 2799 W Grand Blvd, Bldg K Fl 9, Detroit, MI 48202; **Phone:** 313-916-2066; **Board Cert:** Urology 1982; **Med School:** India 1969; **Resid:** Urology, Bryn Mawr Hosp 1974; Urology, Johns Hopkins Hosp 1980; **Fellow:** Transplant Surgery, Johns Hopkins Univ 1977; **Fac Appt:** Prof S, Univ Mass Sch Med

Montague, Drogo K MD [U] - **Spec Exp:** Erectile Dysfunction; Genitourinary Prosthetics; Incontinence; Peyronie's Disease; **Hospital:** Cleveland Clin (page 55); **Address:** Glickmand Urological & Kidney Inst, Cleveland Clinic, 9500 Euclid Ave, Q10-1, Cleveland, OH 44195-5041; **Phone:** 216-444-5600; **Board Cert:** Urology 1995; **Med School:** Univ Mich Med Sch 1968; **Resid:** Surgery, Cleveland Clin 1970; Urology, Cleveland Clin 1973; **Fac Appt:** Prof U, Cleveland Cl Coll Med/Case West Res

Montie, James MD [U] - **Spec Exp:** Bladder Cancer; Prostate Cancer; Genitourinary Cancer; **Hospital:** Univ Michigan Med Ctr; **Address:** Univ of Michigan Cancer Ctr, 1500 E Medical Ctr Drive, SPC 5913, Ann Arbor, MI 48109-5913; **Phone:** 734-647-8903; **Board Cert:** Urology 1978; **Med School:** Univ Mich Med Sch 1971; **Resid:** Urology, Cleveland Clinic Fdn 1976; **Fellow:** Urologic Oncology, Meml Sloan-Kettering Cancer Ctr 1979; **Fac Appt:** Prof U, Univ Mich Med Sch

Nakada, Stephen Y MD [U] - **Spec Exp:** Kidney Stones; Laparoscopic Surgery; Endourology; **Hospital:** Univ WI Hosp & Clins; **Address:** Univ Wisconsin Urology Clinic, 600 Highland Ave, Madison, WI 53705; **Phone:** 608-263-4757; **Board Cert:** Urology 2006; **Med School:** Univ Rochester 1988; **Resid:** Urology, Strong Meml Hosp 1994; **Fellow:** Endourology, Barnes Jewish Hosp 1995; **Fac Appt:** Prof U, Univ Wisc

Nehra, Ajay MD [U] - **Spec Exp:** Erectile Dysfunction; **Hospital:** Rush Univ Med Ctr; **Address:** Rush Univ Urology, Prof Bldg - Ste 762, 1725 W Harrison St, Chicago, IL 60612; **Phone:** 312-563-3447; **Board Cert:** Urology 2006; **Med School:** India 1984; **Resid:** Surgery, Boston Univ Med Ctr 1987; Urology, Maimonides Med Ctr 1993; **Fellow:** Female Urology, Boston Univ Sch Med 1989; Male Infertility, Boston Univ Sch Med 1995; **Fac Appt:** Prof U, Rush Med Coll

O'Donnell, Michael A MD [U] - **Spec Exp:** Bladder Cancer; Immunotherapy; Urologic Cancer; Ureter & Renal Pelvis Cancer; **Hospital:** Univ Iowa Hosp & Clins; **Address:** Univ Iowa Hosp & Clin, Dept Urol, 200 Hawkins Drive, RCP Bldg - Fl 3, Iowa City, IA 52242-1089; **Phone:** 319-353-8939; **Board Cert:** Urology 2005; **Med School:** Duke Univ 1984; **Resid:** Surgery, Brigham & Womens Hosp 1987; Urology, Brigham & Womens Hosp 1991; **Fellow:** Urology, Brigham & Womens Hosp 1993; **Fac Appt:** Prof U, Univ Iowa Coll Med

Ohl, Dana MD [U] - **Spec Exp:** Infertility-Male; Erectile Dysfunction; **Hospital:** Univ Michigan Med Ctr; **Address:** Univ Mich Med Ctr, Div Urology, 1500 E Med Ctr Drive, 3875 Taubman Ctr, Fl 2 Recept C, Ann Arbor, MI 48109-5330; **Phone:** 734-232-4943; **Board Cert:** Urology 2008; **Med School:** Univ Mich Med Sch 1982; **Resid:** Urology, Univ Mich Hosps 1987; **Fac Appt:** Prof U, Univ Mich Med Sch

Ross, Lawrence S MD [U] - **Spec Exp:** Infertility-Male; Erectile Dysfunction; Prostate Disease; **Hospital:** Univ of IL Med Ctr at Chicago; **Address:** Univ Ctr of Urology, 60 E Delaware Pl, Ste 1420, Chicago, IL 60611; **Phone:** 312-440-5127; **Board Cert:** Urology 1974; **Med School:** Univ Chicago-Pritzker Sch Med 1965; **Resid:** Urology, Michael Reese Hosp 1970; **Fac Appt:** Prof U, Univ Chicago-Pritzker Sch Med

Sabanegh Jr, Edmund S MD [U] - **Spec Exp:** Infertility-Male; Microsurgery; Vasectomy; Vasectomy Reversal; **Hospital:** Cleveland Clin (page 55); **Address:** Cleveland Clinic-Urology, 9500 Euclid Ave, MC Q10-1, Cleveland, OH 44195; **Phone:** 216-444-5600; **Board Cert:** Urology 2012; **Med School:** Univ VA Sch Med 1985; **Resid:** Urology, Wilford Hall Med Ctr 1992; **Fellow:** Male Infertility, Cleveland Clin 1994; **Fac Appt:** Assoc Prof U, Cleveland Cl Coll Med/Case West Res

Sandlow, Jay I MD [U] - **Spec Exp:** Infertility-Male; Varicocele Microsurgery; Vasectomy & Vasectomy Reversal; **Hospital:** Froedtert & Med Coll WI, St. Joseph's Hosp; **Address:** Med Coll of WI, Dept Urology, 9200 W Wisconsin Ave, Milwaukee, WI 53226-3522; **Phone:** 414-805-0805; **Board Cert:** Urology 2005; **Med School:** Rush Med Coll 1987; **Resid:** Urology, Univ Iowa Hosps & Clins 1993; **Fellow:** Infertility, Univ Iowa Hosps & Clins 1995; **Fac Appt:** Prof U, Med Coll Wisc

Schaeffer, Anthony MD [U] - **Spec Exp:** Interstitial Cystitis; Incontinence after Prostate Cancer; Urology-Female; Urinary Tract Infections; **Hospital:** Northwestern Meml Hosp; **Address:** Northwestern Med Faculty Foundation, 675 N St Clair St, Fl 20 - rm 150, Chicago, IL 60611; **Phone:** 312-695-8146; **Board Cert:** Urology 1978; **Med School:** Northwestern Univ 1968; **Resid:** Surgery, Northwestern Meml Hosp 1970; Urology, Stanford Med Ctr 1976; **Fac Appt:** Prof U, Northwestern Univ

See, William A MD [U] - **Spec Exp:** Prostate Cancer; Bladder Cancer; Testicular Cancer; **Hospital:** Froedtert & Med Coll WI; **Address:** Clin Canc Ctr-Urology Dept, 9200 W Wisconsin Ave, Milwaukee, WI 53226; **Phone:** 414-805-0805; **Board Cert:** Urology 2008; **Med School:** Univ Chicago-Pritzker Sch Med 1982; **Resid:** Urology, Univ WA Affil Hosps 1988; **Fellow:** Research, Natl Kidney Fdn/Univ Wash 1986; Urologic Oncology, Amer Fdn for Urol Dis/Univ Iowa 1990; **Fac Appt:** Prof U, Med Coll Wisc

Shalhav, Arieh L MD [U] - **Spec Exp:** Minimally Invasive Urologic Surgery; Kidney Cancer; Prostate Cancer; Laparoscopic Surgery; **Hospital:** Univ of Chicago Med; **Address:** 5841 S Maryland Ave, MC 6038, Chicago, IL 60637; **Phone:** 773-834-9889; **Med School:** Israel 1993; **Resid:** Urology, Sheba Med Ctr 1996; **Fellow:** Endourology, Wash Univ Hosp 1998; **Fac Appt:** Prof U, Univ Chicago-Pritzker Sch Med

Silber, Sherman J MD [U] - **Spec Exp:** Infertility-Male; Vasectomy Reversal; Infertility-IVF; Transplant-Ovarian Tissue; **Hospital:** St. Luke's Hosp - Chesterfield, MO; **Address:** St Luke's Hosp, 224 S Woods Mill Rd, Ste 730 S, Chesterfield, MO 63017-3451; **Phone:** 314-576-1400; **Board Cert:** Urology 1977; **Med School:** Univ Mich Med Sch 1966; **Resid:** Internal Medicine, PH Service Comm Corps 1969; Urology, Univ Michigan Hosp 1973; **Fellow:** Microsurgery, Univ Melbourne 1974

Steinberg, Gary D MD [U] - **Spec Exp:** Bladder Cancer; Kidney Cancer; Prostate Cancer; **Hospital:** Univ of Chicago Med; **Address:** Univ Chicago Med Ctr, Div Urology, 5841 S Maryland Ave, rm J-653, MC 6038, Chicago, IL 60637-1447; **Phone:** 773-702-3080; **Board Cert:** Urology 2013; **Med School:** Univ Chicago-Pritzker Sch Med 1985; **Resid:** Surgery, Johns Hopkins Hosp 1987; Urology, Brady Urol Inst/Johns Hopkins 1991; **Fellow:** Clinical Oncology, Johns Hopkins Hosp 1989; **Fac Appt:** Prof U, Univ Chicago-Pritzker Sch Med

Sundaram, Chandru P MD [U] - **Spec Exp:** Kidney Cancer; Prostate Cancer; Adrenal Tumors; Polycystic Kidney Disease; **Hospital:** IU Hlth Univ Hosp; **Address:** IU Health Physicians Urology, Indiana Cancer Pavilion, 535 N Barnhill Drive, Ste 420, Indianapolis, IN 46202; **Phone:** 317-948-3098; **Board Cert:** Urology 2009; **Med School:** India 1985; **Resid:** Urology, Univ MN Med Ctr 1997; **Fellow:** Endourology, Beth Israel Deaconess Med Ctr/Harvard Med Sch 1998; **Fac Appt:** Prof U, Indiana Univ

Wong, Carson MD [U] - **Spec Exp:** Laparoscopic Surgery; Endourology; Prostate Cancer/Robotic Surgery; Urinary Reconstruction; **Hospital:** UH Ahuja Med Ctr (OH); **Address:** 6900 Pearl Rd, Fl 2, Middleburgh Heights, OH 44130; **Phone:** 440-845-0414; **Board Cert:** Urology 2003; **Med School:** Univ Western Ontario 1995; **Resid:** Urology, McGill Univ Affil Hosps 2000; **Fellow:** Endourology, Univ Miami 2001

Wood, David P MD [U] - **Spec Exp:** Genitourinary Cancer; Bladder Cancer; Prostate Cancer; Robotic Surgery; **Hospital:** Beaumont Hosp-Royal Oak; **Address:** 3535 W 13 Mile Rd, Ste 404, Royal Oak, MI 48073; **Phone:** 248-551-3519; **Board Cert:** Urology 2011; **Med School:** Univ Mich Med Sch 1983; **Resid:** Urology, Cleveland Clinic 1988; **Fellow:** Urologic Oncology, Meml Sloan-Kettering Cancer Ctr 1991; **Fac Appt:** Prof U, Univ Mich Med Sch

Great Plains and Mountains

Childs, Stacy J MD [U] - **Spec Exp:** Voiding Dysfunction; Erectile Dysfunction; Prostate Cancer; Bladder Cancer; **Hospital:** Yampa Valley Med Ctr, Memorial Hosp - Craig; **Address:** 501 Anglers Drive, Ste 202, Steamboat Springs, CO 80487-8841; **Phone:** 970-871-9710; **Board Cert:** Urology 1979; **Med School:** Louisiana State U, New Orleans 1972; **Resid:** Urology, Carraway Meth Med Ctr 1977; **Fac Appt:** Clin Prof U, Univ Colorado

Crawford, E. David MD [U] - **Spec Exp:** Prostate Disease; Prostate Cancer; Prostate Cancer-Cryosurgery; Clinical Trials; **Hospital:** Univ Colorado Hosp; **Address:** Univ CO Hosp, Urological Oncology Dept, 1665 Aurora Ct, Ste 1004, MS F710, Aurora, CO 80045; **Phone:** 720-848-0170; **Board Cert:** Urology 1980; **Med School:** Univ Cincinnati 1973; **Resid:** Urology, Good Samaritan Hosp 1977; **Fellow:** Genitourinary Surgery, UCLA Med Ctr 1978; **Fac Appt:** Prof S, Univ Colorado

Davis, Bradley E MD [U] - **Spec Exp:** Prostate Cancer; Bladder Cancer; Kidney Cancer; Vasectomy Reversal; **Hospital:** Overland Pk Regl Med Ctr, Olathe Med Ctr; **Address:** Urologic Surgery Associates, 10550 Quivira Rd, Ste 105, Overland Park, KS 66215; **Phone:** 913-438-3833; **Board Cert:** Urology 2004; **Med School:** Univ Kansas 1986; **Resid:** Surgery, St Lukes Hosp 1991; Urology, Univ Kansas Med Ctr 1991; **Fellow:** Urologic Oncology, Meml Sloan-Kettering Cancer Ctr 1993; **Fac Appt:** Asst Clin Prof U, Univ Kansas

Griebling, Tomas L MD [U] - **Spec Exp:** Urology-Geriatric; Urology-Female; Incontinence; Reconstructive Surgery; **Hospital:** Univ of Kansas Hosp; **Address:** Univ Kansas Hosp-Dept Urology, 3901 Rainbow Blvd, MS 3016, Kansas City, KS 66160; **Phone:** 913-588-6147; **Board Cert:** Urology 2009; **Med School:** Univ Iowa Coll Med 1991; **Resid:** Urology, Univ Iowa Hosp & Clin 1998; **Fellow:** Reconstructive Surgery, Univ Iowa Hosp & Clin 2001; **Fac Appt:** Prof U, Univ Kansas

Hamilton, Blake D MD [U] - **Spec Exp:** Laparoscopic Surgery; Robotic Surgery; Kidney Stones; Endourology; **Hospital:** Univ Utah Hlth Care; **Address:** University Hosps & Clinics, Urology Center, 50 N Medical Drive, Salt Lake City, UT 84132; **Phone:** 801-213-2700; **Board Cert:** Urology 2008; **Med School:** UCSF 1991; **Resid:** Surgery, Univ Utah Med Ctr 1993; Urology, Univ Utah Med Ctr 1996; **Fellow:** Endourology, Cleveland Clinic 1997; Laparoscopic Surgery, Cleveland Clinic 1997; **Fac Appt:** Assoc Prof S, Univ Utah

Lugg, James A MD [U] - **Spec Exp:** Prostate Cancer; Laparoscopic Surgery; Incontinence after Prostate Cancer; **Hospital:** Cheyenne Regl Med Ctr, Univ Colorado Hosp; **Address:** Cheyenne Urological, 2301 House Ave, Ste 502, Cheyenne, WY 82001; **Phone:** 307-635-4131; **Board Cert:** Urology 2008; **Med School:** Northwestern Univ 1990; **Resid:** Urology, UCLA Ronald Reagan Med Ctr 1995; **Fac Appt:** Asst Prof U, Univ Colorado

Meacham, Randall B MD [U] - **Spec Exp:** Infertility-Male; Vasectomy Reversal; Sexual Dysfunction; **Hospital:** Univ Colorado Hosp; **Address:** Univ CO Hosp, Urology Dept, 1635 Aurora Ct, Ste 3500, Aurora, CO 80045; **Phone:** 720-848-1800; **Board Cert:** Urology 2013; **Med School:** Baylor Coll Med 1982; **Resid:** Surgery, Baylor Coll Med 1985; Urology, Baylor Coll Med 1989; **Fellow:** Urolithiasis, Baylor Coll Med 1984; Male Reproductive Medicine/Surgery, Baylor Coll Med 1990; **Fac Appt:** Prof U, Univ Colorado

Thrasher, J Brantley MD [U] - **Spec Exp:** Prostate Cancer; Reconstructive Urologic Surgery; **Hospital:** Univ of Kansas Hosp; **Address:** Univ Kansas Med Ctr, Dept Urology, 3901 Rainbow Blvd, MS 3016, Kansas City, KS 66160; **Phone:** 913-588-6146; **Board Cert:** Urology 2013; **Med School:** Med Univ SC 1986; **Resid:** Urology, Fitzsimons Army Med Ctr 1991; **Fellow:** Urologic Oncology, Duke Univ Med Ctr 1994; **Fac Appt:** Prof U, Univ Kansas

Southwest

Andrews, Paul E MD [U] - **Spec Exp:** Urologic Cancer; Minimally Invasive Urologic Surgery; Robotic Surgery; Laparoscopic Surgery; **Hospital:** Mayo Clinic - Phoenix; **Address:** Mayo Clinic-Urology, 5779 E Mayo Blvd, Phoenix, AZ 85054; **Phone:** 480-342-2951; **Board Cert:** Urology 2003; **Med School:** Texas Tech Univ 1987; **Resid:** Urology, Mayo Clinic 1993; **Fac Appt:** Prof U, Mayo Med Sch

Bans, Larry L MD [U] - **Spec Exp:** Prostate Cancer; Prostate Disease; Men's Health; **Hospital:** Banner Good Samaritan Regl Med Ctr - Phoenix; **Address:** Prostate Solutions of Arizona, 2525 E Arizona Biltmore Cir, Ste C236, Phoenix, AZ 85016; **Phone:** 602-426-9772; **Board Cert:** Urology 2013; **Med School:** Cornell Univ-Weill Med Coll 1978; **Resid:** Urology, Ind Univ Med Ctr 1983

Bardot, Stephen F MD [U] - **Spec Exp:** Urologic Cancer; Prostate Cancer; **Hospital:** Ochsner Med Ctr-New Orleans; **Address:** Ochsner Clinic, 1514 Jefferson Hwy, Fl 4, Atrium 4 West, Dept Urology, New Orleans, LA 70121-2483; **Phone:** 504-842-4083; **Board Cert:** Urology 2012; **Med School:** Univ Kansas 1985; **Resid:** Surgery, St Luke's Hosp 1987; Urology, Kansas City Univ Med Ctr 1990; **Fellow:** Urologic Oncology, Cleveland Clinic 1991

Basler, Joseph W MD [U] - **Spec Exp:** Prostate Cancer; Urologic Cancer; Kidney Stones; **Hospital:** Audie L Murphy Meml Vets Hosp - San Antonio; **Address:** UT Hlth Sci Ctr, Dept Urology, 7703 Floyd Curl Drive, MC 7845, San Antonio, TX 78229-3900; **Phone:** 210-567-5640; **Board Cert:** Urology 2011; **Med School:** Univ MO-Columbia Sch Med 1984; **Resid:** Surgery, Univ MO Affil Hosp 1986; Urology, Washington Univ Phys 1990; **Fac Appt:** Prof U, Univ Tex, San Antonio

Boone, Timothy B MD/PhD [U] - **Spec Exp:** Neuro-Urology; Urinary Reconstruction; Incontinence; **Hospital:** Methodist Hosp - Houston; **Address:** Methodist Hosp, Urology Dept, 6560 Fannin St, Ste 2100, Houston, TX 77030; **Phone:** 713-441-6455; **Board Cert:** Urology 2004; **Med School:** Univ Tex, Houston 1985; **Resid:** Surgery, UT Southwestern Med Ctr 1987; Urology, UT Southwestern Med Ctr 1991; **Fac Appt:** Prof U, Cornell Univ-Weill Med Coll

Buch, Jeffrey Phillip MD [U] - **Spec Exp:** Vasectomy Reversal; Infertility-Male; Sexual Dysfunction; **Hospital:** Baylor Univ Med Ctr-Dallas; **Address:** Legacy Male Hlth Inst, 5616 Warren Pkwy, Ste 101, Frisco, TX 75034; **Phone:** 972-612-7131; **Board Cert:** Urology 2005; **Med School:** Univ Mich Med Sch 1980; **Resid:** Surgery, Albany Med Ctr 1982; Urology, Albany Med Ctr 1985; **Fellow:** Male Infertility, Baylor Coll Med 1987; Microsurgery, Baylor Coll Med 1987; **Fac Appt:** Assoc Clin Prof U, Univ Tex SW, Dallas

Cookson, Michael S MD [U] - **Spec Exp:** Urologic Cancer; Bladder Cancer; Prostate Cancer; Testicular Cancer; **Hospital:** OU Med Ctr-Presbyterian Tower; **Address:** Oklahoma University, Dept Urology, 920 Stanton L Young Blvd, WP Bldg - rm 3150, Oklahoma City, OK 73131; **Phone:** 405-271-6966 x46103; **Board Cert:** Urology 2006; **Med School:** Univ Okla Coll Med 1988; **Resid:** Urology, UTSA Med Ctr 1994; **Fellow:** Urologic Oncology, Meml Sloan-Kettering Cancer Ctr 1996; **Fac Appt:** Prof U, Univ Okla Coll Med

Culkin, Daniel J MD [U] - **Spec Exp:** Voiding Dysfunction; Interstitial Cystitis; Urologic Cancer; Laparoscopic Surgery; **Hospital:** OU Med Ctr; **Address:** OU Medical Ctr, Dept Urology, 825 NE 10th St, Ste 5400, Oklahoma City, OK 73104; **Phone:** 405-271-6452; **Board Cert:** Urology 2006; **Med School:** Creighton Univ 1979; **Resid:** Surgery, Loyola Univ Med Ctr 1981; Urology, Loyola Univ Med Ctr 1983; **Fellow:** Neurourology, Loyola Univ Med Ctr 1984; **Fac Appt:** Prof U, Univ Okla Coll Med

Grossman, H Barton MD [U] - **Spec Exp:** Bladder Cancer; **Hospital:** UT MD Anderson Canc Ctr; **Address:** MD Anderson Cancer Ctr, Dept Urology, Unit 1373, 1515 Holcombe Blvd, Houston, TX 77030-4009; **Phone:** 713-792-3250; **Board Cert:** Urology 1979; **Med School:** Temple Univ 1970; **Resid:** Surgery, St Joseph Mercy Hosp 1974; Urology, Univ Michigan Med Ctr 1977; **Fellow:** Urologic Oncology, Meml Sloan Kettering Cancer Ctr 1979; **Fac Appt:** Clin Prof U, Univ Tex, Houston

Hellstrom, Wayne J MD [U] - **Spec Exp:** Infertility-Male; Erectile Dysfunction; Peyronie's Disease; Penile Prostheses; **Hospital:** Tulane Med Ctr; **Address:** Tulane Med Ctr, Dept Urology, 1415 Tulane Ave Fl 3, New Orleans, LA 70112; **Phone:** 504-988-5271; **Board Cert:** Urology 2007; **Med School:** McGill Univ 1981; **Resid:** Surgery, Montreal Genl/Royal Vistoria Hosp 1983; Urology, UCSF Med Ctr 1985; **Fellow:** Andrology, UC Davis Med Ctr 1988; **Fac Appt:** Prof U, Tulane Univ

Kadmon, Dov MD [U] - **Spec Exp:** Prostate Cancer; **Hospital:** Methodist Hosp - Houston, St. Luke's Episcopal Hosp-Houston; **Address:** Scott Dept of Urology, Baylor College of Medicine, 6620 Main St, Ste 1325, Houston, TX 77030; **Phone:** 713-798-4001; **Board Cert:** Urology 1984; **Med School:** Israel 1970; **Resid:** Surgery, Barnes Jewish Hosp 1977; Urology, Barnes Jewish Hosp 1980; **Fellow:** Urology, Barnes Jewish Hosp 1982; **Fac Appt:** Prof U, Baylor Coll Med

Lerner, Seth P MD [U] - **Spec Exp:** Bladder Cancer; Testicular Cancer; Urinary Reconstruction; **Hospital:** St. Luke's Episcopal Hosp-Houston, Methodist Hosp - Houston; **Address:** 6620 Main St, Ste 1325, Houston, TX 77030; **Phone:** 713-798-4001; **Board Cert:** Urology 2012; **Med School:** Baylor Coll Med 1984; **Resid:** Surgery, Virginia Mason Med Ctr 1986; Urology, Baylor Affil Hosp 1990; **Fellow:** Urologic Oncology, LAC & USC Med Ctr 1992; **Fac Appt:** Prof U, Baylor Coll Med

Lipshultz, Larry I MD [U] - **Spec Exp:** Infertility-Male; Hormone Replacement-Male; Erectile Dysfunction; **Hospital:** St. Luke's Episcopal Hosp-Houston; **Address:** BCM, Urology Dept, 6624 Fannin St, Ste 1700, Houston, TX 77030; **Phone:** 713-798-4001; **Board Cert:** Urology 1977; **Med School:** Univ Pennsylvania 1968; **Resid:** Urology, Hosp Univ Penn 1975; **Fellow:** Male Reproductive Medicine/Surgery, UT Affil Hosp 1977; **Fac Appt:** Prof U, Baylor Coll Med

Miles, Brian J MD [U] - **Spec Exp:** Prostate Cancer; Urologic Cancer; Gene Therapy; **Hospital:** Methodist Hosp - Houston, St. Luke's Episcopal Hosp-Houston; **Address:** Methodist Urology Associates, 6560 Fannin St, Ste 2100, Houston, TX 77030; **Phone:** 713-441-6455; **Board Cert:** Urology 1984; **Med School:** Univ Mich Med Sch 1974; **Resid:** Urology, Walter Reed Army Med Ctr 1982; **Fac Appt:** Clin Prof U, Baylor Coll Med

Pisters, Louis L MD [U] - **Spec Exp:** Prostate Cancer; Genitourinary Cancer; Prostate Cancer/Robotic Surgery; **Hospital:** UT MD Anderson Canc Ctr; **Address:** MD Anderson Canc Ctr, Dept Urology, 1515 Holcombe Blvd, Unit 1373, Houston, TX 77030; **Phone:** 713-792-3250; **Board Cert:** Urology 2013; **Med School:** Univ Western Ontario 1986; **Resid:** Urology, Shands Jacksonville Med Ctr 1992; **Fellow:** Urologic Oncology, MD Anderson Canc Ctr 1994; **Fac Appt:** Prof U, Univ Tex, Houston

Roehrborn, Claus Georg MD [U] - **Spec Exp:** Prostate Cancer; Prostate Disease; Voiding Dysfunction; **Hospital:** UT Southwestern Med Ctr at Dallas, Parkland Hlth & Hosp Sys; **Address:** UTSW Med Ctr, Urology Dept, 5303 Harry Hines Blvd Fl 9 - Ste 110, Dallas, TX 75390; **Phone:** 214-645-8765; **Board Cert:** Urology 2004; **Med School:** Germany 1980; **Resid:** Surgery, W Germany Army Hosp 1982; Urology, UT Southwestern Med Ctr 1989; **Fellow:** Biochemistry, Ameri Fdn 1994; **Fac Appt:** Prof U, Univ Tex SW, Dallas

Sagalowsky, Arthur I MD [U] - **Spec Exp:** Urologic Cancer; Bladder Cancer; Kidney Cancer; Continent Urinary Diversions; **Hospital:** UT Southwestern Med Ctr at Dallas; **Address:** 5303 Harry Hines Blvd, Fl 9, Ste 110, Dallas, TX 75390-9110; **Phone:** 214-645-8765; **Board Cert:** Urology 1980; **Med School:** Indiana Univ 1973; **Resid:** Surgery, Indiana Univ Hosps 1975; Urology, Indiana Univ Hosps 1978; **Fellow:** Clinical Pharmacology, Univ Tex SW Med Ctr 1980; **Fac Appt:** Prof U, Univ Tex SW, Dallas

Slawin, Kevin M MD [U] - **Spec Exp:** Prostate Cancer; Prostate Cancer/Robotic Surgery; Prostate Disease; **Hospital:** Meml Hermann Hosp - Texas Med Ctr, Methodist Hosp - Houston; **Address:** Vanguard Urologic Inst, Meml Hermann Med Plaza, 6400 Fannin, Ste 2300, Houston, TX 77030; **Phone:** 713-366-7847; **Board Cert:** Urology 2005; **Med School:** Columbia P&S 1986; **Resid:** Surgery, Mt Sinai Med Ctr 1988; Urology, Presby/Columbia Univ Med Ctr 1992; **Fellow:** Urologic Oncology, Baylor Coll Med 1994; **Fac Appt:** Clin Prof U, Baylor Coll Med

Thompson Jr, Ian M MD [U] - **Spec Exp:** Prostate Cancer; Prostate Disease; **Hospital:** Univ Hosp-San Antonio; **Address:** Univ Tex Hlth Scis Ctr, Dept Urol, 8300 Floyd Curl Drive, MC 7977, San Antonio, TX 78229; **Phone:** 210-450-1408; **Board Cert:** Urology 2005; **Med School:** Tulane Univ 1980; **Resid:** Urology, Brooke Army Med Ctr 1985; **Fellow:** Medical Oncology, Meml Sloan-Kettering Canc Ctr 1988; **Fac Appt:** Prof S, Univ Tex, San Antonio

Woo, Howard H MD [U] - **Spec Exp:** Pain-Pelvic; Voiding Dysfunction; Incontinence; Urology-Female; **Hospital:** Ochsner Med Ctr-New Orleans; **Address:** Ochsner Clin, Dept Urology, 1514 Jefferson Hwy Fl 4, New Orleans, LA 70121; **Phone:** 504-842-4083; **Board Cert:** Urology 2006; **Med School:** Med Coll Wisc 1989; **Resid:** Surgery, UC Irvine Med Ctr 1991; Urology, Univ Colorado Affil Hosp 1995

West Coast and Pacific

Ahlering, Thomas E MD [U] - **Spec Exp:** Prostate Cancer/Robotic Surgery; **Hospital:** UC Irvine Med Ctr, VA Long Beach Hlthcare Sys; **Address:** UC Irvine Med Ctr, 333 City Blvd W, Ste 2100, Orange, CA 92868; **Phone:** 714-456-6068; **Board Cert:** Urology 2005; **Med School:** St Louis Univ 1979; **Resid:** Urology, LAC-USC Med Ctr 1984; **Fellow:** Urologic Oncology, USC-Norris Comp Cancer Ctr 1986; **Fac Appt:** Prof U, UC Irvine

Amling, Christopher L MD [U] - **Spec Exp:** Prostate Cancer/Robotic Surgery; Kidney Cancer; Bladder Cancer; Testicular Cancer; **Hospital:** OR Hlth & Sci Univ; **Address:** 3303 SW Bond Ave, Portland, OR 97239; **Phone:** 503-346-1500; **Board Cert:** Urology 2008; **Med School:** Oregon Hlth & Sci Univ 1985; **Resid:** Surgery, Duke Univ Med Ctr 1992; Urology, Duke Univ Med Ctr 1996; **Fellow:** Urologic Oncology, Mayo Clinic 1997; **Fac Appt:** Prof U, Oregon Hlth & Sci Univ

Belldegrun, Arie S MD [U] - **Spec Exp:** Urologic Cancer; Gene Therapy; Bladder Cancer; Kidney Cancer; **Hospital:** UCLA Ronald Reagan Med Ctr; **Address:** 200 UCLA Medical Plaza, Ste 140, Los Angeles, CA 90095; **Phone:** 310-206-1434; **Board Cert:** Urology 2011; **Med School:** Israel 1974; **Resid:** Urology, Brigham and Women's Hosp 1985; **Fellow:** Surgery, National Inst of Health 1987; Surgical Oncology, National Inst of Health 1988; **Fac Appt:** Prof U, UCLA

Boyd, Stuart D MD [U] - **Spec Exp:** Urologic Cancer; **Hospital:** USC Norris Cancer Hosp, Keck Med Ctr of USC; **Address:** 1441 Eastlake Ave, Ste 7416, Los Angeles, CA 90089-9178; **Phone:** 323-865-3700 x1; **Board Cert:** Urology 1984; **Med School:** UCLA 1975; **Resid:** Surgery, UCLA Med Ctr 1977; Urology, UCLA Med Ctr 1982; **Fac Appt:** Prof U, USC Sch Med

Carroll, Peter R MD [U] - **Spec Exp:** Testicular Cancer; Prostate Cancer; Bladder Cancer; Bladder Reconstruction; **Hospital:** UCSF - Mt Zion Med Ctr; **Address:** UCSF, Urologic Surgery & Oncology, 1600 Divisadero St Fl 3, San Francisco, CA 94115; **Phone:** 415-353-7171; **Board Cert:** Urology 2006; **Med School:** Georgetown Univ 1979; **Resid:** Surgery, UCSF Med Ctr 1984; **Fellow:** Urology, Meml Sloan-Kettering Cancer Ctr 1986; **Fac Appt:** Prof U, UCSF

Clayman, Ralph V MD [U] - **Spec Exp:** Kidney Stones; Kidney Cancer; Laparoscopic Surgery; Robotic Surgery; **Hospital:** UC Irvine Med Ctr; **Address:** UC Irvine Hlth Ctr for Urological Care, 101 The City Drive S, Pavilion III, Bldg 29, Orange, CA 92868; **Phone:** 714-456-7005; **Board Cert:** Urology 2007; **Med School:** UCSD 1973; **Resid:** Urology, Univ Minn Med Ctr 1979; **Fac Appt:** Prof U, UC Irvine

Dalkin, Bruce L MD [U] - **Spec Exp:** Urologic Cancer; Prostate Cancer; Bladder Cancer; Testicular Cancer; **Hospital:** Univ Wash Med Ctr; **Address:** Univ Wash, Dept Urology, 1959 NE Pacific St, MS 356158, Seattle, WA 98195; **Phone:** 206-598-4294; **Board Cert:** Urology 2013; **Med School:** Northwestern Univ 1985; **Resid:** Surgery, Northwestern Meml Hosp 1987; Urology, Northwestern Meml Hosp 1992; **Fac Appt:** Prof U, Univ Wash

Daneshmand, Sia MD [U] - **Spec Exp:** Bladder Cancer; Testicular Cancer; Kidney Cancer; Prostate Cancer; **Hospital:** Keck Med Ctr of USC; **Address:** 1441 Eastlake Ave, Ste 7416, Los Angeles, CA 90089; **Phone:** 323-865-3700; **Board Cert:** Urology 2006; **Med School:** UC Davis 1996; **Resid:** Surgery, USC Med Ctr 1998; Urology, USC Med Ctr 2002; **Fellow:** Urologic Oncology, USC/Norris Cancer Ctr 2004; **Fac Appt:** Assoc Prof U, USC-Keck School of Medicine

Danoff, Dudley S MD [U] - **Spec Exp:** Urologic Cancer; Erectile Dysfunction; **Hospital:** Cedars-Sinai Med Ctr; **Address:** Tower Urology, 8635 W 3rd St, Ste 1 West, Los Angeles, CA 90048; **Phone:** 310-854-9898; **Board Cert:** Urology 1974; **Med School:** Yale Univ 1963; **Resid:** Surgery, Yale-New Haven Hosp 1965; Urology, Columbia-Presby Med Ctr 1969

DeKernion, Jean B MD [U] - **Spec Exp:** Bladder Cancer; Kidney Cancer; Prostate Cancer; **Hospital:** UCLA Ronald Reagan Med Ctr; **Address:** UCLA, Urology Dept, 200 UCLA Medical Plaza Drive, Ste 140, Los Angeles, CA 90095-1738; **Phone:** 310-794-7700; **Board Cert:** Surgery 1973; Urology 1975; **Med School:** Louisiana State U, New Orleans 1965; **Resid:** Surgery, Univ Hosps-Case West Res 1967; Urology, Univ Hosps-Case West Res 1968; **Fellow:** Urologic Oncology, Natl Cancer Inst 1969; **Fac Appt:** Prof U, UCLA

Ellis, William J MD [U] - **Spec Exp:** Prostate Cancer/Robotic Surgery; Prostate Disease; Kidney Cancer; Urologic Cancer; **Hospital:** Univ Wash Med Ctr; **Address:** Univ Wash Med Ctr, Dept Urology, 1959 NE Pacific St, Box 356510, Seattle, WA 98195; **Phone:** 206-598-4294; **Board Cert:** Urology 2012; **Med School:** Johns Hopkins Univ 1985; **Resid:** Surgery, Northwestern Meml Hosp 1987; Urology, Northwestern Meml Hosp 1993; **Fac Appt:** Assoc Prof U, Univ Wash

Gill, Harcharan Singh MD [U] - **Spec Exp:** Urologic Cancer; Prostate Cancer; **Hospital:** Stanford Univ Hosp & Clins; **Address:** Stanford Univ, Urology Oncology, 875 Blake Wilbur Drive, Clin E, rm 2218, Stanford, CA 94305; **Phone:** 650-725-5544; **Board Cert:** Urology 2004; **Med School:** Kenya 1977; **Resid:** Urology, Inst Urology 1987; Urology, Univ Hosp Penn 1991; **Fac Appt:** Prof U, Stanford Univ

Gill, Inderbir Singh MD [U] - **Spec Exp:** Prostate Cancer; Kidney Cancer; Urologic Cancer; Minimally Invasive Urologic Surgery; **Hospital:** USC Norris Cancer Hosp; **Address:** USC/Norris Cancer Ctr, Dept Urology, 1441 Eastlake Ave, Ste 7416, Los Angeles, CA 90089; **Phone:** 323-865-3700; **Board Cert:** Urology 2008; **Med School:** India 1980; **Resid:** Surgery, All India Inst of Med Sci 1987; Urology, Univ Kentucky Hosp 1995; **Fellow:** Renal Transplant, Cleveland Clinic 1991; **Fac Appt:** Prof U, Univ SC Sch Med

Ginsberg, David A MD [U] - **Spec Exp:** Incontinence; Urinary Reconstruction; Neuro-Urology; Neurogenic Bladder; **Hospital:** Keck Med Ctr of USC; **Address:** USC-Norris Cancer Ctr, 1441 Eastlake Ave, Ste 7416, Los Angeles, CA 90089; **Phone:** 323-865-3700; **Board Cert:** Urology 2008; **Med School:** USC Sch Med 1990; **Resid:** Surgery, LAC-USC Med Ctr 1992; Urology, LAc-USC Med Ctr 1996; **Fellow:** Neurourology, UCLA Med Ctr 1997; **Fac Appt:** Assoc Clin Prof U, USC-Keck School of Medicine

Goldstein, Irwin MD [U] - **Spec Exp:** Sexual Dysfunction-Male & Female; Vulvar Pain; Erectile Dysfunction; Penile Microvascular Bypass Surgery; **Hospital:** Alvarado Hosp & Med Ctr, VA San Diego Hlthcre Sys; **Address:** San Diego Sexual Medicine, 5555 Reservoir Drive, Ste 300, San Diego, CA 92120; **Phone:** 619-265-8865; **Board Cert:** Urology 1982; **Med School:** McGill Univ 1975; **Resid:** Surgery, Boston Univ Med Ctr 1980; **Fellow:** Urology, Boston Univ Med Ctr 1982; **Fac Appt:** Prof S, UCSD

Holden, Stuart MD [U] - **Spec Exp:** Kidney Cancer; Prostate Cancer; **Hospital:** Cedars-Sinai Med Ctr; **Address:** Tower Urology, 8635 W 3rd St, Ste 1 West, Los Angeles, CA 90048; **Phone:** 310-854-9898; **Board Cert:** Urology 1977; **Med School:** Cornell Univ-Weill Med Coll 1968; **Resid:** Surgery, NY Hosp-Cornell 1970; Urology, Emory Univ Hosp 1975; **Fellow:** Urology, Meml Sloan Kettering Cancer Ctr 1978

Kawachi, Mark H MD [U] - **Spec Exp:** Bladder Cancer; Kidney Cancer; Prostate Cancer; Testicular Cancer; **Hospital:** City of Hope Natl Med Ctr; **Address:** Div Urologic Oncology, 1500 E Duarte Rd, Duarte, CA 91010-3012; **Phone:** 626-359-8111 x62655; **Board Cert:** Urology 2004; **Med School:** USC Sch Med 1979; **Resid:** Urology, USC Med Ctr 1984; **Fellow:** Urologic Oncology, USC Med Ctr 1992

Landman, Jaime MD [U] - **Spec Exp:** Minimally Invasive Urologic Surgery; Kidney Stones; Kidney Cancer; **Hospital:** UC Irvine Med Ctr; **Address:** UC Irvine Med Ctr, 333 City Blvd W, Ste 2100, Orange, CA 92868; **Phone:** 714-456-3429; **Board Cert:** Urology 2013; **Med School:** Columbia P&S 1993; **Resid:** Urology, Mount Sinai Hosp 1999; **Fellow:** Urologic Laparoscopic Surg-Endourology, Wash Univ Med Ctr 2001; **Fac Appt:** Prof U, UC Irvine

Lange, Paul H MD [U] - **Spec Exp:** Prostate Cancer; **Hospital:** Univ Wash Med Ctr; **Address:** Univ Wash Med Ctr, Dept Urology, 1959 NE Pacific St, Box 356510, Seattle, WA 98195; **Phone:** 206-598-4294; **Board Cert:** Urology 2006; **Med School:** Washington Univ, St Louis 1967; **Resid:** Surgery, Duke Univ Med Ctr 1972; Urology, Univ Minn Med Ctr 1977; **Fellow:** Research, Natl Inst Hlth 1970; Immunology, Univ Minn Med Ctr 1978; **Fac Appt:** Prof U, Univ Wash

Lieskovsky, Gary MD [U] - **Spec Exp:** Urologic Cancer; **Hospital:** USC Norris Cancer Hosp, Keck Med Ctr of USC; **Address:** 1441 Eastlake Ave, Ste 7416, Los Angeles, CA 90089-0112; **Phone:** 323-865-3702; **Board Cert:** Urology 1980; **Med School:** Canada 1973; **Resid:** Urology, Univ Alberta Hosp 1978; **Fellow:** Endocrinology, Univ Alberta Hosp 1977; Genitourinary Surgery, UCLA Med Ctr 1979; **Fac Appt:** Prof U, USC Sch Med

Lin, Daniel W MD [U] - **Spec Exp:** Urologic Cancer; **Hospital:** Univ Wash Med Ctr; **Address:** UWMC, Urology Clin, 1959 NE Pacific St, Box 356158, Seattle, WA 98195; **Phone:** 206-598-4294; **Board Cert:** Urology 2003; **Med School:** Vanderbilt Univ 1994; **Resid:** Urology, Univ Wash Med Ctr 2000; **Fellow:** Urologic Oncology, Meml Sloan-Kettering Canc Ctr 2001; **Fac Appt:** Assoc Prof U, Univ Wash

Marsh, Christopher L MD [U] - **Spec Exp:** Transplant-Kidney; Transplant-Pancreas; Transplant-Liver; Adrenal Surgery; **Hospital:** Scripps Green Hosp; **Address:** Scripps Green Hosp, 10666 N Torrey Pines Rd, MC N200, La Jolla, CA 92037; **Phone:** 858-554-4310; **Board Cert:** Urology 2006; **Med School:** Loma Linda Univ 1980; **Resid:** Urology, Loma Linda Univ Med Ctr 1986; **Fellow:** Transplant Surgery, Mayo Clinic 1987

McClure, Robert D MD [U] - **Spec Exp:** Infertility-Male; **Address:** Seattle Reproductive Medicine, 1505 Westlake Ave N, Ste 400, Seattle, WA 98109; **Phone:** 206-301-5000; **Board Cert:** Urology 1979; **Med School:** Canada 1968; **Resid:** Urology, McGill Univ Hosp 1975; **Fellow:** Endocrinology, UCLA Med Ctr 1977

Porter, Christopher R MD [U] - **Spec Exp:** Urologic Cancer; Prostate Cancer; Testicular Cancer; Robotic Surgery; **Hospital:** Virginia Mason Med Ctr; **Address:** Virginia Mason Med Ctr, 1100 9th Ave, Seattle, WA 98101; **Phone:** 206-341-0560; **Board Cert:** Urology 2009; **Med School:** Rush Med Coll 1990; **Resid:** Urology, Brown Univ Affil Hosp 1997; **Fellow:** Urologic Oncology, Meml Sloan Kettering Canc Ctr 1999; **Fac Appt:** Assoc Clin Prof U, Univ Wash

Presti Jr, Joseph C MD [U] - **Spec Exp:** Prostate Cancer; Bladder Cancer; Kidney Cancer; Testicular Cancer; **Hospital:** Kaiser Permanente Oakland Med Ctr; **Address:** Kaiser Permanente, Urology Dept, 280 W MacArthur Blvd, Oakland, CA 94611; **Phone:** 510-752-6796; **Board Cert:** Urology 2012; **Med School:** UC Irvine 1984; **Resid:** Surgery, UCSF Med Ctr 1986; Urology, UCSF Med Ctr 1989; **Fellow:** Urologic Oncology, Meml Sloan-Kettering Cancer Ctr 1992

Rajfer, Jacob MD [U] - **Spec Exp:** Erectile Dysfunction; Prostate Cancer; Infertility-Male; Peyronie's Disease; **Hospital:** UCLA Ronald Reagan Med Ctr; **Address:** Frank Clark Urological Center, 200 UCLA Medical Plaza, Ste 140, Los Angeles, CA 90095; **Phone:** 310-206-8164; **Board Cert:** Urology 1980; **Med School:** Northwestern Univ 1972; **Resid:** Surgery, St Josephs Hosp 1974; Urology, Johns Hopkins Hosp 1978; **Fellow:** Research, Johns Hopkins Hosp 1976; **Fac Appt:** Prof U, UCLA

Raz, Shlomo MD [U] - **Spec Exp:** Urinary Reconstruction; Urology-Female; Neurogenic Bladder; **Hospital:** UCLA Ronald Reagan Med Ctr; **Address:** Frank Clark Urological Ctr, 200 UCLA Medical Plaza, Ste 140, Los Angeles, CA 90095; **Phone:** 310-794-0207; **Board Cert:** Urology 1979; **Med School:** Uruguay 1962; **Resid:** Surgery, Poriah Hospital 1967; Urology, Hadassah Medical 1974; **Fellow:** Urology, UCLA Med Ctr 1975; **Fac Appt:** Prof U, UCLA

Sharlip, Ira D MD [U] - **Spec Exp:** Vasectomy Reversal; Erectile Dysfunction; Infertility-Male; **Hospital:** CA Pacific Med Ctr-Pacific Campus, UCSF Med Ctr; **Address:** Golden Gate Urology, 2100 Webster St, Ste 222, San Francisco, CA 94115-2376; **Phone:** 415-202-0250; **Board Cert:** Internal Medicine 1972; Urology 1977; **Med School:** Univ Pennsylvania 1965; **Resid:** Internal Medicine, Hosp Univ Penn 1967; Urology, UCSF Med Ctr 1975; **Fellow:** Urology, Middlesex Hosp 1976; **Fac Appt:** Prof U, UCSF

Skinner, Eila C MD [U] - **Spec Exp:** Urologic Cancer; Bladder Cancer; Testicular Cancer; Urinary Reconstruction; **Hospital:** Stanford Univ Hosp & Clins; **Address:** Urologic Oncology, 875 Blake Wilbur Drive, rm 2200, MC 5826, Stanford, CA 94305; **Phone:** 650-725-5544; **Board Cert:** Urology 2012; **Med School:** USC Sch Med 1983; **Resid:** Urology, LAC-USC Med Ctr 1988; **Fellow:** Urologic Oncology, LAC-USC Med Ctr 1990; **Fac Appt:** Prof U, Stanford Univ

Stoller, Marshall L MD [U] - **Spec Exp:** Laparoscopic Surgery; Kidney Stones; **Hospital:** UCSF Med Ctr; **Address:** Urology Faculty Practice, 400 Parnassus Ave, Ste A-610, San Francisco, CA 94145-0738; **Phone:** 415-353-2200; **Board Cert:** Urology 2009; **Med School:** Baylor Coll Med 1981; **Resid:** Surgery, UCSF Med Ctr 1983; Urology, UCSF Med Ctr 1985; **Fellow:** Urology, Prince Henry Hosp 1987; **Fac Appt:** Prof U, UCSF

Takayama, Thomas K MD [U] - **Spec Exp:** Urologic Cancer; Prostate Cancer; Robotic Surgery; Laparoscopic Surgery; **Hospital:** Overlake Hosp Med Ctr; **Address:** Washington Urology Assocs, 1135 NE 116th Ave, Ste 620, Bellevue, WA 98004; **Phone:** 425-454-8016; **Board Cert:** Urology 2007; **Med School:** Tufts Univ 1985; **Resid:** Surgery, Univ Mass Med Ctr 1987; Urology, Univ Wash Med Ctr 1993; **Fellow:** Urologic Oncology, Univ Wash Med Ctr 1996; **Fac Appt:** Assoc Prof U, Univ Wash

Turek, Paul J MD [U] - **Spec Exp:** Infertility-Male; Vasectomy Reversal; Hormone Replacement-Male; Erectile Dysfunction; **Hospital:** CA Pacific Med Ctr-Pacific Campus, St. Francis Memorial Hosp; **Address:** 55 Francisco St, Ste 300, San Francisco, CA 94133; **Phone:** 415-392-3200; **Board Cert:** Urology 2005; **Med School:** Stanford Univ 1987; **Resid:** Surgery, Hosp Univ Penn 1989; Urology, Hosp Univ Penn 1993; **Fellow:** Microsurgery, Baylor Coll Med 1994; **Fac Appt:** Prof U, UCSF

Wilson, Timothy G MD [U] - **Spec Exp:** Bladder Cancer; Kidney Cancer; Testicular Cancer; Urologic Cancer; **Hospital:** City of Hope Natl Med Ctr; **Address:** Div Urologic Oncology, 1500 E Duarte Rd, Duarte, CA 91010; **Phone:** 626-359-8111 x62655; **Board Cert:** Urology 2012; **Med School:** Oregon Hlth & Sci Univ 1984; **Resid:** Urology, USC Med Ctr 1990; **Fellow:** Urologic Oncology, City Hosp Natl Med Ctr 1992; **Fac Appt:** Assoc Clin Prof U, USC Sch Med

Mount Sinai

THE MOUNT SINAI MEDICAL CENTER

Urogynecology

One Gustave L. Levy Place
Fifth Avenue and 100th Street
New York, NY 10029-6574

Physician Referral: 1-800-MD-SINAI (637-4624)
www.mountsinai.org

Urogynecology: Incontinence and Pelvic Organ Prolapse

Millions of women of all ages suffer from incontinence or overactive bladder in silence and embarrassment, not knowing where to turn for help. By turning to the experts at Mount Sinai, women who have suffered the physical and emotional effects of pelvic floor disorders such as urinary incontinence, pelvic organ prolapse, overactive bladder, stress incontinence, vaginal laxity, labial enlargement, mesh complications, and complications from previous surgery have had their lives restored.

Urinary incontinence affects millions of women. Some women have leakage every day, others occasionally. Incontinence is sometimes easily diagnosed based on a personal history and physical exam. Patients who only leak with a cough or laugh or who demonstrate leakage with a full bladder most likely have SUI. Other patients may need further testing to find the cause of their leakage.

Our urogynecologists (surgeons who are trained in the treatment of pelvic floor disorders) use a wide variety of conservative treatment options including dietary changes, pelvic floor muscle exercises, medication, biofeedback, counseling, physical therapy and electrical stimulation. We also use an Interstim Sacral Nerve Root Stimulator, a tiny pacemaker for the bladder which is placed in the lower back to control urinary urgency and frequency.

For women whose quality of life is bad enough, surgery to reconstruct the vaginal supportive tissues is an option. We treat patients utilizing the latest technology as a matter of course and minimally-invasive techniques—including the use of Robotics—whenever possible. We also provide religious and culturally-sensitive care to a large number of Orthodox Jewish women.

THE MOUNT SINAI MEDICAL CENTER

Urology

Mount Sinai

One Gustave L. Levy Place
Fifth Avenue and 100th Street
New York, NY 10029-6574

Physician Referral: 1-800-MD-SINAI (637-4624)
www.mountsinai.org

THE MILTON AND CARROLL PETRIE DEPARTMENT OF UROLOGY at The Mount Sinai Medical Center offers the latest technologic advances for the diagnosis and treatment of urologic diseases and conditions while supporting a translational and clinical research program.

Prostate Cancer: The Department of Urology's Barbara and Maurice Deane Health and Research Center is at the forefront of diagnosis, treatment and management of localized and advanced prostate cancer. Our surgeons are among the few trained in open, laparoscopic, and robotic surgery. The Robotics Prostatectomy program is one of the world's busiest, with over 4,000 surgeries to date. For men with low grade cancer, we oversee structured and personalized active surveillance. Our research focus is on multi-modal and novel therapies for advanced cancer; our work led to the approval of Provenge®, a cellular immunotherapeutic treatment.

Bladder Cancer: As recognized leaders in the assessment and treatment of all forms of bladder cancer, Mount Sinai urologic oncologists are successfully using tumor markers and new diagnostic techniques. Our surgeons employ robotic and laparoscopic surgery to perform cystectomies (removal of bladder) resulting in minimal impact on quality of life.

Kidney Cancer: Mount Sinai specialists helped pioneer robotic partial nephrectomy for the treatment of small kidney cancers. Other minimally invasive options such as cryoablation (freezing) or radiofrequency ablation (heating) are offered as a means to treat small cancers while preserving maximum kidney function.

Benign Prostatic Hyperplasia (BPH): The Deane Center offers the latest minimally invasive technologies and treatments for BPH, including Holium Laser Enucleation, Greenlight ™ Laser Photoselective Vaporization of the Prostate and bipolar cautery vaporization (Button TURP) in addition to TURP for symptoms of an enlarged prostate. Many of these procedures can be performed on an ambulatory basis.

Reconstructive Urology, Female Urology and Voiding Dysfunction: The Department of Urology provides comprehensive resources for the evaluation and treatment of urinary incontinence, neuro-urologic problems (e.g., spinal cord injury, multiple sclerosis) and pelvic pain syndrome for both men and women. Our specialists are among the few in the country with advanced training in urethral reconstruction. A state-of-the-art continence center provides the convenience of on-site diagnosis and treatment.

Erectile Dysfunction and Infertility: The Mount Sinai Sexual Health Program uses the most advanced techniques available to evaluate the causes of erectile dysfunction. Treatment options are extensive and effective. Importantly, patients and their partners receive the guidance they need to make the appropriate personal decision regarding treatment.

Kidney Stones: Mount Sinai's specialists utilize minimally invasive procedures to treat kidney stones, including laser and ultrasonic lithotripsy techniques. Medical and surgical care is highly customized based on type of stone and stone burden.

Infertility: Mount Sinai's state-of-the-art use of medications, in vitro fertilization techniques and microsurgical repairs have resulted in high success rates.

Pediatric Urology: Mount Sinai excels in treating urologic problems in newborns, infants, children and adolescents, The Division of Pediatric Urology is the highest ranked pediatric urology service in New York City by US News and World Report and noted as "superior" for numerous clinical and family services. Minimally invasive procedures are utilized whenever possible, including robotic assisted surgery.

THE BARBARA AND MAURICE DEANE PROSTATE HEALTH AND RESEARCH CENTER offers a multidisciplinary approach for the assessment and treatment of all aspects of prostate disease, including cancer, benign enlargement, and inflammation. The Center strives to empower the patient and his family and help them better understand various prostate conditions so they can choose the most appropriate treatment for lasting benefits.

Mount Sinai offers a comprehensive Minimally Invasive Urologic Surgery Program and is a recognized leader in the greater New York area for performing complex and laparoscopic procedures to treat urologic cancers. Areas of focus also include the treatment and management of stone disease and reconstructive procedures for various urologic cancers and anatomic abnormalities.

NYU Langone
MEDICAL CENTER

550 First Avenue *(at 31st Street)*
New York, NY 10016

www.NYULMC.org

Physician Referral: **888-7-NYU-MED** *(888-769-8633)*

UROLOGY

Urologists at NYU Langone Medical Center continue to pioneer in the surgical and medical treatment of urological disease and are recognized as a top urology program in the country by U.S. News and World Report.

Smilow Comprehensive Prostate Cancer Center
As part of the NCI-designated NYU Cancer Institute, the Center offers access to a team of uro-oncologic surgeons, radiation oncologists, oncologists and radiologists. Integrative services are available as well.

Benign Prostatic Diseases
Innovative medical and surgical therapies for benign prostatic disease and prostatitis.

Leading Edge Research
We are focused on discovering novel treatments for bladder and prostate cancer, while exploring how cancer markers can be used to determine how cancer treatments are working.

Female Urology and Incontinence
NYU Langone specializes in urological problems unique to women, including recurrent urinary tract infections, pelvic pain, prolapse and sexual dysfunction.

Latest Minimally Invasive Treatments
Advances in prostate imaging and computer biopsy are providing valuable information about tumor location and growth to enable targeted treatment. The latest options are also available to treat kidney stones and other obstructions.

Male Sexual Health
In collaboration with NYU Langone's Fertility Center, urologists use the latest techniques to enable infertile couples to have children. Treatment is also offered to men suffering from erectile dysfunction and low testosterone.

Pediatric Urology and Reconstructive Surgery
Pediatric urologists focus on urinary system disorders in children from birth to early adults.

Robotic Urological Surgery
The Department's robotic surgery program includes prostate and kidney cancers, as well as female incontinence and urinary tract reconstruction.

Urologic Oncology
Because cancer treatment often requires a collaborative approach, urologists work closely with their colleagues at the NYU Cancer Institute to tailor treatments for each patient.

Vascular Surgery

a subspecialty of Surgery

A surgeon with expertise in the management of surgical disorders of the blood vessels, excluding the intercranial vessels or the heart.

Training Required: Five years in surgery *plus* additional training and examination.

Vascular Surgery

New England

Belkin, Michael MD [VascS] - **Spec Exp:** Aneurysm; Arterial Bypass Surgery; Carotid Artery Surgery; Angioplasty & Stent Placement; **Hospital:** Brigham & Women's Hosp, Brigham and Women's Faulkner Hosp; **Address:** Brigham & Women's Hosp, Dept Vasc Surg, 75 Francis St Shapiro Bldg Fl 5, Boston, MA 02115; **Phone:** 857-307-1920; **Board Cert:** Vascular Surgery 2009; **Med School:** Univ Conn 1982; **Resid:** Surgery, Hartford Hosp 1987; **Fellow:** Vascular Surgery, Brigham & Women's Hosp 1989; **Fac Appt:** Assoc Prof S, Harvard Med Sch

Brewster, David C MD [VascS] - **Spec Exp:** Aneurysm-Abdominal Aortic; Endovascular Surgery; Angioplasty & Stent Placement; **Hospital:** Mass Genl Hosp, Newton - Wellesley Hosp; **Address:** MGH, Div Vascular & Endovascular Surgery, 15 Parkman St, WAC 440, Boston, MA 02114; **Phone:** 617-726-3567; **Board Cert:** Surgery 1975; Vascular Surgery 2003; **Med School:** Columbia P&S 1967; **Resid:** Surgery, Mass Genl Hosp 1975; **Fellow:** Vascular Surgery, Mass Genl Hosp 1976; **Fac Appt:** Clin Prof S, Harvard Med Sch

Cambria, Richard P MD [VascS] - **Spec Exp:** Aneurysm-Abdominal Aortic; Cerebrovascular Disease; Renovascular Disease; Aortic Reconstruction; **Hospital:** Mass Genl Hosp; **Address:** MGH, Div Vascular & Endovascular Surgery, 15 Parkman St, WAC 440, Boston, MA 02114; **Phone:** 617-726-8278; **Board Cert:** Vascular Surgery 2006; **Med School:** Columbia P&S 1977; **Resid:** Surgery, Mass Genl Hosp 1978; **Fellow:** Vascular Surgery, Mass Genl Hosp 1984; **Fac Appt:** Prof S, Harvard Med Sch

Chaikof, Elliot L MD/PhD [VascS] - **Spec Exp:** Aneurysm-Aortic; Carotid Artery Disease; Peripheral Vascular Disease; Endovascular Surgery; **Hospital:** Beth Israel Deaconess Med Ctr - Boston; **Address:** BIDMC, Div Vascular Surgery, 110 Francis St NE, Ste 5B, Boston, MA 02215; **Phone:** 617-632-9959; **Board Cert:** Surgery 2002; Vascular Surgery 2003; **Med School:** Johns Hopkins Univ 1982; **Resid:** Surgery, Mass Genl Hosp 1985; Surgery, Mass Genl Hosp 1991; **Fellow:** Vascular Surgery, Emory Univ Hosp 1992; **Fac Appt:** Prof S, Harvard Med Sch

Cronenwett, Jack L MD [VascS] - **Spec Exp:** Peripheral Vascular Disease; Aneurysm-Abdominal Aortic; Carotid Artery Surgery; **Hospital:** Dartmouth - Hitchcock Med Ctr; **Address:** Dartmouth-Hitchcock Med Ctr, Sect Vascular Surgery, One Medical Center Drive, Lebanon, NH 03756; **Phone:** 603-650-8193; **Board Cert:** Vascular Surgery 2003; **Med School:** Stanford Univ 1973; **Resid:** Surgery, Univ Mich Hosp 1979; **Fellow:** Vascular Surgery, Univ Tenn Hosp 1980; **Fac Appt:** Prof S, Dartmouth Med Sch

Iafrati, Mark D MD [VascS] - **Spec Exp:** Endovascular Surgery; Vein Disorders; Wound Healing/Care; Hyperbaric Medicine; **Hospital:** Tufts Med Ctr, Steward Carney Hosp; **Address:** Tufts Medical Center, 185 Harrison Ave, Boston, MA 02111; **Phone:** 617-636-5019; **Board Cert:** Surgery 2005; Vascular Surgery 2005; **Med School:** Tufts Univ 1989; **Resid:** Surgery, Tufts New England Med Ctr 1995; **Fellow:** Vascular Surgery, Tufts New England Med Ctr 1997; **Fac Appt:** Assoc Prof S, Tufts Univ

Kwolek, Christopher J MD [VascS] - **Spec Exp:** Aneurysm-Abdominal & Thoracic Aortic; Endovascular Surgery; Carotid Artery Stent Placement; **Hospital:** Mass Genl Hosp, Newton - Wellesley Hosp; **Address:** MGH, Div Vascular & Endovascular Surgery, 15 Parkman St, Wang Bldg Fl 4, Boston, MA 02114; **Phone:** 617-724-6101; **Board Cert:** Surgery 2003; Vascular Surgery 2006; **Med School:** UCSF 1987; **Resid:** Surgery, New England Deaconess Hosp 1993; Vascular Surgery, Mass Genl Hosp 1995; **Fellow:** Endovascular Surgery, Arizona Heart Inst 1999; **Fac Appt:** Assoc Prof VascS, Harvard Med Sch

LaMuraglia, Glenn M MD [VascS] - **Spec Exp:** Carotid Body Tumors; Aneurysm-Aortic; Endovascular Surgery; Vascular Disease; **Hospital:** Mass Genl Hosp; **Address:** MGH, Div Vascular & Endovascular Surgery, 15 Parkman St, Wang 440, Boston, MA 02114; **Phone:** 617-726-6997; **Board Cert:** Surgery 2004; Vascular Surgery 2007; **Med School:** Harvard Med Sch 1979; **Resid:** Surgery, Mass Genl Hosp 1985; Vascular Surgery, Mass Genl Hosp 1986; **Fac Appt:** Assoc Prof S, Harvard Med Sch

Mackey, William C MD [VascS] - **Spec Exp:** Carotid Artery Surgery; Aneurysm-Abdominal Aortic; Lower Limb Arterial Disease; **Hospital:** Tufts Med Ctr; **Address:** Tufts Medical Center, 800 Washington St, Box 1035, Boston, MA 02111; **Phone:** 617-636-5927; **Board Cert:** Surgery 2002; Vascular Surgery 2004; Surgical Critical Care 2007; **Med School:** Duke Univ 1977; **Resid:** Surgery, NY Presby/Weill Cornell Med Ctr 1982; **Fellow:** Vascular Surgery, Tufts-New Eng Med Ctr 1984; **Fac Appt:** Prof S, Tufts Univ

Pomposelli, Frank B MD [VascS] - **Spec Exp:** Diabetic Leg/Foot; Aortic Surgery; Carotid Artery Disease; Endovascular Surgery; **Hospital:** Steward St Elizabeth's Med Ctr-Boston; **Address:** St Elizabeth's Medical Center, Division of Vascular Surgery, 736 Cambridge St, CCP8, Brighton, MA 02135; **Phone:** 617-789-3309; **Board Cert:** Vascular Surgery 2008; **Med School:** Boston Univ 1979; **Resid:** Surgery, New England Deaconess Hosp 1986; **Fellow:** Peripheral Vascular Surgery, NYU Med Ctr 1987; **Fac Appt:** Prof S, Harvard Med Sch

Sumpio, Bauer E MD/PhD [VascS] - **Spec Exp:** Diabetic Leg/Foot; Endovascular Surgery; Peripheral Vascular Disease; Wound Healing/Care; **Hospital:** Yale-New Haven Hosp; **Address:** Heart & Vascular Ctr, 800 Howard Ave, Yale Physician's Bldg, New Haven, CT 06520; **Phone:** 203-785-6217; **Board Cert:** Vascular Surgery 2009; Surgery 2009; **Med School:** Cornell Univ-Weill Med Coll 1980; **Resid:** Surgery, Yale-New Haven Hosp 1986; **Fellow:** Vascular Surgery, Univ N Carolina Hosp 1987; **Fac Appt:** Prof S, Yale Univ

Mid Atlantic

Adelman, Mark MD [VascS] - **Spec Exp:** Carotid Artery Surgery; Aneurysm-Abdominal Aortic; Vein Disorders; Endovascular Surgery; **Hospital:** NYU Langone Med Ctr (page 68), Bellevue Hosp Ctr; **Address:** NYU Med Ctr, Vascular Surgery Dept, 530 1st Ave, Ste 6F, New York, NY 10016; **Phone:** 212-263-7311; **Board Cert:** Vascular Surgery 2012; **Med School:** NYU Sch Med 1985; **Resid:** Surgery, NYU Med Ctr 1990; **Fellow:** Vascular Surgery, NYU Med Ctr 1991; **Fac Appt:** Prof VascS, NYU Sch Med

Ascher, Enrico MD [VascS] - **Spec Exp:** Endovascular Surgery; Carotid Artery Surgery; Limb Sparing Surgery; Aneurysm; **Hospital:** Lutheran Med Ctr - Brooklyn; **Address:** Vascular Inst, 960 50th St, Brooklyn, NY 11219; **Phone:** 718-438-3800; **Board Cert:** Vascular Surgery 2004; **Med School:** Brazil 1974; **Resid:** Surgery, NY Med Coll 1981; **Fellow:** Vascular Surgery, Montefiore Med Ctr 1982; **Fac Appt:** Prof S, SUNY Downstate

Atnip, Robert G MD [VascS] - **Spec Exp:** Aneurysm-Abdominal Aortic; Peripheral Vascular Disease; Carotid Artery Disease; Endovascular Surgery; **Hospital:** Penn State Milton S Hershey Med Ctr; **Address:** Hershey Med Ctr, Div Vascular Surg, 500 University Drive, MC H053, Hershey, PA 17033-0850; **Phone:** 717-531-4554; **Board Cert:** Surgery 2005; Vascular Surgery 2007; Surgical Critical Care 2010; **Med School:** UAB Sch Med 1978; **Resid:** Surgery, Mass Genl Hosp 1984; **Fellow:** Vascular Surgery, Mass Genl Hosp 1985; **Fac Appt:** Prof S, Penn State Coll Med

Benckart, Daniel MD [VascS] - **Hospital:** Allegheny Genl Hosp; **Address:** Allegheny Genl Hosp-CVI1, 320 E North Ave, Pittsburgh, PA 15212; **Phone:** 412-359-8820; **Board Cert:** Thoracic Surgery 2004; Surgery 2012; Vascular Surgery 2010; **Med School:** Georgetown Univ 1977; **Resid:** Surgery, Vanderbilt Affil Hosp 1982; **Fellow:** Vascular Thoracic Surgery, NYU Med Ctr 1985; **Fac Appt:** Assoc Prof TS, Drexel Univ Coll Med

Benvenisty, Alan I MD [VascS] - **Spec Exp:** Renovascular Disease; Aneurysm-Aortic; Endovascular Surgery; Minimally Invasive Vascular Surgery; **Hospital:** St. Luke's - Roosevelt Hosp Ctr - St Luke's Hosp (page 56), St. Luke's - Roosevelt Hosp Ctr - Roosevelt Div (page 56); **Address:** 1090 Amsterdam Ave Fl 12, New York, NY 10025; **Phone:** 212-523-4706; **Board Cert:** Surgery 2004; Vascular Surgery 2009; **Med School:** Columbia P&S 1978; **Resid:** Surgery, NY-Presby/Columbia Univ Med Ctr 1983; **Fellow:** Vascular Surgery, NY-Presby/Columbia Univ Med Ctr 1984; Transplant Surgery, NY-Presby/Columbia Univ Med Ctr 1984; **Fac Appt:** Prof S, Columbia P&S

Brener, Bruce J MD [VascS] - **Spec Exp:** Endovascular Surgery; Minimally Invasive Vascular Surgery; Carotid Artery Surgery; Aneurysm-Aortic; **Hospital:** Newark Beth Israel Med Ctr, Saint Barnabas Med Ctr; **Address:** Vascular Assocs of NJ, 200 S Orange Ave, Ste 109, Livingston, NJ 07039; **Phone:** 973-322-7233; **Board Cert:** Surgery 1972; Vascular Surgery 2005; **Med School:** Harvard Med Sch 1966; **Resid:** Surgery, Chldns Hosp Med Ctr 1968; Surgery, Peter Bent Brigham Hosp 1972; **Fellow:** Vascular Surgery, Mass Genl Hosp 1973; **Fac Appt:** Assoc Clin Prof S, Columbia P&S

Calligaro, Keith D MD [VascS] - **Spec Exp:** Aneurysm-Abdominal & Thoracic Aortic; Carotid Artery Disease; Varicose Veins; Aortic Stent Grafts; **Hospital:** Pennsylvania Hosp-UPHS (page 69); **Address:** Pennsylvania Vascular Assocs, 700 Spruce St, Ste 101, Philadelphia, PA 19106; **Phone:** 215-829-5000; **Board Cert:** Vascular Surgery 2008; **Med School:** UMDNJ-Rutgers Med Sch 1982; **Resid:** Surgery, Univ Hlth Sci/Chicago Med 1987; **Fellow:** Vascular Surgery, Montefiore Med Ctr/Albert Einstein 1989; **Fac Appt:** Clin Prof VascS, Univ Pennsylvania

Carpenter, Jeffrey P MD [VascS] - **Spec Exp:** Endovascular Surgery; Peripheral Vascular Disease; Aneurysm-Abdominal & Thoracic Aortic; Carotid Artery Surgery; **Hospital:** Cooper Univ Hosp; **Address:** Three Cooper Plaza, Ste 411, Camden, NJ 08103; **Phone:** 856-342-3496; **Board Cert:** Vascular Surgery 2010; **Med School:** Yale Univ 1986; **Resid:** Surgery, Hosp Univ Penn 1991; **Fellow:** Vascular Surgery, Hosp Univ Penn 1993; **Fac Appt:** Prof S

Criado, Frank J MD [VascS] - **Spec Exp:** Endovascular Surgery; Aneurysm-Abdominal & Thoracic Aortic; Carotid Artery Surgery; **Hospital:** MedStar Union Meml Hosp; **Address:** 3333 N Calvert St, Ste 570, Baltimore, MD 21218; **Phone:** 410-554-6400; **Board Cert:** Vascular Surgery 2008; **Med School:** Uruguay 1974; **Resid:** Surgery, Union Meml Hosp 1980; Vascular Surgery, Union Meml Hosp 1985; **Fellow:** Cardiovascular Surgery, Baylor Univ Med Ctr 1981

D'Ayala, Marcus D MD [VascS] - **Spec Exp:** Endovascular Surgery; Aneurysm-Abdominal Aortic; Carotid Artery Disease; Peripheral Vascular Disease; **Hospital:** New York Methodist Hosp; **Address:** NY Methodist Hospital, Vascular Surgery, 506 Sixth St, Brooklyn, NY 11215; **Phone:** 718-780-3288; **Board Cert:** Surgery 2008; Vascular Surgery 2009; **Med School:** Univ Wisc 1992; **Resid:** Surgery, Montefiore Med Ctr 1997; **Fellow:** Vascular Surgery, Mt Sinai Med Ctr 1998; **Fac Appt:** Assoc Clin Prof S, Cornell Univ-Weill Med Coll

Darling III, R Clement MD [VascS] - **Spec Exp:** Aneurysm-Abdominal & Thoracic Aortic; Arterial Bypass Surgery; Carotid Artery Surgery; **Hospital:** Albany Med Ctr, St. Peter's Hosp - Albany; **Address:** AMC, Vascular Grp, 43 New Scotland Ave, MC 157, Albany, NY 12208; **Phone:** 518-262-5640; **Board Cert:** Vascular Surgery 2012; **Med School:** Univ Cincinnati 1984; **Resid:** Surgery, Beth Israel Deaconess Hosp 1989; **Fellow:** Vascular Surgery, Albany Med Ctr 1991; **Fac Appt:** Prof S, Albany Med Coll

Dougherty, Matthew J MD [VascS] - **Spec Exp:** Endovascular Stent Grafts; Aneurysm; Dialysis Access; Minimally Invasive Vascular Surgery; **Hospital:** Pennsylvania Hosp-UPHS (page 69); **Address:** Pennsylvania Vascular Assocs, 700 Spruce St, Ste 101, Philadelphia, PA 19106; **Phone:** 215-829-5000; **Board Cert:** Vascular Surgery 2012; **Med School:** Harvard Med Sch 1984; **Resid:** Surgery, Mass Genl Hosp 1991; **Fellow:** Vascular Surgery, Mayo Clinic 1993; **Fac Appt:** Assoc Clin Prof S, Univ Pennsylvania

Ellozy, Sharif Hamed MD [VascS] - **Spec Exp:** Endovascular Surgery; Aneurysm-Aortic; **Hospital:** Mt Sinai Med Ctr (page 62); **Address:** 5 E 98th St Fl 3, New York, NY 10029; **Phone:** 212-241-5315; **Board Cert:** Surgery 2004; Vascular Surgery 2005; **Med School:** NYU Sch Med 1996; **Resid:** Surgery, Mt Sinai Med Ctr 2002; **Fellow:** Vascular Surgery, Mt Sinai Med Ctr 2003; **Fac Appt:** Assoc Prof S, Mount Sinai Sch Med

Fairman, Ronald M MD [VascS] - **Spec Exp:** Aneurysm-Aortic; Peripheral Vascular Disease; Carotid Artery Surgery; Aneurysm-Abdominal & Thoracic Aortic; **Hospital:** Hosp Univ Penn - UPHS (page 69); **Address:** Penn Heart & Vascular Center, Perelman Ctr for Advanced Medicine, 3400 Civic Center Blvd, Fl 2-East, Philadelphia, PA 19104; **Phone:** 215-615-4949; **Board Cert:** Vascular Surgery 2010; **Med School:** Thomas Jefferson Univ 1977; **Resid:** Surgery, Hosp Univ Penn 1983; **Fellow:** Vascular Surgery, Hosp Univ Penn 1984; **Fac Appt:** Prof S, Univ Pennsylvania

Faries, Peter L MD [VascS] - **Spec Exp:** Aneurysm-Abdominal Aortic; Carotid Artery Surgery; Renovascular Disease; Peripheral Vascular Disease; **Hospital:** Mt Sinai Med Ctr (page 62); **Address:** 1425 Madison Ave, Box 1273, New York, NY 10029; **Phone:** 212-241-5386; **Board Cert:** Surgery 2008; Vascular Surgery 2009; **Med School:** Univ Pennsylvania 1992; **Resid:** Surgery, Montefiore Med Ctr 1998; **Fellow:** Vascular Surgery, Beth Israel Deaconess Med Ctr 2000; **Fac Appt:** Prof S, Mount Sinai Sch Med

Freischlag, Julie A MD [VascS] - **Spec Exp:** Aneurysm-Aortic; Carotid Artery Surgery; Thoracic Outlet Syndrome; **Hospital:** Johns Hopkins Hosp (page 59); **Address:** Johns Hopkins Hosp, Dept Surg, 720 Rutland Ave, Ross Bldg, Ste 759, Baltimore, MD 21205; **Phone:** 443-287-3497; **Board Cert:** Surgery 2005; Vascular Surgery 2005; **Med School:** Rush Med Coll 1980; **Resid:** Surgery, UCLA Med Ctr 1986; **Fellow:** Vascular Surgery, UCLA Med Ctr 1987; **Fac Appt:** Prof S, Johns Hopkins Univ

Golden, Michael A MD [VascS] - **Spec Exp:** Aneurysm; Endovascular Surgery; **Hospital:** Penn Presby Med Ctr - UPHS (page 69); **Address:** Penn Presbyterian Med Ctr, 51 N 39th St, Wright-Saunders Bldg, Ste 266, Philadelphia, PA 19104; **Phone:** 215-662-9660; **Board Cert:** Surgery 2007; Vascular Surgery 2010; **Med School:** Univ Pennsylvania 1981; **Resid:** Surgery, Brigham & Women's Hosp 1987; **Fellow:** Vascular Surgery, Brigham & Women's Hosp 1990; **Fac Appt:** Assoc Prof S, Univ Pennsylvania

Green, Richard M MD [VascS] - **Spec Exp:** Aneurysm-Abdominal Aortic; Carotid Artery Surgery; Percutaneous Vascular Interventions; **Hospital:** NY-Presby/Columbia Univ Med Ctr, NY (page 65); **Address:** NY-Presby, Vascular Surgery Dept, 161 Fort Washington Ave, rm 532, New York, NY 10032; **Phone:** 212-305-1165; **Board Cert:** Vascular Surgery 2003; **Med School:** Univ Rochester 1970; **Resid:** Surgery, Strong Meml Hosp 1976

Harrington, Elizabeth MD [VascS] - **Spec Exp:** Carotid Artery Surgery; Aneurysm-Aortic; Arterial Bypass Surgery-Leg; **Hospital:** Mt Sinai Med Ctr (page 62); **Address:** 2 E 93rd St, New York, NY 10128; **Phone:** 212-876-7400; **Board Cert:** Surgery 2009; Vascular Surgery 2006; **Med School:** NY Med Coll 1975; **Resid:** Surgery, Mount Sinai Med Ctr 1980; **Fellow:** Vascular Surgery, Mount Sinai Med Ctr 1981; **Fac Appt:** Assoc Prof VascS, Mount Sinai Sch Med

Lantis II, John C MD [VascS] - **Spec Exp:** Limb Sparing Surgery; Wound Healing/Care; Endovascular Surgery; Carotid Artery Stent Placement; **Hospital:** St. Luke's - Roosevelt Hosp Ctr - Roosevelt Div (page 56), St. Luke's - Roosevelt Hosp Ctr - St Luke's Hosp (page 56); **Address:** St Lukes-Roosevelt Hosp, Surgery Dept, 1090 Amsterdam Ave, Ste 7A, New York, NY 10025; **Phone:** 212-523-4797; **Board Cert:** Surgery 2009; Vascular Surgery 2010; **Med School:** Albany Med Coll 1993; **Resid:** Surgery, Tufts Med Ctr 1999; **Fellow:** Vascular Surgery, Brigham & Womens Hosp 2000; **Fac Appt:** Asst Prof S, Columbia P&S

Makaroun, Michel S MD [VascS] - **Spec Exp:** Aneurysm-Aortic; Carotid Artery Disease; Endovascular Surgery; Peripheral Vascular Disease; **Hospital:** UPMC Shadyside, UPMC Presby, Pittsburgh; **Address:** Chrmn-Div Vascular Surg, Presby Univ Hosp, Ste A1011, 200 Lothrop St, Pittsburgh, PA 15213; **Phone:** 412-802-3333; **Board Cert:** Surgery 2004; Vascular Surgery 2009; **Med School:** Lebanon 1978; **Resid:** Surgery, American Univ Hosp 1980; Surgery, Univ Pittsburgh Med Ctr 1985; **Fac Appt:** Prof S, Univ Pittsburgh

Marin, Michael L MD [VascS] - **Spec Exp:** Aneurysm-Aortic; Peripheral Vascular Disease; Limb Sparing Surgery; Endovascular Surgery; **Hospital:** Mt Sinai Med Ctr (page 62); **Address:** Mount Sinai Med Ctr, Vascular Surgery, 5 E 98th St Fl 3, Box 1273, New York, NY 10029; **Phone:** 212-241-5315; **Board Cert:** Surgery 2011; **Med School:** Mount Sinai Sch Med 1984; **Resid:** Surgery, NY-Presby/Columbia Univ Med Ctr 1990; **Fellow:** Transplant Surgery, NY-Presby/Columbia Univ Med Ctr 1988; Vascular Surgery, Montefiore Med Ctr 1992; **Fac Appt:** Prof S, Mount Sinai Sch Med

McKinsey, James F MD [VascS] - **Spec Exp:** Aneurysm-Abdominal Aortic; Endovascular Surgery; Carotid Artery Surgery; **Hospital:** NY-Presby/Columbia Univ Med Ctr, NY (page 65); **Address:** NY-Presby, Vascular Surgery Dept, 161 Fort Washington Ave, rm 535, New York, NY 10032; **Phone:** 212-342-3255; **Board Cert:** Surgery 2001; Vascular Surgery 2003; **Med School:** Univ Fla Coll Med 1987; **Resid:** Surgery, Georgia Baptist Med Ctr 1992; **Fellow:** Vascular Surgery, Univ Chicago Hosps 1993; **Fac Appt:** Assoc Prof S, Columbia P&S

Morrissey, Nicholas J MD [VascS] - **Spec Exp:** Endovascular Surgery; Aneurysm-Abdominal & Thoracic Aortic; Carotid Artery Surgery; **Hospital:** NY-Presby/Columbia Univ Med Ctr, NY (page 65); **Address:** 161 Fort Washington Ave, Herbert Irving Pavilion, rm 538, New York, NY 10032; **Phone:** 212-342-2929; **Board Cert:** Surgery 2009; Vascular Surgery 2012; **Med School:** Univ Rochester 1992; **Resid:** Surgery, Strong Meml Hosp 1999; **Fellow:** Vascular Surgery, Mount Sinai Hosp 2001; **Fac Appt:** Assoc Prof S, Columbia P&S

Neville Jr, Richard F MD [VascS] - **Spec Exp:** Endovascular Surgery; Wound Healing/Care; **Hospital:** G Washington Univ Hosp, Inova Mt Vernon Hosp; **Address:** 2150 Pennsylvania Ave NW, Fl 6B, rm 407, PHC Bldg - Fl 4, Washington, DC 20037; **Phone:** 202-741-3210; **Board Cert:** Vascular Surgery 2012; **Med School:** Univ MD Sch Med 1983; **Resid:** Surgery, Georgetown Univ Hosp 1988; **Fellow:** Vascular Surgery, UMDNJ Affil Hosp 1991; **Fac Appt:** Prof S, Geo Wash Univ

Perler, Bruce MD [VascS] - **Spec Exp:** Carotid Artery Surgery; Aneurysm; Arterial Bypass Surgery-Leg; **Hospital:** Johns Hopkins Hosp (page 59), Johns Hopkins Bayview Med Ctr (page 59); **Address:** Johns Hopkins Hosp, Div Vascular Surg, 600 N Wolfe St, Halsted 668, Baltimore, MD 21287; **Phone:** 410-955-2618; **Board Cert:** Vascular Surgery 2008; **Med School:** Duke Univ 1976; **Resid:** Surgery, Mass Genl Hosp 1981; **Fellow:** Vascular Surgery, Mass Genl Hosp 1982; **Fac Appt:** Prof S, Johns Hopkins Univ

Ricotta, John MD [VascS] - **Spec Exp:** Aneurysm; Carotid Artery Surgery; Vein Disorders; **Hospital:** MedStar Washington Hosp Ctr; **Address:** 110 Irving St NW, rm G253, Washington, DC 20010; **Phone:** 202-877-5133; **Board Cert:** Surgery 2004; Vascular Surgery 2003; **Med School:** Johns Hopkins Univ 1973; **Resid:** Surgery, Johns Hopkins Hosp 1980; **Fac Appt:** Prof S, Georgetown Univ

Schneider, Darren B MD [VascS] - **Spec Exp:** Endovascular Surgery; Minimally Invasive Vascular Surgery; Aneurysm-Aortic; Peripheral Vascular Disease; **Hospital:** NY-Presby/Weill Cornell Med Ctr, NY (page 65); **Address:** NY-Presby, Vascular Surgery Dept, 525 E 68th St Starr Bldg Fl 8, New York, NY 10065; **Phone:** 212-746-5192; **Med School:** UCSD 1992; **Resid:** Surgery, UCSF Med Ctr 2000; **Fellow:** Interventional Radiology, UCSF Med Ctr 2001; Vascular Surgery, UCSF Med Ctr 2002; **Fac Appt:** Assoc Prof S, Cornell Univ-Weill Med Coll

Todd, George MD [VascS] - **Spec Exp:** Minimally Invasive Vascular Surgery; Aneurysm-Abdominal Aortic; Carotid Artery Surgery; **Hospital:** St. Luke's - Roosevelt Hosp Ctr - Roosevelt Div (page 56); **Address:** St Lukes Hosp, Vascular Surgery Dept, 1000 10th Ave, rm 5G77, New York, NY 10019; **Phone:** 212-523-7481; **Board Cert:** Surgery 2010; Vascular Surgery 2006; **Med School:** Penn State Coll Med 1974; **Resid:** Surgery, NY-Presby/Columbia Univ Med Ctr 1979; **Fellow:** Vascular Surgery, NY-Presby/Columbia Univ Med Ctr 1980; **Fac Appt:** Prof S, Columbia P&S

Southeast

Cherry Jr, Kenneth J MD [VascS] - **Spec Exp:** Vascular Reconstruction; Aortic Graft Infections; **Hospital:** Univ of Virginia Hlth Sys; **Address:** Heart & Vascular Ctr, 1215 Lee St Fl 2, Charlottesville, VA 22908-0679; **Phone:** 434-243-7052; **Board Cert:** Vascular Surgery 2004; **Med School:** Univ VA Sch Med 1974; **Resid:** Surgery, Univ Virginia Hosp 1980; Vascular Surgery, UCSF Med Ctr 1981; **Fac Appt:** Prof S, Univ VA Sch Med

Dattilo, Jeffery B MD [VascS] - **Spec Exp:** Aneurysm-Abdominal Aortic; Carotid Artery Disease; **Hospital:** Vanderbilt Univ Med Ctr, VA Tennessee Valley Healthcare System-Alvin C. Yor; **Address:** Vanderbilt University Medical Center, 1161 22nd Ave S, D-5237 Medical Center North, Nashville, TN 37232-2735; **Phone:** 615-322-2343; **Board Cert:** Surgery 2011; Vascular Surgery 2005; **Med School:** E Carolina Univ 1993; **Resid:** Surgery, Medical College of Virginia Hosp 2000; **Fellow:** Vascular Surgery, Mass Genl Hosp 2002; **Fac Appt:** Assoc Prof S, Vanderbilt Univ

Eidt, John F MD [VascS] - **Spec Exp:** Aneurysm-Abdominal Aortic; Carotid Artery Stent Placement; Endovascular Surgery; Peripheral Vascular Disease; **Hospital:** Greenville Hlth Sys; **Address:** 200 Patewood Drive, Ste C300, Greenwood, SC 29615; **Phone:** 864-454-8272; **Board Cert:** Surgery 2004; Vascular Surgery 2006; **Med School:** Univ Tex SW, Dallas 1981; **Resid:** Surgery, Brigham-Womens Hosp 1986; **Fellow:** Vascular Surgery, Univ Tex SW Med Ctr 1988

Hakaim, Albert G MD [VascS] - **Spec Exp:** Aneurysm-Abdominal Aortic; Endovascular Surgery; **Hospital:** Mayo - Jacksonville; **Address:** Mayo Clin, Vascular Surgery Dept, 4500 San Pablo Rd, Ste 323N, Jacksonville, FL 32224; **Phone:** 904-953-2077; **Board Cert:** Surgery 2002; Vascular Surgery 2003; **Med School:** Ohio State Univ 1984; **Resid:** Surgery, Cleveland Clin 1989; **Fellow:** Transplant Surgery, Boston Med Ctr 1991; Vascular Surgery, Cleveland Clin 1992; **Fac Appt:** Prof S, Mayo Med Sch

Hallett Jr, John W MD [VascS] - **Spec Exp:** Aneurysm-Abdominal Aortic; Carotid Artery Surgery; Thoracic Outlet Syndrome; **Hospital:** Roper Hosp; **Address:** Roper St Francis Heart & Vascular Ctr, 316 Calhoun St, Charleston, SC 29401; **Phone:** 843-720-5665; **Board Cert:** Vascular Surgery 2003; **Med School:** Duke Univ 1973; **Resid:** Surgery, Wilford Hall USAF Med Ctr 1978; **Fellow:** Vascular Surgery, Mass Genl Hosp-Harvard Med Sch 1979; **Fac Appt:** Assoc Clin Prof VascS, Med Univ SC

Huber, Thomas S MD/PhD [VascS] - **Spec Exp:** Aortic & Visceral Artery Surgery; Aortic Surgery-Complex; Dialysis Access; Endovascular Surgery; **Hospital:** UF Hlth Shands Hosp; **Address:** Shands, Vascular Surgery Dept, 1600 SW Archer Rd, Box 100286, Gainesville, FL 32610; **Phone:** 352-392-9928; **Board Cert:** Surgery 2002; Vascular Surgery 2004; **Med School:** Univ Mich Med Sch 1985; **Resid:** Surgery, Univ Michigan Med Ctr 1992; **Fellow:** Vascular Surgery, Univ Michigan Med Ctr 1994; **Fac Appt:** Prof S, Univ Fla Coll Med

McCann, Richard L MD [VascS] - **Spec Exp:** Endovascular Surgery; **Hospital:** Duke Univ Hosp; **Address:** Duke Univ Med Ctr, Box 2990, Durham, NC 27710; **Phone:** 919-681-2406; **Board Cert:** Surgery 2003; Vascular Surgery 2006; **Med School:** Cornell Univ-Weill Med Coll 1974; **Resid:** Surgery, Duke Univ Med Ctr 1983; **Fac Appt:** Prof S, Duke Univ

Mitchell, Marc E MD [VascS] - **Spec Exp:** Renal Artery Stenosis; Carotid Artery Surgery; Aneurysm-Aortic; Peripheral Vascular Disease; **Hospital:** Univ Mississippi Med Ctr; **Address:** Univ Mississippi Med Ctr, Dept Surgery, 2500 N State St, Jackson, MS 39216; **Phone:** 601-984-5105; **Board Cert:** Surgery 2010; Surgical Critical Care 2005; Vascular Surgery 2007; **Med School:** Georgetown Univ 1984; **Resid:** Surgery, UCSF Med Ctr 1986; Surgery, Univ Mississippi Med Ctr 1991; **Fellow:** Cardiac Surgery, Natl Inst Hlth 1998; Vascular Surgery, Univ Penn 1997; **Fac Appt:** Prof S, Univ Miss

Naslund, Thomas C MD [VascS] - **Spec Exp:** Endovascular Surgery; Aneurysm-Aortic; **Hospital:** Vanderbilt Univ Med Ctr; **Address:** Vanderbilt Vascular Surgery, 1215 21st Ave S, Ste 5209, Nashville, TN 37232; **Phone:** 615-343-2887; **Board Cert:** Vascular Surgery 2011; Surgery 2011; **Med School:** Vanderbilt Univ 1984; **Resid:** Surgery, Vanderbilt Univ Med Ctr 1990; **Fellow:** Vascular Surgery, Ochsner Med Fdn 1992; **Fac Appt:** Prof S, Vanderbilt Univ

Midwest

Acher, Charles W MD [VascS] - **Spec Exp:** Endovascular Surgery; Peripheral Vascular Disease; **Hospital:** Univ WI Hosp & Clins; **Address:** Univ WI Hosp - Div Vascular Surgery, 451 Junction Rd, Madison, WI 53717; **Phone:** 608-265-4420; **Board Cert:** Vascular Surgery 2008; **Med School:** Indiana Univ 1973; **Resid:** Surgery, Univ WI Hosp & Clins 1978; **Fellow:** Peripheral Vascular Surgery, Gloucestershire Royal Hosp 1980; Vascular Surgery, Baylor Coll of Med 1983; **Fac Appt:** Prof S, Univ Wisc

Alexander, J. Jeffrey MD [VascS] - **Spec Exp:** Peripheral Vascular Disease; Carotid Artery Disease; Dialysis Access; **Hospital:** MetroHealth Med Ctr; **Address:** MetroHealth Med Ctr, Heart/Vascular Dept, 2500 MetroHealth Drive, Ste H328, Cleveland, OH 44109-1998; **Phone:** 216-778-4811; **Board Cert:** Surgery 2002; Vascular Surgery 2006; **Med School:** Univ Pittsburgh 1978; **Resid:** Surgery, Univ Chicago Hosps 1983; **Fellow:** Vascular Surgery, Univ Chicago Hosps 1984; **Fac Appt:** Assoc Prof S, Case West Res Univ

Cho, Jae Sung MD [VascS] - **Spec Exp:** Aneurysm; Carotid Artery Disease; Thoracic Outlet Syndrome; Minimally Invasive Vascular Surgery; **Hospital:** Loyola Univ Med Ctr, Gottlieb Meml Hosp; **Address:** 2160 S First Ave, EMS 110 Bldg - rm 3215, Maywood, IL 60153; **Phone:** 708-327-2387; **Board Cert:** Surgery 2006; Vascular Surgery 2009; **Med School:** UC Irvine 1990; **Resid:** Surgery, Univ Rochester Affil Hosp 1996; **Fellow:** Vascular Surgery, Mayo Clinic 1998; **Fac Appt:** Prof S, Loyola Univ-Stritch Sch Med

Clair, Daniel G MD [VascS] - **Spec Exp:** Carotid Artery Surgery; Aneurysm-Abdominal & Thoracic Aortic; Peripheral Vascular Disease; Endovascular Stent Grafts; **Hospital:** Cleveland Clin (page 55); **Address:** Cleveland Clin, Dept Vascular Surg, 9500 Euclid Ave, Desk H32, Cleveland, OH 44195; **Phone:** 216-444-3857; **Board Cert:** Surgery 2011; Vascular Surgery 2004; **Med School:** Univ VA Sch Med 1986; **Resid:** Surgery, Brigham & Women's Hosp 1992; **Fellow:** Oncology, Brigham & Women's Hosp 1991; Vascular Surgery, Brigham & Women's Hosp 1994

Comerota, Anthony J MD [VascS] - **Spec Exp:** Carotid Artery Disease; Gene Therapy; Aneurysm-Aortic; Peripheral Vascular Disease; **Hospital:** Toledo Hosp; **Address:** Jobst Vascular Inst, 2109 Hughes Drive, Ste 400, Toledo, OH 43606; **Phone:** 419-291-2088; **Board Cert:** Vascular Surgery 2003; **Med School:** Temple Univ 1974; **Resid:** Surgery, Temple Univ Hosp 1978; **Fellow:** Vascular Surgery, Good Samaritan Hosp 1981; **Fac Appt:** Clin Prof S, Univ Mich Med Sch

Dalsing, Michael C MD [VascS] - **Spec Exp:** Peripheral Vascular Disease; Carotid Artery Disease; Aortic Reconstruction; Percutaneous Vascular Interventions; **Hospital:** IU Health Methodist Hosp, IU Hlth Univ Hosp; **Address:** 1801 N Senate Blvd, Ste 4400, Indianapolis, IN 46202; **Phone:** 317-962-0280; **Board Cert:** Surgery 2012; Vascular Surgery 2003; Surgical Critical Care 2011; **Med School:** Med Coll Wisc 1978; **Resid:** Surgery, Indiana Univ Med Ctr 1983; **Fellow:** Vascular Surgery, Northwestern Univ Med Ctr 1984; **Fac Appt:** Prof S, Indiana Univ

Eton, Darwin MD [VascS] - **Spec Exp:** Aneurysm; Arterial Reconsatruction; Cerebrovascular Disease; Dialysis Access; **Hospital:** Univ of Chicago Med; **Address:** 5841 S Maryland Ave, MC 5028, Chicago, IL 60637; **Phone:** 773-702-6128; **Board Cert:** Surgery 2007; Vascular Surgery 2011; **Med School:** NYU Sch Med 1982; **Resid:** Surgery, UCLA Med Ctr 1984; Surgery, St Louis Univ Hosp 1988; **Fellow:** Vascular Surgery, Univ IL Med Ctr 1990; Endovascular Surgery, UCLA Med Ctr 1991; **Fac Appt:** Prof S, Univ Chicago-Pritzker Sch Med

Gloviczki, Peter MD [VascS] - **Spec Exp:** Aneurysm-Abdominal Aortic; Lower Limb Arterial Disease; Vein Disorders; **Hospital:** Mayo Med Ctr & Clin - Rochester; **Address:** Mayo Clin, Div Vasc Surg, 200 First St SW, Rochester, MN 55905-0001; **Phone:** 507-284-4652; **Board Cert:** Surgery 2010; Vascular Surgery 2008; **Med School:** Hungary 1972; **Resid:** Vascular Surgery, Semmelweis Med Sch 1980; Surgery, Mayo Clin 1987; **Fellow:** Vascular Surgery, Mayo Clin 1984; **Fac Appt:** Prof S, Mayo Med Sch

Greisler, Howard MD [VascS] - **Spec Exp:** Peripheral Vascular Disease; Aneurysm; Carotid Artery Disease; **Hospital:** Edward Hines, Jr. VA Hosp; **Address:** VA Hospital, 5000 S 5th Ave, Bldg 1, rm C417, Hines, IL 60141; **Phone:** 708-202-2036; **Board Cert:** Vascular Surgery 2003; **Med School:** Penn State Coll Med 1975; **Resid:** Surgery, Columbia Presby Med Ctr 1980; **Fellow:** Vascular Surgery, Columbia Presby Med Ctr 1981; **Fac Appt:** Prof S, Loyola Univ-Stritch Sch Med

Hodgson, Kim John MD [VascS] - **Spec Exp:** Aneurysm; Carotid Artery Surgery; Endovascular Surgery; **Hospital:** Memorial Med Ctr-Springfield, St. John's Hosp - Springfield; **Address:** 747 N Rutledge Fl 5, Box 19638, Springfield, IL 62794; **Phone:** 217-545-8000; **Board Cert:** Vascular Surgery 2005; **Med School:** Univ Pennsylvania 1981; **Resid:** Surgery, Albany Med Ctr 1986; **Fellow:** Vascular Surgery, Southern Ill Univ 1987; **Fac Appt:** Prof VascS, Southern IL Univ

Kazmers, Andris MD [VascS] - **Spec Exp:** Aneurysm-Abdominal & Thoracic Aortic; Carotid Artery Stent Placement; Angioplasty & Stent Placement; Endovascular Surgery; **Hospital:** Northern Michigan Hosp; **Address:** Petoskey Surgeons, 521 Monroe St, Petoskey, MI 49770; **Phone:** 231-487-1900; **Board Cert:** Vascular Surgery 2005; Surgery 2010; Surgical Critical Care 2010; **Med School:** Wayne State Univ 1976; **Resid:** Surgery, Univ Michigan Hosps 1982; **Fellow:** Vascular Surgery, Univ Michigan Hosps 1984

Kent, Kenneth C MD [VascS] - **Spec Exp:** Carotid Artery Surgery; Aneurysm-Abdominal Aortic; Lower Limb Arterial Disease; **Hospital:** Univ WI Hosp & Clins, Meriter Hosp; **Address:** Univ Wisconsin-Madison, Dept Surgery, H4/710D Clinical Sciences Ctr, 600 Highland Ave, Box 7375, Madison, WI 53792-7375; **Phone:** 608-265-8854; **Board Cert:** Surgery 2007; Vascular Surgery 2008; **Med School:** UCSF 1981; **Resid:** Surgery, UCSF Med Ctr 1986; **Fellow:** Vascular Surgery, Brigham & Women's Hosp 1988; **Fac Appt:** Prof VascS, Univ Wisc

Pearce, William H MD [VascS] - **Spec Exp:** Aneurysm-Abdominal Aortic; Peripheral Vascular Disease; Vein Disorders; **Hospital:** Northwestern Meml Hosp, Northwestern Lake Forest Hosp; **Address:** 675 N St Clair St, Ste 19-100, Chicago, IL 60611-2647; **Phone:** 312-695-2714; **Board Cert:** Surgery 2010; Vascular Surgery 2003; **Med School:** Univ Colorado 1975; **Resid:** Surgery, Univ Co Hlth Sci Ctr 1981; **Fellow:** Vascular Surgery, Northwestern Meml Hosp 1982; **Fac Appt:** Prof S, Northwestern Univ

Sanchez, Luis A MD [VascS] - **Spec Exp:** Aneurysm-Abdominal & Thoracic Aortic; Endovascular Stent Grafts; Peripheral Vascular Disease; **Hospital:** Barnes-Jewish Hosp, Barnes-Jewish West County Hosp; **Address:** Washington Univ Sch Med, 660 S Euclid Ave, Box 8109, St Louis, MO 63110; **Phone:** 314-362-7408; **Board Cert:** Surgery 2004; Vascular Surgery 2003; **Med School:** Harvard Med Sch 1987; **Resid:** Surgery, Montefiore Med Ctr 1992; **Fellow:** Vascular Surgery, Montefiore Med Ctr 1994; **Fac Appt:** Prof VascS, Washington Univ, St Louis

Shepard, Alexander D MD [VascS] - **Spec Exp:** Aneurysm-Aortic; Aortic Reconstruction; **Hospital:** Henry Ford Hosp; **Address:** 2799 W Grand Blvd, Ste K8, Detroit, MI 48202-2608; **Phone:** 313-916-3155; **Board Cert:** Surgery 2012; Vascular Surgery 2005; **Med School:** Johns Hopkins Univ 1976; **Resid:** Surgery, Johns Hopkins Hosp 1982; **Fellow:** Vascular Surgery, New England Med Ctr 1985; **Fac Appt:** Prof S, Wayne State Univ

Sicard, Gregorio A MD [VascS] - **Spec Exp:** Aneurysm-Abdominal Aortic; **Hospital:** Barnes-Jewish Hosp; **Address:** Washington Univ Sch Med, 660 S Euclid Ave, Box 8109, St Louis, MO 63110; **Phone:** 314-362-7841; **Board Cert:** Vascular Surgery 2002; **Med School:** Univ Puerto Rico 1972; **Resid:** Surgery, Barnes Hosp 1977; **Fellow:** Transplant Surgery, Wash Univ Hosp 1978; **Fac Appt:** Prof S, Washington Univ, St Louis

Stanley, James C MD [VascS] - **Spec Exp:** Peripheral Vascular Disease; Renovascular Disease; Aneurysm; **Hospital:** Univ Michigan Med Ctr; **Address:** Univ Mich, Dept Vascular Surg, 1500 E Med Ctr Drive, CVC SPC 5167, Ann Arbor, MI 48109-5867; **Phone:** 734-936-5820; **Board Cert:** Surgery 1973; Vascular Surgery 2001; **Med School:** Univ Mich Med Sch 1964; **Resid:** Surgery, Univ Mich Med Ctr 1972; **Fac Appt:** Prof S, Univ Mich Med Sch

Great Plains and Mountains

Annest, Stephen J MD [VascS] - **Spec Exp:** Thoracic Outlet Syndrome; **Hospital:** Presby - St Luke's Med Ctr, Exempla Saint Jos. Hosp.-Denver; **Address:** Vascular Inst of the Rockies, 1601 E 19th Ave, Ste 3950, Denver, CO 80218; **Phone:** 303-539-0736; **Board Cert:** Surgery 2000; Vascular Surgery 2005; **Med School:** Univ Wash 1975; **Resid:** Surgery, Albany Med Ctr 1981; **Fellow:** Trauma, Albany Med Ctr 1980; Vascular Surgery, Baylor Med Ctr 1982

Cooper, Michael A MD [VascS] - **Spec Exp:** Peripheral Vascular Disease; **Hospital:** Rose Med Ctr; **Address:** CO Cardiovascular Surgical Assocs, 4600 E Hale Pkwy, Ste 460, Denver, CO 80220; **Phone:** 303-388-7265; **Board Cert:** Surgery 2008; Vascular Surgery 2012; **Med School:** Univ Nebr Coll Med 1984; **Resid:** Surgery, Univ Kansas Med Ctr 1989; **Fellow:** Vascular Surgery, LSU Med Ctr 1992

Howard, Thomas C MD [VascS] - **Spec Exp:** Aortic Surgery; Aneurysm-Aortic; Carotid Artery Surgery; Lower Limb Arterial Disease; **Hospital:** Nebraska Med Ctr; **Address:** Surgery Ctr of the Heartland, 4242 Farnam St, Ste 490, Omaha, NE 68131; **Phone:** 402-552-3015; **Board Cert:** Surgery 1975; Vascular Surgery 2002; **Med School:** Yale Univ 1969; **Resid:** Surgery, Yale-New Haven Hosp 1974; **Fac Appt:** Assoc Prof S, Univ Nebr Coll Med

Weinstein, Eric S MD [VascS] - **Spec Exp:** Endovascular Surgery; Aneurysm-Abdominal Aortic; Stroke; **Hospital:** Porter Adventist Hosp; **Address:** CO Cardiovascular Surgical Assocs, 950 E Harvard Ave, Ste 550, Denver, CO 80210; **Phone:** 303-778-6257; **Board Cert:** Vascular Surgery 2009; **Med School:** SUNY Buffalo 1981; **Resid:** Surgery, Case Western Reserve Univ 1988; **Fellow:** Research, Case Western Reserve Univ 1985; Vascular Surgery, UCSF Med Ctr 1999

Southwest

Blebea, John MD [VascS] - **Spec Exp:** Endovascular Surgery; Radiofrequency Tumor Ablation; **Hospital:** St. John Med Ctr, OU Med Ctr; **Address:** 1919 S Wheeling Ave, Ste 600, Tulsa, OK 74104; **Phone:** 918-634-7500; **Board Cert:** Vascular Surgery 2012; **Med School:** Case West Res Univ 1982; **Resid:** Surgery, MedStar Georgetown Univ Hosp 1985; Surgery, UMDNJ Affil Hosp 1988; **Fellow:** Vascular Surgery, Univ Rochester Affil Hosp 1991; Endovascular Surgery, Univ Pittsburgh Med Ctr 2001; **Fac Appt:** Prof S, Univ Okla Coll Med

Fowl, Richard J MD [VascS] - **Spec Exp:** Aneurysm-Aortic; Carotid Artery Surgery; Arterial Bypass Surgery-Leg; Endovascular Surgery; **Hospital:** Mayo Clinic - Phoenix; **Address:** Mayo Clinic, Dept Vascular Surgery, 5779 E Mayo Blvd, Phoenix, AZ 85054; **Phone:** 480-342-2868; **Board Cert:** Surgery 2011; Vascular Surgery 2004; **Med School:** Rush Med Coll 1978; **Resid:** Surgery, MCV Affil Hosp 1980; Surgery, Univ Iowa Med Ctr 1983; **Fellow:** Vascular Surgery, Mayo Clinic 1985; Endovascular Surgery, Cornell-Weill Med Coll 2004; **Fac Appt:** Prof S, Mayo Med Sch

Hollier, Larry H MD [VascS] - **Spec Exp:** Aortic Surgery; Carotid Artery Surgery; Endovascular Surgery; Aneurysm; **Hospital:** West Jefferson Med Ctr, LSU Interim Public Hosp; **Address:** 433 Bolivar St, Ste 815, New Orleans, LA 70112; **Phone:** 504-568-4800; **Board Cert:** Surgery 2007; Vascular Surgery 2012; **Med School:** Louisiana State U, New Orleans 1968; **Resid:** Surgery, Charity Hosp 1975; Vascular Surgery, Baylor Univ Med Ctr 1974; **Fellow:** Vascular Surgery, Baylor Univ Med Ctr 1974; **Fac Appt:** Prof S, Louisiana State U, New Orleans

Kougias, Panagiotis MD [VascS] - **Spec Exp:** Vascular Reconstruction; Carotid Artery Surgery; Stroke; Endovascular Surgery; **Hospital:** DeBakey VA Med Ctr-Houston; **Address:** DeBakey VA Med Ctr, Vascular Surgery, 2002 Holcombe Blvd, Houston, TX 77030; **Phone:** 713-794-7892; **Board Cert:** Surgery 2005; Vascular Surgery 2007; **Med School:** Greece 1992; **Resid:** Surgery, E Tenn State Univ Affil Hosp 2004; **Fellow:** Vascular Surgery, Baylor Affil Hosp 2006; **Fac Appt:** Assoc Prof VascS, Baylor Coll Med

Lumsden, Alan B MD [VascS] - **Spec Exp:** Aortic Stent Grafts; Minimally Invasive Surgery; Vein Disorders; **Hospital:** Methodist Hosp - Houston; **Address:** BCM, Vascular Surgery, 6550 Fannin St, Smith Tower, Ste 1401, Houston, TX 77030; **Phone:** 713-441-5200; **Board Cert:** Vascular Surgery 2012; **Med School:** Scotland, UK 1981; **Resid:** Surgery, Emory Univ Hosp 1987; **Fellow:** Vascular Surgery, Emory Univ Hosp 1989; **Fac Appt:** Prof VascS, Baylor Coll Med

Money, Samuel R MD [VascS] - **Spec Exp:** Aneurysm-Abdominal Aortic; Arterial Bypass Surgery-Leg; Endovascular Surgery; Aneurysm; **Hospital:** Mayo Clinic - Phoenix; **Address:** Mayo Clinic, Dept Vascular Surgery, 5779 E Mayo Blvd, Phoenix, AZ 85054; **Phone:** 480-342-2868; **Board Cert:** Vascular Surgery 2002; **Med School:** SUNY Downstate 1983; **Resid:** Surgery, Kings Co Med Ctr 1990; **Fellow:** Vascular Surgery, Ochsner Clinic 1993; **Fac Appt:** Prof S, Mayo Med Sch

West Coast and Pacific

Ahn, Sam S MD [VascS] - **Spec Exp:** Minimally Invasive Vascular Surgery; Endovascular Surgery; Thoracic Outlet Syndrome; Hyperhidrosis; **Hospital:** UCLA Ronald Reagan Med Ctr, St. John's Hlth Ctr, Santa Monica; **Address:** University Vascular Associates, 1082 Glendon Ave, Los Angeles, CA 90024; **Phone:** 310-209-2011 x3; **Board Cert:** Surgery 2004; Vascular Surgery 2008; **Med School:** Univ Tex SW, Dallas 1978; **Resid:** Surgery, UCLA Med Ctr 1984; **Fellow:** Vascular Surgery, UCLA Med Ctr 1986; **Fac Appt:** Prof S, UCLA

Bandyk, Dennis F MD [VascS] - **Spec Exp:** Endovascular Stent Grafts; Lower Limb Arterial Disease; Thoracic Outlet Syndrome; **Hospital:** UCSD Med Ctr; **Address:** 9434 Medical Center Drive, MC 7241, La Jolla, CA 92037; **Phone:** 619-543-6980; **Board Cert:** Vascular Surgery 2012; **Med School:** Univ Mich Med Sch 1975; **Resid:** Surgery, Univ Wash Hosp 1980; **Fellow:** Vascular Surgery, Univ Wash Hosp 1981; **Fac Appt:** Prof S, UCSD

Flanigan, D Preston MD [VascS] - **Spec Exp:** Carotid Artery Surgery; Aneurysm; Vein Disorders; Minimally Invasive Surgery; **Hospital:** St. Joseph's Hosp - Orange; **Address:** Vascular & Interventional Specialists, 1140 W La Veta Ave, Ste 850, Orange, CA 92868; **Phone:** 714-560-4450; **Board Cert:** Vascular Surgery 2011; **Med School:** Jefferson Med Coll 1972; **Resid:** Surgery, St Joseph-Mercy Hosp 1977; **Fellow:** Vascular Surgery, Northwest Med Ctr 1979; **Fac Appt:** Clin Prof S, UC Irvine

Gewertz, Bruce MD [VascS] - **Spec Exp:** Carotid Artery Surgery; Peripheral Vascular Disease; Aneurysm-Aortic; Renovascular Disease; **Hospital:** Cedars-Sinai Med Ctr; **Address:** 8700 Beverly Blvd, Ste 8215, North Tower, Los Angeles, CA 90048; **Phone:** 310-423-5884; **Board Cert:** Vascular Surgery 2012; **Med School:** Jefferson Med Coll 1972; **Resid:** Surgery, Univ Mich Hosp 1977; Vascular Surgery, Univ Mich Hosp 1981; **Fac Appt:** Prof S, UCLA

Pevec, William C MD [VascS] - **Spec Exp:** Vascular Disease; Aortic Reconstruction; Endovascular Surgery; Lower Limb Arterial Disease; **Hospital:** UC Davis Med Ctr; **Address:** UC Davis Vascular Center, 4860 Y St, Ste 2100, Sacramento, CA 95817; **Phone:** 916-734-3800; **Board Cert:** Surgery 1999; Vascular Surgery 2001; **Med School:** Univ Cincinnati 1984; **Resid:** Surgery, Univ Pittsburgh Med Ctr 1990; **Fellow:** Vascular Surgery, Mass Genl Hosp 1992; **Fac Appt:** Prof VascS, UC Davis

White, Rodney A MD [VascS] - **Spec Exp:** Aneurysm; Carotid Artery Surgery; Aortic Surgery-Complex; Endovascular Surgery; **Hospital:** LAC - Harbor - UCLA Med Ctr; **Address:** Harbor-UCLA Med Ctr, 1000 W Carson St, Torrance, CA 90502; **Phone:** 310-222-2704; **Board Cert:** Vascular Surgery 2006; **Med School:** SUNY Upstate Med Univ 1974; **Resid:** Surgery, LAC-Harbor-UCLA Med Ctr 1979; **Fellow:** Vascular Surgery, LAC-Harbor-UCLA Med Ctr 1981; **Fac Appt:** Prof S, UCLA

Maimonides
Medical Center

HEART &
VASCULAR CENTER
4802 Tenth Avenue
Brooklyn, New York 11219
Phone: 718.283.7957 • Fax: 718.283.8599
www.maimonidesmed.org/vascular

The Division of Vascular and Endovascular Surgery and Cardiac Institute and were integrated in 2013 to form the Maimonides Heart & Vascular Center.

Vascular Services
Vascular & Endovascular Surgery, now part of the Maimonides Heart & Vascular Center, offer comprehensive diagnostic, clinical and surgical services for patients with vascular disease and associated conditions. Under the direction of Robert Rhee, MD, our vascular team is renowned for its services in wound care, limb salvage, aneurysm repair, blocked arteries, varicose veins and chronic lower limb ischemia, as well as balloon angioplasties, stents and carotid artery dissections.

In addition to traditional open surgery, Maimonides places a focus on therapeutic options based on minimally invasive, endovascular and catheter-directed techniques. Our team of physicians is board-certified, highly-experienced and makes use of innovative technologies, such as our new hybrid OR. At Maimonides, specialists can combine both surgical and catheter techniques to maximize care.

Vascular Diagnostic Laboratory
Accredited by the Intersocietal Commission for the Accreditation of Vascular Laboratories, the Vascular Diagnostic Laboratory at Maimonides performs screening, diagnostic and post-operative non-invasive imaging using state-of-the-art ultrasound and Doppler machines. We offer sophisticated ultrasound examinations, eliminating the need for invasive angiograms. Precise determinations of blood flow to vital organs and limbs are obtained and serve as the basis for further treatment. These findings are reported within 24 hours, enabling physicians to make timely and informed decisions about the future course of therapy for their patients.

We offer a range of diagnostic services, including:

- Ultrasound Vascular Diagnostic Testing
- Arteriograms
- Magnetic Resonance Angiography
- Plethysmography
- Pulse Volume Recordings
- Transcutaneous Oximetry
- Venograms
- Duplex Ultrasound
- Venous Reflux Evaluation and Venous DVT Studies
- Vein Mapping
- Aortic Aneurysm Studies

Vascular services has received accreditation by the Intersocietal Commission for the Accreditation of Vascular Laboratories, which assures patients that they are receiving the highest standard of care possible at the Vascular Diagnostics Laboratory. Every staff member is committed to excellence in all aspects of service. Our experienced technicians perform precise diagnostic imaging and are leaders in their fields.

Maimonides Medical Center
The right care.
Right here.
www.maimonidesmed.org/vascular

Mount Sinai

THE MOUNT SINAI MEDICAL CENTER

Vascular Surgery

One Gustave L. Levy Place
Fifth Avenue and 100th Street
New York, NY 10029-6574

Physician Referral: 1-800-MD-SINAI (637-4624)
www.mountsinai.org

THE DIVISION OF VASCULAR SURGERY at The Mount Sinai Medical Center is committed to delivering unrivaled patient care and embracing the safest and most effective treatment innovations. Past decades have seen dramatic advances in the treatment of vascular disease, and our surgeons have contributed to this progress by developing new techniques in aneurysm repair and stroke prevention designed to minimize discomfort and improve outcomes.

Peter L. Faries, MD, Chief of the Division of Vascular Surgery, and Michael L. Marin, MD, Chairman of the Department of Surgery, have assembled a team of internationally recognized surgeons dedicated to clinical excellence and comprehensive patient care.

What We Treat

- **Aneurysmal Disease:** We excel in diagnosing and treating aneurysmal disease and offer the most advanced and minimally invasive treatments available to repair aortic aneurysms, thoracic aortic aneurysms and aneurysms of other blood vessels.

- **Carotid Disease and Stroke Prevention:** Having helped pioneer their development, we are proficient in both carotid endarterectomy surgery and carotid stenting. This level of expertise allows us to offer unbiased counseling and tailor the most advanced procedures to the specific needs of each patient.

- **Dialysis Access:** When patients require dialysis, we are adept at providing access points. The three points of access are through a catheter, through an arteriovenous (AV) graft, or an arteriovenous (AV) fistula.

- **Peripheral Vascular Disease:** We are highly skilled in restoring blood flow to the legs and correcting the symptoms of peripheral vascular disease (PVD), through both minimally invasive and traditional techniques.

- **Venous Disease:** We offer multiple treatment options (both surgical and non-surgical) for varicose and spider veins.

Because our expertise encompasses a broad array of patient services, nearly every patient condition can be managed successfully. Our vascular surgeons, together with our award-winning nurses and ancillary staff, are dedicated to achieving unsurpassed quality in patient care. Our emphasis on comprehensive caring for both the mental and physical health of our patients has resulted in more effective therapy. We pride ourselves on providing the highest level of compassion and communication with our patients and families, serving as a model for medical centers worldwide.

NYU Langone
MEDICAL CENTER

CARDIAC AND VASCULAR INSTITUTE
550 First Avenue *(at 31st Street)*
New York, NY 10016
www.NYULMC.org
Physician Referral: **888-7-NYU-MED** *(888-769-8633)*

CARDIAC AND VASCULAR INSTITUTE

The Cardiac and Vascular Institute (CVI) at NYU Langone Medical Center continues to advance new techniques for repairing heart valves, curing heart rhythm disorders, and treating aortic diseases and congestive heart failure. We care for both adults and children. CVI is consistently ranked among the leading heart and heart surgery centers in *U.S. News & World Report's annual 'Best Hospitals'* rankings.

Cardiac Catheterization CVI offers superior catheter-based diagnosis and evaluation of cardiac health. Our laboratory provides a full range of procedures to evaluate, diagnose, and provide treatment options.

Cardiac Rehabilitation and Prevention The Joan and Joel Smilow Cardiopulmonary Rehabilitation and Prevention Center provides individualized treatment plans through NYU Langone's Rusk Rehabilitation, in a state-of-the-art and comfortable facility.

Cardiac Surgery NYU Langone is a nationally recognized leader in advanced surgical treatments for adult and congenital heart disease. We have world-renowned expertise in mitral valve repair, aortic valve replacement and aortic aneurysm repair, as well as specializing in high-risk and elderly patients.

Cardiology The Leon H. Charney Division of Cardiology is a leader in cardiovascular patient care, biomedical research, and education. We are advancing the field of cardiovascular medicine through a variety of innovative collaborations.

Congenital Heart Disease The pediatric and adult congenital cardiac program treats patients of all ages with inherited and acquired cardiac defects. We have a highly experienced team of specialists in pediatric and adult cardiology, pediatric interventional cardiology, congenital cardiac surgery, neonatal and pediatric cardiac intensive care, pediatric cardiac anesthesiology, nursing, and extracorporeal perfusion.

Heart Failure A multidisciplinary team offers the most advanced care for heart failure including echocardiograms, pacemaker and defibrillator implantations, open heart surgeries, and left ventricular assist devices.

Nuclear Cardiology/Stress The Nuclear Cardiology/Stress Laboratory performs a range of tests that assist cardiologists in the assessment and diagnosis of heart disease.

Vascular Surgery We offer diagnostic and treatment for patients with conditions ranging from arterial aneurysms to deep vein thrombosis, as well as carotid stenosis and limb salvage including minimally invasive vein surgery, endovascular aortic surgery, thoracic aneurysm correction and abdominal aneurysm interventions.

Top Doctors Make A Difference

Appendices

Top Doctors Make A Difference

APPENDIX A:
Medical Boards

Introduction to ABMS and Osteopathic Specialties

The following pages contain descriptions of the "official" medical specialties, approved by the American Board of Medical Specialists (for M.D.s) or by the American Osteopathic Association (for D.O.s). These are important because they are the only specialties recognized by the official governing boards. There may be physicians who call themselves one kind of specialist or another, but they may not be certified by the "official" boards. There are, in fact, over 100 such "self-designated" boards, some simply groups of physicians interested in a given area of medicine with no qualifications for membership to other groups with very specific qualifications for membership.

It is important for the medical consumer to seek out physicians certified by the ABMS or AOA to assure their doctor has had the appropriate training and passed the board certification exam.

ABMS

The ABMS is an organization of ABMS Approved medical specialty boards. The mission of the ABMS is to maintain and improve the quality of medical care by assisting the Member Boards in their efforts to develop and utilize professional and educational standards for the evaluation and certification of physician specialists. The intent of certification of physicians is to provide assurance to the public that a physician specialist certified by a Member Board of the ABMS has successfully completed an approved educational program and evaluation process which includes an examination designed to assess the knowledge, skills, and experience required to provide quality patient care in that specialty. The ABMS serves to coordinate the activities of its Member Boards and to provide information to the public, the government, the profession and its Members concerning issues involving specialization and certification in medicine.

Following is a list of the addresses of the various medical specialty boards approved by the ABMS. Note that there are 24 board organizations for 25 medical specialties. Psychiatry and Neurology share the same board.

To find out if a physician is certified, consumers can call the individual boards which may charge a fee for the information, or they can contact the ABMS at (866) 275-2267 (no fee) or www.abms.org.

American Board of Allergy and Immunology
111 S Independence Mall E, Ste 701
Philadelphia, PA 19106
(215) 592-9466, (866) 264-5568

General Certification in Allergy and Immunology. Certifications awarded since 1989 are valid for 10 years. For those certified prior to 1989 there is no recertification requirement.

American Board of Anesthesiology
4208 Six Forks Rd, Ste 1500
Raleigh, NC 27609-5735
(866) 999-7501

General Certification in Anesthesiology; with Special and Added Qualifications in Critical Care Medicine, Hospice & Palliative Medicine, Pain Medicine, Pediatric Anesthesiology and Sleep Medicine. Certifications awarded since 2000 are valid for 10 years.

American Board of Colon and Rectal Surgery
20600 Eureka Road, Suite 600
Taylor, MI 48180
(734) 282-9400

General Certification is in Colon and Rectal Surgery. Certifications awarded since 1990 are valid for 10 years.

American Board of Dermatology
Henry Ford Health System
1 Ford Place
Detroit, MI 48202-3450
(313) 874-1088

General Certification in Dermatology; with Special Qualifications Dermatopathology, and Pediatric Dermatology. Certifications awarded since 1991 are valid for 10 years.

American Board of Emergency Medicine
3000 Coolidge Road
East Lansing, MI 48823-6319
(517) 332-4800

General Certification in Emergency Medicine; with Special and Added Qualifications in Critical Care Medicine, Emergency Medical Services, Hospice & Palliative Medicine, Medical Toxicology, Pediatric Emergency Medicine, Sports Medicine and Undersea and Hyperbaric Medicine. Certifications awarded since 1980 are valid for 10 years

American Board of Family Medicine
1648 McGranthiana Pkwy, Suite 550
Lexington, KY 40511
(859) 269-5626, (888) 995-5700

General Certification in Family Practice; with Added Qualifications in Adolescent Medicine, Geriatric Medicine, Hospice & Palliative Medicine, Sleep Medicine and Sports Medicine. Certifications awarded since 1970 are valid for 7 years.

American Board of Internal Medicine
510 Walnut Street, Suite 1700
Philadelphia, PA 19106-3699
(215) 446-3500, (800) 441-ABIM

General Certification in Internal Medicine; with Special Qualifications in Cardiovascular Disease, Endocrinology, Diabetes and Metabolism, Gastroenterology, Hematology, Infectious Disease, Medical Oncology, Nephrology, Pulmonary Disease, and Rheumatology; and Added Qualifications in Advanced Heart Failure & Transplant Cardiology, Adolescent Medicine, Clinical Cardiac Electrophysiology, Critical Care Medicine, Geriatric Medicine, Hospice and Palliative Medicine, Interventional Cardiology, Sleep Medicine, Sports Medicine and Transplant Hepatology. Certifications awarded since 1990 are valid for 10 years.

American Board of Medical Genetics
9650 Rockville Pike
Bethesda, MD 20814-3998
(301) 634-7315

General Certification in Clinical Genetics (MD), Clinical Biochemical Genetics, Clinical Cytogenetics and Clinical Molecular Genetics; with Added Qualifications in Medical Biochemical Genetics and Molecular Genetic Pathology. Certifications awarded since 2002 are valid for 2 years.

American Board of Neurological Surgery
245 Amity Rd, Suite 208
Woodbridge, CT 06525
(203) 397-2267

General Certification in Neurological Surgery. Certifications awarded since 1999 are valid for 10 years.

American Board of Nuclear Medicine
4555 Forest Park Boulevard, Suite 119
St. Louis, MO 63108
(314) 367-2225

General Certification in Nuclear Medicine. Certifications awarded since 1992 are valid for 10 years.

American Board of Obstetrics and Gynecology
2915 Vine Street, Suite 300
Dallas, TX 75204
(214) 871-1619

General Certification in Obstetrics and Gynecology; with Special Qualifications in Gynecologic Oncology, Maternal and Fetal Medicine, Reproductive Endocrinology/Infertility; and Added Qualifications in Critical Care Medicine, Female Pelvic Medicine and Reconstructive Surgery, and Hospice & Palliative Medicine. Certifications awarded since 1986 are valid for 6 years.

American Board of Ophthalmology
111 Presidential Boulevard, Suite 241
Bala Cynwyd, PA 19004-1075
(610) 664-1175

Certifications Awarded since 1992 are valid for 10 years. For those certified prior to 1992, there is no recertification requirement.

American Board of Orthopaedic Surgery
400 Silver Cedar Court
Chapel Hill, NC 27514
(919) 929-7103

General Certification in Orthopaedic Surgery; with Added Qualification in Hand Surgery and Orthopaedic Sports Medicine. Certifications awarded since 1986 are valid for 10 years.

American Board of Otolaryngology
5615 Kirby Drive, Suite 600
Houston, TX 77005
(713) 850-0399

General Certification in Otolaryngology; with Added Qualifications in Neurotology, Pediatric Otolaryngology, Plastic Surgery within the Head and Neck and Sleep Medicine. Certifications awarded since 2002 are valid for10 years.

American Board of Pathology
P.O. Box 25915
Tampa, FL 33622-5915
(813) 286-2444

General Certification in Anatomic and Clinical Pathology, Anatomic Pathology and Clinical Pathology; with Special Qualifications in Blood Banking/Transfusion Medicine, Chemical Pathology, Clinical Informatics, Dermatopathology, Forensic Pathology, Hematology, Medical Microbiology, Molecular Genetic Pathology, Neuropathology and Pediatric Pathology; and Added Qualifications in Cytopathology. Certifications awarded since 1997 are valid for 10 years.

American Board of Pediatrics
111 Silver Cedar Court
Chapel Hill, NC 27514-1651
(919) 929-0461

General Certification in Pediatrics; with Special Qualifications in Adolescent Medicine, Developmental-Behavioral Pediatrics, Neonatal-Perinatal Medicine, Pediatric Cardiology, Pediatric Critical Care Medicine, Pediatric Emergency Medicine, Pediatric Endocrinology, Pediatric Gastroenterology, Pediatric Hematology-Oncology, Pediatric Infectious Diseases, Pediatric Nephrology, Pediatric Pulmonology, and Pediatric Rheumatology; and Added Qualifications in Child Abuse Pediatrics, Medical Toxicology, Neurodevelopmental Disabilities, Pediatric Transplant Hepatology, Sleep Medicine and Sports Medicine. Certifications awarded since 1988 valid for 7 years.

American Board of Physical Medicine and Rehabilitation
3015 Allegro Park Lane, S.W.
Rochester, MN 55902-4139
(507) 282-1776

General Certification in Physical Medicine and Rehabilitation; with Special Qualifications in Brain Injury Medicine, Hospice & Palliative Medicine, Neuromuscular Medicine, Pain Medicine, Pediatric Rehabilitation Medicine, Spinal Cord Injury Medicine and Sports Medicine. Certifications awarded since 1993 are valid for 10 years.

American Board of Plastic Surgery
Seven Penn Center, Suite 400
1635 Market Street
Philadelphia, PA 19103
(215) 587-9322

General Certification in Plastic Surgery; with Added Qualifications in Hand Surgery and Plastic Surgery within the Head & Neck. Certifications awarded since 1995 are valid for a 10-year period.

American Board of Preventive Medicine
111 W. Jackson Boulevard, Suite 1110
Chicago, IL 60604
(312) 939-ABPM [2276]

General Certification in Aerospace Medicine, Occupational Medicine and Public Health and General Preventive Medicine; with Added Qualifications in Clinical Informatics, Undersea and Hyperbaric Medicine and Medical Toxicology. Certifications awarded since 1997 are valid for 10 years.

American Board of Psychiatry and Neurology
2150 E Lake Cook Rd, Ste 900
Buffalo Grove, IL 60089
(847) 229-6500

General Certification in Psychiatry, Neurology and Neurology with Special Qualification in Child Neurology; with Special Qualifications in Child and Adolescent Psychiatry, Epilepsy, Hospice & Palliative Medicine, Pain Medicine and Sleep Medicine; and Added Qualifications in Addiction Psychiatry, Brain Injury Medicine, Clinical Neurophysiology, Forensic Psychiatry, Geriatric Psychiatry, Neurodevelopmental Disabilities, Neuromuscular Medicine, Psychosomatic Medicine and Vascular Neurology. Certifications awarded since 1994 are valid for 10 years.

American Board of Radiology
5441 E. Williams Circle
Tucson, AZ 85711
(520) 790-2900

General Certification in Diagnostic Radiology, Medical Physics and Radiation Oncology; with Special Competency in Nuclear Radiology; and Added Qualifications in Hospice & Palliative Medicine, Neuroradiology, Nuclear Radiology, Pediatric Radiology and Vascular and Interventional Radiology. Radiological Physics is a non-clinical certification. Certificates are valid for 10 years.

American Board of Surgery
1617 John F. Kennedy Boulevard, Suite 860
Philadelphia, PA 19103-1847
(215) 568-4000

General Certification in Surgery and Vascular Surgery; with Special Qualifications in Pediatric Surgery and Surgery of the Hand; and Added Qualifications in Complex Surgical Oncology, Hospice & Palliative Medicine and Surgical Critical Care. Certifications awarded since 1976 are valid for 10 years.

American Board of Thoracic Surgery

633 North St. Clair Street, Suite 2320
Chicago, IL 60611
(312 202-5900

General Certification in Thoracic and Cardiac Surgery; with Special Qualifications in Congenital Cardiac Surgey. Certifications awarded since 1976 are valid for 10 years and Added Qualifications in Congenital Cardiac Surgery.

American Board of Urology

600 Peter Jefferson Pkwy, Ste 150
Charlottesville, VA 22911
(434) 979-0059

General Certification in Urology; with Special Qualifications in Pediatric Urology and Female Pelvic Medicine & Reconstructive Surgery. Certifications awarded as of 1985 are valid for 10 years with Special Qualifications in Pediatric Urology.

Osteopathic

The American Osteopathic Association (AOA) is a member association representing more than 78,000 osteopathic physicians (D.O.s). The AOA serves as the primary certifying body for D.O.s, and is the accrediting agency for all osetopathic medical colleges and health care facilities. The AOA's mission is to advance the philosophy and practice of osteopathic medicine by promoting excellence in education, research, and the delivery of quality, cost-effective healthcare within a distinct, unified profession. American Osteopathic Association 142 E Ontario Street Chicago, IL 60611.

Consumers may call the American Osteopathic Association at (800) 621-1773 or visit the website, www.osteopathic.org, for general certification information.

American Osteopathic Board of Anesthesiology

General certification in Anesthesiology; with Added Qualifications in Critical Care Medicine, and Pain Management. Certifications awarded since 2004 are valid for 10 years. For those certified prior to 2004 there is no recertification requirement.

American Osteopathic Board of Dermatology

General certification in Dermatology; with Added Qualifications in Dermatopathology and MOHS-Micrographic Surgery. Certifications awarded since 2004 are valid for 10 years.

American Osteopathic Board of Emergency Medicine

General certification in Emergency Medicine; with Added Qualifications in Emergency Medical Services, Medical Toxicology, and Sports Medicine. Certifications awarded since 1994 are valid for 10 years.

American Osteopathic Board of Family Physicians

General certification in Family Practice and Osteopathic Manipulative Treatment (OMT); with Added Qualifications in Adolescent Medicine, Geriatric Medicine, Sports Medicine, Hospice & Palliative Medicine, Sleep Medicine and Undersea & Hyperbaric Medicine. Certifications awarded since March 1,1997 are valid for 8 years.

American Osteopathic Board of Internal Medicine

General certification in Internal Medicine; with Special Qualifications in Allergy/Immunology, Cardiology, Endocrinology, Gastroenterology, Hematology, Infectious Disease, Nephrology, Oncology, Pulmonary Disease, Rheumatology; with Added Qualifications in Addiction Medicine, Critical Care Medicine, Clinical Cardiac Electrophysiology, Geriatric Medicine, Hospice & Palliative Medicine, Interventional Cardiology, Sleep Medicine, Sports Medicine and Undersea & Hyperbaric Medicine. Certifications awarded since 1993 are valid for 10 years.

American Osteopathic Board of Neurology and Psychiatry

General certification in Neurology and Psychiatry; with Special Qualifications in Child/Adolescent Psychiatry and Child/Adolescent Neurology; with Added Qualifications in Addiction Medicine, Geriatric Psychiatry, Hospice & Palliative Medicine, Neurophysiology and Sleep Medicine. Certifications awarded since 1995 are valid for 10 years.

American Osteopathic Board of Neuromusculoskeletal Medicine

(Formerly American Osteopathic Board of Special Proficiency in Osteopathic Manipulative Medicine)

General certification in Neuromusculoskeletal Medicine & Osteopathic Manipulative Medicine with Added Qualifications in Sports Medicine. Certifications awarded since 1995 are valid for 10 years. For those certified prior to 1995 there is no recertification requirement.

American Osteopathic Board of Nuclear Medicine

General certification in Nuclear Medicine. Certifications awarded since 1995 are valid for 10 years

American Osteopathic Board of Obstetrics and Gynecology

General certification in Obstetrics and Gynecology; with Special Qualifications in Gynecologic Oncology; Maternal and Fetal Medicine and Reproductive Endocrinology. Certifications awarded since June, 2002 are valid for 6 years.

American Osteopathic Board of Ophthalmology and Otolaryngology

General certification in Ophthalmology, Otolaryngolgy and Otolaryngology/Facial Plastic Surgery; with Added Qualifications in Otolaryngic Allergy and Sleep Medicine. Certifications awarded in Ophthalmology since 2000 are valid for 10 years. For those certified prior to 2000 there is no recertification requirement. Certifications awarded in Otolaryngology and/or Otolaryngology/Facial Plastic Surgery since 2002 are valid for 10 years.

American Osteopathic Board of Orthopaedic Surgery

General certification in Orthopaedic Surgery; with Added Qualifications in Hand Surgery. Certifications awarded since 1994 are valid for 10 years.

American Osteopathic Board of Pathology

General certification in Laboratory Medicine, Anatomic Pathology and Anatomic Pathology and Laboratory Medicine; with Special Qualifications in Forensic Pathology; and with Added Qualifications in Dermatopathology. Certifications awarded since 1995 are valid for 10 years.

American Osteopathic Board of Pediatrics

General certification in Pediatrics with Special Qualifications in Adolescent and Young Adult Medicine, Neonatology, Pediatric Allergy/Immunology and Pediatric Endocrinology; with Added Qualifications in Sports Medicine. Certifications awarded since 1995 are valid for 7 years.

American Osteopathic Board of Physical Medicine and Rehabilitation Medicine

General certification in Physical Medicine and Rehabilitation; with Added Qualifications in Hospice & Palliative Medicine and Sports Medicine. Certifications awarded since 2004 are valid for 10 years.

American Osteopathic Board of Preventive Medicine

General certification in Preventive Medicine/Aerospace Medicine, Preventive Medicine/Occupational-Environmental Medicine and Preventive Medicine/Public Health; with Added Qualifications in Occupational Medicine and Undersea & Hyperbaric Medicine. Certifications awarded since 1994 are valid for 10 years.

American Osteopathic Board of Proctology

General certification in Proctology. Certifications awarded since 2004 are valid for 10 years.

American Osteopathic Board of Radiology

General certification in Diagnostic Radiology and Radiation Oncology; with Added Qualifications in Angiography and Interventional Radiology, Diagnostic Ultrasound and Pediatric Radiology. Certifications awarded since 2002 are valid for 10 years.

American Osteopathic Board of Surgery

General certification in Surgery, Neurological Surgery, Plastic and Reconstructive Surgery, Thoracic Cardiovascular Surgery, Urological Surgery and General Vascular Surgery; with Added Qualifications in Surgical Critical Care. Certifications awarded since 1997 are valid for 10 years.

Appendix B:
Self-Designated Medical Specialties

This list of self-designated medical specialty groups was obtained from the American Board of Medical Specialties. However, it is important to point out that these groups are not recognized by the ABMS, the governing board for the recognized twenty-four medical specialty boards (listed in Appendix A).

The organizations listed below range from highly organized groups that are attempting to formalize training and certification in their field to informal groups interested in a particular aspect of medicine.

If you wish to obtain information from any of these groups you will have to do some detective work. Because so many are informal, the location, phone and mailing addresses change frequently, depending upon the person who is functioning as secretary or administrator.

The best way to track down one of these groups is to consult the doctor listings to find a doctor who has expressed a special interest in that field, and call his or her office. You might also call a nearby academic health center in the area to see if they have a faculty or staff member known to be involved in that particular medical interest. If that fails, take the same approach with your community hospital.

A

Abdominal Surgeons
Acupuncture Medicine
Addiction Medicine
Addictionology
Adolescent Psychiatry
Aesthetic Plastic Surgery
Alcoholism and Other Drug
Dependencies (AMSAODD)
Algology (Chronic Pain)
Alternative Medicine
Ambulatory Anesthesia
Ambulatory Foot Surgery
Anesthesia
Arthroscopic Surgery
Arthroscopy (Board of North America)

B

Bariatric Medicine
Bionic Psychology
Bloodless Medicine & Surgery

C

Chelation Therapy
Chemical Dependence
Clinical Chemistry
Clinical Ecology
Clinical Medicine and Surgery
Clinical Neurology
Clinical Neurophysiology
Clinical Neurosurgery
Clinical Nutrition
Clinical Orthopaedic Surgery
Clinical Pharmacology
Clinical Polysomnography
Clinical Psychiatry
Clinical Psychology
Clinical Toxicology
Cosmetic Plastic Surgery
Cosmetic Surgery
Council of Non-Board Certified Physicians
Critical Care in Medicine & Surgery

D

Disability Analysis
Disability Evaluating Physicians

E

Electrodiagnostic Medicine
Electroencephalography
Electromyography & Electrodiagnosis
Environmental Medicine
Epidemiology (College)
Eye Surgery

F

Facial Cosmetic Surgery
Facial Plastic & Reconstructive Surgery
Family Practice, Certification
Forensic Examiners
Forensic Psychiatry
Forensic Toxicology

H

Hand Surgery
Head, Facial & Neck Pain & TMJ Orthopaedics
Health Physics
Homeopathic Physicians
Homeotherapeutics
Hypnotic Anesthesiology, National Board for

I

Independent Medical Examiners
Industrial Medicine & Surgery
Insurance Medicine
International Cosmetic & Plastic
Facial Reconstructive Standards
Interventional Radiology

L

Laser Surgery
Law in Medicine
Longevity Medicine/Surgery

M

Malpractice Physicians
Maxillofacial Surgeons
Medical Accreditation (American Federation for)
Medical Hypnosis
Medical Laboratory Immunology
Medical-Legal Analysis of Medicine & Surgery
Medical Legal & Workers Comp. Medicine & Surgery
Medical-Legal Consultants
Medical Management
Medical Microbiology
Medical Preventics (Academy)
Medical Psychotherapists
Medical Toxicology
Microbiology (Medical Microbiology)
Military Medicine
Mohs Micrographic Surgery & Cutaneous Oncology

N

Neuroimaging
Neurologic & Orthopaedic Dental Medicine and Surgery
Neurological & Orthopaedic Medicine
Neurological & Orthopaedic Surgery
Neurological Microsurgery
Neurology
Neuromuscular Thermography
Neuro-Orthopaedic Dental Medicine
Neuro-Orthopaedic Electrodiagnosis
Neuro-Orthopaedic Laser Surgery
Neuro-Orthopaedic Psychiatry
Neuro-Orthopaedic Thoracic Medicine
Neurorehabilitation
Nutrition

O

Orthopaedic Medicine
Orthopaedic Microneurosurgery
Otorhinolaryngology

P

Pain Management (American Academy of)
Pain Management Specialties
Pain Medicine
Palliative Medicine
Percutaneous Diskectomy
Plastic Esthetic Surgeons
Prison Medicine
Professional Disability Consultants Psychiatric Medicine
Psychiatry (American National Board of)
Psychoanalysis (American Examining Board in)
Psychological Medicine (International)

Q

Quality Assurance & Utilization Review

R

Radiology & Medical Imaging
Rheumatologic Surgery
Rheumatological & Reconstructive Medicine
Ringside Medicine & Surgery

S

Skin Specialists
Sleep Medicine (Polysomnography)
Spinal Cord Injury
Spinal Surgery
Sports Medicine
Sports Medicine/Surgery

T

Toxicology
Trauma Surgery
Traumatologic Medicine & Surgery
Tropical Medicine

U

Ultrasound Technology
Urologic Allied Health Professionals
Urological Surgery

W

Weight Reduction Medicine

APPENDIX C:
Hospital Listings

The following is an alphabetical listing of all hospitals that have at least one Castle Connolly Top Doctor in this guide. Institutions listed in **Bold** are profiled in this Guide in association with Castle Connolly's *Partnership for Excellence* program. The abbreviations as they appear in the listings are in italics below. Due to the many changes taking place in the hospital industry, the names on this list may have changed subsequent to publication of this guide.

Abbott - Northwestern Hospital (612) 863-4000
Abbott - Northwestern Hosp
800 E 28th St Minneapolis, MN 55407 MIDWEST

Abington Memorial Hospital (215) 481-2000
Abington Meml Hosp
1200 Old York Rd Abington, PA 19001 MID ATLANTIC

Adventist Hinsdale Hospital (630) 856-9000
Adventist Hinsdale Hosp
120 N Oak St Hinsdale, IL 60521 MIDWEST

Adventist La Grange Memorial Hospital (708) 245-9000
Adventist La Grange Meml Hosp
5101 S Willow Springs Rd La Grange, IL 60525 MIDWEST

Advocate Christ Medical Center (708) 684-8000
Adv Christ Med Ctr
4440 W 95th St Oak Lawn, IL 60453 MIDWEST

Advocate Good Samaritan Hospital (630) 275-5900
Adv Good Samaritan Hosp
3815 Highland Ave Downers Grove, IL 60515 MIDWEST

Advocate Illinois Masonic Medical Center (773) 975-1600
Adv Illinois Masonic Med Ctr
836 W Wellington Ave Chicago, IL 60657-5147 MIDWEST

Advocate Lutheran General Hospital (847) 723-2210
Adv Luth Genl Hosp
1775 Dempster St Park Ridge, IL 60068 MIDWEST

Advocate Sherman Hospital (847) 742-9800
Adv Sherman Hosp
1425 N Randall Rd Elgin, IL 60120 MIDWEST

Advocate South Suburban Hospital (708) 799-8000
Adv S Suburban Hosp
17800 S Kedzie Ave Hazel Crest, IL 60429 MIDWEST

Akron Children's Hospital (330) 543-1000
Akron Children's Hosp
One Perkins Square Akron, OH 44308 MIDWEST

Alamance Regional Med Ctr (336) 538-7000
Alamance Regl Med Ctr
1240 Huffman Mill Rd Burlington, NC 27215 SOUTHEAST

Alameda County Medical Center-Highland Campus (510) 437-4800
Alameda County Med Ctr-Highland Campus
1411 E 31st St Oakland, CA 94602 WEST COAST AND PACIFIC

Albany Medical Center (518) 262-3125
Albany Med Ctr
43 New Scotland Ave Albany, NY 12208 MID ATLANTIC

Albert Lea Medical Center-Mayo Health System (507) 373-2384
Albert Lea Med Ctr-Mayo Hlth Sys
404 W Fountain St Albert Lea, MN 56007 MIDWEST

Alegent Creighton University Medical Center (402) 449-4000
Alegent Creighton Univ Med Ctr
601 N 30th St Omaha, NE 6813 GREAT PLAINS AND MOUNTAINS

Alexian Brothers Medical Center (847) 437-5500
Alexian Brothers Med Ctr
800 Biesterfield Rd Elk Grove Village, IL 60007 MIDWEST

All Children's Hospital (727) 898-7451
All Children's Hosp
501 6th St S St. Petersburg, FL 33701 SOUTHEAST

Allegheny General Hospital (412) 359-3131
Allegheny Genl Hosp
320 E. North Avenue Pittsburgh, PA 15212 MID ATLANTIC

Alta Bates Summit Medical Center-Alta Bates Campus (510) 204-4444
Alta Bates Summit Med Ctr-Alta Bates Campus
2450 Ashby Avenue Berkeley, CA 94705 WEST COAST AND PACIFIC

Alvarado Hospital & Medical Center (619) 287-3270
Alvarado Hosp & Med Ctr
6655 Alvarado Rd San Diego, CA 92120 WEST COAST AND PACIFIC

Andalusia Regional Hospital (334) 222-8466
Andalusia Regl Hosp
849 S Three Notch St Andalusia, AL 36420 SOUTHEAST

Ann & Robert H Lurie Children's Hospital of Chicago (312) 227-4000
Lurie Chldn's Hosp-Chicago
225 E Chicago Ave Chicago, IL 60611 MIDWEST

Anne Arundel Medical Center (443) 481-1000
Anne Arundel Med Ctr
2001 Medical Pkwy Annapolis, MD 21401 MID ATLANTIC

Aria Health - Bucks County Campus (215) 949-5000
Aria Hlth - Bucks County
380 N Oxford Valley Rd Langhorne, PA 19047-8399 MID ATLANTIC

Arkansas Children's Hospital (501) 364-1100
Arkansas Chldns Hosp
1 Children's Way Little Rock, AR 72202 SOUTHWEST

Arthur G. James Cancer Hospital & Research Institute (614) 293-3300
Arthur G James Cancer Hosp & Research Inst
300 W 10th Ave, Ste 519 Columbus, OH 43210 MIDWEST

Ashland Community Hospital (541) 201-4000
Ashland Community Hosp
280 Maple St Ashland, OR 97520 WEST COAST AND PACIFIC

Atlanta VA Medical Center (404) 321-6111
Atlanta VA Med Ctr
1670 Clairmont Rd Decatur, GA 30033 SOUTHEAST

Audie L Murphy Memorial Veterans Hospital - San Antonio (210) 617-5300
Audie L Murphy Meml Vets Hosp - San Antonio
7400 Merton Minter Blvd San Antonio, TX 78229 SOUTHWEST

Austen Riggs Center (413) 298-5511
Austen Riggs Ctr
25 Main Street or PO Box 962 Stockbridge, MA 01262-0962 NEW ENGLAND

Banner Gateway Medical Center (480) 543-2000
Banner Gateway Med Ctr
1900 N Higley Rd Gilbert, AZ 85234 SOUTHWEST

Banner Good Samaritan Regional Medical Center - Phoenix (602) 839-2000
Banner Good Samaritan Regl Med Ctr - Phoenix
1111 E McDowell Rd Phoenix, AZ 85006 SOUTHWEST

Baptist Health System *Baptist Hlth Sys* 615 Soledad	San Antonio, TX 78205	(210) 297-9700 SOUTHWEST
Baptist Hospital - Pensacola *Baptist Hosp - Pensacola* 1000 W Moreno St	Pensacola, FL 32501	(850) 434-4011 SOUTHEAST
Baptist Hospital of Miami *Baptist Hosp of Miami* 8900 N Kendall Dr	Miami, FL 33176	(786) 596-1960 SOUTHEAST
Baptist Medical Center - San Antonio *Baptist Med Ctr - San Antonio* 111 Dallas St	San Antonio, TX 78205	(210) 297-7000 SOUTHWEST
Baptist Medical Center-Jackson *Baptist Med Ctr-Jackson* 1225 N State St	Jackson, MS 39202	(601) 968-1000 SOUTHEAST
Baptist Memorial Hospital-Memphis *Baptist Memorial Hospital-Memphis* 6019 Walnut Grove Rd	Memphis, TN 38120	(901) 226-5000 SOUTHEAST
Barbara Ann Karmanos Cancer Institute *Barbara Ann Karmanos Cancer Inst* 4100 John R	Detroit, MI 48201	(800) 527-6266 MIDWEST
Barnes-Jewish Hospital *Barnes-Jewish Hosp* One Barnes-Jewish Hospital Plaza	St. Louis, MO 63110	(314) 747-3000 MIDWEST
Barnes-Jewish West County Hospital *Barnes-Jewish West County Hosp* 12634 Olive Blvd	St. Louis, MO 63141	(314) 996-8000 MIDWEST
Bascom Palmer Eye Institute *Bascom Palmer Eye Inst* 900 NW 17 St	Miami, FL 33136	(305) 326-6000 SOUTHEAST
Baylor Institute for Rehabilitation *Baylor Inst for Rehabilitation* 3505 Gaston Avenue	Dallas, TX 75246	(800) 422-9567 SOUTHWEST
Baylor Medical Center at Uptown *Baylor Med Ctr at Uptown* 2727 Lemmon Ave	Dallas, TX 75204	(214) 443-3000 SOUTHWEST

Baylor University Medical Center-Dallas (214) 820-0111
Baylor Univ Med Ctr-Dallas
3500 Gaston Avenue Dallas, TX 75246 SOUTHWEST

Baystate Medical Center (413) 794-0000
Baystate Med Ctr
759 Chestnut Street Springfield, MA 01199 NEW ENGLAND

Beaumont Hospital-Royal Oak (248) 898-5000
Beaumont Hosp-Royal Oak
3601 W 13 Mile Rd Royal Oak, MI 48073 MIDWEST

Beaumont Hospital-Troy (248) 964-5000
Beaumont Hosp-Troy
44201 Dequindre Rd Troy, MI 48085 MIDWEST

Ben Taub General Hospital (713) 873-2000
Ben Taub Genl Hosp
1504 Taub Loop Houston, TX 77030 SOUTHWEST

Beth Israel Deaconess Medical Center - Boston (617) 667-7000
Beth Israel Deaconess Med Ctr - Boston
330 Brookline Ave Boston, MA 02215 NEW ENGLAND

Beth Israel Medical Center - Milton & Caroll Petrie Division (212) 420-2000
Beth Israel Med Ctr - Petrie Div
First Avenue at 16th Street New York, NY 10003 MID ATLANTIC

Bethesda North Hospital (513) 865-1111
Bethesda North Hosp
10500 Montgomery Rd Cincinnati, OH 45242-4415 MIDWEST

Boca Raton Regional Hospital (561) 955-7100
Boca Raton Regl Hosp
800 Meadows Road Boca Raton, FL 33486 SOUTHEAST

Bon Secours St Mary's Hospital (804) 285-2011
Bon Secours St Mary's Hosp
5801 Bremo Road Richmond, VA 23226 SOUTHEAST

Boston Medical Center (617) 638-8000
Boston Med Ctr
1 Boston Medical Center Pl Boston, MA 02118 NEW ENGLAND

Botsford Hospital (248) 471-8000
Botsford Hosp
28050 Grand River Ave Farmington Hills, MI 48336 MIDWEST

Boulder Community Hospital		(303) 440-2273
Boulder Community Hospital		
1100 Balsam Ave, Box 9019	Boulder, CO 80301	GREAT PLAINS AND MOUNTAINS
Boys Town National Research Hospital		(402) 498-6511
Boys Town Natl Rsch Hosp		
555 N 30th St	Omaha, NE 68131	GREAT PLAINS AND MOUNTAINS
Brenner Children's Hospital		(336) 716-2011
Brenner Chldrn's Hosp		
Medical Center Blvd	Winston-Salem, NC 27157-1015	SOUTHEAST
Brigham and Women's Hospital		(617) 732-5500
Brigham & Women's Hosp		
75 Francis St	Boston, MA 02115	NEW ENGLAND
Brooklyn Hospital Center		(718) 250-8000
Brooklyn Hosp Ctr		
121 DeKalb Avenue	Brooklyn, NY 11201	MID ATLANTIC
Brookwood Medical Center		(205) 877-1000
Brookwood Med Ctr		
2010 Brookwood Medical Ctr Drive	Birmingham, AL 35209-6804	SOUTHEAST
Broward Health Medical Center		(954) 355-4400
Broward Hlth Med Ctr		
1600 S Andrews Ave	Fort Lauderdale, FL 33316	SOUTHEAST
Bryn Mawr Hospital		(484) 337-3000
Bryn Mawr Hosp		
130 S Bryn Mawr Ave	Bryn Mawr, PA 19010-3143	MID ATLANTIC
Buffalo General Hospital		(716) 859-5600
Buffalo Genl Hosp		
100 High Street	Buffalo, NY 14203	MID ATLANTIC
Burke Rehabilitation Hospital		(914) 597-2500
Burke Rehab Hosp		
785 Mamaroneck Avenue	White Plains, NY 10605	MID ATLANTIC
Butler Hospital		(401) 455-6200
Butler Hosp		
345 Blackstone Blvd	Providence, RI 02906	NEW ENGLAND
Cabell Huntington Hospital		(304) 526-2000
Cabell Huntington Hosp		
1340 Hal Greer Blvd	Huntington, WV 25701-0195	MID ATLANTIC

California Pacific Medical Center - California Campus (415) 600-6000
CA Pacific Med Ctr - CA Campus
3700 California St San Francisco, CA 94114 WEST COAST AND PACIFIC

California Pacific Medical Center - Davies Campus (415) 600-6000
CA Pacific Med Ctr - Davies Campus
Castro at Duboce St San Francisco, CA 94114 WEST COAST AND PACIFIC

California Pacific Medical Center-Pacific Campus (415) 600-6000
CA Pacific Med Ctr-Pacific Campus
2333 Buchanan St, Box 7999 San Francisco, CA 94115 WEST COAST AND PACIFIC

Cape Cod Hospital (508) 771-1800
Cape Cod Hosp
27 Park St Hyannis, MA 02601-5203 NEW ENGLAND

Capital Health Medical Center - Hopewell (609) 303-4000
Capital Health Med Ctr - Hopewell
One Capital Way Pennington, NJ 08534 MID ATLANTIC

Cardon Children's Medical Center (480) 412-5437
Cardon Children's Med Ctr
1400 S Dobson Rd Mesa, AZ 85202 SOUTHWEST

Carilion Roanoke Memorial Hospital (540) 981-7000
Carilion Roanoke Meml Hosp
1906 Belleview Ave, PO Box 13367 Roanoke, VA 24014 SOUTHEAST

Carle Foundation Hospital (217) 383-3311
Carle Foundation Hosp
611 W Park St Urbana, IL 61801 MIDWEST

Carolinas Medical Center (704) 355-2000
Carolinas Med Ctr
1000 Blythe Blvd, PO Box 32861 Charlotte, NC 28203-5871 SOUTHEAST

Carolinas Medical Center-University (704) 863-6000
Carolinas Med Ctr-Univ
8800 N Tryon St Charlotte, NC 28262 SOUTHEAST

Carolinas Specialty Hospital (704) 304-6450
Carolinas Specialty Hosp
2001 Vail Ave 7th Fl South Charlotte, NC 28207 SOUTHEAST

Carteret General Hospital (252) 808-6000
Carteret Genl Hosp
3500 Arendell St Morehead City, NC 28557 SOUTHEAST

Cedars-Sinai Medical Center		(310) 423-3277
Cedars-Sinai Med Ctr		
8700 Beverly Boulevard	Los Angeles, CA 90048	WEST COAST AND PACIFIC
Centennial Medical Center		(615) 342-1000
Centennial Med Ctr		
2300 Patterson Street	Nashville, TN 37203	SOUTHEAST
Central DuPage Hospital		(630) 933-1600
Central DuPage Hosp		
25 N Winfield Rd	Winfield, IL 60190	MIDWEST
Chandler Regional Medical Center		(602) 963-4561
Chandler Regional Med Ctr		
475 S Dobson Rd	Chandler, AZ 85224-5695	SOUTHWEST
Chelsea Community Hospital		(734) 593-6000
Chelsea Comm Hosp		
775 S Main St	Chelsea, MI 48118	MIDWEST
Chestnut Hill Hospital		(212) 248-8200
Chestnut Hill Hosp		
8835 Germantown Ave	Philadelphia, PA 19118	MID ATLANTIC
Cheyenne Regional Medical Center		(307) 634-2273
Cheyenne Regl Med Ctr		
214 E 23rd St	Cheyenne, WY 82001	GREAT PLAINS AND MOUNTAINS
Children's Healthcare of Atlanta at Egleston		(404) 785-6000
Chldns Hlthcare Atlanta @ Egleston		
1405 Clifton Rd NE	Atlanta, GA 30322	SOUTHEAST
Children's Healthcare of Atlanta at Scottish Rite		(404) 785-5252
Chldns Hlthcare Atlanta @ Scottish Rite		
1001 Johnson Ferry Rd NE	Atlanta, GA 30342	SOUTHEAST
Children's Hospital		(804) 321-7474
Children's Hosp		
2924 Brook Rd	Richmond, VA 23220	SOUTHEAST
Children's Hospital - Aurora (Colorado)		(720) 777-1234
Chldn's Hosp - Aurora (CO)		
13123 E 16th Ave	Aurora, CO 80045	GREAT PLAINS AND MOUNTAINS
Children's Hospital - Boston		(617) 355-6000
Children's Hospital - Boston		
300 Longwood Avenue	Boston, MA 02115	NEW ENGLAND

Children's Hospital - Los Angeles (323) 660-2450
Chldns Hosp - Los Angeles
4650 Sunset Blvd Los Angeles, CA 90027 WEST COAST AND PACIFIC

Children's Hospital - New Orleans (504) 899-9511
Children's Hospital - New Orleans
200 Henry Clay Ave New Orleans, LA 70118 SOUTHWEST

Children's Hospital - Oakland (510) 428-3000
Chldns Hosp - Oakland
747 52nd St Oakland, CA 94609 WEST COAST AND PACIFIC

Children's Hospital - Omaha (402) 955-5400
Children's Hosp - Omaha
8200 Dodge St Omaha, NE 68114 GREAT PLAINS AND MOUNTAINS

Children's Hospital at OU Medical Center (405) 271-5437
Chldns Hosp OU Med Ctr
1200 Children's Ave Oklahoma City, OK 73104 SOUTHWEST

Children's Hospital Central California (559) 353-3000
Chldns Hosp Central CA
9300 Valley Children's Pl Madera, CA 93638 WEST COAST AND PACIFIC

Children's Hospital of Alabama (205) 638-9100
Children's Hosp AL
1600 7th Ave South Birmingham, AL 35233 SOUTHEAST

Children's Hospital of Michigan (313) 745-5437
Chldns Hosp of Michigan
3901 Beaubian Blvd Detroit, MI 48201 MIDWEST

Children's Hospital of Orange County (714) 997-3000
Chldns Hosp Orange Co
455 S Main St Orange, CA 92868 WEST COAST AND PACIFIC

Children's Hospital of Philadelphia (215) 590-1000
Chldns Hosp of Philadelphia
34th St & Civic Center Blvd Philadelphia, PA 19104 MID ATLANTIC

Children's Hospital of Pittsburgh - UPMC (412) 692-5325
Chldns Hosp of Pittsburgh - UPMC
4401 Penn Ave Pittsburgh, PA 15224 MID ATLANTIC

Children's Hospital of the King's Daughters (757) 668-7000
Chldns Hosp of King's Daughters
601 Children's Ln Norfolk, VA 23507 SOUTHEAST

Children's Hospital of Wisconsin (414) 266-2000
Chldns Hosp - Wisconsin
9000 W Wisconsin Ave Milwaukee, WI 53226 MIDWEST

Children's Hospitals & Clinics of Minnesota (612) 813-6000
Children's Hosps & Clinics of Minnesota
2525 Chicago Ave Minneapolis, MN 55404 MIDWEST

Children's Medical Center of Dallas (214) 456-7000
Chldns Med Ctr of Dallas
1935 Medical District Drive Dallas, TX 75235 SOUTHWEST

Children's Memorial Hermann Hospital (713) 704-5437
Children's Meml Hermann Hosp
6411 Fannin St Houston, TX 77030 SOUTHWEST

Children's Mercy Hospitals & Clinics (816) 234-3000
Chldns Mercy Hosps & Clinics
2401 Gilham Rd Kansas City, MO 64108 MIDWEST

Children's National Medical Center - DC (202) 476-5000
Chldns Natl Med Ctr
111 Michigan Ave NW Washington, DC 20010 MID ATLANTIC

Christ Hospital, The - Cincinnati (513) 585-2000
Christ Hosp, The - Cincinnati
2139 Auburn Ave Cincinnati, OH 45219 MIDWEST

Christiana Hospital (302) 733-1000
Christiana Hosp
4755 Ogletown-Stanton Rd Newark, DE 19718-0001 MID ATLANTIC

Christus Santa Rosa Children's Hospital (210) 704-2011
Christus Santa Rosa Children's Hosp
333 N Santa Rosa St San Antonio, TX 78207 SOUTHWEST

Christus Santa Rosa Medical Center Hospital (210) 705-6300
Christus Santa Rosa Med Ctr Hosp
2827 Babcock Rd San Antonio, TX 78229-6098 SOUTHWEST

Christus St Vincent Regional Medical Center-Santa Fe (505) 983-3361
Christus St Vincent Reg Med Ctr-Santa Fe
455 St Michaels Dr Santa Fe, NM 87504-2107 SOUTHWEST

CHRISTUS St. Frances Cabrini Hospital (318) 487-1122
CHRISTUS St. Frances Cabrini Hosp
3330 Masonic Dr Alexandria, LA 71301 SOUTHWEST

Cincinnati Children's Hospital Medical Center		(513) 636-4200
Cincinnati Chldns Hosp Med Ctr		
3333 Burnet Ave	Cincinnati, OH 45229-3039	MIDWEST
Cincinnati Shriners Hospital		(513) 872-6000
Cincinnati Shriners Hosp		
3229 Burnet Ave	Cincinnati, OH 45229-3095	MIDWEST
City of Hope National Medical Center		(626) 256-4673
City of Hope Natl Med Ctr		
1500 E Duarte Rd	Duarte, CA 91010	WEST COAST AND PACIFIC
Clara Maass Medical Center		(973) 450-2000
Clara Maass Med Ctr		
One Clara Maass Drive	Belleville, NJ 07109	MID ATLANTIC
Cleveland Clinic		(216) 444-2200
Cleveland Clin		
9500 Euclid Avenue	Cleveland, OH 44195	MIDWEST
Cleveland Clinic Florida - Weston		(954) 659-5000
Cleveland Clin - Weston		
2950 Cleveland Clinic Blvd	Weston, FL 33331	SOUTHEAST
Columbia Medical Center - Plano		(972) 596-6800
Columbia Med Ctr - Plano		
3901 West 15th Street	Plano, TX 75075	SOUTHWEST
Columbia St Mary's Hospital-Milwaukee		(414) 291-1000
Columbia St Mary's Hosp-Milwaukee		
2301 N Lake Drive	Milwaukee, WI 53211-4508	MIDWEST
Community Hospital East - Indianapolis		(317) 355-5411
Community Hosp E - Indianapolis		
1500 N Ritter Ave	Indianapolis, IN 46219	MIDWEST
Community Hospital of Monterey Peninsula		(831) 624-5311
Comm Hosp of Monterey Pen		
23625 Holman Hwy	Monterey, CA 93940	WEST COAST AND PACIFIC
Community Medical Center		(406) 728-4100
Community Med Ctr		
2827 Fort Missoula Rd	Missoula, MT 59804	GREAT PLAINS AND MOUNTAINS
Community Memorial Hospital - Ventura		(805) 652-5011
Comm Meml Hosp - Ventura		
147 N Brent St	Ventura, CA 93003	WEST COAST AND PACIFIC

Concord Hospital (603) 225-2711
Concord Hospital
250 Pleasant St Concord, NH 03301-2598 NEW ENGLAND

Connecticut Children's Medical Center (860) 545-9000
CT Chldns Med Ctr
282 Washington St Hartford, CT 06106 NEW ENGLAND

Cook Children's Medical Center (682) 885-4000
Cook Chldns Med Ctr
801 7th Ave Fort Worth, TX 76104-2796 SOUTHWEST

Cooper University Hospital (856) 342-2000
Cooper Univ Hosp
1 Cooper Plaza Camden, NJ 08103 MID ATLANTIC

Covenant Children's Hospital (806) 725-0000
Covenant Children's Hosp
3610 21st St Lubbock, TX 79410 SOUTHWEST

Covenant HealthCare (517) 583-4000
Covenant HealthCare
1447 N Harrison St Saginaw, MI 48602 MIDWEST

Covenant Medical Center (319) 272-8000
Covenant Med Ctr
3421 W 9th St Waterloo, IA 50702-5499 MIDWEST

Covenant Medical Center (806) 725-0000
Covenant Med Ctr
3615 19th St Lubbock, TX 79410-1203 SOUTHWEST

Crouse Hospital (315) 470-7111
Crouse Hosp
736 Irving Ave Syracuse, NY 13210-1607 MID ATLANTIC

Crozer - Chester Medical Center (610) 447-2000
Crozer - Chester Med Ctr
One Medical Center Boulevard Upland, PA 19013 MID ATLANTIC

CTCA at Midwestern Regional Medical Center (847) 872-4561
CTCA at Midwestern Reg Med Ctr
2520 Elisha Ave Zion, IL 60099 MIDWEST

CTCA at Southeastern Regional Medical Center (770) 400-6000
CTCA at Southeastern Regl Med Ctr
600 Parkway North Newnan, GA 30265 SOUTHEAST

CTCA at Southwestern Regional Medical Center (918) 496-5500
CTCA at Southwestern Regl Med Ctr
10109 E 79th St (81st St & Highway 169) Tulsa, OK 74133 SOUTHWEST

CTCA at Western Regional Medical Center (623) 207-3000
CTCA at Western Regl Med Ctr
14200 W Fillmore St Goodyear, AZ 85338 SOUTHWEST

Dana-Farber Cancer Institute (617) 632-3000
Dana-Farber Cancer Inst
450 Brookline Ave Boston, MA 02215 NEW ENGLAND

Dartmouth - Hitchcock Medical Center (603) 650-5000
Dartmouth - Hitchcock Med Ctr
1 Medical Center Dr Lebanon, NH 03756-0002 NEW ENGLAND

DCH Regional Medical Center (205) 759-7111
DCH Reg Med Ctr
809 University Blvd E Tuscaloosa, AL 35401-2029 SOUTHEAST

Dell Children's Medical Center of Central Texas (512) 324-0000
Dell Children's Med Ctr of Central Texas
4900 Mueller Blvd Austin, TX 78723 SOUTHWEST

Denver Health Medical Center (303) 436-6000
Denver Health Med Ctr
777 Bannock St Denver, CO 80204 GREAT PLAINS AND MOUNTAINS

Desert Regional Medical Center (760) 323-6511
Desert Regl Med Ctr
1150 N Indian Canyon Dr Palm Springs, CA 92262 WEST COAST AND PACIFIC

Detroit Medical Center (313) 578-3930
Detroit Med Ctr
3663 Woodward Ave, Ste 200 Detroit, MI 48201-2403 MIDWEST

DMC Surgery Hospital (248) 733-2200
DMC Surgery Hosp
30671 Stephenson Hwy Madison Heights, MI 48071 MIDWEST

Doctors' Hospital - Coral Gables (FL) (786) 308-3000
Doctors' Hosp - Coral Gables (FL)
5000 University Dr Coral Gables, FL 33146 SOUTHEAST

Doernbecher Children's Hospital/Oregon Health Science University (503) 494-8311
Doernbecher Chldns Hosp/OHSU
3181 SW Sam Jackson Park Rd Portland, OR 97239 WEST COAST AND PACIFIC

Duke Raleigh Hospital | (919) 954-3000
Duke Raleigh Hosp
3400 Wake Forest Rd | Raleigh, NC 27609 | SOUTHEAST

Duke University Hospital | (919) 684-8111
Duke Univ Hosp
2301 Erwin Rd, PO Box 3708 | Durham, NC 27710 | SOUTHEAST

Durham Regional Hospital | (919) 470-4000
Durham Regional Hosp
3643 N Roxboro Rd | Durham, NC 27704 | SOUTHEAST

East Jefferson General Hospital | (504) 454-4000
E Jefferson Genl Hosp
4200 Houma Blvd | Metairie, LA 70006-2973 | SOUTHWEST

Eastern Niagara Hospital-Lockport | (716) 514-5700
Eastern Niagara Hosp-Lockport
521 East Ave | Lockport, NY 14094 | MID ATLANTIC

Edward Hines, Jr. VA Hospital | (708) 202-3800
Edward Hines, Jr. VA Hosp
5000 South 5th Avenue | Hines, IL 60141 | MIDWEST

Einstein Medical Center | (215) 456-6730
Einstein Med Ctr
5501 Old York Rd | Philadelphia, PA 19141 | MID ATLANTIC

Eisenhower Medical Center | (760) 340-3911
Eisenhower Med Ctr
39000 Bob Hope Drive | Rancho Mirage, CA 92270 | WEST COAST AND PACIFIC

El Camino Hospital | (650) 940-7000
El Camino Hosp
2500 Grant Road | Mountain View, CA 94040 | WEST COAST AND PACIFIC

El Paso Children's Hospital | (915) 298-5444
El Paso Chldns Hosp
4845 Alameda Ave | El Paso, TX 79905 | SOUTHWEST

Elliot Hospital | (603) 669-5300
Elliot Hosp
1 Elliot Way | Manchester, NH 03103 | NEW ENGLAND

Elmhurst Hospital Center | (718) 334-4000
Elmhurst Hosp Ctr
79-01 Broadway | Elmhurst, NY 11373 | MID ATLANTIC

Emory University Hospital		(404) 712-2000
Emory Univ Hosp		
1364 Clifton Rd NE	Atlanta, GA 30322	SOUTHEAST
Emory University Hospital Midtown		(404) 686-4411
Emory Univ Hosp Midtown		
550 Peachtree St NE	Atlanta, GA 30308	SOUTHEAST
Englewood Hospital & Medical Center		(201) 894-3000
Englewood Hosp & Med Ctr		
350 Engle Street	Englewood, NJ 07631	MID ATLANTIC
Erie County Medical Center		(716) 898-3000
Erie County Med Ctr		
462 Grider St	Buffalo, NY 14215	MID ATLANTIC
Erlanger Medical Center		(423) 778-7000
Erlanger Med Ctr		
975 E 3rd St	Chattanooga, TN 37403	SOUTHEAST
Evanston Hospital/NorthShore University Health System		(847) 570-2000
Evanston Hosp/NorthShore Univ Hlth Sys		
2650 Ridge Ave	Evanston, IL 60201	MIDWEST
Exempla Saint Joseph Hospital-Denver		(303) 837-7111
Exempla Saint Jos. Hosp.-Denver		
1835 Franklin Street	Denver, CO 80218	GREAT PLAINS AND MOUNTAINS
Fairview Lakes Medical Center		(651) 982-7000
Fairview Lakes Med Ctr		
5200 Fairview Blvd	Wyoming, MN 55092	MIDWEST
Fairview Southdale Hospital		(952) 924-5000
Fairview Southdale Hosp		
6401 France Ave S	Edina, MN 55435-2199	MIDWEST
Fletcher Allen Health Care - Medical Center Campus		(802) 847-0000
FAHC - Med Ctr Campus		
111 Colchester Ave	Burlington, VT 05401	NEW ENGLAND
Floating Hospital for Children at Tufts Medical Center, The		(617) 636-5000
Floating Hosp for Children at Tufts		
755 Washington St	Boston, MA 02111	NEW ENGLAND
Florida Hospital - Celebration Health		(407) 303-4000
Florida Hosp Celebration Hlth		
400 Celebration Pl	Celebration, FL 34747	SOUTHEAST

Florida Hospital - Orlando (407) 303-5600
Florida Hosp - Orlando
601 E Rollins St Orlando, FL 32803 SOUTHEAST

Florida Hospital - Tampa (813) 971-6000
Florida Hosp - Tampa
3100 E Fletcher Avenue Tampa, FL 33613 SOUTHEAST

Floyd Memorial Hospital & Health Services (812) 944-7701
Floyd Meml Hosp & Hlth Svcs
1850 State St New Albany, IN 47150-4997 MIDWEST

Forest Park Medical Center (972) 234-1900
Forest Park Med Ctr
11990 N Central Exprwy Dallas, TX 75243 SOUTHWEST

Forsyth Medical Center (336) 718-5000
Forsyth Med Ctr
3333 Silas Creek Pkwy Winston-Salem, NC 27103 SOUTHEAST

Fort Sanders Regional Medical Center (865) 541-1111
Fort Sanders Reg Med Ctr
1901 Clinch Ave SW Knoxville, TN 37916-2398 SOUTHEAST

Four Winds Hospital (914) 763-8151
Four Winds Hosp
800 Cross River Road Katonah, NY 10536 MID ATLANTIC

Fox Chase Cancer Center (215) 728-6900
Fox Chase Cancer Ctr
333 Cottman Avenue Philadelphia, PA 19111 MID ATLANTIC

Franciscan St. Francis Health-Indianapolis (317) 528-5000
Franciscan St. Francis Hlth-Indianapolis
8111 S Emerson Ave Indianapolis, IN 46237 MIDWEST

Frederick Memorial Hospital (301) 698-3300
Frederick Mem Hospital
400 West 7th Street Frederick, MD 21701 MID ATLANTIC

Froedtert & The Medical College of Wisconsin (414) 805-3000
Froedtert & Med Coll WI
9200 W Wisconsin Ave Milwaukee, WI 53226 MIDWEST

Gaston Memorial Hospital (704) 834-2000
Gaston Meml Hosp
2525 Court Dr Gastonia, NC 28054 SOUTHEAST

George Washington University Hospital (202) 715-4000
G Washington Univ Hosp
900 23rd St NW Washington, DC 20037 MID ATLANTIC

Georgia Regents Medical Center-Augusta (706) 721-0211
Georgia Regents Med Ctr-Augusta
1120 15th Street Augusta, GA 30912 SOUTHEAST

Glenbrook Hospital/NorthShore University Health System (847) 657-5800
Glenbrook Hosp/NorthShore Univ Hlth Syst
2100 Pfingsten Rd Glenview, IL 60026 MIDWEST

Glendale Memorial Hospital & Health Center (818) 502-1900
Glendale Mem Hosp & Hlth Ctr
1420 S Central Ave Glendale, CA 91204-2594 WEST COAST AND PACIFIC

Golisano Children's Hospital (716) 275-2100
Golisano Chldn's Hosp
601 Elmwood Avenue Rochester, NY 14623 MID ATLANTIC

Good Samaritan Hosp - Cincinnati (513) 872-1400
Good Samaritan Hosp - Cincinnati
375 Dixmyth Ave Cincinnati, OH 45220 MIDWEST

Good Samaritan Hospital - Los Angeles (213) 977-2121
Good Samaritan Hosp - LA
1225 Wilshire Boulevard Los Angeles, CA 90017 WEST COAST AND PACIFIC

Good Samaritan Medical Center - West Palm Beach (561) 655-5511
Good Sam Med Ctr - W Palm Beach
1309 N Flagler Dr West Palm Beach, FL 33401 SOUTHEAST

Gottlieb Memorial Hospital (708) 681-3200
Gottlieb Meml Hosp
701 W North Ave Melrose Park, IL 60160 MIDWEST

Grady Health System (404) 616-1000
Grady Hlth Sys
80 Jesse Hill Jr SE Atlanta, GA 30303 SOUTHEAST

Greater Baltimore Medical Center (443) 849-2000
Greater Baltimore Med Ctr
6701 N Charles St Baltimore, MD 21204 MID ATLANTIC

Greenville Health System (864) 455-7000
Greenville Hlth Sys
701 Grove Rd Greenville, SC 29605 SOUTHEAST

Greenville Memorial Hospital		(864) 455-7000
Greenville Meml Hosp		
701 Grove Rd	Greenville, SC 29605	SOUTHEAST
Greenwich Hospital		(203) 863-3000
Greenwich Hosp		
5 Perryridge Rd	Greenwich, CT 06830	NEW ENGLAND
Hackensack University Medical Center		(551) 996-2000
Hackensack Univ Med Ctr		
30 Prospect Avenue	Hackensack, NJ 07601	MID ATLANTIC
Hahnemann University Hospital		(215) 762-7000
Hahnemann Univ Hosp		
Broad & Vine St	Philadelphia, PA 19102	MID ATLANTIC
Harborview Medical Center		(206) 744-3000
Harborview Med Ctr		
325 9th Ave	Seattle, WA 98104	WEST COAST AND PACIFIC
Harper University Hospital		(313) 745-8040
Harper Univ Hosp		
3990 John R St	Detroit, MI 48201-2097	MIDWEST
Harrison Medical Center		(360) 774-3911
Harrison Med Ctr		
2520 Cherry Ave	Bremerton, WA 98310-4270	WEST COAST AND PACIFIC
Hartford Hospital		(860) 545-5000
Hartford Hosp		
80 Seymour St	Hartford, CT 06102-5037	NEW ENGLAND
Healthsouth Lakeshore Rehabilitation Hospital		(205) 868-2000
Healthsouth Lakeshore Rehab Hosp		
3800 Ridgeway Drive	Birmingham, AL 35209	SOUTHEAST
Hennepin County Medical Center		(612) 873-3000
Hennepin Cnty Med Ctr		
701 Park Ave	Minneapolis, MN 55415	MIDWEST
Henrico Doctors Hospital		(804) 289-4500
Henrico Doctors Hosp		
1602 Skipwith Road	Richmond, VA 23229	SOUTHEAST
Henry Ford Hospital		(313) 916-2600
Henry Ford Hosp		
2799 W Grand Blvd	Detroit, MI 48202	MIDWEST

Henry Ford West Bloomfield Hospital (248) 661-4100
Henry Ford- W Bloomfield Hosp
6777 W Maple Rd West Bloomfield, MI 48322 MIDWEST

Henry Mayo Newhall Memorial Hospital (661) 253-8000
Henry Mayo Newhall Memorial Hosp
23845 McBean Parkway Valencia, CA 91355 WEST COAST AND PACIFIC

Highland Hospital of Rochester (585) 473-2200
Highland Hosp of Rochester
1000 South Ave Rochester, NY 14620 MID ATLANTIC

Highland Park Hospital/NorthShore University Health System (847) 432-8000
Highland Park Hosp/NorthShore Univ Hlth Syst
777 Park Ave Highland Park, IL 60035 MIDWEST

Hilton Head Regional Medical Center (843) 681-6122
Hilton Head Reg Med Ctr
25 Hospital Ctr Blvd Hilton Head, SC 29926 SOUTHEAST

Hoag Hospital Irvine (949) 764-4624
Hoag Hosp Irvine
16200 Sand Canyon Ave Irvine, CA 92618 WEST COAST AND PACIFIC

Hoag Memorial Hospital Presbyterian (949) 645-8600
Hoag Meml Hosp Presby
One Hoag Drive Newport Beach, CA 92663 WEST COAST AND PACIFIC

Hollywood Presbyterian Medical Center (213) 413-3000
Hollywood Presby Med Ctr
1300 N Vermont Ave Los Angeles, CA 90027-6069 WEST COAST AND PACIFIC

Holy Cross Hospital - Fort Lauderdale (954) 771-8000
Holy Cross Hosp - Fort Lauderdale
4725 N Federal Hwy Fort Lauderdale, FL 33308 SOUTHEAST

Holy Cross Hospital - Silver Spring (301) 754-7000
Holy Cross Hospital - Silver Spring
1500 Forest Glen Road Silver Spring, MD 20910 MID ATLANTIC

Hospital for Special Surgery (212) 606-1000
Hosp For Special Surgery
535 East 70th Street New York, NY 10021 MID ATLANTIC

Hospital of Central CT at New Britain (860) 224-5011
Hosp of Central CT at New Britain
100 Grand St New Britain, CT 06050 NEW ENGLAND

Hospital of the University of Pennsylvania - UPHS (215) 662-4000
Hosp Univ Penn - UPHS
3400 Spruce Street Philadelphia, PA 19104 MID ATLANTIC

Howard University Hospital (202) 865-6100
Howard Univ Hosp
2041 Georgia Ave NW Washington, DC 20060 MID ATLANTIC

Huntsville Hospital (256) 265-1000
Huntsville Hosp, The
101 Sivley Rd Huntsville, AL 35801-4470 SOUTHEAST

Indian River Medical Center (772) 567-4311
Indian River Med Ctr
1000 36th St Vero Beach, FL 32960 SOUTHEAST

Indiana University Health Methodist Hospital (317) 962-2000
IU Health Methodist Hosp
1701 N Senate Blvd Indianapolis, IN 46202 MIDWEST

Indiana University Health North Hospital (317) 688-2000
IU Health North Hosp
11700 N Meridian St Carmel, IN 46032 MIDWEST

Indiana University Health University Hospital (317) 944-5000
IU Hlth Univ Hosp
550 N University Blvd Indianapolis, IN 46210 MIDWEST

Ingalls Memorial Hospital (708) 333-2300
Ingalls Meml Hosp
1 Ingalls Dr Harvey, IL 60426 MIDWEST

Inova Fair Oaks Hospital (703) 391-3600
Inova Fair Oaks Hosp
3600 Joseph Siewick Dr Fairfax, VA 22033 SOUTHEAST

Inova Fairfax Hospital (703) 776-4001
Inova Fairfax Hosp
3300 Gallows Road Falls Church, VA 22042 SOUTHEAST

Inova Fairfax Hospital for Children (703) 776-4002
Inova Fairfax Hosp for Chldn
3300 Gallows Rd Fairfax, VA 22042 SOUTHEAST

INTEGRIS Baptist Medical Center - Oklahoma (405) 949-3011
INTEGRIS Baptist Med Ctr - OK
3300 NW Expressway Oklahoma City, OK 73112-9028 SOUTHWEST

Intermountain Medical Center (801) 507-7000
Intermountain Med Ctr
5121 S Cottonwood St Murray, UT 84157 GREAT PLAINS AND MOUNTAINS

Jackson Memorial Hospital (305) 585-1111
Jackson Meml Hosp
1611 NW 12th Ave Miami, FL 33136 SOUTHEAST

Jackson North Medical Center (305) 651-1100
Jackson N Med Ctr
160 NW 170 St North Miami Beach, FL 33169 SOUTHEAST

James J. Peters VA Medical Center-Bronx (718) 584-9000
James J. Peters VA Med Ctr-Bronx
130 W Kingsbridge Rd Bronx, NY 10468 MID ATLANTIC

Jeanes Hospital (215) 728-2000
Jeanes Hosp
7600 Central Ave Philadelphia, PA 19111 MID ATLANTIC

Jersey Shore University Medical Center (732) 775-5500
Jersey Shore Univ Med Ctr
1945 Route 33 Neptune, NJ 07753 MID ATLANTIC

Jewish Hospital - Kenwood - Cincinnati (513) 686-3000
Jewish Hosp - Kenwood - Cincinnati
4777 E Galbraith Rd Cincinnati, OH 45236-2891 MIDWEST

Jewish Hospital - Louisville, KY (502) 587-4011
Jewish Hosp (KY)
200 Abraham Flexner Way Louisville, KY 40202 SOUTHEAST

JFK Medical Center - Atlantis (561) 965-7300
JFK Med Ctr - Atlantis
5301 S Congress Ave Atlantis, FL 33462 SOUTHEAST

JFK Medical Center - Edison (732) 321-7000
JFK Med Ctr - Edison
65 James St Edison, NJ 08820 MID ATLANTIC

Joe DiMaggio Children's Hospital (954) 987-2000
Joe DiMaggio Chldns Hosp
1005 Joe Dimaggio Drive Hollywood, FL 33021 SOUTHEAST

John D. Dingell VA Medical Center, Detroit (313) 562-1000
John D. Dingell VA Med Ctr, Detroit
4646 John R. Street Detroit, MI 48201 MIDWEST

Johns Hopkins Bayview Medical Center (410) 550-0100
Johns Hopkins Bayview Med Ctr
4940 Eastern Avenue Baltimore, MD 21224 MID ATLANTIC

Johns Hopkins Hospital (410) 955-5000
Johns Hopkins Hosp
600 N Wolfe St Baltimore, MD 21287 MID ATLANTIC

Kaiser Permanente Baldwin Park Medical Center (626) 851-1011
Kaiser Permanente Baldwin Pk Med Ctr
1011 Baldwin Park Blvd Baldwin Park, CA 91706 WEST COAST AND PACIFIC

Kaiser Permanente Los Angeles Medical Center (323) 783-4011
Kaiser Permanente LA Med Ctr
1526 N Edgemont St Los Angeles, CA 90027 WEST COAST AND PACIFIC

Kaiser Permanente Oakland Medical Center (510) 752-1000
Kaiser Permanente Oakland Med Ctr
280 West MacArthur Boulevard Oakland, CA 94611 WEST COAST AND PACIFIC

Kaiser Permanente South San Francisco Medical Center (650) 742-2000
Kaiser Permanente S San Francisco Med Ctr
1200 El Camino Real South San Francisco, CA 94080 WEST COAST AND PACIFIC

Kaiser Permanente Woodland Hills Medical Center (818) 719-2000
Kaiser Permanente Woodland Hills Med Ctr
5601 De Soto Ave Woodland Hills, CA 91365 WEST COAST AND PACIFIC

Kalispell Regional Medical Center (406) 752-5111
Kalispell Regl Med Ctr
310 Sunnyview Ln Kalispell, MT 59901-3199 GREAT PLAINS AND MOUNTAINS

Kapiolani Medical Center for Women & Children (808) 983-6000
Kapiolani Med Ctr for Women & Chldn
1319 Punahou St Honolulu, HI 96826 WEST COAST AND PACIFIC

Keck Medical Center of USC (323) 442-8500
Keck Med Ctr of USC
1500 San Pablo St Los Angeles, CA 90033 WEST COAST AND PACIFIC

Kessler Institute for Rehabilitation - West Orange (973) 731-3600
Kessler Inst for Rehab - W Orange
1199 Pleasant Valley Way West Orange, NJ 07052-1499 MID ATLANTIC

Kittitas Valley Community Hospital (509) 962-9841
Kittitas Valley Community Hosp
603 S Chestnut St Ellensburg, WA 98926 WEST COAST AND PACIFIC

Kootenai Medical Center *Kootenai Med Ctr* Kootenai Health Way	Coeur d'Alene, ID 83814	(208) 666-2000 GREAT PLAINS AND MOUNTAINS
Kosair Children's Hospital *Kosair Chldn's Hosp* 231 E Chestnut St	Louisville, KY 40202	(502) 629-6000 SOUTHEAST
LAC & USC Medical Center *LAC & USC Med Ctr* 1200 N State St	Los Angeles, CA 90033-4525	(323) 409-1000 WEST COAST AND PACIFIC
LAC - Harbor - UCLA Medical Center *LAC - Harbor - UCLA Med Ctr* 1000 W Carson St, Box 27 PO Box 2910	Torrance, CA 90502	(310) 222-2345 WEST COAST AND PACIFIC
Lafayette General Medical Center *Lafayette Genl Med Ctr* 1214 Coolidge Blvd	Lafayette, LA 70503	(337) 289-7991 SOUTHWEST
Lahey Hospital & Medical Center *Lahey Hosp & Med Ctr* 41 Mall Road	Burlington, MA 01805	(781) 744-5100 NEW ENGLAND
Lakeland Regional Medical Center *Lakeland Regl Med Ctr* 1324 Lakeland Hills Blvd	Lakeland, FL 33805	(863) 687-1100 SOUTHEAST
Lakeland Specialty Hospital *Lakeland Specialty Hosp* 6418 Deans Hill Rd	Berrien Center, MI 49102	(269) 471-7761 MIDWEST
Lankenau Hospital *Lankenau Hosp* 100 Lancaster Ave	Wynnewood, PA 19096-3498	(484) 476-2000 MID ATLANTIC
Largo Medical Center *Largo Med Ctr* 201 14th St SW	Largo, FL 33770	(727) 588-5200 SOUTHEAST
LDS Hospital *LDS Hosp* 8th Ave & C St	Salt Lake City, UT 84143	(801) 408-1100 GREAT PLAINS AND MOUNTAINS
Le Bonheur Children's Medical Center *Le Bonheur Chldns Med Ctr* 50 N Dunlap	Memphis, TN 38103-2893	(901) 287-5437 SOUTHEAST

Lee Memorial Health Systems (239) 343-2000
Lee Memorial Hlth Systems
2776 Cleveland Ave Fort Myers, FL 33901 SOUTHEAST

Legacy Good Samaritan Medical Center (503) 413-7711
Legacy Good Samaritan Med Ctr
1015 NW 22nd Ave Portland, OR 97210-3025 WEST COAST AND PACIFIC

Lehigh Valley Hospital (610) 402-8000
Lehigh Valley Hosp
Cedar Crest & I-78, P.O. Box 689 Allentown, PA 18105 MID ATLANTIC

Lenox Hill Hospital (212) 434-2000
Lenox Hill Hosp
100 East 77th Street New York, NY 10021 MID ATLANTIC

Lenox Hill Hospital (Manhattan Eye, Ear & Throat Hosp) (212) 838-9200
Lenox Hill Hosp (Manh Eye, Ear & Throat Hosp)
210 East 64th Street New York, NY 10021 MID ATLANTIC

Loma Linda Children's Hospital (909) 558-8000
Loma Linda Chldns Hosp
11234 Anderson St Loma Linda, CA 92354 WEST COAST AND PACIFIC

Loma Linda University Medical Center (909) 558-4000
Loma Linda Univ Med Ctr
11234 Anderson St Loma Linda, CA 92354 WEST COAST AND PACIFIC

Long Beach Memorial Medical Center (562) 933-2000
Long Beach Meml Med Ctr
2801 Atlantic Ave Long Beach, CA 90806 WEST COAST AND PACIFIC

Long Island Jewish Medical Center (718) 470-7000
Long Is Jewish Med Ctr
270-05 76th Avenue New Hyde Park, NY 11040 MID ATLANTIC

Los Alamitos Medical Center (562) 598-1311
Los Alamitos Med Ctr
3751 Katella Ave Los Alamitos, CA 90720 WEST COAST AND PACIFIC

Louisiana State University Hospital (318) 675-5000
Louisiana State Univ Hosp
1501 Kings Highway P.O. Box 33932 Shreveport, LA 71130 SOUTHWEST

Loyola University Medical Center (708) 327-3627
Loyola Univ Med Ctr
2160 S 1st Ave Maywood, IL 60153 MIDWEST

Loyola University Medical Center - Ronald McDonald Children's Hospital (708) 216-5437
Loyola Univ - Ronald McDonald Children's Hosp
2160 S First Ave Maywood, IL 60153 MIDWEST

Lucile Packard Children's Hospital (650) 497-8000
Lucile Packard Chldn's Hosp
725 Welch Rd Palo Alto, CA 94304 WEST COAST AND PACIFIC

Lutheran Medical Center - Brooklyn (718) 630-7000
Lutheran Med Ctr - Brooklyn
150 55th Street Brooklyn, NY 11220 MID ATLANTIC

Lutheran Medical Center - Cleveland (216) 696-4300
Lutheran Med Ctr - Cleveland
1730 W 25th St Cleveland, OH 44113 MIDWEST

Magee Rehabilitation Hospital (215) 587-3000
Magee Rehab Hosp
1513 Race St Philadelphia, PA 19102-1177 MID ATLANTIC

Magee-Womens Hospital of UPMC (412) 641-1000
Magee-Womens Hosp - UPMC
300 Halket Street Pittsburgh, PA 15213 MID ATLANTIC

Maimonides Medical Center (718) 283-6000
Maimonides Med Ctr
4802 Tenth Avenue Brooklyn, NY 11219 MID ATLANTIC

Maine Medical Center (207) 662-0111
Maine Med Ctr
22 Bramhall St Portland, ME 04102 NEW ENGLAND

Malcom Randall VA Medical Center (352) 376-1611
Malcom Randall VA Med Ctr
1601 SW Archer Rd Gainesville, FL 32608 SOUTHEAST

Maple Grove Hospital (763) 581-1000
Maple Grove Hosp
9875 Hospital Dr Maple Grove, MN 55369 MIDWEST

Marianjoy Rehabilitation Hospital (630) 462-4000
Marianjoy Rehab Hosp
26 W 171 Roosevelt Rd Wheaton, IL 60187 MIDWEST

Marin General Hospital (415) 925-7000
Marin Genl Hosp
250 Bon Air Rd Greenbrae, CA 94904 WEST COAST AND PACIFIC

Marina Del Rey Hospital (310) 823-8911
Marina Del Rey Hosp
4650 Lincoln Blvd Marina Del Rey, CA 90292 WEST COAST AND PACIFIC

Mary Bridge Children's Hospital & Health Center (253) 403-1000
Mary Bridge Chldns Hosp & Hlth Ctr
317 Martin Luther King Jr Way Tacoma, WA 98405 WEST COAST AND PACIFIC

Maryland General Hospital (410) 225-8000
Maryland Genl Hosp
827 Linden Ave Baltimore, MD 21201 MID ATLANTIC

Massachusetts Eye and Ear Infirmary (617) 523-7900
Mass Eye & Ear Infirm
243 Charles Street Boston, MA 02114 NEW ENGLAND

Massachusetts General Hospital (617) 726-2000
Mass Genl Hosp
55 Fruit St Boston, MA 02114 NEW ENGLAND

Massachusetts Mental Health Center (617) 626-9300
MA Mental Hlth Ctr
180 Morton St Jamaica Plain, MA 02130 NEW ENGLAND

Mattel Children's Hospital at UCLA (310) 825-9111
Mattel Chldns Hosp at UCLA
10833 Le Conte Ave Los Angeles, CA 90095-1752 WEST COAST AND PACIFIC

Maui Memorial Medical Center (808) 244-9056
Maui Meml Med Ctr
221 Mahalani St Wailuku, HI 96793 WEST COAST AND PACIFIC

Mayo Clinic - Jacksonville, FL (904) 953-2000
Mayo - Jacksonville
4500 San Pablo Road Jacksonville, FL 32224 SOUTHEAST

Mayo Clinic - Phoenix (480) 515-6296
Mayo Clinic - Phoenix
5777 E Mayo Blvd Phoenix, AZ 85054 SOUTHWEST

Mayo Clinic - Rochester, MN (507) 284-2511
Mayo Med Ctr & Clin - Rochester
200 First St SW Rochester, MN 55905 MIDWEST

Mayo Clinic - Scottsdale (480) 301-8000
Mayo Clinic - Scottsdale
13400 E Shea Blvd Scottsdale, AZ 85259 SOUTHWEST

McKenzie-Willamette Medical Center (541) 726-4400
McKenzie-Willamette Med Ctr
1460 G St Springfield, OR 97477 WEST COAST AND PACIFIC

McLaren Flint (810) 342-2000
McLaren Flint
401 S. Ballenger Highway Flint, MI 48532 MIDWEST

McLaren Macomb (586) 493-8000
McLaren Macomb
1000 Harrington Blvd Mount Clemens, MI 48043 MIDWEST

McLean Hospital (617) 855-2000
McLean Hosp
115 Mill St Belmont, MA 02478 NEW ENGLAND

MD Anderson Cancer Center-Orlando (407) 648-3800
MD Anderson Cancer Ctr-Orlando
1400 S Orange Ave Orlando, FL 32806 SOUTHEAST

Medical Center of Central Georgia (478) 633-1000
Med Ctr of Central GA
777 Hemlock Street Macon, GA 31201 SOUTHEAST

Medical City Dallas Hospital (972) 566-7000
Med City Dallas Hosp
7777 Forest Ln Dallas, TX 75230-2594 SOUTHWEST

Medical College of Virginia Hospitals (804) 828-9000
Med Coll of VA Hosp
1250 E Marshall St, Box 980510 Richmond, VA 23298 SOUTHEAST

Medical University of South Carolina Children's Hospital (843) 792-1414
MUSC Chldns Hosp
169 Ashley Ave Charleston, SC 29425 SOUTHEAST

Medical University of South Carolina Medical Center (843) 792-2300
MUSC Med Ctr
171 Ashley Ave Charleston, SC 29425 SOUTHEAST

MedStar Franklin Square Hospital (443) 777-7000
MedStar Franklin Square Hosp
9000 Franklin Square Drive Baltimore, MD 21237 MID ATLANTIC

MedStar Georgetown University Hospital (202) 444-2000
MedStar Georgetown Univ Hosp
3800 Reservoir Rd NW Washington, DC 20007 MID ATLANTIC

MedStar Good Samaritan Hospital (443) 444-8000
MedStar Good Samaritan Hosp
5601 Loch Raven Blvd Baltimore, MD 21239 MID ATLANTIC

MedStar National Rehabilitation Hospital (202) 877-1000
MedStar Natl Rehab Hosp
102 Irving St NW Washington, DC 20010 MID ATLANTIC

MedStar Union Memorial Hospital (410) 554-2000
MedStar Union Meml Hosp
201 E University Pkwy Baltimore, MD 21218 MID ATLANTIC

MedStar Washington Hospital Center (202) 877-7000
MedStar Washington Hosp Ctr
110 Irving St NW Washington, DC 20010 MID ATLANTIC

Memorial Health University Medical Center - Savannah (912) 350-8000
Meml Hlth Univ Med Ctr - Savannah
4700 Waters Ave Savannah, GA 31404 SOUTHEAST

Memorial Hermann Hospital - Texas Medical Center (713) 704-4000
Meml Hermann Hosp - Texas Med Ctr
6411 Fannin Houston, TX 77030 SOUTHWEST

Memorial Hermann Southwest Hospital (713) 456-5000
Meml Hermann SW Hosp
7600 Beechnut St Houston, TX 77074-4389 SOUTHWEST

Memorial Hospital (228) 867-4000
Meml Hosp
4500 13th St Gulfport, MS 39501 SOUTHEAST

Memorial Medical Center-Springfield (217) 788-3000
Memorial Med Ctr-Springfield
701 N First St Springfield, IL 62781 MIDWEST

Memorial Regional Hospital (954) 987-2000
Meml Regl Hosp
3501 Johnson Street Hollywood, FL 33021 SOUTHEAST

Memorial Sloan-Kettering Cancer Center (212) 639-2000
Meml Sloan-Kettering Canc Ctr
1275 York Avenue New York, NY 10021 MID ATLANTIC

Menninger Clinic (800) 351-9058
Menninger Clinic
12301 Main St Houston, TX 77035 SOUTHWEST

Mercy General Hospital - Sacramento (916) 453-4545
Mercy General Hosp - Sacramento
4001 J Street Sacramento, CA 95819 WEST COAST AND PACIFIC

Mercy Gilbert Medical Center (480) 728-8000
Mercy Gilbert Med Ctr
3555 S Val Vista Drive Gilbert, AZ 85297 SOUTHWEST

Mercy Health Center - Oklahoma City (405) 755-1515
Mercy Hlth Ctr - Oklahoma City
4300 W Memorial Dr Oklahoma City, OK 73120 SOUTHWEST

Mercy Hospital (305) 854-4400
Mercy Hosp
3663 S Miami Ave Miami, FL 33133 SOUTHEAST

Mercy Hospital - Coon Rapids (763) 236-6000
Mercy Hosp - Coon Rapids
4050 Coon Rapids Blvd Coon Rapids, MN 55433-2522 MIDWEST

Mercy Hospital - Fairfield (513) 870-7000
Mercy Hosp - Fairfield
3000 Mack Rd Fairfield, OH 45014 MIDWEST

Mercy Hospital - St Louis (314) 251-6000
Mercy Hosp - St Louis
615 S New Ballas Rd St Louis, MO 63141 MIDWEST

Mercy Medical Center - Baltimore (410) 332-9000
Mercy Med Ctr - Baltimore
345 St Paul Pl Baltimore, MD 21202 MID ATLANTIC

Methodist Hospital System (713) 790-3311
Methodist Hosp - Houston
6565 Fannin St Houston, TX 77030 SOUTHWEST

Methodist Hospital-Omaha (402) 354-4000
Methodist Hosp - Omaha
8303 Dodge St Omaha, NE 68114 GREAT PLAINS AND MOUNTAINS

Methodist Hospital-San Antonio (210) 575-4000
Methodist Hosp-San Antonio
7700 Floyd Curl Dr San Antonio, TX 78229 SOUTHWEST

Methodist University Hospital - Memphis (901) 516-7000
Methodist Univ Hosp - Memphis
1265 Union Ave Memphis, TN 38104 SOUTHEAST

MetroHealth Medical Center *MetroHealth Med Ctr* 2500 MetroHealth Drive	Cleveland, OH 44109-1998	(216) 778-7800 MIDWEST
Miami Children's Hospital *Miami Children's Hosp* 3100 SW 62nd Ave	Miami, FL 33155	(305) 666-6511 SOUTHEAST
Michael E. DeBakey VA Medical Center - Houston *DeBakey VA Med Ctr-Houston* 2002 Holcombe Blvd	Houston, TX 77030-1414	(713) 791-1414 SOUTHWEST
Michigan State University-Sparrow Hospital *Mich State Univ-Sparrow Hos* 1215 E Michigan Ave, MS 0	Lansing, MI 48912	(517) 364-1000 MIDWEST
Milford Hospital *Milford Hosp* 300 Seaside Ave	Milford, CT 06460	(203) 876-4000 NEW ENGLAND
Mills-Peninsula Medical Center *Mills-Peninsula Med Ctr* 1501 Trousdale Drive	Burlingame, CA 94010	(650) 696-5400 WEST COAST AND PACIFIC
Miriam Hospital *Miriam Hosp* 164 Summit Avenue	Providence, RI 02906-2894	(401) 793-2500 NEW ENGLAND
Mission Hospital-Mission Viejo *Mission Hosp-Mission Viejo* 27700 Medical Center Road	Mission Viejo, CA 92691	(949) 364-1400 WEST COAST AND PACIFIC
Missouri Baptist Medical Center *Missouri Baptist Med Ctr* 3015 N Ballas Rd	St Louis, MO 63131	(314) 996-5000 MIDWEST
Moffitt Cancer Center *Moffitt Canc Ctr* 12902 Magnolia Drive	Tampa, FL 33612-9497	(813) 745-4673 SOUTHEAST
Montefiore Medical Center-Einstein Campus *Montefiore Med Ctr-Einstein Campus* 1825 Eastchester Road	Bronx, NY 10461	(718) 904-2000 MID ATLANTIC
Montefiore Medical Center-Moses Campus *Montefiore Med Ctr-Moses Campus* 111 East 210 Street	Bronx, NY 10467	(718) 920-4321 MID ATLANTIC

Montefiore Medical Center-Wakefield Campus (718) 920-9000
Montefiore Med Ctr-Wakefield Campus
600 E 233rd St Bronx, NY 10466 MID ATLANTIC

Morgan Stanley Children's Hospital of NewYork-Presbyterian, NY (212) 305-5437
Morgan Stanley Children's Hosp of NY-Presby, NY
3959 Broadway New York, NY 10032 MID ATLANTIC

Morristown Medical Center (973) 971-5000
Morristown Med Ctr
100 Madison Avenue Morristown, NJ 07960-6095 MID ATLANTIC

Moss Rehab Hospital (215) 663-6000
Moss Rehab Hosp
60 E Township Line Rd Elkins Park, PA 19027 MID ATLANTIC

Mott Children's Hospital (734) 936-4000
Mott Chldns Hosp
1500 E Medical Center Dr Ann Arbor, MI 48109 MIDWEST

Mount Auburn Hospital (617) 492-3500
Mount Auburn Hosp
330 Mount Auburn St Cambridge, MA 02138 NEW ENGLAND

Mount Carmel West Hospital (614) 234-5000
Mt Carmel W Hosp
793 W State St Columbus, OH 43085 MIDWEST

Mount Sinai Medical Center (212) 241-6500
Mt Sinai Med Ctr
One Gustave L. Levy Pl New York, NY 10029 MID ATLANTIC

Mount Sinai Medical Center - Miami (305) 674-2121
Mount Sinai Med Ctr - Miami
4300 Alton Rd Miami Beach, FL 33140 SOUTHEAST

Mountainview Hospital - Las Vegas (702) 255-5000
Mountainview Hosp - Las Vegas
3100 N Tenaya Way Las Vegas, NV 89128 WEST COAST AND PACIFIC

Munroe Regional Medical Center (352) 351-7200
Munroe Regional Med Ctr
1500 SW 1st Ave Ocala, FL 34471 SOUTHEAST

Nashville General Hospital at Meharry (615) 341-4000
Nashville Genl Hosp
1818 Albion St Nashville, TN 37208 SOUTHEAST

National Institutes of Health - Clinical Center (301) 496-4000
Natl Inst of Hlth - Clin Ctr
10 Center Drive Bethesda, MD 20892-0001 MID ATLANTIC

National Jewish Health (303) 388-4461
Natl Jewish Hlth
1400 Jackson St Denver, CO 80206-2762 GREAT PLAINS AND MOUNTAINS

Nationwide Children's Hospital (614) 722-2000
Nationwide Chldn's Hosp
700 Children's Drive Columbus, OH 43205 MIDWEST

Nebraska Medical Center (402) 552-2000
Nebraska Med Ctr
4350 Dewey Ave Omaha, NE 68198 GREAT PLAINS AND MOUNTAINS

Nebraska Methodist Hospital (402) 354-4000
Nebraska Meth Hosp
8303 Dodge St Omaha, NE 68114 GREAT PLAINS AND MOUNTAINS

Nemours Children's Hospital - Orlando (407) 567-4000
Nemours Chldns Hosp - Orlando
13535 Nemours Pkwy Orlando, FL 32827 SOUTHEAST

Nemours/Alfred I. duPont Hospital for Children (302) 651-4000
Nemours/Alfred I. duPont Hosp for Chldn
1600 Rockland Rd Wilmington, DE 19803 MID ATLANTIC

New England Baptist Hospital (617) 754-5800
New England Bapt Hosp
125 Parker Hill Ave Boston, MA 02120 NEW ENGLAND

New Hanover Regional Medical Center (910) 343-7000
New Hanover Reg Med Ctr
2131 S 17th St Wilmington, NC 28401 SOUTHEAST

New York Eye & Ear Infirmary (212) 979-4000
New York Eye & Ear Infirm
310 East 14th Street New York, NY 10003 MID ATLANTIC

New York Hospital Queens (718) 670-2000
NY Hosp Queens
56-45 Main Street Flushing, NY 11355 MID ATLANTIC

New York Methodist Hospital (718) 780-3000
New York Methodist Hosp
506 Sixth Street Brooklyn, NY 11215 MID ATLANTIC

New York State Psychiatric Institute (212) 543-5000
NY State Psychiatric Inst
1051 Riverside Dr New York, NY 10032 MID ATLANTIC

Newark Beth Israel Medical Center (973) 926-7000
Newark Beth Israel Med Ctr
201 Lyons Ave Newark, NJ 07112 MID ATLANTIC

Newton - Wellesley Hospital (617) 243-6000
Newton - Wellesley Hosp
2014 Washington St Newton, MA 02462 NEW ENGLAND

NewYork-Presbyterian/Columbia University Medical Center, NY (212) 305-2500
NY-Presby/Columbia Univ Med Ctr, NY
622 W 168th St New York, NY 10032 MID ATLANTIC

NewYork-Presbyterian/Weill Cornell Medical Center, NY (212) 746-5454
NY-Presby/Weill Cornell Med Ctr, NY
525 E 68th St New York, NY 10021 MID ATLANTIC

North Carolina Memorial Hospital - UNC (919) 966-4131
NC Memorial Hosp - UNC
101 Manning Drive, Box 7600 Chapel Hill, NC 27514 SOUTHEAST

North Oaks Medical Center (985) 345-2700
North Oaks Med Ctr
15790 Paul Vega MD Dr Hammond, LA 70403 SOUTHWEST

North Shore University Hospital (516) 562-0100
N Shore Univ Hosp
300 Community Dr Manhasset, NY 11030 MID ATLANTIC

North Shore-LIJ Health System (516) 465-2550
NS-LIJ Hlth Sys
125 Community Drive Great Neck, NY 11021 MID ATLANTIC

Northern California Shriners Hospital (916) 453-2000
Northern CA Shriners Hosp
2425 Stockton Blvd Sacramento, CA 95817 WEST COAST AND PACIFIC

Northern Michigan Hospital (231) 487-4000
Northern Michigan Hosp
416 Connable Ave Petoskey, MI 49770 MIDWEST

Northern Nevada Medical Center (775) 331-7000
Northern Nevada Med Ctr
2375 E Prater Way Sparks, NV 89434-9644 WEST COAST AND PACIFIC

Northside Hospital - Atlanta		(404) 851-8000
Northside Hosp		
1000 Johnson Ferry Rd NE	Atlanta, GA 30342	SOUTHEAST
Northwest Hospital - Seattle		(206) 364-0500
Northwest Hosp - Seattle		
1550 N 115th St	Seattle, WA 98133-0806	WEST COAST AND PACIFIC
Northwest Medical Center		(954) 974-0400
Northwest Med Ctr		
2801 N State Rd 7	Margate, FL 33063	SOUTHEAST
Northwestern Memorial Hospital		(312) 926-2000
Northwestern Meml Hosp		
251 E Huron St	Chicago, IL 60611	MIDWEST
Norton Hospital		(502) 629-8000
Norton Hosp		
200 E Chestnut St	Louisville, KY 40202	SOUTHEAST
NYU Hospital for Joint Diseases		(212) 598-6000
NYU Hosp For Joint Dis		
301 East 17th Street	New York, NY 10003	MID ATLANTIC
NYU Langone Medical Center		(212) 263-7300
NYU Langone Med Ctr		
550 First Avenue	New York, NY 10016	MID ATLANTIC
NYU Rusk Institute		(212) 263-1999
NYU Rusk Inst		
400 East 34th Street	New York, NY 10016	MID ATLANTIC
Ochsner Medical Center-Baton Rouge		(225) 752-2470
Ochsner Med Ctr-Baton Rouge		
17000 Medical Center Drive	Baton Rouge, LA 70816	SOUTHWEST
Ochsner Medical Center-Kenner		(504) 468-8600
Ochsner Med Ctr-Kenner		
180 W Esplanade Ave	Kenner, LA 70065-2467	SOUTHWEST
Ochsner Medical Center-New Orleans		(504) 842-3000
Ochsner Med Ctr-New Orleans		
1514 Jefferson Hwy	New Orleans, LA 70121	SOUTHWEST
Ochsner Medical Center-West Bank		(504) 392-3131
Ochsner Med Ctr-West Bank		
2500 Belle Chasse Hwy	Gretna, LA 70056	SOUTHWEST

Ohio State University Hospital East (614) 257-3000
Ohio State U Hosp East
1492 E Broad St Columbus, OH 43085 MIDWEST

Ohio State University Wexner Medical Center (614) 293-8652
OSU Wexner Med Ctr
410 W 10th Avenue Columbus, OH 43210 MIDWEST

Olathe Medical Center (913) 791-4200
Olathe Med Ctr
20333 W 151st St Olathe, KS 66061-5352 GREAT PLAINS AND MOUNTAINS

Olive View-UCLA Medical Center (818) 364-1555
Olive View-UCLA Med Ctr
14445 Olive View Dr Sylmar, CA 91342 WEST COAST AND PACIFIC

Olympia Medical Center (310) 657-5900
Olympia Med Ctr
5900 W Olympic Blvd Los Angeles, CA 90036 WEST COAST AND PACIFIC

Oregon Health & Science University (503) 494-8311
OR Hlth & Sci Univ
3181 SW Sam Jackson Park Rd Portland, OR 97239-3098 WEST COAST AND PACIFIC

Orlando Regional Medical Center (321) 841-5111
Orlando Regl Med Ctr
1414 Kuhl Ave Orlando, FL 32806 SOUTHEAST

Orthopedic Specialty Hospital, The (TOSH) (801) 314-4100
Ortho Spec Hosp, The (TOSH)
5848 Fashion Blvd Salt Lake City, UT 84107 GREAT PLAINS AND MOUNTAINS

OSF Saint Francis Medical Center (309) 655-2000
OSF Saint Francis Med Ctr
530 NE Glen Oak Ave Peoria, IL 61637 MIDWEST

OU Medical Center (405) 271-4700
OU Med Ctr
700 NE 13th St Oklahoma City, OK 73104-5098 SOUTHWEST

Our Lady of Lourdes Regional Medical Center - Lafayette (337) 470-2000
Our Lady of Lourdes Reg Med Ctr - Lafayette
4801 Ambassador Caffery Pkwy Lafayette, LA 70508 SOUTHWEST

Our Lady of the Lake Regional Medical Center (225) 765-6565
Our Lady of the Lake Regl Med Ctr
5000 Hennessy Blvd Baton Rouge, LA 70808-4398 SOUTHWEST

Overlake Hospital Medical Center (425) 688-5000
Overlake Hosp Med Ctr
1035 116th Ave NE Bellevue, WA 98004-4687 WEST COAST AND PACIFIC

Overland Park Regional Medical Center (913) 541-5000
Overland Pk Regl Med Ctr
10500 Quivira Rd Overland Park, KS 66215 GREAT PLAINS AND MOUNTAINS

Palmetto Health Richland Memorial Hospital (803) 434-7000
Palmetto Health Richland Mem Hosp
5 Richland Medical Park Drive Columbia, SC 29203 SOUTHEAST

Park City Medical Center (435) 658-7000
Park City Med Ctr
900 Round Valley Dr Park City, UT 84060 GREAT PLAINS AND MOUNTAINS

Parkland Health & Hospital System (214) 590-8000
Parkland Hlth & Hosp Sys
5201 Harry Hines Blvd Dallas, TX 75235 SOUTHWEST

Penn Presbyterian Medical Center - UPHS (215) 662-8000
Penn Presby Med Ctr - UPHS
51 N 39th St Philadelphia, PA 19104 MID ATLANTIC

Penn State Milton S. Hershey Medical Center (717) 531-8521
Penn State Milton S Hershey Med Ctr
500 University Drive Hershey, PA 17033-0850 MID ATLANTIC

Pennsylvania Hospital - UPHS (215) 829-3000
Pennsylvania Hosp-UPHS
800 Spruce St, Ste 240 Philadelphia, PA 19107 MID ATLANTIC

Penrose Hospital (719) 776-5000
Penrose Hosp
2222 N Nevada Ave Colorado Springs, CO 80907 GREAT PLAINS AND MOUNTAINS

Peyton Manning Children's Hospital at St. Vincent (317) 338-2345
Peyton Manning Children's Hosp at St. Vincent
2001 W 86th St Indianapolis, IN 46260 MIDWEST

Philadelphia Shriners Hospital (215) 430-4000
Philadelphia Shriners Hosp
3551 N Broad St Philadelphia, PA 19140 MID ATLANTIC

Phillips Eye Institute (612) 775-8800
Phillips Eye Inst
2215 Park Ave S Minneapolis, MN 55404 MIDWEST

Phoenix Baptist Hospital & Medical Center (602) 249-0212
Phoenix Baptist Hosp & Med Ctr
2000 West Bethany Home Rd Phoenix, AZ 85015-2184 SOUTHWEST

Phoenix Children's Hospital (602) 933-1000
Phoenix Children's Hosp
1919 E Thomas Rd Phoenix, AZ 85106 SOUTHWEST

Physicians Regional Healthcare System-Pine Ridge (239) 348-4000
Physicians Regl Hlthcare Med Ctr-Pine Ridge
6101 Pine Ridge Rd Naples, FL 34119 SOUTHEAST

Piedmont Hospital (404) 605-5000
Piedmont Hosp
1968 Peachtree Rd NW Atlanta, GA 30309 SOUTHEAST

Pocono Medical Center (570) 421-4000
Pocono Med Ctr
206 E Brown St East Stroudsburg, PA 18301-3094 MID ATLANTIC

Pomerado Hospital (619) 613-4000
Pomerado Hosp
15615 Pomerado Rd Poway, CA 92064 WEST COAST AND PACIFIC

Porter Adventist Hospital (303) 778-1955
Porter Adventist Hosp
2525 S Downing St Denver, CO 80210-5876 GREAT PLAINS AND MOUNTAINS

Portsmouth Regional Hospital (603) 436-5110
Portsmouth Regl Hosp
333 Borthwick Ave Portsmouth, NH 03801-7002 NEW ENGLAND

Presbyterian - St Luke's Medical Center (303) 839-6000
Presby - St Luke's Med Ctr
1719 E 19th Ave Denver, CO 80218 GREAT PLAINS AND MOUNTAINS

Presbyterian Hospital - Charlotte (704) 384-4000
Presby Hosp - Charlotte
200 Hawthorne Ln Charlotte, NC 28204-2528 SOUTHEAST

Presence Saint Francis Hospital - Evanston (847) 316-4000
Presence St Francis Hosp - Evanston
355 Ridge Ave Evanston, IL 60202 MIDWEST

Presence Saint Joseph Hospital (773) 665-3000
Presence St Joseph Hosp
2900 N Lake Shore Dr Chicago, IL 60657 MIDWEST

Primary Children's Medical Center (801) 662-1000
Primary Children's Med Ctr
100 N Mario Capecchi Drive Salt Lake City, UT 84113 GREAT PLAINS AND MOUNTAINS

Providence Alaska Medical Center (907) 562-2211
Providence Alaska Med Ctr
3200 Providence Dr Anchorage, AK 99508-4615 WEST COAST AND PACIFIC

Providence Hospital - Southfield (248) 849-3000
Providence Hosp - Southfield
16001 W Nine Mile Rd Southfield, MI 48075 MIDWEST

Providence Portland Medical Center (503) 215-1111
Providence Portland Med Ctr
4805 NE Glisan Portland, OR 97213-2967 WEST COAST AND PACIFIC

Providence Saint Joseph Medical Center (818) 843-5111
Providence St Joseph Med Ctr
501 S Buena Vista St Burbank, CA 91505 WEST COAST AND PACIFIC

Providence St Vincent Medical Center (503) 216-1234
Providence St Vincent Med Ctr
9205 SW Barnes Rd Portland, OR 97225-6622 WEST COAST AND PACIFIC

Providence St. Joseph's Hospital (509) 935-8211
Providence St. Joseph's Hosp
500 E Webster St Chewelah, WA 99109 WEST COAST AND PACIFIC

Queen's Medical Center - Honolulu (808) 538-9011
Queen's Med Ctr - Honolulu
1301 Punchbowl Street Honolulu, HI 96813 WEST COAST AND PACIFIC

Rady Children's Hospital - San Diego (858) 576-1700
Rady Children's Hosp - San Diego
3020 Children's Way San Diego, CA 92123 WEST COAST AND PACIFIC

Rancho Los Amigos National Rehabilitation Center (562) 401-7111
Rancho Los Amigos Natl Rehab Ctr
7601 East Imperial Highway Downey, CA 90242 WEST COAST AND PACIFIC

Randall Children's Hospital at Legacy Emanuel (503) 276-6500
Randall Chldns Hosp at Legacy
2801 Gantenbein Ave Portland, OR 97227 WEST COAST AND PACIFIC

Reading Hospital (610) 988-8000
Reading Hosp
Sixth and Spruce St, Box 160 West Reading, PA 19611 MID ATLANTIC

Regional Medical Center - Memphis (901) 545-7100
Regional Med Ctr - Memphis
877 Jefferson Avenue Memphis, TN 38103 SOUTHEAST

Regions Hospital - St Paul (651) 254-3456
Regions Hosp - St Paul
640 Jackson Street St Paul, MN 55101 MIDWEST

Rehabilitation Hospital of Indiana (317) 329-2000
Rehab Hosp of Indiana
4141 Shore Drive Indianapolis, IN 46254 MIDWEST

Rehabilitation Institute of Chicago (312) 238-1000
Rehab Inst of Chicago
345 E. Superior Street Chicago, IL 60611 MIDWEST

Rehabilitation Institute of St. Louis (314) 658-3800
Rehab Inst St. Louis
4455 Duncan Ave St. Louis, MO 63110 MIDWEST

Reid Hospital & Health Care Services (765) 983-3000
Reid Hosp & Hlth Care Servs
1100 Reid Pkwy Richmond, IN 47374 MIDWEST

Renown Regional Medical Center (775) 982-4100
Renown Reg Med Ctr
1155 Mill St Reno, NV 89502 WEST COAST AND PACIFIC

Resnick Neuropsychiatric Hospital at UCLA (310) 825-0511
Resnick Neuropsychiatric Hosp at UCLA
760 Westwood Plaza Los Angeles, CA 90095 WEST COAST AND PACIFIC

Reston Hospital Center (703) 689-9000
Reston Hosp Ctr
1850 Town Center Pkwy Reston, VA 20190 SOUTHEAST

Rex HealthCare (919) 784-3100
Rex HlthCare
4420 Lake Boone Trail Raleigh, NC 27607 SOUTHEAST

Rhode Island Hospital (401) 444-4000
Rhode Island Hosp
593 Eddy Street Providence, RI 02903-4923 NEW ENGLAND

Riddle Memorial Hospital (484) 227-9400
Riddle Meml Hosp
1068 W Baltimore Pike Media, PA 19063 MID ATLANTIC

Riley Hospital for Children *Riley Hosp for Children* 705 Riley Hospital Drive	Indianapolis, IN 46202	(317) 944-5000 MIDWEST
Riverside Community Hospital *Riverside Comm Hosp* 4445 Magnolia Avenue	Riverside, CA 92501	(951) 788-3000 WEST COAST AND PACIFIC
Riverview Medical Center *Riverview Med Ctr* 1 Riverview Plaza	Red Bank, NJ 07701	(732) 741-2700 MID ATLANTIC
Robert Packer Hospital *Robert Packer Hosp* 1 Guthrie Sq	Sayre, PA 18840	(570) 888-6666 MID ATLANTIC
Robert Wood Johnson University Hospital - New Brunswick *Robert Wood Johnson Univ Hosp - New Brunswick* 1 Robert Wood Johnson Pl	New Brunswick, NJ 08903	(732) 828-3000 MID ATLANTIC
Rochester General Hospital *Rochester Genl Hosp* 1425 Portland Avenue	Rochester, NY 14621	(585) 922-4000 MID ATLANTIC
Rochester Methodist Hospital *Rochester Methodist Hosp* 201 W Center St	Rochester, MN 55902	(507) 266-7890 MIDWEST
Roger Williams Medical Center *Roger Williams Med Ctr* 825 Chalkstone Avenue	Providence, RI 02908	(401) 456-2000 NEW ENGLAND
Roper Hospital *Roper Hosp* 316 Calhoun St	Charleston, SC 29401	(843) 724-2000 SOUTHEAST
Rose Medical Center *Rose Med Ctr* 4567 E 9th Ave	Denver, CO 80220-3941	(303) 320-2121 GREAT PLAINS AND MOUNTAINS
Roswell Park Cancer Institute *Roswell Park Canc Inst* Elm and Carlton Streets	Buffalo, NY 14263	(716) 845-2300 MID ATLANTIC
Ruby Memorial - WVU Hospital *Ruby Memorial - WVU Hosp* 1 Medical Center Drive	Morgantown, WV 26506	(304) 598-4000 MID ATLANTIC

Rush University Medical Center (312) 942-5000
Rush Univ Med Ctr
1653 W Congress Pkwy Chicago, IL 60612-3833 MIDWEST

Saint Agnes Hospital (410) 368-6000
St. Agnes Hosp
900 Canton Ave Baltimore, MD 21229 MID ATLANTIC

Saint Barnabas Medical Center (973) 322-5000
Saint Barnabas Med Ctr
94 Old Short Hills Rd Livingston, NJ 07039-5672 MID ATLANTIC

Saint Francis Hospital - Memphis (901) 765-1000
St. Francis Hosp - Memphis
5959 Park Ave Memphis, TN 38119 SOUTHEAST

Saint John's Health Center (310) 829-5511
St. John's Hlth Ctr, Santa Monica
2121 Santa Monica Blvd Santa Monica, CA 90404 WEST COAST AND PACIFIC

Saint Joseph's Hospital - Atlanta (678) 843-7001
St. Joseph's Hosp - Atlanta
5665 Peachtree Dunwoody Rd NE Atlanta, GA 30342 SOUTHEAST

Saint Thomas Hospital-Midtown (615) 284-5555
Saint Thomas Hosp-Midtown
2000 Church St Nashville, TN 37236 SOUTHEAST

Saint Thomas West Hospital- Nashville (615) 222-2111
Saint Thomas West Hosp - Nashville
4220 Harding Road Nashville, TN 37205 SOUTHEAST

Salinas Valley Memorial Healthcare Systems (831) 757-4333
Salinas Valley Meml Hlthcare Systs
450 E Romie Ln Salinas, CA 93901 WEST COAST AND PACIFIC

Saline Memorial Hospital (501) 776-6000
Saline Meml Hosp
1 Medical Park Dr Benton, AR 72015 SOUTHWEST

Salt Lake Regional Medical Center (801) 350-4111
Salt Lake Regional Med Ctr
1050 E South Temple Salt Lake City, UT 84102 GREAT PLAINS AND MOUNTAINS

San Francisco General Hospital (415) 206-8000
San Francisco Genl Hosp
1001 Potrero Avenue San Francisco, CA 94110 WEST COAST AND PACIFIC

San Joaquin Community Hospital (661) 395-3000
San Joaquin Community Hosp
2615 Chester Ave Bakersfield, CA 93301 WEST COAST AND PACIFIC

Sanford Medical Center Fargo (701) 234-2000
Sanford Med Ctr Fargo
801 Broadway Drive, PO Box 2010 Fargo, ND 58122 GREAT PLAINS AND MOUNTAINS

Sanford USD Medical Center (605) 333-1000
Sanford USD Med Ctr
1305 W 18th St Sioux Falls, SD 57117 GREAT PLAINS AND MOUNTAINS

Santa Barbara Cottage Hospital (805) 682-7111
Santa Barbara Cottage Hosp
400 W Pueblo St Santa Barbara, CA 93105 WEST COAST AND PACIFIC

Santa Monica - UCLA Medical Center and Orthopaedic Hospital (310) 319-4000
Santa Mónica - UCLA Med Ctr & Ortho Hosp
1250 16th St Santa Monica, CA 90404 WEST COAST AND PACIFIC

Santa Rosa Memorial Hospital (747) 546-3210
Santa Rosa Meml Hosp
1165 Montgomery Drive Santa Rosa, CA 95405 WEST COAST AND PACIFIC

Sarasota Memorial Hospital (941) 917-9000
Sarasota Meml Hosp
1700 S Tamiami Trail Sarasota, FL 34239 SOUTHEAST

Schwab Rehabilitation Hospital (773) 522-2010
Schwab Rehab Hosp
1401 S. California Boulevard Chicago, IL 60608 MIDWEST

Scott & White Memorial Hospital (254) 724-2111
Scott & White Mem Hosp
2401 S 31st St Temple, TX 76508-0001 SOUTHWEST

Scottsdale Healthcare - Osborn (480) 882-4000
Scottsdale Hlthcare - Osborn
7400 E Osborn Rd Scottsdale, AZ 85251-6403 SOUTHWEST

Scottsdale Healthcare - Shea (480) 323-3000
Scottsdale Hlthcare - Shea
9003 E Shea Blvd Scottsdale, AZ 85260 SOUTHWEST

Scottsdale Healthcare Thompson Peak (480) 324-7000
Scottsdale Healthcare Thompson Peak
7400 E Thompson Peak Pkwy Scottsdale, AZ 85255 SOUTHWEST

Scripps Green Hospital		(858) 554-9100
Scripps Green Hosp		
10666 N Torrey Pines Rd	La Jolla, CA 92037	WEST COAST AND PACIFIC
Scripps Memorial Hospital - La Jolla		(858) 626-4123
Scripps Meml Hosp - La Jolla		
9888 Genesee Ave	La Jolla, CA 92037	WEST COAST AND PACIFIC
Scripps Mercy Hospital & Medical Center		(619) 294-8111
Scripps Mercy Hosp & Med Ctr		
4077 Fifth Ave	San Diego, CA 92103	WEST COAST AND PACIFIC
Seattle Children's Hospital		(206) 987-2000
Seattle Chldns Hosp		
4800 Sand Point Way NE	Seattle, WA 98105	WEST COAST AND PACIFIC
Select Specialty Hospital of Pittsburgh-UPMC		(412) 586-9805
Select Specialty Hosp of Pittsburgh-UPMC		
200 Lothrop St 8th Fl	Pittsburgh, PA 15213	MID ATLANTIC
Self Regional Healthcare		(864) 725-4111
Self Regional Healthcare		
1325 Spring St	Greenwood, SC 29646	SOUTHEAST
Sentara Leigh Hospital		(757) 261-6000
Sentara Leigh Hosp		
830 Kempsville Rd	Norfolk, VA 23502-3981	SOUTHEAST
Sentara Norfolk General Hospital		(757) 388-3000
Sentara Norfolk Genl Hosp		
600 Gresham Dr	Norfolk, VA 23507	SOUTHEAST
Sentara Virginia Beach General Hospital		(757) 395-8000
Sentara VA Beach Genl Hosp		
1060 First Colonial Rd	Virginia Beach, VA 23454	SOUTHEAST
Sequoia Hospital		(650) 369-5811
Sequoia Hosp		
170 Alameda de las Pulgas	Redwood, CA 94062	WEST COAST AND PACIFIC
Seton Medical Center		(512) 324-1000
Seton Med Ctr		
1201 W 38th St	Austin, TX 78705	SOUTHWEST
Shady Grove Adventist Hospital		(240) 826-6000
Shady Grove Adven Hosp		
9901 Medical Center Drive	Rockville, MD 20850	MID ATLANTIC

Shawnee Mission Medical Center (913) 676-2000
Shawnee Mission Med Ctr
9100 W 74th St Shawnee Mission, KS 66204 GREAT PLAINS AND MOUNTAINS

Shepherd Center - Atlanta (404) 352-2020
Shepherd Ctr - Atlanta
2020 Peachtree Rd NW Atlanta, GA 30309-1402 SOUTHEAST

Sheppard Pratt Health System (410) 938-3000
Sheppard Pratt Hlth Sys
6501 N Charles St Baltimore, MD 21285-6815 MID ATLANTIC

Shriners Hospitals for Children-Twin Cities (612) 596-6100
Shriners Hosps for Children-Twin Cities
2025 E River Pkwy Minneapolis, MN 55414 MIDWEST

Sibley Memorial Hospital (202) 537-4000
Sibley Mem Hosp
5255 Loughboro Road NW Washington, DC 20016 MID ATLANTIC

Silver Hill Hospital (203) 966-3561
Silver Hill Hosp
208 Valley Rd New Canaan, CT 06840-3899 NEW ENGLAND

Sinai Hospital - Baltimore (410) 601-9000
Sinai Hosp - Baltimore
2401 W Belvedere Ave Baltimore, MD 21215 MID ATLANTIC

Sisters of Charity Hospital, Buffalo (716) 862-1000
Sisters of Charity Hosp, Buffalo
2157 Main St Buffalo, NY 14214-2692 MID ATLANTIC

Sky Ridge Medical Center (720) 225-1000
Sky Ridge Med Ctr
10101 Ridge Gate Pkwy Lone Tree, CO 80124 GREAT PLAINS AND MOUNTAINS

Smilow Cancer Hospital at Yale-New Haven (203) 688-2000
Smilow Cancer Hosp at Yale-New Haven
20 York St New Haven, CT 06510 NEW ENGLAND

South Miami Hospital (786) 662-4000
South Miami Hosp
6200 SW 73 St South Miami, FL 33143 SOUTHEAST

South Nassau Communities Hospital (516) 632-3000
South Nassau Comm Hosp
1 Healthy Way Oceanside, NY 11572 MID ATLANTIC

Southern Arizona VA Health Care System - Tucson (520) 792-1450
Southern AZ VA Health Care Sys - Tucson
3601 S 6th Avenue Tucson, AZ 85723 SOUTHWEST

Southern Hills Hospital & Medical Center (702) 880-2100
Southern Hills Hosp & Med Ctr
9300 W Sunset Rd Las Vegas, NV 89148 WEST COAST AND PACIFIC

Southern New Hampshire Medical Center (603) 577-2000
Southern NH Med Ctr
8 Prospect St Nashua, NH 03061 NEW ENGLAND

Spartanburg Regional Medical Center (803) 560-6000
Spartanburg Reg Med Ctr
101 E Wood St Spartanburg, SC 29303 SOUTHEAST

Spaulding Rehabilitation Hospital (617) 573-7000
Spaulding Rehab Hosp
125 Nashua Street Boston, MA 02114 NEW ENGLAND

Spectrum Health - Blodgett Campus (616) 774-7444
Spectrum Hlth Blodgett Campus
1840 Wealthy St SE Grand Rapids, MI 49506 MIDWEST

Spectrum Health Butterworth Campus (616) 391-1774
Spectrum Hlth Butterworth Campus
100 Michigan St NE Grand Rapids, MI 49503 MIDWEST

SSM Cardinal Glennon Children's Hospital (314) 577-5600
SSM Cardinal Glennon Chldn's Hosp
1465 S Grand Blvd St Louis, MO 63104 MIDWEST

SSM St. Clare Health Ctr (636) 496-2000
SSM St. Clare Hlth Ctr
1015 Bowles Ave Fenton, MO 63026 MIDWEST

St. Alphonsus Regional Medical Center (208) 367-2121
St. Alphonsus Regl Med Ctr
1055 N Curtis Rd Boise, ID 83706-1370 GREAT PLAINS AND MOUNTAINS

St. Anthony Hospital - Oklahoma City (405) 272-7000
St. Anthony Hosp -Oklahoma City
1000 N Lee St Oklahoma City, OK 73102 SOUTHWEST

St. Anthony's Hospital - St Petersburg (727) 825-1100
St. Anthony's Hosp - St Petersburg
1200 7th Avenue North St Petersburg, FL 33705 SOUTHEAST

St. Charles Surgical Hospital (504) 529-6600
St. Charles Surgical Hosp
1717 St. Charles Ave New Orleans, LA 70130 SOUTHWEST

St. Christopher's Hospital for Children (215) 427-5000
St. Christopher's Hosp for Chldn
3601 A St Philadelphia, PA 19134 MID ATLANTIC

St. Clair Hospital (412) 561-4900
St. Clair Hosp
1000 Bower Hill Rd Pittsburgh, PA 15243 MID ATLANTIC

St. David's Medical Center (512) 476-7111
St. David's Med Ctr
919 E 32nd st Austin, TX 78705 SOUTHWEST

St. Elizabeth Healthcare-Edgewood (859) 301-2000
St. Elizabeth Hlthcare-Edgewood
1 Medical Village Dr Edgewood, KY 41017 SOUTHEAST

St. Francis Hospital & Medical Center (860) 714-4000
St. Francis Hosp & Med Ctr
114 Woodland St Hartford, CT 06105 NEW ENGLAND

St. Francis Hospital - The Heart Center (516) 562-6000
St. Francis Hosp - The Heart Ctr
100 Port Washington Boulevard Roslyn, NY 11576 MID ATLANTIC

St. John Medical Center (918) 744-2180
St. John Med Ctr
1923 S Utica Ave Tulsa, OK 74104 SOUTHWEST

St. John's Hospital - Springfield (217) 544-6464
St. John's Hosp - Springfield
800 E Carpenter St Springfield, IL 62769 MIDWEST

St. John's Hospital-Maplewood MN (651) 232-7000
St. John's Hosp-Maplewood MN
1575 Beam Ave Maplewood, MN 55109 MIDWEST

St. Joseph Hospital (360) 734-5400
St. Joseph Hosp - Bellingham
2901 Squalicum Pkwy Bellingham, WA 98225-1898 WEST COAST AND PACIFIC

St. Joseph Hospital & Trauma Center (603) 882-3000
St. Joseph Hosp & Trauma Ctr
172 Kinsley St Nashua, NH 03061 NEW ENGLAND

St. Joseph Medical Center - Tacoma (253) 426-4101
St. Joseph Med Ctr - Tacoma
1717 South J St Tacoma, WA 98405 WEST COAST AND PACIFIC

St. Joseph Mercy Hospital - Ann Arbor (734) 712-3456
St. Joseph Mercy Hosp - Ann Arbor
5301 McAuley Drive Ypsilanti, MI 48197 MIDWEST

St. Joseph Mercy Oakland Hospital (248) 858-3000
St. Joseph Mercy Oakland Hosp
44405 Woodward Ave Pontiac, MI 48341 MIDWEST

St. Joseph's Hospital & Medical Center - Phoenix (602) 406-3000
St. Joseph's Hosp & Med Ctr - Phoenix
350 W Thomas Rd Phoenix, AZ 85013-4496 SOUTHWEST

St. Joseph's Hospital - Orange (714) 633-9111
St. Joseph's Hosp - Orange
1100 West Stewart Drive Orange, CA 92868 WEST COAST AND PACIFIC

St. Joseph's Hospital - Tampa (813) 870-4000
St. Joseph's Hosp - Tampa
3001 W Martin Luther King Jr Blvd Tampa, FL 33607 SOUTHEAST

St. Joseph's Hospital - Tucson (520) 873-3000
St. Joseph's Hosp - Tucson
350 N Wilmot Rd Tucson, AZ 85711 SOUTHWEST

St. Joseph's Regional Medical Center - Paterson (973) 754-2000
St. Joseph's Regl Med Ctr - Paterson
703 Main St Paterson, NJ 07503 MID ATLANTIC

St. Jude Children's Research Hospital (901) 495-3300
St. Jude Children's Research Hosp
262 Danny Thomas Pl Memphis, TN 38105 SOUTHEAST

St. Louis Children's Hospital (314) 454-6000
St. Louis Chldns Hosp
One Children's Pl St Louis, MO 63110 MIDWEST

St. Louis University Hospital (314) 577-8000
St. Louis Univ Hosp
3635 Vista at Grand Blvd St Louis, MO 63110 MIDWEST

St. Luke's - Roosevelt Hospital Center - Roosevelt Division (212) 523-4000
St. Luke's - Roosevelt Hosp Ctr - Roosevelt Div
1000 Tenth Avenue New York, NY 10019 MID ATLANTIC

St. Luke's - Roosevelt Hospital Center - St Luke's Hospital (212) 523-4000
St. Luke's - Roosevelt Hosp Ctr - St Luke's Hosp
1111 Amsterdam Ave New York, NY 10025 MID ATLANTIC

St. Luke's Boise Medical Center (208) 381-2222
St. Luke's Boise Med Ctr
190 E Bannock St Boise, ID 83712 GREAT PLAINS AND MOUNTAINS

St. Luke's Episcopal Hospital-Houston (832) 355-1000
St. Luke's Episcopal Hosp-Houston
6720 Bertner Avenue, PO Box 20269 Houston, TX 77030 SOUTHWEST

St. Luke's Hospital - Allentown Campus (610) 628-8300
St. Luke's Hosp - Allentown
1736 Hamilton St Allentown, PA 18104 MID ATLANTIC

St. Luke's Hospital - Chesterfield, MO (314) 434-1500
St. Luke's Hosp - Chesterfield, MO
232 S Woods Mill Rd Chesterfield, MO 63017 MIDWEST

St. Luke's Hospital - Duluth (218) 249-5555
St. Luke's Hosp - Duluth
915 E 1st St Duluth, MN 55805-2193 MIDWEST

St. Luke's Hospital of Kansas City (816) 932-5100
St. Luke's Hosp of Kansas City
4401 Wornall Rd Kansas City, MO 64111 MIDWEST

St. Mark's Hospital - Salt Lake City (801) 268-7111
St. Mark's Hosp - Salt Lake City
1200 E. 3900 S Salt Lake City, UT 84124 GREAT PLAINS AND MOUNTAINS

St. Mary Medical Center - Long Beach (562) 491-9000
St. Mary Med Ctr - Long Beach
1050 Linden Ave Long Beach, CA 90813 WEST COAST AND PACIFIC

St. Mary's Hospital - Rochester, MN (Mayo Clinic) (507) 255-5123
St. Mary's Hosp - Rochester MN (Mayo)
1216 2nd St SW Rochester, MN 55902 MIDWEST

St. Mary's Medical Center - Huntington (304) 526-1234
St. Mary's Med Ctr - Huntington
2900 First Ave Huntington, WV 25702-1272 MID ATLANTIC

St. Mary's Medical Center - West Palm Beach (561) 844-6300
St. Mary's Med Ctr - W Palm Bch
901 45th St West Palm Beach, FL 33407 SOUTHEAST

St. Peter's Hospital - Albany (518) 525-1550
St. Peter's Hosp - Albany
315 S Manning Blvd Albany, NY 12208 MID ATLANTIC

St. Rose Dominican Hospital - San Martin Campus (702) 492-8000
St. Rose Dom Hosp-San Martin
8280 W Warm Springs Rd Las Vegas, NV 89113 WEST COAST AND PACIFIC

St. Tammany Parish Hospital (985) 898-4000
St. Tammany Parish Hosp
1202 S Tyler St Covington, LA 70433 SOUTHWEST

St. Vincent Carmel Hospital (317) 582-7000
St. Vincent Carmel Hosp
13500 N Meridian St Carmel, IN 46032-1496 MIDWEST

St. Vincent Health System (501) 552-3000
St. Vincent Health System
2 St. Vincent Cir Little Rock, AR 72205 SOUTHWEST

St. Vincent Hospital - Green Bay (920) 433-0111
St. Vincent Hosp - Green Bay
835 S Van Buren St, P.O. Box 13508 Green Bay, WI 54307-3508 MIDWEST

St. Vincent Indianapolis Hospital (317) 338-2345
St. Vincent Indianapolis Hosp
2001 W 86th St Indianapolis, IN 46260-1991 MIDWEST

St. Vincent's Hospital - Birmingham (205) 939-7000
St. Vincent's Hosp - Birmingham
810 St. Vincent's Drive Birmingham, AL 35202-2407 SOUTHEAST

St. Vincent's Medical Center - Los Angeles (213) 484-7111
St. Vincent's Med Ctr - Los Angeles
2131 W 3rd St Los Angeles, CA 90057 WEST COAST AND PACIFIC

St. Vincent's Medical Center- Riverside (Jacksonville) (904) 308-7300
St. Vincent's Med Ctr - Riverside (Jacksonville)
1 Shircliff Way Jacksonville, FL 32204 SOUTHEAST

Stamford Hospital (203) 276-1000
Stamford Hosp
30 Shelburne Rd Stamford, CT 06902 NEW ENGLAND

Stanford University Hospital & Clinics (650) 723-4000
Stanford Univ Hosp & Clins
300 Pasteur Dr Stanford, CA 94305 WEST COAST AND PACIFIC

Steven and Alexandra Cohen Children's Medical Center of New York (718) 470-3000
Steven & Alexandra Cohen Chldn's Med Ctr of NY
269-01 76th Ave New Hyde Park, NY 11040 MID ATLANTIC

Steward St. Elizabeth's Medical Center-Boston (617) 789-3000
Steward St Elizabeth's Med Ctr-Boston
736 Cambridge St Boston, MA 02135 NEW ENGLAND

Stony Brook University Medical Center (631) 444-4000
Stony Brook Univ Med Ctr
101 Nicolls Rd Stony Brook, NY 11794-8410 MID ATLANTIC

Suburban Hospital (301) 896-3100
Suburban Hosp
8600 Old Georgetown Rd Bethesda, MD 20814 MID ATLANTIC

Summerlin Hospital Medical Center (702) 233-7000
Summerlin Hosp Med Ctr
657 Town Center Drive Las Vegas, NV 89144 WEST COAST AND PACIFIC

Sunnyview Hospital & Rehabilitation Center (518) 382-4500
Sunnyview Hosp & Rehab Ctr
1270 Belmont Ave Schenectady, NY 12308-2198 MID ATLANTIC

Sunrise Hospital & Medical Center (702) 731-8000
Sunrise Hosp & Med Ctr
3186 Maryland Pkwy Las Vegas, NV 89109 WEST COAST AND PACIFIC

SUNY Downstate Medical Center (University Hospital of Brooklyn) (718) 270-1000
SUNY Downstate Med Ctr (Univ Hosp Brooklyn)
450 Clarkson Ave Brooklyn, NY 11203 MID ATLANTIC

SUNY Upstate Medical University Hospital (315) 464-5540
SUNY Upstate Med Univ Hosp
750 E Adams St Syracuse, NY 13210-2306 MID ATLANTIC

Sutter Memorial Hospital-Sacramento (916) 454-3333
Sutter Mem Hospital-Sacramento
5151 F St Sacramento, CA 95819-3295 WEST COAST AND PACIFIC

Swedish Covenant Hospital (773) 878-8200
Swedish Covenant Hosp
5145 N California Ave Chicago, IL 60625 MIDWEST

Swedish Medical Center - Denver (303) 788-5000
Swedish Med Ctr - Denver
501 E Hamden Ave Englewood, CO 80110-2795 GREAT PLAINS AND MOUNTAINS

Swedish Medical Center-Cherry Hill Campus (206) 320-2000
Swedish Med Ctr-Cherry Hill Campus
500 17th Ave Seattle, WA 98122 WEST COAST AND PACIFIC

Swedish Medical Center-First Hill Campus - Seattle (206) 386-6000
Swedish Med Ctr-First Hill-Seattle
747 Broadway Seattle, WA 98122 WEST COAST AND PACIFIC

Tampa General Hospital (813) 844-7000
Tampa Genl Hosp
1 Tampa General Cir, PO Box 1289 Tampa, FL 33601 SOUTHEAST

Tanner Medical Center - Carrollton (770) 836-9666
Tanner Med Ctr
705 Dixie Street Carrollton, GA 30117 SOUTHEAST

Temple University Hospital (215) 707-2000
Temple Univ Hosp
3401 N Broad St Philadelphia, PA 19140-5189 MID ATLANTIC

Temple University Hospital-Episcopal Campus (215) 707-1200
Temple University Hosp-Episcopal Campus
100 E Lehigh Ave Philadelphia, PA 19125 MID ATLANTIC

Tennessee Valley Healthcare System - Nashville (615) 327-4751
TN Valley Healthcare Sys-Nashville
1310 24th Ave S Nashville, TN 37212 SOUTHEAST

Texas Children's Hospital (832) 824-1000
Texas Chldns Hosp
6621 Fannin St Houston, TX 77030 SOUTHWEST

Texas Health Presbyterian Hospital Dallas (214) 345-6789
TX Hlth Presby Hosp Dallas
8200 Walnut Hill Ln Dallas, TX 75231 SOUTHWEST

Texas Health Presbyterian Hospital Plano (972) 981-8000
TX Hlth Presby Hosp Plano
6200 West Parker Road Plano, TX 75093 SOUTHWEST

Texas Orthopedic Hospital (713) 799-8600
Texas Ortho Hosp
7401 S Main Houston, TX 77030 SOUTHWEST

Texas Scottish Rite Hospital for Children (214) 559-5000
Texas Scottish Rite Hosp for Chldn
2222 Welborn St Dallas, TX 75219 SOUTHWEST

Thomas Jefferson University Hospital (215) 955-6000
Thomas Jefferson Univ Hosp
111 S 11th St Philadelphia, PA 19107 MID ATLANTIC

TIRR Memorial Hermann (713) 799-5000
TIRR Meml Hermann
1333 Moursund Houston, TX 77030 SOUTHWEST

Toledo Hospital (419) 291-4000
Toledo Hosp
2142 N Cove Blvd Toledo, OH 43606 MIDWEST

Touro Infirmary (504) 897-7011
Touro Infirm
1401 Foucher Street New Orleans, LA 70115 SOUTHWEST

Trinity Mother Frances Hospital (903) 593-8441
Trinity Mother Frances Hosp
800 E Dawson St Tyler, TX 75701-2093 SOUTHWEST

Tucson Medical Center (520) 327-5461
Tucson Med Ctr
5301 E Grant Rd Tucson, AZ 85733-2195 SOUTHWEST

Tufts Medical Center (617) 636-5000
Tufts Med Ctr
800 Washington St Boston, MA 02111 NEW ENGLAND

Tulane Medical Center (504) 988-5800
Tulane Med Ctr
1415 Tulane Ave New Orleans, LA 70112 SOUTHWEST

Tulane-Lakeside Hospital (504) 988-5800
Tulane-Lakeside Hosp
4700 I-10 Service Rd Metairie, LA 70001 SOUTHWEST

UAB Highlands Hospital (205) 930-7000
UAB Highlands Hosp
1201 11th Ave S Birmingham, AL 35205-5299 SOUTHEAST

UAB Hospital (205) 934-4011
UAB Hosp
1802 6th Ave S Birmingham, AL 35249-6544 SOUTHEAST

UAB Medical West (205) 481-7000
UAB Med West
995 9th Ave SW Bessemer, AL 35020 SOUTHEAST

UAB Spain Rehabilitation Center		(205) 934-3450
UAB Spain Rehab Ctr		
1717 6th Ave S	Birmingham, AL 35249	SOUTHEAST
UCLA Ronald Reagan Medical Center		(310) 825-9111
UCLA Ronald Reagan Med Ctr		
757 Westwood Plaza	Los Angeles, CA 90095	WEST COAST AND PACIFIC
UCSD Medical Center		(858) 657-7000
UCSD Med Ctr		
200 W Arbor Drive	San Diego, CA 92103	WEST COAST AND PACIFIC
UCSD Thornton Hospital		(858) 657-7000
UCSD Thornton Hosp		
9300 Campus Point Drive	La Jolla, CA 92037	WEST COAST AND PACIFIC
UCSF - Mount Zion Medical Center		(415) 567-6600
UCSF - Mt Zion Med Ctr		
1600 Divisadero St	San Francisco, CA 94115	WEST COAST AND PACIFIC
UCSF Medical Center		(415) 476-1000
UCSF Med Ctr		
505 Parnassus Ave	San Francisco, CA 94143	WEST COAST AND PACIFIC
UF Health Jacksonville		(904) 244-0411
UF Hlth Jacksonville		
655 W 8th St	Jacksonville, FL 32209	SOUTHEAST
UF Health Shands Children's Hospital		(352) 265-0373
UF Hlth Shands Chldns Hosp		
1600 SW Archer Road	Gainesville, FL 32608	SOUTHEAST
UF Health Shands Hospital		(352) 265-8000
UF Hlth Shands Hosp		
1600 SW Archer Rd	Gainesville, FL 32610	SOUTHEAST
UH Ahuja Medical Center (OH)		(216) 593-5500
UH Ahuja Med Ctr (OH)		
3999 Richmond Rd	Beechwood, OH 44122	MIDWEST
UH Rainbow Babies & Children's Hospital		(216) 844-3991
UH Rainbow Babies & Chldns Hosp		
11100 Euclid Ave	Cleveland, OH 44106	MIDWEST
UMass Memorial Medical Center		(508) 334-1000
UMass Memorial Med Ctr		
55 Lake Ave N	Worcester, MA 01655	NEW ENGLAND

UMass Memorial Medical Center-Memorial Campus (508) 334-1000
UMass Mem Med Ctr-Memorial Campus
119 Belmont St Worcester, MA 01605 NEW ENGLAND

Union Hospital (410)-398-4000
Union Hosp
106 Bow St Elkton, MD 21921 MID ATLANTIC

United Hospital (651) 241-8000
United Hosp
333 N Smith Ave St Paul, MN 55102 MIDWEST

University Health Systems-Vidant Medical Center (252) 847-4100
Univ Hlth Sys-Vidant Med Ctr
2100 Stantonsburg Rd Greenville, NC 27835-6028 SOUTHEAST

University Hospital (Newark) (973) 972-4300
Univ Hosp (Newark)
150 Bergen St Newark, NJ 07103-2406 MID ATLANTIC

University Hospital - New Mexico (505) 272-2111
Univ Hosp - New Mexico
2211 Lomas Blvd NE Albuquerque, NM 87106 SOUTHWEST

University Hospital-San Antonio (210) 358-4000
Univ Hosp-San Antonio
4502 Medical Dr San Antonio, TX 78229 SOUTHWEST

University Hospitals Case Medical Center (216) 844-1000
UH Case Med Ctr
11100 Euclid Ave Cleveland, OH 44106 MIDWEST

University Medical Center of Princeton at Plainsboro (609) 853-7000
Univ Med Ctr Princeton at Plainsboro
One Plainsboro Rd Plainsboro, NJ 08536 MID ATLANTIC

University Medical Center of Southern Nevada - Las Vegas (702) 383-2000
Univ Med Ctr - Las Vegas
1800 W Charleston Blvd Las Vegas, NV 89102 WEST COAST AND PACIFIC

University Medical Center-Lubbock (806) 775-8200
Univ Med Ctr-Lubbock
602 Indiana Ave Lubbock, TX 79408 SOUTHWEST

University of Arizona Medical Center - South Campus (520) 874-2000
Univ Arizona Med Ctr-South Campus
2800 E Ajo Way Tucson, AZ 85713 SOUTHWEST

University of Arizona Medical Center-University Campus (520) 694-0111
Univ Arizona Med Ctr-Univ Campus
1501 N Campbell Ave Tucson, AZ 85724-5128 SOUTHWEST

University of Arkansas for Medical Sciences Medical Center (501) 686-7000
UAMS Med Ctr
4301 W Markham St Little Rock, AR 72205 SOUTHWEST

University of California - Davis Medical Center (916) 734-2011
UC Davis Med Ctr
2315 Stockton Blvd Sacramento, CA 95817 WEST COAST AND PACIFIC

University of California - Irvine Medical Center (714) 456-7890
UC Irvine Med Ctr
101 The City Drive S Orange, CA 92868 WEST COAST AND PACIFIC

University of Chicago Medicine (773) 702-1000
Univ of Chicago Med
5841 S Maryland Ave Chicago, IL 60637 MIDWEST

University of Chicago Medicine-Comer Children's Hospital (773) 702-1000
Univ Chicago Med-Comer Chldn's Hosp
5721 S Maryland Ave Chicago, IL 60637 MIDWEST

University of Cincinnati Medical Center (513) 584-1000
Univ Cincinnati Med Ctr
234 Goodman St Cincinnati, OH 45219 MIDWEST

University of Colorado Hospital (720) 848-4011
Univ Colorado Hosp
12605 E 16th Ave Aurora, CO 80045 GREAT PLAINS AND MOUNTAINS

University of Connecticut Health Center - John Dempsey Hospital (860) 679-2000
Univ of Conn Hlth Ctr, John Dempsey Hosp
263 Farmington Ave Farmington, CT 06030 NEW ENGLAND

University of Illinois at Chicago Eye & Ear Infirmary (312) 996-6500
Univ of IL at Chicago Eye & Ear Infirm
1855 W Taylor St Chicago, IL 60612 MIDWEST

University of Illinois Medical Center at Chicago (312) 355-4000
Univ of IL Med Ctr at Chicago
1740 W Taylor St, Ste 1400 Chicago, IL 60612 MIDWEST

University of Iowa Hospitals and Clinics (319) 356-1616
Univ Iowa Hosp & Clins
200 Hawkins Drive Iowa City, IA 52242 MIDWEST

University of Kansas Hospital (913) 588-5000
Univ of Kansas Hosp
3901 Rainbow Blvd Kansas City, KS 66160 GREAT PLAINS AND MOUNTAINS

University of Kentucky Albert B. Chandler Hospital (859) 323-5000
Univ of Kentucky Albert B. Chandler Hosp
800 Rose Street Lexington, KY 40536 SOUTHEAST

University of Louisville Hospital (502) 562-3000
Univ of Louisville Hosp
530 S Jackson St Louisville, KY 40202 SOUTHEAST

University of Maryland Medical Center (410) 328-8667
Univ of MD Med Ctr
22 S Greene St Baltimore, MD 21201 MID ATLANTIC

University of Maryland-St. Joseph Medical Center (410) 337-1000
Univ of MD-St. Joseph Med Ctr
7601 Osler Rd Towson, MD 21204 MID ATLANTIC

University of Miami Hosp & Clinics/Sylvester Comprehensive Cancer Ctr (305) 243-1000
Univ of Miami Hosp & Clins/Sylvester Comp Canc Ctr
1475 NW 12th Ave Miami, FL 33136 SOUTHEAST

University of Miami Hospital (305) 689-5000
Univ of Miami Hosp
1400 NW 12 Ave Miami, FL 33136 SOUTHEAST

University of Michigan Medical Center (734) 936-4000
Univ Michigan Med Ctr
1500 E Medical Center Dr Ann Arbor, MI 48109 MIDWEST

University of Minnesota Medical Center, Fairview - West Bank Campus (612) 273-3000
Univ Minn Med Ctr, Fairview - West Bank Campus
2450 Riverside Ave S Minneapolis, MN 55454 MIDWEST

University of Mississippi Medical Center (601) 984-1000
Univ Mississippi Med Ctr
2500 N State St Jackson, MS 39216 SOUTHEAST

University of Missouri Health Care (573) 882-4141
Univ of Missouri Hlth Care
1 Hospital Dr Columbia, MO 65212 MIDWEST

University of New Mexico Children's Hospital (505) 272-2111
UNM Chldns Hosp
2211 Lomas Blvd 3rd Fl Albuquerque, NM 87106 SOUTHWEST

University of Rochester Strong Memorial Hospital (585) 275-2100
Univ Rochester Strong Meml Hosp
601 Elmwood Ave Rochester, NY 14642 MID ATLANTIC

University of South Alabama Medical Center (251) 471-7000
Univ of S AL Med Ctr
2451 Fillingim St Mobile, AL 36617 SOUTHEAST

University of Tennesee Medical Center (865) 305-9000
Univ of Tennesee Med Ctr
1924 Alcoa Hwy Knoxville, TN 37920 SOUTHEAST

University of Texas Health Science Center at Tyler (903) 877-7777
Univ of Texas Hlth Sci Ctr at Tyler
11937 US Hwy 271 Tyler, TX 75708 SOUTHWEST

University of Texas MD Anderson Cancer Center (713) 792-2121
UT MD Anderson Canc Ctr
1515 Holcombe Blvd Houston, TX 77030-4095 SOUTHWEST

University of Toledo Medical Center (419) 383-4000
Univ of Toledo Med Ctr
3000 Arlington Ave Toledo, OH 43614 MIDWEST

University of Utah Health Care (801) 581-2121
Univ Utah Hlth Care
50 N Medical Dr Salt Lake City, UT 84132 GREAT PLAINS AND MOUNTAINS

University of Virginia Health System (434) 924-0211
Univ of Virginia Hlth Sys
1215 Lee Street Charlottesville, VA 22903 SOUTHEAST

University of Washington Medical Center (206) 598-3300
Univ Wash Med Ctr
1959 NE Pacific St, PO Box 656355 Seattle, WA 98195 WEST COAST AND PACIFIC

University of Wisconsin Hospital & Clinics (608) 263-6400
Univ WI Hosp & Clins
600 Highland Avenue Madison, WI 53792 MIDWEST

UPMC Hamot (814) 877-6000
UPMC Hamot
201 State Street Erie, PA 16550-0001 MID ATLANTIC

UPMC Mercy (412) 232-8111
UPMC Mercy, Pittsburgh
1400 Locust Street Pittsburgh, PA 15219 MID ATLANTIC

UPMC Montefiore *UPMC Montefiore* 3459 Fifth Ave	Pittsburgh, PA 15213	(412) 647-2345	MID ATLANTIC
UPMC Passavant-McCandless *UPMC Passavant-McCandless* 9100 Babcock Blvd	Pittsburgh, PA 15237	(412) 367-6700	MID ATLANTIC
UPMC Presbyterian *UPMC Presby, Pittsburgh* 200 Lothrop St	Pittsburgh, PA 15213	(412) 647-2345	MID ATLANTIC
UPMC Shadyside *UPMC Shadyside* 5230 Centre Ave	Pittsburgh, PA 15232	(412) 623-2121	MID ATLANTIC
UPMC South Side-Outpatient Center *UPMC South Side-Out Pt Ctr* 2000 Mary St	Pittsburgh, PA 15203	(412) 488-5550	MID ATLANTIC
UPMC St Margaret *UPMC St Margaret* 815 Freeport Rd	Pittsburgh, PA 15215-3301	(412) 784-4000	MID ATLANTIC
USC Norris Cancer Hospital *USC Norris Cancer Hosp* 1441 Eastlake Ave	Los Angeles, CA 90033	(323) 865-3000	WEST COAST AND PACIFIC
UT Medical Branch at Galveston(John Sealy Hospital) *UT Med Br at Galveston(John Sealy Hosp)* 301 University Blvd	Galveston, TX 77555	(409) 772-1011	SOUTHWEST
UT Southwestern Medical Center at Dallas *UT Southwestern Med Ctr at Dallas* 5323 Harry Hines Blvd	Dallas, TX 75390	(214) 648-3111	SOUTHWEST
VA Ann Arbor Healthcare System *VA Ann Arbor Healthcare Sys* 2215 Fuller Rd	Ann Arbor, MI 48105	(734) 769-7100	MIDWEST
VA Connecticut Healthcare System-West Haven Campus *VA Conn Hlthcre Sys-W Haven Campus* 950 Campbell Ave	West Haven, CT 06516	(203) 932-5711	NEW ENGLAND
VA Greater Los Angeles Healthcare System *VA Greater Los Angeles Hlthcare Sys* 11301 Wilshire Blvd	Los Angeles, CA 90073	(310) 478-3711	WEST COAST AND PACIFIC

VA Health Care System - Palo Alto		(650) 493-5000
VA Hlth Care Sys - Palo Alto		
3801 Miranda Ave	Palo Alto, CA 94304	WEST COAST AND PACIFIC
VA Medical Center - Memphis		(901) 523-8990
VA Med Ctr - Memphis		
1030 Jefferson Ave	Memphis, TN 38104	SOUTHEAST
VA Medical Center - Miami		(305) 575-7000
VA Med Ctr - Miami		
1201 NW 16th St	Miami, FL 33125	SOUTHEAST
VA Medical Center - Portland		(503) 220-8262
VA Medical Center - Portland		
3710 SW US Veteran Hospital Rd, PO Box 1034	Portland, OR 97239	WEST COAST AND PACIFIC
VA Medical Center - San Francisco		(415) 221-4810
VA Med Ctr - San Francisco		
4150 Clement St	San Francisco, CA 94121	WEST COAST AND PACIFIC
VA Medical Center - Washington, DC		(202) 745-8000
VA Med Ctr - Washington		
50 Irving St NW	Washington, DC 20422	MID ATLANTIC
VA Puget Sound Health Care System		(206) 762-1010
VA Puget Sound Hlth Care Sys		
1660 S Columbian Way	Seattle, WA 98108	WEST COAST AND PACIFIC
VA San Diego Healthcare System		(858) 552-8585
VA San Diego Hlthcre Sys		
3350 La Jolla Village Drive	San Diego, CA 92161	WEST COAST AND PACIFIC
Vail Valley Medical Center		(970) 476-2451
Vail Valley Med Ctr		
181 W Meadow Dr	Vail, CO 81657-5058	GREAT PLAINS AND MOUNTAINS
Valley Medical Center - Renton,WA		(425) 228-3450
Valley Med Ctr-Renton, WA		
404 S 43 St	Renton, WA 98058-5010	WEST COAST AND PACIFIC
Vanderbilt Monroe Carrell Jr. Children's Hospital		(615) 936-1000
Vanderbilt Monroe Carrell Jr. Chldn's Hosp		
2200 Children's Way	Nashville, TN 37232	SOUTHEAST
Vanderbilt University Medical Center		(615) 322-5000
Vanderbilt Univ Med Ctr		
1211 Medical Center Drive	Nashville, TN 37232	SOUTHEAST

VCU Medical Center (804) 828-9000
VCU Med Ctr
1250 E Marshall St, PO Box 980510 Richmond, VA 23298 SOUTHEAST

Virginia Hospital Center - Arlington (703) 558-5000
Virginia Hosp Ctr - Arlington
1701 N George Mason Dr Arlington, VA 22205-3698 SOUTHEAST

Virginia Mason Medical Center (206) 223-6600
Virginia Mason Med Ctr
1100 Ninth Ave, Box 900 Seattle, WA 98111 WEST COAST AND PACIFIC

Virtua West Jersey Hospital - Voorhees (856) 325-3000
Virtua West Jersey Hosp - Voorhees
101 Carnie Blvd Voorhees, NJ 08043 MID ATLANTIC

Waccamaw Community Hospital (843) 652-1000
Waccamaw Community Hosp
4070 Hwy 17 Bypass Murrells Inlet, SC 29576 SOUTHEAST

Wake Forest Baptist Medical Center (336) 716-2255
Wake Forest Baptist Med Ctr
Medical Center Blvd Winston-Salem, NC 27157-1015 SOUTHEAST

WakeMed Cary Hospital (919) 350-2300
WakeMed Cary
1900 Kildaire Farm Rd Cary, NC 27511-6616 SOUTHEAST

WakeMed-Raleigh Campus (919) 350-8000
WakeMed-Raleigh Campus
3000 New Bern Ave Raleigh, NC 27610 SOUTHEAST

Walter Reed National Military Medical Center (301) 295-4611
Walter Reed Natl Military Med Ctr
8901 Wisconsin Ave Bethesda, MD 20889-5600 MID ATLANTIC

Washington Hospital, The (724) 225-7000
Washington Hosp, The
155 Wilson Ave Washington, PA 15301 MID ATLANTIC

Washington University Physicians (314) 362-6828
Washington Univ Phys
4444 Forest Park Ave St Louis, MO 63108 MIDWEST

Watauga Medical Center (828) 262-4100
Watauga Med Ctr
336 Deerfield Rd Boone, NC 28607 SOUTHEAST

WellStar Windy Hill Hospital (770) 644-1000
WellStar Windy Hill Hosp
2540 Windy Hill Road Marietta, GA 30067 SOUTHEAST

Wesley Woods Geriatric Hospital (404) 728-6200
Wesley Woods Ger Hosp
1821 Clifton Rd Atlanta, GA 30329 SOUTHEAST

West Florida Hospital (850) 494-4000
West FL Hosp
8383 N Davis Hwy Pensacola, FL 32514-6088 SOUTHEAST

West Jefferson Medical Center (504) 347-5511
West Jefferson Med Ctr
1101 Medical Ctr Blvd Marrero, LA 70072 SOUTHWEST

West Palm Hospital (561) 842-6141
West Palm Hosp
2201 45th St West Palm Beach, FL 33407 SOUTHEAST

Westchester Medical Center (914) 493-7000
Westchester Med Ctr
95 Grasslands Road Valhalla, NY 10595 MID ATLANTIC

Western Pennsylvania Hospital (412) 578-5000
West Penn Hosp
4800 Friendship Avenue Pittsburgh, PA 15224 MID ATLANTIC

Western Psychiatric Institute and Clinic-UPMC (412) 624-1000
Western Psych Inst & Clin-UPMC
3811 O'Hara St Pittsburgh, PA 15213 MID ATLANTIC

White River Junction VA Medical Center (802) 295-9363
White River Junction VA Med Ctr
215 North Maine Street White River Junction, VT 05009 NEW ENGLAND

Wills Eye Hospital (215) 928-3000
Wills Eye Hosp
840 Walnut St Philadelphia, PA 19107-5598 MID ATLANTIC

Wilmington Hospital-Christiana Care Health System (302) 733-1000
Wilmington Hosp-Christiana Care
501 W 14th St, P.O. Box 1668 Wilmington, DE 19801 MID ATLANTIC

Winthrop University Hospital (516) 663-0333
Winthrop Univ Hosp
259 1st St Mineola, NY 11501 MID ATLANTIC

Wishard Health Services *Wishard Hlth Srvs* 1001 West 10th Street	Indianapolis, IN 46202	(317) 639-6671	MIDWEST
Wolfson Children's Hospital *Wolfson Chldns Hosp* 800 Prudential Dr	Jacksonville, FL 32207	(904) 202-8000	SOUTHEAST
Women & Infants Hospital of Rhode Island *Women & Infants Hosp of RI* 101 Dudley Street	Providence, RI 02905	(401) 274-1100	NEW ENGLAND
Women and Children's Hospital of Buffalo, The *Women & Chldn's Hosp of Buffalo, The* 219 Bryant St	Buffalo, NY 14222	(716) 878-7000	MID ATLANTIC
Yale New Haven Psychiatric Hospital *Yale New Haven Psychiatric Hosp* 184 Liberty St	New Haven, CT 06519	(203) 688-9907	NEW ENGLAND
Yale-New Haven Hospital *Yale-New Haven Hosp* 20 York St	New Haven, CT 06510	(203) 688-4242	NEW ENGLAND
Yale-New Haven Hospital St Raphael Campus *Yale-New Haven Hosp - St Raphael Campus* 1450 Chapel Street	New Haven, CT 06511	(203) 789-3000	NEW ENGLAND
Yampa Valley Medical Center *Yampa Valley Med Ctr* 1024 Central Park Dr	Steamboat Springs, CO 80487	(970) 879-1322	GREAT PLAINS AND MOUNTAINS
Zucker Hillside Hospital *Zucker Hillside Hosp* 75-59 263rd St	Glen Oaks, NY 11004	(718) 470-8100	MID ATLANTIC

Appendix D:
Selected Resources

GENERAL RESOURCES

AMERICAN AMBULANCE ASSOCIATION (AAA)

The American Ambulance Association represents emergency and non-emergency medical transportation providers, advocating high quality pre-hospital care and keeping these providers aware of legislation and news that may affect them.

8400 West Park Drive, FL2
McLean, VA 22102

800-523-4447
703-610-9018
fax 703-610-0210
www.the-aaa.org/

AMERICA'S HEALTH INSURANCE PLANS (AHIP)

America's Health Insurance Plans is a national trade association representing nearly 1,300 member companies providing health benefits to more than 200 million Americans.

601 Pennsylvania Ave, NW
South Building Suite 500
Washington, DC 20004

202-778-3200
fax: 202-331-7487
www.ahip.org/

AMERICAN BOARD OF MEDICAL SPECIALTIES (ABMS)

The ABMS is the authoritative body for the recognition of medical specialties, coordinating 24 medical specialty boards (including 25 medical specialties) and providing information on the board certification of doctors.

222 N LaSalle, Ste 1500
Chicago, Illinois 60601

312-436-2600 or 866-ASK-ABMS
fax 847-328-3596
www.abms.org

AMERICAN HOSPITAL ASSOCIATION (AHA)

A national health advocacy organization, the AHA represents hospitals and healthcare networks in legislative and regulatory matters. In 1973 the AHA adopted the Patient Bill of Rights to help patients understand their rights and responsibilities.

155 N Wacker Drive
Chicago, IL 60606

800-424-4301 or 312-422-3000
fax 312-422-4796
www.aha.org/

325 7th St. NW
Washington, DC 20004

800-424-4301 or 202-638-1100
fax 202-626-2345

American Medical Association (AMA)

The AMA is an association that maintains information on physicians practicing throughout the nation. Healthcare consumers can use their database to check the location, licensing, education and specialty of many doctors in the United States.

330 N. Wabash Avenue
Chicago, IL 60611

800-621-8335
www.ama-assn.org/

Center for Medical Consumers

Provides volume and outcome data on certain medical procedures performed in New York state.

239 Thompson St.
New York, NY 10012

212-674-7105
fax 212-674-7100
centerformedicalconsumers@gmail.com
www.medicalconsumers.org

Centers for Disease Control and Prevention (CDC)

Part of the Department of Health and Human Services, the CDC's mission is to prevent and manage diseases and illnesses. Its Website contains information on a range of illnesses and the research being pursued to manage them. It also provides free faxed reports on disease risk and prevention in various parts of the world.

Public Inquiries/MASO
Mailstop E11
1600 Clifton Road
Atlanta, GA 30333

800-CDC-INFO
TTY: 888-232-6348

toll free number for international travelers 877 FYI-TRIP or 404-639-3534
fax information service for international travelers 888-232-3299
www.cdc.gov/netinfo.htm

The CenterWatch Clinical Trials Listing Service

Profiles centers conducting clinical research by therapeutic area and geographic region, including more than 41,000 international industry and government-sponsored clinical trials and new FDA approved drug therapies, as well as 5,200 clinical trials that are actively recruiting patients.

10 Winthrop Square
Fl 5
Boston, MA 02110

617-948-5100
fax 617-948-5101
www.centerwatch.com

International Association for Medical Assistance To Travellers (IAMAT)

IAMAT is a non-profit organization that disseminates information on health and sanitary conditions worldwide. Membership is free but donations are appreciated. Members will receive a membership card making them eligible to access English speaking physicians all over the world. The organization also provides information on immunization requirements, malaria, and other tropical diseases, and sanitary and climactic conditions around the world. For information, send request in writing.

1623 Military Road #279
Niagra Falls, New York 14304-1745

716-754-4883
www.iamat.org

Joint Commission on Accreditation of Healthcare Organizations

The Joint Commission (JCAHO) is an independent, not-for-profit organization, which evaluates the quality and safety of care for nearly 17,000 health care organizations. To maintain and earn accreditation, organizations must have an extensive on-site review by a team of JCAHO health care professionals, at least once every three years. JCAHO is governed by a board that includes physicians, nurses, and consumers. JCAHO sets the standards by which health care quality is measured in America and around the world.

One Renaissance Boulevard
Oakbrook Terrace, IL 60181

630-792-5000
fax 630-792-5005
www.jcaho.org

Medic Alert Foundation

The Medic Alert Foundation (a non-profit organization) provides an "ID tag" engraved with personal medical facts, as well as a 24-hour emergency response center which can release additional personal medical details. Membership is $30/year (plus $9.95 initial setup fee) and members need to purchase the "ID tag" which sells for as low as $35.

2323 Colorado Avenue
Turlock, CA 95382

888-633-4298
Fax 209-669-2450
www.medicalert.org

Medline

A medical database including millions of medical references and abstracts from thousands of scientific and medical journals.

One Medline Place
Mundelein, Illinois 60060

1-800-MEDLINE (800-633-5463)
fax 1-800-351-1512
www.medline.com

The National Cancer Institute (NCI)

Part of the NIH, the NCI sponsors cancer clinical trials at more than 100 sites in the United States. Trials are carried out in major medical research centers, such as teaching hospitals, as well as in community hospitals, specialized medical clinics and even in doctors' offices.

Clinical Studies Support Center (CSSC)
6116 Executive Boulevard
Bethesda, MD 20892-8322

800-4-CANCER (800-422-6237)
www.nci.nih.gov
www.cancer.gov
cancergovstaff@mail.nih.gov

National Center for Complementary and Alternative Medicine Clearinghouse (NCCAMC)

The NCCAMC facilitates the evaluation of alternative medical treatment modalities to help determine their effectiveness and bring alternative medicine into mainstream medicine. This agency does not provide referrals.

9000 Rockville Pike
Bethesda, MD 20892

888-644-6226
fax 866-464-3616
www.nccam.nih.gov
info@nccam.nih.gov

National Consumers League (NCL)

NCL is a private, nonprofit consumer advocacy organization. NCL strives to investigate, educate, and advocate on a variety of issues including healthcare. Membership is $20 annually, but individuals can also write to the organization for a list of publications that non-members can purchase.

1701 K Street, NW, Suite 1200
Washington, DC 20006

202-835-3323
fax 202-835-0747
www.nclnet.org
info@nclnet.org

The National Institutes of Health (NIH)

An organization operated by the U.S. government, the NIH operates its own hospital at which the care provided is usually related to clinical studies its researchers are undertaking. Information about the Warren G. Magnuson Clinical Center is also available.

Patient Recruitment Referral Center
9000 Rockville Pike
Bethesda, MD 20892

301-496-4000
www.nih.gov
www.clinicaltrials.gov
nihinfo@od.nih.gov

National Insurance Information Institute

The National Insurance Information Institute Helpline advises consumers on how to choose an insurance company or broker. It also offers an analysis of life insurance and assists in insurance complaints.

110 William St
New York, NY 10038

212-346-5500
www.iii.org

The Patient Advocate Foundation

A national non-profit organization that provides consultation, referrals and case management to patients to ensure that they are not denied access to healthcare, insurance coverage, employment and public assistance programs during an illness. In particular, the organization maintains comprehensive information on cancer treatment options that are available to consumers through a separate Web site: www.oncology.com.

421 Butler Farm Rd
Hampton, VA 23666

800-532-5274
fax 757-873-8999
www.patientadvocate.org/
help@patientadvocate.org

People's Medical Society

The People's Medical Society, a nonprofit organization, is focused on educating the healthcare consumer about healthcare issues and medical rights. Their website provides information on useful books and publications as well as the latest healthcare developments.

P.O. Box 868
Allentown, PA 18105

610-770-1670
fax 610-770-0607
cbi@peoplesmed.org
www.peoplesmed.org

Persons United Limiting Substandards and Errors in Healthcare (P.U.L.S.E.)

A support group for the survivors of medical malpractice and substandard healthcare, this nonprofit group also advocates patient education and patient-doctor communication.

PO Box 353
Wantagh NY 11793-0353

800-96-pulse (800-967-8573) or
516-579-4711
fax: 516-520-8105
www.PULSEamerica.org
www.PULSEofNY.org
pulse516@aol.com

Florida Office

727-712-7370
PULSEofFlorrida@gmail.com
www.PulseofFlorida.org

Public Citizen's Health and Research Group

A non-profit organization, the Public Citizen's Group acts as a watchdog agency by advocating accountability and the open use of doctors' disciplinary backgrounds.

1600 20th Street NW
Washington, D.C. 20009

202-588-1000
www.citizen.org/hrg/

Top Doctors Make A Difference

Appendix E:
Sources of Quality Data on Hospitals

WWW.WHYNOTTHEBEST.ORG

WhyNotTheBest.org was created and is maintained by The Commonwealth Fund, a private foundation working toward a high performance health system. It is a free resource for health care professionals and consumers interested in tracking performance on various measures of health care quality. It enables organizations to compare their performance against that of peer organizations, against a range of benchmarks and over a given period of time. Case studies and improvement tools spotlight successful improvement strategies of the nation's top performers. A regional map shows performance at the county, state and national levels. This site also includes process-of-care measures, patient satisfaction measures, readmission rates, mortality rates and average reimbursement rates. All of these performance measures are publicly reported on the Centers for Medicare and Medicaid Services website, Hospital Compare, and include data from nearly all U.S. hospitals.

THE LEAPFROG GROUP

The Leapfrog Group, http://www.leapfroggroup.org/cp, started in 1998 by a group of large employers. The Leapfrog Hospital Survey compares hospitals' performance on the national standards of safety, quality and efficiency - areas of healthcare that are most relevant to consumers. Hospitals that participate in The Leapfrog Hospital Survey achieve hospital-wide improvements that translate into saving millions of lives and cutting costs for hospitals and consumers. Leapfrog's survey results are later used to inform key employees on purchasing strategies.

HOSPITAL COMPARE

The Hospital Compare website was created through the efforts of the Centers for Medicare & Medicaid Services (CMS), an agency of the U.S. Department of Health and Human Services (DHHS), along with the Hospital Quality Alliance (HQA). The HQA was established to promote reporting on hospital quality of care. The HQA consists of organizations that represent consumers, hospitals, doctors and nurses, employers, accrediting organizations and Federal agencies. The information on this website can be used by patients requiring hospital care. This information helps the consumer and health care providers to compare the quality of care provided in participating hospitals. This information not only helps one to make good decisions about health care, but also encourages hospitals to improve the quality of the care that they provide to their communities. This website can be found at: http://www.hospitalcompare.hhs.gov/hospital-search.aspx or http://bit.ly/jdvCzW

U.S. NEWS AND WORLD REPORT

U.S. News & World Report has been the nation's leading source of information on hospital rankings since 1990. The Best Hospitals rankings evaluate medical centers on their competence in high-stakes situations. Their annual feature on Best Hospitals has become the standard in the field where rankings are concerned and is heavily anticipated and utilized by consumers and members of the health care profession.

Indices

Subject Index

A

Accessibility 18, 19
Admitting Privileges 14
Adverse Reactions 26, 31-33
Ambulatory Care Research Facility 34
American Board of Medical Specialties 5, 10, 41-42, 49-51
American Osteopathic Association 10
Areas of Clinical Study 34
Attendings 14

B

Bedside Manner 19
Benefits and Risks 32-33
Board Certification10-13, 37, 41, 51
Board Eligible 11

C

Cancer Trials 30
Clinical Cancer Centers 27
Clinical Research 2, 4, 25, 27-28, 33-35
Clinical Studies Support Center (CSSC) 35
Clinical Trials 25-28, 30-35
Closed Staffs 14
Comprehensive Cancer Centers 35
Continuing Medical Education (CME) 12
Control Group 28
Cosmetic Surgery 5, 7, 46
Council of Teaching Hospitals 3
Credentialing 14

D

Diplomates of the Board 11
Directory of Graduate Medical Education 10
Doctor-Patient Relationship 19

E

Experimental or Treatment Group 28

Experimental Procedures 30

F

Faculty Appointment 15, 37

Fellow xxix, xxx, 7, 37, 51

Fellowships 13

Follow-up Care 19, 34

Food and Drug Administration 29

Foreign Medical Graduates 9

Foreign Medical Schools 9

G

General Clinical Research Centers 34-35

Grandfathering 12

H

Health Insurance 18

Health Maintenance Organizations (HMO) 18, 27

Health Plan 5, 7, 18, 30-31

Hospital Appointment 2, 14-15

I

Inclusion Criteria 30

Informed Consent 29

Initial Consultation 21

Institutional Review Board 28

L

Laboratory Tests 31

Levels of Recognition 11

Liaison Committee for Medical Education 8

License Histories 4

Long-term Monitoring 19

M

Magnuson Clinical Center, see Warren Grant Magnuson Clinical Center 33-35
Maintenance Trials 31
Major Medical Centers 1-3, 14, 26
Malpractice Insurance 15
Mark O. Hatfield Clinical Research Center 34
Medical Affairs Office 5, 14
Medical College Admissions Tests 9
Medical History 21, 23, 31
Medical Records 21-23, 29, 34
Medical School 2-3, 8-11, 13, 15-16, 37, 49
Medical School Faculty 15
Medical Society Membership 15

N

National Cancer Institute (NCI) 26-27, 30-31, 35
National Institutes of Health (NIH) 25, 27, 33-35
Non-board Certified Doctors 11

O

Office and Practice Arrangements 18
Out-of-Network 18

P

Patient Recruitment and Public Liaison Office (PRPL) 34
Personal Chemistry 19
Placebo 28
Postgraduate Training 10
Prevention Trials 27
Primary Care 1, 3-4, 7, 8, 15, 18-19, 31, 42-44, 49
Private Insurance 29

Professional Reputation 13
Protocol 27-28, 30

R

Recertification 12, 50
Referral 3, 8, 14, 18, 35
Residency 2, 10-11, 16-17, 37, 49-50

S

Second Opinions 17-18
Selection Process 2
Self-Designated Medical Specialties 12
Side Effects 26-27, 32-33
Special Resources 25-26, 28, 30, 32, 34
Specialists 1-10, 12, 14-16, 18, 37, 41, 43, 49-51, 53
Specialties 3-6, 9-12, 14, 24, 38, 41-47, 49-51, 53
Standard Therapies 25
Subspecialties 1, 5-6, 10, 12-13, 15, 41-42, 49-50, 53

T

Therapeutic Approaches 1, 6, 25
Treatment Plan 21, 30
Treatment Studies 25, 30
Trust 19

U

United States Department of Health 33
United States Medical Licensing Exam 9

V

Veritas Medicine 26

W

Warren Grant Magnuson Clinical Center 33-35

Specialty & Special Expertise Index

This index lists the areas that the physicians listed in the Guide have identified as their "special expertise." They are specific elements of disease, procedures, techniques and treatments for which these physicians are best known and are referred patients. Each doctor's medical specialty is also included.

A

Abdominal Imaging

Spec	Name	St	Pg
DR	Berland, L	AL	1013
DR	Coakley, F	OR	1017
DR	Coleman, B	PA	1008
DR	Dachman, A	IL	1014
DR	Dodd, G	CO	1016
DR	Federle, M	CA	1017
DR	Fishman, E	MD	1009
DR	Grant, E	CA	1018
DR	Kruskal, J	MA	1007
DR	Levy, A	DC	1010
DR	Megibow, A	NY	1010
DR	Miller, F	IL	1015
DR	Prince, M	NY	1011
DR	Sivit, C	OH	1015
DR	Weinreb, J	CT	1007
DR	Zagoria, R	CA	1019

Abdominal Wall Reconstruction

Spec	Name	St	Pg
PlS	Dumanian, G	IL	893
PlS	Kuzon, W	MI	894
PlS	Seyfer, A	MD	886
PlS	Stahl, R	CT	879
S	Deitch, E	NJ	1092
S	Fitzgibbons, R	NE	1122

Abdominoplasty

Spec	Name	St	Pg
PlS	Aly, A	CA	901
PlS	Davis, G	NC	889
PlS	Erdmann, D	NC	889
PlS	Eriksson, E	MA	878
PlS	Hunstad, J	NC	890
PlS	Kolker, A	NY	883
PlS	Lesavoy, M	CA	904
PlS	Markowitz, B	CA	904
PlS	Matarasso, A	NY	884
PlS	Nahabedian, M	DC	885
PlS	Ness, J	MN	895
PlS	Pitman, G	NY	885
PlS	Singh, N	MD	886

Abuse/Neglect

Spec	Name	St	Pg
ChAP	Zeanah, C	LA	943
Ger	Lachs, M	NY	265

Achalasia

Spec	Name	St	Pg
Ge	Falk, G	PA	234
Ge	Ravich, W	MD	239
Ge	Vaezi, M	TN	245
S	Pryor, A	NY	1098

Acne

Spec	Name	St	Pg
D	Barbosa, V	IL	194
D	James, W	PA	189
D	Lowitt, M	MD	189
D	Lucky, A	OH	196
D	Woodley, D	CA	202

Acoustic Neuroma

Spec	Name	St	Pg
NS	Eisenberg, H	MD	476
NS	Grubb, R	MO	490
NS	Gutin, P	NY	477
NS	Harsh, G	CA	500
NS	Judy, K	PA	478
NS	Martuza, R	MA	473
NS	Mayberg, M	WA	501
NS	Parsa, A	IL	492
NS	Swaid, S	AL	487
NS	Thompson, B	MI	493
Oto	Arriaga, M	LA	691
Oto	Beatty, C	MN	683
Oto	Brackmann, D	CA	694
Oto	Driscoll, C	MN	684
Oto	Duckert, L	WA	695
Oto	Feghali, J	NY	669
Oto	Haynes, D	TN	679
Oto	Jenkins, H	CO	690
Oto	Kveton, J	CT	666
Oto	Linstrom, C	NY	673
Oto	Miyamoto, R	IN	686
Oto	Oghalai, J	CA	696
Oto	Roland, J	NY	674
Oto	Rubinstein, J	WA	696
Oto	Shelton, C	UT	690
Oto	Telian, S	MI	688
Oto	Wackym, P	OR	697
Oto	Wazen, J	FL	682
Oto	Wiet, R	IL	688
RadRO	Loeffler, J	MA	977

Acromegaly

Spec	Name	St	Pg
EDM	Biller, B	MA	208
EDM	Katznelson, L	CA	225
EDM	Kennedy, L	OH	220
EDM	Melmed, S	CA	225

Acupuncture

Spec	Name	St	Pg
PM	Ngeow, J	NY	707
PMR	Borg-Stein, J	MA	862
PMR	Dillard, J	NY	863

Acute Coronary Syndrome

Spec	Name	St	Pg
IC	Mehran, R	NY	122

Acute Coronary Syndromes

Spec	Name	St	Pg
Cv	Dangas, G	NY	92
Cv	Eagle, K	MI	101
Cv	Rihal, C	MN	104
Cv	Schulman, S	MD	95
Cv	Williams, E	IN	106
IC	Bach, R	MO	125
IC	Fromkin, K	FL	124
IC	Gibson, C	MA	120
IC	Greene, R	CA	128
IC	Henry, T	MN	126
IC	Holmes, D	MN	126

ADD/ADHD

Spec	Name	St	Pg
ChAP	Abright, A	NY	939
ChAP	Alessi, N	MI	941
ChAP	Biederman, J	MA	938
ChAP	Bogrov, M	MD	939
ChAP	Coffey, B	NY	939
ChAP	Dulcan, M	IL	942
ChAP	Heston, J	TN	941
ChAP	Hirsch, G	NY	940
ChAP	Hirsch, S	IL	942
ChAP	Hudziak, J	VT	938
ChAP	Koplewicz, H	NY	940
ChAP	Kwon, H	WA	943
ChAP	Leventhal, B	NY	940
ChAP	Martini, D	UT	942
ChAP	McCracken, J	CA	943
ChAP	Rostain, A	PA	940
ChAP	Slomowitz, M	IL	942
ChAP	Spencer, T	MA	939
ChAP	Turecki, S	NY	941
ChAP	Wilens, T	MA	939
ChiN	Nass, R	NY	146
ChiN	Roddy, S	CA	152
N	Finkel, M	FL	524
Ped	Burgess, D	NJ	740
Ped	Hershorin, E	FL	741
Ped	Roizen, N	OH	742
Psyc	Keepers, G	OR	933

ADD/PTSD

Spec	Name	St	Pg
Psyc	Manevitz, A	NY	925

Addiction Psychiatry

Spec	Name	St	Pg
AdP	Ciraulo, D	MA	936
AdP	Collins, E	NY	936

Spec	Name	St	Pg
AdP	Frances, R	NY	936
AdP	Galanter, I	NY	936
AdP	Greenfield, S	MA	936
AdP	Howell, E	UT	937
AdP	Kampman, K	PA	937
AdP	Kleber, H	NY	937
AdP	Kosten, T	TX	938
AdP	Lawson, W	DC	937
AdP	Nitenson, N	MA	936
AdP	Serota, R	PA	937
AdP	Stine, S	MI	937
AdP	Strain, E	MD	937
AdP	Weiss, R	MA	936

Addiction/Substance Abuse

Spec	Name	St	Pg
AdP	Collins, E	NY	936
AdP	Frances, R	NY	936
AdP	Greenfield, S	MA	936
AdP	Howell, E	UT	937
AdP	Kampman, K	PA	937
AdP	Lawson, W	DC	937
AdP	Nitenson, N	MA	936
AdP	Serota, R	PA	937
AdP	Stine, S	MI	937
AdP	Strain, E	MD	937
AM	Adger, H	MD	76
AM	Sigel, E	CO	78
ChAP	Deas, D	SC	941
ChAP	Wilens, T	MA	939
IM	Selwyn, P	NY	426
Psyc	Rosenthal, R	NY	926
Psyc	Salloum, I	FL	928
Psyc	Weinstock, R	CA	935

Addictive Disorders

Spec	Name	St	Pg
Psyc	Grant, J	IL	929

Addison's Disease

Spec	Name	St	Pg
EDM	Maclaren, N	NY	213

Adolescent Behavior-High Risk

Spec	Name	St	Pg
AM	Ginsburg, K	PA	76
AM	Staggers, B	CA	78

Adolescent Gynecology

Spec	Name	St	Pg
AM	Emans, S	MA	76
AM	Hergenroeder, A	TX	78
AM	Irwin, C	CA	78
AM	Kaplan, D	CO	77
AM	Murray, P	WV	76
ObG	Gilliam, M	IL	564
ObG	Greenfield, M	OH	564
ObG	Merritt, D	MO	565
RE	Ratts, V	MO	1048
RE	Sanfilippo, J	PA	1044

Adolescent Medicine

Spec	Name	St	Pg
AM	Adger, H	MD	76
AM	Anderson, M	CA	78
AM	Bermudez, O	CO	77
AM	Bravender, T	OH	77
AM	Chambers, C	PA	76
AM	Emans, S	MA	76
AM	Garofalo, R	IL	77
AM	Ginsburg, K	PA	76
AM	Hergenroeder, A	TX	78
AM	Irwin, C	CA	78
AM	Kaplan, D	CO	77
AM	Kokotailo, P	WI	77
AM	Murray, P	WV	76
AM	Rudy, B	NY	76
AM	Sigel, E	CO	78
AM	Sigman, G	IL	77
AM	Singh, N	MN	77
AM	Slap, G	PA	76
AM	Staggers, B	CA	78

Adolescent Psychiatry

Spec	Name	St	Pg
Psyc	Weinstock, R	CA	935

Adolescent Sports Medicine

Spec	Name	St	Pg
SM	Metzl, J	NY	1075

Adrenal Cancer

Spec	Name	St	Pg
EDM	Daniels, G	MA	209
EDM	Hammer, G	MI	219
Onc	Oh, W	NY	349
PHO	Wolfe, L	NY	777
S	Lee, J	TX	1127
S	Solorzano, C	TN	1109
U	Coleman, J	NY	1189

Adrenal Disorders

Spec	Name	St	Pg
EDM	Brown, J	TX	222
EDM	Hammer, G	MI	219
EDM	Jacobs, T	NY	213
EDM	Kennedy, L	OH	220
EDM	Lechan, R	MA	210
EDM	Lipson, A	DC	213
EDM	Semenkovich, C	MO	221
Nep	Blumenfeld, J	NY	459
PEn	Kohn, B	NY	758
PEn	New, M	NY	758
PEn	Oberfield, S	NY	758

Adrenal Surgery

Spec	Name	St	Pg
S	Doherty, G	MA	1085
S	Hanks, J	VA	1105
S	Lee, J	NY	1095
S	McHenry, C	OH	1116
S	Schlinkert, R	AZ	1128
S	Weber, C	GA	1110
U	Marsh, C	CA	1212

Adrenal Tumors

Spec	Name	St	Pg
S	Angelos, P	IL	1111
S	Brunt, L	MO	1112
S	Butler, J	CA	1131
S	Duh, Q	CA	1132
S	Gawande, A	MA	1085
S	Grant, C	MN	1114
S	Hanna, N	MD	1094
S	Hodin, R	MA	1086
S	Schulick, R	CO	1123
S	Udelsman, R	CT	1088
U	Libertino, J	MA	1187
U	Sundaram, C	IN	1206

Aggression Disorders

Spec	Name	St	Pg
AM	Sigel, E	CO	78
ChAP	Steiner, H	CA	944

AIDS Related Cancers

Spec	Name	St	Pg
Hem	Levine, A	CA	328
Inf	Palefsky, J	CA	420
Inf	Polsky, B	NY	414
Onc	Aboulafia, D	WA	384
Onc	Abrams, D	CA	384
Onc	Ambinder, R	MD	337
Onc	Henry, D	PA	344
Onc	Mitsuyasu, R	CA	390
Onc	Remick, S	WV	350
Onc	Volberding, P	CA	394
Psyc	Breitbart, W	NY	923

AIDS Related Lymphoma

Spec	Name	St	Pg
Onc	Kaplan, L	CA	389
Onc	Morgan, D	TN	362

AIDS-Neurologic Complications

Spec	Name	St	Pg
N	Simpson, D	NY	521

AIDS/HIV

Spec	Name	St	Pg
AM	Rudy, B	NY	76
Ger	McCormick, W	WA	268
Hem	Levine, A	CA	328
IM	Fischl, M	FL	426
IM	Selwyn, P	NY	426
Inf	Ballon-Landa, G	CA	420
Inf	Bartlett, J	MD	412
Inf	Berkowitz, L	NY	412
Inf	Campbell, J	MO	417
Inf	Cancio, M	FL	415
Inf	Cohn, S	IL	417
Inf	Daar, E	CA	420
Inf	Fichtenbaum, C	OH	417
Inf	Flaherty, J	IL	417
Inf	Flanigan, T	RI	412
Inf	Frank, I	PA	413
Inf	Gorensek, M	FL	416
Inf	Gumprecht, J	NY	413
Inf	Hammer, G	NY	413
Inf	Hammer, S	NY	413
Inf	Johnson, S	CO	419
Inf	Katner, H	GA	416

Spec	Name	St	Pg
Inf	Keiser, P	TX	420
Inf	Kumar, P	DC	413
Inf	Louie, E	NY	414
Inf	McGowan, J	NY	414
Inf	Mildvan, D	NY	414
Inf	Novak, R	IL	418
Inf	O'Keefe, J	IL	418
Inf	Perlman, D	NY	414
Inf	Polsky, B	NY	414
Inf	Pursell, K	IL	418
Inf	Ratzan, K	FL	416
Inf	Richman, D	CA	421
Inf	Romagnoli, M	NY	414
Inf	Saag, M	AL	416
Inf	Salata, R	OH	418
Inf	Sax, P	MA	412
Inf	Scheld, W	VA	416
Inf	Schooley, R	CA	421
Inf	Squires, K	PA	415
Inf	Van Der Horst, C	NC	417
Inf	Wallach, F	NY	415
Inf	Wiviott, L	CA	421
Inf	Wormser, G	NY	415
N	Berger, J	KY	523
N	McArthur, J	MD	519
PA&I	Church, J	CA	746
PA&I	Shearer, W	TX	746
PInf	Andiman, W	CT	792
PInf	Bryson, Y	CA	797
PInf	Durbin, W	MA	792
PInf	Flynn, P	TN	794
PInf	Kline, M	TX	796
PInf	McComsey, G	OH	795
PInf	McKinney, R	NC	794
PInf	Michaels, M	PA	793
PInf	Mitchell, C	FL	795
PInf	Petru, A	CA	797
PInf	Scott, G	FL	795
Pul	Hopewell, P	CA	970
Pul	Huang, L	CA	971

AIDS/HIV in Adolescents

AM	Garofalo, R	IL	77

AIDS/HIV in Elderly

Inf	McGowan, J	NY	414

AIDS/HIV in Pregnancy

MF	Riley, L	MA	433

AIDS/HIV in Women

Inf	Cohn, S	IL	417
Inf	Sha, B	IL	418
Inf	Squires, K	PA	415

AIDS/HIV-Gastrointestinal Complications

Ge	Borum, M	DC	233

Spec	Name	St	Pg
Ge	Dieterich, D	NY	234

Airway Disorders

A&I	Chandler, M	NY	80
A&I	Korenblat, P	MO	84
Oto	Berke, G	CA	694
Oto	Hogikyan, N	MI	685
Oto	Patil, Y	OH	687
Oto	Rassekh, C	PA	674
Oto	Zalzal, G	MD	677
PO	Arnold, J	OH	804
PO	Baroody, F	IL	804
PO	Bower, C	AR	805
PO	Crockett, D	CA	805
PO	Darrow, D	VA	803
PO	Duncan, N	TX	805
PO	Friedman, E	TX	805
PO	Goldsmith, A	NY	802
PO	Holinger, L	IL	804
PO	Inglis, A	WA	805
PO	Miller, R	IL	804
PO	Myer, C	OH	804
PO	Richardson, M	OR	806
PO	Rosbe, K	CA	806
PO	Ward, R	NY	803
PPul	Sherman, J	VA	808
Pul	Goldman, A	FL	962
Pul	Martin, R	CO	968

Airway Reconstruction

Oto	Clark, K	OK	691
Oto	Couch, M	VT	665
Oto	Genden, E	NY	670
PO	Cotton, R	OH	804
PO	Parikh, S	WA	806

Albinism

Oph	Summers, C	MN	599

Alcohol Abuse

AdP	Ciraulo, D	MA	936
AdP	Collins, E	NY	936
AdP	Galanter, I	NY	936
AdP	Greenfield, S	MA	936
AdP	Howell, E	UT	937
AdP	Kampman, K	PA	937
AdP	Kosten, T	TX	938
AdP	Nitenson, N	MA	936

Alcohol Abuse-Consultation

AdP	Weiss, R	MA	936
Psyc	Walker, R	OR	935

Allergic Fungal Sinusitis

Oto	Kuhn, F	GA	679

Spec	Name	St	Pg

Allergic Rhinitis

A&I	Sundy, J	NC	83
PA&I	Burks, A	NC	744

Allergy

A&I	Altman, L	WA	85
A&I	DeShazo, R	MS	82
A&I	Friedman, S	FL	82
A&I	Henderson, W	WA	86
A&I	Korenblat, P	MO	84
A&I	Li, J	MN	84
A&I	MacLean, J	MA	80
A&I	Montanaro, A	OR	86
A&I	Phillips, S	PA	81
A&I	Routes, J	WI	84
A&I	Spector, S	CA	86
Oto	Corey, J	IL	684
PA&I	Gelfand, E	CO	745
PA&I	Lemanske, R	WI	745
PA&I	Schuberth, K	MD	744
PA&I	Shearer, W	TX	746
PA&I	Sly, R	MD	744
PA&I	Wasserman, R	TX	746
PA&I	Wolf, R	IL	745
Pul	Sutherland, E	CO	968
Rhu	Gershwin, M	CA	1067

Allergy & Immunology

A&I	Altman, L	WA	85
A&I	Ballas, Z	IA	83
A&I	Benenati, S	FL	82
A&I	Bernstein, D	OH	83
A&I	Bernstein, J	OH	83
A&I	Buchbinder, E	NY	80
A&I	Castells, M	MA	80
A&I	Chandler, M	NY	80
A&I	Cunningham-Rundles, C	NY	81
A&I	DeShazo, R	MS	82
A&I	Ein, D	DC	81
A&I	Fishman, H	DC	81
A&I	Freeman, T	TX	85
A&I	Friedman, S	FL	82
A&I	Grammer, L	IL	83
A&I	Greenberger, P	IL	84
A&I	Gruchalla, R	TX	85
A&I	Henderson, W	WA	86
A&I	Jost, B	MO	84
A&I	Kaliner, M	MD	81
A&I	Korenblat, P	MO	84
A&I	Ledford, D	FL	82
A&I	Lewis, J	AZ	85
A&I	Li, J	MN	84
A&I	Lieberman, P	TN	82
A&I	Lockey, R	FL	82
A&I	MacLean, J	MA	80
A&I	Markert, M	NC	83
A&I	Mazza, D	NY	81
A&I	Metcalfe, D	MD	81
A&I	Montanaro, A	OR	86
A&I	Ostrom, N	CA	86

Spec	Name	St	Pg
A&I	Pacin, M	FL	83
A&I	Phillips, S	PA	81
A&I	Routes, J	WI	84
A&I	Sanders, G	MI	84
A&I	Schubert, M	AZ	85
A&I	Shepherd, G	NY	81
A&I	Slankard, M	NY	82
A&I	Spector, S	CA	86
A&I	Sundy, J	NC	83
A&I	Tamaroff, M	CA	86
A&I	Tillinghast, J	MO	84
A&I	Tobin, M	IL	84
A&I	Umetsu, D	MA	80
A&I	Wong, D	AZ	85
A&I	Wong, J	MA	80
A&I	Wood, J	MO	85

Allergy up to age 50

Spec	Name	St	Pg
PA&I	Bock, S	CO	745

Alopecia Areata

Spec	Name	St	Pg
D	Duvic, M	TX	198

Alzheimer's Disease

Spec	Name	St	Pg
Ger	Carr, D	MO	266
Ger	Morley, J	MO	266
Ger	Sachs, G	IN	266
GerPsy	Burke, W	NE	946
GerPsy	Grossberg, G	MO	945
GerPsy	Kennedy, G	NY	944
GerPsy	Lyketsos, C	MD	944
GerPsy	Reisberg, B	NY	944
GerPsy	Rovner, B	PA	944
GerPsy	Streim, J	PA	945
GerPsy	Tune, L	GA	945
N	Ahern, G	AZ	535
N	Chui, H	CA	539
N	Cummings, J	NV	539
N	Doody, R	TX	536
N	Farlow, M	IN	529
N	Feinberg, T	NY	515
N	Filley, C	CO	534
N	Henderson, V	CA	540
N	Kirshner, H	TN	525
N	Longo, F	CA	541
N	Marder, K	NY	519
N	Mayeux, R	NY	519
N	Mesulam, M	IL	531
N	Morris, J	MO	531
N	Petersen, R	MN	532
N	Relkin, N	NY	520
N	Sadowsky, C	FL	526
N	Zimmerman, E	NY	522
NRad	Drayer, B	NY	1020
NS	Rezai, A	OH	492
Psyc	Arnold, S	PA	922
Psyc	Kumar, A	IL	930
Psyc	Raskind, M	WA	934

Amblyopia

Spec	Name	St	Pg
Oph	Gallin, P	NY	578
Oph	Miller, J	AZ	602
Oph	Tychsen, L	MO	600
Oph	Warman, R	FL	592
Oph	Weiss, A	WA	610

Amblyopia & Vision Development

Spec	Name	St	Pg
Oph	Burke, M	OH	594

Amniocentesis

Spec	Name	St	Pg
MF	Genc, M	NY	434
MF	Grunebaum, A	NY	434
MF	McLaren, R	VA	437
MF	Nies, B	VA	437
MF	Philipson, E	OH	439
MF	Robinson, J	MA	433
MF	Strassner, H	IL	440

Amputation Surgery

Spec	Name	St	Pg
OrS	Pinzur, M	IL	644
OrS	Smith, D	WA	653

Amputee Rehabilitation

Spec	Name	St	Pg
PMR	Esquenazi, A	PA	863
PMR	Gitller, M	IL	868
PMR	Kuiken, T	IL	869
PMR	Leonard, J	MI	869
PMR	Miknevich, M	PA	865
PMR	Munin, M	PA	865
PMR	Richter, E	CT	862
PMR	Volshteyn, O	MO	870
PMR	Wilson, A	TX	871

Amyloid Heart Disease

Spec	Name	St	Pg
Cv	Follansbee, W	PA	92
Cv	Steingart, R	NY	96
Cv	Young, J	OH	107

Amyloidosis

Spec	Name	St	Pg
H & PM	Davis, M	OH	407
Hem	Comenzo, R	MA	312
Hem	Gertz, M	MN	321
Hem	Stewart, A	AZ	327
Nep	Dember, L	PA	459
Onc	Stadtmauer, E	PA	352
Onc	Vescio, R	CA	394
Pul	Berk, J	MA	954

Amyloidosis/Joint Disease

Spec	Name	St	Pg
Rhu	Gorevic, P	NY	1060

Amyotrophic Lateral Sclerosis (ALS)

Spec	Name	St	Pg
N	Barohn, R	KS	534
N	Cudkowicz, M	MA	510
N	Donofrio, P	TN	524
N	Feldman, E	MI	529
N	Glass, J	GA	524
N	Graves, M	CA	540
N	Harati, Y	TX	537
N	Lacomis, D	PA	517
N	McCluskey, L	PA	519
N	Mitsumoto, H	NY	519
N	Newman, D	MI	531
N	Pascuzzi, R	IN	532
N	Roos, R	IL	533
N	Rutkove, S	MA	512
N	Shefner, J	NY	521
N	Sheikh, K	TX	537
N	Siddique, T	IL	533
N	Weiss, M	WA	542
N	Windebank, A	MN	534
N	Zimnowodzki, S	IL	534
PMR	Bach, J	NJ	863

Anal Cancer

Spec	Name	St	Pg
CRS	Dietz, D	OH	173
CRS	Gorfine, S	NY	170
CRS	Nagle, D	MA	168
CRS	Welton, M	CA	178
DR	Coakley, F	OR	1017
Onc	Berry, J	CA	385
Onc	Eckhardt, S	CO	376
Onc	Goldberg, R	OH	369

Anal Disorders & Reconstruction

Spec	Name	St	Pg
CRS	Blatchford, G	NE	175
CRS	Gorfine, S	NY	170
CRS	Marcet, J	FL	172
CRS	Rafferty, J	OH	174

Anal Sphincter Repair

Spec	Name	St	Pg
CRS	Coutsoftides, T	CA	177
CRS	Lowry, A	MN	174

Anaphylaxis

Spec	Name	St	Pg
A&I	Castells, M	MA	80
A&I	Greenberger, P	IL	84
A&I	Korenblat, P	MO	84
A&I	Lieberman, P	TN	82
A&I	Metcalfe, D	MD	81
PA&I	Burks, A	NC	744

Anemia

Spec	Name	St	Pg
Hem	Blinder, M	MO	321
Hem	Raphael, B	NY	316
Hem	Soff, G	NY	317
Hem	Spivak, J	MD	317
PHO	Beyer, E	IL	781
PHO	Salvi, S	IL	785

Spec	Name	St	Pg
PNep	Ault, B	TN	798

Anemia-Aplastic

Spec	Name	St	Pg
Hem	Isola, L	NY	314
Hem	Maciejewski, J	OH	323
Hem	Mangan, K	PA	315
Hem	Schuster, M	NY	317
Hem	Zuckerman, K	FL	320
Onc	Antin, J	MA	330
Onc	Claxton, D	PA	340
PHO	Boxer, L	MI	782
PHO	Camitta, B	WI	782
PHO	Guinan, E	MA	770
PHO	Wang, W	TN	781

Anemia-Cancer Related

Spec	Name	St	Pg
Hem	Rodgers, G	UT	325
Hem	Schiffman, F	RI	312
Hem	Wisch, N	NY	318

Anemias & Red Cell Disorders

Spec	Name	St	Pg
Hem	Telen, M	NC	320
PHO	Boxer, L	MI	782
PHO	Finklestein, J	CA	789
PHO	Thomas, G	OR	792

Aneurysm

Spec	Name	St	Pg
Cv	Braverman, A	MO	100
N	Biller, J	IL	528
NRad	Christoforidis, G	IL	1023
NRad	Hurst, R	PA	1020
NRad	Lee, S	IL	1024
NRad	Pile-Spellman, J	NY	1021
T&CS	Bolman, R	MA	1146
T&CS	Girardi, L	NY	1153
VascS	Ascher, E	NY	1221
VascS	Belkin, M	MA	1220
VascS	Cho, J	IL	1226
VascS	Dougherty, M	PA	1223
VascS	Eton, D	IL	1227
VascS	Flanigan, D	CA	1230
VascS	Golden, M	PA	1223
VascS	Greisler, H	IL	1227
VascS	Hodgson, K	IL	1227
VascS	Hollier, L	LA	1229
VascS	Money, S	AZ	1229
VascS	Perler, B	MD	1224
VascS	Ricotta, J	DC	1224
VascS	Stanley, J	MI	1228
VascS	White, R	CA	1230
VIR	Dake, M	CA	1032

Aneurysm-Abdominal & Thoracic Aortic

Spec	Name	St	Pg
Cv	Krajcer, Z	TX	108
T&CS	Coselli, J	TX	1173
T&CS	Woo, Y	PA	1160
VascS	Calligaro, K	PA	1222
VascS	Carpenter, J	NJ	1222
VascS	Clair, D	OH	1227
VascS	Criado, F	MD	1222
VascS	Darling, R	NY	1222
VascS	Fairman, R	PA	1223
VascS	Kazmers, A	MI	1227
VascS	Kwolek, C	MA	1220
VascS	Morrissey, N	NY	1224
VascS	Sanchez, L	MO	1228

Aneurysm-Abdominal Aortic

Spec	Name	St	Pg
T&CS	Martin, T	FL	1163
T&CS	Ott, D	TX	1175
T&CS	Safi, H	TX	1176
VascS	Adelman, M	NY	1221
VascS	Atnip, R	PA	1221
VascS	Brewster, D	MA	1220
VascS	Cambria, R	MA	1220
VascS	Cronenwett, J	NH	1220
VascS	D'Ayala, M	NY	1222
VascS	Dattilo, J	TN	1225
VascS	Eidt, J	SC	1225
VascS	Faries, P	NY	1223
VascS	Gloviczki, P	MN	1227
VascS	Green, R	NY	1223
VascS	Hakaim, A	FL	1225
VascS	Hallett, J	SC	1225
VascS	Kent, K	WI	1228
VascS	Mackey, W	MA	1221
VascS	McKinsey, J	NY	1224
VascS	Money, S	AZ	1229
VascS	Pearce, W	IL	1228
VascS	Sicard, G	MO	1228
VascS	Todd, G	NY	1225
VascS	Weinstein, E	CO	1229
VIR	Benenati, J	FL	1029
VIR	Matsumoto, A	VA	1030

Aneurysm-Aortic

Spec	Name	St	Pg
IC	Leya, F	IL	126
T&CS	Bowdish, M	CA	1177
T&CS	Bridges, C	NC	1161
T&CS	Deeb, G	MI	1167
T&CS	Girardi, L	NY	1153
T&CS	Griffith, B	MD	1153
T&CS	Jessen, M	TX	1174
T&CS	Laks, H	CA	1179
T&CS	Loulmet, D	NY	1156
T&CS	Michler, R	NY	1156
T&CS	Shemin, R	CA	1180
T&CS	Stewart, A	NY	1159
VascS	Benvenisty, A	NY	1222
VascS	Brener, B	NJ	1222
VascS	Chaikof, E	MA	1220
VascS	Comerota, A	OH	1227
VascS	Ellozy, S	NY	1223
VascS	Fairman, R	PA	1223
VascS	Fowl, R	AZ	1229
VascS	Freischlag, J	MD	1223
VascS	Gewertz, B	CA	1230
VascS	Harrington, E	NY	1223
VascS	Howard, T	NE	1229
VascS	LaMuraglia, G	MA	1221
VascS	Makaroun, M	PA	1224
VascS	Marin, M	NY	1224
VascS	Mitchell, M	MS	1226
VascS	Naslund, T	TN	1226
VascS	Schneider, D	NY	1225
VascS	Shepard, A	MI	1228
VIR	Hallisey, M	CT	1027
VIR	Hovsepian, D	CA	1033
VIR	Katzen, B	FL	1029
VIR	Murphy, T	RI	1027

Aneurysm-Cerebral

Spec	Name	St	Pg
NRad	Berenstein, A	NY	1020
NRad	Cross, D	MO	1023
NRad	Dion, J	GA	1022
NRad	Frei, D	CO	1025
NRad	Grobelny, T	IL	1023
NRad	Higashida, R	CA	1026
NRad	Jensen, M	VA	1022
NRad	Joseph, G	NC	1022
NRad	Kallmes, D	MN	1023
NRad	Larsen, D	CA	1026
NRad	Masaryk, T	OH	1024
NRad	Moran, C	MO	1024
NRad	Morris, P	NC	1022
NRad	Norbash, A	MA	1019
NRad	Russell, E	IL	1024
NRad	Teitelbaum, G	CA	1026
NS	Barrow, D	GA	484
NS	Bederson, J	NY	474
NS	Charbel, F	IL	489
NS	Dacey, R	MO	489
NS	Dempsey, R	WI	489
NS	Grady, M	PA	477
NS	Guthikonda, M	MI	490
NS	Harbaugh, R	PA	477
NS	Huang, J	MD	478
NS	Kim, D	TX	496
NS	Loftus, C	IL	491
NS	Martin, N	CA	500
NS	Moore, F	NJ	480
NS	Patel, A	NY	480
NS	Riina, H	NY	481
NS	Rosenwasser, R	PA	481
NS	Sekhar, L	WA	501
NS	Selman, W	OH	493
NS	Shapiro, S	IN	493
NS	Solomon, R	NY	482
NS	Steinberg, G	CA	502
NS	Stieg, P	NY	482
NS	Tamargo, R	MD	482
NS	Thompson, B	MI	493
VIR	Kumpe, D	CO	1031

Aneurysm-Thoracic Aortic

Spec	Name	St	Pg
T&CS	Elefteriades, J	CT	1146
T&CS	Liao, K	MN	1169
T&CS	Moon, M	MO	1170
T&CS	Pochettino, A	MN	1171

Specialty & Special Expertise Index

Spec	Name	St	Pg
T&CS	Tranbaugh, R	NY	1159

Angelman Syndrome

Spec	Name	St	Pg
CG	Driscoll, D	FL	159
CG	Shoffner, J	GA	159

Angiogenesis

Spec	Name	St	Pg
IC	Ellis, S	OH	126
IC	Henry, T	MN	126
IC	Perin, E	TX	127

Angiography-Coronary

Spec	Name	St	Pg
Cv	Klein, L	IL	103
IC	Moses, J	NY	122

Angioplasty

Spec	Name	St	Pg
Cv	Coppola, J	NY	91
Cv	Diver, D	CT	88
Cv	Ramee, S	LA	109
Cv	Tobis, J	CA	112
IC	Applegate, R	NC	124
IC	Cohen, H	PA	121
IC	Laham, R	MA	121
IC	Matar, F	FL	125
IC	Morris, D	GA	125
IC	Resar, J	MD	123

Angioplasty & Restenosis

Spec	Name	St	Pg
IC	Holmes, D	MN	126

Angioplasty & Stent Placement

Spec	Name	St	Pg
Cv	Dangas, G	NY	92
Cv	Edelen, J	CA	110
Cv	Pichard, A	DC	95
IC	Bailey, S	TX	127
IC	Chang, G	PA	121
IC	Dieter, R	IL	125
IC	Douglas, J	GA	124
IC	Ellis, S	OH	126
IC	Fromkin, K	FL	124
IC	Herrmann, H	PA	122
IC	Kandzari, D	GA	124
IC	Kleiman, N	TX	127
IC	Moses, J	NY	122
IC	Reddy, B	GA	125
IC	Reiner, J	DC	123
IC	Rosenfield, K	MA	121
IC	Shani, J	NY	123
IC	Sharma, S	NY	123
IC	Stone, G	NY	124
IC	Zelman, R	MA	121
VascS	Belkin, M	MA	1220
VascS	Brewster, D	MA	1220
VascS	Kazmers, A	MI	1227
VIR	Gomes, A	CA	1032
VIR	Kaufman, J	OR	1033
VIR	McLean, G	PA	1028

Angioplasty-Peripheral

Spec	Name	St	Pg
VIR	Smith, S	IL	1031

Ankle Reconstruction

Spec	Name	St	Pg
OrS	Levine, D	NY	628

Ankle Replacement & Revision

Spec	Name	St	Pg
OrS	Brage, M	WA	649
OrS	DeOrio, J	NC	635
OrS	Greisberg, J	NY	624
OrS	Nunley, J	NC	637
OrS	Sangeorzan, B	WA	653

Ankle Surgery

Spec	Name	St	Pg
SM	Micheli, L	MA	1074
SM	Paletta, G	MO	1078
SM	Scheller, A	MA	1074

Ankylosing Spondylitis

Spec	Name	St	Pg
Rhu	Bobrove, A	CA	1067
Rhu	Chang, R	IL	1064
Rhu	Hugenberg, S	IN	1065
Rhu	Kay, J	MA	1058
Rhu	Luthra, H	MN	1065

Anophthalmia

Spec	Name	St	Pg
Oph	Bernardino, C	CA	604
Oph	Tse, D	FL	592

Anorectal Disorders

Spec	Name	St	Pg
CRS	Abcarian, H	IL	173
CRS	Dietz, D	OH	173
CRS	Efron, J	MD	169
CRS	Eisenstat, T	NJ	169
CRS	Fry, R	PA	169
CRS	Heppell, J	AZ	177
CRS	Lederman, E	MO	173
CRS	Procaccino, J	NY	171
CRS	Schoetz, D	MA	169
CRS	Senagore, A	MI	175
CRS	Shah, N	RI	169
CRS	Shellito, P	MA	169
CRS	Trudel, J	MN	175

Anorectal Malformations

Spec	Name	St	Pg
PS	Pena, A	OH	820
PS	Velcek, F	NY	817

Anorexia Nervosa-Severe

Spec	Name	St	Pg
IM	Mehler, P	CO	427

Anterior Segment Surgery

Spec	Name	St	Pg
Oph	Alward, W	IA	593
Oph	Caprioli, J	CA	605
Oph	Cioffi, G	NY	577
Oph	Dhaliwal, D	PA	577
Oph	Lane, S	MN	596
Oph	Page, T	MI	598
Oph	Samuelson, T	MN	599
Oph	Shamie, N	CA	609

Anterior Segment Trauma/Reconstruction

Spec	Name	St	Pg
Oph	Florakis, G	NY	578

Antibiotic Resistance

Spec	Name	St	Pg
Inf	Bartlett, J	MD	412
Inf	Edmond, M	VA	416
Inf	Scheld, W	VA	416
PInf	Alexander, K	IL	795
PInf	Bradley, J	CA	797
PInf	Long, S	PA	793
PInf	McCracken, G	TX	796

Antiphospholipid Syndrome (APS)

Spec	Name	St	Pg
N	Hess, D	GA	525
Rhu	Belmont, H	NY	1059
Rhu	Petri, M	MD	1061
Rhu	Salmon, J	NY	1062

Anxiety & Depression

Spec	Name	St	Pg
AdP	Ciraulo, D	MA	936
AdP	Galanter, I	NY	936
AM	Singh, N	MN	77
ChAP	Slomowitz, M	IL	942
GerPsy	Stein, E	CA	946
Psyc	Bronheim, H	NY	923
Psyc	Goldberg, J	CT	920
Psyc	Sadock, V	NY	927

Anxiety & Mood Disorders

Spec	Name	St	Pg
AdP	Frances, R	NY	936
ChAP	Biederman, J	MA	938
ChAP	Hirsch, G	NY	940
ChAP	Koplewicz, H	NY	940
ChAP	Kwon, H	WA	943
Psyc	Appelbaum, P	NY	922
Psyc	Friedman, M	VT	920
Psyc	Levy, S	GA	928
Psyc	Locala, J	OH	930
Psyc	Pollack, M	IL	930
Psyc	Price, L	RI	921
Psyc	Rosenthal, R	NY	926
Psyc	Roy-Byrne, P	WA	934
Psyc	Sanacora, G	CT	922
Psyc	Schatzberg, A	CA	935
Psyc	Scott, C	PA	927
Psyc	Sussman, N	NY	927
Psyc	Thase, M	PA	927
Psyc	Wait, S	MD	927

Spec	Name	St	Pg
Anxiety Disorders			
AM	Kaplan, D	CO	77
ChAP	Abright, A	NY	939
ChAP	Birmaher, B	PA	939
ChAP	Hagman, J	CO	942
ChAP	Hirsch, S	IL	942
ChAP	McCracken, J	CA	943
ChAP	McKelvey, R	OR	943
ChAP	Riddle, M	MD	940
ChAP	Walkup, J	NY	941
ChAP	Wamboldt, M	CO	942
Psyc	Bystritsky, A	CA	933
Psyc	Cohen, M	PA	923
Psyc	Eaton, J	DC	924
Psyc	Fyer, A	NY	924
Psyc	Hollander, E	NY	925
Psyc	McIntosh, J	UT	931
Psyc	Pi, E	CA	934
Psyc	Saxena, S	CA	934
Psyc	Stein, M	CA	935
Aortic & Visceral Artery Surgery			
VascS	Huber, T	FL	1226
Aortic Diseases & Dissection			
Cv	Braverman, A	MO	100
Cv	Eagle, K	MI	101
Cv	O'Gara, P	MA	89
IC	Lasala, J	MO	126
IC	Schreiber, T	MI	127
Aortic Graft Infections			
VascS	Cherry, K	VA	1225
Aortic Injuries			
S	Moore, E	CO	1122
Aortic Reconstruction			
VascS	Cambria, R	MA	1220
VascS	Dalsing, M	IN	1227
VascS	Pevec, W	CA	1230
VascS	Shepard, A	MI	1228
Aortic Stent Grafts			
VascS	Calligaro, K	PA	1222
VascS	Lumsden, A	TX	1229
VIR	Dake, M	CA	1032
Aortic Surgery			
T&CS	Adams, D	NY	1150
T&CS	Coselli, J	TX	1173
T&CS	Diehl, J	PA	1151
T&CS	Echeverri, L	TX	1174
T&CS	Graver, L	NY	1153
T&CS	Lazar, H	MA	1147
T&CS	Lytle, B	OH	1170
T&CS	Martin, T	FL	1163
T&CS	Merrick, S	CA	1179
T&CS	Miller, D	CA	1180
T&CS	Safi, H	TX	1176
T&CS	Salerno, T	FL	1165
T&CS	Sellke, F	RI	1148
T&CS	Smedira, N	OH	1171
T&CS	Stewart, A	NY	1159
T&CS	Stowe, C	FL	1166
T&CS	Svensson, L	OH	1171
T&CS	Verrier, E	WA	1181
T&CS	Warner, K	MA	1149
VascS	Hollier, L	LA	1229
VascS	Howard, T	NE	1229
VascS	Pomposelli, F	MA	1221
Aortic Surgery-Complex			
T&CS	Bavaria, J	PA	1150
VascS	Huber, T	FL	1226
VascS	White, R	CA	1230
Aortic Thoracic Reconstruction			
T&CS	Bavaria, J	PA	1150
Aortic Valve Disease			
T&CS	Deeb, G	MI	1167
Aortic Valve Replacement			
IC	Shani, J	NY	123
T&CS	DeRose, J	NY	1151
Aphasia			
N	Heilman, K	FL	525
N	Kirshner, H	TN	525
N	Mohr, J	NY	519
Apnea in Infants			
PPul	Givan, D	IN	808
Apnea/Robotic Surgery			
Oto	Thaler, E	PA	676
Appendix Cancer			
S	Bartlett, D	PA	1089
S	Mansfield, P	TX	1127
S	Sugarbaker, P	DC	1101
Arrhythmias			
CE	Anderson, M	IA	117
CE	Buxton, A	MA	112
CE	Callans, D	PA	114
CE	Cannom, D	CA	119
CE	Chinitz, L	NY	114
CE	Cohen, M	NY	114
CE	Curtis, A	NY	114
CE	DeLurgio, D	GA	116
CE	DiMarco, J	VA	116
CE	Donahue, J	MA	113
CE	Ellenbogen, K	VA	116
CE	Epstein, A	PA	114
CE	Epstein, L	MA	113
CE	Estes, N	MA	113
CE	Faddis, M	MO	117
CE	Gang, E	CA	120
CE	Gomes, J	NY	114
CE	Higgins, S	CA	120
CE	Interian, A	FL	116
CE	Iwai, S	NY	115
CE	Josephson, M	MA	113
CE	Knight, B	IL	117
CE	Lerman, B	NY	115
CE	Levine, J	NY	115
CE	Lewkowiez, L	CO	119
CE	Lindsay, B	OH	117
CE	Link, M	MA	113
CE	Marchlinski, F	PA	115
CE	Mehta, D	NY	115
CE	Miller, J	IN	118
CE	Morady, F	MI	118
CE	Naccarelli, G	PA	115
CE	Natale, A	TX	119
CE	Prystowsky, E	IN	118
CE	Ruskin, J	MA	113
CE	Schuger, C	MI	118
CE	Shen, W	AZ	119
CE	Sorrentino, R	GA	116
CE	Stevenson, W	MA	113
CE	Swerdlow, C	CA	120
CE	Tchou, P	OH	118
CE	Tomaselli, G	MD	116
CE	Waldo, A	OH	118
CE	Wang, P	CA	120
Cv	Abi-samra, F	LA	107
Cv	Anderson, J	UT	107
Cv	Borzak, S	FL	97
Cv	Gliklich, J	NY	93
Cv	Slater, W	NY	96
Cv	Volgman, A	IL	106
Cv	Waxman, H	PA	96
IC	Leya, F	IL	126
IC	Mehran, R	NY	122
IC	Shorofsky, S	MD	123
PCd	Beerman, L	PA	748
PCd	Walsh, C	NY	750
PCd	Walsh, E	MA	748
PCd	Young, M	FL	751
T&CS	Bakhos, M	IL	1167
T&CS	Chen, J	NY	1151
T&CS	Harken, A	CA	1178
Arrhythmias-Pediatric & Adult			
PCd	Fish, F	TN	751
Arterial & Venous Stents			
VIR	Keller, F	OR	1033

Specialty & Special Expertise Index

Arterial Bypass Surgery

Spec	Name	St	Pg
VascS	Belkin, M	MA	1220
VascS	Darling, R	NY	1222

Arterial Bypass Surgery-Leg

Spec	Name	St	Pg
VascS	Fowl, R	AZ	1229
VascS	Harrington, E	NY	1223
VascS	Money, S	AZ	1229
VascS	Perler, B	MD	1224

Arterial Reconsatruction

Spec	Name	St	Pg
VascS	Eton, D	IL	1227

Arterial Switch

Spec	Name	St	Pg
PS	Quaegebeur, J	NY	816

Arteriovenous Malformations

Spec	Name	St	Pg
N	Mohr, J	NY	519
NRad	Grobelny, T	IL	1023
NRad	Morris, P	NC	1022
NRad	Norbash, A	MA	1019
NRad	Pile-Spellman, J	NY	1021
NS	Charbel, F	IL	489
NS	Diaz, F	MI	490
NS	Giannotta, S	CA	499
NS	Grady, M	PA	477
NS	Kim, D	TX	496
NS	Loftus, C	IL	491
NS	McCormick, P	NY	480
NS	Morcos, J	FL	486
NS	Patel, A	NY	480
NS	Rosenwasser, R	PA	481
NS	Samson, D	TX	497
NS	Sekhar, L	WA	501
NS	Sisti, M	NY	482
NS	Solomon, R	NY	482
NS	Steinberg, G	CA	502
NS	Stieg, P	NY	482
NS	Tamargo, R	MD	482
NS	Wisoff, J	NY	483
VIR	Coldwell, D	KY	1029
VIR	Smith, S	IL	1031
VIR	Trerotola, S	PA	1029

Arthritis

Spec	Name	St	Pg
HS	Atkinson, R	HI	305
HS	Belsky, M	MA	296
HS	Carlson, M	NY	297
HS	Carneiro, R	FL	301
HS	Friedman, D	FL	301
HS	Godzik, C	CA	306
HS	Greene, T	FL	301
HS	Hastings, H	IN	303
HS	Hunt, T	AL	301
HS	Imbriglia, J	PA	298
HS	Kulick, R	NY	299
HS	Lane, L	NY	299
HS	Light, T	IL	303
HS	Moneim, M	NM	305
HS	Putnam, M	MN	304
HS	Raskin, K	NY	300
HS	Rayan, G	OK	305
OrS	Bozic, K	CA	649
OrS	Bronson, M	NY	621
OrS	Buly, R	NY	622
OrS	Deland, J	NY	623
OrS	Gladstone, J	NY	624
OrS	Goodman, S	CA	651
OrS	Gorab, R	CA	651
OrS	Jiranek, W	VA	636
OrS	Kraay, M	OH	642
OrS	Nunley, J	NC	637
OrS	Stuchin, S	NY	633
OrS	Thornhill, T	MA	619
OrS	Vail, T	CA	654
OrS	Wapner, K	PA	633
PRhu	Lehman, T	NY	812
Rhu	Allman, R	PA	1059
Rhu	Chang, R	IL	1064
Rhu	Fife, R	IN	1065
Rhu	Lipstate, J	LA	1067
Rhu	McAlindon, T	MA	1058
Rhu	Mease, P	WA	1068
Rhu	Schubert, R	DC	1062
Rhu	Sessoms, S	TX	1067
Rhu	Solitar, B	NY	1062
Rhu	Starz, T	PA	1062

Arthritis-Hip & Knee

Spec	Name	St	Pg
OrS	Grelsamer, R	NY	624
OrS	Howe, K	CA	651

Arthritis-Knee

Spec	Name	St	Pg
OrS	Leadbetter, W	MD	627

Arthritis-Septic

Spec	Name	St	Pg
Inf	Bayer, A	CA	420

Arthroplasty Imaging

Spec	Name	St	Pg
DR	Potter, H	NY	1011

Arthroscopic Surgery

Spec	Name	St	Pg
HS	Atkinson, R	HI	305
HS	Beredjiklian, P	PA	297
HS	Greene, T	FL	301
HS	Slutsky, D	CA	306
OrS	Bauman, P	NY	620
OrS	Bigliani, L	NY	621
OrS	Cooper, D	TX	648
OrS	Finerman, G	CA	651
OrS	Garrett, W	NC	636
OrS	Glashow, J	NY	624
OrS	Green, A	RI	617
OrS	Hausman, M	NY	625
OrS	Johnson, D	KY	636
OrS	Kelly, B	NY	627
OrS	Kocher, M	MA	618
OrS	Krackow, K	NY	627
OrS	Lock, T	MI	642
OrS	Millett, P	CO	646
OrS	Minas, T	MA	618
OrS	Nicholas, S	NY	629
OrS	Poehling, G	NC	637
OrS	Schlegel, T	CO	647
OrS	Seltzer, D	AZ	648
OrS	Shelbourne, K	IN	645
OrS	Thomas, B	CA	654
OrS	Vo, P	FL	638
SM	Altchek, D	NY	1074
SM	Bush-Joseph, C	IL	1077
SM	Byrd, J	TN	1076
SM	Ciccotti, M	PA	1075
SM	Fronek, J	CA	1079
SM	Gill, T	MA	1074
SM	Hershman, E	NY	1075
SM	Ho, S	IL	1078
SM	Jones, D	LA	1078
SM	Levine, W	NY	1075
SM	Ma, C	CA	1079
SM	Mirzayan, R	CA	1079
SM	Nisonson, B	NY	1076
SM	Richmond, J	MA	1074
SM	Sennett, B	PA	1076
SM	Steiner, M	MA	1074
SM	Xerogeanes, J	GA	1077

Arthroscopic Surgery-Hip

Spec	Name	St	Pg
OrS	Buly, R	NY	622
OrS	Kocher, M	MA	618
OrS	Mabrey, J	TX	648
OrS	McCarthy, J	OH	643
OrS	Padgett, D	NY	630
OrS	Philippon, M	CO	646
OrS	Rodriguez, J	NY	631
OrS	Westrich, G	NY	634

Arthroscopic Surgery-Knee

Spec	Name	St	Pg
OrS	Bartolozzi, A	PA	620
OrS	Fulkerson, J	CT	617
OrS	Padgett, D	NY	630
OrS	Rodriguez, J	NY	631
OrS	Spindler, K	TN	638
OrS	Steadman, J	CO	647
OrS	Westrich, G	NY	634

Arthroscopic Surgery-Wrist

Spec	Name	St	Pg
OrS	Goldner, R	NC	636

Artificial Heart Devices

Spec	Name	St	Pg
T&CS	Frazier, O	TX	1174
T&CS	Jeevanandam, V	IL	1169
T&CS	Kormos, R	PA	1155
T&CS	Samuels, L	PA	1158

Asbestos-related Lung Disease

Spec	Name	St	Pg
OM	Harber, P	AZ	912

Spec	Name	St	Pg
Pul	Rose, C	CO	968
T&CS	Krellenstein, D	NY	1155

Asherman's Syndrome

Spec	Name	St	Pg
RE	Odem, R	MO	1048
RE	Walmer, D	NC	1046

Asperger's Syndrome

Spec	Name	St	Pg
ChAP	Heston, J	TN	941
ChAP	Rostain, A	PA	940

Asthma

Spec	Name	St	Pg
A&I	Altman, L	WA	85
A&I	Benenati, S	FL	82
A&I	Bernstein, D	OH	83
A&I	Bernstein, J	OH	83
A&I	Chandler, M	NY	80
A&I	Freeman, T	TX	85
A&I	Friedman, S	FL	82
A&I	Grammer, L	IL	83
A&I	Greenberger, P	IL	84
A&I	Korenblat, P	MO	84
A&I	Ledford, D	FL	82
A&I	Lewis, J	AZ	85
A&I	Li, J	MN	84
A&I	Lieberman, P	TN	82
A&I	MacLean, J	MA	80
A&I	Mazza, D	NY	81
A&I	Montanaro, A	OR	86
A&I	Pacin, M	FL	83
A&I	Routes, J	WI	84
A&I	Sanders, G	MI	84
A&I	Slankard, M	NY	82
A&I	Spector, S	CA	86
A&I	Sundy, J	NC	83
A&I	Tamaroff, M	CA	86
A&I	Umetsu, D	MA	80
A&I	Wong, J	MA	80
A&I	Wood, J	MO	85
PA&I	Bahna, S	LA	746
PA&I	Burks, A	NC	744
PA&I	Ehrlich, P	NY	743
PA&I	Gelfand, E	CO	745
PA&I	Josephs, S	MD	743
PA&I	Kelly, C	VA	745
PA&I	Klein, R	RI	743
PA&I	Lemanske, R	WI	745
PA&I	Leung, D	CO	746
PA&I	Pongracic, J	IL	745
PA&I	Schuberth, K	MD	744
PA&I	Shearer, W	TX	746
PA&I	Sicherer, S	NY	744
PA&I	Sly, R	MD	744
PA&I	Spergel, J	PA	744
PA&I	Strunk, R	MO	745
PA&I	Wasserman, R	TX	746
PA&I	Wolf, R	IL	745
PA&I	Wood, R	MD	744
PPul	Dorkin, H	MA	806
PPul	Dovey, M	PA	806
PPul	Dozor, A	NY	807
PPul	Fan, L	CO	810
PPul	Gibson, R	WA	810
PPul	Givan, D	IN	808
PPul	Kattan, M	NY	807
PPul	Kim, Y	IN	809
PPul	Kurachek, S	MN	809
PPul	Lapey, A	MA	806
PPul	McColley, S	IL	809
PPul	McCoy, K	OH	809
PPul	Morgan, W	AZ	810
PPul	Quittell, L	NY	808
PPul	Rubin, B	VA	808
PPul	Sherman, J	VA	808
PPul	Wall, M	OR	811
Pul	Balk, R	IL	964
Pul	Boushey, H	CA	970
Pul	Cooper, W	VA	961
Pul	Doherty, D	KY	961
Pul	Donohue, J	NC	962
Pul	Fahey, P	IL	964
Pul	Fanta, C	MA	954
Pul	Fulkerson, W	NC	962
Pul	Garrity, E	IL	964
Pul	Gerboth, G	AK	970
Pul	Grum, C	MI	964
Pul	Guidry, G	LA	969
Pul	Henke, D	NC	962
Pul	Irwin, R	MA	955
Pul	Jacoby, D	OR	971
Pul	Kaye, M	MN	965
Pul	King, T	CA	971
Pul	Lem, V	MO	965
Pul	Levin, D	OK	969
Pul	Libby, D	NY	957
Pul	Mahler, D	NH	955
Pul	Martin, R	CO	968
Pul	Matuschak, G	MO	966
Pul	Metersky, M	CT	955
Pul	Mosenifar, Z	CA	971
Pul	Nash, T	NY	958
Pul	Rizk, N	CA	971
Pul	Silver, M	IL	966
Pul	Steinberg, H	NY	959
Pul	Vaughey, E	VA	963
Pul	Villanueva, A	MA	955
Pul	Voelkel, N	VA	963
Pul	Wallace, J	CA	972
Pul	Wanner, A	FL	963
Pul	Weissler, J	TX	969
Pul	Wiedemann, H	OH	967

Asthma & Allergy

Spec	Name	St	Pg
A&I	Buchbinder, E	NY	80
A&I	Ein, D	DC	81
A&I	Fishman, H	DC	81
A&I	Gruchalla, R	TX	85
A&I	Henderson, W	WA	86
A&I	Kaliner, M	MD	81
A&I	Lockey, R	FL	82
A&I	Ostrom, N	CA	86
A&I	Schubert, M	AZ	85
PA&I	Epstein, S	CA	747
PA&I	Fanous, Y	CA	747
PA&I	Skoner, D	PA	744
Pul	Wenzel, S	PA	960

Asthma & Chronic Lung Disease

Spec	Name	St	Pg
PPul	Loughlin, G	NY	807
PPul	Sallent, J	FL	808

Asthma up to age 50

Spec	Name	St	Pg
PA&I	Bock, S	CO	745

Ataxia

Spec	Name	St	Pg
N	Reich, S	MD	520

Ataxia Telangiectasia

Spec	Name	St	Pg
ChiN	Crawford, T	MD	145
PHO	Corey, S	IL	782
PPul	McGrath-Morrow, S	MD	807

Atopic Dermatitis

Spec	Name	St	Pg
D	Belsito, D	NY	186
D	Eichenfield, L	CA	200
D	Gottlieb, A	MA	185
D	Hanifin, J	OR	201
D	Paller, A	IL	196
D	Yan, A	PA	191
PA&I	Leung, D	CO	746
PA&I	Sampson, H	NY	743
PA&I	Sly, R	MD	744
PA&I	Spergel, J	PA	744

Atrial Fibrillation

Spec	Name	St	Pg
CE	Asirvatham, S	MN	117
CE	Cannom, D	CA	119
CE	Chinitz, L	NY	114
CE	DeLurgio, D	GA	116
CE	Feld, G	CA	119
CE	Gomes, J	NY	114
CE	Iwai, S	NY	115
CE	Knight, B	IL	117
CE	Lerman, B	NY	115
CE	Levine, J	NY	115
CE	Lewkowiez, L	CO	119
CE	Mehta, D	NY	115
CE	Miller, J	IN	118
CE	Natale, A	TX	119
CE	Onufer, J	VA	116
CE	Prystowsky, E	IN	118
CE	Ruskin, J	MA	113
CE	Swerdlow, C	CA	120
CE	Waldo, A	OH	118
CE	Wang, P	CA	120
CE	Wilber, D	IL	118
Cv	Abi-samra, F	LA	107
Cv	Halperin, J	NY	93

Spec	Name	St	Pg
Cv	Tenenbaum, J	NY	96
Cv	Volgman, A	IL	106
Cv	Zusman, R	MA	90
T&CS	Michler, R	NY	1156
T&CS	Philpott, J	VA	1164

Atrial Septal Defect

Spec	Name	St	Pg
IC	Chang, G	PA	121
IC	Herrmann, H	PA	122
PCd	Sommer, R	NY	750

Attachment Disorders

Spec	Name	St	Pg
ChAP	Zeanah, C	LA	943

Aural Atresia Repair

Spec	Name	St	Pg
Oto	Kesser, B	VA	679

Autism

Spec	Name	St	Pg
ChAP	Alessi, N	MI	941
ChAP	King, B	WA	943
ChAP	Kwon, H	WA	943
ChAP	Leckman, J	CT	938
ChAP	Leventhal, B	NY	940
ChAP	McCracken, J	CA	943
ChAP	Pomeroy, J	NY	940
ChAP	Rostain, A	PA	940
ChAP	Sexson, S	GA	941
ChiN	Filipek, P	TX	150
ChiN	Kosofsky, B	NY	145
ChiN	Mandelbaum, D	RI	144
ChiN	Nass, R	NY	146
ChiN	Trauner, D	CA	152
NRad	Hunter, J	TX	1025
Ped	Burgess, D	NJ	740
Ped	Roizen, N	OH	742
Ped	Walker, W	WA	743
PMR	Keen, M	IL	868
Psyc	Hollander, E	NY	925

Autism & Developmental Disorders

Spec	Name	St	Pg
ChAP	McDougle, C	MA	938

Autism in Infants

Spec	Name	St	Pg
ChiN	Filipek, P	TX	150

Autism Spectrum Disorders-Adult

Spec	Name	St	Pg
Psyc	Brodkin, E	PA	923

Autoimmune Disease

Spec	Name	St	Pg
A&I	Phillips, S	PA	81
D	Anhalt, G	MD	186
D	Mutasim, D	OH	196
D	Werth, V	PA	191
D	Woodley, D	CA	202
Hem	Brodsky, R	MD	313
IM	Burt, R	IL	427
N	Adams, D	FL	523
N	Miller, A	NY	519
Ped	Infante, A	TX	742
Rhu	Gorevic, P	NY	1060
Rhu	Gourley, M	MD	1060
Rhu	Kimberly, R	AL	1064
Rhu	Mease, P	WA	1068
Rhu	Petri, M	MD	1061
Rhu	Sessoms, S	TX	1067
Rhu	Solomon, G	NY	1062
Rhu	Wener, M	WA	1068
Rhu	Wofsy, D	CA	1068

Autoimmune Liver Disease

Spec	Name	St	Pg
Ge	Brown, R	NY	233
Ge	Raiford, D	TN	244
Ge	Vierling, J	TX	255

Autoimmune Lung Disease

Spec	Name	St	Pg
Pul	Brown, K	CO	967
Pul	Wenzel, S	PA	960

Autoimmune Retinopathy

Spec	Name	St	Pg
Oph	Heckenlively, J	MI	595

Autoimmune Rheumatic Disorders

Spec	Name	St	Pg
Rhu	McAlindon, T	MA	1058

Autonomic Disorders

Spec	Name	St	Pg
CE	Shen, W	AZ	119
Cv	Grubb, B	OH	102
PCd	Hanna, B	PA	749

B

Baha Implant

Spec	Name	St	Pg
Oto	Young, N	IL	689

Balance Disorders

Spec	Name	St	Pg
Ger	Studenski, S	PA	265
N	Hain, T	IL	530
Oto	Gianoli, G	LA	692
Oto	Hammerschlag, P	NY	670
Oto	Hoffman, R	NY	671
PO	O'Reilly, R	DE	802

Barrett's Esophagus

Spec	Name	St	Pg
Ge	Chang, K	CA	255
Ge	Cohen, J	NY	233
Ge	Eisen, G	OR	255
Ge	Estores, D	FL	242
Ge	Falk, G	PA	234
Ge	Fang, J	UT	252
Ge	Fleischer, D	AZ	254
Ge	Gerdes, H	NY	234
Ge	Gerson, L	CA	256
Ge	Ginsberg, G	PA	234
Ge	Greenwald, B	MD	235
Ge	Haber, G	NY	235
Ge	Infantolino, A	PA	235
Ge	Katz, P	PA	236
Ge	Lightdale, C	NY	238
Ge	Meiselman, M	IL	249
Ge	Pfau, P	WI	249
Ge	Ravich, W	MD	239
Ge	Reynolds, J	PA	239
Ge	Rothstein, R	NH	232
Ge	Savides, T	CA	257
Ge	Vargo, J	OH	251
Path	Montgomery, E	MD	723
S	Chand, B	IL	1112
S	Pellegrini, C	WA	1135
T&CS	Battafarano, R	MD	1150
T&CS	Ferguson, M	IL	1168

Beckwith-Wiedemann Syndrome

Spec	Name	St	Pg
PIS	Napoli, J	DE	885

Behavioral Disorders

Spec	Name	St	Pg
AM	Ginsburg, K	PA	76
ChAP	King, B	WA	943
ChAP	Ponton, L	CA	943
Psyc	Reus, V	CA	934

Behavioral Neurology

Spec	Name	St	Pg
N	Ahern, G	AZ	535
N	Devinsky, O	NY	514
N	Filley, C	CO	534
N	Heilman, K	FL	525
N	Marshall, R	NY	519
Psyc	Neppe, V	WA	934

Behavioral Problems & Dementia

Spec	Name	St	Pg
GerPsy	Grossberg, G	MO	945
GerPsy	Rovner, B	PA	944

Behavioral Problems in Dementia

Spec	Name	St	Pg
GerPsy	Streim, J	PA	945

Behavorial Disorders

Spec	Name	St	Pg
AM	Sigman, G	IL	77

Spec	Name	St	Pg
Behcet's Syndrome			
D	Fivenson, D	MI	195
Rhu	Spiera, H	NY	1062
Berger's Disease (IgA Nephropathy)			
PNep	Wyatt, R	TN	799
Beryllium-induced Lung Disease			
OM	Harber, P	AZ	912
Pul	Balmes, J	CA	970
Pul	Rossman, M	PA	959
Biliary Cancer			
Onc	Patt, Y	NM	382
Onc	Posey, J	AL	362
Onc	Yen, Y	CA	394
S	Bouvet, M	CA	1130
S	Cameron, J	MD	1090
S	Ellison, E	OH	1113
S	Heslin, M	AL	1105
S	Rosen, C	MN	1118
S	Warren, R	CA	1138
S	Yeo, C	PA	1102
Biliary Disease			
Ge	Barnes, D	OH	246
Ge	Cunningham, J	AZ	253
Ge	Edmundowicz, S	MO	247
Ge	Kowalski, T	PA	237
Ge	Lind, C	TN	243
Ge	Miskovitz, P	NY	238
Biliary Surgery			
PS	Meyers, R	UT	821
PS	Notrica, D	AZ	822
S	Ellison, E	OH	1113
S	Gower, R	AK	1133
S	Levi, J	FL	1106
S	McAneny, D	MA	1087
S	Soper, N	IL	1120
S	Wood, R	TX	1129
Biochemical Genetics			
CG	Charrow, J	IL	160
CG	Craigen, W	TX	161
CG	Northrup, H	TX	162
Bioterrorism Preparedness			
Path	Walker, D	TX	731
Bipolar/Mood Disorders			
AdP	Lawson, W	DC	937
ChAP	Birmaher, B	PA	939
ChAP	Bogrov, M	MD	939
ChAP	Hirsch, G	NY	940
ChAP	Slomowitz, M	IL	942
ChAP	Wilens, T	MA	939
Psyc	Black, D	IA	929
Psyc	Bowden, C	TX	932
Psyc	Calabrese, J	OH	929
Psyc	Davidson, J	TX	932
Psyc	DePaulo, J	MD	924
Psyc	Goldberg, J	CT	920
Psyc	Hirschfeld, R	TX	932
Psyc	Kupfer, D	PA	925
Psyc	McIntosh, J	UT	931
Psyc	Nurnberger, J	IN	930
Psyc	Price, L	RI	921
Psyc	Reus, V	CA	934
Psyc	Roy-Byrne, P	WA	934
Psyc	Salloum, I	FL	928
Psyc	Strakowski, S	OH	931
Psyc	Sussman, N	NY	927
Psyc	Weiner, R	NC	928
Psyc	Weisler, R	NC	928
Birth Defects			
CG	Carey, J	UT	161
CG	Desposito, F	NJ	157
CG	Holmes, L	MA	156
CG	Rosenbaum, K	DC	158
CG	Seaver, L	HI	163
CG	Stevenson, R	SC	159
Ped	Bull, M	IN	741
PNep	Warady, B	MO	800
Birthmarks/Hemangiomas			
D	Alster, T	DC	186
D	Anderson, R	MA	184
D	Cunningham, B	CA	200
D	Orlow, S	NY	190
Oto	Waner, M	NY	677
PlS	Reinisch, J	CA	905
PlS	Zide, B	NY	888
Bladder Cancer			
Onc	Ahmann, F	AZ	378
Onc	Bajorin, D	NY	338
Onc	Dawson, N	DC	341
Onc	Dreicer, R	OH	368
Onc	Garnick, M	MA	332
Onc	Gelmann, E	NY	343
Onc	Godley, P	NC	358
Onc	Hussain, M	MI	370
Onc	Jonasch, E	TX	381
Onc	Levine, E	NY	347
Onc	Logothetis, C	TX	381
Onc	Nanus, D	NY	348
Onc	Natale, R	CA	390
Onc	Parnes, H	MD	349
Onc	Petrylak, D	CT	334
Onc	Quinn, D	CA	391
Onc	Roth, B	MO	373
Onc	Scher, H	NY	351
Onc	Stadler, W	IL	374
Onc	Stein, C	CA	392
Onc	Tagawa, S	NY	352
Onc	Vaughn, D	PA	353
Path	Amin, M	CA	731
Path	Bostwick, D	VA	725
Path	Cote, R	FL	725
Path	Epstein, J	MD	721
Path	Reuter, V	NY	723
Path	True, L	WA	734
RadRO	Rotman, M	NY	982
U	Amling, C	OR	1210
U	Bahnson, R	OH	1202
U	Belldegrun, A	CA	1210
U	Benson, M	NY	1189
U	Campbell, S	OH	1202
U	Carroll, P	CA	1210
U	Chang, S	TN	1197
U	Childs, S	CO	1206
U	Colberg, J	CT	1186
U	Cookson, M	OK	1208
U	Dalkin, B	WA	1211
U	Daneshmand, S	CA	1211
U	Davis, B	KS	1207
U	DeKernion, J	CA	1211
U	Droller, M	NY	1189
U	Flanigan, R	IL	1203
U	Greenberg, R	PA	1190
U	Greene, G	FL	1197
U	Gribetz, M	NY	1190
U	Grossman, H	TX	1208
U	Herr, H	NY	1191
U	Hrebinko, R	PA	1191
U	Kawachi, M	CA	1212
U	Kibel, A	MA	1187
U	Kim, E	TN	1198
U	Kirschenbaum, A	NY	1192
U	Koch, M	IN	1204
U	Lee, C	MI	1204
U	Lerner, S	TX	1209
U	Lockhart, J	FL	1198
U	Loughlin, K	MA	1187
U	Malkowicz, S	PA	1192
U	McDougal, W	MA	1187
U	Montie, J	MI	1204
U	Nieder, A	FL	1199
U	O'Donnell, M	IA	1205
U	Olumi, A	MA	1187
U	Parekh, D	FL	1199
U	Penson, D	TN	1199
U	Presti, J	CA	1213
U	Sagalowsky, A	TX	1209
U	Samadi, D	NY	1194
U	Sanda, M	GA	1200
U	Sawczuk, I	NJ	1194
U	Scardino, P	NY	1194
U	Scherr, D	NY	1194
U	Schoenberg, M	MD	1194
U	See, W	WI	1206
U	Sexton, W	FL	1200
U	Skinner, E	CA	1213
U	Smith, J	TN	1200
U	Soloway, M	FL	1201

Specialty & Special Expertise Index

Spec	Name	St	Pg
U	Steinberg, G	IL	1206
U	Taneja, S	NY	1195
U	Terris, M	GA	1201
U	Weiss, R	NJ	1196
U	Weiss, R	CT	1188
U	Wilson, T	CA	1214
U	Wood, D	MI	1206

Bladder Exstrophy

Spec	Name	St	Pg
Ped Uro	Brock, J	TN	825
Ped Uro	Cain, M	IN	826
Ped Uro	Canning, D	PA	824
Ped Uro	Kirsch, A	GA	826
Ped Uro	Merguerian, P	WA	828
Ped Uro	Mesrobian, H	WI	827

Bladder Reconstruction

Spec	Name	St	Pg
Ped Uro	Canning, D	PA	824
Ped Uro	Docimo, S	PA	825
Ped Uro	Gundeti, M	IL	827
U	Carroll, P	CA	1210

Bleeding/Coagulation Disorders

Spec	Name	St	Pg
Hem	Abrams, C	PA	313
Hem	Allen, S	NY	313
Hem	Baron, J	IL	320
Hem	Blinder, M	MO	321
Hem	Bockenstedt, P	MI	321
Hem	Cobos, E	TX	325
Hem	Cooper, B	TX	326
Hem	DeLoughery, T	OR	328
Hem	Diuguid, D	NY	314
Hem	Kempin, S	NY	315
Hem	Kessler, C	DC	315
Hem	Leung, L	CA	328
Hem	Lin, W	TX	326
Hem	Lind, S	CO	324
Hem	Linenberger, M	WA	328
Hem	Lyons, R	TX	327
Hem	Ortel, T	NC	319
Hem	Palascak, J	OH	323
Hem	Rao, A	PA	316
Hem	Rodgers, G	UT	325
Hem	Schiffman, F	RI	312
Hem	Soff, G	NY	317
Hem	Strauss, J	TX	327
Hem	Streiff, M	MD	317
Onc	Attas, L	NJ	338
Onc	Rosove, M	CA	391
Onc	Silver, S	MI	374
Onc	Waintraub, S	NJ	354
Path	Chesney, C	TN	725
PHO	Beyer, E	IL	781
PHO	Bussel, J	NY	771
PHO	Castle, V	MI	782
PHO	Ducore, J	CA	789
PHO	Kobrinsky, N	ND	787
PHO	Kung, F	CA	790
PHO	Luchtman-Jones, L	DC	775
PHO	Marcus, J	NY	775
PHO	Parker, R	NY	776
PHO	Recht, M	OR	791
PHO	Ritchey, A	PA	776
PHO	Salvi, S	IL	785
PHO	Shapiro, A	IN	785
PHO	Thomas, G	OR	792
PHO	Valentino, L	IL	786
PHO	Weinblatt, M	NY	776
S	Wakefield, T	MI	1121

Blistering Diseases

Spec	Name	St	Pg
D	Anhalt, G	MD	186
D	Fivenson, D	MI	195
D	Levy, M	TX	198
D	Shupack, J	NY	190
D	Stanley, J	PA	191
D	Werth, V	PA	191
D	Woodley, D	CA	202

Body Contouring

Spec	Name	St	Pg
D	Grossman, M	NY	188
PlS	Carraway, J	VA	889
PlS	Cederna, P	MI	893
PlS	Fisher, G	CA	902
PlS	Hardesty, R	CA	903
PlS	Hurwitz, D	PA	883
PlS	Mast, B	FL	890
PlS	Mustoe, T	IL	895
PlS	Pomahac, B	MA	879
PlS	Romano, J	CA	905

Body Contouring after Weight Loss

Spec	Name	St	Pg
PlS	Aly, A	CA	901
PlS	Edwards, M	NV	902
PlS	Erdmann, D	NC	889
PlS	Hammond, D	MI	894
PlS	Hunstad, J	NC	890
PlS	Kenkel, J	TX	899
PlS	Kolker, A	NY	883
PlS	Rappaport, N	TX	900
PlS	Smith, D	FL	891
PlS	Sood, R	IN	896
PlS	Young, V	MO	897

Body Dysmorphic Disorder (BDD)

Spec	Name	St	Pg
Psyc	Hollander, E	NY	925
Psyc	Phillips, K	RI	921
Psyc	Saxena, S	CA	934

Body Image Issues

Spec	Name	St	Pg
Psyc	Bronheim, H	NY	923

Bone & Joint Pathology

Spec	Name	St	Pg
Path	Rosenberg, A	FL	726
Path	Schiller, A	HI	734

Bone & Soft Tissue Pathology

Spec	Name	St	Pg
Path	Brooks, J	PA	720
Path	Mills, S	VA	726
Path	Rubin, B	OH	729

Bone & Soft Tissue Tumors

Spec	Name	St	Pg
HS	Athanasian, E	NY	297
OrS	Brien, E	CA	649
OrS	Brigman, B	NC	635
OrS	Bukata, S	CA	650
OrS	Cheng, E	MN	640
OrS	Friedlaender, G	CT	617
OrS	Joyce, M	OH	642
OrS	Kelly, C	CO	646
OrS	Lee, F	NY	628
OrS	McDonald, D	MO	643
OrS	Parsons, T	MI	644
OrS	Siegel, H	AL	638
OrS	Wurtz, L	IN	645
PHO	Ducore, J	CA	789

Bone Cancer

Spec	Name	St	Pg
DR	Panicek, D	NY	1011
Hem	Milhem, M	IA	323
OrS	Benevenia, J	NJ	620
OrS	Biermann, J	MI	639
OrS	Brigman, B	NC	635
OrS	Buckwalter, J	IA	640
OrS	Bukata, S	CA	650
OrS	Clohisy, D	MN	640
OrS	Dormans, J	PA	623
OrS	Frassica, F	MD	624
OrS	Gitelis, S	IL	641
OrS	Irwin, R	MI	641
OrS	Kelly, C	CO	646
OrS	Kneisl, J	NC	636
OrS	Les, K	MI	642
OrS	Mott, M	MI	643
OrS	O'Donnell, R	CA	652
OrS	Ready, J	MA	618
OrS	Sim, F	MN	645
OrS	Singer, D	HI	653
PHO	Dome, J	DC	772
PHO	Loeb, D	MD	775
PHO	Schwartz, C	RI	770
PHO	Wexler, L	NY	777
PS	Morgan, W	TN	818
RadRO	Marcus, R	FL	985

Bone Disorders-Inherited

Spec	Name	St	Pg
CG	Kronn, D	NY	158
CG	Weaver, D	IN	160

Bone Disorders-Metabolic

Spec	Name	St	Pg
CG	Kronn, D	NY	158
DR	Dalinka, M	PA	1009
DR	Gilsanz, V	CA	1018

Spec	Name	St	Pg
EDM	Bilezikian, J	NY	211
EDM	Bockman, R	NY	211
EDM	Clutter, W	MO	218
EDM	Dalkin, A	VA	216
EDM	Econs, M	IN	219
EDM	Holick, M	MA	209
EDM	Khosla, S	MN	220
EDM	Kronenberg, H	MA	209
EDM	LeBoff, M	MA	209
EDM	Orwoll, E	OR	225
EDM	Siris, E	NY	214
EDM	Watts, N	OH	221
Ger	Lyles, K	NC	265
Nep	Hruska, K	MO	463
Nep	Ott, S	WA	467
Nep	Stern, L	NY	460
OrS	Einhorn, T	MA	616
OrS	Kaplan, F	PA	627
OrS	Lane, J	NY	627
PEn	DiMeglio, L	IN	760
PEn	Gordon, C	RI	757
PEn	Levine, M	PA	758

Bone Infections

Spec	Name	St	Pg
Inf	Nahass, R	NJ	414
Inf	Slama, T	IN	418
OrS	Anglen, J	IN	639
OrS	Browner, B	CT	616
OrS	Ebraheim, N	OH	641
OrS	Swiontkowski, M	MN	645
OrS	Wilkins, R	CO	647

Bone Marrow & Stem Cell Transplant

Spec	Name	St	Pg
Hem	Holland, H	GA	319
Hem	Yeager, A	AZ	327
Onc	Ball, E	CA	385
Onc	Lazarus, H	OH	371
Onc	Maloney, D	WA	389
Onc	Stadtmauer, E	PA	352
Onc	Waller, E	GA	365
PHO	Leung, W	TN	780
PHO	Matthay, K	CA	791

Bone Marrow Failure Disorders

Spec	Name	St	Pg
Onc	Deeg, H	WA	386
PHO	Boxer, L	MI	782
PHO	Coccia, P	NE	786
PHO	Corey, S	IL	782
PHO	Guinan, E	MA	770
PHO	Hord, J	OH	784
PHO	Lipton, J	NY	775
PHO	Wang, W	TN	781

Bone Marrow Pathology

Spec	Name	St	Pg
Path	Arber, D	CA	731
Path	Foucar, M	NM	730
Path	Kurtin, P	MN	728
Path	Orazi, A	NY	723

Bone Marrow Transplant

Spec	Name	St	Pg
Hem	Adams, R	AZ	325
Hem	Ballen, K	MA	312
Hem	Barlogie, B	AR	325
Hem	Bigelow, C	MS	318
Hem	Brenner, M	TX	325
Hem	Champlin, R	TX	325
Hem	Cobos, E	TX	325
Hem	Copelan, E	NC	319
Hem	DiPersio, J	MO	321
Hem	Farag, S	IN	321
Hem	Filicko-O'Hara, J	PA	314
Hem	Forman, S	CA	328
Hem	Juckett, M	WI	322
Hem	Larson, R	IL	322
Hem	Linenberger, M	WA	328
Hem	Litzow, M	MN	322
Hem	Mangan, K	PA	315
Hem	Maziarz, R	OR	329
Hem	McGlave, P	MN	323
Hem	Meehan, K	NH	312
Hem	Milhem, M	IA	323
Hem	Miller, K	MA	312
Hem	Munker, R	LA	327
Hem	Negrin, R	CA	329
Hem	Porter, D	PA	316
Hem	Rondelli, D	IL	323
Hem	Rowley, S	NJ	316
Hem	Savage, D	NY	316
Hem	Schuster, M	NY	317
Hem	Schuster, S	PA	317
Hem	Snyder, D	CA	330
Hem	Spitzer, T	MA	313
Hem	Stiff, P	IL	324
Hem	Strair, R	NJ	317
Hem	Uberti, J	MI	324
Hem	Winter, J	IL	324
Hem	Yanovich, S	MD	318
Onc	Antin, J	MA	330
Onc	Appelbaum, F	WA	385
Onc	Armitage, J	NE	375
Onc	Bierman, P	NE	376
Onc	Bitran, J	IL	366
Onc	Bolwell, B	OH	366
Onc	Camoriano, J	AZ	379
Onc	Carabasi, M	PA	339
Onc	Chao, N	NC	357
Onc	Claxton, D	PA	340
Onc	Fay, J	TX	379
Onc	Flinn, I	TN	357
Onc	Flomenberg, N	PA	342
Onc	Freedman, A	MA	331
Onc	Hurd, D	NC	359
Onc	Jillella, A	GA	359
Onc	Kalaycio, M	OH	370
Onc	Kaminski, M	MI	370
Onc	Kaplan, L	CA	389
Onc	Koczywas, M	CA	389
Onc	Pohlman, B	OH	372
Onc	Press, O	WA	391
Onc	Shea, T	NC	363
Onc	Soiffer, R	MA	335
Onc	Vaughan, W	AL	364
Onc	Wingard, J	FL	365
PA&I	Cowan, M	CA	746
PA&I	Kamani, N	DC	743
PHO	Andrews, R	WA	789
PHO	Arceci, R	AZ	787
PHO	Barredo, J	FL	777
PHO	Bertolone, S	KY	777
PHO	Cairo, M	NY	772
PHO	Camitta, B	WI	782
PHO	Carpenter, P	WA	789
PHO	Chen, A	MD	772
PHO	Coccia, P	NE	786
PHO	Davies, S	OH	782
PHO	Ferrara, J	MI	783
PHO	Garvin, J	NY	773
PHO	Graham, M	AZ	788
PHO	Grupp, S	PA	773
PHO	Guinan, E	MA	770
PHO	Haut, P	IN	783
PHO	Hayashi, R	MO	783
PHO	Horn, B	CA	790
PHO	Kapoor, N	CA	790
PHO	Kurtzberg, J	NC	779
PHO	Kushner, B	NY	775
PHO	Lipton, J	NY	775
PHO	Loeb, D	MD	775
PHO	O'Reilly, R	NY	776
PHO	Olson, J	OR	791
PHO	Rosenthal, J	CA	791
PHO	Rubin, C	IL	785
PHO	Sakamoto, K	CA	791
PHO	Sandler, E	FL	781
RadRO	Wong, J	CA	998

Bone Pathology

Spec	Name	St	Pg
Path	Antonescu, C	NY	720
Path	Kahn, L	NY	722

Bone Tumors

Spec	Name	St	Pg
Onc	Benedetto, P	FL	355
Onc	George, S	MA	332
Onc	Tap, W	NY	352
OrS	Aboulafia, A	MD	620
OrS	Conrad, E	WA	650
OrS	Frassica, F	MD	624
OrS	Gebhardt, M	MA	617
OrS	Healey, J	NY	625
OrS	Henshaw, R	DC	625
OrS	Hornicek, F	MA	617
OrS	Kenan, S	NY	627
OrS	Lane, J	NY	627
OrS	Lewis, V	TX	648
OrS	Malawer, M	MD	628
OrS	Mayerson, J	OH	643
OrS	Menendez, L	CA	652
OrS	O'Keefe, R	NY	630
OrS	Peabody, T	IL	644
OrS	Randall, R	UT	647
OrS	Scarborough, M	FL	638
OrS	Schmidt, R	PA	632
OrS	Schwartz, H	TN	638

Spec	Name	St	Pg
OrS	Walling, A	FL	638
OrS	Ward, W	PA	633
OrS	Wilkins, R	CO	647
OrS	Williams, R	TX	649
OrS	Wittig, J	NY	634
Path	Lucas, D	MI	728
Path	Schiller, A	HI	734
PHO	Aledo, A	NY	771
PHO	Harris, M	NJ	774
PHO	Hawkins, D	WA	790
PHO	Meyers, P	NY	775
PHO	Sandler, E	FL	781

Bone Tumors-Benign

Spec	Name	St	Pg
OrS	Lane, J	NY	627
OrS	Lee, F	NY	628

Bone Tumors-Metastatic

Spec	Name	St	Pg
OrS	Buckwalter, J	IA	640
OrS	Hornicek, F	MA	617
OrS	Lane, J	NY	627
OrS	Lee, F	NY	628
OrS	Schmidt, R	PA	632
OrS	Schwartz, H	TN	638
OrS	Siegel, H	AL	638
RadRO	Meredith, R	AL	986

Bone/Joint Infections

Spec	Name	St	Pg
Inf	Brause, B	NY	412
Inf	Edmond, M	VA	416
Inf	Rao, N	PA	414
Inf	Romagnoli, M	NY	414
Inf	Schmitt, S	OH	418
Inf	Yancovitz, S	NY	415

Botox Therapy

Spec	Name	St	Pg
D	Avram, M	NY	186
D	Brandt, F	NY	187
D	Glogau, R	CA	200
D	Gordon, M	NY	188
N	Sethi, K	GA	527
N	Singer, C	FL	527
N	Stern, M	PA	522
Oph	Capo, H	FL	587
Oph	Carter, K	IA	594
Oto	Becker, F	FL	677
Oto	Blitzer, A	NY	668
Oto	Branham, G	MO	684
Oto	Sulica, R	NY	676
PM	Argoff, C	NY	706
PM	Freitag, F	WI	709
PMR	Robinson, L	WA	872

Brachial Plexus Palsy

Spec	Name	St	Pg
HS	Bishop, A	MN	302
HS	Grossman, J	FL	301
HS	Hentz, V	CA	306
HS	Peljovich, A	GA	301
HS	Steinmann, S	MN	304
HS	Waters, P	MA	296
NS	Spinner, R	MN	493
PMR	Nelson, M	TX	871

Brachial Plexus Palsy-Pediatric

Spec	Name	St	Pg
HS	Kozin, S	PA	298
NS	Park, T	MO	491
NS	Piatt, J	DE	480

Brachytherapy

Spec	Name	St	Pg
RadRO	Anscher, M	VA	983
RadRO	Beitler, J	GA	983
RadRO	Ciezki, J	OH	989
RadRO	D'Amico, A	MA	976
RadRO	Ennis, R	NY	979
RadRO	Gejerman, G	NJ	979
RadRO	Grado, G	AZ	993
RadRO	Harrison, L	NY	980
RadRO	Henderson, R	FL	984
RadRO	Horwitz, E	PA	980
RadRO	Jhingran, A	TX	994
RadRO	Kaplan, I	MA	976
RadRO	Koh, W	WA	996
RadRO	Kudrimoti, M	KY	984
RadRO	Lee, W	NC	985
RadRO	Malcolm, A	TN	985
RadRO	Medbery, C	OK	994
RadRO	Nori, D	NY	981
RadRO	Potters, L	NY	982
RadRO	Vicini, F	MI	992
RadRO	Vijayakumar, S	MS	987
RadRO	Zelefsky, M	NY	983
U	Kane, M	MD	1191
U	Terris, M	GA	1201
VIR	Coldwell, D	KY	1029

Brain & Spinal Cord Tumors

Spec	Name	St	Pg
N	Newton, H	OH	531
NS	Bederson, J	NY	474
NS	Berger, M	CA	498
NS	Bilsky, M	NY	475
NS	Brem, H	MD	475
NS	Caputy, A	DC	475
NS	Carson, B	MD	475
NS	Chen, C	NY	475
NS	Chen, T	CA	499
NS	Frim, D	IL	490
NS	Goumnerova, L	MA	473
NS	Harsh, G	CA	500
NS	Jallo, G	MD	478
NS	Kaufman, B	WI	490
NS	Kobrine, A	DC	479
NS	Lang, F	TX	496
NS	Laske, D	PA	479
NS	Malik, G	MI	491
NS	Moser, R	MA	473
NS	Olivi, A	MD	480
NS	Parsa, A	IL	492
NS	Penar, P	VT	473
NS	Piepmeier, J	CT	473
NS	Reid, W	TN	486
NS	Robertson, J	TN	486
NS	Sills, A	TN	487
NS	Swearingen, B	MA	474
NS	Thompson, R	TN	487
Onc	Friedman, H	NC	358
PHO	Dunkel, I	NY	772
PHO	Kramer, K	NY	774
RadRO	Flickinger, J	PA	979
RadRO	Hartford, A	NH	976
RadRO	Kleinberg, L	MD	981
RadRO	Lewin, A	FL	985
RadRO	Marcus, R	FL	985
RadRO	Regine, W	MD	982
RadRO	Wara, W	CA	998

Brain & Spinal Surgery

Spec	Name	St	Pg
NS	Theodore, N	AZ	497

Brain & Spinal Tumors-Pediatric

Spec	Name	St	Pg
NS	Cohen, A	MA	472
NS	Feldstein, N	NY	476

Brain Development Abnormalities

Spec	Name	St	Pg
NRad	Barkovich, A	CA	1025
NRad	Barnes, P	CA	1026

Brain Imaging

Spec	Name	St	Pg
DR	Mountz, J	PA	1011
NRad	Jarvik, J	WA	1026
NRad	Osborn, A	UT	1025

Brain Imaging-Pediatric

Spec	Name	St	Pg
NRad	Provenzale, J	NC	1022

Brain Infections

Spec	Name	St	Pg
Path	Bollen, A	CA	732

Brain Injury

Spec	Name	St	Pg
ChAP	Martini, D	UT	942
ChiN	Griesemer, D	MA	144
ChiN	Ichord, R	PA	145
ChiN	Noetzel, M	MO	149
N	Fellus, J	NJ	515
N	Jordan, B	NY	516
NP	Delivoria-Papadopoulos, M	PA	449
NRad	Burdette, J	NC	1021
NS	Adelson, P	AZ	495
NS	Bailes, J	IL	488
NS	Carson, B	MD	475
NS	Wilberger, J	PA	483
PMR	Brown, A	MN	867
PS	Nance, M	PA	816

Brain Injury Rehabilitation

Spec	Name	St	Pg
N	Corbetta, M	MO	529
PMR	Apkon, S	WA	872
PMR	Bloch, R	MA	862
PMR	Flanagan, S	NY	864
PMR	Francisco, G	TX	871
PMR	Fried, G	PA	864
PMR	Friedman, A	WA	872
PMR	Glenn, M	MA	862
PMR	Hammond, F	IN	868
PMR	Ivanhoe, C	TX	871
PMR	Mayer, N	PA	865
PMR	Mysiw, W	OH	869
PMR	Ragnarsson, K	NY	865
PMR	Richter, E	CT	862
PMR	Zafonte, R	MA	862

Brain Injury Rehabilitation-Pediatric

Spec	Name	St	Pg
PMR	Massagli, T	WA	872

Brain Injury-Neonatal

Spec	Name	St	Pg
NP	Anday, E	PA	448

Brain Injury-Pediatric

Spec	Name	St	Pg
NRad	Barnes, P	CA	1026
NRad	Hunter, J	TX	1025
NS	Ragheb, J	FL	486
PMR	Matthews, D	CO	870

Brain Injury-Traumatic

Spec	Name	St	Pg
NS	Grady, M	PA	477
NS	Maroon, J	PA	479

Brain Malformations

Spec	Name	St	Pg
N	Kuzniecky, R	NY	517

Brain Mapping

Spec	Name	St	Pg
NRad	Faro, S	PA	1020
NS	Parsa, A	IL	492
NS	Silbergeld, D	WA	502

Brain Radiation Toxicity

Spec	Name	St	Pg
N	Rogers, L	OH	532

Brain Tumor Imaging

Spec	Name	St	Pg
NRad	Hesselink, J	CA	1026
NRad	Koeller, K	MN	1023
NRad	Loevner, L	PA	1021
NRad	Murtagh, F	FL	1022
NRad	Provenzale, J	NC	1022

Brain Tumors

Spec	Name	St	Pg
ChiN	Allen, J	NY	145
ChiN	Fisher, P	CA	151
ChiN	Keating, G	MN	148
ChiN	Packer, R	DC	146
ChiN	Phillips, P	PA	146
ChiN	Pomeroy, S	MA	144
DR	Elster, A	NC	1013
N	Aiken, R	IL	527
N	Barger, G	MI	528
N	Batchelor, T	MA	510
N	Chamberlain, M	WA	539
N	Cloughesy, T	CA	539
N	DeAngelis, L	NY	514
N	Gilbert, M	TX	536
N	Glass, J	PA	516
N	Lassman, A	NY	517
N	Laterra, J	MD	517
N	Mikkelsen, T	MI	531
N	Moots, P	TN	526
N	Nabors, L	AL	526
N	Patchell, R	NJ	520
N	Phuphanich, S	CA	541
N	Posner, J	NY	520
N	Puduvalli, V	OH	532
N	Rogers, L	OH	532
N	Ronan, L	NH	512
N	Rosenfeld, S	OH	533
N	Schiff, D	VA	527
N	Taylor, L	MA	512
N	Vick, N	IL	534
N	Wen, P	MA	512
N	Yung, W	TX	538
NRad	Atlas, S	CA	1025
NRad	Cha, S	CA	1026
NRad	Dillon, W	CA	1026
NRad	Faro, S	PA	1020
NRad	Johnson, A	NC	1022
NRad	Lis, E	NY	1021
NRad	Maldjian, J	NC	1022
NRad	Sze, G	CT	1020
NRad	Vezina, L	DC	1021
NS	Al-Mefty, O	MA	472
NS	Andrews, D	PA	474
NS	Apuzzo, M	CA	498
NS	Asher, A	NC	483
NS	Badie, B	CA	498
NS	Barnett, G	OH	488
NS	Black, K	CA	498
NS	Boop, F	TN	484
NS	Brem, S	PA	475
NS	Chandler, J	IL	489
NS	Charbel, F	IL	489
NS	Cherny, W	ID	494
NS	Chiocca, E	MA	472
NS	Cosgrove, G	RI	472
NS	Dacey, R	MO	489
NS	Danielpour, M	CA	499
NS	David, C	MA	472
NS	Duhaime, A	MA	473
NS	Ellenbogen, R	WA	499
NS	Evans, J	PA	476
NS	Ewend, M	NC	484
NS	Fenstermaker, R	NY	476
NS	Friedman, A	NC	484
NS	Golfinos, J	NY	477
NS	Greene, C	LA	495
NS	Grubb, R	MO	490
NS	Guthrie, B	AL	485
NS	Gutin, P	NY	477
NS	Hankinson, H	NM	495
NS	Heros, R	FL	485
NS	Huang, J	MD	478
NS	Judy, K	PA	478
NS	Kim, D	TX	496
NS	Liau, L	CA	500
NS	Link, M	MN	491
NS	Linskey, M	CA	500
NS	Luken, M	IL	491
NS	Lunsford, L	PA	479
NS	Mamelak, A	CA	500
NS	Markert, J	AL	485
NS	Martuza, R	MA	473
NS	McDermott, M	CA	501
NS	Meyer, F	MN	491
NS	Mickey, B	TX	497
NS	Moore, F	NJ	480
NS	Morcos, J	FL	486
NS	Myseros, J	DC	480
NS	Naff, N	MD	480
NS	Neuwelt, E	OR	501
NS	O'Rourke, D	PA	480
NS	Ojemann, J	WA	501
NS	Olson, J	GA	486
NS	Origitano, T	MT	494
NS	Ott, K	CA	501
NS	Patel, S	SC	486
NS	Pollack, I	PA	481
NS	Quigley, M	PA	481
NS	Raffel, C	CA	501
NS	Rich, K	MO	492
NS	Rigamonti, D	MD	481
NS	Rock, J	MI	492
NS	Rosenblatt, S	IL	492
NS	Rosenblum, M	MI	492
NS	Ruge, J	IL	492
NS	Ryken, T	IA	492
NS	Sampson, J	NC	487
NS	Sawaya, R	TX	497
NS	Schwartz, T	NY	481
NS	Sekhar, L	WA	501
NS	Sen, C	NY	481
NS	Shaffrey, M	VA	487
NS	Shapiro, S	IN	493
NS	Shuer, L	CA	502
NS	Silbergeld, D	WA	502
NS	Spencer, D	CT	474
NS	Spinner, R	MN	493
NS	Sundaresan, N	NY	482
NS	Swaid, S	AL	487
NS	Tatter, S	NC	487
NS	Van Loveren, H	FL	488
NS	Walker, M	UT	495
NS	Warnick, R	OH	493
NS	Weingart, J	MD	483
NS	Wharen, R	FL	488
NS	Yu, J	CA	502
Onc	Buckner, J	MN	367

Specialty & Special Expertise Index

Spec	Name	St	Pg
Onc	Chang, S	CA	385
Onc	Fine, H	NY	342
Onc	Grossman, S	MD	344
Onc	Lesser, G	NC	360
Onc	McClay, E	CA	390
Onc	Peereboom, D	OH	372
Onc	Prados, M	CA	391
Onc	Von Burton, G	LA	384
Onc	Vredenburgh, J	CT	336
Onc	Ward, J	UT	378
Path	Bollen, A	CA	732
Path	Bruner, J	TX	730
Path	Burger, P	MD	721
Path	DeMasters, B	CO	729
Path	Mischel, P	CA	733
Path	Perry, A	CA	734
Path	Rosenblum, M	NY	723
Path	Zagzag, D	NY	725
PHO	Arndt, C	MN	781
PHO	Banerjee, A	CA	789
PHO	Berg, S	TX	787
PHO	Blaney, S	TX	787
PHO	Bruggers, C	UT	786
PHO	Cohen, K	MD	772
PHO	Ducore, J	CA	789
PHO	Dunkel, I	NY	772
PHO	Finlay, J	CA	789
PHO	Fouladi, M	OH	783
PHO	Gajjar, A	TN	778
PHO	Garvin, J	NY	773
PHO	Geyer, J	WA	790
PHO	Gold, S	NC	779
PHO	Goldman, S	IL	783
PHO	Gururangan, S	NC	779
PHO	Halpern, S	NJ	774
PHO	Hetherington, M	MO	783
PHO	Horn, B	CA	790
PHO	Kieran, M	MA	770
PHO	Korones, D	NY	774
PHO	Kuttesch, J	NM	788
PHO	Manera, R	IL	784
PHO	Neuberg, R	SC	780
PHO	Nicholson, H	OR	791
PHO	Olshefski, R	OH	784
PHO	Plautz, G	OH	785
PHO	Puccetti, D	WI	785
PHO	Rood, B	DC	776
PHO	Rubin, C	IL	785
PHO	Russo, C	AL	780
PHO	van Hoff, J	NH	771
PMR	Stewart, P	AL	867
RadRO	Chakravarti, A	OH	988
RadRO	Cmelak, A	TN	984
RadRO	Crocker, I	GA	984
RadRO	Fiveash, J	AL	984
RadRO	Goodman, R	NJ	980
RadRO	Hayman, J	MI	990
RadRO	Herman, T	OK	993
RadRO	Isaacson, S	NY	980
RadRO	Knisely, J	NY	981
RadRO	Kun, L	TN	984
RadRO	Larner, J	VA	985
RadRO	Larson, D	CA	996
RadRO	Loeffler, J	MA	977
RadRO	Mehta, M	MD	981
RadRO	Movsas, B	MI	991
RadRO	Sandler, H	CA	997
RadRO	Schild, S	AZ	994
RadRO	Schomberg, P	WA	997
RadRO	Seung, S	OR	997
RadRO	Shaw, E	NC	987
RadRO	Simpson, J	MO	991
RadRO	St Clair, W	KY	987
RadRO	Stea, B	AZ	995
RadRO	Werner-Wasik, M	PA	983

Brain Tumors & Hemifacial Spasms

NS	Harper, R	TX	495

Brain Tumors-Adult & Pediatric

NS	Butler, W	MA	472
NS	Kondziolka, D	NY	479
NS	Mapstone, T	OK	497
RadRO	Shrieve, D	UT	992
RadRO	Suh, J	OH	992
RadRO	Woo, S	KY	988

Brain Tumors-Benign

NS	Wilberger, J	PA	483
RadRO	Loeffler, J	MA	977

Brain Tumors-Complex

NS	Bruce, J	NY	475
NS	Lang, F	TX	496
NS	Sisti, M	NY	482

Brain Tumors-Metastatic

N	Lassman, A	NY	517
NS	Chen, T	CA	499
NS	Kondziolka, D	NY	479
NS	Laske, D	PA	479
NS	Olivi, A	MD	480
NS	Silbergeld, D	WA	502
Onc	Vredenburgh, J	CT	336
RadRO	Kleinberg, L	MD	981

Brain Tumors-Pediatric

N	Janss, A	GA	525
NS	Edwards, M	CA	499
NS	Sandberg, D	TX	497
NS	Selden, N	OR	502
NS	Souweidane, M	NY	482
NS	Sutton, L	PA	482
NS	Tomita, T	IL	493
NS	Wisoff, J	NY	483
PHO	Hilden, J	CO	786
RadRO	Merchant, T	TN	986
RadRO	Tarbell, N	MA	977

Brain Tumors-Recurrent

PHO	Kuttesch, J	NM	788

Brain/Spinal Cord Injury

PMR	Leslie, D	GA	867

Breast Augmentation

PlS	Meltzer, T	AZ	899
PlS	Stadelmann, W	NH	879
PlS	Young, V	MO	897

Breast Cancer

DR	Abbitt, P	FL	1012
DR	Baker, J	NC	1013
DR	Brem, R	DC	1008
DR	Conant, E	PA	1008
DR	Copit, D	PA	1008
DR	Dershaw, D	NY	1009
DR	Edelstein, B	NY	1009
DR	Evers, K	PA	1009
DR	Feig, S	CA	1017
DR	Freimanis, R	NC	1013
DR	Helvie, M	MI	1015
DR	Hricak, H	NY	1010
DR	Huynh, P	TX	1016
DR	Lehman, C	WA	1018
DR	McDonald, D	CA	1018
DR	Mitnick, J	NY	1010
DR	Monsees, B	MO	1015
DR	Otto, P	TX	1017
DR	Parikh, J	WA	1018
DR	Roth, S	PA	1012
DR	Stough, R	OK	1017
DR	Ulissey, M	WA	1019
DR	Weinreb, J	CT	1007
GO	Braly, P	LA	288
GO	Fiorica, J	FL	281
GO	Kelley, J	PA	278
GO	Runowicz, C	FL	283
Hem	Forman, S	CA	328
Hem	Schwartzberg, L	TN	320
Hem	Wisch, N	NY	318
NuM	Podoloff, D	TX	557
ObG	Goldman, M	CA	567
Onc	Abraham, J	OH	365
Onc	Albain, K	IL	366
Onc	Armstrong, D	MD	337
Onc	Arteaga, C	TN	355
Onc	Arun, B	TX	378
Onc	Astrow, A	NY	337
Onc	Attas, L	NJ	338
Onc	Audeh, M	CA	385
Onc	Balducci, L	FL	355
Onc	Biggs, D	DE	338
Onc	Bitran, J	IL	366
Onc	Blackwell, K	NC	355
Onc	Brenin, C	VA	356
Onc	Brescia, F	SC	356
Onc	Brufsky, A	PA	339
Onc	Budd, G	OH	367

Spec	Name	St	Pg
Onc	Burris, H	TN	356
Onc	Burstein, H	MA	330
Onc	Buys, S	UT	376
Onc	Buzdar, A	TX	379
Onc	Camoriano, J	AZ	379
Onc	Carey, L	NC	356
Onc	Carpenter, J	AL	356
Onc	Celano, P	MD	339
Onc	Chang, J	TX	379
Onc	Chap, L	CA	386
Onc	Chew, H	CA	386
Onc	Chitambar, C	WI	367
Onc	Chlebowski, R	CA	386
Onc	Cobleigh, M	IL	368
Onc	Cohen, G	MD	340
Onc	Cohen, P	DC	340
Onc	Cohen, S	NY	340
Onc	Colon-Otero, G	FL	357
Onc	Come, S	MA	331
Onc	Cowan, K	NE	376
Onc	Cristofanilli, M	PA	340
Onc	Daly, M	PA	341
Onc	Dickler, M	NY	341
Onc	Disis, M	WA	386
Onc	Dizon, D	MA	331
Onc	Domchek, S	PA	341
Onc	Doroshow, J	MD	341
Onc	Elias, A	CO	376
Onc	Ellis, G	WA	387
Onc	Ellis, M	MO	368
Onc	Emens, L	MD	342
Onc	Erban, J	MA	331
Onc	Fabian, C	KS	377
Onc	Fitch, T	AZ	380
Onc	Flynn, P	MN	369
Onc	Forero-Torres, A	AL	358
Onc	Fox, K	PA	343
Onc	Fracasso, P	VA	358
Onc	Ganz, P	CA	388
Onc	Garber, J	MA	332
Onc	Gaynor, E	IL	369
Onc	Geyer, C	VA	358
Onc	Glaspy, J	CA	388
Onc	Glick, J	PA	343
Onc	Goldstein, L	PA	343
Onc	Gradishar, W	IL	369
Onc	Graham, M	NC	358
Onc	Gralow, J	WA	388
Onc	Grana, G	NJ	344
Onc	Grossbard, M	NY	344
Onc	Haley, B	TX	380
Onc	Harris, L	OH	369
Onc	Hayes, D	MI	370
Onc	Hoffman, P	IL	370
Onc	Holland, J	NY	345
Onc	Hollister, D	CT	333
Onc	Hortobagyi, G	TX	380
Onc	Hudis, C	NY	345
Onc	Hutchins, L	AR	380
Onc	Ingle, J	MN	370
Onc	Isaacs, C	DC	345
Onc	Jahanzeb, M	FL	359
Onc	Kaufman, P	NH	333
Onc	Legare, R	RI	333
Onc	Leighton, J	PA	347
Onc	Levine, E	NY	347
Onc	Limentani, S	NC	360
Onc	Lippman, M	FL	360
Onc	Livingston, R	AZ	381
Onc	Loprinzi, C	MN	371
Onc	Lyman, G	NC	361
Onc	Makhoul, I	AR	381
Onc	Marcom, P	NC	361
Onc	Matulonis, U	MA	334
Onc	Mintzer, D	PA	347
Onc	Moore, A	NY	347
Onc	Morginstin, M	PA	347
Onc	Mortimer, J	CA	390
Onc	Muss, H	NC	362
Onc	Nabell, L	AL	362
Onc	Nissenblatt, M	NJ	348
Onc	Northfelt, D	AZ	381
Onc	Norton, L	NY	348
Onc	O'Regan, R	GA	362
Onc	O'Shaughnessy, J	TX	382
Onc	Offit, K	NY	349
Onc	Olopade, O	IL	372
Onc	Oratz, R	NY	349
Onc	Osborne, C	TX	382
Onc	Oster, M	NY	349
Onc	Parker, B	CA	390
Onc	Pasmantier, M	NY	349
Onc	Pegram, M	CA	390
Onc	Perez, E	FL	362
Onc	Pusztai, L	CT	334
Onc	Raptis, G	NY	350
Onc	Robert, N	VA	363
Onc	Romond, E	KY	363
Onc	Rosen, S	IL	373
Onc	Rugo, H	CA	392
Onc	Russell, C	CA	392
Onc	Schnipper, L	MA	334
Onc	Schuchter, L	PA	351
Onc	Schwartz, B	MN	373
Onc	Schwartz, M	FL	363
Onc	Shapiro, C	OH	373
Onc	Shulman, L	MA	335
Onc	Silverman, P	OH	374
Onc	Slamon, D	CA	392
Onc	Smith, T	MD	351
Onc	Somlo, G	CA	392
Onc	Speyer, J	NY	351
Onc	Stockdale, F	CA	393
Onc	Stone, J	FL	364
Onc	Stopeck, A	AZ	383
Onc	Strauss, G	MA	335
Onc	Strenger, R	RI	335
Onc	Sutton, L	NC	364
Onc	Terpenning, M	CA	393
Onc	Thigpen, J	MS	364
Onc	Tkaczuk, K	MD	353
Onc	Toppmeyer, D	NJ	353
Onc	Tripathy, D	CA	393
Onc	Urba, W	OR	393
Onc	Vahdat, L	NY	353
Onc	Valero, V	TX	383
Onc	Vinciguerra, V	NY	353
Onc	Von Burton, G	LA	384
Onc	Von Hoff, D	AZ	384
Onc	Waintraub, S	NJ	354
Onc	Ward, J	UT	378
Onc	Weisberg, T	ME	336
Onc	Wicha, M	MI	375
Onc	Wierman, A	NV	394
Onc	Winer, E	MA	336
Onc	Wolff, A	MD	354
Onc	Yee, D	MN	375
Path	Allred, D	MO	727
Path	Bleiweiss, I	NY	720
Path	Chen, Y	CA	732
Path	Connolly, J	MA	718
Path	Cote, R	FL	725
Path	Hoda, S	NY	722
Path	Ljung, B	CA	733
Path	Masood, S	FL	726
Path	Mies, C	PA	723
Path	Morrow, J	CT	719
Path	Patchefsky, A	PA	723
Path	Rimm, D	CT	719
Path	Ross, J	NY	724
Path	Sahin, A	TX	731
Path	Sanchez, M	NJ	724
Path	Schnitt, S	MA	719
Path	Thor, A	CO	729
Path	Tornos, C	NY	724
Path	Wilczynski, S	CA	735
PlS	Vidal, D	NH	879
RadRO	Awan, A	IL	988
RadRO	Beitler, J	GA	983
RadRO	Buchholz, T	TX	993
RadRO	Chadha, M	NY	978
RadRO	Chakravarthy, A	TN	984
RadRO	Donaldson, S	CA	995
RadRO	Dritschilo, A	DC	979
RadRO	Ennis, R	NY	979
RadRO	Formenti, S	NY	979
RadRO	Fowble, B	CA	995
RadRO	Freedman, G	PA	979
RadRO	Gaffney, D	UT	992
RadRO	Goodman, R	NJ	980
RadRO	Haffty, B	NJ	980
RadRO	Halberg, F	CA	995
RadRO	Halpern, H	IL	989
RadRO	Halyard, M	AZ	993
RadRO	Hancock, S	CA	995
RadRO	Harris, J	MA	976
RadRO	Hayman, J	MI	990
RadRO	Heimann, R	VT	976
RadRO	Herman, T	OK	993
RadRO	Kachnic, L	MA	976
RadRO	Kalnicki, S	NY	980
RadRO	Kuske, R	AZ	994
RadRO	Lee, C	MN	990
RadRO	Lewin, A	FL	985
RadRO	Macklis, R	OH	991
RadRO	Marks, L	NC	985
RadRO	McCormick, B	NY	981
RadRO	Medbery, C	OK	994
RadRO	Mendenhall, N	FL	986

Spec	Name	St	Pg
RadRO	Meredith, R	AL	986
RadRO	Morris, M	VA	986
RadRO	Nicolaou, N	PA	981
RadRO	Nori, D	NY	981
RadRO	Park, C	CA	996
RadRO	Pezner, R	CA	996
RadRO	Pierce, L	MI	991
RadRO	Porrazzo, M	DC	982
RadRO	Prosnitz, L	NC	986
RadRO	Quivey, J	CA	997
RadRO	Rabinovitch, R	CO	992
RadRO	Randolph-Jackson, P	DC	982
RadRO	Recht, A	MA	977
RadRO	Rose, C	CA	997
RadRO	Rosenman, J	NC	987
RadRO	Sailer, S	NC	987
RadRO	Shina, D	NM	995
RadRO	Small, W	IL	991
RadRO	Solin, L	PA	982
RadRO	Taghian, A	MA	977
RadRO	Vicini, F	MI	992
RadRO	Wazer, D	RI	977
RadRO	Weiss, M	PA	983
RadRO	Werner-Wasik, M	PA	983
RadRO	Wilson, J	WI	992
S	Alfonso, A	NY	1089
S	Ames, F	TX	1123
S	Babiera, G	TX	1123
S	Bear, H	VA	1103
S	Beauchamp, R	TN	1103
S	Beitsch, P	TX	1123
S	Bland, K	AL	1103
S	Boraas, M	PA	1090
S	Borgen, P	NY	1090
S	Brooks, A	PA	1090
S	Butler, J	CA	1131
S	Chang, A	MI	1112
S	Chang, H	CA	1131
S	Cole, D	SC	1104
S	Crowe, J	OH	1113
S	Daneker, G	GA	1104
S	Dooley, W	OK	1124
S	Easter, D	CA	1132
S	Eberlein, T	MO	1113
S	Edge, S	TN	1104
S	Edney, J	NE	1122
S	Edwards, M	OH	1113
S	Eisenberg, B	NH	1085
S	Ellenhorn, J	CA	1132
S	Esserman, L	CA	1132
S	Estabrook, A	NY	1093
S	Euhus, D	TX	1124
S	Farrar, W	OH	1114
S	Feig, B	TX	1125
S	Frazier, T	PA	1093
S	Gabram, S	GA	1105
S	Giuliano, A	CA	1132
S	Goodson, W	CA	1133
S	Goulet, R	IN	1114
S	Grant, C	MN	1114
S	Grant, M	TX	1125
S	Gray, R	AZ	1125
S	Herrmann, V	SC	1105
S	Hughes, K	MA	1086
S	Hunt, K	TX	1126
S	Iglehart, J	MA	1086
S	Johnson, R	PA	1094
S	Johnson Miller, D	NJ	1095
S	Kavanah, M	MA	1086
S	Kelley, M	TN	1106
S	Kim, J	OH	1116
S	Klimberg, V	AR	1126
S	Knudson, M	CA	1134
S	Krag, D	VT	1086
S	Krontiras, H	AL	1106
S	Lannin, D	CT	1086
S	Levine, E	NC	1106
S	Li, B	LA	1127
S	Lind, D	PA	1096
S	McGrath, P	KY	1107
S	McMasters, K	KY	1107
S	Morrow, M	NY	1097
S	Nathanson, S	MI	1117
S	Nelson, E	UT	1123
S	Newman, L	MI	1117
S	Nowak, E	NY	1097
S	O'Hea, B	NY	1097
S	Olson, J	MD	1097
S	Paz, I	CA	1135
S	Peterson, L	HI	1135
S	Pockaj, B	AZ	1128
S	Ponn, T	NH	1087
S	Roses, D	NY	1099
S	Ross, M	TX	1128
S	Sataloff, D	PA	1099
S	Sauter, E	TX	1128
S	Schnabel, F	NY	1100
S	Scott-Conner, C	IA	1119
S	Sener, S	CA	1137
S	Shapiro, R	NY	1100
S	Shenk, R	OH	1119
S	Sigurdson, E	PA	1101
S	Simmons, R	NY	1101
S	Skinner, K	NY	1101
S	Smith, B	MA	1088
S	Staren, E	AZ	1129
S	Stolier, A	LA	1129
S	Tafra, L	MD	1101
S	Tartter, P	NY	1101
S	Tchou, J	PA	1102
S	Tuttle, T	MN	1120
S	Urist, M	AL	1110
S	Van Zee, K	NY	1102
S	Walker, A	WI	1121
S	Wallace, A	CA	1138
S	Wapnir, I	CA	1138
S	Ward, B	CT	1088
S	Weigel, R	IA	1121
S	White, R	NC	1110
S	Whitworth, P	TN	1110
S	Willey, S	DC	1102
S	Winchester, D	IL	1121
S	Witt, T	IL	1121
S	Yeung, R	WA	1138
S	Zannis, V	AZ	1129

Breast Cancer & Surgery

Spec	Name	St	Pg
PlS	Fox, J	PA	882
S	Anderson, B	WA	1130
S	Attai, D	CA	1130
S	Borgen, P	NY	1090
S	Brown, E	MI	1112
S	Byrd, D	WA	1131
S	Czerniecki, B	PA	1092
S	Dawson, P	WA	1131
S	Dunnington, G	IN	1113
S	Finlayson, C	CO	1122
S	Graham, R	MA	1085
S	Julian, T	PA	1095
S	Karlan, S	CA	1133
S	Kaufman, C	WA	1134
S	Kirgan, D	NV	1134
S	Leeming, R	OH	1116
S	Leitch, A	TX	1127
S	Meric-Bernstam, F	TX	1127
S	Mesko, T	FL	1107
S	Phillips, E	CA	1135
S	Silverstein, M	CA	1137
S	Swistel, A	NY	1101
S	Thayer, S	MA	1088
S	Tousimis, E	DC	1102
S	Tsangaris, T	CT	1088

Breast Cancer Genetics

Spec	Name	St	Pg
Onc	Armstrong, D	MD	337
Onc	Buys, S	UT	376
Onc	Domchek, S	PA	341
Onc	Garber, J	MA	332
Onc	Graham, M	NC	358
Onc	Olopade, O	IL	372
S	Herrmann, V	SC	1105
S	Hollingsworth, A	OK	1126

Breast Cancer in Elderly

Spec	Name	St	Pg
Onc	Muss, H	NC	362
S	Tartter, P	NY	1101

Breast Cancer Risk Assessment

Spec	Name	St	Pg
GO	Chambers, S	AZ	288
Onc	Buys, S	UT	376
Onc	Chlebowski, R	CA	386
Onc	Daly, M	PA	341
Onc	Domchek, S	PA	341
Onc	Fabian, C	KS	377
Onc	Isaacs, C	DC	345
Onc	Legare, R	RI	333
Onc	O'Regan, R	GA	362
Onc	Perez, E	FL	362
Path	Allred, D	MO	727
S	Attai, D	CA	1130
S	Hansen, N	IL	1114
S	Hollingsworth, A	OK	1126
S	Nathanson, S	MI	1117
S	Sauter, E	TX	1128
S	Tchou, J	PA	1102

Spec	Name	St	Pg
Breast Cancer Vaccine Therapy			
Onc	Serody, J	NC	363
Breast Cancer-High Risk Women			
S	Estabrook, A	NY	1093
S	Gabram, S	GA	1105
S	Hansen, N	IL	1114
S	Johnson Miller, D	NJ	1095
S	Schnabel, F	NY	1100
S	Smith, B	MA	1088
Breast Cancer-Inflammatory			
Onc	Cristofanilli, M	PA	340
Breast Cancer-Male			
Onc	Hortobagyi, G	TX	380
Breast Cancer-Novel Therapies			
Onc	Fleming, G	IL	369
Onc	Goldstein, L	PA	343
Onc	Pegram, M	CA	390
Onc	Rugo, H	CA	392
Onc	Vahdat, L	NY	353
Breast Cosmetic & Reconstructive Surgery			
PlS	Ascherman, J	NY	880
PlS	Edwards, M	NV	902
PlS	Fox, J	PA	882
PlS	Hurwitz, D	PA	883
PlS	Koplin, L	CA	903
PlS	Mast, B	FL	890
PlS	Noone, R	PA	885
PlS	Rappaport, N	TX	900
PlS	Sood, R	IN	896
Breast Disease			
S	Boraas, M	PA	1090
S	Edge, S	TN	1104
S	Finlayson, C	CO	1122
S	Frazier, T	PA	1093
S	Gabram, S	GA	1105
S	Hughes, K	MA	1086
S	Johnson, R	PA	1094
S	Kaufman, C	WA	1134
S	Leeming, R	OH	1116
S	Sataloff, D	PA	1099
S	Tchou, J	PA	1102
S	Tousimis, E	DC	1102
S	Ward, B	CT	1088
S	Witt, T	IL	1121
Breast Imaging			
DR	Abbitt, P	FL	1012
DR	Baker, J	NC	1013
DR	Bassett, L	CA	1017
DR	Brem, R	DC	1008
DR	Cardenosa, G	VA	1013
DR	Conant, E	PA	1008
DR	Copit, D	PA	1008
DR	Dershaw, D	NY	1009
DR	Feig, S	CA	1017
DR	Freimanis, R	NC	1013
DR	Helvie, M	MI	1015
DR	Hricak, H	NY	1010
DR	Jackson, V	IN	1015
DR	Lehman, C	WA	1018
DR	McDonald, D	CA	1018
DR	Otto, P	TX	1017
DR	Parikh, J	WA	1018
DR	Roth, S	PA	1012
DR	Stough, R	OK	1017
DR	Ulissey, M	WA	1019
Breast Pathology			
Path	Allred, D	MO	727
Path	Bleiweiss, I	NY	720
Path	Chen, Y	CA	732
Path	Connolly, J	MA	718
Path	Dahmoush, L	IA	727
Path	De Las Morenas, A	MA	718
Path	Ehya, H	PA	721
Path	Lage, J	MS	726
Path	Masood, S	FL	726
Path	Mies, C	PA	723
Path	Schnitt, S	MA	719
Path	Sewell, C	GA	726
Path	Sibley, R	CA	734
Path	Tavassoli, F	CT	720
Breast Reconstruction			
PlS	Allen, R	NY	880
PlS	Andersen, J	CA	901
PlS	Brandt, K	MO	893
PlS	Bucky, L	PA	881
PlS	Butler, C	TX	898
PlS	Chang, D	TX	899
PlS	Coleman, J	IN	893
PlS	Colen, L	VA	889
PlS	Cordeiro, P	NY	881
PlS	Da Lio, A	CA	902
PlS	Disa, J	NY	881
PlS	Evans, G	CA	902
PlS	Fix, R	AL	889
PlS	Georgiade, G	NC	889
PlS	Grant, R	NY	882
PlS	Grotting, J	AL	890
PlS	Hammond, D	MI	894
PlS	Hansen, J	OR	903
PlS	Hoffman, L	NY	882
PlS	Hultman, C	NC	890
PlS	Isik, F	WA	903
PlS	Jewell, M	OR	903
PlS	Kolker, A	NY	883
PlS	Leipziger, L	NY	883
PlS	Levine, J	NY	883
PlS	Loree, T	NY	884
PlS	Maxwell, G	TN	891
PlS	Mehrara, B	NY	885
PlS	Miller, M	OH	895
PlS	Patel, S	PA	885
PlS	Pomahac, B	MA	879
PlS	Robb, G	TX	900
PlS	Rockwell, W	UT	898
PlS	Schusterman, M	TX	900
PlS	Serletti, J	PA	886
PlS	Sherman, R	CA	905
PlS	Slavin, S	MA	879
PlS	Slezak, S	MD	886
PlS	Smith, D	FL	891
PlS	Smith, P	FL	891
PlS	Song, D	IL	896
PlS	Stadelmann, W	NH	879
PlS	Stahl, R	CT	879
PlS	Sultan, M	NY	887
PlS	Talmor, M	NY	887
PlS	Ting, J	NY	888
PlS	Topham, N	PA	888
PlS	Vasconez, H	KY	892
PlS	Vidal, D	NH	879
PlS	Walton, R	IL	897
PlS	Wilkins, E	MI	897
PlS	Winters, R	NJ	888
PlS	Yetman, R	OH	897
PlS	Yuen, J	AR	901
S	Edington, H	PA	1092
Breast Reconstruction & Augmentation			
PlS	Beasley, M	NC	888
PlS	Nahabedian, M	DC	885
PlS	Neumeister, M	IL	895
Breast Surgery			
PlS	Constantian, M	NH	878
PlS	Puckett, C	MO	896
PlS	Singer, R	CA	905
PlS	Wells, J	CA	906
S	Dawson, P	WA	1131
S	Estabrook, A	NY	1093
S	Goulet, R	IN	1114
S	Gower, R	AK	1133
S	Grant, M	TX	1125
S	Herrmann, V	SC	1105
S	Lannin, D	CT	1086
S	Peterson, L	HI	1135
S	Simmons, R	NY	1101
S	Wapnir, I	CA	1138
S	Ward, B	CT	1088
S	Willey, S	DC	1102
S	Zannis, V	AZ	1129
Breathing Disorders			
NP	Delivoria-Papadopoulos, M	PA	449
NP	Donn, S	MI	452

Spec	Name	St	Pg
NP	Gewolb, I	MI	452
NP	Gross, I	CT	448
NP	Hendricks-Munoz, K	VA	451
NP	Lawson, E	MD	449
NP	Martin, R	OH	452
PPul	Green, T	IL	809
PPul	Keens, T	CA	810
PPul	Kemp, J	MO	809
PPul	Loughlin, G	NY	807
Pul	Mahler, D	NH	955

Bronchiectasis

Pul	Fanta, C	MA	954
Pul	Hansen-Flaschen, J	PA	957
Pul	Metersky, M	CT	955
Pul	O'Donnell, A	DC	958
Pul	Tino, G	PA	960
Pul	Wenzel, S	PA	960

Bronchiolitis Obliterans

Pul	Stover-Pepe, D	NY	960

Bronchopulmonary Dysplasia

PPul	McGrath-Morrow, S	MD	807
PPul	Nielson, D	CA	810

Bronchoscopy

Pul	Maxfield, R	NY	958
Pul	Prakash, U	MN	966

Burn Care

PlS	Cruse, C	FL	889
PlS	Gottlieb, L	IL	893
PlS	Spence, R	MD	886
PMR	Sisung, C	IL	870
PS	Fallat, M	KY	818
S	Bessey, P	NY	1089
S	Buchman, T	GA	1104
S	Cairns, B	NC	1104
S	Deitch, E	NJ	1092
S	Demarest, G	NM	1124
S	Gamelli, R	IL	1114
S	Greenhalgh, D	CA	1133
S	Griswold, J	TX	1125
S	Haith, L	PA	1094
S	Kagan, R	OH	1115
S	Lentz, C	NM	1127
S	Luterman, A	AL	1106
S	Meyer, A	NC	1107
S	Potenza, B	CA	1136
S	Ryan, C	MA	1087
S	Winchell, R	ME	1088
S	Yurt, R	NY	1102

Burns-Reconstructive Plastic Surgery

PlS	Cederna, P	MI	893

Spec	Name	St	Pg
PlS	Cruse, C	FL	889
PlS	Feldman, J	MA	878
PlS	Garner, W	CA	902
PlS	Glat, P	PA	882
PlS	Gottlieb, L	IL	893
PlS	Hultman, C	NC	890
PlS	Lee, R	IL	894
PlS	Leighton, W	AZ	899
PlS	Miller, T	CA	904
PlS	Molnar, J	NC	891
PlS	Orgill, D	MA	878
PlS	Pomahac, B	MA	879
PlS	Rose, E	NY	886
PlS	Smith, D	FL	891
PlS	Sood, R	IN	896
PlS	Spence, R	MD	886

C

Calcium Disorders

EDM	Bergman, D	NY	211
EDM	Clutter, W	MO	218
EDM	Holick, M	MA	209
EDM	Jacobs, T	NY	213

Calcium Disorders in Newborn

PEn	Diamond, F	FL	759

Cancer Chemoembolization

VIR	Cohen, G	PA	1027
VIR	Geschwind, J	MD	1028
VIR	Mauro, M	NC	1030
VIR	Salem, R	IL	1031

Cancer Detection & Staging

NuM	Agress, H	NJ	554
NuM	Siegel, B	MO	556
NuM	Waxman, A	CA	557

Cancer Genetics

CG	Bale, A	CT	156
CG	Bialer, M	NY	157
CG	Chung, W	NY	157
CG	Gilbert, F	NY	157
Ge	Boland, C	TX	253
GO	Fields, A	DC	278
GO	Lancaster, J	FL	282
GO	Lu, K	TX	289
GO	Poliakoff, S	FL	283
Onc	Daly, M	PA	341
Onc	Ford, J	CA	387
Onc	Grana, G	NJ	344
Onc	Gruber, S	CA	388
Onc	Marcom, P	NC	361
Onc	Offit, K	NY	349

Spec	Name	St	Pg
PHO	Tomlinson, G	TX	788
S	Drebin, J	PA	1092

Cancer Immune Therapy

Onc	Brentjens, R	NY	339

Cancer Prevention

Ge	Bresalier, R	TX	253
Ge	Kurtz, R	NY	237
Ge	Weinberg, D	PA	240
GO	Rodriguez, G	IL	286
Onc	Alberts, D	AZ	378
Onc	Arun, B	TX	378
Onc	Daly, M	PA	341
Onc	Fitch, T	AZ	380
Onc	Ganz, P	CA	388
Onc	Grana, G	NJ	344
Onc	O'Regan, R	GA	362
Onc	Parnes, H	MD	349
Onc	Vinciguerra, V	NY	353
Pul	Unger, M	PA	960

Cancer Radiotherapy

VIR	Geschwind, J	MD	1028
VIR	Mauro, M	NC	1030
VIR	Salem, R	IL	1031

Cancer Reconstruction

Oto	Alam, D	OH	682
Oto	Hom, D	OH	685
PlS	Baker, D	NY	880
PlS	Brandt, K	MO	893
PlS	Chang, D	TX	899
PlS	Coleman, J	IN	893
PlS	Cruse, C	FL	889
PlS	Disa, J	NY	881
PlS	Hansen, J	OR	903
PlS	Mehrara, B	NY	885
PlS	Menick, F	AZ	899
PlS	Miller, M	OH	895
PlS	Schusterman, M	TX	900
PlS	Song, D	IL	896
S	Swistel, A	NY	1101

Cancer Rehabilitation

PMR	Cheville, A	MN	867
PMR	DePompolo, R	MN	868
PMR	King, R	GA	866
PMR	Schwartz, L	PA	865
PMR	Stewart, P	AL	867
PMR	Stubblefield, M	NY	866

Cancer Risk Assessment

CG	Plon, S	TX	162
CG	Sutphen, R	FL	159
CRS	Stein, D	PA	171
Ge	Giardiello, F	MD	234
Ge	Hoops, T	PA	235

Spec	Name	St	Pg
Ge	Weinberg, D	PA	240
Onc	Garber, J	MA	332
Onc	Olopade, O	IL	372

Cancer Surgery

Spec	Name	St	Pg
CRS	Weiser, M	NY	171
NS	Kim, J	MS	485
PS	Chwals, W	MA	814
PS	Colombani, P	MD	815
PS	Davidoff, A	TN	818
PS	Hilfiker, M	CA	823
PS	Kandel, J	IL	820
PS	La Quaglia, M	NY	816
PS	Latchaw, L	NH	814
PS	Moss, R	OH	820
PS	Nuchtern, J	TX	822
PS	Rescorla, F	IN	820
PS	Rice, H	NC	818
PS	Ricketts, R	GA	818
PS	Shochat, S	TN	819
S	Averbook, B	OH	1111
S	Bilchik, A	CA	1130
S	Billingsley, K	OR	1130
S	Bland, K	AL	1103
S	Bolton, J	LA	1124
S	Byrd, D	WA	1131
S	Chang, A	MI	1112
S	Chang, H	CA	1131
S	Dunnington, G	IN	1113
S	Edge, S	TN	1104
S	Edney, J	NE	1122
S	Ellenhorn, J	CA	1132
S	Gray, R	AZ	1125
S	Haith, L	PA	1094
S	Kaufman, H	IL	1115
S	Kirgan, D	NV	1134
S	Krag, D	VT	1086
S	Krouse, R	AZ	1126
S	Kuo, P	IL	1116
S	McCabe, D	AZ	1127
S	McGrath, P	KY	1107
S	Pockaj, B	AZ	1128
S	Roh, M	FL	1108
S	Salem, R	CT	1087
S	Schwartzentruber, D	IN	1119
S	Scott-Conner, C	IA	1119
S	Shapiro, R	NY	1100
S	Simeone, D	MI	1119
S	Sondak, V	FL	1109
S	Talamini, M	CA	1137
S	Tuttle, T	MN	1120
S	Urist, M	AL	1110
S	Vetto, J	OR	1137
S	Wallace, A	CA	1138

Cancer Survivors-Late Effects of Therapy

Spec	Name	St	Pg
ChiN	Keating, G	MN	148
H & PM	Friebert, S	OH	408
N	Janss, A	GA	525
Onc	Albain, K	IL	366
Onc	Dizon, D	MA	331
Onc	Ganz, P	CA	388
Onc	Garst, J	NC	358
Ped	Kleinerman, E	TX	742
Ped	Oeffinger, K	NY	741
PEn	Meacham, L	GA	759
PEn	Sklar, C	NY	759
PHO	Barredo, J	FL	777
PHO	Blatt, J	NC	778
PHO	Castellino, S	NC	778
PHO	Castle, V	MI	782
PHO	Diller, L	MA	770
PHO	Dreyer, Z	TX	788
PHO	Finklestein, J	CA	789
PHO	Friedman, D	TN	778
PHO	Gold, S	NC	779
PHO	Green, D	TN	779
PHO	Harris, M	NJ	774
PHO	Hayashi, R	MO	783
PHO	Hudson, M	TN	779
PHO	Kadan-Lottick, N	CT	770
PHO	Marina, N	CA	790
PHO	Neglia, J	MN	784
PHO	Nicholson, H	OR	791
PHO	Plautz, G	OH	785
PHO	Puccetti, D	WI	785
PHO	Rosoff, P	NC	780
PHO	Russo, C	AL	780
PHO	Schwartz, C	RI	770
PHO	Tomlinson, G	TX	788
PHO	Vik, T	IN	786
RadRO	Constine, L	NY	978
RadRO	Hancock, S	CA	995

Cancers-Rare & Unusual

Spec	Name	St	Pg
Onc	Verschraegen, C	VT	336
S	Neifeld, J	VA	1107

Capsule Endoscopy

Spec	Name	St	Pg
Ge	Cello, J	CA	255
Ge	Dea, S	CA	255
Ge	Gerson, L	CA	256
Ge	Kastenberg, D	PA	236
Ge	Leighton, J	AZ	254
Ge	Lewis, B	NY	237

Carcinoid Tumors

Spec	Name	St	Pg
Onc	Ahlgren, J	DC	336
Onc	Anthony, L	KY	354
Onc	Hande, K	TN	359
S	Choti, M	MD	1091
S	Wagman, L	CA	1138

Cardiac Catheterization

Spec	Name	St	Pg
Cv	Cabin, H	CT	88
Cv	Chizner, M	FL	98
Cv	Clements, S	GA	98
Cv	Coppola, J	NY	91
Cv	Corrigan, V	GA	98
Cv	Greenberg, M	NY	93
Cv	Kirshenbaum, J	MA	89
Cv	Kobashigawa, J	CA	111
Cv	Phillips, H	NC	99
Cv	Pichard, A	DC	95
Cv	Rosenbush, S	IL	104
Cv	Schwartz, W	NY	96
Cv	Shlofmitz, R	NY	96
Cv	Tobis, J	CA	112
Cv	Waxman, H	PA	96
Cv	Williams, D	MA	90
IC	Applegate, R	NC	124
IC	Bach, R	MO	125
IC	Bittl, J	FL	124
IC	Chang, G	PA	121
IC	Douglas, J	GA	124
IC	Feldman, M	TX	127
IC	Fromkin, K	FL	124
IC	Greene, R	CA	128
IC	Herrmann, H	PA	122
IC	Jacobs, A	MA	120
IC	Kimmelstiel, C	MA	121
IC	Lasala, J	MO	126
IC	Lee, J	PA	122
IC	Lopez, J	IL	126
IC	Mahmud, E	CA	128
IC	Mehran, R	NY	122
IC	Morris, D	GA	125
IC	Shani, J	NY	123
IC	Whitlow, P	OH	127
PCd	Beekman, R	OH	752
PCd	Biancaniello, T	NY	748
PCd	Cheatham, J	OH	752
PCd	Hanna, B	PA	749
PCd	Hoyer, M	IN	753
PCd	Latson, L	FL	751
PCd	Lock, J	MA	747
PCd	Moskowitz, W	VA	751
PCd	Murphy, J	PA	749
PCd	Perry, S	CA	754
PCd	Radtke, W	DE	749
PCd	Sommer, R	NY	750
PCd	Teitel, D	CA	755
PCd	Velvis, H	NY	750

Cardiac CT Angiography

Spec	Name	St	Pg
Cv	Litwin, S	GA	99
Cv	Poon, M	NY	95
Cv	Raff, G	MI	104
DR	Edelman, R	IL	1014
DR	Zeman, R	DC	1012
NuM	Ziffer, J	FL	556

Cardiac Effects of Cancer/Cancer Therapy

Spec	Name	St	Pg
Cv	Steingart, R	NY	96
PCd	Steinherz, L	NY	750

Cardiac Effects of Chemotherapy

Spec	Name	St	Pg
Cv	Wells, G	NC	100

Spec	Name	St	Pg

Cardiac Electrophysiology

Spec	Name	St	Pg
CE	Anderson, M	IA	117
CE	Asirvatham, S	MN	117
CE	Berger, R	MD	114
CE	Buxton, A	MA	112
CE	Callans, D	PA	114
CE	Cannom, D	CA	119
CE	Chinitz, L	NY	114
CE	Cohen, M	NY	114
CE	Curtis, A	NY	114
CE	DeLurgio, D	GA	116
CE	DiMarco, J	VA	116
CE	Donahue, J	MA	113
CE	Ellenbogen, K	VA	116
CE	Epstein, A	PA	114
CE	Epstein, L	MA	113
CE	Estes, N	MA	113
CE	Faddis, M	MO	117
CE	Feld, G	CA	119
CE	Gang, E	CA	120
CE	Goldberger, J	IL	117
CE	Gomes, J	NY	114
CE	Halperin, H	MD	115
CE	Hayes, D	MN	117
CE	Higgins, S	CA	120
CE	Interian, A	FL	116
CE	Iwai, S	NY	115
CE	Josephson, M	MA	113
CE	Knight, B	IL	117
CE	Lerman, B	NY	115
CE	Levine, J	NY	115
CE	Lewkowiez, L	CO	119
CE	Lindsay, B	OH	117
CE	Link, M	MA	113
CE	Love, C	OH	117
CE	Marchlinski, F	PA	115
CE	Mehta, D	NY	115
CE	Miller, J	IN	118
CE	Morady, F	MI	118
CE	Naccarelli, G	PA	115
CE	Natale, A	TX	119
CE	Onufer, J	VA	116
CE	Prystowsky, E	IN	118
CE	Ruskin, J	MA	113
CE	Sauer, W	CO	119
CE	Schuger, C	MI	118
CE	Shen, W	AZ	119
CE	Sorrentino, R	GA	116
CE	Stevenson, W	MA	113
CE	Swerdlow, C	CA	120
CE	Tchou, P	OH	118
CE	Tomaselli, G	MD	116
CE	Waldo, A	OH	118
CE	Wang, P	CA	120
CE	Wilber, D	IL	118
Cv	Slater, W	NY	96
Cv	Snyder, D	LA	109
PCd	Gullquist, S	VA	751
PCd	Young, M	FL	751

Cardiac Imaging

Spec	Name	St	Pg
Cv	Budoff, M	CA	110
Cv	Cerqueira, M	OH	101
Cv	Kaul, S	OR	111
Cv	Poon, M	NY	95
DR	Bluemke, D	MD	1008
DR	Fishman, E	MD	1009
DR	Rubin, G	NC	1014
DR	White, C	MD	1012
NuM	Sandler, M	TN	555

Cardiac Intensive Care

Spec	Name	St	Pg
Cv	Nissen, S	OH	103

Cardiac MRI

Spec	Name	St	Pg
Cv	Anderson, J	UT	107
Cv	Litwin, S	GA	99
Cv	Raff, G	MI	104
DR	Edelman, R	IL	1014
DR	Flamm, S	OH	1014
PCd	Weinberg, P	PA	750

Cardiac Pathology

Spec	Name	St	Pg
Path	Roberts, W	TX	731

Cardiac Surgery

Spec	Name	St	Pg
T&CS	Athanasuleas, C	AL	1160
T&CS	Dang, M	HI	1178
T&CS	Echeverri, L	TX	1174
T&CS	Girardi, L	NY	1153
T&CS	Harken, A	CA	1178
T&CS	Isom, O	NY	1154
T&CS	Jessen, M	TX	1174
T&CS	Karwande, S	UT	1173
T&CS	Kirklin, J	AL	1163
T&CS	Kopf, G	CT	1147
T&CS	Mack, M	TX	1175
T&CS	Magovern, G	PA	1156
T&CS	Philpott, J	VA	1164
T&CS	Rosengart, T	TX	1176
T&CS	Sanchez, J	MD	1158
T&CS	Singh, A	RI	1148
T&CS	Stuart, R	MO	1171
T&CS	Thistlethwaite, P	CA	1180
T&CS	Trento, A	CA	1180
T&CS	Turner, W	TX	1176
T&CS	Ungerleider, R	NC	1166
T&CS	Vlahakes, G	MA	1148

Cardiac Surgery-Adult

Spec	Name	St	Pg
T&CS	Conte, J	MD	1151
T&CS	Diehl, J	PA	1151
T&CS	Hill, M	WA	1179
T&CS	Joyce, L	MN	1169
T&CS	Krieger, K	NY	1155
T&CS	Panos, A	FL	1164
T&CS	Rastegar, H	MA	1148

Cardiac Surgery-Adult & Pediatric

Spec	Name	St	Pg
T&CS	Calhoon, J	TX	1173
T&CS	Christian, K	TN	1161
T&CS	Drinkwater, D	TN	1162
T&CS	Gundry, S	CA	1178
T&CS	Mullett, T	KY	1164
T&CS	Spray, T	PA	1159
T&CS	Warner, K	MA	1149

Cardiac Surgery-Complex

Spec	Name	St	Pg
T&CS	Savage, E	FL	1165

Cardiac Surgery-Geriatric

Spec	Name	St	Pg
T&CS	Edwards, N	NY	1152

Cardiac Surgery-High Risk

Spec	Name	St	Pg
T&CS	Furukawa, S	PA	1152
T&CS	Gundry, S	CA	1178

Cardiac Surgery-Neonatal

Spec	Name	St	Pg
T&CS	Bichell, D	TN	1160
T&CS	Kirshbom, P	CT	1147
T&CS	Rosenkranz, E	FL	1165
T&CS	Walters, H	MI	1172

Cardiac Surgery-Neonatal & Pediatric

Spec	Name	St	Pg
T&CS	Brown, J	IN	1167

Cardiac Surgery-Pediatric

Spec	Name	St	Pg
T&CS	Bailey, L	CA	1177
T&CS	Bichell, D	TN	1160
T&CS	Fontana, G	NY	1152
T&CS	Harrell, J	TX	1174
T&CS	Turrentine, M	IN	1172

Cardiac Tumors, Myxomas

Spec	Name	St	Pg
T&CS	Grossi, E	NY	1153

Cardiac Tumors/Cancer

Spec	Name	St	Pg
T&CS	Reardon, M	TX	1175
T&CS	Sellke, F	RI	1148

Cardiomyopathy

Spec	Name	St	Pg
Cv	Bonow, R	IL	100
Cv	Fonarow, G	CA	110
Cv	Manning, W	MA	89
Cv	Williams, E	IN	106
PCd	Driscoll, D	MN	752

Cardiomyopathy-Hypertrophic

Spec	Name	St	Pg
IC	Bach, R	MO	125

Cardiothoracic Surgery

Spec	Name	St	Pg
T&CS	Bains, M	NY	1150
T&CS	Bull, D	UT	1172
T&CS	Byrne, J	MA	1146
T&CS	Durham, S	MI	1168
T&CS	Galantowicz, M	OH	1168
T&CS	Glassford, D	TN	1162
T&CS	Lang, S	NY	1155
T&CS	Lanza, L	AZ	1175
T&CS	Love, R	WI	1169
T&CS	Moon, M	MO	1170
T&CS	Oaks, T	NC	1164
T&CS	Salerno, T	FL	1165
T&CS	Stuart, R	MO	1171
T&CS	Toyoda, Y	PA	1159
T&CS	Weiman, D	TN	1166

Cardiovascular Disease

Spec	Name	St	Pg
Cv	Abi-samra, F	LA	107
Cv	Alpert, J	AZ	107
Cv	Andersen, H	NY	91
Cv	Anderson, J	UT	107
Cv	Bairey-Merz, C	CA	110
Cv	Balady, G	MA	88
Cv	Ballantyne, C	TX	107
Cv	Bashore, T	NC	97
Cv	Bass, T	FL	97
Cv	Blanchard, D	CA	110
Cv	Blumenthal, D	NY	91
Cv	Blumenthal, R	MD	91
Cv	Bonow, R	IL	100
Cv	Borer, J	NY	91
Cv	Borzak, S	FL	97
Cv	Bourge, R	AL	97
Cv	Bove, A	PA	91
Cv	Braverman, A	MO	100
Cv	Brozena, S	PA	91
Cv	Budoff, M	CA	110
Cv	Burket, M	OH	101
Cv	Byrd, B	TN	97
Cv	Cabin, H	CT	88
Cv	Califf, R	NC	97
Cv	Carabello, B	TX	108
Cv	Catherwood, E	NH	88
Cv	Cerqueira, M	OH	101
Cv	Chaitman, B	MO	101
Cv	Chizner, M	FL	98
Cv	Clements, S	GA	98
Cv	Connolly, H	MN	101
Cv	Cooper, C	OH	101
Cv	Coppola, J	NY	91
Cv	Corrigan, V	GA	98
Cv	Dangas, G	NY	92
Cv	Davidson, M	IL	101
Cv	DeNofrio, D	MA	88
Cv	Devereux, R	NY	92
Cv	Dichek, D	WA	110
Cv	Diver, D	CT	88
Cv	Eagle, K	MI	101
Cv	Edelen, J	CA	110
Cv	Edmundowicz, D	PA	92
Cv	Eisen, H	PA	92
Cv	Elkayam, U	CA	110
Cv	Fintel, D	IL	101
Cv	Fishbein, D	WA	110
Cv	Follansbee, W	PA	92
Cv	Fonarow, G	CA	110
Cv	Freeman, G	TX	108
Cv	French, W	CA	111
Cv	Friedman, S	NY	92
Cv	Fuster, V	NY	92
Cv	Garcia, M	NY	92
Cv	Gardin, J	NJ	93
Cv	Geltman, E	MO	102
Cv	Gibbons, R	MN	102
Cv	Gliklich, J	NY	93
Cv	Goldberg, N	NY	93
Cv	Goodman, D	NY	93
Cv	Gottdiener, J	MD	93
Cv	Gottlieb, S	MD	93
Cv	Gould, K	TX	108
Cv	Greenberg, M	NY	93
Cv	Grubb, B	OH	102
Cv	Halperin, J	NY	93
Cv	Hare, J	FL	98
Cv	Harrison, J	NC	98
Cv	Hauptman, P	MO	102
Cv	Hayes, S	MN	102
Cv	Herling, I	PA	94
Cv	Heroux, A	IL	102
Cv	Horn, E	NY	94
Cv	Hunt, S	CA	111
Cv	Hutter, A	MA	88
Cv	Inra, L	NY	94
Cv	Iskandrian, A	AL	98
Cv	Jaffe, A	MN	102
Cv	Jessup, M	PA	94
Cv	Johnson, A	CA	111
Cv	Johnson, M	WI	103
Cv	Johnson, P	MA	88
Cv	Judelson, D	CA	111
Cv	Katz, S	NY	94
Cv	Kaul, S	OR	111
Cv	Kereiakes, D	OH	103
Cv	Kirshenbaum, J	MA	89
Cv	Klein, L	IL	103
Cv	Kobashigawa, J	CA	111
Cv	Konstam, M	MA	89
Cv	Kostis, J	NJ	94
Cv	Krajcer, Z	TX	108
Cv	Kuvin, J	MA	89
Cv	Landzberg, J	NJ	94
Cv	Lewis, S	OR	111
Cv	Liang, B	CT	89
Cv	Liao, J	IL	103
Cv	Limacher, M	FL	98
Cv	Lindenfeld, J	CO	107
Cv	Linton, M	TN	98
Cv	Litwin, S	GA	99
Cv	Loscalzo, J	MA	89
Cv	Manning, W	MA	89
Cv	Massin, E	TX	108
Cv	Mather, P	PA	95
Cv	McPherson, D	TX	108
Cv	Mehlman, D	IL	103
Cv	Meller, J	NY	95
Cv	Nagueh, S	TX	108
Cv	Nishimura, R	MN	103
Cv	Nissen, S	OH	103
Cv	Nocero, M	FL	99
Cv	O'Connor, C	NC	99
Cv	O'Gara, P	MA	89
Cv	O'Neill, W	MI	104
Cv	Oparil, S	AL	99
Cv	Pepine, C	FL	99
Cv	Pfeffer, M	MA	90
Cv	Phillips, H	NC	99
Cv	Pichard, A	DC	95
Cv	Poon, M	NY	95
Cv	Powers, E	SC	99
Cv	Quinones, M	TX	108
Cv	Raff, G	MI	104
Cv	Rahko, P	WI	104
Cv	Ramee, S	LA	109
Cv	Redberg, R	CA	112
Cv	Reis, S	PA	95
Cv	Reiss, C	MO	104
Cv	Rich, S	IL	104
Cv	Ridker, P	MA	90
Cv	Rihal, C	MN	104
Cv	Roberts, B	RI	90
Cv	Rogers, J	NC	99
Cv	Rosenbush, S	IL	104
Cv	Russell, S	MD	95
Cv	Safian, R	MI	104
Cv	Sanborn, T	IL	105
Cv	Saunders, E	MD	95
Cv	Schnittger, I	CA	112
Cv	Schulman, S	MD	95
Cv	Schwartz, A	NY	96
Cv	Schwartz, W	NY	96
Cv	Shah, P	CA	112
Cv	Shapiro, J	IL	105
Cv	Shea, R	IN	105
Cv	Shlofmitz, R	NY	96
Cv	Silvestry, F	PA	96
Cv	Simon, D	OH	105
Cv	Skolnick, A	AK	112
Cv	Slater, W	NY	96
Cv	Smart, F	LA	109
Cv	Smith, A	GA	100
Cv	Smith, S	NC	100
Cv	Snyder, D	LA	109
Cv	Sorrentino, M	IL	105
Cv	Stainback, R	TX	109
Cv	Stein, J	WI	105
Cv	Steingart, R	NY	96
Cv	Stevenson, L	MA	90
Cv	Stewart, W	OH	105
Cv	Tenenbaum, J	NY	96
Cv	Thames, M	AZ	109
Cv	Thompson, P	CT	90
Cv	Tobis, J	CA	112
Cv	Topol, E	CA	112
Cv	Vetrovec, G	VA	100
Cv	Vignola, P	NC	100
Cv	Volgman, A	IL	106
Cv	von der Lohe, E	IN	106

Spec	Name	St	Pg
Cv	Wagoner, L	OH	106
Cv	Walsh, M	IN	106
Cv	Waxman, H	PA	96
Cv	Webb, G	OH	106
Cv	Weitz, H	PA	97
Cv	Wells, G	NC	100
Cv	Wilansky, S	AZ	109
Cv	Wilkoff, B	OH	106
Cv	Williams, D	MA	90
Cv	Williams, E	IN	106
Cv	Williams, K	MI	107
Cv	Young, J	OH	107
Cv	Zoghbi, W	TX	109
Cv	Zusman, R	MA	90
EDM	Eckel, R	CO	222
Ger	Wei, J	AR	267

Cardiovascular Disease/Young Adult

Cv	Blumenthal, R	MD	91

Cardiovascular Imaging

Cv	Litwin, S	GA	99
DR	Flamm, S	OH	1014
DR	Rubin, G	NC	1014
DR	Thompson, B	IA	1016
DR	White, R	OH	1016
DR	Zeman, R	DC	1012

Cardiovascular Pathology

Path	Fishbein, M	CA	733

Cardiovascular Surgery

T&CS	Mayer, J	MA	1148
T&CS	Quintessenza, J	FL	1165

Carotid Artery Disease

Cv	Krajcer, Z	TX	108
IC	Schreiber, T	MI	127
N	Goldstein, L	NC	524
NS	Barrow, D	GA	484
VascS	Alexander, J	OH	1226
VascS	Atnip, R	PA	1221
VascS	Calligaro, K	PA	1222
VascS	Chaikof, E	MA	1220
VascS	Cho, J	IL	1226
VascS	Comerota, A	OH	1227
VascS	D'Ayala, M	NY	1222
VascS	Dalsing, M	IN	1227
VascS	Dattilo, J	TN	1225
VascS	Greisler, H	IL	1227
VascS	Makaroun, M	PA	1224
VascS	Pomposelli, F	MA	1221
VIR	Katzen, B	FL	1029
VIR	Matsumoto, A	VA	1030

Carotid Artery Stent Placement

Cv	Ramee, S	LA	109
Cv	Sanborn, T	IL	105
IC	Mahmud, E	CA	128
IC	Petrossian, G	NY	123
IC	Reddy, B	GA	125
IC	Roubin, G	NY	123
NRad	Hurst, R	PA	1020
NRad	Masaryk, T	OH	1024
NRad	Moran, C	MO	1024
NRad	Teitelbaum, G	CA	1026
VascS	Eidt, J	SC	1225
VascS	Kazmers, A	MI	1227
VascS	Kwolek, C	MA	1220
VascS	Lantis, J	NY	1224

Carotid Artery Surgery

NS	David, C	MA	472
NS	Harbaugh, R	PA	477
NS	Loftus, C	IL	491
T&CS	Caskey, M	AZ	1173
T&CS	Ott, D	TX	1175
VascS	Adelman, M	NY	1221
VascS	Ascher, E	NY	1221
VascS	Belkin, M	MA	1220
VascS	Brener, B	NJ	1222
VascS	Carpenter, J	NJ	1222
VascS	Clair, D	OH	1227
VascS	Criado, F	MD	1222
VascS	Cronenwett, J	NH	1220
VascS	Darling, R	NY	1222
VascS	Fairman, R	PA	1223
VascS	Faries, P	NY	1223
VascS	Flanigan, D	CA	1230
VascS	Fowl, R	AZ	1229
VascS	Freischlag, J	MD	1223
VascS	Gewertz, B	CA	1230
VascS	Green, R	NY	1223
VascS	Hallett, J	SC	1225
VascS	Harrington, E	NY	1223
VascS	Hodgson, K	IL	1227
VascS	Hollier, L	LA	1229
VascS	Howard, T	NE	1229
VascS	Kent, K	WI	1228
VascS	Kougias, P	TX	1229
VascS	Mackey, W	MA	1221
VascS	McKinsey, J	NY	1224
VascS	Mitchell, M	MS	1226
VascS	Morrissey, N	NY	1224
VascS	Perler, B	MD	1224
VascS	Ricotta, J	DC	1224
VascS	Todd, G	NY	1225
VascS	White, R	CA	1230

Carotid Body Tumors

Oto	Burkey, B	OH	684
VascS	LaMuraglia, G	MA	1221

Carpal Tunnel Syndrome

HS	Abrams, R	CA	305
HS	Baratz, M	PA	297
HS	Brushart, T	MD	297
HS	Carneiro, R	FL	301
HS	Carroll, C	IL	302
HS	Cendales, L	GA	301
HS	Imbriglia, J	PA	298
HS	Kulick, R	NY	299
HS	Lane, L	NY	299
HS	Nagle, D	IL	303
HS	Raskin, K	NY	300
HS	Rosenwasser, M	NY	300
HS	Thomson, J	CT	296
HS	Weiss, A	RI	297
NS	Taylon, C	NE	494
NS	Zager, E	PA	483
PlS	Derman, G	IL	893

Cartilage Damage

DR	Potter, H	NY	1011
HS	Lee, W	MD	299
OrS	Brage, M	WA	649
OrS	Gladstone, J	NY	624
OrS	Karas, S	GA	636
OrS	Mandelbaum, B	CA	652
OrS	O'Driscoll, S	MN	644
OrS	Zarins, B	MA	619
SM	Bush-Joseph, C	IL	1077
SM	Gambardella, R	CA	1079
SM	Ho, S	IL	1078
SM	Kaplan, L	FL	1077
SM	Miniaci, A	OH	1078
SM	Rodeo, S	NY	1076
SM	Sennett, B	PA	1076

Cartilage Damage & Transplant

OrS	Minas, T	MA	618
OrS	Myerson, M	MD	629
OrS	Plancher, K	NY	631
SM	Jones, D	LA	1078
SM	Williams, R	NY	1076

Castleman's Disease

Hem	Barlogie, B	AR	325
Onc	Camoriano, J	AZ	379
Onc	Sweetenham, J	UT	378

Cataract Surgery

Oph	Afshari, N	CA	604
Oph	Alward, W	IA	593
Oph	Asbell, P	NY	575
Oph	Bouchard, C	IL	594
Oph	Boxer Wachler, B	CA	604
Oph	Braunstein, R	NY	576
Oph	Budenz, D	NC	587
Oph	Caprioli, J	CA	605
Oph	Cioffi, G	NY	577
Oph	Clinch, T	MD	577
Oph	Crandall, A	UT	601
Oph	Cykiert, R	NY	577
Oph	Feder, R	IL	595

Spec	Name	St	Pg
Oph	Foster, C	MA	574
Oph	Gibralter, R	NY	579
Oph	Goldberg, D	NJ	579
Oph	Gorovoy, M	FL	588
Oph	Holland, E	OH	595
Oph	John, T	IL	596
Oph	Koch, D	TX	602
Oph	Lane, S	MN	596
Oph	Lichter, P	MI	596
Oph	Liebmann, J	NY	581
Oph	Lindstrom, R	MN	597
Oph	Mackool, R	NY	581
Oph	Magramm, I	NY	581
Oph	Maloney, R	CA	607
Oph	Masket, S	CA	607
Oph	McCulley, J	TX	602
Oph	Orlin, S	PA	583
Oph	Page, T	MI	598
Oph	Pepose, J	MO	598
Oph	Pflugfelder, S	TX	603
Oph	Robin, A	MD	584
Oph	Rosenberg, M	IL	599
Oph	Salz, J	CA	608
Oph	Samuelson, T	MN	599
Oph	Schein, O	MD	584
Oph	Schuman, J	PA	584
Oph	Seibel, B	CA	609
Oph	Serafano, D	CA	609
Oph	Shamie, N	CA	609
Oph	Shingleton, B	MA	575
Oph	Solomon, K	SC	591
Oph	Sperber, L	NY	585
Oph	Stark, W	MD	585
Oph	Steinert, R	CA	609
Oph	Stulting, R	GA	591
Oph	Wallace, R	LA	603
Oph	Wang, M	TN	592
Oph	Waring, G	GA	592

Cataract Surgery Revision

Oph	Masket, S	CA	607

Cataract Surgery-Lens Implant

Oph	Cionni, R	UT	601
Oph	Culbertson, W	FL	587
Oph	Dodick, J	NY	577
Oph	Greenfield, D	FL	588
Oph	Lass, J	OH	596
Oph	Miller, K	CA	607
Oph	Osher, R	OH	598
Oph	Page, T	MI	598
Oph	Parrish, R	FL	590
Oph	Perez, V	FL	591
Oph	Starr, C	NY	585

Cataract-Pediatric

Oph	Buckley, E	NC	587
Oph	Del Monte, M	MI	594
Oph	Hall, L	NY	579
Oph	Kerr, N	TN	589

Spec	Name	St	Pg
Oph	Lambert, S	GA	589
Oph	Lueder, G	MO	597
Oph	Medow, N	NY	582
Oph	Plager, D	IN	598
Oph	Walton, D	MA	575
Oph	Wilson, M	SC	592
Oph	Wright, K	CA	610

Catheter Ablation

CE	Berger, R	MD	114
CE	Donahue, J	MA	113
CE	Epstein, A	PA	114
CE	Goldberger, J	IL	117
CE	Halperin, H	MD	115
CE	Lerman, B	NY	115
CE	Miller, J	IN	118
CE	Onufer, J	VA	116
CE	Prystowsky, E	IN	118
CE	Sauer, W	CO	119
CE	Shen, W	AZ	119
CE	Wilber, D	IL	118
PCd	Fish, F	TN	751

Celiac Disease

Ge	Di Marino, A	PA	234
Ge	Elliott, D	IA	247
Ge	Forsmark, C	FL	242
Ge	Green, P	NY	235
Ge	Kastenberg, D	PA	236
Ge	Murray, J	MN	249
Ge	Schembre, D	WA	257
Ge	Semrad, C	IL	250
PGe	Baldridge, A	NJ	763
PGe	Benkov, K	NY	763
PGe	Cohen, M	OH	765
PGe	Fasano, A	MA	762
PGe	Guandalini, S	IL	766
PGe	Hill, I	OH	766
PGe	Hoffenberg, E	CO	767
PGe	Leichtner, A	MA	762
PGe	Levy, J	NY	763
PGe	Snyder, J	DC	764

Central Nervous System Cancer

Path	DeMasters, B	CO	729
RadRO	Buatti, J	IA	988
RadRO	Chang, E	CA	995
RadRO	Markoe, A	FL	985
RadRO	Porrazzo, M	DC	982
RadRO	Simpson, J	MO	991

Cerebral Palsy

ChiN	Brunstrom-Hernandez, J	MO	148
ChiN	Darras, B	MA	144
ChiN	Edgar, T	WI	148
ChiN	Noetzel, M	MO	149
HS	Peljovich, A	GA	301
OrS	Oppenheim, W	CA	653
OrS	Otsuka, N	NY	630

Spec	Name	St	Pg
OrS	Strongwater, A	NJ	633
Ped	Walker, W	WA	743
PMR	Alexander, J	NC	866
PMR	Apkon, S	WA	872
PMR	Evans, S	DC	863
PMR	Matthews, D	CO	870
PMR	Webster, H	MA	862

Cerebral Palsy-Select Dorsal Rhizotomy

NS	Park, T	MO	491

Cerebrovascular Disease

N	Adams, H	IA	527
N	Albers, G	CA	538
N	Alexandrov, A	AL	523
N	Brown, R	MN	528
N	Burke, A	IL	528
N	Elkind, M	NY	515
N	Fink, M	NY	515
N	Fisher, M	CA	539
N	Furie, K	RI	511
N	Greer, D	CT	511
N	Kasner, S	PA	516
N	Kent, T	TX	537
N	Levine, S	NY	518
N	Logan, W	MO	531
N	Marshall, R	NY	519
N	Sila, C	OH	533
N	Wechsler, L	PA	522
NRad	Masaryk, T	OH	1024
NRad	Pile-Spellman, J	NY	1021
NS	Amar, A	CA	498
NS	Atkinson, J	MN	488
NS	Bailes, J	IL	488
NS	Barrow, D	GA	484
NS	Hopkins, L	NY	478
NS	Meyer, F	MN	491
NS	Samson, D	TX	497
VascS	Cambria, R	MA	1220
VascS	Eton, D	IL	1227
VIR	Kumpe, D	CO	1031

Cerebrovascular Disease/Stroke

NRad	Frei, D	CO	1025
NRad	Moran, C	MO	1024
NRad	Rowley, H	WI	1024

Cerebrovascular Malformations

ChiN	Sahin, M	MA	144
NRad	Russell, E	IL	1024
NS	Kim, J	MS	485
NS	Riina, H	NY	481

Cerebrovascular Surgery

NS	Al-Mefty, O	MA	472
NS	Bederson, J	NY	474

Spec	Name	St	Pg
NS	Butler, W	MA	472
NS	Dacey, R	MO	489
NS	David, C	MA	472
NS	Giannotta, S	CA	499
NS	Grady, M	PA	477
NS	Heros, R	FL	485
NS	Huang, J	MD	478
NS	Kim, D	TX	496
NS	Lemole, G	AZ	496
NS	Link, M	MN	491
NS	Loftus, C	IL	491
NS	Malik, G	MI	491
NS	Morcos, J	FL	486
NS	Naff, N	MD	480
NS	Rosenblatt, S	IL	492
NS	Rosenwasser, R	PA	481
NS	Spetzler, R	AZ	497
NS	Steinberg, G	CA	502
NS	Van Loveren, H	FL	488
NS	Wilson, J	NC	488
NS	Zager, E	PA	483

Cervical Cancer

Spec	Name	St	Pg
GO	Abbas, F	MD	276
GO	Abu-Rustum, N	NY	276
GO	Alvarez, R	AL	280
GO	Barakat, R	NY	276
GO	Berek, J	CA	290
GO	Berman, M	CA	290
GO	Boice, C	MD	276
GO	Burger, R	PA	277
GO	Cain, J	MA	274
GO	Caputo, T	NY	277
GO	Chi, D	NY	277
GO	Dunton, C	PA	277
GO	Duska, L	VA	281
GO	Edwards, R	PA	278
GO	Finan, M	AL	281
GO	Fromm, G	TX	288
GO	Goff, B	WA	291
GO	Hatch, K	AZ	288
GO	Herzog, T	NY	278
GO	Horowitz, I	GA	282
GO	Hurteau, J	IL	284
GO	Husain, A	CA	291
GO	Johnston, C	MI	284
GO	Kelley, J	PA	278
GO	King, S	PA	278
GO	Kline, R	LA	288
GO	Koulos, J	NY	279
GO	Lambrou, N	FL	282
GO	Levenback, C	TX	289
GO	Lin, J	DC	279
GO	Lucci, J	FL	282
GO	Lurain, J	IL	285
GO	Makhija, S	KY	282
GO	Miller, D	TX	289
GO	Moore, D	IN	285
GO	Muto, M	MA	275
GO	Nagarsheth, N	NY	279
GO	Pejovic, T	OR	291
GO	Penalver, M	FL	283
GO	Plaxe, S	CA	291
GO	Potkul, R	IL	285
GO	Powell, M	MO	285
GO	Rader, J	WI	285
GO	Remmenga, S	NE	287
GO	Reynolds, R	MI	286
GO	Rice, L	WI	286
GO	Rose, P	OH	286
GO	Rotmensch, J	IL	286
GO	Rubin, S	PA	280
GO	Runowicz, C	FL	283
GO	Rutherford, T	CT	275
GO	Schorge, J	MA	275
GO	Schwartz, P	CT	275
GO	Siller, B	TX	289
GO	Smith, D	AZ	289
GO	Soisson, A	UT	287
GO	Valea, F	NC	283
GO	Van Nagell, J	KY	284
GO	Waggoner, S	OH	287
GO	Walker, J	OK	290
GO	Yamada, S	IL	287
ObG	Argenta, P	MN	563
Onc	Schilder, R	PA	351
Onc	Scudder, S	CA	392
Path	Chhieng, D	CT	718
Path	Cho, K	MI	727
Path	Gupta, P	PA	721
RadRO	Eifel, P	TX	993

Charcot Foot

Spec	Name	St	Pg
OrS	Pinzur, M	IL	644

Chemical Exposure

Spec	Name	St	Pg
OM	Gochfeld, M	NJ	912
Pul	Bascom, R	PA	956

Chemo-Radiation Combined Therapy

Spec	Name	St	Pg
RadRO	Cooper, J	NY	978
RadRO	Formenti, S	NY	979

Chemoembolization & Tumor Ablation

Spec	Name	St	Pg
VIR	Cho, K	MI	1030
VIR	Darcy, M	MO	1030
VIR	Gomes, A	CA	1032
VIR	Weintraub, J	NY	1029

Chest Diseases-Benign

Spec	Name	St	Pg
T&CS	Nesbitt, J	TN	1164

Chest Pain-Non Cardiac

Spec	Name	St	Pg
Ge	Rao, S	GA	244

Chest Radiology

Spec	Name	St	Pg
DR	Black, W	NH	1007
DR	Partain, C	TN	1014

Chest Wall Deformities

Spec	Name	St	Pg
PlS	Stahl, R	CT	879
PPul	Redding, G	WA	811
PS	Aiken, J	WI	819
PS	Black, C	TX	821
PS	Cass, D	TX	822
PS	Glick, P	NY	816
PS	Hicks, B	DE	816
PS	Holcomb, G	MO	820
PS	Paidas, C	FL	818
PS	Shochat, S	TN	819
PS	Stylianos, S	NY	817

Chest Wall Reconstruction

Spec	Name	St	Pg
PlS	Seyfer, A	MD	886
PlS	Stahl, R	CT	879
PlS	Yuen, J	AR	901

Chest Wall Tumors

Spec	Name	St	Pg
T&CS	Cerfolio, R	AL	1161
T&CS	Handy, J	OR	1178
T&CS	Kiev, J	WV	1155
T&CS	Kucharczuk, J	PA	1155
T&CS	Marshall, M	DC	1156
T&CS	Naunheim, K	MO	1170
T&CS	Shrager, J	CA	1180
T&CS	Whyte, R	MA	1149

Chiari's Deformity

Spec	Name	St	Pg
ChiN	Keating, G	MN	148
N	Kula, R	NY	517
NS	Butler, W	MA	472
NS	Ellenbogen, R	WA	499
NS	Feldstein, N	NY	476
NS	Frim, D	IL	490
NS	Jallo, G	MD	478
NS	Luken, M	IL	491
NS	Oakes, W	AL	486
NS	Piatt, J	DE	480
NS	Selden, N	OR	502
NS	Shuer, L	CA	502
NS	Weingart, J	MD	483

Child & Adolescent Psychiatry

Spec	Name	St	Pg
ChAP	Abright, A	NY	939
ChAP	Alessi, N	MI	941
ChAP	Biederman, J	MA	938
ChAP	Birmaher, B	PA	939
ChAP	Bleiberg, E	TX	943
ChAP	Bogrov, M	MD	939
ChAP	Brent, D	PA	939
ChAP	Campo, J	OH	941
ChAP	Coffey, B	NY	939
ChAP	Deas, D	SC	941

Spec	Name	St	Pg
ChAP	Dulcan, M	IL	942
ChAP	Emslie, G	TX	943
ChAP	Foley, C	NY	940
ChAP	Fornari, V	NY	940
ChAP	Hagman, J	CO	942
ChAP	Heston, J	TN	941
ChAP	Hirsch, G	NY	940
ChAP	Hirsch, S	IL	942
ChAP	Hudziak, J	VT	938
ChAP	King, B	WA	943
ChAP	Koplewicz, H	NY	940
ChAP	Kwon, H	WA	943
ChAP	Leckman, J	CT	938
ChAP	Leventhal, B	NY	940
ChAP	Luby, J	MO	942
ChAP	Martini, D	UT	942
ChAP	McCracken, J	CA	943
ChAP	McDougle, C	MA	938
ChAP	McKelvey, R	OR	943
ChAP	Pomeroy, J	NY	940
ChAP	Ponton, L	CA	943
ChAP	Riddle, M	MD	940
ChAP	Rostain, A	PA	940
ChAP	Sargent, A	MA	938
ChAP	Sexson, S	GA	941
ChAP	Slomowitz, M	IL	942
ChAP	Spencer, T	MA	939
ChAP	Steiner, H	CA	944
ChAP	Turecki, S	NY	941
ChAP	Walkup, J	NY	941
ChAP	Wamboldt, M	CO	942
ChAP	Wilens, T	MA	939
ChAP	Zeanah, C	LA	943
Psyc	Fox, G	IL	929

Child Abuse

Spec	Name	St	Pg
Ped	Berkowitz, C	CA	742
Ped	Feldman, K	WA	742

Child Neurology

Spec	Name	St	Pg
ChiN	Allen, J	NY	145
ChiN	Ashwal, S	CA	151
ChiN	Bale, J	UT	150
ChiN	Bergman, I	PA	145
ChiN	Brunstrom-Hernandez, J	MO	148
ChiN	Cohen, B	OH	148
ChiN	Crawford, T	MD	145
ChiN	Darras, B	MA	144
ChiN	DeVivo, D	NY	145
ChiN	Dure, L	AL	147
ChiN	Edgar, T	WI	148
ChiN	Epstein, L	IL	148
ChiN	Filipek, P	TX	150
ChiN	Finkel, R	FL	147
ChiN	Fisher, P	CA	151
ChiN	Gospe, S	WA	151
ChiN	Greenwood, R	NC	147
ChiN	Griesemer, D	MA	144
ChiN	Haas, R	CA	151
ChiN	Hartman, A	MD	145
ChiN	Hershey, A	OH	148
ChiN	Holmes, G	VT	144
ChiN	Iannaccone, S	TX	150
ChiN	Ichord, R	PA	145
ChiN	Keating, G	MN	148
ChiN	Kohrman, M	IL	148
ChiN	Kosofsky, B	NY	145
ChiN	Kotagal, S	MN	149
ChiN	Kovnar, E	WI	149
ChiN	Lavenstein, B	VA	147
ChiN	Legido, A	PA	145
ChiN	Lott, I	CA	151
ChiN	Mandelbaum, D	RI	144
ChiN	Maytal, J	NY	146
ChiN	Mink, J	NY	146
ChiN	Mitchell, W	CA	151
ChiN	Nass, R	NY	146
ChiN	Noetzel, M	MO	149
ChiN	Nordli, D	IL	149
ChiN	Packer, R	DC	146
ChiN	Patterson, M	MN	149
ChiN	Phillips, P	PA	146
ChiN	Pinter, J	OR	151
ChiN	Pomeroy, S	MA	144
ChiN	Riviello, J	NY	146
ChiN	Roddy, S	CA	152
ChiN	Rosser, T	CA	152
ChiN	Sahin, M	MA	144
ChiN	Sankar, R	CA	152
ChiN	Santos, C	DC	146
ChiN	Scher, M	OH	149
ChiN	Sharp, G	AR	151
ChiN	Shaywitz, B	CT	144
ChiN	Shinnar, S	NY	147
ChiN	Sivaswamy, L	MI	149
ChiN	Tennison, M	NC	147
ChiN	Tonsgard, J	IL	149
ChiN	Trauner, D	CA	152
ChiN	Tuxhorn, I	OH	150
ChiN	Wheless, J	TN	147
ChiN	Wiznitzer, M	OH	150
ChiN	Wyllie, E	OH	150
ChiN	Yamada, K	MO	150
ChiN	Zupanc, M	CA	152
N	Bebin, E	AL	523

Choanal Atresia

Spec	Name	St	Pg
PO	Ward, R	NY	803

Cholesteatoma

Spec	Name	St	Pg
Oto	Feghali, J	NY	669
Oto	Lambert, P	SC	679
Oto	Linstrom, C	NY	673
Oto	Young, N	IL	689
PO	McGill, T	MA	801

Cholesterol/Lipid Discorders

Spec	Name	St	Pg
Cv	Thompson, P	CT	90

Cholesterol/Lipid Disorders

Spec	Name	St	Pg
Cv	Anderson, J	UT	107
Cv	Ballantyne, C	TX	107
Cv	Borzak, S	FL	97
Cv	Budoff, M	CA	110
Cv	Califf, R	NC	97
Cv	Davidson, M	IL	101
Cv	Edmundowicz, D	PA	92
Cv	Fintel, D	IL	101
Cv	Gardin, J	NJ	93
Cv	Goodman, D	NY	93
Cv	Gould, K	TX	108
Cv	Hayes, S	MN	102
Cv	Herling, I	PA	94
Cv	Inra, L	NY	94
Cv	Judelson, D	CA	111
Cv	Kostis, J	NJ	94
Cv	Liao, J	IL	103
Cv	Linton, M	TN	98
Cv	Nissen, S	OH	103
Cv	Ridker, P	MA	90
Cv	Shah, P	CA	112
Cv	Stein, J	WI	105
Cv	Zusman, R	MA	90
EDM	Blum, C	NY	211
EDM	Eckel, R	CO	222
EDM	Inzucchi, S	CT	209
EDM	Mazzone, T	IL	220
EDM	Semenkovich, C	MO	221
EDM	Seplowitz, A	NY	214
EDM	Sowers, J	MO	221
IM	Cushman, W	TN	426
IM	Rader, D	PA	426
PrM	Pearson, T	FL	913

Chromosome Disorders

Spec	Name	St	Pg
CG	Carey, J	UT	161

Chronic Fatigue Syndrome

Spec	Name	St	Pg
Inf	Cunha, B	NY	413
Inf	Gorensek, M	FL	416
PInf	Krilov, L	NY	793

Chronic Illness

Spec	Name	St	Pg
AM	Slap, G	PA	76
IM	Galland, L	NY	426

Chronic Lung Disease

Spec	Name	St	Pg
PPul	Dovey, M	PA	806
PPul	Kattan, M	NY	807

Chronic Lung Disease of Infancy

Spec	Name	St	Pg
PPul	Sallent, J	FL	808

Chronic Obstructive Lung

Disease (COPD)

Spec	Name	St	Pg
PPul	Panitch, H	PA	807
Pul	Arcasoy, S	NY	956
Pul	Celli, B	MA	954
Pul	Christman, B	TN	961
Pul	Cooper, J	AL	961
Pul	Cooper, W	VA	961
Pul	Criner, G	PA	956
Pul	Deitz, J	PA	957
Pul	Doherty, D	KY	961
Pul	Donahoe, M	PA	957
Pul	Donohue, J	NC	962
Pul	Fahey, P	IL	964
Pul	Fanta, C	MA	954
Pul	Fletcher, E	IN	964
Pul	Fulkerson, W	NC	962
Pul	Guidry, G	LA	969
Pul	Hansen-Flaschen, J	PA	957
Pul	Haynes, J	AL	962
Pul	Henke, D	NC	962
Pul	Hyers, T	MO	965
Pul	Irwin, R	MA	955
Pul	Kaye, M	MN	965
Pul	Levin, D	OK	969
Pul	Libby, D	NY	957
Pul	Mahler, D	NH	955
Pul	Marini, J	MN	965
Pul	Martin, R	CO	968
Pul	Matuschak, G	MO	966
Pul	Mosenifar, Z	CA	971
Pul	Perret, P	LA	969
Pul	Rennard, S	NE	968
Pul	Rochester, C	CT	955
Pul	Sahn, S	SC	963
Pul	Silver, M	IL	966
Pul	Staton, G	GA	963
Pul	Sutherland, E	CO	968
Pul	Thomashow, B	NY	960
Pul	Tino, G	PA	960
Pul	Tobin, M	IL	967
Pul	Villanueva, A	MA	955

Cleft Palate/Lip

Spec	Name	St	Pg
CG	Saal, H	OH	160
Oto	Kriet, J	KS	690
Oto	Senders, C	CA	697
PlS	Ascherman, J	NY	880
PlS	Baker, S	DC	880
PlS	Bauer, B	IL	892
PlS	Billmire, D	OH	893
PlS	Boyajian, M	DC	881
PlS	Bradley, J	CA	901
PlS	Dagum, A	NY	881
PlS	Georgiade, G	NC	889
PlS	Glat, P	PA	882
PlS	Gruss, J	WA	902
PlS	Hoffman, W	CA	903
PlS	Kane, A	TX	899
PlS	Kelly, K	TN	890
PlS	Kirschner, R	OH	894
PlS	Leighton, W	AZ	899
PlS	Losee, J	PA	884
PlS	Low, D	PA	884
PlS	Mackay, D	PA	884
PlS	Magee, W	VA	890
PlS	Marsh, J	MO	894
PlS	Matthews, D	NC	891
PlS	Meara, J	MA	878
PlS	Mulliken, J	MA	878
PlS	Napoli, J	DE	885
PlS	Neumeister, M	IL	895
PlS	Patel, P	IL	895
PlS	Seyfer, A	MD	886
PlS	Staffenberg, D	NY	887
PlS	Stotland, M	NH	879
PlS	Taub, P	NY	887
PlS	Vander Kolk, C	MD	888
PlS	Wells, J	CA	906
PlS	Yu, J	GA	892
PO	Duncan, N	TX	805
PO	Haddad, J	NY	802
PO	Ward, R	NY	803

Clinical Genetics

Spec	Name	St	Pg
CG	Andersson, H	LA	161
CG	Anyane-Yeboa, K	NY	156
CG	Bale, A	CT	156
CG	Bartholomew, D	OH	160
CG	Bialer, M	NY	157
CG	Bianchi, D	MA	156
CG	Boles, R	CA	162
CG	Burton, B	IL	160
CG	Carey, J	UT	161
CG	Cassidy, S	CA	162
CG	Charrow, J	IL	160
CG	Chung, W	NY	157
CG	Craigen, W	TX	161
CG	Cunniff, C	AZ	161
CG	Curry, C	CA	162
CG	Davis, J	NY	157
CG	Desnick, R	NY	157
CG	Desposito, F	NJ	157
CG	Driscoll, D	FL	159
CG	Driscoll, D	PA	157
CG	Falk, R	CA	162
CG	Gilbert, F	NY	157
CG	Graham, J	CA	162
CG	Grody, W	CA	163
CG	Hainline, B	IN	160
CG	Holmes, L	MA	156
CG	Hoyme, H	SD	161
CG	Hudgins, L	CA	163
CG	Jayakar, P	FL	159
CG	Jonas, A	CA	163
CG	Jones, M	CA	163
CG	Korf, B	AL	159
CG	Kronn, D	NY	158
CG	Mahoney, M	CT	156
CG	Marion, R	NY	158
CG	Morris, C	NV	163
CG	Mulvihill, J	OK	161
CG	Northrup, H	TX	162
CG	Nussbaum, R	CA	163
CG	Ostrer, H	NY	158
CG	Pauker, S	MA	156
CG	Pergament, E	IL	160
CG	Plon, S	TX	162
CG	Pyeritz, R	PA	158
CG	Randolph, L	CA	163
CG	Rosenbaum, K	DC	158
CG	Saal, H	OH	160
CG	Seashore, M	CT	156
CG	Seaver, L	HI	163
CG	Shoffner, J	GA	159
CG	Shulman, L	IL	160
CG	Stevenson, R	SC	159
CG	Sutphen, R	FL	159
CG	Ward, J	TN	159
CG	Wasserstein, M	NY	158
CG	Weaver, D	IN	160
CG	Weitzel, J	CA	164
CG	Whelan, A	MO	161
CG	Wilcox, W	CA	164
CG	Zackai, E	PA	158

Clinical Neurophysiology

Spec	Name	St	Pg
N	Bertorini, T	TN	523

Clinical Trials

Spec	Name	St	Pg
A&I	Spector, S	CA	86
AM	Anderson, M	CA	78
ChiN	Santos, C	DC	146
Cv	Fonarow, G	CA	110
D	Bowen, G	UT	197
D	Gottlieb, A	MA	185
EDM	Ahmann, A	OR	223
EDM	Brillon, D	NY	211
Ge	Gish, R	CA	256
Ge	Greenwald, B	MD	235
Ge	Hanauer, S	IL	248
Ge	Okolo, P	MD	238
GO	Chan, J	CA	290
GO	Cornelison, T	MD	277
GO	Creasman, W	SC	281
GO	Edwards, R	PA	278
GO	Ghamande, S	GA	281
GO	Mannel, R	OK	289
GO	Moore, D	IN	285
GO	Odunsi, A	NY	279
GO	Stehman, F	IN	286
GO	Teng, N	CA	292
Hem	Djulbegovic, B	FL	319
Hem	Garcia-Manero, G	TX	326
Hem	Grever, M	OH	322
Hem	Jurcic, J	NY	314
Hem	Komrokji, R	FL	319
Hem	Kraut, E	OH	322
Hem	Maslak, P	NY	315
Hem	Nademanee, A	CA	329
Hem	O'Donnell, M	CA	329
Hem	Slease, R	DE	317
Hem	Stewart, A	AZ	327
Hem	Streiff, M	MD	317
IC	Gibson, C	MA	120
IC	Kandzari, D	GA	124

Spec	Name	St	Pg
IM	Fischl, M	FL	426
Inf	Mildvan, D	NY	414
Inf	Saag, M	AL	416
N	Aiken, R	IL	527
N	Albers, G	CA	538
N	Calabresi, P	MD	514
N	Chamberlain, M	WA	539
N	Cummings, J	NV	539
N	DeAngelis, L	NY	514
N	Janss, A	GA	525
N	Lipton, R	NY	518
N	Mitsumoto, H	NY	519
N	Newton, H	OH	531
N	Pennell, P	MA	511
N	Wolinsky, J	TX	538
NS	Brem, S	PA	475
NS	Levy, E	NY	479
NS	Markert, J	AL	485
NS	Sampson, J	NC	487
NS	Shaffrey, M	VA	487
NS	Yu, J	CA	502
Onc	Abbruzzese, J	TX	378
Onc	Abraham, J	OH	365
Onc	Advani, R	CA	384
Onc	Akerley, W	UT	375
Onc	Arun, B	TX	378
Onc	Audeh, M	CA	385
Onc	Bajorin, D	NY	338
Onc	Bernard, S	NC	355
Onc	Birrer, M	MA	330
Onc	Blackwell, K	NC	355
Onc	Blobe, G	NC	355
Onc	Bunn, P	CO	376
Onc	Burris, H	TN	356
Onc	Carducci, M	MD	339
Onc	Celano, P	MD	339
Onc	Chang, J	TX	379
Onc	Chap, L	CA	386
Onc	Chapman, P	NY	339
Onc	Chu, E	PA	339
Onc	Cohen, R	PA	340
Onc	Czuczman, M	NY	341
Onc	Dickler, M	NY	341
Onc	Disis, M	WA	386
Onc	Ellis, G	WA	387
Onc	Ensminger, W	MI	369
Onc	Estey, E	WA	387
Onc	Ettinger, D	MD	342
Onc	Fine, R	NY	342
Onc	Flaherty, K	MA	331
Onc	Flynn, P	MN	369
Onc	Friedberg, J	NY	343
Onc	Garst, J	NC	358
Onc	Geyer, C	VA	358
Onc	Gold, P	WA	388
Onc	Haas, N	PA	344
Onc	Hauke, R	NE	377
Onc	Herbst, R	CT	332
Onc	Holcombe, R	NY	345
Onc	Hortobagyi, G	TX	380
Onc	Horwitz, S	NY	345
Onc	Hwu, P	TX	380
Onc	Jahanzeb, M	FL	359

Spec	Name	St	Pg
Onc	Kaminski, M	MI	370
Onc	Kaufman, P	NH	333
Onc	Kohn, E	MD	346
Onc	Kraft, A	SC	359
Onc	Limentani, S	NC	360
Onc	Marcom, P	NC	361
Onc	Mitsuyasu, R	CA	390
Onc	Mortimer, J	CA	390
Onc	O'Connor, O	NY	348
Onc	O'Regan, R	GA	362
Onc	Orlowski, R	TX	382
Onc	Perez, E	FL	362
Onc	Perry, D	DC	350
Onc	Pinto, H	CA	391
Onc	Ready, N	NC	363
Onc	Remick, S	WV	350
Onc	Robert-Vizcarrondo, F	AL	363
Onc	Schuchter, L	PA	351
Onc	Serody, J	NC	363
Onc	Sotomayor, E	FL	364
Onc	Triozzi, P	OH	374
Onc	Tripathy, D	CA	393
Onc	Trump, D	NY	353
Onc	Vahdat, L	NY	353
Onc	Wolchok, J	NY	354
Onc	Wolff, R	TX	384
Onc	Worden, F	MI	375
Path	Wilczynski, S	CA	735
Ped Uro	Greenfield, S	NY	825
PEn	DiMeglio, L	IN	760
PGe	Dubinsky, M	CA	768
PHO	Adamson, P	PA	771
PHO	Blaney, S	TX	787
PHO	Brecher, M	NY	771
PHO	Bruggers, C	UT	786
PHO	Cheung, N	NY	772
PHO	Croop, J	IN	782
PHO	Cunningham, J	IL	782
PHO	Goldman, S	IL	783
PHO	Halligan, G	PA	774
PHO	Jakacki, R	PA	774
PHO	Kreissman, S	NC	779
PHO	Maris, J	PA	775
PHO	Neuberg, R	SC	780
PHO	Razzouk, B	IN	785
PHO	Rheingold, S	PA	776
PHO	Ritchey, A	PA	776
PHO	Rosenthal, J	CA	791
PHO	Santana, V	TN	781
PHO	van Hoff, J	NH	771
PInf	Bradley, J	CA	797
PInf	Bryson, Y	CA	797
PInf	Edwards, K	TN	794
PInf	Flynn, P	TN	794
PPul	Borowitz, D	NY	806
Psyc	Mann, J	NY	926
Psyc	Mitchell, J	ND	931
Psyc	Weisler, R	NC	928
Pul	Brown, K	CO	967
RadRO	Blackstock, A	NC	983
RadRO	Bogart, J	NY	978
RadRO	Bradley, J	MO	988
RadRO	Kupelian, P	CA	996

Spec	Name	St	Pg
RadRO	Le, Q	CA	996
RadRO	McGarry, R	KY	986
RadRO	Willett, C	NC	987
Rhu	Wofsy, D	CA	1068
S	Averbook, B	OH	1111
S	Geller, D	PA	1093
S	Julian, T	PA	1095
S	Leeming, R	OH	1116
S	Lowy, A	CA	1134
S	Meric-Bernstam, F	TX	1127
S	Olson, J	MD	1097
S	Ramanathan, R	PA	1099
S	Sauter, E	TX	1128
S	Willey, S	DC	1102
S	Yang, J	MD	1102
T&CS	Pass, H	NY	1157
T&CS	Philpott, J	VA	1164
U	Crawford, E	CO	1207
U	Keane, T	SC	1198
U	Moul, J	NC	1199
U	Shabsigh, R	NY	1195
VIR	Wood, B	MD	1029

Clinical Trials Only

Onc	Arlen, P	MD	337
Onc	Gulley, J	MD	344

Clostridium Difficile Disease

Ge	Brandt, L	NY	233
Ge	La Mont, J	MA	231
Ge	Surawicz, C	WA	257

Clotting Disorders in Pregnancy

MF	Paidas, M	CT	432

Clubfoot

OrS	Aronson, J	AR	647
OrS	Beaty, J	TN	635
OrS	Davidson, R	PA	622
OrS	Herzenberg, J	MD	626
OrS	Morcuende, J	IA	643

Clubfoot/Foot Deformities in Children

OrS	Hyman, J	NY	626

Coarctation of the Aorta

PCd	Hijazi, Z	IL	753
PCd	Moskowitz, W	VA	751

Cocaine Addiction

AdP	Kampman, K	PA	937
AdP	Kleber, H	NY	937
AdP	Kosten, T	TX	938
AdP	Serota, R	PA	937

Coccidioidomycosis

Spec	Name	St	Pg
Inf	Bayer, A	CA	420
Pul	Catanzaro, A	CA	970

Cochlear Implants

Spec	Name	St	Pg
Oto	Arriaga, M	LA	691
Oto	Arts, H	MI	682
Oto	Beatty, C	MN	683
Oto	Driscoll, C	MN	684
Oto	Gantz, B	IA	685
Oto	Hammerschlag, P	NY	670
Oto	Hirsch, B	PA	670
Oto	Hoffman, R	NY	671
Oto	Jenkins, H	CO	690
Oto	Kang, D	NE	690
Oto	Kveton, J	CT	666
Oto	Lalwani, A	NY	672
Oto	Lambert, P	SC	679
Oto	Linstrom, C	NY	673
Oto	Lustig, L	CA	696
Oto	Macias, J	AZ	693
Oto	Mattox, D	GA	679
Oto	McMenomey, S	NY	673
Oto	Miyamoto, R	IN	686
Oto	Niparko, J	CA	696
Oto	O'Leary, M	CA	696
Oto	Pillsbury, H	NC	680
Oto	Roland, J	NY	674
Oto	Rubinstein, J	WA	696
Oto	Shelton, C	UT	690
Oto	Telian, S	MI	688
Oto	Telischi, F	FL	681
Oto	Tucci, D	NC	682
Oto	Wackym, P	OR	697
Oto	Wiet, R	IL	688
Oto	Young, N	IL	689
PO	Arjmand, E	OH	803
PO	Kazahaya, K	PA	802
PO	Lusk, R	NE	805
PO	O'Reilly, R	DE	802
PO	Poe, D	MA	801
PO	Rosbe, K	CA	806

Cognitive Impairment-Mild

Spec	Name	St	Pg
Psyc	Arnold, S	PA	922

Cognitive Impairment/Mild

Spec	Name	St	Pg
N	Petersen, R	MN	532

Cognitive Loss in Aging

Spec	Name	St	Pg
Ger	Raji, M	TX	267
GerPsy	Reisberg, B	NY	944

Cognitive Psychotherapy

Spec	Name	St	Pg
ChAP	Alessi, N	MI	941
Psyc	Eisendrath, S	CA	933
Psyc	Gabbard, G	TX	932
Psyc	Goldberg, J	CT	920

Colon & Rectal Cancer

Spec	Name	St	Pg
CRS	Beart, R	CA	177
CRS	Beck, D	LA	176
CRS	Birnbaum, E	MO	173
CRS	Bleday, R	MA	168
CRS	Church, J	OH	173
CRS	Delaney, C	OH	173
CRS	Dietz, D	OH	173
CRS	Efron, J	MD	169
CRS	Fleshman, J	TX	176
CRS	Foley, E	WI	173
CRS	Fry, R	PA	169
CRS	Galandiuk, S	KY	171
CRS	Goldstein, S	PA	170
CRS	Golub, R	FL	172
CRS	Guillem, J	NY	170
CRS	Haas, E	TX	176
CRS	Harnsberger, J	NH	168
CRS	Heppell, J	AZ	177
CRS	Hicks, T	LA	177
CRS	Huber, P	TX	177
CRS	Hyman, N	VT	168
CRS	Lavery, I	OH	173
CRS	Lederman, E	MO	173
CRS	Longo, W	CT	168
CRS	Madoff, R	MN	174
CRS	Marcet, J	FL	172
CRS	Marks, J	PA	170
CRS	Medich, D	PA	170
CRS	Mutch, M	MO	174
CRS	Nagle, D	MA	168
CRS	Nelson, H	MN	174
CRS	Nogueras, J	FL	172
CRS	Orkin, B	IL	174
CRS	Pello, M	NJ	170
CRS	Pemberton, J	MN	174
CRS	Procaccino, J	NY	171
CRS	Rafferty, J	OH	174
CRS	Ramamoorthy, S	CA	178
CRS	Read, T	MA	168
CRS	Roberts, P	MA	169
CRS	Sands, L	FL	172
CRS	Schoetz, D	MA	169
CRS	Senagore, A	MI	175
CRS	Shah, N	RI	169
CRS	Shellito, P	MA	169
CRS	Stamos, M	CA	178
CRS	Stryker, S	IL	175
CRS	Thorson, A	NE	176
CRS	Trudel, J	MN	175
CRS	Vernava, A	FL	172
CRS	Weiser, M	NY	171
CRS	Welton, M	CA	178
CRS	Wexner, S	FL	172
CRS	Whelan, R	NY	171
CRS	Wolff, B	MN	175
CRS	Worsey, M	CA	178
CRS	Young-Fadok, T	AZ	177
Ge	Cohen, L	NY	233
Ge	Goldberg, M	IL	247
Ge	Itzkowitz, S	NY	236
Onc	Blobe, G	NC	355
Onc	Chu, E	PA	339
Onc	Conry, R	AL	357
Onc	Eckhardt, S	CO	376
Onc	Engstrom, P	PA	342
Onc	Fakih, M	CA	387
Onc	Flynn, P	MN	369
Onc	Ford, J	CA	387
Onc	Goldberg, R	OH	369
Onc	Grem, J	NE	377
Onc	Gruber, S	CA	388
Onc	Hageboutros, A	NJ	344
Onc	Hochster, H	CT	332
Onc	Ilson, D	NY	345
Onc	Krishnamurthi, S	OH	371
Onc	Lacy, J	CT	333
Onc	Markowitz, S	OH	371
Onc	Mayer, R	MA	334
Onc	Messersmith, W	CO	377
Onc	O'Brien, T	OH	372
Onc	O'Reilly, E	NY	348
Onc	Pasche, B	AL	362
Onc	Patt, Y	NM	382
Onc	Saif, M	MA	334
Onc	Saltz, L	NY	350
Onc	Steen, P	ND	377
Onc	Venook, A	CA	394
Onc	Willson, J	TX	384
Onc	Wolff, R	TX	384
RadRO	Minsky, B	TX	994
RadRO	Thomas, C	OR	998
S	Cance, W	NY	1090
S	Curley, S	TX	1124
S	Cusack, J	MA	1084
S	Ellis, L	TX	1124
S	Howe, J	IA	1115
S	Newman, E	NY	1097
S	Paty, P	NY	1098
S	Shibata, D	FL	1109
S	Sigurdson, E	PA	1101
S	Sinanan, M	WA	1137
S	Tanabe, K	MA	1088

Colon & Rectal Cancer & Surgery

Spec	Name	St	Pg
CRS	Ludwig, K	WI	174
CRS	Mantyh, C	NC	172
CRS	Medwell, S	WA	178
CRS	Milsom, J	NY	170
CRS	Remzi, F	OH	175
CRS	Schatz, L	CO	176
CRS	Sokol, T	CA	178
CRS	Stein, D	PA	171
CRS	Steinhagen, R	NY	171
CRS	Varma, M	CA	178
CRS	Wise, P	MO	175
S	Lieberman, M	NY	1096
S	Schraut, W	PA	1100
S	Zinner, M	MA	1088

Colon & Rectal Cancer Detection

Spec	Name	St	Pg
Ge	Boland, C	TX	253

Spec	Name	St	Pg
Ge	Butterly, L	NH	230
Ge	Early, D	MO	247
Ge	Farraye, F	MA	230
Ge	Itzkowitz, S	NY	236
Ge	Levine, J	CO	252
Ge	Pochapin, M	NY	239
Ge	Rex, D	IN	250
Ge	Scudera, P	VA	244
Ge	Smoot, D	TN	245

Colon & Rectal Cancer Risk

Spec	Name	St	Pg
CG	Whelan, A	MO	161

Colon & Rectal Cancer-Familial Polyposis

Spec	Name	St	Pg
CRS	Church, J	OH	173
CRS	Mantyh, C	NC	172
CRS	Procaccino, J	NY	171
CRS	Vernava, A	FL	172
Ge	Butterly, L	NH	230
Ge	Chung, D	MA	230
Ge	Giardiello, F	MD	234
Ge	Hoffman, B	SC	243
Ge	Schembre, D	WA	257
S	Skibber, J	TX	1129

Colon & Rectal Cancer-Hereditary

Spec	Name	St	Pg
CRS	Gearhart, S	MD	170
CRS	Guillem, J	NY	170
CRS	Wise, P	MO	175

Colon & Rectal Surgery

Spec	Name	St	Pg
CRS	Abcarian, H	IL	173
CRS	Bailey, H	TX	176
CRS	Beart, R	CA	177
CRS	Beck, D	LA	176
CRS	Beck, S	KY	171
CRS	Birnbaum, E	MO	173
CRS	Blatchford, G	NE	175
CRS	Bleday, R	MA	168
CRS	Chiu, Y	CA	177
CRS	Church, J	OH	173
CRS	Coutsoftides, T	CA	177
CRS	Delaney, C	OH	173
CRS	Dietz, D	OH	173
CRS	Efron, J	MD	169
CRS	Eisenstat, T	NJ	169
CRS	Fleshman, J	TX	176
CRS	Foley, E	WI	173
CRS	Fry, R	PA	169
CRS	Galandiuk, S	KY	171
CRS	Gearhart, S	MD	170
CRS	Goldstein, S	PA	170
CRS	Golub, R	FL	172
CRS	Gorfine, S	NY	170
CRS	Guillem, J	NY	170
CRS	Haas, E	TX	176
CRS	Hackford, A	MA	168
CRS	Harnsberger, J	NH	168
CRS	Hartmann, R	FL	172
CRS	Heppell, J	AZ	177
CRS	Hicks, T	LA	177
CRS	Huber, P	TX	177
CRS	Hyman, N	VT	168
CRS	Lavery, I	OH	173
CRS	Lederman, E	MO	173
CRS	Lee, P	OR	177
CRS	Longo, W	CT	168
CRS	Lowry, A	MN	174
CRS	Ludwig, K	WI	174
CRS	Madoff, R	MN	174
CRS	Mantyh, C	NC	172
CRS	Marcet, J	FL	172
CRS	Marks, J	PA	170
CRS	Medich, D	PA	170
CRS	Medwell, S	WA	178
CRS	Milsom, J	NY	170
CRS	Mutch, M	MO	174
CRS	Nagle, D	MA	168
CRS	Nelson, H	MN	174
CRS	Nogueras, J	FL	172
CRS	Orkin, B	IL	174
CRS	Pello, M	NJ	170
CRS	Pemberton, J	MN	174
CRS	Procaccino, J	NY	171
CRS	Rafferty, J	OH	174
CRS	Ramamoorthy, S	CA	178
CRS	Read, T	MA	168
CRS	Remzi, F	OH	175
CRS	Roberts, P	MA	169
CRS	Saclarides, T	IL	175
CRS	Sands, L	FL	172
CRS	Schatz, L	CO	176
CRS	Schoetz, D	MA	169
CRS	Senagore, A	MI	175
CRS	Shah, N	RI	169
CRS	Shellito, P	MA	169
CRS	Sokol, T	CA	178
CRS	Stamos, M	CA	178
CRS	Stein, D	PA	171
CRS	Steinhagen, R	NY	171
CRS	Stryker, S	IL	175
CRS	Thorson, A	NE	176
CRS	Trudel, J	MN	175
CRS	Varma, M	CA	178
CRS	Vernava, A	FL	172
CRS	Weiser, M	NY	171
CRS	Welton, M	CA	178
CRS	Wexner, S	FL	172
CRS	Whelan, R	NY	171
CRS	Williams, S	ID	176
CRS	Wise, P	MO	175
CRS	Wolff, B	MN	175
CRS	Wong, R	HI	178
CRS	Worsey, M	CA	178
CRS	Young-Fadok, T	AZ	177
PS	Pena, A	OH	820
S	Baker, C	VA	1103
S	Basson, M	MI	1111
S	Franklin, M	TX	1125
S	Hebert, J	VT	1085
S	Horvath, K	WA	1133
S	Howerton, R	NC	1106

Colon Cancer

Spec	Name	St	Pg
CRS	Blatchford, G	NE	175
CRS	Eisenstat, T	NJ	169
CRS	Hartmann, R	FL	172
DR	Dachman, A	IL	1014
Ge	Giardiello, F	MD	234
Ge	Raju, G	TX	254
Ge	Waye, J	NY	240
Onc	Benson, A	IL	366
Onc	Berlin, J	TN	355
Onc	De Simone, P	KY	357
Onc	Donehower, R	MD	341
Onc	Doroshow, J	MD	341
Onc	Hollister, D	CT	333
Onc	Kemeny, N	NY	346
Onc	Makhoul, I	AR	381
Onc	Meropol, N	OH	371
Onc	Nissenblatt, M	NJ	348
Onc	Posey, J	AL	362
Onc	Ryan, D	MA	334
Path	Morrow, J	CT	719
RadRO	Smalley, S	KS	992
S	Bentley, F	AR	1124
S	Calvo, B	NC	1104
S	Lillemoe, K	MA	1086
S	Mansfield, P	TX	1127
S	Michelassi, F	NY	1096
S	Pachter, H	NY	1097
S	Ramanathan, R	PA	1099
S	Saha, S	MI	1119
S	Salky, B	NY	1099
S	Schirmer, B	VA	1108

Colon Cancer Screening

Spec	Name	St	Pg
Ge	Albert, M	DC	232
Ge	Aronchick, C	PA	232
Ge	Borum, M	DC	233
Ge	Brazer, S	NC	241
Ge	Freiman, H	NY	234
Ge	Peikin, S	NJ	239
Ge	Proctor, D	CT	232
Ge	Vanagunas, A	IL	251
Ge	Yanda, R	GA	245

Colonoscopy

Spec	Name	St	Pg
CRS	Whelan, R	NY	171
Ge	Aronchick, C	PA	232
Ge	Branch, M	NC	241
Ge	Butterly, L	NH	230
Ge	Cello, J	CA	255
Ge	Chung, D	MA	230
Ge	Cohen, J	NY	233
Ge	Green, P	NY	235
Ge	Levine, J	CO	252
Ge	Lipshutz, W	PA	238
Ge	Ostroff, J	CA	257
Ge	Rex, D	IN	250

Spec	Name	St	Pg
Ge	Savides, T	CA	257
Ge	Siegel, C	NH	232
Ge	Waye, J	NY	240
Ge	Weinberg, D	PA	240

Complementary Medicine

Spec	Name	St	Pg
Cv	Goodman, D	NY	93
EDM	Dobs, A	MD	212
Ger	Bloom, P	NY	264
GO	Granai, C	RI	275
IM	Cirigliano, M	PA	426
IM	Galland, L	NY	426
Onc	Abrams, D	CA	384
Onc	Axelrod, R	PA	338
Onc	Rugo, H	CA	392
Oph	Ritch, R	NY	584
Ped	Zeltzer, L	CA	743
PHO	Rheingold, S	PA	776
PHO	Sencer, S	MN	785
PMR	Dillard, J	NY	863
U	Katz, A	NY	1191
U	Lowe, F	NY	1192

Complex Diagnosis

Spec	Name	St	Pg
ChiN	Bergman, I	PA	145
D	Bronin, A	NY	187
D	Jorizzo, J	NC	193
PCd	Mahony, L	TX	754
Ped	Zitelli, B	PA	741

Complex Regional Pain Syndromes

Spec	Name	St	Pg
N	Oaklander, A	MA	511
PM	Audell, L	CA	712
PM	Baumann, P	GA	708
PM	Benzon, H	IL	709
PM	Gharibo, C	NY	707
PM	Jain, S	NY	707
PM	Lubenow, T	IL	710
PM	Prager, J	CA	713
PM	Rauck, R	NC	709
PM	Richman, D	NY	708
PM	Rosenquist, R	OH	710
PM	Weisman, S	WI	711

Concussion

Spec	Name	St	Pg
N	Jordan, B	NY	516
N	Sabo, T	CO	535
NS	Sills, A	TN	487
PMR	Herring, S	WA	872

Congenital Absence of Vas Deferens

Spec	Name	St	Pg
U	Oates, R	MA	1187
U	Shaban, S	NC	1200

Congenital Anomalies

Spec	Name	St	Pg
NS	Mapstone, T	OK	497
Ped Uro	Gundeti, M	IL	827
PS	Arensman, R	IL	819
PS	Chwals, W	MA	814
PS	Dillon, P	MO	819
PS	Grikscheit, T	CA	823
PS	Healey, P	WA	823
PS	Holterman, M	IL	820
PS	McGill, L	AZ	822
PS	Morgan, W	TN	818
PS	Moss, R	OH	820
PS	Nance, M	PA	816
PS	Reynolds, M	IL	820
PS	Sato, T	WI	821
PS	Stylianos, S	NY	817
PS	Waldhausen, J	WA	824
T&CS	Ilbawi, M	IL	1169

Congenital Anomalies-Gastrointestinal

Spec	Name	St	Pg
PS	Alexander, F	NJ	815

Congenital Anomalies-Genitourinary

Spec	Name	St	Pg
PNep	Clardy, C	IL	799
PNep	Zilleruelo, G	FL	799

Congenital Anomalies-Gynecologic

Spec	Name	St	Pg
ObG	Laufer, M	MA	560
ObG	Merritt, D	MO	565
RE	Pfeifer, S	PA	1043

Congenital Anomalies-Limb

Spec	Name	St	Pg
CG	Hudgins, L	CA	163

Congenital Anomalies-Orthopaedic

Spec	Name	St	Pg
OrS	Pizzutillo, P	PA	630

Congenital Breast Anomalies

Spec	Name	St	Pg
PlS	Nichter, L	CA	904

Congenital Cranial Deformities

Spec	Name	St	Pg
NS	Luerssen, T	TX	496

Congenital Eye Disorders-Rare

Spec	Name	St	Pg
Oph	Masket, S	CA	607
Oph	Miller, K	CA	607

Congenital Fibrosis-Extraocular Muscles

Spec	Name	St	Pg
Oph	Hunter, D	MA	574

Congenital Hand Deformities

Spec	Name	St	Pg
HS	Godzik, C	CA	306
HS	Grossman, J	FL	301
HS	Kleinman, W	IN	303
HS	Kozin, S	PA	298
HS	Mih, A	IN	303

Congenital Heart Disease

Spec	Name	St	Pg
Cv	Byrd, B	TN	97
Cv	Connolly, H	MN	101
Cv	Fuster, V	NY	92
Cv	Kuvin, J	MA	89
DR	Flamm, S	OH	1014
IC	Bailey, S	TX	127
IC	Smalling, R	TX	128
PCCM	Easley, R	TX	755
PCd	Agarwala, B	IL	752
PCd	Bernstein, D	CA	754
PCd	Biancaniello, T	NY	748
PCd	Bierman, F	NY	748
PCd	Brenner, J	MD	748
PCd	Caldwell, R	IN	752
PCd	Cetta, F	MN	752
PCd	Cooper, R	NY	748
PCd	Dick, M	MI	752
PCd	Dreyer, W	TX	754
PCd	Feltes, T	OH	753
PCd	Fricker, F	FL	751
PCd	Hanna, B	PA	749
PCd	Hijazi, Z	IL	753
PCd	Mahony, L	TX	754
PCd	Newburger, J	MA	747
PCd	Pahl, E	IL	753
PCd	Parness, I	NY	749
PCd	Rocchini, A	MI	753
PCd	Rogers, J	TX	754
PCd	Rome, J	PA	749
PCd	Rychik, J	PA	749
PCd	Sommer, R	NY	750
PCd	Teitel, D	CA	755
PCd	Velvis, H	NY	750
PCd	Walsh, C	NY	750
PCd	Weinberg, P	PA	750
PCd	Zahn, E	CA	755
T&CS	Abraham, V	IN	1166
T&CS	Brown, J	IN	1167
T&CS	Del-Nido, P	MA	1146
T&CS	Harrell, J	TX	1174
T&CS	Ilbawi, M	IL	1169
T&CS	Jonas, R	DC	1154
T&CS	Kopf, G	CT	1147
T&CS	Mavroudis, C	FL	1163
T&CS	Schaff, H	MN	1171
T&CS	Tedder, M	TN	1166
T&CS	Turrentine, M	IN	1172
T&CS	Ziemer, G	IL	1172

Congenital Heart Disease-Adult

Spec	Name	St	Pg
CE	Mehta, D	NY	115
Cv	Bashore, T	NC	97
Cv	Johnson, A	CA	111
Cv	McPherson, D	TX	108
Cv	Webb, G	OH	106
Cv	Wells, G	NC	100
IC	Carroll, J	CO	127
IC	Resar, J	MD	123
PCd	Cetta, F	MN	752
PCd	Fish, F	TN	751
PCd	Hardin, J	IL	753
PCd	Hoyer, M	IN	753
T&CS	Backer, C	IL	1167
T&CS	Ilbawi, M	IL	1169
T&CS	Verrier, E	WA	1181

Congenital Heart Disease-Adult & Child

Spec	Name	St	Pg
DR	White, R	OH	1016
PCd	Beerman, L	PA	748
PCd	Cheatham, J	OH	752
PCd	Colvin, E	AL	751
PCd	Crosson, J	MD	748
PCd	Latson, L	FL	751
PCd	Moodie, D	TX	754
PCd	Moskowitz, W	VA	751
PCd	Radtke, W	DE	749
T&CS	Chen, J	NY	1151
T&CS	Mosca, R	NY	1157

Congenital Heart Surgery

Spec	Name	St	Pg
PS	Bove, E	MI	819
T&CS	Bacha, E	NY	1150
T&CS	Bailey, L	CA	1177
T&CS	Bichell, D	TN	1160
T&CS	Burke, R	FL	1161
T&CS	Calhoon, J	TX	1173
T&CS	Campbell, D	CO	1172
T&CS	Delius, R	MI	1168
T&CS	Drinkwater, D	TN	1162
T&CS	Fraser, C	TX	1174
T&CS	Gaynor, J	PA	1153
T&CS	Guyton, R	GA	1162
T&CS	Herrington, C	CA	1179
T&CS	Jamieson, S	CA	1179
T&CS	Kirklin, J	AL	1163
T&CS	Kirshbom, P	CT	1147
T&CS	Lamberti, J	CA	1179
T&CS	Mayer, J	MA	1148
T&CS	Mitchell, M	CO	1173
T&CS	Morales, D	OH	1170
T&CS	Quintessenza, J	FL	1165
T&CS	Rosenkranz, E	FL	1165
T&CS	Shemin, R	CA	1180
T&CS	Spray, T	PA	1159
T&CS	Ungerleider, R	NC	1166
T&CS	Warner, K	MA	1149
T&CS	Wells, W	CA	1181

Congenital Heart Surgery-Complex

Spec	Name	St	Pg
T&CS	Christian, K	TN	1161

Congenital Hemolytic Anemia

Spec	Name	St	Pg
PHO	Wolfe, L	NY	777

Congenital Hyperinsulinism

Spec	Name	St	Pg
PS	Adzick, N	PA	814

Congenital Infections

Spec	Name	St	Pg
PInf	Demmler-Harrison, G	TX	796

Congenital Kidney Disease

Spec	Name	St	Pg
PNep	Fouser, L	WA	801

Congenital Limb Deformities

Spec	Name	St	Pg
HS	Peljovich, A	GA	301
HS	Rayan, G	OK	305

Congenital Nervous System Malformations

Spec	Name	St	Pg
NS	Ellenbogen, R	WA	499
NS	Greene, C	LA	495
NS	Myseros, J	DC	480

Congenital Neutropenia-Severe

Spec	Name	St	Pg
PHO	Boxer, L	MI	782

Congenital Reproductive Anomalies

Spec	Name	St	Pg
PS	Graziano, K	AZ	822

Congestive Heart Failure

Spec	Name	St	Pg
Cv	Brozena, S	PA	91
Cv	Eisen, H	PA	92
Cv	Fishbein, D	WA	110
Cv	Geltman, E	MO	102
Cv	Jessup, M	PA	94
Cv	Johnson, A	CA	111
Cv	Johnson, M	WI	103
Cv	Kereiakes, D	OH	103
Cv	Kirshenbaum, J	MA	89
Cv	Kobashigawa, J	CA	111
Cv	Lewis, S	OR	111
Cv	Liang, B	CT	89
Cv	Lindenfeld, J	CO	107
Cv	Massin, E	TX	108
Cv	Rahko, P	WI	104
Cv	Reis, S	PA	95
Cv	Rogers, J	NC	99
Cv	Schwartz, W	NY	96
Cv	Smart, F	LA	109
Cv	Thames, M	AZ	109
Cv	Wagoner, L	OH	106
Cv	Walsh, M	IN	106
PCd	Mahony, L	TX	754

Conjoined Twins

Spec	Name	St	Pg
NP	Muraskas, J	IL	452
PS	Strauch, E	MD	817

Connective Tissue Disorders

Spec	Name	St	Pg
CG	Cassidy, S	CA	162
D	Werth, V	PA	191
Rhu	Chatham, W	AL	1063
Rhu	Oddis, C	PA	1061
Rhu	Paget, S	NY	1061
Rhu	Silver, R	SC	1064

Constipation

Spec	Name	St	Pg
CRS	Sokol, T	CA	178
Ge	Korsten, M	NY	237
Ge	Wald, A	WI	251
PGe	Bishop, W	IA	765

Contact Dermatitis

Spec	Name	St	Pg
D	Belsito, D	NY	186
D	Cohen, S	NY	187
D	DeLeo, V	NY	188
D	Elmets, C	AL	192
D	James, W	PA	189
D	Sherertz, E	SC	194

Continent Urinary Diversions

Spec	Name	St	Pg
U	Bahnson, R	OH	1202
U	Benson, M	NY	1189
U	Hall, S	NY	1190
U	Kozlowski, J	IL	1204
U	Sagalowsky, A	TX	1209

Cornea & External Eye Disease

Spec	Name	St	Pg
Oph	Abbott, R	CA	604
Oph	Carlson, A	NC	587
Oph	Lane, S	MN	596
Oph	Lass, J	OH	596
Oph	Mannis, M	CA	607
Oph	Mondino, B	CA	608
Oph	Perez, V	FL	591

Cornea Transplant

Spec	Name	St	Pg
Oph	Afshari, N	CA	604
Oph	Bouchard, C	IL	594
Oph	Carlson, A	NC	587
Oph	Florakis, G	NY	578
Oph	Gibralter, R	NY	579
Oph	Goldberg, D	NJ	579
Oph	Hersh, P	NJ	579
Oph	Maguire, L	MN	597
Oph	Manche, E	CA	607
Oph	McDonnell, P	MD	582

Spec	Name	St	Pg
Oph	Perez, V	FL	591
Oph	Shamie, N	CA	609
Oph	Sperber, L	NY	585
Oph	Starr, C	NY	585
Oph	Steinert, R	CA	609
Oph	Udell, I	NY	586

Cornea Transplant & Artificial Cornea

Spec	Name	St	Pg
Oph	Alfonso, E	FL	586
Oph	John, T	IL	596
Oph	Mannis, M	CA	607

Corneal & External Eye Disease

Spec	Name	St	Pg
Oph	Culbertson, W	FL	587
Oph	Dhaliwal, D	PA	577
Oph	Irvine, J	CA	606
Oph	McCulley, J	TX	602
Oph	Pepose, J	MO	598

Corneal Disease

Spec	Name	St	Pg
Oph	Durrie, D	KS	601
Oph	Feder, R	IL	595
Oph	Florakis, G	NY	578
Oph	Foster, C	MA	574
Oph	Holland, E	OH	595
Oph	Krueger, R	OH	596
Oph	Lindstrom, R	MN	597
Oph	Mandel, E	NY	581
Oph	McDonnell, P	MD	582
Oph	Pflugfelder, S	TX	603
Oph	Rapuano, C	PA	583
Oph	Smith, R	CA	609
Oph	Solomon, K	SC	591
Oph	Steinert, R	CA	609
Oph	Udell, I	NY	586
Oph	Wilson, S	OH	600

Corneal Disease & Surgery

Spec	Name	St	Pg
Oph	Alfonso, E	FL	586
Oph	Boxer Wachler, B	CA	604
Oph	Gibralter, R	NY	579
Oph	Katowitz, J	PA	580
Oph	Mackool, R	NY	581
Oph	Orlin, S	PA	583
Oph	Schein, O	MD	584
Oph	Starr, C	NY	585
Oph	Updegraff, S	FL	592

Corneal Disease & Transplant

Spec	Name	St	Pg
Oph	Asbell, P	NY	575
Oph	Braunstein, R	NY	576
Oph	Cykiert, R	NY	577
Oph	Dana, R	MA	574
Oph	Gorovoy, M	FL	588
Oph	Stark, W	MD	585
Oph	Stulting, R	GA	591

Corneal Disease-Pediatric

Spec	Name	St	Pg
Oph	Medow, N	NY	582

Corneal Ring Implants

Spec	Name	St	Pg
Oph	Sperber, L	NY	585

Coronary Angioplasty/Stents

Spec	Name	St	Pg
CE	Cohen, M	NY	114
Cv	Chizner, M	FL	98
Cv	Kereiakes, D	OH	103
Cv	Konstam, M	MA	89
Cv	Rosenbush, S	IL	104
IC	Lasala, J	MO	126
IC	Parikh, M	NY	122
IC	Petrossian, G	NY	123
IC	Roubin, G	NY	123
IC	Schreiber, T	MI	127
IC	Teirstein, P	CA	128

Coronary Artery Disease

Spec	Name	St	Pg
Cv	Alpert, J	AZ	107
Cv	Bass, T	FL	97
Cv	Blumenthal, D	NY	91
Cv	Bonow, R	IL	100
Cv	Borer, J	NY	91
Cv	Borzak, S	FL	97
Cv	Burket, M	OH	101
Cv	Califf, R	NC	97
Cv	Cerqueira, M	OH	101
Cv	Chizner, M	FL	98
Cv	Dichek, D	WA	110
Cv	Diver, D	CT	88
Cv	Elkayam, U	CA	110
Cv	Fintel, D	IL	101
Cv	French, W	CA	111
Cv	Fuster, V	NY	92
Cv	Inra, L	NY	94
Cv	Iskandrian, A	AL	98
Cv	Kaul, S	OR	111
Cv	Kirshenbaum, J	MA	89
Cv	Klein, L	IL	103
Cv	Kostis, J	NJ	94
Cv	Landzberg, J	NJ	94
Cv	Loscalzo, J	MA	89
Cv	Massin, E	TX	108
Cv	Mehlman, D	IL	103
Cv	Meller, J	NY	95
Cv	O'Gara, P	MA	89
Cv	Pepine, C	FL	99
Cv	Poon, M	NY	95
Cv	Powers, E	SC	99
Cv	Reiss, C	MO	104
Cv	Ridker, P	MA	90
Cv	Rihal, C	MN	104
Cv	Rosenbush, S	IL	104
Cv	Saunders, E	MD	95
Cv	Schwartz, W	NY	96
Cv	Shah, P	CA	112
Cv	Smith, S	NC	100
Cv	Stainback, R	TX	109
Cv	Tenenbaum, J	NY	96
Cv	Thames, M	AZ	109
Cv	Thompson, P	CT	90
Cv	Williams, K	MI	107
Cv	Zusman, R	MA	90
IC	Bailey, S	TX	127
IC	Carroll, J	CO	127
IC	Douglas, J	GA	124
IC	Fromkin, K	FL	124
IC	Gray, W	NY	122
IC	Lasala, J	MO	126
IC	Leya, F	IL	126
IC	Lopez, J	IL	126
IC	Smalling, R	TX	128
IC	Stone, G	NY	124
IC	Yeung, A	CA	128
NuM	Schelbert, H	CA	557

Coronary Artery Surgery

Spec	Name	St	Pg
T&CS	Acker, M	PA	1149
T&CS	Argenziano, M	NY	1150
T&CS	Boyd, W	CA	1177
T&CS	Caskey, M	AZ	1173
T&CS	Conte, J	MD	1151
T&CS	Damiano, R	MO	1167
T&CS	Fontana, G	NY	1152
T&CS	Galloway, A	NY	1153
T&CS	Graver, L	NY	1153
T&CS	Guyton, R	GA	1162
T&CS	Harken, A	CA	1178
T&CS	Hill, M	WA	1179
T&CS	Isom, O	NY	1154
T&CS	Jamieson, S	CA	1179
T&CS	Krieger, K	NY	1155
T&CS	Kron, I	VA	1163
T&CS	Lansman, S	NY	1156
T&CS	Lazar, H	MA	1147
T&CS	Lytle, B	OH	1170
T&CS	McCarthy, P	IL	1170
T&CS	Michler, R	NY	1156
T&CS	Morris, R	PA	1156
T&CS	Ott, D	TX	1175
T&CS	Pagani, F	MI	1171
T&CS	Quintessenza, J	FL	1165
T&CS	Salerno, T	FL	1165
T&CS	Sellke, F	RI	1148
T&CS	Shemin, R	CA	1180
T&CS	Smith, C	NY	1158
T&CS	Smith, P	NC	1165
T&CS	Swistel, D	NY	1159
T&CS	Toyoda, Y	PA	1159
T&CS	Tranbaugh, R	NY	1159
T&CS	Trento, A	CA	1180
T&CS	Turner, W	TX	1176

Coronary Syndrome-Acute

Spec	Name	St	Pg
Cv	Klein, L	IL	103

Cosmetic & Reconstructive

Surgery

Spec	Name	St	Pg
Oph	Ahmad, A	IL	593
Oph	McCann, J	UT	601
PlS	Derman, G	IL	893
PlS	Leighton, W	AZ	899
PlS	Low, D	PA	884
PlS	Persing, J	CT	879
PlS	Puckett, C	MO	896
PlS	Song, D	IL	896
PlS	Staffenberg, D	NY	887
PlS	Winters, R	NJ	888

Cosmetic & Reconstructive Surgery-Face

Spec	Name	St	Pg
Oto	Branham, G	MO	684
Oto	Graham, H	LA	692

Cosmetic Dermatology

Spec	Name	St	Pg
D	Arndt, K	MA	184
D	Avram, M	NY	186
D	Brandt, F	NY	187
D	Brody, H	GA	191
D	Crutchfield, C	MN	195
D	Dover, J	MA	184
D	Fewkes, J	MA	184
D	Fitzpatrick, R	CA	200
D	Geronemus, R	NY	188
D	Glogau, R	CA	200
D	Gordon, M	NY	188
D	Greenbaum, S	PA	188
D	Grimes, P	CA	201
D	Grossman, M	NY	188
D	Hanke, C	IN	195
D	Kilmer, S	CA	201
D	Lask, G	CA	201
D	Linder, J	AZ	199
D	Menter, M	TX	199
D	Neel, V	MA	185
D	Perone, J	TX	199
D	Rigel, D	NY	190
D	Rubin, M	CA	202
D	Schultz, N	NY	190
D	Sobel, S	FL	194
D	Sokoloff, D	FL	194
D	Swanson, N	OR	202
D	Wheeland, R	AZ	199

Cosmetic Surgery

Spec	Name	St	Pg
D	Hruza, G	MO	195
PlS	Ascherman, J	NY	880
PlS	Dumanian, G	IL	893
PlS	Grossman, J	CO	897
PlS	Hagan, K	TN	890
PlS	Hultman, C	NC	890
PlS	Isik, F	WA	903
PlS	Morgan, R	VA	891
PlS	Serletti, J	PA	886
PlS	Ting, J	NY	888
PlS	Tobin, G	KY	892
PlS	Vasconez, H	KY	892
PlS	Vogt, P	MN	896
PlS	Wilhelmi, B	KY	892
PlS	Wolfe, S	FL	892

Cosmetic Surgery-Breast

Spec	Name	St	Pg
PlS	Aston, S	NY	880
PlS	Barone, C	TX	898
PlS	Barton, F	TX	898
PlS	Bucky, L	PA	881
PlS	Burns, A	TX	898
PlS	Byrd, H	TX	898
PlS	Colen, L	VA	889
PlS	Da Lio, A	CA	902
PlS	Davis, G	NC	889
PlS	Erdmann, D	NC	889
PlS	Eriksson, E	MA	878
PlS	Evans, G	CA	902
PlS	Fisher, G	CA	902
PlS	Fodor, P	CA	902
PlS	Grant, R	NY	882
PlS	Grossman, J	CO	897
PlS	Hagan, K	TN	890
PlS	Hammond, D	MI	894
PlS	Hardesty, R	CA	903
PlS	Herman, C	PA	882
PlS	Hidalgo, D	NY	882
PlS	Horowitz, J	CA	903
PlS	Imber, G	NY	883
PlS	Isik, F	WA	903
PlS	Jewell, M	OR	903
PlS	Kenkel, J	TX	899
PlS	Kolker, A	NY	883
PlS	Leaf, N	CA	903
PlS	Leipziger, L	NY	883
PlS	Lesavoy, M	CA	904
PlS	Maxwell, G	TN	891
PlS	Medalie, D	OH	894
PlS	Metzinger, S	LA	900
PlS	Moses, M	LA	900
PlS	Mustoe, T	IL	895
PlS	Ness, J	MN	895
PlS	Nichter, L	CA	904
PlS	Paul, M	CA	904
PlS	Pitman, G	NY	885
PlS	Rand, R	WA	904
PlS	Romano, J	CA	905
PlS	Rosenberg, H	CA	905
PlS	Slezak, S	MD	886
PlS	Stevens, W	CA	905
PlS	Sullivan, P	RI	879
PlS	Sultan, M	NY	887
PlS	Talmor, M	NY	887
PlS	Tebbetts, J	TX	900
PlS	Vander Kolk, C	MD	888
PlS	Wilcox, R	TX	901

Cosmetic Surgery-Eyes

Spec	Name	St	Pg
Oph	Stefanyszyn, M	PA	585

Cosmetic Surgery-Face

Spec	Name	St	Pg
Oto	Beeson, W	IN	683
Oto	Denenberg, S	NE	690
Oto	Hom, D	OH	685
Oto	Hopping, S	DC	671
Oto	Johnson, C	LA	692
Oto	Keller, G	CA	695
Oto	Kriet, J	KS	690
Oto	Larrabee, W	WA	695
Oto	Moe, K	WA	696
Oto	Papel, I	MD	673
Oto	Ries, W	TN	680
Oto	Spiegel, J	MA	667
Oto	Szachowicz, E	MN	688
Oto	Toriumi, D	IL	688
PlS	Baker, D	NY	880
PlS	Baker, S	DC	880
PlS	Bartlett, S	PA	880
PlS	Barton, F	TX	898
PlS	Bradley, J	CA	901
PlS	Bucky, L	PA	881
PlS	Burns, A	TX	898
PlS	Burstein, F	GA	889
PlS	Byrd, H	TX	898
PlS	Carraway, J	VA	889
PlS	Cederna, P	MI	893
PlS	Cohen, S	CA	901
PlS	Colen, L	VA	889
PlS	Constantian, M	NH	878
PlS	Da Lio, A	CA	902
PlS	Dufresne, C	MD	882
PlS	Evans, G	CA	902
PlS	Fisher, G	CA	902
PlS	Fox, J	PA	882
PlS	Gregory, R	FL	890
PlS	Hamra, S	TX	899
PlS	Herman, C	PA	882
PlS	Hidalgo, D	NY	882
PlS	Hoffman, L	NY	882
PlS	Horowitz, J	CA	903
PlS	Hurwitz, D	PA	883
PlS	Imber, G	NY	883
PlS	Isik, F	WA	903
PlS	Jewell, M	OR	903
PlS	Kenkel, J	TX	899
PlS	Koplin, L	CA	903
PlS	LaBruna, A	NY	883
PlS	Little, J	DC	883
PlS	Mackay, D	PA	884
PlS	Manson, P	MD	884
PlS	Mast, B	FL	890
PlS	Matthews, D	NC	891
PlS	Maxwell, G	TN	891
PlS	Metzinger, S	LA	900
PlS	Miller, T	CA	904
PlS	Moses, M	LA	900
PlS	Mustoe, T	IL	895
PlS	Nahabedian, M	DC	885
PlS	Ness, J	MN	895
PlS	Noone, R	PA	885
PlS	Ousterhout, D	CA	904
PlS	Papay, F	OH	895
PlS	Pitman, G	NY	885

Spec	Name	St	Pg
PlS	Posnick, J	MD	885
PlS	Rand, R	WA	904
PlS	Rappaport, N	TX	900
PlS	Rohrich, R	TX	900
PlS	Rosenberg, H	CA	905
PlS	Siebert, J	WI	896
PlS	Singer, R	CA	905
PlS	Slavin, S	MA	879
PlS	Spinelli, H	NY	887
PlS	Stevens, W	CA	905
PlS	Sullivan, P	RI	879
PlS	Sultan, M	NY	887
PlS	Tabbal, N	NY	887
PlS	Thaller, S	FL	891
PlS	Thorne, C	NY	887
PlS	Vander Kolk, C	MD	888
PlS	Walton, R	IL	897
PlS	Wilcox, R	TX	901
PlS	Zins, J	OH	897

Cosmetic Surgery-Face & Body

PlS	Aston, S	NY	880
PlS	Ducic, I	DC	882
PlS	Grotting, J	AL	890
PlS	Hardesty, R	CA	903
PlS	Markowitz, B	CA	904
PlS	Nichter, L	CA	904
PlS	Rose, E	NY	886

Cosmetic Surgery-Face & Breast

PlS	Beals, S	AZ	898
PlS	Meltzer, T	AZ	899
PlS	Olding, M	DC	885
PlS	Price, G	MD	886
PlS	Schusterman, M	TX	900
PlS	Singh, N	MD	886
PlS	Winters, R	NJ	888

Cosmetic Surgery-Face & Eyes

Oph	Anderson, R	UT	601
Oph	Putterman, A	IL	599
PlS	Gallico, G	MA	878
PlS	Grant, R	NY	882
PlS	Leipziger, L	NY	883
PlS	Matarasso, A	NY	884

Cosmetic Surgery-Face & Neck

Oto	Baker, S	MI	683
Oto	Gliklich, R	MA	665
PlS	Feldman, J	MA	878
PlS	Leaf, N	CA	903
PlS	Lesavoy, M	CA	904
PlS	Marten, T	CA	904
PlS	Paul, M	CA	904
PlS	Stuzin, J	FL	891

Cosmetic Surgery-Head & Neck

PlS	Urata, M	CA	905

Cough

Oto	Aviv, J	NY	668
Pul	Deitz, J	PA	957
Pul	Irwin, R	MA	955
Pul	Nash, T	NY	958

Cough-Chronic

PO	Holinger, L	IL	804
PPul	McColley, S	IL	809
PPul	Rubin, B	VA	808
PPul	Sherman, J	VA	808

Craniocervical Disorders

NS	Menezes, A	IA	491

Craniofacial Disorders

CG	Graham, J	CA	162
CG	Jones, M	CA	163
CG	Saal, H	OH	160

Craniofacial Surgery

NS	Danielpour, M	CA	499
NS	Duhaime, A	MA	473
NS	Johnson, S	CO	494
NS	Origitano, T	MT	494
NS	Pollack, I	PA	481
NS	Sklar, F	TX	497
Oto	Chowdhury, K	CO	689
PlS	Ascherman, J	NY	880
PlS	Barone, C	TX	898
PlS	Beals, S	AZ	898
PlS	Boyajian, M	DC	881
PlS	Buchman, S	MI	893
PlS	Deleyiannis, F	CO	897
PlS	Dufresne, C	MD	882
PlS	Glat, P	PA	882
PlS	Hoffman, W	CA	903
PlS	Kane, A	TX	899
PlS	Kelly, K	TN	890
PlS	Kirschner, R	OH	894
PlS	Mackay, D	PA	884
PlS	Magee, W	VA	890
PlS	Mixter, R	WI	895
PlS	Ousterhout, D	CA	904
PlS	Patel, P	IL	895
PlS	Persing, J	CT	879
PlS	Polley, J	IL	896
PlS	Taub, P	NY	887
PlS	Thorne, C	NY	887

Craniofacial Surgery-Pediatric

PlS	Buchman, S	MI	893
PlS	Burstein, F	GA	889
PlS	Cohen, S	CA	901
PlS	Meara, J	MA	878
PlS	Napoli, J	DE	885
PlS	Stotland, M	NH	879
PlS	Urata, M	CA	905
PlS	Yu, J	GA	892

Craniofacial Surgery/Reconstruction

Oto	Costantino, P	NY	669
PlS	Baker, S	DC	880
PlS	Bartlett, S	PA	880
PlS	Cohen, S	CA	901
PlS	Losee, J	PA	884
PlS	Markowitz, B	CA	904
PlS	Marsh, J	MO	894
PlS	Matthews, D	NC	891
PlS	Papay, F	OH	895
PlS	Posnick, J	MD	885
PlS	Rodriguez, E	MD	886
PlS	Spinelli, H	NY	887
PlS	Tufaro, A	MD	888
PlS	Vander Kolk, C	MD	888
PlS	Vasconez, H	KY	892
PlS	Wolfe, S	FL	892

Craniosynostosis

CG	Zackai, E	PA	158
NS	Dias, M	PA	476
NS	Jimenez, D	TX	496

Creutzfeldt-Jakob Disease (CJD)

Path	Gambetti, P	OH	728

Critical Care

Cv	Tenenbaum, J	NY	96
Inf	Maki, D	WI	418
MF	Norwitz, E	MA	432
N	Becker, K	WA	538
N	Fink, M	NY	515
N	Gress, D	VA	524
N	Suarez, J	TX	538
NP	Gross, I	CT	448
NP	Simmons, C	CA	454
PCCM	Sarnaik, A	MI	755
PCCM	Schwarz, A	CA	756
PCCM	Thompson, A	PA	755
PM	Berde, C	MA	706
PPul	Kurachek, S	MN	809
PS	Gaines, B	PA	815
PS	Karrer, F	CO	821
PS	Reynolds, M	IL	820
Pul	Albertson, T	CA	969
Pul	Arroliga, A	TX	968
Pul	Bellamy, P	CA	970
Pul	Christie, J	PA	956
Pul	Christman, B	TN	961
Pul	Criner, G	PA	956
Pul	Deitz, J	PA	957
Pul	Donahoe, M	PA	957
Pul	Friedman, L	CT	954
Pul	Gerboth, G	AK	970
Pul	Greenberg, H	NY	957
Pul	Hall, J	IL	964

Spec	Name	St	Pg
Pul	Harman, E	FL	962
Pul	Heffner, J	OR	970
Pul	Ingbar, D	MN	965
Pul	Irwin, R	MA	955
Pul	Kaplan, J	KS	968
Pul	King, E	PA	957
Pul	LoRusso, T	VA	963
Pul	Marini, J	MN	965
Pul	Martinez, F	MI	966
Pul	O'Donnell, A	DC	958
Pul	Popovich, J	MI	966
Pul	Rizk, N	CA	971
Pul	Steiger, D	NY	959
Pul	Vaughey, E	VA	963
Pul	Wheeler, A	TN	964
S	Barie, P	NY	1089
S	Buchman, T	GA	1104
S	Burke, P	MA	1084
S	Cioffi, W	RI	1084
S	Cohen, M	PA	1091
S	Cushing, B	ME	1084
S	Deitch, E	NJ	1092
S	Friese, R	AZ	1125
S	Gupta, R	NH	1085
S	Lentz, C	NM	1127
S	Luterman, A	AL	1106
S	McIntyre, R	CO	1122
S	Potenza, B	CA	1136
S	Rhee, P	AZ	1128
S	Weigelt, J	WI	1121
S	Winchell, R	ME	1088
S	Yurt, R	NY	1102

Crohn's Disease

Spec	Name	St	Pg
CRS	Lederman, E	MO	173
CRS	Marcet, J	FL	172
CRS	Medwell, S	WA	178
CRS	Rafferty, J	OH	174
CRS	Roberts, P	MA	169
CRS	Sands, L	FL	172
CRS	Steinhagen, R	NY	171
CRS	Vernava, A	FL	172
CRS	Welton, M	CA	178
CRS	Wolff, B	MN	175
CRS	Young-Fadok, T	AZ	177
Ge	Abreu, M	FL	241
Ge	DeCross, A	NY	233
Ge	Di Marino, A	PA	234
Ge	Hanauer, S	IL	248
Ge	Isaacs, K	NC	243
Ge	Lichtenstein, G	PA	237
Ge	Loftus, E	MN	249
Ge	Magun, A	NY	238
Ge	Plevy, S	NC	244
Ge	Sandborn, W	CA	257
Ge	Scherl, E	NY	240
Ge	Siegel, C	NH	232
Ge	Young, R	NE	252
PGe	Baldassano, R	PA	763
PGe	Dubinsky, M	CA	768
PGe	Piccoli, D	PA	764
PGe	Spivak, W	NY	764

Spec	Name	St	Pg
S	Michelassi, F	NY	1096

Cross Cultural Psychiatry

ChAP	McKelvey, R	OR	943
Psyc	Pi, E	CA	934

Cryoglobulinemia

Rhu	Gorevic, P	NY	1060

CT Body Scan

DR	Erasmus, J	TX	1016
DR	Fishman, E	MD	1009
DR	Megibow, A	NY	1010
DR	Parsons, R	PA	1011
DR	Weinreb, J	CT	1007

CT Chest Scan

DR	Black, W	NH	1007

CT Colonography

DR	Fidler, J	MN	1014

CT Scan

DR	Cohen, B	NY	1008
DR	Yoon, S	NY	1012
NuM	Agress, H	NJ	554
NuM	Freeman, L	NY	554

Cubital Tunnel Syndrome

HS	Nagle, D	IL	303

Cushing's Syndrome

EDM	Biller, B	MA	208
EDM	Katznelson, L	CA	225
EDM	Thorner, M	VA	217
EDM	Weiss, R	IL	221
PEn	Levitsky, L	MA	757

Cutaneous Lymphoma

D	Belsito, D	NY	186
D	Bowen, G	UT	197
D	Duvic, M	TX	198
D	Edelson, R	CT	184
D	Kim, Y	CA	201
D	Kupper, T	MA	185
D	Leffell, D	CT	185
D	Lessin, S	PA	189
D	Lim, H	MI	196
D	Nouri, K	FL	193
D	Olsen, E	NC	193
D	Ramsay, D	NY	190
D	Rook, A	PA	190
D	Shea, C	IL	197
D	Thiers, B	SC	194
D	Wheeland, R	AZ	199

Spec	Name	St	Pg
D	Wood, G	WI	197
Onc	Kuzel, T	IL	371
Path	Le Boit, P	CA	733
RadRO	Hoppe, R	CA	995

Cutaneous T-cell Lymphoma

D	Camisa, C	FL	192
D	Rook, A	PA	190
Hem	Greer, J	TN	319
Hem	Sokol, L	FL	320
Onc	Foss, F	CT	331
Onc	Horwitz, S	NY	345
RadRO	Wilson, L	CT	978

Cystadenocarcinoma

S	Sugarbaker, P	DC	1101

Cystic Fibrosis

Inf	Huitt, G	CO	419
PA&I	Fanous, Y	CA	747
PGe	Baker, R	NY	763
PGe	Narkewicz, M	CO	767
PGe	Sokol, R	CO	767
PPul	Borowitz, D	NY	806
PPul	Dorkin, H	MA	806
PPul	Dovey, M	PA	806
PPul	Dozor, A	NY	807
PPul	Gibson, R	WA	810
PPul	Kattan, M	NY	807
PPul	Konstan, M	OH	809
PPul	Lapey, A	MA	806
PPul	McColley, S	IL	809
PPul	McCoy, K	OH	809
PPul	Morgan, W	AZ	810
PPul	Nielson, D	CA	810
PPul	Orenstein, D	PA	807
PPul	Panitch, H	PA	807
PPul	Quittell, L	NY	808
PPul	Ramsey, B	WA	811
PPul	Rubin, B	VA	808
PPul	Tauber, D	PA	808
PPul	Wall, M	OR	811
PPul	Zeitlin, P	MD	808
Pul	Balk, R	IL	964
Pul	Garrity, E	IL	964
Pul	Grum, C	MI	964
Pul	Padilla, M	NY	958
Pul	Rosenbluth, D	MO	966
Pul	Simon, R	MI	967
Pul	Trulock, E	MO	967
Pul	Young, K	PA	960

Cystic Fibrosis Infection

PInf	Saiman, L	NY	794

Cystinosis

PNep	Jabs, K	TN	799

Spec	Name	St	Pg

Cytogenetic Disorders

CG	Hoyme, H	SD	161
CG	Zackai, E	PA	158

Cytopathology

Path	Cohen, M	UT	729
Path	Ehya, H	PA	721
Path	Leslie, K	AZ	730
Path	Mills, S	VA	726
Path	Nicosia, S	FL	726
Path	Rutgers, J	CA	734
Path	Silverman, J	PA	724

D

Dance Medicine

OrS	Padgett, D	NY	630

Dance/Ballet Injuries

SM	Metzl, J	NY	1075
SM	Micheli, L	MA	1074

Dance/Sports Medicine

OrS	Bauman, P	NY	620

Death & Dying

ChAP	Sexson, S	GA	941

Deep Brain Stimulation

N	Flaherty, A	MA	511
N	Vitek, J	MN	534
NS	Eisenberg, H	MD	476
NS	Liker, M	CA	500
NS	Rezai, A	OH	492
NS	Whiting, D	PA	483

Defibrillator Cable Extraction

CE	Epstein, L	MA	113
CE	Love, C	OH	117
Cv	Wilkoff, B	OH	106

Defibrillators

CE	Chinitz, L	NY	114
CE	Cohen, M	NY	114
CE	Curtis, A	NY	114
CE	DiMarco, J	VA	116
CE	Donahue, J	MA	113
CE	Ellenbogen, K	VA	116
CE	Epstein, A	PA	114
CE	Epstein, L	MA	113
CE	Gang, E	CA	120
CE	Goldberger, J	IL	117
CE	Higgins, S	CA	120
CE	Lerman, B	NY	115
CE	Onufer, J	VA	116
CE	Sauer, W	CO	119
CE	Schuger, C	MI	118
CE	Shen, W	AZ	119
CE	Sorrentino, R	GA	116
CE	Swerdlow, C	CA	120
CE	Wang, P	CA	120

Deformity Reconstruction

OrS	Helfet, D	NY	625
OrS	Strongwater, A	NJ	633

Delirium

Ger	Dyer, C	TX	267

Dementia

Ger	Bloom, P	NY	264
Ger	Callahan, E	NY	264
Ger	Dyer, C	TX	267
Ger	Greganti, M	NC	265
Ger	McCormick, W	WA	268
Ger	Palmer, R	VA	266
Ger	Sachs, G	IN	266
Ger	Tenover, J	CA	268
GerPsy	Burke, W	NE	946
GerPsy	Greenwald, B	NY	944
GerPsy	Holroyd, S	VA	945
GerPsy	Kennedy, G	NY	944
GerPsy	Lyketsos, C	MD	944
GerPsy	Manepalli, J	MO	945
GerPsy	Mellow, A	MI	945
GerPsy	Reisberg, B	NY	944
GerPsy	Stein, E	CA	946
GerPsy	Tune, L	GA	945
N	Ahern, G	AZ	535
N	Chui, H	CA	539
N	Feinberg, T	NY	515
N	Ferrendelli, J	TX	536
N	Foo, S	NY	515
N	Gendelman, S	NY	515
N	Henderson, V	CA	540
N	Kieburtz, K	NY	516
N	Levine, D	NY	518
N	Marder, K	NY	519
N	Mayeux, R	NY	519
N	Mesulam, M	IL	531
N	Relkin, N	NY	520
N	Zimmerman, E	NY	522
Psyc	Arnold, S	PA	922
Psyc	Kumar, A	IL	930
Psyc	Nelson, J	CA	933

Demyelinating Neuropathy

N	Lisak, R	MI	530

Depression

AM	Kaplan, D	CO	77
AM	Sigel, E	CO	78
ChAP	Emslie, G	TX	943
ChAP	Hagman, J	CO	942
ChAP	Heston, J	TN	941
ChAP	McKelvey, R	OR	943
Ger	Tenover, J	CA	268
GerPsy	Burke, W	NE	946
GerPsy	Greenwald, B	NY	944
GerPsy	Grossberg, G	MO	945
GerPsy	Kennedy, G	NY	944
GerPsy	Kramer, B	CA	946
GerPsy	Lyketsos, C	MD	944
GerPsy	Manepalli, J	MO	945
GerPsy	Mellow, A	MI	945
GerPsy	Reisberg, B	NY	944
Psyc	Adler, D	MA	920
Psyc	Alpert, J	MA	920
Psyc	Appelbaum, P	NY	922
Psyc	Canterbury, R	VA	928
Psyc	DePaulo, J	MD	924
Psyc	Eaton, J	DC	924
Psyc	Eisendrath, S	CA	933
Psyc	Greden, J	MI	930
Psyc	Haque, W	TX	932
Psyc	Hirschfeld, R	TX	932
Psyc	Karasu, T	NY	925
Psyc	Leuchter, A	CA	933
Psyc	Levy, S	GA	928
Psyc	Marin, D	NY	926
Psyc	McIntosh, J	UT	931
Psyc	Nelson, J	CA	933
Psyc	Nunes, E	NY	926
Psyc	Nurnberger, J	IN	930
Psyc	Price, L	RI	921
Psyc	Reus, V	CA	934
Psyc	Salloum, I	FL	928
Psyc	Sanacora, G	CT	922
Psyc	Schatzberg, A	CA	935
Psyc	Thase, M	PA	927
Psyc	Weiner, R	NC	928
Psyc	Weisler, R	NC	928

Depression in Cardiovascular Disease

GerPsy	Veith, R	WA	946

Depression in the Elderly

Psyc	Kumar, A	IL	930
Psyc	Marin, D	NY	926
Psyc	Roose, S	NY	926

Depression-TMS Therapy

Psyc	Janicak, P	IL	930
Psyc	Manevitz, A	NY	925

Dermatofibrosarcoma Protruberans

D	Bennett, R	CA	200

Spec	Name	St	Pg

Dermatologic Surgery

Spec	Name	St	Pg
D	Brody, H	GA	191
D	Eichler, C	FL	192
D	Fosko, S	MO	195
D	Greenbaum, S	PA	188
D	Krunic, A	IL	196
D	Maloney, M	MA	185
D	Otley, C	MN	196
D	Russell, M	VA	193

Dermatology

Spec	Name	St	Pg
D	Alster, T	DC	186
D	Amonette, R	TN	191
D	Anderson, R	MA	184
D	Anhalt, G	MD	186
D	Arndt, K	MA	184
D	Arpey, C	MN	194
D	Avram, M	NY	186
D	Bailin, P	OH	194
D	Barbosa, V	IL	194
D	Bayliss, S	MO	194
D	Belsito, D	NY	186
D	Bennett, R	CA	200
D	Berg, D	WA	200
D	Bernstein, R	NY	186
D	Bickers, D	NY	187
D	Bolognia, J	CT	184
D	Bondi, E	PA	187
D	Bowen, G	UT	197
D	Brandt, F	NY	187
D	Braun, M	DC	187
D	Brodland, D	PA	187
D	Brody, H	GA	191
D	Bronin, A	NY	187
D	Brown, M	NY	187
D	Burton, C	NC	191
D	Callen, J	KY	192
D	Camisa, C	FL	192
D	Carney, J	AR	198
D	Cather, J	TX	198
D	Cockerell, C	TX	198
D	Cohen, B	FL	192
D	Cohen, B	MD	187
D	Cohen, S	NY	187
D	Cook, J	NC	192
D	Cornelius, L	MO	195
D	Cotsarelis, G	PA	188
D	Crutchfield, C	MN	195
D	Cunningham, B	CA	200
D	DeLeo, V	NY	188
D	Dover, J	MA	184
D	Dufresne, R	RI	184
D	Duvic, M	TX	198
D	Dzubow, L	PA	188
D	Edelson, R	CT	184
D	Eichenfield, L	CA	200
D	Eichler, C	FL	192
D	Elmets, C	AL	192
D	Fenske, N	FL	192
D	Fewkes, J	MA	184
D	Fitzpatrick, R	CA	200
D	Fivenson, D	MI	195
D	Fosko, S	MO	195
D	Frieden, I	CA	200
D	Friedlander, S	CA	200
D	Garden, J	IL	195
D	Garrett, A	VA	192
D	Gellis, S	MA	185
D	Geronemus, R	NY	188
D	Gilchrest, B	MA	185
D	Glogau, R	CA	200
D	Gordon, M	NY	188
D	Gottlieb, A	MA	185
D	Green, H	FL	192
D	Greenbaum, S	PA	188
D	Greenway, H	CA	201
D	Grichnik, J	FL	193
D	Grimes, P	CA	201
D	Grossman, M	NY	188
D	Halpern, A	NY	188
D	Hanifin, J	OR	201
D	Hanke, C	IN	195
D	Hansen, R	AZ	198
D	Hruza, G	MO	195
D	James, W	PA	189
D	Johnson, T	MI	195
D	Johr, R	FL	193
D	Jorizzo, J	NC	193
D	Kalb, R	NY	189
D	Kane, K	MA	185
D	Kilmer, S	CA	201
D	Kim, Y	CA	201
D	Kirsner, R	FL	193
D	Koo, J	CA	201
D	Kress, D	PA	189
D	Kriegel, D	NY	189
D	Krueger, G	UT	198
D	Krunic, A	IL	196
D	Kupper, T	MA	185
D	Lask, G	CA	201
D	Lebwohl, M	NY	189
D	Leffell, D	CT	185
D	Leshin, B	NC	193
D	Lessin, S	PA	189
D	Levy, M	TX	198
D	Lim, H	MI	196
D	Lim Quan, K	AZ	199
D	Linder, J	AZ	199
D	Liu, V	IA	196
D	Lowitt, M	MD	189
D	Lucky, A	OH	196
D	Maloney, M	MA	185
D	McMichael, A	NC	193
D	Menter, M	TX	199
D	Miller, S	MD	189
D	Mutasim, D	OH	196
D	Neel, V	MA	185
D	Neuburg, M	WI	196
D	Nghiem, P	WA	201
D	Nigra, T	DC	189
D	Nouri, K	FL	193
D	Olbricht, S	MA	186
D	Olsen, E	NC	193
D	Orengo, I	TX	199
D	Orlow, S	NY	190
D	Otley, C	MN	196
D	Paller, A	IL	196
D	Perone, J	TX	199
D	Pitts, J	AZ	199
D	Prioleau, P	NY	190
D	Ramsay, D	NY	190
D	Ratner, D	NY	190
D	Rhodes, A	IL	197
D	Richardson, T	CA	201
D	Rigel, D	NY	190
D	Rook, A	PA	190
D	Rubin, M	CA	202
D	Russell, M	VA	193
D	Schultz, N	NY	190
D	Shea, C	IL	197
D	Sherertz, E	SC	194
D	Shupack, J	NY	190
D	Sobel, S	FL	194
D	Sokoloff, D	FL	194
D	Sontheimer, R	UT	198
D	Soter, N	NY	191
D	Stanley, J	PA	191
D	Stern, R	MA	186
D	Swanson, N	OR	202
D	Swetter, S	CA	202
D	Taylor, R	TX	199
D	Thiers, B	SC	194
D	Treadwell, P	IN	197
D	Tsao, H	MA	186
D	Voorhees, J	MI	197
D	Werth, V	PA	191
D	Wheeland, R	AZ	199
D	Witman, P	OH	197
D	Wood, G	WI	197
D	Woodley, D	CA	202
D	Yan, A	PA	191
D	Zelickson, B	MN	197
D	Zitelli, J	PA	191

Dermatomyositis

Spec	Name	St	Pg
D	Callen, J	KY	192
D	Jorizzo, J	NC	193
D	Sontheimer, R	UT	198
PRhu	Ilowite, N	NY	812
PRhu	McCarthy, P	CT	811
PRhu	Myones, B	TX	813
PRhu	Schanberg, L	NC	812
PRhu	Sills, E	MD	812
PRhu	Wagner-Weiner, L	IL	813
Rhu	Medsger, T	PA	1061
Rhu	Mitnick, H	NY	1061
Rhu	Oddis, C	PA	1061

Dermatopathology

Spec	Name	St	Pg
D	Cockerell, C	TX	198
D	Mutasim, D	OH	196
D	Shea, C	IL	197
Path	Bastian, B	CA	732
Path	Cochran, A	CA	732
Path	Gottlieb, G	MA	718
Path	Le Boit, P	CA	733

Specialty & Special Expertise Index

Spec	Name	St	Pg
Path	Lowe, L	MI	728
Path	Prieto, V	TX	730

DES-Exposed Females

Spec	Name	St	Pg
RE	Haney, A	IL	1047

Desmoid Tumors

Spec	Name	St	Pg
CRS	Church, J	OH	173
Onc	Maki, R	NY	347

Developmental & Behavioral Disorders

Spec	Name	St	Pg
Ped	Burgess, D	NJ	740
Ped	Hofkosh, D	PA	740
Ped	Miller, K	MA	740
Ped	Rappaport, L	MA	740
Ped	Walker, W	WA	743

Developmental & Mood Disorders

Spec	Name	St	Pg
Ped	Hershorin, E	FL	741

Developmental Disorders

Spec	Name	St	Pg
AM	Slap, G	PA	76
CG	Cunniff, C	AZ	161
ChAP	King, B	WA	943
ChAP	Kwon, H	WA	943
ChAP	Pomeroy, J	NY	940
ChiN	Filipek, P	TX	150
ChiN	Kosofsky, B	NY	145
ChiN	Kovnar, E	WI	149
ChiN	Patterson, M	MN	149
N	Kuzniecky, R	NY	517
Ped	Bull, M	IN	741

Diabetes

Spec	Name	St	Pg
EDM	Abrahamson, M	MA	208
EDM	Ahmann, A	OR	223
EDM	Akatsu, H	CA	223
EDM	Axelrod, L	MA	208
EDM	Barrett, E	VA	216
EDM	Beaser, R	MA	208
EDM	Berkson, R	CA	224
EDM	Blum, C	NY	211
EDM	Brennan, M	MN	218
EDM	Brillon, D	NY	211
EDM	Broadstone, V	IN	218
EDM	Brown, J	TX	222
EDM	Buse, J	NC	216
EDM	Clore, J	VA	216
EDM	Cohen, R	OH	218
EDM	Comi, R	NH	208
EDM	Cryer, P	MO	219
EDM	Cunningham, G	TX	222
EDM	D'Alessio, D	OH	219
EDM	Donner, T	MD	212
EDM	Eckel, R	CO	222
EDM	Edelman, S	CA	224
EDM	Ehrmann, D	IL	219
EDM	Emanuele, M	IL	219
EDM	Feinglos, M	NC	216
EDM	Fitzgerald, P	CA	224
EDM	Greene, L	NY	212
EDM	Herman, W	MI	219
EDM	Hirsch, I	WA	224
EDM	Inzucchi, S	CT	209
EDM	Kamdar, V	CA	224
EDM	Kennedy, L	OH	220
EDM	Klonoff, D	CA	225
EDM	Korytkowski, M	PA	213
EDM	Lash, R	MI	220
EDM	Lavis, V	TX	223
EDM	Lipson, A	DC	213
EDM	Maclaren, N	NY	213
EDM	Mazzone, T	IL	220
EDM	McGill, J	MO	220
EDM	McMahon, M	MN	221
EDM	Nathan, D	MA	210
EDM	Nestler, J	VA	217
EDM	Ober, K	NC	217
EDM	Ovalle, F	AL	217
EDM	Peters, A	CA	225
EDM	Philipson, L	IL	221
EDM	Powers, A	TN	217
EDM	Recker, R	NE	222
EDM	Rodbard, H	MD	214
EDM	Rubenfeld, S	TX	223
EDM	Rushakoff, R	CA	225
EDM	Schutta, M	PA	214
EDM	Schwartz, S	PA	214
EDM	Semenkovich, C	MO	221
EDM	Seplowitz, A	NY	214
EDM	Skyler, J	FL	217
EDM	Smith, S	MN	221
EDM	Sowers, J	MO	221
EDM	Weissman, P	FL	218
EDM	Werner, P	IL	221
EDM	Zimmerman, R	OH	222
Ger	Abrass, I	WA	267
Ger	Schwartz, R	CO	267
IM	Braunstein, S	NC	426
PEn	Allen, D	WI	760
PEn	Alter, C	PA	757
PEn	Arslanian, S	PA	757
PEn	Becker, D	PA	757
PEn	Casella, S	NH	756
PEn	DiMeglio, L	IN	760
PEn	Fennoy, I	NY	758
PEn	Foster, C	UT	761
PEn	Freemark, M	NC	759
PEn	Gallagher, M	NY	758
PEn	Gitelman, S	CA	761
PEn	Klingensmith, G	CO	761
PEn	Levitsky, L	MA	757
PEn	Menon, R	MI	760
PEn	Mirmira, R	IN	760
PEn	Norris, A	IA	760
PEn	Plotnick, L	MD	759
PEn	Rogers, D	OH	760
PEn	Rosenthal, S	CA	762
PEn	Silverstein, J	FL	759
PEn	Sperling, M	PA	759
PEn	Tamborlane, W	CT	757
PEn	White, N	MO	761
PEn	Wilson, D	CA	762
S	Oberholzer, J	IL	1117

Diabetes Clinical Trials

Spec	Name	St	Pg
EDM	Korytkowski, M	PA	213

Diabetes in Pregnancy

Spec	Name	St	Pg
EDM	Lash, R	MI	220
EDM	Seely, E	MA	210
MF	Cohen, A	PA	434
MF	Goodman, J	IL	438
MF	Landon, M	OH	439
MF	Landy, H	DC	435
MF	Moore, T	CA	443
MF	Norwitz, E	MA	432
MF	Plante, L	PA	435
MF	Socol, M	IL	440

Diabetes in Women

Spec	Name	St	Pg
EDM	Seely, E	MA	210

Diabetes Prevention

Spec	Name	St	Pg
EDM	Schutta, M	PA	214

Diabetes-Adult & Pediatric

Spec	Name	St	Pg
EDM	Wondisford, F	MD	215

Diabetes-Amputation

Spec	Name	St	Pg
OrS	Pinzur, M	IL	644

Diabetic Eye Disease/Retinopathy

Spec	Name	St	Pg
Oph	Barile, G	NY	576
Oph	Bressler, S	MD	576
Oph	Brown, G	PA	576
Oph	Chang, S	NY	577
Oph	D'Amico, D	NY	577
Oph	Davis, J	FL	587
Oph	Del Priore, L	SC	588
Oph	Duker, J	MA	574
Oph	Edwards, P	MI	594
Oph	Flynn, H	FL	588
Oph	Friberg, T	PA	578
Oph	Fuchs, W	NY	578
Oph	Gentile, R	NY	579
Oph	Hariprasad, S	IL	595
Oph	Ho, A	PA	580
Oph	Humayun, M	CA	606
Oph	Lim, J	IL	597
Oph	Maguire, J	PA	581
Oph	Meredith, T	NC	590
Oph	Muldoon, T	NY	582
Oph	Murray, T	FL	590

Spec	Name	St	Pg
Oph	Nussbaum, J	GA	590
Oph	Olsen, T	GA	590
Oph	Petersen, M	OH	598
Oph	Prenner, J	NJ	583
Oph	Regillo, C	PA	583
Oph	Rosenfeld, P	FL	591
Oph	Sadda, S	CA	608
Oph	Schachat, A	OH	599
Oph	Schiff, W	NY	584
Oph	Schwartz, S	CA	609
Oph	Shabto, U	NY	584
Oph	Spaide, R	NY	585
Oph	Sternberg, P	TN	591
Oph	Vander, J	PA	586
Oph	Walsh, J	NY	586
Oph	Yannuzzi, L	NY	586

Diabetic Kidney Disease

Spec	Name	St	Pg
Nep	Johnston, J	PA	459
Nep	Kasinath, B	TX	465
Nep	Kobrin, S	PA	460
Nep	Lea, J	GA	462
Nep	Pohl, M	OH	464
Nep	Rodby, R	IL	464
Nep	Schreiber, M	OH	464
Nep	Schwartz, G	MN	464
Nep	Seifter, J	MA	458
Nep	Toto, R	TX	466
Nep	Yee, J	MI	465

Diabetic Leg/Foot

Spec	Name	St	Pg
EDM	Kamdar, V	CA	224
OrS	Weinfeld, S	NY	634
PlS	Attinger, C	DC	880
VascS	Pomposelli, F	MA	1221
VascS	Sumpio, B	CT	1221

Diabetic Vascular Disease Prevention

Spec	Name	St	Pg
EDM	Barrett, E	VA	216

Diagnostic Problems

Spec	Name	St	Pg
Ger	Greganti, M	NC	265
Inf	Nahass, R	NJ	414
Inf	Wormser, G	NY	415
N	Adams, D	FL	523
Ped	Gartner, J	DE	740
Pul	Hansen-Flaschen, J	PA	957
Pul	Harman, E	FL	962

Diagnostic Radiology

Spec	Name	St	Pg
DR	Abbitt, P	FL	1012
DR	Adler, R	NY	1008
DR	Austin, J	NY	1008
DR	Bahn, D	CA	1017
DR	Baker, J	NC	1013
DR	Bassett, L	CA	1017
DR	Benson, C	MA	1007
DR	Berland, L	AL	1013
DR	Black, W	NH	1007
DR	Bluemke, D	MD	1008
DR	Brem, R	DC	1008
DR	Cardenosa, G	VA	1013
DR	Charboneau, J	MN	1014
DR	Chiles, C	NC	1013
DR	Coakley, F	OR	1017
DR	Cohen, B	NY	1008
DR	Cohen, H	TN	1013
DR	Coleman, B	PA	1008
DR	Conant, E	PA	1008
DR	Copit, D	PA	1008
DR	Dachman, A	IL	1014
DR	Dalinka, M	PA	1009
DR	Dershaw, D	NY	1009
DR	Dodd, G	CO	1016
DR	Doubilet, P	MA	1007
DR	Edelman, R	IL	1014
DR	Edelstein, B	NY	1009
DR	Elster, A	NC	1013
DR	Erasmus, J	TX	1016
DR	Evers, K	PA	1009
DR	Federle, M	CA	1017
DR	Feig, S	CA	1017
DR	Fidler, J	MN	1014
DR	Filly, R	CA	1017
DR	Fishman, E	MD	1009
DR	Flamm, S	OH	1014
DR	Freimanis, R	NC	1013
DR	Fuhrman, C	PA	1009
DR	Gefter, W	PA	1009
DR	Gilsanz, V	CA	1018
DR	Goodman, L	WI	1015
DR	Grant, E	CA	1018
DR	Helvie, M	MI	1015
DR	Henschke, C	NY	1009
DR	Holliday, R	NY	1009
DR	Hricak, H	NY	1010
DR	Hubbard, A	NE	1016
DR	Huynh, P	TX	1016
DR	Jackson, V	IN	1015
DR	Jaramillo, D	PA	1010
DR	Kanal, E	PA	1010
DR	Kruskal, J	MA	1007
DR	Kurtz, A	PA	1010
DR	Lehman, C	WA	1018
DR	Levy, A	DC	1010
DR	Macmahon, H	IL	1015
DR	Mancuso, A	FL	1013
DR	McDonald, D	CA	1018
DR	Megibow, A	NY	1010
DR	Miller, F	IL	1015
DR	Mirvis, S	MD	1010
DR	Mitnick, J	NY	1010
DR	Monsees, B	MO	1015
DR	Mountz, J	PA	1011
DR	Newman, J	MA	1007
DR	Otto, P	TX	1017
DR	Palmer, W	MA	1007
DR	Panicek, D	NY	1011
DR	Parikh, J	WA	1018
DR	Parsons, R	PA	1011
DR	Partain, C	TN	1014
DR	Pathria, M	CA	1018
DR	Patz, E	NC	1014
DR	Pavlov, H	NY	1011
DR	Potter, H	NY	1011
DR	Prince, M	NY	1011
DR	Rao, V	PA	1011
DR	Reinus, W	PA	1011
DR	Roth, S	PA	1012
DR	Rubin, G	NC	1014
DR	Schwartz, L	NY	1012
DR	Shaw, D	WA	1018
DR	Sivit, C	OH	1015
DR	Stough, R	OK	1017
DR	Swensen, S	MN	1015
DR	Teal, J	DC	1012
DR	Thompson, B	IA	1016
DR	Thurmond, A	OR	1018
DR	Ulissey, M	WA	1019
DR	Weinreb, J	CT	1007
DR	Wells, R	WI	1016
DR	White, C	MD	1012
DR	White, R	OH	1016
DR	Wood, B	CA	1019
DR	Yankelevitz, D	NY	1012
DR	Yoon, S	NY	1012
DR	Zagoria, R	CA	1019
DR	Zeman, R	DC	1012

Diagnostic Second Opinions

Spec	Name	St	Pg
Psyc	Eaton, J	DC	924

Dialectical Behavioral Therapy

Spec	Name	St	Pg
Psyc	Wait, S	MD	927

Dialysis Access

Spec	Name	St	Pg
S	Becker, Y	IL	1111
S	Conti, D	NY	1091
S	Lipkowitz, G	MA	1087
S	Stratta, R	NC	1110
VascS	Alexander, J	OH	1226
VascS	Dougherty, M	PA	1223
VascS	Eton, D	IL	1227
VascS	Huber, T	FL	1226
VIR	Aruny, J	CT	1027
VIR	Denny, D	NJ	1027

Dialysis Care

Spec	Name	St	Pg
Nep	Bernardo, J	PA	459
Nep	Gaston, R	AL	461
Nep	King, A	CA	467
Nep	Kobrin, S	PA	460
Nep	Kraus, M	IN	463
Nep	Lea, J	GA	462
Nep	McCarthy, J	MN	463
Nep	Miller, B	MO	464
Nep	Rodby, R	IL	464
Nep	Schreiber, M	OH	464
Nep	Stern, L	NY	460
Nep	Swartz, R	MI	464

Spec	Name	St	Pg
Nep	Toto, R	TX	466
Nep	Ward, D	CA	467
PNep	Alexander, S	CA	800
PNep	Brophy, P	IA	799
PNep	Conley, S	PA	797
PNep	Flynn, J	WA	800
PNep	Mendley, S	MD	798
PNep	Warady, B	MO	800

Diaphragm Pacing via Laparoscopy

Spec	Name	St	Pg
S	Onders, R	OH	1118

Diarrheal Diseases

Spec	Name	St	Pg
Ge	Farraye, F	MA	230
Ge	Schiller, L	TX	254
Ge	Semrad, C	IL	250
Inf	Bakken, J	MN	417
Inf	DuPont, H	TX	419
PGe	Bishop, W	IA	765
PGe	Cohen, M	OH	765
PGe	Fasano, A	MA	762
PGe	Guandalini, S	IL	766
PGe	Hill, I	OH	766
PGe	Rhoads, J	TX	768
PInf	Kotloff, K	MD	793

DiGeorge Syndrome

Spec	Name	St	Pg
A&I	Markert, M	NC	83

Digestive Disorders

Spec	Name	St	Pg
Ge	Glombicki, A	TX	254
Ge	Owyang, C	MI	249
PGe	Guandalini, S	IL	766

Diplopia

Spec	Name	St	Pg
Oph	Magramm, I	NY	581

Disaster Preparedness

Spec	Name	St	Pg
PCCM	Fuhrman, B	TX	756
PrM	Hoffman, R	NY	913

Disaster Psychiatry

Spec	Name	St	Pg
Psyc	Blumenfield, M	CA	932
Psyc	Pynoos, R	CA	934

Discoid Meniscus

Spec	Name	St	Pg
OrS	Busch, M	GA	635

Dissociative Disorders

Spec	Name	St	Pg
Psyc	Loewenstein, R	MD	925
Psyc	Wait, S	MD	927

Diverticulitis

Spec	Name	St	Pg
CRS	Lederman, E	MO	173
CRS	Ramamoorthy, S	CA	178
CRS	Read, T	MA	168
CRS	Roberts, P	MA	169
CRS	Whelan, R	NY	171

Diving Medicine

Spec	Name	St	Pg
Cv	Bove, A	PA	91

Dizziness/Vertigo

Spec	Name	St	Pg
N	Elkind, M	NY	515
N	Marshall, R	NY	519
Oto	Gianoli, G	LA	692
Oto	Goebel, J	MO	685
Oto	McMenomey, S	NY	673

Down Syndrome

Spec	Name	St	Pg
CG	Marion, R	NY	158
CG	Pergament, E	IL	160
ChiN	Lott, I	CA	151
ChiN	Pinter, J	OR	151
Ped	Bull, M	IN	741
Ped	Roizen, N	OH	742
PHO	Rosoff, P	NC	780

Drug Abuse

Spec	Name	St	Pg
AdP	Galanter, I	NY	936
AdP	Kleber, H	NY	937
AdP	Serota, R	PA	937

Drug Abuse-Consultation

Spec	Name	St	Pg
AdP	Weiss, R	MA	936
Psyc	Walker, R	OR	935

Drug Allergy

Spec	Name	St	Pg
A&I	Bernstein, J	OH	83
A&I	Castells, M	MA	80
A&I	Grammer, L	IL	83
A&I	Greenberger, P	IL	84
A&I	Gruchalla, R	TX	85
A&I	Jost, B	MO	84
D	Stern, R	MA	186

Drug Development

Spec	Name	St	Pg
Hem	Grever, M	OH	322
Hem	Kraut, E	OH	322
Onc	Daud, A	CA	386
Onc	Fine, R	NY	342
Onc	Hande, K	TN	359
Onc	Herbst, R	CT	332
Onc	Kaminski, M	MI	370
Onc	Kraft, A	SC	359
Onc	Marshall, J	DC	347
Onc	O'Connor, O	NY	348
Onc	Peereboom, D	OH	372
Onc	Remick, S	WV	350
Onc	Robert-Vizcarrondo, F	AL	363
Onc	Schilder, R	PA	351
Onc	Spriggs, D	NY	352
Onc	Sznol, M	CT	335
Onc	Wolff, A	MD	354
PHO	Adamson, P	PA	771
PHO	Blaney, S	TX	787
PHO	Furman, W	TN	778
PHO	Gajjar, A	TN	778
PHO	Vik, T	IN	786

Drug Discovery

Spec	Name	St	Pg
Onc	Belani, C	PA	338
Onc	Sosman, J	TN	364
Onc	Verschraegen, C	VT	336
Onc	Von Hoff, D	AZ	384

Drug Discovery & Development

Spec	Name	St	Pg
Onc	Burris, H	TN	356
Onc	Carducci, M	MD	339
Onc	Cohen, R	PA	340
Onc	Doroshow, J	MD	341
Onc	Eckhardt, S	CO	376
Onc	Edelman, M	NM	379
Onc	Ratain, M	IL	373
Onc	Trump, D	NY	353
Onc	Wilding, G	WI	375
PHO	Berg, S	TX	787
PInf	Jacobs, R	AR	796

Drug Induced Lung Disease

Spec	Name	St	Pg
Pul	Cooper, J	AL	961

Drug Sensitivity

Spec	Name	St	Pg
PA&I	Schuberth, K	MD	744
PA&I	Sicherer, S	NY	744

Drug-Resistant Infections

Spec	Name	St	Pg
PInf	Belcher, C	IN	795

Drugs & Aging

Spec	Name	St	Pg
Ger	Flaherty, J	MO	266

Dry Eye Syndrome

Spec	Name	St	Pg
Oph	Dana, R	MA	574
Oph	Kornmehl, E	MA	574
Oph	Pflugfelder, S	TX	603

Dual Diagnosis

Spec	Name	St	Pg
AdP	Collins, E	NY	936
AdP	Lawson, W	DC	937
AdP	Strain, E	MD	937
ChAP	Deas, D	SC	941
Psyc	Norman, K	CA	934
Psyc	Strakowski, S	OH	931

Spec	Name	St	Pg

Dual Diagnosis-Consultation

Spec	Name	St	Pg
AdP	Weiss, R	MA	936

Dupuytren's Contracture

Spec	Name	St	Pg
HS	Belsky, M	MA	296
HS	Carneiro, R	FL	301
HS	Carroll, C	IL	302
HS	Godzik, C	CA	306
HS	Hentz, V	CA	306
HS	Hotchkiss, R	NY	298

Dyskinesias

Spec	Name	St	Pg
N	Goetz, C	IL	529

Dyslexia

Spec	Name	St	Pg
ChiN	Shaywitz, B	CT	144
Ped	Shaywitz, S	CT	740

Dysmorphology

Spec	Name	St	Pg
CG	Anyane-Yeboa, K	NY	156
CG	Gilbert, F	NY	157
CG	Graham, J	CA	162
CG	Hoyme, H	SD	161
CG	Jones, M	CA	163
CG	Northrup, H	TX	162
CG	Seaver, L	HI	163
Ped	Jones, K	CA	742

Dystonia

Spec	Name	St	Pg
ChiN	Mink, J	NY	146
N	Baser, S	PA	513
N	Bressman, S	NY	513
N	DeLong, M	GA	524
N	Lew, M	CA	541
N	Sage, J	NJ	521
N	Tanner, C	CA	542
NS	Baltuch, G	PA	474
NS	Liker, M	CA	500

Dystonia-Botox Therapy

Spec	Name	St	Pg
N	Reich, S	MD	520

E

Ear Disorders/Surgery

Spec	Name	St	Pg
Oto	Brackmann, D	CA	694
Oto	Feghali, J	NY	669
Oto	Gianoli, G	LA	692
Oto	Hoffman, R	NY	671
Oto	Jenkins, H	CO	690
Oto	Johnson, C	LA	692
Oto	Kang, D	NE	690
Oto	Kveton, J	CT	666
Oto	Lalwani, A	NY	672
Oto	Miyamoto, R	IN	686
Oto	Niparko, J	CA	696
Oto	Pillsbury, H	NC	680
Oto	Silverstein, H	FL	681
Oto	Telian, S	MI	688
Oto	Telischi, F	FL	681
Oto	Zalzal, G	MD	677
PO	Eavey, R	TN	803
PO	Miller, R	IL	804
PO	Poe, D	MA	801
PO	Rosenfeld, R	NY	803

Ear Infections

Spec	Name	St	Pg
Oto	Hotaling, A	IL	686
Oto	Jones, J	NY	671
Oto	Paparella, M	MN	687
Oto	Poole, M	GA	680
PInf	Wald, E	WI	796
PO	Baroody, F	IL	804
PO	Casselbrant, M	PA	802
PO	Chan, K	CO	805
PO	Dolitsky, J	NY	802
PO	Haddad, J	NY	802
PO	Katz, R	OH	804

Ear Nose & Throat Imaging

Spec	Name	St	Pg
DR	Rao, V	PA	1011

Ear Reconstruction/Microtia

Spec	Name	St	Pg
PIS	Reinisch, J	CA	905
PIS	Thorne, C	NY	887
PIS	Walton, R	IL	897
PO	Eavey, R	TN	803

Ear Reshaping (Otoplasty)

Spec	Name	St	Pg
Oto	Beeson, W	IN	683
Oto	Farrior, E	FL	678
PIS	Kelly, K	TN	890
PIS	Thorne, C	NY	887

Ear Tumors

Spec	Name	St	Pg
Oto	Bojrab, D	MI	683
Oto	Jackler, R	CA	695
PO	Arnold, J	OH	804

Eating Disorders

Spec	Name	St	Pg
AM	Bermudez, O	CO	77
AM	Bravender, T	OH	77
AM	Hergenroeder, A	TX	78
AM	Irwin, C	CA	78
AM	Sigel, E	CO	78
AM	Sigman, G	IL	77
AM	Singh, N	MN	77
ChAP	Fornari, V	NY	940
ChAP	Hagman, J	CO	942
ChAP	Ponton, L	CA	943
ChAP	Sargent, A	MA	938
ChAP	Steiner, H	CA	944
IM	Mehler, P	CO	427
Psyc	Brandt, H	MD	923
Psyc	Crow, S	MN	929
Psyc	Guarda, A	MD	924
Psyc	Jimerson, D	MA	921
Psyc	McCallum, K	MO	930
Psyc	Mitchell, J	ND	931
Psyc	Powers, P	FL	928
Psyc	Walsh, B	NY	927
Psyc	Weiner, K	CO	931
Psyc	Zerbe, K	OR	935

Eating Disorders/Obesity

Spec	Name	St	Pg
EDM	Eckel, R	CO	222
EDM	Jensen, M	MN	220
Psyc	Norman, K	CA	934

Echocardiography

Spec	Name	St	Pg
Cv	Blanchard, D	CA	110
Cv	Byrd, B	TN	97
Cv	Chaitman, B	MO	101
Cv	Clements, S	GA	98
Cv	Garcia, M	NY	92
Cv	Gardin, J	NJ	93
Cv	Gottdiener, J	MD	93
Cv	Hayes, S	MN	102
Cv	Kaul, S	OR	111
Cv	Kuvin, J	MA	89
Cv	Limacher, M	FL	98
Cv	Litwin, S	GA	99
Cv	Manning, W	MA	89
Cv	McPherson, D	TX	108
Cv	Mehlman, D	IL	103
Cv	Nagueh, S	TX	108
Cv	Nishimura, R	MN	103
Cv	Quinones, M	TX	108
Cv	Rahko, P	WI	104
Cv	Redberg, R	CA	112
Cv	Schnittger, I	CA	112
Cv	Shapiro, J	IL	105
Cv	Shea, R	IN	105
Cv	Silvestry, F	PA	96
Cv	Stein, J	WI	105
Cv	Stewart, W	OH	105
Cv	Wilansky, S	AZ	109
Cv	Williams, E	IN	106
Cv	Zoghbi, W	TX	109
IC	Khawaja, S	GA	124
PCd	Bierman, F	NY	748
PCd	Caldwell, R	IN	752
PCd	Gewitz, M	NY	749
PCd	Lewin, M	WA	754
PCd	Minich, L	UT	753
PCd	Parness, I	NY	749
PCd	Rychik, J	PA	749

Echocardiography-

Specialty & Special Expertise Index

Spec	Name	St	Pg
Transesophageal			
Cv	Garcia, M	NY	92
Cv	McPherson, D	TX	108
Cv	Rahko, P	WI	104
Cv	Schnittger, I	CA	112
Cv	Shea, R	IN	105
Cv	Stainback, R	TX	109
Eczema			
A&I	Bernstein, J	OH	83
A&I	Mazza, D	NY	81
A&I	Umetsu, D	MA	80
D	Bayliss, S	MO	194
D	Crutchfield, C	MN	195
D	Lowitt, M	MD	189
D	Menter, M	TX	199
D	Sherertz, E	SC	194
D	Shupack, J	NY	190
PA&I	Bahna, S	LA	746
PA&I	Sampson, H	NY	743
PA&I	Sicherer, S	NY	744
Ehlers-Danlos Syndrome			
CG	Davis, J	NY	157
Ehrlichiosis			
Inf	Auwaerter, P	MD	412
Inf	Bakken, J	MN	417
Elbow Reconstruction			
HS	Abrams, R	CA	305
HS	Baratz, M	PA	297
HS	Beredjiklian, P	PA	297
HS	Fischer, T	IN	302
HS	Hanel, D	WA	306
HS	Hastings, H	IN	303
HS	Hotchkiss, R	NY	298
HS	Mass, D	IL	303
OrS	Hausman, M	NY	625
SM	Ciccotti, M	PA	1075
Elbow Replacement			
HS	Weiss, A	RI	297
Elbow Surgery			
HS	Badia, A	FL	300
HS	Belsky, M	MA	296
HS	Bozentka, D	PA	297
HS	Carroll, C	IL	302
HS	Cassidy, C	MA	296
HS	Cohen, M	IL	302
HS	Collins, E	TX	305
HS	Culp, R	PA	298
HS	Glickel, S	NY	298
HS	Graham, T	OH	303
HS	Raskin, K	NY	300
HS	Rosenwasser, M	NY	300
HS	Seitz, W	OH	304
HS	Sotereanos, D	PA	300
HS	Steinmann, S	MN	304
HS	Strauch, R	NY	300
HS	Swigart, C	CT	296
HS	Thomson, J	CT	296
HS	Trumble, T	WA	306
OrS	Craig, E	NY	622
OrS	Endrizzi, D	ME	617
OrS	Goitz, H	MI	641
OrS	Green, A	RI	617
OrS	McCann, P	NY	629
OrS	O'Driscoll, S	MN	644
OrS	Plancher, K	NY	631
OrS	Ramsey, M	PA	631
OrS	Romeo, A	IL	644
OrS	Yamaguchi, K	MO	646
SM	Altchek, D	NY	1074
SM	Andrews, J	FL	1076
SM	Ma, C	CA	1079
Elder Abuse			
Ger	Dyer, C	TX	267
Electrical Injury			
S	Cairns, B	NC	1104
Electrical Status Epilepticus Of Sleep			
ChiN	Riviello, J	NY	146
Electroconvulsive Therapy (ECT)			
GerPsy	Kramer, B	CA	946
Psyc	Weiner, R	NC	928
Electrodiagnosis			
N	Sirdofsky, M	DC	521
PMR	Aseff, J	DC	863
PMR	Clairmont, A	OH	867
PMR	Colachis, S	OH	868
PMR	Creamer, M	FL	866
PMR	Dumitru, D	TX	870
PMR	Feinberg, J	NY	864
PMR	Gater, D	PA	864
PMR	Haig, A	MI	868
PMR	Kevorkian, C	TX	871
PMR	King, J	TX	871
PMR	Leonard, J	MI	869
PMR	Mason, K	CO	870
PMR	Miknevich, M	PA	865
PMR	Munin, M	PA	865
PMR	Munin, M	PA	865
PMR	Nelson, M	TX	871
PMR	Nobunaga, A	OH	869
PMR	Robinson, L	WA	872
Electromyography			
N	Bertorini, T	TN	523
N	Busis, N	PA	514
N	Graves, M	CA	540
N	Josephson, D	IN	530
N	Kincaid, J	IN	530
N	Kurtzke, R	VA	525
N	Logigian, E	NY	518
N	Oh, S	AL	526
N	Pula, T	MD	520
N	Zimnowodzki, S	IL	534
PMR	Braddom, R	PA	863
PMR	Feldman, J	IL	868
PMR	LaBan, M	MI	869
PMR	Ma, D	NY	865
PMR	Robinson, L	WA	872
Electroretinograms (ERG)			
Oph	Marmor, M	CA	607
Emphysema			
Pul	Niederman, M	NY	958
Pul	Rennard, S	NE	968
Pul	Rochester, C	CT	955
Pul	Steinberg, H	NY	959
Pul	Sutherland, E	CO	968
Pul	Voelkel, N	VA	963
Pul	Wiedemann, H	OH	967
Emphysema & Asthma			
Pul	Maxfield, R	NY	958
Pul	Thomashow, B	NY	960
Emphysema-Lung Volume Reduction			
Pul	Trulock, E	MO	967
T&CS	Cooper, J	PA	1151
T&CS	DeCamp, M	IL	1167
T&CS	Ginsburg, M	NY	1153
T&CS	Keenan, R	PA	1155
T&CS	Meyers, B	MO	1170
T&CS	Miller, D	GA	1163
T&CS	Mulligan, M	WA	1180
T&CS	Shrager, J	CA	1180
T&CS	Sonett, J	NY	1158
Emphysema/Alpha-1 Antitrypsin Deficiency			
Pul	Stoller, J	OH	967
Encephalitis			
N	Roos, K	IN	533
Encephalocele			
Oto	Linstrom, C	NY	673

Endocarditis

Spec	Name	St	Pg
Inf	Corey, G	NC	416
Inf	Hartman, B	NY	413
Inf	Quagliarello, V	CT	412
Inf	Scheld, W	VA	416
Inf	Yancovitz, S	NY	415

Endocrine Cancers

Spec	Name	St	Pg
EDM	Clutter, W	MO	218
EDM	Kandeel, F	CA	224
EDM	Koch, C	MS	216
EDM	Lechan, R	MA	210
EDM	Lilienfeld, H	FL	216
EDM	Sherman, S	TX	223
Path	LiVolsi, V	PA	722
PS	Skinner, M	TX	822
S	Cance, W	NY	1090
S	Evans, D	WI	1113
S	Fraker, D	PA	1093
S	Lee, J	NY	1095
S	Moley, J	MO	1117
S	Olson, J	MD	1097
S	Solorzano, C	TN	1109
S	Sosa, J	NC	1109
S	Staren, E	AZ	1129

Endocrine Pathology

Spec	Name	St	Pg
Path	Baloch, Z	PA	720

Endocrine Surgery

Spec	Name	St	Pg
PS	Chwals, W	MA	814
S	Bouvet, M	CA	1130
S	Brunicardi, F	CA	1130
S	Carty, S	PA	1091
S	Doherty, G	MA	1085
S	Duh, Q	CA	1132
S	Fahey, T	NY	1093
S	Farley, D	MN	1114
S	Finlayson, C	CO	1122
S	Gawande, A	MA	1085
S	Hanks, J	VA	1105
S	Hodin, R	MA	1086
S	Howe, J	IA	1115
S	Kim, L	AR	1126
S	McIntyre, R	CO	1122
S	Moore, F	MA	1087
S	Norton, J	CA	1135
S	Schlinkert, R	AZ	1128
S	Traynor, M	ND	1123
S	Udelsman, R	CT	1088
S	Weber, C	GA	1110
S	Weigel, R	IA	1121

Endocrine Tumors

Spec	Name	St	Pg
S	Calvo, B	NC	1104
S	Carty, S	PA	1091
S	Lee, J	TX	1127
S	McAneny, D	MA	1087
S	Siperstein, A	OH	1120

Endocrinology

Spec	Name	St	Pg
EDM	Recker, R	NE	222
Ger	Abrass, I	WA	267
Ger	Gambert, S	MD	265
Ger	Morley, J	MO	266

Endocrinology & Joint Disorders

Spec	Name	St	Pg
Rhu	Lahita, R	NJ	1060

Endocrinology, Diabetes & Metabolism

Spec	Name	St	Pg
EDM	Abrahamson, M	MA	208
EDM	Ahmann, A	OR	223
EDM	Ain, K	KY	215
EDM	Akatsu, H	CA	223
EDM	Axelrod, L	MA	208
EDM	Bahn, R	MN	218
EDM	Ball, D	MD	210
EDM	Barrett, E	VA	216
EDM	Beaser, R	MA	208
EDM	Bergman, D	NY	211
EDM	Berkson, R	CA	224
EDM	Bhasin, S	MA	208
EDM	Bilezikian, J	NY	211
EDM	Biller, B	MA	208
EDM	Blum, C	NY	211
EDM	Bockman, R	NY	211
EDM	Braverman, L	MA	208
EDM	Brennan, M	MN	218
EDM	Brillon, D	NY	211
EDM	Broadstone, V	IN	218
EDM	Brown, J	TX	222
EDM	Burman, K	DC	211
EDM	Burmeister, L	MN	218
EDM	Buse, J	NC	216
EDM	Calvi, L	NY	211
EDM	Clore, J	VA	216
EDM	Clutter, W	MO	218
EDM	Cohen, R	OH	218
EDM	Comi, R	NH	208
EDM	Cooper, D	MD	212
EDM	Cryer, P	MO	219
EDM	Cunningham, G	TX	222
EDM	Cushing, G	MA	209
EDM	D'Alessio, D	OH	219
EDM	Dalkin, A	VA	216
EDM	Daniels, G	MA	209
EDM	Davies, T	NY	212
EDM	Dobs, A	MD	212
EDM	Donner, T	MD	212
EDM	Eckel, R	CO	222
EDM	Econs, M	IN	219
EDM	Edelman, S	CA	224
EDM	Ehrmann, D	IL	219
EDM	Emanuele, M	IL	219
EDM	Emanuele, N	IL	219
EDM	Feinglos, M	NC	216
EDM	Fitzgerald, P	CA	224
EDM	Gagel, R	TX	222
EDM	Goodman, N	FL	216
EDM	Greene, L	NY	212
EDM	Greenspan, S	PA	212
EDM	Haber, R	NY	212
EDM	Hammer, G	MI	219
EDM	Heber, D	CA	224
EDM	Herman, W	MI	219
EDM	Hirsch, I	WA	224
EDM	Hoffman, A	CA	224
EDM	Holick, M	MA	209
EDM	Inzucchi, S	CT	209
EDM	Jacobs, T	NY	213
EDM	Jensen, M	MN	220
EDM	Kahn, B	MA	209
EDM	Kamdar, V	CA	224
EDM	Kandeel, F	CA	224
EDM	Katznelson, L	CA	225
EDM	Kennedy, L	OH	220
EDM	Khosla, S	MN	220
EDM	Kleinberg, D	NY	213
EDM	Klonoff, D	CA	225
EDM	Koch, C	MS	216
EDM	Kopp, P	IL	220
EDM	Korytkowski, M	PA	213
EDM	Kronenberg, H	MA	209
EDM	Ladenson, P	MD	213
EDM	Larsen, P	MA	209
EDM	Lash, R	MI	220
EDM	Lavis, V	TX	223
EDM	LeBoff, M	MA	209
EDM	Lechan, R	MA	210
EDM	Levine, R	NH	210
EDM	Lilienfeld, H	FL	216
EDM	Lipson, A	DC	213
EDM	Maclaren, N	NY	213
EDM	Mandel, S	PA	213
EDM	Marshall, J	VA	217
EDM	Mazzone, T	IL	220
EDM	McConnell, R	NY	214
EDM	McGill, J	MO	220
EDM	McMahon, M	MN	221
EDM	Melmed, S	CA	225
EDM	Nathan, D	MA	210
EDM	Nestler, J	VA	217
EDM	Ober, K	NC	217
EDM	Orwoll, E	OR	225
EDM	Ovalle, F	AL	217
EDM	Pearce, E	MA	210
EDM	Peters, A	CA	225
EDM	Philipson, L	IL	221
EDM	Powers, A	TN	217
EDM	Recker, R	NE	222
EDM	Ridgway, E	CO	222
EDM	Robbins, R	TX	223
EDM	Roberts, M	PA	214
EDM	Rodbard, H	MD	214
EDM	Ross, D	MA	210
EDM	Rubenfeld, S	TX	223
EDM	Rushakoff, R	CA	225
EDM	Schutta, M	PA	214
EDM	Schwartz, S	PA	214
EDM	Seely, E	MA	210
EDM	Semenkovich, C	MO	221
EDM	Seplowitz, A	NY	214
EDM	Sherman, S	TX	223

Spec	Name	St	Pg
EDM	Singer, P	CA	225
EDM	Siris, E	NY	214
EDM	Skyler, J	FL	217
EDM	Smith, S	MN	221
EDM	Snyder, P	PA	215
EDM	Sowers, J	MO	221
EDM	Surks, M	NY	215
EDM	Swerdloff, R	CA	226
EDM	Thorner, M	VA	217
EDM	Tuttle, R	NY	215
EDM	Vance, M	VA	217
EDM	Waguespack, S	TX	223
EDM	Wartofsky, L	DC	215
EDM	Watts, N	OH	221
EDM	Weiss, R	IL	221
EDM	Weissman, P	FL	218
EDM	Werner, P	IL	221
EDM	Woeber, K	CA	226
EDM	Wondisford, F	MD	215
EDM	Xing, M	MD	215
EDM	Zimmerman, R	OH	222

Endometrial Cancer

Spec	Name	St	Pg
GO	Cantuaria, G	GA	281
GO	Rosenblum, N	PA	280

Endometriosis

Spec	Name	St	Pg
GO	Magrina, J	AZ	289
ObG	Einarsson, J	MA	560
ObG	Goldstein, M	NY	561
ObG	Jenkins, T	AL	563
ObG	Laufer, M	MA	560
ObG	Merritt, D	MO	565
ObG	Steege, J	NC	563
RE	Adamson, G	CA	1051
RE	Agarwal, S	CA	1051
RE	Clisham, P	IA	1050
RE	Coddington, C	MN	1047
RE	DeVane, G	FL	1045
RE	Dodds, W	MI	1047
RE	Durso, N	VA	1045
RE	Falcone, T	OH	1047
RE	Giudice, L	CA	1052
RE	Hornstein, M	MA	1040
RE	Huang, J	TX	1050
RE	Isaacson, K	MA	1040
RE	Jacobs, L	IL	1048
RE	Johnson, J	MA	1040
RE	Luciano, A	CT	1041
RE	Marrs, R	CA	1052
RE	Mukherjee, T	NY	1043
RE	Ory, S	FL	1046
RE	Petrozza, J	MA	1041
RE	Pfeifer, S	PA	1043
RE	Putman, J	TX	1050
RE	Ratts, V	MO	1048
RE	Schenken, R	TX	1050
RE	Schlaff, W	PA	1044
RE	Sondheimer, S	PA	1044
RE	Soules, M	WA	1053
RE	Surrey, E	CO	1049
RE	Van Voorhis, B	IA	1049
RE	Zinaman, M	MA	1041

Endometriosis-Adolescent

Spec	Name	St	Pg
ObG	Laufer, M	MA	560

Endometriosis-Intestine

Spec	Name	St	Pg
CRS	Bailey, H	TX	176

Endoscopic Sinus Surgery

Spec	Name	St	Pg
Oto	Bhattacharyya, N	MA	665
Oto	Clark, K	OK	691
Oto	Close, L	NY	668
Oto	DiNardo, L	VA	678
Oto	Edelstein, D	NY	669
Oto	Fried, M	NY	669
Oto	Gold, S	NY	670
Oto	Jacobs, J	NY	671
Oto	Josephson, J	NY	671
Oto	Kennedy, D	PA	672
Oto	Kingdom, T	CO	690
Oto	Kuhn, F	GA	679
Oto	Lawson, W	NY	673
Oto	Rosen, M	PA	674
Oto	Schaefer, S	NY	675
Oto	Schaitkin, B	PA	675
Oto	Senders, C	CA	697
Oto	Stankiewicz, J	IL	688
Oto	Vining, E	CT	667

Endoscopic Strip Craniectomy

Spec	Name	St	Pg
NS	Jimenez, D	TX	496

Endoscopic Surgery

Spec	Name	St	Pg
NS	Evans, J	PA	476
NS	Jho, H	PA	478
NS	Martin, N	CA	500
NS	Souweidane, M	NY	482
Oto	Samant, S	TN	681
Oto	Snyderman, C	PA	676
PS	Tracy, T	RI	814
RE	Goldberg, J	OH	1047
S	Herron, D	NY	1094
T&CS	Damiano, R	MO	1167

Endoscopic Surgery/Ventriculoscopy

Spec	Name	St	Pg
NS	Goumnerova, L	MA	473

Endoscopic Therapies

Spec	Name	St	Pg
Ge	Early, D	MO	247
Ge	Haluszka, O	PA	235
Ge	Hoffman, B	SC	243
Ge	Kantsevoy, S	MD	236
Ge	Lichtenstein, D	MA	231
Ge	Wilcox, C	AL	245

Endoscopic Ultrasound

Spec	Name	St	Pg
Ge	Aslanian, H	CT	230
Ge	Canto, M	MD	233
Ge	Chang, K	CA	255
Ge	Das, A	AZ	253
Ge	Dea, S	CA	255
Ge	Early, D	MO	247
Ge	Faigel, D	AZ	253
Ge	Gerdes, H	NY	234
Ge	Ginsberg, G	PA	234
Ge	Gordon, S	NH	231
Ge	Greenwald, B	MD	235
Ge	Haber, G	NY	235
Ge	Haluszka, O	PA	235
Ge	Hawes, R	FL	242
Ge	Hoffman, B	SC	243
Ge	Infantolino, A	PA	235
Ge	Jonnalagadda, S	MO	248
Ge	Kantsevoy, S	MD	236
Ge	Kimmey, M	WA	256
Ge	Kowalski, T	PA	237
Ge	Lambiase, L	TN	243
Ge	Levy, M	MN	249
Ge	Lightdale, C	NY	238
Ge	Mertz, H	TN	243
Ge	Peikin, S	NJ	239
Ge	Pochapin, M	NY	239
Ge	Rex, D	IN	250
Ge	Savides, T	CA	257

Endoscopy

Spec	Name	St	Pg
Ge	Albert, M	DC	232
Ge	Barkin, J	FL	241
Ge	Baron, T	MN	246
Ge	Branch, M	NC	241
Ge	Butterly, L	NH	230
Ge	Canto, M	MD	233
Ge	Carr-Locke, D	NY	233
Ge	Cello, J	CA	255
Ge	Cohen, L	NY	233
Ge	Das, A	AZ	253
Ge	Dea, S	CA	255
Ge	Dieterich, D	NY	234
Ge	Edmundowicz, S	MO	247
Ge	Eisen, G	OR	255
Ge	Elliott, N	GA	242
Ge	Fang, J	UT	252
Ge	Farraye, F	MA	230
Ge	Fisher, R	CT	230
Ge	Fleischer, D	AZ	254
Ge	Forsmark, C	FL	242
Ge	Gerdes, H	NY	234
Ge	Ginsberg, G	PA	234
Ge	Gostout, C	MN	248
Ge	Green, P	NY	235
Ge	Haber, G	NY	235
Ge	Hoops, T	PA	235
Ge	Kalloo, A	MD	236
Ge	Kelsey, P	MA	231
Ge	Kimmey, M	WA	256
Ge	Kochman, M	PA	236
Ge	Konicek, F	IL	248

Spec	Name	St	Pg
Ge	Kurtz, R	NY	237
Ge	Lebwohl, O	NY	237
Ge	Lewis, B	NY	237
Ge	Magun, A	NY	238
Ge	Miskovitz, P	NY	238
Ge	Peikin, S	NJ	239
Ge	Petrini, J	CA	257
Ge	Pfau, P	WI	249
Ge	Proctor, D	CT	232
Ge	Reichelderfer, M	WI	250
Ge	Rothstein, R	NH	232
Ge	Seidner, D	TN	245
Ge	Sherman, S	IN	250
Ge	Shike, M	NY	240
Ge	Vanagunas, A	IL	251
Ge	Vargo, J	OH	251
Ge	Waxman, I	IL	251
Ge	Waye, J	NY	240
Ge	Weinberg, D	PA	240
Ge	Weinstock, J	MA	232
ObG	Bradley, L	OH	564
Oto	Aviv, J	NY	668
PGe	Schwarz, S	NY	764
S	Marks, J	OH	1116
S	Mellinger, J	IL	1117
S	Ponsky, J	OH	1118
S	Stiegmann, G	CO	1123
S	Vitale, G	KY	1110

Endourology

Spec	Name	St	Pg
U	Hamilton, B	UT	1207
U	Nakada, S	WI	1205
U	Wong, C	OH	1206

Endovascular Neurosurgery

Spec	Name	St	Pg
NRad	Morris, P	NC	1022
NS	Patel, A	NY	480

Endovascular Stent Grafts

Spec	Name	St	Pg
T&CS	Szeto, W	PA	1159
VascS	Bandyk, D	CA	1230
VascS	Clair, D	OH	1227
VascS	Dougherty, M	PA	1223
VascS	Sanchez, L	MO	1228
VIR	Dake, M	CA	1032
VIR	Matsumoto, A	VA	1030

Endovascular Surgery

Spec	Name	St	Pg
NRad	Berenstein, A	NY	1020
NRad	Hirsch, J	MA	1019
NS	Hopkins, L	NY	478
NS	Levy, E	NY	479
T&CS	Miller, D	CA	1180
VascS	Acher, C	WI	1226
VascS	Adelman, M	NY	1221
VascS	Ahn, S	CA	1230
VascS	Ascher, E	NY	1221
VascS	Atnip, R	PA	1221
VascS	Benvenisty, A	NY	1222
VascS	Blebea, J	OK	1229
VascS	Brener, B	NJ	1222
VascS	Brewster, D	MA	1220
VascS	Carpenter, J	NJ	1222
VascS	Chaikof, E	MA	1220
VascS	Criado, F	MD	1222
VascS	D'Ayala, M	NY	1222
VascS	Eidt, J	SC	1225
VascS	Ellozy, S	NY	1223
VascS	Fowl, R	AZ	1229
VascS	Golden, M	PA	1223
VascS	Hakaim, A	FL	1225
VascS	Hodgson, K	IL	1227
VascS	Hollier, L	LA	1229
VascS	Huber, T	FL	1226
VascS	Iafrati, M	MA	1220
VascS	Kazmers, A	MI	1227
VascS	Kougias, P	TX	1229
VascS	Kwolek, C	MA	1220
VascS	LaMuraglia, G	MA	1221
VascS	Lantis, J	NY	1224
VascS	Makaroun, M	PA	1224
VascS	Marin, M	NY	1224
VascS	McCann, R	NC	1226
VascS	McKinsey, J	NY	1224
VascS	Money, S	AZ	1229
VascS	Morrissey, N	NY	1224
VascS	Naslund, T	TN	1226
VascS	Neville, R	DC	1224
VascS	Pevec, W	CA	1230
VascS	Pomposelli, F	MA	1221
VascS	Schneider, D	NY	1225
VascS	Sumpio, B	CT	1221
VascS	Weinstein, E	CO	1229
VascS	White, R	CA	1230

Endovascular Therapy

Spec	Name	St	Pg
Cv	Dangas, G	NY	92

Enteroscopy-Small Bowel

Spec	Name	St	Pg
Ge	Elliott, N	GA	242

Environmental Health in Children

Spec	Name	St	Pg
OM	Landrigan, P	NY	912

Environmental Medicine

Spec	Name	St	Pg
OM	Gochfeld, M	NJ	912
OM	Kipen, H	NJ	912
Pul	Bascom, R	PA	956

Eosinophil Disorders

Spec	Name	St	Pg
A&I	Lewis, J	AZ	85

Eosinophilic Esophagitis

Spec	Name	St	Pg
Ge	Falk, G	PA	234
Ge	Gluck, M	WA	256
PA&I	Spergel, J	PA	744
PGe	Gupta, S	IN	766

Epilepsy

Spec	Name	St	Pg
ChiN	Cohen, B	OH	148
ChiN	Edgar, T	WI	148
ChiN	Greenwood, R	NC	147
ChiN	Hartman, A	MD	145
ChiN	Kohrman, M	IL	148
ChiN	Legido, A	PA	145
ChiN	Nordli, D	IL	149
ChiN	Santos, C	DC	146
ChiN	Scher, M	OH	149
ChiN	Sharp, G	AR	151
ChiN	Tennison, M	NC	147
ChiN	Tuxhorn, I	OH	150
ChiN	Yamada, K	MO	150
ChiN	Zupanc, M	CA	152
N	Abou-Khalil, B	TN	523
N	Bebin, E	AL	523
N	Blum, A	RI	510
N	Brick, J	WV	513
N	DeGiorgio, C	CA	539
N	Devinsky, O	NY	514
N	Gross, P	MA	511
N	Heck, C	CA	540
N	Josephson, D	IN	530
N	Labiner, D	AZ	537
N	Luders, H	OH	531
N	Morrell, M	CA	541
N	Nicholl, J	LA	537
N	Oommen, K	TX	537
N	Sperling, M	PA	521
NRad	Faro, S	PA	1020
NRad	Rowley, H	WI	1024
NS	Asher, A	NC	483
NS	Bakay, R	IL	488
NS	Bingaman, W	OH	489
NS	Boop, F	TN	484
NS	Danielpour, M	CA	499
NS	Duhaime, A	MA	473
NS	Ewend, M	NC	484
NS	Goodman, R	NY	477
NS	Jallo, G	MD	478
NS	Liu, C	CA	500
NS	Meyer, F	MN	491
NS	Ojemann, J	WA	501
NS	Ragheb, J	FL	486
NS	Shuer, L	CA	502
NS	Weiner, H	NY	482
NS	Wharen, R	FL	488
NS	Wilberger, J	PA	483

Epilepsy in Pregnancy

Spec	Name	St	Pg
MF	Samuels, P	OH	439
N	Bergey, G	MD	513
N	Liporace, J	PA	518
N	Pennell, P	MA	511
N	Rubin, S	IL	533

Spec Name St Pg

Epilepsy in Tuberous Sclerosis

ChiN Riviello, J NY 146

Epilepsy in Women

N Bergey, G MD 513
N Jobst, B NH 511
N Liporace, J PA 518
N Morrell, M CA 541
N Pennell, P MA 511

Epilepsy-Adult & Pediatric

NS Lee, M TX 496

Epilepsy/Seizure Disorders

ChiN Gospe, S WA 151
ChiN Griesemer, D MA 144
ChiN Holmes, G VT 144
ChiN Kovnar, E WI 149
ChiN Mandelbaum, D RI 144
ChiN Maytal, J NY 146
ChiN Mitchell, W CA 151
ChiN Riviello, J NY 146
ChiN Sankar, R CA 152
ChiN Shinnar, S NY 147
ChiN Wheless, J TN 147
ChiN Wyllie, E OH 150
N Barkley, G MI 528
N Bergey, G MD 513
N Cole, A MA 510
N Ferrendelli, J TX 536
N Fisher, R CA 540
N French, J NY 515
N Hecox, K WI 530
N Jobst, B NH 511
N Krauss, G MD 516
N Krumholz, A MD 517
N Kuzniecky, R NY 517
N Labar, D NY 517
N Strom, L CO 535
NS Adelson, P AZ 495
NS Baltuch, G PA 474
NS Bucholz, R MO 489
NS Caputy, A DC 475
NS Cosgrove, G RI 472
NS Eisenberg, H MD 476
NS Madsen, J MA 473
NS Penar, P VT 473
NS Spencer, D CT 474

Epispadias

Ped Uro Mesrobian, H WI 827

Erectile Dysfunction

EDM Cunningham, G TX 222
U Bar-Chama, N NY 1188
U Broderick, G FL 1197
U Burnett, A MD 1189
U Carson, C NC 1197
U Childs, S CO 1206
U Chun, T NJ 1189
U Danoff, D CA 1211
U Donovan, J OH 1203
U Fraser, L MS 1197
U Goldstein, I CA 1212
U Goldstein, M NY 1190
U Gomery, P MA 1186
U Hellstrom, W LA 1209
U Levine, L IL 1204
U Lipshultz, L TX 1209
U Lloyd, L AL 1198
U McCullough, A NY 1192
U McVary, K IL 1204
U Montague, D OH 1204
U Mulhall, J NY 1193
U Nagler, H NY 1193
U Nehra, A IL 1205
U Ohl, D MI 1205
U Rajfer, J CA 1213
U Ross, L IL 1205
U Sadeghi-Nejad, H NJ 1194
U Shabsigh, R NY 1195
U Sharlip, I CA 1213
U Sigman, M RI 1188
U Steers, W VA 1201
U Turek, P CA 1214

Esophageal Cancer

DR Coakley, F OR 1017
DR Erasmus, J TX 1016
Ge Aslanian, H CT 230
Ge Estores, D FL 242
Ge Fleischer, D AZ 254
Ge Greenwald, B MD 235
Ge Ravich, W MD 239
Ge Schembre, D WA 257
Onc Adelstein, D OH 365
Onc Ajani, J TX 378
Onc Forastiere, A MD 343
Onc Fuchs, C MA 332
Onc Grem, J NE 377
Onc Ilson, D NY 345
Onc Lacy, J CT 333
Onc Loehrer, P IN 371
Onc Masters, G DE 347
Onc Reid, T CA 391
Onc Ross, H AZ 383
Onc Stoopler, M NY 352
Onc Sun, W PA 352
Onc Vokes, E IL 374
Path Chandrasoma, P CA 732
Path Goldblum, J OH 728
Path Odze, R MA 719
RadRO Bradley, J MO 988
RadRO Choi, N MA 976
RadRO Cox, J TX 993
RadRO Greenberger, J PA 980
RadRO Halpern, H IL 989
RadRO Kleinberg, L MD 981
RadRO Komaki, R TX 994
RadRO Konski, A MI 990
RadRO Martenson, J MN 991
RadRO Minsky, B TX 994
RadRO Seung, S OR 997
RadRO Suntharalingam, M MD 983
RadRO Thomas, C OR 998
RadRO Videtic, G OH 992
S Aranha, G IL 1111
S August, D NJ 1089
S Beauchamp, R TN 1103
S Bolton, J LA 1124
S Brodsky, J PA 1090
S Cioffi, W RI 1084
S Karpeh, M NY 1095
S Levine, E NC 1106
S Oelschlager, B WA 1135
S Paz, I CA 1135
S Pellegrini, C WA 1135
S Posner, M IL 1118
S Salo, J NC 1108
T&CS Altorki, N NY 1150
T&CS Baciewicz, F MI 1167
T&CS Bains, M NY 1150
T&CS Bhora, F NY 1151
T&CS Brinckerhoff, L MA 1146
T&CS Bull, D UT 1172
T&CS Cerfolio, R AL 1161
T&CS D'Amico, T NC 1161
T&CS Demmy, T NY 1151
T&CS Deschamps, C MN 1168
T&CS Ferguson, M IL 1168
T&CS Fernando, H MA 1147
T&CS Flores, R NY 1152
T&CS Gaissert, H MA 1147
T&CS Handy, J OR 1178
T&CS Harpole, D NC 1162
T&CS Heitmiller, R MD 1154
T&CS Howington, J IL 1168
T&CS Jones, D NY 1154
T&CS Kaiser, L PA 1154
T&CS Keenan, R PA 1155
T&CS Keller, S NY 1155
T&CS Kernstine, K TX 1175
T&CS Kiev, J WV 1155
T&CS Kucharczuk, J PA 1155
T&CS Landreneau, R LA 1175
T&CS Lau, C VA 1163
T&CS Louie, B WA 1179
T&CS Marshall, M DC 1156
T&CS Mathisen, D MA 1147
T&CS Meyers, B MO 1170
T&CS Miller, D GA 1163
T&CS Moore, J GA 1163
T&CS Mulligan, M WA 1180
T&CS Naunheim, K MO 1170
T&CS Nesbitt, J TN 1164
T&CS Orringer, M MI 1170
T&CS Park, B NJ 1157
T&CS Patterson, G MO 1171
T&CS Pechet, T PA 1157
T&CS Port, J NY 1157
T&CS Putnam, J TN 1165
T&CS Roth, J TX 1176
T&CS Rusch, V NY 1158

Spec	Name	St	Pg
T&CS	Scott, W	PA	1158
T&CS	Soberman, M	MD	1158
T&CS	Sugarbaker, D	MA	1148
T&CS	Swanson, S	MA	1148
T&CS	Swisher, S	TX	1176
T&CS	Wain, J	MA	1149
T&CS	Walsh, G	TX	1177
T&CS	Watson, T	NY	1159
T&CS	Weigel, T	ME	1149
T&CS	Weksler, B	PA	1160
T&CS	Whyte, R	MA	1149
T&CS	Wood, D	WA	1181
T&CS	Wright, C	MA	1149
T&CS	Yang, S	MD	1160
T&CS	Zwischenberger, J	KY	1166

Esophageal Disorders

Spec	Name	St	Pg
Ge	Benjamin, S	DC	232
Ge	Castell, D	SC	241
Ge	Cohen, L	NY	233
Ge	DeVault, K	FL	242
Ge	Di Marino, A	PA	234
Ge	Falk, G	PA	234
Ge	Fang, J	UT	252
Ge	Gerson, L	CA	256
Ge	Kahrilas, P	IL	248
Ge	Katz, P	PA	236
Ge	Koch, K	NC	243
Ge	Kotler, D	NY	237
Ge	Lipshutz, W	PA	238
Ge	Markowitz, D	NY	238
Ge	Mittal, R	CA	257
Ge	Murray, J	MN	249
Ge	Roth, B	CA	257
Ge	Vaezi, M	TN	245
PGe	Gunasekaran, T	IL	766
PGe	Spivak, W	NY	764
S	McFadden, D	CT	1087
S	Richards, W	AL	1108
S	Sharp, K	TN	1109
S	Swanstrom, L	OR	1137
T&CS	Fernando, H	MA	1147

Esophageal Surgery

Spec	Name	St	Pg
PS	Jennings, R	MA	814
S	Crookes, P	CA	1131
S	Dempsey, D	PA	1092
S	Hunter, J	OR	1133
S	Oelschlager, B	WA	1135
S	Pellegrini, C	WA	1135
S	Peters, J	NY	1098
S	Reiner, M	NY	1099
S	Swanstrom, L	OR	1137
S	Unger, S	FL	1110
T&CS	Battafarano, R	MD	1150
T&CS	Cassivi, S	MN	1167
T&CS	DeCamp, M	IL	1167
T&CS	Feins, R	NC	1162
T&CS	Iannettoni, M	IA	1169
T&CS	Jablons, D	CA	1179
T&CS	Johnson, S	TX	1175

Spec	Name	St	Pg
T&CS	Kernstine, K	TX	1175
T&CS	Lazar, H	MA	1147
T&CS	Mitchell, J	CO	1173
T&CS	Mullett, T	KY	1164
T&CS	Sanchez, J	MD	1158
T&CS	Soberman, M	MD	1158
T&CS	Weiman, D	TN	1166

Esthesioneuroblastoma

Spec	Name	St	Pg
Oto	Kennedy, D	PA	672
Oto	Olsen, K	MN	687

Ethics

Spec	Name	St	Pg
Ger	Finucane, T	MD	264
H & PM	Arnold, R	PA	406
H & PM	Levy, M	PA	406
NP	Boyle, R	VA	450
NP	Holzman, I	NY	449
NP	Meadow, W	IL	452
NP	Muraskas, J	IL	452
Onc	Brescia, F	SC	356
Ped	Fost, N	WI	741
Ped	Lantos, J	MO	741
PHO	Morgan, E	IL	784
PHO	Santana, V	TN	781
S	Angelos, P	IL	1111

Ethics Issues in Neonatalogy

Spec	Name	St	Pg
Ped	Lantos, J	MO	741

Ethnic Skin Disorders

Spec	Name	St	Pg
D	Barbosa, V	IL	194
D	Grimes, P	CA	201
D	McMichael, A	NC	193

Ewing's Sarcoma

Spec	Name	St	Pg
Onc	Tap, W	NY	352
OrS	McDonald, D	MO	643
Path	Antonescu, C	NY	720
Ped	Kleinerman, E	TX	742
PHO	Hawkins, D	WA	790
PS	Shamberger, R	MA	814

Exercise Physiology

Spec	Name	St	Pg
PCd	Driscoll, D	MN	752
Rhu	Bunning, R	DC	1059

Eye Diseases-Hereditary

Spec	Name	St	Pg
Oph	Drack, A	IA	594
Oph	Gorin, M	CA	606
Oph	Heckenlively, J	MI	595
Oph	Lewis, R	TX	602
Oph	Stone, E	IA	599
Oph	Summers, C	MN	599

Eye Growth/Development

Spec	Name	St	Pg
Oph	Quinn, G	PA	583

Eye Movement Disorders

Spec	Name	St	Pg
N	Lavin, P	TN	525
Oph	Cheeseman, E	SC	587

Eye Muscle Disorders

Spec	Name	St	Pg
Oph	Choy, A	CA	605
Oph	Ellis, G	LA	601
Oph	Granet, D	CA	606
Oph	Hall, L	NY	579
Oph	Hunter, D	MA	574
Oph	McKeown, C	FL	590
Oph	Mills, M	PA	582
Oph	Nelson, L	PA	582
Oph	Wang, F	NY	586

Eye Muscle Surgery

Spec	Name	St	Pg
Oph	Burke, M	OH	594
Oph	Koller, H	PA	580
Oph	Richard, J	OK	603
Oph	Rosenberg, M	IL	599

Eye Pathology

Spec	Name	St	Pg
Oph	Rao, N	CA	608

Eye Tumors/Cancer

Spec	Name	St	Pg
Oph	Abramson, D	NY	575
Oph	Albert, D	WI	593
Oph	Alward, W	IA	593
Oph	Augsburger, J	OH	593
Oph	Boxrud, C	CA	605
Oph	Char, D	CA	605
Oph	Drack, A	IA	594
Oph	Dutton, J	NC	588
Oph	Finger, P	NY	578
Oph	Haik, B	TN	589
Oph	Harbour, J	FL	589
Oph	Mieler, W	IL	597
Oph	Murphree, A	CA	608
Oph	Murray, T	FL	590
Oph	O'Brien, J	PA	582
Oph	Pulido, J	MN	598
Oph	Shields, J	PA	585
Oph	Soparkar, C	TX	603
Oph	Sternberg, P	TN	591
Oph	Wilson, D	OR	610
Oph	Wilson, M	TN	592
RadRO	Crocker, I	GA	984
RadRO	Markoe, A	FL	985
RadRO	McCormick, B	NY	981
RadRO	Quivey, J	CA	997
RadRO	Rotman, M	NY	982

Eyelid Cancer & Reconstruction

Spec	Name	St	Pg
Oph	Cockerham, K	CA	605

Spec	Name	St	Pg
Oph	Della Rocca, R	NY	577
Oph	Esmaeli-Azad, B	TX	602
Oph	Gigantelli, J	NE	601
Oph	Nerad, J	OH	598
Oph	Rubin, P	MA	575

Eyelid Cosmetic & Reconstructive Surgery

Spec	Name	St	Pg
Oph	Ahmad, A	IL	593
Oph	Lisman, R	NY	581
Oph	Putterman, A	IL	599
Oph	Rubin, P	MA	575

Eyelid Problems/Ptosis/Blepharospasm

Spec	Name	St	Pg
Oph	Anderson, R	UT	601

Eyelid Surgery

Spec	Name	St	Pg
Oph	Cahill, K	OH	594
Oph	Carter, K	IA	594
Oph	Patrinely, J	FL	591
Oph	Stefanyszyn, M	PA	585
Oto	Beeson, W	IN	683
Oto	Larrabee, W	WA	695
PlS	Carraway, J	VA	889
PlS	Imber, G	NY	883
PlS	Miller, T	CA	904
PlS	Sanders, G	CA	905
PlS	Sullivan, P	RI	879
PlS	Tabbal, N	NY	887

Eyelid Surgery/Blepharoplasty

Spec	Name	St	Pg
PlS	Leaf, N	CA	903
PlS	Metzinger, S	LA	900
PlS	Spinelli, H	NY	887

Eyelid Tumors/Cancer

Spec	Name	St	Pg
Oph	Della Rocca, R	NY	577
Oph	Elner, V	MI	595
Oph	Kazim, M	NY	580
Oph	Yeatts, R	NC	592

Eyelid/Tear Duct Reconstruction

Spec	Name	St	Pg
Oph	Cahill, K	OH	594
Oph	Lisman, R	NY	581
Oph	Mawn, L	TN	590

F

Fabry's Disease

Spec	Name	St	Pg
CG	Wasserstein, M	NY	158

Spec	Name	St	Pg
CG	Wilcox, W	CA	164
Nep	Thomas, C	IA	465

Facial Deformities/Reconstruction

Spec	Name	St	Pg
PlS	Bentz, M	WI	892
PlS	LaBruna, A	NY	883

Facial Feminization Surgery (FFS)

Spec	Name	St	Pg
PlS	Ousterhout, D	CA	904

Facial Nerve Disorders

Spec	Name	St	Pg
Oto	Bojrab, D	MI	683
Oto	Brackmann, D	CA	694
Oto	Lalwani, A	NY	672
Oto	Roland, J	NY	674
Oto	Schaitkin, B	PA	675
Oto	Shelton, C	UT	690
Oto	Wax, M	OR	697
PlS	Manders, E	PA	884

Facial Paralysis

Spec	Name	St	Pg
Oto	Hadlock, T	MA	666
Oto	Hom, D	OH	685
Oto	Leonetti, J	IL	686
Oto	Pensak, M	OH	687
PlS	Sherman, R	CA	905

Facial Paralysis Reconstruction

Spec	Name	St	Pg
PlS	Baker, D	NY	880
PlS	Kuzon, W	MI	894
PlS	Rose, E	NY	886

Facial Plastic & Reconstructive Surgery

Spec	Name	St	Pg
Oto	Beeson, W	IN	683
Oto	Gosselin, B	NH	665
Oto	Hayden, R	AZ	692
Oto	Hom, D	OH	685
Oto	Kriet, J	KS	690
Oto	Marentette, L	MI	686
Oto	Moe, K	WA	696
Oto	Shockley, W	NC	681
Oto	Teknos, T	OH	688
Oto	Wax, M	OR	697
Oto	Weisman, R	CA	697
Oto	Wong, B	CA	698
PlS	Bradley, J	CA	901
PlS	Cordeiro, P	NY	881
PlS	Eriksson, E	MA	878
PlS	Hunstad, J	NC	890
PlS	LaBruna, A	NY	883
PlS	Pomahac, B	MA	879
PlS	Rodriguez, E	MD	886
PlS	Rose, E	NY	886
PlS	Siebert, J	WI	896

Spec	Name	St	Pg
PlS	Yu, J	GA	892

Facial Plastic Surgery

Spec	Name	St	Pg
Oph	Seiff, S	CA	609
Oto	Epstein, J	FL	678
Oto	Farrior, E	FL	678
Oto	Hilger, P	MN	685
Oto	Pribitkin, E	PA	674
Oto	Quatela, V	NY	674
PlS	Ness, J	MN	895
PlS	Smith, P	FL	891

Facial Rejuvenation

Spec	Name	St	Pg
D	Brody, H	GA	191
D	Garden, J	IL	195
D	Gordon, M	NY	188
D	Grossman, M	NY	188
D	Kilmer, S	CA	201
Oto	Graham, H	LA	692
PlS	Barton, F	TX	898
PlS	Beasley, M	NC	888
PlS	Burns, A	TX	898
PlS	Cederna, P	MI	893
PlS	Davis, G	NC	889
PlS	Fodor, P	CA	902
PlS	Fox, J	PA	882
PlS	Gregory, R	FL	890
PlS	Grossman, J	CO	897
PlS	Hoffman, L	NY	882
PlS	Koplin, L	CA	903
PlS	Markowitz, B	CA	904
PlS	Marten, T	CA	904
PlS	Rand, R	WA	904
PlS	Rappaport, N	TX	900
PlS	Rohrich, R	TX	900
PlS	Romano, J	CA	905
PlS	Rosenberg, H	CA	905
PlS	Singer, R	CA	905
PlS	Singh, N	MD	886
PlS	Stuzin, J	FL	891
PlS	Zins, J	OH	897

Facial Surgery-Chin & Lip

Spec	Name	St	Pg
PlS	Zide, B	NY	888

Facial Trauma/Fractures

Spec	Name	St	Pg
PlS	Baker, S	DC	880
PlS	Gruss, J	WA	902
PlS	Manson, P	MD	884
PlS	Matthews, D	NC	891

Facial Tumors

Spec	Name	St	Pg
PlS	Yu, J	GA	892

Falls in the Elderly

Spec	Name	St	Pg
Ger	Lipsitz, L	MA	264
Ger	Studenski, S	PA	265
Ger	Tinetti, M	CT	264

Family Therapy

Spec	Name	St	Pg
ChAP	Sargent, A	MA	938
ChAP	Wamboldt, M	CO	942
Psyc	Shapiro, E	MA	922

Fanconi Aplastic Anemia

Spec	Name	St	Pg
Ped	Berman, B	MI	741

Female Genital Cutting (FGC) Education

Spec	Name	St	Pg
ObG	Nour, N	MA	560

Fertility in Cancer Survivors

Spec	Name	St	Pg
CG	Mulvihill, J	OK	161
PHO	Green, D	TN	779

Fertility Preservation

Spec	Name	St	Pg
RE	Toth, T	MA	1041

Fertility Preservation in Cancer

Spec	Name	St	Pg
GO	Burnett, A	AR	288
GO	Fields, A	DC	278
GO	Gershenson, D	TX	288
GO	Reynolds, R	MI	286
Onc	Matulonis, U	MA	334
RE	Cohen, D	IL	1047
RE	Copperman, A	NY	1041
RE	Crowley, W	MA	1040
RE	Ginsburg, E	MA	1040
RE	Gracia, C	PA	1042
RE	Grazi, R	NY	1042
RE	Grifo, J	NY	1042
RE	Kuo, J	CA	1052
RE	Licciardi, F	NY	1043
RE	Marshall, L	WA	1052
RE	McGovern, P	NJ	1043
RE	Molo, M	IL	1048
RE	Noyes, N	NY	1043
RE	Patrizio, P	CT	1041
RE	Rosenwaks, Z	NY	1044
RE	Sauer, M	NY	1044
RE	Seifer, D	NY	1044
RE	Smikle, C	CA	1052
U	Schlegel, P	NY	1194
U	Sheinfeld, J	NY	1195

Fetal Abnormalities

Spec	Name	St	Pg
CG	Bianchi, D	MA	156
CG	Driscoll, D	PA	157
MF	Dooley, S	IL	438
MF	Genc, M	NY	434
MF	Robichaux, A	LA	441
CG	Morris, C	NV	163
CG	Seaver, L	HI	163

Fetal Alcohol Syndrome

Spec	Name	St	Pg
CG	Cunniff, C	AZ	161
CG	Hoyme, H	SD	161

Fetal Cardiology

Spec	Name	St	Pg
PCd	Lewin, M	WA	754
PCd	Rychik, J	PA	749
PCd	Sherman, F	PA	750

Fetal Diagnosis & Therapy

Spec	Name	St	Pg
MF	Blakemore, K	MD	433
MF	Copel, J	CT	432
MF	Goldberg, J	CA	442
MF	Koos, B	CA	443
MF	MacGregor, S	IL	439
MF	Moore, T	CA	443
MF	Silver, R	IL	439
MF	Tabsh, K	CA	443
MF	Treadwell, M	MI	440
MF	Wilkins-Haug, L	MA	433
ObG	Corteville, J	OH	564
ObG	Evans, M	NY	561

Fetal Echocardiography

Spec	Name	St	Pg
MF	Copel, J	CT	432
MF	Reed, K	AZ	441
MF	Robinson, J	MA	433
PCd	Biancaniello, T	NY	748
PCd	Bierman, F	NY	748
PCd	Colvin, E	AL	751
PCd	Crosson, J	MD	748
PCd	Parness, I	NY	749

Fetal Imaging

Spec	Name	St	Pg
DR	Hubbard, A	NE	1016

Fetal Macrosomia

Spec	Name	St	Pg
MF	Benedetti, T	WA	442

Fetal MRI

Spec	Name	St	Pg
DR	Hubbard, A	NE	1016

Fetal Neuroradiology

Spec	Name	St	Pg
NRad	Barnes, P	CA	1026

Fetal Neurosurgery

Spec	Name	St	Pg
NS	Sutton, L	PA	482

Fetal Pathology

Spec	Name	St	Pg
Path	Faye-Petersen, O	AL	726

Fetal Surgery

Spec	Name	St	Pg
MF	Carr, S	RI	432
MF	Chmait, R	CA	442
MF	Robichaux, A	LA	441
MF	Wilkins-Haug, L	MA	433
ObG	De Lia, J	WI	564
PS	Adzick, N	PA	814
PS	Albanese, C	CA	823
PS	Bond, S	KY	817
PS	Cass, D	TX	822
PS	Crombleholme, T	CO	821
PS	Farmer, D	CA	823
PS	Flake, A	PA	815
PS	Glick, P	NY	816
PS	Krummel, T	CA	823
PS	Proctor, M	WA	823
PS	Tracy, T	RI	814

Fetal Surgical Imaging

Spec	Name	St	Pg
DR	Benson, C	MA	1007

Fetal Therapy

Spec	Name	St	Pg
CG	Mahoney, M	CT	156
MF	Berkowitz, R	NY	433
MF	Cheng, E	WA	442
MF	Eddleman, K	NY	434
MF	Mari, G	TN	437

Fetal Ultrasound

Spec	Name	St	Pg
MF	Parry, S	PA	435

Fetal Ultrasound/Obstetrical Imaging

Spec	Name	St	Pg
DR	Cohen, H	TN	1013

Fetal Urology

Spec	Name	St	Pg
Ped Uro	Maizels, M	IL	827
Ped Uro	Rushton, H	DC	825

Fever in Returning Travelers

Spec	Name	St	Pg
Inf	Wallace, M	FL	417

Fevers of Unknown Origin

Spec	Name	St	Pg
Inf	Auwaerter, P	MD	412
Inf	Cunha, B	NY	413
Inf	Trenholme, G	IL	419
PInf	Alexander, K	IL	795
PInf	McKinney, R	NC	794

Fevers-Periodic

Spec	Name	St	Pg
Ped	Infante, A	TX	742

Fibrodysplasia Ossificans Progressiv FOP

Spec	Name	St	Pg
OrS	Kaplan, F	PA	627

Fibromyalgia

Spec	Name	St	Pg
Rhu	Crofford, L	TN	1063

Specialty & Special Expertise Index

Spec	Name	St	Pg
Rhu	Katz, R	IL	1065
Rhu	Rothenberg, R	MD	1062
Rhu	Solitar, B	NY	1062

Fine Needle Aspiration Biopsy

Spec	Name	St	Pg
Path	Ehya, H	PA	721
Path	Gupta, P	PA	721
Path	Ljung, B	CA	733
Path	Silverman, J	PA	724

Fluid/Electrolyte Balance

Spec	Name	St	Pg
Nep	Coe, F	IL	463
Nep	Gluck, S	CA	466
Nep	Olivero, J	TX	466
Nep	Weiner, I	FL	462

Food & Drug Allergy

Spec	Name	St	Pg
A&I	Buchbinder, E	NY	80
A&I	Shepherd, G	NY	81
PA&I	Bahna, S	LA	746

Food Allergy

Spec	Name	St	Pg
A&I	Castells, M	MA	80
A&I	Ein, D	DC	81
A&I	Grammer, L	IL	83
A&I	Greenberger, P	IL	84
A&I	Slankard, M	NY	82
A&I	Tobin, M	IL	84
A&I	Umetsu, D	MA	80
PA&I	Bock, S	CO	745
PA&I	Burks, A	NC	744
PA&I	Ehrlich, P	NY	743
PA&I	Epstein, S	CA	747
PA&I	Josephs, S	MD	743
PA&I	Leung, D	CO	746
PA&I	Pongracic, J	IL	745
PA&I	Sampson, H	NY	743
PA&I	Schuberth, K	MD	744
PA&I	Sicherer, S	NY	744
PA&I	Spergel, J	PA	744
PA&I	Wasserman, R	TX	746
PA&I	Wood, R	MD	744
PPul	Lapey, A	MA	806

Food Allergy & Eczema

Spec	Name	St	Pg
A&I	Sanders, G	MI	84

Foodborne Illnesses

Spec	Name	St	Pg
Inf	Lorber, B	PA	413

Foot & Ankle Surgery

Spec	Name	St	Pg
OrS	Bauman, P	NY	620
OrS	Brodsky, J	TX	648
OrS	Coughlin, M	ID	646
OrS	Deland, J	NY	623
OrS	DeOrio, J	NC	635
OrS	DiGiovanni, C	RI	616
OrS	Levine, D	NY	628
OrS	Manoli, A	MI	643
OrS	Myerson, M	MD	629
OrS	Nunley, J	NC	637
OrS	Pinzur, M	IL	644
OrS	Saltzman, C	UT	647
OrS	Sangeorzan, B	WA	653
OrS	Smith, D	WA	653
OrS	Walling, A	FL	638
OrS	Wapner, K	PA	633
OrS	Weinfeld, S	NY	634
SM	Teitz, C	WA	1079

Foot & Ankle Surgery-Complex

Spec	Name	St	Pg
OrS	Brage, M	WA	649
OrS	Greisberg, J	NY	624
OrS	Myerson, M	MD	629

Foot Deformities

Spec	Name	St	Pg
OrS	Davidson, R	PA	622
OrS	DeOrio, J	NC	635
OrS	Weinfeld, S	NY	634

Forensic Pathology

Spec	Name	St	Pg
Path	Mark, E	MA	719

Forensic Psychiatry

Spec	Name	St	Pg
AdP	Frances, R	NY	936
Psyc	Appelbaum, P	NY	922
Psyc	Eth, S	FL	928
Psyc	Greiner, C	NE	931
Psyc	Neppe, V	WA	934
Psyc	Wilson, D	FL	929

Fracture Deformities/Arm

Spec	Name	St	Pg
HS	Putnam, M	MN	304

Fractures

Spec	Name	St	Pg
HS	Idler, R	CO	304
HS	Melone, C	NY	299
HS	Wolfe, S	NY	300
OrS	Brage, M	WA	649
OrS	Dirschl, D	IL	640
OrS	Sethi, P	CT	619
SM	Veitch, A	NM	1078

Fractures & Tendon Transfers

Spec	Name	St	Pg
HS	Abrams, R	CA	305
HS	Hastings, H	IN	303

Fractures in the Elderly

Spec	Name	St	Pg
OrS	Tornetta, P	MA	619

Fractures-Complex

Spec	Name	St	Pg
HS	Fischer, T	IN	302
OrS	Browner, B	CT	616
OrS	Rodriguez, J	NY	631
OrS	Tornetta, P	MA	619

Fractures-Complex & Non Union

Spec	Name	St	Pg
OrS	Anglen, J	IN	639
OrS	Ebraheim, N	OH	641
OrS	Friedlaender, G	CT	617
OrS	Helfet, D	NY	625
OrS	Joyce, M	OH	642
OrS	Lowenberg, D	CA	652
OrS	Muschler, G	OH	643
OrS	Rozbruch, S	NY	631
OrS	Webb, L	GA	639

Fractures-Non Union

Spec	Name	St	Pg
HS	Jupiter, J	MA	296
OrS	Browner, B	CT	616
OrS	Swiontkowski, M	MN	645
OrS	Wilkins, R	CO	647

Fractures-Pediatric

Spec	Name	St	Pg
OrS	Beaty, J	TN	635
OrS	Hyman, J	NY	626

Fractures-Stress

Spec	Name	St	Pg
OrS	Helfet, D	NY	625

Frail Elderly

Spec	Name	St	Pg
Ger	Callahan, E	NY	264
Ger	Thomas, D	MO	266

Frailty Syndrome

Spec	Name	St	Pg
Ger	Hanson, L	NC	265
Ger	Morley, J	MO	266

Frbromyalgia Syndrome (FMS)

Spec	Name	St	Pg
Psyc	Manevitz, A	NY	925

Fungal Infections

Spec	Name	St	Pg
Inf	Galgiani, J	AZ	420
Inf	O'Keefe, J	IL	418
Inf	Sobel, J	MI	419
Inf	Van Der Horst, C	NC	417
PInf	Belcher, C	IN	795
PInf	Saiman, L	NY	794

G

Gait Disorders

Spec	Name	St	Pg
PMR	De Lateur, B	MD	863
PMR	Kuiken, T	IL	869

Gallbladder & Biliary Cancer

Spec	Name	St	Pg
S	DeMatteo, R	NY	1092
S	Espat, N	RI	1085
S	Hiotis, S	NY	1094
S	Jarnagin, W	NY	1094
S	Pawlik, T	MD	1098
S	Sielaff, T	MN	1119
S	Vauthey, J	TX	1129

Gallbladder & Biliary Disease

Spec	Name	St	Pg
S	Drebin, J	PA	1092

Gallbladder Surgery

Spec	Name	St	Pg
S	Vitale, G	KY	1110

Gastroenterology

Spec	Name	St	Pg
Ge	Abreu, M	FL	241
Ge	Al-Kawas, F	DC	232
Ge	Albert, M	DC	232
Ge	Anderson, K	TX	252
Ge	Aronchick, C	PA	232
Ge	Aslanian, H	CT	230
Ge	Bacon, B	MO	246
Ge	Baillie, J	NC	241
Ge	Balart, L	LA	253
Ge	Barkin, J	FL	241
Ge	Barnes, D	OH	246
Ge	Baron, T	MN	246
Ge	Benjamin, S	DC	232
Ge	Berg, C	NC	241
Ge	Bloomer, J	AL	241
Ge	Boland, C	TX	253
Ge	Borum, M	DC	233
Ge	Boyer, T	AZ	253
Ge	Branch, M	NC	241
Ge	Brandt, L	NY	233
Ge	Brazer, S	NC	241
Ge	Bresalier, R	TX	253
Ge	Brown, K	MI	246
Ge	Brown, R	NY	233
Ge	Bulat, R	LA	253
Ge	Butterly, L	NH	230
Ge	Canto, M	MD	233
Ge	Carr-Locke, D	NY	233
Ge	Castell, D	SC	241
Ge	Cello, J	CA	255
Ge	Chang, K	CA	255
Ge	Chari, S	MN	246
Ge	Chey, W	MI	246
Ge	Chung, D	MA	230
Ge	Chung, R	MA	230
Ge	Cohen, J	NY	233
Ge	Cohen, L	NY	233
Ge	Cominelli, F	OH	246
Ge	Crippin, J	MO	247
Ge	Cunningham, J	AZ	253
Ge	Das, A	AZ	253
Ge	Dea, S	CA	255
Ge	DeCross, A	NY	233
Ge	DeVault, K	FL	242
Ge	Di Bisceglie, A	MO	247
Ge	Di Marino, A	PA	234
Ge	Diehl, A	NC	242
Ge	Dienstag, J	MA	230
Ge	Dieterich, D	NY	234
Ge	Drossman, D	NC	242
Ge	Early, D	MO	247
Ge	Edmundowicz, S	MO	247
Ge	Eisen, G	OR	255
Ge	Elliott, D	IA	247
Ge	Elliott, N	GA	242
Ge	Ellis, J	CA	255
Ge	Elta, G	MI	247
Ge	Estores, D	FL	242
Ge	Faigel, D	AZ	253
Ge	Falk, G	PA	234
Ge	Fallon, M	TX	254
Ge	Fang, J	UT	252
Ge	Farraye, F	MA	230
Ge	Fennerty, M	OR	256
Ge	Fisher, R	PA	234
Ge	Fisher, R	CT	230
Ge	Fleischer, D	AZ	254
Ge	Forsmark, C	FL	242
Ge	Freiman, H	NY	234
Ge	Fried, M	NC	242
Ge	Friedman, L	MA	231
Ge	Galati, J	TX	254
Ge	Gerdes, H	NY	234
Ge	Gerson, L	CA	256
Ge	Gholam, P	OH	247
Ge	Giardiello, F	MD	234
Ge	Ginsberg, G	PA	234
Ge	Gish, R	CA	256
Ge	Glombicki, A	TX	254
Ge	Gluck, M	WA	256
Ge	Goggins, M	MD	235
Ge	Goldberg, M	IL	247
Ge	Gordon, S	NH	231
Ge	Gostout, C	MN	248
Ge	Green, P	NY	235
Ge	Greenwald, B	MD	235
Ge	Haber, G	NY	235
Ge	Haluszka, O	PA	235
Ge	Han, S	CA	256
Ge	Hanauer, S	IL	248
Ge	Hawes, R	FL	242
Ge	Herrine, S	PA	235
Ge	Hoffman, B	SC	243
Ge	Hoops, T	PA	235
Ge	Hunter, E	ID	252
Ge	Infantolino, A	PA	235
Ge	Isaacs, K	NC	243
Ge	Itzkowitz, S	NY	236
Ge	Jacobson, I	NY	236
Ge	Jensen, D	IL	248
Ge	Jonnalagadda, S	MO	248
Ge	Kahrilas, P	IL	248
Ge	Kalloo, A	MD	236
Ge	Kantsevoy, S	MD	236
Ge	Kaplan, L	MA	231
Ge	Kastenberg, D	PA	236
Ge	Katz, P	PA	236
Ge	Kelsey, P	MA	231
Ge	Kimmey, M	WA	256
Ge	Koch, K	NC	243
Ge	Kochman, M	PA	236
Ge	Konicek, F	IL	248
Ge	Korsten, M	NY	237
Ge	Kotler, D	NY	237
Ge	Kowalski, T	PA	237
Ge	Kozarek, R	WA	256
Ge	Kurtz, R	NY	237
Ge	Kwo, P	IN	248
Ge	La Mont, J	MA	231
Ge	La Russo, N	MN	248
Ge	Lambiase, L	TN	243
Ge	Lashner, B	OH	249
Ge	Lebwohl, O	NY	237
Ge	Leighton, J	AZ	254
Ge	Levine, J	CO	252
Ge	Levy, M	MN	249
Ge	Lewis, B	NY	237
Ge	Lichtenstein, D	MA	231
Ge	Lichtenstein, G	PA	237
Ge	Liddle, R	NC	243
Ge	Lightdale, C	NY	238
Ge	Lind, C	TN	243
Ge	Lipshutz, W	PA	238
Ge	Loftus, E	MN	249
Ge	Loomba, R	CA	256
Ge	Lucey, M	WI	249
Ge	Magun, A	NY	238
Ge	Markowitz, D	NY	238
Ge	Martin, P	FL	243
Ge	Mason, J	MA	231
Ge	Meiselman, M	IL	249
Ge	Mertz, H	TN	243
Ge	Metz, D	PA	238
Ge	Miskovitz, P	NY	238
Ge	Mittal, R	CA	257
Ge	Murray, J	MN	249
Ge	Nunes, D	MA	231
Ge	Okolo, P	MD	238
Ge	Ostroff, J	CA	257
Ge	Owyang, C	MI	249
Ge	Pasricha, P	MD	239
Ge	Peikin, S	NJ	239
Ge	Petrini, J	CA	257
Ge	Pezzone, M	PA	239
Ge	Pfau, P	WI	249
Ge	Plevy, S	NC	244
Ge	Pochapin, M	NY	239
Ge	Poordad, F	TX	254
Ge	Porayko, M	TN	244
Ge	Proctor, D	CT	232
Ge	Raiford, D	TN	244
Ge	Raju, G	TX	254
Ge	Rao, S	GA	244
Ge	Ravich, W	MD	239
Ge	Reddy, K	PA	239

Spec	Name	St	Pg
Ge	Reichelderfer, M	WI	250
Ge	Reuben, A	SC	244
Ge	Rex, D	IN	250
Ge	Reynolds, J	PA	239
Ge	Roth, B	CA	257
Ge	Rothstein, R	NH	232
Ge	Sandborn, W	CA	257
Ge	Sartor, R	NC	244
Ge	Sass, D	PA	240
Ge	Savides, T	CA	257
Ge	Schembre, D	WA	257
Ge	Scherl, E	NY	240
Ge	Schiano, T	NY	240
Ge	Schiller, L	TX	254
Ge	Schulze, K	IA	250
Ge	Scudera, P	VA	244
Ge	Seidner, D	TN	245
Ge	Semrad, C	IL	250
Ge	Shah, R	CO	252
Ge	Shaker, R	WI	250
Ge	Sherman, S	IN	250
Ge	Shiffman, M	VA	245
Ge	Shike, M	NY	240
Ge	Siegel, C	NH	232
Ge	Silverman, W	IA	250
Ge	Slivka, A	PA	240
Ge	Smoot, D	TN	245
Ge	Sorrell, M	NE	252
Ge	Speeg, K	TX	255
Ge	Stump, D	TX	255
Ge	Surawicz, C	WA	257
Ge	Targan, S	CA	258
Ge	Te, H	IL	250
Ge	Tobias, H	NY	240
Ge	Tremaine, W	MN	251
Ge	Vaezi, M	TN	245
Ge	Vanagunas, A	IL	251
Ge	Vargo, J	OH	251
Ge	Vege, S	MN	251
Ge	Vierling, J	TX	255
Ge	Wald, A	WI	251
Ge	Waxman, I	IL	251
Ge	Waye, J	NY	240
Ge	Weinberg, D	PA	240
Ge	Weinstock, J	MA	232
Ge	Wiesner, R	MN	251
Ge	Wilcox, C	AL	245
Ge	Wolfe, M	OH	251
Ge	Yanda, R	GA	245
Ge	Young, R	NE	252
Ge	Younossi, Z	VA	245
Ge	Zaman, A	OR	258

Gastroesophageal Reflux Disease (GERD)

Spec	Name	St	Pg
Ge	Benjamin, S	DC	232
Ge	Brazer, S	NC	241
Ge	Chey, W	MI	246
Ge	Cohen, L	NY	233
Ge	DeVault, K	FL	242
Ge	Di Marino, A	PA	234
Ge	Fennerty, M	OR	256
Ge	Freiman, H	NY	234
Ge	Gerson, L	CA	256
Ge	Katz, P	PA	236
Ge	Levine, J	CO	252
Ge	Lind, C	TN	243
Ge	Lipshutz, W	PA	238
Ge	Markowitz, D	NY	238
Ge	Metz, D	PA	238
Ge	Rao, S	GA	244
Ge	Reynolds, J	PA	239
Ge	Roth, B	CA	257
Ge	Rothstein, R	NH	232
Ge	Schulze, K	IA	250
Ge	Shaker, R	WI	250
Ge	Vaezi, M	TN	245
NP	Gewolb, I	MI	452
Oto	Schley, W	NY	675
PGe	Baker, R	NY	763
PGe	Baker, S	NY	763
PGe	Gunasekaran, T	IL	766
PGe	Gupta, S	IN	766
PGe	Heyman, M	CA	769
PGe	Levy, J	NY	763
PGe	Mousa, H	OH	766
PGe	Schwarz, S	NY	764
PGe	Snyder, J	DC	764
PS	Holcomb, G	MO	820
S	Chand, B	IL	1112
S	Crookes, P	CA	1131
S	Dunkin, B	TX	1124
S	Hawn, M	AL	1105
S	Hunter, J	OR	1133
S	Park, A	MD	1098
S	Peters, J	NY	1098
S	Pryor, A	NY	1098
S	Rattner, D	MA	1087
S	Salky, B	NY	1099
S	Soper, N	IL	1120
S	Sweeney, J	GA	1110
T&CS	Deschamps, C	MN	1168
T&CS	Louie, B	WA	1179
T&CS	Watson, T	NY	1159

Gastroesophageal Reflux Disease(GERD)

Spec	Name	St	Pg
S	Holzman, M	TN	1106

Gastroesophageal Reflux-LINX device

Spec	Name	St	Pg
T&CS	Louie, B	WA	1179

Gastrointestinal Cancer

Spec	Name	St	Pg
CRS	Nelson, H	MN	174
Ge	Barkin, J	FL	241
Ge	Bresalier, R	TX	253
Ge	Chang, K	CA	255
Ge	Cohen, J	NY	233
Ge	Crippin, J	MO	247
Ge	Das, A	AZ	253
Ge	Faigel, D	AZ	253
Ge	Gerdes, H	NY	234
Ge	Haluszka, O	PA	235
Ge	Hoffman, B	SC	243
Ge	Hoops, T	PA	235
Ge	Infantolino, A	PA	235
Ge	Kastenberg, D	PA	236
Ge	Kochman, M	PA	236
Ge	Kurtz, R	NY	237
Ge	Lebwohl, O	NY	237
Ge	Lightdale, C	NY	238
Ge	Meiselman, M	IL	249
Ge	Okolo, P	MD	238
Ge	Savides, T	CA	257
Ge	Shike, M	NY	240
Ge	Smoot, D	TN	245
Ge	Waxman, I	IL	251
Hem	Gruenstein, S	NY	314
Onc	Abbruzzese, J	TX	378
Onc	Ahlgren, J	DC	336
Onc	Ajani, J	TX	378
Onc	Anthony, L	KY	354
Onc	Back, A	WA	385
Onc	Benedetto, P	FL	355
Onc	Benson, A	IL	366
Onc	Berlin, J	TN	355
Onc	Bernard, S	NC	355
Onc	Boston, B	TN	356
Onc	Brescia, F	SC	356
Onc	Chu, E	PA	339
Onc	Chung, K	SC	357
Onc	Crocenzi, T	OR	386
Onc	Eckhardt, S	CO	376
Onc	Engstrom, P	PA	342
Onc	Ensminger, W	MI	369
Onc	Fakih, M	CA	387
Onc	Fisher, G	CA	387
Onc	Ford, J	CA	387
Onc	Fuchs, C	MA	332
Onc	Gaynor, E	IL	369
Onc	Glaspy, J	CA	388
Onc	Gold, P	WA	388
Onc	Goldberg, R	OH	369
Onc	Grossbard, M	NY	344
Onc	Hageboutros, A	NJ	344
Onc	Hochster, H	CT	332
Onc	Holcombe, R	NY	345
Onc	Kane, M	CO	377
Onc	Kelsen, D	NY	346
Onc	Kindler, H	IL	370
Onc	Krishnamurthi, S	OH	371
Onc	Lacy, J	CT	333
Onc	Laheru, D	MD	346
Onc	Leighton, J	PA	347
Onc	Makhoul, I	AR	381
Onc	Marshall, J	DC	347
Onc	Mayer, R	MA	334
Onc	Meropol, N	OH	371
Onc	Messersmith, W	CO	377
Onc	Mintzer, D	PA	347
Onc	O'Brien, T	OH	372
Onc	Oster, M	NY	349
Onc	Pasche, B	AL	362
Onc	Patt, Y	NM	382

Spec	Name	St	Pg
Onc	Perry, D	DC	350
Onc	Picozzi, V	WA	391
Onc	Posey, J	AL	362
Onc	Reid, T	CA	391
Onc	Ruggiero, J	NY	350
Onc	Ryan, D	MA	334
Onc	Saif, M	MA	334
Onc	Sun, W	PA	352
Onc	Taetle, R	AZ	383
Onc	Tempero, M	CA	393
Onc	Venook, A	CA	394
Onc	Vinciguerra, V	NY	353
Onc	Ward, J	UT	378
Onc	Weiner, L	DC	354
Onc	Weiss, G	VA	365
Onc	Willson, J	TX	384
Onc	Wolff, R	TX	384
Path	Crawford, J	NY	721
RadRO	Abrams, R	IL	988
RadRO	Blackstock, A	NC	983
RadRO	Chakravarthy, A	TN	984
RadRO	Crane, C	TX	993
RadRO	Heimann, R	VT	976
RadRO	Kachnic, L	MA	976
RadRO	Koh, W	WA	996
RadRO	Konski, A	MI	990
RadRO	Landry, J	GA	985
RadRO	Lawrence, T	MI	990
RadRO	Lee, C	MN	990
RadRO	Martenson, J	MN	991
RadRO	Mendenhall, W	FL	986
RadRO	Minsky, B	TX	994
RadRO	Randolph-Jackson, P	DC	982
RadRO	Regine, W	MD	982
RadRO	Shrieve, D	UT	992
RadRO	Small, W	IL	991
RadRO	Smalley, S	KS	992
RadRO	Tepper, J	NC	987
RadRO	Thomas, C	OR	998
RadRO	Wazer, D	RI	977
RadRO	Willett, C	NC	987
S	Bear, H	VA	1103
S	Beauchamp, R	TN	1103
S	Becker, J	MA	1084
S	Bilchik, A	CA	1130
S	Brodsky, J	PA	1090
S	Brooks, A	PA	1090
S	Chang, A	MI	1112
S	Cole, D	SC	1104
S	Curcillo, P	PA	1091
S	Cusack, J	MA	1084
S	Daneker, G	GA	1104
S	Easter, D	CA	1132
S	Ellenhorn, J	CA	1132
S	Feig, B	TX	1125
S	Finlayson, C	CO	1122
S	Gibbs, J	NY	1093
S	Goodman, M	MA	1085
S	Graham, R	MA	1085
S	Heslin, M	AL	1105
S	Hoffman, J	PA	1094
S	Holzman, M	TN	1106
S	Howe, J	IA	1115
S	Hurst, R	IL	1115
S	Jackson, G	TX	1126
S	Karpeh, M	NY	1095
S	Kim, J	OH	1116
S	Krouse, R	AZ	1126
S	Li, B	LA	1127
S	Libutti, S	NY	1096
S	Lieberman, M	NY	1096
S	Lillemoe, K	MA	1086
S	Lowy, A	CA	1134
S	McCabe, D	AZ	1127
S	Michelassi, F	NY	1096
S	Mulvihill, S	UT	1122
S	Nagorney, D	MN	1117
S	Nakakura, E	CA	1134
S	Neifeld, J	VA	1107
S	Newman, E	NY	1097
S	Onders, R	OH	1118
S	Paty, P	NY	1098
S	Pawlik, T	MD	1098
S	Pisters, P	TX	1127
S	Posner, M	IL	1118
S	Reber, H	CA	1136
S	Salem, R	CT	1087
S	Salo, J	NC	1108
S	Sarr, M	MN	1119
S	Sasson, A	NE	1123
S	Schwartz, M	NY	1100
S	Shen, P	NC	1109
S	Sinanan, M	WA	1137
S	Talamini, M	CA	1137
S	Tyler, D	NC	1110
S	Wagman, L	CA	1138
S	Warren, R	CA	1138
S	Weber, S	WI	1121
VIR	Mauro, M	NC	1030
VIR	Weintraub, J	NY	1029

Gastrointestinal Cancer & Rare Tumors

Onc	Saltz, L	NY	350
S	Staley, C	GA	1109

Gastrointestinal Cancer & Surgery

S	Alexander, H	MD	1089
S	Ashley, S	MA	1084
S	Behrns, K	FL	1103
S	Bentrem, D	IL	1112
S	Brown, C	IL	1112
S	Duncan, M	MD	1092
S	Lee, K	PA	1096
S	Mahvi, D	IL	1116
S	McAneny, D	MA	1087
S	McIntyre, R	CO	1122
S	Nguyen, N	CA	1134
S	Norton, J	CA	1135
S	Pellegrini, C	WA	1135
S	Rattner, D	MA	1087
S	Schraut, W	PA	1100
S	Sundaram, M	IL	1120
S	Talamonti, M	IL	1120
S	Thayer, S	MA	1088

Gastrointestinal Disorders

NuM	Freeman, L	NY	554
PS	Dillon, P	MO	819

Gastrointestinal Disorders-Neonatal

PGe	Thomas, D	CA	769

Gastrointestinal Functional Disorders

Ge	Chey, W	MI	246
Ge	Drossman, D	NC	242
Ge	Fisher, R	PA	234
Ge	Schiller, L	TX	254
PGe	Di Lorenzo, C	OH	765
PGe	Mousa, H	OH	766

Gastrointestinal Imaging

DR	Berland, L	AL	1013
DR	Dachman, A	IL	1014
DR	Federle, M	CA	1017
DR	Fidler, J	MN	1014
DR	Levy, A	DC	1010
DR	Megibow, A	NY	1010
DR	Miller, F	IL	1015

Gastrointestinal Metabolic Surgery

S	Bessler, M	NY	1089

Gastrointestinal Motility Disorders

CRS	Sokol, T	CA	178
Ge	Benjamin, S	DC	232
Ge	Chey, W	MI	246
Ge	Drossman, D	NC	242
Ge	Fisher, R	PA	234
Ge	Koch, K	NC	243
Ge	Korsten, M	NY	237
Ge	Lind, C	TN	243
Ge	Metz, D	PA	238
Ge	Mittal, R	CA	257
Ge	Owyang, C	MI	249
Ge	Pasricha, P	MD	239
Ge	Rao, S	GA	244
Ge	Reynolds, J	PA	239
Ge	Schiller, L	TX	254
Ge	Shaker, R	WI	250
Ge	Wald, A	WI	251
PGe	Di Lorenzo, C	OH	765
PGe	Mousa, H	OH	766
PS	Caty, M	CT	813
S	Sarr, M	MN	1119
S	Swanstrom, L	OR	1137

Spec	Name	St	Pg
Gastrointestinal Pathology			
Path	Appelman, H	MI	727
Path	Bostwick, D	VA	725
Path	Chandrasoma, P	CA	732
Path	Crawford, J	NY	721
Path	Fogt, F	PA	721
Path	Goldblum, J	OH	728
Path	Greenson, J	MI	728
Path	Hamilton, S	TX	730
Path	Hruban, R	MD	722
Path	Klimstra, D	NY	722
Path	Montgomery, E	MD	723
Path	Odze, R	MA	719
Path	Petras, R	OH	729
Path	Rashid, A	TX	731
Path	Rimm, D	CT	719
Path	Rutgers, J	CA	734
Path	Silverman, J	PA	724
Gastrointestinal Stromal Tumor			
S	Singer, S	NY	1101
Gastrointestinal Stromal Tumors			
Hem	Heinrich, M	OR	328
Onc	Maki, R	NY	347
Onc	von Mehren, M	PA	353
PHO	Wexler, L	NY	777
S	Zinner, M	MA	1088
Gastrointestinal Surgery			
CRS	Longo, W	CT	168
CRS	Schatz, L	CO	176
PS	Alexander, F	NJ	815
PS	Barksdale, E	OH	819
PS	Chen, M	AL	818
PS	Ginsburg, H	NY	815
PS	Gittes, G	PA	815
PS	Midulla, P	NY	816
PS	Oldham, K	WI	820
PS	Rescorla, F	IN	820
PS	Ricketts, R	GA	818
PS	Schwartz, M	PA	817
PS	Warner, B	MO	821
S	Barie, P	NY	1089
S	Basson, M	MI	1111
S	Becker, J	MA	1084
S	Brody, F	DC	1090
S	Brooks, D	MA	1084
S	Dempsey, D	PA	1092
S	Essner, R	CA	1132
S	Eubanks, W	FL	1105
S	Fitzgibbons, R	NE	1122
S	Galloway, J	GA	1105
S	Hawn, M	AL	1105
S	Hebert, J	VT	1085
S	Horvath, K	WA	1133
S	Hunter, J	OR	1133
S	Hurst, R	IL	1115
S	Katkhouda, N	CA	1133
S	Koruda, M	NC	1106
S	MacDonald, K	NC	1107
S	Marks, J	OH	1116
S	Matthews, J	IL	1116
S	Mellinger, J	IL	1117
S	Mulvihill, S	UT	1122
S	Nowak, E	NY	1097
S	Oelschlager, B	WA	1135
S	Pachter, H	NY	1097
S	Ponsky, J	OH	1118
S	Rege, R	TX	1128
S	Richards, W	AL	1108
S	Rogers, S	CA	1136
S	Rosemurgy, A	FL	1108
S	Rosen, M	OH	1118
S	Sarosi, G	FL	1108
S	Satava, R	WA	1136
S	Schirmer, B	VA	1108
S	Schlinkert, R	AZ	1128
S	Sharp, K	TN	1109
S	Sinanan, M	WA	1137
S	Stiegmann, G	CO	1123
S	Vickers, S	MN	1120
S	Walsh, R	OH	1121
S	Yeo, C	PA	1102
Gastroparesis			
Ge	Koch, K	NC	243
Ge	Pasricha, P	MD	239
Ge	Schulze, K	IA	250
Gaucher Disease			
CG	Desnick, R	NY	157
Hem	Allen, S	NY	313
Onc	Attas, L	NJ	338
Gay & Lesbian Issues			
Psyc	Grant, J	IL	929
Gay/Lesbian/Transgender Health			
AM	Garofalo, R	IL	77
Gender Reassignment Surgery			
PlS	Alter, G	CA	901
PlS	Kuzon, W	MI	894
PlS	Medalie, D	OH	894
PlS	Meltzer, T	AZ	899
PlS	Ousterhout, D	CA	904
Gene Therapy			
Cv	Dichek, D	WA	110
GO	Chan, J	CA	290
GO	Lancaster, J	FL	282
Hem	Brenner, M	TX	325
Hem	Porter, D	PA	316
IC	Mahmud, E	CA	128
Onc	Hortobagyi, G	TX	380
Onc	Sotomayor, E	FL	364
PHO	Neuberg, R	SC	780
Pul	Sterman, D	PA	959
T&CS	Roth, J	TX	1176
U	Belldegrun, A	CA	1210
U	Malkowicz, S	PA	1192
U	Miles, B	TX	1209
VascS	Comerota, A	OH	1227
Gene Therapy Delivery Systems			
VIR	Wood, B	MD	1029
Gene Therapy-Cardiac Angiogenesis			
Cv	Sanborn, T	IL	105
T&CS	Rosengart, T	TX	1176
Genetic Arrhythmias			
CE	Epstein, A	PA	114
Cv	Topol, E	CA	112
Genetic Disorders			
CG	Bartholomew, D	OH	160
CG	Desposito, F	NJ	157
CG	Grody, W	CA	163
CG	Jonas, A	CA	163
CG	Mulvihill, J	OK	161
CG	Nussbaum, R	CA	163
CG	Ostrer, H	NY	158
CG	Sutphen, R	FL	159
CG	Weaver, D	IN	160
MF	Bahado-Singh, R	MI	437
MF	Cheng, E	WA	442
MF	Pridjian, G	LA	441
MF	Wapner, R	NY	435
MF	Wilkins-Haug, L	MA	433
Ped	Jones, K	CA	742
RE	Rosenwaks, Z	NY	1044
Genetic Disorders-Blood			
PHO	Glader, B	CA	790
Genetic Disorders-Eye			
Oph	Kerr, N	TN	589
Genetic Disorders-Skin			
D	Levy, M	TX	198
D	Paller, A	IL	196
D	Yan, A	PA	191
Genetic Preimplantation Diagnosis			
CG	Pergament, E	IL	160

Spec	Name	St	Pg

Genital Birth Defects

Ped Uro	Hatch, D	IL	827

Genital Enhancement

PlS	Alter, G	CA	901
PlS	Medalie, D	OH	894

Genital Reconstruction

Ped Uro	Merguerian, P	WA	828
Ped Uro	Rink, R	IN	828

Genital Reconstruction-Pediatric

Ped Uro	Cheng, E	IL	826
Ped Uro	Maizels, M	IL	827
Ped Uro	Poppas, D	NY	825

Genitalia Ambiguity

Ped Uro	Rushton, H	DC	825

Genitourinary Cancer

DR	Parsons, R	PA	1011
Onc	Bajorin, D	NY	338
Onc	Balducci, L	FL	355
Onc	Benedetto, P	FL	355
Onc	Boston, B	TN	356
Onc	Celano, P	MD	339
Onc	Clinton, S	OH	368
Onc	DiPaola, R	NJ	341
Onc	Ernstoff, M	NH	331
Onc	Glode, L	CO	377
Onc	Haas, N	PA	344
Onc	Higano, C	WA	388
Onc	Hogan, T	WV	345
Onc	Hussain, M	MI	370
Onc	Jonasch, E	TX	381
Onc	Kantoff, P	MA	333
Onc	Kucuk, O	GA	360
Onc	Loehrer, P	IN	371
Onc	Mathew, P	MA	334
Onc	Nanus, D	NY	348
Onc	Oh, W	NY	349
Onc	Picozzi, V	WA	391
Onc	Scher, H	NY	351
Onc	Sweeney, C	MA	335
Onc	Taplin, M	MA	335
Onc	Trump, D	NY	353
Onc	Twardowski, P	CA	393
Onc	Vaughn, D	PA	353
Onc	Vogelzang, N	NV	394
Onc	Weiss, G	VA	365
Onc	Wilding, G	WI	375
Path	Wheeler, T	TX	731
RadRO	Ciezki, J	OH	989
RadRO	Forman, J	MI	989
RadRO	Kestin, L	MI	990
RadRO	Kuban, D	TX	994
RadRO	Kupelian, P	CA	996
RadRO	Lee, A	TX	994
RadRO	Pollack, A	FL	986
RadRO	Roach, M	CA	997
RadRO	Russell, K	WA	997
RadRO	Sailer, S	NC	987
RadRO	Sandler, H	CA	997
RadRO	Schild, S	AZ	994
RadRO	Shrieve, D	UT	992
U	Keane, T	SC	1198
U	Montie, J	MI	1204
U	Pisters, L	TX	1209
U	Wood, D	MI	1206

Genitourinary Congenital Anomalies

Ped Uro	Canning, D	PA	824
Ped Uro	Kaefer, M	IN	827

Genitourinary Imaging

DR	Miller, F	IL	1015

Genitourinary Pathology

Path	Amin, M	CA	731
Path	Reuter, V	NY	723
Path	Tomaszewski, J	NY	724

Genitourinary Prosthetics

U	Montague, D	OH	1204

Genitourinary Radiology

DR	Parsons, R	PA	1011
DR	Zagoria, R	CA	1019

Genitourinary Reconstruction

Ped Uro	Bloom, D	MI	826
Ped Uro	Cain, M	IN	826
Ped Uro	Coplen, D	MO	827
PlS	Alter, G	CA	901
U	Burnett, A	MD	1189

Geriatric Cardiology

Cv	Gardin, J	NJ	93

Geriatric Endocrinology

Ger	Abrass, I	WA	267

Geriatric Functional Assessment

Ger	Cooney, L	CT	264
Ger	Duthie, E	WI	266
Ger	Dyer, C	TX	267
Ger	Palmer, R	VA	266
Ger	Reuben, D	CA	268
Ger	Supiano, M	UT	267
Ger	Tinetti, M	CT	264

Geriatric Medicine

Ger	Abrass, I	WA	267
Ger	Bloom, P	NY	264
Ger	Burton, J	MD	264
Ger	Callahan, E	NY	264
Ger	Carr, D	MO	266
Ger	Cooney, L	CT	264
Ger	Dale, L	MN	266
Ger	Duthie, E	WI	266
Ger	Dyer, C	TX	267
Ger	Finucane, T	MD	264
Ger	Flaherty, J	MO	266
Ger	Gambert, S	MD	265
Ger	Greganti, M	NC	265
Ger	Hanson, L	NC	265
Ger	Lachs, M	NY	265
Ger	Lipschitz, D	AR	267
Ger	Lipsitz, L	MA	264
Ger	Lyles, K	NC	265
Ger	McCormick, W	WA	268
Ger	Morley, J	MO	266
Ger	Palmer, R	VA	266
Ger	Raji, M	TX	267
Ger	Resnick, N	PA	265
Ger	Reuben, D	CA	268
Ger	Sachs, G	IN	266
Ger	Schwartz, R	CO	267
Ger	Studenski, S	PA	265
Ger	Supiano, M	UT	267
Ger	Tenover, J	CA	268
Ger	Thomas, D	MO	266
Ger	Tinetti, M	CT	264
Ger	Wei, J	AR	267

Geriatric Ophthalmology

Oph	Sterns, G	NY	586

Geriatric Psychiatry

GerPsy	Burke, W	NE	946
GerPsy	Greenwald, B	NY	944
GerPsy	Grossberg, G	MO	945
GerPsy	Holroyd, S	VA	945
GerPsy	Kennedy, G	NY	944
GerPsy	Kramer, B	CA	946
GerPsy	Lyketsos, C	MD	944
GerPsy	Manepalli, J	MO	945
GerPsy	Mellow, A	MI	945
GerPsy	Reisberg, B	NY	944
GerPsy	Rovner, B	PA	944
GerPsy	Stein, E	CA	946
GerPsy	Streim, J	PA	945
GerPsy	Tune, L	GA	945
GerPsy	Veith, R	WA	946
Psyc	Blazer, D	NC	927
Psyc	Ellison, J	MA	920
Psyc	Eth, S	FL	928
Psyc	Kumar, A	IL	930
Psyc	Marin, D	NY	926
Psyc	Nelson, J	CA	933
Psyc	Raskind, M	WA	934
Psyc	Roth, A	NY	926

Spec	Name	St	Pg
Geriatric Rehabilitation			
PMR	Bloch, R	MA	862
PMR	De Lateur, B	MD	863
PMR	Diamond, P	VA	866
PMR	Frost, F	OH	868
PMR	Miknevich, M	PA	865
PMR	Roth, E	IL	869
Germ Cell Tumors			
Onc	Margolin, K	WA	389
PHO	Marina, N	CA	790
PHO	Olson, T	GA	780
PS	Morgan, W	TN	818
Gestational Trophoblastic Disease			
GO	Burger, R	PA	277
GO	Clarke-Pearson, D	NC	281
GO	Curtin, J	NY	277
GO	Fromm, G	TX	288
GO	Giuntoli, R	MD	278
GO	Kohler, M	SC	282
GO	Lurain, J	IL	285
GO	Muntz, H	WA	291
GO	Plaxe, S	CA	291
GO	Soper, J	NC	283
Glaucoma			
Oph	Alward, W	IA	593
Oph	Baerveldt, G	CA	604
Oph	Budenz, D	NC	587
Oph	Caprioli, J	CA	605
Oph	Cioffi, G	NY	577
Oph	Crandall, A	UT	601
Oph	Gorovoy, M	FL	588
Oph	Greenfield, D	FL	588
Oph	Heuer, D	WI	595
Oph	Iwach, A	CA	606
Oph	Katz, L	PA	580
Oph	Kaufman, P	WI	596
Oph	Kwon, Y	IA	596
Oph	Lee, P	MI	596
Oph	Levin, A	PA	581
Oph	Lichter, P	MI	596
Oph	Liebmann, J	NY	581
Oph	Mills, M	PA	582
Oph	Myers, J	PA	582
Oph	Parrish, R	FL	590
Oph	Quigley, H	MD	583
Oph	Ritch, R	NY	584
Oph	Robin, A	MD	584
Oph	Samuelson, T	MN	599
Oph	Schuman, J	PA	584
Oph	Serafano, D	CA	609
Oph	Sergott, R	PA	584
Oph	Sherwood, M	FL	591
Oph	Shingleton, B	MA	575
Oph	Spaeth, G	PA	585
Oph	Tsai, J	CT	575
Oph	Vajaranant, T	IL	600
Oph	Varma, R	IL	600
Oph	Wallace, R	LA	603
Oph	Weinreb, R	CA	610
Glaucoma-Pediatric			
Oph	Freedman, S	NC	588
Oph	Hodapp, E	FL	589
Oph	Jaafar, M	VA	589
Oph	Lueder, G	MO	597
Oph	Medow, N	NY	582
Oph	Plager, D	IN	598
Oph	Traboulsi, E	OH	599
Oph	Walton, D	MA	575
Oph	Weiss, A	WA	610
Gliomas			
N	Batchelor, T	MA	510
N	Lassman, A	NY	517
N	Laterra, J	MD	517
N	Mikkelsen, T	MI	531
N	Puduvalli, V	OH	532
N	Rosenfeld, S	OH	533
N	Taylor, L	MA	512
NS	Chen, T	CA	499
NS	Friedman, A	NC	484
NS	Lang, F	TX	496
NS	Liau, L	CA	500
NS	Lillehei, K	CO	494
NS	Mamelak, A	CA	500
NS	Markert, J	AL	485
NS	Weingart, J	MD	483
Onc	Friedman, H	NC	358
Onc	Vredenburgh, J	CT	336
RadRO	Isaacson, S	NY	980
RadRO	Simpson, J	MO	991
Glomerulonephritis			
Nep	Appel, G	NY	458
Nep	Berns, J	PA	459
Nep	Bolton, W	VA	461
Nep	Cho, K	CA	466
Nep	Cohen, D	NY	459
Nep	Falk, R	NC	461
Nep	Holzman, L	PA	459
Nep	Kasinath, B	TX	465
Nep	Rodby, R	IL	464
Nep	Torres, V	MN	465
Nep	Winston, J	NY	461
PNep	Andreoli, S	IN	799
PNep	Benfield, M	AL	798
PNep	Clardy, C	IL	799
PNep	Fouser, L	WA	801
PNep	Mendley, S	MD	798
PNep	Roskes, S	MD	798
Gorham-Stout Disease			
EDM	Watts, N	OH	221
Gout			
A&I	Sundy, J	NC	83
Rhu	Davis, W	LA	1066
Rhu	Fields, T	NY	1060
Rhu	Lawry, G	CA	1068
Rhu	Massarotti, E	MA	1058
Rhu	Weinstein, A	DC	1063
Rhu	Wise, C	VA	1064
Graft vs Host Disease			
Hem	Brodsky, R	MD	313
Hem	Rowley, S	NJ	316
Hem	Yeager, A	AZ	327
Onc	Appelbaum, F	WA	385
Onc	Deeg, H	WA	386
Onc	Foss, F	CT	331
PGe	Molleston, J	IN	766
PHO	Carpenter, P	WA	789
PHO	Chen, A	MD	772
PHO	Ferrara, J	MI	783
Graves' Disease			
EDM	Bahn, R	MN	218
EDM	Burmeister, L	MN	218
EDM	Davies, T	NY	212
T&CS	Weigel, T	ME	1149
Graves' Disease-Eye			
EDM	Bahn, R	MN	218
Oto	Lanza, D	FL	679
Gravet Syndrome			
ChiN	Tuxhorn, I	OH	150
Growth Disorders			
PEn	Allen, D	WI	760
PEn	Alter, C	PA	757
PEn	DeLuca, F	PA	758
PEn	Diamond, F	FL	759
PEn	Freemark, M	NC	759
PEn	Garibaldi, L	PA	758
PEn	Geffner, M	CA	761
PEn	Kohn, B	NY	758
PEn	Oberfield, S	NY	758
PEn	Plotnick, L	MD	759
PEn	Wilson, D	CA	762
Growth Disorders in Childhood Cancer			
PEn	Meacham, L	GA	759
PEn	Sklar, C	NY	759
PEn	Zimmerman, D	IL	761
Growth Hormone Disorder-Adult			
EDM	Inzucchi, S	CT	209

Spec	Name	St	Pg
EDM	Thorner, M	VA	217

Growth/Development Disorders

Spec	Name	St	Pg
PEn	Casella, S	NH	756
PEn	Eugster, E	IN	760
PEn	Fennoy, I	NY	758
PEn	Foster, C	UT	761
PEn	Kappy, M	CO	761
PEn	Levitsky, L	MA	757
PEn	Menon, R	MI	760
PEn	New, M	NY	758
PEn	Rogers, D	OH	760
PEn	Silverstein, J	FL	759
PEn	Sperling, M	PA	759
PEn	Zimmerman, D	IL	761

Guillain-Barre Syndrome

Spec	Name	St	Pg
N	Arnason, B	IL	528
N	Barohn, R	KS	534
N	Graves, M	CA	540
N	Ropper, A	MA	512

Gynecologic Cancer

Spec	Name	St	Pg
DR	Hricak, H	NY	1010
GO	Abbas, F	MD	276
GO	Alvarez, R	AL	280
GO	Barnes, W	DC	276
GO	Berkowitz, R	MA	274
GO	Berman, M	CA	290
GO	Brewer, M	CT	274
GO	Bristow, R	CA	290
GO	Burnett, A	AR	288
GO	Carlson, J	NJ	277
GO	Carney, M	HI	290
GO	Chambers, S	AZ	288
GO	Clarke-Pearson, D	NC	281
GO	Cliby, W	MN	284
GO	Copeland, L	OH	284
GO	Cornelison, T	MD	277
GO	Davidson, S	CO	287
GO	DeMars, L	NH	274
GO	Dottino, P	NY	277
GO	Duska, L	VA	281
GO	Edwards, R	PA	278
GO	Fishman, D	NY	278
GO	Fowler, J	OH	284
GO	Giuntoli, R	MD	278
GO	Granai, C	RI	275
GO	Greer, B	WA	291
GO	Herzog, T	NY	278
GO	Kelley, J	PA	278
GO	Kohler, M	SC	282
GO	Lentz, S	NC	282
GO	Levenback, C	TX	289
GO	Lin, J	DC	279
GO	Magrina, J	AZ	289
GO	McGonigle, K	WA	291
GO	Miller, D	TX	289
GO	Modesitt, S	VA	283
GO	Morgan, M	PA	279
GO	Mutch, D	MO	285
GO	Odunsi, A	NY	279
GO	Orr, J	FL	283
GO	Penalver, M	FL	283
GO	Randall, T	PA	280
GO	Remmenga, S	NE	287
GO	Rotmensch, J	IL	286
GO	Singh, D	AZ	289
GO	Sood, A	TX	290
GO	Soper, J	NC	283
GO	Spann, C	GA	283
GO	Spirtos, N	NV	292
GO	Stehman, F	IN	286
GO	Tarraza, H	ME	275
GO	Walker, J	OK	290
ObG	Morgan, L	FL	563
Onc	Aghajanian, C	NY	336
Onc	Armstrong, D	MD	337
Onc	Birrer, M	MA	330
Onc	Celano, P	MD	339
Onc	Chap, L	CA	386
Onc	Dizon, D	MA	331
Onc	Fleming, G	IL	369
Onc	Fracasso, P	VA	358
Onc	Hochster, H	CT	332
Onc	Kohn, E	MD	346
Onc	Matulonis, U	MA	334
Onc	McGuire, W	VA	361
Onc	Morgan, R	CA	390
Onc	Muggia, F	NY	348
Onc	Schilder, R	PA	351
Onc	Spriggs, D	NY	352
Onc	Terpenning, M	CA	393
Onc	Thigpen, J	MS	364
Onc	Verschraegen, C	VT	336
Path	LiVolsi, V	PA	722
Path	Ronnett, B	MD	723
Path	Silva, E	TX	731
Path	Thor, A	CO	729
Path	Tornos, C	NY	724
Path	Wilczynski, S	CA	735
Path	Young, R	MA	720
RadRO	Chadha, M	NY	978
RadRO	Gaffney, D	UT	992
RadRO	Grigsby, P	MO	989
RadRO	Halpern, H	IL	989
RadRO	Henderson, R	FL	984
RadRO	Jhingran, A	TX	994
RadRO	Jose, B	IN	990
RadRO	Koh, W	WA	996
RadRO	Malcolm, A	TN	985
RadRO	Mendenhall, W	FL	986
RadRO	Mundt, A	CA	996
RadRO	Randall, M	KY	986
RadRO	Recht, A	MA	977
RadRO	Rotman, M	NY	982
RadRO	Russell, A	MA	977
RadRO	Schiff, P	NY	982
RadRO	Small, W	IL	991
RadRO	Wolfson, A	FL	988
S	Kavanah, M	MA	1086

Gynecologic Cancer Risk

Spec	Name	St	Pg
CG	Whelan, A	MO	161

Gynecologic Cancer-Rare

Spec	Name	St	Pg
GO	Brewer, M	CT	274
GO	Copeland, L	OH	284
GO	Creasman, W	SC	281
GO	Pejovic, T	OR	291
GO	Rubin, S	PA	280

Gynecologic Imaging

Spec	Name	St	Pg
DR	Benson, C	MA	1007
DR	Thurmond, A	OR	1018

Gynecologic Oncology

Spec	Name	St	Pg
GO	Abbas, F	MD	276
GO	Abu-Rustum, N	NY	276
GO	Alexander, M	MD	276
GO	Alvarez, R	AL	280
GO	Azodi, M	CT	274
GO	Barakat, R	NY	276
GO	Barnes, W	DC	276
GO	Barter, J	MD	276
GO	Berchuck, A	NC	280
GO	Berek, J	CA	290
GO	Berkowitz, R	MA	274
GO	Berman, M	CA	290
GO	Bicher, A	VA	280
GO	Bodurka, D	TX	287
GO	Boice, C	MD	276
GO	Borst, M	AZ	287
GO	Braly, P	LA	288
GO	Brewer, M	CT	274
GO	Bristow, R	CA	290
GO	Burger, R	PA	277
GO	Burke, T	TX	288
GO	Burnett, A	AR	288
GO	Cain, J	MA	274
GO	Cantuaria, G	GA	281
GO	Caputo, T	NY	277
GO	Carlson, J	NJ	277
GO	Carney, M	HI	290
GO	Chambers, S	AZ	288
GO	Chan, J	CA	290
GO	Chi, D	NY	277
GO	Clarke-Pearson, D	NC	281
GO	Cliby, W	MN	284
GO	Copeland, L	OH	284
GO	Cornelison, T	MD	277
GO	Cosin, J	CT	274
GO	Creasman, W	SC	281
GO	Curtin, J	NY	277
GO	Davidson, S	CO	287
GO	DeMars, L	NH	274
GO	Dottino, P	NY	277
GO	Dunton, C	PA	277
GO	Duska, L	VA	281
GO	Edwards, R	PA	278
GO	Fields, A	DC	278
GO	Finan, M	AL	281

Spec	Name	St	Pg
GO	Fiorica, J	FL	281
GO	Fishman, D	NY	278
GO	Fowler, J	OH	284
GO	Fromm, G	TX	288
GO	Gershenson, D	TX	288
GO	Ghamande, S	GA	281
GO	Giuntoli, R	MD	278
GO	Goff, B	WA	291
GO	Gostout, B	MN	284
GO	Granai, C	RI	275
GO	Greer, B	WA	291
GO	Hatch, K	AZ	288
GO	Havrilesky, L	NC	282
GO	Herzog, T	NY	278
GO	Horowitz, I	GA	282
GO	Hurteau, J	IL	284
GO	Husain, A	CA	291
GO	Johnston, C	MI	284
GO	Kelley, J	PA	278
GO	King, S	PA	278
GO	Kline, R	LA	288
GO	Kohler, M	SC	282
GO	Koulos, J	NY	279
GO	Lambrou, N	FL	282
GO	Lancaster, J	FL	282
GO	Lele, S	NY	279
GO	Lengyel, E	IL	285
GO	Lentz, S	NC	282
GO	Levenback, C	TX	289
GO	Lin, J	DC	279
GO	Lu, K	TX	289
GO	Lucci, J	FL	282
GO	Lurain, J	IL	285
GO	Magrina, J	AZ	289
GO	Makhija, S	KY	282
GO	Mannel, R	OK	289
GO	Martino, M	PA	279
GO	McGonigle, K	WA	291
GO	Miller, D	TX	289
GO	Modesitt, S	VA	283
GO	Moore, D	IN	285
GO	Morgan, M	PA	279
GO	Muntz, H	WA	291
GO	Mutch, D	MO	285
GO	Muto, M	MA	275
GO	Nagarsheth, N	NY	279
GO	Odunsi, A	NY	279
GO	Orr, J	FL	283
GO	Pejovic, T	OR	291
GO	Penalver, M	FL	283
GO	Plaxe, S	CA	291
GO	Poliakoff, S	FL	283
GO	Potkul, R	IL	285
GO	Powell, M	MO	285
GO	Rader, J	WI	285
GO	Randall, T	PA	280
GO	Remmenga, S	NE	287
GO	Reynolds, R	MI	286
GO	Rice, L	WI	286
GO	Rodriguez, G	IL	286
GO	Rose, P	OH	286
GO	Rosenblum, N	PA	280
GO	Rotmensch, J	IL	286

Spec	Name	St	Pg
GO	Rubin, S	PA	280
GO	Runowicz, C	FL	283
GO	Rutherford, T	CT	275
GO	Santin, A	CT	275
GO	Schink, J	IL	286
GO	Schorge, J	MA	275
GO	Schwartz, P	CT	275
GO	Silasi, D	CT	275
GO	Siller, B	TX	289
GO	Singh, D	AZ	289
GO	Smith, D	AZ	289
GO	Smith, L	CA	291
GO	Soisson, A	UT	287
GO	Sood, A	TX	290
GO	Soper, J	NC	283
GO	Spann, C	GA	283
GO	Spirtos, N	NV	292
GO	Stehman, F	IN	286
GO	Steren, A	MD	280
GO	Stern, J	CA	292
GO	Tarraza, H	ME	275
GO	Teng, N	CA	292
GO	Valea, F	NC	283
GO	Van Nagell, J	KY	284
GO	Waggoner, S	OH	287
GO	Walker, J	OK	290
GO	Yamada, S	IL	287

Gynecologic Pathology

ObG	Bartholomew, D	OH	563
Path	Balla, A	IL	727
Path	Bell, D	MN	727
Path	Cho, K	MI	727
Path	Dahmoush, L	IA	727
Path	De Las Morenas, A	MA	718
Path	Heller, D	NJ	721
Path	Kurman, R	MD	722
Path	Lage, J	MS	726
Path	Ronnett, B	MD	723
Path	Rutgers, J	CA	734
Path	Silva, E	TX	731
Path	Soslow, R	NY	724
Path	Tavassoli, F	CT	720
Path	Ulbright, T	IN	729
Path	Young, R	MA	720

Gynecologic Surgery

GO	McGonigle, K	WA	291
ObG	Parker, W	CA	567
ObG	Snyder, R	TX	566
ObG	Steege, J	NC	563
RE	De Cherney, A	MD	1042

Gynecologic Surgery-Complex

GO	Carlson, J	NJ	277
GO	Chi, D	NY	277
GO	Clarke-Pearson, D	NC	281
GO	Dunton, C	PA	277
GO	Duska, L	VA	281
GO	Ghamande, S	GA	281

Spec	Name	St	Pg
GO	Goff, B	WA	291
GO	Johnston, C	MI	284
GO	Kohler, M	SC	282
GO	Morgan, M	PA	279
GO	Muntz, H	WA	291
GO	Schwartz, P	CT	275
GO	Soper, J	NC	283
ObG	Eschenbach, D	WA	567

Gynecology Only

ObG	Carson, D	PA	561
ObG	Richardson, M	KS	566

Gynecology-African women only

ObG	Nour, N	MA	560

Gynecomastia

EDM	Rodbard, H	MD	214
PIS	Medalie, D	OH	894

H

Hair Loss

D	Barbosa, V	IL	194
D	Cohen, B	FL	192
D	Cotsarelis, G	PA	188
D	McMichael, A	NC	193
D	Nigra, T	DC	189
D	Olsen, E	NC	193

Hair Loss in Women

D	Bernstein, R	NY	186

Hair Restoration/Transplant

D	Avram, M	NY	186
D	Berg, D	WA	200
D	Bernstein, R	NY	186
D	Cohen, B	FL	192
D	Fitzpatrick, R	CA	200
Oto	Epstein, J	FL	678
Oto	Hopping, S	DC	671
Oto	Quatela, V	NY	674
S	Rassman, W	CA	1136

Hair Transplant-Robotic Surgery

D	Bernstein, R	NY	186

Hand & Elbow Nerve Disorders

HS	Strauch, R	NY	300

Hand & Fingers Vascular Surgery

Spec	Name	St	Pg
HS	Sampson, C	MA	296

Hand & Microvascular Surgery

Spec	Name	St	Pg
HS	Chung, K	MI	302
PlS	Chiu, D	NY	881

Hand & Upper Extremity Surgery

Spec	Name	St	Pg
HS	Abrams, R	CA	305
HS	Badia, A	FL	300
HS	Bozentka, D	PA	297
HS	Brushart, T	MD	297
HS	Carlson, M	NY	297
HS	Cassidy, C	MA	296
HS	Chang, J	CA	305
HS	Collins, E	TX	305
HS	Culp, R	PA	298
HS	Eglseder, W	MD	298
HS	Goitz, R	PA	298
HS	Hentz, V	CA	306
HS	Kulick, R	NY	299
HS	Seitz, W	OH	304
HS	Sotereanos, D	PA	300
OrS	Levin, L	PA	628

Hand & Upper Extremity Tumors

Spec	Name	St	Pg
HS	Athanasian, E	NY	297
HS	Szabo, R	CA	306
OrS	Singer, D	HI	653

Hand & Wrist Reconstrction

Spec	Name	St	Pg
OrS	Goldner, R	NC	636

Hand & Wrist Surgery

Spec	Name	St	Pg
HS	Beredjiklian, P	PA	297
HS	Carneiro, R	FL	301
HS	Glickel, S	NY	298
HS	Graham, T	OH	303
HS	Hunt, T	AL	301
HS	Meals, R	CA	306
HS	Stern, P	OH	304
HS	Strauch, R	NY	300
HS	Swigart, C	CT	296
HS	Trumble, T	WA	306
OrS	Goldner, R	NC	636

Hand Injuries

Spec	Name	St	Pg
HS	Moneim, M	NM	305
HS	Sampson, C	MA	296
HS	Szabo, R	CA	306

Hand Injuries-Pediatric

Spec	Name	St	Pg
HS	Light, T	IL	303

Hand Reconstruction

Spec	Name	St	Pg
HS	Eglseder, W	MD	298
HS	Failla, J	MI	302
HS	Friedman, D	FL	301
HS	Hunt, T	AL	301
HS	Kleinman, W	IN	303
HS	Lane, L	NY	299
HS	Strauch, R	NY	300
HS	Thomson, J	CT	296
OrS	Hausman, M	NY	625
OrS	Weiland, A	NY	633
PlS	Yuen, J	AR	901

Hand Reconstruction-Pediatric

Spec	Name	St	Pg
HS	Ezaki, M	TX	305
HS	Jones, N	CA	306
HS	Mih, A	IN	303

Hand Surgery

Spec	Name	St	Pg
HS	Abrams, R	CA	305
HS	Athanasian, E	NY	297
HS	Atkinson, R	HI	305
HS	Badia, A	FL	300
HS	Baratz, M	PA	297
HS	Belsky, M	MA	296
HS	Beredjiklian, P	PA	297
HS	Bishop, A	MN	302
HS	Bozentka, D	PA	297
HS	Breidenbach, W	AZ	304
HS	Brushart, T	MD	297
HS	Carlson, M	NY	297
HS	Carneiro, R	FL	301
HS	Carroll, C	IL	302
HS	Cassidy, C	MA	296
HS	Cendales, L	GA	301
HS	Chang, J	CA	305
HS	Chung, K	MI	302
HS	Cohen, M	IL	302
HS	Cohen, M	IL	302
HS	Collins, E	TX	305
HS	Culp, R	PA	298
HS	DeSilva, S	MI	302
HS	Eglseder, W	MD	298
HS	Ezaki, M	TX	305
HS	Failla, J	MI	302
HS	Fischer, T	IN	302
HS	Friedman, D	FL	301
HS	Gelberman, R	MO	302
HS	Glickel, S	NY	298
HS	Godzik, C	CA	306
HS	Goitz, R	PA	298
HS	Graham, T	OH	303
HS	Greene, T	FL	301
HS	Grossman, J	FL	301
HS	Hanel, D	WA	306
HS	Hastings, H	IN	303
HS	Hentz, V	CA	306
HS	Hotchkiss, R	NY	298
HS	Hunt, T	AL	301
HS	Idler, R	CO	304
HS	Imbriglia, J	PA	298
HS	Jones, N	CA	306
HS	Jupiter, J	MA	296
HS	Jupiter, J	MA	296
HS	Kleinman, W	IN	303
HS	Koman, L	NC	301
HS	Kozin, S	PA	298
HS	Kulick, R	NY	299
HS	Lane, L	NY	299
HS	Lee, W	MD	299
HS	Light, T	IL	303
HS	Lubahn, J	PA	299
HS	Mass, D	IL	303
HS	Meals, R	CA	306
HS	Melone, C	NY	299
HS	Mih, A	IN	303
HS	Moneim, M	NM	305
HS	Nagle, D	IL	303
HS	Osterman, A	PA	299
HS	Peljovich, A	GA	301
HS	Putnam, M	MN	304
HS	Raphael, J	PA	299
HS	Raskin, K	NY	300
HS	Rayan, G	OK	305
HS	Rosenwasser, M	NY	300
HS	Sampson, C	MA	296
HS	Seitz, W	OH	304
HS	Slutsky, D	CA	306
HS	Sotereanos, D	PA	300
HS	Steinmann, S	MN	304
HS	Stern, P	OH	304
HS	Strauch, R	NY	300
HS	Swigart, C	CT	296
HS	Szabo, R	CA	306
HS	Thoder, J	PA	300
HS	Thomson, J	CT	296
HS	Trumble, T	WA	306
HS	Waters, P	MA	296
HS	Weiss, A	RI	297
HS	Wolfe, S	NY	300
OrS	Poehling, G	NC	637
OrS	Singer, D	HI	653
OrS	Stuchin, S	NY	633
OrS	Weiland, A	NY	633
PlS	Chang, B	PA	881
PlS	Constantian, M	NH	878
PlS	Dagum, A	NY	881
PlS	Derman, G	IL	893
PlS	Erdmann, D	NC	889
PlS	Fix, R	AL	889
PlS	MacKinnon, S	MO	894
PlS	Molnar, J	NC	891
PlS	Morgan, R	VA	891
PlS	Neumeister, M	IL	895
PlS	Rockwell, W	UT	898
PlS	Sanger, J	WI	896
PlS	Wilhelmi, B	KY	892

Hand-Congenital Anomaly

Spec	Name	St	Pg
HS	Ezaki, M	TX	305
HS	Hanel, D	WA	306
HS	Light, T	IL	303
HS	Waters, P	MA	296

Spec	Name	St	Pg

Hashimoto's Disease

Spec	Name	St	Pg
EDM	Burmeister, L	MN	218
EDM	Davies, T	NY	212

Head & Neck Autoimmune Disease

Spec	Name	St	Pg
Oto	Lebovics, R	NY	673

Head & Neck Cancer

Spec	Name	St	Pg
NRad	Loevner, L	PA	1021
NRad	Sze, G	CT	1020
Onc	Adelstein, D	OH	365
Onc	Algazy, K	PA	337
Onc	Argiris, A	TX	378
Onc	Axelrod, R	PA	338
Onc	Brockstein, B	IL	367
Onc	Clark, J	IL	367
Onc	Cleary, J	WI	368
Onc	Cohen, R	PA	340
Onc	Cullen, K	MD	340
Onc	Dunphy, F	NC	357
Onc	Forastiere, A	MD	343
Onc	Glisson, B	TX	380
Onc	Haddad, R	MA	332
Onc	Hong, W	TX	380
Onc	Kane, M	CO	377
Onc	Khuri, F	GA	359
Onc	Kies, M	TX	381
Onc	Langer, C	PA	346
Onc	Mintzer, D	PA	347
Onc	Nabell, L	AL	362
Onc	Oster, M	NY	349
Onc	Pfister, D	NY	350
Onc	Pinto, H	CA	391
Onc	Posner, M	NY	350
Onc	Ready, N	NC	363
Onc	Shin, D	GA	364
Onc	Troner, M	FL	364
Onc	Urba, S	MI	374
Onc	Vokes, E	IL	374
Onc	Worden, F	MI	375
Oto	Akervall, J	MI	682
Oto	Bradford, C	MI	684
Oto	Browne, J	NC	678
Oto	Bumpous, J	KY	678
Oto	Burkey, B	OH	684
Oto	Califano, J	MD	668
Oto	Campbell, B	WI	684
Oto	Caruana, S	NY	668
Oto	Chalian, A	PA	668
Oto	Chowdhury, K	CO	689
Oto	Civantos, F	FL	678
Oto	Clayman, G	TX	691
Oto	Costantino, P	NY	669
Oto	Couch, M	VT	665
Oto	Davidson, B	DC	669
Oto	Day, T	SC	678
Oto	Deschler, D	MA	665
Oto	Diaz, E	TX	691
Oto	DiNardo, L	VA	678
Oto	Donovan, D	TX	692
Oto	Eisele, D	MD	669
Oto	Ferris, R	PA	669
Oto	Funk, G	IA	684
Oto	Goodwin, W	FL	679
Oto	Gosselin, B	NH	665
Oto	Grandis, J	PA	670
Oto	Grillone, G	MA	665
Oto	Har-El, G	NY	670
Oto	Hartig, G	WI	685
Oto	Haughey, B	MO	685
Oto	Hoffman, H	IA	685
Oto	Johnson, J	PA	671
Oto	Kaplan, M	CA	695
Oto	Koch, W	MD	672
Oto	Kraus, D	NY	672
Oto	Lavertu, P	OH	686
Oto	Leonetti, J	IL	686
Oto	Levine, P	VA	679
Oto	Lydiatt, D	NE	690
Oto	Lydiatt, W	NE	690
Oto	Myers, J	TX	693
Oto	Netterville, J	TN	680
Oto	Newkirk, K	DC	673
Oto	Nuss, D	LA	693
Oto	O'Malley, B	PA	673
Oto	Otto, R	TX	693
Oto	Ozer, E	OH	687
Oto	Pelzer, H	IL	687
Oto	Persky, M	NY	674
Oto	Peters, G	AL	680
Oto	Rassekh, C	PA	674
Oto	Rice, D	CA	696
Oto	Rosenthal, E	AL	681
Oto	Sasaki, C	CT	667
Oto	Schantz, S	NY	675
Oto	Shapshay, S	NY	675
Oto	Siegel, G	IL	687
Oto	Singer, M	CA	697
Oto	Sinha, U	CA	697
Oto	Smith, R	NE	691
Oto	Snyderman, C	PA	676
Oto	Song, J	CO	691
Oto	Strome, S	MD	676
Oto	Suen, J	AR	693
Oto	Teknos, T	OH	688
Oto	Tufano, R	MD	676
Oto	Valentino, J	KY	682
Oto	Wang, S	CA	697
Oto	Weber, R	TX	694
Oto	Weinstein, G	PA	677
Oto	Weisman, R	CA	697
Oto	Weissler, M	NC	682
Oto	Weymuller, E	WA	698
Oto	Wong, R	NY	677
Oto	Yarbrough, W	CT	667
Oto	Yueh, B	MN	689
PlS	Loree, T	NY	884
PlS	Tufaro, A	MD	888
PMR	Schwartz, L	PA	865
PO	Crockett, D	CA	805
RadRO	Beitler, J	GA	983
RadRO	Brizel, D	NC	984
RadRO	Cooper, J	NY	978
RadRO	Eisbruch, A	MI	989
RadRO	Emami, B	IL	989
RadRO	Haffty, B	NJ	980
RadRO	Halyard, M	AZ	993
RadRO	Haraf, D	IL	989
RadRO	Harari, P	WI	989
RadRO	Harrison, L	NY	980
RadRO	Johnstone, P	IN	990
RadRO	Jose, B	IN	990
RadRO	Kalnicki, S	NY	980
RadRO	Kudrimoti, M	KY	984
RadRO	Laramore, G	WA	996
RadRO	Le, Q	CA	996
RadRO	Lee, C	MN	990
RadRO	Machtay, M	OH	990
RadRO	Mendenhall, W	FL	986
RadRO	Mittal, B	IL	991
RadRO	Morrison, W	TX	994
RadRO	Quivey, J	CA	997
RadRO	Sailer, S	NC	987
RadRO	Song, S	VA	987
RadRO	Streeter, O	CA	998
RadRO	Suntharalingam, M	MD	983
RadRO	Tripuraneni, P	CA	998
RadRO	Wilson, L	CT	978
RadRO	Zelefsky, M	NY	983
S	Flynn, M	KY	1105
S	Neifeld, J	VA	1107
S	Paramo, J	FL	1108

Head & Neck Cancer & Surgery

Spec	Name	St	Pg
Oto	Andersen, P	OR	694
Oto	Blackwell, K	CA	694
Oto	Blair, E	IL	683
Oto	Futran, N	WA	695
Oto	Genden, E	NY	670
Oto	Goldenberg, D	PA	670
Oto	Hanna, E	TX	692
Oto	Hicks, W	NY	670
Oto	Keane, W	PA	672
Oto	Krespi, Y	NY	672
Oto	Kuhel, W	NY	672
Oto	Olsen, K	MN	687
Oto	Patil, Y	OH	687
Oto	Petruzzelli, G	GA	680
Oto	Pitman, K	AZ	693
Oto	Samant, S	TN	681
Oto	Silverman, D	VT	667
Oto	Singh, B	NY	675
Oto	Stenson, K	IL	688
Oto	Strome, M	NY	676
Oto	Urken, M	NY	676
Oto	Wilson, K	OH	688
Oto	Zeitels, S	MA	667
S	Jackson, G	TX	1126
S	Ridge, J	PA	1099
S	Saha, S	MI	1119
S	Shah, J	NY	1100

Head & Neck Cancer

Spec	Name	St	Pg

Reconstruction

Spec	Name	St	Pg
Oto	Futran, N	WA	695
Oto	Genden, E	NY	670
Oto	Stenson, K	IL	688
Oto	Strome, M	NY	676
Oto	Urken, M	NY	676
PlS	Yuen, J	AR	901

Head & Neck Imaging

Spec	Name	St	Pg
DR	Holliday, R	NY	1009
NRad	Russell, E	IL	1024

Head & Neck Infectious Disease

Spec	Name	St	Pg
Oto	Lebovics, R	NY	673

Head & Neck Inflammatory Disorders

Spec	Name	St	Pg
Oto	Lebovics, R	NY	673

Head & Neck Pathology

Spec	Name	St	Pg
Path	Kahn, L	NY	722
Path	Wang, B	NY	725

Head & Neck Radiology

Spec	Name	St	Pg
DR	Mancuso, A	FL	1013
NRad	Curtin, H	MA	1019
NRad	Mukherji, S	MI	1024
NRad	Osborn, A	UT	1025
NRad	Zinreich, S	MD	1021

Head & Neck Reconstruction

Spec	Name	St	Pg
Oto	Akervall, J	MI	682
Oto	Alam, D	OH	682
Oto	Blackwell, K	CA	694
Oto	Browne, J	NC	678
Oto	Bumpous, J	KY	678
Oto	Chalian, A	PA	668
Oto	Deschler, D	MA	665
Oto	Funk, G	IA	684
Oto	Gosselin, B	NH	665
Oto	Haughey, B	MO	685
Oto	Picken, C	DC	674
Oto	Strome, S	MD	676
PlS	Andersen, J	CA	901
PlS	Deleyiannis, F	CO	897
PlS	Disa, J	NY	881
PlS	Miller, M	OH	895
PlS	Patel, S	PA	885
PlS	Serletti, J	PA	886
PlS	Topham, N	PA	888

Head & Neck Surgery

Spec	Name	St	Pg
Oto	Baim, H	IL	683
Oto	Hayden, R	AZ	692
Oto	Hilger, P	MN	685
Oto	Johnson, J	PA	671
Oto	Kaplan, M	CA	695
Oto	Kim, D	MA	666
Oto	Miller, F	TX	693
Oto	Netterville, J	TN	680
Oto	Orloff, L	CA	696
Oto	Ozer, E	OH	687
Oto	Rebeiz, E	MA	667
Oto	Schaefer, S	NY	675
Oto	Schantz, S	NY	675
Oto	Shindo, M	OR	697
Oto	Singer, M	CA	697
Oto	Spiegel, J	MA	667
Oto	Stewart, M	NY	676
Oto	Wackym, P	OR	697
Oto	Wang, S	CA	697
Oto	Weber, S	TX	694
Oto	Wong, B	CA	698
PlS	Coleman, J	IN	893
PO	Cotton, R	OH	804
PO	Drake, A	NC	803
PO	Duncan, N	TX	805
PO	Rosenfeld, R	NY	803
PO	Tunkel, D	MD	803
PS	Holterman, M	IL	820
PS	Rescorla, F	IN	820
S	Alfonso, A	NY	1089
S	Flynn, M	KY	1105
S	Sosa, J	NC	1109

Head & Neck Trauma

Spec	Name	St	Pg
NS	Fessler, R	IL	490

Head & Neck Tumors

Spec	Name	St	Pg
Oto	Fried, M	NY	669
PO	Cunningham, M	MA	801
PO	McGill, T	MA	801
PO	Myer, C	OH	804

Head & Neck Tumors Imaging

Spec	Name	St	Pg
DR	Rao, V	PA	1011
NRad	Koeller, K	MN	1023
NRad	Mukherji, S	MI	1024

Head Injury

Spec	Name	St	Pg
S	Britt, L	VA	1103

Headache

Spec	Name	St	Pg
ChiN	Hershey, A	OH	148
ChiN	Sankar, R	CA	152
ChiN	Shaywitz, B	CT	144
ChiN	Sivaswamy, L	MI	149
ChiN	Tennison, M	NC	147
N	Buchholz, D	MD	513
N	Charles, A	CA	539
N	Charney, J	NY	514
N	Corbett, J	MS	524
N	Cutrer, F	MN	529
N	Dodick, D	AZ	536
N	Finkel, A	NC	524
N	Foo, S	NY	515
N	Gendelman, S	NY	515
N	Lane, J	CO	535
N	Lavin, P	TN	525
N	Lipton, R	NY	518
N	Newman, L	NY	520
N	Petito, F	NY	520
N	Rothrock, J	NV	541
N	Sabo, T	CO	535
N	Saper, J	MI	533
N	Silberstein, S	PA	521
N	Swanson, J	MN	533
N	Weinberg, H	NY	522
NRad	Khandji, A	NY	1020
PM	Argoff, C	NY	706
PM	Freitag, F	WI	709
PM	Loder, E	MA	706
PM	Robbins, L	IL	710
PM	Rosenquist, R	OH	710

Headache in Women

Spec	Name	St	Pg
N	Finkel, M	FL	524
N	Rubin, S	IL	533

Headache/Facial Pain

Spec	Name	St	Pg
PM	Racz, G	TX	711

Hearing & Balance Disorders

Spec	Name	St	Pg
Oto	Amedee, R	LA	691
Oto	Dornhoffer, J	AR	692
Oto	Harris, J	CA	695
Oto	Pensak, M	OH	687
Oto	Rauch, S	MA	666
Oto	Shelton, C	UT	690
Oto	Tucci, D	NC	682
Oto	Wazen, J	FL	682

Hearing Disorders

Spec	Name	St	Pg
Oto	Carey, J	MD	668
Oto	Feghali, J	NY	669
Oto	Goebel, J	MO	685
Oto	Hirsch, B	PA	670
Oto	Paparella, M	MN	687
PO	Chan, K	CO	805
PO	Parikh, S	WA	806

Hearing Loss

Spec	Name	St	Pg
CG	Carey, J	UT	161
N	Hecox, K	WI	530
Oto	Arts, H	MI	682
Oto	Dornhoffer, J	AR	692
Oto	Farrior, J	FL	678
Oto	Gianoli, G	LA	692
Oto	Grundfast, K	MA	666
Oto	Hammerschlag, P	NY	670
Oto	Kveton, J	CT	666
Oto	Lustig, L	CA	696
Oto	Macias, J	AZ	693

Spec	Name	St	Pg
Oto	Mattox, D	GA	679
Oto	McMenomey, S	NY	673
Oto	Niparko, J	CA	696
Oto	Oghalai, J	CA	696
Oto	Rubinstein, J	WA	696
Oto	Telischi, F	FL	681
Oto	Wiet, R	IL	688
Oto	Young, N	IL	689
Oto	Yueh, B	MN	689
PO	Arjmand, E	OH	803
PO	Eavey, R	TN	803
PO	Goldsmith, A	NY	802
PO	Katz, R	OH	804
PO	O'Reilly, R	DE	802

Heart Attack

Spec	Name	St	Pg
CE	Gomes, J	NY	114
Cv	Eagle, K	MI	101
Cv	Gibbons, R	MN	102
IC	Holmes, D	MN	126

Heart Disease & Depression

Spec	Name	St	Pg
Cv	Jaffe, A	MN	102

Heart Disease in Athletes

Spec	Name	St	Pg
CE	Link, M	MA	113

Heart Disease in Cancer Patients

Spec	Name	St	Pg
Cv	Steingart, R	NY	96

Heart Disease in Diabetic Patients

Spec	Name	St	Pg
EDM	Donner, T	MD	212

Heart Disease in Down Syndrome

Spec	Name	St	Pg
PCd	Velvis, H	NY	750

Heart Disease in Pregnancy

Spec	Name	St	Pg
Cv	Connolly, H	MN	101
Cv	Elkayam, U	CA	110
Cv	Meller, J	NY	95
Cv	Wells, G	NC	100
Cv	Wilansky, S	AZ	109
MF	Adam, K	TX	440
MF	Hibbard, J	IL	438

Heart Disease in Women

Spec	Name	St	Pg
Cv	Bairey-Merz, C	CA	110
Cv	Brozena, S	PA	91
Cv	Goldberg, N	NY	93
Cv	Hayes, S	MN	102
Cv	Johnson, P	MA	88
Cv	Judelson, D	CA	111
Cv	Lewis, S	OR	111
Cv	Limacher, M	FL	98
Cv	Lindenfeld, J	CO	107
Cv	Oparil, S	AL	99
Cv	Pepine, C	FL	99
Cv	Redberg, R	CA	112
Cv	Reis, S	PA	95
Cv	Roberts, B	RI	90
Cv	Volgman, A	IL	106
Cv	von der Lohe, E	IN	106
Cv	Wagoner, L	OH	106
Cv	Walsh, M	IN	106
Cv	Wilansky, S	AZ	109
IC	Jacobs, A	MA	120

Heart Failure

Spec	Name	St	Pg
CE	DeLurgio, D	GA	116
CE	Mehta, D	NY	115
CE	Sorrentino, R	GA	116
Cv	Borer, J	NY	91
Cv	Borzak, S	FL	97
Cv	Bourge, R	AL	97
Cv	Bove, A	PA	91
Cv	Califf, R	NC	97
Cv	Clements, S	GA	98
Cv	DeNofrio, D	MA	88
Cv	Elkayam, U	CA	110
Cv	Fonarow, G	CA	110
Cv	French, W	CA	111
Cv	Gottlieb, S	MD	93
Cv	Hare, J	FL	98
Cv	Hauptman, P	MO	102
Cv	Heroux, A	IL	102
Cv	Horn, E	NY	94
Cv	Katz, S	NY	94
Cv	Konstam, M	MA	89
Cv	Landzberg, J	NJ	94
Cv	Mather, P	PA	95
Cv	Nagueh, S	TX	108
Cv	O'Connor, C	NC	99
Cv	Rich, S	IL	104
Cv	Rosenbush, S	IL	104
Cv	Russell, S	MD	95
Cv	Smith, A	GA	100
Cv	Steingart, R	NY	96
Cv	Stevenson, L	MA	90
Cv	Young, J	OH	107
IC	Kimmelstiel, C	MA	121
PCd	Bernstein, D	CA	754
PCd	Dreyer, W	TX	754
PCd	Fricker, F	FL	751
PCd	Gewitz, M	NY	749
PCd	Hsu, D	NY	749
PCd	Pahl, E	IL	753
PCd	Shaddy, R	PA	750
T&CS	Athanasuleas, C	AL	1160
T&CS	Byrne, J	MA	1146
T&CS	Cohen, G	CA	1177
T&CS	Savage, E	FL	1165

Heart Failure & Ventricular Containment

Spec	Name	St	Pg
T&CS	Bolman, R	MA	1146
T&CS	Furukawa, S	PA	1152
T&CS	Naka, Y	NY	1157

Heart Failure in Kidney Disease

Spec	Name	St	Pg
Nep	Schreiber, M	OH	464

Heart Laser Revascularization

Spec	Name	St	Pg
T&CS	Horvath, K	MD	1154

Heart Valve Disease

Spec	Name	St	Pg
Cv	Bashore, T	NC	97
Cv	Blumenthal, D	NY	91
Cv	Bonow, R	IL	100
Cv	Borer, J	NY	91
Cv	Braverman, A	MO	100
Cv	Byrd, B	TN	97
Cv	Carabello, B	TX	108
Cv	Elkayam, U	CA	110
Cv	Fuster, V	NY	92
Cv	Gliklich, J	NY	93
Cv	Greenberg, M	NY	93
Cv	Harrison, J	NC	98
Cv	Herling, I	PA	94
Cv	Iskandrian, A	AL	98
Cv	Kobashigawa, J	CA	111
Cv	Landzberg, J	NJ	94
Cv	Liang, B	CT	89
Cv	Manning, W	MA	89
Cv	McPherson, D	TX	108
Cv	Mehlman, D	IL	103
Cv	Meller, J	NY	95
Cv	O'Gara, P	MA	89
Cv	O'Neill, W	MI	104
Cv	Powers, E	SC	99
Cv	Quinones, M	TX	108
Cv	Rahko, P	WI	104
Cv	Reiss, C	MO	104
Cv	Sanborn, T	IL	105
Cv	Shah, P	CA	112
Cv	Shea, R	IN	105
Cv	Silvestry, F	PA	96
Cv	Slater, W	NY	96
Cv	Stainback, R	TX	109
Cv	Stewart, W	OH	105
Cv	Tenenbaum, J	NY	96
Cv	Tobis, J	CA	112
Cv	Waxman, H	PA	96
Cv	Wells, G	NC	100
Cv	Wilansky, S	AZ	109
IC	Bailey, S	TX	127
IC	Carroll, J	CO	127
IC	Herrmann, H	PA	122
IC	Leya, F	IL	126
IC	Lopez, J	IL	126
IC	Morris, D	GA	125
IC	Moses, J	NY	122
IC	Sharma, S	NY	123
IC	Smalling, R	TX	128

Spec	Name	St	Pg
IC	Teirstein, P	CA	128
T&CS	Merrick, S	CA	1179
T&CS	Szeto, W	PA	1159

Heart Valve Surgery

Spec	Name	St	Pg
PS	Quaegebeur, J	NY	816
T&CS	Acker, M	PA	1149
T&CS	Adams, D	NY	1150
T&CS	Aldea, G	WA	1177
T&CS	Bavaria, J	PA	1150
T&CS	Bridges, C	NC	1161
T&CS	Brown, J	IN	1167
T&CS	Byrne, J	MA	1146
T&CS	Caskey, M	AZ	1173
T&CS	Chitwood, W	NC	1161
T&CS	Cohen, R	CA	1178
T&CS	Drinkwater, D	TN	1162
T&CS	Filsoufi, F	NY	1152
T&CS	Furukawa, S	PA	1152
T&CS	Graver, L	NY	1153
T&CS	Griffith, B	MD	1153
T&CS	Hargrove, W	PA	1154
T&CS	Hashim, S	CT	1147
T&CS	Horvath, K	MD	1154
T&CS	Isom, O	NY	1154
T&CS	Jessen, M	TX	1174
T&CS	Joyce, L	MN	1169
T&CS	Krieger, K	NY	1155
T&CS	Lamberti, J	CA	1179
T&CS	Lang, S	NY	1155
T&CS	Lansman, S	NY	1156
T&CS	Lazar, H	MA	1147
T&CS	Loulmet, D	NY	1156
T&CS	Love, R	WI	1169
T&CS	Lytle, B	OH	1170
T&CS	McCarthy, P	IL	1170
T&CS	Michler, R	NY	1156
T&CS	Mill, M	NC	1163
T&CS	Mitchell, M	CO	1173
T&CS	Murphy, D	GA	1164
T&CS	Ott, D	TX	1175
T&CS	Oz, M	NY	1157
T&CS	Pochettino, A	MN	1171
T&CS	Rastegar, H	MA	1148
T&CS	Salerno, T	FL	1165
T&CS	Schaff, H	MN	1171
T&CS	Sellke, F	RI	1148
T&CS	Shemin, R	CA	1180
T&CS	Smedira, N	OH	1171
T&CS	Smith, P	NC	1165
T&CS	Starnes, V	CA	1180
T&CS	Swistel, D	NY	1159
T&CS	Tedder, M	TN	1166
T&CS	Toyoda, Y	PA	1159
T&CS	Tranbaugh, R	NY	1159
T&CS	Verrier, E	WA	1181
T&CS	Warner, K	MA	1149
T&CS	Williams, M	NY	1160
T&CS	Yuh, D	CT	1149

Heart Valve Surgery-Aortic

Spec	Name	St	Pg
T&CS	Diehl, J	PA	1151
T&CS	Reardon, M	TX	1175
T&CS	Stewart, A	NY	1159

Heart Valve Surgery-Mitral

Spec	Name	St	Pg
T&CS	Diehl, J	PA	1151

Heart Valve Surgery-Pediatric

Spec	Name	St	Pg
T&CS	Del-Nido, P	MA	1146
T&CS	Forbess, J	TX	1174

Heart Valve Surgery-Percutaneous

Spec	Name	St	Pg
T&CS	Guyton, R	GA	1162
T&CS	Svensson, L	OH	1171

Hemangiomas

Spec	Name	St	Pg
D	Cohen, B	MD	187
D	Frieden, I	CA	200
D	Yan, A	PA	191
PO	Cunningham, M	MA	801
PO	McGill, T	MA	801

Hemangiomas/Birthmarks

Spec	Name	St	Pg
D	Bayliss, S	MO	194
PIS	Kane, A	TX	899

Hematologic Disorders

Spec	Name	St	Pg
PHO	O'Reilly, R	NY	776
PHO	Pendergrass, T	WA	791
PHO	Recht, M	OR	791

Hematologic Disorders in Cancer Patients

Spec	Name	St	Pg
Hem	Soff, G	NY	317

Hematologic Infections

Spec	Name	St	Pg
Inf	Slama, T	IN	418

Hematologic Malignancies

Spec	Name	St	Pg
Hem	Anderson, K	MA	312
Hem	Blaustein, A	FL	318
Hem	Brodsky, R	MD	313
Hem	Cheson, B	DC	313
Hem	DiPersio, J	MO	321
Hem	Filicko-O'Hara, J	PA	314
Hem	Greer, J	TN	319
Hem	Grever, M	OH	322
Hem	Gruenstein, S	NY	314
Hem	Heinrich, M	OR	328
Hem	Holland, H	GA	319
Hem	Kessler, C	DC	315
Hem	Kraut, E	OH	322
Hem	Lill, M	CA	328
Hem	Lin, W	TX	326
Hem	Maciejewski, J	OH	323
Hem	Mangan, K	PA	315
Hem	Millenson, M	PA	316
Hem	Mitchell, B	CA	329
Hem	Munker, R	LA	327
Hem	Nademanee, A	CA	329
Hem	Rondelli, D	IL	323
Hem	Roodman, G	IN	323
Hem	Schiffman, F	RI	312
Hem	Schuster, M	NY	317
Hem	Slease, R	DE	317
Hem	Sokol, L	FL	320
Onc	Advani, R	CA	384
Onc	Algazy, K	PA	337
Onc	Armitage, J	NE	375
Onc	Bashevkin, M	NY	338
Onc	Beatty, P	MT	376
Onc	Bergsagel, P	AZ	379
Onc	Bolwell, B	OH	366
Onc	Carabasi, M	PA	339
Onc	Chow, W	CA	386
Onc	Claxton, D	PA	340
Onc	Cohen, G	MD	340
Onc	Colon-Otero, G	FL	357
Onc	Druker, B	OR	387
Onc	Erban, J	MA	331
Onc	Flomenberg, N	PA	342
Onc	Flynn, P	MN	369
Onc	Gabrilove, J	NY	343
Onc	Mitsuyasu, R	CA	390
Onc	Morginstin, M	PA	347
Onc	Picozzi, V	WA	391
Onc	Rosen, S	IL	373
Onc	Rosove, M	CA	391
Onc	Shields, P	OH	374
Onc	Silver, S	MI	374
Onc	Somlo, G	CA	392
Onc	Strenger, R	RI	335
Onc	Taetle, R	AZ	383
Onc	Terpenning, M	CA	393
Onc	Vaughan, W	AL	364
PHO	Carroll, W	NY	772
PHO	Hord, J	OH	784
PHO	O'Reilly, R	NY	776
PHO	Ritchey, A	PA	776

Hematology

Spec	Name	St	Pg
Hem	Abrams, C	PA	313
Hem	Adams, R	AZ	325
Hem	Adams-Graves, P	TN	318
Hem	Allen, S	NY	313
Hem	Anderson, K	MA	312
Hem	Baer, M	MD	313
Hem	Ballen, K	MA	312
Hem	Barlogie, B	AR	325
Hem	Baron, J	IL	320
Hem	Bigelow, C	MS	318
Hem	Blaustein, A	FL	318
Hem	Blinder, M	MO	321
Hem	Blum, K	OH	321

Spec	Name	St	Pg
Hem	Bockenstedt, P	MI	321
Hem	Brenner, M	TX	325
Hem	Brodsky, R	MD	313
Hem	Byrd, J	OH	321
Hem	Champlin, R	TX	325
Hem	Cheson, B	DC	313
Hem	Cobos, E	TX	325
Hem	Comenzo, R	MA	312
Hem	Cooper, B	TX	326
Hem	Copelan, E	NC	319
Hem	Cortes, J	TX	326
Hem	Damon, L	CA	327
Hem	DeLoughery, T	OR	328
Hem	DiPersio, J	MO	321
Hem	Diuguid, D	NY	314
Hem	Djulbegovic, B	FL	319
Hem	Emanuel, P	AR	326
Hem	Farag, S	IN	321
Hem	Filicko-O'Hara, J	PA	314
Hem	Fonseca, R	AZ	326
Hem	Forman, S	CA	328
Hem	Friedman, A	PA	314
Hem	Fruchtman, S	NY	314
Hem	Garcia-Manero, G	TX	326
Hem	Gertz, M	MN	321
Hem	Goldberg, J	PA	314
Hem	Gordon, L	IL	321
Hem	Greer, J	TN	319
Hem	Gregory, S	IL	322
Hem	Grever, M	OH	322
Hem	Gruenstein, S	NY	314
Hem	Habermann, T	MN	322
Hem	Heinrich, M	OR	328
Hem	Holland, H	GA	319
Hem	Isola, L	NY	314
Hem	Juckett, M	WI	322
Hem	Jurcic, J	NY	314
Hem	Kantarjian, H	TX	326
Hem	Keating, M	TX	326
Hem	Kempin, S	NY	315
Hem	Kessler, C	DC	315
Hem	Kipps, T	CA	328
Hem	Komrokji, R	FL	319
Hem	Kraut, E	OH	322
Hem	Kuriakose, P	MI	322
Hem	Larson, R	IL	322
Hem	Leung, L	CA	328
Hem	Levine, A	CA	328
Hem	Lill, M	CA	328
Hem	Lin, W	TX	326
Hem	Lind, S	CO	324
Hem	Linenberger, M	WA	328
Hem	Litzow, M	MN	322
Hem	Luger, S	PA	315
Hem	Lyons, R	TX	327
Hem	Maciejewski, J	OH	323
Hem	Mangan, K	PA	315
Hem	Marks, S	PA	315
Hem	Maslak, P	NY	315
Hem	Maziarz, R	OR	329
Hem	McGlave, P	MN	323
Hem	Mears, J	NY	315
Hem	Meehan, K	NH	312
Hem	Mesa, R	AZ	327
Hem	Milhem, M	IA	323
Hem	Millenson, M	PA	316
Hem	Miller, K	MA	312
Hem	Mitchell, B	CA	329
Hem	Munker, R	LA	327
Hem	Nademanee, A	CA	329
Hem	Nand, S	IL	323
Hem	Negrin, R	CA	329
Hem	O'Donnell, M	CA	329
Hem	Ortel, T	NC	319
Hem	Palascak, J	OH	323
Hem	Petersdorf, S	WA	329
Hem	Porcu, P	OH	323
Hem	Porter, D	PA	316
Hem	Powell, B	NC	319
Hem	Rai, K	NY	316
Hem	Rao, A	PA	316
Hem	Raphael, B	NY	316
Hem	Rapoport, A	MD	316
Hem	Richardson, P	MA	312
Hem	Rodgers, G	UT	325
Hem	Rondelli, D	IL	323
Hem	Roodman, G	IN	323
Hem	Rosenblatt, J	FL	320
Hem	Rowley, S	NJ	316
Hem	Savage, D	NY	316
Hem	Saven, A	CA	329
Hem	Schiffman, F	RI	312
Hem	Schiller, G	CA	329
Hem	Schuster, M	NY	317
Hem	Schuster, S	PA	317
Hem	Schwartzberg, L	TN	320
Hem	Singhal, S	IL	324
Hem	Slease, R	DE	317
Hem	Snyder, D	CA	330
Hem	Soff, G	NY	317
Hem	Sokol, L	FL	320
Hem	Spitzer, T	MA	313
Hem	Spivak, J	MD	317
Hem	Stewart, A	AZ	327
Hem	Stiff, P	IL	324
Hem	Stock, W	IL	324
Hem	Stone, R	MA	313
Hem	Strair, R	NJ	317
Hem	Strauss, J	TX	327
Hem	Streiff, M	MD	317
Hem	Tallman, M	NY	318
Hem	Tefferi, A	MN	324
Hem	Telen, M	NC	320
Hem	Uberti, J	MI	324
Hem	Van Besien, K	NY	318
Hem	Vose, J	NE	325
Hem	Williams, M	VA	320
Hem	Winter, J	IL	324
Hem	Wisch, N	NY	318
Hem	Yanovich, S	MD	318
Hem	Yeager, A	AZ	327
Hem	Zuckerman, K	FL	320
Onc	Koczywas, M	CA	389
Onc	Lim, D	CA	389
Onc	Reckamp, K	CA	391
Onc	Twardowski, P	CA	393

Hematopathology

Spec	Name	St	Pg
Hem	Rodgers, G	UT	325
Path	Bagg, A	PA	720
Path	Banks, P	NC	725
Path	Behm, F	IL	727
Path	Chesney, C	TN	725
Path	Harris, N	MA	718
Path	Kinney, M	TX	730
Path	Morrow, J	CT	719
Path	Nathwani, B	CA	734
Path	Orazi, A	NY	723
Path	Swerdlow, S	PA	724
Path	Warnke, R	CA	734
Path	Weisenburger, D	CA	735
Path	Weiss, L	CA	735

Hemochromatosis

Spec	Name	St	Pg
PHO	Wolfe, L	NY	777

Hemolytic Uremic Syndrome

Spec	Name	St	Pg
PNep	Ault, B	TN	798
PNep	Kaplan, B	PA	798

Hemophagocytic Syndrome

Spec	Name	St	Pg
PHO	Morgan, E	IL	784

Hemophilia

Spec	Name	St	Pg
Hem	Kessler, C	DC	315
Hem	Palascak, J	OH	323
Hem	Streiff, M	MD	317
Onc	Romond, E	KY	363
Onc	Stopeck, A	AZ	383
PHO	Buchanan, G	TX	787
PHO	Giardina, P	NY	773
PHO	Glader, B	CA	790
PHO	Halpern, S	NJ	774
PHO	Hoots, W	MD	774
PHO	Johnston, J	GA	779
PHO	Kobrinsky, N	ND	787
PHO	Luchtman-Jones, L	DC	775
PHO	Manco-Johnson, M	CO	787
PHO	Recht, M	OR	791
PHO	Shapiro, A	IN	785
PHO	Tebbi, C	FL	781
PHO	Valentino, L	IL	786

Hemorrhoids

Spec	Name	St	Pg
CRS	Eisenstat, T	NJ	169
CRS	Golub, R	FL	172
CRS	Gorfine, S	NY	170
CRS	Steinhagen, R	NY	171

Hepatic Iron Metabolism

Spec	Name	St	Pg
Ge	Bacon, B	MO	246

Spec	Name	St	Pg
Hepatitis			
Ge	Barnes, D	OH	246
Ge	Boyer, T	AZ	253
Ge	Brown, R	NY	233
Ge	Di Bisceglie, A	MO	247
Ge	Dienstag, J	MA	230
Ge	Dieterich, D	NY	234
Ge	Freiman, H	NY	234
Ge	Fried, M	NC	242
Ge	Gish, R	CA	256
Ge	Glombicki, A	TX	254
Ge	Hunter, E	ID	252
Ge	Jacobson, I	NY	236
Ge	Kotler, D	NY	237
Ge	Magun, A	NY	238
Ge	Martin, P	FL	243
Ge	Nunes, D	MA	231
Ge	Reddy, K	PA	239
Ge	Schiano, T	NY	240
Ge	Sorrell, M	NE	252
Ge	Te, H	IL	250
Ge	Zaman, A	OR	258
PGe	Jonas, M	MA	762
PGe	Molleston, J	IN	766
PGe	Suchy, F	CO	768
Hepatitis B			
Ge	Bloomer, J	AL	241
Hepatitis B & C			
Ge	Han, S	CA	256
Ge	Kwo, P	IN	248
Ge	Poordad, F	TX	254
Ge	Tobias, H	NY	240
Ge	Vierling, J	TX	255
Inf	Nahass, R	NJ	414
PGe	Murray, K	WA	769
PGe	Schwarz, K	MD	764
PGe	Squires, R	PA	764
Hepatitis B-Immune Response			
Rhu	Cupps, T	DC	1060
Hepatitis C			
Ge	Bacon, B	MO	246
Ge	Balart, L	LA	253
Ge	Brown, K	MI	246
Ge	Chung, R	MA	230
Ge	Di Bisceglie, A	MO	247
Ge	Fallon, M	TX	254
Ge	Galati, J	TX	254
Ge	Herrine, S	PA	235
Ge	Jacobson, I	NY	236
Ge	Jensen, D	IL	248
Ge	Reuben, A	SC	244
Ge	Shiffman, M	VA	245
Inf	Kumar, P	DC	413
Hepatitis-Chronic			
Ge	Porayko, M	TN	244
Ge	Scudera, P	VA	244
Hepatobiliary Cancer			
S	Curley, S	TX	1124
S	Espat, N	RI	1085
Hepatobiliary Surgery			
PS	Superina, R	IL	821
PS	Tracy, T	RI	814
S	Adams, R	VA	1103
S	Billingsley, K	OR	1130
S	Brems, J	IL	1112
S	Busuttil, R	CA	1130
S	Colquhoun, S	CA	1131
S	Deziel, D	IL	1113
S	Eckhoff, D	AL	1104
S	Emond, J	NY	1093
S	Emre, S	CT	1085
S	Farley, D	MN	1114
S	Galloway, J	GA	1105
S	Hemming, A	CA	1133
S	Hoffman, J	PA	1094
S	Howerton, R	NC	1106
S	Jarnagin, W	NY	1094
S	Kendrick, M	MN	1115
S	Kinkhabwala, M	NY	1095
S	Kuo, P	IL	1116
S	Lieberman, M	NY	1096
S	Nagorney, D	MN	1117
S	Oberholzer, J	IL	1117
S	Philosophe, B	MD	1098
S	Reed, A	IA	1118
S	Reich, D	PA	1099
S	Reyes, J	WA	1136
S	Schwartz, M	NY	1100
S	Shaked, A	PA	1100
S	Teperman, L	NY	1102
S	Thayer, S	MA	1088
S	Vauthey, J	TX	1129
S	Walsh, R	OH	1121
Hepatopulmonary Syndrome			
Pul	Krowka, M	MN	965
Hereditary Angioedema			
A&I	Lockey, R	FL	82
Hereditary Cancer			
CG	Grody, W	CA	163
CG	Ostrer, H	NY	158
CG	Plon, S	TX	162
CG	Sutphen, R	FL	159
CG	Weitzel, J	CA	164
CG	Whelan, A	MO	161
Ge	Boland, C	TX	253
Ge	Itzkowitz, S	NY	236
Onc	Markowitz, S	OH	371
Onc	Nissenblatt, M	NJ	348
Onc	Olopade, O	IL	372
Onc	Pasche, B	AL	362
Onc	Terpenning, M	CA	393
Onc	Toppmeyer, D	NJ	353
S	Hughes, K	MA	1086
Hereditary Colon Cancer			
CRS	Nogueras, J	FL	172
Hereditary Endocrine Cancers			
EDM	Waguespack, S	TX	223
Hereditary Hemorrhagic Telangiectasia			
CG	Pyeritz, R	PA	158
PHO	Valentino, L	IL	786
VIR	Trerotola, S	PA	1029
Hernia			
Ped Uro	Atala, A	NC	825
PS	Aiken, J	WI	819
PS	Crombleholme, T	CO	821
PS	Midulla, P	NY	816
PS	Paidas, C	FL	818
PS	Stolar, C	CA	824
PS	Velcek, F	NY	817
S	Baker, C	VA	1103
S	Barie, P	NY	1089
S	Brody, F	DC	1090
S	Brunt, L	MO	1112
S	Chand, B	IL	1112
S	Dunkin, B	TX	1124
S	Farley, D	MN	1114
S	Fitzgibbons, R	NE	1122
S	Hawn, M	AL	1105
S	Hebert, J	VT	1085
S	Meyers, W	PA	1096
S	Nowak, E	NY	1097
S	Pomp, A	NY	1098
S	Rege, R	TX	1128
S	Reiner, M	NY	1099
S	Rosen, M	OH	1118
Hernia-Complex			
S	Park, A	MD	1098
Hernia-Sports			
S	Brunt, L	MO	1112
Herpetic Neuralgia (Shingles)			
PM	Audell, L	CA	712
PM	Raja, S	MD	707

Specialty & Special Expertise Index

Spec Name St Pg

Hidradenitis Suppurativa
D Bennett, R CA 200

High Intensity Focused Ultrasound(HIFU)
U Robertson, C NC 1200

High Risk Pregnancy
MF Koos, B CA 443

Hip & Knee Reconstruction
OrS Bostrom, M NY 621
OrS Caillouette, J CA 650
OrS Einhorn, T MA 616
OrS Garvin, K NE 646
OrS Kress, K GA 637
OrS McDonald, D MO 643
OrS Oakes, D CA 653
OrS Smith, E MA 619
OrS Weiner, R FL 639

Hip & Knee Replacement
OrS Bucholz, R TX 648
OrS Callaghan, J IA 640
OrS Copp, S CA 650
OrS Einhorn, T MA 616
OrS Finerman, G CA 651
OrS Gorab, R CA 651
OrS Hozack, W PA 626
OrS Kress, K GA 637
OrS Oakes, D CA 653
OrS Padgett, D NY 630
OrS Ready, J MA 618
OrS Rodriguez, J NY 631
OrS Schmalzried, T CA 653
OrS Siegel, H AL 638
OrS Smith, E MA 619
OrS Stuchin, S NY 633
OrS Stulberg, S IL 645
OrS Thornhill, T MA 619
OrS Vail, T CA 654
OrS Weiner, R FL 639
OrS Wixson, R IL 645

Hip & Knee Replacement in Bone Tumors
OrS Healey, J NY 625
OrS Ready, J MA 618

Hip & Knee Surgery
OrS Ward, W PA 633

Hip Disorders & Dysplasia
OrS Aronson, J AR 647
OrS Clohisy, J MO 640
OrS Sponseller, P MD 633
OrS Weinstein, S IA 645

Hip Disorders-Pediatric
OrS Beaty, J TN 635
OrS Herman, M PA 626
OrS McCarthy, J OH 643
OrS Roye, D NY 631
OrS Weinstein, S IA 645

Hip Replacement
OrS Bozic, K CA 649
OrS Brick, G MA 616
OrS Bronson, M NY 621
OrS Burke, D MA 616
OrS Cornell, C NY 622
OrS Dorr, L CA 651
OrS Gitelis, S IL 641
OrS Goldstein, W IL 641
OrS Howe, K CA 651
OrS Hume, E PA 626
OrS Jiranek, W VA 636
OrS Johnson, E CA 651
OrS Lieberman, J CA 652
OrS Macaulay, W NY 628
OrS Muschler, G OH 643
OrS Pellicci, P NY 630
OrS Reilly, D MA 618
OrS Robinson, R FL 637
OrS Rothman, R PA 631
OrS Salvati, E NY 631
OrS Sculco, T NY 632
OrS Sharkey, P PA 632
OrS Zuckerman, J NY 635

Hip Replacement & Revision
OrS Berry, D MN 639
OrS Bostrom, M NY 621
OrS Buly, R NY 622
OrS Clohisy, J MO 640
OrS Hungerford, M MD 626
OrS Jacobs, J IL 642
OrS Johanson, N PA 626
OrS Krackow, K NY 627
OrS Mabrey, J TX 648
OrS Meere, P NY 629
OrS Moucha, C NY 629
OrS Parvizi, J PA 630
OrS Thomas, B CA 654
OrS Westrich, G NY 634

Hip Replacement-Young Adults
OrS Clohisy, J MO 640
OrS Pellicci, P NY 630

Hip Resurfacing
OrS Clohisy, J MO 640
OrS Stuchin, S NY 633
OrS Vail, T CA 654

Hip Surgery
OrS Bono, J MA 616
OrS Crossett, L PA 622
OrS Hanssen, A MN 641
OrS Kelly, B NY 627
SM Byrd, J TN 1076

Hirschsprung's Disease
PS Doody, D MA 814
PS Notrica, D AZ 822
PS Proctor, M WA 823
PS Ricketts, R GA 818
PS Tracy, T RI 814

Hirsutism
D Olsen, E NC 193

Histiocytoma
PHO Arceci, R AZ 787
PHO Nicholson, H OR 791

Histoplasmosis
PInf Belcher, C IN 795
PInf Christenson, J IN 795

HIV
Inf Longworth, D OH 417
Inf Nahass, R NJ 414
Inf Schooley, R CA 421
Inf Wallace, M FL 417

HIV & Blood Transfusions
Inf Wallach, F NY 415

HIV & Hepatitis co-infection
Inf McGowan, J NY 414

HIV in Adolescents
AM Rudy, B NY 76

HIV in Pregnancy
Inf Cohn, S IL 417
Inf McGowan, J NY 414

HIV Related Kidney Disease
Nep Winston, J NY 461

Hives
A&I Buchbinder, E NY 80

Hoarding-Compulsive
Psyc Saxena, S CA 934

Spec	Name	St	Pg

Hodgkin's Disease Consultation

Spec	Name	St	Pg
Onc	DeVita, V	CT	331
Onc	Lynch, J	FL	361
Onc	Offit, K	NY	349

Hodgkin's Disease-Second Opinion

Spec	Name	St	Pg
Onc	Canellos, G	MA	330

Hodgkin's Lymphoma

Spec	Name	St	Pg
Hem	Emanuel, P	AR	326
Hem	Gordon, L	IL	321
Hem	Habermann, T	MN	322
Hem	Isola, L	NY	314
Hem	Slease, R	DE	317
Hem	Winter, J	IL	324
Onc	Ambinder, R	MD	337
Onc	Coleman, M	NY	340
Onc	Come, S	MA	331
Onc	Czuczman, M	NY	341
Onc	Fisher, R	PA	342
Onc	Friedberg, J	NY	343
Onc	Glick, J	PA	343
Onc	Goy, A	NJ	343
Onc	Hochberg, E	MA	332
Onc	Horwitz, S	NY	345
Onc	Lossos, I	FL	360
Onc	Lynch, J	FL	361
Onc	Moore, J	NC	361
Onc	Morgan, D	TN	362
Onc	O'Connor, O	NY	348
Onc	Smith, M	OH	374
Onc	Straus, D	NY	352
PHO	Billett, A	MA	769
PHO	Brecher, M	NY	771
PHO	Chen, A	MD	772
PHO	Fallon, R	IN	783
PHO	Friedman, D	TN	778
PHO	Halpern, S	NJ	774
PHO	Hudson, M	TN	779
PHO	Hutchinson, R	MI	784
PHO	Keller, F	GA	779
PHO	Olson, J	OR	791
PHO	Schwartz, C	RI	770
PHO	Tebbi, C	FL	781
PHO	Weinstein, H	MA	771
RadRO	Donaldson, S	CA	995
RadRO	Hoppe, R	CA	995
RadRO	Mendenhall, N	FL	986
RadRO	Nicolaou, N	PA	981
RadRO	Rabinovitch, R	CO	992
RadRO	Roberts, K	CT	977
RadRO	Yahalom, J	NY	983

Hormonal Disorders

Spec	Name	St	Pg
EDM	Dobs, A	MD	212
EDM	Goodman, N	FL	216
EDM	Korytkowski, M	PA	213
Ger	Schwartz, R	CO	267
ObG	Richardson, M	KS	566
RE	Chang, R	CA	1051
RE	Dumesic, D	CA	1051
RE	Ory, S	FL	1046
RE	Winer, S	CA	1053
RE	Zacur, H	MD	1045

Hormone Replacement-Male

Spec	Name	St	Pg
U	Lipshultz, L	TX	1209
U	Turek, P	CA	1214

Hormone Secreting Tumors

Spec	Name	St	Pg
Ge	Liddle, R	NC	243

Hospice & Palliative Medicine

Spec	Name	St	Pg
H & PM	Abrahm, J	MA	406
H & PM	Arnold, R	PA	406
H & PM	Block, S	MA	406
H & PM	Bricker, L	MI	407
H & PM	Davis, M	OH	407
H & PM	Ferris, F	OH	407
H & PM	Fine, R	TX	408
H & PM	Friebert, S	OH	408
H & PM	Jackson, V	MA	406
H & PM	Kutner, J	CO	408
H & PM	Levy, M	PA	406
H & PM	Pantilat, S	CA	408
H & PM	Portenoy, R	NY	407
H & PM	Quill, T	NY	407
H & PM	Ritchie, C	CA	409
H & PM	Santa-Emma, P	OH	408
H & PM	Selvaggi, K	MA	406
H & PM	Tucker, R	AL	407
H & PM	Tulsky, J	NC	407
H & PM	Von Gunten, C	OH	408
H & PM	Weinstein, S	UT	408

Hospital Acquired Infections

Spec	Name	St	Pg
Inf	Ballon-Landa, G	CA	420
Inf	Edmond, M	VA	416
Inf	Hammer, G	NY	413
Inf	Louie, E	NY	414
Inf	Sepkowitz, K	NY	415
PInf	Baltimore, R	CT	792

HPV-Human Papilloma Virus

Spec	Name	St	Pg
GO	Alexander, M	MD	276
GO	Lucci, J	FL	282
GO	Soisson, A	UT	287
Onc	Berry, J	CA	385
PInf	Alexander, K	IL	795

Human Granulocytic Anaplasmosis

Spec	Name	St	Pg
Inf	Bakken, J	MN	417

Huntington's Disease

Spec	Name	St	Pg
ChiN	Dure, L	AL	147
N	Ashizawa, T	FL	523
N	Baser, S	PA	513
N	Corey-Bloom, J	CA	539
N	Kieburtz, K	NY	516
N	Longo, F	CA	541
N	Louis, E	NY	518
N	Marder, K	NY	519
N	Perlmutter, J	MO	532
Path	Gambetti, P	OH	728

Hydrocephalus

Spec	Name	St	Pg
NS	Bierbrauer, K	OH	489
NS	Bierbrauer, K	OH	489
NS	Dias, M	PA	476
NS	Feldstein, N	NY	476
NS	Frim, D	IL	490
NS	Ojemann, J	WA	501
NS	Ruge, J	IL	492
NS	Sandberg, D	TX	497
NS	Sklar, F	TX	497
NS	Sutton, L	PA	482
NS	Tomita, T	IL	493
NS	Walker, M	UT	495
Ped	Walker, W	WA	743

Hydrocephalus-Adult

Spec	Name	St	Pg
NS	Goodman, R	NY	477
NS	Rigamonti, D	MD	481

Hydronephrosis

Spec	Name	St	Pg
Ped Uro	Elder, J	MI	827
Ped Uro	Kass, E	MI	827
Ped Uro	Rushton, H	DC	825

Hydronephrosis-Prenatal

Spec	Name	St	Pg
Ped Uro	Cain, M	IN	826
Ped Uro	Kaefer, M	IN	827
Ped Uro	Rink, R	IN	828

Hyperbaric Medicine

Spec	Name	St	Pg
S	Yurt, R	NY	1102
VascS	Iafrati, M	MA	1220

Hyperhidrosis

Spec	Name	St	Pg
VascS	Ahn, S	CA	1230

Hyperhidrosis-Palmar

Spec	Name	St	Pg
T&CS	Keller, S	NY	1155
T&CS	Nugent, W	NH	1148
T&CS	Vigneswaran, W	IL	1172

Hyperhydrosis-Palmar

Spec	Name	St	Pg
T&CS	Cohen, N	MD	1151

Specialty & Special Expertise Index

Spec	Name	St	Pg

Hyperinsulinism

Spec	Name	St	Pg
PEn	Lustig, R	CA	762

Hypertension

Spec	Name	St	Pg
Cv	Blanchard, D	CA	110
Cv	Blumenthal, R	MD	91
Cv	Inra, L	NY	94
Cv	Judelson, D	CA	111
Cv	Kostis, J	NJ	94
Cv	Oparil, S	AL	99
Cv	Pepine, C	FL	99
Cv	Sorrentino, M	IL	105
Cv	Thompson, P	CT	90
Cv	Zusman, R	MA	90
EDM	Sowers, J	MO	221
Ge	Zaman, A	OR	258
Ger	Lipsitz, L	MA	264
Ger	Supiano, M	UT	267
IM	Cushman, W	TN	426
IM	Fischbein, L	MO	427
IM	Mehler, P	CO	427
IM	Wright, J	OH	427
Nep	Ahmad, S	WA	466
Nep	August, P	NY	459
Nep	Bakris, G	IL	462
Nep	Bazari, H	MA	458
Nep	Berns, J	PA	459
Nep	Blumenfeld, J	NY	459
Nep	Coffman, T	NC	461
Nep	Fadem, S	TX	465
Nep	Fulop, T	MS	461
Nep	Gluck, S	CA	466
Nep	Johnston, J	PA	459
Nep	Josephson, M	IL	463
Nep	King, A	CA	467
Nep	Kobrin, S	PA	460
Nep	Nolan, C	TX	466
Nep	Olivero, J	TX	466
Nep	Perrone, R	MA	458
Nep	Piraino, B	PA	460
Nep	Pohl, M	OH	464
Nep	Rudnick, M	PA	460
Nep	Schwartz, G	MN	464
Nep	Textor, S	MN	464
Nep	Tolkoff-Rubin, N	MA	458
Nep	Weiner, I	FL	462
Nep	Williams, G	NY	460
Nep	Yee, J	MI	465
PNep	Benfield, M	AL	798
PNep	Ellis, D	PA	797
PNep	Flynn, J	WA	800
PNep	Jabs, K	TN	799
PNep	Mendley, S	MD	798
PNep	Neiberger, R	FL	799

Hypertension in Children

Spec	Name	St	Pg
PNep	Ettenger, R	CA	800
PNep	Fouser, L	WA	801

Hypertension in Obesity

Spec	Name	St	Pg
PCd	Rocchini, A	MI	753

Hypertension in Pregnancy

Spec	Name	St	Pg
MF	Genc, M	NY	434
MF	Hankins, G	TX	441
MF	Repke, J	PA	435
MF	Saade, G	TX	441
MF	Samuels, P	OH	439
Nep	August, P	NY	459

Hypertension-Complex

Spec	Name	St	Pg
Cv	Saunders, E	MD	95
Nep	Lea, J	GA	462
Nep	Townsend, R	PA	460

Hypertension-Drug Resistent

Spec	Name	St	Pg
Nep	Wilcox, C	DC	460

Hypertension-Renovascular

Spec	Name	St	Pg
Nep	Wilcox, C	DC	460
VIR	Murphy, T	RI	1027

Hypertension/Kidney Disease

Spec	Name	St	Pg
Nep	Kelepouris, E	PA	460
Nep	Toto, R	TX	466

Hyperthermia Treatment of Cancer

Spec	Name	St	Pg
RadRO	Prosnitz, L	NC	986

Hypertrophic Cardiomyopathy

Spec	Name	St	Pg
PCd	Ackerman, M	MN	752
T&CS	Swistel, D	NY	1159

Hypnosis

Spec	Name	St	Pg
Psyc	Spiegel, D	CA	935

Hypoglycemia

Spec	Name	St	Pg
EDM	Clore, J	VA	216
EDM	Comi, R	NH	208
EDM	Cryer, P	MO	219
EDM	Schutta, M	PA	214
PEn	Sperling, M	PA	759

Hypogonadism

Spec	Name	St	Pg
EDM	Cunningham, G	TX	222
U	Shabsigh, R	NY	1195

Hypogonadism-Male

Spec	Name	St	Pg
EDM	Dobs, A	MD	212

Hypoplastic Left Heart Syndrome

Spec	Name	St	Pg
PS	Bove, E	MI	819
T&CS	Huddleston, C	MO	1168

Hypospadias

Spec	Name	St	Pg
Ped Uro	Atala, A	NC	825
Ped Uro	Baskin, L	CA	828
Ped Uro	Bloom, D	MI	826
Ped Uro	Caldamone, A	RI	824
Ped Uro	Canning, D	PA	824
Ped Uro	Cartwright, P	UT	828
Ped Uro	Cheng, E	IL	826
Ped Uro	Elder, J	MI	827
Ped Uro	Ewalt, D	TX	828
Ped Uro	Kass, E	MI	827
Ped Uro	Kolon, T	PA	825
Ped Uro	Maizels, M	IL	827
Ped Uro	Pope, J	TN	826
Ped Uro	Rushton, H	DC	825
Ped Uro	Strand, W	TX	828
Ped Uro	Sutherland, R	NC	826
U	Hensle, T	NJ	1191

Hypotension

Spec	Name	St	Pg
Ger	Lipsitz, L	MA	264

Hypothalamic Dysfunction

Spec	Name	St	Pg
EDM	Lechan, R	MA	210

Hysterectomy Alternatives

Spec	Name	St	Pg
GO	Magrina, J	AZ	289

Hysteroscopic Surgery

Spec	Name	St	Pg
ObG	Bradley, L	OH	564
ObG	Jenkins, T	AL	563
ObG	Parker, W	CA	567
RE	Copperman, A	NY	1041
RE	Dumesic, D	CA	1051
RE	Falcone, T	OH	1047
RE	Grifo, J	NY	1042
RE	Grunfeld, L	NY	1042
RE	Hickok, L	WA	1052
RE	Hornstein, M	MA	1040
RE	Huang, J	TX	1050
RE	Scoccia, H	IL	1048
RE	Stewart, E	MN	1049
RE	Yee, B	CA	1053

I

Iliac Vein Obstruction

Spec	Name	St	Pg
VIR	Khilnani, N	NY	1028

Immune Deficiencies-Primary

Spec	Name	St	Pg
Inf	Segal, B	NY	415
Ped	Infante, A	TX	742

Immune Deficiency

Spec	Name	St	Pg
A&I	Ein, D	DC	81
A&I	Lockey, R	FL	82
A&I	Tamaroff, M	CA	86
A&I	Umetsu, D	MA	80
A&I	Wong, J	MA	80
Inf	Van Der Horst, C	NC	417
PA&I	Bahna, S	LA	746
PA&I	Fanous, Y	CA	747
PA&I	Gelfand, E	CO	745
PA&I	Lemanske, R	WI	745
PA&I	Shearer, W	TX	746
PA&I	Sullivan, K	PA	744
PA&I	Wolf, R	IL	745
PHO	Kapoor, N	CA	790
PRhu	Haines, K	NJ	811

Immune Deficiency-Skin Disorders

Spec	Name	St	Pg
D	Edelson, R	CT	184
D	Jorizzo, J	NC	193
D	Mutasim, D	OH	196
D	Paller, A	IL	196
D	Rook, A	PA	190
D	Sontheimer, R	UT	198

Immunodeficiency Disorders

Spec	Name	St	Pg
A&I	Cunningham-Rundles, C	NY	81
A&I	DeShazo, R	MS	82
A&I	Gruchalla, R	TX	85
A&I	Markert, M	NC	83
A&I	Montanaro, A	OR	86
A&I	Phillips, S	PA	81
A&I	Routes, J	WI	84
PA&I	Church, J	CA	746
PA&I	Cowan, M	CA	746
PA&I	Orange, J	TX	746
PA&I	Wasserman, R	TX	746
Rhu	Lahita, R	NJ	1060

Immunopathology

Spec	Name	St	Pg
Path	Bhan, A	MA	718
Path	Tomaszewski, J	NY	724
Path	Weiss, L	CA	735

Immunotherapy

Spec	Name	St	Pg
A&I	Cunningham-Rundles, C	NY	81
A&I	Sundy, J	NC	83
DR	Bahn, D	CA	1017
GO	Giuntoli, R	MD	278
GO	Odunsi, A	NY	279
GO	Santin, A	CT	275
Hem	Maziarz, R	OR	329
Hem	Porcu, P	OH	323
IM	Fischl, M	FL	426
Nep	Ward, D	CA	467
Onc	Albertini, M	WI	366
Onc	Atkins, M	DC	337
Onc	Ball, E	CA	385
Onc	Chapman, P	NY	339
Onc	Emens, L	MD	342
Onc	Figlin, R	CA	387
Onc	Hwu, P	TX	380
Onc	Kirkwood, J	PA	346
Onc	Kwak, L	TX	381
Onc	Maloney, D	WA	389
Onc	Mitsuyasu, R	CA	390
Onc	Peace, D	IL	372
Onc	Pecora, A	NJ	349
Onc	Pfister, D	NY	350
Onc	Scheinberg, D	NY	351
Onc	Scher, H	NY	351
Onc	Sosman, J	TN	364
Onc	Sznol, M	CT	335
Onc	von Mehren, M	PA	353
Onc	Weiner, G	IA	375
Onc	Weiner, L	DC	354
Onc	Wolchok, J	NY	354
PA&I	Kamani, N	DC	743
PHO	Chen, A	MD	772
PHO	Cooper, L	TX	788
PHO	Horn, B	CA	790
PHO	Kobrinsky, N	ND	787
PHO	Kushner, B	NY	775
PHO	Sondel, P	WI	785
S	Czerniecki, B	PA	1092
S	Eberlein, T	MO	1113
S	Kaufman, H	IL	1115
S	Kim, J	OH	1116
S	Slingluff, C	VA	1109
S	White, R	NC	1110
S	Yang, J	MD	1102
U	O'Donnell, M	IA	1205

Imperforate Anus

Spec	Name	St	Pg
PS	Pena, A	OH	820

Impulse-Control Disorders

Spec	Name	St	Pg
Psyc	Burt, V	CA	932
Psyc	Grant, J	IL	929

Inborn Errors of Metabolism

Spec	Name	St	Pg
CG	Burton, B	IL	160
CG	Hainline, B	IN	160
CG	Seashore, M	CT	156
CG	Ward, J	TN	159
CG	Wilcox, W	CA	164

Incontinence

Spec	Name	St	Pg
Ger	Resnick, N	PA	265
GO	Lentz, S	NC	282
ObG	Brodman, M	NY	560
ObG	De Lancey, J	MI	564
ObG	Hullfish, K	VA	562
ObG	Maynard, S	DC	561
ObG	Sand, P	IL	565
ObG	Valaitis, S	IL	565
Ped Uro	Kaefer, M	IN	827
U	Badlani, G	NC	1196
U	Boone, T	TX	1208
U	Foster, H	CT	1186
U	Ginsberg, D	CA	1211
U	Griebling, T	KS	1207
U	Kaplan, S	NY	1191
U	Kennelly, M	NC	1198
U	Klutke, C	MO	1203
U	Lloyd, L	AL	1198
U	Lockhart, J	FL	1198
U	Montague, D	OH	1204
U	Shabsigh, R	NY	1195
U	Shenot, P	PA	1195
U	Steers, W	VA	1201
U	Vapnek, J	NY	1196
U	Woo, H	LA	1210

Incontinence after Prostate Cancer

Spec	Name	St	Pg
U	Blaivas, J	NY	1189
U	Fraser, L	MS	1197
U	Kane, M	MD	1191
U	Kaplan, S	NY	1191
U	Lugg, J	WY	1207
U	Schaeffer, A	IL	1205

Incontinence-Fecal

Spec	Name	St	Pg
CRS	Abcarian, H	IL	173
CRS	Bailey, H	TX	176
CRS	Church, J	OH	173
CRS	Efron, J	MD	169
CRS	Gearhart, S	MD	170
CRS	Haas, E	TX	176
CRS	Ludwig, K	WI	174
CRS	Mantyh, C	NC	172
CRS	Nogueras, J	FL	172
CRS	Sands, L	FL	172
CRS	Schoetz, D	MA	169
CRS	Sokol, T	CA	178
CRS	Thorson, A	NE	176
CRS	Wexner, S	FL	172
Ge	Rao, S	GA	244
Ge	Wald, A	WI	251
GO	Lentz, S	NC	282
S	Baker, C	VA	1103

Incontinence-Female

Spec	Name	St	Pg
ObG	Einarsson, J	MA	560
ObG	Karram, M	OH	565
ObG	Lucente, V	PA	561
ObG	Walters, M	OH	566
U	Chancellor, M	MI	1203
U	Loughlin, K	MA	1187

Specialty & Special Expertise Index

Incontinence-Male & Female

Spec	Name	St	Pg
U	Bales, G	IL	1202
U	Nitti, V	NY	1193

Incontinence/Pelvic Floor Disorders

Spec	Name	St	Pg
CRS	Madoff, R	MN	174
CRS	Mutch, M	MO	174
CRS	Ramamoorthy, S	CA	178

Infant-Toddler Psychiatry

Spec	Name	St	Pg
ChAP	Zeanah, C	LA	943

Infantile Spasms-West Syndrome

Spec	Name	St	Pg
ChiN	Shinnar, S	NY	147

Infection Control

Spec	Name	St	Pg
Inf	Galgiani, J	AZ	420
Inf	Wallach, F	NY	415

Infections in Cancer Patients

Spec	Name	St	Pg
Inf	Freifeld, A	NE	419
Inf	Polsky, B	NY	414
Inf	Segal, B	NY	415
Inf	Sepkowitz, K	NY	415
PHO	Siegel, S	CA	792
PHO	Wiley, J	MD	777

Infections in Immunocompromised Patients

Spec	Name	St	Pg
Inf	Cunha, B	NY	413
Inf	Pursell, K	IL	418
PInf	Alexander, K	IL	795
PInf	Flynn, P	TN	794
PInf	McComsey, G	OH	795
PInf	McKinney, R	NC	794
PInf	Michaels, M	PA	793

Infections in Int'l Adopted Children

Spec	Name	St	Pg
PInf	Krilov, L	NY	793

Infections in Pregnancy

Spec	Name	St	Pg
MF	Duff, W	FL	436
MF	Ismail, M	IL	438
MF	Parry, S	PA	435

Infections in Prosthetic Devices

Spec	Name	St	Pg
Inf	Brause, B	NY	412
Inf	Slama, T	IN	418
OrS	Moucha, C	NY	629

Infections-CNS

Spec	Name	St	Pg
N	Gilden, D	CO	535
N	Simpson, D	NY	521

Infections-Congenital

Spec	Name	St	Pg
ChiN	Bale, J	UT	150

Infections-Emerging

Spec	Name	St	Pg
Path	Walker, D	TX	731

Infections-Neonatal

Spec	Name	St	Pg
MF	Ismail, M	IL	438
NP	Davis, J	MA	448
NP	Simmons, C	CA	454

Infections-Neurologic

Spec	Name	St	Pg
ChiN	Bale, J	UT	150
N	Coyle, P	NY	514
N	McArthur, J	MD	519
N	Roos, K	IN	533
NS	Rosenblum, M	MI	492

Infections-Respiratory

Spec	Name	St	Pg
PInf	Bradley, J	CA	797
PInf	Krilov, L	NY	793
PInf	Meissner, H	MA	792
PInf	Wald, E	WI	796
Pul	Jacoby, D	OR	971
Pul	Niederman, M	NY	958

Infections-Surgical

Spec	Name	St	Pg
Inf	Gumprecht, J	NY	413
Inf	Hammer, G	NY	413
Inf	Hartman, B	NY	413
Inf	Kumar, P	DC	413
Inf	O'Keefe, J	IL	418
T&CS	Mitchell, J	CO	1173

Infections-Transplant

Spec	Name	St	Pg
Inf	Alvarez-Elcoro, S	FL	415
Inf	Gorensek, M	FL	416
Inf	Kumar, P	DC	413
Inf	Pursell, K	IL	418
PInf	Green, M	PA	793

Infectious & Demyelinating Diseases

Spec	Name	St	Pg
N	Berger, J	KY	523
N	Cook, S	NJ	514

Infectious Diarrhea

Spec	Name	St	Pg
Ge	Surawicz, C	WA	257

Infectious Disease

Spec	Name	St	Pg
D	Friedlander, S	CA	200
IM	Fischl, M	FL	426
Inf	Alvarez-Elcoro, S	FL	415
Inf	Auwaerter, P	MD	412
Inf	Bakken, J	MN	417
Inf	Ballon-Landa, G	CA	420
Inf	Bartlett, J	MD	412
Inf	Bayer, A	CA	420
Inf	Berkowitz, L	NY	412
Inf	Brause, B	NY	412
Inf	Campbell, J	MO	417
Inf	Cancio, M	FL	415
Inf	Cohn, S	IL	417
Inf	Corey, G	NC	416
Inf	Cunha, B	NY	413
Inf	Daar, E	CA	420
Inf	DuPont, H	TX	419
Inf	Edmond, M	VA	416
Inf	Fichtenbaum, C	OH	417
Inf	Flaherty, J	IL	417
Inf	Flanigan, T	RI	412
Inf	Frank, I	PA	413
Inf	Freifeld, A	NE	419
Inf	Galgiani, J	AZ	420
Inf	Gorensek, M	FL	416
Inf	Gumprecht, J	NY	413
Inf	Hammer, G	NY	413
Inf	Hammer, S	NY	413
Inf	Hartman, B	NY	413
Inf	Huitt, G	CO	419
Inf	Johnson, S	CO	419
Inf	Katner, H	GA	416
Inf	Keiser, P	TX	420
Inf	Kumar, P	DC	413
Inf	Longworth, D	OH	417
Inf	Lorber, B	PA	413
Inf	Louie, E	NY	414
Inf	Luby, J	TX	420
Inf	Maki, D	WI	418
Inf	McGowan, J	NY	414
Inf	Mildvan, D	NY	414
Inf	Nahass, R	NJ	414
Inf	Novak, R	IL	418
Inf	O'Keefe, J	IL	418
Inf	Palefsky, J	CA	420
Inf	Pearson, R	VA	416
Inf	Perlman, D	NY	414
Inf	Polsky, B	NY	414
Inf	Pursell, K	IL	418
Inf	Quagliarello, V	CT	412
Inf	Rao, N	PA	414
Inf	Ratzan, K	FL	416
Inf	Richman, D	CA	421
Inf	Romagnoli, M	NY	414
Inf	Saag, M	AL	416
Inf	Salata, R	OH	418
Inf	Sax, P	MA	412
Inf	Scheld, W	VA	416
Inf	Schmitt, S	OH	418
Inf	Schooley, R	CA	421
Inf	Segal, B	NY	415
Inf	Sepkowitz, K	NY	415

Spec	Name	St	Pg
Inf	Sha, B	IL	418
Inf	Slama, T	IN	418
Inf	Sobel, J	MI	419
Inf	Squires, K	PA	415
Inf	Tomford, J	OH	419
Inf	Trenholme, G	IL	419
Inf	Van Der Horst, C	NC	417
Inf	Wallace, M	FL	417
Inf	Wallace, R	TX	420
Inf	Wallach, F	NY	415
Inf	Wiviott, L	CA	421
Inf	Wormser, G	NY	415
Inf	Yancovitz, S	NY	415
MF	Andrews, W	AL	436
MF	Landers, D	MN	439
PInf	Kotloff, K	MD	793

Infectious Disease during Chemotherapy

Inf	Freifeld, A	NE	419

Infectious Disease in Pregnancy

MF	Gibbs, R	CO	440
MF	Gonik, B	MI	438
MF	Riley, L	MA	433

Infectious Disease-Lung

Pul	Campbell, G	MS	961
Pul	Hopewell, P	CA	970

Infectious Disease-Perinatal

MF	Gravett, M	WA	442
PInf	Michaels, M	PA	793

Infectious Diseases-Gynecologic

ObG	Wiesenfeld, H	PA	562

Infectious Mononucleosis

PInf	Andiman, W	CT	792

Infective Endocarditis

Inf	Bayer, A	CA	420

Infertility

EDM	Goodman, N	FL	216
ObG	Berga, S	NC	562
ObG	Simon, J	DC	562
ObG	Young, B	NY	562
RE	Adamson, G	CA	1051
RE	Cohen, D	IL	1047
RE	De Cherney, A	MD	1042
RE	Dodds, W	MI	1047
RE	Isaacson, K	MA	1040
RE	Kutteh, W	TN	1046
RE	Licciardi, F	NY	1043
RE	Luciano, A	CT	1041
RE	Milad, M	IL	1048
RE	Noyes, N	NY	1043
RE	Odem, R	MO	1048
RE	Sanfilippo, J	PA	1044
RE	Schenken, R	TX	1050
RE	Schlaff, W	PA	1044
RE	Thomas, M	OH	1049
RE	Toth, T	MA	1041
RE	Weiss, G	NJ	1044
RE	Wilson, E	TX	1050
RE	Zinaman, M	MA	1041

Infertility-Advanced Maternal Age

RE	Keefe, D	NY	1042
RE	Paulson, R	CA	1052
RE	Seifer, D	NY	1044

Infertility-Female

RE	Azziz, R	GA	1045
RE	Blackwell, R	AL	1045
RE	Carr, B	TX	1049
RE	Dumesic, D	CA	1051
RE	Haney, A	IL	1047
RE	Hill, J	NH	1040
RE	Marrs, R	CA	1052
RE	Pfeifer, S	PA	1043
RE	Sondheimer, S	PA	1044

Infertility-IVF

RE	Agarwal, S	CA	1051
RE	Baker, V	CA	1051
RE	Barnes, R	IL	1046
RE	Bateman, B	VA	1045
RE	Buster, J	MA	1040
RE	Cedars, M	CA	1051
RE	Chenette, P	CA	1051
RE	Clisham, P	LA	1050
RE	Coddington, C	MN	1047
RE	Copperman, A	NY	1041
RE	DeVane, G	FL	1045
RE	Dickey, R	LA	1050
RE	Durso, N	VA	1045
RE	Falcone, T	OH	1047
RE	Friedman, C	OH	1047
RE	Fritz, M	NC	1046
RE	Ginsburg, E	MA	1040
RE	Giudice, L	CA	1052
RE	Goldberg, J	OH	1047
RE	Grazi, R	NY	1042
RE	Grunfeld, L	NY	1042
RE	Hickok, L	WA	1052
RE	Hill, J	NH	1040
RE	Hornstein, M	MA	1040
RE	Huang, J	TX	1050
RE	Jacobs, L	IL	1048
RE	Johnson, J	MA	1040
RE	Kazer, R	IL	1048
RE	Keefe, D	NY	1042
RE	Keltz, M	NY	1042
RE	Kuo, J	CA	1052
RE	Legro, R	PA	1043
RE	Licciardi, F	NY	1043
RE	Marshall, L	WA	1052
RE	Marut, E	IL	1048
RE	McClamrock, H	MD	1043
RE	McGovern, P	NJ	1043
RE	Moffitt, D	AZ	1050
RE	Molo, M	IL	1048
RE	Mukherjee, T	NY	1043
RE	Noyes, N	NY	1043
RE	Ory, S	FL	1046
RE	Oskowitz, S	MA	1041
RE	Patrizio, P	CT	1041
RE	Paulson, R	CA	1052
RE	Petrozza, J	MA	1041
RE	Putman, J	TX	1050
RE	Ratts, V	MO	1048
RE	Rosenwaks, Z	NY	1044
RE	Sauer, M	NY	1044
RE	Schriock, E	CA	1052
RE	Scoccia, H	IL	1048
RE	Seifer, D	NY	1044
RE	Session, D	GA	1046
RE	Smikle, C	CA	1052
RE	Smith, Y	MI	1049
RE	Sondheimer, S	PA	1044
RE	Soules, M	WA	1053
RE	Steinkampf, M	AL	1046
RE	Stewart, E	MN	1049
RE	Surrey, E	CO	1049
RE	Thomas, M	OH	1049
RE	Toth, T	MA	1041
RE	Van Voorhis, B	IA	1049
RE	Walmer, D	NC	1046
RE	Widra, E	DC	1045
RE	Winer, S	CA	1053
RE	Yee, B	CA	1053
RE	Zacur, H	MD	1045
U	Silber, S	MO	1206

Infertility-Male

U	Bar-Chama, N	NY	1188
U	Buch, J	TX	1208
U	Donovan, J	OH	1203
U	Fisch, H	NY	1190
U	Goldstein, M	NY	1190
U	Hellstrom, W	LA	1209
U	Kim, E	TN	1198
U	Levine, L	IL	1204
U	Lipshultz, L	TX	1209
U	McClure, R	WA	1212
U	McCullough, A	NY	1192
U	Meacham, R	CO	1207
U	Mulhall, J	NY	1193
U	Nagler, H	NY	1193
U	Oates, R	MA	1187
U	Ohl, D	MI	1205
U	Rajfer, J	CA	1213
U	Ross, L	IL	1205
U	Sabanegh, E	OH	1205
U	Sadeghi-Nejad, H	NJ	1194

Specialty & Special Expertise Index

Spec	Name	St	Pg
U	Sandlow, J	WI	1205
U	Schlegel, P	NY	1194
U	Seftel, A	NJ	1194
U	Shaban, S	NC	1200
U	Sharlip, I	CA	1213
U	Sigman, M	RI	1188
U	Silber, S	MO	1206
U	Turek, P	CA	1214
U	Van Arsdalen, K	PA	1196

Infertility-Male in Spinal Cord Injury

Spec	Name	St	Pg
U	Linsenmeyer, T	NJ	1192

Infertility/Genetics

Spec	Name	St	Pg
ObG	Simpson, J	NY	562

Inflammation in Critical Illness

Spec	Name	St	Pg
PCCM	Zimmerman, J	WA	756

Inflammatory Arthritis

Spec	Name	St	Pg
Rhu	Peng, S	WA	1068

Inflammatory Arthritis-Consult

Spec	Name	St	Pg
Rhu	Chang-Miller, A	AZ	1066

Inflammatory Bowel Disease

Spec	Name	St	Pg
CRS	Abcarian, H	IL	173
CRS	Bailey, H	TX	176
CRS	Beck, D	LA	176
CRS	Coutsoftides, T	CA	177
CRS	Efron, J	MD	169
CRS	Eisenstat, T	NJ	169
CRS	Fleshman, J	TX	176
CRS	Goldstein, S	PA	170
CRS	Harnsberger, J	NH	168
CRS	Hartmann, R	FL	172
CRS	Heppell, J	AZ	177
CRS	Huber, P	TX	177
CRS	Hyman, N	VT	168
CRS	Lavery, I	OH	173
CRS	Longo, W	CT	168
CRS	Lowry, A	MN	174
CRS	Madoff, R	MN	174
CRS	Marks, J	PA	170
CRS	Mutch, M	MO	174
CRS	Pello, M	NJ	170
CRS	Ramamoorthy, S	CA	178
CRS	Read, T	MA	168
CRS	Remzi, F	OH	175
CRS	Roberts, P	MA	169
CRS	Saclarides, T	IL	175
CRS	Shah, N	RI	169
CRS	Stamos, M	CA	178
CRS	Stein, D	PA	171
CRS	Stryker, S	IL	175
CRS	Varma, M	CA	178
CRS	Vernava, A	FL	172
CRS	Wise, P	MO	175
CRS	Wolff, B	MN	175
Ge	Abreu, M	FL	241
Ge	Albert, M	DC	232
Ge	Brandt, L	NY	233
Ge	DeCross, A	NY	233
Ge	Farraye, F	MA	230
Ge	Gluck, M	WA	256
Ge	Hanauer, S	IL	248
Ge	Isaacs, K	NC	243
Ge	Itzkowitz, S	NY	236
Ge	Kimmey, M	WA	256
Ge	Kozarek, R	WA	256
Ge	La Mont, J	MA	231
Ge	Lashner, B	OH	249
Ge	Leighton, J	AZ	254
Ge	Lichtenstein, G	PA	237
Ge	Loftus, E	MN	249
Ge	Mason, J	MA	231
Ge	Mertz, H	TN	243
Ge	Pezzone, M	PA	239
Ge	Plevy, S	NC	244
Ge	Proctor, D	CT	232
Ge	Reichelderfer, M	WI	250
Ge	Rex, D	IN	250
Ge	Sandborn, W	CA	257
Ge	Sartor, R	NC	244
Ge	Scherl, E	NY	240
Ge	Siegel, C	NH	232
Ge	Targan, S	CA	258
Ge	Weinstock, J	MA	232
Ge	Young, R	NE	252
PGe	Baldassano, R	PA	763
PGe	Baldridge, A	NJ	763
PGe	Bishop, W	IA	765
PGe	Christie, D	WA	768
PGe	Cohen, M	OH	765
PGe	Dubinsky, M	CA	768
PGe	Gunasekaran, T	IL	766
PGe	Hill, I	OH	766
PGe	Hoffenberg, E	CO	767
PGe	Piccoli, D	PA	764
PGe	Rhoads, J	TX	768
PGe	Rothbaum, R	MO	767
PGe	Schwarz, S	NY	764
PGe	Thomas, D	CA	769
PGe	Ulshen, M	NC	765
PS	Doody, D	MA	814
PS	Notrica, D	AZ	822
PS	Schwartz, M	PA	817
PS	Shamberger, R	MA	814
S	Becker, J	MA	1084
S	Hodin, R	MA	1086
S	Koruda, M	NC	1106

Inflammatory Bowel Disease/Crohn's

Spec	Name	St	Pg
CRS	Birnbaum, E	MO	173
CRS	Delaney, C	OH	173
CRS	Galandiuk, S	KY	171
CRS	Gearhart, S	MD	170
CRS	Haas, E	TX	176
CRS	Medich, D	PA	170
CRS	Milsom, J	NY	170
CRS	Nogueras, J	FL	172
CRS	Pemberton, J	MN	174
CRS	Procaccino, J	NY	171
CRS	Schoetz, D	MA	169
CRS	Senagore, A	MI	175
CRS	Wexner, S	FL	172
Ge	Cominelli, F	OH	246
Ge	Elliott, D	IA	247
Ge	Fisher, R	CT	230
Ge	Konicek, F	IL	248
Ge	Lebwohl, O	NY	237
Ge	Lipshutz, W	PA	238
Ge	Roth, B	CA	257
Ge	Tremaine, W	MN	251
PGe	Benkov, K	NY	763
PGe	Berman, J	IL	765
PGe	Heyman, M	CA	769
PGe	Kirschner, B	IL	766
PGe	Levy, J	NY	763
PGe	Oliva-Hemker, M	MD	763
PGe	Wyllie, R	OH	767
PS	Dolgin, S	NY	815
S	Hurst, R	IL	1115

Inflammatory Cytokines

Spec	Name	St	Pg
PHO	Ferrara, J	MI	783

Inflammatory Pulmonary Diseases

Spec	Name	St	Pg
Pul	Wenzel, S	PA	960

Inherited Disorders

Spec	Name	St	Pg
CG	Holmes, L	MA	156
CG	Korf, B	AL	159
CG	Morris, C	NV	163
CG	Pyeritz, R	PA	158
CG	Weaver, D	IN	160
Hem	Rao, A	PA	316

Inherited Metabolic Disorders

Spec	Name	St	Pg
CG	Andersson, H	LA	161
CG	Desnick, R	NY	157
CG	Jonas, A	CA	163
CG	Seashore, M	CT	156
Nep	Hruska, K	MO	463

Insect Allergies

Spec	Name	St	Pg
A&I	Freeman, T	TX	85
A&I	Pacin, M	FL	83
A&I	Shepherd, G	NY	81

Intensity Modulated Radiotherapy (IMRT)

Spec	Name	St	Pg
RadRO	Chao, K	NY	978

Spec	Name	St	Pg
RadRO	Cooper, J	NY	978
RadRO	Gejerman, G	NJ	979
RadRO	Horwitz, E	PA	980
RadRO	Lee, W	NC	985
RadRO	Mundt, A	CA	996
RadRO	Potters, L	NY	982
RadRO	Quivey, J	CA	997
RadRO	Rose, C	CA	997
RadRO	Russell, A	MA	977
RadRO	St Clair, W	KY	987
RadRO	Wong, J	CA	998

Internal Medicine

Spec	Name	St	Pg
IM	Bissell, D	CA	427
IM	Braunstein, S	NC	426
IM	Burt, R	IL	427
IM	Cirigliano, M	PA	426
IM	Cushman, W	TN	426
IM	Fischbein, L	MO	427
IM	Fischl, M	FL	426
IM	Galland, L	NY	426
IM	Mehler, P	CO	427
IM	Rabow, M	CA	427
IM	Rader, D	PA	426
IM	Selwyn, P	NY	426
IM	Wright, J	OH	427

International Health

Spec	Name	St	Pg
GO	Granai, C	RI	275
Inf	Keiser, P	TX	420
PMR	Haig, A	MI	868
PrM	Cahill, J	NY	912

Interstitial Cystitis

Spec	Name	St	Pg
U	Culkin, D	OK	1208
U	Lloyd, L	AL	1198
U	O'Leary, M	MA	1187
U	Schaeffer, A	IL	1205

Interstitial Lung Disease

Spec	Name	St	Pg
Path	Katzenstein, A	NY	722
PPul	Fan, L	CO	810
PPul	Redding, G	WA	811
Pul	Arcasoy, S	NY	956
Pul	Berk, J	MA	954
Pul	Brown, K	CO	967
Pul	Doherty, D	KY	961
Pul	Enelow, R	NH	954
Pul	Fahey, P	IL	964
Pul	Hansen-Flaschen, J	PA	957
Pul	King, T	CA	971
Pul	Kotloff, R	PA	957
Pul	Libby, D	NY	957
Pul	Loyd, J	TN	963
Pul	Lynch, J	CA	971
Pul	Mosenifar, Z	CA	971
Pul	Popovich, J	MI	966
Pul	Raghu, G	WA	971
Pul	Rossman, M	PA	959
Pul	Sahn, S	SC	963
Pul	Staton, G	GA	963
Pul	Stover-Pepe, D	NY	960
Pul	Thomashow, B	NY	960
Pul	Tino, G	PA	960
Pul	Weissler, J	TX	969

Interventional Bronchoscopy

Spec	Name	St	Pg
T&CS	Pechet, T	PA	1157

Interventional Cardiology

Spec	Name	St	Pg
Cv	Bass, T	FL	97
Cv	Cabin, H	CT	88
Cv	Cooper, C	OH	101
Cv	Corrigan, V	GA	98
Cv	Edelen, J	CA	110
Cv	Freeman, G	TX	108
Cv	French, W	CA	111
Cv	Greenberg, M	NY	93
Cv	Harrison, J	NC	98
Cv	Kereiakes, D	OH	103
Cv	Klein, L	IL	103
Cv	O'Neill, W	MI	104
Cv	Pichard, A	DC	95
Cv	Powers, E	SC	99
Cv	Ramee, S	LA	109
Cv	Rihal, C	MN	104
Cv	Safian, R	MI	104
Cv	Sanborn, T	IL	105
Cv	Shlofmitz, R	NY	96
Cv	Simon, D	OH	105
Cv	Tobis, J	CA	112
Cv	Vetrovec, G	VA	100
Cv	Vignola, P	NC	100
Cv	von der Lohe, E	IN	106
IC	Applegate, R	NC	124
IC	Bach, R	MO	125
IC	Bailey, S	TX	127
IC	Bittl, J	FL	124
IC	Carroll, J	CO	127
IC	Chang, G	PA	121
IC	Cohen, H	PA	121
IC	Dieter, R	IL	125
IC	Douglas, J	GA	124
IC	Ellis, S	OH	126
IC	Feldman, M	TX	127
IC	Feldman, T	IL	126
IC	Fromkin, K	FL	124
IC	Gibson, C	MA	120
IC	Gray, W	NY	122
IC	Greene, R	CA	128
IC	Henry, T	MN	126
IC	Herrmann, H	PA	122
IC	Holmes, D	MN	126
IC	Jacobs, A	MA	120
IC	Kandzari, D	GA	124
IC	Khawaja, S	GA	124
IC	Kimmelstiel, C	MA	121
IC	Kleiman, N	TX	127
IC	Laham, R	MA	121
IC	Lasala, J	MO	126
IC	Lee, J	PA	122
IC	Leesar, M	AL	125
IC	Leon, M	NY	122
IC	Leya, F	IL	126
IC	Lopez, J	IL	126
IC	Mahmud, E	CA	128
IC	Matar, F	FL	125
IC	Mehran, R	NY	122
IC	Morris, D	GA	125
IC	Moses, J	NY	122
IC	Palacios, I	MA	121
IC	Palacios, I	MA	121
IC	Parikh, M	NY	122
IC	Perin, E	TX	127
IC	Petrossian, G	NY	123
IC	Reddy, B	GA	125
IC	Reiner, J	DC	123
IC	Resar, J	MD	123
IC	Rosenfield, K	MA	121
IC	Roubin, G	NY	123
IC	Schreiber, T	MI	127
IC	Shani, J	NY	123
IC	Sharma, S	NY	123
IC	Shorofsky, S	MD	123
IC	Smalling, R	TX	128
IC	Stone, G	NY	124
IC	Teirstein, P	CA	128
IC	Whitlow, P	OH	127
IC	Yeung, A	CA	128
IC	Zelman, R	MA	121
PCd	Beekman, R	OH	752
PCd	Biancaniello, T	NY	748
PCd	Cheatham, J	OH	752
PCd	De Moor, M	MA	747
PCd	Hellenbrand, W	CT	747
PCd	Hijazi, Z	IL	753
PCd	Hsu, D	NY	749
PCd	Latson, L	FL	751
PCd	Murphy, J	PA	749
PCd	Radtke, W	DE	749
PCd	Rocchini, A	MI	753
PCd	Rome, J	PA	749
PCd	Velvis, H	NY	750
PCd	Zahn, E	CA	755
T&CS	Williams, M	NY	1160

Interventional Endoscopy

Spec	Name	St	Pg
Ge	Chang, K	CA	255
Ge	Infantolino, A	PA	235
Ge	Jonnalagadda, S	MO	248
Ge	Waxman, I	IL	251
Ge	Yanda, R	GA	245

Interventional Neuroradiology

Spec	Name	St	Pg
NRad	Berenstein, A	NY	1020
NRad	Christoforidis, G	IL	1023
NRad	Cross, D	MO	1023
NRad	Dion, J	GA	1022
NRad	Frei, D	CO	1025
NRad	Grobelny, T	IL	1023
NRad	Hirsch, J	MA	1019
NRad	Hurst, R	PA	1020

Specialty & Special Expertise Index

Spec	Name	St	Pg
NRad	Jensen, M	VA	1022
NRad	Larsen, D	CA	1026
NRad	Lee, S	IL	1024
NRad	Mawad, M	TX	1025
NRad	Moran, C	MO	1024
NRad	Morris, P	NC	1022
NRad	Norbash, A	MA	1019
NRad	Orbach, D	MA	1020
NRad	Pile-Spellman, J	NY	1021
NRad	Teitelbaum, G	CA	1026
NS	Amar, A	CA	498
NS	Patel, A	NY	480
VIR	Kumpe, D	CO	1031
VIR	Yakes, W	CO	1032

Interventional Pulmonology

Spec	Name	St	Pg
Pul	Kovitz, K	IL	965
Pul	Nader, D	OK	969
Pul	Sterman, D	PA	959
Pul	Unger, M	PA	960

Interventional Radiology

Spec	Name	St	Pg
DR	Abbitt, P	FL	1012
DR	Conant, E	PA	1008
DR	Mirvis, S	MD	1010
DR	Shaw, D	WA	1018
DR	Teal, J	DC	1012
DR	Yoon, S	NY	1012
DR	Zagoria, R	CA	1019
VIR	Lewis, C	GA	1030

Intestinal Disorders

Spec	Name	St	Pg
PGe	Rhoads, J	TX	768
PGe	Squires, R	PA	764

Intestinal Parasites

Spec	Name	St	Pg
Ge	Elliott, D	IA	247

Intracranial Angioplasty & Stent

Spec	Name	St	Pg
NRad	Dion, J	GA	1022
NRad	Higashida, R	CA	1026
NRad	Hurst, R	PA	1020
NRad	Joseph, G	NC	1022

Intraoperative MRI

Spec	Name	St	Pg
NS	Goumnerova, L	MA	473

Intravascular Ultrasound

Spec	Name	St	Pg
Cv	Nissen, S	OH	103
IC	Reddy, B	GA	125

Invasive Cardiology

Spec	Name	St	Pg
Cv	Smith, S	NC	100
IC	Bittl, J	FL	124

Irritable Bowel Syndrome

Spec	Name	St	Pg
A&I	Tobin, M	IL	84
Ge	Fang, J	UT	252
Ge	Freiman, H	NY	234
Ge	Mertz, H	TN	243
Ge	Pezzone, M	PA	239
Ge	Roth, B	CA	257
Ge	Tremaine, W	MN	251
Ge	Wald, A	WI	251
PGe	Ulshen, M	NC	765

Ischemic Heart Disease

Spec	Name	St	Pg
Cv	Bairey-Merz, C	CA	110
Cv	Jaffe, A	MN	102
Cv	Liang, B	CT	89
Cv	Reiss, C	MO	104
Cv	Williams, E	IN	106

J

Jaw Tumors

Spec	Name	St	Pg
Path	Kahn, L	NY	722

Joint Infections

Spec	Name	St	Pg
OrS	Meere, P	NY	629

Joint Reconstruction

Spec	Name	St	Pg
HS	Collins, E	TX	305
OrS	Parvizi, J	PA	630

Joint Replacement

Spec	Name	St	Pg
OrS	Bronson, M	NY	621
OrS	Bucholz, R	TX	648
OrS	Caillouette, J	CA	650
OrS	Endrizzi, D	ME	617
OrS	Goodman, S	CA	651
OrS	Hozack, W	PA	626
OrS	Kraay, M	OH	642
OrS	Lieberman, J	CA	652
OrS	Minas, T	MA	618
OrS	Oakes, D	CA	653
OrS	Pellicci, P	NY	630
OrS	Pettrone, F	VA	637
OrS	Rothman, R	PA	631
OrS	Sculco, T	NY	632
OrS	Thornhill, T	MA	619
OrS	Vo, P	FL	638

Juvenile Arthritis

Spec	Name	St	Pg
OrS	Johanson, N	PA	626
PRhu	Finkel, T	FL	812
PRhu	Goldsmith, D	PA	811
PRhu	Haines, K	NJ	811
PRhu	Ilowite, N	NY	812
PRhu	Klein-Gitelman, M	IL	813
PRhu	McCarthy, P	CT	811
PRhu	Onel, K	IL	813
PRhu	Schanberg, L	NC	812
PRhu	Sherry, D	PA	812
PRhu	Sills, E	MD	812
PRhu	Wagner-Weiner, L	IL	813
PRhu	Warren, R	SC	813

K

Kallmann's Syndrome

Spec	Name	St	Pg
RE	Crowley, W	MA	1040

Kasabach-Merritt Syndrome (KMS)

Spec	Name	St	Pg
PHO	Bertolone, S	KY	777

Kawasaki Disease

Spec	Name	St	Pg
PCd	Bierman, F	NY	748
PCd	Cooper, R	NY	748
PCd	Gewitz, M	NY	749
PCd	Newburger, J	MA	747
PCd	Pahl, E	IL	753
PInf	Meissner, H	MA	792
PInf	Shulman, S	IL	796
PRhu	Myones, B	TX	813

Keinbocks Disease

Spec	Name	St	Pg
HS	Slutsky, D	CA	306

Keratoconus

Spec	Name	St	Pg
Oph	Asbell, P	NY	575
Oph	Boxer Wachler, B	CA	604
Oph	Cykiert, R	NY	577
Oph	Florakis, G	NY	578
Oph	Hersh, P	NJ	579
Oph	Kornmehl, E	MA	574
Oph	Shamie, N	CA	609
Oph	Stulting, R	GA	591
Oph	Udell, I	NY	586

Kidney Cancer

Spec	Name	St	Pg
Onc	Antonia, S	FL	355
Onc	Atkins, M	DC	337
Onc	Biggs, D	DE	338
Onc	Clark, J	IL	367
Onc	Dawson, N	DC	341
Onc	Dreicer, R	OH	368
Onc	Figlin, R	CA	387
Onc	Gelmann, E	NY	343
Onc	George, D	NC	358

Spec	Name	St	Pg
Onc	Haas, N	PA	344
Onc	Hogan, T	WV	345
Onc	Jonasch, E	TX	381
Onc	Kuzel, T	IL	371
Onc	Logie, K	IN	371
Onc	Margolin, K	WA	389
Onc	Motzer, R	NY	348
Onc	Petrylak, D	CT	334
Onc	Quinn, D	CA	391
Onc	Roth, B	MO	373
Onc	Samlowski, W	NV	392
Onc	Stadler, W	IL	374
Onc	Tagawa, S	NY	352
Onc	Thompson, J	WA	393
Onc	Vogelzang, N	NV	394
Onc	Wilding, G	WI	375
Path	Morrow, J	CT	719
PHO	Steinherz, P	NY	776
PHO	Tomlinson, G	TX	788
S	Rosenberg, S	MD	1099
S	Schwartzentruber, D	IN	1119
S	Yang, J	MD	1102
U	Amling, C	OR	1210
U	Babayan, R	MA	1186
U	Belldegrun, A	CA	1210
U	Benson, M	NY	1189
U	Campbell, S	OH	1202
U	Carpinito, G	MA	1186
U	Chang, S	TN	1197
U	Ciancio, G	FL	1197
U	Clayman, R	CA	1211
U	Colberg, J	CT	1186
U	Coleman, J	NY	1189
U	Daneshmand, S	CA	1211
U	Davis, B	KS	1207
U	DeKernion, J	CA	1211
U	Donovan, J	OH	1203
U	Droller, M	NY	1189
U	Ellis, W	WA	1211
U	Flanigan, R	IL	1203
U	Gill, I	CA	1211
U	Gluckman, G	IL	1203
U	Greenberg, R	PA	1190
U	Holden, S	CA	1212
U	Hrebinko, R	PA	1191
U	Jackman, S	PA	1191
U	Kavoussi, L	NY	1191
U	Kawachi, M	CA	1212
U	Kibel, A	MA	1187
U	Kirschenbaum, A	NY	1192
U	Klein, E	OH	1203
U	Landman, J	CA	1212
U	Libertino, J	MA	1187
U	Malkowicz, S	PA	1192
U	Olumi, A	MA	1187
U	Palese, M	NY	1193
U	Parekh, D	FL	1199
U	Patel, V	FL	1199
U	Presti, J	CA	1213
U	Richie, J	MA	1188
U	Robertson, C	NC	1200
U	Sagalowsky, A	TX	1209
U	Samadi, D	NY	1194
U	Sanda, M	GA	1200
U	Sawczuk, I	NJ	1194
U	Schulam, P	CT	1188
U	Sexton, W	FL	1200
U	Shalhav, A	IL	1206
U	Siegelbaum, M	MD	1195
U	Singh, D	CT	1188
U	Smith, J	TN	1200
U	Soloway, M	FL	1201
U	Steinberg, G	IL	1206
U	Su, L	FL	1201
U	Sundaram, C	IN	1206
U	Taneja, S	NY	1195
U	Teigland, C	NC	1201
U	Uzzo, R	PA	1195
U	Weiss, R	NJ	1196
U	Wilson, T	CA	1214
VIR	Brown, D	TN	1029
VIR	McGahan, J	CA	1033
VIR	Solomon, S	NY	1028
VIR	Soulen, M	PA	1028

Kidney Cancer-Cryosurgery

U	Katz, A	NY	1191

Kidney Disease

Nep	August, P	NY	459
Nep	Bakris, G	IL	462
Nep	Bernardo, J	PA	459
Nep	Butterly, D	NC	461
Nep	Cho, K	CA	466
Nep	Delmez, J	MO	463
Nep	Gaston, R	AL	461
Nep	Gluck, S	CA	466
Nep	Kliger, A	CT	458
Nep	Pohl, M	OH	464
Nep	Rudnick, M	PA	460
Nep	Venkat, K	MI	465
PNep	Chandar, J	FL	798
PNep	Ettenger, R	CA	800
PNep	Flynn, J	WA	800
PNep	McDonald, R	WA	801
PNep	Roskes, S	MD	798

Kidney Disease-Autoimmune

Nep	Helderman, J	TN	462
Nep	Salant, D	MA	458
PNep	Wyatt, R	TN	799

Kidney Disease-Chronic

Nep	Berns, J	PA	459
Nep	Bolton, W	VA	461
Nep	Fadem, S	TX	465
Nep	King, A	CA	467
Nep	Kraus, M	IN	463
Nep	Lea, J	GA	462
Nep	Perrone, R	MA	458
Nep	Schwartz, G	MN	464
Nep	Townsend, R	PA	460
Nep	Weiner, I	FL	462
Nep	Winston, J	NY	461
Nep	Yee, J	MI	465
PNep	Cohn, R	IL	800
PNep	Warady, B	MO	800

Kidney Disease-Genetic

PNep	Kashtan, C	MN	800
PNep	Neiberger, R	FL	799

Kidney Disease-Geriatric

Nep	Kasiske, B	MN	463

Kidney Disease-Glomerular

Nep	Bolton, W	VA	461
Nep	Helderman, J	TN	462
Nep	Rakowski, T	VA	462
Nep	Salant, D	MA	458

Kidney Disease-Metabolic

Nep	Kliger, A	CT	458

Kidney Disease-Pediatric & Adult

Nep	Hruska, K	MO	463

Kidney Failure

Nep	Fadem, S	TX	465
Nep	Kobrin, S	PA	460
Nep	Piraino, B	PA	460
Nep	Swartz, R	MI	464
Nep	Winston, J	NY	461
PNep	Alexander, S	CA	800
PNep	Andreoli, S	IN	799
PNep	Ault, B	TN	798
PNep	Fouser, L	WA	801
PNep	Neiberger, R	FL	799

Kidney Failure-Acute

Nep	Bazari, H	MA	458
Nep	Kraus, M	IN	463
Nep	Okusa, M	VA	462
Nep	Olivero, J	TX	466
Nep	Perrone, R	MA	458
Nep	Rudnick, M	PA	460
Nep	Tolkoff-Rubin, N	MA	458
Nep	Toto, R	TX	466

Kidney Failure-Chronic

Nep	Ahmad, S	WA	466
Nep	Brennan, S	TX	465
Nep	Dember, L	PA	459
Nep	McCarthy, J	MN	463
Nep	Miller, B	MO	464
Nep	Okusa, M	VA	462
Nep	Olivero, J	TX	466
Nep	Roth, D	FL	462

Spec	Name	St	Pg
Nep	Seifter, J	MA	458
Nep	Stern, L	NY	460
Nep	Williams, G	NY	460
PNep	Andreoli, S	IN	799
PNep	Jabs, K	TN	799

Kidney Pathology

Spec	Name	St	Pg
Path	Koss, M	CA	733
Path	Rennke, H	MA	719
Path	Sibley, R	CA	734
Path	Tomaszewski, J	NY	724

Kidney Stones

Spec	Name	St	Pg
Nep	Ahmad, S	WA	466
Nep	Brennan, S	TX	465
Nep	Coe, F	IL	463
Nep	Fulop, T	MS	461
Nep	Gluck, S	CA	466
Nep	Hruska, K	MO	463
Nep	Kelepouris, E	PA	460
Nep	Rudnick, M	PA	460
Nep	Seifter, J	MA	458
PNep	Langman, C	IL	800
U	Albala, D	NY	1188
U	Basler, J	TX	1208
U	Carson, C	NC	1197
U	Chun, T	NJ	1189
U	Clayman, R	CA	1211
U	Grasso, M	NY	1190
U	Hamilton, B	UT	1207
U	Irby, P	NC	1198
U	Jackman, S	PA	1191
U	Janeiro, J	NH	1186
U	Landman, J	CA	1212
U	Loo, M	NY	1192
U	Lowe, F	NY	1192
U	Nakada, S	WI	1205
U	Palese, M	NY	1193
U	Patterson, A	TN	1199
U	Preminger, G	NC	1200
U	Sanders, W	GA	1200
U	Schulam, P	CT	1188
U	Stoller, M	CA	1213
U	Winfield, H	AL	1201

Klinefelter's Syndrome

Spec	Name	St	Pg
PEn	Fennoy, I	NY	758

Klippel-Trenaunay Syndrome

Spec	Name	St	Pg
PCd	Driscoll, D	MN	752

Knee Cartilage/Meniscus Transplants

Spec	Name	St	Pg
OrS	Anderson, L	CA	649
OrS	Miller, M	VA	637

Knee Injuries

Spec	Name	St	Pg
OrS	Johnson, D	KY	636
OrS	Scott, W	NY	632
OrS	Sethi, P	CT	619
SM	Arendt, E	MN	1077
SM	Burke, C	PA	1075
SM	Fronek, J	CA	1079
SM	Gill, T	MA	1074
SM	Harner, C	PA	1075
SM	Hershman, E	NY	1075
SM	Levine, W	NY	1075
SM	Mirzayan, R	CA	1079
SM	Rodeo, S	NY	1076
SM	Steiner, M	MA	1074

Knee Injuries/ACL

Spec	Name	St	Pg
OrS	Ahmad, C	NY	620
OrS	Anderson, L	CA	649
OrS	Busch, M	GA	635
OrS	Cooper, D	TX	648
OrS	Diduch, D	VA	635
OrS	Kaeding, C	OH	642
OrS	Mandelbaum, B	CA	652
OrS	Souryal, T	TX	649
OrS	Wickiewicz, T	NY	634
OrS	Zarins, B	MA	619
SM	Bach, B	IL	1077
SM	Fu, F	PA	1075
SM	Micheli, L	MA	1074
SM	Taft, T	NC	1077
SM	Williams, R	NY	1076
SM	Xerogeanes, J	GA	1077

Knee Injuries/ACL/Meniscus Tears

Spec	Name	St	Pg
OrS	Goitz, H	MI	641
OrS	Karas, S	GA	636
OrS	Meere, P	NY	629
OrS	Steadman, J	CO	647
SM	Veitch, A	NM	1078

Knee Injuries/Ligament Surgery

Spec	Name	St	Pg
OrS	Hannafin, J	NY	625
OrS	Marx, R	NY	628
OrS	Warren, R	NY	633

Knee Ligament Reconstruction

Spec	Name	St	Pg
OrS	Bartolozzi, A	PA	620
OrS	Booth, R	PA	621
OrS	Johnson, D	KY	636
OrS	Miller, M	VA	637
OrS	Shelbourne, K	IN	645
OrS	Spindler, K	TN	638
SM	Arendt, E	MN	1077
SM	Garth, W	AL	1077

Knee Reconstruction

Spec	Name	St	Pg
OrS	Garrett, W	NC	636
OrS	Krackow, K	NY	627
SM	Bush-Joseph, C	IL	1077
SM	Ciccotti, M	PA	1075
SM	Miniaci, A	OH	1078

Knee Reconstruction & Revision

Spec	Name	St	Pg
OrS	Moucha, C	NY	629

Knee Rehabilitation (Non-Surgical)

Spec	Name	St	Pg
OrS	Shelbourne, K	IN	645

Knee Repacement

Spec	Name	St	Pg
OrS	Bozic, K	CA	649

Knee Replacement

Spec	Name	St	Pg
OrS	Blaha, J	MI	640
OrS	Brick, G	MA	616
OrS	Bronson, M	NY	621
OrS	Buly, R	NY	622
OrS	Burke, D	MA	616
OrS	Cornell, C	NY	622
OrS	Goldstein, W	IL	641
OrS	Haas, S	NY	625
OrS	Hume, E	PA	626
OrS	Jiranek, W	VA	636
OrS	Krackow, K	NY	627
OrS	Lieberman, J	CA	652
OrS	Macaulay, W	NY	628
OrS	Marx, R	NY	628
OrS	Muschler, G	OH	643
OrS	Pellicci, P	NY	630
OrS	Reilly, D	MA	618
OrS	Robinson, R	FL	637
OrS	Rothman, R	PA	631
OrS	Salvati, E	NY	631
OrS	Scott, R	MA	619
OrS	Scott, W	NY	632
OrS	Sculco, T	NY	632
OrS	Sharkey, P	PA	632
OrS	Zuckerman, J	NY	635
SM	Nisonson, B	NY	1076

Knee Replacement & Revision

Spec	Name	St	Pg
OrS	Bartolozzi, A	PA	620
OrS	Berry, D	MN	639
OrS	Booth, R	PA	621
OrS	Bostrom, M	NY	621
OrS	Hungerford, M	MD	626
OrS	Jacobs, J	IL	642
OrS	Johanson, N	PA	626
OrS	Mabrey, J	TX	648
OrS	Meere, P	NY	629
OrS	Moucha, C	NY	629
OrS	Parvizi, J	PA	630
OrS	Thomas, B	CA	654
OrS	Westrich, G	NY	634

Spec	Name	St	Pg

Knee Surgery

Spec	Name	St	Pg
OrS	Bauman, P	NY	620
OrS	Bono, J	MA	616
OrS	Crossett, L	PA	622
OrS	Elattrache, N	CA	651
OrS	Estwanik, J	NC	636
OrS	Garrett, W	NC	636
OrS	Glashow, J	NY	624
OrS	Haas, S	NY	625
OrS	Hanssen, A	MN	641
OrS	Heiden, E	UT	646
OrS	Jokl, P	CT	617
OrS	Kenter, K	OH	642
OrS	Millett, P	CO	646
OrS	Rosenberg, T	UT	647
OrS	Scott, W	NY	632
OrS	Shelbourne, K	IN	645
SM	Altchek, D	NY	1074
SM	Andrews, J	FL	1076
SM	Bach, B	IL	1077
SM	Bradley, J	PA	1075
SM	Gambardella, R	CA	1079
SM	Hershman, E	NY	1075
SM	Ma, C	CA	1079
SM	Paletta, G	MO	1078
SM	Richmond, J	MA	1074
SM	Scheller, A	MA	1074
SM	Teitz, C	WA	1079
SM	Williams, R	NY	1076
SM	Xerogeanes, J	GA	1077

Knee-Microfracture Surgery

Spec	Name	St	Pg
OrS	Steadman, J	CO	647

Knee-Patella Problems

Spec	Name	St	Pg
OrS	Fulkerson, J	CT	617
OrS	Gladstone, J	NY	624
OrS	Leadbetter, W	MD	627

Knee-Patella Problems Consult

Spec	Name	St	Pg
OrS	Grelsamer, R	NY	624

L

Lacrimal Gland Disorders

Spec	Name	St	Pg
Oph	Gallin, P	NY	578
Oph	Kikkawa, D	CA	606
Oph	Lueder, G	MO	597
Oph	Tse, D	FL	592

Langerhans Cell Histiocytosis (LCH)

Spec	Name	St	Pg
Hem	Winter, J	IL	324
PHO	Razzouk, B	IN	785

Laparoscopic Abdominal Surgery

Spec	Name	St	Pg
S	Frantzides, C	IL	1114
S	Hunter, J	OR	1133
S	Petelin, J	KS	1123
S	Pomp, A	NY	1098
S	Salky, B	NY	1099
S	Satava, R	WA	1136
S	Shikora, S	MA	1088

Laparoscopic Surgery

Spec	Name	St	Pg
CRS	Coutsoftides, T	CA	177
CRS	Delaney, C	OH	173
CRS	Fleshman, J	TX	176
CRS	Goldstein, S	PA	170
CRS	Golub, R	FL	172
CRS	Haas, E	TX	176
CRS	Hartmann, R	FL	172
CRS	Marks, J	PA	170
CRS	Milsom, J	NY	170
CRS	Nagle, D	MA	168
CRS	Orkin, B	IL	174
CRS	Pello, M	NJ	170
CRS	Read, T	MA	168
CRS	Remzi, F	OH	175
CRS	Saclarides, T	IL	175
CRS	Senagore, A	MI	175
CRS	Stamos, M	CA	178
CRS	Stein, D	PA	171
CRS	Stryker, S	IL	175
CRS	Thorson, A	NE	176
CRS	Varma, M	CA	178
CRS	Weiser, M	NY	171
CRS	Wexner, S	FL	172
CRS	Whelan, R	NY	171
CRS	Wong, R	HI	178
CRS	Young-Fadok, T	AZ	177
GO	Alexander, M	MD	276
GO	Azodi, M	CT	274
GO	Barter, J	MD	276
GO	Bicher, A	VA	280
GO	Burnett, A	AR	288
GO	Curtin, J	NY	277
GO	DeMars, L	NH	274
GO	Dottino, P	NY	277
GO	Fowler, J	OH	284
GO	Herzog, T	NY	278
GO	Horowitz, I	GA	282
GO	Mannel, R	OK	289
GO	Morgan, M	PA	279
GO	Reynolds, R	MI	286
GO	Stern, J	CA	292
GO	Valea, F	NC	283
ObG	Argenta, P	MN	563
ObG	Brodman, M	NY	560
ObG	Goldstein, M	NY	561
ObG	Steege, J	NC	563
Ped Uro	Gundeti, M	IL	827
Ped Uro	Strand, W	TX	828
PS	Albanese, C	CA	823
PS	Caty, M	CT	813
PS	Nuchtern, J	TX	822
PS	Waldhausen, J	WA	824
RE	Adamson, G	CA	1051
RE	Clisham, P	LA	1050
RE	Cohen, D	IL	1047
RE	Grifo, J	NY	1042
RE	Hornstein, M	MA	1040
RE	Pfeifer, S	PA	1043
RE	Smikle, C	CA	1052
RE	Yee, B	CA	1053
S	Bessler, M	NY	1089
S	Bilchik, A	CA	1130
S	Blackstone, R	AZ	1124
S	Brody, F	DC	1090
S	Callery, M	MA	1084
S	Crookes, P	CA	1131
S	Daneker, G	GA	1104
S	Dempsey, D	PA	1092
S	Deziel, D	IL	1113
S	Doherty, G	MA	1085
S	Farley, D	MN	1114
S	Franklin, M	TX	1125
S	Frantzides, C	IL	1114
S	Fung, J	OH	1114
S	Geller, D	PA	1093
S	Hawn, M	AL	1105
S	Herron, D	NY	1094
S	Howerton, R	NC	1106
S	Jackson, G	TX	1126
S	Jones, D	MA	1086
S	Katkhouda, N	CA	1133
S	Kendrick, M	MN	1115
S	Marks, J	OH	1116
S	Mellinger, J	IL	1117
S	Melvin, W	OH	1117
S	Nguyen, N	CA	1134
S	Onders, R	OH	1118
S	Pappas, T	NC	1107
S	Park, A	MD	1098
S	Phillips, E	CA	1135
S	Rege, R	TX	1128
S	Reiner, M	NY	1099
S	Richards, W	AL	1108
S	Sarosi, G	FL	1108
S	Schaffer, R	CA	1137
S	Schirmer, B	VA	1108
S	Schlinkert, R	AZ	1128
S	Scott-Conner, C	IA	1119
S	Sharp, K	TN	1109
S	Shibata, D	FL	1109
S	Siperstein, A	OH	1120
S	Soper, N	IL	1120
S	Sweeney, J	GA	1110
S	Unger, S	FL	1110
S	Wood, R	TX	1129
U	Albala, D	NY	1188
U	Andrews, P	AZ	1207
U	Andriole, G	MO	1202
U	Chen, D	PA	1189
U	Clayman, R	CA	1211
U	Culkin, D	OK	1208
U	Grasso, M	NY	1190
U	Hamilton, B	UT	1207
U	Hemal, A	NC	1198

Spec	Name	St	Pg
U	Jackman, S	PA	1191
U	Kozlowski, J	IL	1204
U	Lugg, J	WY	1207
U	Nakada, S	WI	1205
U	Nieder, A	FL	1199
U	Palese, M	NY	1193
U	Patterson, A	TN	1199
U	Sexton, W	FL	1200
U	Shalhav, A	IL	1206
U	Siegelbaum, M	MD	1195
U	Singh, D	CT	1188
U	Stoller, M	CA	1213
U	Su, L	FL	1201
U	Takayama, T	WA	1213
U	Teigland, C	NC	1201
U	Trabulsi, E	PA	1195
U	Wallen, E	NC	1201
U	Winfield, H	AL	1201
U	Wong, C	OH	1206

Laparoscopic Surgery-Advanced

PS	Notrica, D	AZ	822
S	Dunkin, B	TX	1124
S	Pryor, A	NY	1098
S	Scott, D	TX	1128

Laryngeal & Tracheal Disorders

Oto	Burns, J	MA	665
Oto	Weissler, M	NC	682
Oto	Zalzal, G	MD	677

Laryngeal & Vocal Cord Surgery

Oto	Burns, J	MA	665
Oto	Sulica, R	NY	676

Laryngeal & Voice Disorders

Oto	Benninger, M	OH	683
Oto	Fried, M	NY	669
PO	Thompson, D	IL	804

Laryngeal Cancer

Onc	Pfister, D	NY	350
Oto	Andersen, P	OR	694
Oto	Courey, M	CA	694
Oto	Diaz, E	TX	691
Oto	Ferris, R	PA	669
Oto	Grillone, G	MA	665
Oto	Shapshay, S	NY	675
Oto	Strome, S	MD	676
Oto	Weinstein, G	PA	677
Oto	Woo, P	NY	677
Oto	Yoo, G	MI	689
Oto	Zeitels, S	MA	667
S	Ridge, J	PA	1099

Laryngeal Cancer-Organ Preservation

Oto	Diaz, E	TX	691

Laryngeal Disorders

Oto	Bastian, R	IL	683
Oto	Berke, G	CA	694
Oto	Courey, M	CA	694
Oto	Flint, P	OR	695
Oto	Grillone, G	MA	665
Oto	Koufman, J	NY	672
Oto	Mirza, N	PA	673
Oto	Sataloff, R	PA	675
Oto	Stasney, C	TX	693
Oto	Suen, J	AR	693
Oto	Woo, P	NY	677
PO	April, M	NY	802
PO	Tunkel, D	MD	803

Laser Surgery

D	Anderson, R	MA	184
D	Cunningham, B	CA	200
Oph	Wang, M	TN	592
Oto	Caruana, S	NY	668
PlS	Hardesty, R	CA	903
PlS	Kenkel, J	TX	899

Laser Vision Surgery

Oph	Caster, A	CA	605
Oph	Clinch, T	MD	577
Oph	Dodick, J	NY	577
Oph	Gibralter, R	NY	579
Oph	McCulley, J	TX	602
Oph	Stulting, R	GA	591

LASIK-Refractive Surgery

Oph	Afshari, N	CA	604
Oph	Asbell, P	NY	575
Oph	Azar, D	IL	593
Oph	Boxer Wachler, B	CA	604
Oph	Braunstein, R	NY	576
Oph	Carlson, A	NC	587
Oph	Caster, A	CA	605
Oph	Clinch, T	MD	577
Oph	Culbertson, W	FL	587
Oph	Cykiert, R	NY	577
Oph	Dhaliwal, D	PA	577
Oph	Durrie, D	KS	601
Oph	Feder, R	IL	595
Oph	Goldberg, D	NJ	579
Oph	Gorovoy, M	FL	588
Oph	Hersh, P	NJ	579
Oph	Kornmehl, E	MA	574
Oph	Krauss, H	CA	607
Oph	Mackool, R	NY	581
Oph	Maloney, R	CA	607
Oph	Manche, E	CA	607
Oph	Mandel, E	NY	581
Oph	Pepose, J	MO	598
Oph	Pflugfelder, S	TX	603
Oph	Salz, J	CA	608
Oph	Serafano, D	CA	609
Oph	Sperber, L	NY	585
Oph	Starr, C	NY	585
Oph	Updegraff, S	FL	592
Oph	Wang, M	TN	592
Oph	Waring, G	GA	592
Oph	Wilson, S	OH	600

Latex Allergy

A&I	Benenati, S	FL	82
PA&I	Pongracic, J	IL	745

Learning Disorders

ChiN	Nass, R	NY	146
ChiN	Shaywitz, B	CT	144
Ped	Hershorin, E	FL	741
Ped	Shaywitz, S	CT	740

Left Ventricular Assist Device (LVAD)

T&CS	Bowdish, M	CA	1177
T&CS	Pagani, F	MI	1171
T&CS	Pochettino, A	MN	1171

Leg Ulcers

D	Kirsner, R	FL	193

Lens Implants

Oph	Goldberg, D	NJ	579
Oph	John, T	IL	596
Oph	Serafano, D	CA	609
Oph	Waring, G	GA	592

Lens Implants-Multifocal

Oph	Mackool, R	NY	581
Oph	Solomon, K	SC	591

Lens Implants-Pediatric

Oph	Wilson, M	SC	592

Leukemia

Hem	Baer, M	MD	313
Hem	Ballen, K	MA	312
Hem	Bigelow, C	MS	318
Hem	Bockenstedt, P	MI	321
Hem	Cooper, B	TX	326
Hem	Copelan, E	NC	319
Hem	Cortes, J	TX	326
Hem	Damon, L	CA	327
Hem	DiPersio, J	MO	321
Hem	Emanuel, P	AR	326
Hem	Forman, S	CA	328
Hem	Garcia-Manero, G	TX	326
Hem	Goldberg, J	PA	314

Spec	Name	St	Pg
Hem	Gregory, S	IL	322
Hem	Grever, M	OH	322
Hem	Habermann, T	MN	322
Hem	Jurcic, J	NY	314
Hem	Kantarjian, H	TX	326
Hem	Kempin, S	NY	315
Hem	Kipps, T	CA	328
Hem	Kraut, E	OH	322
Hem	Kuriakose, P	MI	322
Hem	Litzow, M	MN	322
Hem	Luger, S	PA	315
Hem	Marks, S	PA	315
Hem	Maslak, P	NY	315
Hem	Maziarz, R	OR	329
Hem	McGlave, P	MN	323
Hem	Mears, J	NY	315
Hem	Mesa, R	AZ	327
Hem	Miller, K	MA	312
Hem	Mitchell, B	CA	329
Hem	Nand, S	IL	323
Hem	O'Donnell, M	CA	329
Hem	Petersdorf, S	WA	329
Hem	Porter, D	PA	316
Hem	Powell, B	NC	319
Hem	Rai, K	NY	316
Hem	Raphael, B	NY	316
Hem	Rapoport, A	MD	316
Hem	Rosenblatt, J	FL	320
Hem	Saven, A	CA	329
Hem	Schiller, G	CA	329
Hem	Snyder, D	CA	330
Hem	Spitzer, T	MA	313
Hem	Spivak, J	MD	317
Hem	Stiff, P	IL	324
Hem	Stock, W	IL	324
Hem	Stone, R	MA	313
Hem	Strair, R	NJ	317
Hem	Strauss, J	TX	327
Hem	Tallman, M	NY	318
Hem	Tefferi, A	MN	324
Hem	Williams, M	VA	320
Hem	Wisch, N	NY	318
Hem	Yeager, A	AZ	327
Hem	Zuckerman, K	FL	320
Onc	Brentjens, R	NY	339
Onc	Chao, N	NC	357
Onc	Chitambar, C	WI	367
Onc	Claxton, D	PA	340
Onc	Dakhil, S	KS	376
Onc	Druker, B	OR	387
Onc	Estey, E	WA	387
Onc	Flinn, I	TN	357
Onc	Gabrilove, J	NY	343
Onc	Gerson, S	OH	369
Onc	Hurd, D	NC	359
Onc	Jillella, A	GA	359
Onc	Kalaycio, M	OH	370
Onc	List, A	FL	360
Onc	Lossos, I	FL	360
Onc	Moore, J	NC	361
Onc	O'Brien, S	TX	382
Onc	Orlowski, R	TX	382
Onc	Peterson, B	MN	372
Onc	Saiki, J	NM	383
Onc	Scheinberg, D	NY	351
Onc	Schiffer, C	MI	373
Onc	Shea, T	NC	363
Onc	Soiffer, R	MA	335
Onc	Waller, E	GA	365
Onc	Weiner, G	IA	375
Onc	Wetzler, M	NY	354
Onc	Wingard, J	FL	365
Path	Chang, K	CA	732
Path	Foucar, M	NM	730
Path	Kinney, M	TX	730
Path	Nathwani, B	CA	734
PHO	Aledo, A	NY	771
PHO	Altman, A	CT	769
PHO	Andrews, R	WA	789
PHO	Angiolillo, A	DC	771
PHO	Arceci, R	AZ	787
PHO	Barredo, J	FL	777
PHO	Brecher, M	NY	771
PHO	Buchanan, G	TX	787
PHO	Cairo, M	NY	772
PHO	Camitta, B	WI	782
PHO	Carroll, W	NY	772
PHO	Castellino, S	NC	778
PHO	Corey, S	IL	782
PHO	Davies, S	OH	782
PHO	Felix, C	PA	773
PHO	Frantz, C	DE	773
PHO	Friedman, A	MD	773
PHO	Godder, K	VA	778
PHO	Gold, S	NC	779
PHO	Goldman, S	TX	788
PHO	Graham, M	AZ	788
PHO	Guarini, L	NY	773
PHO	Haut, P	IN	783
PHO	Hawkins, D	WA	790
PHO	Hayani, A	IL	783
PHO	Hayashi, R	MO	783
PHO	Homans, A	VT	770
PHO	Hutchinson, R	MI	784
PHO	Johnston, J	GA	779
PHO	Keller, F	GA	779
PHO	Kuttesch, J	NM	788
PHO	Luchtman-Jones, L	DC	775
PHO	Marcus, J	NY	775
PHO	Morgan, E	IL	784
PHO	Pui, C	TN	780
PHO	Razzouk, B	IN	785
PHO	Rheingold, S	PA	776
PHO	Ritchey, A	PA	776
PHO	Rosoff, P	NC	780
PHO	Sakamoto, K	CA	791
PHO	Sallan, S	MA	770
PHO	Sandler, E	FL	781
PHO	Small, D	MD	776
PHO	Tebbi, C	FL	781
PHO	Vik, T	IN	786
PHO	Wayne, A	CA	792
PHO	Weiner, M	NY	777
PHO	Weinstein, H	MA	771
PHO	Winick, N	TX	789
PHO	Yaddanapudi, R	MI	786
PHO	York, T	MD	777

Leukemia & Lymphoma

Spec	Name	St	Pg
Hem	Allen, S	NY	313
Hem	Champlin, R	TX	325
Hem	Cheson, B	DC	313
Hem	Farag, S	IN	321
Hem	Filicko-O'Hara, J	PA	314
Hem	Friedman, A	PA	314
Hem	Greer, J	TN	319
Hem	Larson, R	IL	322
Hem	Linenberger, M	WA	328
Hem	Lyons, R	TX	327
Hem	Millenson, M	PA	316
Hem	Munker, R	LA	327
Onc	Aboulafia, D	WA	384
Onc	Ball, E	CA	385
Onc	Bishop, M	IL	366
Onc	Carabasi, M	PA	339
Onc	Coleman, M	NY	340
Onc	Fay, J	TX	379
Onc	Flomenberg, N	PA	342
Onc	Himelstein, A	DE	344
Onc	Hollister, D	CT	333
Onc	Lazarus, H	OH	371
Onc	Logie, K	IN	371
Onc	Morgan, D	TN	362
Onc	Peace, D	IL	372
Onc	Petruska, P	MO	372
Onc	Rosen, S	IL	373
Onc	Silverman, L	NY	351
Onc	Stadtmauer, E	PA	352
Path	Bagg, A	PA	720
PHO	Coccia, P	NE	786
PHO	Halpern, S	NJ	774
PHO	Harris, M	NJ	774
PHO	Hilden, J	CO	786
PHO	Kung, F	CA	790
PHO	Manera, R	IL	784
PHO	Plautz, G	OH	785
PHO	Ribeiro, R	TN	780
PHO	Salvi, S	IL	785
PHO	Steinherz, P	NY	776
PHO	Wechsler, D	NC	781
PHO	Weinblatt, M	NY	776

Leukemia in Down Syndrome

Spec	Name	St	Pg
PHO	Hilden, J	CO	786

Leukemia in Infants

Spec	Name	St	Pg
PHO	Dreyer, Z	TX	788
PHO	Felix, C	PA	773
PHO	Hilden, J	CO	786

Leukemia-Acute Lymphoblastic

Spec	Name	St	Pg
Hem	Stone, R	MA	313

Leukemia-Chronic Lymphocytic

Spec	Name	St	Pg
Hem	Byrd, J	OH	321

Specialty & Special Expertise Index

Spec	Name	St	Pg
Hem	Gordon, L	IL	321
Hem	Keating, M	TX	326
Hem	Sokol, L	FL	320
Onc	Brentjens, R	NY	339
Onc	Chanan-Khan, A	FL	356
Onc	Czuczman, M	NY	341
Onc	Smith, M	OH	374

Leukemia-Chronic Myeloid

Spec	Name	St	Pg
Hem	Luger, S	PA	315
Onc	Druker, B	OR	387
Onc	Wetzler, M	NY	354

Leukemia-Myeloid

Spec	Name	St	Pg
Hem	Garcia-Manero, G	TX	326
Hem	Komrokji, R	FL	319
Onc	Appelbaum, F	WA	385
Onc	Estey, E	WA	387

Leukoencephalopathy

Spec	Name	St	Pg
N	Kesari, S	CA	540

Li-Fraumeni Syndrome

Spec	Name	St	Pg
Onc	Ford, J	CA	387

Lichen Planus

Spec	Name	St	Pg
D	Camisa, C	FL	192

Ligament Reconstruction

Spec	Name	St	Pg
OrS	Hannafin, J	NY	625
SM	Hershman, E	NY	1075
SM	Kaplan, L	FL	1077
SM	Mirzayan, R	CA	1079

Limb Deformities

Spec	Name	St	Pg
OrS	Aronson, J	AR	647
OrS	Davidson, R	PA	622
OrS	Feldman, D	NY	623
OrS	Gugenheim, J	TX	648
OrS	Herzenberg, J	MD	626
OrS	Lowenberg, D	CA	652
OrS	Rozbruch, S	NY	631

Limb Lengthening

Spec	Name	St	Pg
OrS	Rozbruch, S	NY	631

Limb Lengthening (Ilizarov Procedure)

Spec	Name	St	Pg
OrS	Aronson, J	AR	647
OrS	Davidson, R	PA	622
OrS	Gugenheim, J	TX	648
OrS	Herzenberg, J	MD	626
OrS	Lowenberg, D	CA	652

Limb Sparing Surgery

Spec	Name	St	Pg
OrS	Aboulafia, A	MD	620
OrS	Benevenia, J	NJ	620
OrS	Biermann, J	MI	639
OrS	Gitelis, S	IL	641
OrS	Irwin, R	MI	641
OrS	Kenan, S	NY	627
OrS	Malawer, M	MD	628
OrS	Peabody, T	IL	644
OrS	Schmidt, R	PA	632
OrS	Smith, D	WA	653
OrS	Wilkins, R	CO	647
OrS	Wurtz, L	IN	645
VascS	Ascher, E	NY	1221
VascS	Lantis, J	NY	1224
VascS	Marin, M	NY	1224

Limb Surgery/Reconstruction

Spec	Name	St	Pg
HS	Raphael, J	PA	299
OrS	Friedlaender, G	CT	617
OrS	Mayerson, J	OH	643
OrS	Rozbruch, S	NY	631
PlS	Attinger, C	DC	880
PlS	Sherman, R	CA	905

Liposuction

Spec	Name	St	Pg
PlS	Matarasso, A	NY	884
PlS	Nahabedian, M	DC	885
PlS	Sanders, G	CA	905
PlS	Tebbetts, J	TX	900

Liposuction & Body Contouring

Spec	Name	St	Pg
PlS	Aston, S	NY	880
PlS	Barone, C	TX	898
PlS	Barton, F	TX	898
PlS	Beals, S	AZ	898
PlS	Beasley, M	NC	888
PlS	Bucky, L	PA	881
PlS	Byrd, H	TX	898
PlS	Da Lio, A	CA	902
PlS	Davis, G	NC	889
PlS	Dufresne, C	MD	882
PlS	Edwards, M	NV	902
PlS	Evans, G	CA	902
PlS	Fodor, P	CA	902
PlS	Gallico, G	MA	878
PlS	Gregory, R	FL	890
PlS	Grossman, J	CO	897
PlS	Grotting, J	AL	890
PlS	Hoffman, L	NY	882
PlS	Jewell, M	OR	903
PlS	Koplin, L	CA	903
PlS	Leipziger, L	NY	883
PlS	Maxwell, G	TN	891
PlS	Moses, M	LA	900
PlS	Nichter, L	CA	904
PlS	Noone, R	PA	885
PlS	Olding, M	DC	885
PlS	Orgill, D	MA	878
PlS	Paul, M	CA	904
PlS	Pitman, G	NY	885
PlS	Price, G	MD	886
PlS	Rand, R	WA	904
PlS	Rohrich, R	TX	900
PlS	Rosenberg, H	CA	905
PlS	Schusterman, M	TX	900
PlS	Singer, R	CA	905
PlS	Singh, N	MD	886
PlS	Slavin, S	MA	879
PlS	Stevens, W	CA	905
PlS	Sultan, M	NY	887
PlS	Wilcox, R	TX	901

Liver & Biliary Cancer

Spec	Name	St	Pg
S	Calvo, B	NC	1104
S	Cioffi, W	RI	1084
S	Emond, J	NY	1093
S	Fong, Y	NY	1093
S	Fung, J	OH	1114
S	Jenkins, R	MA	1086
S	Kinkhabwala, M	NY	1095
S	Mulvihill, S	UT	1122
S	Newman, E	NY	1097
S	Pinson, C	TN	1108
S	Schulick, R	CO	1123
S	Shen, P	NC	1109
S	Sinanan, M	WA	1137
S	Staley, C	GA	1109
S	Sundaram, M	IL	1120
S	Yeung, R	WA	1138

Liver & Biliary Disease

Spec	Name	St	Pg
Ge	Jacobson, I	NY	236
Ge	Jensen, D	IL	248
Ge	La Russo, N	MN	248
Ge	Tobias, H	NY	240

Liver & Biliary Imaging

Spec	Name	St	Pg
DR	Grant, E	CA	1018

Liver & Biliary Surgery

Spec	Name	St	Pg
PS	Dunn, S	DE	815
S	Chabot, J	NY	1091
S	Chapman, W	MO	1112
S	Cronin, D	WI	1113
S	Kinkhabwala, M	NY	1095
S	Matthews, J	IL	1116
S	Melvin, W	OH	1117
S	Meyers, W	PA	1096
S	Olthoff, K	PA	1097
S	Pinson, C	TN	1108
S	Selby, R	CA	1137

Liver Cancer

Spec	Name	St	Pg
DR	Charboneau, J	MN	1014
DR	Coakley, F	OR	1017
DR	Dodd, G	CO	1016
Ge	Brown, K	MI	246
Ge	Di Bisceglie, A	MO	247

Spec	Name	St	Pg
Ge	Galati, J	TX	254
Ge	Gish, R	CA	256
Ge	Jensen, D	IL	248
Ge	Okolo, P	MD	238
Ge	Porayko, M	TN	244
Ge	Shiffman, M	VA	245
Onc	Benson, A	IL	366
Onc	Berlin, J	TN	355
Onc	Ensminger, W	MI	369
Onc	Holcombe, R	NY	345
Onc	Kemeny, N	NY	346
Onc	Leighton, J	PA	347
Onc	Patt, Y	NM	382
Onc	Posey, J	AL	362
Onc	Reid, T	CA	391
Onc	Venook, A	CA	394
Onc	Weiner, L	DC	354
Onc	Yen, Y	CA	394
Path	Bhan, A	MA	718
Path	Greenson, J	MI	728
PHO	Furman, W	TN	778
PHO	Tomlinson, G	TX	788
PS	La Quaglia, M	NY	816
RadRO	Lawrence, T	MI	990
S	Abecassis, M	IL	1111
S	Abouljoud, M	MI	1111
S	Adams, R	VA	1103
S	Ascher, N	CA	1130
S	Bartlett, D	PA	1089
S	Bolton, J	LA	1124
S	Brems, J	IL	1112
S	Busuttil, R	CA	1130
S	Callery, M	MA	1084
S	Cameron, J	MD	1090
S	Chapman, W	MO	1112
S	Colquhoun, S	CA	1131
S	Curley, S	TX	1124
S	DeMatteo, R	NY	1092
S	Drebin, J	PA	1092
S	Eason, J	TN	1104
S	Emond, J	NY	1093
S	Emre, S	CT	1085
S	Espat, N	RI	1085
S	Fraker, D	PA	1093
S	Geller, D	PA	1093
S	Gibbs, J	NY	1093
S	Hemming, A	CA	1133
S	Hiotis, S	NY	1094
S	Hoffman, J	PA	1094
S	Jarnagin, W	NY	1094
S	Karpeh, M	NY	1095
S	Kendrick, M	MN	1115
S	Klein, A	CA	1134
S	Kuhn, J	TX	1126
S	Levi, J	FL	1106
S	Mahvi, D	IL	1116
S	Marsh, J	PA	1096
S	McMasters, K	KY	1107
S	Millis, J	IL	1117
S	Nakakura, E	CA	1134
S	Nissen, N	CA	1135
S	Olthoff, K	PA	1097
S	Pawlik, T	MD	1098
S	Philosophe, B	MD	1098
S	Reich, D	PA	1099
S	Roh, M	FL	1108
S	Salem, R	CT	1087
S	Sasson, A	NE	1123
S	Schwartz, M	NY	1100
S	Selby, R	CA	1137
S	Sielaff, T	MN	1119
S	Sigurdson, E	PA	1101
S	Staren, E	AZ	1129
S	Talamonti, M	IL	1120
S	Tanabe, K	MA	1088
S	Teperman, L	NY	1102
S	Vauthey, J	TX	1129
S	Vickers, S	MN	1120
S	Wagman, L	CA	1138
S	Warren, R	CA	1138
S	Weber, S	WI	1121
S	Wood, R	TX	1129
S	Yeatman, T	SC	1111
S	Yeung, R	WA	1138
VIR	Brown, K	NY	1027
VIR	Durham, J	CO	1031
VIR	Goodwin, S	CA	1032
VIR	Hicks, M	TX	1032
VIR	McGahan, J	CA	1033
VIR	Solomon, S	NY	1028

Liver Cancer-Metastatic

S	Alexander, H	MD	1089
S	Choti, M	MD	1091

Liver Cancer/Chemoembolization

VIR	Geschwind, J	MD	1028
VIR	Hallisey, M	CT	1027
VIR	Haskal, Z	MD	1028
VIR	Rilling, W	WI	1031
VIR	Salem, R	IL	1031
VIR	Soulen, M	PA	1028

Liver Cancer/Radioembolization

VIR	Brown, D	TN	1029

Liver Disease

Ge	Anderson, K	TX	252
Ge	Bacon, B	MO	246
Ge	Balart, L	LA	253
Ge	Barnes, D	OH	246
Ge	Berg, C	NC	241
Ge	Bloomer, J	AL	241
Ge	Borum, M	DC	233
Ge	Boyer, T	AZ	253
Ge	Brown, K	MI	246
Ge	Brown, R	NY	233
Ge	Chung, R	MA	230
Ge	Crippin, J	MO	247
Ge	Diehl, A	NC	242
Ge	Dienstag, J	MA	230
Ge	Dieterich, D	NY	234
Ge	Eisen, G	OR	255
Ge	Fallon, M	TX	254
Ge	Fried, M	NC	242
Ge	Friedman, L	MA	231
Ge	Galati, J	TX	254
Ge	Gholam, P	OH	247
Ge	Han, S	CA	256
Ge	Herrine, S	PA	235
Ge	Hunter, E	ID	252
Ge	Kaplan, L	MA	231
Ge	Konicek, F	IL	248
Ge	Korsten, M	NY	237
Ge	Kwo, P	IN	248
Ge	Lambiase, L	TN	243
Ge	Loomba, R	CA	256
Ge	Lucey, M	WI	249
Ge	Martin, P	FL	243
Ge	Miskovitz, P	NY	238
Ge	Nunes, D	MA	231
Ge	Poordad, F	TX	254
Ge	Porayko, M	TN	244
Ge	Reddy, K	PA	239
Ge	Reuben, A	SC	244
Ge	Sass, D	PA	240
Ge	Schiano, T	NY	240
Ge	Shiffman, M	VA	245
Ge	Silverman, W	IA	250
Ge	Sorrell, M	NE	252
Ge	Te, H	IL	250
Ge	Tobias, H	NY	240
Ge	Vierling, J	TX	255
Ge	Younossi, Z	VA	245
Ge	Zaman, A	OR	258
PGe	Baker, S	NY	763
PGe	Baldridge, A	NJ	763
PGe	Benkov, K	NY	763
PGe	Bishop, W	IA	765
PGe	El-Youssef, M	MN	765
PGe	Hoffenberg, E	CO	767
PGe	Jonas, M	MA	762
PGe	McDiarmid, S	CA	769
PGe	Mittal, N	TX	768
PGe	Molleston, J	IN	766
PGe	Murray, K	WA	769
PGe	Narkewicz, M	CO	767
PGe	Novak, D	FL	765
PGe	Piccoli, D	PA	764
PGe	Schwarz, K	MD	764
PGe	Sokol, R	CO	767
PGe	Squires, R	PA	764
PGe	Suchy, F	CO	768
PGe	Ulshen, M	NC	765
PGe	Whitington, P	IL	767
S	Levi, J	FL	1106
S	Millis, J	IL	1117
S	Stiegmann, G	CO	1123

Liver Failure

Ge	Crippin, J	MO	247
Ge	Reuben, A	SC	244

Spec	Name	St	Pg
S	Klein, A	CA	1134
Liver Pathology			
Path	Appelman, H	MI	727
Path	Bhan, A	MA	718
Path	Crawford, J	NY	721
Path	Demetris, A	PA	721
Path	Ferrell, L	CA	732
Path	Govindarajan, S	CA	733
Path	Greenson, J	MI	728
Path	Hamilton, S	TX	730
Path	Kanel, G	CA	733
Path	Odze, R	MA	719
Path	Rashid, A	TX	731
Path	Sibley, R	CA	734
Liver Surgery			
PS	Karrer, F	CO	821
S	Aboulјoud, M	MI	1111
S	Halff, G	TX	1125
S	Johnson, L	DC	1094
Liver Surgery-Complex			
S	Reich, D	PA	1099
Liver Trauma			
S	Moore, E	CO	1122
Liver Tumors			
DR	Kruskal, J	MA	1007
Ge	Sorrell, M	NE	252
S	Billingsley, K	OR	1130
VIR	Johnson, M	IN	1030
VIR	Nemcek, A	IL	1031
Long QT Interval Syndrome			
CE	Waldo, A	OH	118
PCd	Ackerman, M	MN	752
Low Vision			
Oph	Sterns, G	NY	586
Lower Limb Arterial Disease			
VascS	Bandyk, D	CA	1230
VascS	Gloviczki, P	MN	1227
VascS	Howard, T	NE	1229
VascS	Kent, K	WI	1228
VascS	Mackey, W	MA	1221
VascS	Pevec, W	CA	1230
Lower Limb Reconstruction			
PlS	Attinger, C	DC	880
PlS	Wilkins, E	MI	897
Lower Limb Surgery in Children			
OrS	McCarthy, J	OH	643
Lung Cancer			
DR	Austin, J	NY	1008
DR	Black, W	NH	1007
DR	Chiles, C	NC	1013
DR	Erasmus, J	TX	1016
DR	Henschke, C	NY	1009
DR	Macmahon, H	IL	1015
DR	Patz, E	NC	1014
DR	Swensen, S	MN	1015
DR	White, C	MD	1012
DR	Yankelevitz, D	NY	1012
Hem	Gruenstein, S	NY	314
Hem	Schwartzberg, L	TN	320
Onc	Adelstein, D	OH	365
Onc	Aisner, J	NJ	337
Onc	Akerley, W	UT	375
Onc	Albain, K	IL	366
Onc	Algazy, K	PA	337
Onc	Antonia, S	FL	355
Onc	Argiris, A	TX	378
Onc	Axelrod, R	PA	338
Onc	Azzoli, C	MA	330
Onc	Belani, C	PA	338
Onc	Bitran, J	IL	366
Onc	Bonomi, P	IL	366
Onc	Bunn, P	CO	376
Onc	Carbone, D	OH	367
Onc	Chachoua, A	NY	339
Onc	Chapman, R	MI	367
Onc	Clamon, G	IA	367
Onc	Cohen, R	PA	340
Onc	Cohen, S	NY	340
Onc	Conry, R	AL	357
Onc	Crawford, J	NC	357
Onc	Dowlati, A	OH	368
Onc	Dunphy, F	NC	357
Onc	Edelman, M	NM	379
Onc	Einhorn, L	IN	368
Onc	Ettinger, D	MD	342
Onc	Figlin, R	CA	387
Onc	Fossella, F	TX	380
Onc	Gandara, D	CA	388
Onc	Garst, J	NC	358
Onc	Glisson, B	TX	380
Onc	Greco, F	TN	359
Onc	Hageboutros, A	NJ	344
Onc	Herbst, R	CT	332
Onc	Hoffman, P	IL	370
Onc	Hollister, D	CT	333
Onc	Hong, W	TX	380
Onc	Jahanzeb, M	FL	359
Onc	Johnson, B	MA	333
Onc	Kalemkerian, G	MI	370
Onc	Kelly, K	CA	389
Onc	Khuri, F	GA	359
Onc	Kies, M	TX	381
Onc	Koczywas, M	CA	389
Onc	Kressel, B	DC	346
Onc	Kris, M	NY	346
Onc	Langer, C	PA	346
Onc	Lilenbaum, R	CT	333
Onc	Lynch, T	CT	333
Onc	Martins, R	WA	389
Onc	Masters, G	DE	347
Onc	Miller, A	NC	361
Onc	Miller, D	KY	361
Onc	Natale, R	CA	390
Onc	Nissenblatt, M	NJ	348
Onc	O'Brien, T	OH	372
Onc	Oster, M	NY	349
Onc	Pao, W	TN	362
Onc	Pasmantier, M	NY	349
Onc	Perry, D	DC	350
Onc	Pisters, K	TX	382
Onc	Ready, N	NC	363
Onc	Reckamp, K	CA	391
Onc	Robert-Vizcarrondo, F	AL	363
Onc	Ross, H	AZ	383
Onc	Salgia, R	IL	373
Onc	Schiller, J	TX	383
Onc	Sherman, C	SC	363
Onc	Shin, D	GA	364
Onc	Simon, G	TX	383
Onc	Socinski, M	PA	351
Onc	Steen, P	ND	377
Onc	Stone, J	FL	364
Onc	Stoopler, M	NY	352
Onc	Strauss, G	MA	335
Onc	Taetle, R	AZ	383
Onc	Tester, W	PA	353
Onc	Thigpen, J	MS	364
Onc	Vinciguerra, V	NY	353
Onc	Vokes, E	IL	374
Onc	Wierman, A	NV	394
Path	Cagle, P	TX	730
Path	Hammar, S	WA	733
Path	Katzenstein, A	NY	722
Path	Koss, M	CA	733
Path	Moran, C	TX	730
Path	Myers, J	MI	728
Path	Travis, W	NY	724
Path	Yousem, S	PA	725
Pul	Alberts, W	FL	961
Pul	Cooper, W	VA	961
Pul	Garver, R	AL	962
Pul	Goldman, A	FL	962
Pul	Guidry, G	LA	969
Pul	Kern, J	CO	968
Pul	King, E	PA	957
Pul	Libby, D	NY	957
Pul	Maxfield, R	NY	958
Pul	Nader, D	OK	969
Pul	Silver, M	IL	966
Pul	Steinberg, H	NY	959
Pul	Sterman, D	PA	959
Pul	Unger, M	PA	960
RadRO	Beitler, J	GA	983
RadRO	Blackstock, A	NC	983
RadRO	Bogart, J	NY	978
RadRO	Bradley, J	MO	988
RadRO	Choi, N	MA	976
RadRO	Choy, H	TX	993

Spec	Name	St	Pg
RadRO	Cox, J	TX	993
RadRO	Emami, B	IL	989
RadRO	Greenberger, J	PA	980
RadRO	Hahn, S	PA	980
RadRO	Haraf, D	IL	989
RadRO	Hayman, J	MI	990
RadRO	Heimann, R	VT	976
RadRO	Jose, B	IN	990
RadRO	Kalnicki, S	NY	980
RadRO	Kestin, L	MI	990
RadRO	Komaki, R	TX	994
RadRO	Kudrimoti, M	KY	984
RadRO	Le, Q	CA	996
RadRO	Lewin, A	FL	985
RadRO	Marks, L	NC	985
RadRO	McGarry, R	KY	986
RadRO	Mehta, M	MD	981
RadRO	Movsas, B	MI	991
RadRO	Nori, D	NY	981
RadRO	Randolph-Jackson, P	DC	982
RadRO	Roach, M	CA	997
RadRO	Rosenman, J	NC	987
RadRO	Schiff, P	NY	982
RadRO	Schild, S	AZ	994
RadRO	Seung, S	OR	997
RadRO	Stevens, C	FL	987
RadRO	Streeter, O	CA	998
RadRO	Suntharalingam, M	MD	983
RadRO	Videtic, G	OH	992
RadRO	Werner-Wasik, M	PA	983
RadRO	Wilson, L	CT	978
T&CS	Altorki, N	NY	1150
T&CS	Baciewicz, F	MI	1167
T&CS	Bains, M	NY	1150
T&CS	Battafarano, R	MD	1150
T&CS	Bhora, F	NY	1151
T&CS	Brinckerhoff, L	MA	1146
T&CS	Bueno, R	MA	1146
T&CS	Cameron, R	CA	1177
T&CS	Cerfolio, R	AL	1161
T&CS	Colson, Y	MA	1146
T&CS	D'Amico, T	NC	1161
T&CS	Demmy, T	NY	1151
T&CS	Deschamps, C	MN	1168
T&CS	Downey, R	NY	1152
T&CS	Feins, R	NC	1162
T&CS	Ferguson, M	IL	1168
T&CS	Fernando, H	MA	1147
T&CS	Flores, R	NY	1152
T&CS	Friedberg, J	PA	1152
T&CS	Gaissert, H	MA	1147
T&CS	Gharagozloo, F	AZ	1174
T&CS	Ginsburg, M	NY	1153
T&CS	Grannis, F	CA	1178
T&CS	Handy, J	OR	1178
T&CS	Harpole, D	NC	1162
T&CS	Heitmiller, R	MD	1154
T&CS	Howington, J	IL	1168
T&CS	Iannettoni, M	IA	1169
T&CS	Jablons, D	CA	1179
T&CS	Johnstone, D	WI	1169
T&CS	Jones, D	NY	1154
T&CS	Kaiser, L	PA	1154
T&CS	Karwande, S	UT	1173
T&CS	Keenan, R	PA	1155
T&CS	Keller, S	NY	1155
T&CS	Kernstine, K	TX	1175
T&CS	Kiev, J	WV	1155
T&CS	Krellenstein, D	NY	1155
T&CS	Kucharczuk, J	PA	1155
T&CS	Landreneau, R	LA	1175
T&CS	Lanza, L	AZ	1175
T&CS	Lau, C	VA	1163
T&CS	Louie, B	WA	1179
T&CS	Marshall, M	DC	1156
T&CS	Mason, D	OH	1170
T&CS	Mathisen, D	MA	1147
T&CS	Meyers, B	MO	1170
T&CS	Miller, D	GA	1163
T&CS	Mitchell, J	CO	1173
T&CS	Moore, J	GA	1163
T&CS	Mullett, T	KY	1164
T&CS	Mulligan, M	WA	1180
T&CS	Naunheim, K	MO	1170
T&CS	Nesbitt, J	TN	1164
T&CS	Nguyen, D	FL	1164
T&CS	Oaks, T	NC	1164
T&CS	Orringer, M	MI	1170
T&CS	Orringer, M	MI	1170
T&CS	Park, B	NJ	1157
T&CS	Pass, H	NY	1157
T&CS	Patterson, G	MO	1171
T&CS	Pechet, T	PA	1157
T&CS	Pierson, R	MD	1157
T&CS	Port, J	NY	1157
T&CS	Putnam, J	TN	1165
T&CS	Robinson, L	FL	1165
T&CS	Roth, J	TX	1176
T&CS	Rusch, V	NY	1158
T&CS	Scott, W	PA	1158
T&CS	Shrager, J	CA	1180
T&CS	Smythe, W	TX	1176
T&CS	Soberman, M	MD	1158
T&CS	Swanson, S	MA	1148
T&CS	Swisher, S	TX	1176
T&CS	Vallieres, E	WA	1181
T&CS	Wain, J	MA	1149
T&CS	Watson, T	NY	1159
T&CS	Weigel, T	ME	1149
T&CS	Weiman, D	TN	1166
T&CS	Weksler, B	PA	1160
T&CS	Whyte, R	MA	1149
T&CS	Wood, D	WA	1181
T&CS	Wright, C	MA	1149
T&CS	Yang, S	MD	1160
T&CS	Zwischenberger, J	KY	1166
VIR	Hicks, M	TX	1032
VIR	Solomon, S	NY	1028

Lung Cancer (advanced)

H & PM	Davis, M	OH	407
Onc	Azzoli, C	MA	330

Lung Cancer in Women

Pul	Unger, M	PA	960

Lung Cancer-Early Detection

Pul	Mazzone, P	OH	966

Lung Disease

DR	Goodman, L	WI	1015
DR	Henschke, C	NY	1009
DR	Swensen, S	MN	1015
Pul	Christie, J	PA	956
Pul	Enelow, R	NH	954
Pul	Garver, R	AL	962
Pul	Greenberg, H	NY	957
Pul	Martinez, F	MI	966
Pul	Popovich, J	MI	966
Pul	Redlich, C	CT	955

Lung Disease in Newborns

NP	Adams, J	TX	453
NP	Davidson, D	NY	449
NP	Davis, J	MA	448
NP	Dennery, P	PA	449
NP	Ehrenkranz, R	CT	448
NP	Frantz, I	MA	448
NP	Garcia-Prats, J	TX	453
NP	Holtzman, R	NC	451
NP	Perlman, J	NY	450
NP	Van Marter, L	MA	448
PS	Latchaw, L	NH	814

Lung Disease in Newborns-Genetic

NP	Hamvas, A	MO	452
NP	Nogee, L	MD	450
NP	Whitsett, J	OH	452

Lung Disease-Complex

Pul	Kotloff, R	PA	957

Lung Injuries-Inhalation Induced

Pul	Boushey, H	CA	970

Lung Injuries-RSV related

PPul	Sallent, J	FL	808

Lung Injury-Neonatal

PPul	McGrath-Morrow, S	MD	807

Lung Injury/ARDS

Pul	Balk, R	IL	964

Lung Pathology

Spec	Name	St	Pg
Path	Ehya, H	PA	721
Path	Gupta, P	PA	721
Path	Myers, J	MI	728

Lung Pathology-Rare Tumors

Spec	Name	St	Pg
Path	Mark, E	MA	719

Lung Surgery

Spec	Name	St	Pg
T&CS	Cooper, J	PA	1151
T&CS	DeCamp, M	IL	1167
T&CS	Frazier, O	TX	1174
T&CS	Oaks, T	NC	1164
T&CS	Sanchez, J	MD	1158
T&CS	Thistlethwaite, P	CA	1180

Lupus Nephritis

Spec	Name	St	Pg
Nep	Appel, G	NY	458
Nep	Falk, R	NC	461
Nep	Holzman, L	PA	459
Nep	Rodby, R	IL	464
Nep	Salant, D	MA	458

Lupus/SLE

Spec	Name	St	Pg
D	Callen, J	KY	192
D	Fivenson, D	MI	195
D	Sontheimer, R	UT	198
D	Werth, V	PA	191
PA&I	Sullivan, K	PA	744
PRhu	Finkel, T	FL	812
PRhu	Haines, K	NJ	811
PRhu	Ilowite, N	NY	812
PRhu	Klein-Gitelman, M	IL	813
PRhu	Lehman, T	NY	812
PRhu	McCarthy, P	CT	811
PRhu	Onel, K	IL	813
PRhu	Schanberg, L	NC	812
PRhu	Sherry, D	PA	812
PRhu	Sills, E	MD	812
PRhu	Wagner-Weiner, L	IL	813
PRhu	Warren, R	SC	813
Rhu	Adams, E	IL	1064
Rhu	Allen, N	NC	1063
Rhu	Belmont, H	NY	1059
Rhu	Blume, R	NY	1059
Rhu	Bobrove, A	CA	1067
Rhu	Chatham, W	AL	1063
Rhu	Coblyn, J	MA	1058
Rhu	Crofford, L	TN	1063
Rhu	Curran, J	IL	1065
Rhu	Davis, W	LA	1066
Rhu	Ehresmann, G	CA	1067
Rhu	Gourley, M	MD	1060
Rhu	Katz, R	IL	1065
Rhu	Kimberly, R	AL	1064
Rhu	Lahita, R	NJ	1060
Rhu	Manzi, S	PA	1061
Rhu	Massarotti, E	MA	1058
Rhu	McCune, W	MI	1065
Rhu	Moder, K	MN	1066
Rhu	Moore, W	GA	1064
Rhu	Paget, S	NY	1061
Rhu	Peng, S	WA	1068
Rhu	Petri, M	MD	1061
Rhu	Rothenberg, R	MD	1062
Rhu	Salmon, J	NY	1062
Rhu	Sessoms, S	TX	1067
Rhu	Spiera, H	NY	1062
Rhu	Steen, V	DC	1062
Rhu	Tsokos, G	MA	1059
Rhu	Wallace, D	CA	1068
Rhu	Weinstein, A	DC	1063
Rhu	Wener, M	WA	1068
Rhu	Wofsy, D	CA	1068

Lupus/SLE in Menopause

Spec	Name	St	Pg
Rhu	Buyon, J	NY	1060

Lupus/SLE in Pregnancy

Spec	Name	St	Pg
MF	Druzin, M	CA	442
MF	Witter, F	MD	436
Rhu	Buyon, J	NY	1060

Lupus/SLE in Women

Spec	Name	St	Pg
Rhu	Manzi, S	PA	1061

Lyme Disease

Spec	Name	St	Pg
Inf	Auwaerter, P	MD	412
Inf	Louie, E	NY	414
Inf	Perlman, D	NY	414
Inf	Wormser, G	NY	415
Inf	Yancovitz, S	NY	415
N	Coyle, P	NY	514
N	Logigian, E	NY	518
N	Petito, F	NY	520
PInf	Andiman, W	CT	792
PInf	Christenson, J	IN	795
PInf	Durbin, W	MA	792
PInf	Krilov, L	NY	793
PInf	Shapiro, E	CT	793
PRhu	Ilowite, N	NY	812
Rhu	Magid, S	NY	1061
Rhu	Schoen, R	CT	1058
Rhu	Shadick, N	MA	1059
Rhu	Simms, R	MA	1059
Rhu	Weinstein, A	DC	1063

Lyme Disease-Neuro Complications

Spec	Name	St	Pg
Psyc	Fallon, B	NY	924

Lymph Node Pathology

Spec	Name	St	Pg
Path	Arber, D	CA	731
Path	Cote, R	FL	725
Path	Foucar, M	NM	730
Path	Kurtin, P	MN	728
Path	Orazi, A	NY	723

Lymphangioleiomyomatosis(LAM)

Spec	Name	St	Pg
Pul	Ahya, V	PA	956
Pul	Kotloff, R	PA	957
Pul	Lynch, J	CA	971

Lymphatic Malformations-Head & Neck

Spec	Name	St	Pg
PO	Friedman, E	TX	805
PO	McGill, T	MA	801

Lymphedema

Spec	Name	St	Pg
PMR	Cheville, A	MN	867
PMR	DePompolo, R	MN	868
PMR	Feldman, J	IL	868
PMR	Francis, K	NJ	864
PMR	King, R	GA	866
PMR	Richter, E	CT	862
PMR	Schwartz, L	PA	865
PMR	Stewart, P	AL	867
S	Sener, S	CA	1137

Lymphoma

Spec	Name	St	Pg
Hem	Baron, J	IL	320
Hem	Blaustein, A	FL	318
Hem	Blum, K	OH	321
Hem	Cooper, B	TX	326
Hem	Damon, L	CA	327
Hem	Djulbegovic, B	FL	319
Hem	Emanuel, P	AR	326
Hem	Forman, S	CA	328
Hem	Goldberg, J	PA	314
Hem	Gregory, S	IL	322
Hem	Habermann, T	MN	322
Hem	Kempin, S	NY	315
Hem	Levine, A	CA	328
Hem	Lill, M	CA	328
Hem	Lind, S	CO	324
Hem	Marks, S	PA	315
Hem	Maziarz, R	OR	329
Hem	Mears, J	NY	315
Hem	Mitchell, B	CA	329
Hem	Nademanee, A	CA	329
Hem	Petersdorf, S	WA	329
Hem	Porcu, P	OH	323
Hem	Porter, D	PA	316
Hem	Rai, K	NY	316
Hem	Raphael, B	NY	316
Hem	Rapoport, A	MD	316
Hem	Rosenblatt, J	FL	320
Hem	Savage, D	NY	316
Hem	Saven, A	CA	329
Hem	Schuster, S	PA	317
Hem	Sokol, L	FL	320
Hem	Strair, R	NJ	317
Hem	Strauss, J	TX	327
Hem	Van Besien, K	NY	318

Spec	Name	St	Pg
Hem	Vose, J	NE	325
Hem	Williams, M	VA	320
Hem	Wisch, N	NY	318
Onc	Advani, R	CA	384
Onc	Ambinder, R	MD	337
Onc	Armitage, J	NE	375
Onc	Attas, L	NJ	338
Onc	Beatty, P	MT	376
Onc	Bierman, P	NE	376
Onc	Camoriano, J	AZ	379
Onc	Chao, N	NC	357
Onc	Chitambar, C	WI	367
Onc	Cohen, S	NY	340
Onc	Dakhil, S	KS	376
Onc	Fisher, R	PA	342
Onc	Flinn, !	TN	357
Onc	Forero-Torres, A	AL	358
Onc	Freedman, A	MA	331
Onc	Friedberg, J	NY	343
Onc	Glaspy, J	CA	388
Onc	Goy, A	NJ	343
Onc	Grossbard, M	NY	344
Onc	Hochberg, E	MA	332
Onc	Hurd, D	NC	359
Onc	Jillella, A	GA	359
Onc	Kaminski, M	MI	370
Onc	Kaplan, L	CA	389
Onc	Kwak, L	TX	381
Onc	Lossos, I	FL	360
Onc	Lynch, J	FL	361
Onc	Maloney, D	WA	389
Onc	Miller, T	AZ	381
Onc	Northfelt, D	AZ	381
Onc	Northfelt, D	AZ	381
Onc	O'Brien, S	TX	382
Onc	Offit, K	NY	349
Onc	Ozer, H	IL	372
Onc	Pasmantier, M	NY	349
Onc	Peterson, B	MN	372
Onc	Pohlman, B	OH	372
Onc	Press, O	WA	391
Onc	Romaguera, J	TX	382
Onc	Saiki, J	NM	383
Onc	Schiffer, C	MI	373
Onc	Schwartz, B	MN	373
Onc	Schwartz, M	FL	363
Onc	Serody, J	NC	363
Onc	Shea, T	NC	363
Onc	Smith, M	OH	374
Onc	Soiffer, R	MA	335
Onc	Sotomayor, E	FL	364
Onc	Straus, D	NY	352
Onc	Strenger, R	RI	335
Onc	Sweetenham, J	UT	378
Onc	Weiner, G	IA	375
Onc	Wierman, A	NV	394
Onc	Wilson, W	MD	354
Onc	Wingard, J	FL	365
Onc	Yunus, F	TN	365
Onc	Zelenetz, A	NY	354
Path	Banks, P	NC	725
Path	Chang, K	CA	732
Path	Harris, N	MA	718
Path	Kinney, M	TX	730
Path	Kurtin, P	MN	728
Path	Nathwani, B	CA	734
Path	Swerdlow, S	PA	724
Path	Warnke, R	CA	734
Path	Weisenburger, D	CA	735
PHO	Aledo, A	NY	771
PHO	Andrews, R	WA	789
PHO	Angiolillo, A	DC	771
PHO	Brecher, M	NY	771
PHO	Cairo, M	NY	772
PHO	Castellino, S	NC	778
PHO	Fallon, R	IN	783
PHO	Goldman, S	TX	788
PHO	Hayani, A	IL	783
PHO	Hutchinson, R	MI	784
PHO	Johnston, J	GA	779
PHO	Link, M	CA	790
PHO	Marcus, J	NY	775
PHO	Parker, R	NY	776
PHO	Pui, C	TN	780
PHO	Razzouk, B	IN	785
PHO	Small, D	MD	776
PHO	Wayne, A	CA	792
PHO	Weiner, M	NY	777
RadRO	Abrams, R	IL	988
RadRO	Constine, L	NY	978
RadRO	Goodman, R	NJ	980
RadRO	Hoppe, R	CA	995
RadRO	Lee, C	MN	990
RadRO	Macklis, R	OH	991
RadRO	Markoe, A	FL	985
RadRO	McGarry, R	KY	986
RadRO	Mendenhall, N	FL	986
RadRO	Mittal, B	IL	991
RadRO	Nicolaou, N	PA	981
RadRO	Park, C	CA	996
RadRO	Prosnitz, L	NC	986
RadRO	Roberts, K	CT	977
RadRO	Russell, K	WA	997
RadRO	Song, S	VA	987
RadRO	Stea, B	AZ	995
RadRO	Tripuraneni, P	CA	998
RadRO	Wolfson, A	FL	988
RadRO	Yahalom, J	NY	983

Lymphoma Consultation

Onc	DeVita, V	CT	331

Lymphoma, Non-Hodgkin's

Hem	Blum, K	OH	321
Hem	Gordon, L	IL	321
Hem	Kipps, T	CA	328
Hem	Komrokji, R	FL	319
Hem	Nand, S	IL	323
Hem	Porcu, P	OH	323
Hem	Winter, J	IL	324
NuM	Lamonica, D	NY	554
NuM	Podoloff, D	TX	557
NuM	Wiseman, G	MN	556
Onc	Bishop, M	IL	366
Onc	Gerson, S	OH	369
Onc	Glick, J	PA	343
Onc	Horwitz, S	NY	345
Onc	Lynch, J	FL	361
Onc	Miller, T	AZ	381
Onc	Moore, J	NC	361
Onc	O'Connor, O	NY	348
Onc	Orlowski, R	TX	382
Onc	Pohlman, B	OH	372
PHO	Billett, A	MA	769
PHO	Laver, J	NY	775
PHO	Weiner, M	NY	777
PHO	Weinstein, H	MA	771

Lymphoma-Ocular (eye)

Oph	Gigantelli, J	NE	601

Lymphoma-Second Opinion

Onc	Canellos, G	MA	330

Lymphomas-Rare

Hem	Blum, K	OH	321
Hem	Rosenblatt, J	FL	320
Onc	Lossos, I	FL	360

Lymphomatoid Granulomatosis

Onc	Hochberg, E	MA	332

Lysosomal Diseases

CG	Andersson, H	LA	161
CG	Burton, B	IL	160
CG	Charrow, J	IL	160
CG	Desnick, R	NY	157

M

Macular Degeneration

Oph	Blumenkranz, M	CA	604
Oph	Bressler, S	MD	576
Oph	Brown, G	PA	576
Oph	Brucker, A	PA	576
Oph	Davis, J	FL	587
Oph	Del Priore, L	SC	588
Oph	Edwards, P	MI	594
Oph	Friberg, T	PA	578
Oph	Gentile, R	NY	579
Oph	Gorin, M	CA	606
Oph	Handa, J	MD	579
Oph	Hariprasad, S	IL	595
Oph	Ho, A	PA	580
Oph	Lewis, R	TX	602
Oph	Lim, J	IL	597
Oph	Maguire, J	PA	581
Oph	Meredith, T	NC	590

Specialty & Special Expertise Index

Spec	Name	St	Pg
Oph	Miller, J	MA	574
Oph	Murray, T	FL	590
Oph	Nussbaum, J	GA	590
Oph	Olsen, T	GA	590
Oph	Petersen, M	OH	598
Oph	Prenner, J	NJ	583
Oph	Puliafito, C	CA	608
Oph	Regillo, C	PA	583
Oph	Sadda, S	CA	608
Oph	Schwartz, S	CA	609
Oph	Spaide, R	NY	585
Oph	Sternberg, P	TN	591
Oph	Vander, J	PA	586
Oph	Walsh, J	NY	586
Oph	Williams, G	MI	600

Macular Disease/Degeneration

Spec	Name	St	Pg
Oph	Abrams, G	MI	593
Oph	Barile, G	NY	576
Oph	Chang, S	NY	577
Oph	Flynn, H	FL	588
Oph	Fuchs, W	NY	578
Oph	Grossniklaus, H	GA	588
Oph	Mieler, W	IL	597
Oph	Muldoon, T	NY	582
Oph	Rosenfeld, P	FL	591
Oph	Schiff, W	NY	584
Oph	Shabto, U	NY	584
Oph	Yannuzzi, L	NY	586

Malabsorption Syndrome

Spec	Name	St	Pg
Ge	Green, P	NY	235
Ge	Seidner, D	TN	245
Ge	Semrad, C	IL	250
PGe	Baker, R	NY	763
PGe	Hill, I	OH	766
PGe	Oliva-Hemker, M	MD	763

Malaria

Spec	Name	St	Pg
Inf	Trenholme, G	IL	419
Inf	Wallace, M	FL	417

Mammography

Spec	Name	St	Pg
DR	Baker, J	NC	1013
DR	Copit, D	PA	1008
DR	Dershaw, D	NY	1009
DR	Evers, K	PA	1009
DR	Helvie, M	MI	1015
DR	Huynh, P	TX	1016
DR	Jackson, V	IN	1015
DR	Lehman, C	WA	1018
DR	Mitnick, J	NY	1010
DR	Monsees, B	MO	1015
DR	Parikh, J	WA	1018
DR	Ulissey, M	WA	1019

Mantle Cell Lymphoma

Spec	Name	St	Pg
Hem	Gordon, L	IL	321
Hem	Williams, M	VA	320

Marfan's Syndrome

Spec	Name	St	Pg
CG	Bialer, M	NY	157
CG	Burton, B	IL	160
CG	Davis, J	NY	157
CG	Marion, R	NY	158
CG	Pauker, S	MA	156
CG	Pyeritz, R	PA	158
Cv	Braverman, A	MO	100
Cv	Devereux, R	NY	92
PCd	Gelb, B	NY	748
PCd	Hardin, J	IL	753
PCd	Mahony, L	TX	754
PCd	Moodie, D	TX	754
T&CS	Coselli, J	TX	1173
T&CS	Girardi, L	NY	1153
T&CS	Svensson, L	OH	1171

Marital/Family/Sex Therapy

Spec	Name	St	Pg
Psyc	Fox, G	IL	929
Psyc	Giustra, L	GA	928
Psyc	Manevitz, A	NY	925
Psyc	Sadock, V	NY	927

Mast Cell Diseases

Spec	Name	St	Pg
A&I	Castells, M	MA	80
A&I	Lewis, J	AZ	85
A&I	Metcalfe, D	MD	81

Maternal & Fetal Medicine

Spec	Name	St	Pg
MF	Abuhamad, A	VA	436
MF	Adam, K	TX	440
MF	Adashek, J	NV	441
MF	Andrews, W	AL	436
MF	Bahado-Singh, R	MI	437
MF	Baker, E	NH	432
MF	Bartelsmeyer, J	MO	438
MF	Benedetti, T	WA	442
MF	Berkowitz, R	NY	433
MF	Blakemore, K	MD	433
MF	Caritis, S	PA	433
MF	Carr, S	RI	432
MF	Cheng, E	WA	442
MF	Chmait, R	CA	442
MF	Cohen, A	PA	434
MF	Copel, J	CT	432
MF	D'Alton, M	NY	434
MF	Dooley, S	IL	438
MF	Druzin, M	CA	442
MF	Duff, W	FL	436
MF	Dugoff, L	PA	434
MF	Eddleman, K	NY	434
MF	Ferguson, J	VA	436
MF	Fox, H	MD	434
MF	Genc, M	NY	434
MF	Gibbs, R	CO	440
MF	Goldberg, J	CA	442
MF	Gonik, B	MI	438
MF	Goodman, J	IL	438
MF	Grandis, A	NC	436
MF	Gravett, M	WA	442
MF	Greene, M	MA	432
MF	Grunebaum, A	NY	434
MF	Hankins, G	TX	441
MF	Heyl, P	KY	436
MF	Hibbard, J	IL	438
MF	Hussey, M	IL	438
MF	Ismail, M	IL	438
MF	Johnson, T	MI	438
MF	Kelly, T	CA	442
MF	Koos, B	CA	443
MF	Kuller, J	NC	437
MF	Landers, D	MN	439
MF	Landon, M	OH	439
MF	Landy, H	DC	435
MF	Leslie, K	IA	439
MF	MacGregor, S	IL	439
MF	Macones, G	MO	439
MF	Mari, G	TN	437
MF	Mastrobattista, J	TX	441
MF	McLaren, R	VA	437
MF	Moore, T	CA	443
MF	Nies, B	VA	437
MF	Norwitz, E	MA	432
MF	Paidas, M	CT	432
MF	Parry, S	PA	435
MF	Philipson, E	OH	439
MF	Pinckert, T	MD	435
MF	Plante, L	PA	435
MF	Platt, L	CA	443
MF	Pridjian, G	LA	441
MF	Reed, K	AZ	441
MF	Repke, J	PA	435
MF	Riley, L	MA	433
MF	Robertson, P	CA	443
MF	Robichaux, A	LA	441
MF	Robinson, J	MA	433
MF	Saade, G	TX	441
MF	Samuels, P	OH	439
MF	Silver, R	IL	439
MF	Socol, M	IL	440
MF	Strassner, H	IL	440
MF	Tabsh, K	CA	443
MF	Thomas, R	PA	435
MF	Thorp, J	NC	437
MF	Tomich, P	NE	440
MF	Treadwell, M	MI	440
MF	Van Dorsten, J	SC	437
MF	Wapner, R	NY	435
MF	Wenstrom, K	RI	433
MF	Wilkins-Haug, L	MA	433
MF	Winn, H	MO	440
MF	Witter, F	MD	436
MF	Zalud, I	HI	443
ObG	Corteville, J	OH	564
ObG	Ordorica, S	NY	561

Maxillofacial & Craniofacial Surgery

Spec	Name	St	Pg
PIS	Gruss, J	WA	902
PIS	Staffenberg, D	NY	887

Maxillofacial Surgery

Spec	Name	St	Pg
Oto	Chowdhury, K	CO	689
PlS	Burstein, F	GA	889
PlS	Deleyiannis, F	CO	897
PlS	Napoli, J	DE	885
PlS	Papay, F	OH	895
PlS	Polley, J	IL	896
PlS	Posnick, J	MD	885
PlS	Taub, P	NY	887
PlS	Urata, M	CA	905
PlS	Wolfe, S	FL	892
PlS	Zins, J	OH	897

Maze Procedure for Atrial Fibrillation

Spec	Name	St	Pg
T&CS	Argenziano, M	NY	1150
T&CS	Bridges, C	NC	1161
T&CS	Caskey, M	AZ	1173
T&CS	DeFilippi, V	CA	1178
T&CS	Fullerton, D	CO	1172
T&CS	Hashim, S	CT	1147
T&CS	Schaff, H	MN	1171
T&CS	Vlahakes, G	MA	1148

McCune-Albright Syndrome

Spec	Name	St	Pg
EDM	Kopp, P	IL	220

Mechanical Ventilation

Spec	Name	St	Pg
PCCM	Easley, R	TX	755
PCCM	Perez Fontan, J	TX	756
PCCM	Thompson, A	PA	755
Pul	Celli, B	MA	954
Pul	Harman, E	FL	962
Pul	Marini, J	MN	965
Pul	Tobin, M	IL	967

Mediastinal Fibrosis

Spec	Name	St	Pg
Pul	Loyd, J	TN	963

Mediastinal Tumors

Spec	Name	St	Pg
Onc	Kris, M	NY	346
Path	Moran, C	TX	730
Path	Suster, S	WI	729
T&CS	Kaiser, L	PA	1154
T&CS	Keenan, R	PA	1155
T&CS	Keller, S	NY	1155
T&CS	Kucharczuk, J	PA	1155
T&CS	Orringer, M	MI	1170
T&CS	Park, B	NJ	1157
T&CS	Scott, W	PA	1158
T&CS	Vallieres, E	WA	1181

Medical Oncology

Spec	Name	St	Pg
Onc	Abbruzzese, J	TX	378
Onc	Aboulafia, D	WA	384
Onc	Abraham, J	OH	365
Onc	Abrams, D	CA	384
Onc	Adelstein, D	OH	365
Onc	Advani, R	CA	384
Onc	Aghajanian, C	NY	336
Onc	Ahlgren, J	DC	336
Onc	Ahmann, F	AZ	378
Onc	Aisner, J	NJ	337
Onc	Ajani, J	TX	378
Onc	Akerley, W	UT	375
Onc	Albain, K	IL	366
Onc	Albertini, M	WI	366
Onc	Alberts, D	AZ	378
Onc	Algazy, K	PA	337
Onc	Ambinder, R	MD	337
Onc	Anthony, L	KY	354
Onc	Antin, J	MA	330
Onc	Antonia, S	FL	355
Onc	Appelbaum, F	WA	385
Onc	Argiris, A	TX	378
Onc	Arlen, P	MD	337
Onc	Armitage, J	NE	375
Onc	Armstrong, D	MD	337
Onc	Arteaga, C	TN	355
Onc	Arun, B	TX	378
Onc	Astrow, A	NY	337
Onc	Atkins, M	DC	337
Onc	Attas, L	NJ	338
Onc	Audeh, M	CA	385
Onc	Axelrod, R	PA	338
Onc	Azzoli, C	MA	330
Onc	Back, A	WA	385
Onc	Bajorin, D	NY	338
Onc	Balducci, L	FL	355
Onc	Ball, E	CA	385
Onc	Bashevkin, M	NY	338
Onc	Beatty, P	MT	376
Onc	Beer, T	OR	385
Onc	Belani, C	PA	338
Onc	Belenkov, E	NY	338
Onc	Benedetto, P	FL	355
Onc	Benjamin, R	TX	379
Onc	Bensinger, W	WA	385
Onc	Benson, A	IL	366
Onc	Bergsagel, P	AZ	379
Onc	Berlin, J	TN	355
Onc	Bernard, S	NC	355
Onc	Berry, J	CA	385
Onc	Bierman, P	NE	376
Onc	Biggs, D	DE	338
Onc	Birrer, M	MA	330
Onc	Bishop, M	IL	366
Onc	Bitran, J	IL	366
Onc	Blackwell, K	NC	355
Onc	Blobe, G	NC	355
Onc	Bolger, G	AL	356
Onc	Bolwell, B	OH	366
Onc	Bonomi, P	IL	366
Onc	Bosl, G	NY	338
Onc	Boston, B	TN	356
Onc	Brenin, C	VA	356
Onc	Brentjens, R	NY	339
Onc	Brescia, F	SC	356
Onc	Brockstein, B	IL	367
Onc	Bruera, E	TX	379
Onc	Brufsky, A	PA	339
Onc	Bubley, G	MA	330
Onc	Buckner, J	MN	367
Onc	Budd, G	OH	367
Onc	Bunn, P	CO	376
Onc	Burris, H	TN	356
Onc	Burstein, H	MA	330
Onc	Buys, S	UT	376
Onc	Buzdar, A	TX	379
Onc	Camoriano, J	AZ	379
Onc	Canellos, G	MA	330
Onc	Carabasi, M	PA	339
Onc	Carbone, D	OH	367
Onc	Carducci, M	MD	339
Onc	Carey, L	NC	356
Onc	Carpenter, J	AL	356
Onc	Celano, P	MD	339
Onc	Chachoua, A	NY	339
Onc	Chanan-Khan, A	FL	356
Onc	Chang, J	TX	379
Onc	Chang, S	CA	385
Onc	Chao, N	NC	357
Onc	Chap, L	CA	386
Onc	Chapman, P	NY	339
Onc	Chapman, R	MI	367
Onc	Chew, H	CA	386
Onc	Chitambar, C	WI	367
Onc	Chlebowski, R	CA	386
Onc	Chow, W	CA	386
Onc	Chu, E	PA	339
Onc	Chung, K	SC	357
Onc	Clamon, G	IA	367
Onc	Clark, J	IL	367
Onc	Claxton, D	PA	340
Onc	Cleary, J	WI	368
Onc	Clinton, S	OH	368
Onc	Cobleigh, M	IL	368
Onc	Cohen, G	MD	340
Onc	Cohen, P	DC	340
Onc	Cohen, R	PA	340
Onc	Cohen, S	NY	340
Onc	Coleman, M	NY	340
Onc	Colon-Otero, G	FL	357
Onc	Come, S	MA	331
Onc	Conry, R	AL	357
Onc	Cooney, K	MI	368
Onc	Cowan, K	NE	376
Onc	Crawford, J	NC	357
Onc	Cristofanilli, M	PA	340
Onc	Crocenzi, T	OR	386
Onc	Cullen, K	MD	340
Onc	Czuczman, M	NY	341
Onc	Dakhil, S	KS	376
Onc	Daly, M	PA	341
Onc	Daud, A	CA	386
Onc	Dawson, N	DC	341
Onc	De Simone, P	KY	357
Onc	Deeg, H	WA	386
Onc	DeVita, V	CT	331
Onc	Dickler, M	NY	341
Onc	DiPaola, R	NJ	341
Onc	Disis, M	WA	386
Onc	Dizon, D	MA	331

Spec	Name	St	Pg
Onc	Domchek, S	PA	341
Onc	Donehower, R	MD	341
Onc	Doroshow, J	MD	341
Onc	Dowlati, A	OH	368
Onc	Dreicer, R	OH	368
Onc	Druker, B	OR	387
Onc	Dunphy, F	NC	357
Onc	Eckhardt, S	CO	376
Onc	Edelman, M	NM	379
Onc	Einhorn, L	IN	368
Onc	Eisenberger, M	MD	342
Onc	Elias, A	CO	376
Onc	Ellis, G	WA	387
Onc	Ellis, M	MO	368
Onc	Emens, L	MD	342
Onc	Engstrom, P	PA	342
Onc	Ensminger, W	MI	369
Onc	Erban, J	MA	331
Onc	Ernstoff, M	NH	331
Onc	Estey, E	WA	387
Onc	Ettinger, D	MD	342
Onc	Fabian, C	KS	377
Onc	Fakih, M	CA	387
Onc	Fay, J	TX	379
Onc	Figlin, R	CA	387
Onc	Fine, H	NY	342
Onc	Fine, R	NY	342
Onc	Fisher, G	CA	387
Onc	Fisher, R	PA	342
Onc	Fitch, T	AZ	380
Onc	Flaherty, K	MA	331
Onc	Fleming, G	IL	369
Onc	Flinn, I	TN	357
Onc	Flomenberg, N	PA	342
Onc	Flynn, P	MN	369
Onc	Forastiere, A	MD	343
Onc	Ford, J	CA	387
Onc	Forero-Torres, A	AL	358
Onc	Forscher, C	CA	387
Onc	Foss, F	CT	331
Onc	Fossella, F	TX	380
Onc	Fox, K	PA	343
Onc	Fracasso, P	VA	358
Onc	Freedman, A	MA	331
Onc	Friedberg, J	NY	343
Onc	Friedman, H	NC	358
Onc	Fuchs, C	MA	332
Onc	Gabrilove, J	NY	343
Onc	Gandara, D	CA	388
Onc	Ganz, P	CA	388
Onc	Garber, J	MA	332
Onc	Garnick, M	MA	332
Onc	Garst, J	NC	358
Onc	Gaynor, E	IL	369
Onc	Gelmann, E	NY	343
Onc	George, D	NC	358
Onc	George, S	MA	332
Onc	Gerson, S	OH	369
Onc	Geyer, C	VA	358
Onc	Glaspy, J	CA	388
Onc	Glick, J	PA	343
Onc	Glisson, B	TX	380
Onc	Glode, L	CO	377
Onc	Godley, P	NC	358
Onc	Gold, P	WA	388
Onc	Goldberg, R	OH	369
Onc	Goldstein, L	PA	343
Onc	Goy, A	NJ	343
Onc	Gradishar, W	IL	369
Onc	Graham, M	NC	358
Onc	Gralow, J	WA	388
Onc	Grana, G	NJ	344
Onc	Greco, F	TN	359
Onc	Grem, J	NE	377
Onc	Grosh, W	VA	359
Onc	Grossbard, M	NY	344
Onc	Grossman, S	MD	344
Onc	Gruber, S	CA	388
Onc	Gulley, J	MD	344
Onc	Haas, N	PA	344
Onc	Haddad, R	MA	332
Onc	Hageboutros, A	NJ	344
Onc	Haley, B	TX	380
Onc	Hande, K	TN	359
Onc	Harris, L	OH	369
Onc	Hauke, R	NE	377
Onc	Hayes, D	MI	370
Onc	Henry, D	PA	344
Onc	Herbst, R	CT	332
Onc	Higano, C	WA	388
Onc	Himelstein, A	DE	344
Onc	Hochberg, E	MA	332
Onc	Hochster, H	CT	332
Onc	Hoffman, P	IL	370
Onc	Hogan, T	WV	345
Onc	Holcombe, R	NY	345
Onc	Holland, J	NY	345
Onc	Hollister, D	CT	333
Onc	Hong, W	TX	380
Onc	Hortobagyi, G	TX	380
Onc	Horwitz, S	NY	345
Onc	Hudis, C	NY	345
Onc	Hurd, D	NC	359
Onc	Hussain, M	MI	370
Onc	Hutchins, L	AR	380
Onc	Hwu, P	TX	380
Onc	Ilson, D	NY	345
Onc	Ingle, J	MN	370
Onc	Isaacs, C	DC	345
Onc	Jacobs, C	CA	388
Onc	Jahanzeb, M	FL	359
Onc	Jillella, A	GA	359
Onc	Johnson, B	MA	333
Onc	Jonasch, E	TX	381
Onc	Kalaycio, M	OH	370
Onc	Kalemkerian, G	MI	370
Onc	Kaminski, M	MI	370
Onc	Kane, M	CO	377
Onc	Kantoff, P	MA	333
Onc	Kaplan, L	CA	389
Onc	Kaufman, P	NH	333
Onc	Kelly, K	CA	389
Onc	Kelly, W	PA	345
Onc	Kelsen, D	NY	346
Onc	Kemeny, N	NY	346
Onc	Khuri, F	GA	359
Onc	Kies, M	TX	381
Onc	Kindler, H	IL	370
Onc	Kirkwood, J	PA	346
Onc	Koczywas, M	CA	389
Onc	Kohn, E	MD	346
Onc	Kraft, A	SC	359
Onc	Kressel, B	DC	346
Onc	Kris, M	NY	346
Onc	Krishnamurthi, S	OH	371
Onc	Kucuk, O	GA	360
Onc	Kuzel, T	IL	371
Onc	Kwak, L	TX	381
Onc	Lacy, J	CT	333
Onc	Laheru, D	MD	346
Onc	Langer, C	PA	346
Onc	Lawson, D	GA	360
Onc	Lazarus, H	OH	371
Onc	Legare, R	RI	333
Onc	Leighton, J	PA	347
Onc	Leong, L	CA	389
Onc	Lesser, G	NC	360
Onc	Levine, E	NY	347
Onc	Lilenbaum, R	CT	333
Onc	Lim, D	CA	389
Onc	Limentani, S	NC	360
Onc	Lippman, M	FL	360
Onc	List, A	FL	360
Onc	Livingston, R	AZ	381
Onc	Loehrer, P	IN	371
Onc	Logie, K	IN	371
Onc	Logothetis, C	TX	381
Onc	Loprinzi, C	MN	371
Onc	Lossos, I	FL	360
Onc	Lutzky, J	FL	360
Onc	Lyckholm, L	VA	361
Onc	Lyman, G	NC	361
Onc	Lynch, J	FL	361
Onc	Lynch, T	CT	333
Onc	Makhoul, I	AR	381
Onc	Maki, R	NY	347
Onc	Maloney, D	WA	389
Onc	Marcom, P	NC	361
Onc	Margolin, K	WA	389
Onc	Markowitz, S	OH	371
Onc	Marshall, J	DC	347
Onc	Martins, R	WA	389
Onc	Masters, G	DE	347
Onc	Mathew, P	MA	334
Onc	Matulonis, U	MA	334
Onc	Mayer, R	MA	334
Onc	McClay, E	CA	390
Onc	McGuire, W	VA	361
Onc	Meropol, N	OH	371
Onc	Messersmith, W	CO	377
Onc	Meyskens, F	CA	390
Onc	Miller, A	NC	361
Onc	Miller, D	KY	361
Onc	Miller, T	AZ	381
Onc	Mintzer, D	PA	347
Onc	Mitsuyasu, R	CA	390
Onc	Moore, A	NY	347
Onc	Moore, J	NC	361
Onc	Morgan, D	TN	362

Spec	Name	St	Pg
Onc	Morgan, R	CA	390
Onc	Morginstin, M	PA	347
Onc	Mortimer, J	CA	390
Onc	Motzer, R	NY	348
Onc	Muggia, F	NY	348
Onc	Muss, H	NC	362
Onc	Nabell, L	AL	362
Onc	Nanus, D	NY	348
Onc	Natale, R	CA	390
Onc	Nissenblatt, M	NJ	348
Onc	Northfelt, D	AZ	381
Onc	Norton, L	NY	348
Onc	O'Brien, S	TX	382
Onc	O'Brien, T	OH	372
Onc	O'Connor, O	NY	348
Onc	O'Regan, R	GA	362
Onc	O'Reilly, E	NY	348
Onc	O'Shaughnessy, J	TX	382
Onc	Offit, K	NY	349
Onc	Oh, W	NY	349
Onc	Olopade, O	IL	372
Onc	Oratz, R	NY	349
Onc	Orlowski, R	TX	382
Onc	Osborne, C	TX	382
Onc	Oster, M	NY	349
Onc	Ozer, H	IL	372
Onc	Pao, W	TN	362
Onc	Parker, B	CA	390
Onc	Parnes, H	MD	349
Onc	Pasche, B	AL	362
Onc	Pasmantier, M	NY	349
Onc	Patel, S	TX	382
Onc	Patt, Y	NM	382
Onc	Pavlick, A	NY	349
Onc	Peace, D	IL	372
Onc	Pecora, A	NJ	349
Onc	Peereboom, D	OH	372
Onc	Pegram, M	CA	390
Onc	Perez, E	FL	362
Onc	Perry, D	DC	350
Onc	Peterson, B	MN	372
Onc	Petruska, P	MO	372
Onc	Petrylak, D	CT	334
Onc	Pfister, D	NY	350
Onc	Picozzi, V	WA	391
Onc	Pienta, K	MD	350
Onc	Pinto, H	CA	391
Onc	Pisters, K	TX	382
Onc	Pohlman, B	OH	372
Onc	Posey, J	AL	362
Onc	Posner, M	NY	350
Onc	Prados, M	CA	391
Onc	Press, O	WA	391
Onc	Pusztai, L	CT	334
Onc	Quinn, D	CA	391
Onc	Raptis, G	NY	350
Onc	Ratain, M	IL	373
Onc	Ready, N	NC	363
Onc	Reckamp, K	CA	391
Onc	Reid, T	CA	391
Onc	Remick, S	WV	350
Onc	Richards, J	IL	373
Onc	Robert, N	VA	363
Onc	Robert-Vizcarrondo, F	AL	363
Onc	Romaguera, J	TX	382
Onc	Romond, E	KY	363
Onc	Rosen, S	IL	373
Onc	Rosove, M	CA	391
Onc	Ross, H	AZ	383
Onc	Roth, B	MO	373
Onc	Ruggiero, J	NY	350
Onc	Rugo, H	CA	392
Onc	Russell, C	CA	392
Onc	Ryan, D	MA	334
Onc	Saif, M	MA	334
Onc	Saiki, J	NM	383
Onc	Salgia, R	IL	373
Onc	Saltz, L	NY	350
Onc	Samlowski, W	NV	392
Onc	Samuels, B	ID	377
Onc	Scheinberg, D	NY	351
Onc	Scher, H	NY	351
Onc	Schiffer, C	MI	373
Onc	Schilder, R	PA	351
Onc	Schiller, J	TX	383
Onc	Schnipper, L	MA	334
Onc	Schuchter, L	PA	351
Onc	Schwartz, B	MN	373
Onc	Schwartz, M	FL	363
Onc	Scudder, S	CA	392
Onc	Serody, J	NC	363
Onc	Shapiro, C	OH	373
Onc	Shea, T	NC	363
Onc	Sherman, C	SC	363
Onc	Shields, P	OH	374
Onc	Shin, D	GA	364
Onc	Shulman, L	MA	335
Onc	Silver, S	MI	374
Onc	Silverman, L	NY	351
Onc	Silverman, P	OH	374
Onc	Simon, G	TX	383
Onc	Slamon, D	CA	392
Onc	Small, E	CA	392
Onc	Smith, M	MA	335
Onc	Smith, M	OH	374
Onc	Smith, T	MD	351
Onc	Socinski, M	PA	351
Onc	Soiffer, R	MA	335
Onc	Somlo, G	CA	392
Onc	Sosman, J	TN	364
Onc	Sotomayor, E	FL	364
Onc	Speyer, J	NY	351
Onc	Spriggs, D	NY	352
Onc	Staddon, A	PA	352
Onc	Stadler, W	IL	374
Onc	Stadtmauer, E	PA	352
Onc	Steen, P	ND	377
Onc	Stein, C	CA	392
Onc	Stewart, F	WA	393
Onc	Stockdale, F	CA	393
Onc	Stone, J	FL	364
Onc	Stoopler, M	NY	352
Onc	Stopeck, A	AZ	383
Onc	Straus, D	NY	352
Onc	Strauss, G	MA	335
Onc	Strenger, R	RI	335
Onc	Sun, W	PA	352
Onc	Sutton, L	NC	364
Onc	Sweeney, C	MA	335
Onc	Sweetenham, J	UT	378
Onc	Sznol, M	CT	335
Onc	Taetle, R	AZ	383
Onc	Tagawa, S	NY	352
Onc	Tap, W	NY	352
Onc	Taplin, M	MA	335
Onc	Tempero, M	CA	393
Onc	Terpenning, M	CA	393
Onc	Tester, W	PA	353
Onc	Thigpen, J	MS	364
Onc	Thompson, J	WA	393
Onc	Tkaczuk, K	MD	353
Onc	Toppmeyer, D	NJ	353
Onc	Torti, F	CT	336
Onc	Triozzi, P	OH	374
Onc	Tripathy, D	CA	393
Onc	Troner, M	FL	364
Onc	Trump, D	NY	353
Onc	Twardowski, P	CA	393
Onc	Urba, S	MI	374
Onc	Urba, W	OR	393
Onc	Vahdat, L	NY	353
Onc	Valero, V	TX	383
Onc	Varadhachary, G	TX	383
Onc	Vaughan, W	AL	364
Onc	Vaughn, D	PA	353
Onc	Venook, A	CA	394
Onc	Verschraegen, C	VT	336
Onc	Vescio, R	CA	394
Onc	Vinciguerra, V	NY	353
Onc	Vogelzang, N	NV	394
Onc	Vokes, E	IL	374
Onc	Volberding, P	CA	394
Onc	Von Burton, G	LA	384
Onc	Von Hoff, D	AZ	384
Onc	von Mehren, M	PA	353
Onc	Vredenburgh, J	CT	336
Onc	Waintraub, S	NJ	354
Onc	Waller, E	GA	365
Onc	Ward, J	UT	378
Onc	Weber, J	FL	365
Onc	Weiner, G	IA	375
Onc	Weiner, L	DC	354
Onc	Weisberg, T	ME	336
Onc	Weiss, G	VA	365
Onc	Wetzler, M	NY	354
Onc	Wicha, M	MI	375
Onc	Wierman, A	NV	394
Onc	Wilding, G	WI	375
Onc	Willson, J	TX	384
Onc	Wilson, W	MD	354
Onc	Winer, E	MA	336
Onc	Wingard, J	FL	365
Onc	Wolchok, J	NY	354
Onc	Wolff, A	MD	354
Onc	Wolff, R	TX	384
Onc	Wolin, E	CA	394
Onc	Worden, F	MI	375
Onc	Yee, D	MN	375
Onc	Yen, Y	CA	394

Specialty & Special Expertise Index

Spec	Name	St	Pg
Onc	Yunus, F	TN	365
Onc	Zelenetz, A	NY	354

Medulloblastoma

Spec	Name	St	Pg
NS	Raffel, C	CA	501
PHO	Gajjar, A	TN	778
PHO	O'Dorisio, M	IA	784

Melanoma

Spec	Name	St	Pg
D	Bolognia, J	CT	184
D	Bondi, E	PA	187
D	Bowen, G	UT	197
D	Bronin, A	NY	187
D	Brown, M	NY	187
D	Cornelius, L	MO	195
D	Dzubow, L	PA	188
D	Fenske, N	FL	192
D	Gellis, S	MA	185
D	Gilchrest, B	MA	185
D	Greenway, H	CA	201
D	Grichnik, J	FL	193
D	Halpern, A	NY	188
D	Johnson, T	MI	195
D	Johr, R	FL	193
D	Krunic, A	IL	196
D	Kupper, T	MA	185
D	Leffell, D	CT	185
D	Miller, S	MD	189
D	Orengo, I	TX	199
D	Pitts, J	AZ	199
D	Prioleau, P	NY	190
D	Rhodes, A	IL	197
D	Rigel, D	NY	190
D	Shea, C	IL	197
D	Swetter, S	CA	202
D	Taylor, R	TX	199
D	Tsao, H	MA	186
D	Wood, G	WI	197
D	Zitelli, J	PA	191
Hem	Milhem, M	IA	323
Onc	Albertini, M	WI	366
Onc	Atkins, M	DC	337
Onc	Biggs, D	DE	338
Onc	Brockstein, B	IL	367
Onc	Chapman, P	NY	339
Onc	Chow, W	CA	386
Onc	Clark, J	IL	367
Onc	Cohen, G	MD	340
Onc	Cohen, S	NY	340
Onc	Conry, R	AL	357
Onc	Daud, A	CA	386
Onc	Ernstoff, M	NH	331
Onc	Fay, J	TX	379
Onc	Glaspy, J	CA	388
Onc	Grosh, W	VA	359
Onc	Gruber, S	CA	388
Onc	Hutchins, L	AR	380
Onc	Hwu, P	TX	380
Onc	Kirkwood, J	PA	346
Onc	Kuzel, T	IL	371
Onc	Lawson, D	GA	360
Onc	Lutzky, J	FL	360
Onc	Margolin, K	WA	389
Onc	McClay, E	CA	390
Onc	Meyskens, F	CA	390
Onc	Miller, D	KY	361
Onc	Pavlick, A	NY	349
Onc	Pecora, A	NJ	349
Onc	Richards, J	IL	373
Onc	Samlowski, W	NV	392
Onc	Schuchter, L	PA	351
Onc	Sosman, J	TN	364
Onc	Strauss, G	MA	335
Onc	Sznol, M	CT	335
Onc	Thompson, J	WA	393
Onc	Triozzi, P	OH	374
Onc	von Mehren, M	PA	353
Onc	Weber, J	FL	365
Onc	Weiss, G	VA	365
Onc	Wolchok, J	NY	354
Oto	Califano, J	MD	668
Oto	Singer, M	CA	697
Path	Bastian, B	CA	732
Path	Cochran, A	CA	732
Path	Gottlieb, G	MA	718
Path	Prieto, V	TX	730
Path	Rimm, D	CT	719
PHO	Rodriguez-Galindo, C	MA	770
PlS	Chang, B	PA	881
PlS	Yetman, R	OH	897
PlS	Zide, B	NY	888
RadRO	Wazer, D	RI	977
RadRO	Werner-Wasik, M	PA	983
S	Averbook, B	OH	1111
S	Bear, H	VA	1103
S	Beauchamp, R	TN	1103
S	Bland, K	AL	1103
S	Brady, M	NY	1090
S	Brown, C	IL	1112
S	Byrd, D	WA	1131
S	Chang, A	MI	1112
S	Coit, D	NY	1091
S	Cusack, J	MA	1084
S	Dooley, W	OK	1124
S	Eberlein, T	MO	1113
S	Edington, H	PA	1092
S	Edney, J	NE	1122
S	Edwards, M	OH	1113
S	Eisenberg, B	NH	1085
S	Essner, R	CA	1132
S	Graham, R	MA	1085
S	Gray, R	AZ	1125
S	Huth, J	TX	1126
S	Johnson Miller, D	NJ	1095
S	Kaufman, H	IL	1115
S	Kavanah, M	MA	1086
S	Kelley, M	TN	1106
S	Kim, J	OH	1116
S	Krag, D	VT	1086
S	Kuhn, J	TX	1126
S	Lee, J	TX	1127
S	Leitch, A	TX	1127
S	Lind, D	PA	1096
S	Loggie, B	NE	1122
S	Mansfield, P	TX	1127
S	McCabe, D	AZ	1127
S	McMasters, K	KY	1107
S	Mesko, T	FL	1107
S	Moley, J	MO	1117
S	Nathanson, S	MI	1117
S	Neifeld, J	VA	1107
S	Olson, J	MD	1097
S	Paramo, J	FL	1108
S	Pockaj, B	AZ	1128
S	Rosenberg, S	MD	1099
S	Roses, D	NY	1099
S	Ross, M	TX	1128
S	Schwartzentruber, D	IN	1119
S	Sener, S	CA	1137
S	Shapiro, R	NY	1100
S	Shen, P	NC	1109
S	Shenk, R	OH	1119
S	Sigurdson, E	PA	1101
S	Slingluff, C	VA	1109
S	Sondak, V	FL	1109
S	Tanabe, K	MA	1088
S	Tyler, D	NC	1110
S	Tyler, D	NC	1110
S	Urist, M	AL	1110
S	Wallace, A	CA	1138
S	White, R	NC	1110
S	Yang, J	MD	1102
S	Yeung, R	WA	1138

Melanoma Early Detection/Prevention

Spec	Name	St	Pg
D	Halpern, A	NY	188
D	Rhodes, A	IL	197
D	Schultz, N	NY	190
D	Swetter, S	CA	202

Melanoma Genetics

Spec	Name	St	Pg
D	Tsao, H	MA	186

Melanoma Risk Assessment

Spec	Name	St	Pg
D	Lessin, S	PA	189
D	Rhodes, A	IL	197

Melanoma-Advanced

Spec	Name	St	Pg
Onc	Albertini, M	WI	366
Onc	Flaherty, K	MA	331

Melanoma-Choroidal (eye)

Spec	Name	St	Pg
Oph	Abramson, D	NY	575
Oph	Augsburger, J	OH	593
Oph	Dutton, J	NC	588
Oph	Finger, P	NY	578
Oph	Grossniklaus, H	GA	588
Oph	Handa, J	MD	579
Oph	Harbour, J	FL	589
Oph	Schachat, A	OH	599
Oph	Shields, C	PA	584

Spec	Name	St	Pg
Oph	Shields, J	PA	585
Oph	Wilson, M	TN	592
RadRO	Crocker, I	GA	984

Melanoma-Head & Neck

Spec	Name	St	Pg
D	Fewkes, J	MA	184
Oto	Bradford, C	MI	684
Oto	Myers, J	TX	693
PlS	Stadelmann, W	NH	879

Memory Disorders

Spec	Name	St	Pg
Ger	Raji, M	TX	267
GerPsy	Stein, E	CA	946
N	Doody, R	TX	536
N	Heilman, K	FL	525
N	Henderson, V	CA	540
N	Jordan, B	NY	516
N	Relkin, N	NY	520
N	Sadowsky, C	FL	526
N	Weinberg, H	NY	522
NRad	Murtagh, F	FL	1022
Psyc	Arnold, S	PA	922
Psyc	Marin, D	NY	926

Memory Loss

Spec	Name	St	Pg
GerPsy	Rovner, B	PA	944

Men's Health

Spec	Name	St	Pg
U	Bans, L	AZ	1208

Meniere's Disease

Spec	Name	St	Pg
N	Hain, T	IL	530
Oto	Arriaga, M	LA	691
Oto	Beatty, C	MN	683
Oto	Farrior, J	FL	678
Oto	Hammerschlag, P	NY	670
Oto	Harris, J	CA	695
Oto	Mattox, D	GA	679
Oto	Paparella, M	MN	687
Oto	Rauch, S	MA	666
Oto	Silverstein, H	FL	681
Oto	Wazen, J	FL	682

Meningioma

Spec	Name	St	Pg
NS	Bederson, J	NY	474
NS	Bruce, J	NY	475
NS	Gutin, P	NY	477
NS	Krisht, A	AR	496
NS	Liau, L	CA	500
NS	McDermott, M	CA	501
NS	Olivi, A	MD	480
NS	Sen, C	NY	481
NS	Sisti, M	NY	482
NS	Stieg, P	NY	482
RadRO	Loeffler, J	MA	977

Meningioma-Orbital (eye)

Spec	Name	St	Pg
Oph	Cockerham, K	CA	605

Meningitis

Spec	Name	St	Pg
Inf	Quagliarello, V	CT	412
Inf	Scheld, W	VA	416
PInf	Kaplan, S	TX	796
PInf	McCracken, G	TX	796
PInf	Wald, E	WI	796

Menopause Problems

Spec	Name	St	Pg
ObG	Berga, S	NC	562
ObG	Richardson, M	KS	566
ObG	Simon, J	DC	562
Psyc	Joffe, H	MA	921
RE	Blackwell, R	AL	1045
RE	Fritz, M	NC	1046
RE	Johnson, J	MA	1040
RE	Luciano, A	CT	1041
RE	Smith, Y	MI	1049
RE	Weiss, G	NJ	1044

Menopause-Male

Spec	Name	St	Pg
Ger	Morley, J	MO	266

Menstrual Disorders

Spec	Name	St	Pg
AM	Murray, P	WV	76
ObG	Berga, S	NC	562
ObG	Bradley, L	OH	564
ObG	Bradshaw, K	TX	566
ObG	Gilliam, M	IL	564
RE	Chang, R	CA	1051
RE	Legro, R	PA	1043
RE	Marut, E	IL	1048

Mental Retardation

Spec	Name	St	Pg
CG	Davis, J	NY	157
CG	Falk, R	CA	162
CG	Graham, J	CA	162
CG	Stevenson, R	SC	159
ChAP	McDougle, C	MA	938
ChAP	Pomeroy, J	NY	940

Mercury Toxic Exposure

Spec	Name	St	Pg
OM	Gochfeld, M	NJ	912

Merkel Cell Carcinoma

Spec	Name	St	Pg
D	Nghiem, P	WA	201
Onc	Kelsen, D	NY	346
Onc	Samlowski, W	NV	392
PlS	Tufaro, A	MD	888
RadRO	Morrison, W	TX	994
S	Brady, M	NY	1090
S	Cusack, J	MA	1084

Mesothelioma

Spec	Name	St	Pg
Onc	Aisner, J	NJ	337
Onc	Bonomi, P	IL	366
Onc	Bunn, P	CO	376
Onc	Carbone, D	OH	367
Onc	Dakhil, S	KS	376
Onc	Ilson, D	NY	345
Onc	Johnson, B	MA	333
Onc	Kalemkerian, G	MI	370
Onc	Kindler, H	IL	370
Onc	Langer, C	PA	346
Onc	Martins, R	WA	389
Onc	Robert-Vizcarrondo, F	AL	363
Onc	Ross, H	AZ	383
Onc	Salgia, R	IL	373
Onc	Shin, D	GA	364
Onc	Simon, G	TX	383
Onc	Vogelzang, N	NV	394
Path	Cagle, P	TX	730
Path	Moran, C	TX	730
Pul	Sterman, D	PA	959
RadRO	Choi, N	MA	976
RadRO	Videtic, G	OH	992
S	Loggie, B	NE	1122
T&CS	Battafarano, R	MD	1150
T&CS	Bueno, R	MA	1146
T&CS	Cameron, R	CA	1177
T&CS	Colson, Y	MA	1146
T&CS	Flores, R	NY	1152
T&CS	Friedberg, J	PA	1152
T&CS	Handy, J	OR	1178
T&CS	Harpole, D	NC	1162
T&CS	Jablons, D	CA	1179
T&CS	Landreneau, R	LA	1175
T&CS	Mason, D	OH	1170
T&CS	Miller, D	GA	1163
T&CS	Pass, H	NY	1157
T&CS	Rice, D	TX	1176
T&CS	Robinson, L	FL	1165
T&CS	Rusch, V	NY	1158
T&CS	Smythe, W	TX	1176
T&CS	Sugarbaker, D	MA	1148
T&CS	Swisher, S	TX	1176
T&CS	Vallieres, E	WA	1181
T&CS	Vigneswaran, W	IL	1172
T&CS	Weigel, T	ME	1149
T&CS	Wood, D	WA	1181
T&CS	Yang, S	MD	1160

Metabolic Disorders

Spec	Name	St	Pg
ChiN	DeVivo, D	NY	145
ChiN	Patterson, M	MN	149
EDM	Akatsu, H	CA	223
EDM	Cohen, R	OH	218
EDM	Dobs, A	MD	212
EDM	Rodbard, H	MD	214
IM	Rader, D	PA	426
Ped	Jones, K	CA	742

Metabolic Genetic Disorders

Spec	Name	St	Pg
CG	Bialer, M	NY	157

Spec	Name	St	Pg
CG	Chung, W	NY	157
CG	Hainline, B	IN	160
CG	Ward, J	TN	159
CG	Wasserstein, M	NY	158

Metabolic Syndrome

Spec	Name	St	Pg
AM	Chambers, C	PA	76
Cv	Linton, M	TN	98
Cv	Reis, S	PA	95
EDM	Schwartz, S	PA	214
EDM	Thorner, M	VA	217
PEn	DeLuca, F	PA	758
PEn	Lustig, R	CA	762

Metastatic Cancer

Spec	Name	St	Pg
S	Ellis, L	TX	1124

Microdiscectomy

Spec	Name	St	Pg
NS	Haid, R	GA	485
NS	Maroon, J	PA	479
OrS	Boden, S	GA	635

Microscopic Colitis

Spec	Name	St	Pg
Ge	Loftus, E	MN	249

Microsurgery

Spec	Name	St	Pg
CRS	Orkin, B	IL	174
HS	Bishop, A	MN	302
HS	Cendales, L	GA	301
HS	Culp, R	PA	298
HS	Fischer, T	IN	302
HS	Friedman, D	FL	301
HS	Idler, R	CO	304
HS	Lubahn, J	PA	299
HS	Mih, A	IN	303
HS	Moneim, M	NM	305
HS	Rayan, G	OK	305
HS	Slutsky, D	CA	306
HS	Stern, P	OH	304
HS	Thomson, J	CT	296
NS	Black, K	CA	498
NS	Chen, C	NY	475
NS	Khan, A	MD	478
NS	Reid, W	TN	486
NS	Selman, W	OH	493
Oto	Strome, S	MD	676
Ped Uro	Atala, A	NC	825
PIS	Allen, R	NY	880
PIS	Andersen, J	CA	901
PIS	Brandt, K	MO	893
PIS	Chang, B	PA	881
PIS	Chang, D	TX	899
PIS	Dagum, A	NY	881
PIS	Disa, J	NY	881
PIS	Dumanian, G	IL	893
PIS	Fix, R	AL	889
PIS	Levine, J	NY	883
PIS	Low, D	PA	884
PIS	Mehrara, B	NY	885
PIS	Neumeister, M	IL	895
PIS	Rockwell, W	UT	898
PIS	Rodriguez, E	MD	886
PIS	Sanger, J	WI	896
PIS	Siebert, J	WI	896
PIS	Siemionow, M	OH	896
PIS	Topham, N	PA	888
PIS	Wilkins, E	MI	897
PIS	Yetman, R	OH	897
RE	Goldberg, J	OH	1047
RE	Yee, B	CA	1053
U	Fisch, H	NY	1190
U	Sabanegh, E	OH	1205

Microvascular Surgery

Spec	Name	St	Pg
NS	Martin, N	CA	500
Oto	Couch, M	VT	665
Oto	Hayden, R	AZ	692
Oto	Rosenthal, E	AL	681
Oto	Wax, M	OR	697

Migraine

Spec	Name	St	Pg
ChiN	Epstein, L	IL	148
ChiN	Hershey, A	OH	148
ChiN	Maytal, J	NY	146
ChiN	Nass, R	NY	146
ChiN	Sankar, R	CA	152
ChiN	Sivaswamy, L	MI	149
N	Buchholz, D	MD	513
N	Charles, A	CA	539
N	Cutrer, F	MN	529
N	Dodick, D	AZ	536
N	Finkel, A	NC	524
N	Lane, J	CO	535
N	Rothrock, J	NV	541
N	Sabo, T	CO	535
N	Saper, J	MI	533
N	Silberstein, S	PA	521
N	Swanson, J	MN	533
N	Wright, R	IL	534
PM	Loder, E	MA	706
PM	Robbins, L	IL	710

Migraine in Women

Spec	Name	St	Pg
N	Rubin, S	IL	533

Migraine-Chronic

Spec	Name	St	Pg
PM	Freitag, F	WI	709

Minimally Invasive Cardiac Surgery

Spec	Name	St	Pg
T&CS	Adams, D	NY	1150
T&CS	Aldea, G	WA	1177
T&CS	Bacha, E	NY	1150
T&CS	Bakhos, M	IL	1167
T&CS	Bichell, D	TN	1160
T&CS	Boyd, W	CA	1177
T&CS	Bridges, C	NC	1161
T&CS	Chitwood, W	NC	1161
T&CS	Damiano, R	MO	1167
T&CS	DeFilippi, V	CA	1178
T&CS	Furukawa, S	PA	1152
T&CS	Graver, L	NY	1153
T&CS	Grossi, E	NY	1153
T&CS	Guyton, R	GA	1162
T&CS	Hargrove, W	PA	1154
T&CS	Horvath, K	MD	1154
T&CS	Joyce, L	MN	1169
T&CS	Lang, S	NY	1155
T&CS	Loulmet, D	NY	1156
T&CS	Merrick, S	CA	1179
T&CS	Murphy, D	GA	1164
T&CS	Oz, M	NY	1157
T&CS	Panos, A	FL	1164
T&CS	Rastegar, H	MA	1148
T&CS	Smith, C	NY	1158
T&CS	Woo, Y	PA	1160
T&CS	Yuh, D	CT	1149

Minimally Invasive Esophageal Surgery

Spec	Name	St	Pg
T&CS	Bueno, R	MA	1146

Minimally Invasive Gynecologic Surgery

Spec	Name	St	Pg
GO	Cantuaria, G	GA	281
GO	King, S	PA	278
ObG	Kenton, K	IL	565
RE	Haney, A	IL	1047

Minimally Invasive Heart Valve Surgery

Spec	Name	St	Pg
T&CS	DeRose, J	NY	1151
T&CS	Filsoufi, F	NY	1152
T&CS	Galloway, A	NY	1153
T&CS	Guber, M	CO	1173
T&CS	Guy, T	PA	1154
T&CS	Jeevanandam, V	IL	1169
T&CS	Savage, E	FL	1165

Minimally Invasive Knee Replacement

Spec	Name	St	Pg
OrS	Haas, S	NY	625

Minimally Invasive Spinal Surgery

Spec	Name	St	Pg
NRad	Hirsch, J	MA	1019
NS	Branch, C	NC	484
NS	Bray, R	CA	499
NS	El-Kadi, H	PA	476
NS	Fessler, R	IL	490
NS	Foley, K	TN	484
NS	Haid, R	GA	485
NS	Hartl, R	NY	477
NS	Jenkins, A	NY	478

Spec	Name	St	Pg
NS	Kaiser, M	NY	478
NS	Levi, A	FL	485
NS	Maroon, J	PA	479
NS	Reid, W	TN	486
NS	Rodts, G	GA	487
NS	Sekhon, L	NV	501
NS	Traynelis, V	IL	493
OrS	Cammisa, F	NY	622
OrS	Cappuccino, A	NY	622
OrS	Delamarter, R	CA	650
OrS	Garfin, S	CA	651
OrS	Goldstein, J	NY	624
OrS	Hecht, A	NY	625
OrS	Hilibrand, A	PA	626
OrS	Kim, C	CA	652
OrS	Parazin, S	MA	618
OrS	Riew, K	MO	644
OrS	Sandhu, H	NY	632

Minimally Invasive Surgery

Spec	Name	St	Pg
CRS	Beck, D	LA	176
CRS	Marks, J	PA	170
CRS	Wise, P	MO	175
GO	Carney, M	HI	290
GO	Fishman, D	NY	278
GO	Hurteau, J	IL	284
GO	Martino, M	PA	279
GO	Poliakoff, S	FL	283
GO	Schorge, J	MA	275
GO	Yamada, S	IL	287
NS	Bauer, J	IL	488
NS	Caputy, A	DC	475
NS	Cohen, A	MA	472
NS	Ellenbogen, R	WA	499
NS	Jho, H	PA	478
NS	Lemole, G	AZ	496
NS	Sandberg, D	TX	497
NS	Schwartz, T	NY	481
NS	Souweidane, M	NY	482
NS	Theodore, N	AZ	497
ObG	Bartholomew, D	OH	563
ObG	Einarsson, J	MA	560
ObG	Famuyide, A	MN	564
ObG	Jenkins, T	AL	563
ObG	Maynard, S	DC	561
ObG	Visco, A	NC	563
ObG	Young, B	NY	562
OrS	Caillouette, J	CA	650
OrS	Gorab, R	CA	651
OrS	Jiranek, W	VA	636
OrS	Macaulay, W	NY	628
OrS	McAfee, P	MD	628
OrS	Sculco, T	NY	632
OrS	Tornetta, P	MA	619
OrS	Vo, P	FL	638
OrS	Wetzel, F	PA	634
Oto	Akervall, J	MI	682
Oto	Kennedy, D	PA	672
Oto	Orloff, L	CA	696
Oto	Rosenthal, E	AL	681
PCd	Zahn, E	CA	755
Ped Uro	Docimo, S	PA	825
Ped Uro	Merguerian, P	WA	828
PS	Barksdale, E	OH	819
PS	Black, C	TX	821
PS	Doody, D	MA	814
PS	Flake, A	PA	815
PS	Ford, H	CA	823
PS	Gaines, B	PA	815
PS	Holcomb, G	MO	820
PS	Holterman, M	IL	820
PS	Kane, T	DC	816
PS	Krummel, T	CA	823
PS	Midulla, P	NY	816
PS	Moss, R	OH	820
PS	Rodgers, B	VA	818
PS	Spigland, N	NY	817
PS	Voigt, R	MD	817
PS	Waldhausen, J	WA	824
RE	Falcone, T	OH	1047
RE	Isaacson, K	MA	1040
RE	Petrozza, J	MA	1041
RE	Putman, J	TX	1050
RE	Sanfilippo, J	PA	1044
S	Brodsky, J	PA	1090
S	Brooks, A	PA	1090
S	Brunt, L	MO	1112
S	Courcoulas, A	PA	1091
S	Curcillo, P	PA	1091
S	Duh, Q	CA	1132
S	Duncan, M	MD	1092
S	Easter, D	CA	1132
S	Fahey, T	NY	1093
S	Fitzgibbons, R	NE	1122
S	Frantzides, C	IL	1114
S	Holzman, M	TN	1106
S	Horvath, K	WA	1133
S	Ikramuddin, S	MN	1115
S	Jones, D	MA	1086
S	Koruda, M	NC	1106
S	Lee, K	PA	1096
S	McFadden, D	CT	1087
S	Mesko, T	FL	1107
S	Morton, J	CA	1134
S	Nissen, N	CA	1135
S	Oelschlager, B	WA	1135
S	Pachter, H	NY	1097
S	Park, A	MD	1098
S	Ponsky, J	OH	1118
S	Ramanathan, R	PA	1099
S	Rattner, D	MA	1087
S	Rogers, S	CA	1136
S	Rosemurgy, A	FL	1108
S	Rosen, M	OH	1118
S	Schauer, P	OH	1119
S	Schraut, W	PA	1100
S	Shibata, D	FL	1109
S	Soper, N	IL	1120
S	Swanstrom, L	OR	1137
S	Sweeney, J	GA	1110
S	Talamini, M	CA	1137
S	Tousimis, E	DC	1102
S	Tuttle, T	MN	1120
T&CS	Burke, R	FL	1161
T&CS	Cassivi, S	MN	1167
T&CS	Cohen, R	CA	1178
T&CS	Del-Nido, P	MA	1146
T&CS	Ferguson, M	IL	1168
T&CS	Fontana, G	NY	1152
T&CS	Lazzaro, R	NY	1156
T&CS	Liao, K	MN	1169
T&CS	Mack, M	TX	1175
T&CS	Rice, D	TX	1176
T&CS	Rosengart, T	TX	1176
T&CS	Swistel, D	NY	1159
U	Balaji, K	NC	1197
U	Coleman, J	NY	1189
U	Irby, P	NC	1198
U	Kane, M	MD	1191
U	Kibel, A	MA	1187
U	McVary, K	IL	1204
U	Schulam, P	CT	1188
VascS	Flanigan, D	CA	1230
VascS	Lumsden, A	TX	1229

Minimally Invasive Surgery-Advanced

Spec	Name	St	Pg
S	Eubanks, W	FL	1105

Minimally Invasive Surgery-Pediatric

Spec	Name	St	Pg
Ped Uro	Poppas, D	NY	825

Minimally Invasive Thoracic Surgery

Spec	Name	St	Pg
T&CS	Baciewicz, F	MI	1167
T&CS	Brinckerhoff, L	MA	1146
T&CS	Bueno, R	MA	1146
T&CS	Cohen, N	MD	1151
T&CS	Demmy, T	NY	1151
T&CS	Fernando, H	MA	1147
T&CS	Howington, J	IL	1168
T&CS	Jones, D	NY	1154
T&CS	Krellenstein, D	NY	1155
T&CS	Mason, D	OH	1170
T&CS	Nesbitt, J	TN	1164
T&CS	Nguyen, D	FL	1164
T&CS	Sonett, J	NY	1158
T&CS	Thistlethwaite, P	CA	1180
T&CS	Weksler, B	PA	1160

Minimally Invasive Urologic Surgery

Spec	Name	St	Pg
U	Andrews, P	AZ	1207
U	Carpinito, G	MA	1186
U	Gill, I	CA	1211
U	Gluckman, G	IL	1203
U	Gomella, L	PA	1190
U	Hall, S	NY	1190
U	Landman, J	CA	1212
U	Miller, S	GA	1199
U	Moul, J	NC	1199
U	Shalhav, A	IL	1206

Spec	Name	St	Pg
U	Strup, S	KY	1201
U	Trabulsi, E	PA	1195

Minimally Invasive Vascular Surgery

Spec	Name	St	Pg
VascS	Ahn, S	CA	1230
VascS	Benvenisty, A	NY	1222
VascS	Brener, B	NJ	1222
VascS	Cho, J	IL	1226
VascS	Dougherty, M	PA	1223
VascS	Schneider, D	NY	1225
VascS	Todd, G	NY	1225

Miscarriage-Recurrent

Spec	Name	St	Pg
MF	Druzin, M	CA	442
MF	Koos, B	CA	443
MF	Landy, H	DC	435
MF	Paidas, M	CT	432
ObG	Ordorica, S	NY	561
ObG	Young, B	NY	562
RE	Barnes, R	IL	1046
RE	DeVane, G	FL	1045
RE	Hill, J	NH	1040
RE	Kutteh, W	TN	1046
RE	Marut, E	IL	1048
RE	Odem, R	MO	1048
RE	Ratts, V	MO	1048
RE	Scoccia, H	IL	1048
RE	Walmer, D	NC	1046

Mitochondrial Disorders

Spec	Name	St	Pg
CG	Boles, R	CA	162
CG	Craigen, W	TX	161
CG	Hainline, B	IN	160
CG	Shoffner, J	GA	159
ChiN	Cohen, B	OH	148
ChiN	Haas, R	CA	151
ChiN	Legido, A	PA	145

Mitral Valve Prolapse

Spec	Name	St	Pg
Cv	Andersen, H	NY	91

Mitral Valve Robotic Surgery

Spec	Name	St	Pg
T&CS	Hargrove, W	PA	1154
T&CS	Murphy, D	GA	1164
T&CS	Smith, J	OH	1171
T&CS	Woo, Y	PA	1160

Mitral Valve Surgery

Spec	Name	St	Pg
IC	Gray, W	NY	122
IC	Yeung, A	CA	128
T&CS	Adams, D	NY	1150
T&CS	Bakhos, M	IL	1167
T&CS	Bolman, R	MA	1146
T&CS	Chitwood, W	NC	1161
T&CS	DeFilippi, V	CA	1178
T&CS	DeRose, J	NY	1151
T&CS	Filsoufi, F	NY	1152
T&CS	Fontana, G	NY	1152
T&CS	Fullerton, D	CO	1172
T&CS	Galloway, A	NY	1153
T&CS	Grossi, E	NY	1153
T&CS	Hashim, S	CT	1147
T&CS	Hill, M	WA	1179
T&CS	Jamieson, S	CA	1179
T&CS	Merrick, S	CA	1179
T&CS	Miller, D	CA	1180
T&CS	Moon, M	MO	1170
T&CS	Naka, Y	NY	1157
T&CS	Savage, E	FL	1165
T&CS	Slaughter, M	KY	1165
T&CS	Smith, C	NY	1158

Mobility Evaluation & Treatment

Spec	Name	St	Pg
Ger	Cooney, L	CT	264
Ger	Studenski, S	PA	265
PMR	Esquenazi, A	PA	863

Mohs' Surgery

Spec	Name	St	Pg
D	Amonette, R	TN	191
D	Arpey, C	MN	194
D	Bailin, P	OH	194
D	Bennett, R	CA	200
D	Berg, D	WA	200
D	Bowen, G	UT	197
D	Brodland, D	PA	187
D	Brown, M	NY	187
D	Carney, J	AR	198
D	Cook, J	NC	192
D	Dufresne, R	RI	184
D	Dzubow, L	PA	188
D	Fewkes, J	MA	184
D	Fosko, S	MO	195
D	Garrett, A	VA	192
D	Geronemus, R	NY	188
D	Glogau, R	CA	200
D	Green, H	FL	192
D	Greenbaum, S	PA	188
D	Greenway, H	CA	201
D	Hanke, C	IN	195
D	Hruza, G	MO	195
D	Johnson, T	MI	195
D	Kriegel, D	NY	189
D	Krunic, A	IL	196
D	Lask, G	CA	201
D	Leffell, D	CT	185
D	Leshin, B	NC	193
D	Lim Quan, K	AZ	199
D	Linder, J	AZ	199
D	Maloney, M	MA	185
D	Miller, S	MD	189
D	Neel, V	MA	185
D	Neuburg, M	WI	196
D	Nouri, K	FL	193
D	Olbricht, S	MA	186
D	Orengo, I	TX	199
D	Otley, C	MN	196
D	Perone, J	TX	199
D	Pitts, J	AZ	199
D	Prioleau, P	NY	190
D	Ratner, D	NY	190
D	Richardson, T	CA	201
D	Russell, M	VA	193
D	Swanson, N	OR	202
D	Taylor, R	TX	199
D	Wheeland, R	AZ	199
D	Zitelli, J	PA	191
PIS	Imber, G	NY	883

Mood Disorders

Spec	Name	St	Pg
AdP	Howell, E	UT	937
ChAP	Abright, A	NY	939
ChAP	Alessi, N	MI	941
ChAP	Foley, C	NY	940
ChAP	Hirsch, S	IL	942
ChAP	Luby, J	MO	942
ChAP	Riddle, M	MD	940
GerPsy	Holroyd, S	VA	945
GerPsy	Manepalli, J	MO	945
Psyc	Blazer, D	NC	927
Psyc	Gitlin, M	CA	933
Psyc	Janicak, P	IL	930
Psyc	Mann, J	NY	926
Psyc	Pi, E	CA	934

Motion Sickness

Spec	Name	St	Pg
N	Hain, T	IL	530

Motor Control Analysis

Spec	Name	St	Pg
PMR	Mayer, N	PA	865

Movement Disorders

Spec	Name	St	Pg
ChiN	Dure, L	AL	147
ChiN	Lavenstein, B	VA	147
ChiN	Mink, J	NY	146
ChiN	Noetzel, M	MO	149
N	Ahlskog, J	MN	527
N	Aminoff, M	CA	538
N	Ashizawa, T	FL	523
N	Azizi, S	PA	513
N	Baser, S	PA	513
N	Bressman, S	NY	513
N	Bruno, M	HI	538
N	Busis, N	PA	514
N	DeLong, M	GA	524
N	Fahn, S	NY	515
N	Flaherty, A	MA	511
N	Goetz, C	IL	529
N	Golbe, L	NJ	516
N	Hauser, R	FL	525
N	Hurtig, H	PA	516
N	Jankovic, J	TX	537
N	Langston, J	CA	540
N	Lew, M	CA	541
N	Maraganore, D	IL	531
N	Montgomery, E	PA	520
N	Nutt, J	OR	541
N	Olanow, C	NY	520

Spec	Name	St	Pg
N	Perlmutter, J	MO	532
N	Reich, S	MD	520
N	Samii, A	WA	542
N	Sethi, K	GA	527
N	Shulman, L	MD	521
N	Singer, C	FL	527
N	Stern, M	PA	522
N	Tanner, C	CA	542
N	Tetrud, J	CA	542
N	Waters, C	NY	522
N	Watts, R	AL	527
N	Wooten, G	VA	527
NS	Apuzzo, M	CA	498
NS	Baltuch, G	PA	474
NS	Burchiel, K	OR	499
NS	Burchiel, K	OR	499
NS	Kondziolka, D	NY	479
NS	Lunsford, L	PA	479
NS	Nazzaro, J	KS	494
NS	Penar, P	VT	473
NS	Whiting, D	PA	483
PMR	Ivanhoe, C	TX	871

Movement Disorders-Botox Therapy

N	Shulman, L	MD	521

Movement Disorders-Lower Limb

N	Finkel, M	FL	524

MoyaMoya Disease

N	Mohr, J	NY	519
NS	Feldstein, N	NY	476
NS	Harbaugh, R	PA	477
NS	Steinberg, G	CA	502
NS	Wilson, J	NC	488

MRI

DR	Bluemke, D	MD	1008
DR	Cohen, B	NY	1008
DR	Dalinka, M	PA	1009
DR	Edelman, R	IL	1014
DR	Elster, A	NC	1013
DR	Fidler, J	MN	1014
DR	Kanal, E	PA	1010
DR	Miller, F	IL	1015
DR	Partain, C	TN	1014
DR	Reinus, W	PA	1011
DR	Schwartz, L	NY	1012
DR	Weinreb, J	CT	1007
DR	Yoon, S	NY	1012
DR	Zagoria, R	CA	1019
N	Kuzniecky, R	NY	517
NRad	Barkovich, A	CA	1025
NRad	Burdette, J	NC	1021
NRad	Johnson, A	NC	1022
NRad	Khandji, A	NY	1020
NRad	Lis, E	NY	1021
NRad	Modic, M	OH	1024
NRad	Quencer, R	FL	1023
NRad	Sze, G	CT	1020
NRad	Thulborn, K	IL	1024

MRI & CT of Brain & Spine

NRad	Drayer, B	NY	1020
NRad	Hesselink, J	CA	1026

MRI Angiography

DR	Mirvis, S	MD	1010
DR	Prince, M	NY	1011

MRI-Brain & Spine

NRad	Atlas, S	CA	1025

MRI-Breast

DR	Evers, K	PA	1009
DR	Lehman, C	WA	1018
DR	Stough, R	OK	1017

Mucositis

RadRO	Martenson, J	MN	991

Muir-Torre Syndrome

D	Olbricht, S	MA	186

Multiple Gestation

MF	Abuhamad, A	VA	436
MF	Bartelsmeyer, J	MO	438
MF	Berkowitz, R	NY	433
MF	Carr, S	RI	432
MF	D'Alton, M	NY	434
MF	Dooley, S	IL	438
MF	Fox, H	MD	434
MF	Greene, M	MA	432
MF	Hussey, M	IL	438
MF	Socol, M	IL	440
MF	Thorp, J	NC	437
MF	Wapner, R	NY	435
MF	Winn, H	MO	440
MF	Witter, F	MD	436
NP	Muraskas, J	IL	452
ObG	Evans, M	NY	561

Multiple Myeloma

Hem	Allen, S	NY	313
Hem	Anderson, K	MA	312
Hem	Barlogie, B	AR	325
Hem	Copelan, E	NC	319
Hem	Djulbegovic, B	FL	319
Hem	Emanuel, P	AR	326
Hem	Farag, S	IN	321
Hem	Fonseca, R	AZ	326
Hem	Friedman, A	PA	314
Hem	Gertz, M	MN	321
Hem	Goldberg, J	PA	314
Hem	Gregory, S	IL	322
Hem	Isola, L	NY	314
Hem	Linenberger, M	WA	328
Hem	Lyons, R	TX	327
Hem	Marks, S	PA	315
Hem	Mears, J	NY	315
Hem	Rai, K	NY	316
Hem	Raphael, B	NY	316
Hem	Rapoport, A	MD	316
Hem	Richardson, P	MA	312
Hem	Roodman, G	IN	323
Hem	Rosenblatt, J	FL	320
Hem	Singhal, S	IL	324
Hem	Stewart, A	AZ	327
Hem	Strair, R	NJ	317
Hem	Williams, M	VA	320
NuM	Wiseman, G	MN	556
Onc	Aboulafia, D	WA	384
Onc	Ball, E	CA	385
Onc	Bensinger, W	WA	385
Onc	Bergsagel, P	AZ	379
Onc	Bishop, M	IL	366
Onc	Chanan-Khan, A	FL	356
Onc	Coleman, M	NY	340
Onc	Czuczman, M	NY	341
Onc	Fay, J	TX	379
Onc	Flinn, I	TN	357
Onc	Foss, F	CT	331
Onc	Gerson, S	OH	369
Onc	Jillella, A	GA	359
Onc	Kwak, L	TX	381
Onc	Lazarus, H	OH	371
Onc	O'Brien, T	OH	372
Onc	Orlowski, R	TX	382
Onc	Schiffer, C	MI	373
Onc	Silverman, L	NY	351
Onc	Smith, M	OH	374
Onc	Somlo, G	CA	392
Onc	Stadtmauer, E	PA	352
Onc	Straus, D	NY	352
Onc	Vescio, R	CA	394
Onc	Wingard, J	FL	365
Onc	Yunus, F	TN	365
OrS	Biermann, J	MI	639
OrS	Frassica, F	MD	624
RadRO	Meredith, R	AL	986
RadRO	Yahalom, J	NY	983

Multiple Sclerosis

N	Apatoff, B	NY	512
N	Arnason, B	IL	528
N	Berger, J	KY	523
N	Brooks, B	NC	523
N	Calabresi, P	MD	514
N	Cohen, J	OH	529
N	Cook, S	NJ	514
N	Corey-Bloom, J	CA	539
N	Coyle, P	NY	514
N	Elias, S	MI	529
N	Frohman, E	TX	536
N	Galetta, S	NY	515
N	Gilden, D	CO	535

Spec	Name	St	Pg
N	Goodin, D	CA	540
N	Hauser, S	CA	540
N	Lisak, R	MI	530
N	Lublin, F	NY	518
N	McArthur, J	MD	519
N	Miller, A	NY	519
N	Morgenlander, J	NC	526
N	Petito, F	NY	520
N	Pulst, S	UT	535
N	Reder, A	IL	532
N	Reed, R	OH	532
N	Roos, R	IL	533
N	Sadiq, S	NY	521
N	Swerdlow, M	NY	522
N	Vas, G	NY	522
N	Vollmer, T	CO	535
N	Weiner, L	CA	542
N	Windebank, A	MN	534
N	Wolinsky, J	TX	538
PMR	Sliwa, J	IL	870

Multiple Sclerosis Imaging

NRad	Provenzale, J	NC	1022

Multiple Sclerosis in Women

N	Rubin, S	IL	533

Multiple Sclerosis/Visual Disorders

N	Balcer, L	NY	513
N	Schatz, N	FL	526

Multisystem Disorders

Ped	Gartner, J	DE	740

Multisystem Inflammatory Disease

PRhu	Goldsmith, D	PA	811

Munchausen Syndrome

Psyc	Eisendrath, S	CA	933

Muscle Disorders

N	Busis, N	PA	514
N	Lacomis, D	PA	517

Muscle Pain-Stress Related

SM	Schechter, D	CA	1079

Muscular Dystrophy

ChiN	Crawford, T	MD	145
N	Amato, A	MA	510
N	Donofrio, P	TN	524
N	Graves, M	CA	540
N	Siddique, T	IL	533
Path	Moore, S	IA	728
PCd	Hardin, J	IL	753
PMR	Matthews, D	CO	870
PMR	Palmer, J	MD	865
PMR	Webster, H	MA	862

Musculoskeletal Disorders

PMR	Bloch, R	MA	862
PMR	Braddom, R	PA	863
PMR	De Lateur, B	MD	863
PMR	Herring, S	WA	872
PMR	Ma, D	NY	865
Rhu	Bunning, R	DC	1059
Rhu	Coblyn, J	MA	1058
Rhu	Hadler, N	NC	1063

Musculoskeletal Imaging

DR	Adler, R	NY	1008
DR	Dalinka, M	PA	1009
DR	Newman, J	MA	1007
DR	Palmer, W	MA	1007
DR	Pathria, M	CA	1018
DR	Pavlov, H	NY	1011
DR	Potter, H	NY	1011
DR	Reinus, W	PA	1011

Musculoskeletal Infections

OrS	Bostrom, M	NY	621
OrS	Garvin, K	NE	646
OrS	Webb, L	GA	639

Musculoskeletal Injuries

OrS	Dirschl, D	IL	640
PMR	Mason, K	CO	870
PMR	Press, J	IL	869

Musculoskeletal Injuries in Dancers

SM	Teitz, C	WA	1079

Musculoskeletal Tissue Banking

OrS	Joyce, M	OH	642

Musculoskeletal Tumors

DR	Panicek, D	NY	1011
OrS	Bos, G	WA	649
OrS	Brigman, B	NC	635
OrS	Bukata, S	CA	650
OrS	Gebhardt, M	MA	617
OrS	Henshaw, R	DC	625
OrS	Kneisl, J	NC	636
OrS	Mayerson, J	OH	643
OrS	Menendez, L	CA	652
OrS	Mott, M	MI	643
OrS	Schwartz, H	TN	638
OrS	Walling, A	FL	638

Myasthenia Gravis

N	Arnason, B	IL	528
N	Ashizawa, T	FL	523
N	Barohn, R	KS	534
N	Elias, S	MI	529
N	Harati, Y	TX	537
N	Kula, R	NY	517
N	Lacomis, D	PA	517
N	Lisak, R	MI	530
N	Pascuzzi, R	IN	532
N	Reder, A	IL	532
N	Swerdlow, M	NY	522
N	Vollmer, T	CO	535
N	Weiss, M	WA	542
N	Wright, R	IL	534
N	Zimnowodzki, S	IL	534
T&CS	Cassivi, S	MN	1167
T&CS	Kaiser, L	PA	1154

Mycobacterial Infections

Inf	Huitt, G	CO	419
Pul	Catanzaro, A	CA	970
Pul	Friedman, L	CT	954
Pul	Nardell, E	MA	955

Mycosis Fungoides

D	Lessin, S	PA	189
D	Ramsay, D	NY	190
D	Rook, A	PA	190

Myelodysplastic Syndromes

Hem	Baer, M	MD	313
Hem	Copelan, E	NC	319
Hem	Cortes, J	TX	326
Hem	Friedman, A	PA	314
Hem	Garcia-Manero, G	TX	326
Hem	Jurcic, J	NY	314
Hem	Komrokji, R	FL	319
Hem	Larson, R	IL	322
Hem	Luger, S	PA	315
Hem	Maslak, P	NY	315
Hem	Mesa, R	AZ	327
Hem	Miller, K	MA	312
Hem	Nand, S	IL	323
Hem	Petersdorf, S	WA	329
Hem	Powell, B	NC	319
Hem	Schuster, M	NY	317
Hem	Stock, W	IL	324
Hem	Zuckerman, K	FL	320
Onc	Antin, J	MA	330
Onc	Deeg, H	WA	386
Onc	Estey, E	WA	387
Onc	Gabrilove, J	NY	343
Onc	List, A	FL	360
Onc	Pecora, A	NJ	349
Onc	Rosove, M	CA	391
Onc	Silverman, L	NY	351
Onc	Wetzler, M	NY	354
Path	Bagg, A	PA	720
PHO	Corey, S	IL	782

Spec	Name	St	Pg

Myeloproliferative Disorders

Spec	Name	St	Pg
Hem	Baer, M	MD	313
Hem	Baron, J	IL	320
Hem	Cortes, J	TX	326
Hem	DeLoughery, T	OR	328
Hem	Djulbegovic, B	FL	319
Hem	Filicko-O'Hara, J	PA	314
Hem	Fruchtman, S	NY	314
Hem	Mesa, R	AZ	327
Hem	Nand, S	IL	323
Hem	Snyder, D	CA	330
Hem	Spivak, J	MD	317
Hem	Tefferi, A	MN	324
Hem	Zuckerman, K	FL	320
Onc	Aboulafia, D	WA	384
Onc	Deeg, H	WA	386
Onc	Gabrilove, J	NY	343
Onc	Rosove, M	CA	391
Onc	Silver, S	MI	374
Onc	Wetzler, M	NY	354

N

Nail Diseases

Spec	Name	St	Pg
D	Russell, M	VA	193

Nail Surgery

Spec	Name	St	Pg
HS	Chung, K	MI	302

Narcolepsy

Spec	Name	St	Pg
Psyc	Doghramji, K	PA	924

Nasal & Sinus Cancer & Surgery

Spec	Name	St	Pg
Oto	Andersen, P	OR	694

Nasal & Sinus Disorders

Spec	Name	St	Pg
Oto	Benninger, M	OH	683
Oto	Corey, J	IL	684
Oto	Josephson, J	NY	671
Oto	Kern, R	IL	686
Oto	Kingdom, T	CO	690
Oto	Schley, W	NY	675
Oto	Siegel, G	IL	687
Oto	Sillers, M	AL	681
Oto	Stankiewicz, J	IL	688
Oto	Stewart, M	NY	676

Nasal & Sinus Surgery

Spec	Name	St	Pg
Oto	Benninger, M	OH	683
Oto	Blitzer, A	NY	668
Oto	Krespi, Y	NY	672
Oto	Setzen, M	NY	675
Oto	Weber, S	TX	694

Nasal Allergy

Spec	Name	St	Pg
A&I	Benenati, S	FL	82
Oto	Hurst, M	WV	671
Oto	Senior, B	NC	681

Nasal Reconstruction

Spec	Name	St	Pg
Oto	Alam, D	OH	682
Oto	Edelstein, D	NY	669
Oto	Graham, H	LA	692
PlS	Menick, F	AZ	899
PlS	Miller, T	CA	904
PlS	Walton, R	IL	897

Nasal Surgery

Spec	Name	St	Pg
Oto	Bolger, W	FL	677
Oto	Branham, G	MO	684
Oto	Johnson, C	LA	692
Oto	Larrabee, W	WA	695

Natural Orifice Surgery (NOTES)

Spec	Name	St	Pg
S	Bessler, M	NY	1089
S	Marks, J	OH	1116
S	Morton, J	CA	1134
S	Rattner, D	MA	1087

Neck Masses

Spec	Name	St	Pg
Oto	Andersen, P	OR	694
Oto	Eisele, D	MD	669
Oto	Hotaling, A	IL	686
PO	April, M	NY	802
PO	Darrow, D	VA	803
PO	Dolitsky, J	NY	802
PO	Myer, C	OH	804
PO	Rosbe, K	CA	806

Necrotizing Enterocolitis

Spec	Name	St	Pg
NP	Holzman, I	NY	449
NP	La Gamma, E	NY	449
PS	Chwals, W	MA	814
PS	Grikscheit, T	CA	823

Neonatal & Infant Cardiac Surgery

Spec	Name	St	Pg
T&CS	Bacha, E	NY	1150
T&CS	Dabal, R	AL	1162
T&CS	Spray, T	PA	1159
T&CS	Ziemer, G	IL	1172

Neonatal Cardiology

Spec	Name	St	Pg
NP	Bucciarelli, R	FL	451
PCd	Gewitz, M	NY	749

Neonatal Cholestasis

Spec	Name	St	Pg
PGe	Suchy, F	CO	768

Neonatal Chronic Lung Disease (CLD)

Spec	Name	St	Pg
NP	Cole, F	MO	451
NP	Seidner, S	TX	453
NP	Van Marter, L	MA	448

Neonatal Critical Care

Spec	Name	St	Pg
NP	Bell, E	IA	451
NP	Gleason, C	WA	453
NP	Lawson, E	MD	449
NP	Perlman, J	NY	450
NP	Zach, T	NE	453

Neonatal Diabetes

Spec	Name	St	Pg
PEn	Sperling, M	PA	759

Neonatal Hemochromatosis

Spec	Name	St	Pg
NP	Bell, E	IA	451

Neonatal Infections

Spec	Name	St	Pg
NP	La Gamma, E	NY	449
NP	Meadow, W	IL	452
NP	Polin, R	NY	450
PInf	Baker, C	TX	796
PInf	Baltimore, R	CT	792
PInf	Jacobs, R	AR	796

Neonatal Neurology

Spec	Name	St	Pg
ChiN	Legido, A	PA	145
ChiN	Mandelbaum, D	RI	144
ChiN	Scher, M	OH	149
NP	Hendricks-Munoz, K	VA	451
NP	Perlman, J	NY	450

Neonatal Nutrition

Spec	Name	St	Pg
NP	Holzman, I	NY	449

Neonatal Pathology

Spec	Name	St	Pg
Path	Faye-Petersen, O	AL	726

Neonatal Surgery

Spec	Name	St	Pg
PS	Adzick, N	PA	814
PS	Black, C	TX	821
PS	Cass, D	TX	822
PS	Caty, M	CT	813
PS	Dolgin, S	NY	815
PS	Doody, D	MA	814
PS	Flake, A	PA	815
PS	Ginsburg, H	NY	815
PS	Glick, P	NY	816
PS	Grikscheit, T	CA	823

Spec	Name	St	Pg
PS	Hicks, B	DE	816
PS	Hilfiker, M	CA	823
PS	Holterman, M	IL	820
PS	Jackson, R	AR	822
PS	Kandel, J	IL	820
PS	Kane, T	DC	816
PS	Karrer, F	CO	821
PS	Latchaw, L	NH	814
PS	Midulla, P	NY	816
PS	Nance, M	PA	816
PS	Oldham, K	WI	820
PS	Proctor, M	WA	823
PS	Rescorla, F	IN	820
PS	Rice, H	NC	818
PS	Ricketts, R	GA	818
PS	Rodgers, B	VA	818
PS	Sato, T	WI	821
PS	Schwartz, M	PA	817
PS	Spigland, N	NY	817
PS	Stolar, C	CA	824
PS	Strauch, E	MD	817
PS	Stylianos, S	NY	817
PS	Velcek, F	NY	817
PS	Voigt, R	MD	817
PS	Waldhausen, J	WA	824
PS	Warner, B	MO	821
T&CS	Abraham, V	IN	1166
T&CS	Cohen, G	CA	1177

Neonatal Surgery-Gastrointestinal

Spec	Name	St	Pg
PS	Sawin, R	WA	824

Neonatal-Perinatal Medicine

Spec	Name	St	Pg
NP	Adams, J	TX	453
NP	Anday, E	PA	448
NP	Bell, E	IA	451
NP	Boyle, R	VA	450
NP	Bucciarelli, R	FL	451
NP	Cole, F	MO	451
NP	Davidson, D	NY	449
NP	Davis, J	MA	448
NP	Delivoria-Papadopoulos, M	PA	449
NP	Dennery, P	PA	449
NP	Dhanireddy, R	TN	451
NP	Donn, S	MI	452
NP	Ehrenkranz, R	CT	448
NP	Escobedo, M	OK	453
NP	Frantz, I	MA	448
NP	Garcia-Prats, J	TX	453
NP	Gewolb, I	MI	452
NP	Gleason, C	WA	453
NP	Gross, I	CT	448
NP	Hamvas, A	MO	452
NP	Hendricks-Munoz, K	VA	451
NP	Holtzman, R	NC	451
NP	Holzman, I	NY	449
NP	Hurt, H	PA	449
NP	La Gamma, E	NY	449
NP	Lawson, E	MD	449
NP	Martin, R	OH	452
NP	Meadow, W	IL	452
NP	Milley, J	UT	452
NP	Muraskas, J	IL	452
NP	Nogee, L	MD	450
NP	Odom, M	TX	453
NP	Perlman, J	NY	450
NP	Polin, R	NY	450
NP	Seidner, S	TX	453
NP	Short, B	DC	450
NP	Silverman, G	PA	450
NP	Simmons, C	CA	454
NP	Stevenson, D	CA	454
NP	Stiles, A	NC	451
NP	Van Marter, L	MA	448
NP	Watchko, J	PA	450
NP	Whitsett, J	OH	452
NP	Zach, T	NE	453
NP	Zubrow, A	PA	450

Neonatology

Spec	Name	St	Pg
NP	Boyle, R	VA	450
NP	Delivoria-Papadopoulos, M	PA	449
NP	Dhanireddy, R	TN	451
NP	Escobedo, M	OK	453
NP	Holtzman, R	NC	451
NP	Hurt, H	PA	449
NP	Odom, M	TX	453
NP	Stevenson, D	CA	454
NP	Stiles, A	NC	451
NP	Zubrow, A	PA	450

Nephrogenic Systemic Fibrosis

Spec	Name	St	Pg
Rhu	Kay, J	MA	1058

Nephrology

Spec	Name	St	Pg
Nep	Ahmad, S	WA	466
Nep	Allon, M	AL	461
Nep	Appel, G	NY	458
Nep	August, P	NY	459
Nep	Bakris, G	IL	462
Nep	Bazari, H	MA	458
Nep	Bennett, W	OR	466
Nep	Bernardo, J	PA	459
Nep	Berns, J	PA	459
Nep	Blumenfeld, J	NY	459
Nep	Bolton, W	VA	461
Nep	Brennan, D	MO	463
Nep	Brennan, S	TX	465
Nep	Butterly, D	NC	461
Nep	Cho, K	CA	466
Nep	Coe, F	IL	463
Nep	Coffman, T	NC	461
Nep	Cohen, D	NY	459
Nep	Delmez, J	MO	463
Nep	Dember, L	PA	459
Nep	Fadem, S	TX	465
Nep	Falk, R	NC	461
Nep	Fulop, T	MS	461
Nep	Gaston, R	AL	461
Nep	Gluck, S	CA	466
Nep	Helderman, J	TN	462
Nep	Holzman, L	PA	459
Nep	Hruska, K	MO	463
Nep	Johnston, J	PA	459
Nep	Josephson, M	IL	463
Nep	Kasinath, B	TX	465
Nep	Kasiske, B	MN	463
Nep	Kelepouris, E	PA	460
Nep	King, A	CA	467
Nep	Kliger, A	CT	458
Nep	Kobrin, S	PA	460
Nep	Kraus, M	IN	463
Nep	Lea, J	GA	462
Nep	McCarthy, J	MN	463
Nep	Miller, B	MO	464
Nep	Nolan, C	TX	466
Nep	Okusa, M	VA	462
Nep	Olivero, J	TX	466
Nep	Ott, S	WA	467
Nep	Perrone, R	MA	458
Nep	Piraino, B	PA	460
Nep	Pohl, M	OH	464
Nep	Rakowski, T	VA	462
Nep	Riordan, J	CA	467
Nep	Rodby, R	IL	464
Nep	Roth, D	FL	462
Nep	Rudnick, M	PA	460
Nep	Salant, D	MA	458
Nep	Scandling, J	CA	467
Nep	Schreiber, M	OH	464
Nep	Schwartz, G	MN	464
Nep	Seifter, J	MA	458
Nep	Somerville, J	MN	464
Nep	Stern, L	NY	460
Nep	Swartz, R	MI	464
Nep	Textor, S	MN	464
Nep	Thomas, C	IA	465
Nep	Tolkoff-Rubin, N	MA	458
Nep	Torres, V	MN	465
Nep	Toto, R	TX	466
Nep	Townsend, R	PA	460
Nep	Venkat, K	MI	465
Nep	Ward, D	CA	467
Nep	Weiner, I	FL	462
Nep	Wilcox, C	DC	460
Nep	Williams, G	NY	460
Nep	Winston, J	NY	461
Nep	Yee, J	MI	465

Nephrotic Syndrome

Spec	Name	St	Pg
Nep	Appel, G	NY	458
Nep	Bazari, H	MA	458
Nep	Dember, L	PA	459
Nep	Okusa, M	VA	462
PNep	Alexander, S	CA	800
PNep	Benfield, M	AL	798
PNep	Clardy, C	IL	799
PNep	Cohn, R	IL	800
PNep	Harmon, W	MA	797
PNep	Kaplan, B	PA	798

Spec	Name	St	Pg
PNep	Zilleruelo, G	FL	799

Nerve Disorders/Surgery

Spec	Name	St	Pg
HS	Atkinson, R	HI	305
HS	Jones, N	CA	306
HS	Putnam, M	MN	304
HS	Trumble, T	WA	306
HS	Wolfe, S	NY	300

Nerve Injuries

Spec	Name	St	Pg
N	Oaklander, A	MA	511
N	Zimnowodzki, S	IL	534

Nerve Injuries/Surgery

Spec	Name	St	Pg
PlS	Lee, R	IL	894

Nerve Surgery & Transplantation

Spec	Name	St	Pg
NS	Belzberg, A	MD	474
NS	Freeman, T	FL	484
PlS	MacKinnon, S	MO	894

Nerve Tumors

Spec	Name	St	Pg
NS	Belzberg, A	MD	474

Neuro-Immunology

Spec	Name	St	Pg
N	Apatoff, B	NY	512
N	Becker, K	WA	538
N	Cohen, J	OH	529
N	Coyle, P	NY	514
N	Latov, N	NY	517

Neuro-Oncology

Spec	Name	St	Pg
ChiN	Allen, J	NY	145
ChiN	Bergman, I	PA	145
ChiN	Fisher, P	CA	151
ChiN	Phillips, P	PA	146
ChiN	Pomeroy, S	MA	144
N	Aiken, R	IL	527
N	Barger, G	MI	528
N	Cascino, T	MN	528
N	Chamberlain, M	WA	539
N	Cloughesy, T	CA	539
N	DeAngelis, L	NY	514
N	Gilbert, M	TX	536
N	Glass, J	PA	516
N	Kesari, S	CA	540
N	Lassman, A	NY	517
N	Laterra, J	MD	517
N	Moots, P	TN	526
N	Nabors, L	AL	526
N	Newton, H	OH	531
N	Patchell, R	NJ	520
N	Phuphanich, S	CA	541
N	Posner, J	NY	520
N	Puduvalli, V	OH	532
N	Rogers, L	OH	532
N	Ronan, L	NH	512
N	Rosenfeld, S	OH	533
N	Schiff, D	VA	527
N	Shapiro, W	AZ	537
N	Taylor, L	MA	512
N	Vick, N	IL	534
N	Wen, P	MA	512
N	Yung, W	TX	538
NRad	Murtagh, F	FL	1022
NS	Berger, M	CA	498
NS	Brem, S	PA	475
NS	Chandler, J	IL	489
NS	De Monte, F	TX	495
NS	Evans, J	PA	476
NS	Guthrie, B	AL	485
NS	Liau, L	CA	500
NS	Lillehei, K	CO	494
NS	Neuwelt, E	OR	501
NS	O'Rourke, D	PA	480
NS	Olson, J	GA	486
NS	Park, T	MO	491
NS	Piepmeier, J	CT	473
NS	Pollack, I	PA	481
NS	Quigley, M	PA	481
NS	Rock, J	MI	492
NS	Rosenblum, M	MI	492
NS	Sundaresan, N	NY	482
NS	Thompson, R	TN	487
NS	Warnick, R	OH	493
Onc	Buckner, J	MN	367
Onc	Fine, H	NY	342
Onc	Friedman, H	NC	358
Onc	Grossman, S	MD	344
Onc	Lesser, G	NC	360
Onc	Lyckholm, L	VA	361
Onc	Peereboom, D	OH	372
Onc	Prados, M	CA	391
PHO	Blaney, S	TX	787
PHO	Fouladi, M	OH	783
PHO	Gajjar, A	TN	778
PHO	Geyer, J	WA	790
PHO	Goldman, S	IL	783
PHO	Gururangan, S	NC	779
PHO	Jakacki, R	PA	774
PHO	Kieran, M	MA	770
PHO	Olson, J	OR	791
PHO	Puccetti, D	WI	785
RadRO	Flickinger, J	PA	979
RadRO	Isaacson, S	NY	980
RadRO	Larner, J	VA	985
RadRO	Larson, D	CA	996
RadRO	Mehta, M	MD	981

Neuro-Ophthalmology

Spec	Name	St	Pg
N	Balcer, L	NY	513
N	Corbett, J	MS	524
N	Frohman, E	TX	536
N	Galetta, S	NY	515
N	Gizzi, M	NJ	516
N	Goodwin, J	IL	530
N	Lavin, P	TN	525
N	Liu, G	PA	518
N	Newman, N	GA	526
N	Schatz, N	FL	526
Oph	Arnold, A	CA	604
Oph	Biousse, V	GA	587
Oph	Buckley, E	NC	587
Oph	Capo, H	FL	587
Oph	Cockerham, K	CA	605
Oph	Feldon, S	NY	578
Oph	Guy, J	FL	589
Oph	Hedges, T	MA	574
Oph	Krauss, H	CA	607
Oph	Kupersmith, M	NY	581
Oph	Lee, A	TX	602
Oph	Mawn, L	TN	590
Oph	Miller, N	MD	582
Oph	Mizen, T	IL	598
Oph	Odel, J	NY	583
Oph	Rizzo, J	MA	575
Oph	Savino, P	CA	608
Oph	Schiffman, J	TX	603
Oph	Sergott, R	PA	584
Oph	Siatkowski, R	OK	603
Oph	Trobe, J	MI	600
Oph	Volpe, N	IL	600
Oph	Walton, D	MA	575

Neuro-Otology

Spec	Name	St	Pg
N	Hain, T	IL	530
N	Lavin, P	TN	525
Oto	Arts, H	MI	682
Oto	Carey, J	MD	668
Oto	Dornhoffer, J	AR	692
Oto	Gantz, B	IA	685
Oto	Harris, J	CA	695
Oto	Haynes, D	TN	679
Oto	Hirsch, B	PA	670
Oto	Holliday, M	MD	671
Oto	Jackler, R	CA	695
Oto	Jenkins, H	CO	690
Oto	Kesser, B	VA	679
Oto	Lambert, P	SC	679
Oto	Leonetti, J	IL	686
Oto	Macias, J	AZ	693
Oto	Mattox, D	GA	679
Oto	McKenna, M	MA	666
Oto	Miyamoto, R	IN	686
Oto	Niparko, J	CA	696
Oto	O'Leary, M	CA	696
Oto	Oghalai, J	CA	696
Oto	Paparella, M	MN	687
Oto	Pillsbury, H	NC	680
Oto	Rauch, S	MA	666
Oto	Roland, J	NY	674
Oto	Rubinstein, J	WA	696
Oto	Sataloff, R	PA	675
Oto	Telischi, F	FL	681
PO	Friedman, E	TX	805
PO	O'Reilly, R	DE	802
PO	Poe, D	MA	801

Neuro-Pathology

Spec	Name	St	Pg
N	Filley, C	CO	534
Path	Bollen, A	CA	732
Path	Bruner, J	TX	730
Path	Burger, P	MD	721
Path	Chandrasoma, P	CA	732
Path	DeMasters, B	CO	729
Path	Gambetti, P	OH	728
Path	Mischel, P	CA	733
Path	Moore, S	IA	728
Path	Perry, A	CA	734
Path	Petito, C	FL	726
Path	Rosenblum, M	NY	723
Path	Smith, T	MA	719
Path	Zagzag, D	NY	725

Neuro-Psychiatry

Spec	Name	St	Pg
GerPsy	Lyketsos, C	MD	944
N	Cummings, J	NV	539
N	Kent, T	TX	537
Psyc	Black, K	MO	929
Psyc	Fann, J	WA	933
Psyc	Keepers, G	OR	933
Psyc	Locala, J	OH	930
Psyc	Neppe, V	WA	934
Psyc	Wilson, D	FL	929

Neuro-Rehabilitation

Spec	Name	St	Pg
N	Corbetta, M	MO	529
N	Fellus, J	NJ	515
N	Kirshner, H	TN	525
PMR	Currie, D	TX	870
PMR	Diamond, P	VA	866
PMR	Palmer, J	MD	865
PMR	Richter, E	CT	862

Neuro-Urology

Spec	Name	St	Pg
Ped Uro	Bauer, S	MA	824
Ped Uro	Joseph, D	AL	826
U	Bodner, D	OH	1202
U	Boone, T	TX	1208
U	Bushman, W	WI	1202
U	Chancellor, M	MI	1203
U	Ginsberg, D	CA	1211
U	Gomery, P	MA	1186
U	Wein, A	PA	1196

Neuroblastoma

Spec	Name	St	Pg
PHO	Blatt, J	NC	778
PHO	Castle, V	MI	782
PHO	Cheung, N	NY	772
PHO	Cohn, S	IL	782
PHO	Diller, L	MA	770
PHO	Frantz, C	DE	773
PHO	Furman, W	TN	778
PHO	Grupp, S	PA	773
PHO	Hutchinson, R	MI	784
PHO	Kramer, K	NY	774
PHO	Kreissman, S	NC	779
PHO	Kushner, B	NY	775
PHO	Maris, J	PA	775
PHO	Matthay, K	CA	791
PHO	O'Dorisio, M	IA	784
PHO	Park, J	WA	791
PHO	Sondel, P	WI	785
PHO	Vik, T	IN	786
PHO	Wechsler, D	NC	781
PS	Barksdale, E	OH	819
PS	Davidoff, A	TN	818
PS	Kandel, J	IL	820
PS	La Quaglia, M	NY	816
PS	Morgan, W	TN	818
PS	Shamberger, R	MA	814

Neurocutaneous Disorders

Spec	Name	St	Pg
CG	Cassidy, S	CA	162
ChiN	Rosser, T	CA	152

Neurodegenerative Disorders

Spec	Name	St	Pg
ChiN	Mitchell, W	CA	151
N	Farlow, M	IN	529
Path	Gambetti, P	OH	728

Neurodevelopmental Disabilities

Spec	Name	St	Pg
PMR	Keen, M	IL	868

Neuroendocrine Disorders

Spec	Name	St	Pg
PEn	Oberfield, S	NY	758

Neuroendocrine Tumors

Spec	Name	St	Pg
EDM	Katznelson, L	CA	225
EDM	Snyder, P	PA	215
Ge	Metz, D	PA	238
NS	Parent, A	MS	486
NS	Swearingen, B	MA	474
Onc	Ahlgren, J	DC	336
Onc	Ajani, J	TX	378
Onc	Anthony, L	KY	354
Onc	Engstrom, P	PA	342
Onc	Fisher, G	CA	387
Onc	Goldberg, R	OH	369
Onc	Grosh, W	VA	359
Onc	Kane, M	CO	377
Onc	Kelsen, D	NY	346
Onc	Moore, J	NC	361
Onc	O'Reilly, E	NY	348
Onc	Saltz, L	NY	350
Onc	Taetle, R	AZ	383
Onc	Wolin, E	CA	394
PHO	O'Dorisio, M	IA	784
S	Clark, O	CA	1131
S	Johnson Miller, D	NJ	1095
S	Libutti, S	NY	1096
S	Sasson, A	NE	1123
S	Solorzano, C	TN	1109
S	Woltering, E	LA	1129

Neuroendocrinology

Spec	Name	St	Pg
EDM	Calvi, L	NY	211
EDM	Hoffman, A	CA	224
EDM	Kandeel, F	CA	224
EDM	Kleinberg, D	NY	213
EDM	Marshall, J	VA	217
EDM	Vance, M	VA	217
PEn	Lustig, R	CA	762

Neurofibromatosis

Spec	Name	St	Pg
CG	Bialer, M	NY	157
CG	Charrow, J	IL	160
CG	Davis, J	NY	157
CG	Korf, B	AL	159
CG	Mulvihill, J	OK	161
CG	Saal, H	OH	160
ChiN	Allen, J	NY	145
ChiN	Greenwood, R	NC	147
ChiN	Packer, R	DC	146
ChiN	Phillips, P	PA	146
ChiN	Rosser, T	CA	152
ChiN	Tonsgard, J	IL	149
N	Moots, P	TN	526
N	Roos, K	IN	533
NRad	Vezina, L	DC	1021
PHO	Fouladi, M	OH	783

Neurogenetics

Spec	Name	St	Pg
CG	Jayakar, P	FL	159
CG	Korf, B	AL	159
CG	Northrup, H	TX	162
CG	Shoffner, J	GA	159
ChiN	Patterson, M	MN	149
ChiN	Tennison, M	NC	147
N	Siddique, T	IL	533
NRad	Hunter, J	TX	1025

Neurogenic Bladder

Spec	Name	St	Pg
Ped Uro	Bauer, S	MA	824
Ped Uro	Bloom, D	MI	826
Ped Uro	Cheng, E	IL	826
Ped Uro	Ewalt, D	TX	828
Ped Uro	Greenfield, S	NY	825
Ped Uro	Rink, R	IN	828
PMR	Cardenas, D	FL	866
PMR	Fried, G	PA	864
U	Blaivas, J	NY	1189
U	Ginsberg, D	CA	1211
U	Kennelly, M	NC	1198
U	Lloyd, L	AL	1198
U	Raz, S	CA	1213
U	Vapnek, J	NY	1196

Neurologic Rehabilitation

Spec	Name	St	Pg
PMR	Ahn, J	NY	862
PMR	Mason, K	CO	870
PMR	Roth, E	IL	869

Neurological Aspects of

Systemic Disease

Spec	Name	St	Pg
N	Samuels, M	MA	512

Neurological Complications of Cancer

Spec	Name	St	Pg
N	Moots, P	TN	526
N	Schiff, D	VA	527

Neurological Imaging

Spec	Name	St	Pg
DR	Elster, A	NC	1013
DR	Mountz, J	PA	1011
N	Burke, A	IL	528
N	Corbetta, M	MO	529
N	Greer, D	CT	511
NuM	Strashun, A	NY	555

Neurological Surgery

Spec	Name	St	Pg
NS	Adelson, P	AZ	495
NS	Al-Mefty, O	MA	472
NS	Amar, A	CA	498
NS	Ames, C	CA	498
NS	Anderson, R	NY	474
NS	Andrews, D	PA	474
NS	Apuzzo, M	CA	498
NS	Asher, A	NC	483
NS	Atkinson, J	MN	488
NS	Badie, B	CA	498
NS	Bailes, J	IL	488
NS	Bakay, R	IL	488
NS	Baltuch, G	PA	474
NS	Barnett, G	OH	488
NS	Barrow, D	GA	484
NS	Bauer, J	IL	488
NS	Bederson, J	NY	474
NS	Belzberg, A	MD	474
NS	Benzel, E	OH	489
NS	Berger, M	CA	498
NS	Bierbrauer, K	OH	489
NS	Bilsky, M	NY	475
NS	Bingaman, W	OH	489
NS	Black, K	CA	498
NS	Boggan, J	CA	498
NS	Boop, F	TN	484
NS	Borges, L	MA	472
NS	Branch, C	NC	484
NS	Bray, R	CA	499
NS	Brem, H	MD	475
NS	Brem, S	PA	475
NS	Brockmeyer, D	UT	494
NS	Bruce, J	NY	475
NS	Bucholz, R	MO	489
NS	Burchiel, K	OR	499
NS	Butler, W	MA	472
NS	Caputy, A	DC	475
NS	Carson, B	MD	475
NS	Chandler, J	IL	489
NS	Charbel, F	IL	489
NS	Chen, C	NY	475
NS	Chen, T	CA	499
NS	Cherny, W	ID	494
NS	Chiocca, E	MA	472
NS	Cohen, A	MA	472
NS	Cosgrove, G	RI	472
NS	Couldwell, W	UT	494
NS	Dacey, R	MO	489
NS	Danielpour, M	CA	499
NS	David, C	MA	472
NS	De Monte, F	TX	495
NS	Dempsey, R	WI	489
NS	Di Giacinto, G	NY	476
NS	Dias, M	PA	476
NS	Diaz, F	MI	490
NS	Duhaime, A	MA	473
NS	Edwards, M	CA	499
NS	Eisenberg, H	MD	476
NS	El-Kadi, H	PA	476
NS	Ellenbogen, R	WA	499
NS	Evans, J	PA	476
NS	Ewend, M	NC	484
NS	Feldstein, N	NY	476
NS	Fenstermaker, R	NY	476
NS	Fessler, R	IL	490
NS	Foley, K	TN	484
NS	Freeman, T	FL	484
NS	Friedman, A	NC	484
NS	Frim, D	IL	490
NS	Giannotta, S	CA	499
NS	Gokaslan, Z	MD	477
NS	Golfinos, J	NY	477
NS	Goodman, R	NY	477
NS	Goumnerova, L	MA	473
NS	Grady, M	PA	477
NS	Green, B	FL	484
NS	Greene, C	LA	495
NS	Grubb, R	MO	490
NS	Gupta, N	CA	499
NS	Guthikonda, M	MI	490
NS	Guthrie, B	AL	485
NS	Gutin, P	NY	477
NS	Hadley, M	AL	485
NS	Haid, R	GA	485
NS	Hankinson, H	NM	495
NS	Harbaugh, R	PA	477
NS	Harper, R	TX	495
NS	Harrop, J	PA	477
NS	Harsh, G	CA	500
NS	Hartl, R	NY	477
NS	Heilman, C	MA	473
NS	Heros, R	FL	485
NS	Hopkins, L	NY	478
NS	Huang, J	MD	478
NS	Jallo, G	MD	478
NS	Jenkins, A	NY	478
NS	Jho, H	PA	478
NS	Jimenez, D	TX	496
NS	Johnson, S	CO	494
NS	Judy, K	PA	478
NS	Kaiser, M	NY	478
NS	Kaufman, B	WI	490
NS	Khan, A	MD	478
NS	Kim, D	TX	496
NS	Kim, D	TX	496
NS	Kim, J	MS	485
NS	Kobrine, A	DC	479
NS	Kondziolka, D	NY	479
NS	Kotapka, M	PA	479
NS	Krisht, A	AR	496
NS	Kuntz, C	OH	490
NS	Landy, H	FL	485
NS	Lang, F	TX	496
NS	Laske, D	PA	479
NS	Lavyne, M	NY	479
NS	Lee, M	TX	496
NS	Lemole, G	AZ	496
NS	Levi, A	FL	485
NS	Levy, E	NY	479
NS	Levy, M	CA	500
NS	Liau, L	CA	500
NS	Liker, M	CA	500
NS	Lillehei, K	CO	494
NS	Link, M	MN	491
NS	Linskey, M	CA	500
NS	Liu, C	CA	500
NS	Loftus, C	IL	491
NS	Luerssen, T	TX	496
NS	Luken, M	IL	491
NS	Lunsford, L	PA	479
NS	Madsen, J	MA	473
NS	Malik, G	MI	491
NS	Mamelak, A	CA	500
NS	Mapstone, T	OK	497
NS	Markert, J	AL	485
NS	Maroon, J	PA	479
NS	Martin, N	CA	500
NS	Martuza, R	MA	473
NS	Mayberg, M	WA	501
NS	McCormick, P	NY	480
NS	McDermott, M	CA	501
NS	Menezes, A	IA	491
NS	Meyer, F	MN	491
NS	Mickey, B	TX	497
NS	Moore, F	NJ	480
NS	Morcos, J	FL	486
NS	Moser, R	MA	473
NS	Myseros, J	DC	480
NS	Naff, N	MD	480
NS	Nagib, M	MN	491
NS	Nazzaro, J	KS	494
NS	Neuwelt, E	OR	501
NS	O'Rourke, D	PA	480
NS	Oakes, W	AL	486
NS	Ojemann, J	WA	501
NS	Olivi, A	MD	480
NS	Olson, J	GA	486
NS	Origitano, T	MT	494
NS	Ott, K	CA	501
NS	Parent, A	MS	486
NS	Park, T	MO	491
NS	Parsa, A	IL	492
NS	Patel, A	NY	480
NS	Patel, S	SC	486
NS	Penar, P	VT	473
NS	Piatt, J	DE	480
NS	Piepmeier, J	CT	473
NS	Pollack, I	PA	481
NS	Quigley, M	PA	481

Specialty & Special Expertise Index

Spec	Name	St	Pg
NS	Raffel, C	CA	501
NS	Ragheb, J	FL	486
NS	Reid, W	TN	486
NS	Rezai, A	OH	492
NS	Rich, K	MO	492
NS	Rigamonti, D	MD	481
NS	Riina, H	NY	481
NS	Robertson, J	TN	486
NS	Rock, J	MI	492
NS	Rodts, G	GA	487
NS	Rosenblatt, S	IL	492
NS	Rosenblum, M	MI	492
NS	Rosenwasser, R	PA	481
NS	Ruge, J	IL	492
NS	Ryken, T	IA	492
NS	Sampson, J	NC	487
NS	Samson, D	TX	497
NS	Sandberg, D	TX	497
NS	Sawaya, R	TX	497
NS	Schwartz, T	NY	481
NS	Sekhar, L	WA	501
NS	Sekhon, L	NV	501
NS	Selden, N	OR	502
NS	Selman, W	OH	493
NS	Sen, C	NY	481
NS	Shaffrey, C	VA	487
NS	Shaffrey, M	VA	487
NS	Shapiro, S	IN	493
NS	Shuer, L	CA	502
NS	Silbergeld, D	WA	502
NS	Sills, A	TN	487
NS	Sisti, M	NY	482
NS	Sklar, F	TX	497
NS	Solomon, R	NY	482
NS	Souweidane, M	NY	482
NS	Spencer, D	CT	474
NS	Spetzler, R	AZ	497
NS	Spinner, R	MN	493
NS	Steinberg, G	CA	502
NS	Stieg, P	NY	482
NS	Sun, P	CA	502
NS	Sundaresan, N	NY	482
NS	Sutton, L	PA	482
NS	Swaid, S	AL	487
NS	Swearingen, B	MA	474
NS	Tamargo, R	MD	482
NS	Tatter, S	NC	487
NS	Taylon, C	NE	494
NS	Theodore, N	AZ	497
NS	Thompson, B	MI	493
NS	Thompson, R	TN	487
NS	Tomita, T	IL	493
NS	Traynelis, V	IL	493
NS	Van Loveren, H	FL	488
NS	Walker, M	UT	495
NS	Warnick, R	OH	493
NS	Weiner, H	NY	482
NS	Weingart, J	MD	483
NS	Welch, W	PA	483
NS	Wharen, R	FL	488
NS	Whiting, D	PA	483
NS	Wilberger, J	PA	483
NS	Wilson, J	NC	488
NS	Wisoff, J	NY	483
NS	Yonas, H	NM	498
NS	Yu, J	CA	502
NS	Zager, E	PA	483
NS	Zimmerman, C	ID	495

Neurology

Spec	Name	St	Pg
N	Abou-Khalil, B	TN	523
N	Adams, D	FL	523
N	Adams, H	IA	527
N	Adornato, B	CA	538
N	Ahern, G	AZ	535
N	Ahlskog, J	MN	527
N	Aiken, R	IL	527
N	Albers, G	CA	538
N	Alberts, M	TX	536
N	Alexandrov, A	AL	523
N	Amato, A	MA	510
N	Aminoff, M	CA	538
N	Apatoff, B	NY	512
N	Arnason, B	IL	528
N	Ashizawa, T	FL	523
N	Azizi, S	PA	513
N	Balcer, L	NY	513
N	Barger, G	MI	528
N	Barkley, G	MI	528
N	Barohn, R	KS	534
N	Baser, S	PA	513
N	Batchelor, T	MA	510
N	Bebin, E	AL	523
N	Becker, K	WA	538
N	Bell, R	PA	513
N	Berger, J	KY	523
N	Bergey, G	MD	513
N	Bernstein, R	IL	528
N	Bertorini, T	TN	523
N	Biller, J	IL	528
N	Blum, A	RI	510
N	Bressman, S	NY	513
N	Brick, J	WV	513
N	Broderick, J	OH	528
N	Bromberg, M	UT	534
N	Brooks, B	NC	523
N	Brown, R	MN	528
N	Bruno, M	HI	538
N	Buchholz, D	MD	513
N	Burke, A	IL	528
N	Busis, N	PA	514
N	Calabresi, P	MD	514
N	Caplan, L	MA	510
N	Cascino, T	MN	528
N	Chamberlain, M	WA	539
N	Charles, A	CA	539
N	Charney, J	NY	514
N	Chelimsky, T	WI	529
N	Chui, H	CA	539
N	Cloughesy, T	CA	539
N	Cohen, J	OH	529
N	Cohen, J	NH	510
N	Cole, A	MA	510
N	Cook, S	NJ	514
N	Corbett, J	MS	524
N	Corbetta, M	MO	529
N	Corey-Bloom, J	CA	539
N	Cornblath, D	MD	514
N	Coull, B	AZ	536
N	Coyle, P	NY	514
N	Cudkowicz, M	MA	510
N	Cummings, J	NV	539
N	Cutrer, F	MN	529
N	DeAngelis, L	NY	514
N	DeGiorgio, C	CA	539
N	DeLong, M	GA	524
N	Devinsky, O	NY	514
N	Dewberry, R	MD	514
N	Dodick, D	AZ	536
N	Donofrio, P	TN	524
N	Doody, R	TX	536
N	Elias, S	MI	529
N	Elkind, M	NY	515
N	Engstrom, J	CA	539
N	Fahn, S	NY	515
N	Farlow, M	IN	529
N	Feinberg, T	NY	515
N	Feldman, E	MI	529
N	Fellus, J	NJ	515
N	Ferrendelli, J	TX	536
N	Filley, C	CO	534
N	Fink, M	NY	515
N	Finkel, A	NC	524
N	Finkel, M	FL	524
N	Fisher, M	CA	539
N	Fisher, R	CA	540
N	Flaherty, A	MA	511
N	Foo, S	NY	515
N	French, J	NY	515
N	Frohman, E	TX	536
N	Furie, K	RI	511
N	Furlan, A	OH	529
N	Galetta, S	NY	515
N	Gendelman, S	NY	515
N	Gilbert, M	TX	536
N	Gilden, D	CO	535
N	Gizzi, M	NJ	516
N	Glass, J	PA	516
N	Glass, J	GA	524
N	Goetz, C	IL	529
N	Golbe, L	NJ	516
N	Goldstein, L	NC	524
N	Goodin, D	CA	540
N	Goodwin, J	IL	530
N	Graves, M	CA	540
N	Greer, D	CT	511
N	Gress, D	VA	524
N	Gross, P	MA	511
N	Grotta, J	TX	536
N	Guilleminault, C	CA	540
N	Hain, T	IL	530
N	Haley, E	VA	525
N	Harati, Y	TX	537
N	Hauser, R	FL	525
N	Hauser, S	CA	540
N	Heck, C	CA	540
N	Hecox, K	WI	530
N	Heilman, K	FL	525

Spec	Name	St	Pg
N	Henderson, V	CA	540
N	Hess, D	GA	525
N	Hiesiger, E	NY	516
N	Homer, D	IL	530
N	Hurtig, H	PA	516
N	Jankovic, J	TX	537
N	Janss, A	GA	525
N	Jobst, B	NH	511
N	Jordan, B	NY	516
N	Josephson, D	IN	530
N	Kase, C	MA	511
N	Kasner, S	PA	516
N	Katirji, B	OH	530
N	Kent, T	TX	537
N	Kesari, S	CA	540
N	Kieburtz, K	NY	516
N	Kincaid, J	IN	530
N	Kirshner, H	TN	525
N	Krauss, G	MD	516
N	Krumholz, A	MD	517
N	Kula, R	NY	517
N	Kurtzke, R	VA	525
N	Kuzniecky, R	NY	517
N	Labar, D	NY	517
N	Labiner, D	AZ	537
N	Lacomis, D	PA	517
N	Lane, J	CO	535
N	Langston, J	CA	540
N	Lassman, A	NY	517
N	Laterra, J	MD	517
N	Latov, N	NY	517
N	Lavin, P	TN	525
N	Levine, D	NY	518
N	Levine, S	NY	518
N	Lew, M	CA	541
N	Lewis, R	CA	541
N	Liporace, J	PA	518
N	Lipton, R	NY	518
N	Lisak, R	MI	530
N	Liu, G	PA	518
N	Logan, W	MO	531
N	Logigian, E	NY	518
N	Longo, F	CA	541
N	Louis, E	NY	518
N	Lublin, F	NY	518
N	Luders, H	OH	531
N	Lutsep, H	OR	541
N	Maraganore, D	IL	531
N	Marder, K	NY	519
N	Marshall, R	NY	519
N	Mayeux, R	NY	519
N	McArthur, J	MD	519
N	McCluskey, L	PA	519
N	Mesulam, M	IL	531
N	Mikkelsen, T	MI	531
N	Miller, A	NY	519
N	Mitsumoto, H	NY	519
N	Mohr, J	NY	519
N	Montgomery, E	PA	520
N	Moots, P	TN	526
N	Morgenlander, J	NC	526
N	Morrell, M	CA	541
N	Morris, J	MO	531
N	Nabors, L	AL	526
N	Newman, D	MI	531
N	Newman, L	NY	520
N	Newman, N	GA	526
N	Newton, H	OH	531
N	Nicholl, J	LA	537
N	Nolan, B	FL	526
N	Nutt, J	OR	541
N	Oaklander, A	MA	511
N	Oh, S	AL	526
N	Olanow, C	NY	520
N	Oommen, K	TX	537
N	Pascuzzi, R	IN	532
N	Patchell, R	NJ	520
N	Pennell, P	MA	511
N	Perlmutter, J	MO	532
N	Pestronk, A	MO	532
N	Petersen, R	MN	532
N	Petito, F	NY	520
N	Phuphanich, S	CA	541
N	Posner, J	NY	520
N	Puduvalli, V	OH	532
N	Pula, T	MD	520
N	Pulst, S	UT	535
N	Reder, A	IL	532
N	Reed, R	OH	532
N	Reich, S	MD	520
N	Relkin, N	NY	520
N	Richerson, G	IA	532
N	Ringel, S	CO	535
N	Rogers, L	OH	532
N	Ronan, L	NH	512
N	Roos, K	IN	533
N	Roos, R	IL	533
N	Ropper, A	MA	512
N	Rosenbaum, R	OR	541
N	Rosenfeld, S	OH	533
N	Rothrock, J	NV	541
N	Rubin, S	IL	533
N	Rutkove, S	MA	512
N	Sabo, T	CO	535
N	Sacco, R	FL	526
N	Sadiq, S	NY	521
N	Sadowsky, C	FL	526
N	Sage, J	NJ	521
N	Samii, A	WA	542
N	Samuels, M	MA	512
N	Saper, C	MA	512
N	Saper, J	MI	533
N	Saver, J	CA	542
N	Schatz, N	FL	526
N	Schiff, D	VA	527
N	Sethi, K	GA	527
N	Shapiro, W	AZ	537
N	Shefner, J	NY	521
N	Sheikh, K	TX	537
N	Shulman, L	MD	521
N	Siddique, T	IL	533
N	Sila, C	OH	533
N	Silberstein, S	PA	521
N	Simpson, D	NY	521
N	Singer, C	FL	527
N	Sirdofsky, M	DC	521
N	Smith, W	CA	542
N	Sperling, M	PA	521
N	Stern, M	PA	522
N	Strom, L	CO	535
N	Suarez, J	TX	538
N	Swanson, J	MN	533
N	Swerdlow, M	NY	522
N	Tanner, C	CA	542
N	Tayal, A	PA	522
N	Taylor, L	MA	512
N	Tetrud, J	CA	542
N	Vas, G	NY	522
N	Vick, N	IL	534
N	Vitek, J	MN	534
N	Vollmer, T	CO	535
N	Waters, C	NY	522
N	Watts, R	AL	527
N	Wechsler, L	PA	522
N	Weinberg, H	NY	522
N	Weiner, L	CA	542
N	Weiss, M	WA	542
N	Wen, P	MA	512
N	Windebank, A	MN	534
N	Wolinsky, J	TX	538
N	Wooten, G	VA	527
N	Wright, R	IL	534
N	Yung, W	TX	538
N	Zimmerman, E	NY	522
N	Zimnowodzki, S	IL	534

Neurometabolic Disorders

ChiN	Haas, R	CA	151

Neuromuscular Disorder & Vision Problems

N	Goodwin, J	IL	530

Neuromuscular Disorders

ChiN	Crawford, T	MD	145
ChiN	Darras, B	MA	144
ChiN	DeVivo, D	NY	145
ChiN	Edgar, T	WI	148
ChiN	Finkel, R	FL	147
ChiN	Gospe, S	WA	151
ChiN	Iannaccone, S	TX	150
ChiN	Lavenstein, B	VA	147
HS	Osterman, A	PA	299
N	Amato, A	MA	510
N	Bertorini, T	TN	523
N	Bromberg, M	UT	534
N	Brooks, B	NC	523
N	Busis, N	PA	514
N	Cohen, J	NH	510
N	Cudkowicz, M	MA	510
N	Feldman, E	MI	529
N	Glass, J	GA	524
N	Harati, Y	TX	537
N	Katirji, B	OH	530
N	Kincaid, J	IN	530
N	Kula, R	NY	517

Spec	Name	St	Pg
N	Kurtzke, R	VA	525
N	Lacomis, D	PA	517
N	Lewis, R	CA	541
N	Logigian, E	NY	518
N	Mitsumoto, H	NY	519
N	Morgenlander, J	NC	526
N	Newman, D	MI	531
N	Oh, S	AL	526
N	Pascuzzi, R	IN	532
N	Pestronk, A	MO	532
N	Ringel, S	CO	535
N	Roos, R	IL	533
N	Rosenbaum, R	OR	541
N	Rutkove, S	MA	512
N	Shefner, J	NY	521
N	Sheikh, K	TX	537
N	Simpson, D	NY	521
N	Sirdofsky, M	DC	521
N	Weinberg, H	NY	522
N	Weiss, M	WA	542
OrS	Otsuka, N	NY	630
OrS	Roye, D	NY	631
Path	Bollen, A	CA	732
PMR	Apkon, S	WA	872
PMR	Bach, J	NJ	863
PMR	Ballard, P	DC	863
PMR	Friedman, A	WA	872
PMR	Kevorkian, C	TX	871
PMR	Kirschner, K	IL	869
PMR	LaBan, M	MI	869
PMR	Massagli, T	WA	872
PMR	Matthews, D	CO	870

Neurophysiology

ChiN	Kovnar, E	WI	149
ChiN	Tennison, M	NC	147
N	Abou-Khalil, B	TN	523
N	Pula, T	MD	520

Neuroradiology

DR	Kanal, E	PA	1010
DR	Mancuso, A	FL	1013
DR	Teal, J	DC	1012
DR	Yoon, S	NY	1012
NRad	Atlas, S	CA	1025
NRad	Barkovich, A	CA	1025
NRad	Barnes, P	CA	1026
NRad	Berenstein, A	NY	1020
NRad	Burdette, J	NC	1021
NRad	Cha, S	CA	1026
NRad	Christoforidis, G	IL	1023
NRad	Cross, D	MO	1023
NRad	Curtin, H	MA	1019
NRad	Dillon, W	CA	1026
NRad	Dion, J	GA	1022
NRad	Drayer, B	NY	1020
NRad	Faro, S	PA	1020
NRad	Frei, D	CO	1025
NRad	Grobelny, T	IL	1023
NRad	Hackney, D	MA	1019
NRad	Haughton, V	WI	1023
NRad	Hesselink, J	CA	1026
NRad	Higashida, R	CA	1026
NRad	Hirsch, J	MA	1019
NRad	Hunter, J	TX	1025
NRad	Hurst, R	PA	1020
NRad	Jarvik, J	WA	1026
NRad	Jensen, M	VA	1022
NRad	Johnson, A	NC	1022
NRad	Joseph, G	NC	1022
NRad	Kallmes, D	MN	1023
NRad	Khandji, A	NY	1020
NRad	Koeller, K	MN	1023
NRad	Larsen, D	CA	1026
NRad	Lee, S	IL	1024
NRad	Lis, E	NY	1021
NRad	Loevner, L	PA	1021
NRad	Maldjian, J	NC	1022
NRad	Masaryk, T	OH	1024
NRad	Mawad, M	TX	1025
NRad	Modic, M	OH	1024
NRad	Moran, C	MO	1024
NRad	Morris, P	NC	1022
NRad	Mukherji, S	MI	1024
NRad	Murtagh, F	FL	1022
NRad	Norbash, A	MA	1019
NRad	Orbach, D	MA	1020
NRad	Osborn, A	UT	1025
NRad	Pile-Spellman, J	NY	1021
NRad	Provenzale, J	NC	1022
NRad	Quencer, R	FL	1023
NRad	Rowley, H	WI	1024
NRad	Russell, E	IL	1024
NRad	Sze, G	CT	1020
NRad	Teitelbaum, G	CA	1026
NRad	Thulborn, K	IL	1024
NRad	Vezina, L	DC	1021
NRad	Yousem, D	MD	1021
NRad	Zimmerman, R	PA	1021
NRad	Zinreich, S	MD	1021
NS	Riina, H	NY	481

Neurosarcoidosis

N	Corbett, J	MS	524

Neurotoxicology

ChiN	Gospe, S	WA	151
N	Brooks, B	NC	523

Neurovascular Surgery

NRad	Lee, S	IL	1024
NS	Rich, K	MO	492
NS	Tamargo, R	MD	482
NS	Thompson, B	MI	493
NS	Thompson, R	TN	487

Neutron Therapy for Advanced Cancer

RadRO	Forman, J	MI	989
RadRO	Laramore, G	WA	996

Nipple Sparing Mastectomy

PIS	Talmor, M	NY	887
S	Swistel, A	NY	1101
S	Tsangaris, T	CT	1088

Nocardia Infection

Inf	Wallace, R	TX	420

Non Tuberculous Mycobacteria

Inf	Wallace, R	TX	420

Non-Invasive Cardiology

Cv	Geltman, E	MO	102
Cv	Liao, J	IL	103

Noonan Syndrome

PCd	Gelb, B	NY	748

Nuclear Cardiology

Cv	Borer, J	NY	91
Cv	Bourge, R	AL	97
Cv	Cerqueira, M	OH	101
Cv	Chaitman, B	MO	101
Cv	Fintel, D	IL	101
Cv	Follansbee, W	PA	92
Cv	Follansbee, W	PA	92
Cv	Gibbons, R	MN	102
Cv	Iskandrian, A	AL	98
Cv	Nocero, M	FL	99
Cv	Shea, R	IN	105
Cv	Skolnick, A	AK	112
Cv	Walsh, M	IN	106
Cv	Williams, K	MI	107
IC	Khawaja, S	GA	124
NuM	Appelbaum, D	IL	556
NuM	Dae, M	CA	557
NuM	Dillehay, G	IL	556
NuM	Goldsmith, S	NY	554
NuM	Neumann, D	OH	556
NuM	Sanger, J	NY	555
NuM	Schelbert, H	CA	557
NuM	Strashun, A	NY	555
NuM	Ziffer, J	FL	556

Nuclear Endocrinology

NuM	Carrasquillo, J	NY	554
NuM	Sandler, M	TN	555

Nuclear Medicine

NuM	Agress, H	NJ	554
NuM	Alavi, A	PA	554
NuM	Alazraki, N	GA	555
NuM	Appelbaum, D	IL	556
NuM	Carrasquillo, J	NY	554
NuM	Dae, M	CA	557
NuM	Dillehay, G	IL	556

Spec	Name	St	Pg
NuM	Freeman, L	NY	554
NuM	Goldsmith, S	NY	554
NuM	Klaas, V	WA	557
NuM	Lamonica, D	NY	554
NuM	Neumann, D	OH	556
NuM	Neumann, R	MD	555
NuM	Pandit-Taskar, N	NY	555
NuM	Podoloff, D	TX	557
NuM	Sandler, M	TN	555
NuM	Sanger, J	NY	555
NuM	Schelbert, H	CA	557
NuM	Siegel, B	MO	556
NuM	Strashun, A	NY	555
NuM	Wahl, R	MD	555
NuM	Waxman, A	CA	557
NuM	Wiseman, G	MN	556
NuM	Ziffer, J	FL	556

Nuclear Oncology

Spec	Name	St	Pg
NuM	Agress, H	NJ	554
NuM	Alazraki, N	GA	555
NuM	Appelbaum, D	IL	556
NuM	Freeman, L	NY	554
NuM	Neumann, D	OH	556
NuM	Neumann, R	MD	555
NuM	Sanger, J	NY	555

Nuclear Radiology

Spec	Name	St	Pg
DR	Partain, C	TN	1014
NuM	Klaas, V	WA	557

Nutrition

Spec	Name	St	Pg
AM	Bermudez, O	CO	77
AM	Bravender, T	OH	77
AM	Singh, N	MN	77
EDM	Holick, M	MA	209
EDM	Jensen, M	MN	220
EDM	Kahn, B	MA	209
EDM	McMahon, M	MN	221
Ge	Fisher, R	CT	230
Ge	Peikin, S	NJ	239
Ge	Seidner, D	TN	245
Ge	Semrad, C	IL	250
Ger	Dale, L	MN	266
Ger	Lipschitz, D	AR	267
Ger	Schwartz, R	CO	267
Ger	Thomas, D	MO	266
IM	Galland, L	NY	426
NP	Ehrenkranz, R	CT	448
NP	Escobedo, M	OK	453
NP	Milley, J	UT	452
PEn	Ludwig, D	MA	757
PGe	Baker, R	NY	763
PGe	Baker, S	NY	763
PGe	Berman, J	IL	765
PGe	Black, D	TN	764
PGe	Fasano, A	MA	762
PGe	Gupta, S	IN	766
PGe	Heyman, M	CA	769
PGe	Kleinman, R	MA	762
PGe	Krebs, N	CO	767
PGe	Leichtner, A	MA	762
PGe	Novak, D	FL	765
PGe	Schwarz, S	NY	764
PGe	Sokol, R	CO	767
PGe	Spivak, W	NY	764
PGe	Vanderhoof, J	NE	768
PMR	Dillard, J	NY	863
PPul	Borowitz, D	NY	806

Nutrition & AIDS

Spec	Name	St	Pg
Ge	Kotler, D	NY	237

Nutrition & Cancer Prevention

Spec	Name	St	Pg
EDM	Heber, D	CA	224
Ge	Kastenberg, D	PA	236
Ge	Mason, J	MA	231
Ge	Shike, M	NY	240
U	Katz, A	NY	1191

Nutrition & Cancer Prevention/Control

Spec	Name	St	Pg
Onc	Clinton, S	OH	368
Onc	Kucuk, O	GA	360
S	Herrmann, V	SC	1105

Nutrition & Disease Prevention/Control

Spec	Name	St	Pg
EDM	Heber, D	CA	224

Nutrition & Obesity

Spec	Name	St	Pg
EDM	Heber, D	CA	224

Nutrition in Acute Illness

Spec	Name	St	Pg
Ge	Mason, J	MA	231

Nutrition in Autism

Spec	Name	St	Pg
PGe	Levy, J	NY	763

Nutrition in Bowel Disorders

Spec	Name	St	Pg
Ge	Fisher, R	CT	230
Ge	Mason, J	MA	231
Ge	Seidner, D	TN	245
PGe	Thomas, D	CA	769
PS	Barksdale, E	OH	819

Nutrition in Cancer Therapy

Spec	Name	St	Pg
Onc	Kucuk, O	GA	360
Onc	Parker, B	CA	390

Nystagmus

Spec	Name	St	Pg
Oph	Demer, J	CA	605
Oph	Granet, D	CA	606
Oph	Mitchell, P	CT	575

O

Obesity

Spec	Name	St	Pg
AM	Anderson, M	CA	78
AM	Bermudez, O	CO	77
AM	Hergenroeder, A	TX	78
AM	Sigman, G	IL	77
EDM	Kahn, B	MA	209
EDM	Maclaren, N	NY	213
Ge	Kaplan, L	MA	231
GO	Modesitt, S	VA	283
PEn	Arslanian, S	PA	757
PEn	Diamond, F	FL	759
PEn	Fennoy, I	NY	758
PEn	Ludwig, D	MA	757
PEn	Lustig, R	CA	762
PEn	Silverstein, J	FL	759
PGe	Baker, S	NY	763
PGe	Black, D	TN	764
PGe	Gupta, S	IN	766
PGe	Krebs, N	CO	767
PGe	Novak, D	FL	765
PNep	Flynn, J	WA	800
Psyc	Crow, S	MN	929
Psyc	Powers, P	FL	928
Psyc	Walsh, B	NY	927
RE	Jacobs, L	IL	1048

Obesity-Pediatric

Spec	Name	St	Pg
CG	Driscoll, D	FL	159

Obesity/Bariatric Surgery

Spec	Name	St	Pg
S	Bessler, M	NY	1089
S	Blackstone, R	AZ	1124
S	Chand, B	IL	1112
S	Courcoulas, A	PA	1091
S	Crookes, P	CA	1131
S	Dallal, R	PA	1092
S	Dempsey, D	PA	1092
S	Frantzides, C	IL	1114
S	Herron, D	NY	1094
S	Ikramuddin, S	MN	1115
S	Jayaseelan, N	TX	1126
S	Jones, D	MA	1086
S	Katkhouda, N	CA	1133
S	MacDonald, K	NC	1107
S	Morton, J	CA	1134
S	Nguyen, N	CA	1134
S	Phillips, E	CA	1135
S	Pomp, A	NY	1098
S	Posselt, A	CA	1136
S	Pryor, A	NY	1098
S	Ramanathan, R	PA	1099
S	Richards, W	AL	1108
S	Rogers, S	CA	1136
S	Sarr, M	MN	1119
S	Schauer, P	OH	1119
S	Schirmer, B	VA	1108
S	Scott, D	TX	1128

Spec	Name	St	Pg
S	Shikora, S	MA	1088
S	Sweeney, J	GA	1110

Obsessive-Compulsive Disorder

Spec	Name	St	Pg
ChAP	Coffey, B	NY	939
ChAP	Hudziak, J	VT	938
ChAP	Leckman, J	CT	938
ChAP	McCracken, J	CA	943
ChAP	McDougle, C	MA	938
Psyc	Black, D	IA	929
Psyc	Bystritsky, A	CA	933
Psyc	Davidson, J	TX	932
Psyc	Fallon, B	NY	924
Psyc	Greenberg, B	RI	920
Psyc	Hollander, E	NY	925
Psyc	Jenike, M	MA	921
Psyc	Phillips, K	RI	921
Psyc	Price, L	RI	921
Psyc	Rasmussen, S	RI	921
Psyc	Saxena, S	CA	934

Obstetric Pathology

Spec	Name	St	Pg
Path	Lage, J	MS	726

Obstetric Ultrasound

Spec	Name	St	Pg
DR	Benson, C	MA	1007
DR	Doubilet, P	MA	1007
DR	Filly, R	CA	1017
DR	Kurtz, A	PA	1010
MF	Bahado-Singh, R	MI	437
MF	Eddleman, K	NY	434
MF	Mari, G	TN	437
MF	Platt, L	CA	443
MF	Strassner, H	IL	440
MF	Zalud, I	HI	443
ObG	Corteville, J	OH	564

Obstetrics & Gynecology

Spec	Name	St	Pg
ObG	Amundsen, C	NC	562
ObG	Andersen, G	VA	562
ObG	Argenta, P	MN	563
ObG	Bartholomew, D	OH	563
ObG	Berga, S	NC	562
ObG	Bradley, L	OH	564
ObG	Bradshaw, K	TX	566
ObG	Brodman, M	NY	560
ObG	Byrne, J	UT	566
ObG	Carson, D	PA	561
ObG	Cornella, J	AZ	566
ObG	Corteville, J	OH	564
ObG	Cramer, D	MA	560
ObG	Culbertson, S	IL	564
ObG	De Lancey, J	MI	564
ObG	De Lia, J	WI	564
ObG	Eckler, K	MA	560
ObG	Einarsson, J	MA	560
ObG	Eschenbach, D	WA	567
ObG	Evans, M	NY	561
ObG	Famuyide, A	MN	564
ObG	Gilliam, M	IL	564
ObG	Goldman, M	CA	567
ObG	Goldstein, M	NY	561
ObG	Greenfield, M	OH	564
ObG	Hale, D	IN	565
ObG	Hockstein, S	NY	561
ObG	Hullfish, K	VA	562
ObG	Iglesia, C	DC	561
ObG	Jenkins, T	AL	563
ObG	Karram, M	OH	565
ObG	Kenton, K	IL	565
ObG	King, A	ID	566
ObG	Laufer, M	MA	560
ObG	Levine, E	IL	565
ObG	Lucente, V	PA	561
ObG	Maynard, S	DC	561
ObG	Merritt, D	MO	565
ObG	Morgan, L	FL	563
ObG	Myers, D	RI	560
ObG	Niebyl, J	IA	565
ObG	Nour, N	MA	560
ObG	Ordorica, S	NY	561
ObG	Parker, W	CA	567
ObG	Richardson, M	KS	566
ObG	Sand, P	IL	565
ObG	Sanz, L	VA	563
ObG	Simon, J	DC	562
ObG	Simpson, J	NY	562
ObG	Snyder, R	TX	566
ObG	Steege, J	NC	563
ObG	Valaitis, S	IL	565
ObG	Visco, A	NC	563
ObG	Walters, M	OH	566
ObG	Wiesenfeld, H	PA	562
ObG	Young, B	NY	562

Occult Spinal Dysraphism (OSD)

Spec	Name	St	Pg
NS	Oakes, W	AL	486

Occupational Asthma

Spec	Name	St	Pg
A&I	Bernstein, D	OH	83
A&I	Bernstein, J	OH	83
OM	Harber, P	AZ	912
Pul	Sutherland, E	CO	968

Occupational Lung Disease

Spec	Name	St	Pg
OM	Harber, P	AZ	912
OM	Kipen, H	NJ	912
Path	Mark, E	MA	719
Pul	Bascom, R	PA	956
Pul	Christiani, D	MA	954
Pul	Cooper, J	AL	961
Pul	Goldman, A	FL	962
Pul	Hyers, T	MO	965
Pul	Maxfield, R	NY	958
Pul	Redlich, C	CT	955
Pul	Rose, C	CO	968
Pul	Shellito, J	LA	969

Occupational Medicine

Spec	Name	St	Pg
OM	Gochfeld, M	NJ	912
OM	Harber, P	AZ	912
OM	Kipen, H	NJ	912
OM	Landrigan, P	NY	912

Occupational Musculoskeletal Disorders

Spec	Name	St	Pg
Rhu	Hadler, N	NC	1063

Occupational Skin Diseases

Spec	Name	St	Pg
D	Cohen, S	NY	187
D	Sherertz, E	SC	194

Oculoplastic & Orbital Surgery

Spec	Name	St	Pg
Oph	Ahmad, A	IL	593
Oph	Carter, K	IA	594
Oph	Choy, A	CA	605
Oph	Eiseman, A	SC	588
Oph	Katowitz, J	PA	580
Oph	Kikkawa, D	CA	606
Oph	Lucarelli, M	WI	597
Oph	Ng, J	OR	608
Oph	Putterman, A	IL	599
Oph	Stefanyszyn, M	PA	585
PlS	Spinelli, H	NY	887

Oculoplastic Surgery

Spec	Name	St	Pg
Oph	Bernardino, C	CA	604
Oph	Boxrud, C	CA	605
Oph	Cahill, K	OH	594
Oph	Char, D	CA	605
Oph	Della Rocca, R	NY	577
Oph	Dutton, J	NC	588
Oph	Esmaeli-Azad, B	TX	602
Oph	Iliff, N	MD	580
Oph	Kazim, M	NY	580
Oph	Kidwell, E	DC	580
Oph	Kim, J	CA	607
Oph	Krauss, H	CA	607
Oph	Lisman, R	NY	581
Oph	McCann, J	UT	601
Oph	Nerad, J	OH	598
Oph	Nunery, W	KY	590
Oph	Rubin, P	MA	575
Oph	Seiff, S	CA	609
Oph	Soparkar, C	TX	603
Oph	Tse, D	FL	592
Oph	Yeatts, R	NC	592
PlS	Carraway, J	VA	889

Ophthalmic Genetics

Spec	Name	St	Pg
Oph	Del Monte, M	MI	594
Oph	Edwards, P	MI	594
Oph	Levin, A	PA	581
Oph	Lewis, R	TX	602
Oph	Mets, M	IL	597
Oph	Murphree, A	CA	608

Ophthalmic Pathology

Spec	Name	St	Pg
Oph	Albert, D	WI	593
Oph	Alfonso, E	FL	586
Oph	Eagle, R	PA	578
Oph	Grossniklaus, H	GA	588
Oph	Wilson, D	OR	610
Path	Fogt, F	PA	721

Ophthalmic Plastic Surgery

Spec	Name	St	Pg
Oph	Kikkawa, D	CA	606
Oph	Lucarelli, M	WI	597
Oph	Patrinely, J	FL	591

Ophthalmology

Spec	Name	St	Pg
Oph	Abbott, R	CA	604
Oph	Abrams, G	MI	593
Oph	Abramson, D	NY	575
Oph	Afshari, N	CA	604
Oph	Ahmad, A	IL	593
Oph	Albert, D	WI	593
Oph	Alfonso, E	FL	586
Oph	Alward, W	IA	593
Oph	Anderson, R	UT	601
Oph	Archer, S	MI	593
Oph	Arnold, A	CA	604
Oph	Asbell, P	NY	575
Oph	Augsburger, J	OH	593
Oph	Azar, D	IL	593
Oph	Azar, N	IL	593
Oph	Baerveldt, G	CA	604
Oph	Baker, J	MI	594
Oph	Barile, G	NY	576
Oph	Bernardino, C	CA	604
Oph	Biousse, V	GA	587
Oph	Blumenkranz, M	CA	604
Oph	Borchert, M	CA	604
Oph	Bouchard, C	IL	594
Oph	Boxer Wachler, B	CA	604
Oph	Boxrud, C	CA	605
Oph	Braunstein, R	NY	576
Oph	Bressler, N	MD	576
Oph	Bressler, S	MD	576
Oph	Brown, G	PA	576
Oph	Brucker, A	PA	576
Oph	Buckley, E	NC	587
Oph	Budenz, D	NC	587
Oph	Burke, M	OH	594
Oph	Cahill, K	OH	594
Oph	Campochiaro, P	MD	576
Oph	Capo, H	FL	587
Oph	Caprioli, J	CA	605
Oph	Caputo, A	NJ	576
Oph	Carlson, A	NC	587
Oph	Carter, K	IA	594
Oph	Caster, A	CA	605
Oph	Chang, S	NY	577
Oph	Char, D	CA	605
Oph	Cheeseman, E	SC	587
Oph	Choy, A	CA	605
Oph	Cioffi, G	NY	577
Oph	Cionni, R	UT	601
Oph	Clinch, T	MD	577
Oph	Cockerham, K	CA	605
Oph	Crandall, A	UT	601
Oph	Culbertson, W	FL	587
Oph	Cykiert, R	NY	577
Oph	D'Amico, D	NY	577
Oph	Dana, R	MA	574
Oph	Davis, J	FL	587
Oph	Day, S	CA	605
Oph	De Juan, E	CA	605
Oph	Del Monte, M	MI	594
Oph	Del Priore, L	SC	588
Oph	Della Rocca, R	NY	577
Oph	Demer, J	CA	605
Oph	Dhaliwal, D	PA	577
Oph	Dodick, J	NY	577
Oph	Drack, A	IA	594
Oph	Duker, J	MA	574
Oph	Durrie, D	KS	601
Oph	Dutton, J	NC	588
Oph	Eagle, R	PA	578
Oph	Edwards, P	MI	594
Oph	Eggers, H	NY	578
Oph	Eiseman, A	SC	588
Oph	Ellis, G	LA	601
Oph	Elner, V	MI	595
Oph	Esmaeli-Azad, B	TX	602
Oph	Eustis, H	LA	602
Oph	Feder, R	IL	595
Oph	Feldon, S	NY	578
Oph	Finger, P	NY	578
Oph	Fishman, G	IL	595
Oph	Florakis, G	NY	578
Oph	Flynn, H	FL	588
Oph	Foster, C	MA	574
Oph	Freedman, S	NC	588
Oph	Freeman, W	CA	606
Oph	Friberg, T	PA	578
Oph	Fuchs, W	NY	578
Oph	Gallin, P	NY	578
Oph	Gentile, R	NY	579
Oph	Gibralter, R	NY	579
Oph	Gigantelli, J	NE	601
Oph	Goldberg, D	NJ	579
Oph	Gorin, M	CA	606
Oph	Gorovoy, M	FL	588
Oph	Granet, D	CA	606
Oph	Greenfield, D	FL	588
Oph	Greenwald, M	IL	595
Oph	Grossniklaus, H	GA	588
Oph	Guy, J	FL	589
Oph	Guyton, D	MD	579
Oph	Haik, B	TN	589
Oph	Hall, L	NY	579
Oph	Haller, J	PA	579
Oph	Handa, J	MD	579
Oph	Harbour, J	FL	589
Oph	Hariprasad, S	IL	595
Oph	Heckenlively, J	MI	595
Oph	Hedges, T	MA	574
Oph	Hersh, P	NJ	579
Oph	Hess, J	FL	589
Oph	Heuer, D	WI	595
Oph	Ho, A	PA	580
Oph	Hodapp, E	FL	589
Oph	Holland, E	OH	595
Oph	Humayun, M	CA	606
Oph	Hunter, D	MA	574
Oph	Iliff, N	MD	580
Oph	Irvine, J	CA	606
Oph	Isenberg, S	CA	606
Oph	Iwach, A	CA	606
Oph	Jaafar, M	VA	589
Oph	Jabs, D	NY	580
Oph	John, T	IL	596
Oph	Katowitz, J	PA	580
Oph	Katz, L	PA	580
Oph	Kaufman, P	WI	596
Oph	Kazim, M	NY	580
Oph	Kerr, N	TN	589
Oph	Kidwell, E	DC	580
Oph	Kikkawa, D	CA	606
Oph	Kim, J	CA	607
Oph	Koch, D	TX	602
Oph	Koller, H	PA	580
Oph	Kornmehl, E	MA	574
Oph	Krauss, H	CA	607
Oph	Krueger, R	OH	596
Oph	Kupersmith, M	NY	581
Oph	Kushner, B	WI	596
Oph	Kwon, Y	IA	596
Oph	Lambert, S	GA	589
Oph	Lane, S	MN	596
Oph	Lass, J	OH	596
Oph	Lee, A	TX	602
Oph	Lee, P	MI	596
Oph	Levin, A	PA	581
Oph	Lewis, R	TX	602
Oph	Lichter, P	MI	596
Oph	Liebmann, J	NY	581
Oph	Lim, J	IL	597
Oph	Lindstrom, R	MN	597
Oph	Lisman, R	NY	581
Oph	Lucarelli, M	WI	597
Oph	Lueder, G	MO	597
Oph	Mackool, R	NY	581
Oph	Magramm, I	NY	581
Oph	Maguire, J	PA	581
Oph	Maguire, L	MN	597
Oph	Maloney, R	CA	607
Oph	Manche, E	CA	607
Oph	Mandel, E	NY	581
Oph	Mannis, M	CA	607
Oph	Marmor, M	CA	607
Oph	Masket, S	CA	607
Oph	Mawn, L	TN	590
Oph	McCann, J	UT	601
Oph	McCulley, J	TX	602
Oph	McDonnell, J	IL	597
Oph	McDonnell, P	MD	582
Oph	McKeown, C	FL	590
Oph	Medow, N	NY	582
Oph	Meredith, T	NC	590
Oph	Mets, M	IL	597
Oph	Mieler, W	IL	597
Oph	Miller, J	MA	574

Spec	Name	St	Pg
Oph	Miller, J	AZ	602
Oph	Miller, K	CA	607
Oph	Miller, N	MD	582
Oph	Mills, M	PA	582
Oph	Mims, J	TX	603
Oph	Mitchell, P	CT	575
Oph	Mizen, T	IL	598
Oph	Mondino, B	CA	608
Oph	Muldoon, T	NY	582
Oph	Murphree, A	CA	608
Oph	Murray, T	FL	590
Oph	Myers, J	PA	582
Oph	Nelson, L	PA	582
Oph	Nerad, J	OH	598
Oph	Ng, J	OR	608
Oph	Nunery, W	KY	590
Oph	Nussbaum, J	GA	590
Oph	O'Brien, J	PA	582
Oph	Odel, J	NY	583
Oph	Olitsky, S	MO	598
Oph	Olsen, T	GA	590
Oph	Orlin, S	PA	583
Oph	Osher, R	OH	598
Oph	Page, T	MI	598
Oph	Parrish, R	FL	590
Oph	Patrinely, J	FL	591
Oph	Paul, T	CA	608
Oph	Pepose, J	MO	598
Oph	Perez, V	FL	591
Oph	Petersen, M	OH	598
Oph	Pflugfelder, S	TX	603
Oph	Plager, D	IN	598
Oph	Pollard, Z	GA	591
Oph	Prenner, J	NJ	583
Oph	Puliafito, C	CA	608
Oph	Pulido, J	MN	598
Oph	Putterman, A	IL	599
Oph	Quigley, H	MD	583
Oph	Quinn, G	PA	583
Oph	Rao, N	CA	608
Oph	Rapuano, C	PA	583
Oph	Regillo, C	PA	583
Oph	Reynolds, J	NY	583
Oph	Richard, J	OK	603
Oph	Ritch, R	NY	584
Oph	Rizzo, J	MA	575
Oph	Robin, A	MD	584
Oph	Rogers, G	OH	599
Oph	Rosenberg, M	IL	599
Oph	Rosenfeld, P	FL	591
Oph	Rubin, P	MA	575
Oph	Sadda, S	CA	608
Oph	Salz, J	CA	608
Oph	Samuelson, T	MN	599
Oph	Savino, P	CA	608
Oph	Schachat, A	OH	599
Oph	Schein, O	MD	584
Oph	Schiff, W	NY	584
Oph	Schiffman, J	TX	603
Oph	Schuman, J	PA	584
Oph	Schwartz, S	CA	609
Oph	Seibel, B	CA	609
Oph	Seiff, S	CA	609
Oph	Serafano, D	CA	609
Oph	Sergott, R	PA	584
Oph	Shabto, U	NY	584
Oph	Shamie, N	CA	609
Oph	Sherwood, M	FL	591
Oph	Shields, C	PA	584
Oph	Shields, J	PA	585
Oph	Shingleton, B	MA	575
Oph	Siatkowski, R	OK	603
Oph	Simon, J	NY	585
Oph	Smith, R	CA	609
Oph	Solomon, K	SC	591
Oph	Soparkar, C	TX	603
Oph	Spaeth, G	PA	585
Oph	Spaide, R	NY	585
Oph	Sperber, L	NY	585
Oph	Stark, W	MD	585
Oph	Starr, C	NY	585
Oph	Stefanyszyn, M	PA	585
Oph	Steinert, R	CA	609
Oph	Sternberg, P	TN	591
Oph	Sterns, G	NY	586
Oph	Stone, E	IA	599
Oph	Stout, J	OR	609
Oph	Stulting, R	GA	591
Oph	Summers, C	MN	599
Oph	Traboulsi, E	OH	599
Oph	Trese, M	MI	600
Oph	Trobe, J	MI	600
Oph	Tsai, J	CT	575
Oph	Tse, D	FL	592
Oph	Tychsen, L	MO	600
Oph	Udell, I	NY	586
Oph	Updegraff, S	FL	592
Oph	Vajaranant, T	IL	600
Oph	Vander, J	PA	586
Oph	Varma, R	IL	600
Oph	Volpe, N	IL	600
Oph	Wallace, R	LA	603
Oph	Walsh, J	NY	586
Oph	Walton, D	MA	575
Oph	Wang, F	NY	586
Oph	Wang, M	TN	592
Oph	Waring, G	GA	592
Oph	Warman, R	FL	592
Oph	Weinreb, R	CA	610
Oph	Weiss, A	WA	610
Oph	Williams, G	MI	600
Oph	Wilson, D	OR	610
Oph	Wilson, M	SC	592
Oph	Wilson, M	TN	592
Oph	Wilson, S	OH	600
Oph	Wright, K	CA	610
Oph	Yannuzzi, L	NY	586
Oph	Yeatts, R	NC	592

Opiate Addiction

AdP	Collins, E	NY	936
AdP	Howell, E	UT	937
AdP	Kampman, K	PA	937
AdP	Kleber, H	NY	937
AdP	Kosten, T	TX	938
AdP	Serota, R	PA	937
AdP	Stine, S	MI	937
AdP	Strain, E	MD	937
AM	Adger, H	MD	76

Opsoclonus-Ataxia in Children

ChiN	Mitchell, W	CA	151

Optic Nerve Disorders

N	Galetta, S	NY	515
N	Goodwin, J	IL	530
N	Miller, A	NY	519
N	Newman, N	GA	526
Oph	Biousse, V	GA	587
Oph	Borchert, M	CA	604
Oph	Lee, A	TX	602
Oph	Mizen, T	IL	598
Oph	Odel, J	NY	583
Oph	Rizzo, J	MA	575
Oph	Sergott, R	PA	584
Oph	Trobe, J	MI	600

Optic Nerve Tumors

Oph	Lee, A	TX	602

Oral Cancer

Oto	Yoo, G	MI	689

Oral Dermatology

D	Anhalt, G	MD	186
D	Camisa, C	FL	192

Orbital & Eyelid Tumors/Cancer

Oph	Anderson, R	UT	601
Oph	Esmaeli-Azad, B	TX	602
Oph	Iliff, N	MD	580
Oph	Lisman, R	NY	581
Oph	Rubin, P	MA	575
Oph	Soparkar, C	TX	603

Orbital Diseases

Oph	Boxrud, C	CA	605
Oph	Haik, B	TN	589
Oph	McCann, J	UT	601
Oph	Miller, N	MD	582
Oph	Yeatts, R	NC	592

Orbital Surgery

Oph	Bernardino, C	CA	604
Oph	Cahill, K	OH	594
Oph	Feldon, S	NY	578
Oph	Mawn, L	TN	590
Oph	Nunery, W	KY	590
Oph	Patrinely, J	FL	591

Spec	Name	St	Pg
Orbital Tumors/Cancer			
Oph	Abramson, D	NY	575
Oph	Choy, A	CA	605
Oph	Cockerham, K	CA	605
Oph	Della Rocca, R	NY	577
Oph	Elner, V	MI	595
Oph	Finger, P	NY	578
Oph	Gigantelli, J	NE	601
Oph	Kazim, M	NY	580
Oph	Kim, J	CA	607
Oph	Nerad, J	OH	598
Oph	Seiff, S	CA	609
Oph	Shields, C	PA	584
Oph	Tse, D	FL	592
Oph	Yeatts, R	NC	592
RadRO	Markoe, A	FL	985
Orthopaedic Imaging			
DR	Pavlov, H	NY	1011
Orthopaedic Infectious Disease			
Inf	Flaherty, J	IL	417
Orthopaedic Surgery			
OrS	Abdu, W	NH	616
OrS	Aboulafia, A	MD	620
OrS	Agarwal, A	TX	647
OrS	Ahmad, C	NY	620
OrS	Albert, T	PA	620
OrS	Albright, J	IA	639
OrS	An, H	IL	639
OrS	Anderson, L	CA	649
OrS	Anglen, J	IN	639
OrS	Archdeacon, M	OH	639
OrS	Aronson, J	AR	647
OrS	Balderston, R	PA	620
OrS	Bartolozzi, A	PA	620
OrS	Bauman, P	NY	620
OrS	Beaty, J	TN	635
OrS	Benevenia, J	NJ	620
OrS	Berry, D	MN	639
OrS	Betz, R	PA	621
OrS	Biermann, J	MI	639
OrS	Bigliani, L	NY	621
OrS	Bitan, F	NY	621
OrS	Blaha, J	MI	640
OrS	Boachie-Adjei, O	NY	621
OrS	Boden, S	GA	635
OrS	Bono, J	MA	616
OrS	Booth, R	PA	621
OrS	Bos, G	WA	649
OrS	Bostrom, M	NY	621
OrS	Bozic, K	CA	649
OrS	Brage, M	WA	649
OrS	Brick, G	MA	616
OrS	Bridwell, K	MO	640
OrS	Brien, E	CA	649
OrS	Brigman, B	NC	635
OrS	Brodsky, J	TX	648
OrS	Bronson, M	NY	621
OrS	Browner, B	CT	616
OrS	Bucholz, R	TX	648
OrS	Buckwalter, J	IA	640
OrS	Bukata, S	CA	650
OrS	Buly, R	NY	622
OrS	Burke, D	MA	616
OrS	Busch, M	GA	635
OrS	Caillouette, J	CA	650
OrS	Callaghan, J	IA	640
OrS	Cammisa, F	NY	622
OrS	Cappuccino, A	NY	622
OrS	Carragee, E	CA	650
OrS	Chapman, J	WA	650
OrS	Cheng, E	MN	640
OrS	Clohisy, D	MN	640
OrS	Clohisy, J	MO	640
OrS	Conrad, E	WA	650
OrS	Cooper, D	TX	648
OrS	Copp, S	CA	650
OrS	Cornell, C	NY	622
OrS	Coughlin, M	ID	646
OrS	Craig, E	NY	622
OrS	Crossett, L	PA	622
OrS	Davidson, R	PA	622
OrS	Delahay, J	DC	622
OrS	Delamarter, R	CA	650
OrS	Deland, J	NY	623
OrS	DeOrio, J	NC	635
OrS	Diduch, D	VA	635
OrS	DiGiovanni, C	RI	616
OrS	Dillingham, M	CA	650
OrS	Dines, D	NY	623
OrS	Dirschl, D	IL	640
OrS	Donaldson, W	PA	623
OrS	Dormans, J	PA	623
OrS	Dorr, L	CA	651
OrS	Ebraheim, N	OH	641
OrS	Einhorn, T	MA	616
OrS	Eismont, F	FL	636
OrS	Elattrache, N	CA	651
OrS	Endrizzi, D	ME	617
OrS	Errico, T	NY	623
OrS	Estwanik, J	NC	636
OrS	Farmer, J	NY	623
OrS	Feldman, D	NY	623
OrS	Finerman, G	CA	651
OrS	Flatow, E	NY	624
OrS	Frassica, F	MD	624
OrS	Friedlaender, G	CT	617
OrS	Fulkerson, J	CT	617
OrS	Garfin, S	CA	651
OrS	Garrett, W	NC	636
OrS	Garvin, K	NE	646
OrS	Gebhardt, M	MA	617
OrS	Gitelis, S	IL	641
OrS	Gladstone, J	NY	624
OrS	Glashow, J	NY	624
OrS	Goitz, H	MI	641
OrS	Goldner, R	NC	636
OrS	Goldstein, J	NY	624
OrS	Goldstein, W	IL	641
OrS	Goodman, S	CA	651
OrS	Gorab, R	CA	651
OrS	Graf, B	WI	641
OrS	Green, A	RI	617
OrS	Greisberg, J	NY	624
OrS	Grelsamer, R	NY	624
OrS	Gugenheim, J	TX	648
OrS	Haas, S	NY	625
OrS	Hannafin, J	NY	625
OrS	Hanssen, A	MN	641
OrS	Hausman, M	NY	625
OrS	Healey, J	NY	625
OrS	Hecht, A	NY	625
OrS	Heiden, E	UT	646
OrS	Helfet, D	NY	625
OrS	Henshaw, R	DC	625
OrS	Herman, M	PA	626
OrS	Herzenberg, J	MD	626
OrS	Hilibrand, A	PA	626
OrS	Hochschuler, S	TX	648
OrS	Hornicek, F	MA	617
OrS	Howe, K	CA	651
OrS	Hozack, W	PA	626
OrS	Hume, E	PA	626
OrS	Hungerford, M	MD	626
OrS	Hyman, J	NY	626
OrS	Iannotti, J	OH	641
OrS	Irwin, R	MI	641
OrS	Jacobs, J	IL	642
OrS	Jiranek, W	VA	636
OrS	Johanson, N	PA	626
OrS	Johnson, D	KY	636
OrS	Johnson, E	CA	651
OrS	Jokl, P	CT	617
OrS	Joyce, M	OH	642
OrS	Kaeding, C	OH	642
OrS	Kaplan, F	PA	627
OrS	Karas, S	GA	636
OrS	Kasser, J	MA	617
OrS	Kelly, B	NY	627
OrS	Kelly, C	CO	646
OrS	Kenan, S	NY	627
OrS	Kenter, K	OH	642
OrS	Kim, C	CA	652
OrS	Kneisl, J	NC	636
OrS	Kocher, M	MA	618
OrS	Kraay, M	OH	642
OrS	Krackow, K	NY	627
OrS	Kress, K	GA	637
OrS	Lane, J	NY	627
OrS	Lauerman, W	DC	627
OrS	Laurencin, C	CT	618
OrS	Leadbetter, W	MD	627
OrS	Lebwohl, N	FL	637
OrS	Lee, F	NY	628
OrS	Lenke, L	MO	642
OrS	Les, K	MI	642
OrS	Levin, L	PA	628
OrS	Levine, D	NY	628
OrS	Lewis, V	TX	648
OrS	Lieberman, J	CA	652
OrS	Lock, T	MI	642
OrS	Lowenberg, D	CA	652
OrS	Luck, J	CA	652
OrS	Mabrey, J	TX	648

Spec	Name	St	Pg
OrS	Macaulay, W	NY	628
OrS	Malawer, M	MD	628
OrS	Mandelbaum, B	CA	652
OrS	Manoli, A	MI	643
OrS	Marsh, J	CT	618
OrS	Marx, R	NY	628
OrS	Matsen, F	WA	652
OrS	Mayerson, J	OH	643
OrS	McAfee, P	MD	628
OrS	McCance, S	NY	629
OrS	McCann, P	NY	629
OrS	McCarthy, J	OH	643
OrS	McDonald, D	MO	643
OrS	McFarland, E	MD	629
OrS	Medvecky, M	CT	618
OrS	Meere, P	NY	629
OrS	Menendez, L	CA	652
OrS	Miller, M	VA	637
OrS	Millett, P	CO	646
OrS	Minas, T	MA	618
OrS	Morcuende, J	IA	643
OrS	Mott, M	MI	643
OrS	Moucha, C	NY	629
OrS	Muschler, G	OH	643
OrS	Myerson, M	MD	629
OrS	Nepola, J	IA	643
OrS	Neuwirth, M	NY	629
OrS	Nicholas, S	NY	629
OrS	Nunley, J	NC	637
OrS	O'Donnell, R	CA	652
OrS	O'Driscoll, S	MN	644
OrS	O'Keefe, R	NY	630
OrS	O'Leary, P	NY	630
OrS	Oakes, D	CA	653
OrS	Oppenheim, W	CA	653
OrS	Otsuka, N	NY	630
OrS	Padgett, D	NY	630
OrS	Parazin, S	MA	618
OrS	Parsons, T	MI	644
OrS	Parvizi, J	PA	630
OrS	Peabody, T	IL	644
OrS	Pellicci, P	NY	630
OrS	Peterson, D	AK	653
OrS	Pettrone, F	VA	637
OrS	Philippon, M	CO	646
OrS	Pinzur, M	IL	644
OrS	Pizzutillo, P	PA	630
OrS	Plancher, K	NY	631
OrS	Poehling, G	NC	637
OrS	Polly, D	MN	644
OrS	Rajacich, N	WA	653
OrS	Ramsey, M	PA	631
OrS	Randall, R	UT	647
OrS	Ready, J	MA	618
OrS	Reilly, D	MA	618
OrS	Richardson, W	NC	637
OrS	Riew, K	MO	644
OrS	Robinson, R	FL	637
OrS	Rodriguez, J	NY	631
OrS	Romeo, A	IL	644
OrS	Rosenberg, T	UT	647
OrS	Rothman, R	PA	631
OrS	Roye, D	NY	631

Spec	Name	St	Pg
OrS	Rozbruch, S	NY	631
OrS	Saltzman, C	UT	647
OrS	Salvati, E	NY	631
OrS	Sandhu, H	NY	632
OrS	Sangeorzan, B	WA	653
OrS	Scarborough, M	FL	638
OrS	Schafer, M	IL	644
OrS	Schlegel, T	CO	647
OrS	Schlesinger, I	NY	632
OrS	Schmalzried, T	CA	653
OrS	Schmidt, R	PA	632
OrS	Schuler, T	VA	638
OrS	Schwab, F	NY	632
OrS	Schwartz, H	TN	638
OrS	Scott, R	MA	619
OrS	Scott, W	NY	632
OrS	Sculco, T	NY	632
OrS	Seltzer, D	AZ	648
OrS	Sethi, P	CT	619
OrS	Sharkey, P	PA	632
OrS	Shelbourne, K	IN	645
OrS	Siegel, H	AL	638
OrS	Sim, F	MN	645
OrS	Singer, D	HI	653
OrS	Smith, D	WA	653
OrS	Smith, E	MA	619
OrS	Souryal, T	TX	649
OrS	Spengler, D	TN	638
OrS	Spindler, K	TN	638
OrS	Spivak, J	NY	632
OrS	Sponseller, P	MD	633
OrS	Steadman, J	CO	647
OrS	Strongwater, A	NJ	633
OrS	Stuchin, S	NY	633
OrS	Stulberg, S	IL	645
OrS	Swiontkowski, M	MN	645
OrS	Thomas, B	CA	654
OrS	Thompson, G	OH	645
OrS	Thornhill, T	MA	619
OrS	Tornetta, P	MA	619
OrS	Vaccaro, A	PA	633
OrS	Vail, T	CA	654
OrS	Vo, P	FL	638
OrS	Walling, A	FL	638
OrS	Wang, J	CA	654
OrS	Wapner, K	PA	633
OrS	Ward, W	PA	633
OrS	Warren, R	NY	633
OrS	Watkins, R	CA	654
OrS	Webb, L	GA	639
OrS	Weiland, A	NY	633
OrS	Weiner, R	FL	639
OrS	Weinfeld, S	NY	634
OrS	Weinstein, J	NH	619
OrS	Weinstein, S	IA	645
OrS	Westrich, G	NY	634
OrS	Wetzel, F	PA	634
OrS	Wickiewicz, T	NY	634
OrS	Wiesel, S	DC	634
OrS	Wilkins, R	CO	647
OrS	Williams, G	PA	634
OrS	Williams, R	TX	649
OrS	Wirth, M	TX	649

Spec	Name	St	Pg
OrS	Wittig, J	NY	634
OrS	Wixson, R	IL	645
OrS	Wurtz, L	IN	645
OrS	Yamaguchi, K	MO	646
OrS	Yoo, J	OR	654
OrS	Zarins, B	MA	619
OrS	Zdeblick, T	WI	646
OrS	Zuckerman, J	NY	635

Osteoarthritis

Rhu	Fields, T	NY	1060
Rhu	Fife, R	IN	1065
Rhu	Hochberg, M	MD	1060
Rhu	Hugenberg, S	IN	1065
Rhu	Magid, S	NY	1061
Rhu	O'Dell, J	NE	1066
Rhu	Shadick, N	MA	1059

Osteodystrophy

PNep	Andreoli, S	IN	799

Osteomyelitis

OrS	Browner, B	CT	616
OrS	Lowenberg, D	CA	652
OrS	Swiontkowski, M	MN	645

Osteonecrosis

OrS	Einhorn, T	MA	616
OrS	Kelly, C	CO	646
OrS	Oakes, D	CA	653
OrS	Vail, T	CA	654

Osteopetrosis

PHO	Coccia, P	NE	786

Osteoporosis

EDM	Bergman, D	NY	211
EDM	Bilezikian, J	NY	211
EDM	Bockman, R	NY	211
EDM	Brown, J	TX	222
EDM	Dalkin, A	VA	216
EDM	Econs, M	IN	219
EDM	Emanuele, M	IL	219
EDM	Greene, L	NY	212
EDM	Greenspan, S	PA	212
EDM	Holick, M	MA	209
EDM	Khosla, S	MN	220
EDM	Lash, R	MI	220
EDM	LeBoff, M	MA	209
EDM	Orwoll, E	OR	225
EDM	Recker, R	NE	222
EDM	Roberts, M	PA	214
EDM	Siris, E	NY	214
EDM	Watts, N	OH	221
Ger	Gambert, S	MD	265
Ger	Lyles, K	NC	265
Nep	Ott, S	WA	467
ObG	Simon, J	DC	562

Spec	Name	St	Pg
PEn	DeLuca, F	PA	758
PEn	Levine, M	PA	758
RE	Luciano, A	CT	1041
Rhu	Hochberg, M	MD	1060
Rhu	Lindsey, S	LA	1067
Rhu	Lipstate, J	LA	1067
Rhu	Mease, P	WA	1068
Rhu	Mitnick, H	NY	1061
Rhu	Schoen, R	CT	1058

Osteoporosis in Men

Spec	Name	St	Pg
EDM	Greenspan, S	PA	212
EDM	Orwoll, E	OR	225

Osteoporosis Spine-Kyphoplasty

Spec	Name	St	Pg
NRad	Norbash, A	MA	1019

Osteoporosis Spine-Vertebroplasty

Spec	Name	St	Pg
NRad	Hirsch, J	MA	1019
NRad	Jensen, M	VA	1022
NRad	Kallmes, D	MN	1023

Osteoporosis-Juvenile

Spec	Name	St	Pg
PNep	Langman, C	IL	800

Otolaryngology

Spec	Name	St	Pg
Oto	Abaza, M	CO	689
Oto	Akervall, J	MI	682
Oto	Alam, D	OH	682
Oto	Amedee, R	LA	691
Oto	Andersen, P	OR	694
Oto	Arriaga, M	LA	691
Oto	Arts, H	MI	682
Oto	Aviv, J	NY	668
Oto	Baim, H	IL	683
Oto	Baker, S	MI	683
Oto	Bastian, R	IL	683
Oto	Beatty, C	MN	683
Oto	Becker, F	FL	677
Oto	Beeson, W	IN	683
Oto	Benninger, M	OH	683
Oto	Berke, G	CA	694
Oto	Bhattacharyya, N	MA	665
Oto	Blackwell, K	CA	694
Oto	Blair, E	IL	683
Oto	Blitzer, A	NY	668
Oto	Bojrab, D	MI	683
Oto	Bolger, W	FL	677
Oto	Brackmann, D	CA	694
Oto	Bradford, C	MI	684
Oto	Branham, G	MO	684
Oto	Browne, J	NC	678
Oto	Bumpous, J	KY	678
Oto	Burkey, B	OH	684
Oto	Burns, J	MA	665
Oto	Califano, J	MD	668
Oto	Campbell, B	WI	684
Oto	Carey, J	MD	668
Oto	Caruana, S	NY	668
Oto	Chalian, A	PA	668
Oto	Chowdhury, K	CO	689
Oto	Civantos, F	FL	678
Oto	Clark, K	OK	691
Oto	Clayman, G	TX	691
Oto	Close, L	NY	668
Oto	Corey, J	IL	684
Oto	Costantino, P	NY	669
Oto	Couch, M	VT	665
Oto	Courey, M	CA	694
Oto	Davidson, B	DC	669
Oto	Day, T	SC	678
Oto	Denenberg, S	NE	690
Oto	Deschler, D	MA	665
Oto	Diaz, E	TX	691
Oto	DiNardo, L	VA	678
Oto	Donovan, D	TX	692
Oto	Dornhoffer, J	AR	692
Oto	Driscoll, C	MN	684
Oto	Duckert, L	WA	695
Oto	Edelstein, D	NY	669
Oto	Eisele, D	MD	669
Oto	Epstein, J	FL	678
Oto	Farrior, E	FL	678
Oto	Farrior, J	FL	678
Oto	Feghali, J	NY	669
Oto	Ferris, R	PA	669
Oto	Flint, P	OR	695
Oto	Fried, M	NY	669
Oto	Friedman, M	IL	684
Oto	Funk, G	IA	684
Oto	Futran, N	WA	695
Oto	Gantz, B	IA	685
Oto	Genden, E	NY	670
Oto	Gianoli, G	LA	692
Oto	Gliklich, R	MA	665
Oto	Goebel, J	MO	685
Oto	Gold, S	NY	670
Oto	Goldenberg, D	PA	670
Oto	Goodwin, W	FL	679
Oto	Gosselin, B	NH	665
Oto	Graham, H	LA	692
Oto	Grandis, J	PA	670
Oto	Grillone, G	MA	665
Oto	Grundfast, K	MA	666
Oto	Hadlock, T	MA	666
Oto	Hammerschlag, P	NY	670
Oto	Hanna, E	TX	692
Oto	Har-El, G	NY	670
Oto	Harris, J	CA	695
Oto	Hartig, G	WI	685
Oto	Haughey, B	MO	685
Oto	Hayden, R	AZ	692
Oto	Haynes, D	TN	679
Oto	Hicks, W	NY	670
Oto	Hilger, P	MN	685
Oto	Hirsch, B	PA	670
Oto	Hoffman, H	IA	685
Oto	Hoffman, R	NY	671
Oto	Hogikyan, N	MI	685
Oto	Holliday, M	MD	671
Oto	Hom, D	OH	685
Oto	Hopping, S	DC	671
Oto	Hotaling, A	IL	686
Oto	Hurst, M	WV	671
Oto	Jackler, R	CA	695
Oto	Jacobs, J	NY	671
Oto	Jenkins, H	CO	690
Oto	Johnson, C	LA	692
Oto	Johnson, J	PA	671
Oto	Jones, J	NY	671
Oto	Jones, P	IL	686
Oto	Josephson, J	NY	671
Oto	Kang, D	NE	690
Oto	Kaplan, M	CA	695
Oto	Keane, W	PA	672
Oto	Keller, G	CA	695
Oto	Kennedy, D	PA	672
Oto	Kern, R	IL	686
Oto	Kesser, B	VA	679
Oto	Kim, D	MA	666
Oto	Kingdom, T	CO	690
Oto	Koch, W	MD	672
Oto	Koufman, J	NY	672
Oto	Kraus, D	NY	672
Oto	Krespi, Y	NY	672
Oto	Kriet, J	KS	690
Oto	Kuhel, W	NY	672
Oto	Kuhn, F	GA	679
Oto	Kveton, J	CT	666
Oto	Lalwani, A	NY	672
Oto	Lambert, P	SC	679
Oto	Lanza, D	FL	679
Oto	Larrabee, W	WA	695
Oto	Lavertu, P	OH	686
Oto	Lawson, W	NY	673
Oto	Lebovics, R	NY	673
Oto	Leonetti, J	IL	686
Oto	Levine, P	VA	679
Oto	Linstrom, C	NY	673
Oto	Lustig, L	CA	696
Oto	Lydiatt, D	NE	690
Oto	Lydiatt, W	NE	690
Oto	Macias, J	AZ	693
Oto	Marentette, L	MI	686
Oto	Mattox, D	GA	679
Oto	McKenna, M	MA	666
Oto	McMenomey, S	NY	673
Oto	Metson, R	MA	666
Oto	Miller, F	TX	693
Oto	Mirza, N	PA	673
Oto	Miyamoto, R	IN	686
Oto	Moe, K	WA	696
Oto	Myers, J	TX	693
Oto	Naclerio, R	IL	686
Oto	Netterville, J	TN	680
Oto	Newkirk, K	DC	673
Oto	Niparko, J	CA	696
Oto	Nuss, D	LA	693
Oto	O'Leary, M	CA	696
Oto	O'Malley, B	PA	673
Oto	Oghalai, J	CA	696
Oto	Olsen, K	MN	687
Oto	Orloff, L	CA	696

Spec	Name	St	Pg
Oto	Ossoff, R	TN	680
Oto	Otto, R	TX	693
Oto	Ozer, E	OH	687
Oto	Paparella, M	MN	687
Oto	Papel, I	MD	673
Oto	Patil, Y	OH	687
Oto	Pelzer, H	IL	687
Oto	Pensak, M	OH	687
Oto	Persky, M	NY	674
Oto	Peters, G	AL	680
Oto	Petruzzelli, G	GA	680
Oto	Piccirillo, J	MO	687
Oto	Picken, C	DC	674
Oto	Pillsbury, H	NC	680
Oto	Pitman, K	AZ	693
Oto	Poole, M	GA	680
Oto	Postma, G	GA	680
Oto	Pribitkin, E	PA	674
Oto	Quatela, V	NY	674
Oto	Randolph, G	MA	666
Oto	Rassekh, C	PA	674
Oto	Rauch, S	MA	666
Oto	Rebeiz, E	MA	667
Oto	Rice, D	CA	696
Oto	Ries, W	TN	680
Oto	Roland, J	NY	674
Oto	Rosen, C	PA	674
Oto	Rosen, M	PA	674
Oto	Rosenthal, E	AL	681
Oto	Rubinstein, J	WA	696
Oto	Samant, S	TN	681
Oto	Sasaki, C	CT	667
Oto	Sataloff, R	PA	675
Oto	Schaefer, S	NY	675
Oto	Schaitkin, B	PA	675
Oto	Schantz, S	NY	675
Oto	Schley, W	NY	675
Oto	Senders, C	CA	697
Oto	Senior, B	NC	681
Oto	Setzen, M	NY	675
Oto	Shapshay, S	NY	675
Oto	Shelton, C	UT	690
Oto	Shindo, M	OR	697
Oto	Shockley, W	NC	681
Oto	Siegel, G	IL	687
Oto	Sillers, M	AL	681
Oto	Silverman, D	VT	667
Oto	Silverstein, H	FL	681
Oto	Singer, M	CA	697
Oto	Singh, B	NY	675
Oto	Sinha, U	CA	697
Oto	Smith, R	NE	691
Oto	Snyderman, C	PA	676
Oto	Song, J	CO	691
Oto	Spiegel, J	MA	667
Oto	Stankiewicz, J	IL	688
Oto	Stasney, C	TX	693
Oto	Stenson, K	IL	688
Oto	Stewart, M	NY	676
Oto	Stringer, S	MS	681
Oto	Strome, M	NY	676
Oto	Strome, S	MD	676
Oto	Suen, J	AR	693
Oto	Sulica, R	NY	676
Oto	Szachowicz, E	MN	688
Oto	Teknos, T	OH	688
Oto	Telian, S	MI	688
Oto	Telischi, F	FL	681
Oto	Terris, D	GA	682
Oto	Thaler, E	PA	676
Oto	Toriumi, D	IL	688
Oto	Tucci, D	NC	682
Oto	Tufano, R	MD	676
Oto	Urken, M	NY	676
Oto	Valentino, J	KY	682
Oto	Vining, E	CT	667
Oto	Wackym, P	OR	697
Oto	Waner, M	NY	677
Oto	Wang, S	CA	697
Oto	Wax, M	OR	697
Oto	Wazen, J	FL	682
Oto	Weber, R	TX	694
Oto	Weber, S	TX	694
Oto	Weinstein, G	PA	677
Oto	Weisman, R	CA	697
Oto	Weissler, M	NC	682
Oto	Weymuller, E	WA	698
Oto	Wiet, R	IL	688
Oto	Wilson, K	OH	688
Oto	Wong, B	CA	698
Oto	Wong, R	NY	677
Oto	Woo, P	NY	677
Oto	Woodson, B	WI	689
Oto	Woodson, G	IL	689
Oto	Yarbrough, W	CT	667
Oto	Yoo, G	MI	689
Oto	Young, N	IL	689
Oto	Yueh, B	MN	689
Oto	Zalzal, G	MD	677
Oto	Zeitels, S	MA	667
Oto	Zwillenberg, S	PA	677

Otology

Spec	Name	St	Pg
Oto	Farrior, J	FL	678
Oto	Haynes, D	TN	679
Oto	Holliday, M	MD	671
Oto	Macias, J	AZ	693
Oto	McKenna, M	MA	666
Oto	Tucci, D	NC	682
PO	Arnold, J	OH	804
PO	Darrow, D	VA	803
PO	Eavey, R	TN	803
PO	Kazahaya, K	PA	802
PO	Tunkel, D	MD	803

Otology & Neuro-Otology

Spec	Name	St	Pg
Oto	Amedee, R	LA	691
Oto	Beatty, C	MN	683
Oto	Bojrab, D	MI	683
Oto	Duckert, L	WA	695
Oto	Goebel, J	MO	685
Oto	McMenomey, S	NY	673

Otosclerosis/Stapedectomy

Spec	Name	St	Pg
Oto	Brackmann, D	CA	694
Oto	Duckert, L	WA	695
Oto	Farrior, J	FL	678
Oto	Wiet, R	IL	688

Ovarian Cancer

Spec	Name	St	Pg
CG	Shulman, L	IL	160
GO	Abbas, F	MD	276
GO	Abu-Rustum, N	NY	276
GO	Alvarez, R	AL	280
GO	Barakat, R	NY	276
GO	Barter, J	MD	276
GO	Berchuck, A	NC	280
GO	Berek, J	CA	290
GO	Bicher, A	VA	280
GO	Bodurka, D	TX	287
GO	Boice, C	MD	276
GO	Borst, M	AZ	287
GO	Braly, P	LA	288
GO	Brewer, M	CT	274
GO	Bristow, R	CA	290
GO	Burger, R	PA	277
GO	Cain, J	MA	274
GO	Cantuaria, G	GA	281
GO	Caputo, T	NY	277
GO	Carlson, J	NJ	277
GO	Chambers, S	AZ	288
GO	Chan, J	CA	290
GO	Chi, D	NY	277
GO	Cliby, W	MN	284
GO	Copeland, L	OH	284
GO	Cornelison, T	MD	277
GO	Creasman, W	SC	281
GO	Curtin, J	NY	277
GO	Dottino, P	NY	277
GO	Dunton, C	PA	277
GO	Duska, L	VA	281
GO	Edwards, R	PA	278
GO	Finan, M	AL	281
GO	Fromm, G	TX	288
GO	Ghamande, S	GA	281
GO	Giuntoli, R	MD	278
GO	Goff, B	WA	291
GO	Havrilesky, L	NC	282
GO	Herzog, T	NY	278
GO	Horowitz, I	GA	282
GO	Hurteau, J	IL	284
GO	Kelley, J	PA	278
GO	King, S	PA	278
GO	Kline, R	LA	288
GO	Koulos, J	NY	279
GO	Lambrou, N	FL	282
GO	Lancaster, J	FL	282
GO	Lele, S	NY	279
GO	Lengyel, E	IL	285
GO	Lin, J	DC	279
GO	Lu, K	TX	289
GO	Lurain, J	IL	285
GO	Makhija, S	KY	282
GO	Mannel, R	OK	289
GO	Modesitt, S	VA	283

Spec	Name	St	Pg
GO	Moore, D	IN	285
GO	Muntz, H	WA	291
GO	Muto, M	MA	275
GO	Nagarsheth, N	NY	279
GO	Odunsi, A	NY	279
GO	Pejovic, T	OR	291
GO	Plaxe, S	CA	291
GO	Poliakoff, S	FL	283
GO	Potkul, R	IL	285
GO	Powell, M	MO	285
GO	Rader, J	WI	285
GO	Remmenga, S	NE	287
GO	Rice, L	WI	286
GO	Rodriguez, G	IL	286
GO	Rose, P	OH	286
GO	Rosenblum, N	PA	280
GO	Rotmensch, J	IL	286
GO	Rubin, S	PA	280
GO	Runowicz, C	FL	283
GO	Rutherford, T	CT	275
GO	Santin, A	CT	275
GO	Schink, J	IL	286
GO	Schorge, J	MA	275
GO	Schwartz, P	CT	275
GO	Singh, D	AZ	289
GO	Smith, D	AZ	289
GO	Smith, L	CA	291
GO	Sood, A	TX	290
GO	Spann, C	GA	283
GO	Spirtos, N	NV	292
GO	Teng, N	CA	292
GO	Van Nagell, J	KY	284
GO	Waggoner, S	OH	287
GO	Walker, J	OK	290
GO	Yamada, S	IL	287
Hem	Stiff, P	IL	324
ObG	Argenta, P	MN	563
Onc	Aghajanian, C	NY	336
Onc	Alberts, D	AZ	378
Onc	Astrow, A	NY	337
Onc	Audeh, M	CA	385
Onc	Birrer, M	MA	330
Onc	Colon-Otero, G	FL	357
Onc	Disis, M	WA	386
Onc	Fleming, G	IL	369
Onc	Kohn, E	MD	346
Onc	Matulonis, U	MA	334
Onc	McGuire, W	VA	361
Onc	Pasmantier, M	NY	349
Onc	Schilder, R	PA	351
Onc	Scudder, S	CA	392
Onc	Slamon, D	CA	392
Onc	Speyer, J	NY	351
Onc	Spriggs, D	NY	352
Path	Bell, D	MN	727
Path	Cho, K	MI	727
Path	Dubeau, L	CA	732
Path	Kurman, R	MD	722
Path	Nicosia, S	FL	726
Path	Tornos, C	NY	724
Path	Wilczynski, S	CA	735
S	Sugarbaker, P	DC	1101

Ovarian Cancer-Early Detection

Spec	Name	St	Pg
GO	Azodi, M	CT	274
GO	Fishman, D	NY	278
GO	Lu, K	TX	289
GO	Rodriguez, G	IL	286
GO	Rutherford, T	CT	275
GO	Singh, D	AZ	289
Onc	Armstrong, D	MD	337

Ovarian Cancer-High Risk Consult

Spec	Name	St	Pg
ObG	Cramer, D	MA	560

Ovarian Failure

Spec	Name	St	Pg
ObG	Simpson, J	NY	562
RE	Legro, R	PA	1043

Ovarian Masses in Children/Adolescents

Spec	Name	St	Pg
PS	Dolgin, S	NY	815

Ovarian Rare & Borderline Tumors

Spec	Name	St	Pg
GO	Gershenson, D	TX	288

Oxalosis

Spec	Name	St	Pg
PNep	Langman, C	IL	800

P

Pacemakers

Spec	Name	St	Pg
CE	Callans, D	PA	114
CE	Chinitz, L	NY	114
CE	Cohen, M	NY	114
CE	Curtis, A	NY	114
CE	DiMarco, J	VA	116
CE	Ellenbogen, K	VA	116
CE	Epstein, L	MA	113
CE	Gang, E	CA	120
CE	Goldberger, J	IL	117
CE	Gomes, J	NY	114
CE	Halperin, H	MD	115
CE	Hayes, D	MN	117
CE	Interian, A	FL	116
CE	Knight, B	IL	117
CE	Levine, J	NY	115
CE	Love, C	OH	117
CE	Marchlinski, F	PA	115
CE	Naccarelli, G	PA	115
CE	Onufer, J	VA	116
CE	Sauer, W	CO	119
CE	Sorrentino, R	GA	116
CE	Swerdlow, C	CA	120
Cv	Wilkoff, B	OH	106
PCd	Crosson, J	MD	748
PCd	Fish, F	TN	751

Paget's Disease of Bone

Spec	Name	St	Pg
EDM	Bergman, D	NY	211
EDM	Bockman, R	NY	211
EDM	Econs, M	IN	219
EDM	Siris, E	NY	214
EDM	Watts, N	OH	221
OrS	Bukata, S	CA	650
OrS	Frassica, F	MD	624
Rhu	Seton, M	MA	1058

Pain & Spasticity

Spec	Name	St	Pg
NS	Whiting, D	PA	483

Pain Management

Spec	Name	St	Pg
DR	Palmer, W	MA	1007
Ger	Finucane, T	MD	264
H & PM	Levy, M	PA	406
H & PM	Portenoy, R	NY	407
NS	Berger, M	CA	498
NS	Di Giacinto, G	NY	476
Ped	Zeltzer, L	CA	743
PM	Argoff, C	NY	706
PM	Fuller, N	CA	713
PM	Noe, C	TX	711
PM	Prager, J	CA	713
PM	Robbins, L	IL	710
PM	Rosner, H	CA	713
PM	Vetter, T	AL	709
PMR	Borg-Stein, J	MA	862
PMR	Creamer, M	FL	866
PMR	Dillard, J	NY	863
PMR	Friedman, A	WA	872

Pain Management-Pediatric

Spec	Name	St	Pg
PM	Anghelescu, D	TN	708
PM	Berde, C	MA	706
PM	Koh, J	OR	713
PM	Weisman, S	WI	711

Pain Medicine

Spec	Name	St	Pg
PM	Abram, S	WI	709
PM	Anghelescu, D	TN	708
PM	Argoff, C	NY	706
PM	Audell, L	CA	712
PM	Ballantyne, J	WA	712
PM	Baumann, P	GA	708
PM	Bedder, M	WA	712
PM	Benzon, H	IL	709
PM	Berde, C	MA	706
PM	Burton, A	TX	711
PM	Christo, P	MD	706
PM	Cope, D	MD	706
PM	Covington, E	OH	709
PM	DeLeon, O	NY	707
PM	Diwan, S	NY	707

Spec	Name	St	Pg
PM	Driver, L	TX	711
PM	Falco, F	DE	707
PM	Ferrante, F	CA	712
PM	Fine, P	UT	711
PM	Fishman, S	CA	712
PM	Fitzgibbon, D	WA	713
PM	Freitag, F	WI	709
PM	Fuller, N	CA	713
PM	Gharibo, C	NY	707
PM	Gobrial, W	FL	708
PM	Green, C	MI	709
PM	Hooten, W	MN	710
PM	Huntoon, M	TN	708
PM	Jain, S	NY	707
PM	Jasmin, L	OR	713
PM	Koh, J	OR	713
PM	Kreitzer, J	NY	707
PM	Loder, E	MA	706
PM	Lubenow, T	IL	710
PM	Macadaeg, K	IN	710
PM	Mackey, S	CA	713
PM	Mays, K	TN	709
PM	Mekhail, N	OH	710
PM	Ngeow, J	NY	707
PM	Noe, C	TX	711
PM	Peeters-Asdourian, C	MA	706
PM	Prager, J	CA	713
PM	Racz, G	TX	711
PM	Raja, S	MD	707
PM	Ramamurthy, S	TX	712
PM	Rauck, R	NC	709
PM	Richman, D	NY	708
PM	Robbins, L	IL	710
PM	Rosenquist, R	OH	710
PM	Rosner, H	CA	713
PM	Ross, E	MA	706
PM	Schnapp, M	TN	709
PM	Slatkin, N	CA	713
PM	Staats, P	NJ	708
PM	Suresh, S	IL	710
PM	Swarm, R	MO	710
PM	Vetter, T	AL	709
PM	Wallace, M	CA	714
PM	Walsh, N	TX	712
PM	Weinberger, M	NY	708
PM	Weisman, S	WI	711
PM	Wellington, J	IN	711

Pain-Abdominal Recurrent

PGe	Gunasekaran, T	IL	766
PGe	Kirschner, B	IL	766

Pain-Abdominal/Functional

Ge	Drossman, D	NC	242
Ge	Lambiase, L	TN	243

Pain-Acute

PM	Swarm, R	MO	710

Pain-after Spinal Intervention

PM	Diwan, S	NY	707
PM	Huntoon, M	TN	708
PM	Racz, G	TX	711

Pain-Back

N	Hiesiger, E	NY	516
NS	Bauer, J	IL	488
NS	Fessler, R	IL	490
OrS	Lauerman, W	DC	627
OrS	Schwab, F	NY	632
OrS	Weinstein, J	NH	619
PM	Baumann, P	GA	708
PM	Benzon, H	IL	709
PM	Kreitzer, J	NY	707
PM	Ramamurthy, S	TX	712
PM	Rosenquist, R	OH	710
PM	Rosner, H	CA	713
PM	Staats, P	NJ	708
PM	Walsh, N	TX	712
PM	Weinberger, M	NY	708
PMR	Harris, D	TX	871
PMR	Kezar, L	AL	866
PMR	LaBan, M	MI	869
PMR	Press, J	IL	869
PMR	Sliwa, J	IL	870
Rhu	Hadler, N	NC	1063
SM	Schechter, D	CA	1079

Pain-Back & Neck

PM	Ferrante, F	CA	712
PM	Gharibo, C	NY	707
PM	Mekhail, N	OH	710
PM	Noe, C	TX	711
PM	Richman, D	NY	708
PMR	Haig, A	MI	868
PMR	Ragnarsson, K	NY	865

Pain-Back & Shoulder

N	Smith, W	CA	542

Pain-Back, Head & Neck

PM	Racz, G	TX	711

Pain-Cancer

H & PM	Abrahm, J	MA	406
H & PM	Levy, M	PA	406
H & PM	Selvaggi, K	MA	406
H & PM	Weinstein, S	UT	408
Onc	Grossman, S	MD	344
PM	Anghelescu, D	TN	708
PM	Ballantyne, J	WA	712
PM	Burton, A	TX	711
PM	DeLeon, O	NY	707
PM	Diwan, S	NY	707
PM	Driver, L	TX	711
PM	Ferrante, F	CA	712
PM	Fine, P	UT	711
PM	Fishman, S	CA	712
PM	Fitzgibbon, D	WA	713
PM	Huntoon, M	TN	708
PM	Jain, S	NY	707
PM	Jasmin, L	OR	713
PM	Kreitzer, J	NY	707
PM	Mackey, S	CA	713
PM	Mekhail, N	OH	710
PM	Rauck, R	NC	709
PM	Ross, E	MA	706
PM	Slatkin, N	CA	713
PM	Staats, P	NJ	708
PM	Swarm, R	MO	710
PM	Wallace, M	CA	714
PM	Weinberger, M	NY	708
PM	Weisman, S	WI	711
PM	Wellington, J	IN	711
PMR	Cheville, A	MN	867
PMR	Stubblefield, M	NY	866
Psyc	Breitbart, W	NY	923
Psyc	Strouse, T	CA	935

Pain-Cancer, Spine

N	Hiesiger, E	NY	516

Pain-Chronic

NS	Cosgrove, G	RI	472
NS	Rezai, A	OH	492
PM	Ballantyne, J	WA	712
PM	Covington, E	OH	709
PM	Falco, F	DE	707
PM	Fine, P	UT	711
PM	Fishman, S	CA	712
PM	Gharibo, C	NY	707
PM	Mackey, S	CA	713
PM	Mekhail, N	OH	710
PM	Ramamurthy, S	TX	712
PM	Swarm, R	MO	710
PM	Vetter, T	AL	709
PM	Wallace, M	CA	714
PMR	King, J	TX	871
Psyc	Cohen, M	PA	923

Pain-Chronic after Head Injury

N	Saper, J	MI	533

Pain-Chronic Pelvic

RE	Petrozza, J	MA	1041

Pain-Facial

N	Cutrer, F	MN	529
N	Finkel, A	NC	524
N	Kincaid, J	IN	530
N	Newman, L	NY	520
NS	Patel, S	SC	486
PM	Rosenquist, R	OH	710

Pain-HIV patients

Spec	Name	St	Pg
H & PM	Arnold, R	PA	406

Pain-Interventional Techniques

Spec	Name	St	Pg
PM	Argoff, C	NY	706
PM	Gobrial, W	FL	708
PM	Hooten, W	MN	710
PM	Macadaeg, K	IN	710
PM	Mays, K	TN	709
PM	Schnapp, M	TN	709

Pain-Low Back

Spec	Name	St	Pg
PM	Christo, P	MD	706
PMR	Braddom, R	PA	863
PMR	Lutz, C	NY	864
PMR	Lutz, G	NY	864

Pain-Lower Back (IDET procedure)

Spec	Name	St	Pg
PMR	Saal, J	CA	872

Pain-Musculoskeletal

Spec	Name	St	Pg
PM	Diwan, S	NY	707
PMR	Schwartz, L	PA	865
PRhu	Passo, M	SC	812
PRhu	Sherry, D	PA	812

Pain-Musculoskeletal-Spine

Spec	Name	St	Pg
PM	Falco, F	DE	707

Pain-Musculoskeletal-Spine & Neck

Spec	Name	St	Pg
PM	Ngeow, J	NY	707

Pain-Neck

Spec	Name	St	Pg
PMR	Braddom, R	PA	863

Pain-Nerve Injury

Spec	Name	St	Pg
HS	Koman, L	NC	301

Pain-Neuropathic

Spec	Name	St	Pg
N	Donofrio, P	TN	524
N	Oaklander, A	MA	511
PM	Baumann, P	GA	708
PM	Bedder, M	WA	712
PM	Benzon, H	IL	709
PM	Diwan, S	NY	707
PM	Gharibo, C	NY	707
PM	Kreitzer, J	NY	707
PM	Mays, K	TN	709
PM	Mekhail, N	OH	710
PM	Ngeow, J	NY	707
PM	Raja, S	MD	707
PM	Richman, D	NY	708
PM	Rosner, H	CA	713
PM	Schnapp, M	TN	709
PM	Wellington, J	IN	711
PMR	Stubblefield, M	NY	866

Pain-Pediatric

Spec	Name	St	Pg
PM	Wellington, J	IN	711

Pain-Pelvic

Spec	Name	St	Pg
Ge	Pezzone, M	PA	239
PM	Jain, S	NY	707
U	Woo, H	LA	1210

Pain-Pelvic & Perineal

Spec	Name	St	Pg
ObG	Steege, J	NC	563

Pain-Soft Tissue

Spec	Name	St	Pg
PMR	Aseff, J	DC	863

Pain-Spine

Spec	Name	St	Pg
N	Hiesiger, E	NY	516
NRad	Lis, E	NY	1021
PM	Bedder, M	WA	712
PM	Christo, P	MD	706
PM	Cope, D	MD	706
PM	Gobrial, W	FL	708
PM	Macadaeg, K	IN	710
PM	Wellington, J	IN	711
PMR	Harris, D	TX	871
PMR	Kezar, L	AL	866
PMR	Lutz, C	NY	864

Palliative Care

Spec	Name	St	Pg
Ger	Hanson, L	NC	265
Ger	Sachs, G	IN	266
GerPsy	Manepalli, J	MO	945
H & PM	Abrahm, J	MA	406
H & PM	Arnold, R	PA	406
H & PM	Block, S	MA	406
H & PM	Bricker, L	MI	407
H & PM	Davis, M	OH	407
H & PM	Ferris, F	OH	407
H & PM	Fine, R	TX	408
H & PM	Friebert, S	OH	408
H & PM	Jackson, V	MA	406
H & PM	Kutner, J	CO	408
H & PM	Levy, M	PA	406
H & PM	Pantilat, S	CA	408
H & PM	Portenoy, R	NY	407
H & PM	Quill, T	NY	407
H & PM	Ritchie, C	CA	409
H & PM	Santa-Emma, P	OH	408
H & PM	Selvaggi, K	MA	406
H & PM	Tucker, R	AL	407
H & PM	Tulsky, J	NC	407
H & PM	Von Gunten, C	OH	408
H & PM	Weinstein, S	UT	408
IM	Rabow, M	CA	427
IM	Selwyn, P	NY	426
N	Taylor, L	MA	512
Onc	Back, A	WA	385
Onc	Bernard, S	NC	355
Onc	Brescia, F	SC	356
Onc	Bruera, E	TX	379
Onc	Carducci, M	MD	339
Onc	Clamon, G	IA	367
Onc	Cleary, J	WI	368
Onc	Fitch, T	AZ	380
Onc	Himelstein, A	DE	344
Onc	Lyckholm, L	VA	361
Onc	Mintzer, D	PA	347
Onc	Smith, T	MD	351
Onc	Steen, P	ND	377
Onc	Sutton, L	NC	364
Onc	Worden, F	MI	375
PHO	Godder, K	VA	778
PHO	Jakacki, R	PA	774
PHO	Kane, J	TX	788
PHO	Korones, D	NY	774
PHO	Morgan, E	IL	784
PHO	Russo, C	AL	780
PHO	Thomas, G	OR	792
PHO	Wolfe, L	NY	777
PM	Burton, A	TX	711
PM	Driver, L	TX	711
PM	Fine, P	UT	711
PM	Huntoon, M	TN	708
PM	Slatkin, N	CA	713
PM	Wallace, M	CA	714
PM	Weinberger, M	NY	708
Psyc	Breitbart, W	NY	923
Psyc	Strouse, T	CA	935
Psyc	Valentine, A	TX	932
Pul	Nelson, J	NY	958
S	Hinshaw, D	MI	1115
T&CS	Grannis, F	CA	1178
VIR	Coldwell, D	KY	1029

Pancreatic & Biliary Disease

Spec	Name	St	Pg
Ge	Al-Kawas, F	DC	232
Ge	Barkin, J	FL	241
Ge	Branch, M	NC	241
Ge	Carr-Locke, D	NY	233
Ge	Elta, G	MI	247
Ge	Faigel, D	AZ	253
Ge	Gluck, M	WA	256
Ge	Gordon, S	NH	231
Ge	Kelsey, P	MA	231
Ge	Lichtenstein, D	MA	231
Ge	Meiselman, M	IL	249
Ge	Sherman, S	IN	250
Ge	Slivka, A	PA	240
Ge	Wilcox, C	AL	245

Pancreatic & Biliary Surgery

Spec	Name	St	Pg
S	Abecassis, M	IL	1111
S	Adams, R	VA	1103
S	Aranha, G	IL	1111
S	Hebert, J	VT	1085

Spec	Name	St	Pg
S	Lillemoe, K	MA	1086
S	Stiegmann, G	CO	1123
S	Vitale, G	KY	1110

Pancreatic Cancer

Spec	Name	St	Pg
DR	Dachman, A	IL	1014
Ge	Aslanian, H	CT	230
Ge	Cunningham, J	AZ	253
Ge	Edmundowicz, S	MO	247
Ge	Goldberg, M	IL	247
Ge	Okolo, P	MD	238
Ge	Pochapin, M	NY	239
Ge	Schembre, D	WA	257
Ge	Slivka, A	PA	240
Ge	Waxman, I	IL	251
Onc	Abbruzzese, J	TX	378
Onc	Benedetto, P	FL	355
Onc	Benson, A	IL	366
Onc	Berlin, J	TN	355
Onc	Blobe, G	NC	355
Onc	Burris, H	TN	356
Onc	De Simone, P	KY	357
Onc	Donehower, R	MD	341
Onc	Fine, R	NY	342
Onc	Fisher, G	CA	387
Onc	Grem, J	NE	377
Onc	Holcombe, R	NY	345
Onc	Holland, J	NY	345
Onc	Kindler, H	IL	370
Onc	Lacy, J	CT	333
Onc	Laheru, D	MD	346
Onc	Loehrer, P	IN	371
Onc	Meropol, N	OH	371
Onc	O'Reilly, E	NY	348
Onc	Picozzi, V	WA	391
Onc	Reid, T	CA	391
Onc	Ryan, D	MA	334
Onc	Saif, M	MA	334
Onc	Sun, W	PA	352
Onc	Tempero, M	CA	393
Onc	Varadhachary, G	TX	383
Onc	Von Hoff, D	AZ	384
Onc	Wolff, R	TX	384
Onc	Wolin, E	CA	394
Path	Chhieng, D	CT	718
Path	Hruban, R	MD	722
RadRO	Konski, A	MI	990
RadRO	Lawrence, T	MI	990
RadRO	Minsky, B	TX	994
RadRO	Small, W	IL	991
S	Alexander, H	MD	1089
S	August, D	NJ	1089
S	Bartlett, D	PA	1089
S	Behrns, K	FL	1103
S	Bolton, J	LA	1124
S	Bouvet, M	CA	1130
S	Brems, J	IL	1112
S	Brodsky, J	PA	1090
S	Brunicardi, F	CA	1130
S	Callery, M	MA	1084
S	Cameron, J	MD	1090
S	Cance, W	NY	1090
S	Chabot, J	NY	1091
S	Choti, M	MD	1091
S	Coit, D	NY	1091
S	Colquhoun, S	CA	1131
S	DeMatteo, R	NY	1092
S	Drebin, J	PA	1092
S	Ellison, E	OH	1113
S	Evans, D	WI	1113
S	Fahey, T	NY	1093
S	Fisher, W	TX	1125
S	Fong, Y	NY	1093
S	Gibbs, J	NY	1093
S	Hanna, N	MD	1094
S	Hemming, A	CA	1133
S	Heslin, M	AL	1105
S	Hiotis, S	NY	1094
S	Hoffman, J	PA	1094
S	Jarnagin, W	NY	1094
S	Jenkins, R	MA	1086
S	Karpeh, M	NY	1095
S	Kendrick, M	MN	1115
S	Leach, S	MD	1095
S	Lee, J	TX	1127
S	Lee, K	PA	1096
S	Levi, J	FL	1106
S	Lieberman, M	NY	1096
S	Lillemoe, K	MA	1086
S	Lowy, A	CA	1134
S	Mahvi, D	IL	1116
S	Marsh, J	PA	1096
S	McAneny, D	MA	1087
S	McFadden, D	CT	1087
S	Melvin, W	OH	1117
S	Nagorney, D	MN	1117
S	Nakakura, E	CA	1134
S	Nissen, N	CA	1135
S	Norton, J	CA	1135
S	Pachter, H	NY	1097
S	Pawlik, T	MD	1098
S	Pinson, C	TN	1108
S	Pisters, P	TX	1127
S	Posner, M	IL	1118
S	Postier, R	OK	1128
S	Reber, H	CA	1136
S	Rosemurgy, A	FL	1108
S	Salem, R	CT	1087
S	Sarr, M	MN	1119
S	Sasson, A	NE	1123
S	Schulick, R	CO	1123
S	Shen, P	NC	1109
S	Shenk, R	OH	1119
S	Sielaff, T	MN	1119
S	Simeone, D	MI	1119
S	Staley, C	GA	1109
S	Sundaram, M	IL	1120
S	Talamonti, M	IL	1120
S	Thayer, S	MA	1088
S	Tyler, D	NC	1110
S	Vickers, S	MN	1120
S	Vitale, G	KY	1110
S	Walsh, R	OH	1121
S	Weber, S	WI	1121
S	Yeo, C	PA	1102
S	Zinner, M	MA	1088

Pancreatic Cancer (Familial)

Spec	Name	St	Pg
Ge	Chung, D	MA	230
Ge	Kurtz, R	NY	237

Pancreatic Cancer-Acinar Cell

Spec	Name	St	Pg
Onc	Colon-Otero, G	FL	357

Pancreatic Cancer-Early Detection

Spec	Name	St	Pg
Ge	Canto, M	MD	233
Ge	Goggins, M	MD	235
S	Postier, R	OK	1128

Pancreatic Disease

Spec	Name	St	Pg
Ge	Chari, S	MN	246
Ge	Edmundowicz, S	MO	247
Ge	Forsmark, C	FL	242
Ge	Hawes, R	FL	242
Ge	Kalloo, A	MD	236
Ge	Kantsevoy, S	MD	236
Ge	Kochman, M	PA	236
Ge	Konicek, F	IL	248
Ge	Kowalski, T	PA	237
Ge	Kozarek, R	WA	256
Ge	Lambiase, L	TN	243
Ge	Liddle, R	NC	243
Ge	Ostroff, J	CA	257
Ge	Pasricha, P	MD	239
Ge	Vargo, J	OH	251
Ge	Vege, S	MN	251
PGe	Hoffenberg, E	CO	767

Pancreatic Endocrine Tumors

Spec	Name	St	Pg
Ge	Chung, D	MA	230
S	Yeo, C	PA	1102

Pancreatic Islet Cell Transplant

Spec	Name	St	Pg
EDM	Clore, J	VA	216
S	Brunicardi, F	CA	1130
S	Eckhoff, D	AL	1104
S	Fisher, J	CA	1132
S	Galloway, J	GA	1105
S	Markmann, J	MA	1087
S	Oberholzer, J	IL	1117
S	Posselt, A	CA	1136
S	Shapiro, R	PA	1100
S	Weber, C	GA	1110

Pancreatic Surgery

Spec	Name	St	Pg
PS	Meyers, R	UT	821
S	Billingsley, K	OR	1130
S	Cameron, J	MD	1090
S	Chabot, J	NY	1091
S	Cronin, D	WI	1113
S	DeMatteo, R	NY	1092

Spec	Name	St	Pg
S	Deziel, D	IL	1113
S	Galloway, J	GA	1105
S	Halff, G	TX	1125
S	Horvath, K	WA	1133
S	Howerton, R	NC	1106
S	Johnson, L	DC	1094
S	Lee, J	NY	1095
S	MacDonald, K	NC	1107
S	Matthews, J	IL	1116
S	Pappas, T	NC	1107
S	Postier, R	OK	1128
S	Reber, H	CA	1136
S	Reiner, M	NY	1099
S	Sharp, K	TN	1109

Pancreatic/Biliary Endoscopy (ERCP)

Spec	Name	St	Pg
Ge	Baillie, J	NC	241
Ge	Baron, T	MN	246
Ge	Branch, M	NC	241
Ge	Carr-Locke, D	NY	233
Ge	Cello, J	CA	255
Ge	Cohen, J	NY	233
Ge	Cunningham, J	AZ	253
Ge	Das, A	AZ	253
Ge	Dea, S	CA	255
Ge	Faigel, D	AZ	253
Ge	Forsmark, C	FL	242
Ge	Ginsberg, G	PA	234
Ge	Gluck, M	WA	256
Ge	Gordon, S	NH	231
Ge	Haber, G	NY	235
Ge	Haluszka, O	PA	235
Ge	Hawes, R	FL	242
Ge	Jonnalagadda, S	MO	248
Ge	Kantsevoy, S	MD	236
Ge	Kimmey, M	WA	256
Ge	Kochman, M	PA	236
Ge	Kowalski, T	PA	237
Ge	Kozarek, R	WA	256
Ge	Levy, M	MN	249
Ge	Ostroff, J	CA	257
Ge	Scudera, P	VA	244
Ge	Shah, R	CO	252
Ge	Shaker, R	WI	250
Ge	Sherman, S	IN	250
Ge	Silverman, W	IA	250
Ge	Slivka, A	PA	240
Ge	Vargo, J	OH	251
Ge	Wilcox, C	AL	245
Ge	Yanda, R	GA	245
S	Dunkin, B	TX	1124
S	Mellinger, J	IL	1117

Panic Disorder

Spec	Name	St	Pg
GerPsy	Burke, W	NE	946
Psyc	Canterbury, R	VA	928
Psyc	Fyer, A	NY	924
Psyc	Haque, W	TX	932
Psyc	Pollack, M	IL	930
Psyc	Roy-Byrne, P	WA	934
Psyc	Stein, M	CA	935

Pap Smear Abnormalities

Spec	Name	St	Pg
ObG	Gilliam, M	IL	564
ObG	Snyder, R	TX	566

Paraneoplastic Syndromes

Spec	Name	St	Pg
N	Posner, J	NY	520

Parapsoriasis

Spec	Name	St	Pg
D	Wood, G	WI	197

Parasitic Infections

Spec	Name	St	Pg
Inf	Hartman, B	NY	413
Inf	Pearson, R	VA	416
Inf	Slama, T	IN	418
PrM	Cahill, J	NY	912

Parathyroid Cancer

Spec	Name	St	Pg
EDM	Haber, R	NY	212
Oto	Kuhel, W	NY	672
Oto	Shindo, M	OR	697
Oto	Weber, S	TX	694
S	Clark, O	CA	1131
S	Sosa, J	NC	1109
S	Udelsman, R	CT	1088

Parathyroid Disease

Spec	Name	St	Pg
EDM	Bockman, R	NY	211
EDM	Daniels, G	MA	209
EDM	Emanuele, M	IL	219
EDM	Haber, R	NY	212
EDM	Kopp, P	IL	220
EDM	Kronenberg, H	MA	209
Ger	Lyles, K	NC	265
NuM	Neumann, D	OH	556
Oto	Randolph, G	MA	666
Oto	Song, J	CO	691
Oto	Terris, D	GA	682

Parathyroid Surgery

Spec	Name	St	Pg
Oto	Funk, G	IA	684
Oto	Keane, W	PA	672
Oto	Shindo, M	OR	697
Oto	Tufano, R	MD	676
S	Carty, S	PA	1091
S	Gosnell, J	CA	1133
S	Kim, L	AR	1126
S	McHenry, C	OH	1116
S	Norman, J	FL	1107

Parent Guidance in Parental Cancer

Spec	Name	St	Pg
Psyc	Rauch, P	MA	922

Parenting Issues

Spec	Name	St	Pg
ChAP	Turecki, S	NY	941

Parkinson's Disease

Spec	Name	St	Pg
N	Ahlskog, J	MN	527
N	Aminoff, M	CA	538
N	Ashizawa, T	FL	523
N	Azizi, S	PA	513
N	Baser, S	PA	513
N	Bressman, S	NY	513
N	Bruno, M	HI	538
N	DeLong, M	GA	524
N	Fahn, S	NY	515
N	Flaherty, A	MA	511
N	Foo, S	NY	515
N	Gendelman, S	NY	515
N	Goetz, C	IL	529
N	Golbe, L	NJ	516
N	Hauser, R	FL	525
N	Hurtig, H	PA	516
N	Jankovic, J	TX	537
N	Kieburtz, K	NY	516
N	Langston, J	CA	540
N	Lew, M	CA	541
N	Maraganore, D	IL	531
N	Montgomery, E	PA	520
N	Nutt, J	OR	541
N	Olanow, C	NY	520
N	Perlmutter, J	MO	532
N	Pulst, S	UT	535
N	Reich, S	MD	520
N	Ropper, A	MA	512
N	Rosenbaum, R	OR	541
N	Sage, J	NJ	521
N	Samii, A	WA	542
N	Sethi, K	GA	527
N	Shulman, L	MD	521
N	Singer, C	FL	527
N	Stern, M	PA	522
N	Tanner, C	CA	542
N	Tetrud, J	CA	542
N	Waters, C	NY	522
N	Watts, R	AL	527
N	Wooten, G	VA	527
NS	Baltuch, G	PA	474
NS	Burchiel, K	OR	499
NS	Freeman, T	FL	484
NS	Liker, M	CA	500
NS	Nazzaro, J	KS	494
NS	Rezai, A	OH	492
NS	Wharen, R	FL	488

Parkinson's Disease/Aging Brain

Spec	Name	St	Pg
NRad	Drayer, B	NY	1020

Parkinson's Disease/Movement Disorders

Spec	Name	St	Pg
N	Louis, E	NY	518
N	Vitek, J	MN	534

Spec	Name	St	Pg
NS	Bakay, R	IL	488
NS	Goodman, R	NY	477
NS	Guthrie, B	AL	485

Parkinson's Disease/Visual Disorders

Spec	Name	St	Pg
N	Balcer, L	NY	513

Parotid Gland Tumors

Spec	Name	St	Pg
Oto	Alam, D	OH	682
Oto	Burkey, B	OH	684
Oto	Johnson, J	PA	671

Paroxysmal Nocturnal Hemoglobinuria

Spec	Name	St	Pg
Hem	Goldberg, J	PA	314
Hem	Mangan, K	PA	315
Hem	Miller, K	MA	312

Patent Foramen Ovale

Spec	Name	St	Pg
IC	Feldman, T	IL	126
PCd	Moskowitz, W	VA	751

Pathology

Spec	Name	St	Pg
Path	Allred, D	MO	727
Path	Amin, M	CA	731
Path	Antonescu, C	NY	720
Path	Appelman, H	MI	727
Path	Arber, D	CA	731
Path	Bagg, A	PA	720
Path	Balla, A	IL	727
Path	Baloch, Z	PA	720
Path	Banks, P	NC	725
Path	Bastian, B	CA	732
Path	Behm, F	IL	727
Path	Bell, D	MN	727
Path	Bhan, A	MA	718
Path	Bleiweiss, I	NY	720
Path	Bollen, A	CA	732
Path	Bostwick, D	VA	725
Path	Brooks, J	PA	720
Path	Bruner, J	TX	730
Path	Burger, P	MD	721
Path	Cagle, P	TX	730
Path	Chandrasoma, P	CA	732
Path	Chang, K	CA	732
Path	Chen, Y	CA	732
Path	Chesney, C	TN	725
Path	Chhieng, D	CT	718
Path	Cho, K	MI	727
Path	Cochran, A	CA	732
Path	Cohen, M	UT	729
Path	Connolly, J	MA	718
Path	Cote, R	FL	725
Path	Crawford, J	NY	721
Path	Dahmoush, L	IA	727
Path	De Las Morenas, A	MA	718
Path	DeMasters, B	CO	729
Path	Demetris, A	PA	721
Path	Dubeau, L	CA	732
Path	Ehya, H	PA	721
Path	Epstein, J	MD	721
Path	Faye-Petersen, O	AL	726
Path	Ferrell, L	CA	732
Path	Fishbein, M	CA	733
Path	Fletcher, C	MA	718
Path	Fogt, F	PA	721
Path	Foucar, M	NM	730
Path	Gambetti, P	OH	728
Path	Goldblum, J	OH	728
Path	Gottlieb, G	MA	718
Path	Govindarajan, S	CA	733
Path	Greenson, J	MI	728
Path	Gupta, P	PA	721
Path	Hamilton, S	TX	730
Path	Hammar, S	WA	733
Path	Harris, N	MA	718
Path	Heller, D	NJ	721
Path	Hoda, S	NY	722
Path	Hruban, R	MD	722
Path	Kahn, L	NY	722
Path	Kanel, G	CA	733
Path	Katzenstein, A	NY	722
Path	Kaufman, R	MA	718
Path	Kinney, M	TX	730
Path	Klimstra, D	NY	722
Path	Koss, M	CA	733
Path	Kurman, R	MD	722
Path	Kurtin, P	MN	728
Path	Lage, J	MS	726
Path	Le Boit, P	CA	733
Path	Leslie, K	AZ	730
Path	LiVolsi, V	PA	722
Path	Ljung, B	CA	733
Path	Lowe, L	MI	728
Path	Lucas, D	MI	728
Path	Mark, E	MA	719
Path	Masood, S	FL	726
Path	Melamed, J	NY	722
Path	Mies, C	PA	723
Path	Mills, S	VA	726
Path	Mischel, P	CA	733
Path	Montgomery, E	MD	723
Path	Moore, S	IA	728
Path	Moran, C	TX	730
Path	Morrow, J	CT	719
Path	Myers, J	MI	728
Path	Nathwani, B	CA	734
Path	Nicosia, S	FL	726
Path	O'Brien, M	MA	719
Path	Odze, R	MA	719
Path	Orazi, A	NY	723
Path	Patchefsky, A	PA	723
Path	Perry, A	CA	734
Path	Petito, C	FL	726
Path	Petras, R	OH	729
Path	Prieto, V	TX	730
Path	Rashid, A	TX	731
Path	Rennke, H	MA	719
Path	Reuter, V	NY	723
Path	Rimm, D	CT	719
Path	Roberts, W	TX	731
Path	Ronnett, B	MD	723
Path	Rosenberg, A	FL	726
Path	Rosenblum, M	NY	723
Path	Ross, J	NY	724
Path	Rubin, B	OH	729
Path	Rutgers, J	CA	734
Path	Sahin, A	TX	731
Path	Sanchez, M	NJ	724
Path	Schiller, A	HI	734
Path	Schnitt, S	MA	719
Path	Sewell, C	GA	726
Path	Sibley, R	CA	734
Path	Silva, E	TX	731
Path	Silverman, J	PA	724
Path	Smith, T	MA	719
Path	Soslow, R	NY	724
Path	Suster, S	WI	729
Path	Swerdlow, S	PA	724
Path	Tavassoli, F	CT	720
Path	Thor, A	CO	729
Path	Tomaszewski, J	NY	724
Path	Tornos, C	NY	724
Path	Travis, W	NY	724
Path	Triche, T	CA	734
Path	True, L	WA	734
Path	Ulbright, T	IN	729
Path	Walker, D	TX	731
Path	Wang, B	NY	725
Path	Warnke, R	CA	734
Path	Weisenburger, D	CA	735
Path	Weiss, L	CA	735
Path	Weiss, S	GA	727
Path	Wheeler, T	TX	731
Path	Wilczynski, S	CA	735
Path	Young, R	MA	720
Path	Yousem, S	PA	725
Path	Zagzag, D	NY	725

Pediatric & Adolescent Gynecology

Spec	Name	St	Pg
ObG	Bradshaw, K	TX	566
RE	Smith, Y	MI	1049
RE	Wilson, E	TX	1050

Pediatric & Adolescent Sports Medicine

Spec	Name	St	Pg
AM	Hergenroeder, A	TX	78

Pediatric & Adult Plastic Surgery

Spec	Name	St	Pg
PlS	Glat, P	PA	882

Pediatric Allergy & Immunology

Spec	Name	St	Pg
A&I	DeShazo, R	MS	82
A&I	Sanders, G	MI	84
A&I	Wong, D	AZ	85
PA&I	Bahna, S	LA	746
PA&I	Bock, S	CO	745

Spec	Name	St	Pg
PA&I	Burks, A	NC	744
PA&I	Church, J	CA	746
PA&I	Cowan, M	CA	746
PA&I	Ehrlich, P	NY	743
PA&I	Epstein, S	CA	747
PA&I	Fanous, Y	CA	747
PA&I	Gelfand, E	CO	745
PA&I	Josephs, S	MD	743
PA&I	Kamani, N	DC	743
PA&I	Kelly, C	VA	745
PA&I	Klein, R	RI	743
PA&I	Lemanske, R	WI	745
PA&I	Leung, D	CO	746
PA&I	Orange, J	TX	746
PA&I	Pongracic, J	IL	745
PA&I	Sampson, H	NY	743
PA&I	Schuberth, K	MD	744
PA&I	Shearer, W	TX	746
PA&I	Sicherer, S	NY	744
PA&I	Skoner, D	PA	744
PA&I	Sly, R	MD	744
PA&I	Spergel, J	PA	744
PA&I	Strunk, R	MO	745
PA&I	Sullivan, K	PA	744
PA&I	Wasserman, R	TX	746
PA&I	Wolf, R	IL	745
PA&I	Wood, R	MD	744

Pediatric Cancers

Path	Triche, T	CA	734
PHO	Adamson, P	PA	771
PHO	Beyer, E	IL	781
PHO	Cheung, N	NY	772
PHO	Cohn, S	IL	782
PHO	Drachtman, R	NJ	772
PHO	Dunkel, I	NY	772
PHO	Frangoul, H	TN	778
PHO	Friedman, D	TN	778
PHO	Garvin, J	NY	773
PHO	Geyer, J	WA	790
PHO	Hord, J	OH	784
PHO	Kane, J	TX	788
PHO	Kobrinsky, N	ND	787
PHO	Korones, D	NY	774
PHO	Meyer, W	OK	788
PHO	Meyers, P	NY	775
PHO	Neuberg, R	SC	780
PHO	Park, J	WA	791
PHO	Parker, R	NY	776
PHO	Pendergrass, T	WA	791
PHO	Sakamoto, K	CA	791
PHO	Sallan, S	MA	770
PHO	Sencer, S	MN	785
PHO	Siegel, S	CA	792
PHO	Sondel, P	WI	785
PHO	Steinherz, P	NY	776
PHO	Weinstein, H	MA	771
PS	Bond, S	KY	817
PS	Dillon, P	MO	819
PS	Ehrlich, P	MI	819
PS	Farmer, D	CA	823
PS	Glick, P	NY	816
PS	Jackson, R	AR	822
PS	Paidas, C	FL	818
PS	Reynolds, M	IL	820
PS	Sawin, R	WA	824
PS	Shochat, S	TN	819
PS	Spigland, N	NY	817
PS	Stolar, C	CA	824
PS	Strauch, E	MD	817
PS	Warner, B	MO	821
RadRO	Buatti, J	IA	988
RadRO	Constine, L	NY	978
RadRO	Donaldson, S	CA	995
RadRO	Dritschilo, A	DC	979
RadRO	Fiveash, J	AL	984
RadRO	Kun, L	TN	984
RadRO	Marcus, R	FL	985
RadRO	Michalski, J	MO	991
RadRO	Roberts, K	CT	977
RadRO	Schomberg, P	WA	997
RadRO	Stea, B	AZ	995
RadRO	Wara, W	CA	998
RadRO	Woo, S	KY	988

Pediatric Cardiac Surgery

PS	Jennings, R	MA	814
PS	Quaegebeur, J	NY	816
T&CS	Bacha, E	NY	1150
T&CS	Burke, R	FL	1161
T&CS	Dabal, R	AL	1162
T&CS	Delius, R	MI	1168
T&CS	Herrington, C	CA	1179
T&CS	Ilbawi, M	IL	1169
T&CS	Kanter, K	GA	1162
T&CS	Lamberti, J	CA	1179
T&CS	Mavroudis, C	FL	1163
T&CS	Mayer, J	MA	1148
T&CS	Mill, M	NC	1163
T&CS	Mitchell, M	CO	1173
T&CS	Mosca, R	NY	1157
T&CS	Rosenkranz, E	FL	1165
T&CS	Trento, A	CA	1180
T&CS	Ungerleider, R	NC	1166
T&CS	Walters, H	MI	1172
T&CS	Ziemer, G	IL	1172

Pediatric Cardiology

PCd	Ackerman, M	MN	752
PCd	Agarwala, B	IL	752
PCd	Beekman, R	OH	752
PCd	Beerman, L	PA	748
PCd	Bernstein, D	CA	754
PCd	Biancaniello, T	NY	748
PCd	Bierman, F	NY	748
PCd	Brenner, J	MD	748
PCd	Caldwell, R	IN	752
PCd	Cetta, F	MN	752
PCd	Cheatham, J	OH	752
PCd	Colvin, E	AL	751
PCd	Cooper, R	NY	748
PCd	Crosson, J	MD	748
PCd	De Moor, M	MA	747
PCd	Dick, M	MI	752
PCd	Dreyer, W	TX	754
PCd	Driscoll, D	MN	752
PCd	Feltes, T	OH	753
PCd	Fish, F	TN	751
PCd	Fricker, F	FL	751
PCd	Gelb, B	NY	748
PCd	Gewitz, M	NY	749
PCd	Gullquist, S	VA	751
PCd	Hanna, B	PA	749
PCd	Hardin, J	IL	753
PCd	Hellenbrand, W	CT	747
PCd	Hijazi, Z	IL	753
PCd	Hoyer, M	IN	753
PCd	Hsu, D	NY	749
PCd	Lang, P	MA	747
PCd	Latson, L	FL	751
PCd	Lewin, M	WA	754
PCd	Lock, J	MA	747
PCd	Mahony, L	TX	754
PCd	Minich, L	UT	753
PCd	Moodie, D	TX	754
PCd	Moskowitz, W	VA	751
PCd	Murphy, J	PA	749
PCd	Newburger, J	MA	747
PCd	Pahl, E	IL	753
PCd	Parness, I	NY	749
PCd	Perry, S	CA	754
PCd	Radtke, W	DE	749
PCd	Rocchini, A	MI	753
PCd	Rogers, J	TX	754
PCd	Rome, J	PA	749
PCd	Rychik, J	PA	749
PCd	Shaddy, R	PA	750
PCd	Sherman, F	PA	750
PCd	Sommer, R	NY	750
PCd	Steinherz, L	NY	750
PCd	Teitel, D	CA	755
PCd	Velvis, H	NY	750
PCd	Walsh, C	NY	750
PCd	Walsh, E	MA	748
PCd	Weinberg, P	PA	750
PCd	Young, M	FL	751
PCd	Zahn, E	CA	755

Pediatric Cardiothoracic Surgery

PS	Bove, E	MI	819
PS	Colombani, P	MD	815
T&CS	Abraham, V	IN	1166
T&CS	Backer, C	IL	1167
T&CS	Campbell, D	CO	1172
T&CS	Chen, J	NY	1151
T&CS	Cohen, G	CA	1177
T&CS	Forbess, J	TX	1174
T&CS	Fraser, C	TX	1174
T&CS	Gaynor, J	PA	1153
T&CS	Hanley, F	CA	1178
T&CS	Jonas, R	DC	1154
T&CS	Kirshbom, P	CT	1147
T&CS	Kopf, G	CT	1147
T&CS	Morales, D	OH	1170

Pediatric Clinical Genetics

Spec	Name	St	Pg
CG	Andersson, H	LA	161

Pediatric Critical Care Medicine

Spec	Name	St	Pg
PCCM	Dean, J	UT	755
PCCM	Easley, R	TX	755
PCCM	Fuhrman, B	TX	756
PCCM	Perez Fontan, J	TX	756
PCCM	Sarnaik, A	MI	755
PCCM	Schwarz, A	CA	756
PCCM	Taylor, R	TX	756
PCCM	Thompson, A	PA	755
PCCM	Zimmerman, J	WA	756

Pediatric Dermatology

Spec	Name	St	Pg
D	Anderson, R	MA	184
D	Bayliss, S	MO	194
D	Cohen, B	MD	187
D	Cunningham, B	CA	200
D	Eichenfield, L	CA	200
D	Frieden, I	CA	200
D	Friedlander, S	CA	200
D	Gellis, S	MA	185
D	Hansen, R	AZ	198
D	Johr, R	FL	193
D	Kane, K	MA	185
D	Kress, D	PA	189
D	Levy, M	TX	198
D	Lucky, A	OH	196
D	Orlow, S	NY	190
D	Paller, A	IL	196
D	Rhodes, A	IL	197
D	Treadwell, P	IN	197
D	Witman, P	OH	197
D	Yan, A	PA	191

Pediatric Endocrinology

Spec	Name	St	Pg
EDM	Weiss, R	IL	221
PEn	Allen, D	WI	760
PEn	Alter, C	PA	757
PEn	Arslanian, S	PA	757
PEn	Becker, D	PA	757
PEn	Casella, S	NH	756
PEn	DeLuca, F	PA	758
PEn	Diamond, F	FL	759
PEn	DiMeglio, L	IN	760
PEn	Eugster, E	IN	760
PEn	Fennoy, I	NY	758
PEn	Foster, C	UT	761
PEn	Freemark, M	NC	759
PEn	Gallagher, M	NY	758
PEn	Garibaldi, L	PA	758
PEn	Geffner, M	CA	761
PEn	Gitelman, S	CA	761
PEn	Gordon, C	RI	757
PEn	Gutai, J	MI	760
PEn	Kappy, M	CO	761
PEn	Klingensmith, G	CO	761
PEn	Kohn, B	NY	758
PEn	Levine, M	PA	758
PEn	Levitsky, L	MA	757
PEn	Ludwig, D	MA	757
PEn	Lustig, R	CA	762
PEn	Meacham, L	GA	759
PEn	Menon, R	MI	760
PEn	Mirmira, R	IN	760
PEn	New, M	NY	758
PEn	Norris, A	IA	760
PEn	Oberfield, S	NY	758
PEn	Plotnick, L	MD	759
PEn	Rogers, D	OH	760
PEn	Rosenthal, S	CA	762
PEn	Silverstein, J	FL	759
PEn	Sklar, C	NY	759
PEn	Spack, N	MA	757
PEn	Sperling, M	PA	759
PEn	Tamborlane, W	CT	757
PEn	White, N	MO	761
PEn	Wilson, D	CA	762
PEn	Zimmerman, D	IL	761

Pediatric Facial Plastic Surgery

Spec	Name	St	Pg
Oto	Waner, M	NY	677

Pediatric Gastroenterology

Spec	Name	St	Pg
PGe	Baker, R	NY	763
PGe	Baker, S	NY	763
PGe	Baldassano, R	PA	763
PGe	Baldridge, A	NJ	763
PGe	Benkov, K	NY	763
PGe	Berman, J	IL	765
PGe	Bishop, W	IA	765
PGe	Black, D	TN	764
PGe	Christie, D	WA	768
PGe	Cohen, M	OH	765
PGe	Di Lorenzo, C	OH	765
PGe	Dubinsky, M	CA	768
PGe	El-Youssef, M	MN	765
PGe	Fasano, A	MA	762
PGe	Guandalini, S	IL	766
PGe	Gunasekaran, T	IL	766
PGe	Gupta, S	IN	766
PGe	Heyman, M	CA	769
PGe	Hill, I	OH	766
PGe	Hoffenberg, E	CO	767
PGe	Jonas, M	MA	762
PGe	Kirschner, B	IL	766
PGe	Kleinman, R	MA	762
PGe	Krebs, N	CO	767
PGe	Leichtner, A	MA	762
PGe	Levy, J	NY	763
PGe	McDiarmid, S	CA	769
PGe	Mittal, N	TX	768
PGe	Molleston, J	IN	766
PGe	Mousa, H	OH	766
PGe	Murray, K	WA	769
PGe	Narkewicz, M	CO	767
PGe	Novak, D	FL	765
PGe	Oliva-Hemker, M	MD	763
PGe	Piccoli, D	PA	764
PGe	Rhoads, J	TX	768
PGe	Rothbaum, R	MO	767
PGe	Schwarz, K	MD	764
PGe	Schwarz, S	NY	764
PGe	Snyder, J	DC	764
PGe	Sokol, R	CO	767
PGe	Spivak, W	NY	764
PGe	Squires, R	PA	764
PGe	Suchy, F	CO	768
PGe	Thomas, D	CA	769
PGe	Ulshen, M	NC	765
PGe	Vanderhoof, J	NE	768
PGe	Whitington, P	IL	767
PGe	Wyllie, R	OH	767

Pediatric Gastrointestinal Surgery

Spec	Name	St	Pg
CRS	Lavery, I	OH	173

Pediatric Gynecology

Spec	Name	St	Pg
AM	Emans, S	MA	76
ObG	Gilliam, M	IL	564
ObG	Merritt, D	MO	565
PS	Velcek, F	NY	817
RE	Sanfilippo, J	PA	1044

Pediatric Hand Surgery

Spec	Name	St	Pg
HS	Carlson, M	NY	297
HS	Chang, J	CA	305
HS	Hentz, V	CA	306
HS	Koman, L	NC	301
HS	Lee, W	MD	299
HS	Mih, A	IN	303
PlS	Bentz, M	WI	892
PlS	Sood, R	IN	896

Pediatric Hematology-Oncology

Spec	Name	St	Pg
PHO	Abromowitch, M	NE	786
PHO	Adamson, P	PA	771
PHO	Albritton, K	TX	787
PHO	Aledo, A	NY	771
PHO	Altman, A	CT	769
PHO	Andrews, R	WA	789
PHO	Angiolillo, A	DC	771
PHO	Arceci, R	AZ	787
PHO	Arndt, C	MN	781
PHO	Banerjee, A	CA	789
PHO	Barredo, J	FL	777
PHO	Berg, S	TX	787
PHO	Bertolone, S	KY	777
PHO	Beyer, E	IL	781
PHO	Billett, A	MA	769
PHO	Blaney, S	TX	787
PHO	Blatt, J	NC	778
PHO	Boxer, L	MI	782
PHO	Brecher, M	NY	771
PHO	Bruggers, C	UT	786
PHO	Buchanan, G	TX	787
PHO	Bussel, J	NY	771

Spec	Name	St	Pg
PHO	Cairo, M	NY	772
PHO	Camitta, B	WI	782
PHO	Carpenter, P	WA	789
PHO	Carroll, W	NY	772
PHO	Castellino, S	NC	778
PHO	Castle, V	MI	782
PHO	Chen, A	MD	772
PHO	Cheung, N	NY	772
PHO	Coccia, P	NE	786
PHO	Cohen, K	MD	772
PHO	Cohn, S	IL	782
PHO	Cooper, L	TX	788
PHO	Corey, S	IL	782
PHO	Croop, J	IN	782
PHO	Cunningham, J	IL	782
PHO	Davies, S	OH	782
PHO	Diller, L	MA	770
PHO	Dome, J	DC	772
PHO	Drachtman, R	NJ	772
PHO	Dreyer, Z	TX	788
PHO	Ducore, J	CA	789
PHO	Dunkel, I	NY	772
PHO	Fallon, R	IN	783
PHO	Felix, C	PA	773
PHO	Ferrara, J	MI	783
PHO	Finklestein, J	CA	789
PHO	Finlay, J	CA	789
PHO	Fouladi, M	OH	783
PHO	Frangoul, H	TN	778
PHO	Frantz, C	DE	773
PHO	Friedman, A	MD	773
PHO	Friedman, D	TN	778
PHO	Furman, W	TN	778
PHO	Gajjar, A	TN	778
PHO	Garvin, J	NY	773
PHO	Geyer, J	WA	790
PHO	Giardina, P	NY	773
PHO	Glader, B	CA	790
PHO	Godder, K	VA	778
PHO	Gold, S	NC	779
PHO	Goldman, S	TX	788
PHO	Goldman, S	IL	783
PHO	Graham, M	AZ	788
PHO	Green, D	TN	779
PHO	Greenberg, J	DC	773
PHO	Grupp, S	PA	773
PHO	Guarini, L	NY	773
PHO	Guinan, E	MA	770
PHO	Gururangan, S	NC	779
PHO	Halligan, G	PA	774
PHO	Halpern, S	NJ	774
PHO	Harris, M	NJ	774
PHO	Haut, P	IN	783
PHO	Hawkins, D	WA	790
PHO	Hayani, A	IL	783
PHO	Hayashi, R	MO	783
PHO	Helman, L	MD	774
PHO	Hetherington, M	MO	783
PHO	Hilden, J	CO	786
PHO	Homans, A	VT	770
PHO	Hoots, W	MD	774
PHO	Hord, J	OH	784
PHO	Horn, B	CA	790
PHO	Hsu, L	IL	784
PHO	Hudson, M	TN	779
PHO	Hutchinson, R	MI	784
PHO	Jakacki, R	PA	774
PHO	Johnston, J	GA	779
PHO	Kadan-Lottick, N	CT	770
PHO	Kane, J	TX	788
PHO	Kapoor, N	CA	790
PHO	Keller, F	GA	779
PHO	Kieran, M	MA	770
PHO	Kobrinsky, N	ND	787
PHO	Korones, D	NY	774
PHO	Kramer, K	NY	774
PHO	Kreissman, S	NC	779
PHO	Kung, F	CA	790
PHO	Kurtzberg, J	NC	779
PHO	Kushner, B	NY	775
PHO	Kuttesch, J	NM	788
PHO	Laver, J	NY	775
PHO	Leung, W	TN	780
PHO	Link, M	CA	790
PHO	Lipton, J	NY	775
PHO	Loeb, D	MD	775
PHO	Luchtman-Jones, L	DC	775
PHO	Manco-Johnson, M	CO	787
PHO	Manera, R	IL	784
PHO	Marcus, J	NY	775
PHO	Marina, N	CA	790
PHO	Maris, J	PA	775
PHO	Matthay, K	CA	791
PHO	McLean, T	NC	780
PHO	Meyer, W	OK	788
PHO	Meyers, P	NY	775
PHO	Morgan, E	IL	784
PHO	Neglia, J	MN	784
PHO	Neuberg, R	SC	780
PHO	Nicholson, H	OR	791
PHO	O'Dorisio, M	IA	784
PHO	O'Reilly, R	NY	776
PHO	Olshefski, R	OH	784
PHO	Olson, J	OR	791
PHO	Olson, T	GA	780
PHO	Park, J	WA	791
PHO	Parker, R	NY	776
PHO	Pendergrass, T	WA	791
PHO	Plautz, G	OH	785
PHO	Puccetti, D	WI	785
PHO	Pui, C	TN	780
PHO	Razzouk, B	IN	785
PHO	Recht, M	OR	791
PHO	Rheingold, S	PA	776
PHO	Ribeiro, R	TN	780
PHO	Ritchey, A	PA	776
PHO	Rodriguez-Galindo, C	MA	770
PHO	Rood, B	DC	776
PHO	Rosenthal, J	CA	791
PHO	Rosoff, P	NC	780
PHO	Rubin, C	IL	785
PHO	Russo, C	AL	780
PHO	Sakamoto, K	CA	791
PHO	Sallan, S	MA	770
PHO	Salvi, S	IL	785
PHO	Sandler, E	FL	781
PHO	Santana, V	TN	781
PHO	Schwartz, C	RI	770
PHO	Sencer, S	MN	785
PHO	Shapiro, A	IN	785
PHO	Siegel, S	CA	792
PHO	Small, D	MD	776
PHO	Sondel, P	WI	785
PHO	Steinherz, P	NY	776
PHO	Tebbi, C	FL	781
PHO	Thomas, G	OR	792
PHO	Tomlinson, G	TX	788
PHO	Valentino, L	IL	786
PHO	van Hoff, J	NH	771
PHO	Vik, T	IN	786
PHO	Wang, W	TN	781
PHO	Wayne, A	CA	792
PHO	Wechsler, D	NC	781
PHO	Weinblatt, M	NY	776
PHO	Weiner, M	NY	777
PHO	Weinstein, H	MA	771
PHO	Wexler, L	NY	777
PHO	Wiley, J	MD	777
PHO	Williams, J	AZ	789
PHO	Winick, N	TX	789
PHO	Wolfe, L	NY	777
PHO	Yaddanapudi, R	MI	786
PHO	York, T	MD	777

Pediatric Infectious Disease

Inf	Gorensek, M	FL	416
PInf	Alexander, K	IL	795
PInf	Andiman, W	CT	792
PInf	Baker, C	TX	796
PInf	Baltimore, R	CT	792
PInf	Belcher, C	IN	795
PInf	Bell, L	PA	793
PInf	Bradley, J	CA	797
PInf	Bryson, Y	CA	797
PInf	Christenson, J	IN	795
PInf	Demmler-Harrison, G	TX	796
PInf	Durbin, W	MA	792
PInf	Edwards, K	TN	794
PInf	Flynn, P	TN	794
PInf	Givner, L	NC	794
PInf	Green, M	PA	793
PInf	Ingram, D	NC	794
PInf	Jacobs, R	AR	796
PInf	Kaplan, S	TX	796
PInf	Kline, M	TX	796
PInf	Kotloff, K	MD	793
PInf	Krilov, L	NY	793
PInf	Leonard, E	OH	795
PInf	Long, S	PA	793
PInf	McComsey, G	OH	795
PInf	McCracken, G	TX	796
PInf	McKinney, R	NC	794
PInf	Meissner, H	MA	792
PInf	Michaels, M	PA	793
PInf	Mitchell, C	FL	795
PInf	Petru, A	CA	797
PInf	Raszka, W	VT	793
PInf	Saiman, L	NY	794

Spec	Name	St	Pg
PInf	Scott, G	FL	795
PInf	Shapiro, E	CT	793
PInf	Shulman, S	IL	796
PInf	Singh, N	DC	794
PInf	Starke, J	TX	797
PInf	Wald, E	WI	796

Pediatric Nephrology

Spec	Name	St	Pg
PNep	Alexander, S	CA	800
PNep	Andreoli, S	IN	799
PNep	Ault, B	TN	798
PNep	Benfield, M	AL	798
PNep	Brophy, P	IA	799
PNep	Chandar, J	FL	798
PNep	Clardy, C	IL	799
PNep	Cohn, R	IL	800
PNep	Conley, S	PA	797
PNep	Ellis, D	PA	797
PNep	Ettenger, R	CA	800
PNep	Fivush, B	MD	798
PNep	Flynn, J	WA	800
PNep	Fouser, L	WA	801
PNep	Harmon, W	MA	797
PNep	Jabs, K	TN	799
PNep	Jordan, S	CA	801
PNep	Kaplan, B	PA	798
PNep	Kashtan, C	MN	800
PNep	Langman, C	IL	800
PNep	McDonald, R	WA	801
PNep	Mendley, S	MD	798
PNep	Neiberger, R	FL	799
PNep	Roskes, S	MD	798
PNep	Warady, B	MO	800
PNep	Wyatt, R	TN	799
PNep	Zilleruelo, G	FL	799

Pediatric Neuro-Ophthalmology

Spec	Name	St	Pg
N	Liu, G	PA	518
Oph	Borchert, M	CA	604
Oph	Warman, R	FL	592

Pediatric Neurology

Spec	Name	St	Pg
N	Hecox, K	WI	530
N	Hess, D	GA	525
N	Sabo, T	CO	535

Pediatric Neuroradiology

Spec	Name	St	Pg
DR	Shaw, D	WA	1018
NRad	Barkovich, A	CA	1025
NRad	Barnes, P	CA	1026
NRad	Hunter, J	TX	1025
NRad	Vezina, L	DC	1021
NRad	Zimmerman, R	PA	1021

Pediatric Neurosurgery

Spec	Name	St	Pg
NS	Adelson, P	AZ	495
NS	Anderson, R	NY	474
NS	Bierbrauer, K	OH	489
NS	Boggan, J	CA	498
NS	Boop, F	TN	484
NS	Brockmeyer, D	UT	494
NS	Butler, W	MA	472
NS	Carson, B	MD	475
NS	Cherny, W	ID	494
NS	Cohen, A	MA	472
NS	Danielpour, M	CA	499
NS	Dias, M	PA	476
NS	Duhaime, A	MA	473
NS	Edwards, M	CA	499
NS	Ewend, M	NC	484
NS	Frim, D	IL	490
NS	Goumnerova, L	MA	473
NS	Greene, C	LA	495
NS	Gupta, N	CA	499
NS	Jallo, G	MD	478
NS	Jimenez, D	TX	496
NS	Kaufman, B	WI	490
NS	Lang, F	TX	496
NS	Lee, M	TX	496
NS	Levy, M	CA	500
NS	Luerssen, T	TX	496
NS	Madsen, J	MA	473
NS	Mapstone, T	OK	497
NS	Menezes, A	IA	491
NS	Myseros, J	DC	480
NS	Nagib, M	MN	491
NS	Oakes, W	AL	486
NS	Ojemann, J	WA	501
NS	Parent, A	MS	486
NS	Park, T	MO	491
NS	Pollack, I	PA	481
NS	Raffel, C	CA	501
NS	Ragheb, J	FL	486
NS	Ruge, J	IL	492
NS	Sandberg, D	TX	497
NS	Selden, N	OR	502
NS	Sklar, F	TX	497
NS	Souweidane, M	NY	482
NS	Sun, P	CA	502
NS	Tomita, T	IL	493
NS	Walker, M	UT	495
NS	Weiner, H	NY	482
NS	Wisoff, J	NY	483
NS	Zager, E	PA	483

Pediatric Nuclear Medicine

Spec	Name	St	Pg
NuM	Dae, M	CA	557

Pediatric Ophthalmology

Spec	Name	St	Pg
Oph	Archer, S	MI	593
Oph	Azar, N	IL	593
Oph	Baker, J	MI	594
Oph	Buckley, E	NC	587
Oph	Burke, M	OH	594
Oph	Capo, H	FL	587
Oph	Caputo, A	NJ	576
Oph	Cheeseman, E	SC	587
Oph	Day, S	CA	605
Oph	Del Monte, M	MI	594
Oph	Demer, J	CA	605
Oph	Drack, A	IA	594
Oph	Eggers, H	NY	578
Oph	Ellis, G	LA	601
Oph	Eustis, H	LA	602
Oph	Freedman, S	NC	588
Oph	Gallin, P	NY	578
Oph	Granet, D	CA	606
Oph	Greenwald, M	IL	595
Oph	Guyton, D	MD	579
Oph	Haik, B	TN	589
Oph	Hall, L	NY	579
Oph	Hess, J	FL	589
Oph	Hunter, D	MA	574
Oph	Isenberg, S	CA	606
Oph	Jaafar, M	VA	589
Oph	Katowitz, J	PA	580
Oph	Kerr, N	TN	589
Oph	Koller, H	PA	580
Oph	Kushner, B	WI	596
Oph	Lambert, S	GA	589
Oph	Levin, A	PA	581
Oph	Magramm, I	NY	581
Oph	McDonnell, J	IL	597
Oph	McKeown, C	FL	590
Oph	Mets, M	IL	597
Oph	Miller, J	AZ	602
Oph	Mills, M	PA	582
Oph	Mims, J	TX	603
Oph	Mitchell, P	CT	575
Oph	Murphree, A	CA	608
Oph	Nelson, L	PA	582
Oph	Olitsky, S	MO	598
Oph	Paul, T	CA	608
Oph	Plager, D	IN	598
Oph	Pollard, Z	GA	591
Oph	Quinn, G	PA	583
Oph	Reynolds, J	NY	583
Oph	Richard, J	OK	603
Oph	Shields, C	PA	584
Oph	Shields, J	PA	585
Oph	Siatkowski, R	OK	603
Oph	Simon, J	NY	585
Oph	Traboulsi, E	OH	599
Oph	Tychsen, L	MO	600
Oph	Wang, F	NY	586
Oph	Warman, R	FL	592
Oph	Weiss, A	WA	610
Oph	Wilson, M	SC	592
Oph	Wright, K	CA	610

Pediatric Orthopaedic Cancers

Spec	Name	St	Pg
OrS	Kelly, C	CO	646
OrS	O'Donnell, R	CA	652
OrS	Peabody, T	IL	644
OrS	Wittig, J	NY	634
OrS	Wurtz, L	IN	645

Pediatric Orthopaedic Surgery

Spec	Name	St	Pg
OrS	Ahmad, C	NY	620
OrS	Beaty, J	TN	635
OrS	Brigman, B	NC	635

Spec	Name	St	Pg
OrS	Busch, M	GA	635
OrS	Conrad, E	WA	650
OrS	Delahay, J	DC	622
OrS	Dormans, J	PA	623
OrS	Errico, T	NY	623
OrS	Feldman, D	NY	623
OrS	Gugenheim, J	TX	648
OrS	Herman, M	PA	626
OrS	Herzenberg, J	MD	626
OrS	Hyman, J	NY	626
OrS	Kasser, J	MA	617
OrS	Kenan, S	NY	627
OrS	Kocher, M	MA	618
OrS	Lee, F	NY	628
OrS	Malawer, M	MD	628
OrS	Marsh, J	CT	618
OrS	McCarthy, J	OH	643
OrS	Morcuende, J	IA	643
OrS	Oppenheim, W	CA	653
OrS	Otsuka, N	NY	630
OrS	Pizzutillo, P	PA	630
OrS	Rajacich, N	WA	653
OrS	Randall, R	UT	647
OrS	Roye, D	NY	631
OrS	Schlesinger, I	NY	632
OrS	Sponseller, P	MD	633
OrS	Strongwater, A	NJ	633
OrS	Thompson, G	OH	645

Pediatric Otolaryngology

Spec	Name	St	Pg
Oto	Grundfast, K	MA	666
Oto	Hotaling, A	IL	686
Oto	Jones, J	NY	671
Oto	Jones, P	IL	686
Oto	Naclerio, R	IL	686
Oto	Poole, M	GA	680
Oto	Senders, C	CA	697
Oto	Zwillenberg, S	PA	677
PO	April, M	NY	802
PO	Arjmand, E	OH	803
PO	Arnold, J	OH	804
PO	Baroody, F	IL	804
PO	Bower, C	AR	805
PO	Casselbrant, M	PA	802
PO	Chan, K	CO	805
PO	Cotton, R	OH	804
PO	Crockett, D	CA	805
PO	Cunningham, M	MA	801
PO	Darrow, D	VA	803
PO	Dolitsky, J	NY	802
PO	Drake, A	NC	803
PO	Duncan, N	TX	805
PO	Eavey, R	TN	803
PO	Friedman, E	TX	805
PO	Goldsmith, A	NY	802
PO	Haddad, J	NY	802
PO	Harley, E	DC	802
PO	Holinger, L	IL	804
PO	Inglis, A	WA	805
PO	Katz, R	OH	804
PO	Kazahaya, K	PA	802
PO	Lusk, R	NE	805
PO	McGill, T	MA	801
PO	Miller, R	IL	804
PO	Myer, C	OH	804
PO	O'Reilly, R	DE	802
PO	Parikh, S	WA	806
PO	Poe, D	MA	801
PO	Richardson, M	OR	806
PO	Rosbe, K	CA	806
PO	Rosenfeld, R	NY	803
PO	Thompson, D	IL	804
PO	Tunkel, D	MD	803
PO	Ward, R	NY	803

Pediatric Pathology

Spec	Name	St	Pg
Path	Faye-Petersen, O	AL	726
Path	Heller, D	NJ	721
Path	Triche, T	CA	734

Pediatric Plastic Surgery

Spec	Name	St	Pg
PlS	Bartlett, S	PA	880
PlS	Beals, S	AZ	898
PlS	Bentz, M	WI	892
PlS	Boyajian, M	DC	881
PlS	Bradley, J	CA	901
PlS	Buchman, S	MI	893
PlS	Chang, B	PA	881
PlS	Coleman, J	IN	893
PlS	Deleyiannis, F	CO	897
PlS	Gruss, J	WA	902
PlS	Hoffman, W	CA	903
PlS	Kane, A	TX	899
PlS	Kelly, K	TN	890
PlS	Losee, J	PA	884
PlS	Mackay, D	PA	884
PlS	Marsh, J	MO	894
PlS	Mulliken, J	MA	878
PlS	Papay, F	OH	895
PlS	Patel, P	IL	895
PlS	Polley, J	IL	896
PlS	Reinisch, J	CA	905
PlS	Staffenberg, D	NY	887
PlS	Stotland, M	NH	879
PlS	Taub, P	NY	887
PlS	Thaller, S	FL	891
PlS	Vasconez, H	KY	892

Pediatric Pulmonology

Spec	Name	St	Pg
PPul	Borowitz, D	NY	806
PPul	Cooper, D	CA	810
PPul	Dorkin, H	MA	806
PPul	Dovey, M	PA	806
PPul	Dozor, A	NY	807
PPul	Fan, L	CO	810
PPul	Gibson, R	WA	810
PPul	Givan, D	IN	808
PPul	Green, T	IL	809
PPul	Kattan, M	NY	807
PPul	Keens, T	CA	810
PPul	Kemp, J	MO	809
PPul	Kim, Y	IN	809
PPul	Konstan, M	OH	809
PPul	Kurachek, S	MN	809
PPul	Kurland, G	PA	807
PPul	Lapey, A	MA	806
PPul	Loughlin, G	NY	807
PPul	Marcus, C	PA	807
PPul	McColley, S	IL	809
PPul	McCoy, K	OH	809
PPul	McGrath-Morrow, S	MD	807
PPul	Morgan, W	AZ	810
PPul	Nielson, D	CA	810
PPul	Orenstein, D	PA	807
PPul	Panitch, H	PA	807
PPul	Quittell, L	NY	808
PPul	Ramsey, B	WA	811
PPul	Redding, G	WA	811
PPul	Rubin, B	VA	808
PPul	Sallent, J	FL	808
PPul	Sherman, J	VA	808
PPul	Tauber, D	PA	808
PPul	Wall, M	OR	811
PPul	Warren, R	AR	810
PPul	Zeitlin, P	MD	808

Pediatric Radiology

Spec	Name	St	Pg
DR	Cohen, H	TN	1013
DR	Gilsanz, V	CA	1018
DR	Hubbard, A	NE	1016
DR	Jaramillo, D	PA	1010
DR	Sivit, C	OH	1015
DR	Wells, R	WI	1016
DR	Wood, B	CA	1019

Pediatric Rehabilitation

Spec	Name	St	Pg
PMR	Alexander, J	NC	866
PMR	Currie, D	TX	870
PMR	Evans, S	DC	863
PMR	Keen, M	IL	868
PMR	Massagli, T	WA	872
PMR	Nelson, M	TX	871
PMR	Webster, H	MA	862

Pediatric Rheumatology

Spec	Name	St	Pg
PRhu	Finkel, T	FL	812
PRhu	Goldsmith, D	PA	811
PRhu	Haines, K	NJ	811
PRhu	Ilowite, N	NY	812
PRhu	Klein-Gitelman, M	IL	813
PRhu	Lehman, T	NY	812
PRhu	McCarthy, P	CT	811
PRhu	Myones, B	TX	813
PRhu	Onel, K	IL	813
PRhu	Passo, M	SC	812
PRhu	Schanberg, L	NC	812
PRhu	Sherry, D	PA	812
PRhu	Sills, E	MD	812
PRhu	Wagner-Weiner, L	IL	813
PRhu	Warren, R	SC	813
Rhu	Albert, D	NH	1058
Rhu	Silver, R	SC	1064

Spec	Name	St	Pg

Pediatric Sports Medicine

Spec	Name	St	Pg
OrS	Busch, M	GA	635
OrS	Kocher, M	MA	618
SM	Micheli, L	MA	1074

Pediatric Surgery

Spec	Name	St	Pg
PS	Adzick, N	PA	814
PS	Aiken, J	WI	819
PS	Albanese, C	CA	823
PS	Alexander, F	NJ	815
PS	Andrews, W	MO	819
PS	Arensman, R	IL	819
PS	Barksdale, E	OH	819
PS	Black, C	TX	821
PS	Bond, S	KY	817
PS	Bove, E	MI	819
PS	Cass, D	TX	822
PS	Caty, M	CT	813
PS	Chen, M	AL	818
PS	Chwals, W	MA	814
PS	Colombani, P	MD	815
PS	Crombleholme, T	CO	821
PS	Davidoff, A	TN	818
PS	Dillon, P	MO	819
PS	Dolgin, S	NY	815
PS	Doody, D	MA	814
PS	Dunn, S	DE	815
PS	Ehrlich, P	MI	819
PS	Fallat, M	KY	818
PS	Farmer, D	CA	823
PS	Flake, A	PA	815
PS	Foglia, R	TX	822
PS	Ford, H	CA	823
PS	Gaines, B	PA	815
PS	Ginsburg, H	NY	815
PS	Gittes, G	PA	815
PS	Glick, P	NY	816
PS	Graziano, K	AZ	822
PS	Grikscheit, T	CA	823
PS	Healey, P	WA	823
PS	Hicks, B	DE	816
PS	Hilfiker, M	CA	823
PS	Holcomb, G	MO	820
PS	Holterman, M	IL	820
PS	Jackson, R	AR	822
PS	Jan, D	NY	816
PS	Jennings, R	MA	814
PS	Kandel, J	IL	820
PS	Kane, T	DC	816
PS	Karrer, F	CO	821
PS	Krummel, T	CA	823
PS	La Quaglia, M	NY	816
PS	Latchaw, L	NH	814
PS	McGill, L	AZ	822
PS	Meyers, R	UT	821
PS	Midulla, P	NY	816
PS	Morgan, W	TN	818
PS	Moss, R	OH	820
PS	Nance, M	PA	816
PS	Notrica, D	AZ	822
PS	Nuchtern, J	TX	822
PS	Oldham, K	WI	820
PS	Paidas, C	FL	818
PS	Pena, A	OH	820
PS	Proctor, M	WA	823
PS	Quaegebeur, J	NY	816
PS	Rescorla, F	IN	820
PS	Reynolds, M	IL	820
PS	Rice, H	NC	818
PS	Ricketts, R	GA	818
PS	Rodgers, B	VA	818
PS	Sato, T	WI	821
PS	Sawin, R	WA	824
PS	Schwartz, M	PA	817
PS	Shamberger, R	MA	814
PS	Shochat, S	TN	819
PS	Skinner, M	TX	822
PS	Spigland, N	NY	817
PS	Stein, J	CA	824
PS	Stolar, C	CA	824
PS	Strauch, E	MD	817
PS	Stylianos, S	NY	817
PS	Superina, R	IL	821
PS	Tracy, T	RI	814
PS	Velcek, F	NY	817
PS	Voigt, R	MD	817
PS	Waldhausen, J	WA	824
PS	Warner, B	MO	821

Pediatric Thoracic Surgery

Spec	Name	St	Pg
PS	Latchaw, L	NH	814
PS	Nuchtern, J	TX	822
PS	Oldham, K	WI	820
PS	Rodgers, B	VA	818
PS	Sawin, R	WA	824
PS	Spigland, N	NY	817

Pediatric Urology

Spec	Name	St	Pg
Ped Uro	Atala, A	NC	825
Ped Uro	Baskin, L	CA	828
Ped Uro	Bauer, S	MA	824
Ped Uro	Bloom, D	MI	826
Ped Uro	Brock, J	TN	825
Ped Uro	Cain, M	IN	826
Ped Uro	Caldamone, A	RI	824
Ped Uro	Canning, D	PA	824
Ped Uro	Cartwright, P	UT	828
Ped Uro	Cheng, E	IL	826
Ped Uro	Coplen, D	MO	827
Ped Uro	Docimo, S	PA	825
Ped Uro	Elder, J	MI	827
Ped Uro	Ewalt, D	TX	828
Ped Uro	Gonzales, E	TX	828
Ped Uro	Greenfield, S	NY	825
Ped Uro	Gundeti, M	IL	827
Ped Uro	Hatch, D	IL	827
Ped Uro	Joseph, D	AL	826
Ped Uro	Kaefer, M	IN	827
Ped Uro	Kass, E	MI	827
Ped Uro	Kirsch, A	GA	826
Ped Uro	Kolon, T	PA	825
Ped Uro	Maizels, M	IL	827
Ped Uro	Merguerian, P	WA	828
Ped Uro	Mesrobian, H	WI	827
Ped Uro	Pope, J	TN	826
Ped Uro	Poppas, D	NY	825
Ped Uro	Rink, R	IN	828
Ped Uro	Rushton, H	DC	825
Ped Uro	Strand, W	TX	828
Ped Uro	Sutherland, R	NC	826
PS	Ginsburg, H	NY	815
PS	Voigt, R	MD	817
U	Gearhart, J	MD	1190
U	Hensle, T	NJ	1191
U	Siegelbaum, M	MD	1195
U	Weiss, R	CT	1188

Pediatrics

Spec	Name	St	Pg
Ped	Berkowitz, C	CA	742
Ped	Berlin, C	PA	740
Ped	Berman, B	MI	741
Ped	Bull, M	IN	741
Ped	Burgess, D	NJ	740
Ped	Feldman, K	WA	742
Ped	Fost, N	WI	741
Ped	Gartner, J	DE	740
Ped	Hershorin, E	FL	741
Ped	Hofkosh, D	PA	740
Ped	Infante, A	TX	742
Ped	Jones, K	CA	742
Ped	Kleinerman, E	TX	742
Ped	Lantos, J	MO	741
Ped	Miller, K	MA	740
Ped	Oeffinger, K	NY	741
Ped	Rappaport, L	MA	740
Ped	Roizen, N	OH	742
Ped	Shaywitz, S	CT	740
Ped	Sheldon, S	IL	742
Ped	Walker, W	WA	743
Ped	Zeltzer, L	CA	743
Ped	Zitelli, B	PA	741

Pelvic & Acetabular Fractures

Spec	Name	St	Pg
OrS	Archdeacon, M	OH	639
OrS	Helfet, D	NY	625
OrS	Johnson, E	CA	651
OrS	Joyce, M	OH	642
OrS	Webb, L	GA	639

Pelvic Congestion Syndrome

Spec	Name	St	Pg
VIR	Roberts, A	CA	1033
VIR	Shlansky-Goldberg, R	PA	1028

Pelvic Floor Disorders

Spec	Name	St	Pg
CRS	Dietz, D	OH	173
CRS	Varma, M	CA	178

Pelvic Floor Reconstruction

Spec	Name	St	Pg
ObG	Hale, D	IN	565
ObG	Karram, M	OH	565
ObG	Lucente, V	PA	561

Spec	Name	St	Pg
Pelvic Organ Prolapse			
CRS	Birnbaum, E	MO	173
CRS	Ludwig, K	WI	174
Pelvic Organ Prolapse Repair			
GO	Hatch, K	AZ	288
ObG	Amundsen, C	NC	562
ObG	Brodman, M	NY	560
ObG	Culbertson, S	IL	564
ObG	De Lancey, J	MI	564
ObG	Einarsson, J	MA	560
ObG	Goldstein, M	NY	561
ObG	Hullfish, K	VA	562
ObG	Kenton, K	IL	565
ObG	Lucente, V	PA	561
ObG	Sand, P	IL	565
ObG	Valaitis, S	IL	565
ObG	Visco, A	NC	563
ObG	Walters, M	OH	566
U	Badlani, G	NC	1196
U	Bales, G	IL	1202
U	Kennelly, M	NC	1198
Pelvic Pain Syndrome			
U	O'Leary, M	MA	1187
Pelvic Reconstruction			
GO	Fields, A	DC	278
GO	Fowler, J	OH	284
GO	Lentz, S	NC	282
GO	Mutch, D	MO	285
ObG	Amundsen, C	NC	562
ObG	Cornella, J	AZ	566
ObG	Culbertson, S	IL	564
ObG	Eckler, K	MA	560
ObG	Hullfish, K	VA	562
ObG	Kenton, K	IL	565
ObG	Sanz, L	VA	563
ObG	Young, B	NY	562
Pelvic Reconstruction After Cancer			
PlS	Tobin, G	KY	892
Pelvic Surgery			
S	Moore, E	CO	1122
Pelvic Surgery-Complex			
GO	Bodurka, D	TX	287
GO	Carney, M	HI	290
GO	Lele, S	NY	279
Pelvic Tumors			
GO	Barnes, W	DC	276
GO	Penalver, M	FL	283
S	Paty, P	NY	1098
Pemphigus			
D	Anhalt, G	MD	186
D	Sobel, S	FL	194
D	Stanley, J	PA	191
Penile Cancer			
Onc	Godley, P	NC	358
RadRO	Anscher, M	VA	983
U	Loughlin, K	MA	1187
U	McDougal, W	MA	1187
U	Weiss, R	CT	1188
Penile Inversion Technique			
PlS	Meltzer, T	AZ	899
Penile Microvascular Bypass Surgery			
U	Goldstein, I	CA	1212
Penile Prostheses			
U	Hellstrom, W	LA	1209
U	Mulhall, J	NY	1193
Peptic Acid Disorders			
Ge	Bresalier, R	TX	253
Ge	Chey, W	MI	246
Ge	Fisher, R	PA	234
Ge	Lichtenstein, D	MA	231
Ge	Metz, D	PA	238
Ge	Schulze, K	IA	250
Ge	Smoot, D	TN	245
Ge	Vanagunas, A	IL	251
Percutaneous ASD/PFO Closure			
PCd	Rome, J	PA	749
Percutaneous Coronary Intervention			
IC	Leesar, M	AL	125
IC	Resar, J	MD	123
Percutaneous Valve Repair			
Cv	Pichard, A	DC	95
Cv	Silvestry, F	PA	96
IC	Gray, W	NY	122
IC	Resar, J	MD	123
IC	Shani, J	NY	123
Percutaneous Vascular Interventions			
Cv	Burket, M	OH	101
Cv	Dangas, G	NY	92
VascS	Dalsing, M	IN	1227
VascS	Green, R	NY	1223
Pericardial Disease			
Cv	Bashore, T	NC	97
Cv	Nishimura, R	MN	103
Perinatal Medicine			
MF	Ismail, M	IL	438
MF	Wapner, R	NY	435
PCCM	Sarnaik, A	MI	755
Perinatal Pathology			
Path	Faye-Petersen, O	AL	726
Path	Heller, D	NJ	721
Peripheral Nerve Disorders			
N	Sheikh, K	TX	537
N	Sirdofsky, M	DC	521
NS	Belzberg, A	MD	474
NS	Levi, A	FL	485
NS	Zager, E	PA	483
PMR	Robinson, L	WA	872
Peripheral Nerve Surgery			
HS	Brushart, T	MD	297
HS	Chang, J	CA	305
HS	Gelberman, R	MO	302
HS	Glickel, S	NY	298
HS	Greene, T	FL	301
HS	Grossman, J	FL	301
HS	Moneim, M	NM	305
HS	Szabo, R	CA	306
NS	Anderson, R	NY	474
NS	Chiocca, E	MA	472
NS	Kim, D	TX	496
NS	Kuntz, C	OH	490
NS	Lillehei, K	CO	494
NS	Naff, N	MD	480
NS	Spinner, R	MN	493
PlS	Chiu, D	NY	881
PlS	Ducic, I	DC	882
PlS	Dumanian, G	IL	893
PlS	MacKinnon, S	MO	894
PlS	Siemionow, M	OH	896
Peripheral Neuropathy			
N	Adornato, B	CA	538
N	Amato, A	MA	510
N	Barohn, R	KS	534
N	Bromberg, M	UT	534
N	Cohen, J	NH	510
N	Cornblath, D	MD	514
N	Donofrio, P	TN	524
N	Engstrom, J	CA	539
N	Feldman, E	MI	529
N	Glass, J	GA	524
N	Kincaid, J	IN	530
N	Latov, N	NY	517
N	Logigian, E	NY	518
N	Oaklander, A	MA	511

Spec	Name	St	Pg
N	Pestronk, A	MO	532
N	Simpson, D	NY	521
N	Weiss, M	WA	542
N	Windebank, A	MN	534
PMR	Feinberg, J	NY	864

Peripheral Vascular Disease

Spec	Name	St	Pg
Cv	Burket, M	OH	101
Cv	Eagle, K	MI	101
Cv	Krajcer, Z	TX	108
Cv	Liao, J	IL	103
Cv	Loscalzo, J	MA	89
IC	Dieter, R	IL	125
IC	Gray, W	NY	122
IC	Kandzari, D	GA	124
IC	Khawaja, S	GA	124
IC	Leesar, M	AL	125
IC	Matar, F	FL	125
IC	Petrossian, G	NY	123
IC	Reddy, B	GA	125
IC	Roubin, G	NY	123
IC	Smalling, R	TX	128
S	Mannella, W	PA	1096
T&CS	Dang, M	HI	1178
VascS	Acher, C	WI	1226
VascS	Alexander, J	OH	1226
VascS	Atnip, R	PA	1221
VascS	Carpenter, J	NJ	1222
VascS	Chaikof, E	MA	1220
VascS	Clair, D	OH	1227
VascS	Comerota, A	OH	1227
VascS	Cooper, M	CO	1228
VascS	Cronenwett, J	NH	1220
VascS	D'Ayala, M	NY	1222
VascS	Dalsing, M	IN	1227
VascS	Eidt, J	SC	1225
VascS	Fairman, R	PA	1223
VascS	Faries, P	NY	1223
VascS	Gewertz, B	CA	1230
VascS	Greisler, H	IL	1227
VascS	Makaroun, M	PA	1224
VascS	Marin, M	NY	1224
VascS	Mitchell, M	MS	1226
VascS	Pearce, W	IL	1228
VascS	Sanchez, L	MO	1228
VascS	Schneider, D	NY	1225
VascS	Stanley, J	MI	1228
VascS	Sumpio, B	CT	1221
VIR	Benenati, J	FL	1029
VIR	Cho, K	MI	1030
VIR	Durham, J	CO	1031
VIR	Hallisey, M	CT	1027
VIR	Katzen, B	FL	1029
VIR	Roberts, A	CA	1033

Peritoneal Carcinomatosis

Spec	Name	St	Pg
S	Bartlett, D	PA	1089
S	Brown, C	IL	1112
S	Ellis, L	TX	1124
S	Goodman, M	MA	1085
S	Hanna, N	MD	1094
S	Kuhn, J	TX	1126
S	Levine, E	NC	1106
S	Lowy, A	CA	1134
S	Sugarbaker, P	DC	1101

Peritoneal Mucinous Carcinomatosis

Spec	Name	St	Pg
CRS	Guillem, J	NY	170

Personality Disorders

Spec	Name	St	Pg
ChAP	Bleiberg, E	TX	943
Psyc	Adler, D	MA	920
Psyc	Black, D	IA	929
Psyc	Cloninger, C	MO	929
Psyc	Karasu, T	NY	925
Psyc	Norman, K	CA	934
Psyc	Samberg, E	NY	927

Personality Disorders, Consults

Spec	Name	St	Pg
Psyc	Gunderson, J	MA	921

Personality Disorders-Borderline

Spec	Name	St	Pg
Psyc	Gabbard, G	TX	932

PET Imaging

Spec	Name	St	Pg
Cv	Gould, K	TX	108
DR	Cohen, B	NY	1008
DR	Erasmus, J	TX	1016
DR	Patz, E	NC	1014
NuM	Agress, H	NJ	554
NuM	Appelbaum, D	IL	556
NuM	Carrasquillo, J	NY	554
NuM	Freeman, L	NY	554
NuM	Goldsmith, S	NY	554
NuM	Lamonica, D	NY	554
NuM	Pandit-Taskar, N	NY	555
NuM	Sandler, M	TN	555
NuM	Siegel, B	MO	556
NuM	Wahl, R	MD	555

PET Imaging-Brain

Spec	Name	St	Pg
NuM	Alavi, A	PA	554
NuM	Strashun, A	NY	555
NuM	Waxman, A	CA	557

PET Imaging-Breast

Spec	Name	St	Pg
NuM	Wahl, R	MD	555

Peyronie's Disease

Spec	Name	St	Pg
U	Broderick, G	FL	1197
U	Carson, C	NC	1197
U	Hellstrom, W	LA	1209
U	Levine, L	IL	1204
U	Montague, D	OH	1204
U	Mulhall, J	NY	1193
U	Rajfer, J	CA	1213
U	Sadeghi-Nejad, H	NJ	1194
U	Seftel, A	NJ	1194

Phenylketonuria (PKU)

Spec	Name	St	Pg
CG	Burton, B	IL	160
CG	Ward, J	TN	159
CG	Wasserstein, M	NY	158
Ped	Berlin, C	PA	740

Pheochromocytoma

Spec	Name	St	Pg
EDM	Fitzgerald, P	CA	224
NuM	Neumann, D	OH	556
S	Angelos, P	IL	1111
S	Fahey, T	NY	1093

Photoaging

Spec	Name	St	Pg
D	Gilchrest, B	MA	185
D	Voorhees, J	MI	197

Photodynamic Therapy

Spec	Name	St	Pg
D	Elmets, C	AL	192
D	Hanke, C	IN	195
RadRO	Hahn, S	PA	980

Photosensitive Skin Diseases

Spec	Name	St	Pg
D	Koo, J	CA	201

Phototherapy

Spec	Name	St	Pg
D	Elmets, C	AL	192
D	Kalb, R	NY	189
D	Koo, J	CA	201
D	Lim, H	MI	196
D	Soter, N	NY	191
D	Stern, R	MA	186

Physical Medicine & Rehabilitation

Spec	Name	St	Pg
PMR	Ahn, J	NY	862
PMR	Alexander, J	NC	866
PMR	Apkon, S	WA	872
PMR	Aseff, J	DC	863
PMR	Bach, J	NJ	863
PMR	Ballard, P	DC	863
PMR	Bloch, R	MA	862
PMR	Borg-Stein, J	MA	862
PMR	Braddom, R	PA	863
PMR	Brown, A	MN	867
PMR	Cardenas, D	FL	866
PMR	Chen, D	IL	867
PMR	Cheville, A	MN	867
PMR	Clairmont, A	OH	867
PMR	Colachis, S	OH	868
PMR	Creamer, M	FL	866
PMR	Currie, D	TX	870
PMR	De Lateur, B	MD	863
PMR	DePompolo, R	MN	868
PMR	Diamond, P	VA	866

Spec	Name	St	Pg
PMR	Dillard, J	NY	863
PMR	Dumitru, D	TX	870
PMR	Esquenazi, A	PA	863
PMR	Evans, S	DC	863
PMR	Feinberg, J	NY	864
PMR	Feldman, J	IL	868
PMR	Flanagan, S	NY	864
PMR	Francis, K	NJ	864
PMR	Francisco, G	TX	871
PMR	Fried, G	PA	864
PMR	Friedman, A	WA	872
PMR	Frost, F	OH	868
PMR	Gater, D	PA	864
PMR	Gittler, M	IL	868
PMR	Glenn, M	MA	862
PMR	Haig, A	MI	868
PMR	Hammond, F	IN	868
PMR	Harris, D	TX	871
PMR	Herring, S	WA	872
PMR	Ivanhoe, C	TX	871
PMR	Keen, M	IL	868
PMR	Kevorkian, C	TX	871
PMR	Kezar, L	AL	866
PMR	King, J	TX	871
PMR	King, R	GA	866
PMR	Kirschner, K	IL	869
PMR	Kirshblum, S	NJ	864
PMR	Kuiken, T	IL	869
PMR	LaBan, M	MI	869
PMR	Leonard, J	MI	869
PMR	Leslie, D	GA	867
PMR	Lutz, C	NY	864
PMR	Lutz, G	NY	864
PMR	Ma, D	NY	865
PMR	Marino, R	PA	865
PMR	Mason, K	CO	870
PMR	Massagli, T	WA	872
PMR	Matthews, D	CO	870
PMR	Mayer, N	PA	865
PMR	McKinley, W	VA	867
PMR	McLain, A	AL	867
PMR	Miknevich, M	PA	865
PMR	Munin, M	PA	865
PMR	Mysiw, W	OH	869
PMR	Nelson, M	TX	871
PMR	Nobunaga, A	OH	869
PMR	Palmer, J	MD	865
PMR	Press, J	IL	869
PMR	Ragnarsson, K	NY	865
PMR	Richter, E	CT	862
PMR	Robinson, L	WA	872
PMR	Roth, E	IL	869
PMR	Saal, J	CA	872
PMR	Schwartz, L	PA	865
PMR	Sisung, C	IL	870
PMR	Sliwa, J	IL	870
PMR	Stewart, P	AL	867
PMR	Stubblefield, M	NY	866
PMR	Volshteyn, O	MO	870
PMR	Webster, H	MA	862
PMR	Wilson, A	TX	871
PMR	Zafonte, R	MA	862

Pigmented Lesions

Spec	Name	St	Pg
D	Barbosa, V	IL	194
D	Gellis, S	MA	185
D	Grimes, P	CA	201
D	Johr, R	FL	193
D	McMichael, A	NC	193
D	Neuburg, M	WI	196
D	Shea, C	IL	197

Pilonidal Disease

Spec	Name	St	Pg
S	Buchman, T	GA	1104

Pineal Tumors

Spec	Name	St	Pg
NS	Black, K	CA	498

Pituitary Disorders

Spec	Name	St	Pg
EDM	Biller, B	MA	208
EDM	Calvi, L	NY	211
EDM	Comi, R	NH	208
EDM	Greene, L	NY	212
EDM	Hoffman, A	CA	224
EDM	Inzucchi, S	CT	209
EDM	Jacobs, T	NY	213
EDM	Katznelson, L	CA	225
EDM	Kennedy, L	OH	220
EDM	Kleinberg, D	NY	213
EDM	Koch, C	MS	216
EDM	Kopp, P	IL	220
EDM	Lechan, R	MA	210
EDM	Lipson, A	DC	213
EDM	Marshall, J	VA	217
EDM	Melmed, S	CA	225
EDM	Ridgway, E	CO	222
EDM	Robbins, R	TX	223
EDM	Singer, P	CA	225
EDM	Swerdloff, R	CA	226
EDM	Thorner, M	VA	217
EDM	Vance, M	VA	217
EDM	Weiss, R	IL	221
NRad	Khandji, A	NY	1020
PEn	Geffner, M	CA	761
PEn	Kohn, B	NY	758
RE	Crowley, W	MA	1040

Pituitary Surgery

Spec	Name	St	Pg
NS	Atkinson, J	MN	488
NS	Liu, C	CA	500
NS	Mamelak, A	CA	500
NS	Mayberg, M	WA	501
NS	Rock, J	MI	492
NS	Selman, W	OH	493

Pituitary Tumors

Spec	Name	St	Pg
EDM	Fitzgerald, P	CA	224
EDM	Hoffman, A	CA	224
EDM	Melmed, S	CA	225
EDM	Robbins, R	TX	223
EDM	Snyder, P	PA	215
EDM	Waguespack, S	TX	223
NS	Berger, M	CA	498
NS	Brem, H	MD	475
NS	Brem, S	PA	475
NS	Bruce, J	NY	475
NS	Couldwell, W	UT	494
NS	David, C	MA	472
NS	Ewend, M	NC	484
NS	Fenstermaker, R	NY	476
NS	Guthikonda, M	MI	490
NS	Harsh, G	CA	500
NS	Kotapka, M	PA	479
NS	Laske, D	PA	479
NS	Lillehei, K	CO	494
NS	Maroon, J	PA	479
NS	Meyer, F	MN	491
NS	Mickey, B	TX	497
NS	Origitano, T	MT	494
NS	Parent, A	MS	486
NS	Reid, W	TN	486
NS	Schwartz, T	NY	481
NS	Shapiro, S	IN	493
NS	Swaid, S	AL	487
NS	Swearingen, B	MA	474
NS	Tatter, S	NC	487
Onc	Fine, R	NY	342
Oto	O'Leary, M	CA	696
Oto	Petruzzelli, G	GA	680
RE	Chang, R	CA	1051

Plasma Cell Disorders

Spec	Name	St	Pg
Hem	Barlogie, B	AR	325
Hem	Comenzo, R	MA	312
Hem	Gertz, M	MN	321
Hem	Gregory, S	IL	322

Plastic Bronchitis

Spec	Name	St	Pg
PPul	Rubin, B	VA	808

Plastic Surgery

Spec	Name	St	Pg
PlS	Allen, R	NY	880
PlS	Alter, G	CA	901
PlS	Aly, A	CA	901
PlS	Andersen, J	CA	901
PlS	Ascherman, J	NY	880
PlS	Aston, S	NY	880
PlS	Attinger, C	DC	880
PlS	Baker, D	NY	880
PlS	Baker, S	DC	880
PlS	Barone, C	TX	898
PlS	Bartlett, S	PA	880
PlS	Barton, F	TX	898
PlS	Bauer, B	IL	892
PlS	Beals, S	AZ	898
PlS	Beasley, M	NC	888
PlS	Bentz, M	WI	892
PlS	Billmire, D	OH	893
PlS	Boyajian, M	DC	881
PlS	Bradley, J	CA	901
PlS	Brandt, K	MO	893

Spec	Name	St	Pg
PlS	Buchman, S	MI	893
PlS	Bucky, L	PA	881
PlS	Burns, A	TX	898
PlS	Burstein, F	GA	889
PlS	Butler, C	TX	898
PlS	Byrd, H	TX	898
PlS	Carraway, J	VA	889
PlS	Cederna, P	MI	893
PlS	Chang, B	PA	881
PlS	Chang, D	TX	899
PlS	Chiu, D	NY	881
PlS	Cohen, S	CA	901
PlS	Coleman, J	IN	893
PlS	Colen, L	VA	889
PlS	Constantian, M	NH	878
PlS	Cordeiro, P	NY	881
PlS	Cruse, C	FL	889
PlS	Da Lio, A	CA	902
PlS	Dagum, A	NY	881
PlS	Daniel, R	CA	902
PlS	Davis, G	NC	889
PlS	Deleyiannis, F	CO	897
PlS	Derman, G	IL	893
PlS	Disa, J	NY	881
PlS	Ducic, I	DC	882
PlS	Dufresne, C	MD	882
PlS	Dumanian, G	IL	893
PlS	Edwards, M	NV	902
PlS	Erdmann, D	NC	889
PlS	Eriksson, E	MA	878
PlS	Evans, G	CA	902
PlS	Feldman, J	MA	878
PlS	Fisher, G	CA	902
PlS	Fix, R	AL	889
PlS	Fodor, P	CA	902
PlS	Fox, J	PA	882
PlS	Gallico, G	MA	878
PlS	Garner, W	CA	902
PlS	Georgiade, G	NC	889
PlS	Glat, P	PA	882
PlS	Gottlieb, L	IL	893
PlS	Grant, R	NY	882
PlS	Gregory, R	FL	890
PlS	Grossman, J	CO	897
PlS	Grotting, J	AL	890
PlS	Gruss, J	WA	902
PlS	Hagan, K	TN	890
PlS	Hammond, D	MI	894
PlS	Hamra, S	TX	899
PlS	Hansen, J	OR	903
PlS	Hardesty, R	CA	903
PlS	Herman, C	PA	882
PlS	Hidalgo, D	NY	882
PlS	Hoffman, L	NY	882
PlS	Hoffman, W	CA	903
PlS	Horowitz, J	CA	903
PlS	Hultman, C	NC	890
PlS	Hunstad, J	NC	890
PlS	Hurwitz, D	PA	883
PlS	Imber, G	NY	883
PlS	Isik, F	WA	903
PlS	Jewell, M	OR	903
PlS	Kane, A	TX	899
PlS	Kelly, K	TN	890
PlS	Kenkel, J	TX	899
PlS	Kirschner, R	OH	894
PlS	Kolker, A	NY	883
PlS	Koplin, L	CA	903
PlS	Kronowitz, S	TX	899
PlS	Kuzon, W	MI	894
PlS	LaBruna, A	NY	883
PlS	Leaf, N	CA	903
PlS	Lee, R	IL	894
PlS	Leighton, W	AZ	899
PlS	Leipziger, L	NY	883
PlS	Lesavoy, M	CA	904
PlS	Levine, J	NY	883
PlS	Little, J	DC	883
PlS	Loree, T	NY	884
PlS	Losee, J	PA	884
PlS	Low, D	PA	884
PlS	Mackay, D	PA	884
PlS	MacKinnon, S	MO	894
PlS	Magee, W	VA	890
PlS	Manders, E	PA	884
PlS	Manson, P	MD	884
PlS	Markowitz, B	CA	904
PlS	Marsh, J	MO	894
PlS	Marten, T	CA	904
PlS	Mast, B	FL	890
PlS	Matarasso, A	NY	884
PlS	Matthews, D	NC	891
PlS	Maxwell, G	TN	891
PlS	Meara, J	MA	878
PlS	Medalie, D	OH	894
PlS	Mehrara, B	NY	885
PlS	Meltzer, T	AZ	899
PlS	Menick, F	AZ	899
PlS	Metzinger, S	LA	900
PlS	Miller, M	OH	895
PlS	Miller, T	CA	904
PlS	Mixter, R	WI	895
PlS	Molnar, J	NC	891
PlS	Morgan, R	VA	891
PlS	Moses, M	LA	900
PlS	Mulliken, J	MA	878
PlS	Mustoe, T	IL	895
PlS	Nahabedian, M	DC	885
PlS	Napoli, J	DE	885
PlS	Ness, J	MN	895
PlS	Neumeister, M	IL	895
PlS	Nichter, L	CA	904
PlS	Noone, R	PA	885
PlS	Olding, M	DC	885
PlS	Orgill, D	MA	878
PlS	Ousterhout, D	CA	904
PlS	Papay, F	OH	895
PlS	Patel, P	IL	895
PlS	Patel, S	PA	885
PlS	Paul, M	CA	904
PlS	Persing, J	CT	879
PlS	Pitman, G	NY	885
PlS	Polley, J	IL	896
PlS	Pomahac, B	MA	879
PlS	Posnick, J	MD	885
PlS	Price, G	MD	886
PlS	Puckett, C	MO	896
PlS	Rand, R	WA	904
PlS	Rappaport, N	TX	900
PlS	Reinisch, J	CA	905
PlS	Robb, G	TX	900
PlS	Rockwell, W	UT	898
PlS	Rodriguez, E	MD	886
PlS	Rohrich, R	TX	900
PlS	Romano, J	CA	905
PlS	Rose, E	NY	886
PlS	Rosenberg, H	CA	905
PlS	Sanders, G	CA	905
PlS	Sanger, J	WI	896
PlS	Schusterman, M	TX	900
PlS	Serletti, J	PA	886
PlS	Seyfer, A	MD	886
PlS	Sherman, R	CA	905
PlS	Siebert, J	WI	896
PlS	Siemionow, M	OH	896
PlS	Singer, R	CA	905
PlS	Singh, N	MD	886
PlS	Slavin, S	MA	879
PlS	Slezak, S	MD	886
PlS	Smith, D	FL	891
PlS	Smith, P	FL	891
PlS	Song, D	IL	896
PlS	Sood, R	IN	896
PlS	Spence, R	MD	886
PlS	Spinelli, H	NY	887
PlS	Stadelmann, W	NH	879
PlS	Staffenberg, D	NY	887
PlS	Stahl, R	CT	879
PlS	Stevens, W	CA	905
PlS	Stotland, M	NH	879
PlS	Stuzin, J	FL	891
PlS	Sullivan, P	RI	879
PlS	Sultan, M	NY	887
PlS	Tabbal, N	NY	887
PlS	Talmor, M	NY	887
PlS	Taub, P	NY	887
PlS	Tebbetts, J	TX	900
PlS	Thaller, S	FL	891
PlS	Thorne, C	NY	887
PlS	Ting, J	NY	888
PlS	Tobin, G	KY	892
PlS	Topham, N	PA	888
PlS	Tufaro, A	MD	888
PlS	Urata, M	CA	905
PlS	Vander Kolk, C	MD	888
PlS	Vasconez, H	KY	892
PlS	Vidal, D	NH	879
PlS	Vogt, P	MN	896
PlS	Walton, R	IL	897
PlS	Wells, J	CA	906
PlS	Wilcox, R	TX	901
PlS	Wilhelmi, B	KY	892
PlS	Wilkins, E	MI	897
PlS	Winters, R	NJ	888
PlS	Wolfe, S	FL	892
PlS	Yetman, R	OH	897
PlS	Young, V	MO	897
PlS	Yu, J	GA	892
PlS	Yuen, J	AR	901

Spec	Name	St	Pg
PlS	Zide, B	NY	888
PlS	Zins, J	OH	897

Platelet Disorders

Spec	Name	St	Pg
Hem	DeLoughery, T	OR	328
Hem	Lyons, R	TX	327
Hem	Rao, A	PA	316
PHO	Bussel, J	NY	771
PHO	Parker, R	NY	776

Pleural Disease

Spec	Name	St	Pg
Pul	Light, R	TN	963
Pul	Sahn, S	SC	963
Pul	Villanueva, A	MA	955
T&CS	Friedberg, J	PA	1152

Pneumococcal Infections

Spec	Name	St	Pg
PInf	Kaplan, S	TX	796
PInf	McCracken, G	TX	796

Pneumoconiosis

Spec	Name	St	Pg
Pul	Rose, C	CO	968

Pneumocystis Carinii Pneumonia (PCP)

Spec	Name	St	Pg
Pul	Huang, L	CA	971

Pneumonia

Spec	Name	St	Pg
Inf	Bartlett, J	MD	412
Inf	Cunha, B	NY	413
Inf	Quagliarello, V	CT	412
PPul	Wall, M	OR	811
Pul	Guidry, G	LA	969
Pul	Nash, T	NY	958
Pul	Niederman, M	NY	958

POEMS Syndrome

Spec	Name	St	Pg
Hem	Comenzo, R	MA	312

Poison Control

Spec	Name	St	Pg
PrM	Hoffman, R	NY	913

Polycystic Kidney Disease

Spec	Name	St	Pg
Nep	Blumenfeld, J	NY	459
Nep	Fadem, S	TX	465
Nep	Kelepouris, E	PA	460
Nep	Perrone, R	MA	458
Nep	Rakowski, T	VA	462
Nep	Tolkoff-Rubin, N	MA	458
Nep	Torres, V	MN	465
PNep	Brophy, P	IA	799
PNep	Kaplan, B	PA	798
U	Sundaram, C	IN	1206

Polycystic Ovarian Syndrome

Spec	Name	St	Pg
EDM	Ehrmann, D	IL	219
EDM	Goodman, N	FL	216
EDM	Marshall, J	VA	217
EDM	Nestler, J	VA	217
RE	Azziz, R	GA	1045
RE	Barnes, R	IL	1046
RE	Cedars, M	CA	1051
RE	Chang, R	CA	1051
RE	Dumesic, D	CA	1051
RE	Friedman, C	OH	1047
RE	Jacobs, L	IL	1048
RE	Kazer, R	IL	1048
RE	Legro, R	PA	1043
RE	Marut, E	IL	1048
RE	Scoccia, H	IL	1048
RE	Session, D	GA	1046
RE	Smith, Y	MI	1049
RE	Soules, M	WA	1053
RE	Walmer, D	NC	1046
RE	Wilson, E	TX	1050

Polycythemia Rubra Vera

Spec	Name	St	Pg
Hem	Fruchtman, S	NY	314
Hem	Spivak, J	MD	317
Hem	Streiff, M	MD	317

Polymyalgia Rheumatica

Spec	Name	St	Pg
Rhu	Magid, S	NY	1061

Polymyositis

Spec	Name	St	Pg
Rhu	Curran, J	IL	1065
Rhu	Medsger, T	PA	1061
Rhu	Oddis, C	PA	1061
Rhu	Steen, V	DC	1062

Polypharmacology

Spec	Name	St	Pg
Ger	Carr, D	MO	266
Ger	Tenover, J	CA	268

Porphyria

Spec	Name	St	Pg
CG	Desnick, R	NY	157
Ge	Anderson, K	TX	252
Ge	Bloomer, J	AL	241
IM	Bissell, D	CA	427
Onc	Silver, S	MI	374

Portal Hypertension

Spec	Name	St	Pg
S	Ascher, N	CA	1130
S	Emre, S	CT	1085
S	Rosemurgy, A	FL	1108
VIR	Cohen, G	PA	1027
VIR	Darcy, M	MO	1030
VIR	Johnson, M	IN	1030

Post Polio Syndrome

Spec	Name	St	Pg
N	Pascuzzi, R	IN	532

Post Polio Syndrome/Rehabilitation

Spec	Name	St	Pg
PM	Walsh, N	TX	712
PMR	Bach, J	NJ	863
PMR	Sliwa, J	IL	870

Post Traumatic Stress Disorder

Spec	Name	St	Pg
ChAP	Fornari, V	NY	940
ChAP	Martini, D	UT	942
ChAP	Zeanah, C	LA	943
Psyc	Eth, S	FL	928
Psyc	Friedman, M	VT	920
Psyc	Greiner, C	NE	931
Psyc	Loewenstein, R	MD	925
Psyc	Pollack, M	IL	930
Psyc	Pynoos, R	CA	934
Psyc	Raskind, M	WA	934
Psyc	Roy-Byrne, P	WA	934
Psyc	Spiegel, D	CA	935
Psyc	Stein, M	CA	935
Psyc	Wait, S	MD	927

Postpartum Depression

Spec	Name	St	Pg
Psyc	Burt, V	CA	932

Power Doppler Imaging

Spec	Name	St	Pg
DR	Adler, R	NY	1008

Prader-Willi Syndrome

Spec	Name	St	Pg
CG	Cassidy, S	CA	162
CG	Driscoll, D	FL	159
CG	Shoffner, J	GA	159
PEn	Freemark, M	NC	759
PEn	Garibaldi, L	PA	758

Praxis Functional Electrical Stim (FES)

Spec	Name	St	Pg
OrS	Betz, R	PA	621

Pregnancy & Endocrine Disorders

Spec	Name	St	Pg
EDM	Seely, E	MA	210

Pregnancy & Hematologic Abnormalities

Spec	Name	St	Pg
MF	Berkowitz, R	NY	433
MF	Samuels, P	OH	439

Pregnancy Loss-Recurrent

Spec	Name	St	Pg
RE	Keltz, M	NY	1042
RE	Stephenson, M	IL	1049

Specialty & Special Expertise Index

Pregnancy-African women only

Spec	Name	St	Pg
ObG	Nour, N	MA	560

Pregnancy-High Risk

Spec	Name	St	Pg
MF	Adam, K	TX	440
MF	Adashek, J	NV	441
MF	Bahado-Singh, R	MI	437
MF	Baker, E	NH	432
MF	Bartelsmeyer, J	MO	438
MF	Blakemore, K	MD	433
MF	Caritis, S	PA	433
MF	Cohen, A	PA	434
MF	Copel, J	CT	432
MF	D'Alton, M	NY	434
MF	Dooley, S	IL	438
MF	Duff, W	FL	436
MF	Dugoff, L	PA	434
MF	Eddleman, K	NY	434
MF	Ferguson, J	VA	436
MF	Fox, H	MD	434
MF	Genc, M	NY	434
MF	Gibbs, R	CO	440
MF	Goodman, J	IL	438
MF	Grandis, A	NC	436
MF	Gravett, M	WA	442
MF	Greene, M	MA	432
MF	Grunebaum, A	NY	434
MF	Hankins, G	TX	441
MF	Heyl, P	KY	436
MF	Hibbard, J	IL	438
MF	Ismail, M	IL	438
MF	Kelly, T	CA	442
MF	Landy, H	DC	435
MF	MacGregor, S	IL	439
MF	Macones, G	MO	439
MF	Mari, G	TN	437
MF	Mastrobattista, J	TX	441
MF	McLaren, R	VA	437
MF	Nies, B	VA	437
MF	Paidas, M	CT	432
MF	Parry, S	PA	435
MF	Philipson, E	OH	439
MF	Pinckert, T	MD	435
MF	Plante, L	PA	435
MF	Platt, L	CA	443
MF	Pridjian, G	LA	441
MF	Repke, J	PA	435
MF	Riley, L	MA	433
MF	Robertson, P	CA	443
MF	Robichaux, A	LA	441
MF	Saade, G	TX	441
MF	Silver, R	IL	439
MF	Strassner, H	IL	440
MF	Tabsh, K	CA	443
MF	Thomas, R	PA	435
MF	Tomich, P	NE	440
MF	Treadwell, M	MI	440
MF	Van Dorsten, J	SC	437
MF	Wenstrom, K	RI	433
MF	Wilkins-Haug, L	MA	433
MF	Winn, H	MO	440
MF	Witter, F	MD	436
MF	Zalud, I	HI	443
ObG	Ordorica, S	NY	561

Preimplantation Genetic Diagnosis

Spec	Name	St	Pg
RE	Grazi, R	NY	1042
RE	Grifo, J	NY	1042
RE	Kuo, J	CA	1052

Preiser's Disease

Spec	Name	St	Pg
HS	Slutsky, D	CA	306

Premature Labor

Spec	Name	St	Pg
MF	Ferguson, J	VA	436
MF	Macones, G	MO	439
MF	Parry, S	PA	435
MF	Saade, G	TX	441
MF	Socol, M	IL	440
MF	Thorp, J	NC	437
ObG	Niebyl, J	IA	565

Prematurity Prevention

Spec	Name	St	Pg
MF	Adashek, J	NV	441
MF	Benedetti, T	WA	442
MF	Fox, H	MD	434
MF	Gravett, M	WA	442
MF	MacGregor, S	IL	439
MF	Norwitz, E	MA	432

Prematurity/Low Birth Weight Infants

Spec	Name	St	Pg
MF	Andrews, W	AL	436
MF	Gravett, M	WA	442
NP	Bell, E	IA	451
NP	Cole, F	MO	451
NP	Delivoria-Papadopoulos, M	PA	449
NP	Dhanireddy, R	TN	451
NP	Ehrenkranz, R	CT	448
NP	Gleason, C	WA	453
NP	Holzman, I	NY	449
NP	La Gamma, E	NY	449
NP	Lawson, E	MD	449
NP	Muraskas, J	IL	452
NP	Perlman, J	NY	450
NP	Simmons, C	CA	454

Prenatal Diagnosis

Spec	Name	St	Pg
CG	Anyane-Yeboa, K	NY	156
CG	Falk, R	CA	162
CG	Holmes, L	MA	156
CG	Hudgins, L	CA	163
CG	Mahoney, M	CT	156
CG	Pauker, S	MA	156
CG	Seaver, L	HI	163
CG	Shulman, L	IL	160
MF	Abuhamad, A	VA	436
MF	Adashek, J	NV	441
MF	Cheng, E	WA	442
MF	Copel, J	CT	432
MF	D'Alton, M	NY	434
MF	Dugoff, L	PA	434
MF	Goldberg, J	CA	442
MF	Gonik, B	MI	438
MF	Goodman, J	IL	438
MF	Hibbard, J	IL	438
MF	Hussey, M	IL	438
MF	Johnson, T	MI	438
MF	Kuller, J	NC	437
MF	Mastrobattista, J	TX	441
MF	McLaren, R	VA	437
MF	Pinckert, T	MD	435
MF	Platt, L	CA	443
MF	Pridjian, G	LA	441
MF	Reed, K	AZ	441
MF	Robinson, J	MA	433
ObG	Byrne, J	UT	566
ObG	Simpson, J	NY	562

Prenatal Genetic Diagnosis

Spec	Name	St	Pg
CG	Bianchi, D	MA	156
CG	Driscoll, D	PA	157
CG	Falk, R	CA	162
CG	Pergament, E	IL	160
CG	Randolph, L	CA	163
ObG	Corteville, J	OH	564
RE	McClamrock, H	MD	1043

Prenatal Ultrasound

Spec	Name	St	Pg
MF	Abuhamad, A	VA	436
MF	Goodman, J	IL	438
MF	Pridjian, G	LA	441
MF	Tomich, P	NE	440

Preventive Cardiology

Spec	Name	St	Pg
Cv	Andersen, H	NY	91
Cv	Bairey-Merz, C	CA	110
Cv	Balady, G	MA	88
Cv	Ballantyne, C	TX	107
Cv	Blumenthal, D	NY	91
Cv	Blumenthal, R	MD	91
Cv	Budoff, M	CA	110
Cv	Chizner, M	FL	98
Cv	Davidson, M	IL	101
Cv	Edmundowicz, D	PA	92
Cv	Fonarow, G	CA	110
Cv	Friedman, S	NY	92
Cv	Fuster, V	NY	92
Cv	Gardin, J	NJ	93
Cv	Goldberg, N	NY	93
Cv	Goodman, D	NY	93
Cv	Gould, K	TX	108
Cv	Hayes, S	MN	102
Cv	Herling, I	PA	94
Cv	Inra, L	NY	94
Cv	Judelson, D	CA	111
Cv	Kaul, S	OR	111

Spec	Name	St	Pg
Cv	Kuvin, J	MA	89
Cv	Landzberg, J	NJ	94
Cv	Lewis, S	OR	111
Cv	Limacher, M	FL	98
Cv	Linton, M	TN	98
Cv	Meller, J	NY	95
Cv	Redberg, R	CA	112
Cv	Reis, S	PA	95
Cv	Reiss, C	MO	104
Cv	Ridker, P	MA	90
Cv	Roberts, B	RI	90
Cv	Shah, P	CA	112
Cv	Shapiro, J	IL	105
Cv	Sorrentino, M	IL	105
Cv	Stein, J	WI	105
Cv	Thompson, P	CT	90
Cv	Volgman, A	IL	106
Cv	Weitz, H	PA	97
IM	Cushman, W	TN	426
IM	Rader, D	PA	426
PrM	Pearson, T	FL	913

Preventive Medicine

Spec	Name	St	Pg
AM	Garofalo, R	IL	77
Ger	Callahan, E	NY	264
Ger	Lipschitz, D	AR	267
IM	Braunstein, S	NC	426
IM	Cirigliano, M	PA	426
IM	Fischbein, L	MO	427
ObG	Bradshaw, K	TX	566
PrM	Cahill, J	NY	912
PrM	Hoffman, R	NY	913
PrM	Pearson, T	FL	913
Rhu	Rothenberg, R	MD	1062

Prion Diseases

Spec	Name	St	Pg
N	Farlow, M	IN	529

PRK-Refractive Surgery

Spec	Name	St	Pg
Oph	Afshari, N	CA	604
Oph	Kornmehl, E	MA	574
Oph	Manche, E	CA	607
Oph	Mandel, E	NY	581
Oph	Wilson, S	OH	600

Progressive Osseous Heteroplasia POH

Spec	Name	St	Pg
OrS	Kaplan, F	PA	627

Progressive Supranuclear Palsy (PSP)

Spec	Name	St	Pg
N	Gizzi, M	NJ	516
N	Golbe, L	NJ	516

Prolactin Disorders

Spec	Name	St	Pg
RE	Zacur, H	MD	1045

PROSE Contact Lens

Spec	Name	St	Pg
Oph	Udell, I	NY	586

Prostate Cancer

Spec	Name	St	Pg
DR	Schwartz, L	NY	1012
NuM	Podoloff, D	TX	557
Onc	Ahmann, F	AZ	378
Onc	Beer, T	OR	385
Onc	Bolger, G	AL	356
Onc	Boston, B	TN	356
Onc	Bubley, G	MA	330
Onc	Clinton, S	OH	368
Onc	Dawson, N	DC	341
Onc	DiPaola, R	NJ	341
Onc	Donehower, R	MD	341
Onc	Dreicer, R	OH	368
Onc	Eisenberger, M	MD	342
Onc	Garnick, M	MA	332
Onc	Gaynor, E	IL	369
Onc	Gelmann, E	NY	343
Onc	George, D	NC	358
Onc	Glode, L	CO	377
Onc	Haas, N	PA	344
Onc	Hauke, R	NE	377
Onc	Higano, C	WA	388
Onc	Hussain, M	MI	370
Onc	Kantoff, P	MA	333
Onc	Kelly, W	PA	345
Onc	Kraft, A	SC	359
Onc	Kucuk, O	GA	360
Onc	Levine, E	NY	347
Onc	Logothetis, C	TX	381
Onc	Lutzky, J	FL	360
Onc	Mathew, P	MA	334
Onc	Nanus, D	NY	348
Onc	Natale, R	CA	390
Onc	Oh, W	NY	349
Onc	Parnes, H	MD	349
Onc	Peace, D	IL	372
Onc	Petrylak, D	CT	334
Onc	Pienta, K	MD	350
Onc	Quinn, D	CA	391
Onc	Roth, B	MO	373
Onc	Scher, H	NY	351
Onc	Schwartz, M	FL	363
Onc	Small, E	CA	392
Onc	Smith, M	MA	335
Onc	Stadler, W	IL	374
Onc	Stein, C	CA	392
Onc	Sweeney, C	MA	335
Onc	Tagawa, S	NY	352
Onc	Taplin, M	MA	335
Onc	Tester, W	PA	353
Onc	Torti, F	CT	336
Onc	Trump, D	NY	353
Onc	Vaughn, D	PA	353
Onc	Vogelzang, N	NV	394
Onc	Wilding, G	WI	375
Path	Amin, M	CA	731
Path	Balla, A	IL	727
Path	Bostwick, D	VA	725
Path	Epstein, J	MD	721
Path	Melamed, J	NY	722
Path	Reuter, V	NY	723
Path	Ross, J	NY	724
Path	True, L	WA	734
RadRO	Anscher, M	VA	983
RadRO	Awan, A	IL	988
RadRO	Bogart, J	NY	978
RadRO	Ciezki, J	OH	989
RadRO	D'Amico, A	MA	976
RadRO	DeWeese, T	MD	979
RadRO	Dicker, A	PA	979
RadRO	Dritschilo, A	DC	979
RadRO	Ennis, R	NY	979
RadRO	Fiveash, J	AL	984
RadRO	Forman, J	MI	989
RadRO	Gejerman, G	NJ	979
RadRO	Goodman, R	NJ	980
RadRO	Grado, G	AZ	993
RadRO	Hahn, S	PA	980
RadRO	Hancock, S	CA	995
RadRO	Haraf, D	IL	989
RadRO	Hartford, A	NH	976
RadRO	Henderson, R	FL	984
RadRO	Horwitz, E	PA	980
RadRO	Johnstone, P	IN	990
RadRO	Jose, B	IN	990
RadRO	Kalnicki, S	NY	980
RadRO	Kaplan, I	MA	976
RadRO	Kuettel, M	NY	981
RadRO	Lee, A	TX	994
RadRO	Lee, W	NC	985
RadRO	Malcolm, A	TN	985
RadRO	Medbery, C	OK	994
RadRO	Mendenhall, N	FL	986
RadRO	Michalski, J	MO	991
RadRO	Movsas, B	MI	991
RadRO	Nori, D	NY	981
RadRO	Peschel, R	CT	977
RadRO	Pollack, A	FL	986
RadRO	Porrazzo, M	DC	982
RadRO	Potters, L	NY	982
RadRO	Roach, M	CA	997
RadRO	Rose, C	CA	997
RadRO	Rosenman, J	NC	987
RadRO	Rossi, C	CA	997
RadRO	Rotman, M	NY	982
RadRO	Russell, K	WA	997
RadRO	Sandler, H	CA	997
RadRO	Schiff, P	NY	982
RadRO	Schild, S	AZ	994
RadRO	Stock, R	NY	982
RadRO	Tripuraneni, P	CA	998
RadRO	Vicini, F	MI	992
RadRO	Vijayakumar, S	MS	987
RadRO	Wong, J	CA	998
RadRO	Zelefsky, M	NY	983
RadRO	Zietman, A	MA	978
U	Albertsen, P	CT	1186
U	Alexander, R	MD	1188
U	Andriole, G	MO	1202
U	Babayan, R	MA	1186
U	Bahnson, R	OH	1202
U	Balaji, K	NC	1197

Spec	Name	St	Pg
U	Bans, L	AZ	1208
U	Bardot, S	LA	1208
U	Basler, J	TX	1208
U	Beall, M	VA	1197
U	Brendler, C	IL	1202
U	Burnett, A	MD	1189
U	Busby, J	SC	1197
U	Campbell, S	OH	1202
U	Carpinito, G	MA	1186
U	Carroll, P	CA	1210
U	Carter, H	MD	1189
U	Catalona, W	IL	1202
U	Chang, S	TN	1197
U	Childs, S	CO	1206
U	Chun, T	NJ	1189
U	Cohen, J	PA	1189
U	Colberg, J	CT	1186
U	Coleman, J	NY	1189
U	Cookson, M	OK	1208
U	Crawford, E	CO	1207
U	Dalkin, B	WA	1211
U	Daneshmand, S	CA	1211
U	Davis, B	KS	1207
U	DeKernion, J	CA	1211
U	Droller, M	NY	1189
U	Flanigan, R	IL	1203
U	Fraser, L	MS	1197
U	Gill, H	CA	1211
U	Gill, I	CA	1211
U	Gluckman, G	IL	1203
U	Gomella, L	PA	1190
U	Greenberg, R	PA	1190
U	Hall, S	NY	1190
U	Heney, N	MA	1186
U	Herr, H	NY	1191
U	Holden, S	CA	1212
U	Hrebinko, R	PA	1191
U	Jones, J	OH	1203
U	Kadmon, D	TX	1209
U	Kane, M	MD	1191
U	Kavoussi, L	NY	1191
U	Kawachi, M	CA	1212
U	Keane, T	SC	1198
U	Kibel, A	MA	1187
U	Kim, E	TN	1198
U	Kirschenbaum, A	NY	1192
U	Klein, E	OH	1203
U	Koch, M	IN	1204
U	Lange, P	WA	1212
U	Lepor, H	NY	1192
U	Levine, L	IL	1204
U	Libertino, J	MA	1187
U	Loo, M	NY	1192
U	Loughlin, K	MA	1187
U	Lowe, F	NY	1192
U	Lugg, J	WY	1207
U	Malkowicz, S	PA	1192
U	McConnell, J	NC	1198
U	McCullough, A	NY	1192
U	McDougal, W	MA	1187
U	McGovern, F	MA	1187
U	McVary, K	IL	1204
U	Miles, B	TX	1209
U	Mohler, J	NY	1193
U	Montie, J	MI	1204
U	Mostwin, J	MD	1193
U	Moul, J	NC	1199
U	Naslund, M	MD	1193
U	Nelson, J	PA	1193
U	Nieder, A	FL	1199
U	Olumi, A	MA	1187
U	Parekh, D	FL	1199
U	Partin, A	MD	1193
U	Penson, D	TN	1199
U	Pisters, L	TX	1209
U	Porter, C	WA	1213
U	Pow-Sang, J	FL	1199
U	Presti, J	CA	1213
U	Rajfer, J	CA	1213
U	Richie, J	MA	1188
U	Robertson, C	NC	1200
U	Roehrborn, C	TX	1209
U	Sanda, M	GA	1200
U	Sanders, W	GA	1200
U	Scardino, P	NY	1194
U	Schlegel, P	NY	1194
U	Schulam, P	CT	1188
U	See, W	WI	1206
U	Shalhav, A	IL	1206
U	Siegelbaum, M	MD	1195
U	Singh, D	CT	1188
U	Slawin, K	TX	1210
U	Soloway, M	FL	1201
U	Steinberg, G	IL	1206
U	Su, L	FL	1201
U	Sundaram, C	IN	1206
U	Takayama, T	WA	1213
U	Taneja, S	NY	1195
U	Terris, M	GA	1201
U	Thompson, I	TX	1210
U	Thrasher, J	KS	1207
U	Wallen, E	NC	1201
U	Walsh, P	MD	1196
U	Wein, A	PA	1196
U	Wood, D	MI	1206
VIR	Wood, B	MD	1029

Prostate Cancer (advanced)

Spec	Name	St	Pg
Onc	Godley, P	NC	358
Onc	Taplin, M	MA	335

Prostate Cancer-Cryosurgery

Spec	Name	St	Pg
DR	Bahn, D	CA	1017
U	Crawford, E	CO	1207
U	Katz, A	NY	1191

Prostate Cancer-MR Spectroscopy (MRSI)

Spec	Name	St	Pg
DR	Hricak, H	NY	1010

Prostate Cancer-Vaccine Therapy

Spec	Name	St	Pg
Onc	Arlen, P	MD	337
Onc	Gulley, J	MD	344

Prostate Cancer/Robotic Surgery

Spec	Name	St	Pg
U	Ahlering, T	CA	1210
U	Albala, D	NY	1188
U	Amling, C	OR	1210
U	Benson, M	NY	1189
U	Donovan, J	OH	1203
U	Ellis, W	WA	1211
U	Greenberg, R	PA	1190
U	Jackman, S	PA	1191
U	Lanteri, V	NJ	1192
U	Menon, M	MI	1204
U	Miller, S	GA	1199
U	Patel, V	FL	1199
U	Pisters, L	TX	1209
U	Samadi, D	NY	1194
U	Sawczuk, I	NJ	1194
U	Scherr, D	NY	1194
U	Slawin, K	TX	1210
U	Smith, J	TN	1200
U	Steers, W	VA	1201
U	Teigland, C	NC	1201
U	Tewari, A	NY	1195
U	Trabulsi, E	PA	1195
U	Wong, C	OH	1206

Prostate Disease

Spec	Name	St	Pg
U	Alexander, R	MD	1188
U	Bans, L	AZ	1208
U	Catalona, W	IL	1202
U	Crawford, E	CO	1207
U	Ellis, W	WA	1211
U	Gribetz, M	NY	1190
U	Kaplan, S	NY	1191
U	Loo, M	NY	1192
U	Lowe, F	NY	1192
U	McVary, K	IL	1204
U	Moul, J	NC	1199
U	Naslund, M	MD	1193
U	Nieder, A	FL	1199
U	O'Leary, M	MA	1187
U	Partin, A	MD	1193
U	Penson, D	TN	1199
U	Roehrborn, C	TX	1209
U	Ross, L	IL	1205
U	Sadeghi-Nejad, H	NJ	1194
U	Seftel, A	NJ	1194
U	Slawin, K	TX	1210
U	Thompson, I	TX	1210

Prosthesis Control

Spec	Name	St	Pg
PMR	Kuiken, T	IL	869

Proton Beam Therapy

Spec	Name	St	Pg
RadRO	DeLaney, T	MA	976

Spec	Name	St	Pg
RadRO	Henderson, R	FL	984
RadRO	Johnstone, P	IN	990
RadRO	Lee, A	TX	994
RadRO	Marcus, R	FL	985
RadRO	Rossi, C	CA	997
RadRO	Russell, A	MA	977
RadRO	Tarbell, N	MA	977
RadRO	Woo, S	KY	988
RadRO	Zietman, A	MA	978

Pseudomyxoma Peritonei

Spec	Name	St	Pg
S	Loggie, B	NE	1122

Pseudotumor Cerebri

Spec	Name	St	Pg
N	Adams, D	FL	523
N	Corbett, J	MS	524

Pseudoxanthoma Elasticum

Spec	Name	St	Pg
D	Lebwohl, M	NY	189
Oph	Fuchs, W	NY	578

Psoriasis

Spec	Name	St	Pg
D	Belsito, D	NY	186
D	Callen, J	KY	192
D	Camisa, C	FL	192
D	Cather, J	TX	198
D	Cohen, S	NY	187
D	Crutchfield, C	MN	195
D	Fenske, N	FL	192
D	Gottlieb, A	MA	185
D	Kalb, R	NY	189
D	Krueger, G	UT	198
D	Lebwohl, M	NY	189
D	Lowitt, M	MD	189
D	Menter, M	TX	199
D	Nigra, T	DC	189
D	Shupack, J	NY	190
D	Soter, N	NY	191
D	Stern, R	MA	186
D	Thiers, B	SC	194
D	Voorhees, J	MI	197
D	Woodley, D	CA	202

Psoriasis/Eczema

Spec	Name	St	Pg
D	Elmets, C	AL	192
D	Koo, J	CA	201
D	Orlow, S	NY	190

Psoriatic Arthritis

Spec	Name	St	Pg
D	Gottlieb, A	MA	185
Rhu	Bobrove, A	CA	1067
Rhu	Hugenberg, S	IN	1065
Rhu	Kay, J	MA	1058
Rhu	Massarotti, E	MA	1058
Rhu	Mitnick, H	NY	1061
Rhu	Pope, R	IL	1066
Rhu	Solomon, G	NY	1062

Psychiatric Barriers to Physical Rehab

Spec	Name	St	Pg
GerPsy	Streim, J	PA	945

Psychiatric Genetics

Spec	Name	St	Pg
Psyc	Nurnberger, J	IN	930

Psychiatry

Spec	Name	St	Pg
Psyc	Adler, D	MA	920
Psyc	Akhtar, S	PA	922
Psyc	Alpert, J	MA	920
Psyc	Appelbaum, P	NY	922
Psyc	Arnold, S	PA	922
Psyc	Baile, W	TX	931
Psyc	Basch, S	NY	923
Psyc	Bialer, P	NY	923
Psyc	Black, D	IA	929
Psyc	Black, K	MO	929
Psyc	Blazer, D	NC	927
Psyc	Blumenfield, M	CA	932
Psyc	Bowden, C	TX	932
Psyc	Brandt, H	MD	923
Psyc	Breitbart, W	NY	923
Psyc	Brodkin, E	PA	923
Psyc	Bronheim, H	NY	923
Psyc	Burt, V	CA	932
Psyc	Buysse, D	PA	923
Psyc	Bystritsky, A	CA	933
Psyc	Calabrese, J	OH	929
Psyc	Canterbury, R	VA	928
Psyc	Cloninger, C	MO	929
Psyc	Cohen, M	PA	923
Psyc	Crow, S	MN	929
Psyc	Davidson, J	TX	932
Psyc	DePaulo, J	MD	924
Psyc	Doghramji, K	PA	924
Psyc	Eaton, J	DC	924
Psyc	Eisendrath, S	CA	933
Psyc	Ellison, J	MA	920
Psyc	Eth, S	FL	928
Psyc	Fallon, B	NY	924
Psyc	Fann, J	WA	933
Psyc	First, M	NY	924
Psyc	Fox, G	IL	929
Psyc	Friedman, B	CA	933
Psyc	Friedman, M	VT	920
Psyc	Fyer, A	NY	924
Psyc	Gabbard, G	TX	932
Psyc	Gitlin, M	CA	933
Psyc	Giustra, L	GA	928
Psyc	Goff, D	NY	924
Psyc	Goldberg, J	CT	920
Psyc	Grant, J	IL	929
Psyc	Greden, J	MI	930
Psyc	Greenberg, B	RI	920
Psyc	Greenberg, D	MA	920
Psyc	Greenberg, W	MA	920
Psyc	Greiner, C	NE	931
Psyc	Guarda, A	MD	924
Psyc	Gunderson, J	MA	921
Psyc	Haque, W	TX	932
Psyc	Henderson, D	MA	921
Psyc	Hirschfeld, R	TX	932
Psyc	Hollander, E	NY	925
Psyc	Janicak, P	IL	930
Psyc	Jenike, M	MA	921
Psyc	Jimerson, D	MA	921
Psyc	Joffe, H	MA	921
Psyc	Kafka, M	MA	921
Psyc	Karasu, T	NY	925
Psyc	Keepers, G	OR	933
Psyc	Klagsbrun, S	NY	925
Psyc	Klapheke, M	FL	928
Psyc	Krueger, R	NY	925
Psyc	Kumar, A	IL	930
Psyc	Kunkel, E	PA	925
Psyc	Kupfer, D	PA	925
Psyc	Leuchter, A	CA	933
Psyc	Levine, S	OH	930
Psyc	Levy, S	GA	928
Psyc	Locala, J	OH	930
Psyc	Loewenstein, R	MD	925
Psyc	Manevitz, A	NY	925
Psyc	Mann, J	NY	926
Psyc	Marder, S	CA	933
Psyc	Marin, D	NY	926
Psyc	McCallum, K	MO	930
Psyc	McCann, M	MD	926
Psyc	McIntosh, J	UT	931
Psyc	Mitchell, J	ND	931
Psyc	Moench, L	UT	931
Psyc	Mohl, P	TX	932
Psyc	Nelson, J	CA	933
Psyc	Neppe, V	WA	934
Psyc	Norman, K	CA	934
Psyc	Nunes, E	NY	926
Psyc	Nurnberger, J	IN	930
Psyc	Phillips, K	RI	921
Psyc	Pi, E	CA	934
Psyc	Pollack, M	IL	930
Psyc	Powers, P	FL	928
Psyc	Price, L	RI	921
Psyc	Pynoos, R	CA	934
Psyc	Raskind, M	WA	934
Psyc	Rasmussen, S	RI	921
Psyc	Rauch, P	MA	922
Psyc	Reus, V	CA	934
Psyc	Riba, M	MI	930
Psyc	Roose, S	NY	926
Psyc	Rosenthal, N	MD	926
Psyc	Rosenthal, R	NY	926
Psyc	Rosse, R	DC	926
Psyc	Roth, A	NY	926
Psyc	Roy-Byrne, P	WA	934
Psyc	Sadock, V	NY	927
Psyc	Salloum, I	FL	928
Psyc	Salzman, C	MA	922
Psyc	Samberg, E	NY	927
Psyc	Sanacora, G	CT	922
Psyc	Saxena, S	CA	934
Psyc	Schatzberg, A	CA	935
Psyc	Scott, C	PA	927
Psyc	Shapiro, E	MA	922
Psyc	Spiegel, D	CA	935

Spec	Name	St	Pg
Psyc	Stein, M	CA	935
Psyc	Strakowski, S	OH	931
Psyc	Strouse, T	CA	935
Psyc	Summergrad, P	MA	922
Psyc	Sussman, N	NY	927
Psyc	Thase, M	PA	927
Psyc	Valentine, A	TX	932
Psyc	Wait, S	MD	927
Psyc	Walker, R	OR	935
Psyc	Walsh, B	NY	927
Psyc	Weiner, K	CO	931
Psyc	Weiner, R	NC	928
Psyc	Weinstock, R	CA	935
Psyc	Weisler, R	NC	928
Psyc	Wilson, D	FL	929
Psyc	Wooten, V	OH	931
Psyc	Zerbe, K	OR	935

Psychiatry in Cancer

Spec	Name	St	Pg
H & PM	Block, S	MA	406
Psyc	Baile, W	TX	931
Psyc	Basch, S	NY	923
Psyc	Breitbart, W	NY	923
Psyc	Fann, J	WA	933
Psyc	Greenberg, D	MA	920
Psyc	Greiner, C	NE	931
Psyc	Klagsbrun, S	NY	925
Psyc	Kunkel, E	PA	925
Psyc	Riba, M	MI	930
Psyc	Spiegel, D	CA	935
Psyc	Strouse, T	CA	935
Psyc	Valentine, A	TX	932

Psychiatry in Head & Neck Cancer

Spec	Name	St	Pg
Psyc	Bialer, P	NY	923

Psychiatry in Physical Illness

Spec	Name	St	Pg
ChAP	Campo, J	OH	941
ChAP	Martini, D	UT	942
GerPsy	Streim, J	PA	945
Psyc	Bialer, P	NY	923
Psyc	Bronheim, H	NY	923
Psyc	Cohen, M	PA	923
Psyc	Fallon, B	NY	924
Psyc	Fann, J	WA	933
Psyc	Greiner, C	NE	931
Psyc	Kunkel, E	PA	925
Psyc	Locala, J	OH	930
Psyc	Rauch, P	MA	922
Psyc	Strouse, T	CA	935

Psychiatry in Pregnancy

Spec	Name	St	Pg
Psyc	Burt, V	CA	932
Psyc	Joffe, H	MA	921

Psychiatry in Terminal Illness

Spec	Name	St	Pg
Psyc	Klagsbrun, S	NY	925

Psychiatry in Transplant Patients

Spec	Name	St	Pg
ChAP	Sexson, S	GA	941
Psyc	Locala, J	OH	930

Psychiatry of Prostate Cancer

Spec	Name	St	Pg
Psyc	Roth, A	NY	926

Psychoanalysis

Spec	Name	St	Pg
Psyc	Akhtar, S	PA	922
Psyc	Basch, S	NY	923
Psyc	Friedman, B	CA	933
Psyc	Gabbard, G	TX	932
Psyc	Klapheke, M	FL	928
Psyc	Levy, S	GA	928
Psyc	Roose, S	NY	926
Psyc	Samberg, E	NY	927
Psyc	Scott, C	PA	927
Psyc	Shapiro, E	MA	922
Psyc	Zerbe, K	OR	935

Psychodermatology

Spec	Name	St	Pg
D	Koo, J	CA	201

Psychopharmacology

Spec	Name	St	Pg
AdP	Ciraulo, D	MA	936
AdP	Kosten, T	TX	938
ChAP	Biederman, J	MA	938
ChAP	Coffey, B	NY	939
ChAP	Hirsch, S	IL	942
ChAP	Hudziak, J	VT	938
ChAP	Koplewicz, H	NY	940
ChAP	Leventhal, B	NY	940
ChAP	Riddle, M	MD	940
GerPsy	Tune, L	GA	945
PM	Robbins, L	IL	710
Psyc	Alpert, J	MA	920
Psyc	Basch, S	NY	923
Psyc	Blumenfield, M	CA	932
Psyc	Bystritsky, A	CA	933
Psyc	First, M	NY	924
Psyc	Friedman, B	CA	933
Psyc	Friedman, M	VT	920
Psyc	Goff, D	NY	924
Psyc	Goldberg, J	CT	920
Psyc	Henderson, D	MA	921
Psyc	Janicak, P	IL	930
Psyc	Kafka, M	MA	921
Psyc	Loewenstein, R	MD	925
Psyc	Marder, S	CA	933
Psyc	Mohl, P	TX	932
Psyc	Nelson, J	CA	933
Psyc	Neppe, V	WA	934
Psyc	Pi, E	CA	934
Psyc	Pollack, M	IL	930
Psyc	Reus, V	CA	934
Psyc	Salzman, C	MA	922
Psyc	Schatzberg, A	CA	935
Psyc	Sussman, N	NY	927
Psyc	Thase, M	PA	927
Psyc	Wilson, D	FL	929

Psychoses-Late Onset

Spec	Name	St	Pg
GerPsy	Holroyd, S	VA	945

Psychosocial Support in Childhood Cancer

Spec	Name	St	Pg
PHO	Siegel, S	CA	792

Psychosomatic Disorders

Spec	Name	St	Pg
ChAP	Campo, J	OH	941
ChAP	Steiner, H	CA	944
ChAP	Wamboldt, M	CO	942
Psyc	Blumenfield, M	CA	932
Psyc	Fallon, B	NY	924

Psychotherapy

Spec	Name	St	Pg
Psyc	Basch, S	NY	923
Psyc	Blumenfield, M	CA	932
Psyc	First, M	NY	924
Psyc	Giustra, L	GA	928
Psyc	Karasu, T	NY	925
Psyc	Mohl, P	TX	932
Psyc	Sadock, V	NY	927
Psyc	Salzman, C	MA	922
Psyc	Samberg, E	NY	927

Psychotic Disorders

Spec	Name	St	Pg
Psyc	Black, D	IA	929
Psyc	Janicak, P	IL	930
Psyc	Strakowski, S	OH	931

Pubertal Disorders

Spec	Name	St	Pg
PEn	Allen, D	WI	760
PEn	Alter, C	PA	757
PEn	Eugster, E	IN	760
PEn	Foster, C	UT	761
PEn	Freemark, M	NC	759
PEn	Garibaldi, L	PA	758
PEn	Geffner, M	CA	761
PEn	Kappy, M	CO	761
PEn	Plotnick, L	MD	759

Pulmonary Complications-Cancer Therapy

Spec	Name	St	Pg
PPul	Kim, Y	IN	809

Pulmonary Complications-Neurodisability

Spec	Name	St	Pg
PPul	Givan, D	IN	808
PPul	Warren, R	AR	810

Pulmonary Complications-Sickle

Spec	Name	St	Pg

Cell Dis

Spec	Name	St	Pg
PPul	Kim, Y	IN	809

Pulmonary Disease

Spec	Name	St	Pg
Pul	Ahya, V	PA	956
Pul	Alberts, W	FL	961
Pul	Albertson, T	CA	969
Pul	Antony, V	AL	961
Pul	Arcasoy, S	NY	956
Pul	Arroliga, A	TX	968
Pul	Auger, W	CA	970
Pul	Balk, R	IL	964
Pul	Balmes, J	CA	970
Pul	Bascom, R	PA	956
Pul	Bellamy, P	CA	970
Pul	Berk, J	MA	954
Pul	Bijwadia, J	MN	964
Pul	Boushey, H	CA	970
Pul	Brown, K	CO	967
Pul	Burschtin, O	NY	956
Pul	Campbell, G	MS	961
Pul	Catanzaro, A	CA	970
Pul	Celli, B	MA	954
Pul	Christiani, D	MA	954
Pul	Christie, J	PA	956
Pul	Christman, B	TN	961
Pul	Cooper, J	AL	961
Pul	Cooper, W	VA	961
Pul	Criner, G	PA	956
Pul	Deitz, J	PA	957
Pul	Doherty, D	KY	961
Pul	Donahoe, M	PA	957
Pul	Donohue, J	NC	962
Pul	Elliott, C	UT	967
Pul	Enelow, R	NH	954
Pul	Fahey, P	IL	964
Pul	Fanta, C	MA	954
Pul	Fletcher, E	IN	964
Pul	Friedman, L	CT	954
Pul	Fulkerson, W	NC	962
Pul	Garrity, E	IL	964
Pul	Garver, R	AL	962
Pul	Gerboth, G	AK	970
Pul	Goldman, A	FL	962
Pul	Greenberg, H	NY	957
Pul	Grum, C	MI	964
Pul	Guidry, G	LA	969
Pul	Hall, J	IL	964
Pul	Hansen-Flaschen, J	PA	957
Pul	Harman, E	FL	962
Pul	Haynes, J	AL	962
Pul	Heffner, J	OR	970
Pul	Henke, D	NC	962
Pul	Hertz, M	MN	965
Pul	Hill, N	MA	954
Pul	Hopewell, P	CA	970
Pul	Huang, L	CA	971
Pul	Hyers, T	MO	965
Pul	Ingbar, D	MN	965
Pul	Irwin, R	MA	955
Pul	Jacoby, D	OR	971
Pul	Johnson, B	VA	962
Pul	Kaplan, J	KS	968
Pul	Kaye, M	MN	965
Pul	Kern, J	CO	968
Pul	King, E	PA	957
Pul	King, T	CA	971
Pul	Kotloff, R	PA	957
Pul	Kovitz, K	IL	965
Pul	Krowka, M	MN	965
Pul	Lem, V	MO	965
Pul	Levin, D	OK	969
Pul	Libby, D	NY	957
Pul	Light, R	TN	963
Pul	LoRusso, T	VA	963
Pul	Loyd, J	TN	963
Pul	Lynch, J	CA	971
Pul	Mahler, D	NH	955
Pul	Marini, J	MN	965
Pul	Martin, R	CO	968
Pul	Martinez, F	MI	966
Pul	Matuschak, G	MO	966
Pul	Maxfield, R	NY	958
Pul	Mazzone, P	OH	966
Pul	Metersky, M	CT	955
Pul	Millman, R	RI	955
Pul	Mosenifar, Z	CA	971
Pul	Nader, D	OK	969
Pul	Nardell, E	MA	955
Pul	Nash, T	NY	958
Pul	Nelson, J	NY	958
Pul	Niederman, M	NY	958
Pul	O'Donnell, A	DC	958
Pul	Pack, A	PA	958
Pul	Padilla, M	NY	958
Pul	Palevsky, H	PA	959
Pul	Perret, P	LA	969
Pul	Popovich, J	MI	966
Pul	Prakash, U	MN	966
Pul	Raghu, G	WA	971
Pul	Redlich, C	CT	955
Pul	Rennard, S	NE	968
Pul	Rizk, N	CA	971
Pul	Rochester, C	CT	955
Pul	Rose, C	CO	968
Pul	Rosenbluth, D	MO	966
Pul	Rossman, M	PA	959
Pul	Sahn, S	SC	963
Pul	Schluger, N	NY	959
Pul	Schraufnagel, D	IL	966
Pul	Schwab, R	PA	959
Pul	Shellito, J	LA	969
Pul	Silver, M	IL	966
Pul	Simon, R	MI	967
Pul	Staton, G	GA	963
Pul	Steiger, D	NY	959
Pul	Steinberg, H	NY	959
Pul	Sterman, D	PA	959
Pul	Stoller, J	OH	967
Pul	Stover-Pepe, D	NY	960
Pul	Strollo, P	PA	960
Pul	Sutherland, E	CO	968
Pul	Thomashow, B	NY	960
Pul	Tino, G	PA	960
Pul	Tobin, M	IL	967
Pul	Trulock, E	MO	967
Pul	Unger, M	PA	960
Pul	Vaughey, E	VA	963
Pul	Villanueva, A	MA	955
Pul	Voelkel, N	VA	963
Pul	Wallace, J	CA	972
Pul	Wanner, A	FL	963
Pul	Weissler, J	TX	969
Pul	Wenzel, S	PA	960
Pul	Wheeler, A	TN	964
Pul	White, D	MA	956
Pul	Wiedemann, H	OH	967
Pul	Wolfe, R	CA	972
Pul	Young, K	PA	960

Pulmonary Disease/Immunocompromised

Spec	Name	St	Pg
Pul	Stover-Pepe, D	NY	960

Pulmonary Embolism

Spec	Name	St	Pg
DR	Goodman, L	WI	1015
Pul	Arcasoy, S	NY	956
Pul	Popovich, J	MI	966
S	Wakefield, T	MI	1121

Pulmonary Fibrosis

Spec	Name	St	Pg
Pul	Bascom, R	PA	956
Pul	Berk, J	MA	954
Pul	Brown, K	CO	967
Pul	Criner, G	PA	956
Pul	Donohue, J	NC	962
Pul	Fulkerson, W	NC	962
Pul	King, T	CA	971
Pul	Loyd, J	TN	963
Pul	Lynch, J	CA	971
Pul	Raghu, G	WA	971
Pul	Rossman, M	PA	959
Pul	Sahn, S	SC	963
Pul	Staton, G	GA	963
Pul	Tino, G	PA	960

Pulmonary Hypertension

Spec	Name	St	Pg
Cv	Bashore, T	NC	97
Cv	Bourge, R	AL	97
Cv	Catherwood, E	NH	88
Cv	Horn, E	NY	94
Cv	Poon, M	NY	95
Cv	Rich, S	IL	104
Cv	Smart, F	LA	109
Cv	von der Lohe, E	IN	106
Cv	Wagoner, L	OH	106
PCd	Hanna, B	PA	749
Pul	Arroliga, A	TX	968
Pul	Auger, W	CA	970
Pul	Criner, G	PA	956
Pul	Elliott, C	UT	967
Pul	Hertz, M	MN	965
Pul	Hill, N	MA	954
Pul	Krowka, M	MN	965

Specialty & Special Expertise Index

Spec	Name	St	Pg
Pul	Mosenifar, Z	CA	971
Pul	Padilla, M	NY	958
Pul	Palevsky, H	PA	959
Pul	Steiger, D	NY	959
Pul	Steinberg, H	NY	959
Pul	Trulock, E	MO	967
Pul	Voelkel, N	VA	963

Pulmonary Hypertension of Newborn (PPHN)

Spec	Name	St	Pg
NP	Donn, S	MI	452
NP	Seidner, S	TX	453
NP	Van Marter, L	MA	448

Pulmonary Infections

Spec	Name	St	Pg
PPul	Gibson, R	WA	810
Pul	Ingbar, D	MN	965
Pul	Metersky, M	CT	955
Pul	Rizk, N	CA	971
Pul	Schraufnagel, D	IL	966
Pul	Shellito, J	LA	969
Pul	Stover-Pepe, D	NY	960
Pul	Wallace, J	CA	972

Pulmonary Pathology

Spec	Name	St	Pg
Path	Cagle, P	TX	730
Path	Fishbein, M	CA	733
Path	Hammar, S	WA	733
Path	Katzenstein, A	NY	722
Path	Klimstra, D	NY	722
Path	Koss, M	CA	733
Path	Leslie, K	AZ	730
Path	Mark, E	MA	719
Path	Patchefsky, A	PA	723
Path	Travis, W	NY	724
Path	Yousem, S	PA	725

Pulmonary Rehabilitation

Spec	Name	St	Pg
PPul	Warren, R	AR	810

Pulmonary Vascular Disease

Spec	Name	St	Pg
Pul	Garrity, E	IL	964
Pul	Palevsky, H	PA	959
Pul	Schraufnagel, D	IL	966

R

Radiation Oncology

Spec	Name	St	Pg
RadRO	Abrams, R	IL	988
RadRO	Anscher, M	VA	983
RadRO	Awan, A	IL	988
RadRO	Beitler, J	GA	983
RadRO	Blackstock, A	NC	983
RadRO	Bogart, J	NY	978
RadRO	Bradley, J	MO	988
RadRO	Brizel, D	NC	984
RadRO	Buatti, J	IA	988
RadRO	Buchholz, T	TX	993
RadRO	Chadha, M	NY	978
RadRO	Chakravarthy, A	TN	984
RadRO	Chakravarti, A	OH	988
RadRO	Chang, E	CA	995
RadRO	Chao, K	NY	978
RadRO	Choi, N	MA	976
RadRO	Choy, H	TX	993
RadRO	Ciezki, J	OH	989
RadRO	Cmelak, A	TN	984
RadRO	Constine, L	NY	978
RadRO	Cooper, J	NY	978
RadRO	Cox, J	TX	993
RadRO	Crane, C	TX	993
RadRO	Crocker, I	GA	984
RadRO	D'Amico, A	MA	976
RadRO	DeLaney, T	MA	976
RadRO	DeWeese, T	MD	979
RadRO	Dicker, A	PA	979
RadRO	Donaldson, S	CA	995
RadRO	Dritschilo, A	DC	979
RadRO	Eifel, P	TX	993
RadRO	Eisbruch, A	MI	989
RadRO	Emami, B	IL	989
RadRO	Ennis, R	NY	979
RadRO	Fiveash, J	AL	984
RadRO	Flickinger, J	PA	979
RadRO	Forman, J	MI	989
RadRO	Formenti, S	NY	979
RadRO	Fowble, B	CA	995
RadRO	Freedman, G	PA	979
RadRO	Gaffney, D	UT	992
RadRO	Gejerman, G	NJ	979
RadRO	Goodman, R	NJ	980
RadRO	Grado, G	AZ	993
RadRO	Greenberger, J	PA	980
RadRO	Grigsby, P	MO	989
RadRO	Haffty, B	NJ	980
RadRO	Hahn, S	PA	980
RadRO	Halberg, F	CA	995
RadRO	Halpern, H	IL	989
RadRO	Halyard, M	AZ	993
RadRO	Hancock, S	CA	995
RadRO	Haraf, D	IL	989
RadRO	Harari, P	WI	989
RadRO	Harris, J	MA	976
RadRO	Harrison, L	NY	980
RadRO	Hartford, A	NH	976
RadRO	Hayman, J	MI	990
RadRO	Heimann, R	VT	976
RadRO	Henderson, R	FL	984
RadRO	Herman, T	OK	993
RadRO	Hoppe, R	CA	995
RadRO	Horwitz, E	PA	980
RadRO	Isaacson, S	NY	980
RadRO	Jhingran, A	TX	994
RadRO	Johnstone, P	IN	990
RadRO	Jose, B	IN	990
RadRO	Kachnic, L	MA	976
RadRO	Kalnicki, S	NY	980
RadRO	Kaplan, I	MA	976
RadRO	Kestin, L	MI	990
RadRO	Kleinberg, L	MD	981
RadRO	Knisely, J	NY	981
RadRO	Koh, W	WA	996
RadRO	Komaki, R	TX	994
RadRO	Konski, A	MI	990
RadRO	Kuban, D	TX	994
RadRO	Kudrimoti, M	KY	984
RadRO	Kuettel, M	NY	981
RadRO	Kun, L	TN	984
RadRO	Kupelian, P	CA	996
RadRO	Kuske, R	AZ	994
RadRO	Landry, J	GA	985
RadRO	Laramore, G	WA	996
RadRO	Larner, J	VA	985
RadRO	Larson, D	CA	996
RadRO	Lawrence, T	MI	990
RadRO	Le, Q	CA	996
RadRO	Lee, A	TX	994
RadRO	Lee, C	MN	990
RadRO	Lee, W	NC	985
RadRO	Lepanto, P	WV	981
RadRO	Lewin, A	FL	985
RadRO	Loeffler, J	MA	977
RadRO	Machtay, M	OH	990
RadRO	Macklis, R	OH	991
RadRO	Malcolm, A	TN	985
RadRO	Marcus, R	FL	985
RadRO	Markoe, A	FL	985
RadRO	Marks, L	NC	985
RadRO	Martenson, J	MN	991
RadRO	McCormick, B	NY	981
RadRO	McGarry, R	KY	986
RadRO	Medbery, C	OK	994
RadRO	Mehta, M	MD	981
RadRO	Mendenhall, N	FL	986
RadRO	Mendenhall, W	FL	986
RadRO	Merchant, T	TN	986
RadRO	Meredith, R	AL	986
RadRO	Michalski, J	MO	991
RadRO	Minsky, B	TX	994
RadRO	Mittal, B	IL	991
RadRO	Morris, M	VA	986
RadRO	Morrison, W	TX	994
RadRO	Movsas, B	MI	991
RadRO	Mundt, A	CA	996
RadRO	Nicolaou, N	PA	981
RadRO	Nori, D	NY	981
RadRO	Park, C	CA	996
RadRO	Peschel, R	CT	977
RadRO	Pezner, R	CA	996
RadRO	Pierce, L	MI	991
RadRO	Pollack, A	FL	986
RadRO	Porrazzo, M	DC	982
RadRO	Potters, L	NY	982
RadRO	Prosnitz, L	NC	986
RadRO	Quivey, J	CA	997
RadRO	Rabinovitch, R	CO	992
RadRO	Randall, M	KY	986
RadRO	Randolph-Jackson, P	DC	982
RadRO	Recht, A	MA	977

Spec	Name	St	Pg
RadRO	Regine, W	MD	982
RadRO	Roach, M	CA	997
RadRO	Roberts, K	CT	977
RadRO	Rose, C	CA	997
RadRO	Rosenman, J	NC	987
RadRO	Rossi, C	CA	997
RadRO	Rotman, M	NY	982
RadRO	Russell, A	MA	977
RadRO	Russell, K	WA	997
RadRO	Sailer, S	NC	987
RadRO	Sandler, H	CA	997
RadRO	Schiff, P	NY	982
RadRO	Schild, S	AZ	994
RadRO	Schomberg, P	WA	997
RadRO	Seung, S	OR	997
RadRO	Shaw, E	NC	987
RadRO	Shina, D	NM	995
RadRO	Shrieve, D	UT	992
RadRO	Simpson, J	MO	991
RadRO	Small, W	IL	991
RadRO	Smalley, S	KS	992
RadRO	Solin, L	PA	982
RadRO	Song, S	VA	987
RadRO	St Clair, W	KY	987
RadRO	Stea, B	AZ	995
RadRO	Stevens, C	FL	987
RadRO	Stock, R	NY	982
RadRO	Streeter, O	CA	998
RadRO	Suh, J	OH	992
RadRO	Suntharalingam, M	MD	983
RadRO	Taghian, A	MA	977
RadRO	Tarbell, N	MA	977
RadRO	Tepper, J	NC	987
RadRO	Thomas, C	OR	998
RadRO	Tripuraneni, P	CA	998
RadRO	Vicini, F	MI	992
RadRO	Videtic, G	OH	992
RadRO	Vijayakumar, S	MS	987
RadRO	Wara, W	CA	998
RadRO	Wazer, D	RI	977
RadRO	Weiss, M	PA	983
RadRO	Werner-Wasik, M	PA	983
RadRO	Willett, C	NC	987
RadRO	Wilson, J	WI	992
RadRO	Wilson, L	CT	978
RadRO	Wolfson, A	FL	988
RadRO	Wong, J	CA	998
RadRO	Woo, S	KY	988
RadRO	Yahalom, J	NY	983
RadRO	Zelefsky, M	NY	983
RadRO	Zietman, A	MA	978

Radiation Therapy-Intraoperative

Spec	Name	St	Pg
RadRO	Harrison, L	NY	980

Radiofrequency Ablation

Spec	Name	St	Pg
CE	Iwai, S	NY	115

Radiofrequency Tumor Ablation

Spec	Name	St	Pg
DR	Charboneau, J	MN	1014
S	Klimberg, V	AR	1126
VascS	Blebea, J	OK	1229
VIR	Brown, D	TN	1029
VIR	Brown, K	NY	1027
VIR	Coldwell, D	KY	1029
VIR	Kay, D	LA	1032
VIR	McGahan, J	CA	1033
VIR	Nemcek, A	IL	1031
VIR	Solomon, S	NY	1028
VIR	Soulen, M	PA	1028
VIR	Wood, B	MD	1029

Radioimmunotherapy of Cancer

Spec	Name	St	Pg
NuM	Carrasquillo, J	NY	554
NuM	Lamonica, D	NY	554
NuM	Pandit-Taskar, N	NY	555
NuM	Wahl, R	MD	555
NuM	Wiseman, G	MN	556
RadRO	Macklis, R	OH	991
RadRO	Wong, J	CA	998

Radionuclide Therapy

Spec	Name	St	Pg
RadRO	Meredith, R	AL	986

Rare Genetic Disorders

Spec	Name	St	Pg
CG	Wilcox, W	CA	164

Rare Lung Disease-Pediatric

Spec	Name	St	Pg
PPul	Kim, Y	IN	809

Rare Skin Disorders

Spec	Name	St	Pg
D	Shupack, J	NY	190

Rare Tumors

Spec	Name	St	Pg
PHO	Rodriguez-Galindo, C	MA	770

Rasmussen's Syndrome

Spec	Name	St	Pg
N	Cole, A	MA	510

Raynaud's Disease

Spec	Name	St	Pg
Rhu	Clements, P	CA	1067
Rhu	Medsger, T	PA	1061
Rhu	Wigley, F	MD	1063

Reconstructive Microsurgery

Spec	Name	St	Pg
OrS	Levin, L	PA	628

Reconstructive Microvascular Surgery

Spec	Name	St	Pg
HS	Hanel, D	WA	306
HS	Raphael, J	PA	299
HS	Steinmann, S	MN	304
OrS	Hausman, M	NY	625
Oto	Day, T	SC	678
Oto	Teknos, T	OH	688
Oto	Valentino, J	KY	682
PlS	Molnar, J	NC	891

Reconstructive Plastic Surgery

Spec	Name	St	Pg
Oph	Lucarelli, M	WI	597
Oto	Toriumi, D	IL	688
PlS	Bauer, B	IL	892
PlS	Billmire, D	OH	893
PlS	Dagum, A	NY	881
PlS	Gottlieb, L	IL	893
PlS	Grant, R	NY	882
PlS	Hultman, C	NC	890
PlS	Loree, T	NY	884
PlS	Siemionow, M	OH	896
PlS	Thaller, S	FL	891
PlS	Tobin, G	KY	892
PlS	Wilhelmi, B	KY	892
PlS	Zide, B	NY	888

Reconstructive Surgery

Spec	Name	St	Pg
GO	Lele, S	NY	279
HS	Cendales, L	GA	301
HS	Chang, J	CA	305
HS	Chung, K	MI	302
HS	Lee, W	MD	299
ObG	Hale, D	IN	565
Oph	Mawn, L	TN	590
Oph	Ng, J	OR	608
OrS	Agarwal, A	TX	647
OrS	Bos, G	WA	649
OrS	Burke, D	MA	616
OrS	Cheng, E	MN	640
OrS	Cooper, D	TX	648
OrS	Ebraheim, N	OH	641
OrS	Goodman, S	CA	651
OrS	Greisberg, J	NY	624
OrS	Kraay, M	OH	642
OrS	Luck, J	CA	652
OrS	Macaulay, W	NY	628
OrS	Manoli, A	MI	643
OrS	Menendez, L	CA	652
OrS	O'Keefe, R	NY	630
OrS	Parsons, T	MI	644
OrS	Ward, W	PA	633
OrS	Wittig, J	NY	634
Oto	Baker, S	MI	683
Oto	Burkey, B	OH	684
Oto	Hicks, W	NY	670
Oto	Quatela, V	NY	674
Oto	Ries, W	TN	680
Oto	Rosenthal, E	AL	681
Oto	Spiegel, J	MA	667
Ped Uro	Atala, A	NC	825
Ped Uro	Brock, J	TN	825
Ped Uro	Kaefer, M	IN	827
Ped Uro	Strand, W	TX	828
PlS	Bentz, M	WI	892

Spec	Name	St	Pg
PlS	Chiu, D	NY	881
PlS	Cordeiro, P	NY	881
PlS	Dufresne, C	MD	882
PlS	Feldman, J	MA	878
PlS	Hagan, K	TN	890
PlS	Hoffman, W	CA	903
PlS	Kronowitz, S	TX	899
PlS	Lee, R	IL	894
PlS	Lesavoy, M	CA	904
PlS	MacKinnon, S	MO	894
PlS	Manson, P	MD	884
PlS	Sanger, J	WI	896
PlS	Serletti, J	PA	886
PlS	Seyfer, A	MD	886
PlS	Smith, D	FL	891
PlS	Talmor, M	NY	887
S	Edington, H	PA	1092
S	Wallace, A	CA	1138
SM	Bradley, J	PA	1075
U	Foster, R	IN	1203
U	Griebling, T	KS	1207
U	Miller, S	GA	1199

Reconstructive Surgery-Complex

Spec	Name	St	Pg
OrS	Copp, S	CA	650
OrS	Kenan, S	NY	627
PlS	Brandt, K	MO	893
PlS	Patel, P	IL	895

Reconstructive Surgery-Face

Spec	Name	St	Pg
Oto	Chalian, A	PA	668
Oto	Haughey, B	MO	685
Oto	Papel, I	MD	673
PlS	Baker, D	NY	880
PlS	Bartlett, S	PA	880
PlS	Mehrara, B	NY	885
PlS	Menick, F	AZ	899
PlS	Smith, P	FL	891

Reconstructive Surgery-Skin

Spec	Name	St	Pg
D	Brodland, D	PA	187
D	Cook, J	NC	192
D	Swanson, N	OR	202
D	Zitelli, J	PA	191

Reconstructive Urologic Surgery

Spec	Name	St	Pg
Ped Uro	Greenfield, S	NY	825
Ped Uro	Rink, R	IN	828
U	Bales, G	IL	1202
U	Greene, G	FL	1197
U	Hemal, A	NC	1198
U	Koch, M	IN	1204
U	Shenot, P	PA	1195
U	Thrasher, J	KS	1207

Rectal Cancer

Spec	Name	St	Pg
CRS	Gorfine, S	NY	170
Ge	Aslanian, H	CT	230
Onc	Kemeny, N	NY	346
RadRO	Konski, A	MI	990
RadRO	Tepper, J	NC	987
S	Calvo, B	NC	1104

Rectal Cancer/Sphincter Preservation

Spec	Name	St	Pg
CRS	Abcarian, H	IL	173
CRS	Bailey, H	TX	176
CRS	Beart, R	CA	177
CRS	Delaney, C	OH	173
CRS	Fry, R	PA	169
CRS	Guillem, J	NY	170
CRS	Ludwig, K	WI	174
CRS	Mantyh, C	NC	172
CRS	Saclarides, T	IL	175
CRS	Stamos, M	CA	178
CRS	Thorson, A	NE	176
S	Skibber, J	TX	1129

Rectovaginal Fistula

Spec	Name	St	Pg
CRS	Birnbaum, E	MO	173
CRS	Hartmann, R	FL	172
CRS	Lowry, A	MN	174
CRS	Mutch, M	MO	174

Reflex Sympathetic Dystrophy (RSD)

Spec	Name	St	Pg
N	Reder, A	IL	532
PM	Audell, L	CA	712
PM	Berde, C	MA	706
PM	Christo, P	MD	706
PM	Ferrante, F	CA	712
PM	Jain, S	NY	707
PM	Ngeow, J	NY	707
PM	Racz, G	TX	711
PM	Raja, S	MD	707
PM	Richman, D	NY	708
PRhu	Sherry, D	PA	812

Refractive Surgery

Spec	Name	St	Pg
Oph	Cionni, R	UT	601
Oph	Holland, E	OH	595
Oph	John, T	IL	596
Oph	Koch, D	TX	602
Oph	Krueger, R	OH	596
Oph	Lane, S	MN	596
Oph	Lindstrom, R	MN	597
Oph	Maguire, L	MN	597
Oph	Maloney, R	CA	607
Oph	McDonnell, P	MD	582
Oph	Miller, K	CA	607
Oph	Orlin, S	PA	583
Oph	Page, T	MI	598
Oph	Rapuano, C	PA	583
Oph	Rosenberg, M	IL	599
Oph	Samuelson, T	MN	599
Oph	Solomon, K	SC	591
Oph	Stark, W	MD	585
Oph	Steinert, R	CA	609
Oph	Updegraff, S	FL	592
Oph	Wallace, R	LA	603

Rehabilitation for Rheumatic Diseases

Spec	Name	St	Pg
Rhu	Ehresmann, G	CA	1067

Reiter's Syndrome

Spec	Name	St	Pg
Rhu	Solitar, B	NY	1062

Relapsing Polychondritis

Spec	Name	St	Pg
Rhu	Luthra, H	MN	1065

Relationship Problems

Spec	Name	St	Pg
Psyc	Bronheim, H	NY	923
Psyc	Levine, S	OH	930

Renal Artery Stenosis

Spec	Name	St	Pg
IC	Dieter, R	IL	125
Nep	Textor, S	MN	464
Nep	Townsend, R	PA	460
VascS	Mitchell, M	MS	1226

Renal Replacement Therapy

Spec	Name	St	Pg
Nep	Fulop, T	MS	461
PNep	Chandar, J	FL	798

Renovascular Disease

Spec	Name	St	Pg
Cv	Ramee, S	LA	109
IC	Petrossian, G	NY	123
VascS	Benvenisty, A	NY	1222
VascS	Cambria, R	MA	1220
VascS	Faries, P	NY	1223
VascS	Gewertz, B	CA	1230
VascS	Stanley, J	MI	1228

Reproductive Endocrinology

Spec	Name	St	Pg
EDM	Goodman, N	FL	216
EDM	Marshall, J	VA	217
ObG	Berga, S	NC	562
ObG	Richardson, M	KS	566
RE	Adamson, G	CA	1051
RE	Agarwal, S	CA	1051
RE	Azziz, R	GA	1045
RE	Baker, V	CA	1051
RE	Barnes, R	IL	1046
RE	Bateman, B	VA	1045
RE	Blackwell, R	AL	1045
RE	Buster, J	MA	1040
RE	Carr, B	TX	1049
RE	Cedars, M	CA	1051
RE	Chang, R	CA	1051
RE	Chenette, P	CA	1051
RE	Clisham, P	LA	1050
RE	Coddington, C	MN	1047
RE	Cohen, D	IL	1047

Spec	Name	St	Pg
RE	Copperman, A	NY	1041
RE	Crowley, W	MA	1040
RE	De Cherney, A	MD	1042
RE	DeVane, G	FL	1045
RE	Dickey, R	LA	1050
RE	Dodds, W	MI	1047
RE	Dumesic, D	CA	1051
RE	Durso, N	VA	1045
RE	Falcone, T	OH	1047
RE	Friedman, C	OH	1047
RE	Fritz, M	NC	1046
RE	Ginsburg, E	MA	1040
RE	Giudice, L	CA	1052
RE	Goldberg, J	OH	1047
RE	Gracia, C	PA	1042
RE	Grazi, R	NY	1042
RE	Grifo, J	NY	1042
RE	Grunfeld, L	NY	1042
RE	Haney, A	IL	1047
RE	Hickok, L	WA	1052
RE	Hill, J	NH	1040
RE	Hornstein, M	MA	1040
RE	Huang, J	TX	1050
RE	Isaacson, K	MA	1040
RE	Jacobs, L	IL	1048
RE	Johnson, J	MA	1040
RE	Kazer, R	IL	1048
RE	Keefe, D	NY	1042
RE	Keltz, M	NY	1042
RE	Kuo, J	CA	1052
RE	Kutteh, W	TN	1046
RE	Legro, R	PA	1043
RE	Licciardi, F	NY	1043
RE	Luciano, A	CT	1041
RE	Marrs, R	CA	1052
RE	Marshall, L	WA	1052
RE	Marut, E	IL	1048
RE	McClamrock, H	MD	1043
RE	McGovern, P	NJ	1043
RE	Milad, M	IL	1048
RE	Moffitt, D	AZ	1050
RE	Molo, M	IL	1048
RE	Mukherjee, T	NY	1043
RE	Noyes, N	NY	1043
RE	Odem, R	MO	1048
RE	Ory, S	FL	1046
RE	Oskowitz, S	MA	1041
RE	Patrizio, P	CT	1041
RE	Paulson, R	CA	1052
RE	Petrozza, J	MA	1041
RE	Pfeifer, S	PA	1043
RE	Putman, J	TX	1050
RE	Ratts, V	MO	1048
RE	Rosenwaks, Z	NY	1044
RE	Sanfilippo, J	PA	1044
RE	Sauer, M	NY	1044
RE	Schenken, R	TX	1050
RE	Schlaff, W	PA	1044
RE	Schriock, E	CA	1052
RE	Scoccia, H	IL	1048
RE	Seifer, D	NY	1044
RE	Session, D	GA	1046
RE	Smikle, C	CA	1052
RE	Smith, Y	MI	1049
RE	Sondheimer, S	PA	1044
RE	Soules, M	WA	1053
RE	Steinkampf, M	AL	1046
RE	Stephenson, M	IL	1049
RE	Stewart, E	MN	1049
RE	Surrey, E	CO	1049
RE	Thomas, M	OH	1049
RE	Toth, T	MA	1041
RE	Van Voorhis, B	IA	1049
RE	Walmer, D	NC	1046
RE	Weiss, G	NJ	1044
RE	Widra, E	DC	1045
RE	Wilson, E	TX	1050
RE	Winer, S	CA	1053
RE	Yee, B	CA	1053
RE	Zacur, H	MD	1045
RE	Zinaman, M	MA	1041

Reproductive Endocrinology-Male

Spec	Name	St	Pg
EDM	Bhasin, S	MA	208
EDM	Snyder, P	PA	215
EDM	Swerdloff, R	CA	226

Reproductive Genetics

Spec	Name	St	Pg
CG	Ward, J	TN	159
MF	Dugoff, L	PA	434
MF	Eddleman, K	NY	434
MF	Wenstrom, K	RI	433
ObG	Byrne, J	UT	566
ObG	Evans, M	NY	561
U	Oates, R	MA	1187

Reproductive Surgery

Spec	Name	St	Pg
RE	Azziz, R	GA	1045
RE	Coddington, C	MN	1047
RE	Licciardi, F	NY	1043
RE	Milad, M	IL	1048
RE	Moffitt, D	AZ	1050
RE	Odem, R	MO	1048
RE	Session, D	GA	1046

Respiratory Distress Syndrome (ARDS)

Spec	Name	St	Pg
Pul	Arroliga, A	TX	968
Pul	Christman, B	TN	961
Pul	Donahoe, M	PA	957
Pul	Hyers, T	MO	965
Pul	Wheeler, A	TN	964
Pul	Wiedemann, H	OH	967

Respiratory Distress Syndrome (RDS)

Spec	Name	St	Pg
NP	Cole, F	MO	451
NP	Donn, S	MI	452
NP	Lawson, E	MD	449
NP	Seidner, S	TX	453

Respiratory Failure

Spec	Name	St	Pg
PCCM	Perez Fontan, J	TX	756
PCCM	Schwarz, A	CA	756
PCCM	Thompson, A	PA	755
PPul	Green, T	IL	809
Pul	Balk, R	IL	964
Pul	Celli, B	MA	954
Pul	Deitz, J	PA	957
Pul	Hall, J	IL	964
Pul	Heffner, J	OR	970
Pul	Ingbar, D	MN	965
Pul	Niederman, M	NY	958
Pul	Strollo, P	PA	960
Pul	Thomashow, B	NY	960
T&CS	Zwischenberger, J	KY	1166

Restless Legs Syndrome

Spec	Name	St	Pg
N	Sethi, K	GA	527
Psyc	Doghramji, K	PA	924

Retina-Artificial

Spec	Name	St	Pg
Oph	Del Priore, L	SC	588

Retina/Vitreous Consultation

Spec	Name	St	Pg
Oph	Barile, G	NY	576

Retina/Vitreous Surgery

Spec	Name	St	Pg
Oph	Abrams, G	MI	593
Oph	Brucker, A	PA	576
Oph	Campochiaro, P	MD	576
Oph	Chang, S	NY	577
Oph	Davis, J	FL	587
Oph	De Juan, E	CA	605
Oph	Flynn, H	FL	588
Oph	Gentile, R	NY	579
Oph	Haller, J	PA	579
Oph	Ho, A	PA	580
Oph	Humayun, M	CA	606
Oph	Lim, J	IL	597
Oph	Meredith, T	NC	590
Oph	Mieler, W	IL	597
Oph	Muldoon, T	NY	582
Oph	Prenner, J	NJ	583
Oph	Pulido, J	MN	598
Oph	Rosenfeld, P	FL	591
Oph	Schachat, A	OH	599
Oph	Spaide, R	NY	585
Oph	Trese, M	MI	600
Oph	Yannuzzi, L	NY	586

Retinal Detachment

Spec	Name	St	Pg
Oph	D'Amico, D	NY	577
Oph	Del Priore, L	SC	588
Oph	Hariprasad, S	IL	595
Oph	Lim, J	IL	597
Oph	Olsen, T	GA	590
Oph	Petersen, M	OH	598
Oph	Prenner, J	NJ	583

Spec	Name	St	Pg
Oph	Rosenfeld, P	FL	591
Oph	Schiff, W	NY	584
Oph	Schwartz, S	CA	609
Oph	Shabto, U	NY	584

Retinal Disorders

Spec	Name	St	Pg
Oph	Barile, G	NY	576
Oph	Blumenkranz, M	CA	604
Oph	Bressler, N	MD	576
Oph	Bressler, S	MD	576
Oph	Brown, G	PA	576
Oph	Brucker, A	PA	576
Oph	Chang, S	NY	577
Oph	D'Amico, D	NY	577
Oph	Duker, J	MA	574
Oph	Edwards, P	MI	594
Oph	Freeman, W	CA	606
Oph	Friberg, T	PA	578
Oph	Fuchs, W	NY	578
Oph	Gentile, R	NY	579
Oph	Gorin, M	CA	606
Oph	Grossniklaus, H	GA	588
Oph	Haller, J	PA	579
Oph	Hariprasad, S	IL	595
Oph	Heckenlively, J	MI	595
Oph	Humayun, M	CA	606
Oph	Lewis, R	TX	602
Oph	Maguire, J	PA	581
Oph	Marmor, M	CA	607
Oph	Mets, M	IL	597
Oph	Miller, J	MA	574
Oph	Murray, T	FL	590
Oph	Odel, J	NY	583
Oph	Puliafito, C	CA	608
Oph	Regillo, C	PA	583
Oph	Schwartz, S	CA	609
Oph	Spaide, R	NY	585
Oph	Stone, E	IA	599
Oph	Vander, J	PA	586
Oph	Walsh, J	NY	586
Oph	Williams, G	MI	600

Retinal Disorders-Inherited

Spec	Name	St	Pg
Oph	Fishman, G	IL	595
Oph	Sadda, S	CA	608

Retinal Disorders-Pediatric

Spec	Name	St	Pg
Oph	Duker, J	MA	574
Oph	Olsen, T	GA	590
Oph	Stout, J	OR	609
Oph	Trese, M	MI	600

Retinal Drug Toxicity

Spec	Name	St	Pg
Oph	Marmor, M	CA	607

Retinal Dystrophies

Spec	Name	St	Pg
Oph	Heckenlively, J	MI	595
Oph	Marmor, M	CA	607

Retinal Vascular Diseases

Spec	Name	St	Pg
Oph	Brown, G	PA	576
Oph	Haller, J	PA	579
Oph	Humayun, M	CA	606
Oph	Sadda, S	CA	608

Retinitis Pigmentosa

Spec	Name	St	Pg
Oph	Fishman, G	IL	595

Retinoblastoma

Spec	Name	St	Pg
Oph	Abramson, D	NY	575
Oph	Augsburger, J	OH	593
Oph	Finger, P	NY	578
Oph	Handa, J	MD	579
Oph	Harbour, J	FL	589
Oph	Kim, J	CA	607
Oph	Murphree, A	CA	608
Oph	O'Brien, J	PA	582
Oph	Shields, C	PA	584
Oph	Shields, J	PA	585
Oph	Stout, J	OR	609
Oph	Wilson, M	TN	592
PHO	Dunkel, I	NY	772
PHO	Friedman, D	TN	778
PHO	Olson, T	GA	780
PHO	Pendergrass, T	WA	791
PHO	Rodriguez-Galindo, C	MA	770
PHO	Rubin, C	IL	785

Retinopathy of Prematurity

Spec	Name	St	Pg
NP	Hendricks-Munoz, K	VA	451
Oph	Freedman, S	NC	588
Oph	McDonnell, J	IL	597
Oph	Nussbaum, J	GA	590
Oph	Quinn, G	PA	583
Oph	Reynolds, J	NY	583
Oph	Shabto, U	NY	584
Oph	Siatkowski, R	OK	603
Oph	Stout, J	OR	609
Oph	Vander, J	PA	586

Retroperitoneal Fibrosis

Spec	Name	St	Pg
Rhu	Solitar, B	NY	1062

Rhabdomyosarcoma

Spec	Name	St	Pg
PHO	Adamson, P	PA	771
PHO	Hawkins, D	WA	790
PHO	Wexler, L	NY	777

Rheumatic Diseases of Childhood

Spec	Name	St	Pg
PMR	Sisung, C	IL	870

Rheumatic Heart Disease

Spec	Name	St	Pg
PCd	Cooper, R	NY	748

Rheumatoid Arthritis

Spec	Name	St	Pg
PRhu	Lehman, T	NY	812
Rhu	Adams, E	IL	1064
Rhu	Albert, D	NH	1058
Rhu	Belmont, H	NY	1059
Rhu	Blume, R	NY	1059
Rhu	Bobrove, A	CA	1067
Rhu	Bunning, R	DC	1059
Rhu	Chang, R	IL	1064
Rhu	Chatham, W	AL	1063
Rhu	Coblyn, J	MA	1058
Rhu	Crofford, L	TN	1063
Rhu	Curran, J	IL	1065
Rhu	Davis, W	LA	1066
Rhu	Ehresmann, G	CA	1067
Rhu	Fields, T	NY	1060
Rhu	Gershwin, M	CA	1067
Rhu	Hochberg, M	MD	1060
Rhu	Hugenberg, S	IN	1065
Rhu	Katz, R	IL	1065
Rhu	Kay, J	MA	1058
Rhu	Kimberly, R	AL	1064
Rhu	Lawry, G	CA	1068
Rhu	Lindsey, S	LA	1067
Rhu	Luthra, H	MN	1065
Rhu	Magid, S	NY	1061
Rhu	Massarotti, E	MA	1058
Rhu	McCune, W	MI	1065
Rhu	Mitnick, H	NY	1061
Rhu	Moder, K	MN	1066
Rhu	Moore, W	GA	1064
Rhu	O'Dell, J	NE	1066
Rhu	Paget, S	NY	1061
Rhu	Pope, R	IL	1066
Rhu	Rothenberg, R	MD	1062
Rhu	Salmon, J	NY	1062
Rhu	Schoen, R	CT	1058
Rhu	Shadick, N	MA	1059
Rhu	Simms, R	MA	1059
Rhu	Solomon, G	NY	1062
Rhu	Wallace, D	CA	1068
Rhu	Weinblatt, M	MA	1059
Rhu	Weinstein, A	DC	1063
Rhu	Wise, C	VA	1064
Rhu	Wofsy, D	CA	1068

Rheumatologic Dermatology

Spec	Name	St	Pg
D	Jorizzo, J	NC	193

Rheumatologic Diseases of the Lung

Spec	Name	St	Pg
Pul	Steiger, D	NY	959

Rheumatology

Spec	Name	St	Pg
A&I	DeShazo, R	MS	82
Ger	Cooney, L	CT	264
IM	Fischbein, L	MO	427
Rhu	Adams, E	IL	1064
Rhu	Albert, D	NH	1058
Rhu	Allen, N	NC	1063

Spec	Name	St	Pg
Rhu	Allman, R	PA	1059
Rhu	Belmont, H	NY	1059
Rhu	Blume, R	NY	1059
Rhu	Bobrove, A	CA	1067
Rhu	Brasington, R	MO	1064
Rhu	Bunning, R	DC	1059
Rhu	Buyon, J	NY	1060
Rhu	Chang, R	IL	1064
Rhu	Chang-Miller, A	AZ	1066
Rhu	Chatham, W	AL	1063
Rhu	Clements, P	CA	1067
Rhu	Coblyn, J	MA	1058
Rhu	Crofford, L	TN	1063
Rhu	Cupps, T	DC	1060
Rhu	Curran, J	IL	1065
Rhu	Davis, W	LA	1066
Rhu	Ehresmann, G	CA	1067
Rhu	Farber, M	NY	1060
Rhu	Fields, T	NY	1060
Rhu	Fife, R	IN	1065
Rhu	Gershwin, M	CA	1067
Rhu	Gorevic, P	NY	1060
Rhu	Gourley, M	MD	1060
Rhu	Hadler, N	NC	1063
Rhu	Hochberg, M	MD	1060
Rhu	Hugenberg, S	IN	1065
Rhu	Katz, R	IL	1065
Rhu	Kay, J	MA	1058
Rhu	Kimberly, R	AL	1064
Rhu	Lahita, R	NJ	1060
Rhu	Langford, C	OH	1065
Rhu	Lawry, G	CA	1068
Rhu	Lindsey, S	LA	1067
Rhu	Lipstate, J	LA	1067
Rhu	Luggen, M	OH	1065
Rhu	Luthra, H	MN	1065
Rhu	Magid, S	NY	1061
Rhu	Manzi, S	PA	1061
Rhu	Massarotti, E	MA	1058
Rhu	Mayes, M	TX	1067
Rhu	McAlindon, T	MA	1058
Rhu	McCune, W	MI	1065
Rhu	Mease, P	WA	1068
Rhu	Medsger, T	PA	1061
Rhu	Merkel, P	PA	1061
Rhu	Mitnick, H	NY	1061
Rhu	Moder, K	MN	1066
Rhu	Moore, W	GA	1064
Rhu	O'Dell, J	NE	1066
Rhu	Oddis, C	PA	1061
Rhu	Paget, S	NY	1061
Rhu	Peng, S	WA	1068
Rhu	Petri, M	MD	1061
Rhu	Pope, R	IL	1066
Rhu	Rothenberg, R	MD	1062
Rhu	Salmon, J	NY	1062
Rhu	Schoen, R	CT	1058
Rhu	Schubert, R	DC	1062
Rhu	Sergent, J	TN	1064
Rhu	Sessoms, S	TX	1067
Rhu	Seton, M	MA	1058
Rhu	Shadick, N	MA	1059
Rhu	Silver, R	SC	1064
Rhu	Simms, R	MA	1059
Rhu	Solitar, B	NY	1062
Rhu	Solomon, G	NY	1062
Rhu	Spiera, H	NY	1062
Rhu	Starz, T	PA	1062
Rhu	Steen, V	DC	1062
Rhu	Tsokos, G	MA	1059
Rhu	Varga, J	IL	1066
Rhu	Vivino, F	PA	1063
Rhu	Wallace, D	CA	1068
Rhu	Warner, A	MO	1066
Rhu	Weinblatt, M	MA	1059
Rhu	Weinstein, A	DC	1063
Rhu	Wener, M	WA	1068
Rhu	Wigley, F	MD	1063
Rhu	Wise, C	VA	1064
Rhu	Wofsy, D	CA	1068

Rhinitis

Spec	Name	St	Pg
A&I	Buchbinder, E	NY	80
A&I	Freeman, T	TX	85
A&I	Kaliner, M	MD	81
A&I	Lieberman, P	TN	82
A&I	Lockey, R	FL	82
A&I	Pacin, M	FL	83
A&I	Sanders, G	MI	84
A&I	Tamaroff, M	CA	86
Oto	Lanza, D	FL	679
Oto	Naclerio, R	IL	686
Oto	Rice, D	CA	696
Oto	Stringer, S	MS	681
PA&I	Kelly, C	VA	745
PA&I	Skoner, D	PA	744

Rhinoplasty

Spec	Name	St	Pg
Oto	Denenberg, S	NE	690
Oto	Farrior, E	FL	678
Oto	Gliklich, R	MA	665
Oto	Kriet, J	KS	690
Oto	Larrabee, W	WA	695
Oto	Papel, I	MD	673
Oto	Pribitkin, E	PA	674
Oto	Quatela, V	NY	674
Oto	Ries, W	TN	680
Oto	Setzen, M	NY	675
Oto	Shockley, W	NC	681
Oto	Szachowicz, E	MN	688
Oto	Toriumi, D	IL	688
PlS	Aston, S	NY	880
PlS	Barone, C	TX	898
PlS	Burstein, F	GA	889
PlS	Byrd, H	TX	898
PlS	Cohen, S	CA	901
PlS	Constantian, M	NH	878
PlS	Daniel, R	CA	902
PlS	Fisher, G	CA	902
PlS	Gallico, G	MA	878
PlS	Grotting, J	AL	890
PlS	Hamra, S	TX	899
PlS	Herman, C	PA	882
PlS	Hidalgo, D	NY	882
PlS	Hurwitz, D	PA	883
PlS	Matarasso, A	NY	884
PlS	Menick, F	AZ	899
PlS	Metzinger, S	LA	900
PlS	Moses, M	LA	900
PlS	Mustoe, T	IL	895
PlS	Orgill, D	MA	878
PlS	Rohrich, R	TX	900
PlS	Stuzin, J	FL	891
PlS	Sullivan, P	RI	879
PlS	Tabbal, N	NY	887
PlS	Tebbetts, J	TX	900
PlS	Thaller, S	FL	891
PlS	Winters, R	NJ	888
PlS	Zins, J	OH	897

Rhinoplasty Revision

Spec	Name	St	Pg
Oto	Josephson, J	NY	671
Oto	Kuhn, F	GA	679
PlS	LaBruna, A	NY	883

Rhinosinusitis

Spec	Name	St	Pg
A&I	Bernstein, D	OH	83
A&I	Lewis, J	AZ	85
A&I	Wong, J	MA	80
Oto	Schaitkin, B	PA	675
Oto	Stankiewicz, J	IL	688

Rhinosinusitis & Asthma

Spec	Name	St	Pg
A&I	Shepherd, G	NY	81

Robotic Cardiac Surgery

Spec	Name	St	Pg
T&CS	Argenziano, M	NY	1150
T&CS	Boyd, W	CA	1177
T&CS	Brunsting, L	AL	1161
T&CS	Chitwood, W	NC	1161
T&CS	DeFilippi, V	CA	1178
T&CS	DeRose, J	NY	1151
T&CS	Filsoufi, F	NY	1152
T&CS	Guber, M	CO	1173
T&CS	Guy, T	PA	1154
T&CS	Loulmet, D	NY	1156
T&CS	Smith, C	NY	1158
T&CS	Stuart, R	MO	1171
T&CS	Woo, Y	PA	1160

Robotic Hysterectomy

Spec	Name	St	Pg
ObG	Visco, A	NC	563

Robotic Surgery

Spec	Name	St	Pg
CRS	Fleshman, J	TX	176
CRS	Orkin, B	IL	174
GO	Alvarez, R	AL	280
GO	Barakat, R	NY	276
GO	Barter, J	MD	276
GO	Cantuaria, G	GA	281
GO	Cliby, W	MN	284
GO	Fields, A	DC	278

Spec	Name	St	Pg
GO	Fowler, J	OH	284
GO	Lambrou, N	FL	282
GO	Magrina, J	AZ	289
GO	Martino, M	PA	279
GO	Moore, D	IN	285
GO	Muntz, H	WA	291
GO	Muto, M	MA	275
GO	Poliakoff, S	FL	283
GO	Potkul, R	IL	285
GO	Randall, T	PA	280
GO	Silasi, D	CT	275
GO	Spann, C	GA	283
GO	Steren, A	MD	280
NS	Theodore, N	AZ	497
ObG	Bartholomew, D	OH	563
ObG	Cornella, J	AZ	566
ObG	Hale, D	IN	565
ObG	Sanz, L	VA	563
OrS	Kress, K	GA	637
Oto	Caruana, S	NY	668
Oto	Weinstein, G	PA	677
Ped Uro	Elder, J	MI	827
PS	Jackson, R	AR	822
PS	Jennings, R	MA	814
PS	Krummel, T	CA	823
S	Bouvet, M	CA	1130
S	Newman, E	NY	1097
S	Ridge, J	PA	1099
S	Talamini, M	CA	1137
T&CS	Bhora, F	NY	1151
T&CS	Del-Nido, P	MA	1146
T&CS	Feins, R	NC	1162
T&CS	Galloway, A	NY	1153
T&CS	Gharagozloo, F	AZ	1174
T&CS	Lazzaro, R	NY	1156
T&CS	Moore, J	GA	1163
T&CS	Murphy, D	GA	1164
T&CS	Park, B	NJ	1157
T&CS	Pass, H	NY	1157
T&CS	Yang, S	MD	1160
U	Andrews, P	AZ	1207
U	Balaji, K	NC	1197
U	Busby, J	SC	1197
U	Chen, D	PA	1189
U	Clayman, R	CA	1211
U	Gluckman, G	IL	1203
U	Hamilton, B	UT	1207
U	Hemal, A	NC	1198
U	Kavoussi, L	NY	1191
U	Koch, M	IN	1204
U	Kozlowski, J	IL	1204
U	Miller, S	GA	1199
U	Mohler, J	NY	1193
U	Palese, M	NY	1193
U	Parekh, D	FL	1199
U	Porter, C	WA	1213
U	Pruthi, R	NC	1200
U	Scherr, D	NY	1194
U	Singh, D	CT	1188
U	Strup, S	KY	1201
U	Su, L	FL	1201
U	Takayama, T	WA	1213
U	Uzzo, R	PA	1195
U	Wallen, E	NC	1201
U	Weiss, R	NJ	1196
U	Winfield, H	AL	1201
U	Wood, D	MI	1206

Robotic Surgery-Pediatric

Spec	Name	St	Pg
Ped Uro	Gundeti, M	IL	827
Ped Uro	Poppas, D	NY	825

RoboticSurgery

Spec	Name	St	Pg
T&CS	Yuh, D	CT	1149

Rocky Mountain Spotted Fever

Spec	Name	St	Pg
PInf	Givner, L	NC	794

Rosacea

Spec	Name	St	Pg
D	James, W	PA	189

Ross Procedure for Aortic Valve Disease

Spec	Name	St	Pg
T&CS	Fullerton, D	CO	1172
T&CS	Starnes, V	CA	1180

Rotator Cuff Surgery

Spec	Name	St	Pg
HS	Imbriglia, J	PA	298
OrS	Anderson, L	CA	649
OrS	Bigliani, L	NY	621
OrS	Diduch, D	VA	635
OrS	Endrizzi, D	ME	617
OrS	Flatow, E	NY	624
OrS	Goitz, H	MI	641
OrS	Green, A	RI	617
OrS	Iannotti, J	OH	641
OrS	Kaeding, C	OH	642
OrS	Matsen, F	WA	652
OrS	McFarland, E	MD	629
OrS	Medvecky, M	CT	618
OrS	Warren, R	NY	633
OrS	Wickiewicz, T	NY	634
OrS	Williams, G	PA	634
OrS	Yamaguchi, K	MO	646
OrS	Zarins, B	MA	619
OrS	Zuckerman, J	NY	635
SM	Bush-Joseph, C	IL	1077
SM	Fronek, J	CA	1079
SM	Richmond, J	MA	1074
SM	Rodosky, M	PA	1076

Running Injuries

Spec	Name	St	Pg
SM	Metzl, J	NY	1075

S

Salivary Gland Tumors

Spec	Name	St	Pg
Onc	Khuri, F	GA	359
Onc	Martins, R	WA	389
Oto	Blair, E	IL	683
Oto	Ferris, R	PA	669
Oto	Hanna, E	TX	692
Oto	Urken, M	NY	676
Oto	Weissler, M	NC	682
Oto	Yarbrough, W	CT	667
RadRO	Laramore, G	WA	996

Salivary Gland Tumors & Surgery

Spec	Name	St	Pg
Oto	Clayman, G	TX	691
Oto	Deschler, D	MA	665
Oto	Eisele, D	MD	669
Oto	Goldenberg, D	PA	670
Oto	Hoffman, H	IA	685
Oto	Lydiatt, W	NE	690
Oto	Olsen, K	MN	687
Oto	Rassekh, C	PA	674
Oto	Shockley, W	NC	681
Oto	Weber, R	TX	694
S	Shah, J	NY	1100

Sarcoidosis

Spec	Name	St	Pg
Pul	Donohue, J	NC	962
Pul	King, T	CA	971
Pul	Padilla, M	NY	958
Pul	Raghu, G	WA	971
Pul	Rose, C	CO	968
Pul	Rossman, M	PA	959
Pul	Staton, G	GA	963

Sarcoma

Spec	Name	St	Pg
Hem	Adams, R	AZ	325
Hem	Heinrich, M	OR	328
Hem	Milhem, M	IA	323
Onc	Benjamin, R	TX	379
Onc	Brockstein, B	IL	367
Onc	Conry, R	AL	357
Onc	Elias, A	CO	376
Onc	Ettinger, D	MD	342
Onc	Fitch, T	AZ	380
Onc	Grosh, W	VA	359
Onc	Hande, K	TN	359
Onc	Jacobs, C	CA	388
Onc	Kraft, A	SC	359
Onc	Maki, R	NY	347
Onc	Meyskens, F	CA	390
Onc	Patel, S	TX	382
Onc	Pavlick, A	NY	349
Onc	Samlowski, W	NV	392
Onc	Samuels, B	ID	377
Onc	Staddon, A	PA	352
Onc	Stewart, F	WA	393
Onc	Tap, W	NY	352
Onc	Verschraegen, C	VT	336
Onc	Von Burton, G	LA	384
Onc	von Mehren, M	PA	353

Spec	Name	St	Pg
OrS	Aboulafia, A	MD	620
OrS	Biermann, J	MI	639
OrS	Bos, G	WA	649
OrS	Healey, J	NY	625
OrS	Hornicek, F	MA	617
OrS	Malawer, M	MD	628
OrS	McDonald, D	MO	643
OrS	Scarborough, M	FL	638
OrS	Schwartz, H	TN	638
OrS	Sim, F	MN	645
OrS	Wurtz, L	IN	645
Oto	Kraus, D	NY	672
Path	Brooks, J	PA	720
Path	Fletcher, C	MA	718
Path	Goldblum, J	OH	728
Path	Patchefsky, A	PA	723
Path	Rubin, B	OH	729
Path	Triche, T	CA	734
Path	Weiss, S	GA	727
PHO	Albritton, K	TX	787
PHO	Arndt, C	MN	781
PHO	Link, M	CA	790
PHO	Marina, N	CA	790
PHO	Meyer, W	OK	788
PHO	Meyers, P	NY	775
PHO	Olson, T	GA	780
PHO	Rodriguez-Galindo, C	MA	770
PlS	Rockwell, W	UT	898
RadRO	Brizel, D	NC	984
RadRO	Constine, L	NY	978
RadRO	DeLaney, T	MA	976
RadRO	Donaldson, S	CA	995
RadRO	Hahn, S	PA	980
RadRO	Herman, T	OK	993
RadRO	Michalski, J	MO	991
RadRO	Pollack, A	FL	986
RadRO	Prosnitz, L	NC	986
RadRO	Tepper, J	NC	987
RadRO	Wara, W	CA	998
RadRO	Wolfson, A	FL	988
S	Brown, C	IL	1112
S	Dooley, W	OK	1124
S	Eilber, F	CA	1132
S	Eisenberg, B	NH	1085
S	Feig, B	TX	1125
S	Fraker, D	PA	1093
S	Gray, R	AZ	1125
S	Leitch, A	TX	1127
S	Levine, E	NC	1106
S	Li, B	LA	1127
S	Nakakura, E	CA	1134
S	Nathanson, S	MI	1117
S	Pollock, R	OH	1118
S	Sondak, V	FL	1109
S	Talamonti, M	IL	1120
S	Urist, M	AL	1110
S	Weber, S	WI	1121
S	White, R	NC	1110

Sarcoma-Soft Tissue

Spec	Name	St	Pg
Onc	Chow, W	CA	386
Onc	Forscher, C	CA	387
Onc	George, S	MA	332
Onc	Tap, W	NY	352
OrS	Benevenia, J	NJ	620
OrS	Buckwalter, J	IA	640
OrS	Healey, J	NY	625
OrS	Irwin, R	MI	641
OrS	Mayerson, J	OH	643
OrS	O'Donnell, R	CA	652
OrS	Randall, R	UT	647
OrS	Ready, J	MA	618
OrS	Schmidt, R	PA	632
OrS	Wittig, J	NY	634
Path	Antonescu, C	NY	720
PHO	Wexler, L	NY	777
RadRO	Awan, A	IL	988
RadRO	Landry, J	GA	985
RadRO	Pezner, R	CA	996
S	August, D	NJ	1089
S	Brady, M	NY	1090
S	Hanna, N	MD	1094
S	Heslin, M	AL	1105
S	Hunt, K	TX	1126
S	Huth, J	TX	1126
S	Pisters, P	TX	1127
S	Singer, S	NY	1101
T&CS	Putnam, J	TN	1165

Scalp Disorders

Spec	Name	St	Pg
D	Cotsarelis, G	PA	188

Scar Revision

Spec	Name	St	Pg
D	Alster, T	DC	186
D	Lask, G	CA	201

Schizophrenia

Spec	Name	St	Pg
Psyc	Adler, D	MA	920
Psyc	Davidson, J	TX	932
Psyc	Goff, D	NY	924
Psyc	Henderson, D	MA	921
Psyc	Hirschfeld, R	TX	932
Psyc	Marder, S	CA	933
Psyc	McIntosh, J	UT	931
Psyc	Weiner, R	NC	928

Scleroderma

Spec	Name	St	Pg
Cv	Follansbee, W	PA	92
PRhu	Haines, K	NJ	811
PRhu	Lehman, T	NY	812
PRhu	Myones, B	TX	813
Rhu	Clements, P	CA	1067
Rhu	Ehresmann, G	CA	1067
Rhu	Mayes, M	TX	1067
Rhu	Medsger, T	PA	1061
Rhu	Merkel, P	PA	1061
Rhu	Peng, S	WA	1068
Rhu	Simms, R	MA	1059
Rhu	Spiera, H	NY	1062
Rhu	Steen, V	DC	1062
Rhu	Varga, J	IL	1066
Rhu	Wallace, D	CA	1068
Rhu	Wigley, F	MD	1063

Scleroderma & Lung Disease

Spec	Name	St	Pg
Rhu	Silver, R	SC	1064

Scoliosis

Spec	Name	St	Pg
NS	Jenkins, A	NY	478
OrS	An, H	IL	639
OrS	Balderston, R	PA	620
OrS	Betz, R	PA	621
OrS	Boachie-Adjei, O	NY	621
OrS	Bridwell, K	MO	640
OrS	Cammisa, F	NY	622
OrS	Dormans, J	PA	623
OrS	Errico, T	NY	623
OrS	Feldman, D	NY	623
OrS	Goldstein, J	NY	624
OrS	Herman, M	PA	626
OrS	Hyman, J	NY	626
OrS	Kim, C	CA	652
OrS	Lauerman, W	DC	627
OrS	Lebwohl, N	FL	637
OrS	Lenke, L	MO	642
OrS	McAfee, P	MD	628
OrS	McCance, S	NY	629
OrS	Neuwirth, M	NY	629
OrS	Parazin, S	MA	618
OrS	Polly, D	MN	644
OrS	Roye, D	NY	631
OrS	Schafer, M	IL	644
OrS	Schwab, F	NY	632
OrS	Spivak, J	NY	632
OrS	Sponseller, P	MD	633
OrS	Thompson, G	OH	645
OrS	Weinstein, S	IA	645

Seizure Disorders

Spec	Name	St	Pg
ChiN	Kohrman, M	IL	148
N	Cloughesy, T	CA	539
N	DeGiorgio, C	CA	539
N	Labiner, D	AZ	537
N	Nicholl, J	LA	537

Seizure Disorders & Pregnancy

Spec	Name	St	Pg
MF	Greene, M	MA	432

Sentinel Node Surgery

Spec	Name	St	Pg
Oto	Pitman, K	AZ	693
S	Czerniecki, B	PA	1092
S	Essner, R	CA	1132
S	Giuliano, A	CA	1132
S	Hansen, N	IL	1114
S	Klimberg, V	AR	1126
S	Krag, D	VT	1086
S	Nowak, E	NY	1097
S	O'Hea, B	NY	1097
S	Ross, M	TX	1128
S	Saha, S	MI	1119
S	Tartter, P	NY	1101

Specialty & Special Expertise Index

Spec	Name	St	Pg

Sepsis

Spec	Name	St	Pg
PCCM	Schwarz, A	CA	756
PCCM	Zimmerman, J	WA	756
Pul	Christman, B	TN	961
Pul	Wheeler, A	TN	964

Septic Shock

Spec	Name	St	Pg
PCCM	Schwarz, A	CA	756
PCCM	Zimmerman, J	WA	756

Sex Cord-Stromal Tumors

Spec	Name	St	Pg
GO	Gershenson, D	TX	288

Sex Development Disorders

Spec	Name	St	Pg
PEn	Eugster, E	IN	760

Sexual Addiction

Spec	Name	St	Pg
Psyc	First, M	NY	924
Psyc	Kafka, M	MA	921

Sexual Anomalies

Spec	Name	St	Pg
PS	Graziano, K	AZ	822

Sexual Behavior-Compulsive

Spec	Name	St	Pg
Psyc	First, M	NY	924
Psyc	Kafka, M	MA	921
Psyc	Krueger, R	NY	925

Sexual Differentiation Disorders

Spec	Name	St	Pg
CG	Cunniff, C	AZ	161

Sexual Dysfunction

Spec	Name	St	Pg
EDM	Bhasin, S	MA	208
ObG	Levine, E	IL	565
ObG	Simon, J	DC	562
Psyc	Grant, J	IL	929
Psyc	Levine, S	OH	930
Psyc	Sadock, V	NY	927
U	Buch, J	TX	1208
U	Gribetz, M	NY	1190
U	Meacham, R	CO	1207
U	Milam, D	TN	1198
U	O'Leary, M	MA	1187
U	Seftel, A	NJ	1194

Sexual Dysfunction-Male & Female

Spec	Name	St	Pg
U	Goldstein, I	CA	1212

Sexual Health in Cancer Survivors

Spec	Name	St	Pg
Onc	Dizon, D	MA	331

Sexual Identity Issues

Spec	Name	St	Pg
Psyc	Eaton, J	DC	924
Psyc	Levine, S	OH	930

Sexually Transmitted Diseases

Spec	Name	St	Pg
AM	Chambers, C	PA	76
AM	Garofalo, R	IL	77
ObG	Levine, E	IL	565
ObG	Wiesenfeld, H	PA	562
PInf	Kotloff, K	MD	793

Short Bowel Syndrome

Spec	Name	St	Pg
PGe	Mittal, N	TX	768
PGe	Vanderhoof, J	NE	768
PS	Grikscheit, T	CA	823
PS	Warner, B	MO	821

Shoulder & Elbow Surgery

Spec	Name	St	Pg
OrS	Elattrache, N	CA	651
OrS	Thornhill, T	MA	619
SM	Gambardella, R	CA	1079
SM	Levine, W	NY	1075
SM	Mirzayan, R	CA	1079
SM	Paletta, G	MO	1078

Shoulder & Knee Injuries

Spec	Name	St	Pg
OrS	Schlegel, T	CO	647

Shoulder & Knee Reconstruction

Spec	Name	St	Pg
OrS	Lock, T	MI	642

Shoulder & Knee Surgery

Spec	Name	St	Pg
OrS	Gladstone, J	NY	624
OrS	Laurencin, C	CT	618
OrS	Nicholas, S	NY	629
OrS	Pettrone, F	VA	637
OrS	Schlegel, T	CO	647
SM	Ho, S	IL	1078
SM	Nisonson, B	NY	1076

Shoulder and Elbow Surgery

Spec	Name	St	Pg
OrS	Ahmad, C	NY	620

Shoulder Arthroscopic Surgery

Spec	Name	St	Pg
OrS	Craig, E	NY	622
OrS	Dines, D	NY	623
OrS	Flatow, E	NY	624
OrS	Fulkerson, J	CT	617
OrS	Hannafin, J	NY	625
OrS	Hungerford, M	MD	626
OrS	Miller, M	VA	637
SM	Miniaci, A	OH	1078
SM	Rodosky, M	PA	1076
SM	Williams, R	NY	1076

Shoulder Cartilage Implant

Spec	Name	St	Pg
OrS	Williams, G	PA	634

Shoulder Injuries

Spec	Name	St	Pg
OrS	Flatow, E	NY	624
OrS	Kaeding, C	OH	642
OrS	Karas, S	GA	636
OrS	Sethi, P	CT	619
OrS	Zarins, B	MA	619
SM	Burke, C	PA	1075
SM	Fronek, J	CA	1079
SM	Fu, F	PA	1075
SM	Gill, T	MA	1074
SM	Richmond, J	MA	1074
SM	Steiner, M	MA	1074
SM	Veitch, A	NM	1078

Shoulder Problems-Complex

Spec	Name	St	Pg
OrS	Romeo, A	IL	644

Shoulder Reconstruction

Spec	Name	St	Pg
HS	Mass, D	IL	303
HS	Szabo, R	CA	306
OrS	Diduch, D	VA	635
OrS	Kenter, K	OH	642
OrS	Nepola, J	IA	643
OrS	Romeo, A	IL	644
OrS	Williams, G	PA	634
SM	Ciccotti, M	PA	1075
SM	Garth, W	AL	1077
SM	Miniaci, A	OH	1078

Shoulder Replacement

Spec	Name	St	Pg
OrS	Craig, E	NY	622
OrS	Dines, D	NY	623
OrS	Flatow, E	NY	624
OrS	Matsen, F	WA	652
OrS	Plancher, K	NY	631
OrS	Siegel, H	AL	638
OrS	Thomas, B	CA	654
OrS	Warren, R	NY	633
OrS	Williams, G	PA	634
OrS	Wirth, M	TX	649

Shoulder Surgery

Spec	Name	St	Pg
HS	Badia, A	FL	300
HS	Carroll, C	IL	302
HS	Imbriglia, J	PA	298
HS	Seitz, W	OH	304
HS	Steinmann, S	MN	304
OrS	Bigliani, L	NY	621
OrS	Dines, D	NY	623
OrS	Endrizzi, D	ME	617
OrS	Glashow, J	NY	624
OrS	Green, A	RI	617
OrS	Iannotti, J	OH	641
OrS	Jokl, P	CT	617
OrS	Marx, R	NY	628

Spec	Name	St	Pg
OrS	McCann, P	NY	629
OrS	McFarland, E	MD	629
OrS	Medvecky, M	CT	618
OrS	Millett, P	CO	646
OrS	O'Driscoll, S	MN	644
OrS	Plancher, K	NY	631
OrS	Ramsey, M	PA	631
OrS	Warren, R	NY	633
OrS	Wickiewicz, T	NY	634
OrS	Wirth, M	TX	649
OrS	Yamaguchi, K	MO	646
OrS	Zuckerman, J	NY	635
SM	Altchek, D	NY	1074
SM	Andrews, J	FL	1076
SM	Bach, B	IL	1077
SM	Bradley, J	PA	1075
SM	Kaplan, L	FL	1077
SM	Ma, C	CA	1079
SM	Rodeo, S	NY	1076
SM	Scheller, A	MA	1074
SM	Taft, T	NC	1077
SM	Xerogeanes, J	GA	1077

Shoulder Surgery-Complex

OrS	Seltzer, D	AZ	648

Sickle Cell Disease

Hem	Adams-Graves, P	TN	318
Hem	Bigelow, C	MS	318
Hem	Blinder, M	MO	321
Hem	Rondelli, D	IL	323
Hem	Telen, M	NC	320
Ped	Berman, B	MI	741
PHO	Bertolone, S	KY	777
PHO	Buchanan, G	TX	787
PHO	Cunningham, J	IL	782
PHO	Drachtman, R	NJ	772
PHO	Giardina, P	NY	773
PHO	Hord, J	OH	784
PHO	Hsu, L	IL	784
PHO	Kung, F	CA	790
PHO	Luchtman-Jones, L	DC	775
PHO	Sandler, E	FL	781
PHO	Tebbi, C	FL	781
PHO	Wang, W	TN	781
PHO	Weinblatt, M	NY	776

Sickle Cell Disease-Lung

Pul	Haynes, J	AL	962
Pul	Schraufnagel, D	IL	966

Single Port Surgery

S	Curcillo, P	PA	1091

Sinus Disorders

A&I	Benenati, S	FL	82
A&I	Chandler, M	NY	80
A&I	Ein, D	DC	81
A&I	Friedman, S	FL	82
A&I	Mazza, D	NY	81
A&I	Schubert, M	AZ	85
A&I	Slankard, M	NY	82
A&I	Tamaroff, M	CA	86
Oto	Baim, H	IL	683
Oto	Bhattacharyya, N	MA	665
Oto	Miller, F	TX	693
Oto	Newkirk, K	DC	673
Oto	Poole, M	GA	680
PO	April, M	NY	802
PO	Arjmand, E	OH	803
PO	Baroody, F	IL	804
PO	Cunningham, M	MA	801
PO	Darrow, D	VA	803
PO	Duncan, N	TX	805
PO	Haddad, J	NY	802
PO	Miller, R	IL	804
PO	Richardson, M	OR	806

Sinus Disorders/Surgery

Oto	Amedee, R	LA	691
Oto	Bolger, W	FL	677
Oto	Close, L	NY	668
Oto	DiNardo, L	VA	678
Oto	Fried, M	NY	669
Oto	Friedman, M	IL	684
Oto	Gold, S	NY	670
Oto	Jacobs, J	NY	671
Oto	Jones, J	NY	671
Oto	Kern, R	IL	686
Oto	Kim, D	MA	666
Oto	Lanza, D	FL	679
Oto	Lawson, W	NY	673
Oto	Metson, R	MA	666
Oto	Naclerio, R	IL	686
Oto	Otto, R	TX	693
Oto	Piccirillo, J	MO	687
Oto	Picken, C	DC	674
Oto	Rebeiz, E	MA	667
Oto	Rice, D	CA	696
Oto	Rosen, M	PA	674
Oto	Schaefer, S	NY	675
Oto	Schaitkin, B	PA	675
Oto	Senior, B	NC	681
Oto	Sillers, M	AL	681
Oto	Thaler, E	PA	676
Oto	Vining, E	CT	667
Oto	Weymuller, E	WA	698
PO	Bower, C	AR	805
PO	Katz, R	OH	804
PO	Lusk, R	NE	805
PO	Parikh, S	WA	806
PO	Rosbe, K	CA	806
PO	Rosenfeld, R	NY	803
PO	Ward, R	NY	803

Sinus Surgery-Revision

Oto	Jacobs, J	NY	671

Sinus Tumors

Oto	Bolger, W	FL	677
Oto	Har-El, G	NY	670
Oto	Koch, W	MD	672
Oto	O'Malley, B	PA	673
Oto	Snyderman, C	PA	676
Oto	Yoo, G	MI	689

Sinusitis

A&I	Altman, L	WA	85
A&I	Grammer, L	IL	83
A&I	Jost, B	MO	84
A&I	Kaliner, M	MD	81
PA&I	Kelly, C	VA	745
PO	Chan, K	CO	805
PO	Lusk, R	NE	805

Sjogren's Syndrome

Rhu	Curran, J	IL	1065
Rhu	Pope, R	IL	1066
Rhu	Vivino, F	PA	1063
Rhu	Wise, C	VA	1064

Skeletal Dysplasia

CG	Wilcox, W	CA	164

Skin Cancer

D	Amonette, R	TN	191
D	Arpey, C	MN	194
D	Bailin, P	OH	194
D	Bennett, R	CA	200
D	Berg, D	WA	200
D	Bolognia, J	CT	184
D	Bondi, E	PA	187
D	Braun, M	DC	187
D	Brodland, D	PA	187
D	Bronin, A	NY	187
D	Brown, M	NY	187
D	Carney, J	AR	198
D	Cook, J	NC	192
D	Crutchfield, C	MN	195
D	Dufresne, R	RI	184
D	Duvic, M	TX	198
D	Dzubow, L	PA	188
D	Eichler, C	FL	192
D	Fenske, N	FL	192
D	Fosko, S	MO	195
D	Garrett, A	VA	192
D	Geronemus, R	NY	188
D	Gilchrest, B	MA	185
D	Green, H	FL	192
D	Greenbaum, S	PA	188
D	Greenway, H	CA	201
D	Grichnik, J	FL	193
D	Halpern, A	NY	188
D	Johnson, T	MI	195
D	Kim, Y	CA	201
D	Kriegel, D	NY	189
D	Krunic, A	IL	196

Spec	Name	St	Pg
D	Kupper, T	MA	185
D	Lebwohl, M	NY	189
D	Leshin, B	NC	193
D	Lessin, S	PA	189
D	Lim, H	MI	196
D	Lim Quan, K	AZ	199
D	Linder, J	AZ	199
D	Lowitt, M	MD	189
D	Maloney, M	MA	185
D	McMichael, A	NC	193
D	Miller, S	MD	189
D	Neel, V	MA	185
D	Neuburg, M	WI	196
D	Nghiem, P	WA	201
D	Nigra, T	DC	189
D	Nouri, K	FL	193
D	Olbricht, S	MA	186
D	Orengo, I	TX	199
D	Otley, C	MN	196
D	Pitts, J	AZ	199
D	Prioleau, P	NY	190
D	Ramsay, D	NY	190
D	Ratner, D	NY	190
D	Richardson, T	CA	201
D	Rigel, D	NY	190
D	Russell, M	VA	193
D	Sobel, S	FL	194
D	Sokoloff, D	FL	194
D	Stern, R	MA	186
D	Swanson, N	OR	202
D	Swetter, S	CA	202
D	Taylor, R	TX	199
D	Thiers, B	SC	194
D	Tsao, H	MA	186
D	Wood, G	WI	197
D	Zitelli, J	PA	191
Onc	Biggs, D	DE	338
Onc	Daud, A	CA	386
Onc	Ernstoff, M	NH	331
Onc	Pavlick, A	NY	349
Onc	Sosman, J	TN	364
Oto	Shockley, W	NC	681
Oto	Weber, R	TX	694
Path	Bastian, B	CA	732
Path	Le Boit, P	CA	733
Path	Lowe, L	MI	728
Path	Prieto, V	TX	730
PlS	Manson, P	MD	884
RadRO	Cooper, J	NY	978
RadRO	Laramore, G	WA	996
RadRO	Machtay, M	OH	990
RadRO	Mittal, B	IL	991
RadRO	Morrison, W	TX	994
RadRO	Wilson, J	WI	992
RadRO	Wolfson, A	FL	988
S	Huth, J	TX	1126
S	Trisal, V	CA	1137

Skin Cancer in Transplant Patients

Spec	Name	St	Pg
D	Otley, C	MN	196

Skin Cancer Reconstruction

Spec	Name	St	Pg
PlS	Mast, B	FL	890

Skin Cancer-Consult by Referral Only

Spec	Name	St	Pg
D	Bickers, D	NY	187

Skin Cancer-Head & Neck

Spec	Name	St	Pg
D	Fewkes, J	MA	184
Onc	Posner, M	NY	350
Oto	Bradford, C	MI	684
PlS	Tufaro, A	MD	888

Skin Cancer/Facial Reconstruction

Spec	Name	St	Pg
Oto	Papel, I	MD	673

Skin Healing

Spec	Name	St	Pg
PlS	Garner, W	CA	902

Skin Laser Surgery

Spec	Name	St	Pg
D	Alster, T	DC	186
D	Arndt, K	MA	184
D	Arpey, C	MN	194
D	Avram, M	NY	186
D	Bailin, P	OH	194
D	Berg, D	WA	200
D	Burton, C	NC	191
D	Cohen, B	MD	187
D	Cook, J	NC	192
D	Dover, J	MA	184
D	Garden, J	IL	195
D	Glogau, R	CA	200
D	Grossman, M	NY	188
D	Hanke, C	IN	195
D	Hruza, G	MO	195
D	Leffell, D	CT	185
D	Pitts, J	AZ	199
D	Rubin, M	CA	202
D	Schultz, N	NY	190
D	Sobel, S	FL	194
D	Wheeland, R	AZ	199
D	Zelickson, B	MN	197
PlS	Gregory, R	FL	890

Skin Laser Surgery-Resurfacing

Spec	Name	St	Pg
D	Brody, H	GA	191
D	Fitzpatrick, R	CA	200
D	Kilmer, S	CA	201
D	Lask, G	CA	201
Oto	Branham, G	MO	684
Oto	Gliklich, R	MA	665
PlS	Stuzin, J	FL	891
PlS	Young, V	MO	897

Skin/Soft Tissue Infections

Spec	Name	St	Pg
Inf	Brause, B	NY	412
Inf	Edmond, M	VA	416

Skull Base Surgery

Spec	Name	St	Pg
NS	Al-Mefty, O	MA	472
NS	Bruce, J	NY	475
NS	Chandler, J	IL	489
NS	Chen, C	NY	475
NS	Couldwell, W	UT	494
NS	Eisenberg, H	MD	476
NS	Evans, J	PA	476
NS	Fenstermaker, R	NY	476
NS	Giannotta, S	CA	499
NS	Heilman, C	MA	473
NS	Heros, R	FL	485
NS	Khan, A	MD	478
NS	Kotapka, M	PA	479
NS	Krisht, A	AR	496
NS	Lemole, G	AZ	496
NS	Linskey, M	CA	500
NS	Martuza, R	MA	473
NS	Mickey, B	TX	497
NS	Nagib, M	MN	491
NS	Patel, S	SC	486
NS	Rock, J	MI	492
NS	Rosenblatt, S	IL	492
NS	Tamargo, R	MD	482
NS	Van Loveren, H	FL	488
NS	Wilson, J	NC	488
NS	Yonas, H	NM	498
Oto	Amedee, R	LA	691
Oto	Arriaga, M	LA	691
Oto	Browne, J	NC	678
Oto	Carey, J	MD	668
Oto	Civantos, F	FL	678
Oto	Day, T	SC	678
Oto	DiNardo, L	VA	678
Oto	Duckert, L	WA	695
Oto	Gantz, B	IA	685
Oto	Harris, J	CA	695
Oto	Holliday, M	MD	671
Oto	Jackler, R	CA	695
Oto	Kaplan, M	CA	695
Oto	Kingdom, T	CO	690
Oto	Lalwani, A	NY	672
Oto	McKenna, M	MA	666
Oto	Moe, K	WA	696
Oto	Rassekh, C	PA	674
Oto	Rebeiz, E	MA	667
Oto	Samant, S	TN	681
Oto	Stringer, S	MS	681
Oto	Tucci, D	NC	682
Oto	Wazen, J	FL	682
Oto	Weisman, R	CA	697
PO	Kazahaya, K	PA	802

Skull Base Tumors

Spec	Name	St	Pg
NS	Bilsky, M	NY	475
NS	Brem, H	MD	475
NS	Charbel, F	IL	489

Spec	Name	St	Pg
NS	Chen, C	NY	475
NS	Couldwell, W	UT	494
NS	Friedman, A	NC	484
NS	Golfinos, J	NY	477
NS	Grubb, R	MO	490
NS	Guthikonda, M	MI	490
NS	Harsh, G	CA	500
NS	Judy, K	PA	478
NS	Link, M	MN	491
NS	Mayberg, M	WA	501
NS	McDermott, M	CA	501
NS	Olivi, A	MD	480
NS	Olson, J	GA	486
NS	Parsa, A	IL	492
NS	Robertson, J	TN	486
NS	Sekhar, L	WA	501
NS	Sen, C	NY	481
NS	Thompson, R	TN	487
Oto	Blair, E	IL	683
Oto	Bojrab, D	MI	683
Oto	Califano, J	MD	668
Oto	Costantino, P	NY	669
Oto	Driscoll, C	MN	684
Oto	Har-El, G	NY	670
Oto	Hartig, G	WI	685
Oto	Haynes, D	TN	679
Oto	Hirsch, B	PA	670
Oto	Kraus, D	NY	672
Oto	Lanza, D	FL	679
Oto	Lavertu, P	OH	686
Oto	Levine, P	VA	679
Oto	Netterville, J	TN	680
Oto	O'Malley, B	PA	673
Oto	Olsen, K	MN	687
Oto	Pensak, M	OH	687
Oto	Persky, M	NY	674
Oto	Petruzzelli, G	GA	680
Oto	Smith, R	NE	691
Oto	Song, J	CO	691
Oto	Vining, E	CT	667
RadRO	Knisely, J	NY	981
RadRO	Machtay, M	OH	990
S	Shah, J	NY	1100

Skull Base Tumors & Surgery

Spec	Name	St	Pg
NS	Ames, C	CA	498
NS	Boggan, J	CA	498
NS	De Monte, F	TX	495
NS	Johnson, S	CO	494
NS	Liu, C	CA	500
NS	Morcos, J	FL	486
NS	Origitano, T	MT	494
NS	Spetzler, R	AZ	497
NS	Thompson, B	MI	493
Oto	Arts, H	MI	682
Oto	Chowdhury, K	CO	689
Oto	Futran, N	WA	695
Oto	Hanna, E	TX	692
Oto	Kennedy, D	PA	672
Oto	Kim, D	MA	666
Oto	Leonetti, J	IL	686
Oto	Marentette, L	MI	686
Oto	Nuss, D	LA	693
Oto	O'Leary, M	CA	696
Oto	Snyderman, C	PA	676
Oto	Wax, M	OR	697

Sleep Apnea

Spec	Name	St	Pg
Oto	Bhattacharyya, N	MA	665
Oto	Josephson, J	NY	671
PO	April, M	NY	802
PO	Goldsmith, A	NY	802

Sleep Disorders

Spec	Name	St	Pg
ChiN	Kohrman, M	IL	148
ChiN	Santos, C	DC	146
N	Gross, P	MA	511
Oto	Corey, J	IL	684
Oto	Senior, B	NC	681
PO	Dolitsky, J	NY	802
PPul	Gibson, R	WA	810
PPul	Kemp, J	MO	809
PPul	Tauber, D	PA	808
Psyc	Buysse, D	PA	923
Psyc	Wooten, V	OH	931

Sleep Disorders/Apnea

Spec	Name	St	Pg
ChiN	Kotagal, S	MN	149
N	Adornato, B	CA	538
N	Guilleminault, C	CA	540
N	Krumholz, A	MD	517
N	Nolan, B	FL	526
N	Saper, C	MA	512
Oto	Baim, H	IL	683
Oto	Edelstein, D	NY	669
Oto	Edelstein, D	NY	669
Oto	Hotaling, A	IL	686
Oto	Hurst, M	WV	671
Oto	Piccirillo, J	MO	687
Oto	Poole, M	GA	680
Oto	Senders, C	CA	697
Oto	Setzen, M	NY	675
Oto	Stewart, M	NY	676
Oto	Woodson, B	WI	689
Ped	Sheldon, S	IL	742
PO	Baroody, F	IL	804
PO	Bower, C	AR	805
PO	Lusk, R	NE	805
PPul	Givan, D	IN	808
PPul	Loughlin, G	NY	807
PPul	Marcus, C	PA	807
Psyc	Doghramji, K	PA	924
Pul	Burschtin, O	NY	956
Pul	Fletcher, E	IN	964
Pul	Greenberg, H	NY	957
Pul	Johnson, B	VA	962
Pul	Kaplan, J	KS	968
Pul	King, E	PA	957
Pul	LoRusso, T	VA	963
Pul	Millman, R	RI	955
Pul	Pack, A	PA	958
Pul	Schwab, R	PA	959
Pul	Strollo, P	PA	960
Pul	Vaughey, E	VA	963
Pul	Wallace, J	CA	972
Pul	White, D	MA	956

Sleep Disorders/Apnea/Snoring

Spec	Name	St	Pg
Oto	Friedman, M	IL	684
Oto	Johnson, J	PA	671
Oto	Krespi, Y	NY	672

Sleep Medicine

Spec	Name	St	Pg
N	Nolan, B	FL	526
Pul	Bijwadia, J	MN	964
Pul	Burschtin, O	NY	956
Pul	O'Donnell, A	DC	958

Small Bowel Cancer

Spec	Name	St	Pg
S	Butler, J	CA	1131

Smoking Cessation

Spec	Name	St	Pg
Pul	Levin, D	OK	969

Snoring/Sleep Apnea

Spec	Name	St	Pg
Oto	Graham, H	LA	692
Oto	Kern, R	IL	686
Oto	Setzen, M	NY	675

Soft Tissue Pathology

Spec	Name	St	Pg
Path	Goldblum, J	OH	728
Path	Montgomery, E	MD	723
Path	Schiller, A	HI	734
Path	Weiss, S	GA	727

Soft Tissue Radiation Necrosis

Spec	Name	St	Pg
PMR	King, R	GA	866

Soft Tissue Radiation Necrosis-Breast

Spec	Name	St	Pg
PMR	King, R	GA	866

Soft Tissue Tumors

Spec	Name	St	Pg
DR	Panicek, D	NY	1011
OrS	Aboulafia, A	MD	620
OrS	Gitelis, S	IL	641
OrS	Hornicek, F	MA	617
OrS	Lewis, V	TX	648
OrS	Mott, M	MI	643
OrS	O'Keefe, R	NY	630
OrS	Peabody, T	IL	644
OrS	Walling, A	FL	638
OrS	Ward, W	PA	633
Path	Fletcher, C	MA	718
Path	Kahn, L	NY	722

Spec	Name	St	Pg
Path	Lucas, D	MI	728

Solid Tumors

Spec	Name	St	Pg
Onc	Aisner, J	NJ	337
Onc	Bashevkin, M	NY	338
Onc	Belenkov, E	NY	338
Onc	Chachoua, A	NY	339
Onc	Kelly, W	PA	345
Onc	Logie, K	IN	371
Onc	Petruska, P	MO	372
Onc	Ratain, M	IL	373
PHO	Berg, S	TX	787
PHO	Croop, J	IN	782
PHO	Dome, J	DC	772
PHO	Frantz, C	DE	773
PHO	Guarini, L	NY	773
PHO	Halligan, G	PA	774
PHO	Hayani, A	IL	783
PHO	Helman, L	MD	774
PHO	Kuttesch, J	NM	788
PHO	Marcus, J	NY	775
PHO	Salvi, S	IL	785
PHO	Santana, V	TN	781
PHO	Williams, J	AZ	789
PS	Aiken, J	WI	819
PS	Alexander, F	NJ	815
S	Loggie, B	NE	1122

Spasticity & Movement Disorders

Spec	Name	St	Pg
NS	Kaufman, B	WI	490
NS	Piatt, J	DE	480
NS	Walker, M	UT	495
PM	Jasmin, L	OR	713

Spasticity Management

Spec	Name	St	Pg
N	Siddique, T	IL	533
PMR	Ballard, P	DC	863
PMR	Clairmont, A	OH	867
PMR	Esquenazi, A	PA	863
PMR	Francisco, G	TX	871
PMR	Glenn, M	MA	862
PMR	Ivanhoe, C	TX	871
PMR	Keen, M	IL	868
PMR	Kirshblum, S	NJ	864
PMR	Marino, R	PA	865
PMR	Mayer, N	PA	865
PMR	Miknevich, M	PA	865
PMR	Munin, M	PA	865
PMR	Stubblefield, M	NY	866
PMR	Webster, H	MA	862

Speech Disorders

Spec	Name	St	Pg
ChiN	Trauner, D	CA	152
N	Heilman, K	FL	525

Spina Bifida

Spec	Name	St	Pg
CG	Marion, R	NY	158
CG	Northrup, H	TX	162
NS	Anderson, R	NY	474
NS	Bierbrauer, K	OH	489
NS	Cherny, W	ID	494
NS	Dias, M	PA	476
NS	Selden, N	OR	502
Ped Uro	Brock, J	TN	825
PMR	Alexander, J	NC	866
PMR	Cardenas, D	FL	866
PMR	Evans, S	DC	863
PS	Farmer, D	CA	823

Spina Bifida-Adult

Spec	Name	St	Pg
PMR	Kirschner, K	IL	869

Spinal Cord Disorders

Spec	Name	St	Pg
N	Engstrom, J	CA	539
N	Levine, D	NY	518
PM	Audell, L	CA	712

Spinal Cord Injury

Spec	Name	St	Pg
NRad	Dillon, W	CA	1026
NRad	Faro, S	PA	1020
NRad	Quencer, R	FL	1023
NS	Adelson, P	AZ	495
NS	Green, B	FL	484
NS	Harrop, J	PA	477
NS	Levi, A	FL	485
NS	Shapiro, S	IN	493
NS	Traynelis, V	IL	493
OrS	Abdu, W	NH	616
OrS	Chapman, J	WA	650
OrS	Hecht, A	NY	625
OrS	Vaccaro, A	PA	633
OrS	Wang, J	CA	654
PMR	Ahn, J	NY	862
PMR	Ballard, P	DC	863
PMR	Bloch, R	MA	862
PMR	Cardenas, D	FL	866
PMR	Chen, D	IL	867
PMR	Colachis, S	OH	868
PMR	Creamer, M	FL	866
PMR	Fried, G	PA	864
PMR	Frost, F	OH	868
PMR	Gater, D	PA	864
PMR	Gittler, M	IL	868
PMR	Harris, D	TX	871
PMR	King, J	TX	871
PMR	Kirshblum, S	NJ	864
PMR	Marino, R	PA	865
PMR	McKinley, W	VA	867
PMR	McLain, A	AL	867
PMR	Nobunaga, A	OH	869
PMR	Ragnarsson, K	NY	865
PMR	Volshteyn, O	MO	870
PMR	Zafonte, R	MA	862

Spinal Cord Injury & Colonic Motility

Spec	Name	St	Pg
Ge	Korsten, M	NY	237

Spinal Cord Injury-Pediatric

Spec	Name	St	Pg
HS	Kozin, S	PA	298
OrS	Betz, R	PA	621
PMR	Massagli, T	WA	872

Spinal Cord Stimulation

Spec	Name	St	Pg
PM	Bedder, M	WA	712
PM	Christo, P	MD	706
PM	Ferrante, F	CA	712
PM	Jasmin, L	OR	713
PM	Lubenow, T	IL	710
PM	Noe, C	TX	711
PM	Prager, J	CA	713
PM	Rauck, R	NC	709
PM	Rosner, H	CA	713
PM	Ross, E	MA	706

Spinal Cord Surgery

Spec	Name	St	Pg
NS	Kim, J	MS	485
NS	Kobrine, A	DC	479

Spinal Cord Tumors

Spec	Name	St	Pg
N	Schiff, D	VA	527
NRad	Lis, E	NY	1021
NRad	Sze, G	CT	1020
NS	Ames, C	CA	498
NS	Bilsky, M	NY	475
NS	Chiocca, E	MA	472
NS	Edwards, M	CA	499
NS	Harrop, J	PA	477
NS	Kaiser, M	NY	478
NS	Lavyne, M	NY	479
NS	Moore, F	NJ	480
NS	Quigley, M	PA	481
NS	Shaffrey, M	VA	487
Onc	Chang, S	CA	385
PHO	Gururangan, S	NC	779
PMR	Stewart, P	AL	867

Spinal Cord Tumors-Pediatric

Spec	Name	St	Pg
NS	Ragheb, J	FL	486

Spinal Deformity

Spec	Name	St	Pg
OrS	Albert, T	PA	620
OrS	Bitan, F	NY	621
OrS	Bridwell, K	MO	640
OrS	Garfin, S	CA	651
OrS	Lebwohl, N	FL	637
OrS	Lenke, L	MO	642
OrS	Neuwirth, M	NY	629
OrS	Richardson, W	NC	637
OrS	Schwab, F	NY	632
OrS	Weinstein, S	IA	645

Spinal Deformity-Pediatric

Spec	Name	St	Pg
OrS	Betz, R	PA	621
OrS	Sponseller, P	MD	633
OrS	Thompson, G	OH	645

Spinal Deformity-Pediatric & Adult

Spec	Name	St	Pg
OrS	Lauerman, W	DC	627

Spinal Disc Replacement

Spec	Name	St	Pg
NS	Haid, R	GA	485
NS	Hartl, R	NY	477
NS	Kaiser, M	NY	478
NS	Sekhon, L	NV	501
OrS	Balderston, R	PA	620
OrS	Bitan, F	NY	621
OrS	Boden, S	GA	635
OrS	Cammisa, F	NY	622
OrS	Cappuccino, A	NY	622
OrS	Carragee, E	CA	650
OrS	Delamarter, R	CA	650
OrS	Goldstein, J	NY	624
OrS	Richardson, W	NC	637
OrS	Watkins, R	CA	654

Spinal Disorders

Spec	Name	St	Pg
N	Swerdlow, M	NY	522
N	Weinberg, H	NY	522
NS	Anderson, R	NY	474
NS	Bailes, J	IL	488
NS	Chandler, J	IL	489
NS	Harrop, J	PA	477
NS	Huang, J	MD	478
NS	Kuntz, C	OH	490
NS	O'Rourke, D	PA	480
NS	Rigamonti, D	MD	481
NS	Weingart, J	MD	483
OrS	Abdu, W	NH	616
OrS	Boden, S	GA	635
OrS	Chapman, J	WA	650
OrS	Eismont, F	FL	636
OrS	Hochschuler, S	TX	648
PM	Baumann, P	GA	708
PM	Falco, F	DE	707
PM	Macadaeg, K	IN	710

Spinal Disorders-Degenerative

Spec	Name	St	Pg
NS	Bray, R	CA	499
NS	Hadley, M	AL	485
NS	Kotapka, M	PA	479
NS	Sekhon, L	NV	501
OrS	Balderston, R	PA	620
OrS	Bitan, F	NY	621
OrS	Farmer, J	NY	623

Spinal Imaging

Spec	Name	St	Pg
NRad	Haughton, V	WI	1023
NRad	Jarvik, J	WA	1026
NRad	Modic, M	OH	1024
NRad	Osborn, A	UT	1025
NRad	Russell, E	IL	1024

Spinal Microdiscectomy

Spec	Name	St	Pg
OrS	An, H	IL	639
OrS	Balderston, R	PA	620
OrS	Riew, K	MO	644

Spinal Muscular Atrophy (SMA)

Spec	Name	St	Pg
ChiN	DeVivo, D	NY	145

Spinal Reconstructive Surgery

Spec	Name	St	Pg
NS	Ames, C	CA	498
NS	Branch, C	NC	484
NS	El-Kadi, H	PA	476
NS	Gokaslan, Z	MD	477
NS	Whiting, D	PA	483
OrS	Boachie-Adjei, O	NY	621
OrS	Delamarter, R	CA	650
OrS	Lenke, L	MO	642
OrS	McAfee, P	MD	628

Spinal Rehabilitation

Spec	Name	St	Pg
PMR	Borg-Stein, J	MA	862
PMR	Feinberg, J	NY	864
PMR	Friedman, A	WA	872
PMR	Harris, D	TX	871
PMR	Herring, S	WA	872
PMR	Lutz, G	NY	864
PMR	Saal, J	CA	872
SM	Saint-Phard, D	CO	1078

Spinal Surgery

Spec	Name	St	Pg
NS	Bauer, J	IL	488
NS	Belzberg, A	MD	474
NS	Benzel, E	OH	489
NS	Bilsky, M	NY	475
NS	Bingaman, W	OH	489
NS	Borges, L	MA	472
NS	Caputy, A	DC	475
NS	Cosgrove, G	RI	472
NS	Di Giacinto, G	NY	476
NS	Diaz, F	MI	490
NS	El-Kadi, H	PA	476
NS	Fessler, R	IL	490
NS	Foley, K	TN	484
NS	Freeman, T	FL	484
NS	Green, B	FL	484
NS	Haid, R	GA	485
NS	Harper, R	TX	495
NS	Jenkins, A	NY	478
NS	Jho, H	PA	478
NS	Jimenez, D	TX	496
NS	Khan, A	MD	478
NS	Kim, D	TX	496
NS	Kobrine, A	DC	479
NS	Kuntz, C	OH	490
NS	Levi, A	FL	485
NS	Liker, M	CA	500
NS	Luken, M	IL	491
NS	McCormick, P	NY	480
NS	Moore, F	NJ	480
NS	Rodts, G	GA	487
NS	Rosenblum, M	MI	492
NS	Ryken, T	IA	492
NS	Sekhon, L	NV	501
NS	Shaffrey, C	VA	487
NS	Sun, P	CA	502
NS	Sundaresan, N	NY	482
NS	Swearingen, B	MA	474
NS	Traynelis, V	IL	493
NS	Welch, W	PA	483
NS	Wilson, J	NC	488
NS	Yu, J	CA	502
OrS	Abdu, W	NH	616
OrS	Albert, T	PA	620
OrS	An, H	IL	639
OrS	Boachie-Adjei, O	NY	621
OrS	Boden, S	GA	635
OrS	Brick, G	MA	616
OrS	Bridwell, K	MO	640
OrS	Cammisa, F	NY	622
OrS	Cappuccino, A	NY	622
OrS	Carragee, E	CA	650
OrS	Delamarter, R	CA	650
OrS	Donaldson, W	PA	623
OrS	Eismont, F	FL	636
OrS	Errico, T	NY	623
OrS	Farmer, J	NY	623
OrS	Feldman, D	NY	623
OrS	Garfin, S	CA	651
OrS	Goldstein, J	NY	624
OrS	Hecht, A	NY	625
OrS	Hilibrand, A	PA	626
OrS	Hochschuler, S	TX	648
OrS	Kim, C	CA	652
OrS	Lauerman, W	DC	627
OrS	Lebwohl, N	FL	637
OrS	Lenke, L	MO	642
OrS	McCance, S	NY	629
OrS	Neuwirth, M	NY	629
OrS	O'Leary, P	NY	630
OrS	Parazin, S	MA	618
OrS	Peterson, D	AK	653
OrS	Polly, D	MN	644
OrS	Richardson, W	NC	637
OrS	Sandhu, H	NY	632
OrS	Schafer, M	IL	644
OrS	Schwab, F	NY	632
OrS	Spengler, D	TN	638
OrS	Spivak, J	NY	632
OrS	Vaccaro, A	PA	633
OrS	Wang, J	CA	654
OrS	Watkins, R	CA	654
OrS	Wetzel, F	PA	634
OrS	Wiesel, S	DC	634
OrS	Yoo, J	OR	654
OrS	Zdeblick, T	WI	646

Spec	Name	St	Pg

Spinal Surgery-Cervical

Spec	Name	St	Pg
NS	Taylon, C	NE	494
OrS	Albert, T	PA	620
OrS	Chapman, J	WA	650
OrS	Hecht, A	NY	625
OrS	Hilibrand, A	PA	626
OrS	McAfee, P	MD	628
OrS	Riew, K	MO	644
OrS	Schuler, T	VA	638

Spinal Surgery-Complex

Spec	Name	St	Pg
NS	Bray, R	CA	499
NS	Gokaslan, Z	MD	477
NS	Hadley, M	AL	485
NS	Hartl, R	NY	477
NS	Kaiser, M	NY	478
NS	Zimmerman, C	ID	495

Spinal Surgery-Low Back

Spec	Name	St	Pg
NS	Taylon, C	NE	494
OrS	Schuler, T	VA	638

Spinal Surgery-Pediatric

Spec	Name	St	Pg
NS	Brockmeyer, D	UT	494
NS	Menezes, A	IA	491
NS	Shaffrey, C	VA	487
OrS	Dormans, J	PA	623

Spinal Surgery-Pediatric & Adult

Spec	Name	St	Pg
OrS	Bitan, F	NY	621

Spinal Trauma

Spec	Name	St	Pg
NS	Ames, C	CA	498
NS	Hartl, R	NY	477
NS	Rodts, G	GA	487
OrS	Eismont, F	FL	636
OrS	Hilibrand, A	PA	626
OrS	Richardson, W	NC	637
OrS	Vaccaro, A	PA	633
OrS	Wang, J	CA	654

Spinal Tumor Imaging

Spec	Name	St	Pg
DR	Elster, A	NC	1013
NRad	Koeller, K	MN	1023
NRad	Loevner, L	PA	1021
NRad	Murtagh, F	FL	1022

Spinal Tumors

Spec	Name	St	Pg
ChiN	Keating, G	MN	148
N	Glass, J	PA	516
N	Patchell, R	NJ	520
N	Phuphanich, S	CA	541
NS	Badie, B	CA	498
NS	Borges, L	MA	472
NS	Chen, T	CA	499
NS	El-Kadi, H	PA	476
NS	Gokaslan, Z	MD	477
NS	Green, B	FL	484
NS	Guthikonda, M	MI	490
NS	Harrop, J	PA	477
NS	Jenkins, A	NY	478
NS	McCormick, P	NY	480
NS	Rodts, G	GA	487
NS	Shaffrey, M	VA	487
NS	Shuer, L	CA	502
NS	Sun, P	CA	502
NS	Traynelis, V	IL	493
NS	Yu, J	CA	502
OrS	Eismont, F	FL	636
OrS	Wang, J	CA	654
OrS	Weinstein, J	NH	619
PHO	Cohen, K	MD	772

Spine Imaging & Intervention

Spec	Name	St	Pg
NRad	Khandji, A	NY	1020

Spleen Pathology

Spec	Name	St	Pg
Path	Arber, D	CA	731
Path	Orazi, A	NY	723

Spondylitis

Spec	Name	St	Pg
Rhu	Hadler, N	NC	1063

Spondyloarthritis-Consult

Spec	Name	St	Pg
Rhu	Chang-Miller, A	AZ	1066

Spondyloarthropathies

Spec	Name	St	Pg
PRhu	Schanberg, L	NC	812
Rhu	Adams, E	IL	1064

Sports Injuries

Spec	Name	St	Pg
HS	Belsky, M	MA	296
HS	Carlson, M	NY	297
HS	Friedman, D	FL	301
HS	Godzik, C	CA	306
HS	Graham, T	OH	303
HS	Lane, L	NY	299
HS	Rosenwasser, M	NY	300
NS	Sills, A	TN	487
SM	Kaplan, L	FL	1077
SM	Schechter, D	CA	1079
SM	Scheller, A	MA	1074
SM	Sennett, B	PA	1076
SM	Teitz, C	WA	1079

Sports Injuries-Foot & Ankle

Spec	Name	St	Pg
OrS	DiGiovanni, C	RI	616
OrS	Nunley, J	NC	637

Sports Medicine

Spec	Name	St	Pg
Cv	Bove, A	PA	91
OrS	Ahmad, C	NY	620
OrS	Albright, J	IA	639
OrS	Bartolozzi, A	PA	620
OrS	Bigliani, L	NY	621
OrS	Callaghan, J	IA	640
OrS	Cooper, D	TX	648
OrS	Craig, E	NY	622
OrS	Deland, J	NY	623
OrS	Diduch, D	VA	635
OrS	Dillingham, M	CA	650
OrS	Dines, D	NY	623
OrS	Elattrache, N	CA	651
OrS	Finerman, G	CA	651
OrS	Fulkerson, J	CT	617
OrS	Garrett, W	NC	636
OrS	Glashow, J	NY	624
OrS	Goitz, H	MI	641
OrS	Graf, B	WI	641
OrS	Heiden, E	UT	646
OrS	Johnson, D	KY	636
OrS	Jokl, P	CT	617
OrS	Kaeding, C	OH	642
OrS	Karas, S	GA	636
OrS	Kelly, B	NY	627
OrS	Kenter, K	OH	642
OrS	Kress, K	GA	637
OrS	Laurencin, C	CT	618
OrS	Lock, T	MI	642
OrS	Mandelbaum, B	CA	652
OrS	Marx, R	NY	628
OrS	McFarland, E	MD	629
OrS	Medvecky, M	CT	618
OrS	Miller, M	VA	637
OrS	Millett, P	CO	646
OrS	Nicholas, S	NY	629
OrS	O'Driscoll, S	MN	644
OrS	Pettrone, F	VA	637
OrS	Philippon, M	CO	646
OrS	Pizzutillo, P	PA	630
OrS	Poehling, G	NC	637
OrS	Ramsey, M	PA	631
OrS	Romeo, A	IL	644
OrS	Rosenberg, T	UT	647
OrS	Schafer, M	IL	644
OrS	Schlegel, T	CO	647
OrS	Scott, W	NY	632
OrS	Seltzer, D	AZ	648
OrS	Sethi, P	CT	619
OrS	Souryal, T	TX	649
OrS	Spindler, K	TN	638
OrS	Steadman, J	CO	647
OrS	Vo, P	FL	638
OrS	Watkins, R	CA	654
OrS	Wickiewicz, T	NY	634
PMR	Borg-Stein, J	MA	862
PMR	Feinberg, J	NY	864
PMR	Herring, S	WA	872
PMR	Lutz, C	NY	864
PMR	Lutz, G	NY	864
PMR	Press, J	IL	869
PMR	Saal, J	CA	872
SM	Altchek, D	NY	1074
SM	Andrews, J	FL	1076

Spec	Name	St	Pg
SM	Arendt, E	MN	1077
SM	Arendt, E	MN	1077
SM	Bach, B	IL	1077
SM	Bach, B	IL	1077
SM	Bradley, J	PA	1075
SM	Burke, C	PA	1075
SM	Bush-Joseph, C	IL	1077
SM	Byrd, J	TN	1076
SM	Ciccotti, M	PA	1075
SM	Fronek, J	CA	1079
SM	Fu, F	PA	1075
SM	Fu, F	PA	1075
SM	Gambardella, R	CA	1079
SM	Garth, W	AL	1077
SM	Gill, T	MA	1074
SM	Harner, C	PA	1075
SM	Hershman, E	NY	1075
SM	Ho, S	IL	1078
SM	Jones, D	LA	1078
SM	Kaplan, L	FL	1077
SM	Levine, W	NY	1075
SM	Ma, C	CA	1079
SM	Metzl, J	NY	1075
SM	Micheli, L	MA	1074
SM	Miniaci, A	OH	1078
SM	Mirzayan, R	CA	1079
SM	Nisonson, B	NY	1076
SM	Paletta, G	MO	1078
SM	Richmond, J	MA	1074
SM	Rodeo, S	NY	1076
SM	Rodosky, M	PA	1076
SM	Rodosky, M	PA	1076
SM	Saint-Phard, D	CO	1078
SM	Schechter, D	CA	1079
SM	Scheller, A	MA	1074
SM	Sennett, B	PA	1076
SM	Steiner, M	MA	1074
SM	Taft, T	NC	1077
SM	Taft, T	NC	1077
SM	Teitz, C	WA	1079
SM	Veitch, A	NM	1078
SM	Veitch, A	NM	1078
SM	Williams, R	NY	1076
SM	Xerogeanes, J	GA	1077

Sports Medicine Back Injuries

OrS	Schuler, T	VA	638
OrS	Spivak, J	NY	632

Sports Medicine Radiology

DR	Palmer, W	MA	1007
DR	Pavlov, H	NY	1011

Sports Medicine-Women

OrS	Hannafin, J	NY	625
SM	Saint-Phard, D	CO	1078

Sports Neurology

N	Jordan, B	NY	516

Staphylococcal Infections

Inf	Corey, G	NC	416

Steatohepatitis

Ge	Raiford, D	TN	244

Stem Cell Therapy

N	Kesari, S	CA	540

Stem Cell Therapy & Biosurgery

T&CS	Boyd, W	CA	1177

Stem Cell Therapy in Heart Failure

Cv	Hare, J	FL	98
IC	Mahmud, E	CA	128
IC	Perin, E	TX	127

Stem Cell Transplant

Hem	Adams, R	AZ	325
Hem	Champlin, R	TX	325
Hem	Comenzo, R	MA	312
Hem	Damon, L	CA	327
Hem	Farag, S	IN	321
Hem	Greer, J	TN	319
Hem	Lill, M	CA	328
Hem	Luger, S	PA	315
Hem	Maciejewski, J	OH	323
Hem	Maslak, P	NY	315
Hem	Rondelli, D	IL	323
Hem	Rowley, S	NJ	316
Hem	Savage, D	NY	316
Hem	Schwartzberg, L	TN	320
Hem	Slease, R	DE	317
Hem	Uberti, J	MI	324
Hem	Van Besien, K	NY	318
Onc	Antin, J	MA	330
Onc	Bensinger, W	WA	385
Onc	Bishop, M	IL	366
Onc	Carabasi, M	PA	339
Onc	Cohen, G	MD	340
Onc	Erban, J	MA	331
Onc	Flomenberg, N	PA	342
Onc	Foss, F	CT	331
Onc	Freedman, A	MA	331
Onc	Gerson, S	OH	369
Onc	Pecora, A	NJ	349
Onc	Soiffer, R	MA	335
Onc	Sweetenham, J	UT	378
Onc	Wicha, M	MI	375
PA&I	Kamani, N	DC	743
PHO	Arndt, C	MN	781
PHO	Barredo, J	FL	777
PHO	Cairo, M	NY	772
PHO	Cunningham, J	IL	782
PHO	Davies, S	OH	782
PHO	Fallon, R	IN	783
PHO	Frangoul, H	TN	778
PHO	Godder, K	VA	778
PHO	Goldman, S	TX	788
PHO	Graham, M	AZ	788
PHO	Grupp, S	PA	773
PHO	Haut, P	IN	783
PHO	Horn, B	CA	790
PHO	Kurtzberg, J	NC	779
PHO	Laver, J	NY	775
PHO	Link, M	CA	790
PHO	Lipton, J	NY	775
PHO	O'Reilly, R	NY	776
PHO	Sondel, P	WI	785

Stem Cell Transplant in Lupus/Crohn's

IM	Burt, R	IL	427

Stem Cell Transplant in MS

IM	Burt, R	IL	427

Stem Cell Transplant-Fetal

PA&I	Cowan, M	CA	746
PS	Flake, A	PA	815

Stem Cells in Orthopedics

OrS	Anderson, L	CA	649

Stereotactic Body Radiation Therapy

RadRO	Kestin, L	MI	990
RadRO	Kupelian, P	CA	996
RadRO	Mundt, A	CA	996
RadRO	Suh, J	OH	992

Stereotactic Radiosurgery

NS	Andrews, D	PA	474
NS	Apuzzo, M	CA	498
NS	Asher, A	NC	483
NS	Bakay, R	IL	488
NS	Barnett, G	OH	488
NS	Branch, C	NC	484
NS	Bucholz, R	MO	489
NS	Edwards, M	CA	499
NS	Fenstermaker, R	NY	476
NS	Giannotta, S	CA	499
NS	Guthrie, B	AL	485
NS	Khan, A	MD	478
NS	Kondziolka, D	NY	479
NS	Landy, H	FL	485
NS	Laske, D	PA	479
NS	Lemole, G	AZ	496
NS	Linskey, M	CA	500
NS	Liu, C	CA	500
NS	Lunsford, L	PA	479
NS	Markert, J	AL	485
NS	McDermott, M	CA	501
NS	Moser, R	MA	473

Spec	Name	St	Pg
NS	Nazzaro, J	KS	494
NS	Ott, K	CA	501
NS	Penar, P	VT	473
NS	Rich, K	MO	492
NS	Robertson, J	TN	486
NS	Swaid, S	AL	487
NS	Tatter, S	NC	487
PM	Jasmin, L	OR	713
RadRO	Cmelak, A	TN	984
RadRO	Ennis, R	NY	979
RadRO	Isaacson, S	NY	980
RadRO	Kleinberg, L	MD	981
RadRO	Knisely, J	NY	981
RadRO	Kupelian, P	CA	996
RadRO	Larson, D	CA	996
RadRO	McGarry, R	KY	986
RadRO	Medbery, C	OK	994
RadRO	Mendenhall, W	FL	986
RadRO	Movsas, B	MI	991
RadRO	Pezner, R	CA	996
RadRO	Porrazzo, M	DC	982
RadRO	Randall, M	KY	986
RadRO	Regine, W	MD	982
RadRO	Seung, S	OR	997
RadRO	Shaw, E	NC	987
RadRO	Simpson, J	MO	991
RadRO	Stea, B	AZ	995
RadRO	Suh, J	OH	992
RadRO	Woo, S	KY	988

Stomach Cancer

Spec	Name	St	Pg
Onc	Ajani, J	TX	378
Onc	Grem, J	NE	377
RadRO	Hayman, J	MI	990
S	Aranha, G	IL	1111
S	August, D	NJ	1089
S	Coit, D	NY	1091
S	Fong, Y	NY	1093
S	Gibbs, J	NY	1093
S	Hiotis, S	NY	1094
S	Mansfield, P	TX	1127
S	Pockaj, B	AZ	1128
S	Shenk, R	OH	1119
S	Sundaram, M	IL	1120
S	Zinner, M	MA	1088

Strabismus

Spec	Name	St	Pg
Oph	Azar, N	IL	593
Oph	Buckley, E	NC	587
Oph	Burke, M	OH	594
Oph	Capo, H	FL	587
Oph	Caputo, A	NJ	576
Oph	Cheeseman, E	SC	587
Oph	Demer, J	CA	605
Oph	Drack, A	IA	594
Oph	Eustis, H	LA	602
Oph	Feldon, S	NY	578
Oph	Freedman, S	NC	588
Oph	Gallin, P	NY	578
Oph	Granet, D	CA	606
Oph	Greenwald, M	IL	595
Oph	Guyton, D	MD	579
Oph	Hess, J	FL	589
Oph	Hunter, D	MA	574
Oph	Isenberg, S	CA	606
Oph	Kerr, N	TN	589
Oph	Koller, H	PA	580
Oph	Lambert, S	GA	589
Oph	Levin, A	PA	581
Oph	Lueder, G	MO	597
Oph	Magramm, I	NY	581
Oph	Mets, M	IL	597
Oph	Miller, J	AZ	602
Oph	Mills, M	PA	582
Oph	Mitchell, P	CT	575
Oph	Nelson, L	PA	582
Oph	Olitsky, S	MO	598
Oph	Plager, D	IN	598
Oph	Pollard, Z	GA	591
Oph	Reynolds, J	NY	583
Oph	Siatkowski, R	OK	603
Oph	Simon, J	NY	585
Oph	Tychsen, L	MO	600
Oph	Volpe, N	IL	600
Oph	Wang, F	NY	586
Oph	Weiss, A	WA	610
Oph	Wilson, M	SC	592

Strabismus-Adult & Pediatric

Spec	Name	St	Pg
Oph	Day, S	CA	605
Oph	Del Monte, M	MI	594
Oph	Eggers, H	NY	578
Oph	Hall, L	NY	579
Oph	Jaafar, M	VA	589
Oph	Kushner, B	WI	596
Oph	McDonnell, J	IL	597
Oph	McKeown, C	FL	590
Oph	Mims, J	TX	603
Oph	Paul, T	CA	608
Oph	Rogers, G	OH	599
Oph	Warman, R	FL	592

Streptococcal Infections

Spec	Name	St	Pg
PInf	Baker, C	TX	796
PInf	Givner, L	NC	794
PInf	Shulman, S	IL	796

Stress Management

Spec	Name	St	Pg
GerPsy	Stein, E	CA	946
Psyc	Sanacora, G	CT	922

Stroke

Spec	Name	St	Pg
ChiN	Kosofsky, B	NY	145
Cv	Diver, D	CT	88
Cv	Stainback, R	TX	109
N	Adams, H	IA	527
N	Adornato, B	CA	538
N	Albers, G	CA	538
N	Alexandrov, A	AL	523
N	Azizi, S	PA	513
N	Bell, R	PA	513
N	Broderick, J	OH	528
N	Brown, R	MN	528
N	Caplan, L	MA	510
N	Charney, J	NY	514
N	Chui, H	CA	539
N	Corbetta, M	MO	529
N	Coull, B	AZ	536
N	Elkind, M	NY	515
N	Fink, M	NY	515
N	Fisher, M	CA	539
N	Foo, S	NY	515
N	Furie, K	RI	511
N	Furlan, A	OH	529
N	Gizzi, M	NJ	516
N	Gizzi, M	NJ	516
N	Goldstein, L	NC	524
N	Greer, D	CT	511
N	Gress, D	VA	524
N	Grotta, J	TX	536
N	Haley, E	VA	525
N	Hess, D	GA	525
N	Homer, D	IL	530
N	Josephson, D	IN	530
N	Kase, C	MA	511
N	Kasner, S	PA	516
N	Kent, T	TX	537
N	Kirshner, H	TN	525
N	Levine, D	NY	518
N	Levine, S	NY	518
N	Logan, W	MO	531
N	Marshall, R	NY	519
N	Mohr, J	NY	519
N	Morgenlander, J	NC	526
N	Reed, R	OH	532
N	Rothrock, J	NV	541
N	Sacco, R	FL	526
N	Saver, J	CA	542
N	Smith, W	CA	542
N	Suarez, J	TX	538
N	Tayal, A	PA	522
N	Vas, G	NY	522
N	Vollmer, T	CO	535
N	Wechsler, L	PA	522
NRad	Christoforidis, G	IL	1023
NRad	Cross, D	MO	1023
NRad	Grobelny, T	IL	1023
NRad	Hesselink, J	CA	1026
NRad	Higashida, R	CA	1026
NRad	Joseph, G	NC	1022
NRad	Kallmes, D	MN	1023
NRad	Larsen, D	CA	1026
NRad	Lee, S	IL	1024
NRad	Maldjian, J	NC	1022
NS	Amar, A	CA	498
NS	Atkinson, J	MN	488
NS	Barrow, D	GA	484
NS	Dempsey, R	WI	489
NS	Hopkins, L	NY	478
NS	Levy, E	NY	479
NS	Riina, H	NY	481
NS	Selman, W	OH	493
NS	Stieg, P	NY	482
NS	Yonas, H	NM	498

Spec	Name	St	Pg
PMR	Brown, A	MN	867
VascS	Kougias, P	TX	1229
VascS	Weinstein, E	CO	1229
VIR	Kumpe, D	CO	1031

Stroke in Children

Spec	Name	St	Pg
ChiN	Ichord, R	PA	145
ChiN	Santos, C	DC	146
N	Biller, J	IL	528
NRad	Orbach, D	MA	1020

Stroke Prevention

Spec	Name	St	Pg
N	Greer, D	CT	511
N	Lutsep, H	OR	541
N	Sacco, R	FL	526
N	Saver, J	CA	542
NRad	Larsen, D	CA	1026

Stroke Rehabilitation

Spec	Name	St	Pg
PMR	Ahn, J	NY	862
PMR	Flanagan, S	NY	864
PMR	Francisco, G	TX	871
PMR	Frost, F	OH	868
PMR	Kevorkian, C	TX	871
PMR	King, J	TX	871
PMR	Mason, K	CO	870
PMR	Palmer, J	MD	865
PMR	Roth, E	IL	869
PMR	Wilson, A	TX	871

Stroke-Neonatal

Spec	Name	St	Pg
NRad	Barkovich, A	CA	1025

Stroke-Young Adults

Spec	Name	St	Pg
N	Becker, K	WA	538
N	Sila, C	OH	533

Stroke/Cerebrovascular Disease

Spec	Name	St	Pg
N	Alberts, M	TX	536
N	Becker, K	WA	538
N	Bernstein, R	IL	528
N	Biller, J	IL	528
N	Lutsep, H	OR	541

Sturge-Weber Syndrome

Spec	Name	St	Pg
ChiN	Sahin, M	MA	144

Subglottic Stenosis

Spec	Name	St	Pg
Oto	Benninger, M	OH	683

Substance Abuse

Spec	Name	St	Pg
IM	Mehler, P	CO	427
Psyc	Canterbury, R	VA	928
Psyc	Nunes, E	NY	926

Substance Abuse in ADHD Patients

Spec	Name	St	Pg
ChAP	Deas, D	SC	941

Substance Abuse-Consultation

Spec	Name	St	Pg
Psyc	Walker, R	OR	935

Sudden Death Prevention

Spec	Name	St	Pg
CE	DeLurgio, D	GA	116
CE	Interian, A	FL	116
CE	Levine, J	NY	115
CE	Link, M	MA	113
CE	Tomaselli, G	MD	116
CE	Wilber, D	IL	118

Sudden Infant Death Syndrome (SIDS)

Spec	Name	St	Pg
PCd	Ackerman, M	MN	752
PCd	Walsh, C	NY	750
PPul	Keens, T	CA	810
PPul	Kemp, J	MO	809

Sudden Unexplained Death Syndrome (SUDS)

Spec	Name	St	Pg
PCd	Ackerman, M	MN	752

Suicidal Behavior

Spec	Name	St	Pg
Psyc	Mann, J	NY	926

Suicide

Spec	Name	St	Pg
ChAP	Brent, D	PA	939
ChAP	McKelvey, R	OR	943
ChAP	Sargent, A	MA	938
Psyc	Hirschfeld, R	TX	932

Surfactant Biology

Spec	Name	St	Pg
NP	Cole, F	MO	451
NP	Donn, S	MI	452

Surgery

Spec	Name	St	Pg
S	Abecassis, M	IL	1111
S	Abouljoud, M	MI	1111
S	Adams, R	VA	1103
S	Alexander, H	MD	1089
S	Alfonso, A	NY	1089
S	Ames, F	TX	1123
S	Anderson, B	WA	1130
S	Andreoni, K	FL	1103
S	Angelos, P	IL	1111
S	Aranha, G	IL	1111
S	Ascher, N	CA	1130
S	Ashley, S	MA	1084
S	Attai, D	CA	1130
S	August, D	NJ	1089
S	Averbook, B	OH	1111
S	Babiera, G	TX	1123
S	Baker, C	VA	1103
S	Barie, P	NY	1089
S	Bartlett, D	PA	1089
S	Bartlett, S	MD	1089
S	Basson, M	MI	1111
S	Bear, H	VA	1103
S	Beauchamp, R	TN	1103
S	Becker, J	MA	1084
S	Becker, Y	IL	1111
S	Behrns, K	FL	1103
S	Beitsch, P	TX	1123
S	Benedetti, E	IL	1112
S	Bentley, F	AR	1124
S	Bentrem, D	IL	1112
S	Bessey, P	NY	1089
S	Bessler, M	NY	1089
S	Bilchik, A	CA	1130
S	Billingsley, K	OR	1130
S	Blackstone, R	AZ	1124
S	Bland, K	AL	1103
S	Bolton, J	LA	1124
S	Boraas, M	PA	1090
S	Borgen, P	NY	1090
S	Bouvet, M	CA	1130
S	Brady, M	NY	1090
S	Brems, J	IL	1112
S	Britt, L	VA	1103
S	Brodsky, J	PA	1090
S	Brody, F	DC	1090
S	Bromberg, J	MD	1090
S	Brooks, A	PA	1090
S	Brooks, D	MA	1084
S	Brown, C	IL	1112
S	Brown, E	MI	1112
S	Brunicardi, F	CA	1130
S	Brunt, L	MO	1112
S	Buchman, T	GA	1104
S	Burke, P	MA	1084
S	Busuttil, R	CA	1130
S	Butler, J	CA	1131
S	Byrd, D	WA	1131
S	Cairns, B	NC	1104
S	Callery, M	MA	1084
S	Calvo, B	NC	1104
S	Cameron, J	MD	1090
S	Cance, W	NY	1090
S	Carty, S	PA	1091
S	Chabot, J	NY	1091
S	Chand, B	IL	1112
S	Chang, A	MI	1112
S	Chang, H	CA	1131
S	Chapman, W	MO	1112
S	Choti, M	MD	1091
S	Cioffi, W	RI	1084
S	Clark, O	CA	1131
S	Cohen, M	PA	1091
S	Coit, D	NY	1091
S	Cole, D	SC	1104
S	Colquhoun, S	CA	1131
S	Conti, D	NY	1091
S	Cornwell, E	DC	1091
S	Courcoulas, A	PA	1091

Spec	Name	St	Pg
S	Cronin, D	WI	1113
S	Crookes, P	CA	1131
S	Crowe, J	OH	1113
S	Curcillo, P	PA	1091
S	Curley, S	TX	1124
S	Cusack, J	MA	1084
S	Cushing, B	ME	1084
S	Czerniecki, B	PA	1092
S	Dallal, R	PA	1092
S	Daneker, G	GA	1104
S	Dawson, P	WA	1131
S	Deitch, E	NJ	1092
S	Demarest, G	NM	1124
S	DeMatteo, R	NY	1092
S	Dempsey, D	PA	1092
S	Deziel, D	IL	1113
S	Dixon, S	NV	1131
S	Doherty, G	MA	1085
S	Dooley, W	OK	1124
S	Drebin, J	PA	1092
S	Duh, Q	CA	1132
S	Dulchavsky, S	MI	1113
S	Duncan, M	MD	1092
S	Dunkin, B	TX	1124
S	Dunnington, G	IN	1113
S	Eason, J	TN	1104
S	Easter, D	CA	1132
S	Eberlein, T	MO	1113
S	Eckhoff, D	AL	1104
S	Edge, S	TN	1104
S	Edington, H	PA	1092
S	Edney, J	NE	1122
S	Edwards, M	OH	1113
S	Eilber, F	CA	1132
S	Eisenberg, B	NH	1085
S	Ellenhorn, J	CA	1132
S	Ellis, L	TX	1124
S	Ellison, E	OH	1113
S	Emond, J	NY	1093
S	Emre, S	CT	1085
S	Espat, N	RI	1085
S	Esquivel, C	CA	1132
S	Esserman, L	CA	1132
S	Essner, R	CA	1132
S	Estabrook, A	NY	1093
S	Eubanks, W	FL	1105
S	Euhus, D	TX	1124
S	Evans, D	WI	1113
S	Fahey, T	NY	1093
S	Farley, D	MN	1114
S	Farrar, W	OH	1114
S	Feig, B	TX	1125
S	Finlayson, C	CO	1122
S	Fisher, J	CA	1132
S	Fisher, W	TX	1125
S	Fitzgibbons, R	NE	1122
S	Flynn, M	KY	1105
S	Fong, Y	NY	1093
S	Fraker, D	PA	1093
S	Franklin, M	TX	1125
S	Frantzides, C	IL	1114
S	Frazier, T	PA	1093
S	Friese, R	AZ	1125
S	Fung, J	OH	1114
S	Gabram, S	GA	1105
S	Galloway, J	GA	1105
S	Gamelli, R	IL	1114
S	Gawande, A	MA	1085
S	Geller, D	PA	1093
S	Gibbs, J	NY	1093
S	Giuliano, A	CA	1132
S	Goodman, M	MA	1085
S	Goodson, W	CA	1133
S	Gosnell, J	CA	1133
S	Goulet, R	IN	1114
S	Gower, R	AK	1133
S	Graham, R	MA	1085
S	Grant, C	MN	1114
S	Grant, M	TX	1125
S	Gray, R	AZ	1125
S	Greenhalgh, D	CA	1133
S	Griswold, J	TX	1125
S	Gupta, R	NH	1085
S	Haith, L	PA	1094
S	Halff, G	TX	1125
S	Hanks, J	VA	1105
S	Hanna, N	MD	1094
S	Hansen, N	IL	1114
S	Hawn, M	AL	1105
S	Hebert, J	VT	1085
S	Hemming, A	CA	1133
S	Herrmann, V	SC	1105
S	Herron, D	NY	1094
S	Heslin, M	AL	1105
S	Hinshaw, D	MI	1115
S	Hiotis, S	NY	1094
S	Hodin, R	MA	1086
S	Hoffman, J	PA	1094
S	Holcomb, J	TX	1125
S	Hollingsworth, A	OK	1126
S	Holzman, M	TN	1106
S	Horvath, K	WA	1133
S	Howe, J	IA	1115
S	Howerton, R	NC	1106
S	Hughes, K	MA	1086
S	Hunt, K	TX	1126
S	Hunter, J	OR	1133
S	Hurst, R	IL	1115
S	Huth, J	TX	1126
S	Iglehart, J	MA	1086
S	Ikramuddin, S	MN	1115
S	Jackson, G	TX	1126
S	Jarnagin, W	NY	1094
S	Jayaseelan, N	TX	1126
S	Jenkins, R	MA	1086
S	Johnson, L	DC	1094
S	Johnson, R	PA	1094
S	Johnson Miller, D	NJ	1095
S	Jones, D	MA	1086
S	Julian, T	PA	1095
S	Kagan, R	OH	1115
S	Kapur, S	NY	1095
S	Karlan, S	CA	1133
S	Karpeh, M	NY	1095
S	Katkhouda, N	CA	1133
S	Kato, T	NY	1095
S	Kaufman, C	WA	1134
S	Kaufman, D	WI	1115
S	Kaufman, H	IL	1115
S	Kavanah, M	MA	1086
S	Kelley, M	TN	1106
S	Kendrick, M	MN	1115
S	Kim, J	OH	1116
S	Kim, L	AR	1126
S	Kinkhabwala, M	NY	1095
S	Kirgan, D	NV	1134
S	Klein, A	CA	1134
S	Klimberg, V	AR	1126
S	Knechtle, S	GA	1106
S	Knudson, M	CA	1134
S	Koruda, M	NC	1106
S	Krag, D	VT	1086
S	Krontiras, H	AL	1106
S	Krouse, R	AZ	1126
S	Kuhn, J	TX	1126
S	Kuo, P	IL	1116
S	Lannin, D	CT	1086
S	Leach, S	MD	1095
S	Lee, J	NY	1095
S	Lee, J	TX	1127
S	Lee, K	PA	1096
S	Leeming, R	OH	1116
S	Leitch, A	TX	1127
S	Lentz, C	NM	1127
S	Levi, J	FL	1106
S	Levine, E	NC	1106
S	Li, B	LA	1127
S	Libutti, S	NY	1096
S	Lieberman, M	NY	1096
S	Lillemoe, K	MA	1086
S	Lind, D	PA	1096
S	Lipkowitz, G	MA	1087
S	Loggie, B	NE	1122
S	Lowy, A	CA	1134
S	Luterman, A	AL	1106
S	MacDonald, K	NC	1107
S	Mahvi, D	IL	1116
S	Mannella, W	PA	1096
S	Mansfield, P	TX	1127
S	Markmann, J	MA	1087
S	Marks, J	OH	1116
S	Marsh, J	PA	1096
S	Matas, A	MN	1116
S	Matthews, J	IL	1116
S	McAneny, D	MA	1087
S	McCabe, D	AZ	1127
S	McFadden, D	CT	1087
S	McGrath, P	KY	1107
S	McHenry, C	OH	1116
S	McIntyre, R	CO	1122
S	McMasters, K	KY	1107
S	Mellinger, J	IL	1117
S	Melvin, W	OH	1117
S	Meric-Bernstam, F	TX	1127
S	Mesko, T	FL	1107
S	Meyer, A	NC	1107
S	Meyers, W	PA	1096
S	Michelassi, F	NY	1096
S	Millis, J	IL	1117

Spec	Name	St	Pg
S	Mistry, B	ND	1122
S	Moley, J	MO	1117
S	Montgomery, R	MD	1097
S	Moore, E	CO	1122
S	Moore, F	MA	1087
S	Morrow, M	NY	1097
S	Morton, J	CA	1134
S	Mulvihill, S	UT	1122
S	Nagorney, D	MN	1117
S	Nakakura, E	CA	1134
S	Nathanson, S	MI	1117
S	Neifeld, J	VA	1107
S	Nelson, E	UT	1123
S	Newell, K	GA	1107
S	Newman, E	NY	1097
S	Newman, L	MI	1117
S	Nguyen, N	CA	1134
S	Nissen, N	CA	1135
S	Norman, J	FL	1107
S	Norton, J	CA	1135
S	Nowak, E	NY	1097
S	O'Hea, B	NY	1097
S	Oberholzer, J	IL	1117
S	Oelschlager, B	WA	1135
S	Olson, J	MD	1097
S	Olthoff, K	PA	1097
S	Onders, R	OH	1118
S	Pachter, H	NY	1097
S	Pappas, T	NC	1107
S	Paramo, J	FL	1108
S	Park, A	MD	1098
S	Paty, P	NY	1098
S	Pawlik, T	MD	1098
S	Paz, I	CA	1135
S	Peitzman, A	PA	1098
S	Pellegrini, C	WA	1135
S	Perkins, J	WA	1135
S	Petelin, J	KS	1123
S	Peters, J	NY	1098
S	Peterson, L	HI	1135
S	Phillips, E	CA	1135
S	Philosophe, B	MD	1098
S	Pinson, C	TN	1108
S	Pisters, P	TX	1127
S	Pockaj, B	AZ	1128
S	Pollock, R	OH	1118
S	Pomp, A	NY	1098
S	Ponn, T	NH	1087
S	Ponsky, J	OH	1118
S	Posner, M	IL	1118
S	Posselt, A	CA	1136
S	Postier, R	OK	1128
S	Potenza, B	CA	1136
S	Pryor, A	NY	1098
S	Ramanathan, R	PA	1099
S	Rassman, W	CA	1136
S	Rattner, D	MA	1087
S	Reber, H	CA	1136
S	Reed, A	IA	1118
S	Rege, R	TX	1128
S	Reich, D	PA	1099
S	Reiner, M	NY	1099
S	Renz, J	IL	1118
S	Reyes, J	WA	1136
S	Rhee, P	AZ	1128
S	Richards, W	AL	1108
S	Ridge, J	PA	1099
S	Roberts, J	CA	1136
S	Rogers, S	CA	1136
S	Roh, M	FL	1108
S	Rosemurgy, A	FL	1108
S	Rosen, C	MN	1118
S	Rosen, M	OH	1118
S	Rosenberg, S	MD	1099
S	Roses, D	NY	1099
S	Ross, M	TX	1128
S	Ryan, C	MA	1087
S	Saha, S	MI	1119
S	Salem, R	CT	1087
S	Salky, B	NY	1099
S	Salo, J	NC	1108
S	Sarosi, G	FL	1108
S	Sarr, M	MN	1119
S	Sasson, A	NE	1123
S	Sataloff, D	PA	1099
S	Satava, R	WA	1136
S	Sauter, E	TX	1128
S	Scantlebury, V	DE	1100
S	Schaffer, R	CA	1137
S	Schauer, P	OH	1119
S	Schirmer, B	VA	1108
S	Schlinkert, R	AZ	1128
S	Schnabel, F	NY	1100
S	Schraut, W	PA	1100
S	Schulick, R	CO	1123
S	Schwartz, M	NY	1100
S	Schwartzentruber, D	IN	1119
S	Scott, D	TX	1128
S	Scott-Conner, C	IA	1119
S	Selby, R	CA	1137
S	Sener, S	CA	1137
S	Shah, J	NY	1100
S	Shaked, A	PA	1100
S	Shapiro, R	NY	1100
S	Shapiro, R	PA	1100
S	Sharp, K	TN	1109
S	Shen, P	NC	1109
S	Shenk, R	OH	1119
S	Shibata, D	FL	1109
S	Shikora, S	MA	1088
S	Sielaff, T	MN	1119
S	Sigurdson, E	PA	1101
S	Silverstein, M	CA	1137
S	Simeone, D	MI	1119
S	Simmons, R	NY	1101
S	Sinanan, M	WA	1137
S	Singer, S	NY	1101
S	Siperstein, A	OH	1120
S	Skibber, J	TX	1129
S	Skinner, K	NY	1101
S	Slingluff, C	VA	1109
S	Smith, B	MA	1088
S	Solorzano, C	TN	1109
S	Sondak, V	FL	1109
S	Soper, N	IL	1120
S	Sosa, J	NC	1109
S	Staley, C	GA	1109
S	Staren, E	AZ	1129
S	Stewart, R	TX	1129
S	Stiegmann, G	CO	1123
S	Stolier, A	LA	1129
S	Stratta, R	NC	1110
S	Sugarbaker, P	DC	1101
S	Sundaram, M	IL	1120
S	Swanstrom, L	OR	1137
S	Sweeney, J	GA	1110
S	Swistel, A	NY	1101
S	Tafra, L	MD	1101
S	Talamini, M	CA	1137
S	Talamonti, M	IL	1120
S	Tanabe, K	MA	1088
S	Tartter, P	NY	1101
S	Tchou, J	PA	1102
S	Teperman, L	NY	1102
S	Thayer, S	MA	1088
S	Thistlethwaite, J	IL	1120
S	Tousimis, E	DC	1102
S	Traynor, M	ND	1123
S	Trisal, V	CA	1137
S	Tsangaris, T	CT	1088
S	Tuttle, T	MN	1120
S	Tyler, D	NC	1110
S	Tzakis, A	OH	1120
S	Udelsman, R	CT	1088
S	Unger, S	FL	1110
S	Urist, M	AL	1110
S	Van Zee, K	NY	1102
S	Vauthey, J	TX	1129
S	Vetto, J	OR	1137
S	Vickers, S	MN	1120
S	Vitale, G	KY	1110
S	Wagman, L	CA	1138
S	Wakefield, T	MI	1121
S	Walker, A	WI	1121
S	Wallace, A	CA	1138
S	Walsh, R	OH	1121
S	Wapnir, I	CA	1138
S	Ward, B	CT	1088
S	Warren, R	CA	1138
S	Weber, C	GA	1110
S	Weber, S	WI	1121
S	Weigel, R	IA	1121
S	Weigelt, J	WI	1121
S	White, R	NC	1110
S	Whitworth, P	TN	1110
S	Willey, S	DC	1102
S	Winchell, R	ME	1088
S	Winchester, D	IL	1121
S	Witt, T	IL	1121
S	Woltering, E	LA	1129
S	Wood, R	TX	1129
S	Yang, J	MD	1102
S	Yeatman, T	SC	1111
S	Yeo, C	PA	1102
S	Yeung, R	WA	1138
S	Yurt, R	NY	1102
S	Zannis, V	AZ	1129
S	Zinner, M	MA	1088

Surgical Pathology

Spec	Name	St	Pg
Path	Chandrasoma, P	CA	732
Path	Fishbein, M	CA	733
Path	Fletcher, C	MA	718
Path	Hoda, S	NY	722
Path	Leslie, K	AZ	730
Path	Lucas, D	MI	728
Path	Mills, S	VA	726
Path	Mischel, P	CA	733
Path	Sewell, C	GA	726
Path	Silverman, J	PA	724
Path	Suster, S	WI	729
Path	Weiss, L	CA	735
Path	Weiss, S	GA	727

Swallowing Disorders

Spec	Name	St	Pg
Ge	Castell, D	SC	241
Ge	Estores, D	FL	242
Ge	Kahrilas, P	IL	248
Ge	Katz, P	PA	236
Ge	Lind, C	TN	243
Ge	Mittal, R	CA	257
Ge	Ravich, W	MD	239
Ge	Rothstein, R	NH	232
Ge	Shaker, R	WI	250
Ger	Finucane, T	MD	264
Oto	Abaza, M	CO	689
Oto	Aviv, J	NY	668
Oto	Bastian, R	IL	683
Oto	Berke, G	CA	694
Oto	Blitzer, A	NY	668
Oto	Courey, M	CA	694
Oto	Hogikyan, N	MI	685
Oto	Mirza, N	PA	673
Oto	Pelzer, H	IL	687
Oto	Sasaki, C	CT	667
Oto	Sinha, U	CA	697
Oto	Strome, M	NY	676
Oto	Woodson, G	IL	689
PMR	Palmer, J	MD	865
PO	Holinger, L	IL	804
PO	Thompson, D	IL	804
PPul	Loughlin, G	NY	807
PPul	McGrath-Morrow, S	MD	807
S	Holzman, M	TN	1106

Swallowing Disorders-Botox Therapy

Spec	Name	St	Pg
Ge	Pasricha, P	MD	239

Syncope

Spec	Name	St	Pg
CE	Waldo, A	OH	118
Ger	Lipsitz, L	MA	264
PCd	Crosson, J	MD	748
PCd	Walsh, C	NY	750
PCd	Young, M	FL	751

Syringomyelia & Spinal Cord Diseases

Spec	Name	St	Pg
N	Kula, R	NY	517
N	Levine, D	NY	518
NS	Piatt, J	DE	480

T

T cell Immune Therapy

Spec	Name	St	Pg
Onc	Brentjens, R	NY	339

Taste & Smell Disorders

Spec	Name	St	Pg
Oto	Kern, R	IL	686

Tattoo Removal

Spec	Name	St	Pg
D	Schultz, N	NY	190
PlS	Mixter, R	WI	895

Tear Duct Problems

Spec	Name	St	Pg
Oph	Ahmad, A	IL	593
Oph	Pollard, Z	GA	591

Tearing Disorders

Spec	Name	St	Pg
Oph	Bouchard, C	IL	594

Temperamentally Difficult Child

Spec	Name	St	Pg
ChAP	Turecki, S	NY	941

Temporal Arteritis

Spec	Name	St	Pg
Rhu	Allen, N	NC	1063
Rhu	Merkel, P	PA	1061

Tendon Surgery

Spec	Name	St	Pg
HS	Gelberman, R	MO	302
HS	Greene, T	FL	301
HS	Jones, N	CA	306
HS	Kozin, S	PA	298
HS	Kulick, R	NY	299
HS	Mass, D	IL	303
OrS	Wapner, K	PA	633

Testicular Cancer

Spec	Name	St	Pg
Onc	Ahmann, F	AZ	378
Onc	Bajorin, D	NY	338
Onc	Bolger, G	AL	356
Onc	Bosl, G	NY	338
Onc	Bubley, G	MA	330
Onc	Dreicer, R	OH	368
Onc	Einhorn, L	IN	368
Onc	Garnick, M	MA	332
Onc	Godley, P	NC	358
Onc	Hauke, R	NE	377
Onc	Higano, C	WA	388
Onc	Hussain, M	MI	370
Onc	Jonasch, E	TX	381
Onc	Kantoff, P	MA	333
Onc	Levine, E	NY	347
Onc	Motzer, R	NY	348
Onc	Nanus, D	NY	348
Onc	Oh, W	NY	349
Onc	Petrylak, D	CT	334
Onc	Quinn, D	CA	391
Onc	Roth, B	MO	373
Onc	Stadler, W	IL	374
Onc	Sweeney, C	MA	335
Onc	Vaughn, D	PA	353
Onc	Waller, E	GA	365
Path	Reuter, V	NY	723
Path	Ulbright, T	IN	729
RadRO	Anscher, M	VA	983
RadRO	DeWeese, T	MD	979
RadRO	Peschel, R	CT	977
U	Amling, C	OR	1210
U	Beall, M	VA	1197
U	Carroll, P	CA	1210
U	Chang, S	TN	1197
U	Colberg, J	CT	1186
U	Cookson, M	OK	1208
U	Dalkin, B	WA	1211
U	Daneshmand, S	CA	1211
U	Foster, R	IN	1203
U	Grasso, M	NY	1190
U	Herr, H	NY	1191
U	Hrebinko, R	PA	1191
U	Kawachi, M	CA	1212
U	Klein, E	OH	1203
U	Lerner, S	TX	1209
U	Olumi, A	MA	1187
U	Porter, C	WA	1213
U	Presti, J	CA	1213
U	Richie, J	MA	1188
U	Robertson, C	NC	1200
U	Scherr, D	NY	1194
U	Schlegel, P	NY	1194
U	See, W	WI	1206
U	Sheinfeld, J	NY	1195
U	Skinner, E	CA	1213
U	Weiss, R	NJ	1196
U	Weiss, R	CT	1188
U	Wilson, T	CA	1214

Testicular Cancer-Pediatric

Spec	Name	St	Pg
Ped Uro	Coplen, D	MO	827

Tetanus

Spec	Name	St	Pg
N	Reder, A	IL	532

Thalassemia

Spec	Name	St	Pg
Ped	Berman, B	MI	741
PHO	Cunningham, J	IL	782
PHO	Giardina, P	NY	773
PHO	Weinblatt, M	NY	776

Thoracic & Cardiac Surgery

Spec	Name	St	Pg
T&CS	Abraham, V	IN	1166
T&CS	Acker, M	PA	1149
T&CS	Adams, D	NY	1150
T&CS	Aldea, G	WA	1177
T&CS	Altorki, N	NY	1150
T&CS	Argenziano, M	NY	1150
T&CS	Athanasuleas, C	AL	1160
T&CS	Bacha, E	NY	1150
T&CS	Baciewicz, F	MI	1167
T&CS	Backer, C	IL	1167
T&CS	Bailey, L	CA	1177
T&CS	Bains, M	NY	1150
T&CS	Bakhos, M	IL	1167
T&CS	Battafarano, R	MD	1150
T&CS	Bavaria, J	PA	1150
T&CS	Bhora, F	NY	1151
T&CS	Bichell, D	TN	1160
T&CS	Bolman, R	MA	1146
T&CS	Bowdish, M	CA	1177
T&CS	Boyd, W	CA	1177
T&CS	Bridges, C	NC	1161
T&CS	Brinckerhoff, L	MA	1146
T&CS	Brown, J	IN	1167
T&CS	Brunsting, L	AL	1161
T&CS	Bueno, R	MA	1146
T&CS	Bull, D	UT	1172
T&CS	Burke, R	FL	1161
T&CS	Byrne, J	MA	1146
T&CS	Calhoon, J	TX	1173
T&CS	Cameron, R	CA	1177
T&CS	Campbell, D	CO	1172
T&CS	Caskey, M	AZ	1173
T&CS	Cassivi, S	MN	1167
T&CS	Cerfolio, R	AL	1161
T&CS	Chen, J	NY	1151
T&CS	Chitwood, W	NC	1161
T&CS	Christian, K	TN	1161
T&CS	Cohen, G	CA	1177
T&CS	Cohen, N	MD	1151
T&CS	Cohen, R	CA	1178
T&CS	Colson, Y	MA	1146
T&CS	Conte, J	MD	1151
T&CS	Cooper, J	PA	1151
T&CS	Coselli, J	TX	1173
T&CS	D'Amico, T	NC	1161
T&CS	Dabal, R	AL	1162
T&CS	Damiano, R	MO	1167
T&CS	Dang, M	HI	1178
T&CS	DeCamp, M	IL	1167
T&CS	Deeb, G	MI	1167
T&CS	DeFilippi, V	CA	1178
T&CS	Del-Nido, P	MA	1146
T&CS	Delius, R	MI	1168
T&CS	Demmy, T	NY	1151
T&CS	DeRose, J	NY	1151
T&CS	Deschamps, C	MN	1168
T&CS	Diehl, J	PA	1151
T&CS	Downey, R	NY	1152
T&CS	Drinkwater, D	TN	1162
T&CS	Durham, S	MI	1168
T&CS	Echeverri, L	TX	1174
T&CS	Edwards, N	NY	1152
T&CS	Elefteriades, J	CT	1146
T&CS	Feins, R	NC	1162
T&CS	Ferguson, M	IL	1168
T&CS	Fernando, H	MA	1147
T&CS	Filsoufi, F	NY	1152
T&CS	Flores, R	NY	1152
T&CS	Fontana, G	NY	1152
T&CS	Forbess, J	TX	1174
T&CS	Fraser, C	TX	1174
T&CS	Frazier, O	TX	1174
T&CS	Friedberg, J	PA	1152
T&CS	Fullerton, D	CO	1172
T&CS	Furukawa, S	PA	1152
T&CS	Gaissert, H	MA	1147
T&CS	Galantowicz, M	OH	1168
T&CS	Galloway, A	NY	1153
T&CS	Gaynor, J	PA	1153
T&CS	Gharagozloo, F	AZ	1174
T&CS	Ginsburg, M	NY	1153
T&CS	Girardi, L	NY	1153
T&CS	Glassford, D	TN	1162
T&CS	Grannis, F	CA	1178
T&CS	Graver, L	NY	1153
T&CS	Griffith, B	MD	1153
T&CS	Grossi, E	NY	1153
T&CS	Guber, M	CO	1173
T&CS	Gundry, S	CA	1178
T&CS	Guy, T	PA	1154
T&CS	Guyton, R	GA	1162
T&CS	Handy, J	OR	1178
T&CS	Hanley, F	CA	1178
T&CS	Hargrove, W	PA	1154
T&CS	Harken, A	CA	1178
T&CS	Harpole, D	NC	1162
T&CS	Harrell, J	TX	1174
T&CS	Hashim, S	CT	1147
T&CS	Heitmiller, R	MD	1154
T&CS	Herrington, C	CA	1179
T&CS	Hill, M	WA	1179
T&CS	Horvath, K	MD	1154
T&CS	Howington, J	IL	1168
T&CS	Huddleston, C	MO	1168
T&CS	Iannettoni, M	IA	1169
T&CS	Ilbawi, M	IL	1169
T&CS	Isom, O	NY	1154
T&CS	Jablons, D	CA	1179
T&CS	Jamieson, S	CA	1179
T&CS	Jeevanandam, V	IL	1169
T&CS	Jessen, M	TX	1174
T&CS	Johnson, S	TX	1175
T&CS	Johnstone, D	WI	1169
T&CS	Jonas, R	DC	1154
T&CS	Jones, D	NY	1154
T&CS	Joyce, L	MN	1169
T&CS	Kaiser, L	PA	1154
T&CS	Kanter, K	GA	1162
T&CS	Karwande, S	UT	1173
T&CS	Keenan, R	PA	1155
T&CS	Keller, S	NY	1155
T&CS	Kernstine, K	TX	1175
T&CS	Kiev, J	WV	1155
T&CS	Kirklin, J	AL	1163
T&CS	Kirshbom, P	CT	1147
T&CS	Kopf, G	CT	1147
T&CS	Kormos, R	PA	1155
T&CS	Krellenstein, D	NY	1155
T&CS	Krieger, K	NY	1155
T&CS	Kron, I	VA	1163
T&CS	Kucharczuk, J	PA	1155
T&CS	Laks, H	CA	1179
T&CS	Lamberti, J	CA	1179
T&CS	Landreneau, R	LA	1175
T&CS	Lang, S	NY	1155
T&CS	Lansman, S	NY	1156
T&CS	Lanza, L	AZ	1175
T&CS	Lau, C	VA	1163
T&CS	Lazar, H	MA	1147
T&CS	Lazzaro, R	NY	1156
T&CS	Liao, K	MN	1169
T&CS	Louie, B	WA	1179
T&CS	Loulmet, D	NY	1156
T&CS	Love, R	WI	1169
T&CS	Lytle, B	OH	1170
T&CS	Mack, M	TX	1175
T&CS	Magovern, G	PA	1156
T&CS	Marshall, M	DC	1156
T&CS	Martin, T	FL	1163
T&CS	Mason, D	OH	1170
T&CS	Mathisen, D	MA	1147
T&CS	Mavroudis, C	FL	1163
T&CS	Mayer, J	MA	1148
T&CS	McCarthy, P	IL	1170
T&CS	Merrick, S	CA	1179
T&CS	Meyers, B	MO	1170
T&CS	Michler, R	NY	1156
T&CS	Mill, M	NC	1163
T&CS	Miller, D	CA	1180
T&CS	Miller, D	GA	1163
T&CS	Mitchell, J	CO	1173
T&CS	Mitchell, M	CO	1173
T&CS	Moon, M	MO	1170
T&CS	Moore, J	GA	1163
T&CS	Morales, D	OH	1170
T&CS	Morris, R	PA	1156
T&CS	Mosca, R	NY	1157
T&CS	Mullett, T	KY	1164
T&CS	Mulligan, M	WA	1180
T&CS	Murphy, D	GA	1164
T&CS	Naka, Y	NY	1157
T&CS	Naunheim, K	MO	1170
T&CS	Nesbitt, J	TN	1164
T&CS	Nguyen, D	FL	1164
T&CS	Nugent, W	NH	1148
T&CS	Oaks, T	NC	1164
T&CS	Orringer, M	MI	1170
T&CS	Ott, D	TX	1175
T&CS	Oz, M	NY	1157
T&CS	Pagani, F	MI	1171
T&CS	Panos, A	FL	1164
T&CS	Park, B	NJ	1157
T&CS	Pass, H	NY	1157
T&CS	Patterson, G	MO	1171
T&CS	Pechet, T	PA	1157
T&CS	Philpott, J	VA	1164
T&CS	Pierson, R	MD	1157
T&CS	Pochettino, A	MN	1171

Spec	Name	St	Pg
T&CS	Port, J	NY	1157
T&CS	Putnam, J	TN	1165
T&CS	Quintessenza, J	FL	1165
T&CS	Rastegar, H	MA	1148
T&CS	Reardon, M	TX	1175
T&CS	Rice, D	TX	1176
T&CS	Robinson, L	FL	1165
T&CS	Rosengart, T	TX	1176
T&CS	Rosenkranz, E	FL	1165
T&CS	Roth, J	TX	1176
T&CS	Rusch, V	NY	1158
T&CS	Safi, H	TX	1176
T&CS	Salerno, T	FL	1165
T&CS	Samuels, L	PA	1158
T&CS	Sanchez, J	MD	1158
T&CS	Savage, E	FL	1165
T&CS	Schaff, H	MN	1171
T&CS	Scott, W	PA	1158
T&CS	Sellke, F	RI	1148
T&CS	Shemin, R	CA	1180
T&CS	Shrager, J	CA	1180
T&CS	Singh, A	RI	1148
T&CS	Slaughter, M	KY	1165
T&CS	Smedira, N	OH	1171
T&CS	Smith, C	NY	1158
T&CS	Smith, J	OH	1171
T&CS	Smith, P	NC	1165
T&CS	Smythe, W	TX	1176
T&CS	Soberman, M	MD	1158
T&CS	Sonett, J	NY	1158
T&CS	Spray, T	PA	1159
T&CS	Staples, E	FL	1166
T&CS	Starnes, V	CA	1180
T&CS	Stewart, A	NY	1159
T&CS	Stowe, C	FL	1166
T&CS	Stuart, R	MO	1171
T&CS	Sugarbaker, D	MA	1148
T&CS	Svensson, L	OH	1171
T&CS	Swanson, S	MA	1148
T&CS	Swisher, S	TX	1176
T&CS	Swistel, D	NY	1159
T&CS	Szeto, W	PA	1159
T&CS	Tedder, M	TN	1166
T&CS	Thistlethwaite, P	CA	1180
T&CS	Toyoda, Y	PA	1159
T&CS	Tranbaugh, R	NY	1159
T&CS	Trento, A	CA	1180
T&CS	Turner, W	TX	1176
T&CS	Turrentine, M	IN	1172
T&CS	Ungerleider, R	NC	1166
T&CS	Vallieres, E	WA	1181
T&CS	Verrier, E	WA	1181
T&CS	Vigneswaran, W	IL	1172
T&CS	Vlahakes, G	MA	1148
T&CS	Wain, J	MA	1149
T&CS	Walsh, G	TX	1177
T&CS	Walters, H	MI	1172
T&CS	Warner, K	MA	1149
T&CS	Watson, T	NY	1159
T&CS	Weigel, T	ME	1149
T&CS	Weiman, D	TN	1166
T&CS	Weksler, B	PA	1160
T&CS	Wells, W	CA	1181
T&CS	Whyte, R	MA	1149
T&CS	Williams, M	NY	1160
T&CS	Woo, Y	PA	1160
T&CS	Wood, D	WA	1181
T&CS	Wright, C	MA	1149
T&CS	Yang, S	MD	1160
T&CS	Yuh, D	CT	1149
T&CS	Ziemer, G	IL	1172
T&CS	Zwischenberger, J	KY	1166

Thoracic Aortic Surgery

Spec	Name	St	Pg
S	Moore, E	CO	1122
T&CS	Aldea, G	WA	1177
T&CS	Bowdish, M	CA	1177
T&CS	Cohen, R	CA	1178
T&CS	Miller, D	CA	1180
T&CS	Szeto, W	PA	1159

Thoracic Cancers

Spec	Name	St	Pg
Onc	Antonia, S	FL	355
Onc	Chachoua, A	NY	339
Onc	Dowlati, A	OH	368
Onc	Edelman, M	NM	379
Onc	Garst, J	NC	358
Onc	Herbst, R	CT	332
Onc	Hong, W	TX	380
Onc	Johnson, B	MA	333
Onc	Kris, M	NY	346
Onc	Langer, C	PA	346
Onc	Lilenbaum, R	CT	333
Onc	Lynch, T	CT	333
Onc	Masters, G	DE	347
Onc	Pao, W	TN	362
Onc	Reckamp, K	CA	391
Onc	Ross, H	AZ	383
Onc	Salgia, R	IL	373
Onc	Sherman, C	SC	363
Onc	Strauss, G	MA	335
RadRO	Bogart, J	NY	978
RadRO	Bradley, J	MO	988
RadRO	Cox, J	TX	993
RadRO	Kachnic, L	MA	976
RadRO	Kestin, L	MI	990
RadRO	Le, Q	CA	996
T&CS	Altorki, N	NY	1150
T&CS	Bhora, F	NY	1151
T&CS	Colson, Y	MA	1146
T&CS	Demmy, T	NY	1151
T&CS	Downey, R	NY	1152
T&CS	Feins, R	NC	1162
T&CS	Grannis, F	CA	1178
T&CS	Johnson, S	TX	1175
T&CS	Johnstone, D	WI	1169
T&CS	Karwande, S	UT	1173
T&CS	Moore, J	GA	1163
T&CS	Nguyen, D	FL	1164
T&CS	Nugent, W	NH	1148
T&CS	Rice, D	TX	1176
T&CS	Rusch, V	NY	1158
T&CS	Soberman, M	MD	1158
T&CS	Sonett, J	NY	1158
T&CS	Swisher, S	TX	1176
T&CS	Vallieres, E	WA	1181
T&CS	Vigneswaran, W	IL	1172
T&CS	Zwischenberger, J	KY	1166

Thoracic Imaging

Spec	Name	St	Pg
DR	Fuhrman, C	PA	1009
DR	Gefter, W	PA	1009
DR	Goodman, L	WI	1015
DR	Macmahon, H	IL	1015
DR	White, C	MD	1012

Thoracic Insufficiency Syndrome

Spec	Name	St	Pg
PPul	Redding, G	WA	811

Thoracic Outlet Syndrome

Spec	Name	St	Pg
VascS	Ahn, S	CA	1230
VascS	Annest, S	CO	1228
VascS	Bandyk, D	CA	1230
VascS	Cho, J	IL	1226
VascS	Freischlag, J	MD	1223
VascS	Hallett, J	SC	1225

Thoracic Radiology

Spec	Name	St	Pg
DR	Austin, J	NY	1008
DR	Chiles, C	NC	1013
DR	Henschke, C	NY	1009
DR	Macmahon, H	IL	1015
DR	Patz, E	NC	1014
DR	Rubin, G	NC	1014
DR	Yankelevitz, D	NY	1012

Thoracic Surgery

Spec	Name	St	Pg
PS	Alexander, F	NJ	815
PS	Caty, M	CT	813
PS	Hilfiker, M	CA	823
T&CS	Cassivi, S	MN	1167
T&CS	Guber, M	CO	1173
T&CS	Hill, M	WA	1179
T&CS	Lazzaro, R	NY	1156
T&CS	Lazzaro, R	NY	1156

Throat Disorders

Spec	Name	St	Pg
Oto	Sataloff, R	PA	675
Oto	Schley, W	NY	675
Oto	Silverman, D	VT	667

Thromboembolic Disorders

Spec	Name	St	Pg
Hem	Millenson, M	PA	316
Hem	Rao, A	PA	316
Pul	Auger, W	CA	970
Pul	Elliott, C	UT	967
Pul	Hyers, T	MO	965
Pul	Palevsky, H	PA	959
Pul	Steiger, D	NY	959
Pul	Wheeler, A	TN	964

Spec	Name	St	Pg
Thrombolytic Therapy			
N	Furlan, A	OH	529
VIR	Aruny, J	CT	1027
VIR	Valji, K	WA	1033
Thrombotic Disorders			
Hem	Abrams, C	PA	313
Hem	DeLoughery, T	OR	328
Hem	Kempin, S	NY	315
Hem	Ortel, T	NC	319
Hem	Palascak, J	OH	323
Hem	Soff, G	NY	317
Onc	Stopeck, A	AZ	383
Ped	Berman, B	MI	741
PHO	Buchanan, G	TX	787
PHO	Manco-Johnson, M	CO	787
PHO	Valentino, L	IL	786
S	Wakefield, T	MI	1121
Thumb-Absence			
HS	Light, T	IL	303
Thymoma			
Onc	Aisner, J	NJ	337
Onc	Bonomi, P	IL	366
Onc	Bunn, P	CO	376
Onc	Carbone, D	OH	367
Onc	Kalemkerian, G	MI	370
Onc	Kris, M	NY	346
Onc	Loehrer, P	IN	371
Onc	Shin, D	GA	364
Onc	Simon, G	TX	383
RadRO	Cox, J	TX	993
RadRO	Komaki, R	TX	994
RadRO	Videtic, G	OH	992
T&CS	Gaissert, H	MA	1147
T&CS	Howington, J	IL	1168
T&CS	Marshall, M	DC	1156
T&CS	Sanchez, J	MD	1158
T&CS	Shrager, J	CA	1180
T&CS	Weksler, B	PA	1160
Thyroid & Parathyroid Cancer & Surgery			
Oto	Bumpous, J	KY	678
Oto	Caruana, S	NY	668
Oto	Couch, M	VT	665
Oto	Ferris, R	PA	669
Oto	Genden, E	NY	670
Oto	Goldenberg, D	PA	670
Oto	Orloff, L	CA	696
Oto	Otto, R	TX	693
Oto	Patil, Y	OH	687
Oto	Peters, G	AL	680
Oto	Pitman, K	AZ	693
Oto	Samant, S	TN	681
Oto	Urken, M	NY	676
Oto	Weber, R	TX	694
Oto	Weisman, R	CA	697
S	Angelos, P	IL	1111
S	Bland, K	AL	1103
S	Duh, Q	CA	1132
S	Edney, J	NE	1122
S	Grant, C	MN	1114
S	Lee, J	NY	1095
S	Mesko, T	FL	1107
S	Siperstein, A	OH	1120
S	Solorzano, C	TN	1109
Thyroid & Parathyroid Surgery			
Oto	Blair, E	IL	683
Oto	Clayman, G	TX	691
Oto	Friedman, M	IL	684
Oto	Har-El, G	NY	670
Oto	Hayden, R	AZ	692
Oto	Kim, D	MA	666
Oto	Kraus, D	NY	672
Oto	Miller, F	TX	693
S	Chabot, J	NY	1091
S	Flynn, M	KY	1105
S	Hanks, J	VA	1105
S	Jackson, G	TX	1126
S	Roses, D	NY	1099
S	Shapiro, R	NY	1100
S	Traynor, M	ND	1123
S	Weber, C	GA	1110
Thyroid Cancer			
DR	Charboneau, J	MN	1014
EDM	Ain, K	KY	215
EDM	Akatsu, H	CA	223
EDM	Ball, D	MD	210
EDM	Burman, K	DC	211
EDM	Daniels, G	MA	209
EDM	Davies, T	NY	212
EDM	Gagel, R	TX	222
EDM	Haber, R	NY	212
EDM	Kandeel, F	CA	224
EDM	Koch, C	MS	216
EDM	Kopp, P	IL	220
EDM	Ladenson, P	MD	213
EDM	Levine, R	NH	210
EDM	Lilienfeld, H	FL	216
EDM	Mandel, S	PA	213
EDM	Ridgway, E	CO	222
EDM	Robbins, R	TX	223
EDM	Ross, D	MA	210
EDM	Rubenfeld, S	TX	223
EDM	Sherman, S	TX	223
EDM	Tuttle, R	NY	215
EDM	Waguespack, S	TX	223
EDM	Wartofsky, L	DC	215
EDM	Xing, M	MD	215
NRad	Loevner, L	PA	1021
NuM	Dillehay, G	IL	556
NuM	Goldsmith, S	NY	554
NuM	Lamonica, D	NY	554
NuM	Pandit-Taskar, N	NY	555
NuM	Waxman, A	CA	557
NuM	Ziffer, J	FL	556
Onc	Khuri, F	GA	359
Onc	Pfister, D	NY	350
Onc	Remick, S	WV	350
Oto	Browne, J	NC	678
Oto	Califano, J	MD	668
Oto	Chalian, A	PA	668
Oto	Eisele, D	MD	669
Oto	Keane, W	PA	672
Oto	Krespi, Y	NY	672
Oto	Kuhel, W	NY	672
Oto	Lavertu, P	OH	686
Oto	Lydiatt, W	NE	690
Oto	Persky, M	NY	674
Oto	Petruzzelli, G	GA	680
Oto	Randolph, G	MA	666
Oto	Schantz, S	NY	675
Oto	Singh, B	NY	675
Oto	Smith, R	NE	691
Oto	Suen, J	AR	693
Oto	Teknos, T	OH	688
Oto	Terris, D	GA	682
Oto	Valentino, J	KY	682
Oto	Weber, S	TX	694
Oto	Wong, R	NY	677
Oto	Yoo, G	MI	689
Path	Baloch, Z	PA	720
Path	Chhieng, D	CT	718
Path	LiVolsi, V	PA	722
Path	Sanchez, M	NJ	724
Path	Suster, S	WI	729
Path	Wheeler, T	TX	731
PEn	Zimmerman, D	IL	761
PlS	Loree, T	NY	884
PS	Ehrlich, P	MI	819
PS	Skinner, M	TX	822
RadRO	Grigsby, P	MO	989
S	Alfonso, A	NY	1089
S	Butler, J	CA	1131
S	Byrd, D	WA	1131
S	Evans, D	WI	1113
S	Farrar, W	OH	1114
S	Gawande, A	MA	1085
S	Giuliano, A	CA	1132
S	Graham, R	MA	1085
S	Hodin, R	MA	1086
S	Kim, L	AR	1126
S	Kuhn, J	TX	1126
S	Moore, F	MA	1087
S	Sener, S	CA	1137
S	Shah, J	NY	1100
S	Sosa, J	NC	1109
S	Udelsman, R	CT	1088
Thyroid Cancer & Surgery			
Oto	Clayman, G	TX	691
Oto	Shindo, M	OR	697
S	Clark, O	CA	1131
S	Gosnell, J	CA	1133
S	McIntyre, R	CO	1122
S	Moley, J	MO	1117
S	Ridge, J	PA	1099

Spec	Name	St	Pg
Thyroid Disorders			
EDM	Ain, K	KY	215
EDM	Akatsu, H	CA	223
EDM	Barrett, E	VA	216
EDM	Bergman, D	NY	211
EDM	Berkson, R	CA	224
EDM	Blum, C	NY	211
EDM	Braverman, L	MA	208
EDM	Brennan, M	MN	218
EDM	Brillon, D	NY	211
EDM	Brown, J	TX	222
EDM	Burman, K	DC	211
EDM	Burmeister, L	MN	218
EDM	Comi, R	NH	208
EDM	Cooper, D	MD	212
EDM	Cushing, G	MA	209
EDM	Daniels, G	MA	209
EDM	Emanuele, M	IL	219
EDM	Feinglos, M	NC	216
EDM	Fitzgerald, P	CA	224
EDM	Greene, L	NY	212
EDM	Haber, R	NY	212
EDM	Jacobs, T	NY	213
EDM	Kamdar, V	CA	224
EDM	Ladenson, P	MD	213
EDM	Larsen, P	MA	209
EDM	Lash, R	MI	220
EDM	Levine, R	NH	210
EDM	Lipson, A	DC	213
EDM	Maclaren, N	NY	213
EDM	Mandel, S	PA	213
EDM	McConnell, R	NY	214
EDM	McGill, J	MO	220
EDM	Pearce, E	MA	210
EDM	Powers, A	TN	217
EDM	Ridgway, E	CO	222
EDM	Ross, D	MA	210
EDM	Rubenfeld, S	TX	223
EDM	Schwartz, S	PA	214
EDM	Semenkovich, C	MO	221
EDM	Seplowitz, A	NY	214
EDM	Singer, P	CA	225
EDM	Surks, M	NY	215
EDM	Weiss, R	IL	221
EDM	Werner, P	IL	221
EDM	Woeber, K	CA	226
EDM	Xing, M	MD	215
NuM	Goldsmith, S	NY	554
NuM	Siegel, B	MO	556
NuM	Strashun, A	NY	555
NuM	Ziffer, J	FL	556
Oto	Davidson, B	DC	669
Oto	Donovan, D	TX	692
Oto	Picken, C	DC	674
Oto	Pribitkin, E	PA	674
Oto	Randolph, G	MA	666
Oto	Sinha, U	CA	697
Oto	Song, J	CO	691
Oto	Tufano, R	MD	676
Path	Baloch, Z	PA	720
Path	De Las Morenas, A	MA	718
Path	Suster, S	WI	729
Path	Wheeler, T	TX	731
PEn	Alter, C	PA	757
PEn	Casella, S	NH	756
PEn	Geffner, M	CA	761
PEn	Kappy, M	CO	761
PEn	Kohn, B	NY	758
PEn	Plotnick, L	MD	759
PEn	Rogers, D	OH	760
PEn	Zimmerman, D	IL	761
Thyroid Disorders in Pregnancy			
EDM	Davies, T	NY	212
EDM	Mandel, S	PA	213
EDM	Seely, E	MA	210
Thyroid Eye Disease			
Oph	Bernardino, C	CA	604
Oph	Char, D	CA	605
Oph	Feldon, S	NY	578
Oph	Kazim, M	NY	580
Oph	Kikkawa, D	CA	606
Oph	Lucarelli, M	WI	597
Oph	McCann, J	UT	601
Oph	Miller, N	MD	582
Oph	Nunery, W	KY	590
Oph	Putterman, A	IL	599
Oph	Sergott, R	PA	584
Thyroid Surgery			
Oto	Campbell, B	WI	684
Oto	Hurst, M	WV	671
Oto	Terris, D	GA	682
Oto	Thaler, E	PA	676
PO	Kazahaya, K	PA	802
S	Britt, L	VA	1103
S	Doherty, G	MA	1085
S	Gower, R	AK	1133
S	McHenry, C	OH	1116
Thyroid Ultrasound			
DR	Benson, C	MA	1007
DR	Grant, E	CA	1018
EDM	Levine, R	NH	210
EDM	Mandel, S	PA	213
EDM	McConnell, R	NY	214
Tick-borne Diseases			
Inf	Auwaerter, P	MD	412
Inf	Bakken, J	MN	417
PInf	Saiman, L	NY	794
Tissue Banking			
OrS	Friedlaender, G	CT	617
PlS	Spence, R	MD	886
TMJ Imaging			
DR	Rao, V	PA	1011
Tobacco Abuse			
Ger	Dale, L	MN	266
T&CS	Grannis, F	CA	1178
Toe-to-Hand Transfer			
HS	Jones, N	CA	306
OrS	Levin, L	PA	628
Tongue Cancer			
Oto	Diaz, E	TX	691
Oto	Myers, J	TX	693
Tonsil/Adenoid Disorders			
PO	Dolitsky, J	NY	802
PO	Miller, R	IL	804
Tourette's Syndrome			
ChAP	Coffey, B	NY	939
ChAP	Hirsch, G	NY	940
ChAP	Leckman, J	CT	938
ChAP	Rostain, A	PA	940
ChiN	Dure, L	AL	147
ChiN	Mink, J	NY	146
ChiN	Pinter, J	OR	151
ChiN	Roddy, S	CA	152
N	Bruno, M	HI	538
N	Flaherty, A	MA	511
N	Jankovic, J	TX	537
N	Mesulam, M	IL	531
Ped	Berlin, C	PA	740
Toxic Epidermal Necrolysis			
S	Ryan, C	MA	1087
Toxicology			
Pul	Albertson, T	CA	969
Toxoplasmosis			
PInf	Bryson, Y	CA	797
Tracheal Reconstruction			
PO	Thompson, D	IL	804
Tracheal Surgery			
PO	Cotton, R	OH	804
T&CS	Backer, C	IL	1167
T&CS	Cerfolio, R	AL	1161
T&CS	Gaissert, H	MA	1147
T&CS	Kernstine, K	TX	1175
T&CS	Mathisen, D	MA	1147
T&CS	Wood, D	WA	1181
T&CS	Wright, C	MA	1149

Spec	Name	St	Pg

Tracheal Surgery-Pediatric

Spec	Name	St	Pg
T&CS	Wells, W	CA	1181

Transfusion Free Surgery

Spec	Name	St	Pg
T&CS	Rosengart, T	TX	1176

Transfusion Medicine

Spec	Name	St	Pg
Hem	Telen, M	NC	320
Path	Kaufman, R	MA	718
PNep	Conley, S	PA	797

Transgender Issues

Spec	Name	St	Pg
PEn	Spack, N	MA	757

Transplant Immunology

Spec	Name	St	Pg
PGe	McDiarmid, S	CA	769
S	Knechtle, S	GA	1106

Transplant Medicine-Bowel

Spec	Name	St	Pg
Ge	Schiano, T	NY	240
PGe	McDiarmid, S	CA	769

Transplant Medicine-Heart

Spec	Name	St	Pg
Cv	Bourge, R	AL	97
Cv	Brozena, S	PA	91
Cv	Corrigan, V	GA	98
Cv	DeNofrio, D	MA	88
Cv	Eisen, H	PA	92
Cv	Fishbein, D	WA	110
Cv	Geltman, E	MO	102
Cv	Gottlieb, S	MD	93
Cv	Heroux, A	IL	102
Cv	Hunt, S	CA	111
Cv	Jessup, M	PA	94
Cv	Johnson, M	WI	103
Cv	Katz, S	NY	94
Cv	Kobashigawa, J	CA	111
Cv	Konstam, M	MA	89
Cv	Lindenfeld, J	CO	107
Cv	Massin, E	TX	108
Cv	Mather, P	PA	95
Cv	Rogers, J	NC	99
Cv	Russell, S	MD	95
Cv	Smart, F	LA	109
Cv	Smith, A	GA	100
Cv	Stevenson, L	MA	90
Cv	Wagoner, L	OH	106
Cv	Walsh, M	IN	106
Cv	Young, J	OH	107
PCd	Bernstein, D	CA	754
PCd	Caldwell, R	IN	752
PCd	Colvin, E	AL	751
PCd	Dreyer, W	TX	754
PCd	Fricker, F	FL	751
PCd	Hsu, D	NY	749
PCd	Pahl, E	IL	753
PCd	Shaddy, R	PA	750

Transplant Medicine-Heart & Lung

Spec	Name	St	Pg
Pul	Hertz, M	MN	965

Transplant Medicine-Kidney

Spec	Name	St	Pg
Nep	Bennett, W	OR	466
Nep	Brennan, D	MO	463
Nep	Brennan, S	TX	465
Nep	Butterly, D	NC	461
Nep	Coffman, T	NC	461
Nep	Cohen, D	NY	459
Nep	Gaston, R	AL	461
Nep	Helderman, J	TN	462
Nep	Josephson, M	IL	463
Nep	Kasiske, B	MN	463
Nep	Miller, B	MO	464
Nep	Nolan, C	TX	466
Nep	Roth, D	FL	462
Nep	Scandling, J	CA	467
Nep	Stern, L	NY	460
Nep	Textor, S	MN	464
Nep	Thomas, C	IA	465
Nep	Tolkoff-Rubin, N	MA	458
Nep	Venkat, K	MI	465
Nep	Ward, D	CA	467
Nep	Williams, G	NY	460
PNep	Alexander, S	CA	800
PNep	Benfield, M	AL	798
PNep	Brophy, P	IA	799
PNep	Chandar, J	FL	798
PNep	Clardy, C	IL	799
PNep	Cohn, R	IL	800
PNep	Conley, S	PA	797
PNep	Ellis, D	PA	797
PNep	Ettenger, R	CA	800
PNep	Fivush, B	MD	798
PNep	Jabs, K	TN	799
PNep	Jordan, S	CA	801
PNep	Kashtan, C	MN	800
PNep	McDonald, R	WA	801
PNep	Mendley, S	MD	798
PNep	Warady, B	MO	800
PNep	Zilleruelo, G	FL	799

Transplant Medicine-Liver

Spec	Name	St	Pg
Ge	Barnes, D	OH	246
Ge	Berg, C	NC	241
Ge	Bloomer, J	AL	241
Ge	Boyer, T	AZ	253
Ge	Brown, K	MI	246
Ge	Brown, R	NY	233
Ge	Chung, R	MA	230
Ge	Crippin, J	MO	247
Ge	Dienstag, J	MA	230
Ge	Fried, M	NC	242
Ge	Galati, J	TX	254
Ge	Gholam, P	OH	247
Ge	Gish, R	CA	256
Ge	Glombicki, A	TX	254
Ge	Han, S	CA	256
Ge	Herrine, S	PA	235
Ge	Hunter, E	ID	252
Ge	Jensen, D	IL	248
Ge	Kwo, P	IN	248
Ge	La Russo, N	MN	248
Ge	Loomba, R	CA	256
Ge	Lucey, M	WI	249
Ge	Martin, P	FL	243
Ge	Poordad, F	TX	254
Ge	Porayko, M	TN	244
Ge	Raiford, D	TN	244
Ge	Reddy, K	PA	239
Ge	Sass, D	PA	240
Ge	Schiano, T	NY	240
Ge	Shiffman, M	VA	245
Ge	Sorrell, M	NE	252
Ge	Speeg, K	TX	255
Ge	Te, H	IL	250
Ge	Vierling, J	TX	255
Ge	Wiesner, R	MN	251
PGe	Jonas, M	MA	762
PGe	Kleinman, R	MA	762
PGe	McDiarmid, S	CA	769
PGe	Mittal, N	TX	768
PGe	Molleston, J	IN	766
PGe	Narkewicz, M	CO	767
PGe	Schwarz, K	MD	764
PGe	Sokol, R	CO	767
PGe	Thomas, D	CA	769
PGe	Whitington, P	IL	767

Transplant Medicine-Lung

Spec	Name	St	Pg
PPul	Kurland, G	PA	807
Pul	Ahya, V	PA	956
Pul	Arcasoy, S	NY	956
Pul	Christie, J	PA	956
Pul	Garrity, E	IL	964
Pul	Hertz, M	MN	965
Pul	Kotloff, R	PA	957
Pul	Loyd, J	TN	963
Pul	Lynch, J	CA	971
Pul	Padilla, M	NY	958
Pul	Trulock, E	MO	967
Pul	Young, K	PA	960

Transplant Medicine-Pancreas

Spec	Name	St	Pg
Nep	Nolan, C	TX	466
Nep	Scandling, J	CA	467

Transplant Pathology

Spec	Name	St	Pg
Path	Demetris, A	PA	721
Path	Swerdlow, S	PA	724

Transplant Surgery

Spec	Name	St	Pg
S	Becker, Y	IL	1111
S	Johnson, L	DC	1094
S	Kaufman, D	WI	1115
S	Kuo, P	IL	1116
S	Renz, J	IL	1118
S	Reyes, J	WA	1136
S	Shaked, A	PA	1100

Spec	Name	St	Pg

Transplant Surgery-Pediatric

Spec	Name	St	Pg
PS	Chen, M	AL	818
PS	Healey, P	WA	823
PS	Jan, D	NY	816
PS	Paidas, C	FL	818
PS	Superina, R	IL	821
S	Cronin, D	WI	1113
S	Kato, T	NY	1095
S	Reyes, J	WA	1136
S	Roberts, J	CA	1136
S	Thistlethwaite, J	IL	1120

Transplant-Auto Transplantation

Spec	Name	St	Pg
S	Kato, T	NY	1095

Transplant-Bile Duct

Spec	Name	St	Pg
S	Rosen, C	MN	1118

Transplant-Bowel

Spec	Name	St	Pg
PS	Jan, D	NY	816
S	Benedetti, E	IL	1112
S	Tzakis, A	OH	1120

Transplant-Face

Spec	Name	St	Pg
PlS	Rodriguez, E	MD	886
PlS	Siemionow, M	OH	896

Transplant-Hand

Spec	Name	St	Pg
HS	Breidenbach, W	AZ	304
HS	Cendales, L	GA	301
HS	Lee, W	MD	299
PlS	Tobin, G	KY	892

Transplant-Heart

Spec	Name	St	Pg
T&CS	Acker, M	PA	1149
T&CS	Backer, C	IL	1167
T&CS	Brown, J	IN	1167
T&CS	Byrne, J	MA	1146
T&CS	Christian, K	TN	1161
T&CS	Cohen, R	CA	1178
T&CS	Conte, J	MD	1151
T&CS	Dang, M	HI	1178
T&CS	Echeverri, L	TX	1174
T&CS	Edwards, N	NY	1152
T&CS	Frazier, O	TX	1174
T&CS	Harrell, J	TX	1174
T&CS	Jeevanandam, V	IL	1169
T&CS	Jessen, M	TX	1174
T&CS	Kormos, R	PA	1155
T&CS	Kron, I	VA	1163
T&CS	Lansman, S	NY	1156
T&CS	Liao, K	MN	1169
T&CS	Mayer, J	MA	1148
T&CS	Morris, R	PA	1156
T&CS	Naka, Y	NY	1157
T&CS	Oz, M	NY	1157
T&CS	Pagani, F	MI	1171
T&CS	Panos, A	FL	1164
T&CS	Pierson, R	MD	1157
T&CS	Quintessenza, J	FL	1165
T&CS	Samuels, L	PA	1158
T&CS	Slaughter, M	KY	1165
T&CS	Smedira, N	OH	1171
T&CS	Toyoda, Y	PA	1159
T&CS	Trento, A	CA	1180
T&CS	Turrentine, M	IN	1172
T&CS	Vlahakes, G	MA	1148

Transplant-Heart & Lung

Spec	Name	St	Pg
T&CS	Bakhos, M	IL	1167
T&CS	Bavaria, J	PA	1150
T&CS	Calhoon, J	TX	1173
T&CS	Fullerton, D	CO	1172
T&CS	Gaynor, J	PA	1153
T&CS	Griffith, B	MD	1153
T&CS	Jamieson, S	CA	1179
T&CS	Kirklin, J	AL	1163
T&CS	Laks, H	CA	1179
T&CS	Love, R	WI	1169
T&CS	Mack, M	TX	1175
T&CS	Mavroudis, C	FL	1163
T&CS	Mill, M	NC	1163
T&CS	Mullett, T	KY	1164
T&CS	Patterson, G	MO	1171
T&CS	Spray, T	PA	1159
T&CS	Staples, E	FL	1166
T&CS	Starnes, V	CA	1180
T&CS	Thistlethwaite, P	CA	1180

Transplant-Heart-Adult & Pediatric

Spec	Name	St	Pg
T&CS	Mill, M	NC	1163

Transplant-Heart-Pediatric

Spec	Name	St	Pg
T&CS	Bailey, L	CA	1177
T&CS	Campbell, D	CO	1172
T&CS	Cohen, G	CA	1177
T&CS	Herrington, C	CA	1179
T&CS	Huddleston, C	MO	1168
T&CS	Kanter, K	GA	1162
T&CS	Laks, H	CA	1179
T&CS	Morales, D	OH	1170
T&CS	Rosenkranz, E	FL	1165
T&CS	Starnes, V	CA	1180
T&CS	Walters, H	MI	1172

Transplant-Kidney

Spec	Name	St	Pg
Ped Uro	Hatch, D	IL	827
PS	Andrews, W	MO	819
PS	Colombani, P	MD	815
PS	Dunn, S	DE	815
PS	Healey, P	WA	823
PS	Schwartz, M	PA	817
PS	Superina, R	IL	821
S	Abecassis, M	IL	1111
S	Ascher, N	CA	1130
S	Bartlett, S	MD	1089
S	Becker, Y	IL	1111
S	Benedetti, E	IL	1112
S	Bentley, F	AR	1124
S	Bromberg, J	MD	1090
S	Conti, D	NY	1091
S	Eason, J	TN	1104
S	Eckhoff, D	AL	1104
S	Fisher, J	CA	1132
S	Fung, J	OH	1114
S	Kapur, S	NY	1095
S	Kaufman, D	WI	1115
S	Knechtle, S	GA	1106
S	Kuo, P	IL	1116
S	Lipkowitz, G	MA	1087
S	Markmann, J	MA	1087
S	Matas, A	MN	1116
S	Mistry, B	ND	1122
S	Montgomery, R	MD	1097
S	Newell, K	GA	1107
S	Perkins, J	WA	1135
S	Reed, A	IA	1118
S	Roberts, J	CA	1136
S	Scantlebury, V	DE	1100
S	Schaffer, R	CA	1137
S	Shapiro, R	PA	1100
S	Stratta, R	NC	1110
S	Teperman, L	NY	1102
S	Thistlethwaite, J	IL	1120
U	Ciancio, G	FL	1197
U	Marsh, C	CA	1212
U	Menon, M	MI	1204

Transplant-Kidney-Adult & Pediatric

Spec	Name	St	Pg
S	Andreoni, K	FL	1103

Transplant-Liver

Spec	Name	St	Pg
PS	Andrews, W	MO	819
PS	Colombani, P	MD	815
PS	Dunn, S	DE	815
PS	Healey, P	WA	823
PS	Jan, D	NY	816
PS	Karrer, F	CO	821
PS	Meyers, R	UT	821
PS	Sawin, R	WA	824
PS	Superina, R	IL	821
S	Abecassis, M	IL	1111
S	Abouljoud, M	MI	1111
S	Benedetti, E	IL	1112
S	Brems, J	IL	1112
S	Busuttil, R	CA	1130
S	Colquhoun, S	CA	1131
S	Cronin, D	WI	1113
S	Eckhoff, D	AL	1104
S	Emond, J	NY	1093
S	Fisher, J	CA	1132
S	Fung, J	OH	1114
S	Halff, G	TX	1125
S	Hemming, A	CA	1133
S	Jenkins, R	MA	1086

Spec	Name	St	Pg
S	Kato, T	NY	1095
S	Kinkhabwala, M	NY	1095
S	Klein, A	CA	1134
S	Knechtle, S	GA	1106
S	Markmann, J	MA	1087
S	Marsh, J	PA	1096
S	Mistry, B	ND	1122
S	Nissen, N	CA	1135
S	Perkins, J	WA	1135
S	Philosophe, B	MD	1098
S	Pinson, C	TN	1108
S	Reed, A	IA	1118
S	Reich, D	PA	1099
S	Renz, J	IL	1118
S	Reyes, J	WA	1136
S	Roberts, J	CA	1136
S	Rosen, C	MN	1118
S	Schaffer, R	CA	1137
S	Schwartz, M	NY	1100
S	Shaked, A	PA	1100
S	Teperman, L	NY	1102
S	Thistlethwaite, J	IL	1120
S	Tzakis, A	OH	1120
U	Marsh, C	CA	1212

Transplant-Liver-Adult & Pediatric

Spec	Name	St	Pg
S	Andreoni, K	FL	1103
S	Ascher, N	CA	1130
S	Chapman, W	MO	1112
S	Emre, S	CT	1085
S	Esquivel, C	CA	1132
S	Millis, J	IL	1117
S	Olthoff, K	PA	1097
S	Posselt, A	CA	1136
S	Renz, J	IL	1118

Transplant-Lung

Spec	Name	St	Pg
Path	Yousem, S	PA	725
Pul	Raghu, G	WA	971
T&CS	Campbell, D	CO	1172
T&CS	Conte, J	MD	1151
T&CS	Cooper, J	PA	1151
T&CS	Ginsburg, M	NY	1153
T&CS	Iannettoni, M	IA	1169
T&CS	Johnson, S	TX	1175
T&CS	Lau, C	VA	1163
T&CS	Liao, K	MN	1169
T&CS	Mason, D	OH	1170
T&CS	Meyers, B	MO	1170
T&CS	Mitchell, J	CO	1173
T&CS	Mitchell, M	CO	1173
T&CS	Mulligan, M	WA	1180
T&CS	Patterson, G	MO	1171
T&CS	Pierson, R	MD	1157
T&CS	Pochettino, A	MN	1171
T&CS	Sonett, J	NY	1158
T&CS	Sugarbaker, D	MA	1148
T&CS	Turrentine, M	IN	1172
T&CS	Vigneswaran, W	IL	1172
T&CS	Wain, J	MA	1149

Transplant-Lung-Pediatric

Spec	Name	St	Pg
T&CS	Huddleston, C	MO	1168
T&CS	Kanter, K	GA	1162
T&CS	Laks, H	CA	1179
T&CS	Morales, D	OH	1170

Transplant-Multi Organ

Spec	Name	St	Pg
S	Kato, T	NY	1095

Transplant-Ovarian Tissue

Spec	Name	St	Pg
U	Silber, S	MO	1206

Transplant-Pancreas

Spec	Name	St	Pg
S	Andreoni, K	FL	1103
S	Bartlett, S	MD	1089
S	Becker, Y	IL	1111
S	Benedetti, E	IL	1112
S	Bromberg, J	MD	1090
S	Conti, D	NY	1091
S	Fisher, J	CA	1132
S	Kapur, S	NY	1095
S	Kaufman, D	WI	1115
S	Markmann, J	MA	1087
S	Millis, J	IL	1117
S	Mistry, B	ND	1122
S	Newell, K	GA	1107
S	Oberholzer, J	IL	1117
S	Olthoff, K	PA	1097
S	Perkins, J	WA	1135
S	Philosophe, B	MD	1098
S	Posselt, A	CA	1136
S	Reed, A	IA	1118
S	Schaffer, R	CA	1137
S	Shapiro, R	PA	1100
S	Stratta, R	NC	1110
S	Thistlethwaite, J	IL	1120
U	Ciancio, G	FL	1197
U	Marsh, C	CA	1212

Transplant-Pancreas & Liver

Spec	Name	St	Pg
S	Eason, J	TN	1104

Transplantation Psychiatry

Spec	Name	St	Pg
Psyc	Klapheke, M	FL	928

Transumbilical Breast Augmentation(TUBA)

Spec	Name	St	Pg
PlS	Horowitz, J	CA	903

Trauma

Spec	Name	St	Pg
HS	Eglseder, W	MD	298
HS	Hunt, T	AL	301
HS	Peljovich, A	GA	301
HS	Rosenwasser, M	NY	300
HS	Thoder, J	PA	300
N	Finkel, M	FL	524
NS	Kotapka, M	PA	479
NS	Taylon, C	NE	494
Oph	Mieler, W	IL	597
Oph	Ng, J	OR	608
Oph	Sternberg, P	TN	591
OrS	Agarwal, A	TX	647
OrS	Anglen, J	IN	639
OrS	Archdeacon, M	OH	639
OrS	Delahay, J	DC	622
OrS	Dirschl, D	IL	640
OrS	Ebraheim, N	OH	641
OrS	Farmer, J	NY	623
OrS	Greisberg, J	NY	624
OrS	Herman, M	PA	626
OrS	Johnson, E	CA	651
OrS	Kim, C	CA	652
OrS	Nepola, J	IA	643
OrS	Otsuka, N	NY	630
OrS	Sangeorzan, B	WA	653
OrS	Seltzer, D	AZ	648
OrS	Smith, E	MA	619
OrS	Swiontkowski, M	MN	645
OrS	Tornetta, P	MA	619
OrS	Webb, L	GA	639
OrS	Weiner, R	FL	639
Oto	Stenson, K	IL	688
PS	Bond, S	KY	817
PS	Dillon, P	MO	819
PS	Fallat, M	KY	818
PS	Ford, H	CA	823
PS	Gaines, B	PA	815
PS	Hicks, B	DE	816
PS	Hilfiker, M	CA	823
PS	Nance, M	PA	816
PS	Reynolds, M	IL	820
PS	Stylianos, S	NY	817
S	Barie, P	NY	1089
S	Bessey, P	NY	1089
S	Britt, L	VA	1103
S	Buchman, T	GA	1104
S	Burke, P	MA	1084
S	Cioffi, W	RI	1084
S	Cohen, M	PA	1091
S	Cornwell, E	DC	1091
S	Cushing, B	ME	1084
S	Demarest, G	NM	1124
S	Dulchavsky, S	MI	1113
S	Friese, R	AZ	1125
S	Gupta, R	NH	1085
S	Holcomb, J	TX	1125
S	Knudson, M	CA	1134
S	Lentz, C	NM	1127
S	Meyer, A	NC	1107
S	Peitzman, A	PA	1098
S	Rhee, P	AZ	1128
S	Stewart, R	TX	1129
S	Weigelt, J	WI	1121
S	Winchell, R	ME	1088

Trauma Psychiatry

Spec	Name	St	Pg
ChAP	Bleiberg, E	TX	943
ChAP	Fornari, V	NY	940

Spec	Name	St	Pg
ChAP	Sargent, A	MA	938
ChAP	Steiner, H	CA	944
Psyc	Loewenstein, R	MD	925

Trauma Radiology

Spec	Name	St	Pg
DR	Mirvis, S	MD	1010
DR	Sivit, C	OH	1015

Trauma Rehabilitation

Spec	Name	St	Pg
PM	Walsh, N	TX	712
PMR	Sisung, C	IL	870

Trauma-Reconstructive Plastic Surgery

Spec	Name	St	Pg
PlS	Lee, R	IL	894

Trauma/Critical Care

Spec	Name	St	Pg
S	Baker, C	VA	1103
S	Gamelli, R	IL	1114
S	Mistry, B	ND	1122

Travel Medicine

Spec	Name	St	Pg
D	James, W	PA	189
Inf	Alvarez-Elcoro, S	FL	415
Inf	Ballon-Landa, G	CA	420
Inf	Corey, G	NC	416
Inf	DuPont, H	TX	419
Inf	Flaherty, J	IL	417
Inf	Gumprecht, J	NY	413
Inf	O'Keefe, J	IL	418
Inf	Pearson, R	VA	416
Inf	Perlman, D	NY	414
Inf	Rao, N	PA	414
Inf	Wallace, M	FL	417
PInf	Belcher, C	IN	795
PInf	Christenson, J	IN	795
PInf	Raszka, W	VT	793
PrM	Cahill, J	NY	912

Tremor

Spec	Name	St	Pg
N	Langston, J	CA	540
N	Tetrud, J	CA	542

Tremor & Dystonia

Spec	Name	St	Pg
N	Hauser, R	FL	525
N	Louis, E	NY	518
N	Samii, A	WA	542
N	Vitek, J	MN	534
N	Wooten, G	VA	527

Trigeminal Neuralgia

Spec	Name	St	Pg
NS	Carson, B	MD	475
NS	Goodman, R	NY	477
NS	Grubb, R	MO	490
NS	Linskey, M	CA	500
NS	Malik, G	MI	491
NS	Patel, S	SC	486
NS	Van Loveren, H	FL	488
NS	Yonas, H	NM	498

Trophoblastic Tumors

Spec	Name	St	Pg
Onc	Aghajanian, C	NY	336

Tropical Diseases

Spec	Name	St	Pg
Inf	Corey, G	NC	416
Inf	DuPont, H	TX	419
Inf	Pearson, R	VA	416
Inf	Rao, N	PA	414
Inf	Trenholme, G	IL	419
Path	Walker, D	TX	731
PrM	Cahill, J	NY	912

Tuberculosis

Spec	Name	St	Pg
Inf	Alvarez-Elcoro, S	FL	415
Inf	Huitt, G	CO	419
Inf	Perlman, D	NY	414
Inf	Sepkowitz, K	NY	415
Inf	Yancovitz, S	NY	415
PInf	Baltimore, R	CT	792
PInf	Mitchell, C	FL	795
PInf	Saiman, L	NY	794
PInf	Starke, J	TX	797
Pul	Catanzaro, A	CA	970
Pul	Friedman, L	CT	954
Pul	Hopewell, P	CA	970
Pul	Nardell, E	MA	955
Pul	Schluger, N	NY	959
Pul	Schraufnagel, D	IL	966

Tuberous Breasts

Spec	Name	St	Pg
PlS	Romano, J	CA	905

Tuberous Sclerosis

Spec	Name	St	Pg
ChiN	Kohrman, M	IL	148
ChiN	Rosser, T	CA	152
ChiN	Sahin, M	MA	144
N	Bebin, E	AL	523
N	Devinsky, O	NY	514
NS	Weiner, H	NY	482

Tumor Banking

Spec	Name	St	Pg
Path	Balla, A	IL	727

Tumor Banking-Brain

Spec	Name	St	Pg
Path	Zagzag, D	NY	725

Tumor Banking-Prostate

Spec	Name	St	Pg
Path	Melamed, J	NY	722

Tumor Surgery

Spec	Name	St	Pg
PS	Aiken, J	WI	819
PS	Ginsburg, H	NY	815
PS	Meyers, R	UT	821
S	Crowe, J	OH	1113

Tumoral Calcinosis

Spec	Name	St	Pg
Ger	Lyles, K	NC	265

Tumors-Rare & Multiple

Spec	Name	St	Pg
S	Dooley, W	OK	1124

Turner Syndrome

Spec	Name	St	Pg
PEn	Eugster, E	IN	760

Twin to Twin Transfusion Syndrome (TTTS)

Spec	Name	St	Pg
CG	Bianchi, D	MA	156
MF	Abuhamad, A	VA	436
MF	Bahado-Singh, R	MI	437
MF	Carr, S	RI	432
MF	Chmait, R	CA	442
ObG	De Lia, J	WI	564
PS	Adzick, N	PA	814
PS	Albanese, C	CA	823
PS	Crombleholme, T	CO	821
PS	Farmer, D	CA	823

U

Ulcerative Colitis

Spec	Name	St	Pg
CRS	Foley, E	WI	173
CRS	Fry, R	PA	169
CRS	Medich, D	PA	170
CRS	Medwell, S	WA	178
CRS	Rafferty, J	OH	174
CRS	Shellito, P	MA	169
CRS	Steinhagen, R	NY	171
CRS	Welton, M	CA	178
CRS	Williams, S	ID	176
CRS	Young-Fadok, T	AZ	177
Ge	Abreu, M	FL	241
Ge	Albert, M	DC	232
Ge	Cominelli, F	OH	246
Ge	DeCross, A	NY	233
Ge	Hanauer, S	IL	248
Ge	Isaacs, K	NC	243
Ge	Lebwohl, O	NY	237
Ge	Leighton, J	AZ	254
Ge	Lichtenstein, G	PA	237
Ge	Loftus, E	MN	249
Ge	Magun, A	NY	238
Ge	Plevy, S	NC	244
Ge	Sandborn, W	CA	257
Ge	Scherl, E	NY	240
Ge	Siegel, C	NH	232

Spec	Name	St	Pg
Ge	Tremaine, W	MN	251
PGe	Baldassano, R	PA	763
PGe	Berman, J	IL	765
PGe	Dubinsky, M	CA	768
PGe	Kirschner, B	IL	766
PGe	Oliva-Hemker, M	MD	763
PGe	Spivak, W	NY	764
PGe	Wyllie, R	OH	767
PS	Dolgin, S	NY	815
S	Hurst, R	IL	1115
S	Michelassi, F	NY	1096
S	Salky, B	NY	1099

Ultrasound

Spec	Name	St	Pg
DR	Abbitt, P	FL	1012
DR	Adler, R	NY	1008
DR	Bahn, D	CA	1017
DR	Cohen, H	TN	1013
DR	Coleman, B	PA	1008
DR	Doubilet, P	MA	1007
DR	Grant, E	CA	1018
DR	Kurtz, A	PA	1010
DR	Pathria, M	CA	1018
MF	Baker, E	NH	432
MF	Blakemore, K	MD	433
MF	Dugoff, L	PA	434
MF	Ferguson, J	VA	436
MF	Hibbard, J	IL	438
MF	Mastrobattista, J	TX	441
MF	Reed, K	AZ	441
MF	Robinson, J	MA	433
MF	Treadwell, M	MI	440
ObG	Byrne, J	UT	566
ObG	Evans, M	NY	561
RE	Session, D	GA	1046

Unknown Primary Cancer

Spec	Name	St	Pg
Onc	Greco, F	TN	359
Onc	Hande, K	TN	359
Onc	Ilson, D	NY	345
Onc	Jacobs, C	CA	388
Onc	Kelsen, D	NY	346
Onc	Saltz, L	NY	350
Onc	Stewart, F	WA	393
Onc	Stoopler, M	NY	352
Onc	Varadhachary, G	TX	383
Onc	Ward, J	UT	378

Upper Extremity Surgery

Spec	Name	St	Pg
HS	Baratz, M	PA	297
HS	Idler, R	CO	304
HS	Osterman, A	PA	299

Upper Extremity Surgery-Pediatric

Spec	Name	St	Pg
HS	Kleinman, W	IN	303

Upper Extremity Trauma

Spec	Name	St	Pg
HS	Chung, K	MI	302
HS	Jupiter, J	MA	296
HS	Raphael, J	PA	299
HS	Trumble, T	WA	306
SM	Sennett, B	PA	1076

Ureter & Renal Pelvis Cancer

Spec	Name	St	Pg
U	O'Donnell, M	IA	1205

Urinary Reconstruction

Spec	Name	St	Pg
Ped Uro	Cheng, E	IL	826
Ped Uro	Elder, J	MI	827
Ped Uro	Ewalt, D	TX	828
Ped Uro	Kirsch, A	GA	826
Ped Uro	Maizels, M	IL	827
U	Boone, T	TX	1208
U	Ginsberg, D	CA	1211
U	Hensle, T	NJ	1191
U	Lerner, S	TX	1209
U	Lockhart, J	FL	1198
U	Milam, D	TN	1198
U	Raz, S	CA	1213
U	Scardino, P	NY	1194
U	Schoenberg, M	MD	1194
U	Skinner, E	CA	1213
U	Uzzo, R	PA	1195
U	Wong, C	OH	1206

Urinary Reflux

Spec	Name	St	Pg
Ped Uro	Docimo, S	PA	825
Ped Uro	Kirsch, A	GA	826

Urinary Tract Infections

Spec	Name	St	Pg
Inf	Maki, D	WI	418
Inf	Sobel, J	MI	419
Ped Uro	Greenfield, S	NY	825
PInf	Wald, E	WI	796
PMR	Cardenas, D	FL	866
PNep	Ettenger, R	CA	800
U	Schaeffer, A	IL	1205

Urinary Tract Interventions

Spec	Name	St	Pg
VIR	Keller, F	OR	1033

Uro-Gynecology

Spec	Name	St	Pg
GO	Hatch, K	AZ	288
GO	Morgan, M	PA	279
ObG	Amundsen, C	NC	562
ObG	Brodman, M	NY	560
ObG	Cornella, J	AZ	566
ObG	Culbertson, S	IL	564
ObG	De Lancey, J	MI	564
ObG	Eckler, K	MA	560
ObG	Hale, D	IN	565
ObG	Hullfish, K	VA	562
ObG	Iglesia, C	DC	561
ObG	Karram, M	OH	565
ObG	Kenton, K	IL	565
ObG	Lucente, V	PA	561
ObG	Myers, D	RI	560
ObG	Parker, W	CA	567
ObG	Sand, P	IL	565
ObG	Sanz, L	VA	563
ObG	Valaitis, S	IL	565
ObG	Visco, A	NC	563
ObG	Walters, M	OH	566
U	Blaivas, J	NY	1189

Urodynamics

Spec	Name	St	Pg
Ped Uro	Joseph, D	AL	826
U	Bushman, W	WI	1202
U	Foster, H	CT	1186
U	Klutke, C	MO	1203
U	Milam, D	TN	1198
U	Nitti, V	NY	1193
U	Vapnek, J	NY	1196
U	Wein, A	PA	1196

Urodynamics in Spinal Cord Injury

Spec	Name	St	Pg
U	Linsenmeyer, T	NJ	1192

Urologic Cancer

Spec	Name	St	Pg
Onc	Carducci, M	MD	339
Onc	DiPaola, R	NJ	341
Onc	Einhorn, L	IN	368
Onc	Figlin, R	CA	387
Onc	Hauke, R	NE	377
Onc	Hogan, T	WV	345
Onc	Kelly, W	PA	345
Onc	Small, E	CA	392
Onc	Stein, C	CA	392
Onc	Tagawa, S	NY	352
Onc	Torti, F	CT	336
Onc	Troner, M	FL	364
Path	Cohen, M	UT	729
Path	Ross, J	NY	724
RadRO	D'Amico, A	MA	976
RadRO	DeWeese, T	MD	979
RadRO	Dicker, A	PA	979
RadRO	Gejerman, G	NJ	979
RadRO	Nicolaou, N	PA	981
RadRO	St Clair, W	KY	987
RadRO	Stock, R	NY	982
RadRO	Zietman, A	MA	978
U	Andrews, P	AZ	1207
U	Andriole, G	MO	1202
U	Balaji, K	NC	1197
U	Bardot, S	LA	1208
U	Basler, J	TX	1208
U	Belldegrun, A	CA	1210
U	Bodner, D	OH	1202
U	Boyd, S	CA	1210
U	Chen, D	PA	1189
U	Cohen, J	PA	1189
U	Cookson, M	OK	1208

Spec	Name	St	Pg
U	Culkin, D	OK	1208
U	Dalkin, B	WA	1211
U	Danoff, D	CA	1211
U	Droller, M	NY	1189
U	Ellis, W	WA	1211
U	Flanigan, R	IL	1203
U	Gill, H	CA	1211
U	Gill, I	CA	1211
U	Gomella, L	PA	1190
U	Grasso, M	NY	1190
U	Greene, G	FL	1197
U	Hall, S	NY	1190
U	Hemal, A	NC	1198
U	Heney, N	MA	1186
U	Janeiro, J	NH	1186
U	Kavoussi, L	NY	1191
U	Keane, T	SC	1198
U	Klein, E	OH	1203
U	Kozlowski, J	IL	1204
U	Lanteri, V	NJ	1192
U	Lee, C	MI	1204
U	Lieskovsky, G	CA	1212
U	Lin, D	WA	1212
U	McDougal, W	MA	1187
U	McGovern, F	MA	1187
U	Menon, M	MI	1204
U	Miles, B	TX	1209
U	O'Donnell, M	IA	1205
U	Penson, D	TN	1199
U	Porter, C	WA	1213
U	Pruthi, R	NC	1200
U	Sagalowsky, A	TX	1209
U	Samadi, D	NY	1194
U	Sanda, M	GA	1200
U	Sanders, W	GA	1200
U	Scardino, P	NY	1194
U	Sexton, W	FL	1200
U	Skinner, E	CA	1213
U	Strup, S	KY	1201
U	Takayama, T	WA	1213
U	Terris, M	GA	1201
U	Trabulsi, E	PA	1195
U	Uzzo, R	PA	1195
U	Van Arsdalen, K	PA	1196
U	Verghese, M	DC	1196
U	Wallen, E	NC	1201
U	Wein, A	PA	1196
U	Wilson, T	CA	1214

Urologic Cancer-Pediatric

Spec	Name	St	Pg
Ped Uro	Bloom, D	MI	826
Ped Uro	Cain, M	IN	826
Ped Uro	Cartwright, P	UT	828
Ped Uro	Coplen, D	MO	827
Ped Uro	Ewalt, D	TX	828
Ped Uro	Joseph, D	AL	826
Ped Uro	Kirsch, A	GA	826
Ped Uro	Kolon, T	PA	825
Ped Uro	Merguerian, P	WA	828
Ped Uro	Pope, J	TN	826

Urologic Pathology

Spec	Name	St	Pg
Path	Amin, M	CA	731
Path	Bostwick, D	VA	725
Path	Dahmoush, L	IA	727
Path	Epstein, J	MD	721
Path	True, L	WA	734
U	Soloway, M	FL	1201

Urology

Spec	Name	St	Pg
U	Ahlering, T	CA	1210
U	Albala, D	NY	1188
U	Albertsen, P	CT	1186
U	Alexander, R	MD	1188
U	Amling, C	OR	1210
U	Andrews, P	AZ	1207
U	Andriole, G	MO	1202
U	Babayan, R	MA	1186
U	Badlani, G	NC	1196
U	Bahnson, R	OH	1202
U	Balaji, K	NC	1197
U	Bales, G	IL	1202
U	Bans, L	AZ	1208
U	Bar-Chama, N	NY	1188
U	Bardot, S	LA	1208
U	Basler, J	TX	1208
U	Beall, M	VA	1197
U	Belldegrun, A	CA	1210
U	Benson, M	NY	1189
U	Blaivas, J	NY	1189
U	Bodner, D	OH	1202
U	Boone, T	TX	1208
U	Boyd, S	CA	1210
U	Brendler, C	IL	1202
U	Broderick, G	FL	1197
U	Buch, J	TX	1208
U	Burnett, A	MD	1189
U	Busby, J	SC	1197
U	Bushman, W	WI	1202
U	Campbell, S	OH	1202
U	Carpinito, G	MA	1186
U	Carroll, P	CA	1210
U	Carson, C	NC	1197
U	Carter, H	MD	1189
U	Catalona, W	IL	1202
U	Chancellor, M	MI	1203
U	Chang, S	TN	1197
U	Chen, D	PA	1189
U	Childs, S	CO	1206
U	Chun, T	NJ	1189
U	Ciancio, G	FL	1197
U	Clayman, R	CA	1211
U	Cohen, J	PA	1189
U	Colberg, J	CT	1186
U	Coleman, J	NY	1189
U	Cookson, M	OK	1208
U	Crawford, E	CO	1207
U	Culkin, D	OK	1208
U	Dalkin, B	WA	1211
U	Daneshmand, S	CA	1211
U	Danoff, D	CA	1211
U	Davis, B	KS	1207
U	DeKernion, J	CA	1211
U	Donovan, J	OH	1203
U	Droller, M	NY	1189
U	Ellis, W	WA	1211
U	Fisch, H	NY	1190
U	Flanigan, R	IL	1203
U	Foster, H	CT	1186
U	Foster, R	IN	1203
U	Fraser, L	MS	1197
U	Gearhart, J	MD	1190
U	Gill, H	CA	1211
U	Gill, I	CA	1211
U	Ginsberg, D	CA	1211
U	Gluckman, G	IL	1203
U	Goldstein, I	CA	1212
U	Goldstein, M	NY	1190
U	Gomella, L	PA	1190
U	Gomery, P	MA	1186
U	Grasso, M	NY	1190
U	Greenberg, R	PA	1190
U	Greene, G	FL	1197
U	Gribetz, M	NY	1190
U	Griebling, T	KS	1207
U	Grossman, H	TX	1208
U	Gujral, S	MN	1203
U	Hall, S	NY	1190
U	Hamilton, B	UT	1207
U	Hellstrom, W	LA	1209
U	Hemal, A	NC	1198
U	Heney, N	MA	1186
U	Hensle, T	NJ	1191
U	Herr, H	NY	1191
U	Holden, S	CA	1212
U	Hrebinko, R	PA	1191
U	Irby, P	NC	1198
U	Jackman, S	PA	1191
U	Janeiro, J	NH	1186
U	Jones, J	OH	1203
U	Kadmon, D	TX	1209
U	Kane, M	MD	1191
U	Kaplan, S	NY	1191
U	Katz, A	NY	1191
U	Kavoussi, L	NY	1191
U	Kawachi, M	CA	1212
U	Keane, T	SC	1198
U	Kennelly, M	NC	1198
U	Kibel, A	MA	1187
U	Kim, E	TN	1198
U	Kirschenbaum, A	NY	1192
U	Klein, E	OH	1203
U	Klutke, C	MO	1203
U	Koch, M	IN	1204
U	Kozlowski, J	IL	1204
U	Landman, J	CA	1212
U	Lange, P	WA	1212
U	Lanteri, V	NJ	1192
U	Lee, C	MI	1204
U	Lepor, H	NY	1192
U	Lerner, S	TX	1209
U	Levine, L	IL	1204
U	Libertino, J	MA	1187
U	Lieskovsky, G	CA	1212
U	Lin, D	WA	1212
U	Linsenmeyer, T	NJ	1192

Spec	Name	St	Pg
U	Lipshultz, L	TX	1209
U	Lloyd, L	AL	1198
U	Lockhart, J	FL	1198
U	Loo, M	NY	1192
U	Loughlin, K	MA	1187
U	Lowe, F	NY	1192
U	Lugg, J	WY	1207
U	Malkowicz, S	PA	1192
U	Marsh, C	CA	1212
U	McClure, R	WA	1212
U	McConnell, J	NC	1198
U	McCullough, A	NY	1192
U	McDougal, W	MA	1187
U	McGovern, F	MA	1187
U	McVary, K	IL	1204
U	Meacham, R	CO	1207
U	Menon, M	MI	1204
U	Milam, D	TN	1198
U	Miles, B	TX	1209
U	Miller, S	GA	1199
U	Mohler, J	NY	1193
U	Montague, D	OH	1204
U	Montie, J	MI	1204
U	Mostwin, J	MD	1193
U	Moul, J	NC	1199
U	Mulhall, J	NY	1193
U	Nagler, H	NY	1193
U	Nakada, S	WI	1205
U	Naslund, M	MD	1193
U	Nehra, A	IL	1205
U	Nelson, J	PA	1193
U	Nieder, A	FL	1199
U	Nitti, V	NY	1193
U	O'Donnell, M	IA	1205
U	O'Leary, M	MA	1187
U	Oates, R	MA	1187
U	Ohl, D	MI	1205
U	Olumi, A	MA	1187
U	Palese, M	NY	1193
U	Parekh, D	FL	1199
U	Partin, A	MD	1193
U	Patel, V	FL	1199
U	Patterson, A	TN	1199
U	Penson, D	TN	1199
U	Pisters, L	TX	1209
U	Porter, C	WA	1213
U	Pow-Sang, J	FL	1199
U	Preminger, G	NC	1200
U	Presti, J	CA	1213
U	Pruthi, R	NC	1200
U	Rajfer, J	CA	1213
U	Raz, S	CA	1213
U	Richie, J	MA	1188
U	Robertson, C	NC	1200
U	Roehrborn, C	TX	1209
U	Ross, L	IL	1205
U	Sabanegh, E	OH	1205
U	Sadeghi-Nejad, H	NJ	1194
U	Sagalowsky, A	TX	1209
U	Samadi, D	NY	1194
U	Sanda, M	GA	1200
U	Sanders, W	GA	1200
U	Sandlow, J	WI	1205
U	Sawczuk, I	NJ	1194
U	Scardino, P	NY	1194
U	Schaeffer, A	IL	1205
U	Scherr, D	NY	1194
U	Schlegel, P	NY	1194
U	Schoenberg, M	MD	1194
U	Schulam, P	CT	1188
U	See, W	WI	1206
U	Seftel, A	NJ	1194
U	Sexton, W	FL	1200
U	Shaban, S	NC	1200
U	Shabsigh, R	NY	1195
U	Shalhav, A	IL	1206
U	Sharlip, I	CA	1213
U	Sheinfeld, J	NY	1195
U	Shenot, P	PA	1195
U	Siegelbaum, M	MD	1195
U	Sigman, M	RI	1188
U	Silber, S	MO	1206
U	Singh, D	CT	1188
U	Skinner, E	CA	1213
U	Slawin, K	TX	1210
U	Smith, J	TN	1200
U	Soloway, M	FL	1201
U	Steers, W	VA	1201
U	Steinberg, G	IL	1206
U	Stoller, M	CA	1213
U	Strup, S	KY	1201
U	Su, L	FL	1201
U	Sundaram, C	IN	1206
U	Takayama, T	WA	1213
U	Taneja, S	NY	1195
U	Teigland, C	NC	1201
U	Terris, M	GA	1201
U	Tewari, A	NY	1195
U	Thompson, I	TX	1210
U	Thrasher, J	KS	1207
U	Trabulsi, E	PA	1195
U	Turek, P	CA	1214
U	Uzzo, R	PA	1195
U	Van Arsdalen, K	PA	1196
U	Vapnek, J	NY	1196
U	Verghese, M	DC	1196
U	Wallen, E	NC	1201
U	Walsh, P	MD	1196
U	Wein, A	PA	1196
U	Weiss, R	NJ	1196
U	Weiss, R	CT	1188
U	Wilson, T	CA	1214
U	Winfield, H	AL	1201
U	Wong, C	OH	1206
U	Woo, H	LA	1210
U	Wood, D	MI	1206
U	Yu, G	MD	1196

Urology-Female

U	Bales, G	IL	1202
U	Blaivas, J	NY	1189
U	Bushman, W	WI	1202
U	Chancellor, M	MI	1203
U	Foster, H	CT	1186
U	Gribetz, M	NY	1190
U	Griebling, T	KS	1207
U	Klutke, C	MO	1203
U	Nitti, V	NY	1193
U	Raz, S	CA	1213
U	Schaeffer, A	IL	1205
U	Vapnek, J	NY	1196
U	Woo, H	LA	1210

Urology-Geriatric

U	Griebling, T	KS	1207

Urticaria

A&I	Altman, L	WA	85
A&I	MacLean, J	MA	80
A&I	Shepherd, G	NY	81
A&I	Wong, J	MA	80
D	Soter, N	NY	191

Uterine Cancer

GO	Abu-Rustum, N	NY	276
GO	Azodi, M	CT	274
GO	Barakat, R	NY	276
GO	Berchuck, A	NC	280
GO	Berek, J	CA	290
GO	Burger, R	PA	277
GO	Burke, T	TX	288
GO	Cain, J	MA	274
GO	Caputo, T	NY	277
GO	Chi, D	NY	277
GO	Cliby, W	MN	284
GO	Copeland, L	OH	284
GO	Creasman, W	SC	281
GO	Curtin, J	NY	277
GO	Dottino, P	NY	277
GO	Dunton, C	PA	277
GO	Finan, M	AL	281
GO	Fiorica, J	FL	281
GO	Goff, B	WA	291
GO	Hurteau, J	IL	284
GO	King, S	PA	278
GO	Kline, R	LA	288
GO	Koulos, J	NY	279
GO	Lambrou, N	FL	282
GO	Lengyel, E	IL	285
GO	Lu, K	TX	289
GO	Lurain, J	IL	285
GO	Makhija, S	KY	282
GO	Miller, D	TX	289
GO	Nagarsheth, N	NY	279
GO	Pejovic, T	OR	291
GO	Plaxe, S	CA	291
GO	Rader, J	WI	285
GO	Rice, L	WI	286
GO	Rose, P	OH	286
GO	Rosenblum, N	PA	280
GO	Rotmensch, J	IL	286
GO	Rubin, S	PA	280
GO	Rutherford, T	CT	275
GO	Schorge, J	MA	275
GO	Schwartz, P	CT	275

Spec	Name	St	Pg
GO	Smith, L	CA	291
GO	Waggoner, S	OH	287
GO	Walker, J	OK	290
GO	Yamada, S	IL	287
MF	Leslie, K	IA	439
Onc	Scudder, S	CA	392
Onc	Spriggs, D	NY	352
Path	Kurman, R	MD	722
RadRO	Eifel, P	TX	993

Uterine Fibroid Embolization

Spec	Name	St	Pg
VIR	Benenati, J	FL	1029
VIR	Cohen, G	PA	1027
VIR	Durham, J	CO	1031
VIR	Gomes, A	CA	1032
VIR	Hallisey, M	CT	1027
VIR	Haskal, Z	MD	1028
VIR	Hovsepian, D	CA	1033
VIR	Johnson, M	IN	1030
VIR	Kaufman, J	OR	1033
VIR	Keller, F	OR	1033
VIR	McLean, G	PA	1028
VIR	Murphy, T	RI	1027
VIR	Shlansky-Goldberg, R	PA	1028
VIR	Smith, S	IL	1031
VIR	Trerotola, S	PA	1029
VIR	Vogelzang, R	IL	1031
VIR	Weintraub, J	NY	1029

Uterine Fibroids

Spec	Name	St	Pg
ObG	Bradley, L	OH	564
ObG	Famuyide, A	MN	564
ObG	Goldstein, M	NY	561
ObG	Hockstein, S	NY	561
ObG	Jenkins, T	AL	563
ObG	Parker, W	CA	567
RE	Clisham, P	LA	1050
RE	Durso, N	VA	1045
RE	Huang, J	TX	1050
RE	Marrs, R	CA	1052
RE	Milad, M	IL	1048
RE	Molo, M	IL	1048
RE	Mukherjee, T	NY	1043
RE	Ory, S	FL	1046
RE	Putman, J	TX	1050
RE	Stewart, E	MN	1049
RE	Van Voorhis, B	IA	1049
RE	Wilson, E	TX	1050
RE	Zacur, H	MD	1045
RE	Zinaman, M	MA	1041
VIR	Denny, D	NJ	1027
VIR	Goodwin, S	CA	1032
VIR	Roberts, A	CA	1033

Uterine Leiomyosarcoma

Spec	Name	St	Pg
Onc	McGuire, W	VA	361

Uveitis

Spec	Name	St	Pg
Oph	Dana, R	MA	574
Oph	Davis, J	FL	587
Oph	Foster, C	MA	574
Oph	Jabs, D	NY	580
Oph	Perez, V	FL	591
Oph	Petersen, M	OH	598
Oph	Smith, R	CA	609
PRhu	Onel, K	IL	813

Uveitis/AIDS

Spec	Name	St	Pg
Oph	Rao, N	CA	608

V

Vaccinations in Pregnancy

Spec	Name	St	Pg
MF	Gonik, B	MI	438

Vaccine Therapy

Spec	Name	St	Pg
GO	Alexander, M	MD	276
Hem	Stiff, P	IL	324
Onc	Chapman, P	NY	339
Onc	Kwak, L	TX	381
Onc	Laheru, D	MD	346
Onc	Maloney, D	WA	389
Onc	Peace, D	IL	372
Onc	Scheinberg, D	NY	351
Onc	Small, E	CA	392
Onc	Sotomayor, E	FL	364
Onc	Triozzi, P	OH	374
Onc	Wolchok, J	NY	354
S	Cole, D	SC	1104
S	Huth, J	TX	1126
S	Kaufman, H	IL	1115
S	Schulick, R	CO	1123

Vaccine Therapy-Clinical Trials Only

Spec	Name	St	Pg
Onc	Arlen, P	MD	337
Onc	Gulley, J	MD	344

Vaccines

Spec	Name	St	Pg
PInf	Baker, C	TX	796
PInf	Demmler-Harrison, G	TX	796
PInf	Edwards, K	TN	794
PInf	Long, S	PA	793
PInf	Meissner, H	MA	792
PInf	Shapiro, E	CT	793

Vaginal Cancer

Spec	Name	St	Pg
GO	Nagarsheth, N	NY	279
GO	Smith, L	CA	291
RadRO	Eifel, P	TX	993

Vaginal Reconstruction

Spec	Name	St	Pg
ObG	Cornella, J	AZ	566
ObG	Sanz, L	VA	563
ObG	Walters, M	OH	566

Vaginal/Uterine Abnormalities

Spec	Name	St	Pg
RE	DeVane, G	FL	1045
RE	Schlaff, W	PA	1044

Vaginitis

Spec	Name	St	Pg
Inf	Sobel, J	MI	419
RE	Winer, S	CA	1053

Valley Fever

Spec	Name	St	Pg
Inf	Galgiani, J	AZ	420

Varicocele

Spec	Name	St	Pg
Ped Uro	Caldamone, A	RI	824
Ped Uro	Cartwright, P	UT	828
Ped Uro	Kolon, T	PA	825
Ped Uro	Pope, J	TN	826
Ped Uro	Sutherland, R	NC	826

Varicocele Embolization

Spec	Name	St	Pg
VIR	Johnson, M	IN	1030
VIR	Shlansky-Goldberg, R	PA	1028
VIR	Smith, S	IL	1031
VIR	Vogelzang, R	IL	1031

Varicocele in Adolescents

Spec	Name	St	Pg
Ped Uro	Kass, E	MI	827

Varicocele Microsurgery

Spec	Name	St	Pg
U	Bar-Chama, N	NY	1188
U	Goldstein, M	NY	1190
U	Nagler, H	NY	1193
U	Sandlow, J	WI	1205
U	Van Arsdalen, K	PA	1196

Varicose Veins

Spec	Name	St	Pg
VascS	Calligaro, K	PA	1222
VIR	Khilnani, N	NY	1028

Vascular & Interventional Radiology

Spec	Name	St	Pg
VIR	Aruny, J	CT	1027
VIR	Benenati, J	FL	1029
VIR	Brown, D	TN	1029
VIR	Brown, K	NY	1027
VIR	Cho, K	MI	1030
VIR	Cohen, G	PA	1027
VIR	Coldwell, D	KY	1029
VIR	Dake, M	CA	1032
VIR	Darcy, M	MO	1030
VIR	Denny, D	NJ	1027
VIR	Durham, J	CO	1031
VIR	Funaki, B	IL	1030

Spec	Name	St	Pg
VIR	Geschwind, J	MD	1028
VIR	Gomes, A	CA	1032
VIR	Goodwin, S	CA	1032
VIR	Hallisey, M	CT	1027
VIR	Haskal, Z	MD	1028
VIR	Hicks, M	TX	1032
VIR	Hovsepian, D	CA	1033
VIR	Johnson, M	IN	1030
VIR	Katzen, B	FL	1029
VIR	Kaufman, J	OR	1033
VIR	Kay, D	LA	1032
VIR	Keller, F	OR	1033
VIR	Khilnani, N	NY	1028
VIR	Kumpe, D	CO	1031
VIR	Lewis, C	GA	1030
VIR	Matsumoto, A	VA	1030
VIR	Mauro, M	NC	1030
VIR	McGahan, J	CA	1033
VIR	McLean, G	PA	1028
VIR	Murphy, T	RI	1027
VIR	Nemcek, A	IL	1031
VIR	Rilling, W	WI	1031
VIR	Roberts, A	CA	1033
VIR	Salem, R	IL	1031
VIR	Shlansky-Goldberg, R	PA	1028
VIR	Smith, S	IL	1031
VIR	Solomon, S	NY	1028
VIR	Soulen, M	PA	1028
VIR	Trerotola, S	PA	1029
VIR	Valji, K	WA	1033
VIR	Vogelzang, R	IL	1031
VIR	Weintraub, J	NY	1029
VIR	Wood, B	MD	1029
VIR	Yakes, W	CO	1032

Vascular Birthmarks

Spec	Name	St	Pg
D	Eichenfield, L	CA	200
D	Frieden, I	CA	200
D	Garden, J	IL	195
D	Levy, M	TX	198
D	Treadwell, P	IN	197
PIS	Burns, A	TX	898

Vascular Disease

Spec	Name	St	Pg
Cv	Halperin, J	NY	93
N	Roos, K	IN	533
VascS	LaMuraglia, G	MA	1221
VascS	Pevec, W	CA	1230
VIR	Aruny, J	CT	1027
VIR	Dake, M	CA	1032
VIR	Matsumoto, A	VA	1030
VIR	Nemcek, A	IL	1031

Vascular Disease-Upper Extremity

Spec	Name	St	Pg
HS	Koman, L	NC	301

Vascular Lesions of the CNS

Spec	Name	St	Pg
NRad	Masaryk, T	OH	1024
NRad	Teitelbaum, G	CA	1026

Vascular Lesions-Head & Neck

Spec	Name	St	Pg
Oto	Persky, M	NY	674
Oto	Suen, J	AR	693

Vascular Malformations

Spec	Name	St	Pg
CG	Graham, J	CA	162
D	Bayliss, S	MO	194
D	Cohen, B	MD	187
NRad	Berenstein, A	NY	1020
NRad	Orbach, D	MA	1020
NS	Amar, A	CA	498
NS	Lunsford, L	PA	479
Oto	Waner, M	NY	677
Oto	Wong, B	CA	698
PIS	Boyajian, M	DC	881
PIS	Low, D	PA	884
PIS	Mulliken, J	MA	878
PIS	Persing, J	CT	879
PO	Cunningham, M	MA	801
VIR	Cho, K	MI	1030
VIR	Gomes, A	CA	1032
VIR	Haskal, Z	MD	1028
VIR	Hovsepian, D	CA	1033
VIR	Rilling, W	WI	1031
VIR	Vogelzang, R	IL	1031
VIR	Weintraub, J	NY	1029
VIR	Yakes, W	CO	1032

Vascular Medicine

Spec	Name	St	Pg
IC	Dieter, R	IL	125
IC	Khawaja, S	GA	124

Vascular Neurology

Spec	Name	St	Pg
N	Tayal, A	PA	522
NRad	Drayer, B	NY	1020

Vascular Neurosurgery

Spec	Name	St	Pg
NS	Couldwell, W	UT	494
NS	Dempsey, R	WI	489
NS	Krisht, A	AR	496
NS	Martin, N	CA	500
NS	Rigamonti, D	MD	481
NS	Samson, D	TX	497
NS	Yonas, H	NM	498

Vascular Reconstruction

Spec	Name	St	Pg
VascS	Cherry, K	VA	1225
VascS	Kougias, P	TX	1229

Vascular Surgery

Spec	Name	St	Pg
S	Bartlett, S	MD	1089
S	Mannella, W	PA	1096
S	Traynor, M	ND	1123
T&CS	Aldea, G	WA	1177
T&CS	Martin, T	FL	1163
T&CS	Safi, H	TX	1176
VascS	Acher, C	WI	1226
VascS	Adelman, M	NY	1221
VascS	Ahn, S	CA	1230
VascS	Alexander, J	OH	1226
VascS	Annest, S	CO	1228
VascS	Ascher, E	NY	1221
VascS	Atnip, R	PA	1221
VascS	Bandyk, D	CA	1230
VascS	Belkin, M	MA	1220
VascS	Benckart, D	PA	1222
VascS	Benvenisty, A	NY	1222
VascS	Blebea, J	OK	1229
VascS	Brener, B	NJ	1222
VascS	Brewster, D	MA	1220
VascS	Calligaro, K	PA	1222
VascS	Cambria, R	MA	1220
VascS	Carpenter, J	NJ	1222
VascS	Chaikof, E	MA	1220
VascS	Cherry, K	VA	1225
VascS	Cho, J	IL	1226
VascS	Clair, D	OH	1227
VascS	Comerota, A	OH	1227
VascS	Cooper, M	CO	1228
VascS	Criado, F	MD	1222
VascS	Cronenwett, J	NH	1220
VascS	D'Ayala, M	NY	1222
VascS	Dalsing, M	IN	1227
VascS	Darling, R	NY	1222
VascS	Dattilo, J	TN	1225
VascS	Dougherty, M	PA	1223
VascS	Eidt, J	SC	1225
VascS	Ellozy, S	NY	1223
VascS	Eton, D	IL	1227
VascS	Fairman, R	PA	1223
VascS	Faries, P	NY	1223
VascS	Flanigan, D	CA	1230
VascS	Fowl, R	AZ	1229
VascS	Freischlag, J	MD	1223
VascS	Gewertz, B	CA	1230
VascS	Gloviczki, P	MN	1227
VascS	Golden, M	PA	1223
VascS	Green, R	NY	1223
VascS	Greisler, H	IL	1227
VascS	Hakaim, A	FL	1225
VascS	Hallett, J	SC	1225
VascS	Harrington, E	NY	1223
VascS	Hodgson, K	IL	1227
VascS	Hollier, L	LA	1229
VascS	Howard, T	NE	1229
VascS	Huber, T	FL	1226
VascS	Iafrati, M	MA	1220
VascS	Kazmers, A	MI	1227
VascS	Kent, K	WI	1228
VascS	Kougias, P	TX	1229
VascS	Kwolek, C	MA	1220
VascS	LaMuraglia, G	MA	1221
VascS	Lantis, J	NY	1224
VascS	Lumsden, A	TX	1229
VascS	Mackey, W	MA	1221
VascS	Makaroun, M	PA	1224
VascS	Marin, M	NY	1224
VascS	McCann, R	NC	1226

Spec	Name	St	Pg
VascS	McKinsey, J	NY	1224
VascS	Mitchell, M	MS	1226
VascS	Money, S	AZ	1229
VascS	Morrissey, N	NY	1224
VascS	Naslund, T	TN	1226
VascS	Neville, R	DC	1224
VascS	Pearce, W	IL	1228
VascS	Perler, B	MD	1224
VascS	Pevec, W	CA	1230
VascS	Pomposelli, F	MA	1221
VascS	Ricotta, J	DC	1224
VascS	Sanchez, L	MO	1228
VascS	Schneider, D	NY	1225
VascS	Shepard, A	MI	1228
VascS	Sicard, G	MO	1228
VascS	Stanley, J	MI	1228
VascS	Sumpio, B	CT	1221
VascS	Todd, G	NY	1225
VascS	Weinstein, E	CO	1229
VascS	White, R	CA	1230

Vasculitis

D	Callen, J	KY	192
D	Soter, N	NY	191
N	Lisak, R	MI	530
Nep	Falk, R	NC	461
Nep	Fulop, T	MS	461
Nep	Holzman, L	PA	459
Nep	Salant, D	MA	458
PRhu	Finkel, T	FL	812
PRhu	McCarthy, P	CT	811
PRhu	Myones, B	TX	813
PRhu	Onel, K	IL	813
PRhu	Sills, E	MD	812
PRhu	Wagner-Weiner, L	IL	813
Pul	Henke, D	NC	962
Rhu	Albert, D	NH	1058
Rhu	Allen, N	NC	1063
Rhu	Blume, R	NY	1059
Rhu	Coblyn, J	MA	1058
Rhu	Cupps, T	DC	1060
Rhu	Katz, R	IL	1065
Rhu	Kimberly, R	AL	1064
Rhu	Lahita, R	NJ	1060
Rhu	Langford, C	OH	1065
Rhu	Lawry, G	CA	1068
Rhu	Merkel, P	PA	1061
Rhu	Paget, S	NY	1061
Rhu	Peng, S	WA	1068
Rhu	Sergent, J	TN	1064
Rhu	Spiera, H	NY	1062
Rhu	Wener, M	WA	1068

Vasculitis of the Nervous System

N	Vollmer, T	CO	535

Vasectomy

U	Irby, P	NC	1198
U	Sabanegh, E	OH	1205
U	Sanders, W	GA	1200

Vasectomy & Vasectomy Reversal

U	Goldstein, M	NY	1190
U	Sandlow, J	WI	1205

Vasectomy Reversal

U	Bar-Chama, N	NY	1188
U	Beall, M	VA	1197
U	Buch, J	TX	1208
U	Davis, B	KS	1207
U	Fisch, H	NY	1190
U	Janeiro, J	NH	1186
U	Meacham, R	CO	1207
U	Nagler, H	NY	1193
U	Oates, R	MA	1187
U	Sabanegh, E	OH	1205
U	Sharlip, I	CA	1213
U	Sigman, M	RI	1188
U	Silber, S	MO	1206
U	Turek, P	CA	1214
U	Van Arsdalen, K	PA	1196

Vein Disorders

VascS	Adelman, M	NY	1221
VascS	Flanigan, D	CA	1230
VascS	Gloviczki, P	MN	1227
VascS	Iafrati, M	MA	1220
VascS	Lumsden, A	TX	1229
VascS	Pearce, W	IL	1228
VascS	Ricotta, J	DC	1224
VIR	Aruny, J	CT	1027
VIR	Khilnani, N	NY	1028
VIR	Lewis, C	GA	1030

Ventilation Management-Long Term

PPul	Redding, G	WA	811
PPul	Warren, R	AR	810

Ventricular Assist Device (LVAD)

Cv	Horn, E	NY	94
Cv	Smart, F	LA	109
Cv	Young, J	OH	107
IC	Cohen, H	PA	121
T&CS	Acker, M	PA	1149
T&CS	Bolman, R	MA	1146
T&CS	Elefteriades, J	CT	1146
T&CS	Lansman, S	NY	1156
T&CS	Magovern, G	PA	1156
T&CS	McCarthy, P	IL	1170
T&CS	Morris, R	PA	1156
T&CS	Naka, Y	NY	1157
T&CS	Samuels, L	PA	1158
T&CS	Slaughter, M	KY	1165
T&CS	Smedira, N	OH	1171
T&CS	Staples, E	FL	1166
T&CS	Szeto, W	PA	1159
T&CS	Tedder, M	TN	1166

Ventricular Septal Defect (Amplatzer R)

PCd	Zahn, E	CA	755

Ventricular Tachycardia Ablation

CE	Donahue, J	MA	113
CE	Lewkowiez, L	CO	119
CE	Link, M	MA	113
CE	Miller, J	IN	118

Video Assisted Thoracic Surgery (VATS)

T&CS	Cohen, N	MD	1151
T&CS	Flores, R	NY	1152
T&CS	Friedberg, J	PA	1152
T&CS	Gharagozloo, F	AZ	1174
T&CS	Landreneau, R	LA	1175
T&CS	Naunheim, K	MO	1170
T&CS	Pechet, T	PA	1157
T&CS	Scott, W	PA	1158
T&CS	Swanson, S	MA	1148

Viral Infections

Inf	Luby, J	TX	420
Inf	Polsky, B	NY	414
Inf	Van Der Horst, C	NC	417
PInf	Andiman, W	CT	792
PInf	Christenson, J	IN	795
PInf	Jacobs, R	AR	796
PInf	Mitchell, C	FL	795
Pul	Jacoby, D	OR	971

Vision-Unexplained Loss

N	Schatz, N	FL	526
Oph	Borchert, M	CA	604

Visual Perception & Learning Disorders

Oph	Koller, H	PA	580

Vitiligo

D	Grimes, P	CA	201
D	Lim, H	MI	196
D	Nigra, T	DC	189

Vocal Cord Disorders

Oto	Donovan, D	TX	692
Oto	Hogikyan, N	MI	685
Oto	Mirza, N	PA	673
Oto	Netterville, J	TN	680
Oto	Ossoff, R	TN	680

Spec	Name	St	Pg
Oto	Stasney, C	TX	693
Oto	Stenson, K	IL	688
Oto	Stewart, M	NY	676
Oto	Sulica, R	NY	676
PO	Parikh, S	WA	806
Pul	Martin, R	CO	968

Vocal Cord Disorders-Botox Therapy

Spec	Name	St	Pg
Oto	Clark, K	OK	691

Voice after Laryngeal Cancer Surgery

Spec	Name	St	Pg
Oto	Deschler, D	MA	665

Voice Disorders

Spec	Name	St	Pg
Oto	Abaza, M	CO	689
Oto	Aviv, J	NY	668
Oto	Bastian, R	IL	683
Oto	Berke, G	CA	694
Oto	Blitzer, A	NY	668
Oto	Burns, J	MA	665
Oto	Clark, K	OK	691
Oto	Corey, J	IL	684
Oto	Donovan, D	TX	692
Oto	Flint, P	OR	695
Oto	Grillone, G	MA	665
Oto	Hoffman, H	IA	685
Oto	Hogikyan, N	MI	685
Oto	Koufman, J	NY	672
Oto	Mirza, N	PA	673
Oto	Ossoff, R	TN	680
Oto	Postma, G	GA	680
Oto	Rosen, C	PA	674
Oto	Sasaki, C	CT	667
Oto	Sataloff, R	PA	675
Oto	Schley, W	NY	675
Oto	Silverman, D	VT	667
Oto	Sinha, U	CA	697
Oto	Stasney, C	TX	693
Oto	Strome, M	NY	676
Oto	Sulica, R	NY	676
Oto	Weissler, M	NC	682
Oto	Wilson, K	OH	688
Oto	Woo, P	NY	677
Oto	Woodson, G	IL	689
Oto	Zeitels, S	MA	667
PO	Goldsmith, A	NY	802
PO	Holinger, L	IL	804
PO	Inglis, A	WA	805

Voiding Dysfunction

Spec	Name	St	Pg
Ger	Resnick, N	PA	265
ObG	Sand, P	IL	565
Ped Uro	Docimo, S	PA	825
U	Broderick, G	FL	1197
U	Childs, S	CO	1206
U	Culkin, D	OK	1208
U	Foster, H	CT	1186
U	Gomery, P	MA	1186
U	Kaplan, S	NY	1191
U	Kennelly, M	NC	1198
U	Lockhart, J	FL	1198
U	Loo, M	NY	1192
U	Milam, D	TN	1198
U	Nitti, V	NY	1193
U	Roehrborn, C	TX	1209
U	Shenot, P	PA	1195
U	Woo, H	LA	1210

Voiding Dysfunction/Spinal Cord Injury

Spec	Name	St	Pg
U	Linsenmeyer, T	NJ	1192
U	Shenot, P	PA	1195

Vomiting-Cyclic

Spec	Name	St	Pg
CG	Boles, R	CA	162
MF	Wapner, R	NY	435
ObG	Niebyl, J	IA	565

Von Hippel-Lindau Disease

Spec	Name	St	Pg
NS	Barnett, G	OH	488
NS	Olson, J	GA	486
S	Carty, S	PA	1091

Von Willebrand's Disease

Spec	Name	St	Pg
Hem	Bockenstedt, P	MI	321

Vulvar & Vaginal Cancer

Spec	Name	St	Pg
GO	Azodi, M	CT	274
GO	Berek, J	CA	290
GO	Burke, T	TX	288
GO	Clarke-Pearson, D	NC	281
GO	Kline, R	LA	288
GO	Koulos, J	NY	279
GO	Muto, M	MA	275
GO	Potkul, R	IL	285
GO	Powell, M	MO	285
GO	Santin, A	CT	275
RadRO	Randall, M	KY	986

Vulvar & Vaginal Disorders

Spec	Name	St	Pg
ObG	Eschenbach, D	WA	567
ObG	Levine, E	IL	565
ObG	Snyder, R	TX	566

Vulvar Disease/Cancer

Spec	Name	St	Pg
GO	Abu-Rustum, N	NY	276
GO	Caputo, T	NY	277
GO	Levenback, C	TX	289
GO	Modesitt, S	VA	283
GO	Rosenblum, N	PA	280
GO	Smith, L	CA	291
GO	Stern, J	CA	292
RadRO	Eifel, P	TX	993

Vulvar Pain

Spec	Name	St	Pg
ObG	Levine, E	IL	565
U	Goldstein, I	CA	1212

W

Waldenstrom's Macroglobulinemia

Spec	Name	St	Pg
Hem	Gertz, M	MN	321
Hem	Stewart, A	AZ	327
Onc	Coleman, M	NY	340

Weaver Syndrome

Spec	Name	St	Pg
CG	Weaver, D	IN	160

Wegener's Granulomatosis

Spec	Name	St	Pg
Nep	Falk, R	NC	461
Oto	Lebovics, R	NY	673
Rhu	Allen, N	NC	1063
Rhu	Belmont, H	NY	1059

Weight Management

Spec	Name	St	Pg
EDM	Broadstone, V	IN	218
Ge	Kaplan, L	MA	231
PEn	Wilson, D	CA	762
PGe	Krebs, N	CO	767

White Matter Disorders

Spec	Name	St	Pg
N	Filley, C	CO	534
PMR	Evans, S	DC	863

Whooping Cough

Spec	Name	St	Pg
PInf	Long, S	PA	793

Williams Syndrome

Spec	Name	St	Pg
CG	Marion, R	NY	158
CG	Morris, C	NV	163

Wilms' Tumor

Spec	Name	St	Pg
Ped Uro	Kolon, T	PA	825
PHO	Dome, J	DC	772
PHO	Green, D	TN	779
PHO	Plautz, G	OH	785
PHO	Steinherz, P	NY	776
PS	Ehrlich, P	MI	819
PS	Kandel, J	IL	820
PS	La Quaglia, M	NY	816
PS	Shamberger, R	MA	814
U	Hensle, T	NJ	1191

Spec	Name	St	Pg

Wiskott-Aldrich Syndrome

Spec	Name	St	Pg
PHO	Bussel, J	NY	771

Women & Addiction

Spec	Name	St	Pg
AdP	Greenfield, S	MA	936

Women's Eye Health

Spec	Name	St	Pg
Oph	Vajaranant, T	IL	600

Women's Health

Spec	Name	St	Pg
Cv	Andersen, H	NY	91
Cv	Goldberg, N	NY	93
Cv	Johnson, P	MA	88
Cv	Limacher, M	FL	98
Ge	Borum, M	DC	233
GO	Cain, J	MA	274
GO	Husain, A	CA	291
IM	Cirigliano, M	PA	426
Inf	Cohn, S	IL	417
MF	Gibbs, R	CO	440
MF	Repke, J	PA	435
N	Liporace, J	PA	518
ObG	Argenta, P	MN	563
ObG	Bradshaw, K	TX	566
ObG	King, A	ID	566
ObG	Morgan, L	FL	563
Onc	Chlebowski, R	CA	386
RE	Blackwell, R	AL	1045
Rhu	Fife, R	IN	1065

Women's Health-Mental Health

Spec	Name	St	Pg
Psyc	Burt, V	CA	932
Psyc	Joffe, H	MA	921
Psyc	Zerbe, K	OR	935

Women's Health/Disabilities

Spec	Name	St	Pg
PMR	Kirschner, K	IL	869

Women's Imaging

Spec	Name	St	Pg
DR	Edelstein, B	NY	1009
DR	Thurmond, A	OR	1018

Wound Healing/Care

Spec	Name	St	Pg
D	Arpey, C	MN	194
D	Fivenson, D	MI	195
D	Kirsner, R	FL	193
Ger	Thomas, D	MO	266
PlS	Attinger, C	DC	880
PlS	Cruse, C	FL	889
PlS	Garner, W	CA	902
PlS	Molnar, J	NC	891
PlS	Orgill, D	MA	878
S	Bessey, P	NY	1089
S	Cairns, B	NC	1104
S	Dixon, S	NV	1131
S	Edington, H	PA	1092
S	Greenhalgh, D	CA	1133
S	Lentz, C	NM	1127
S	Luterman, A	AL	1106
S	Mannella, W	PA	1096
S	Ryan, C	MA	1087
S	Yurt, R	NY	1102
VascS	Iafrati, M	MA	1220
VascS	Lantis, J	NY	1224
VascS	Neville, R	DC	1224
VascS	Sumpio, B	CT	1221

WPW Syndrome

Spec	Name	St	Pg
CE	Morady, F	MI	118

Wrist Reconstruction

Spec	Name	St	Pg
HS	Kleinman, W	IN	303

Wrist Surgery

Spec	Name	St	Pg
HS	Badia, A	FL	300
HS	Cohen, M	IL	302
HS	Fischer, T	IN	302
HS	Hastings, H	IN	303
HS	Hotchkiss, R	NY	298
HS	Mass, D	IL	303
HS	Melone, C	NY	299
HS	Nagle, D	IL	303
HS	Osterman, A	PA	299
HS	Putnam, M	MN	304
HS	Seitz, W	OH	304
HS	Weiss, A	RI	297
HS	Wolfe, S	NY	300

Wrist/Hand Injuries

Spec	Name	St	Pg
HS	Collins, E	TX	305
HS	Graham, T	OH	303
HS	Raskin, K	NY	300
HS	Thoder, J	PA	300
OrS	Weiland, A	NY	633

X

Xeroderma Pigmentosum

Spec	Name	St	Pg
D	Hruza, G	MO	195

Z

Zenker Diverticulum

Spec	Name	St	Pg
Oto	Miller, F	TX	693
Oto	Sasaki, C	CT	667

Zollinger-Ellison Syndrome

Spec	Name	St	Pg
Ge	Wilcox, C	AL	245

Alphabetical Listing of Doctors

Name	Specialty	Pg
A		
Abaza, Mona (CO)	Oto	689
Abbas, Fouad (MD)	GO	276
Abbitt, Patricia (FL)	DR	1012
Abbott, Richard (CA)	Oph	604
Abbruzzese, James (TX)	Onc	378
Abcarian, Herand (IL)	CRS	173
Abdu, William (NH)	OrS	616
Abecassis, Michael (IL)	S	1111
Abi-samra, Freddy (LA)	Cv	107
Abou-Khalil, Bassel (TN)	N	523
Aboulafia, Albert (MD)	OrS	620
Aboulafia, David (WA)	Onc	384
Abouljoud, Marwan (MI)	S	1111
Abraham, Jame (OH)	Onc	365
Abraham, V. (IN)	T&CS	1166
Abrahamson, Martin (MA)	EDM	208
Abrahm, Janet (MA)	H & PM	406
Abram, Stephen (WI)	PM	709
Abrams, Charles (PA)	Hem	313
Abrams, Donald (CA)	Onc	384
Abrams, Gary (MI)	Oph	593
Abrams, Reid (CA)	HS	305
Abrams, Ross (IL)	RadRO	988
Abramson, David (NY)	Oph	575
Abrass, Itamar (WA)	Ger	267
Abreu, Maria (FL)	Ge	241
Abright, A. Reese (NY)	ChAP	939
Abromowitch, Minnie (NE)	PHO	786
Abu-Rustum, Nadeem (NY)	GO	276
Abuhamad, Alfred (VA)	MF	436
Acher, Charles (WI)	VascS	1226
Acker, Michael (PA)	T&CS	1149
Ackerman, Michael (MN)	PCd	752
Adam, Karolina (TX)	MF	440
Adams, David (FL)	N	523
Adams, David (NY)	T&CS	1150
Adams, Elaine (IL)	Rhu	1064
Adams, Harold (IA)	N	527
Adams, James (TX)	NP	453
Adams, Reid (VA)	S	1103
Adams, Roberta (AZ)	Hem	325
Adams-Graves, Patricia (TN)	Hem	318
Adamson, G. David (CA)	RE	1051
Adamson, Peter (PA)	PHO	771
Adashek, Joseph (NV)	MF	441
Adelman, Mark (NY)	VascS	1221
Adelson, P David (AZ)	NS	495
Adelstein, David (OH)	Onc	365
Adger, Hoover (MD)	AM	76
Adler, David (MA)	Psyc	920
Adler, Ronald (NY)	DR	1008
Adornato, Bruce (CA)	N	538
Advani, Ranjana (CA)	Onc	384
Adzick, N. Scott (PA)	PS	814
Afshari, Natalie (CA)	Oph	604
Agarwal, Animesh (TX)	OrS	647
Agarwal, Sanjay (CA)	RE	1051
Agarwala, Brojendra (IL)	PCd	752
Aghajanian, Carol (NY)	Onc	336
Agress, Harry (NJ)	NuM	554
Ahern, Geoffrey (AZ)	N	535
Ahlering, Thomas (CA)	U	1210
Ahlgren, James (DC)	Onc	336
Ahlskog, J Eric (MN)	N	527
Ahmad, Amjad (IL)	Oph	593
Ahmad, Christopher (NY)	OrS	620
Ahmad, Suhail (WA)	Nep	466
Ahmann, Andrew (OR)	EDM	223
Ahmann, Frederick (AZ)	Onc	378
Ahn, Jung (NY)	PMR	862
Ahn, Sam (CA)	VascS	1230
Ahya, Vivek (PA)	Pul	956
Aiken, John (WI)	PS	819
Aiken, Robert (IL)	N	527
Ain, Kenneth (KY)	EDM	215
Aisner, Joseph (NJ)	Onc	337
Ajani, Jaffer (TX)	Onc	378
Akatsu, Haruko (CA)	EDM	223
Akerley, Wallace (UT)	Onc	375
Akervall, Jan (MI)	Oto	682
Akhtar, Salman (PA)	Psyc	922
Al-Kawas, Firas (DC)	Ge	232
Al-Mefty, Ossama (MA)	NS	472
Alam, Daniel (OH)	Oto	682
Alavi, Abass (PA)	NuM	554
Alazraki, Naomi (GA)	NuM	555
Albain, Kathy (IL)	Onc	366
Albala, David (NY)	U	1188
Albanese, Craig (CA)	PS	823
Albers, Gregory (CA)	N	538
Albert, Daniel (WI)	Oph	593
Albert, Daniel (NH)	Rhu	1058
Albert, Michael (DC)	Ge	232
Albert, Todd (PA)	OrS	620
Albertini, Mark (WI)	Onc	366
Alberts, David (AZ)	Onc	378

Alphabetical Listing of Doctors

Name	Specialty	Pg
Alberts, Mark (TX)	N	536
Alberts, W. Michael (FL)	Pul	961
Albertsen, Peter (CT)	U	1186
Albertson, Timothy (CA)	Pul	969
Albright, John (IA)	OrS	639
Albritton, Karen (TX)	PHO	787
Aldea, Gabriel (WA)	T&CS	1177
Aledo, Alexander (NY)	PHO	771
Alessi, Norman (MI)	ChAP	941
Alexander, Frederick (NJ)	PS	815
Alexander, H. Richard (MD)	S	1089
Alexander, J. Jeffrey (OH)	VascS	1226
Alexander, Joshua (NC)	PMR	866
Alexander, Kenneth (IL)	PInf	795
Alexander, Margaret (MD)	GO	276
Alexander, Richard (MD)	U	1188
Alexander, Steven (CA)	PNep	800
Alexandrov, Andrei (AL)	N	523
Alfonso, Antonio (NY)	S	1089
Alfonso, Eduardo (FL)	Oph	586
Algazy, Kenneth (PA)	Onc	337
Allen, David (WI)	PEn	760
Allen, Jeffrey (NY)	ChiN	145
Allen, Nancy (NC)	Rhu	1063
Allen, Robert (NY)	PlS	880
Allen, Steven (NY)	Hem	313
Allman, Richard (PA)	Rhu	1059
Allon, Michael (AL)	Nep	461
Allred, D. (MO)	Path	727
Alpert, Jonathan (MA)	Psyc	920
Alpert, Joseph (AZ)	Cv	107
Alster, Tina (DC)	D	186
Altchek, David (NY)	SM	1074
Alter, Craig (PA)	PEn	757
Alter, Gary (CA)	PlS	901
Altman, Arnold (CT)	PHO	769
Altman, Leonard (WA)	A&I	85
Altorki, Nasser (NY)	T&CS	1150
Alvarez, Ronald (AL)	GO	280
Alvarez-Elcoro, Salvador (FL)	Inf	415
Alward, Wallace (IA)	Oph	593
Aly, Al (CA)	PlS	901
Amar, Arun (CA)	NS	498
Amato, Anthony (MA)	N	510
Ambinder, Richard (MD)	Onc	337
Amedee, Ronald (LA)	Oto	691
Ames, Christopher (CA)	NS	498
Ames, Frederick (TX)	S	1123
Amin, Mahul (CA)	Path	731
Aminoff, Michael (CA)	N	538
Amling, Christopher (OR)	U	1210
Amonette, Rex (TN)	D	191
Amundsen, Cindy (NC)	ObG	562
An, Howard (IL)	OrS	639
Anday, Endla (PA)	NP	448
Andersen, Glenna (VA)	ObG	562
Andersen, Holly (NY)	Cv	91
Andersen, James (CA)	PlS	901
Andersen, Peter (OR)	Oto	694
Anderson, Benjamin (WA)	S	1130
Anderson, Jeffrey (UT)	Cv	107
Anderson, Karl (TX)	Ge	252
Anderson, Kenneth (MA)	Hem	312
Anderson, Lesley (CA)	OrS	649
Anderson, Mark (IA)	CE	117
Anderson, Martin (CA)	AM	78
Anderson, Richard (MA)	D	184
Anderson, Richard (UT)	Oph	601
Anderson, Richard (NY)	NS	474
Andersson, Hans (LA)	CG	161
Andiman, Warren (CT)	PInf	792
Andreoli, Sharon (IN)	PNep	799
Andreoni, Kenneth (FL)	S	1103
Andrews, David (PA)	NS	474
Andrews, James (FL)	SM	1076
Andrews, Paul (AZ)	U	1207
Andrews, Robert (WA)	PHO	789
Andrews, Walter (MO)	PS	819
Andrews, William (AL)	MF	436
Andriole, Gerald (MO)	U	1202
Angelos, Peter (IL)	S	1111
Anghelescu, Doralina (TN)	PM	708
Angiolillo, Anne (DC)	PHO	771
Anglen, Jeffrey (IN)	OrS	639
Anhalt, Grant (MD)	D	186
Annest, Stephen (CO)	VascS	1228
Anscher, Mitchell (VA)	RadRO	983
Anthony, Lowell (KY)	Onc	354
Antin, Joseph (MA)	Onc	330
Antonescu, Cristina (NY)	Path	720
Antonia, Scott (FL)	Onc	355
Antony, Veena (AL)	Pul	961
Anyane-Yeboa, Kwame (NY)	CG	156
Apatoff, Brian (NY)	N	512
Apkon, Susan (WA)	PMR	872
Appel, Gerald (NY)	Nep	458
Appelbaum, Daniel (IL)	NuM	556
Appelbaum, Frederick (WA)	Onc	385
Appelbaum, Paul (NY)	Psyc	922
Appelman, Henry (MI)	Path	727
Applegate, Robert (NC)	IC	124
April, Max (NY)	PO	802

Name	Specialty	Pg
Apuzzo, Michael (CA)	NS	498
Aranha, Gerard (IL)	S	1111
Arber, Daniel (CA)	Path	731
Arcasoy, Selim (NY)	Pul	956
Arceci, Robert (AZ)	PHO	787
Archdeacon, Michael (OH)	OrS	639
Archer, Steven (MI)	Oph	593
Arendt, Elizabeth (MN)	SM	1077
Arensman, Robert (IL)	PS	819
Argenta, Peter (MN)	ObG	563
Argenziano, Michael (NY)	T&CS	1150
Argiris, Athanassios (TX)	Onc	378
Argoff, Charles (NY)	PM	706
Arjmand, Ellis (OH)	PO	803
Arlen, Philip (MD)	Onc	337
Armitage, James (NE)	Onc	375
Armstrong, Deborah (MD)	Onc	337
Arnason, Barry (IL)	N	528
Arndt, Carola (MN)	PHO	781
Arndt, Kenneth (MA)	D	184
Arnold, Anthony (CA)	Oph	604
Arnold, James (OH)	PO	804
Arnold, Robert (PA)	H & PM	406
Arnold, Steven (PA)	Psyc	922
Aronchick, Craig (PA)	Ge	232
Aronson, James (AR)	OrS	647
Arpey, Christopher (MN)	D	194
Arriaga, Moises (LA)	Oto	691
Arroliga, Alejandro (TX)	Pul	968
Arslanian, Silva (PA)	PEn	757
Arteaga, Carlos (TN)	Onc	355
Arts, H Alexander (MI)	Oto	682
Arun, Banu (TX)	Onc	378
Aruny, John (CT)	VIR	1027
Asbell, Penny (NY)	Oph	575
Ascher, Enrico (NY)	VascS	1221
Ascher, Nancy (CA)	S	1130
Ascherman, Jeffrey (NY)	PlS	880
Aseff, John (DC)	PMR	863
Asher, Anthony (NC)	NS	483
Ashizawa, Tetsuo (FL)	N	523
Ashley, Stanley (MA)	S	1084
Ashwal, Stephen (CA)	ChiN	151
Asirvatham, Samuel (MN)	CE	117
Aslanian, Harry (CT)	Ge	230
Aston, Sherrell (NY)	PlS	880
Astrow, Alan (NY)	Onc	337
Atala, Anthony (NC)	Ped Uro	825
Athanasian, Edward (NY)	HS	297
Athanasuleas, Constantine (AL)	T&CS	1160
Atkins, Michael (DC)	Onc	337
Atkinson, John (MN)	NS	488
Atkinson, Robert (HI)	HS	305
Atlas, Scott (CA)	NRad	1025
Atnip, Robert (PA)	VascS	1221
Attai, Deanna (CA)	S	1130
Attas, Lewis (NJ)	Onc	338
Attinger, Christopher (DC)	PlS	880
Audeh, M William (CA)	Onc	385
Audell, Laura (CA)	PM	712
Auger, William (CA)	Pul	970
Augsburger, James (OH)	Oph	593
August, David (NJ)	S	1089
August, Phyllis (NY)	Nep	459
Ault, Bettina (TN)	PNep	798
Austin, John (NY)	DR	1008
Auwaerter, Paul (MD)	Inf	412
Averbook, Bruce (OH)	S	1111
Aviv, Jonathan (NY)	Oto	668
Avram, Marc (NY)	D	186
Awan, Azhar (IL)	RadRO	988
Axelrod, Lloyd (MA)	EDM	208
Axelrod, Rita (PA)	Onc	338
Azar, Dimitri (IL)	Oph	593
Azar, Nathalie (IL)	Oph	593
Azizi, S Ausim (PA)	N	513
Azodi, Masoud (CT)	GO	274
Azziz, Ricardo (GA)	RE	1045
Azzoli, Christopher (MA)	Onc	330

B

Name	Specialty	Pg
Babayan, Richard (MA)	U	1186
Babiera, Gildy (TX)	S	1123
Bach, Bernard (IL)	SM	1077
Bach, John (NJ)	PMR	863
Bach, Richard (MO)	IC	125
Bacha, Emile (NY)	T&CS	1150
Baciewicz, Frank (MI)	T&CS	1167
Back, Anthony (WA)	Onc	385
Backer, Carl (IL)	T&CS	1167
Bacon, Bruce (MO)	Ge	246
Badia, Alejandro (FL)	HS	300
Badie, Behnam (CA)	NS	498
Badlani, Gopal (NC)	U	1196
Baer, Maria (MD)	Hem	313
Baerveldt, George (CA)	Oph	604
Bagg, Adam (PA)	Path	720
Bahado-Singh, Ray (MI)	MF	437
Bahn, Duke (CA)	DR	1017
Bahn, Rebecca (MN)	EDM	218

Alphabetical Listing of Doctors

Name	Specialty	Pg
Bahna, Sami (LA)	PA&I	746
Bahnson, Robert (OH)	U	1202
Baile, Walter (TX)	Psyc	931
Bailes, Julian (IL)	NS	488
Bailey, H Randolph (TX)	CRS	176
Bailey, Leonard (CA)	T&CS	1177
Bailey, Steven (TX)	IC	127
Bailin, Philip (OH)	D	194
Baillie, John (NC)	Ge	241
Baim, Howard (IL)	Oto	683
Bains, Manjit (NY)	T&CS	1150
Bairey-Merz, Cathleen Noel (CA)	Cv	110
Bajorin, Dean (NY)	Onc	338
Bakay, Roy (IL)	NS	488
Baker, Carol (TX)	PInf	796
Baker, Christopher (VA)	S	1103
Baker, Daniel (NY)	PIS	880
Baker, Emily (NH)	MF	432
Baker, Jay (NC)	DR	1013
Baker, John (MI)	Oph	594
Baker, Robert (NY)	PGe	763
Baker, Shan (MI)	Oto	683
Baker, Stephen (DC)	PIS	880
Baker, Susan (NY)	PGe	763
Baker, Valerie (CA)	RE	1051
Bakhos, Mamdouh (IL)	T&CS	1167
Bakken, Johan (MN)	Inf	417
Bakris, George (IL)	Nep	462
Balady, Gary (MA)	Cv	88
Balaji, K. C. (NC)	U	1197
Balart, Luis (LA)	Ge	253
Balcer, Laura (NY)	N	513
Baldassano, Robert (PA)	PGe	763
Balderston, Richard (PA)	OrS	620
Baldridge, Alan (NJ)	PGe	763
Balducci, Lodovico (FL)	Onc	355
Bale, Allen (CT)	CG	156
Bale, James (UT)	ChiN	150
Bales, Gregory (IL)	U	1202
Balk, Robert (IL)	Pul	964
Ball, Douglas (MD)	EDM	210
Ball, Edward (CA)	Onc	385
Balla, Andre (IL)	Path	727
Ballantyne, Christie (TX)	Cv	107
Ballantyne, Jane (WA)	PM	712
Ballard, Pamela (DC)	PMR	863
Ballas, Zuhair (IA)	A&I	83
Ballen, Karen (MA)	Hem	312
Ballon-Landa, Gonzalo (CA)	Inf	420
Balmes, John (CA)	Pul	970
Baloch, Zubair (PA)	Path	720
Baltimore, Robert (CT)	PInf	792
Baltuch, Gordon (PA)	NS	474
Bandyk, Dennis (CA)	VascS	1230
Banerjee, Anuradha (CA)	PHO	789
Banks, Peter (NC)	Path	725
Bans, Larry (AZ)	U	1208
Bar-Chama, Natan (NY)	U	1188
Barakat, Richard (NY)	GO	276
Baratz, Mark (PA)	HS	297
Barbosa, Victoria (IL)	D	194
Bardot, Stephen (LA)	U	1208
Barger, Geoffrey (MI)	N	528
Barie, Philip (NY)	S	1089
Barile, Gaetano (NY)	Oph	576
Barkin, Jamie (FL)	Ge	241
Barkley, Gregory (MI)	N	528
Barkovich, A James (CA)	NRad	1025
Barksdale, Edward (OH)	PS	819
Barlogie, Bart (AR)	Hem	325
Barnes, David (OH)	Ge	246
Barnes, Patrick (CA)	NRad	1026
Barnes, Randall (IL)	RE	1046
Barnes, Willard (DC)	GO	276
Barnett, Gene (OH)	NS	488
Barohn, Richard (KS)	N	534
Baron, Joseph (IL)	Hem	320
Baron, Todd (MN)	Ge	246
Barone, Constance (TX)	PIS	898
Baroody, Fuad (IL)	PO	804
Barredo, Julio (FL)	PHO	777
Barrett, Eugene (VA)	EDM	216
Barrow, Daniel (GA)	NS	484
Bartelsmeyer, James (MO)	MF	438
Barter, James (MD)	GO	276
Bartholomew, Deborah (OH)	ObG	563
Bartholomew, Dennis (OH)	CG	160
Bartlett, David (PA)	S	1089
Bartlett, John (MD)	Inf	412
Bartlett, Scott (PA)	PIS	880
Bartlett, Stephen (MD)	S	1089
Bartolozzi, Arthur (PA)	OrS	620
Barton, Fritz (TX)	PIS	898
Basch, Samuel (NY)	Psyc	923
Bascom, Rebecca (PA)	Pul	956
Baser, Susan (PA)	N	513
Bashevkin, Michael (NY)	Onc	338
Bashore, Thomas (NC)	Cv	97
Baskin, Laurence (CA)	Ped Uro	828
Basler, Joseph (TX)	U	1208
Bass, Theodore (FL)	Cv	97
Bassett, Lawrence (CA)	DR	1017

Name	Specialty	Pg
Basson, Marc (MI)	S	1111
Bastian, Boris (CA)	Path	732
Bastian, Robert (IL)	Oto	683
Batchelor, Tracy (MA)	N	510
Bateman, Bruce (VA)	RE	1045
Battafarano, Richard (MD)	T&CS	1150
Bauer, Bruce (IL)	PlS	892
Bauer, Jerry (IL)	NS	488
Bauer, Stuart (MA)	Ped Uro	824
Bauman, Phillip (NY)	OrS	620
Baumann, Patricia (GA)	PM	708
Bavaria, Joseph (PA)	T&CS	1150
Bayer, Arnold (CA)	Inf	420
Bayliss, Susan (MO)	D	194
Bazari, Hasan (MA)	Nep	458
Beall, Michael (VA)	U	1197
Beals, Stephen (AZ)	PlS	898
Bear, Harry (VA)	S	1103
Beart, Robert (CA)	CRS	177
Beaser, Richard (MA)	EDM	208
Beasley, Michael (NC)	PlS	888
Beatty, Charles (MN)	Oto	683
Beatty, Patrick (MT)	Onc	376
Beaty, James (TN)	OrS	635
Beauchamp, R Daniel (TN)	S	1103
Bebin, E Martina (AL)	N	523
Beck, David (LA)	CRS	176
Beck, Sandra (KY)	CRS	171
Becker, Dorothy (PA)	PEn	757
Becker, Ferdinand (FL)	Oto	677
Becker, James (MA)	S	1084
Becker, Kyra (WA)	N	538
Becker, Yolanda (IL)	S	1111
Bedder, Marshall (WA)	PM	712
Bederson, Joshua (NY)	NS	474
Beekman, Robert (OH)	PCd	752
Beer, Tomasz (OR)	Onc	385
Beerman, Lee (PA)	PCd	748
Beeson, William (IN)	Oto	683
Behm, Frederick (IL)	Path	727
Behrns, Kevin (FL)	S	1103
Beitler, Jonathan (GA)	RadRO	983
Beitsch, Peter (TX)	S	1123
Belani, Chandra (PA)	Onc	338
Belcher, Christopher (IN)	PInf	795
Belenkov, Elliot (NY)	Onc	338
Belkin, Michael (MA)	VascS	1220
Bell, Debra (MN)	Path	727
Bell, Edward (IA)	NP	451
Bell, Louis (PA)	PInf	793
Bell, Rodney (PA)	N	513
Bellamy, Paul (CA)	Pul	970
Belldegrun, Arie (CA)	U	1210
Belmont, H. Michael (NY)	Rhu	1059
Belsito, Donald (NY)	D	186
Belsky, Mark (MA)	HS	296
Belzberg, Allan (MD)	NS	474
Benckart, Daniel (PA)	VascS	1222
Benedetti, Enrico (IL)	S	1112
Benedetti, Thomas (WA)	MF	442
Benedetto, Pasquale (FL)	Onc	355
Benenati, James (FL)	VIR	1029
Benenati, Susan (FL)	A&I	82
Benevenia, Joseph (NJ)	OrS	620
Benfield, Mark (AL)	PNep	798
Benjamin, Robert (TX)	Onc	379
Benjamin, Stanley (DC)	Ge	232
Benkov, Keith (NY)	PGe	763
Bennett, Richard (CA)	D	200
Bennett, William (OR)	Nep	466
Benninger, Michael (OH)	Oto	683
Bensinger, William (WA)	Onc	385
Benson, Al (IL)	Onc	366
Benson, Carol (MA)	DR	1007
Benson, Mitchell (NY)	U	1189
Bentley, Frederick (AR)	S	1124
Bentrem, David (IL)	S	1112
Bentz, Michael (WI)	PlS	892
Benvenisty, Alan (NY)	VascS	1222
Benzel, Edward (OH)	NS	489
Benzon, Honorio (IL)	PM	709
Berchuck, Andrew (NC)	GO	280
Berde, Charles (MA)	PM	706
Beredjiklian, Pedro (PA)	HS	297
Berek, Jonathan (CA)	GO	290
Berenstein, Alejandro (NY)	NRad	1020
Berg, Carl (NC)	Ge	241
Berg, Daniel (WA)	D	200
Berg, Stacey (TX)	PHO	787
Berga, Sarah (NC)	ObG	562
Berger, Joseph (KY)	N	523
Berger, Mitchel (CA)	NS	498
Berger, Ronald (MD)	CE	114
Bergey, Gregory (MD)	N	513
Bergman, Donald (NY)	EDM	211
Bergman, Ira (PA)	ChiN	145
Bergsagel, Peter (AZ)	Onc	379
Berk, John (MA)	Pul	954
Berke, Gerald (CA)	Oto	694
Berkowitz, Carol (CA)	Ped	742
Berkowitz, Leonard (NY)	Inf	412
Berkowitz, Richard (NY)	MF	433

Alphabetical Listing of Doctors

Name	Specialty	Pg
Berkowitz, Ross (MA)	GO	274
Berkson, Richard (CA)	EDM	224
Berland, Lincoln (AL)	DR	1013
Berlin, Cheston (PA)	Ped	740
Berlin, Jordan (TN)	Onc	355
Berman, Brian (MI)	Ped	741
Berman, James (IL)	PGe	765
Berman, Michael (CA)	GO	290
Bermudez, Ovidio (CO)	AM	77
Bernard, Stephen (NC)	Onc	355
Bernardino, Carlo (CA)	Oph	604
Bernardo, Jose (PA)	Nep	459
Berns, Jeffrey (PA)	Nep	459
Bernstein, Daniel (CA)	PCd	754
Bernstein, David (OH)	A&I	83
Bernstein, Jonathan (OH)	A&I	83
Bernstein, Richard (IL)	N	528
Bernstein, Robert (NY)	D	186
Berry, Daniel (MN)	OrS	639
Berry, John (CA)	Onc	385
Bertolone, Salvatore (KY)	PHO	777
Bertorini, Tulio (TN)	N	523
Bessey, Palmer (NY)	S	1089
Bessler, Marc (NY)	S	1089
Betz, Randal (PA)	OrS	621
Beyer, Eric (IL)	PHO	781
Bhan, Atul (MA)	Path	718
Bhasin, Shalender (MA)	EDM	208
Bhattacharyya, Neil (MA)	Oto	665
Bhora, Faiz (NY)	T&CS	1151
Bialer, Martin (NY)	CG	157
Bialer, Philip (NY)	Psyc	923
Biancaniello, Thomas (NY)	PCd	748
Bianchi, Diana (MA)	CG	156
Bichell, David (TN)	T&CS	1160
Bicher, Annette (VA)	GO	280
Bickers, David (NY)	D	187
Biederman, Joseph (MA)	ChAP	938
Bierbrauer, Karin (OH)	NS	489
Bierman, Fredrick (NY)	PCd	748
Bierman, Philip (NE)	Onc	376
Biermann, J Sybil (MI)	OrS	639
Bigelow, Carolyn (MS)	Hem	318
Biggs, David (DE)	Onc	338
Bigliani, Louis (NY)	OrS	621
Bijwadia, Jagdeep (MN)	Pul	964
Bilchik, Anton (CA)	S	1130
Bilezikian, John (NY)	EDM	211
Biller, Beverly (MA)	EDM	208
Biller, Jose (IL)	N	528
Billett, Amy (MA)	PHO	769
Billingsley, Kevin (OR)	S	1130
Billmire, David (OH)	PIS	893
Bilsky, Mark (NY)	NS	475
Bingaman, William (OH)	NS	489
Biousse, Valerie (GA)	Oph	587
Birmaher, Boris (PA)	ChAP	939
Birnbaum, Elisa (MO)	CRS	173
Birrer, Michael (MA)	Onc	330
Bishop, Allen (MN)	HS	302
Bishop, Michael (IL)	Onc	366
Bishop, Warren (IA)	PGe	765
Bissell, Dwight (CA)	IM	427
Bitan, Fabien (NY)	OrS	621
Bitran, Jacob (IL)	Onc	366
Bittl, John (FL)	IC	124
Black, C Thomas (TX)	PS	821
Black, Dennis (TN)	PGe	764
Black, Donald (IA)	Psyc	929
Black, Keith (CA)	NS	498
Black, Kevin (MO)	Psyc	929
Black, William (NH)	DR	1007
Blackstock, A. William (NC)	RadRO	983
Blackstone, Robin (AZ)	S	1124
Blackwell, Keith (CA)	Oto	694
Blackwell, Kimberly (NC)	Onc	355
Blackwell, Richard (AL)	RE	1045
Blaha, John (MI)	OrS	640
Blair, Elizabeth (IL)	Oto	683
Blaivas, Jerry (NY)	U	1189
Blakemore, Karin (MD)	MF	433
Blanchard, Daniel (CA)	Cv	110
Bland, Kirby (AL)	S	1103
Blaney, Susan (TX)	PHO	787
Blatchford, Garnet (NE)	CRS	175
Blatt, Julie (NC)	PHO	778
Blaustein, Arnold (FL)	Hem	318
Blazer, Dan (NC)	Psyc	927
Blebea, John (OK)	VascS	1229
Bleday, Ronald (MA)	CRS	168
Bleiberg, Efrain (TX)	ChAP	943
Bleiweiss, Ira (NY)	Path	720
Blinder, Morey (MO)	Hem	321
Blitzer, Andrew (NY)	Oto	668
Blobe, Gerard (NC)	Onc	355
Bloch, Rina (MA)	PMR	862
Block, Susan (MA)	H & PM	406
Bloom, David (MI)	Ped Uro	826
Bloom, Patricia (NY)	Ger	264
Bloomer, Joseph (AL)	Ge	241
Bluemke, David (MD)	DR	1008
Blum, Andrew (RI)	N	510

Name	Specialty	Pg
Blum, Conrad (NY)	EDM	211
Blum, Kristie (OH)	Hem	321
Blume, Ralph (NY)	Rhu	1059
Blumenfeld, Jon (NY)	Nep	459
Blumenfield, Michael (CA)	Psyc	932
Blumenkranz, Mark (CA)	Oph	604
Blumenthal, David (NY)	Cv	91
Blumenthal, Roger (MD)	Cv	91
Boachie-Adjei, Oheneba (NY)	OrS	621
Bobrove, Arthur (CA)	Rhu	1067
Bock, Samuel (CO)	PA&I	745
Bockenstedt, Paula (MI)	Hem	321
Bockman, Richard (NY)	EDM	211
Boden, Scott (GA)	OrS	635
Bodner, Donald (OH)	U	1202
Bodurka, Diane (TX)	GO	287
Bogart, Jeffrey (NY)	RadRO	978
Boggan, James (CA)	NS	498
Bogrov, Michael (MD)	ChAP	939
Boice, Charles (MD)	GO	276
Bojrab, Dennis (MI)	Oto	683
Boland, Clement (TX)	Ge	253
Boles, Richard (CA)	CG	162
Bolger, Graeme (AL)	Onc	356
Bolger, William (FL)	Oto	677
Bollen, Andrew (CA)	Path	732
Bolman, Ralph Morton (MA)	T&CS	1146
Bolognia, Jean (CT)	D	184
Bolton, John (LA)	S	1124
Bolton, W Kline (VA)	Nep	461
Bolwell, Brian (OH)	Onc	366
Bond, Sheldon (KY)	PS	817
Bondi, Edward (PA)	D	187
Bono, James (MA)	OrS	616
Bonomi, Philip (IL)	Onc	366
Bonow, Robert (IL)	Cv	100
Boone, Timothy (TX)	U	1208
Boop, Frederick (TN)	NS	484
Booth, Robert (PA)	OrS	621
Boraas, Marcia (PA)	S	1090
Borchert, Mark (CA)	Oph	604
Borer, Jeffrey (NY)	Cv	91
Borg-Stein, Joanne (MA)	PMR	862
Borgen, Patrick (NY)	S	1090
Borges, Lawrence (MA)	NS	472
Borowitz, Drucy (NY)	PPul	806
Borst, Matthew (AZ)	GO	287
Borum, Marie (DC)	Ge	233
Borzak, Steven (FL)	Cv	97
Bos, Gary (WA)	OrS	649
Bosl, George (NY)	Onc	338
Boston, Barry (TN)	Onc	356
Bostrom, Mathias (NY)	OrS	621
Bostwick, David (VA)	Path	725
Bouchard, Charles (IL)	Oph	594
Bourge, Robert (AL)	Cv	97
Boushey, Homer (CA)	Pul	970
Bouvet, Michael (CA)	S	1130
Bove, Alfred (PA)	Cv	91
Bove, Edward (MI)	PS	819
Bowden, Charles (TX)	Psyc	932
Bowdish, Michael (CA)	T&CS	1177
Bowen, Glen (UT)	D	197
Bower, Charles (AR)	PO	805
Boxer, Laurence (MI)	PHO	782
Boxer Wachler, Brian (CA)	Oph	604
Boxrud, Cynthia (CA)	Oph	605
Boyajian, Michael (DC)	PlS	881
Boyd, Stuart (CA)	U	1210
Boyd, Walter (CA)	T&CS	1177
Boyer, Thomas (AZ)	Ge	253
Boyle, Robert (VA)	NP	450
Bozentka, David (PA)	HS	297
Bozic, Kevin (CA)	OrS	649
Brackmann, Derald (CA)	Oto	694
Braddom, Randall (PA)	PMR	863
Bradford, Carol (MI)	Oto	684
Bradley, James (PA)	SM	1075
Bradley, James (CA)	PlS	901
Bradley, Jeffrey (MO)	RadRO	988
Bradley, John (CA)	PInf	797
Bradley, Linda (OH)	ObG	564
Bradshaw, Karen (TX)	ObG	566
Brady, Mary (NY)	S	1090
Brage, Michael (WA)	OrS	649
Braly, Patricia (LA)	GO	288
Branch, Charles (NC)	NS	484
Branch, Malcolm (NC)	Ge	241
Brandt, Fredric (NY)	D	187
Brandt, Harry (MD)	Psyc	923
Brandt, Keith (MO)	PlS	893
Brandt, Lawrence (NY)	Ge	233
Branham, Gregory (MO)	Oto	684
Brasington, Richard (MO)	Rhu	1064
Braun, Martin (DC)	D	187
Braunstein, Richard (NY)	Oph	576
Braunstein, Seth (NC)	IM	426
Brause, Barry (NY)	Inf	412
Bravender, Terrill (OH)	AM	77
Braverman, Alan (MO)	Cv	100
Braverman, Lewis (MA)	EDM	208
Bray, Robert (CA)	NS	499

Alphabetical Listing of Doctors

Name	Specialty	Pg
Brazer, Scott (NC)	Ge	241
Brecher, Martin (NY)	PHO	771
Breidenbach, Warren (AZ)	HS	304
Breitbart, William (NY)	Psyc	923
Brem, Henry (MD)	NS	475
Brem, Rachel (DC)	DR	1008
Brem, Steven (PA)	NS	475
Brems, John (IL)	S	1112
Brendler, Charles (IL)	U	1202
Brener, Bruce (NJ)	VascS	1222
Brenin, Christiana (VA)	Onc	356
Brennan, Daniel (MO)	Nep	463
Brennan, Michael (MN)	EDM	218
Brennan, Stephen (TX)	Nep	465
Brenner, Joel (MD)	PCd	748
Brenner, Malcolm (TX)	Hem	325
Brent, David (PA)	ChAP	939
Brentjens, Renier (NY)	Onc	339
Bresalier, Robert (TX)	Ge	253
Brescia, Frank (SC)	Onc	356
Bressler, Neil (MD)	Oph	576
Bressler, Susan (MD)	Oph	576
Bressman, Susan (NY)	N	513
Brewer, Molly (CT)	GO	274
Brewster, David (MA)	VascS	1220
Brick, Gregory (MA)	OrS	616
Brick, John (WV)	N	513
Bricker, Leslie (MI)	H & PM	407
Bridges, Charles (NC)	T&CS	1161
Bridwell, Keith (MO)	OrS	640
Brien, Earl (CA)	OrS	649
Brigman, Brian (NC)	OrS	635
Brillon, David (NY)	EDM	211
Brinckerhoff, Laurence (MA)	T&CS	1146
Bristow, Robert (CA)	GO	290
Britt, L D (VA)	S	1103
Brizel, David (NC)	RadRO	984
Broadstone, Vasti Lima (IN)	EDM	218
Brock, John (TN)	Ped Uro	825
Brockmeyer, Douglas (UT)	NS	494
Brockstein, Bruce (IL)	Onc	367
Broderick, Gregory (FL)	U	1197
Broderick, Joseph (OH)	N	528
Brodkin, Edward (PA)	Psyc	923
Brodland, David (PA)	D	187
Brodman, Michael (NY)	ObG	560
Brodsky, James (TX)	OrS	648
Brodsky, Jeffrey (PA)	S	1090
Brodsky, Robert (MD)	Hem	313
Brody, Fred (DC)	S	1090
Brody, Harold (GA)	D	191
Bromberg, Jonathan (MD)	S	1090
Bromberg, Mark (UT)	N	534
Bronheim, Harold (NY)	Psyc	923
Bronin, Andrew (NY)	D	187
Bronson, Michael (NY)	OrS	621
Brooks, Ari (PA)	S	1090
Brooks, Benjamin (NC)	N	523
Brooks, David (MA)	S	1084
Brooks, John (PA)	Path	720
Brophy, Patrick (IA)	PNep	799
Brown, Allen (MN)	PMR	867
Brown, Charles (IL)	S	1112
Brown, Daniel (TN)	VIR	1029
Brown, Eric (MI)	S	1112
Brown, Gary (PA)	Oph	576
Brown, Jeffrey (TX)	EDM	222
Brown, John (IN)	T&CS	1167
Brown, Karen (NY)	VIR	1027
Brown, Kevin (CO)	Pul	967
Brown, Kimberly (MI)	Ge	246
Brown, Marc (NY)	D	187
Brown, Robert (MN)	N	528
Brown, Robert (NY)	Ge	233
Browne, J. (NC)	Oto	678
Browner, Bruce (CT)	OrS	616
Brozena, Susan (PA)	Cv	91
Bruce, Jeffrey (NY)	NS	475
Brucker, Alexander (PA)	Oph	576
Bruera, Eduardo (TX)	Onc	379
Brufsky, Adam (PA)	Onc	339
Bruggers, Carol (UT)	PHO	786
Bruner, Janet (TX)	Path	730
Brunicardi, F Charles (CA)	S	1130
Bruno, Michiko (HI)	N	538
Brunsting, Louis (AL)	T&CS	1161
Brunstrom-Hernandez, Janice (MO)	ChiN	148
Brunt, L Michael (MO)	S	1112
Brushart, Thomas (MD)	HS	297
Bryson, Yvonne (CA)	PInf	797
Buatti, John (IA)	RadRO	988
Bubley, Glenn (MA)	Onc	330
Bucciarelli, Richard (FL)	NP	451
Buch, Jeffrey (TX)	U	1208
Buchanan, George (TX)	PHO	787
Buchbinder, Ellen (NY)	A&I	80
Buchholz, David (MD)	N	513
Buchholz, Thomas (TX)	RadRO	993
Buchman, Steven (MI)	PIS	893
Buchman, Timothy (GA)	S	1104
Bucholz, Richard (MO)	NS	489
Bucholz, Robert (TX)	OrS	648

Name	Specialty	Pg
Buckley, Edward (NC)	Oph	587
Buckner, Jan (MN)	Onc	367
Buckwalter, Joseph (IA)	OrS	640
Bucky, Louis (PA)	PlS	881
Budd, G. Thomas (OH)	Onc	367
Budenz, Donald (NC)	Oph	587
Budoff, Matthew (CA)	Cv	110
Bueno, Raphael (MA)	T&CS	1146
Bukata, Susan (CA)	OrS	650
Bulat, Robert (LA)	Ge	253
Bull, David (UT)	T&CS	1172
Bull, Marilyn (IN)	Ped	741
Buly, Robert (NY)	OrS	622
Bumpous, Jeffrey (KY)	Oto	678
Bunn, Paul (CO)	Onc	376
Bunning, Robert (DC)	Rhu	1059
Burchiel, Kim (OR)	NS	499
Burdette, Jonathan (NC)	NRad	1021
Burger, Peter (MD)	Path	721
Burger, Robert (PA)	GO	277
Burgess, David (NJ)	Ped	740
Burke, Allan (IL)	N	528
Burke, Charles (PA)	SM	1075
Burke, Dennis (MA)	OrS	616
Burke, Miles (OH)	Oph	594
Burke, Peter (MA)	S	1084
Burke, Redmond (FL)	T&CS	1161
Burke, Thomas (TX)	GO	288
Burke, William (NE)	GerPsy	946
Burket, Mark (OH)	Cv	101
Burkey, Brian (OH)	Oto	684
Burks, A Wesley (NC)	PA&I	744
Burman, Kenneth (DC)	EDM	211
Burmeister, Lynn (MN)	EDM	218
Burnett, Alexander (AR)	GO	288
Burnett, Arthur (MD)	U	1189
Burns, A Jay (TX)	PlS	898
Burns, James (MA)	Oto	665
Burris, Howard (TN)	Onc	356
Burschtin, Omar (NY)	Pul	956
Burstein, Fernando (GA)	PlS	889
Burstein, Harold (MA)	Onc	330
Burt, Richard (IL)	IM	427
Burt, Vivien (CA)	Psyc	932
Burton, Allen (TX)	PM	711
Burton, Barbara (IL)	CG	160
Burton, Claude (NC)	D	191
Burton, John (MD)	Ger	264
Busby, Joseph (SC)	U	1197
Busch, Michael (GA)	OrS	635
Buse, John (NC)	EDM	216
Bush-Joseph, Charles (IL)	SM	1077
Bushman, Wade (WI)	U	1202
Busis, Neil (PA)	N	514
Bussel, James (NY)	PHO	771
Buster, John (MA)	RE	1040
Busuttil, Ronald (CA)	S	1130
Butler, Charles (TX)	PlS	898
Butler, John (CA)	S	1131
Butler, William (MA)	NS	472
Butterly, David (NC)	Nep	461
Butterly, Lynn (NH)	Ge	230
Buxton, Alfred (MA)	CE	112
Buyon, Jill (NY)	Rhu	1060
Buys, Saundra (UT)	Onc	376
Buysse, Daniel (PA)	Psyc	923
Buzdar, Aman (TX)	Onc	379
Byrd, Benjamin (TN)	Cv	97
Byrd, David (WA)	S	1131
Byrd, H Stephenson (TX)	PlS	898
Byrd, J.W. (TN)	SM	1076
Byrd, John (OH)	Hem	321
Byrne, Janice (UT)	ObG	566
Byrne, John (MA)	T&CS	1146
Bystritsky, Alexander (CA)	Psyc	933

C

Name	Specialty	Pg
Cabin, Henry (CT)	Cv	88
Cagle, Philip (TX)	Path	730
Cahill, John (NY)	PrM	912
Cahill, Kenneth (OH)	Oph	594
Caillouette, James (CA)	OrS	650
Cain, Joanna (MA)	GO	274
Cain, Mark (IN)	Ped Uro	826
Cairns, Bruce (NC)	S	1104
Cairo, Mitchell (NY)	PHO	772
Calabrese, Joseph (OH)	Psyc	929
Calabresi, Peter (MD)	N	514
Caldamone, Anthony (RI)	Ped Uro	824
Caldwell, Randall (IN)	PCd	752
Calhoon, John (TX)	T&CS	1173
Califano, Joseph (MD)	Oto	668
Califf, Robert (NC)	Cv	97
Callaghan, John (IA)	OrS	640
Callahan, Eileen (NY)	Ger	264
Callans, David (PA)	CE	114
Callen, Jeffrey (KY)	D	192
Callery, Mark (MA)	S	1084
Calligaro, Keith (PA)	VascS	1222
Calvi, Laura (NY)	EDM	211

Alphabetical Listing of Doctors

Name	Specialty	Pg
Calvo, Benjamin (NC)	S	1104
Cambria, Richard (MA)	VascS	1220
Cameron, John (MD)	S	1090
Cameron, Robert (CA)	T&CS	1177
Camisa, Charles (FL)	D	192
Camitta, Bruce (WI)	PHO	782
Cammisa, Frank (NY)	OrS	622
Camoriano, John (AZ)	Onc	379
Campbell, Bruce (WI)	Oto	684
Campbell, David (CO)	T&CS	1172
Campbell, Guy Douglas (MS)	Pul	961
Campbell, J William (MO)	Inf	417
Campbell, Steven (OH)	U	1202
Campo, John (OH)	ChAP	941
Campochiaro, Peter (MD)	Oph	576
Cance, William (NY)	S	1090
Cancio, Margarita (FL)	Inf	415
Canellos, George (MA)	Onc	330
Canning, Douglas (PA)	Ped Uro	824
Cannom, David (CA)	CE	119
Canterbury, Randolph (VA)	Psyc	928
Canto, Marcia (MD)	Ge	233
Cantuaria, Guilherme (GA)	GO	281
Caplan, Louis (MA)	N	510
Capo, Hilda (FL)	Oph	587
Cappuccino, Andrew (NY)	OrS	622
Caprioli, Joseph (CA)	Oph	605
Caputo, Anthony (NJ)	Oph	576
Caputo, Thomas (NY)	GO	277
Caputy, Anthony (DC)	NS	475
Carabasi, Matthew (PA)	Onc	339
Carabello, Blase (TX)	Cv	108
Carbone, David (OH)	Onc	367
Cardenas, Diana (FL)	PMR	866
Cardenosa, Gilda (VA)	DR	1013
Carducci, Michael (MD)	Onc	339
Carey, John (UT)	CG	161
Carey, John (MD)	Oto	668
Carey, Lisa (NC)	Onc	356
Caritis, Steve (PA)	MF	433
Carlson, Alan (NC)	Oph	587
Carlson, John (NJ)	GO	277
Carlson, Michelle (NY)	HS	297
Carneiro, Ronaldo (FL)	HS	301
Carney, John (AR)	D	198
Carney, Michael (HI)	GO	290
Carpenter, Jeffrey (NJ)	VascS	1222
Carpenter, John (AL)	Onc	356
Carpenter, Paul (WA)	PHO	789
Carpinito, Gennaro (MA)	U	1186
Carr, Bruce (TX)	RE	1049
Carr, David (MO)	Ger	266
Carr, Stephen (RI)	MF	432
Carr-Locke, David (NY)	Ge	233
Carragee, Eugene (CA)	OrS	650
Carrasquillo, Jorge (NY)	NuM	554
Carraway, James (VA)	PIS	889
Carroll, Charles (IL)	HS	302
Carroll, John (CO)	IC	127
Carroll, Peter (CA)	U	1210
Carroll, William (NY)	PHO	772
Carson, Benjamin (MD)	NS	475
Carson, Culley (NC)	U	1197
Carson, Donald (PA)	ObG	561
Carter, H. Ballentine (MD)	U	1189
Carter, Keith (IA)	Oph	594
Cartwright, Patrick (UT)	Ped Uro	828
Carty, Sally (PA)	S	1091
Caruana, Salvatore (NY)	Oto	668
Cascino, Terrence (MN)	N	528
Casella, Samuel (NH)	PEn	756
Caskey, Michael (AZ)	T&CS	1173
Cass, Darrell (TX)	PS	822
Casselbrant, Margaretha (PA)	PO	802
Cassidy, Charles (MA)	HS	296
Cassidy, Suzanne (CA)	CG	162
Cassivi, Stephen (MN)	T&CS	1167
Castell, Donald (SC)	Ge	241
Castellino, Sharon (NC)	PHO	778
Castells, Maria (MA)	A&I	80
Caster, Andrew (CA)	Oph	605
Castle, Valerie (MI)	PHO	782
Catalona, William (IL)	U	1202
Catanzaro, Antonino (CA)	Pul	970
Cather, Jennifer (TX)	D	198
Catherwood, Edward (NH)	Cv	88
Caty, Michael (CT)	PS	813
Cedars, Marcelle (CA)	RE	1051
Cederna, Paul (MI)	PIS	893
Celano, Paul (MD)	Onc	339
Celli, Bartolome (MA)	Pul	954
Cello, John (CA)	Ge	255
Cendales, Linda (GA)	HS	301
Cerfolio, Robert (AL)	T&CS	1161
Cerqueira, Manuel (OH)	Cv	101
Cetta, Frank (MN)	PCd	752
Cha, Soonmee (CA)	NRad	1026
Chabot, John (NY)	S	1091
Chachoua, Abraham (NY)	Onc	339
Chadha, Manjeet (NY)	RadRO	978
Chaikof, Elliot (MA)	VascS	1220
Chaitman, Bernard (MO)	Cv	101

Name	Specialty	Pg
Chakravarthy, Anuradha (TN)	RadRO	984
Chakravarti, Arnab (OH)	RadRO	988
Chalian, Ara (PA)	Oto	668
Chamberlain, Marc (WA)	N	539
Chambers, Christopher (PA)	AM	76
Chambers, Setsuko (AZ)	GO	288
Champlin, Richard (TX)	Hem	325
Chan, John (CA)	GO	290
Chan, Kenny (CO)	PO	805
Chanan-Khan, Asher (FL)	Onc	356
Chancellor, Michael (MI)	U	1203
Chand, Bipan (IL)	S	1112
Chandar, Jayanthi (FL)	PNep	798
Chandler, James (IL)	NS	489
Chandler, Michael (NY)	A&I	80
Chandrasoma, Parakrama (CA)	Path	732
Chang, Alfred (MI)	S	1112
Chang, Benjamin (PA)	PlS	881
Chang, David (TX)	PlS	899
Chang, Eric (CA)	RadRO	995
Chang, Gene (PA)	IC	121
Chang, Helena (CA)	S	1131
Chang, James (CA)	HS	305
Chang, Jenny (TX)	Onc	379
Chang, Karen (CA)	Path	732
Chang, Kenneth (CA)	Ge	255
Chang, R Jeffrey (CA)	RE	1051
Chang, Rowland (IL)	Rhu	1064
Chang, Sam (TN)	U	1197
Chang, Stanley (NY)	Oph	577
Chang, Susan (CA)	Onc	385
Chang-Miller, April (AZ)	Rhu	1066
Chao, K.S. Clifford (NY)	RadRO	978
Chao, Nelson (NC)	Onc	357
Chap, Linnea (CA)	Onc	386
Chapman, Jens (WA)	OrS	650
Chapman, Paul (NY)	Onc	339
Chapman, Robert (MI)	Onc	367
Chapman, William (MO)	S	1112
Char, Devron (CA)	Oph	605
Charbel, Fady (IL)	NS	489
Charboneau, J William (MN)	DR	1014
Chari, Suresh (MN)	Ge	246
Charles, Andrew (CA)	N	539
Charney, Jonathan (NY)	N	514
Charrow, Joel (IL)	CG	160
Chatham, W. Winn (AL)	Rhu	1063
Cheatham, John (OH)	PCd	752
Cheeseman, Edward (SC)	Oph	587
Chelimsky, Thomas (WI)	N	529
Chen, Allen (MD)	PHO	772
Chen, Chun (NY)	NS	475
Chen, David (PA)	U	1189
Chen, David (IL)	PMR	867
Chen, Jonathan (NY)	T&CS	1151
Chen, Mike (AL)	PS	818
Chen, Thomas (CA)	NS	499
Chen, Yunn-Yi (CA)	Path	732
Chenette, Philip (CA)	RE	1051
Cheng, Earl (IL)	Ped Uro	826
Cheng, Edith (WA)	MF	442
Cheng, Edward (MN)	OrS	640
Cherny, W Bruce (ID)	NS	494
Cherry, Kenneth (VA)	VascS	1225
Chesney, Carolyn (TN)	Path	725
Cheson, Bruce (DC)	Hem	313
Cheung, Nai-Kong (NY)	PHO	772
Cheville, Andrea (MN)	PMR	867
Chew, Helen (CA)	Onc	386
Chey, William (MI)	Ge	246
Chhieng, David (CT)	Path	718
Chi, Dennis (NY)	GO	277
Childs, Stacy (CO)	U	1206
Chiles, Caroline (NC)	DR	1013
Chinitz, Larry (NY)	CE	114
Chiocca, E. Antonio (MA)	NS	472
Chitambar, Christopher (WI)	Onc	367
Chitwood, W Randolph (NC)	T&CS	1161
Chiu, David (NY)	PlS	881
Chiu, Yanek (CA)	CRS	177
Chizner, Michael (FL)	Cv	98
Chlebowski, Rowan (CA)	Onc	386
Chmait, Ramen (CA)	MF	442
Cho, Jae (IL)	VascS	1226
Cho, Kathleen (MI)	Path	727
Cho, Kerry (CA)	Nep	466
Cho, Kyung (MI)	VIR	1030
Choi, Noah (MA)	RadRO	976
Choti, Michael (MD)	S	1091
Chow, Warren (CA)	Onc	386
Chowdhury, Khalid (CO)	Oto	689
Choy, Andrew (CA)	Oph	605
Choy, Hak (TX)	RadRO	993
Christenson, John (IN)	PInf	795
Christian, Karla (TN)	T&CS	1161
Christiani, David (MA)	Pul	954
Christie, Dennis (WA)	PGe	768
Christie, Jason (PA)	Pul	956
Christman, Brian (TN)	Pul	961
Christo, Paul (MD)	PM	706
Christoforidis, Gregory (IL)	NRad	1023
Chu, Edward (PA)	Onc	339

Alphabetical Listing of Doctors

Name	Specialty	Pg
Chui, Helena (CA)	N	539
Chun, Thomas (NJ)	U	1189
Chung, Daniel (MA)	Ge	230
Chung, Kevin (MI)	HS	302
Chung, Ki Young (SC)	Onc	357
Chung, Raymond (MA)	Ge	230
Chung, Wendy (NY)	CG	157
Church, James (OH)	CRS	173
Church, Joseph (CA)	PA&I	746
Chwals, Walter (MA)	PS	814
Ciancio, Gaetano (FL)	U	1197
Ciccotti, Michael (PA)	SM	1075
Ciezki, Jay (OH)	RadRO	989
Cioffi, George (NY)	Oph	577
Cioffi, William (RI)	S	1084
Cionni, Robert (UT)	Oph	601
Ciraulo, Domenic (MA)	AdP	936
Cirigliano, Michael (PA)	IM	426
Civantos, Francisco (FL)	Oto	678
Clair, Daniel (OH)	VascS	1227
Clairmont, Albert (OH)	PMR	867
Clamon, Gerald (IA)	Onc	367
Clardy, Christopher (IL)	PNep	799
Clark, Joseph (IL)	Onc	367
Clark, Keith (OK)	Oto	691
Clark, Orlo (CA)	S	1131
Clarke-Pearson, Daniel (NC)	GO	281
Claxton, David (PA)	Onc	340
Clayman, Gary (TX)	Oto	691
Clayman, Ralph (CA)	U	1211
Cleary, James (WI)	Onc	368
Clements, Philip (CA)	Rhu	1067
Clements, Stephen (GA)	Cv	98
Cliby, William (MN)	GO	284
Clinch, Thomas (MD)	Oph	577
Clinton, Steven (OH)	Onc	368
Clisham, P. Ronald (LA)	RE	1050
Clohisy, Denis (MN)	OrS	640
Clohisy, John (MO)	OrS	640
Cloninger, C Robert (MO)	Psyc	929
Clore, John (VA)	EDM	216
Close, Lanny (NY)	Oto	668
Cloughesy, Timothy (CA)	N	539
Clutter, William (MO)	EDM	218
Cmelak, Anthony (TN)	RadRO	984
Coakley, Fergus (OR)	DR	1017
Cobleigh, Melody (IL)	Onc	368
Coblyn, Jonathan (MA)	Rhu	1058
Cobos, Everardo (TX)	Hem	325
Coccia, Peter (NE)	PHO	786
Cochran, Alistair (CA)	Path	732
Cockerell, Clay (TX)	D	198
Cockerham, Kimberly (CA)	Oph	605
Coddington, Charles (MN)	RE	1047
Coe, Fredric (IL)	Nep	463
Coffey, Barbara (NY)	ChAP	939
Coffman, Thomas (NC)	Nep	461
Cohen, Alan (MA)	NS	472
Cohen, Arnold (PA)	MF	434
Cohen, Bernard (FL)	D	192
Cohen, Bernard (MD)	D	187
Cohen, Bruce (OH)	ChiN	148
Cohen, Burton (NY)	DR	1008
Cohen, David (IL)	RE	1047
Cohen, David (NY)	Nep	459
Cohen, Gary (PA)	VIR	1027
Cohen, Gary (MD)	Onc	340
Cohen, Gordon (CA)	T&CS	1177
Cohen, Harris (TN)	DR	1013
Cohen, Howard (PA)	IC	121
Cohen, Jeffrey (NH)	N	510
Cohen, Jeffrey (PA)	U	1189
Cohen, Jeffrey (OH)	N	529
Cohen, Jonathan (NY)	Ge	233
Cohen, Kenneth (MD)	PHO	772
Cohen, Lawrence (NY)	Ge	233
Cohen, Mark (IL)	HS	302
Cohen, Martin (NY)	CE	114
Cohen, Michael (UT)	Path	729
Cohen, Mitchell (OH)	PGe	765
Cohen, Mitchell (PA)	Psyc	923
Cohen, Murray (PA)	S	1091
Cohen, Neri (MD)	T&CS	1151
Cohen, Philip (DC)	Onc	340
Cohen, Robbin (CA)	T&CS	1178
Cohen, Robert (OH)	EDM	218
Cohen, Roger (PA)	Onc	340
Cohen, Seymour (NY)	Onc	340
Cohen, Steven (NY)	D	187
Cohen, Steven (CA)	PlS	901
Cohn, Richard (IL)	PNep	800
Cohn, Susan (IL)	PHO	782
Cohn, Susan (IL)	Inf	417
Coit, Daniel (NY)	S	1091
Colachis, Samuel (OH)	PMR	868
Colberg, John (CT)	U	1186
Coldwell, Douglas (KY)	VIR	1029
Cole, Andrew (MA)	N	510
Cole, David (SC)	S	1104
Cole, Francis (MO)	NP	451
Coleman, Beverly (PA)	DR	1008
Coleman, John (IN)	PlS	893

Name	Specialty	Pg
Coleman, Jonathan (NY)	U	1189
Coleman, Morton (NY)	Onc	340
Colen, Lawrence (VA)	PlS	889
Collins, Eric (NY)	AdP	936
Collins, Evan (TX)	HS	305
Colombani, Paul (MD)	PS	815
Colon-Otero, Gerardo (FL)	Onc	357
Colquhoun, Steven (CA)	S	1131
Colson, Yolonda (MA)	T&CS	1146
Colvin, Edward (AL)	PCd	751
Come, Steven (MA)	Onc	331
Comenzo, Raymond (MA)	Hem	312
Comerota, Anthony (OH)	VascS	1227
Comi, Richard (NH)	EDM	208
Cominelli, Fabio (OH)	Ge	246
Conant, Emily (PA)	DR	1008
Conley, Susan (PA)	PNep	797
Connolly, Heidi (MN)	Cv	101
Connolly, James (MA)	Path	718
Conrad, Ernest (WA)	OrS	650
Conry, Robert (AL)	Onc	357
Constantian, Mark (NH)	PlS	878
Constine, Louis (NY)	RadRO	978
Conte, John (MD)	T&CS	1151
Conti, David (NY)	S	1091
Cook, Jonathan (NC)	D	192
Cook, Stuart (NJ)	N	514
Cookson, Michael (OK)	U	1208
Cooney, Kathleen (MI)	Onc	368
Cooney, Leo (CT)	Ger	264
Cooper, Barry (TX)	Hem	326
Cooper, Christopher (OH)	Cv	101
Cooper, Dan (CA)	PPul	810
Cooper, Daniel (TX)	OrS	648
Cooper, David (MD)	EDM	212
Cooper, J Allen (AL)	Pul	961
Cooper, Jay (NY)	RadRO	978
Cooper, Joel (PA)	T&CS	1151
Cooper, Laurence (TX)	PHO	788
Cooper, Michael (CO)	VascS	1228
Cooper, Rubin (NY)	PCd	748
Cooper, William (VA)	Pul	961
Cope, Doris (MD)	PM	706
Copel, Joshua (CT)	MF	432
Copelan, Edward (NC)	Hem	319
Copeland, Larry (OH)	GO	284
Copit, Debra (PA)	DR	1008
Coplen, Douglas (MO)	Ped Uro	827
Copp, Steven (CA)	OrS	650
Copperman, Alan (NY)	RE	1041
Coppola, John (NY)	Cv	91
Corbett, James (MS)	N	524
Corbetta, Maurizio (MO)	N	529
Cordeiro, Peter (NY)	PlS	881
Corey, G Ralph (NC)	Inf	416
Corey, Jacquelynne (IL)	Oto	684
Corey, Seth (IL)	PHO	782
Corey-Bloom, Jody (CA)	N	539
Cornblath, David (MD)	N	514
Cornelison, Terri (MD)	GO	277
Cornelius, Lynn (MO)	D	195
Cornell, Charles (NY)	OrS	622
Cornella, Jeffrey (AZ)	ObG	566
Cornwell, Edward (DC)	S	1091
Corrigan, Victor (GA)	Cv	98
Cortes, Jorge (TX)	Hem	326
Corteville, Jane (OH)	ObG	564
Coselli, Joseph (TX)	T&CS	1173
Cosgrove, Garth (RI)	NS	472
Cosin, Jonathan (CT)	GO	274
Costantino, Peter (NY)	Oto	669
Cote, Richard (FL)	Path	725
Cotsarelis, George (PA)	D	188
Cotton, Robin (OH)	PO	804
Couch, Marion (VT)	Oto	665
Coughlin, Michael (ID)	OrS	646
Couldwell, William (UT)	NS	494
Coull, Bruce (AZ)	N	536
Courcoulas, Anita (PA)	S	1091
Courey, Mark (CA)	Oto	694
Coutsoftides, Theodore (CA)	CRS	177
Covington, Edward (OH)	PM	709
Cowan, Kenneth (NE)	Onc	376
Cowan, Morton (CA)	PA&I	746
Cox, James (TX)	RadRO	993
Coyle, Patricia (NY)	N	514
Craig, Edward (NY)	OrS	622
Craigen, William (TX)	CG	161
Cramer, Daniel (MA)	ObG	560
Crandall, Alan (UT)	Oph	601
Crane, Christopher (TX)	RadRO	993
Crawford, E. David (CO)	U	1207
Crawford, James (NY)	Path	721
Crawford, Jeffrey (NC)	Onc	357
Crawford, Thomas (MD)	ChiN	145
Creamer, Michael (FL)	PMR	866
Creasman, William (SC)	GO	281
Criado, Frank (MD)	VascS	1222
Criner, Gerard (PA)	Pul	956
Crippin, Jeffrey (MO)	Ge	247
Cristofanilli, Massimo (PA)	Onc	340
Crocenzi, Todd (OR)	Onc	386

Alphabetical Listing of Doctors

Name	Specialty	Pg
Crocker, Ian (GA)	RadRO	984
Crockett, Dennis (CA)	PO	805
Crofford, Leslie (TN)	Rhu	1063
Crombleholme, Timothy (CO)	PS	821
Cronenwett, Jack (NH)	VascS	1220
Cronin, David (WI)	S	1113
Crookes, Peter (CA)	S	1131
Croop, James (IN)	PHO	782
Cross, Dewitte (MO)	NRad	1023
Crossett, Lawrence (PA)	OrS	622
Crosson, Jane (MD)	PCd	748
Crow, Scott (MN)	Psyc	929
Crowe, Joseph (OH)	S	1113
Crowley, William (MA)	RE	1040
Cruse, C. Wayne (FL)	PIS	889
Crutchfield, Charles (MN)	D	195
Cryer, Philip (MO)	EDM	219
Cudkowicz, Merit (MA)	N	510
Culbertson, Sandra (IL)	ObG	564
Culbertson, William (FL)	Oph	587
Culkin, Daniel (OK)	U	1208
Cullen, Kevin (MD)	Onc	340
Culp, Randall (PA)	HS	298
Cummings, Jeffrey (NV)	N	539
Cunha, Burke (NY)	Inf	413
Cunniff, Christopher (AZ)	CG	161
Cunningham, Bari (CA)	D	200
Cunningham, Glenn (TX)	EDM	222
Cunningham, John (AZ)	Ge	253
Cunningham, John (IL)	PHO	782
Cunningham, Michael (MA)	PO	801
Cunningham-Rundles, Charlotte (NY)	A&I	81
Cupps, Thomas (DC)	Rhu	1060
Curcillo, Paul (PA)	S	1091
Curley, Steven (TX)	S	1124
Curran, James (IL)	Rhu	1065
Currie, Donald (TX)	PMR	870
Curry, Cynthia (CA)	CG	162
Curtin, Hugh (MA)	NRad	1019
Curtin, John (NY)	GO	277
Curtis, Anne (NY)	CE	114
Cusack, James (MA)	S	1084
Cushing, Brad (ME)	S	1084
Cushing, Gary (MA)	EDM	209
Cushman, William (TN)	IM	426
Cutrer, F Michael (MN)	N	529
Cykiert, Robert (NY)	Oph	577
Czerniecki, Brian (PA)	S	1092
Czuczman, Myron (NY)	Onc	341

D

Name	Specialty	Pg
D'Alessio, David (OH)	EDM	219
D'Alton, Mary (NY)	MF	434
D'Amico, Anthony (MA)	RadRO	976
D'Amico, Donald (NY)	Oph	577
D'Amico, Thomas (NC)	T&CS	1161
D'Ayala, Marcus (NY)	VascS	1222
Da Lio, Andrew (CA)	PIS	902
Daar, Eric (CA)	Inf	420
Dabal, Robert (AL)	T&CS	1162
Dacey, Ralph (MO)	NS	489
Dachman, Abraham (IL)	DR	1014
Dae, Michael (CA)	NuM	557
Dagum, Alexander (NY)	PIS	881
Dahmoush, Laila (IA)	Path	727
Dake, Michael (CA)	VIR	1032
Dakhil, Shaker (KS)	Onc	376
Dale, Lowell (MN)	Ger	266
Dalinka, Murray (PA)	DR	1009
Dalkin, Alan (VA)	EDM	216
Dalkin, Bruce (WA)	U	1211
Dallal, Ramsey (PA)	S	1092
Dalsing, Michael (IN)	VascS	1227
Daly, Mary (PA)	Onc	341
Damiano, Ralph (MO)	T&CS	1167
Damon, Lloyd (CA)	Hem	327
Dana, Reza (MA)	Oph	574
Daneker, George (GA)	S	1104
Daneshmand, Sia (CA)	U	1211
Dang, Michael (HI)	T&CS	1178
Dangas, George (NY)	Cv	92
Daniel, Rollin (CA)	PIS	902
Danielpour, Moise (CA)	NS	499
Daniels, Gilbert (MA)	EDM	209
Danoff, Dudley (CA)	U	1211
Darcy, Michael (MO)	VIR	1030
Darling, R Clement (NY)	VascS	1222
Darras, Basil (MA)	ChiN	144
Darrow, David (VA)	PO	803
Das, Ananya (AZ)	Ge	253
Dattilo, Jeffery (TN)	VascS	1225
Daud, Adil (CA)	Onc	386
David, Carlos (MA)	NS	472
Davidoff, Andrew (TN)	PS	818
Davidson, Bruce (DC)	Oto	669
Davidson, Dennis (NY)	NP	449
Davidson, Joyce (TX)	Psyc	932
Davidson, Michael (IL)	Cv	101
Davidson, Richard (PA)	OrS	622
Davidson, Susan (CO)	GO	287
Davies, Stella (OH)	PHO	782

Name	Specialty	Pg
Davies, Terry (NY)	EDM	212
Davis, Bradley (KS)	U	1207
Davis, Glenn (NC)	PlS	889
Davis, Janet (FL)	Oph	587
Davis, Jessica (NY)	CG	157
Davis, Jonathan (MA)	NP	448
Davis, Mellar (OH)	H & PM	407
Davis, William (LA)	Rhu	1066
Dawson, Nancy (DC)	Onc	341
Dawson, Patricia (WA)	S	1131
Day, Susan (CA)	Oph	605
Day, Terry (SC)	Oto	678
De Cherney, Alan (MD)	RE	1042
De Juan, Eugene (CA)	Oph	605
De Lancey, John (MI)	ObG	564
De Las Morenas, Antonio (MA)	Path	718
De Lateur, Barbara (MD)	PMR	863
De Lia, Julian (WI)	ObG	564
De Monte, Franco (TX)	NS	495
De Moor, Michael (MA)	PCd	747
De Simone, Philip (KY)	Onc	357
Dea, Stanley (CA)	Ge	255
Dean, J. Michael (UT)	PCCM	755
DeAngelis, Lisa (NY)	N	514
Deas, Deborah (SC)	ChAP	941
DeCamp, Malcolm (IL)	T&CS	1167
DeCross, Arthur (NY)	Ge	233
Deeb, G. Michael (MI)	T&CS	1167
Deeg, H. Joachim (WA)	Onc	386
DeFilippi, Vincent (CA)	T&CS	1178
DeGiorgio, Christopher (CA)	N	539
Deitch, Edwin (NJ)	S	1092
Deitz, Joel (PA)	Pul	957
DeKernion, Jean (CA)	U	1211
Del Monte, Monte (MI)	Oph	594
Del Priore, Luciano (SC)	Oph	588
Del-Nido, Pedro (MA)	T&CS	1146
Delahay, John (DC)	OrS	622
Delamarter, Rick (CA)	OrS	650
Deland, Jonathan (NY)	OrS	623
Delaney, Conor (OH)	CRS	173
DeLaney, Thomas (MA)	RadRO	976
DeLeo, Vincent (NY)	D	188
DeLeon, Oscar (NY)	PM	707
Deleyiannis, Frederic (CO)	PlS	897
Delius, Ralph (MI)	T&CS	1168
Delivoria-Papadopoulos, Maria (PA)	NP	449
Della Rocca, Robert (NY)	Oph	577
Delmez, James (MO)	Nep	463
DeLong, Mahlon (GA)	N	524
DeLoughery, Thomas (OR)	Hem	328
DeLuca, Francesco (PA)	PEn	758
DeLurgio, David (GA)	CE	116
Demarest, Gerald (NM)	S	1124
DeMars, Leslie (NH)	GO	274
DeMasters, Bette (CO)	Path	729
DeMatteo, Ronald (NY)	S	1092
Dember, Laura (PA)	Nep	459
Demer, Joseph (CA)	Oph	605
Demetris, Anthony (PA)	Path	721
Demmler-Harrison, Gail (TX)	PInf	796
Demmy, Todd (NY)	T&CS	1151
Dempsey, Daniel (PA)	S	1092
Dempsey, Robert (WI)	NS	489
Denenberg, Steven (NE)	Oto	690
Dennery, Phyllis (PA)	NP	449
Denny, Donald (NJ)	VIR	1027
DeNofrio, David (MA)	Cv	88
DeOrio, James (NC)	OrS	635
DePaulo, J Raymond (MD)	Psyc	924
DePompolo, Robert (MN)	PMR	868
Derman, Gordon (IL)	PlS	893
DeRose, Joseph (NY)	T&CS	1151
Dershaw, D David (NY)	DR	1009
Deschamps, Claude (MN)	T&CS	1168
Deschler, Daniel (MA)	Oto	665
DeShazo, Richard (MS)	A&I	82
DeSilva, Stephen (MI)	HS	302
Desnick, Robert (NY)	CG	157
Desposito, Franklin (NJ)	CG	157
DeVane, Gary (FL)	RE	1045
DeVault, Kenneth (FL)	Ge	242
Devereux, Richard (NY)	Cv	92
Devinsky, Orrin (NY)	N	514
DeVita, Vincent (CT)	Onc	331
DeVivo, Darryl (NY)	ChiN	145
Dewberry, Robert (MD)	N	514
DeWeese, Theodore (MD)	RadRO	979
Deziel, Daniel (IL)	S	1113
Dhaliwal, Deepinder (PA)	Oph	577
Dhanireddy, Ramasubbareddy (TN)	NP	451
Di Bisceglie, Adrian (MO)	Ge	247
Di Giacinto, George (NY)	NS	476
Di Lorenzo, Carlo (OH)	PGe	765
Di Marino, Anthony (PA)	Ge	234
Diamond, Frank (FL)	PEn	759
Diamond, Paul (VA)	PMR	866
Dias, Mark (PA)	NS	476
Diaz, Eduardo (TX)	Oto	691
Diaz, Fernando (MI)	NS	490
Dichek, David (WA)	Cv	110

Alphabetical Listing of Doctors

Name	Specialty	Pg
Dick, Macdonald (MI)	PCd	752
Dicker, Adam (PA)	RadRO	979
Dickey, Richard (LA)	RE	1050
Dickler, Maura (NY)	Onc	341
Diduch, David (VA)	OrS	635
Diehl, Anna Mae (NC)	Ge	242
Diehl, James (PA)	T&CS	1151
Dienstag, Jules (MA)	Ge	230
Dieter, Robert (IL)	IC	125
Dieterich, Douglas (NY)	Ge	234
Dietz, David (OH)	CRS	173
DiGiovanni, Christopher (RI)	OrS	616
Dillard, James (NY)	PMR	863
Dillehay, Gary (IL)	NuM	556
Diller, Lisa (MA)	PHO	770
Dillingham, Michael (CA)	OrS	650
Dillon, Patrick (MO)	PS	819
Dillon, William (CA)	NRad	1026
DiMarco, John (VA)	CE	116
DiMeglio, Linda (IN)	PEn	760
DiNardo, Laurence (VA)	Oto	678
Dines, David (NY)	OrS	623
Dion, Jacques (GA)	NRad	1022
DiPaola, Robert (NJ)	Onc	341
DiPersio, John (MO)	Hem	321
Dirschl, Douglas (IL)	OrS	640
Disa, Joseph (NY)	PlS	881
Disis, Mary (WA)	Onc	386
Diuguid, David (NY)	Hem	314
Diver, Daniel (CT)	Cv	88
Diwan, Sudhir (NY)	PM	707
Dixon, Sherwood (NV)	S	1131
Dizon, Don (MA)	Onc	331
Djulbegovic, Benjamin (FL)	Hem	319
Dobs, Adrian (MD)	EDM	212
Docimo, Steven (PA)	Ped Uro	825
Dodd, Gerald (CO)	DR	1016
Dodds, William (MI)	RE	1047
Dodick, David (AZ)	N	536
Dodick, Jack (NY)	Oph	577
Doghramji, Karl (PA)	Psyc	924
Doherty, Dennis (KY)	Pul	961
Doherty, Gerard (MA)	S	1085
Dolgin, Stephen (NY)	PS	815
Dolitsky, Jay (NY)	PO	802
Domchek, Susan (PA)	Onc	341
Dome, Jeffrey (DC)	PHO	772
Donahoe, Michael (PA)	Pul	957
Donahue, J. Kevin (MA)	CE	113
Donaldson, Sarah (CA)	RadRO	995
Donaldson, William (PA)	OrS	623
Donehower, Ross (MD)	Onc	341
Donn, Steven (MI)	NP	452
Donner, Thomas (MD)	EDM	212
Donofrio, Peter (TN)	N	524
Donohue, James (NC)	Pul	962
Donovan, Donald (TX)	Oto	692
Donovan, James (OH)	U	1203
Doody, Daniel (MA)	PS	814
Doody, Rachelle (TX)	N	536
Dooley, Sharon (IL)	MF	438
Dooley, William (OK)	S	1124
Dorkin, Henry (MA)	PPul	806
Dormans, John (PA)	OrS	623
Dornhoffer, John (AR)	Oto	692
Doroshow, James (MD)	Onc	341
Dorr, Lawrence (CA)	OrS	651
Dottino, Peter (NY)	GO	277
Doubilet, Peter (MA)	DR	1007
Dougherty, Matthew (PA)	VascS	1223
Douglas, John (GA)	IC	124
Dover, Jeffrey (MA)	D	184
Dovey, Mark (PA)	PPul	806
Dowlati, Afshin (OH)	Onc	368
Downey, Robert (NY)	T&CS	1152
Dozor, Allen (NY)	PPul	807
Drachtman, Richard (NJ)	PHO	772
Drack, Arlene (IA)	Oph	594
Drake, Amelia (NC)	PO	803
Drayer, Burton (NY)	NRad	1020
Drebin, Jeffrey (PA)	S	1092
Dreicer, Robert (OH)	Onc	368
Dreyer, William (TX)	PCd	754
Dreyer, ZoAnn (TX)	PHO	788
Drinkwater, Davis (TN)	T&CS	1162
Driscoll, Colin (MN)	Oto	684
Driscoll, Daniel (FL)	CG	159
Driscoll, David (MN)	PCd	752
Driscoll, Deborah (PA)	CG	157
Dritschilo, Anatoly (DC)	RadRO	979
Driver, Larry (TX)	PM	711
Droller, Michael (NY)	U	1189
Drossman, Douglas (NC)	Ge	242
Druker, Brian (OR)	Onc	387
Druzin, Maurice (CA)	MF	442
Dubeau, Louis (CA)	Path	732
Dubinsky, Marla (CA)	PGe	768
Ducic, Ivica (DC)	PlS	882
Duckert, Larry (WA)	Oto	695
Ducore, Jonathan (CA)	PHO	789
Duff, William (FL)	MF	436
Dufresne, Craig (MD)	PlS	882

Name	Specialty	Pg
Dufresne, Raymond (RI)	D	184
Dugoff, Lorraine (PA)	MF	434
Duh, Quan-Yang (CA)	S	1132
Duhaime, Ann (MA)	NS	473
Duker, Jay (MA)	Oph	574
Dulcan, Mina (IL)	ChAP	942
Dulchavsky, Scott (MI)	S	1113
Dumanian, Gregory (IL)	PlS	893
Dumesic, Daniel (CA)	RE	1051
Dumitru, Daniel (TX)	PMR	870
Duncan, Mark (MD)	S	1092
Duncan, Newton (TX)	PO	805
Dunkel, Ira (NY)	PHO	772
Dunkin, Brian (TX)	S	1124
Dunn, Stephen (DE)	PS	815
Dunnington, Gary (IN)	S	1113
Dunphy, Frank (NC)	Onc	357
Dunton, Charles (PA)	GO	277
DuPont, Herbert (TX)	Inf	419
Durbin, William (MA)	PInf	792
Dure, Leon (AL)	ChiN	147
Durham, Janette (CO)	VIR	1031
Durham, Samuel (MI)	T&CS	1168
Durrie, Daniel (KS)	Oph	601
Durso, Nancy (VA)	RE	1045
Duska, Linda (VA)	GO	281
Duthie, Edmund (WI)	Ger	266
Dutton, Jonathan (NC)	Oph	588
Duvic, Madeleine (TX)	D	198
Dyer, Carmel (TX)	Ger	267
Dzubow, Leonard (PA)	D	188

E

Name	Specialty	Pg
Eagle, Kim (MI)	Cv	101
Eagle, Ralph (PA)	Oph	578
Early, Dayna (MO)	Ge	247
Easley, Ronald (TX)	PCCM	755
Eason, James (TN)	S	1104
Easter, David (CA)	S	1132
Eaton, James (DC)	Psyc	924
Eavey, Roland (TN)	PO	803
Eberlein, Timothy (MO)	S	1113
Ebraheim, Nabil (OH)	OrS	641
Echeverri, Luis (TX)	T&CS	1174
Eckel, Robert (CO)	EDM	222
Eckhardt, S Gail (CO)	Onc	376
Eckhoff, Devin (AL)	S	1104
Eckler, Kristen (MA)	ObG	560
Econs, Michael (IN)	EDM	219
Eddleman, Keith (NY)	MF	434
Edelen, John (CA)	Cv	110
Edelman, Martin (NM)	Onc	379
Edelman, Robert (IL)	DR	1014
Edelman, Steven (CA)	EDM	224
Edelson, Richard (CT)	D	184
Edelstein, Barbara (NY)	DR	1009
Edelstein, David (NY)	Oto	669
Edgar, Terence (WI)	ChiN	148
Edge, Stephen (TN)	S	1104
Edington, Howard (PA)	S	1092
Edmond, Michael (VA)	Inf	416
Edmundowicz, Daniel (PA)	Cv	92
Edmundowicz, Steven (MO)	Ge	247
Edney, James (NE)	S	1122
Edwards, Kathryn (TN)	PInf	794
Edwards, Michael (OH)	S	1113
Edwards, Michael (CA)	NS	499
Edwards, Michael (NV)	PlS	902
Edwards, Niloo (NY)	T&CS	1152
Edwards, Paul (MI)	Oph	594
Edwards, Robert (PA)	GO	278
Efron, Jonathan (MD)	CRS	169
Eggers, Howard (NY)	Oph	578
Eglseder, W. Andrew (MD)	HS	298
Ehrenkranz, Richard (CT)	NP	448
Ehresmann, Glenn (CA)	Rhu	1067
Ehrlich, Paul (NY)	PA&I	743
Ehrlich, Peter (MI)	PS	819
Ehrmann, David (IL)	EDM	219
Ehya, Hormoz (PA)	Path	721
Eichenfield, Lawrence (CA)	D	200
Eichler, Craig (FL)	D	192
Eidt, John (SC)	VascS	1225
Eifel, Patricia (TX)	RadRO	993
Eilber, Frederick (CA)	S	1132
Ein, Daniel (DC)	A&I	81
Einarsson, Jon (MA)	ObG	560
Einhorn, Lawrence (IN)	Onc	368
Einhorn, Thomas (MA)	OrS	616
Eisbruch, Avraham (MI)	RadRO	989
Eisele, David (MD)	Oto	669
Eiseman, Andrew (SC)	Oph	588
Eisen, Glenn (OR)	Ge	255
Eisen, Howard (PA)	Cv	92
Eisenberg, Burton (NH)	S	1085
Eisenberg, Howard (MD)	NS	476
Eisenberger, Mario (MD)	Onc	342
Eisendrath, Stuart (CA)	Psyc	933
Eisenstat, Theodore (NJ)	CRS	169
Eismont, Frank (FL)	OrS	636

Alphabetical Listing of Doctors

Name	Specialty	Pg
El-Kadi, Hikmat (PA)	NS	476
El-Youssef, Mounif (MN)	PGe	765
Elattrache, Neal (CA)	OrS	651
Elder, Jack (MI)	Ped Uro	827
Elefteriades, John (CT)	T&CS	1146
Elias, Anthony (CO)	Onc	376
Elias, Stanton (MI)	N	529
Elkayam, Uri (CA)	Cv	110
Elkind, Mitchell (NY)	N	515
Ellenbogen, Kenneth (VA)	CE	116
Ellenbogen, Richard (WA)	NS	499
Ellenhorn, Joshua (CA)	S	1132
Elliott, C. (UT)	Pul	967
Elliott, David (IA)	Ge	247
Elliott, Norman (GA)	Ge	242
Ellis, Demetrius (PA)	PNep	797
Ellis, George (LA)	Oph	601
Ellis, Georgiana (WA)	Onc	387
Ellis, Jonathan (CA)	Ge	255
Ellis, Lee (TX)	S	1124
Ellis, Matthew (MO)	Onc	368
Ellis, Stephen (OH)	IC	126
Ellis, William (WA)	U	1211
Ellison, E. Christopher (OH)	S	1113
Ellison, James (MA)	Psyc	920
Ellozy, Sharif (NY)	VascS	1223
Elmets, Craig (AL)	D	192
Elner, Victor (MI)	Oph	595
Elster, Allen (NC)	DR	1013
Elta, Grace (MI)	Ge	247
Emami, Bahman (IL)	RadRO	989
Emans, Sarah (MA)	AM	76
Emanuel, Peter (AR)	Hem	326
Emanuele, Mary Ann (IL)	EDM	219
Emanuele, Nicholas (IL)	EDM	219
Emens, Leisha (MD)	Onc	342
Emond, Jean (NY)	S	1093
Emre, Sukru (CT)	S	1085
Emslie, Graham (TX)	ChAP	943
Endrizzi, Donald (ME)	OrS	617
Enelow, Richard (NH)	Pul	954
Engstrom, John (CA)	N	539
Engstrom, Paul (PA)	Onc	342
Ennis, Ronald (NY)	RadRO	979
Ensminger, William (MI)	Onc	369
Epstein, Andrew (PA)	CE	114
Epstein, Jeffrey (FL)	Oto	678
Epstein, Jonathan (MD)	Path	721
Epstein, Laurence (MA)	CE	113
Epstein, Leon (IL)	ChiN	148
Epstein, Stuart (CA)	PA&I	747
Erasmus, Jeremy (TX)	DR	1016
Erban, John (MA)	Onc	331
Erdmann, Detlev (NC)	PlS	889
Eriksson, Elof (MA)	PlS	878
Ernstoff, Marc (NH)	Onc	331
Errico, Thomas (NY)	OrS	623
Eschenbach, David (WA)	ObG	567
Escobedo, Marilyn (OK)	NP	453
Esmaeli-Azad, Bita (TX)	Oph	602
Espat, N. Joseph (RI)	S	1085
Esquenazi, Alberto (PA)	PMR	863
Esquivel, Carlos (CA)	S	1132
Esserman, Laura (CA)	S	1132
Essner, Richard (CA)	S	1132
Estabrook, Alison (NY)	S	1093
Estes, N.A. Mark (MA)	CE	113
Estey, Elihu (WA)	Onc	387
Estores, David (FL)	Ge	242
Estwanik, Joseph (NC)	OrS	636
Eth, Spencer (FL)	Psyc	928
Eton, Darwin (IL)	VascS	1227
Ettenger, Robert (CA)	PNep	800
Ettinger, David (MD)	Onc	342
Eubanks, W Stephen (FL)	S	1105
Eugster, Erica (IN)	PEn	760
Euhus, David (TX)	S	1124
Eustis, H. 504Sprague (LA)	Oph	602
Evans, Douglas (WI)	S	1113
Evans, Gregory (CA)	PlS	902
Evans, James (PA)	NS	476
Evans, Mark (NY)	ObG	561
Evans, Sarah (DC)	PMR	863
Evers, Kathryn (PA)	DR	1009
Ewalt, David (TX)	Ped Uro	828
Ewend, Matthew (NC)	NS	484
Ezaki, Marybeth (TX)	HS	305

F

Name	Specialty	Pg
Fabian, Carol (KS)	Onc	377
Faddis, Mitchell (MO)	CE	117
Fadem, Stephen (TX)	Nep	465
Fahey, Patrick (IL)	Pul	964
Fahey, Thomas (NY)	S	1093
Fahn, Stanley (NY)	N	515
Faigel, Douglas (AZ)	Ge	253
Failla, Joseph (MI)	HS	302
Fairman, Ronald (PA)	VascS	1223
Fakih, Marwan (CA)	Onc	387
Falco, Frank (DE)	PM	707

Name	Specialty	Pg
Falcone, Tommaso (OH)	RE	1047
Falk, Gary (PA)	Ge	234
Falk, Rena (CA)	CG	162
Falk, Ronald (NC)	Nep	461
Fallat, Mary (KY)	PS	818
Fallon, Brian (NY)	Psyc	924
Fallon, Michael (TX)	Ge	254
Fallon, Robert (IN)	PHO	783
Famuyide, Abimbola (MN)	ObG	564
Fan, Leland (CO)	PPul	810
Fang, John (UT)	Ge	252
Fann, Jesse (WA)	Psyc	933
Fanous, Yvonne (CA)	PA&I	747
Fanta, Christopher (MA)	Pul	954
Farag, Sherif (IN)	Hem	321
Farber, Martin (NY)	Rhu	1060
Faries, Peter (NY)	VascS	1223
Farley, David (MN)	S	1114
Farlow, Martin (IN)	N	529
Farmer, Diana (CA)	PS	823
Farmer, James (NY)	OrS	623
Faro, Scott (PA)	NRad	1020
Farrar, William (OH)	S	1114
Farraye, Francis (MA)	Ge	230
Farrior, Edward (FL)	Oto	678
Farrior, Joseph (FL)	Oto	678
Fasano, Alessio (MA)	PGe	762
Fay, Joseph (TX)	Onc	379
Faye-Petersen, Ona (AL)	Path	726
Feder, Robert (IL)	Oph	595
Federle, Michael (CA)	DR	1017
Feghali, Joseph (NY)	Oto	669
Feig, Barry (TX)	S	1125
Feig, Stephen (CA)	DR	1017
Feinberg, Joseph (NY)	PMR	864
Feinberg, Todd (NY)	N	515
Feinglos, Mark (NC)	EDM	216
Feins, Richard (NC)	T&CS	1162
Feld, Gregory (CA)	CE	119
Feldman, David (NY)	OrS	623
Feldman, Eva (MI)	N	529
Feldman, Joel (MA)	PlS	878
Feldman, Joseph (IL)	PMR	868
Feldman, Kenneth (WA)	Ped	742
Feldman, Marc (TX)	IC	127
Feldman, Ted (IL)	IC	126
Feldon, Steven (NY)	Oph	578
Feldstein, Neil (NY)	NS	476
Felix, Carolyn (PA)	PHO	773
Fellus, Jonathan (NJ)	N	515
Feltes, Timothy (OH)	PCd	753
Fennerty, M. Brian (OR)	Ge	256
Fennoy, Ilene (NY)	PEn	758
Fenske, Neil (FL)	D	192
Fenstermaker, Robert (NY)	NS	476
Ferguson, James (VA)	MF	436
Ferguson, Mark (IL)	T&CS	1168
Fernando, Hiran (MA)	T&CS	1147
Ferrante, F Michael (CA)	PM	712
Ferrara, James (MI)	PHO	783
Ferrell, Linda (CA)	Path	732
Ferrendelli, James (TX)	N	536
Ferris, Frank (OH)	H & PM	407
Ferris, Robert (PA)	Oto	669
Fessler, Richard (IL)	NS	490
Fewkes, Jessica (MA)	D	184
Fichtenbaum, Carl (OH)	Inf	417
Fidler, Jeff (MN)	DR	1014
Fields, Abbie (DC)	GO	278
Fields, Theodore (NY)	Rhu	1060
Fife, Rose (IN)	Rhu	1065
Figlin, Robert (CA)	Onc	387
Filicko-O'Hara, Joanne (PA)	Hem	314
Filipek, Pauline (TX)	ChiN	150
Filley, Christopher (CO)	N	534
Filly, Roy (CA)	DR	1017
Filsoufi, Farzan (NY)	T&CS	1152
Finan, Michael (AL)	GO	281
Fine, Howard (NY)	Onc	342
Fine, Perry (UT)	PM	711
Fine, Robert (TX)	H & PM	408
Fine, Robert (NY)	Onc	342
Finerman, Gerald (CA)	OrS	651
Finger, Paul (NY)	Oph	578
Fink, Matthew (NY)	N	515
Finkel, Alan (NC)	N	524
Finkel, Michael (FL)	N	524
Finkel, Richard (FL)	ChiN	147
Finkel, Terri (FL)	PRhu	812
Finklestein, Jerry (CA)	PHO	789
Finlay, Jonathan (CA)	PHO	789
Finlayson, Christina (CO)	S	1122
Fintel, Dan (IL)	Cv	101
Finucane, Thomas (MD)	Ger	264
Fiorica, James (FL)	GO	281
First, Michael (NY)	Psyc	924
Fisch, Harry (NY)	U	1190
Fischbein, Lewis (MO)	IM	427
Fischer, Thomas (IN)	HS	302
Fischl, Margaret (FL)	IM	426
Fish, Frank (TN)	PCd	751
Fishbein, Daniel (WA)	Cv	110

Name	Specialty	Pg
Fishbein, Michael (CA)	Path	733
Fisher, Garth (CA)	PlS	902
Fisher, George (CA)	Onc	387
Fisher, Jonathan (CA)	S	1132
Fisher, Mark (CA)	N	539
Fisher, Paul (CA)	ChiN	151
Fisher, Richard (PA)	Onc	342
Fisher, Robert (PA)	Ge	234
Fisher, Robert (CA)	N	540
Fisher, Rosemarie (CT)	Ge	230
Fisher, William (TX)	S	1125
Fishman, David (NY)	GO	278
Fishman, Elliot (MD)	DR	1009
Fishman, Gerald (IL)	Oph	595
Fishman, Henry (DC)	A&I	81
Fishman, Scott (CA)	PM	712
Fitch, Tom (AZ)	Onc	380
Fitzgerald, Paul (CA)	EDM	224
Fitzgibbon, Dermot (WA)	PM	713
Fitzgibbons, Robert (NE)	S	1122
Fitzpatrick, Richard (CA)	D	200
Fiveash, John (AL)	RadRO	984
Fivenson, David (MI)	D	195
Fivush, Barbara (MD)	PNep	798
Fix, Richard (AL)	PlS	889
Flaherty, Alice (MA)	N	511
Flaherty, John (IL)	Inf	417
Flaherty, Joseph (MO)	Ger	266
Flaherty, Keith (MA)	Onc	331
Flake, Alan (PA)	PS	815
Flamm, Scott (OH)	DR	1014
Flanagan, Steven (NY)	PMR	864
Flanigan, D Preston (CA)	VascS	1230
Flanigan, Robert (IL)	U	1203
Flanigan, Timothy (RI)	Inf	412
Flatow, Evan (NY)	OrS	624
Fleischer, David (AZ)	Ge	254
Fleming, Gini (IL)	Onc	369
Fleshman, James (TX)	CRS	176
Fletcher, Christopher (MA)	Path	718
Fletcher, Eugene (IN)	Pul	964
Flickinger, John (PA)	RadRO	979
Flinn, Ian (TN)	Onc	357
Flint, Paul (OR)	Oto	695
Flomenberg, Neal (PA)	Onc	342
Florakis, George (NY)	Oph	578
Flores, Raja (NY)	T&CS	1152
Flynn, Harry (FL)	Oph	588
Flynn, Joseph (WA)	PNep	800
Flynn, Michael (KY)	S	1105
Flynn, Patricia (TN)	PInf	794

Name	Specialty	Pg
Flynn, Patrick (MN)	Onc	369
Fodor, Peter (CA)	PlS	902
Foglia, Robert (TX)	PS	822
Fogt, Franz (PA)	Path	721
Foley, Carmel (NY)	ChAP	940
Foley, Eugene (WI)	CRS	173
Foley, Kevin (TN)	NS	484
Follansbee, William (PA)	Cv	92
Fonarow, Gregg (CA)	Cv	110
Fong, Yuman (NY)	S	1093
Fonseca, Rafael (AZ)	Hem	326
Fontana, Gregory (NY)	T&CS	1152
Foo, Sun-Hoo (NY)	N	515
Forastiere, Arlene (MD)	Onc	343
Forbess, Joseph (TX)	T&CS	1174
Ford, Henri (CA)	PS	823
Ford, James (CA)	Onc	387
Forero-Torres, Andres (AL)	Onc	358
Forman, Jeffrey (MI)	RadRO	989
Forman, Stephen (CA)	Hem	328
Formenti, Silvia (NY)	RadRO	979
Fornari, Victor (NY)	ChAP	940
Forscher, Charles (CA)	Onc	387
Forsmark, Christopher (FL)	Ge	242
Fosko, Scott (MO)	D	195
Foss, Francine (CT)	Onc	331
Fossella, Frank (TX)	Onc	380
Fost, Norman (WI)	Ped	741
Foster, C (MA)	Oph	574
Foster, Carol (UT)	PEn	761
Foster, Harris (CT)	U	1186
Foster, Richard (IN)	U	1203
Foucar, M Kathryn (NM)	Path	730
Fouladi, Maryam (OH)	PHO	783
Fouser, Laurie (WA)	PNep	801
Fowble, Barbara (CA)	RadRO	995
Fowl, Richard (AZ)	VascS	1229
Fowler, Jeffrey (OH)	GO	284
Fox, Geraldine (IL)	Psyc	929
Fox, Harold (MD)	MF	434
Fox, James (PA)	PlS	882
Fox, Kevin (PA)	Onc	343
Fracasso, Paula (VA)	Onc	358
Fraker, Douglas (PA)	S	1093
Frances, Richard (NY)	AdP	936
Francis, Kathleen (NJ)	PMR	864
Francisco, Gerard (TX)	PMR	871
Frangoul, Haydar (TN)	PHO	778
Frank, Ian (PA)	Inf	413
Franklin, Morris (TX)	S	1125
Frantz, Christopher (DE)	PHO	773

Name	Specialty	Pg
Frantz, Ivan (MA)	NP	448
Frantzides, Constantine (IL)	S	1114
Fraser, Charles (TX)	T&CS	1174
Fraser, Lionel (MS)	U	1197
Frassica, Frank (MD)	OrS	624
Frazier, O. Howard (TX)	T&CS	1174
Frazier, Thomas (PA)	S	1093
Freedman, Arnold (MA)	Onc	331
Freedman, Gary (PA)	RadRO	979
Freedman, Sharon (NC)	Oph	588
Freeman, Gregory (TX)	Cv	108
Freeman, Leonard (NY)	NuM	554
Freeman, Theodore (TX)	A&I	85
Freeman, Thomas (FL)	NS	484
Freeman, William (CA)	Oph	606
Freemark, Michael (NC)	PEn	759
Frei, Donald (CO)	NRad	1025
Freifeld, Alison (NE)	Inf	419
Freiman, Hal (NY)	Ge	234
Freimanis, Rita (NC)	DR	1013
Freischlag, Julie (MD)	VascS	1223
Freitag, Frederick (WI)	PM	709
French, Jacqueline (NY)	N	515
French, William (CA)	Cv	111
Friberg, Thomas (PA)	Oph	578
Fricker, F. Jay (FL)	PCd	751
Friebert, Sarah (OH)	H & PM	408
Fried, Guy (PA)	PMR	864
Fried, Marvin (NY)	Oto	669
Fried, Michael (NC)	Ge	242
Friedberg, Jonathan (NY)	Onc	343
Friedberg, Joseph (PA)	T&CS	1152
Frieden, Ilona (CA)	D	200
Friedlaender, Gary (CT)	OrS	617
Friedlander, Sheila (CA)	D	200
Friedman, Alan (MD)	PHO	773
Friedman, Alan (PA)	Hem	314
Friedman, Allan (NC)	NS	484
Friedman, Andrew (WA)	PMR	872
Friedman, Barry (CA)	Psyc	933
Friedman, Chad (OH)	RE	1047
Friedman, David (FL)	HS	301
Friedman, Debra (TN)	PHO	778
Friedman, Ellen (TX)	PO	805
Friedman, Henry (NC)	Onc	358
Friedman, Lawrence (MA)	Ge	231
Friedman, Lloyd (CT)	Pul	954
Friedman, Matthew (VT)	Psyc	920
Friedman, Michael (IL)	Oto	684
Friedman, Sanford (NY)	Cv	92
Friedman, Stuart (FL)	A&I	82
Friese, Randall (AZ)	S	1125
Frim, David (IL)	NS	490
Fritz, Marc (NC)	RE	1046
Frohman, Elliot (TX)	N	536
Fromkin, Kenneth (FL)	IC	124
Fromm, Geri-Lynn (TX)	GO	288
Fronek, Jan (CA)	SM	1079
Frost, Frederick (OH)	PMR	868
Fruchtman, Steven (NY)	Hem	314
Fry, Robert (PA)	CRS	169
Fu, Freddie (PA)	SM	1075
Fuchs, Charles (MA)	Onc	332
Fuchs, Wayne (NY)	Oph	578
Fuhrman, Bradley (TX)	PCCM	756
Fuhrman, Carl (PA)	DR	1009
Fulkerson, John (CT)	OrS	617
Fulkerson, William (NC)	Pul	962
Fuller, Nicholas (CA)	PM	713
Fullerton, David (CO)	T&CS	1172
Fulop, Tibor (MS)	Nep	461
Funaki, Brian (IL)	VIR	1030
Fung, John (OH)	S	1114
Funk, Gerry (IA)	Oto	684
Furie, Karen (RI)	N	511
Furlan, Anthony (OH)	N	529
Furman, Wayne (TN)	PHO	778
Furukawa, Satoshi (PA)	T&CS	1152
Fuster, Valentin (NY)	Cv	92
Futran, Neal (WA)	Oto	695
Fyer, Abby (NY)	Psyc	924

G

Name	Specialty	Pg
Gabbard, Glen (TX)	Psyc	932
Gabram, Sheryl (GA)	S	1105
Gabrilove, Janice (NY)	Onc	343
Gaffney, David (UT)	RadRO	992
Gagel, Robert (TX)	EDM	222
Gaines, Barbara (PA)	PS	815
Gaissert, Henning (MA)	T&CS	1147
Gajjar, Amar (TN)	PHO	778
Galandiuk, Susan (KY)	CRS	171
Galanter, I Marc (NY)	AdP	936
Galantowicz, Mark (OH)	T&CS	1168
Galati, Joseph (TX)	Ge	254
Galetta, Steven (NY)	N	515
Galgiani, John (AZ)	Inf	420
Gallagher, Mary (NY)	PEn	758
Galland, Leo (NY)	IM	426
Gallico, G Gregory (MA)	PlS	878

Alphabetical Listing of Doctors

Name	Specialty	Pg
Gallin, Pamela (NY)	Oph	578
Galloway, Aubrey (NY)	T&CS	1153
Galloway, John (GA)	S	1105
Gambardella, Ralph (CA)	SM	1079
Gambert, Steven (MD)	Ger	265
Gambetti, Pierluigi (OH)	Path	728
Gamelli, Richard (IL)	S	1114
Gandara, David (CA)	Onc	388
Gang, Eli (CA)	CE	120
Gantz, Bruce (IA)	Oto	685
Ganz, Patricia (CA)	Onc	388
Garber, Judy (MA)	Onc	332
Garcia, Mario (NY)	Cv	92
Garcia-Manero, Guillermo (TX)	Hem	326
Garcia-Prats, Joseph (TX)	NP	453
Garden, Jerome (IL)	D	195
Gardin, Julius (NJ)	Cv	93
Garfin, Steven (CA)	OrS	651
Garibaldi, Luigi (PA)	PEn	758
Garner, Warren (CA)	PlS	902
Garnick, Marc (MA)	Onc	332
Garofalo, Robert (IL)	AM	77
Garrett, Algin (VA)	D	192
Garrett, William (NC)	OrS	636
Garrity, Edward (IL)	Pul	964
Garst, Jennifer (NC)	Onc	358
Garth, William (AL)	SM	1077
Gartner, J. Carlton (DE)	Ped	740
Garver, Robert (AL)	Pul	962
Garvin, James (NY)	PHO	773
Garvin, Kevin (NE)	OrS	646
Gaston, Robert (AL)	Nep	461
Gater, David (PA)	PMR	864
Gawande, Atul (MA)	S	1085
Gaynor, Ellen (IL)	Onc	369
Gaynor, J William (PA)	T&CS	1153
Gearhart, John (MD)	U	1190
Gearhart, Susan (MD)	CRS	170
Gebhardt, Mark (MA)	OrS	617
Geffner, Mitchell (CA)	PEn	761
Gefter, Warren (PA)	DR	1009
Gejerman, Glen (NJ)	RadRO	979
Gelb, Bruce (NY)	PCd	748
Gelberman, Richard (MO)	HS	302
Gelfand, Erwin (CO)	PA&I	745
Geller, David (PA)	S	1093
Gellis, Stephen (MA)	D	185
Gelmann, Edward (NY)	Onc	343
Geltman, Edward (MO)	Cv	102
Genc, Mehmet (NY)	MF	434
Gendelman, Seymour (NY)	N	515
Genden, Eric (NY)	Oto	670
Gentile, Ronald (NY)	Oph	579
George, Daniel (NC)	Onc	358
George, Suzanne (MA)	Onc	332
Georgiade, Gregory (NC)	PlS	889
Gerboth, Gregory (AK)	Pul	970
Gerdes, Hans (NY)	Ge	234
Geronemus, Roy (NY)	D	188
Gershenson, David (TX)	GO	288
Gershwin, Merrill (CA)	Rhu	1067
Gerson, Lauren (CA)	Ge	256
Gerson, Stanton (OH)	Onc	369
Gertz, Morie (MN)	Hem	321
Geschwind, Jean-Francois (MD)	VIR	1028
Gewertz, Bruce (CA)	VascS	1230
Gewitz, Michael (NY)	PCd	749
Gewolb, Ira (MI)	NP	452
Geyer, Charles (VA)	Onc	358
Geyer, J. Russell (WA)	PHO	790
Ghamande, Sharad (GA)	GO	281
Gharagozloo, Farid (AZ)	T&CS	1174
Gharibo, Christopher (NY)	PM	707
Gholam, Pierre (OH)	Ge	247
Giannotta, Steven (CA)	NS	499
Gianoli, Gerard (LA)	Oto	692
Giardiello, Francis (MD)	Ge	234
Giardina, Patricia (NY)	PHO	773
Gibbons, Raymond (MN)	Cv	102
Gibbs, John (NY)	S	1093
Gibbs, Ronald (CO)	MF	440
Gibralter, Richard (NY)	Oph	579
Gibson, C (MA)	IC	120
Gibson, Ronald (WA)	PPul	810
Gigantelli, James (NE)	Oph	601
Gilbert, Fred (NY)	CG	157
Gilbert, Mark (TX)	N	536
Gilchrest, Barbara (MA)	D	185
Gilden, Donald (CO)	N	535
Gill, Harcharan (CA)	U	1211
Gill, Inderbir (CA)	U	1211
Gill, Thomas (MA)	SM	1074
Gilliam, Melissa (IL)	ObG	564
Gilsanz, Vicente (CA)	DR	1018
Ginsberg, David (CA)	U	1211
Ginsberg, Gregory (PA)	Ge	234
Ginsburg, Elizabeth (MA)	RE	1040
Ginsburg, Howard (NY)	PS	815
Ginsburg, Kenneth (PA)	AM	76
Ginsburg, Mark (NY)	T&CS	1153
Girardi, Leonard (NY)	T&CS	1153
Gish, Robert (CA)	Ge	256

Name	Specialty	Pg
Gitelis, Steven (IL)	OrS	641
Gitelman, Stephen (CA)	PEn	761
Gitlin, Michael (CA)	Psyc	933
Gittes, George (PA)	PS	815
Gittler, Michelle (IL)	PMR	868
Giudice, Linda (CA)	RE	1052
Giuliano, Armando (CA)	S	1132
Giuntoli, Robert (MD)	GO	278
Giustra, Lawrence (GA)	Psyc	928
Givan, Deborah (IN)	PPul	808
Givner, Laurence (NC)	PInf	794
Gizzi, Martin (NJ)	N	516
Glader, Bertil (CA)	PHO	790
Gladstone, James (NY)	OrS	624
Glashow, Jonathan (NY)	OrS	624
Glaspy, John (CA)	Onc	388
Glass, Jon (PA)	N	516
Glass, Jonathan (GA)	N	524
Glassford, David (TN)	T&CS	1162
Glat, Paul (PA)	PlS	882
Gleason, Christine (WA)	NP	453
Glenn, Mel (MA)	PMR	862
Glick, John (PA)	Onc	343
Glick, Philip (NY)	PS	816
Glickel, Steven (NY)	HS	298
Gliklich, Jerry (NY)	Cv	93
Gliklich, Richard (MA)	Oto	665
Glisson, Bonnie (TX)	Onc	380
Glode, L. Michael (CO)	Onc	377
Glogau, Richard (CA)	D	200
Glombicki, Alan (TX)	Ge	254
Gloviczki, Peter (MN)	VascS	1227
Gluck, Michael (WA)	Ge	256
Gluck, Stephen (CA)	Nep	466
Gluckman, Gordon (IL)	U	1203
Gobrial, Wagih (FL)	PM	708
Gochfeld, Michael (NJ)	OM	912
Godder, Kamar (VA)	PHO	778
Godley, Paul (NC)	Onc	358
Godzik, Cathleen (CA)	HS	306
Goebel, Joel (MO)	Oto	685
Goetz, Christopher (IL)	N	529
Goff, Barbara (WA)	GO	291
Goff, Donald (NY)	Psyc	924
Goggins, Michael (MD)	Ge	235
Goitz, Henry (MI)	OrS	641
Goitz, Robert (PA)	HS	298
Gokaslan, Ziya (MD)	NS	477
Golbe, Lawrence (NJ)	N	516
Gold, Philip (WA)	Onc	388
Gold, Scott (NY)	Oto	670
Gold, Stuart (NC)	PHO	779
Goldberg, Daniel (NJ)	Oph	579
Goldberg, Jack (PA)	Hem	314
Goldberg, James (CA)	MF	442
Goldberg, Jeffrey (OH)	RE	1047
Goldberg, Joseph (CT)	Psyc	920
Goldberg, Michael (IL)	Ge	247
Goldberg, Nieca (NY)	Cv	93
Goldberg, Richard (OH)	Onc	369
Goldberger, Jeffrey (IL)	CE	117
Goldblum, John (OH)	Path	728
Golden, Michael (PA)	VascS	1223
Goldenberg, David (PA)	Oto	670
Goldman, Allan (FL)	Pul	962
Goldman, Mindy (CA)	ObG	567
Goldman, Stanton (TX)	PHO	788
Goldman, Stewart (IL)	PHO	783
Goldner, Richard (NC)	OrS	636
Goldsmith, Ari (NY)	PO	802
Goldsmith, Donald (PA)	PRhu	811
Goldsmith, Stanley (NY)	NuM	554
Goldstein, Irwin (CA)	U	1212
Goldstein, Jeffrey (NY)	OrS	624
Goldstein, Larry (NC)	N	524
Goldstein, Lori (PA)	Onc	343
Goldstein, Marc (NY)	U	1190
Goldstein, Martin (NY)	ObG	561
Goldstein, Scott (PA)	CRS	170
Goldstein, Wayne (IL)	OrS	641
Golfinos, John (NY)	NS	477
Golub, Richard (FL)	CRS	172
Gomella, Leonard (PA)	U	1190
Gomery, Pablo (MA)	U	1186
Gomes, Antoinette (CA)	VIR	1032
Gomes, Joseph (NY)	CE	114
Gonik, Bernard (MI)	MF	438
Gonzales, Edmond (TX)	Ped Uro	828
Goodin, Douglas (CA)	N	540
Goodman, Dennis (NY)	Cv	93
Goodman, Jean (IL)	MF	438
Goodman, Lawrence (WI)	DR	1015
Goodman, Martin (MA)	S	1085
Goodman, Neil (FL)	EDM	216
Goodman, Robert (NJ)	RadRO	980
Goodman, Robert (NY)	NS	477
Goodman, Stuart (CA)	OrS	651
Goodson, William (CA)	S	1133
Goodwin, James (IL)	N	530
Goodwin, Scott (CA)	VIR	1032
Goodwin, W. Jarrard (FL)	Oto	679
Gorab, Robert (CA)	OrS	651

Name	Specialty	Pg
Gordon, Catherine (RI)	PEn	757
Gordon, Leo (IL)	Hem	321
Gordon, Marsha (NY)	D	188
Gordon, Stuart (NH)	Ge	231
Gorensek, Margaret (FL)	Inf	416
Gorevic, Peter (NY)	Rhu	1060
Gorfine, Stephen (NY)	CRS	170
Gorin, Michael (CA)	Oph	606
Gorovoy, Mark (FL)	Oph	588
Gosnell, Jessica (CA)	S	1133
Gospe, Sidney (WA)	ChiN	151
Gosselin, Benoit (NH)	Oto	665
Gostout, Bobbie (MN)	GO	284
Gostout, Christopher (MN)	Ge	248
Gottdiener, John (MD)	Cv	93
Gottlieb, Alice (MA)	D	185
Gottlieb, Geoffrey (MA)	Path	718
Gottlieb, Lawrence (IL)	PlS	893
Gottlieb, Stephen (MD)	Cv	93
Gould, K Lance (TX)	Cv	108
Goulet, Robert (IN)	S	1114
Goumnerova, Liliana (MA)	NS	473
Gourley, Mark (MD)	Rhu	1060
Govindarajan, Sugantha (CA)	Path	733
Gower, Roland (AK)	S	1133
Goy, Andre (NJ)	Onc	343
Gracia, Clarisa (PA)	RE	1042
Gradishar, William (IL)	Onc	369
Grado, Gordon (AZ)	RadRO	993
Grady, M Sean (PA)	NS	477
Graf, Ben (WI)	OrS	641
Graham, H. Devon (LA)	Oto	692
Graham, John (CA)	CG	162
Graham, Mark (NC)	Onc	358
Graham, Michael (AZ)	PHO	788
Graham, Roger (MA)	S	1085
Graham, Thomas (OH)	HS	303
Gralow, Julie (WA)	Onc	388
Grammer, Leslie (IL)	A&I	83
Grana, Generosa (NJ)	Onc	344
Granai, Cornelius (RI)	GO	275
Grandis, Arnold (NC)	MF	436
Grandis, Jennifer (PA)	Oto	670
Granet, David (CA)	Oph	606
Grannis, Frederic (CA)	T&CS	1178
Grant, Clive (MN)	S	1114
Grant, Edward (CA)	DR	1018
Grant, Jon (IL)	Psyc	929
Grant, Michael (TX)	S	1125
Grant, Robert (NY)	PlS	882
Grasso, Michael (NY)	U	1190

Name	Specialty	Pg
Graver, L. Michael (NY)	T&CS	1153
Graves, Michael (CA)	N	540
Gravett, Michael (WA)	MF	442
Gray, Richard (AZ)	S	1125
Gray, William (NY)	IC	122
Grazi, Richard (NY)	RE	1042
Graziano, Kathleen (AZ)	PS	822
Greco, F Anthony (TN)	Onc	359
Greden, John (MI)	Psyc	930
Green, Andrew (RI)	OrS	617
Green, Barth (FL)	NS	484
Green, Carmen (MI)	PM	709
Green, Daniel (TN)	PHO	779
Green, Howard (FL)	D	192
Green, Michael (PA)	PInf	793
Green, Peter (NY)	Ge	235
Green, Richard (NY)	VascS	1223
Green, Thomas (IL)	PPul	809
Greenbaum, Steven (PA)	D	188
Greenberg, Benjamin (RI)	Psyc	920
Greenberg, Donna (MA)	Psyc	920
Greenberg, Harly (NY)	Pul	957
Greenberg, Jay (DC)	PHO	773
Greenberg, Mark (NY)	Cv	93
Greenberg, Richard (PA)	U	1190
Greenberg, William (MA)	Psyc	920
Greenberger, Joel (PA)	RadRO	980
Greenberger, Paul (IL)	A&I	84
Greene, Clarence (LA)	NS	495
Greene, Graham (FL)	U	1197
Greene, Loren (NY)	EDM	212
Greene, Michael (MA)	MF	432
Greene, Robert (CA)	IC	128
Greene, Thomas (FL)	HS	301
Greenfield, David (FL)	Oph	588
Greenfield, Marjorie (OH)	ObG	564
Greenfield, Saul (NY)	Ped Uro	825
Greenfield, Shelly (MA)	AdP	936
Greenhalgh, David (CA)	S	1133
Greenson, Joel (MI)	Path	728
Greenspan, Susan (PA)	EDM	212
Greenwald, Blaine (NY)	GerPsy	944
Greenwald, Bruce (MD)	Ge	235
Greenwald, Mark (IL)	Oph	595
Greenway, Hubert (CA)	D	201
Greenwood, Robert (NC)	ChiN	147
Greer, Benjamin (WA)	GO	291
Greer, David (CT)	N	511
Greer, John (TN)	Hem	319
Greganti, Mac (NC)	Ger	265
Gregory, Richard (FL)	PlS	890

Name	Specialty	Pg
Gregory, Stephanie (IL)	Hem	322
Greiner, Carl (NE)	Psyc	931
Greisberg, Justin (NY)	OrS	624
Greisler, Howard (IL)	VascS	1227
Grelsamer, Ronald (NY)	OrS	624
Grem, Jean (NE)	Onc	377
Gress, Daryl (VA)	N	524
Grever, Michael (OH)	Hem	322
Gribetz, Michael (NY)	U	1190
Grichnik, James (FL)	D	193
Griebling, Tomas (KS)	U	1207
Griesemer, David (MA)	ChiN	144
Griffith, Bartley (MD)	T&CS	1153
Grifo, James (NY)	RE	1042
Grigsby, Perry (MO)	RadRO	989
Grikscheit, Tracy (CA)	PS	823
Grillone, Gregory (MA)	Oto	665
Grimes, Pearl (CA)	D	201
Griswold, John (TX)	S	1125
Grobelny, Thomas (IL)	NRad	1023
Grody, Wayne (CA)	CG	163
Grosh, William (VA)	Onc	359
Gross, Ian (CT)	NP	448
Gross, Paul (MA)	N	511
Grossbard, Michael (NY)	Onc	344
Grossberg, George (MO)	GerPsy	945
Grossi, Eugene (NY)	T&CS	1153
Grossman, H Barton (TX)	U	1208
Grossman, John (CO)	PIS	897
Grossman, John (FL)	HS	301
Grossman, Melanie (NY)	D	188
Grossman, Stuart (MD)	Onc	344
Grossniklaus, Hans (GA)	Oph	588
Grotta, James (TX)	N	536
Grotting, James (AL)	PIS	890
Grubb, Blair (OH)	Cv	102
Grubb, Robert (MO)	NS	490
Gruber, Stephen (CA)	Onc	388
Gruchalla, Rebecca (TX)	A&I	85
Gruenstein, Steven (NY)	Hem	314
Grum, Cyril (MI)	Pul	964
Grundfast, Kenneth (MA)	Oto	666
Grunebaum, Amos (NY)	MF	434
Grunfeld, Lawrence (NY)	RE	1042
Grupp, Stephan (PA)	PHO	773
Gruss, Joseph (WA)	PIS	902
Guandalini, Stefano (IL)	PGe	766
Guarda, Angela (MD)	Psyc	924
Guarini, Ludovico (NY)	PHO	773
Guber, Myles (CO)	T&CS	1173
Gugenheim, Joseph (TX)	OrS	648
Guidry, George (LA)	Pul	969
Guillem, Jose (NY)	CRS	170
Guilleminault, Christian (CA)	N	540
Guinan, Eva (MA)	PHO	770
Gujral, Saroj (MN)	U	1203
Gulley, James (MD)	Onc	344
Gullquist, Scott (VA)	PCd	751
Gumprecht, Jeffrey (NY)	Inf	413
Gunasekaran, T S (IL)	PGe	766
Gunderson, John (MA)	Psyc	921
Gundeti, Mohan (IL)	Ped Uro	827
Gundry, Steven (CA)	T&CS	1178
Gupta, Nalin (CA)	NS	499
Gupta, Prabodh (PA)	Path	721
Gupta, Rajan (NH)	S	1085
Gupta, Sandeep (IN)	PGe	766
Gururangan, Sridharan (NC)	PHO	779
Gutai, James (MI)	PEn	760
Guthikonda, Murali (MI)	NS	490
Guthrie, Barton (AL)	NS	485
Gutin, Philip (NY)	NS	477
Guy, John (FL)	Oph	589
Guy, T Sloane (PA)	T&CS	1154
Guyton, David (MD)	Oph	579
Guyton, Robert (GA)	T&CS	1162

H

Name	Specialty	Pg
Haas, Eric (TX)	CRS	176
Haas, Naomi (PA)	Onc	344
Haas, Richard (CA)	ChiN	151
Haas, Steven (NY)	OrS	625
Haber, Gregory (NY)	Ge	235
Haber, Richard (NY)	EDM	212
Habermann, Thomas (MN)	Hem	322
Hackford, Alan (MA)	CRS	168
Hackney, David (MA)	NRad	1019
Haddad, Joseph (NY)	PO	802
Haddad, Robert (MA)	Onc	332
Hadler, Nortin (NC)	Rhu	1063
Hadley, Mark (AL)	NS	485
Hadlock, Theresa (MA)	Oto	666
Haffty, Bruce (NJ)	RadRO	980
Hagan, Kevin (TN)	PIS	890
Hageboutros, Alexandre (NJ)	Onc	344
Hagman, Jennifer (CO)	ChAP	942
Hahn, Stephen (PA)	RadRO	980
Haid, Regis (GA)	NS	485
Haig, Andrew (MI)	PMR	868
Haik, Barrett (TN)	Oph	589

Alphabetical Listing of Doctors

Name	Specialty	Pg
Hain, Timothy (IL)	N	530
Haines, Kathleen (NJ)	PRhu	811
Hainline, Bryan (IN)	CG	160
Haith, Linwood (PA)	S	1094
Hakaim, Albert (FL)	VascS	1225
Halberg, Francine (CA)	RadRO	995
Hale, Douglass (IN)	ObG	565
Haley, Barbara (TX)	Onc	380
Haley, Elliott (VA)	N	525
Halff, Glenn (TX)	S	1125
Hall, Jesse (IL)	Pul	964
Hall, Lisabeth (NY)	Oph	579
Hall, Simon (NY)	U	1190
Haller, Julia (PA)	Oph	579
Hallett, John (SC)	VascS	1225
Halligan, Gregory (PA)	PHO	774
Hallisey, Michael (CT)	VIR	1027
Halperin, Henry (MD)	CE	115
Halperin, Jonathan (NY)	Cv	93
Halpern, Allan (NY)	D	188
Halpern, Howard (IL)	RadRO	989
Halpern, Steven (NJ)	PHO	774
Haluszka, Oleh (PA)	Ge	235
Halyard, Michele (AZ)	RadRO	993
Hamilton, Blake (UT)	U	1207
Hamilton, Stanley (TX)	Path	730
Hammar, Samuel (WA)	Path	733
Hammer, Gary (MI)	EDM	219
Hammer, Glenn (NY)	Inf	413
Hammer, Scott (NY)	Inf	413
Hammerschlag, Paul (NY)	Oto	670
Hammond, Dennis (MI)	PlS	894
Hammond, Flora (IN)	PMR	868
Hamra, Sameer (TX)	PlS	899
Hamvas, Aaron (MO)	NP	452
Han, Steven-Huy (CA)	Ge	256
Hanauer, Stephen (IL)	Ge	248
Hancock, Steven (CA)	RadRO	995
Handa, James (MD)	Oph	579
Hande, Kenneth (TN)	Onc	359
Handy, John (OR)	T&CS	1178
Hanel, Douglas (WA)	HS	306
Haney, Arthur (IL)	RE	1047
Hanifin, Jon (OR)	D	201
Hanke, C. William (IN)	D	195
Hankins, Gary (TX)	MF	441
Hankinson, Hal (NM)	NS	495
Hanks, John (VA)	S	1105
Hanley, Frank (CA)	T&CS	1178
Hanna, Brian (PA)	PCd	749
Hanna, Ehab (TX)	Oto	692
Hanna, Nader (MD)	S	1094
Hannafin, Jo (NY)	OrS	625
Hansen, Juliana (OR)	PlS	903
Hansen, Nora (IL)	S	1114
Hansen, Ronald (AZ)	D	198
Hansen-Flaschen, John (PA)	Pul	957
Hanson, Laura (NC)	Ger	265
Hanssen, Arlen (MN)	OrS	641
Haque, Waheedul (TX)	Psyc	932
Har-El, Gady (NY)	Oto	670
Haraf, Daniel (IL)	RadRO	989
Harari, Paul (WI)	RadRO	989
Harati, Yadollah (TX)	N	537
Harbaugh, Robert (PA)	NS	477
Harber, Philip (AZ)	OM	912
Harbour, J William (FL)	Oph	589
Hardesty, Robert (CA)	PlS	903
Hardin, Joel (IL)	PCd	753
Hare, Joshua (FL)	Cv	98
Hargrove, W Clark (PA)	T&CS	1154
Hariprasad, Seenu (IL)	Oph	595
Harken, Alden (CA)	T&CS	1178
Harley, Earl (DC)	PO	802
Harman, Eloise (FL)	Pul	962
Harmon, William (MA)	PNep	797
Harner, Christopher (PA)	SM	1075
Harnsberger, Jeffrey (NH)	CRS	168
Harper, Richard (TX)	NS	495
Harpole, David (NC)	T&CS	1162
Harrell, James (TX)	T&CS	1174
Harrington, Elizabeth (NY)	VascS	1223
Harris, David (TX)	PMR	871
Harris, Jay (MA)	RadRO	976
Harris, Jeffrey (CA)	Oto	695
Harris, Lyndsay (OH)	Onc	369
Harris, Michael (NJ)	PHO	774
Harris, Nancy (MA)	Path	718
Harrison, J Kevin (NC)	Cv	98
Harrison, Louis (NY)	RadRO	980
Harrop, James (PA)	NS	477
Harsh, Griffith (CA)	NS	500
Hartford, Alan (NH)	RadRO	976
Hartig, Gregory (WI)	Oto	685
Hartl, Roger (NY)	NS	477
Hartman, Adam (MD)	ChiN	145
Hartman, Barry (NY)	Inf	413
Hartmann, Rene (FL)	CRS	172
Hashim, Sabet (CT)	T&CS	1147
Haskal, Ziv (MD)	VIR	1028
Hastings, Hill (IN)	HS	303
Hatch, David (IL)	Ped Uro	827

Name	Specialty	Pg
Hatch, Kenneth (AZ)	GO	288
Haughey, Bruce (MO)	Oto	685
Haughton, Victor (WI)	NRad	1023
Hauke, Ralph (NE)	Onc	377
Hauptman, Paul (MO)	Cv	102
Hauser, Robert (FL)	N	525
Hauser, Stephen (CA)	N	540
Hausman, Michael (NY)	OrS	625
Haut, Paul (IN)	PHO	783
Havrilesky, Laura (NC)	GO	282
Hawes, Robert (FL)	Ge	242
Hawkins, Douglas (WA)	PHO	790
Hawn, Mary (AL)	S	1105
Hayani, Ammar (IL)	PHO	783
Hayashi, Robert (MO)	PHO	783
Hayden, Richard (AZ)	Oto	692
Hayes, Daniel (MI)	Onc	370
Hayes, David (MN)	CE	117
Hayes, Sharonne (MN)	Cv	102
Hayman, James (MI)	RadRO	990
Haynes, David (TN)	Oto	679
Haynes, Johnson (AL)	Pul	962
Healey, John (NY)	OrS	625
Healey, Patrick (WA)	PS	823
Heber, David (CA)	EDM	224
Hebert, James (VT)	S	1085
Hecht, Andrew (NY)	OrS	625
Heck, Christianne (CA)	N	540
Heckenlively, John (MI)	Oph	595
Hecox, Kurt (WI)	N	530
Hedges, Thomas (MA)	Oph	574
Heffner, John (OR)	Pul	970
Heiden, Eric (UT)	OrS	646
Heilman, Carl (MA)	NS	473
Heilman, Kenneth (FL)	N	525
Heimann, Ruth (VT)	RadRO	976
Heinrich, Michael (OR)	Hem	328
Heitmiller, Richard (MD)	T&CS	1154
Helderman, J Harold (TN)	Nep	462
Helfet, David (NY)	OrS	625
Hellenbrand, William (CT)	PCd	747
Heller, Debra (NJ)	Path	721
Hellstrom, Wayne (LA)	U	1209
Helman, Lee (MD)	PHO	774
Helvie, Mark (MI)	DR	1015
Hemal, Ashok (NC)	U	1198
Hemming, Alan (CA)	S	1133
Henderson, David (MA)	Psyc	921
Henderson, Randal (FL)	RadRO	984
Henderson, Victor (CA)	N	540
Henderson, William (WA)	A&I	86
Hendricks-Munoz, Karen (VA)	NP	451
Heney, Niall (MA)	U	1186
Henke, David (NC)	Pul	962
Henry, David (PA)	Onc	344
Henry, Timothy (MN)	IC	126
Henschke, Claudia (NY)	DR	1009
Henshaw, Robert (DC)	OrS	625
Hensle, Terry (NJ)	U	1191
Hentz, Vincent (CA)	HS	306
Heppell, Jacques (AZ)	CRS	177
Herbst, Roy (CT)	Onc	332
Hergenroeder, Albert (TX)	AM	78
Herling, Irving (PA)	Cv	94
Herman, Charles (PA)	PlS	882
Herman, Martin (PA)	OrS	626
Herman, Terence (OK)	RadRO	993
Herman, William (MI)	EDM	219
Heros, Roberto (FL)	NS	485
Heroux, Alain (IL)	Cv	102
Herr, Harry (NY)	U	1191
Herrine, Steven (PA)	Ge	235
Herring, Stanley (WA)	PMR	872
Herrington, Cynthia (CA)	T&CS	1179
Herrmann, Howard (PA)	IC	122
Herrmann, Virginia (SC)	S	1105
Herron, Daniel (NY)	S	1094
Hersh, Peter (NJ)	Oph	579
Hershey, Andrew (OH)	ChiN	148
Hershman, Elliott (NY)	SM	1075
Hershorin, Eugene (FL)	Ped	741
Hertz, Marshall (MN)	Pul	965
Herzenberg, John (MD)	OrS	626
Herzog, Thomas (NY)	GO	278
Heslin, Martin (AL)	S	1105
Hess, David (GA)	N	525
Hess, Jeffrey (FL)	Oph	589
Hesselink, John (CA)	NRad	1026
Heston, Jerry (TN)	ChAP	941
Hetherington, Maxine (MO)	PHO	783
Heuer, Dale (WI)	Oph	595
Heyl, Peter (KY)	MF	436
Heyman, Melvin (CA)	PGe	769
Hibbard, Judith (IL)	MF	438
Hickok, Lee (WA)	RE	1052
Hicks, Barry (DE)	PS	816
Hicks, Marshall (TX)	VIR	1032
Hicks, Terry (LA)	CRS	177
Hicks, Wesley (NY)	Oto	670
Hidalgo, David (NY)	PlS	882
Hiesiger, Emile (NY)	N	516
Higano, Celestia (WA)	Onc	388

Name	Specialty	Pg
Higashida, Randall (CA)	NRad	1026
Higgins, Steven (CA)	CE	120
Hijazi, Ziyad (IL)	PCd	753
Hilden, Joanne (CO)	PHO	786
Hilfiker, Mary (CA)	PS	823
Hilger, Peter (MN)	Oto	685
Hilibrand, Alan (PA)	OrS	626
Hill, Ivor (OH)	PGe	766
Hill, Joseph (NH)	RE	1040
Hill, Mark (WA)	T&CS	1179
Hill, Nicholas (MA)	Pul	954
Himelstein, Andrew (DE)	Onc	344
Hinshaw, Daniel (MI)	S	1115
Hiotis, Spiros (NY)	S	1094
Hirsch, Barry (PA)	Oto	670
Hirsch, Glenn (NY)	ChAP	940
Hirsch, Irl (WA)	EDM	224
Hirsch, Joshua (MA)	NRad	1019
Hirsch, Sharon (IL)	ChAP	942
Hirschfeld, Robert (TX)	Psyc	932
Ho, Allen (PA)	Oph	580
Ho, Sherwin (IL)	SM	1078
Hochberg, Ephraim (MA)	Onc	332
Hochberg, Marc (MD)	Rhu	1060
Hochschuler, Stephen (TX)	OrS	648
Hochster, Howard (CT)	Onc	332
Hockstein, Steven (NY)	ObG	561
Hoda, Syed (NY)	Path	722
Hodapp, Elizabeth (FL)	Oph	589
Hodgson, Kim (IL)	VascS	1227
Hodin, Richard (MA)	S	1086
Hoffenberg, Edward (CO)	PGe	767
Hoffman, Andrew (CA)	EDM	224
Hoffman, Brenda (SC)	Ge	243
Hoffman, Henry (IA)	Oto	685
Hoffman, John (PA)	S	1094
Hoffman, Lloyd (NY)	PIS	882
Hoffman, Philip (IL)	Onc	370
Hoffman, Robert (NY)	PrM	913
Hoffman, Ronald (NY)	Oto	671
Hoffman, William (CA)	PIS	903
Hofkosh, Dena (PA)	Ped	740
Hogan, Thomas (WV)	Onc	345
Hogikyan, Norman (MI)	Oto	685
Holcomb, George (MO)	PS	820
Holcomb, John (TX)	S	1125
Holcombe, Randall (NY)	Onc	345
Holden, Stuart (CA)	U	1212
Holick, Michael (MA)	EDM	209
Holinger, Lauren (IL)	PO	804
Holland, Edward (OH)	Oph	595
Holland, H Kent (GA)	Hem	319
Holland, James (NY)	Onc	345
Hollander, Eric (NY)	Psyc	925
Holliday, Michael (MD)	Oto	671
Holliday, Roy (NY)	DR	1009
Hollier, Larry (LA)	VascS	1229
Hollingsworth, Alan (OK)	S	1126
Hollister, Dickerman (CT)	Onc	333
Holmes, David (MN)	IC	126
Holmes, Gregory (VT)	ChiN	144
Holmes, Lewis (MA)	CG	156
Holroyd, Suzanne (VA)	GerPsy	945
Holterman, Mark (IL)	PS	820
Holtzman, Ronald (NC)	NP	451
Holzman, Ian (NY)	NP	449
Holzman, Lawrence (PA)	Nep	459
Holzman, Michael (TN)	S	1106
Hom, David (OH)	Oto	685
Homans, Alan (VT)	PHO	770
Homer, Daniel (IL)	N	530
Hong, Waun (TX)	Onc	380
Hoops, Timothy (PA)	Ge	235
Hooten, William (MN)	PM	710
Hoots, William (MD)	PHO	774
Hopewell, Philip (CA)	Pul	970
Hopkins, L. Nelson (NY)	NS	478
Hoppe, Richard (CA)	RadRO	995
Hopping, Steven (DC)	Oto	671
Hord, Jeffrey (OH)	PHO	784
Horn, Biljana (CA)	PHO	790
Horn, Evelyn (NY)	Cv	94
Hornicek, Francis (MA)	OrS	617
Hornstein, Mark (MA)	RE	1040
Horowitz, Ira (GA)	GO	282
Horowitz, Jed (CA)	PIS	903
Hortobagyi, Gabriel (TX)	Onc	380
Horvath, Karen (WA)	S	1133
Horvath, Keith (MD)	T&CS	1154
Horwitz, Eric (PA)	RadRO	980
Horwitz, Steven (NY)	Onc	345
Hotaling, Andrew (IL)	Oto	686
Hotchkiss, Robert (NY)	HS	298
Hovsepian, David (CA)	VIR	1033
Howard, Thomas (NE)	VascS	1229
Howe, James (IA)	S	1115
Howe, Kevin (CA)	OrS	651
Howell, Elizabeth (UT)	AdP	937
Howerton, Russell (NC)	S	1106
Howington, John (IL)	T&CS	1168
Hoyer, Mark (IN)	PCd	753
Hoyme, H Eugene (SD)	CG	161

Name	Specialty	Pg
Hozack, William (PA)	OrS	626
Hrebinko, Ronald (PA)	U	1191
Hricak, Hedvig (NY)	DR	1010
Hruban, Ralph (MD)	Path	722
Hruska, Keith (MO)	Nep	463
Hruza, George (MO)	D	195
Hsu, Daphne (NY)	PCd	749
Hsu, Lewis (IL)	PHO	784
Huang, Jaou-Chen (TX)	RE	1050
Huang, Judy (MD)	NS	478
Huang, Laurence (CA)	Pul	971
Hubbard, Anne (NE)	DR	1016
Huber, Philip (TX)	CRS	177
Huber, Thomas (FL)	VascS	1226
Huddleston, Charles (MO)	T&CS	1168
Hudgins, Louanne (CA)	CG	163
Hudis, Clifford (NY)	Onc	345
Hudson, Melissa (TN)	PHO	779
Hudziak, James (VT)	ChAP	938
Hugenberg, Steven (IN)	Rhu	1065
Hughes, Kevin (MA)	S	1086
Huitt, Gwen (CO)	Inf	419
Hullfish, Kathie (VA)	ObG	562
Hultman, C Scott (NC)	PlS	890
Humayun, Mark (CA)	Oph	606
Hume, Eric (PA)	OrS	626
Hungerford, Marc (MD)	OrS	626
Hunstad, Joseph (NC)	PlS	890
Hunt, Kelly (TX)	S	1126
Hunt, Sharon (CA)	Cv	111
Hunt, Thomas (AL)	HS	301
Hunter, David (MA)	Oph	574
Hunter, Ellen (ID)	Ge	252
Hunter, Jill (TX)	NRad	1025
Hunter, John (OR)	S	1133
Huntoon, Marc (TN)	PM	708
Hurd, David (NC)	Onc	359
Hurst, Michael (WV)	Oto	671
Hurst, Robert (PA)	NRad	1020
Hurst, Roger (IL)	S	1115
Hurt, Hallam (PA)	NP	449
Hurteau, Jean (IL)	GO	284
Hurtig, Howard (PA)	N	516
Hurwitz, Dennis (PA)	PlS	883
Husain, Amreen (CA)	GO	291
Hussain, Maha (MI)	Onc	370
Hussey, Michael (IL)	MF	438
Hutchins, Laura (AR)	Onc	380
Hutchinson, Raymond (MI)	PHO	784
Huth, James (TX)	S	1126
Hutter, Adolph (MA)	Cv	88
Huynh, Phan (TX)	DR	1016
Hwu, Patrick (TX)	Onc	380
Hyers, Thomas (MO)	Pul	965
Hyman, Joshua (NY)	OrS	626
Hyman, Neil (VT)	CRS	168

I

Name	Specialty	Pg
Iafrati, Mark (MA)	VascS	1220
Iannaccone, Susan (TX)	ChiN	150
Iannettoni, Mark (IA)	T&CS	1169
Iannotti, Joseph (OH)	OrS	641
Ichord, Rebecca (PA)	ChiN	145
Idler, Richard (CO)	HS	304
Iglehart, James (MA)	S	1086
Iglesia, Cheryl (DC)	ObG	561
Ikramuddin, Sayeed (MN)	S	1115
Ilbawi, Michel (IL)	T&CS	1169
Iliff, Nicholas (MD)	Oph	580
Ilowite, Norman (NY)	PRhu	812
Ilson, David (NY)	Onc	345
Imber, Gerald (NY)	PlS	883
Imbriglia, Joseph (PA)	HS	298
Infante, Anthony (TX)	Ped	742
Infantolino, Anthony (PA)	Ge	235
Ingbar, David (MN)	Pul	965
Ingle, James (MN)	Onc	370
Inglis, Andrew (WA)	PO	805
Ingram, David (NC)	PInf	794
Inra, Lawrence (NY)	Cv	94
Interian, Alberto (FL)	CE	116
Inzucchi, Silvio (CT)	EDM	209
Irby, Pierce (NC)	U	1198
Irvine, John (CA)	Oph	606
Irwin, Charles (CA)	AM	78
Irwin, Richard (MA)	Pul	955
Irwin, Ronald (MI)	OrS	641
Isaacs, Claudine (DC)	Onc	345
Isaacs, Kim (NC)	Ge	243
Isaacson, Keith (MA)	RE	1040
Isaacson, Steven (NY)	RadRO	980
Isenberg, Sherwin (CA)	Oph	606
Isik, F. (WA)	PlS	903
Iskandrian, Ami (AL)	Cv	98
Ismail, Mahmoud (IL)	MF	438
Isola, Luis (NY)	Hem	314
Isom, O. Wayne (NY)	T&CS	1154
Itzkowitz, Steven (NY)	Ge	236
Ivanhoe, Cindy (TX)	PMR	871
Iwach, Andrew (CA)	Oph	606

Name	Specialty	Pg
Iwai, Sei (NY)	CE	115

J

Name	Specialty	Pg
Jaafar, Mohamad (VA)	Oph	589
Jablons, David (CA)	T&CS	1179
Jabs, Douglas (NY)	Oph	580
Jabs, Kathy (TN)	PNep	799
Jackler, Robert (CA)	Oto	695
Jackman, Stephen (PA)	U	1191
Jackson, Gilchrist (TX)	S	1126
Jackson, Richard (AR)	PS	822
Jackson, Valerie (IN)	DR	1015
Jackson, Vicki (MA)	H & PM	406
Jacobs, Alice (MA)	IC	120
Jacobs, Charlotte (CA)	Onc	388
Jacobs, Joseph (NY)	Oto	671
Jacobs, Joshua (IL)	OrS	642
Jacobs, Laurence (IL)	RE	1048
Jacobs, Richard (AR)	PInf	796
Jacobs, Thomas (NY)	EDM	213
Jacobson, Ira (NY)	Ge	236
Jacoby, David (OR)	Pul	971
Jaffe, Allan (MN)	Cv	102
Jahanzeb, Mohammad (FL)	Onc	359
Jain, Subhash (NY)	PM	707
Jakacki, Regina (PA)	PHO	774
Jallo, George (MD)	NS	478
James, William (PA)	D	189
Jamieson, Stuart (CA)	T&CS	1179
Jan, Dominique (NY)	PS	816
Janeiro, John (NH)	U	1186
Janicak, Philip (IL)	Psyc	930
Jankovic, Joseph (TX)	N	537
Janss, Anna (GA)	N	525
Jaramillo, Diego (PA)	DR	1010
Jarnagin, William (NY)	S	1094
Jarvik, Jeffrey (WA)	NRad	1026
Jasmin, Luc (OR)	PM	713
Jayakar, Parul (FL)	CG	159
Jayaseelan, Nirmal (TX)	S	1126
Jeevanandam, Valluvan (IL)	T&CS	1169
Jenike, Michael (MA)	Psyc	921
Jenkins, Arthur (NY)	NS	478
Jenkins, Herman (CO)	Oto	690
Jenkins, Roger (MA)	S	1086
Jenkins, Todd (AL)	ObG	563
Jennings, Russell (MA)	PS	814
Jensen, Donald (IL)	Ge	248
Jensen, Mary (VA)	NRad	1022
Jensen, Michael (MN)	EDM	220
Jessen, Michael (TX)	T&CS	1174
Jessup, Mariell (PA)	Cv	94
Jewell, Mark (OR)	PlS	903
Jhingran, Anuja (TX)	RadRO	994
Jho, Hae-Dong (PA)	NS	478
Jillella, Anand (GA)	Onc	359
Jimenez, David (TX)	NS	496
Jimerson, David (MA)	Psyc	921
Jiranek, William (VA)	OrS	636
Jobst, Barbara (NH)	N	511
Joffe, Hadine (MA)	Psyc	921
Johanson, Norman (PA)	OrS	626
John, Thomas (IL)	Oph	596
Johnson, Allen (CA)	Cv	111
Johnson, Annette (NC)	NRad	1022
Johnson, Bruce (MA)	Onc	333
Johnson, Bruce (VA)	Pul	962
Johnson, Calvin (LA)	Oto	692
Johnson, Darren (KY)	OrS	636
Johnson, Eric (CA)	OrS	651
Johnson, Jonas (PA)	Oto	671
Johnson, Julia (MA)	RE	1040
Johnson, Lynt (DC)	S	1094
Johnson, Maryl (WI)	Cv	103
Johnson, Matthew (IN)	VIR	1030
Johnson, Paula (MA)	Cv	88
Johnson, Ronald (PA)	S	1094
Johnson, Scott (TX)	T&CS	1175
Johnson, Stephen (CO)	NS	494
Johnson, Steven (CO)	Inf	419
Johnson, Timothy (MI)	D	195
Johnson, Timothy (MI)	MF	438
Johnson Miller, Denise (NJ)	S	1095
Johnston, Carolyn (MI)	GO	284
Johnston, J Martin (GA)	PHO	779
Johnston, James (PA)	Nep	459
Johnstone, David (WI)	T&CS	1169
Johnstone, Peter (IN)	RadRO	990
Johr, Robert (FL)	D	193
Jokl, Peter (CT)	OrS	617
Jonas, Adam (CA)	CG	163
Jonas, Maureen (MA)	PGe	762
Jonas, Richard (DC)	T&CS	1154
Jonasch, Eric (TX)	Onc	381
Jones, Daniel (MA)	S	1086
Jones, David (NY)	T&CS	1154
Jones, Deryk (LA)	SM	1078
Jones, J (OH)	U	1203
Jones, Jacqueline (NY)	Oto	671
Jones, Kenneth (CA)	Ped	742

Name	Specialty	Pg
Jones, Marilyn (CA)	CG	163
Jones, Neil (CA)	HS	306
Jones, Paul (IL)	Oto	686
Jonnalagadda, Sreenivasa (MO)	Ge	248
Jordan, Barry (NY)	N	516
Jordan, Stanley (CA)	PNep	801
Jorizzo, Joseph (NC)	D	193
Jose, Baby (IN)	RadRO	990
Joseph, David (AL)	Ped Uro	826
Joseph, Gregory (NC)	NRad	1022
Josephs, Shelby (MD)	PA&I	743
Josephson, David (IN)	N	530
Josephson, Jordan (NY)	Oto	671
Josephson, Mark (MA)	CE	113
Josephson, Michelle (IL)	Nep	463
Jost, Barbara (MO)	A&I	84
Joyce, Lyle (MN)	T&CS	1169
Joyce, Michael (OH)	OrS	642
Juckett, Mark (WI)	Hem	322
Judelson, Debra (CA)	Cv	111
Judy, Kevin (PA)	NS	478
Julian, Thomas (PA)	S	1095
Jupiter, Jesse (MA)	HS	296
Jurcic, Joseph (NY)	Hem	314

K

Name	Specialty	Pg
Kachnic, Lisa (MA)	RadRO	976
Kadan-Lottick, Nina (CT)	PHO	770
Kadmon, Dov (TX)	U	1209
Kaeding, Christopher (OH)	OrS	642
Kaefer, Martin (IN)	Ped Uro	827
Kafka, Martin (MA)	Psyc	921
Kagan, Richard (OH)	S	1115
Kahn, Barbara (MA)	EDM	209
Kahn, Leonard (NY)	Path	722
Kahrilas, Peter (IL)	Ge	248
Kaiser, Larry (PA)	T&CS	1154
Kaiser, Michael (NY)	NS	478
Kalaycio, Matt (OH)	Onc	370
Kalb, Robert (NY)	D	189
Kalemkerian, Gregory (MI)	Onc	370
Kaliner, Michael (MD)	A&I	81
Kallmes, David (MN)	NRad	1023
Kalloo, Anthony (MD)	Ge	236
Kalnicki, Shalom (NY)	RadRO	980
Kamani, Naynesh (DC)	PA&I	743
Kamdar, Vikram (CA)	EDM	224
Kaminski, Mark (MI)	Onc	370
Kampman, Kyle (PA)	AdP	937
Kanal, Emanuel (PA)	DR	1010
Kandeel, Fouad (CA)	EDM	224
Kandel, Jessica (IL)	PS	820
Kandzari, David (GA)	IC	124
Kane, Alex (TX)	PIS	899
Kane, Javier (TX)	PHO	788
Kane, Kay (MA)	D	185
Kane, Madeleine (CO)	Onc	377
Kane, Michael (MD)	U	1191
Kane, Timothy (DC)	PS	816
Kanel, Gary (CA)	Path	733
Kang, Dong-Kyoo (NE)	Oto	690
Kantarjian, Hagop (TX)	Hem	326
Kanter, Kirk (GA)	T&CS	1162
Kantoff, Philip (MA)	Onc	333
Kantsevoy, Sergey (MD)	Ge	236
Kaplan, Bernard (PA)	PNep	798
Kaplan, David (CO)	AM	77
Kaplan, Frederick (PA)	OrS	627
Kaplan, Irving (MA)	RadRO	976
Kaplan, James (KS)	Pul	968
Kaplan, Lawrence (CA)	Onc	389
Kaplan, Lee (FL)	SM	1077
Kaplan, Lee (MA)	Ge	231
Kaplan, Michael (CA)	Oto	695
Kaplan, Sheldon (TX)	PInf	796
Kaplan, Steven (NY)	U	1191
Kapoor, Neena (CA)	PHO	790
Kappy, Michael (CO)	PEn	761
Kapur, Sandip (NY)	S	1095
Karas, Spero (GA)	OrS	636
Karasu, T Byram (NY)	Psyc	925
Karlan, Scott (CA)	S	1133
Karpeh, Martin (NY)	S	1095
Karram, Mickey (OH)	ObG	565
Karrer, Frederick (CO)	PS	821
Karwande, Shreekanth (UT)	T&CS	1173
Kase, Carlos (MA)	N	511
Kashtan, Clifford (MN)	PNep	800
Kasinath, Balakuntalam (TX)	Nep	465
Kasiske, Bertram (MN)	Nep	463
Kasner, Scott (PA)	N	516
Kass, Evan (MI)	Ped Uro	827
Kasser, James (MA)	OrS	617
Kastenberg, David (PA)	Ge	236
Katirji, Bashar (OH)	N	530
Katkhouda, Namir (CA)	S	1133
Katner, Harold (GA)	Inf	416
Kato, Tomoaki (NY)	S	1095
Katowitz, James (PA)	Oph	580
Kattan, Meyer (NY)	PPul	807

Alphabetical Listing of Doctors

Name	Specialty	Pg
Katz, Aaron (NY)	U	1191
Katz, L. Jay (PA)	Oph	580
Katz, Philip (PA)	Ge	236
Katz, Robert (OH)	PO	804
Katz, Robert (IL)	Rhu	1065
Katz, Stuart (NY)	Cv	94
Katzen, Barry (FL)	VIR	1029
Katzenstein, Anna-Luise (NY)	Path	722
Katznelson, Laurence (CA)	EDM	225
Kaufman, Bruce (WI)	NS	490
Kaufman, Cary (WA)	S	1134
Kaufman, Dixon (WI)	S	1115
Kaufman, Howard (IL)	S	1115
Kaufman, John (OR)	VIR	1033
Kaufman, Paul (WI)	Oph	596
Kaufman, Peter (NH)	Onc	333
Kaufman, Richard (MA)	Path	718
Kaul, Sanjiv (OR)	Cv	111
Kavanah, Maureen (MA)	S	1086
Kavoussi, Louis (NY)	U	1191
Kawachi, Mark (CA)	U	1212
Kay, Dennis (LA)	VIR	1032
Kay, Jonathan (MA)	Rhu	1058
Kaye, Mitchell (MN)	Pul	965
Kazahaya, Ken (PA)	PO	802
Kazer, Ralph (IL)	RE	1048
Kazim, Michael (NY)	Oph	580
Kazmers, Andris (MI)	VascS	1227
Keane, Thomas (SC)	U	1198
Keane, William (PA)	Oto	672
Keating, Gesina (MN)	ChiN	148
Keating, Michael (TX)	Hem	326
Keefe, David (NY)	RE	1042
Keen, Mary (IL)	PMR	868
Keenan, Robert (PA)	T&CS	1155
Keens, Thomas (CA)	PPul	810
Keepers, George (OR)	Psyc	933
Keiser, Philip (TX)	Inf	420
Kelepouris, Ellie (PA)	Nep	460
Keller, Frank (GA)	PHO	779
Keller, Frederick (OR)	VIR	1033
Keller, Gregory (CA)	Oto	695
Keller, Steven (NY)	T&CS	1155
Kelley, Joseph (PA)	GO	278
Kelley, Mark (TN)	S	1106
Kelly, Bryan (NY)	OrS	627
Kelly, Cynthia (VA)	PA&I	745
Kelly, Cynthia (CO)	OrS	646
Kelly, Karen (CA)	Onc	389
Kelly, Kevin (TN)	PlS	890
Kelly, Thomas (CA)	MF	442
Kelly, W Kevin (PA)	Onc	345
Kelsen, David (NY)	Onc	346
Kelsey, Peter (MA)	Ge	231
Keltz, Martin (NY)	RE	1042
Kemeny, Nancy (NY)	Onc	346
Kemp, James (MO)	PPul	809
Kempin, Sanford (NY)	Hem	315
Kenan, Samuel (NY)	OrS	627
Kendrick, Michael (MN)	S	1115
Kenkel, Jeffrey (TX)	PlS	899
Kennedy, David (PA)	Oto	672
Kennedy, Gary (NY)	GerPsy	944
Kennedy, Laurence (OH)	EDM	220
Kennelly, Michael (NC)	U	1198
Kent, Kenneth (WI)	VascS	1228
Kent, Thomas (TX)	N	537
Kenter, Keith (OH)	OrS	642
Kenton, Kimberly (IL)	ObG	565
Kereiakes, Dean (OH)	Cv	103
Kern, Jeffrey (CO)	Pul	968
Kern, Robert (IL)	Oto	686
Kernstine, Kemp (TX)	T&CS	1175
Kerr, Natalie (TN)	Oph	589
Kesari, Santosh (CA)	N	540
Kesser, Bradley (VA)	Oto	679
Kessler, Craig (DC)	Hem	315
Kestin, Larry (MI)	RadRO	990
Kevorkian, Charles (TX)	PMR	871
Kezar, Laura (AL)	PMR	866
Khan, Agha (MD)	NS	478
Khandji, Alexander (NY)	NRad	1020
Khawaja, Shazib (GA)	IC	124
Khilnani, Neil (NY)	VIR	1028
Khosla, Sundeep (MN)	EDM	220
Khuri, Fadlo (GA)	Onc	359
Kibel, Adam (MA)	U	1187
Kidwell, Earl (DC)	Oph	580
Kieburtz, Karl (NY)	N	516
Kieran, Mark (MA)	PHO	770
Kies, Merrill (TX)	Onc	381
Kiev, Jonathan (WV)	T&CS	1155
Kikkawa, Don (CA)	Oph	606
Kilmer, Suzanne (CA)	D	201
Kim, Choll (CA)	OrS	652
Kim, Daniel (MA)	Oto	666
Kim, Daniel (TX)	NS	496
Kim, Dong (TX)	NS	496
Kim, Edward (TN)	U	1198
Kim, Jhinho (MS)	NS	485
Kim, Jonathan (CA)	Oph	607
Kim, Julian (OH)	S	1116

Name	Specialty	Pg
Kim, Lawrence (AR)	S	1126
Kim, Youn (CA)	D	201
Kim, Young-Jee (IN)	PPul	809
Kimberly, Robert (AL)	Rhu	1064
Kimmelstiel, Carey (MA)	IC	121
Kimmey, Michael (WA)	Ge	256
Kincaid, John (IN)	N	530
Kindler, Hedy (IL)	Onc	370
King, Aileen (ID)	ObG	566
King, Andrew (CA)	Nep	467
King, Bryan (WA)	ChAP	943
King, Earl (PA)	Pul	957
King, John (TX)	PMR	871
King, Richard (GA)	PMR	866
King, Stephanie (PA)	GO	278
King, Talmadge (CA)	Pul	971
Kingdom, Todd (CO)	Oto	690
Kinkhabwala, Milan (NY)	S	1095
Kinney, Marsha (TX)	Path	730
Kipen, Howard (NJ)	OM	912
Kipps, Thomas (CA)	Hem	328
Kirgan, Daniel (NV)	S	1134
Kirklin, James (AL)	T&CS	1163
Kirkwood, John (PA)	Onc	346
Kirsch, Andrew (GA)	Ped Uro	826
Kirschenbaum, Alexander (NY)	U	1192
Kirschner, Barbara (IL)	PGe	766
Kirschner, Kristi (IL)	PMR	869
Kirschner, Richard (OH)	PIS	894
Kirshblum, Steven (NJ)	PMR	864
Kirshbom, Paul (CT)	T&CS	1147
Kirshenbaum, James (MA)	Cv	89
Kirshner, Howard (TN)	N	525
Kirsner, Robert (FL)	D	193
Klaas, Virginia (WA)	NuM	557
Klagsbrun, Samuel (NY)	Psyc	925
Klapheke, Martin (FL)	Psyc	928
Kleber, Herbert (NY)	AdP	937
Kleiman, Neal (TX)	IC	127
Klein, Andrew (CA)	S	1134
Klein, Eric (OH)	U	1203
Klein, Lloyd (IL)	Cv	103
Klein, Robert (RI)	PA&I	743
Klein-Gitelman, Marisa (IL)	PRhu	813
Kleinberg, David (NY)	EDM	213
Kleinberg, Lawrence (MD)	RadRO	981
Kleinerman, Eugenie (TX)	Ped	742
Kleinman, Ronald (MA)	PGe	762
Kleinman, William (IN)	HS	303
Kliger, Alan (CT)	Nep	458
Klimberg, Vicki (AR)	S	1126
Klimstra, David (NY)	Path	722
Kline, Mark (TX)	PInf	796
Kline, Richard (LA)	GO	288
Klingensmith, Georgeanna (CO)	PEn	761
Klonoff, David (CA)	EDM	225
Klutke, Carl (MO)	U	1203
Knechtle, Stuart (GA)	S	1106
Kneisl, Jeffrey (NC)	OrS	636
Knight, Bradley (IL)	CE	117
Knisely, Jonathan (NY)	RadRO	981
Knudson, Mary (CA)	S	1134
Kobashigawa, Jon (CA)	Cv	111
Kobrin, Sidney (PA)	Nep	460
Kobrine, Arthur (DC)	NS	479
Kobrinsky, Nathan (ND)	PHO	787
Koch, Christian (MS)	EDM	216
Koch, Douglas (TX)	Oph	602
Koch, Kenneth (NC)	Ge	243
Koch, Michael (IN)	U	1204
Koch, Wayne (MD)	Oto	672
Kocher, Mininder (MA)	OrS	618
Kochman, Michael (PA)	Ge	236
Koczywas, Marianna (CA)	Onc	389
Koeller, Kelly (MN)	NRad	1023
Koh, Jeffrey (OR)	PM	713
Koh, Wui-Jin (WA)	RadRO	996
Kohler, Matthew (SC)	GO	282
Kohn, Brenda (NY)	PEn	758
Kohn, Elise (MD)	Onc	346
Kohrman, Michael (IL)	ChiN	148
Kokotailo, Patricia (WI)	AM	77
Kolker, Adam (NY)	PIS	883
Koller, Harold (PA)	Oph	580
Kolon, Thomas (PA)	Ped Uro	825
Komaki, Ritsuko (TX)	RadRO	994
Koman, L. Andrew (NC)	HS	301
Komrokji, Rami (FL)	Hem	319
Kondziolka, Douglas (NY)	NS	479
Konicek, Frank (IL)	Ge	248
Konski, Andre (MI)	RadRO	990
Konstam, Marvin (MA)	Cv	89
Konstan, Michael (OH)	PPul	809
Koo, John (CA)	D	201
Koos, Brian (CA)	MF	443
Kopf, Gary (CT)	T&CS	1147
Koplewicz, Harold (NY)	ChAP	940
Koplin, Lawrence (CA)	PIS	903
Kopp, Peter (IL)	EDM	220
Korenblat, Phillip (MO)	A&I	84
Korf, Bruce (AL)	CG	159
Kormos, Robert (PA)	T&CS	1155

Name	Specialty	Pg
Kornmehl, Ernest (MA)	Oph	574
Korones, David (NY)	PHO	774
Korsten, Mark (NY)	Ge	237
Koruda, Mark (NC)	S	1106
Korytkowski, Mary (PA)	EDM	213
Kosofsky, Barry (NY)	ChiN	145
Koss, Michael (CA)	Path	733
Kosten, Thomas (TX)	AdP	938
Kostis, John (NJ)	Cv	94
Kotagal, Suresh (MN)	ChiN	149
Kotapka, Mark (PA)	NS	479
Kotler, Donald (NY)	Ge	237
Kotloff, Karen (MD)	PInf	793
Kotloff, Robert (PA)	Pul	957
Koufman, Jamie (NY)	Oto	672
Kougias, Panagiotis (TX)	VascS	1229
Koulos, John (NY)	GO	279
Kovitz, Kevin (IL)	Pul	965
Kovnar, Edward (WI)	ChiN	149
Kowalski, Thomas (PA)	Ge	237
Kozarek, Richard (WA)	Ge	256
Kozin, Scott (PA)	HS	298
Kozlowski, James (IL)	U	1204
Kraay, Matthew (OH)	OrS	642
Krackow, Kenneth (NY)	OrS	627
Kraft, Andrew (SC)	Onc	359
Krag, David (VT)	S	1086
Krajcer, Zvonimir (TX)	Cv	108
Kramer, Barry (CA)	GerPsy	946
Kramer, Kim (NY)	PHO	774
Kraus, Dennis (NY)	Oto	672
Kraus, Michael (IN)	Nep	463
Krauss, Gregory (MD)	N	516
Krauss, Howard (CA)	Oph	607
Kraut, Eric (OH)	Hem	322
Krebs, Nancy (CO)	PGe	767
Kreissman, Susan (NC)	PHO	779
Kreitzer, Joel (NY)	PM	707
Krellenstein, Daniel (NY)	T&CS	1155
Krespi, Yosef (NY)	Oto	672
Kress, Douglas (PA)	D	189
Kress, Kenneth (GA)	OrS	637
Kressel, Bruce (DC)	Onc	346
Kriegel, David (NY)	D	189
Krieger, Karl (NY)	T&CS	1155
Kriet, John (KS)	Oto	690
Krilov, Leonard (NY)	PInf	793
Kris, Mark (NY)	Onc	346
Krishnamurthi, Smitha (OH)	Onc	371
Krisht, Ali (AR)	NS	496
Kron, Irving (VA)	T&CS	1163
Kronenberg, Henry (MA)	EDM	209
Kronn, David (NY)	CG	158
Kronowitz, Steven (TX)	PIS	899
Krontiras, Helen (AL)	S	1106
Krouse, Robert (AZ)	S	1126
Krowka, Michael (MN)	Pul	965
Krueger, Gerald (UT)	D	198
Krueger, Richard (NY)	Psyc	925
Krueger, Ronald (OH)	Oph	596
Krumholz, Allan (MD)	N	517
Krummel, Thomas (CA)	PS	823
Krunic, Aleksandar (IL)	D	196
Kruskal, Jonathan (MA)	DR	1007
Kuban, Deborah (TX)	RadRO	994
Kucharczuk, John (PA)	T&CS	1155
Kucuk, Omer (GA)	Onc	360
Kudrimoti, Mahesh (KY)	RadRO	984
Kuettel, Michael (NY)	RadRO	981
Kuhel, William (NY)	Oto	672
Kuhn, Frederick (GA)	Oto	679
Kuhn, Joseph (TX)	S	1126
Kuiken, Todd (IL)	PMR	869
Kula, Roger (NY)	N	517
Kulick, Roy (NY)	HS	299
Kuller, Jeffrey (NC)	MF	437
Kumar, Anand (IL)	Psyc	930
Kumar, Princy (DC)	Inf	413
Kumpe, David (CO)	VIR	1031
Kun, Larry (TN)	RadRO	984
Kung, Faith (CA)	PHO	790
Kunkel, Elisabeth (PA)	Psyc	925
Kuntz, Charles (OH)	NS	490
Kuo, John (CA)	RE	1052
Kuo, Paul (IL)	S	1116
Kupelian, Patrick (CA)	RadRO	996
Kupersmith, Mark (NY)	Oph	581
Kupfer, David (PA)	Psyc	925
Kupper, Thomas (MA)	D	185
Kurachek, Stephen (MN)	PPul	809
Kuriakose, Philip (MI)	Hem	322
Kurland, Geoffrey (PA)	PPul	807
Kurman, Robert (MD)	Path	722
Kurtin, Paul (MN)	Path	728
Kurtz, Alfred (PA)	DR	1010
Kurtz, Robert (NY)	Ge	237
Kurtzberg, Joanne (NC)	PHO	779
Kurtzke, Robert (VA)	N	525
Kushner, Brian (NY)	PHO	775
Kushner, Burton (WI)	Oph	596
Kuske, Robert (AZ)	RadRO	994
Kutner, Jean (CO)	H & PM	408

Name	Specialty	Pg
Kutteh, William (TN)	RE	1046
Kuttesch, John (NM)	PHO	788
Kuvin, Jeffrey (MA)	Cv	89
Kuzel, Timothy (IL)	Onc	371
Kuzniecky, Ruben (NY)	N	517
Kuzon, William (MI)	PlS	894
Kveton, John (CT)	Oto	666
Kwak, Larry (TX)	Onc	381
Kwo, Paul (IN)	Ge	248
Kwolek, Christopher (MA)	VascS	1220
Kwon, Hower (WA)	ChAP	943
Kwon, Young (IA)	Oph	596

L

Name	Specialty	Pg
La Gamma, Edmund (NY)	NP	449
La Mont, J Thomas (MA)	Ge	231
La Quaglia, Michael (NY)	PS	816
La Russo, Nicholas (MN)	Ge	248
LaBan, Myron (MI)	PMR	869
Labar, Douglas (NY)	N	517
Labiner, David (AZ)	N	537
LaBruna, Anthony (NY)	PlS	883
Lachs, Mark (NY)	Ger	265
Lacomis, David (PA)	N	517
Lacy, Jill (CT)	Onc	333
Ladenson, Paul (MD)	EDM	213
Lage, Janice (MS)	Path	726
Laham, Roger (MA)	IC	121
Laheru, Daniel (MD)	Onc	346
Lahita, Robert (NJ)	Rhu	1060
Laks, Hillel (CA)	T&CS	1179
Lalwani, Anil (NY)	Oto	672
Lambert, Paul (SC)	Oto	679
Lambert, Scott (GA)	Oph	589
Lamberti, John (CA)	T&CS	1179
Lambiase, Louis (TN)	Ge	243
Lambrou, Nicholas (FL)	GO	282
Lamonica, Dominick (NY)	NuM	554
LaMuraglia, Glenn (MA)	VascS	1221
Lancaster, Johnathan (FL)	GO	282
Landers, Daniel (MN)	MF	439
Landman, Jaime (CA)	U	1212
Landon, Mark (OH)	MF	439
Landreneau, Rodney (LA)	T&CS	1175
Landrigan, Philip (NY)	OM	912
Landry, Jerome (GA)	RadRO	985
Landy, Helain (DC)	MF	435
Landy, Howard (FL)	NS	485
Landzberg, Joel (NJ)	Cv	94
Lane, Joseph (NY)	OrS	627
Lane, Judy (CO)	N	535
Lane, Lewis (NY)	HS	299
Lane, Stephen (MN)	Oph	596
Lang, Frederick (TX)	NS	496
Lang, Peter (MA)	PCd	747
Lang, Samuel (NY)	T&CS	1155
Lange, Paul (WA)	U	1212
Langer, Corey (PA)	Onc	346
Langford, Carol (OH)	Rhu	1065
Langman, Craig (IL)	PNep	800
Langston, J William (CA)	N	540
Lannin, Donald (CT)	S	1086
Lansman, Steven (NY)	T&CS	1156
Lanteri, Vincent (NJ)	U	1192
Lantis, John (NY)	VascS	1224
Lantos, John (MO)	Ped	741
Lanza, Donald (FL)	Oto	679
Lanza, Louis (AZ)	T&CS	1175
Lapey, Allen (MA)	PPul	806
Laramore, George (WA)	RadRO	996
Larner, James (VA)	RadRO	985
Larrabee, Wayne (WA)	Oto	695
Larsen, Donald (CA)	NRad	1026
Larsen, Philip Reed (MA)	EDM	209
Larson, David (CA)	RadRO	996
Larson, Richard (IL)	Hem	322
Lasala, John (MO)	IC	126
Lash, Robert (MI)	EDM	220
Lashner, Bret (OH)	Ge	249
Lask, Gary (CA)	D	201
Laske, Douglas (PA)	NS	479
Lass, Jonathan (OH)	Oph	596
Lassman, Andrew (NY)	N	517
Latchaw, Laurie (NH)	PS	814
Laterra, John (MD)	N	517
Latov, Norman (NY)	N	517
Latson, Larry (FL)	PCd	751
Lau, Christine (VA)	T&CS	1163
Lauerman, William (DC)	OrS	627
Laufer, Marc (MA)	ObG	560
Laurencin, Cato (CT)	OrS	618
Lavenstein, Bennett (VA)	ChiN	147
Laver, Joseph (NY)	PHO	775
Lavertu, Pierre (OH)	Oto	686
Lavery, Ian (OH)	CRS	173
Lavin, Patrick (TN)	N	525
Lavis, Victor (TX)	EDM	223
Lavyne, Michael (NY)	NS	479
Lawrence, Theodore (MI)	RadRO	990
Lawry, George (CA)	Rhu	1068

Alphabetical Listing of Doctors

Name	Specialty	Pg
Lawson, David (GA)	Onc	360
Lawson, Edward (MD)	NP	449
Lawson, William (NY)	Oto	673
Lawson, William (DC)	AdP	937
Lazar, Harold (MA)	T&CS	1147
Lazarus, Hillard (OH)	Onc	371
Lazzaro, Richard (NY)	T&CS	1156
Le, Quynh-Thu (CA)	RadRO	996
Le Boit, Philip (CA)	Path	733
Lea, Janice (GA)	Nep	462
Leach, Steven (MD)	S	1095
Leadbetter, Wayne (MD)	OrS	627
Leaf, Norman (CA)	PlS	903
LeBoff, Meryl (MA)	EDM	209
Lebovics, Robert (NY)	Oto	673
Lebwohl, Mark (NY)	D	189
Lebwohl, Nathan (FL)	OrS	637
Lebwohl, Oscar (NY)	Ge	237
Lechan, Ronald (MA)	EDM	210
Leckman, James (CT)	ChAP	938
Lederman, Eric (MO)	CRS	173
Ledford, Dennis (FL)	A&I	82
Lee, Andrew (TX)	Oph	602
Lee, Andrew (TX)	RadRO	994
Lee, Cheryl (MI)	U	1204
Lee, Chung (MN)	RadRO	990
Lee, Francis (NY)	OrS	628
Lee, James (NY)	S	1095
Lee, Jeffrey (TX)	S	1127
Lee, Joon (PA)	IC	122
Lee, Kenneth (PA)	S	1096
Lee, Mark (TX)	NS	496
Lee, Patrick (OR)	CRS	177
Lee, Paul (MI)	Oph	596
Lee, Raphael (IL)	PlS	894
Lee, Seon Kyu (IL)	NRad	1024
Lee, W. P. Andrew (MD)	HS	299
Lee, W. Robert (NC)	RadRO	985
Leeming, Rosemary (OH)	S	1116
Leesar, Massoud (AL)	IC	125
Leffell, David (CT)	D	185
Legare, Robert (RI)	Onc	333
Legido, Agustin (PA)	ChiN	145
Legro, Richard (PA)	RE	1043
Lehman, Constance (WA)	DR	1018
Lehman, Thomas (NY)	PRhu	812
Leichtner, Alan (MA)	PGe	762
Leighton, John (PA)	Onc	347
Leighton, Jonathan (AZ)	Ge	254
Leighton, William (AZ)	PlS	899
Leipziger, Lyle (NY)	PlS	883
Leitch, A. Marilyn (TX)	S	1127
Lele, Shashikant (NY)	GO	279
Lem, Vincent (MO)	Pul	965
Lemanske, Robert (WI)	PA&I	745
Lemole, G Michael (AZ)	NS	496
Lengyel, Ernst (IL)	GO	285
Lenke, Lawrence (MO)	OrS	642
Lentz, Christopher (NM)	S	1127
Lentz, Samuel (NC)	GO	282
Leon, Martin (NY)	IC	122
Leonard, Ethan (OH)	PInf	795
Leonard, James (MI)	PMR	869
Leonetti, John (IL)	Oto	686
Leong, Lucille (CA)	Onc	389
Lepanto, Philip (WV)	RadRO	981
Lepor, Herbert (NY)	U	1192
Lerman, Bruce (NY)	CE	115
Lerner, Seth (TX)	U	1209
Les, Kimberly (MI)	OrS	642
Lesavoy, Malcolm (CA)	PlS	904
Leshin, Barry (NC)	D	193
Leslie, Donald (GA)	PMR	867
Leslie, Kevin (AZ)	Path	730
Leslie, Kimberly (IA)	MF	439
Lesser, Glenn (NC)	Onc	360
Lessin, Stuart (PA)	D	189
Leuchter, Andrew (CA)	Psyc	933
Leung, Donald (CO)	PA&I	746
Leung, Lawrence (CA)	Hem	328
Leung, Wing (TN)	PHO	780
Levenback, Charles (TX)	GO	289
Leventhal, Bennett (NY)	ChAP	940
Levi, Allan (FL)	NS	485
Levi, Joe (FL)	S	1106
Levin, Alex (PA)	Oph	581
Levin, David (OK)	Pul	969
Levin, L. Scott (PA)	OrS	628
Levine, Alexandra (CA)	Hem	328
Levine, David (NY)	N	518
Levine, David (NY)	OrS	628
Levine, Edward (NC)	S	1106
Levine, Elliot (IL)	ObG	565
Levine, Ellis (NY)	Onc	347
Levine, Joel (CO)	Ge	252
Levine, Joseph (NY)	CE	115
Levine, Joshua (NY)	PlS	883
Levine, Laurence (IL)	U	1204
Levine, Michael (PA)	PEn	758
Levine, Paul (VA)	Oto	679
Levine, Robert (NH)	EDM	210
Levine, Stephen (OH)	Psyc	930

Name	Specialty	Pg
Levine, Steven (NY)	N	518
Levine, William (NY)	SM	1075
Levitsky, Lynne (MA)	PEn	757
Levy, Angela (DC)	DR	1010
Levy, Elad (NY)	NS	479
Levy, Joseph (NY)	PGe	763
Levy, Michael (PA)	H & PM	406
Levy, Michael (MN)	Ge	249
Levy, Michael (CA)	NS	500
Levy, Moise (TX)	D	198
Levy, Steven (GA)	Psyc	928
Lew, Mark (CA)	N	541
Lewin, Alan (FL)	RadRO	985
Lewin, Mark (WA)	PCd	754
Lewis, Blair (NY)	Ge	237
Lewis, Curtis (GA)	VIR	1030
Lewis, John (AZ)	A&I	85
Lewis, Richard (TX)	Oph	602
Lewis, Richard (CA)	N	541
Lewis, Sandra (OR)	Cv	111
Lewis, Valerae (TX)	OrS	648
Lewkowiez, Laurent (CO)	CE	119
Leya, Fred (IL)	IC	126
Li, Benjamin (LA)	S	1127
Li, James Tung-Chieh (MN)	A&I	84
Liang, Bruce (CT)	Cv	89
Liao, James (IL)	Cv	103
Liao, Kenneth (MN)	T&CS	1169
Liau, Linda (CA)	NS	500
Libby, Daniel (NY)	Pul	957
Libertino, John (MA)	U	1187
Libutti, Steven (NY)	S	1096
Licciardi, Frederick (NY)	RE	1043
Lichtenstein, David (MA)	Ge	231
Lichtenstein, Gary (PA)	Ge	237
Lichter, Paul (MI)	Oph	596
Liddle, Rodger (NC)	Ge	243
Lieberman, Jay (CA)	OrS	652
Lieberman, Michael (NY)	S	1096
Lieberman, Phillip (TN)	A&I	82
Liebmann, Jeffrey (NY)	Oph	581
Lieskovsky, Gary (CA)	U	1212
Light, Richard (TN)	Pul	963
Light, Terry (IL)	HS	303
Lightdale, Charles (NY)	Ge	238
Liker, Mark (CA)	NS	500
Lilenbaum, Rogerio (CT)	Onc	333
Lilienfeld, Howard (FL)	EDM	216
Lill, Michael (CA)	Hem	328
Lillehei, Kevin (CO)	NS	494
Lillemoe, Keith (MA)	S	1086
Lim, Dean (CA)	Onc	389
Lim, Henry (MI)	D	196
Lim, Jennifer (IL)	Oph	597
Lim Quan, Katherine (AZ)	D	199
Limacher, Marian (FL)	Cv	98
Limentani, Steven (NC)	Onc	360
Lin, Daniel (WA)	U	1212
Lin, Jeffrey (DC)	GO	279
Lin, Weei-Chin (TX)	Hem	326
Lind, Christopher (TN)	Ge	243
Lind, D Scott (PA)	S	1096
Lind, Stuart (CO)	Hem	324
Lindenfeld, JoAnn (CO)	Cv	107
Linder, Jennifer (AZ)	D	199
Lindsay, Bruce (OH)	CE	117
Lindsey, Stephen (LA)	Rhu	1067
Lindstrom, Richard (MN)	Oph	597
Linenberger, Michael (WA)	Hem	328
Link, Mark (MA)	CE	113
Link, Michael (CA)	PHO	790
Link, Michael (MN)	NS	491
Linsenmeyer, Todd (NJ)	U	1192
Linskey, Mark (CA)	NS	500
Linstrom, Christopher (NY)	Oto	673
Linton, MacRae (TN)	Cv	98
Lipkowitz, George (MA)	S	1087
Liporace, Joyce (PA)	N	518
Lippman, Marc (FL)	Onc	360
Lipschitz, David (AR)	Ger	267
Lipshultz, Larry (TX)	U	1209
Lipshutz, William (PA)	Ge	238
Lipsitz, Lewis (MA)	Ger	264
Lipson, Ace (DC)	EDM	213
Lipstate, James (LA)	Rhu	1067
Lipton, Jeffrey (NY)	PHO	775
Lipton, Richard (NY)	N	518
Lis, Eric (NY)	NRad	1021
Lisak, Robert (MI)	N	530
Lisman, Richard (NY)	Oph	581
List, Alan (FL)	Onc	360
Little, John (DC)	PlS	883
Litwin, Sheldon (GA)	Cv	99
Litzow, Mark (MN)	Hem	322
Liu, Charles (CA)	NS	500
Liu, Grant (PA)	N	518
Liu, Vincent (IA)	D	196
Livingston, Robert (AZ)	Onc	381
LiVolsi, Virginia (PA)	Path	722
Ljung, Britt-Marie (CA)	Path	733
Lloyd, L. Keith (AL)	U	1198
Locala, Joseph (OH)	Psyc	930

Name	Specialty	Pg
Lock, James (MA)	PCd	747
Lock, Terrence (MI)	OrS	642
Lockey, Richard (FL)	A&I	82
Lockhart, Jorge (FL)	U	1198
Loder, Elizabeth (MA)	PM	706
Loeb, David (MD)	PHO	775
Loeffler, Jay (MA)	RadRO	977
Loehrer, Patrick (IN)	Onc	371
Loevner, Laurie (PA)	NRad	1021
Loewenstein, Richard (MD)	Psyc	925
Loftus, Christopher (IL)	NS	491
Loftus, Edward (MN)	Ge	249
Logan, William (MO)	N	531
Loggie, Brian (NE)	S	1122
Logie, Keith (IN)	Onc	371
Logigian, Eric (NY)	N	518
Logothetis, Christopher (TX)	Onc	381
Long, Sarah (PA)	PInf	793
Longo, Frank (CA)	N	541
Longo, Walter (CT)	CRS	168
Longworth, David (OH)	Inf	417
Loo, Marcus (NY)	U	1192
Loomba, Rohit (CA)	Ge	256
Lopez, John (IL)	IC	126
Loprinzi, Charles (MN)	Onc	371
Lorber, Bennett (PA)	Inf	413
Loree, Thom (NY)	PIS	884
LoRusso, Thomas (VA)	Pul	963
Loscalzo, Joseph (MA)	Cv	89
Losee, Joseph (PA)	PIS	884
Lossos, Izidore (FL)	Onc	360
Lott, Ira (CA)	ChiN	151
Loughlin, Gerald (NY)	PPul	807
Loughlin, Kevin (MA)	U	1187
Louie, Brian (WA)	T&CS	1179
Louie, Eddie (NY)	Inf	414
Louis, Elan (NY)	N	518
Loulmet, Didier (NY)	T&CS	1156
Love, Charles (OH)	CE	117
Love, Robert (WI)	T&CS	1169
Low, David (PA)	PIS	884
Lowe, Franklin (NY)	U	1192
Lowe, Lori (MI)	Path	728
Lowenberg, David (CA)	OrS	652
Lowitt, Mark (MD)	D	189
Lowry, Ann (MN)	CRS	174
Lowy, Andrew (CA)	S	1134
Loyd, James (TN)	Pul	963
Lu, Karen (TX)	GO	289
Lubahn, John (PA)	HS	299
Lubenow, Timothy (IL)	PM	710
Lublin, Fred (NY)	N	518
Luby, James (TX)	Inf	420
Luby, Joan (MO)	ChAP	942
Lucarelli, Mark (WI)	Oph	597
Lucas, David (MI)	Path	728
Lucci, Joseph (FL)	GO	282
Lucente, Vincent (PA)	ObG	561
Lucey, Michael (WI)	Ge	249
Luchtman-Jones, Lori (DC)	PHO	775
Luciano, Anthony (CT)	RE	1041
Luck, James (CA)	OrS	652
Lucky, Anne (OH)	D	196
Luders, Hans (OH)	N	531
Ludwig, David (MA)	PEn	757
Ludwig, Kirk (WI)	CRS	174
Lueder, Gregg (MO)	Oph	597
Luerssen, Thomas (TX)	NS	496
Luger, Selina (PA)	Hem	315
Lugg, James (WY)	U	1207
Luggen, Michael (OH)	Rhu	1065
Luken, Martin (IL)	NS	491
Lumsden, Alan (TX)	VascS	1229
Lunsford, L Dade (PA)	NS	479
Lurain, John (IL)	GO	285
Lusk, Rodney (NE)	PO	805
Lustig, Lawrence (CA)	Oto	696
Lustig, Robert (CA)	PEn	762
Luterman, Arnold (AL)	S	1106
Luthra, Harvinder (MN)	Rhu	1065
Lutsep, Helmi (OR)	N	541
Lutz, Christopher (NY)	PMR	864
Lutz, Gregory (NY)	PMR	864
Lutzky, Jose (FL)	Onc	360
Lyckholm, Laurel (VA)	Onc	361
Lydiatt, Daniel (NE)	Oto	690
Lydiatt, William (NE)	Oto	690
Lyketsos, Constantine (MD)	GerPsy	944
Lyles, Kenneth (NC)	Ger	265
Lyman, Gary (NC)	Onc	361
Lynch, James (FL)	Onc	361
Lynch, Joseph (CA)	Pul	971
Lynch, Thomas (CT)	Onc	333
Lyons, Roger (TX)	Hem	327
Lytle, Bruce (OH)	T&CS	1170

M

Name	Specialty	Pg
Ma, C Benjamin (CA)	SM	1079
Ma, Dong (NY)	PMR	865
Mabrey, Jay (TX)	OrS	648

Name	Specialty	Pg
Macadaeg, Kevin (IN)	PM	710
Macaulay, William (NY)	OrS	628
MacDonald, Kenneth (NC)	S	1107
MacGregor, Scott (IL)	MF	439
Machtay, Mitchell (OH)	RadRO	990
Macias, John (AZ)	Oto	693
Maciejewski, Jaroslaw (OH)	Hem	323
Mack, Michael (TX)	T&CS	1175
Mackay, Donald (PA)	PlS	884
Mackey, Sean (CA)	PM	713
Mackey, William (MA)	VascS	1221
MacKinnon, Susan (MO)	PlS	894
Macklis, Roger (OH)	RadRO	991
Mackool, Richard (NY)	Oph	581
Maclaren, Noel (NY)	EDM	213
MacLean, James (MA)	A&I	80
Macmahon, Heber (IL)	DR	1015
Macones, George (MO)	MF	439
Madoff, Robert (MN)	CRS	174
Madsen, Joseph (MA)	NS	473
Magee, William (VA)	PlS	890
Magid, Steven (NY)	Rhu	1061
Magovern, George (PA)	T&CS	1156
Magramm, Irene (NY)	Oph	581
Magrina, Javier (AZ)	GO	289
Maguire, Joseph (PA)	Oph	581
Maguire, Leo (MN)	Oph	597
Magun, Arthur (NY)	Ge	238
Mahler, Donald (NH)	Pul	955
Mahmud, Ehtisham (CA)	IC	128
Mahoney, Maurice (CT)	CG	156
Mahony, Lynn (TX)	PCd	754
Mahvi, David (IL)	S	1116
Maizels, Max (IL)	Ped Uro	827
Makaroun, Michel (PA)	VascS	1224
Makhija, Sharmila (KY)	GO	282
Makhoul, Issam (AR)	Onc	381
Maki, Dennis (WI)	Inf	418
Maki, Robert (NY)	Onc	347
Malawer, Martin (MD)	OrS	628
Malcolm, Arnold (TN)	RadRO	985
Maldjian, Joseph (NC)	NRad	1022
Malik, Ghaus (MI)	NS	491
Malkowicz, S. Bruce (PA)	U	1192
Maloney, David (WA)	Onc	389
Maloney, Mary (MA)	D	185
Maloney, Robert (CA)	Oph	607
Mamelak, Adam (CA)	NS	500
Manche, Edward (CA)	Oph	607
Manco-Johnson, Marilyn (CO)	PHO	787
Mancuso, Anthony (FL)	DR	1013

Name	Specialty	Pg
Mandel, Eric (NY)	Oph	581
Mandel, Susan (PA)	EDM	213
Mandelbaum, Bert (CA)	OrS	652
Mandelbaum, David (RI)	ChiN	144
Manders, Ernest (PA)	PlS	884
Manepalli, Jothika (MO)	GerPsy	945
Manera, Ricarchito (IL)	PHO	784
Manevitz, Alan (NY)	Psyc	925
Mangan, Kenneth (PA)	Hem	315
Mann, J. John (NY)	Psyc	926
Mannel, Robert (OK)	GO	289
Mannella, William (PA)	S	1096
Manning, Warren (MA)	Cv	89
Mannis, Mark (CA)	Oph	607
Manoli, Arthur (MI)	OrS	643
Mansfield, Paul (TX)	S	1127
Manson, Paul (MD)	PlS	884
Mantyh, Christopher (NC)	CRS	172
Manzi, Susan (PA)	Rhu	1061
Mapstone, Timothy (OK)	NS	497
Maraganore, Demetrius (IL)	N	531
Marcet, Jorge (FL)	CRS	172
Marchlinski, Francis (PA)	CE	115
Marcom, Paul (NC)	Onc	361
Marcus, Carole (PA)	PPul	807
Marcus, Judith (NY)	PHO	775
Marcus, Robert (FL)	RadRO	985
Marder, Karen (NY)	N	519
Marder, Stephen (CA)	Psyc	933
Marentette, Lawrence (MI)	Oto	686
Margolin, Kim (WA)	Onc	389
Mari, Giancarlo (TN)	MF	437
Marin, Deborah (NY)	Psyc	926
Marin, Michael (NY)	VascS	1224
Marina, Neyssa (CA)	PHO	790
Marini, John (MN)	Pul	965
Marino, Ralph (PA)	PMR	865
Marion, Robert (NY)	CG	158
Maris, John (PA)	PHO	775
Mark, Eugene (MA)	Path	719
Markert, James (AL)	NS	485
Markert, M Louise (NC)	A&I	83
Markmann, James (MA)	S	1087
Markoe, Arnold (FL)	RadRO	985
Markowitz, Bernard (CA)	PlS	904
Markowitz, David (NY)	Ge	238
Markowitz, Sanford (OH)	Onc	371
Marks, Jeffrey (OH)	S	1116
Marks, John (PA)	CRS	170
Marks, Lawrence (NC)	RadRO	985
Marks, Stanley (PA)	Hem	315

Name	Specialty	Pg
Marmor, Michael (CA)	Oph	607
Maroon, Joseph (PA)	NS	479
Marrs, Richard (CA)	RE	1052
Marsh, Christopher (CA)	U	1212
Marsh, James (PA)	S	1096
Marsh, James (CT)	OrS	618
Marsh, Jeffrey (MO)	PlS	894
Marshall, John (VA)	EDM	217
Marshall, John (DC)	Onc	347
Marshall, Lorna (WA)	RE	1052
Marshall, M. Blair (DC)	T&CS	1156
Marshall, Randolph (NY)	N	519
Marten, Timothy (CA)	PlS	904
Martenson, James (MN)	RadRO	991
Martin, Neil (CA)	NS	500
Martin, Paul (FL)	Ge	243
Martin, Richard (CO)	Pul	968
Martin, Richard (OH)	NP	452
Martin, Tomas (FL)	T&CS	1163
Martinez, Fernando (MI)	Pul	966
Martini, D Richard (UT)	ChAP	942
Martino, Martin (PA)	GO	279
Martins, Renato (WA)	Onc	389
Martuza, Robert (MA)	NS	473
Marut, Edward (IL)	RE	1048
Marx, Robert (NY)	OrS	628
Masaryk, Thomas (OH)	NRad	1024
Masket, Samuel (CA)	Oph	607
Maslak, Peter (NY)	Hem	315
Mason, David (OH)	T&CS	1170
Mason, Joel (MA)	Ge	231
Mason, Kristin (CO)	PMR	870
Masood, Shahla (FL)	Path	726
Mass, Daniel (IL)	HS	303
Massagli, Teresa (WA)	PMR	872
Massarotti, Elena (MA)	Rhu	1058
Massin, Edward (TX)	Cv	108
Mast, Bruce (FL)	PlS	890
Masters, Gregory (DE)	Onc	347
Mastrobattista, Joan (TX)	MF	441
Matar, Fadi (FL)	IC	125
Matarasso, Alan (NY)	PlS	884
Matas, Arthur (MN)	S	1116
Mather, Paul (PA)	Cv	95
Mathew, Paul (MA)	Onc	334
Mathisen, Douglas (MA)	T&CS	1147
Matsen, Frederick (WA)	OrS	652
Matsumoto, Alan (VA)	VIR	1030
Matthay, Katherine (CA)	PHO	791
Matthews, David (NC)	PlS	891
Matthews, Dennis (CO)	PMR	870
Matthews, Jeffrey (IL)	S	1116
Mattox, Douglas (GA)	Oto	679
Matulonis, Ursula (MA)	Onc	334
Matuschak, George (MO)	Pul	966
Mauro, Matthew (NC)	VIR	1030
Mavroudis, Constantine (FL)	T&CS	1163
Mawad, Michel (TX)	NRad	1025
Mawn, Louise (TN)	Oph	590
Maxfield, Roger (NY)	Pul	958
Maxwell, G Patrick (TN)	PlS	891
Mayberg, Marc (WA)	NS	501
Mayer, John (MA)	T&CS	1148
Mayer, Nathaniel (PA)	PMR	865
Mayer, Robert (MA)	Onc	334
Mayerson, Joel (OH)	OrS	643
Mayes, Maureen (TX)	Rhu	1067
Mayeux, Richard (NY)	N	519
Maynard, Steven (DC)	ObG	561
Mays, Kit (TN)	PM	709
Maytal, Joseph (NY)	ChiN	146
Maziarz, Richard (OR)	Hem	329
Mazza, David (NY)	A&I	81
Mazzone, Peter (OH)	Pul	966
Mazzone, Theodore (IL)	EDM	220
McAfee, Paul (MD)	OrS	628
McAlindon, Timothy (MA)	Rhu	1058
McAneny, David (MA)	S	1087
McArthur, Justin (MD)	N	519
McCabe, Daniel (AZ)	S	1127
McCallum, Kimberli (MO)	Psyc	930
McCance, Sean (NY)	OrS	629
McCann, John (UT)	Oph	601
McCann, Merle (MD)	Psyc	926
McCann, Peter (NY)	OrS	629
McCann, Richard (NC)	VascS	1226
McCarthy, James (MN)	Nep	463
McCarthy, James (OH)	OrS	643
McCarthy, Patrick (IL)	T&CS	1170
McCarthy, Paul (CT)	PRhu	811
McClamrock, Howard (MD)	RE	1043
McClay, Edward (CA)	Onc	390
McClure, Robert (WA)	U	1212
McCluskey, Leo (PA)	N	519
McColley, Susanna (IL)	PPul	809
McComsey, Grace (OH)	PInf	795
McConnell, John (NC)	U	1198
McConnell, Robert (NY)	EDM	214
McCormick, Beryl (NY)	RadRO	981
McCormick, Paul (NY)	NS	480
McCormick, Wayne (WA)	Ger	268
McCoy, Karen (OH)	PPul	809

Name	Specialty	Pg
McCracken, George (TX)	PInf	796
McCracken, James (CA)	ChAP	943
McCulley, James (TX)	Oph	602
McCullough, Andrew (NY)	U	1192
McCune, W. Joseph (MI)	Rhu	1065
McDermott, Michael (CA)	NS	501
McDiarmid, Suzanne (CA)	PGe	769
McDonald, Dennis (CA)	DR	1018
McDonald, Douglas (MO)	OrS	643
McDonald, Ruth (WA)	PNep	801
McDonnell, James (IL)	Oph	597
McDonnell, Peter (MD)	Oph	582
McDougal, W Scott (MA)	U	1187
McDougle, Christopher (MA)	ChAP	938
McFadden, David (CT)	S	1087
McFarland, Edward (MD)	OrS	629
McGahan, John (CA)	VIR	1033
McGarry, Ronald (KY)	RadRO	986
McGill, Janet (MO)	EDM	220
McGill, Leigh (AZ)	PS	822
McGill, Trevor (MA)	PO	801
McGlave, Philip (MN)	Hem	323
McGonigle, Kathryn (WA)	GO	291
McGovern, Francis (MA)	U	1187
McGovern, Peter (NJ)	RE	1043
McGowan, Joseph (NY)	Inf	414
McGrath, Patrick (KY)	S	1107
McGrath-Morrow, Sharon (MD)	PPul	807
McGuire, William (VA)	Onc	361
McHenry, Christopher (OH)	S	1116
McIntosh, J Michael (UT)	Psyc	931
McIntyre, Robert (CO)	S	1122
McKelvey, Robert (OR)	ChAP	943
McKenna, Michael (MA)	Oto	666
McKeown, Craig (FL)	Oph	590
McKinley, William (VA)	PMR	867
McKinney, Ross (NC)	PInf	794
McKinsey, James (NY)	VascS	1224
McLain, Amie (AL)	PMR	867
McLaren, Rodney (VA)	MF	437
McLean, Gordon (PA)	VIR	1028
McLean, Thomas (NC)	PHO	780
McMahon, M Molly (MN)	EDM	221
McMasters, Kelly (KY)	S	1107
McMenomey, Sean (NY)	Oto	673
McMichael, Amy (NC)	D	193
McPherson, David (TX)	Cv	108
McVary, Kevin (IL)	U	1204
Meacham, Lillian (GA)	PEn	759
Meacham, Randall (CO)	U	1207
Meadow, William (IL)	NP	452
Meals, Roy (CA)	HS	306
Meara, John (MA)	PlS	878
Mears, John Gregory (NY)	Hem	315
Mease, Philip (WA)	Rhu	1068
Medalie, Daniel (OH)	PlS	894
Medbery, Clinton (OK)	RadRO	994
Medich, David (PA)	CRS	170
Medow, Norman (NY)	Oph	582
Medsger, Thomas (PA)	Rhu	1061
Medvecky, Michael (CT)	OrS	618
Medwell, Steven (WA)	CRS	178
Meehan, Kenneth (NH)	Hem	312
Meere, Patrick (NY)	OrS	629
Megibow, Alec (NY)	DR	1010
Mehler, Philip (CO)	IM	427
Mehlman, David (IL)	Cv	103
Mehran, Roxana (NY)	IC	122
Mehrara, Babak (NY)	PlS	885
Mehta, Davendra (NY)	CE	115
Mehta, Minesh (MD)	RadRO	981
Meiselman, Mick (IL)	Ge	249
Meissner, H Cody (MA)	PInf	792
Mekhail, Nagy (OH)	PM	710
Melamed, Jonathan (NY)	Path	722
Meller, Jose (NY)	Cv	95
Mellinger, John (IL)	S	1117
Mellow, Alan (MI)	GerPsy	945
Melmed, Shlomo (CA)	EDM	225
Melone, Charles (NY)	HS	299
Meltzer, Toby (AZ)	PlS	899
Melvin, W. Scott (OH)	S	1117
Mendenhall, Nancy (FL)	RadRO	986
Mendenhall, William (FL)	RadRO	986
Mendley, Susan (MD)	PNep	798
Menendez, Lawrence (CA)	OrS	652
Menezes, Arnold (IA)	NS	491
Menick, Frederick (AZ)	PlS	899
Menon, Mani (MI)	U	1204
Menon, Ram (MI)	PEn	760
Menter, M (TX)	D	199
Merchant, Thomas (TN)	RadRO	986
Meredith, Ruby (AL)	RadRO	986
Meredith, Travis (NC)	Oph	590
Merguerian, Paul (WA)	Ped Uro	828
Meric-Bernstam, Funda (TX)	S	1127
Merkel, Peter (PA)	Rhu	1061
Meropol, Neal (OH)	Onc	371
Merrick, Scot (CA)	T&CS	1179
Merritt, Diane (MO)	ObG	565
Mertz, Howard (TN)	Ge	243
Mesa, Ruben (AZ)	Hem	327

Name	Specialty	Pg
Mesko, Thomas (FL)	S	1107
Mesrobian, Hrair-George (WI)	Ped Uro	827
Messersmith, Wells (CO)	Onc	377
Mesulam, Marsel (IL)	N	531
Metcalfe, Dean (MD)	A&I	81
Metersky, Mark (CT)	Pul	955
Mets, Marilyn (IL)	Oph	597
Metson, Ralph (MA)	Oto	666
Metz, David (PA)	Ge	238
Metzinger, Stephen (LA)	PlS	900
Metzl, Jordan (NY)	SM	1075
Meyer, Anthony (NC)	S	1107
Meyer, Fredric (MN)	NS	491
Meyer, William (OK)	PHO	788
Meyers, Bryan (MO)	T&CS	1170
Meyers, Paul (NY)	PHO	775
Meyers, Rebecka (UT)	PS	821
Meyers, William (PA)	S	1096
Meyskens, Frank (CA)	Onc	390
Michaels, Marian (PA)	PInf	793
Michalski, Jeff (MO)	RadRO	991
Michelassi, Fabrizio (NY)	S	1096
Micheli, Lyle (MA)	SM	1074
Michler, Robert (NY)	T&CS	1156
Mickey, Bruce (TX)	NS	497
Midulla, Peter (NY)	PS	816
Mieler, William (IL)	Oph	597
Mies, Carolyn (PA)	Path	723
Mih, Alexander (IN)	HS	303
Mikkelsen, Tom (MI)	N	531
Miknevich, Mary Ann (PA)	PMR	865
Milad, Magdy (IL)	RE	1048
Milam, Douglas (TN)	U	1198
Mildvan, Donna (NY)	Inf	414
Miles, Brian (TX)	U	1209
Milhem, Mohammed (IA)	Hem	323
Mill, Michael (NC)	T&CS	1163
Millenson, Michael (PA)	Hem	316
Miller, Aaron (NY)	N	519
Miller, Antonius (NC)	Onc	361
Miller, Brent (MO)	Nep	464
Miller, D Craig (CA)	T&CS	1180
Miller, Daniel (GA)	T&CS	1163
Miller, David (TX)	GO	289
Miller, Donald (KY)	Onc	361
Miller, Frank (TX)	Oto	693
Miller, Frank (IL)	DR	1015
Miller, Joan (MA)	Oph	574
Miller, John (IN)	CE	118
Miller, Joseph (AZ)	Oph	602
Miller, Karen (MA)	Ped	740
Miller, Kenneth (MA)	Hem	312
Miller, Kevin (CA)	Oph	607
Miller, Mark (VA)	OrS	637
Miller, Michael (OH)	PlS	895
Miller, Neil (MD)	Oph	582
Miller, Robert (IL)	PO	804
Miller, Scott (GA)	U	1199
Miller, Stanley (MD)	D	189
Miller, Thomas (AZ)	Onc	381
Miller, Timothy (CA)	PlS	904
Millett, Peter (CO)	OrS	646
Milley, J Ross (UT)	NP	452
Millis, J Michael (IL)	S	1117
Millman, Richard (RI)	Pul	955
Mills, Monte (PA)	Oph	582
Mills, Stacey (VA)	Path	726
Milsom, Jeffrey (NY)	CRS	170
Mims, James (TX)	Oph	603
Minas, Tom (MA)	OrS	618
Miniaci, Anthony (OH)	SM	1078
Minich, Lois (UT)	PCd	753
Mink, Jonathan (NY)	ChiN	146
Minsky, Bruce (TX)	RadRO	994
Mintzer, David (PA)	Onc	347
Mirmira, Raghu (IN)	PEn	760
Mirvis, Stuart (MD)	DR	1010
Mirza, Natasha (PA)	Oto	673
Mirzayan, Raffy (CA)	SM	1079
Mischel, Paul (CA)	Path	733
Miskovitz, Paul (NY)	Ge	238
Mistry, Bhargav (ND)	S	1122
Mitchell, Beverly (CA)	Hem	329
Mitchell, Charles (FL)	PInf	795
Mitchell, James (ND)	Psyc	931
Mitchell, John (CO)	T&CS	1173
Mitchell, Marc (MS)	VascS	1226
Mitchell, Max (CO)	T&CS	1173
Mitchell, Paul (CT)	Oph	575
Mitchell, Wendy (CA)	ChiN	151
Mitnick, Hal (NY)	Rhu	1061
Mitnick, Julie (NY)	DR	1010
Mitsumoto, Hiroshi (NY)	N	519
Mitsuyasu, Ronald (CA)	Onc	390
Mittal, Bharat (IL)	RadRO	991
Mittal, Naveen (TX)	PGe	768
Mittal, Ravinder (CA)	Ge	257
Mixter, Roger (WI)	PlS	895
Miyamoto, Richard (IN)	Oto	686
Mizen, Thomas (IL)	Oph	598
Moder, Kevin (MN)	Rhu	1066
Modesitt, Susan (VA)	GO	283

Name	Specialty	Pg
Modic, Michael (OH)	NRad	1024
Moe, Kristen (WA)	Oto	696
Moench, Louis (UT)	Psyc	931
Moffitt, Drew (AZ)	RE	1050
Mohl, Paul (TX)	Psyc	932
Mohler, James (NY)	U	1193
Mohr, JP (NY)	N	519
Moley, Jeffrey (MO)	S	1117
Molleston, Jean (IN)	PGe	766
Molnar, Joseph (NC)	PlS	891
Molo, Mary (IL)	RE	1048
Mondino, Bartly (CA)	Oph	608
Moneim, Moheb (NM)	HS	305
Money, Samuel (AZ)	VascS	1229
Monsees, Barbara (MO)	DR	1015
Montague, Drogo (OH)	U	1204
Montanaro, Anthony (OR)	A&I	86
Montgomery, Elizabeth (MD)	Path	723
Montgomery, Erwin (PA)	N	520
Montgomery, Robert (MD)	S	1097
Montie, James (MI)	U	1204
Moodie, Douglas (TX)	PCd	754
Moon, Marc (MO)	T&CS	1170
Moore, Anne (NY)	Onc	347
Moore, David (IN)	GO	285
Moore, Ernest (CO)	S	1122
Moore, Francis (MA)	S	1087
Moore, Frank (NJ)	NS	480
Moore, John (GA)	T&CS	1163
Moore, Joseph (NC)	Onc	361
Moore, Steven (IA)	Path	728
Moore, Thomas (CA)	MF	443
Moore, Walter (GA)	Rhu	1064
Moots, Paul (TN)	N	526
Morady, Fred (MI)	CE	118
Morales, David (OH)	T&CS	1170
Moran, Cesar (TX)	Path	730
Moran, Christopher (MO)	NRad	1024
Morcos, Jacques (FL)	NS	486
Morcuende, Jose (IA)	OrS	643
Morgan, David (TN)	Onc	362
Morgan, Elaine (IL)	PHO	784
Morgan, Linda (FL)	ObG	563
Morgan, Mark (PA)	GO	279
Morgan, Raymond (VA)	PlS	891
Morgan, Robert (CA)	Onc	390
Morgan, Walter (TN)	PS	818
Morgan, Wayne (AZ)	PPul	810
Morgenlander, Joel (NC)	N	526
Morginstin, Mark (PA)	Onc	347
Morley, John (MO)	Ger	266

Name	Specialty	Pg
Morrell, Martha (CA)	N	541
Morris, Colleen (NV)	CG	163
Morris, Douglas (GA)	IC	125
Morris, John (MO)	N	531
Morris, Monica (VA)	RadRO	986
Morris, P. Pearse (NC)	NRad	1022
Morris, Rohinton (PA)	T&CS	1156
Morrison, William (TX)	RadRO	994
Morrissey, Nicholas (NY)	VascS	1224
Morrow, Jon (CT)	Path	719
Morrow, Monica (NY)	S	1097
Mortimer, Joanne (CA)	Onc	390
Morton, John (CA)	S	1134
Mosca, Ralph (NY)	T&CS	1157
Mosenifar, Zab (CA)	Pul	971
Moser, Richard (MA)	NS	473
Moses, Jeffrey (NY)	IC	122
Moses, Michael (LA)	PlS	900
Moskowitz, William (VA)	PCd	751
Moss, R Lawrence (OH)	PS	820
Mostwin, Jacek (MD)	U	1193
Mott, Michael (MI)	OrS	643
Motzer, Robert (NY)	Onc	348
Moucha, Calin (NY)	OrS	629
Moul, Judd (NC)	U	1199
Mountz, James (PA)	DR	1011
Mousa, Hayat (OH)	PGe	766
Movsas, Benjamin (MI)	RadRO	991
Muggia, Franco (NY)	Onc	348
Mukherjee, Tanmoy (NY)	RE	1043
Mukherji, Suresh (MI)	NRad	1024
Muldoon, Thomas (NY)	Oph	582
Mulhall, John (NY)	U	1193
Mullett, Timothy (KY)	T&CS	1164
Mulligan, Michael (WA)	T&CS	1180
Mulliken, John (MA)	PlS	878
Mulvihill, John (OK)	CG	161
Mulvihill, Sean (UT)	S	1122
Mundt, Arno (CA)	RadRO	996
Munin, Michael (PA)	PMR	865
Munker, Reinhold (LA)	Hem	327
Muntz, Howard (WA)	GO	291
Muraskas, Jonathan (IL)	NP	452
Murphree, A Linn (CA)	Oph	608
Murphy, Douglas (GA)	T&CS	1164
Murphy, John (PA)	PCd	749
Murphy, Timothy (RI)	VIR	1027
Murray, Joseph (MN)	Ge	249
Murray, Karen (WA)	PGe	769
Murray, Pamela (WV)	AM	76
Murray, Timothy (FL)	Oph	590

Name	Specialty	Pg
Murtagh, F. Reed (FL)	NRad	1022
Muschler, George (OH)	OrS	643
Muss, Hyman (NC)	Onc	362
Mustoe, Thomas (IL)	PlS	895
Mutasim, Diya (OH)	D	196
Mutch, David (MO)	GO	285
Mutch, Matthew (MO)	CRS	174
Muto, Michael (MA)	GO	275
Myer, Charles (OH)	PO	804
Myers, Deborah (RI)	ObG	560
Myers, Jeffrey (TX)	Oto	693
Myers, Jeffrey (MI)	Path	728
Myers, Jonathan (PA)	Oph	582
Myerson, Mark (MD)	OrS	629
Myones, Barry (TX)	PRhu	813
Myseros, John (DC)	NS	480
Mysiw, W. Jerry (OH)	PMR	869

N

Name	Specialty	Pg
Nabell, Lisle (AL)	Onc	362
Nabors, Louis (AL)	N	526
Naccarelli, Gerald (PA)	CE	115
Naclerio, Robert (IL)	Oto	686
Nademanee, Auayporn (CA)	Hem	329
Nader, Daniel (OK)	Pul	969
Naff, Neal (MD)	NS	480
Nagarsheth, Nimesh (NY)	GO	279
Nagib, Mahmoud (MN)	NS	491
Nagle, Daniel (IL)	HS	303
Nagle, Deborah (MA)	CRS	168
Nagler, Harris (NY)	U	1193
Nagorney, David (MN)	S	1117
Nagueh, Sherif (TX)	Cv	108
Nahabedian, Maurice (DC)	PlS	885
Nahass, Ronald (NJ)	Inf	414
Naka, Yoshifumi (NY)	T&CS	1157
Nakada, Stephen (WI)	U	1205
Nakakura, Eric (CA)	S	1134
Nance, Michael (PA)	PS	816
Nand, Sucha (IL)	Hem	323
Nanus, David (NY)	Onc	348
Napoli, Joseph (DE)	PlS	885
Nardell, Edward (MA)	Pul	955
Narkewicz, Michael (CO)	PGe	767
Nash, Thomas (NY)	Pul	958
Naslund, Michael (MD)	U	1193
Naslund, Thomas (TN)	VascS	1226
Nass, Ruth (NY)	ChiN	146
Natale, Andrea (TX)	CE	119
Natale, Ronald (CA)	Onc	390
Nathan, David (MA)	EDM	210
Nathanson, S David (MI)	S	1117
Nathwani, Bharat (CA)	Path	734
Naunheim, Keith (MO)	T&CS	1170
Nazzaro, Jules (KS)	NS	494
Neel, Victor (MA)	D	185
Neglia, Joseph (MN)	PHO	784
Negrin, Robert (CA)	Hem	329
Nehra, Ajay (IL)	U	1205
Neiberger, Richard (FL)	PNep	799
Neifeld, James (VA)	S	1107
Nelson, Edward (UT)	S	1123
Nelson, Heidi (MN)	CRS	174
Nelson, J Craig (CA)	Psyc	933
Nelson, Joel (PA)	U	1193
Nelson, Judith (NY)	Pul	958
Nelson, Leonard (PA)	Oph	582
Nelson, Maureen (TX)	PMR	871
Nemcek, Albert (IL)	VIR	1031
Nepola, James (IA)	OrS	643
Neppe, Vernon (WA)	Psyc	934
Nerad, Jeffrey (OH)	Oph	598
Nesbitt, Jonathan (TN)	T&CS	1164
Ness, John (MN)	PlS	895
Nestler, John (VA)	EDM	217
Netterville, James (TN)	Oto	680
Neuberg, Ronnie (SC)	PHO	780
Neuburg, Marcelle (WI)	D	196
Neumann, Donald (OH)	NuM	556
Neumann, Ronald (MD)	NuM	555
Neumeister, Michael (IL)	PlS	895
Neuwelt, Edward (OR)	NS	501
Neuwirth, Michael (NY)	OrS	629
Neville, Richard (DC)	VascS	1224
New, Maria (NY)	PEn	758
Newburger, Jane (MA)	PCd	747
Newell, Kenneth (GA)	S	1107
Newkirk, Kenneth (DC)	Oto	673
Newman, Daniel (MI)	N	531
Newman, Elliot (NY)	S	1097
Newman, Joel (MA)	DR	1007
Newman, Lawrence (NY)	N	520
Newman, Lisa (MI)	S	1117
Newman, Nancy (GA)	N	526
Newton, Herbert (OH)	N	531
Ng, John (OR)	Oph	608
Ngeow, Jeffrey (NY)	PM	707
Nghiem, Paul (WA)	D	201
Nguyen, Dao (FL)	T&CS	1164
Nguyen, Ninh (CA)	S	1134

Name	Specialty	Pg
Nicholas, Stephen (NY)	OrS	629
Nicholl, Jeffrey (LA)	N	537
Nicholson, H. Stacy (OR)	PHO	791
Nichter, Larry (CA)	PlS	904
Nicolaou, Nicos (PA)	RadRO	981
Nicosia, Santo (FL)	Path	726
Niebyl, Jennifer (IA)	ObG	565
Nieder, Alan (FL)	U	1199
Niederman, Michael (NY)	Pul	958
Nielson, Dennis (CA)	PPul	810
Nies, Barbara (VA)	MF	437
Nigra, Thomas (DC)	D	189
Niparko, John (CA)	Oto	696
Nishimura, Rick (MN)	Cv	103
Nisonson, Barton (NY)	SM	1076
Nissen, Nicholas (CA)	S	1135
Nissen, Steven (OH)	Cv	103
Nissenblatt, Michael (NJ)	Onc	348
Nitenson, Nancy (MA)	AdP	936
Nitti, Victor (NY)	U	1193
Nobunaga, Austin (OH)	PMR	869
Nocero, Michael (FL)	Cv	99
Noe, Carl (TX)	PM	711
Noetzel, Michael (MO)	ChiN	149
Nogee, Lawrence (MD)	NP	450
Nogueras, Juan (FL)	CRS	172
Nolan, Bruce (FL)	N	526
Nolan, Charles (TX)	Nep	466
Noone, R Barrett (PA)	PlS	885
Norbash, Alexander (MA)	NRad	1019
Nordli, Douglas (IL)	ChiN	149
Nori, Dattatreyudu (NY)	RadRO	981
Norman, James (FL)	S	1107
Norman, Kim (CA)	Psyc	934
Norris, Andrew (IA)	PEn	760
Northfelt, Donald (AZ)	Onc	381
Northrup, Hope (TX)	CG	162
Norton, Jeffrey (CA)	S	1135
Norton, Larry (NY)	Onc	348
Norwitz, Errol (MA)	MF	432
Notrica, David (AZ)	PS	822
Nour, Nawal (MA)	ObG	560
Nouri, Keyvan (FL)	D	193
Novak, Donald (FL)	PGe	765
Novak, Richard (IL)	Inf	418
Nowak, Eugene (NY)	S	1097
Noyes, Nicole (NY)	RE	1043
Nuchtern, Jed (TX)	PS	822
Nugent, William (NH)	T&CS	1148
Nunery, William (KY)	Oph	590
Nunes, David (MA)	Ge	231
Nunes, Edward (NY)	Psyc	926
Nunley, James (NC)	OrS	637
Nurnberger, John (IN)	Psyc	930
Nuss, Daniel (LA)	Oto	693
Nussbaum, Julian (GA)	Oph	590
Nussbaum, Robert (CA)	CG	163
Nutt, John (OR)	N	541

O

Name	Specialty	Pg
O'Brien, Joan (PA)	Oph	582
O'Brien, Michael (MA)	Path	719
O'Brien, Susan (TX)	Onc	382
O'Brien, Timothy (OH)	Onc	372
O'Connor, Christopher (NC)	Cv	99
O'Connor, Owen (NY)	Onc	348
O'Dell, James (NE)	Rhu	1066
O'Donnell, Anne (DC)	Pul	958
O'Donnell, Margaret (CA)	Hem	329
O'Donnell, Michael (IA)	U	1205
O'Donnell, Richard (CA)	OrS	652
O'Dorisio, M Sue (IA)	PHO	784
O'Driscoll, Shawn (MN)	OrS	644
O'Gara, Patrick (MA)	Cv	89
O'Hea, Brian (NY)	S	1097
O'Keefe, J Paul (IL)	Inf	418
O'Keefe, Regis (NY)	OrS	630
O'Leary, Michael (MA)	U	1187
O'Leary, Michael (CA)	Oto	696
O'Leary, Patrick (NY)	OrS	630
O'Malley, Bert (PA)	Oto	673
O'Neill, William (MI)	Cv	104
O'Regan, Ruth (GA)	Onc	362
O'Reilly, Eileen (NY)	Onc	348
O'Reilly, Richard (NY)	PHO	776
O'Reilly, Robert (DE)	PO	802
O'Rourke, Donald (PA)	NS	480
O'Shaughnessy, Joyce (TX)	Onc	382
Oakes, Daniel (CA)	OrS	653
Oakes, W. Jerry (AL)	NS	486
Oaklander, Anne Louise (MA)	N	511
Oaks, Timothy (NC)	T&CS	1164
Oates, Robert (MA)	U	1187
Ober, K Patrick (NC)	EDM	217
Oberfield, Sharon (NY)	PEn	758
Oberholzer, Jose (IL)	S	1117
Oddis, Chester (PA)	Rhu	1061
Odel, Jeffrey (NY)	Oph	583
Odem, Randall (MO)	RE	1048
Odom, Michael (TX)	NP	453

Name	Specialty	Pg
Odunsi, Adekunle (NY)	GO	279
Odze, Robert (MA)	Path	719
Oeffinger, Kevin (NY)	Ped	741
Oelschlager, Brant (WA)	S	1135
Offit, Kenneth (NY)	Onc	349
Oghalai, John (CA)	Oto	696
Oh, Shin (AL)	N	526
Oh, William (NY)	Onc	349
Ohl, Dana (MI)	U	1205
Ojemann, Jeffrey (WA)	NS	501
Okolo, Patrick (MD)	Ge	238
Okusa, Mark (VA)	Nep	462
Olanow, C Warren (NY)	N	520
Olbricht, Suzanne (MA)	D	186
Oldham, Keith (WI)	PS	820
Olding, Michael (DC)	PlS	885
Olitsky, Scott (MO)	Oph	598
Oliva-Hemker, Maria (MD)	PGe	763
Olivero, Juan (TX)	Nep	466
Olivi, Alessandro (MD)	NS	480
Olopade, Olufunmilayo (IL)	Onc	372
Olsen, Elise (NC)	D	193
Olsen, Kerry (MN)	Oto	687
Olsen, Timothy (GA)	Oph	590
Olshefski, Randal (OH)	PHO	784
Olson, Janice (OR)	PHO	791
Olson, Jeffrey (GA)	NS	486
Olson, John (MD)	S	1097
Olson, Thomas (GA)	PHO	780
Olthoff, Kim (PA)	S	1097
Olumi, Aria (MA)	U	1187
Onders, Raymond (OH)	S	1118
Onel, Karen (IL)	PRhu	813
Onufer, John (VA)	CE	116
Oommen, Kalarickal (TX)	N	537
Oparil, Suzanne (AL)	Cv	99
Oppenheim, William (CA)	OrS	653
Orange, Jordan (TX)	PA&I	746
Oratz, Ruth (NY)	Onc	349
Orazi, Attilio (NY)	Path	723
Orbach, Darren (MA)	NRad	1020
Ordorica, Steven (NY)	ObG	561
Orengo, Ida (TX)	D	199
Orenstein, David (PA)	PPul	807
Orgill, Dennis (MA)	PlS	878
Origitano, Thomas (MT)	NS	494
Orkin, Bruce (IL)	CRS	174
Orlin, Stephen (PA)	Oph	583
Orloff, Lisa (CA)	Oto	696
Orlow, Seth (NY)	D	190
Orlowski, Robert (TX)	Onc	382
Orr, James (FL)	GO	283
Orringer, Mark (MI)	T&CS	1170
Ortel, Thomas (NC)	Hem	319
Orwoll, Eric (OR)	EDM	225
Ory, Steven (FL)	RE	1046
Osborn, Anne (UT)	NRad	1025
Osborne, C. Kent (TX)	Onc	382
Osher, Robert (OH)	Oph	598
Oskowitz, Selwyn (MA)	RE	1041
Ossoff, Robert (TN)	Oto	680
Oster, Martin (NY)	Onc	349
Osterman, A Lee (PA)	HS	299
Ostrer, Harry (NY)	CG	158
Ostroff, James (CA)	Ge	257
Ostrom, Nancy (CA)	A&I	86
Otley, Clark (MN)	D	196
Otsuka, Norman (NY)	OrS	630
Ott, David (TX)	T&CS	1175
Ott, Kenneth (CA)	NS	501
Ott, Susan (WA)	Nep	467
Otto, Pamela (TX)	DR	1017
Otto, Randal (TX)	Oto	693
Ousterhout, Douglas (CA)	PlS	904
Ovalle, Fernando (AL)	EDM	217
Owyang, Chung (MI)	Ge	249
Oz, Mehmet (NY)	T&CS	1157
Ozer, Enver (OH)	Oto	687
Ozer, Howard (IL)	Onc	372

P

Name	Specialty	Pg
Pachter, H Leon (NY)	S	1097
Pacin, Michael (FL)	A&I	83
Pack, Allan (PA)	Pul	958
Packer, Roger (DC)	ChiN	146
Padgett, Douglas (NY)	OrS	630
Padilla, Maria (NY)	Pul	958
Pagani, Francis (MI)	T&CS	1171
Page, Timothy (MI)	Oph	598
Paget, Stephen (NY)	Rhu	1061
Pahl, Elfriede (IL)	PCd	753
Paidas, Charles (FL)	PS	818
Paidas, Michael (CT)	MF	432
Palacios, Igor (MA)	IC	121
Palascak, Joseph (OH)	Hem	323
Palefsky, Joel (CA)	Inf	420
Palese, Michael (NY)	U	1193
Paletta, George (MO)	SM	1078
Palevsky, Harold (PA)	Pul	959
Paller, Amy (IL)	D	196

Name	Specialty	Pg
Palmer, Jeffrey (MD)	PMR	865
Palmer, Robert (VA)	Ger	266
Palmer, William (MA)	DR	1007
Pandit-Taskar, Neeta (NY)	NuM	555
Panicek, David (NY)	DR	1011
Panitch, Howard (PA)	PPul	807
Panos, Anthony (FL)	T&CS	1164
Pantilat, Steven (CA)	H & PM	408
Pao, William (TN)	Onc	362
Paparella, Michael (MN)	Oto	687
Papay, Francis (OH)	PlS	895
Papel, Ira (MD)	Oto	673
Pappas, Theodore (NC)	S	1107
Paramo, Juan (FL)	S	1108
Parazin, Stephen (MA)	OrS	618
Parekh, Dipen (FL)	U	1199
Parent, Andrew (MS)	NS	486
Parikh, Jay (WA)	DR	1018
Parikh, Manish (NY)	IC	122
Parikh, Sanjay (WA)	PO	806
Park, Adrian (MD)	S	1098
Park, Bernard (NJ)	T&CS	1157
Park, Catherine (CA)	RadRO	996
Park, Julie (WA)	PHO	791
Park, Tae Sung (MO)	NS	491
Parker, Barbara (CA)	Onc	390
Parker, Robert (NY)	PHO	776
Parker, William (CA)	ObG	567
Parnes, Howard (MD)	Onc	349
Parness, Ira (NY)	PCd	749
Parrish, Richard (FL)	Oph	590
Parry, Samuel (PA)	MF	435
Parsa, Andrew (IL)	NS	492
Parsons, Rosaleen (PA)	DR	1011
Parsons, Theodore (MI)	OrS	644
Partain, Clarence (TN)	DR	1014
Partin, Alan (MD)	U	1193
Parvizi, Javad (PA)	OrS	630
Pasche, Boris (AL)	Onc	362
Pascuzzi, Robert (IN)	N	532
Pasmantier, Mark (NY)	Onc	349
Pasricha, P. Jay (MD)	Ge	239
Pass, Harvey (NY)	T&CS	1157
Passo, Murray (SC)	PRhu	812
Patchefsky, Arthur (PA)	Path	723
Patchell, Roy (NJ)	N	520
Patel, Aman (NY)	NS	480
Patel, Pravin (IL)	PlS	895
Patel, Sameer (PA)	PlS	885
Patel, Shreyaskumar (TX)	Onc	382
Patel, Sunil (SC)	NS	486
Patel, Vipul (FL)	U	1199
Pathria, Mini (CA)	DR	1018
Patil, Yash (OH)	Oto	687
Patrinely, James (FL)	Oph	591
Patrizio, Pasquale (CT)	RE	1041
Patt, Yehuda (NM)	Onc	382
Patterson, Anthony (TN)	U	1199
Patterson, G Alexander (MO)	T&CS	1171
Patterson, Marc (MN)	ChiN	149
Paty, Philip (NY)	S	1098
Patz, Edward (NC)	DR	1014
Pauker, Susan (MA)	CG	156
Paul, Malcolm (CA)	PlS	904
Paul, T Otis (CA)	Oph	608
Paulson, Richard (CA)	RE	1052
Pavlick, Anna (NY)	Onc	349
Pavlov, Helene (NY)	DR	1011
Pawlik, Timothy (MD)	S	1098
Paz, Isaac (CA)	S	1135
Peabody, Terrance (IL)	OrS	644
Peace, David (IL)	Onc	372
Pearce, Elizabeth (MA)	EDM	210
Pearce, William (IL)	VascS	1228
Pearson, Richard (VA)	Inf	416
Pearson, Thomas (FL)	PrM	913
Pechet, Taine (PA)	T&CS	1157
Pecora, Andrew (NJ)	Onc	349
Peereboom, David (OH)	Onc	372
Peeters-Asdourian, Christine (MA)	PM	706
Pegram, Mark (CA)	Onc	390
Peikin, Steven (NJ)	Ge	239
Peitzman, Andrew (PA)	S	1098
Pejovic, Tanja (OR)	GO	291
Peljovich, Allan (GA)	HS	301
Pellegrini, Carlos (WA)	S	1135
Pellicci, Paul (NY)	OrS	630
Pello, Mark (NJ)	CRS	170
Pelzer, Harold (IL)	Oto	687
Pemberton, John (MN)	CRS	174
Pena, Alberto (OH)	PS	820
Penalver, Manuel (FL)	GO	283
Penar, Paul (VT)	NS	473
Pendergrass, Thomas (WA)	PHO	791
Peng, Stanford (WA)	Rhu	1068
Pennell, Page (MA)	N	511
Pensak, Myles (OH)	Oto	687
Penson, David (TN)	U	1199
Pepine, Carl (FL)	Cv	99
Pepose, Jay (MO)	Oph	598
Perez, Edith (FL)	Onc	362
Perez, Victor (FL)	Oph	591

Alphabetical Listing of Doctors

Name	Specialty	Pg
Perez Fontan, Jose (TX)	PCCM	756
Pergament, Eugene (IL)	CG	160
Perin, Emerson (TX)	IC	127
Perkins, James (WA)	S	1135
Perler, Bruce (MD)	VascS	1224
Perlman, David (NY)	Inf	414
Perlman, Jeffrey (NY)	NP	450
Perlmutter, Joel (MO)	N	532
Perone, Jennifer (TX)	D	199
Perret, Philip (LA)	Pul	969
Perrone, Ronald (MA)	Nep	458
Perry, Arie (CA)	Path	734
Perry, David (DC)	Onc	350
Perry, Stanton (CA)	PCd	754
Persing, John (CT)	PlS	879
Persky, Mark (NY)	Oto	674
Peschel, Richard (CT)	RadRO	977
Pestronk, Alan (MO)	N	532
Petelin, Joseph (KS)	S	1123
Peters, Anne (CA)	EDM	225
Peters, Glenn (AL)	Oto	680
Peters, Jeffrey (NY)	S	1098
Petersdorf, Stephen (WA)	Hem	329
Petersen, Michael (OH)	Oph	598
Petersen, Ronald (MN)	N	532
Peterson, Bruce (MN)	Onc	372
Peterson, Davis (AK)	OrS	653
Peterson, Laura (HI)	S	1135
Petito, Carol (FL)	Path	726
Petito, Frank (NY)	N	520
Petras, Robert (OH)	Path	729
Petri, Michelle (MD)	Rhu	1061
Petrini, John (CA)	Ge	257
Petrossian, George (NY)	IC	123
Petrozza, John (MA)	RE	1041
Petru, Ann (CA)	PInf	797
Petruska, Paul (MO)	Onc	372
Petruzzelli, Guy (GA)	Oto	680
Petrylak, Daniel (CT)	Onc	334
Pettrone, Frank (VA)	OrS	637
Pevec, William (CA)	VascS	1230
Pezner, Richard (CA)	RadRO	996
Pezzone, Michael (PA)	Ge	239
Pfau, Patrick (WI)	Ge	249
Pfeffer, Marc (MA)	Cv	90
Pfeifer, Samantha (PA)	RE	1043
Pfister, David (NY)	Onc	350
Pflugfelder, Stephen (TX)	Oph	603
Philippon, Marc (CO)	OrS	646
Philipson, Elliot (OH)	MF	439
Philipson, Louis (IL)	EDM	221
Phillips, Edward (CA)	S	1135
Phillips, Harry (NC)	Cv	99
Phillips, Katharine (RI)	Psyc	921
Phillips, Peter (PA)	ChiN	146
Phillips, S. Michael (PA)	A&I	81
Philosophe, Benjamin (MD)	S	1098
Philpott, Jonathan (VA)	T&CS	1164
Phuphanich, Surasak (CA)	N	541
Pi, Edmond (CA)	Psyc	934
Piatt, Joseph (DE)	NS	480
Piccirillo, Jay (MO)	Oto	687
Piccoli, David (PA)	PGe	764
Pichard, Augusto (DC)	Cv	95
Picken, Catherine (DC)	Oto	674
Picozzi, Vincent (WA)	Onc	391
Pienta, Kenneth (MD)	Onc	350
Piepmeier, Joseph (CT)	NS	473
Pierce, Lori (MI)	RadRO	991
Pierson, Richard (MD)	T&CS	1157
Pile-Spellman, John (NY)	NRad	1021
Pillsbury, Harold (NC)	Oto	680
Pinckert, Thomas (MD)	MF	435
Pinson, C Wright (TN)	S	1108
Pinter, Joseph (OR)	ChiN	151
Pinto, Harlan (CA)	Onc	391
Pinzur, Michael (IL)	OrS	644
Piraino, Beth (PA)	Nep	460
Pisters, Katherine (TX)	Onc	382
Pisters, Louis (TX)	U	1209
Pisters, Peter (TX)	S	1127
Pitman, Gerald (NY)	PlS	885
Pitman, Karen (AZ)	Oto	693
Pitts, Jeanette (AZ)	D	199
Pizzutillo, Peter (PA)	OrS	630
Plager, David (IN)	Oph	598
Plancher, Kevin (NY)	OrS	631
Plante, Lauren (PA)	MF	435
Platt, Lawrence (CA)	MF	443
Plautz, Gregory (OH)	PHO	785
Plaxe, Steven (CA)	GO	291
Plevy, Scott (NC)	Ge	244
Plon, Sharon (TX)	CG	162
Plotnick, Leslie (MD)	PEn	759
Pochapin, Mark (NY)	Ge	239
Pochettino, Alberto (MN)	T&CS	1171
Pockaj, Barbara (AZ)	S	1128
Podoloff, Donald (TX)	NuM	557
Poe, Dennis (MA)	PO	801
Poehling, Gary (NC)	OrS	637
Pohl, Marc (OH)	Nep	464
Pohlman, Brad (OH)	Onc	372

Name	Specialty	Pg
Poliakoff, Steven (FL)	GO	283
Polin, Richard (NY)	NP	450
Pollack, Alan (FL)	RadRO	986
Pollack, Ian (PA)	NS	481
Pollack, Mark (IL)	Psyc	930
Pollard, Zane (GA)	Oph	591
Polley, John (IL)	PlS	896
Pollock, Raphael (OH)	S	1118
Polly, David (MN)	OrS	644
Polsky, Bruce (NY)	Inf	414
Pomahac, Bohdan (MA)	PlS	879
Pomeroy, John (NY)	ChAP	940
Pomeroy, Scott (MA)	ChiN	144
Pomp, Alfons (NY)	S	1098
Pomposelli, Frank (MA)	VascS	1221
Pongracic, Jacqueline (IL)	PA&I	745
Ponn, Teresa (NH)	S	1087
Ponsky, Jeffrey (OH)	S	1118
Ponton, Lynn (CA)	ChAP	943
Poole, Michael (GA)	Oto	680
Poon, Michael (NY)	Cv	95
Poordad, Fred (TX)	Ge	254
Pope, John (TN)	Ped Uro	826
Pope, Richard (IL)	Rhu	1066
Popovich, John (MI)	Pul	966
Poppas, Dix (NY)	Ped Uro	825
Porayko, Michael (TN)	Ge	244
Porcu, Pierluigi (OH)	Hem	323
Porrazzo, Michael (DC)	RadRO	982
Port, Jeffrey (NY)	T&CS	1157
Portenoy, Russell (NY)	H & PM	407
Porter, Christopher (WA)	U	1213
Porter, David (PA)	Hem	316
Posey, James (AL)	Onc	362
Posner, Jerome (NY)	N	520
Posner, Marshall (NY)	Onc	350
Posner, Mitchell (IL)	S	1118
Posnick, Jeffrey (MD)	PlS	885
Posselt, Andrew (CA)	S	1136
Postier, Russell (OK)	S	1128
Postma, Gregory (GA)	Oto	680
Potenza, Bruce (CA)	S	1136
Potkul, Ronald (IL)	GO	285
Potter, Hollis (NY)	DR	1011
Potters, Louis (NY)	RadRO	982
Pow-Sang, Julio (FL)	U	1199
Powell, Bayard (NC)	Hem	319
Powell, Matthew (MO)	GO	285
Powers, Alvin (TN)	EDM	217
Powers, Eric (SC)	Cv	99
Powers, Pauline (FL)	Psyc	928
Prados, Michael (CA)	Onc	391
Prager, Joshua (CA)	PM	713
Prakash, Udaya (MN)	Pul	966
Preminger, Glenn (NC)	U	1200
Prenner, Jonathan (NJ)	Oph	583
Press, Joel (IL)	PMR	869
Press, Oliver (WA)	Onc	391
Presti, Joseph (CA)	U	1213
Pribitkin, Edmund (PA)	Oto	674
Price, G Wesley (MD)	PlS	886
Price, Lawrence (RI)	Psyc	921
Pridjian, Gabriella (LA)	MF	441
Prieto, Victor (TX)	Path	730
Prince, Martin (NY)	DR	1011
Prioleau, Philip (NY)	D	190
Procaccino, John (NY)	CRS	171
Proctor, Deborah (CT)	Ge	232
Proctor, Monja (WA)	PS	823
Prosnitz, Leonard (NC)	RadRO	986
Provenzale, James (NC)	NRad	1022
Pruthi, Raj (NC)	U	1200
Pryor, Aurora (NY)	S	1098
Prystowsky, Eric (IN)	CE	118
Puccetti, Diane (WI)	PHO	785
Puckett, Charles (MO)	PlS	896
Puduvalli, Vinay (OH)	N	532
Pui, Ching-Hon (TN)	PHO	780
Pula, Thaddeus (MD)	N	520
Puliafito, Carmen (CA)	Oph	608
Pulido, Jose (MN)	Oph	598
Pulst, Stefan (UT)	N	535
Pursell, Kenneth (IL)	Inf	418
Pusztai, Lajos (CT)	Onc	334
Putman, John (TX)	RE	1050
Putnam, Joe (TN)	T&CS	1165
Putnam, Matthew (MN)	HS	304
Putterman, Allen (IL)	Oph	599
Pyeritz, Reed (PA)	CG	158
Pynoos, Robert (CA)	Psyc	934

Q

Name	Specialty	Pg
Quaegebeur, Jan (NY)	PS	816
Quagliarello, Vincent (CT)	Inf	412
Quatela, Vito (NY)	Oto	674
Quencer, Robert (FL)	NRad	1023
Quigley, Harry (MD)	Oph	583
Quigley, Matthew (PA)	NS	481
Quill, Timothy (NY)	H & PM	407
Quinn, David (CA)	Onc	391

Name	Specialty	Pg
Quinn, Graham (PA)	Oph	583
Quinones, Miguel (TX)	Cv	108
Quintessenza, James (FL)	T&CS	1165
Quittell, Lynne (NY)	PPul	808
Quivey, Jeanne (CA)	RadRO	997

R

Name	Specialty	Pg
Rabinovitch, Rachel (CO)	RadRO	992
Rabow, Michael (CA)	IM	427
Racz, Gabor (TX)	PM	711
Rader, Daniel (PA)	IM	426
Rader, Janet (WI)	GO	285
Radtke, Wolfgang (DE)	PCd	749
Raff, Gilbert (MI)	Cv	104
Raffel, Corey (CA)	NS	501
Rafferty, Janice (OH)	CRS	174
Ragheb, John (FL)	NS	486
Raghu, Ganesh (WA)	Pul	971
Ragnarsson, Kristjan (NY)	PMR	865
Rahko, Peter (WI)	Cv	104
Rai, Kanti (NY)	Hem	316
Raiford, David (TN)	Ge	244
Raja, Srinivasa (MD)	PM	707
Rajacich, Nicholas (WA)	OrS	653
Rajfer, Jacob (CA)	U	1213
Raji, Mukaila (TX)	Ger	267
Raju, Gottumukkala (TX)	Ge	254
Rakowski, Thomas (VA)	Nep	462
Ramamoorthy, Sonia (CA)	CRS	178
Ramamurthy, Somayaji (TX)	PM	712
Ramanathan, Ramesh (PA)	S	1099
Ramee, Stephen (LA)	Cv	109
Ramsay, David (NY)	D	190
Ramsey, Bonnie (WA)	PPul	811
Ramsey, Matthew (PA)	OrS	631
Rand, Richard (WA)	PlS	904
Randall, Marcus (KY)	RadRO	986
Randall, R. Lor (UT)	OrS	647
Randall, Thomas (PA)	GO	280
Randolph, Gregory (MA)	Oto	666
Randolph, Linda (CA)	CG	163
Randolph-Jackson, Pamela (DC)	RadRO	982
Rao, A Koneti (PA)	Hem	316
Rao, Nalini (PA)	Inf	414
Rao, Narsing (CA)	Oph	608
Rao, Satish (GA)	Ge	244
Rao, Vijay (PA)	DR	1011
Raphael, Bruce (NY)	Hem	316
Raphael, James (PA)	HS	299
Rapoport, Aaron (MD)	Hem	316
Rappaport, Leonard (MA)	Ped	740
Rappaport, Norman (TX)	PlS	900
Raptis, George (NY)	Onc	350
Rapuano, Christopher (PA)	Oph	583
Rashid, Asif (TX)	Path	731
Raskin, Keith (NY)	HS	300
Raskind, Murray (WA)	Psyc	934
Rasmussen, Steven (RI)	Psyc	921
Rassekh, Christopher (PA)	Oto	674
Rassman, William (CA)	S	1136
Rastegar, Hassan (MA)	T&CS	1148
Raszka, William (VT)	PInf	793
Ratain, Mark (IL)	Onc	373
Ratner, Desiree (NY)	D	190
Rattner, David (MA)	S	1087
Ratts, Valerie (MO)	RE	1048
Ratzan, Kenneth (FL)	Inf	416
Rauch, Paula (MA)	Psyc	922
Rauch, Steven (MA)	Oto	666
Rauck, Richard (NC)	PM	709
Ravich, William (MD)	Ge	239
Rayan, Ghazi (OK)	HS	305
Raz, Shlomo (CA)	U	1213
Razzouk, Bassem (IN)	PHO	785
Read, Thomas (MA)	CRS	168
Ready, John (MA)	OrS	618
Ready, Neal (NC)	Onc	363
Reardon, Michael (TX)	T&CS	1175
Rebeiz, Elie (MA)	Oto	667
Reber, Howard (CA)	S	1136
Recht, Abram (MA)	RadRO	977
Recht, Michael (OR)	PHO	791
Reckamp, Karen (CA)	Onc	391
Recker, Robert (NE)	EDM	222
Redberg, Rita (CA)	Cv	112
Redding, Gregory (WA)	PPul	811
Reddy, Bhagat (GA)	IC	125
Reddy, K Rajender (PA)	Ge	239
Reder, Anthony (IL)	N	532
Redlich, Carrie (CT)	Pul	955
Reed, Alan (IA)	S	1118
Reed, Kathryn (AZ)	MF	441
Reed, Robert (OH)	N	532
Rege, Robert (TX)	S	1128
Regillo, Carl (PA)	Oph	583
Regine, William (MD)	RadRO	982
Reich, David (PA)	S	1099
Reich, Stephen (MD)	N	520
Reichelderfer, Mark (WI)	Ge	250
Reid, Tony (CA)	Onc	391

Name	Specialty	Pg
Reid, William (TN)	NS	486
Reilly, Donald (MA)	OrS	618
Reiner, Jonathan (DC)	IC	123
Reiner, Mark (NY)	S	1099
Reinisch, John (CA)	PlS	905
Reinus, William (PA)	DR	1011
Reis, Steven (PA)	Cv	95
Reisberg, Barry (NY)	GerPsy	944
Reiss, Craig (MO)	Cv	104
Relkin, Norman (NY)	N	520
Remick, Scot (WV)	Onc	350
Remmenga, Steven (NE)	GO	287
Remzi, Feza (OH)	CRS	175
Rennard, Stephen (NE)	Pul	968
Rennke, Helmut (MA)	Path	719
Renz, John (IL)	S	1118
Repke, John (PA)	MF	435
Resar, Jon (MD)	IC	123
Rescorla, Frederick (IN)	PS	820
Resnick, Neil (PA)	Ger	265
Reuben, Adrian (SC)	Ge	244
Reuben, David (CA)	Ger	268
Reus, Victor (CA)	Psyc	934
Reuter, Victor (NY)	Path	723
Rex, Douglas (IN)	Ge	250
Reyes, Jorge (WA)	S	1136
Reynolds, James (PA)	Ge	239
Reynolds, James (NY)	Oph	583
Reynolds, Marleta (IL)	PS	820
Reynolds, R (MI)	GO	286
Rezai, Ali (OH)	NS	492
Rhee, Peter (AZ)	S	1128
Rheingold, Susan (PA)	PHO	776
Rhoads, J Marc (TX)	PGe	768
Rhodes, Arthur (IL)	D	197
Riba, Michelle (MI)	Psyc	930
Ribeiro, Raul (TN)	PHO	780
Rice, Dale (CA)	Oto	696
Rice, David (TX)	T&CS	1176
Rice, Henry (NC)	PS	818
Rice, Laurel (WI)	GO	286
Rich, Keith (MO)	NS	492
Rich, Stuart (IL)	Cv	104
Richard, James (OK)	Oph	603
Richards, Jon (IL)	Onc	373
Richards, William (AL)	S	1108
Richardson, Marilyn (KS)	ObG	566
Richardson, Mark (OR)	PO	806
Richardson, Paul (MA)	Hem	312
Richardson, Timothy (CA)	D	201
Richardson, William (NC)	OrS	637
Richerson, George (IA)	N	532
Richie, Jerome (MA)	U	1188
Richman, Daniel (NY)	PM	708
Richman, Douglas (CA)	Inf	421
Richmond, John (MA)	SM	1074
Richter, Edwin (CT)	PMR	862
Ricketts, Richard (GA)	PS	818
Ricotta, John (DC)	VascS	1224
Riddle, Mark (MD)	ChAP	940
Ridge, John (PA)	S	1099
Ridgway, Eli (CO)	EDM	222
Ridker, Paul (MA)	Cv	90
Ries, W Russell (TN)	Oto	680
Riew, K Daniel (MO)	OrS	644
Rigamonti, Daniele (MD)	NS	481
Rigel, Darrell (NY)	D	190
Rihal, Charanjit (MN)	Cv	104
Riina, Howard (NY)	NS	481
Riley, Laura (MA)	MF	433
Rilling, William (WI)	VIR	1031
Rimm, David (CT)	Path	719
Ringel, Steven (CO)	N	535
Rink, Richard (IN)	Ped Uro	828
Riordan, John (CA)	Nep	467
Ritch, Robert (NY)	Oph	584
Ritchey, A Kim (PA)	PHO	776
Ritchie, Christine (CA)	H & PM	409
Riviello, James (NY)	ChiN	146
Rizk, Norman (CA)	Pul	971
Rizzo, Joseph (MA)	Oph	575
Roach, Mack (CA)	RadRO	997
Robb, Geoffrey (TX)	PlS	900
Robbins, Larry (IL)	PM	710
Robbins, Richard (TX)	EDM	223
Robert, Nicholas (VA)	Onc	363
Robert-Vizcarrondo, Francisco (AL)	Onc	363
Roberts, Anne (CA)	VIR	1033
Roberts, Barbara (RI)	Cv	90
Roberts, John (CA)	S	1136
Roberts, Kenneth (CT)	RadRO	977
Roberts, Michelle (PA)	EDM	214
Roberts, Patricia (MA)	CRS	169
Roberts, William (TX)	Path	731
Robertson, Cary (NC)	U	1200
Robertson, Jon (TN)	NS	486
Robertson, Patricia (CA)	MF	443
Robichaux, Alfred (LA)	MF	441
Robin, Alan (MD)	Oph	584
Robinson, Julian (MA)	MF	433
Robinson, Lary (FL)	T&CS	1165
Robinson, Lawrence (WA)	PMR	872

Name	Specialty	Pg
Robinson, Raymond (FL)	OrS	637
Rocchini, Albert (MI)	PCd	753
Rochester, Carolyn (CT)	Pul	955
Rock, Jack (MI)	NS	492
Rockwell, William (UT)	PlS	898
Rodbard, Helena (MD)	EDM	214
Rodby, Roger (IL)	Nep	464
Roddy, Sarah (CA)	ChiN	152
Rodeo, Scott (NY)	SM	1076
Rodgers, Bradley (VA)	PS	818
Rodgers, George (UT)	Hem	325
Rodosky, Mark (PA)	SM	1076
Rodriguez, Eduardo (MD)	PlS	886
Rodriguez, Gustavo (IL)	GO	286
Rodriguez, Jose (NY)	OrS	631
Rodriguez-Galindo, Carlos (MA)	PHO	770
Rodts, Gerald (GA)	NS	487
Roehrborn, Claus (TX)	U	1209
Rogers, Douglas (OH)	PEn	760
Rogers, Gary (OH)	Oph	599
Rogers, James (TX)	PCd	754
Rogers, Joseph (NC)	Cv	99
Rogers, Lisa (OH)	N	532
Rogers, Stanley (CA)	S	1136
Roh, Mark (FL)	S	1108
Rohrich, Rod (TX)	PlS	900
Roizen, Nancy Jean (OH)	Ped	742
Roland, J Thomas (NY)	Oto	674
Romagnoli, Mario (NY)	Inf	414
Romaguera, Jorge (TX)	Onc	382
Romano, James (CA)	PlS	905
Rome, Jonathan (PA)	PCd	749
Romeo, Anthony (IL)	OrS	644
Romond, Edward (KY)	Onc	363
Ronan, Lara (NH)	N	512
Rondelli, Damiano (IL)	Hem	323
Ronnett, Brigitte (MD)	Path	723
Rood, Brian (DC)	PHO	776
Roodman, G. David (IN)	Hem	323
Rook, Alain (PA)	D	190
Roos, Karen (IN)	N	533
Roos, Raymond (IL)	N	533
Roose, Steven (NY)	Psyc	926
Ropper, Allan (MA)	N	512
Rosbe, Kristina (CA)	PO	806
Rose, Cecile (CO)	Pul	968
Rose, Christopher (CA)	RadRO	997
Rose, Elliott (NY)	PlS	886
Rose, Peter (OH)	GO	286
Rosemurgy, Alexander (FL)	S	1108
Rosen, Charles (MN)	S	1118
Rosen, Clark (PA)	Oto	674
Rosen, Marc (PA)	Oto	674
Rosen, Michael (OH)	S	1118
Rosen, Steven (IL)	Onc	373
Rosenbaum, Kenneth (DC)	CG	158
Rosenbaum, Richard (OR)	N	541
Rosenberg, Andrew (FL)	Path	726
Rosenberg, Howard (CA)	PlS	905
Rosenberg, Michael (IL)	Oph	599
Rosenberg, Steven (MD)	S	1099
Rosenberg, Thomas (UT)	OrS	647
Rosenblatt, Joseph (FL)	Hem	320
Rosenblatt, Szymon (IL)	NS	492
Rosenblum, Marc (NY)	Path	723
Rosenblum, Mark (MI)	NS	492
Rosenblum, Norman (PA)	GO	280
Rosenbluth, Daniel (MO)	Pul	966
Rosenbush, Stuart (IL)	Cv	104
Rosenfeld, Philip (FL)	Oph	591
Rosenfeld, Richard (NY)	PO	803
Rosenfeld, Steven (OH)	N	533
Rosenfield, Kenneth (MA)	IC	121
Rosengart, Todd (TX)	T&CS	1176
Rosenkranz, Eliot (FL)	T&CS	1165
Rosenman, Julian (NC)	RadRO	987
Rosenquist, Richard (OH)	PM	710
Rosenthal, Eben (AL)	Oto	681
Rosenthal, Joseph (CA)	PHO	791
Rosenthal, Norman (MD)	Psyc	926
Rosenthal, Richard (NY)	Psyc	926
Rosenthal, Stephen (CA)	PEn	762
Rosenwaks, Zev (NY)	RE	1044
Rosenwasser, Melvin (NY)	HS	300
Rosenwasser, Robert (PA)	NS	481
Roses, Daniel (NY)	S	1099
Roskes, Saul (MD)	PNep	798
Rosner, Howard (CA)	PM	713
Rosoff, Philip (NC)	PHO	780
Rosove, Michael (CA)	Onc	391
Ross, Douglas (MA)	EDM	210
Ross, Edgar (MA)	PM	706
Ross, Helen (AZ)	Onc	383
Ross, Jeffrey (NY)	Path	724
Ross, Lawrence (IL)	U	1205
Ross, Merrick (TX)	S	1128
Rosse, Richard (DC)	Psyc	926
Rosser, Tena (CA)	ChiN	152
Rossi, Carl (CA)	RadRO	997
Rossman, Milton (PA)	Pul	959
Rostain, Anthony (PA)	ChAP	940
Roth, Andrew (NY)	Psyc	926

Name	Specialty	Pg
Roth, Bennett (CA)	Ge	257
Roth, Bruce (MO)	Onc	373
Roth, David (FL)	Nep	462
Roth, Elliot (IL)	PMR	869
Roth, Jack (TX)	T&CS	1176
Roth, Susan (PA)	DR	1012
Rothbaum, Robert (MO)	PGe	767
Rothenberg, Russell (MD)	Rhu	1062
Rothman, Richard (PA)	OrS	631
Rothrock, John (NV)	N	541
Rothstein, Richard (NH)	Ge	232
Rotman, Marvin (NY)	RadRO	982
Rotmensch, Jacob (IL)	GO	286
Roubin, Gary (NY)	IC	123
Routes, John (WI)	A&I	84
Rovner, Barry (PA)	GerPsy	944
Rowley, Howard (WI)	NRad	1024
Rowley, Scott (NJ)	Hem	316
Roy-Byrne, Peter (WA)	Psyc	934
Roye, David (NY)	OrS	631
Rozbruch, S Robert (NY)	OrS	631
Rubenfeld, Sheldon (TX)	EDM	223
Rubin, Brian (OH)	Path	729
Rubin, Bruce (VA)	PPul	808
Rubin, Charles (IL)	PHO	785
Rubin, Geoffrey (NC)	DR	1014
Rubin, Mark (CA)	D	202
Rubin, Peter (MA)	Oph	575
Rubin, Stephen (PA)	GO	280
Rubin, Susan (IL)	N	533
Rubinstein, Jay (WA)	Oto	696
Rudnick, Michael (PA)	Nep	460
Rudy, Bret (NY)	AM	76
Ruge, John (IL)	NS	492
Ruggiero, Joseph (NY)	Onc	350
Rugo, Hope (CA)	Onc	392
Runowicz, Carolyn (FL)	GO	283
Rusch, Valerie (NY)	T&CS	1158
Rushakoff, Robert (CA)	EDM	225
Rushton, H Gil (DC)	Ped Uro	825
Ruskin, Jeremy (MA)	CE	113
Russell, Anthony (MA)	RadRO	977
Russell, Christy (CA)	Onc	392
Russell, Eric (IL)	NRad	1024
Russell, Kenneth (WA)	RadRO	997
Russell, Mark (VA)	D	193
Russell, Stuart (MD)	Cv	95
Russo, Carolyn (AL)	PHO	780
Rutgers, Joanne (CA)	Path	734
Rutherford, Thomas (CT)	GO	275
Rutkove, Seward (MA)	N	512
Ryan, Colleen (MA)	S	1087
Ryan, David (MA)	Onc	334
Rychik, Jack (PA)	PCd	749
Ryken, Timothy (IA)	NS	492

S

Name	Specialty	Pg
Saade, George (TX)	MF	441
Saag, Michael (AL)	Inf	416
Saal, Howard (OH)	CG	160
Saal, Jeffrey (CA)	PMR	872
Sabanegh, Edmund (OH)	U	1205
Sabo, Tonia (CO)	N	535
Sacco, Ralph (FL)	N	526
Sachs, Greg (IN)	Ger	266
Saclarides, Theodore (IL)	CRS	175
Sadda, SriniVas (CA)	Oph	608
Sadeghi-Nejad, Hossein (NJ)	U	1194
Sadiq, Saud (NY)	N	521
Sadock, Virginia (NY)	Psyc	927
Sadowsky, Carl (FL)	N	526
Safi, Hazim (TX)	T&CS	1176
Safian, Robert (MI)	Cv	104
Sagalowsky, Arthur (TX)	U	1209
Sage, Jacob (NJ)	N	521
Saha, Sukamal (MI)	S	1119
Sahin, Aysegul (TX)	Path	731
Sahin, Mustafa (MA)	ChiN	144
Sahn, Steven (SC)	Pul	963
Saif, M (MA)	Onc	334
Saiki, John (NM)	Onc	383
Sailer, Scott (NC)	RadRO	987
Saiman, Lisa (NY)	PInf	794
Saint-Phard, Deborah (CO)	SM	1078
Sakamoto, Kathleen (CA)	PHO	791
Salant, David (MA)	Nep	458
Salata, Robert (OH)	Inf	418
Salem, Riad (IL)	VIR	1031
Salem, Ronald (CT)	S	1087
Salerno, Tomas (FL)	T&CS	1165
Salgia, Ravi (IL)	Onc	373
Salky, Barry (NY)	S	1099
Sallan, Stephen (MA)	PHO	770
Sallent, Jorge (FL)	PPul	808
Salloum, Ihsan (FL)	Psyc	928
Salmon, Jane (NY)	Rhu	1062
Salo, Jonathan (NC)	S	1108
Saltz, Leonard (NY)	Onc	350
Saltzman, Charles (UT)	OrS	647
Salvati, Eduardo (NY)	OrS	631

Alphabetical Listing of Doctors

Name	Specialty	Pg
Salvi, Sharad (IL)	PHO	785
Salz, James (CA)	Oph	608
Salzman, Carl (MA)	Psyc	922
Samadi, David (NY)	U	1194
Samant, Sandeep (TN)	Oto	681
Samberg, Eslee (NY)	Psyc	927
Samii, Ali (WA)	N	542
Samlowski, Wolfram (NV)	Onc	392
Sampson, Christian (MA)	HS	296
Sampson, Hugh (NY)	PA&I	743
Sampson, John (NC)	NS	487
Samson, Duke (TX)	NS	497
Samuels, Brian (ID)	Onc	377
Samuels, Louis (PA)	T&CS	1158
Samuels, Martin (MA)	N	512
Samuels, Philip (OH)	MF	439
Samuelson, Thomas (MN)	Oph	599
Sanacora, Gerard (CT)	Psyc	922
Sanborn, Timothy (IL)	Cv	105
Sanchez, Juan (MD)	T&CS	1158
Sanchez, Luis (MO)	VascS	1228
Sanchez, Miguel (NJ)	Path	724
Sand, Peter (IL)	ObG	565
Sanda, Martin (GA)	U	1200
Sandberg, David (TX)	NS	497
Sandborn, William (CA)	Ge	257
Sanders, George (CA)	PlS	905
Sanders, Georgiana (MI)	A&I	84
Sanders, William (GA)	U	1200
Sandhu, Harvinder (NY)	OrS	632
Sandler, Eric (FL)	PHO	781
Sandler, Howard (CA)	RadRO	997
Sandler, Martin (TN)	NuM	555
Sandlow, Jay (WI)	U	1205
Sands, Laurence (FL)	CRS	172
Sanfilippo, Joseph (PA)	RE	1044
Sangeorzan, Bruce (WA)	OrS	653
Sanger, James (WI)	PlS	896
Sanger, Joseph (NY)	NuM	555
Sankar, Raman (CA)	ChiN	152
Santa-Emma, Philip (OH)	H & PM	408
Santana, Victor (TN)	PHO	781
Santin, Alessandro (CT)	GO	275
Santos, Cesar (DC)	ChiN	146
Sanz, Luis (VA)	ObG	563
Saper, Clifford (MA)	N	512
Saper, Joel (MI)	N	533
Sargent, Albert (MA)	ChAP	938
Sarnaik, Ashok (MI)	PCCM	755
Sarosi, George (FL)	S	1108
Sarr, Michael (MN)	S	1119
Sartor, Ryan (NC)	Ge	244
Sasaki, Clarence (CT)	Oto	667
Sass, David (PA)	Ge	240
Sasson, Aaron (NE)	S	1123
Sataloff, Dahlia (PA)	S	1099
Sataloff, Robert (PA)	Oto	675
Satava, Richard (WA)	S	1136
Sato, Thomas (WI)	PS	821
Sauer, Mark (NY)	RE	1044
Sauer, William (CO)	CE	119
Saunders, Elijah (MD)	Cv	95
Sauter, Edward (TX)	S	1128
Savage, David (NY)	Hem	316
Savage, Edward (FL)	T&CS	1165
Saven, Alan (CA)	Hem	329
Saver, Jeffrey (CA)	N	542
Savides, Thomas (CA)	Ge	257
Savino, Peter (CA)	Oph	608
Sawaya, Raymond (TX)	NS	497
Sawczuk, Ihor (NJ)	U	1194
Sawin, Robert (WA)	PS	824
Sax, Paul (MA)	Inf	412
Saxena, Sanjaya (CA)	Psyc	934
Scandling, John (CA)	Nep	467
Scantlebury, Velma (DE)	S	1100
Scarborough, Mark (FL)	OrS	638
Scardino, Peter (NY)	U	1194
Schachat, Andrew (OH)	Oph	599
Schaefer, Steven (NY)	Oto	675
Schaeffer, Anthony (IL)	U	1205
Schafer, Michael (IL)	OrS	644
Schaff, Hartzell (MN)	T&CS	1171
Schaffer, Randolph (CA)	S	1137
Schaitkin, Barry (PA)	Oto	675
Schanberg, Laura (NC)	PRhu	812
Schantz, Stimson (NY)	Oto	675
Schatz, Lisa (CO)	CRS	176
Schatz, Norman (FL)	N	526
Schatzberg, Alan (CA)	Psyc	935
Schauer, Philip (OH)	S	1119
Schechter, David (CA)	SM	1079
Schein, Oliver (MD)	Oph	584
Scheinberg, David (NY)	Onc	351
Schelbert, Heinrich (CA)	NuM	557
Scheld, W Michael (VA)	Inf	416
Scheller, Arnold (MA)	SM	1074
Schembre, Drew (WA)	Ge	257
Schenken, Robert (TX)	RE	1050
Scher, Howard (NY)	Onc	351
Scher, Mark (OH)	ChiN	149
Scherl, Ellen (NY)	Ge	240

Name	Specialty	Pg
Scherr, Douglas (NY)	U	1194
Schiano, Thomas (NY)	Ge	240
Schiff, David (VA)	N	527
Schiff, Peter (NY)	RadRO	982
Schiff, William (NY)	Oph	584
Schiffer, Charles (MI)	Onc	373
Schiffman, Fred (RI)	Hem	312
Schiffman, Jade (TX)	Oph	603
Schild, Steven (AZ)	RadRO	994
Schilder, Russell (PA)	Onc	351
Schiller, Alan (HI)	Path	734
Schiller, Gary (CA)	Hem	329
Schiller, Joan (TX)	Onc	383
Schiller, Lawrence (TX)	Ge	254
Schink, Julian (IL)	GO	286
Schirmer, Bruce (VA)	S	1108
Schlaff, William (PA)	RE	1044
Schlegel, Peter (NY)	U	1194
Schlegel, Theodore (CO)	OrS	647
Schlesinger, Iris (NY)	OrS	632
Schley, W Shain (NY)	Oto	675
Schlinkert, Richard (AZ)	S	1128
Schluger, Neil (NY)	Pul	959
Schmalzried, Thomas (CA)	OrS	653
Schmidt, Richard (PA)	OrS	632
Schmitt, Steven (OH)	Inf	418
Schnabel, Freya (NY)	S	1100
Schnapp, Moacir (TN)	PM	709
Schneider, Darren (NY)	VascS	1225
Schnipper, Lowell (MA)	Onc	334
Schnitt, Stuart (MA)	Path	719
Schnittger, Ingela (CA)	Cv	112
Schoen, Robert (CT)	Rhu	1058
Schoenberg, Mark (MD)	U	1194
Schoetz, David (MA)	CRS	169
Schomberg, Paula (WA)	RadRO	997
Schooley, Robert (CA)	Inf	421
Schorge, John (MA)	GO	275
Schraufnagel, Dean (IL)	Pul	966
Schraut, Wolfgang (PA)	S	1100
Schreiber, Martin (OH)	Nep	464
Schreiber, Theodore (MI)	IC	127
Schriock, Eldon (CA)	RE	1052
Schubert, Mark (AZ)	A&I	85
Schubert, Richard (DC)	Rhu	1062
Schuberth, Kenneth (MD)	PA&I	744
Schuchter, Lynn (PA)	Onc	351
Schuger, Claudio (MI)	CE	118
Schulam, Peter (CT)	U	1188
Schuler, Thomas (VA)	OrS	638
Schulick, Richard (CO)	S	1123
Schulman, Steven (MD)	Cv	95
Schultz, Neal (NY)	D	190
Schulze, Konrad (IA)	Ge	250
Schuman, Joel (PA)	Oph	584
Schuster, Michael (NY)	Hem	317
Schuster, Stephen (PA)	Hem	317
Schusterman, Mark (TX)	PlS	900
Schutta, Mark (PA)	EDM	214
Schwab, Frank (NY)	OrS	632
Schwab, Richard (PA)	Pul	959
Schwartz, Allan (NY)	Cv	96
Schwartz, Burton (MN)	Onc	373
Schwartz, Cindy (RI)	PHO	770
Schwartz, Gary (MN)	Nep	464
Schwartz, Herbert (TN)	OrS	638
Schwartz, Lawrence (NY)	DR	1012
Schwartz, Linden (PA)	PMR	865
Schwartz, Marshall (PA)	PS	817
Schwartz, Michael (FL)	Onc	363
Schwartz, Myron (NY)	S	1100
Schwartz, Peter (CT)	GO	275
Schwartz, Robert (CO)	Ger	267
Schwartz, Stanley (PA)	EDM	214
Schwartz, Steven (CA)	Oph	609
Schwartz, Theodore (NY)	NS	481
Schwartz, William (NY)	Cv	96
Schwartzberg, Lee (TN)	Hem	320
Schwartzentruber, Douglas (IN)	S	1119
Schwarz, Adam (CA)	PCCM	756
Schwarz, Kathleen (MD)	PGe	764
Schwarz, Steven (NY)	PGe	764
Scoccia, Humberto (IL)	RE	1048
Scott, C Paul (PA)	Psyc	927
Scott, Daniel (TX)	S	1128
Scott, Gwendolyn (FL)	PInf	795
Scott, Richard (MA)	OrS	619
Scott, W Norman (NY)	OrS	632
Scott, Walter (PA)	T&CS	1158
Scott-Conner, Carol (IA)	S	1119
Scudder, Sidney (CA)	Onc	392
Scudera, Peter (VA)	Ge	244
Sculco, Thomas (NY)	OrS	632
Seashore, Margretta (CT)	CG	156
Seaver, Laurie (HI)	CG	163
See, William (WI)	U	1206
Seely, Ellen (MA)	EDM	210
Seftel, Allen (NJ)	U	1194
Segal, Brahm (NY)	Inf	415
Seibel, Barry (CA)	Oph	609
Seidner, Douglas (TN)	Ge	245
Seidner, Steven (TX)	NP	453

Name	Specialty	Pg
Seifer, David (NY)	RE	1044
Seiff, Stuart (CA)	Oph	609
Seifter, Julian (MA)	Nep	458
Seitz, William (OH)	HS	304
Sekhar, Laligam (WA)	NS	501
Sekhon, Lali (NV)	NS	501
Selby, Robert (CA)	S	1137
Selden, Nathan (OR)	NS	502
Sellke, Frank (RI)	T&CS	1148
Selman, Warren (OH)	NS	493
Seltzer, Dana (AZ)	OrS	648
Selvaggi, Kathy (MA)	H & PM	406
Selwyn, Peter (NY)	IM	426
Semenkovich, Clay (MO)	EDM	221
Semrad, Carol (IL)	Ge	250
Sen, Chandranath (NY)	NS	481
Senagore, Anthony (MI)	CRS	175
Sencer, Susan (MN)	PHO	785
Senders, Craig (CA)	Oto	697
Sener, Stephen (CA)	S	1137
Senior, Brent (NC)	Oto	681
Sennett, Brian (PA)	SM	1076
Sepkowitz, Kent (NY)	Inf	415
Seplowitz, Alan (NY)	EDM	214
Serafano, Donald (CA)	Oph	609
Sergent, John (TN)	Rhu	1064
Sergott, Robert (PA)	Oph	584
Serletti, Joseph (PA)	PlS	886
Serody, Jonathan (NC)	Onc	363
Serota, Ronald (PA)	AdP	937
Session, Donna (GA)	RE	1046
Sessoms, Sandra (TX)	Rhu	1067
Sethi, Kapil (GA)	N	527
Sethi, Paul (CT)	OrS	619
Seton, Margaret (MA)	Rhu	1058
Setzen, Michael (NY)	Oto	675
Seung, Steven (OR)	RadRO	997
Sewell, C. Whitaker (GA)	Path	726
Sexson, Sandra (GA)	ChAP	941
Sexton, Wade (FL)	U	1200
Seyfer, Alan (MD)	PlS	886
Sha, Beverly (IL)	Inf	418
Shaban, Stephen (NC)	U	1200
Shabsigh, Ridwan (NY)	U	1195
Shabto, Uri (NY)	Oph	584
Shaddy, Robert (PA)	PCd	750
Shadick, Nancy (MA)	Rhu	1059
Shaffrey, Christopher (VA)	NS	487
Shaffrey, Mark (VA)	NS	487
Shah, Jatin (NY)	S	1100
Shah, Nishit (RI)	CRS	169
Shah, Prediman (CA)	Cv	112
Shah, Raj (CO)	Ge	252
Shaked, Abraham (PA)	S	1100
Shaker, Reza (WI)	Ge	250
Shalhav, Arieh (IL)	U	1206
Shamberger, Robert (MA)	PS	814
Shamie, Neda (CA)	Oph	609
Shani, Jacob (NY)	IC	123
Shapiro, Amy (IN)	PHO	785
Shapiro, Charles (OH)	Onc	373
Shapiro, Edward (MA)	Psyc	922
Shapiro, Eugene (CT)	PInf	793
Shapiro, Jerrold (IL)	Cv	105
Shapiro, Richard (NY)	S	1100
Shapiro, Ron (PA)	S	1100
Shapiro, Scott (IN)	NS	493
Shapiro, William (AZ)	N	537
Shapshay, Stanley (NY)	Oto	675
Sharkey, Peter (PA)	OrS	632
Sharlip, Ira (CA)	U	1213
Sharma, Samin (NY)	IC	123
Sharp, Gregory (AR)	ChiN	151
Sharp, Kenneth (TN)	S	1109
Shaw, Dennis (WA)	DR	1018
Shaw, Edward (NC)	RadRO	987
Shaywitz, Bennett (CT)	ChiN	144
Shaywitz, Sally (CT)	Ped	740
Shea, Christopher (IL)	D	197
Shea, Richard (IN)	Cv	105
Shea, Thomas (NC)	Onc	363
Shearer, William (TX)	PA&I	746
Shefner, Jeremy (NY)	N	521
Sheikh, Kazim (TX)	N	537
Sheinfeld, Joel (NY)	U	1195
Shelbourne, K Donald (IN)	OrS	645
Sheldon, Stephen (IL)	Ped	742
Shellito, Judd (LA)	Pul	969
Shellito, Paul (MA)	CRS	169
Shelton, Clough (UT)	Oto	690
Shemin, Richard (CA)	T&CS	1180
Shen, Perry (NC)	S	1109
Shen, Win-Kuang (AZ)	CE	119
Shenk, Robert (OH)	S	1119
Shenot, Patrick (PA)	U	1195
Shepard, Alexander (MI)	VascS	1228
Shepherd, Gillian (NY)	A&I	81
Sherertz, Elizabeth (SC)	D	194
Sherman, Carol (SC)	Onc	363
Sherman, Frederick (PA)	PCd	750
Sherman, James (VA)	PPul	808
Sherman, Randolph (CA)	PlS	905

Name	Specialty	Pg
Sherman, Steven (TX)	EDM	223
Sherman, Stuart (IN)	Ge	250
Sherry, David (PA)	PRhu	812
Sherwood, Mark (FL)	Oph	591
Shibata, David (FL)	S	1109
Shields, Carol (PA)	Oph	584
Shields, Jerry (PA)	Oph	585
Shields, Peter (OH)	Onc	374
Shiffman, Mitchell (VA)	Ge	245
Shike, Moshe (NY)	Ge	240
Shikora, Scott (MA)	S	1088
Shin, Dong Moon (GA)	Onc	364
Shina, Donald (NM)	RadRO	995
Shindo, Maisie (OR)	Oto	697
Shingleton, Bradford (MA)	Oph	575
Shinnar, Shlomo (NY)	ChiN	147
Shlansky-Goldberg, Richard (PA)	VIR	1028
Shlofmitz, Richard (NY)	Cv	96
Shochat, Stephen (TN)	PS	819
Shockley, William (NC)	Oto	681
Shoffner, John (GA)	CG	159
Shorofsky, Stephen (MD)	IC	123
Short, Billie (DC)	NP	450
Shrager, Joseph (CA)	T&CS	1180
Shrieve, Dennis (UT)	RadRO	992
Shuer, Lawrence (CA)	NS	502
Shulman, Lawrence (MA)	Onc	335
Shulman, Lee (IL)	CG	160
Shulman, Lisa (MD)	N	521
Shulman, Stanford (IL)	PInf	796
Shupack, Jerome (NY)	D	190
Siatkowski, R Michael (OK)	Oph	603
Sibley, Richard (CA)	Path	734
Sicard, Gregorio (MO)	VascS	1228
Sicherer, Scott (NY)	PA&I	744
Siddique, Teepu (IL)	N	533
Siebert, John (WI)	PlS	896
Siegel, Barry (MO)	NuM	556
Siegel, Corey (NH)	Ge	232
Siegel, Gordon (IL)	Oto	687
Siegel, Herrick (AL)	OrS	638
Siegel, Stuart (CA)	PHO	792
Siegelbaum, Marc (MD)	U	1195
Sielaff, Timothy (MN)	S	1119
Siemionow, Maria (OH)	PlS	896
Sigel, Eric (CO)	AM	78
Sigman, Garry (IL)	AM	77
Sigman, Mark (RI)	U	1188
Sigurdson, Elin (PA)	S	1101
Sila, Cathy (OH)	N	533
Silasi, Dan-Arin (CT)	GO	275
Silber, Sherman (MO)	U	1206
Silbergeld, Daniel (WA)	NS	502
Silberstein, Stephen (PA)	N	521
Siller, Barry (TX)	GO	289
Sillers, Michael (AL)	Oto	681
Sills, Allen (TN)	NS	487
Sills, Edward (MD)	PRhu	812
Silva, Elvio (TX)	Path	731
Silver, Michael (IL)	Pul	966
Silver, Richard (IL)	MF	439
Silver, Richard (SC)	Rhu	1064
Silver, Samuel (MI)	Onc	374
Silverman, Damon (VT)	Oto	667
Silverman, Gary (PA)	NP	450
Silverman, Jan (PA)	Path	724
Silverman, Lewis (NY)	Onc	351
Silverman, Paula (OH)	Onc	374
Silverman, William (IA)	Ge	250
Silverstein, Herbert (FL)	Oto	681
Silverstein, Janet (FL)	PEn	759
Silverstein, Melvin (CA)	S	1137
Silvestry, Frank (PA)	Cv	96
Sim, Franklin (MN)	OrS	645
Simeone, Diane (MI)	S	1119
Simmons, Charles (CA)	NP	454
Simmons, Rache (NY)	S	1101
Simms, Robert (MA)	Rhu	1059
Simon, Daniel (OH)	Cv	105
Simon, George (TX)	Onc	383
Simon, James (DC)	ObG	562
Simon, John (NY)	Oph	585
Simon, Richard (MI)	Pul	967
Simpson, David (NY)	N	521
Simpson, Joe (NY)	ObG	562
Simpson, Joseph (MO)	RadRO	991
Sinanan, Mika (WA)	S	1137
Singer, Carlos (FL)	N	527
Singer, Daniel (HI)	OrS	653
Singer, Mark (CA)	Oto	697
Singer, Peter (CA)	EDM	225
Singer, Robert (CA)	PlS	905
Singer, Samuel (NY)	S	1101
Singh, Arun (RI)	T&CS	1148
Singh, Bhuvanesh (NY)	Oto	675
Singh, Diljeet (AZ)	GO	289
Singh, Dinesh (CT)	U	1188
Singh, Nalini (DC)	PInf	794
Singh, Navin (MD)	PlS	886
Singh, Nimi (MN)	AM	77
Singhal, Seema (IL)	Hem	324
Sinha, Uttam (CA)	Oto	697

Alphabetical Listing of Doctors

Name	Specialty	Pg
Siperstein, Allan (OH)	S	1120
Sirdofsky, Michael (DC)	N	521
Siris, Ethel (NY)	EDM	214
Sisti, Michael (NY)	NS	482
Sisung, Charles (IL)	PMR	870
Sivaswamy, Lalitha (MI)	ChiN	149
Sivit, Carlos (OH)	DR	1015
Skibber, John (TX)	S	1129
Skinner, Eila (CA)	U	1213
Skinner, Kristin (NY)	S	1101
Skinner, Michael (TX)	PS	822
Sklar, Charles (NY)	PEn	759
Sklar, Frederick (TX)	NS	497
Skolnick, Alan (AK)	Cv	112
Skoner, David (PA)	PA&I	744
Skyler, Jay (FL)	EDM	217
Slama, Thomas (IN)	Inf	418
Slamon, Dennis (CA)	Onc	392
Slankard, Marjorie (NY)	A&I	82
Slap, Gail (PA)	AM	76
Slater, William (NY)	Cv	96
Slatkin, Neal (CA)	PM	713
Slaughter, Mark (KY)	T&CS	1165
Slavin, Sumner (MA)	PIS	879
Slawin, Kevin (TX)	U	1210
Slease, Robert (DE)	Hem	317
Slezak, Sheri (MD)	PIS	886
Slingluff, Craig (VA)	S	1109
Slivka, Adam (PA)	Ge	240
Sliwa, James (IL)	PMR	870
Slomowitz, Marcia (IL)	ChAP	942
Slutsky, David (CA)	HS	306
Sly, R Michael (MD)	PA&I	744
Small, Donald (MD)	PHO	776
Small, Eric (CA)	Onc	392
Small, William (IL)	RadRO	991
Smalley, Stephen (KS)	RadRO	992
Smalling, Richard (TX)	IC	128
Smart, Frank (LA)	Cv	109
Smedira, Nicholas (OH)	T&CS	1171
Smikle, Collin (CA)	RE	1052
Smith, Andrew (GA)	Cv	100
Smith, Barbara (MA)	S	1088
Smith, Craig (NY)	T&CS	1158
Smith, David (FL)	PIS	891
Smith, Donna (AZ)	GO	289
Smith, Douglas (WA)	OrS	653
Smith, Eric (MA)	OrS	619
Smith, John (OH)	T&CS	1171
Smith, Joseph (TN)	U	1200
Smith, Lloyd (CA)	GO	291
Smith, Matthew (MA)	Onc	335
Smith, Mitchell (OH)	Onc	374
Smith, Paul (FL)	PIS	891
Smith, Peter (NC)	T&CS	1165
Smith, Ronald (CA)	Oph	609
Smith, Russell (NE)	Oto	691
Smith, Sidney (NC)	Cv	100
Smith, Steven (MN)	EDM	221
Smith, Steven (IL)	VIR	1031
Smith, Thomas (MA)	Path	719
Smith, Thomas (MD)	Onc	351
Smith, Wade (CA)	N	542
Smith, Yolanda (MI)	RE	1049
Smoot, Duane (TN)	Ge	245
Smythe, W. Roy (TX)	T&CS	1176
Snyder, David (LA)	Cv	109
Snyder, David (CA)	Hem	330
Snyder, John (DC)	PGe	764
Snyder, Peter (PA)	EDM	215
Snyder, Russell (TX)	ObG	566
Snyderman, Carl (PA)	Oto	676
Sobel, Jack (MI)	Inf	419
Sobel, Stuart (FL)	D	194
Soberman, Mark (MD)	T&CS	1158
Socinski, Mark (PA)	Onc	351
Socol, Michael (IL)	MF	440
Soff, Gerald (NY)	Hem	317
Soiffer, Robert (MA)	Onc	335
Soisson, Andrew (UT)	GO	287
Sokol, Lubomir (FL)	Hem	320
Sokol, Ronald (CO)	PGe	767
Sokol, Thomas (CA)	CRS	178
Sokoloff, Daniel (FL)	D	194
Solin, Lawrence (PA)	RadRO	982
Solitar, Bruce (NY)	Rhu	1062
Solomon, Gary (NY)	Rhu	1062
Solomon, Kerry (SC)	Oph	591
Solomon, Robert (NY)	NS	482
Solomon, Stephen (NY)	VIR	1028
Solorzano, Carmen (TN)	S	1109
Soloway, Mark (FL)	U	1201
Somerville, James (MN)	Nep	464
Somlo, George (CA)	Onc	392
Sommer, Robert (NY)	PCd	750
Sondak, Vernon (FL)	S	1109
Sondel, Paul (WI)	PHO	785
Sondheimer, Steven (PA)	RE	1044
Sonett, Joshua (NY)	T&CS	1158
Song, David (IL)	PIS	896
Song, John (CO)	Oto	691
Song, Shiyu (VA)	RadRO	987

Name	Specialty	Pg
Sontheimer, Richard (UT)	D	198
Sood, Anil (TX)	GO	290
Sood, Rajiv (IN)	PlS	896
Soparkar, Charles (TX)	Oph	603
Soper, John (NC)	GO	283
Soper, Nathaniel (IL)	S	1120
Sorrell, Michael (NE)	Ge	252
Sorrentino, Matthew (IL)	Cv	105
Sorrentino, Robert (GA)	CE	116
Sosa, Julie (NC)	S	1109
Soslow, Robert (NY)	Path	724
Sosman, Jeffrey (TN)	Onc	364
Soter, Nicholas (NY)	D	191
Sotereanos, Dean (PA)	HS	300
Sotomayor, Eduardo (FL)	Onc	364
Soulen, Michael (PA)	VIR	1028
Soules, Michael (WA)	RE	1053
Souryal, Tarek (TX)	OrS	649
Souweidane, Mark (NY)	NS	482
Sowers, James (MO)	EDM	221
Spack, Norman (MA)	PEn	757
Spaeth, George (PA)	Oph	585
Spaide, Richard (NY)	Oph	585
Spann, Cyril (GA)	GO	283
Spector, Sheldon (CA)	A&I	86
Speeg, Kermit (TX)	Ge	255
Spence, Robert (MD)	PlS	886
Spencer, Dennis (CT)	NS	474
Spencer, Thomas (MA)	ChAP	939
Spengler, Dan (TN)	OrS	638
Sperber, Laurence (NY)	Oph	585
Spergel, Jonathan (PA)	PA&I	744
Sperling, Mark (PA)	PEn	759
Sperling, Michael (PA)	N	521
Spetzler, Robert (AZ)	NS	497
Speyer, James (NY)	Onc	351
Spiegel, David (CA)	Psyc	935
Spiegel, Jeffrey (MA)	Oto	667
Spiera, Harry (NY)	Rhu	1062
Spigland, Nitsana (NY)	PS	817
Spindler, Kurt (TN)	OrS	638
Spinelli, Henry (NY)	PlS	887
Spinner, Robert (MN)	NS	493
Spirtos, Nicola (NV)	GO	292
Spitzer, Thomas (MA)	Hem	313
Spivak, Jeffrey (NY)	OrS	632
Spivak, Jerry (MD)	Hem	317
Spivak, William (NY)	PGe	764
Sponseller, Paul (MD)	OrS	633
Spray, Thomas (PA)	T&CS	1159
Spriggs, David (NY)	Onc	352
Squires, Kathleen (PA)	Inf	415
Squires, Robert (PA)	PGe	764
St Clair, William (KY)	RadRO	987
Staats, Peter (NJ)	PM	708
Staddon, Arthur (PA)	Onc	352
Stadelmann, Wayne (NH)	PlS	879
Stadler, Walter (IL)	Onc	374
Stadtmauer, Edward (PA)	Onc	352
Staffenberg, David (NY)	PlS	887
Staggers, Barbara (CA)	AM	78
Stahl, Richard (CT)	PlS	879
Stainback, Raymond (TX)	Cv	109
Staley, Charles (GA)	S	1109
Stamos, Michael (CA)	CRS	178
Stankiewicz, James (IL)	Oto	688
Stanley, James (MI)	VascS	1228
Stanley, John (PA)	D	191
Staples, Edward (FL)	T&CS	1166
Staren, Edgar (AZ)	S	1129
Stark, Walter (MD)	Oph	585
Starke, Jeffrey (TX)	PInf	797
Starnes, Vaughn (CA)	T&CS	1180
Starr, Christopher (NY)	Oph	585
Starz, Terence (PA)	Rhu	1062
Stasney, C Richard (TX)	Oto	693
Staton, Gerald (GA)	Pul	963
Stea, Baldassarre (AZ)	RadRO	995
Steadman, J Richard (CO)	OrS	647
Steege, John (NC)	ObG	563
Steen, Preston (ND)	Onc	377
Steen, Virginia (DC)	Rhu	1062
Steers, William (VA)	U	1201
Stefanyszyn, Mary (PA)	Oph	585
Stehman, Frederick (IN)	GO	286
Steiger, David (NY)	Pul	959
Stein, Cy (CA)	Onc	392
Stein, David (PA)	CRS	171
Stein, Elliott (CA)	GerPsy	946
Stein, James (CA)	PS	824
Stein, James (WI)	Cv	105
Stein, Murray (CA)	Psyc	935
Steinberg, Gary (CA)	NS	502
Steinberg, Gary (IL)	U	1206
Steinberg, Harry (NY)	Pul	959
Steiner, Hans (CA)	ChAP	944
Steiner, Mark (MA)	SM	1074
Steinert, Roger (CA)	Oph	609
Steingart, Richard (NY)	Cv	96
Steinhagen, Randolph (NY)	CRS	171
Steinherz, Laurel (NY)	PCd	750
Steinherz, Peter (NY)	PHO	776

Alphabetical Listing of Doctors

Name	Specialty	Pg
Steinkampf, Michael (AL)	RE	1046
Steinmann, Scott (MN)	HS	304
Stenson, Kerstin (IL)	Oto	688
Stephenson, Mary (IL)	RE	1049
Steren, Albert (MD)	GO	280
Sterman, Daniel (PA)	Pul	959
Stern, Jeffrey (CA)	GO	292
Stern, Leonard (NY)	Nep	460
Stern, Matthew (PA)	N	522
Stern, Peter (OH)	HS	304
Stern, Robert (MA)	D	186
Sternberg, Paul (TN)	Oph	591
Sterns, Gwen (NY)	Oph	586
Stevens, Craig (FL)	RadRO	987
Stevens, W. Grant (CA)	PlS	905
Stevenson, David (CA)	NP	454
Stevenson, Lynne (MA)	Cv	90
Stevenson, Roger (SC)	CG	159
Stevenson, William (MA)	CE	113
Stewart, Alexander (AZ)	Hem	327
Stewart, Allan (NY)	T&CS	1159
Stewart, Elizabeth (MN)	RE	1049
Stewart, F. Marc (WA)	Onc	393
Stewart, Michael (NY)	Oto	676
Stewart, Paula (AL)	PMR	867
Stewart, Ronald (TX)	S	1129
Stewart, William (OH)	Cv	105
Stieg, Philip (NY)	NS	482
Stiegmann, Gregory (CO)	S	1123
Stiff, Patrick (IL)	Hem	324
Stiles, Alan (NC)	NP	451
Stine, Susan (MI)	AdP	937
Stock, Richard (NY)	RadRO	982
Stock, Wendy (IL)	Hem	324
Stockdale, Frank (CA)	Onc	393
Stolar, Charles (CA)	PS	824
Stolier, Alan (LA)	S	1129
Stoller, James (OH)	Pul	967
Stoller, Marshall (CA)	U	1213
Stone, Edwin (IA)	Oph	599
Stone, Gregg (NY)	IC	124
Stone, Joel (FL)	Onc	364
Stone, Richard (MA)	Hem	313
Stoopler, Mark (NY)	Onc	352
Stopeck, Alison (AZ)	Onc	383
Stotland, Mitchell (NH)	PlS	879
Stough, Rebecca (OK)	DR	1017
Stout, J. Timothy (OR)	Oph	609
Stover-Pepe, Diane (NY)	Pul	960
Stowe, Cary (FL)	T&CS	1166
Strain, Eric (MD)	AdP	937
Strair, Roger (NJ)	Hem	317
Strakowski, Stephen (OH)	Psyc	931
Strand, William (TX)	Ped Uro	828
Strashun, Arnold (NY)	NuM	555
Strassner, Howard (IL)	MF	440
Stratta, Robert (NC)	S	1110
Strauch, Eric (MD)	PS	817
Strauch, Robert (NY)	HS	300
Straus, David (NY)	Onc	352
Strauss, Gary (MA)	Onc	335
Strauss, James (TX)	Hem	327
Streeter, Oscar (CA)	RadRO	998
Streiff, Michael (MD)	Hem	317
Streim, Joel (PA)	GerPsy	945
Strenger, Rochelle (RI)	Onc	335
Stringer, Scott (MS)	Oto	681
Strollo, Patrick (PA)	Pul	960
Strom, Laura (CO)	N	535
Strome, Marshall (NY)	Oto	676
Strome, Scott (MD)	Oto	676
Strongwater, Allan (NJ)	OrS	633
Strouse, Thomas (CA)	Psyc	935
Strunk, Robert (MO)	PA&I	745
Strup, Stephen (KY)	U	1201
Stryker, Steven (IL)	CRS	175
Stuart, Richard (MO)	T&CS	1171
Stubblefield, Michael (NY)	PMR	866
Stuchin, Steven (NY)	OrS	633
Studenski, Stephanie (PA)	Ger	265
Stulberg, S David (IL)	OrS	645
Stulting, R. Doyle (GA)	Oph	591
Stump, David (TX)	Ge	255
Stuzin, James (FL)	PlS	891
Stylianos, Steven (NY)	PS	817
Su, Li-Ming (FL)	U	1201
Suarez, Jose (TX)	N	538
Suchy, Frederick (CO)	PGe	768
Suen, James (AR)	Oto	693
Sugarbaker, David (MA)	T&CS	1148
Sugarbaker, Paul (DC)	S	1101
Suh, John (OH)	RadRO	992
Sulica, Radu (NY)	Oto	676
Sullivan, Kathleen (PA)	PA&I	744
Sullivan, Patrick (RI)	PlS	879
Sultan, Mark (NY)	PlS	887
Summergrad, Paul (MA)	Psyc	922
Summers, C Gail (MN)	Oph	599
Sumpio, Bauer (CT)	VascS	1221
Sun, Peter (CA)	NS	502
Sun, Weijing (PA)	Onc	352
Sundaram, Chandru (IN)	U	1206

Name	Specialty	Pg
Sundaram, Magesh (IL)	S	1120
Sundaresan, Narayan (NY)	NS	482
Sundy, John (NC)	A&I	83
Suntharalingam, Mohan (MD)	RadRO	983
Superina, Riccardo (IL)	PS	821
Supiano, Mark (UT)	Ger	267
Surawicz, Christina (WA)	Ge	257
Suresh, Santhanam (IL)	PM	710
Surks, Martin (NY)	EDM	215
Surrey, Eric (CO)	RE	1049
Sussman, Norman (NY)	Psyc	927
Suster, Saul (WI)	Path	729
Sutherland, Everett (CO)	Pul	968
Sutherland, Richard (NC)	Ped Uro	826
Sutphen, Rebecca (FL)	CG	159
Sutton, Leslie (PA)	NS	482
Sutton, Linda (NC)	Onc	364
Svensson, Lars (OH)	T&CS	1171
Swaid, Swaid (AL)	NS	487
Swanson, Jerry (MN)	N	533
Swanson, Neil (OR)	D	202
Swanson, Scott (MA)	T&CS	1148
Swanstrom, Lee (OR)	S	1137
Swarm, Robert (MO)	PM	710
Swartz, Richard (MI)	Nep	464
Swearingen, Brooke (MA)	NS	474
Sweeney, Christopher (MA)	Onc	335
Sweeney, John (GA)	S	1110
Sweetenham, John (UT)	Onc	378
Swensen, Stephen (MN)	DR	1015
Swerdloff, Ronald (CA)	EDM	226
Swerdlow, Charles (CA)	CE	120
Swerdlow, Michael (NY)	N	522
Swerdlow, Steven (PA)	Path	724
Swetter, Susan (CA)	D	202
Swigart, Carrie (CT)	HS	296
Swiontkowski, Marc (MN)	OrS	645
Swisher, Stephen (TX)	T&CS	1176
Swistel, Alexander (NY)	S	1101
Swistel, Daniel (NY)	T&CS	1159
Szabo, Robert (CA)	HS	306
Szachowicz, Edward (MN)	Oto	688
Sze, Gordon (CT)	NRad	1020
Szeto, Wilson (PA)	T&CS	1159
Sznol, Mario (CT)	Onc	335

T

Name	Specialty	Pg
Tabbal, Nicolas (NY)	PlS	887
Tabsh, Khalil (CA)	MF	443
Taetle, Raymond (AZ)	Onc	383
Tafra, Lorraine (MD)	S	1101
Taft, Timothy (NC)	SM	1077
Tagawa, Scott (NY)	Onc	352
Taghian, Alphonse (MA)	RadRO	977
Takayama, Thomas (WA)	U	1213
Talamini, Mark (CA)	S	1137
Talamonti, Mark (IL)	S	1120
Tallman, Martin (NY)	Hem	318
Talmor, Mia (NY)	PlS	887
Tamargo, Rafael (MD)	NS	482
Tamaroff, Marc (CA)	A&I	86
Tamborlane, William (CT)	PEn	757
Tanabe, Kenneth (MA)	S	1088
Taneja, Samir (NY)	U	1195
Tanner, Caroline (CA)	N	542
Tap, William (NY)	Onc	352
Taplin, Mary Ellen (MA)	Onc	335
Tarbell, Nancy (MA)	RadRO	977
Targan, Stephan (CA)	Ge	258
Tarraza, Hector (ME)	GO	275
Tartter, Paul (NY)	S	1101
Tatter, Stephen (NC)	NS	487
Taub, Peter (NY)	PlS	887
Tauber, Danna (PA)	PPul	808
Tavassoli, Fattaneh (CT)	Path	720
Tayal, Ashis (PA)	N	522
Taylon, Charles (NE)	NS	494
Taylor, Lynne (MA)	N	512
Taylor, R. (TX)	D	199
Taylor, Richard (TX)	PCCM	756
Tchou, Julia (PA)	S	1102
Tchou, Patrick (OH)	CE	118
Te, Helen (IL)	Ge	250
Teal, James (DC)	DR	1012
Tebbetts, John (TX)	PlS	900
Tebbi, Cameron (FL)	PHO	781
Tedder, Mark (TN)	T&CS	1166
Tefferi, Ayalew (MN)	Hem	324
Teigland, Chris (NC)	U	1201
Teirstein, Paul (CA)	IC	128
Teitel, David (CA)	PCd	755
Teitelbaum, George (CA)	NRad	1026
Teitz, Carol (WA)	SM	1079
Teknos, Theodoros (OH)	Oto	688
Telen, Marilyn (NC)	Hem	320
Telian, Steven (MI)	Oto	688
Telischi, Fred (FL)	Oto	681
Tempero, Margaret (CA)	Onc	393
Tenenbaum, Joseph (NY)	Cv	96
Teng, Nelson (CA)	GO	292

Name	Specialty	Pg
Tennison, Michael (NC)	ChiN	147
Tenover, Joyce (CA)	Ger	268
Teperman, Lewis (NY)	S	1102
Tepper, Joel (NC)	RadRO	987
Terpenning, Marilou (CA)	Onc	393
Terris, David (GA)	Oto	682
Terris, Martha (GA)	U	1201
Tester, William (PA)	Onc	353
Tetrud, James (CA)	N	542
Tewari, Ashutosh (NY)	U	1195
Textor, Stephen (MN)	Nep	464
Thaler, Erica (PA)	Oto	676
Thaller, Seth (FL)	PlS	891
Thames, Marc (AZ)	Cv	109
Thase, Michael (PA)	Psyc	927
Thayer, Sarah (MA)	S	1088
Theodore, Nicholas (AZ)	NS	497
Thiers, Bruce (SC)	D	194
Thigpen, James (MS)	Onc	364
Thistlethwaite, J Richard (IL)	S	1120
Thistlethwaite, Patricia (CA)	T&CS	1180
Thoder, Joseph (PA)	HS	300
Thomas, Bert (CA)	OrS	654
Thomas, Charles (OR)	RadRO	998
Thomas, Christie (IA)	Nep	465
Thomas, Dan (CA)	PGe	769
Thomas, David (MO)	Ger	266
Thomas, Gregory (OR)	PHO	792
Thomas, Michael (OH)	RE	1049
Thomas, Ronald (PA)	MF	435
Thomashow, Byron (NY)	Pul	960
Thompson, Ann (PA)	PCCM	755
Thompson, B (MI)	NS	493
Thompson, Brad (IA)	DR	1016
Thompson, Dana (IL)	PO	804
Thompson, George (OH)	OrS	645
Thompson, Ian (TX)	U	1210
Thompson, John (WA)	Onc	393
Thompson, Paul (CT)	Cv	90
Thompson, Reid (TN)	NS	487
Thomson, J Grant (CT)	HS	296
Thor, Ann (CO)	Path	729
Thorne, Charles (NY)	PlS	887
Thorner, Michael (VA)	EDM	217
Thornhill, Thomas (MA)	OrS	619
Thorp, John (NC)	MF	437
Thorson, Alan (NE)	CRS	176
Thrasher, J Brantley (KS)	U	1207
Thulborn, Keith (IL)	NRad	1024
Thurmond, Amy (OR)	DR	1018
Tillinghast, Jeffrey (MO)	A&I	84
Tinetti, Mary (CT)	Ger	264
Ting, Jess (NY)	PlS	888
Tino, Gregory (PA)	Pul	960
Tkaczuk, Katherine (MD)	Onc	353
Tobias, Hillel (NY)	Ge	240
Tobin, Gordon (KY)	PlS	892
Tobin, Martin (IL)	Pul	967
Tobin, Mary (IL)	A&I	84
Tobis, Jonathan (CA)	Cv	112
Todd, George (NY)	VascS	1225
Tolkoff-Rubin, Nina (MA)	Nep	458
Tomaselli, Gordon (MD)	CE	116
Tomaszewski, John (NY)	Path	724
Tomford, J Walton (OH)	Inf	419
Tomich, Paul (NE)	MF	440
Tomita, Tadanori (IL)	NS	493
Tomlinson, Gail (TX)	PHO	788
Tonsgard, James (IL)	ChiN	149
Topham, Neal (PA)	PlS	888
Topol, Eric (CA)	Cv	112
Toppmeyer, Deborah (NJ)	Onc	353
Toriumi, Dean (IL)	Oto	688
Tornetta, Paul (MA)	OrS	619
Tornos, Carmen (NY)	Path	724
Torres, Vicente (MN)	Nep	465
Torti, Frank (CT)	Onc	336
Toth, Thomas (MA)	RE	1041
Toto, Robert (TX)	Nep	466
Tousimis, Eleni (DC)	S	1102
Townsend, Raymond (PA)	Nep	460
Toyoda, Yoshiya (PA)	T&CS	1159
Traboulsi, Elias (OH)	Oph	599
Trabulsi, Edouard (PA)	U	1195
Tracy, Thomas (RI)	PS	814
Tranbaugh, Robert (NY)	T&CS	1159
Trauner, Doris (CA)	ChiN	152
Travis, William (NY)	Path	724
Traynelis, Vincent (IL)	NS	493
Traynor, Michael (ND)	S	1123
Treadwell, Marjorie (MI)	MF	440
Treadwell, Patricia (IN)	D	197
Tremaine, William (MN)	Ge	251
Trenholme, Gordon (IL)	Inf	419
Trento, Alfredo (CA)	T&CS	1180
Trerotola, Scott (PA)	VIR	1029
Trese, Michael (MI)	Oph	600
Triche, Timothy (CA)	Path	734
Triozzi, Pierre (OH)	Onc	374
Tripathy, Debasish (CA)	Onc	393
Tripuraneni, Prabhakar (CA)	RadRO	998
Trisal, Vijay (CA)	S	1137

Name	Specialty	Pg
Trobe, Jonathan (MI)	Oph	600
Troner, Michael (FL)	Onc	364
Trudel, Judith (MN)	CRS	175
True, Lawrence (WA)	Path	734
Trulock, Elbert (MO)	Pul	967
Trumble, Thomas (WA)	HS	306
Trump, Donald (NY)	Onc	353
Tsai, James (CT)	Oph	575
Tsangaris, Theodore (CT)	S	1088
Tsao, Hensin (MA)	D	186
Tse, David (FL)	Oph	592
Tsokos, George (MA)	Rhu	1059
Tucci, Debara (NC)	Oto	682
Tucker, Rodney (AL)	H & PM	407
Tufano, Ralph (MD)	Oto	676
Tufaro, Anthony (MD)	PIS	888
Tulsky, James (NC)	H & PM	407
Tune, Larry (GA)	GerPsy	945
Tunkel, David (MD)	PO	803
Turecki, Stanley (NY)	ChAP	941
Turek, Paul (CA)	U	1214
Turner, William (TX)	T&CS	1176
Turrentine, Mark (IN)	T&CS	1172
Tuttle, R Michael (NY)	EDM	215
Tuttle, Todd (MN)	S	1120
Tuxhorn, Ingrid (OH)	ChiN	150
Twardowski, Przemyslaw (CA)	Onc	393
Tychsen, Lawrence (MO)	Oph	600
Tyler, Douglas (NC)	S	1110
Tzakis, Andreas (OH)	S	1120

U

Name	Specialty	Pg
Uberti, Joseph (MI)	Hem	324
Udell, Ira (NY)	Oph	586
Udelsman, Robert (CT)	S	1088
Ulbright, Thomas (IN)	Path	729
Ulissey, Michael (WA)	DR	1019
Ulshen, Martin (NC)	PGe	765
Umetsu, Dale (MA)	A&I	80
Unger, Michael (PA)	Pul	960
Unger, Stephen (FL)	S	1110
Ungerleider, Ross (NC)	T&CS	1166
Updegraff, Stephen (FL)	Oph	592
Urata, Mark (CA)	PIS	905
Urba, Susan (MI)	Onc	374
Urba, Walter (OR)	Onc	393
Urist, Marshall (AL)	S	1110
Urken, Mark (NY)	Oto	676
Uzzo, Robert (PA)	U	1195

V

Name	Specialty	Pg
Vaccaro, Alexander (PA)	OrS	633
Vaezi, Michael (TN)	Ge	245
Vahdat, Linda (NY)	Onc	353
Vail, Thomas (CA)	OrS	654
Vajaranant, Thasarat (IL)	Oph	600
Valaitis, Sandra (IL)	ObG	565
Valea, Fidel (NC)	GO	283
Valentine, Alan (TX)	Psyc	932
Valentino, Joseph (KY)	Oto	682
Valentino, Leonard (IL)	PHO	786
Valero, Vicente (TX)	Onc	383
Valji, Karim (WA)	VIR	1033
Vallieres, Eric (WA)	T&CS	1181
Van Arsdalen, Keith (PA)	U	1196
Van Besien, Koen (NY)	Hem	318
Van Der Horst, Charles (NC)	Inf	417
Van Dorsten, J Peter (SC)	MF	437
van Hoff, Jack (NH)	PHO	771
Van Loveren, Harry (FL)	NS	488
Van Marter, Linda (MA)	NP	448
Van Nagell, John (KY)	GO	284
Van Voorhis, Bradley (IA)	RE	1049
Van Zee, Kimberly (NY)	S	1102
Vanagunas, Arvydas (IL)	Ge	251
Vance, Mary Lee (VA)	EDM	217
Vander, James (PA)	Oph	586
Vander Kolk, Craig (MD)	PIS	888
Vanderhoof, Jon (NE)	PGe	768
Vapnek, Jonathan (NY)	U	1196
Varadhachary, Gauri (TX)	Onc	383
Varga, John (IL)	Rhu	1066
Vargo, John (OH)	Ge	251
Varma, Madhulika (CA)	CRS	178
Varma, Rohit (IL)	Oph	600
Vas, George (NY)	N	522
Vasconez, Henry (KY)	PIS	892
Vaughan, William (AL)	Onc	364
Vaughey, Ellen (VA)	Pul	963
Vaughn, David (PA)	Onc	353
Vauthey, Jean-Nicholas (TX)	S	1129
Vege, Santhi (MN)	Ge	251
Veitch, Andrew (NM)	SM	1078
Veith, Richard (WA)	GerPsy	946
Velcek, Francisca (NY)	PS	817
Velvis, Harmannus (NY)	PCd	750
Venkat, K. K. (MI)	Nep	465
Venook, Alan (CA)	Onc	394
Verghese, Mohan (DC)	U	1196
Vernava, Anthony (FL)	CRS	172
Verrier, Edward (WA)	T&CS	1181

Name	Specialty	Pg
Verschraegen, Claire (VT)	Onc	336
Vescio, Robert (CA)	Onc	394
Vetrovec, George (VA)	Cv	100
Vetter, Thomas (AL)	PM	709
Vetto, John (OR)	S	1137
Vezina, Louis (DC)	NRad	1021
Vicini, Frank (MI)	RadRO	992
Vick, Nicholas (IL)	N	534
Vickers, Selwyn (MN)	S	1120
Vidal, Dale (NH)	PIS	879
Videtic, Gregory (OH)	RadRO	992
Vierling, John (TX)	Ge	255
Vigneswaran, Wickii (IL)	T&CS	1172
Vignola, Paul (NC)	Cv	100
Vijayakumar, Srinivasan (MS)	RadRO	987
Vik, Terry (IN)	PHO	786
Villanueva, Andrew (MA)	Pul	955
Vinciguerra, Vincent (NY)	Onc	353
Vining, Eugenia (CT)	Oto	667
Visco, Anthony (NC)	ObG	563
Vitale, Gary (KY)	S	1110
Vitek, Jerrold (MN)	N	534
Vivino, Frederick (PA)	Rhu	1063
Vlahakes, Gus (MA)	T&CS	1148
Vo, Phuc (FL)	OrS	638
Voelkel, Norbert (VA)	Pul	963
Vogelzang, Nicholas (NV)	Onc	394
Vogelzang, Robert (IL)	VIR	1031
Vogt, Peter (MN)	PIS	896
Voigt, Roger (MD)	PS	817
Vokes, Everett (IL)	Onc	374
Volberding, Paul (CA)	Onc	394
Volgman, Annabelle (IL)	Cv	106
Vollmer, Timothy (CO)	N	535
Volpe, Nicholas (IL)	Oph	600
Volshteyn, Oksana (MO)	PMR	870
Von Burton, Gary (LA)	Onc	384
von der Lohe, Elisabeth (IN)	Cv	106
Von Gunten, Charles (OH)	H & PM	408
Von Hoff, Daniel (AZ)	Onc	384
von Mehren, Margaret (PA)	Onc	353
Voorhees, John (MI)	D	197
Vose, Julie (NE)	Hem	325
Vredenburgh, James (CT)	Onc	336

W

Name	Specialty	Pg
Wackym, P Ashley (OR)	Oto	697
Waggoner, Steven (OH)	GO	287
Wagman, Lawrence (CA)	S	1138
Wagner-Weiner, Linda (IL)	PRhu	813
Wagoner, Lynne (OH)	Cv	106
Waguespack, Steven (TX)	EDM	223
Wahl, Richard (MD)	NuM	555
Wain, John (MA)	T&CS	1149
Waintraub, Stanley (NJ)	Onc	354
Wait, Susan (MD)	Psyc	927
Wakefield, Thomas (MI)	S	1121
Wald, Arnold (WI)	Ge	251
Wald, Ellen (WI)	PInf	796
Waldhausen, John (WA)	PS	824
Waldo, Albert (OH)	CE	118
Walker, Alonzo (WI)	S	1121
Walker, David (TX)	Path	731
Walker, Joan (OK)	GO	290
Walker, Marion (UT)	NS	495
Walker, R. Dale (OR)	Psyc	935
Walker, William (WA)	Ped	743
Walkup, John (NY)	ChAP	941
Wall, Michael (OR)	PPul	811
Wallace, Anne Marie (CA)	S	1138
Wallace, Daniel (CA)	Rhu	1068
Wallace, Jeanne (CA)	Pul	972
Wallace, Mark (FL)	Inf	417
Wallace, Mark (CA)	PM	714
Wallace, Richard (TX)	Inf	420
Wallace, Robert (LA)	Oph	603
Wallach, Frances (NY)	Inf	415
Wallen, Eric (NC)	U	1201
Waller, Edmund (GA)	Onc	365
Walling, Arthur (FL)	OrS	638
Walmer, David (NC)	RE	1046
Walsh, B. Timothy (NY)	Psyc	927
Walsh, Christine (NY)	PCd	750
Walsh, Edward (MA)	PCd	748
Walsh, Garrett (TX)	T&CS	1177
Walsh, Joseph (NY)	Oph	586
Walsh, Mary (IN)	Cv	106
Walsh, Nicolas (TX)	PM	712
Walsh, Patrick (MD)	U	1196
Walsh, R. Matthew (OH)	S	1121
Walters, Henry (MI)	T&CS	1172
Walters, Mark (OH)	ObG	566
Walton, David (MA)	Oph	575
Walton, Robert (IL)	PIS	897
Wamboldt, Marianne (CO)	ChAP	942
Waner, Milton (NY)	Oto	677
Wang, Beverly (NY)	Path	725
Wang, Frederick (NY)	Oph	586
Wang, Jeffrey (CA)	OrS	654
Wang, Ming (TN)	Oph	592

Name	Specialty	Pg
Wang, Paul (CA)	CE	120
Wang, Steven (CA)	Oto	697
Wang, Winfred (TN)	PHO	781
Wanner, Adam (FL)	Pul	963
Wapner, Keith (PA)	OrS	633
Wapner, Ronald (NY)	MF	435
Wapnir, Irene (CA)	S	1138
Wara, William (CA)	RadRO	998
Warady, Bradley (MO)	PNep	800
Ward, Barbara (CT)	S	1088
Ward, David (CA)	Nep	467
Ward, Jewell (TN)	CG	159
Ward, John (UT)	Onc	378
Ward, Robert (NY)	PO	803
Ward, William (PA)	OrS	633
Waring, George (GA)	Oph	592
Warman, Roberto (FL)	Oph	592
Warner, Ann (MO)	Rhu	1066
Warner, Brad (MO)	PS	821
Warner, Kenneth (MA)	T&CS	1149
Warnick, Ronald (OH)	NS	493
Warnke, Roger (CA)	Path	734
Warren, Robert (CA)	S	1138
Warren, Robert (SC)	PRhu	813
Warren, Robert (AR)	PPul	810
Warren, Russell (NY)	OrS	633
Wartofsky, Leonard (DC)	EDM	215
Wasserman, Richard (TX)	PA&I	746
Wasserstein, Melissa (NY)	CG	158
Watchko, Jon (PA)	NP	450
Waters, Cheryl (NY)	N	522
Waters, Peter (MA)	HS	296
Watkins, Robert (CA)	OrS	654
Watson, Thomas (NY)	T&CS	1159
Watts, Nelson (OH)	EDM	221
Watts, Ray (AL)	N	527
Wax, Mark (OR)	Oto	697
Waxman, Alan (CA)	NuM	557
Waxman, Harvey (PA)	Cv	96
Waxman, Irving (IL)	Ge	251
Waye, Jerome (NY)	Ge	240
Wayne, Alan (CA)	PHO	792
Wazen, Jack (FL)	Oto	682
Wazer, David (RI)	RadRO	977
Weaver, David (IN)	CG	160
Webb, Gary (OH)	Cv	106
Webb, Lawrence (GA)	OrS	639
Weber, Collin (GA)	S	1110
Weber, Jeffrey (FL)	Onc	365
Weber, Randal (TX)	Oto	694
Weber, Samuel (TX)	Oto	694
Weber, Sharon (WI)	S	1121
Webster, Harry (MA)	PMR	862
Wechsler, Daniel (NC)	PHO	781
Wechsler, Lawrence (PA)	N	522
Wei, Jeanne (AR)	Ger	267
Weigel, Ronald (IA)	S	1121
Weigel, Tracey (ME)	T&CS	1149
Weigelt, John (WI)	S	1121
Weiland, Andrew (NY)	OrS	633
Weiman, Darryl (TN)	T&CS	1166
Wein, Alan (PA)	U	1196
Weinberg, David (PA)	Ge	240
Weinberg, Harold (NY)	N	522
Weinberg, Paul (PA)	PCd	750
Weinberger, Michael (NY)	PM	708
Weinblatt, Mark (NY)	PHO	776
Weinblatt, Michael (MA)	Rhu	1059
Weiner, George (IA)	Onc	375
Weiner, Howard (NY)	NS	482
Weiner, I David (FL)	Nep	462
Weiner, Kenneth (CO)	Psyc	931
Weiner, Leslie (CA)	N	542
Weiner, Louis (DC)	Onc	354
Weiner, Michael (NY)	PHO	777
Weiner, Richard (FL)	OrS	639
Weiner, Richard (NC)	Psyc	928
Weinfeld, Steven (NY)	OrS	634
Weingart, Jon (MD)	NS	483
Weinreb, Jeffrey (CT)	DR	1007
Weinreb, Robert (CA)	Oph	610
Weinstein, Arthur (DC)	Rhu	1063
Weinstein, Eric (CO)	VascS	1229
Weinstein, Gregory (PA)	Oto	677
Weinstein, Howard (MA)	PHO	771
Weinstein, James (NH)	OrS	619
Weinstein, Sharon (UT)	H & PM	408
Weinstein, Stuart (IA)	OrS	645
Weinstock, Joel (MA)	Ge	232
Weinstock, Robert (CA)	Psyc	935
Weintraub, Joshua (NY)	VIR	1029
Weisberg, Tracey (ME)	Onc	336
Weisenburger, Dennis (CA)	Path	735
Weiser, Martin (NY)	CRS	171
Weisler, Richard (NC)	Psyc	928
Weisman, Robert (CA)	Oto	697
Weisman, Steven (WI)	PM	711
Weiss, Arnold-Peter (RI)	HS	297
Weiss, Avery (WA)	Oph	610
Weiss, Geoffrey (VA)	Onc	365
Weiss, Gerson (NJ)	RE	1044
Weiss, Lawrence (CA)	Path	735

Alphabetical Listing of Doctors

Name	Specialty	Pg
Weiss, Marisa (PA)	RadRO	983
Weiss, Michael (WA)	N	542
Weiss, Robert (CT)	U	1188
Weiss, Robert (NJ)	U	1196
Weiss, Roger (MA)	AdP	936
Weiss, Roy (IL)	EDM	221
Weiss, Sharon (GA)	Path	727
Weissler, Jonathan (TX)	Pul	969
Weissler, Mark (NC)	Oto	682
Weissman, Peter (FL)	EDM	218
Weitz, Howard (PA)	Cv	97
Weitzel, Jeffrey (CA)	CG	164
Weksler, Benny (PA)	T&CS	1160
Welch, William (PA)	NS	483
Wellington, Joshua (IN)	PM	711
Wells, Gretchen (NC)	Cv	100
Wells, James (CA)	PlS	906
Wells, Robert (WI)	DR	1016
Wells, Winfield (CA)	T&CS	1181
Welton, Mark (CA)	CRS	178
Wen, Patrick (MA)	N	512
Wener, Mark (WA)	Rhu	1068
Wenstrom, Katharine (RI)	MF	433
Wenzel, Sally (PA)	Pul	960
Werner, Phillip (IL)	EDM	221
Werner-Wasik, Maria (PA)	RadRO	983
Werth, Victoria (PA)	D	191
Westrich, Geoffrey (NY)	OrS	634
Wetzel, F. Todd (PA)	OrS	634
Wetzler, Meir (NY)	Onc	354
Wexler, Leonard (NY)	PHO	777
Wexner, Steven (FL)	CRS	172
Weymuller, Ernest (WA)	Oto	698
Wharen, Robert (FL)	NS	488
Wheeland, Ronald (AZ)	D	199
Wheeler, Arthur (TN)	Pul	964
Wheeler, Thomas (TX)	Path	731
Whelan, Alison (MO)	CG	161
Whelan, Richard (NY)	CRS	171
Wheless, James (TN)	ChiN	147
White, Charles (MD)	DR	1012
White, David (MA)	Pul	956
White, Neil (MO)	PEn	761
White, Richard (OH)	DR	1016
White, Richard (NC)	S	1110
White, Rodney (CA)	VascS	1230
Whiting, Donald (PA)	NS	483
Whitington, Peter (IL)	PGe	767
Whitlow, Patrick (OH)	IC	127
Whitsett, Jeffrey (OH)	NP	452
Whitworth, Pat (TN)	S	1110
Whyte, Richard (MA)	T&CS	1149
Wicha, Max (MI)	Onc	375
Wickiewicz, Thomas (NY)	OrS	634
Widra, Eric (DC)	RE	1045
Wiedemann, Herbert (OH)	Pul	967
Wierman, Ann (NV)	Onc	394
Wiesel, Sam (DC)	OrS	634
Wiesenfeld, Harold (PA)	ObG	562
Wiesner, Russell (MN)	Ge	251
Wiet, Richard (IL)	Oto	688
Wigley, Frederick (MD)	Rhu	1063
Wilansky, Susan (AZ)	Cv	109
Wilber, David (IL)	CE	118
Wilberger, James (PA)	NS	483
Wilcox, C. Mel (AL)	Ge	245
Wilcox, Christopher (DC)	Nep	460
Wilcox, Robert (TX)	PlS	901
Wilcox, William (CA)	CG	164
Wilczynski, Sharon (CA)	Path	735
Wilding, George (WI)	Onc	375
Wilens, Timothy (MA)	ChAP	939
Wiley, Joseph (MD)	PHO	777
Wilhelmi, Bradon (KY)	PlS	892
Wilkins, Edwin (MI)	PlS	897
Wilkins, Ross (CO)	OrS	647
Wilkins-Haug, Louise (MA)	MF	433
Wilkoff, Bruce (OH)	Cv	106
Willett, Christopher (NC)	RadRO	987
Willey, Shawna (DC)	S	1102
Williams, David (MA)	Cv	90
Williams, Eric (IN)	Cv	106
Williams, Gail (NY)	Nep	460
Williams, George (MI)	Oph	600
Williams, Gerald (PA)	OrS	634
Williams, James (AZ)	PHO	789
Williams, Kim (MI)	Cv	107
Williams, Mathew (NY)	T&CS	1160
Williams, Michael (VA)	Hem	320
Williams, Riley (NY)	SM	1076
Williams, Ronald (TX)	OrS	649
Williams, Shauna (ID)	CRS	176
Willson, James (TX)	Onc	384
Wilson, Amy (TX)	PMR	871
Wilson, Daniel (FL)	Psyc	929
Wilson, Darrell (CA)	PEn	762
Wilson, David (OR)	Oph	610
Wilson, Ellen (TX)	RE	1050
Wilson, J. Frank (WI)	RadRO	992
Wilson, John (NC)	NS	488
Wilson, Keith (OH)	Oto	688
Wilson, Lynn (CT)	RadRO	978

Name	Specialty	Pg
Wilson, Marion (SC)	Oph	592
Wilson, Matthew (TN)	Oph	592
Wilson, Steven (OH)	Oph	600
Wilson, Timothy (CA)	U	1214
Wilson, Wyndham (MD)	Onc	354
Winchell, Robert (ME)	S	1088
Winchester, David (IL)	S	1121
Windebank, Anthony (MN)	N	534
Winer, Eric (MA)	Onc	336
Winer, Sharon (CA)	RE	1053
Winfield, Howard (AL)	U	1201
Wingard, John (FL)	Onc	365
Winick, Naomi (TX)	PHO	789
Winn, Hung (MO)	MF	440
Winston, Jonathan (NY)	Nep	461
Winter, Jane (IL)	Hem	324
Winters, Richard (NJ)	PlS	888
Wirth, Michael (TX)	OrS	649
Wisch, Nathaniel (NY)	Hem	318
Wise, Christopher (VA)	Rhu	1064
Wise, Paul (MO)	CRS	175
Wiseman, Gregory (MN)	NuM	556
Wisoff, Jeffrey (NY)	NS	483
Witman, Patricia (OH)	D	197
Witt, Thomas (IL)	S	1121
Witter, Frank (MD)	MF	436
Wittig, James (NY)	OrS	634
Wiviott, Lory (CA)	Inf	421
Wixson, Richard (IL)	OrS	645
Wiznitzer, Max (OH)	ChiN	150
Woeber, Kenneth (CA)	EDM	226
Wofsy, David (CA)	Rhu	1068
Wolchok, Jedd (NY)	Onc	354
Wolf, Raoul (IL)	PA&I	745
Wolfe, Lawrence (NY)	PHO	777
Wolfe, M Michael (OH)	Ge	251
Wolfe, Robert (CA)	Pul	972
Wolfe, S. Anthony (FL)	PlS	892
Wolfe, Scott (NY)	HS	300
Wolff, Antonio (MD)	Onc	354
Wolff, Bruce (MN)	CRS	175
Wolff, Robert (TX)	Onc	384
Wolfson, Aaron (FL)	RadRO	988
Wolin, Edward (CA)	Onc	394
Wolinsky, Jerry (TX)	N	538
Woltering, Eugene (LA)	S	1129
Wondisford, Frederic (MD)	EDM	215
Wong, Brian (CA)	Oto	698
Wong, Carson (OH)	U	1206
Wong, Duane (AZ)	A&I	85
Wong, Jeffrey (CA)	RadRO	998
Wong, Johnson (MA)	A&I	80
Wong, Richard (NY)	Oto	677
Wong, Ronald (HI)	CRS	178
Woo, Howard (LA)	U	1210
Woo, Peak (NY)	Oto	677
Woo, Shiao (KY)	RadRO	988
Woo, Y Joseph (PA)	T&CS	1160
Wood, Beverly (CA)	DR	1019
Wood, Bradford (MD)	VIR	1029
Wood, David (MI)	U	1206
Wood, Douglas (WA)	T&CS	1181
Wood, Gary (WI)	D	197
Wood, John (MO)	A&I	85
Wood, R. Patrick (TX)	S	1129
Wood, Robert (MD)	PA&I	744
Woodley, David (CA)	D	202
Woodson, B. Tucker (WI)	Oto	689
Woodson, Gayle (IL)	Oto	689
Wooten, George (VA)	N	527
Wooten, Virgil (OH)	Psyc	931
Worden, Francis (MI)	Onc	375
Wormser, Gary (NY)	Inf	415
Worsey, Michael (CA)	CRS	178
Wright, Cameron (MA)	T&CS	1149
Wright, Jackson (OH)	IM	427
Wright, Kenneth (CA)	Oph	610
Wright, Robert (IL)	N	534
Wurtz, L Daniel (IN)	OrS	645
Wyatt, Robert (TN)	PNep	799
Wyllie, Elaine (OH)	ChiN	150
Wyllie, Robert (OH)	PGe	767

X

Name	Specialty	Pg
Xerogeanes, John (GA)	SM	1077
Xing, Michael (MD)	EDM	215

Y

Name	Specialty	Pg
Yaddanapudi, Ravindranath (MI)	PHO	786
Yahalom, Joachim (NY)	RadRO	983
Yakes, Wayne (CO)	VIR	1032
Yamada, Kelvin (MO)	ChiN	150
Yamada, S (IL)	GO	287
Yamaguchi, Ken (MO)	OrS	646
Yan, Albert (PA)	D	191
Yancovitz, Stanley (NY)	Inf	415
Yanda, Randy (GA)	Ge	245

Alphabetical Listing of Doctors

Name	Specialty	Pg
Yang, James (MD)	S	1102
Yang, Stephen (MD)	T&CS	1160
Yankelevitz, David (NY)	DR	1012
Yannuzzi, Lawrence (NY)	Oph	586
Yanovich, Saul (MD)	Hem	318
Yarbrough, Wendell (CT)	Oto	667
Yeager, Andrew (AZ)	Hem	327
Yeatman, Timothy (SC)	S	1111
Yeatts, R. Patrick (NC)	Oph	592
Yee, Billy (CA)	RE	1053
Yee, Douglas (MN)	Onc	375
Yee, Jerry (MI)	Nep	465
Yen, Yun (CA)	Onc	394
Yeo, Charles (PA)	S	1102
Yetman, Randall (OH)	PlS	897
Yeung, Alan (CA)	IC	128
Yeung, Raymond (WA)	S	1138
Yonas, Howard (NM)	NS	498
Yoo, George (MI)	Oto	689
Yoo, Jung (OR)	OrS	654
Yoon, Sydney (NY)	DR	1012
York, Teresa (MD)	PHO	777
Young, Bruce (NY)	ObG	562
Young, James (OH)	Cv	107
Young, K Randall (PA)	Pul	960
Young, Ming-Lon (FL)	PCd	751
Young, Nancy (IL)	Oto	689
Young, Renee (NE)	Ge	252
Young, Robert (MA)	Path	720
Young, V Leroy (MO)	PlS	897
Young-Fadok, Tonia (AZ)	CRS	177
Younossi, Zobair (VA)	Ge	245
Yousem, David (MD)	NRad	1021
Yousem, Samuel (PA)	Path	725
Yu, George (MD)	U	1196
Yu, Jack (GA)	PlS	892
Yu, John (CA)	NS	502
Yueh, Bevan (MN)	Oto	689
Yuen, James (AR)	PlS	901
Yuh, David (CT)	T&CS	1149
Yung, W.K. Alfred (TX)	N	538
Yunus, Furhan (TN)	Onc	365
Yurt, Roger (NY)	S	1102

Z

Name	Specialty	Pg
Zach, Terence (NE)	NP	453
Zackai, Elaine (PA)	CG	158
Zacur, Howard (MD)	RE	1045
Zafonte, Ross (MA)	PMR	862
Zager, Eric (PA)	NS	483
Zagoria, Ronald (CA)	DR	1019
Zagzag, David (NY)	Path	725
Zahn, Evan (CA)	PCd	755
Zalud, Ivica (HI)	MF	443
Zalzal, George (MD)	Oto	677
Zaman, Atif (OR)	Ge	258
Zannis, Victor (AZ)	S	1129
Zarins, Bertram (MA)	OrS	619
Zdeblick, Thomas (WI)	OrS	646
Zeanah, Charles (LA)	ChAP	943
Zeitels, Steven (MA)	Oto	667
Zeitlin, Pamela (MD)	PPul	808
Zelefsky, Michael (NY)	RadRO	983
Zelenetz, Andrew (NY)	Onc	354
Zelickson, Brian (MN)	D	197
Zelman, Richard (MA)	IC	121
Zeltzer, Lonnie (CA)	Ped	743
Zeman, Robert (DC)	DR	1012
Zerbe, Kathryn (OR)	Psyc	935
Zide, Barry (NY)	PlS	888
Ziemer, Gerhard (IL)	T&CS	1172
Zietman, Anthony (MA)	RadRO	978
Ziffer, Jack (FL)	NuM	556
Zilleruelo, Gaston (FL)	PNep	799
Zimmerman, Christian (ID)	NS	495
Zimmerman, Donald (IL)	PEn	761
Zimmerman, Earl (NY)	N	522
Zimmerman, Jerry (WA)	PCCM	756
Zimmerman, Robert (PA)	NRad	1021
Zimmerman, Robert (OH)	EDM	222
Zimnowodzki, Simon (IL)	N	534
Zinaman, Michael (MA)	RE	1041
Zinner, Michael (MA)	S	1088
Zinreich, S. James (MD)	NRad	1021
Zins, James (OH)	PlS	897
Zitelli, Basil (PA)	Ped	741
Zitelli, John (PA)	D	191
Zoghbi, William (TX)	Cv	109
Zubrow, Alan (PA)	NP	450
Zuckerman, Joseph (NY)	OrS	635
Zuckerman, Kenneth (FL)	Hem	320
Zupanc, Mary (CA)	ChiN	152
Zusman, Randall (MA)	Cv	90
Zwillenberg, Seth (PA)	Oto	677
Zwischenberger, Joseph (KY)	T&CS	1166

Acknowledgments

The publishers would like to thank the entire staff for their many hours and days of intense and precise work on this guide in order to further its goal of assisting consumers in making the best healthcare choices.

Castle Connolly Executive Management:

Chairman	John K. Castle
President & CEO	John J. Connolly, Ed.D.
Vice President, Chief Medical & Research Officer	Jean Morgan, M.D.
Vice President, Chief Strategy & Operations Officer	William Liss-Levinson, Ph.D.

Vice President, Advertising	Mark McGinty
Senior Research & Healthcare Associate	Maryann Hynd, RN

Research Coordinators

Terysia Browne	Najette Miller
Anicia Buite	Yuliya Nagdimova
Catherine Hoffman-Freiria	Zachary Preneta
Maitry Gandhi	Maria Salvador
Samiya Ikram	Mariadiep Vu

Book Layout, Database Management	Russell Hodgson
Office Manager	Marcie Samartino
Director, Client Relations & Research Operations	Nicki Hughes
Client Relations	Adam Akmal-Gonzalez

We also would like to extend our gratitude to the American Board of Medical Specialties (ABMS) for allowing us to use excerpts, especially the descriptions of medical specialties and subspecialties, from the text of their publication "Which Medical Specialist for You?"

Other Publications from Castle Connolly Medical Ltd.:
America's Top Doctors® for Cancer*; *Top Doctors: New York Metro Area*; *Top Doctors: Chicago Metro Area; Top Doctors Southern California; Top Doctors Washington-Baltimore; Cancer Made Easier: New York—Metro Area*, *Eldercare and others...
Order online at http://www.castleconnolly.com/books

Top Doctors Make A Difference

Corporate Membership for Employers

This service enables an employer to assist employees in identifying Top Doctors to care for themselves and their families. It is a low-cost, non-intrusive service that will result in better care and, ultimately, lower healthcare costs. For as low as a few dollars per year, employees can have complete access to the Castle Connolly website and database of Top Doctors who were nominated by their peers and screened by the Castle Connolly physician-led research team.

Instead of simply choosing a doctor's name from the phone book or a plan directory, the employee can compare physician names to the Castle Connolly database of 34,000 plus Top Doctors and select from among the best doctors in the country. This will result in overall better care, lower costs and improved morale. Once an employee logs on to the Castle Connolly database, valuable background information is available on every Top Doctor such as: medical school, board certifications, fellowships, hospital affiliations, residencies and much more, to allow them to make the best informed decision they can make when selecting a doctor.

Top Doctors can have an enormous impact. For patients and their families, the value of receiving first-class medical care is not measured in dollars – it is measured in quality and even length of life. Employers, however, can see the results in their bottom line. Faulty diagnoses and improper treatment take a toll in productivity and ripple out into higher workplace costs. No company should have to "make do" for weeks or months without a key employee or executive, when a Top Doctor may have solved the patient's problem quickly and efficiently. The effort to identify the best doctors from ordinary ones is justified by the money saved on incorrect treatments, unnecessary surgery and days lost from work.

The Corporate Membership is suited for employers of varying sizes and can also be of great value to professional, social, civic, fraternal and religious associations. Castle Connolly may also be able to adapt and tailor the presentation of the database to meet the specific corporate client's needs.

New Movers Program

The Castle Connolly New Movers Program is designed to alleviate that concern, or even fear, as well as the time-consuming struggle to identify the right – and best – doctors and hospitals in one's new community or region. The service can be provided on a family basis (those living in the household) or for a single client. The service includes identifying primary care physicians, including Pediatricians, OB/GYN's, Internists and Family Practitioners as well as other specialists that may be needed: for example, Ophthalmologists, Allergists, Endocrinologists, Surgeons or others as required.

Perhaps nothing is more challenging to a family that has relocated to a new community than finding appropriate healthcare resources, especially physicians. While they can turn to recommendations from new neighbors and friends, or select names from the phone book or a plan directory, that is hardly adequate, especially if there are special healthcare needs in the family.

A Castle Connolly Health Advisor will identify two or three recommendations for up to six different medical specialties. If, for some reason the client wishes to change doctors within two months, Castle Connolly will identify new physicians in the same specialty. After the selection process occurs, the Health Advisor will make an introductory phone call to the physician's office. This typically facilitates faster appointments.

Healthcare Solutions

Castle Connolly's Healthcare Solutions is designed to help your employees and their loved ones navigate through the healthcare system with less stress, faster service and better outcomes. It is a high touch service with a hands-on health advocate to serve as a guide and dedicated healthcare champion 24 hours a day, 7 days a week, 365 days a year. Why have your most valued employees, your most critical asset, spend their time -- and possibly company time –coping with difficult and complex medical issues they may know little about, when Castle Connolly's Healthcare Solutions professionals can resolve them quickly and expertly. With one phone call, your employees will gain priority access to a global network of best-in-class medical professionals, Castle Connolly Top Doctors™, and higher quality patient resources. Our professional staff coordinates the entire process to provide consistency and support during their time of need.

Services include, but are not limited to, the following:

» Identifying top physicians and hospitals (nationally)

» Identifying reputable non-physician providers, such as Dieticians, Physical and Occupational Therapists, etc.

» Facilitating second opinions

» Defining complex medical terminology and situations

» Providing a list of tailored questions to discuss with your medical team

» Conducting medical research on your health condition

» Navigating the healthcare system

» Assisting with medical record retrieval and/or arranging a medical record review

» Identifying and assisting with eldercare issues

» Coordinating a hospital transfer

» Arranging medical transport or evacuation for travelers

» Coordinating with the employers' other vendors for continuity of care

Healthcare Solutions can be made available to your organization as a specific number of cases during the course of the year with the option to obtain more, or as a yearly retainer. Organizations may opt to make this service available for all of their employees, or to select groups such as high level executives or partners.

For further information on Healthcare Solutions, Corporate Membership, New Movers, and Doctor-Patient Advisor Program, please contact:

Michael D. Wolf, Ph.D.
Executive Vice President
Castle Connolly Graduate Medical Publishing, Ltd.
212-644-9696
or
mwolf@ccgmp.com

Thora Eidsdottir, Ed.D.
Account Executive
Castle Connolly Medical Ltd.
42 W. 24th St.
New York, NY 10010
teidsdottir@castleconnolly.com

Top Doctors Make A Difference

Strategic Relationships

Castle Connolly Medical Ltd. has a number of strategic relationships that may be of interest to consumers and physicians.

Everyday Health, Inc. comprises some of the nation's leading online health information resources. With over 25 comprehensive health websites including www.EverydayHealth.com, www.Carepages.com, PDRHealth.com and www.WhatToExpect.com, information and knowledge is accessible on a wide range of health topics such as lifestyle offerings in pregnancy, diet and fitness to in-depth medical content for condition prevention and management.

In addition to their commitment to provide consumers with health solutions that span the health spectrum, they also provide a wide range of content and advertising-based services to healthcare entities including hospitals, physicians and other healthcare professionals. Castle Connolly has formed a strategic relationship with Everyday Health to offer one of these services in particular; Reputation Management Solutions.

More than 150 million people search listings and online healthcare directories each month making it imperative for physicians and hospitals to consistently update and manage their information on local directories, reviews sites and social networks. Understandably, this is, at times, an unfeasible commitment. Everyday Health's Reputation Management Solutions provides online visibility information which shows exactly where listings appear on the web, information across hundreds of directory sites, identifying and tips on how to respond to negative reviews and much more.

For more information, please contact our Manager of Client Relations at (212) 367-8400 Ext. 123.

sharecare

Sharecare is an interactive, social Q&A platform designed to greatly simplify the search for quality healthcare information and help consumers live their healthiest life. Sharecare has enlisted the nation's leading health experts, care providers, organizations, and brands to join the health and wellness conversation and empowering users with high-quality, relevant answers to their health questions from multiple expert perspectives and with interactive health and wellness tools to take action on what they've learned.

The website was launched in 2010 by Jeff Arnold, founder of WebMD, and Emmy–award winning host, Dr. Mehmet Oz, in partnership with Harpo Studios, Sony Pictures Television and Discovery Communications.

Castle Connolly teamed up with Sharecare in 2011. Dr. John Connolly, President and CEO of CCML, is one of the featured experts on Sharecare for healthcare choice questions. Find out more at www.sharecare.com

Vitals (www.vitals.com), an innovative online doctor review and comparison service from MDx Medical Inc., is the comprehensive source for vital information, peer evaluations and patient feedback on more than 700,000 doctors nationwide. Drawing upon prestigious information repositories, cutting-edge search and comparison technologies, and a robust patient feedback mechanism, Vitals has organized key information to help patients make an informed choice in their search for the right doctor. Castle Connolly and Vitals have a branding relationship in which those physicians who are Castle Connolly Top Doctors™ and appear on Vitals web sites have an icon indicating their status and recognition as a Castle Connolly Top Doctor.

In 2012, Castle Connolly will begin displaying insurance plans that are accepted by all physicians listed as Castle Connolly Top Doctors. An appointment scheduling feature will also appear on our site for those physicians who wish to participate in this feature. Additional information can be found at www.vitals.com.

CASTLE CONNOLLY

LIFESTREAM MD

Castle Connolly Medical Ltd. has a strategic relationship with Castle Connolly LifeStream MD to provide a unique health advisory service designed for families and executives, especially those who travel regularly or may have more than one residence.

Each client is assigned a Castle Connolly LifeStream MD physician who is available to them by phone 24/7/365. A client call from anywhere in the world is answered promptly and the client is connected with their Castle Connolly LifeStream MD physician advisor.

The Castle Connolly LifeStream MD physician acts as a health manager assisting in navigation of an increasingly complex health care environment. The Castle Connolly LifeStream MD physician does not replace the member's primary physician or specialists, but provides additional independent counsel and services that provide security to our members either at home or while traveling.

In the United States, the Castle Connolly LifeStream MD physician will use the Castle Connolly database of Top Doctors to assure that the client is cared for in the best medical facilities by the top doctors. Assistance in securing timely appointments with specialists and records transfers is facilitated as needed. Outside of the United States, Castle Connolly LifeStream MD has an affiliation with International SOS, the world's largest and leading provider of travel medical assistance to assure the LifeStream MD member is cared for by the best doctors and hospitals available in that region or, if necessary, is transported to a place where that care is available.

EMPOWERED MEDICAL

Empowered Doctor is a media, news and marketing service. Empowered Doctor produces syndicated consumer health reports. Its video and text news stories appear on major media websites, including CBS. Empowered Doctor also provides marketing services to hospitals, clinics and individual physicians by generating visibility in online search and social media. Empowered Doctor's clients benefit from the company's efficient methodologies for generating new patient referrals.

For more information call 888-333-1027 or visit www.empowereddoctor.com

DrScore.com

PATIENTS SPEAK, DOCTORS LISTEN

Founded by Steven Feldman, M.D., DrScore.com is an interactive online survey site where patients can rate their physicians, as well as find a physician based on their service level preference.

The mission of DrScore.com is to improve medical care by giving patients a forum for rating their physician and by giving doctors an affordable, objective, non-intrusive means of documenting the quality of care that they provide. Visitors on Castle Connolly's website who are searching for "top doctors" have the option to also rate these and other physicians they have been to as patients, as well as to see if these physicians have been rated previously by other consumers on DrScore.com. Visitors to DrScore.com will be able to see if their doctors and/or other doctors are Castle Connolly "top doctors."

For more information, visit www.drscore.com.

grandparents.com®
it's great to be grand.

Grandparents.com is dedicated to enhancing the lives of America's 70 million grandparents by fostering family connections, via child- and grandparent-friendly activities, travel ideas, compelling lifestyle features, expert advice, gift ideas, recipes, and more. Visitors have access to a range of tools, including groups, discussions, a homepage blog, photo sharing, and a Facebook page and Twitter feeds. Through the Grandparents.com Benefits Club, catering to America's 120 million grandparents, Boomers and seniors, members benefit from discounts and incentives they can use every day, in categories like gifts, clothes, and vitamins, plus exclusive opportunities to save on hotels, cruises, auto rentals, theme park trips, theatrical productions, and insurance. Grandparents can share their membership benefits with four extended family and household members. In 2010, Grandparents.com was ranked as the No. 3 website for seniors, boomers, and grandparents, following the U.S. Government and AARP. Castle Connolly provides access to its Top Doctors' database, its Doctor-Patient Advisor and New Movers programs for Grandparents.com members.

CONSUMER'S MEDICAL RESOURCE

Turning Patients Into Informed Consumers®

Consumer's Medical Resource was started in 1996 to offer high-quality, high-impact employee benefit programs to help employees and their dependents, and has been a pioneer in Medical Decision Support® services. CMR addresses all medical conditions at any point within the continuum of care, by providing personalized, evidence-based medical research, information, access to genuine, in-person second opinions and support services to employees who face serious, complicated, and chronic illness, or would like to become well-informed healthcare consumers.

Leveraging a state-of-the-art integrated model of web, phone, and print-based services, CMR enables employees to fully understand and evaluate their options so they can make the most informed medical decisions possible with their doctors. The company is privately held and currently provides services to more than 750,000 Americans, achieving extremely high levels of user and customer satisfaction, improved clinical quality outcomes, and generated excellent ROI.

Castle Connolly and CMR are working together to provide Castle Connolly's various corporate services to CMR client companies and their employees.

For more information, please visit: http://www.consumersmedical.com.

Gluten-Free RESOURCE DIRECTORY

The Gluten-Free Resource Directory is a unique and easy, one-stop guide to all things Gluten-Free. Each category on this site has been carefully selected to provide you with products and services that simplify and demystify the Gluten-Free shopping experience. The Gluten-Free Resource Directory is dynamic in that it is constantly evolving, growing, changing and being updated with new products and services every day. So, be sure to check the site often to take advantage of some great promotions and new-to-market products available to you and your family.

Castle Connolly has entered into a strategic partnership with Directory Media Group, publishers of The Gluten-Free Resource Directory, to provide more than 1,900 doctors listings at www.glutenfreeresourcedirectory.com, free of charge. The listings include profiles of the nation's most distinguished gastroenterology, pediatric allergy and immunology, allergy and immunology and pediatric gastroenterology physicians.

Visitors to the Gluten-Free Resource Directory can search the more than 1,900 Castle Connolly Top Doctor profiles for each physician's contact information, specialty, training and faculty appointments, along with which medical school and residency program they attended. The profiles also include information for the insurance plans accepted by each Castle Connolly Top Doctor.

For more information, please visit: http://GlutenFreeResourceDirectory.com.

National Physician of the Year Awards

Castle Connolly Medical Ltd. proudly hosted its seventh annual ***National Physician of the Year Awards*** on March 18, 2013 at The Pierre Hotel in New York City. It was a spectacular evening which allowed us to recognize both the outstanding honorees and the excellence of the many thousands of physicians throughout the nation.

The Genesis of the National Physician of the Year Award.

Each year we receive thousands of nominations from physicians and the medical leadership of major medical centers, specialty hospitals, teaching hospitals and regional and community medical centers across the United States as an integral part of our research, screening and selection process to identify ***America's Top Doctors®***. The selected physicians, while spread across all fifty states and involved in more than 70 medical specialties and subspecialties, all share one distinguishing professional attribute: an unwavering dedication to their patients and to medicine as a whole. Each and every one of these outstanding medical professionals is a symbol of the clinical excellence that characterizes American medicine. In honor of these exemplary physicians, Castle Connolly Medical Ltd. has created the ***National Physician of the Year Awards*** to recognize the thousands of excellent, dedicated physicians across the United States. Our Medical Advisory Board selected the honorees from the hundreds nominated in a special nomination process conducted months before the event.

The honorees, Drs. Gopal Badlani, Jo A. Hannafin, and Jerry A. Shields, are superb examples of excellence in clinical medical practice. In addition to these awards for Clinical Excellence, Castle Connolly Medical Ltd. honored Drs. Michael Harrison and Sterling B. Williams for their lifetime achievement in medicine. Ms. Dawn Halfaker is a tireless fundraiser for The Wounded Warrior Project and an exemplary recipient for the seventh National Health Leadership Award.

Each honoree received a beautiful and distinctive porcelain figurine created by the Boehm Porcelain Company exclusively for the National Physician of the Year Awards. The award features a golden caduceus, the symbol of the medical community, surrounded by a golden laurel wreath. Laurel wreaths were used by the ancients to crown and honor their leaders.

The caduceus and laurel rest upon a column accented by the signature Castle Connolly logo. By combining the caduceus and the laurel wreaths, the award embodies the excellence in medical achievement that the National Physician of the Year Awards celebrates each year.

2013 National Physician of the Year Awards Honorees

"Top Doctors Make a Difference™"

For Clinical Excellence

Gopal Badlani, M.D.
Professor and Vice Chair for Clinical Affairs
Department of Urology
Wake Forest Baptist Medical Center

Jo A. Hannafin, M.D., Ph.D.
Hospital for Special Surgry
Professor of Orthopaedic Surgery
Weill Cornell Medical College

Jerry A. Shields, M.D.
Professor of Ophthalmology
Thomas Jefferson University
Director, Oncology Service
Wills Eye Institute

For Lifetime Achievement

Michael R. Harrison, M.D.
Professor Emeritus of Surgery, Pediatrics,
Obstetrics, Gynecology & Reproductive Sciences
Founding Director, Fetal Treatment Center
University of California, San Francisco

Sterling Williams, M.S., M.D., Ph.D.
Clinical Professor of Obstetrics & Gynecology
George Washington University Medical School
Vice President of Education
American College of Obstetricians & Gynecologists

National Health Leadership

Dawn Halfaker
President and CEO
Halfaker and Associated, LLC
President, Board of Directors, Wounded Warrior Project

2012 National Physician of the Year Awards Honorees

"Top Doctors Make a Difference™"

For Clinical Excellence

Richard Edelson, M.D.
Aaron B. and Marguerite Lerner Professor
Chairman of the Department of Dermatology
Yale School of Medicine.

Susan Mackinnon, M.D.
Chief of Plastic and Reconstructive Surgery
Washington University School of Medicine

John M. Morton, M.D., M.P.H., F.A.C.S.
Associate Professor of Surgery
Stanford University
Chief of Minimally Invasive Surgery,
Director of Bariatric Surgery and Surgical Quality

For Lifetime Achievement

Robert L. Brent, M.D., Ph.D., D.Sc.
Distinguished Professor of Pediatrics, Radiology and Pathology
Louis and Bess Stein Professor of Pediatrics at the Jefferson Medical College
and the Nemours/Alfred I. DuPont Hospital for Children

John G. Clarkson, M.D.
Dean Emeritus and Professor of Ophthalmology
Anne Bates Leach Eye Hospital/Bascom Palmer Eye Institute
Department of Ophthalmology
Miller School of Medicine at the University of Miami

National Health Leadership

Marlo Thomas
National Outreach Director
St. Jude Children's Research Hospital

2011 National Physician of the Year Awards Honorees

"Doctors Make a Difference"

For Clinical Excellence

Armando E. Giuliano, M.D., FACS, FRCSED
Chief of Science and Medicine
John Wayne Cancer Institute at Saint John's Health Center,
Santa Monica, CA

O. Wayne Isom, M.D.
Chairman of the Dept. of Cardiothoracic Surgery
New York Presbyterian-Weill Cornell Medical College

David W. Kennedy, M.D.
Otorhinolaryngology Professor at the
University of Pennsylvania

For Lifetime Achievement

George P. Canellos, M.D.
Served as Founding Chief of Medical Oncology at
Dana-Farber Cancer Institute;

Matthew D. Davis, M.D.
University of Wisconsin Medical Center
Chair, UW Opthalmology

National Health Leadership

Evelyn H. Lauder
Chairman of The Breast Cancer Research Foundation®

Previous National Physician of the Year Award Honorees

2010

Clinical Excellence

John B. Buse, M.D., Ph.D.

Director of the Diabetes Care Center, Professor, Chief of the Division of Endocrinology and Executive Associate Dean for Clinical Research, University of North Carolina School of Medicine, Chapel Hill

Larry Norton, M.D.

Deputy Physician-in-Chief, Memorial Hospital, Memorial Sloan-Kettering Cancer Center, for Breast Cancer Programs
Medical Director of the MSKCC's Breast and Imaging Center, Evelyn H. Lauder Breast Center

Ching-Hon Pui, M.D.

Department Chair of Oncology, St. Jude Children's Research Hospital
Medical Director of the St. Jude International Outreach China Program, holder of the Fahad Nassar Al-Rashid Chair of Leukemia Research

Lifetime Achievement

Basil I Hirschowitz, M.D.

Director, Gastroenterology Division, The University of Alabama
Receipient of the Kettering Medal from the General Motors Cancer Foundation; Friedenwald Medal of the AGA; the Schindler Medal and the Crystal Award for lifetime contributions to Endoscopy by the ASGE; honorary doctorate of Gothenburg University; honorary fellow of the Royal Society of Medicine

Leonard Apt, M.D.

Professor of Ophthalmology Emeritus; Director Emeritus and Founder of the Division of Pediatric Opthalmology and Strabismus, and Co-Director of UCLA's Center for Child Blindness

National Health Leadership

Alexandra Reeve Givens and Matthew Reeve

Trustees, The Christopher & Dana Reeve Foundation

2009

Clinical Excellence
Carol R. Bradford, M.D.,
Professor and Chair
Department of Otolaryngology
University of Michigan Medical System

Diane E. Meier, M.D.,
Director, Center to Advance Palliative Care
Mount Sinai School of Medicine

Judd W. Moul, M.D.,
Chief of Urology
Duke University Medical Center

Lifetime Achievement
Emil J. Freireich, M.D., D. Sc. (Hon.),
Ruth Harriet Ainsworth Chair, Distinguished Teaching Professor
Director, Special Medical Education Programs
Director, Adult Leukemia Research Program
The University of Texas M.D. Anderson Cancer Center

Thomas E. Starzl, M.D., Ph.D.
Professor of Surgery, Emeritus
Distinguished Service Professor
University of Pittsburgh Medical Center

National Health Leadership
Page Morton Black
Chairman of the Board, Parkinson's Disease Foundation

****

2008

Clinical Excellence

Robert W. Carlson, M.D.
Medical Oncology
Stanford University Medical Center

Stanley Chang, M.D.
Ophthalmology
New York-Presbyterian Hospital

L. Dade Lunsford, M.D.
Neurological Surgery
University of Pittsburgh Medical Center

Lifetime Achievement

Jacqueline A. Noonan, M.D.
Pediatric Cardiology
University of Kentucky Medical Center

Robert W. Schrier, M.D.
Nephrology
University of Colorado Health Sciences Center

National Health Leadership

Suzanne and Robert Wright
Vice-Chair of the Board, General Electric Company
Co-founders of Autism Speaks™

****

2007

Clinical Excellence

Delos M. Cosgrove, M.D.
Chairman, Board of Governors
CEO and President
The Cleveland Clinic

Joseph G. McCarthy, M.D.
Lawrence D. Bell Professor of Plastic Surgery
Director, The Institute of Reconstructive Plastic Surgery
NYU Medical Center

Patrick C. Walsh, M.D.
University Distinguished Service Professor and Director of Urology
The James Buchanan Brady Urological Institute
The Johns Hopkins Hospital

Lifetime Achievement

Maria Delivoria-Papadopoulos, M.D.
Director, The Neonatal Intensive Care Unit
St. Christopher's Hospital for Children;
Professor of Pediatrics, Physiology and Obstetrics/Gynecology
Drexel University College of Medicine

National Health Leadership

The Honorable Nancy G. Brinker
Founder of Susan G. Komen for the Cure
Former U.S. Ambassador to Hungary

****

2006

Clinical Excellence

Bart Barlogie, M.D., Ph.D.
Director, Myeloma Institute for Research Therapy
University of Arkansas for Medical Services

Marilyn J. Bull, M.D.
Morris Green Professor of Pediatrics
Riley Hospital for Children

Michael J. Zinner, M.D.
Moseley Professor of Surgery
Harvard Medical School
Surgeon-in-Chief, Brigham & Women's Hospital

Lifetime Achievement

Michael E. DeBakey, M.D.
Chancellor Emeritus, Baylor College of Medicine

National Health Leadership

Princess Yasmin Aga Khan
Honorary Vice Chair
Alzheimer's Association

Castle Connolly maintains Facebook, Twitter, LinkedIn and Sharecare accounts in an effort to keep consumers informed of the latest news not only regarding Castle Connolly Medical Ltd., its Top Doctors and Top Hospitals, but also reports on various health observances and events. A live Twitter feed can also be found on the homepage of www.castleconnolly.com.

Consumers who use our print guides, online database or refer to our regional magazine features can find up-to-date information about Castle Connolly, healthcare and medical news by logging onto these social networking sites:

Find us on Facebook

www.facebook.com/TopDoctors

Follow Us On twitter

www.twitter.com/CastleConnolly

Blog - Ask America's Top Doctors™
www.castleconnolly.com/blog

LinkedIn

http://linkd.in/mP4Lmb (case sensitive)

Do you have a story about a Castle Connolly Top Doctor or Top Hospital that you want to share? If so, please email a link to the article to:

Nicki Hughes
Director of Client Relations and Research Operations
nhughes@castleconnolly.com

Top Doctors Make A Difference

Doctor-Patient Advisor for Individual Consumers

Doctor-Patient Advisor is a Castle Connolly Medical Ltd. service providing one-on-one consultations with a physician or nurse practitioner to individuals who have serious or complex medical problems or to anyone who feels he/she needs assistance finding the right physician for any purpose. Each client will receive personalized assistance in identifying the appropriate specialists for his/her condition, utilizing the Castle Connolly Medical Ltd. database of physicians and hospitals, as well as individual searches, to locate the best resources to meet the client's needs.

Fee: $375. For further information call (212) 367-8400 x 116.

Premium Membership at www.CastleConnolly.com

Reap the benefits of membership with Castle Connolly. Gain access to ALL online top doctor listings and get discounts on book purchases from our extensive catalog.

- Search among more than 34,000 Castle Connolly Top Doctor listings
- Search among select hospitals and centers of excellence
- Receive a 30% discount on all book purchases

Membership Levels:
- Monthly - $1.99
- One year - $24.95
- Two years - $34.95

For more information visit: www.CastleConnolly.com/membership

Other Products From Castle Connolly

Castle Connolly Guides

Titles Include:

- ***America's Top Doctors® for Cancer***
- ***Top Doctors: New York Metro Area***

And Many More

To order other Castle Connolly guides at a 15% discount please visit
http://www.CastleConnolly.com/books
When ordering use discount code: **ATD13VAN**

Castle Connolly's Top Doctors Available Online

- Free Access to 20 -25% of Castle Connolly's Top Doctors
- Purchase Access to the entire database of more than 34,000 doctor profiles

http://www.castleconnolly.com/membership

Customer Feedback

We appreciate your comments regarding our guides. Please email us at info@castleconnolly.com